# WHO'S WHO
# 1971

# WHO *WAS* WHO

Six volumes containing the biographies removed from WHO'S WHO each year on account of death, with final details and date of death added.

VOL. I. 1897–1915

VOL. II. 1916–1928

VOL. III. 1929–1940

VOL. IV. 1941–1950

VOL. V. 1951–1960

VOL. VI. 1961–1970
*(ready Autumn 1971)*

ADAM & CHARLES BLACK : LONDON

# WHO'S WHO
# 1971

AN
ANNUAL BIOGRAPHICAL DICTIONARY

ONE HUNDRED AND TWENTY-THIRD
YEAR OF ISSUE

ADAM AND CHARLES BLACK
LONDON

# EDITORIAL NOTE

Some occurrences of a date later than November 1970, when this edition had to go to press, could not be recorded in the relevant entries; a number of these, of the most general interest, are listed in a supplement preceding the first page of the biographies. This includes also the names of those who, having no entry as yet in the body of the book, received titles gazetted on 1 January 1971. The obituary, on pages 25–30, includes the deaths reported up to mid-November 1970.

A proof of each entry is posted to its subject every year for personal revision, but this cannot be sent unless an address is given. It should be pointed out that the numbers given of the children of a marriage are, unless otherwise indicated, those of the sons and daughters now living; also, that it is the practice to print the names of London clubs unaccompanied by the word London. Forenames printed within brackets are those which the subject of the entry does not commonly use. While every care is taken to ensure accuracy, neither the publishers nor the printers can admit liability for any loss incurred through misprint or other circumstances.

It cannot be stated too emphatically that inclusion in *Who's Who* has never at any time been a matter for payment or of obligation to purchase the volume.

PUBLISHED BY A. & C. BLACK LIMITED
4, 5, & 6 SOHO SQUARE LONDON W.1

---



ISBN 0 7136 1140 5

PRINTED IN GREAT BRITAIN

# ABBREVIATIONS USED IN THIS BOOK

Some of the designatory letters in this list are used merely for economy of space and do not necessarily imply any professional or other qualification

## A

**AA** . . Anti-Aircraft; Automobile Association; Architectural Association; Augustinians of the Assumption
**AAA** . . Amateur Athletic Association
**AA&QMG** . Assistant Adjutant and Quartermaster-General
**AAAS** . . American Association for Advancement of Science
**AACCA** . . Associate of the Association of Certified and Corporate Accountants
**AAF** . . Auxiliary Air Force (now RAux AF)
**AAG** . . Assistant Adjutant-General
**AAI** . . Associate of Chartered Auctioneers' and Estate Agents' Institute
**AAMC** . . Australian Army Medical Corps
**A&AEE** . Aeroplane and Armament Experimental Establishment
**AASA** . . Associate of Australian Society of Accountants
**AAUQ** . . Associate in Accountancy, University of Queensland
**AB** . . Bachelor of Arts (US); able-bodied seaman
**ABA** . . Amateur Boxing Association
**ABC** . . Australian Broadcasting Commission
**ABCA** . . Army Bureau of Current Affairs
**ABCFM** . . American Board of Commissioners for Foreign Missions
**Abp** . . Archbishop
**AC** . . *Ante Christum* (before Christ)
**ACA** . . Associate of the Institute of Chartered Accountants
**Acad.** . . Academy
**ACAS** . . Assistant Chief of the Air Staff
**ACCM** . . Advisory Council for the Church's Ministry (formerly CACTM)
**ACCS** . . Associate of Corporation of Secretaries (formerly of Certified Secretaries)
**ACDS** . . Assistant Chief of Defence Staff
**ACF** . . Army Cadet Force
**ACG** . . Assistant Chaplain-General
**ACGI** . . Associate of City and Guilds of London Institute
**ACII** . . Associate of the Chartered Insurance Institute
**ACIS** . . Associate of the Chartered Institute of Secretaries
**ACOS** . . Assistant Chief of Staff
**ACS** . . Additional Curates Society
**ACSEA** . . Allied Command SE Asia
**ACSM** . . Associate of the Camborne School of Mines
**ACT** . . Australian Capital Territory; Australian College of Theology; Associate of the College of Technology
**ACWA** . . Associate of the Institute of Cost and Works Accountants
**AD** . . *Anno Domini*
**ADC** . . Aide-de-camp
**ADCM** . . Archbishop of Canterbury's Diploma in Church Music
**AD Corps** . Army Dental Corps
**Ad eund.** . . *Ad eundem gradum* (admitted to the same degree); and *see under* a e g
**ADFW** . . Assistant Director of Fortifications and Works
**ADGB** . . Air Defence of Great Britain
**ADGMS** . . Assistant Director-General of Medical Services
**ADH** . . Assistant Director of Hygiene
**Adjt** . . Adjutant
**ADJAG** . . Assistant Deputy Judge Advocate General
**Adm.** . . Admiral
**ADMS** . . Assistant Director of Medical Services
**ADOS** . . Assistant Director of Ordnance Services
**ADPR** . . Assistant Director of Public Relations
**ADS&T** . . Assistant Director of Supplies and Transport
**Adv.** . . Advisory; Advocate
**ADVS** . . Assistant Director of Veterinary Services
**ADWE&M** . Assistant Director of Works, Electrical and Mechanical
**AEA** . . Atomic Energy Authority; Air Efficiency Award
**AEAF** . . Allied Expeditionary Air Force
**AEC** . . Agricultural Executive Council; Army Educational Corps (now RAEC)
**AEF** . . Amalgamated Union of Engineering and Foundry Workers; American Expeditionary Forces
**a e g** . . *ad eundem gradum* (to the same degree—of the admission of a graduate of one university to the same degree at another without examination)
**AEGIS** . . Aid for the Elderly in Government Institutions
**AEI** . . Associated Electrical Industries
**AEM** . . Air Efficiency Medal
**AER** . . Army Emergency Reserve
**AERE** . . Atomic Energy Research Establishment (Harwell)
**Æt., Ætat.** . *Ætatis* (aged)
**AEU** . . Amalgamated Engineering Union
**AFA** . . Amateur Football Alliance
**AFAIAA** . Associate Fellow of American Institute of Aeronautics and Astronautics (and *see under* AFIAS)
**AFC** . . Air Force Cross; Association Football Club
**AFCAI** . . Associate Fellow of the Canadian Aeronautical Institute
**AFD** . . Doctor of Fine Arts (US)
**AFHQ** . . Allied Force Headquarters
**AFIA** . . Associate of Federal Institute of Accountants (Australia)
**AFIAS** . . (now *see under* AFAIAA) (formerly) Associate Fellow Institute of Aeronautical Sciences (US)
**AFICD** . . Associate Fellow Institute of Civil Defence
**AFM** . . Air Force Medal
**AFRAeS** . . Associate Fellow Royal Aeronautical Society
**AFV** . . Armoured Fighting Vehicles
**AG** . . Attorney-General
**AGH** . . Australian General Hospital
**AGI** . . Artistes Graphiques Internationales; Associate of the Institute of Certificated Grocers
**AGSM** . . Associate of Guildhall School of Music
**AHQ** . . Army Headquarters
**AH-WC** . . Associate of Heriot-Watt College, Edinburgh

**AIA** . . Associate of the Institute of Actuaries; American Institute of Architects
**AIAL** . . Associate Member of the International Institute of Arts and Letters
**AIB** . . Associate of the Institute of Bankers
**AIBD** . . Associate of the Institute of British Decorators
**AIBP** . . Associate of the Institute of British Photographers
**AIC** . . Agricultural Improvement Council; also formerly Associate of the Institute of Chemistry (*see* ARIC)
**AICA** . . Associate Member Commonwealth Institute of Accountants; Association Internationale des Critiques d'Art
**AICE** . . Associate of the Institution of Civil Engineers
**AICTA** . . Associate of the Imperial College of Tropical Agriculture
**AIEE** . . Associate of the Institution of Electrical Engineers
**AIF** . . Australian Imperial Forces
**AIG** . . Adjutant-Inspector-General
**AIIA** . . Associate Insurance Institute of America
**AIL** . . Associate of the Institute of Linguists
**AILA** . . Associate of the Institute of Landscape Architects
**AILocoE** . . Associate of Institution of Locomotive Engineers
**AIME** . . American Institute of Mechanical Engineers
**AIMarE** . . Associate of the Institute of Marine Engineers
**AIOB** . . Associate of the Institute of Builders
**AInstP** . . Associate of Institute of Physics
**AInstPI** . . Associate of the Institute of Patentees (Incorporated)
**AISA** . . Associate of the Incorporated Secretaries' Association
**AIWSP** . . Associate Member of Institute of Work Study Practitioners
**AJAG** . . Assistant Judge Advocate General
**AKC** . . Associate of King's College (London)
**ALA** . . Associate of the Library Association
**Ala** . . Alabama (US)
**ALAS** . . Associate of Chartered Land Agents' Society
**ALCD** . . Associate of London College of Divinity
**ALCM** . . Associate of London College of Music
**ALFSEA** . . Allied Land Forces South-East Asia
**ALI** . . Argyll Light Infantry
**ALS** . . Associate of the Linnaean Society
**Alta** . . Alberta
**AM** . . Albert Medal; Master of Arts (US); Alpes Maritimes
**AMA** . . Associate of the Museums Association; Australian Medical Association
**Amb.** . . Ambulance
**AMBritIRE** . (now *see under* AMIERE) (formerly) Associate Member of British Institution of Radio Engineers
**AMC** . . Association of Municipal Corporations
**AMet** . . Associate of Metallurgy (Sheffield University)
**AMF** . . Australian Military Forces
**AMGOT** . . Allied Military Government of Occupied Territory
**AMIAgrE** . Associate Member of Institution of Agricultural Engineers
**AMICE** . . Associate Member of Institution of Civil Engineers (formerly lower rank of corporate membership of Instn, now *see under* MICE; change dated July 1968)
**AMIChemE** . Associate Member of Institution of Chemical Engineers
**AMIEA** . . Associate Member of Institute of Engineers, Australia
**AMIED** . . Associate Member of Institution of Engineering Designers
**AMIEE** . . Associate Member of Institution of Electrical Engineers (formerly lower rank of corporate membership of Instn, now *see under* MIEE; change dated Dec. 1966)
**AMIE(Ind)** . Associate Member, Institution of Engineers, India
**AMIERE** . . Associate Member of Institution of Electronic and Radio Engineers (and *see under* AMBritIRE)
**AMIMechE** . Associate Member of Institution of Mechanical Engineers (formerly lower rank of corporate membership of Instn, now *see under* MIMechE, change dated April 1968)
**AMIMinE** . Associate Member of Institution of Mining Engineers
**AMIMM** . . Associate Member of Institution of Mining and Metallurgy
**AMInstBE** . Associate Member of Institution of British Engineers
**AMInstCE** . Associate Member of Institution of Civil Engineers (changed 1946 to AMICE)
**AmInstEE** . American Institute of Electrical Engineers
**AMInstR** . . Associate Member of Institute of Refrigeration
**AMInstT** . . Associate Member of the Institute of Transport
**AMIStructE** . Associate Member of the Institution of Structural Engineers
**AMRINA** . Associate Member of Royal Institution of Naval Architects
**AMS** . . Assistant Military Secretary; Army Medical Service
**AMTPI** . . Associate of Town Planning Institute
**ANA** . . Associate National Academician (America)
**Anat.** . . Anatomy; Anatomical
**ANECInst** . Associate of NE Coast Institution of Engineers and Shipbuilders
**Anon.** . . Anonymously
**ANU** . . Australian National University
**ANZAAS** . Australian and New Zealand Association for the Advancement of Science
**AO** . . Air Officer
**AOA** . . Air Officer in charge of Administration
**AOC** . . Air Officer Commanding
**AOC-in-C** . Air Officer Commanding-in-Chief
**AOD** . . Army Ordnance Department
**AOER** . . Army Officers Emergency Reserve
**APD** . . Army Pay Department
**APS** . . Aborigines Protection Society
**APTC** . . Army Physical Training Corps
**AQMG** . . Assistant Quartermaster-General
**AR** . . Associated Rediffusion (Television)
**ARA** . . Associate of the Royal Academy
**ARAD** . . Associate of the Royal Academy of Dancing
**ARAeS** . . Associate of the Royal Aeronautical Society
**ARAM** . . Associate of the Royal Academy of Music
**ARAS** . . Associate of the Royal Astronomical Society
**ARBA** . . Associate of the Royal Society of British Artists
**ARBC** . . Associate Royal British Colonial Society of Artists
**ARBS** . . Associate Royal Society of British Sculptors
**ARC** . . Architects' Registration Council; Agricultural Research Council; Aeronautical Research Council
**ARCA** . . Associate Royal College of Art; Associate Royal Canadian Academy

**ARCamA** . Associate Royal Cambrian Academy (formerly ARCA)
**ARCE** . . Academical Rank of Civil Engineers
**Archt** . . Architect
**ARCM** . . Associate Royal College of Music
**ARCO** . . Associate Royal College of Organists
**ARCO(CHM)** . Associate Royal College of Organists with Diploma in Choir Training
**ARCS** . . Associate Royal College of Science
**ARCST** . . Associate Royal College of Science and Technology (Glasgow)
**ARCVS** . . Associate of Royal College of Veterinary Surgeons
**ARE** . . Associate of Royal Society of Painter-Etchers and Engravers
**ARIBA** . . Associate of the Royal Institute of British Architects
**ARIC** . . Associate of the Royal Institute of Chemistry
**ARICS** . . Professional Associate of the Royal Institution of Chartered Surveyors
**Ark** . . Arkansas (US)
**ARMS** . . Associate of the Royal Society of Miniature Painters
**ARP** . . Air Raid Precautions
**ARPS** . . Associate of the Royal Photographic Society
**ARRC** . . Associate of the Royal Red Cross
**ARSA** . . Associate Royal Scottish Academy
**ARSM** . . Associate Royal School of Mines
**ARTC** . . Associate Royal Technical College (Glasgow) (name changed) *see under* ARCST
**ARVIA** . . Associate Royal Victorian Institute of Architects
**ARWA** . . Associate Royal West of England Academy
**ARWS** . . Associate Royal Society of Painters in Water-Colours
**AS** . . Anglo-Saxon
**ASAA** . . Associate of the Society of Incorporated Accountants and Auditors
**ASAM** . . Associate of the Society of Art Masters
**AScW** . . Association of Scientific Workers
**ASE** . . Amalgamated Society of Engineers
**ASIA(Ed)** . Associate, Society of Industrial Artists (Education)
**ASLEF** . . Associated Society of Locomotive Engineers and Firemen
**ASLIB** . . Association of Special Libraries and Information Bureaux
**ASO** . . Air Staff Officer
**ASSET** . . Association of Supervisory Staffs, Executives and Technicians
**AssocISI** . Associate of Iron and Steel Institute
**AssocMCT** . Associateship of Manchester College of Technology
**AssocMIAeE** . Associate Member Institution of Aeronautical Engineers
**AssocRINA** . Associate of the Royal Institution of Naval Architects
**AssocSc** . Associate in Science
**Asst** . . Assistant
**ASTMS** . . Association of Scientific, Technical and Managerial Staffs
**Astr.** . . Astronomy
**ASW** . . Association of Scientific Workers
**ATA** . . Air Transport Auxiliary
**ATC** . . Air Training Corps
**ATCL** . . Associate of Trinity College of Music, London
**ATD** . . Art Teachers' Diploma
**ATI** . . Associate of Textile Institute
**ATII** . . Associate Member of the Institute of Taxation
**ATS** . . Auxiliary Territorial Service
**ATV** . . Associated TeleVision
**AUS** . . Army of the United States
**AVD** . . Army Veterinary Department
**AVR** . . Army Volunteer Reserve

## B

**b** . . . born; brother
**BA** . . Bachelor of Arts
**B&FBS** . . British and Foreign Bible Society
**BAFO** . . British Air Forces of Occupation
**BAI** . . Bachelor of Engineering (*Baccalarius in Arte Ingeniaria*)
**BALPA** . . British Air Line Pilots' Association
**BAO** . . Bachelor of Art of Obstetrics
**BAOR** . . British Army of the Rhine (formerly *on* the Rhine)
**BARC** . . British Automobile Racing Club
**Bart** or **Bt** . Baronet
**BAS** . . Bachelor in Agricultural Science
**BASc** . . Bachelor of Applied Science
**Batt.** . . Battery
**BB&CIRly** . Bombay, Baroda and Central India Railway
**BBC** . . British Broadcasting Corporation
**BC** . . Before Christ; British Columbia
**BCE (Melb)** . Bachelor of Civil Engineering (Melbourne Univ.)
**BCh** or **BChir** . Bachelor of Surgery
**BCL** . . Bachelor of Civil Law
**BCMS** . . Bible Churchmen's Missionary Society
**BCOF** . . British Commonwealth Occupation Force
**BCom** . . Bachelor of Commerce
**BComSc** . . Bachelor of Commercial Science
**BCS** . . Bengal Civil Service
**BCURA** . . British Coal Utilization Research Association
**BD** . . Bachelor of Divinity
**Bd** . . Board
**BDA** . . British Dental Association
**Bde** . . Brigade
**BDS** . . Bachelor of Dental Surgery
**BDSc** . . Bachelor of Dental Science
**BE** . . Bachelor of Engineering; British Element
**BEA** . . British East Africa; British European Airways
**BEAMA** . . British Electrical and Allied Manufacturers' Association
**BEc** . . Bachelor of Economics (Australian)
**BEd** . . Bachelor of Education
**Beds** . . Bedfordshire
**BEE** . . Bachelor of Electrical Engineering
**BEF** . . British Expeditionary Force
**BEM** . . British Empire Medal
**BEngEE** . . Bachelor of Electrical Engineering (Canada)
**Berks** . . Berkshire
**BFPO** . . British Forces Post Office
**BGS** . . Brigadier General Staff
**BHS** . . British Horse Society
**BIF** . . British Industries Fair
**BIM** . . British Institute of Management
**BIS** . . Bank for International Settlements
**BISF** . . British Iron and Steel Federation
**BISFA** . . British Industrial and Scientific Film Association
**BISRA** . . British Iron and Steel Research Association
**BJ** . . Bachelor of Journalism
**BJSM** . . British Joint Services Mission
**BL** . . Bachelor of Law
**BLA** . . British Liberation Army
**BLE** . . Brotherhood of Locomotive Engineers
**BLitt** . . Bachelor of Letters
**BM** . . British Museum; Bachelor of Medicine
**BMA** . . British Medical Association
**BMH** . . British Military Hospital
**BMJ** . . British Medical Journal
**Bn** . . Battalion
**BNAF** . . British North Africa Force
**BNC** . . Brasenose College
**BNEC** . . British National Export Council
**BNOC** . . British National Opera Company
**BOAC** . . British Overseas Airways Corporation
**BomCS** . . Bombay Civil Service
**BomSC** . . Bombay Staff Corps

**BoT** . . Board of Trade
**Bot.** . . Botany; Botanical
**Bp** . . Bishop
**BPharm** . . Bachelor of Pharmacy
**BR** . . British Rail
**Br.** . . Branch
**BRA** . . Brigadier Royal Artillery
**BRCS** . . British Red Cross Society
**Brig.** . . Brigadier
**BritIRE** . . (now *see under* IERE) (formerly) British Institution of Radio Engineers
**BRS** . . British Road Services
**BS** . . Bachelor of Surgery; Bachelor of Science
**BSA** . . Bachelor of Scientific Agriculture; Birmingham Small Arms
**BSAA** . . British South American Airways
**BSAP** . . British South Africa Police
**BSC** . . British Steel Corporation; Bengal Staff Corps
**BSc** . . Bachelor of Science
**BSc (Dent)** . Bachelor of Science in Dentistry
**BSE** . . Bachelor of Science in Engineering (US)
**BSF** . . British Salonica Force
**BSI** . . British Standards Institution
**BSJA** . . British Show Jumping Association
**Bt** . . Baronet; Brevet
**BTA** . . British Tourist Authority (*formerly* British Travel Association)
**BTC** . . British Transport Commission
**BTh** . . Bachelor of Theology
**BVM** . . Blessed Virgin Mary
**Bucks** . . Buckinghamshire
**BWI** . . British West Indies (now WI; West Indies)
**BWM** . . British War Medal

# C

**(C)** . . Conservative; 100
**c** . . Child; cousin
**CA** . . Central America; County Alderman; Chartered Accountant (Scotland, and Canada)
**CACTM** . . Central Advisory Council of Training for the Ministry (*now see* ACCM)
**CALE** . . Canadian Army Liaison Executive
**Cambs** . . Cambridgeshire
**CAMC** . . Canadian Army Medical Corps
**CAMW** . . Central Association for Mental Welfare
**Cantab** . . Of Cambridge University
**CAS** . . Chief of the Air Staff
**CASI** . . Canadian Aeronautics and Space Institute
**Cav.** . . Cavalry
**CB** . . Companion of the Bath
**CBE** . . Commander Order of the British Empire
**CBI** . . Confederation of British Industry (and *see under* FBI)
**CBSA** . . Clay Bird Shooting Association
**CC** . . Companion of the Order of Canada; City Council; County Council; Cricket Club; Cycling Club; County Court
**CCC** . . Corpus Christi College; Central Criminal Court; County Cricket Club
**CCF** . . Combined Cadet Force
**CCG** . . Control Commission Germany
**CCPR** . . Central Council of Physical Recreation
**CCRA** . . Commander Corps Royal Artillery
**CCS** . . Casualty Clearing Station; Ceylon Civil Service
**CD** . . Canadian Forces Decoration
**CDEE** . . Chemical Defence Experimental Establishment
**Cdre** . . Commodore
**CDS** . . Chief of the Defence Staff
**CE** . . Civil Engineer
**CEF** . . Canadian Expeditionary Force
**CEGB** . . Central Electricity Generating Board
**CEI** . . Council of Engineering Institutions
**CEIR** . . Corporation for Economic and Industrial Research
**CEMA** . . Council for the Encouragement of Music and the Arts
**CEMS** . . Church of England Men's Society
**CEng** . . Chartered Engineer
**Cento** . . Central Treaty Organisation
**CERN** . . Conseil (now Organisation) Européenne pour la Recherche Nucléaire
**CETS** . . Church of England Temperance Society
**CF** . . Chaplain to the Forces
**CFA** . . Canadian Field Artillery
**CFE** . . Central Fighter Establishment
**CFR** . . Commander of Federal Republic of Nigeria
**CFS** . . Central Flying School
**CGIA** . . City and Guilds of London Insignia Award
**CGS** . . Chief of the General Staff
**CH** . . Companion of Honour
**Chanc.** . . Chancellor; Chancery
**Chap.** . . Chaplain
**ChapStJ** . . Chaplain of Order of St John of Jerusalem (now ChStJ)
**ChB** . . Bachelor of Surgery
**Ch. Ch.** . . Christ Church
**Ch. Coll.** . . Christ's College
**(CHM)** . . *See under* ARCO(CHM), FRCO(CHM)
**ChM** . . Master of Surgery
**Chm.** . . Chairman
**ChStJ** . . Chaplain of Order of St John of Jerusalem
**CI** . . Imperial Order of the Crown of India; Channel Islands
**CIAD** . . Central Institute of Art and Design
**CIAgrE** . . Companion, Institution of Agricultural Engineers
**CIAL** . . Corresponding Member of the International Institute of Arts and Letters
**CID** . . Criminal Investigation Department
**CIE** . . Companion of the Order of the Indian Empire
**CIGRE** . . Conférence Internationale des Grands Réseaux Electriques
**CIGS** . . (formerly) Chief of the Imperial General Staff (now CGS)
**CIMarE** . . Companion of the Institute of Marine Engineers
**CIMechE** . Companion of the Institution of Mechanical Engineers
**C-in-C** . . Commander-in-Chief
**CIR** . . Commission on Industrial Relations
**CIV** . . City Imperial Volunteers
**CJ** . . Chief Justice
**CJM** . . Congregation of Jesus and Mary (Eudist Fathers)
**CL** . . Commander of Order of Leopold
**c.l.** . . *cum laude*
**Cl.** . . Class
**CLA** . . Country Landowners' Association
**CLit** . . Companion of Literature (Royal Society of Literature Award)
**CM** . . Medal of Courage (Canada); Congregation of the Mission (Vincentians); Master in Surgery; Certificated Master; Canadian Militia
**CMA** . . Canadian Medical Association
**CMB** . . Central Midwives' Board
**CMF** . . Commonwealth Military Forces; Central Mediterranean Force
**CMG** . . Companion of St Michael and St George
**CMO** . . Chief Medical Officer
**CMS** . . Church Missionary Society
**CNAA** . . Council for National Academic Awards
**CNR** . . Canadian National Railways
**CO** . . Commanding Officer; Commonwealth Office (from Aug. 1966) (*see also* FCO); Colonial Office (before Aug. 1966); Conscientious Objector

**Co.** . . County; Company
**C of E** . . Church of England
**C of S** . . Chief of Staff
**CoID** . . Council of Industrial Design
**Co.L** or **Coal.L** Coalition Liberal
**Col** . . Colonel
**Coll.** . . College; Collegiate
**Colo** . . Colorado (US)
**Col.-Sergt** . Colour-Sergeant
**Com** . . Communist
**Comd** . . Command
**Comdg** . . Commanding
**Comdr** . . Commander
**Comdt** . . Commandant
**Commn** . . Commission
**Commnd** . . Commissioned
**CompIEE** . Companion of the Institution of Electrical Engineers
**CompIERE** . Companion of the Institution of Electronic and Radio Engineers
**CompTI** . . Companion of the Textile Institute
**Comr** . . Commissioner
**Comy-Gen.** . Commissary-General
**CON** . . Cross of Order of the Niger
**Conn** . . Connecticut (US)
**Const.** . . Constitutional
**COPEC** . . Conference of Politics, Economics and Christianity
**Corp.** . . Corporation; Corporal
**Corr. Mem.** or **Fell.** . Corresponding Member or Fellow
**COS** . . Charity Organization Society
**COSA** . . Colliery Officials and Staffs Association
**COSSAC** . Chief of Staff to Supreme Allied Commander
**COTC** . . Canadian Officers' Training Corps
**Co.U** or **Coal.U** Coalition Unionist
**CP** . . Central Provinces; Cape Province
**CPA** . . Commonwealth Parliamentary Association; Chartered Patent Agent; also (formerly) Certified Public Accountant (Canada) (now merged with CA)
**CPR** . . Canadian Pacific Railway
**CPRE** . . Council for the Preservation of Rural England
**CPSU** . . Communist Party of the Soviet Union
**CR** . . Community of the Resurrection
**cr** . . created or creation
**CRA** . . Commander, Royal Artillery
**CRASC** . . Commander, Royal Army Service Corps
**CRE** . . Commander, Royal Engineers
**Cres.** . . Crescent
**CRO** . . Commonwealth Relations Office (before Aug. 1966; *now see* CO)
**CS** . . Civil Service
**CSB** . . Bachelor of Christian Science
**CSC** . . Conspicuous Service Cross
**CSI** . . Companion of the Order of the Star of India
**CSIR** . . Commonwealth Council for Scientific and Industrial Research (re-named: Commonwealth Scientific and Industrial Research Organisation; *see* below)
**CSIRO** . . Commonwealth Scientific and Industrial Research Organization (and *see* above)
**CSO** . . Chief Scientific Officer; Chief Signal Officer
**CSP** . . Chartered Society of Physiotherapists; Civil Service of Pakistan
**CSSp** . . Holy Ghost Father
**CSSR** . . Congregation of the Most Holy Redeemer (Redemptorist Order)
**CStJ** . . Commander of the Order of St John of Jerusalem
**CTA** . . Chaplain Territorial Army
**CTC** . . Cyclists' Touring Club
**CTR** (Harwell) Controlled Thermonuclear Research
**CU** . . Cambridge University
**CUAC** . . Cambridge University Athletic Club
**CUAFC** . . Cambridge University Association Football Club
**CUBC** . . Cambridge University Boat Club
**CUCC** . . Cambridge University Cricket Club
**CUF** . . Common University Fund
**CUHC** . . Cambridge University Hockey Club
**CUP** . . Cambridge University Press
**CURUFC** . Cambridge University Rugby Union Football Club
**CVO** . . Commander of the Royal Victorian Order
**CWS** . . Co-operative Wholesale Society

# D

**D** . . . Duke
**d** . . . Died; daughter
**DA** . . Diploma in Anaesthesia; Diploma in Art
**DAA&QMG** . Deputy Assistant Adjutant and Quartermaster-General
**DAAG** . . Deputy Assistant Adjutant-General
**DA&QMG** . Deputy Adjutant and Quartermaster-General
**DACG** . . Deputy Assistant Chaplain-General
**DAD** . . Deputy Assistant Director
**DADMS** . . Deputy Assistant Director of Medical Services
**DADOS** . . Deputy Assistant Director of Ordnance Services
**DADQ** . . Deputy Assistant Director of Quartering
**DADST** . . Deputy Assistant Director of Supplies and Transport
**DAG** . . Deputy Adjutant-General
**DAMS** . . Deputy Assistant Military Secretary
**DAQMG** . Deputy Assistant Quartermaster-General
**DASc** . . Doctor in Agricultural Sciences
**DATA** . . Draughtsmen's and Allied Technicians' Association
**DBE** . . Dame Commander Order of the British Empire
**DC** . . District of Columbia (US)
**DCAe** . . Diploma of College of Aeronautics
**DCAS** . . Deputy Chief of the Air Staff
**DCG** . . Deputy Chaplain-General
**DCGS** . . Deputy Chief of the General Staff
**DCh** . . Doctor of Surgery
**DCH** . . Diploma in Child Health
**DCIGS** . . (formerly) Deputy Chief of the Imperial General Staff (now DCGS)
**DCL** . . Doctor of Civil Law
**DCLI** . . Duke of Cornwall's Light Infantry
**DCM** . . Distinguished Conduct Medal
**DCMG** . . Dame Commander of St Michael and St George
**DCnL** . . Doctor of Canon Law
**DCS** . . Deputy Chief of Staff; Doctor of Commercial Sciences
**DCSO** . . Deputy Chief Scientific Officer
**DCT** . . Doctor of Christian Theology
**DCVO** . . Dame Commander of Royal Victorian Order
**DD** . . Doctor of Divinity
**DDL** . . Deputy Director of Labour
**DDME** . . Deputy Director of Mechanical Engineering
**DDMI** . . Deputy Director of Military Intelligence
**DDMS** . . Deputy Director of Medical Services
**DDMT** . . Deputy Director of Military Training
**DDNI** . . Deputy Director of Naval Intelligence
**DDO** . . Diploma in Dental Orthopædics
**DDPR** . . Deputy Director of Public Relations
**DDPS** . . Deputy Director of Personal Services
**DDRA** . . Deputy Director Royal Artillery

**DDS** . . Doctor of Dental Surgery; Director of Dental Services
**DDSc** . . Doctor of Dental Science
**DDSD** . . Deputy Director Staff Duties
**DDST** . . Deputy Director of Supplies and Transport
**DDWE&M** . Deputy Director of Works, Electrical and Mechanical
**DE** . . Doctor of Engineering
**DEA** . . Department of Economic Affairs
**Decd** . . Deceased
**DEconSc** . . Doctor of Economic Science
**DEd** . . Doctor of Education
**Del** . . Delaware (US)
**Deleg.** . . Delegate
**DEng** . . Doctor of Engineering
**DenM** . . Docteur en Médicine
**DEOVR** . . Duke of Edinburgh's Own Volunteer Rifles
**DEP** . . Department of Employment and Productivity
**Dep.** . . Deputy
**DèsL** . . Docteur ès lettres
**DèsS** . . Docteur ès sciences
**DesRCA** . . Designer of the Royal College of Art
**DFA** . . Doctor of Fine Arts
**DFC** . . Distinguished Flying Cross
**DFM** . . Distinguished Flying Medal (Canada)
**DG** . . Dragoon Guards
**DGAMS** . . Director-General Army Medical Services
**DGMS** . . Director-General of Medical Services
**DGMT** . . Director-General of Military Training
**DGMW** . . Director-General of Military Works
**DGNPS** . . Director-General of Naval Personal Services
**DGP** . . Director-General of Personnel
**DGS** . . Diploma in Graduate Studies
**DGStJ** . . (formerly) Dame of Grace, Order of St John of Jerusalem (now DStJ)
**DHL** . . Doctor of Humane Letters; Doctor of Hebrew Literature
**DHQ** . . District Headquarters
**DIC** . . Diploma of the Imperial College
**DIG** . . Deputy Inspector-General
**DIH** . . Diploma in Industrial Health
**Dio.** . . Diocese
**DipCD** . . Diploma in Civic Design
**DipEd** . . Diploma in Education
**DipPA** . . Diploma of Practitioners in Advertising
**DipTPT** . . Diploma in Theory and Practice of Teaching
**DisTP** . . Distinction Town Planning
**Div.** . . Division; divorced
**DJAG** . . Deputy Judge Advocate General
**DJStJ** . . formerly Dame of Justice of St John of Jerusalem (now DStJ)
**DJur** . . Doctor Juris
**DL** . . Deputy-Lieutenant
**DLC** . . Diploma Loughborough College
**DLES** . . Doctor of Letters in Economic Studies
**DLI** . . Durham Light Infantry
**DLitt** or **DLit** . Doctor of Literature; Doctor of Letters
**DLO** . . Diploma in Laryngology and Otology
**DM** . . Doctor of Medicine
**DMD** . . Doctor of Medical Dentistry (Australia)
**DME** . . Director of Mechanical Engineering
**DMI** . . Director of Military Intelligence
**DMJ** . . Diploma in Medical Jurisprudence
**DMR** . . Diploma in Medical Radiology
**DMRE** . . Diploma in Medical Radiology and Electrology
**DMRT** . . Diploma in Medical Radio-Therapy
**DMS** . . Director of Medical Services
**DMus** . . Doctor of Music
**DMT** . . Director of Military Training
**DNB** . . Dictionary of National Biography
**DNE** . . Director of Naval Equipment
**DNI** . . Director of Naval Intelligence
**DO** . . Diploma in Ophthalmology
**DObstRCOG** . Diploma Royal College of Obstetricians and Gynaecologists
**DOC** . . District Officer Commanding
**DocEng** . . Doctor of Engineering
**DOL** . . Doctor of Oriental Learning
**Dom.** . . *Dominus*
**DOMS** . . Diploma in Ophthalmic Medicine and Surgery
**DOR** . . Director of Operational Requirements
**DOS** . . Director of Ordnance Services
**Dow.** . . Dowager
**DPed** . . Doctor of Pedagogy
**DPA** . . Diploma in Public Administration; Discharged Prisoners' Aid
**DPEc** . . Doctor of Political Economy
**DPH** . . Diploma in Public Health
**DPh** or **DPhil** . Doctor of Philosophy
**DPM** . . Diploma in Psychological Medicine
**DPR** . . Director of Public Relations
**DPS** . . Director of Postal Services; also (formerly) Director of Personal Services
**DQMG** . . Deputy Quartermaster-General
**Dr** . . Doctor
**DRAC** . . Director Royal Armoured Corps
**DrIng** . . Doctor of Engineering (Germany)
**DrOEcPol** . Doctor OEconomiæ Politicæ
**DSAO** . . Diplomatic Service Administration Office
**DSC** . . Distinguished Service Cross
**DSc** . . Doctor of Science
**DScA** . . Docteur en sciences agricoles
**DSD** . . Director Staff Duties
**DSIR** . . Dept. of Scientific and Industrial Research (now *see under* SRC)
**DSM** . . Distinguished Service Medal
**DSO** . . Companion of the Distinguished Service Order
**DSP** . . Director of Selection of Personnel; Docteur en sciences politiques (Montreal)
**d.s.p.** . . *decessit sine prole* (died without issue)
**DSS** . . Doctor of Sacred Scripture
**DSSc** . . Doctor of Social Science (USA)
**DST** . . Director of Supplies and Transport
**DStJ** . . Dame of Grace, Order of St John of Jerusalem; Dame of Justice, Order of St John of Jerusalem; and *see* GCStJ
**DTD** . . Dekoratie voor Trouwe Dienst (Decoration for Devoted Service)
**DTech** . . Doctor of Technology
**DTH** . . Diploma in Tropical Hygiene
**DTheol** . . Doctor of Theology
**DThPT** . . Diploma in Theory and Practice of Teaching (Durham University)
**DTM&H** . . Diploma in Tropical Medicine and Hygiene
**DUniv** . . Doctor of the University
**DUP** . . Docteur de l'Université de Paris
**DVH** . . Diploma in Veterinary Hygiene
**DVM** . . Doctor of Veterinary Medicine
**DVSM** . . Diploma in Veterinary State Medicine

# E

**E** . . . East; Earl
**e** . . . eldest
**EAP** . . East Africa Protectorate
**Ebor** . . (*Eboracensis*) of York
**EC** . . . East Central (postal district); Emergency Commission
**ECA** . . Economic Co-operation Administration
**ECAFE** . . Economic Commission for Asia and the Far East
**ECE** . . Economic Commission for Europe

**ECGD** . . Export Credits Guarantee Department
**ECSC** . . European Coal and Steel Community
**ECU** . . English Church Union
**ED** . . Efficiency Decoration; Doctor of Engineering (US)
**EdB** . . Bachelor of Education
**EDC** . . Economic Development Committee
**EdD** . . Doctor of Education
**Edin.** . . Edinburgh
**Edn** . . Edition
**Educ** . . Educated
**Educn** . . Education
**EEC** . . European Economic Community
**EEF** . . Egyptian Expeditionary Force
**EETS** . . Early English Text Society
**EFTA** . . European Free Trade Association
**e.h.** . . *ehrenhalber*; see under *h.c.*
**EI** . . East Indian; East Indies
**EICS** . . East India Company's Service
**E-in-C** . . Engineer-in-Chief
**EMS** . . Emergency Medical Service
**Ency.Brit.** . Encyclopaedia Britannica
**Eng.** . . England
**Engr** . . Engineer
**ENSA** . . Entertainments National Service Association
**ENT** . . Ear, Nose and Throat
**er** . . elder
**ER** . . Eastern Region (BR)
**ERC** . . Electronics Research Council
**ERD** . . Emergency Reserve Decoration (Army)
**ESRO** . . European Space Research Organization
**ESU** . . English-Speaking Union
**Euratom** . . European Atomic Energy Commission
**Ext.** . . Extinct

# F

**FA** . . Football Association
**FAA** . . Fellow of the Australian Academy of Science; also (formerly) Fleet Air Arm
**FAAAS** . . Fellow of the American Association for the Advancement of Science
**FACC** . . Fellow of the American College of Cardiology
**FACCA** . . Fellow of the Association of Certified and Corporate Accountants
**FACCP** . . Fellow of American College of Chest Physicians
**FACD** . . Fellow of the American College of Dentistry
**FACE** . . Fellow of the Australian College of Education
**FACI** . . (Changed to) FRACI
**FACP** . . Fellow of American College of Physicians
**FACR** . . Fellow of American College of Radiology
**FACS** . . Fellow of American College of Surgeons
**FAGS** . . Fellow American Geographical Society
**FAHA** . . Fellow, Australian Academy of the Humanities
**FAI** . . Fellow of Chartered Auctioneers' and Estate Agents' Institute
**FAIA** . . Fellow of American Institute of Architects
**FAIAA** . . Fellow of American Institute of Aeronautics and Astronautics (and *see under* FIAS)
**FAIAS** . . Fellow of Australian Institute of Agricultural Science
**FAIM** . . Fellow of the Australian Institute of Management
**FAIP** . . Fellow of Australian Institute of Physics
**FAMS** . . Fellow of the Ancient Monuments Society
**FAmSCE** . Fellow of the American Society of Civil Engineers
**FANY** . . First Aid Nursing Yeomanry
**FAO** . . Food and Agriculture Organization
**FAPHA** . . Fellow American Public Health Association
**FAPI** . . Fellow of the Australian Planning Institute
**FARELF** . Far East Land Forces
**FAS** . . Fellow of the Antiquarian Society
**FASA** . . Fellow of Australian Society of Accountants
**FASCE** . . Fellow of the American Society of Civil Engineers
**FBA** . . Fellow of the British Academy
**FBCS** . . Fellow of the British Computer Society
**FBHI** . . Fellow of the British Horological Institute
**FBI** . . Federation of British Industries (*see under* CBI, in which now merged)
**FBIM** . . Fellow of the British Institute of Management (formerly FIIA: Fellow of the Institute of Industrial Administration)
**FBOA** . . Fellow of British Optical Association
**FBOU** . . Fellow British Ornithologists Union
**FBritIRE** . (formerly) Fellow of British Institution of Radio Engineers
**FBPsS** . . Fellow of British Psychological Society
**FBS** . . Fellow Building Societies Institute
**FBSI** . . Fellow of Boot and Shoe Institution
**FBSM** . . Fellow of the Birmingham School of Music
**FCA** . . Fellow of the Institute of Chartered Accountants
**FCASI** . . (formerly FCAI) Fellow of the Canadian Aeronautics and Space Institute
**FCCS** . . Fellow of Corporation of Secretaries (formerly of Certified Secretaries)
**FCGI** . . Fellow of City and Guilds of London Institute
**FCGP** . . Fellow of the College of General Practitioners
**FCH** . . Fellow of Coopers Hill College
**FChS** . . Fellow of the Society of Chiropodists
**FCIC** . . Fellow Chemical Institute of Canada (formerly Canadian Institute of Chemistry)
**FCII** . . Fellow of the Chartered Insurance Institute
**FCIPA** . . (formerly used for) Fellow of the Chartered Institute of Patent Agents (now *see* CPA)
**FCIS** . . Fellow of the Chartered Institute of Secretaries
**FCO** . . Foreign and Commonwealth Office (departments merged Oct. 1968)
**FCP** . . Fellow College of Preceptors
**FCPath** . . Fellow of the College of Pathologists (now *see* FRCPath)
**FCP(SoAf)** . Fellow of the College of Physicians, South Africa
**FCPSO(SoAf)** (and *see* FCP(SoAf) and FCS(SoAf) Fellow of the College of Physicians and Surgeons and Obstetricians, South Africa
**FCRA** . . Fellow of the College of Radiologists of Australia
**FCS** or **FChemSoc** Fellow of the Chemical Society
**FCSP** . . Fellow of the Chartered Society of Physiotherapy
**FCS(SoAf)** . Fellow of the College of Surgeons, South Africa
**FCST** . . Fellow of the College of Speech Therapists
**FCT** . . Federal Capital Territory (now ACT)
**FCTB** . . Fellow of the College of Teachers of the Blind

**FCU** . . Fighter Control Unit
**FCWA** . . Fellow of the Institute of Cost and Works Accountants
**FDS** . . Fellow in Dental Surgery
**FDSRCS** . Fellow in Dental Surgery, Royal College of Surgeons of England
**FDSRCSE** . Fellow in Dental Surgery, Royal College of Surgeons of Edinburgh
**FEAF** . . Far East Air Force
**FEIS** . . Fellow of the Educational Institute of Scotland
**FES** . . Fellow of the Entomological Society; Fellow of the Ethnological Society
**FF** . . Field Force
**FFA** . . Fellow of Faculty of Actuaries (in Scotland)
**FFARACS** . Fellow of Faculty of Anaesthetists, Royal Australian College of Surgeons
**FFARCS** . Fellow of Faculty of Anaesthetists, Royal College of Surgeons of England
**FFARCSI** . Fellow of Faculty of Anaesthetists, Royal College of Surgeons in Ireland
**FFAS** . . Fellow of Faculty of Architects and Surveyors, London
**FFDRCSI** . Fellow of Faculty of Dentistry, Royal College of Surgeons in Ireland
**FFF** . . Free French Forces
**FFHom** . . Fellow of Faculty of Homœopathy
**FFI** . . French Forces of the Interior
**FFR** . . Fellow of Faculty of Radiologists
**FGA** . . Fellow Gemmological Association
**FGI** . . Fellow of the Institute of Certificated Grocers
**FGS** . . Fellow of Geological Society
**FGSM** . . Fellow of Guildhall School of Music
**FHA** . . Fellow of the Institute of Hospital Administrators
**FHAS** . . Fellow of Highland and Agricultural Society of Scotland
**FH-WC** . . Fellow of Heriot-Watt College (now University), Edinburgh
**FIA** . . Fellow of Institute of Actuaries
**FIAAS** . . Fellow of the Institute of Australian Agricultural Science
**FIAA&S** . . Fellow of the Incorporated Association of Architects and Surveyors
**FIAgrE** . . Fellow of the Institution of Agricultural Engineers
**FIAI** . . Fellow of the Institute of Industrial and Commercial Accountants
**FIAL** . . Fellow of the International Institute of Arts and Letters
**FIArb** . . Fellow of Institute of Arbitrators
**FIAS** . . (now *see under* FAIAA) (formerly) Fellow Institute of Aeronautical Sciences (US)
**FIB** . . Fellow of Institute of Bankers
**FIBD** . . Fellow of the Institute of British Decorators
**FIBP** . . Fellow of the Institute of British Photographers
**FIBiol** . . Fellow of Institute of Biology
**FIC** . . *See* FRIC
**FICA** . . Fellow of the Commonwealth Institute of Accountancy; Fellow of the Institute of Chartered Accountants in England and Wales (but *see* FCA)
**FICD** . . Fellow of the Institute of Civil Defence; Fellow of the Indian College of Dentists
**FICE** . . Fellow of the Institution of Civil Engineers (*see also* MICE)
**FICeram** . . Fellow of the Institute of Ceramics
**FICI** . . Fellow of the Institute of Chemistry of Ireland; Fellow of the International Colonial Institute
**FICS** . . Fellow of Institute of Chartered Shipbrokers; Fellow of the International College of Surgeons
**FIE** . . Fellow of Institute of Engineers
**FIEE** . . Fellow of the Institution of Electrical Engineers (*see also* MIEE)
**FIEEE** . . Fellow of Institute of Electrical and Electronics Engineers (NY)
**FIEI** . . Fellow of the Institution of Engineering Inspection
**FIES** . . Fellow of Illuminating Engineering Society
**FIFST** . . Fellow of Institute of Food Science and Technology
**FIGCM** . . Fellow Incorporated Guild of Church Musicians
**FIHsg** . . (formerly) Fellow of Institute of Housing (now *see under* FIHM)
**FIHE** . . Fellow of Institute of Health Education
**FIHM** . . Fellow of Institute of Housing Managers
**FIIA** . . Fellow of Institute of Industrial Administration (now FBIM: Fellow of the British Institute of Management)
**FIInst** . . Fellow of the Imperial Institute
**FIL** . . Fellow of the Institute of Linguists
**FILA** . . Fellow of the Institute of Landscape Architects
**FIM** . . Fellow of the Institution of Metallurgists
**FIMA** . . Fellow of the Institute of Mathematics and its Applications
**FIMechE** . Fellow of the Institution of Mechanical Engineers (*see also* MIMechE)
**FIMI** . . Fellow of the Institute of the Motor Industry (formerly FIMT: Fell. Inst. of Motor Trade)
**FIMinE** . . Fellow of the Institution of Mining Engineers
**FIMIT** . . Fellow of the Institute of Music Instrument Technology
**FIMTA** . . Fellow of the Institute of Municipal Treasurers and Accountants
**FIN** . . Fellow of the Institute of Navigation
**FInstBiol** . . Fellow of Institute of Biology (now *see* FIBiol)
**FInstD** . . Fellow of Institute of Directors
**FInstF** . . Fellow of Institute of Fuel
**FInstM** . . Fellow of the Institute of Meat
**FInstMSM** . Fellow of the Institute of Marketing and Sales Management (formerly FSMA)
**FInstMet** . Fellow of Institute of Metals
**FInstP** . . Fellow of Institute of Physics
**FInstPet** . . Fellow of the Institute of Petroleum
**FInstPI** . . Fellow of the Institute of Patentees (Incorporated)
**FInstPS** . . Fellow of Institute of Purchasing and Supply
**FInstW** . . Fellow of the Institute of Welding
**FIOB** . . Fellow of Institute of Builders
**FIPA** . . Fellow of the Institute of Practitioners in Advertising
**FIPHE** . . Fellow of the Institution of Public Health Engineers
**FIPM** . . Fellow of the Institute of Personnel Management
**FIPR** . . Fellow of Institute of Public Relations
**FIRA(Ind)** . Fellow of Institute of Railway Auditors and Accountants (India)
**FIRE(Aust)** . (now *see under* FIREE (Aust)); (formerly) Fellow of the Institution of Radio Engineers (Australia)

**FIREE(Aust)** . . Fellow of the Institution of Radio and Electronics Engineers (Australia) (and *see under* FIRE(Aust))
**FIRI** . . Fellow of the Institution of the Rubber Industry
**FIS** . . Fellow of the Institute of Statisticians (formerly Assoc. of Incorporated Statisticians)
**FISA** . . Fellow of the Incorporated Secretaries' Association
**FISE** . . Fellow Institution of Sanitary Engineers
**FIST** . . Fellow of the Institute of Science Technology
**FIWM** . . Fellow of the Institution of Works Managers
**FIWSc** . . Fellow of the Institute of Wood Science
**FJI** . . Fellow of Institute of Journalists
**FKC** . . Fellow of King's College (London)
**FLA** . . Fellow of Library Association
**Fla** . . Florida (US)
**FLAS** . . Fellow of the Chartered Land Agents' Society
**FLCM** . . Fellow of the London College of Music
**FLHS** . . Fellow of the London Historical Society
**FLS** . . Fellow of the Linnaean Society
**Flt** . . Flight
**FM** . . Field-Marshal
**FMA** . . Fellow of the Museums Association
**FMS** . . Federated Malay States
**FMSA** . . Fellow of the Mineralogical Society of America
**FNI** . . Fellow of National Institute of Sciences in India
**FNZIA** . . Fellow of the New Zealand Institute of Architects
**FNZIAS** . . Fellow of the New Zealand Institute of Agricultural Science
**FNZIC** . . Fellow of the New Zealand Institute of Chemistry
**FNZIE** . . Fellow of the New Zealand Institution of Engineers
**FO** . . Foreign Office (*see also* FCO); Field Officer; Flying Officer
**FOIC** . . Flag Officer in charge
**FPhS** . . Fellow of the Philosophical Society of England
**FPS** . . Fellow of the Pharmaceutical Society
**FPhysS** . . Fellow of the Physical Society
**FRACI** . . Fellow of the Royal Australian Chemical Institute (formerly FACI)
**FRACP** . . Fellow of the Royal Australasian College of Physicians
**FRACS** . . Fellow of the Royal Australasian College of Surgeons
**FRAD** . . Fellow of the Royal Academy of Dancing
**FRAeS** . . Fellow of the Royal Aeronautical Society
**FRAgSs** . . Fellow of the Royal Agricultural Societies (*i e* of England, Scotland and Wales)
**FRAHS** . . Fellow Royal Australian Historical Society
**FRAI** . . Fellow of the Royal Anthropological Institute
**FRAIA** . . Fellow of the Royal Australian Institute of Architects
**FRAIC** . . Fellow of the Royal Architectural Institute of Canada
**FRAM** . . Fellow of the Royal Academy of Music
**FRAS** . . Fellow of the Royal Astronomical Society; Fellow of the Royal Asiatic Society
**FRASB** . . Fellow of Royal Asiatic Society of Bengal
**FRASE** . . Fellow of the Royal Agricultural Society of England
**FRBS** . . Fellow of Royal Society of British Sculptors; Fellow of The Royal Botanic Society
**FRCGP** . . Fellow of the Royal College of General Practitioners
**FRCM** . . Fellow of the Royal College of Music
**FRCO** . . Fellow of the Royal College of Organists
**FRCO(CHM)** . . Fellow of the Royal College of Organists with Diploma in Choir Training
**FRCOG** . . Fellow of the Royal College of Obstetricians and Gynaecologists
**FRCP** . . Fellow of the Royal College of Physicians, London
**FRCPath.** . Fellow of the Royal College of Pathologists
**FRCP(C)** . . Fellow of the Royal College of Physicians of Canada
**FRCPE** and **FRCPEd** . . Fellow of the Royal College of Physicians of Edinburgh
**FRCPGlas** . . Fellow of the Royal College (formerly Faculty) of Physicians and Surgeons, Glasgow (and *see under* FRFPSG)
**FRCPI** . . Fellow of the Royal College of Physicians in Ireland
**FRCPS(Hon)** . . Hon. Fellow of Royal College Physicians and Surgeons (Glasgow)
**FRCS** . . Fellow of the Royal College of Surgeons of England
**FRCSE** and **FRCSEd** . . Fellow of the Royal College of Surgeons of Edinburgh
**FRCSGlas** . . Fellow of the Royal College of Surgeons of Glasgow
**FRCSI** . . Fellow of the Royal College of Surgeons in Ireland
**FRCSoc** . . Fellow of the Royal Commonwealth Society
**FRCUS** . . Fellow of the Royal College of University Surgeons (Denmark)
**FRCVS** . . Fellow of the Royal College of Veterinary Surgeons
**FREconS** . . Fellow of Royal Economic Society
**FREI** . . Fellow of the Real Estate Institute (Australia)
**FRES** . . Fellow of Royal Entomological Society of London
**FRFPSG** . . (formerly) Fellow of Royal Faculty of Physicians and Surgeons, Glasgow (now Royal College of Physicians and Surgeons, Glasgow) (and *see under* FRCPGlas)
**FRGS** . . Fellow of the Royal Geographical Society
**FRHistS** . . Fellow of Royal Historical Society
**FRHS** . . Fellow of the Royal Horticultural Society
**FRIAS** . . Fellow of the Royal Incorporation of Architects of Scotland
**FRIBA** . . Fellow of the Royal Institute of British Architects
**FRIC** . . (formerly FIC) Fellow of Royal Institute of Chemistry
**FRICS** . . Fellow of the Royal Institution of Chartered Surveyors
**FRIH** . . Fellow of Royal Institute of Horticulture (NZ)
**FRIPHH** . . Fellow of the Royal Institute of Public Health and Hygiene
**FRMCM** . . Fellow of Royal Manchester College of Music
**FRMedSoc** . . Fellow of Royal Medical Society
**FRMetS** . . Fellow of the Royal Meteorological Society
**FRMS** . . Fellow of the Royal Microscopical Society
**FRNS** . . Fellow of Royal Numismatic Society
**FRNSA** . . Fellow Royal School Naval Architecture
**FRPS** . . Fellow of the Royal Photographic Society
**FRPSL** . . Fellow of the Royal Philatelic Society, London
**FRS** . . Fellow of the Royal Society
**FRSA** . . Fellow of Royal Society of Arts
**FRSAI** . . Fellow of the Royal Society of Antiquaries of Ireland

**FRSanI** . . Fellow of Royal Sanitary Institute (*see* FRSH)
**FRSC** . . Fellow of the Royal Society of Canada
**FRSCM** . . Fellow of the Royal School of Church Music
**FRSE** . . Fellow of the Royal Society of Edinburgh
**FRSGS** . . Fellow of the Royal Scottish Geographical Society
**FRSH** . . Fellow of the Royal Society for the Promotion of Health (formerly FRSanI)
**FRSL** . . Fellow of the Royal Society of Literature
**FRSM** or **FRSocMed** . Fellow of Royal Society of Medicine
**FRSNZ** . . Fellow of Royal Society of New Zealand
**FRSSAf** . . Fellow of Royal Society of South Africa
**FRST** . . Fellow of the Royal Society of Teachers
**FRSTM&H** . Fellow of Royal Society of Tropical Medicine and Hygiene
**FRVIA** . . Fellow Royal Victorian Institute of Architects
**FRZSScot** . Fellow of the Royal Zoological Society of Scotland
**fs** . . . Graduate of Royal Air Force Staff College
**FSA** . . Fellow of the Society of Antiquaries
**FSAA** . . Fellow of the Society of Incorporated Accountants and Auditors
**FSAM** . . Fellow of the Society of Art Masters
**FSArc** . . Fellow of Society of Architects (merged with the RIBA, 1925)
**FSAScot** . Fellow of the Society of Antiquaries of Scotland
**FSASM** . . Fellow of the South Australian School of Mines
**fsc** . . . Foreign Staff College
**FSDC** . . Fellow of Society of Dyers and Colourists
**FSE** . . Fellow Society of Engineers
**FSG** . . Fellow of the Society of Genealogists
**FSGT** . . Fellow Society of Glass Technology
**FSI** . . Fellow of Royal Institution of Chartered Surveyors (changed Aug. 1947 to FRICS)
**FSIA** . . Fellow of Society of Industrial Artists and Designers
**FSMA** . . Fellow Incorporated Sales Managers' Association; *see* FInstMSM
**FSMC** . . Freeman of the Spectacle-Makers' Company
**FSS** . . Fellow of the Royal Statistical Society
**FTCD** . . Fellow of Trinity College, Dublin
**FTCL** . . Fellow of Trinity College of Music, London
**FTI** . . Fellow of the Textile Institute
**FTII** . . Fellow of the Institute of Taxation
**FTS** . . Flying Training School
**FUMIST** . . Fellow of University of Manchester Institute of Science and Technology
**FWA** . . Fellow of the World Academy of Arts and Sciences
**FZS** . . Fellow of the Zoological Society
**FZSScot** . . (Changed to) FRZSScot

# G

**Ga** . . . Georgia (US)
**GAPAN** . . Guild of Air Pilots and Air Navigators
**GATT** . . General Agreement on Tariffs and Trade
**GB** . . Great Britain
**GBA** . . Governing Bodies Association
**GBE** . . Knight or Dame Grand Cross Order of the British Empire
**GC** . . George Cross
**GCB** . . Knight Grand Cross of the Bath
**GCH** . . Knight Grand Cross of Hanover
**GCIE** . . Knight Grand Commander of the Indian Empire
**GCMG** . . Knight or Dame Grand Cross of St Michael and St George
**GCON** . . Grand Cross, Order of the Niger
**GCSI** . . Knight Grand Commander of the Star of India
**GCStJ** . . Bailiff or Dame Grand Cross of the Order of St John of Jerusalem
**GCVO** . . Knight or Dame Grand Cross of Royal Victorian Order
**GDC** . . General Dental Council
**Gdns** . . Gardens
**Gen.** . . General
**Ges.** . . Gesellschaft
**GFS** . . Girls' Friendly Society
**g g s** . . Great grandson
**GHQ** . . General Headquarters
**Gib.** . . Gibraltar
**GIMechE** . Graduate Institution of Mechanical Engineers
**GL** . . Grand Lodge
**GLC** . . Greater London Council
**Glos** . . Gloucestershire
**GM** . . George Medal; Grand Medal (Ghana)
**GMC** . . General Medical Council; Guild of Memorial Craftsmen
**GMIE** . . Grand Master of Indian Empire
**GMSI** . . Grand Master of Star of India
**GOC** . . General Officer Commanding
**GOC-in-C** . General Officer Commanding-in-Chief
**GOE** . . General Ordination Examination
**Gov.** . . Governor
**Govt** . . Government
**GP** . . General Practitioner; Grand Prix
**GPDST** . . Girls' Public Day School Trust
**GPO** . . General Post Office
**GQG** . . Grand Quartier Général (French GHQ)
**Gr.** . . Greek
**Gram. Sch.** . Grammar School
**GRSM** . . Graduate of the Royal Schools of Music
**GS** . . General Staff
**g s** . . Grandson
**GSM** . . Guildhall School of Music
**GSO** . . General Staff Officer
**GTS** . . General Theological Seminary (New York)
**GUI** . . Golfing Union of Ireland
**GWR** . . Great Western Railway

# H

**HAA** . . Heavy Anti-Aircraft
**HAC** . . Honourable Artillery Company
**Hants** . . Hampshire
**HARCVS** . Honorary Associate of the Royal College of Veterinary Surgeons
**Harv.** . . Harvard
**HBM** . . His (or Her) Britannic Majesty (Majesty's)
**hc** . . . *honoris causa*
**HCF** . . Hon. Chaplain to the Forces
**HDA** . . Hawkesbury Diploma in Agriculture (Australian)
**HDD** . . Higher Dental Diploma
**HE** . . His Excellency; His Eminence
**HEH** . . His Exalted Highness
**HEIC** . . Honourable East India Company
**HEICS** . . Honourable East India Company's Service
**Heir-pres.** . Heir-presumptive
**Herts** . . Hertfordshire
**HFARA** . . Honorary Foreign Associate of the Royal Academy
**HFRA** . . Honorary Foreign Member of the Royal Academy
**HG** . . Home Guard
**HH** . . His (or Her) Highness; His Holiness

**HHD** . . Doctor of Humanities (US)
**HIH** . . His (or Her) Imperial Highness
**HIM** . . His (or Her) Imperial Majesty
**HJ** . . Hilal-e-Jurat (Pakistan)
**HLI** . . Highland Light Infantry
**HM** . . His (or Her) Majesty, or Majesty's
**HMAS** . . His (or Her) Majesty's Australian Ship
**HMC** . . Headmasters' Conference; Hospital Management Committee
**HMHS** . . His (or Her) Majesty's Hospital Ship
**HMI** . . His (or Her) Majesty's Inspector
**HMOCS** . . His (or Her) Majesty's Overseas Civil Service
**HMS** . . His (or Her) Majesty's Ship
**HMSO** . . His (or Her) Majesty's Stationery Office
**Hon.** . . Honourable; Honorary
**HP** . . House Physician
**HPk** . . Hilal-e-Pakistan
**HQ** . . Headquarters
**(HR)** . . Home Ruler
**HRCA** . . Honorary Royal Cambrian Academician
**HRH** . . His (or Her) Royal Highness
**HRHA** . . Honorary Member of Royal Hibernian Academy
**HRI** . . Honorary Member of Royal Institute of Painters in Water Colours
**HROI** . . Honorary Member of Royal Institute of Oil Painters
**HRSA** . . Honorary Member of Royal Scottish Academy
**HRSW** . . Honorary Member of Royal Scottish Water Colour Society
**HS** . . House Surgeon
**HSH** . . His (or Her) Serene Highness
**Hum.** . . Humanity, Humanities (Latin)
**Hunts** . . Huntingdonshire
**Hy** . . Heavy

# I

**I** . . . . Island
**Ia** . . . Iowa (US)
**IA** . . . Indian Army
**IAF** . . Indian Air Force; Indian Auxiliary Force
**IAHM** . . Incorporated Association of Headmasters
**IAMC** . . Indian Army Medical Corps
**IAMTACT** . Institute of Advanced Machine Tool and Control Technology
**IAOC** . . Indian Army Ordnance Control
**IAPS** . . Incorporated Association of Preparatory Schools
**IARO** . . Indian Army Reserve of Officers
**IAS** . . Indian Administrative Service
**IATA** . . International Air Transport Association
**Ib.** or **Ibid.** . *Ibidem* (in the same place)
**IBRD** . . International Bank for Reconstruction and Development (World Bank)
**i/c** . . . In charge
**ICA** . . Institute of Contemporary Arts
**ICAA** . . Invalid Children's Aid Association
**ICAO** . . International Civil Aviation Organization
**ICE** . . Institution of Civil Engineers
**Icel.** . . Icelandic
**ICFTU** . . International Confederation of Free Trade Unions
**IChemE** . . Institution of Chemical Engineers
**ICI** . . Imperial Chemical Industries
**ICOM** . . International Council of Museums
**ICRC** . . International Committee of the Red Cross
**ICS** . . Indian Civil Service
**ICSV** . . International Council of Scientific Unions
**ICT** . . International Computers and Tabulators Ltd
**Id** . . Idaho (US)
**IDA** . . International Development Association
**idc** . . Completed a Course at, or served for a year on the Staff of, the Imperial Defence College
**IEE** . . Institution of Electrical Engineers
**IEEE** . . Institute of Electrical and Electronics Engineers (NY)
**IERE** . . Institution of Electronic and Radio Engineers (and *see under* BritIRE)
**IES** . . Indian Educational Service; Illuminating Engineering Society
**IFS** . . Irish Free State; Indian Forest Service
**IG** . . Instructor in Gunnery
**IGU** . . International Geographical Union
**ILEC** . . Inner London Education Committee
**Ill** . . Illinois (US)
**ILO** . . International Labour Office
**ILP** . . Independent Labour Party
**IMA** . . International Music Association
**IMEA** . . Incorporated Municipal Electrical Association
**IMechE** . . Institution of Mechanical Engineers
**IMinE** . . Institution of Mining Engineers
**IMF** . . International Monetary Fund
**IMMTS** . . Indian Mercantile Marine Training Ship
**Imp.** . . Imperial
**IMS** . . Indian Medical Service
**IMTA** . . Institute of Municipal Treasurers and Accountants
**IMunE** . . Institution of Municipal Engineers
**IN** . . Indian Navy
**Inc.** . . Incorporated
**Incog.** . . *Incognito* (in secret)
**Ind.** . . Independent; Indiana (US)
**Insp.** . . Inspector
**Inst.** . . Institute
**InstT** . . Institute of Transport
**Instn** . . Institution
**InstnMM** . Institution of Mining and Metallurgy
**IODE** . . Imperial Order of the Daughters of the Empire
**I of M** . . Isle of Man
**IOGT** . . International Order of Good Templars
**IOM** . . Isle of Man; Indian Order of Merit
**IOOF** . . Independent Order of Oddfellows
**IOP** . . Inst. of Painters in Oil Colours
**IoW** . . Isle of Wight
**IPCS** . . Institution of Professional Civil Servants
**IPI** . . International Press Institute
**IPM** . . Institute of Personnel Management
**IPPS** . . Institute of Physics and The Physical Society
**IPS** . . Indian Police Service; Indian Political Service
**IPU** . . Inter-Parliamentary Union
**IRA** . . Irish Republican Army
**IRC** . . Industrial Reorganization Corporation
**IREE(Aust)** . Institution of Radio and Electronics Engineers (Australia)
**IRO** . . International Refugee Organization
**Is** . . . Island(s)
**IS** . . . International Society of Sculptors, Painters and Gravers
**ISC** . . Imperial Service College, Haileybury; Indian Staff Corps
**ISE** . . Indian Service of Engineers
**ISMRC** . . Inter-Services Metallurgical Research Council
**ISO** . . Imperial Service Order
**IStructE** . . Institution of Structural Engineers
**IT** . . . Indian Territory (US)
**ITA** . . Independent Television Authority
**Ital.** or **It.** . Italian

**ITO** . . International Trade Organization
**IUCW** . . International Union for Child Welfare
**IUP** . . Association of Independent Unionist Peers
**IW** . . . Isle of Wight
**IWGC** . . Imperial War Graves Commission
**IY** . . . Imperial Yeomanry
**IZ** . . . I Zingari

## J

**JA** . . . Judge Advocate
**JAG** . . Judge Advocate General
**Jas** . . . James
**JCB** . . *Juris Canonici Bachelor* (Bachelor of Canon Law)
**JCS** . . Journal of the Chemical Society
**JCD** . . *Juris Canonici Doctor* (Doctor of Canon Law)
**JD** . . . Doctor of Jurisprudence
**JDipMA** . Joint Diploma in Management Accounting Services
**JInstE** . . Junior Institution of Engineers
**jls** . . . Journals
**JMN** . . *Johan Mangku Negara* (Malaysian Honour)
**Joh.** or **Jno.** . John
**JP** . . . Justice of the Peace
**Jr** . . . Junior
**jsc** . . . Qualified at a Junior Staff Course, or the equivalent, 1942–46
**JSLS** . . Joint Services Liaison Staff
**jssc** . . . Joint Services Staff Course
**JWS** or **jws** . Joint Warfare Staff
**JUD** . . *Juris Utriusque Doctor,* Doctor of Both Laws (Canon and Civil)
**Jun.** . . Junior
**Jun. Opt.** . . Junior Optime

## K

**Kans** . . Kansas (US)
**KAR** . . King's African Rifles
**KBE** . . Knight Commander Order of the British Empire
**KC** . . . King's Counsel
**KCB** . . Knight Commander of the Bath
**KCC** . . Commander of Order of Crown, Belgian and Congo Free State
**KCH** . . King's College Hospital; Knight Commander of Hanover
**KCIE** . . Knight Commander of the Indian Empire
**KCL** . . King's College, London
**KCMG** . . Knight Commander of St Michael and St George
**KCSG** . . Knight Commander of St Gregory
**KCSI** . . Knight Commander of the Star of India
**KCSS** . . Knight Commander of St Silvester
**KCVO** . . Knight Commander of the Royal Victorian Order
**KDG** . . King's Dragoon Guards
**KEH** . . King Edward's Horse
**KG** . . . Knight of the Order of the Garter
**KGStJ** . . formerly Knight of Grace, Order of St John of Jerusalem (now KStJ)
**KH** . . . Knight of Hanover
**KHC** . . Hon. Chaplain to the King
**KHDS** . . Hon. Dental Surgeon to the King
**KHNS** . . Hon. Nursing Sister to the King
**KHP** . . Hon. Physician to the King
**KHS** . . Hon. Surgeon to the King; Knight of the Holy Sepulchre
**K-i-H** . . Kaisar-i-Hind
**KJStJ** . . formerly Knight of Justice, Order of St John of Jerusalem (now KStJ)
**KORR** . . King's Own Royal Regiment
**KOSB** . . King's Own Scottish Borderers
**KOYLI** . . King's Own Yorkshire Light Infantry
**KP** . . . Knight of the Order of St Patrick (now held only by Dukes of Windsor and Gloucester)
**KRRC** . . King's Royal Rifle Corps
**KStJ** . . Knight of Order of St John of Jerusalem; and *see* GCStJ
**KS** . . . King's Scholar
**KSG** . . Knight of St Gregory
**KSLI** . . King's Shropshire Light Infantry
**KSS** . . Knight of St Silvester
**KT** . . . Knight of the Order of the Thistle
**Kt** or **Knt** . Knight
**Ky** . . . Kentucky (US)

## L

**(L)** . . . Liberal
**LA** . . . Los Angeles; Literate in Arts; Liverpool Academy
**La** . . . Louisiana (US)
**(Lab)** . . Labour
**LAC** . . London Athletic Club
**L-Corp.** or **Lance-Corp.** Lance-Corporal
**Lancs** . . Lancashire
**LCC** . . London County Council (now *see under* GLC)
**LCh** . . Licentiate in Surgery
**LCJ** . . Lord Chief Justice
**LCL** . . Licentiate of Canon Law
**LCP** . . Licentiate of the College of Preceptors
**LDiv** . . Licentiate in Divinity
**LDS** . . Licentiate in Dental Surgery
**LDV** . . Local Defence Volunteers
**LEA** . . Local Education Authority
**LesL** . . Licencié ès lettres
**LH** . . . Light Horse
**LHD** . . (*Literarum Humaniorum Doctor*) Doctor of Literature
**LI** . . . Light Infantry; Long Island
**LicMed** . . Licentiate in Medicine
**Lieut** . . Lieutenant
**Lincs** . . Lincolnshire
**Lit.** . . . Literature; Literary
**LitD** . . Doctor of Literature; Doctor of Letters
**Lit. Hum.** . *Literae Humaniores* (Classics)
**LittD** . . Doctor of Literature; Doctor of Letters
**LJ** . . . Lord Justice
**LLA** . . Lady Literate in Arts
**LLB** . . Bachelor of Laws
**LLCM** . . Licentiate London College of Music
**LLD** . . Doctor of Laws
**LLL** . . Licentiate in Laws
**LLM** . . Master of Laws
**LM** . . . Licentiate in Midwifery
**LMBC** . . Lady Margaret Boat Club
**LMCC** . . Licentiate of Medical Council of Canada
**LMR** . . London Midland Region (BR)
**LMS** . . London, Midland and Scottish Railway (*see* BR); London Missionary Society
**LMSSA** . . Licentiate in Medicine and Surgery, Society of Apothecaries
**LMTPI** . . Legal Member of the Town Planning Institute
**(LNat)** . . Liberal National
**LNER** . . London and North Eastern Railway (*see* BR)
**LRAM** . . Licentiate of the Royal Academy of Music
**LRCP** . . Licentiate of the Royal College
**LRAD** . . Licentiate of the Royal Academy of Dancing
**L of C** . . Lines of Communication
**LPTB** . . London Passenger Transport Board
Physicians, London
**LRCPE** . . Licentiate Royal College of Physicians, Edinburgh
**LRCS** . . Licentiate of the Royal College of Surgeons of England

**LRCSE** . . Licentiate of the Royal College of Surgeons, Edinburgh
**LRFPS(G)** . (formerly) Licentiate of the Royal Faculty of Physicians and Surgeons, Glasgow (now Royal College of Physicians and Surgeons, Glasgow)
**LRIBA** . . Licentiate Royal Institute of British Architects
**LSA** . . Licentiate of the Society of Apothecaries
**LSE** . . London School of Economics
**Lt** . . . Light (*e.g.* Light Infantry)
**Lt** or **Lieut** . Lieutenant
**LT** . . . Licentiate in Teaching
**LTB** . . London Transport Board
**LTCL** . . Licentiate of Trinity College of Music, London
**Lt-Col** . . Lieutenant-Colonel
**Lt-Gen.** . . Lieutenant-General
**LTh** . . Licentiate in Theology
**(LU)** . . Liberal Unionist
**LUOTC** . . London University Officers' Training Corps
**LXX** . . Septuagint

# M

**M** . . . Marquess; Member; Monsieur
**m** . . . married
**MA** . . Master of Arts
**MAAF** . . Mediterranean Allied Air Forces
**MACE** . . Member of the Australian College of Education
**MACI** . . Member of the American Concrete Institute
**MACS** . . Member of the American Chemical Society
**MAEE** . . Marine Aircraft Experimental Establishment
**Mag.** . . Magnetism or Magazine
**MAI** . . Master of Engineering (*Magister in Arte Ingeniaria*)
**MAIAA** . . Member of American Institute of Aeronautics and Astronautics (and *see under* MIAS)
**MAICE** . . Member of American Institute of Consulting Engineers
**MAIChE** . Member of the American Institute of Chemical Engineers
**Maj.-Gen.** . Major-General
**Man** . . Manitoba (Canada)
**MAO** . . Master of Obstetric Art
**MAOU** . . Member American Ornithologists' Union
**MAP** . . Ministry of Aircraft Production
**MArch** . . Master of Architecture
**Marq.** . . Marquess
**MASAE** . . Member American Society of Agricultural Engineering
**MASCE** . . Member American Society of Civil Engineers
**MASME** . . Member American Society of Mechanical Engineers
**Mass** . . Massachusetts (US)
**Math.** . . Mathematics; Mathematical
**MB** . . Bachelor of Medicine
**MBE** . . Member of the Order of the British Empire
**MBIM** . . Member of the British Institute of Management (formerly MIIA: Member of the Institute of Industrial Administration)
**MBOU** . . Member British Ornithologists' Union
**MBritIRE** . (now *see under* MIERE) (formerly) Member of British Institution of Radio Engineers
**MC** . . . Military Cross
**MCC** . . Marylebone Cricket Club
**MCE(Melb)** . Master of Civil Engineering (Melbourne University)
**MCh** or **MChir** Master in Surgery
**MChOrth** . Master of Orthopaedic Surgery
**MChemA** . Master in Chemical Analysis
**MCL** . . Master of Civil Law
**MCMES** . . Member of Civil and Mechanical Engineers' Society
**MCom** . . Master of Commerce
**MConsE** . . Master of Association of Consulting Engineers
**MCP** . . Master of City Planning (US)
**MCPA** . . Member of the College of Pathologists of Australia
**MCPath** . . Member of College of Pathologists
**MCPS** . . Member College of Physicians and Surgeons
**MCS** . . Madras Civil Service; Malayan Civil Service
**MD** . . Doctor of Medicine; Military District
**Md** . . Maryland (US)
**MDS** . . Master of Dental Surgery
**Me** . . Maine (US)
**ME** . . Mining Engineer; Middle East
**MEAF** . . Middle East Air Force
**MEC** . . Member of Executive Council
**MEc** . . Master of Economics
**Mech.** . . Mechanics; Mechanical
**Med.** . . Medical
**MEd** . . Master of Education
**MEF** . . Middle East Force
**MEIC** . . Member Engineering Institute of Canada
**MELF** . . Middle East Land Forces
**MEng** . . Master of Engineering
**MetR** . . Metropolitan Railway
**MEXE** . . Military Engineering Experimental Establishment
**MFGB** . . Miners' Federation of Great Britain
**MFH** . . Master of Foxhounds
**MGA** . . Maj.-Gen. i/c Administration
**MGC** . . Machine Gun Corps
**MGGS** . . Major-General, General Staff
**MGI** . . Member of the Institute of Certificated Grocers
**Mgr** . . Monsignor
**MHA** . . Member of House of Assembly
**MHR** . . Member House of Representatives
**MI** . . . Military Intelligence
**MIAeE** . . Member Institute of Aeronautical Engineers
**MIAgrE** . . Member of Institution of Agricultural Engineers
**MIAS** . . (now *see under* MAIAA) (formerly) Member Institute of Aeronautical Science (US)
**MIBF** . . Member Institute of British Foundrymen
**MIBritishE** . Member Institute of British Engineers
**MICE** . . Member of Institution of Civil Engineers (formerly the higher rank of corporate membership of the Institution, now the lower rank; *see also* FICE; change dated July 1968)
**MICEI** . . Member of Institution of Civil Engineers of Ireland
**Mich** . . Michigan (US)
**MIChemE** . Member of the Institution of Chemical Engineers
**MIEAust** . Member Institution of Engineers, Australia
**MIEE** . . Member of Institution of Electrical Engineers (formerly the higher rank of corporate membership of the Institution, now the lower rank; *see also* FIEE; change dated Dec. 1966)
**MIEEE** . . Member of Institute of Electrical and Electronics Engineers (NY)
**MIEI** . . Member of Institution of Engineering Inspection
**MIE(Ind)** . Member of Institution of Engineers, India
**MIERE** . . Member of Institution of Electronic and Radio Engineers (and *see under* MBritIRE)
**MIES** . . Member Institution of Engineers and Shipbuilders, Scotland
**MIEx** . . Member Institute of Export
**MIH** . . Member Institute of Hygiene
**MIHVE** . . Member Institution of Heating and Ventilating Engineers
**MIIA** . . Member of the Institute of In-

dustrial Administration (now *see under* MBIM)

**Mil.** . . Military
**MILocoE** . Member of Institution of Locomotive Engineers
**MIMarE** . Member of the Institute of Marine Engineers
**MIMechE** . Member of Institution of Mechanical Engineers (formerly the higher rank of corporate membership of the Institution, now the lower rank; *see also* FIMechE: change dated April 1968)
**MIMI** . . Member of Institute of Motor Industry
**MIMinE** . . Member of the Institution of Mining Engineers
**MIMM** . . Member Institution of Mining and Metallurgy
**MIMunE** . Member Institution of Municipal Engineers
**Min.** . . Ministry
**MIN** . . Member of the Institute of Navigation
**Minn** . . Minnesota (US)
**MInstCE** . Member of Institution of Civil Engineers (changed Feb. 1940 to MICE)
**MInstF** . . Member of Institute of Fuel
**MInstGasE** . Member Institution of Gas Engineers
**MInstHE** . Member of the Institution of Highway Engineers
**MInstM** . . Member of Institute of Marketing
**MInstME** . Member of Institution of Mining Engineers
**MInstMet** . Member of the Institute of Metals
**MInstPet** . Member of the Institute of Petroleum
**MInstPI** . . Member of the Institute of Patentees (Inc.)
**MInstR** . . Member of the Institute of Refrigeration
**MInstRA** . Member of the Institute of Registered Architects
**MInstT** . . Member of the Institute of Transport
**MInstW** . . Member Institute of Welding
**MInstWE** . Member of the Institution of Water Engineers (now MIWE)
**MINucE** . . Member of Institution of Nuclear Engineers
**MIOB** . . Member of the Institute of Builders
**MIPA** . . Member of the Institute of Practitioners in Advertising
**MIPlantE** . Member of the Institution of Plant Engineers
**MIPM** . . Member of the Institute of Personnel Management
**MIPR** . . Member of the Institute of Public Relations
**MIProdE** . (formerly MIPE) Member of the Institution of Production Engineers
**MIRE** . . (now *see under* MIERE) (formerly) Member of the Institution of Radio Engineers
**MIREE(Aust)** Member of the Institution of Radio and Electronics Engineers (Australia)
**MIRTE** . . Member of Institute of Road Transport Engineers
**MIS(India)** . Member of the Institution of Surveyors of India
**MISI** . . Member of Iron and Steel Institute
**Miss** . . Mississippi (US)
**MIStructE** . Member of the Institution of Structural Engineers
**MIT** . . Massachusetts Institute of Technology
**MIWE** . . Member of the Institution of Water Engineers
**MJI** . . Member of Institute of Journalists
**MJIE** . . Member of the Junior Institute of Engineers
**MJS** . . Member of the Japan Society
**ML** . . Licentiate in Medicine; Master of Laws
**MLA** . . Member of Legislative Assembly
**MLC** . . Member of Legislative Council
**MLitt** . . Master of Letters
**Mlle** . . *Mademoiselle* (Miss)
**MLO** . . Military Liaison Officer
**MM** . . Military Medal
**MME** . . Master of Mining Engineering
**MMechE** . . Master of Mechanical Engineering
**Mme** . . Madame
**MMet** . . Master of Metallurgy
**MMGI** . . Member of the Mining, Geological and Metallurgical Institute of India
**MMSA** . . Master of Midwifery Society of Apothecaries
**MN** . . Merchant Navy
**MNAS** . . Member of the National Academy of Sciences (US)
**MO** . . Medical Officer
**Mo** . . Missouri (US)
**MoD** . . Ministry of Defence
**Mods** . . Moderations (Oxford)
**MOH** . . Medical Officer(s) of Health
**MOI** . . Ministry of Information
**Mon** . . Monmouthshire
**Mont** . . Montana (US); Montgomeryshire
**MOP** . . Ministry of Power
**Most Rev.** . Most Reverend
**MoT** . . Ministry of Transport
**MP** . . Member of Parliament
**MPBW** . . Ministry of Public Building and Works
**MPP** . . Member Provincial Parliament
**MPS** . . Member of Pharmaceutical Society
**MR** . . Master of the Rolls; Municipal Reform
**MRAIC** . . Member Royal Architectural Institute of Canada
**MRAS** . . Member of Royal Asiatic Society
**MRC** . . Medical Research Council
**MRCOG** . Member of Royal College of Obstetricians and Gynaecologists.
**MRCP** . . Member of the Royal College of Physicians, London
**MRCPE** . . Member of the Royal College of Physicians, Edinburgh
**MRCPGlas** . Member of the Royal College (formerly Faculty) of Physicians and Surgeons, Glasgow
**MRCS** . . Member Royal College of Surgeons of England
**MRCSE** . . Member of the Royal College of Surgeons, Edinburgh
**MRCVS** . Member of the Royal College of Veterinary Surgeons
**MREmpS** . Member of the Royal Empire Society
**MRI** . . Member Royal Institution
**MRIA** . . Member Royal Irish Academy
**MRIAI** . . Member of the Royal Institute of the Architects of Ireland
**MRICS** . . Member of the Royal Institution of Chartered Surveyors
**MRINA** . . Member of Royal Institution of Naval Architects
**MRSanI** . . Member of Royal Sanitary Institute (*see* MRSH)
**MRSH** . . Member of the Royal Society for the Promotion of Health (formerly MRSanI)
**MRST** . . Member of Royal Society of Teachers
**MRUSI** . . Member of the Royal United Service Institution
**MS** . . Master of Surgery; Master of Science (US)
**MS, MSS** . Manuscript, Manucripts
**MSA** . . Master of Science, Agriculture (US); Mineralogical Society of America
**MSAE** . . Member of the Society of Automotive Engineers (US)
**MSAICE** . Member of South African Institution of Civil Engineers
**MSAInstMM** . Member of South African Institute of Mining and Metallurgy
**MS&R** . . Merchant Shipbuilding and Repairs

**MSAutE** . . Member of the Society of Automobile Engineers
**MSC** . . Madras Staff Corps
**MSc** . . Master of Science
**MScD** . . Master of Dental Science
**MSE** . . Master of Science in Chemical Engineering (US)
**MSH** . . Master of Stag Hounds
**MSIA** . . Member Society of Industrial Artists
**MSINZ** . . Member Surveyors' Institute New Zealand
**MSIT** . . Member Society of Instrument Technology
**MSM** . . Meritorious Service Medal; Madras Sappers and Miners
**MSR** . . Member Society of Radiographers
**Mt** . . Mountain
**MT** . . Mechanical Transport
**MTAI** . . Member of Institute of Travel Agents
**MTCA** . . Ministry of Transport and Civil Aviation
**MTPI** . . Member of Town Planning Institute
**MusB** . . Bachelor of Music
**MusD** . . Doctor of Music
**MusM** . . Master of Music
**MV** . . Merchant Vessel, Motor Vessel (naval)
**MVO** . . Member of the Royal Victorian Order
**Mx** . . Middlesex

# N

**(N)** . . Nationalist; Navigating Duties
**N** . . North
**n** . . Nephew
**NA** . . National Academician (America)
**NAACP** . . National Association for the Advancement of Colored People
**NAAFI** . . Navy, Army and Air Force Institutes
**NABC** . . National Association of Boys' Clubs
**NALGO (Nalgo)** . National and Local Government Officers' Association
**NAPT** . . National Association for the Prevention of Tuberculosis
**NASA** . . National Aeronautics and Space Administration (US)
**NATCS** . . National Air Traffic Control Services
**NATO** . . North Atlantic Treaty Organisation
**Nat.Sci.** . . Natural Sciences
**NB** . . New Brunswick
**NBA** . . North British Academy
**NBC** . . National Book Council (now National Book League); National Broadcasting Company (of America)
**NBL** . . National Book League (formerly National Book Council)
**NBPI** . . National Board for Prices and Incomes
**NC** . . North Carolina (US)
**NCB** . . National Coal Board
**NCLC** . . National Council of Labour Colleges
**NCU** . . National Cyclists' Union
**NDA** . . National Diploma in Agriculture
**NDak** . . North Dakota (US)
**ndc** . . National Defence College (Canada)
**NDD** . . National Diploma in Dairying; National Diploma in Design
**NDH** . . National Diploma in Horticulture
**NE** . . North-east
**NEAC** . . New English Art Club
**NEAF** . . Near East Air Force
**Neb** . . Nebraska (US)
**NECInst** . North-East Coast Institution of Engineers and Shipbuilders
**NEDC** . . National Economic Development Council; North East Development Council
**NEL** . . National Engineering Laboratory
**NERC** . . National Environment Research Council
**Nev** . . Nevada (US)
**New M** . . New Mexico (US)
**NFER** . . National Foundation for Educational Research
**NFS** . . National Fire Service
**NFU** . . National Farmers' Union
**NFWI** . . National Federation of Women's Institutes
**NH** . . New Hampshire (US)
**NI** . . Northern Ireland; Native Infantry
**NIAB** . . National Institute of Agricultural Botany
**NID** . . Naval Intelligence Division; National Institute for the Deaf; Northern Ireland District
**NJ** . . New Jersey (US)
**NL** . . National Liberal
**NLF** . . National Liberal Federation
**Northants** . Northamptonshire
**Notts** . . Nottinghamshire
**NP** . . Notary Public
**NPFA** . . National Playing Fields Association
**NPk** . . Nishan-e-Pakistan
**NPL** . . National Physical Laboratory
**NRA** . . National Rifle Association; National Recovery Administration
**NRD** . . National Registered Designer
**NRDC** . . National Research Development Corporation
**NRR** . . Northern Rhodesia Regiment
**NS** . . Nova Scotia; New Style in the Calendar (in Great Britain since 1752); National Society
**ns** . . Graduate of Royal Naval Staff College, Greenwich
**NSA** . . National Skating Association
**NSPCC** . . National Society for Prevention of Cruelty to Children
**N/SSF** . . Novice, Society of St Francis
**NSW** . . New South Wales
**NT** . . New Testament; Northern Territory of South Australia
**NTDA** . . National Trade Development Association
**NUGMW** . National Union of General and Municipal Workers
**NUI** . . National University of Ireland
**NUM** . . National Union of Mineworkers
**NUPE** . . National Union of Public Employees
**NUR** . . National Union of Railwaymen
**NUT** . . National Union of Teachers
**NUTG** . . National Union of Townswomen's Guilds
**NUTN** . . National Union of Trained Nurses
**NW** . . North-west
**NWFP** . . North-West Frontier Province
**NWP** . . North-Western Provinces
**NWT** . . North-Western Territories
**NY** . . New York—City or State
**NYC** . . New York City
**NZ** . . New Zealand
**NZEF** . . New Zealand Expeditionary Force
**NZIA** . . New Zealand Institute of Architects

# O

**O** . . Ohio (US)
**o** . . only
**OA** . . Officier d'Académie
**OAS** . . On Active Service
**O & E** . . Operations and Engineering (US)
**O & O** . . Oriental and Occidental (Steamship Co)
**ob.** . . died
**OBE** . . Officer Order of the British Empire

**OBI** . . Order of British India
**o c** . . only child
**OC and o/c** . Officer Commanding
**OCF** . . Officiating Chaplain to the Forces
**OCTU** . . Officer Cadet Training Unit
**ODA** . . Overseas Development Administration
**ODI** . . Overseas Development Institute
**ODM** . . Ministry of Overseas Development
**OECD** . . Organization for Economic Co-operation and Development (formerly OEEC)
**OEEC** . . Organization for European Economic Co-operation: *see* OECD
**OFM** . . Order of Friars Minor
**OFS** . . Orange Free State
**OHMS** . . On His (or Her) Majesty's Service
**OL** . . Officer of the Order of Leopold
**OM** . . Order of Merit
**OMI** . . Oblate of Mary Immaculate
**Ont** . . Ontario
**OON** . . Officer of the Order of Niger
**OP** . . *Ordinis Praedicatorum*—of the Order of Preachers (Dominican Ecclesiastical Title); Observation Post
**ORC** . . Orange River Colony
**Ore** . . Oregon (US)
**o s** . . only son
**OSA** . . Ontario Society of Artists
**OSB** . . Order of St Benedict
**OSFC** . . Franciscan (Capuchin) Order
**OSNC** . . Orient Steam Navigation Co.
**OSRD** . . Office of Scientific Research and Development
**OStJ** . . Officer of Order of St John of Jerusalem
**OT** . . Old Testament
**OTC** . . Officers' Training Corps
**OU** . . Oxford University
**OUAC** . . Oxford University Athletic Club
**OUAFC** . . Oxford University Association Football Club
**OUBC** . . Oxford University Boat Club
**OUCC** . . Oxford University Cricket Club
**OUDS** . . Oxford University Dramatic Society
**OUP** . . Oxford University Press
**OURC** . . Oxford Union Rifle Club
**OURFC** . . Oxford University Rugby Football Club
**Oxon** . . Oxfordshire; of Oxford

# P

**PA** . . Pakistan Army
**Pa** . . Pennsylvania (US)
**pac** . . passed the final examination of the Advanced Class, The Military College of Science
**PASI** . . Professional Associate Chartered Surveyors' Institution (changed August 1947 to ARICS)
**PC** . . Privy Councillor; Police Constable; Perpetual Curate; Peace Commissioner (Ireland)
**pc** . . *per centum* (by the hundred)
**PCMO** . . Principal Colonial Medical Officer
**PdD** . . Doctor of Pedagogy (US)
**PEI** . . Prince Edward Island
**PEN** . . (Name of Club: Poets, Playwrights, Editors, Essayists, Novelists)
**PEng** . . Registered Professional Engineer (Canada)
**PEP** . . Political and Economic Planning
**PEST** . . Pressure for Economic and Social Toryism
**PF** . . Procurator-Fiscal
**pfc** . . Graduate of RAF Flying College
**PH** . . Presidential Medal of Honour (Botswana)
**PhB** . . Bachelor of Philosophy
**PhC** . . Pharmaceutical Chemist
**PhD** . . Doctor of Philosophy
**Phil.** . . Philology, Philological; Philosophy, Philosophical
**PhM** . . Master of Philosophy (USA)
**Phys.** . . Physical
**PIB** . . Prices and Incomes Board (*see* NBPI)
**PICAO** . . Provisional International Civil Aviation Organization
**pinx.** . . (He) painted it
**Pl** . . Place; Plural
**PLA** . . Port of London Authority
**Plen.** . . Plenipotentiary
**PMG** . . Postmaster-General
**PMN** . . *Panglima Mangku Negara* (Malaysian Honour)
**PMO** . . Principal Medical Officer
**PMRAFNS** . Princess Mary's Royal Air Force Nursing Service
**PMS** . . President Miniature Society
**PNBS** . . *Panglima Negara Bintang Sarawak*
**PNEU** . . Parents' National Educational Union
**P&O** . . Peninsular and Oriental Steamship Co.
**P&OSNCo.** . Peninsular and Oriental Steam Navigation Co.
**PO** . . Post Office
**Pop.** . . Population
**POW** . . Prisoner of War; Prince of Wales's
**PP** . . Parish Priest; Past President
**Pp** . . Pages
**PPCLI** . . Princess Patricia's Canadian Light Infantry
**PPE** . . Philosophy, Politics and Economics (Oxford Univ.)
**PPIStructE** . Past President of the Institution of Structural Engineers
**PPRA** . . Past President of the Royal Academy
**PPRBA** . . Past President of the Royal Society of British Artists
**PPRE** . . Past President of the Royal Society of Painter-Etchers and Engravers
**PPS** . . Parliamentary Private Secretary
**PPSIA** . . Past President of the Society of Industrial Artists
**PPTPI** . . Past President Town Planning Institute
**PQ** . . Province of Quebec
**PRA** . . President of the Royal Academy
**PRCS** . . President of the Royal College of Surgeons
**PRE** . . President of the Royal Society of Painter-Etchers and Engravers
**Preb.** . . Prebendary
**Pres.** . . President
**PRHA** . . President of the Royal Hibernian Academy
**PRI** . . President of the Royal Institute of Painters in Water Colours
**PRIA** . . President of the Royal Irish Academy
**Prin.** . . Principal
**PRO** . . Public Relations Officer; Public Records Office
**Proc.** . . Proctor; Proceedings
**Prof.** . . Professor
**PROI** . . President of the Royal Institute of Oil Painters
**Pro tem.** . . *Pro tempore* (for the time being)
**Prov.** . . Provost; Provincial
**Prox.** . . *Proximo* (next)
**Prox. acc.** . *Proxime accessit* (next in order of merit to the winner, or a very close second)
**PRS** . . President of the Royal Society; Performing Right Society Ltd
**PRSA** . . President of the Royal Scottish Academy
**PRSE** . . President of the Royal Society of Edinburgh
**PRSH** . . President of the Royal Society for the Promotion of Health
**PRSW** . . President of the Royal Scottish Water Colour Society

**PRUAA** . . President of the Royal Ulster Academy of Arts
**PRWS** . . President of the Royal Society of Painters in Water Colours
**PS** . . Pastel Society
**ps** . . . passed School of Instruction (of Officers)
**psa** . . . Graduate of RAF Staff College
**psc** . . . Graduate of Staff College († indicated Graduate of Senior Wing Staff College)
**PSIA** . . President of the Society of Industrial Artists
**psm** . . Certificate of Royal Military School of Music
**PSMA** . . President of Society of Marine Artists
**PSNC** . . Pacific Steam Navigation Co.
**Pte** . . . Private (soldier)
**Pty** . . . Proprietary
**PWD** . . Public Works Department
**PWO** . . Prince of Wales's Own

# Q

**Q** . . . Queen
**QAIMNS** . Queen Alexandra's Imperial Military Nursing Service
**QALAS** . . Qualified Associate Chartered Land Agents' Society
**QARANC** . Queen Alexandra's Royal Army Nursing Corps
**QARNNS** . Queen Alexandra's Royal Naval Nursing Service
**QC** . . Queen's Counsel
**QHC** . . Queen's Honorary Chaplain
**QHDS** . . Queen's Honorary Dental Surgeon
**QHNS** . . Queen's Honorary Nursing Sister
**QHP** . . Queen's Honorary Physician
**QHS** . . Queen's Honorary Surgeon
**Qld** . . Queensland
**QMAAC** . Queen Mary's Army Auxiliary Corps
**QMC** . . Queen Mary College (London)
**QMG** . . Quartermaster-General
**Q(ops)** . . Quartering (operations)
**QPM** . . Queen's Police Medal
**Qr** . . . Quarter
**QRV** . . Qualified Valuer, Real Estate Institute of New South Wales
**QS** . . . Quarter Sessions
**qs** . . . RAF graduates of the Military or Naval Staff College (symbol omitted if subsequently qualified psa)
**QUB** . . Queen's University, Belfast
**qv** . . . *quod vide* (which see)

# R

**(R)** . . . Reserve
**RA** . . . Royal Academician; Royal Artillery
**RAAF** . . Royal Australian Air Force
**RAAMC** . Royal Australian Army Medical Corps
**RAC** . . Royal Automobile Club; Royal Agricultural College; Royal Armoured Corps
**RACGP** . . Royal Australian College of General Practitioners
**RAChD** . . Royal Army Chaplains' Dept
**RACP** . . Royal Australasian College of Physicians
**RACS** . . Royal Australasian College of Surgeons
**RADA** . . Royal Academy of Dramatic Art
**RAE** . . . Royal Australian Engineers; Royal Aircraft Establishment
**RAEC** . . Royal Army Educational Corps
**RAeS** . . Royal Aeronautical Society
**RAF** . . . Royal Air Force
**RAFO** . . Reserve of Air Force Officers (now Royal Air Force Reserve of Officers)
**RAFRO** . . Royal Air Force Reserve of Officers
**RAFVR** . . Royal Air Force Volunteer Reserve
**RAIA** . . Royal Australian Institute of Architects
**RAIC** . . Royal Architectural Institute of Canada
**RAM** . . (Member of) Royal Academy of Music
**RAMC** . . Royal Army Medical Corps
**RAN** . . Royal Australian Navy
**R&D** . . Research and Development
**RANVR** . . Royal Australian Naval Volunteer Reserve
**RAOC** . . Royal Army Ordnance Corps
**RAPC** . . Royal Army Pay Corps
**RARO** . . Regular Army Reserve of Officers
**RAS** . . . Royal Astronomical or Asiatic Society
**RASC** . . (formerly) Royal Army Service Corps (now *see under* RCT)
**RASE** . . Royal Agricultural Society of England
**RAuxAF** . Royal Auxiliary Air Force
**RAVC** . . Royal Army Veterinary Corps
**RB** . . . Rifle Brigade
**RBA** . . Member Royal Society of British Artists
**RBC** . . Royal British Colonial Society of Artists
**RBS** . . Royal Society of British Sculptors
**RBSA** . . Royal Birmingham Soc. of Artists
**RC** . . . Roman Catholic
**RCA** . . Member Royal Canadian Academy; Royal College of Art
**RCAF** . . Royal Canadian Air Force
**RCAC** . . Royal Canadian Armoured Corps
**RCamA** . . Member Royal Cambrian Academy (formerly RCA)
**RCAS** . . Royal Central Asian Society
**RCGP** . . Royal College of General Practitioners
**RCHA** . . Royal Canadian Horse Artillery
**RCHM** . . Royal Commission on Historical Monuments
**RCM** . . Royal College of Music
**RCN** . . Royal Canadian Navy
**RCNC** . . Royal Corps of Naval Constructors
**RCNR** . . Royal Canadian Navy Retd
**RCNVR** . . Royal Canadian Naval Volunteer Reserve
**RCO** . . Royal College of Organists
**RCOG** . . Royal College of Obstetricians and Gynaecologists
**RCP** . . . Royal College of Physicians, London
**RCPath** . . Royal College of Pathologists
**RCPE** and **RCPEd** . Royal College of Physicians of Edinburgh
**RCPGlas**. . Royal College of Physicians and Surgeons, Glasgow
**RCS** . . . Royal College of Surgeons of England; Royal Corps of Signals; Royal College of Science
**RCSE** and **RCSEd** . Royal College of Surgeons of Edinburgh
**RCSI** . . Royal College of Surgeons in Ireland
**RCT** . . . Royal Corps of Transport
**RCVS** . . Royal College of Veterinary Surgeons
**RD** . . . Rural Dean; Royal Navy Reserve Decoration
**Rd** . . . Road
**RDA** . . Royal Defence Academy
**RDC** . . Rural District Council
**RDF** . . Royal Dublin Fusiliers
**RDI** . . . Royal Designer for Industry (Royal Society of Arts)
**RDS** . . Royal Dublin Society
**RE** . . . Royal Engineers; Fellow of Royal Society of Painter-Etchers and Engravers
**Rear-Adm.** . Rear-Admiral
**REconS** . . Royal Economic Society
**Rect.** . . Rector
**Reg. Prof.** . Regius Professor
**Regt** . . Regiment

**REME** . . Royal Electrical and Mechanical Engineers
**RERO** . . Royal Engineers Reserve of Officers
**RES** . . Royal Empire Society (now Royal Commonwealth Society)
**Res.** . . Resigned; Reserve; Resident; Research
**Rev.** . . Reverend; Review
**RFA** . . Royal Field Artillery
**RFC** . . Royal Flying Corps (now RAF); Rugby Football Club
**RFPS(G)** . *see under* FRFPSG (formerly)
**RFU** . . Rugby Football Union
**RGA** . . Royal Garrison Artillery
**RGS** . . Royal Geographical Society
**RHA** . . Royal Hibernian Academy; Royal Horse Artillery
**RHB** . . Regional Hospitals Board
**RHG** . . Royal Horse Guards
**RHR** . . Royal Highland Regiment
**RHS** . . Royal Horticultural Society; Royal Humane Society
**RI** . . . Member Royal Institute of Painters in Water Colours; Rhode Island
**RIA** . . Royal Irish Academy
**RIAM** . . Royal Irish Academy of Music
**RIAS** . . Royal Incorporation of Architects in Scotland
**RIASC** . . Royal Indian Army Service Corps
**RIBA** . . Royal Institute of British Architects
**RIBI** . . Rotary International in Great Britain and Ireland
**RIC** . . Royal Irish Constabulary; Royal Institute of Chemistry
**RICS** . . Royal Institution of Chartered Surveyors
**RIE** . . Royal Indian Engineering (College)
**RIF** . . Royal Irish Fusiliers
**RIIA** . . Royal Institute of International Affairs
**RIM** . . Royal Indian Marine
**RIN** . . Royal Indian Navy
**RINA** . . Royal Institution of Naval Architects
**RIPH&H** . Royal Institute of Public Health and Hygiene
**RM** . . RoyalMarines;ResidentMagistrate
**RMA** . . Royal Marine Artillery; Royal Military Academy Sandhurst (now incorporating Royal Military Academy, Woolwich)
**RMC** . . Royal Military College Sandhurst (now Royal Military Academy)
**RMCS** . . Royal Military College of Science
**RMedSoc** . Royal Medical Society, Edinburgh
**RMetS** . Royal Meteorological Society
**RMFVR** . . Royal Marine Forces Volunteer Reserve
**RMLI** . . Royal Marine Light Infantry
**RMO** . . Resident Medial Officer(s)
**RMPA** . . Royal Medico-Psychological Association
**RMS** . . Royal Microscopical Society; Royal Mail Steamer; Royal Society of Miniature Painters
**RN** . . Royal Navy; Royal Naval
**RNAS** . . Royal Naval Air Services
**RNAY** . . Royal Naval Air Yard
**RNC** . . Royal Naval College
**RNEC** . . Royal Naval Engineering College
**RNIB** . . Royal National Institute for the Blind
**RNLI** . . Royal National Life-boat Institution
**RNR** . . Royal Naval Reserve
**RNT** . . Registered Nurse Tutor
**RNVR** . . Royal Naval Volunteer Reserve
**RNVSR** . . Royal Naval Volunteer Supplementary Reserve
**RNZN** . . Royal New Zealand Navy
**RNZNVR** . Royal New Zealand Naval Volunteer Reserve
**ROC** . . Royal Observer Corps
**ROF** . . Royal Ordnance Factories
**R of O** . . Reserve of Officers
**ROI** . . Royal Institute of Oil Painters
**RoSPA** . . Royal Society for the Prevention of Accidents
**(Rot.)** . . Rotunda Hospital, Dublin (after degree)
**Roy.** . . Royal
**RP** . . Member Royal Society of Portrait Painters
**RPC** . . Royal Pioneer Corps
**RPGMS** . . Royal Postgraduate Medical School (formerly PGMS)
**RPS** . . Royal Photographic Society
**RRC** . . Royal Red Cross
**RRE** . . Royal Radar Establishment (formerly TRE)
**RRS** . . Royal Research Ship
**RSA** . . Royal Scottish Academician; Royal Society of Arts
**RSAI** . . Royal Society of Antiquaries of Ireland
**RSanI** . . *See* RSH
**RSC** . . Royal Society of Canada
**RSCM** . . Royal School of Church Music
**RSCN** . . Registered Sick Children's Nurse
**RSE** . . Royal Society of Edinburgh
**RSF** . . Royal Scots Fusiliers
**RSFSR** . . Russian Socialist Federated Soviet Republic
**RSGS** . . Royal Scottish Geographical Society
**RSH** . . Royal Society for the Promotion of Health (formerly Royal Sanitary Institute)
**RSL** . . Royal Society of Literature
**RSM** . . Royal Society of Medicine; Royal School of Mines
**RSMA** . . (formerly SMA) Royal Society of Marine Artists
**RSO** . . Rural Sub-Office; Railway Sub-Office; Resident Surgical Officer.
**RSPB** . . Royal Society for Protection of Birds
**RSPCA** . . Royal Society for Prevention of Cruelty to Animals
**RSSAILA** . Returned Sailors, Soldiers and Airmen's Imperial League of Australia
**RSW** . . Member Royal Scottish Water Colour Society
**Rt Hon.** . . Right Honourable
**RTO** . . Railway Transport Officer
**RTR** . . Royal Tank Regiment
**Rt Rev.** . . Right Reverend
**RTS** . . Religious Tract Society; Royal Toxophilite Society
**RU** . . Rugby Union
**RUI** . . Royal University of Ireland
**RUSI** . . Royal United Services Institute for Defence Studies (formerly Royal United Service Institution)
**RWA (RWEA)** Member of Royal West of England Academy
**RWAFF** . Royal West African Frontier Force
**RWF** . . Royal Welch Fusiliers
**RWS** . . Member Royal Society of Painters in Water Colours
**RYA** . . Royal Yachting Association
**RYS** . . Royal Yacht Squadron

# S

**(S)** . . . (in Navy) Paymaster
**S** . . . Succeeded; South; Saint
**s** . . . Son
**SA** . . . South Australia; South Africa; Société Anonyme
**SAAF** . . South African Air Force
**SACSEA** . Supreme Allied Command, SE Asia
**SADG** . . Société des Architectes Diplômés par le Gouvernement
**Salop** . . Shropshire
**SAMC** . . South African Medical Corps
**Sarum** . . Salisbury
**SAS** . . Special Air Service
**SASO** . . Senior Air Staff Officer

**SB** . . . Bachelor of Science (US)
**SBAC** . . Society of British Aircraft Constructors
**SBStJ** . . Serving Brother, Order of St John of Jerusalem
**SC** . . . Senior Counsel (Eire); South Carolina (US)
**sc** . . . Student at the Staff College
**SCAO** . . Senior Civil Affairs Officer
**SCAPA** . . Society for Checking the Abuses of Public Advertising
**ScD** . . Doctor of Science
**SCF** . . Senior Chaplain to the Forces
**Sch.** . . School
**SCL** . . Student in Civil Law
**SCM** . . State Certified Midwife; Student Christian Movement
**Sculpt.** . . Sculptor
**SDak** . . South Dakota (US)
**SDB** . . Salesian of Don Bosco
**SDF** . . Sudan Defence Force; Social Democratic Federation
**SE** . . South-east
**SEAC** . . South-East Asia Command
**SEALF** . . South-East Asia Land Forces
**SEATO** . . South-East Asia Treaty Organization
**Sec.** . . Secretary
**SEN** . . State Enrolled Nurse
**SESO** . . Senior Equipment Staff Officer
**SG** . . Solicitor-General
**SGA** . . Member Society of Graphic Art
**Sgt** . . Sergeant
**SHAEF** . . Supreme Headquarters, Allied Expeditionary Force
**SHAPE** . . Supreme Headquarters, Allied Powers, Europe
**SIB** . . Shipbuilding Industry Board
**SITA** . . Société Internationale de Télécommunications Aéronautiques
**SJ** . . Society of Jesus (Jesuits)
**SJAB** . . St John Ambulance Brigade
**SJD** . . Doctor of Juristic Science
**SL** . . Serjeant-at-Law
**SM** . . Medal of Service (Canada); Master of Science; Officer qualified for Submarine Duties
**SMA** . . Society of Marine Artists (now *see under* RSMA)
**SME** . . School of Military Engineering
**SMIEEE** . Senior Member of Institution of Electrical and Electronic Engineering (US)
**SMIRE** . . Senior Member Institution of Radio Engineers (New York)
**SMMT** . . Society of Motor Manufacturers and Traders Ltd
**SMO** . . Senior Medical Officer; Sovereign Military Order
**SNCF** . . Société Nationale des Chemins de Fer Français
**SNP** . . Scottish Nationalist Party
**SO** . . Staff Officer
**SOAS** . . School of Oriental and African Studies
**Soc.** . . Society
**SOE** . . Special Operations Executive
**s.p.** . . *sine prole* (without issue)
**SP** . . Self-Propelled (Anti-Tank Regt)
**SPCK** . . Society for Promoting Christian Knowledge
**SPD** . . Salisbury Plain District
**SPG** . . Society for the Propagation of the Gospel (now USPG)
**SPk** . . Sitara-e-Pakistan
**SPRC** . . Society for Prevention and Relief of Cancer
**sprl** . . *société pour responsabilité limité*
**Sq.** . . Square
**SR** . . Special Reserve; Southern Railway (*see* BR); Southern Region (BR)
**SRC** . . Science Research Council (formerly DSIR)
**SRN** . . State Registered Nurse
**SRO** . . Supplementary Reserve of Officers
**SRP** . . State Registered Physiotherapist
**SS** . . Saints; Straits Settlements; Steamship
**SSA** . . Society of Scottish Artists
**SS&AFA** . Soldiers', Sailors', and Airmen's Families Association
**SSC** . . Solicitor before Supreme Court (Scotland); Sculptors Society of Canada
**SSJE** . . Society of St John the Evangelist
**SSM** . . Society of the Sacred Mission
**SSO** . . Senior Supply Officer
**SSRC** . . Social Science Research Council
**SSStJ** . . Serving Sister, Order of St John of Jerusalem
**St** . . Street; Saint
**STB** . . *Sacrae Theologiae Bachelor* (Bachelor of Sacred Theology)
**STC** . . Senior Training Corps
**STD** . . *Sacrae Theologiae Doctor* (Doctor of Sacred Theology)
**STh** . . Scholar in Theology
**Stip.** . . Stipend; Stipendiary
**STL** . . *Sacrae Theologiae Lector* (Reader or a Professor of Sacred Theology)
**STM** . . *Sacrae Theologiae Magister*
**STP** . . *Sacrae Theologiae Professor* (Professor of Divinity, old form of DD)
**STRIVE** . Society for Preservation of Rural Industries and Village Enterprises
**STSO** . . Senior Technical Staff Officer
**Supp. Res.** . Supplementary Reserve (of Officers)
**Supt** . . Superintendent
**Surg.** . . Surgeon
**Surv.** . . Surviving
**SW** . . South-west
**Syd.** . . Sydney

# T

**T** . . . Telephone; Territorial
**TA** . . Telegraphic Address; Territorial Army
**TAA** . . Territorial Army Association
**TAF** . . Tactical Air Force
**T&AFA** . . Territorial and Auxiliary Forces Association
**TANS** . . Territorial Army Nursing Service
**TANU** . . Tanganyika African National Union
**TARO** . . Territorial Army Reserve of Officers
**T&AVR** . . Territorial and Army Volunteer Reserve
**TA&VRA** . Territorial Auxiliary and Volunteer Reserve Association
**TC** . . Order of the Trinity Cross (Trinidad and Tobago)
**TCD** . . Trinity College, Dublin (University of Dublin, Trinity College)
**TCF** . . Temporary Chaplain to the Forces
**TD** . . Territorial Efficiency Decoration; Efficiency Decoration (T&AVR) (since April 1967); (Teachta Dala) Member of the Dail, Eire
**Temp.** . . Temperature; Temporary
**Tenn** . . Tennessee (US)
**Tex** . . Texas (US)
**TF** . . Territorial Forces
**TFR** . . Territorial Force Reserve
**TGO** . . Timber Growers Organisation
**TGWU** . . Transport and General Workers' Union
**ThL** . . Theological Licentiate
**TP** . . Transvaal Province
**TPI** . . Town Planning Institute
**Trans.** . . Translation, Translated
**Transf.** . . Transferred
**TRC** . . Thames Rowing Club
**TRE** . . (now *see under* RRE) (formerly Telecommunications Research Establishment
**TRH** . . Their Royal Highnesses
**Trin.** . . Trinity
**tsc** . . passed a Territorial Army Course in Staff Duties
**TSD** . . Tertiary of St Dominick
**TUC** . . Trades Union Congress
**TV** . . Television
**TYC** . . Thames Yacht Club

# U

| | |
|---|---|
| **(U)** | Unionist |
| **u** | Uncle |
| **UAR** | United Arab Republic |
| **UC** | University College |
| **UCH** | University College Hospital (London) |
| **UCL** | University College, London |
| **UCW** | University College of Wales |
| **UDC** | Urban District Council |
| **UDF** | Union Defence Force |
| **UF** | United Free Church |
| **UGC** | University Grants Committee |
| **UJD** | *Utriusque Juris Doctor,* Doctor of both Laws (Doctor of Canon and Civil Law) |
| **UK** | United Kingdom |
| **UKAC** | United Kingdom Automation Council |
| **UKAEA** | United Kingdom Atomic Energy Authority |
| **UN** | United Nations |
| **UNA** | United Nations Association |
| **UNCIO** | United Nations Conference on International Organisation |
| **UNCSAT** | United Nations Conference on the Application of Science and Technology |
| **UNCTAD (Unctad)** | United Nations Commission for Trade and Development |
| **UNDP** | United Nations Development Programme |
| **UNESCO (Unesco)** | United Nations Educational, Scientific and Cultural Organisation |
| **UNICEF (Unicef)** | United Nations Children's Fund (formerly United Nations International Children's Emergency Fund) |
| **Univ.** | University |
| **UNRRA** | United Nations Relief and Rehabilitation Administration |
| **UNRWA** | United Nations Relief Works Agency |
| **UNSCOB** | United Nations Special Commission on the Balkans |
| **UP** | United Provinces; Uttar Pradesh; United Presbyterian |
| **US** | United States |
| **USA** | United States of America |
| **USAAF** | United States Army Air Forces |
| **USAF** | United States Air Force |
| **USAR** | United States Army Reserve |
| **USDAW** | Union of Shop Distributive and Allied Workers |
| **USMA** | United States Military Academy |
| **USN** | United States Navy |
| **USNR** | United States Naval Reserve |
| **USPG** | United Society for the Propagation of the Gospel (formerly SPG) |
| **USS** | United States Ship |
| **USSR** | Union of Soviet Socialist Republics |
| **UTC** | University Training Corps |
| **(UU)** | Ulster Unionist |

# V

| | |
|---|---|
| **V** | Five (Roman numerals); Version; Vicar; Viscount; *Vice* |
| **v** | *Versus* (against) |
| **v or vid.** | *Vide* (see) |
| **V&A** | Victoria and Albert |
| **Va** | Virginia (US) |
| **VAD** | Voluntary Aid Detachment |
| **VC** | Victoria Cross |
| **VCAS** | Vice-Chief of the Air Staff |
| **VD** | Royal Naval Volunteer Reserve Officers' Decoration (now VRD); Volunteer Officers' Decoration; Victorian Decoration |
| **VDC** | Volunteer Defence Corps |
| **Ven.** | Venerable (of an Archdeacon) |
| **Very Rev.** | Very Reverend (of a Dean) |
| **Vet.** | Veterinary |
| **VG** | Vicar-General |
| **VHS** | Hon Surgeon to Viceroy of India |
| **Vice-Adm.** | Vice-Admiral |
| **Visc.** | Viscount |
| **VM** | Victory Medal |
| **VMH** | Victoria Medal of Honour (Royal Horticultural Society) |
| **Vol.** | Volume; Volunteers |
| **VP** | Vice-President |
| **VQMG** | Vice-Quartermaster-General |
| **VR** | *Victoria Regina* (Queen Victoria) |
| **VRD** | Royal Naval Volunteer Reserve Officers' Decoration |
| **VSO** | Voluntary Service Overseas |
| **Vt** | Vermont (US) |

# W

| | |
|---|---|
| **W** | West |
| **WA** | Western Australia |
| **WAAF** | Women's Auxiliary Air Force (now WRAF) |
| **Wash** | Washington State (US) |
| **W/Cdr** | Wing Commander |
| **WEA** | Workers' Educational Association; Royal West of England Academy |
| **WEU** | Western European Union |
| **WFTU** | World Federation of Trade Unions |
| **WHO** | World Health Organization |
| **WhSch** | Whitworth Scholar |
| **WI** | West Indies (formerly BWI: British West Indies) |
| **Wilts** | Wiltshire |
| **Wis** | Wisconsin (US) |
| **WLA** | Women's Land Army |
| **WLF** | Women's Liberal Federation |
| **Wm** | William |
| **WO** | War Office |
| **Worcs** | Worcestershire |
| **WOSB** | War Office Selection Board |
| **WR** | West Riding; Western Region (BR) |
| **WRAC** | Women's Royal Army Corps |
| **WRAF** | Women's Royal Air Force (formerly WAAF) |
| **WRNS** | Women's Royal Naval Service |
| **WRVS** | Women's Royal Voluntary Service (previously WVS) |
| **WS** | Writer to the Signet |
| **WSPU** | Women's Social and Political Union |
| **WVa** | West Virginia (US) |
| **WVS** | Women's Voluntary Services (*now see* WRVS) |
| **Wyo** | Wyoming (US) |

# X

| | |
|---|---|
| **X** | Ten (Roman numerals) |

# Y

| | |
|---|---|
| **y** | youngest |
| **Yeo.** | Yeomanry |
| **YHA** | Youth Hostels Association |
| **YMCA** | Young Men's Christian Association |
| **Yorks** | Yorkshire |
| **yr** | younger |
| **yrs** | years |
| **YWCA** | Young Women's Christian Association |

# OBITUARY

Deaths notified from January to mid-November 1970

**Agnon,** (Shmuel) Yosef Halevi, 17 Feb. 1970.
**Ainsworth,** Harry [*Deceased.*
**Alexander,** Rear-Adm. Charles Otway, 13 April 1970.
**Alexander,** Henry Clay, 14 Dec. 1969.
**Allen,** Sir George Vance, 2 Oct. 1970.
**Allen,** William Gilbert, 27 Feb. 1970.
**Anderson,** Ian, OBE, MC, 11 May 1970.
**Annaly,** 4th Baron; Luke Henry White, 4 May 1970.
**Appleton,** Brig. Gilbert Leonard, CB, OBE, 23 Oct. 1970.
**Archer,** Norman Ernest, CMG, OBE, 15 Feb. 1970.
**Archibald,** John Gordon, 8 June 1970.
**Arnold,** Ralph Crispian Marshall, 23 Sept. 1970.
**Ashley-Brown,** Ven. William, 2 Sept. 1970.
**Atcherley,** Air Marshal Sir Richard Llewellyn Roger, KBE, CB, AFC, 18 April 1970.
**Atukorala,** Nandasara Wijetilaka, CMG, CBE [*Deceased.*
**Awbery,** Stanley Stephen [*Deceased.*

**Baker,** Bryant, 29 March 1970.
**Baker,** Prof. Henry Wright [*Deceased.*
**Balchin,** Brig. Nigel Marlin, 17 May 1970.
**Bannatyne,** Maj.-Gen. Neil Charles, CB, CIE, 22 Aug. 1970.
**Bannister,** Frederick Allan, 4 Oct. 1970.
**Barbirolli,** Sir John (Giovanni Battista), CH, 29 July 1970.
**Barnett,** Prof. Cyril Harry, 23 Oct. 1970.
**Barnett,** Sir Geoffrey Morris, 18 May 1970.
**Barry,** Sir (Claude) Francis, 3rd Bt, 25 Oct. 1970.
**Bateman,** Henry Mayo, 11 Feb. 1970.
**Bathurst,** Hon. William Ralph Seymour, TD, 10 Sept. 1970.
**Beazley,** Sir John Davidson, CH, 6 May 1970.
**Beckett,** James, CIE, 16 Jan. 1970.
**Beer,** Harry, CB, 3 Jan. 1970.
**Belcher,** Sir Charles Frederic, OBE, 7 Feb. 1970.
**Bell,** Dr Arthur Doyne Courtenay, 16 Sept. 1970.
**Bell,** Sir Francis Gordon, KBE, MC, 28 Feb. 1970.
**Bell,** Sir Hugh Francis, 4th Bt, 6 Aug. 1970.
**Bennett,** Captain (Eugene) Paul, VC, MC, 4 April 1970.
**Bentinck,** Baron, Adolph Willem Carel, 7 March 1970.
**Bentley,** Rt Rev. David Williams Bentley, CBE, 14 Nov. 1970.
**Bertram,** Lt-Col William Robert, CMG, DSO, 8 Aug. 1970.
**Besicovitch,** Prof. Abram Samoilovitch, FRS, 2 Nov. 1970.
**Bevan,** Ven. Hugh Henry Molesworth, 15 Jan. 1970.
**Biddle,** Sir Reginald Poulton, CBE, TD, 11 Sept. 1970.
**Bigland,** Eileen Anne Carstairs, (Mrs E. W. Bigland), 11 April 1970.
**Binns,** Kenneth, CBE [*Deceased.*
**Black,** Hon. George, PC (Can.), QC (Can.) [*Deceased.*
**Blackburn,** Sir Arthur Dickinson, KCMG, CBE, 5 March 1970.
**Blond,** Neville, CMG, OBE, 4 Aug. 1970.
**Bonnetard,** Sir (Nicholas Patrick) France [*Deceased.*
**Boon,** Sir Geoffrey Pearl, CBE, QC (WI), 26 April 1970.
**Booth,** Sir Charles Sylvester, CBE, 27 June 1970.
**Born,** Prof. Max, FRS, 5 Jan. 1970.
**Bottomley,** Air Chief Marshal Sir Norman Howard, KCB, CIE, DSO, AFC, 13 Aug. 1970.
**Bourdillon,** Francis Bernard, CBE, 9 June 1970.
**Bowstead,** John, CSI, CIE, MC [*Deceased.*
**Boyd,** Prof. James, 30 Oct. 1970.
**Braddell,** (Thomas Arthur) Darcy, 20 Feb. 1970.
**Braddock,** Mrs Elizabeth Margaret, 13 Nov. 1970.
**Brambell,** Francis William Rogers, CBE, FRS, 6 June 1970.
**Brayne,** Albert Frederic Lucas, CIE, 18 June 1970.
**Brittain,** Vera, 29 March 1970.
**Brock,** Captain Donald Carey, CBE, RN, 29 July 1970.
**Brown,** Rear-Adm. Sydney, CB, 14 Aug. 1970.
**Brown,** Tom, (Thomas James), 10 Nov. 1970.
**Brown,** Very Rev. William James, 13 May 1970.
**Browne,** Prof. George Stephenson, MC, 23 May 1970.
**Bruce Lockhart,** Sir Robert Hamilton, KCMG, 27 Feb. 1970.
**Brüning,** Prof. Heinrich, 27 March 1970.
**Buesst,** Captain Aylmer, 25 Jan. 1970.
**Bull,** Archibald William Major, CB, 11 Feb. 1970.
**Bulleid,** Oliver Vaughan Snell, CBE, 25 April 1970.
**Burden,** 1st Baron; Thomas William Burden, CBE, 27 May 1970.
**Burn,** Col Harold Septimus, CB, MC, TD, 25 Oct. 1970.
**Burne,** Ven. Richard Vernon Higgins, 9 Oct. 1970.
**Burns,** William, CIE, 8 April 1970.
**Burrows,** Lionel Burton, CBE, 13 Oct. 1970.
**Busk,** Air Cdre Clifford Westly, CB, MC, AFC, 23 Oct. 1970.
**Butler,** Maj.-Gen. Hon. Theobald Patrick Probyn, DSO, 18 Oct. 1970.
**Butters,** Sir John Henry, CMG, MBE, VD [*Deceased.*
**Buxton,** Major Anthony, DSO, 9 Aug. 1970.
**Buxton,** Captain Roden Henry Victor, CBE, RN, 10 Nov. 1970.

**Cable,** Eric Grant, CMG, 7 May 1970.
**Cambon,** Roger, Hon. KCVO, 18 July 1970.
**Cameron,** John Gordon Patrick, CIE, 16 July 1970.
**Campbell,** Sir Louis Hamilton, 14th Bt, 13 Oct. 1970.
**Campbell,** His Honour (William) Lawson, 26 Sept. 1970.
**Capps,** Frederick Cecil Wray, 12 June 1970.
**Carmichael,** George Chapman, MC, QC (Scot.), 10 Sept. 1970.
**Carr,** Henry Marvell, RA, 16 March 1970.
**Carr,** His Honour Norman Alexander, 29 Sept. 1970.
**Cawdor,** 5th Earl; John Duncan Vaughan Campbell, TD, 9 Jan. 1970.
**Cawthorne,** Sir Terence Edward, 22 Jan. 1970.
**Central Africa,** Archbishop of; Most Rev. Francis Oliver Green-Wilkinson, CBE, MC, 26 Aug. 1970.
**Cerny,** Prof. Jaroslav, FBA, 29 May 1970.
**Chadwick,** Brig. Cecil Arthur Harrop, CBE, 3 Sept. 1970.
**Chamberlain,** Francis Walter, CBE, 2 April 1970.
**Chambers,** Prof. Jonathan David, 12 April 1970.
**Chance,** P. V., CIE, 12 April 1970.
**Chapman,** Captain Alex Colin, CBE, RN, 4 Sept. 1970.
**Chapman,** Sydney, FRS, 16 June 1970.
**Chaworth-Musters,** Col John Nevile, DSO, OBE, TD, 12 March 1970.
**Chelmsford,** 2nd Viscount; Andrew Charles Gerald Thesiger, 27 Sept. 1970.
**Cheng,** Tien-Hsi, (F. T. Cheng), 31 Jan. 1970.
**Chew,** Frederic Robert Gansel, CVO, 11 Sept. 1970.
**Churchill,** Rev. Robert Reginald, CBE, 27 Jan. 1970.
**Churchman,** Air Cdre Allan Robert, CB, DFC, 13 Jan. 1970.

**Clare**, Mary, (Mrs L. Mawhood), 29 Aug. 1970.
**Clarke**, Col Sir Ralph Stephenson, KBE, TD, DL, 9 May 1970.
**Cleminson**, Henry Millican, 30 March 1970.
**Clifford**, Col Esmond Humphrey Miller, CBE, MC, 3 Sept. 1970.
**Clunes**, Alec Sheriff de Moro, 13 March 1970.
**Clutton**, Sir George Lisle, KCMG, 9 Sept. 1970.
**Cockburn**, Captain William, DSO, MC, 4 Feb. 1970.
**Collingwood**, Sir Edward Foyle, CBE, FRS, 25 Oct. 1970.
**Collins**, Seymour John, 28 Jan. 1970.
**Columbia, British**, Bishop of; Rt Rev. John Ogle Anderson, MC, Nov. 1969.
**Conan Doyle**, Adrian Malcolm, 3 June 1970.
**Cooch Behar**, Maharaja of; Lt-Col HH Sir Jagaddipendra Narayan Bhup Bahadur, KCIE, 11 April 1970.
**Cook**, Lt-Col Sir Thomas Russell Albert Mason, 12 Aug. 1970.
**Cooke**, Roger Gresham, CBE, MP, 22 Feb. 1970.
**Cooper**, Sir William Herbert, 3rd Bt, 8 June 1970.
**Corbin**, (André) Charles, Hon. GCVO, Hon. GCB, 25 Sept. 1970.
**Costin**, William Conrad, OBE, MC, 6 Oct. 1970.
**Cox**, Alfred Innes, CIE, OBE, 7 Aug. 1970.
**Craig**, John Manson, VC, 17 Feb. 1970.
**Craig**, Thomas Joseph Alexander, CIE, 7 March 1970.
**Craufurd**, Sir James Gregan, 8th Bt, 7 April 1970.
**Creagh Coen**, Sir Terence Bernard, KBE, CIE, 27 Sept. 1970.
**Cremer**, Herbert William, CBE, 11 Feb. 1970.
**Cressy-Marcks**, Violet Olivia, 10 Sept. 1970.
**Crick**, Very Rev. Thomas, CB, CBE, MVO, 13 Nov. 1970.
**Cross**, Rev. Robert Nicol, 20 Sept. 1970.
**Cuff**, Maj.-Gen. Brian, CB, CBE, 12 March 1970.
**Curtis**, Amy, CBE, 29 July 1970.
**Cusack-Smith**, Sir (William Robert) Dermot (Joshua), 6th Bt, 10 April 1970 (*ext*).

**Daladier**, Edouard, 10 Oct. 1970.
**Davenport**, Hon. Sir George Arthur, KBE, CMG, 17 Sept. 1970.
**Davidson**, Charles Rundle, FRS, 18 June 1970.
**Davies**, Evan Thomas, 25 Dec. 1969.
**Davies**, Richard Humphrey, CB, 16 June 1970.
**Dawson**, Prof. Christopher, FBA, 25 May 1970.
**Day**, Vice-Adm. Sir Archibald, KBE, CB, DSO, 17 July 1970.
**Dean**, Hon. Sir Arthur, 25 Sept. 1970.
**Deane**, Lt-Col Robert, CBE [*Deceased.*
**de Gaulle**, Général Charles André Joseph Marie, 9 Nov. 1970.
**Delhi**, Bishop of; Rt Rev. Philip Parmar, 9 May 1970.
**Denham**, Humphrey John, CBE, 20 May 1970.
**de Silva**, Sir Albert Ernest [*Deceased.*
**Dick**, Bt Col Alan Macdonald, CBE, 20 March 1970.
**Dick**, Prof. John, 3 Nov. 1970.
**Dobbs**, Cecil Moore, CMG, OBE [*Deceased.*
**Dobell**, Sir William, OBE, 14 May 1970.
**Donachy**, Frank, OBE, 1 Feb. 1970.
**Donnelly**, Harry Hill, CB [*Deceased.*
**Dorté**, Philip Hoghton, OBE, 26 July 1970.
**Dos Passos**, John, 28 Sept. 1970.
**Dowding**, 1st Baron; Air Chief Marshal Hugh Caswall Tremenheere Dowding, GCB, GCVO, CMG, 15 Feb. 1970.
**Drucquer**, His Honour Maurice Nathaniel, 21 July 1970.
**Drummond**, Sir James Hamlyn Williams Williams-, 5th Bt, 7 Jan. 1970.
**Dryden**, Sir Noel Percy Hugh, 7th and 10th Bt, 23 March 1970.
**Dudgeon**, Major Cecil Randolph, CBE, 4 Nov. 1970.
**Duff**, Sir James Fitzjames, 24 April 1970.
**Duguid-McCombie**, Col William McCombie, DSO, 24 May 1970.
**Dunbar**, Robert, CMG, MC, 1 Feb. 1970.
**Dunne**, Sir Laurence Rivers, MC, 30 June 1970.
**Dunstan**, Victor Joseph, 15 Feb. 1970.
**Durham**, 5th Earl of; John Frederick Lambton, 4 Feb. 1970.

**Eager**, Sir Clifden Henry Andrews, KBE, QC [*Deceased.*
**Eardley-Wilmot**, Sir John, 4th Bt, 9 Feb. 1970.
**Eardley-Wilmot**, May, 3 June 1970.
**Edwards**, Sir Ifan ab Owen, 23 Jan. 1970.
**Eisenschitz**, Prof. Robert Karl [*Deceased.*
**Elderton**, Sir Thomas Howard, KCIE, 14 Feb. 1970.
**Elliott**, (Colin) Fraser, CMG, 19 Dec. 1969.
**Ellis**, Major Lionel Frederic, CVO, CBE, DSO, MC, 19 Oct. 1970.
**Ellis**, Thomas Iorwerth, OBE, 20 April 1970.
**Elliston**, Julian Clement Peter, CB, TD, 4 March 1970.
**Emlyn-Jones**, His Honour Hugh, 9 June 1970.
**England**, Sir Russell, CBE, 13 Jan. 1970.
**Enock**, Charles Reginald, 7 April 1970.
**Evans**, Sir Evelyn Ward, 3rd Bt, 1 Feb. 1970 (*ext*).
**Evans**, Sir Lincoln, CBE, 3 Aug. 1970.
**Evans**, Stanley Norman, 25 June 1970.
**Evans-Jones**, Rev. Sir Cynan, CBE, 26 Jan. 1970.

**Farren**, Sir William Scott, CB, MBE, FRS, 3 July 1970.
**Felton**, Mrs Monica, 3 March 1970.
**Finney**, Victor Harold, 10 April 1970.
**Fischer**, Louis, 15 Jan. 1970.
**Fisher**, James Maxwell McConnell, 25 Sept. 1970.
**Foley**, Guy Francis, CMG, OBE, MC, 13 Oct. 1970.
**Folley**, Prof. Sydney John, FRS, 29 June 1970.
**Forrester-Brown**, Maud Frances, 12 Jan. 1970.
**Forster**, Edward Morgan, OM, CH, 7 June 1970.
**Forsyth**, James Alexander, QC (Scot.) [*Deceased.*
**Fosdick**, Raymond Blaine [*Deceased.*
**Foster**, Thomas Henry, 5 Feb. 1970.
**Fox**, William Sherwood [*Deceased.*
**Fox-Williams**, Captain Jack, MC, 27 June 1970.
**Fraenkel**, Prof. Eduard, 5 Feb. 1970.
**Francis-Williams**, Baron (Life Peer); Edward Francis Williams, CBE, 5 June 1970.
**Fraser**, Rear-Adm. Hon. George, DSO, 13 June 1970.
**Freeth**, Francis Arthur, OBE, FRS, 15 July 1970.
**French**, Lt-Col Hon. (Edward) Gerald, DSO, 17 Sept. 1970.
**Fuller**, Maj.-Gen. Algernon Clement, CBE, 6 Aug. 1970.
**Fullerton**, Prof. Harold Williams, 14 July 1970.

**Gadsby**, John, CBE, 14 June 1970.
**Gamble**, Brig. Geoffrey Massey, CMG, OBE, 12 Jan. 1970.
**Gardner**, Erle Stanley, 11 March 1970.
**Gardner**, James Clark Molesworth, CIE, 7 March 1970.
**Gascoigne**, Sir Alvary Douglas Frederick, GBE, KCMG, 18 April 1970.
**Gawsworth**, John, (Terence Ian Fytton Armstrong), 23 Sept. 1970.
**Gedye**, George Eric Rowe, MBE, 21 March 1970.
**Genée-Isitt**, Dame Adeline, DBE, 23 April 1970.
**Gerard**, Amelia Louise, 5 Nov. 1970.
**Gerhard**, Roberto Juan René, CBE, 5 Jan. 1970.
**Gibraltar**, Bishop of; Rt Rev. Stanley Albert Hallam Eley, 7 April 1970.
**Gibson**, John Gibson, CB, 13 June 1970.
**Gibson**, Rt Rev. Percival William, CBE, 3 April 1970.
**Giles**, Lt-Col Sir Oswald Bissill, 4 Aug. 1970.
**Gilliat**, Algernon Earle, CIE, 25 May 1970.
**Ginsberg**, Prof. Morris, FBA, 31 Aug. 1970.
**Glenday**, Sir Vincent Gonçalves, KCMG, OBE, 30 April 1970.
**Glenn**, Air Vice-Marshal Robert William Lowry, CB, CBE, 7 April 1970.
**Goldsworthy**, Captain Ivan Ernest Goodman, RD, 10 June 1970.
**Goodchild**, Norman Walter, CBE, 4 May 1970.
**Goosman**, Hon. Sir (William) Stanley [*Deceased.*
**Gourlay**, Brig. Kenneth Ian, DSO, OBE, MC, 14 March 1970.
**Grafton**, 10th Duke of; Captain Charles Alfred Euston FitzRoy, 11 Nov. 1970.
**Graham**, Henry Archibald Roger, 25 Feb. 1970.
**Gray**, Sir John Milner, 15 Jan. 1970.
**Griffin**, Sir Arthur Cecil, KCIE, KBE, 28 Jan. 1970.
**Griffiths**, Albert Edward, 13 Feb. 1970.
**Guggenheim**, Prof. Edward Armand, FRS, 9 Aug. 1970.
**Guise**, Sir Anselm William Edward, 6th Bt, 12 Sept. 1970.
**Gunther**, John, 29 May 1970.
**Gurney-Dixon**, Sir Samuel, 30 April 1970.
**Guthrie**, Hon. Lord; Henry Wallace Guthrie, 11 March 1970.

**Haigh,** Frank Fraser, CIE, 27 Jan. 1970.
**Hall,** Captain Geoffrey Fowler, CIE, MC, 8 Aug. 1970.
**Halls,** Arthur Norman, (Michael), MBE, TD, 3 April 1970.
**Hallstrom,** Sir Edward John Lees, 27 Feb. 1970.
**Halsey,** Captain Sir Thomas Edgar, 3rd Bt, DSO, 30 Aug. 1970.
**Hanafin,** Lt-Col John Berchmans, CIE, 25 Aug. 1970.
**Hannay,** Rt Rev. Thomas, DD, 31 Jan. 1970.
**Hardy,** Rt Rev. Alexander Ogilvy, DD, 14 Sept. 1970.
**Hare,** Maj.-Gen. James Francis, CB, DSO, 28 Aug. 1970.
**Harman,** Rt Hon. Sir Charles Eustace, PC, 14 Nov. 1970.
**Harris,** Brig. Lawrence Anstie, CBE, DSO, MC, 19 Jan. 1970.
**Hart,** Cecil Augustus, CMG, TD, 27 July 1970.
**Hart,** Sir Robert, 3rd Bt, 15 Oct. 1970 (*ext*).
**Harting,** Prof. Pieter, 11 Aug. 1970.
**Hartley,** Lt-Col Donald Reginald Cavendish, CIE, CBE, DSO, ED, 25 March 1970.
**Hartwell,** Maj.-Gen. John Redmond, CB, DSO, 19 Sept. 1970.
**Hatchard,** Caroline, (Caroline Langford), 7 Jan. 1970.
**Hawksley,** Dorothy Webster, 1 July 1970.
**Haydon,** Maj.-Gen. Joseph Charles, CB, DSO, OBE, 8 Nov. 1970.
**Hayward,** Lt-Col Reginald Frederick Johnson, VC, MC, 17 Jan. 1970.
**Healy,** Cahir, 8 Feb. 1970.
**Heathcote,** Robert Evelyn Manners, DSO, 17 July 1970.
**Henry,** Prof. Robert Francis Jack, 28 Aug. 1970.
**Henson,** John, 12 Dec. 1969.
**Herbert,** Sir Charles Gordon, KCIE, CSI, 4 April 1970.
**Hewat,** Air Cdre Harry Aitken, CBE, 4 April 1970.
**Hewer,** Maj.-Gen. Reginald Kingscote, CB, CBE, MC, 15 Nov. 1970.
**Hezlet,** Lt-Col Charles Owen, DSO [*Deceased.*
**Hinton,** Captain Eric Perceval, DSO, MVO, 30 March 1970.
**Hiscox,** Ralph, CBE, 6 May 1970.
**Hoare,** Michael Richard, 20 Feb. 1970.
**Hobart,** Brig. James Wilfred Lang Stanley, CBE, DSO, MC, 10 March 1970.
**Hobson,** Sir Patrick, 30 July 1970.
**Hofstadter,** Richard, 24 Oct. 1970.
**Holbein,** Arthur Montague, CBE, 8 Feb. 1970.
**Hope,** Brig.-Gen. John Frederic Roundell, CBE, DSO, 26 July 1970.
**Hornyold-Strickland,** Hon. Mary Constance Elizabeth Christina, CBE, 18 Jan. 1970.
**Horton,** Percy Frederick, 4 Nov. 1970.
**Hosie,** Ian, 15 Aug. 1970.
**Hounsell,** Maj.-Gen. Harold Arthur, CB, CBE, 14 March 1970.
**Howard,** Sir Algar Henry Stafford, KCB, KCVO, MC, TD, 14 Feb. 1970.
**Howard,** Sir Harry, (Henry Rudolph), KBE, 11 Aug. 1970.
**Howe,** Air Cdre Thomas Edward Barham, CBE, AFC, 2 Jan. 1970.
**Hubback,** Vice-Adm. Sir Arthur Gordon Voules, KBE, CB, 25 Aug. 1970.
**Hudson,** Rt Rev. Noel Baring, DSO, MC, 5 Oct. 1970.
**Hudson,** Walter Richard Austen, CBE, 21 Aug. 1970.
**Hugh-Jones,** Llewelyn Arthur, OBE, 8 Jan. 1970.
**Hughes,** Hector, QC, 23 June 1970.
**Hughes,** Sir Richard Edgar, 13th Bt, 29 Aug. 1970.
**Hughes,** Hon. Sir Wilfrid Selwyn Kent, KBE, MVO, MC, ED, 30 July 1970.
**Huish,** Sir Raymond Douglas, CBE, 26 Jan. 1970.
**Hull,** Surgeon Rear-Adm. Herbert Richard Barnes, CB, 31 May 1970.
**Hulme-Taylor,** Col Jack, OBE, 3 Nov. 1970.
**Humphrey,** George Magoffin, 20 Jan. 1970.
**Hunt,** Alan Henderson, 4 July 1970.
**Hunt,** Col John Philip, TD, 9 July 1970.
**Hunt,** Sir Reuben James, 22 Jan. 1970.
**Hunter,** Andrew, CBE [*Deceased.*
**Hunton,** Gen. Sir Thomas Lionel, KCB, MVO, OBE, 20 April 1970.
**Huron,** Bishop of; Rt Rev. George Nasmith Luxton, DD, 2 Oct. 1970.
**Hurwitz,** Alter Max, 20 Oct. 1970.
**Hussey,** Christopher Edward Clive, CBE, 20 March 1970.
**Hutchison,** Sir William Oliphant, 5 Feb. 1970.
**Hutton,** Sir Maurice Inglis, CMG, 1 May 1970.
**Hutton,** Prof. Robert Salmon, 5 Aug. 1970.
**Hyland,** Hon. Sir Herbert John Thornhill, 18 March 1970.

**Iddesleigh,** 3rd Earl of; Henry Stafford Northcote, 16 Feb. 1970.
**Ilchester,** 8th Earl of; Walter Angelo Fox-Strangways, 4 Oct. 1970.
**Irving,** Sir Stanley Gordon, KBE, CMG, 16 May 1970.

**Jackson of Burnley,** Baron (Life Peer); Willis Jackson, FRS, 17 Feb. 1970.
**Jaipur,** Maharaja of; HH Sir Sawai Man Singh Bahadur, GCSI, GCIE, 24 June 1970.
**James,** Richard Bush, QC, 20 June 1970.
**Jamieson,** Stanley Wyndham, CBE, 26 April 1970.
**Jensen,** Sir John Klunder, OBE, 20 Feb. 1970.
**Johnston,** Carruthers Melvill, CMG, 13 Nov. 1970.
**Jones,** Prof. Arnold Hugh Martin, 9 April 1970.
**Jones,** Sir Cyril Edgar, KCIE, CSI, 21 June 1970.
**Jones,** Jack, CBE, 7 May 1970.
**Jones,** Maj.-Gen. Roderick Idrisyn, CB, CBE, 10 July 1970.
**Jones,** Prof. William Richard, CBE, 9 June 1970.
**Joslin,** Prof. David Maelgwyn, 15 Oct. 1970.

**Kaula,** Sir Ganga, CIE, July 1970.
**Kay,** Arthur William, OBE, 18 March 1970.
**Kennedy,** Maj.-Gen. Sir John Noble, GCMG, KCVO, KBE, CB, MC, 15 June 1970.
**Kent-Lemon,** Brig. Arthur Leslie, CBE, 13 July 1970.
**Kenyon-Slaney,** Sybil Agnes, CVO, 10 June 1970.
**Kermack,** Prof. William Ogilvy, FRS, 20 July 1970.
**Keyes,** Frances Parkinson, (Mrs Henry Wilder Keyes), 3 July 1970.
**King,** Prof. Kenneth Charles, 3 Nov. 1970.
**Kingsley,** Brig. Harold Evelyn William Bell, CIE, DSO, 15 April 1970.
**Kinnear,** Her Honour Helen Alice, 25 April 1970.
**Kinvig,** Prof. Robert Henry [*Deceased.*
**Kirkwood,** 2nd Baron; David Kirkwood, 9 March 1970.
**Kirwan,** Geoffrey Dugdale, CB, CMG, MC, 11 Nov. 1970.
**Knight,** Dame Laura, DBE, RA, 7 July 1970.
**Knighton-Hammond,** Arthur Henry, 28 Feb. 1970.
**Knittel,** John Herman Emanuel, 26 April 1970.
**Knox,** Walter Ernest, CMG, MM, 28 June 1970.
**Knox-Shaw,** Harold, 11 April 1970.
**Koenig,** Général d'Armée Marie-Pierre, Hon. CB, DSO, 2 Sept. 1970.
**Kronberger,** Hans, CBE, FRS, 29 Sept. 1970.
**Krug,** Julius Albert, 26 March 1970.

**La Dell,** Edwin, ARA, 27 June 1970.
**Lane,** Sir Allen Lane Williams, CH, 7 July 1970.
**Lang,** Robert Buntin, OBE, 12 March 1970.
**Langley,** Very Rev. Henry Thomas [*Deceased.*
**Langmaid,** Brig. Thomas John Robert, CVO, MC [*Deceased.*
**Larking,** Captain Dennis Augustus Hugo, CMG, RN, 20 April 1970.
**Latham,** 1st Baron; Charles Latham, 31 March 1970.
**Laurence,** Admiral Sir Noel Frank, KCB, DSO, 26 Jan. 1970.
**Leake,** Henry Dashwood Stucley, CB, 2 June 1970.
**Ledger,** Air Vice-Marshal Arthur Percy, CB, CBE, 6 May 1970.
**Leeds,** Comdr Sir Reginald Arthur St John, 6th Bt, RN, 18 Jan. 1970.
**Lemass,** Edwin Stephen, 12 April 1970.
**Leonard,** William [*Deceased.*
**Lever,** Sir Ernest Harry, 4 Sept. 1970.
**Lewis,** Prof. Michael Arthur, CBE, 27 Feb. 1970.
**Lewis,** Sir (William) Hawthorne, KCSI, KCIE, 19 Oct. 1970.
**Liddell Hart,** Sir Basil Henry, 29 Jan. 1970.
**Lindemann,** Brig. Charles Lionel, DSO, 13 Aug. 1970.
**Livesey,** Rev. Herbert, 14 Oct. 1970.

**Livingstone**, Dame Adelaide Lord, DBE, 14 Sept. 1970.
**Llewellyn**, Captain Llewellyn Evan Hugh, CB, OBE, RN, 4 Feb. 1970.
**Lloyd**, Col Edward Prince, CBE, DSO, 14 May 1970.
**Lloyd**, Sir Robert Owen, OBE, 10 March 1970.
**London**, Dr Heinz, FRS, 3 Aug. 1970.
**Lough**, Brig. John Robertson Stewart, CBE, DSO, MC, VD, 26 Jan. 1970.
**Low**, Dr William Alexander, MC, 26 May 1970.
**Lumsden**, Sir James Robert, CBE, 30 Oct. 1970.
**Lyne**, Maj.-Gen. Lewis Owen, CB, DSO, 4 Nov. 1970.
**Lysaght**, Desmond Royse, 1 Jan. 1970.

**Macan-Markar**, Hadji Sir Mohamed [*Deceased*.
**McCall**, Robert Clark, CMG, 16 Oct. 1970.
**McCarthy**, Sir Leslie Ernest Vivian, 20 June 1970.
**MacCracken**, Henry Noble, 7 May 1970.
**McCulloch**, Norman George, CBE [*Deceased*.
**McDonald**, Sir Charles George, KBE, 23 April 1970.
**McDonald**, Thomas Pringle, QC (Scot.) [*Deceased*.
**McDougall**, Sir Malcolm, 25 June 1970.
**Macfarlane-Grieve**, Lt-Col Angus Alexander, MC, TD, 2 Aug. 1970.
**McGeough**, Most Rev. Joseph F., 12 Oct. 1970.
**MacGregor**, Alasdair Alpin, 15 April 1970.
**Macintosh**, Edward Hyde, CBE, 15 Sept. 1970.
**MacIver**, Prof. Robert Morrison, 15 June 1970.
**Mackay**, Lt-Col Hon. John Keiller, SM, DSO, VD, QC (Canada), 13 June 1970.
**Mackay**, John Martin, 29 Jan. 1970.
**Mackenzie**, Alasdair Roderick, 8 Nov. 1970.
**Mackenzie**, Rev. Francis Scott, 26 April 1970.
**Mackenzie**, Helen Margaret [*Deceased*.
**Mackenzie**, Rear-Adm. Kenneth H. L., CBE, 30 Oct. 1970.
**McKittrick**, Thomas Harrington, 21 Jan. 1970.
**Mackness**, Lt-Comdr George John, CBE, DSC, 27 Oct. 1970.
**MacLean**, Col Archibald Campbell Holms, CBE, 30 April 1970.
**MacLeod**, Douglas Hamilton, 27 Jan. 1970.
**Macleod**, Rt Hon. Iain Norman, PC, MP, 20 July 1970.
**MacMillan**, Rear-Adm. Donald Baxter, 7 Sept. 1970.
**Macnab of Macnab**, Archibald Corrie, CIE, 13 Nov. 1970.
**McNeil**, Kenneth Gordon, CBE, 7 Feb. 1970.
**Macneil of Barra, The**; Robert Lister, 24 June 1970.
**MacOrlan**, Pierre, 27 June 1970.
**Macpherson**, Colin Francis, CIE, 8 Jan. 1970.
**McSparran**, James, QC (NI), 15 April 1970.
**McWhae**, Brig. Douglas Murray, CMG, CBE, VD [*Deceased*.
**Madsen**, Prof. Sir John Percival Vissing [*Deceased*.
**Mahadeva**, Sir Arunachalam, KCMG [*Deceased*.
**Mahir**, Thomas Edward, CBE, GM, 29 Jan. 1970.
**Malone**, Surgeon Rear-Adm. Albert Edward, CB, 19 May 1970.
**Mandeville**, Rt Rev. Gay Lisle Griffith [*Deceased*.
**Mansergh**, Gen. Sir (E. C.) Robert, GCB, KBE, MC, 8 Nov. 1970.
**Maplestone**, Philip Alan, DSO [*Deceased*.
**Mardy Jones**, Thomas Isaac, 26 Aug. 1970.
**Marshall**, Dr John, MC, TD, 9 Aug. 1970.
**Marshall**, Robert Ian, 5 April 1970.
**Martin**, Reginald James, 2 Nov. 1970.
**Martyn**, David Forbes, FRS, 5 March 1970.
**Mason**, Sir Laurence, CIE, OBE, MC, 4 June 1970.
**Mauriac**, François, 1 Sept. 1970.
**Mavrogordato**, Prof. John Nicholas, 24 July 1970.
**Maxwell**, Vice-Adm. Hon. Sir Denis Crichton, KCB, CBE, 16 Jan. 1970.
**Maxwell**, James Robert, CMG [*Deceased*.
**Mayers**, Thomas Henry, QC (Jam.), 20 Sept. 1970.
**Maynard**, Charles Gordon, CBE, 1 April 1970.
**Meadon**, Ernest John, CB, 6 May 1970.
**Mercer**, Rev. Dr. Samuel Alfred Browne [*Deceased*.
**Meredith**, Rev. Canon Ralph Creed, 10 Jan. 1970.
**Merewether**, Edward Rowland Alworth, CB, CBE, 13 Feb. 1970.
**Michell**, Humfrey, 5 May 1970.
**Micks**, Dr Robert Henry, 9 Feb. 1970.
**Middleton**, 11th Baron; Michael Guy Percival Willoughby, 16 Nov. 1970.
**Mifsud**, Edward Robert, CMG, OBE, 6 May 1970.
**Miles**, Sir Charles Watt, OBE, 20 Oct. 1970.
**Milford Haven**, 3rd Marquess of; David Michael Mountbatten, OBE, DSC, 14 April 1970.
**Miller**, Dr Emanuel, 29 July 1970.
**Minor**, Clark Haynes, Hon. GBE [*Deceased*.
**Mitchison**, Baron (Life Peer); Gilbert Richard Mitchison, CBE, QC, 14 Feb. 1970.
**Montgomery**, Bo Gabriel de, Count [*Deceased*.
**Moody**, Dr Robert Ley, 26 Aug. 1970.
**Moray, Ross and Caithness**, Bishop of; Rt Rev Duncan MacInnes, MBE, MC, 9 Aug. 1970.
**Morley**, Austin, 22 Jan. 1970.
**Morris**, Gen. Sir Edwin Logie, KCB, OBE, MC, 29 June 1970.
**Morris**, Robert Schofield [*Deceased*.
**Morrison**, Col Frank Stanley, CMG, DSO [*Deceased*.
**Moysey**, Edward Luttrell, CIE, 17 Sept. 1970.
**Muller**, Walter Angus, CMG, 18 Jan. 1970.
**Murdoch**, Sir Walter, KCMG, CBE, 30 July 1970.
**Murray**, George McIntosh, CBE, 2 Nov. 1970.
**Murray**, (William Ewart) Gladstone, DFC, MC, 28 Feb. 1970.
**Musgrave**, Sir Charles, 14th Bt, 26 July 1970.

**Nairn**, Sir Douglas Leslie Spencer-, 2nd Bt, TD, 8 Nov. 1970.
**Nall**, John Spencer, CMG [*Deceased*.
**Narang**, Sir Gokul Chand [*Deceased*.
**Nasser**, President Gamal Abdel, 28 Sept. 1970.
**Neave**, James Stephen, 3 Sept. 1970.
**Newnham**, Hubert Ernest, CMG, VD, 1 Oct. 1970.
**Nicholls**, John Ralph, CBE, 17 Feb. 1970.
**Nicholls**, Sir John Walter, GCMG, OBE, 25 Oct. 1970.
**Nicholls**, Hon. Sir Robert Dove, 18 Jan. 1970.
**Nicholls**, William, 8 March 1970.
**Nickolls**, Lewis Charles, CBE, 2 March 1970.
**Nixon**, Wilfred Ernest, 26 Sept. 1970.
**Norris**, His Honour Richard Hill, 25 March 1970.
**Nugent**, Sir (George) Guy Bulwer, 4th Bt, 17 Aug. 1970.

**Obeyesekere**, Sir James Peter [*Deceased*.
**O'Brien**, Richard Alfred, CBE, 19 Oct. 1970.
**O'Brien**, Sir Tom, 5 May 1970.
**O'Connell**, Thomas J. [*Deceased*.
**O'Hara**, John Henry, 11 April 1970.
**Ontario**, Bishop of; Rt Rev. Kenneth Charles Evans, DD, 13 Feb. 1970.
**Oppenheimer**, Joseph [*Deceased*.
**Ottawa**, Bishop of; Rt Rev. Ernest Samuel Reed, 28 Feb. 1970.
**Overstreet**, Prof. Harry Allen, 17 Aug. 1970.
**Owen**, Sir (Arthur) David Kemp, KCMG, 29 June 1970.

**Palmer**, Reginald Howard Reed, MC, 15 Feb. 1970.
**Panapa**, Rt Rev. Wiremu Netana, CBE, 10 June 1970.
**Pass**, (Alfred) Douglas, OBE, 9 March 1970.
**Paterson**, John Wilson, CVO, MBE [*Deceased*.
**Patrick**, Prof. Adam, 19 Sept. 1970.
**Paul**, Leslie Douglas, 12 Oct. 1970.
**Peacey**, Rt Rev. Basil William [*Deceased*.
**Peacock**, Frederick Hood, CMG, 29 Dec. 1969.
**Peacock**, Rev. Canon Wilfrid Morgan, 25 Jan. 1970.
**Peake**, Frederick Gerald, CMG, CBE, 30 March 1970.
**Peirse**, Air Chief Marshal Sir Richard Edmund Charles, KCB, DSO, AFC, 5 Aug. 1970.
**Penney**, Air Cdre Howard Wright, CB, CBE, 19 June 1970.
**Pickford**, Sir Anthony Frederick Ingham, 16 Sept. 1970.
**Pierce**, Robert [*Deceased*.
**Plender**, Mabel Agnes, (Lady Plender), 12 June 1970.
**Potter**, Rupert Barnadiston, 19 Aug. 1970.
**Pratt**, Sir John Thomas, KBE, CMG, 23 Jan. 1970.
**Prempeh, II**, Otumfuo Sir Osei Agyeman, KBE, May 1970.
**Preston**, Frank Sansome, 8 Feb. 1970.
**Price**, Allen, CMG, 27 Jan. 1970.
**Price**, (Lilian) Nancy (Bache), CBE, 31 March 1970.
**Prichard**, Katharine Susannah [*Deceased*.

**Prower**, Brig. John Mervyn, DSO [*Deceased.*
**Pullinger**, Henry Robert, 10 Aug. 1970.

**Raeburn**, Sir Colin, CBE, 27 Oct. 1970.
**Rattenbury**, Robert Mantle, 29 July 1970.
**Rau**, Sir Benegal Rama, CIE, 13 Dec. 1969.
**Read**, Prof. Herbert Harold, FRS, 29 March 1970.
**Rees**, Sir Richard Lodowick Edward Montagu, 2nd Bt, 24 July 1970 (*ext*).
**Reeve**, Russell, 1 April 1970.
**Reid**, Brig. Sir Francis Smith, CBE, 18 Jan. 1970.
**Reid**, Helen Rogers, (Mrs Ogden Reid), 27 July 1970.
**Relf**, Ernest Frederick, CBE, FRS, 25 Feb. 1970.
**Remarque**, Erich Maria, 25 Sept. 1970.
**Reuther**, Walter Philip, 9 May 1970.
**Rhodes**, Harold Vale, CB, 23 Feb. 1970.
**Rich**, Roy, 24 March 1970.
**Richardson**, Prof. John Henry, CMG, 8 June 1970.
**Riddoch**, John William, MC, 31 Dec. 1969.
**Riggall**, Robert Marmaduke, 3 Oct. 1970.
**Rivalland**, Sir Michel Jean Joseph Laval, MBE, 29 Jan. 1970.
**Rivett-Carnac**, Vice-Adm. James William, CB, CBE, DSC, 9 Oct. 1970.
**Roberts**, Ven. Richard Henry, 6 July 1970.
**Robertson**, Prof. Alexander, FRS, 9 Feb. 1970.
**Robertson**, Sir David, 3 June 1970.
**Robertson**, Prof. Donald James, 22 Aug. 1970.
**Robertson**, Sir James Jackson, OBE, 9 June 1970.
**Robertson**, Thomas Logan, CMG [*Deceased.*
**Robinson**, Joseph, CBE, 4 Jan. 1970.
**Robinson**, Rev. Canon Reginald Henry, DD, 19 Aug. 1970.
**Roe-Thompson**, Edwin Reginald, 20 June 1970.
**Roscoe**, Prof. Kenneth Harry, MC, TD, 10 April 1970.
**Ross**, Rev. Kenneth Needham, 8 June 1970.
**Roth**, Cecil, 21 June 1970.
**Rothko**, Mark, 25 Feb. 1970.
**Rous**, Francis Peyton, 16 Feb. 1970.
**Rowland**, Sir Wentworth Lowe, 2nd Bt, 19 Sept. 1970 (*ext*).
**Runge**, Rev. Charles Herman Schmettau, DSO, MC, 13 Sept. 1970.
**Runge**, Sir Peter Francis, 19 Aug. 1970.
**Runnett**, Henry Brian, 20 Aug. 1970.
**Rushton**, Prof. Martin Amsler, CBE, 16 Nov. 1970.
**Rushworth**, Geoffrey Harrington, CMG [*Deceased.*
**Russell**, 3rd Earl; Bertrand Arthur William Russell, OM, FRS, 2 Feb. 1970.
**Russell**, George Clifford Dowsett, 12 June 1970.
**Russell**, John Eaton Nevill, 15 July 1970.
**Ryan**, Dr James, 25 Sept. 1970.

**Sachs**, Nelly Leonie, 12 May 1970.
**Sadler**, Prof. Arthur Lindsay, 13 July 1970.
**St George**, Frederick Ferris Bligh, CVO, 4 April 1970.
**Salazar**, Dr Antonio de Oliveira, 27 July 1970.
**Salt**, Sir Edward William, 8 Sept. 1970.
**Salt**, Henry Edwin, QC, 11 June 1970.
**Sands**, Ven. Havilland Hubert Allport, 22 March 1970.
**Savage**, John Percival, 22 Feb. 1970.
**Scallan**, Eugene Kevin [*Deceased.*
**Scarff**, Prof. Robert Wilfred, CBE, 19 Jan. 1970.
**Schacht**, Dr Hjalmar Horace Greely, 4 June 1970.
**Schreiber**, Ricardo Rivera, Hon. GBE [*Deceased.*
**Scoggins**, Air Vice-Marshal Roy, CB, CBE, 19 Jan. 1970.
**Scothern**, Col Albert Edward, CMG, DSO, 20 March 1970.
**Scott**, Prof. James Henderson, 14 Nov. 1970.
**Shakerley**, Major Sir Cyril Holland, 5th Bt, 21 Aug. 1970.
**Sharman**, Col Charles Henry Ludovic, CMG, CBE, ISO, 15 May 1970.
**Sheldon**, Christine Mary, CBE, 7 June 1970.
**Sheridan**, Clare Consuelo, 31 May 1970.
**Sherwood**, 1st Baron; Hugh Michael Seely, 1 April 1970 (*ext*).
**Sidgwick**, Ethel, 29 April 1970.
**Simon**, André Louis, Hon. CBE, 5 Sept. 1970.
**Simpson**, Rev. John E., 20 Jan. 1970.
**Sinclair-Lockhart**, Sir John Beresford, 13th Bt, ED, 11 March 1970.
**Sladen**, Francis Farquhar, CIE, 17 Sept. 1970.
**Slater**, Sir William Kershaw, KBE, FRS, 19 April 1970.
**Smail**, James Cameron, OBE, 26 April 1970.
**Smith**, Sir Frank Edward, GCB, GBE, FRS, 1 July 1970.
**Smith**, Thomas James, 3 Aug. 1970.
**Snedden**, Sir Richard, CVO, CBE, 9 March 1970.
**Sondes**, 4th Earl; George Henry Milles-Lade, 30 April 1970.
**Sopwith**, Douglas George, CBE, 20 Oct. 1970.
**Southgate**, Margaret Cecil Irene, 3 Jan. 1970.
**Sowerby**, Katherine Githa, (Mrs John Kendall), 30 June 1970.
**Speares**, Denis James, CMG, 24 March 1970.
**Sperring**, Digby [*Deceased.*
**Starkie**, Enid Mary, CBE, 22 April 1970.
**Stephens**, Lt-Col Rupert, 5 Oct. 1970.
**Stevenson**, Sheriff Alexander James, 2 Sept. 1970.
**Stewart**, Brig.-Gen. John Smith, CMG, DSO, ED, 14 Aug. 1970.
**Stewart**, Sir Robert Sproul, CBE [*Deceased.*
**Stowell**, Thomas Edmund Alex, CBE, 8 Nov. 1970.
**Straker-Smith**, Sir Thomas D., 6 April 1970.
**Strang**, John Martin, CBE, 28 Jan. 1970.
**Strathalmond**, 1st Baron; William Fraser, CBE, 1 April 1970.
**Street**, Maj.-Gen. Vivian Wakefield, CMG, CBE, DSO, MC, 4 April 1970.
**Stuart**, Rear-Adm. Charles Gage, DSO, DSC, 2 July 1970.
**Sturges**, Lt-Gen. Sir Robert Grice, KBE, CB, DSO, 12 Sept. 1970.
**Sutherland**, George Arthur, 1 March 1970.
**Swainson**, Willan, 28 Sept. 1970.
**Swift**, Sir Brian Herbert, MC [*Deceased.*
**Swiney**, Maj.-Gen. Sir (George Alexander) Neville, KBE, CB, MC, 21 May 1970.

**Talbot**, Vice-Adm. Sir Cecil Ponsonby, KCB, KBE, DSO, 17 March 1970.
**Taschereau**, Rt Hon. Robert, CC (Can.), PC (Can.), 26 July 1970.
**Taylor**, Rear-Adm. Bertram Wilfrid, CB, DSC, 30 Sept. 1970.
**Templar-Smith**, Col Sir Harold Charles, KBE, 6 Sept. 1970.
**Thomas**, Prof. David Winton, FBA, 18 June 1970.
**Thompson**, Prof. Eric, CBE [*Deceased.*
**Thompson**, Sir Ivan, 22 July 1970.
**Thomson**, Eng. Capt. Alan Leslie, CBE, 16 March 1970.
**Thomson**, David, 24 Feb. 1970.
**Thomson**, Major George, CBE, DSO, 16 Oct. 1970.
**Thorne**, Gen. Sir (Augustus Francis) Andrew Nicol, KCB, CMG, DSO, 25 Sept. 1970.
**Thorneycroft**, Thomas Hamo, 5 March 1970.
**Thornhill**, Arthur Horace, 9 Jan. 1970.
**Thorold**, Sir Guy Frederick, KCMG, 16 Jan. 1970.
**Thorpe**, Col Sir Fred Garner, MC, ED, 29 March 1970.
**Thring**, Captain Ernest Walsham Charles, CB, RN, 17 March 1970.
**Thurso**, 1st Viscount; Archibald Henry Macdonald Sinclair, KT, CMG, 15 June 1970.
**Timoshenko**, Marshal Semyon Konstantinovich, 1 April 1970.
**Tod**, Sir Alan Cecil, CBE, TD, 7 Sept. 1970.
**Todd**, Lt-Col Alfred John Kennett, 27 Aug. 1970.
**Todd**, Sir Desmond Henry, 5 Aug. 1970.
**Tozer**, Major Sir James Clifford, 8 June 1970.
**Tresidder**, Lt-Col Alfred Geddes, CIE, 9 July 1970.
**Treston**, Col Maurice Lawrence, CBE, 14 April 1970.
**Tuite**, Sir Brian Hugh Morgan, 12th Bt, 26 Aug. 1970.
**Tunstall**, (William Cuthbert) Brian, 27 Sept. 1970.
**Turing**, Sir Robert Andrew Henry, 10th Bt, 6 Jan. 1970.
**Tuttle**, Wilbur C. [*Deceased.*
**Twysden**, Sir William Adam Duncan, 12th Bt, 17 Feb. 1970 (*ext*).

**Uvarov**, Sir Boris Petrovitch, KCMG, FRS, 18 March 1970.

**Valentine**, Alfred Buyers, CB, 21 Feb. 1970.
**Vallery-Radot Pasteur**, Louis, 9 Oct. 1970.
**Valluy**, Général d'Armée Jean Etienne, 4 Jan. 1970.
**Vaskess**, Henry Harrison, CMG, OBE [*Deceased.*
**Velázquez**, Dr Carlos María, 3 July 1970.

**Venning**, Brig. Francis Esmond Wingate, CB, CBE, DSO, 28 Aug. 1970.
**Verity**, Sir John, 9 April 1970.
**Vevers**, Geoffrey Marr, 9 Jan. 1970.
**Vickers**, Harold James, CBE, 22 Sept. 1970.
**Villar**, Captain George, CBE, RN, 18 April 1970.

**Waddy**, Dorothy Knight, QC, 8 Jan. 1970.
**Wadely**, Frederick William, OBE, 28 May 1970.
**Waight**, Leonard, CMG, 15 Jan. 1970.
**Wainewright**, Brig.-Gen. Arthur Reginald, CMG, DSO, 23 July 1970.
**Wakehurst**, 2nd Baron; John de Vere Loder, KG, KCMG, 30 Oct. 1970.
**Walkden**, Evelyn, 12 Sept. 1970.
**Walker**, Cyril Herbert, CBE, MC, 5 Sept. 1970.
**Walker**, Prof. Thomas Kennedy, 29 June 1970.
**Walkey**, Rear-Adm. Howarth Seymour, CBE, 20 Aug. 1970.
**Wallace**, William Stewart, 11 March 1970.
**Wallace of that Ilk**, Col Robert Francis Hurter, CMG, 1 June 1970.
**Walwyn**, Algernon Edward Vere, CMG, 23 June 1970.
**Warburg**, Prof. Otto Heinrich, 1 Aug. 1970.
**Ward**, Sir Joseph George Davidson, 3rd Bt, 4 Aug. 1970.
**Wass**, Samuel Hall, 10 Feb. 1970.
**Waterhouse**, Prof. Walter Lawry, CMG, MC, 9 Dec. 1969.
**Watkin**, Prof. Morgan, 7 Sept. 1970.
**Watkins**, Rear-Adm. John Kingdon, CB, OBE, 13 May 1970.
**Watson**, Elliot Lovegood Grant, 21 May 1970.
**Webb**, Prof. Geoffrey Fairbank, CBE, FBA, 17 July 1970.
**Wedgwood**, 3rd Baron; Hugh Everard Wedgwood, 25 April 1970.
**Welby**, Hugh Robert Everard Earle, CMG, 18 April 1970.
**Wenham**, Sir John Henry, 25 Aug. 1970.
**Westall**, Bernard Clement, CBE, 18 Jan. 1970.
**Wheeler**, Rear-Adm. Aubrey John, CB, 16 March 1970.
**Whiddington**, Prof. Richard, CBE, FRS, 7 June 1970.
**Whiteley**, Gen. Sir John Francis Martin, GBE, KCB, MC, 20 May 1970.
**Whiteley**, Wilfrid, CBE, 4 April 1970.
**Whitham**, Gilbert Shaw, CMG, CBE, 20 Aug. 1970.
**Whyte**, Sir (Alexander) Frederick, KCSI, 30 July 1970.
**Wickham**, Brig. John Charles, DSO, 12 May 1970.
**Wicks**, Margaret Campbell Walker, 27 May 1970.
**Wigley**, Rev. Henry Townsend, 26 May 1970.
**Wijeyeratne**, Sir Edwin Aloysius Perera, KBE [*Deceased.*
**Wilde**, Prof. Johannes, CBE, FBA, 13 Sept. 1970.
**Wildman-Lushington**, Maj.-Gen. Godfrey Edward, CB, CBE, 3 Feb. 1970.
**Wilkes**, Richard Leslie Vaughan, CMG, 19 Oct. 1970.
**Wilkinson**, Frank, CBE, 21 Oct. 1970.
**Williams**, Bernard Warren, 24 Sept. 1970.
**Williams**, Sir David Philip, 3rd Bt, 31 Oct. 1970.
**Williams**, Brig. Frederick Christian, CB, CBE, MC, 16 Jan. 1970.
**Williams**, William Daniel, OBE, 9 March 1970.
**Wills**, Edith Agnes, OBE, 7 April 1970.
**Wilson**, Charles Paul, CVO, 12 March 1970.
**Wilson**, George Frederick, CBE, 6 Aug. 1970.
**Wilson**, Rt Rev. John Leonard, KCMG, 18 Aug. 1970.
**Wiltshire**, Aubrey Roy Liddon, CMG, DSO, MC, VD [*Deceased.*
**Wishart**, Rear-Adm. John Webster, CB, CBE [*Deceased.*
**Wodeman**, Guy Stanley, CMG, 5 May 1970.
**Wolfe**, Herbert Robert Inglewood, VRD, 18 Feb. 1970.
**Wood**, Ernest Clement, CIE, 5 Oct. 1970.
**Wood**, Mrs Ethel Mary, CBE, 29 June 1970.
**Wood**, William Alfred Rae, CMG, CIE, 22 Jan. 1970.
**Wooll**, Edward, OBE, QC, 20 May 1970.
**Wootten**, Maj.-Gen. Sir George Frederick, KBE, CB, DSO, ED, 30 March 1970.
**Worthington**, Charles Edward, CBE, 26 April 1970.
**Wright**, Frank Joseph Henry, 16 Nov. 1970.
**Wright**, Sir Norman Charles, CB, 16 July 1970.
**Wright**, Phillip Arundell, CMG, 30 Aug. 1970.
**Wykes**, John Arthur, 25 Jan. 1970.
**Wymark**, Patrick Carl, (A. K. A. Cheeseman), 20 Oct. 1970.

**Yerbury**, Francis Rowland, OBE, 7 July 1970.
**York**, Thomas John Pinches, 25 May 1970.

**Zealley**, Sir Alec Thomas Sharland, 20 April 1970.

# WHO'S WHO 1971

## THE ROYAL FAMILY

### THE SOVEREIGN

| | Born |
|---|---|
| **Her Majesty Queen Elizabeth II** . . . . . . . . . . | 21 Apr. 1926 |

Succeeded her father, King George VI, 6 February 1952.

Married 20 Nov. 1947, HRH The Duke of Edinburgh (*now* HRH The Prince Philip, Duke of Edinburgh). *b* 10 June 1921; *s* of HRH Prince Andrew of Greece (*d* 1944) and of HRH Princess Andrew of Greece (*d* 1969), *g g-d* of Queen Victoria.

*Residences:* Buckingham Palace, London, SW1; Windsor Castle, Berkshire; Sandringham House, Norfolk; Balmoral Castle, Aberdeenshire.

### SONS AND DAUGHTER OF HER MAJESTY

| | |
|---|---|
| **HRH The Prince of Wales (Prince Charles Philip Arthur George)** . . | 14 Nov. 1948 |
| **HRH The Prince Andrew (Albert Christian Edward)** . . . . . | 19 Feb. 1960 |
| **HRH The Prince Edward (Antony Richard Louis)** . . . . . | 10 Mar. 1964 |
| **HRH The Princess Anne (Elizabeth Alice Louise)**. . . . . | 15 Aug. 1950 |

### SISTER OF HER MAJESTY

| | |
|---|---|
| **HRH The Princess Margaret, Countess of Snowdon** . . . . . | 21 Aug. 1930 |

Married 6 May 1960, Antony Charles Robert Armstrong-Jones (*now* 1st Earl of Snowdon, *qv*) and has issue—

| | |
|---|---|
| DAVID ALBERT CHARLES ARMSTRONG-JONES (VISCOUNT LINLEY, *qv*) | 3 Nov. 1961 |
| SARAH FRANCES ELIZABETH ARMSTRONG-JONES (LADY SARAH ARMSTRONG-JONES) . . . . . . . . . . . | 1 May 1964 |

*Residence:* Kensington Palace, W8.

### MOTHER OF HER MAJESTY

| | |
|---|---|
| **Her Majesty Queen Elizabeth The Queen Mother** . . . . . | 4 Aug. 1900 |

Married 26 April 1923 (as Lady Elizabeth Bowes-Lyon, *d* of 14th Earl of Strathmore), HRH The Duke of York (Prince ALBERT), who succeeded as KING GEORGE VI, 11 Dec. 1936; he died 6 Feb. 1952.

*Residences:* Clarence House, St James's, SW1; Royal Lodge, Windsor Great Park, Berkshire; Castle of Mey, Caithness-shire.

### UNCLES OF HER MAJESTY

| | |
|---|---|
| **HRH The Duke of Gloucester (Prince Henry William Frederick Albert)**. | 31 Mar. 1900 |

Governor-General of the Commonwealth of Australia, 1945–47.

Married 6 Nov. 1935, Lady Alice Montagu-Douglas-Scott, *b* 25 Dec. 1901, 3rd *d* of 7th Duke of Buccleuch, and has issue—

| | |
|---|---|
| HRH PRINCE WILLIAM HENRY ANDREW FREDERICK . . . | 18 Dec. 1941 |
| HRH PRINCE RICHARD ALEXANDER WALTER GEORGE . . . | 26 Aug. 1944 |

*Residences:* York House, St James's Palace, SW1; Barnwell Manor, near Peterborough, Northamptonshire.

**HRH The Duke of Windsor (Prince Edward Albert Christian George Andrew Patrick David)** . . . . . . . . 23 June 1894

Governor and Commander-in-Chief of the Bahama Islands, 1940–45.

Succeeded his father, King George V, 20 January 1936 as King Edward VIII; abdicated 11 December 1936.

Married 3 June 1937, Mrs Wallis Warfield.

*Residences:* 4 Route du Champ d'Entraînement, Paris XVI; Moulin de la Tuilerie, Gif-sur-Yvette, Essonne, France.

## COUSINS OF HER MAJESTY

Children of HRH The Duke of Kent (Prince George Edward Alexander Edmund, *b* 20 Dec. 1902, *d* 25 Aug. 1942) and HRH Princess Marina, Duchess of Kent (*b* 13 Dec. 1906, *d* 27 Aug. 1968), *y d* of late Prince Nicolas of Greece.

**HRH The Duke of Kent (Prince Edward George Nicholas Patrick)**. . 9 Oct. 1935

Married 8 June 1961, Katharine, *b* 22 Feb. 1933, *o d* of Sir William Worsley, *qv*, and has issue—

GEORGE PHILIP NICHOLAS (EARL OF ST ANDREWS, *qv*) . . 26 June 1962

NICHOLAS CHARLES EDWARD JONATHAN (LORD NICHOLAS WINDSOR) . . . . . . . . . . . . . . . 25 July 1970

HELEN MARINA LUCY (LADY HELEN WINDSOR) . . . 28 Apr. 1964

*Residence:* Coppins, Iver, Bucks.

**HRH Prince Michael George Charles Franklin** . . . . . . 4 July 1942

*Residences:* Kensington Palace, W8; Barnwell Manor, near Peterborough, Northamptonshire.

**HRH Princess Alexandra, the Hon. Mrs Angus Ogilvy** . . . . . 25 Dec. 1936

Married 24 April 1963, Hon. Angus James Bruce Ogilvy, *qv*; one *s*, James Robert Bruce Ogilvy, *b* 29 Feb. 1964; one *d*, Marina Victoria Alexandra Ogilvy, *b* 31 July 1966.

*Residence:* Thatched House Lodge, Richmond, Surrey.

# SUPPLEMENT
## TO WHO'S WHO, 1971

PART I of this Supplement contains a selection of the alterations and additions too late for inclusion in the body of the book, noted up to late December 1970.

PART II of the Supplement contains a selection of names included in the New Year Honours List, 1971.

## SUPPLEMENT: PART I

**ACKNER, Desmond James Conrad; Hon. Mr Justice Ackner.** Judge of the High Court of Justice, Queen's Bench Division, since 1971.

**ACLAND, Sir Hubert Guy Dyke,** 4th Bt. Succeeded to baronetcy of brother; *see infra.*

**ACLAND, Sir William Henry Dyke,** 3rd Bt. Died 4 Dec. 1970. *See supra.*

**ADAMS, Mary Grace.** Deputy Chairman, Consumers' Association, 1958–70.

**ADAMS, Sir Philip (George Doyne).** Deputy Secretary, Cabinet Office, since 1971.

**ALLEN, Alfred Walter Henry.** Member, Commission on Industrial Relations, 1969–70.

**ALLEN, Sir Peter (Christopher).** Chairman, Imperial Chemical Industries Ltd, 1968–71.

**ANDREW, Sir (George) Herbert.** *Address:* Heathfield, Kirkbymoorside, York YO6 6DN.

**ASHBY, Sir Eric.** Chancellor, Queen's University, Belfast, since 1970.

**ASHMORE, Vice-Adm. Sir Edward Beckwith.** Admiral, Nov. 1970.

**BAKER, Gen. Sir Geoffrey Harding.** Master Gunner, St James's Park, since 1970.

**BALLANTYNE, Alexander Hanson.** Consultant, Organisation for Economic Co-operation and Development, since 1971.

**BARLOW, Harold Everard Monteagle.** *Address:* 13 Hookfield, Epsom, Surrey. *T:* Epsom 21586.

**BENNION, Francis Alan Roscoe.** *Address:* (office) 50 The Green, Warlingham, Surrey CR3 9NA. *T:* Upper Warlingham 4961.

**BILSLAND,** 1st Baron. Died 10 Dec. 1970. Barony and Baronetcy extinct.

**BLACKETT,** Baron. President of the Royal Society, 1965–70.

**BLACKMAN, Dr Lionel Cyril Francis.** Head of Glass Fibre Technology Group, Pilkington Brothers Ltd, St Helens, Lancs.

**BLUNDELL, Commandant Daphne Mary.** *Address:* 22 Marsham Court, Marsham Street, SW1,

**BONDI, Hermann.** Chief Scientific Adviser in the Ministry of Defence, since 1971.

**BONHAM CARTER, Hon. Mark Raymond.** Chairman, Community Relations Commission, since 1971; Chairman, Race Relations Board, 1966–70.

**BOWES-LYON, Maj.-Gen. Francis James Cecil.** GOC London District, and Major-General commanding the Household Division, since 1971.

**BOYD, Prof. Alexander Michael.** Professor of Surgery, University of Manchester, 1947–70, now Professor Emeritus.

**BRADLEY, Richard Alan.** Warden of St Edward's School, Oxford, 1966–71.

**BRIDGE, George Wilfred.** *Address:* Hazel Croft, Deans Lane, Walton-on-the-Hill, Tadworth, Surrey. *T:* Tadworth 2846.

**BRUCE, Robert Elton Spencer.** Editor, *Woman's Own*, 1968–70.

**BURKITT, Robert William.** *Address:* 26 Charlwood Road, SW15. Telephone unchanged.

**BUXTON, Sir Thomas Fowell Victor,** 6th Bt. Heir now *cousin* Jocelyn Charles Roden Buxton [*b* 8 Aug. 1924; *m* 1960, Ann Frances, *d* of Frank Smitherman, *qv*; three *d*].

**CALLARD, Eric John.** Chairman, Imperial Chemical Industries Ltd, since 1971.

**CARNOCHAN, John Golder.** *Address:* Pine Cottage, 5 Fenton Terrace, Pitlochry, Perthshire.

**CARTER, John (Waynflete).** *Address:* 113 Dovehouse Street, SW3. Telephone unchanged.

**CHELMSFORD, Bishop of,** 1962–71; **Rt. Rev. John Gerhard Tiarks.**

**CHRISTIE, Charles Henry.** Warden of St Edward's School, Oxford, from Sept. 1971.

**CLARK, Michael William.** Managing Director, Plessey Co. Ltd, since 1970.

**CLEARY, Sir Joseph Jackson.** Deputy Chairman, Mersey Docks and Harbour Board, 1964–70.

**CLIFFORD, Rev. Sir Lewis Arthur Joseph,** 5th Bt. Died 8 Dec. 1970. *See p* 608 for heir.

**COLE,** Baron. Chairman, Rolls Royce Ltd, since Nov. 1970.

**COMPTON, Sir Edmund (Gerald).** Parliamentary Commissioner for Administration, 1967–71; Parliamentary Commissioner in Northern Ireland, since 1969.

**COOK, Sir William Richard Joseph.** Chief Adviser (Projects and Research) to the Minister for Defence (Equipment), 1968–70.

**COUSINS, Rt. Hon. Frank.** Chairman, Community Relations Commission, 1968–70.

**CROMER,** Earl of. British Ambassador in Washington, since 1971.

**CROSS, James Richard.** Senior British Trade Commissioner, Montreal, 1968–70.

**CURRIE, George Boyle Hanna.** *Address:* (chambers) 34 Castle Street, Liverpool. *T:* 051-236 5072; Wyncote, Roscote Close, Lower Village, Heswall, Wirral. *T:* Heswall 1444.

**DAHL, Robert Henry.** Head Master of Wrekin College, 1952–71.

**DALRYMPLE, Sir (Charles) Mark,** Bt. *Address:* 12a Inver Court, Inverness Terrace, Bayswater, W2 6JB. *T:* 01–727 9993.

**DAVIDSON,** 1st Viscount. Died 11 Dec. 1970. *See p* 778 for heir.

**de la MARE, Sir Arthur (James).** Ambassador to Thailand, since 1970.

**DENBIGH and DESMOND,** Earl of. Heir now *s* (Viscount Feilding), *b* 4 Nov. 1970.

**DROGHEDA,** Earl of. Chairman of Financial Times Ltd, since 1971.

**DUNDAS, Sir Thomas Calderwood, 7th Bt. Died 2 Dec. 1970.** Baronetcy extinct.

**DYE, Maj.-Gen. Jack Bertie.** Director, Volunteers, Territorials and Cadets, since 1971.

**EAST, Frederick Henry.** Director, Royal Armament Research and Development Establishment, since 1971. *Address:* Fort Halstead, Sevenoaks, Kent. *T:* Sevenoaks 55211.

**ECCLES, Maj.-Gen. Ronald Whalley.** Assistant Master General of the Ordnance (Inspection), 1967–70, retired.

**EDWARDS, Joseph Robert.** Resigned as Chairman, Harland and Wolff Ltd, 1970.

**EDWARDS, Prof. Kenneth Charles.** Professor of Geography in the University of Nottingham, 1948–70, now Emeritus Professor.

**EUSTON, Earl of.** Succeeded father as 11th Duke of Grafton. *See p* 993 and *infra* **Ipswich.**

**EUSTON, Countess of.** Now Duchess of Grafton.

**EXMOUTH,** 9th Viscount. Died 2 Dec. 1970. *See p* 1012 for heir.

**FAIRFIELD, Sir Ronald McLeod.** Managing Director, British Insulated Callender's Cables Ltd. 1964–70, Deputy Chairman since 1964.

**FINLAY, Bernard.** A County Court Judge, since 1970.

**FORSTER, Sir (Samuel Alexander) Sadler.** Chairman, English Industrial Estates Corporation, 1960–70.

**FOXLEY-NORRIS, Air Marshal Sir Christopher (Neil).** Air Chief Marshal, Dec. 1970.

**FRASER, Thomas Cameron.** Director, Commission of Inquiry into Industrial Representation, since 1970.

**FREEMAN, Rt. Hon. John.** British Ambassador in Washington, 1969–70.

**FREYBERG,** Baron. Heir now *son*, *b* 15 Dec. 1970.

**GELLERT, Leon.** *Address:* 21 Lerwick Avenue, Hazelwood Park, South Australia 5066.

**GERRARD, Basil Harding.** A County Court Judge, since 1970.

**GILES, Very Rev. Alan Stanley.** Dean of Jersey and Rector of St Helier, 1959–70.

**GRAFTON,** 10th Duke of. *See* Obituary, and *infra* **Euston.**

**GRANVILLE, Keith.** Chairman, BOAC, since 1971.

**GRIFFITHS, (William) Hugh; Hon. Mr Justice Griffiths.** Judge of the High Court of Justice, Queen's Bench Division, since 1971.

**GUTHRIE, Sir (William) Tyrone.** Chancellor, Queen's University, Belfast, 1963–70.

**HALL,** Viscount. Chairman of the Post Office Corporation, 1969–70.

**HAMILTON, (Charles) Denis.** Chairman, since 1971, and Editor-in-Chief since 1967, Times Newspapers Ltd (Chief Executive, 1967–70).

**HAMILTON, James Arnot.** Deputy Secretary, Ministry of Aviation Supply, since 1971.

**HARDIE, Sir Charles Edgar Mathewes.** Chairman of BOAC, 1968–70.

**HARMER, Sir Frederick (Evelyn).** Deputy Chairman, P&OSN Co., 1957–70.

**HAYDON, Walter Robert.** High Commissioner in Malawi, since 1971.

**HEDDY, Brian Huleatt.** HM Consul-General in Durban since 1971.

**HELLINGS, Lt-Gen. Peter William Cradock.** General, Nov. 1970.

**HERSEY, John.** Master, Pierson College, Yale University, 1965–70. *Address:* 420 Humphrey Street, New Haven, Conn. 06511, USA.

**HEWISH, Antony.** Professor of Radioastronomy, University of Cambridge, since 1971.

**HIDAYATULLAH, Hon. Mr. Justice M.,** Chief Justice, Supreme Court of India, 1968–70.

**HODGKIN, Alan Lloyd.** President of the Royal Society, since 1970.

**HODSON, Dr Cecil John.** Professor of Radiology, Faculty of Medicine, Memorial University of Newfoundland, since 1970. *Address:* 45 Fox Avenue, St John's, Newfoundland, Canada. *T:* Area Code 709 722 7673.

**HORSLEY, Air Vice-Marshal (Beresford) Peter (Torrington).** Assistant Chief of the Air Staff (Operations), 1968–70.

**HUMPHREY, Air Marshal Sir Andrew (Henry).** Air Chief Marshal, Jan. 1971.

**HUNT, Sir Joseph Anthony.** Chairman, The Fairey Company Ltd, since 1970.

**IPSWICH, Viscount.** Title now Earl of Euston. *See supra.*

**JORDAN-MOSS, Norman.** Deputy Under-Secretary of State, Department of Health and Social Security, since 1971.

**KENNEDY, David Matthew.** Secretary of the Treasury, USA, 1969–70; Ambassador-at-Large, since 1970.

**KING, Rt. Hon. Horace Maybray.** Speaker of the House of Commons, 1965–70; MP, 1950–70.

**LAMBERT, Richard Stanton.** *Address:* Apartment 401, 11 Valley Woods Road, Don Mills, Ontario, Canada.

**LANDA, Hon. Abram.** Agent-General for NSW, 1965–70.

**LEAHY, John Henry Gladstone.** Head of News Department, Foreign and Commonwealth Office, since 1971.

**LLOYD, Rt. Hon. (John) Selwyn (Brooke).** Speaker of the House of Commons, since 1971.

**MAAZEL, Lorin.** Associate Principal Conductor, New Philharmonia Orchestra, since 1971.

**MACDERMOT, Niall.** Secretary General, International Commission of Jurists, since Dec. 1970. *Additional address:* 2 quai du Cheval-Blanc, 1211 Geneva 24, Switzerland.

**MACDONALD, 7th Baron.** *See* Obituary, and *p* 1964 for heir.

**MACEY, John Percival.** Director of Housing to the Greater London Council, 1964–71.

**McINTOSH, Rear-Adm. Ian Stewart.** Vice-Admiral, Nov. 1970.

**MACKINTOSH, Duncan Robert.** *Address:* Woodfolds, Oaksey, Malmesbury, Wilts.

**MALCOLM, Dugald.** Ambassador to Panama, since 1970.

**MARKING, Henry Ernest.** Chairman and Chief Executive, BEA, since 1971.

**MARRE, Sir Alan Samuel.** Parliamentary Commissioner for Administration, since 1971.

**MATTHEWS, Prof. Ernest.** Director of Prosthetics, University of Manchester, 1935–70.

**MAYER, Col Edward Rudolph.** Member, Thames Conservancy, since 1970.

**MENAUL, Air Vice-Marshal Stewart William Blacker.** Director-General, Royal United Services Institute for Defence Studies (title changed 1971).

**MIDDLETON,** 11th Baron. *See* Obituary, and *infra* **Willoughby.**

**MILLOTT, Prof. Norman.** Director, University Marine Biological Station, Millport, since 1970.

**MORRIS, Walter Frederick.** Head of Claims Department, Foreign and Commonwealth Office, since 1971.

**MUIR MACKENZIE, Sir Robert Henry, 6th Bt.** Died 4 Dec. 1970. *See p* 2258 for heir.

**MURRAY, James Dalton.** Reemployed, 1970, as First Secretary and Consul (Chargé d'Affaires) resident in Port-au-Prince, Haiti.

**NAIRN, Sir Douglas (Leslie) Spencer-, 2nd Bt.** *See* Obituary, and *p* 2281 for heir.

**NORMAN, Sir Arthur (Gordon).** Deputy Chairman, BOAC, since 1970.

**NORWICH, Bishop of; Rt. Rev. William Launcelot Scott Fleming.** Dean of Windsor, from July 1971.

**PAGAN, Sir John Ernest.** Agent-General for NSW in London, since Nov. 1971.

**PARKER, Vice-Adm. Sir (Wilfred) John.** Deputy Director, Incorporated Society of British Advertisers, 1969–70.

**PARSONS, Sir Maurice (Henry).** Chairman, Bank of London and South America, July–Dec. 1970.

**PAYNTER, (Thomas) William.** Member, Commission on Industrial Relations, 1969–70.

**PEARSON, Sir (James) Denning.** Deputy Chairman, Rolls Royce Ltd, since Nov. 1970.

**PLUMBE, William John Conway.** HM Chief Inspector of Factories, 1967–71.

**PORTER, Walter Stanley.** Headmaster of Framlingham College, 1955–71.

**PRIDEAUX, John Francis.** Chairman, National Westminster Bank Ltd, since 1971.

**PRITCHARD, Sir Neil.** Ambassador to Thailand, 1967–70.

**RIDDELSDELL, Mildred.** Second Permanent Under-Secretary of State, Department of Health and Social Security, since 1971.

**ROBARTS, David John.** Director, National Westminster Bank Ltd (Chairman, 1969–70).

**ROBBINS, Baron.** Chairman of Financial Times Ltd, 1961–70.

**ROBERTS, Rear-Adm. Cedric Kenelm.** Flag Officer Naval Flying Training, 1968–70, retired.

**ROSS, Prof. Claud Richard.** Member, Central Policy Review Staff, Cabinet Office, since 1971.

**SANTA CRUZ, Victor (Rafael Andrés).** Chilean Ambassador to the Court of St James's, 1959–70.

**SCRIVENER, Ronald Stratford.** Ambassador to Panama, 1969–70.

**SEKERS, Sir Nicholas (Thomas).** Managing Director, West Cumberland Silk Mills Ltd, 1938–70.

**SHEFFIELD, Bishop of,** 1962–71; **Rt. Rev. Francis John Taylor.**

**SLIM,** 1st Viscount. Died 14 Dec. 1970. *See p* 2912 for heir.

**SMITH, Roderick Philip.** Recorder of Newcastle upon Tyne, since 1970.

**SPRING, Frank Stuart.** Director, Laporte Industries Ltd, 1959–70.

**STANTON, Rev. John Maurice.** Headmaster, Blundell's School, 1959–71.

**STAPLES, Sir Robert George Alexander,** 13th Bt. Died 9 Dec. 1970. *Heir:* John Richard Staples, *b* 5 April 1906.

**STARK, Andrew Alexander Steel.** Ambassador to Denmark, since 1971.

**STEVENSON, Sir Matthew.** Deputy Chairman, Mersey Docks and Harbour Board, since Dec. 1970.

**STEWART, Sir Michael (Norman Francis).** Ambassador to Greece, 1967–71.

**SUTCLIFFE, Kenneth Edward.** Headmaster, Latymer Upper School, 1958–71.

**TAVERNE, Dick.** Director, Institute for Fiscal Studies, since 1970.

**TAYLOR, Lt-Col Eustace Trevor Neave.** *Address:* Berkeley Square, Suite 40, Main Road, Rondebosch, Cape Province, South Africa.

**TAYLOR, Leon Eric Manners.** Hon. Visiting Fellow, Centre for Contemporary European Studies, University of Sussex; Economic Counsellor, British High Commission, Malaysia, 1966–70.

**TAYLOR, Peter Murray.** Recorder of Teesside, since 1970.

**TEJAN-SIE, Sir Banja.** GCMG 1970; Governor General of Sierra Leone, since 1970.

**THOMAS, Lt-Gen. Sir (John) Noel.** Master-General of the Ordnance, with the rank of General, since 1971.

**THOMSON, Hon. Kenneth (Roy).** Joint Chairman, Thomson Organisation, since 1971; Co-President, Times Newspapers Ltd, since 1971.

**TRITTON, Arthur Stanley.** *Address:* 11 Rusthall Road, Tunbridge Wells, Kent.

**TULL, Thomas Stuart.** High Commissioner in Malawi, 1967–70.

**TWINING, Gen. Nathan Farragut.** *Address:* 25 North Live Oak Road, Hilton Head Island, S Carolina 29928, USA.

**TWISS, Adm. Sir Frank (Roddam).** Serjeant-at-Arms, House of Lords (as well as Gentleman Usher of the Black Rod) since 1971.

**VEALL, Harry Truman.** *Address:* 20 Wincombe Drive, Ferndown, Dorset BH22 8HX. *T:* Ferndown 4726.

**WALKER, Sir (Charles) Michael.** Secretary, Overseas Development Administration, since 1970.

**WALLER, Sir (John) Keith.** Secretary, Department of Foreign Affairs, Canberra, since 1970.

**WALTERS, Sir Roger Talbot.** Architect to the Greater London Council, since 1971.

**WEARING, John Frederick.** Counsellor and Deputy Head of UK Delegation to OECD, since 1970.

**WHEELER, Dr Denis Edward.** Consultant to the Wellcome Foundation, since 1970 (Deputy Chairman, 1967–70).

**WHEELER, Maj.-Gen. Thomas Norman Samuel.** Chief of Staff, HQ BAOR, 1969–71, retired.

**WIGGLESWORTH, Walter Somerville.** Dean of the Arches Court of Canterbury, Auditor of the Chancery Court of York, and Master of the Faculties, since 1971.

**WILLINK, Rt. Hon. Sir Henry Urmston.** Dean of the Arches, Auditor of the Chancery Court of York, and Master of the Faculties, 1955–70.

**WILLOUGHBY, Hon. Digby Michael Godfrey John.** Succeeded father as 12th Baron Middleton. See *p* 3419 and *supra* **Middleton.**

**WILSON, Sir Reginald (Holmes).** Deputy Chairman, Transport Development Group, since Dec. 1970; Chairman, National Freight Corporation, 1969–70.

**WROTTESLEY,** Baron. Son, Hon. Richard Francis Gerard Wrottesley died 1970. Heir now *g s* Clifton Hugh Lancelot de Verdon Wrottesley, *b* 10 Aug. 1968.

**WYNDHAM WHITE, Sir Eric.** Ceased to be Chairman, Investors Overseas Service, Nov. 1970.

**WYNNE MASON, Walter.** Director of External Relations and Records, Commonwealth War Graves Commission, 1956–70.

**YOST, Charles Woodruff.** Ambassador, and Permanent Representative of the United States to the United Nations, 1969–70.

# SUPPLEMENT: PART II

## A SELECTION OF NAMES IN THE NEW YEAR HONOURS LIST: JAN. 1971

**ANDERSON, Rear-Adm. (Charles) Courtney.** CB 1971.
**ANDERSON, Maj.-Gen. Sir John Evelyn.** KBE 1971.
**ARDIZZONE, Edward Jeffrey Irving.** CBE 1971.
**ARNOTT, Sir William Melville.** Kt 1971.
**ASHMORE, Adm. Sir Edward Beckwith.** KCB 1971.
**ATKINSON, Frederick John.** CB 1971.

***BANKS, Sir Maurice Alfred Lister.** Kt 1971. For services to Patent Law.
**BANNISTER, Prof. Frank Kenneth.** CBE 1971.
**BARCLAY-SMITH, (Ida) Phyllis.** CBE 1971.
**BARRAN, Sir David (Haven).** Kt 1971.
***BARRATT-BOYES, Sir Brian Gerald.** KBE 1971. For outstanding services as surgeon-in-charge of the cardiac-thoracic unit at Green Lane Hospital, Auckland, NZ.
**BAYLIS, Clifford Henry.** CB 1971.
**BECKETT, Maj.-Gen. Denis Arthur.** CB 1971.
**BELLAMY, Basil Edmund.** CB 1971.
**BENSON, Sir Henry (Alexander).** GBE 1971.
**BOGGIS-ROLFE, Hume.** CB 1971.
**BOOTH, Eric Stuart.** CBE 1971.
**BOWRA, Sir (Cecil) Maurice.** CH 1971.
**BRAMWELL-BOOTH, Catherine.** CBE 1971.
***BREARLEY, Sir Norman.** Kt 1971. For services to aviation, Western Australia.
**BRECHIN, Sir Herbert Archbold.** KBE 1971.
**BROOKES, Sir Raymond Percival.** Kt 1971.
**BROWN, Gillian Gerda.** CMG 1971.
**BROWN, William.** CBE 1971.
**BROWNE, Air Commodore Charles Duncan Alfred.** CB 1971.
***BRYCE, Sir William Gordon.** Kt 1971. Chief Justice, Bahama Islands.
**BUNTING, Prof. Arthur Hugh.** CMG 1971.
**BUSHELL, John Christopher Wyndowe.** CMG 1971.

***CAKOBAU, Ratu Sir Etuate Tuivanuavou Tugi.** KBE 1971. Minister of Labour, Fiji.
**CAMERON, Air Vice-Marshal Neil.** CB 1971.
**CAMPBELL, Dame Kate Isabel.** DBE 1971.
**CATHERWOOD, Sir Henry Frederick Ross.** Kt 1971.
**CHISHOLM, Sir Henry.** Kt 1971.
**CHRISTIE, Dame Agatha Mary Clarissa.** DBE 1971.
**CLARK, Prof. John Grahame Douglas.** CBE 1971.
***COLE, Sir Noel.** Kt 1971. For outstanding services to the community in New Zealand.
**COLERIDGE, Baron.** KBE 1971.
**COLES, Norman.** CB 1971.
**COTTRELL, Sir Alan (Howard).** Kt 1971.
**COWLEY, Maj.-Gen. John Cain.** CB 1971.
**COX, Peter Richmond.** CB 1971.
***CRIPPS, Sir Cyril Thomas.** Kt 1971. For public and charitable services.
**CRIPPS, (Matthew) Anthony Leonard.** CBE 1971.
**CROSS, James Richard.** CMG 1971.

**DAINTON, Sir Frederick (Sydney).** Kt 1971.
**DARLING, Prof. Arthur Ivan.** CBE 1971.
***DARVALL, Sir Charles Roger.** Kt 1971. For public service, Victoria, Australia.
**DEACON, Sir George (Edward Raven).** Kt 1971
**DEAVIN, Stanley Gwynne.** CBE 1971.

* The current edition contains no entry under this name, which will appear with the usual details in *WHO'S WHO*, 1972.

***DOUGHTY, Dame Adelaide Baillieu.** DBE 1971. For political services in the South East.
**DUCKMANTON, Talbot Sydney.** CBE 1971.
**DUFFUS, Hon. Sir William Algernon Holwell.** Kt 1971.
***DUNLOP, Sir John Wallace.** KBE 1971. For distinguished services to industry in Australia.

**FITZER, Herbert Clyde.** CB 1971.
**FITZPATRICK, Gen. Sir (Geoffrey Richard) Desmond.** GCB 1971.
**FLETCHER, Leonard Ralph.** CB 1971.
***FORGET, Sir Joseph Guy.** Kt 1971. Mauritius Ambassador to France.
***FUNG Ping-fan, Hon. Sir Kenneth.** Kt 1971. For public and social services in Hong Kong.

***GLOVER, Sir Gerald Alfred.** Kt 1971. For political and public services.
**GODBER, Sir George (Edward).** GCB 1971.
**GORDON, Brig. Barbara (Masson).** CB 1971.
**GORDON, Ian Alistair.** CBE 1971.
**GOWANS, Prof. James Learmonth.** CBE 1971.
**GREEN, Thomas Charles.** CB 1971.
***GRIFFIN, Sir Francis Frederick.** Kt 1971. Alderman, Birmingham City Council.

**HALLINAN, Sir (Adrian) Lincoln.** Kt 1971.
***HANNAH, Air Marshal Sir Colin Thomas, RAAF.** KBE 1971.
**HAY, Lady Margaret Katharine.** DCVO 1971.
**HAYMAN, Sir Peter Telford.** KCMG 1971.
**HEWER, Prof. Humphrey Robert.** CBE 1971.
***HEWITT, Sir Cyrus Lenox Simson.** Kt 1971. Secretary, Prime Minister's Department, Australia.
**HILL, Prof. Dorothy.** CBE 1971.
**HODGKINSON, Air Marshal Sir William Derek.** KCB 1971.
**HOPKIN, Sir William Aylsham Bryan.** Kt 1971.
***HULME, Hon. Sir Alan Shallcross.** KBE 1971. Postmaster-General, Australia.
**HUNTER-TOD, Air Marshal Sir John Hunter.** KBE 1971.
**HUTCHISON, Prof. James Holmes.** CBE 1971.

**IBBOTSON, Lancelot William Cripps.** CBE 1971.

**JACKSON, Lt-Gen. Sir William Godfrey Fothergill.** KCB 1971.
***JOEL, Hon. Sir Asher Alexander.** Kt. 1971. For services to the community, New South Wales.
***JOHN, Sir Rupert Godfrey.** Kt 1971. Governor of Saint Vincent.
**JOHNSON-MARSHALL, Sir Stirrat Andrew William.** Kt 1971.
**JOHNSTON, Sir Charles (Hepburn).** GCMG 1971.
**JOLLIFFE, Christopher.** CBE 1971.

***KENT, Rear-Adm. Derrick George.** CB 1971.
**KING, Maj.-Gen. Frank Douglas.** CB 1971.
**KLEINWORT, Sir Cyril Hugh.** Kt 1971.
**KNIGHT, Gerald Hocken.** CBE 1971.

***LATOUR-ADRIEN, Sir Maurice.** Kt 1971. Chief Justice, Mauritius.
**LAVER, Frederick John Murray.** CBE 1971.
**LESLIE, Ian (William) Murray.** CBE 1971.
**LEWIS, Vice-Adm. Sir Andrew Mackenzie.** KCB 1971.
***LEWIS, Eric William Charles.** CB 1971. Controller of Death Duties, Board of Inland Revenue.
**LIDDLE, Sir Donald Ross.** Kt 1971.
***LLOYD, Sir John Peter Daniel.** Kt 1971. For distinguished services to finance, commerce and government, Australia.
**LLOYD OWEN, Maj.-Gen. David Lanyon.** CB 1971.
***LORD, Sir Ackland Archibald.** Kt 1971. For distinguished services to the community in Victoria and Tasmania.

**McEWEN, Rt. Hon. Sir John.** GCMG 1971.
**McGRATH, John Cornelius.** CBE 1971.
**MACKIE, George Yull.** CBE 1971.
**McKISSOCK, Sir Wylie.** Kt 1971.
**MACLEAN, Sir Charles Hector Fitzroy, Bt.** Life Peer (Baron) *cr* 1971. *Title unknown at time of going to press.*
**MALIM, Rear-Adm. Nigel Hugh.** CB 1971.
**MANCE, Sir Henry Stenhouse.** Kt 1971.
**MARSHALL, Sir Frank Shaw.** Kt 1971.
***MARTIN, Air Marshal Sir Harold Brownlow.** KCB 1971.
**MAYNARD, Air Vice-Marshal Nigel Martin.** CB 1971.
**MILNE, Kenneth Lancelot.** CBE 1971.

**MOORE, Henry Roderick.** CBE 1971.
***MORGAN, Sir Ernest Dunstan.** KBE 1971. For outstanding public service in Sierra Leone.
**MOULTON, Air Vice-Marshal Leslie Howard.** CB 1971.

**NEAL, Leonard Francis.** CBE 1971.
**NUNN, Jean Josephine.** CB 1971.

***O'NEILL, Sir Matthew John.** Kt 1971. For services to commerce and charity, New South Wales.
***OSMOND, Sir Douglas.** Kt 1971. Chief Constable, Hampshire Constabulary.
**OWEN, John Glendwr.** CB 1971.

**PACE, George Gaze.** CVO 1971.
**PACKER, Sir (Douglas) Frank (Hewson).** KBE 1971.
**PAGAN, Brig. Sir John Ernest.** Kt 1971.
**PAGE, Sir Denys Lionel.** Kt 1971.
**PAGET, Paul Edward.** CVO 1971.
**PARK, Daphne Margaret Sybil Désirée.** CMG 1971.
***PARKER, Rear-Adm. Douglas Granger.** CB 1971.
**PARSONS, Ian Macnaghten.** CBE 1971.
***PEEK, Vice-Adm. Richard Innes.** CB 1971. Chief of Naval Staff, Royal Australian Navy.
**PILE, Sir William Dennis.** KCB 1971.
**POLLOCK, Adm. Sir Michael (Patrick).** GCB 1971.
**POPE-HENNESSY, Sir John Wyndham.** Kt 1971.
**PORTER, Rt. Hon. Sir Robert Wilson.** Kt 1971.
**PRIDEAUX, Sir Humphrey Povah Treverbian.** Kt 1971.
**PROCTOR, Sir George Philip.** KBE 1971. For outstanding services to manufacturing and the community, Wellington, NZ.
**PURVES, James Grant.** CMG 1971.
***PURVES, Sir Raymond Edgar.** Kt 1971. For services to the community, New South Wales.

**RADFORD, Ronald Walter.** CB 1971.
***RAMSAY, Sir William Clark.** Kt 1971. For services to Rugby football.
**RHODES, John Ivor McKinnon.** CMG 1971.
***RICHTER, Hon. Sir Harold.** Kt 1971. For oustanding public services, Queensland, Australia.
**RIDLER, Vivian Hughes.** CBE 1971.
**ROSKILL, Captain Stephen Wentworth.** CBE 1971.
**ROSS, Sir Alexander.** Kt 1971.
***RUSHTON, Sir Reginald Fielding.** Kt 1971. For outstanding service to the community, Western Australia.

**SEAMAN, Clarence Milton Edwards.** CBE 1971.
**SIEFF, Hon. Sir Marcus (Joseph).** Kt 1971.
**SIMON, Rt. Hon. Sir Jocelyn Edward Salis.** Life Peer (Baron) *cr* 1971. *Title unknown at time of going to press.*
**SOMERVILLE, Mrs (Katherine) Lilian.** CMG 1971.
**SPOTSWOOD, Air Chief Marshal Sir Denis (Frank).** GCB 1971.
***SPRINGER, Sir Hugh Worrell.** KCMG 1971. For services to higher education in Barbados and the Commonwealth.

**TAYLOR, Arnold Joseph.** CBE 1971.
**THOMAS, Sir (William) Miles (Webster).** Life Peer (Baron) *cr* 1971. *Title unknown at time of going to press.*
**THORNTON, Peter Eustace.** CB 1971.
***TOWNSEND, Sir Sydney Lance.** Kt 1971. Professor of Obstetrics and Gynaecology, University of Melbourne.
**TRIPP, John Peter.** CMG 1971.

**WALKER, Prof. James.** CBE 1971.
**WALSH, Rt. Hon. Sir Cyril Ambrose.** PC 1971.
**WALTERS, Sir Roger Talbot.** KBE 1971.
**WARD, Lt-Gen. Sir Richard Erskine.** KCB 1971.
**WARE, Henry Gabriel.** CB 1971.
**WARWICK, Captain William Eldon.** CBE 1971.
**WHITE, Hon. Sir Alfred John.** Kt 1971.
**WILSON, Prof. Andrew.** CBE 1971.
**WORCESTER, Bishop of; Rt. Rev. Robert Wilmer Woods.** KCVO 1971.

**YOUNG, Maj.-Gen. Alexander.** CB 1971.
**YOUNG, Col Sir Arthur (Edwin).** KBE 1971.

* The current edition contains no entry under this name, which will appear with the usual details in *WHO'S WHO*, 1972.

# A

**AALTO, Prof. (Hugo) Alvar (Henrik);** Finnish Architect; furniture designer; Founder-Director, Aalto Architectural Office, since 1923; *b* 3 Feb. 1898; *m* 1924 (wife *d* 1949); one *s* one *d*; *m* 1952. *Educ:* Jyräskylän Lyseo and Inst. of Technology, Helsinki. Architect, 1921. In partnership with wife for twenty years; founded furniture firm; Prof., Massachusetts Institute of Technology, 1946-48. Work in Finland includes: Sanatorium at Paimio, library at Viipuri, factory at Sunila, university buildings at Oulu and Jyväskulä, government and commercial buildings in Helsinki and many other municipal buildings, country houses, and housing projects, also churches, in Finland. Abroad: dormitory at Massachusetts Institute of Technology, flats in Berlin, Cultural centre and a 22 floor flat-building in Germany, country house in France. Finnish Pavilions at Paris Exhibition, 1937, and New York World Fair, etc, 1939. Member: Finnish Acad. (Pres., 1963-68); Det Kongelige Akademi för de Skønne Kunster; Academie de l'Architecture; Les Congrès Internationaux d'Architecture Moderne; Akademie der Künste, Berlin; Hon. RDI (RSA Lond.); Hon. Member: Royal College of Art (Lond.); Associazone per l'Architettura Organica; Instituto de Arquitetos do Brasil; Södra Sveriges Byggnadstekn. Samfund; Assoc. of Finnish Architects; Norkse Arkitekters Landsforbund; Accademia di Belle Arti di Venezia; Amer. Acad. of Arts and Sciences; Invited Member: Kungliga Akademin för de Fria Konsterna; Koninklijke Vlaamse Academie; Fell. Mem. World Acad. of Art and Science (Israel); Corresp. Mem. Accademia Nazionale di San Luca; Hon. Corresp. Mem. RIBA; Hon. Fell., Amer. Inst. of Architects. Dr *hc*: Princeton University (US); Inst. of Technology, Helsinki; Inst. of Technology, Trondheim, Norway; Swiss Federal Institute of Technology; Columbia University, New York; Technische Hochschule, Wien; Laurea *hc*, Polytechnic Inst. of Milan. Royal Gold Medal for Architecture, RIBA, 1957; Gold Medal, Amer. Inst. of Architects, 1963; Gold Cube, Svenska Arkitekters Riksförbund, 1963. Chevalier de la Légion d'Honneur; Akademisk Arkitektførenings Aeres-medaille; Prins Eugen medal; Medaglia d'Oro della Città di Firenze; Grande Ufficiale al Merito della Repubblica Italiana; Suomen Leijonan. Ritarikunnan Suurristi; Comdr of Dannebrog, etc. *Address:* Tiilimäki 20, Helsinki 33, Finland.

**AARON, Richard Ithamar,** MA, DPhil; Professor of Philosophy, University College of Wales, Aberystwyth, 1932-69; *b* 6 Nov. 1901; *s* of William and Margaret Aaron, Ynystawe, Swansea; *m* Rhiannon, *d* of Dr M. J. Morgan, Aberystwyth; two *s* three *d*. *Educ:* Ystalyfera Grammar School; Cardiff University College; Oriel College, Oxford. Fellow, Univ. of Wales, 1923; Lectr at Swansea, 1926; Chm., Central Adv. Coun. for Educn (Wales), 1946-52; Mem., Coun. for Wales, 1956-63 (Chm., 1960-63); Chm. Library Advisory Council (Wales), 1965-; Mem. Gen. Advisory Council, BBC, 1962-, and TV Research Council, 1963-69; Mem. Council, National Library of Wales; Vice-Chm., Coleg Harlech Residential Coll.; Chm., Pembroke and Cardigan Agricultural Wages Cttee, 1962-. Vis. Prof. in Philosophy, Yale Univ., US, 1952-53 (Fell. of Pierson Coll.). Pres., Mind Assoc., 1955-56; Pres., Aristotelian Society, London, 1957-58. FBA 1955. *Publications:* The Nature of Knowing, 1930; Hanes Athroniaeth, 1932; An Early Draft of Locke's Essay (with Jocelyn Gibb), 1936; John Locke, 1937, 2nd rev. edn 1955; The Limitations of Locke's Rationalism, in Seventeenth Century Studies, 1938; Our Knowledge of Universals, Annual Philosophical Lecture to British Academy, 1945; The Theory of Universals, 1952, 2nd rev. edn 1967; The True and the Valid, Friends of Dr Williams's Library Lecture, 1954; Knowing and the Function of Reason, 1971; Editor, Efrydiau Athronyddol, 1938-68; contributor to Mind, Proc. Arist. Soc., Philosophy, Mod. Lang. Rev., Llenor, etc. *Address:* Garth Celyn, Aberystwyth, Cards. *T:* 3535.

**AARONS, Sir Daniel (Sidney),** Kt 1970; OBE 1966; MC 1917 and Bar, 1918; retired; *b* 1 Aug. 1885; *s* of Solomon Aarons and Hannah Hart; *m* 1925, Jessie Chaddock Stronach; no *c*. *Educ:* North Broken Hill Public School. Joined Vacuum Oil Co. Australia in West Australia, 1903; enlisted AIF, 1915; returned 1920, after spending 7 months in USA for advanced knowledge in oil marketing with parent company and on return joined Head Office of Company, Melbourne, as Australasian Sales Manager; transf. to Sydney as Gen. Man. NSW, 1935; retd 1947; Director: Yellow Cab Co. Ltd; Yellow Express Carriers Ltd; Hardy & Sons Ltd, Timber Merchants; Chm., Butler Air Transport Co., 1946-55 (when taken over by another co.). Foundn Mem., Liberal Party of Australia, 1945; subseq. Chm. of Finance Cttee; treas. 1969. Past Pres., Legacy Club of Sydney; Mem. Federal Council, Legacy Clubs of Australia; Past Pres., Civic Reform Assoc. (local govt). *Recreations:* lawn bowls; formerly rowing (Mem. King's Cup 8-oared Crew WA 1912), lacrosse (Player Man., WA Interstate Lacrosse Team, 1912) and golf. *Address:* Australian Club, 31 Bligh Street, Sydney, NSW, Australia. *T:* 284914. *Club:* Australian (Sydney).

**AARVOLD, Sir Carl (Douglas),** Kt 1968; OBE 1945; TD 1950; **His Honour Judge Aarvold;** Recorder of London since 1964; Chairman, National Advisory Council on the Training of Magistrates, since 1964; Chairman, City of London Quarter Sessions, since 1969; *b* 7 June 1907; *s* of late O. P. Aarvold and late J. M. Aarvold, West Hartlepool, County Durham; *m* 1934, Noeline Etrenne Hill, Denton Park,

Yorks; three *s*. *Educ:* Durham Sch.; Emmanuel College, Cambridge. Called to the Bar, Inner Temple, 1932; North Eastern Circuit. Master of the Bench, Inner Temple, 1959. Recorder of Pontefract, 1951-54; a Judge of the Mayor's and City of London Court, 1954-; Common Serjeant, City of London, 1959-64. Hon. LLD Dalhousie, 1962; Hon. DCL Durham, 1965. Pres., Lawn Tennis Assoc., 1962-. *Recreations:* golf, tennis, gardening. *Address:* Foxbury, Westhumble, Dorking, Surrey. *T:* Dorking 2771.

**ABAYOMI, Sir Kofo Adekunle,** Kt 1951; MD, ChB, DTM&H; DOMS (Eng.); FRSA; Member Privy Council, Nigeria, 1951; Chief Ona Ishokun of Oyo since 1949; Chief Baba Isale of Lagos since 1952; is an Eye Specialist; *b* 10 July 1896; *s* of Joseph N. John and Aiyelagbe Davies; *m* 1932, Oyinkan Morenikeji, MBE, *o d* of Sir Kitoyi Ajasa, OBE; five *s* one *d*. *Educ:* Methodist Boys' High School, Lagos; Edinburgh Univ. Served European War, 1914-17 (medals). Pharmacist, 1917-22; Edinburgh Univ., 1922; MB, ChB 1928. Demonstrator in Physiological Methods, Edinburgh Univ., 1927-30; DTM&H Edinburgh 1929; MD with speciality in Tropical Medicine, 1936; FRSA 1934; Rhodes Scholar in Ophthalmology, 1941; studied also at Moorfields Eye Hosp., 1940-41; DOMS England 1941. MLC, Nigeria, 1938-40; MEC, Nigeria, 1949-51; Member: Government and educational committees; Univ. Coll. Council, Ibadan, 1947-; Dep. Chm., Univ. Coll. Hosp., Ibadan, 1953-; Chm. Bd of Management, Univ. Teaching Hosp., Ibadan; President: Nigeria Federal Soc. for the Blind, 1953-; Assoc. of Medical Practitioners, 1946-; Nigeria Br., BMA, 1953-; Nigeria Medical Assoc., 1960; Chm., Lagos Exec. Development Board; Director: Barclays Bank, DCO (Nigeria); ICI (Nigeria); P & Z Co. Ltd; Vice-Chm., British Bata Shoe Co. (Nigeria); Chm. Bd of Trustees, Glover Memorial Hall. Hon. LLD Mount Allison Univ., Canada, 1958; Hon. LLD Univ. of Ibadan, 1963. *Recreation:* walking. *Address:* PO Box 300, Lagos, Nigeria. *Clubs:* Royal Commonwealth Society; Dining, Metropolitan, Ikoyi (Lagos).

**ABBADO, Claudio;** Permanent Conductor of La Scala Orchestra, Milan, since 1968; *b* 26 June 1933. *Educ:* Conservatorio G. Verdi, Milan; Musical Academy, Vienna. Guest Conductor of principal orchestras in Europe and America; Conductor at: Vienna Festival, 1961-; Salzburg Festival, 1965-; Edinburgh Festival, 1966-; Prague Spring, 1966-; Lucerne Festival, 1966-; Holland Festival, 1966-; Venice Festival, 1966-. Sergei Koussewitzky Prize, Berkshire Music Festival (USA), 1958; Dimitri Mitropoulos Prize, 1963; Philips Prize, Salzburg, 1965; Diapason Prize, 1966, 1967; Grand Prix du Disque, 1967; Deutscher Schalplatten-Preis, 1968. *Address:* Via Speronari 8, 20123 Milan, Italy. *T:* 890477.

**ABBOT, Charles Greeley,** DSc, LLD; Research Associate, Smithsonian Institution, since 1944; *b* 31 May 1872; *s* of Harris Abbot and Ann Caroline Greeley; *m* 1897, Lillian Elvira Moore (*d* 1944); no *c*; *m* 1954, Virginia Andes Johnston. *Educ:* Massachusetts Inst. of Technology. Continuously employed by Smithsonian Instn of Washington from 1895; Asst, 1895-1906, Director, 1907-44, of Smithsonian Astrophysical Observatory; Asst Sec., 1918-27, Sec., 1928-44, Smithsonian Institution. Research on solar radiation, atmospheric transparency, the weather, applications of solar radiation, stellar radiation. Member Nat. Acad. of Sciences, Am. Assoc. for Advancement of Sciences, and many socs and acads in America and abroad. *Publications:* Vols. 1-6 Annals Astrophysical Observatory; The Sun, 1911, 2nd edn 1929; Everyday Mysteries, 1925; The Earth and the Stars, 1926, 2nd edn 1946; The Sun and the Welfare of Man, 1928, 2nd edn 1944; Great Inventions, 1932; papers on scientific subjects. *Recreations:* reading; music; games, especially golf, tennis, bridge. *Address:* 4409 Beechwood Road, Hyattsville, Md 20782, USA; Smithsonian Institution, Washington, DC. *T:* National 8-1810. *Clubs:* Cosmos, Abracadabra (Washington, DC).

**ABBOT, Dermot Charles Hyatt,** CB 1959; Assistant Under-Secretary of State, Department of Health and Social Security, 1968-69 (Under-Secretary, Ministry of Pensions and National Insurance, 1955-66, Ministry of Social Security, 1966-68); retired 1969; *b* 8 Sept. 1908; *e s* of late Reginald Arthur Brame Abbot and late Sarah Ethel Abbot; *m* 1947, Elsie Myrtle Arnott (*see* Dame Elsie Abbot). *Educ:* High School, Newcastle-under-Lyme; High School, Southend-on-Sea; University College, London. Post Office, 1929-40 and 1945-49; transferred to Ministry of Pensions and National Insurance, 1949. *Recreations:* gardening, fishing, travel. *Address:* 4 Constable Close, NW11. *T:* 01-455 9413. *Club:* Royal Automobile.

**ABBOT, Dame Elsie (Myrtle),** DBE 1966 (CBE 1957); Third Secretary, HM Treasury, 1958-67; *b* 3 Sept. 1907; *d* of Leonard and Frances Tostevin, Streatham, London; *m* 1st, 1938, E. A. Arnott, *s* of R. E. Arnott, Pontypridd; one *s* one *d*; 2nd, 1947, D. C. H. Abbot, *qv*. *Educ:* Clapham County Secondary School; St Hugh's College, Oxford. 1st Class Hons Modern History, 1929; 1st Class Hons Philosophy, Politics and Economics, 1930. Entered Administrative Class of Home Civil Service, 1930; Post Office, 1930-47; transferred to HM Treasury, 1947. *Address:* 4 Constable Close, NW11. *T:* 01-455 9413.

**ABBOTT, Arthur William,** CMG 1956; CBE 1949; FRHistS; *b* 5 Feb. 1893; *s* of late William Henry Abbott, Southampton, sometime President, Hampshire Law Society; *m* 1926, Kathleen, *d* of Richard Way; one *s*. *Educ:* Blundell's School, Tiverton. Entered Crown Agents' Office, 1912; served European War, 1914-18, Hampshire Regt, North Russia, 1917-19; Secretary, East African Currency Board, 1930-38; Head of Department, 1938; Establishment Officer, 1948; Secretary to the Crown Agents (for oversea governments and administrations), 1954-58. *Publications:* History of the Crown Agents (printed for private circulation, 1960); review and magazine articles. *Address:* Frithys Orchard, West Clandon, Surrey. *T:* Clandon 565

**ABBOTT, Hon. Charles Lydiard Aubrey;** *b* Sydney, 4 May 1886; *s* of Thomas Kingsmill Abbott, Chief Stipendiary Magistrate at Sydney; *m* Hilda, *d* of John Harnett, Monaro, NSW; two *d*. *Educ:* The King's School, Parramatta. Pastoralist; served with AIF, Aug. 1914-Oct. 1919 (wounded); promoted to commissioned rank, and returned to Australia with rank of captain; Member House of Representatives for Gwydir, NSW, 1925-29 and 1931-37; Minister for Home Affairs, Commonwealth of Australia, 1928-29; Administrator of Northern Territory of Australia, 1937-46. *Publication:* Australia's Frontier Province (The Northern Territory), 1950; addressed RGS on N Territory, 1946. *Recreations:* gardening, writing, historical research. *Address:* Carpe Diem, Merrigang Street, Bowral, NSW 2576, Australia. *Club:* Imperial Service (Sydney).

**ABBOTT, Claude Colleer,** MA London, BA, PhD Cantab; Professor of English Language and Literature in the University of Durham, 1932-54, Emeritus Professor, 1954; *b* 17 April 1889; *er s* of George Henry Abbott and Mary Matilda Colleer; unmarried. *Educ:* King Edward VI Sch., Chelmsford; Gonville and Caius Coll., Cambridge. Asst Master at the Grammar School, Sudbury, Suffolk, and the High School, Middlesbrough; BA London, 1913; MA London, 1915; Artists' Rifles OTC, 1918; Household Brigade OCB; 2nd Lieut Irish Guards (Special Reserve); BA Cantab, 1921; PhD Cantab, 1926; Lecturer in English Language and Literature in the University of Aberdeen, 1921-32; Censor of University College, Durham, 1932-41; Dean of the Faculty of Arts, 1943-45; Chm. Univ. Publications Bd, 1948-50, 1952-54; Editor Durham Univ. Journal, 1939-52. Visited and lectured at many univs in USA, 1949 (Goldwin Smith Lecture at Cornell, Lamont Lecture at Yale); Visiting Professor Univ. of Virginia, Feb.-June 1953; Resident, Yale: lectured at univs in South USA, Oct. 1956-March 1957. Member of Boswell Papers Advisory Committee. *Publications:* Youth and Age, 1918; Nine Songs from the Old French, 1920; Poems, 1921; Miss Bedell and Other Poems, 1924; Life and Letters of George Darley, 1928 (repr. 1967); Ploughed Earth, Poems, 1930; Early Mediæval French Lyrics, 1932; Letters of Gerard Manley Hopkins to Robert Bridges, 1935; Correspondence of Gerard Manley Hopkins and Richard Watson Dixon, 1935; A Catalogue of Papers relating to Boswell, Johnson and Sir William Forbes, 1936; Further Letters of Gerard Manley Hopkins, including his correspondence with Patmore, 1938 (2nd edn revised and enlarged, 1956); Early Verses, 1938; Further Letters of George Darley (Durham University journal, Dec. 1940); The Parents of Thomas Lovell Beddoes (DUJ, June 1942); Versions of Old English Elegies (DUJ, June 1943, June 1944); The Sand Castle and other Poems, 1946; Boswell (Spence Watson Memorial Lecture), 1946; (ed. with introd.) Poems and Plays by Gordon Bottomley, 1953; Poet and Painter: the Correspondence of Gordon Bottomley and Paul Nash, 1955; Summer Love Poems, 1958; Collected Poems, 1963. *Recreations:* walking, book-hunting, gardening. *Address:* 7 Church Street, Durham. *T:* Durham 2853. *Club:* Athenæum.

**ABBOTT, Hon. Douglas Charles,** PC (Can.) 1945; QC 1939; BCL (McGill); Hon. LLD, Hon. DCL; Justice of the Supreme Court, Canada, since 1954; *b* Lennoxville, PQ, 29 May 1899; *s* of Lewis Duff Abbott and Mary Jane Pearce; *m* 1925, Mary Winifred Chisholm; two *s* one *d*. *Educ:* Bishop's College; McGill University; Dijon University, France. Elected to House of Commons, 1940; re-elected, 1945, 1949 and 1953. Minister of National Defence for Naval Services, April 1945; Minister of National Defence (Army), Aug. 1945; Min. of Finance, Canada, 1946-54. Practised law in Montreal with firm of Robertson, Abbott, Brierley and O'Connor. Chancellor, Bishop's Univ., 1958-68. *Recreations:* fishing, curling, golf. *Address:* 124 Springfield Road, Ottawa, Canada. *TA:* Ottawa Canada. *T:* 745-6250. *Clubs:* University, Royal Montreal Curling (Montreal); Rideau (Ottawa).

**ABBOTT, Very Rev. Eric Symes,** KCVO 1966; DD (Lambeth); MA Cantab and Oxon (by incorporation); Dean of Westminster since 1959; *b* 26 May 1906; *s* of William Henry and Mary Abbott, Nottingham. *Educ:* Nottingham High School; Jesus College, Cambridge. Curate, St John's, Smith Square, Westminster, 1930-32; Chaplain, King's College, London, 1932-36; Chaplain to Lincoln's Inn, 1935-36; Warden of the Scholae Cancellarii, Lincoln, 1936-45; Canon and Prebendary of Lincoln Cathedral, 1940-60. Dean of King's College, London, 1945-55; Warden of Keble College, Oxford, 1956-60; Chaplain to King George VI, 1948-52, and to the Queen, 1952-59. Chaplain and Sub-Prelate, Order of St John of Jerusalem, 1969-. FKC, London, 1946-; Hon. Fellow: Keble Coll., Oxford, 1960-61; Jesus Coll., Cambridge, 1966. Hon. DD London, 1966. *Address:* The Deanery, Westminster, SW1. *Club:* Athenæum.

**ABBOTT, John Sutherland,** JP; Director, The Bank of Scotland, Royal Exchange Assurance (Chairman Glasgow Local Board) and other Companies; Chairman and Managing Director, Saxone Lilley & Skinner (Holdings) Ltd, 1938-64; Director, Glenfield and Kennedy Holdings Ltd, 1952-65; Hon. President, Kilmarnock and District Chamber of Industries; Governor, Welbeck College; Member, Scottish National Committee, English-speaking Union; Member of Kennel Club Committee; *b* 24 August 1900; 2nd *s* of late George Sutherland Abbott, JP, Middleton House, Ayr; *m* 1928, Winifred May, 2nd *d* of George Thomas, Wolverhampton; one *s*. *Educ:* Bedales School; Pembroke College, Cambridge. JP Ayrshire 1942. *Recreations:* shooting, racing, breeding and exhibiting wire-haired foxterriers. *Address:* Whitehill of Coodham, Symington, Ayrshire. *Clubs:* East India and Sports, Kennel; Leander.

**ABBOTT, Sir Myles (John),** Kt 1964; **Hon. Mr Justice Abbott;** Chief Justice of Bermuda since 1961; *b* 27 Feb. 1906; *s* of Edmund Rushworth Abbott, 13 Victoria Street, London, Solicitor; *m* 1st, 1932, Grace Ada Jeffery; one *d*; 2nd, 1960, Dorothy Anne Campbell, *widow* of Robert Currie Campbell. *Educ:* King's Sch., Canterbury. Admitted Solicitor, 1929; Partner, Chas Rogers Sons & Abbott, 1930. 2nd Lieut 9th Middlesex Regt. (TA), 1933. Selected for appointment to Colonial Legal Service, 1935; Lieut 9th Middx Regt and transferred to TARO, 1936; Asst Crown Solicitor, Hong Kong, 1936; called to the Bar, 1940; Official Receiver and Registrar of Trade Marks, Hong Kong, 1941. Served War of 1939-45 (prisoner); released, 1945. President, High Court of Ethiopia, Oct. 1946-Oct. 1949; Puisne Judge, Nigeria, 1950-55; Judge of High Court of Lagos, 1955-57; Federal Justice of Federal Supreme Court of Nigeria, 1957-61. *Publications:* (ed) West African Court of Appeal Reports, 1946-49; (ed) Federal Supreme Court Reports, Nigeria, Vol. 4, 1959, 1960. *Address:* Supreme Court, Hamilton, Bermuda. *T:* Bermuda 20263. *Clubs:* Naval and Military; Royal Hamilton Amateur Dinghy (Bermuda).

**ABDELA, Jack Samuel Ronald,** TD 1948; QC 1966; **His Honour Judge Abdela;** Deputy Chairman, Inner London Quarter Sessions, since 1970; *b* 9 Oct. 1913; *s* of Joseph and Dorothy Abdela, Manchester; *m* 1942, Enid Hope Russell, *y d* of Edgar Dodd Russell, London; two *s*. *Educ:* Manchester Gram. Sch.; Milton Sch., Bulawayo; Fitzwilliam House, Cambridge (BA Hons). Called to the Bar, Gray's Inn, 1935. 2nd Lieut, Lancashire Fusiliers (TA), 1938; Lieut-Col. Comdt 55 Div. Battle School, 1943; 7th Bn Royal Welch Fusiliers, NW Europe, 1944-46; Major, Inns of Court Regt. (TA), 1946-52. *Recreations:* swimming, tennis, gardening. *Address:* 5 Raymond Buildings, Gray's Inn, WC1. *T:* 01-242 2764; Lamb Building, Temple, EC4. *T:* 01-583 6094. *Club:* Savage.

**ABDOOLCADER, Sir Husein Hasanally,** Kt 1948; CBE 1938; LLD (Malaya); Barrister-at-Law, Advocate and Solicitor; formerly Member Advisory Council of Governor of The Malayan Union; *b* Surat, Bombay Presidency, 10 Sept. 1890; *e s* of H. A. Cader, JP, merchant; *m* 1914, Manubai Mohamedally, *yr d* of late Mohamedally Mulla Abdullhusein Hakimji, Surat; five *s* two *d*. *Educ:* Raffles Institution, Singapore; Penang Free School, Penang; County High School, Ilford, Essex; Christ's College, Cambridge; Lincoln's Inn. Indian Member Straits Settlements Legislative Council from 1928 until outbreak of war with Japan; Member of Indian Immigration Cttee, 1935-53; Pres. Third All Malaya Indian Conf., 1929-30; Indian Mem. of Municipal Commn, Georgetown, Penang, 1925-51; Past Pres., Penang Soc. for Prevention of Cruelty to Animals; Past Pres., Mohammedan Football Assoc.; Silver Jubilee Medal, 1935; Coronation Medal, 1937. Hon. LLD Univ. of Malaya, 1963. *Recreations:* tennis, rowing, walking. *Address:* Surat Lodge, 3R Tarjong Tokong Road, Mukim 18, Penang; Georgetown Chambers, 39 Beach Street, Penang. *TA:* Sir Abdoolcader Penang. *T:* 60690, (office) 63275.

**ABDUL RAHMAN PUTRA, Tunku (Prince),** CH 1961; Order of the National Crown, Malaysia; Kedah Order of Merit; Prime Minister of Malaysia, 1963-70; *b* 1903; *m* 3rd, 1939, Puan Sharifah Rodziah binti Syed Alwi Barakbah; one *s* one *d* (both by 1st wife); one *s* three *d* (all adopted). *Educ:* Alor Star; Bangkok; St Catharine's Coll., Cambridge; Inner Temple, London. Joined Kedah State Civil Service, 1931, District Officer. During the occupation, when the Japanese returned Kedah to Siam, he served as Supt of Educn and Dir of Passive Defence until the reoccupation, Sept. 1945; opposed British Govt fusion of States and Colonies to form the Malayan Union and took a leading part in formation of United Malays National Organisation (UMNO); when the Malayan Union gave way to the Federation of Malaya in 1949, he became Chairman of UMNO in Kedah; after being called to Bar (Inner Temple), he returned to Kedah and was seconded to Federal Legal Dept as a Dep. Public Prosecutor, 1949; President of UMNO, 1951; resigned from CS and a year later was apptd an unofficial Mem. Federal Executive and Legislative Councils; leader of the Alliance Party (UMNO, Malayan Chinese Association, Malayan Indian Congress), 1954; elected to Federal Legislative Council, 1955; became Chief Minister and Minister of Home Affairs; in reshuffle of 1956 also took portfolio of Minister for Internal Defence and Security; was also Chm. Emergency Ops Council which decides on policy in fighting Malayan Communist Party; headed Alliance deleg. to London to negotiate Independence for the Federation, Dec. 1955; after Independence on 31 Aug. 1957, became Prime Minister and Minister of External Affairs and continued to be Chm. Emergency Ops Council; resigned as Prime Minister in Feb. 1959 to prepare for general elections in Aug.; became Prime Minister for second time, Aug. 1959, and in Sept. initiated Min. of Rural Development; became also Minister of Ext. Affairs, Nov. 1960, and Minister of Information and Broadcasting, June 1961; Prime Minister, Federation of Malaya, until it became Malaysia, 1963; became Prime Minister for third time, April 1964, following Gen. Elections in States of Malaya, also Minister of External Affairs and Minister of Culture, Youth and Sports. Attended Prime Ministers' Conferences in London, May 1960 and March 1961; Head of mission to London to discuss and agree in principle proposed formation of Federation of Malaysia, Nov. 1961; Head of second mission to London on formation of Malaysia, July 1962; attended Prime Ministers' Confs, London, 1965, 1966. Apptd Chancellor, Univ. Malaya, 1962. Pres., Football Assoc. of Malaya; Pres., Asian Football Confedn; Vice-Pres. (for life), Royal Commonwealth Society. Dr of Law, Univ. of Malaya; Hon. LLD: Araneta Univ., 1958; Cambridge Univ., 1960; Univ. of Sydney, 1960; Univ. of Saigon, 1961; Aligarh Muslim Univ., 1962; Hon. DLitt, Seoul National Univ., 1965; Hon. DCL Oxford, 1970. Holds various foreign Orders. *Publications:* Mahsuri (imaginary play of Malaya; performed on stage in North Malaya throughout 1941; filmed in Malaya, 1958); Raja Bersiong (filmed 1966). *Relevant publication:* Prince and Premier (Biography) by Harry Miller, 1959. *Recreations:* golf, football, tennis, walking, swimming, racing, motor-boating, photography (both cine and still); collector of ancient weapons, particularly the Malay kris. *Address:* c/o Office of the Prime Minister, Jalan Dato Onn, Kuala Lumpur, Malaysia. *T:* Kuala Lumpur 88228 and 84432.

**ABDY, Sir Robert (Henry Edward),** 5th Bt, *cr* 1850; late 15th Hussars; *b* 11 Sept. 1896; *s* of 4th Bt and Anna Adele Coronna; *S* father, 1921; *m* 1st, 1923, Iya Jongeyans (who obtained a divorce, 1928); 2nd, 1930, Lady Diana Bridgeman (marr. diss., 1962; she *d* 1967), *e d* of 5th Earl of Bradford; one *s*; 3rd, 1962, Jane Noble. *Educ:* Sandhurst. *Heir:* *s* Valentine Robert Duff Abdy, *b* 11 Sept. 1937. *Address:* Newton Ferrers, Callington, Cornwall.

*See also Earl of Lanesborough.*

**ABEL, Arthur Lawrence,** MS; MD(*hc*); FRCS; Consulting Surgeon: Princess Beatrice Hospital; Gordon Hospital (Westminster Hospital Group); Royal Marsden Hospital and Institute of Cancer Research, Royal Cancer Hospital; Hon. Consulting Surgeon: Woolwich War Memorial Hospital; Wood Green and Southgate Hospital; Hounslow Hospital; Vice-President, British Medical Association; *b* 15 Nov. 1895; *s* of Rev. A. E. Abel; *m* (wife *d* 1963); three *s* one *d*. *Educ:* University Coll., London; University Coll. Hospital. MB, BS 1917; MS Lond. 1921; MRCS, LRCP 1917; FRCS 1920; MD(*hc*) Bristol 1967. Jacksonian Prize 1924 and Hunterian Professor 1926, RCS; Fellowes Silver Medal in Clinical Medicine; First Prize in Clinical Surgery, UCH Bradshaw Lectr, 1957. Member: Council RCS, 1947-63 (Vice-Pres., 1956-57); Grand Council British Empire Cancer Campaign for Research; former Member, Bd of Governors: Westminster Hosp.; Royal Marsden Hosp. and Inst. of Cancer Research, Royal Cancer Hospital; Fellow Royal Society of Medicine; Fell. Chelsea Clinical Soc.; Hon. Fellow, Member Council and Past Pres. Metropolitan Cos Br., BMA; Hon. Fellow and Auditor, Hunterian Soc. (Pres., 1963; Orator, 1962). Fellow and Trustee, Harveian Society. Visiting Professor: Royal North Shore Hospital, Sydney; Marquette Univ., Milwaukee; Brooklyn Med. Centre, NY. Lectr, Cook County Graduate Sch. of Medicine, Chicago. Hon. Mem., Soc. of Surgeons of Madrid. Hon. Fellow: Amer. Med. Assoc.; Amer. Proctol. Soc.; Argentine Proctol. Soc. Late House Surg. and House Physician, Univ. Coll. Hosp. and Hosp. for Sick Children, Gt Ormond Street; Surg. Registrar (5 years) Cancer Hosp.; Temp. Surg. Lieut RN. *Publications:* contribs to med. jls. *Address:* 48 Harley Street, W1. *T:* 01-580 4118.

**ABEL SMITH, Sir Alexander,** Kt 1968; TD; JP; Consultant, J. Henry Schroder Wagg and Co. Ltd; Chairman: Provident Mutual Life

Assurance Association; BHD Engineers Ltd; Director of other companies; *b* 18 Sept. 1904; *s* of late Lieut-Col Francis Abel Smith, DL; *m* 1st, 1936, Elizabeth (*d* 1948), *d* of David B. Morgan, Biltmore, North Carolina, USA; one *s* one *d*; 2nd, 1953, Henriette Alice, CVO, JP (Lady-in-waiting to HRH Princess Elizabeth and subsequently to HM The Queen, 1949-53; Extra Woman of the Bedchamber to HM The Queen since 1953), *widow* of Sir Anthony Palmer, 4th Bt, and *d* of Comdr Francis Cadogan, Royal Navy, Quenington Old Rectory, Cirencester; one *s* one *d*. *Educ:* Eton College; Magdalen College, Oxford. Served War of 1939-45, AA Command and British Army Staff, Washington (hon. Brigadier). Order of Legion of Merit, USA. Knight (1st Class) Order of Dannebrog (Denmark). *Recreations:* shooting and fishing. *Address:* Houndsell Place, Mark Cross, Crowborough, Sussex. *T:* Rotherfield 347; 63 Cadogan Gardens, SW3. *Club:* Buck's.
*See also Col Sir Henry Abel Smith.*

**ABEL-SMITH, Prof. Brian;** Professor of Social Administration, University of London, at the London School of Economics, since 1965, half-time since 1968; Senior Adviser to Secretary of State for Health and Social Security, 1968–70; *b* 6 Nov. 1926; *s* of late Brig.-Gen. Lionel Abel-Smith. *Educ:* Haileybury Coll.; Clare Coll., Cambridge. MA, PhD, 1955. Served Army: Private 1945; commissioned Oxford and Bucks Light Inf., 1946; Mil. Asst to Dep. Comr, Allied Commn for Austria (Capt.), 1947-48. Res. Fellow, Nat. Inst. of Economic and Social Res., collecting economic evidence for Guillebaud Cttee (cost of Nat. Health Service), 1953-55. LSE: Asst Lectr in Social Science, 1955; Lecturer, 1957; Reader in Social Administration, University of London, 1961. Assoc. Professor, Yale Law Sch., Yale Univ., 1961. Consultant and Expert Adv. to WHO on costs of med. care, 1957-; Consultant: to Social Affairs Div. of UN, 1959, 1961; to ILO, 1967. Member: SW Metrop. Reg. Hosp. Bd, 1956-63; Cent. Health Services Coun. Sub-Cttee on Prescribing Statistics, 1960-64; Sainsbury Cttee (Relationship of Pharmaceut. Industry with Nat. Health Service), 1965-67; Long-term Study Group (to advise on long-term develt of NHS), 1965-. Chm., Chelsea and Kensington Hosp. Man. Cttee, 1961-62; Governor: St Thomas' Hosp., 1957-; Maudsley Hosp. and Inst. of Psychiatry, 1963-67. *Publications:* (with R. M. Titmuss) The Cost of the National Health Service in England and Wales, 1956; A History of the Nursing Profession, 1960; (with R. M. Titmuss) Social Policy and Population Growth in Mauritius, 1961; Paying for Health Services (for WHO), 1963; The Hospitals, 1800-1948, 1964; (with R. M. Titmuss *et al.*) The Health Services of Tanganyika, 1964; (with K. Gales) British Doctors at Home and Abroad, 1964; (with P. Townsend) The Poor and the Poorest, 1965; (with R. Stevens) Lawyers and the Courts, 1967; An International Study of Health Expenditure (for WHO), 1967; (with R. Stevens) In Search of Justice, 1968; pamphlets for Fabian Soc., 1953-; articles. *Recreations:* skiing, swimming. *Address:* London School of Economics, Houghton Street, WC2. *T:* 01-405 7686.

**ABEL SMITH, Desmond,** MC 1916; Major, late Grenadier Guards; Director: Borax Consolidated Ltd, 1937-69; National Westminster Bank Ltd (formerly National Provincial Bank Ltd), 1948-70; Equitable Life Assurance Society, 1930-70, and other companies; *b* 2 Sept. 1892; *e s* of Eustace Abel Smith, Longhills, Lincoln, and Ailleen, *d* of Col J. A. Conolly, VC, Coldstream Guards; *m* Elizabeth Barbara Peace, JP Bucks, *d* of General Hon. Sir H. A. Lawrence, GCB; one *s* four *d*. *Educ:* Eton; Trinity College, Cambridge. Served European War, 1914-18, Grenadier Guards, 1918-19; Adjutant Guards Machine Gun Regt (twice wounded, despatches, MC); War of 1939-45, GSO2 London District, 1939-43; Senior Military Liaison Officer, London Region. *Recreations:* shooting, ornithology. *Address:* Hampden Old Rectory, Great Missenden, Bucks; Longhills, Branston, Lincoln. *Club:* Travellers'.
*See also Vice-Adm. Sir E. M. C. Abel Smith.*

**ABEL SMITH, Vice-Adm. Sir (Edward Michael) Conolly,** GCVO 1958 (KCVO 1954; CVO 1946); CB 1951; RN retd; HM Lieutenant for Selkirk since 1958; Extra Equerry to the Queen since 1952; *b* 3 Dec. 1899; 2nd *s* of Eustace Abel Smith, Longhills, Lincoln, and Ailleen Geta, *d* of Col. John A. Conolly, VC, Coldstream Guards; *m* 1932, Lady Mary Elizabeth Carnegie, *d* of 10th Earl of Southesk; one *s* one *d*. *Educ:* Royal Naval Colleges, Osborne and Dartmouth. Mid. HMS Princess Royal, 1915; Qualified Pilot, 1924; Comdr 1933; Naval Equerry to the King, 1939; Capt. 1940; HMS Biter, 1942; Naval Attaché, British Embassy, Washington, DC, 1944-46; HMS Triumph, 1947; Naval ADC to the King, 1949; Rear-Adm. 1949; Vice-Controller (Air), Chief of Naval Air Equipment and Chief Naval Representative, Min. of Supply, 1950; Vice-Adm. 1952; Flag Officer, Royal Yachts, 1953-58. Grand Cross of St Olav, 1955. *Recreations:* hunting, shooting. *Address:* Ashiestiel, Galashiels, Scotland. *T:* Clovenfords 214. *Clubs:* Brooks's, Buck's.
*See also D. Abel Smith.*

**ABEL SMITH, Col Sir Henry,** KCMG 1961; KCVO 1950; DSO 1945; late Royal Horse Guards; Governor of Queensland, 1958-66; Administrator, Australian Commonwealth, during part of 1965; *b* 8 March 1900; *er s* of late Francis Abel Smith and Madeline St Maur, *d* of late Rev. Henry Seymour; *m* 1931, Lady May Cambridge, *o surv. c* of Earl of Athlone, KG, PC, GCB, GCMG, GCVO, DSO, FRS (*d* 1957), and of Princess Alice, Countess of Athlone, *qv*; one *s* two *d*. *Educ:* RMC, Sandhurst. Entered RHG, 1919; Capt. 1930; Major, 1934; Temp. Lieut-Col 1941; Lieut-Col 1944; Acting Colonel, Corps of Household Cavalry, 1946; retired, 1950. ADC to Earl of Athlone, Governor-General of S Africa, 1928-31. KStJ 1958; Hon. LLD Univ. of Queensland, 1962. Hon. Air Cdre, RAAF, 1966. *Recreations:* hunting, shooting, fishing, polo. *Address:* Barton Lodge, Winkfield, Windsor, Berks. *T:* Winkfield Row 2632. *Club:* Turf.
*See also Sir Alexander Abel Smith.*

**ABELL, Sir Anthony (Foster),** KCMG 1952 (CMG 1950); part-time Member, Civil Service Commission; *b* 11 Dec. 1906; 2nd *s* of late G. F. Abell, JP, Foxcote Manor, Andoversford, Glos; unmarried. *Educ:* Repton; Magdalen Coll., Oxford. Joined Colonial Admin. Service, Nigeria, 1929. Resident, Oyo Province, Nigeria, 1949; Governor and C-in-C, Sarawak, 1950-59; High Commissioner, Brunei, 1950-58. Member: Council, Royal Over-Seas League; Advisory Council, Overseas Services Resettlement Bureau. Family Order of Brunei (First Class), 1954. *Address:* Foxcote Manor, Andoversford, Glos. *Clubs:* MCC, Royal Over-Seas League, Bath.
*See also Sir George Abell.*

**ABELL, Sir George (Edmond Brackenbury),** KCIE 1947 (CIE 1946); OBE 1943; Hon. LLD (Aberdeen), 1947; *b* 22 June 1904; *s* of late G. F. Abell, JP, Foxcote Manor, Andoversford, Glos; *m* 1928, Susan Norman-Butler; two *s* one *d. Educ:* Marlborough; Corpus Christi Coll., Oxford (Charles Oldham Schol., 1st Cl. Hon. Mods, 2nd Cl. Lit. Hum., MA). Joined Indian Civil Service, 1928; Private Sec. to the Viceroy, 1945-47. Advisor, 1948-52, Director, 1952-64, Bank of England; First Civil Service Comr, 1964-67. Dir, Portals Holdings Ltd. Mem. Council: Reading Univ. (Pres., 1969-); Marlborough Coll.; Cheltenham Coll.; Rhodes Trustee (Chm., 1969-). *Recreations:* fishing, shooting; previously games (Blues for Rugby football (Capt. 1926), cricket and hockey). *Address:* Whittonditch House, Ramsbury, Wilts. *T:* Ramsbury 449. *Clubs:* Oriental, MCC.

*See also Sir Anthony Abell.*

**ABERCONWAY,** 3rd Baron, *cr* 1911, of Bodnant; **Charles Melville McLaren,** Bt 1902; Chairman: John Brown & Co. Ltd; Sheepbridge Engineering Ltd; English China Clays Ltd; Vice-Chairman, Sun Alliance & London Insurance Ltd; President, Royal Horticultural Society, since 1961; *b* 16 April 1913; *e s* of 2nd Baron Aberconway, CBE, LLD and Christabel, *y d* of Sir Melville Macnaghten, CB; *S* father, 1955; *m* 1st, 1941, Deirdre Knewstub (marriage dissolved, 1949); one *s* two *d*; 2nd, 1949, Ann Lindsay Bullard, *o d* of Mrs A. L. Aymer, New York City; one *s*. *Educ:* Eton; New Coll., Oxford. Barrister, Middle Temple, 1937. Served War of 1939-45, 2nd Lieut RA. Director: National Westminster Bank Ltd; Westland Aircraft Ltd; Sub-Gov., London Assce. JP Denbighshire 1946; High Sheriff of Denbighshire 1950. *Heir: s* Hon. Henry Charles McLaren, *b* 26 May 1948. *Address:* 25 Egerton Terrace, SW3; Bodnant, Tal-y-cafn, North Wales.

*See also K. R. M. Carlisle.*

**ABERCORN,** 4th Duke of, *cr* 1868; **James Edward Hamilton;** Baron of Paisley, 1587; Baron Abercorn, 1603; Baron Hamilton and Earl of Abercorn, 1606; Baron of Strabane, 1617; Viscount of Strabane, 1701; Viscount Hamilton, 1786; Marquess of Abercorn, 1790; Marquess of Hamilton, 1868; Bt 1660; HM Lieutenant for County of Tyrone since 1951; Captain Grenadier Guards; Member: Tyrone County Council, 1946; of Senate, Government of Northern Ireland, 1949-62; *b* 29 Feb. 1904; *er s* of 3rd Duke of Abercorn, KG, KP, and Lady Rosalind Cecilia Caroline Bingham (*d* 1958, as Dowager Duchess of Abercorn, DBE), *o d* of 4th Earl of Lucan; *S* father, 1953; *m* 1928, Lady Mary Kathleen Crichton (Duchess of Abercorn, DCVO 1969); two *s* one *d*. *Educ:* Eton; RMC Sandhurst. High Sheriff, Co. Tyrone, 1946. Chm. Trustees, Ulster Museum, 1962; Chancellor, University of Ulster at Coleraine, 1970-; President: Royal Forestry Soc. of England, Wales and N Ireland, 1964; Internat. Dendrological Union, 1964; N Ireland Council of YMCAs; Army Cadet Force Assoc. for N Ireland; Not Forgotten Assoc., N Ireland; RN Lifeboat Inst., N Ireland; Royal UK Beneficent Assoc.; Nat. Playing Fields Assoc., N Ireland; Vice-Pres., N Ireland Area, British Legion. Hon. Col, 5th Bn The Royal Inniskilling Fusiliers (TA), 1963. *Heir: s* Marquess of Hamilton, *qv*. *Address:* Barons Court, Co. Tyrone, Northern Ireland. *Club:* Turf.

*See also Earl of Erne, Sir John L. Gilmour, Bt, Lady Katharine Seymour, Countess Spencer.*

**ABERCROMBIE, Prof. David;** Professor of Phonetics, Edinburgh University, since 1964; *b* 19 Dec. 1909; *e s* of Lascelles and Catherine Abercrombie; *m* 1944, Mary, *d* of Eugene and Mary Marble, Carmel, Calif; no *c*. *Educ:* Leeds Grammar Sch.; Leeds Univ.; University Coll., London; Sorbonne. Asst Lectr in English, LSE, 1934-38; Dir of Studies, Inst. of English Studies, Athens, 1938-40; Lectr in English: Cairo Univ., 1940-45; LSE, 1945-47; Lectr in Phonetics, Leeds Univ., 1947-48; Edinburgh Univ.: Lectr in Phonetics, 1948-51; Sen. Lectr 1951-57; Reader, 1957-63. *Publications:* Isaac Pitman: a Pioneer in the Scientific Study of Language, 1937; Problems and Principles in Language Study, 1956; English Phonetic Texts, 1964; Studies in Phonetics and Linguistics, 1965; Elements of General Phonetics, 1967. *Address:* 13 Grosvenor Crescent, Edinburgh 12. *T:* 031-337 4864. *Club:* Scottish Arts (Edinburgh).

*See also Prof. Michael Abercrombie.*

**ABERCROMBIE, George Francis,** VRD 1940; MA, MD Cambridge; Surgeon Captain, RNVR, retired; in General Practice, 1924-66; *b* 25 June 1896; *o s* of late George Kennedy Abercrombie, Solicitor, London, and Margaret Jane (*née* Forbes); *m* 1932, Marie, *yr d* of late Frank Underhill, JP, Plympton, S Devon; one *s* two *d*. *Educ:* Charterhouse Sch.; Gonville and Caius Coll., Cambridge. MA, BCh 1922; MB 1924, MD 1935. House Surg. and Resident Midwifery Asst, St Bartholomew's Hosp.; House Phys., Hosp. for Sick Children, Gt Ormond Street. FRSocMed (first Pres., Sect. of Gen. Practice, 1950): Mem. of Management Cttee, 1963-67, and Chm., Emerg. Bed Service Cttee, King Edward's Hosp. Fund for London, 1951-67; Lectr on Gen. Practice, St Bart's Hosp. Med. Sch., 1953-66. Foundn Mem., Coll. of Gen. Practitioners (Chm. Coun., 1952-55; James Mackenzie Lectr, 1958; Pres., 1959-62). Formerly Surg. Probationer, RNVR (HMS Warwick, Zeebrugge, 1918, despatches); Surg. Lieut 1922; Surg. Comdr 1935. War of 1939-45 (VRD): HMS Birmingham; HMS Anson. Surg. Captain 1948; KHP 1950; retired, 1951. *Publications:* papers in Alpine and med. jls; Joint Editor, The Encyclopædia of General Practice, 1963. *Recreations:* country walking, chess. *Address:* Walton Gorse, Mogador Lane, Lower Kingswood, Surrey. *T:* Reigate 47066.

**ABERCROMBIE, Prof. Michael,** FRS 1958; MA, BSc; Director, Strangeways Research Laboratory, Cambridge, since 1970; *b* 14 Aug. 1912; *s* of Lascelles and Catherine Abercrombie; *m* 1939, Minnie Louie Johnson; one *s*. *Educ:* Leeds Grammar Sch.; The Queen's Coll., Oxford (Hastings Scholar, 1931; Taberdar, 1935; Junior Research Fellow, 1937). Beit Memorial Fellow for Medical Research, 1940; Lecturer in Zoology, Birmingham University, 1945; Reader in Embryology, UCL, 1950-59, Professor, 1959-62, Jodrell Prof. of Zoology, 1962-70. Mem. Council, Royal Soc., 1967-69. Jt Editor, Advances in Morphogenesis. *Publications:* Dictionary of Biology (with C. J. Hickman and M. L. Johnson), 1951; papers on embryology, tissue culture and wound healing. *Address:* Strangeways Research Laboratory, Wort's Causeway, Cambridge.

*See also Prof. David Abercrombie.*

**ABERCROMBIE, Nigel James;** Chief Regional Adviser, Arts Council of Great Britain, since 1968; *b* 5 Aug. 1908; 2nd *s* of late Lieutenant-Colonel A. W. Abercrombie; *m* 1931, Elisabeth Brownlees; one *s* one *d*. *Educ:* Haileybury; Oriel College, Oxford. BA 1929; DPhil 1933; MA 1934. Lecturer in French, Magdalen College, Oxford, 1931-36; Paget Toynbee Prize, 1934; Professor of French and Head of Mod. Lang. Dept, University College, Exeter, 1936-40. Entered Secretary's Department, Admiralty, 1940; Asst Sec., 1942; Under-Secretary, 1956; Cabinet Office, 1962-63; Secretary-General, Arts Council of Great Britain, 1963-68. Editor, Dublin Review, 1953-55. *Publications:*

The Origins of Jansenism, 1936; St Augustine and French Classical Thought, 1938; editions of Le Misanthrope and Tartuffe, 1938; Life and Work of Edmund Bishop, 1959; articles and reviews in theological, philological and literary periodicals. *Recreations:* The 3 R's. *Address:* Baldy's Garden, Lewes, Sussex. *T:* Lewes 3833.

*See also J. L. Gardner.*

**ABERCROMBIE, Robert James,** CMG 1964; General Manager, Bank of New South Wales, 1962-64, retired; *b* 9 July 1898; *s* of P. M. Abercrombie, Whitburn, Scotland; *m* 1924, Dorothy, *d* of H. F. Oldham; two *d. Educ:* Sydney Grammar School; Scotch Coll., Melbourne. Chairman, Consultative Council of Export Payments Insurance Corporation, 1958-64; Chairman, Australian Bankers' Assoc., 1964. Director: Bank of New South Wales; Associated Portland Cement Manufrs (Australia) Ltd; London Australia Investment Co. Ltd. *Recreation:* golf. *Address:* 2 Wentworth Road, Vaucluse, NSW, Australia. *Clubs:* Union, Australian (Sydney); Australian, Athenæum (Melbourne).

**ABERCROMBY, Sir Robert (Alexander),** 9th Bt, *cr* 1636, of Birkenbog; MC 1918; JP; Vice-Lieutenant of Banffshire since 1965; *b* (posthumous) 15 Aug. 1895; 2nd *s* of Sir Robert John Abercromby, 7th Bt; *S* brother, Sir George Abercromby, 8th Bt, DSO, 1964; *m* 1st, 1923, Hon. Diamond Hardinge (*d* 1927); 2nd, 1929, Pamela (*d* 1944), *d* of late John Lomax; 3rd, 1951, Elizabeth, *d* of Major James Corcoran. *Educ:* Eton; RMC. Served European War, 1914-18, France, Belgium, Germany, Scots Guards. Major, retired 1933. Served War of 1939-45, Scots Guards, East Africa, Italy. JP 1940, DL 1947, Banffshire. *Recreations:* fishing, shooting. *Heir: kinsman* Ian George Abercromby [*b* 30 June 1925; *m* 1st, 1950, Joyce Beryl (marr. diss.), *d* of Leonard Griffiths; 2nd, 1959, Fanny Mary, *o d* of Dr Graham Udale-Smith]. *Address:* Dunlugas, Turriff, Aberdeenshire. *Clubs:* Guards, Pratt's; Royal Northern (Aberdeen).

**ABERDARE,** 4th Baron, *cr* 1873, of Duffryn; **Morys George Lyndhurst Bruce,** DL; Minister of State, Department of Health and Social Security, since 1970; Prior for Wales, Order of St John; *b* 16 June 1919; *s* of 3rd Baron Aberdare, GBE, and Margaret Bethune (*née* Black); *S* father 1957; *m* 1946, Maud Helen Sarah, *o d* of Sir John Dashwood, 10th Bt, CVO; four *s. Educ:* Winchester; New College, Oxford (MA). Welsh Guards, 1939-46. DL Glamorgan, 1966. KStJ. *Publication:* The Story of Tennis, 1959. *Recreations:* real tennis and rackets. *Heir: s* Hon. Alastair John Lyndhurst Bruce, *b* 2 May 1947. *Address:* 1 St Peter's Square, W6. *T:* 01-748 1403. *Clubs:* Lansdowne, MCC.

**ABERDEEN, Bishop of, (RC),** since 1965; **Rt. Rev. Michael Foylan;** *b* 29 June 1907; *s* of James Foylan and Anne Foylan (*née* Murphy). *Educ:* Blairs College, Aberdeen; St Sulpice, Paris. Curate, St Andrew's Cathedral, Dundee, 1931-37; Curate, St Joseph's, Dundee, 1937-46; Parish Priest, St Serf's, Highvalleyfield, Fife, 1946–49; Administrator of St Andrew's Cathedral, Dundee, 1949-65; Vicar General of Diocese of Dunkeld, 1952-65. Domestic Prelate of His Holiness the Pope, 1953. JP, County of City of Dundee, 1957. *Recreations:* walking, golf. *Address:* Bishop's House, 156 King's Gate, Aberdeen. *T:* Aberdeen 39154.

**ABERDEEN, Provost of** (St Andrew's Cathedral); *see* Hodgkinson, Very Rev. A. E.

**ABERDEEN and ORKNEY, Bishop of,** since 1956; **Rt. Rev. Edward Frederick Easson;** *b* 29 July 1905; *s* of Edward Easson and Ada Jessie Easson (*née* Betsworth); *m* 1937, Mary Forbes Macdonald; two *s. Educ:* Morgan Academy, Dundee; St Andrews Univ.; Edinburgh Theological College. Maths and Science Master at Lasswade Secondary School, 1929-31; Assistant Curate of St Peter's, Lutton Place, 1933-36, with charge of St Aidan's, Craigmillar, 1936-39; Rector of St Peter's, Peterhead, and Chaplain to HM Prison, 1940-48; Diocesan Inspector of Schools, 1945-55; Canon of St Andrew's Cathedral, Aberdeen, 1946; Rector of St Devenick's, Bieldside, 1948-56; Dean of Aberdeen and Orkney, 1953-56. Hon. DD, St Andrews, 1962. *Address:* 46 Queens Road, Aberdeen AB9 2PP. *T:* Aberdeen 33563.

**ABERDEEN and ORKNEY, Dean of;** *see* Begg, Very Rev. I. F.

**ABERDEEN and TEMAIR,** 3rd Marquis of, *cr* 1916; **Dudley Gladstone Gordon,** DSO 1917; Viscount Formatine, Lord Haddo, Methlic, Tarves and Kellie, Earl of Aberdeen, 1682, Peerage of Scotland; Viscount Gordon, 1814, and Earl of Haddo, 1916, Peerage of the United Kingdom; Baronet of Nova Scotia, 1642; Hon. LLD (Aberdeen); MIMechE; President: Hadfields Ltd (Chairman 1945-62, Director 1943); Allied Circle; Engineering Section British Association for the Advancement of Science, 1953; Institute of Refrigeration; The Bach Choir; *b* 6 May 1883; 2nd *s* of 1st Marquis of Aberdeen and Temair, KT, PC, GCMG, GCVO; *S* brother, 1965; *m* 1st, 1907, Cécile Elizabeth (*d* 1948), *d* of George Drummond, Swaylands, Penshurst, Kent; three *s* (and one killed in action) one *d*; 2nd, 1949, Margaret Gladys, ARRC, JP, Member East Grinstead UDC, 1947-62 (Chm. 1953, 1960), *d* of late Lieutenant-Colonel R. G. Munn, CMG, East Grinstead. *Educ:* Cargilfield; Harrow. After leaving Harrow served apprenticeship in Hall, Russell & Co.'s shipbuilding yard at Aberdeen, and afterwards to W. H. Allen, Son & Co., engineers, Bedford; joined J. & E. Hall, Ltd, 1907; Past President: British Iron & Steel Research Association; Hall Thermotank Ltd; British Assoc. of Refrigeration; British Engineers Assoc.; FBI; President: Instn of Mech. Engrs Centenary (1847-1947), 1947-48; Highland Society of London, 1955-58. Formerly: Director of British Overseas Fairs; Director, Industrial and Commercial Finance Corp.; Mem. Exec. Cttee British Iron and Steel Federation; Chairman J. & E. Hall Ltd, Engineers, Dartford, 1936-60; Director: Phœnix Assurance Co. Ltd, 1942-59; Barclays Bank, 1943-58; Governor of Harrow School, 1950-65. Hon. Member, Amer. Soc. of Mech. Engrs. Captain 2nd VB Gordon Hldrs, 1902-5; served European War, 1914-18 (DSO): Lieut-Col Comdg 8/10th Bn Gordon Highlanders. Chm., Dartford Urban District Coun., 1924. *Recreations:* choral singing, swimming, golf, shooting. *Heir: s* Earl of Haddo, *qv. Address:* Bullards, East Grinstead, Sussex. *T:* 25446. *Clubs:* Bath, Allied Circle (Pres.); Royal & Ancient Golf, Royal St George's Golf, Royal Ashdown Forest Golf (Pres.).

**ABERDEEN, David du Rieu,** FRIBA, AMTPI; Architect (Private Practice); *b* 13 Aug. 1913; *s* of David Aberdeen and Lilian du Rieu; *m* 1940, Phyllis Irene Westbrook (*née* Buller), *widow*; two *step c. Educ:* privately; Sch. of Architecture, London Univ. (BA Hons, Arch.). RIBA Donaldson Medallist, 1934; RIBA Alfred Bossom Research Fell., 1946-47. Works include: Brabazon Hangars, Filton, for Bristol Aeroplane Co.; TUC Headquarters,

London, won in open architectural competition, 1948 (RIBA London Architecture Bronze Medal, 1958); 13-storey point block flats, New Southgate; housing for Basildon and Harlow New Towns. Architect for: new headquarters in City for Swiss Bank Corp.; redevelopment of Paddington Gen. Hosp.; New Gen. Market Hall, Shrewsbury; Swiss Centre, cultural and trade Headquarters, Leicester Square. Lectr, Atelier of Advanced Design, Sch. of Architecture, London Univ., 1947-53. *Publications:* contrib. to architectural press. *Address:* 20 Green Moor Link, N21; 19 Southampton Place, WC1.

**ABERGAVENNY,** 5th Marquess of, *cr* 1876; **John Henry Guy Nevill,** OBE 1945; Baron Abergavenny, 1450; Earl of Abergavenny and Viscount Nevill, 1784; Earl of Lewes, 1876; Lt-Col late Life Guards; Vice-Lieutenant of Sussex, since 1970; *b* 8 Nov. 1914; *er s* of 4th Marquess and Isabel Nellie (*d* 1953), *d* of James Walker Larnach; *S* father, 1954; *m* 1938, Patricia (CVO 1970), *d* of Major and Hon. Mrs J. F. Harrison, King's Walden Bury, Hitchin; three *d* (and one *s* one *d* decd). *Educ:* Eton; Trinity College Cambridge. Served War of 1939-45 (OBE). JP 1949, DL 1956, Sussex. *Heir: b* Lord Rupert Charles Montacute Nevill, *qv. Address:* (seat) Eridge Park, Tunbridge Wells, Sussex. *T:* Tunbridge Wells 27378; 19 Lowndes Square, SW1. *T:* 01-235 7486. *Clubs:* Turf, White's.
*See also Earl of Cottenham.*

**ABERNETHY, James Smart;** *b* 3 Oct. 1907; *s* of J. J. Abernethy, JP, Balmain, Fettercairn; *m* 1st, 1936, Winifred M. J. Marr (*d* 1960); two *d*; 2nd, 1960, Margaret P. Campbell; one *s*. *Educ:* Private Prep. Sch.; Sedbergh, Yorks; Aberdeen Grammar Sch.; Aberdeen and Edinburgh Univs. MA, LLB Aberdeen; WS. Legal Adviser, Commissioner of Lands and Protector of Labour, North Borneo (Chartered Co.), 1936; Food Controller, North Borneo, 1941; interned by Japanese, 1942; actg Attorney-General, 1946, Commissioner of Lands, 1947, Circuit Magistrate and Sessions Judge, 1948, Colony of N Borneo; Resident Magistrate, Tanganyika, 1949; Puisne Judge, Tanganyika Territory, 1951-58, retired. In South Africa and Australia, 1958-61; Town Clerk: Tanga, Tanganyika, 1961-63; Thurso, Caithness, 1963-65; Registrar and Legal Officer, Lands and Surveys Dept, Sarawak, 1965-. *Recreations:* gardening, cooking. *Address:* c/o Royal Bank of Scotland, 42 St Andrew Square, Edinburgh.

**ABERNETHY, William Leslie,** FCA; Chartered Municipal Treasurer; Treasurer to the Greater London Council since 1964 and Chief Financial Officer, Inner London Education Authority, since 1967; *b* 10 June 1910; *s* of Robert and Margaret Abernethy; *m* 1937, Irene Holden; one *s*. *Educ:* Darwen Grammar Sch., Lancs. Hindle & Jepson, Chartered Accts, Darwen, 1925-31; Borough Treasurer's Dept, Darwen, 1931-37; Derbyshire CC, Treasurer's Dept, 1937-48 (Dep. Co. Treas., 1944-48); 1st Treas., Newcastle upon Tyne Regional Hosp. Bd, 1948-50. LCC: Asst Comptroller, 1950-56; Dep. Comptroller, 1956-64; Comptroller, Sept. 1964-Mar. 1965. Investment Manager, Teachers' Family Benefits Fund; Treasurer, London Orchestral Concert Board Ltd. A Vice-Pres., Roy. Inst. of Public Admin (Chm. Exec. Coun., 1959-60). Mem. Council, IMTA. *Publications:* Housing Finance and Accounts (with A. R. Holmes), 1953; Internal Audit in Local Authorities and Hospitals, 1957; Internal Audit in the Public Boards, 1957; contribs professional jls. *Address:* 10 Woodcote Green Road, Epsom, Surrey. *T:* Epsom 26075.

**ABINGDON, Earl of;** *see* Lindsey and Abingdon, Earl of.

**ABINGER,** 8th Baron, *cr* 1835; **James Richard Scarlett,** DL; Lt-Col, late Royal Artillery; farmer and company director; *b* 28 Sept. 1914; *e s* of 7th Baron and Marjorie (*d* 1965), 2nd *d* of John McPhillamy, Blair Athol, Bathurst, NSW; *S* father, 1943; *m* 1957, Isla Carolyn, *o d* of late Vice-Adm. J. W. Rivett-Carnac, CB, CBE, DSC; two *s*. *Educ:* Eton; Magdalene College, Cambridge (MA 1952). India, France, Airborne Corps, and attached RAF; RNXS, 1968. Governor, ESU; Chairman: Keats Shelley Memorial Assoc.; Exec. Cttee, CPRE. DL Essex, 1968. OStJ. *Heir: s* Hon. James Harry Scarlett, *b* 28 May 1959. *Address:* 40 Draycott Place, SW3. *T:* 01-589 9311; Clees Hall, Bures, Suffolk. *T:* Bures 227. *Clubs:* Carlton, Royal Automobile.

**ABNEY-HASTINGS,** family name of **Countess of Loudoun.**

**ABOYNE, Earl of; Granville Charles Gomer Gordon;** *b* 4 Feb. 1944; *s* of 12th Marquess of Huntly, *qv*. *Educ:* Gordonstoun. *Address:* 34 Groom Place, SW1. *T:* 01-235 4709; Aboyne Castle, Aberdeenshire. *T:* Aboyne 2118.

**ABRAHALL, Rt. Rev. A. L. E. H.;** *see* Lancaster, Suffragan Bishop of.

**ABRAHALL, Sir T. C. H.;** *see* Hoskyns-Abrahall.

**ABRAHAM, Edward Penley,** FRS 1958; MA, DPhil (Oxon); Fellow of Lincoln College, Oxford, since 1948; Professor of Chemical Pathology, Oxford, since 1964; *b* 10 June 1913; *s* of Albert Penley Abraham and Mary Abraham (*née* Hearn); *m* 1939, Asbjörg Harung, Bergen, Norway; one *s*. *Educ:* King Edward VI School, Southampton; The Queen's College, Oxford. Rockefeller Foundation Travelling Fellow at Universities of Stockholm (1939) and California (1948). Ciba lecturer at Rutgers University, NJ, 1957; Guest lecturer, Univ. of Sydney, 1960; Reader in Chemical Pathology, Oxford, 1960-64; Rennebohm Lecturer, Univ. of Wisconsin, 1966-67. *Publications:* Biochemistry of Some Peptide and Steroid Antibiotics, 1957; contribs to: Antibiotics, 1949; The Chemistry of Penicillin, 1949; General Pathology, 1957, 4th edn 1970; scientific papers on the biochemistry of natural products. *Recreations:* walking, ski-ing. *Address:* Badger's Wood, Bedwells Heath, Boars Hill, Oxford. *T:* Oxford 35395. *Club:* Athenæum.

**ABRAHAM, Gerald Ernest Heal,** MA, FTCL; President, Royal Musical Association; *b* 9 March 1904; *s* of Ernest and Dorothy Mary Abraham; *m* 1936, Isobel Patsie Robinson; one *d*. Asst Editor, Radio Times, 1935-39; Dep. Editor, The Listener, 1939-42; Director of Gramophone Dept, BBC, 1942-47; James and Constance Alsop Prof. of Music, Liverpool Univ., 1947-62; BBC Asst Controller of Music, 1962-67; Music Critic, The Daily Telegraph, 1967-68; Ernest Bloch Prof. of Music, Univ. of Calif (Berkeley), 1968-69. Chairman, Music Section of the Critics' Circle, 1944-46. Editor, Monthly Musical Record, 1945-60; Editor, Music of the Masters (series of books); General Editor, The History of Music in Sound (gramophone records and handbooks); Chm., Editorial Bd, Grove's Dictionary of Music; Sec. Editorial Board, New Oxford History of Music; Chm., Early English Church Music Cttee; Mem. Editorial

Cttee, Musica Britannica. President, International Society for Music Education, 1958-61; Dep. Chm. Haydn Institute (Cologne), 1961-68; Governor, Dolmetsch Foundn, 1970-. FRSA 1968; Hon. RAM 1970. Hon. DMus Dunelm, 1961; Hon. Dr of Fine Arts, California (Berkeley), 1969. *Publications:* This Modern Stuff, 1933; Nietzsche, 1933; Studies in Russian Music, 1935; Tolstoy, 1935; Masters of Russian Music (with M. D. Calvocoressi), 1936; Dostoevsky, 1936; A Hundred Years of Music, 1938; On Russian Music, 1939; Chopin's Musical Style, 1939; Beethoven's Second-Period Quartets, 1942; Eight Soviet Composers, 1943; Tchaikovsky, 1944; Rimsky-Korsakov, 1945; Design in Music, 1949; Slavonic and Romantic Music, 1968; (ed, with Dom Anselm Hughes) New Oxford History of Music, Vol. III (Ars Nova and the Renaissance), 1960; (ed) New Oxford History of Music, Vol. IV (The Age of Humanism), 1968. *Recreations:* walking, languages, military history. *Address:* The Old School House, Ebernoe, near Petworth, Sussex. *T:* North Chapel 325.

**ABRAHAM, Louis Arnold,** CB 1956; CBE 1950; *b* 26 Nov. 1893; *y s* of late William Abraham, MP, Limerick; *m* 1921, Irene, *yr d* of late Frederick George Kerin, Ennis, County Clare. *Educ:* Owen's School, London; Peterhouse, Cambridge (Exhibr). BA 1915; Pres., Cambridge Union, 1920. Asst Clerk, House of Commons, 1920; called to the Bar (certif. of honour), 1928; Pres., Hardwicke Soc., 1928; Senior Clerk, House of Commons, 1932; Clerk of Private Bills, 1945-52; Examr of Petitions for Private Bills and Taxing Officer, 1946-52; Principal Clerk of Committees, 1952-58. *Publications:* (with S. C. Hawtrey) A Parliamentary Dictionary; Palgrave's Chairman's Handbook, 1964. *Address:* 13 Lushington Road, Eastbourne, Sussex. *T:* Eastbourne 32223.

**ABRAHAM, Maj.-Gen. Sutton Martin O'Heguerty,** MC 1942 and Bar, 1943; Director of Combat Development (Army), Ministry of Defence, since 1968; *b* 26 Jan. 1919; *s* of Capt. E. G. F. Abraham, CB, late Indian Civil Service, and Ruth Eostre Abraham; *m* 1950, Iona Margaret, *d* of Sir John Stirling, *qv*; two *s* one *d*. *Educ:* Durnford; Eton; Trinity Coll., Cambridge (BA Modern Languages). Commissioned in RA, 1939; transf. to 12th Royal Lancers, 1941; disembarked Egypt, 1941; Armoured Car Troop Leader, desert campaigns; Armoured Car Sqdn 2nd-in-Comd, Italian campaign, Sangro Valley, Rimini, Po Valley; accepted surrender of Trieste (Sqdn Ldr); Mil. Asst to C-in-C Austria, and accompanied him to BAOR, 1946; psc 1948; Mem. Chiefs of Staff Secretariat, 1949-52; Sqdn Ldr 12th Lancers, Malaya, 1953-54; Mem. Staff Coll. Directing Staff, 1955-57; 2nd-in-Comd 12th Lancers, 1957-58; CO 12th Lancers, 1958-62 (Cyprus, 1959-60); Asst Mil. Sec., Southern Comd, 1960-62; GSO1, Staff Coll. (Minley Div.), 1960-62; Comdr RAC (Brig.), 1st Brit. Corps, Germany, 1964-66; idc 1967. *Recreations:* painting, riding occasionally, reading, sundry practical country pursuits and chores, shooting. *Address:* Mangerton House, near Bridport, Dorset. *T:* Powerstock 301. *Club:* Cavalry.

**ABRAHAM, William Ernest Victor,** CBE 1942; Lay Member of Restrictive Practices Court; *b* 21 Aug. 1897; *s* of John and Frances Abraham, Enniskillen; *m* 1928, Susan Jeanette Bidwell (*d* 1965), Kinsley, Kansas, USA; one *s* two *d*; *m* 1966, Rosemary Eustace, *d* of Louis H. King, Berrow, Somerset. *Educ:* Methodist Coll., Belfast; Royal Coll. of Science, Dublin. In Burma and India as Geologist, 1920-37. Commanded Upper Burma Bn, Burma Auxiliary Force, 1932-37; rejoined army, 1940, as 2nd Lieut and rose to rank of Major-General, after service in Greece, Middle East (OBE, despatches twice), Burma, Tunisia (CBE), Sicily; Controller General of Mil. Economy, India, 1945. Formerly Managing Director of Burmah Oil Co. Ltd, retd 1955. National Chm., Burma Star Assoc., 1966-. *Address:* Kencot Manor, Lechlade, Glos. *T:* Filkins 212. *Clubs:* East India and Sports, Royal Automobile.

**ABRAHAMS, Allan Rose,** CMG 1962; company director; *b* 29 Nov. 1908; *s* of late Mr and Mrs Frank Abrahams; *m* 1948, Norma Adeline Neita; one *s* two *d*. *Educ:* Jamaica College, Jamaica. Joined Civil Service, 1927; Permanent Secretary, Ministry of Communications and Works, Jamaica, 1955-64, retired. Chairman Working Cttee to stimulate Production of Flowers and Ornamental Shrubs for Export, 1964-. *Recreation:* gardening. *Address:* 20 Widcombe Road, Kingston 6, Jamaica. *T:* 78214. *Club:* Kingston (Kingston, Jamaica).

**ABRAHAMS, Sir Charles (Myer),** KCVO 1970; Deputy Chairman and Joint Managing Director, Aquascutum and associated companies; *b* 25 April 1914; *s* of late Isidor and Eva Abrahams; *m* 1940, Luisa (*née* Kramer); two *d*. *Educ:* Westminster School. Hon. Chairman, Friends of the Duke of Edinburgh's Award Scheme, 1969-; Vice-President, Jewish Welfare Board, 1968-70; Member: Board of Governors, Cutty Sark Society, 1964-; Advisory Panel, World Wildlife Fund, 1969-. Served War of 1939-45 in Italy, Flt-Lt RAFVR. *Recreations:* golf and sculpture. *Address:* The Birches, Coombe Park, Kingston Hill, Surrey. *T:* 01-546 9808. *Clubs:* Coombe Hill Golf (Surrey); Sunningdale Golf (Berks).

**ABRAHAMS, Harold Maurice,** CBE 1957; MA, LLB; Secretary of National Parks Commission, 1950-63; *b* 15 December 1899; *s* of late Isaac Abrahams; *m* 1936, Sybil Marjorie (*d* 1963), *er d* of late C. P. Evers; one adopted *s* one adopted *d*. *Educ:* Repton; Gonville and Caius Coll., Cambridge. Hons Law Tripos, Cambridge, 1923; called to Bar, 1924; Ministry of Economic Warfare, 1939, Head of Statistics Section, 1941-42; Temp. Asst Sec., 1942-44; Assistant Secretary, Ministry of Town and Country Planning, 1946. Pres. Cambridge Univ. Athletic Club, 1922-23; represented Cambridge against Oxford, 1920-23, winning eight events in all; represented Great Britain in the Olympic Games, 1920 and 1924, winner 100 metres 1924; Captain British Athletic Team Olympic Games, 1928; Mem., Gen. Cttee of Amateur Athletic Assoc., 1926- (Vice-Pres., 1948; Life Vice-Pres., 1958); British Amateur Athletic Board: Asst Hon. Sec., 1939-48; Hon. Treas., 1948-68; Chm., 1968-. Hon. Pres., World Assoc. of Track and Field Statisticians, 1950; Athletics Corresp. Sunday Times, 1925-67; has broadcast regularly every year since 1924. JP Essex, 1956-63. *Publications:* Sprinting, 1925; Athletics, 1926; Training for Athletics (with late A. Abrahams and others), 1928; Oxford *v* Cambridge (with late J. Bruce Kerr), 1931; Training for Health and Athletics (with late A. Abrahams), 1936; Official Records of 1928 and 1936 Olympic Games; Track and Field Olympic Records, 1948; The Olympic Games, 1896-1952, 1956; Empire and Commonwealth Games, 1930-58, 1958; The Rome Olympiad, 1960. *Recreations:* photography, statistics. *Address:* 64 Abingdon Road, W8. *T:* 01-937 5668. *Clubs:* Achilles (Chm., 1947-61), Garrick; Cambridge University Pitt.

**ABRAMS, Mark Alexander,** PhD; Director of Survey Research Unit, Social Science Research Council, since 1970; Member: Metrication Board, since 1969; Health Education Council, since 1969; *b* 27 April 1906; *s* of Abram Abrams and Anne (*née* Jackson); *m* 1st, 1931, Una Strugnell (marr. diss. 1951); one *s* one *d*; 2nd, 1951, Jean Bird; one *d*. *Educ:* Latymer Sch., Edmonton; London Sch. of Economics, Univ. of London. Fellow, Brookings Institute, Washington, DC, 1931-33; Research Department, London Press Exchange, 1933-39; BBC Overseas Dept, 1939-41; Psychological Warfare Board and SHAEF, 1941-46; Man. Dir, then Chm., Research Services Ltd, 1946-70. Chairman Executive Committee, PEP, 1964-. *Publications:* Condition of the British People, 1911-1946, 1947; Social Surveys and Social Action, 1951. *Recreation:* listening to music. *Address:* 5a The Boltons, SW10. *T:* 01-373 7957. *Club:* Reform.

**ABSE, Leo;** MP (Lab) Pontypool, since Nov. 1958; *b* 22 April 1917; *s* of Rudolph and Kate Abse; *m* 1955, Marjorie (*née* Davies); one *s* one *d*. *Educ:* Howard Gardens High School; London School of Economics. Solicitor; Chairman: Cardiff City Labour Party, 1952-53; Cardiff Watch Cttee, 1958. Member: Cardiff City Council, 1953-58; Home Office Adv. Council on the Penal System; Council of Inst. for Study and Treatment of Delinquency; Nat. Council for Unmarried Mother and her Child. Sponsor or Co-sponsor of Private Members Acts relating to divorce, homosexuality, family planning and legitimacy. *Address:* Merchaviah, 396 Cyncoed Road, Cardiff. *T:* 751844 and 23252; Beulah, 13 Cavendish Avenue, NW8. *T:* 01-286 7440.

**ABUBAKAR, Sir;** *see* Sokoto, Sultan of.

**ABUZEID, Salah;** Order of the Star of Jordan (1st class); Minister of Information, Jordan, 1964-65, 1967, and since 1969 (Minister of Culture and Information, 1967-68); *b* 21 April 1925; *m* 1954, Nimat Abuzeid; two *s* five *d*; *m* 1964, Fomia Batshone; two *d*. *Educ:* Syrian Univ. Law Coll., Damascus; Syracuse Univ., Syracuse, USA. Govt Official, 1950-58; Director, Amman Radio Station, 1958-59; Asst Director-Gen., Hashemite Broadcasting Service, 1959-62; Director-Gen., Hashemite Broadcasting Service, and Chief of National Guidance, 1962-64; Jordan Ambassador to Court of St James's, 1969. Holds numerous foreign decorations. *Recreations:* reading, music, sports. *Address:* Ministry of Information, Amman, Jordan.

**ACHARD, Marcel;** Officier de la Légion d'Honneur; dramatic author; Member of the French Academy since 1959; *b* 5 July 1899; *m* 1925, Juliette Marty. Awarded Prix de l'Humour français, 1924. *Publications:* La Messe est dite, 1923; Voulez-vous jouer avec moi?, 1923; Malbrough s'en va t'en guerre, 1924; La Femme silencieuse, 1925; Je ne vous aime pas, 1926; La Vie est belle, 1928; Jean de la Lune, 1929; La Belle Marinière, 1929; Mistigri, 1930; Domino, 1931; La Femme en blanc, 1932; Petrus, 1935; Noix de Coco, 1935; Le Corsaire, 1938; Adam, 1939; Mademoiselle de Panama, 1942; Colinette, 1947; Auprès de ma blonde, 1948; Nous irons à Valparaiso, 1949; La Demoiselle de petite vertu, 1949; Le Moulin de la Galette, 1951; Les Compagnons de la Marjolaine, 1953; Le Mal d'amour, 1955; Patate, 1957; La Bagatelle, 1959; L'Idiote, 1960; La Polka des Lampions; the scenarios of 73 pictures. *Address:* 8 rue de Courty, Paris 7, France.

**ACHEBE, Chinua;** author; Senior Research Fellow, University of Nigeria, Nsukka; *b* 16 Nov. 1930; *s* of Isaiah and Janet Achebe; *m* 1961, Christiana Okoli; two *s* two *d*. *Educ:* Univ. of Ibadan. Nigerian Broadcasting Corp.: Talks Producer, 1954; Controller, 1959; Dir, 1961-66. Rockefeller Fellowship, 1960; Unesco Fellowship, 1963. Chairman, Soc. of Nigerian Authors, 1966. Member of Council, Univ. of Lagos, 1966. Jock Campbell New Statesman Award, 1965. *Publications:* Things Fall Apart, 1958; No Longer at Ease, 1960; Arrow of God, 1964; A Man of the People, 1966; *for children:* Chike and the River, 1966. *Recreation:* music. *Address:* Institute of African Studies, University of Nigeria, Nsukka, Nigeria.

**ACHESON,** family name of **Earl of Gosford.**

**ACHESON, Dean;** lawyer, United States of America; *b* 11 April 1893; *s* of Edward Campion Acheson and Eleanor Gooderham; *m* 1917, Alice Stanley; one *s* two *d*. *Educ:* Groton; Yale (AB 1915); Harvard Law School (LLB 1918). Hon. MA, Yale, 1936; Hon. LLD: Wesleyan Univ., 1947; Harvard, 1950; Cambridge, 1958; Yale, 1962; Johns Hopkins, 1963; Hon. DCL: Oxford, 1952; Michigan, 1967; Hon. LHD, Brandeis Univ., 1956. Private Sec. to Associate Justice Brandeis of US Supreme Court, 1919-21; with law firm Covington, Burling and Rublee, 1921-33; Under-Sec. of Treasury, 1933; Covington, Burling and Rublee, Acheson and Shorb, 1934-41, 1947-49, and Covington & Burling since Jan. 1953; Assistant Sec. of State, 1941-45, Under-Secretary of State, 1945-47, Secretary of State, 1949-Jan. 1953, USA. *Publications:* An American Vista, 1956; A Citizen Looks at Congress, 1957; Power and Diplomacy, 1958; Sketches from Life of Men I Have Known, 1961; Morning and Noon, 1967; Present at the Creation: My Years in the State Department, 1969. *Address:* 2805 P Street, Washington, DC, USA. *Clubs:* Metropolitan (Washington); Century (NYC).

**ACHESON, Sir James Glasgow,** Kt 1945; CIE 1929; ICS (retired); *b* 1889; *s* of John Acheson, JP, Portadown, County Armagh; *m* 1917, Violet Catharine French, K-i-H Gold Medal, *d* of Lieut-Col C. W. Field, IA; one *s* one *d* (and one *s* one *d* decd). *Educ:* St Andrew's College and Trinity College, Dublin. Entered ICS, 1913; Political Service, 1917; UP, 1913; Baluchistan, 1917; Anglo-Afghan Conference, 1920; British Mission to Kabul, 1921; Deputy Secretary to Government of India in the Foreign Department, 1927-29 (officiated as Foreign Secretary, 1928, 1931, and 1935); Imperial Defence College, 1929-30; Deputy Commissioner, Peshawar, 1932-34; Resident in Waziristan, 1935-37; Political Resident on the North West Frontier, 1937-39; Revenue and Judicial Commissioner in Baluchistan, 1939-42; Resident in Kashmir, 1943-45; retired from ICS 1945; Control Commission for Germany, Schleswig-Holstein, 1946-48. *Recreations:* shooting, fishing, chess. *Address:* Holly Bush House, Much Birch, Hereford. *T:* Wormelow 260.

**ACHONRY, Bishop of, (RC),** since 1947; **Most Rev. James Fergus,** DD; *b* Louisburgh, Co. Mayo, 23 Dec. 1895. *Educ:* St Jarlath's College, Tuam; and at Maynooth. Ordained priest, 1920; studied Dunboyne; Curate, Glenamaddy, 1921, Tuam, 1924; Archbishop's secretary, 1926; Administrator, Westport, 1943; Parish Priest, Ballinrobe, 1944. *Address:* St Nathy's, Ballaghaderreen, Co. Roscommon, Eire.

**ACKLAND, Rodney;** Playwright; *b* 18 May 1908; *m* 1952, Mab, *d* of Frederick Lonsdale. First play, Improper People, Arts, 1929;

Marionella, Players, 1930; Dance With No Music, Arts and Embassy, 1931; Strange Orchestra, Embassy and St Martin's, 1932; Ballerina, adapted from Lady Eleanor Smith's novel, Gaiety, 1933; Birthday, Cambridge, 1934; The Old Ladies, adapted from Sir Hugh Walpole's novel, New and St Martin's, 1935; After October, Criterion and Aldwych, 1936; Plot Twenty-One, Embassy, 1936; The White Guard, adapted from the Russian play by Michael Bulgakov, Phœnix, 1938; Remembrance of Things Past, Globe, 1938; Sixth Floor, adapted from the French play by Alfred Gehri, St James's, 1939; The Dark River, Whitehall, 1943; Crime and Punishment, adapted from Dostoevsky, New, 1946; (with Robert G. Newton) Cupid and Mars, Arts, 1947; Diary of a Scoundrel, based on a comedy by Ostrovsky, Arts, 1949; Before the Party, adapted from Somerset Maugham's short story, St Martin's, 1949; The Pink Room, Lyric, Hammersmith, 1952; A Dead Secret, Piccadilly, 1957; adapted Farewell, Farewell, Eugene, Garrick, 1959. *Publications:* Improper People; Dance With No Music; Strange Orchestra; The Old Ladies; Birthday; After October; The Dark River; Crime and Punishment; Cupid and Mars; Diary of a Scoundrel; Before the Party; Farewell, Farewell, Eugene; The Celluloid Mistress (autobiography); The Other Palace. *Address:* c/o Eric Glass Ltd, 28 Berkeley Square, W1.

**ACKNER, Conrad A.;** Knight Commander of Order of St Olav (Norway); Commander of the Crown of Rumania; Mag. Pharm., Vienna, 1902; PhD (Pharmocol), Bern, 1904; LDS, RCS, England (Guy's), 1912; Dental Surgeon to late Queen Maud of Norway and to the late Princess Louise, Duchess of Argyll; naturalised British subject; *m* 1956, Mrs V. Lewis; four *s* by previous marriage. *Educ:* Vienna. Late Dental Radiographer, Guy's Hosp.; Post-Graduate: Bacteriology, Zürich; Berlin Univ. Hosp. in Radiology and Surgery of the Jaws; Member; BDA; Fédération Dentaire Internationale. FRSocMed. *Publications:* X-Ray Observations on Abscesses, Cysts and Root Resections, 6th International Dental Congress, 1914; A Maxillary Splint, Lancet and Dental Record, 1915. *Recreations:* golf, motoring, photography, and collection of old ivories. *Address:* Yew Tree House, Jordans, Bucks. *Clubs:* Beaconsfield Golf; Wentworth.

**ACKNER, Desmond James Conrad,** QC 1961; Recorder of Swindon since Dec. 1962; Judge of the Courts of Appeal of Jersey and Guernsey, 1967; *b* 18 Sept. 1920; *s* of Dr Conrad and Rhoda Ackner; *m* 1946, Joan, *d* of late John Evans, JP, and widow of K. B. Spence; one *s* two *d*. *Educ:* Highgate Sch.; Clare Coll., Cambridge. MA Economics and Law. Served in RA, 1941-42; Admty Naval Law Br., 1942-45. Called to Bar, Middle Temple, 1945; Mem. Gen. Council of Bar, 1957-61, 1963- (Hon. Treas., 1964-65; Vice-Chm., 1966-68; Chm., 1968-70); Bencher Middle Temple, 1965; Mem. Senate of the Four Inns of Court, 1966- (Vice-Pres., 1968-). *Recreations:* swimming, sailing, theatre. *Address:* 4 Pump Court, Temple, EC4. *T:* 01-353 5913; 21 Carlyle Mansions, Cheyne Walk, Chelsea, SW3. *T:* 01-352 8796; Browns House, Sutton, Petworth, Sussex. *T:* Sutton (Sussex) 206. *Clubs:* Bath; Bar Yacht, Birdham Yacht.

**ACKRILL, Prof. John Lloyd;** Professor of the History of Philosophy, Oxford University, since Oct. 1966; *b* 30 Dec. 1921; *s* of late Frederick William Ackrill and Jessie Anne Ackrill; *m* 1953, Margaret Walker Kerr; one *s* three *d*. *Educ:* Reading School; St John's Coll., Oxford (Scholar) (1940-41 and 1945-48). War service (Royal Berks Regt and GS, Capt.), 1941-45. Assistant Lecturer in Logic, Glasgow Univ., 1948-49; Univ. Lectr in Ancient Philosophy, Oxford, 1951-52; Fell. and Tutor, Brasenose Coll., 1953-66. Mem., Inst. for Adv. Study, Princeton, 1950-51, 1961-62; Fell. Coun. of Humanities, and Vis. Prof., Princeton Univ., 1955, 1964. *Publications:* Aristotle's *Categories* and *De Interpretatione* (trans. with notes), 1963. Articles in philos. and class. jls. *Address:* 51 Park Town, Oxford. *T:* 56098.

**ACKROYD, Sir Cuthbert (Lowell),** 1st Bt, *cr* 1956, of Dewsbury, Co. York; DL; Alderman (Cordwainer Ward) and JP City of London, 1945-70; one of HM Lieutenants for City of London, 1945-70; Commissioner of Assize, City of London, 1945-70; retired; *b* 1892; *y s* of Benjamin Batley Ackroyd and Emily Armitage, Dewsbury, Yorks; *m* 1927, Joyce Wallace Whyte, MA (Cantab); two *s*. *Educ:* Dewsbury; Univ. of London. Served European War, 1914-19, Hon. Captain RA; HG, 1940-44 and on Advisory Council Eastern Command Welfare of Troops, 1939-44; Veteran, Hon. Artillery Company. Member Corporation of London, 1940-70; Chm. Guildhall Library Cttee and Art Gallery, 1945; Sheriff, City of London, 1945-50; Lord Mayor of London, 1955-56. Underwriting Mem. of Lloyd's; Chm., Licensing Sessions, City of London, 1957-62; Vice-President Victoria League (Chairman, 1958-62); Hon. Treasurer UNICEF, British Section, 1956-59. Visiting Magistrate Holloway Prison, 1945-55. Governor and Almoner, Christ's Hosp. (Blue Coat School), 1945-69; Governor: Charing Cross Hospital; Hospital for Incurables, Putney; Hospital for Sick Children, 1934-47; Royal Hospitals, 1945-48; Royal Bridewell Hospital; Royal Society for Deaf and Dumb; National Corporation for Care of Old People, 1954-63; Trustee: Morden College; Sir John Soane's Museum, 1959-64; Pres., Metropolitan Institute for the Blind; Bromley Churchill Homes for the Aged. Church Commissioner for England, 1947-63; Church Warden Bow Church (Bow Bells); President, Nat. Brotherhood Movement (Inc.), 1947-48; Vice-Pres., British and Foreign Bible Soc.; Vice-Pres., Boys' Brigade; Pres., Nat. Sunday School Union, 1954; Governor: Royal Coll. of Art; RNLBI; The Hon. Irish Society, 1964-67. FRSA; Mem., The Pilgrims of Gt Britain. Past Grand Warden, United Grand Lodge of England; Pres., Ward of Cordwainer Club, 1945-70; Master, Worshipful Co. of Carpenters, 1952-53; Hon. Freeman, Worshipful Co. of Woolmen; Freeman: City of Belfast; City of Washington, USA; Richmond, Virginia. Hon. Colonel 290 Field Regt RA, 1956-. Hon. LLD Leeds University. DL Kent, 1962; High Sheriff of Kent, 1964; Charter Mayor, Greater London Coun. Borough of Bromley (19), 1964. Comdr Royal Order Orange-Nassau; Officer Legion of Honour; Knight Grand Cross Order of El Rafidain, 1st Class, Iraq; 5 Star Bronze Medal, New York City; Grand Officer Order of Merit, Italy. KStJ. *Recreations:* cricket, literature, pictures. *Heir: s* John Robert Whyte Ackroyd [*b* 2 March 1932; *m* 1956, Jennifer, *d* of H. G. S. Bishop; two *s* two *d*]. *Address:* 48 Bow Lane, Cheapside, EC4; Finches, Bromley, Kent. *T:* 01-460 1443. *Clubs:* Athenæum, City Livery, City Lieutenants', Eccentric.

**ACKROYD, Dame (Dorothy) Elizabeth,** DBE 1970; MA, BLitt (Oxon); Director, Consumer Council, 1963-71; *d* of late Major Charles Harris Ackroyd, MC. *Educ:* privately; St Hugh's Coll., Oxford. Research Asst, Barnett House, Oxford, 1936-39; Min. of Supply, 1940-42, 1946-49, 1951-52 (Under-Sec., 1952); Min.

of Prodn, 1942-45; BoT, 1945-46, 1955-61; Commonwealth Fund Fell., 1949-50; Dir of Steel and Power Div., Economic Commn for Europe, 1950–51; UK Delegn to High Authority of ECSC, 1952-55; MoT, 1961-63. *Address:* 73 St James's Street, SW1. *T:* 01-493 6686.

**ACKROYD, Rev. Prof. Peter Runham,** MA, PhD Cantab, BD, MTh, DD London; Samuel Davidson Professor of Old Testament Studies, University of London, since 1961; *b* 15 Sept. 1917; *s* of Jabez Robert Ackroyd and Winifred (*née* Brown); *m* 1940, Evelyn Alice Nutt, BSc (Manch.), *d* of William Young Nutt; two *s* three *d*. *Educ:* Harrow County School for Boys; Downing and Trinity Colleges, Cambridge. Open Exhibition in Modern Languages, Downing Coll., Cambridge, 1935; Mod. and Med. Langs Tripos, Pt I, 1936, Pt II, 1938; BDHons London, 1940; Stanton Student, Trin. Coll., Cambridge, 1941-43; Dr Williams's Trust Exhibnr, 1941; MTh London, 1942; PhD Cambridge, 1945; DD London, 1970. Minister of: Roydon Congregational Church, Essex, 1943-47; Balham Congregational Church, London, 1947-48; Lectr in Old Testament and Biblical Hebrew, Leeds Univ., 1948-52; Cambridge University: Univ. Lectr in Divinity, 1952-61; Select Preacher, 1955; Mem. Council of Senate, 1957-61; Hulsean Lectr, 1960-62; Select Preacher, Oxford, 1962; Dean of Faculty of Theology, King's Coll., London, 1968-69; FKC 1969. Vis. Prof., Lutheran Sch. of Theology, Chicago, 1967; Selwyn Lectr, NZ, 1970. External Examiner, Belfast, Bristol, Durham, Cambridge, Edinburgh. Ordained Deacon, 1957; Priest, 1958. Hon. Curate, Holy Trinity, Cambridge, 1957-61. Proctor in Convocation, Cambridge Univ., 1960-64. Examining Chaplain to the Bishop of Salisbury; Hon. Sec., Palestine Exploration Fund, 1962-70. Hon. DD St Andrews, 1970. *Publications:* Freedom in Action, 1951; The People of the Old Testament, 1959; Continuity, 1962; The Old Testament Tradition, 1963; Exile and Restoration, 1968; Israel under Babylon and Persia, 1970; 1 & 2 Chronicles, Ezra, Nehemiah, Ruth, Jonah, Maccabees, 1970; 1 Samuel (Cambridge Bible Commentary), 1971; articles and reviews in various learned jls, dictionaries, etc; *Translations:* E. Würthwein's The Text of the Old Testament, 1957; L. Köhler's Hebrew Man, 1957; O. Eissfeldt's The Old Testament: An Introduction, 1965; *editor:* Faith, Law, Hope, Wrath, Life and Death (Bible Key Words), 1961-64; Society for OT Study Book List, 1967-; *joint editor:* SCM Press OT Library, 1960-; Cambridge Bible Commentary, 1961-; SCM Studies in Biblical Theol., 1962-; Words and Meanings: Essays presented to D. W. Thomas, 1968; Cambridge History of the Bible: from the beginnings to Jerome, 1970. *Recreations:* reading, music. *Address:* 34 Half Moon Lane, SE24. *T:* 01-733 1898.

**ACLAND, Lieut-Gen. Arthur N. F.;** *see* Floyer-Acland.

**ACLAND, Captain Hubert Guy Dyke,** DSO 1920; *b* 1890; *y s* of Sir William Alison Dyke Acland, 2nd Bt, and *heir-pres.* to 3rd Bt; *m* 1915, Lalage Mary Kathleen (*d* 1961), *e d* of Captain John Edward Acland; two *s*. Lieutenant 1910; Lieutenant Commander, 1918; Commander, 1925; Captain 1932; served European War, 1914-19 (despatches, DSO); Commanded 1st Minesweeping Flotilla, 1934-35 and Fishery Protection and Minesweeping Flotilla, 1935-36; lent to Royal Australian Navy, 1937-38, and commanded HMAS Australia, 1937-38 and HMAS Albatross, 1938; Senior Officer of Reserve Fleet, Devonport, 1939; Gunnery School, Chatham, Nov. 1939; commanded HMS Vindictive, 1941-42; retired list, 1942; on staff of C-in-C Rosyth, 1943 and of Flag Officer in Charge N Ireland, 1943-45. *Address:* Sunny Bank, Totland Bay, Isle of Wight. *Clubs:* United Service; Royal Yacht Squadron.

**ACLAND, Sir (Hugh) John (Dyke),** KBE 1968; Chairman, New Zealand Wool Board; Vice-Chairman, International Wool Secretariat; *b* 18 Jan. 1904; *e s* of Sir Hugh Acland, CMG, CBE, FRCS, and Lady Acland; *m* 1935, Katherine Wilder Ormond; three *s* three *d*. *Educ:* Christ's College, Christchurch, NZ. *Address:* Mount Peel, Peel Forest, South Canterbury, New Zealand.

**ACLAND, Sir John;** *see* Acland, Sir H. J. D.

**ACLAND, Brigadier Peter Bevil Edward,** OBE 1945; MC 1941; TD; Vice-Lieutenant of Devon, since 1962; *b* 9 July 1902; *s* of late Col A. D. Acland, CBE; *m* 1927, Susan Bridget Barnett, *d* of late Canon H. Barnett; two *s*. *Educ:* Eton; Christ Church, Oxford. Sudan Political Service, 1924-40. Served War of 1939-45: Abyssinia, Western Desert, Ægean (wounded, despatches). Comd Royal Devon Yeomanry, 1947-51, Hon. Col, 1953; Chairman, Devon AEC, 1948-58; Member, National Parks Commission, 1953-60; Chairman, Devon T&AFA, 1960. DL Devon, 1948; High Sheriff for Devon, 1961; JP 1962. 4th Class Order of the Nile; Greek War Cross. *Address:* Feniton Court, Honiton, Devon. *Club:* English-Speaking Union.

**ACLAND, Sir Richard Thomas Dyke,** 15th Bt, *cr* 1644; Lecturer, St Luke's Training College, Exeter, since 1959; *b* 26 Nov. 1906; *e s* of Rt Hon. Sir Francis Acland, 14th Bt, MP; *S* father, 1939; *m* 1936, Anne Stella Alford; three *s*. *Educ:* Rugby; Balliol Coll., Oxford. MP Barnstaple Div. Devon, 1935-45; contested: Torquay Div., 1929; Barnstaple, 1931; Putney, 1945; MP (Lab) Gravesend Division of Kent, 1947-55. Second Church Estates Commissioner, 1950-51. *Publications:* Unser Kampf, 1940; The Forward March, 1941; What it will be like, 1943; How it can be done, 1943; Public Speaking, 1946; Nothing Left to Believe?, 1949; Why So Angry?, 1958; Waging Peace, 1958; We Teach Them Wrong, 1963; Curriculum and Life, 1966. *Heir:* *s* John Dyke Acland [*b* 13 May 1939; *m* 1961, Virginia, *d* of Roland Forge; two *s*]. *Address:* Killerton, Exeter. *TA:* Budlake. *T:* Hele 280.

**ACLAND, Sir William Henry Dyke,** 3rd Bt *cr* 1890; MC; AFC; *b* 16 May 1888; *s* of 2nd Bt and late Emily Anna (author of several novels), *d* of late Viscountess Hambleden and late Rt Hon. W. H. Smith; *S* father, 1924; *m* 1916, Margaret (*d* 1967), *d* of late Theodore Barclay, Fanshaws, Hertford; three *d* (and one *d* decd). *Educ:* Eton; Christ Church, Oxford. MA 1909. Royal Scots Greys; late Col, Royal Devon Yeomanry Artillery, RFC and RAF; Imperial Defence Coll., 1939; served European War (MC, AFC, 4th Class Order of St George, despatches); served War of 1939-45. JP and DL Herts, retd from Aldermanic Bench, Herts CC, 1966. High Sheriff of Hertfordshire, 1951; Governor, Police College. *Heir:* *b* Capt. Hubert Guy Dyke Acland, *qv*. *Address:* Ellacombe, Seaview, Isle of Wight. *Clubs:* Athenæum; Royal Yacht Squadron, Seaview Yacht.

**A'COURT;** *see* Holmes A'Court.

**ACTON,** 3rd Baron, *cr* 1869; **John Emerich Henry Lyon-Dalberg-Acton,** Bt, *cr* 1643; CMG 1963; MBE 1945; TD; Major RA, TA; Chairman: Swaziland Board, Standard Bank

Ltd; Neopac (Swaziland) Ltd; British and Continental Holdings (Insurance Brokers) Ltd; Director, Swaziland Building Society; *b* 15 Dec. 1907; *s* of 2nd Baron and Dorothy (*d* 1923), *d* of late T. H. Lyon, Appleton Hall, Cheshire; *S* father, 1924; *m* 1931, Hon. Daphne Strutt, *o d* of 4th Baron Rayleigh, FRS; five *s* five *d*. *Educ:* Downside; Trinity Coll., Cambridge. Served War of 1939-45 (MBE). Dir, Swaziland Br., BRCS. *Recreation:* horse racing. *Heir:* *s* Hon. Richard Gerald Acton [*b* 30 July 1941; *m* 1965, Hilary Juliet Sarah Cookson; one *s*]. *Address:* PO Box 583, Mbabane, Swaziland. *T:* Mbabane 1840. *Clubs:* Mbabane; Salisbury; Shrewsbury.

*See also J. D. Woodruff.*

**ACTON, Dame (Ellen) Marian,** DBE 1951 (CBE 1920; OBE 1918); Deputy Controller from 1921, Comptroller, 1936-63, Forces Help Society and Lord Roberts Workshops: retd Sept. 1963. Formerly Member: Central Adv. Cttee to Ministry of Pensions and National Insurance; Ministry of Labour National Advisory Council on the Employment of the Disabled until 1965. *Address:* c/o Barclays Bank, 137 Brompton Road, SW3.

**ACTON, Harold Mario,** CBE 1965; author; *b* 5 July 1904; *s* of Arthur Mario Acton and Hortense Mitchell, La Pietra, Florence. *Educ:* Eton Coll.; Ch. Ch., Oxford (BA). FRSL. Lectr in English Literature, National University of Peking and Peking Normal College, 1933-35. Lived for seven years in Peking, devoting much time to Chinese Classical Theatre. Served in RAF during War of 1939-45, chiefly in Far East. Grand Officer, Republic of Italy; Kt of the Constantinian Order. *Publications:* Aquarium, 1923; An Indian Ass, 1925; Five Saints and an Appendix, 1927; Humdrum, 1928; Cornelian, 1928; This Chaos, 1930; The Last Medici, 1932, new edn 1958; (in collab.) Modern Chinese Poetry, 1936; (in collab.) Famous Chinese Plays, 1937; Peonies and Ponies, 1941; Glue and Lacquer, 1941 (Four Cautionary Tales, 1947, reprint of former); Memoirs of an Aesthete, 1948; Prince Isidore, 1950; The Bourbons of Naples, 1956; The Last Bourbons of Naples, 1961; Florence (an essay), 1961; Old Lamps for New, 1965; More Memoirs of an Aesthete, 1970. *Recreations:* jettatura; hunting the Philistines. *Address:* La Pietra, Florence, Italy. *T:* 496-156. *Club:* Savile.

**ACTON, Harry Burrows;** Professor of Moral Philosophy, University of Edinburgh, since 1964; *b* 2 June 1908; *s* of Henry James Acton and Elizabeth Jane (*née* Burrows); *m* 1938, Barbara James; no *c*. *Educ:* St Olave's Grammar School, London; Magdalen Coll., Oxford. 1st Cl. Hons PPE 1930; DPhil (Oxon) 1935. Demy, 1927, Senior Demy 1930, Magdalen Coll., Oxford. Asst Lectr in Philosophy, Univ. Coll. of Swansea, 1931; Lectr in Philosophy, Bedford Coll., 1935; Min. of Supply, 1940-45; Prof. of Philosophy, Bedford Coll., Univ. of London, 1945-64. Visiting Professor of Philosophy, University of Chicago, 1949; President, Aristotelian Soc., 1952-53; Editor, Philosophy, 1956-. Gave Dawes Hicks Lecture, 1959; Director, Royal Inst. of Philosophy, 1962-64. *Publications:* The Illusion of the Epoch: MarxismLeninism as a Philosophical Creed, 1955; What Marx Really Said, 1967; (ed) The Philosophy of Punishment, 1969; Kant's Moral Philosophy, 1970; articles and reviews in Mind, Philosophy, Proc. Aristotelian Soc., etc. *Address:* 5 Abbotsford Park, Edinburgh 10. *T:* 031-447 4026. *Club:* Reform.

**ACTON, Dame Marian;** *see* Acton, Dame E. M.

**ACTON, Murray A.;** *see* Adams-Acton.

**ACTON, Maj.-Gen. Thomas Heward,** CBE 1963 (OBE 1957); Chief of Staff to the GOC and Director of Operations, Northern Ireland, since 1970; *b* 12 June 1917; *s* of Lt-Col W. M. Acton, DSO. *Educ:* Eton; RMA Sandhurst. Commissioned Rifle Brigade, 1937; served War of 1939-45 (despatches); Mil. Asst to Governor of Cyprus, 1955-57; Lt-Col, King's Royal Rifle Corps, 1959; Maj.-Gen. 1967; GOC SW District, 1967-70; Dep. Comdr Army in N Ireland, 1970. *Recreations:* fishing, shooting. *Club:* Naval and Military.

**ACTON, William Antony;** *b* 8 April 1904; *o s* of late William Walter Acton, Wolverton Hall, Pershore, Worcs; *m* 1932, Joan, *o c* of late Hon. Francis Geoffrey Pearson; one *d*. *Educ:* Eton; Trinity College, Cambridge. HM Treasury, 1939-45. Managing Director, Lazard Bros & Co. Ltd, 1945-53; Director: The National Bank Ltd, 1945-70 (Chm., 1964-70); Bank of London and South America Ltd, 1953-70; Standard Bank Ltd, 1953-70; Ottoman Bank, 1953-58; Bank of London and Montreal Ltd., 1959-64; Bank of West Africa Ltd, 1954-70; Bank of Ireland, 1966-70; National Commercial Bank of Scotland, 1967-70; National and Commercial Banking Group Ltd, 1969-70; The Whitehall Trust, 1945-70. High Sheriff, County of London, 1955. *Recreation:* travelling. *Address:* c/o The National Bank Ltd, 13-17 Old Broad Street, EC2. *Club:* White's.

**ACUTT, Sir Keith (Courtney),** KBE 1962 (CBE 1957); Deputy Chairman, Anglo-American Corporation of South Africa Ltd; Director: Charter Consolidated Ltd; De Beers Consolidated Mines Ltd; director of several other finance and mining companies; *b* 6 October 1909; *s* of late Guy Courtney Acutt. *Educ:* in South Africa. Served War of 1939-45 (despatches, 1944). *Address:* 44 Main Street, Johannesburg, South Africa. *T:* 838-8111.

**ADAIR, Maj.-Gen. Sir Allan (Henry Shafto),** 6th Bt, *cr* 1838; KCVO 1967 (CVO 1957); CB 1945; DSO 1940; MC; DL; JP; Lieutenant of HM Bodyguard of the Yeomen of the Guard, 1951-67; *b* 3 Nov. 1897; *o s* of Sir R. Shafto Adair, 5th Bt and Mary (*d* 1950), *d* of Henry Anstey Bosanquet; *S* father, 1949; *m* Enid, *d* of late Hon. Mrs Dudley Ward; three *d* (one *s* killed in action, 1943). *Educ:* Harrow. Grenadier Guards, 1916-41; commanded 3rd Battalion, 1940; Comdr 30 Guards Brigade, 1941; Comdr 6 Guards Brigade, 1942; Comdr Guards Armoured Division 1942-45; retired pay, 1947. Colonel of the Grenadier Guards, 1961-. DL for Co. Antrim, JP for Suffolk. Governor of Harrow School, 1947-52. Dep. Grand Master, Grand Lodge of Freemasons. *Recreations:* shooting, golf. *Address:* 55 Green Street, W1. *T:* 01-629 3860; Ballymena, Co. Antrim. *Clubs:* Turf, Guards.

*See also Brig. Sir J. L. Darell, Bt.*

**ADAIR, Arthur Robin,** CVO 1961; MBE 1947; British High Commissioner in Brunei since 1968; *b* 10 Feb. 1913; *s* of late Francis Robin Adair and Ethel Anne Adair, Grove House, Youghal, Eire; *m* 1952, Diana Theodora Synnott; one *s*. *Educ:* abroad; Emmanuel College, Cambridge. Indian Civil Service, 1937-47 (incl. 3 yrs in Army in charge of recruitment for Bihar Prov.); Dist Magistrate and Dep. Comr, 1944-47; Treasury, July 1947; transferred to CRO, Oct. 1947; First Secretary: Dacca, 1947-50; Colombo, 1952-56; British Deputy High Commissioner in: Dacca, 1960-64; Cyprus, 1964-68. *Recreation:* flying as private pilot. *Address:* Providence Corner, Well Road, Hampstead, NW3. *T:* 01-435 4351.

*Clubs:* Royal Aero, Royal Commonwealth Society.

**ADAIR, Gilbert Smithson,** FRS 1939; MA; Reader in Biophysics, Physiological Laboratory, Cambridge, 1947-63; *b* 21 Sept. 1896; *s* of Harold Adair, JP; *m* 1931, Muriel Elaine Robinson; no *c*. *Educ:* Bootham School, York; King's College, Cambridge. Scholar and Fellow of King's College, Cambridge; Hon. Fellow, 1963; engaged in research on thermodynamical properties of proteins. *Publications:* papers in scientific periodicals. *Recreation:* climbing. *Address:* 92 Grantchester Meadows, Cambridge. *Club:* Fell and Rock Climbing.

**ADAM, Hon. Sir Alexander Duncan Grant** (known as Hon. Sir Alistair Adam), Kt 1970; MA, LLM; **Hon. Mr Justice Adam;** Judge Supreme Court of Victoria, since 1957; *b* Greenock, Scotland, 30 Nov. 1902; *s* of late Rev. Prof. Adam and of Mrs D. S. Adam; *m* 1930, Nora Laver; one *s* two *d*. *Educ:* Scotch Coll., Melbourne; Melbourne Univ. Associate to Mr Justice Starke, 1927-28; Victorian Bar, 1928-57; Independent Lecturer in Real Property, Melbourne Univ., 1932-51; Defence Dept, 1942-45; QC 1950; Mem. Council, Melbourne Univ., 1957-69; Trustee, Nat. Museum of Victoria, 1962-. *Publications:* contributor to learned jls. *Recreation:* golf. *Address:* 39 Walsh Street, Balwyn, Victoria, Australia. *T:* 801524. *Clubs:* Australian (Melbourne); Royal Automobile Club of Victoria.

**ADAM, Captain Charles Keith,** DSO 1942; RN (retired); *b* Perth, West Australia, 29 April 1891; 2nd *s* of William Keith Adam and Jane Emily Leake; *m* 1939, Barbara Eunice, *y d* of Maj.-Gen. A. H. Marindin and Gertrude Florence Evelyn Wilmot-Chetwode, Fordel, Glenfarg; one *s* three *d*. *Educ:* RN Colleges Osborne and Dartmouth. Naval Cadet, 1903; Sub-Lieut, 1911; served European War, 1914-19; commanded destroyers, 1916-19; Brit. Mil. Mission, S. Russia, 1919-20; retd list, rank of Comdr, 1934; Colombian Navy (Capitan di Navio), 1934-37; recalled to RN (staff), 1939; served War of 1939-46, in command: HMS Rion, 1941; HMS Ulster Queen, 1942-43 (DSO); HMS Beachy Head, 1945; HMS Caradoc, 1945; Captain (actg), 1942; Captain, 1946. Convener, Kinross-shire County Council, 1954-60. Mem. of Queen's Body Guard for Scotland (Royal Company of Archers), 1941. JP Kinross-shire, 1937; Lord Lieutenant of County of Kinross, 1955-56. Order of St Anne of Russia, 3rd Class, 1920; Cross of Boyaca (Colombia), 1936. *Recreations:* shooting, fishing, golf. *Address:* Blair Adam, Kinross-shire. *T:* Kelty 239. *Clubs:* Naval and Military; New (Edinburgh).

**ADAM, Colin Gurdon Forbes,** CSI 1924; *b* 18 Dec. 1889; *y s* of Sir Frank Forbes Adam, 1st Bt; *m* 1920, Hon. Irene Constance Lawley, *o c* of 3rd Baron Wenlock; two *s* one *d* (and one *s* decd). *Educ:* Eton; King's Coll., Cambridge (BA). Entered Indian Civil Service, 1912; Asst Collector and Magistrate, Poona, 1913-15; Under-Sec. to Government of Bombay, 1919; Private Sec. to Governor of Bombay, 1920; Dep. Sec. to Govt, 1925; retired, 1927; District Comr for Special Area of Durham and Tyneside, 1934-39; Chairman, Yorkshire Conservative Newspaper Co., 1960-65. Served Indian Army Reserve of Officers, 1915-18; Indian Expeditionary Force, Mesopotamia and Palestine, 1916-18. DL Kingston upon Hull, 1958-66. *Publication:* Life of Lord Lloyd, 1948. *Address:* 9 Dickens Close, Sudbrook Lane, Petersham, Surrey. *Club:* Yorkshire.

*See also Gen. Sir R. F. Adam, H. F. G. Charteris.*

**ADAM, Kenneth,** CBE 1962; MA; FRSA; Overseas Visitor to Temple University, Philadelphia, since 1969; *b* 1 March 1908; *s* of Edward Percy Adam and Ethel Jane Saunders; *m* 1932, Ruth Augusta King; three *s* one *d*. *Educ:* Nottingham High Sch.; St John's Coll., Cambridge (Senior Scholar and Prizeman). Editorial Staff, Manchester Guardian, 1930-34; Home News Editor, BBC, 1934-36; Special Corresp. of The Star, 1936-40; Press Officer, BOAC, 1940-41; Dir of BBC Publicity, 1941-50; Controller, Light Programme, BBC, 1950-55; Gen. Manager (Joint), Hulton Press, 1955-57; Controller of Television Programmes, BBC, 1957-61; Dir of BBC Television, 1961-68. Vis. Prof. of Communications, Temple Univ., Philadelphia, 1968; Danforth Travelling Fellow, USA, 1969. Governor, Charing Cross Hosp., 1960-66; Governor, British Film Inst., 1961; Member: (co-opted), Extra Mural Delegacy, Oxford, 1962; London Topographical Soc., 1962; Brit. Travel Assoc. Council, 1966; Council of Industrial Design, 1967; Council, Nat. Youth Theatre, 1967; Council, Tavistock Inst., 1968; Inst. of Public Relations, 1969-. Hon. Mem., Anglo-Danish Soc., 1952-. FAMS 1962. *Address:* 19 Old Court House, W8. *T:* 01-937 0369; Annenberg Hall, Philadelphia, Pa, USA. *T:* (215) 787-8421. *Clubs:* Caledonian, Press; Union Society (Cambridge).

**ADAM, Madge Gertrude,** MA, DPhil; FRAS; University Lecturer (Astronomy), Department of Astrophysics, University Observatory, Oxford; Research Fellow of St Hugh's College, 1957; *b* 6 March 1912; 2nd *d* of late John Gill Simpson and late Gertrude Adam; unmarried. *Educ:* Municipal High School, Doncaster; St Hugh's College, Oxford (Scholar). Research Scholar, Lady Margaret Hall, 1935-37; Junior British Scholarship, 1936-37; Assistant Tutor of St Hugh's College and Research Assistant at Oxford University Observatory, 1937; lately Fellow and Tutor, St Hugh's College. *Publications:* papers in Monthly Notices of Royal Astronomical Society from 1937. *Address:* Department of Astro-physics, The University Observatory, South Parks Road, Oxford.

**ADAM, Neil Kensington,** FRS 1935; FRIC; MA, ScD (Cantab); Emeritus Professor of Chemistry, University of Southampton (Professor, 1937-57); formerly Lecturer and Hon. Research Associate, University College, London; *s* of James Adam, MA, LittD and Adela Marion Adam, MA; *m* 1916, Winifred Wright; one *s* one *d*. *Educ:* Winchester; Trinity College, Cambridge (Fellow, 1915-23). Royal Society Sorby Research Fellow at Sheffield University, 1921-29. *Publications:* The Physics and Chemistry of Surfaces; Physical Chemistry; numerous papers in scientific periodicals. *Recreations:* camping, sailing, ducks. *Address:* 95 Highfield Lane, Southampton SO2 1NN. *Club:* Athenæum.

**ADAM, Randle R.;** *see* Reid-Adam.

**ADAM, General Sir Ronald Forbes,** 2nd Bt, *cr* 1917; GCB 1946 (KCB 1941; CB 1939); DSO 1918; OBE 1919; RA; Hon. LLD (Aberdeen); Hon. Fellow, Worcester College, Oxford; President, United Nations Association; Trustee, National Central Library; *b* 30 Oct. 1885; *e s* of Sir Frank Forbes Adam, 1st Bt, and Rose Frances (*d* 1944), *d* of C. G. Kemball, late Judge, High Court, Bombay; *S* father, 1926; *m* 1915, Anna Dorothy, *d* of late F. I. Pitman; three *d*. *Educ:* Eton; RMA, Woolwich. Served European War (France and Flanders,

Italy), 1914-18 (despatches, DSO, OBE); GSO1, Staff College, Camberley, 1932-35; GSO1, War Office, 1935-36; Deputy Director of Military Operations, War Office, 1936; Commander Royal Artillery, 1st Division, 1936-37; Commandant of Staff College, Camberley, 1937; Deputy Chief of Imperial General Staff, 1938-39; Commanding 3rd Army Corps, 1939-40; General Officer Commanding-in-Chief, Northern Command, 1940-41; Adjutant-General to the Forces, 1941-46; General, 1942; retired pay, 1946. Col Comdt of RA and of Army Educational Corps, 1940-50; Col Comdt Royal Army Dental Corps, 1945-51 (Representative, 1950). President: MCC, 1946-47; Library Assoc., 1949; Nat. Inst. of Adult Education, 1949-64; Chairman: Linoleum Working Party, 1946; Nat. Inst. Industrial Psychology, 1947-52; Council, Inst. of Education, London Univ., 1948-67; Mem., Miners Welfare Commn, 1946-52; Chm. and Dir-Gen., British Council, 1946-54; Executive Board UNESCO, 1950-54, Chm., 1952-54; Principal, Working Men's Coll., 1956-61. *Heir: n* Christopher Eric Forbes Adam, *b* 1920. *Address:* Carylls Lea, Faygate, Sussex. *Clubs:* Athenæum, United Service.

*See also C. G. F. Adam, Sir P. D. Proctor.*

**ADAM SMITH, Janet (Buchanan), (Mrs John Carleton);** author and journalist; *b* 9 Dec. 1905; *d* of late Very Rev. Sir George Adam Smith, Principal of Aberdeen Univ. and late Lady Adam Smith; *m* 1st, 1935, Michael Roberts (*d* 1948); three *s* one *d*; 2nd, 1965, John Carleton, *qv*. *Educ:* Cheltenham Ladies' College (scholar); Somerville College, Oxford (exhibitioner). BBC, 1928-35; Asst Editor, The Listener, 1930-35; Asst Literary Editor, New Statesman and Nation, 1949-52, Literary Editor, 1952-60. Virginia Gildersleeve Vis. Prof., Barnard Coll., New York, 1961 and 1964. Trustee, National Library of Scotland, 1950-. Hon. LLD Aberdeen, 1962. *Publications:* Poems of Tomorrow (ed), 1935; R. L. Stevenson, 1937; Mountain Holidays, 1946; Life Among the Scots, 1946; Henry James and Robert Louis Stevenson (ed) 1948; Collected Poems of R. L. Stevenson (ed), 1950; Faber Book of Children's Verse (ed), 1953; Collected Poems of Michael Roberts (ed), 1958; John Buchan: a Biography, 1965; (ed) The Living Stream, 1969. *Recreation:* mountaineering. *Address:* 57 Lansdowne Road, W11. *T:* 01-727 9324. *Clubs:* Ladies' Alpine (President, 1962-65); Club Alpin Français.

*See also Baron Balerno.*

**ADAMS, Alec Cecil Stanley,** CMG 1960; CBE 1952; *b* 25 July 1909; *e s* of late Stanley A. Adams. *Educ:* King's School, Canterbury; Corpus Christi Coll., Cambridge. One of HM Vice-Consuls in Siam, 1933; served in Portuguese East Africa (acting Consul at Beira, June 1936-Feb. 1937); local rank 2nd Secretary, Bangkok Legation, 1937; Acting Consul, Sourabaya, 1938; Bangkok Legation, 1939-40; Foreign Office, Ministry of Information, 1940; Consul, in Foreign Office, 1945; Bangkok, 1946, Acting Consul-General and Chargé d'Affaires, 1948; Consul, Cincinnati, 1949; HM Chargé d'Affaires in Korea, 1950; HM Consul-General at Houston, Texas, 1953-55; Counsellor and Consul-General at HM Embassy, Bangkok, 1956-62; Deputy Commissioner-General for South East Asia, 1962-63; Political Advisor to C-in-C (Far East) at Singapore, 1963-67; retired from HM Diplomatic Service, 1967. *Address:* Flat 513, 97 Southampton Row, WC1B 4HH. *Club:* Royal Automobile.

**ADAMS, Air Vice-Marshal Alexander Annan,** CB 1957; DFC 1944; *b* 14 Nov. 1908; *s* of Capt. Norman Anderson Adams, Durham; *m* 1933, Eileen Mary O'Neill; one *s* one *d*. *Educ:* Beechmont, Sevenoaks; Bellerive, Switzerland; Austria. Commnd RAF, 1930; 54 Fighter Sqdn, 1931-32; 604 Aux. Sqdn, Hendon, 1933-35; CFS, 1935; Asst Air Attaché, Berlin, Brussels, The Hague, Berne, 1938-40; Ops, Air Min., 1940; British Embassy, Washington, 1941-42; in comd 49 (Lancaster) Sqdn, 1943-44; RAF Staff Coll., 1945; Head of RAF Intelligence, Germany, 1946-48; in comd RAF Binbrook, 1948-50; NATO Standing Gp, Washington, DC, 1951-53; idc, 1954; Air Attaché, Bonn, 1955; Min. of Defence, 1956; Chief of Staff, Far East Air Force, 1957-59. Hawker Siddeley Aviation, 1961-66; retired 1966. Comdr Order of Orange Nassau, 1950. *Recreations:* golf, painting. *Address:* Upper Mayes, Middleton-on-Sea, Sussex. *T:* Middleton-on-Sea 2414. *Club:* Royal Air Force.

**ADAMS, Captain Bryan Fullerton,** DSO 1919; Royal Navy, retired; *b* 22 July 1887; *s* of late G. H. Adams, Portglenone, Co. Down, and Melbourne, Australia; *m* 1st, 1921, Audrey (*d* 1929), *d* of C. E. Marshall, Thurlestone, Devon; one *d*; 2nd, 1937, Pamela Jocelyne, *o d* of late Vice-Adm. Sidney Drury-Lowe, CMG; one *d*. *Educ:* Sherborne; HMS Britannia. Served European War, 1914-18 (despatches, DSO); Comdr, 1918; retired list, 1933. *Recreation:* gardening. *Address:* Cherry Tree, Hacheston, Suffolk. *Clubs:* United Service, MCC.

*See also Wayland Young (Baron Kennet).*

**ADAMS, Charles Kingsley,** CBE 1954; FSA; Director, Keeper and Secretary of the National Portrait Gallery, 1951-64, retd; *b* 17 June 1899; *s* of late Albert Edward Adams; *m* 1927, Lily Eva Brewer; one *s* two *d*. *Educ:* King's School, Worcester. Served European War, Temp. 2nd Lieut, E Surrey Regt, 1918-19. Assistant Keeper, National Portrait Gallery, 1919-51. Chairman: National Loan Collection Trust, 1953-; Exec. Cttee, Soc. of Genealogists, 1964-68. *Publications:* compiled Catalogue of Pictures in the Garrick Club, 1936; edited Catalogue of Pictures in the Collection of the Duke of Portland, 1936. *Address:* 9 St Mary Abbots Terrace, W14. *T:* 01-602 3726. *Club:* Athenæum.

**ADAMS, Prof. Colin Wallace Maitland;** Sir William Dunn Professor of Pathology, Guy's Hospital Medical School, since 1965; *b* 17 Feb. 1928; *s* of Sidney Ewart Adams and Gladys Alethea Fletcher Adams; *m* 1953, Anne Brownhill; one *s*. *Educ:* Oundle School; Christ's College, Cambridge. Sir Lionel Whitby Medal, Cambridge Univ., 1959-60. Visiting Scientist, National Institutes of Health, Bethesda, USA, 1960-61. *Publications:* Neurohistochemistry, 1965; Vascular Histochemistry, 1967; papers on arterial diseases, neuropathology and microscopical chemistry in medical and biological journals. *Address:* The Knoll, Rayleigh, Essex. *T:* Rayleigh 6489.

**ADAMS, Air Commodore Cyril Douglas,** CB 1948; OBE 1942; retired; *b* 18 Sept. 1897; British; *m* 1927, D. M. Le Brocq (*d* 1957), Highfield, Jersey; one *s* one *d*; *m* 1968, Mrs K. E. Webster, NZ. *Educ:* Parkstone Grammar School. Served European War in Army, 1915-18, Egypt, Palestine; Commissioned RFC, 1918; Flying Instructor, 1918-25; Staff Duties, Iraq Command, 1925-27; Staff and Flying Duties, Halton Comd, 1928-35; CO 15 Sqdn, 1936-38; HQ Bomber Comd, 1938; CO 38 Sqdn, 1938-39; Sen. Officer i/c

Administration, No 3 Group, 1939-40; Station Comdr, Kemble, Oakington, Abingdon, 1940-44; Base Comdr, Marston Moor and North Luffenham, 1944-45; India Command, AOA, AHQ, 1945-46; Base Comdr, Bombay, 1946; AOC No 2 Indian Group, 1946-47 (despatches 6 times, OBE); Air Officer Commanding No 85 Group, BAFO, 1948-49; retired, 1949. *Recreations:* represented: RAF (Rugby, cricket, athletics); Hampshire (Rugby); Dorset and minor counties (cricket); keen golfer. *Address:* Meadow Way, Barton-on-Sea, Hants. *T:* New Milton 5441.

**ADAMS, Sir Ernest (Charles),** Kt 1949; CBE 1945 (MBE 1935); *b* 5 May 1886; *s* of William D. Adams; *m* 1911, Agnes S. Fortune (*d* 1965); one *d. Educ:* Roan Sch., Greenwich. Inland Revenue Dept, 1905; Customs and Excise, 1909; Min. of Pensions, 1919; Export Credits Guarantee Dept, 1928; Comptroller General, Export Credits Guarantee Dept, 1946-49. *Address:* Cleevers, Ham Lane, Shepton Mallet, Somerset. *T:* Shepton Mallet 2646.

**ADAMS, Hon. Sir Francis Boyd,** Kt 1961; retired as Judge of Supreme Court of New Zealand (1950-60); *b* 25 Nov. 1888; *s* of Hon. Alexander Samuel Adams, Supreme Court Judge; *m* 1st, 1917, Olive Evelyn (*née* Chandler) (*d* 1950); four *d*; 2nd, 1960, Joyce Ellen Gilbert (*née* Terry), Sydney. *Educ:* Otago Boys' High School, Dunedin; Victoria University College, Wellington; University of Otago, Dunedin. BA, LLM. Admitted to Bar, 1911. Served European War, 1914-18, in 1st New Zealand Expeditionary Force, 1916-19 (wounded, 1918). Home Service in War of 1939-45, to rank of Lieut-Colonel. Crown Solicitor and Crown Prosecutor at Dunedin, NZ, 1921-50; occasional service as a Judge of Fiji Court of Appeal, 1960-. Consulting Editor, Adams' Criminal Law and Practice in NZ. *Publications:* Criminal Onus and Exculpations, 1968; contribs to law jls. *Recreation:* bowls. *Address:* 27 Makora Street, Christchurch 4, New Zealand. *T:* 517-217.

**ADAMS, Frank Alexander,** CB 1964; Member, Public Health Laboratory Service Board, since 1968; *b* 9 July 1907; *m* 1928, Esther Metcalfe; two *d. Educ:* Selhurst Grammar Sch.; London School of Economics, Univ. of London. HM Inspector of Taxes, 1928; Assistant Secretary, Board of Inland Revenue, 1945; Counsellor (Economic and Financial), UK Delegation to OEEC, Paris, 1957-59; Director, Civil Service Pay Research Unit, 1960-63; Under-Sec. (Finance) and Accountant-General, Min. of Health, 1963-67. *Address:* The Red House, Speldhurst, Kent. *T:* Speldhurst 2987. *Clubs:* Royal Automobile, Climbers'; Swiss Alpine, (Geneva).

**ADAMS, Frederick Baldwin, Jr;** Director, Pierpont Morgan Library, since 1948; *b* 28 March 1910; *s* of Frederick B. Adams and Ellen Walters Delano; *m* 1st, 1933, Ruth Potter; 2nd, 1941, Betty Abbott; four *d. Educ:* St Paul's Sch.; Yale Univ. (BA). Empl. Air Reduction Co. Inc., 1933-48. Director, Atlantic Coast Line Co.; Pres., New-York Historical Society; Pres. Bd Govs, Yale University Press; Trustee: Yale Univ.; Carnegie Corporation; Brooklyn Museum; Fellow: Amer. Acad. Arts and Sciences; Amer. Philosophical Soc.; Amer. Antiquarian Soc.; Mass. Historical Soc.; Mem., Phi Beta Kappa. Hon. degrees: LittD: Hofstra Coll., 1959; Williams Coll., 1966; DFA, Union Coll., 1959; MA, Yale Univ., 1965; LHD, New York Univ., 1966. Chevalier, Légion d'Honneur, 1950. *Publications:* Radical Literature in America, 1939; One Hundred Influential American Books (with Streeter and Wilson), 1947; To Russia with Frost, 1963; contrib. to books and jls in bibliography, printing, collecting. *Address:* 435 East 52 Street, New York, NY 10022, USA. *Clubs:* Athenæum, Roxburghe; Century, Grolier (NY).

**ADAMS, Sir Grantley Herbert,** Kt 1957; CMG 1952; QC (Barbados) 1953; *b* 28 April 1898; *s* of Fitzherbert Adams; *m* Grace Thorne; one *s. Educ:* Harrison Coll., Barbados; Oxford University. Called to the Bar, Gray's Inn, 1923. Premier of Barbados, 1954-58; Prime Minister of the West Indies, 1958-62. Formerly: Leader of the House of Assembly and Member of the Executive Committee, Barbados, British West Indies; Mem., Colonial Parlt, 1934-54. Mem., ILO Cttee of Experts, 1949-. Hon. DLitt Mount Allison 1958. *Recreations:* cricket (Barbados XI), gardening. *Address:* Codrington Hill, St Michael, Barbados.

**ADAMS, (Harold) Richard;** Management Consultant, since 1938; *b* 8 Oct. 1912; *s* of late A. Adams; *m* 1938, Joyce Love (marr. diss. 1955); two *d*; *m* 1956, P. Fribbins; one *s. Educ:* elementary; Emanuel School; London University; Middle Temple. Member Wandsworth Borough Council before War of 1939-45. Served War of 1939-45: joined East Surrey Regt, 1940; with 25 Army Tank Bde in N Africa and Italy; later, Staff Officer Land Forces Adriatic. Experience as business consultant; one time Asst Comr for National Savings; Lectr in Economics. MP (Lab) Balham and Tooting Div. of Wandsworth, 1945-50, Central Div., 1950-55; Asst Whip (unpaid), 1947-49; a Lord Comr of the Treasury, 1949-50. FIS. Mem., Fabian Soc. *Recreations:* antiques, politics. *Address:* 1 Darlaston Road, SW19.

**ADAMS, Herbert Louis,** CMG 1961; TD 1945; retired as Permanent Secretary, Civil Aviation, East African Common Services Organization (1962-64); Appointments Officer, Ministry of Overseas Development; *b* 29 May 1910; *s* of late Herbert Adams, author, and Jessie Louise Cooper; *m* 1934, Margherita Anna Henley Wareing; one *d. Educ:* Haileybury College. 2nd Lieut, 24th London Regt (The Queen's) TA, 1929. Partner, Adams & Watts, Surveyors and Estate Agents, SW1, 1934-38. Military Service, 1938-45: Staff College, Camberley, War Course; Lt-Col, GSO1, 1945. Joined Colonial Service as Cadet, Kenya, 1946; Sec. for Commerce and Industry, 1949; Economic Sec., E Africa High Commn, 1954; Chief Administrative Secretary, 1958. *Recreations:* photography, gardening. *Address:* Corner Cottage, Badlesmere, Faversham, Kent. *Clubs:* East India and Sports; Nairobi.

**ADAMS, Hervey Cadwallader,** RBA 1932; FRSA 1951; landscape painter and portrait painter; lecturer on art; *b* Kensington, 1903; *o s* of Cadwallader Edmund Adams and Dorothy Jane, *y d* of Rev. J. W. Knight; *m* 1928, Iris Gabrielle, *y d* of late F. V. Bruce, St Fagans, Glamorgan; two *s. Educ:* Charterhouse. Studied languages and singing in France and Spain, 1922-26; studied painting under Bernard Adams, 1929. Art Master, Tonbridge Sch., 1940-63. *Publications:* The Student's Approach to Landscape Painting, 1938; Art and Everyman, 1945; Eighteenth Century Painting, 1949; Nineteenth Century Painting, 1949; The Adventure of Looking, 1949. *Address:* Pummel, Houndscroft, near Stroud, Glos.

**ADAMS, Professor James Whyte Leitch;** Professor of Education, University of Dundee (formerly Queen's College), since 1955; *b* 7 Nov. 1909; *o s* of Charles and Helen Adams,

Stirling; *m* 1939, Isobel Margaret, ARIBA, *d* of Robert Gordon, Fraserburgh; one *s* two *d*. *Educ:* Arbroath High School; St Andrews University; Oxford University. Harkness Scholar, St Andrews, 1928; Guthrie Scholar, 1931; 1st cl. hons Classics, 1932; Marshall Prizeman, Miller Prizeman, Lewis Campbell Medallist, etc; Waugh Scholar, Exeter Coll., Oxford, 1932; 1st cl. Classical Mods, 1934; 1st cl. Lit. Hum., 1936; Craven Fellowship, 1936; Dipl. in Educn, St Andrews Univ., 1937. Teacher of Classics, Golspie Senior Secondary Sch., 1937-39; Educn Officer (Scotland), BBC, 1939-47; RAF Education Service, 1942-45; HM Inspector of Schools, 1947-50; Lecturer in Humanity, Aberdeen University, 1950-55. *Publications:* various contributions, especially on Renaissance Latin Poetry. *Recreations:* golf and "brither" Scots. *Address:* Wentworth, Broughty Ferry, Dundee. *T:* Dundee 78138.

**ADAMS, Dr John Bertram,** CMG 1962; FRS 1963; Director, 300 GeV Accelerator Project, European Organisation for Nuclear Research (CERN), since 1969; *b* 24 May 1920; *s* of John A. Adams and Emily Searles; *m* 1943, Renie Warburton; one *s* two *d*. *Educ:* Eltham College; Research Laboratory, Siemens. Telecommunications Research Establishment, Swanage and Malvern, 1940-45; Atomic Energy Research Establishment, Harwell, 1945-53; European Organisation for Nuclear Research (CERN), Geneva, 1953, Dir of Proton Synchrotron Division, 1954-60; Director-Gen., CERN, 1960-61; Director, Culham Laboratory, AEA, Oxford, 1960-67; Controller, Min. of Technology, 1965-66; Member: Council for Scientific Policy, 1965-68; UKAEA, 1966-69; Adv. Council on Technology, 1966-69. Fellow, Wolfson College, Oxford, 1966 (MA). Guthrie Lecturer, Phys. Soc., 1965. DSc *hc*: Univ. of Geneva, 1960; Birmingham Univ., 1961; Univ. of Surrey, 1966. Röntgen Prize, Univ. of Giessen, 1960; Duddell Medal, Physical Soc., 1961. *Publications:* contributions to Nature, Nuovo Cimento, etc. *Recreations:* swimming, ski-ing. *Address:* (home) 8 chemin aux Folies, 1293 Bellevue, Geneva, Switzerland; (office) European Organisation for Nuclear Research (CERN), 1211 Geneva 23, Switzerland.

**ADAMS, John Crawford,** MD, MS, FRCS; Consultant Orthopædic Surgeon: St Mary's Hospital, London; Paddington Green Children's Hospital; St Vincent's Orthopædic Hospital, Pinner; Civil Consultant in Orthopædic Surgery, Royal Air Force; Deputy Editor, Journal of Bone and Joint Surgery. MB, BS 1937; MRCS 1937; LRCP 1937; FRCS 1941; MD (London) 1943; MS (London) 1965. Formerly: Chief Asst, Orthopædic and Accident Dept, London Hosp.; Orthopædic Specialist, RAFVR; Resident Surgical Officer, Wingfield-Morris Orthopædic Hosp., Oxford. FRSM; Fellow and Hon. Sec. of the British Orthopædic Association. *Publications:* Outline of Orthopædics, 1956, 1958, 1967; Outline of Fractures, 1957, 1967; Ischio-femoral Arthrodesis, 1966; Recurrent Dislocation of Shoulder (chapter in Techniques in British Surgery, ed Maingot), 1950; Associate Editor and Contributor Operative Surgery (ed Rob and Smith); contributions to the Journal of Bone and Joint Surgery, etc. *Address:* St Mary's Hospital, W2.

**ADAMS, Prof. John Frank,** MA, PhD; FRS 1964; Lowndean Professor of Astronomy and Geometry, Cambridge University, since 1970; Fellow of Trinity College, Cambridge; *b* 5 Nov. 1930; *m* 1953, Grace Rhoda, BA, BD; one *s* three *d*. *Educ:* Bedford School; Trinity College, Cambridge; The Institute for Advanced Study, Princeton. Junior Lecturer, Oxford, 1955-56; Research Fellow, Trinity College, Cambridge, 1955-58; Commonwealth Fund Fellow, 1957-58; Assistant Lecturer, Cambridge, and Director of Studies in Mathematics, Trinity Hall, Cambridge, 1958-61; Reader, Manchester, 1962-64; Fielden Prof. of Pure Mathematics, Manchester Univ., 1964-70. *Publications:* Stable Homotopy Theory, 1964; Lectures on Lie Groups, 1969; papers in mathematical jls. *Recreations:* walking, climbing. *Address:* Trinity College, Cambridge.

**ADAMS, Rear-Adm. John Harold,** CB 1967; MVO 1957; *b* Newcastle-on-Tyne, 19 Dec. 1918; *m* 1st, 1943, Mary Parker (marr. diss. 1961); one *s*; 2nd, 1961, Ione Eadie, MVO; two *s* one *d*. *Educ:* Glenalmond. Joined Navy, 1936; Home Fleet, 1937-39; Western Approaches, Channel and N Africa, 1939-42 (despatches); Staff Capt. (D), Liverpool, 1943-45; Staff Course, Greenwich, 1945; jssc 1949; Comdr, HM Yacht Britannia, 1954-57; Asst Dir, Underwater Weapons Matériel Dept, 1957-58; Capt. (SM) 3rd Submarine Sqdn, HMS Adamant, 1958-60; Captain Supt, Underwater Detection Estab., Portland, subseq. Admty Underwater Weapons Estab., 1960-62; idc 1963; comd HMS Albion, 1964-66; Asst Chief of Naval Staff (Policy), 1966-68; retd 1968. Lieut 1941; Lieut-Comdr 1949; Comdr 1951; Capt. 1957; Rear-Adm. 1966. Dir, Paper and Paper Products Industry Training Bd. MIEE; MBIM; MIPM. *Recreations:* sailing, photography. *Address:* The Oxdrove House, Burghclere, Newbury, Berks. *T:* Burghclere 385. *Club:* Royal Automobile.

**ADAMS, John Kenneth;** Editor of Country Life; Editorial Director, Country Life Ltd; *b* 3 June 1915; *o s* of late Thomas John Adams and late Mabel Adams (*née* Jarvis), Oxford; *m* 1944, Margaret, *o d* of late Edward Claude Fortescue, Banbury, Oxon. *Educ:* City of Oxford Sch.; Balliol Coll., Oxford. Asst Master, Stonyhurst Coll., 1939-40; served with RAFVR, 1940-41 (invalided); Asst Master, Wellington Coll., 1941-44; attached to Manchester Guardian as Leader-writer, 1942-44; Leader-writer, The Scotsman, 1944-46; joined editorial staff of Country Life, 1946; Asst Editor, 1952; Deputy Editor, 1956; Editor, 1958; Editorial Director, 1959. *Recreations:* gardening, ornithology, travel. *Address:* 95 Alleyn Park, West Dulwich, SE21. *T:* 01-693 1736. *Clubs:* Athenæum, United University.

**ADAMS, (John) Roland,** QC 1949; *b* 24 July 1900; *s* of late Alfred Courthope Adams and Sabina Newberry; *m* 1946, Violet, *d* of late Sir Francis Hanson, London; no *c*. *Educ:* Charterhouse; New College, Oxford. Hon. Exhibitioner of New College, 1919; BA 1922; MA 1926. Barrister, Inner Temple, 1925; Master of the Bench, Inner Temple, 1957. Essex County Council, 1930-39; Vice-Chm., Essex Rivers Catchment Bd, 1935-39. Major, The Essex Regt, 1939-45; GSO3, War Office, 1939-40; DAAG, War Office, 1940-42; specially employed, 1942-45. Member: panel of Lloyd's arbitrators in salvage cases, 1950; panel from which Wreck Comrs are chosen, 1950-70; A Dep. Chm., Essex QS, 1950-56, Chairman, 1956. *Recreation:* staying at home. *Address:* Gubbions Hall, Great Leighs, Chelmsford, Essex. *T:* Great Leighs 248. *Club:* Carlton.

**ADAMS, Mary Grace, (Mrs Vyvyan Adams),** OBE 1953; Deputy-Chairman, Consumers' Association, since 1958; Member, Independent Television Authority, 1965-70; *b* Hermitage, Berks; *o d* of late Catherine Elizabeth Mary and Edward Bloxham Campin;

*m* 1925, S. Vyvyan T. Adams (*d* 1951), sometime MP for W Leeds; one *d*. *Educ:* Godolphin Sch.; University Coll., Cardiff (1st class Hons BSc); Newnham Coll., Cambridge. 1851 Res. Scholar and Bathurst Student, Univ. of Cambridge, 1921-25; Lectr and Tutor under Cambridge Extra-Mural Board and Board of Civil Service Studies, and broadcaster, 1925-30; joined staff of BBC, 1930; Producer, BBC TV, 1936-39; Dir, Home Intelligence, Min. of Information, 1939-41; N Amer. Broadcasting, 1942-45; Head of Talks and Current Affairs, 1945-54; Asst to Controller of Television Programmes, BBC, 1954-58, retired. Chm., Telephone Users Assoc. Vice-Chairman: Nat. Council for the Unmarried Mother and her Child; Women's Group on Public Welfare; Soc. for Anglo-Chinese Understanding. Member: Council, Nat. Assoc. for Mental Health; Design Panel, British Railways Board; BMA Planning Unit. Trustee: Res. Inst. for Consumer Affairs; Galton Foundn; Anglo-Chinese Educational Inst. *Publications:* papers on genetical cytology; Talks on Heredity; (ed) various symposia. *Recreation:* children. *Address:* 3 Gloucester Gate, Regent's Park, NW1. *T:* 01-935 5337.

**ADAMS, Sir Maurice (Edward),** KBE 1958 (OBE 1943); FInstCE; company director; *b* 20 Aug. 1901; *s* of Herbert William and Minnie Adams; *m* 1924, Hilda May Williams; one *s* one *d*. *Educ:* Bristol. Served European War, Midshipman, RNR. Entered Admty as Asst Civil Engr, 1927; HM Dockyards: Devonport, 1927-30; Malta, 1930-33; Portsmouth, 1933-35; Civil Engr: Trincomalee, 1935-37; Aden, 1937-38; Portsmouth, 1938-39; Superintending CE, Lower grade, 1939, Higher grade, 1940; served War of 1939-45: Admty, 1939-41; Singapore, from 1941 to evacuation; Simonstown, 1942-43; Asst CE-in-Chief, 1943; Eastern Theatre, 1943-45; Admty, 1945-46; Dep. CE-in-Chief, 1946; resigned to take up appt with Balfour Beatty & Co. Ltd, Public Works Contractors, 1949; re-entered Admty service, 1954; Civil Engr-in-Chief, Admty, 1954-59. Mem. Council, Instn of Civil Engrs, 1955. *Recreations:* big game, yachting. *Address:* 44 Marlborough Court, Pembroke Road, W8. *Clubs:* Royal Automobile, Caledonian.

**ADAMS, Surg. Rear-Adm. Maurice Henry,** CB 1965; MB, BCh, DOMS; *b* 16 July 1908; *s* of Henry Adams and Dorothea (*née* Whitehouse); *m* 1938, Kathleen Mary (*née* Hardy); one *s* two *d*. *Educ:* Campbell Coll.; Queen's University, Belfast. MB, BCh, 1930. RN Medical Service 1933; HMS Cornwall, 1934; HMS Barham, 1936; Central Air Medical Board, 1940; HMS Activity, 1942; RN Hospital, Haslar, 1944; Med. Dept, Admiralty, 1946; RN Hospital: Malta, 1950; Chatham, 1952; MO i/c Trincomalee, 1957; Med. Dept, Admiralty, 1958; Medical Officer-in-Charge, Royal Naval Hosp., Malta, 1963; QHS, 1963-66; retd 1966. *Recreations:* sailing, golf. *Address:* Canberra, Rock, Cornwall. *Club:* Army and Navy.

**ADAMS, Norman (Edward Albert),** ARA 1967; ARCA 1951; Head of the School of Painting, Manchester College of Art and Design, since 1962; Artist (Painter); *b* 9 Feb. 1927; *s* of Albert Henry Adams and Winifred Elizabeth Rose Adams; *m* 1947, Anna Theresa; two *s*. *Educ:* Royal Coll. of Art. Exhibitions in most European capitals, also in America (New York, Pittsburgh); Retrospective exhibn, Royal College of Art, 1969. Paintings in collections of: most British Provincial Art Galleries; Tate Gall., London; Nat. Galls, New Zealand; work purchased by: Arts Coun. of Gt Brit.; Contemp. Art Soc.; Chantrey Bequest; various Educn. Authorities. Murals at Broad Lane Comprehensive Sch., Coventry; decor for ballets, Covent Garden and Sadlers Wells. *Address:* Butts, Horton-in-Ribblesdale, Settle, Yorks. *T:* Horton-in-Ribblesdale 284; 98 Ladybarn Lane, Fallowfield, Manchester 14. *T:* 061-224 5640.

**ADAMS, Paul,** TD; Chief Taxing Master of Supreme Court since 1954 (Master, 1950-54); *b* 16 March 1903; *s* of late Herbert Adams; *m* 1929, Joan Madeline Corfield; two *s*. *Educ:* Haileybury College. Admitted Solicitor, 1925; partner in firm of A. J. Adams & Adams, 1935. Lieut-Col TA; commanded, War of 1939-45: 1/7 Bn, then 15th Bn The Queen's Royal Regt; 2nd Bn, Lincolnshire Regt; 13th Infantry Bn Sudan Defence Force. Resumed Practice, Oct. 1945; partner in combined firms of Bridges Sawtell & Co. and A. J. Adams & Adams, 1946; Mem. Lord Chancellor's Advisory Cttee (Legal Aid and Advice Act, 1949), 1961; Chairman: MoD Cttee on pay etc of Officers of Army and RAF Legal Services, 1965; Lord Chancellor's Cttee on Civil Judicial Statistics, 1966; an Editor of Annual Practice, 1961, and Supreme Court Practice, 1967. *Recreations:* growing roses, fly-fishing. *Address:* Royal Courts of Justice, WC2; The Croft, Tangmere, Sussex.

**ADAMS, Sir Philip (George Doyne),** KCMG 1969 (CMG 1959); HM Ambassador to Jordan since 1966; *b* 17 Dec. 1915; *s* of late George Basil Doyne Adams, MD, and of Arline Maud Adams (*née* Dodgson); *m* 1954, Hon. (Mary) Elizabeth Lawrence, *e d* of Baron Trevethin and Oaksey (3rd and 1st Baron respectively), *qv*; two *s* two *d*. *Educ:* Lancing Coll.; Christ Church, Oxford. Entered Foreign Service, 1939; served at: Beirut, 1939; Cairo, 1941; Jedda, 1945; FO, 1947; First Sec., 1948; Vienna, 1951; Counsellor, Khartoum, 1954; Beirut, 1956; FO, 1959; Chicago, 1963. *Address:* Wortley Cottage, Wotton-under-Edge, Glos; British Embassy, Amman, Jordan. *Club:* Brooks's.

**ADAMS, Richard;** *see* Adams, (Harold) Richard.

**ADAMS, Richard John Moreton G.;** *see* Goold-Adams.

**ADAMS, Robert;** Sculptor and Designer; works in wood, stone, bronze, steel; *b* 5 Oct. 1917; *s* of Arthur Adams; *m* 1951, Patricia Devine; one *d*. *Educ:* Northampton School of Art. Instructor, Central School of Arts and Crafts, London, 1949-60. One man exhibitions: Gimpel Fils, London, 1947-68; Galerie Jeanne Bucher, Paris, 1949; Passedoit Gall., New York, 1950; Victor Waddington Gall., Dublin, 1955; Douglas Coll., NJ, USA, 1955; Galerie Parnass, Wuppertal, Germany, 1957; Nebelung Galerie, Düsseldorf, 1957; Galerie Vertiko, Bonn, 1957; Museum am Ostwall, Dortmund, 1957; Bertha Schaefer Gall., New York, 1963. International Biennales: São Paulo, Brazil, 1950-57; Antwerp, 1951-53; Venice, 1952; Holland Park, London, 1954-57; Battersea Park, 1961; Venice, 1962; 7th Tokyo, 1963; work in British Sculpture in the 'Sixties' exhibn, Tate Gall., 1965. Various Arts Council and British Council travelling exhibns in Europe, USA and Japan. Works in permanent collections: Arts Council; British Council; Tate Gallery; Museums of Modern Art: New York, Rome and Turin; New York Public Library; São Paulo Museum; Univ. of Michigan, Ann Arbor; and many private collections. Commissions include sculptures for: Kings Heath Sch., Northampton; Sconce Hills Secondary Sch., Newark; The State Theatre, Gelsenkirchen; LCC Comprehensive Sch., Eltham; Hull City Centre; P & O Liner Canberra; Sekers Showroom, London; BP Building, Moorgate; London Airport; Maths

Building, University Coll., London. *Address:* 1 Rosslyn Hill, Hampstead, NW3. *T:* 01-435 9617.

**ADAMS, Roland;** *see* Adams, J. R.

**ADAMS, Sherman;** President, Loon Mountain Corporation; *b* 8 Jan. 1899; *s* of Clyde H. Adams and Winnie Marion (*née* Sherman); *m* 1923, Rachel Leona White; one *s* three *d.* *Educ:* Dartmouth College. Graduated, 1920; Manager, timberland and lumber operations, The Parker-Young Co., Lincoln, NH, 1928-45. Mem., New Hampshire House of Representatives, 1941-44; Chm. Cttee on Labor, 1941-42; Speaker of House, 1943-44; mem. 79th Congress, 2nd New Hampshire Dist; Gov. of New Hampshire, 1949-53; Chief of White House Staff, Asst to President of US, 1953-58, resigned. Chm., Conf. of New England Govs, 1951-52. Director (life), Northeastern Lumber Mfrs Assoc., New England Council. Served with US Marine Corps, 1918. First Robert Frost Award, Plymouth State Coll., 1970. Holds several hon. degrees. *Publications:* First Hand Report, 1961 (Gt Brit. 1962); articles in Life, American Forests, Appalachia, 1958-70. *Recreations:* golf, fishing, ski-ing. *Address:* Pollard Road, Lincoln, New Hampshire, USA.

**ADAMS, Sydney,** MA (Oxon); Headmaster, Bancroft's School, 1944-65, retired; *b* 13 Sept. 1905; *s* of A. S. and H. R. Adams; *m* 1933, Evelyn Mary Evanson; one *d.* *Educ:* City of Oxford School (Head of School); St John's College, Oxford (Scholar). 1st cl. Maths Mods, 1926; 2nd cl. Maths Finals, 1928; Diploma in Educn, Oxford, 1929. Sixth Form Maths Master: Aldenham, 1929-31; Sedbergh, 1931-44. *Recreations:* gardening, walking. *Address:* Walden, 28 Roman Way, Glastonbury, Somerset. *T:* Glastonbury 3276.

**ADAMS, Mrs Vyvyan;** *see* Adams, Mary Grace.

**ADAMS, Sir Walter,** Kt 1970; CMG 1952; OBE 1945; Director, London School of Economics and Political Science, since Oct. 1967; Fellow, University College, London; *b* 16 Dec. 1906; *m* 1933, Tatiana Makaroff; three *s* one *d.* *Educ:* Brighton, Hove and Sussex Grammar School; University College, London. Lecturer in History, Univ. Coll., London, 1926-34; Rockefeller Fellow in USA, 1929-30; Organizing Sec., Second International Congress of the History of Science and Technology, 1931; Secretary: Academic Assistance Council, 1933-38; London School of Economics and Political Science, 1938-46. Dep. Head, British Political Warfare Mission, USA, 1942-44; Asst Dep. Director-General, Political Intelligence Dept, Foreign Office, 1945; Secretary, Inter-University Council for Higher Education in the Colonies, 1946-55; Principal, University College of Rhodesia and Nyasaland, 1955-67. Hon. LLD (Malta, Melbourne). *Publication:* (with H. W. Robinson) The Diary of Robert Hooke, 1672-80, 1935. *Address:* London School of Economics and Political Science, Houghton Street, Aldwych, WC2. *Club:* Athenæum.

**ADAMS-ACTON, Murray,** FIRA, FIAL, FRSA; *b* 1886; godson of Mr and Mrs W. E. Gladstone; *s* of John Adams-Acton, sculptor, and Marion Hamilton, authoress; *m* Ailsa Stevenson (*d* 1955); one *d.* *Educ:* London, abroad. Authority on art and architecture; exhibited at RA; medal at Salon, 1926; elected to Heraldic and Historical Institute of France; Internat. Inst. of Arts and Letters; late Mem. Architectural Cttee, Royal Soc. of Arts; late Chm., Institute of British Decorators; Member of Committee, The Society for the Preservation of Ancient Cottages; donor of works of art to English and Canadian Museums, etc; held commission in Scots Guards during war. *Publications:* Domestic Architecture and Old Furniture; Portals and Doorways of France; contributor to all leading art journals, England and America, daily Press, etc. *Recreations:* horticulture, fishing, shooting. *Address:* 37 Palace Gate, W8; Beach House, Cooden Beach, Sussex. *Clubs:* Royal London Yacht, Pilgrim's, St John's Wood Arts.

**ADAMSON, Campbell;** *see* Adamson, W. O. C.

**ADAMSON, Prof. Colin,** DSc; Director, The Polytechnic of Central London, since 1970; *b* 23 Nov. 1922; British; *m* 1946, Janet Marjory Conyers; one *s* one *d.* *Educ:* Pocklington Sch., Yorks. BSc 1947, MSc(Eng.) 1952, London; DSc Manchester, 1961. REME (Capt.), 1942-46. Asst Lectr, Bradford Techn. College, 1946-49; Research unit, A. Reyrolle & Co. (power system analysis), 1949-52; Sen. Lectr, then Reader, in Electrical Power Systems Engrg, UMIST, 1952-61; Chm., Dept of Electrical Engineering and Electronics, Univ. of Manchester Institute of Science and Technology, 1961-70. Mem., Conférence Internationale des Grands Réseaux Electriques. Vis. Professor: Univ. of Roorkee, India, 1954-55; Univs of Washington and Wisconsin, 1959; Middle East Techn. Univ., Ankara, 1967-68. Cons. Editor, Internat. Jl of Electrical Engrg Educn; Editor, Direct Current. *Publications:* (jtly) High Voltage Direct Current Power Transmission, 1960; High Voltage DC Power Convertors and Systems, 1963; contribs to Proc. IEE and other learned jls. *Recreation:* yachting. *Address:* 309 Regent Street, W1. *Clubs:* Llanbedr and Pensarn Yacht; Royal Mersey Yacht.

**ADAMSON, Estelle Inez Ommanney,** OBE 1962; Director of Nursing, St Thomas' Hospital, London, 1965-70, retired; *b* 21 May 1910; *d* of late R. O. Adamson, MA, MD, and late Evelyn Mary Ommanney. *Educ:* Benenden School, Cranbrook, Kent. Nurse training, St Thomas's Hosp., 1932-35; Sister, etc, St Thomas' Hosp., 1936-43; Asst Matron, King Edward VII Sanatorium, Midhurst, Sussex, 1943-45; Secretary, Nursing Recruitment Service, Nuffield Provincial Hospitals Trust, Scotland, 1946-51; Matron, Western General Hosp., Edinburgh, 1951-65. *Address:* 19 Millers Close, Goring-on-Thames, Oxon. *Club:* Sesame.

**ADAMSON, Joy-Friederike Victoria;** painter since 1938, research on wild animals since 1956, and author since 1958; *b* 20 Jan. 1910; *d* of Victor and Traute Gessner; *m* 1st, 1935, Victor von Klarwill (Austrian); 2nd, 1938, Peter Bally (Swiss); 3rd, 1943, George Adamson (British). *Educ:* Vienna. Staatspruefung Piano, 1927; Diploma (Gremium) in dress-making, 1928; sculpting, 1929-30; metal work at Kunstgewerbe Schule, 1931-32; graduate course to study medicine, 1933-35; living in Kenya, 1938-; painted indigenous flora, Kenya, 1938-43; Gold Grenfell Medal, RHS, 1947; illustrated seven books; painted tribes of Kenya, 1944-52; about 500 paintings exhibited in Nat. Museum, Nairobi, and State House, Nairobi. Elsa Wild Animal Appeal, UK 1961, USA 1969. *Publications:* Born Free: a lioness of two worlds, 1960, 1964, new edn 1965 (filmed 1966); Elsa, 1961; Living Free, 1961, 1964; Forever Free, 1962, 1966; Elsa and Her Cubs, 1965; The Story of Elsa, 1966; The Peoples of Kenya, 1967; The Spotted Sphinx, 1969; Pippa and her Cubs, 1970; articles in Jl of RGS,

Field, Country Life, Blackwood-Magazine, German Anthropolog. Jl, E African Annuals, Brit. Geographical Magazine, and in several popular magazines in England, USA and Austria. *Recreations:* riding, ski-ing, tennis, mountaineering, swimming, photography, sketching, painting. *Address:* Lake Naivasha, PO Naivasha, Kenya. *Clubs:* Nanyuki, Nairobi.

**ADAMSON, Sir Kenneth Thomas,** Kt 1968; CMG 1963; Specialist Orthodontic Practice since 1929; Senior Lecturer, Department of Orthodontics, Dental School, University of Melbourne, 1935-68; Hon. Consultant in Orthodontics, Dental Hospital of Melbourne, 1943-68, Hon. Consulting Orthodontist, since 1969; *b* 19 June 1904; *s* of late Thomas Cartwright Adamson, Melbourne; *m* 1932, Jean Isobel, *d* of Dr John Daniel King-Scott; one *s* two *d*. *Educ:* Wesley Coll., Melb.; Univ. of Melbourne. BDSc 1927; DDSc 1929. Hon. Dental Surgeon: Royal Melb. Hosp., 1927-29; Alfred Hosp., 1939-47; Royal Children's, 1927-53. Austr. Dental Assoc. (Victorian Br.): Pres., 1934-35; Vice-Pres., 1962-69; Federal Pres., Austr. Dental Assoc., 1954-60; President: Dental Bd of Victoria, 1964-66; Austr. Soc. of Orthodontists; Austr. Coll. of Dental Surgeons, 1969-70. Mem. Bd, Dental Hosp. of Melbourne. Fellow, Amer. Coll. of Dentists, 1952; FDSRCS 1957; Hon. Life Member: Amer. Dental Assoc., 1964; British Soc. of Orthodontists, 1969. *Publications:* numerous, 1927-62, in various dental jls throughout world. *Recreations:* golf, fishing, gardening. *Address:* 12 Hill Street, Toorak, Victoria 3142, Australia. *T:* 24-2257. *Clubs:* Athenæum, Melbourne, Naval and Military, Frankston Golf (all in Melbourne).

**ADAMSON, Rt. Rev. Mgr. Canon Thomas;** Canon, Liverpool Metropolitan Cathedral, since 1950; Parish Priest of St Clare's, Liverpool 17, since 1945; *b* 30 Sept. 1901; *s* of George and Teresa Adamson, Alston Lane, near Preston. *Educ:* St Edward's College, Liverpool; Upholland College; Oscott College, Birmingham; Gregorian University, Rome. Ordained Priest, 1926; Beda College, Rome, 1926-28; Principal Private Secretary to Archbishop of Liverpool, 1928-45; Privy Chamberlain to Pope Pius XI, 1932; Domestic Prelate to the Pope, 1955; Protonotary Apostolic to the Pope, 1966. *Address:* St Clare's Presbytery, Arundel Avenue, Liverpool 17. *T:* 051-733 2374.

**ADAMSON, (William Owen) Campbell;** Director-General, Confederation of British Industry, since 1969; *b* 26 June 1922; *o s* of late John Adamson, CA; *m* 1945, Gilvray Adamson (*née* Allan); two *s* two *d*. *Educ:* Rugby Sch.; Corpus Christi Coll., Cambridge. Royal Inst. of Internat. Affairs, 1944-45; Baldwins Ltd as Management Trainee, 1945; successive managerial appts with Richard Thomas & Baldwins Ltd and Steel Co. of Wales Ltd, 1947-69; Gen. Man. i/c of construction and future operation of Spencer Steelworks, Llanwern; Dir, Richard Thomas & Baldwins Ltd, 1959-69, seconded as Dep. Under-Sec. of State, and Co-ordinator of Industrial Advisers, DEA, 1967-69. Member: BBC Adv. Cttee, 1964-67 and 1967-; Social Science Res. Coun. (on formation), 1965-; NEDC, 1969-; Coun., Industrial Soc.; Coun., Iron and Steel Inst.; Iron and Steel Industry Delegn to Russia, 1956, and to India, 1968. *Publications:* various technical articles. *Recreations:* brass rubbing, tennis, swimming, arguing. *Address:* Birchamp House, Newland, Glos. *T:* Coleford 3143; 31 Chesham Street, Belgravia, SW1. *T:* 01-235 8623. *Club:* Bath.

**ADCOCK, Sir Robert (Henry),** Kt 1950; CBE 1941; DL; retired as Clerk of County Council, Lancashire (1944-60), also as Clerk of the Peace for Lancashire and Clerk of the Lancashire Lieutenancy; *b* 27 Sept. 1899; *s* of late Henry Adcock, Polesworth, Warwicks; *m* Mary, *d* of late R. K. Wadsworth, Handforth Hall, Cheshire; one *s* two *d*. *Educ:* Atherstone, Warwicks. Asst Solicitor, Manchester, 1923; Asst Solicitor and Asst Clerk of the Peace, Notts CC, 1926; Senior Asst Solicitor, Manchester, 1929; Deputy Town Clerk, Manchester, 1931; Town Clerk, Manchester, 1938. *Recreation:* golf. *Address:* Summer Place, Rock End, Torquay, Devon. *T:* 22775.

**ADDERLEY,** family name of **Baron Norton.**

**ADDINGTON,** family name of **Viscount Sidmouth.**

**ADDINGTON,** 4th Baron, *cr* 1887; **Raymond Egerton Hubbard;** *b* 11 Nov. 1884; 2nd *s* of 2nd Baron Addington and Mary Adelaide (*d* 1933), *d* of Sir Wyndham S. Portal, 1st Bt; *S* brother, 1966; *m* 1926, Margaret Favre (*d* 1963), *widow* of Edward Marriott Gibson. *Educ:* Eton; Magdalen College, Oxford (BA). *Heir: kinsman* James Hubbard [*b* 3 Nov. 1930; *m* 1961, Alexandra Patricia, *yr d* of Norman Fordill Mar; two *s* two *d*]. *Address:* House of Lords, Westminster, SW1; Lesmoyne Hotel, Fleet, Hampshire. *Club:* Bath.

**ADDINSELL, Richard Stewart;** composer; *b* London, 13 Jan. 1904. *Educ:* privately; Hertford Coll., Oxford; Royal Coll. of Music. Spent four years in Berlin and Vienna. Contributed to Charlot's Revue, 1926; composed Adam's Opera, 1928. Has since written songs and incidental music for many stage productions including: The Good Companions, Alice in Wonderland, L'Aiglon, The Happy Hypocrite, Trespass, Ring Round the Moon, Penny Plain, Lyric Revue, Globe Revue, Airs on a Shoestring, Joyce Grenfell Requests the Pleasure; Living for Pleasure (Revue). Musical scores for *films* include: South Riding, Good-bye Mr Chips, The Lion Has Wings, Dangerous Moonlight, Love on the Dole, Blithe Spirit, The Passionate Friends, Under Capricorn, Tom Brown's Schooldays, The Prince and the Showgirl, A Tale of Two Cities, The Greengage Summer, The Roman Spring of Mrs Stone, The Waltz of the Toreadors, The War Lover. During War of 1939-45 wrote music for many documentary films. Also composes for radio and TV. *Address:* 30 Launceston Place, W8.

**ADDIS, John Mansfield,** CMG 1959; Senior Civilian Instructor, Royal College of Defence Studies (formerly Imperial Defence College), since 1970; *b* 11 June 1914; 5th *s* and 12th *c* of late Sir Charles and Lady Addis. *Educ:* Rugby School; Christ Church, Oxford. 3rd Sec., Foreign Office, 1938; with Allied Force HQ (Mediterranean), 1942-44; Junior Private Sec. to Prime Minister (Mr Attlee), 1945-47; 1st Sec., Nanking, 1947-50, Peking, 1950; Counsellor, Peking, 1954-57; Counsellor in the Foreign Office, 1957-60; Ambassador to Laos, 1960-62; Fellow at Harvard Centre for Internat. Affairs, 1962-63; Ambassador to the Philippines, 1963-70. *Address:* Woodside, Frant, Sussex. *T:* Frant 202. *Club:* Boodle's. *See also Sir William Addis.*

**ADDIS, Sir William,** KBE 1955; CMG 1948; MA; *b* 5 Sept. 1901; 3rd *s* of late Sir Charles Addis, KCMG, LLD, Woodside, Frant, Sussex; *m* 1929, Rosemary (*d* 1964), *d* of late Rev. R. T. Gardner; four *s*. *Educ:* Rugby; Magdalene College, Cambridge. Mechanical Science Tripos, 1923. Entered Colonial

Administrative Service, 1924; served in Zanzibar and Northern Rhodesia; seconded to Dominions Office during 1933; Private Sec. to Sultan of Zanzibar, 1939-45. Served in Zanzibar Naval Volunteer Force, 1939-45. Colonial Secretary, Bermuda, 1945-50; acting Governor, Bermuda, during 1945 and 1946; Deputy Commissioner-General for Colonial Affairs, South-East Asia, 1950-53; Governor and Commander-in-Chief, Seychelles, 1953-58, retired; temporary appointment in Foreign Office, 1958-66. 3rd Class Order of Brilliant Star of Zanzibar, 1945. *Address:* Woodside, Frant, Sussex. *T:* 202. *Club:* Travellers'. *See also J. M. Addis.*

**ADDISON,** family name of **Viscount Addison.**

**ADDISON,** 2nd Viscount, *cr* 1945, of Stallingborough; **Christopher Addison;** Baron Addison, 1937; Director of several Companies; *b* 8 Dec. 1904; *s* of 1st Viscount Addison, KG, PC, MD, FRCS, and Isobel (*d* 1934), *d* of late Archibald Gray; *S* father 1951; *m* 1928, Brigit Helen Christine, *d* of Ernest Edwin George Williams, Wimbledon; two *d. Educ:* University College School, Hampstead; Newton College, Newton Abbot, Devon. Trained Mechanical Engineering, 1922-27; Automobile Industry, 1927-34 (Past President, Inst. Motor Industry; Hon. Mem. Inst. Auto. Assessors); formerly Member London Stock Exchange, retd 1969. 2nd Lieut, Territorial Army, 1939; served War of 1939-45; discharged, disabled, 1945, with rank of Major. Chm., S-W Metropolitan Regional Hosp. Bd, 1965-68. *Recreations:* formerly boxing, cricket, tennis and sailing. *Heir: b* Hon. Michael Addison [*b* 12 April 1914; *m* 1936, Kathleen, *d* of Rt Rev. J. W. C. Wand, *qv*; one *s* two *d*]. *Address:* The Mount, Uffculme, Devon. *T:* Craddock 459. *Clubs:* Naval and Military, Buck's; (Past Cdre) Birdham Yacht.

**ADDISON, Prof. Cyril Clifford,** PhD, DSc (Dunelm); FRS 1970; FInstP; FRIC; Professor of Inorganic Chemistry, University of Nottingham, since 1960; *b* 28 Nov. 1913; *s* of late Edward Thomas Addison and Olive Clifford; *m* 1939, Marjorie Whineray Thompson; one *s* one *d. Educ:* Workington and Millom Grammar Schools, Cumberland; University of Durham (Hatfield College). Scientific Officer, British Launderers' Research Assoc., 1936-38; Lectr, Harris Inst., Preston, 1938-39; Ministry of Supply, Chemical Inspection Dept, 1939-45; Chemical Defence Research Establ., 1945; Univ. of Nottingham: Lectr, 1946; Reader in Inorganic Chemistry, 1952. Corday-Morgan Lectr, E Africa, 1969. Member: Chemical Soc. Council, 1954-57; Inst. of Chemistry Council, 1948-51 and 1962-65 (Vice-Pres., 1965-67). *Publications:* numerous papers in Jl Chemical Soc., Trans. Faraday Soc., etc. *Recreations:* mountain walking, gardening. *Address:* Department of Chemistry, The University, Nottingham. *T:* Nottingham 56101.

**ADDISON, Air Vice-Marshal Edward Barker,** CB 1945; CBE 1942 (OBE 1938); MA; CEng, FIEE; RAF, retired; *b* 4 Oct. 1898; *m* 1926, Marie-Blanche Marguerite Rosain; one *s* one *d. Educ:* Sidney Sussex Coll., Cambridge. Served European War, 1915-18, RFC and RAF; Cambridge Univ., 1918-21; BA (Cantab), 1921; MA (Cantab), 1926; Ingénieur Diplomé de l'Ecole Supérieure d'Electricité, Paris, 1927; re-commissioned RAF, 1921; retd from RAF, 1955; Dir and Div. Manager, Redifon Ltd, 1956-63, retd; Director, Intercontinental Technical Services Ltd, 1964; Consultant to Vocational Guidance Assoc., 1966. AMIEE 1933; MIEE 1941; FIEE 1966. Commander of US Legion of Merit, 1947. *Address:* 7 Hall Place Drive, Weybridge, Surrey. *T:* Weybridge 47450. *Clubs:* Royal Societies, Royal Automobile.

**ADDISON, Brig. Leonard Joseph Lancelot,** CMG 1952; CBE 1947; *b* 27 Sept. 1902; *s* of Joseph Lancelot Addison; *m* 1927, Phyllis Mabel, *d* of late E. E. Coombs, OBE; one *s* one *d. Educ:* Dulwich; RMC Sandhurst. 2nd Lieut The Queen's Own Royal West Kent Regt, 1923; Indian Army, 1926. Served War of 1939-45 (despatches); Brigadier, 1945; retired 1948. Chief Director of Purchase, Dept of Food, Govt of India, 1946; Counsellor, UK High Commn, Calcutta, 1947; Acting Deputy High Commissioner, March-Aug., 1948; Deputy High Commissioner for the UK in India, Calcutta, 1949-52. *Address:* Flat B, 23 Pembroke Gardens, W8.

**ADDISON, Dr Philip Harold,** MRCS, LRCP; Secretary, The Medical Defence Union, since 1959; *b* 28 June 1909; 2nd *s* of late Dr Joseph Bartlett Addison and Mauricia Renée Addison; *m* 1934, Mary Norah Ryan; one *s* one *d. Educ:* Clifton Coll., Bristol; St Mary's Hosp. Medical Sch. MRCS, LRCP 1933; Gold Medallist, Military Medicine and Bronze Medallist Pathology, Army Medical Sch., Millbank, SW1, 1935. Permanent Commission, IMS, 1935; served Burma Campaign, 1943-45 (despatches). Chm., Ethical Cttee of Family Planning Assoc., 1956-60; Vice-Pres., Medico-Legal Soc. 1965-. *Publications:* contrib. Brit. Med. Jl, Proc. R.Soc.Med, Medico-Legal Jl, Lancet; Professional Negligence, chap. in Compendium of Emergencies, 1965; (jointly) chap. in General Anaesthesia 1969. *Recreations:* fishing, golf, bridge. *Address:* Medical Defence Union, Tavistock House South, Tavistock Square, WC1H 9LP. *T:* 01-387 4244; Red-Wyn-Byn, Monkmead Lane, West Chiltington, Pulborough, Sussex. *T:* West Chiltington 3047. *Clubs:* East India and Sports; Shark Angling Club of Gt Britain; West Sussex Golf; BMA Duplicate Bridge.

**ADDLESHAW, Very Rev. George William Outram;** Dean of Chester since 1963; *b* 1 Dec. 1906; *s* of late Canon Stanley Addleshaw and late Mrs Rose Elgood Addleshaw. *Educ:* Bromsgrove School; Trinity College, Oxford; Cuddesdon College, Oxford. 2nd cl. hons Modern History, 1928; BA 1929; MA 1932; BD 1935; FSA 1945; FRHistS 1949. Curate of Christ Church, Highfield, Southampton, 1930-36; Curate of Basingstoke, 1936-39; Vice-Principal and Fellow of St Chad's College, Durham, 1939-46; Treasurer and Canon Residentiary of York Minster, and Prebendary of Tockerington in York Minster, 1946-63. Examining Chaplain to Archbishop of York, 1942-63; Hon. Secretary Archbishops' Canon Law Commn 1943-47; Lecturer, Leeds, Parish Church, 1947-54; Proctor in Convocation of York, 1945-; a Deputy Prolocutor, Lower House of Convocation of York, 1957-66; Prolocutor, Lower House of Convocation of York, 1966; Hon. Treas., York Minster Appeal, 1950-63. Select Preacher: Univ. of Oxford, 1954-56; Univ. of Cambridge, 1955; Examining Chaplain to Bp of Chester, 1955; Chaplain to the Queen, 1957-63; Hon. Chaplain, Cheshire Regt, 1969. *Publications:* Jocism, 1939; Dogma and Youth Work, 1941; The High Church Tradition, 1941; Divine Humanity and the Young Worker, 1942; (with Frederick Etchells) The Architectural Setting of Anglican Worship, 1948; The Beginnings of the Parochial System, 1953; The Parochial System from Charlemagne to Urban II, 1954; Rectors, Vicars and Patrons, 1956; The Early Parochial System and the Divine Office, 1957; contrib. to: The History of Christian Thought,

1937; The Priest as Student, 1939; The Mission of the Anglican Communion, 1948; Architectural History, 1967. *Recreations:* travel, ecclesiology. *Address:* The Deanery, 7 Abbey Street, Chester. *T:* Chester 25920. *Clubs:* Athenæum; Yorkshire (York).

**ADDLESHAW, John Lawrence; His Honour Judge Addleshaw;** County Court Judge, No 10 Circuit, since 1960; *b* 30 Oct. 1902; *s* of Harold Pope Addleshaw, Solicitor and Mary Gertrude (*née* Shore), Manchester; unmarried. *Educ:* Shrewsbury School; University College, Oxford (BA). Called to the Bar, Inner Temple, 1925. Auxiliary Air Force, 1939-45. *Recreations:* golf, walking. *Address:* College House, Bowdon, Cheshire, *T:* Altrincham 2139. *Club:* Clarendon (Manchester).

**ADEANE, Lt-Col Rt. Hon. Sir Michael Edward,** PC 1953; GCB 1968 (KCB 1955; CB 1947); GCVO 1962 (KCVO 1951; MVO 1946); MA; Private Secretary to the Queen and Keeper of HM's Archives; *b* 30 Sept. 1910; *s* of late Capt. H. R. A. Adeane, Coldstream Guards (killed in action, 1914), and Hon. Victoria Eugenie Bigge (*d* 1969); *m* 1939, Helen Chetwynd-Stapylton; one *s* (one *d* decd). *Educ:* Eton; Magdalene Coll., Cambridge (1st Cl. Hons Historical Tripos Part II). 2nd Lieut Coldstream Guards, 1931; ADC to Governor-General of Canada, 1934-36; Major, 1941; Lieut-Col 1942. Served War of 1939-45: with 2nd Bn Coldstream Guards, 1940-42; on Joint Staff Mission, Washington, 1942-43; 5th Bn Coldstream Guards, 1943-45; in NW Europe from 1944 (wounded, despatches). Page of honour to King George V; Equerry and Assistant Private Secretary to the Queen, 1952-53 (to King George VI, 1937-52). Lieut-Col (R of O) 1954. Governor, Wellington College. *Recreations:* shooting and fishing. *Address:* St James's Palace, SW1. *T:* 01-930 1418. *Clubs:* Brooks's, Beefsteak.

**ADEANE, Col Sir Robert (Philip Wyndham),** Kt 1961; OBE 1943; Chairman: Securities Agency Ltd; Consolidated Trust Ltd; *b* 1905; 2nd and *o surv. s* of late Charles Robert Whorwood Adeane, CB, Babraham Hall, Cambridge; *m* 1st, 1929, Joyce Violet, *d* of Rev. Cyril Burnett; one *s* one *d* (and one *s* decd); 2nd, 1947, Kathleen, (*d* 1969), *d* of Sir James Dunn, Bt; one *s* one *d*. *Educ:* Eton; Trinity Coll., Cambridge. 2nd Lieut RA (TA), 1938; Lt-Col 1941; Temp. Col 1943. Chairman: Municipal Trust Co. Ltd; New York & General Trust Ltd; International Financial Society; Government Stock & Other Securities Investment Co. Ltd, etc. Trustee, Tate Gallery, 1955-62. *Address:* 18 Cheyne Walk, Chelsea, SW3. *T:* 01-352 8250; Loudham Hall, near Wickham Market, Suffolk. *Clubs:* Brooks's, Bath, Beefsteak.

**ADEBO, Simeon Olaosebikan, (Chief), The Okanlomo of Itoko,** CMG 1959; United Nations Under-Secretary-General and Executive Director of United Nations Institute for Training and Research since 1968; *b* 5 Oct. 1913; *s* of late Chief Adebo, the Okanlomo of Itoko, Abeokuta; *m* 1941, Regina Abimbola, *d* of Chief D. A. Majekodunmi, Abeokuta; three *s* one *d*. *Educ:* St Peter's Sch., Ake, Abeokuta; Abeokuta Grammar Sch.; King's Coll., Lagos, Nigeria. BA Hons (London) 1939; LLB Hons (London) 1946. Called to Bar, Gray's Inn, 1949. Accountant in trg, Nigerian Rly, 1933; Admin. Officer Cadet, Nigerian Govt, 1942; Asst Fin. Sec. to Govt of Nigeria, 1954; Western Nigeria: Admin. Officer, Class I, 1955; Perm. Sec., Min. of Finance, 1957; Perm. Sec. to Treasury and Head of Civil Service, 1958; Head of Civil Service and Chief Secretary to Government, 1961; Permanent Representative of Nigeria at UN and Comr-Gen. for Economic Affairs, 1962-67. Hon. LLD: Western, 1963; Nigeria, Nsukka, 1965; Fordham, 1966; Lincoln, 1966; Beaver Coll., 1966; Ife, 1968; Ibadan, 1969; Hon. DCL, Union Coll., 1965. *Publication:* (with Sir Sydney Phillipson) Report on the Nigerianisation of the Nigerian Civil Service, 1953. *Recreations:* tennis and cricket. *Address:* UNITAR, 801 UN Plaza, New York, NY 10017, USA. *Clubs:* Royal Commonwealth Society; Island, Lisabi (Lagos, Nigeria); Ibadan Tennis.

**ADELAIDE, Archbishop of, (RC),** since 1940; **Most Rev. Matthew Beovich,** DD, PhD; *b* 1896; *s* of Matthew and Elizabeth Beovich, Melbourne. *Educ:* Melbourne; Propaganda College, Rome. *Address:* Archbishop's House, West Terrace, Adelaide, South Australia.

**ADELAIDE, Bishop of,** since 1957; **Rt. Rev. Thomas Thornton Reed,** MA, DLitt, ThD; *b* Eastwood, South Australia, 9 Sept. 1902; *s* of Alfred Ernest Reed, Avoca, Vic; *m* 1932, Audrey Airlie, *d* of Major Harry Lort Spencer Balfour-Ogilvy, MBE, DCM, Tannadice, Renmark, South Australia; two *d* (and one *d* decd). *Educ:* Collegiate Sch. of St Peter, Adelaide; Trinity College, University of Melbourne (Hon. Schol., BA, MA); St Barnabas' Theol. Coll., Adelaide. ThL, ATC, 1st cl. hons. Fred Johns Schol. for Biography, Univ. of Adelaide, 1950. Deacon, 1926; Priest, 1927; Curate, St Augustine's, Unley, 1926-28; Priest in Charge, Berri Mission, 1928-29; Resident Tutor, St Mark's Coll., Univ. of Adelaide, and Area Padre, Toc H, 1929-31; Asst Chaplain, Melbourne Grammar Sch., 1932-36; Rector, St Michael's, Henley Beach, 1936-44; Rector, St Theodore's, Rose Park, 1944-54. Chaplain, Australian Mil. Forces, 1939-57; Chaplain, AIF with HQ, New Guinea Force, 1944-45; Asst Tutor, St Barnabas' Coll., 1940-46; Senior Chaplain, RAAChD, HQ, C Command, South Australia, 1953-56; Editor Adelaide Church Guardian, 1940-44; Rural Dean, Western Suburbs, 1944; Priest Comr, Adelaide Dio. Centenary, 1947; Canon of Adelaide, 1947-49; Archdeacon of Adelaide, 1949-53; Dean of Adelaide, 1953-57. Pres., Toc H, S Aust., 1960; Pres., St Mark's Coll., Univ. of Adelaide, 1961. Hon. ThD, Australian Coll., of Theology, 1955; DLitt, Univ. of Adelaide, 1954. Chaplain and Sub Prelate of Venerable Order of St John of Jerusalem, 1965. *Publications:* Henry Kendall: A Critical Appreciation, 1960; Sonnets and Songs, 1962; (ed) The Poetical Works of Henry Kendall, 1966; A History of the Cathedral Church of St Peter, Adelaide, 1969. *Recreations:* golf, research on Australian literature, heraldry, and genealogy. *Address:* Bishop's Court, North Adelaide, South Australia. *T:* 672364. *Clubs:* Adelaide, Naval, Military and Air Force, Royal Adelaide Golf (Adelaide).

**ADELAIDE, Coadjutor Bishop of, (RC);** *see* Gleeson, Most Rev. J. W.

**ADEMOLA, Rt. Hon. Sir Adetokunbo (Adegboyega),** PC 1963; KBE 1963; CFR 1963; Kt 1947; **Hon. Chief Justice Ademola;** Chief Justice of Nigeria, since 1958; *b* 1 Feb. 1906; *e s* of late Sir Ladapo Ademola, Alake of Abeokuta, KBE, CMG; *m* 1939, Kofoworola, *yr d* of late Eric Olawolu Moore, CBE; three *s* two *d*. *Educ:* King's Coll., Lagos, Nigeria; Selwyn Coll., Cambridge. Attached to Attorney-General's Chambers, Lagos, Nigeria, 1934-35; Assistant Secretary, Secretariat, Southern Provinces, Nigeria, 1935-36; private law practice, Nigeria, 1936-39; Magistrate, Nigeria, 1939; served on commn for Revision of Courts Legislation,

Nigeria, 1948; served on commn to enquire into Enugu (Nigeria) disturbances, 1949; Puisne Judge, Nigeria, 1949; Chief Justice, Western Region, Nigeria, 1955-58. Hon. Bencher, Middle Temple, 1959-. *Recreations:* golf, horse racing. *Address:* 15 Ikoyi Crescent, Lagos, Nigeria. *T:* Lagos 23260; Supreme Court, Lagos, Nigeria. *T:* (chambers) Lagos 21307. *Clubs:* Island, Metropolitan, Yoruba Tennis (Lagos); Ibadan Recreation, Ibadan (Ibadan).

**ADEREMI I;** *see* Ife.

**ADERMANN, Rt. Hon. Charles Frederick,** PC 1966; Member House of Representatives, for Fisher, Queensland, since Dec. 1949 (Maranoa, 1943-49); *b* 3 Aug. 1896; *s* of late Charles and Emilie Adermann; *m* 1926, Mildred, *d* of late S. T. and Mrs Turner, Wooroolin, Qld; two *s* two *d.* Chm., Peanut Marketing Bd, 1925-30, 1933-52, retd; Chm., Kingaroy Shire Council, 1939-46, retd; Chm. cttees, House of Reps, 1950-58; Dep. Speaker, periods 1950, 1955, 1956; Minister of State for Primary Industry, in Australian Cabinet, Dec. 1958-Oct. 1967. Dep. Leader, Aust. Country Party, 1964-66. Leader, Aust. Delegn to Commonwealth Parly Conf., Wellington, Nov.-Dec. 1965. *Address:* PO Box 182, Kingaroy, Queensland, Australia. *T:* 12 Kingaroy.

**ADIE, Edward Percival,** MC 1918; *b* 1890; *s* of late W. J. Adie, Voe, Shetland; *m* 1924, Grace Dorothy, *d* of late Thomas Anderson, Hillswick, Shetland. *Educ:* Edinburgh Academy. Served European War, 1914-18, Canadian Scottish Regiment. Convener of Zetland, 1938-44. DL 1939, JP 1951, Zetland; Vice-Lieutenant of Zetland, 1953, retd 1965. *Recreation:* fishing. *Address:* Voe, Shetland. *T:* Voe 202.

**ADIE, Jack Jesson,** CMG 1962; BA (Oxon); *b* 1 May 1913; *s* of late P. J. Adie; *m* 1940, Patricia McLoughlin; one *s* two *d. Educ:* Shrewsbury Sch.; Magdalen Coll., Oxford. Entered Colonial Administrative Service, 1938; served in Zanzibar, 1938-48 (on military service, 1940-42 in Kenya Regt, KAR and Occupied Territory Administration), posts included: Private Sec. to The Sultan, Private Sec. to British Resident and Sen. Asst Sec.; seconded to Colonial Office, 1949-51, as Principal; Asst Sec., Kenya, 1951; Sec. for Educn and Labour, Kenya, 1952; Sec. for Educn, Labour and Lands, Kenya, 1954; acted as Minister for Educn, Labour and Lands, Kenya, Sept. 1955-Feb. 1956; Chief Sec., Barbados, 1957; Perm. Sec. for Forest Development, Game and Fisheries, Kenya, April-Dec. 1958; for Agriculture, Animal Husbandry and Water Resources, and Chm. African Land Development Bd, Dec. 1958-July 1959; for Housing, and Chm. Central Housing Bd, Nov. 1959-April 1960; for Housing, Common Services, Probation and Approved Schools, April 1960-April 1961; for Labour and Housing, 1961-62; acted as Minister for Labour and Housing, Jan.-April 1962; Perm. Sec. for Labour, 1962-63; retd from HMOCS, Jan 1964; Temp. Principal, Min. of Overseas Develt, 1964-69. Brilliant Star of Zanzibar, 4th class, 1947. *Address:* Capricorn, Qawra Road, St Paul's Bay, Malta.

**ADIE-SHEPHERD, His Honour Harold Richard Bowman,** QC 1950; County Court Judge, Circuit No 59 (Cornwall, etc), 1955-62; *b* 24 July 1904; *yr s* of late Richard Atkinson Shepherd, Barrister-at-law, and Mabel Shepherd, Cumberland Priory, Headingley, Leeds; *m* 1928, Magaret Rohesia Gundred Mayo, West Lodge, Pinner; two *d*; *m* 1962, Phyllis Margaret Adie. *Educ:* Uppingham Sch.; Trinity Coll., Oxford. Called to Bar, Inner Temple, 1928; joined North-Eastern Circuit; practised at 39 Park Square, Leeds. Served War of 1939-45, in Army, Aug. 1939-Aug. 1945, including North Africa, Sicily and Italy. Recorder of Pontefract, 1948-50; Recorder of York, 1950-55; Solicitor-General of the County Palatine of Durham, 1950-55; JP Herts, 1952; Dep. Chm., Herts QS, 1953-55; Chm., Cornwall QS, 1966- (Dep. Chm., 1955-66). Pres., Devon and Cornwall Rent Assessment Panel, 1965-. *Recreations:* boats, cars, gardening. *Address:* Sealand Court, Newton Ferrers, Plymouth. *T:* Newton Ferrers 399. *Club:* Royal Western Yacht (Plymouth).

**ADJAYE, Sir Edward;** *see* Asafu-Adjaye.

**ADLAM, Lt-Col Tom Edwin,** VC 1916; formerly Headmaster, Blackmoor Church of England School; retired, 1952; late RE; *b* 21 Oct. 1893; *s* of late John Adlam, Salisbury; *m* 1916, Ivy Annette, *y d* of late W. H. Mace, South Farnborough, Hants; two *s* two *d.* Served European War, 1914-18 (VC); awarded the Italian Silver Medal for Military Valour, June 1917 (demobilised 15 Nov. 1919, with hon. rank of Capt.); Army Education Corps; retired March 1923 with hon. rank of Captain. Recalled to Army from RARO, 1939; War of 1939-45; RE (Movement Control Section), 1939-46, Embarkation Comdt Tilbury, and later Glasgow, with rank of Lt-Col; demobilised 1946 with hon. rank of Lt-Col. *Address:* School House, Blackmoor, Liss, Hants.

**ADLER, Larry, (Lawrence Cecil Adler);** composer, writer, performer; *b* 10 Feb. 1914; *s* of Louis Adler and Sadie Hack; *m* 1st, 1938, Eileen Walser (marr. diss. 1961); one *s* two *d*; 2nd, 1969, Sally Cline, one *d. Educ:* Baltimore City Coll. Won Maryland Harmonica Championship, 1927; first stage appearance, 1928 (NY); first British appearance, 1934 (in C. B. Cochran's Streamline revue); first appearance as soloist with Symphony Orchestra, Sydney, Australia, 1939; jt recital tours with dancer Paul Draper, US, 1941-49; soloist with NY Philharmonic and other major US Orchestras, also orchestras in England, Japan and Europe; war tours for Allied Troops, 1943, 1944, 1945; Germany, 1947, 1949; Korea (Brit. Commonwealth Div.), 1951; Israel (Six-Day War), 1967; soloist, Edinburgh Festival, playing first performance of unpublished Gerschwin quartet (MS gift to Adler from I. Gerschwin), 1963; works composed for Adler by: Dr Ralph Vaughan Williams, Malcolm Arnold, Darius Milhaud, Arthur Benjamin, Gordon Jacob and others. *Compositions:* film scores: Genevieve; King and Country; High Wind in Jamaica; The Great Chase, etc; TV scores: Midnight Men (BBC serial); various TV plays and documentaries; music for TV commercials, children's records, stage plays, etc; concert music: Theme and Variations; Camera III; One Man Show, From Hand to Mouth, Edinburgh Festival, 1965 (other festivals, 1965-70); numerous TV One Man Shows. *Publications:* How I Play, 1937; Larry Adler's Own Arrangements, 1960; Jokes and How to Tell Them, 1963. *Recreations:* tennis, journalism, cycling, conversation. *Address:* 75 Upper Lewes Road, Brighton, Sussex. *Clubs:* Thursday, English-Speaking Union; Campden Hill Lawn Tennis.

**ADLEY, Robert James;** MP (C) Bristol (North East) since 1970; Director of Marketing (Europe), Commonwealth Holiday Inns of Canada Ltd; *b* 2 March 1935; *s* of Harry Adley and Marie Adley (*née* Isaacs); *m* 1961, Jane

Elizabeth Pople; two *s*. *Educ:* Falconbury; Uppingham. Joined Pearl & Dean Ltd and lived and worked in: Malaya, Singapore, Thailand; established Pearl & Dean (Thailand) Ltd, 1956; Sales Director, May Fair Hotel, 1960-64. Holiday Inns: various appts within this Group; responsible for establishing BRAMBEC (British & American Hotels & Institutional Buildings Equipment Co. Ltd), a joint venture Co. between Holiday Inns and Great Universal Stores. Mem., Railway Correspondence and Travel Soc.; Chm., Brunel Soc. *Publication:* Hotels, the Case for Aid, 1966. *Recreations:* railway photography, railway enthusiast. *Address:* 13 Orchard Street, Bristol 1. *T:* Bristol 27817. *Clubs:* Carlton; Constitutional, Fishponds Conservative (Bristol).

**ADOO**; *see* Sarkodee-Adoo.

**ADRIAN,** family name of **Baron Adrian.**

**ADRIAN,** 1st Baron, *cr* 1955, of Cambridge; **Edgar Douglas Adrian,** OM 1942; FRS 1923; FRCP; Chancellor: University of Cambridge, since 1968 (Vice-Chancellor, 1957-59); University of Leicester, since 1957; *b* 30 Nov. 1889; *s* of late Alfred Douglas Adrian, CB, KC, of Local Govt Bd; *m* 1923, Hester Agnes, DBE 1965 (*d* 1966), *o d* of late Hume C. and Dame Ellen Pinsent, DBE, Birmingham; one *s* two *d*. *Educ:* Westminster; Trinity Coll., Cambridge (MA, MD; Fellow, 1913); St Bartholomew's Hosp. Foulerton Res. Prof., Royal Soc., 1929-37; Prof. of Physiology, Cambridge Univ., 1937-51; Master of Trinity Coll., Cambridge, 1951-65. Pres., University Coll. of Leicester, 1955-57. Romanes Lectr, Oxford Univ., 1960. Royal Society: Foreign Sec., 1946-50; Pres., 1950-55. President: British Assoc. for the Advancement of Science, 1954; RSM, 1960-61. Mem., BBC Gen. Adv. Council, 1952-56. Trustee, Rockefeller Inst., 1962-65. Member: Amer. Philosophical Soc.; Kungl. Vetenshaps. Soc., Uppsala; Royal Acad. of Science, Amsterdam; Royal Danish Acad. of Science and Letters. Foreign Member: Royal Acad. of Lincei; Swedish Royal Acad. of Science; Acad. of Science, Bologna. Foreign Associate: Nat. Acad. of Sci., USA; Acad. Nacional de Medicina, Buenos Aires; Acad. de Médicine, Paris; Soc. Française de Psychologie; Royal Acad., Belgium. Corres. Member: Acad. de Science, Paris; Société de Biologie and Société Philomathique, France. Hon. Member: RSM; Amer. Physiological Soc.; New York Neurological Soc.; Acad. Royale de Médicine Belgique; Amer. Acad. of Arts and Sciences; Sociedad Argentina de Biologia; Deutsche Gesellschaft für Neurol. Hon. Foreign Mem., Royal Flemish Acad. of Medicine. Hon. Life Mem., NY Acad. of Sciences. Hon. Fellow: Darwin Coll., Cambridge, 1966; RSM; RSE; British Psychological Soc.; Soc. Italiana di Biologia; Academia Nacional de Medicina, Mexico. Hon. Liveryman, Dyers Co. Hon. DSc: Pennsylvania; Oxon; Harvard; Lyon; London; Manchester; Durham; Johns Hopkins; Belfast; Wales; New York; Sheffield; Hull; Brazil; Bologna; Freiburg; Paris; Leicester; Allahabad; Rockefeller; Cracow; Strathclyde. Hon. ScD Cambridge. Hon. LLD: McGill; St Andrews; Glasgow; Liverpool; Dalhousie; Edinburgh; Buckwell. Hon. MD: Brussels; Louvain; Montreal. Baly Medal, 1929; Nobel Laureate (Medicine), 1932; Royal Medal, Royal Soc., 1934; Copley Medal, 1946; Gold Medal, RSM, 1950; Albert Gold Medal, RSA, 1953; Harben Medal, 1955; Conway Evans Prize, 1956. Chevalier de la Légion d'Honneur. *Publications:* The Basis of Sensation, 1928; The Mechanism of Nervous Action, 1932; The Physical Basis of Perception, 1947; papers on the physiology of the nervous system in Jl of Physiology, Brain, etc. *Heir:* *s* Hon. Richard Hume Adrian [*b* 16 Oct. 1927; *m* 1967, Lucy, *er d* of Alban Caroe]. *Address:* Trinity College, Cambridge. *Club:* Athenæum.

*See also R. D. Keynes.*

**ADRIAN, Max;** actor; *b* Ireland, 1 Nov. 1903; *s* of Edward Norman Cavendish Bor and Mabel Lloyd Thornton. *Educ:* Portora Royal School, Enniskillen. First appearance on English stage in Katja, the Dancer, 1925; subsequently West End parts and tours; appeared in First Episode, Comedy, 1934, playing same part in New York, 1935; continued in West End. Joined Old Vic, 1939. 1940-56: appearances in London included Haymarket season (Hamlet, A Midsummer Night's Dream, The Circle, The Duchess of Malfi, Love for Love) and Revues: Tuppence Coloured; Oranges and Lemmons; Penny Plain; Airs on a Shoestring; Fresh Airs. Candide, New York, 1956; appeared in America until 1959 (The Would Be Gentleman, No Laughing Matter, Mary Stuart, The Lesson, The Merchant of Venice, The School for Scandal, Pygmalion); Look after Lulu, London, 1959; The Deadly Game, NY, 1960. Joined Royal Shakespeare Company, 1960 (Twelfth Night, Troilus and Cressida, The Duchess of Malfi, The Devils, The Hollow Crown, As You Like It, Romeo and Juliet); played The Hollow Crown in Europe and USA, 1962-63; Chichester Festival, 1963-64 (St Joan, Uncle Vanya) also National Theatre (Hamlet, The Recruiting Officer, The Master Builder, Uncle Vanya, St Joan); Guildford Festival, 1965 (A Month in the Country, Samson Agonistes, Lionel and Clarissa); The Doctor's Dilemma, Guildford and London, 1966; GBS, Edinburgh Festival, London, and tours in England, Northern Ireland, Far and Middle East and US, 1966, 1967, World Tour, 1968; Yvonne Arnaud, Guildford: The Viaduct, 1967; The Cardinal of Spain, 1969; Gilbert and Sullivan, 1969; GBS and Gilbert and Sullivan, World Tour, 1970. Films include: Kipps, The Young Mr Pitt, Henry V, Pool of London, The Pickwick Papers, Border Story, The Primrose Path. Television in New York, Hollywood and London, from 1937; Delius in Song of Summer, TV film, 1968. Radio from 1933. Recorded verse, prose and plays, 1960-69. *Address:* Smarkham Orchard, Shamley Green, Surrey. *T:* Bramley 2187.

*See also N. L. Bor.*

**ADSHEAD, Mary, (Mrs Stephen Bone);** *b* 15 Feb. 1904; *d* of late Prof. S. D. Adshead; *m* 1929, Stephen Bone (*d* 1958); two *s* one *d*. *Educ:* Lycée Victor Duruy, Paris; Slade School of Art (under Prof. Henry Tonks). Began career as decorative painter in 1923 with mural paintings at the Highways Club, Shadwell, and in the Basilica at Wembley Exhibition; Subsequently executed various murals and paintings in private houses, restaurants and exhibitions; East wall of St Christopher's, Withington completed, 1936; The Restaurant, Wernher Museum, Luton Hoo; Jungle Restaurant, Selfridges; mural in Restaurant of Messrs Lewis's new building, Bristol; mural in Civic Centre, Plymouth, 1962; mural in St Francis' Church, Vauxhall Park, Luton, 1962. Designed stamps for GPO, 1951; 8d to 11d permanent issue, 1953; special issue GPO twopence-halfpenny postage stamp, Boy Scout Jubilee Jamboree, Aug. 1957. Hon. Sec. Soc. of Mural Painters; Women's International Association. Exhibitor Royal Academy, Society for Education in Art (SEA), etc. *Recreation:* travel. *Address:* 140 Haverstock Hill, NW3.

**AFSHAR, Amir Khosrow;** Order of Homayoun, third, second and first class, Order of the Crown, fourth and third class, Iran; HIM's Ambassador to the Court of St James's, since 1969; *b* 1920; *m*; one *s* two *d*. *Educ:* American Coll., Tehran; Faculty of Law, Paris Univ.; Univ. of Geneva. Served in various Depts of Foreign Ministry; First Sec., Imperial Iranian Embassy, Washington, 1947; First Sec., Permanent Iranian Delegn to UN, 1948-50; Head of UN Dept, Min. of Foreign Affairs, Tehran, 1950; Head of 3rd Political Dept, MFO, 1951; Head of 4th Political Dept, MFO, 1953; appointed Chargé d'Affaires in London, after resumption of diplomatic relations, 1953; Minister Plenipotentiary, London, 1954-57; Dir Gen. (Political Affairs), MFO, 1958; Political and Parly Under-Sec., MFO, 1959; HIM's Ambassador in Germany, 1961; HIM's Ambassador in Paris, 1963; Deputy and Acting Foreign Minister, 1967. Hon. KCMG (UK), 1961; Grand Officier de la légion d'Honneur (France); Commander's Cross of the Order of Merit (Federal Republic of Germany). *Recreations:* horse breeding, riding. *Address:* 26 Princes Gate, SW7.

**AGA KHAN (IV), His Highness Shah Karim;** granted title His Highness by the Queen, 1957, granted title His Royal Highness by the Shah of Iran, 1959; *b* 13 Dec. 1936; *s* of late Prince Aly Khan, and of Princess Joan Aly Khan (marriage dissolved, 1949) (*née* Hon. Joan Barbara Yarde-Buller, *e d* of 3rd Baron Churston, MVO, OBE); became Aga Khan, spiritual leader and Imam of Ismaili Muslims all over the world, on the death of his grandfather, Sir Sultan Mohamed Shah, Aga Khan III, GCSI, GCIE, GCVO, 11 July 1957; *m* 1969, Sarah Frances Crichton-Stuart, *o d* of Lt-Col A. E. Croker Poole; one *d*. *Educ:* Le Rosey, Switzerland; Harvard University, USA. Commander, Ordre du Mérite Mauritanien, 1960; Grand Croix de l'Ordre National: Côte d'Ivoire, 1965; de la Haute-Volta, 1965; Malgache, 1966; Grand Croix de l'Ordre du Croissant Vert des Comores, 1966; Grand Cordon de l'Ordre du Tadj de l'Empire d'Iran, 1967; Doctor of Laws (*hc*) Peshawar Univ., Pakistan, 1967. *Recreations:* tennis, skiing. *Address:* 1 rue des Ursins, Paris 4, France.

**AGA KHAN, Prince Sadruddin;** United Nations High Commissioner for Refugees since Dec. 1965; *b* 17 Jan. 1933; *s* of His late Highness Sir Sultan Mohamed Shah, Aga Khan III, GCSI, GCIE, GCVO and of Andrée Joséphine Caron; *m* 1957, Nina Sheila Dyer (marriage dissolved, 1962). *Educ:* Harvard Univ. (BA); Harvard Grad. Sch. Arts and Sciences; Centre of Middle Eastern Studies. Unesco Consultant for Afro-Asian Projects, 1958; Head of Mission and Adviser to UN High Comr for Refugees, 1959-60; Unesco Special Consultant to Dir-Gen., 1961; Exec. Sec., Internat. Action Cttee for Preservation of Nubian Monuments, 1961; UN Dep. High Comr for Refugees, 1962-65. Grand Cross: Order of St Silvestro (Papal), 1963; Order of Homayoun (Iran), 1967. *Recreations:* Islamic art, sailing, ski-ing, photography, travel. *Address:* Château de Bellerive, Collonge-Bellerive, Canton of Geneva, Switzerland. *Clubs:* Travellers' (Paris); Knickerbocker (New York).

**AGAR,** family name of **Earl of Normanton.**

**AGAR, Herbert Sebastian;** author; *b* New Rochelle, NY, 29 Sept. 1897; *s* of John Giraud Agar and Agnes Louise Macdonough; *m* 1st, 1918, Adeline Scott; one *s* one *d*; 2nd, 1933, Eleanor Carroll Chilton (*d* 1949); 3rd, 1945, Mrs Euan Wallace, *widow* of Capt. Euan Wallace and *e d* of late Sir Edwyn Lutyens. *Educ:* Columbia Univ. (BA 1919); Princeton Univ. (MA 1920, PhD 1922). London Correspondent, Louisville Courier-Journal and Louisville Times, 1929-34; Literary Editor, English Review, 1930-34; Editor, Louisville Courier-Journal, 1939-42; Special Assistant to American Ambassador in London, 1942-46; Counsellor for Public Affairs, US Embassy, 1945-46; President of Freedom House, New York, 1941-43; Director: Rupert Hart-Davis Ltd, publishers, 1953-63; TWW Ltd (Independent Television, S Wales and W of England), 1957-68. Served as seaman, later Chief Quartermaster, USNR, 1917-18; Lt-Comdr USNR, 1942. *Publications:* Milton and Plato, 1928; Bread and Circuses, 1930; The Defeat of Baudelaire (trans.), 1932; American Presidents, 1933; What is America, 1936; Pursuit of Happiness, 1938; A Time for Greatness, 1943; The Price of Union, 1950 (Eng. title The United States, 1950); Declaration of Faith, 1952; Abraham Lincoln, 1952; The Unquiet Years, 1957; The Saving Remnant, 1960; The Perils of Democracy, 1965. *Address:* Beechwood, Petworth, Sussex. *T:* Graffham 213. *Clubs:* Savile; National Arts, Century (New York).

**AGAR-ROBARTES,** family name of **Viscount Clifden.**

**AGARWALA, Sir Clifford Manmohan,** Kt 1943; *b* 5 Feb. 1890; *e s* of Dr M. L. Agarwala, barrister-at-law, Allahabad, UP; *m* 1918, Dorrie Muriel Lall; two *d*. *Educ:* Aldenham School, Elstree. Called to Bar, Gray's Inn, 1911; barrister at Patna, 1912; official law reporter in the High Court, 1916; Standing Counsel to the Income Tax Dept, 1925; Asst Govt Advocate, 1927; Puisne Judge, High Court, Patna, 1932-46; Chief Justice, 1946-50. Chairman, Central Board of Film Censors, Govt of India, 1951-54. *Publications:* Trial by Jury (India); Law of Evidence (India); Law of Limitation (India). *Address:* 17 Hill Drive, Hove 4, Sussex. *Club:* Royal Over-Seas League. *See also Thomas Whitworth.*

**AGGEY, Most Rev. John Kwao Amuzu;** *see* Lagos, Archbishop of, (RC).

**AGHNIDES, Thanassis;** Chairman Advisory Committee on Administrative and Budgetary Questions of UNO, 1946-64; *b* Nigdé, Asia Minor, 1889; *s* of Prodromos and Anastasia Aghnides. *Educ:* Superior National Greek Coll., Phanar, Istanbul; Anatolia Coll. (Asia Minor); Univ. of Istanbul; University of Paris. Directed Greek Press Bureau at Greek Legation, London, 1918-19; worked for League of Nations, 1919-42; Dir of Disarmament Section, 1930, and Under Secretary-General of the League, 1939; Secretary of Disarmament Conference, 1932-34; Secretary-General Montreux Conference concerning the Straits, May 1936; Secretary-General Conference for the suppression of Egyptian Capitulations, 1937; Secretary-General Nyon Conference for the suppression of piracy in the Mediterranean, 1937; Permanent Under-Secretary for Foreign Affairs in Greek Cabinet, 1942-43; Greek Ambassador to the Court of St James's, 1942-47; Greek Delegate to San Francisco Conference on International Organisation, 1945; Chief Delegate for Greece on Preparatory Commission of UNO; Chm. 6th Committee, on organisation of UNO Secretariat, Dec. 1945; Delegate to the 1st Assembly of UNO; Rapporteur of its 5th Cttee (on organisation), Jan. 1946; rep. Greece on Security Council when it dealt with question of presence of British troops in Greece, 1-6 Feb. 1946; Chairman Greek Deleg. to Gen. Assembly of UNO, Oct.-Dec. 1946; Chm. Cttee on Admin of UNESCO, Feb.-

April 1948. Member Curatorium Acad. of Internat. Law of the Hague, 1948-68. *Recreation:* music. *Address:* 3 Avenue Bertrand, Geneva, Switzerland. *T:* 463602. *Club:* St James' (London).

**AGLEN, Anthony John,** CB 1957; FRSE; Joint Deputy Secretary, Department of Agriculture and Fisheries for Scotland, also Fisheries Secretary for Scotland since 1946; *b* 30 May 1911; 2nd *s* of late Sir Francis A. Aglen, GCMG, KBE, Alyth, Perthshire; *m* 1946, Audrey Louise Murray, *o d* of late Andrew E. Murray, WS, Edinburgh; one *s* one *d. Educ:* Marlborough; Trinity Coll., Cambridge (Scholar). First Class Mathematical Tripos, Part I, 1931, and Part II 1933, BA 1933. Entered Civil Service (Scottish Office), 1934; Private Secretary to successive Secretaries of State for Scotland, 1939-41; Assistant Secretary, Scottish Home Dept, 1942; Under-Sec., 1953; Dep. Sec., 1956-60. President, North East Atlantic Fisheries Commission, 1963-66. *Recreations:* gardening, fishing. *Address:* Birkhill, Earlston, Berwickshire. *T:* Earlston 307. *Club:* New (Edinburgh).

**AGNELLI, Dr Giovanni;** industrialist; car manufacturer, Italy; Chairman of FIAT; Chairman of RIV-SKF; *b* Turin, Italy, 12 March 1921; *s* of Edoardo Agnelli, and *g s* of Giovanni Agnelli, founder of Fabbrica Italiana Automobile Torino (FIAT); *m* 1953, Princess Marella Caracciolo di Castagneto; one *s* one *d. Educ:* Turin. DrJur, Univ. of Turin, 1943. *Address:* 10 Corso Marconi, Turin, Italy. *T:* 6565.

**AGNEW, Sir Anthony Stuart;** *see* Agnew, Sir J. A. S.

**AGNEW, Sir Fulque Melville Gerald Noel,** 10th Bt, *cr* 1629; *b* 1900; *s* of late Major Charles Hamlyn Agnew, 3rd *s* of 8th Bt, and Lilian Ann, *d* of late Lt-Gen. Sir J. Wolfe Murray, KCB; *S* uncle, 1928; *m* 1937, Swanzie, *d* of late Major Esmé Nourse Erskine, CMG, MC; one *s. Heir: s* Crispin Hamlyn Agnew, *b* 13 May 1944. *Address:* Cambridge University Department of Education, 17 Brookside, Cambridge.

*See also Lord Kinnaird.*

**AGNEW, Geoffrey William Gerald;** Chairman, Thos Agnew & Sons, Ltd (Fine Art Dealers), since 1965; *b* 11 July 1908; *er s* of late Charles Gerald Agnew and Olive Mary (*née* Danks); *m* 1934, Hon. Doreen Maud Jessel, *y d* of 1st Baron Jessel, CB, CMG; two *s* one *d. Educ:* Eton; Trinity College, Cambridge (BA 1930); Munich. Joined Thos Agnew & Sons (Fine Art Dealers), 1931; Managing Director, 1937-. Assistant master (History), Eton College, and Captain (acting) and Company Commander, Eton College JTC, 1939-45. Chairman, Evelyn (Agnew) Nursing Home, Cambridge, 1955-. A Permanent Steward, 1955- and a Vice-Pres., 1968-, Artists' General Benevolent Institution; President, Fine Art Provident Institution, 1963-66; Chairman: St George's Arts Trust, King's Lynn, 1966-; Society of London Art Dealers, 1970-; Friends of the Courtauld Institute, 1970-. *Publications:* Agnew's 1817-1967, 1967; various broadcasts on art published in the Listener. *Recreations:* works of art, travel, gardening. *Address:* 11 Alexander Square, SW3. *T:* 01-589 5916; Egmere Farm House, Walsingham, Norfolk. *T:* Walsingham 247. *Clubs:* Brooks's, Garrick.

**AGNEW, Sir Godfrey;** *see* Agnew, Sir W. G.

**AGNEW, Commander Hugh Ladas,** RN (retired); Chairman of Thos Agnew & Sons Ltd, 1955-65; *b* 6 June 1894; 4th *s* of Charles Morland Agnew and Evelyn Mary (*née* Naylor); *m* 1st, 1920, Mary Violet Maud Davies (*d* 1932); one *d* (one *s* killed in action, 1943; and one *d* decd); 2nd, 1934, Gwendolen Ford Low. *Educ:* Warren Hill, Eastbourne; RN College, Dartmouth. Served RN (including European War, 1914-18), Sub-Lieut and Lieut, 1912-20. Joined Thos Agnew & Sons Ltd (fine art dealers), 1920; Managing Dir, 1931. Lt-Comdr RN, staff of RNC Dartmouth, 1939-45; Comdr RN (retd), 1946. Chm. of Governors, Bloxham School, 1948-60. *Recreations:* shooting, walking, reading. *Address:* 59 Cranmer Court, Chelsea, SW3. *T:* 01-589 1169. *Clubs:* Bath; Royal Navy Club of 1765 and 1785.

**AGNEW, Sir (John) Anthony Stuart,** 4th Bt, *cr* 1895; *b* 25 July 1914; *s* of Sir John Stuart Agnew, 3rd Bt, TD, DL, and Kathleen, 3rd *d* of late I. W. H. White, Leeds; *S* father, 1957. *Educ:* privately in Switzerland. *Heir: b* Major George Keith Agnew, TD [*b* 25 Nov. 1918; *m* 1948, Anne Merete Louise, *yr d* of Baron Johann Schaffalitzky de Muckadell, Fyn, Denmark; two *s*]. *Address:* c/o Moat Farm, Rougham, Bury St Edmunds, Suffolk.

**AGNEW, Sir Norris (Montgomerie),** Kt 1967; CBE 1957; Chairman of Board of Governors of United Manchester Hospitals, 1953-67; Chairman of Manchester Regional Hospital Board, 1953-62; *b* 2 Dec. 1895; *yr s* of late Harold Agnew; *m* 1923, Mona Christine Nimmo Duggan; one *s* two *d. Educ:* Wellington College; Brasenose College, Oxford (BA). Practised as Solicitor in Manchester, 1920-52. Hon. LLD Univ. of Manchester, 1968. *Recreation:* gardening. *Address:* Yew Tree Cottage, Nether Alderley, Macclesfield, Cheshire. *T:* Alderley 2320.

**AGNEW, Commander Sir Peter (Garnett),** 1st Bt *cr* 1957; *b* 1900; *s* of late C. L. Agnew; *m* 1928, Enid Frances, *d* of late Henry Boan, Perth, Western Australia; one *s. Educ:* Repton. Entered Royal Navy, 1918; ADC to Governor of Jamaica, 1927-28; retired, 1931; returned to service at sea, Aug. 1939 (despatches). MP (C) Camborne Div. of Cornwall, 1931-50; PPS to Rt Hon. Walter Runciman, President of Board of Trade, 1935-37, and to Rt Hon. Sir Philip Sassoon, First Commissioner of Works, 1937-39; an Assistant Government Whip, May-July, 1945; a Conservative Whip, Aug. 1945-Feb. 1950; contested (C) Falmouth and Camborne Div., Feb. 1950; MP (C) South Worcs, 1955-66. Member of House of Laity Church Assembly, 1935-65; a Church Comr for England, 1948-68; Trustee, Historic Churches Preservation Trust, 1968-. Chm., Iran Society, 1966-. *Recreation:* travelling. *Heir; s* Quentin Charles Agnew-Somerville [*b* 8 March 1929; *m* 1963, Hon. April, *y d* of 15th Baron Strange, *qv*; one *s* two *d. Educ:* RNC Dartmouth]. *Address:* 2 Smith Square, SW1. *T:* 01-222 7179. *Club:* Carlton.

**AGNEW, Peter Graeme,** MBE 1946; BA; Deputy Chairman, Bradbury Agnew & Co. Ltd (Proprietors of Punch), since 1969; *b* 7 April 1914; *s* of late Alan Graeme Agnew; *m* 1937, Mary Diana (*née* Hervey); two *s* two *d. Educ:* Kingsmead, Seaford; Stowe School; Trinity College, Cambridge. Student Printer, 1935-37. Joined Bradbury Agnew & Co. Ltd, 1937. RAFVR 1937. Served War of 1939-45; Demobilised, 1945, as Wing Commander. *Recreations:* shooting, sailing, gardening. *Address:* Roscaddon, Manaccan, Nr Helston, Cornwall. *T:* Manaccan 223.

**AGNEW, Spiro Theodore, (Ted);** Vice-President of the United States since 1969; *b* Baltimore, Md, 9 Nov. 1918; *s* of Theodore S. Agnew and

Margaret Akers; *m* 1942, Elinor Isabel Judefind; one *s* three *d*. *Educ:* Forest Park High Sch., Baltimore; Johns Hopkins Univ.; Law Sch., Univ. Baltimore (LLB). Served War of 1939-45 with 8th and 10th Armd Divs, 1941-46, company combat comdr in France and Germany (Bronze Star). Apptd to Zoning Bd of Appeals of Baltimore County, 1957 (Chm., 1958-61); Chief Executive, Baltimore County, 1962-67; Governor of Maryland, 1967-68. Republican. *Recreations:* golf, tennis. *Address:* White House, Washington, DC, USA.

**AGNEW, Sir (William) Godfrey,** KCVO 1965 (CVO 1953); Clerk of the Privy Council since 1953; *b* 11 Oct. 1913; *o s* of late Lennox Edelsten Agnew and of Elsie Blyth Nott, Tunbridge Wells; *m* 1st, 1939, Ruth Mary (*d* 1962), *e d* of late Charles J. H. O'H. Moore, CVO, MC, and late Lady Dorothie Moore; three *s* three *d*; 2nd, 1965, Lady (Nancy Veronica) Tyrwhitt, *widow* of Adm. Sir St John Reginald Joseph Tyrwhitt, 2nd Bt, KCB, DSO, DSC; two step *s* one step *d*. *Educ:* Tonbridge. Solicitor, 1935; entered Public Trustee Office, 1936. Served RA and Surrey and Sussex Yeomanry, 1939-46; Major, 1945. Senior Clerk, Privy Council Office, 1946-51; Deputy Clerk of the Privy Council, 1951-53. Chairman, Sembal Trust. Hon. FIMechE, 1968. *Address:* Pinehurst, South Ascot, Berks. *T:* Ascot 20036. *Club:* Army and Navy.
*See also Baron Davies.*

**AGRA, Archbishop of, (RC),** since 1956; **Most Rev. Dominic Romuald Athaide,** DD; OFMCap; *b* Bandra, India, 7 Feb. 1909. *Educ:* Holland; France; Pontifical Gregorian University, Rome. Priest, 1932. Lecturer in Philosophy and theology, Quilon, India, 1937; Missionary, Aden, 1940; subsequently Director of St Joseph's High School, and Parish Priest, Aden. Member Order of Friars Minor (Capuchins). *Address:* Cathedral House, Wazirpura Road, Agra 3, UP, India. *T:* 7-24-07. *TA:* Cathedral.

**AHERN, Most Rev. John;** *see* Cloyne, Bishop of, (RC).

**AHERN, Maj.-Gen. Timothy Michael Richard,** CBE 1959 (OBE 1945); Director of Medical Services, British Army of the Rhine, 1966-69, retired; *b* 16 Aug. 1908; *s* of late Lieut-Col M. D. Ahern and late Mrs Ahern, formerly of Glanmire, Co. Cork, Eire; *m* 1943, Joan Aisne, *d* of late S. Blencowe, and of Mrs Blencowe, Latmus, Bishopsteignton, S Devon; two *s* one *d*. *Educ:* Ampleforth College; Trinity College, Dublin. ADMS, Eighth Army, 1944-45. Chief of Medical Plans and Ops, SHAPE, 1953-56; Comdt, RAMC Field Training Centre, 1956-59; Exchange Officer, Brooke Army Medical Center, Texas, USA, 1959-60; DDMS: 1 (British) Corps, 1960-63; Eastern Comd, 1965-66. Col Comdt, RAMC, 1969-. *Publications:* contribs to Proc. Roy. Soc. Med. and Jl of Assoc. of Military Surgeons of USA. *Address:* c/o Glyn Mills & Co., Kirkland House, 22 Whitehall, SW1.

**AHLMANN, Prof. Hans Wilhelmson;** *b* 14 Nov. 1889; *s* of Col W. Ahlmann and Mais Bergqvist; *m* 1920, Erica (Lillemor) Harloff. *Educ:* Stockholm and Uppsala Universities. DrPh and Docent Stockholm Univ., 1915; Docent Uppsala Univ., 1920; Prof. and Dir of Geographical Inst., Stockholm Univ., 1929-50; Swedish Ambassador to Norway, 1950-56. Leader of Swedish-Norwegian Arctic Expedn, 1931; leader (with H. U. Sverdrup) of Norwegian-Swedish Spitzbergen Expedn, 1934; leader (with Jón Eythórsson and Sigurdur Thorarinsson) of Swedish-Icelandic Vatnajökull Investigations, 1936-37-38; leader of Swedish glaciological investigations in North-East Greenland, 1939-40; initiator and Swedish representative of board of Norwegian-British-Swedish Antarctic Expedn, 1949-52. Pres., Internat. Geogr. Union, 1956-60; Gold Medallist: Swedish Geographical Soc.; Roy. Geographical Soc.; American Geographical Soc.; Gesellschaft für Erdkunde, Berlin; Tokyo Geographical Soc.; Russian Geographical Soc., Leningrad. *Publications:* Sommar vid Polhavet, 1931; Land of Ice and Fire, London, 1937; Norge, natur och näringsliv, 1943, 1957; Scientific Results of the Expeditions in 1931, 1934, and 1936-37-38, 39-40, Geografiska Annaler, 1933, 1935-43; Glaciological Research on the North Atlantic Coast; R. Geog. Soc., Research Series I, London, 1948; Glacier Variations and Climatic Fluctuations, Bowman Memorial Lectures, Amer. Geog. Society, New York, 1953. *Address:* Geogr. Inst., Drottninggt. 120, Stockholm, Sweden.

**AHMED, Jamal Mohammed;** writer; Ambassador from the Republic of the Sudan to the Court of St James's, 1969, retired; *b* Wadi Halfa, Sudan, 14 April 1917; *s* of Mohammed Ahmed and Fatima Hassan; *m*; four *s* three *d*. *Educ:* Sudan; Oxford Univ. (BLitt). Teacher, Sudan Govt schs and Teacher Trng Coll., 1936-44; Editor, children's magazines and writer of books for children, 1946-49; Students Warden, Univ. Coll., Khartoum, 1949-51; Sen. Warden, Univ. of Khartoum, 1954-56; Sudan Ambassador: to Arab Countries and Turkey, 1957-59; to Ethiopia, 1959-64; Perm. Delegate to UN, 1964-66; Sudan Ambassador to UK, 1966-67; Permanent Under-Sec., Min. of Foreign Affairs, Sudan, 1967-69. Holds foreign orders from Ethiopia, Iraq, Syria and Jordan. *Publications:* (trans. into Arabic) The Federalist Papers, 1959; (trans. into Arabic) Old Africa Rediscovered, 1961; Intellectual Origins of Egyptian Nationalism, 1961; Readings in African Literature and Thought; Sali Fu Hamar: a collection of African stories, 1970. *Address:* PO Box 83, Khartoum, Sudan. *T:* 41200, 41854, 80191. *Club:* Cultural Centre (Sudan).

**AIERS, David Pascoe;** Head of South-West Pacific Department, Foreign and Commonwealth Office, since Sept. 1968; *b* 19 Sept. 1922; *s* of late George Aiers and Sarah Adshead; *m* 1948, Pauleen Victoria Brittain-Jones; one *s* one *d*. *Educ:* Stationers' Company's Sch.; Trinity Coll., Oxford. Royal Artillery, 1942-46; Third Sec., Warsaw, 1946-48; FO, 1948; Second Sec., Copenhagen, 1951-53, Buenos Aires, 1953-55; FO, 1955; First Sec. (Commercial), Manila, 1958-62; First Sec. and Head of Chancery, Ankara, 1962-65; Counsellor and Head of Chancery, Political Adviser's Office, Singapore, 1965-68. *Address:* Burnside, Littleworth Road, Esher, Surrey. *T:* Esher 63861. *Clubs:* Royal Automobile, Royal Commonwealth Society.

**AIKEN, Conrad Potter;** Poet; *b* Savannah, Georgia, 5 Aug. 1889; *s* of William Ford and Anna Potter Aitken; *m* 1st, 1912, Jessie McDonald (marr. diss. 1929); one *s* two *d*; 2nd, 1930, Clarice Mary Lorenz (marr. diss. 1937); 3rd, Mary Augusta Hoover. *Educ:* Middlesex Sch., Concord, Mass; Harvard Coll. (AB). Contributing Editor, The Dial, 1917-19. Library of Congress: Fellow, 1948; Consultant in Poetry, 1950-51, 1951-52. Fellow, Acad. of Amer. Poets, 1957; Mem., Amer. Acad. of Arts and Letters, 1957. Pulitzer Prize for Selected Poems, 1930; Shelley Memorial Award, 1930; Nat. Book Award for Collected Poems, 1954; Bollingen Prize, 1956; Gold Medal for Poetry, Nat. Inst. of Arts and Letters, 1958; Nat. Medal for Literature, 1969. *Publications:*

Poems: Earth Triumphant, 1914; Turns and Movies, 1916; The Jig of Forslin, 1916; Nocturne of Remembered Spring, 1917; The Charnel Rose, 1918; The House of Dust, 1920; Punch, the Immortal Liar, 1921; Priapus and the Pool, 1922; Modern American Poets (ed), 1922; The Pilgrimage of Festus, 1923; Selected Poems of Emily Dickinson (ed), 1924; Senlin: A Biography, 1925; Prose: Scepticisms; Notes on Contemporary Poetry, 1919; Bring!, Bring!, and other Stories, 1925; Blue Voyage, a novel, 1927; Costumes by Eros (short stories), 1928; American Poetry, 1671-1928; A Comprehensive Anthology (ed), 1929; Selected Poems, 1929; John Deth and Other Poems, 1930; The Coming Forth by Day of Osiris Jones, 1931; Preludes for Memnon, 1931; Great Circle, a novel, 1933; Among the Lost People (short stories), 1934; Landscape West of Eden (poem), 1934; King Coffin (novel), 1935; Time in the Rock (poems), 1936; A Heart for the Gods of Mexico (novel), 1939; The Conversation, or Pilgrims' Progress (novel), 1939; And in the Human Heart (poems), 1940; Brownstone Eclogues (poems), 1942; The Soldier (poem), 1944; The Kid (poem), 1947; The Divine Pilgrim (poem), 1949; Skylight One (Poems), 1949; The Short Stories of Conrad Aiken, 1950; Ushant: an Essay (autobiography), 1952; Collected Poems, 1953; A Letter from Li Po (poems), 1955; Mr Arcularis (play), 1957; Sheepfold Hill (poems), 1958; A Reviewer's ABC; Collected Criticism, 1958; Collected Short Stories, 1960; Selected Poems, 1961; The Morning Song of Lord Zero (poems), 1963; The Collected Novels of Conrad Aiken, 1964; A Seizure of Limericks, 1964; Cats and Bats and Things with Wings (poems), 1965; Poets on Poetry (contrib. essay), 1965; Tom, Sue and the Clock (poems), 1966; Preludes (poems), 1966; Collected Criticism (Preface by I. A. Richards), 1967; Thee (poem), 1967. *Recreations:* gardening, tennis, travel, chess. *Address:* Brewster, Mass, USA. *T:* Dennis, (Mass) 385. *Clubs:* Authors'; Harvard (Boston); Oglethorpe (Savannah, Ga).

**AIKEN, Frank;** Tánaiste (Deputy Prime Minister) in the Government of Ireland, 1965-69; Member Dail for County Louth since 1923; *b* Camlough Co. Armagh, 13 Feb. 1898; *y s* of James Aiken and Mary McGeeny; *m* 1934, Maud Davin; two *s* one *d*. *Educ:* Christian Brothers' Schools, Newry. Joined Irish Volunteers, 1913; Captain, Camlough Co., IRA, 1918; Comdt, Camlough Bn, IRA, 1919; Vice-Brig., Newry Bde, IRA, 1920; Comdt, 4th Northern Div., IRA, 1921; Chief of Staff, IRA, 1923. Secretary: Camlough Br., Gaelic League, 1914; Sinn Fein Organisation, S Armagh, 1917. Local and CCs, 1920. Minister for: Defence, Ireland, 1932-39; Lands, June-Nov. 1936; Co-ordination of Defensive Measures, 1939-45; Finance, 1945-48; External Affairs, 1951-54 and 1957-69; Agriculture, March-May 1957. Leader, Irish Delegn to Council of Europe, 1969. Hon. LLD: NUI; St John's Univ., Jamaica, New York; Dublin Univ. Military Service Medal with Bar. Grand Cross: Pian Order; Order of Merit of Federal Republic of Germany; Belgian Order of Crown. Grand Officer with plaque, Order of St Charles. *Address:* Dungaoithe, Sandyford, Co. Dublin.

**AIKEN, Air Vice-Marshal John Alexander Carlisle,** CB 1967; Royal Air Force; Deputy Commander, RAF, Germany, since 1969; *b* 22 Dec. 1921; *s* of Thomas Leonard and Margaret Aiken; *m* 1948, Pamela Jane (*née* Bartlett); one *s* one *d*. *Educ:* Birkenhead School. Joined RAF, 1941; Fighter Sqdns, Europe and Far East, 1942-45; Fighter Comd, 1946-47; CFS, 1948; Staff of RAF Coll., Cranwell, 1948-50; OC Univ. of Birmingham Air Sqdn, 1950-52; Staff Coll., 1953; HQ Fighter Comd, 1954-55; OC 29 Fighter Sqdn, 1956-57; jssc 1958; Headquarters AF North, 1958-60; Air Min., 1960-63; Station Comdr, RAF Finningley, 1963-64; Air Cdre Intelligence, Min. of Defence, 1965-67; idc 1968. *Recreations:* ski-ing, music. *Address:* Headquarters, RAF Germany, BFPO 40. *Club:* Royal Air Force.

**AILESBURY,** 7th Marquess of, *cr* 1821; **Chandos Sydney Cedric Brudenell-Bruce,** Bt, 1611; Baron Brudenell, 1628; Earl of Cardigan, 1661; Baron Bruce, 1746; Earl of Ailesbury, 1776; Viscount Savernake, 1821; *b* 26 Jan. 1904; *o s* of 6th Marquess of Ailesbury, DSO, TD, and Sydney (*d* 1941), *o d* of John Madden, Hilton Park, Co. Monagh; *S* father 1961; *m* 1st, 1924, Joan (*d* 1937), *d* of S. Salter, Ryde, Isle of Wight; two *s*; 2nd, 1944, Mrs Joyce Frances Quennell (marriage dissolved, 1948), *d* of Charles Warwick-Evans; 3rd, 1950, Jean Frances, *widow* of Sqdn Ldr Williamson, MBE; one *s*. *Educ:* Eton; Christ Church, Oxford. Served War of 1939-45 RASC and Military Government (prisoner, escaped, despatches). CC Wiltshire 1961-64. JP Wilts, 1938, DL 1950-69. CStJ 1964. *Publications:* Youth goes East, 1928; Amateur Pilot, 1933; Wardens of Savernake Forest, 1949; I Walked Alone, 1950; Life and Loyalties of Thomas Bruce, 1951. *Heir: s* Viscount Savernake, *qv*. *Address:* Bel au Vent, St Lawrence, Jersey, Channel Islands.

**AILSA,** 7th Marquess of, *cr* 1831; **Archibald David Kennedy,** OBE 1968; Baron Kennedy, 1452; Earl of Cassillis, 1509; Baron Ailsa (UK), 1806; *b* 3 Dec. 1925; *s* of 6th Marquess of Ailsa and Gertrude Millicent (*d* 1957), *d* of Gervas Weir Cooper, Wordwell Hall, Bury St Edmunds; *S* father 1957; *m* 1954, Mary, 7th *c* of John Burn, Amble; two *s* one *d*. *Educ:* Nautical Coll., Pangbourne. Scots Guards, 1943-47; Royal Northumberland Fusiliers, 1950-52. National Trust for Scotland, 1953-56. Territorial Army, 1958-68. *Recreations:* walking, motoring, modelling. *Heir: s* Earl of Cassillis, *qv*. *Address:* Cassillis House, Maybole, Ayrshire. *Clubs:* Carlton; New (Edinburgh).

**AILWYN,** 3rd Baron, *cr* 1921, of Honingham, Norfolk; **Eric William Edward Fellowes,** CBE 1962; Captain RN retired; a Deputy Chairman of Committees and a Deputy Speaker, House of Lords, since 1957; *b* 24 Nov. 1887; 2nd *s* of 1st Baron Ailwyn, PC, KCVO, KBE, 2nd *s* of 1st Baron de Ramsey, and Hon. Agatha Eleanor Augusta Jolliffe, *d* of 2nd Lord Hylton; *S* brother, 1936; *m* 1935, Cecil Lorna, *d* of late Hugh G. Barclay, Colney Hall, Norwich, and *widow* of Col Malise Graham, DSO. *Educ:* Stubbington; HMS Britannia. Entered RN, 1902; served throughout European War, 1914-18, in North Sea; retired 1934 with rank of Captain; War of 1939-45; Member of British Parliamentary Mission to China, 1942; Pres. of China Assoc., 1943-48. DL and JP Suffolk. Hon. Col 419 Coast Regt RA (Suffolk TA), 1947-54. Order of Brilliant Star of China. *Heir: b* Hon. Carol Arthur Fellowes, *b* 23 Nov. 1896. *Address:* Sweffling Grange, Saxmundham, Suffolk. *T:* Rendham 496. *Club:* United Service.

**AINLEY, Sir (Alfred) John,** Kt 1957; MC 1940; Chief Justice, Kenya, 1963-68; retired; *b* 10 May 1906; *o s* of late Rev. A. Ainley, Cockermouth, Cumb; *m* 1935, Mona Sybil Wood; one *s* two *d*. *Educ:* St Bees Sch.; Corpus Christi, Oxford. Called to Bar, 1928; Magistrate, Gold Coast, 1935; Crown Counsel (Gold Coast), 1936; Puisne Judge, Uganda, 1946-55; Chief Justice of Eastern Region, Nigeria, 1955-59; Combined Judiciary of

Sarawak, N Borneo and Brunei, 1959-62. Served War of 1939-45, West African Forces, E Africa and Burma. *Address:* Horrock Wood, Watermillock, Penrith, Cumberland.

**AINLEY, Eric Stephen;** Under-Secretary, Centralised Licensing Group, Ministry of Transport, since 1968; *b* 15 Sept. 1918; *s* of Capt. Eric E. Ainley and late Dorothy Ainley (*née* Sharp); *m* 1946, Pamela, *d* of late Mr and Mrs Philip G. Meadows; two *s*. *Educ:* Giggleswick Sch.; Trinity Coll., Cambridge. BA, Classics and English; MA. Served War of 1939-45: RA, RIASC, and Civil Affairs (Malaya), 1940-46. Asst Principal, Min. of Civil Aviation, 1948; Principal, 1950; Civil Air Adviser and Attaché, Singapore and Far East, 1955-58; Asst Sec., Min. of Transport, 1960; seconded as the Traffic Manager, GLC, 1965-67. *Recreations:* mathematics, golf. *Address:* 27 Long Shepherd's Drive, Caswell Bay, Swansea. *T:* Swansea 67672. *Clubs:* Arts; Dulwich and Sydenham Hill Golf.

**AINLEY, Sir John;** *see* Ainley, Sir A. J.

**AINSCOUGH, Sir Thomas Martland,** Kt 1932; CBE 1925 (OBE 1918); MCom; FRGS; *b* 12 Aug. 1886; *e s* of late James M. Ainscough, JP, of Lindley Mount, Parbold, Lancs; *m* 1st, 1918, Mabel (*d* 1956), 3rd *d* of late Wm Lincolne, of Ely, Cambs; one *s* (and one killed in action, 1941) one *d*; 2nd, 1956, Mrs Marjorie Jones, Bourne House, 15 Westbourne Grove, W2. *Educ:* Manchester Grammar Sch.; Switzerland; Manchester University. In business in Manchester and China, 1906-12; travelled widely in Western China, 1913; Special Commissioner to the Board of Trade in China, 1914-16; Secretary to the Board of Trade Textile Committee, 1916-17; Secretary to the Empire Cotton Growing Committee, 1917; HM Senior Trade Commissioner in India, Burma, and Ceylon, 1918-44; retired, 1944; Ministry of War Transport Rep. in India, 1942; attached to the Persian Tariff Revision Commission, 1920; attached to the United Kingdom Delegation at the Imperial Economic Conference, Ottawa, 1932. *Address:* Royal Glen Hotel, Sidmouth, Devon. *Club:* Oriental.

**AINSLEY, John William;** *b* 30 June 1899; *s* of John George and Jane Ainsley, Co. Durham; *m* 1924; two *d*. *Educ:* elementary school; evening classes. corespondence courses. Enlisted in Durham Light Infantry, 1916. A miner. Labour Party agent at general elections. Chairman Durham County Council (Member, 1942-); Chairman County Education Committee, Durham; Chairman Northern Advisory Council for Further Education, 1951-55. MP (Lab) North-West Division of Durham, 1955-64. Methodist local preacher. *Address:* 5 Reservoir Road, Wooley Terrace PO, Crook, Co. Durham.

**AINSLIE, James Percival,** CMG 1962; Consultant Surgeon, Royal Perth Hospital, Western Australia, since 1952; Consultant Neuro-surgeon, Royal Perth Hospital, since 1959; Consultant Neuro-surgeon, Repatriation Hospital, Perth; *b* 14 Aug. 1899; *s* of James W. Ainslie; *m* 1930, Jean W., *d* of Dr G. E. Clemons; one *s* two *d*. *Educ:* Hale School, Perth; Univ. of Western Australia; Trinity Coll., Univ. of Melbourne. MB, BS 1923, MD 1924 (Melb.); FRCS 1927, FRACS 1929. Royal Melb. Hosp.: House appts, 1923-24; Med. Supt, 1925-26; Royal Perth Hosp.: Surgeon to out-patients, 1929-35; to in-patients, 1935-51; Neuro-surgeon, 1949-59. Pres. BMA, WA Br., 1941; Mem. of Senate, Univ. of WA, 1933-58; Pres., Medical Bd of WA, 1959- (Mem. 1951-); Mem. Australiasian Soc. of Neuro-surgeons (Pres. 1960); Fellow Aust. Med. Assoc., 1964. Hon. Lt-Col retd list. *Publications:* various to surgical journals. *Recreations:* golf, tennis, fishing. *Address:* 252 St George's Terrace, Perth, Western Australia. *T:* 214497. *Club:* Weld (Perth).

**AINSWORTH, Mrs Robert;** *see* Brunskill, Muriel.

**AINSWORTH, Sir Thomas,** 2nd Bt, *cr* 1916; late Lieutenant 11th Hussars; *b* 8 Feb. 1886; *s* of 1st Bt and Margaret Catherine (*d* 1918), *d* of Robert Reid Macredie; *S* father, 1923; *m* 1st, 1911, Lady Edina Dorothy Hope (who obtained a divorce, 1925), 4th *d* of 4th Marquess Conyngham; one *s* one *d*; 2nd, 1925, May Hope Johnstone (*d* 1969), 14 Grove Court, Drayton Gardens, SW; one *s*. *Heir: s* John Francis Ainsworth [*b* 1912; *m* 1st, 1938, Josephine (marr. diss. 1946), *er d* of Commander W. R. Bernard; 2nd, 1946, Anita, *e d* of late H. A. Lett, Enniscorthy, Co. Wexford]. *Address:* Ballinakill, Kilfinny, Adare, Co. Limerick. *T:* Croom 18. *Clubs:* Cavalry; Kildare Street (Dublin).
*See also Viscount Massereene and Ferrard.*

**AINSWORTH-DAVIS, John Creyghton,** MA, MD, BCh (Cantab); FRCSE; FRCS; LRCP; Consulting Urological Surgeon; Emeritus Consulting Urological Surgeon, Lord Mayor Treloar's Hospital, Alton; Hon. Consulting Urological Surgeon, King Edward VII's Hospital for Officers, Beaumont House; Senior Member British Association of Urological Surgeons; Fellow and late Secretary of Council Royal Society of Medicine (Ex-Vice-President Section of Urology); late President Hunterian Society; Vice-President and Hon. Fellow, Royal Institute of Public Health and Hygiene (late Chairman Executive Council); *b* 23 April 1895; *s* of late Prof. J. R. Ainsworth-Davis; *m* 1920; one *s* two *d*; *m* 1947, Irene, *d* of late Alfred Hope. *Educ:* Westminster Sch.; Christ's Coll., Cambridge (Closed and Open Exhibition). Served European War 1914-19 as Captain in the Rifle Brigade and RFC, France, Salonica, Palestine, Egypt; World War, 1939-45, as Wing Commander in charge of a Surgical Division, RAFVR Medical Services. Qualified at St Bartholomew's Hospital in 1923, and subsequently held the following appointments: Junior and Senior House-Surgeon, Surgical Registrar and Hon. Asst Surg. to All Saints' Hospital for Genito-Urinary Diseases; Clinical Asst, Hon. Surgical Registrar and Urological Surg. to the Royal Waterloo Hosp. for Women and Children; Clinical Asst, Surgical Registrar and Deputy Surgeon to St Paul's Hospital for Genito-Urinary Diseases. Late Consultant Urological Surg., The Bolingbroke Hospital, Royal Waterloo Hospital, London, Kettering and District General Hospital. *Publications:* Essentials of Urology, 1950; Articles in Postgraduate Surgery, Vol. II, and in Maingot's (1957) Management of Abdominal Operations; many papers contributed to medical journals. *Recreations:* athletics (Olympic Gold Medallist, 1920), fishing. *Address:* Townsend Farmhouse, Stockland, Nr Honiton, Devon. *T:* Stockland 257.

**AIRD, Colonel Sir John Renton,** 3rd Bt, *cr* 1901; MVO 1936; MC; JP; DL; Extra Equerry to the Queen since 1952 (and to King George VI, 1937-52); *b* 7 Aug. 1898; *e s* of Sir John Aird, 2nd Bt; *S* father 1934; *m* 1939, Lady Priscilla Willoughby, *yr d* of 2nd Earl of Ancaster, GCVO; one *s* three *d*. *Educ:* Eton; Sandhurst. Served European War, 1917-18; Staff of Governor of Bombay, 1921-23; Staff of High Comr for Egypt, 1926-27; Equerry to the

Prince of Wales, 1929-36. Commanded 3rd Bn Grenadier Guards, 1937-40; General Staff, 1940-45. Alderman, Berks CC; Member, Court of Assistants, Drapers' Company; Governor, Queen Mary's Coll., E1. Order of St Olav. *Heir: s* George John Aird [*b* 30 Jan. 1940; *m* 1968, Margaret, *yr d* of Sir John Muir, Bt, *qv*; one *d*]. *Address:* Forest Lodge, The Great Park, Windsor. *T:* Windsor 61262; 43 Clabon Mews, SW1. *T:* 01-584 5942.

*See also Baron Willoughby de Broke.*

**AIRD, Ronald,** MC 1942; TD; Secretary Marylebone Cricket Club, 1952-62, retired; *b* 4 May 1902; 2nd *s* of late Malcolm R. Aird; *m* 1925, Viola Mary (*d* 1965), 2nd *d* of late Sir Godfrey Baring, Bt; one *d*. *Educ:* Eton; Clare College, Cambridge. Stock Exchange, 1924-26; Assistant Secretary, MCC, 1926-52; Pres., MCC, 1968-69. *Recreations:* cricket, rackets, real tennis, golf, National Hunt racing. *Address:* Champlain's Well, Great Mongeham, Deal, Kent. *T:* Deal 3461. *Clubs:* White's, Oriental, MCC.

**AIREDALE,** 4th Baron, *cr* 1907; **Oliver James Vandeleur Kitson,** Bt, *cr* 1886; Deputy Chairman of Committees, House of Lords, since 1961; Deputy Speaker, House of Lords, since 1962; *b* 22 April 1915; *o s* of 3rd Baron Airedale, DSO, MC, and Sheila Grace (*d* 1935), *d* of late Frank E. Vandeleur, London; *S* father, 1958; unmarried. *Educ:* Eton; Trinity College, Cambridge. Is Major, The Green Howards. Called to the Bar, Inner Temple, 1941. *Heir:* none. *Address:* (seat) Ufford Hall, Stamford, Lincs.

**AIREY, Lawrence;** Under-Secretary, HM Treasury, since 1969; *b* 10 March 1926; *s* of late Lawrence Clark Airey and Isabella Marshall Pearson; *m* 1953, Patricia Anne, *d* of late Edward George Williams and Mary Selway; two *s* one *d*. *Educ:* Newcastle Royal Grammar Sch.; Peterhouse, Cambridge. Entered Civil Service, 1949; General Register Office, 1949-56; Cabinet Office, 1956-58; HM Treasury, 1958-; Research Fellow, Nuffield Coll., Oxford, 1961-62. *Recreations:* collecting books; music. *Address:* 41 Fairdene Road, Coulsdon, Surrey. *T:* Downland 54191.

**AIREY, Lt-Gen. Sir Terence (Sydney),** KCMG *cr* 1951; CB 1944; CBE 1943 (OBE 1941). psc; retired; *b* 9 July 1900; *s* of late Sydney Airey, Orchard Cottage, Holbrook, Suffolk; *m* 1934, Constance Hedley (marr. diss. 1947); one *s*; *m* 1947, Bridget Georgiana, *d* of late Col the Hon. Thomas Vesey. 2nd Lieutenant Durham Light Infantry, 1919; Capt. 1933; Major 1938; Temp. Lieut-Col 1940; War Subst. Lieut-Col; Col 1945; Temp. Maj.-Gen. 1944; Brig. Sept. 1945; Maj.-Gen. 1947; Lieut-Gen. 1952. Served War of 1939-45 (despatches, OBE, CBE, CB): Acting Deputy Supreme Allied Commander, Italy, 1946; Allied Commander and Military Gov., British-US Zone of Free Territory, Trieste, 1947-51; Assistant Chief of Staff, Supreme HQ, Allied Powers, Europe, 1951-52; Commdr, British Forces, Hong-Kong, 1952-54; representative Col Light Inf. Bde, 1954-55; retd 1954. Col The Durham Light Infantry, 1952-56. Commander, Order of Merit (US); Officer, Légion d'Honneur (France). *Address:* Fritton Old Rectory, Fritton, near Norwich, Norfolk. *T:* Hempnall 214.

**AIRLIE,** 13th Earl of, *cr* 1639 (*de facto* 10th Earl, 13th but for the Attainder); **David George Coke Patrick Ogilvy,** DL; Baron Ogilvy of Airlie, 1491; Capt. late Scots Guards; Director: J. Henry Schroder Wagg & Co. Ltd; Schroder Investment Co. Ltd; Corporacion Espanola Financiacion Internacional SA; General Accident Fire & Life Assurance Corp. Ltd; Schroder Executor & Trustee Co. Ltd; Anlage-Gesellschaft MbH für englische und hollandische Aktienwerte (Anglo Dutch Fund); The Trading Investment Co. Ltd; Yorkshire General Life Assurance Co.; Scottish & Newcastle Breweries Ltd; G. and A. Unit Trust Managers Ltd; Chairman: The Westpool Investment Trust Ltd; Trans Europe Investment Trust Ltd; Ashdown Investment Trust; *b* 17 May 1926; *e s* of 12th (*de facto* 9th) Earl of Airlie, KT, GCVO, MC, and of Lady Alexandra Marie Bridget Coke, *d* of 3rd Earl of Leicester, GCVO; *S* father, 1968; *m* 1952, Virginia Fortune Ryan, Moorland Farm, Newport, RI, USA; two *s* three *d*. *Educ:* Eton. Lieutenant Scots Guards, 1944; serving 2nd Battalion Germany, 1945; Captain, ADC to High Comr and C-in-C Austria, 1947-48; Malaya, 1948-49; resigned commission, 1950. DL Angus, 1964. *Heir: s* Lord Ogilvy, *qv*. *Address:* Cortachy Castle, Kirriemuir, Angus, Scotland. *T:* Cortachy 231; 13 St Leonards Terrace, SW3. *T:* 01-730 8741.

*See also Hon. Angus Ogilvy.*

**AISHER, Owen A(rthur);** Chairman of Marley Tile Companies; *b* 28 May 1900; *s* of late Owen Aisher, Little Marley, Western Avenue, Branksome Park, Poole; *m* 1921, Ann Allingham; two *s* two *d*. Mem. Court of Paviors; Pres., RYA; has had many successes in off-shore racing; was elected Yachtsman of the Year, 1958. *Recreations:* sailing, fishing, shooting. *Address:* Faygate, South Godstone, Surrey; Yeomans, Queen's Road, Cowes. *Clubs:* Reform; Royal Thames Yacht; RORC (Adm.); Ranelagh Sailing; Little Ship (Pres.); Royal Southern Yacht (Hamble); Royal London Yacht, Island Sailing (Adm.) (Cowes); Bembridge Sailing; Royal Motor Yacht (Poole); Seawanhaka Corinthian Yacht (USA); Royal St George Yacht (Eire); Royal Cape Yacht (S Africa).

**AITCHISON, Sir Charles (Walter de Lancey),** 4th Bt, *cr* 1938; *b* 27 May 1951; *er s* of Sir Stephen Charles de Lancey Aitchison, 3rd Bt, and (Elizabeth) Anne (Milburn), *er d* of late Lt-Col Edward Reed, Ghyllheugh, Longhorsley, Northumberland; *S* father 1958. *Heir: b* (Stephen) Edward Aitchison, *b* 27 March 1954. *Address:* The Brow, Wylam, Northumberland.

**AITCHISON, Sir David,** KCVO 1954; Captain SS Southern Cross, 1955, retired, 1957; *b* 26 Sept. 1892; *s* of Adam Aitchison and Annie Richardson Aitchison, Sunderland, County Durham; *m* 1924, Mary Alethea, *d* of Samuel William Moscrip, Morebattle, Roxburgh; no *c*. *Educ:* Sunderland. Commanded: MV Empire Grace, 1941-47; SS Athenic, 1947-50; SS New Australia, 1950-51; MV Dominion Monarch, 1951-53; SS Gothic, 1953-54, including Royal Tour; SS New Australia, 1954. *Publication:* Royal Standard: Red Ensign, 1958. *Address:* The Garth, Great Easton, Dunmow, Essex. *T:* Great Easton 268.

**AITHRIE, Viscount; Andrew Victor Arthur Charles Hope;** *b* 22 May 1969; *s* and *heir* of Earl of Hopetoun, *qv*.

**AITKEN,** family name of **Beaverbrook Barony.**

**AITKEN, Sir Arthur Percival Hay, (Sir Peter Aitken),** Kt 1968; Deputy-Chairman, Stone-Platt Industries Ltd; *b* 2 Oct. 1905; *e s* of late Canon R. A. Aitken, Great Yarmouth; *m* 1937, Ursula Wales, *d* of Herbert Wales, MB; one *s* one *d*. *Educ:* Norwich Gram. Sch.; Trinity Coll., Oxford. Man. Dir Textile Machinery Makers Ltd, 1949, Chm. 1960; Director: Norwich Union Insurance Group; Norwich Union Life Insurance Soc.; Norwich Union

Fire Insurance Soc.; Scottish Union and National Insurance Co.; Maritime Insurance Co.; Skefko Ball Bearing Co. Ltd. Chm., BNEC's Australia Cttee, 1966-69; Bd Mem., Commonwealth Develt Corp., 1960-69. *Recreations:* golf, shooting, fishing, sailing. *Address:* Longlands Hall, Stonham Aspal, Stowmarket, Suffolk. *T:* Stonham 242. *Clubs:* Royal Thames Yacht; Aldeburgh Golf, Aldeburgh Yacht.

**AITKEN, Janet Kerr,** CBE 1950; MD London; FRCP; retired; late Consulting Physician: Elizabeth Garrett Anderson Hospital; Princess Louise Kensington Hospital for Children; Mothers' (Salvation Army) Hospital; *b* Buenos Aires, 1886, Scottish parents. *Educ:* St Leonard's School, St Andrews; London School of Medicine for Women (Royal Free Hospital). LRCP, MRCS and MB, BS, London 1922; MD London 1924; MRCP 1926; FRCP 1943; Vice-Dean London Royal Free Hospital School of Medicine for Women, 1930-34; President, Medical Women's Federation, 1942-44; late Pres., Med. Women's Internat. Assoc.; late Councillor Royal College of Physicians; late Council Mem. BMA; late Member: Central Health Services Council; General Medical Council. *Publications:* papers in medical journals. *Recreation:* music; LRAM (piano), Gold Medallist (singing). *Address:* 70 Viceroy Court, Prince Albert Road, Regents Park, NW8. *T:* 01-722 3833.

**AITKEN, Prof. John Thomas;** Professor of Anatomy, University College, London, since 1965; *b* 16 May 1913; *s* of David and Helen Aitken; *m* 1941, Doreen Violet Whitaker; two *s* two *d. Educ:* High School, Glasgow; Grammar School, Hull; Glasgow University. MB, ChB 1936, MD 1950. University College, London, 1940-. *Publications:* Manual of Human Anatomy (in collab.); Essential Anatomy (in collab.); papers on regeneration of nerves and muscles, in various jls. *Recreation:* gardening. *Address:* 13 Russell Hill, Purley, Surrey. *T:* 01-660 8660.

**AITKEN, Sir (John William) Max,** 2nd Bt, *cr* 1916; DSO 1942; DFC 1940; Director and Chairman Beaverbrook Newspapers Limited; Director: Price Company Limited; Associated Television Ltd; *b* Montreal, 15 February 1910; *e s* of 1st Baron Beaverbrook (Bt 1916), PC, ED, CD; *S* father, 1964; disclaimed the barony, 11 June 1964; *m* 1st, 1939, Cynthia Monteith (who obtained a divorce, 1944); 2nd, 1946, Mrs Jane Lindsay (who obtained a divorce, 1950); two *d*; 3rd, 1951, Violet, *d* of Sir Humphrey de Trafford, *qv*; one *s* one *d*. *Educ:* Westminster; Pembroke Coll., Cambridge. Joined RAuxAF, 1935. Served War of 1939-45, RAF (despatches, DSO, DFC, Czech War Cross); day fighter pilot during Battle of Britain; comd night fighter squadron, 1941-42; Group Capt. comdg Strike Mosquito Wing, Norwegian waters, 1943. MP (C) Holborn, 1945-50. President, Newspaper Press Fund, 1965. Chancellor, Univ. of New Brunswick, Fredericton, NB, 1966-. Hon. LLD, New Brunswick, 1966. *Recreations:* Cambridge Assoc. Football Blue, 1930, 1931; golf, sailing. *Heir: s* Hon. (*as heir to disclaimed barony*) Maxwell William Humphrey Aitken, *b* 29 Dec. 1951. *Address:* The Garden House, Cherkley, Leatherhead, Surrey. *T:* Leatherhead 3162. *Clubs:* White's, Buck's, Royal Yacht Squadron.

**AITKEN, Sir Max;** *see* Aitken, Sir J. W. M.

**AITKEN, Sir Peter;** *see* Aitken, Sir A. P. H.

**AITKEN, Air Vice-Marshal (Robert) Stanley,** CB 1945; CBE 1942 (OBE 1938); MC 1917; AFC 1918; retired; *b* 4 April 1896; *s* of late Robert Aitken, Newcastle, and late Emma Louise Townsend, Manchester; *m* 1st, 1925, Jeanie Allison (*d* 1963), *o d* of late Rev. David Tweedie, Stitchill, Roxburghshire; one *s* (and one *s* decd); 2nd, 1964, Laura Barler, *widow* of Arthur Sewall. *Educ:* Highgate; Wiesbaden. Enlisted 15th London Regt, 1914; commnd 1/1st (Essex) RGA, 1915; seconded RFC, July 1916; served France with 41, 52 and 7 Sqdns; Flying Instructor, 1918-21; Comd 41(F) and 25(F) Sqdns, 1928-30; British Air Attaché, China, 1938-40; Air Staff signals duties, Air Ministry, and CSO, varying periods, Air Defence of GB and Fighter Comd, 1940-42; AOC 60 (Radar) Group, 1942-43; ASO in C, HQ, MAAF, 1944-45; retired 1946. Legion of Merit (USA). *Address:* Stone House Farm, Bath, Maine 04530, USA. *Club:* United Service.

**AITKEN, Sir Robert (Stevenson),** Kt 1960; MD (New Zealand), DPhil (Oxford); FRCP, FRACP; DL; Deputy Chairman, University Grants Committee, since 1968; *b* NZ; *s* of late Rev. James Aitken; *m* 1929, Margaret G. Kane; one *s* two *d. Educ:* Gisborne High School, Gisborne, NZ; University of Otago, Dunedin, NZ; Oxford. Medical Qualification in New Zealand, 1922; Rhodes Scholar, Balliol College, Oxford, 1924-26; attached to Medical Unit, The London Hospital, 1926-34; Reader in Medicine, British Post-Graduate Medical School, Univ. of London, 1935-38; Regius Prof. of Medicine, Univ. of Aberdeen, 1939-48; Vice-Chancellor, Univ. of Otago, Dunedin, NZ, 1948-53; Vice-Chancellor, Univ. of Birmingham, 1953-68. Vice-Chm. Association of Univs of the British Commonwealth, 1955-58; Chairman: Committee of Vice-Chancellors and Principals, 1958-61; Birmingham Repertory Theatre, 1962-. DL Co. Warwick, 1967. Hon FRCPE; Hon. DCL Oxford; Hon. LLD: Dalhousie, Melbourne, Panjab, McGill, Pennsylvania, Aberdeen, Newfoundland, Leicester, Birmingham, Otago; Hon. DSc: Sydney, Liverpool. *Publications:* papers in medical and scientific Journals. *Address:* 6 Hintlesham Avenue, Birmingham 15. *Club:* Athenæum.

**AITKEN, Air Vice-Marshal Stanley;** *see* Aitken, R. S.

**AITKEN, Ven. William Aubrey;** Archdeacon of Norwich since 1961; *b* 2 Aug. 1911; *s* of late Canon R. A. Aitken, Great Yarmouth; *m* 1937, Margaret Cunningham; three *s* two *d. Educ:* Norwich Grammar School; Trinity College, Oxford (MA Modern History, 2nd class Hons). Curate of: Tynemouth, 1934-37; Kingston, Jamaica, 1937-40; Rector of Kessingland, 1940-43; Vicar of: Sprowston, 1943-53; St Margaret's, King's Lynn, 1953-61. Proctor in Convocation, 1944-; Hon. Canon of Norwich, 1958. *Recreations:* football, cricket, sailing. *Address:* 57 The Close, Norwich, Norfolk.

**AIYAR, Mrs Robert Duray;** *see* Carlyle, Joan Hildred.

**AKENHEAD, David,** OBE 1950; MA Oxon, BSc London; *b* 23 Feb. 1894; *s* of Edmund Akenhead, sometime Prebendary of Lincoln Cathedral, and Lucy Collingwood Akenhead; *m* 1933, Beatrice Carter. *Educ:* Rugby; New College, Oxford; (post-war) South Eastern Agricultural College, Wye. Served European War, 1914-18. On staff: Royal Agricultural Coll., 1922-24; Internat. Inst. of Agriculture, Rome, 1926-28; helped to start what is now known as the Commonwealth Bureau of Horticulture and Plantation Crops, East

Malling, Kent, in 1929, and was Director thereof, 1945-59. *Address:* Three Roods, Offham, Maidstone, Kent. *T:* West Malling 2171. *Club:* United University.

**AKERMAN, Major-General William Philip Jopp,** CB 1941; DSO 1918; MC late RA; *b* 16 Jan. 1888; *s* of late W. S. Akerman of the Mount, Burnham, Som.; *m* 1st, 1920, Olga Phyllis (*d* 1922), *o d* of late Major-Gen. Sir John Steevens, KCB; one *d*; 2nd, 1925, Annie, *er d* of late Major-Gen. E. W. Alexander, VC, CB, CMG; two *d. Educ:* Oundle School; RMA, Woolwich. Served India, 1908-14; Mesopotamia, 1914-16 (MC); France and Belgium, 1917-18 (DSO and bar); Staff College, Camberley, 1922-23; Imperial Defence College, 1933; Assistant Dir of Artillery, War Office, 1934-36; Assistant Master-General of Ordnance, War Office, 1936-38; Major-Gen. Royal Artillery, AHQ, India, 1939-42; retired pay, 1942. *Address:* Rotherwood, Churt, Surrey.

**AKERS-DOUGLAS,** family name of **Viscount Chilston.**

**AKHURST, Instructor Captain Algernon Frederic,** CBE 1944; MA; RN retired; *b* 13 Nov. 1893; *s* of late Herbert Akhurst, Civil Servant, and late Florence Akhurst; unmarried. *Educ:* Merchant Taylors' School, London; Jesus College, Cambridge, Math. Tripos, Wrangler. Joined RN 1915; HMS Minotaur, 1916-19; HMS Cornwall, 1919; HMS Barham, 1920-22; RN Engineering College, 1922-26; RN College, Greenwich, 1926; HMS Warspite, 1926-28; RN College, Greenwich, 1928-31; HMS Nelson, 1931-33; Fleet Education Officer, Home Fleet, 1933-36; RN Engineering College, Keyham, 1936-39; Education Dept, Admiralty, 1939-40; HMS Ganges, 1940; HMS St George, 1940-42. Dean of RNC, Greenwich, 1942-47; HMS Ganges, 1947-48; retired list, 1948. Cravat of the Order of the Cloud and Banner, China. *Recreations:* golf, gardening, walking, music. *Address:* Downscroft, 49 Headland Avenue, Seaford, Sussex. *T:* Seaford 2751. *Club:* United Service.

**ALAM, Hon. Anthony Alexander;** Member of Legislative Council, 1925-59, and since 1963; Member of the Upper House, NSW, since 1925; Director: Alam Homes Pty Ltd; Alam Stores Pty Ltd; Mala Homes Pty Ltd; Latec Ltd; *b* Wallsend, NSW, 23 Jan. 1898; parents born Republic Lebanon; *m*; no *c. Educ:* De La Salle College, Armidale, NSW. King George V Silver Jubilee Medal; Merit of Lebanon; Commander Nichan Iftikar; King George VI Coronation Medal; Commander Toile Noir; Chevalier, Legion of Honour; Commander Order Cedars (Liban); Queen Elizabeth Coronation Medal; Grand Cross; Order of Torsani; Order of St Mark; Grand Officer, Order of Phoenix, Greece. *Recreations:* bowls, billiards, tennis, motoring, horse-racing. *Address:* Parliament House, Sydney, Australia. *TA:* Alam Parliament, Sydney. *Club:* Commercial Travellers' (Sydney).

**ALANBROOKE,** 2nd Viscount, *cr* 1946; **Thomas Brooke;** Baron Alanbrooke, *cr* 1945; *b* 9 Jan. 1920; *e s* of 1st Viscount Alanbrooke, KG, GCB, OM, GCVO, DSO; *S* father, 1963. *Educ:* Wellington College. Served War of 1939-45, RA. *Heir: half-b* Hon. Alan Victor Harold Brooke, *b* 24 Nov. 1932. *Address:* c/o Lloyds Bank Ltd, 6 Pall Mall, SW1.

**ALBEE, Edward;** American dramatist; *b* 12 March 1928. *Publications: plays:* The Zoo Story, 1958; The Death of Bessie Smith, 1959; The Sandbox, 1959; The American Dream, 1960; Who's Afraid of Virginia Woolf?, 1962; (adapted from Carson McCullers' novella) The Ballad of the Sad Café, 1963; Tiny Alice, 1964; Malcolm, 1965; A Delicate Balance, 1966 (Pulitzer Prize, 1967); Everything in the Garden, 1967; Box and Quotations from Chairman Mao Tse-Tung, 1968. *Address:* 969 Fifth Avenue, New York, NY, USA.

**ALBEMARLE,** 9th Earl of, *cr* 1696; **Walter Egerton George Lucian Keppel;** MC; Baron Ashford, 1696; Viscount Bury, 1696; *b* 28 Feb. 1882; *e s* of 8th Earl and Lady Gertrude Lucia Egerton (*d* 1943), *o c* of 1st Earl Egerton of Tatton; *S* father, 1942; *m* 1st, 1909, Lady Judith Sydney Myee Carrington (*d* 1928), 4th *d* of 1st Marquis of Lincolnshire; one *s* two *d* (and two *s* decd); 2nd, 1931, Diana Cicely (*see* Countess of Albemarle), *o c* of late John Archibald Grove; one *d. Educ:* Eton. Late Lieut PWO Norfolk Artillery; ADC to Gov.-Gen. of Canada, 1904-05; to Viceroy of India, 1906-07; to Governor of Orange River Colony, 1907-08; Major Special Reserve Scots Guards, 1918; late commanding PWO Civil Service Rifles; commanded Norfolk Yeo. 108th Brigade RFA until 1926; contested (U) Altrincham Division, Cheshire, 1910; Vice-Lieut County of Norfolk, 1940-44; elected LCC for Central Wandsworth, 1919; elected Norfolk CC and to Church Assembly, 1943; Alderman Norfolk CC, 1957. Formerly Pres. St John Amb. Bde, Norfolk (KStJ 1963); Pres. Norwich Philharmonic Soc.; Pres. Tatton Park Gardens Soc.; Vice-Pres. Assoc. of River Authorities; Anglo-Netherlands Soc., 1943. Grand Cross, Order of Orange Nassau. *Heir: g s* Viscount Bury, *qv. Address:* Beacon Hill, Woodbridge, Suffolk. *Club:* Carlton.

*See also Sir Hew Hamilton-Dalrymple, Bt, Sir T. A. Matheson, Bt, Prof. M. Postan.*

**ALBEMARLE, Countess of; (Diana Cicely),** DBE 1956; Chairman: Development Commission, since 1948; The Drama Board, since 1964; *b* 6 Aug. 1909; *o c* of John Archibald Grove; *m* 1931, 9th Earl of Albemarle, *qv*; one *d. Educ:* Sherborne Sch. for Girls. Norfolk County Organiser, WVS, 1939-44. Chairman: Exec. Cttee, Nat. Fedn of Women's Institutes, 1946-51; Departmental Cttee on Youth Service, 1958-60; Nat. Youth Employment Council, 1962-68. Vice-Chm., British Council, 1959-. Member: Arts Council, 1951; Royal Commn on Civil Service, 1954; Harkness Fellowship Cttee of Award, 1963-69; UGC, 1956-70; Standing Commn on Museums and Galleries, 1958-; Youth Develt Council, 1960-68; Council, Univ. of E Anglia, 1964-. Life Trustee, Carnegie UK Trust; Trustee of: The Observer; Glyndebourne Arts Trust, 1968-. RD Councillor, Wayland, Norfolk, 1935-46. Hon. DLitt Reading, 1959; Hon. DCL Oxon, 1960; Hon. LLD London, 1960. *Recreations:* gardening, reading. *Address:* 204 Cranmer Court, SW3. *T:* 01-589 8073; Beacon Hill, Martlesham, Woodbridge, Suffolk. *T:* Woodbridge 264.

**ALBERT, Alexis Francois,** CMG 1967; VRD 1942; Chairman and Governing Director: J. Albert & Son Pty Ltd, Sydney, since 1962; The Australian Broadcasting Company Pty Ltd, Sydney; *b* 15 Oct. 1904; *s* of M. F. and M. E. Albert, Sydney; *m* 1934, Elsa K. R., *d* of late Capt. A. E. Lundgren, Sydney; three *s. Educ:* Knox College, Sydney; St Paul's College, University of Sydney. BEc 1930. Director: Amalgamated Television Services Pty Ltd, 1955-; Brisbane TV Limited, 1958-; Australasian Performing Right Association Ltd, 1946-. Underwriting Member of Lloyd's, 1944-; President, Royal Blind Soc. of NSW, 1962; Fellow of Council, St Paul's Coll., Univ. of Sydney, 1965-; Council, Nat. Heart Foundn of Aust., NSW Div. 1959. RANR, 1918-49; Lt-

Comdr, retd. Hon. ADC to Governors of NSW, 1937-57. *Recreations:* swimming, yachting. *Address:* 25 Coolong Road, Vaucluse, NSW 2030, Australia; (office) 139 King Street, Sydney, NSW 2000. *T:* 28 2141. *Clubs:* United Service; Australian, University (Sydney); Royal Sydney Golf, Royal Sydney Yacht Squadron (Vice-Commodore); New York Yacht.

**ALBERY, Sir Bronson (James),** Kt, *cr* 1949; theatre director; *b* 6 March 1881; *s* of James Albery and Mary Moore, afterwards Lady Wyndham; *m* 1912, Una G. Rolleston; two *s* two *d. Educ:* Uppingham; Balliol Coll., Oxford. Barrister-at-law; Lieut RNVR, 1917-19. Jt Man. Dir (with Howard Wyndham) The Wyndham Theatres Ltd, 1925-47, controlling Criterion, New and Wyndham's Theatres; Man. Dir The Wyndham Theatres Ltd, 1947-50; Jt Man. Dir (with his son, Donald Albery) of The Wyndham Theatres Ltd, 1950-62; appointed Chm., upon resignation of Sir Irving Albery, Jan. 1962; apptd Exec. Dir, upon his resignation as Jt Man. Dir, Sept. 1962; resigned as Chm. and Exec. Dir, Oct. 1965. Governor, Old Vic, 1936-41; Chm., Old Vic Trust, Dec. 1951-Sept. 1959. Presented (in partnership with Lewis Casson and Sybil Thorndyke) Advertising April, Criterion, 1923; Saint Joan, New, 1924 (subsequent revivals); The Lie, New, 1923, and Wyndham's, 1925; 1932-36 (in partnership with John Gielgud) presented: Musical Chairs, Criterion; Richard of Bordeaux, New; Sheppey, Wyndham's; Hamlet, New; Romeo and Juliet, New; The Seagull, New. Presented La Compagnie des Quinze in Noé, New, 1935, Le Viol de Lucrece, and other plays, subsequently. Administrator Sadler's Wells Ballet, 1941-42; Administrator, jointly with Tyrone Guthrie, of Old Vic and Sadler's Wells, 1942-44; Mem. Exec. Cttee Arts Council of Great Britain and Chm. of Drama Panel, 1948-52, Chm. British Council Drama Advisory Cttee, 1952-61; Pres. Society of West End Theatre Managers, 1941-45 and 1952-53; Chairman Theatres' War Service Council, 1942-46. Pres., Theatrical Traders Assoc.; Vice-Pres., Actors' Benevolent Fund. Chevalier de la Légion d'Honneur. *Recreations:* bridge, maps. *Address:* 8 Lees Place, W1. *T:* 01-629 0901. *Club:* Garrick.

**ALBERY, Michael James,** QC 1955; *b* 12 March 1910; *s* of late Sir Irving Albery, MC; *m* 1934, Mary Laughton Isaac; one *s* two *d. Educ:* Uppingham; Exeter Coll., Oxford (Scholar). 1st Cl. Jurisprudence, 1933, Cholmondeley Studentship, called to Bar, 1934. Served with Royal Artillery from outbreak of War until discharged on account of wounds in June 1942. Director, The Wyndham Theatres Ltd, 1947-62. Bencher of Lincoln's Inn, 1962. *Publication:* Cellar for Six, 1943. *Recreations:* ski-ing, golf, gardening, bridge. *Address:* 35 Falmouth House, Hyde Park Place, W2. *T:* 01-262 3909. *Club:* Garrick.

**ALBRECHT, Ralph Gerhart;** American lawyer, barrister and international legal consultant; *b* Jersey City, NJ, 11 Aug. 1896; *s* of J. Robert Albrecht and Gertrude A. F. Richter; *m* 1936, Aillinn, *d* of late William Elderkin Leffingwell, Watkins Glen, NY; one *s. Educ:* Pennsylvania Univ. (AB); Harvard Univ. (JD). Admitted to Bar of NY, 1924, US Supreme Court, 1927; senior partner, Peaslee, Albrecht & McMahon, 1931-61, counsel to firm, 1961-; gen. practice, specializing in foreign causes and internat. law. Special Dep. Attorney-Gen. of New York, 1926; Special Asst to US Attorney-Gen., 1945; Mem. US War Crimes Commn and leading trial counsel in Prosecution of Major Nazi War Criminals, before Internat. Mil. Tribunal, Nuremberg, 1945-46, prosecuted Hermann Goering; counsel to German steel, coal and chem. industries in decartelization procs before Allied High Commn for Germany, 1950-53. Mem. Republican County Cttee, NY Co., 1933-35; Harvard Univ. Overseers' Visiting Cttee to Faculty of Germanic Langs and Lits, 1949-63. Apprentice Seaman, USN Res. Force, 1918; served with Sqdn A (101st Cavalry, NY Nat. Guard), 1924-30; Comdr USNR, on active duty, 1941-45; Naval Observer, American Embassy, London, 1942 (letter of commendation from Chief of Naval Ops); Asst Dir OSS (War Crimes), 1945. Member: NY City Bar Assoc.; Amer. Bar Assoc.; Amer. Soc. of Internat. Law (Chm. Manley O. Hudson Medal Cttee); Internat. Bar Assoc.; International Law Assoc.; World Peace Through Law Center (Cttee on Conciliation and Mediation of Disputes); NY, Nat. and Internat., Legal Aid Assocs, etc. Fellow: Nat. Audubon Society; Massachusetts Audubon Soc.; Amer. Geog. Soc., etc. Delegate, First Internat. Congress Comparative Law, The Hague, 1932. Republican; Mason. *Publications:* (with Prof. Walter B. Pitkin) Studies for Vocational Guidance of Recent School and College Graduates; contrib. Peter Markham's (pseud.) America Next, 1940. *Address:* 520 East 86th Street, New York, NY 10028, USA. *Clubs:* University, Harvard, Pilgrims, Squadron A (all in NY).

**ALBRIGHT, Prof. William Foxwell;** Professor emeritus of Semitic Languages, Johns Hopkins University, since 1958; W. W. Spence Professor of Semitic Languages, 1929-58; *b* Chile, 24 May 1891; *s* of Rev. Wilbur Finley Albright and Zephine Viola (*née* Foxwell); *m* 1921, Ruth Norton; four *s. Educ:* Upper Iowa Univ. (AB); Johns Hopkins Univ. (PhD). Dir, American Sch. of Oriental Research in Jerusalem, 1920-29, 1933-36; first vice-pres. American Schools of Oriental Research, 1937-65; pres., Internat. Organisation Old Testament Scholars, 1956-59. Jordan Lectr, Univ. of London, 1965. Holds thirty hon. degrees inc. Yale, Harvard, St Andrews, TCD, Utrecht, Oslo, Uppsala, Hebrew Univ. (Jerusalem). Corresp. FBA, 1967. Member: Nat. Acad. of Sciences, Washington; American Philosophical Soc., Philadelphia; American Acad. of Arts and Sciences, Cambridge (Mass); Royal-Danish Acad. (for.); Royal Flemish Acad. (for.); Royal Irish Acad. (hon.). Corr. Member: Inst. of France (Acad. des Inscriptions et Belles Lettres); Austrian Acad. of Sciences. Hon. Fellow, Royal Asiatic Soc. Hon. Member: Société Asiatique; Brit. Soc. for Old Testament Study; Glasgow Oriental Soc., etc. Hon. Fellow German Archaeolog. Inst. *Publications:* Excavations at Gibeah of Benjamin, 1924; The Archaeology of Palestine and the Bible, 1932; The Excavation of Tell Beit Mirsim I-III, 1932-43; The Vocalization of the Egyptian Syllabic Orthography, 1934; From the Stone Age to Christianity, 1940; Archaeology and the Religion of Israel, 1942; The Archaeology of Palestine, 1949; Recent Discoveries in Bible Lands, 1956; The Biblical Period from Abraham to Ezra, 1963; History, Archaeology and Christian Humanism, 1964; The Proto-Sinaitic Inscriptions, 1966; Yahweh and the Gods of Canaan, 1968, etc. *Address:* 3401 Greenway, Baltimore, Md 21218, USA. *T:* Hopkins 7-9859; Johns Hopkins University, Baltimore, Md 21218.

**ALBROW, Desmond;** Editor, Catholic Herald, since Oct. 1966; *b* 22 Jan. 1925; *er s* of Frederick and Agnes Albrow; *m* 1950, Aileen Mary Jennings; one *s* three *d. Educ:* St Bede's Grammar Sch., Bradford; Keble Coll., Oxford (MA). On the Editorial Staff of the Yorkshire

Observer, 1950-51, Manchester Guardian, 1951-56, Daily Telegraph, 1956-60; Sunday Telegraph, 1960-66: Chief Sub-Editor, News Editor, and Night Editor. *Recreations:* drinking in moderation and talking to excess; watching other people cultivate their gardens. *Address:* 1 St James Road, Hampton Hill, Middlesex. *T:* 01-979 2661.

**ALBU, Austen Harry,** BSc (Eng.); FCGI, MIMechE; MP (Lab) Edmonton, since 1948; *b* London, 21 Sept. 1903; *s* of Ferdinand and Beatrice Rachel Albu; *m* 1st, 1929, Rose (*d* 1956), *d* of Simon Marks, Newcastle; two *s*; 2nd, 1958, Dr Marie Jahoda, New York City. *Educ:* Tonbridge School; City and Guilds College (Imperial College of Science and Technology). Works Manager, Aladdin Industries, Greenford, 1930-46. Dep. Pres., Govtl Sub-Commn, CCG, 1946-47. Dep. Dir, British Institute of Management, Feb.-Nov. 1948. Minister of State, Dept of Economic Affairs, 1965-67. Fellow, Imp. Coll. of Science and Technology. DUniv Surrey, 1966. *Address:* House of Commons, SW1.

**ALBU, Sir George,** 3rd Bt, *cr* (UK) 1912, of Grosvenor Place, City of Westminster, and Johannesburg, Province of Transvaal, South Africa; *b* 5 June 1944; *o s* of Major Sir George Werner Albu, 2nd Bt, and Kathleen Betty (*d* 1956), *d* of Edward Charles Dicey, Parktown, Johannesburg; *S* father, 1963; *m* 1969, Joan Valerie Millar, London. *Heir:* none. *Address:* 16 4th Avenue, Melville, Johannesburg, South Africa.

**ALDEN, John H.,** MA, DMus. (Oxon), FRCO, ARCM; Secretary of the Music Masters' Association since 1956; part-time Tutor, Education Department, Reading University; *b* 22 Feb. 1900; *s* of late Herbert E. Alden; *m* 1953, Caroline Patricia, *yr d* of late Lieut-Colonel H. W. Worsley-Gough, CMG; one *s* (one *d* decd). *Educ:* New and Magdalen College Schools, Oxford; New College, Oxford. Dir of Music, Diocesan College, Capetown, 1923-26; Assistant Director of Music, Harrow School, 1927-30; Director of Music, Bradfield College, Berks, 1931-34; Organist, St Martin-in-the-Fields, 1935-38; Acting-Head of Cambridge House, Camberwell, 1939; Director of Music, Eastbourne College, 1940-45; Royal Naval College, Dartmouth, 1945-46; Chairman, Slatter & Rose, Ltd, Oxford, 1942-47; Director of Music, Bradfield College, Berks, 1947-53. Chairman, Berks County Music Cttee. *Address:* Cray Cottage, Bradfield, Reading RG7 6BT. *T:* Bradfield 310.

**ALDENHAM,** 5th Baron *cr* 1896, and **HUNSDON OF HUNSDON,** 3rd Baron *cr* 1923; **Antony Durant Gibbs;** Director, Antony Gibbs & Sons, Ltd, since 1954; *b* 18 May 1922; *s* of 4th Baron and of Beatrix Elinor, *d* of Herbert Paul; *S* father, 1969; *m* 1947, Mary Elizabeth, *o d* of late Walter Parkyns Tyser; three *s* one *d*. *Educ:* Eton; Christ Church, Oxford. RNVR, 1940-46. Antony Gibbs & Sons, Ltd, 1947 (Chile, 1948-51). *Recreations:* shooting, fishing. *Heir: s* Hon. Vicary Tyser Gibbs, *b* 8 June 1948. *Address:* Stanstead Lodge, Stanstead Abbots, Herts. *T:* Roydon 3101. *Clubs:* Brooks's, Pratt's, City University; Cannonsbrook Golf; Brickendon Grange Golf.

*See also C. H. Villiers.*

**ALDERSEY, Captain Ralph,** JP; Landowner, Chester; land agent to Col E. Royds, Stubton, Lincolnshire, from 1919; *b* 1890; 2nd *s* of Hugh Aldersey of Aldersey; *m* 1st, 1927, Rachel (*d* 1948), *d* of Commander Gaussen, Brookman's Park, Herts; two *s* two *d*; 2nd, 1949, Beatrice Maude, *e d* of late Charles Stonor, Trearddur Bay, Anglesey; one *s*. *Educ:* Radley College. Business, 1908-14; Army, 1914-19 (twice wounded, despatches). *Recreations:* hunting, shooting, etc. *Address:* Aldersey, Chester. *TA:* Clutton. *T:* Broxton 265 (Aldersey Estate Office), 279.

**ALDERSON, Sir Harold George,** Kt 1956; MBE 1938; Chairman of the Olympic Federation of Australia; Hon. Secretary Anniversary Day Regatta since 1920; President New South Wales Olympic Council since 1926; *b* Balmain, NSW, 18 Aug. 1891; *s* of J. B. Alderson, Sydney; *m* 1915, Rose Stella, *d* of W. F. Wills; one *d*. *Educ:* Mosman Sup. Public School, NSW. Hon. Manager Australian Olympic Team, Berlin, 1936; Member Organising Council, British Empire Games, Sydney, 1938; President Australian Rowing Club, 1928, 1934, 1939-52, 1958, 1964; Chm., NSW Rowing Assoc. 1921-68, Hon. Sec., 1918-20; Member Executive Organising Committee Olympic Games, Melbourne, 1956. Member Council National Fitness, NSW; Hon. Treasurer St John Ambulance Assoc. KStJ. *Address:* 29 Bligh Street, Sydney, NSW, Australia. *Clubs:* NSW Sports, Union of Old Oarsmen.

**ALDERTON, George Edwin Lisle,** CMG 1954; High Commissioner for New Zealand in the Commonwealth of Australia, 1950-58; *b* Whangarei, New Zealand, 11 Jan. 1888; *s* of G. E. Alderton; *m* 1945, Kathleen, *d* of J. Leonard. *Educ:* Whangarei High Sch.; Grammar Sch. and University Coll., Auckland. Barrister and Solicitor (Lisle, Alderton and Kingston), Auckland. Judge, Auckland Racing Club, 1947-49; Transport Appeal Board and Co-ordination Board, 1934-36; Dir Devonport Ferry Co. and North Shore Transport Co.; Chairman Auckland Division, National Party, 1936-37; Vice-President, New Zealand National Party, 1938. In RNVR, 1915-18, and RNZNVR, 1939-42. *Address:* 33 Portland Road, Auckland, SE2, New Zealand. *Clubs:* Northern, Officers, Auckland Golf (all in NZ).

**ALDINGTON,** 1st Baron, *cr* 1962; **Toby (Austin Richard William) Low,** PC 1954; KCMG 1957; CBE 1945 (MBE 1944); DSO 1941; TD and clasp, 1950; Chairman: National and Grindlays Bank Ltd; General Electric Co. Ltd; AEI Ltd; Exporters Refinance Corp. Ltd; United Power Co. Ltd; Deputy Chairman: General Electric and English Electric Companies Ltd; Sun Alliance and London Insurance Ltd; Director: John Brown and Co.; English China Clays Ltd; Lloyds Bank; Wm Brandt's Sons & Co. Ltd; Genard & Reid Ltd, and other companies; Barrister-at-law; *b* 25 May 1914; *s* of Col Stuart Low, DSO (killed at sea by enemy action, Dec. 1942), and of late Hon. Mrs Spear; *m* 1947, Araminta Bowman, *e d* of late Sir Harold MacMichael, GCMG, DSO; one *s* two *d*. *Educ:* Winchester; New Coll., Oxford. Called to the Bar, 1939. TA; 2nd Lieut 1934; Brig. BGS 5 Corps Italy, Aug. 1944-June 1945; served Greece, Crete, Egypt, Libya, Tunisia, Sicily, Italy, Austria (DSO, MBE, CBE, Croix de guerre avec palmes, Commander of Legion of Merit, USA); Hon. Col 288 LAA Regt RA (TA), 1947-59. MP (C) Blackpool North, 1945-62; Parliamentary Secretary, Ministry of Supply, 1951-54; Minister of State, Board of Trade, 1954-57; Deputy-Chairman of the Conservative Party Organisation, Oct. 1959-63. Member Board of Governors, National Hospital for Nervous Diseases; Committee of Management, Inst. of Neurology (Chm.). *Recreation:* golf. *Heir: s* Hon. Charles Harold Stuart Low, *b* 22 June 1948. *Address:* 21d Cadogan Gardens, SW3. *T:* 01-730 1356; Knoll Farm, Aldington, Kent. *T:* Aldington 292. *Clubs:* Carlton, Brooks's.

**ALDINGTON, Sir Geoffrey (William),** KBE 1965 (OBE 1946); CMG 1958; *b* 1 June 1907; *s* of late Henry William Aldington; *m* 1932, Roberta Finch; two *d. Educ:* City of London School; Magdalen Coll., Oxford. Student Interpreter, China Consular Service, 1929; Vice-Consul (Grade II), China, 1931; Vice-Consul, Peking, 1931-33; Private Secretary to HM Minister, Peking, 1933-35; Foreign Office, 1936-37; Acting Consul, Chungking, 1937-39; Consul, Tsingtao, 1939-41; seconded to Min. of Information, 1943-45; Actg Consul-Gen., Hankow, 1945-46; Suptg Consul, Shanghai, 1946-47; Foreign Office, 1947-50; Political Adviser to Hong Kong Govt, 1950-53; Consul-Gen. Zagreb, Yugoslavia, 1954-56; Consul-General at Philadelphia, Pa, USA, 1956-61; HM Ambassador to Luxembourg, 1961-66; also Consul-General, Luxembourg, 1962-66; retd from HM Diplomatic Service, Dec. 1966. *Recreations:* tennis, riding, reading. *Address:* The Copse, Pound Lane, Sonning, Berks. *T:* Sonning 3202.

**ALDINGTON, John Norman,** BSc, PhD; FRIC; FInstP; CEng; FIEE; Director: Royal Worcester Ltd, since 1968; Welwyn Electric Co. Ltd, since 1968; Worcester Industrial Ceramics Ltd, since 1968; Worcester Royal Porcelain Co. Ltd, since 1969; *b* 2 March 1905; *s* of Allen Aldington, Preston, Lancashire; *m* 1930, Edna, *d* of late John James Entwisle; one *s. Educ:* Balshaws Grammar Sch., Leyland; Harris Inst., Preston. Joined Siemens Electric Lamps and Supplies Ltd, 1923; Head of Laboratories, 1935; Dir of Research, 1948; Dir of the firm, 1948; Dir Alfred Graham & Co. Ltd, 1950; Man. Dir of Siemens Bros & Co. Ltd, 1955; former Director: AEI Ltd; LEW Ltd; Sub. Cables Ltd, etc. Fellow and Past Pres., Illuminating Engrg Soc.; Leon Gaster Memorial Award, IES, 1945 and 1947; Crompton Award, IEE, 1949; Mem. Amer. Illum. Eng Soc., 1950; Chm. of Light Sources Secretariat, Internat. Commn on Illumination, 1945-54; Mem. various BSI Cttees. Part-time Lectr Harris Inst., Preston, 1928-38; Gov., Preston Grammar Sch., 1950-55; JP Duchy of Lancaster, 1953-55. MRI 1958. *Publications:* The High Current Density Mercury Vapour Arc, 1944 (thesis, London Univ. Library); numerous papers, particularly on light sources and kindred devices, and on high current discharges and xenon gas arc. *Recreations:* gardening and golf. *Address:* White Oaks, 39 Forest Drive, Keston, Kent. *T:* Farnborough 52904. *Club:* Athenæum.

**ALDISS, Brian Wilson;** writer; critic; *b* 18 Aug. 1925; *s* of Stanley and Elizabeth May Aldiss; *m* 1965, Margaret Manson; one *s* one *d*, and one *s* one *d* by previous marr. *Educ:* Framlingham Coll.; West Buckland School. Royal Signals, 1943-47; book-selling, 1947-56; writer, 1956-; Literary Editor, Oxford Mail, 1958-69. Pres., British Science Fiction Assoc., 1960-64. Editor, SF Horizons, 1964-. Chairman, Oxford Branch Conservation Soc., 1968-69. Observer Book Award for Science Fiction, 1956; Ditmar Award for Best Contemporary Writer of Science Fiction, 1969. *Publications:* The Brightfount Diaries, 1955; Space, Time and Nathaniel, 1957; Non-Stop, 1958; Canopy of Time, 1959; The Male Response, 1961; Hothouse, 1962 (Hugo Award, 1961); Best Fantasy Stories, 1962; The Airs of Earth, 1963; The Dark Light Years, 1964; Introducing SF, 1964; Greybeard, 1964; Best SF Stories of Brian W. Aldiss, 1965; Earthworks, 1965; The Saliva Tree, 1966 (Nebula Award, 1965); Cities and Stones: A Traveller's Jugoslavia, 1966; An Age, 1967; Report on Probability A, 1968; Farewell, Fantastic Venus!, 1968; Intangibles Inc. and other Stories, 1969; A Brian Aldiss Omnibus, 1969; Barefoot in the Head, 1969; The Hand-Reared Boy, 1970; The Shape of Further Things, 1970; The Moment of Eclipse, 1970. *Recreations:* travel, introspection. *Address:* Heath House, Southmoor, near Abingdon, Berks. *T:* Longworth 215.

**ALDOUS, Guy Travers,** QC 1956; *b* 30 Aug 1906; *s* of H. G. Aldous, Gedding Hall, Suffolk; *m* 1932, Elizabeth Angela Paul; four *s* one *d. Educ:* Harrow; Trinity College, Cambridge. Retired Bar, 1967. Director, Showerings Ltd, 1968-. MFH Suffolk, 1958-60, Essex and Suffolk, 1967-. *Recreation:* hunting. *Address:* 5 King's Bench Walk, Temple, EC4; Freston House, Suffolk. *T:* Woolverstone 243. *Club:* Royal Automobile.

**ALDREN TURNER, Dr J. W.;** *see* Turner.

**ALDRICH, Winthrop Williams;** US lawyer, banker, diplomat; retired; Hon. Trustee: Presbyterian Hospital, New York; Riverside Church, New York; Vice-President and Trustee, The Pilgrims of the United States; Member Advisory Council, School of International Affairs, Columbia University; retired as Member Visiting Committee Harvard Center for International Affairs; Hon. Bencher, Middle Temple, 1953; *b* Providence, Rhode Island, 2 Nov. 1885; *s* of Nelson Wilmarth Aldrich and Abby Pierce Chapman Greene; *m* 1916, Harriet, *d* of Charles B. Alexander, New York; one *s* four *d* (and one *s* decd). *Educ:* Harvard University (AB); Harvard Law School (JD). Admitted to New York State Bar, 1912; Mem. law firm Byrne, Cutcheon and Taylor, 1916-17; served as Lieut US Naval Reserve, 1917-18; Mem. law firm Murray, Aldrich & Webb, 1919; Pres. Equitable Trust Co., 1929; President, 1930-34, Chairman of Board of Directors, 1934-53, of the Chase National Bank; Ambassador to the Court of St James's, 1953-57. Honorary Degrees: LLD: Colgate University, 1937; North-eastern University, 1938; Washington and Jefferson College, 1939; Brown University, 1944; Lafayette Coll., 1945; Columbia Univ., 1946; Bryant Coll., 1947; Georgetown Univ., 1952; Harvard Univ., 1953; Queen's Univ., Belfast, 1955; Univ. of Liverpool, England, 1956; Univ. of Rhode Island, 1965; Tuskegee Inst., 1967; DBS New York Univ., 1950; DSc Stevens Inst. of Technology, 1957. *Decorations:* Medal for Merit, US; Knight Grand Cross of the Order of the British Empire (Hon. GBE); Associate KStJ; King's Medal for Service in the Cause of Freedom, GB; Comdr Légion d'Honneur, France; Comdr Order of Leopold, Grand Officer of Order of the Crown, Belgium; Grand Officer of the Order of Orange Nassau, Netherlands; Grand Officer of Oak Crown, Luxembourg; Knight Comdr of Order of Pius IX, Vatican. *Clubs:* St James', White's (London); Royal Yacht Squadron (Cowes); Royal and Ancient Golf (St Andrews); Metropolitan (Washington, DC); Hope (RI), Racquet, Harvard, Pilgrims of the US, Knickerbocker, Piping Rock, The Brook, Century, Links, New York Yacht (New York). *Address:* 960 Fifth Avenue, New York, NY 10021, USA.

**ALDRIDGE, Frederick Jesse;** Assistant Under-Secretary of State and Controller of Supply, Department of Health and Social Security, since Nov. 1968; *b* 13 Oct. 1915; *s* of late Jesse and Clara Amelia Aldridge; *m* 1940, Grace Hetty Palser; two *d. Educ:* Westminster City Sch. Clerical Off., Air Min., 1933; Exec. Off., Min. of Health, 1935; RAF, 1940-46; Acct-General's Div., Min. of Health: Asst Acct-Gen., 1956; Dep. Acct-Gen., 1958; Asst Sec. for Finance and Dep. Acct-Gen., 1964; Asst

Sec., Food, Health and Nutrition, also Civil Defence, 1966. *Recreation:* music. *Address:* 33 Court Road, SE25. *T:* 01-653 4939.

**ALDRIDGE, (Harold Edward) James;** author; *b* 10 July 1918; *s* of William Thomas Aldridge and Edith Quayle Aldridge; *m* 1942, Dina Mitchnik; two *s.* With Herald and Sun, Melbourne, 1937-38; Daily Sketch, and Sunday Dispatch, London, 1939; subsequently Australian Newspaper Service and North American Newspaper Alliance (war correspondent), Finland, Norway, Middle East, Greece, USSR, until 1945; also correspondent for Time and Life, Teheran, 1944. *Publications:* Signed With Their Honour; The Sea Eagle; Of Many Men; The Diplomat; The Hunter; Heroes of the Empty View; I Wish He Would Not Die; The Last Exile; Underwater Hunting for Inexperienced Englishmen; A Captive in the Land; The Statesman's Game; My Brother Tom; Cairo: Biography of a City; The Flying 19. *Recreations:* underwater, trout fishing, hunting, etc. *Address:* 21 Kersley Street, SW11. *Club:* British Sub-Aqua.

**ALDRIDGE, James;** *see* Aldridge, Harold Edward James.

**ALDRIDGE, John Arthur Malcolm,** RA 1963 (ARA 1954); painter; Assistant at The Slade School of Fine Art, 1949-67, Lecturer (part-time), 1967-70; *b* 26 July 1905; *s* of Major John Bartelott Aldridge, DSO, RHA, and Margaret Jessica (*née* Goddard); *m* 1st, 1940, Cecilia Lucie Leeds Brown (*née* Saunders) (marr. diss. 1970); no *c*; 2nd, 1970, Margareta Anna Maria Cameron (*née* Bajardi). *Educ:* Uppingham Sch.; Corpus Christi Coll., Oxford (MA). London, 1928-33; Essex, 1933-. Served, 1941-45, Army (N Africa and Italy, 1943-45). Member of 7 and 5 Soc.; Exhibitions at Leicester Galleries, 1933, 1936, 1940, 1947; exhibited Royal Acad. 1948 onwards. Pictures acquired by: Nat. Portrait Gallery; Royal Acad. of Arts, Tate Gallery, Min. of Works, Italian Min. of Education, Aberdeen, Leeds, Manchester, Newport, Northampton, British Council, Contemporary Art Society. *Publications:* Illustrations: The Life of the Dead (text by Laura Riding), 1933; Adam was a Ploughman (text by C. Henry Warren), 1948. *Recreation:* gardening. *Address:* The Place House, Great Bardfield, Essex. *T:* Great Bardfield 275.

**ALDRIN, Col Edwin E., Jr,** DFC (US) (with oak leaf cluster); Air Medal (with 2 oak leaf clusters), etc; NASA Astronaut; Lunar Module Pilot, Apollo 11 rocket flight to the Moon; Second man to walk on the Moon, 20 July 1969 (Neil Armstrong being the first); *b* Montclair, NJ, USA, 20 Jan. 1930; *s* of Col Edwin E. Aldrin, USAF retd, Brielle, NJ, and of late Marion Aldrin (*née* Moon); *m* 1954, Joan A., *d* of Michael Archer, Ho-Ho-Kus, NJ; two *s* one *d. Educ:* Montclair High Sch., Montclair, NJ (grad.); US Mil. Academy, West Point, NY (BSc); Mass Inst. of Technology (DSc in Astronautics). Received wings (USAF), 1952. Served in Korea (66 combat missions) with 51st Fighter Interceptor Wing. Aerial Gunnery Instr, Nellis Air Force Base, Nevada; attended Sqdn Officers Sch., Air Univ., Maxwell Air Force Base, Alabama; Aide to Dean of Faculty, USAF Academy; Flt Comdr with 36th Tactical Fighter Wing, Bitburg, Germany. Subseq. assigned to Gemini Target Office of Air Force Space Systems Div., Los Angeles, Calif; later transf. to USAF Field Office, Manned Spacecraft Center. One of 3rd group of astronauts named by NASA, Oct. 1963; served as back up pilot, Gemini 9 Mission and prime pilot, Gemini 12 Mission (launched into space, with James Lovell, 11 Nov. 1966), 4 day 59 revolution flight which brought Gemini Program to successful close; he established a new record for extravehicular activity and obtained first pictures taken from space of an eclipse of the sun; also made a rendezvous with the previously launched Agena; later assigned to 3rd manned Apollo flight. Mem., Soc. of Experimental Test Pilots; AFAIAA; Tau Beta Pi, Sigma Xi, Sigma Gamma Tau. Further honours include Presidential Medal of Freedom, NASA Exceptional Service Medal and NASA Group Achievement Award. Various hon. memberships and hon. doctorates. *Recreations:* athletics, scuba diving, etc. *Address:* c/o NASA, Manned Spacecraft Center, Houston, Texas 77058, USA.

**ALEMAYEHOU, Haddis;** Chevalier, Order of Menelik II, Ethiopia; Cordon of Star of Honour, Ethiopia; Minister of Planning and Development, Ethiopia, since 1966; *b* 17 Oct. 1913; *m* Kibebe Tsehai (*d* 1962). *Educ:* in Ethiopia; (night sch.) Amer. Univ., Washington. Taught in Ethiopia, 1932; served Italo-Ethiopian War as volunteer, Ethiopian Army, 1935 (POW in Italy, 1936-43). Dep. Dir in Press and Information Office, 1944; Dir Amer. Div. of Min. of Foreign Affairs, 1945; Consul in Jerusalem, 1945-47; Plen. Rep. of Ethiopia to World Telecomm. Conf., USA, and First Sec. to Ethiopian Legation in Washington, 1947; Ethiopian Rep. at Gen. Conf. of FAO of UN, 1948; Alternate Deleg. to 4th Sess. Gen. Ass. of UN, 1949, and Ethiopian Rep. to Interim Cttee, 1949-50; Dir Gen. at Min. of Foreign Affairs, and Ethiopian Deleg., 6th and 7th Assemblies, un, 1950-62; Vice-Min. of Foreign Affairs, 1952-56; Ambassador and Perm. Rep. to UN, 1956-60; Minister of State: Min. of Foreign Affairs, 1960, Min. of Education and Fine Arts, 1961; Ambassador of Ethiopia to the Court of St James's, 1961-65. Holds foreign decorations. *Address:* Ministry of Planning and Development, Addis Ababa, Ethiopia.

**ALEXANDER,** family name of **Earl Alexander of Tunis,** and of **Earl of Caledon.**

**ALEXANDER OF TUNIS,** 2nd Earl *cr* 1952; **Shane William Desmond Alexander;** Viscount, 1946; Baron Rideau, 1952; Lieutenant Irish Guards, retired, 1958; *b* 30 June 1935; *er s* of 1st Earl Alexander of Tunis, KG, PC, GCB, OM, GCMG, CSI, DSO, MC, and of Lady Margaret Diana Bingham (Countess Alexander of Tunis), GBE, DStJ, *yr d* of 5th Earl of Lucan, PC, GCVO, KBE, CB; *S* father, 1969. *Educ:* Ashbury Coll., Ottawa, Canada; Harrow. Liveryman, Mercers Company. *Heir:* *b* Hon. Brian James Alexander, *b* 31 July 1939. *Address:* Winkfield Lodge, Windsor Forest, Berks. *T:* Winkfield Row 2240.

**ALEXANDER, Viscount; Nicholas James Alexander;** *b* 6 May 1955; *s* and *heir* of 6th Earl of Caledon, *qv.*

**ALEXANDER, Alexander Sandor;** Managing Director and Chief Executive since 1967, and Chairman, Ross Group Ltd, since 1969 (Director, 1954); Director, Imperial Tobacco Group since 1969; *b* 21 Nov. 1916; *m* 1946, Margaret Irma; two *s* two *d. Educ:* Charles Univ., Prague. Part-time Member, Eastern Gas Bd, 1967-. *Recreations:* tennis, shooting, painting. *Address:* Westwick Hall, Westwick, Norwich. *T:* Swanton Abbot 664.

**ALEXANDER, Sir Charles G(undry),** 2nd Bt *cr* 1945; MA, AIMarE; Chairman, Alexander

Shipping Co. Ltd; Director: Houlder Bros and Co. Ltd; Ore Carriers Ltd; Houlder Line Ltd; Furness-Houlder Insurance Ltd; Leadenhall Transport Ltd; South American Stevedoring & Lighterage Co. Ltd; Hull, Blyth & Co. Ltd; South American Saint Line Ltd; AIR; Brooks & Walker Ltd; Trent Valve Co. Ltd; Bergl Australia Ltd; Ocean Gas Transport Ltd; Geo. Taylor & Son (Engineers) Ltd; *b* 5 May 1923; *s* of Sir Frank Alexander, 1st Bt, and Elsa Mary (*d* 1959), *d* of Sir Charles Collett, 1st Bt; *S* father 1959; *m* 1944, Mary Neale, *o c* of S. R. Richardson; one *s* one *d*. *Educ:* Bishop's Stortford College; St John's College, Cambridge. Served War as Lieut (E), RN, 1943-46. Mem. Court of Common Council, 1969; Alderman (Bridge Ward), 1970. *Recreation:* farming. *Heir:* *s* Richard Alexander, *b* 1 Sept. 1947. *Address:* 53 Leadenhall Street, EC3. *T:* 01-481 2020; Norsted Manor, Orpington, Kent. *T:* Knockholt 2288. *Club:* Royal Automobile.

**ALEXANDER of Ballochmyle, Sir Claud Hagart-,** 3rd Bt, *cr* 1886 of Ballochmyle; *b* 6 Jan. 1927; *s* of late Wilfred Archibald Alexander (2nd *s* of 2nd Bt) and Mary Prudence, *d* of late Guy Acheson; *S* grandfather, 1945; assumed additional surname of Hagart, 1949; *m* 1959, Hilda Etain, 2nd *d* of Miles Malcolm Acheson, Ganges, BC, Canada; two *s* two *d*. *Educ:* Sherborne; Corpus Christi Coll., Cambridge (BA 1948). *Heir:* *s* Claud Hagart-Alexander, *b* 5 Nov. 1963. *Address:* Kingencleugh House, Mauchline, Ayrshire. *Club:* New (Edinburgh).

**ALEXANDER, Conel Hugh O'Donel,** CMG 1970; CBE 1955 (OBE 1946); Government Communications Headquarters, Foreign Office, Cheltenham, since 1946; *b* Cork, 19 April 1909; *s* of late Prof. C. W. L. Alexander and late H. B. Alexander (*née* Bennett); *m* 1934, Enid Constance Crichton Neate; two *s*. *Educ:* King Edward's High Sch., Birmingham; King's Coll., Cambridge. 1st cl. hons Maths 1931. Schoolmaster, Winchester Coll., 1932-38; John Lewis Partnership, 1938-39 and 1945-46; Foreign Office, 1939-45; idc 1956. Chess Correspondent, Sunday Times, Evening News and Spectator; British Chess Champion, 1938 and 1956; British team, 1931-58; non-playing Captain, 1964-. *Publications:* Chess, 1937; Alekhine's Best Games of Chess, Vol. III, 1946; (with T. J. Beach) Learn Chess: a new way for all, 1963. *Recreations:* chess, bridge, croquet, philately, reading. *Address:* 28 King's Road, Cheltenham, GL52 6BG. *T:* Cheltenham 23647. *Club:* Savile.

**ALEXANDER, David;** Director: National and Commercial Banking Group Ltd, since 1968; The Royal Bank of Scotland Ltd (Vice-Chairman); Brown Brothers & Co. Ltd (Chairman); Life Association of Scotland Ltd; National Commercial & Glyns Ltd; William Bain & Co. Ltd; Beneficial Finance Corporation Ltd, Adelaide, Australia; *b* 26 April 1906; *s* of David Alexander and Helen Burns; *m* 1937, Jessie Paton McMillan; two *d*. *Educ:* The White House Sch., Brampton, Cumberland. Joined service of The National Bank of Scotland Ltd, 1923; Gen. Manager, 1955; Dir, 1958; National Commercial Bank of Scotland Ltd: Gen. Manager, 1959-67; Dir, 1959; Vice-Chm., 1968. *Recreations:* shooting, fishing, gardening. *Address:* Bridge Bank, Oxton, Lauder, Berwickshire. *T:* Oxton 255. *Club:* Caledonian.

**ALEXANDER, Sir Desmond William Lionel C.;** *see* Cable-Alexander.

**ALEXANDER, Sir Douglas (Hamilton),** 2nd Bt, *cr* 1921; *b* 6 June 1900; *e s* of Sir Douglas Alexander, 1st Bt, and Helen Hamilton (*d* 1923); *d* of George Hamilton Gillespie, Hamilton; *S* father, 1949. *Educ:* Appleby College; Phillips Exeter Academy; Princeton University. BA 1921. The Singer Manufacturing Company, 1922; Secretary of the Company, 1946; now retired. *Heir:* *b* Archibald Gillespie Alexander [*b* 29 March 1907; *m* 1932, Margery Isabel Griffith, Media, Pa, USA; two *s* one *d*]. *Address:* Palmers Hill, Stamford, Conn 06902, USA.

**ALEXANDER, Duncan Hubert David,** OBE 1959; TD; DL; Senior Partner, Stephenson & Alexander, Chartered Surveyors, Chartered Auctioneers and Estate Agents, Cardiff; *b* 15 June 1911; *e c* of Hubert G. and Edith Alexander; *m* 1937, Dorothy Evelyn, 3rd *d* of late Edmund L. Hann; three *d*. *Educ:* Sherborne School, Dorset; Trinity College, Cambridge (MA). Family business of Stephenson & Alexander, 1933- (except War Service, 1939-45). Mem., Cwmbran New Town Corporation, 1960. National Pres. of Chartered Auctioneers' and Estate Agents' Institute, 1964-65; Member, Housing Corporation, 1964-. DL 1958, High Sheriff 1960, Glamorgan. *Recreations:* golf, shooting, gardening. *Address:* Star House, Capel Llanilterne, Glamorgan. *T:* Pentyrch 332; (business) 5 High Street, Cardiff. *Clubs:* MCC, United Service; Cardiff and County (Cardiff).

**ALEXANDER, Henry Joachim,** Dr phil, Dr jur Breslau; Vice-President, Fédération Internationale des Communautés d'Enfants, Paris, since 1967 (Secrétaire Général Adjoint, 1960-67); Chairman, UK Section, since 1960; *b* 4 Jan. 1897; *s* of Bruno and Lisbeth Alexander-Katz; *m* 1925, Hilda (*née* Speyer); two *s*. *Educ:* Gymnasium Augustum Germany; Univs of Göttingen and Breslau. Member, Berlin Bar, 1925-37. Member, European Service of BBC, 1942-56. Chm., British Pestalozzi Children's Village Assoc., 1947-57; Chm. Pestalozzi Children's Village Trust, 1957-62 (Exec. Vice-Pres., 1962-63); Mem. Council, Pestalozzi Children's Village Foundation, Trogen, Switzerland, 1954-; Mem. Exec. Cttee, Lifeline, an Internat. Refugee Cttee, 1965-; Mem. Exec. Cttee, Residential Child Care Assoc., and Chm. of its Internat. Cttee, 1965-. FZS. *Publications:* International Trade Mark Law, 1935. *Recreations:* music, hill walking. *Address:* Hildings, Pett, Hastings, Sussex. *T:* Pett 3055.

**ALEXANDER, Maj.-Gen. Henry Templer,** CB 1961; CBE 1960 (OBE 1942); DSO 1954; *b* 17 May 1911; *s* of Maj.-Gen. H. L. Alexander, CB, CMG, DSO, and Mrs Dorothy Alexander; *m* 1938, Maribel, *d* of W. A. Sedgwick Rough; one *s* two *d*. *Educ:* Sedbergh School. Gazetted to Cameronians (Scottish Rifles), 1931; served 1st Cameronians (Scottish Rifles), 1931-38; Instructor Royal Military College, Sandhurst, 1938-39. Served War of 1939-45 (despatches, 1941 and 1943, OBE, DSO): saw service in NW Europe, N Africa, Italy, India and Burma, comdg 2nd Cameronians (Scottish Rifles) and serving with General Wingate. Chief Instructor, School of Combined Ops, 1946-48; comdg 1st Cameronians (Scottish Rifles), 1954-55; since War has also commanded 26 Gurkha Bde, 1955-57, and been a Senior Instructor, Staff College; Chief of Defence Staff, Ghana, 1960-61; Chief of Staff, Northern Command HQ, York, 1962-65, retd. Col, The Cameronians (Scottish Rifles), 1969. Hon. Sec., Middleton Hunt, 1970-. *Publication:* African Tightrope, 1965. *Recreations:* horse racing, hunting. *Address:* The Old Rectory, Brandsby, York. *Clubs:* White's, United Service.

**ALEXANDER, Rt. Hon. Sir James Ulick F. C.;** *see* Alexander, Rt Hon. Sir Ulick.

**ALEXANDER, (John) Lindsay,** MA; JP; Managing Director, Ocean Steam Ship Co. Ltd, since 1955; *b* 12 Sept. 1920; *e s* of Ernest Daniel Alexander and Florence Mary Mainsmith; *m* 1944, Maud Lilian, 2nd *d* of Oliver Ernest and Bridget Collard; two *s* one *d*. *Educ:* Alleyn's Sch.; Brasenose Coll., Oxford (Thomas Wall Schol.). Royal Engineers, 1940-45 (Capt.); served Middle East and Italy. Chm., Liverpool Port Employers' Assoc., 1964-67; Vice-Chm., Nat. Assoc. of Port Employers, 1965-69; Dir, Lloyds Bank, 1970-. MInstT 1968. JP Cheshire, 1965. *Recreations:* gardening, music, photography. *Address:* Baskervyle, Heswall, Cheshire. *T:* 051-342 3043.

**ALEXANDER, Prof. John Malcolm;** Professor of Applied Mechanics, Imperial College, London University, since 1969; *b* 14 Oct. 1921; *s* of Robert Henry Alexander and Gladys Irene Lightfoot Alexander (*née* Domville); *m* 1946, Margaret, *d* of F. A. Ingram; two *s*. *Educ:* Ipswich Sch.; City and Guilds Coll. (Imperial Coll., London Univ.). DSc (Eng) London; PhD; FCGI; FIMechE; FIProdE; FIM. Practical trng, Ransomes Sims & Jefferies Ltd, Ipswich, 1937-42; REME commn, 1942-47; res. in plasticity and applied mechanics, City and Guilds Coll., 1950-53; Head of Metal Deformation Section, Aluminium Labs Ltd, 1953-55; Head of Mech. Engrg Res. Labs and Nuclear Reactor Mechanical Design, English Electric, 1955-57; Reader in Plasticity, Univ. of London, 1957-63; Prof. of Engrg Plasticity, Univ. of London, 1963-69. Vice-Pres., Inst. of Metals, 1968-; Chm. Board of Studies in Civil and Mech. Engrg, Univ. of London, 1966-68; Gov., Reigate Grammar Sch., 1964-67; Engrg Adviser, Van Nostrand, 1964-; Mem. Editorial Board: Jl Strain Analysis, 1965-; Internat. Jl Mech. Sciences, 1968-. Joseph Bramah Medal, IMechE, 1970. *Publications:* Advanced Mechanics of Materials, Manufacturing Properties of Materials, 1963; papers to Royal Soc., IMechE, Iron and Steel Inst., Inst. Metals. *Recreations:* music, gardening, golf. *Address:* Mansard Cottage, Shere Road, West Horsley, Surrey. *T:* East Horsley 2260; 79 Princes Gate Mews, South Kensington, SW7. *Club:* Athenæum.

**ALEXANDER, Prof. Kenneth John Wilson,** BSc (Econ.); Professor of Economics and Head of Department of Economics, University of Strathclyde, since 1963; *b* Edinburgh, 14 March 1922; *o s* of late William Wilson Alexander; *m* 1949, Angela-May, *d* of late Capt. G. H. Lane, RN; one *s* four *d*. *Educ:* George Heriot's Sch., Edinburgh; Sch. of Economics, Dundee. Research Asst, Univ. of Leeds, 1949-51; Lectr, Univ. of Sheffield, 1951-56; Lectr, Univ. of Aberdeen, 1957-62. Umpire, N Derbyshire District Conciliation Bd, 1963; Mem. Adv. Cttee on University of the Air, 1965; Director: Fairfields (Glasgow) Ltd, 1966-68; Upper Clyde Shipbuilders Ltd, 1968-; Glasgow Chamber of Commerce, 1969-; Economic Consultant to Sec. of State for Scotland, 1968-; Chm., Cttee on Adult Educn in Scotland, 1970; Mem. Exec. Cttee, Scottish Council (Develt and Industry), 1968-; Mem., part-time, Scottish Transport Gp, 1969-. Governor, Newbattle Abbey Coll., 1967-. *Publications:* The Economist in Business, 1967; articles in Oxford Econ. Papers, Quarterly Jl of Econ., Scottish Jl of Pol. Econ., Economica, Yorkshire Bulletin Economics, and other jls. *Recreation:* Scottish antiquarianism. *Address:* Ardnacraggan, Callander, Perthshire. *T:* Callander 307.

**ALEXANDER, Lindsay;** *see* Alexander, J. L.

**ALEXANDER, Sir Norman (Stanley),** Kt 1966; CBE 1959; Vice-Chancellor, Ahmadu Bello University, Nigeria, 1961-66, retired; *b* 25 Oct. 1906; *s* of late Charles Monrath Alexander; *m* 1st, 1935, Frances Elizabeth Somerville, *d* of late K. S. Caldwell; one *s* two *d*; 2nd, 1959, Constance Lilian Helen, *d* of late H. V. Geary. *Educ:* Univ. of Auckland, NZ (MSc); Trinity Coll., Cambridge (PhD). Professor of Physics: Raffles Coll., Singapore, 1936-49; Univ. of Malaya, Singapore, 1949-52; University Coll., Ibadan, Nigeria, 1952-60. Hon. DSc Malaya, 1952; Hon. LLD Ahmadu Bello, 1965. Hon. Mem., Order of the Niger, 1965. *Recreation:* music. *Address:* 34 Belitha Villas, N1. *T:* 01-607 1218.

**ALEXANDER, Rear-Adm. Robert Love,** CB 1964; DSO 1943; DSC 1944; *b* 29 April 1913; *o s* of Captain R. L. Alexander, Edinburgh; *m* 1936, Margaret Elizabeth, *o d* of late George Conrad Spring, and Mrs Maurice House; one *s* four *d*. *Educ:* Merchiston Castle; Royal Naval College, Dartmouth. Joined RNC, 1927; Cadet HMS Repulse, 1930; Midshipman HMS Kent, 1931-33; Sub-Lieut, qualified in submarines, 1935. Served throughout War of 1939-45 in submarines; first command HMS H32, 1940; later commands: HMS Proteus, 1942; HMS Truculent, 1942-44; HMS Tuna, 1945. Second in command and in temp. command HMS Glory, Korean War, 1951-52; in command First Destroyer Squadron, 1957; Imperial Defence College, 1959; in command HMS Forth and 1st Submarine Squadron, 1960; Captain Submarines and Minesweepers, Mediterranean, and NATO Commander Submarines, Mediterranean, HMS Narvik, 1960-62. Vice Naval Deputy to the Supreme Allied Commander Europe, 1962-65. Lieut 1936; Comdr 1946; Capt. 1952; Rear-Adm. 1962; retd, 1965. *Recreation:* shooting. *Address:* Crofton Manor, Stubbington, Fareham, Hants. *T:* Stubbington 2014. *Clubs:* Army and Navy; Hampshire (Winchester).

**ALEXANDER, Stanley Walter,** MBE 1918; Proprietor and Editor, 1951-66, City Press, the City of London newspaper; continuing contributor; *b* 16 Nov. 1895; *s* of Walter Henry Alexander; *m* 1919, Doris Emily Kibble; two *s*. *Educ:* Roan School, Greenwich. Entered Lord Beaverbrook's office, 1910; Canadian War Records Office, 1915-17; Ministry of Information, 1918; Financial Editor, Daily Express, Sunday Express, Evening Standard, 1923-46; contested, as Free Trade candidate, City of London, 1945, North Ilford, 1950. One of founders with late Sir Ernest Benn of Soc. of Individualists; President: Free Trade League; Cobden Club. Liveryman, Worshipful Co. of Tallow Chandlers; Mem. Council, Kipling Soc.; a Governor, Cripplegate Foundn. *Publications:* author of the Hannibal pamphlets (on free trade, sound money, against the coercion of the people by the State, and on the economics of sea power), including The Kingdom of Bevin, The Price We Pay, Tariffs Mean War, 1933-44. *Recreation:* watching cricket. *Address:* 44 Speed House, Barbican, EC2. *Clubs:* Reform, City Livery.

**ALEXANDER, Rt. Hon. Sir Ulick,** PC 1952; GCB 1953 (KCB 1947); GCVO 1948 (KCVO 1937; CVO 1932; MVO 1925); CMG 1934; OBE 1919; an Extra Equerry to the Queen since 1952; Director: Tanganyika Concessions Ltd, 1957-63 (Chairman, 1952-57); The Benguela Railway Co., 1952-64; Union Minière du Haut Katanga, 1954-63; Banque Belge Ltd since 1957; *b* 10 Feb. 1889; *e s* of James Dalison and The Lady Emily Alexander, *e d* of 9th Earl of Cork; *m* 1947, Lady Mary Beatrice (*née*

Thynne), *d* of 5th Marquess of Bath, KG, PC, CB (she married 1st, 1927, 3rd Baron Nunburnholme, *qv*). *Educ:* Eton; Sandhurst. Joined Coldstream Guards, 1909; served European War in France (1914 star), Egypt and Palestine; and on expedition to Darfur, 1916 (medal and clasp); served in Egyptian Army, 1915-21 (Order of the Nile, 4th Class, despatches); Military Secretary, Egyptian Army, 1920-21; Political Secretary to the Governor-General of the Union of South Africa (Lord Athlone), 1923-25; Comptroller of the Household of the Duke and Duchess of Kent, 1928-36; Keeper of the Privy Purse and Extra Equerry to King Edward VIII, 1936; Financial Secretary to the King, 1936-37; Chief of Staff to Prince George during official visit to South Africa, 1934; Keeper of the Privy Purse, 1936-52; Extra Equerry to the King, 1937-52; Keeper of the Privy Purse and Treasurer to the King, 1941-52, to the Queen in 1952. Receiver-General to Duchy of Lancaster, 1936-52; a Trustee of the Ascot Authority, 1939-52. Sec. to Royal Victorian Order, 1942-52. Chairman Rhodesian Board of Standard Bank of South Africa, 1953-57. *Address:* 3 Cadogan Gardens, SW3. *T:* 01-730 6767. *Clubs:* White's, Guards.

**ALEXANDER, William Gemmell,** MBE 1945; Director-General, Royal Society for the Prevention of Accidents, since 1968; *b* 19 Aug. 1918; *s* of Harold Gemmell Alexander and Winifred Ada Alexander (*née* Stott); *m* 1945, Janet Rona Page Alexander (*née* Elias); four *s* one *d*. *Educ:* Tre Arddur Bay Sch.; Sedbergh Sch.; Oxford Univ. (MA). Served War of 1939-45 (despatches, war stars and clasps): Driver Mechanic, 2nd Lieut, Lieut, Capt., Maj.; served in France, S Africa, Eritrea, Egypt, Middle East, Sicily, Italy, Algeria, NW Europe. HM Overseas Civil Service, 1946-59: Gilbert and Ellice Is, 1946-51; Mauritius, 1951-55; Cyprus, 1955-59; Man., Cooperative Wholesale Soc., Agricultural Dept, 1960-63; Dir, Internat. Cooperative Alliance 1963-68. Associate Mem., BIM, 1963. *Recreations:* all sports and walking. *Address:* Sheepcote, North Park, Gerrards Cross, Bucks. *T:* Gerrards Cross 84040. *Club:* Royal Commonwealth Society.

**ALEXANDER, Sir William (Picken),** Kt 1961; LHD, PhD, MEd, MA, BSc, FBPsS; General Secretary, Association of Education Committees (England, Wales, Northern Ireland, Isle of Man and Channel Islands) since 1945; *b* 13 Dec. 1905; *y s* of Thomas and Joan Alexander; *m* 1949, Joan Mary, *d* of Robert and Margaret Williamson; two *s*. *Educ:* Paisley Grammar School; Glasgow Univ. Schoolmaster in Scotland, 1929-31; Asst Lectr in Education, Glasgow Univ., 1931-32; Rockefeller Research Fellow, 1932-33; Deputy Director of Education, Walthamstow, 1934-35; Director of Education, Margate, 1935-39, Sheffield, 1939-44. Joint Sec. to Management Panel of Burnham Committees and Associated Committees negotiating salaries of teachers. Mem., Nat. Council for Educn Technology, 1968-. *Publications:* Intelligence, Concrete and Abstract, 1935; The Educational Needs of Democracy, 1940; A Performance Scale for the Measurement of Technical Ability, 1947; A Parents' Guide to the Education Act, 1944, 1947; Education in England, 1953; Towards a new Education Act, 1969, etc. *Recreations:* golf and contract bridge. *Address:* 10 Queen Anne Street, W1. *T:* 01-580 4064. *Clubs:* National Liberal; Moor Park Golf (Herts).

**ALEXANDER, Colonel Hon. William Sigismund Patrick,** DSO 1917; Irish Guards; *b* 1895; *y s* of 4th Earl of Caledon; *m* 1934, Jane Hermione (*d* 1967), *o d* of late Comdr Bernard Buxton, RN; two *s* one *d*. *Educ:* Harrow; RMC Sandhurst. Served European War, 1914-19 (wounded, despatches, DSO); retired pay, 1936. Served War of 1939-45, Irish Guards and General Staff, 1939-46. DL, Essex, 1956-67. *Address:* Gobions House Farm, Mowsley, Nr Rugby, Warwickshire. *T:* Fleckney 358.

**ALEXANDER-SINCLAIR, John Alexis Clifford Cerda;** Inter Executive Vice-Chairman, Human Rights Trust (Founder and Chairman, 1969); Chairman, Art Registration Committee, since 1969; *b* 22 Feb. 1906; *s* of Col C. H. Alexander, Jacob's Horse, and Donna Lyta Alexander dei Marchesi della Cerda; *m* 1st, 1927, Baroness von Gottberg; one *d*; 2nd, 1933, Stella Tucker; one *s* one *d*; 3rd, 1950, Simonne de Rougemont (*née* Vion); 4th, 1965, Maureen Dover (*née* Wood); one step *s*. *Educ:* Charterhouse; Goettingen and Munich Univs. Entered HM Foreign Service, 1928; served in China as Vice-Consul and Consul (POW Shanghai, 1942); despatches (Admiralty) 1938; Liaison Free French Headquarters, Far East, 1941; served in Washington as 1st Sec.; seconded to UNRRA, London and Paris, 1944; CCG as Controller (Col) Economic Plans, 1945; 1st Sec. UK Delegation, UN, NY, 1946, 1947, 1948; Vice-Chm. UNICEF, 1946, 1947; Sec. Gen. UK Delegation Geneva Red Cross Conf., 1949; served UN, NY, 1950; Dir UN Office of High Comr for refugees, Geneva, 1951-52; transf. UN High Comr for Refugees Rep. (local rank Minister), Rome, 1953-55; European Dir (Paris), International Rescue Cttee, NY, 1957-58; UN Tech. Assistance Adviser to Min. of Finance, Govt of Thailand, Jan.-Feb. 1959, to Nat. Iranian Oil Co., Tehran, Iran, 1959-60; Head of Oil Industry Labour Re-deployment Unit, 1960; Manpower Expert, FAO (UN Special Fund) in the Rif, Morocco, 1961-62. Executive Sec. Liberal International, London, 1963-64; Hon. Campaign Dir, UK Cttee for Human Rights Year, 1967, 1968, 1969; Mem. Cttee, Anti-Slavery Soc., 1965-. Knight of Magistral Grace, British Assoc. of SMO Malta, 1957. Distinguished Service Award (Internat. Rescue Cttee), 1959. FRSA 1964. *Address:* 5 Aysgarth Road, Dulwich Village, SE21. *T:* 01-733 1666; John Alexander Chevalier de Sinclair, La Source de Marcoury, Chemin des Moulins, 06 Valbonne, France. *T:* Valbonne 67/0126. *Clubs:* Athenæum, Royal Automobile.

**ALEXANDROWICZ, Prof. Charles Henry,** LLD; Chairman and Director of Studies, Grotian Society; Visiting Fellow, Centre of International Studies, Cambridge, since 1969; *b* 13 Oct. 1902; *s* of Gen. Francis de Alexandrowicz; *m* 1945, Marguerite Gabrielle Drabble. *Educ:* Scottish Coll., Vienna; Jagellonian Univ., Cracow; Inns of Court Law Sch., London. Barrister-at-Law, Lincoln's Inn. Chm., London Bd of National Econ. Bank of Poland, 1941-46; Chm., European Central Inland Transport Org., 1946-48. Prof. of International Law, Univ. of Madras, Editor of Indian Year Book of International Affairs and Hon. Legal Adviser to Govt of India, 1951-61; Prof., Univ. of Sydney, 1961-68; Visiting Prof.: Sorbonne, 1963; Hague Acad. of Internat. Law, 1960, 1968; Institut des Hautes Etudes Internationales, Paris, 1969; Professorial Fellow, Ecole Pratique des Hautes Etudes, Sorbonne, 1969-70. Grotius Memorial Medal, 1961. *Publications:* International Economic Organisations, 1952; Constitutional Developments in India, 1957; World Economic Agencies - Law and Practice, 1962; History of the Law of Nations in the East Indies, 1967; The Afro-Asian World and the Law of Nations, 1969 (Hague Academy). Articles in BYIL, AJIL, etc. *Recreations:*

music, alpinism. *Address:* 8 Rochester Gardens, Croydon, Surrey. *T:* 01-686 2004.

**ALFORD, Sir Robert (Edmund),** KBE 1960; CMG 1951; *b* 10 Sept. 1904; 2nd *s* of late R. G. Alford and of Mrs Alford, 11 Oakley Gardens, SW3; *m* 1st, 1934, Teresa Margaret Riddell (*d* 1964); one *s*; 2nd, 1967, Eileen Mary Riddell. *Educ:* Winchester Coll.; University Coll., Oxford. Colonial Administrative Service, Nigeria, 1928; Sen. District Officer, 1946; Financial Sec., Zanzibar, 1947; Chief Secretary, 1952; Governor and C-in-C of St Helena, 1958-62. Served War of 1939-45 in RNVR, 1940-45. Brilliant Star of Zanzibar, 1958. *Address:* The Barn, Staple Cross, Sussex.

**ALFRED, Arnold Montague;** Director, British Printing Corporation, since 1969; *b* 21 March 1925; *s* of Reuben Alfred and Bessie Alfred (*née* Arbesfield); *m* 1947, Sheila Jacqueline Gold; three *s*. *Educ:* Central Foundation Boys' Sch.; Imperial Coll., London; London Sch. of Economics. Head of Economics Dept., Courtaulds Ltd, 1953-69; Director, CELON Div., Courtaulds Ltd, 1964-69. *Publications:* Discounted Cash Flow (jointly), 1965; Business Economics (jointly), 1968. Numerous articles in: Accountant, Textile Jl, Investment Analyst, etc. *Recreation:* active in Jewish community affairs. *Address:* 179 Ramsden Road, SW12. *T:* 01-673 6694.

**ALGAR, Claudius Randleson,** JP; barrister-at-law; Deputy Chairman Wiltshire Quarter Sessions since 1945; *b* 18 May 1900; *s* of Claudius G. Algar; *m* 1930, Constance, *d* of Edgar Tucker, Carmarthen; one *s*. *Educ:* Highgate School. Barrister-at-law, Inner Temple, 1925. Member of the Corporation of London, 1930-48. JP Wiltshire, 1941. *Address:* Rye Hill, Longbridge Deverill, Warminster, Wilts. *T:* Maiden Bradley 316.

**ALGIE, Hon. Sir Ronald (Macmillan),** Kt 1964; MP (N) for Remuera, New Zealand, 1943-66; Speaker, House of Representatives, 1961-66; *b* 22 Oct. 1888; *s* of John Alexander Algie and Agnes Macmillan Algie; *m* 1st, 1917, Helen Adair McMaster (*d* 1944); 2nd, 1947, Mary Joan Gray Stewart; one *s* one *d*. *Educ:* primary and secondary schools in NZ; Auckland University College. Barrister, 1913. Auckland University: Lectr in Law, 1913; Prof. of Law, 1919-37. Minister of Education, New Zealand, 1950-57. Hon. LLD Univ. of Auckland, 1968. *Publications:* articles in professional jls. *Recreation:* mountaineering (Mem. Alpine Club). *Address:* 261 Remuera Road, Remuera, Auckland, New Zealand. *T:* 50.274. *Club:* Northern (Auckland, NZ).

**ALGOMA, Archbishop of,** since 1955; **Most Rev. William Lockridge Wright,** DD, DCL, LLD; Metropolitan of Ontario, since 1955, and Acting Primate of the Anglican Church of Canada, since 1970; *b* 8 Sept. 1904; *s* of Rev. Canon J. de Pencier Wright and Lucy Lockridge; *m* 1936, Margaret Clare, BA; two *s* two *d*. *Educ:* Queen's University, Kingston, Ontario; Trinity College, Toronto. LTh 1927. Curate St George's, Toronto, 1926-28; Incumbent St James', Tweed, 1928-32; Curate Christ's Church Cathedral, Hamilton, 1932-36; Rector St George's Church, Toronto, 1936-40; Rector St Luke's Cathedral, Sault Ste Marie, 1940-44; Dean St Luke's Cathedral, 1941-44; Bishop of Algoma, 1944-55. DD (juris dig.) 1941; DCL (Bishop's University, Lennoxville), 1953; DD (*hc*): Wycliffe Coll., Toronto, 1956; Huron Coll., 1957; Montreal Diocesan Coll., 1958; LLD (*hc*) Laurentian University of Sudbury, Ont, 1964. *Address:* Box 637, Sault Ste Marie, Ontario, Canada.

**ALI, (Chaudri) Mohamad;** Politician, Pakistan; *b* Jullundur, India, 15 July 1905; *m*; four *s* one *d*. *Educ:* Punjab University, Lahore (MSc). Lecturer in Chemistry, Islamia College, Lahore, 1927-28; Indian Audit and Accounting Service, 1928; Accountant-Gen., Bahawalpur, 1932; Private Secretary to Finance Minister, Government of India, 1936; Under Secretary Finance Dept, 1938; Deputy Financial Adviser, 1939; Addtl Financial Adviser, Dept of Supply, 1943; Financial Adviser of War and Supply, 1945; Mem. Steering Cttee of Partition Council, 1947; Secretary-General, Govt of Pakistan, 1947; Minister of Finance, 1951. Alternate Deleg. to UN Security Council. 1948; Deleg. to Commonwealth Consultative Cttee, Colombo Plan Confs, 1951-; Head of Pakistan Delegation to Commonwealth Finance Ministers' Confs, 1952, 1953, 1954; Chairman Bd of Governors of International Monetary Fund and International Bank for Reconstruction and Development, 1953; Prime Minister, Pakistan, 1955-56, resigned, also as Minister of Defence. *Publication:* The Emergence of Pakistan, 1967. *Address:* 86-D/1, Gulberg III, Lahore, Pakistan.

**ALI, Salman Ahmad;** Sitari-i-Quaid-i-Azam (SQA) 1966; High Commissioner for Pakistan in the UK since Nov. 1969; *b* 29 Sept. 1913; *s* of Chaudri Mohammad Ali, Talukdar (Oudh); *m* 1940, Itrat Fatima Bilgrami; two *s*. *Educ:* Oxford Univ. In Pakistan Govt Service, 1941-; Min. of Commerce, later MoI and in broadcasting, 1947-49; Press Attaché, Pakistani High Commn, London, 1949-53; served in: Canada, Netherlands, Turkey, 1953-58; Counsellor: Moscow, 1958-61, Washington, 1961-63; Dir-Gen., Min. of Foreign Affairs, Pakistan, 1963-66; Ambassador, USSR, Nov. 1966-69. *Recreation:* tennis. *Address:* 56 Avenue Road, London, NW8. *T:* 01-235 2044.

**ALI, S. Warisa;** *see* Ameer Ali.

**ALICE, HRH Princess;** *see* Athlone, Countess of.

**ALIKHAN, Kunwer Hajee Ismaiel,** CIE 1944; OBE 1933; Nominated non-official Member of Legislative Assembly (Central), India, 1940-45; Deputy Government Whip, 1944; Chief Government Whip, 1945; Rais of Asrauli Estate, District Bulandshahr; *b* 18 Dec. 1897; *s* of Hajee Ibrahim Alikhan; *m* 1st, 1913, Shafi-un-Nisa Begam, *d* of Kunwer Abdul Shakur Khan of Dharampur Estate; 2nd, Gauhar Zaman, *d* of Khan Qutab Ahmad Khan of Basti Guzan (Jullundur); four *s* one *d* (and one *s* decd). *Educ:* Persian and Arabic at home; English, St Peter's College, Agra. Extensively toured Western and Eastern countries. MLC, United Provinces (under Montford Reforms), 1926; Pres. and Founder of several Public Institutions at Mussoorie, 1920-42; MLA (Central) from Meerut Div. Muhammad Rural Constituency, 1930-34; Chief Whip and Founder of United India Party in Central Assembly, 1931-34; Member several Standing and Select Committees; nominated non-official Member, Council of State, 1936-40; one of founders of National Agriculturist Party in UP to work Reforms of 1935; Vice-Pres. All India Muslim Rajput Conf. *Recreations:* travelling, reading and bridge. *Address:* Darulsalam, Civil Lines, Aligarh, Uttar Pradesh, India.

**ALISON, Sir Frederick (Black),** 5th Bt *cr* 1852; RN, retired; *b* 5 Aug. 1893; *s* of Sir Archibald Alison, 3rd Bt, and Georgina (*d* 1939), *y d* of late J. Bond Cabbell, Cromer Hall, Norfolk; *S* brother, 1967; *m* 1919, Lilian Phoebe, *d* of late

L. C. Phillips, S Africa; one *d. Educ:* RN Colleges, Osborne and Dartmouth. *Heir:* none. *Address:* Dormers, Camber, Rye, Sussex.

**ALISON, Michael James Hugh;** MP (C) Barkston Ash since 1964; Parliamentary Under-Secretary of State, Department of Health and Social Security, since 1970; *b* 27 June 1926; *m* 1958, Sylvia Mary Haigh; two *s* one *d. Educ:* Eton; Wadham Coll., Oxford. Coldstream Guards, 1944-48; Wadham Coll., Oxford, 1948-51; Lazard Bros & Co. Ltd, 1951-53; London Municipal Soc., 1954-58; Conservative Research Dept, 1958-64. *Address:* Flat 7, Sheridan Court, Barkston Gardens, SW5.

**ALIYU, Alhaji Makama of Bida,** CMG 1961; CBE 1959 (OBE 1958); CFR (Nigeria) 1964; ONO 1962; Minister of Finance, Northern Nigeria, from 1957; *b* 1906; *m*; four *s* two *d. Educ:* Koran Sch., Bida; Provincial Sch., Bida; Katsina Training College. Teacher and Headmaster, Niger Middle Sch., 1927-42; Councillor for Dist. Admin. and Educn, Bida Native Authority, 1942-51; Minister of Education, Northern Nigeria, 1952-57. Mem. Niger Prov. Develt Cttee, 1945-; MLC (Nigeria), 1947; Mem. all Constitutional Confs, London and Lagos, 1953-. Makama of Bida, 1938. Hon. LLD, Ahmadu Bello Univ., 1963. *Recreation:* formerly sports (holder 100 yds record, Northern Nigeria, for 30 years). *Heir: s* Abubakr Dan-Iya, *b* 2 Nov. 1938. *Address:* Ministry of Finance, PMB 2008, Kaduna, Northern Nigeria. *T:* (office) 2405, (house) 23201.

**ALKER, Thomas,** CBE 1958; LLM Liverpool (Hon.); Town Clerk of Liverpool and Legal and Parliamentary Officer to the Mersey Tunnel Joint Committee, 1947-67, retired; *b* 25 Aug. 1904; *m* 1930, Marion Eckersley Dove; four *d. Educ:* Wigan Grammar School; Manchester University. Asst Solicitor, Wigan, 1928-30; Sen. Asst Solicitor and Dep. Town Clerk, Kingston-upon-Hull, 1930-37; Town Clerk and Clerk of the Peace, Oldham, 1937-47. President Society of Town Clerks, 1954-55. Hon. Solicitor for England, National and Local Government Officers Association, 1957-61. *Recreations:* music, photography. *Address:* 278 Allerton Road, Liverpool 18. *T:* 051-724 2768. *Club:* National Liberal.

**ALLAM, Peter John;** The Director, Saltire Society, Gladstone's Land, Lawnmarket, Edinburgh, since 1968; *b* 17 June 1927; *er s* of Leslie Francis Allam and Annette Farquharson (*née* Lawson); *m* 1961, Pamela Mackie Haynes; two *d. Educ:* Royal High Sch., Edinburgh; Glasgow Sch. of Architecture. War service, 1944-48, Far East; commnd in Seaforth Highlanders, 1946. Architectural trng, 1948-53. Bahrain Petroleum Co., Engrg Div., 1954-55; Asst in private architectural practices, 1956-64; Principal, own practice, 1964-68. ARIBA 1964; Associate, RIAS, 1964. *Recreations:* study and practice of conservation, both architectural and natural; music; Rugby. *Address:* The Stick House, 43 Ravelston Dykes Road, Edinburgh EH4 3PA. *T:* 031-337 4022.

**ALLAN, (Charles) Lewis (Cuthbert),** MA, CEng, FICE, FIEE; Chairman, South of Scotland Electricity Board, since 1967 (Deputy Chairman., 1964-67); *b* 22 July 1911; *s* of Charles W. Allan, Edinburgh, and Isabella H. Young; *m* 1938, Kathleen Mary Robinson, Chesterfield, Derbyshire; one *s* three *d. Educ:* Merchiston Castle School, Edinburgh; Pembroke College, Cambridge (Mechanical Sciences Tripos). Bruce Peebles & Co. Ltd, Edinburgh, 1933-35; Balfour Beatty & Co. Ltd, 1935-38; Central Electricity Board, 1938-41; Ipswich Corp. Electric Supply and Transport Dept, 1941-44; North of Scotland Hydro-Electric Board, 1944-63 (Chief Electrical and Mechanical Engineer, 1954-63). *Publications:* articles in the electrical techincal press and for World Power Conference. *Recreations:* gardening, walking, fishing, piping, Church work. *Address:* Cathcart House, Inverlair Avenue, Glasgow S4. *T:* 041-637 7177. *Club:* Royal Scottish Automobile (Glasgow).

**ALLAN, Colin Faulds;** Chief Housing and Planning Inspector, Ministry of Housing and Local Government since 1967; *b* Newcastle upon Tyne, 1917; *s* of late Jack Stanley and Ruth Allan; *m* 1940, Aurea, 2nd *d* of Algernon Noble, Hexham; one *s* one *d. Educ:* Royal Grammar Sch., Newcastle upon Tyne; King's Coll. (Newcastle), Durham Univ. DipArch, ARIBA, DipTP (Distinction), MTPI. Capt., RA, 1940-45; served in Iraq, India, Burma (despatches). Chief Asst to Dr Thomas Sharp, Planning Consultant, 1945-47; Area Planning Officer, Cumberland and Staffs CC, 1947-57; joined Housing and Planning Inspectorate, 1957. *Recreations:* reading philosophy and poetry; bird-watching; eighteenth-century glass. *Address:* Orchard Lea Cottage, 25 Ganghill, Guildford, Surrey. *T:* Guildford 61528.

**ALLAN, Colin Hamilton,** CMG 1968; OBE 1959; British Resident Commissioner, New Hebrides, since 1966; *b* 23 Oct. 1921; *yr s* of late John Calder Allan, Cambridge, NZ; *m* 1955, Betty Dorothy, *e d* of late A. C. Evans, Brisbane, Australia; three *s. Educ:* Hamilton High Sch., NZ; Christchurch College, Canterbury Univ., NZ; Magdalene College, Cambridge. Military Service, NZ, 1942-44. Cadet, Colonial Admin. Service, British Solomon Is, 1945; District Comr, Western Solomons, 1946; District Comr, Malaita, 1950; Special Lands Comr, 1953; Sen. Asst Sec., Western Pacific High Commn, 1957; Asst Resident Comr, New Hebrides, 1959. Commandeur, l'Ordre Nationale du Mérite (France), 1966. *Publications:* Land Tenure in the British Solomon Islands Protectorate, 1958; papers on Colonial Administration. *Recreation:* malacology. *Address:* British Residency, Iririki, Vila, New Hebrides. *Club:* Royal Commonwealth Society.

**ALLAN, Professor Donald James;** Professor of Greek, University of Glasgow, since Oct. 1957; Dean of the Faculty of Arts, 1968-70; *b* 22 Dec. 1907; *s* of J. B. Allan and Ethel Allan (*née* Bullen). *Educ:* Christ's Hospital, Horsham; Christ Church, Oxford. BA 1930, MA 1933. Fellow and Tutor in Classics, Balliol College, 1931-47; Reader in Ancient Philosophy, Edinburgh Univ., 1948-57. Held temporary post at Foreign Office, 1940-45. Fellow of British Academy, 1955. Pres., Mind Assoc., 1964-65. *Publications:* Aristotle, de Caelo, 1936; Plato, Republic book I, 1940; The Philosophy of Aristotle, 1952; articles in classical and philosophical journals. *Address:* The University, Glasgow W2; 83 Bainton Road, Oxford.

**ALLAN, Sir Henry Ralph M. H.;** *see* Havelock-Allan.

**ALLAN, Captain Henry Samuel,** RD 1929; Commodore, Royal Naval Reserve and Peninsular and Oriental Steam Navigation Co. (retired); *b* 13 Dec. 1892; *o s* of John M. and Beatrice Allan, Saltcoats, Ayrshire, Scotland; *m* 1st, 1916, Ida Mary Poole, Stourbridge, Worcs; one *s*; 2nd, 1947, Isabel M. A. Fairweather, Cust, NZ. *Educ:* Ardrossan

Academy, Ayrshire, Scotland. Apprentice George Smith & Sons, City Line, Glasgow, 1908-13. Joined P & OSN Co., as Junior Officer, Dec. 1913. Served European War, in RN as Sub-Lieut RNR, 1914-19, War of 1939-45 as Comdr, Capt. and Actg Cdre, RNR, 1939-46 (despatches); Commodore of Convoys, Captain HMS Largs, Normandy and South of France landings, and HMS Artifex, British Pacific Fleet. Commander, P&OSN Co., 1946; Command P&O SS Strathaird, 1947-Dec. 1952; Commodore P&OSN Co., Dec. 1951-Dec. 1952 (retd). Order of St Stanislas, 3rd Class, 1915. *Address:* 136 North Road, Hythe, Kent. *T:* Hythe 66916.

**ALLAN, Commissioner Janet Laurie;** retired 1957; *b* 20 March 1892; *d* of Thomas Alexander Allan, chemist, Strathaven, Scotland. *Educ:* in Scotland. Entered Salvation Army Training Coll., 1911; commissioned as sergeant to the College, 1912; opened Salvation Army work in Castle Douglas, Scotland, 1913; returned to Training College as a Brigade Officer, 1915; Home Officer at Training Coll., 1918; with "Calypso" Party sailed to India (South Travancore, South India), 1921; returned to England, 1929, and appointed to slum and goodwill work in British Isles; returned to India; served in Travancore, Calcutta, and Eastern India; also Madras and Telegu country as Territorial Comdr; Territorial Comdr of Western India, 1951-54; Territorial Comdr of Southern India, 1954-57, Salvation Army. Leader Salvation Army Women's Social Work, Great Britain and Ireland, 1947; Comr, 1951. *Address:* Slavanka, 42 Belle Vue Road, Southbourne, Bournemouth, Hants BH6 3DS. *T:* Bournemouth 46256.

**ALLAN, John;** Sheriff-Substitute of Fife and Kinross at Kirkcaldy since 1966; *b* 14 Aug. 1927; *s* of Dr John Allan, Cathcart, Glasgow; *m* 1955, Janet Evelyne Geddes; two *s*. *Educ:* Glasgow Academy; Glasgow University. Admitted a Member of the Faculty of Advocates, 1953; Sheriff-Substitute of Inverness, Moray, Nairn and Ross and Cromarty at Stornoway and Lochmaddy, 1961-66. *Recreations:* sailing, fishing. *Address:* Sheriff's Chambers, Kirkcaldy, Fife.

**ALLAN, John Arthur Briscoe,** CMG 1965; Adviser on Prison Services, Ministry of Overseas Development, since 1964 (on loan to Kenya Government); *b* 30 Nov. 1911; Scottish; *er s* of Eng. Capt. (Retd) George Allan, New Malden; *m* 1935, Dorothy Mary; one *d*. *Educ:* Douai School. Served with HM Forces, 1940-48 (despatches); Lt-Col; Dep. Comr Prisons, 1958; Comr Prisons, HMOCS, Kenya, 1961-64. *Recreations:* the arts, golf, swimming. *Address:* c/o Ministry of Home Affairs, PO Box 30175, Nairobi, Kenya. *T:* Nairobi 24221. *Club:* Special Forces.

**ALLAN, John Gray;** Legal Adviser and Solicitor to the Crown Estate Commissioners since 1961; *b* 10 Nov. 1915; *s* of late John Allan, CB, FSA, FBA, LLD, and Ida Mary (*née* Law). *Educ:* Charterhouse; Oriel College, Oxford. Called to Bar, Middle Temple, 1940. War Service, 1940-46: The Black Watch, GSO2 (War Office and Allied Land Headquarters, Melbourne), 1942-46. Legal Branch, Min. of Agriculture, Fisheries and Food, 1946-57. Deputy Legal Adviser, Crown Estate Office, 1957. *Recreations:* golf, bridge. *Address:* 5 Rheidol Terrace, N1. *T:* 01-226 7616. *Clubs:* Boodles; Royal Mid-Surrey Golf.

**ALLAN, Captain John Steele,** CBE 1956; DL; company director; *b* 25 Dec. 1889; *s* of late Andrew Allan, JP, Chirnside, Berwickshire; *m* 1915, Margaret, *d* of late Joseph Mason, Dunbar; one *s*. *Educ:* Berwickshire High School, Duns. Served War of 1914-18: 1/4 KOSB, Gallipoli, Egypt, and Palestine, 1915-17; wounded in Palestine, 1917. Pres., Aberdeen Chamber of Commerce, 1937-38. Chairman: Technical Section, Paper Makers' Assoc., 1932-34, and 1939-50; North of Scotland Bank Ltd, 1942-50. Dep. Chm., White Fish Authority, 1954-56 (Chm., Scottish Cttee). Director: Home Flax Production, Min. of Supply, 1941-42; Aberdeen Steam Navigation Co. Ltd, 1940-64; (Chm., 1944-64); Burns & Laird Lines Ltd, 1955-64; Clydesdale Bank Ltd, 1950-67 (Dep. Chm., 1950-56); Wiggins Teape & Co. Ltd, 1931-51; Alex. Pirie & Sons Ltd, 1931-51; Dartford Paper Mills, 1931-51; Midland Bank Ltd, 1944-67; Midland Bank Executor and Trustee Co. Ltd, 1944-67. Rector's Assessor, Univ. of Aberdeen, 1949-50. FRIC 1926. DL Aberdeenshire, 1945. Chevalier 1st Class Royal Order of Vasa (Sweden), 1950. *Publication:* The Young Angler, 1949. *Recreation:* angling. *Address:* Kinord, Links Road, North Berwick. *T:* North Berwick 2868. *Club:* New (North Berwick).

**ALLAN, Lewis;** *see* Allan, C. L. C.

**ALLAN, Philip Bertram Murray,** MBE 1945; FSA; FRES; Editor-in-chief, The Journal of Criminal Law, since 1937; *b* 1884; *y s* of Alexander Allan, Bylands, and Frances Ann Hamilton-Beattie; *m* 1914, Elsie Kate, *d* of James Whitehead; one *s* two *d*. *Educ:* Charterhouse; Clare College, Cambridge (MA); Middlesex Hospital. Reader at Smith, Elder & Co., 1912; Asst Editor, Cornhill Magazine, 1912-14. Served European War (Infantry Captain), 1914-19 (despatches). Head of Philip Allan & Co., 1919-32. Founded The Police Journal at request of Home Office, 1928, and edited it until Dec. 1958; founded The Journal of Criminal Law, 1937. FSA 1921; FRES 1944. *Publications:* Book-Hunter at Home, 1920; Boy's Book of Verse, 1924; Book of Loneliness, 1926; Prison Breakers, 1927; Golden Ladies of Pampeluna, 1934; Trout Heresy, 1936; Moth-Hunter's Gossip, 1937; Talking of Moths, 1943; Moths and Memories, 1948; edited and annotated many other volumes. *Recreations:* formerly shooting and fishing; now reading and writing. *Address:* 4 Windhill, Bishop's Stortford, Herts.

**ALLAN, Robert Alexander,** DSO 1944; OBE 1942; Vice-Chairman, Longman Group of Companies; Director: Pearson/Longman; Bank of Scotland; Financial Times, and other companies; *b* 11 July 1914; *yr s* of late Claud A. Allan, VL, JP, Kilmahew Castle, Cardross, Dunbartonshire, and of Adeline Allan; *m* 1947, Maureen, *d* of late Harold Stuart-Clark, Singapore; one *s* one *d*. *Educ:* Harrow (Rothschild Schol.); Clare Coll., Cambridge (Mellon Fellow; ran cross-country for Cambridge, 1935, 1936); Yale University. Served War of 1939-45, mostly in Coastal Forces in Mediterranean, until 1946; Lieut RNVR July 1939, Commander, 1943; Senior Officer Inshore Squadron, 1944-45; Dep. Chief of Naval Information, Washington, 1945-46. Pres. Scottish Junior Unionists, 1948-51; contested (U) Dunbartonshire, 1945 and West Dunbartonshire, general election and bye-election, 1950; MP (C) South Paddington, 1951-66; Assistant Whip, 1953-55; PPS to the Prime Minister, 1955-58; Parly and Financial Sec., Admiralty, Jan. 1958-Jan. 1959; Parly Under-Sec., Foreign Office, 1959-60. A Treasurer, Conservative and Unionist Party Organization, 1960-65; Chm., Conservative Central Board of Finance, 1961-66. A Governor of Harrow School, 1968-; a Trustee and Governor, Lord Mayor Treloar Schools.

Commander Légion d'Honneur, 1943, Croix de Guerre, 1943 (France); Officer of Legion of Merit, 1944 (USA); despatches (5 times). *Publication:* The Open Door Policy in China, 1939. *Recreation:* sailing. *Address:* 5 Campden House Terrace, W8. *T:* 01-727 9515.

**ALLAN, Sir Robert George,** Kt, *cr* 1945; CIE 1936; MA Cantab; FRSE; late Indian Agricultural Service; *b* 7 Nov. 1879; *s* of Alexander Allan and Jemina Dalmahoy, Glenmore Estate, Coonoor, S. India, and 4 Hillside Crescent, Edinburgh; *m* 1911, Mabel Isabel Anderson; three *d. Educ:* Haileybury; Loretto School, Musselburgh; Pembroke College, Cambridge. Principal Agricultural College, Nagpur, CP, 1907; officiating Director of Agriculture, Central Provinces, 1926 and 1930; Director of Agriculture, United Provinces, 1931; retired 1935. Commissioner of Agriculture, Baroda State, India, 1935-44; Minister for Agriculture and Post-war Development, 1944-46, retired 1946. Services to cultivators of State-commemorated by endowment of a gold medal to be awarded annually under his name at Univ. of Bombay. *Publications:* An Outline of Indian Agriculture; chapters on Indian agriculture in Social Service in India (HMSO); numerous agricultural bulletins and papers. *Address:* 33 Drumsheugh Gardens, Edinburgh. *Club:* Caledonian United Service (Edinburgh).

**ALLAN, William Nimmo,** CMG 1948; MC 1917; FICE; engineering consultant; *b* 10 Nov. 1896; *s* of late Rev. W. G. Allan, MA, BD, Callander, Perthshire; *m* 1932, Mary Helen Burnett, *o d* of late Rev. T. Burnett Peter, MA, BD, Callander, Perthshire; two *s. Educ:* George Watson's Boys' College, Edinburgh. Served European War, 1914-19, 9th (Ser.) Bn The Gordon Highlanders, Captain (MC). BSC(Eng) Glasgow Univ., 1921. AMICE 1923, MICE 1944. Engineer with Kassala Cotton Co., Sudan, 1924; Irrigation Dept of Sudan Govt, 1927; Asst Director, 1941; Director, 1944; Irrigation Consultant to Sudan Govt, 1946-69; Consultant to FAO of UNO, Rome, 1959-67. *Address:* Garth, Oakley Close, East Grinstead, Sussex. *T:* East Grinstead 21403.

**ALLANSON-WINN,** family name of **Baron Headley.**

**ALLARD, General Jean Victor,** CC (Canada) 1968; CBE 1946; DSO 1943 (Bars 1944, 1945); ED 1946; CD 1958; Chief of Canadian Defence Staff, 1966-69; *b* Nicolet, PQ, 12 June 1913; *s* of late Ernest Allard and Victorine Trudel; *m* 1939, Simone, *d* of Gustave Piche, OBE; two *d. Educ:* St Laurent Coll., Montreal; St Jerome Coll., Kitchener, Ont. Joined Three Rivers Regt, 1933; Capt., 1938; Major, 1939; War of 1939-45: Co. of London Yeomanry, 1940-41; Canadian Army Staff Coll., Kingston, 1941-42 (Instructor, 1942); 5th Canadian Armoured Div.; second in command: Régt de la Chaudière; Royal 22e Regt, 1943 (Italy); Lt-Col 1944; CO Royal 22e Regt; Brig. 1945; Comd 6th Canadian Infantry Brigade, 1945 (Holland); Military Attaché Canadian Embassy, Moscow, 1945-48; Comd Eastern Quebec Area, 1948-50; idc 1951; Vice Quarter-Master Gen., Canada, 1952; Comdr, 25th Canadian Infantry Brigade Group, in Korea, 1953; Comdr 3rd Canadian Infantry Brigade, 1954; Comd Eastern Quebec Area, 1956; Maj.-Gen. 1958; Vice Chief of the General Staff, Canada, 1958; Comdr 4th Division, BAOR, 1961-63 (first Canadian to command a British Div.); Maj.-Gen. Survival, Ottawa, 1963; Lt-Gen. 1964; Chief of Operational Readiness, Canada, 1964-65; Comdr, Mobile Command, Canada, Oct. 1965-June 1966; General, 1966. Member: Royal Canadian Military Inst.; Royal 22e Regt Assoc.; La Régie du 22e; Royal Canadian Air Force Assoc.; Royal Canadian Naval Service Assoc.; Cercle Universitaire d'Ottawa; Chm. Bd of Governors, Ottawa Univ., 1966-69, Member Bd, 1969-. Hon. DSS Laval, 1958; Hon. LLD: Ottawa, 1959; St Thomas, 1966. FRSA. Bronze Lion (Netherlands), 1945; Légion d'Honneur and Croix de Guerre (France), 1945; Legion of Merit (US), 1954. Kt of Magistral Grace, Sovereign and Military Order of Malta, 1967. *Recreations:* golf, music, fishing, hunting. *Address:* Casa Belvedere, 251 Chemin du Sommet Bleu, Ste-Adèle, Québec; (office) 1015 Beaver Hall Hill, Suite 350, Montreal 128, Québec. *Clubs:* Quebec Garrison, Quebec Winter; Mount Royal, Canadian (Montreal); Laval-sur-le-Lac Golf.

**ALLASON, Lt-Col James Harry,** OBE 1953; MP (C) Hemel Hempstead since 1959; *b* 6 Sept. 1912; *s* of late Brigadier-General Walter Allason, DSO; *m* 1946, Nuala Elveen, *d* of late J. A. McArevey, Foxrock, Co. Dublin; two *s. Educ:* Haileybury; RMA, Woolwich. Commissioned RA, 1932; transferred 3rd DG, 1937; War Service India and Burma, 1939-44; retired 1953. Member Kensington Borough Council, 1956-65. Contested (C) Hackney Central, General Election, 1955. PPS to Sec. of State for War, 1960-64. *Recreations:* ski-ing, sailing. *Address:* 15 Cheyne Walk, SW1. *T:* 01-352 4782; Hillside Cottage, Markyate, Herts. *Clubs:* White's; Royal Yacht Squadron.

**ALLAUN, Frank;** MP (Lab), East Salford, since 1955; *b* 27 Feb. 1913; *s* of Harry and Hannah Allaun; *m* 1941, Lilian Ball; one *s* one *d. Educ:* Manchester Grammar Sch. BA (Com); ACA. Town Hall Correspondent, and later Industrial Correspondent, Manchester Evening News; Northern Industrial Correspondent; Daily Herald; Editor, Labour's Northern Voice, 1951-67. Mem., NUJ; formerly Mem. AEU and Shop Assistants' Union; National Chm. Labour Peace Fellowship; helped organise first Aldermaston march. Vice-Pres. Assoc. of Public Health Inspectors. PPS to the Secretary of State for the Colonies, Oct. 1964-March 1965, resigned. Chm., NW Group of Labour MPs; Mem., Labour Party National Executive, 1967-. *Publications:* Heartbreak Housing; Stop the H Bomb Race; Your Trade Union and You, etc; numerous broadcasts. *Recreations:* walking, camping, swimming, dancing. *Address:* 1 South Drive, Manchester 21. *T:* 061-881 7547.

**ALLCOCK, John Gladding Major,** CB 1964; *b* 20 July 1905; *o s* of Rev. William Gladding Allcock, MA (TCD), and Ada Allcock (*née* Hall); *m* 1936, Eileen, *d* of Dr Ll. A. Baiss, OBE, Swanage, Dorset; one *s* one *d. Educ:* St Paul's School; Jesus College, Cambridge. Classical Tripos Cl. II in Pts I and II, BA 1927; MA 1931. Asst Master: Exeter School, 1927-28; Liverpool College, 1928-35. HM Inspector of Schools, 1935. Awarded Commonwealth Fund Fellowship, 1939. War Service in Admiralty, 1939-44. Divisional Inspector (NW Div.), 1949, Chief Inspector 1959; HM Inspector of Schools, Department of Education and Science and Chief Inspector for Educational Developments, 1959-66, retired. *Recreations:* music, theatre, foreign travel. *Address:* Russet Cottage, Corfe Castle, Dorset. *T:* Corfe Castle 574. *Club:* English-Speaking Union.

**ALLCROFT, Sir Philip Magnus-;** *see* Magnus-Allcroft, Sir Philip.

**ALLDRITT, Walter,** JP; Regional Secretary, National Union of General and Municipal Workers, in Liverpool, North Wales, and Northern Ireland, since Oct. 1970; *b* 4 July 1918; *s* of late Henry and Bridget Alldritt; *m* 1945, Mary Teresa, *d* of W. H. McGuinness; four *s* one *d*. *Educ:* St Francis de Sales; Liverpool University (WEA). Served with HM Forces, 1939-46. Trade Union Officer. MP (Lab) Scotland Div. of Liverpool, June 1964-Oct. 1970. Member various public bodies. Councillor 1955, JP 1958, Liverpool. *Address:* 104 Longmeadow Road, Knowsley, Prescot, Lancs. *T:* 051-546 5703.

**ALLEGRO, John Marco;** author; *b* 17 Feb. 1923; *s* of late John Marco Allegro and Mabel Jessie (*née* Perry); *m* 1948, Joan Ruby Lawrence; one *s* one *d*. *Educ:* Wallington County Grammar Sch.; Univ. of Manchester. Royal Navy, 1941-46; Manchester Univ. 1947-52; BA 1st cl. Hons Oriental Studies, 1951; MA 1952; Bles Hebrew Prize, 1950; Scarborough Sen. Studentship, 1951-54; Leverhulme Research Award, 1958; Oxford Univ. (Magdalen), research in Hebrew dialects, 1952-53; University of Manchester: Lectureship in Comparative Semitic Philology and in Hebrew, 1954-62; Lectr in Old Testament and Intertestamental Studies, 1962-70. Brit. rep. on Internat. editing team for Dead Sea Scrolls, Jerusalem, 1953-; Adviser to Jordanian Govt on Dead Sea Scrolls, 1961-; Trustee and Hon. Sec. of Dead Sea Scrolls Fund, 1962-70. Organiser and leader of archaeological expedns to Jordan, 1959-. Popular lectr and broadcaster on archaeological subjects. TV films include: Dead Sea Scrolls, BBC, 1957; Search in the Kidron, BBC, 1963. *Publications:* The Dead Sea Scrolls (Pelican), 1956 (revised edn 1964); The People of the Dead Sea Scrolls, 1958; The Treasure of the Copper Scroll, 1960 (revised edn 1964); Search in the Desert, 1964; The Shapira Affair, 1964; Discoveries in the Judæan Desert, V, 1968; The Sacred Mushroom and the Cross, 1970; The End of a Road, 1970; articles in learned jls on Semitic philology. *Recreations:* ciné and still photography; sketching. *Address:* The Old Parsonage, St Mark's, Ballasalla, Isle of Man. *T:* Castletown 2345.

**ALLEN OF HURTWOOD, Lady, (Marjory),** FILA; *b* 10 May 1897; *d* of George and Sarah Shorey Gill; *m* 1921, Lord Allen of Hurtwood (*d* 1939); one *d*. *Educ:* Bedales School; Reading University. Landscape Architect; Vice-President Institute Landscape Architects, 1939-46; Hon. Vice-President ILA 1962; Governor Bedales School; Chairman Nursery School Assoc. of Great Britain, 1942-48 (Pres., 1948-51); Vice-Pres. British Assoc., 1948; Founder-President World Organisation Early Childhood Education; Member Central Advisory Council for Education (England), 1945-49; Chairman Advisory Council on Children's Entertainment Films, 1944-50; United Nations Children's Fund (Child Welfare in Europe and Middle East), 1950-51; Member Advisory Council Child Care (Home Office); Governor, British Film Institute, 1949-50; Chairman Coronation Planting Committee, 1937-39. Chairman: Lollard Adventure Playground Assoc., 1954-60; London Adventure Playground Association; Handicapped Adventure Playground Assoc. JP 1946. *Publications:* Gardens, 1953; Whose Children?, 1944; Adventure Playgrounds, 1954; The New Small Garden, 1956 (with Susan Jellicoe); Play Parks, 1960; Design for Play, 1962; New Playgrounds, 1964; Planning for Play, 1968. *Address:* 10 Selwood Terrace, SW7. *T:* 01-373 4144.

**ALLEN, Alfred Walter Henry,** CBE 1967; General Secretary, Union of Shop Distributive & Allied Workers, since 1962; a Crown Estate Commissioner since 1965; a Commissioner, Commission on Industrial Relations, since 1969; *b* Bristol, 7 July 1914; *m* 1940, Ruby Millicent Hounsell; one *s* one *d*. *Educ:* East Bristol Sch. Bristol Co-operative Society, 1931-40. RAF (Sergeant), 1940-45. Apptd Area Organiser, Nat. Union Distributive & Allied Workers, 1946; Nat. Officer, Union of Shop Distributive & Allied Workers, 1951. Member: Gen. Council of TUC; Brit. Productivity Council; Central Training Council; Government Cttee of Inquiry into Statutory Smallholdings, 1963; Council of the Manchester Business Sch.; NEDC; CIR, 1969-; Dir Industrial Training Service. *Recreations:* reading, theatre, gardening, cricket. *Address:* Oakley, 188 Wilmslow Road, Fallowfield, Manchester 14. *T:* 061-224 2804; 83 Manley Road, Sale, Cheshire. *T:* 061-973 3058.

**ALLEN, Arnold Millman;** Authority Personnel and Programmes Officer, UKAEA; *b* 30 Dec. 1924; *s* of Wilfrid Millman and Edith Muriel Allen; *m* 1947, Beatrice Mary Whitaker; three *s* one *d*. *Educ:* Hackney Downs Sec. Sch.; Peterhouse, Cambridge (Scholar). Entered HM Treasury, 1945; Private Sec. to Financial Secretary, 1951-52; Principal, HM Treasury, 1953-55; Private Sec. to Chm. of UKAEA (Lord Plowden), 1956-57; HM Treasury, 1958; Dir of Personnel and Admin., Development and Engineering Group (subseq. Reactor Group), UKAEA, 1959-63; Gen. Manager, British Waterways Bd, 1963-68, and Mem. of Bd 1965-68. *Address:* 34 Brookmans Avenue, Brookmans Park, Herts. *T:* Potters Bar 55986.

**ALLEN, Arthur Cecil;** retired as MP (Lab) Market Bosworth Division of Leicestershire (1945-Sept. 1959), and Opposition Whip (1951); *b* 10 Jan. 1887; *s* of Charles Allen; *m* 1914, Polly Mary Bradshaw; one *s* one *d*. *Educ:* Elementary School; Ruskin College. Parliamentary Private Sec. to Chancellor of Exchequer and to Minister of State for Economic Affairs, 1950-51, to Leader of the Opposition, 1955-59. *Recreation:* reading. *Address:* Nenehurst, Thrift Street, Higham Ferrers, Northants.

**ALLEN, Air Vice-Marshal Charles Edward Hamilton,** CB 1945; DFC 1918; *b* 1899; *s* of Edward Allen, Capetown, South Africa, and Louise Henrietta Arendse; *m* 1923, Marion, *d* of Walter Burke, Caythorpe, Lincs; one *s*. *Educ:* Sea Point Boys' High Sch., Cape Town; St Catharine's Coll., Cambridge. RFC 1917, as a cadet from S Africa; 2nd Lieut Sept. 1917. Permanent commission RAF 1919. Director-General of Technical Services, Air Ministry, 1952-54. Retired, 1954. Lately Liaison Officer, Aviation Division, Dunlop Rubber Company. *Address:* 49a Lillington Road, Leamington Spa, Warwicks.

**ALLEN, Charles Peter Selwyn,** CMG 1963; MVO 1954; OBE 1959; *b* New Zealand, 29 Sept. 1917; *yr s* of late John Allen; *m* 1947, Joan Audrey Cundall; no *c*. *Educ:* Wanganui Collegiate Sch., NZ; Gonville and Caius Coll., Cambridge. Administrative Service, Uganda, 1940-63; Dist Officer, 1940-52; Asst Chief Sec., 1952-55. Seconded to British Embassy Washington, 1955-56, Permanent Sec., 1955. Permanent Sec. to Prime Minister of Uganda (Sec. to Cabinet and Head of Uganda Civil Service), 1962-63; Local Dir (Zambia), The British South Africa Company, 1963-65; Anglo-American Corporation, Johannesburg, 1965-. *Address:* 2a Woolston Road, Westcliff, Johannesburg, South Africa. *T:* 41-3195. *Club:* Royal Commonwealth Society.

**ALLEN, Professor Clabon Walter;** Professor of Astronomy at University College, London University, since 1951; *b* 28 Dec. 1904; *s* of J. B. Allen and A. H. Allen; *m* 1937, Rose M. Smellie; five *s. Educ:* Perth High School; University of Western Australia. DSc (WA), 1935. Assistant at Commonwealth Observatory, Canberra, 1926-51. Solar Eclipse Expeditions, 1936, 1940, 1954, 1955 and 1959; Hackett Research Studentship, 1935-37. *Publications:* Astrophysical Quantities, 1955, rev. edn 1963; papers in Monthly Notices of Royal Astronomical Soc., Astro-physical Jl, Memoirs of Commonwealth Observatory, etc. *Address:* 43 Lawrence Gardens, Mill Hill, NW7. *T:* 01-959 4206.

**ALLEN, Sir Denis;** *see* Allen, Sir W. D.

**ALLEN, Derek Fortrose,** CB 1967; FBA 1963; Secretary of the British Academy, since 1969; *b* 29 May 1910; *s* of late Ernest Allen and late Elsie Mackenzie Allen (*née* Skues); *m* 1938, Godythe Winifred (*née* Gell); three *s. Educ:* Wellington Coll., Berkshire; Magdalen Coll., Oxford (MA); British School at Rome. British Museum, Assistant Keeper, Department of Coins and Medals, 1935-39; Min. of Shipping (later War Transport): Dept of Foreign Shipping Relations, 1940-46; marine insurance, 1946-47; UK Shipping Rep., Far East, 1947-52; Min. of Transport (later Min. of Aviation): Asst Sec., Vehicle Regulations, 1952-53, Road Traffic, 1953-58, Aerodrome Lands, 1958-59, Aviation General Policy, 1959-61; Under-Sec., Min. of Aviation, 1961-66, Civil Aviation Div., BoT, 1966-68. FSA 1947. President: Oxford Musical Club, 1932; British Numismatic Soc., 1959-63; Royal Numismatic Soc., 1966. Rhind Lectr, 1963-64. Chevalier, Ordre de Mérite Maritime, 1950. *Publications:* Major Ports of Malaya, 1951; British Museum Catalogue of Coins of Henry II, 1952; Minor Ports of Malaya, 1953; Origins of Coinage in Britain, a Reappraisal, 1961; Coins of the Coritani, 1962. Articles in Jl of Walpole Soc., Archaeologia, Proc. of Prehistoric Soc., Numismatic Chronicle, Brit. Numismatic Jl, Revue Numismatique, Jahrb. für Num. und Geldgeschichte, etc. *Recreations:* playing string quartets, numismatics. *Address:* Grenna House, Chilson, Oxon. *Clubs:* Athenæum, Savage; Hong Kong (Hong Kong).
*See also R. S. S. Allen and Prof. P. G. H. Gell.*

**ALLEN, Rev. Derek William;** Principal, St Stephen's House, Oxford, since 1962; *b* 2 Nov. 1925. *Educ:* Eastbourne College; Oriel College, Oxford. Curate of Christ the Saviour, Ealing, 1952-54. Tutor, 1954-56, Chaplain, 1956-60, St Stephen's House, Oxford. Asst Chaplain, Pembroke College, Oxford, 1955-60. Sub-Warden, King's College Hostel and Lecturer in Theology, King's College, London, 1960-62. *Publications:* Articles in: Theology, Church Quarterly Review, Internat. Rev. of Missions, Lambeth Essays on Unity. *Address:* St Stephen's House, Oxford. *T:* 55891.

**ALLEN, Prof. Deryck Norman de Garrs;** Professor of Applied Mathematics in the University of Sheffield since 1955; Pro-Vice-Chancellor, since 1966; *b* 22 April 1918; *s* of Leonard Lincoln Allen and Dorothy Allen (*née* Asplin). *Educ:* King Edward VII School, Sheffield; Christ Church, Oxford. Messrs Rolls Royce, 1940; Research Asst to Sir Richard Southwell, FRS, 1941; Lectr in Applied Mathematics at Imperial Coll., London, 1945; Visiting Prof. in Dept of Mechanical Engineering, Massachusetts Inst. of Technology, 1949; Reader in Applied Mathematics at Imperial Coll. in Univ. of London, 1950. *Publications:* Relaxation Methods, 1954 (US); papers on Applied Maths and Engineering Maths in: Proc. Royal Soc.; Philosophical Trans. of Royal Soc.; Quarterly Jl of Mechanics and Applied Maths; Jl of Instn of Civil Engineers. *Recreations:* travel, tennis. *Address:* Ranmoor House, Sheffield, Yorkshire. *T:* Sheffield 66645.

**ALLEN, Sir Donald (Richard),** Kt, 1954; OBE 1944; MC and Bar 1917; Clerk to Trustees of London Parochial Charities, 1930-65; *b* 31 Aug. 1894; *s* of Thomas Allen and Elizabeth (*née* Willett); *m* 1918, Irene Dora Andrews (*d* 1965); one *s* one *d. Educ:* William Morris School, Walthamstow. Served European War, RFA, 1914-18; Ministry of Health, 1919-25; Assistant Clerk, London Parochial Charities, 1925: Barrister-at-Law, Inner Temple, 1928; Mem. Cttee on Charitable Trusts, 1950-52. *Publication:* History City Parochial Foundation, 1951. *Address:* Sprigg's Court, Epping, Essex. *Club:* Reform.

**ALLEN, Sir Douglas (Albert Vivian),** KCB 1967 (CB 1963); Permanent Secretary, Treasury, since 1968; *b* 15 Dec. 1917; *s* of late Albert Allen; *m* 1941, Sybil Eileen Allegro; two *s* one *d. Educ:* Wallington County Gram. Sch.; London School of Economics. BSc (Econ.) First Class Hons, 1938. Entered Board of Trade, 1939; Royal Artillery, 1940-45; Cabinet Office, 1947; Treasury, 1948-58; Under-Secretary, Ministry of Health, 1958-60; Under-Secretary, Treasury 1960-62, Third Secretary, 1962-64; Dept of Economic Affairs: Dep. Under-Sec. of State, 1964-66; Second Permanent Under-Sec. of State, May-Oct. 1966; Permanent Under-Sec. of State, 1966-68. FBIM 1969. Hon. Fellow, LSE, 1969. *Recreations:* tennis, bridge, woodwork. *Address:* 9 Manor Way, South Croydon, Surrey. *Club:* Reform.

**ALLEN, Fergus Hamilton,** CB 1969; ScD, MA, MAI, FICE; a Civil Service Commissioner, and Scientific and Technological Adviser to the Civil Service Department, since 1969; *b* 3 Sept. 1921; *s* of Charles Winckworth Allen and Marjorie Helen, *d* of F. J. S. Budge; *m* 1947, Margaret Joan, *d* of Prof. M. J. Gorman; two *d. Educ:* Newtown Sch., Waterford; Trinity Coll., Dublin. ScD 1966. Asst Engineer, Sir Cyril Kirkpatrick and Partners, 1944-48; Engineer in charge, Thames Model Investigation, Port of London Authority, 1949-52; Asst Director, Hydraulics Research Station, DSIR, 1952-58; Dir of Hydraulics Research, DSIR, 1958-65; Chief Scientific Officer, Cabinet Office, 1965-69. Instn Civil Engrs: Telford Gold Medal, 1958; Mem. Council, 1962-. *Publications:* papers in technical journals; poems. *Address:* Dundrum, Church Lane, Wallingford, Berkshire. *T:* Wallingford 3012. *Club:* Athenæum.

**ALLEN, Frederick Martin Brice,** MD, FRCP; *b* 20 June 1898; *m* Anne Evelyn Maud, *d* of James Calvert, Lurgan. Formerly Hospital Officer, Ministry of Home Affairs, Northern Ireland, Member Northern Ireland Hospitals Authority and Northern Ireland Tuberculosis Authority; Fellow of Ulster Med. Society (President 1955-56); Member British Pædiatric Association (President, 1955-56), Hon. Member, The Canadian Pædiatric Society; formerly Chairman Northern Ireland Regional Committee of Inst. of Almoners; Member of: Ministry Advisory Committee on Child Guidance and Speech Therapy; Nuffield Regionalisation Council, and of Medical Planning Commission; Pres., Section Diseases of Children, British Medical Association, 1938 and Northern Ireland Branch, 1951; Pres. Queen's University Association. Surgeon Lieutenant-Comdr RNVR, retd. Emeritus

Professor of Child Health, Queen's University, Belfast, 1948-63; Pædiatrician, Royal Belfast Hospital for Sick Children, 1924-63; Physician in charge of Infants to Royal Maternity Hospital, Belfast, 1927-63. Dawson Williams Prize, 1963. *Publications:* Diseases of Children; Aids to Disease of Children; contributions to Medical Journals. *Recreation:* golf. *Address:* Lenaghmore, Cultra, Holywood, Co. Down. *T:* Holywood 3134.

**ALLEN, Rt. Rev. Geoffrey Francis,** DD; *b* 25 August 1902; 2nd *s* of late John Edward Taylor Allen, Holt House, Mobberley, Cheshire, and Mabel Saunders; *m* 1932, Madeline, *d* of Rev. R. J. S. Gill, Tadworth, Surrey. *Educ:* Rugby (Scholar); University College, Oxford (Scholar); Ripon Hall, Oxford (1st Class Philosophy, Politics, and Economics, 1924; 2nd Class Theology, 1926). Liverpool Intercollegiate Secretary of the Student Christian Movement, 1926; Curate of St Saviour's, Liverpool, 1927; Chaplain of Ripon Hall, Oxford, 1928; Fellow and Chaplain of Lincoln College, Oxford, 1930-35; Union Theological College, Canton, 1935; Deputy Provost, Birmingham Cathedral, 1941; Sec. National Christian Council of China and Chaplain to British Embassy, Chungking, 1942-44; Archdeacon of Birmingham, 1944-47; Bishop in Egypt, 1947-52; Principal of Ripon Hall, Oxford, 1952-59; Bishop of Derby, 1959-69. *Publications:* Tell John, 1932 (part author); He that Cometh, 1932; Christ the Victorious, 1935; The Courage to be Real, 1938; Law with Liberty, 1942; The Theology of Missions, 1943. Contributor, The Churches and Christian Unity (ed) R. J. W. Bevan), 1963. *Recreations:* the company of our friends, our garden. *Address:* The Knowle, Deddington, Oxford OX5 4TB. *T:* Deddington 225. *Clubs:* Athenæum, English-Speaking Union.

**ALLEN, Prof. George Cyril,** CBE 1958; FBA 1965; MCom, PhD; Emeritus Professor of Political Economy in the University of London; *b* Kenilworth, Warwickshire, 28 June 1900; *s* of late George Henry and late Elizabeth Allen; *m* 1929, Eleanora, *d* of late David Shanks, JP, Moseley, Birmingham. *Educ:* King Henry VIII School, Coventry; University of Birmingham. Lecturer in Economics at the Higher Commercial College, Nagoya, Japan, 1922-25; Research Fellow and Lecturer in the Faculty of Commerce, University of Birmingham, 1925-29; Professor of Economics and Commerce, University College, Hull, 1929-33; Brunner Professor of Economic Science, University of Liverpool, 1933-47; Prof. of Political Economy, Univ. of London, 1947-67; Temp. Asst Sec., Board of Trade, 1941-44. Member of Central Price Regulation Cttee, 1944-53; Temp. Counsellor, Foreign Office, Oct. 1945-April 1946. President of Economics Section, British Association, 1950; Mem. of Monopolies (and Restrictive Practices) Commn, 1950-62; Vice-Pres., Royal Economic Soc. Order of the Rising Sun (Third Class) (Japan). *Publications:* The Industrial Development of Birmingham and the Black Country, 1860-1927, 1929, repr. 1966; British Industries and their Organization, 1933 (rev. edn 1970); Japan: the Hungry Guest, 1938; Japanese Industry: Its Recent Development and Present Condition, 1939; (part-author) The Industrialization of Japan and Manchukuo, 1930-1940, 1940; A Short Economic History of Japan, 1946 (rev. edn 1962); (jt) Western Enterprise in Far Eastern Economic Development: China and Japan, 1954; (jt) Western Enterprise in Indonesia and Malaya, 1957; Japan's Economic Expansion, 1965; The Structure of Industry in Britain, 1961 (rev. edn 1970); Japan as a Market and Source of Supply, 1967; Monopoly and Restrictive Practices, 1968. *Recreations:* painting, gardening. *Address:* Quinces, Beech Close, Cobham, Surrey. *T:* Cobham 4744. *Club:* Reform.

**ALLEN, Rev. George Kendall,** MA; *b* 15 Feb. 1883; *s* of Rev. Dr Allen, sometime Headmaster, Cranleigh Sch.; *m* 1910, Mary Ellen Blake. *Educ:* Wellington College; Trinity College, Cambridge. Assistant Master, Christ's Hospital, 1906-24; Chaplain to the Forces, 1916-18; Headmaster The London Orphan School, Watford, 1924-30; Rector of Hampton Lovett and Elmley Lovett, 1930-36. *Publication:* Selections from Tennyson. *Recreations:* gardening, walking. *Address:* St Barnabas Homes, Dormans, Lingfield, Surrey.

**ALLEN, George Oswald Browning,** CBE 1962; TD 1945; *b* 31 July 1902; *s* of late Sir Walter M. Allen, KBE. *Educ:* Eton; Trinity College, Cambridge. GSO1, . War Office, 1943-45. Member of London Stock Exchange. Cricket: Eton XI, 1919-21; Cambridge Univ., 1922-23; represented England in 25 Test Matches; Captain *v* India, 1936, *v* Australia, 1936-37, *v* West Indies, 1948; Chm. Selection Cttee, 1955-61; Chm. MCC cricket sub cttee, 1956-63; President, MCC, 1963-64; Treasurer, 1964. Legion of Merit (USA). *Recreations:* cricket, golf. *Address:* 4 Grove End Road, NW8. *T:* 01-286 4601. *Club:* White's.

**ALLEN, Godfrey;** *see* Allen, W. G.

**ALLEN, Harold Major,** QC 1965; *b* 2 Oct 1911; *o s* of Arthur Major Allen, journalist, and Minnie Emily (*née* Camfield); *m* 1942, Joan Renée (*née* Boesche); one *d*. *Educ:* Merchant Taylors' School. Inland Revenue Dept, 1935-50. Called to Bar, Gray's Inn, 1949; commenced practice at Bar, 1950. *Recreations:* boats, walking and conversation. *Address:* 83 Hillway, Highgate, N6. *T:* 01-348 1159; 10 St Thomas Park, Lymington, Hants. *Club:* Royal Lymington Yacht.

**ALLEN, Professor Harry Cranbrook,** MC 1944; Commonwealth Fund Professor of American History, University College, London, 1955-71; Director, Institute of United States Studies, University of London, 1966-71; Professor of American Studies, University of East Anglia, from Oct. 1971; *b* 23 March 1917; *s* of Christopher Albert Allen and Margaret Enid (*née* Hebb); *m* 1947, Mary Kathleen Andrews; one *s* two *d*. *Educ:* Bedford School; Pembroke College, Oxford (Open Scholar; 1st cl. hons Modern History; MA). Elected Fellow, Commonwealth Fund of New York, 1939 (held Fellowship, Harvard Univ., Jan-Sept. 1946). Served War of 1939-45, with Hertfordshire and Dorsetshire Regts, in France and Germany (Major); comdt 43rd Division Educational Coll., June-Nov. 1945. fellow and Tutor in Modern History, Lincoln College, Oxford. 1946-55; Senior Research Fellow, Austr. Nat. Univ., Canberra, and Visiting Scholar, Univ. of California, Berkeley, 1953-54; Schouler Lecturer, The Johns Hopkins University, April 1956; American Studies Fellow, Commonwealth Fund of New York, 1957, at the University of Virginia; Vis. Mem., Inst. for Advanced Study, Princeton, NJ, 1959; Vis. Professor: Univ. of Rochester, New York, 1963; Univ. of Michigan, Ann Arbor, 1966. Member: Dartmouth Royal Naval College Review Cttee, 1958, Naval Education Adv. Cttee, 1960-66; Academic Planning Board, Univ. of Essex, 1962. *Publications:* Great Britain and the United States, 1955; Bush and Backwoods, 1959; The Anglo-American Relationship since 1783, 1960; The Anglo–American

Predicament, 1960; The United States of America, 1964. Joint Editor, British Essays in American History, 1957. *Recreation:* travel. *Address:* (till Oct. 1971) Northwold, Beechwood Avenue, Little Chalfont, Amersham, Bucks. *T:* Little Chalfont 2837; (from Oct. 1971) University of East Anglia, Earlham Hall, Norwich NOR 88C. *Club:* Athenæum.

**ALLEN, Brigadier Henry Isherwood,** CBE 1943; DSO 1917; Commander, Legion of Merit (USA), 1946; psc; *b* 18 Nov. 1887; *s* of late Rev. Dr George Cantrell Allen; *m* 1921, Rachel Alice Houssemayne, *d* of late Col Woodford George Du Boulay of Cheltenham and *widow* of Capt. William Haire Forster, Royal Irish Fusiliers; (*er s* killed in action, Normandy, 1944 and one *s* decd). *Educ:* Wellington College. Gazetted North Staffordshire Regt, 1908; served European War, France, 1915; Mesopotamia, 1916-19 (DSO, Bt. Majority, despatches five times); General Staff, War Office, 1921; transferred to Royal Corps of Signals; Student Staff Coll., Camberley, 1922-23; DAA and QMG 48th Div., 1924-25; GSO2, AHQ, India, 1926-27; Brigade Major 3rd (Jhelum) Infantry Brigade, 1927-29; Bt Lieut-Col 1927; Commandant School of Signals, Catterick, 1930-32; British Military Mission, Iraq Army, 1934-35; General Staff Officer, 1st Grade, War Office, 1936-38; retired pay, 1938; War Service, General Staff, 1939-45. *Address:* Beverley, Dunsfold, Surrey. *T:* Dunsfold 259.

**ALLEN, Jack,** DSc, LLD; FICE; FRSE; Professor of Engineering, Aberdeen University, 1946-69; *b* 19 Sept. 1905; *s* of late John and Phoebe Annie Allen, Heywood; *m* 1933, Elizabeth, *d* of late Samuel and Frances Hall, Heaton Park, Lancs. *Educ:* Elton Council School; Bury Grammar School; Manchester University, BSc (First Class Hons in Engineering) 1926; Vulcan Research Fellow, 1928-29; Asst Lecturer, 1929-35, Lecturer, 1935-43; DSc 1939; Senior Lecturer, 1943-46 (Manchester Univ.). Engaged on investigations of Severn Barrage Scheme, Liverpool Bay training walls, proposed Humber Bridge, improvement of rivers Mersey, Dee and Parrett, Scapa Flow causeways (all as Asst to Prof. A. H. Gibson); flood relief in river Great Ouse, harbour developments at Dundee and Aberdeen, spillways on hydro-electric schemes, etc. MICE 1946; FRSE 1951. James Forest Lecturer, Institution of Civil Engineers, 1947. Member of: Hydraulics Research Bd (DSIR), 1946-53, 1957-61, 1962-65; Hydraulics Research Station Steering Cttee, 1965-68; Research Advisory Council, British Transport Commn, 1957-64; Academic Advisory Council, Univs of St Andrews and Dundee, 1964-66. Hon. LLD Manchester, 1968 *Publications:* Scale Models in Hydraulic Engineering, 1947; many papers in Jl ICE, Phil. Mag., etc. *Address:* End Wing Flat, Holker Hall, Cark-in-Cartmel, Lancs.

**ALLEN, James Godfrey Colquhoun,** CMG 1956; Secretary, Nigeria Timber Association, 1961-69, retired; *b* 26 May 1904; *s* of Dr J. D. C. Allen and F. D. L. Allen (*née* Beckett), Bath; unmarried. *Educ:* Blundell's Sch.; Ecole Supérieure de Commerce, Lausanne; Univ. of Munich. Asst Master, Alleyn Court School, Westcliff-on-Sea, 1926. Cadet, Nigerian Administrative Service, 1926; Asst District Officer and District Officer, 1929-45; Resident, 1947; Senior Resident, 1953. Anglo-French Cameroons Boundary Commissioner, 1937-39; Nigerian Rep. with Free French, Douala, 1940; Chief Censor and Chief of Military Intelligence, Nigeria, 1940-41; W African Liaison Officer with Free French forces in Equatorial Africa, 1942-43; Political Sec. to Resident Minister, W Africa, 1943; Dep. Commissioner of the Colony, Lagos, 1946-52; Senior Resident, Rivers Province, Nigeria, 1953. Director of Administration, Nigerian Broadcasting Corporation, 1957-61. Coronation Medal, 1953. *Publications:* A Native Court Handbook, 1955; The Organisation and Procedure of Local Government Councils, 1956. *Recreations:* golf, music. *Address:* c/o Lloyds Bank Ltd, 23 Milsom Street, Bath, Somerset. *Club:* Royal Commonwealth Society.

**ALLEN, Prof. John F.,** FRS 1949; Professor of Natural Philosophy in the School of Physical Sciences, University of St Andrews, since 1947; *b* 6 May 1908; *s* of late Prof. Frank Allen, FRSC; *m* 1933, Elfriede Hiebert (marriage dissolved, 1951); one *s*. *Educ:* Public schools of Winnipeg, Canada. BA (University of Manitoba, 1928), MA (University of Toronto, 1930), PhD (University of Toronto, 1933). Bursar, Student and Fellow of National Research Council of Canada, 1930-33; Fellow of National Research Council of USA, 1933-35; Research Assistant, Royal Society Mond Laboratory, Cambridge, 1935-44; MA Cantab, 1936; Lecturer in Physics, Univ. of Cambridge and Fellow and Lecturer of St John's College, Cambridge, 1944-47. *Publications:* numerous scientific papers and articles, mainly on experimental low temperature physics. *Recreation:* golf. *Address:* 2 Shorehead, St Andrews, Fife. *T:* St Andrews 2717. *See also W. A. Allen.*

**ALLEN, Prof. Joseph Stanley;** (first) Professor and Head of Department of Town and Country Planning, University of Newcastle upon Tyne (formerly King's College, Durham University), 1946-63; Senior Partner, J. S. Allen, Architects & Town Planning Consultants; *b* 15 March 1898; *s* of late Harry Charles Allen and of Elizabeth S. Allen; *m* 1931, Guinevere Mary Aubrey Pugh; one *s* one *d*. *Educ:* Liverpool Collegiate School; Liverpool University. RIBA Athens Bursar, Post-graduate Study in USA; Lecturer in Architecture, Univ. of Liverpool, 1929; Head, Leeds School of Architecture, 1933-45. Vice-Chm. RIBA Bd of Architectural Education and Chm. Recognised Schools Cttee, 1943-45; Member of Council RIBA, 1943-50; Pres. Town Planning Institute, 1959 (Vice-Pres. 1957-59). Architect and Town Planning Consultant for hospitals, churches, neighbourhood units, university and industrial undertakings. Consultant, Snowdonia National Park; Member, North of England Regional Advisory Committee, Forestry Commission; Member Diocesan Committees for Care of Churches: Ripon, Newcastle and York Dioceses. *Publications:* (with R. H. Mattocks): Report and Plan for West Cumberland; Report and Plan for Accrington (Industry and Prudence), 1950. Founder-Editor, Planning Outlook (founded 1948); contrib. to professional journals on architecture and town and country planning. *Recreations:* motoring and walking in the countryside; music. *Address:* Bleach Green Farm, Ovingham, Northumberland.

**ALLEN, Sir Kenneth;** *see* Allen, Sir William Kenneth G.

**ALLEN, Prof. Kenneth William;** Professor of Nuclear Structure, and Fellow of Balliol College, University of Oxford, since Oct. 1963; *b* 17 Nov. 1923; *m* 1947, Josephine E. Boreham; two *s*. *Educ:* Ilford County High School; London University (Drapers' Scholar); St Catharine's College, Cambridge University. PhD (Cantab) 1947. Physics Division, Atomic Energy of Canada, Chalk River, 1947-51;

Leverhulme Research Fellow and Lecturer, Liverpool University, 1951-54; Superintendent, later (1958) Senior Superintendent, Nuclear Research Division, Atomic Weapons Research Establishment, 1954-63. *Publications:* contribs to Proc. Physical Soc., Physical Review, Review of Scientific Instruments, Nature, etc. *Recreations:* tennis, chess. *Address:* Ridgeway, Lincombe Lane, Boars Hill, Oxford.

**ALLEN, Mark Echalaz,** CMG 1966; CVO 1961; United Kingdom Representative on Economic and Social Council of the United Nations, since 1968; *b* 19 Mar. 1917; *s* of late Lancelot John Allen and of Eleanor Mary (*née* Carlisle); *m* 1948, Elizabeth Joan, *d* of late Richard Hope Bowdler and Elsie (*née* Bryning); two *s* one *d* (and one *d* decd). *Educ:* Charterhouse; Christ Church, Oxford (MA). Appointed Asst Principal, Dominions Office, 1939. Served War of 1939-45 in Western Desert, Sicily and Italy. Office of UK Representative to Eire, 1945; First Sec., Office of UK Deputy High Comr, Bombay, 1948; First Secretary, UK Permanent Delegation to United Nations, New York, 1953; Dep. High Comr for the UK in Madras, S India, 1960; Counsellor (Political), Office of British High Commissioner to India, New Delhi, 1961; Diplomatic Service Inspector, 1964-66; Dep. Chief of Administration, DSAO, 1966-68. *Address:* 830 Park Avenue, New York, NY 10021, USA. *Club:* Oxford and Cambridge University.

**ALLEN, Milton Pentonville,** OBE 1964; Acting Governor, St Kitts/Nevis/Anguilla, since July 1969; *b* St Kitts, WI, 22 June 1888; *m* 1937, Annie Matilda (*née* Locker), MBE; no *c. Educ:* (primary) Palmetto Point, St Kitts; then (for tailoring) studied at David Mitchell designing and cutting Academy, NY (diploma). Worked at trade of tailor until the Depression, 1929. Nominated Member, 1957, Speaker, 1962, House of Assembly, St Kitts. Patron: St Kitts Cricket Assoc.; St Kitts Net Ball Assoc.; Boy Scouts Assoc. *Publication:* Chosen Poems (a collection), (New York) 1945. *Recreations:* reading, music, gardening; interested in Arts Festival of Basseterre (one of his chosen poems set to music for a choir, by Dr Leon Forrester, FRCO). *Address:* Government House, Basseterre, St Kitts, West Indies.

**ALLEN, Dr Norman Percy,** CB 1966; FRS 1956; DSc; Deputy Director (A), National Physical Laboratory, 1966-67; *b* 5 June 1903; *s* of Sidney Edward Allen and Emily Eliza Davies; *m* 1929, Olive Gwendolen Williams; two *s* one *d. Educ:* Grammar School, Burton-upon-Trent; Sheffield University. BMet (Sheffield), 1923; MMet (Sheffield), 1924; DSc (Birmingham), 1934. British Non-Ferrous Metals Research Assoc., 1923-28; Lecturer in Metallurgy, Univ. of Birmingham, 1928-35; Senior Research Metallurgist, Research and Development Dept, Mond Nickel Co. Ltd, 1935-44; Supt, Metallurgy Div., National Physical Laboratory, 1944-66. President: Birmingham Metallurgical Soc., 1935-36; Inst. of Metallurgists, 1961; Chm., Inter-Services Metallurgical Council, 1963-69. Osmond Medal Société Française de Métallurgie, 1963; Bessemer Medal Iron and Steel Institute, 1965; Platinum Medal, Inst. of Metals, 1967; Luigi Losana Medal, Associazione Italiana di Metallurgia, 1968. Hon. Dr of Technical Science, Technical Univ. of Prague, 1964; Hon. DMet Sheffield, 1966. *Publications:* papers in Jl of Iron and Steel Institute and Institute of Metals; Hatfield Memorial Lecture (1958). *Address:* 10 Firlands, off Ellesmere Road, Weybridge, Surrey. *T:* Weybridge 49944.

**ALLEN, Prof. Percival;** Professor of Geology, University of Reading, since 1952; Director, Sedimentology Research Laboratory since 1965; *b* 15 March 1917; British; *m* 1941, Frances Margaret Hepworth; three *s* one *d. Educ:* Brede Council Sch.; Rye Grammar School; University of Reading. BSc 1939, PhD 1943, Reading; MA St Catharine's College, Cambridge, 1946. Univ. Demonstrator, 1942-45, Univ. Asst Lectr, 1945-46, Reading; University Demonstrator, 1946-47, Univ. Lectr, 1947-52, Cambridge; Dean of Science Faculty, Reading, 1963-66. Vis. Prof., Univ. of Kuwait, 1970. Served War of 1939-45. In Royal Air Force, 1941-42. Sedgwick Prize, Univ. of Cambridge, 1952; Daniel Pidgeon Fund, Geological Soc. of London, 1944; Leverhulme Fellowships Research Grant, 1948, 1949. Hon. Member, American Soc. of Economic Paleontologists and Mineralogists, 1949 (Keynote Speaker, SEPM Meeting, Toronto, 1964); Mem. Council, Geological Soc. of London, 1964-67. UK Editor, Sedimentology, 1961-67. Chm., Org. Cttee, VII Internat. Sedimentological Congress, 1967; Sec.-Gen., Internat. Assoc. Sedimentologists, 1967-; Algerian Sahara Glacials Expedn, 1970. *Publications:* papers in various scientific journals. *Recreations:* chess, natural history. *Address:* 6 St Barnabas Road, Emmer Green, Reading RG4 8RA.

**ALLEN, Sir Peter (Christopher),** Kt 1967; MA, BSc (Oxon); Chairman, Imperial Chemical Industries Ltd, since 1968 (Director, 1951-63, a Deputy Chairman, 1963-68); Director, Bank of Montreal, since 1968; *b* Ashtead, Surrey, 8 Sept. 1905; *s* of late Sir Ernest King Allen and Florence Mary (*née* Gellatly); *m* 1st, 1931, Violet Sylvester Wingate-Saul (*d* 1951); two *d*; 2nd, 1952, Consuelo Maria Linares Rivas. *Educ:* Harrow; Trinity Coll., Oxford (Hon. Fellow 1969). Joined Brunner, Mond & Co., Ltd, 1928; Chm., Plastics Div. of ICI Ltd, 1948-51 (Man. Dir, 1942-48); Dir, British Nylon Spinners Ltd, 1954-58; Pres. and Chm., ICI of Canada Ltd, 1961-68; Pres., Canadian Industries Ltd, 1959-62, Chm., 1962-68; Director, Royal Trust Co., Canada, 1961-64. Vice-President: Inst. of Manpower Studies, 1968-; Manufacturing Chemists' Assoc., USA, 1961-62 (Dir, 1959-62); Mem. and Vice-Chairman: Council of Assoc. of Brit. Chem. Manufacturers, 1963-65; Bd of Dirs, Société de Chimie Industrielle, 1968; President: Plastics Inst., 1950-52; Brit. Plastics Fedn, 1963-65; Univ. of Manchester Inst. of Sci. and Technology, 1968-; Vice-Pres., British Assoc. for Commercial and Industrial Educn, 1969-; Mem. of Council: Canadian Chamber of Commerce in Gt Brit. Inc., 1964-68 (Associate Mem., 1963-68); CBI, 1965-67. Chm., BNEC (Mem., 1964-67; Chm., Cttee for Exports to Canada, 1964-67). Governor, Nat. Coll. of Rubber Technology, 1964-68; Member: Court, British Shippers' Council, 1968-; Export Council for Europe, 1962-65; Overseas Development Inst. Council, 1963-64; Iron and Steel Holding and Realisation Agency, 1963-67; NEDC for Chemical Industry, 1964-67; Commonwealth Export Council, 1964-67; Industrial Policy Group, 1969-. FBIM 1968-; FInstD 1969-. Hon. Member: Chemical Industries Assoc., 1968- (Pres., 1965-67; Mem. Council, 1967-68); ICE, 1968-; Canadian Chemical Producers' Assoc., 1962-. Trustee: Civic Trust; British Industry Roads Campaign, 1970-. Governor, Harrow School, 1969-. *Publications:* The Railways of the Isle of Wight, 1928; Locomotives of Many Lands, 1954; On the Old Lines, 1957; (with P. B. Whitehouse) Narrow Gauge Railways of Europe, 1959; (with R. A. Wheeler) Steam on the Sierra, 1960; (with P. B. Whitehouse) Round the World on the Narrow Gauge, 1966;

(with Consuelo Allen) The Curve of Earth's Shoulder, 1966; (with A. B. MacLeod) Rails in the Isle of Wight, 1967; Famous Fairways, 1968. *Recreations:* foreign travel, railways, golf, writing, philately. *Address:* c/o Imperial Chemical Industries Ltd, IC House, Millbank, SW1; Telham Hill House, near Battle, Sussex. *Clubs:* Junior Carlton; Mount Royal (Montreal); Royal and Ancient, Royal Cinque Ports, Rye, Royal St George's, Oxford and Cambridge Golfing Soc.; Augusta National (Ga, USA); Pine Valley (NJ, USA).

**ALLEN, Sir Philip,** GCB 1970 (KCB 1964; CB 1954); Permanent Under-Secretary of State, Home Office, since 1966; *b* 8 July 1912; *yr s* of late Arthur Allen and Louie Tipper, Sheffield; *m* 1938, Marjorie Brenda Coe. *Educ:* King Edward VII Sch., Sheffield; Queens' Coll., Cambridge. Entered Home Office, 1934; Offices of War Cabinet, 1943-44; Commonwealth Fellowship in USA, 1948-49; Deputy Chm. of Prison Commn for England and Wales, 1950-52; Asst Under Sec. of State, Home Office, 1952-55; Deputy Sec., Ministry of Housing and Local Government, 1955-60; Deputy Under Secretary of State, Home Office, 1960-62; Second Secretary, HM Treasury, 1963-66. *Address:* Holly Lodge, Englefield Green, Surrey. *T:* Egham 2291. *Clubs:* Brooks's, Oxford and Cambridge.

**ALLEN, Raymond Seaforth Stirling,** TD; *b* 30 May 1905; *s* of late Ernest Allen, Solicitor, and late Elsie Mackenzie Allen (*née* Skues); unmarried. *Educ:* Wellington College (Scholar); Queens' College, Cambridge (Scholar). MA, LLB. Admitted Solicitor (Hons), 1931; with E. F. Turner & Sons, Solicitors, 1931-39 and 1955-68. Trustee, Northern Arts and Sciences Foundation, 1965-68. Served Westminster Dragoons (TA) at home, War Office General Staff, Combined Chiefs of Staff, Washington, DC (1939-45); Lieutenant-Colonel 1943; Legion of Merit (US Army), 1945. Joined Legal Department of National Coal Board on its formation, 1946, Legal Adviser and Solicitor to the Board, 1948-53. Institute of International Air Law, McGill University, Montreal, 1953-54. *Publication:* The Legal Relationships of a Nationalised Industry, 1954. *Recreations:* reading, travel, the arts. *Address:* 46 Redhill Drive, Brighton BN1 5FL. *Club:* Royal Automobile.

*See also D. F. Allen.*

**ALLEN, Sir Richard (Hugh Sedley),** KCMG 1960 (CMG 1953); retired; *b* 3 Feb. 1903; *s* of late Sir Hugh Allen, GCVO; *m* 1945, Juliet Home Thomson; one *s* one step *s. Educ:* Royal Naval Colleges, Osborne and Dartmouth; New College, Oxford. Junior Asst Sec., Govt of Palestine, 1925-27. Entered Foreign Office and Diplomatic Service, 1927; Second Sec., 1932; First Sec., 1939; Counsellor, 1946; Minister, British Embassy, Buenos Aires, 1950-54; Minister to Guatemala, 1954-56; British Ambassador to Burma, 1956-62. *Publications:* Malaysia: Prospect and Retrospect, 1968; A Short Introduction to the History and Politics of Southeast Asia, 1969. *Recreation:* sailing. *Address:* 27 Wellington Square, SW3. *T:* 01-730 1597. *Clubs:* St James', Oriental, Royal Automobile.

**ALLEN, Maj.-Gen. Robert Hall,** CB 1942; *b* 11 June 1886; *s* of R. Allen, LLD, Barrister-at-Law; *m* 1916, Magaret Lawrence, *d* of Maj.-Gen. Sir David Mercer, KCB; one *d. Educ:* Charterhouse; RMA, Woolwich. Retired pay, 1942. *Recreation:* solving simple chess problems. *Address:* The Pound House, Chinnor, Oxon.

**ALLEN, Sir Roger,** KCMG 1957 (CMG 1950); Director-General Middle East Association, since 1970; *b* 17 Aug. 1909; *s* of late Herbert Charles Goodeve and Winifred Frances Allen; *m* 1954, Jocelyn, *d* of late Comdr A. H. de Kantzow, DSO, RN, and Mrs de Kantzow; one *s* one *d. Educ:* Repton; Corpus Christi College, Cambridge. Called to the Bar, Inner Temple, 1937; employed temp. in the Foreign Office, 1940-; transferred to Moscow, April 1946; granted Civil Service Certificate, February 1947, and appointed to be a Foreign Service Officer, Grade 7, January 1946; transferred to the Foreign Office, May 1948; promoted to be a Foreign Service Officer, Grade 6 (Head of United Nations (Political) Department), January 1949; Head of African Dept, 1950; Asst Under Sec. of State, 1953-54; UK Dep. High Comr in Germany, 1954; HM Minister, Bonn, 1955-56; HM Ambassador: to Greece, 1957-61; to Iraq, 1961-65; Dep. Under-Sec. of State, FO, 1965-67; HM Ambassador to Turkey, 1967-69. *Address:* 5 William Street House, William Street, SW1. *Club:* Travellers'.

**ALLEN, Brig. Ronald Lewis,** CBE 1970 (OBE 1956); Deputy Commander, Base Organisation RAOC, and Head of Inventory Systems Development, since 1967; *b* 2 April 1916; *s* of W. J. Allen and M. B. Allen (*née* Lewis); *m* 1st, 1945, Jirina Georgette (*née* Valachova) (marr. diss. 1952); one *d*; 2nd, 1956, Christine Maude (*née* Scott); one *s* one *d. Educ:* Polytechnic, London; Univ. of South Wales and Monmouthshire. BSc Hons London 1939. Scientist, Safety in Mines Research Bd; Birmingham Univ., 1939; Imperial Chemical Industries, 1939. War of 1939-45: commissioned, RAOC, 1940; served UK, 1940-42; MEF, 1942-44 (despatches, 1943); CMF, 1944-45. Egypt, 1949-50; USA, 1951-52; Cyprus, 1960-61; BAOR, 1961-62; Principal Ammunition Technical Officer, 1962-66; Comdr Ammunition Organisation and Chief Inspector, Land Service Ammunition, 1966-67. FRIC, 1962 (ARIC 1939); MBIM, 1967; Fellow Brit. Computer Soc. 1969. Queen's Commendation for Brave Conduct, 1964. *Recreations:* bridge, tennis, computers, travel. *Address:* c/o Messrs Glyn Mills & Co., Kirkland House, Whitehall, SW1.

**ALLEN, Rowland Lancelot,** CB 1968; Principal Assistant Treasury Solicitor, 1963-69, retired; *b* 17 Feb. 1908; *s* of Rowland Allen and Maud Annie Allen (*née* Bacon); *m* 1934, Elizabeth Ethel (*née* Lewis); two *s* one *d. Educ:* Eton College. Called to the Bar, Inner Temple, 1931; Public Trustee Office, 1934; Treasury Solicitor's Dept, 1940; Foreign Compensation Commission, 1950-53; Treasury Solicitor's Dept, 1953. *Recreation:* golf. *Address:* Herries, Crastock, Woking, Surrey. *T:* Brookwood 2312.

**ALLEN, Sir Roy George Douglas,** Kt 1966; CBE 1954 (OBE 1946); MA, DSc (Econ.); FBA 1952; Professor of Statistics, University of London, since 1944; *b* 3 June 1906; *er s* of G. H. Allen, Worcester; *m* 1936; two *s* one *d. Educ:* Royal Grammar School, Worcester; Sidney Sussex College, Cambridge (Wrangler, 1927). DSc (Econ.) London, 1943; Assistant and later Lecturer in Statistics, London School of Economics, 1928-39; Reader in Economic Statistics, Univ. of London, 1939-44; Statistician, HM Treasury, 1939-41; Dir of Records and Statistics, British Supply Council, Washington, 1941-42; British Dir of Research and Statistics, Combined Production and Resources Board, Washington, 1942-45; Statistical Adviser, HM Treasury, 1947-48; Consultant, UN Statistical Office, 1949-50 and 1952. Visiting Professor, Univ. of California, 1958-59. Treasurer,

British Academy; Part-time Mem., Air Transport Licensing Bd, 1960-; Mem., Cttee of Inquiry on Decimal Currency, 1962-63; Chm., Impact of Rates Cttee, 1963-65; Mem. Research Council, DSIR, 1964-65; Mem., Social Science Research Council, 1967-. Hon. DSc (Soc. Sci.) Southampton, 1970. *Publications:* Family Expenditure (with Sir Arthur Bowley), 1935; Mathematical Analysis for Economists, 1938; Statistics for Economists, 1949; International Trade Statistics (with J. Edward Ely), 1953; Mathematical Economics, 1956; Basic Mathematics, 1962; Marco-economic Theory, 1967. Articles in economic and statistical journals. *Address:* 11 The Limes, Linden Gardens, W2. *T:* 01-727 9979; Greyfriars, South Green, Southwold, Suffolk. *T:* Southwold 3307. *Club:* Arts Theatre.

**ALLEN, Sydney Scholefield,** QC 1945; JP; MP (Lab) Crewe Division of Cheshire since 1945; *b* 8 Jan. 1898; *e s* of Joseph William and Annie Edith Scholefield Allen, Birkenhead; *m* 1928, F. Mona Irving, Meols, Wirral; two *s*. *Educ:* Birkenhead Institute; Univ. of Liverpool (LLB 1st cl. Hons 1922). Served European War, 1915-19, first in the ranks and later as an officer in RFA in 55th (West Lancs) Division; called to Bar, Gray's Inn, 1923; joined Northern Circuit practising on that Circuit and in North Wales; Recorder of Blackburn, 1947-69. Pres. Merseyside Fabian Soc.; Chm. Birkenhead Branch, League of Nations Union. Member Manx Bar. Commercial and Insurance Practice. Vice-Chm., Brit. Branch of Inter-Parly Union; Delegate: Inter-Parly Union, Rio de Janeiro, 1958, 1962; Brazilia, 1962; Belgrade, 1963; Copenhagen, 1964; Canada, 1965; Tehran, 1966; Dakar, Senegal, 1968. Member Exec. Cttee, Commonwealth Parly Assoc. (British Branch); Member Exec. Cttee and Jt Treas., Brit. Amer. Parly Gp. Delegate, Council of Europe and Western European Union, 1959-62. Vice-Chm. Legal Cttee, Council of Europe, 1960-62; Mem. Fabian Delegation to Poland (1958), Rumania (1960), Greece (1963), Turkey (1967). JP Lancashire, 1947. Hon. Freeman of Crewe, 1967. *Recreations:* walking, reading, music, drama, politics. *Address:* 2 Romney Close, Hampstead Way, NW11. *T:* 01-455 4385. *Club:* University (Liverpool).

**ALLEN, Prof. Thomas Palmer,** MSc; CEng; FIEE; Professor of Light Electrical Engineering, The Queen's University, Belfast, 1955-65, Emeritus Professor since 1965; *b* 9 Aug. 1899; *s* of William Palmer Allen and Mary Jane Allen; *m* 1925, Dorothy Margaret Mathews; two *d*. *Educ:* Rosetta School, Belfast; Trades Preparatory School, Belfast; The Queen's University, Belfast. Apprenticeship Elect. Eng, 1914-18; Lectr in Physics and Elect. Eng, Walthamstow Technical Inst., 1922; Asst Lectr in Mathematics, College of Technology, Belfast (CTB), 1923; Asst Lectr in Elect. Eng, CTB, 1924; Extra-Mural Lectr in Wireless Telegraphy and Telephony, QUB, 1927; Lectr in Elect. Eng, CTB, and Extra-Mural Lectr in Elect. Eng, QUB, 1936; Senior Lectr in Elect. Eng, CTB, 1942; Adviser of Studies, Faculty of Applied Science, QUB, 1938-52; Director of Higher Technological Studies, CTB, 1955; Dean of Faculty of Applied Science and Technology, QUB, 1958-61. Chm., N Ireland Centre of IEE, 1946-47. Senator, The Queen's Univ., Belfast, 1964-69; Gov., City of Belfast College of Technology, 1965-. *Publications:* various contributions to technical press, and many book reviews. *Recreations:* angling, cryptanalysis, amateur radio transmission (call Sign Gi6YW). *Address:* 62 Balmoral Avenue, Belfast BT9 6NY. *T:* Belfast 665982.

**ALLEN, Walter Ernest;** author, literary journalist and broadcaster; Professor of English in the New University of Ulster since 1967; Berg Professor of English, New York University, 1970-71; *b* Birmingham, 23 Feb. 1911; 4th *s* of Charles Henry Allen and Annie Maria Thomas; *m* 1944, Peggy Yorke, 3rd *d* of Guy Lionel Joy and Dorothy Yorke Maundrell, Calne, Wilts; two *s* two *d*. *Educ:* King Edward's Grammar School, Aston, Birmingham; Birmingham University. Assistant Master, King Edward's Grammar School, Aston, Birmingham, 1934; Visiting Lecturer in English, State University of Iowa, USA, 1935; Features Editor, Cater's News Agency, Birmingham, 1935-37; Assistant Technical Officer, Wrought Light Alloys Development Assoc., 1943-45. Asst Literary Editor, New Statesman, 1959-60, Literary Editor, 1960-61. Margaret Pilcher Vis. Prof. of English, Coe Coll., Iowa, 1955-56; Visiting Professor of English: Vassar College, New York, 1963-64; University of Kansas, 1967; Univ. of Washington, 1967. FRSL. *Publications:* Innocence is Drowned, 1938; Blind Man's Ditch, 1939; Living Space, 1940; Rogue Elephant, 1946; The Black Country, 1946; Writers on Writing, 1948; Arnold Bennett, 1948; Reading a Novel, 1949; Dead Man Over All, 1950; The English Novel–A Short Critical History, 1954; Six Great Novelists, 1955; All in a Lifetime, 1959; Tradition and Dream, 1964; George Eliot, 1964; The Urgent West: an Introduction to the Idea of the United States, 1969. *Address:* 6 Canonbury Square, N1. *T:* 01-226 7085; The New University of Ulster, Coleraine, Northern Ireland. *T:* Coleraine 4141. *Club:* Savile.

**ALLEN, W(alter) Godfrey,** FSA, MA, FRIBA; Hon. DLitt (Oxford), 1963; Surveyor of the Fabric of St Paul's Cathedral, 1931-56; Consulting Architect to Southwark Cathedral, 1932-55, to Exeter Cathedral, 1942-52, to Gloucester Cathedral since 1953; architect in private practice; *b* 21 Oct. 1891; *s* of Walter Allen and Frances Baker; *m* 1931, Phyllis Seyler Gill. *Educ:* Berkhampstead Sch.; Slade Sch.; King's Coll., London. Articled, later Asst to Sir Mervyn Macartney; Sec. to Commn of architects and engrs apptd in 1921 to investigate and report on condition of St Paul's Cathedral, Asst Architect to the Dean and Chapter, 1925-31. Member of: Royal Commn on Historical Monuments (Eng.), 1952-60; Exec. Cttee of Wren Soc., 1933-43; Advisory Panel of Specialist Architects, Historic Churches Preservation Trust (London Region); Chairman Church Roofing Committee set up by Central Council for the Care of Churches and Society for the Protection of Ancient Buildings, 1952; Commander of St Paul's Watch, 1939-45; Prime Warden Goldsmiths' Co., 1951-53; Master of Art Workers' Guild, 1953-54; Hon. Mem., City and Guilds of London Inst. *Works include:* restoration of St Bride's, Fleet Street; St Giles, Cripplegate; St Mary Abchurch; St Dunstan-in-the-West; St James, Louth; St James's Chapel, Exeter Cathedral; Chapter-House, St Paul's Cathedral; Sheldonian Theatre; Old Ashmolean Building and Radcliffe Camera, Oxford. *Publications:* The Preservation of St Paul's Cathedral, RIBA Jl; A Survey of Views of St Paul's Cathedral; numerous articles. *Recreation:* walking. *Address:* 21 Carmel Court, Birchington, Kent.

**ALLEN, William Alexander,** FRIBA; Chairman, Bickerdike Allen and Partners; *b* 29 June 1914; *s* of late Professor Frank Allen, FRSC; *m* 1938, Beatrice Mary Teresa Pearson; two *s* one *d*. *Educ:* public schools in Winnipeg; University of Manitoba. Royal Architectural Inst. of

Canada Silver Medal, 1935. Univ. Gold Medal in Architecture, 1936. Appointed to Min. of Tech. Building Research Station, Watford, 1937; Chief Architect, Bldg Res. Stn, 1953-61; Principal of the Architectural Assoc. School of Architecture, 1961-66. Member Council RIBA, 1953-70 (Chairman various committees; ARIBA 1937; FRIBA 1965). Hon. Associate NZIA. *Publications:* (with R. Fitzmaurice) Sound Transmission in Buildings, 1939. Papers, etc., on scientific and technical aspects of architecture, professionalism, and modern architectural history and education. *Recreations:* writing, drawing, music. *Address:* 4 Ashley Close, Welwyn Garden City, Herts. *T:* Welwyn Garden 24178. *Club:* Athenæum. *See also Prof. J. F. Allen.*

**ALLEN, Sir (William) Denis,** GCMG 1969 (KCMG 1958; CMG 1950); CB 1955; Deputy Under-Secretary, Foreign Office, 1967-68; *b* 24 Dec. 1910; *s* of John Allen; *m* 1939, Elizabeth Helen (*née* Watkin Williams); one *s*. *Educ:* Wanganui, New Zealand; Cambridge. Entered HM Diplomatic Service, 1934. Deputy Commissioner General for South East Asia, 1959-62; Ambassador to Turkey, 1963-67. *Address:* Stockland, Honiton, Devon.

**ALLEN, William Edward David,** OBE 1948; Chairman of David Allen & Sons Ltd; Director of Mills & Allen Ltd; Hon. Vice-President of British Poster Advertising Association; *b* 6 Jan. 1901; *e s* of William Edward Allen, Commonwood House, Chipperfield, Herts, and *g s* of late David Allen, JP, Belfast; *m* 1922, Lady Phyllis Edith King (marr. diss. 1932; she *d* 1947), 2nd *d* of 3rd Earl of Lovelace; one *d*; *m* 1943, Nathalie (*d* 1966), *e d* of late Maxime Kossovsky, formerly of the Moscow Bar; *m* 1969, Anne, *d* of P. Pentland, Heyfield, Vic, Australia. *Educ:* Eton. MP (U) West Belfast, 1929-31; resigned from Unionist Party, 1931. Captain Life Guards, active service Middle East and Africa, 1940-42 (despatches). Press Attaché British Legation, Beirut, 1943-44; Information Officer, N Iraq, 1944; Press Attaché, British Embassy, Angora, 1945. Counsellor (Information), 1947-49. Mem. Council, Brit. Inst. of Archaeology, Ankara, 1951-67; Mem. Council, Hakluyt Soc.; FSA (Ireland and London); FRAS; Mem. Société Asiatique (Paris). *Publications:* History of the Georgian People, 1932; The Ukraine: A History, 1940; Guerilla War in Abyssinia, 1943; The Russian Campaigns of 1941-45 (2 vols) (with late Paul Muratoff), 1944-46; Caucasian Battlefields, 1953; David Allens: The History of a Family Firm, 1957: The Poet and the Spae-Wife, 1960; Problems of Turkish Power in the Sixteenth Century, 1963; Russian Embassies to the Georgian Kings, 2 vols (for Hakluyt Soc.), 1970. *Address:* Whitechurch House, Cappagh, Co. Waterford, Ireland; 34 Lad Lane, Dublin. *Clubs:* Turf; Kildare Street (Dublin); Cercle d'Orient (Istanbul).

**ALLEN, Sir (William) Kenneth (Gwynne),** Kt 1961; Director, Electrolux, since 1970; *b* 23 May 1907; *er s* of Harold Gwynne Allen and Hilda Allen, Bedford; *m* 1931, Eleanor Mary (*née* Eeles); one *s* one *d*. *Educ:* Westminster Sch.; Univ. of Neuchâtel, Switzerland. Started as engineering pupil, Harland & Wolff Ltd, Glasgow and Belfast; subsequently at W. H. Allen, Sons & Co. Ltd, Bedford; Dir, 1937-70, Man. Dir, 1946-70, Chm., 1955-70, W. H. Allen, Sons & Co. Ltd; Chm., Amalgamated Power Engineering, 1968-70. Mem. Beds CC, 1945-55; High Sheriff, Beds, 1958-59. Past Chairman: Brit. Internal Combustion Engine Manufacturers' Assoc. (1955-57); Mem. Council Brit. Engineers' Assoc. (now Brit. Mechanical Engineering Fedn; Past Pres., 1957-59); Counsellor, BEAMA (Chm. Council, 1959-61); Pres., Engineering Employers' Fedn, 1962-64; Chm., Labour and Social Affairs Cttee of CBI, 1965-67. MIMarE; AMRINA; MIBritishE. Freeman of City of London. Liveryman, Worshipful Company of Shipwrights. *Address:* Manor Close, Aspley Guise, Beds. *T:* Woburn Sands 3161. *Club:* Brooks's.

**ALLEN, William Maurice;** Executive Director, Bank of England, 1964-70; *b* 16 April 1908; *s* of David Allen. *Educ:* Dulwich College; London School of Economics. Army 1940-45. Asst Dir of Research, International Monetary Fund, 1947-49; Adviser, Bank of England, 1950-64. Fellow of Balliol Coll., Oxford, 1931-48; Visiting Fellow Nuffield Coll., Oxford, 1954-62. Hon. Fellow, LSE, 1963. Gov., LSE, 1951. *Address:* Bank of England, EC2. *Club:* Reform.

**ALLEN, Prof. William Sidney,** MA, PhD (Cantab); Professor of Comparative Philology in the University of Cambridge since Oct. 1955; *b* 18 March 1918; *er s* of late W. P. Allen and of Ethel (*née* Pearce); *m* 1955, Aenea, *yr d* of late Rev. D. McCallum and Mrs McCallum, Invergordon. *Educ:* Christ's Hosp.; Trinity Coll., Cambridge (Classical Scholar); Porson Scholarship, 1939. War of 1939-45: RTR and General Staff (Int) (despatches). Lecturer in Phonetics, 1948-51, and in Comparative Linguistics, 1951-55, School of Oriental and African Studies, Univ. of London. Dialect research in India, 1952; Fellow of Rockefeller Foundation, USA, 1953; Brit. Council visitor, Univ. of W Indies, 1959. Linguistic Soc. of America's Professor, 1961; Collitz Professor, Linguistic Institute, USA, 1962. Pres., Philological Soc., 1965-67. Fellow of Trinity Coll., Cambridge, 1955-. *Publications:* Phonetics in Ancient India, 1953; On the Linguistic Study of Languages (inaugural lecture), 1957; Sandhi, 1962; Vox Latina, 1965; Vox Graeca, 1968; articles on general and comparative linguistics, phonetics, and classical, Indian and Caucasian languages. *Address:* 14 Applecourt, Newton Road, Cambridge. *T:* Cambridge 56739.

**ALLEN-JONES, Air Vice-Marshal John Ernest,** CBE 1966; Director of RAF Legal Services, 1961-70, retired; *b* 13 Oct. 1909; *s* of Rev. John Allen-Jones, Llanyblodwel Vicarage, Oswestry; *m* 1937, Margaret Rix, Sawbridgeworth; one *s* two *d*. *Educ:* Rugby; Worcester Coll., Oxford (MA). Solicitor (Honours), 1934; Partner with Vaudrey, Osborne & Mellor, Manchester. Joined RAF, 1939. Air Vice-Marshal, 1967. Gordon-Shepherd Memorial Prizeman, 1963. *Recreations:* tennis, bridge. *Address:* Little Bursteads, Little Hallingbury, Essex. *T:* Sawbridgeworth 2363. *Club:* Royal Automobile.

**ALLENBY,** family name of **Viscount Allenby.**

**ALLENBY,** 2nd Viscount, *cr* 1919, of Megiddo and of Felixstowe; **Dudley Jaffray Hynman Allenby;** late 11th Hussars; *b* 8 Jan. 1903; *e s* of late Capt. Frederick Claude Hynman Allenby, CBE, RN, JP; *S* uncle 1936; *m* 1st, 1930, Mary (marr. diss. 1949), *d* of Edward Champneys, Otterpool Manor, Kent; one *s*; 2nd, 1949, Mrs Daisy Neame, CStJ, White Walls, Aldington, Kent. *Educ:* Eton; RMC, Sandhurst. Joined 11th Hussars, 1923; served in India, 1923-26; Adjutant, 11th Hussars, 1926-30; Instructor, Royal Military College, Sandhurst, 1930-34; Captain, 1936; served Egypt, 1934-37; Adjutant, Army Fighting Vehicles School, 1937-40; Major, 1938; 2nd in Command Royal Gloucestershire Hussars, 1940-42; Lt-Col 2nd Derbyshire Yeomanry, 1942; retd (Lt-Col)

1946. *Heir:* *s* Major Hon. Michael Jaffray Hynman Allenby, 11th Hussars [*b* 20 April 1931; *m* 1965, Sara Margaret Wiggin; one *s*]. *Address:* Parsonage Farm, Westwell, Ashford, Kent. *T:* Ashford 24783. *Club:* Cavalry.

**ALLENBY, Rt. Rev. David Howard Nicholas;** Assistant Bishop of Worcester since 1968; *b* 28 Jan. 1909; *s* of late William Allenby; unmarried. *Educ:* Kelham Theological College. MA (Lambeth), 1957. Deacon, 1934; Priest, 1935. Curate of St Jude, West Derby, 1934-36; Tutor, Kelham Theological College and Public Preacher, Diocese of Southwell, 1936-44; Rector of Averham with Kelham, 1944-57; Proctor in Convocation, Southwell, 1950-57; Editor of Diocesan News and Southwell Review, 1950-55; Hon. Canon of Southwell, 1953-57, Canon Emeritus, 1957; Personal Chaplain to Bishop of Southwell, 1954-57; Rural Dean of Newark, 1955-57; Provincial of Society of Sacred Mission in Australia, 1957-62; Commissary, Melanesia, 1958-62; Warden of Community of Holy Name, City and Diocese of Melbourne, 1961-62; Bishop of Kuching, 1962-68; Commissary, Kuching, 1969. *Publication:* Pray with the Church, 1937 (jointly). *Address:* 90 Wells Road, Malvern, Worcs. *T:* Malvern 4644. *Club:* Royal Commonwealth Society.

**ALLENDALE,** 3rd Viscount, *cr* 1911; **Wentworth Hubert Charles Beaumont,** DL; Baron, 1906; *b* 12 Sept. 1922; *e s* of 2nd Viscount Allendale, KG, CB, CBE, MC, and Violet, *d* of Sir Charles Seely, 2nd Bt; *S* father 1956; *m* 1948, Hon. Sarah Ismay, 2nd *d* of 1st Baron Ismay, KG, PC, GCB, CH, DSO; three *s*. *Educ:* Eton. RAFVR, 1940; Flight-Lieutenant 1943; ADC to Viceroy of India, 1946-47. DL Northumberland, 1961. *Heir:* *s* Hon. Wentworth Peter Ismay Beaumont, *b* 13 Nov. 1948. *Address:* Bywell Hall, Stocksfield on Tyne, Northumberland. *T:* Stocksfield 3169; Allenheads, Hexham, Northumberland. *T:* Allenheads 205. *Clubs:* Turf, White's; Northern Counties (Newcastle upon Tyne).
*See also Hon. R. E. B. Beaumont, Earl of Carlisle.*

**ALLERTON,** 3rd Baron of Chapel Allerton, *cr* 1902; **George William Lawies Jackson;** Squadron-Leader Auxiliary Air Force, retired; late Lieutenant Coldstream Guards; *b* 23 July 1903; *s* of 2nd Baron and Katherine Louisa (*d* 1956), *y d* of W. W. Wickham, JP, of Chestnut Grove, Boston Spa; *S* father, 1925; *m* 1st, 1926, Joyce (who obtained a divorce, 1934; *d* 1953), *o c* of late J. R. Hatfeild, Thorp Arch Hall, Yorks; one *s*; 2nd, 1934, Mrs Hope Aline Whitelaw; 3rd, 1947, Anne, *er d* of James Montagu, Skippetts, nr Basingstoke; one *d*. *Educ:* Eton; RMC, Sandhurst. *Recreations:* shooting, golf. *Heir:* *s* Hon. Edward Lawies Jackson, Capt. RHG (retd) [*b* 23 March 1928; *m* 1953, Sally Moore, *o d* of late Ian Hezlett, Cranbourne Corner, Ascot; two *d*]. *Address:* Loddington Hall, Leicestershire. *T:* Belton 220. *Clubs:* White's, Turf.
*See also Sir J. M. Brocklebank.*

**ALLERTON, Air Commodore Ord Denny,** CB 1960; CBE 1953 (OBE 1945); Royal Air Force; *s* of Charles Hedley and Elizabeth Allerton; *m* 1935, Kathleen Mary Tucker; two *s*. *Educ:* Professor Ludicker's Private School, Felixtowe; Ipswich School. Group Captain, 1947; Air Commodore, 1957. Lately Director of Movements, Air Ministry. *Address:* Rags Corner, Nether Wallop, Stockbridge, Hampshire. *T:* Nether Wallop 276. *Club:* United Hunts.

**ALLERTON, Reginald John,** CBE 1964; FRICS, FIHM; *b* 20 June 1898; 3rd *s* of late Robert Sterry Allerton, Lowestoft, and Mary Maria (*née* Bailey); *m* 1924, Dorothy Rose Saunders; one *s*. *Educ:* Lowestoft Grammar School. Entered Local Government Service, 1915; on Active Service with RNVR, 1917-19. Various urban and borough appointments until 1926; Chief Architectural and Building Asst, Reading Borough Council, 1926-30; Estates Surveyor, City of Norwich, 1930-39; Housing Manager and Sec., City of Bristol, 1939-51; Housing Manager, City of Birmingham, 1951-54; Director of Housing to the London County Council, 1954-63. Pres., Inst. of Housing, 1949-50, 1960-61. Apptd (by Minister of Housing and Local Govt) as Vice-Pres., Surrey and Sussex Rent Assessment Panel, 1965. Served on Govt Cttees on Housing and Immigration, and Housing in Greater London (Sir Milner Holland Cttee); Founder Mem., Hanover Housing Assoc. *Publications:* many papers and lectures to professional societies and conferences dealing mainly with municipal housing work. *Recreations:* gardening, fishing. *Address:* 10 Mill Mead, Wendover, Bucks. *T:* Wendover 2691.

**ALLEY, Ronald Edgar;** Keeper of the Modern Collection, Tate Gallery, London, since 1965; *b* 12 March 1926; *s* of late Edgar Thomas Alley; *m* 1955, Anthea Oswell (now painter and sculptor, as Anthea Alley); two *d*. *Educ:* Bristol Grammar School; Courtauld Institute of Art, London University. Tate Gallery staff as Asst Keeper II, 1951-54; Deputy Keeper, 1954-65. Member: Museum Board, Cecil Higgins Art Gallery, Bedford, 1957-; Art Committee Ulster Museum, Belfast, 1962-; Art Panel of Arts Council, 1963-. *Publications:* Tate Gallery: Foreign Paintings, Drawings and Sculpture, 1959; Gauguin, 1962; William Scott, 1963; Ben Nicholson, 1963; Francis Bacon (with Sir John Rothenstein), 1964; British Painting since 1945, 1966; Picasso's "Three Dancers" 1967; Barbara Hepworth, 1968; Recent American Art, 1969. *Recreation:* ornithology. *Address:* 61 Deodar Road, SW15. *T:* 01-874 2016. *Club:* Institute of Contemporary Arts.

**ALLEYNE, Captain Sir John (Meynell),** 4th Bt, *cr* 1769; DSO 1918; DSC; RN retired; *b* 11 Aug. 1889; *s* of Reynold Alleyne, *e s* of 3rd Bt and Susanna, *d* of late John Meynell of Meynell Langley, Derbyshire; *S* grandfather, 1912; *m* 1920, Alice Violet, *d* of late James Campbell, and Mrs Campbell, 12 Cornwall Gardens, SW; one *s* two *d*. Served European War; was navigator of HMS Vindictive when sunk to block Ostend Harbour, May 1918 (severely wounded); retired list, 1936. Served War of 1939-45. *Heir:* *s* Rev. John Olpherts Campbell Alleyne, [*b* 18 Jan. 1928; *m* 1968, Honor Irwin]. *Address:* South Lynch, Hursley, near Winchester. *T:* Hursley 239. *Club:* United Service.

**ALLHUSEN, Major Derek Swithin,** DL; farmer; *b* 9 Jan. 1914; 2nd *s* of late Lt-Col F. H. Allhusen, CMG, DSO, Fulmer House, Fulmer, Bucks; *m* 1937, Hon. Claudia Violet Betterton, *yr d* of 1st and last Baron Rushcliffe, PC, GBE (*d* 1949); one *s* one *d* (and one *s* decd). *Educ:* Eton; Chillon Coll., Montreux, Switzerland; Trinity Coll., Cambridge. Lieut, 9th Queen's Royal Lancers, 1935. Served War of 1939-45: France, 1940 (wounded), North Africa, Italy (Silver Star Medal of USA, 1944); Major 1942; retired, 1949. One of HM's Body Guard of Hon. Corps of Gentlemen-at-Arms, 1963-. High Sheriff, 1958, DL 1969, Norfolk. *Recreations:* riding, shooting, skiing. Represented GB: Winter Pentathlon Olympic Games, 1948; Equestrianism European Championships Three-Day Event, 1957, 1959, 1965, 1967,

1969 (Winners of Team Championship, 1957, 1967, 1969); Olympic Games, Mexico, 1968 (Gold Medal, Team; Silver Medal, Individual). *Address:* Manor House, Claxton, Norwich, Norfolk. *T:* Thurton 228; Flat 1, 22 St James's Square, SW1. *T:* 01-839 3390. *Clubs:* Cavalry, Junior Carlton.

**ALLIBONE, Thomas Edward,** CBE 1960; FRS 1948; DSc Sheffield; Chief Scientist, Central Electricity Generating Board, 1963-70; External Professor of Electrical Engineering, University of Leeds, since 1967; *b* 11 Nov. 1903; *s* of Henry J. Allibone; *m* 1931, Dorothy Margery, *d* of Frederick Boulden, BSc, MEng, MIMechE; two *d. Educ:* Central Sch., Sheffield (Birley Scholar); Sheffield Univ. (Linley Scholar); Gonville and Caius Coll., Cambridge (Wollaston Scholar). PhD Sheffield; PhD Cantab. 1851 Exhibition Sen. Student, Cavendish Laboratory, Cambridge, 1926-30; i/c High-Voltage Laboratory, Metropolitan-Vickers Electrical Co., Manchester, 1930-46; Director: Res. Laboratory, AEI, Aldermaston, 1946-63; AEI (Woolwich) Ltd, 1948-63; Scientific Adviser, AEI, 1963. Mem., British Mission on Atomic Energy, Berkeley, Calif, and Oakridge, Tenn, 1944-45; Visitor: BISRA, 1949-55; ASLIB, 1955-62. Lectures: Faraday, 1946, 1956; Royal Instn Christmas, 1959; Wm Menelaus, 1959; Bernard Price, 1959; Trotter Patterson, 1963; Fison Memorial, 1963; Royal Soc. Rutherford Memorial, 1964; Baird Memorial, 1967; Melchett, 1970. President: Section A, British Assoc., 1958; EIBA, 1958-59; Inst. of Information Scientists, 1964-67. Vice-President: Inst. of Physics, 1948-52; Royal Instn, 1955-57. Chm., Res. Cttee, British Electrical and Allied Industries Res. Assoc., 1955-62. Member: Council, British Inst. of Radiology, 1935-38; Council, IEE, 1937-40, 1946-49, 1950-53; Cttee, Nat. Physical Laboratory, 1950-60; Govt Cttee on Copyright, 1951; DSIR (Mem., Industrial Grants Cttee, 1950-58); Council, Physical Soc., 1953-56; Council, Southern Electricity Bd, 1953-62; Adv. Council, Science Museum; Adv. Council, RMC; Adv. Court, AEA; Nuclear Safety Adv. Council, Min. of Power, 1959-. Trustee, British Museum, 1968-. Governor, Downe House, 1959-69; Chm. Governors, Reading Technical Coll., 1959-68. FInstP; FIEE; Fellow, Amer. Inst. of Electrical Engineers. Hon. DSc Reading; Hon. DEng Sheffield. Röntgen Medal, British Inst. of Radiology; Thornton and Cooper Hill Medals, IEE; Melchett Medal, Inst. of Fuel. *Publications:* The Release and Use of Nuclear Energy, 1961; papers on high voltage and transient electrical phenomena, fission and fusion. *Address:* Little Grange, Hurst, near Reading, Berks. *T:* Hurst 104. *Club:* Athenæum.

**ALLIGHAN, Garry;** Journalist and Author; Principal, Premier School of Journalism, Johannesburg, 1963-69; *b* 16 Feb. 1900; *s* of George and Catherine Allighan, Wickford, Essex; *m*; one *s* one *d. Educ:* St James School, Enfield; Enfield Grammar School. Naval service in European War; joined Luton News, 1919; Assistant Editor John Bull, 1921-25; Feature Editor Toronto Evening Telegram, 1925-28; Feature Writer Daily Express, 1928-31; Radio Editor Evening Standard, 1931-39; War Correspondent Toronto Star, 1939-41; News Editor Daily Mirror, 1941-44; Industrial Editor Daily Mail, 1944-46; MP (Lab) Gravesend Div. of Kent, 1945-47. Has also acted as Press Consultant to Advertising Assoc. and Radio Manufacturers Assoc. *Publications:* Priceless Treasure (Canada), 1926; Romance of the Talkies, 1929; Reith of the BBC, 1937; De Valera Revealed (USA), 1937; The First Thirteen, 1941; Curtain-Up on South Africa, 1960; Verwoerd–The End, 1961; The Welensky Story, 1962; Four Bonnets to Golgotha, 1963; The 65th Defendant, 1963; The Moving Finger, 1964. *Recreations:* motoring and photography. *Clubs:* Press, Eccentric; Union, Wanderers (Johannesburg); Owl (Cape Town).

**ALLIN, Norman,** CBE 1958; Hon. RAM, FRMCM; Professor of Singing at Royal Academy of Music, London, 1935-60; *b* Lancashire, 1884; two *d. Educ:* privately; Royal Manchester Coll. of Music. Principal Bass Covent Garden, English and Internat. Seasons, 1918-48; Roles include: Boris, Gurnemanz, Osmin, Mephistopheles, Hagen, Hunding, Sarastro, Baron Ochs, Ramphis, King Mark, etc; Principal Bass at all leading British Musical Festivals, Choral and Orchestral Socs; Principal Bass at Melbourne (Australia) Centenary Season of Grand Opera, 1934-35. *Recreations:* country pursuits *Address:* Newbury, Berks. *Club:* Savage.

**ALLINSON, Air Vice-Marshal Norman Stuart,** CB 1946; DL; retired; *b* 19 April 1904; *s* of late Rev. H. C. W. Allinson, Hinxhill, Kent; *m* 1928, Florence Muriel Hall; one *s* one *d. Educ:* Trent Coll.; RAF, Cranwell. Served with No 13 Sqdn, 1924-29; in HMS Hermes, 1930-32; Dept of Air Member of Personnel, 1933-35; RAF Staff Coll., 1936; comd No 269 Sqdn, 1937-38; HQ Coastal Comd, 1938-39; served War of 1939-45, Armament duties, Air Min. and MAP, 1940-41; HQ Army Co-operation Comd, 1942; served in Middle East, 1943-45, on planning duties, as AOC No 212 Group and Force 438 and as Dep. SASO, HQ Middle East; Dir of Operational Trng, Air Min., 1945-47; Imperial Defence Coll., 1948; AOC Rhodesian Air Trng Group, Bulawayo, S Rhodesia, 1949-51; Director-General of Manning, 1951-52; Director-General of Personnel I, 1953-54; Air Officer i/c Administration, Flying Training Command, 1954-56; retired, 1956. DL, Essex, 1964. *Recreation:* sailing. *Address:* Dene House, Layer de la Haye, Colchester, Essex. *Club:* RAF.

**ALLINSON, Walter Leonard,** MVO 1961; Counsellor and Head of Chancery, British High Commission, Nairobi, since 1970; *b* 1 May 1926; *o s* of Walter Allinson and Alice Frances Cassidy; *m* 1951, Margaret Patricia Watts; three *d* (of whom two are twins). *Educ:* Friern Barnet Grammar Sch.; Merton Coll., Oxford. First class in History, 1947; MA. Asst Principal, Ministry of Fuel and Power (Petroleum Div.), 1947-48; Asst Principal, later Principal, Min. of Education, 1948-58 (Asst Private Sec. to Minister, 1953-54); transf. CRO, 1958; First Sec. in Lahore and Karachi, 1960-62, Madras and New Delhi, 1963-66; Counsellor and Head of Political Affairs Dept, March 1968; Dep. Head, later Head, of Permanent Under Secretary's Dept, FCO, 1968-70. *Recreations:* gardening, scouting, piping, local history. *Address:* c/o Foreign and Commonwealth Office, King Charles Street, SW1. *Clubs:* Travellers', Madras Boat (India).

**ALLISON, Charles Ralph,** MA; Secretary, Lord Kitchener National Memorial Fund; Headmaster of Brentwood School, 1945-65; *b* 26 May 1903; *s* of Harry A. Allison, FCA, and Gertrude Wolfsberger; *m* 1930, Winifred Rita, *d* of A. C. Williams; two *s* one *d. Educ:* Caterham Sch.; University Coll., London; St Catharine's College, Cambridge (Exhibitioner). Assistant Master, Worksop College, 1928; Malvern College, 1929-36; English Tutor, Stowe School, 1936-38; Headmaster of Reigate Grammar School,

1938-40, and Alleyn's School, 1940-45. Formerly Mem. Cttee, Headmasters' Conf. (Vice-Chm. 1965). Governor: Covenantors' Educational Trust (Chm.); Lindisfarne Coll., Ruabon (Vice-Chm.); Brentwood Sch.; Stowe Sch. Vice-Chm., Commonwealth Youth Exchange Cttee. Mem., Nat. Commn for UNESCO, 1954-65; UK Delegate to Gen. Confs, 1958 and 1960. Mem., Essex Education Cttee. Reader in the Parish of St Mary's, Great Warley. *Address:* Barn Meadow, Great Warley, near Brentwood, Essex. *T:* Brentwood 4211. *Club:* Public Schools.

**ALLISON, Sir Charles William,** Kt 1966; CBE 1959 (OBE 1947); JP; former Chairman of Tees Valley and Cleveland Water Board; *b* 29 July 1886; *s* of John and Sarah Allison; *m* 1906, Hetty, *d* of William Burn; one *d* (one *s* decd). *Educ:* Stockton Sec. Sch.; Labour College. Trades Union Secretary with late Ernest Bevin for 36 years. JP, Stockton-on-Tees. *Publications:* contrib. to TUC History. *Recreations:* fishing, football and cricket. *Address:* 32 Winston Street, Stockton-on-Tees, Durham. *T:* Stockton 63189.

**ALLISON, James Anthony,** CMG 1966; OBE 1960; PH (Botswana); *b* 31 Jan. 1915; *s* of John Schiller Allison, Edinburgh and Union of South Africa, and Anna Elizabeth Christina (*née* van Velden); *m* 1946, Dorothy Patricia Kerr; one *d. Educ:* Boys' High School, Pretoria, SA; St John's College, Johannesburg, SA; Witwatersrand University, Johannesburg, SA (BA Hons); Colonial Service Course, Cambridge. Assistant District Officer, Colonial Service, 1938-39; War of 1939-45: Military Service, 3 West African Infantry Brigade, 1939-46 (Major). Asst District Officer and District Officer, Nigeria, 1946-50; District Commissioner, Secretariat, Finance Secretary, Administration Secretary, and Sec. to Cabinet, Bechuanaland, 1950-65; Sen. Permanent Sec. and Sec. to the Cabinet, Botswana (formerly Bechuanaland), 1965-Jan. 1970, retired. *Recreations:* golf, birds, shells, literature, music, travelling. *Address:* 11 Victory Place, Amanzimtoti, Natal, South Africa.

**ALLISON, Rt. Rev. O. C.;** *see* Sudan, Bishop in the.

**ALLISON, Prof. Philip Rowland,** FRCS; FACS; MA, DM Oxon; DSc; ChM Leeds; LRCP; Nuffield Professor of Surgery, University of Oxford, since 1954; Hon. Consulting Surgeon General Infirmary, Leeds, since 1955; *b* 2 June 1907; *s* of Jesse Rhodes Allison, Selby, and Rhoda Allison; *m* 1937, Kathleen Greaves; two *s* one *d. Educ:* Hymers College, Hull; University of Leeds. General Infirmary, Leeds: House Surgeon, 1931; Res. Orthop. Officer, 1931-32; Res. Surgical Officer, 1932-33; Hon. Asst Surg., 1936-41, and Senior Thoracic Surgeon, 1941. University of Leeds: Surgical Tutor and Registrar, 1933-36; Clin. Lectr in Surgery, 1936-41; Sen. Lectr in Thoracic Surgery, 1941. Corresp. Mem. Roman Soc. of Surgeons, 1949; Hon. Fellow: Soc. Med. of Pernambuco, 1953; American Surgical Assoc.; American Soc. of Thoracic and Cardiovascular Surgeons; Hon. Mem., Coll. of Surgeons of Brazil, 1953. *Publications:* chapters contrib. to Textbook of Medicine by Garland and Phillips, 1953. Contrib. to surgical and med. jls and text-books. *Address:* Balliol College, Oxford. *T:* Oxford 49601; Wincote, Steeple Aston, Oxon. *T:* Steeple Aston 230.

**ALLISON, Ralph Victor,** CMG 1967; Advisor (manufacturing and export industry), Australia; *b* 20 Feb. 1900; *s* of late Albert John and Edith Victoria Allison; *m* 1923, Myrtle Ellen Birch; two *d. Educ:* public and night schools, Milang, SA. General Store, A. H. Landseer Ltd: Milang, 1916-19; Adelaide, 1919-26; R. J. Finlayson Ltd, Adelaide: Company Sec., 1926-39; Dir, 1939-64; Man. Dir, 1954-64; Chm. Dirs of subsidiaries, 1954-64. Mem. Council: Royal Agric. and Hort. Soc. of SA, 1937- (Exec. Mem. 8 yrs); SA Chamber of Manufactures, 1948- (Pres. 1962, 1963). Mem. SA Dairy Bd, 1957-. Pres. Aust. Chamber of Manufactures, 1964; Mem. Aust. Export Develt Council, 1964-; Director, Australian Export Promotions Ltd and various other Australian Cos until 1966. Mem., many Aust. Commonwealth Cttees. *Recreations:* formerly tennis and bowls; latterly golf. *Address:* 18 Taylor Terrace, Rosslyn Park, South Australia. *T:* 31.2538. *Clubs:* Commonwealth, Commerce (both SA).

**ALLISON, Dr Richard Sydney,** VRD; MD (Belfast); FRCP; DPM; Consulting Neurologist (retired) to Royal Victoria and Claremont Street Hospitals, Belfast; *b* 15 May 1899; *s* of William Lowcock and Eliza Russell Allison; *m* 1925, Elizabeth Newett Barnett Steen; one *s* two *d. Educ:* Royal Belfast Academical Institution; Queen's University, Belfast. RNVR Surg.-Prob. 1918-19; Surg.-Lt 1926, retd 1950 (Surg.-Comdr). Actg Surg.-Capt. and Consultant to SW and W Approaches, 1944-45. Consultant in Medicine to Admiralty, N Ireland. Asst Physician, Ruthin Castle, 1925-30; appointed Asst Physician: Royal Victoria Hospital, 1930; Claremont Street Hospital, 1938. Clinical Examiner in Medicine, Queen's University, Belfast, 1931-; External Examiner in Neurology, Victoria Univ., Manchester, 1959-62. Visiting Professor: Medical College of South Carolina, 1957; Dalhousie Univ., Nova Scotia, 1958; Visiting Consultant Neurologist to Thailand Govt, 1965. Pres. Ulster Neuropsych. Soc., 1950-52, 1961-63; Pres. Sect. Neurology, RSM, London, 1962-63. For. Corresp. Mem., French Soc. of Neurology; Past Pres., Assoc. Brit. Neurologists. *Publications:* Sea Diseases: The Story of a Great Natural Experiment in Preventive Medicine in The Royal Navy, 1943; The Senile Brain, 1962. (Jt) Whitla's Dictionary of Treatment (8th edn), 1938, (ed jtly) *ibid* (9th edn), 1957; papers in scientific jls. *Recreations:* travel, fly fishing, naval history. *Address:* Waringstown, Lurgan, Co. Armagh, Northern Ireland. *T:* Waringstown 353.

**ALLISON, Rt. Rev. Sherard Falkner;** *see* Winchester, Bishop of.

**ALLITT, Sir (John) William,** Kt 1966; MBE 1955; retired Shop Manager; *b* 2 April 1896; *s* of George and Mary Allitt; *m* 1919, Minnie Parker; two *s. Educ:* Village School, Leadenham, Lincs and WEA Classes. Member of Labour Party for 50 years. 40 years public life. *Recreations:* public work; schools and school concerts. *Address:* Brelade, Holly Bank Close, Newhall, Burton-upon-Trent, Staffs. *T:* Swadlincote 6788. *Club:* Newhall Labour.

**ALLNUTT, Colonel Edward Bruce,** CBE 1944; MC 1915; late RAMC; *b* Embleton, 16 Sept. 1885; *s* of Rev. W. Bruce Allnutt and Edith Hawks; *m* 1916, Joan Cicely (*d* 1964), *e d* of Rev. G. B. Gainsford, MA, VD; one *s* two *d* (and one *s* decd). *Educ:* Bedford; Alleyne's Sch., Stevenage; St Bartholomew's Hosp. Served in London Scottish Rifles. MRCS; LRCP; DPH (London), 1923. House Physician, Westminster Hospital, 1911; Lieutenant RAMC 1912; De Chaumont Prize, Hygiene, at Royal Army Medical College, 1912. Served European War, 1914-18 (wounded, despatches thrice, MC, OStJ). Served in India; DAD Hygiene and Pathology, Bermuda Command, 1924-28; OC Military Hospital, Gibraltar, 1934-37; ADH Northern Comd, 1937-38. War of 1939-45 (CBE, King Haakon VII Liberty Cross of Norway, 2 Medals). Commandant Army School of Hygiene; Member Army Hygiene Advisory Cttee, War Office, 1939-46; retired, 1947. *Publications:* various articles in Lancet, Journal of RAMC, etc. *Recreations:* rowing, hunting, tennis, hockey, etc (past); music, motoring, watching all forms of sport (present). *Address:* Woodside, Lynch Road, Farnham, Surrey. *T:* Farnham 5047. *Club:* Leander.

**ALLOTT, Prof. Antony Nicolas,** JP; Professor of African Law, in the University of London, since 1964; *b* 30 June 1924; *s* of late Reginald William Allott and of Dorothy Allott (*née* Dobson); *m* 1952, Anna Joan Sargant; two *s* two *d.* *Educ:* Downside Sch.; New Coll., Oxford. Lieut Royal Northumberland Fusiliers and King's African Rifles, 1944-46. BA Oxon (1st class Hons Jurispudence), 1948; Lecturer in African Law, School of Oriental and African Studies, London, 1948-60; Reader in African Law, Univ. of London, 1960-64; PhD London 1954. Editor, Journal of African Law, 1957-; Dir, Restatement of African Law Project, 1959-; Lectr in African Law, Council of Legal Educn, 1960-; Hon. Director, Africa Centre, 1963-66; Pres., African Studies Assoc. of UK, 1969-70 (past Hon. Treas.); Vice-Pres., Internat. African Law Assoc., 1967. Governor: Sch. of Oriental and African Studies, London; Plater Coll., Oxford; Polytechnic of Central London. *Publications:* Essays in African Law, with special reference to the Law of Ghana, 1960; (ed) Judicial and Legal Systems in Africa, 1962; New Essays in African Law, 1970; articles in legal and other jls. *Recreations:* music, gardening, travel, carpentry. *Address:* 21 Windsor Road, Finchley, N3. *T:* 01-346 7245.

**ALLOTT, Eric Newmarch,** DM, FRCP, FRIC; Consultant Adviser in Chemical Pathology, Ministry of Health, 1963-68; Director, Group Laboratory, Lewisham Hospital, 1931-64; *b* 28 May 1899; *e s* of Henry Newmarch Allott, Stretford, Manchester; *m* 1930, Edith Mary Kydd; one *d.* *Educ:* Manchester Grammar Sch.; Balliol Coll., Oxford (Brackenbury Scholar). St Bartholomew's Hospital, BA 1920; BM Oxford, 1925. Demonstrator in Chemistry, Univ. of Oxford, 1920-22; Beit Memorial Fellow in Medical Research, 1925-27; Asst Physiologist, Sheffield Royal Hosp., 1928; Chief Asst, Medical Professorial Unit, St Barts Hosp., 1929-31. Chm. of Council, 1957-61, and former Pres., Assoc. of Clinical Pathologists; FRSocMed (Sec., 1937-44 Pres., 1944-46, Section of Experimental Medicine); Chm., Section of Chemical Pathology, 1st Internat. Congress of Clinical Pathology, 1951; Mem., Biochemical Soc. (Cttee, 1948-52); Member Council: Royal Institute of Chemistry, 1962-65; College of Pathologists, 1963-66; Member Editorial Board, Journal of Clinical Pathology; Hon. Lecturer in Pathology, KCH and RCS. *Publications:* Richter's Organic Chemistry (3rd English edn), 1934; Section Editor, Recent Advances in Clinical Pathology; papers on medical and chemical pathological subjects. *Recreation:* gardening. *Address:* Flat 2, 65 Carlisle Road, Eastbourne, Sussex. *T:* Eastbourne 31452. *Club:* Athenæum.

**ALLSOP, Kenneth;** author, journalist, television commentator; Rector of University of Edinburgh, since 1968; *b* 29 Jan. 1920; *s* of John Allsop and late Mary Ann Allsop (*née* Halliday); *m* 1942, Hilda Betty Creak; two *s* one *d.* *Educ:* St Andrew's College. Served RAF, 1940-44. Staff editorial posts: Jun. Reporter, Slough Observer, 1938-39; Sub-Editor, John Bull, 1945; Reporter, Evening Advertiser, Swindon, 1946; Reporter, Sunday Express, 1946-47; Law Courts Reporter, Press Assoc., 1948-50; Feature-writer and Foreign Corresp., Picture Post, 1950-55; Feature-writer, Evening Standard, 1955-56; Literary Editor and Columnist, Daily Mail, 1956-64. Has contrib. to most leading newspapers and periodicals, incl. articles for The Spectator, The Sunday Times and Weekend Telegraph; film criticism for The Observer, and literary criticism for The New York Times Book Review; writes regularly for The New Statesman, Nova, Encounter and Punch; now does weekly book review for The Evening News. On television: reporter for ITN, 1955; ed The Bookman for ABC, 1958; presented fortnightly documentary, Searchlight, for Granada, 1959-60; joined BBC as studio interviewer and film reporter for Tonight, 1960; also presented This Nation Tomorrow, 1963, and Life, 1968; now sen. presenter and interviewer on BBC's nightly current affairs programme, Twenty-Four Hours. On radio: Mem. The Critics, 1966-67; presented: The World of Jazz, 1963; The World of Books, 1966-67; Wildlife Review, 1967-68; Now Read On, 1970. Elected Vis. Research Fellow of Merton Coll., Oxford, 1968; MA (special status), Oxon, 1969; Mem., Standing Adv. Cttee on Artificial Limbs, 1968-; Founder Mem. (now Hon. Life Mem.), Middle Thames Natural Hist. Soc.; Mem., Llewellyn Rhys Memorial Prize Cttee, 1958-64. *Publications:* (include): Adventure Lit Their Star, 1949 (John Llewellyn Rhys Memorial Prize for 1950) (repr. 1962); The Sun Himself Must Die, 1949; The Daybreak Edition, 1951; The Last Voyages of the Mayflower, 1955 (US only); The Angry Decade, 1958; The Bootleggers, 1961 (repr. 1968); Scan, 1965; Hard Travellin', 1967; Countryside and Conservation, 1970. Is incl. in anthologies and collections both Brit. and Amer., 1951-, notably in The Saturday Book, nos 19, 21 and 28; The Annals of America (Encyc. Brit.), 1968; The Negro in American History (Encyc. Brit.), 1969. *Recreations:* ornithology, walking, music (esp. jazz and folk). *Address:* The Mill House, West Milton, Bridport, Dorset. *T:* Powerstock 342. *Clubs:* Ronnie Scott's, Savile.

**ALLSOPP,** family name of **Baron Hindlip.**

**ALLSOPP, Bruce;** *see* Allsopp, H. B.

**ALLSOPP, Prof. Cecil Benjamin,** MA, PhD, DSc; FInstP; Professor of Physics Applied to Medicine, University of London at Guy's Hospital Medical School, 1953-70; Hon. Consulting Physicist to Guy's Hospital; *b* 2 Sept. 1904; *m* 1935, Ivy Kathleen Johns; one *s* one *d.* *Educ:* Emmanuel College, Cambridge; University of Frankfurt-am-Main. MA, Cambridge, 1930; PhD, Cambridge, 1932; DSc, London, 1951. Pres., British Institute of Radiology, 1963-64; Silvanus Thompson Memorial Lectr, 1955. *Publications:* Absorption Spectrophotometry (with F. Twyman, FRS), 1934. Papers in Proc. of the Royal Soc., Jl of the Chemical Soc., Trans of the Faraday Soc., British Journal of Radiology, British Journal of Experimental Pathology, Cancer Research, etc. *Address:* 40 Queen Edith's Way, Cambridge.

**ALLSOPP, (Harold) Bruce,** BArch, DipCD, FSA, FRIBA, AMTPI; Senior Lecturer in History of Architecture, University of Newcastle upon Tyne, since 1969; Chairman, Oriel Press Ltd, since 1962; *b* Oxford, 4 July

1912; *s* of Henry Allsopp and Elizabeth May Allsopp (*née* Robertson); *m* 1935, Florence Cyrilla Woodroffe; two *s*. *Educ:* Manchester Grammar Sch.; Liverpool School of Architecture. BArch (1st Cl. Hons), Liverpool, 1933; Rome Finalist, 1934; Diploma in Civic Design 1935; ARIBA 1935; AMTPI 1936; FRIBA 1955; FSA 1968. Asst Architect in Chichester and London, 1934-35; Lecturer, Leeds Coll. of Art, 1935-40. War Service 1940-46, N Africa, Italy, Captain RE. Lecturer in Architecture, Univ. of Durham, 1946; Sen. Lecturer, 1955; Sen. Lecturer, Univ. of Newcastle upon Tyne, 1963, Dir of Architectural Studies, 1965-69. Chairman, Soc. of Architectural Historians of Gt Brit., 1959-65; Master, Art Workers Guild, 1970. *Publications:* Art and the Nature of Architecture, 1952; Decoration and Furniture, Vol. 1 1952, Vol. 2 1953; A General History of Architecture, 1955; Style in the Visual Arts, 1957; Possessed, 1959; The Future of the Arts, 1959; A History of Renaissance Architecture, 1959; The Naked Flame, 1962; Architecture, 1964; To Kill a King, 1965; A History of Classical Architecture, 1965; Historic Architecture of Newcastle upon Tyne, 1967; Civilization, the Next Stage, 1969; The Romanesque Achievement, 1970; The Study of Architectural History, 1970; (ed) Modern Architecture of Northern England, 1970; (with Ursula Clark): Oriel Guides: Architecture of France, 1963; Architecture of Italy, 1964; Architecture of England, 1964; Photography for Tourists, 1966; (with U. Clark and H. W. Booton): The Great Tradition of Western Architecture, 1966. *Recreations:* piano and harpsichord; skiing. *Address:* Woodburn, Batt House Road, Stocksfield, Northumberland. *T:* Stocksfield 2323; 32 Ridley Place, Newcastle upon Tyne NE1 8LH. *T:* Newcastle 20892. *Clubs:* Arts, Ski of Great Britain.

**ALLSOPP, Samuel Ranulph,** CBE 1954 (MBE 1942); DL; Merchant Banker, Arbuthnot Latham & Co. Ltd, 1929-69; Member, Hops Marketing Board (Chairman, 1947-69); *b* 7 March 1899; *s* of Lt-Col Hon. Ranulph Allsopp, 4th *s* of 1st Baron Hindlip, and Margaret, *d* of William Whitbread; *m* 1923, Hon. Norah Hyacinthe Littleton, *d* of 4th Baron Hatherton; two *s* two *d*. *Educ:* Eton; King's Coll., Cambridge. Served European War, 1918-19 (2nd Lt); served Home Guard, 1940-44 (Major); Lt-Col OC 12th Essex Cadet Bn, 1945-47; Lt-Col OC 12th Bn Essex Home Guard, 1952-55. Anglo-Austrian Bank, Vienna and London, 1922-28; Hon. Sec. Eton Coll. War Memorial and Bursary Funds, 1943-69. DL Essex, 1946; High Sheriff of Essex, 1955. *Recreation:* shooting. *Address:* Alsa Lodge, Stansted, Essex. *T:* Stansted 3244. *Clubs:* Pratt's, City University.

*See also Sir John FitzHerbert, Bt.*

**ALLUM, Sir John (Andrew Charles),** Kt 1950; CBE 1946; *b* 27 Jan. 1889; *s* of John Allum, London; *m* Annie, *d* of Thomas William Attwood; two *s* three *d*. Mayor of the City of Auckland, New Zealand, 1941-53. *Address:* 158 Aberdeen Road, Auckland 9, New Zealand.

**ALMEDINGEN, E. M.;** novelist and poet; *b* St Petersburg, 21 July 1898; *y d* of late Prof. A. N. von Almedingen. *Educ:* Xenia Nobility School; The University, Petrograd. Lecturer on English Mediaeval History and Literature, The University, Petrograd, 1920-22; came to England, 1923; has supported herself by writing and lecturing since then. Lecturer on Russian Literature, Univ. of Oxford, 1951. Member Faculty (Historico-Philological), Univ. of Petrograd, 1922. FRSL, 1951. *Publications: poetry:* Rus, 1939; Poloniae Testamentum, 1942; Out of Seir, 1943; Storm at Westminster, 1952; The Unnamed Stream, 1965; *autobiography:* Tomorrow Will Come, 1941; The Almond Tree, 1947; Within the Harbour, 1950; St Petersburg, 1969; *novels:* Frossia, 1943; Dasha, 1945; The Inmost Heart, 1948; Flame under the Water, 1951; The Rock, 1953; Stand Fast, Beloved City, 1954; Fair Haven, 1956; Stephen's Light, 1957; The Scarlet Goose, 1958; The Little Stairway, 1960; Dark Splendour, 1961; The Ladies of St Hedwig's, 1965; Too Early Lilac, 1970; *biography:* Life of Many Colours, 1958; So Dark a Stream (a Study of Emperor Paul I), 1959; The Empress Alexandra (1872-1918), 1961; The Emperor Alexander II (1818-1881), 1962; Catherine the Great, 1963; The Emperor Alexander I, 1964; An Unbroken Unity (A Study of Grand-Duchess Serge of Russia), 1964; The Romanovs (1613-1917), 1966; Francis of Assisi, 1967; Charlemagne, 1968; Leonardo Da Vinci: a Portrait, 1969; *children's books:* The Young Pavlova, 1961; The Young Leonardo da Vinci, 1963; The Knights of the Golden Table, 1963; The Treasure of Siegfried, 1964; The Young Catherine the Great, 1965; Little Katia, 1966; The Retreat from Moscow, 1812, 1966; Young Mark, 1967 (1st Prize, Children's Books World Council, USA); Gudrun, 1968; One Little Tree, 1968; A Candle at Dusk, 1969; Fanny, 1969; I Remember St Petersburg, 1969; Ellen, 1970. *Recreations:* reading, embroidery. *Address:* c/o Messrs Anthony Sheil Associates, 47 Dean Street, W1.

**ALPHAND, Herve;** Grand Officier, Légion d'Honneur, 1968; Secretary-General, Ministry of Foreign Affairs, France, since 1965; *b* 1907; *s* of Charles Hervé and Jeanne Alphand; *m* 1958, Nicole Merenda. *Educ:* Lycée Janson de Sailly; Ecole des Sciences Politiques. Inspector of Finances and Dir Dept of Treaties, Min. of Commerce, 1937-38; Financial Attaché to Embassy, Washington, 1940-41; Dir of Economic Affairs for French National Cttee in London, 1941-44; Director-General, Economic, Financial and Technical Affairs (Min. of Foreign Affairs), 1945; French Ambassador to OEEC; French Dep. to Atlantic Council, 1950, and Mem. NATO Perm. Council, 1952-54; Ambassador: to UN, 1955-56; to USA, 1956-65. *Address:* 37 Quai d'Orsay, Paris, VIIe.

**ALPORT,** family name of **Baron Alport.**

**ALPORT,** Baron, *cr* 1961, of Colchester (Life Peer); **Cuthbert James McCall Alport,** PC 1960; TD, 1949; *b* 22 March 1912; *o s* of late Prof. Arthur Cecil Alport, MD, FRCP, and of Janet, *y d* of James McCall, Dumfriesshire; *m* 1945, Rachel Cecilia, *o d* of Lt-Col R. C. Bingham, *qv*; one *s* two *d*. *Educ:* Haileybury; Pembroke Coll., Cambridge. MA History and Law; Pres., Cambridge Union Society, 1935. Tutor Ashridge Coll., 1935-37. Barrister-at-Law, Middle Temple. Joined Artists Rifles, 1934. Served War of 1939-45: Hon. Lieut-Col; Director Conservative Political Centre, 1945-50. MP (C) Colchester division of Essex, 1950-61; Chairman Joint East and Central African Board, 1953-55; Governor, Charing Cross Hospital, 1954-55. Asst Postmaster-General, Dec. 1955-Jan. 1957; Parliamentary Under-Secretary of State, Commonwealth Relations Office, 1957-59; Minister of State, Commonwealth Relations Office, Oct. 1959-March 1961; British High Commissioner in the Federation of Rhodesia and Nyasaland, 1961-63; Mem. of Council of Europe, 1964-65; British Govt Representative to Rhodesia, June-July 1967. A Dir of Industrial Finance and Investment Ltd and other companies, 1965. FBIM, 1967. Governor, Haileybury

Coll. Master Skinners' Co., 1969-70. High Steward of Colchester, 1967-. *Publications:* Kingdoms in Partnership, 1937; Hope in Africa, 1952; The Sudden Assignment, 1965. *Address:* The Cross House, Layer de la Haye, Colchester, Essex. *T:* Layer de la Haye 217. *Clubs:* Farmers', Pratt's.

**ALSTEAD, Stanley,** CBE 1960; MD, FRCP; Professor Emeritus, Regius Chair of Materia Medica, University of Glasgow; Senior Visiting Physician, Stobhill Hospital, Glasgow; *b* 6 June 1905; *s* of late Robert Alstead, OBE, and Anne Alstead; *m* 1932, Nora, 2nd *d* of late M. W. Sowden and late Nell Sowden; one *s*. *Educ:* Wigan Grammar Sch.; Liverpool Univ. Held various appts in north of England, Glasgow and Inverness. Appointed Pollok Lecturer in Pharmacology, Univ. of Glasgow, 1932, and became interested in clinical aspects of subject; Regius Prof. of Materia Medica and Therapeutics, Univ. of Glasgow, 1948-70; External Examiner in Univs of St Andrews, Glasgow, Aberdeen, London, Manchester, Liverpool, Cairo, Malta. Hon. Prof., Univ. of East Africa (Makerere University Coll.) and Hon. Physician to Kenyatta Nat. Hosp., Nairobi, Kenya, 1965-66. Served War of 1939-45, in RAMC as medical specialist to 5 CCS in Tunisia and Sicily, and in Belgium and Egypt as Officer in Charge of Med. Div. 67 Gen. Hosp. and 63 Gen. Hosp. with rank of Lt-Col (despatches). MD Liverpool (N. E. Roberts Prize); FRCP; FRCPGlas.; FRCPE; FRSE. Pres. RFPSG (now RCPGlas), 1956-58. Member: British Pharmacopœia Commn, 1953-57; Standing Jt Cttee on Classification of Proprietary Preparations; Commn. on Spiritual Healing (General Assembly of Church of Scotland). Jt Editor: Dilling's Clinical Pharmacology; Textbook of Medical Treatment. *Publications:* papers in med. jls on results of original research in clinical pharmacology. *Recreations:* gardening, music (violin) and reading poetry. *Address:* 33 Ochlochy Park, Dunblane, Perthshire. *Clubs:* Western, RASC (Glasgow).

**ALSTON, (Arthur) Rex;** Freelance Broadcaster, Journalist and Lecturer; BBC Commentator, 1943-61, retired; *b* 2 July 1901; *e s* of late Arthur Fawssett Alston, Suffragan Bishop of Middleton, and late Mary Isabel Alston; *m* 1932, Elspeth, *d* of late Sir Stewart Stockman and of Lady Stockman; one *s* one *d*. *Educ:* Trent College; Clare College, Cambridge. Assistant Master, Bedford School, 1924-41. Joined BBC, Jan. 1942. *Publications:* Taking the Air, 1950; Over to Rex Alston, 1953; Test Commentary, 1956; Watching Cricket, 1962. *Recreations:* golf, gardening. *Address:* Ryders, Oakwood Hill, Ockley, Surrey. *T:* Oakwood Hill 410. *Clubs:* East India and Sports, MCC.

**ALSTON, Rt. Rev. Mgr. Joseph Leo;** Rector of Venerable English College, Rome, since 1964; *b* 17 Dec. 1917; *s* of Benjamin Alston and Mary Elizabeth (*née* Moss). *Educ:* St Mary's School, Chorley; Upholland College, Wigan; English Coll., Rome; Christ's College, Cambridge. Priest, 1942; Licentiate in Theology, Gregorian Univ., Rome, 1942; BA (1st Cl Hons Classics) Cantab 1945. Classics Master, Upholland Coll., Wigan, 1945-52, Headmaster, 1952-64. *Recreation:* music. *Address:* Venerabile Collegio Inglese, Via Monserrato 45, Rome, Italy. *T:* Roma 651829.

**ALSTON, Rex;** *see* Alston, A. R.

**ALSTON, Dr Robin Carfrae;** Lecturer in Philology, Leeds University, since 1964; *b* 29 Jan. 1933; *s* of Wilfred Louis Alston; *m* 1957, Joanna Dorothy Ormiston; two *s* one *d*. *Educ:* Rugby Sch.; Univs of British Columbia (BA), Oxford (MA), Toronto (MA) and London (PhD). Teaching Fellow, University Coll., Toronto, 1956-58; Lectr, New Brunswick Univ., 1958-60. Jt Editor Leeds Studies in English and Leeds Texts and Monographs; Editor Studies in Early Modern English. Founder, Chm. and principal Editor, Scolar Press Ltd, 1966-. *Publications:* An Introduction to Old English, 1961 (rev. edn 1966); A Catalogue of Books relating to the English Language (1500-1800) in Swedish Libraries, 1965; English Language and Medieval English Literature: a Select Reading-List for Students, 1966; A Bibliography of the English Language from the Invention of Printing to the Year 1800: Vol. I, 1965; Vols V and VIII, 1966; Vols VII and IV, 1967; Vol. II, 1968; Vol. VI, 1969; Vol. III, 1970; Alexander Gil's Logonomia Anglica (1619): a translation into Modern English, 1968; (jtly) The Works of William Bullokar, Vol. I, 1966; English Studies (rev. edn of Vol. III, Cambridge Bibl. Eng. Lit.), 1968; English Linguistics 1500-1800: a Collection of Texts in Facsimile, 1967-; European Linguistics 1500-1700: a Collection of Texts in Facsimile, 1968-; numerous articles, etc. *Recreations:* music, photography. *Address:* Alva Cottage, Kettlewell, Yorks. *T:* Kettlewell 289.

**ALSTON ROBERTS WEST, General Sir Michael M.;** *see* West.

**ALTAMONT, Earl of; Jeremy Ulick Browne;** *b* 4 June 1939; *s* of 10th Marquess of Sligo, *qv*; *m* 1961, Jennifer June, *d* of Major Derek Cooper, Dunlewey, Co. Donegal, and Mrs C. Heber Percy, Pophleys, Radnage; three *d*. *Educ:* St Columba's College, Eire; Royal Agricultural College, Cirencester. *Address:* Westport House, Co. Mayo, Eire.

**ALTHAUS, Frederick Rudolph,** CBE 1970; Senior Partner, Pember & Boyle, Stockbrokers; *b* 6 Sept. 1895; *s* of late T. F. Althaus, London; *m* 1927, Margaret, *d* of late C. F. Twist, London; two *s* one *d*. *Educ:* Rugby; Balliol College, Oxford. Served Suffolk Regt, 1914-18 (wounded, despatches). Mem. Stock Exchange, London, 1922 (Mem. Council, 1949-; Deputy-Chairman, 1959-63); London Del. to Conf. of European Stock Exchanges (now Fédération Internationale des Bourses de Valeurs), 1957-, Vice-Pres., 1968-69, Pres., 1970; Member Jenkins Cttee on Company Law, 1959; a Comr, Public Works Loan Board, 1965-69. *Publications:* (Originator and Editor) British Government Securities in the Twentieth Century, 1945-. *Recreations:* music, painting, golf. *Address:* Yew Place, Farnham Royal, Bucks. *T:* Farnham Common 3102. *Clubs:* Oriental, City University.

**ALTHORP, Viscount; Edward John Spencer,** MVO 1954; DL; President, Northamptonshire Association of Boys' Clubs; Chairman National Association of Boys' Clubs; *b* 24 Jan. 1924; *o s* of 7th Earl Spencer, *qv*; *m* 1954, Hon. Frances Ruth Burke Roche (marr. diss. 1969), *yr d* of 4th Baron Fermoy; one *s* three *d* (and one *s* decd). *Educ:* Eton; RMC Sandhurst and RAC, Cirencester. ADC to Gov. of South Australia, 1947-50; Equerry to the Queen, 1952-54 (to King George VI, 1950-52). Formerly Capt. RS Greys. Hon. Col The Northamptonshire Regt (Territorials), T&AVR, 1967-. CC Northants; High Sheriff of Northants, 1959; DL Northants, 1961. *Heir:* *s* Hon. Charles Edward Maurice Spencer, *b* 20 May 1964. *Address:* Park House, Sandringham, Norfolk. *T:* Dersingham 203; 107 Eaton Square, SW1. *T:* 01-235 8798. *Clubs:* Turf, Brooks's, MCC, Royal Over-Seas League, Farmers'.

**ALTON, Euan Beresford Seaton,** MBE 1945; MC 1943; Assistant Under Secretary of State, Department of Health and Social Security, since 1968; *b* 22 April 1919; *y s* of late William Lester St John Alton and Ellen Seaton Alton; *m* 1953, Diana Margaret Ede; one *s* one *d*. *Educ:* St Paul's Sch.; Magdalen Coll., Oxford. Served with Army, 1939-45; Major RA. Admin. Officer, Colonial Service and HM OCS, Gold Coast and Ghana, 1946-58; Admin. Officer, Class 1, 1957. Entered Civil Service as Asst Principal, Min. of Health, 1958; Principal, 1958; Asst Sec., 1961; Under Sec., 1968. *Recreations:* sailing, rifle shooting, golf. *Address:* Broad Sawyers, 57 Loom Lane, Radlett, Herts. *T:* Radlett 5276. *Clubs:* Royal Commonwealth Society; Aldenham Sailing (Aldenham, Herts).

**ALTRINCHAM,** Barony of, *cr* 1945, of Tormarton; title disclaimed by 2nd Baron; *see under* Grigg, John Edward Poynder.

**ALTY, Thomas,** DSc Liverpool; PhD Cantab; DCL Dunelm; LLD Glasgow, Toronto, Rhodes; FInstP; FRSC, FRSE; Deputy Principal, University of Birmingham, 1963-69; *b* 30 Sept. 1899; *s* of James Alty, Rufford, Lancashire; *m* 1925, Stella West, *d* of W. Harris, solicitor, Liverpool; no *c*. *Educ:* Univ. of Liverpool (Oliver Lodge Fellow, 1921); University of Cambridge. Lecturer in Physics, University of Durham, 1924-25; Prof. of Physics, Univ. of Saskatchewan, Canada, 1925-29; Research Physicist, Imperial Chemical Industries, Northwich, Cheshire, 1929-30; Prof. of Physics, Univ. of Saskatchewan, 1930-32; Research Prof. of Physics, Univ. of Saskatchewan, 1932-35; Cargill Prof. of Applied Physics, Univ. of Glasgow, 1935-45; Cargill Prof. of Natural Philosophy, Univ. of Glasgow, 1945-48; Master of Rhodes University Coll., 1948-51; Principal and Vice-Chancellor of Rhodes Univ., Grahamstown, S Africa, 1951-63. Chm. Assoc. of Univs of British Commonwealth, 1958-60. Mem., SA Council for Scientific and Industrial Research, 1956-63. Member, SA National Council for Social Research, 1955-63. *Publications:* scientific papers. *Address:* c/o The University of Birmingham, Birmingham 15.

**ALUWIHARE, Sir Richard,** KCMG 1950; Kt 1948; CBE 1945; High Commissioner of Ceylon in India, 1957-63, retired; *b* 23 May 1895; *m* 1921, Lucille Moonemalle (*d* 1961); two *d*. *Educ:* Trinity Coll., Kandy. Served European War, 1914-18, Somme, France (wounded); welfare work with Indian Army (despatches). Joined Ceylon Civil Service, 1920; (appointed by Governor) Actg Police Magistrate, Dandagamuwa, 1923; HM Customs, 1926; District Judge, Kegalle, 1928, Nuwara Eliya, 1931; Class II of Civil Service; Controller of Finance and Supply, General Treasury, 1934; Asst Govt Agent, Kegalle, 1937; Dep. Collector of Customs, 1939; Actg Govt Agent, North Central Prov., 1941; Class I Civil Service; Govt Agent, Central Prov., 1946; Inspector-General of Police, Ceylon, 1947-53, retd. *Recreations:* cricket, Rugby football, swimming, riding. *Address:* Aluwihare, Matale, Ceylon. *Clubs:* Singhalese Sports, Orient.

**ALVAREZ, Alfred;** writer; Poetry Editor, The Observer; Advisory Editor, Penguin Modern European Poets; *b* London, 1929; *s* of Bertie Alvarez and Katie Alvarez (*née* Levy); *m* 1st, 1956, Ursula Barr (marr. diss. 1962); one *s*; 2nd, 1966, Anne Adams; one *s*. *Educ:* Oundle Sch.; Corpus Christi Coll., Oxford. BA (Oxon) 1952, MA 1956. Sen. Research Schol., CCC, Oxon, and Research Schol. of Goldsmiths' Company, 1952-53, 1954-55. Procter Visiting Fellowship, Princeton, 1953-54; Vis. Fellow of Rockefeller Foundn, USA, 1955-56, 1958; gave Christian Gauss Seminars in Criticism, Princeton, and was Lectr in Creative Writing, 1957-58; D. H. Lawrence Fellowship, New Mexico, 1958; Drama Critic, The New Statesman, 1958-60. Visiting Prof.: Brandeis Univ., 1960; New York State Univ., Buffalo, 1966. Vachel Lindsay Prize for Poetry (from Poetry, Chicago), 1961. *Publications:* The Shaping Spirit (US title, Stewards of Excellence), 1958; The School of Donne, 1961; The New Poetry (ed and introd), 1962; Under Pressure, 1965; Beyond All This Fiddle, 1968; Lost (poems), 1968; (ed) Penguin Modern Poets, No 18, 1970. Three pamphlets of poetry: 1952, 1958, 1968. The Anarchist (film script), 1969. *Recreations:* rock-climbing, poker, cinema. *Address:* c/o The Observer, 160 Queen Victoria Street, EC4. *Club:* Climbers'.

**ALVAREZ, Prof. Luis W.;** Professor of Physics, University of California, Berkeley, since 1945; *b* 13 June, 1911; *s* of Dr Walter C. Alvarez and Harriet Smyth; *m* 1st, 1936, Geraldine Smithwick; one *s* one *d*; 2nd, 1958, Janet Landis; one *s* one *d*. *Educ:* University of Chicago. SB 1932, PhD 1936. Radiation Lab., Univ. of California, 1936-; MIT Radiation Lab., 1940-43; Metallurgical Lab., Univ. of Chicago, 1943-44; Los Alamos Sci. Lab., 1944-45; Associate Dir, Lawrence Rad. Lab., 1954-59. Member: Nat. Acad. of Sciences; Nat. Acad. of Engineering; Am. Phil. Soc.; Am. Acad. of Arts and Sciences. Awarded: Collier Trophy, 1946; John Scott Medal, 1953; US Medal for Merit, 1947; Einstein Medal, 1961; Pioneer Award, AIEEE, 1963; Nat. Medal of Science, 1964; Michelson Award, 1965; Nobel Prize in Physics, 1968. Hon. ScD: Chicago, 1967; Carnegie-Mellon, 1968; Kenyon, 1969. *Publications:* nearly 100 contributions to Physics Literature, largely in Nuclear Physics and High Energy Physics; 22 US Patents, largely in Electronics and Optics. *Recreations:* flying, golf, music. *Address:* (business) Lawrence Radiation Laboratory, University of California, Berkeley, Calif 94720, USA. *T:* 415-843-2740; (home) 131 Southampton Avenue, Berkeley, Calif 94707, USA. *T:* 415-525-0590. *Clubs:* Bohemian (San Francisco); Faculty (Berkeley); Miravista Golf (El Cerrito).

**ALVIN, Madame Juliette;** violoncellist and viola de gamba player; registered Music Therapist (USA); 2nd *d* of Jeanne and Henri Alvin, Paris; *m* William A. Robson, *qv*; two *s* one *d*. *Educ:* Lycée de Versailles; Conservatoire National de Musique, Paris (First prix d'Excellence); later studied with Pablo Casals; has played in principal musical centres of Europe, including London, Paris, Berlin, Vienna, Brussels, Prague, Buda Pesth, Belgrade, Bucarest, The Hague, Warsaw, Stockholm, etc; often with the Philharmonic Orchestra; toured USA frequently, 1932-68. Has broadcast as a soloist in BBC programmes from London and provinces; musical activities during War of 1939-45 included war factory tours and other concerts organised by the Arts Council (CEMA); also recitals in military and Red Cross hospitals and service concerts; more than 200 recitals in aid of War Charities. Recognised as a leading authority on musical education in England through special recitals for school children, and a teacher of internat. reputation. Appointed for winter session, 1950-51, in music dept of North Carolina Univ., USA. Has lectured at numerous universities and colleges in Great Britain, on the Continent, in USA, Canada, S America, and Japan, esp., in recent years, on her experiments in music therapy with handicapped children and mental patients; has televised and made films on her work in music therapy. Member American National Assoc. for Music Therapy; Hon. Mem., Argentine Assoc. for Music Therapy; Hon. Adviser, Japanese Soc. for Music Therapy; Founder and Hon. Sec., British Society for Music Therapy (formerly Soc. for Music Therapy and Remedial Music), London, 1958-; Dir, Diploma Course in Music Therapy, Guildhall School of Music and Drama, London. *Publications:* The Logic of Casals' Technique; Introducing music to children; Class Teaching of Instruments; Bach and the 'Cello; Musical Theory and Instrumental Technique, 1953; Casals, a great teacher; A Musical Experiment on Backward Children, 1954; 'Cello Tutor for Beginners, 1955 (2nd volume, 1958); Music for the Handicapped Child, 1965; Music Therapy, 1966; Report on a Research Project on Music Therapy, 1970. Contrib. to American Jl of Mental Deficiency, Cerebral Palsy Bulletin and other learned jls. *Recreations:* tennis and swimming. *Address:* 49 Lanchester Road, N6. *T:* 01-883 1331. *Club:* London Violoncello.

**ALVINGHAM,** 2nd Baron, *cr* 1929, of Woodfold; **Robert Guy Eardley Yerburgh;** *b* 16 Dec. 1926; *s* of 1st Baron and Dorothea Gertrude (*d* 1927), *d* of late J. Eardley Yerburgh; *S* father 1955; *m* 1952, Beryl Elliot, *d* of late W. D. Williams; one *s* one *d*. *Educ:* Eton. Lt-Col, Coldstream Guards. *Heir: s* Robert Richard Guy Yerburgh, *b* 10 Dec. 1956. *Address:* Bix Hall, Henley-on-Thames, Oxfordshire. *Club:* Guards.

**ALWYN, William;** composer; Professor of Composition, Royal Academy of Music, 1926-55; *b* Northampton, 1905. *Educ:* Northampton Sch.; Royal Acad. of Music. FRAM 1936; Collard Fellow, Worshipful Company of Musicians, 1938; Chm. of Composers' Guild of Gt Britain, 1949, 1950 and 1954; Fellow, British Film Acad., 1958. *Works:* Five Orchestral Preludes (Proms., 1927); Divertimento for Flute (Internat. Contemp. Music Festival, New York, 1940); Concerto Grosso No I (commissioned by BBC, 1942); Symphony No I (Cheltenham Festival, 1950, London, 1953); Concerto Grosso No II (LSO and Proms, 1951); Festival March (commissioned by Arts Council for Festival of Britain, 1951); Symphonic Prelude, The Magic Island (Hallé Concerts, 1953); Symphony No II (Hallé Concerts, Manchester, 1953, BBC, Festival Hall, 1954); Lyra Angelica, Concerto for Harp Proms, 1954; Autumn Legend, for cor anglais and strings (Cheltenham Festival and Proms, 1955); Symphony No III (commissioned by BBC, 1956); Elizabethan Dances (commissioned by BBC, Festival Hall 1957); Symphony No IV (Promenade Concerts, 1959); Overture: Derby Day (commissioned by BBC, Proms, 1960); Concerto Grosso No III (commissioned by BBC, Proms, 1964); Sinfonietta for Strings (commissioned by Cheltenham Festival, 1970). *Film Music* since 1936 includes: Odd Man Out, The Way Ahead, The True Glory, World of Plenty, The Magic Box, etc. *Publications: orchestral:* 4 symphonies, 2 concerti grossi, Oboe Concerto, Festival March, The Magic Island, Scottish Dances, Harp Concerto (Lyra Angelica); *chamber music:* Rhapsody for Piano Quartet, String Quartet in D Minor, Sonata alla Toccata for Piano, Divertimento for Solo Flute, Fantasy-Waltzes for Piano, 12 Preludes for Piano; String Trio; Movements for Piano; Sonata for Clarinet and Piano. *Publications:* Ariel to Miranda *in* Adam Internat. Review, 1968; Anthology of 20th Century French Poetry, 1969. *Address:* Lark Rise, Blythburgh, Suffolk. *T:* Blythburgh 331. *Clubs:* Savile; Island Sailing (Cowes).

**AMALDI, Prof. Edoardo,** PhD; Italian physicist; Professor of General Physics, University of Rome, since 1937; *b* Carpaneto, Piacenza, 5 Sept. 1908; *s* of Ugo Amaldi and Luisa Basini; *m* 1933, Ginestra Giovene; two *s* one *d*. *Educ:* Rome Univ. Dr of Physics, 1929. Sec.-Gen., European Org. for Nuclear Research, 1952-54; Pres., Internat. Union of Pure and Applied Physics, 1957-60; Pres., Istituto Nazionale di Fisica Nucleare; Fellow, Acad. Naz. dei Lincei; Member: Royal Soc. of Sciences, Uppsala; Acad. of Sciences, USSR; Amer. Philos. Soc.; Amer. Acad. of Arts and Sciences; Nat. Acad. of Sciences, USA; Royal Acad., Netherlands; Acad. Leopoldino; Foreign Member: Royal Instn of GB; Royal Society, London, 1968; Royal Acad. Sweden, 1968. *Publications:* The production and slowing down of neutrons, 1959; contributor many papers on atomic, molecular and nuclear physics to learned jls. *Address:* Istituto di Fisica, Città Universitaria, Rome, Italy; (home) Viale Parioli 50, Rome.

**AMAN,** family name of **Baron Marley.**

**AMAND de MENDIETA, Rev. Dr Emmanuel Alexandre,** DD; Residentiary Canon of Winchester since Oct. 1962; *b* Bouvignes-sur-Meuse, Belgium, 11 Nov. 1907; *e s* of Ludovic Amand de Mendieta and of the Baroness Jeanne de Bonhome; *m* 1956, Ginette Christiane Bosc; one *s*. *Educ:* Coll. Notre-Dame de Bellevue, Dinant; Univ. catholique de Louvain. Entered Benedictine Abbey of Maredsous, Belgium, Oct. 1925; Mont-César, Louvain, 1927-33 (course in philos. and theol.); Priestly ordination in Namur Cathedral, 1932; Univ. of Louvain (courses in Class. Philol., 1933-36; Dr Philosophy and Letters 1939). Regular Contrib. to Revue Bénédictine, 1940-55. Reception into Church of England, 1956; Bye-Fellow of Gonville and Caius Coll., Cambridge, 1957-62. DD Cambridge 1966. *Publications:* (as Dom David Amand): Fatalisme et liberté dans l'antiquité grecque, 1945 (Louvain); L'ascèse monastique de saint Basile, essai historique, 1949 (Maredsous); (as E. Amand de Mendieta): La Presqu'île des Caloyers, le Mont-Athos, 1955 (Bruges-Paris); (collab. Dr Stig Y. Rudberg) Eustathius, Ancienne version latine des neuf homélies sur l'Hexaéméron de Basile de Césarée, 1958 (Berlin); Rome and Canterbury, A Biblical and Free Catholicism, 1962 (London); contrib. to Biblical and Patristic Studies in Memory of R. P. Casey, 1963; The "Unwritten" and "Secret" Apostolic Traditions in the Theological Thought of St Basil of Caesarea, 1965 (Edinburgh); The Garden of the Panaghia, Mount Athos, 1970 (Berlin). Contribs to L'Antiquité Classique (Brussels), Jl of Theological Studies (Oxford), Byzantinische Zeitschrift (Munich). *Address:* 1 The Close, Winchester, Hants. *T:* Winchester 4148.

**AMBARTSUMIAN, Victor;** Hero of Socialist Labour; Order of Lenin (twice); Order of Labour Red Banner (twice); President, Academy of Sciences of Armenian Soviet Socialist Republic, USSR, since 1947; *b* 18 Sept. 1908; *m* 1931, Vera Ambartsumian; two *s* two *d*. *Educ:* Univ. of Leningrad. Lecturer in Astronomy, 1931-34, Prof. of Astrophysics, 1934-44, Univ. of Leningrad; Prof. of Astrophysics, Univ. of Erevan, 1944-. Full Mem., Academy of Sciences of USSR, 1953-. Pres., Internat. Council of Scientific Unions, 1968-70. Hon. Dr of Science: Univs of Canberra, 1963; Paris, 1965; Liege, 1967; Prague, 1967; Foreign Member of Academies of Science: Washington, Paris, Rome, Vienna,

Berlin; Foreign Member of Royal Society, London. *Publications:* Theoretical Astrophysics, 1953 (in Russian; trans. into German, English, Chinese); about 100 papers in learned jls. Editor of jl, Astrofizika. *Address:* Academy of Sciences of Armenian SSR, Barekamutyan Street 24, Erevan, Armenia, USSR.

**AMBLER, Eric;** novelist and screenwriter; *b* 28 June 1909; *s* of Alfred Percy and Amy Madeleine Ambler; *m* 1st, 1939, Louise Crombie; 2nd, 1958, Joan Harrison. *Educ:* Colfe's Grammar Sch.; London Univ. Apprenticeship in engineering, 1927-28; advertisement copywriter, 1929-35; professional writer, 1936-. Served War of 1939-45: RA, 1940; commissioned, 1941; served in Italy, 1943; Lt-Col, 1944; Asst Dir of Army Kinematography, War Office, 1944-46, when released. US Bronze Star, 1946. Wrote and produced film, The October Man, 1947 and resumed writing career. Film Scenarios include: The Way Ahead, 1944; The October Man, 1947; The Passionate Friends, 1948; Highly Dangerous, 1950; The Magic Box, 1951; Gigolo and Gigolette, in Encore, 1952; The Card, 1952; Rough Shoot, 1953; The Cruel Sea, 1953; Lease of Life, 1954; The Purple Plain, 1954; Yangtse Incident, 1957; A Night to Remember, 1958; Wreck of the Mary Deare, 1959. *Publications:* The Dark Frontier, 1936; Uncommon Danger, 1937; Epitaph for a Spy, 1938; Cause for Alarm, 1938; The Mask of Dimitrios, 1939; Journey into Fear, 1940; Judgment on Deltchev, 1951; The Schirmer Inheritance, 1953; The Night-comers, 1956; Passage of Arms, 1959; The Light of Day, 1962; The Ability to Kill (essays), 1963; (Ed and introd) To Catch a Spy, 1964; A Kind of Anger, 1964; Dirty Story, 1967; The Intercom Conspiracy, 1969; numerous short stories, magazine and newspaper articles. *Address:* c/o Peter Janson-Smith Ltd, 42 Great Russell Street, WC1. *Clubs:* Garrick, Savile.

**AMBLER, Air Vice-Marshal Geoffrey Hill,** CB 1946; CBE 1944 (OBE 1941); AFC; DL; *b* 1904; *s* of late Fred Ambler; *m* 1940, Phoebe, *d* of Edgar Gaunt, Hawksworth Hall, Guiseley; three *d*. *Educ:* Cambridge University. Joined Auxiliary Air Force, 1931. DL West Riding, Yorks, 1949. *Address:* Brae Top, Curly Hill, Ilkley, Yorks.

**AMBLER, Harry,** OBE 1963; QPM 1955; Chief Constable, City of Bradford Police, since Dec. 1957; *b* 27 June 1908; *m* 1934, Kathleen Freda Muriel Mitchell; one *d*. *Educ:* Hanson Secondary Sch., Bradford; Oulton Sch., Liverpool. Joined City of Bradford Police as a Constable, 1930; Inspector, 1940; Staff Officer to HM Inspector of Constabulary, 1941-43; Superintendent, 1943; Asst and Dep. Chief Constable, 1952; Chief Constable, 1957. President: Bradford Development Cttee of Yorkshire Assoc. of Boys' Clubs; Police Boys' Club. Police Long Service and Good Conduct Medal, 1952; Coronation Medal, 1953. *Address:* Park House, Park Road, Thackley, Bradford, Yorkshire. *T:* Bradford 613267.

**AMBO, Rt. Rev. George Somboba;** an Assistant Bishop of New Guinea since Oct. 1960 (first Papuan-born Anglican Bishop); *b* Gona, Nov. 1925; *s* of late J. O. Ambo, Gona; *m* 1946, Marcella O., *d* of Karau; two *s* two *d*. *Educ:* St Aidan's College, Dogura; Newton Theological Coll., Dogura. Deacon, 1955; Priest, 1958. Curate of: Menapi, 1955-57; Dogura, 1957-58; Priest in charge of Boianai, Diocese of New Guinea, 1958-60. *Publication:* St John's Gospel in Ewage. *Recreations:* reading, carpentry. *Address:* Anglican Mission, Wamira, Dogura, Samarai, Papua; c/o Rev. J. D. Bodger (New Guinea Mission), Holcot Rectory, Northampton, England.

**AMBROSE, Prof. Edmund Jack,** MA (Cantab), DSc (London); Professor of Cell Biology, University of London, Institute of Cancer Research, since 1967; Staff of Chester Beatty Research Institute, Institute of Cancer Research: Royal Cancer Hospital since 1952; *b* 2 March 1914; *s* of Alderman Harry Edmund Ambrose and Kate (*née* Stanley); *m* 1943, Andrée (*née* Huck), Seine, France; one *s* one *d*. *Educ:* Perse Sch., Cambridge; Emmanuel Coll., Cambridge. Wartime research for Admiralty on infra-red detectors, 1940-45; subseq. research on structure of proteins using infra-red radiation at Courtauld Fundamental Research Laboratory. Convener of Brit. Soc. for Cell Biology. Chm., Scientific Adv. Cttee, Tate Memorial Centre, Bombay. Research on structure of proteins, on structure of normal and cancer cells, and on characteristics of surface of cancer cells. *Publications:* Cell Electrophoresis, 1965; The Biology of Cancer, 1966; The Cancer Cell *in vitro*, 1967. Publications on Protein Structure and Cell Biology, in Proc. Royal Soc., biological and chemical and scientific jls. *Recreation:* sailing. *Address:* 10 Calcott Street, Campden Hill, W8. *T:* 01-727 3356. *Clubs:* Royal Thames Yacht; Royal Bombay Yacht.

**AMBROSE, James Walter Davy;** Judge, Supreme Court Singapore, 1958-68; *b* 5 Dec. 1909; *s* of Samuel Ambrose; *m* 1945, Theresa Kamala Ambrose; no *c*. *Educ:* Free Sch., Penang; Oxford Univ. Asst Official Assignee, Singapore, 1936; Police Magistrate and Asst District Judge, Malacca, 1940; Registrar, Superior Court, Malacca, 1945; Dep. Public Prosecutor, 1946; Sen. Asst Registrar, Supreme Courts of Ipoh, Penang, and Kuala Lumpur, 1947-52; President, Sessions Court, Penang, 1953; Acting District Judge and First Magistrate, Singapore, 1955; Official Assignee, Public Trustee, and Comr of Estate Duties, Singapore 1957. *Address:* Unit 7, 101 Esplanade, South Perth, Western Australia 6151, Australia.

**AMBROSE, Brig. Robert Denis,** CIE 1947; OBE 1938; MC 1917; retired 1961, as Public Relations manager, Smith Kline and French International Company; *b* 3 Feb. 1896; *s* of Dr T. D. Ambrose, Dewsbury, Yorks; *m* 1938, Miriam Tilden, Philadelphia, USA; one *s* two *d*. *Educ:* Mount St Mary's College, Derbyshire; Wellington Military College, India. Commissioned in 104th Wellesley's Rifles, Indian Army, 1916; served European War, 1914-18, Palestine Campaign, 1917-18 (MC); NW Frontier, India, 1923-26 and 1930-38; commanded Tochi Scouts, 1933-36. Served War of 1939-45, in Middle East, Hong Kong and Burma; commanded 5th Bn (Napier's) Rajputana Rifles, 1940-43, Bde Comdr, 1943-45; Inspector Gen., Frontier Corps, 1945-47. *Address:* 109 Kenilworth Court, Lower Richmond Road, SW15. *T:* 01-789 8719. *Clubs:* Naval and Military, Challoner.
*See also Sir Edmund Paston-Bedingfeld.*

**AMCOTTS;** *see* Cracroft-Amcotts.

**AMEER ALI, (Syed) Waris,** CIE 1942; Indian Civil Service (retired); *b* 12 Oct. 1886; *e s* of late Rt Hon. Syed Ameer Ali, PC, CIE, and late Isabelle Ida Ameer Ali, 2 Cadogan Place, SW1; *m* 1st, 1918, Anne Marguerite (*d* 1943), *d* of late Walter Thomas Hindmarsh Radford, 25 Park Crescent, Portland Place; no *c*; 2nd, 1951, Lady Eleanor Szanto, *y d* of 3rd Earl of Dartrey. *Educ:* Wellington College; Balliol College, Oxford. Served in the United Provinces of Agra and Oudh. Closed Indian

Service as District and Sessions Judge of Gonda-cum-Bahraich in Oudh; retired, 1929; War Services Adviser to High Commissioner for India, 1939-45. *Publications:* articles, etc. *Recreations:* shooting, golf, target shooting (India Rifle Team, Bisley, 1930-38). *Address:* 1 Alexandra Court, Queen's Gate, SW7. *T:* 01-589 1556. *Club:* Reform.

**AMEER ALI, Sir Torick,** Kt 1941; *b* 9 June 1891; *y s* of late Rt Hon. Syed Ameer Ali, PC, CIE, etc, and Isabelle Ida Ameer Ali; *m* 1925, Mary Louise, *d* of late Roderick Edmond Carter, Indian Imperial Service of Engineers; one *s* one *d*. *Educ:* Marlborough; Christ Church, Oxford. Called to Bar Inner Temple; Puisne Judge, High Court, Calcutta, 1931-44; acting Chief Justice, 1944; an Adviser to Secretary of State for India, 1944. *Publications:* Memoirs of the Chevalier de Melville, etc. *Address:* Gregory Arms, Doccombe, Moretonhampstead, Devon.

**AMERS, Maj.-Gen. John Henry,** OBE 1941; *b* 8 July 1904; *s* of John Amers; *m* 1933, Muriel Henrietta Ethel Haeberlin; one *d*. *Educ:* Christ's Hospital; Royal Military Acad., Woolwich; Cambridge Univ. Commissioned 2nd Lieut into Royal Engineers, 1925. Served War of 1939-45, E Africa, Middle East and Italy. Col 1951; Brig. 1955; Maj.-Gen. 1958. Served HQ, BCOF, Japan, 1947-48; Chief Engineer, Salisbury Plain District, 1951-54; Deputy Director of Works, BAOR, 1955-57; Director of Fortification and Works, 1958-59; retired, 1959. *Address:* c/o Messrs Coutts and Co., 440 Strand, WC2. *Club:* Royal Commonwealth.

**AMERY, Rt. Hon. Julian,** PC 1960; MP (C) Brighton Pavilion since 1969; Minister for Housing and Construction, Department of the Environment, since Oct. 1970; *b* 27 March 1919; *s* of late Rt Hon. Leopold Amery, PC, CH; *m* 1950, Catherine, *d* of Rt Hon. Harold Macmillan, *qv*; one *s* three *d*. *Educ:* Summerfields; Eton; Balliol Coll., Oxford. War Corresp. in Spanish Civil War, 1938-39; Attaché HM Legation, Belgrade, and on special missions in Bulgaria, Turkey, Roumania and Middle East, 1939-40; Sergeant in RAF, 1940-41; commissioned and transferred to army, 1941; on active service, Egypt, Palestine and Adriatic, 1941-42; liaison officer to Albanian resistance movement, 1944; served on staff of Gen. Carton de Wiart, VC, Mr Churchill's personal representative with Generalissimo Chiang Kai-Shek, 1945. Contested Preston in Conservative interest, July 1945; MP (C) Preston North, 1950-66; Delegate to Consultative Assembly of Council of Europe, 1950-53 and 1956. Member Round Table Conference on Malta, 1955. Parliamentary Under-Sec. of State and Financial Secretary, War Office, 1957-58: Parliamentary Under-Sec. of State, Colonial Office, 1958-60; Secretary of State for Air, Oct. 1960-July 1962; Minister of Aviation, 1962-64; Minister of Public Building and Works, June-Oct. 1970. *Publications:* Sons of the Eagle, 1948; The Life of Joseph Chamberlain: vol. IV, 1901-3: At the Height of his Power, 1951; vols V and VI, 1901-14: Joseph Chamberlain and the Tariff Reform Campaign, 1969; articles in National Review, Nineteenth Century and Daily Telegraph. *Recreations:* ski-ing, mountaineering, travel. *Address:* 112 Eaton Square, SW1. *T:* 01-235 1543, 01-235 7409; Forest Farm House, Chelwood Gate, Sussex. *Clubs:* White's, Beefsteak, Carlton, Buck's.

**AMES, Sir Cecil (Geraint),** Kt 1965; *b* 5 Aug. 1897; *s* of late Herbert Edmund Ames, solicitor, Frome; *m* 1938, Jean Munro Miller; one *d*. *Educ:* Elstree Prep. School; Dover College. Somerset LI, 1916-18. Solicitor, 1921; Nigerian Administrative Service, 1922-33; Registrar, Supreme Court of Nigeria, 1933-34; Asst Judge, High Court of Protectorate of Nigeria, 1934-44; Puisne Judge, Supreme Court of Nigeria, 1944-50; retd 1950. Colonial Magistrate, Gambia, 1953-58; Comr for Law Revision, Sierra Leone, 1958-60; Pres. (part-time) Sierra Leone and Gambia Court of Appeal, 1960-61; Comr for Revision of Laws, Eastern Nigeria, 1960-64; Presiding Judge, Sierra Leone Court of Appeal (part-time), 1961-65; President, Gambia Court of Appeal (part-time position), 1961-67; Comr for Revision of Laws, Gambia, 1965-67; retd 1967. *Publications:* Gazetteer of the Plateau Province of Nigeria, 1934 (publ. Nigeria). Editor, Nigeria Law Reports, Vols XIV-XVIII. *Address:* 5 St Mary's Close, Bath, Somerset. *T:* Bath 64089.

**AMES, Jennifer;** *see* Greig, Maysie.

**AMES, Mrs Kenneth;** *see* Gainham, S. R.

**AMHERST,** family name of **Earl Amherst.**

**AMHERST,** 5th Earl, *cr* 1826; **Jeffery John Archer Amherst,** MC 1918; Baron Amherst of Montreal, 1788; Viscount Holmesdale, 1826; Major, late Coldstream Guards; Manager, External Affairs, BEA, 1946; later Director of Associated Companies, retd, Dec. 1966; Hon. Commission as Wing Commander, RAF, 1942; *b* 13 Dec. 1896; *e s* of 4th Earl and Hon. Eleanor Clementina St Aubyn (*d* 1960), *d* of 1st Baron St Levan; *S* father, 1927. *Educ:* Eton; RMC Sandhurst. Served European War, 1914-18, with Coldstream Guards (MC); placed on RARO 1921; recalled 1940, served Middle East, 1940-44. Reportorial Staff, New York Morning World, 1923-29; Commercial Air Pilot and General Manager Air Line Company, 1929-39; Asst Air Adviser to British Railways, 1945-46. *Heir:* *b* Hon. Humphrey William Amherst, *b* 25 July 1903. *Clubs:* Guards, Travellers', Pratt's, Garrick.

**AMHERST of Hackney,** 3rd Baron, *cr* 1829; **William Alexander Evering Cecil,** CBE 1963; Major late Royal Horse Guards; *b* 31 May 1912; *s* of Capt. Hon. William Amherst Cecil, MC (*d* 1914), Grenadier Guards, and Gladys (*d* 1947), *o c* of Col H. C. Baggalay, of Heatherhurst Grange, Frimley; *S* grandmother, 1919; *m* 1939, Margaret E. Clifton, *y d* of late Brig.-Gen. Howard Clifton Brown; two *s* one *d*. *Educ:* Eton; Trinity College, Cambridge. Royal Horse Guards, 1933; served War of 1939-45, MEF, 1940-45. CStJ. *Heir:* *s* Hon. William Hugh Amherst Cecil [*b* 28 Dec. 1940; *m* 1965, Elisabeth, *d* of Hugh H. Merriman; one *s* one *d*]. *Address:* Shroner Wood, Martyr Worthy, Winchester, Hants. *T:* Winchester 2803; 29 Eaton Mews South, SW1. *T:* 01-235 1421. *Clubs:* Buck's, Carlton, Royal Yacht Squadron.

**AMIES, Sir Arthur (Barton Pilgrim),** Kt 1957; CMG 1949; Emeritus Professor of Dental Medicine and Surgery, University of Melbourne; *b* 17 Oct. 1902; *s* of late Arthur P. Amies, Melbourne; *m* 1930, Geraldine C., *d* of Peter Collee, Linlithgow, Scotland. *Educ:* Modern Sch., Perth, Western Australia; Queen's College, Univ. of Melbourne; Edinburgh Royal Colls. DDSc (Melbourne) 1929; DLO Melbourne 1933; FRCSE 1948; FRACS 1934; FDSRCS 1948; FDSRCS Edinburgh, 1950; FRSE 1939. Formerly Member Council and Pro-Vice-Chancellor, University of Melbourne; Hon. Fellow of Queen's College; Hon. Consulting Oral Surgeon, Alfred Hospital, Eye and Ear

Hospital and Dental Hospital, Melbourne; Federal President, Australian Dental Association, 1937-39. Served War of 1939-45, with 4th Australian General Hospital in Western Desert and Tobruk, and later with Maxillo-Facial and Plastic Surgery Unit, 2nd Aust. Gen. Hosp. Kantara. Hon. LLD Glasgow, 1963. *Address:* Upper Kinneil, Yarra Glen, Victoria 3775, Australia. *T:* 7376278. *Clubs:* Melbourne, Naval and Military (Melbourne).

**AMIES, (Edwin) Hardy,** RDI 1964; FRSA 1965; Dressmaker by Appointment to HM The Queen; Director Hardy Amies Ltd, since 1946; Vice-President, Clothing Institute, since 1957; Hon. Senior Lecturer Royal College of Art, since 1964; Design Consultant to: J. Hepworth & Son, Ltd, since 1960; C. & J. Clark Ltd (Men's shoe Division), since 1963; D. Byford & Co. Ltd since 1963; Bonsoir Ltd since 1966, and to overseas manufacturers in USA, Canada, Australia, New Zealand and Japan; *b* 17 July 1909; *s* of late Herbert William Amies and Mary (*née* Hardy). *Educ:* Brentwood. Studied languages in France and Germany, 1927-30; trainee at W. & T. Avery Ltd, Birmingham, 1930-34; managing designer at Lachasse, Farm Street, W1, 1934-39. War Service, 1939-45: joined Intelligence Corps, 1939, becoming Lt-Col and head of Special Forces Mission to Belgium, 1944; founded dressmaking business, 1946; opened Hardy Amies' Boutique Ltd, 1950. Chairman, Incorporated Society of London Fashion Designers, 1959-60 (Vice-Chm., 1954-56): Mem., Cttee of Management, Friends of Covent Garden. Awards: Harper's Bazaar, 1962; Caswell-Massey, 1962, 1964, 1968; Ambassador Magazine, 1964; Sunday Times Special Award, 1965. Officier de l'Ordre de la Couronne (Belgium), 1946. *Publications:* Just So Far, 1954; ABC of Men's Fashion, 1964. *Recreations:* lawn tennis, gardening, opera. *Address:* 17b Eldon Road, W8; Hardy Amies Ltd, 14 Savile Row, W1. *T:* 01-734 2436. *Club:* Queen's.

**AMIES, Hardy;** *see* Amies, E. H.

**AMIS, Kingsley;** author; *b* 16 April 1922; *o c* of William Robert and Rosa Amis; *m* 1st, 1948, Hilary Ann, *d* of Leonard Sidney and Margery Bardwell; two *s* one *d*; 2nd, 1965, Elizabeth Jane Howard, *qv*. *Educ:* City of London School; St John's, Oxford. Served in Army, 1942-45. Lectr in English, University Coll. of Swansea, 1949-61; Fellow of Peterhouse, Cambridge, 1961-63. *Publications:* A Frame of Mind (verse), 1953; Lucky Jim (novel), 1954, filmed, 1957; That Uncertain Feeling (novel), 1955, filmed (Only Two Can Play), 1962; A Case of Samples (verse), 1956; I Like it Here (novel), 1958; Take a Girl Like You (novel), 1960; New Maps of Hell (belles-lettres), 1960; My Enemy's Enemy (short stories), 1962; One Fat Englishman (novel), 1963; The James Bond Dossier (belles-lettres), 1965; The Egyptologists (novel), with Robert Conquest, 1965; The Anti-Death League (novel), 1966; A Look Round the Estate (poems), 1967; (as Robert Markham) Colonel Sun (novel), 1968; I Want it Now (novel), 1968; The Green Man (novel), 1969; What Became of Jane Austen? (belles-lettres), 1970. *Recreations:* music, films, television. *Address:* Lemmons, Hadley Common, Barnet, Herts. *Club:* Travellers'.

**AMOORE, Rt. Rev. Frederick Andrew;** *see* Bloemfontein, Bishop of.

**AMOROSO, Prof. Emmanuel Ciprian,** CBE 1969; FRS 1957; FRCP; FRCS; FRCOG; DSc(London), PhD, MD, BCh, BAO; Professor of Physiology, Royal Veterinary College, University of London, 1947-68, Emeritus since 1968; *Educ:* University Coll., Dublin (Grad. in Medicine); Kaiser Wilhelm Inst. für Zellforschung, Berlin; University Coll., London. McArdle Medal in Surgery and a travelling fellowship in science at NUI, 1929; then appointed to staff of Royal Veterinary Coll. Lectures: Goldwin Smith, Cornell, 1954; Holme, UCL, 1956; Keibel, Free Univ., Berlin, 1957; Josiah Macey, Harvard, 1958; Ingleby, Birmingham, 1958; Leoherb, Washington Univ., St Louis, 1958; Terry, Washington Univ., St Louis, 1961; Liebig, Univ. of Geissen, 1964; Darwin, Eugenics Soc., 1967; Sir James Mackenzie Oration, Burnley, 1970. Hon. ARCVS 1959; Fellow: Royal Veterinary Coll., 1969; UCL, 1970. Hon. ScD NUI, 1963; Hon. DSc Illinois; Hon DVetMed Santiago, 1967; Hon. DSc Nottingham, 1970. *Publications:* chapter on the Placenta, in 3rd edn of Marshall's Physiology of Reproduction, 1952; papers in Proc. Royal Soc., Jl of Physiol., Jl of Anat. *Address:* Agricultural Research Council Institute of Animal Physiology, Brabaham, Cambridge. *T:* Sawston 2312; 29 Derwent Close, Cherry Hinton Road, Cambridge. *T:* Cambridge 47825.

**AMORY,** *see* Heathcoat Amory.

**AMORY,** 1st Viscount, *cr* 1960: **Derick Heathcoat Amory,** KG 1968; PC 1953; GCMG 1961; TD; DL; Lieutenant-Colonel (hon. rank); RA (TA) retired; *b* 26 Dec. 1899; *s* of Sir Ian Murray Heathcoat Amory, 2nd Bt, CBE, and *heir-pres.* to brother, Sir John Heathcoat-Amory, 3rd Bt, *qv*. *Educ:* Eton; Christ Church, Oxford (MA). Served war of 1939-45. Governor, Hudson's Bay Co.; Director: Lloyds Bank, 1948-51 and 1964-70; John Heathcoat & Co. (Chm., 1966-); ICI, 1964-70. Member Devon CC, 1932-51; MP (C) Tiverton Div. of Devon, 1945-60; Minister of Pensions, Nov. 1951-Sept. 1953; Minister of State, Board of Trade, 1953-54; Minister of Agriculture and Fisheries, July 1954; Minister of Agriculture and Fisheries and Minister of Food, Oct. 1954; Minister of Agriculture, Fisheries and Food, April 1955-Jan. 1958; Chancellor of the Exchequer, Jan. 1958-July 1960; High Commissioner for the United Kingdom in Canada, 1961-63. Jt Pro-Chancellor, University of Exeter, 1966-. Chairman: Medical Research Council, 1960-61, and 1965-69; Voluntary Service Overseas, 1964-; President: County Councils Assoc., 1961-; London Federation of Boys' Clubs; Jt Hon. Treas., YMCA. High Steward Borough of South Molton, 1959. DL Devon, 1962. Hon. LLD: Exeter Univ., 1959; McGill Univ. *Address:* 150 Marsham Court, SW1; The Wooden House, Chevithorne, Tiverton, Devon. *Clubs:* Carlton; Royal Yacht Squadron.

**AMORY, Major Sir John Heathcoat-,** 3rd Bt, *cr* 1874; Major Home Guard; *b* 2 May 1894; *e s* of Sir Ian Murray Heathcoat Amory, 2nd Bt, CBE, and Alexandra Georgina, OBE (*d* 1942), *e d* of late Vice-Adm. G. H. Seymour, CB; *S* father 1931; *m* 1937, Joyce, *o d* of Newton Wethered, Brook, Surrey. *Educ:* Christ Church, Oxford. Served European War, 1914-19, with 4th Devon Regt in India and Mesopotamia and in Persia and the Caucasus with the Dunster Force (despatches, two medals); President of John Heathcoat & Co.; High Sheriff of Devon, 1942-43; JP Devon, 1922; DL Devon, 1952. *Recreations:* gardening, shooting. *Heir:* *b* Viscount Amory, *qv*. *Address:* Knightshayes Court, Tiverton, Devon. *T:* 2438; Glenfernate Lodge, Enochdhu, Blairgowrie, Perthshire. *Club:* Buck's.

**AMPLEFORTH, Abbot of;** *see* Hume, Rt Rev. G. B.

**AMPTHILL,** 3rd Baron, *cr* 1881; **John Hugo Russell,** CBE 1945; Captain RN, retired; recalled for Service, 1939; *b* 4 Oct. 1896; *e s* of 2nd Baron and Lady Margaret Lygon, CI, GCVO, GBE (*d* 1957), *d* of 6th Earl Beauchamp; *S* father, 1935; *m* 1st, 1918, Christabel Hulme Hart (who obtained a divorce 1937); one *s*; 2nd, 1937, Sibell Faithfull (*d* 1947), *yr d* of Thomas Wilkinson Lumley; 3rd, 1948, Adeline, *e d* of Canon H. E. Hone; one *s* one *d*. *Heir:* *s* Hon. Geoffrey Denis Erskine Russell [*b* 15 Oct. 1921; *m* 1946, Susan Mary, *d* of Hon. Charles John Frederic Winn; two *s* one *d* (and one *s* decd)]. *Address:* 6 Springfield Road, St John's Wood, NW8. *T:* 01-624 3475. *Club:* United Service.
*See also Adm. Hon. Sir G. H. E. Russell.*

**AMULREE,** 2nd Baron, *cr* 1929; **Basil William Sholto Mackenzie,** MD; FRCP; Liberal Whip, House of Lords, since 1955; *b* 25 July 1900; *o s* of 1st Baron and Lilian (*d* 1916), *e d* of late W. H. Bradbury; *S* father, 1942. *Educ:* Lancing Coll.; Gonville and Caius Coll., Cambridge (MA 1925); Paris; University Coll. Hosp. MRCS, LRCP 1925; MRCP 1928; MD Cantab 1936; FRCP 1946. Asst Pathologist: University Coll. Hosp., 1929-31; Royal Northern Hosp., 1931-36; MO, Min. of Health, 1936-50; Physician, University Coll. Hosp., 1949-66. President: London Co. Div., British Red Cross, 1945-60; Assoc. of Occupational Therapists, 1956-60; Soc. of Chiropodists, 1963; Assoc. of Welfare Officers, 1960-68; British Geriatric Soc. Chm., Invalid Meals for London, 1956-59. Vice-Chm., Chadwick Trust. Member: Nat. Radium Commn, 1942-45; (professional) Assoc. of Water Engineers; Royal Inst. of Health. Hon. Mem. Faculty of Radiologists; Hon. FCCP. Star of Ethiopia (1st class), 1952. *Publications:* Adding Life to Years; Min. of Health Report on Public Health and Medical Subjects, No 89; various articles in periodicals. *Recreation:* walking. *Heir:* none. *Address:* 18 Egerton Terrace, SW3. *Club:* Reform.

**AMWELL,** 2nd Baron *cr* 1947, of Islington; **Frederick Norman Montague;** *b* 6 Nov. 1912; *o s* of 1st Baron Amwell, CBE, and Constance (*d* 1964), *d* of James Craig; *S* father, 1966; *m* 1939, Kathleen Elizabeth Fountain; one *s* one *d*. *Educ:* Highbury Grammar School; Northampton Coll. of Technology. Aircraft Design Engineer (Apprenticeship in 1930). AFRAeS. *Heir:* *s* Hon. Keith Norman Montague, BSc, AMInstHE, *b* 1 April 1943. *Address:* 34 Halliford Road, Sunbury-on-Thames, Middx. *T:* Sunbury-on-Thames 85413.

**ANCASTER,** 3rd Earl of, *cr* 1892; **Gilbert James Heathcote-Drummond-Willoughby,** TD; Baron Willoughby de Eresby, 1313; Baron Aveland, 1856; Lord Lieutenant of County of Lincoln since 1950; *b* 8 Dec. 1907; *s* of 2nd Earl of Ancaster, GCVO, and late Eloise, *e d* of W. L. Breese, New York; *S* father 1951; *m* 1933, Hon. Nancy Phyllis Louise Astor, *o d* of 2nd Viscount Astor; one *d* (one *s* decd). *Educ:* Eton; Magdalene Coll., Cambridge (MA). Served War of 1939-45: Leicestershire Yeomanry and Major RA (wounded, despatches). MP (C) Rutland and Stamford, 1933-50; summoned to the Upper House of Parliament as Baron Willoughby de Eresby, 1951; Lord Great Chamberlain of England, 1950-52. JP 1937, CC 1950, Alderman, 1954, Kesteven; DL 1947, Co. Lincoln. KStJ 1957. *Heir:* (to Barony of Willoughby de Eresby): *d* Lady Nancy Jane Marie Heathcote-Drummond-Willoughby, *b* 1 Dec. 1934; (to Baronetcy) (Gilbert) Simon Heathcote, CBE [*b* 21 Sept. 1913; *m* 1939, Patricia Margaret, *d* of Brig. James Travers Leslie, MC; one *s* one *d*]. *Address:* Grimsthorpe, Bourne, Lincs. *T:* Edenham 222; Drummond Castle, Crieff. *T:* Muthill 321. *Club:* Turf.
*See also Sir John Aird, Earl of Dalhousie.*

**ANCRAM, Earl of; Michael Andrew Foster Jude Kerr;** *b* 7 July 1945: *s* and *heir* of 12th Marquess of Lothian, *qv*. *Educ:* Ampleforth; Christ Church, Oxford. *Recreations:* ski-ing, shooting and fishing. *Address:* Melbourne Hall, Derby; 3 Chesterfield Street, W1; Monteviot, Ancrum, Roxburghshire. *T:* Ancrum 288. *Club:* Turf.

**ANDA, Géza;** pianist; *b* Budapest, 19 Nov. 1921; *s* of Géza Anda, Headmaster; became Swiss citizen, 1955; *m* 1964, Hortense Bührle. *Educ:* Budapest Academy of Music. Made début with Mengelberg, 1939; has played with numerous orchestras, including: Berlin Philharmonic; Vienna Philharmonic; New York Philharmonic; Amsterdam Concertgebouw; Philharmonia, London; Paris Conservatoire; Santa Cecilia, Rome; Philadelphia Symphony; Chicago Symphony; San Francisco Symphony, etc. Has played at Salzburg, Lucerne, Edinburgh and Vienna Festivals; makes annual appearances at Festival Hall; frequent tours of United States and Canada. Hon. RAM, 1969. Grand Prix des Disques, 1961, 1962, 1963, 1966; Preis der Deutschen Schallplattenkritik, Berlin; Franz Liszt Prize; Wiener Flötenuhr, 1969-70. Ordre des Arts et des Lettres (France). *Recreations:* bookbinding, sailing, walking tours. *Address:* Zollikerstrasse 178, Zürich, Switzerland.

**ANDERSEN, Valdemar Jens,** CMG 1965; OBE 1960 (MBE 1955); VRD 1962; Resident Commissioner, Gilbert and Ellice Islands Colony, 1962-70, retired; *b* 21 March 1919; 2nd *s* of Max Andersen, Maraenui, NZ; *m* 1946, Alison Leone, 2nd *d* of G. A. Edmonds, Remuera, Auckland, NZ; one *s* one *d*. *Educ:* Napier Boys High Sch., NZ; Auckland University Coll. (BSc). Lieut, RNZNVR, 1940-46; Lieut, RANVR, 1947-62. British Solomon Islands Protectorate: Administrative Officer, 1947; Class A, Administrative Officer, 1954; Secretary Protectorate Affairs, 1958. *Recreations:* tennis, golf, poetry and orchids. *Address:* Morris Road, Manurewa, New Zealand. *Club:* Pakuranga Country.

**ANDERSON,** family name of **Viscount Waverley.**

**ANDERSON, Archibald Stirling Kennedy,** DSO 1918; MC; MA, MB, ChB, DPH; retired; *b* 1887; *s* of late Alex. Anderson, Aberdeen; *m* 1925, Joyce (*d* 1954), *e d* of W. S. Wharton, Southtown, Great Yarmouth; twin *s*. *Educ:* Aberdeen Grammar Sch.; Aberdeen Univ. Served European War, 1914-19 (DSO, MC with bar, despatches, Hon. Lieut-Col RAMC). *Address:* 1 Marine Parade, Gorleston, Great Yarmouth. *T:* Great Yarmouth 61438.

**ANDERSON, Arthur Ingham;** Chairman, The United Africa Co. Ltd, since 1969; Director of Unilever Ltd since 1970; *b* 4 April 1916; *s* of John Fraser Anderson and Jane (*née* Millie); *m* 1954, Rolande Marie Bois-Meyer; one *s* one *d*. *Educ:* George Watson's Boys' Coll., Edinburgh; Univs of Edinburgh and Glasgow (MA). Joined Unilever, 1935; Management Trainee, 1937-39. Served War of 1939-45, HAC: Captain 19th Field Regt RA, N Africa, Sicily, Italy, Palestine, 1940-46 (despatches). The United Africa Co. Ltd, 1946-: Germany, 1947; Nigeria, 1948; Company Rep. in US, 1952-54; Merchandise Man., 1955; Dir, 1957; Dep. Chm. and Jt Man. Dir, 1968. *Recreations:* military history, photography, golf. *Address:*

12 Barham Road, West Wimbledon, SW20. *T:* 01-946 3671.

**ANDERSON, Sir Austin (Innes),** Kt 1956; Chairman Orient Line, 1952-60 (Director 1950); Chairman Anderson, Green & Co. Ltd, 1950-63 (Director, 1924); Director: Peninsular and Oriental Steam Navigation Co., 1955-62; University Life Assurance Ltd, 1943-67; Westminster Bank, 1950-68; *b* 16 Mar. 1897; *s* of Sir Hugh Anderson, FRS; *m* Alison Royse, *d* of W. R. Lysaght, CBE; one *s* two *d. Educ:* Harrow; King's Coll., Cambridge. Served in Army, 1915-18. Member Food Investigation Board, 1934-38; Assistant Director Liner Division, Ministry of War Transport, 1940-43, and of Sea Transport Division, 1943-45. Chairman, Refrigerated Cargo Research Council, 1946-58; Pres., Chamber of Shipping, 1955; Chm., General Council of British Shipping, 1955; Mem. Cttee Lloyds Register of Shipping, 1951-62; Member: Ministry of Transport Cttee on application of Nuclear Power to Marine Purposes, 1957-62; Air Min. Meteorological Cttee, 1959-65; Central Transport Users Consultative Cttee for Gt Britain, 1952-54. *Address:* Summers, West Clandon, Surrey. *T:* Clandon 512.

**ANDERSON, Betty H.;** *see* Harvie Anderson.

**ANDERSON, Carl David,** PhD; Professor of Physics, California Institute of Technology, since 1939; Chairman, Division of Physics, Mathematics and Astronomy, since 1962; *b* 3 Sept. 1905; *s* of Carl David Anderson and Emma Adolfina Ajaxson; *m* 1946, Lorraine Bergman; two *s. Educ:* California Institute of Technology. BS 1927, PhD 1930. War activities on projects, 1941-45; Presidential Certificate of Merit, 1945. Has conducted research on X-rays, gamma rays, cosmic rays, elementary particles, etc. Member: Nat. Acad. of Sciences; Amer. Philosoph. Soc.; Amer. Acad. of Arts and Sciences. Nobel prize in Physics, 1936; Elliott Cresson Medal of the Franklin Inst., 1937; John Ericsson Medal of Amer. Soc. of Swedish Engineers, 1960, etc. Holds hon. degrees. *Address:* California Institute of Technology, Pasadena, Calif 91109, USA.

**ANDERSON, Rear-Adm. (Charles) Courtney;** Flag Officer, Admiralty Interview Board, since 1969; *b* 8 Nov. 1916; *s* of late Lt-Col Charles Anderson, Australian Light Horse, and Mrs Constance Powell-Anderson, OBE, JP; *m* 1940, Pamela Ruth Miles; three *s. Educ:* RNC, Dartmouth. Joined RN, 1930. Served War of 1939-45: in command of Motor Torpedo Boats, Destroyers and Frigates. Naval Intelligence, 1946-49 and 1955-57; Commanded HMS Contest, 1949-51; Comdr, 1952; BJSM, Washington, 1953-55; Capt., 1959; Naval Attaché, Bonn, 1962-65; Director, Naval Recruiting, 1966-68; ADC to Queen, 1968; Rear-Adm., 1969. *Publications:* The Drum Beats Still, 1951. Numerous articles and short stories. *Recreations:* gardening, do-it-yourself. *Address:* Timbercroft, 5 Southborough Close, Surbiton, Surrey. *T:* 01-399 3652. *Club:* United Service.

**ANDERSON, Lt-Col Charles Groves Wright,** VC 1942; MC; Member House of Representatives, for Hume, New South Wales, 1949-51 and 1955-61; grazier; *b* Capetown, South Africa, 12 Feb. 1897; *s* of A. G. W. Anderson; *m* 1931, Edith M. Tout; two *s* two *d.* Served European War, 1914-18 (MC), KAR, E Africa. Served War of 1939-45 (VC, POW), 2nd AIF, Malaya. *Recreation:* motoring. *Address:* Springfield, Young, New South Wales 2594, Australia. *Club:* Commonwealth (Canberra).

**ANDERSON, Clinton Presba;** US Senator since 1948; *b* Centerville, SD, 23 Oct. 1895; *s* of Andrew Jay Anderson and Hattie Belle Presba; *m* 1921, Henrietta McCartney; one *s* one *d. Educ:* Dakota Wesleyan University; University of Michigan. Hon. LHD Dakota Wesleyan Univ., 1933; hon. DAgr New Mexico Coll. of Agric. and Mechanic Arts, 1946; hon. LLD: Univ. of Michigan, St Lawrence Univ., Canton, NY, 1946; Missouri Valley Coll., Marshall, Mo., 1949; Univ. of Alaska, 1965. Newspaper reporter and editor, Albuquerque, New Mexico, 1918-22; owner insurance agency, Albuquerque, New Mexico, 1925-63; Treasurer, State of New Mexico, 1933-34; Mem. 77th, 78th and 79th Congresses (1941-45), New Mexico at large. Secretary of Agriculture, United States, 1945-48, when resigned to enter Democratic primary for US Senator. Member Delta Theta Phi; Democrat; Presbyterian; Mason, Elk. *Address:* (home) 3621 Camino Alameda, SW, Albuquerque, New Mexico, USA; 6 Wesley Circle NW, Washington, DC, USA; (office) 215-5th Street SW, Albuquerque, New Mexico, 87101, New Senate Office Building, Washington, DC 20510, USA. *Club:* Rotary (Pres. Rotary Internat., 1932-33).

**ANDERSON, Sir Colin (Skelton),** KBE 1969; Kt 1950; Director, P & O Steam Navigation Co., 1960-69; *b* 15 July 1904; *s* of late Sir Alan Anderson, GBE; *m* 1932, Morna Campbell, 2nd *d* of Sir Alexander MacCormick, KCMG; two *d* (and one *d* decd). *Educ:* Eton; Trinity College, Oxford. Director: Midland Bank Ltd, 1950-; Marine Insurance Co. Ltd, 1950-70; Orient Steam Navigation Co. Ltd, 1950-69; Australia & New Zealand Bank Ltd, 1951-70; Royal Opera House, Covent Garden, Ltd, 1961-; City Arts Trust Ltd, 1962-; English Opera Group Ltd, 1963-. Chairman: London Shipowners' Dock Labour Cttee, 1944-45; London Port Employers (and a Member of London Bd of Nat. Dock Labour Bd), 1945-47; Nat. Assoc. of Port Employers, 1947-48, 1950-54; General Council of British Shipping, 1949-50; British Liner Cttee, 1949-50; Internat. Chamber of Shipping, 1949-63; Min. of Transport's Advisory Cttee on Traffic Signs for Motor Roads, 1957-61; Min. of Education's Cttee on Grants to Students, 1958-60; Gray, Dawes, Westray & Co. Ltd, 1960-70; Trustees of Tate Gall., 1960-67 (Vice-Chm., 1953-59); Ocean Travel Development, 1961-68; Anderson Green & Co. Ltd, 1963-70 (Dir, 1930); HMS Victory Adv. Technical Cttee, 1964-; Sea Transport Commn of Internat. Chamber of Commerce, 1965-; Hampstead Heath and Old Hampstead Protection Soc., 1960-67. President: Seamen's Hospital Soc., 1962-; Chamber of Shipping of the UK, 1949-50 (Vice-Pres., 1948-49); British Employers' Confederation, 1956-58 (Vice-Pres., 1952-56); Hon. Pres., Internat. Chamber of Shipping, 1963-. Member: Min. of Transport's Cttee on the Prevention of Pollution of the Sea by Oil, 1954-64; Commonwealth Office's Oversea Migration Board, 1953-66; Court of Enquiry into National Railway Strike (with Sir J. Cameron and Mr H. Douglas), 1954; Contemporary Art Soc. (Chairman, 1956-60); Council of Royal College of Art (Chairman, 1952-56; Provost, 1967-); National Council of Design and Industries Association (President, 1950-53); Council of Industrial Design, 1951-60; Royal Fine Art Commn, 1959- (Chairman, 1968-). Trustee, Nat. Gall. (representing Tate Gall.), 1963-67. Prime Warden of the Fishmongers' Company, 1963-64. Corres. Mem., Bayerische Akademie der Schönen Künste, 1969-. Hon. ARIBA 1957; Hon. Fellow, Trinity College, Oxford, 1963. Hon. LLD, Aberdeen, 1963. Hon. Designer, RCA, 1953; Hon. Dr, RCA,

1967. Jubilee Medal, RSA, 1954. Officer of the Order of Orange Nassau, 1948. *Recreations:* the home, the arts, the garden. *Address:* Admiral's House, Hampstead, NW3. *T:* 01-435 0597. *Clubs:* Brooks's, City of London.

**ANDERSON, Courtney;** *see* Anderson, (Charles) Courtney.

**ANDERSON, Rev. Canon David;** Senior Lecturer, Wall Hall College, Aldenham, Herts, since 1970; *b* 30 Oct. 1919; *s* of William and Nancy Anderson, Newcastle upon Tyne; *m* 1953, Helen Finlay Robinson, 3rd *d* of Johnson and Eleanor Robinson, Whitley Bay, Northumberland; one *s* two *d. Educ:* Royal Grammar Sch. Newcastle upon Tyne; Selwyn Coll., Cambridge. Served in RA, 1940-42, Intelligence Corps, 1942-46, Lieut. Deacon, 1949, Priest, 1950; Curate of parish of St Gabriel, Sunderland, 1949-52; Tutor of St Aidan's Coll., Birkenhead, 1952-56; Warden of Melville Hall, Ibadan, Nigeria, 1956-58; Principal of: Immanuel Coll., Ibadan, Nigeria, 1958-62; Wycliffe Hall, Oxford, 1962-69. Examining Chaplain to Bishop of Liverpool, 1969-. *Publications:* The Tragic Protest, 1969; Simone Weil, 1970. *Recreations:* listening to music, hi-fi gramophones. *Address:* Wall Hall College, Aldenham, Watford, Herts.

**ANDERSON, David Colville,** QC (Scotland) 1957; VRD 1947, and Clasp, 1958; *b* 8 Sept. 1916; *yr s* of late J. L. Anderson of Pittormie, Fife, Solicitor and Farmer, and late Etta Colville; *m* 1948, Juliet, *yr d* of late Hon. Lord Hill Watson, MC, LLD; two *s* one *d. Educ:* Trinity Coll., Glenalmond; Pembroke Coll., Oxford; Edinburgh Univ. BA (Hons) Oxford 1938; LLB (Distinction) 1946. Thow Scholar, Maclagan Prizeman, Dalgety Prizeman, Edinburgh Univ. Lecturer in Scots Law, Edinburgh Univ., 1947-60; Advocate, 1946; Standing Junior Counsel to Ministry of Works, 1954-55, and to War Office, 1955-57. Contested (C) Coatbridge and Airdrie, 1955, and East Dunbartonshire, 1959; MP (C) Dumfries, Dec. 1963-Sept. 1964. Solicitor-General for Scotland, 1960-64; Vice-Chairman, Commissioners of Northern Lighthouses, 1963-64; Hon. Sheriff-Substitute, Lothians and Peebles, 1965-. Joined RNVR, 1935. In VIII awarded Ashburton Shield, Bisley, 1933 (Trinity Coll., Glenalmond; schools event); Inter-Services XX at Bisley, 1936-38. Served War of 1939-45 in destroyers (despatches); Lieut 1940; Egerton Prizeman in Naval Gunnery, 1943; Gunnery Officer, Rosyth Escort Force, 1943-45; Norway, 1945; Lt-Comdr 1948. King Haakon VII Liberty Medal, 1946. *Address:* 8 Arboretum Road, Edinburgh EH3 5PD. *T:* 031-552 3003. *Club:* New (Edinburgh).

**ANDERSON, David Dick,** CBE 1951; MC 1916 (and Bar, 1918); retired as HM Chief Inspector of Schools, Scottish Education Department, 1954; *b* 26 March 1889; *m* 1930; three *s. Educ:* Glasgow High School and University. Teacher: Queen's Park Senior Secondary School, Glasgow; Madras College, St Andrews; Daniel Stewart's College, Edinburgh. Served European War; officer, 1914-19, in East Yorkshire Regiment; retired with rank of Major. *Recreations:* golf, gardening, foreign travel. *Address:* 12 Ross Road, Edinburgh EH16 5QN. *T:* 031-667 8873. *Clubs:* Royal Over-Seas League; Royal Scots (Edinburgh).

**ANDERSON, David Fyfe,** MD, ChB, FRCOG, FRCPGlas; Muirhead Professor of Obstetrics and Gynæcology, University of Glasgow, 1946-70; Obstetric Surgeon, Royal Maternity Hospital, Glasgow; Gynæcological Surgeon, Royal Infirmary, Glasgow; *b* 8 June 1904; *o s* of David Fyfe Anderson and Mary Ann Mackay, Viewfield, Strathaven, Lanarkshire; *m* 1945, Elizabeth Rose, 2nd *d* of W. F. McAusland, Wyndyknowe, Scotstounhill, Glasgow; three *s* one *d. Educ:* Strathaven Academy (Dux); High Sch. of Glasgow (Dux, Modern Side); Univ. of Glasgow (Gardiner Bursary); Johns Hopkins Univ. MB, ChB (Commendation), Univ. of Glasgow, 1926; McCunn Research Scholar, 1929-31; MRCOG 1932; FRFPSG 1935; MD (Hons) 1935; FRCOG 1940; Rockefeller Travelling Fellowship 1935-36; FRSM; FRCPGlas 1964; Fellow of Glasgow Obstetrical and Gynæcological Soc. and of Edinburgh Obstetrical Soc.; formerly Examiner to Central Midwives Board for Scotland; lately Professor of Midwifery and Diseases of Women at Anderson College of Medicine, Glasgow. Freeman of City of Glasgow. Member of Incorporations of: Barbers, Bonnetmakers and Dyers, and Tailors (Ex-Deacon). *Publications:* Medical papers and verse. *Address:* 6 Cleveden Drive, Glasgow W2. *T:* 041-339 8345.

**ANDERSON, Prof. David Steel;** Emeritus Professor of Accounting and Business Method, Edinburgh University; *b* 27 Oct. 1902; *s* of David Anderson and Jessie Marian Steel; *m* 1931, Cicely Bouskell Hockin; one *s. Educ:* Viewpark School; George Watson's College, Edinburgh. Mem. Soc. of Accountants in Edinburgh, 1925; private practice as Chartered Accountant, 1927-29; joined firm of Wallace & Somerville, Edinburgh, as partner, 1929; partner of Whinney Murray & Co. External Examiner in Accounting, Faculty of Law, Edinburgh Univ., 1938-41; Mem. Gen. Examining Bd, Chartered Accountants of Scotland, 1939; Mem. Council Soc. of Accountants in Edinburgh, 1942-46; Mem. Advisory Cttee, Gen. Examining Bd, Inst. of Chartered Accountants of Scotland, 1937-57; Mem. Council Inst. of Chartered Accountants of Scotland, 1955-57, Vice-Pres., 1966, President, 1967-68. Hon. MA (Edinburgh Univ.), 1957. *Recreations:* golf, tennis, fishing. *Address:* 12 Succoth Gardens, Edinburgh. *T:* 031-337 3617. *Club:* Caledonian United Service and Northern (Edinburgh).

**ANDERSON, Sir David (Stirling),** Kt 1957; PhD, LLD Glasgow and Strathclyde; FRSE; FIMechE; *b* 25 Sept. 1895; *s* of Alexander Anderson and Sarah Stirling; *m* 1932, Grace Boyd. *Educ:* Royal Technical College, Glasgow (Greenock Research Schol.). Engineering experience with North British Locomotive Company and Fullerton, Hodgart and Barclay; 2nd Lieut RAF 1918; Head of Dept of Mech. Engineering, Derby Tech. Coll., 1924-26, Principal, 1926-30; Principal, Coll. of Technology, Birmingham, 1930-46; Dir, Royal College of Science and Technology, Glasgow, 1946-59; part-time Mem., S of Scotland Electricity Bd, 1960-67; Mem., Cttee on Higher Education, 1961-63; Chm., Scottish Certificate of Education Examination Bd, 1964-69. Pres. Assoc. of Principals of Technical Institutions, 1937; Chm. of Council, Assoc. of Tech. Instns, 1951; Mem. Council, Inst. Mech. Engrs, 1941-42, 1948-50. Hon. DSc (Aston), 1966. *Publications:* numerous papers and contributions on technical education. *Recreation:* climbing. Address: Braehead, Helensburgh, Dunbartonshire. *T:* 2227. *Clubs:* Royal Automobile; Royal Scottish Automobile, Western (Glasgow); Scottish Mountaineering (Edinburgh).

**ANDERSON, Prof. Declan John;** Professor of Oral Biology, University of Bristol, since 1966; *b* 20 June 1920; *s* of Arthur John Anderson and Katherine Mary Coffey; *m* 1947, Vivian Joy

Dunkerton; four *s* three *d*. *Educ:* Christ's Hospital; Guy's Hospital Medical School, Univ. of London. BDS (London) 1942; LDSRCS 1943, BSc 1946, MSc 1947, PhD 1955. Prof. of Physiology, Univ. of Oregon, USA, 1957-58; Prof. of Physiology in Relation to Dentistry, Univ. of London, 1963-66. *Publications:* Physiology for Dental Students, 1952. Scientific papers in professional Jls. *Recreations:* silversmithing and music. *Address:* 32 Downleaze, Bristol BS9 1LY. *T:* 684589.

**ANDERSON, Donald**; barrister-at-law; *b* 17 June 1939; *s* of David Robert Anderson and Eva (*née* Mathias); *m* 1963, Dorothy Trotman, BSc, PhD; two *s*. *Educ:* Swansea Grammar Sch.; University Coll. of Swansea. 1st cl. hons Modern History and Politics, Swansea, 1960. Barrister; called to Bar, Inner Temple, 1969. Member of HM Foreign Service, 1960-64: Foreign Office, 1960-63; 3rd Sec., British Embassy, Budapest, 1963-64; lectured in Dept of Political Theory and Govt, University Coll., Swansea, 1964-66. MP (Lab) Monmouth, 1966-70; Mem. Estimates Cttee, 1966-68; Vice-Chm., Welsh Labour Group, 1969-70; PPS to Min. of Defence (Administration), 1969-70. Dir, Campaign for European Political Community, 1967. Methodist local preacher. *Recreations:* church work, walking and talking. *Address:* Lamb Building, Temple, EC4; 8 Portobello Road, W11.

**ANDERSON, Sir Donald (Forsyth)**, Kt 1954; DL; Chairman and a Managing Director of P&OSN Co. since 1960 (formerly Deputy Chairman, and a Managing Director); Director: National Westminster Bank Ltd; Australia and New Zealand Bank Ltd; Times Newspapers Ltd; *b* 3 Sept. 1906; 2nd *s* of late Sir Alan Garrett Anderson, GBE; *m* 1935, Margaret Elaine, *e d* of Sir David R. Llewellyn, 1st Bt; four *d*. *Educ:* Eton; Trinity Coll., Oxford (MA). Entered Anderson Green & Co. Ltd; P&OSN Co. in 1934. In Min. of Shipping (subsequently Min. of War Transport), Sept. 1939-June 1943; Washington, DC, with British Merchant Shipping Mission, 1941-43. Chm. Council, Royal Free Hospital Sch. of Medicine; Mem. Governing Body, London Graduate Sch. of Business Studies; Pres. Seafarers' Education Service; Chm. Shipping Federation, 1950-62 (Pres., 1963-); Joint Chm., National Maritime Board, 1950-62; President International Shipping Federation, 1950-62; Pres. Chamber of Shipping, 1953-54; Chm. General Council of British Shipping, 1953-54; Pres. Inst. of Shipping and Forwarding Agents, 1955; Pres. Inst. of Marine Engineers, 1956; Chm. British Liner Cttee, 1956-58; Pres., Institute of Export, 1961-63; Mem. Minister of Transport's Shipping Advisory Panel, 1962-64. Elder Brother of Trinity House and Hon. Brother of Hull Trinity House. Hon. Captain, RNR; Hon. Mem., Hon. Co. of Master Mariners. DL Glos, 1969. Officer, Order of Orange Nassau; Commendatore, Order Al Merito della Repubblica Italiana. *Address:* 55 Cranmer Court, Sloane Avenue, SW3. *T:* 01-589 8866. *Clubs:* City of London, Brooks's. *See also Earl of Darnley.*

**ANDERSON, Sir Donald (George)**, Kt 1967; CBE 1959; Director-General of Civil Aviation, Australia, since 1956; *b* 1 March 1917; *s* of Alick Gibb Anderson and Clara Katherine Anderson; *m* 1941, Monica Mary Porker; two *d*. *Educ:* Adelaide High Sch; Adelaide Teachers' Coll.; Adelaide Univ. Served RAF, 1940-46, Flt Lt (Pilot). Asst Dir-Gen., Dept of Civil Aviation, 1951; Deputy Dir-Gen., 1955. *Address:* c/o Department of Civil Aviation, Aviation House, 188 Queen Street, Melbourne, Victoria 3000, Australia. *T:* 62.0131. *Club:* Savage (Melbourne).

**ANDERSON, Sir Duncan (Law)**, KBE 1960 (CBE 1944); TD; CEng, FICE; Director; British Overseas Airways Corporation; Airways Housing Trust (Chairman); British Oxygen Company; Thomas Tilling Ltd; *b* 10 June 1901; *s* of J. D. Anderson, MA, Aberdeen, and L. Anderson; *m* 1947, Edens Alcyone, *er d* of Wallace McMullen; no *c*. *Educ:* Robert Gordon's Coll., Aberdeen. Practised as Civil Engineer on railway, road, bridge and tunnel construction, 1922-39. TA Officer, 1923-61; served with Royal Engineers, War of 1939-45 (despatches, CBE); Deputy Dir of Works, Gen. Eisenhower's staff, N African Campaign, and Dir of Works (Brig.), FM Alexander's Staff, Italian Campaign. Concerned latterly with rehabilitation of Italian Industry as Dep. Vice-Pres. Allied Commn, Rome. Chm. Jt Anglo-American/Jugo-Slav Econ. Commn, Trieste. CCG, 1946-50; Vice-Pres. Econ. Sub-Commn, Berlin, and Dep. Chm. US/UK Control Office, Frankfurt; Mem. two Foreign Office Missions led by Lord Strang to Washington, 1947 (first on rehabilitation of Ruhr coal industry, second, on finance and control of German foreign trade). Gen. Manager, Overseas Food Corp., Southern Prov., Tanganyika, 1950-51; responsible for re-organising and cutting down "Ground-nuts scheme" in that area after its failure. Controller, Caribbean Region, Colonial Development Corp., 1951-53, in charge of the Corporation's interest in Islands of West Indies, Br. Honduras and Br. Guiana; Controller in charge of Corporation's interests in Nyasaland, Rhodesias, Bechuanaland and Swaziland, 1953-55; Chm. Federal Power Bd of Rhodesia and Nyasaland (responsible for construction of £80 m. Kariba Hydro-electric project on the Zambezi), 1955-61. First Chm., Commn for the New Towns, 1961-64. *Address:* Flat 7, Woodsford, 14 Melbury Road, Holland Park, W14. *T:* 01-937 4141. *Club:* Athenæum.

**ANDERSON, Sir Edward (Arthur)**, Kt 1952; JP; Managing Director of A. Anderson & Son (Electrical Engineers) Ltd, Middlesbrough; *b* 4 Jan. 1908; *s* of Arthur and Florence Anderson; *m* 1937, Elsa Mary French; no *c*. *Educ:* Middlesbrough High Sch.; South Shields Marine Engineering Coll. Entire working life spent in family business, A. Anderson & Son. AIEE 1937. Director: P. A. Mudd Ltd; Lionweld Ltd. Councillor for County Borough of Middlesbrough, 1945-56; Chairman Middlesbrough Conservative Assoc., 1947-60; JP Middlesbrough, 1950-. *Recreations:* swimming, walking, reading, music and travel. *Address:* Spring Lodge, Guisborough, North Yorkshire. *T:* Guisborough 2581. *Clubs:* Carlton; Cleveland (Middlesbrough).

**ANDERSON, Prof. Edward William**, MD, FRCP; Hon. MSc; Lord Chancellor's Visitor since 1965; retired as Professor of Psychiatry, Victoria University of Manchester and Director of Department of Psychiatry, Manchester Royal Infirmary (1949-65), now Professor Emeritus; *b* 8 July 1901; *s* of Edward Ross Anderson and Elizabeth Leith (*née* Dow); *m* 1934, Margaret Mottram Hutton; two *s* one *d*. *Educ:* Daniel Stewart's Coll., Edinburgh; Univs of Edinburgh, London and Frankfurt-on-Main. MD Edinburgh 1927, MB, ChB 1923, FRCP 1946; DPM London 1925. Junior hosp. appts in medicine and surgery, 1923-24; various mental hosp. appts, 1924-29; Asst MO, The Maudsley Hosp., 1929-35; Med. Dir Cassel Hosp. for Functional Nervous Disorders, 1935-37; Cons.

Psychiatrist, Devon CC, 1938-47; Neuropsychiatric Specialist, Royal Navy (Temp. Actg Surg. Comdr, RNVR), 1940-45. Physician, The Maudsley Hospital and Lecturer in Psychiatry, The Institute of Psychiatry, 1947-49. Rockefeller Fellow in Psychiatry, 1937-38. Visiting Professor, Univs of Witwatersrand and Cape Town, 1964. Examiner in Psychological Medicine, Univ. of London, 1950-58, and in Psychological Medicine (Pt I), Conjoint Examining Bd, England, 1956-60; also (in the Membership) to RCP, 1964-. Pres. Sect. Psychiatry RSM, 1961-62; Pres. (1964) Sect. Med., Manchester Med. Society. Hon. MSc (Vict.) 1953; Hon. Fellow (Psychiatry), Coll. of Physicians, Surgeons and Gynæcologists, of S Africa, 1964. *Publications:* Psychiatry, 1964, 2nd edn (jointly with W. H. Trethowan), 1967; various articles on psychiatric topics in professional journals. *Address:* Lord Chancellor's Visitors' Office, Staffordshire House, 25 Store Street, WC1. *T:* 01-636 6877. *Club:* Reform.

**ANDERSON, Dr Ephraim Saul,** FRS 1968; Director, Enteric Reference Laboratory, Public Health Laboratory Service, since 1954; *b* 1911; *e s* of Benjamin and Ada Anderson, Newcastle upon Tyne; *m* 1959, Carol Jean (*née* Thompson); three *s*. *Educ:* Rutherford Coll., and King's Coll. Med. Sch. (Univ. of Durham), Newcastle upon Tyne. MB, BS (2nd cl. hons), 1934; MD Durham, 1953; Dip.Bact. London, 1948; Founder Fellow, Royal Coll. of Pathologists, 1963. GP, 1935-39; RAMC, 1940-46; Pathologist 1943-46; Registrar in Bacteriology, Postgrad. Med. Sch., 1946-47; Staff, Enteric Reference Lab., 1947-52, Dep. Dir, 1952-54. WHO Fellow, 1953. Chm., Internat. Cttee for Enteric Phage Typing of Internat. Assoc. of Microbiol. Socs, 1966- (Jt Chm., 1958-66); Dir, Internat. Ref. Lab. for Enteric Phage Typing of Internat. Cttee for Enteric Phage Typing, 1954-; Dir, Internat. Centre for Enteric Phage Typing of WHO, 1960-; Mem., WHO Expert Adv. Panel for Enteric Diseases. *Publications:* contrib. to: The Bacteriophages (Mark Adams), 1959; The World Problem of Salmonellosis (Van Oye), 1964; numerous articles on bacteriophage typing and its genetic basis, microbial ecology, transferable drug resistance, and epidemiology. *Recreations:* music, photography. *Address:* Enteric Reference Laboratory, Public Health Laboratory Service, Colindale Avenue, NW9. *T:* 01-205 7041.

**ANDERSON, Dame Frances Margaret;** *see* Anderson, Dame Judith.

**ANDERSON, George David,** CMG 1967; British High Commissioner to Botswana, since 1969; *b* 11 Sept. 1913; *m* 1950, Audrey Rowena Money; one *d*. *Educ:* King Edward VII Gram. Sch., King's Lynn; Emmanuel Coll., Cambridge. National Association of Boys' Clubs, 1935-37; Macgregor and Co., Rangoon, Burma, 1937-41. Army Service, Burma Rifles, 1941-44; Combined Services Detailed Interrogation Centre (India), 1944-46. Min. of Food, 1946; CRO 1947. Office of British High Commission in New Delhi and Calcutta, 1947-51; British Embassy, Dublin, 1957-60; Dep. High Comr, Ceylon, 1961-66; Diplomatic Service, 1964; Head of Chancery, British High Commn, Lagos, Nigeria, 1967-69. *Recreations:* gardening, photography. *Address:* c/o Foreign and Commonwealth Office, SW1.

**ANDERSON, Major George Denis;** *b* 15 Nov. 1885; *s* of George and Alice Anderson; *m* 1926, Mary Myddleton-Evans (*d* 1968); one *d*. *Educ:* Eton; Christ Church, Oxford. High Sheriff of Northumberland, 1935. Dep. Chm. Northumberland QS, 1935-55; Chairman, 1955-60. *Address:* Little Harle Tower, Harle, Northumberland. *T:* Kirkwhelpington 229. *Clubs:* Junior Carlton; Northern Counties (Newcastle upon Tyne).

**ANDERSON, Rev. Prof. George Wishart;** Professor of Hebrew and Old Testament Studies, University of Edinburgh, since 1968 (Professor of Old Testament Literature and Theology, 1962-68); *b* 25 Jan. 1913; *s* of George Anderson and Margaret Gordon Wishart; *m* 1st, 1941, Edith Joyce Marjorie Walter (decd); one *s* one *d*; 2nd, 1959, Anne Phyllis Walter. *Educ:* Arbroath High Sch.; Univs of St Andrews, Cambridge, Lund. United Coll., St Andrews: Harkness Scholar; MA 1st Cl. Hons Classics, 1935. Fitzwilliam House and Wesley House, Cambridge: 1st Cl. Theol Tripos Part I, 1937; 2nd Cl. Theol Tripos Part II, 1938; BA 1937; MA 1946. Asst Tutor, Richmond Coll., 1939-41. Chaplain, RAF, 1941-46; Tutor in Old Testament Lang. and Lit., Handsworth Coll., 1946-56; Lecturer in O.T. Lit. and Theol., Univ. of St Andrews, 1956-58; Prof. of Old Testament Studies, Univ. of Durham, 1958-62. Hon. Sec., Internat. Organization of Old Testament Scholars, 1953-; Mem. Editorial Bd of Vetus Testamentum, 1950-; Editor, Book List of Soc. for O.T. Study, 1957-66; President, Soc. for O.T. Study, 1963; Hon. Sec. (Foreign Correspondence), soc. for O.T. Study, 1964-; Charles Ryder Smith Mem. Lectr, 1964; Fernley-Hartley Lectr, 1969; Hon. DD St Andrews, 1959. *Publications:* He That Cometh (trans. from Norwegian of S. Mowinckel), 1956; A Critical Introduction to the Old Testament, 1959; The Ras Shamra Discoveries and the Old Testament (trans. from Norwegian of A. S. Kapelrud, US 1963, UK 1965); The History and Religion of Israel, 1966; articles in: The Old Testament and Modern Study (ed H. H. Rowley), 1951; The New Peake Commentary (ed M. Black and H. H. Rowley), 1962; The Cambridge History of the Bible, Vol. I (ed P. R. Ackroyd and C. F. Evans), 1970, and in various learned jls. *Recreations:* reading, music, walking. *Address:* 51 Fountainhall Road, Edinburgh 9.

**ANDERSON, Sir Gilmour M.;** *see* Menzies Anderson.

**ANDERSON, Rev. Hector David,** MVO 1951; MA, BD; Chaplain to the Queen since 1955; Rector of Swanage, Dorset, since 1961; Rector of Sandringham, 1942-55; *b* 16 Aug. 1906; *s* of Rev. David Anderson, LLD, Dublin; *m* 1931, Muriel Louise Peters; one *s*. *Educ:* The Abbey, Tipperary; Trinity Coll., Dublin. Schol. 1928, BA Mods 1929, MA 1932, BD 1949. Curate, Shirley, Croydon, 1930-33; St Michael's, Chester Square, SW1, 1933-39; CF, Sept. 1939-42; Domestic Chaplain to King George VI, 1942-52, to the Queen, 1952-55; Rector: Sandringham, 1942-55; Lutterworth, 1955-61; Swanage, 1961-69. *Address:* Adare, The Hyde, Langton Matravers, Swanage, Dorset. *T:* Swanage 3206.

**ANDERSON, H(ector) John,** FRCP; Physician, St Thomas' Hospital, since 1948, Governor since 1968; Physician, Lambeth Hospital, South Western Hospital and French Hospital; *b* Central Provinces, India, 5 Jan. 1915; *s* of H. J. Anderson; *m* 1st, 1940, Frances Pearce (marr. diss.), *er d* of Rev. W. P. Putt; one *s* one *d*; 2nd, 1956, Pauline Mary, *d* of A. Hammond. *Educ:* Exeter Sch.; St Catharine's Coll., Cambridge; St Thomas' Hospital. MA, MB (Cantab), FRCP. Medical Registrar and Res. Asst Physician, St Thomas' Hospital, 1941 and 1942. Hon. Lt-Col RAMC; served MEF, 1944-47. Kitchener Scholar; Mead Prizeman, St Thomas' Hospital; Murchison Scholar, RCP,

1942; Goulstonian Lectr, RCP, 1951; Examiner: MB London; Medicine, Conjoint Bd, London and England; RCP. Member: Assoc. of Physicians of Gt Britain; Thoracic Soc.; FRSoc.Med. *Publications:* Brim of Day, 1944; contrib. to medical literature. *Address:* 5 Coombe Rise, Kingston Hill, Surrey; 3 Upper Wimpole Street, W1. *T:* 01-935 5873; 102 Lambeth Road, SE1. *T:* 01-928 1533.

**ANDERSON, Hugh Fraser,** MA, FRCS; Urological Surgeon, St George's Hospital, London, since 1948; Surgeon, West Park Hospital, Epsom, since 1939; *b* 19 April 1910; *s* of late William Thomson Anderson and late Madeline Bertha (*née* Grubb); *m* 1942, Nancy Singleton; one *s* one *d*. *Educ:* King William's Coll., I of M; Gonville and Caius Coll., Cambridge (Open Exhibition, 1929); St George's Hospital (Anne Selina Fernee Exhibition, 1932). MA (Cantab) 1939; MB, BCh (Cantab) 1935; LRCP 1935; FRCS 1940. Allingham Prize in Surgery, St George's Hospital, 1938. Served War of 1939-45 (Major, RAMC) (despatches). Examiner in Surgery, Univ. of London, 1958; Mem., Court of Examiners, Royal Coll. of Surgeons, 1966. Member: Assoc. of Surgeons; British Association of Urological Surgeons; International Soc. of Urology. *Publications:* articles on urological subjects and the infected hand in learned journals and textbooks. *Recreations:* golf, railways, gardening. *Address:* 13 Durrington Park Road, Wimbledon, SW20. *T:* 01-946 2114; 1 Harley Street, W1. *T:* 01-580 4850. *Clubs:* MCC, Ski Club of Great Britain; Walton Heath Golf, St Enodoc Golf (Rock, Cornwall).

**ANDERSON, Prof. James Norman Dalrymple,** OBE 1945 (MBE 1943); BA 1930, LLB 1931, MA 1934, LLD 1955 (Cantab); FBA 1970; Professor of Oriental Laws in the University of London and Head of Department of Law, School of Oriental and African Studies, since 1953; Director of the Institute of Advanced Legal Studies in the University of London, since Oct. 1959; Lecturer in Mohammedan Law, Council of Legal Education, since 1954; *b* 29 Sept. 1908; *s* of late William Dalrymple Anderson; *m* 1933, Patricia Hope, *d* of A. Stock Givan; one *s* two *d*. *Educ:* St Lawrence Coll., Ramsgate; Trinity Coll., Cambridge (Senior Scholar). 1st Class, Law Tripos Parts I and II (distinction in Part I); 1st Class LLB. Missionary, Egypt General Mission, 1932; served War of 1939-45 in Army as Arab Liaison Officer, Libyan Arab Force, 1940 (Capt.); Sec. for Sanusi Affairs, Civil Affairs Branch, GHQ, MEF, 1941 (Major); Sec. for Arab Affairs, 1943 (Lieut-Col); Political Sec., 1943; Chief Sec. (Col), 1944; Lectr in Islamic Law, Sch. of Oriental and African Studies, 1947; Reader in Oriental Laws in Univ. of London, 1951-53; Dean of Faculty of Laws, Univ. of London, 1965-69. Mem. Colonial Native Law Advisory Panel; Chm. UK Nat. Cttee of Comparative Law, 1957-59; Vice-Chm. Internat. African Law Assoc.; Visiting Prof., Princeton Univ. and New York Univ. Law Sch., 1958; Harvard Law Sch., 1966; Mem., Denning Cttee on Legal Education for Students from Africa, 1960. Conducted survey of application of Islamic Law in British African possessions for Colonial Office, 1950-51. Pres.: BCMS; Soc. of Public Teachers of Law, 1968-69. Chm. Middle East General Mission; Mem., House of Laity in Church Assembly; Anglican delegate to the World Council of Churches. Libyan Order of Istiqlal, Class II, 1959. *Publications:* Islamic Law in Africa, 1954; Islamic Law in the Modern World, 1959; Into the World: The Need and Limits of Christian Involvement, 1968; Editor: Changing Law in Developing Countries, 1963; Family Law in Asia and Africa, 1968; Christianity: The Witness of History, 1969; numerous articles in periodicals. *Address:* 12 Constable Close, NW11. *T:* 01-455 0309. *Club:* Athenæum.

**ANDERSON, James S.,** MA, MB, ChB, MD, DPH; retired as Physician, St George's Hospital, also Director, Infectious Diseases Unit, Grove Hospital, and External Examiner Epidemiology and Infectious Diseases, University of Edinburgh; *b* 3 Dec. 1891; *s* of William Anderson and Annie Carrie; *m* 1928, Mary Stirk, MRCS, LRCP; one *s* one *d*. *Educ:* Robert Gordon's Coll., Aberdeen; Univ. of Aberdeen. House Physician and House Surg., Aberdeen Royal Infirmary; Resident Physician, City Hospital, Aberdeen; Asst MOH, Aberdeen; Dep. Medical Supt, Monsall Hospital, Manchester; Medical Supt, City Hospitals, Leeds; Lectr in Infectious Diseases, Univ. of Leeds; War service 4th Bn Gordon Highlanders, 1914-16; ed. Aberdeen Univ. Magazine. *Publications:* articles in British Medical Journal, Lancet, Journal of Pathology and Bacteriology, Archives of Disease in Childhood, Public Health and Clinical Journal. *Recreations:* golf, fishing. *Address:* Elm House, Arncliffe, near Skipton, Yorks. *T:* Arncliffe 231.

**ANDERSON, John,** CB 1956; CBE 1950; CEng, FIEE; retired as Chief Scientist, Admiralty Surface Weapons Establishment, Portsmouth, 1961; *b* 29 Aug. 1896; *s* of John Anderson, Beith, Ayrshire; *m* 1928, Isabella Mary Morton Crerar; no *c*. *Educ:* Spiers Sch., Beith, Ayrshire; Royal Technical Coll., Glasgow (Diploma). Joined RN Scientific Service, 1918; Chief Scientist, HM Underwater Detection Establishment, Portland, 1943-51; Chief Scientist, Admiralty Signal and Radar Establishment, Portsmouth, 1951. American Medal of Freedom, 1946. *Address:* Blue Hills, Denbigh Road, Haslemere. *T:* Haslemere 3575.

**ANDERSON, General Sir John (D'Arcy),** GBE 1967 (CBE 1945); KCB 1961 (CB 1957); DSO 1940; DL; Colonel Commandant, The Ulster Defence Regiment, since 1969; Pro-Chancellor, Queen's University, Belfast, since 1969; *b* 23 Sept. 1908; *s* of late Major Reginald D'Arcy Anderson, RGA, and Mrs Anderson, Ballyhossett, Downpatrick, Co. Down; *m* 1937, Elizabeth, *d* of late Augustus M. Walker. *Educ:* Winchester; New Coll., Oxford (MA). 2nd Lieut 5th Royal Inniskilling Dragoon Guards, 1930; served War of 1939-45, France, Middle East and Italy (wounded twice, despatches twice); GOC 11th Armoured Div., BAOR, 1955-56. Chief of Staff, Headquarters Northern Army Group and BAOR, 1956-58; Director, RAC, WO, 1958-59; Dir-Gen. of Military Training, 1959-61; DCIGS, 1961-63; Military Sec. to: Sec. of State for War, 1963-64; Min. of Defence, 1964-65. Commandant IDC, 1966-68; Col 5th Royal Inniskilling Dragoon Guards, 1962-67; Col Comdt, RAEC, 1964-70; Hon. Col: Oxford Univ. OTC, 1961-67; Queen's Univ., Belfast, OTC, 1964. ADC General to the Queen, 1966-68. Mem., Commonwealth War Graves Commn, 1963-. Chm., Army Museums Ogilby Trust; Vice-Pres. Sandes Soldiers' and Airmen's Homes. DL Co. Down. Grand Officer, Order of the Crown (Belgium), 1963. Grand Officer, Order of Leopold (Belgium), 1966. *Recreations:* horses, painting. *Address:* Ballyhossett, Downpatrick, Co. Down, Northern Ireland. *T:* Ardglass 227. *Clubs:* Cavalry; Ulster (Belfast).

**ANDERSON, Maj.-Gen. John Evelyn,** CBE 1963; FIEE; Assistant Chief of Defence Staff (Signals), since 1969; *b* 28 June 1916; *e s* of Lt-Col John Gibson Anderson, Christchurch,

NZ, and Margaret (*née* Scott), Edinburgh; *m* 1944, Jean Isobel, *d* of Charles Tait, farmer, Aberdeenshire; one *s* one *d*. *Educ:* King's Sch., Rochester; RMA, Woolwich. Commissioned in Royal Signals, 1936; Lt-Col 1956; Col 1960; Brig. 1964; Maj.-Gen. 1967; Signal Officer in Chief (Army), MoD, 1967-69. Col Comdt, Royal Corps of Signals, 1969-. MBIM. *Recreation:* fishing. *Address:* The Cottage, Broad Layings, Woolton Hill, Newbury, Berks. *T:* Highclere 361. *Club:* United Service.

**ANDERSON, Prof. John Kinloch;** Professor of Classical Archaeology, University of California, Berkeley, since 1958; *b* 3 Jan. 1924; *s* of late Sir James Anderson, KCIE, and of Lady Anderson; *m* 1954, Esperance, *d* of Guy Batham, Dunedin, NZ; one *s* two *d*. *Educ:* Trinity Coll., Glenalmond; Christ Church, Oxford (MA). Served War, in Black Watch (RHR) and Intelligence Corps, 1942-46 (final rank, Lieut). Student, British Sch. at Athens, 1949-52; Lecturer in Classics, Univ. of Otago, NZ, 1953-58. *Publications:* Greek Vases in the Otago Museum, 1955; Ancient Greek Horsemanship, 1961; Military Theory and Practice in the Age of Xenophon, 1970; articles and reviews in Annual of British Sch. at Athens; Jl of Hellenic Studies, etc. *Recreations:* gardening, riding. *Address:* 1020 Middlefield Road, Berkeley, California 94708, USA. *T:* Berkeley 841-5335.

**ANDERSON, Sir John (Muir),** Kt 1969; CMG 1957; Commissioner of State Savings Bank of Victoria, since 1962, Chairman of Commissioners, 1967; *b* 14 Sept. 1914; *s* of John Weir Anderson; *m* 1949, Audrey Drayton Jamieson; two *s* one *d*. *Educ:* Brighton Grammar Sch.; Melbourne Univ. 2/6th Commando Co., 1941; Lieut, 1st Australian Parachute Bn, 1944; served SE Asia, 1941-45. Established John M. Anderson & Co., Manufacturers, Agents and Importers, 1951; Director: Victoria Insurance Co. Ltd; Bly's (Australia) Pty Ltd; Managing Director, King Oscar Fine Foods Pty Ltd. Pres. of Liberal and Country Party of Victoria, 1952-56 (Treasurer, 1957-61). Trustee, Melbourne Exhibn, 1960, Chm. of Trustees, 1968. *Recreations:* swimming, fishing. *Address:* 25 Cosham Street, Brighton, Victoria, Australia. *T:* XB 4790.

**ANDERSON, Professor John Neil;** Professor of Dental Prosthetics, University of Dundee, since 1964; *b* 11 Feb. 1922; *s* of J. Anderson and Mrs A. Anderson, Sheffield; *m* 1945, Mary G. Croll; one *s* one *d*. *Educ:* High Storrs Gram. Sch., Sheffield; Sheffield Univ. Asst Lectr, Sheffield Univ., 1945-46; Lectr, Durham Univ., 1946-48; Lectr, Birmingham Univ., 1948-52; Sen. Lectr, St Andrews Univ., 1952-64. *Publications:* Applied Dental Materials, (3rd edn) 1967; (with R. Storer) Immediate and Replacement Dentures, 1966; contribs to British Dental Jl, Dental Practitioner, Dental Progress. *Recreations:* music, gardening, carpentry. *Address:* The Bensil, Carnoustie, Angus, Scotland. *T:* Carnoustie 2133. *Club:* University (Dundee).

**ANDERSON, Prof. John Russell;** Professor of Pathology at the Western Infirmary, Glasgow University, since Oct. 1967; *b* 31 May 1918; *s* of William Gregg Anderson and Mary Gordon Adam; *m* 1956, Audrey Margaret Shaw Wilson; two *s* two *d*. *Educ:* Worksop Coll.; St Andrews Univ. BSc (St Andrews) 1939, MB, ChB (St Andrews) 1942, MD (St Andrews) 1955; MRCP 1961; FRCPGlas 1965; FRCPath 1966; FRSE 1968. RAMC, 1944-47 (Emergency Commn). Lecturer and Senior Lecturer in Pathology, Glasgow Univ., 1947-65; George Holt Prof. of Pathology, Liverpool Univ., 1965-67. Rockefeller travelling fellowship in Medicine, at Rochester, NY, 1953-54. *Publications:* Autoimmunity, Clinical and Experimental (jointly), 1967; various papers on immunopathology in scientific jls. *Recreations:* squash, ski-ing, gardening. *Address:* Pathology Department, Western Infirmary, Glasgow, W1. *T:* 041-339 8822.

**ANDERSON, Prof. John Stuart,** FRS 1953; MA, PhD, MSc; Professor of Inorganic Chemistry, Oxford University, since Oct. 1963; *b* 9 Jan. 1908; *m* 1935, Joan Taylor; one *s* three *d*. Formerly Dep. Chief Scientific Officer, Chemistry Div., Atomic Energy Research Establishment, Harwell, Berks; Prof. of Inorganic and Physical Chemistry and Head of the Dept of Chemistry, Univ. of Melbourne, Australia, 1954-59; Director of the National Chemical Laboratory (Department of Scientific and Industrial Research), Teddington, 1959-63. *Address:* Inorganic Chemistry Laboratory, South Parks Road, Oxford. *T:* Oxford 57387.

**ANDERSON, Dame Judith,** DBE 1960; (**Dame Frances Margaret Anderson**); Actress; *b* Adelaide, South Australia, 10 Feb. 1898; *d* of James Anderson Anderson and Jessie Saltmarsh; *m* 1937, Prof. B. H. Lehman (divorced 1939); *m* 1946, Luther Greene. *Educ:* Norwood High Sch., South Australia. Started Theatre with Julius Knight; toured Australia and America, 1918; has played in: The Dove, 1925; Behold the Bridegroom, 1927; Strange Interlude, 1930; Mourning becomes Electra, 1931; Come of Age, 1934; The Old Maid, 1935; Hamlet, 1936; Macbeth (London), 1937; Family Portrait, 1939; Three Sisters, 1942; Medea (New York, 1947-48; toured America, 1948-49; Paris Internat. Drama Festival, 1955); The Seagull, Edin. Fest., 1960, Sept. at Old Vic. *Films:* Rebecca, Edge of Darkness, Laura, King's Row, Spectre of the Rose, The Red House, Pursued, Tycoon, Cat on a Hot Tin Roof, Macbeth, Don't Bother to Knock. *Recreation:* gardening. *Address:* Famous Artists Corporation, California Bank Building, Beverly Hills, California, USA.

**ANDERSON, Sir Kenneth,** KBE 1962 (CBE 1946); CB 1955; *b* 5 June 1906; *s* of Walter Anderson, Exmouth; *m* 1932, Helen Veronica Grose; one *s* one *d*. *Educ:* Swindon Secondary Sch.; Wadham Coll., Oxford (BA). Entered India Office, 1928; Asst Sec., 1942; Dep. Financial Adviser to British Military Governor, Germany, 1947-48; Imperial Defence Coll., 1949; Under-Sec., HM Treasury, 1950-51; Dep. Director-General, 1954-66 and Comptroller and Accountant-General, 1952-66, GPO. Officer, Order of Orange-Nassau, 1947. *Address:* 7 Milton Close, N2. *T:* 01-455 8701. *Club:* United University.

**ANDERSON, Dame Kitty,** DBE 1961; BA London; PhD London; Chairman, Girls' Public Day School Trust, since 1965; Director, Longmans Young Books; *b* 4 July 1903; *d* of J. H. Anderson, FCA, and L. Anderson. *Educ:* High Sch. for Girls, Saltburn-by-the-Sea; Royal Holloway Coll., Univ. of London. Head Mistress King's Norton Girls' Grammar Sch., Birmingham, 1939-44; Head Mistress, North London Collegiate Sch., 1944-65. FCP, 1966. Hon. LLD, Hull, 1967. *Address:* 61 Lake View, Edgware, Middlesex.

**ANDERSON, Lindsay (Gordon);** film and theatre director; Co-Director, Royal Court Theatre, since 1969; Governor, British Film Institute, 1969-70; *b* 17 April 1923; 2nd *s* of late Maj.-Gen. A. V. Anderson and Estelle Bell Sleigh. *Educ:* Cheltenham Coll.; Wadham Coll., Oxford. *Films include:* Wakefield

Express, 1953; Thursday's Children (with Guy Brenton), 1954; O Dreamland, 1954; Every Day Except Christmas, 1957; This Sporting Life, 1963; The White Bus, 1966; Raz, Dwa, Trzy (The Singing Lesson), for Warsaw Documentary Studio, 1967; If . . . ., 1968. *Productions in theatre:* The Waiting of Lester Abbs, 1957; The Long and the Short and the Tall; Progress to the Park; Jazzetry; Serjeant Musgrave's Dance, 1959; The Lily White Boys; Billy Liar; Trials by Logue, 1960; The Fire-Raisers, 1961; The Diary of a Madman, 1963; Andorra, 1964; Julius Caesar, 1964; The Cherry Orchard, 1966; first Polish production of Inadmissible Evidence (Nie Do Obrony), Warsaw, 1966; In Celebration, 1969; The Contractor, 1969; Home, 1970; Editor, film quarterly, Sequence, 1947-51. *Publications:* Making a Film, 1952; contrib. to Declaration, 1957. *Address:* 57 Greencroft Gardens, NW6.

**ANDERSON, Marian; (Mrs Orpheus H. Fisher);** American contralto; *b* Philadelphia, Pa; *m* 1943, Orpheus H. Fisher. *Educ:* Philadelphia; New York; Chicago; and in Europe. MusD Howard Univ., 1938. Singing career began in 1924; 1st prize at Lewisohn Stadium competition, New York, 1925. Has made numerous tours in the United States, Europe, Japan, Israel, India, Pakistan, Korea, etc. Ulrica in Verdi's The Masked Ball, Metropolitan Opera House, New York, 1955. US Delegate to UN, 1958. Has made many recordings. Holds numerous American and other hon. doctorates; Bok Award, 1940. Finnish decoration, 1940; Litteris et Artibus Medal, Sweden, 1952; Yukusho Medal, Japan, 1953; Gimbel Award, 1958; Gold Medal, US Inst. of Arts and Sciences, 1958; US Presidential Medal of Freedom, 1963. *Publication:* My Lord, What a Morning, 1957. *Address:* Danbury, Conn, USA.

**ANDERSON, Brig. Hon. Dame Mary Mackenzie,** DBE 1970 (MBE 1958); Director, Women's Royal Army Corps, 1967-Aug. 1970; *b* 3 Feb. 1916; *d* of Sir John Anderson, later 1st Viscount Waverley, PC, GCB, OM, GCSI, GCIE, FRS, and Christina Mackenzie Anderson. *Educ:* Sutton High Sch.; Villa Brillantmont, Lausanne. Joined Auxiliary Territorial Service, 1941; transferred to Women's Royal Army Corps, 1949. Hon. ADC to the Queen, 1967-70. *Address:* c/o National Westminster Bank Ltd, West End Branch, 78 High Street, Reigate, Surrey. *Club:* English-Speaking Union.

**ANDERSON, Lt-Gen. Sir Richard (Neville),** KCB 1961 (CB 1957); CBE 1949; DSO and Bar, 1944; Colonel, The King's Own Royal Border Regiment, since 1961; Colonel, 10th Princess Mary's Own Gurkha Rifles, 1960-66; *b* 28 April 1907; *s* of Col Sir Neville Anderson, CBE; *m* 1942, Dorrie Norah Wybergh; two *s*. *Educ:* Tonbridge; Royal Mil. Coll., Sandhurst; idc. Served Palestine, 1938-39; War of 1939-45; Italy campaign, 1944-45; Palestine, 1946-48; GOC 17 Gurkha Div., 1955-57; GOC Overseas Forces, Malaya, 1957-58; Vice-Adj.-Gen., War Office, 1958-60; GOC-in-C, MELF, 1960-63; GOC-in-C, NI Command, 1963-65, retd 1965. Director, Civil Defence for Wales, 1965-68. Hon. Fellow Inst. of Civil Defence, 1966. CC Dorset, 1970-. *Recreation:* golf. *Address:* Tarrant Keynston House, Blandford, Dorset. *Club:* Brooks's.

**ANDERSON, Robert Bernard;** lawyer and statesman, United States; *b* Burleson, Texas, 4 June 1910; *s* of Robert Lee and Elizabeth (*née* Haskew); *m* 1935, Ollie Mae Anderson; two *s*. *Educ:* Weatherford Coll., Texas; Univ. of Texas (LLB). Admitted to Texas Bar, and began law practice, Fort Worth, Texas, 1932; elected to Texas legislature, 1932; Asst Attorney-Gen., Texas, 1932; Prof. of Law, Univ. of Texas, 1933; State Tax Commr, Texas, 1934; Racing Commr, Texas, 1934; Member State Tax Board, 1934; Chm. and Executive Director, Texas Unemployment Commn, 1936; Gen. Counsel for the Waggoner Estate (oil and ranching), 1937- (Gen. Man., 1941-53). Secretary of US Navy, 1953-54; Dep. Secretary of Defense, 1954-55; Secretary of the Treasury, 1957-61. Director: Ventures Ltd (Past Pres.); Dresser Industries (Chm. Exec. Cttee); Greenwich Trust Co.; Webb & Knapp (Canada) Ltd; Missouri Pacific Railroad Co.; NY Capital Fund of Canada Ltd; Pan American World Airways; Partner, Carl M. Loeb, Rhoades and Co., 1961-. Mem. Texas Bar Assoc.; Associate of Bar of City of New York. *Address:* c/o Carl M. Loeb, Rhoades & Co., 230 Park Avenue, New York, NY, USA.

**ANDERSON, Roger Charles,** LittD; FSA, FRHistSoc; Chairman of Trustees, National Maritime Museum, 1959-62 (Trustee, 1927-62); *b* 23 July 1883; *o c* of John Rodgerson Anderson, and Edith, *d* of Edward Tayloe; *m* 1916, Romola Urquhart, *d* of Robert Fowler Mackenzie; no *c*. *Educ:* Winchester; Clare Coll., Cambridge. RNVR as Midshipman and Sub-Lieut, 1905-11; Lieut and Lt-Comdr 1914-19; Hon. Editor The Mariner's Mirror (Soc. for Nautical Research), 1914, 1919-22, 1931-32, and 1939-46; Joint Hon. Gen. Editor Southampton Record Soc., 1930-39; Pres. Soc. for Nautical Research, 1951-60. *Publications:* Naval Wars in the Baltic, 1910; Canoeing and Camping Adventures, 1910; The Naval Pocket Book, 1912-15; The Sailing Ship (with R. U. Anderson), 1926; The Rigging of Ships (1600-1720), 1927; Naval Wars in the Levant, 1952; Catalogue of Ship Models (National Maritime Museum), 1952; Seventeenth Century Rigging, 1955; Oared Fighting Ships, 1962. For Southampton Record Society: Letters of 15th and 16th Centuries, 1921-22; Assize of Bread Book, 1923; Book of Examinations, 1926; Examinations and Depositions, 1931-36. For Navy Records Society: Journal of the Earl of Sandwich, 1929; Journals of Thomas Allin, 1939-40; Journals and Narratives of the Third Dutch War, 1946; A Memoir of James Trevenen (with C. C. Lloyd), 1959. For Society for Nautical Research: A Treatise on Rigging (1625), 1921; Lists of English Men-of-War (1649-1702), 1935; Index to the Mariners' Mirror (Vols 1-35), 1956; List of English Men-of-War (1509-1649), 1959; List of English Naval Captains (1642-60), 1964. *Address:* Gorley Firs, South Gorley, Fordingbridge, Hants.

**ANDERSON, Dr Theodore Farnworth,** CMG 1956; OBE 1943; HM Overseas Medical Service, retired; *b* 22 Oct. 1901; *s* of Rev. J. F. Anderson; *m* 1928, Isabel Cecile Downey; two *d*. *Educ:* Rugby Sch.; Trinity Hall, Cambridge; University Coll. Hospital. MA (Cantab), MD, BCh, MRCS, LRCP, DTM & H. General Practice, Kenya, 1925; appointed Medical Officer, Colonial Medical Service, Kenya, 1928. North Persian Forces Memorial Medal, 1930. Commn RAMC, 1939 (despatches); demobilised, 1945, rank of Col. Director of Medical Services, Somaliland Protectorate, 1945-49; Director of Medical Services, HM Overseas Medical Services, Kenya, 1949-57, retd. *Publications:* numerous articles in medical press. *Recreations:* golf, fishing, gardening. *Address:* The Clearing, Hawkhurst, Kent. *T:* Hawkhurst 2217; Limuru, Kenya. *Clubs:* East India and Sports, Royal Commonwealth Society; Rye Golf; Nairobi; Limuru Country; Muthaiga Country.

**ANDERSON, Prof. Thomas,** MD, FRCPE, FRCPGlas; Henry Mechan Professor of Public Health, University of Glasgow, since 1964 (Professor of Infectious Diseases, 1959-64); *b* 7 Dec. 1904; *e s* of Thomas Anderson and Mary (*née* Johnstone); *m* 1935, Helen Turner Massey; one *s* three *d*. *Educ:* The High Sch. of Glasgow; Glasgow Univ. (MB, ChB 1928; MD, Hons and Bellahouston Gold Medal, 1945); MRCPE 1934; FRCPE 1940; FRCPGlas 1947. Dep. Phys., Ruchill Hosp., 1933-41; Phys. Supt, Knightswood Hosp., 1941-47; Sen. Lectr, subseq. Reader, Infectious Diseases, Glasgow Univ., 1947-59. Consultant in Infectious Diseases to Western Region of Scotland; Chm. Bd of Management, Scottish Med. Jl. *Publications:* various, on Infectious Diseases, in med. scientific jls. Contributor to Conybeare and Mann, Textbook of Medicine, 1957. *Recreation:* bowls. *Address:* 52 Kingsborough Gardens, Glasgow, W2. *Club:* Royal Scottish Automobile (Glasgow).

**ANDERSON, Maj.-Gen. Thomas Victor,** DSO 1918; psc 1920; *b* Ottawa, 4 July 1881; *s* of late Col William P. Anderson, CMG; *m* 1910, Elizabeth Grace, 2nd *d* of late Col W. D. Gordon, Kingston, Canada; three *d*. *Educ:* Royal Military Coll., Canada; McGill Univ. Graduated with Hons from RMC Canada, 1900; McGill, 1901 (BSc); Instructor in Civil Engineering, RMC, Canada, 1902-06; entered Canadian Permanent Force (Royal Canadian Engineers), 1905; in charge of Military Survey of Canada, 1910-14; served European War in France, Feb. 1915-April 1917; CRE 3rd Canadian Div., 1916-17; Commandant, Canadian Engineers' Training Centre, England, 1917-19; (severely wounded, DSO, Russian Order of St Anne, 2nd class, with swords, despatches four times, 1914-15 Star, British War Medal and Victory Medal, Canadian Volunteer Service Medal, War Medal, 1939-45); GSO, RMC, Kingston, 1921-25; Director Military Training and Staff Duties at National Defence Headquarters, Canada, 1925-29; District Officer Commanding Military District No 10, Winnipeg, 1929-33, Military District No 2, Toronto, 1933-35; Quarter Master General, Canada, 1935-38; Chief of Gen. Staff, Canada, 1938-40; Inspector-Gen. Central Canada, 1940-42, retd 1943. Hon. Col 2nd Fd Eng. Regt Royal Canadian Engineers, 1963-67. DSc Mil., 1963. *Address:* 34 Russell Hill Road, Toronto 7, Ontario.

**ANDERSON, Walter Charles,** CBE 1968; Solicitor; General Secretary, National and Local Government Officers Association, since 1957; Member, General Council of TUC, since 1965; *b* 3 Dec. 1910; *s* of William Walter John Anderson and Mary Theresa McLoughlin; *m* 1941, Doris Jessie Deacon; two *s*. *Educ:* Bootle Grammar Sch. and Wigan Grammar Sch.; Liverpool Univ. (LLB). Articled Clerk, J. W. Wall & Co., Solicitors, Bootle, Liverpool, 1930-33; Asst Solicitor, Bootle, 1933-34; Dep. Town Clerk, Heywood, 1934-37; Asst Solicitor, Nalgo, 1937-41; Royal Air Force, 1941-45; Legal Officer, Nalgo, 1945-50; Dep. Gen. Sec., Nalgo, 1950-57. Mem., Fulton Cttee on Civil Service Recruitment, Structure, Management and Training, 1966-68. *Publications:* Simonds' Local Government Superannuation Act, 1937 (rev. and ed), 1947. *Recreations:* football, cricket, tennis, gardening. *Address:* Nalgo House, Harewood Row, NW1. *T:* 01-262 8030.

**ANDERSON, Major-General Warren Melville,** CBE 1946; DSO 1919; *b* 1894; *e s* of late Marsham Ambrose Anderson, Flowerbank, Singleton, NSW; *m* 1928, Violet, *o d* of Nathaniel Josslyn Clark, Allowah, New Lambton, NSW. *Educ:* RMC Duntroon, Australia. Served European War, 1914-18: with 6th Light Horse Regt, AIF, in Egypt, Gallipoli and Palestine (despatches twice, DSO). Served War of 1939-45, Middle East and SW Pacific. Adjutant-Gen., Australian Military Forces, and Second Mem., Military Board, 1947-51; Maj.-Gen. (retd) Australian Staff Corps. *Address:* 1 Marathon Road, Darling Point, Sydney, Australia.

**ANDERSON, William Alexander,** CIE 1946; MICE; Parish Councillor, retired; *b* Forfar, Scotland, 29 Jan. 1890; *s* of late W. Anderson, OBE, JP, Aberdeen; *m* 1917, Margaret Grace Dalley; one *s* one *d*. *Educ:* Robert Gordon's Coll.; Aberdeen Univ. Asst Engineer, Indian State Rlys, 1913, posted NW Rly; Executive Rank, 1920; Administrative Rank, 1938; Gen. Manager, NW Rly, 1944-46; retired finally, from the Railway service, 1948. OStJ. *Publications:* various technical papers and articles. *Recreations:* gardening; organ. *Address:* The Anchorage, 27 Seal Road, Sussex. *T:* Selsey 2686.

**ANDERSON, Professor William Ferguson,** OBE 1961; David Cargill Professor of Geriatric Medicine, University of Glasgow, since 1965; Physician in Geriatric Medicine, Stobhill General Hospital and Adviser in Diseases of Old Age and Chronic Sickness, Western Regional Hospital Board, Scotland, since 1952; *b* 8 April 1914; *s* of James Kirkwood Anderson, Capt. 7th Scottish Rifles (killed on active service Gaza 1917) and late Sarah Barr Anderson; *m* 1940, Margaret Battison Gebbie; one *s* two *d*. *Educ:* Merchiston Castle Sch.; Glasgow Academy; Glasgow Univ. (MB Hons 1936; MD Hons 1942, with Bellahouston Gold Medal). FRFPSG 1939 (now FRCPG); FRCPE 1961; FRCP 1964. Med. Registrar, Univ. Med. Clinic, 1939-41; Army Service, 1941-46, Major (Med. Specialist). Sen. Lectr, Dept of Materia Medica and Therapeutics, Univ. of Glasgow, and Asst Phys., Univ. Med. Clinic, Stobhill Hosp., Glasgow, 1946-49; Sen. Univ. Lectr, Medical Unit, also Hon. Cons. Phys., Cardiff Royal Infirmary, 1949-52. Chairman: Glasgow Retirement Council; Glasgow and W of Scotland Hosp. Sunday Fund; Strathclyde House, Marie Curie Foundn, Glasgow; St Mungo's Old Folks' Club, Glasgow. St Mungo Prize, Glasgow, 1968. *Publications:* Practical Management of the Elderly, 1967; Current Achievements in Geriatrics (ed with Dr B. Isaacs), 1964. Articles on Geriatic Medicine and Preventive aspects of Geriatrics in current med. jls. *Recreations:* walking; interest in English Crown Coinage. *Address:* Broadgate House, Strathblane, Glasgow. *T:* Blanefield 525. *Clubs:* Western, University Staff (Glasgow).

**ANDERSON, William Galloway Macdonald,** CBE 1957; CEng, FICE; Director-General of Works, Air Ministry, 1959-63, retired; *b* 27 Feb. 1905; *s* of late Andrew Syme Anderson, Dundee and of late Mary Anderson (*née* McDonald), Dundee; *m* 1934, Ivy Walker, York; one *s* one *d*. *Educ:* Dundee High Sch., Dundee; St Andrews Univ. Chief Engineer (Air Ministry) W African Command, 1942-44; Chief Supt Designs, Air Ministry (Works), 1944-46; Chief Engineer (Group Capt.) Far East Command, 1947-48; Deputy Dir of Works, Ministry of Civil Aviation, 1948-52; Dir of Works, Air Ministry, 1952-59. *Recreations:* golfing, motoring and gardening. *Address:* 39 The Barnhams, Bexhill-on-Sea, Sussex. *T:* Cooden 4212. *Club:* Rye Golf.

**ANDERSON, Right Reverend William Louis,** DD (Lambeth); *b* Tezpur, Assam, India, 11 Feb. 1892; *s* of late James Drummond Anderson,

LittD, ICS, and Frances Louisa Cordue; *m* 1st, 1921, Gwendoline Victoria Mary Jones (*d* 1957); two *s*; 2nd, 1963, Jessie Vida Hearn. *Educ:* St Paul's Sch. (Scholar); Gonville and Caius College, Cambridge (Exhibitioner); Ridley Hall, Cambridge. Hon. Fellow, Gonville and Caius Coll., Cambridge, 1950. BA 1914: MA 1920. 1st King Edward's Horse, 1911-16, Squadron Sergeant-Major; Royal Naval Air Service, Flight Lieut; Royal Air Force, 1918-19; Captain (DSC). Deacon, 1920; Priest, 1921; Chaplain of Caius Coll. and Curate of Holy Trinity, Cambridge, 1920; Chaplain, Royal Navy, 1922-28; HMS Antrim, 1922; HMS Thunderer, 1922-24; HMS Royal Oak, 1924-25; HMS Britannia for RNC Dartmouth, 1926-28; Vicar of St John's, Sparkhill, Birmingham, 1928-32; Rural Dean of Bordesley, 1930; Vicar of St John's, Meads, Eastbourne, 1932-37; Rural Dean of Eastbourne, 1937; Bishop Suffragan, Vicar, Rural Dean and Archdeacon of Croydon, 1937-42; Bishop of Portsmouth, 1942-49; Bishop of Salisbury, 1949-62; resigned, Dec. 1962. *Recreations:* sketching, bird-watching. *Address:* Woodriding, Hale Purlieu, Fordingbridge, Hants. *T:* Breamore 279. *Club:* United Service.

**ANDERTON, Col Geoffrey,** OBE 1944; *b* 23 Jan. 1902; *s* of late Frederic Anderton, Embsay, Yorks, and Jersey, CI; *m* 1930, Edyth Cecile Hastings; two *s* one *d*. *Educ:* Ermysted's Sch., Skipton-in-Craven, Yorks; St Mary's Hospital, Paddington, W2. MRCS, LRCP 1924; MB, BS London 1925; DRCOG 1947. Entered RAMC Jan. 1927; War of 1939-45 (despatches twice: Tunisia, 1943; Italy, 1944); Korean War (despatches, Cross of Honour of Norwegian Red Cross, 1952); retd Dec. 1952. Comdt Star and Garter Home for Disabled Sailors, Soldiers and Airmen, Richmond, Surrey, 1953-67. Officer, Legion of Merit (USA), 1954; OStJ 1960. *Recreation:* sailing. *Address:* Spring Corner, Spring Road, Lymington, Hants. *T:* Lymington 3488. *Club:* Royal Lymington Yacht.

**ANDERTON, James,** CBE 1966 (OBE 1956); CEng, MIMinE; *b* 3 Nov. 1904; *s* of Richard and Rebecca Anderton; *m* 1st, 1931, Margaret Asbridge (*d* 1945); no *c*; 2nd, 1949, Lucy Mackie; no *c*. *Educ:* Wigan and District Mining and Technical Coll. Manager of various collieries. On nationalisation of mining industry in 1947 became Asst Agent for a group of collieries in St Helens, Lancs; later made Prod. Man., St Helens Area, N Western Div.; Area Gen. Man., St Helens Area, 1949; Dep. Chm., Scottish Div., NCB, 1958. Chm., North Western Div., NCB, 1961-67. Dir, Gullick Ltd, Wigan, 1967-. Mem. Assoc. of Mining, Elec. and Mech. Engineers; Hon. MIMinE, 1968. Governor: Wigan and District Mining and Technical Coll.; Leigh Technical Coll.; Mem. Ct. of Govs, Manchester Coll. of Science and Technology. Medal, Instn of Mining Engineers, 1965. *Recreation:* golf. *Address:* The Knoll, Mere Road, Newton-le-Willows, Lancs. *T:* Newton-le-Willows 5901.

**ANDRADE, Prof. Edward Neville da Costa,** FRS 1935; FInstP; DSc London, PhD Heidelberg; Hon. LLD Edinburgh; Hon. DSc Durham, Manchester; Chevalier Légion d'Honneur; Correspondant, Académie des Sciences, Institut de France; Membre d'Honneur, Société Française de Physique; *b* London, 27 Dec. 1887; 2nd *s* of S. H. da C. Andrade; *m* 1st, 1917, Katherine Barbara, *d* of T. T. Evans, Manchester; two *s*; 2nd, 1938, Mona, *widow* of Clennell Wilkinson. *Educ:* St Dunstan's Coll.; University Coll., London; Univ. of Heidelberg; Cavendish Laboratory, Cambridge; Univ. of Manchester. BSc London, 1st class hons physics, 1907; Trouton scholar, Ellen Watson scholar, Jessel scholar, University Coll., London, 1907-10; 1851 Exhibition scholar, 1910-13; Heidelberg Univ. 1910-11; PhD (*summa cum laude*), 1911; Cavendish Lab., Cambridge, 1911-12; University Coll. London, 1912-13; Univ. of Manchester, John Harling Fellow, 1913-14. 2nd Lieut to Captain, RGA, 1914-19; active service, France, 1915-17 (despatches). Fellow of University Coll., London, 1916; Scientific Adviser to Dir of Scientific Research, Min. of Supply, 1939-43, Member Advisory Council of Scientific Research and Technical Development to Ministry of Supply from its inception to 1942; Professor of Physics, Artillery Coll., Woolwich, 1920-28; Quain Prof. of Physics, Univ. of London, 1928-50; Emeritus Prof., 1950; Dir in the Royal Institution, Resident Prof. and Dir of Davy Faraday Research Laboratory, 1950-52. Christmas Lectr, Royal Institution, 1927, 1943 and 1950; Guthrie Lectr, Physical Society, James Forrest Lectr, Institution of Civil Engineers, 1941; Rutherford Memorial Lectr, Royal Society, 1957; President, Physical Society, 1943-45; Council Royal Society, 1942-44; Hon. Mem. Inst. of Metals; Holweck Prizeman, 1947; Grande Médaille Osmond, Société Française de Métallurgie, 1951; Hughes Medallist, Royal Society, 1958. Editor for Physics, Encyclopædia Britannica, Fourteenth Edition. *Publications:* The Structure of the Atom (3rd edn, 1927); Airs; The Atom (Burmese Translation, 1928); Engines (Polish Translation, 1932); The Mechanism of Nature (translated into French, Italian, Polish, Dutch, Danish and Swedish); (with Julian Huxley) Simple Science; The New Chemistry; The Atom and its Energy; Poems and Songs; Isaac Newton; An Approach to Modern Physics (translated into Italian, Dutch and Polish); A Brief History of the Royal Society; Physics for the Modern World; Rutherford (trans. into German, Norwegian and Japanese); papers on physical and mathematical subjects in Royal Soc. Proceedings and Transactions, Proceedings Physical Society, Philosophical Magazine, Annalen der Physik, and other technical journals; numerous articles in Encyclopædia Britannica and elsewhere. *Recreations:* poetry, collecting old scientific books and useless knowledge. *Address:* Flat 3, 19 The Boltons, SW10. *Clubs:* Athenæum, Savage, Chelsea Arts.

**ANDRE, Brigadier James Richard Glencoe,** CBE 1950; DSO 1945; retired; *b* 20 Oct. 1899; *s* of Dr J. E. F. André and Mrs D. K. André (*née* Fowler); *m* 1929, Grace Douglas Darbyshire; two *s* one *d* (and one *s* decd). *Educ:* Killcott; RMC, Sandhurst. Commissioned, 1918, Royal Lincolns. Served European War, with Royal Lincolns, France, 1918-19; Ireland, 1919 and 1920; India, 1920-27; UK, 1927-34; seconded for service with Colonial Office, 1934; served with Malay Regt, 1935-42. Commanded 1st Bn The Malay Regt during Malaya Campaign, 1941-42; in battle for Singapore (DSO); despatches, 1946; Commandant (Col), Malay Regt, 1947; despatches, 1949; Brig. (temp.) 1948, (subs.) 1952; retired 1953. *Recreations:* gardening, handicraft. *Address:* Peaked Croft, Sidlesham Common, Chichester, Sussex. *T:* Sidlesham 260.

**ANDREW, Prof. Edward Raymond,** MA, PhD, ScD (Cambridge); FInstP; FRSE; Lancashire-Spencer Professor of Physics, University of Nottingham, since 1964; *b* Boston, Lincs, 27 June 1921; *o s* of late Edward Richard Andrew and Anne Andrew; *m* 1948, Mary Ralph Farnham (*d* 1965); two *d*. *Educ:* Wellingborough Sch.; Christ's (Open

Scholarship) and Pembroke Colls, Univ. of Cambridge. Scientific Officer, RRDE (now Royal Radar Establishment), Malvern, 1942-45; Cavendish Laboratory, Cambridge, 1945-48; Stokes Student, Pembroke Coll., Cambridge, 1947-49; Commonwealth Fund Fellow, Harvard Univ., 1948-49; Lectr in Natural Philosophy, St Salvator's Coll., Univ. of St Andrews, 1949-54; Prof. of Physics, University Coll. of North Wales, Bangor, 1954-63; Prof. of Experimental Physics, Univ. of Nottingham, 1963-64. Vis. Prof. of Physics, Univ. of Florida, 1969-70. *Publications:* Nuclear Magnetic Resonance, 1955; scientific papers in learned jls. *Address:* Department of Physics, University of Nottingham, University Park, Nottingham. *T:* Nottingham 56101.

**ANDREW, Sir (George) Herbert,** KCMG 1963; CB 1956; Permanent Under-Secretary of State for Education and Science, 1964-70, retired; *b* 19 March 1910; *s* of James Andrew and Harriet Rose, Woodley, Cheshire; *m* 1936, Irene Jones; two *s* two *d*. *Educ:* Godley Sch.; Manchester Grammar Sch.; Corpus Christi Coll., Oxford. Patent Office (Asst Examiner), 1931; Transf. to Board of Trade headquarters, 1938; Asst Sec., 1945; Second Secretary: (General) 1955-60, (Overseas) 1960-63, Bd of Trade; Mem., UK delegn to Common Market Conf., 1961-63; Deputy Secretary, Ministry of Education, during 1963, Permanent Secretary, 1963-64. Hon. Fellow, Corpus Christi Coll., Oxford, 1965. *Recreations:* walking, talking, playing the piano. *Address:* 9 Kynance Place, SW7. *T:* 01-584 6049. *Club:* Oxford and Cambridge.

**ANDREW, Sir Herbert;** *see* Andrew, Sir G. H.

**ANDREW, His Honour William Monro,** MBE 1946; BCL, MA Oxon; Judge of Marylebone County Court (Circuit 43), 1958-67; *b* 21 Feb. 1895; *s* of James Andrew, LLD Glasgow, and Jeannie Jackson, *d* of William Monro, MD; unmarried. *Educ:* Glasgow Academy; Oriel Coll., Oxford. Called to Bar, Lincoln's Inn, 1921; joined the Oxford Circuit; Recorder of Dudley, 1934-36; Recorder of Walsall, 1936-46; Judge of County Courts, Circuit No. 58, 1946-50, Circuit No. 40 (Bow), 1950-58. Formerly a mem. of the County Court Rule Cttee. Asst Judge Advocate General, 1944. Served European War in 9th Bn HLI (wounded and prisoner in 1917); War of 1939-45, Squadron Leader in RAF (VR), 1940; Wing Comdr 1944. *Address:* 20 Eaton Mansions, SW1. *T:* 01-730 2860; Crossloan, Gullane, East Lothian. *T:* Gullane 3169.

**ANDREWES, Antony,** MBE 1945; FBA 1957; Wykeham Professor of Ancient History, Oxford, since 1953; *b* 12 June 1910; *s* of late P. L. Andrewes; *m* 1938, Alison Blakeway (*née* Hope); two *d*. *Educ:* Winchester; New College, Oxford. Fellow of Pembroke Coll., Oxford, 1933-46. Intelligence Corps, 1941-45. Fellow of New Coll., Oxford, 1946-. *Publications:* articles in Classical Quarterly, etc.; (with R. Meiggs) revised edition of Sir George Hill's Sources for Greek History, 1951; The Greek Tyrants, 1955; The Greeks, 1967. *Address:* New College, Oxford; 13 Manor Place, Oxford. *T:* Oxford 48807.

**ANDREWES, Sir Christopher (Howard),** Kt 1961; FRS 1939; Deputy Director, National Institute for Medical Research, 1952-June 1961 (Member of Scientific Staff from 1927) and in charge of World Influenza Centre (WHO) until June 1961; *b* 7 June 1896; *s* of late Sir Frederick William Andrewes, MD, FRS and Phyllis Mary Hamer; *m* 1927, Kathleen Helen Lamb; three *s*. *Educ:* Highgate Sch.; St Bartholomew's Hospital. Surgeon Sub-Lt (RNVR), 1918-19; MRCS, LRCP, 1921, MB BS London (Univ. Gold Medal), 1921, MD London (Univ. Gold Medal), 1922, MRCP, 1923; FRCP, 1935; House Physician and Asst to Medical Unit St Bartholomew's Hospital, 1921-23 and 1925-26; Assistant Resident Physician, Hospital of the Rockefeller Institute, New York City, 1923-25; William Julius Mickle Fellowship, Univ. of London, 1931; Oliver-Sharpey Lectureship, Royal Coll. of Physicians, 1934; Bisset-Hawkins Medal, RCP, 1947; Stewart Prize, BMA, 1952. Hon LLD Aberdeen 1963; Hon. MD Lund, 1968. *Publications:* Viruses of Vertebrates, 1964, 2nd edn (with H. G. Pereira), 1967; The Common Cold, 1965; Viruses and Evolution (Huxley lecture), 1966; Natural History of Viruses, 1967; The Lives of Wasps and Bees, 1969. *Recreation:* natural history, especially entomology. *Address:* Overchalke, Coombe Bissett, Salisbury, Wilts. *T:* Coombe Bissett 201.

**ANDREWES, Admiral Sir William (Gerrard),** KBE *cr* 1951 (CBE 1945); CB 1949; DSO 1944; retired; *b* 3 Nov. 1899; 2nd *s* of late Reverend Canon G. T. Andrewes, Winchester; *m* 1927, Frances Audrey, *e d* of H. G. Welchman, Grove House, Winchester; one *s* one *d*. *Educ:* Twyford Sch., Winchester; RNC, Osborne and Dartmouth. Midshipman and Sub-Lt in European War, 1914-18 (Jutland). Comdr 1932; Capt. 1938; Joint Planning Staff, 1939 and 1940-42. Served War of 1939-45; Atlantic, Mediterranean invasion of Sicily (despatches) and Italy (DSO); Chief Staff Officer for administration and turn round invasion duties to C-in-C Portsmouth, 1944 (CBE); Chief of Staff to Vice-Adm. (Q) Pacific, 1944-45; Chief of Staff to C-in-C Portsmouth, 1947; ADC to the King, 1947; Rear-Adm, 1948; Senior Naval Member directing Staff Imperial Defence Coll., 1948-49; Vice-Admiral, 1951; Flag Officer Commanding 5th Cruiser Squadron and Flag Officer, Second-in-Command, Far East Station, 1950-51; comd British and Commonwealth Naval Forces in Korean war, 1950, and UN Task Force 95, 1951 (KBE); Commander-in-Chief, America and West Indies Station, 1951-53, and Deputy Supreme Allied Commander, Atlantic, 1952-53; Admiral, 1954; Pres., RN Coll., Greenwich, 1954-56; retired Dec. 1956. Chartered Electrical Engineer, MIEE, 1956. Officer American Legion of Merit, 1946, and Silver Star, 1950; Greek Military Cross, 1947; Commander, Legion of Merit, 1953; Knight Commander of Royal Order of Sword of Sweden, 1954. CStJ 1964. *Recreations:* gardening and painting. *Address:* Sparkford House, Winchester. *T:* 3977. *Club:* United Service.

**ANDREWS;** *see* Fox-Andrews.

**ANDREWS, Albert Andrew,** CBE 1951 (OBE 1942); *b* 14 July 1896; *s* of late T. F. Andrews, Bath; *m* 1st, 1919, Rose Mabel Nickolds (*d* 1965); one *s* one *d*; 2nd, 1969, Sheila Betty Joyner Mawbey, *widow* of H. R. Mawbey. *Educ:* Victoria Coll., Bath. Served European War, 1914-18; commissioned 7th (Service) Bn Somerset Light Infantry, 1915; Captain, 1916; invalided, 1919. Joined Soldiers', Sailors' and Airmen's Families Association, 1919 (Asst Secretary); Secretary, 1927; Controller, 1944-61, retired. *Address:* 7 Ebbisham Court, Epsom, Surrey. *T:* Epsom 23346.

**ANDREWS, (Arthur) John (Francis),** CBE 1970; Chairman, Clark Equipment Ltd, UK, since 1962; Vice-President, Clark Equipment Co., USA, since 1963; Chairman, All Wheel Drive Ltd, since 1954; *b* 15 May 1906; *s* of Arthur

Andrews and Gertrude Ellen Andrews (*née* Francis); *m* 1936, Elsy Maud (*née* Johns); one *d*. *Educ:* Malvern; Paris. Development Engineer, AC Cars Ltd, 1926; Chief Purchasing Manager, Gardner Diesel Engines, 1935. *Recreations:* sailing, golf. *Address:* Pembroke House, Valley End, Chobham, Surrey. *T:* Chobham 8019. *Clubs:* Royal Automobile, Royal Thames Yacht, Cruising Assoc.; Royal Naval Sailing Assoc. (Portsmouth); Royal Motor Yacht (Poole); Royal Fowey Yacht (Fowey); Berkshire Golf (Ascot); Ferndown Golf (Ferndown).

**ANDREWS, Air Cdre Charles Beresford Eaton B.;** *see* Burt-Andrews.

**ANDREWS, Dame Cicily;** *see* West, Dame Rebecca.

**ANDREWS, Cyril Frank Wilton,** *b* 22 Dec. 1892; *s* of late Robert Parsons and Mariannellen Wilton Gleadhill Andrews; *m* 1929, Dorothy Constance Lascelles, *d* of late Major George Thomas and Mrs Pickering; no *c*. *Educ:* abroad. Served European War, RE; Foreign Service, 1920; Vice-Consul at Antwerp, 1920-21; Tunis, 1921-23; Paris, 1923-24; Genoa, 1924-28; Montevideo (with rank of 2nd Sec.), 1929; Naples, 1929-30; Katowice, 1930-32; Philadelphia, 1933-35; Consul and 1st Sec. at Panama, 1935-38; Chargé d'Affaires, 1936 and 1938; Consul at Madeira, 1939-42; Minister to Dominican Republic, 1943-45; Special Ambassador for celebration of Centenary of Independence of Dominican Republic, Feb. 1944; Consul-General at Lourenço Marques, 1946-49; Consul-General at Algiers, 1949-53; retired from HM Foreign Service, 1953; Coronation Medal, 1953. Grand Cross of Dominican Order of Merit Juan Pablo Duarte. *Recreations:* golf, reading. *Address:* c/o Lloyds Bank, Ltd, Lansdowne, Bournemouth, Hants.

**ANDREWS, Eamonn,** CBE (Hon.) 1970; Television Compère; Broadcaster; Writer; *b* 19 Dec. 1922; *s* of William and Margaret Andrews; *m* 1951, Gráinne Bourke; one *s* two *d*. *Educ:* Irish Christian Brothers, Synge Street, Dublin. Radio Eireann broadcaster (boxing commentaries, general sports commentating, interview programmes, etc.), 1941-50; first broadcast for the BBC, 1950; first appeared on BBC Television, 1951; BBC programmes included: What's My Line?, This Is Your Life, Sports Report, Crackerjack, Playbox; also boxing commentaries, variety, interview and general sports programmes. Chm. Radio Eireann Statutory Authority, charged with establishment of television in Ireland, 1960-66; joined ABC Television, 1964, Thames Television, 1968. Director, Butlin's Ltd, 1970- . Former All-Ireland Amateur Junior Boxing Champion (Middle Weight). Knight of St Gregory, 1964. *Publications:* Play, The Moon is Black, 1941; This Is My Life (autobiog.), 1963: articles for magazines and newspapers; Empire News (general columnist); formerly contrib. to: Irish Independent (radio columnist), The Star (general columnist), Sunday Dispatch (boxing columnist). *Recreations:* walking and talking. *Address:* 4 Golden Square, W1. *T:* 01-437 0292. *Clubs:* Irish, Royal Automobile.

**ANDREWS, Sir Edwin Arthur C.;** *see* Chapman-Andrews.

**ANDREWS, Brig. George Lewis Williams,** CBE 1960; DSO 1944; *b* 1 July 1910; *o s* of Captain C. G. W. Andrews, The Border Regt (killed in action, 1914) and of late Mrs Diana Gambier-Parry (*née* Norrington); *m* 1938, Marianne, *d* of late Carl Strindberg, Stockholm and Fru Greta Winbergh (*née* Skjöldebrand); one *s*. *Educ:* Haileybury; Sandhurst. Commissioned 2nd Lieut, The Seaforth Highlanders, 1930; active service, Palestine, 1936. Served War of 1939-45; BEF, 1939, MEF, 1941-43, BLA, 1944-45; Comd 2nd Bn The Seaforth Highlanders, 1943-45. Comd 1st Bn Seaforth Highlanders, 1953-54; Comd 152nd Highland Infantry Brigade (TA), 1954-57; Assistant Commandant, RMA Sandhurst, 1957-60. Lieut-Col, 1953; Colonel, 1955; Hon. Brig., 1960; psc 1940; jssc 1948. Chevalier, Order of Leopold, Belgium, 1945; Croix de Guerre with palm, Belgium, 1945. *Recreations:* shooting, ski-ing. *Address:* West Kingsteps, Nairn, Scotland. *T:* Nairn 3231.

**ANDREWS, Lt-Col Harold Marcus E.;** *see* Ervine-Andrews.

**ANDREWS, Harry (Fleetwood),** CBE 1966; Actor since 1933; *b* 10 Nov. 1911. *Educ:* Tonbridge; Wrekin Coll. With Liverpool Repertory, 1933-35. Played Horatio in Hamlet, New York 1936; John Gielgud's Season, 1937; with Old Vic, 1945-49; Bolingbroke, Mirabel, Warwick in St Joan; Shakespeare Memorial Theatre; Wolsey, Macduff Brutus, Bolingbroke in Henry IV Pts I and II, 1949-51; Enobarbus, Buckingham, Kent, 1953; Othello, Claudius, 1956; Menenius in Coriolanus, 1959; Casanova in Camino Real, Phoenix, 1957; Henry VIII, Old Vic, 1958; Allenby in Ross, Haymarket, 1960; Rockhart in The Lizard on the Rock, Phoenix, 1962; Ekhart in Baal, Phoenix, 1963; Crampton in You Never Can Tell, Haymarket, 1966. *Films:* Red Beret, Helen of Troy, Alexander the Great, Hill in Korea, Moby Dick, St Joan, Dreyfus, Ice Cold in Alex, Solomon and Sheba, Question of Larceny, Circle of Deception, The Best of Enemies, The Inspector, Barabbas, Reach for Glory, Nine Hours to Rama, 55 Days at Peking, The Snout, The Best of Everything, The Hill, The Agony and the Ecstasy, The Sands of Kalahari, Modesty Blaise, The Deadly Affair, The Jokers, The Long Duel, A Dandy in Aspic, The Charge of The Light Brigade, The Night They Raided Minsky's, The Southern Star, The Seagull, A Nice Girl Like Me; Too Late The Hero; The Gaunt Woman. Served War of 1939-45 (despatches). *Recreations:* cricket, tennis, sailing, gardening. *Address:* Church Farm Oast, Salehurst, Robertsbridge, Sussex; Flat 7, 1 Bryanston Square, W1.

**ANDREWS, Harry Thomson;** Director: Consolidated Diamond Mines of South West Africa (De Beers Group); Welkom GM Co. (Anglo-American Corp. of South Africa); French Bank of Southern Africa, 1958; Union Liquid Air Co.; *b* Capetown, South Africa, 11 Dec. 1897; *s* of late H. Andrews, Capetown; *m* 1926, R. D. Williams, Pretoria; one *d*. *Educ:* Observatory High Sch., Capetown; Marist Brothers' Coll., Capetown; Univ. of Pretoria. Served European War, 1917-19, in France, South African Signals, RE. Advocate, Supreme Court (Transvaal), 1927; Political Secretary South Africa House, London, 1930-35; Accredited Representative of Union of South Africa to League of Nations, Geneva, 1936-40; Asst Sec. for Defence, Pretoria; Under-Sec. for External Affairs, Pretoria; Head of South Africa Govt Supply Mission to USA, 1942-45; Ambassador of South Africa to USA, 1945-49; Permanent Representative of SA to United Nations, 1945-49; South African Ambassador to France, 1949-57; Minister to Switzerland, 1954-56. Member French-Commonwealth War Graves Commission, 1954-57. Trustee, S Africa Foundn, 1960. *Recreation:* golf. *Address:* 214 Bretton Woods, Killarney, Johannesburg, S Africa. *Clubs:* Kimberley (Kimberley); Rand, Bryanston

Country (Johannesburg); West Province Sports (Cape Town).

**ANDREWS, John;** *see* Andrews, Arthur John Francis.

**ANDREWS, Rt. Hon. John Lawson Ormrod,** PC (Northern Ireland) 1957; DL; Senator since 1964; Minister and Leader in the Senate, Northern Ireland, since 1964; also Deputy Prime Minister; *b* 15 July 1903; *o s* of late Right Hon. John Miller Andrews, CH, DL, LLD, MP, Maxwell Court, Comber, Co. Down, and Jessie, *er d* of Joseph Ormrod, Morelands, Heaton, Bolton; *m* 1928, Marjorie Elaine Maynard James, *d* of Alfred Morgan James, The Fields, Newport, Mon; three *s* one *d*. *Educ:* Mourne Grange Preparatory Sch., Kilkeel, Co. Down; Shrewsbury. Served apprenticeship to flax spinning trade and joined family firm, John Andrews & Co. Ltd, Comber, 1922; now Chm. and Man. Dir. Ex-Chm. Flax Spinners Association for Northern Ireland. Northern Ireland Government: MP (U) Mid-Down, 1953-64; Minister of Health and Local Govt, 1957-61; Minister of Commerce, 1961-63; Minister of Finance, 1963-64. President: Ulster Unionist Council, 1969; Comber Br., Mid-Down Unionist Assoc.; Chm., Mid-Down Unionist Assoc. DL Co. Down, N Ireland, 1961. *Recreation:* yachting (Commodore Strangford Lough Yacht Club). *Address:* Maxwell Court, Comber, Co. Down. *T:* Comber 263. *Clubs:* Ulster Reform (Belfast); Royal Ulster Yacht.

**ANDREWS, Air Vice-Marshal John Oliver,** CB 1942; DSO 1917; MC; idc; *b* 1896; *s* of John Andrews, Waterloo, Lancs; *m* 1923, Bertha, *d* of Wilfred Bisdée, Hambrook, Glos; two *s*. Lieut Royal Scots; seconded RFC, 1914; served France, 1914-18; S Russia, 1919; India, 1920 (MC and bar, Montenegrin Silver Medal for bravery, DSO, despatches thrice); transferred to RAF, 1919; retired, 1945.

**ANDREWS, Julie Elizabeth;** Actress; *b* 1 Oct. 1935; *m* 1st, Anthony J. Walton (marr. diss. 1968); one *d*; 2nd, 1969, Blake Edwards. *Educ:* Woodbrook Girls' Sch., Beckenham and private governess. Appeared in The Boy Friend, Broadway, New York, 1954; My Fair Lady: New York, 1956, London, 1958; Camelot, New York, 1960. *Films:* (Walt Disney) Mary Poppins, 1963 (Academy Award, 1964); Americanisation of Emily, 1964; Sound of Music, 1964; Hawaii, 1965; Torn Curtain, 1966; Thoroughly Modern Millie, 1966; Star, 1967; Darling Lili, 1970. *Recreations:* boating, ski-ing, riding. *Address:* Chasin-Park-Citron Agency, 10889 Wilshire Boulevard, Los Angeles, Calif 90024, USA.

**ANDREWS, Rev. Canon Leonard Martin,** CVO 1946; MBE; MC 1917; Rector of Stoke Climsland, Cornwall, 1922-68; Chaplain to the Queen, 1952-69 (to King George VI, 1936-52); Hon. Canon of Truro since 1932; *b* 24 Sept. 1886. *Educ:* Queens' Coll., Cambridge. BA 1909; MA 1921; Deacon, 1909; Priest, 1910; Rector of Brewarrina, NSW, 1913-14; Vice-Principal Brotherhood of the Good Shepherd, NSW, 1914-15; Temp. CF, 1914-19; Chaplain at Khartoum, 1920-22; Rural Dean of Trigg Major, 1929-32. *Address:* Climsland, Downderry, Torpoint, Callington, Cornwall. *Club:* United University.

**ANDREWS, Sir Linton;** *see* Andrews, Sir William Linton.

**ANDREWS, Stanley George B.;** *see* Burt-Andrews.

**ANDREWS, Wilfrid,** CBE 1968; Chairman Royal Automobile Club since 1946; *b* 15 Jan. 1892; *s* of late Norris Andrews, Sittingbourne, and Harriet, *d* of Chilman Taylor, Sittingbourne; *m* 1917, Ruth Eleanor (*d* 1968), *d* of W. F. Goodhew, Sittingbourne; one *s* two *d*. *Educ:* Wreight's Sch., Faversham. President: Fédération Internationale de l'Automobile; Organisation Mondiale de Tourisme et de l'Automobile; Chm., RAC Buildings Co. Ltd, Golf Club and Country House Ltd, RAC Travel Ltd, and other cos. Founder and Chm. Roads Campaign Council. Pres. Rotary International Association of Great Britain and Ireland, 1930-31; Chm., Aims and Objects Cttee, 1931-32 and Board of Dirs, 1932-33, Rotary International. Founder Vice-Chm. American British Commonwealth Association. Widely travelled USA and Europe. Order of the Crown of Belgium, 1947; Swedish Royal Order of Vasa, 1947; Danish Order of the Dannebrog, 1948; Royal Order of St Olav, Norway, 1949; Officer, Order of Grimaldi, Monaco. *Publications:* articles upon Rotary, Highways and Motoring. *Recreations:* painting, motoring, yachting, golf. *Clubs:* Royal Automobile, Royal Motor Yacht.

**ANDREWS, Sir (William) Linton,** Kt 1954; Editor Emeritus, Yorkshire Post, 1968 (Editor, 1939-60 and Director of Yorkshire Post Group, 1950-68); *b* Hull, 1886; *s* of late William Andrews, author; *m* 1915, Gertrude (*d* 1958), *e d* of Alexander Douglas, Dundee. *Educ:* Hull Grammar Sch.; Christ's Hospital. Began journalistic career at Hull and continued it at Huddersfield, Sheffield, Portsmouth, Dundee, Paris, and London. Served in Black Watch throughout World War 1, three years on Western Front. Sub-Editor, Daily Mail, 1919-23; Editor of the Leeds Mercury, 1923-39. President: Guild of British Newspaper Editors, 1952-53; Inst. of Journalists, 1946. Chairman: Brontë Society Council, 1940-70; editorial cttee of Newspaper Soc., etc, 1943-50; Press Council, 1955-59 (Foundation Mem. and first Vice-Chm., 1953); Yorkshire Centre, RSA, 1966-67. Mem. cttee of 6th Imperial Press Conf., and Delegate to Conf. in Canada, 1950; Delegate to Commonwealth Press Union Conf. in India and Pakistan, 1961; helped to set up national scheme of Press training; has often broadcast on North Country and International topics. Pres. Leeds Philosophical and Literary Society, 1948-50, and Bradford English Soc., 1956-57; Vice-Chm. of Leeds Centenary Musical Festival, 1958, and Jt Vice-Chm., 1961 and 1964. Mem. Court and Council, Leeds Univ., 1943-59. Vis. Professor, Southern Illinois Univ., 1967. FRSA; FJI. Hon. LLD, Leeds Univ.; Hon. DLitt, Emerson Coll., Boston, Mass. Médaille d'Argent de la Reconnaissance Française (War of 1939-45). *Publications:* Old English Towns and Picturesque York and the North Riding (with the late W. Andrews); Haunting Years; Wayside Pageant (with A. P. Maguire); Yorkshire Folk; Englands Presserad (Copenhagen); Problems of an Editor; Autobiography of a Journalist; Lords and Labourers of the Press (with H. A. Taylor). Contributor to Has the Church Failed? and If I Had My Time Again. Edited, The Yorkshire PostTwo Centuries. Many articles on humours and pathos of North Country industrial life and English political commentaries for American readers. *Recreations:* books and the country. *Address:* 28 North Parade, West Park, Leeds 16. *T:* Leeds 52973. *Clubs:* Athenæum, Devonshire, Press, Christ's Hospital; Leeds, Leeds and County Conservative (Leeds); Alwoodley Golf.

**ANDRIC, Ivo;** author; *b* Travnik, Bosnia, 10 Oct. 1892; *m* 1959, Milica Babić, painter and theatre designer. *Educ:* secondary sch., Sarajevo; Universities of Zagreb, Vienna, Cracow, Graz. Political prisoner for 3 years during European War, 1914-18. Joined diplomatic service of his country, 1919; served in Rome, Bucharest, Trieste, Graz, Berlin (Ambassador), etc. Deputy to Yugoslav Parl., 1949-55. Pres., Federation of Writers of Yugoslavia, 1946-52. Prize for Life Work, Yugoslavia, 1956; Nobel Prize for Literature, 1961. Dr (*hc*), Kraków University, 1964. *Publications:* Ex Ponto (prison meditations); Gospodjica (Eng. trans. The Woman from Sarajevo, 1966); Travnička Kronika (Eng. trans. A Bosnian Story, 1959), Na Drini čuprija (Eng. trans. The Bridge on the Drina, 1959); Prokleta avlija (Eng. trans. Devil's Yard, 1962); poems, essays, several vols of stories, etc. *Address:* Proleterskih brigada 2a, Belgrade, Yugoslavia.

**ANFOM, Emmanuel E.;** *see* Evans-Anfom.

**ANGAS, Sir (John) Keith,** Kt 1952; Hon. Treasurer of Royal Agricultural Society of South Australia (President 1951-59); Chairman of Council, Institute of Medical and Veterinary Science, 1952-62; Vice-President Royal Zoological Society of South Australia and Royal Automobile Association of South Australia; Former Chairman of Council, St Mark's College, University of Adelaide; *b* 30 Jan. 1900; *s* of Charles H. Angas, Lindsay Park, Angaston, South Australia; *m* 1924, Gwynnyth Fay, *d* of Dr J. E. Good; one *s* one *d*. *Educ:* Geelong Grammar Sch., Corio, Victoria. War of 1939-45: Capt. 1st Australian Armoured Div., 1941-42; Staff, 1942-44. Pres., Stockowners Assoc. of SA, 1937-40, 1945-46; Chm., Grazier's Federal Council of Australia, 1939-40; Chm., South Australian Jockey Club, 1940-42, 1947-50; President: Liberal & Country League of SA, 1947-50. Chairman: Bagots Executor and Trustee Company; Colonial Mutual Life Assce Soc. (SA); Mem. Cttee on Future of Tertiary Educn, Austr. Univs Commn, 1961. *Address:* Bagot House, North Terrace, Adelaide, South Australia. *Clubs:* Adelaide, Naval and Military (Adelaide); Melbourne (Melbourne).

**ANGAS, Major Lawrence Lee Bazley,** MC; MA; Financial Consultant and writer on economic fluctuations; *b* 22 Feb. 1893; *m* Catherine Lowe; one *s* two *d*. *Educ:* Charterhouse; Magdalen Coll., Oxford. Major 1st Cheshire Regt; served France and Italy (MC, Croix de Guerre, despatches twice, twice wounded); resigned 1919. Student of unemployment, currency and the Business Cycle. *Publications:* Reparations, Trade and Foreign Exchange; Germany and Her Debts; Investment for Appreciation; L'Art du Placement des Capitaux; The Problems of the Foreign Exchanges; and various other books on economic and Stock Exchange subjects. *Recreations:* rackets, ski-ing, tennis, golf. *Address:* (Private and Office) Academy Avenue, Saxtons River, Vermont, USA. *Clubs:* Bath, Leander; Vincent's (Oxford).

**ANGELES, Victoria de los;** *see* De los Angeles.

**ANGELL JAMES, John;** *see* James, J. A.

**ANGLESEY,** 7th Marquess of, *cr* 1815; **George Charles Henry Victor Paget;** Baron Paget, of Beau Desert, 1549; Earl of Uxbridge, 1784; Bt 1730; Vice-Lieutenant of Anglesey, since 1960; *b* 8 Oct. 1922; *o s* of 6th Marquess of Anglesey, GCVO, and Lady Victoria Marjorie Harriet Manners (*d* 1946), *d* of 8th Duke of Rutland; *S* father, 1947; *m* 1948, Elizabeth Shirley Vaughan Morgan (*see* Marchioness of Anglesey); two *s* three *d*. *Educ:* Wixenford, Wokingham; Eton Coll. Major, RHG, 1946. President: Anglesey Conservative Assoc.; Nat. Museum of Wales, 1962-68; Friends of Friendless Churches. Dir, Welsh Nat. Opera Co. Treasurer, Danilo Dolci Trust (Britain). Member: Welsh Cttee, Nat. Trust; Historic Buildings Council for Wales, 1953-; Royal Fine Art Commn, 1965-; Redundant Churches Fund, 1969-. FSA 1952. Cdre, Royal Welsh Yacht Club, 1948. Anglesey: CC, 1951-67; JP, 1959-68; DL, 1960. Hon. Fellow, Royal Cambrian Acad. Lord of the Manor of Burton-upon-Trent; Freeman of the City of London. *Publications:* (ed) The Capel Letters, 1814-1817, 1955; One-Leg: the Life and Letters of 1st Marquess of Anglesey, 1961; (ed) Sergeant Pearman's Memoirs, 1968. *Recreations:* gardening, music. *Heir:* *s* Earl of Uxbridge, *qv*. *Address:* Plâs-Newydd, Llanfairpwll, Anglesey. *T:* Llanfairpwll 330.

*See also Sir C. M. R. V. Duff, Bt.*

**ANGLESEY, Marchioness of; (Elizabeth) Shirley Vaughan Paget;** *b* 4 Dec. 1924; *d* of late Charles Morgan, novelist, and of Hilda Vaughan, *qv*; *m* 1948, Marquess of Anglesey, *qv*; two *s* three *d*. *Educ:* Francis Holland Sch., London; St James', West Malvern; Kent Place Sch., USA. Personal Secretary to Gladwyn Jebb, FO, until marriage. Member, Civic Trust for Wales, 1967; Member Award Panel, Duke of Edinburgh's Award for Elegant Design, CoID, 1967-70; Chairman, Nat. Federation of Women's Institutes, 1966-69; Vice-Chairman, Govt Working Party on Methods of Sewage Disposal, 1969-70; Mem. Council, University Coll. of N Wales, Bangor, 1970. *Address:* Plâs-Newydd, Llanfairpwll, Anglesey. *T:* Llanfairpwll 330.

**ANGLIN, Prof. Douglas (George);** Professor of Political Science, Carleton University, Ottawa, Canada, since 1958; *b* Toronto, Canada, 16 Dec. 1923; *s* of George Chambers Anglin, MD, and Ruth Cecilia Cale, MD; *m* 1948, Mary Elizabeth Watson; two *d*. *Educ:* Toronto Univ.; Corpus Christi and Nuffield Colls, Oxford Univ. BA Toronto; MA, DPhil Oxon. Lieut, RCNVR, 1943-45. Asst (later Associate) Prof. of Polit. Sci. and Internat. Relations, Univ. of Manitoba, Winnipeg, 1951-58; Associate Prof. (later Prof.), Carleton Univ., 1958. Vice-Chancellor, Univ. of Zambia, Lusaka, Zambia, 1965-69; Associate Research Fellow, Nigerian Inst. of Social and Economic Research, Univ. of Ibadan, Ibadan, Nigeria, 1962-63; Research Associate, Center of Internat. Studies, Princeton Univ., Princeton, NJ, 1969-70. *Publications:* The St. Pierre and Miquelon Affair of 1941: a study in diplomacy in the North Atlantic quadrangle, 1966; (ed jtly) Africa: Problems and Prospects 1961; articles on Internat. and African affairs in a variety of learned jls. *Address:* Carleton University, Ottawa, Canada.

**ANGUS, Col Edmund Graham,** CBE 1944; MC; TD; DL, JP; President: George Angus & Co. Ltd, Newcastle upon Tyne (Chairman, 1933-64); Newcastle upon Tyne Permanent Building Society, since 1969; Director: Newcastle & Gateshead Water Co.; Royal Insurance Co. Ltd (Local); *b* 9 June 1889; *s* of Col W. M. Angus, CB; *m* 1922, Bridget E. I. Spencer; one *s* one *d* (and two *s* decd, of whom *e s* was presumed killed in action, Anzio, Italy, 1944). *Educ:* Felsted Sch. Joined George Angus & Co. Ltd, 1906. Commissioned in Volunteer Forces (RA). Served in firm's Boston office, 1910-11, mobilised Aug. 1914; served in France and Flanders with 50th Div. Artillery till Feb. 1919; demobilised with rank of Major; rejoined

G. Angus & Co. Ltd, Dir. 1920. Rejoined TA 1920; commanded 74th Northumbrian Field Regt, 1925-32; subst. Col with effect, 1929. DL Co. Durham, 1945; JP Northumberland, 1948. KStJ 1966. *Recreation:* horticulture. *Address:* Ravenstone, Corbridge, Northumberland. *T:* Corbridge 2122. *Clubs:* Carlton; Northern Counties, Union (Newcastle upon Tyne).

**ANGUS, Brig. (hon.) Tom Hardy,** DSO 1938; psc†; fs; late Indian Army; *b* 22 May 1899; *s* of late J. B. Angus and M. S. D. Hardy; *m* 1954, Lilian Maud, *er d* of late John Emil and Ada Hyort. *Educ:* privately; RMC, Sandhurst. First Commission, 1918; Joined 45th Rattray's Sikhs, now 3rd Bn 11th Sikh Regt (Rattray's Sikhs), 1918; Regimental duty until 1932; Staff Coll., Quetta, 1932-33; RAF Staff Coll., Andover, 1935; Brigade Major, 1st Infantry Brigade, Abbottabad, NWFP, 1936-40; served Waziristan (DSO); Instructor (GSO2) Staff Coll., Quetta, 1940; Brig. Gen. Staff, Ceylon, 1942; Commander 51 Indian Infantry Brigade, 1943-44; DDMT, GHQ, India, 1945; Director of Air, India, 1946-47; retired 1948. *Recreation:* golf. *Address:* c/o Lloyds Bank Ltd, St Mary Street, Weymouth, Dorset. *Club:* Royal Dorset Yacht (Weymouth).

**ANKOLE, Omugabe of;** *see* Gasyonga II, Sir C. G.

**ANNALY,** 5th Baron *cr* 1863; **Luke Robert White;** Partner, W. Greenwell & Co., Members of London Stock Exchange; *b* 15 March 1927; *o s* of 4th Baron Annaly and Lady Annaly (formerly Lady Lavinia Spencer); *S* father, 1970; *m* 1st, 1953, Lady Marye Pepys (marr. diss. 1957; she *d* 1958); one *s*; 2nd, 1960, Jennifer Carey (marr. diss. 1967); two *d*. *Educ:* Eton. RAF, 1944-48; RAuxAF, 1948-51; Flying Officer (601 Sqdn). Livery, Haberdashers' Company; Freeman of City of London, 1953. *Recreations:* cricket, golf, theatre. *Heir:* *s* Hon. Luke Richard White, *b* 29 June 1954. *Address:* Welches, Bentley, Farnham, Surrey. *T:* Bentley (Hants) 2107. *Clubs:* Turf, Royal Air Force, MCC.

**ANNAMUNTHODO, Sir Harry,** Kt 1967; FRCS, FACS; Professor of Surgery, University of the West Indies, since 1961; *b* 26 April 1920; *s* of George Annamunthodo and Rosaline (*née* Viapree); *m* 1953, Margaret Pullman; one *s* three *d*. *Educ:* Queen's Coll., Guyana; London Hospital Medical Coll. MB, BS London, 1946; DTM&H, 1947; FRCS, 1951; FACS, 1961. Lectr in Surg., Univ. of the W Indies, 1955-57; Sen. Lectr in Surg., UWI, 1957-61. Rockefeller Research Fellow, 1959-60; Hunterian Prof., Royal Coll. of Surgeons, 1960. *Publications:* (Co-author) Lymphogranuloma Venereum, 1962; papers on: various cancers and diseases of stomach, rectum, etc in British and American Med. Jls. *Recreation:* horticulture. *Address:* 44 Hope Boulevard, Kingston 6, Jamaica, WI. *T:* 70716.

**ANNAN,** family name of **Baron Annan.**

**ANNAN,** Baron, *cr* 1965 (Life Peer); **Noël Gilroy Annan,** OBE 1946; Provost of University College, London, since Oct. 1966; *b* 25 Dec. 1916; *s* of late James Gilroy Annan; *m* 1950, Gabriele, *d* of Louis Ferdinand Ullstein, Berlin; two *d*. *Educ:* Stowe Sch.; King's Coll., Cambridge (Exhibitioner and Scholar). Served War of 1939-45: WO, War Cabinet Offices, and Military Intelligence, 1940-44; France and Germany, 1944-46; GSO1, Political Div. of British Control Commn, 1945-46. University of Cambridge: Fellow of King's Coll., 1944-56; Asst Tutor, 1947; Lectr in Politics, 1948-66; Provost of King's Coll., 1956-66. Romanes Lectr, Oxford, 1965. Chairman: Departmental Cttee on Teaching of Russian in Schools, 1960; Academic Planning Bd, Univ. of Essex, 1962; Member: Academic Adv. Cttee, Brunel Coll., 1964; Academic Planning Bd, Univ. of East Anglia, 1960; Public Schools Commn, 1966-70. Sen. Fellow Eton Coll., 1956-66. Governor: Stowe Sch., 1945-66; Queen Mary Coll., London, 1959-60. Trustee: Churchill Coll., 1958; British Museum, 1963. Dir, Royal Opera House, Covent Garden; Mem., Arts Cttee, Gulbenkian Foundn, 1957-64. FRHistS; Fellow, Berkeley Coll., Yale, 1963; Hon. Fellow, University Coll., London, 1968. Hon. DLitt: York; Toronto; DUniv Essex. Le Bas Prize, 1948. Comdr, Royal Order of King George I of the Hellenes (Greece), 1962. *Publications:* Leslie Stephen: His thought and character in relation to his time, 1951 (awarded James Tait Black Memorial Prize, 1951); The Intellectual Aristocracy (in Studies in Social History, a tribute to G. M. Trevelyan, 1956); Kipling's Place in the History of Ideas (in Kipling's Mind and Art, 1964); The Curious Strength of Positivism in English Political Thought, 1959; Roxburgh of Stowe, 1965; articles in Victorian Studies and other periodicals. *Recreation:* Mediterranean travel. *Address:* University College, Gower Street, WC1E 6BT. *T:* 01-387 7050.

**ANNAN, Robert;** President, Consolidated Gold Fields Ltd, since 1960 (Chairman, 1944-60); director of mining companies; *b* 16 May 1885; *er s* of John and Marion Annan; *m* 1911, Dely (*d* 1967), *yr d* of Everett Loraine Weston, New York; two *s*. *Educ:* Uppingham Sch.; Columbia Univ., New York City. Served European War, 1915-18, in France, with Royal Engineers (TF). Institution of Mining and Metallurgy: Mem. 1920; Pres. 1936-37; Hon. Treas., 1946-68; Gold Medallist, 1949; Hon. Fellow, Imperial Coll. of Science and Technology, 1951; Egleston Medal, Columbia Univ., 1957. Mem.: South African Institute of Mining and Metallurgy, 1936; Newcomen Soc. *Recreations:* history and early literature of mining and metallurgy; book collecting. *Address:* 132 Bickenhall Mansions, W1. *T:* 01-935 2065. *Club:* Caledonian.

**ANNAND, Richard Wallace,** VC 1940; DL; Personnel Officer at Finchale Abbey Training Centre for the Disabled, near Durham, since 1948; late Captain Durham Light Infantry (RARO); *b* 5 Nov. 1914; *s* of Lt-Comdr Wallace Moir Annand, Royal Naval Division (killed Gallipoli 1915), and late Dora Elizabeth Chapman, South Shields; *m* 1940, Shirley Osborne, JP 1957. *Educ:* Pocklington, East Yorks. Staff of National Provincial Bank, 1933-37; commissioned in RNVR 1933 (Tyne and London Divisions); transferred to Durham Light Infantry, Jan. 1938; served in France and Belgium, 1939-40 (wounded, VC). Invalided, Dec. 1948. Hon. Freeman Co. Borough of South Shields, 1940; Hon. Representative of The Officers' Assoc.; DL Co. of Durham, 1956. *Recreations:* Rugby football, golf; interest: general welfare of the deafened. *Address:* Springwell House, Whitesmocks, Durham City. *Club:* County (Durham).

**ANNENBERG, Walter H.;** US Ambassador to the Court of St James's, since 1969; *b* 13 March 1908; *s* of M. L. Annenberg; *m* 1951, Leonore Cohn; one *d*. *Educ:* Peddie Sch.; Univ. of Pennsylvania. President, Triangle Publications Inc., Philadelphia, Pa; Publisher: Seventeen Magazine; TV Guide; Daily Telegraph (NY); Daily Racing Form. Holds foreign decorations. *Address:* American Embassy, 24 Grosvenor Square, London, W1.

*T:* 01-499 9000. *Clubs:* Turf, Buck's, St James'; Lyford Cay (Bahamas); National Press (Washington, DC); etc.

**ANNESLEY,** family name of **Earl Annesley** and **Viscount Valentia.**

**ANNESLEY,** 9th Earl, *cr* 1789; **Robert Annesley;** Baron Annesley, 1758; Viscount Glerawly, 1766; Civil Servant, retired; *b* 20 Feb. 1900; *s* of Arthur Albert O'Donel Valentia Annesley (*d* 1947) and Elizabeth Mary (*d* 1909), *d* of late Embertus van Ooms, Consul for the Netherlands; *S* kinsman, 8th Earl of Annesley, 1957; *m* 1922, Nora, *y d* of late Walter Harrison, Sapperton, near Cirencester, Glos; three *s.* Served European War, 1914-18, with Royal Navy; War of 1939-45 with Royal Corps of Signals, France and West Africa. *Heir: s* Viscount Glerawly, *qv. Address:* 67 Vegal Crescent, Englefield Green, Surrey. *T:* Egham 2162.

**ANNETT, David Maurice,** MA; Headmaster of King's School, Worcester, since 1959; *b* 27 April 1917; *s* of late M. W. Annett and Marguerite, *d* of Rev. W. M. Hobson; *m* 1953, Evelyn Rosemary, *d* of late W. M. Gordon, Headmaster of Wrekin Coll., and *widow* of R. E. Upcott; one *d* (one step-*s* two step-*d*). *Educ:* Haileybury Coll.; Queens' Coll., Cambridge. Head of Classical Dept at Oundle Sch., 1939-53, and Housemaster, 1948-53; Headmaster of Marling Sch., Stroud, 1953-59. Served with 27th Field Regt, RA, in India and Burma (Capt.), 1941-45. *Address:* 14 College Green, Worcester. *T:* Worcester 24989.

**ANNETT, Engineer-Captain George Lewis,** CIE 1941; RIN, retired; *b* 1887; *s* of late George Samuel Annett, MC; *m* 1918, Hessie Mary (*d* 1963), *d* of late Robert Felpts, Ulverston. Arms Traffic Operations, Persian Gulf, 1909-14; served European War, 1914-19 (despatches twice); Head of Engineering Branch, Royal Indian Navy; retired, 1941. CA Lancs. *Address:* Rakehead, Ulverston, Lancs.

**ANNIGONI, Pietro,** RP; Italian painter; artist in oil, tempera, etching and fresco; *b* Milan, 7 June 1910; *s* of Ricciardo Annigoni, engineer; *m* Anna Maggini (*d* 1969); one *s* one *d. Educ:* Accademia delle Belle Arti, Florence. Member of: Accademia di S Luca, Rome; Accademia delle Arti del Disegno, Florence; Academy of Design, New York. Portraits exhibited at Royal Academy, London: The Queen (for the Fishmongers' Company), 1955; Dame Margot Fonteyn, 1956; The Duke of Edinburgh (for the Fishmongers' Company), 1957; Maharanee of Jaipur, 1958. Other works exhibited recently: Exhibition (Wildenstein Gall., London), 1954; Exhibition (Royal Acad., London), 1956; Exhibition (Wildenstein, New York), 1957; Portrait of Princess Margaret, 1958; Exhibition (Galleries of the Federation of British Artists), 1961; The Immaculate Heart of Mary, 1962; Retrospective Exhbn, New York and San Francisco, 1969. Permanent collections showing his works include: Uffizi (Print Room), Florence; Galleria Arte Moderna, Milan; National Portrait Gallery, London (HM the Queen, 1970); Frescoes: S Martino, Florence; Madonna del Consiglio, Pistoia; Basilica of S Lorenzo, Florence. Has also exhibited in Rome, Turin, Paris, Florence, Milan, etc. *Address:* Borgo degli Albizi 8, Florence, Italy.

**ANNIS, Air Marshal Clare Levi,** OBE 1943; CD 1952; RCAF, Retired; General Manager, Canadian Patents and Development Ltd, since 1966; *b* 22 Jan. 1912; *s* of late Levi Chester Annis, Highland Creek, Ont.; *m* 1939, Fern Beatrice, *d* of John Thomas Atkinson, Calgary, Alberta; three *s. Educ:* Univ. of Toronto. Joined RCAF, 1936. Served War of 1939-45, Coastal and Bomber Comd Ops. AOC Air Material Cmd, 1958-62; VCAS 1962-64; Chief of Logistics and Engineering, Min. of Defence, Canada, 1964-66. Air Cdre, 1952; Air Vice-Marshal, 1957; Air Marshal, 1964. *Recreations:* fishing, sailing, hobbycrafts. *Club:* Royal Ottawa Golf and Country.

**ANOUILH, Jean;** French dramatic author; *b* Bordeaux, 23 June 1910. *Educ:* Collège Chaptal; Univ. of Paris. *Plays include:* L'Ermine, 1934 (prod Nottingham, 1955, as The Ermine); Y'avait un prisonnier, 1935; Le Voyageur sans bagages, 1937; Le Bal des Voleurs, 1938 (prod London, 1952, as Thieves' Carnival); La Sauvage, 1938 (prod London, 1957, as Restless Heart); Cavalcade d'Amour, 1941; Le Rendez-vous de Senlis, 1942: Léocadia, 1942 (prod London, 1954, as Time Remembered); Eurydice, 1942 (prod London as Point of Departure, 1950); Humulus le Muet (in collaboration with Jean Aurenche), 1945; Oreste, 1945; Antigone, 1946 (prod London, 1949); Jézébel, 1946; Roméo et Jeannette, 1946 (prod London, 1949, as Fading Mansion); Médée, 1946; L'Invitation au château, 1948 (prod London, 1950, 1968, as Ring Round the Moon); Ardèle ou la Marguerite, 1949; La Répétition, ou l'amour puni, 1950 (prod Edinburgh Festival 1957, and London, 1961); Colombe, 1950 (prod London, 1951); La Valse des toréadors, 1952 (prod London, 1956); L'Alouette, 1953 (prod London, 1955, as The Lark); Ornifle, 1955; L'Hurluberlu, 1958 (prod Chichester and London, 1966, as The Fighting Cock); La Foire d'Empoigne, 1960; Becket (prod London, 1961); La Grotte, 1961 (prod London, 1965, as The Cavern); Poor Bitos (prod London, 1963-64); Le Boulanger, la Boulangère et le Petit Mitson, 1968; Cher Antoine, 1969; Les Poissons Rouges, 1969; Ne Réveillez Pas, Madame, 1970. *Films include:* Monsieur Vincent (awarded Grand Prix du Cinéma Français); Pattes blanches; Caprice de Caroline, etc. *Address:* c/o Les Editions de la Table Ronde, 40 rue du Bac, Paris VIIe, France.

**ANSCOMBE, Gertrude Elizabeth Margaret,** FBA 1967; Professor of Philosopny, University of Cambridge, since 1970; Fellow, New Hall, Cambridge, since 1970; Fellow, Somerville College, Oxford, 1964-70, Hon. Fellow since 1970; Adjunct Professor, University of Pennsylvania, since 1968; *b* 1919; *d* of Allen Wells Anscombe and Gertrude Elizabeth Anscombe (*née* Thomas); *m* 1941, Prof. Peter Thomas Geach, *qv*; three *s* four *d. Educ:* Sydenham High Sch.; St Hugh's Coll., Oxford (Schol.); Newnham Coll., Cambridge. 2nd cl. Hon. Mods 1939, 1st cl. Greats 1941, Oxford. Research studentships, Oxford and Cambridge, 1941-44; research fellowships, Somerville Coll., 1946-64. *Publications:* Intention, 1957; An Introduction to Wittgenstein's Tractatus, 1959; (with Peter Geach) Three Philosophers, 1961; translator and co-editor of posthumous works of Ludwig Wittgenstein. *Recreation:* sitting around. *Address:* New Hall, Cambridge.

**ANSELL, James Lawrence Bunting,** MRCS, LRCP; lately Surgeon Apothecary to HM Household at Sandringham. *Educ:* Cambridge Univ.; St Thomas' Hospital. BA Cambridge; MRCS, LRCP, 1940. Formerly: Casualty Officer, Ear, Nose and Throat House Surgeon at St Thomas' Hospital; House Physician and Opthalmic House Surgeon, Royal Hants County Hospital, Winchester; House Physician and Resident Medical Officer,

London Chest Hospital. *Address:* The Surgery, Sandringham, Norfolk. *T:* King's Lynn 2675.

**ANSELL, Sir Michael Picton,** Kt 1968; CBE 1951; DSO 1944; DL; Chairman, British Show Jumping Association, 1945-64 and since 1970 (President, 1964-66); Show Director, Royal International Horse Show, since 1951, and Horse of the Year Show; (first) Chairman, British Horse Society Council, since 1963 (Hon. Director, British Horse Society, 1952-63); *b* 26 March 1905; *s* of Lieut-Col G. K. Ansell and K. Cross; *m* 1936, Victoria Jacintha Fleetwood Fuller (*d* 1969); two *s* one *d*. *Educ:* Wellington; RMC Sandhurst. Gazetted 5th Royal Inniskilling Dragoon Guards, 1924, Col, 1957-62. War of 1939-45: Lieut-Col to command 1st Lothian & Border Yeo., 1940 (severely wounded and prisoner, 1940); discharged disabled, 1944. Yeoman, Worshipful Co. of Saddlers, 1963; Freeman: Worshipful Co. of Farriers, 1962, Worshipful Co. of Loriners, 1962. A Vice-Pres., St Dunstan's, 1970- (Mem. Council, 1958-). DL 1966, High Sheriff 1967, Devon. Chevalier, Order of Leopold, Belgium, 1932. *Recreations:* Show Jumping (International, 1931-39), Polo International, fishing. *Address:* Pillhead House, Bideford, N Devon. *T:* Bideford 2574. *Club:* Cavalry.

**ANSETT, Sir Reginald (Myles),** KBE 1969; Chairman and Managing Director, Ansett Transport Industries Ltd and subsidiary cos; *b* 13 Feb. 1909; *s* of late Charles John and Mary Ann Ansett; *m* 1944, Joan McAuliffe Adams; three *d*. *Educ:* State Sch. and Swinbourne Techn. Coll., Victoria. Founded Ansett Roadways, 1931, and Ansett Airways Ltd, 1936; Managing Dir, Ansett Airways Ltd, 1936, later Ansett Transport Industries Ltd, 1946. Subsidiary cos include: Ansett Transport Industries (Ops) Pty Ltd (operating as Ansett Airlines of Australia, Airlines of NSW, Ansett Flying Boat Services, Ansett Airlines of S Australia, MacRobertson Miller Airline Services, Ansett Freight Express, Aviation Engineering Supplies, N.I.C. Instrument Co.; Ansett-Pioneer, Mildura Bus Lines, Barrier Reef Islands); Ansair Pty Ltd; Ansett Hotels Pty Ltd; Ansett Airlines of Papua, New Guinea; Ansett Motors Pty Ltd; Provincial Motors (Bendigo) Pty Ltd; Ansett General Aviation Pty Ltd; Austarama Television Pty Ltd; Universal Telecasters (Qld) Ltd. Director: Woolcord Fabrics Ltd (Vic); Cathay Holdings Ltd (Hong Kong); Cathay Pacific Airways Ltd (Hong Kong); Pacific Air Maintenance & Supplies Co. Ltd (Hong Kong). Chairman, Peninsula Church of England Sch. Council, 1965. *Recreations:* horse racing (Chm., Port Phillip Dist Racing Assoc., 1965); game shooting. *Address:* (private) Gunyong Valley, Mount Eliza, Victoria, Australia. *T:* 78-71551; (business) 489 Swanston Street, Melbourne, Victoria, Australia. *T:* 34-0401. *Clubs:* Victorian, Victoria Racing, Victoria Amateur Turf, Moonee Valley Racing, (Chm. 1947) Mornington Racing (all in Victoria).

**ANSON,** family name of **Earl of Lichfield.**

**ANSON, Sir (George) Wilfrid,** Kt 1951; MBE 1919; MC 1916; Director of the Imperial Tobacco Co. Ltd, 1941-66, and Deputy Chairman, 1948-58, retired; *b* 2 June 1893; *s* of late G. E. Anson and of Mrs Mabel Anson; *m* 1916, Dinah Maud Lilian, *d* of late A. A. Bourne, Cheltenham; two *s* one *d*. *Educ:* Winchester; Trinity Coll., Oxford. MA 2nd Class Hons Lit. Hum. Served European War, 1914-18, commissioned in Loyal Regt, 1914; France, 1915-17, Major (wounded). Joined Imperial Tobacco Co. Ltd, 1919, Company's Leaf Manager, 1926, Sec., 1936, Dir, 1941; Mem. of Board of Trade Tobacco Manufacturers' Advisory Cttee, 1940-58. Mem. of Council, Bristol Univ., 1942, Dep. Chm., 1955, Chm., 1956-68, Chm. of Appointments Board, 1948-56. Member: Appointments Committee, Oxford Univ., 1943-63; Newson-Smith Cttee on Training for Business Administration, 1945; SW Regional Board for Industry, 1945-48; Council, Public Schools Appointments Bureau, 1950-54 and 1956-58; Council, Outward Bound Trust, 1951; Council, British Institute of Management, 1952-58; Chm. Oxford Univ. Business Summer Sch. Cttee, 1954-56 and 1959; Pres., Incorporated Association of Preparatory Schools, 1958-64; Mem. Gov. Body BTC Staff Coll., 1959; Chm. Advisory Council on Employment for Prisoners, 1960-66. JP Somerset, 1948; High Sheriff, Somerset, 1958. Hon. LLD Bristol, 1963. *Recreations:* mountaineering, ski-ing, shooting, swimming, tennis. *Address:* West Hay, Wrington, Bristol. *T:* Wrington 274. *Clubs:* Athenæum, Alpine, Alpine Ski.

**ANSON, John;** Financial Counsellor, British Embassy, Paris, since 1968; *b* 3 Aug. 1930; *yr s* of Sir Edward Anson, 6th Bt, and of Dowager Lady Anson, Little Orchard, Church Lane, Haslemere, Surrey; *m* 1957, Myrica Fergie-Woods; two *s* two *d*. *Educ:* Winchester, Magdalene Coll., Cambridge. Asst Principal, HM Treasury, 1954-59; Asst Private Sec. to Chancellor of the Exchequer, 1957-58; Private Sec. to Economic Sec. to the Treasury, 1958-59; Principal, 1959-67, Asst Sec., 1967-68, HM Treasury. *Address:* 37 rue La Pérouse, Paris 16. *T:* 553.27.87; 4 Montana Road, SW20. *T:* 01-946 9320. *Club:* Union Interalliée (Paris). *See also Sir Peter Anson, Bt.*

**ANSON, Sir Peter,** 7th Bt, *cr* 1831; Commodore, Royal Navy; Commander, Naval Forces Gulf, since 1970; *b* 31 July 1924; *er s* of Sir Edward R. Anson, 6th Bt, and Alison, *o d* of late Hugh Pollock; *S* father 1951; *m* 1955, Elizabeth Audrey, *o d* of late Rear-Adm. Sir Philip Clarke, KBE, CB, DSO; two *s* two *d*. *Educ:* RNC, Dartmouth. Joined RN 1938; Lieut 1944. Served War of 1939-45, HMS Prince of Wales, HMS Exeter. Lieut-Comdr, 1952; Comdr 1956. Commanding Officer, HMS Alert, 1957-58; Staff of RN Tactical Sch., Woolwich, 1959-61; Commanding Officer, HMS Broadsword, 1961-62; Captain, 1963; Director Weapons, Radio (Naval), 1965-66 (Dep. Director, 1963-65); CO HMS Naiad and Captain (D) Londonderry Squadron, 1966-68; Captain, HM Signal School, 1968-70. *Heir: s* Philip Roland Anson, *b* 4 Oct. 1957. *Address:* Rosefield, Rowledge, Farnham, Surrey. *T:* Frensham 2724. *Club:* United Service. *See also John Anson.*

**ANSON, Sir Wilfrid;** *see* Anson, Sir G. W.

**ANSORGE, Sir Eric Cecil,** Kt 1946; CSI 1942; CIE 1937; MA (Oxon); FRES; Fellow, Ancient Monuments Society; Indian Civil Service (retired); *b* 6 March 1887; *s* of late Dr W. J. Ansorge; *m* 1915, Wenonah, *d* of late Major J. W. Leather. *Educ:* St Paul's Sch.; St John's Coll., Oxford (Schol.). Entered ICS 1910 and posted to Bengal, 1911; served under Government of India (Commercial Intelligence Dept, 1918-19, Commerce and Finance Depts, 1919-24); Sec. to Government of Bihar and Orissa, 1926-29; Registrar of Co-operative Societies, 1930-34; Commissioner of Tirhut, 1935-38; revenue Commissioner, Orissa, 1938; Adviser to Governor of Orissa, 1939-Nov. 1941; Chief Commissioner Designate Andaman and Nicobar Islands, 1941; Supervisor ICS Probationers' Training

Camp, 1941; Adviser to Governor of Bihar, 1943-46; Mem. Board of Revenue, Bihar, 1946; retired. Employed under Colonial Office in Nyasaland, 1948-50. *Publications:* Silk in India (with late Prof. Maxwell Lefroy); The Macrolepidoptera of Buckinghamshire; articles in Entomological journals. *Recreations:* entomology, philately. *Address:* Timbers, Welders Lane, Chalfont St Peter, Bucks. *Club:* Oxford and Cambridge University.

**ANSTEY, Edgar,** MA, PhD; Deputy Chief Scientific Officer, Civil Service Department, and Head of Research Division, since 1969; *b* 5 March 1917; British; *s* of late Percy Lewis Anstey and of Vera Anstey, *qv*; *m* 1939, Zoë Lilian Robertson; one *s*. *Educ:* Winchester Coll.; King's Coll, Cambridge. Assistant Principal, Dominions Office, 1938; Private Sec. to Duke of Devonshire, 1939. 2nd Lieut Dorset Regt, 1940; Major, War Office (DSP), 1941. Founder-Head of Civil Service Commission Research Unit, 1945; Principal, Home Office, 1951; Senior Principal Psychologist, Min. of Defence, 1958; Chief Psychologist, Civil Service Commn, 1964-69. *Publications:* Interviewing for the Selection of Staff (with Dr E. O. Mercer), 1956; Staff Reporting and Staff Development, 1961; Committees–How they work and how to work them, 1962; Psychological Tests, 1966; The Techniques of Interviewing, 1968; articles in Brit. Jl of Psychology, Occupational Psychology, etc. *Recreations:* fell-walking, lawn tennis, bridge. *Address:* 27 Cumberland Drive, Esher, Surrey. *T:* 01-398 3129. *Club:* Royal Commonwealth Society.

**ANSTEY, Edgar (Harold Macfarlane),** OBE 1969; Documentary Film Producer and Critic; Chief Officer (Films), British Railways Board; *b* 16 Feb. 1907; *s* of Percy Edgar Macfarlane Anstey and Kate Anstey (*née* Clowes); *m* 1949, Daphne Lilly, Canadian film-maker; one *s* one *d*. *Educ:* Watford Grammar Sch. Empire Marketing Board Film Unit, 1931; associated with Grierson group in develt of sociological and scientific documentaries, 1931-; organised Shell Film Unit, 1934; March of Time: London Dir of Productions, later Foreign Editor, NY, 1936-38. Produced wartime films for Ministries and Services, 1940-46. Film planning and prod. for BOAC, for oil industry in Venezuela and for CO in WI, 1946-49; rep. short films on Cinematograph Films Council, 1947-49; org. and acted as producer-in-charge, British Transport Films, 1949-. Formerly film critic of The Spectator. Chairman: Brit. Film Acad., 1956; and again (with Soc. of Film and Television Arts), 1967; Pres., Internat. Scientific Film Assoc., 1961-63; Mem. Council RCA, 1963-70 (Sen. Fellow, RCA, 1970); led Brit. cultural delegns to USSR, 1964, 1966; Chm., Brit. Industrial and Scientific Film Assoc.; Governor: Brit. Film Inst. Film prizes include: (for Journey into Spring, and Terminus) Brit. Film Acad. and Venice Awards; (for Between the Tides) Venice Award; (for Wild Wings) Hollywood Oscar. *Publication:* The Development of Film Technique in Britain (Experiment in the Film), 1948. *Recreations:* formerly football, tennis and walking, now international relations and giving public advice to professional footballers and referees (at Watford and Highbury). *Address:* 6 Hurst Close, Hampstead Garden Suburb, NW11. *T:* 01-455 2385. *Club:* Savile.

**ANSTEY, Gilbert T.,** CB 1949; *b* 31 Jan. 1889; *s* of Robert and Elizabeth Mary Anstey; *m* 1914, Eva Alice Simpson; one *s* one *d*. *Educ:* Sexey's Sch., Blackford, Somerset. Entered Civil Service (Post Office), 1908; Asst Accountant-General, 1940; Dep. Comptroller and Accountant-General, 1945; Comptroller and Accountant-General, 1947-50; Accounting Adviser, S Rhodesian Post Office, 1951-52; representative of Federal Government of Rhodesia and Nyasaland on Commonwealth Telecommunications Board, 1952-63. *Address:* Malham, Vann Road, Fernhurst, Haslemere, Surrey. *T:* Fernhurst 340.

**ANSTEY, Brigadier John,** CBE 1946; TD; DL; retired as Chairman and Managing Director, John Player & Sons; Director, Imperial Tobacco Co., Ltd, 1949-67; *b* 3 Jan. 1907; *s* of late Major Alfred Anstey, Matford House, Exeter, Devon; *m* 1935, Elizabeth Mary, *d* of late William Garnett, Backwell, Somerset; one *s* one *d*. *Educ:* Clifton; Trinity Coll., Oxford. Served War of 1939-45: N Africa, France, SEAC (despatches); Lt-Col 1944; Brig. 1944. Chm., Nottingham Savings Cttee; Vice-Chm., Nat. Savings Cttee; Mem. of Council Nottingham Univ.; Hon. Col, Nottingham Univ. OTC; Mem. (part-time) East Midlands Gas Board, 1968-. Governor, Clifton Coll. High Sheriff of Nottinghamshire, 1967; DL Notts 1970. Legion of Honour; Croix de Guerre (France); Legion of Merit (USA). *Address:* The Old House, Epperstone, Notts.

**ANSTEY, Sidney Herbert;** HM Diplomatic Service, retired; Consul-General, Atlanta, 1968-70; *b* 4 June 1910; *m* 1937, Winifred Mary Gray; three *s* one *d*. Foreign Office, 1940-49; Vice-Consul, Nantes, 1950; First Sec. and Consul, Port-au-Prince, 1951; Belgrade, 1952; Vienna, 1953; Dep. Finance Officer, Foreign Office, 1957; First Sec., Paris, 1960, Counsellor, 1963; Consul, Bilbao, 1965; Consul-Gen., Bilbao, 1966. *Address:* 97 Roehampton Vale, Putney, SW15.

**ANSTEY, Vera,** DSc(Econ.); *b* 1889; 2nd *d* of James and Mary Powell; *m* 1913, Percy L. Anstey (*d* 1920); one *s* one *d*. *Educ:* Ladies' Coll., Cheltenham; Bedford Coll. for Women; London Sch. of Economics and Political Science. Studied music and German at Frankfurt a/M, 1907-8; Hygiene Diploma, Bedford Coll. for Women, 1910; Gerstenberg Scholar in Economics, 1912; BSc(Econ.) with 1st Class Hons in Economic History, 1913; resided in Bombay, India, 1914-20; Assistant, 1921, Lecturer in Commerce, 1929, London Sch. of Economics and Political Science; Sir Ernest Cassel Reader in Commerce, London Univ., 1941-54 (retired). Part-time Mem. of Academic Staff, London Sch. of Economics, 1954-64, retd 1964. DSc(Econ.) London Univ., 1930, Dean, Faculty of Economics, 1950-54; Mem. of Royal Commission on the Taxation of Profits and Income, Dec. 1950-55. Hon. Fellow, London Sch. of Economics and Political Science, 1964. *Publications:* The Trade of the Indian Ocean, 1929; The Economic Development of India, 1929, Revised Edn, 1936 and 1952; Introduction to Economics for Students in India and Pakistan, 1964. *Address:* Startforth Mews, The Green, Esher, Surrey. *T:* Esher 63124.

*See also Edgar Anstey.*

**ANSTICE, Vice-Adm. Sir Edmund (Walter),** KCB 1953 (CB 1950); retired; *b* 5 May 1899; 2nd *s* of late Major J. C. A. Anstice; *m* 1928, Lesley, *d* of late L. Ritchie, Sydney, NSW; two *s*. *Educ:* RNC, Osborne and Dartmouth. Lieut, 1920; Comdr, 1932; Capt., 1939; Rear-Adm., 1948; Vice-Adm., 1951. Served European War, 1914-18; specialised Naval Aviation, 1924; War of 1939-45, Admty; comd HMS Fencer; Chief of Staff Flag Officer, Carrier Training; 4th Naval Mem. Australian Naval Board, 1946-48; Flag Officer Training Squadron, 1948-49; Flag Officer Flying Training, 1949-51; a Lord

Commissioner of the Admiralty, Fifth Sea Lord and Dep. Chief of Naval Staff (Air), 1951-54; retd 1954. *Recreations:* fishing, shooting. *Address:* Inverdunning House, Dunning, Perthshire. *T:* 207. *Club:* Royal Perth (Perth).

**ANSTRUTHER, Sir Ralph Hugo,** 7th Bt, *cr* 1694; CVO 1967; MC 1943; DL; Equerry to the Queen Mother since 1959, also Treasurer, since 1961; *b* 13 June 1921; *o s* of late Capt. Robert Edward Anstruther, MC, The Black Watch, *o s* of 6th Bt; *S* grandfather, 1934. *Educ:* Eton; Magdalene Coll., Cambridge (BA). Major, RARO Coldstream Gds. Served Malaya, 1950 (despatches). Mem. Queen's Body Guard for Scotland (Royal Co. of Archers). DL Fife, 1960, Caithness-shire, 1965. *Heir: cousin,* Ian Fife Campbell Anstruther, Capt. late Royal Corps of Signals [*b* 11 May 1922; *m* 1st, 1951, Honor (marr. diss., 1963), *er d* of late Capt. Gerald Blake, MC; one *d*; 2nd, 1963, Susan Margaret Walker, *e d* of H. St J. B. Paten; one *s* one *d*]. *Address:* Balcaskie, Pittenweem, Fife; Watten, Caithness.
*See also Sir T. D. Erskine.*

**ANSTRUTHER, Sir Windham Eric Francis Carmichael-,** 12th Bt, *cr* 1694 and 1798; Hereditary Carver to Royal Household in Scotland; one of the Hereditary Masters of the Household for Scotland; *b* 1900; *s* of late Gerald Yorke Anstruther and Ellen Caroline, *d* of J. Milne, Cradock, Cape Colony; *S* cousin, 1928; *m* 1st, 1932, Fay Sibyl Marie (marriage dissolved), *o c* of Ernest Rechnitzer, Berkeley Square (she *m* 1948, Capt. Jerzy Bondorowski); 2nd, 1948, Joan Coates. *Educ:* Marlborough; RMC, Sandhurst. *Heir:* none. *Address:* Carmichael, Thankerton, Biggar, Lanarks.

**ANSTRUTHER-GOUGH-CALTHORPE, Brig. Sir Richard (Hamilton),** 2nd Bt *cr* 1929; CBE 1946 (OBE 1940); DL, JP, CA; Croix de Guerre, 1947; Hon. LLD Birmingham 1950; MA (Cantab); Brigadier the Greys, retired; *b* 28 March 1908; *o s* of Sir FitzRoy Anstruther-Gough-Calthorpe, 1st Bt; *S* father 1957; *m* 1939, Nancy Moireach, *o d* of late Vernon Austen Malcolmson, MA, JP, Aston Bury, Stevenage, Herts; two *s* (and one *s* decd). *Educ:* Harrow; Magdalene Coll., Cambridge (MA). 2nd Lieut Royal Scots Greys, 1930, Capt., 1938. Served War of 1939-45, Norway and Middle East; Dep. Director Military Operations, War Office, 1944-47; retd 1947. CC 1949, JP 1950, DL 1955, CA 1956, Chm. CC 1967, Hants. Director: Artagen Co. Ltd; Rowton Houses Ltd. *Heir: g s* Euan Hamilton Anstruther-Gough-Calthorpe, *b* 22 June 1966. *Address:* Elvetham Farm House, Hartley Wintney, Hants. *T:* Hartley Wintney 2117. *Clubs:* Turf, Royal Yacht Squadron.
*See also Baron Luke.*

**ANSTRUTHER-GRAY,** family name of **Baron Kilmany.**

**ANTHONY,** Archbishop, Metropolitan of Sourozh, (*né* **André Borisovich Bloom**); Exarch of the Patriarch of Moscow and all Russia in Western Europe, since 1965; *b* Lausanne, Switzerland, 19 June 1914; *o c* of Boris Edwardovich Bloom (Russian Imperial Diplomatic Service) and Xenia Nikolaevna Scriabina (sister of the composer Alexander Scriabin). *Educ:* Lycée Condorcet and Sorbonne, Paris. Dr of Med., Sorbonne, 1943. Army service, med. corps French Army and Resistance, 1939-45. Gen. Practitioner, 1945-49. Took monastic vows, 1943; Priest, Russian Orthodox Church in Paris, 1948; Chaplain to Fellowship of St Alban and St Sergius, London, 1949-50; Vicar, Russian Orthodox Church of St Philip, London, 1950; apptd Hegumen, 1953, Archimandrite, 1956; consecrated Bishop of Sergievo, Suffragan Bishop, Exarchate of Western Europe, 1957; Archbishop of Sourozh, 1960, acting Exarch, 1962-65; Metropolitan of Sourozh and Exarch, 1965. Member: Ecumenical Commn of Russian Orthodox Church; Central Cttee and Christian Medical Commn of World Council of Churches, 1968. Médaille de Bronze de la Société d'encouragement au Bien (France), 1945; Orders of: St Vladimir 1st Cl. (Russia), 1962; St Andrew (Ecumenical Patriarchate), 1963. *Publications:* Asceticism, 1948; Living Prayer, 1965; School of Prayer, 1970. *Address:* 34 Upper Addison Gardens, W14. *T:* 01-603 5200.

**ANTHONY, C. L.;** *see* Smith, Dodie.

**ANTHONY, Irvin;** Author; (serving as Lieutenant US Coast Guard Reserve, but placed in inactive duty status); *b* 5 March 1890; *s* of Samuel Anthony and Eliza Conquest; *m* 1918, Eleanor L. Cooper, BS and MA, University of Pennsylvania. *Publications:* Down to the Sea in Ships, 1925; Three Ships in Azure, 1927; Paddle Wheels and Pistols, 1929; Voyagers Unafraid, 1930; Decatur, 1931; Ralegh and His World, 1934; The Saga of the Bounty, 1935; Revolt at Sea, 1937; contributor to The Bookman, Saturday Evening Post, Rudder, Sea Stories, Yachting, Motorboating, etc. *Recreations:* swimming, yachting, travel. *Address:* 45 H Street, Seaside Park, New Jersey 08752, USA.

**ANTHONY, John;** *see* Beckett, R. B.

**ANTHONY, Sir Mobolaji B.;** *see* Bank-Anthony.

**ANTONIO;** *see* Ruiz Soler, Antonio.

**ANTONIONI, Michelangelo;** Film Director; *b* Ferrara, Italy, 29 Sept. 1912; *s* of Ismaele and Elisabetta Roncagli; *m* (marr. diss.). *Educ:* degree in Economics and Commerce, Univ. of Bologna. Formerly an Asst Dir, Film Critic to newspapers, and Script Writer. Films directed include: 8 documentaries, etc, 1945-50; subseq. long films: Cronaca di un Amore, 1950; I Vinti, 1952; La Signora Senza Camelie, 1953; Le Amiche, 1955; Il Grido, 1957; L'Avventura, 1959-60; La Notte, 1961; L'Eclisse, 1962; Il Deserto Rosso, 1964; Blow-Up, 1967; Zabriskie Point, 1969. *Recreations:* collecting blown glass; tennis. *Address:* Via Vincenzo Tiberio 18, Rome, Italy.

**ANTONY, Jonquil;** Author; *b* 5 Oct. 1916; *m* 1941, John Wyse. *Educ:* Worthing High Sch. Began writing for BBC in 1937 and has since written over 4,000 scripts: daily serials, plays, adaptations, features for radio and television; wrote The Robinson Family (jointly) for four years, also initiated Mrs Dale's Diary, 1948 and wrote it (jointly) until 1963. *Publications:* The Robinson Family, 1948; The Malindens, 1951; Mrs Dale's Bedside Book, 1951; Paradise Square, 1952; Mrs Dale At Home, 1952; Mrs Dale, 1958; The Dales of Parkwood Hill, 1959; Hark! Hark! The Ark!, 1960; Mrs Dale's Friendship Book, 1961; Eaglemania, 1966. *Recreations:* reading, theatres, the country. *Address:* 14 Rugby Street, WC1. *T:* 01-405 0137.

**ANTRIM,** 13th Earl of, *cr* 1620; **Randal John Somerled McDonnell** KBE 1970; Viscount Dunluce, 1785; Vice-Lieutenant, Co. Antrim, since 1955; Chairman, National Trust, since 1965; *b* 22 May 1911; *er s* of 12th Earl of Antrim, and Margaret, *y d* of Rt Hon. J. G. Talbot; *S* father, 1932; *m* 1934, Angela

Christina, *d* of Sir Mark Sykes, 6th Bt; two *s* one *d*. *Educ:* Eton; Christ Church, Oxford. Served War of 1939-45 in RN. Hon. Attaché, HM Legation, Tehran, 1932; Clerk in the House of Lords, 1933-34; Captain RNVR, i/c Ulster Div., 1954-57, retd. Chairman: Gen. Purposes Cttee, Nat. Trust; Nat. Trust in NI, 1948-64; Ulster Television Ltd; St Peter's Group of Hospitals, London. Co. Antrim: JP 1934-, DL 1934-. Hon. Col, 429 Coast Regt RA (TA), 1952-58. *Heir:* *s* Viscount Dunluce, *qv*. *Address:* Glenarm Castle, Ballymena, Co. Antrim, Northern Ireland. *T:* Glenarm 229; 14 Moore Street, SW3. *T:* 01-584 6039. *Clubs:* Beefsteak, Brooks's, White's; Ulster (Belfast).

*See also Lady Rose Baring.*

**ANTROBUS, Maurice Edward,** CMG 1943; OBE 1938; *b* 20 July 1895; *er s* of late Sir Reginald Antrobus and late Dame Edith Antrobus, DBE; *m* 1929, Betty, *er d* of late Sir Llewelyn Dalton; two *s*. *Educ:* Winchester; Trinity Coll., Cambridge (Exhibitioner). BA 1920; served European War, 1914-19, KRRC (wounded twice); Asst Principal, Colonial Office, 1920; Private Sec. to Governor of Ceylon, 1927-30; Principal Dominions Office, 1930; Political Sec., Office of UK High Comr in Union of S Africa, 1935-39; Asst Sec., Colonial Office, 1939; Principal Sec., Office of UK Representative to Eire, 1939-41; Official Sec., Office of UK High Comr in Commonwealth of Australia, 1941-44; Official Sec., Office of UK High Commissioner in New Zealand, 1944-45; Asst Sec., Commonwealth Relations Office, 1945; retd 1955. *Recreations:* golf, gardening. *Address:* Quorndon, Forest Row, Sussex. *T:* Forest Row 2159. *Clubs:* United University; Royal Ashdown Forest Golf (Forest Row).

**ANTROBUS, Sir Philip Coutts,** 7th Bt, *cr* 1815; *b* 10 April 1908; *s* of late Geoffrey Edward Antrobus and Mary Atherstone, *d* of Hilton Barber, JP, Halesowen, Cradock, Cape Province; *S* cousin, 1968; *m* 1937, Dorothy Margaret Mary, *d* of late Rev. W. G. Davis; two *s* one *d*. Served War, 1939-45 (POW). *Heir:* *s* Edward Philip Antrobus [*b* 28 Sept. 1938; *m* 1966, Janet, *d* of Philip Sceales; one *d*]. *Address:* Longacre, PO Baroda, Cradock District, Cape Province, South Africa.

**ANTROBUS, Lieutenant-Colonel Ronald Henry,** MC 1916; DL; *b* 8 Nov. 1891; *s* of John Coutts Antrobus and Mary, *d* of Lieut-Gen. Hon. Sir James Lindsay, KCMG; *m* 1921, Muriel, *d* of R. H. Gosling, Hawthorn Hill, Berks, and *widow* of Capt. Miles Chetwynd Stapylton (killed in action); one *s*. *Educ:* Charterhouse. Royal Artillery Special Reserve, 1910-13; Royal Artillery, 1913-44. DL Cheshire, 1952; High Sheriff of Cheshire, 1960. *Address:* Eaton Hall, Congleton, Cheshire. *T:* Congleton 3123.

**ANWYL-DAVIES, Marcus John,** MA, QC 1967; *b* 11 July 1923; *s* of Thomas Anwyl-Davies, *qv*, and of Kathleen Beryl Anwyl-Davies (*née* Oakshott); *m* 1954, Eva Hilda Elisabeth Paulson; one *s* one *d*. *Educ:* Harrow Sch.; Christ Church, Oxford. Royal Artillery, including service with Hong Kong and Singapore RA, 1942-47 (despatches 1945). Called to Bar, Inner Temple, 1949. Legal Assessor, GMC and GDC, 1969-. *Recreations:* farming, flying, photography. *Address:* 2 Garden Court, Temple, EC4; 29 Clareville Street, SW7; Great Buckstepe, Bodle Street, Sussex.

**ANWYL-DAVIES, Thomas,** MD London; FRCP; Hon. Consulting Physician to St Thomas' Hospital; Hon. Secretary Royal Medical Benevolent Fund; Member of Lloyd's; *m* 1922, Kathleen Beryl, *o d* of P. G. Oakshott, Barham House, East Hoathly; one *s*; *m* 1946, Elizabeth, MRCS, LRCP, *e d* of J. S. Counsell, Lympsham Manor, Somerset; one *d*. *Educ:* Bonn; Marburg; Lille; St Thomas' Hospital; University of London (MD, gold Medal). BS 1917 (London); MD 1930; FRCP 1937; FRSocMed; Fellow Med. Soc. of London; Mem. various medical advisory cttees. Formerly: Dir and Physician in Charge of the Dept of Venereal Diseases, St Thomas' Hospital; London University Lecturer at St Thomas's Hospital Medical Sch.; Dir, London Hospital (Whitechapel) Clinic for Venereal Diseases; Lectr on Venereal Diseases to London Hosp. Med. Coll.; Cons. and Venereologist to LCC (which is now GLC); Vice-Pres. Med. Soc. for Study of Venereal diseases; Hon. Sec., Royal Med. Benevolent Fund, 1956-70. Mem. (Pall Mall and St James's) Westminster City Council, 1951-65. Served European War, 1914-18, in RAMC, and was MO with Royal Fusiliers and Field Ambulances. *Publications:* various books and papers on research into therapeutic and administrative problems of venereology; yearly contrib. for venereal diseases to The Medical Annual, 1937-59; articles in med. press and trans of med. socs. *Recreations:* painting, philately. *Address:* 149 Harley Street, W1. *T:* 01-935 4444; Great Buckstepe, Herstmonceux, Sussex. *T:* Herstmonceux 3101. *Clubs:* Royal Automobile, 1900.

**AOTEAROA, Bishop of,** since 1968; **Rt. Rev. Manu Augustus Bennett,** DD; *b* 10 Feb. 1916; *s* of Rt Rev. F. A. Bennett, Bishop of Aotearoa, 1928-50, and Alice Rangione Bennett; *m* 1944, Kathleen Clark; one *d*. *Educ:* Victoria Univ. Coll., Univ. of Hawaii. BSc 1954. Deacon, 1939; Priest, 1940; Vicar of Tauranga, Te Puke Maori District, Dio. Waiapu, 1940-44; Chaplain to 2 NZEF, 1944-46; Pastor of Rangitikei South-Manawatu Pastorate, Dio. Wellington, 1946-52; Asst Vicar of Church of Holy Nativity, Honolulu, 1953-54; Pastor of Wellington Pastorate, 1952-57; Vicar of Ohinemutu Pastorate, 1957-64; Associate Chaplain, Waikeria Youth Centre, Dio. Waikato, 1964-68; Nat. Council of Churches Chaplain, Dept of Justice. Hon. DD Jackson Coll., 1964. *Address:* PO Box 227, Napier, New Zealand.

**APPEL, Karel Christian;** Netherlands Artist (Painter); *b* 25 April 1921; *s* of Jan Appel and Johanna Chevallier. *Educ:* Royal Academy of Art, Amsterdam. Began career as artist in 1938. Has had one-man exhibitions in Europe and America including the following in London: Inst. of Contemporary Art, 1957; Gimpel Fils, 1959, 1960, 1964. UNESCO Prize, Venice Biennale, 1953; Lissone Prize, Italy, 1958; Acquisition Prize, Sao Paulo Biennale, Brazil, 1959; Graphique Internat. Prize, Ljubljana, Jugoslavia, 1959; Guggenheim National Prize, Holland, 1961; Guggenheim International Prize, 1961. *Publications:* Illustrations: De Blijde en Onvoorziene Week, by Hugo Claus, 1950; Atonaal, by Simon Vinkenoog, 1951; De Ronde Kant van de Aarde, by Hans Andreus, 1952; Het Bloed Stroomt Door, by Bert Schierbeek, 1954; Haine, by E. Looten, 1954; Cogne Ciel, by E. Looten, 1954; Rhapsodie de ma Nuit, by E. Looten, 1958; Unteilbare Teil, by André Frénaud, 1960; Een Dier Heeft een Mens Getekend, by B. Schierbeek, 1961. *Address:* 7 Rue Brézin, Paris 14e, France. *T:* Ségur 1484.

**APPLEBY, Lt-Col Charles Bernard,** DSO 1944; FSA; FMA; FRAS; first Director, National Army Museum, from 1960 (when founded) until 1966; *b* 4 July 1905; *s* of Alfred James Appleby and Florence Nightingale; *m* 1st,

1937, Hilary Agnes Branch; two *s* one *d*; 2nd, 1948, Pauline Margaret Brough-Maltby (*d* 1950). *Educ:* Culford Sch. 2nd Lieut 54th Divisional Train, RASC (TA), 1926; RMC Sandhurst; IA, 1928, Burma Rifles; Burma Ops 1930-32 (despatches); Adjt 1936; Instructor, Officers' Trng Sch., Maymyo, 1939-40; psc Quetta, 1941; Bde Major, Burma, 1941; Burma Ops, 1941-42 (despatches); DAAG 25 Ind. Burma Ops., 1941-42 (despatches); DAAG 25 Ind Div., 1942; Asst Comdt, 1st Punjab Regtl Centre (lieut-Col), 1943; comd. 2/1st Punjab Regt in Burma Ops, 1944-45 (despatches, DSO); Asst Adjt Gen., Bihar and Orissa Area, 1946; AA&QMG, Malaya, 1947; retired, 1948. Wing Commander RAF Regiment, 1950-55. Curator RMA Sandhurst Museum, 1956. CC Oxon, 1967-. *Publications:* Victoria Crosses and George Crosses of the Honourable East India Company and the Indian Army, 1962; articles on military history, genealogy and museum technique, TV and radio broadcasts. *Address:* The Old Malt House, Middle Barton, Oxford. *T:* Steeple Aston 252. *Club:* United Service.

**APPLEBY, Robert,** CBE 1969; Chairman and Managing Director, Black & Decker Ltd, Maidenhead, Berks, and Deputy-Chairman, The Black & Decker Manufacturing Co., Maryland, USA; *b* 1913; *s* of Robert James Appleby; *m* 1957, Elisabeth Friederike, *d* of Prof. Eidmann. *Educ:* Graham Sea Training and Engineering Sch., Scarborough. CEng, FIProdE, FBIM. *Address:* Ridgewood House, Ridgemead, Englefield Green, Surrey. *Clubs:* Reform; Baltimore Country (Baltimore, Md).

**APPLETON, Most Rev. George;** *see* Jerusalem, Archbishop in, and Metropolitan.

**APSLEY, Lord; Allen Christopher Bertram Bathurst;** *b* 11 March 1961; *s* and *heir* of 8th Earl Bathurst, *qv*.

**AQUILECCHIA, Prof. Giovanni;** Professor of Italian, University of London, since 1970; *b* 28 Nov. 1923; *s* of late Gen. Vincenzo Aquilecchia and Maria L. Filibeck; *m* 1951, Constantina M. Bacchetta; two *s* one *d*. *Educ:* Liceo T. Tasso, Rome; Univ. of Rome. Dott. Lett., 1946, Diploma of Perfezionamento in Filologia Moderna, 1948, Univ. of Rome. Asst in Italian, Univ. of Rome, 1946-49; Boursier du Gouvernement Français at Collège de France, Univ. of Paris, 1949-50; British Council Scholar, Warburg Inst., Univ. of London, 1950-51; Asst, Dept of Italian Studies, Univ. of Manchester, 1951-53; Asst Lectr in Italian, University Coll., London, 1953-55, Lectr, 1955-59; Libero Docente di Letteratura Italiana, Univ. of Rome, 1958-; Reader in Italian, Univ. of London, at University Coll., 1959-61; Prof. of Italian Lang. and Lit., Univ. of Manchester, 1961-70. Corr. Fellow, Arcadia, 1961. MA (Manchester) 1965. *Publications:* Giordano Bruno: La Cena de le Ceneri, 1955; Due Dialoghi sconosciuti, 1957; Dialoghi Italiani, 1958; Praelectiones geometricæ e Ars deformationum, 1964; Pietro Aretino: Sei Giornate, 1969; contrib.: Atti dell'Accad. dei Lincei, Atti e Memorie dell'Arcadia, Bull. dell'Accad. della Crusca, Bull. John Rylands Library, Cultura Neolatina, Encyclopædia Britannica, English Miscellany, Giornale storico della letteratura italiana, Studi Secenteschi, Studi Tassiani, etc. *Address:* Department of Italian, Bedford College, Regent's Park, NW1.

**ARAGON, Louis;** poet; novelist; essayist; leader Socialistic Realism Movement; formerly leader Surrealist Movement; Managing Editor, Ce Soir, Paris, 1950; *b* 1897. Served European War, 1914-18, Infantry; War of 1939-45, Tank Div., 1939-40 (prisoner, escaped to unoccupied France); one of leaders of intellectual Resistance. *Publications: poems:* Feudejoie, Le Mouvement perpétuel, La grande Gaité, Persécuté persécuteur, Hourra l'Oural, Le Crève-Cœur, Les Yeux d'Elsa, Brocéliande, Le Musée Grévin, La Diane française; *novels:* Anicet, Le Libertinage, Le Paysan de Paris, Les cloches de Bâle, Les Beaux Quartiers (awarded Prix Renaudot), Les Voyageurs de l'Impériale, Aurélien, La Semaine Sainte (Eng. trans. as Holy Week, 1961); *essays:* Traité du Style, Les aventures de Télémaque, Pour un réalisme Socialiste, La Culture et les Hommes, Chroniques du Bel-Canto, Matisse ou Comme il vous plaira. *Address:* (business) 37 Rue du Louvre, Paris 2e.

**ARAM, Abbas;** *b* Yazd, Iran, August 1905. *Educ:* Calcutta Univ. (BA). Entered Foreign Service 1935; Sec., Consulate-Gen., New Delhi; 3rd Sec., London, 1938-43; Min. of Foreign Affairs, 1943; 1st Sec., Berne, 1945; 1st Sec. Counsellor, and Chargé d'Affaires, Washington, 1946, 1949, 1950; Min. of Foreign Affairs, 1951; Counsellor, Baghdad, 1953; Chargé d'Affaires and Minister, Washington, 1953 and 1954-56; Dir-Gen. of Political Affairs, Min. of Foreign Affairs, 1958; Ambassador: to Japan 1958 (concurrently to Rep. of China); to Iraq, 1960-62; Minister of Foreign Affairs, 1959-60, 1962-67; Ambassador to the Court of St James's, 1967-69; returned to Teheran, 1969. Leader of Iranian Delegn to Gen. Assembly of UN, 1959, 1960, 1963, 1964, 1966. *Address:* c/o Ministry of Foreign Affairs, Teheran, Iran.

**ARBUTHNOT, Clifford William Ernest,** CIE 1930; ED 1945; Superintending Engineer (retired) Bombay Public Works Department; *s* of late William H. Arbuthnot, Belfast; *m* 1921, Josephine Turton (*d* 1922). *Educ:* Campbell Coll., Belfast; Queen's University, Belfast, BA, BE. Entered Indian Service of Engineers, 1908; served European War, 1914-18, Lieut, 53rd Sikhs (FF), Capt., 3rd Sappers and Miners, Egypt, Aden, Mesopotamia and India; Member Bombay and Sind Public Service Commn 1937-42; Rent Controller, Bombay, 1942-47. *Clubs:* East India and Sports; Royal Bombay Yacht; Sind (Karachi).

**ARBUTHNOT, Sir Hugh Fitz-Gerald,** 7th Bt, *cr* 1823; Master, Duke of Buccleuch's Hounds, since 1964; late Temporary Captain Welsh Guards; *b* 2 Jan. 1922; *s* of Brig.-Gen. Sir Dalrymple Arbuthnot, 5th Bt, CMG, DSO, and Alice Maude (*d* 1969), *d* of Hugh Arbuthnot; *S* brother 1944; *m* 1949, Elizabeth K., *e d* of Sqdn Ldr G. G. A. Williams, Curral Hall, Tenbury Wells; two *s* one *d*. *Educ:* Eton. MFH: Ludlow Hounds, 1948-52; Cotswold Hounds, 1952-64. *Heir:* *s* Keith Robert Charles Arbuthnot, *b* 23 Sept. 1951. *Address:* Mount Ulston, Jedburgh, Roxburghshire.

**ARBUTHNOT, Sir John (Sinclair-Wemyss),** 1st Bt *cr* 1964; MBE 1944; TD 1951; Chairman, HANIPHA (Ceylon) Tea & Rubber Co. Ltd; Director, Ecclesiastical Insurance Office Ltd, and other companies; a Church Commissioner for England since 1962, Deputy Chairman of Assets Committee since 1966 and Member of Board of Governors since 1968; a Vice-President, Trustee Savings Banks Association since 1962; Member House of Laity, Church Assembly, since 1955; A Trustee of Lambeth Palace Library, since 1964; Underwriting Member of Lloyd's; *b* 11 Feb. 1912; *s* of late Major K. W. Arbuthnot, the Seaforth Highlanders; *m* 1943, Margaret Jean, *y d* of Alexander G. Duff; two *s* three *d*. *Educ:* Eton; Trinity Coll., Cambridge. MA Hons in Nat.

Sciences. Served throughout War of 1939-45, in RA, with rank of Major (wounded); TARO, 1948-62. Prospective Conservative candidate, Don Valley Div. of Yorks, 1934-35, Dunbartonshire, 1936-45, Dover Div. of Kent, 1945-50, contesting elections in 1935 and 1945. MP (C) Dover Div. of Kent, 1950-64; PPS to Parly Sec., Min. of Pensions, 1952-53, to Minister of Pensions, 1953-56, and Minister of Health, 1956-57; a Chm. of Committees and a Temporary Chm. of the House, 1958-64; Second Church Estates Comr, 1962-64; Chm., Archbp of Canterbury's Commn to inquire into the organisation of the Church by dioceses in London and the SE of England, 1965-67. Member: Crathorne Cttee on Sunday Observance, 1961-64; Hodson Commn on Synodical Government for the Church of England, 1964-66; Parliamentary Chm. Dock & Harbour Authorities Assoc., 1962-64; Member: Public Accounts Cttee, 1955-64; Standing Cttee, Ross Inst., 1951-62; Council, Ceylon Assoc., 1951-62; Cttee, South Indian Assoc., 1951-62. Member Parliamentary Delegations: to the Iron and Steel Community, 1955; to West Africa, 1956; to USA, 1957; to The West Indies, 1958; to Zanzibar, Mauritius and Madagascar, 1961; Leader of Parliamentary Delegation to Bulgaria, 1963. Chm., Estates & Agency Holdings Ltd, 1955-70; Joint Hon. Sec. Assoc. of British Chambers of Commerce, 1953-59. *Recreations:* shooting, ski-ing. *Heir:* *s* William Reierson Arbuthnot, *b* 2 Sept. 1950. *Address:* Poulton Manor, Ash, Canterbury, Kent. *T:* Ash 516; 7 Fairholt Street, SW7. *T:* 01-589 1727. *Clubs:* Carlton, City of London.

**ARBUTHNOTT,** family name of **Viscount of Arbuthnott.**

**ARBUTHNOTT,** 16th Viscount of, *cr* 1641; **John Campbell Arbuthnott,** DSC 1945; Chairman, The Red Deer Commission, since 1969; Member, The Countryside Commission for Scotland, since 1968; *b* 26 Oct. 1924; *e s* of 15th Viscount of Arbuthnott, CB, CBE, DSO, MC, and Ursula Collingwood; *S* father, 1966; *m* 1949, Mary Elizabeth Darley (*née* Oxley); one *s* one *d*. *Educ:* Fettes Coll.; Gonville and Caius Coll., Cambridge. Served RNVR (Fleet Air Arm), 1942-46; Near and Far East, British Pacific Fleet, 1945. Cambridge University, 1946-49 (Estate Management), MA 1967. Chartered Surveyor and Land Agent; Agricultural Land Service, 1949-55; Land Agent, The Nature Conservancy, Scotland, 1955-67. *Recreations:* countryside activities, historical research. *Heir:* *s* Master of Arbuthnott, *qv*. *Address:* Arbuthnott House, by Laurencekirk, Kincardineshire, Scotland. *T:* Inverbervie 226. *Clubs:* Army and Navy; Royal Northern (Aberdeen).

**ARBUTHNOTT, Master of; Hon. John Keith Oxley Arbuthnott;** *b* 18 July 1950; *s* and *heir* of 16th Viscount of Arbuthnott, *qv*. *Educ:* Fettes College.

**ARBUTHNOTT, Robert,** MBE 1945; TD 1941; HM Lieutenant for the County of Dunbarton, since 1968; *b* 22 Sept. 1900; *s* of Hugh Corsar Arbuthnott and Marianne Arbuthnott (*née* Gibson); unmarried. *Educ:* Cheltenham Coll. Served War of 1939-45: The Manchester Regt; RAC; REME. Mem. Queen's Body Guard for Scotland, Royal Company of Archers. DL Dunbartonshire, 1961. *Address:* Ardmoy, Rhu, Dunbartonshire. *T:* Rhu 230. *Clubs:* Caledonian; Royal Northern Yacht.

**ARCHDALE, Captain Sir Edward (Folmer),** 3rd Bt, *cr* 1928; DSC 1943; Captain, HM Dockyard, Chatham; *b* 8 Sept. 1921; *s* of Vice-Adm. Sir Nicholas Edward Archdale, 2nd Bt, CBE, and Gerda (*d* 1969), 2nd *d* of late F. C. Sievers, Copenhagen; *S* father 1955; *m* 1954, Elizabeth Ann Stewart, *d* of late Maj-Gen. Wilfrid Boyd Fellowes Lukis, CBE; one *s* two *d*. *Educ:* Royal Naval Coll., Dartmouth. Joined Royal Navy, 1935; served War of 1939-45 (despatches, DSC); Capt., 1962. *Recreations:* shooting, tennis. *Heir:* *s* Nicholas Edward Archdale, *b* 2 Dec. 1965. *Address:* c/o The National Westminster Bank, 24 Marlborough Street, Devonport, Devon. *Club:* United Service.

*See also P. M. Tottenham.*

**ARCHDALL, Rev. Canon Henry Kingsley,** MA, ThD; Chancellor, St David's Cathedral, 1940-56; Canon Emeritus, 1956; *b* Balmain, Sydney, 1886; *s* of late Rev. Canon Mervyn Archdall, MA, Sydney; *m* Laura Madden (*d* 1953), one *s* (and two lost in War of 1939-45) one *d*. *Educ:* Sydney Grammar Sch.; Sydney Univ. (First class honours in philosophy and classics, Woolley Travelling Scholarship); Trinity Coll., Cambridge (First Class, philosophy of religion Tripos); Fellow and Lectr, Corpus Christi Coll., Cambridge, 1911-15; Dean 1915; Dean of Newcastle, NSW, 1915-19; Fellow Australian Coll. of Theology (ThD), 1916; Headmaster, Armidale School, NSW, 1919-26; Headmaster King's Coll., Auckland, NZ, 1926-35; Chaplain, Wellington Coll., Berks, 1935-38; Principal and Professor of Theology, St David's Coll., Lampeter, Cards, 1938-53; Fellow of Jesus Coll., Oxford, 1941. Select Preacher, Cambridge, 1940, Oxford, 1947-48. Visiting Fellow, Yale Univ., USA, 1954-55; Visiting Prof., Berkeley Divinity Sch., New Haven, USA, 1954-57. Episcopal Chaplain, Heidelberg, 1957-59. *Publication:* A Christian Instruction, 1933. *Address:* 51 Victoria Avenue, Porthcawl, South Wales.

**ARCHER, Archibald,** CMG 1961; grazier; company director; Land Consultant to Queensland Government, 1961-63; *b* 10 Jan. 1902; *s* of late Robert Stubbs Archer and Alice Manon Archer, Gracemere Station, Queensland; *m* 1930, Sarah Beatrice Cameron Crombie, *er d* of late Donald Charles Cameron Crombie and Mildred Ida Lloyd Crombie, Greenhills Station, Longreach, Qld; one *s* two *d*. *Educ:* Church of England Grammar Sch., Sydney, NSW, Australia. Member, Picture Theatre and Films Commission, 1957-; Vice-Pres., Royal National Assoc., 1961-; Pres., Qld Chamber of Agricultural Societies, 1965-. *Address:* 11 Glasnevin Street, Indooroopilly, Brisbane, Queensland, Australia. *T:* Brisbane 70-1853. *Clubs:* Queensland (Brisbane); Australasian Pioneers (Sydney).

**ARCHER, Sir Clyde Vernon Harcourt,** Kt 1962; *b* 12 Nov. 1904. *Educ:* Harrison Coll., Barbados; Cambridge Univ. Barrister-at-Law, Gray's Inn; clerk to the Attorney-General Barbados, 1930; police magistrate Barbados, 1935; Judge, Bridgetown Petty Debt Court, 1938; Legal Draftsman, Trinidad and Tobago, 1944; Solicitor-General, Trinidad and Tobago, 1953; Puisne Judge, Trinidad and Tobago, 1954; Chief Justice of the Windward Islands and Leeward Islands, 1958; a Federal Justice, WI, 1958-62. *Publication:* (jointly) Revised Edition of the Laws of Barbados, 1944. *Address:* Belleville, St Michael, Barbados.

**ARCHER, Frank Joseph,** RE 1960 (ARE 1940); Head of School of Fine Art, Kingston College of Art, Kingston upon Thames, since 1962; *b* 30 June 1912; *s* of Joseph and Alberta Archer; *m* 1939, Celia Cole; one *s* one *d*. *Educ:* Eastbourne Grammar Sch.; Eastbourne Sch. of Art; Royal Coll. of Art. ARCA 1937; Rome Scholar, Engraving, 1938; British Sch. at Rome, 1938. Paintings bought by numerous local authorities and private collectors. *Address:* Delichon, 65 Hampton Road, Teddington, Middx. *T:* 01-977 3796.

**ARCHER, Maj.-Gen. Gilbert Thomas Lancelot,** CB 1960; FRCPI; retired; *b* 6 April 1903; *s* of Gilbert Archer, Dublin, Ireland, and Kate Archer (*née* Lamb); *m* 1928, Catherine, *d* of Edward O'Malley, Louisburgh, Westport, Co. Mayo, Ireland; two *s* one *d*. *Educ:* St Andrews Coll., Dublin; Dublin Univ. (TCD). MB 1926; Lieut RAMC, 1928; Major, 1937; Deputy Asst Dir of Pathology, China Command, 1937-40; Asst Dir of Pathology, West Africa, 1943-45; Reader in Pathology, Royal Army Medical Coll., 1946-48; Asst Dir of Pathology, Middle East Land Forces, 1949-52; MRCPI, 1953; Officer Commanding David Bruce Laboratories, 1952-53; QHS 1953-61; Dir of Pathology and Consulting Pathologist to the Army, 1953-61; Brig., 1956; Major-General, 1958; FRCPI 1958. *Publications:* Articles on bacteriology, immunity, etc., in Jl of the RAMC, Brit. Med. Jl, etc. *Address:* 7 Nutley Avenue, Ballsbridge, Dublin, Eire.

**ARCHER, Jeffrey Howard;** MP (C) Louth since Dec. 1969; Chairman, Arrow Enterprises Public Relations Co., since 1968; Managing Director Archer Gallery, since 1969; *b* 15 April 1940; *s* of William Archer and Lola Archer (*née* Cook); *m* 1966, Mary Weeden. *Educ:* Wellington Sch., Somerset; Brasenose Coll., Oxford. Athletics Blues, 1963-65, Half Blue, Gymnastics, 1965, Pres. OUAC 1965; ran for Great Britain (very badly). Freelance Journalist and Public Relations work, 1966-68. Mem. GLC for Havering, 1966-70. *Recreation:* theatre. *Address:* 18 Lancaster Mews, W2. *T:* 01-499 9746. *Clubs:* Carlton, MCC; Louth Working Men's.

**ARCHER, Peter Kingsley;** MP (Lab) Rowley Regis and Tipton since 1966; Parliamentary Private Secretary to Attorney-General since 1967; Vice-Chairman, Amnesty International (British Section); *b* 20 Nov. 1926; *s* of Cyril Kingsley Archer and May (*née* Baker); *m* 1954, Margaret Irene (*née* Smith); one *s*. *Educ:* Wednesbury Boys' High Sch.; LSE; University Coll., London. Called to Bar, 1952; commenced practice, 1953. UK Deleg. to UN Gen. Assembly (Third Cttee), 1969. *Publications:* The Queen's Courts, 1956; ed Social Welfare and the Citizen, 1957; Communism and the Law, 1963; contrib. Trends in Social Welfare, 1965; contrib. Atkins, Court Forms, 1965; (with Lord Reay) Freedom at Stake, 1966; contrib. The International Protection of Human Rights, 1967; Human Rights, 1969. *Recreations:* music, writing, talking. *Address:* Arvika, 44 Clements Road, Chorleywood, Herts. *T:* Chorleywood 3103.

**ARCHER, William George,** OBE 1947; MA; FRAS; Keeper Emeritus, Indian Section, Victoria and Albert Museum, since 1959; *b* 11 Feb. 1907; *s* of William Archer; *m* 1934, Mildred Bell; one *s* one *d*. *Educ:* Strand Sch.; Emmanuel Coll., Cambridge. Entered ICS, 1930; posted Bihar, 1931; District Magistrate, Purnea, 1938-39; Superintendent of Census Operations, Bihar, 1939-41; Dist Magistrate Patna, 1941-42; Deputy Commissioner, Santal Parganas, 1942-45; Special Officer, Santal Law, 1945-46; Additional Deputy Commissioner, Naga Hills, 1946-48; retired ICS, 1948; Keeper, Indian Section, Victoria and Albert Museum, 1949-59; re-visited India, 1954, as lecturer (Indian Painting), Govt of India, British Council; research tours India, Ceylon, 1960, 1966, 1968; Visiting Lecturer, USA, 1958, 1963, 1970. Editor, Man in India, 1942-49; Contrib. Editor, Marg, 1956-; Mem. Editorial Bd, Roopa Lekha, 1959-. Hon. DLitt Punjab Univ., Chandigarh. *Publications:* The Blue Grove, 1940; The Vertical Man, 1947; The Plains of the Sun, 1948; The Dove and the Leopard, 1948; Forty Thousand Years of Modern Art (with Robert Melville), 1948; Indian Painting in the Punjab Hills, 1952; Kangra Painting, 1952; Bazaar Paintings of Calcutta, 1953; Garhwal Painting, 1954; Indian Painting for the British (with Mildred Archer), 1955; Indian Painting, 1957; The Loves of Krishna, 1957; Indian Paintings from Rajasthan, 1957; Ceylon: Paintings from Temple, Shrine and Rock, 1958; Central Indian Painting, 1958; India and Modern Art, 1959; Indian Painting in Bundi and Kotah, 1960; Indian Miniatures, 1960; Kalighat Drawings, 1962; The Kama Sutra (ed), 1963; Love Songs of Vidyapati (jt), 1963; Kangra Paintings of the Gita Govinda (jt), 1964; The Rose Garden of Sa'di (ed), 1964; The Koka Shastra (preface), 1964; Paintings of the Sikhs, 1966; Rajput Miniatures, 1968; Kalighat Paintings, 1970. *Recreations:* films, foreign travel. *Address:* 18 Provost Road, NW3. *T:* 01-722 2713.

**ARCHER HOUBLON, Mrs Doreen,** CVO 1969 (MVO 1954); *b* 1899; *d* of Lt-Col Walter Charles Lindsay, MVO, and Lady Kathleen Lindsay, *d* of 6th Earl of Carrick; *m* 1929, Major Richard Archer Houblon, DSO (*d* 1957); no *c*. Spent many years training and remaking horses with her father, and studying in depth the art of horsemanship and adapting it to the side saddle. Has lectured with films, and officiated as a judge at Internat. Horse Shows at Olympia, etc. *Publication:* Side Saddle, 1938. *Address:* Kilmurry, Thomastown, Co. Kilkenny, Ireland. *T:* Thomastown 230. *Clubs:* English-Speaking Union; Service Women's.

**ARCHEY, Sir Gilbert (Edward),** Kt 1963; CBE 1958 (OBE 1919); retired; *b* York, England, 4 Aug. 1890; *s* of late Thomas Archey, Christchurch, New Zealand; *m* 1915, Myrtle, *d* of William Gee, Christchurch NZ; three *d*. *Educ:* West Christchurch Sch.; Canterbury Coll., Univ. of New Zealand. MA 1914; DSc 1940. Lecturer, Canterbury Coll. and Asst Curator, Canterbury Museum, 1914-24; Dir, Auckland Institute and Museum, 1924-64, retd. Mem. of Senate, Univ. of New Zealand, 1940-61; Mem., Univ. Grants Committee, 1948-51 and 1954-60; Fellow, Royal Soc. of New Zealand (Pres., 1941-42); Mem. Auckland Cathedral Chapter; President, Auckland Branch of Royal Commonwealth Soc., 1956-59. Served European War, 1916-18 (OBE), capt. New Zealand Field Artillery; War of 1939-45: CO (Lt-Col) 4 Bn Auckland Regt, NZ Service; Staff Officer, (Lt-Col) British Military Admin., Malaya. *Publications:* South Sea Folk; Sculpture and Design, An Outline of Maori Art; Art Forms of Polynesia; contributions to Trans. Royal Society of New Zealand, Journal Polynesian Soc., Records (also Bulletin) Auckland Inst. and Museum. *Recreation:* gardening. *Address:* 20 Bassett Road, Remuera, Auckland 5, New Zealand. *T:* 52.262. *Club:* Northern (Auckland).

**ARCHIBALD,** family name of **Baron Archibald.**

**ARCHIBALD,** 1st Baron, *cr* 1949, of Woodside in the City of Glasgow; **George Archibald,** CBE 1968; Deputy President, Film Production Association of Great Britain, 1967-68; late Director: J. Arthur Rank Productions Ltd and This Modern Age Ltd; *b* 21 July 1898; *m* 1st, 1926, Dorothy Holroyd Edwards (*d* 1960); one *s*; 2nd, 1961, Mrs Catherine Edith Mary Colwell, *d* of late Rt Hon. Andrew Bonar Law, MP. *Educ:* elementary and secondary schs. Deputy Regional Commissioner for the

Midlands, 1941-42; Director Films Div., British Information Services, New York, 1942-44; Controller MOI, 1944-45. Mem. Cinematograph Films Council, 1963-67. Labour Mem. of Glasgow City Council, 1920-28; Magistrate of the City of Glasgow, 1925-28; contested (Lab) South Aberdeen, 1924, Sparkbrook, Birmingham, 1931; Capt. of HM Bodyguard of the Yeomen of the Guard, June-Oct. 1951. Was Asst Government Whip, House of Lords, June-Oct. 1951. Chm. Fedn of British Film Makers, 1957-66. *Heir:* *s* Hon. George Christopher Archibald [*b* 30 Dec. 1926; *m* 1951, Liliana Barou (marr. diss., 1964)]. *Address:* 3 Martlett Lodge, Oak Hill Park, Frognal, NW3.

**ARCTIC, Bishop of the,** since 1950; **Rt. Rev. Donald Ben Marsh,** DD; *b* 24 Nov. 1903; *s* of William John Marsh and Kathleen Daisy (*née* Peters); *m* 1933, Winifred Florence (*née* Petchey); one *s* two *d. Educ:* Emmanuel Coll., Saskatchewan; Hon. DD 1950. Deacon, 1926; priest, 1929, Keewatin. Missionary at Eskimo Point, 1926-44; Incumbent of All Saints Cathedral, Aklavik, Diocese of the Arctic, 1944-47; Archdeacon of Baffin Land, 1939-44; Archdeacon of Aklavik, 1944-50; Administrator of Diocese of the Arctic, 1949-50. *Recreation:* photography. *Address:* 30 Westwood Lane, Thornhill, Ont., Canada; 1055 Avenue Road, Toronto, Ont., Canada. *T:* HU 51016.

**ARCULUS, Ronald,** CMG 1968; Head of Science and Technology Department, Foreign and Commonwealth Office, since 1970; *b* 11 Feb. 1923; *s* of late Cecil and of Ethel L. Arculus; *m* 1953, Sheila Mary Faux; one *s* one *d. Educ:* Solihull; Exeter Coll., Oxford (BA). 4th Queen's Own Hussars (now Queen's Royal Irish Hussars), 1942-45 (Capt.). Joined HM Diplomatic Service, 1947; FO, 1947; San Francisco, 1948; La Paz, 1950; FO, 1951; Ankara, 1953; FO, 1957; Washington, 1961; Counsellor, 1965; New York, 1965-68; IDC, 1969. *Recreations:* travel, music and fine arts. *Address:* c/o Lloyds Bank Ltd, Cox's & King's Branch, Guards and Cavalry Section, 6 Pall Mall, SW1. *Club:* Cavalry.

**ARDAGH and CLONMACNOIS, Bishop of, (RC),** since 1967; **Most Rev. Cahal Brendan Daly;** *b* 1917. *Educ:* St Malachy's, Belfast; Queen's Univ., Belfast (BA Hons, Classics, MA); St Patrick's, Maynooth (DD); Institut Catholique, Paris (LPh). Ordained, 1941. Lecturer in Scholastic Philosophy, Queen's Univ., Belfast, 1946-62; Reader, 1962-67; consecrated Bishop, 1967. *Publications:* Morals, Law and Life; Natural Law Morality Today; chapters in Prospect for Metaphysics, Intellect and Hope. *Address:* St Michael's, Longford, Ireland.

**ARDEE, Lord; John Anthony Brabazon;** *b* 11 May 1941; *e s* of 14th Earl of Meath, *qv. Educ:* Harrow. Page of Honour to the Queen, 1956-57. Served Grenadier Guards, 1959-62. *Address:* Killruddery, Bray, Co. Wicklow, Ireland.

**ARDEN, Rt. Rev. Donald Seymour;** *see* Malawi, Bishop of.

**ARDEN, John;** Playwright; *b* 26 Oct. 1930; *s* of C. A. Arden and A. E. Layland; *m* 1957, Margaretta Ruth D'Arcy; four *s* (and one *s* decd). *Educ:* Sedbergh Sch.; King's Coll., Cambridge; Edinburgh Coll. of Art. Plays produced include: All Fall Down, 1955; The Life of Man, 1956; The Waters of Babylon, 1957; Live Like Pigs, 1958; Serjeant Musgrave's Dance, 1959; Soldier, Soldier, 1960; The Happy Haven, 1960; The Business of Good Government, 1960; Wet Fish, 1962; The Workhouse Donkey, 1963; Ironhand, 1963; Ars Longa Vita Brevis (with Margaretta D'Arcy), 1964; Armstrong's Last Goodnight, 1964; Left-Handed Liberty, 1965; Friday's Hiding (with Margaretta D'Arcy), 1966; The Royal Pardon (with Margaretta D'Arcy), 1966; The Hero Rises Up, 1968; The True History of Squire Jonathan and his unfortunate Treasure, 1968. *Recreations:* antiquarianism, mythology. *Address:* c/o Margaret Ramsay Ltd, 14 Goodwin's Court, WC2.

**ARDIZZONE, Edward Jeffrey Irving,** RA 1970 (ARA 1962); Hon. ARCA; FSIA; Artist; *b* 16 Oct. 1900; *s* of Auguste Ardizzone and Margaret Irving; *m* 1929, Catherine Berkley Anderson; two *s* one *d. Educ:* Clayesmore Sch. Worked for 6 years for Eastern Telegraph Co.; studied art at Westminster and Central Schools of Art; Official War Artist, 1940-46; pictures purchased by Tate Gallery, Sheffield, Leeds and Liverpool Art Galleries and Contemporary Art Society. *Publications:* Little Tim and the Brave Sea Captain, 1936; Lucy Brown and Mr Grimes, 1937; Tim and Lucy go to Sea, 1938; Baggage to the Enemy, 1941; Nicholas and the Fast Moving Diesel, 1947; Paul the Hero of the Fire, 1947; Tim to the Rescue, 1949; Tim and Charlotte, 1951; Tim in Danger, 1953; Tim All Alone, 1956 (Kate Greenaway medal of Library Association, for best illustrated children's book in 1956); Johnny the Clockmaker, 1960; Tim's Friend Towser, 1962; Peter the Wanderer, 1963; Diana and Her Rhinoceros, 1964; Tim and Ginger, 1965; Sarah and Simon and No Red Paint, 1965; Tim to the Lighthouse, 1968; *illustrated:* more than 120 books which include: In a Glass Darkly, 1929; My Uncle Silas, 1939; The Local, 1939; Peacock Pie, 1947; The Poems of François Villon, 1947; The Pilgrim's Progress, 1947; The Blackbird in the Lilac, 1952; The Warden, 1952; The Little Bookroom, 1955; Henry Esmond, 1956; Ding Dong Bell, 1957; Titus in Trouble, 1959; contrib. Oxford Illustrated Old Testament, 1968; The Young Ardizzone: an autobiographical fragment, 1970. *Address:* 130 Elgin Avenue, Maida Vale, W9. *T:* 01-286 7006.

**ARDWICK,** Baron *cr* 1970 (Life Peer), of Barnes; **John Cowburn Beavan;** *b* 1910; *s* of late Silas Beavan and Alderman Emily Beavan, JP; *m* 1934, Gladys (*née* Jones); one *d. Educ:* Manchester Grammar Sch. Blackpool Times, 1927; Evening Chronicle, Manchester, 1928; Manchester Evening News, 1930; London staff, Manchester Evening News, 1933; News Editor, Manchester Evening News, Manchester, 1936; Asst Editor, Londoner's Diary, Evening Standard, and leader writer, 1940; News Editor and Chief Sub, Observer, 1942; Editor, Manchester Evening News; Dir, Manchester Guardian and Evening News Ltd, 1943; London Editor, Manchester Guardian, 1946; Asst Dir, Nuffield Foundation, 1955; Editor, Daily Herald, 1960-62; Political Adviser to the Daily Mirror Group, 1962-69, Staff Writer 1970. *Address:* 10 Chester Close, SW13. *T:* 01-789 3490. *Clubs:* Garrick, Press.

**ARGENTI, Philip Pandely,** CVO (Hon.) 1963; MBE (Hon.) 1920; formerly cultural Counsellor at the Royal Greek Embassy in London; Commander, Order of George I (Greece); Commander, Order of Phoenix (Greece); 4th *s* of late Pandely Leonidas Argenti and late Fanny, 3rd *d* of late John Stephen Schilizzi; *m* 1930, Alexandra Helen Schilizzi (Grand Officer of the Holy Sepulchre; Officer Order of *Ευποῖιας*; Greek Commemorative Naval Medal), 3rd *d* of late Stephen John Schilizzi, formerly of

Loddington Hall, and Julia, 2nd *d* of Sir Lucas Ralli, 1st Bt; one *s* two *d*. *Educ:* Winchester Coll.; Christ Church, Oxford; Athens Univ. BA, MA 1919, and DLitt 1941 (Oxon); LLB 1920 (Athens); Silver Medallist, Athens Academy, 1938; Corresp. Mem. Athens Academy, 1947; Barrister-at-law, 1922, Athens. Entered Greek Diplomatic Service, 1923; Counsellor to Greek Legations to exiled Govts of Poland, Belgium and Luxemburg. Served European War, 1914-18, in 3rd Greek cavalry regt and as Adj. to GOC 2nd Greek Army Corps (despatches, Greek MC and Greek MM, 1919). Freeman of town of Chios, 1920 and 1953; Gold Medal of town of Chios. Grand Officer, Order of Holy Sepulchre, 1928, etc. *Publications:* Massacres of Chios, 1822, 1932; The Expedition of Colonel Fabvier to Chios, 1827, 1933; Chius Liberata, 1912, 1933; The Expedition of the Florentines to Chios, 1599, 1934; The Occupation of Chios by the Venetians, 1694, 1935; Bibliography of Chios, 1940; Chius Vincta, 1566, 1941; (with Prof. Stilpon Kyriakides) *'Η Χίος παρὰ τοῖς Γεωγράφοις καὶ Περιηγηταῖς* (Chios according to the Geographers and Travellers) (3 vols, Athens), 1946; (with Prof. H. J. Rose) The Folklore of Chios, 1949; The Costumes of Chios, 1953; Diplomatic Archive of Chios 1577-1841 (2 vols), 1954; Libro d'Oro de la Noblesse de Chio (2 vols), 1955; The Occupation of Chios by the Genoese, 1346-1566 (3 vols), 1958; ed The Architecture of Chios, by Arnold Smith, 1962; The Occupation of Chios by the Germans and Their Administration of the Island, 1966. *Recreations:* riding, travelling. *Address:* 16 via Tevere, Rome, Italy; Argentikon, Campos, Chios. *Clubs:* Turf, St James'; Athenien (Athens); La Caccia (Rome).

**ARGENTINA AND EASTERN SOUTH AMERICA, with the FALKLAND ISLANDS, Bishop in,** since 1963; **Rt. Rev. Cyril James Tucker;** *b* 17 Nov. 1911; British; *s* of Henry Castledine and Lilian Beatrice Tucker; *m* 1936, Kathleen Mabel, *d* of Major Merry; one *s* two *d*. *Educ:* Highgate Sch.; St Catharine's Coll., Cambridge (MA); Ridley Hall, Cambridge. MA Oxford (by Incorporation), 1951. Deacon, 1935; Priest, 1936; Curate, St Mark's, Dalston (in charge Highgate Sch. Mission), 1935; Curate, St Barnabas, Cambridge, 1937; Youth Sec., British and Foreign Bible Soc., 1938. Chaplain, RAFVR, 1939-46. Warden of Monmouth Sch., 1946; Chaplain, Wadham Coll., Oxford, and Chaplain of the Oxford Pastorate, 1949; Vicar of Holy Trinity, Cambridge, 1957-63; Rural Dean of Cambridge, 1959-63; Chaplain of the Cambridge Pastorate, 1957-63. *Recreations:* sailing; Amateur Athletics Administration (Cambridge Athletic Blue). *Address:* 25 de Mayo, 282, Buenos Aires, Argentina. *Clubs:* Hawk's (Cambridge); Hurlingham (Buenos Aires).

**ARGYLE, Major Michael Victor,** MC 1945; QC 1961; **His Honour Judge Argyle;** an Additional Judge of the Central Criminal Court, since 1970; *b* 31 Aug. 1915; *e s* of late Harold Victor Argyle and Elsie Marion, Repton, Derbyshire; *m* 1951, Ann Norah, *d* of late Charles Newton, and of Mrs V. Jobson, Duffield, Nr Derby; three *d*. *Educ:* Shardlow Hall, Derbyshire; Westminster Sch.; Trinity Coll., Cambridge (MA). Served War of 1939-45: with 7th QO Hussars in India, ME and Italy (immediate MC), 1939-47. Called to Bar, Lincoln's Inn, 1938, Bencher, 1967; resumed practice at Bar, 1947 (Midland Circuit); Recorder of Northampton, 1962-65, of Birmingham, 1965-70; Dep. Chm., Holland QS, 1965-70. Dep. Sen. Judge in Sovereign Base Areas of Akrotiri and Dhekelia, Cyprus, 1969. Lay Judge, Arches Court, Province of Canterbury, 1968-. Legal Mem., Mental Health Review Tribunal, Sheffield Area. General Elections, contested (C) Belper, 1950, and Loughborough, 1955. *Publications:* (ed) Phipson on Evidence, 10th edn. *Recreations:* chess, boxing. *Address:* The Red House, Fiskerton, Notts. *T:* Bleasby 267. *Clubs:* Carlton, Cavalry, Kennel; County (Derby); County (Nottingham); County (Northampton); Abbey (Burton-upon-Trent); St Paul's (Birmingham); Kildare Street (Dublin).

**ARGYLL,** 11th Duke of, *cr* 1701 (Scotland), 1892 (UK); **Ian Douglas Campbell,** TD; DL; Marquess of Lorne and Kintyre; Earl of Campbell and Cowal; Viscount Lochow and Glenisla; Baron Inveraray, Mull, Morvern, and Tiry, 1701; Baron Campbell, 1445; Earl of Argyll, 1457; Baron Lorne, 1470; Baron Kintyre, 1633 (Scotland); Baron Sundridge, 1766; Baron Hamilton, 1776; Baronet, 1627; 35th Baron and 45th Knight of Lochow; Celtic title, Mac Cailein Mor, Chief of Clan Campbell (from Sir Colin Campbell, knighted 1286); Hereditary Master of the Royal Household, Scotland; Hereditary High Sheriff of the County of Argyll; Admiral of the Western Coast and Isles; Keeper of the Great Seal of Scotland and of the Castles of Dunstaffnage, Dunoon, and Carrick and Tarbert; formerly Capt. Argyll and Sutherland Highlanders; *b* Paris, 18 June 1903; *s* of late Douglas Walter Campbell (*gs* of 8th Duke), and Aimée, 3rd *d* of John Lawrence, New York; *S* cousin 1949; *m* 1st, 1927, Hon. Janet Gladys Aitken (who obtained a divorce, 1934), *d* of 1st Baron Beaverbrook, CD; one *d*; 2nd, 1935, Hon. Mrs Louise Vanneck (who obtained a divorce, 1951, and *m* 3rd, 1954, Robert C. L. Timpson, New York, and *d* 1970), *o d* of Henry Clews; two *s*; 3rd, 1951, Margaret (marr. diss., 1963), *d* of George Hay Whigham; 4th, 1963, Mrs Mathilda Coster Mortimer. *Educ:* Milton, Massachusetts; Christ Church, Oxford. Served War of 1939-45 (prisoner). FRSA 1953. DL Argyllshire, 1950. KStJ. *Heir:* *s* Marquess of Lorne, *qv*. *Address:* Inveraray Castle, Argyll. *T:* Inveraray 2275. *Clubs:* MCC, Pratt's; New (Edinburgh); Travellers' (Paris).

**ARGYLL AND THE ISLES, Bishop of,** since 1963; **Rt. Rev. Richard Knyvet Wimbush;** *b* 18 March 1909; *s* of late Rev. Canon J. S. Wimbush, Terrington, Yorks, and late Judith Isabel Wimbush, *d* of Sir Douglas Fox; *m* 1937, Mary Margaret, *d* of Rev. E. H. Smith; three *s* one *d*. *Educ:* Haileybury Coll.; Oriel Coll., Oxford; Cuddesdon Coll. 2nd cl. Classical Mods 1930; BA 1st cl. Theol. 1932; MA 1935. Deacon, 1934; Priest, 1935; Chaplain, Cuddesdon Coll., Oxon, 1934-37; Curate: Pocklington, Yorks, 1937-39; St Wilfrid, Harrogate, 1939-42. Rector, Melsonby, Yorks, 1942-48; Principal, Edinburgh Theological Coll., 1948-63. Canon of St Mary's Cathedral, Edinburgh, 1948-63; Exam. Chap. to Bp of Edinburgh, 1949-62. *Recreations:* gardening, walking. *Address:* Letterwalton, Connel, Argyll. *T:* Ledaig 206.

**ARGYLL AND THE ISLES, Bishop of, (RC),** since 1968; **Rt. Rev. Colin MacPherson;** *b* Lochboisdale, South Uist, 5 Aug. 1917; *e s* of Malcolm MacPherson and Mary MacPherson (*née* MacMillan). *Educ:* Lochboisdale School; Daliburgh H. G. School; Blairs Coll., Aberdeen; Pontificium Athenæum Urbanum, Rome. Bachelor of Philosophy 1936; Bachelor of Theology 1938; Licentiate of Theology 1940 (Rome). Assistant Priest, St Columba's Cathedral, Oban, 1940-42. Parish Priest: Knoydart, 1942-51; Eriskay, 1951-56; Benbecula, 1956-66; Fort William, 1966-68.

*Address:* Bishop's House, Esplanade, Oban, Argyll. *T:* Oban 2010.

**ARGYLL AND THE ISLES, Dean of;** *see* Douglas, Very Reverend G. J. C.

**ARGYRIS, Prof. John,** DScEng, DE Munich; Professor of Aeronautical Structures in the University of London, at Imperial College of Science and Technology, since 1955; *b* 19 Aug. 1913; *s* of Nicolas and Lucie Argyris; *m* 1953, Inga-Lisa (*née* Johansson). *Educ:* 3rd Gymnasium, Athens; Technical Universities, Athens, Munich and Zurich. With J. Gollnow u. Son, Stettin, Research in Structures, 1937-39; Royal Aeronautical Soc., Research and Technical Officer, 1943-49; Univ. of London, Imperial Coll. of Science and Technology, Dept of Aeronautics: Senior Lecturer, 1949; Reader in Theory of Aeronautical Structures, 1950. Hon. ACGI; Hon. Dott Ing Genoa. *Publications:* Handbook of Aeronautics, Vol. I, 1952: Energy Theorems and Structural Analysis, 1960; Modern Fuselage Analysis and the Elastic Aircraft, 1963; Recent Advances in Matrix Methods of Structural Analysis, 1964; articles and publications in Ingenieur Archiv, Reports and Memoranda of Aeronautical Research Council, Journal of Royal Aeronautical Society and Aircraft Engineering, etc. *Recreations:* reading, music, hiking, archæology. *Address:* Imperial College, Prince Consort Road, SW7.. *T:* 01-589 5111. *Club:* English-Speaking Union.

**ARIAS, Dame Margot Fonteyn de (Margot Fonteyn),** DBE 1956 (CBE 1951); Prima Ballerina, Royal Ballet (Guest Artist), London; President of the Royal Academy of Dancing, since 1954; *b* 18 May 1919; *m* 1955, Roberto E. Arias, *qv*. Hon. degrees: LittD, Leeds; DMus, London and Oxon; LLD Cantab; DLitt, Manchester. Order of Finnish Lion, 1960. *Address:* c/o Royal Opera House, Covent Garden, WC2.

**ARIAS, Roberto Emilio;** *b* 1918; *s* of Harmodio Arias and Rosario Guardia de Arias; *m* 1955, Margot Fonteyn (*see* Dame Margot Fonteyn de Arias). *Educ:* Peddie Sch., New Jersey, USA; St John's Coll., Cambridge. Called to the Bar, Panama, 1939; Fifth Circuit, Court of Appeals, US, 1941; Editor, El Panama-America, 1942-46; Counsellor to Panama Embassy, Chile, 1947; Publisher, La Hora, since 1948; Delegate to UN Assembly, New York, 1953; Panamanian Ambassador to the Court of St James's, 1955-58, 1960-62; Elected Dep. to the Nat. Assembly of Panama, Oct. 1964-Sept. 1968. *Address:* Apartado 6307, Panama, Republic of Panama.

**ARKELL, Rev. Anthony John,** MBE 1928; MC 1918; DLitt; FSA; Vicar of Cuddington with Dinton, in the Diocese of Oxford, since Oct. 1963; Reader in Egyptian Archæology in the Univ. of London, 1953-63; Curator of the Flinders Petrie Collection of Egyptian Antiquities at Univ. Coll., London, 1948-63; Hon. Asst Curate, Great Missenden, 1960-63; *b* Hinxhill, Kent, 29 July 1898; *s* of late Rev. John Norris Arkell and late Eleanor Jessy (*née* Bunting); *m* 1st, 1928, Dorothy (*d* 1945), *d* of late John Davidson; one *s* one *d*; 2nd, 1950, Joan Margaret Burnell, *d* of late Col Louis James Andrews, Indian Army. *Educ:* Bradfield Coll. (Schol.); Queen's Coll., Oxford (Jodrell Schol. in Classics). DLitt. (Oxon) 1955; Cuddesdon Coll.; deacon, 1960, priest, 1961. Served European War: RFC 1916-18; RAF 1918-19. Joined Sudan Political Service, 1920; Asst Dist Commr, Darfur Province, 1921-24; Actg Res., Dar Masalit, 1925-26; Dist Comr, Kosti (White Nile Province), 1926-29; Sennar (Blue Nile Province), 1929-32; Actg Dep.-Governor, Darfur Province, 1932-37; Comr for Archæology and Anthropology, Sudan Govt, 1938-48; Chief Transport Officer, Sudan Govt, 1940-44; Ed., Sudan Notes and Records, 1945-48; Archæological Adviser to Sudan Govt, 1948-53; Lecturer in Egyptology, Univ. Coll., London, 1948-53. British Ennedi Expedition, 1957. First Pres., Philosophical Soc. of Sudan, 1947 (Hon. Life Mem., 1949); Hon. Mem., German Archæological Inst., 1953; Mem. Council, Soc. of Antiquaries, 1956-57; Mem. Cttee Egypt Exploration Soc. Order of the Nile, 4th Class (Egypt), 1931. *Publications:* Early Khartoum, 1949; The Old Stone Age in the Anglo-Egyptian Sudan, 1949; Shaheinab, 1953; The History of the Sudan from the earliest times to 1821, 1955; Wanyanga, 1964. Articles in Enc. Britannica; numerous articles in Sudan Notes and Records and other learned jls. *Recreations:* travel, photography, natural history and gardening. *Address:* The Vicarage, Cuddington, Aylesbury, Bucks. *T:* Haddenham 243. *Club:* Athenæum.

**ARKELL, John Heward,** CBE 1961; Director, Boots Pure Drug Co., since 1970; *b* 20 May 1909; *s* of Rev. H. H. Arkell, MA, and Gertrude Mary Arkell; *m* 1st, 1940, Helen Birgit Huitfeldt; two *s* one *d*; 2nd, 1956, Meta Bachke Grundtvig; one *s*. *Educ:* Dragon Sch.; Radley Coll.; Christ Church, Oxford (MA). Sir Max Michaelis (Investment) Trust, 1931-37. Asst Sec., CPRE, 1937-39, Mem. of Exec. Cttee, 1945-, Vice-Chm., 1967. Commissioned Territorial Officer, KRRC 1939; served War of 1939-45; demobilised 1945, Major. Personnel Manager to the Company of Messrs J. Lyons, 1945-49; Controller, Staff Administration, BBC, 1949-58; Director: Staff Administration, BBC, 1958-60; Administration, BBC, 1960-70. Gen. Hon. Sec. Christ Church (Oxford) United Clubs, then Chm. London Exec. Cttee, then Exec. Pres., 1932-. Fellow, Mem. and Vice-Chm. of Council British Institute of Management (Chm. Exec. Cttee until 1970); Chm., Cttee of British Council of Churches responsible for report on further educn of young people, 1960-61; Trustee, Visnews, 1960-69. *Recreations:* walking, swimming, music. *Address:* Pinnocks, Fawley, near Henley-on-Thames. *T:*Henley 3017. *Clubs:* Savile, Leander.

**ARKELL, Sir Noël;** *see* Arkell, Sir T. N.

**ARKELL, Captain Sir (Thomas) Noël,** Kt 1937; DL Wiltshire; Joint Managing Director of J. Arkell and Sons, Ltd, Swindon, Wiltshire; Local Director, Royal Insurance Group; *b* 25 Dec. 1893; 2nd *s* of James Arkell, Redlands Court, Highworth, Wilts, and Laura Jane Rixon; *m* 1919, Olive Arscott Quick, Tiverton, Devon; two *s* three *d* (and one *s* killed in action). *Educ:* Bradfield Coll. Joined 4th Wiltshire Regt (Territorials) in 1912 as 2nd Lieut; served European War in India, Mesopotamia and Palestine (thrice wounded); invalided with rank of Captain, 1919; Chm., Swindon Conservative Assoc., 1927-47, Pres. 1947-52; Chm. Wessex Provincial Area of Conservative Party, 1933-35; Mem. of National Executive Cttee of Conservative Party, 1933-38; High Sheriff of Wiltshire, 1953-54. *Recreation:* fishing. *Address:* Hillcrest, Highworth, near Swindon, Wilts. *T:* Highworth 216.

**ARKLE, Harry;** *b* 7 April 1893; *m* 1928, Nell V. Coventry; no *c*. *Educ:* various schools and privately. Freight Traffic Department, Canadian Pacific Railway, Winnipeg, 1912; General Freight Traffic Manager, Canadian Pacific Railway, Montreal, Que., 1953; European General Manager, Canadian Pacific

Railway Co., London, 1954; Managing Director, Europe, Canadian Pacific Railway Co., London, and Chairman, Canadian Pacific Steamships Ltd, 1961-63. *Recreation:* golf. *Address:* 49 Bryanston Court, W1. *T:* 01-723 6344. *Clubs:* Travellers'; Denham; Hurlingham; Manitoba (Winnipeg).

**ARKWRIGHT, Maj.-Gen. Robert Harry Bertram,** CB 1945; DSO 1943; *b* 30 July 1903; *s* of late Bertram Harry Godfrey Arkwright; *m* 1927, Kathleen Gladys, *d* of late Major E. E. Hanbury, Scots Gds; one *s* one *d* (and one *s* decd). *Educ:* Eton; RMC, Sandhurst. Joined 12th Royal Lancers, 1924; Staff Coll., Camberley, 1934-35; Bde Major 1st Cavalry Bde, 1936-39; GSO2 War Office, June-Dec. 1939; DAAG 1st Armoured Div., 1940 (France); GSO1 8th Armoured Div., 1940-42; Brig. AFV Eighth Army, 1942-43; Comdr 23rd Armoured Bde, 1943-46 (DSO and Bar, CB); Comdr 2nd Div., 1946; DRAC War Office, 1947-48; Comdr, 56th (London) Armoured Div., TA, 1948-49; Comdr 7th Armoured Div., 1949-51. *Recreations:* hunting, fishing. *Address:* The Nether House, Poulton, Cirencester, Glos. *Club:* Cavalry.

**ARLOTT, John;** *see* Arlott, L. T. J.

**ARLOTT (Leslie Thomas) John,** OBE 1970; Cricket Correspondent and General Writer of The Guardian; Leader-Writer of Hampshire County Magazine; broadcaster; topographer; *b* Basingstoke, 25 Feb. 1914; *s* of William John and Nellie Jenvey Arlott; *m* 1st, Dawn Rees; one *s* (and one *s* decd); 2nd, Valerie France; one *s*. *Educ:* Queen Mary's Sch., Basingstoke. Clerk in Mental Hospital, 1930-34; Police (Detective), 1934-45; Producer, BBC, 1945-50; General Instructor, BBC Staff Training School, 1951-53. Contested (L) Epping Division, Gen. Election, 1955 and 1959. President: Cricketers' Assoc., 1968-; Hampshire Schools Cricket Assoc., 1966-. *Publications:* Landmarks (with G. R. Hamilton), 1943; Of Period and Place (poems), 1944; Clausentum (poems), 1945; First Time In America (anthology), 1949; Concerning Cricket, 1949; How to Watch Cricket, 1949; Maurice Tate, 1951; Concerning Soccer, 1952; (ed) Cricket (Pleasures of Life series), 1953; The Picture of Cricket, 1955; English Cheeses of the South and West, 1956; Jubilee History of Cricket, 1965; Vintage Summer, 1967; (with Sir Neville Cardus) The Noblest Game, 1969, etc. *Recreations:* watching cricket, drinking wine, talking, sleeping, golf, collecting aquatints, engraved glass, and books about Gladstone. *Address:* The Old Sun, Alresford, Hants. *T:* Alresford 2197. *Clubs:* National Liberal, MCC; Master's, Forty, Hampshire CC.

**ARMAGH, Archbishop of, and Primate of All Ireland,** since 1969; **Most Rev. George Otto Simms,** DD; MRIA 1957; *b* 4 July 1910; 3rd *s* of John F. A. Simms, Crown Solicitor, County Tyrone, and Mrs Simms, Combermore, Lifford, County Donegal; *m* 1941, Mercy Felicia, *o d* of Brian James Gwynn, Temple Hill, Terenure, Dublin; three *s* two *d*. *Educ:* St Edmund's School, Hindhead; Cheltenham College; Trinity College, Dublin; Scholar, 1930; Moderator in Classics, and History and Political Science, 1932; Berkeley Medallist; Vice-Chancellor's Latin Medallist; Theological Exhibnr. MA 1935; BD 1936; PhD 1950; DD (*jure dignitatis*, Dublin), 1952; DD (*hc* Huron), 1963; Deacon, 1935; Priest, 1936; Curate-asst, St Bartholomew's Church, Dublin, 1935-38; Chaplain Lincoln Theol. Coll., 1938-39; Dean of Residence, Trinity Coll., Dublin, 1939-52; Asst Lectr to Archbishop King's Prof. of Divinity, Dublin Univ., 1939-52; Chaplain-Secretary, Church of Ireland Training Coll., 1943-52; Hon. Clerical Vicar, Christ Church Cathedral, Dublin, 1937-52; Dean of Cork, 1952; Bishop of Cork, Cloyne, and Ross, 1952-56; Archbishop of Dublin and Primate of Ireland, 1956-69; also Bishop of Glendalough and Bishop of Kildare. Member Governing Body, University College, Cork, 1953-57. *Publications:* joint-editor (with E. H. Alton and P. Meyer), The Book of Kells (fac. edn), Berne, 1951; For Better, for Worse, 1945; The Book of Kells: a short description, 1950; The Bible in Perspective, 1953; contributor, The Book of Durrow (fac. edn), 1960; Memoir of Michael Lloyd Ferrar, 1962; articles in Hermathena, Theology, and Dublin Magazine, JTS; contrib. to New Divinity. *Address:* The Palace, Armagh.

**ARMAGH, Cardinal Archbishop of,** since 1965; **His Eminence Cardinal William Conway;** Archbishop of Armagh and Primate of All Ireland (RC), since 1963; *b* 22 Jan. 1913; *s* of Patrick Joseph and Annie (*née* Donnelly) Conway. *Educ:* Christian Brothers, Belfast; Queen's Univ., Belfast; St Patrick's Coll., Maynooth; Gregorian Univ., Rome. Prof. of Moral Theology and Canon Law, Maynooth, 1942; Vice-Pres., Maynooth, 1957; Auxiliary Bishop to the Archbishop of Armagh, 1958. *Publications:* Problems in Canon Law, 1956; The Child and the Catechism, 1959; articles in Irish Theological Quarterly, Irish Ecclesiastical Record, Christus Rex, The Furrow, etc. *Recreations:* walking; local history and archeology. *Address:* Ara Coeli, Armagh, Ireland. *T:* Armagh 2045.

**ARMAGH, Dean of;** *see* Lillie, Very Rev. H. A.

**ARMAND, Louis,** KBE (Hon.), 1957; Grand Officier de la Légion d'Honneur, 1956; Compagnon de la Libération, 1944; Membre de l'Académie Française, 1963; Membre de l'Académie des Sciences Morales et Politiques, 1960; *b* 17 Jan. 1905; *m* 1925; two *s* two *d*. *Educ:* Ecole Polytechnique. Mining Engineer, Clermont-Ferrand, 1926; Engineer, PLM Railways Company, 1934; Director of Works, SNCF, 1944; Director-Gen., SNCF, 1946; President: Board of Directors, SNCF, 1955; European Atomic Energy Commission, 1958-59; Ecole Polytechnique, 1956-68. Past Pres. and Gen. Sec. of Internat. Union of Railways, 1961; Pres. Channel Tunnel Company, 1957; Vice-Pres. European Foundation of Culture, 1961; Director, number of Companies. Medal of Freedom (US), 1946; Comdr of the Order of Leopold (Belgium), 1952; Comdr of the Order of Orange-Nassau (Netherlands), 1953; Comdr of the Order of San Tiego (Portugal), 1958. *Publications:* Plaidoyer pour l'Avenir; Simples Propos, 1968; Le Pari européen, 1968; Propos ferroviaires, 1970; various papers on mineral waters, on the treatment of feed waters for boilers, on the direct utilisation of the industrial current for electric propulsion, on the building of Europe, on education, on perspective thought, etc. *Recreations:* reading, walking. *Address:* 30 Avenue de Villiers, Paris 17e.

**ARMER, Sir Frederick;** *see* Armer, Sir I. F.

**ARMER, Sir (Isaac) Frederick,** KBE 1954; CB 1945; MC 1918; *b* 1891; 2nd *s* of William and Gwenllian Armer; *m* 1925, Elsie Maude Neale; one *s* two *d*. *Educ:* University Coll., South Wales and Monmouth. BSc (Hons). Served European War, 1914-19. Entered Civil Service Sept. 1919 as Assistant Principal; Sec. Royal Commission on London Squares, 1928; Assistant Sec., 1938; Chm. Welsh Board of Health, 1940-44; Under Sec., Min. of Health, 1946, Dep. Sec., 1951-56; Chm., Board of

Control, 1952-60. *Address:* Hurley House, Broom Road, Teddington, Middx.

**ARMFIELD, Maxwell Ashby,** RWS; Writer, Lecturer, Designer and Painter; *s* of Joseph J. Armfield and Margaret Maxwell; *m* Constance Smedley (*d* 1941). *Educ:* Sidcot and Leighton Park; Birmingham Sch. of Art; Paris; Italy. Exhibitor, RA, Salons NEAC, Venice International, Berlin, New York, Chicago, and all principal exhibitions; Lectures on Design and Stage Decoration at the Univs of Columbia, California, New Mexico, etc; Special Studies, Esoteric Symbolism, Design, Tempera Painting; represented: National Collection, Paris, British Museum, Bath, Bournemouth, Derby, Nottingham, etc. *Publications:* The Hanging Garden, 1914; White Horses; An Artist in America, 1925; An Artist in Italy, 1926; (technical) Rhythmic Shape; Stencil-Printing; A Manual of Tempera Painting, 1930; Tempera Painting Today, 1946; 3 Rhythmic Plays: Homage to Masters, 1949; Hermes in the Zodiac; articles in art journals. *Recreation:* musical composition. *Address:* Teddington House, Warminster, Wilts.

**ARMIDALE (NSW), Bishop of,** since 1965; **Rt. Rev. Ronald Clive Kerle;** *b* 28 Dec. 1915; *s* of William Alfred Ronald Kerle and Isabel Ada (*née*Turner); *m* 1940, Helen Marshall Jackson; one *s* one *d*. *Educ:* Univ. of Sydney (BA); Moore Theological Coll., Sydney. Sydney ACT, ThL 1937; BA 1942. Deacon, 1939; Priest, 1940; Curate, St Paul's, Sydney, 1939; St Anne, Ryde, 1939-41; Rector, Kangaroo Valley, 1941-43; St Stephen, Port Kembla, 1943-47; Chaplain, AIF, 1945-47; Gen. Sec., NSW Branch, Church Missionary Society, 1947-54; Rector of Summer Hill, 1954-57; Archdeacon of Cumberland, 1954-60; Bishop Co-adjutor of Sydney, 1956-65. *Address:* Bishopscourt, Armidale, NSW, Australia.

**ARMITAGE, Arthur Llewellyn,** MA, LLB; JP; Vice-Chancellor, Victoria University of Manchester, since 1970; Deputy Chairman of Quarter Sessions, Co. Huntingdon and Peterborough, since 1965 (Co. Huntingdon, 1963-65); *b* 1 Aug. 1916; *s* of Kenyon Armitage and Lucy Amelia Armitage (*née* Beaumont), Rhos-on-Sea, N Wales; *m* 1940, Joan Kenyon, *e d* of late Harold Marcroft, Oldham; two *d*. *Educ:* Oldham Hulme Grammar Sch.; Queens' Coll., Cambridge. Law Tripos (both parts) 1935, 1936; LLB 1937; Commonwealth Fund Fellow, Yale Univ., USA, 1937-39; called to the Bar, 1940, Inner Temple. Served Army, 1940-45, KRRC and 2nd Army, temp. Major. Fellow Queens' Coll., Cambridge, 1945-58; Asst Tutor, 1945; Tutor, 1946; Senior Tutor, 1957; President, 1958-70. University Lectr in Law, 1947-70; Vice-Chancellor, Univ. of Cambridge, 1965-67, Dep. Vice-Chancellor, 1967-70. Mem. and Chm., Wages Councils, 1955-; Chairman: Trustee Savings Bank Arbitration Tribunal, 1964-; Cttee on Pay of Postmen, 1964; British Cttee of Award of Commonwealth Fund, 1969-; Member: Departmental Cttee on Summary Trial of Minor Offences, 1954-55; Chm.'s Panel Industrial Ct, 1962-; Agric. Wages Bd for England and Wales, 1967- (Chm., 1968-); Nat. Adv. Council on Training of Magistrates, 1964-; UGC, 1967-70; Lord Chancellor's Cttee on Legal Educn, 1967-; UNESCO Adv. Mission for Develt of Univ. of W Indies, 1968; Standing Adv. Cttee on Grants to Students, 1961-65. Pres., Soc. of Public Teachers of Law, 1967-68; Trustee, Henry Fund, 1961-70. Hon. Bencher, Inner Temple. JP City of Cambridge, 1950-70. Order of Andrés Bello 1st Class (Venezuela), 1968. *Publications:* Case Book on Criminal Law (with J. W. C. Turner), 1952, 1958, 1964; Jt Editor Clerk and Lindsell on Torts, 1954, 1961. *Address:* The Firs, Manchester 14. *Club:* Athenaeum.

**ARMITAGE, Bernard William,** MA Cambridge; FBPsS; MRCS, LRCP; *b* 6 July 1890; *s* of William Armitage, FZS, and Clara, *niece* of late Sir Jonathan Hutchinson of Inval, Haslemere, Surrey; *m* 1938, Lucy Mitchell, *d* of late John Charles Molteno, MP (SA) and of Mrs Molteno, Virginia, USA, and *gd* of late Sir John Molteno, Prime Minister of Cape Colony. *Educ:* Gresham's Sch., Holt; St John's Coll., Cambridge; St Bartholomew's Hosp., London. Fellow and Tutor of St John's Coll., Cambridge, 1919-25; Demonstrator of Anatomy, Cambridge Univ., 1919-23; Director of Psychotherapy, Bethlem Royal Hospital, 1935-41; Medico-Psychological dept, St Bartholomew's Hospital; Mem. of the British Repatriation Commission, 1918; Medical Adviser, Olympic Games, Antwerp, 1920; FRSocMed, Mem. Council and Chm. Parly Cttee of Royal Medico-Psychological Assoc.; Mem. of Anatomical Assoc. of Great Britain and Ireland; Mem. of Cttee, Psychological Section, British Assoc. Has represented British Psychiatry abroad. Liveryman of Fishmongers' Company, Freeman of the City of London. *Publications:* occasional articles. *Recreations:* represented Cambridge in 3 miles *v.* Oxford, 1910-12, and Oxford and Cambridge *v.* Harvard and Yale, USA; Past Pres. Cambridge Univ. Ski and Ice Hockey Club; Hon. Vice-Pres. Cambridge Univ. Shipping Club; painting, music, field sports and country pursuits, travel. *Address:* Herons Gate, 24 Haig Road, Cambridge. *T:* Cambridge 55510. *Clubs:* Athenæum, Savage, Royal Automobile, Achilles, Royal Corinthian Yacht, Royal Victoria Yacht, Royal Solent Yacht, Royal Yachting Association; University Pitt, Hawks, Alverstone, Cambridge University Cruising.

**ARMITAGE, General Sir (Charles) Clement,** KCB 1938 (CB 1933); CMG 1918; DSO 1916; DL; Colonel Commandant, RA; *b* 12 Dec. 1881; *s* of late C. I. Armitage of High Royd, Honley, Yorks; *m* 1st, 1915, Hilda Caroline (*d* 1931), *d* of late T. J. Hirst, Meltham Hall, Yorks; two *s* one *d*; 2nd, 1933, Eileen, *widow* of Lieut-Col F. A. W. Armitage. Served South African War, 1901-2; European War, 1914-18 (Croix de Guerre, DSO and bar, CMG, Chevalier of the Legion of Honour, Officer of the Order of Leopold, despatches seven times); Comdt Sch. of Artillery, 1927-29; Comdr 7th Inf. Bde, 1929-32; ADC to King George V, 1930-32; Comdt Staff Coll., Camberley, 1934-36; Comdr 1st Div., 1936-38; Master General of the Ordnance, India, 1938-42; retired, 1942. DL Glos, 1950. *Address:* Downington House, Lechlade, Glos. *Club:* United Service.

*See also Lieut-Gen. Sir I. H. Freeland.*

**ARMITAGE, Edward;** Comptroller-General of Patents Designs and Trade Marks, since 1969; *b* 16 July 1917; *s* of Harry and Florence Armitage; *m* 1940, Marjorie Pope; one *s* two *d*. *Educ:* Huddersfield Coll.; St Catharine's Coll., Cambridge. Patent Office, BoT: Asst Examr 1939; Examr 1944; Sen. Examr 1949; Principal Examr 1960; Suptg Examr 1962; Asst Comptroller 1966. *Recreations:* tennis, bridge, gardening. *Address:* 218 Crofton Lane, Orpington, Kent. *T:* Orpington 28188.

**ARMITAGE, Maj.-Gen. Geoffrey Thomas Alexander,** CBE 1968 (MBE 1945); GOC, Northumbrian District, since 1970; *b* 5 July 1917; *s* of late Lt-Col H. G. P. Armitage and late Mary Madeline (*née* Drought); *m* 1949, Monica Wall Kent (*widow, née* Poat); one *s* one step *d*. *Educ:* Haileybury Coll.; RMA,

Woolwich (Sword of Honour). Commissioned Royal Artillery, 1937. Served War of 1939-45 (despatches, MBE), BEF, Middle East, Italy, NW Europe. Transferred to Royal Dragoons (1st Dragoons), 1951, comd 1956-59; Instructor (GSO1), Imp. Def. Coll., 1959-60; Col GS, War Office, 1960-62; Comdt RAC Centre, 1962-65; Chief of Staff, HQ1 (BR) Corps, 1966-68; Dir, Royal Armoured Corps, 1968-70. *Recreation:* field sports. *Address:* c/o Lloyds Bank (Cox's & King's Branch), 6 Pall Mall, SW1. *Club:* Cavalry.

**ARMITAGE, John;** Editor and Bookseller; *b* 25 Sept. 1910; *s* of C. V. and C. C. Armitage, Lincoln; *m* 1934, Margaret Rosa, *y d* of W. G. Watkins; three *s. Educ:* Bedford Sch; Emmanuel Coll., Cambridge. Editor Rackets Publications Ltd, 1932-39; Asst Editor, The Fortnightly, 1937-39, Editor, 1939-54; RAF 1942, Educational Service, Squadron Leader, 1943-46; Times Educational Supplement, 1946-49; Editor, Encyclopædia Britannica Ltd, 1949-67. Councillor, Surbiton Borough Council, 1942-46; Chm. Education Advisory Cttee, Liberal Party, 1948-56; Education Cttee, RAF Benevolent Fund, 1951-; Gov., Letchworth Secondary Schs; Pres. Rugby Fives Assoc., 1956-60; Dir, David's Bookshops (Letchworth) Ltd. *Publications:* A History of Ball Games and Rugby Fives (Lonsdale Library), 1934; To Christian England, 1942; Europe in Bondage, 1943; Our Children's Education, 1960; contributor to: Partnership in Education, 1948, The Unservile State, 1957. *Address:* 100 Wilbury Road, Letchworth, Herts. *Clubs:* Athenæum, PEN.

**ARMITAGE, Kenneth,** CBE 1969; Sculptor; *b* 18 July 1916; *m* 1940. Studied at Slade Sch., London, 1937-39. Served War of 1939-45 in the Army. Teacher of Sculpture, Bath Academy of Art, 1946-56. Regular one-man exhibitions, Gimpel Fils, London, since 1952, and New York since 1954, the last at Paul Rosenberg & Co., 1958; joined Marlborough Fine Art Ltd, London, 1959. Gregory Fellowship in sculpture, Leeds Univ., 1953-55; Guest Artist: Caracas, Venezuela, 1963; City of Berlin, 1967-69. Representations of work shown in: Exhibn of Recent Sculpture in British Pavilion at 26th Venice Biennale, 1952; Internat. Open-Air Exhibns of sculpture in Antwerp, London, Sonsbeek, Varese, and Sydney; British Council Exhibns of sculpture since 1952, which have toured Denmark, Germany, Holland, Norway, Sweden, Switzerland, Canada, USA, and S America; New Decade Exhibn, Museum of Modern Art, New York, 1955; British Section of 4th Internat. São Paulo Biennial, Brazil, 1957; 5th Internat. Exhibn of Drawings and Engravings, Lugano, 1958 (prize-winner); British Pavilion at 29th Venice Biennale, 1958; Art since 1945, Kassel Exhibition, 1959; work in British Sculpture in the 'Sixties' exhibition, Tate Gallery, 1965. Work represented in: Victoria and Albert Museum, Tate Gallery; Museum of Modern Art, Brooklyn Museum, New York; Musée D'Art Moderne, Paris; Galleria Nazionale d' Arti Moderne, Rome, etc. Hon. Dr RCA, 1969. *Address:* 22a Avonmore Road, W14. *T:* 01-385 5800.

**ARMITAGE, Prof. Peter;** Professor of Medical Statistics in the University of London, since 1961; *b* 15 June 1924; *s* of Harry and Florence Armitage, Huddersfield; *m* 1947, Phyllis Enid Perry, London: one *s* two *d. Educ:* Huddersfield Coll.; Trinity Coll., Cambridge. Wrangler, 1947; MA Cambridge, 1952; PhD London, 1951; Ministry of Supply, 1943-45; National Physical Laboratory, 1945-46; Mem. Statistical Research Unit of Med. Research Council, London Sch. of Hygiene and Trop. Med., 1947-61. Hon. Sec., Royal Statistical Society, 1958-64; Mem., International Statistical Institute, 1961. *Publications:* Sequential Medical Trials, 1960; Statistical Methods in Medical Research, 1970; papers in statistical and medical journals. *Recreation:* music. *Address:* London School of Hygiene and Tropical Medicine, Keppel Street, WC1. *T:* 01-636 8636; 7 Plymouth Park, Sevenoaks, Kent. *T:* Sevenoaks 51758.

**ARMITAGE, Sir Robert (Perceval),** KCMG 1954 (CMG 1951); MBE 1944; MA; *b* 21 Dec. 1906; *s* of late F. Armitage, CIE; *m* 1930, Gwladys Lyona, *d* of late Lt-Col H. M. Meyler, CBE, DSO, MC, Croix de Guerre; two *s. Educ:* Winchester; New Coll. District Officer, Kenya Colony, 1929; Sec. to Mem. for Agriculture and Natural Resources, 1945; Administrative Sec., 1947; Under Sec., Gold Coast, 1948; Financial Sec., 1948; Min. for Finance, Gold Coast, 1951-53; Governor and C-in-C, Cyprus, 1954-55; Governor of Nyasaland, 1956-61, retired. Trustee of the Beit Trust, 1963-. KStJ 1954. *Recreations:* golf and gardening. *Address:* South Well, Marnhull, Sturminster Newton, Dorset. *T:* Marnhull 294. *Club:* Royal Commonwealth Society.

**ARMITAGE, (William) Kenneth;** *see* Armitage, Kenneth.

**ARMOUR, Mary Nicol Neill,** RSA 1958 (ARSA 1940); RSW 1956; Teacher of Still Life, Glasgow School of Art, 1952-62, retd; *b* 27 March 1902; *d* of William Steel; *m* 1927, William Armour, *qv. Educ:* Glasgow Sch. of Art. Has exhibited at Royal Academy, Royal Scottish Academy, Soc. of Scottish Artists, and Royal Glasgow Institute. Work in permanent collections: Glasgow Municipal Gallery; Edinburgh Corporation; Art Galleries of Aberdeen, Perth, Dundee, Newport, Paisley, Greenock and Victoria (Australia). *Recreations:* weaving, gardening. *Address:* 2 Gateside, Kilbarchan, Renfrewshire. *T:* Kilbarchan 2873. *Club:* Lady Artists' (Glasgow).

**ARMOUR, William,** RSA 1966 (ARSA 1958); RSW; painter; formerly Head of Drawing and Painting, School of Art, Glasgow, retired; *b* 1903; *s* of Hugh T. Armour; *m* 1927, Mary Nicol Neill (*see* M. N. N. Armour), *d* of William Steel. *Educ:* Camphill Sch., Paisley. Has exhibited: RSA, RSW, etc. *Address:* Kilbarchan, Renfrewshire. *Club:* Glasgow Art.

**ARMSTRONG,** 2nd Baron, *cr* 1903, of Bamburgh and Cragside; **William John Montagu Watson-Armstrong,** late Captain 7th Battalion Northumberland Fusiliers (TF); *b* 10 Oct. 1892; *o surv c* of 1st Baron Armstrong (2nd *cr* 1903) and Winifreda, *d* of late Sir John Adye, GCB; *S* father 1941; *m* 1917, Zaida Cecile, *e d* of Cecil Drummond-Wolff, Caplanne, Billere, Pau, France; one *s. Educ:* Eton College; Trinity Coll., Cambridge; MA, first-class honours Historical Tripos, 1914; Bowen Modern History Prize, etc. Contested Berwick-on-Tweed Division as Independent Candidate, 1918; obtained commission in 7th NF (TF), 1913; served abroad France, and Belgium (severely wounded, April 1915, 2nd battle, Ypres, despatches); invalided home, Nov. 1917; served in India, 1918-19; Siamese Consul in Canada, 1924-29; Siamese Consul-General in Canada, 1929-42; Consul of the Netherlands for British Columbia and Yukon Territory, 1942-46; Commander of the Order of the Crown of Siam; Commander of the Order of the White Elephant; Commander Order of Orange-Nassau (Netherlands). *Publications:* various articles in the Press; My First Week in Flanders (2nd battle Ypres), etc. *Recreations:* travel and exploration; fishing, motoring, cricket. *Heir: s* Hon. William Henry Cecil John Robin Watson-Armstrong [*b* 6 Mar. 1919; *m* 1947, Baroness Maria-Teresa du Four Chiodelli Manzoni, *o c* of late Mme Ruegger (*see* Paul J. Ruegger)]. *Address:* Cragside, Rothbury, Morpeth, Northumberland. *T:* Rothbury 333; Bamburgh Castle, Bamburgh, Northumberland. *T:* Bamburgh 245. *Clubs:* International Sportsmen's, MCC; Canadian, Vancouver (Vancouver); Surrey County Cricket.

**ARMSTRONG, Andrew Clarence Francis,** CMG 1959; Permanent Secretary, Ministry of Mines and Power, Federation of Nigeria, retired; *b* 1 May 1907; *s* of E. R. C. Armstrong, FSA, MRIA (Keeper of Irish Antiquities and later Bluemantle Pursuivant, Herald's Coll.) and Mary Frances, *d* of Sir Francis Cruise; *cousin* and *heir-pres.* to Sir Andrew St Clare Armstrong, 5th Bt, *qv*; *m* 1st, 1930, Phyllis Marguerite (*d* 1930), *e d* of Lt-Col H. Waithman, DSO; 2nd, 1932, Laurel May, *d* of late A. W. Stuart; one *s* (and one *s* decd). *Educ:* St Edmund's Coll., Old Hall, Ware; Christ's Coll., Cambridge (BA). Colonial Administrative Service : Western Pacific, 1929; Nigeria, 1940. *Recreation:* golf. *Address:* Fernacre, Little Marlow, Bucks. *T:* Bourne End 22784.

**ARMSTRONG, Sir Andrew St Clare,** 5th Bt *cr* 1841; *b* 20 Dec. 1912; *s* of Sir Nesbitt William Armstrong, 4th Bt, and Clarice Amy, *d* of John Carter Hodkinson, Maryborough, Victoria, Australia; *S* father 1953. *Educ:* Waitaki; Wellesley Coll. Served War of 1939-45 with RAE, 2nd AIF. *Heir: cousin* Andrew Clarence Francis Armstrong, *qv*.

**ARMSTRONG, Anthony (A. A.);** *see* Willis, A. A.

**ARMSTRONG, His Honour Arthur Henry;** Deputy Chairman Dorset Quarter Sesssions since 1953; *b* 19 Dec. 1893; *s* of Rev. W. D. H. Armstrong, Ilchester, Somerset; *m* 1917, Monica Clare (*d* 1969), *d* of Rev. C. F. Benthall, Cofton, Devon; one *s* two *d. Educ:* Eton; Christ Church, Oxford. Somerset LI and MGC, 1914-18. Called to Bar, 1919; Western Circuit. Wiltshire Regt, 1940-45. Judge of County Courts, Dorset Circuit, 1946-63. *Recreations:* "The meanest chares". *Address:* The Old Vicarage, Queen Camel, Som. *T:* Marston Magna 210.

**ARMSTRONG, Prof. Arthur Hilary,** MA Cantab; FBA 1970; Gladstone Professor of Greek in the University of Liverpool since 1950; *b* 13 Aug. 1909; *s* of the Rev. W. A. Armstrong and Mrs E. M. Armstrong (*née* Cripps); *m* 1933, Deborah, *d* of Alfred Wilson and Agnes Claudia Fox Pease; two *s* two *d* (and one *d* decd). *Educ:* Lancing Coll.; Jesus Coll., Cambridge. Asst Lectr in Classics, University Coll., Swansea, 1936-39; Professor of Classics, Royal University of Malta, Valletta, 1939-43; Classical VIth Form Master, Beaumont Coll., Old Windsor, Berks, 1943-46; Lectr in Latin, University Coll., Cardiff, 1946-50. *Publications:* The Architecture of the Intelligible Universe in the Philosophy of Plotinus, 1940, repr. 1967; An Introduction to Ancient Philosophy, 1947 (American edn, 1949, 4th edn, 1965); Plotinus, 1953 (American edn, 1963); Christian Faith and Greek Philosophy (with R. A. Markus), 1960 (American edn, 1964); Plotinus I-III (Loeb Classical Library), 1966-67; Cambridge History of Later Greek and Early Mediæval Philosophy (Editor and part author), 1967; St Augustine and Christian Platonism, 1968. Has contributed to Classical Quarterly, Mind, Journal of Hellenic Studies, Tablet, Downside Review, etc. *Recreations:* travel, gardening. *Address:* Flat 1, 11 North Road, Grassendale Park, Liverpool L19 0LP.

**ARMSTRONG, Arthur Leopold,** CMG 1944; OBE 1939; *b* 1888. Cadet, Fiji, 1915; Principal Assistant Colonial Secretary, 1936; Agent and Consul, Tonga, 1937; Commissioner for Reconstruction, Fiji, 1943; retired, 1946. *Address:* Bexley, Selwyn Corner, Howich, Auckland, New Zealand.

**ARMSTRONG, Brig. Charles Douglas,** CBE 1945; DSO 1940; MC 1919; late East Surrey Regiment; *b* 11 June 1897; *s* of late C. F. Armstrong, Kitale, Kenya Colony; *m* 1935, Sylvia Holden Earl Bailey; one *s* three *d. Educ:* Cheltenham Coll.; RMC, Sandhurst. Served European War (wounded twice, MC): France, 1916-18; North Russia, Mesopotamia, 1920-21; NWF India, 1930-31; War of 1939-45 (wounded twice, DSO, Africa Star, CBE): France, 1939-40; N Africa, 1943; Jugoslavia, 1943-44. Retired 1948. *Address:* Wix's Farm, Kingsnorth, Ashford, Kent. *T:* Ashford 20707. *Club:* Special Forces.

**ARMSTRONG, Christopher Wyborne,** OBE 1943; farming in Kenya since 1959; *b* 9 May 1899; *s* of Rt Hon. H. B. Armstrong, Dean's Hill, Armagh; *m* 1956, Hilde Ingeburg Kolz, Lübeck; one *s* one *d. Educ:* Winchester; Trinity Coll., Cambridge (MA). Leiutenant RFA, BEF, France, 1918; Burmah Oil Co., Burma, 1922-39; Royal Engineers, BEF, France, 1939-40; Burmah Oil Co., Burma, 1940-42; Member, House of Representatives, Burma, 1942; Controller of Petroleum Industry, Burma, 1942; AQMG, MEF, Egypt, 1942-43; GHQ, India, 1944-45; Commissioner, Magwe Division, Burma, 1945-46; farming in Kenya, 1947-54 and 1959-. MP (UU) Co. Armagh, 1954-59. *Address:* Kwetu Farm, Gilgil, Kenya. *Clubs:* Carlton, United University.

**ARMSTRONG, Rev. Claude Blakeley,** MA, BD; Canon residentiary of Worcester, 1947-70, Canon Emeritus 1970; Vice-Dean and Treasurer, 1965-70; *b* 31 Oct. 1889; *e s* of late Rev. J. B. Armstrong, MA; *m* 1914, Hester (*d* 1968), *d* of late Sir Samuel Dill, LittD; one *d. Educ:* St Stephen's Green School and Trinity Coll., Dublin (First Classical Scholar). Senior Moderator in Classics and Philosophy; Fellowship prizeman; Vice-Chancellor's prizeman and Medallist. Lieut, OTC, 1914-18; Observer Officer, ROC, 1940-45. Deputy for the Professor of Greek, Queen's Univ. Belfast, 1913-14; Headmaster of Cork Grammar Sch., 1914-19; Warden of St Columba's Coll., Rathfarnham, 1920-33; Headmaster of St Andrew's Coll., Grahamstown, SA, 1934-38; Rector of Clannaborough, near Exeter, 1940-43; Rector of Clyst St George, 1943-47; Lectr in Classics, University Coll. of the South-West, Exeter, 1940-47. Pres. Irish Schoolmasters Assoc., 1929; Pres. Exeter Clerical Soc., 1942; Vice-Pres. Classical Assoc. (Chm. Council). Examining Chaplain to the Bishop of Worcester, and Director of Training, 1948; Warden, Worcester Ordination Coll., 1952-64; Founder, Worcester Ordination Coll., 1965. *Publications:* The Persians of Aeschylus translated into English verse; Outline of Western Philosophy, 1964; Foundations Unshaken, 1966; Creeds and Credibility, 1969; contributor to Reviews and Punch; Editor Sir S. Dill's Roman Society in Gaul in the Merovingian Age. *Address:* 12a College Green, Worcester. *T:* Worcester 25837. *Club:* University (Dublin).

**ARMSTRONG, Ernest;** MP (Lab) North West Durham since 1964; an Opposition Whip, since 1970; *b* 12 Jan. 1915; *s* of John and Elizabeth Armstrong; *m* 1941, Hannah P. Lamb; one *s* one *d*. *Educ:* Wolsingham Grammar Sch. Schoolmaster, 1937-52; Headmaster, 1952-64. Asst Govt Whip, 1967-69; Lord Comr, HM Treasury, 1969-70; Mem., Public Accounts Cttee, 1964-. *Recreation:* walking. *Address:* Penny Well, Witton-le-Wear, Bishop Auckland, Co. Durham. *T:* Witton-le-Wear 397.

**ARMSTRONG, Francis William,** MVO 1953; Assistant Under-Secretary of State, Ministry of Defence, since 1969; *b* 11 July 1919; *s* of late W. T. Armstrong, Gravesend, Kent; *m* 1st, 1945, Brenda Gladys de Wardt (*d* 1967); one *d*; 2nd, 1969, Muriel Ernestine Hockaday, MBE. *Educ:* King's Sch., Rochester; Brasenose Coll., Oxford (Open Scholarship in Classics) (MA). Served War of 1939-45: RA (commissioned, 1940); Western Desert, India, Burma. Asst Principal, War Office, 1947; Private Sec. to Permanent Under-Sec., War Office, 1948-50; Principal Private Sec. to Sec. of State for War, 1957-60; Director of Finance, Metropolitan Police, 1968-69. *Recreations:* walking, reading. *Address:* 50 Nork Way, Banstead, Surrey. *T:* Burgh Heath 54602.

**ARMSTRONG, George James,** CMG 1953; CBE 1946 (OBE 1942; MBE 1938); *b* 15 June 1901; *s* of late P. G. Armstrong, Magistrate, Union of South Africa Public Service; *m* 1936, Viva Pearl Rhodes Forrester; three *s* one *d*. *Educ:* St Andrew's Coll., Grahamstown. Entered South-West Africa Protectorate Admin., Jan. 1920; Colonial Service, Basutoland, July 1920; District Commissioner, Basutoland, 1938; Financial Secretary, Swaziland, 1940; Dep. Resident Commissioner and Govt Sec., Swaziland, 1943-48; Deputy Resident Commissioner and Government Secretary, Basutoland, 1948-53; Retired, 1953, and re-appointed as Agent for the High Commission Territories at Johannesburg, S Africa. Retired, 1963. *Recreation:* fishing. *Address:* Glengariff Hotel, PO Box 709, East London, S Africa.

**ARMSTRONG, Hamilton Fish;** Editor of Foreign Affairs since 1928; Writer; *b* New York, 7 April 1893; *s* of late David Maitland Armstrong and Helen Neilson; *m* 1st, 1918, Helen Macgregor Byrne (divorced 1938); one *d*; 2nd, 1945, Carman Barnes; 3rd, 1951, Christa von Tippelskirch. *Educ:* Princeton Univ. 1st Lieut US Army, 1917; Acting Military Attaché, American Legation, Belgrade, Serbia, 1918-19; Member of Editorial Staff of New York Evening Post, 1919-22; Managing Editor of Foreign Affairs, 1922-28; Director, Council on Foreign Relations; Member, Advisory Cttee on Post-war Problems, State Dept, 1942-44; Special Assistant to Mr Winant, 1944; Special Adviser to Secretary of State, USA, 1944-45; Adviser to US Delegation, San Francisco Conference, 1945; Vice-Pres., Woodrow Wilson Foundation, 1928-30; Pres., 1935-37; Trustee, New York Society Library; Member of President's Advisory Cttee on Political Refugees; BA Princeton, 1916; Hon. LLD, Brown Univ., 1942; Hon. LittD, Yale Univ., 1957; Hon. Dr rer. pol., Univ. of Basel, 1960; Hon. LittD Princeton Univ., 1961; Hon. LLD, Columbia Univ., 1963; Hon. LittD, Harvard Univ., 1963. Order of White Eagle (Serbian), 1919; Legion of Honour (French), Officer 1937, Commander 1947; Order of the White Lion (Czechoslovakia), 1937. *Publications:* The New Balkans, 1926; Where the East Begins, 1929; Hitler's Reich; The First Phase, 1933; Europe Between Wars?, 1934; Can We Be Neutral? (with A. W. Dulles), 1936; We or They, 1937; When There is no Peace, 1939; Can America Stay Neutral? (with A. W. Dulles), 1939; Chronology of Failure, 1940; The Calculated Risk, 1947; Tito and Goliath, 1951; Those Days, 1963. *Address:* 58 East 68th Street, New York, NY 10021, USA. *TA:* Foraffairs, New York. *T:* Lehigh 5-3300. *Club:* Century (NY).

**ARMSTRONG, James Shelley Phipps;** Director, Imperial Life Assurance Co. of Canada, since 1968; *b* 28 Dec. 1899; *s* of Joseph E. Armstrong, MP, Petrolia, Ontario, and Margaret Phipps Armstrong, Petrolia and Philadelphia; *m* 1924, Helen Strawn, *d* of late C. W. I. Woodland, Toronto; one *s* one *d*; *m* 1948, Eileen Mary, *widow* of Harry Lascelles Carr, and *d* of Sir Bracewell Smith, 1st Bt, KCVO; one *d*. *Educ:* Ashbury Coll., Ottawa; Univ. of Toronto Schools. Superintendent of Agencies, Norwich Union Fire Insurance Soc., 1922-29; Agency Manager of Dominion of Canada General Insurance Company and Casualty Company of Canada, 1930-39; Agent-Gen. for Ontario in UK, 1944-67. Past President: Life Underwriters Assoc. of Toronto; Canadian Veterans' Assoc. in UK; Canadian Ch. of Commerce in UK; Vice-President: Insurance Inst., Toronto; Empire Club; Past Hon. Sec. Canada Club. Member, Canada Committee, BNEC, 1968. Hon. Life Mem. The Board of Trade of Metropolitan Toronto. AIIA. Major, 48th Highlanders of Canada. *Address:* 14 Ennismore Gardens, SW7; National Trust Company, Toronto, Canada.

**ARMSTRONG, John,** ARA 1966; Painter; *b* Nov. 1893. Has had one-man exhibitions during many years at Leicester and Lefevre Galleries, the most recent being at Leicester Galls, 1957. Designer of costumes, etc, for numerous films, theatrical productions and ballet; paintings in the Tate Gallery, Birmingham, Newport (Mon), Aberdeen, Preston, Glasgow and Newcastle galleries, etc. Murals in Festival of Britain Exhibn, ceiling of Bristol Council Chamber, Shell Centre, etc. Paintings purchased by V&A, Arts Council, and Chantrey Bequest. *Address:* 40 Erpingham Road, SW15. *T:* 01-788 5958.

**ARMSTRONG, Rt. Rev. John,** CB 1962; OBE 1942; Vicar of Yarcombe, Honiton, since 1969; Commissary of the Lord Bishop of Exeter; *b* 4 Oct. 1905; *y s* of late John George and Emily Armstrong; *m* 1942, Diana Gwladys Prowse, *widow* of Lieut Geoffrey Vernon Prowse, and 2nd *d* of late Admiral Sir Geoffrey Layton, GBE, KCB, KCMG, DSO; one step *s*. *Educ:* Durham School and St Francis Coll., Nundah, Brisbane, Qld. LTh, 2nd Class Hons, Australian College of Theology, 1932. Ordained 1933; Mem. Communion of Ascension, Goulburn, 1932-33; Curate, St Martin, Scarborough, 1933-35; Chaplain RN, HMS Victory, 1935; Courageous, 1936-39; 6th Destroyer Flotilla, 1939-41 (despatches 1940); RM Div., 1941-43; Commando Group, 1943-45; HMS Nelson, 1945; Sen. Naval Chaplain, Germany, 1946-48; Excellent, 1948-50; RM Barracks, Portsmouth, 1950-53; Indomitable, 1953; RN Rhine Sqdn, 1953-54; HMS Vanguard, 1954; Tyne, 1954; HM Dockyard, Malta, and Asst to Chaplain of the Fleet, Mediterranean, 1955-57; HMS Bermuda, 1957-59; RM Barracks, Portsmouth, 1959-60; Chaplain of the Fleet and Archdeacon of the Royal Navy, 1960-63; Bishop of Bermuda, 1963-68. Hon. Chaplain to the Queen, 1958-63. *Address:* Yarcombe Vicarage, Honiton, Devon. *T:* Up Ottery 244. *Club:* United Service.

**ARMSTRONG, Rt. Rev. John Ward;** *see* Cashel and Emly, Waterford and Lismore, Bishop of.

**ARMSTRONG, Louis;** jazz musician; trumpeter, singer and band leader; *b* New Orleans, 4 July 1900; *s* of Willie and Mary Ann Armstrong; *m* 1st, 1917, Daisy Parker (marr. diss.); 2nd, 1924, Lillian Hardin (marr. diss.); 3rd, Alpha Smith (marr. diss.); 4th, Lucille Wilson. Began professional career with Kid Ory's Band, in the United States, 1917; formed own band, 1925; has since toured USA and Europe, and has made two tours for the State Department of the USA in Africa and South America. First appeared in films, 1938. Has made very numerous recordings, particularly as trumpeter and singer. *Address:* c/o Associated Booking Corporation, 50 West 57th Street, New York City, NY, USA.

**ARMSTRONG, Martin Donisthorpe;** author; *b* Newcastle upon Tyne, Oct. 1882; *s* of late Charles Armstrong, Brisco Hill, Carlisle; *m* 1930, Jessie McDonald Aiken (*d* 1970); one *s*. *Educ:* Charterhouse Sch.; Pembroke Coll., Cambridge (BA). Private in 2nd Batt. Artists Rifles, 1914-15; Commissioned in 8th Batt. Middlesex Regt, 1915-19; served in France; Associate Literary Editor of The Spectator, 1922-24. *Publications:* Exodus, and other poems, 1912; Thirty New Poems, 1918; The Buzzards, 1921; The Puppet Show, 1922; Jeremy Taylor, a Selection from his Works, 1923; The Bazaar, 1924; The Goat and Compasses, 1925; Desert, 1926; Sir Pompey and Madame Juno, 1927; The Stepson, 1927; Saint Hercules, 1927; St Christopher's Day, 1928; The Birdcatcher (poems) and The Sleeping Fury, 1929; Adrian Glynde, 1930; Collected Poems, Mr Darby, and The Paintbox, 1931; Lover's Leap, 1932; The Foster-Mother and Fifty Four Conceits, 1933; General Buntop's Miracle, 1934; (Ed) The Major Pleasures of Life, 1934; Venus over Lannery, 1936; A Case of Conscience, 1937; Spanish Circus (1788-1808), 1937; The Snake in the Grass, 1938; Victorian Peep-Show, 1938; Simplicity Jones, 1940; The Butterfly, 1941; Chichester Concert (An Ode), 1944; Said the Cat to the Dog, 1945; Said the Dog to the Cat, 1948; George Borrow, 1950; Selected Stories, 1951. *Address:* Sutton, near Pulborough, Sussex.

**ARMSTRONG, Rt. Rev. Mervyn,** OBE 1946; Adviser on Industry to the Archbishop of York, and Assistant Bishop of York, 1964-70; *b* 10 Mar. 1906; *o s* of Rev. Evan Armstrong and Sarah Armstrong; *m* 1st, 1933, Charlotte Stewart (*d* 1961), *y d* of Rev. A. Irvine-Robertson, DD, Clackmannan; 2nd, 1963, Mrs Barbara Newborn, *widow* of G. R. Newborn, Epworth. *Educ:* Balliol Coll., Oxford. In business in China, 1928-37; ordained 1938; served War of 1939-45 as Chaplain, RNVR, 1940-43; Adviser on Seamen's Welfare, Min. of War Transport and Dir of Seamen's Welfare, Govt of India, 1944-45; Vicar of Margate, 1946-49; Chaplain to Archbishop of Canterbury, 1949-51; Archdeacon of Stow and Rector of Epworth and of Wroot, 1951-54; Provost of Leicester, 1954-58; Bishop Suffragan of Jarrow, 1958-64. *Address:* Glen Brathay, Skelwith Fold, Ambleside, Westmorland. *T:* Ambleside 3249. *Club:* Savile.

**ARMSTRONG, Neil A.;** NASA Astronaut; Commander, Apollo 11 rocket flight to the Moon; First man to land on the Moon, 20 July 1969 (Edwin Aldrin being the second); Deputy Associate Administrator of Aeronautics, Space Headquarters, Washington, since 1970; *b* Wapakoneta, Ohio, USA, 5 Aug. 1930; *s* of Stephen and Viola Armstrong, Wapakoneta; *m* 1956, Janet Shearon, Evanston, Ill, *d* of Mrs Louise Shearon, Pasadena, Calif; two *s*. *Educ:* High Sch., Wapakoneta, Ohio; Univ. of Southern California (grad.); Purdue Univ. (BSc). Pilot's licence obtained at age of 16. Served in Korea (78 combat missions) being a naval aviator, 1949-52. He joined NASA's Lewis Research Center, 1955 (then NACA Lewis Flight Propulsion Lab.) and later transf. to NASA High Speed Flight Station (now Flight Research Center) at Edwards Air Force Base, Calif, as an aeronautical research pilot for NACA and NASA; in this capacity, he performed as an X-15 project pilot, flying that aircraft to over 200,000 feet and approximately 4,000 miles per hour; other flight test work included piloting the X-1 rocket airplane, the F-100, F-101, F-102, F-104, F5D, B-47, the paraglider, and others; as pilot of the B-29 "drop" aircraft, he participated in the launches of over 100 rocket airplane flights. Selected as an astronaut by NASA, Sept. 1962; served as backup Command Pilot for Gemini 5 flight; as Command Pilot for Gemini 8 mission, launched 16 March 1966; he performed the first successful docking of 2 vehicles in space; served as backup Command Pilot for Gemini 11 mission; assigned as backup Comdr for Apollo VIII Flight, 1969. Fellow, Soc. of Experimental Test Pilots; AFAIAA Honours include NASA Exceptional Service Medal, and AIAA Astronautics Award for 1966; RGS Gold Medal, 1970. Presidential Medal for Freedom, 1960. *Recreation:* soaring (FAI gold badge). *Address:* c/o NASA, Manned Spacecraft Center, Houston, Texas, USA.

**ARMSTRONG, Robert George,** MC 1946; TD 1958; Deputy Director and Controller, Savings Bank, Department for National Savings, since 1969 (Deputy Director and Controller, Post Office Savings Bank, 1964); *b* 26 Oct. 1913; *s* of late George William Armstrong; *m* 1947, Clara Christine Hyde; one *s* one *d*. *Educ:* Marylebone Grammar Sch.; University Coll., London. Post Office Engineering Dept, 1936-50. Served War of 1939-45, Royal Signals. Principal, PO Headquarters, 1950; Asst Sec., 1962; Dep. Dir of Savings, 1963. *Address:* Barryleigh, Wheelers Lane, Brockham, Betchworth, Surrey. *T:* Betchworth 3217.

**ARMSTRONG, Robert Temple;** Principal Private Secretary to the Prime Minister, since 1970; *b* 30 March 1927; *o s* of Sir Thomas (Henry Wait) Armstrong, *qv*; *m* 1953, Serena Mary Benedicta, *er d* of Sir Roger Chance, 3rd Bt, *qv*; two *d*. *Educ:* Dragon Sch., Oxford; Eton; Christ Church, Oxford. Asst Principal, Treasury, 1950-55; Private Secretary to: Rt Hon. Reginald Maudling, MP (when Economic Sec. to Treasury), 1953-54; Rt Hon. R. A. Butler, CH, MP (when Chancellor of the Exchequer), 1954-55; Principal, Treasury, 1955-57; Sec., Radcliffe Cttee on Working of Monetary System, 1957-59; returned to Treasury as Principal, 1959-64; Sec., Armitage Cttee on Pay of Postmen, 1964; Asst Sec., Cabinet Office, 1964-66; Sec. of Kindersley Review Body on Doctors' and Dentists' Remuneration and of Franks Cttee on Pay of Higher Civil Service, 1964-66; Asst Sec., Treasury, 1967-68; Jt Princ. Private Sec. to Rt Hon. Roy Jenkins, MP (Chancellor of the Exchequer), 1968; Under Secretary (Home Finance), Treasury, 1968-70. *Recreation:* music. *Address:* 6 Woronzow Road, NW8. *T:* 01-722 6393. *Club:* Athenæum.

**ARMSTRONG, Thomas;** Author; *b* 3 Sept. 1899; *s* of late Charles Plaxton and late Alice Lily Armstrong, Airedale, Yorks; *m* 1930, Una Dulcie, *er d* of late Edgar and late Amy Jane Bray, Huddersfield. *Educ:* Queen Elizabeth's Sch., Wakefield; Royal Naval Coll., Keyham. Served in Royal Navy during European War, 1914-19. *Publications:* The Crowthers of Bankdam, 1940 (filmed as Master of

Bankdam); Dover Harbour, 1942; King Cotton, 1947; Adam Brunskill, 1952; Pilling Always Pays, 1954; A Ring Has No End, 1958; Sue Crowther's Marriage, 1961; The Face of a Madonna, 1964; Our London Office, 1966. *Recreations:* reading, mediæval architecture, outdoor constructional work, country pursuits, any ball game, racing. *Address:* Lawn House, Low Row, Swaledale, North Yorks. *T:* Gunnerside 247.

**ARMSTRONG, Sir Thomas Henry Wait,** Kt 1958; MA, DMus; FRCM; Hon. FRCO, Hon. RAM; Principal, Royal Academy of Music, 1955-68; Organist of Christ Church, Oxford, 1933-55; Student of Christ Church, 1939-55; Student Emeritus, 1955; Choragus of the University and University lecturer in music, 1937-54; Conductor of the Oxford Bach Choir and the Oxford Orchestral Society; Musical Director of the Balliol Concerts; Trustee, The Countess of Munster Musical Trust; *b* 15 June 1898; *o s* of A. E. Armstrong, Peterborough, Northants; *m* 1926, Hester, 2nd *d* of late Rev. W. H. Draper; one *s* one *d*. *Educ:* Choir Sch., Chapel Royal, St James's; King's Sch., Peterborough; Keble Coll., Oxford; Royal Coll. of Music. Organist, Thorney Abbey, 1914; sub-organist, Peterborough Cathedral, 1915; Organ Scholar, Keble Coll., Oxford 1916, Hon. Fellow, 1955; served in RA, BEF, France, 1917-19; sub-organist, Manchester Cathedral, 1922; organist, St Peter's, Eaton Square, 1923; organist of Exeter Cathedral, 1928. Cramb Lectr in music, Univ. of Glasgow, 1949. Vice-President, Bruckner-Mahler Chorale, 1970. *Compositions:* various, the larger ones remain unpublished. *Publications:* include choral music, songs and church music, together with many occasional writings on music. *Address:* The Old Rectory, Newton Blossomville, near Turvey, Beds. *Club:* Athenæum.

*See also R. T. Armstrong.*

**ARMSTRONG, Prof. Wallace Edwin,** MA Cantab; Professor Emeritus since 1961; *b* 24 Feb. 1896; *s* of William Wallace Armstrong and Alice Imeson; *m* 1928, Mary Agnes Canavan; one *s* one *d*. *Educ:* Dulwich Coll.; (Exhibitioner) Sidney Sussex College, Cambridge. Volunteered as Private in RAMC, 1914 (wounded, 1915, with loss of leg). BA Cantab Moral Sciences Tripos, 1918; Anthony Wilkin Studentship for ethnological research in New Guinea, 1919-22; Asst Anthropologist to Papuan Govt, 1921-22; Lecturer in Social Anthropology, Cambridge, 1922-26; Supervisor and occasional lecturer in Economics, Cambridge, 1926-39; Lecturer in Economics, University Coll., Southampton, 1939, Senior Lecturer, 1949; Reader, Univ. of Southampton, 1953; Professor of Economic Theory, Univ. of Southampton, 1958-61. *Publications:* Rossel Island, 1928; Saving and Investment, 1936. Numerous articles in: Man, Anthropos, Economic Journal, Oxford Economic Papers, Review of Economic Studies. *Recreations:* gardening, building. *Address:* Ballards Wood, Straight Mile, Ampfield, near Romsey, Hants. *T:* Romsey 3234.

**ARMSTRONG, Sir William,** GCB 1968 (KCB 1963; CB 1957); MVO 1945; Permanent Secretary, Civil Service Department, since 1968; Official Head of the Home Civil Service since 1968; *b* 3 March 1915; *s* of William Armstrong, Stirling, Scotland; *m* 1942, Gwendoline Enid Bennett; one *s* one *d*. *Educ:* Bec Sch., London; Exeter Coll., Oxford. Assistant Principal, Board of Education, 1938; Asst Private Secretary, to President of Board of Education, 1940; Private Sec. to Sec. of War Cabinet, 1943-46; Prin. Private Sec. to successive Chancellors of the Exchequer, 1949-53; Under-Sec., Overseas Finance Div., HM Treasury, 1953-57, and Home Finance Div., 1957-58; Third Secretary and Treasury Officer of Acccounts, 1958-62; Jt Permanent Secretary, 1962-68. Hon. Fellow, Exeter Coll., Oxford, 1963; Visiting Fellow, Nuffield Coll., Oxford, 1964. *Recreations:* reading, walking, sailing. *Address:* 54 Bilton Towers, Great Cumberland Place, W1. *T:* 01-262 1750. *Club:* Athenæum.

**ARMSTRONG COWAN, Sir Christopher;** *see* Cowan, Sir C. G. A.

**ARMSTRONG-JONES,** family name of **Earl of Snowdon.**

**ARMYTAGE, Captain Sir John Lionel,** 8th Bt *cr* 1738; *b* 23 Nov. 1901; *s* of Brig.-Gen. Sir George (Ayscough) Armytage, 7th Bt, CMG, DSO, and Aimée (*d* 1955), 3rd *d* of Sir Lionel Milborne Swinnerton-Pilkington, 11th Bt; *S* father 1953; *m* 1st, 1927, Evelyne Mary Jessamine (marr. diss., 1946); *d* of Edward Herbert Fox, Adbury Park, Newbury; one *s* one *d*; 2nd, 1949, Maria Margarete, *o d* of Paul Hugo Tenhaeff, Bruenen, Niederrhein; one *d*. *Educ:* Eton; Royal Military Coll., Sandhurst. Joined King's Royal Rifle Corps, 1921; retired owing to ill-health, 1940. *Heir: s* John Martin Armytage, *b* 26 Feb. 1933. *Address:* (seat) Kirklees Park, Brighouse, Yorks. *T:* Brighouse 3016. *Clubs:* Naval and Military, Oriental.

**ARMYTAGE, Rear-Adm. Reginald William,** CBE 1959; AM 1928; retired; *b* 18 May 1903; *s* of Sir George Ayscough Armytage, 7th Bart, CMG, DSO, Kirklees Park, Brighouse; *m* 1928, Sylvia Beatrice Staveley; three *s*. *Educ:* Osborne and Dartmouth. Entered Royal Navy, 1917. Served in HMS: Royal Oak, 1921; Capetown, 1922-24; Emergency Destroyers, 1925; Warspite, 1926-28. Qualified in Gunnery, 1929. Served HMS: Devonshire, 1930-32; Mackay, 1932-34; Frobisher, 1935. Took up Naval Ordnance Design, Experiment and Inspection Duties, 1935; Head of Gun Design and Senior Naval Representative at Armament Design Estab., 1946; Deputy Chief Inspector of Naval Ordnance, 1949; Chief Inspector of Naval Ordnance, 1956; Vice-Pres. (Naval), Ordnance Board, 1959; President of The Ordnance Board, 1961-62. *Address:* Wick Cottage, Downton, Wilts. *Club:* United Service.

**ARMYTAGE, Prof. Walter Harry Green;** Professor of Education, University of Sheffield, since 1954; *b* 22 Nov. 1915; *e s* of Walter Green Armytage and Harriet Jane May Armytage; *m* 1948, Lucy Frances Horsfall; one *s*. *Educ:* Redruth County School; Downing Coll., Cambridge. 1st Cl. Hist. Trip. 1937, Cert. in Educ., 1938. History Master, Dronfield Grammar Sch., 1938-39; served War of 1939-45 (despatches); Captain, London Irish Rifles. Univ. of Sheffield: Lectr, 1946; Sen. Lectr, 1952; Pro-Vice-Chancellor, 1964-68. Visiting Lectr, Univ. of Michigan, USA, 1955, 1959, 1961, 1963; Ballard-Matthews Lectr, University Coll. of North Wales, 1963; Cantor Lectr, RSA, 1969; Hawkesley Lectr, IMechE, 1969. *Publications:* A. J. Mundella 1825-1897; The Liberal Background of the Labour Movement, 1951; Thomas Hughes: The Life of the Author of Tom Brown's Schooldays, 1953 (with E. C. Mack); Civic Universities: Aspects of a British Tradition, 1955; Sir Richard Gregory: his Life and Work, 1957; A Social History of Engineering, 1961; Heavens Below: Utopian Experiments in England, 1560-1960, 1962; Four Hundred Years of English Education, 1964; The Rise of the Technocracy, 1965; The American

Influence on English Education, 1967; Yesterday's Tomorrows: A Historical Survey of Future Societies, 1968; The French Influence on English Education, 1968; The German Influence on English Education, 1969; The Russian Influence on English Education, 1969. *Recreations:* walking and gardening. *Address:* 3 The Green, Totley, Sheffield, Yorks. *T:* Sheffield 362515. *Clubs:* National Liberal; University Staff (Sheffield).

**ARNASON, Fru Barbara;** *see* Moray Williams, B.

**ARNELL, Richard Anthony Sayer;** Hon. FTCL; Composer; Conductor; Teacher of Composition, Trinity College, London, since 1949; *b* 15 Sept. 1917; *s* of late Richard Sayer Arnell and of Helène Marie Sherf; *m* 1967, Maxine Leah (De Felice). *Educ:* The Hall, Hampstead; University Coll. Sch., NW3; Royal Coll. of Music. Music Consultant, BBC North American Service, 1943-46; Lectr, Royal Ballet Sch., 1958-59. Editor, The Composer, 1961-64; Chm., Composers' Guild of Great Britain, 1965. Vis. Lectr (Fulbright Exchange), bowdoin Coll., Maine, 1967-68; Vis. Prof. hofstra Univ., New York, 1968-69. Composer of the Year 1966 (Music Teachers Assoc. Award). Compositions include: 5 symphonies; 2 concertos for violin; concerto for harpsichord; concerto for piano; 5 string quartets; 2 quintets; piano trio; piano works; songs; cantatas; organ works; music for string orchestra, wind ensembles, brass ensembles. *Opera:* Love in Transit; Moonflowers; Rain Folly. *Ballet scores:* Punch and the Child, for Ballet Soc., NY, 1947; Harlequin in April, for Arts Council, 1951; The Great Detective, for Sadler's Wells Theatre Ballet, 1953; The Angels, for Royal Ballet, 1957; Giselle (Adam) re-orchestrated, for Ballet Rambert, 1965. *Film Scores:* The Land, 1941; The Third Secret, 1963; The Visit, 1964; The Man Outside, 1966; Topsail Schooner, 1966; Bequest for a Village, 1969. *Other works:* Symphonic Portrait, Lord Byron, for Sir Thomas Beecham, 1953; Landscapes and Figures, for Sir Thomas Beecham, 1956; Petrified Princess, puppet operetta, for BBC, 1959; Robert Flaherty Impression for Radio Eireann, 1960; Musica Pacifica for Edward Benjamin, 1963; Festival Flourish, for Salvation Army, 1965; 2nd piano concerto, for RPO, 1967; Overture, Food of Love, for Portland Symph. Orch., 1968; My Ladye Greene Sleeves, for Hofstra Univ., 1968. *Recreation:* film production. *Address:* c/o Westminster Bank Ltd, 115 Old Brompton Road, SW7. *Clubs:* Savile, Le Petit Club Français.

**ARNEY, Frank Douglas,** CBE 1959; *b* 4 Feb. 1899; *s* of Frank Charles Arney; *m* 1925, Mildred, *d* of W. J. Dallin; three *s*. *Educ:* Grammar Sch., Bristol. Formerly: General Manager, Port of Bristol Authority, for 16 years until retd Oct. 1961; Part-time Chm. British Waterways Board, Dec. 1962-June 1963; Mem., National Ports Council, 1963-. Chm., West of England Freight Terminal Ltd, 1968; Director: Butlers Warehousing & Distribution Ltd, 1963-; Wharf Holdings Ltd, 1965-. *Recreations:* fly fishing, golf. *Address:* Glenleven, Northumbria Drive, Henleaze, Bristol. *T:* Bristol 628810.

**ARNOLD, Mrs Elliott;** *see* Johns, Glynis.

**ARNOLD, John Lewis,** QC 1958; Barrister-at-Law, Middle Temple; *b* 6 May 1915; *s* of late A. L. Arnold and E. K. Arnold; *m* 1940, Alice Margaret Dorothea (*née* Cookson) (marr. diss., 1963); one *s* one *d*; *m* 1963, Florence Elizabeth, *d* of H. M. Hague, Montreal; one *s* two *d*. *Educ:* Wellington Coll.; abroad. Called to Bar, Middle Temple, 1937; served War of 1939-45 in Army (despatches, 1945); resumed practice at Bar, 1946; Chm., Bar Council, 1970-. Chm., Plant Variety Rights Tribunal for proceedings in England and Wales, 1969-. *Recreations:* cricket, travel. *Address:* Little Horse Leas, Bradfield, Berks. *T:* Bradfield 442; 7 Clareville Grove, SW7. *T:* 01-373 7707. *Club:* Bath.

**ARNOLD, Malcolm,** CBE 1970; composer; *b* 21 Oct. 1921; *s* of William and Annie Arnold, Northampton; *m*; two *s* one *d*. *Educ:* Royal Coll. of Music, London (Schol., 1938). Principal Trumpet, London Philharmonic Orchestra, 1941-44; served in the Army, 1944-45; Principal Trumpet, London Philharmonic Orchestra, 1945-48; Mendelssohn Schol. (study in Italy), 1948; Coronation Ballet, Homage to the Queen, performed Royal Opera House, 1953. Awarded Oscar for music for film Bridge on the River Kwai, 1957. Bard of the Cornish Gorsedd, 1969. Hon. DMus Exeter, 1970. *Publications:* Beckus the Dandipratt, overture, 1943; Symphony No 1, 1949; Symphony No 2, 1953; Tam O'Shanter, overture, 1955; Symphony No 3, 1957; Symphony No 4, 1960; Symphony No 5, 1961; Symphony No 6, 1967; Peterloo, overture, 1967; ten concertos; five ballets; two one-act operas; one string quartet; vocal music; chamber music. *Recreations:* conducting, reading and foreign travel. *Address:* Primrose Cottage, St Merryn, Padstow, Cornwall.

**ARNOLD, Vere Arbuthnot,** CBE 1970; MC 1945; TD 1953; JP; DL; Chairman and Managing Director of Ross T. Smyth & Co. Ltd, since 1957; *b* 23 May 1902; *s* of Rev. H. A. Arnold, Wolsingham Rectory, Co. Durham; *m* 1928, Joan Kathleen, *d* of C. J. Tully, Wairarapa, NZ; one *s* one *d*. *Educ:* Haileybury Coll.; Jesus Coll., Cambridge (BA). Ross T. Smyth & Co. Ltd, 1924, Director, 1931; President Liverpool Corn Trade Association, 1947-48 and 1951-52; Mem. of Mersey Docks and Harbour Bd; Chairman: Liverpool Grain Storage and Transit Co. Ltd; Runcorn Development Corporation; Dir, Joseph Heap & Sons Ltd; Regional Dir, Lloyds Bank Ltd. Served War of 1939-45 as Major (MC, TD). JP County of Chester; High Sheriff, Cheshire, 1958; DL Cheshire, 1969. *Recreations:* shooting, fishing. *Address:* Ardmore, Great Barrow, Near Chester. *T:* Tarvin 257. *Clubs:* Army and Navy; Palatine (Liverpool).

**ARNOLD, Sir William (Henry),** Kt 1963; CBE 1955; Bailiff of Guernsey since 1960; *b* 5 Aug. 1903; *s* of William John Arnold and Emma Elizabeth Le Patourel; *m* 1933, Christine Beryl Carré; two *s* one *d*. *Educ:* Guernsey Gram. Sch.; Univ. of Caen. Bachelier en Droit, Caen, 1923; Barrister-at-Law, Gray's Inn, 1926; Advocate of the Royal Court, Guernsey, 1927; HM Attorney-General for the Bailiwick of Guernsey, 1946-60. Docteur en Droit (*hc*), Caen, 1967; Hon. LLD Brock Univ., Canada, 1969. KStJ. *Recreation:* gardening. *Address:* The Royal Court House, Guernsey. *T:* Guernsey 20015 and 23670. *Clubs:* Savage; Royal Guernsey Golf, Royal Channel Islands Yacht.

**ARNOTT, Most Rev. Felix Raymond;** *see* Brisbane, Archbishop of.

**ARNOTT, Sir John (Robert Alexander),** 5th Bt *cr* 1896, of Woodlands, Shandon, Co. Cork; *b* 9 April 1927; *er s* of Sir Robert John Arnott, 4th Bt, and Emita Amelia (*d* 1948), *d* of Francis James, formerly of Royston, Herts; *S* father, 1966; unmarried. *Educ:* Harrow. Formerly Lt, Royal Irish Fusiliers. Chm., Phoenix Park

Racecourse, Dublin. *Heir:* *b* Eric John Arnott, FRCS, DO England [*b* 12 June 1929; *m* 1960, Veronica Mary, *o d* of Captain Arvid Langué, Hartley Wintney, Hants; one *s* one *d*. *Educ:* Harrow; Trinity Coll., Dublin (MB, BCh, BAO)]. *Address:* Woodlands, Lucan, Co. Dublin, Ireland. *Club:* Kildare Street (Dublin).

**ARNOTT, Maj.-Gen. Stanley,** CB 1948; CBE 1944; DSO 1937; MD; County Director and Hon. Secretary City of Edinburgh Branch of British Red Cross Society, 1956-64; retired; *b* 16 Dec. 1888; British. *Educ:* Durham Sch., Edinburgh Univ. MB, ChB 1913; MD 1920, Edin. Lieut RAMC 1913. Served throughout European War, 1914-18, in France and Egypt (despatches); Soudan Service, 1918 for 4 years (despatches, 4th Order of Nile); served North West Frontier, India (DSO); 13 years (on and off) in India; War of 1939-45 (despatches, CBE): ADMS, 4th Div., in France (Dunkirk); War Office; then DDMS, 13th Corps (Sicily and Italy); DDMS, 8th Army (Italy); DMS, Southern Army, India, as Maj.-Gen., 1944; retired 1948, after 36 years' service. Formerly Medical Superintendent, Borders Hospitals Board of Management. *Clubs:* New, Royal Scots (Edinburgh); Hon. Company of Edinburgh Golfers (Muirfield); Gullane Golf.

**ARNOTT, Prof. W(illiam) Melville,** TD (and clasps) 1944; MD; FRCP, FRCPE, FRCPath; William Withering Professor of Medicine, University of Birmingham, since 1946; Physician, United Birmingham Hospitals, since 1946; *b* 14 Jan. 1909; *s* of Rev. Henry and Jeanette Main Arnott; *m* 1938, Dorothy Eleanor, *er d* of G. F. S. Hill, Edinburgh; one *s*. *Educ:* George Watson's Coll., Edinburgh; Univ. of Edinburgh. MB, ChB (Hons), 1931, BSc (1st Cl. Hons Path.), 1934, MD (Gold Medal and Gunning Prize in Path.), 1937, Edinburgh; McCunn Res. Schol. in Path., 1933-35, Crichton Res. Schol. in Path., 1935, Shaw Macfie Lang Res. Fellow, 1936-38, Edinburgh. MD Birmingham, 1947. 2nd Lieut RA, 1929; TA 1929-39; War of 1939-45, served as specialist physician; five years foreign service (Siege of Tobruk; despatches, NW Europe); Lt-Col 1942. Asst Physician, Edinburgh Municipal Hosps, 1934-36; Hon. Asst Physician: Church of Scotland Deaconess Hosp., Edinburgh, 1938-46; Edinburgh Royal Infirmary, 1946. Dir, Post-grad. studies in Medicine, Edinburgh Univ., 1945-46. Associate Examr in Medicine, London Univ., 1948-49; Examr in Medicine, to Univs of Cambridge, 1950-56, London, 1951-54, Wales, 1954-57, Queen's, Belfast, 1956-59, Edinburgh, 1959-62, Leeds, 1959-62, St Andrews, 1961-63, Oxford, 1961-68, Newcastle, 1964-67, Manchester, 1964, Singapore, 1965, East Africa, 1965. Member: UGC, 1954-63; MRC, 1965-69; Council, University Coll. of Rhodesia, 1964-70; UGC Hong Kong, 1966-. Dep. Pres., First Internat. Conf. on Med. Educn, 1953. Editor, Clinical Science, 1953-58, and Mem., Ed. Bd of Brit. Jl of Social Medicine. RCPE: Mem., 1933; Fellow, 1937; John Matheson Shaw Lectr, 1958; Cullen Prize, 1958. RCP: Mem., 1947; Fellow, 1951; Mem. Council, 1954-56; Oliver-Sharpey Lectr, 1955; Examr for Membership, 1957-66; Croonian Lectr, 1963; Censor, 1969-71. Foundation Fellow, Royal Coll. of Pathologists. FRMedSoc 1929 (late Senior Pres.); Hon. FRCP(C), 1957; Hon. FACP, 1968 (Lilly Lectr, 1968). Member: Assoc. of Physicians; Physiological Soc.; Pathological Soc.; Med. Res. Soc.; Cardiac Soc.; Thoracic Soc.; Internat. Soc. of Internal Medicine. Sir Arthur Sims Commonwealth Trav. Prof. of Medicine, 1957. Lectures: Frederick Price, Trinity Coll., Dublin, 1959; Hall, Cardiac Soc. of Aust. and NZ, 1962; Henry Cohen, Hebrew Univ. of Jerusalem, 1964. Pres., Edinburgh Harveian Soc., 1955. Research: Originally into experimental path. of renal hypertension and peripheral vascular disease; at present, into physiology and path. of cardio-respiratory function. *Publications:* some 50 scientific papers, principally in Lancet, Jl of Physiol., Jl of Path., Brit. Jl of Social Medicine, Edinburgh Med. Jl, etc. *Recreation:* travel. *Address:* 40 Carpenter Road, Edgbaston, Birmingham 15. *T:* 021-440 2195. *Clubs:* Athenæum, Naval and Military.

**ARON, Prof. Raymond Claude Ferdinand;** Chevalier de la Légion d'Honneur; author; Professor at Ecole Pratique des Hautes Etudes, Paris, since 1960; Professor at the Collège de France, since 1970; Columnist, Figaro, since 1947; *b* Paris, 14 March 1905; *m* 1933, Suzanne Gauchon; two *d* (and one *d* decd). *Educ:* Ecole Normale Supérieur and Sorbonne, Paris. Lectr, Univ. of Cologne, 1931; French Academic House, Berlin, 1931-33; Lycée du Havre, 1933-34; Centre Documentation sociale ENS, 1934-39; Maître de Conférences, Univ. of Toulouse, 1939; Editor, La France Libre, in London, 1940-44; Columnist, Combat, 1946-47; Professor of Sociology at the Sorbonne, 1955-68. Several hon. doctorates from foreign univs, 1958-; For. Hon. Mem., Amer. Acad. of Arts and Sciences, Boston, 1962; Mem., Académie des Sciences Morales et Politiques, Paris, 1963; Mem., Philosophical Soc., Philadelphia, 1967; Corres. Fellow, British Acad., 1970. *Publications:* Introduction à la philosophie de l'histoire, 1938 (Introduction to the Philosophy of History, 1961); Le grand schisme, 1948; Les guerres en chaîne, 1951 (Century of Total War, 1954); L'Opium des intellectuels, 1955 (Opium of the Intellectuels, 1957); Espoir et peur du siècle, 1957 (Part III trans. as On War: atomic weapons and global diplomacy, 1958); Diversity of Worlds, 1957; La tragédie algérienne, 1957; Immuable et changeante, 1959 (France: steadfast and changing, 1960); La société industrielle et la guerre; Dimensions de la conscience historique, 1960 (parts trans. in Evidence and Inference, ed Aron, 1959, and The Dawn of Universal History, 1961); (ed) The Human Meaning of the Social Sciences, 1959; France: the new republic, 1960; Imperialism and Colonialism, 1960; Paix et guerre entre les nations, 1962 (Peace and War, 1967); Dix-huit leçons sur la société industrielle, 1963 (Eighteen Lectures in Industrial Society, 1968); Le grand débat, 1963 (The Great Debate: theories of nuclear strategy, 1965); (ed) World Technology and Human Destiny, 1963; La lutte des classes, 1964; Démocratie et totalitarisme, 1965 (Democracy and Totalitarianism, 1968); Trois essais sur la société industrielle, 1966 (The Industrial Society, 1967); Les étapes de la pensée sociologique, 1967 (Main Currents in Sociological Thought: I, Montesquieu, Comte, Marx, Tocqueville, the sociologist and the revolution of 1848, 1965; II, Durkheim, Pareto, Weber, 1968); De Gaulle, Israël et les juifs, 1968 (De Gaulle, Israel and the Jews, 1969); La révolution introuvable, 1968 (The Elusive Revolution: anatomy of a student revolt, 1970); Les désillusions du progrès, 1969 Progress and Disillusion, 1968). *Address:* 87 Boulevard Saint-Michel, Paris 5, France.

**ARON, Robert;** Chevalier, Légion d'Honneur; French author; *b* Vesinet, S-et-O, 25 May 1898; *s* of Georges Aron and Louise Aron (*née* Lippmann); *m* 1929, Sabine Pelletier (nom de plume Sabine Berritz). *Educ:* Lycée Condorcet; Faculty of letters, Sorbonne, Paris. Served European War, 1914-18 (Croix de Guerre). Founder (with Arnaud Dandieu) of Personalist Movement (Ordre Nouveau), 1930. In War of 1939-45, escaped to Algeria, 1943, after arrest by forces of occupation, and worked with govts of Giraud and de Gaulle, 1943-44. Dir of Theorectical Studies, in Mouvement Fédéraliste Français and La Fédération, 1946-; Literary Dir, Librairie Fayard. Prix Femina-Vacaresco, 1961; Prix Eve-Delacroix, 1967. *Publications:* La Révolution nécessaire (with A. Dandieu), 1934; Victoire à Waterloo, 1937, new edn 1968; Le Piège où nous a pris l'Histoire, 1950; Histoire de Vichy, 1954; Ce que je crois, 1955; Histoire de la Libération de la France, 1959; Les Années obscures de Jésus, 1960 (Eng. trans: Jesus of Nazareth: The Hidden Years, 1962); Les Grands Dossiers de l'Histoire contemporaine, 1962; Les Nouveaux Grands Dossiers de l'Histoire contemporaine, 1963; Le Dieu des origines des cavernes du Sinaï, 1964; Charles de Gaulle, 1964; Histoire de l'épuration, 1967; Ainsi priait Jésus enfant, 1968. *Address:* 2 rue Michel-Ange, Paris 16e, France.

**ARRAN,** 8th Earl of, *cr* 1762; **Arthur Kattendyke Strange David Archibald Gore;** Bt 1662; Viscount Sudley, Baron Saunders, 1758; Earl of Arran of the Arran Islands, Co. Galway, 1762; Baron Sudley (UK) 1884; journalist; broadcaster on radio and television; *b* 5 July 1910; *s* of 6th Earl of Arran, KP, PC(Ire.), and Maud, *o d* of Baron Huyssen van Kattendijke; *S* brother, 1958; *m* 1937, Fiona Bryde, *d* of Sir Iain Colquhoun, 7th Bt, of Luss, KT, DSO; two *s. Educ:* Eton; Balliol Coll., Oxford. Assistant Press Attaché, British Legation, Berne, 1939-40; Attaché, British Embassy, Lisbon, 1941-42; Deputy Dir, Overseas General Div., MOI, 1943-45; Dir of Secretariat, Central Office of Information, 1945-49. Introduced Sexual Offences Bill (now Act) 3 times in House of Lords. Director, Daily Mail and General Trust Ltd; Chm., Children's Country Holidays Fund; Governor and Hon. Treasurer of Moorfields Eye Hospital. *Publications:* Lord Arran Writes, 1964; columnist, Evening News; contributions to Punch, The Observer, Manchester Guardian, Daily Mail and Evening Standard. *Recreations:* shooting and tennis. *Heir: s* Viscount Sudley, *qv. Address:* Pimlico House, Hemel Hempstead, Herts. *Clubs:* Turf, Beefsteak.

**ARRAU, Claudio;** Concert Pianist; *b* Chillan, Chile, 6 Feb. 1903; *m*; one *s* one *d.* Gave first recital at Santiago at age of 5; musical education in Europe financed by Chilean Govt; studied at Stern Conservatoire, Berlin, under Martin Krause; won Liszt prize, Schulhoff prize, Ibach prize (1917), and, in 1925, first place in International Congress of Pianists in Switzerland. Has appeared in US, Canada, England, France, Holland, Italy, Germany, Scandinavia, Russia, South America, Mexico, Cuba, Hawaii, South Africa, Australia, Israel, Singapore, Ceylon and Bombay. Cycle performances include: all keyboard works of Bach in 12 recitals, Berlin, 1935; all Beethoven Sonatas, 8 recitals, Berlin, Buenos Aires, Santiago; all Beethoven Sonatas, Diabelli Variations, first BBC broadcast from London, 1952; all Beethoven, NY Season, 1953-54. *Address:* Management:– Columbia Artists Management, 113 W 57 Street, New York City, NY, USA.

**ARROWSMITH, Sir Edwin (Porter),** KCMG 1959 (CMG 1950); Director of Overseas Services Resettlement Bureau, since 1965; *b* 23 May 1909; *s* of late Edwin Arrowsmith; *m* 1936, Clondagh, *e d* of late Dr W. G. Connor; two *d. Educ:* Cheltenham Coll.; Trinity Coll., Oxford (MA). Assistant District Commissioner, Bechuanaland Protectorate, 1932; in various District posts, Bechuanaland Protectorate, 1933-38; Commissioner, Turks and Caicos Islands, BWI, 1940-46; Administrator, Dominica, BWI, 1946-52; Resident Commissioner, Basutoland, 1952-56; Governor and Commander-in-Chief, Falkland Islands, 1957-64, and High Commissioner, British Antarctic Territory, 1962-64. Chm., Royal Commonwealth Soc. for the Blind, 1970-. *Recreations:* golf, fishing. *Address:* 25 Rivermead Court, Hurlingham, SW6. *T:* 01-736 4757. *Clubs:* Flyfishers' (Pres.), Hurlingham.

**ARROWSMITH, Hugh,** CBE 1953; *b* 2 June 1888; *s* of late P. R. Arrowsmith; *m* 1914, Edith (*d* 1963), *d* of John Jaques; no *c. Educ:* Marlborough. Cotton Broker, 1910-40; Asst Controller, Min. of Supply, 1940-47; Independent Mem., Raw Cotton Commission, 1951-54. *Recreation:* gardening. *Address:* Ribby Cottage, Wood Lane, Neston, Wirral, Cheshire. *T:* Neston 1355.

**ARTHUR,** family name of **Baron Glenarthur.**

**ARTHUR, Sir Basil Malcolm,** 5th Bt, *cr* 1841; MP (Lab) for Timaru, New Zealand, since 1962; *b* 18 Sept. 1928; *o s* of Sir George Malcolm Arthur, 4th Bt, and Doris Fay, *y d* of Joseph Wooding, JP, Woodland Grange, Woodbury, Geraldine, New Zealand; *S* father 1949; *m* 1950, Elizabeth Rita, *d* of late Alan Wells, Wakefield, Nelson, New Zealand; one *s* two *d. Heir: s* Stephen John Arthur, *b* 1 July 1953. *Address:* Seadown, No. 3 RD, Timaru, New Zealand.

**ARTHUR, Prof. Donald Ramsay,** MSc, PhD, DSc; Professor of Zoology, King's College, London University, since 1963; *b* 1 May 1917; *s* of Henry and Rachel Arthur; *m* 1945, Iris Doreen (*née* Gingell); one *d. Educ:* Amman Valley Gram. Sch.; UCW, Aberystwyth. School Master, Brockley Co. Sch., London, 1938-39; Scientist, Royal Ordnance Factory, 1939-42; Sen. Entomologist, University Coll. South Wales (working under grant from ARC), 1943-47; Sen. Biology Master, City of Cardiff High Sch., 1947-48; King's Coll., London: Lectr in Zoology, 1948-59; Leverhulme Research Award, 1954-55; Reader in Zoology, 1959-63; Dean, Faculty of Science, 1968-70; Consultant US Naval Med. Res. Unit, Cairo, 1955-62. Vis. Prof., Univ. of Rhodesia, 1962; Mem. Council, Brit. Soc. Parasitol., 1962-64; Chm., Bd of Studies in Zoology, Univ. of London, 1965-67; Pres., London Branch of Assoc. for Science Educn, 1965-66; Member: Exec. Cttee and Finance and Admin. Cttee, Field Studies Council, 1963-; Council of Environmental Educn, 1968-; Editorial Bd, Parasitology, 1964-; Editorial Bd, Internat. Jl of Environmental Sciences, 1970-; Council, John Cass Coll., 1965-69; Delegacy, King's Coll., 1970-; Finance Cttee, King's Coll., 1970; Cleaner Thames Consultative Cttee, 1968-; Adv. Cttee of Pollution by oil of the sea, 1970-. Editor, Biological Science Texts, 1966-. President: London Old Aberystwythians, 1967-68; London Carms Soc., 1970-71. FIBiol, 1965. *Publications:* Ticks: a Monograph of the Ixodoidea, Pt V, 1960; Ticks and Disease, 1962; (ed) Aspects of Disease Transmission by Ticks, 1962; British Ticks, 1963; Ticks of the Genus Ixodes in Africa, 1965; (ed) Looking at Animals Again, 1966; Survival: Man and his Environment, 1969; (ed with J. D. Carthy) Oil Pollution and Littoral Organisms, 1968; Joint Editor, Symposium vol., 2nd Internat. Acarological Congress, 1969; Adv. Editor, Encyclopaedia of Zoology, 1970; papers in Parasitology, Jl Parasitology, Proc. Zool.

Soc., Bulletin Entomological Research, etc. *Recreation:* Rugby football. *Address:* 57 Rushgrove Avenue, NW9. *T:* 01-205 6375.

**ARTHUR, Geoffrey George,** CMG 1963; Political Resident in the Persian Gulf, since 1970; *b* 19 March 1920; *s* of G. J. Arthur; *m* 1946, Margaret, *d* of late T. A. Woodcock, OBE; no *c*. *Educ:* Ashby de la Zouch Grammar Sch.; Christ Church, Oxford. Served in Army, 1940-45. Joined HM Foreign Service, 1947. Served in: Baghdad, 1948-50; Ankara, 1950-53; Foreign Office, 1953-55; Bonn, 1956-58; Cairo, 1959-63; Counsellor in Foreign Office, 1963-67; Ambassador to Kuwait, 1967-68; Asst Under-Sec. of State, FCO, 1968-70. *Address:* c/o Foreign and Commonwealth Office, SW1. *Club:* United University.

**ARTHUR, Prof. Geoffrey Herbert;** Professor of Veterinary Obstetrics and Diseases of Reproduction, University of London, since 1965; *b* 6 March 1916; *s* of William Gwyn Arthur and Ethel Jessie Arthur; *m* 1948, Lorna Isabel Simpson; four *s* one *d*. *Educ:* Abersychan Secondary Sch.; Liverpool Univ. BVSc 1939; MRCVS 1939; MVSc 1945; DVSc 1957; FRCVS 1957. Lectr in Veterinary Medicine, Liverpool Univ., 1941-48; Reader in Veterinary Surgery, Royal Veterinary Coll., 1949-51; Reader in Veterinary Surgery and Obstetrics, Univ. of London, 1952-65. Examiner to Univs of Cambridge, Dublin, Edinburgh, Glasgow, Liverpool, London, Reading, Bristol and Ceylon. Visiting Prof., Univ. of Khartoum, 1964. *Publications:* Wright's Veterinary Obstetrics, 1964; papers on medicine and reproduction in Veterinary Record, Veterinary Jl, Jl of Comparative Pathology, Jl Reprod. Fert. and Vet. Jl. *Recreation:* observing natural phenomena. *Address:* 142 North Road, Hertford, Herts. *T:* Hertford 2080.

**ARTHUR, James Stanley;** Counsellor, British High Commission, Kenya, since 1967; *b* 3 Feb. 1923; *s* of Lawrence and Catherine Arthur, Lerwick, Shetland; *m* 1950, Marion North; two *s* two *d*. *Educ:* Trinity Academy, Edinburgh; Liverpool Univ. (BSc). Scientific Civil Service, 1944-46; Asst Principal, Scottish Educn Dept, 1946; Min. of Educn/Dept of Educn and Science, 1947-66: Private Sec. to Parly Sec., 1948-50; Principal Private Sec. to Minister, 1960-62; Counsellor, FO, 1966; Nairobi, 1967. *Recreations:* golf, music. *Address:* Foreign and Commonwealth Office, King Charles Street, SW1. *T:* 01-930 8440. *Clubs:* English-Speaking Union; Muthaiga Country, Muthaiga Golf (Nairobi).

**ARTHUR, Sir (Oswald) Raynor,** KCMG 1957 (CMG 1953); CVO 1953; JP; retired as Governor and Commander-in-Chief, The Bahamas (1957-60); *b* 1905; *s* of late Sigismund Raynor Arthur, ICS, and of Constance Eleanor (*née* Hobhouse); *m* 1935, Mary Elizabeth, *d* of late Rt Hon. Sir Cecil Spring Rice, PC, GCMG, GCVO; one *s* one *d*. *Educ:* Charterhouse; Corpus Christi Coll., Cambridge. Entered Nigerian Political Service, 1928; transferred to Cyprus as administrative officer, 1937; Commissioner, 1947; Chief Commissioner, 1948. Colonial Sec., Bermuda, 1951; Governor and Commander-in-Chief, Falkland Islands, 1954. JP East Sussex, 1962. *Recreations:* tennis, hunting. *Address:* 36 Argyll Road, W8. *T:* 01-937 5912; The Glebe House, Burwash, Sussex. *T:* Burwash 224. *Club:* East India and Sports.

**ARTHUR, Sir Raynor;** *see* Arthur, Sir O. R.

**ARTHUR, Rt. Rev. Robert Gordon;** *see* Grafton, NSW, Bishop of.

**ARTHURE, Humphrey George Edgar,** CBE 1969; MD, FRCS, FRCOG; Senior Obstetric Physician, Charing Cross Hospital; Obstetric Surgeon, Queen Charlotte's Hospital; Gynæcologist, Mount Vernon Hospital. MRCS, LRCP 1931; MB, BS 1933; FRCS 1935; MD London 1938; FRCOG 1950 (Hon. Sec. 1949-56; Vice-Pres. 1964-67); FRSM (Pres., Section of Obstetrics and Gynaecology, 1969); co-opted Mem. Council, RCS 1960; Pres., West London Medico-Chirurgical Soc., 1964; Chm., Central Midwives Board; Mem., Standing Maternity and Midwifery Advisory Cttee. Formerly: Resident Obstetric Officer and Obstetrical Registrar, Charing Cross Hospital; Resident Medical Officer, Chelsea Hospital for Women. Served War of 1939-45, temp. Lt-Col, RAMC. *Publications:* contribs med. jls. *Address:* 78 Harley Street, W1. *T:* 01-580 6166.

**ARTON, Major A. T. B.-;** *see* Bourne-Arton.

**ARUNDEL AND BRIGHTON, Bishop of, (RC),** since 1965; **Rt. Rev. David (John) Cashman;** *b* 27 Dec. 1912; *s* of Philip and Norah Cashman (*née* McSwiney). *Educ:* Cotton Coll., North Staffordshire; English Coll., Rome. Assistant, St Mary and Angels, Stoke on Trent, 1939; Sec., Apostolic Delegation, London, 1940; Parish Priest, Arundel, and Chaplain to Duke of Norfolk, 1956-58; Parish Priest, St Mary's Cadogan Street, SW3, 1958-65; Auxiliary Bishop of Westminster, (RC), 1958-65, and Titular Bishop of Cantano. Canon Metropolitan Chapter of Westminster and Canon Theologian, 1961. Commander Polonia Restituta (Poland), 1945; Knight of Malta (Sovereign Military Order), 1947; Commander Order of Holy Sepulchre, 1952; Cruz Distinguida San Ramón de Peñafort (Spain), 1956. *Recreation:* shooting. *Address:* St Joseph's Hall, Greyfriars Lane, Storrington, Pulborough, Sussex. *T:* Storrington 2172. *Clubs:* Royal Automobile, Turf.

**ARUNDEL AND BRIGHTON, Coadjutor Bishop of, (RC);** *see* Bowen, Rt Rev. M. G.

**ARUNDELL, Dennis Drew** (formerly D. D. Arundel); actor, composer, producer, writer for theatre, radio, films and television, since 1926; *b* 22 July 1898; *s* of Arundel Drew Arundel and Rose Lucy Campbell. *Educ:* Tonbridge Sch.; St John's Coll., Cambridge. Lieut, RGA, 1917-19 (gassed, 1918). St John's Coll., 1919-29 (Sizarship, 1917; Strathcona Studentship, 1922); BA (Classics) 1922, MusB 1923, MA 1924. Fellow of St John's Coll., Cambridge, 1923-29; Lecturer in Music and English Drama, Deputy Organist St John's, 1924. First appeared on professional stage at Lyric, Hammersmith, 1926; subseq. joined Old Vic Company, and has since taken many parts, directed and composed music for plays in West End theatres, films, radio and television. As an opera director his work has been especially with Sadler's Wells and the BBC; producer of over 50 operas; translator of some 15 operas; has also directed both operas and plays in Australia and Finland. *Publications:* Henry Purcell, 1927; Dryden and Howard, 1929; The Critic at the Opera, 1957; The Story of Sadler's Wells, 1965. Ed Congreve's Semele, 1925; (trans.) Morax and Honegger's King David, 1929; (trans.) Weinberger's Schwanda the Bagpiper, 1946; (trans.) Claudel's Jeanne d'Arc au Bûcher, 1939. Various musical compositions and musical articles. *Recreation:* operatic research. *Address:* 21 Lloyd Square, WC1. *T:* 01-837 2942.

**ARUNDELL, Brigadier Sir Robert (Duncan Harris),** KCMG 1950 (CMG 1947); OBE 1943; retired as Governor and Commander-in-Chief,

Barbados (1953-59) (Acting Governor-General and C-in-C, The West Indies, 1959); Zanzibar Delimitation Commissioner, 1962; *b* Lifton, Devon, 22 July 1904; *s* of late C. H. Arundell; *m* 1929, Joan, *d* of late Capt. J. A. Ingles, RN; one *s. Educ:* Blundell's Sch.; Brasenose Coll., Oxford. Colonial Administrative Service, Tanganyika Territory, 1927; seconded Colonial Office, 1935-37; Sec. Nyasaland Financial Commission, 1937-38; Tanganyika Territory, 1938-39; Assistant Chief Sec. Uganda, 1939; Army, Civil Affairs, 1941-45; served War of 1939-45 in Middle East and East Africa (despatches, OBE); Chief Civil Affairs Officer MEF (Brig.), 1944-45; British Resident Mem. in Washington of Caribbean Commission, 1946-47; Governor and C-in-C, Windward Islands, 1948-53. KStJ 1952. *Address:* Wakehill, Ilminster, Somerset. *Club:* East India and Sports.

**ARUP, Ove Nyquist,** CBE 1953; MICE, MIStructE, MICEI, MSAICE; Senior Partner of Ove Arup & Partners, Consulting Engineers, since 1949; *b* Newcastle upon Tyne, 16 April 1895; *s* of Jens Simon Johannes Arup and Mathilde B. Nyquist; *m* 1925, Ruth Sørensen; one *s* two *d. Educ:* Preparatory Sch., Hamburg, Germany; Public Sch., Sorø; Univ. of Copenhagen, Denmark. MIngF (Medlem Ingeniør Forening), Copenhagen. Designer Christiani & Nielsen, GmbH, Hamburg, 1922; Chief Designer, Christiani & Nielsen, Ltd, London, 1925-34 (Designer, 1923-25); Director and Chief Designer, J. L. Kier & Co., Ltd, London, 1934-38; Consulting Engineer for: schools, flats, air raid shelters, industrial projects, marine work (Air Min.); Director: Arup Designs, Ltd; Arup & Arup, Ltd; Pipes, Ltd, 1938-45; Chm. Soc. of Danish Civil Engineers in Gt Britain and Ireland, 1955-59; Visiting Lectr, Harvard Univ., 1955; Alfred Bossom Lectr, RSA, 1970; Maitland Lecture, IStructE, 1968. RIBA Royal Gold Medal for Architecture for 1966. Hon. DSc Durham, 1967; Hon. ScD East Anglia, 1968. Chevalier (First Class), Order of the Dannebrog, 1965. *Publications:* Design, Cost, Construction and Relative Safety of Trench, Surface, Bomb-proof and other Air Raid Shelters, 1939; Safe Housing in War-Time, 1941; various contribs to technical jls. *Recreations:* music and reading. *Address:* 6 Fitzroy Park, Highgate, N6. *T:* 01-340 3388. *Clubs:* Athenæum; Danish.

**ARWYN,** Baron, *cr* 1964 (Life Peer); **Arwyn Randall Arwyn;** Deputy Chairman, Bath and Portland Group Ltd; Director of various other companies; Member, China Clay Council; Past President, Institute of Cornish Mining Engineers. Changed name by deed poll from Davies to Arwyn, 1964. Served Wars of 1914-18 and 1939-45: Army, Air Force, and specialist duties. Member, Mineral Development Committee, 1946-49. CEng, MIMinE. *Address:* Greenbank, Falmouth, Cornwall. *Clubs:* Reform; Royal Automobile; Royal Cornwall Yacht, House of Lords Yacht, Flushing Sailing.

**ASAFU-ADJAYE, Sir Edward (Okyere),** Kt 1960; Fellow of University College, London, since 1959; Member, Ghana Board, Barclays Bank DCO, since 1961; *b* 1903; *m* 1930, Martha Violet Randolph; several *s* and *d. Educ:* Kumasi Government Primary Boys' Sch.; SPG Grammar Sch. (now Adisadel Coll.), Cape Coast; University Coll., London Univ. Hons Philosophy, 1925; Law, 1926. Profumo prize, Inner Temple; called to Bar, Inner Temple, 1927; enrolled as member Gold Coast Bar (now the Bar of Ghana), 1927. Practised principally in Accra Courts until 1934, when Kumasi Courts were opened and his Accra Chambers moved to Kumasi. Formerly: Dir Ghana Commercial Bank; Councillor in the old Kumasi Town Council; Mem. Asanteman Council; Mem. Council University Coll. of Ghana. Served on CNC delegation to London, 1934; a representative of the Gold Coast at the Coronations: of King George VI, 1937; and of Queen Elizabeth II, 1953; attended Commonwealth Parly Conf., Ottawa, 1949. MLC 1946; MLA 1951; Minister of Local Govt, 1951-55 (MLA as Convention People's Party candidate, 1954); Minister of Trade and Labour, 1955: did not seek election in 1956, and resumed his legal practice until his appt as Ghana's first High Commissioner to the UK; also first Ambassador of Ghana to France; High Commissioner for Ghana in London, 1957-61. Director, Consolidated African Selection Trust, 1961-66. *Recreations:* golf and walking. *Address:* c/o Bank of West Africa Ltd, PO Box 564, 37 Gracechurch Street, EC3.

**ASEA, Dr Solomon Bayo,** MB, ChB, DTM&H, DPH; High Commissioner for Uganda, in London, 1966-68; *b* 1924; *m*; five *s* three *d. Educ:* Medical Sch., Makerere Univ., Uganda (MB, ChB); Liverpool Sch. of Tropical Medicine; London Sch. of Hygiene and Tropical Medicine. BMA Essay Prize for Colonial Medical Schools 1951. DTM&H Liverpool, 1958, DPH London, 1962. Joined Uganda Civil Service, as a Medical Officer, 1952; subsequently Senior MO and PMO; after a year at Medical Headquarters, Entebbe, he was transferred to Ministry of Internal Affairs as an Under-Sec., 1964; later he moved to Ministry of Foreign Affairs; first Uganda Ambassador to the USA, 1964-66. *Recreations:* reading, photography; enjoys listening to classical music. *Address:* c/o Ministry of Foreign Affairs, PO Box 122, Entebbe, Uganda.

**ASH, Graham Baron;** *b* 18 Aug. 1889; *s* of Alfred James Ash, OBE. *Educ:* Radley. Served European War with RFC and RAF, and with RAF, 1939-40; High Sheriff of Warwickshire, 1938-39. *Recreation:* shooting. *Address:* Wingfield Castle, Diss, Norfolk. *Club:* Royal Automobile.

**ASH, Maurice Anthony,** BSc (Econ); Chairman of Executive, Town and Country Planning Association, since 1969; *b* 31 Oct. 1917; *s* of Wilfred Cracroft and Beatrice Ash; *m* 1947, Ruth Whitney Elmhirst, *o d* of Leonard Knight Elmhirst, *qv*; three *d* (one *s* decd). *Educ:* Gresham's Sch., Holt; LSE; Yale. Served War of 1939-45, armoured forces in Western Desert, Italy, Greece (despatches 1944). Mem. Executive, TCPA, 1956-; Trustee, Dartington Hall and Dir associated companies, 1964-; Mem., SW Regional Economic Planning Council, 1965-68. Founder, Harlow Arts Trust. Chm., Adams & Dart, publishers, 1969-. *Publications:* The Human Cloud, 1962; Who are the Progressives Now?, 1969; Regions of Tomorrow, 1969; articles on land use, education, international relations. *Recreations:* sailing, philosophy. *Address:* Sharpham House, Ashprington, Totnes, Devon. *T:* Harbertonford 216. *Clubs:* Reform, Royal Ocean Racing.

**ASH, Rear-Admiral Walter William Hector,** CB 1962; WhSch; FIEE; *b* Portsmouth, Hants, 2 May 1906; *s* of Hector Sidney and Mabel Jessy Ash; *m* 1932, Louisa Adelaide Salt, Jarrow-on-Tyne; three *d. Educ:* City & Guilds Coll., Kensington; Royal Naval Coll., Greenwich. Whitworth Scholar, 1926; John Samuel Scholar, 1927. Asst Elect. Engr, Admiralty (submarine design), 1932-37; Elect. Engr, Admiralty (battleship design), 1937-39; Fleet Elect. Engr, Staff C-in-C Med., 1939-40; Supt

Elect. Engr, Admiralty (supply and prod.), 1940-45; Supt Elect. Engr, HM Dockyard, Hong Kong, 1945-48; Supt Elect. Engr, Admiralty Engineering Lab., 1948-49; Comdr RN, HMS Montclare, 1950-51; Capt. RN, Admiralty (weapon control design), 1951-54; Capt. RN, Elect. Engr Manager, HM Dockyard, Devonport, 1954-58; Capt. RN, Ship Design Dept, Admiralty, 1959-60; Rear-Adm. 1960; subseq. Ship Dept Directorate, Admty, retd Aug. 1963. Vis. Lectr in electrical machinery design, RN Coll., Greenwich, 1934-37. Chairman IEE, SW Sub Centre, 1957-58. ADC to the Queen, 1958-60. *Recreations:* golf, music, (piano and organ). *Address:* Saltash, 14 Beacon Drive, Highcliffe-on-Sea, Christchurch, Hants BH23 5DH. *T:* Highcliffe 5261.

**ASHBOURNE,** 3rd Baron, *cr* 1885; **Edward Russell Gibson;** CB 1950; DSO 1943; Vice-Admiral, retired; *b* 1 June 1901; *s* of Hon. Edward Graves Mayne Gibson (3rd *s* of 1st Baron Ashbourne) and Mary Philips Greg; *S* uncle, 1942; *m* 1929, Reta Frances Manning, *e d* of E. M. Hazeland of Hong Kong; one *s* one *d*. *Educ:* Osborne; Dartmouth; Caius Coll., Cambridge. Entered Osborne, 1915; Midshipman, 1917; served in HMS Superb, Dreadnought, Monarch, in War of 1914-18; Lieut, 1922; specialised in submarines, 1925; Commander 1934; served on staff of Admiral of the Fleet Sir Dudley Pound in Mediterranean, 1938-39; Capt., 1939; served War of 1939-45 (DSO, Legion of Merit, US); served on staff of Adm. Sir Max Horton, 1940-42; Sicily Assault (DSO), 1943; commanded HMS Ariadne (Legion of Merit, US), 1943-45; commanded 3rd Submarine Flotilla, 1945; served on Naval Staff at Admiralty, 1946-47; commanded HMS Mauritius, 1947-48; Rear-Adm., 1948; Naval Representative on Military Staff Cttee, UN, 1949-50; Flag Officer, Gibraltar, and Admiral Supt, HM Dockyard, Gibraltar, 1950-52; Vice-Adm. 1952; retired list, 1952. JP Co. of Devon, 1955; DL County of Devon, 1962-65. County Pres., St John Ambulance Brigade for Devon, 1963. OStJ 1964. *Heir: s* Lieut-Comdr Hon. Edward Barry Greynville Gibson, Royal Navy [*b* 28 Jan. 1933; *m* 1967, Yvonne Georgina, *d* of late Major G. W. Ham; two *s*]. *Address:* 56 Chiltley Way, Liphook, Hampshire. *Club:* United Service.

**ASHBRIDGE, Sir Noel,** Kt 1935; BSc; MICE; MIEE; FKC; FIRE; Knight of Royal Order of Dannebrog (Danish); *b* 10 Dec. 1889; 4th *s* of John Ashbridge, Wanstead; *m* 1926, Olive Maude (*d* 1948), *d* of Rowland Strickland, Erith; two *d*. *Educ:* Forest Sch.; King's Coll., London. Engineering training with Yarrow and Co., Ltd, and British Thomson-Houston Co., Ltd; served European War, 1914-19, Royal Fusiliers and RE; six years Marconi's, at Writtle Experimental Station; joined BBC 1926 as Assistant Chief Engineer; late Controller of Engineering, BBC; Deputy Dir-Gen., BBC, 1943-48; Dir of Technical Services, BBC, 1948-52; Chm., Radio Research Bd, 1952-57. President Institution of Electrical Engineers, 1941-42; Member of Television Cttee, 1934 and 1943, and Television Advisory Cttee, 1935; Vice-Pres. Inst. of Radio Engineers, 1947; Pres. Junior Inst. of Engineers, 1949-50. *Publications:* various technical and scientific papers. *Address:* Tyneham, Highview Road, Sidcup, Kent. *Club:* Athenæum.

**ASHBROOK,** 10th Viscount, *cr* 1751; **Desmond Llowarch Edward Flower,** MBE 1945; DL; Baron of Castle Durrow, 1733; Member of Council of Duchy of Lancaster, since 1957; *b* 9 July 1905; *o s* of 9th Viscount and late Gladys, *d* of late Gen. Sir George Wentworth A. Higginson, GCB, GCVO; *S* father, 1936; *m* 1934, Elizabeth, *er d* of late Capt. John Egerton-Warburton, and of late Hon. Mrs Waters; two *s* one *d*. *Educ:* Eton; Balliol Coll., Oxford (BA 1927). Served War of 1939-45, RA. Formerly a Chartered Accountant. JP, 1946-67, DL 1949-, Vice-Lieutenant, 1961-67, Cheshire. *Heir: s* Hon. Michael Llowarch Warburton Flower, *b* 9 Dec. 1935. *Address:* Arley Hall, Northwich, Cheshire. *T:* Arley 204. *Club:* Travellers'.

**ASHBURNHAM, Captain Sir Denny Reginald,** 12th Bt *cr* 1661; Captain South Staffordshire Regiment; *b* 24 March 1916; *o surv s* of Sir Fleetwood Ashburnham, 11th Bt, and Elfrida, *d* of late James Kirkley, JP, Cleadon Park, Co. Durham; *S* father 1953; *m* 1946, Mary Frances, *d* of Major Robert Pascoe Mair, Wick, Udimore, Sussex; one *s* two *d*. *Heir: s* John Anchitel Fleetwood Ashburnham, *b* 25 June 1951. *Address:* Little Broomham, Guestling, Hastings, Sussex; (seat) Broomham, Hastings.

**ASHBURTON,** 6th Baron, *cr* 1835; **Alexander Francis St Vincent Baring,** KG 1969; KCVO 1961; JP; Lord Lieutenant and Custos Rotulorum of Hampshire since 1960; High Steward of Winchester, since 1967; Receiver-General to the Duchy of Cornwall since 1961; Chairman, Hampshire Police Authority, since 1967 (Chairman, Hampshire & Isle of Wight Police Authority, 1961-67); *b* 7 April 1898; *o s* of 5th Baron and Hon. Mabel Edith Hood (*d* 1904), *d* of 4th Viscount Hood; *S* father, 1938; *m* 1924, Hon. Doris Mary Thérèse Harcourt, *e d* of 1st Viscount Harcourt; two *s*. *Educ:* Eton; Royal Military Coll. Lieut The Grays, 1917-23; Flt-Lt AAF, 1939, retd as Group Captain, 1944. Director: Baring Brothers & Co. Ltd, 1962-68 (Managing Director, 1928-62); Alliance Assurance, 1932-68; Pressed Steel Co. Ltd, 1944-66; Mem. London Cttee, Hongkong & Shanghai Banking Corp., 1935-39. Treasurer, King Edward VII Hospital Fund for London, 1955-64; Trustee: King George's Jubilee Trust, 1949-68; Chantrey Bequest, 1963-; St Cross Hospital of Noble Poverty, Winchester, 1961-. President: Hampshire & Isle of Wight Territorial Assoc., 1960-67 (Mem., 1951-60); Eastern Wessex Territorial Assoc., 1968-. CC 1945-, CA 1955-, JP 1951, Vice-Lieut, 1951-60, Hants. KStJ 1960. *Heir: s* Hon. John Francis Harcourt Baring, *qv*. *Address:* Itchen Stoke House, Alresford, Hants. *T:* Alresford 2479. *Club:* Turf.

**ASHBY, Sir Eric,** Kt 1956; FRS 1963; DSc London, MA Cantab; DIC; Master of Clare College, Cambridge, since July 1959; Fellow of Clare College, 1958; Chairman, Royal Commission on Environmental Pollution, since 1970; *b* 1904; *s* of Herbert Charles Ashby, Bromley, Kent, and Helena Chater; *m* 1931, Elizabeth Helen Farries, Castle-Douglas, Scotland; two *s*. *Educ:* City of London Sch.; Imperial Coll. of Science, Univ. of London; Univ. of Chicago. Demonstrator at Imperial Coll., 1926-29; Commonwealth Fund Fellow in Univ. of Chicago and Desert Laboratory of Carnegie Institution, 1929-31; Lectr, Imperial Coll. of Science, 1931-35; Reader in Botany, Bristol Univ., 1935-37; Prof. of Botany, Univ. of Sydney, Australia, 1938-46; Harrison Prof. of Botany and Dir of Botanical Labs, Univ. of Manchester, 1946-50; Pres. and Vice-Chancellor, Queen's Univ., Belfast, 1950-59. Chm., Aust. National Research Council, 1940-42; Chm., Professorial Board, Univ. of Sydney, 1942-44; Mem., Power Alcohol Committee of Enquiry, 1940-41; conducted enquiry for Prime Minister into enlistment of scientific resources in war, 1942; Trustee, Aust. Museum, 1942-46; Dir, Scientific

Liaison Bureau, 1942-43; Counsellor and Chargé d'Affaires at Australian Legation, Moscow, USSR, 1945-46; Member of: Advisory Council on Scientific Policy, 1950-53; Nuffield Provincial Hospitals Trust, 1951-59; Advisory Council on Scientific and Industrial Research, 1954-60; Chairman: Scientific Grants Cttee, DSIR, 1955-56; Postgraduate Grants Cttee, DSIR, 1956-60; Northern Ireland Adv. Council for Education, 1953-58; Adult Education Cttee, 1953-54; Cttee of Award of Commonwealth Fund, 1963- (Member, 1956-61); Member: Univ. Grants Cttee, 1959-67; Commonwealth Scholarship Commn, 1960-; Council of Royal Soc., 1964-65; Governing Body, Sch. of Oriental and African Studies, Univ. of London, 1965-; Chm., Commn for post-secondary and higher education in Nigeria, 1959-61; Vice-Chm. Assoc. of Univs of Brit. Commonwealth, 1959-61; Vice-Chancellor, Cambridge Univ., 1967-69; Pres., Brit. Assoc. for the Advancement of Science, 1963. Godkin Lectr, Harvard Univ., 1964; Whidden Lectr, Hamilton Univ., 1970; Trustee: Ciba Foundation, 1966-; British Museum, 1969-, Fellow: Imperial Coll. of Science; Davenport Coll., Yale Univ.; Hon. Fellow, Royal Inst. of Chemistry. Hon. LLD: St Andrews's; Aberdeen; Rand; London; Wales; Colombia; Chicago; Hon. ScD, Dublin; Hon. DSc: NUI; Univ. of Nigeria; Southampton; Hon. DLitt, W Ont; Hon. DPhil, Tech. Univ. Berlin; Hon. DCL, East Anglia; Hon. DHL Yale. *Publications:* papers on aspects of experimental botany and on education; Environment and Plant Development, translated from German; German-English Botanical Terminology (with Elizabeth Helen Ashby); Food Shipment from Australia in Wartime; Challenge to Education; Scientist in Russia; Technology and the Academics; Community of Universities; African Universities and Western Tradition; Universities: British, Indian, African (with Mary Anderson); Masters and Scholars; the rise of the student estate (with Mary Anderson). *Recreations:* chamber music, mountain walking. *Address:* Clare College, Cambridge. *Club:* Athenæum.

**ASHBY, Dame Margery I. C.;** *see* Corbett Ashby.

**ASHCOMBE,** 4th Baron, *cr* 1892; **Henry Edward Cubitt;** late RAF; Chairman, Cubitt Estates Ltd; *b* 31 March 1924; *er s* of 3rd Baron Ashcombe; *S* father, 1962; *m* 1955, Ghislaine (marr. diss. 1968), *o d* of Cornelius Willem Dresselhuys, Long Island, New York. *Educ:* Eton. Served War of 1939-45, RAF. Consul-General in London for the Principality of Monaco, 1961-68. *Heir: uncle,* Hon. Archibald Edward Cubitt [*b* 16 Jan. 1901; *m* 1st, 1926, Lady Irene Helen Pratt (marr. diss., 1933), *d* of 4th Marquess Camden; one *s*; 2nd, 1934, Sibell Margaret (marr. diss., 1949), *er d* of R. C. Norman, JP; one *s* one *d* (and one *d* decd)]. *Address:* Denbies, Dorking, Surrey. *Clubs:* White's, St James'.

*See also Earl of Harrington.*

**ASHCROFT, David,** TD 1957; MA Cantab; Headmaster, Cheltenham College, since 1959; *b* 20 May 1920; *s* of late A. H. Ashcroft, DSO; *m* 1949, Joan Elizabeth Young; two *s* three *d*. *Educ:* Rugby Sch.; Gonville and Caius Coll., Cambridge. War Service, 1940-46 (despatches). Asst Master, Rossall Sch., 1946-50; Asst Master, Rugby Sch., 1950-59. *Recreations:* most in general, none in particular. *Address:* College House, Cheltenham, Glos. *T:* Cheltenham 24841.

**ASHCROFT, Reverend Lawrence;** retired as Archdeacon of Stow and Vicar of Burton-on-Stather (1954-62); *b* 1901; *s* of Lawrence Ashcroft; *m* 1927, Barbara Louise Casson; two *s* three *d*. *Educ:* University Coll., Durham; Lichfield Theological Coll. Deacon, 1926; Priest, 1927; Curate of Ulverston, 1926-29, of Egremont, 1929-30; District Sec., Brit. and Foreign Bible Society, 1930-33; Vicar of St Saviour's, Retford, 1934-40; Chaplain to the Forces (Emergency Commission), 1940-43; Rector of St Michael Stoke, Coventry, 1943; Rural Dean of Coventry, 1949; Hon. Canon of Coventry, 1952; Hon. Canon of Lincoln, 1954. *Address:* c/o Lloyds Bank Ltd, St Helier, Jersey, Channel Islands.

**ASHCROFT, Dame Peggy, (Edith Margaret Emily),** DBE 1956 (CBE 1951); actress; Director, Royal Shakespeare Co., since 1968; *b* 22 Dec. 1907; *d* of William Worsley Ashcroft and Violet Maud Bernheim; *m* 1st, 1929, Rupert Hart-Davis (marr. diss.; he was knighted, 1967); 2nd, 1934, Theodore Komisarjevsky (marr. diss.); 3rd, 1940, Jeremy Hutchinson, QC (marr. diss., 1966); one *s* one *d*. *Educ:* Woodford Sch., Croydon; Central Sch. of Dramatic Art. Member of the Arts Council, 1962-64. First appeared as Margaret in Dear Brutus, Birmingham Repertory Theatre, 1926; parts include: Bessie in One Day More, Everyman, Eve in When Adam Delved, Wyndham's, 1927, Mary Bruin in The Land of Heart's Desire, Hester in The Silver Cord, 1928; Constance Neville in She Stoops to Conquer, Naomi in Jew Süss, 1929; Desdemona in Othello with Paul Robeson, 1930; Fanny in Sea Fever, 1931; Cleopatra, Imogen, Rosalind, etc, at Old Vic and Sadler's Wells, 1932; Juliet at New, 1935; Nina in Seagull, New, 1936; Portia, Lady Teazle, and, Irina in Three Sisters, Queen's, 1937-38; Yeliena in White Guard and Viola, Phoenix, 1938-39; Cecily Cardew in The Importance of Being Earnest, 1939-40, and Dinah in Cousin Muriel, 1940, both at Globe; revival of Importance of Being Earnest, Phoenix, 1942; Catherine in The Dark River, Whitehall, 1943; Ophelia, Titania, Duchess of Malfi, Haymarket Repertory Season, 1944-45; Evelyn Holt in Edward my Son, His Majesty's, 1947; Catherine Sloper in The Heiress, Haymarket, 1949; Beatrice and Cordelia, Memorial Theatre, Stratford-on-Avon, 1950; Viola, Electra and Mistress Page, Old Vic 1950-51; Hester Collyer in the Deep Blue Sea, Duchess, 1952; Cleopatra, Stratford-on-Avon and Princes, 1953; title-rôle, Hedda Gabler, Lyric, Hammersmith and Westminster, 1954; Beatrice in Much Ado About Nothing, Stratford Festival Company, 1955 (London, provinces and continental tour); Miss Madrigal in The Chalk Garden, Haymarket, 1956; Shen Te in The Good Woman of Setzuan, Royal Court, 1956; Rosalind, Imogen, Cymbeline, Stratford-on-Avon, 1957; Julia Rajk in Shadow of Heroes, Piccadilly, 1958; Stratford-on-Avon Season, 1960: Katharina in The Taming of the Shrew; Paulina in The Winter's Tale; The Hollow Crown, Aldwych, 1961; title rôle in The Duchess of Malfi, Aldwych, 1961; Emilia in Othello, Stratford-on-Avon, 1961, also Madame Ranevskaya in the Cherry Orchard, subseq. Aldwych; Margaret of Anjou in Henry VI and Margaret in Edward IV, also Margaret in Richard III, Stratford-on-Avon, 1963, Aldwych, 1964; Mme Arkadina in The Seagull, Queen's, 1964; Mother in Days in the Trees, Aldwych, 1966; Mrs Alving in Ghosts, 1967; A Delicate Balance, Aldwych, 1969; Beth in Landscape, Aldwych, 1969; Katharine of Aragon in Henry VIII, Stratford-on-Avon, 1969; The Plebeians Rehearse the Uprising, Aldwych, 1970. Entered films 1933;

subsequent films include: The Wandering Jew, The Thirty-nine Steps, The Nun's Story (played Mother Mathilde), etc. King's Gold Medal, Norway, 1955; Hon. DLitt: Oxford, 1961; Leicester, 1964; Hon. DLit London, 1965. Hon. Fellow, St Hugh's College, Oxford, 1964. *Address:* Manor Lodge, Frognal Lane, NW3.

**ASHDOWN, Rt. Rev. Hugh Edward;** *see* Newcastle, Bishop of.

**ASHE, Derick Rosslyn,** CMG 1966; HM Diplomatic Service; Minister, Tokyo, since 1969; *b* 20 Jan. 1919; *s* of late Frederick Allen Ashe and late Rosalind Ashe (*née* Mitchell); *m* 1957, Rissa Guinness, *d* of Capt. Hon. Trevor Tempest Parker, DSC, Royal Navy (retd) and late Mrs Parker; one *s* one *d*. *Educ:* Bradfield Coll.; Trinity Coll., Oxford. HM Forces, 1940-46 (despatches 1945). Second Sec., Berlin and Frankfurt-am-Main, 1947-49; Private Sec. to Permanent Under-Sec. of State for German Section of FO, 1950-53; First Sec., La Paz, 1953-55; FO, 1955-57; First Sec. (Information), Madrid, 1957-61; FO, 1961-62; Counsellor and Head of Chancery: Addis Ababa, 1962-64; Havana, 1964-66; Head of Security Dept, FCO (formerly FO), 1966-69. Knight of the Order of Orange-Nassau (with swords), 1945. *Recreation:* riding. *Address:* 30 Gloucester Square, W2. *T:* 01-262 4647. *Club:* Travellers'.

**ASHENHEIM, Sir Neville (Noel),** Kt 1963; CBE 1958; Leader of Government Business in the Senate and Minister without Portfolio, Jamaica, since 1967; *b* 18 Dec. 1900; *s* of Lewis Ashenheim and Estelle Lillian de Cordova; *m* 1926, Leonie Vivienne Delevante; three *s*. *Educ:* Jamaica Coll.; Munro Coll.; Wadham Coll., Oxford. BA 1922, MA 1944. Admitted Solicitor of Supreme Court, 1926, and joined father's firm of Milholland, Ashenheim & Stone. HM's Jamaican Ambassador to the USA, 1962-67. Chairman: "The Gleaner" Company, 1946-67 (newspaper in Caribbean founded by his forbears in 1834); Jamaica Industrial Development Corporation, 1952-57; Caribbean Cement Co.; Caribbean Steel Co.; Consolidated Internat. Corp.; Standard Life Assurance Co. (Jamaican Branch); Jamaica Housing Develt Co.; Abdel Lighting Products Ltd; Blinds & Furnishings Ltd. Director: Lascelles de Merado & Co. Ltd; Henriques Brothers Ltd; West Indies Glass Co. Ltd. Hon. DHL Hebrew Union Coll., 1964. *Address:* The British American Building, Knutsford Boulevard, Kingston 5, Jamaica. *Clubs:* Jamaica, Liguanea, St Andrew, Kingston Cricket, Jamaica Jockey (all in Jamaica).

**ASHER, Florence May,** RBA; FRSA 1950; figure and landscape painter; *b* Nottingham, 2 May 1888; 2nd *d* of Joseph William and Ruth Asher. *Educ:* Nottingham. Studied at the Royal Academy Schs (Silver Medallist and Landseer Scholarship); exhibited Royal Academy, International Exhibition, America, Stockholm, Toronto, Paris Salon, Australia, New Zealand; sold picture, In the Tyrol, to Canadian Government for permanent collection at Toronto. *Recreations:* reading, gardening, and scientific interests. *Address:* 28 Rushworth Road, Reigate, Surrey.

**ASHER, Mrs Peter;** *see* Shuard, Amy.

**ASHERSON, Nehemiah,** MA Cape; MB, BS London; FRCS, LRCP; FZS; MRI, etc; Fellow International College of Surgeons; Hon. Fellow Surgical Academy, Madrid; Associate, Royal Institute of Chemistry, 1919; Hon. Cons. Surgeon, The Royal National (Central London) Throat, Nose, and Ear Hospital (late Member of Board of Governors, 1948-49-50-58); late Hon. Secretary to the Medical Council; Lecturer to the Institute of Otology and Laryngology (Member Academic Board); Teacher in Oto-laryngology in the University of London; Consulting Surgeon for Diseases of the Ear, Nose, and Throat to the NE, NW and SE regional hospital boards, including the Queen Elizabeth Hospital for Children; Fellow Royal Society of Medicine (late President, Section of Laryngology; Member Council, Section History of Medicine; late Member Council Section Otology, and Library Committee); Trustee Hunterian Society; Fellow, late Councillor, Medical Society of London; *b* 1897; *s* of Isaac Asherson; *m*; one *s* one *d*. *Educ:* South African Coll.; Univ. of Cape Town (Entrance Scholar); University Coll. and Hospital, London; postgraduate study in speciality in London and Vienna. Medallist in Chemistry; exhibitioner at the BA examination; Jamieson Scholar at MA; Alexander Bruce Gold Medallist in Surgery and Liston Gold Medal in Surgical Pathology, University Coll. Hosp.; Geoffrey Duveen Travelling Scholar of the Univ. of London in Oto-rhino Laryngology; late Harker Smith Cancer (radium) Registrar and Casualty Surgical Officer at University Coll. Hosp.; Chief Asst to the Royal Ear Hospital, University Coll. Hosp.; Chief Asst to the Ear, Nose, and Throat Dept of the Bolingbroke Hospital, etc; Late: Ear Consultant to Army Medical Boards; Surgeon Emergency Medical Service; Consulting Surgeon to LCC and to the Charterhouse Rheumatism Clinic; Pres., Hunterian Soc. Hunterian Prof., RCS, 1942. Mem. Bd of Visitors, Royal Instn. *Publications:* Diagnosis and Treatment of Foreign Bodies in the Upper Food and Respiratory Passages, 1932; Acute Otitis and Mastoiditis in General Practice, 1934; Chronic Ear Discharge (Otorrhœa) and its complications, 1936; Otogenic Cerebellar Abscess, Hunterian Lecture, 1942; Identification by Frontal Sinus Prints, 1965; The Deafness of Beethoven, 1965; communications in Jl of Laryngology, of the Royal Society of Medicine, in The Lancet and in medical journals on subjects relating to the speciality. *Address:* 21 Harley Street, W1. *T:* 01-580 3197; Green Shutters, West Kingston, West Sussex. *Clubs:* Reform, Savage.

**ASHFORD, (Albert) Reginald,** CMG 1962; Assistant Secretary, Board of Customs and Excise, since 1952; *b* 30 June 1914; *s* of late Ernest Ashford; *m* 1946, Mary Anne Ross Davidson, *d* of late Thomas Davidson; one *s*. *Educ:* Ealing Grammar Sch.; London Sch. of Economics. *Address:* Sandy Lodge, Westbury Road, Northwood, Middlesex. *T:* 21956. *Club:* Reform.

**ASHFORD, George Francis,** OBE 1945; a Managing Director, The British Petroleum Co. Ltd, since 1969 (a Director since 1967); *b* 5 July 1911; *s* of G. W. Ashford and L. M. Redfern; *m* 1950, Eleanor Vera Alexander; two *s*. *Educ:* Malvern Coll.; Trinity Hall, Cambridge; Birmingham Univ. Served War of 1939-45, Army, N Africa and Italy (despatches 1944). Distillers Co. Ltd, 1937-67: Solicitor, 1937; Legal Adviser, 1945; Dir, 1956; Management Cttee, 1963-67. Pres., British Plastics Fedn, 1966-67; Vice-Pres., Soc. of Chemical Industry, 1966-69; Mem. Economic Policy Cttee for Chemical Industry, 1967-. *Recreation:* gardening. *Address:* Meadow House, Kingston Hill, Surrey. *T:* 01-546 6589. *Club:* Royal Automobile.

**ASHFORD, Reginald;** *see* Ashford, A. R.

**ASHIOTIS, Costas;** High Commissioner of Cyprus in London since 1966; *b* 1908; *m. Educ:* Pancyprian Gymnasium, Nicosia; London Sch. of Economics. Journalist and editor; joined Govt Service, 1942; Asst Comr of Labour, 1948; Dir-Gen., Min. of Foreign Affairs, 1960. Mem. Cyprus delegns to UN and to internat. confs. MBE 1952. *Publications:* Labour Conditions in Cyprus during the War Years, 1939-45; literary articles. *Address:* Cyprus High Commission, 93 Park Street, W1. *T:* 01-499 8272.

**ASHKANASY, Maurice,** CMG 1961; QC (Victoria); LLM; *b* 16 Oct. 1901; *s* of late Aaron Solomon Ashkanasy and Annie Ashkanasy; *m* 1927, Heather Helen Epstein; two *s* one *d. Educ:* South Melbourne Coll.; Melbourne High Sch.; Melbourne Univ. Admitted to Victorian Bar, 1924; KC Victoria, 1940, NSW, 1949; QC Tasmania, 1959. Served War of 1939-45 (despatches): Lieut-Col, AAG, AIF, Malaya, 1st Aust. Corps, 2nd and 3rd Aust. Corps and New Guinea Forces. Past Chm. Victorian Bar Council, 1952-55. Pres. Melbourne High School Old Boys, 1924-28. Past Pres. Victorian Jewish Board of Deputies; Dep. Pres. Executive Council of Australian Jewry; Vice-Pres. Aust. Section Internat. Commn of Jurists. *Recreation:* fishing. *Address:* 205 William Street, Melbourne Victoria 3000, Australia. *T:* BL 7161. *Clubs:* Naval and Military; Constitutional (Melbourne) (Pres. 1958).

**ASHKENAZY, Vladimir;** concert pianist; *b* Gorky, Russia, 6 July 1937; *m* 1961, Thorunn Tryggvason, Iceland; two *s* one *d. Educ:* Central Musical Sch., Moscow; Conservatoire, Moscow. Studied under Sumbatyan; Lev Oborin class, 1955: grad 1960. Internat. Chopin Comp., Warsaw, at age of 17 (gained 2nd prize); won Queen Elizabeth Internat. Piano Comp., Brussels, at age of 18 (gold medal). Joint winner (with John Ogdon) of Tchaikovsky Piano Comp., Moscow, 1962. London debut with London Symph. Orch. under George Hurst, and subseq. solo recital, Festival Hall, 1963. Has played in many countries. Makes recordings. *Address:* Brekkugerdi 22, Reykjavik, Iceland.

**ASHLEY;** *see* Havinden, A. E.

**ASHLEY, Francis Noel,** CMG 1937; Squadron Leader RAFVR; *b* 11 Dec. 1884; *s* of Frederick Moorewood Ashley and Edith. *d* of J. O. Hodges, Penny Hill Park, Bagshot; *m* 1913, Marjorie, *d* of James Wills Robinson, Barrister-at-law; one *d. Educ:* Westminster. Sussex Militia Artillery, 1902-04; Cape Colonial Mounted Forces, 1904-08; Cadet, Political Service, Nigeria, 1908; West Africa Frontier Force, 1915; Resident, Southern Provinces, Nigeria, 1924-28; Resident Commissioner British Solomon Islands Protectorate, 1929-39; RAFVR, 1940-44; employed by Bahamas Government, 1944-46. *Recreations:* cricket, golf. *Address:* Flat 21, Southbury, Lawn Road, Guildford. *T:* Guildford 62480.

**ASHLEY, Jack;** MP (Lab) Stoke-on-Trent, South, since 1966; *b* 6 Dec. 1922; *s* of John Ashley and Isabella Bridge; *m* 1951, Pauline Kay Crispin; three *d. Educ:* St Patrick's Elem. Sch., Widnes, Lancs; Ruskin Coll., Oxford; Gonville and Caius Coll., Cambridge. Labourer and cranedriver, 1936-46; Shop Steward, Convener and Nat. Exec. Mem., Chemical Workers' Union, 1946; Scholarship, Ruskin Coll., 1946-48 and Caius Coll., 1948-51 (Chm. Cambridge Labour Club, 1950; Pres. Cambridge Union, 1951); BBC Radio Producer, 1951-57; Commonwealth Fund Fellow, 1955; BBC Senior Television Producer, 1957-66; Mem., General Advisory Council, BBC, 1967-69. Councillor, Borough of Widnes, 1945. *Recreations:* walking, golf, reading. *Address:* 17 Bridge Road, Epsom, Surrey. *T:* Epsom 23784.

**ASHLEY, Maurice Percy;** *b* 4 Sept. 1907; *s* of Sir Percy Ashley, KBE, and Lady Ashley (*née* Hayman); *m* 1935, Phyllis Mary Griffiths; one *s* one *d. Educ:* St Paul's Sch., London; New Coll., Oxford (History Scholar). 1st Class Hons Modern History; DPhil Oxon. Historical Research Asst to Sir Winston Churchill, 1929-33; Editorial Staff, The Manchester Guardian, 1933-37; Editorial Staff, The Times, 1937-39; Editor, Britain Today, 1939-40. Served in Army, 1940-45 (Major, Intelligence Corps). Deputy Editor, The Listener, 1946-58, Editor, 1958-67; Research Fellow, Loughborough Univ. of Technology, 1968-70. Pres. Cromwell Association, 1961. *Publications:* Financial and Commercial Policy under the Cromwellian Protectorate, 1934 (revised, 1962); Marlborough, 1939; Louis XIV and the Greatness of France, 1946; John Wildrman: Plotter and Postmaster, 1947; Mr President, 1948; England in the Seventeenth Century, 1952 (revised, 1967); Cromwell's Generals, 1954; The Greatness of Oliver Cromwell, 1957 (revised 1967); Oliver Cromwell and the Puritan Revolution, 1958; Great Britain to 1688, 1961; The Stuarts in Love, 1963; Life in Stuart England, 1964; The Glorious Revolution of 1688, 1966 (revised, 1968); Churchill as Historian, 1968; A Golden Century, 1598-1715, 1969. *Recreations:* bridge, gardening, painting. *Address:* 34 Wood Lane, Ruislip, Middlesex. *T:* Ruislip 35993. *Club:* Reform.

**ASHLEY-COOPER,** family name of **Earl of Shaftesbury.**

**ASHLEY-SCARLETT, Lt-Col Henry,** DSO 1918; JP; Past Councillor Hampstead Borough Council (which is now in Camden Borough Council); *b* Jan. 1886; *m* 1928, Marjorie Laird, *d* of Percy Collins, JP, Frinton-on-Sea, Essex. *Educ:* Berkhampstead Sch.; Lycée Carnot, Paris. Capt. and Adjutant, 13th Royal Fusiliers; Major, 2nd in Command, 9th Royal Fusiliers; Lieut-Col, 7th Norfolk Regt; Lt-Col, Royal Fusiliers (Reserve of Officers); served European War, 1914-19 (despatches thrice, DSO); War of 1939-45, attached to RAF, 1943-45; Sch. Manager, Fitzjohns, Fleet and New End Primary Schs; Governor of Royal Soldiers' Daughters' Sch.; ex-Council Royal Society St George; Mayor, Borough of Hampstead, 1957-59 (Deputy Mayor, 1959-61, 1962-63); Member: London Magistrates Club; past Chairman, HM Prison, Wormwood Scrubs; past Visiting Magistrate, HM Prison, Wandsworth; President, Hampstead Old People's Homesteads. Vice-Pres. Hampstead Conservative Assoc. Managing Director: Hillpath Ltd; Trowchurch Ltd. JP London. *Recreation:* golf. *Address:* 43 Ferncroft Avenue, NW3.

**ASHMOLE, Professor Bernard,** CBE 1957; MC; MA, BLitt; Hon. ARIBA, FBA; Fellow of Lincoln College, Oxford; Hon. Fellow, Hertford College, Oxford, 1961; *b* Ilford, 22 June 1894; 2nd *s* of late William Ashmole and Caroline Wharton Tiver; *m* 1920, Dorothy Irene, 2nd *d* of late Everard de Peyer, Newent Court, Glos; one *s* two *d. Educ:* Forest; privately; Hertford Coll., Oxford (Classical Scholar). 11th Royal Fusiliers, 1914-18; Craven Fellow, and Student of the British schools at Athens and Rome, 1920-22; Asst Curator of Coins, Ashmolean Museum, 1923-25; Director of the British Sch. at Rome, 1925-

28; Florence Bursar, RIBA, 1937; Hon. Member of the Archæological Institute of America, 1940; RAF 1940-45, Adjutant of 84 Sqdn in Greece, Iraq, Western Desert, Sumatra and India (despatches twice, Hellenic Flying Cross). Yates Professor of Archæology, University of London, 1929-48; Keeper of Greek and Roman Antiquities, British Museum, 1939-56; Lincoln Professor of Classical Archæology, Univ. of Oxford, 1956-61; Geddes-Harrower Professor of Greek Art and Archæology, Univ. of Aberdeen, 1961-63; Visiting Professor in Archæology, Univ. of Yale, 1964. Rhind Lectr, 1952; Myres Memorial Lectr, Oxford, 1961; Norton Lectr, Archæological Inst. of America, 1963; Wrightsman Lectr, New York, 1967. Hon. LLD Aberdeen, 1968. *Publications:* Catalogue of Ancient Marbles at Ince Blundell, 1929; Greek Sculpture and Painting (with Beazley), 1932, repr. 1966; The Ancient World (with Groenewegen-Frankfort), 1967; Olympia: sculptures of the temple of Zeus (with Yalouris and Frantz), 1967; articles on Greek sculpture in the Journal of Hellenic Studies and other periodicals. *Address:* The Mill House, Iffley, Oxford. *T:* Oxford 78310. *Club:* Athenæum.

**ASHMORE, Prof. Alick;** Director Daresbury Nuclear Physics Laboratory, Science Research Council, since 1970; *b* 7 Nov. 1920; *s* of Frank Owen Ashmore and Beatrice Maud Swindells; *m* 1947, Eileen Elsie Fuller; two *s* three *d*. *Educ:* King Edward VII Sch., Lytham; King's Coll., London. Experimental Officer, RRDE, Malvern, 1941-47; Lecturer in physics, University of Liverpool, 1947-59; Queen Mary Coll., London: Reader in experimental physics, 1960-64; Prof. of Nuclear Physics, 1964-70, also Head of Physics Dept, 1968-70. *Publications:* research publications on nuclear and elementary-particle physics in Proc. Phys. Soc., Nuclear Physics, Physical Review. *Recreations:* walking, camping. *Address:* 3 Dane Bank Road, Lymm, Cheshire. *T:* Lymm 3735.

**ASHMORE, Vice-Adm. Edward Beckwith,** CB 1966; DSC 1942; Vice-Chief of the Naval Staff, 1969-71; *b* 11 Dec. 1919; *er s* of Vice-Admiral L. H. Ashmore, *qv*; *m* 1942, Elizabeth Mary Doveton Sturdee, *d* of Rear-Admiral Sir Lionel Sturdee, Bt, *qv*; one *s* one *d* (and one *d* decd). *Educ:* RNC, Dartmouth. Served HMS Birmingham, Jupiter, Middleton, 1938-42; qualified in Signals, 1943; Staff of C-in-C Home Fleet, Flag Lieut, 4th Cruiser Sqdn, 1944-45; qualified Interpreter in Russian, 1946; Asst Naval Attaché, Moscow, 1946-47; Squadron Communications Officer, 3rd Aircraft Carrier Squadron, 1950; Commander 1950; comd HMS Alert, 1952-53; Captain 1955; Captain (F) 6th Frigate Sqdn, and CO HMS Blackpool, 1958; Director of Plans, Admiralty and Min. of Defence, 1960-62; Commander British Forces Caribbean Area, 1963-64; Rear-Admiral, 1965; Vice-Adm. 1968; Asst Chief of the Defence Staff, Signals, 1965-67; Flag Officer, Second-in-Command, Far East Fleet, 1967-68. *Recreations:* usual. *Address:* South Cottage, Headley Down, near Bordon, Hants. *T:* Headley Down 3236. *Club:* United Service.

*See also Vice-Adm. L. H. Ashmore, Vice-Adm. P. W. B. Ashmore, Sir Francis Sykes, Bt.*

**ASHMORE, Vice-Adm. Leslie Haliburton,** CB 1947; DSO 1944; *b* 21 Feb. 1893; *e s* of late Arthur Haliburton Ashmore, Shanklin, IoW; *m* 1919, Tamara Vasilevna Shutt, Petrograd; two *s*. *Educ:* Sandroyd; RN Colleges, Osborne and Dartmouth. Lieut 1915; European War, 1914-18: served in submarines; commanded HM Submarines C35, V3, E46, and subsequently L52. Comdr 1928; RN Staff Coll.; commanded HM ships Wallflower and Cyclamen; Capt. 1934; Imperial Defence Coll.; commanded HM ships Kent, Valiant and Malaya; Rear-Admiral, 1944; Flag Officer commanding Reserve Fleet, 1945-47; retired list, 1947; Vice-Adm. retd, 1948. *Address:* Godden Green Lodge, Godden Green, near Sevenoaks, Kent. *T:* Sevenoaks 61594.

*See also Vice-Adm. E. B. Ashmore, Vice-Adm. P. W. B. Ashmore.*

**ASHMORE, Vice-Adm. Peter William Beckwith,** CB 1968; MVO (4th Class) 1948; DSC 1942; Chief of Allied Staff in NATO Naval HQ, Southern Europe, since March 1970; *b* 4 Feb. 1921; *yr s* of Vice-Adm. L. H. Ashmore, *qv*; *m* 1952, Patricia Moray Buller, *o d* of late Admiral Sir Henry Buller, GCVO, CB; one *s* three *d*. *Educ:* Yardley Court; RN Coll., Dartmouth. Midshipman, 1939. Served War of 1939-45, principally in destroyers (despatches); Lieut, 1941; Comdr, 1951; Capt., 1957. Equerry (temp.) to King George VI, 1946-48; Extra Equerry, 1948; Extra Equerry to the Queen, 1952-. Deputy Director, RN Staff Coll., Greenwich, 1957; Capt. (F) Dartmouth Training Squadron, 1960-61; Imperial Defence Coll., 1962; Admiralty, Plans Division, 1963; Rear-Adm. 1966; Flag Officer, Admiralty Interview Board, 1966-67; Chief of Staff to C-in-C Western Fleet and to NATO C-in-C Eastern Atlantic, 1967-69. *Recreations:* fishing, golf, squash. *Address:* c/o Ministry of Defence (Navy), SW1. *Club:* United Service.

*See also Vice-Adm. E. B. Ashmore, Vice-Adm. L. H. Ashmore.*

**ASHMORE, Prof. Philip George;** Professor of Physical Chemistry, The University of Manchester Institute of Science and Technology, since 1963; *b* 5 May 1916; *m* 1943, Ann Elizabeth Scott; three *s* one *d*. *Educ:* Emmanuel Coll., Cambridge. Fellow, Asst Tutor and Dir of Studies of Natural Sciences, Emmanuel Coll., Cambridge, 1949-59; Lecturer in Physical Chem., Univ. of Cambridge, 1953-63; Fellow and Tutor to Advanced Students, Churchill Coll., Cambridge, 1959-63. *Publications:* The Catalysis and Inhibition of Chemical Reactions, 1963; RIC Monographs for Teachers: No 5 and No 9; many papers in: TFS, International Symposium on Combustion, Jl of Catalysis. *Address:* Department of Chemistry, University of Manchester Institute of Science and Technology, Manchester M60 1QD. *T:* 061-236 3311.

**ASHTON,** family name of **Baron Ashton of Hyde.**

**ASHTON OF HYDE,** 2nd Baron *cr* 1911; **Thomas Henry Raymond Ashton,** DL, JP; Major, late 1st Royal Gloucestershire Hussars, RAC, TA; Joint Master, Heythrop, 1934-36, sole Master, 1936-48, Joint Master, 1948-52; *b* 2 Oct. 1901; *s* of 1st Baron and Eva Margaret (*d* 1938) *d* of J. H. James Kingswood, Watford, Herts; *S* father, 1933; *m* 1925, Marjorie Nell, *d* of late Hon. Marshall Brooks; one *s* (two *d* decd). *Educ:* Eton; New Coll., Oxford (MA). DL, JP Glos. *Recreations:* hunting, shooting, deerstalking. *Heir: s* Hon. Thomas John Ashton [*b* 19 Nov. 1926; *m* 1957, Pauline Trewlove, *er d* of Lieut-Col R. H. L. Brackenbury, Yerdley House, Long Compton, Shipston-on-Stour; two *s* two *d*]. *Address:* Broadwell Hill, Moreton-in-Marsh, Glos. *TA:* Broadwell Hill, Stow-on-the-Wold. *T:* Stow-on-the-Wold 626. *Clubs:* Boodle's, Farmer's.

**ASHTON, Anthony Southcliffe;** Member of Board (Finance and Corporate Planning), Post Office Corporation, since 1970; *b* 5 July 1916; *s* of late Prof. Thomas Southcliffe Ashton, FBA, and of Mrs Marion Hague Ashton; *m* 1939, Katharine Marion Louise Vivian; two *d*. *Educ:* Manchester Grammar Sch.; Hertford Coll., Oxford (MA). Economist, Export Credits Guarantee Dept, 1937. Served War of 1939-45, as driver and Lt-Col, RASC. Asst Financial Editor, Manchester Guardian, 1945; Dep. Asst Dir of Marketing, NCB, 1947; Manager, various depts of Vacuum Oil Co. (later Mobil Oil Co.), 1949-; attended Advanced Management Programme, Harvard Business Sch., 1961; Treasurer, and later Finance Director, Esso Petroleum Co., 1961. Member: Shipbuilding Industry Bd; Council of Manchester Business Sch. *Publications:* numerous articles and broadcasts on economic and business subjects. *Recreation:* mountain walking. *Address:* 215 Ashley Gardens, SW1. *T:* 01-828 8538; Quarry Field, Newton Lane, Norton, near Presteigne, Radnorshire. *T:* Presteigne 447.

**ASHTON, Sir (Arthur) Leigh (Bolland),** Kt 1948; Director and Secretary, Victoria and Albert Museum, 1945-55, retired; *b* London, 20 Oct. 1897; *o s* of late A. J. Ashton, KC, Recorder of Manchester; *m* 1952, Mrs Madge Garland. *Educ:* Horris Hill; Winchester; Balliol Coll., Oxford, BA (war degree). Served European War, Lieut RGA, 1916-19. Victoria and Albert Musuem: Asst Keeper (2nd class), Dept of Architecture and Sculpture, 1922-25; Dept of Textiles, 1925-31; Dept of Ceramics, 1931-37; Keeper of Special Collections, 1937, Secretary of the Advisory Council, 1935, and Asst to Dir, 1937; Asst Keeper, 1st class, 1932; Keeper (1st class) 1938. Mem. Committee, City Companies Exhibition, 1927; Asst Dir International Exhibition of Persian Art, RA, 1931; Executive Committee and arranger of the Exhibition of Chinese Art, RA, 1935-36; Executive Committee, Exhibition of 17th Century Art, RA, 1937; Dir, Exhibition of the Arts of India and Pakistan, RA, 1947-48; loaned to Ministry of Information, April 1939; Officer i/c Finance, 1939; Dep.-Dir of Foreign Division, 1940; Director of Neutral Countries Division, 1941; Dir of British Information Office, Istanbul, 1942, and head of Press Office, HM Embassy, Ankara, with rank of Counsellor. Comdr of the Dannebrog. *Publications:* Introduction to the History of Chinese Sculpture, 1922; Samplers, 1927; Memoirs of the Prince de Ligne, 1928; Chinese Art (with Basil Gray), 1935; Chinese Art (with others), 1935; (ed) Commemoration Catalogue of Chinese Exhibition, 1936; (ed) Commemorative Catalogue of the Exhibition of the Arts of India and Pakistan, 1950; numerous articles and lectures on the decorative arts. *Recreations:* music, the theatre, travel, bridge.

**ASHTON, Lt-Col Edward Malcolm,** CIE 1947; OBE 1945; Indian Army (retired); *b* 21 May 1895; 3rd *s* of late H. Bankes Ashton, Bury St Edmunds; *m* 1927, Gwyneth Ena Darcy Smith; one *s* two *d*. *Educ:* Falconbury Sch., Purley; King Edward VI Sch., Bury St Edmunds. Indian Army; Mil. Officer in Civil Employ; Dir Military Lands and Cantonments; Defence Dept, Govt of India. Served European War, 1914-18 (despatches). *Recreations:* fishing, shooting, tennis. *Address:* 8 Angel Hill, Bury St Edmunds. *T:* Bury St Edmunds 2719. *Club:* National Liberal.

**ASHTON, Sir Frederick (William Mallandaine),** CH 1970; Kt 1962; CBE 1950; Founder-choreographer to the Royal Ballet (Principal Choreographer, 1933-70, and Director, 1963-70); *b* Guayaquil, Ecuador, 17 Sept. 1906; *s* of George Ashton and Georgiana Fulcher. *Educ:* The Dominican Fathers, Lima, Peru; Dover Coll., Dover. Best known ballets: Les Patineurs, Apparitions, Horoscope, Symphonic Variations, Façade, Wedding Bouquet, Scènes de Ballet, Cinderella (first English choreographer to do a 3-act ballet), Illuminations, Sylvia, Romeo and Juliet, Ondine, La Fille Mal Gardée, Les Deux Pigeons, Marguerite and Armand, The Dream, Sinfonietta, Jazz Calendar, Enigma Variations, etc. Served in Royal Air Force during War as Flight Lieut. Queen Elizabeth II Coronation Award, Royal Academy of Dancing, 1959. Hon. DLitt: Durham, 1962; East Anglia, 1967. Legion of Honour (France), 1960; Order of Dannebrog (Denmark), 1964. *Recreation:* dancing. *Address:* Royal Opera House, Covent Garden, WC2; Chandos Lodge, Eye, Suffolk.

**ASHTON, Gilbert,** MC 1916; MA Cantab; DL; Headmaster, Abberley Hall (Preparatory School), near Worcester, 1921-61; *b* 27 Sept. 1896; *s* of Hubert Shorrock Ashton and Victoria Alexandrina, *d* of Maj.-Gen, Sir John Inglis, KCB; *m* 1921, Joan Mary, *d* of Rev. H. R. Huband; four *d*. *Educ:* Winchester Coll.; Trinity Coll., Cambridge. Served European War (wounded, MC): 2nd Lieut RFA, 1915; Instructor Army Signal Sch., 1918. Underwriter, Lloyd's, 1936. Chm. Incorporated Association of Preparatory Schs, 1937 and 1946. Major, Home Guard, 1940-45; Governor: Tudor Hall Sch., 1958-; Abberley Hall Sch., 1961-. Pres., Worcs CC 1967-69. JP 1934, DL 1968-, Worcs. *Recreations:* golf, formerly cricket (CU Cricket XI, 1919-21, Capt.; CU Assoc. XI, 1919-20, Capt.). *Address:* Abberley Lodge, near Worcester. *T:* Great Witley 305. *Clubs:* United University, MCC; Worcestershire County (Worcester).

**ASHTON, Sir Hubert,** KBE 1959; MC; MA Cantab; DL; Third Church Estates Commissioner since 1962; *b* 13 Feb. 1898; *s* of late H. S. Ashton, Trueloves, Ingatestone, Essex, and Mrs V. A. Ashton; *m* 1927, Dorothy Margaret Gaitskell; one *s* two *d* (and one *s* decd). *Educ:* Winchester Coll.; Trinity Coll., Cambridge (Blues for cricket (captain), football and hockey). Royal Field Artillery, 1916-19. Burmah Oil Co., 1922-45; Underwriter at Lloyd's, 1936. MP (C) Chelmsford Division of Essex, 1950-64; Parliamentary Private Secretary to the Chancellor of the Exchequer, 1951-55, to the Lord Privy Seal, Oct. 1955 and to Lord Privy Seal and Home Sec., 1957; Second Church Estates Commissioner, 1957-62. Governor: Brentwood Sch., 1948- (Chm., 1962-); London Hosp., 1948-70 (Dep. Chm., 1967-70; Vice-Patron, 1970-); Mem. GBA, 1963-, Vice-Chm. 1966-. Cttee Mem., MCC, 1947-50, 1952-55 and 1957-64, Pres. 1961; Pres., Essex CCC, 1948-70. Church Warden, St Peter's Church, S Weald, 1940-70. High Sheriff of Essex, 1943; Essex County Councillor, 1946, Vice-Chm., 1949-52; Alderman Essex CC, 1950-61. Dir of public cos. *Recreations:* walking, grandchildren. *Address:* Wealdside, South Weald, Brentwood, Essex. *T:* Coxtie Green 324. *Clubs:* City of London, Oriental, Carlton.

**ASHTON, Joseph William;** MP (Lab) Bassetlaw Division of Notts since Nov. 1968; *b* 9 Oct. 1933; *s* of Arthur and Nellie Ashton, Sheffield; *m* 1957, Margaret Patricia Lee; no *c*. *Educ:* High Storrs Grammar Sch.; Rotherham Technical Coll. Engineering Apprentice, 1949-54; RAF National Service, 1954-56; Cost Control Design Engineer, 1956-68; Sheffield City Councillor, 1962-69. Former Chief Whip and Chm. of Public Works, and Dep. Chm. of Finance and Housing Cttees; PPS to Minister of State for Housing and Sport, 1969-70.

*Recreations:* watching Sheffield Wednesday, reading, do-it-yourself, motoring, arguing in pubs. *Address:* 475 Richmond Road, Sheffield 13. *T:* Sheffield 396137. *Clubs:* Foundry Working Men's (Sheffield); Doncaster Road Working Men's (Langold); various Miners' Institutes, etc.

**ASHTON, Sir Leigh;** *see* Ashton, Sir A. L. B.

**ASHTON, Ven. Leonard (James),** CB 1970; Chaplain in Chief, Royal Air Force (with relative rank of Air Vice-Marshal), and Archdeacon of RAF, since 1969; also Hon. Canon and Prebendary of St Botolph, Lincoln Cathedral, since 1969; *b* 27 June 1915; *s* of late Henry Ashton and Sarah Ashton (*née* Ing). *Educ:* Tyndale Hall, Bristol. Ordained, Chester, 1942; Curate, Cheadle, 1942-45; Chap. RAF, 1945-; N Wales, 1945; AHQ Malaya and Singapore, 1946; BC Air Forces, Japan, 1947-48; Halton, 1948-49; Feltwell, 1949-50; Chap. and Lectr, RAF Chap. Sch., Cheltenham, 1950-53; Sen. Chap., AHQ Iraq, 1954-55; RAF Coll., Cranwell, 1956-60; Br. Forces Arabian Peninsular and Mid. East Command, 1960-61; Asst Chap. Chief, Trng Commands, 1962-65; Res. Chap., St Clement Danes, Strand, 1965-69. Hon. Chaplain to The Queen, 1967-. *Recreations:* gardening, photography. *Address:* c/o Ministry of Defence, Adastral House, Theobalds Road, WC1. *T:* Holborn 3434 (ext. 7268). *Clubs:* United Service, Royal Air Force.

**ASHTON, Prof. Norman (Henry),** DSc (London), FRCP, MRCS; FCPath; Professor of Pathology, University of London since 1957; Director, Department of Pathology, Institute of Ophthalmology, University of London, since 1948; Consultant Pathologist, Moorfields Eye Hospital, since 1948; *b* 11 Sept. 1913; 2nd *s* of Henry James and Margaret Ann Ashton. *Educ:* King's Coll. and Westminster Hosp. Med. Sch., Univ. of London. Westminster Hospital: Prize in Bacteriology, 1938; Editor Hosp. Gazette, 1939-40; House Surg., House Phys., Sen. Casualty Officer and RMO, 1939-41. Asst Pathologist, Princess Beatrice Hosp., 1939; Dir of Pathology, Kent and Canterbury Hosp., and Blood Transfusion Officer of East Kent, 1941. Lieut-Col RAMC, Asst Dir of Pathology and Officer i/c Central Pathological Lab., Middle East, 1946. Pathologist to the Gordon Hosp., 1947; Reader in Pathology, Univ. of London, 1953; Fellow in Residence, Johns Hopkins Hosp., Baltimore, 1953, and Visiting Prof. there, 1959. Edward Nettleship Prize for Research in Ophthalmology, 1953; BMA Middlemore Prize, 1955; Proctor Medal for Research in Ophthalmology (USA), 1957; Walter Wright Lectr, 1959; Banting Lectr, 1960; Doyne Medal (Oxford), 1960; William Julius Mickle Fellow, Univ. London, 1961; Bowman Medal, 1965; Proctor Lecture (USA), 1965; Donder's Medal, 1967; Wm Mackenzie Memorial Medal, 1967; Member: Pathological Soc. of Great Britain and Ireland; Assoc. of Clinical Pathologists; BMA; British Microcirculation Soc.; European Assoc. for Study of Diabetes; Assoc. for Eye Research; Vice-Pres. Ophth. Soc. of UK and Ophth. Sect., RSM; Oxford Ophth. Congress; Council, Coll. of Pathology, 1963-66 (Founder Fellow); Ophth. Hosp. Cttee of Order of St John. Hon. Life Mem., British Diabetic Association; Life Pres. European Ophth. Pathology Soc.; Past Pres. Brit. Div. Internat. Acad. of Pathology, 1962. Hon. Member: Amer. Acad. Ophthal. and Otolaryng.; Hellenic Ophth. Soc. Chm. Council Postgrad. Fedn, Univ. London. Examr in Ophthalmic Pathology, RCSI, 1963-. Mem. Ed. Bd, Brit. Jl Ophthalmology. FRSocMed; Liveryman of the Soc. of Apothecaries of London. CStJ. *Publications:* contrib. to books and numerous scientific articles in Jl of Pathology and Bacteriology, Brit. Jl of Ophthalmology, and Amer. Jl of Ophthalmology. *Recreations:* painting, gardening. *Address:* 2 The Cloisters, Westminster Abbey, SW1. *T:* 01-222 4982. *Clubs:* Athenæum, Garrick.

**ASHTON, Rev. Patrick Thomas,** MVO; Chaplain to the Queen since 1968; Rector, Swanborough Team of Parishes, Salisbury Diocese, since 1970; *b* 27 July 1916; *s* of Lieut-Col S. E. Ashton, OBE; *m* 1942, Mavis St Clair Brown, New Zealand; three *d* (one *s* decd). *Educ:* Stowe; Christ Church, Oxford (MA); Westcott House, Cambridge. Served War of 1939-45 as Captain, Oxfordshire Yeomanry; Curate, St Martin-in-the-Fields, 1947-51; Rector of All Saints, Clifton, Beds, 1951-55; Rector of Sandringham with West Newton and Appleton, and Domestic Chaplain to the Queen, 1955-70; Rector, Sandringham Group of Eight Parishes, 1963-70. *Address:* The Rectory, Wilcot, Pewsey, Wilts.

**ASHTON, Prof. Robert,** PhD; Professor of English History, University of East Anglia, since 1963; *b* 21 July 1924; *s* of Joseph and late Edith F. Ashton; *m* 1946, Margaret Alice Sedgwick; two *d*. *Educ:* Magdalen Coll. Sch., Oxford; University Coll., Southampton (1942-43, 1946-49); London Sch. of Economics (1949-52). BA 1st Cl. hons (London) 1949; PhD (London) 1953; Asst Lecturer in Economic History, Univ. of Nottingham, 1952; Lecturer, 1954; Senior Lecturer, 1961; Vis. Associate Prof. in History, Univ. of California, Berkeley, 1962; Prof. of English History, 1963, and Dean of Sch. of English Studies, 1964-67, Univ. of East Anglia. FRHistS 1960. *Publications:* The Crown and the Money Market, 1603-1640, 1960; Charles I and the City, in Essays in the Economic and Social History of Tudor and Stuart England in honour of R. H. Tawney (ed F. J. Fisher), 1961; James I by his Contemporaries, 1969; The Civil War and the Class Struggle, in The English Civil War and After 1642-1658 (ed R. H. Parry), 1970; articles in learned periodicals. *Recreations:* music, looking at old buildings, walking. *Address:* The Manor House, Brundall, Norwich NOR 86Z. *T:* Brundall 3368.

**ASHTON-GWATKIN, Frank Trelawny Arthur,** CB 1939; CMG 1933; *b* 14 April 1889; *s* of late Rev. Canon W. H. T. Ashton-Gwatkin; *m* Nancy Violet Butler (*d* 1953), Melbourne, Australia. *Educ:* Eton; Balliol Coll., Oxford. Entered HM Consular Service (Far East), 1913; 2nd Sec., Foreign Office, 1921; 1st Sec., 1924; Acting Counsellor of Embassy, Moscow, 1929; 1st Sec., Foreign Office, 1930; Counsellor, 1934; attached to suite of Crown Prince of Japan on his visit to England, 1921; attached to United Kingdom Delegation, Disarmament Conference at Washington, 1921-22; Imperial Economic Conference at Ottawa, 1932; World Monetary and Economic Conference at London, 1933; Lord Runciman's Mission to Czecho-Slovakia, 1938; Policy Adviser, Min. of Economic Warfare, 1939; Asst Under-Sec. and Chief Clerk, Foreign Office, 1940; Sen. Insp. of Diplomatic Missions (with rank of Minister), 1944; Asst Under-Sec. FO, 1947; retired on pension, 1947; Associate Director of Studies, Royal Institute of International Affairs, 1947-52. FSA. *Publications:* Michelangelo (Newdigate Prize Poem for English verse, 1909); The British Foreign Service (Syracuse Univ. lectures, USA 1949); contributions to the RIIA History of The War; (under *nom de plume* of John Paris) Kimono, 1921; Sayonara, 1924; Banzai, 1925; A Japanese Don Juan (poems), 1926; The Island beyond Japan, 1930; Matsu, 1932. *Address:* 9 Barton Close, Nyetimber, Sussex. *T:* Pagham 2058. *Club:* Brooks's.

**ASHTOWN,** 5th Baron *cr* 1800; **Dudley Oliver Trench,** OBE 1961; retired as Assistant Chief Constable, War Department Constabulary, 1964; late KRRC; *b* 11 July 1901; *yr s* of 3rd Baron Ashtown (*d* 1946), and Violet Grace (*d* 1945), *d* of Col R. G. Cosby; *S* brother, 1966; *m* 1st, 1932, Ellen Nancy (*d* 1949), *y d* of late William Garton, Brixedone, Bursledon, Hants; two *d*; 2nd, 1955, Sheelah A. S. (*d* 1963), *yr d* of late Brig.-Gen. L. F. Green-Wilkinson, CMG, DSO; 3rd, 1966, Natalie *widow* of Major James de Sales La Terrière. *Educ:* Wellington Coll.; RMC Sandhurst. Adjutant 11th London Regt, 1934-35, and Queen's Westminsters, 1936-38; retd pay, 1939. Served War of 1939-45 (despatches). *Heir: kinsman* Christopher Oliver Trench, *b* 23 March 1931. *Address:* Woodlawn, King's Somborne, Near Stockbridge, Hants. *T:* King's Somborne 333.

**ASHWELL, Major Arthur Lindley,** DSO 1916; OBE 1946; TD 1926; DL; late 8th Battalion Sherwood Foresters; *b* 19 Jan. 1886; *o s* of Arthur Thomas Ashwell, solicitor, Nottingham; *m* 1932, Sylvia Violet, *widow* of Harold Gallatly, MC, and *d* of Philip Scratchley. *Educ:* Lambrook, Bracknell; Winchester Coll. Served European War, 1915 (wounded thrice, despatches, DSO). DL Notts, 1941-. *Address:* Flat 3, 19 The Vale, SW3. *Clubs:* Naval and Military, Royal Automobile.

**ASHWIN, Sir Bernard Carl,** KBE 1956; CMG 1946; company director; Director: Coulls, Somerville, Wilkie Ltd; Thomas Ballinger & Co. Ltd, 1955; Holland and Hannen and Cubitts (NZ) Ltd, 1959; Reid NZ Rubber Mills Ltd, 1959; Chairman: Colonial Mutual Life Assurance Society Ltd, 1964-67; C. & A. Odlin Timber & Hardware Co. Ltd, 1965-69; *b* Paeroa, NZ, 1896; *s* of Manley John Ashwin; *m* 1926, Rachel Robinson, *d* of William Turnbull; one *s* two *d*. *Educ:* Cambridge Dist High Sch.; Victoria University Coll. (MCom Hons). Cadet Educ. Dept, 1912; served European War, 1914-18, with NZEF; qualified as public accountant 1921; transferred to Treasury, 1922; Sec. to Treasury, and Director, Reserve Bank of NZ, 1939-55, retired. *Recreation:* golf. *Address:* 122 Woburn Road, Lower Hutt, New Zealand.

**ASHWORTH, Harold Kenneth,** TD and Clasp 1951; Hon. Consultant Anaesthetist, Charing Cross and Moorfields Hospitals, since 1968; *b* 16 May 1903; *s* of Dr J. H. Ashworth, Manchester. *Educ:* Sedbergh; Manchester Univ. MB, ChB (Vic) 1925; MRCS, LRCP 1925; DA 1934; FFARCS 1948. Formerly: Visiting Anaesthetist, Royal Infirmary, Manchester; Clinical Lecturer in Anaesthesia, Univ. of Manchester; Senior Anaesthetist, Charing Cross and Moorfields Hosps; Director, Dept of Anaesthesia, Charing Cross Hosp. Med. Sch., 1956-68; Consulting Anaesthetist to the Kingdom of Libya, 1968-69. RAMC (TA) 1939-45, BEF France, 1940; Brig., Cons. Anaesthetist, India Command, 1944-45. Councillor: St Marylebone Borough Council, 1949-65; Westminster City Council, 1964-68. Examiner for DA (RCP & S), 1962-68. Sen. Mem., Assoc. of Anæsthetists of Great Britain and Ireland, 1968. *Publications:* Practical Points in Anaesthesia, 1936. Contributions to Medical Journals. *Recreations:* watching cricket; formerly Rugby football (Manchester Univ. XV, 1922-26). *Address:* c/o Glyn Mills & Co., Whitehall, SW1. *Clubs:* MCC; XXI (Manchester University).

**ASHWORTH, Herbert;** Chairman, Housing Corporation, since 1968 (Deputy Chairman, 1964-68); Deputy Chairman, Co-operative Permanent Building Society, since 1968; *b* 30 Jan. 1910; *s* of Joseph Hartley Ashworth; *m* 1936, Barbara Helen Mary, *d* of late Douglas D. Henderson; two *s* one *d*. *Educ:* Burnley Grammar Sch.; London Univ. (grad. econ. and law). General Manager, Portman Building Soc., 1938-50; General Manager, Co-operative Permanent Building Soc., 1950-61; Director and General Manager, Hallmark Securities Ltd, 1961-66. *Publications:* Housing in Great Britain, 1951; Building Society Work Explained, (current edn), 1970. *Address:* Buckles, Buckles Gap, Epsom Downs, Surrey. *T:* Burgh Heath 52608. *Club:* Reform.

**ASHWORTH, James Louis,** FIMechE, FIEE, ARTC (Salford); Full-Time Member for Operations, Central Electricity Generating Board, 1966-70, retired; *b* 7 March 1906; *s* of late James and late Janet Ashworth; *m* 1931 Clara Evelyn Arnold; one *s* two *d*. *Educ:* Stockport Grammar Sch.; Salford Royal Coll. of Technology. Apprenticeship with Mirrlees, Bickerton & Day Ltd, Stockport (Diesel Oil Engine Manufrs), 1924-29; Metro-Vickers Electrical Co. Ltd, 1929; Manchester Corp. Elec. Dept, Stuart Street Gen. Stn, 1930-32; Hull Corp. Elec. Dept, 1932-35; Halifax Corp. Elec. Dept, 1935-40; Mersey Power Co. Ltd, Runcorn, 1940-48; British Elec. Authority, N West: Chief Generation Engr (O), 1948-57; Dep. Divisional Controller, 1957-58; Central Elec. Gen. Bd, N West, Merseyside and N Wales Region: Dep. Regional Dir, 1958-62; Regional Dir, 1962-66. *Recreations:* gardening, photography, travel, reading. *Address:* Chase Cottage, 23 The Chase, Reigate, Surrey. *T:* Redhill 61279.

**ASHWORTH, Brigadier John Blackwood,** CBE 1962; DSO 1944; retired 1965; *b* 7 Dec. 1910; *s* of Lieut-Col H. S. Ashworth, Royal Sussex Regt (killed in action, 1917) and late Mrs E. M. Ashworth; *m* 1946, Eileen Patricia, *d* of late Major H. L. Gifford (Royal Ulster Rifles) and of Lady Gooch; one *d*. *Educ:* Wellington Coll.; RMC, Sandhurst. Commissioned Royal Sussex Regt, 1930; Instructor RMC, 1938; War of 1939-45 (despatches twice); OC Training Centre, 1942; OC 1/5 Queen's Royal Regt (wounded, DSO), 1944; GSO1, War Office, 1944; OC 4/5 Royal Sussex, 1945; OC 1st Royal Sussex, 1946; GSO1, Brit. Middle East Office, 1947; AMS War Office, 1948; OC 1st Royal Sussex, 1951; Comdt Joint Sch. of Chemical Warfare, 1954; Commander 133rd Inf. Bde (TA), 1957; Director of Military Training, War Office, 1959-62; Inspector of Boys' Training, War Office, 1962-65. ADC to the Queen, 1961-65. Col The Royal Sussex Regt, 1963-66; Dep. Col, The Queen's Regt (Royal Sussex), 1967-68. OStJ 1950. Grand Officer, Order of House of Orange, 1967. *Recreation:* gardening. *Address:* West Common Drive, Hayward's Heath, Sussex. *T:* Hayward's Heath 52371. *Club:* United Service.

**ASHWORTH, Hon. Sir John (Percy),** Kt 1954; MBE 1944; **Hon. Mr Justice Ashworth;** Judge of Queen's Bench Division, High Court of Justice, since Oct. 1954; Chairman, Staffordshire Quarter Sessions since 1963 (Deputy Chairman Staffordshire Quarter Sessions, 1951); Presiding Judge, Midland Circuit, since 1970; *b* 3 Feb. 1906; *s* of Percy Ashworth, Ollerton, Bolton; unmarried. *Educ:* Winchester; Christ Church, Oxford. Junior Counsel: to the Post Office, 1936; to the Treasury (Common Law), 1950-54. Chancellor of Diocese: of Rochester, 1943-54; of London, 1944-54; of Lichfield, 1947-54. Served War of 1939-45, Intelligence Corps, 1940-45 (despatches). *Address:* Fradswell Hall, Stafford. *T:* Weston (Staffs) 210; 26 Stourcliffe Close, W1. *T:* 01-723 3766. *Club:* United Service.

**ASHWORTH, Air Commandant Dame Veronica Margaret,** DBE 1964; RRC 1959 (ARRC 1944); Air Commandant-Matron-in-Chief, PMRAFNS, 1963-66; *b* 25 Dec. 1910; *d* of late Dr and Mrs F. H. S. Ashworth. *Educ:* St Katharine's Sch., Wantage, Berks. Trained at St Bartholomew's Hosp., London, 1930-34 (SRN); Midwifery Training, Leeds Maternity Hosp., 1935 (SCM). Joined Princess Mary's Royal Air Force Nursing Service, 1936; Group Officer-Principal Matron, PMRAFNS, 1960-63. QHNS, 1963-66. *Recreations:* riding, tennis, music. *Address:* Flat 6, Kenilworth Court, Hempstead Road, Watford, Herts. *T:* Watford 29893.

**ASHWORTH, Prof. William;** Professor of Economic and Social History, University of Bristol, since 1958; Dean, Faculty of Social Sciences, 1968-70; *b* 11 March 1920; *s* of Harold and Alice Ashworth; unmarried. *Educ:* Todmorden Grammar Sch.; London Sch. of Economics and Political Science. Served 1941-45, RAPC and REME. BSc (Econ.) 1946; PhD 1950. Research Assistant, London Sch. of Economics and Political Science, 1946-47; on staff of Cabinet Office (Historical Section), 1947-48; Assistant Lecturer and Lecturer in Economic History, London Sch. of Economics and Political Science, 1948-55; Reader in Economic History in the Univ. of London, 1955-58. *Publications:* A Short History of the International Economy, 1952 (revised 1962); Contracts and Finance (History of the Second World War: UK Civil Series), 1953; The Genesis of Modern British Town Planning, 1954; An Economic History of England, 1870-1939, 1960; contributor to: London, Aspects of Change, ed by Centre for Urban Studies, 1964; Victoria County History of Essex, 1966. Articles and reviews in Economic History Review and other jls. *Address:* 3rd floor flat, 12a Royal York Crescent, Bristol BS8 4JY. *T:* Bristol 37851; 54 Queens Grove Road, Chingford, E4.

**ASKE, Rev. Sir Conan,** 2nd Bt *cr* 1922; Assistant Curate of Hagley, Stourbridge, Worcs, since 1970; *b* 22 April 1912; *s* of Sir Robert William Aske, 1st Bt, TD, QC, LLD, and Edith (*d* 1918), *d* of Sir Walter Herbert Cockerline; *S* father 1954; *m* 1st, 1948, Vera (*d* 1960), *yr d* of George Rowbotham, Iffley, Oxon; 2nd, 1965, Rebecca Grant. *Educ:* Rugby; Balliol Coll., Oxford. TA, London Irish Rifles, 1939; served, 1939-49, with East York Regt, Sudan Defence Force, Somalia Gendarmerie. Major, Civil Affairs Officer, Reserved Area of Ethiopia and The Ogaden, 1949-51; Schoolmaster, Hillstone, Malvern, 1952-69. *Heir: b* Robert Edward Aske [*b* 21 March 1915; *m* 1940, Joan Bingham, *o d* of Captain Bingham Ackerley, Cobham; one *s*]. *Address:* 3 Park Road, West Hagley, Stourbridge, Worcs. *T:* Hagley 4883. *Club:* Malvern (Malvern).

**ASKEW, Herbert Royston,** QC 1955; BSc; MICE; *e s* of late Leonard Askew; *m* 1st, 1919, Christiana Rachel (decd), *o d* of late C. Wolryche Dixon, Great Roke, Witley, Surrey; one *d* (one *s* killed on active service, 1942; and one *d* decd); 2nd, 1948, Dorothy Beatrice, *o d* of late J. Gale Wilson, Aberdour, Fife. *Educ:* Alleyn's Sch., Dulwich; London Univ. Served European War 1914-18, Capt. Middlesex Regt and Royal Tank Corps. Called to the Bar, Middle Temple, 1926; Master of the Bench, 1963. Mem. Kensington Borough Council, 1931-39. Served War of 1939-45, Lieut-Col, Gen. List (GSO1). *Address:* 24 Palace Court, W2. *T:* 01-727 6033. *Club:* Reform.

**ASKEW, John Marjoribanks Eskdale;** *b* 22 Sept. 1908; *o s* of late William Haggerston Askew, JP, Ladykirk, Berwicks, and Castle Hills, Berwick-on-Tweed; *m* 1st, 1933, Lady Susan Egerton (marr. diss., 1966), 4th *d* of 4th Earl of Ellesmere, MVO; one *s* one *d*; 2nd, 1967, Mrs Rona Trotter, Cleughhead, Berwicks, *widow* of Major H. R. Trotter. *Educ:* Eton; Magdalene Coll., Cambridge (BA). Lieut 2 Bn Grenadier Guards, 1932; Capt. 1940; Major 1943. Royal Company of Archers, Queen's Body Guard for Scotland. Convener Berwicks CC, 1961. *Address:* Ladykirk, Berwicks. *T:* Norham 229; Castle Hills, Berwick-on-Tweed. *Clubs:* Boodle's; New (Edinburgh).

*See also Baron Faringdon, Duke of Sutherland.*

**ASKEY, Arthur Bowden,** OBE 1969; theatrical artiste; *b* 6 June 1900; *s* of Samuel Askey, Liverpool, and Betty Askey (*née* Bowden), Knutsford, Cheshire; *m* 1925, Elizabeth May Swash; one *d*. *Educ:* Liverpool Institute. Liverpool Education Offices, 1916-24; concert parties, pantomimes, broadcasts, London and Provincial Concerts, 1924-38. *Films:* Band Waggon, Charlie's Big-Hearted Aunt, The Ghost Train, I Thank You, Back-Room Boy, King Arthur was a Gentleman, Miss London Ltd, Bees in Paradise, 1939-44; The Love Match; Ramsbottom Rides Again; Make Mine a Million; Friends and Neighbours. *Broadcast Series:* Band Waggon, 1938-39; Big's Broadcast, 1940; Big Time, 1942; Forever Arthur, 1945; How Do You Do, 1949; Arthur's Inn, 1952; Hello, Playmates, 1954; Askey Galore, 1957; The Arthur Askey Show, 1958. *Television Series:* Before Your Very Eyes, 1953, 1955, 1956, 1957; Living it up, 1958; Arthur's Treasured Volumes, 1960; The Arthur Askey Show, 1961; Raise Your Glasses, 1962. *London Theatres:* The Boy Who Lost His Temper, Garrick, 1937, Cambridge, 1938; Band Waggon, London Palladium, 1939; Jack and Jill, Palace, 1941, His Majesty's, 1942; The Love Racket, Victoria Palace, Prince's and Adelphi, 1944-45; Follow the Girls, His Majesty's, 1945-47; Cinderella, London Casino, 1948; The Kid from Stratford, Prince's, Winter Garden, 1948-49; Goody Two Shoes, London Casino, 1950; Bet Your Life, London Hippodrome, 1951-52; The Love Match, Palace, 1953-54; Babes in the Wood, Golders Green, 1954; Babes in the Wood, Streatham Hill, 1955; Humpty Dumpty, Golders Green Hippodrome, 1956; Robinson Crusoe, Palladium, 1957; Dick Whittington, Golders Green Hippodrome, 1958; Dick Whittington, Streatham Hill Theatre, 1959-60; Cinderella, Golders Green Hippodrome, 1961-62; Pantomime: Robin Hood, Coventry Theatre, 1963-64; Babes in the Wood, Wimbledon, 1966-67; Sleeping Beauty, Wimbledon, 1969-70. London Palladium: Aladdin, 1964-65; Babes in the Wood, 1965-66; Robinson Crusoe, 1967-68; Jack and the Beanstalk, 1968-69. Royal Command Performance (Palladium), 1946, 1948, 1952, 1954, 1955, 1957, 1968; Command Performance (Manchester), 1959. Australian tour, 1949-50; various radio and television broadcasts and provincial variety tours. Summer seasons: Blackpool, Bournemouth, Southsea, Margate, Shanklin, Hastings, Rhyl, Torquay, etc. Past Pres., Stage Golfing Soc. *Recreations:* golfing, motoring. *Club:* Savage.

**ASKWITH, Arthur Vivian,** CSI 1945; CIE 1941; *b* 16 Nov. 1893; *s* of Preb. Henry Askwith, Ripon and Hereford. *Educ:* Bedford Sch. Joined India Police, 1913; War of 1914-18, served with 28th

Light Cavalry and on General Staff; joined Indian Civil Service, 1921; Sec. to Government of the Punjab, Home Dept, 1935-40; Chief Commissioner, Delhi, 1940-45. *Address:* 13 Loder Drive, Aylestone Hill, Hereford; c/o Lloyds Bank Ltd (Cox and King's Branch), 6 Pall Mall, SW1.

**ASKWITH, Hon. Betty Ellen,** FRSL; *b* 26 June 1909; *o d* of late Baron Askwith, KCB, KC, LLD, and Lady Askwith, CBE; *m* 1950, Keith Miller Jones, *qv*. *Educ:* Lycée Français, London; North Foreland Lodge, Broadstairs. *Publications:* First Poems, 1928; If This Be Error, 1932; Poems, 1933; Green Corn, 1933; Erinna, 1937; Keats, 1940; The Admiral's Daughters, 1947; A Broken Engagement, 1950; The Blossoming Tree, 1954; The Tangled Web, 1960; A Step Out of Time, 1966; Lady Dilke, 1969. With Theodora Benson: Lobster Quadrille, 1930; Seven Basketfuls, 1932; Foreigners, 1935; Muddling Through, 1936; How to Be Famous, 1937. *Translations:* The Tailor's Cake, 1947; A Hard Winter, 1947; Meeting, 1950. *Recreations:* travelling, reading. *Address:* 8 Egerton Terrace, SW3. *T:* 01-589 7126.

**ASPIN, Norman,** CMG 1968; Counsellor, HM Diplomatic Service; Imperial Defence College, since 1970; *b* 9 Nov. 1922; *s* of Thomas and Eleanor Aspin; *m* 1948, Elizabeth Irving; three *s*. *Educ:* Darwen Grammar Sch.; Durham Univ. (MA). War Service, 1942-45, Lieut RNVR. Demonstrator in Geography, Durham Univ., 1947-48; Asst Principal, Commonwealth Relations Office, 1948; served in India, 1948-51; Principal, Commonwealth Relations Office, 1952; served in Federation of Rhodesia and Nyasaland, 1954-57; British Deputy High Commissioner in Sierra Leone, 1961-63; Commonwealth Relations Office, 1963-65; British Embassy, Tel Aviv, 1966-69. *Recreations:* sailing, tennis. *Address:* c/o Foreign and Commonwealth Office, King Charles Street, SW1. *Club:* Naval and Military.

**ASPINALL, Arthur,** CVO 1965; MA, DLitt; Professor of Modern History, University of Reading, 1947-65; Professor Emeritus since 1965; *b* 11 July 1901; *m* 1st, 1931, Gladys Shaw (*d* 1965); one *s* one *d*; 2nd, 1968, Beryl Johnson. *Educ:* Manchester Univ. Lecturer in History, Univ. of Rangoon, 1925-31; Lecturer in Modern History, Univ. of Reading, 1931-47. Raleigh Lecturer, British Academy, 1952. External Examiner in Final Hon. Sch. of Mod. Hist., Oxford Univ., 1947-49. *Publications:* Lord Brougham and the Whig Party, 1927; Cornwallis in Bengal, 1931; The Formation of Canning's Ministry, 1937; The Letters of King George IV, 1812-1830 (3 vols), 1938; (with the Earl of Bessborough) Lady Bessborough and her Family Circle, 1940; The Correspondence of Charles Arbuthnot, 1941; The Diary of Henry Hobhouse, 1820-1827, 1947; Politics and the Press, *c* 1780-1850, 1949; The Letters of Princess Charlotte, 1811-1817, 1949; The Early English Trade Unions, 1949; Mrs Jordan and her Family, 1951; Three Early Nineteenth Century Diaries, 1952; The Cabinet Council, 1783-1835, 1954; The reporting of the House of Commons' Debates, 1771-1834, in Essays presented to Sir Lewis Namier, 1956; English Historical Documents, Vol. XI, 1783-1832 (with E. A. Smith), 1959; The Later Correspondence of George III, Vols I-V, 1962-70; Parliament through Seven Centuries: Reading and its MPs (with others), 1962; The Correspondence of George, Prince of Wales, Vols I-VII, 1963-70; articles in the Eng. Hist. Review, etc. *Address:* Highlands, Belle Vue, Maughold, Isle of Man. *T:* Ramsey 3343.

**ASPINALL, William Briant Philip,** OBE 1945; Headmaster, Queen's School, HQ Northern Army Group, Rheindahlen, since 1960; *b* 1912; *s* of William Pryce Aspinall and Ethel Eleanor (*née* Ravenscroft); *m* 1st, Aileen, *d* of Major R. FitzGerald; one *s*; 2nd, Phyllis, *d* of Leopold Hill. *Educ:* Royal Masonic Sch.; St John's Coll., Cambridge; Headmaster, Sutton Valence Sch., 1950-53; Windsor Sch., Hamm, BAOR, 1953-58; King Richard Sch., Cyprus, 1959. *Recreations:* cricket, hockey, golf, etc. *Address:* Queen's School, BFPO 40. *Clubs:* Oxford and Cambridge, MCC.

**ASQUITH,** family name of **Earl of Oxford and Asquith.**

**ASQUITH, Viscount; Raymond Benedict Bartholomew Michael Asquith;** *b* 24 Aug. 1952; *er s* and *heir* of 2nd Earl of Oxford and Asquith, *qv*.

**ASSHETON,** family name of **Baron Clitheroe.**

**ASTAIRE, Fred;** actor, motion pictures; *b* 10 May 1899; *s* of F. E. Astaire and Ann Geilus; *m* 1933, Phyllis Livingston Potter (*d* 1954); two *s* one *d*. *Educ:* private. Stage musical comedy-vaudeville until 1933, then motion pictures. First appearance in London, 1923, in Stop Flirting; American and English successes: Lady Be Good, Funny Face, The Band Waggon, Gay Divorce. *Films:* Flying Down to Rio, Top Hat, Roberta, Gay Divorce, Follow the Fleet, Swingtime, Shall We Dance?, Story of Vernon and Irene Castle, Holiday Inn, Ziegfeld Follies, Blue Skies, Easter Parade, The Barkleys of Broadway, Three Little Words, Let's Dance, Daddy Longlegs, Funny Face, Silk Stockings, On the Beach, The Pleasure of His Company, Finian's Rainbow, The Midas Run, A Run on Gold, etc. *Television Shows:* An Evening with Fred Astaire, 1958; Another Evening with Fred Astaire, 1959; Astaire Time, 1960; The Fred Astaire Show, 1968. *Publication:* Autobiography, Steps in Time, 1959. *Recreations:* golf, thoroughbred racing. *Address:* Beverly Hills, California 90210, USA. *Clubs:* Racquet and Tennis, The Brook, Lamb's (New York).

**ASTBURY, Arthur Ralph,** CSI 1933; CIE 1928; FInstCE; *b* 5 June 1880; *o s* of Arthur Kingsby Astbury; *m* 1908, Friede Hildegard von Schoenberg; one *s* one *d*. *Educ:* Westminster; Royal Indian Engineering College, Coopers Hill. Assistant Engineer, Indian Public Works Dept, 1900; Superintending Engineer, 1920; Chief Engineer and Sec. to Government, 1925; retired, 1935; Ministry of Home Security, 1938; Ministry of Works, 1945-50, retired, 1950. *Address:* Hampdenleaf, Dunsmore, Aylesbury, Bucks. *Club:* Athenæum.

**ASTBURY, Sir George,** Kt 1966; JP; *b* 10 May 1902; 2nd *s* of Thomas Astbury, Longton, Stoke-on-Trent; *m* 1930, Nellie, 2nd *d* of Albert Bagnall, Sandford Hill, Longton; two *s*. *Educ:* St James's, Longton. Retired as Co-operative Soc. Insurance Agent. Mem. Nat. Wages Bd of Co-op. Union. CC 1937, JP 1938, CA 1951, Cheshire. *Address:* West Winds, Strawberry Roundabout, Backford, near Chester.

**ASTBURY, Norman Frederick,** CBE 1968; MA, ScD Cantab, CEng, FIEE, FInstP, FICeram, FRSA; Director, British Ceramic Research Association, since 1960; *b* 1 Dec. 1908; *y c* of William and Clara Astbury, Normacot, Staffs; *m* 1933, Nora Enid, *yr d* of William and Mary Wilkinson; three *s* one *d*. *Educ:* Longton High Sch.; St John's Coll., Cambridge (Scholar and Prizeman). National Physical Laboratory,

1929-39; HM Anti-Submarine Experimental Establishment, 1939-45; Dir of Research, J. Sankey & Sons Ltd and Guest, Keen & Nettlefold Ltd, 1945-49; Prof. of Applied Physics, NSW Univ. of Technology, 1949-51; Prof. of Physics, Univ. of Khartoum, 1951-56; Royal Aircraft Establishment, 1956-57; Dep. Dir of Research, Brit. Ceram. Research Assoc., 1957-60. Pres., Brit. Ceram. Soc., 1969; Member: Coun. Inst. of Physics and Phys. Soc., 1963-66; Nat. Coun. for Technological Awards, 1958-64; Coun. for Nat. Academic Awards, 1964-66; Inter-services Metallurgical Research Coun., 1962-64; Joint Services Non-metallic Materials Research Board, 1964-69; Chm. Cttee of Directors of Research Assocs, 1964-66; Vice-Pres., Parly and Sci. Cttee, 1965-68; Member: Governing Body, N Staffs Polytechnic; Construction Res. Adv. Council, MPBW, 1968-. *Publications:* Industrial Magnetic Testing, 1952; Electrical Applied Physics, 1952; numerous papers in scientific jls. *Recreations:* music, model railways. *Address:* 13 Allerton Road, Trentham, Staffs. *T:* Stoke-on-Trent 57912. *Clubs:* Athenæum, United Service; Federation (Stoke-on-Trent).

**ASTLEY,** family name of **Baron Hastings.**

**ASTLEY, Sir Francis Jacob Dugdale,** 6th Bt, *cr* 1821; Head of Classics Department, The Atlantic College, St Donat's Castle, Glamorgan, 1962-69; *b* 26 Oct. 1908; *s* of Rev. Anthony Aylmer Astley (6th *s* of 2nd Bt); *S* kinsman 1943; *m* 1934, Brita Margareta Josefina Nyström, Stockholm; one *d. Educ:* Marlborough; Trinity Coll., Oxford. Sen. Lectr, University Coll. of Ghana, 1948-61. *Heir:* none. *Address:* 21a Lindfield Gardens, NW3. *T:* 01-435 9945.

**ASTLEY, Mrs Reginald,** CBE 1920; Kathleen Mary, *e d* of Thomas Mercer Cliffe Vigors, Burgage, Co. Carlow; *m* 1st, 1909, Hon. Wilfred Thesiger, DSO (*d* 1920); three *s* (and one *s* killed on active service, 1942); 2nd, 1931, Reginald Basil Astley (*d* 1942). *Address:* 15 Shelley Court, Tite Street, Chelsea, SW3. *T:* 01-352 7213. *Club:* Guards.

*See also R. M. D. Thesiger and W. P. Thesiger.*

**ASTON, Bishop Suffragan of,** since 1962; **Rt. Rev. David Brownfield Porter;** *b* 10 May 1906; *s* of Sydney Lawrence Porter and Edith Alice Porter; *m* 1936, Violet Margaret Eliot (*d* 1956); one *s*; *m* 1961, Mrs Pamela Cecil (*née* Lightfoot), *widow* of Neil McNeill. *Educ:* Hertford Coll., Oxford. Curate of St Augustine's, Leeds, 1929; Tutor of Wycliffe Hall, Oxford, 1931; Chaplain, 1933; Chaplain of Wadham Coll., Oxford, 1934; Vicar of All Saints', Highfield, Oxford, 1935; Vicar of Darlington, 1943; Rector of St John's, Princes Street, Edinburgh, 1947-61; Dean of Edinburgh, 1954-61; Select Preacher, Oxford Univ., 1964. *Recreations:* fishing and painting. *Address:* Park Mount, 259 Bristol Road, Birmingham 5.

**ASTON, Archdeacon of;** *see* Warman, Venerable Francis Frederick Guy.

**ASTON, Arthur Vincent,** CMG 1950; MC 1917; *b* 5 Nov. 1896; *m* 1922, Rita Bethia Walker Simpson; two *s. Educ:* King's Sch., Chester; Queen's Coll., Oxford. Malayan Civil Service, 1919; ADC to Officer Administering the Govt, 1929; Resident Commissioner, Pahang, 1946, Perak, 1947, Penang, 1948-51; retired, 1951. Served European War, 1914-18 (MC); War of 1939-45 (despatches). *Address:* Croylands, Hindon, Salisbury, Wilts. *T:* Hindon 285.

**ASTON, Thomas William,** CMG 1969; Director, International Affairs Division, Commonwealth Secretariat, since 1966; *b* 14 May 1922; *s* of late Henry Herbert Aston, Birmingham, and of Lilian Perks; *m* 1947, Eve Dunning; one *d. Educ:* Saltley Grammar Sch., Birmingham. Entered Civil Service as Employment Clerk, Ministry of Labour, 1939. Served with RAF, 1941-46: Middle East, Palestine, Persian Gulf, Egypt, South Africa; Navigator, 1942; Flight-Lieut, 1944. Executive Officer (Inspector), Ministry of National Insurance, 1947; Assistant Principal, Commonwealth Relations Office, 1951; Delhi, 1953-54; Principal, 1954; seconded to Joint Intelligence Cttee, 1954-56; First Secretary, South Africa, 1957-60; CO, 1961-63; First Sec., Kenya, 1963-64; Deputy British High Commissioner, Kampala, 1964-65. *Recreations:* tennis, cricket, gardening, bird watching. *Address:* c/o Commonwealth Secretariat, Marlborough House, SW1. *Clubs:* Royal Commonwealth Society, Royal Over-Seas League.

**ASTON, Hon. Sir William (John),** KCMG 1970; Speaker, House of Representatives, Australia, since 1967; MP for Phillip since 1963 (also 1955-61); *b* 19 Sept. 1916; *s* of Harold John Aston and Dorothea (*née* McKeown); *m* 1941, Beatrice Delaney Burrett; one *s* two *d. Educ:* Randwick Boys' High School. Mayor of Waverley, 1952-53. Dep. Govt Whip, 1959-61 and 1963-64; Chief Govt Whip, 1964-67; Trustee, Parlt Retiring Allowances, 1964-67; Mem. and Dep. Chm., Joint Select Cttee on New and Perm. Parlt House, 1965-; Chairman: House of Reps Standing Orders Cttee; Joint House Cttee; Library Cttee, 1967-; Joint Cttee on Broadcasting of Parly Proceedings, 1967-; Jt Chm., Inter-Parliamentary Union (Commonwealth of Aust. Br.) and Commonwealth Parly Assoc. (Aust. Br.); Leader, Aust. Delegn to IPU Conf., Ottawa, 1964; Convenor and Chm., First Conf. of Aust. Presiding Officers, 1968; rep. Australia at: opening of Zambian Parlt Bldg; Funeral of Israeli Prime Minister Eshkol and IPU Symposium, Geneva, 1968; Conf. of Commonwealth Presiding Officers, Ottawa, 1969. Korean Order of Distinguished Service Merit (1st Class), 1969. *Recreations:* cricket, golf, football, fishing, bowls. *Address:* 46 Carrington Road, Waverley, NSW 2024, Australia. *T:* 38-6737; House of Representatives, Canberra, ACT. *T:* Canberra 705. *Clubs:* Royal Automobile of Australia (Sydney); Waverley Bowling.

**ASTOR,** family name of **Viscount Astor** and **Baron Astor of Hever.**

**ASTOR,** 4th Viscount, *cr* 1917, of Hever Castle; Baron *cr* 1916; **William Waldorf Astor;** student; *b* 27 Dec. 1951; *s* of 3rd Viscount Astor and Hon. Sarah Katherine Elinor Norton (now Hon. Mrs Sarah Baring), *d* of 6th Baron Grantley; *S* father 1966. *Educ:* Eton Coll. *Heir: uncle* Hon. (Francis) David (Langhorne) Astor, *qv. Address:* 23 Scarsdale Villas, W8; Ginge Manor, Wantage, Berks.

**ASTOR OF HEVER,** 1st Baron, *cr* 1956, of Hever Castle; **Colonel John Jacob Astor;** Chief Proprietor of The Times Newspaper, 1922-66; *b* 20 May 1886; *y s* of 1st Viscount Astor; *m* 1916, Lady Violet Mary Elliot, (DStJ) (*d* 1965), *y d* of 4th Earl of Minto, and *widow* of Major Lord Charles Mercer Nairne, *s* of 5th Marquess of Lansdowne; three *s. Educ:* Eton Coll. Joined 1st Life Guards, 1906; ADC to Viceroy of India, 1911-14; served European War, 1914-18; commanded Household Siege Battery; Hon. Colonel: 23rd London Regt (TA), 1928-49; Kent and Sussex RGA (TA),

1927-46; Lieut-Col 5th Bn City of London Home Guard, 1940-44. MP (U) Dover Division of Kent, 1922-45. Director: GWR, 1929-48; Barclays Bank, 1942-52; Hambros Bank, 1934-60. Dir until Oct. 1962 when resigned: The Times Publishing Co., Phoenix Assurance Co. (Dep. Chm., 1941-52, Chm. 1952-58), and London Guarantee and Accident Co. Ltd. Member: Govt Broadcasting Cttee, 1923; Gen. Advisory Council, BBC, 1937; Council, St Dunstan's, 1922-62. President: Press Club; Commonwealth Press Union; Nat. Assoc. for Employment of Regular Sailors, Soldiers and Airmen, 1936-62; Kent Council, British Legion, 1934-62; MCC, 1937; Kent County Cricket Club, 1929. Past Pres., Newspaper Press Fund. Vice-Pres., Royal Coll. of Music, 1934-62. Chairman: 4th, 5th, 6th and 7th Imperial Press Confs; Middlesex Hosp., 1938-62; Middlesex Hosp. Medical Sch., 1945-62; Old Etonian Assoc., 1939-49; Hurlingham Club, 1929-49. Master of Guild, St Bride's Church (Fleet Street), 1955-62. DL, Kent, 1936-62, JP, Kent, 1929-62. Hon. Freeman, Borough of Dover. Holds hon. degrees at Univs of Perth (Australia), 1925, London, 1939, McGill, 1950. Chevalier, Legion of Honour, 1918. *Recreations:* Eton XI, 1904-05; Public Sch. Racquets, 1904-05 (winner); Army Racquets, 1908 (singles and doubles). *Heir: e s* Hon. Gavin Astor, *qv*. *Address:* Les Terres Blanches, Pegomas, (AM), France. *Club:* Royal Yacht Squadron.

*See also Hon. H. W. and Hon. John Astor.*

**ASTOR, Hon. (Francis) David (Langhorne);** Editor of the Observer since 1948; *b* 5 March 1912; *s* of 2nd Viscount Astor and *heir-pres.* to 4th Viscount Astor, *qv*; *m* 1st, 1945, Melanie Hauser; one *d*; 2nd, 1952, Bridget Aphra Wreford; two *s* three *d*. *Educ:* Eton; Balliol, Oxford. Yorkshire Post, 1936. Served War of 1939-45, with Royal Marines, 1940-45. Foreign Editor of the Observer, 1946-48. Croix de Guerre, 1944. *Address:* 12 Elm Tree Road, St John's Wood, NW8. *T:* 01-286 0223/4; Manor House, Sutton Courtenay, Berks. *T:* Sutton Courtenay 221. *Clubs:* Athenæum, Boodle's, Royal Automobile.

**ASTOR, Hon. Gavin;** President, Times Newspapers Ltd, since 1967; Director: Monotype Corporation Ltd, 1952; Alliance Assurance Co. Ltd, 1954; Chairman of Council, Commonwealth Press Union, since 1959; *b* 1 June 1918; *e s* and *heir* of 1st Baron Astor of Hever, *qv*; *m* 1945, Lady Irene Haig, *d* of late Field Marshal Earl Haig, KT, GCB, OM, GCVO, KCIE; two *s* three *d*. *Educ:* Eton; New Coll., Oxford. Served with The Life Guards, 1940-46. Director: C. Townsend Hook Ltd, 1954-65; Reuters Ltd, 1955-61; Electrolux Ltd, 1959-70; Chm., The Times Publishing Co. Ltd, 1959-66 (Dir, 1952-66); Co-Chief Proprietor of The Times, 1962-66. Chairman: 9th Commonwealth Press Conf., India and Pakistan, 1961; 10th Conf., West Indies, 1965; Exec. Cttee, Pilgrims Soc. of Gt Britain, 1967-. High Sheriff of Sussex, 1955-56, DL 1956; DL Kent 1966. FRSA 1965. *Address:* 11 Lyall Street, SW1 *T:* 01-235 4755; Hever Castle, Edenbridge, Kent. *T:* Edenbridge 2204; Tillypronie, Tarland, Aberdeenshire. *T:* Tarland 238. *Clubs:* Bath, White's.

*See also Hon. H. W. and Hon. John Astor.*

**ASTOR, Hon. Hugh Waldorf,** JP; Director: Hambro's Bank; Phœnix Assurance; Hutchinson Ltd; Winterbottom Trust Ltd; Olympia Ltd; *b* 20 Nov. 1920; 2nd *s* of 1st Baron Astor of Hever, *qv*; *m* 1950, Emily Lucy, *d* of Sir Alexander Kinloch, 12th Bt, *qv*; two *s* three *d*. *Educ:* Eton; New Coll., Oxford. Served War of 1939-45; Intelligence Corps, Europe and SE Asia (Lieut-Col). Joined The Times as Asst Middle East Correspondent, 1947; elected to Board of The Times, 1956; Dep. Chm., 1959, resigned 1967; Chm., The Times Book Co. Ltd, 1960, resigned 1967. Chm., Times Trust; Member of Council, Trust Houses Group Ltd. Dep. Chm., Middlesex Hosp.; Governor: Bradfield Coll.; Gresham Coll.; Hon. Treasurer, Franco-British Soc., 1969-. JP Berks, 1953; High Sheriff of Berks, 1963. *Recreations:* sailing, flying, shooting, diving. *Address:* Folly Farm, Sulhamstead, Berks. *T:* Theale 326; 14 Culross Street, W1. *T:* 01-629 4601. *Clubs:* Brooks's, Buck's, Royal Aero, Royal Yacht Squadron, Royal Ocean Racing.

*See also Hon. Gavin and Hon. John Astor.*

**ASTOR, Hon. John;** MP (C) Newbury since 1964; a Director, TPC (Investments) Ltd; *b* 26 Sept. 1923; 3rd *s* of 1st Baron Astor of Hever, *qv*; *m* 1950, Diana Kathleen Drummond; two *s* one *d*. *Educ:* Summerfields, Hastings; Eton Coll. RAFVR, 1942-45. Berkshire County Council, 1953; Alderman, 1960; Chairman, Education Cttee, 1961-66. Vice-Chm., South Berkshire Conservative Assoc., 1958 until 1963, when adopted as candidate. *Recreations:* fishing, shooting. *Address:* Kirby House, Inkpen, Berks. *T:* Inkpen 284. *Clubs:* Buck's; Royal Yacht Squadron.

*See also Hon. Gavin Astor, Hon. H. W. Astor.*

**ASTOR, Major Hon. John Jacob,** MBE 1945; DL, JP; Major, Life Guards; *b* 29 Aug. 1918; 4th *s* of 2nd Viscount Astor; *m* 1944, Ana Inez, *yr d* of Senor Dr Don Miguel Carcano, *qv*; one *s* one *d*. *Educ:* Eton; New Coll., Oxford. Served War of 1939-45: Italy, France, Germany, Norway; North-West Europe, 1944-45 (MBE, Legion of Honour, French Croix de Guerre). Contested (C) Sutton Div. of Plymouth, 1950; MP (C) Sutton Div. of Plymouth, 1951-Sept. 1959. Chm., Agric. Res. Council, 1968-. DL 1962, JP 1960, Cambs. *Address:* Hatley Park, Hatley St George, Sandy, Beds. *T:* Gamlingay 266. *Clubs:* Boodle's, Buck's, White's, Royal Automobile.

**ASTOR, Hon. Michael Langhorne;** *b* 10 April 1916; *s* of 2nd Viscount Astor; *m* 1st, 1942, Barbara Mary Colonsay (marr. diss., 1961; she *m* 1962, 1st Viscount Ward of Witley, *qv*), *o d* of late Capt. Ronald Fitzroy Rous McNeill; two *s* two *d*; 2nd, 1961, Mrs Pandora Jones (marr. diss. 1968), *d* of late Sir Bede Clifford, GCMG, CB, MVO; *m* 1970, Judy, *d* of Paul Innes. *Educ:* Eton; New College, Oxford. Served in Berkshire Yeomanry TA and GHQ Liaison Regt Sept. 1939-June 1945. MP (C) Eastern Division of Surrey, 1945-51. Farms 1000 acres Oxfordshire. Member: Arts Council, 1968-; Cttee, The London Library. *Publications:* Tribal Feeling (biog.), 1963; Brand (novel), 1967. *Address:* 1 Swan Walk, SW3. *T:* 01-352 1155; Bruern, Churchill, Oxfordshire. *Clubs:* Beefsteak, Garrick, White's.

**ASTURIAS, Miguel Angel;** Guatemalan writer and diplomat; Guatemalan Ambassador in Paris, since 1966; *b* 19 Oct. 1899. *Educ:* Instituto Nacional de Guatemala, University of Guatemala. Cultural Attaché, Guatemalan Embassy, Mexico, 1946-47; Counsellor, 1947-52; Minister, Paris, 1952-53; Ambassador to El Salvador, 1953. Founder, General Students' Association, and Popular Univ., Guatemala. Prizes: Sylla Monsegur, Paris, 1931; du Meilleur Roman Etranger, Paris, 1952; Lenin Peace Prize, 1966; Nobel Prize for Literature, 1967. *Publications:* El Problema Social del Indio, 1923; Arquitectura de la Vida Nueva (Lectures), 1928; Layendas de Guatemala, 1930; El Señor Presidente, 1946; Sien de Alondra (anthology of poetry 1918-48), 1948;

Hombres de Maiz, 1949; Viento Fuerte, 1950; El Papa Verde, 1953; Week-end en Guatemala, 1955; Los Ojos de los Enterrados, 1960; El Alhajadito, 1961; Mulata de Tal, 1963; Antologia Teatral, 1964; Clarivigilia Primaveral (poems), 1965; Le Miroir de Lida Sal, 1967. *Address:* Ambassade de Guatemala, rue de Courcelles 73, Paris 8e, France.

**ATHABASCA, Bishop of,** since 1950; **Rt. Rev. Reginald James Pierce,** Hon. DD (Winnipeg), 1947; *b* 1909; *s* of James Reginald Pierce and Clara (*née* Whitehand), Plymouth; *m* 1932, Ivy Bell, *d* of Edward and Lucy Jackson, Saskatoon, Canada; one *d*. *Educ:* University of Saskatchewan (BA 1931); Emmanuel Coll., Saskatoon (LTh 1932); Univ. of London (BD 1942). Deacon, 1932; priest, 1934; Curate of Colinton, 1932-33; Priest-in-charge, 1933-34; Rector and Rural Dean of Grande Prairie, 1934-38; Rector of South Saanich, 1938-41; Rector of St Barnabas, Calgary, 1941-43; Canon of St John's Cathedral, Winnipeg, and Warden of St John's Coll., 1943-50; Priest-in-charge of St Barnabas, Winnipeg, 1946-50. Examining Chaplain: to Bishop of Athabasca, 1935-38; to Archbishop of Rupertsland, 1943-50. *Address:* Bishop's Lodge, Peace River, Alberta, Canada.

**ATHABASCA, Bishop Suffragan of,** since 1966; called locally Bishop of Mackenzie since 1967; **Rt. Rev. Henry George Cook;** *b* Walthamstow, London, England, 12 Oct. 1906; *s* of Henry G. Cook and Ada Mary Evans; *m* 1935, Opal May Thompson, Sarnia, Ont, *d* of Wesley Thompson and Charity Ellen Britney; two *s* one *d*. *Educ:* Ingersoll Collegiate Inst., Ont; Huron Coll. (LTh); Univ. of Western Ont, London, Canada (BA). Deacon, 1935, Priest, 1936; Missionary at Fort Simpson, 1935-43; Canon of Athabasca, 1940-43; Incumbent S Porcupine, Ont., 1943-44; Archdeacon of James Bay, 1945-48; Principal, Bp Horden Sch., Moose Factory, 1945-48; Mem., Gen. Synod Exec., 1943-47; Supt of Indian Sch. Admin., 1948-62; Bishop Suffragan of the Arctic, 1963-66. RCN(R) Chaplain, 1949-. Hon. DD Huron Coll. and Univ. of Western Ont, 1946. *Recreations:* fishing, coin collecting, model carving. *Address:* Box 158, Yellowknife, Northwest Territories, Canada.

**ATHAIDE, Most Rev. D. R.;** *see* Agra, Archbishop of, (RC).

**ATHENAGORAS, Spyrou;** Oecumenical Patriarch, also Archbishop of Constantinople and New Rome, since Nov. 1948; *b* 1886. *Educ:* Theological Academy of Halki, Istanbul, Turkey. Metropolitan of Corfu, 1923-30; Archbishop of North and South America, 1930-48. *Address:* Rum Ortodoks Patrikhanesi, Fener, Istanbul, Turkey. *T:* 212532-211921.

**ATHENAGORAS, Theodoritos,** (*né* **Theodoros G. Kokkinakis**), STM, MA, STD; Archbishop Athenagoras, Metropolitan of Thyateira and Great Britain, since 1964; Exarch of Sweden, Norway, Ireland, Iceland, and Malta; *b* Patmos, Dodecanese, 1912. *Educ:* schs in Patmos and Cyprus; Patriarchal Theological Seminary; Gen. Theolog. Seminary, NY; Northwestern Univ., Chicago. Went to USA 1936. Priest, Greek Orthodox Church, 1940. Formerly: served Patriarchal Church of St Sava, Alexandria, St Andrew's Church, Chicago and St Demetrios Church, Astoria, NY; taught theology at Acad. of Pomfret, Conn. and at Acad. of St Basil; Dean and then Pres., Holy Cross Theolog. Sch., Brookline, Mass; rep. The Ecumenical Patriarchate of Constantinople at World Council of Churches Conferences: Amsterdam, Evanston, New Delhi, Uppsala; Bishop, Western States Dio., 1950; Metropolitan Bishop of Canada, 1960-63. Pres. 4th Panorthodox Conference, Belgrade, 1967. Editor, Orthodox Herald; past Editor, Orthodox Observer and Greek Orthodox Theolog. Review. Hon. DD Edinburgh, 1970. *Publications:* several books in English and in Greek. *Address:* Greek Archdiocese, 5 Craven Hill, W2. *T:* 01-723 4787.

**ATHERTON, Ernest;** Regional Director (NW Region), Ministry of Technology; *b* 27 Oct. 1916; 2nd *s* of E. Atherton; *m* 1967, Christel Gertrud Posselt; one *s*. *Educ:* Manchester Grammar Sch.; King's Coll., Cambridge. Served War, Royal Armoured Corps, 1940-46, Captain. Board of Trade, 1947-69. *Recreations:* music, sport. *Address:* Ministry of Technology, Sunley Building, Piccadilly Plaza, Manchester 1. *T:* 061-832 9111. *Club:* Leeds (Leeds).

**ATHLONE, Countess of; (HRH Princess Alice Mary Victoria Augusta Pauline; Princess Alice, Countess of Athlone),** VA 1898; GCVO 1948; GBE 1937; *b* 25 Feb. 1883; *d* of HRH Prince Leopold George Duncan Albert, 1st Duke of Albany, KG, PC, KT, GCSI, GCMG (4th *s* of Queen Victoria) and HSH Princess Helene Friederike Auguste, VA, CI, RRC (*d* 1922); *m* 1904, Maj.-Gen. the 1st Earl of Athlone, KG, PC, GCB, GCMG, GCVO, DSO, FRS (*d* 1957), 3rd *s* of HH the 1st Duke of Teck, GCB, and brother of HM Queen Mary; one *d* (two *s* decd). Commandant-in-Chief, Women's Transport Service (FANY). Chairman of Governors, Royal Holloway Coll., 1936-Dec. 1958, resigned; Chancellor, Univ. of West Indies, 1950-. Hon. DLitt: London Univ., 1933; Queen's Univ., Kingston, Ont., 1943; McGill Univ., 1944; Birmingham Univ., 1946; Hon. LLD St Andrews Univ., 1951. Hon. Freeman: Weavers' Co., 1947; Vintners' Co., 1956; Royal Borough of Kensington, 1961. DGStJ. Grand Cross, Legion of Honour, France. *Address:* Clock House, Kensington Palace, W8.

*See also Col Sir Henry Abel Smith.*

**ATHOLL,** 10th Duke of, *cr* 1703; **George Iain Murray;** Lord Murray of Tullibardine, 1604; Earl of Tullibardine, Lord Gask and Balquhidder, 1606; Earl of Atholl, 1629; Marquess of Atholl, Viscount Balquhidder, Lord Balvenie, 1676; Marquess of Tullibardine, Earl of Strathtay, Earl of Strathardle, Viscount Glenalmond, Viscount Glenlyon, 1703-all in the peerage of Scotland; Representative Peer for Scotland in the House of Lords, 1958-63; *b* 19 June 1931; *s* of Lieut-Col George Anthony Murray, OBE, Scottish Horse (killed in action, Italy, 1945), and of Hon. Mrs Angela Campbell-Preston, *qv*; *S* kinsman 1957. *Educ:* Eton; Christ Church, Oxford. Convener, Scottish Lifeboat Council; Chm., Tridant Group Printers; Dir, Westminster Press. *Heir:* *cousin* Arthur Stewart Pakington Murray, *b* 9 Sept. 1899. *Address:* Blair Castle, Blair Atholl, Perthshire. *T:* Blair Atholl 212; 31 Marlborough Hill, NW8. *Clubs:* Buck's, Turf, White's.

**ATIYAH, Michael Francis,** MA, PhD Cantab; FRS 1962; Professor of Mathematics, The Institute for Advanced Study, Princeton, NJ, since 1969; *b* 22 April 1929; *e s* of late Edward Atiyah and Jean Levens; *m* 1955, Lily Brown; three *s*. *Educ:* Victoria Coll., Egypt; Manchester Grammar Sch.; Trinity Coll., Cambridge. Research Fellow, Trinity Coll., Camb., 1954-58; First Smith's Prize, 1954; Commonwealth Fund Fellow, 1955-56; Mem. Inst. for Advanced Study, Princeton, 1955-56, 1959-60, 1967-68; Asst Lectr in Mathematics,

1957-58, Lectr 1958-61, Univ. of Cambridge; Fellow Pembroke Coll., Cambridge, 1958-61; Reader in Mathematics, Univ. of Oxford, and Professorial Fellow of St Catherine's Coll., Oxford, 1961-63; Savilian Prof. of Geometry, and Fellow of New College, Oxford, 1963-69. Visiting Lecturer, Harvard, 1962-63 and 1964-65. Mem. Exec. Cttee, Internat. Mathematical Union, 1966. Hon. DSc: Bonn; Warwick. Fields Medal, Internat. Congress of Mathematicians, Moscow, 1966; Royal Medal, Royal Soc., 1968. *Publications:* papers in mathematical journals. *Recreation:* gardening. *Address:* School of Mathematics, Institute for Advanced Study, Princeton, NJ 08540, USA; 56 Maxwell Lane, Princeton, NJ.

**ATKINS, Professor Sir Hedley (John Barnard),** KBE 1967; DM, MCh, FRCS, FRCP; Professor of Surgery, University of London, since 1961; Director of the Department of Surgery, Guy's Hospital, since 1947; *b* 30 Dec. 1905; *s* of Col Sir John Atkins, KCMG, KCVO, FRCS; *m* 1933, Gladwys Gwendolen, *e d* of Frank Harding Jones; two *s*. *Educ:* Rugby; Trinity Coll., Oxford; Guy's Hospital. War of 1939-45 (despatches): Temp. Lieut-Col RAMC, 1941. Surgeon to Guy's Hosp., 1936; Hunterian Professor, RCS, 1936; Examiner in Surgery at: Cambridge Univ., 1947; London Univ., 1948; Durham Univ., 1950; Univ. of The W Indies 1960; Member: Court of Examiners, RCS, 1950, Council, 1952; Gen. Dental Council, 1954; Gen. Medical Council, 1955; Central Health Services Council, 1956; Dean of the Institute of Basic Med. Sciences, 1957-62; Clinical Research Bd, Med. Research Council, 1959; Pres. Surgical Research Soc., 1960. Visiting Professor: Johns Hopkins Hosp., 1947; UCLA, 1954; Univ. of California, 1956; Sims Commonwealth Travelling Prof., 1961. Lectures: Arton, Middlesex Hosp., 1970; Cavendish, W London Med. Chir. Soc., 1970; Gidson de Laune, Soc. of Apothecaries, 1970. Mem. Med. Advisory Cttee of British Council, 1962; Chm., MRC working party, on Tristan da Cunha, 1962; Mem. Med. Consultative Cttee of Nuffield Provincial Hosps Trust, 1962; Chm., Med. Res. Council Cttee on Uses of High Oxygen Tension, 1963, and on Gastric Hypothermia, 1963; Mem., Med. Research Council, 1963; Thomas Vicary Lecturer, Royal Coll. of Surgeons, 1964; Examr in Surgery, at Birmingham Univ., 1964; Vice-Chm., Standing Med. Adv. Cttee (of Central Health Services Council), 1964; Chairman: (MRC) Cttee on Endolymphatic Therapy, 1965; Jt Bd, Clinical Nursing Studies, 1969-; Med. Bd, St John, 1969. Chm. Council, Queen Elizabeth Coll., Univ. of London, 1969-. Pres., Section of Measurement in Medicine of Royal Soc. Med., 1965; Pres., RCS, 1966-69 (Vice-Pres. 1964-66); Bradshaw Lectr, RCS, 1965; Hunterian Orator, RCS, 1971. Governor, Strangeways Research Laboratory, Cambridge, 1968. Hon. FACS, 1956; Hon. FRACS, 1961; Hon. FCS (So. Af.), 1968; Hon. FRCP&S (Can.) 1969; Hon. Fellow: Trinity Coll., Oxford, 1968; Queen Elizabeth Coll., Univ. of London, 1968; American Surgical Assoc., 1966; New England Surgical Soc. Thomas and Edith Dixon Medal, 1965. Hon. DSc East Anglia, 1968. KStJ 1968. *Publications:* After-Treatment, 1942; (author of Biographical introduction) Hilton's Rest and Pain, 1950; (ed) Tools of Biological Research, 1959; The Surgeon's Craft; numerous articles in med. jls. *Recreation:* gardening. *Address:* Down House, Downe, Kent BR6 7JT. *Clubs:* Athenæum, Garrick; Vincent's (Oxford); Royal Cruising.

**ATKINS, Henry St J.,** DSc; President, University College, Cork, 1954-63, retired; *b* 19 March 1896; *s* of Patrick Atkins and Agnes Egan, Cork; *m* 1929, Agnes E. O'Regan (*d* 1960), MB, BCh; one *s* one *d*. *Educ:* Christian Brothers, North Monastery, Cork; University Coll., Cork. BSc (Math. Science) 1915; post-grad. scholar, MSc 1923. Prof. of Pure Maths, University Coll., Cork, 1936-54; Registrar, 1943-54. Hon. DSc 1955. MRIA, 1957. *Recreations:* golf, fishing. *Address:* Knockrea Park, Cork. *T:* Cork 32448. *Clubs:* National University of Ireland; Cork City and County (Cork).

**ATKINS, Humphrey Edward,** MP (C) Spelthorne since 1970 (Merton and Morden, Surrey, 1955-70); Treasurer of HM Household, since 1970; *b* 12 Aug. 1922; *s* of late Capt. E. D. Atkins, Nyeri, Kenya Colony; *m* 1944, Margaret, *d* of Sir Robert Spencer-Nairn, 1st Bt; one *s* three *d*. *Educ:* Wellington Coll. Special entry cadetship, RN, 1940; Lieut RN, 1943; resigned, 1948. Parliamentary Private Sec. to Civil Lord of the Admiralty, 1959-62; Hon.. Sec. Conservative Parly Defence Cttee, 1965-67; Opposition Whip, 1967-. Vice-Chm., Management Cttee, Outward Bound Trust, 1966-70. *Address:* 3 North Court, Great Peter Street, SW1; Beech House, Bembridge, IOW. *Club:* Brooks's.

**ATKINS, Ian Robert,** OBE 1963; Controller, Programme Services, Television, BBC, since 1963; *b* 22 Jan. 1912; *s* of Robert Atkins, *qv*, and late Mary (*née* Sumner); *m* 1939, Freda Bamford; one *s* one *d*. *Educ:* St Paul's Sch. Film cameraman, 1930-33; theatre stage manager, 1934-36; asst film dir, 1936-37; theatre stage manager, 1937-39. Royal Artillery, 1939-46; seconded to Min. of Supply, 1942-46. Television, BBC: Television Studio Manager, BBC, 1939 and 1946; Producer, Drama Dept, 1946-58; Asst to Controller, Programme Services, 1958-62; Asst Controller, Programme Services, 1962-63. *Recreations:* gardening, caravanning. *Address:* Ash Cottage, Blacksmith Lane, London Street, Chertsey, Surrey. *T:* Chertsey 3161.

**ATKINS, John Spencer,** DSO 1945; TD; DL; Chairman, Atkins Brothers (Hosiery) Ltd, since 1965; *b* 28 Oct. 1905; 3rd *s* of late Col E. C. Atkins, CB, DL; *m* 1936, Monica Lucy Standish; one *s* two *d*. *Educ:* Uppingham Sch. DL 1946; Vice-Lieutenant County of Leicestershire, 1966-. *Recreations:* shooting, hunting, fishing. *Address:* White House, Ullesthorpe, Rugby. *T:* Leire 274. *Clubs:* Naval and Military; Leicestershire (Leicester).

**ATKINS, Leonard B. W.;** *see* Walsh Atkins.

**ATKINS, Robert,** CBE 1949; actor and producer; *b* Dulwich, 10 Aug. 1886; *s* of Robert Atkins and Annie Evans; *m* 1st, Mary Sumner (marr. diss.); *m* 2nd, Ethel Davey. *Educ:* privately; Academy of Dramatic Art. First appearance His Majesty's, 1906; three years with Sir Herbert Tree; one season with Glasgow Repertory Company; with Martin Harvey on tour and at Lyceum, 1911; with Forbes Robertson on tour, at Drury Lane, 1913, and in America; toured with Sir Frank Benson's Shakespearean Companies; joined Old Vic Company, 1915; war service; after demobilisation, 1919, toured with Ben Greet's Company; Dir of the Plays at Old Vic, 1920-25; produced and appeared in many plays since 1926 at London Theatres; took his own Shakespearean Repertory Company to Egypt, 1927 and 1928; Dir of British Empire Shakespeare Society, 1927; produced and played lead in Mussolini's Napoleon, New Theatre, 1932 (Cavaliere of Order of Crown of Italy); produced plays at Open Air Theatre, 1933-39, and appeared in many of them; managed and produced the plays in Regent's Park during war years including 1944, also subsequently, continuing annual seasons of producing and playing in Shakespearean and other productions there. Produced Henry V at Stratford-on-Avon, 1934; Dir of Stratford-on-Avon Shakespeare Memorial Theatre Festival Company, 1944-45; produced adaptation of an Elizabethan masque, in the hall of Gray's Inn, 1956. First appeared in films, 1935, in Peg of Old Drury.

*See also I. R. Atkins.*

**ATKINS, Ronald Henry;** *b* Barry, Glam, 13 June 1916; *s* of Frank and Elizabeth Atkins; *m*; three *s* two *d*. *Educ:* Barry County Sch.; London Univ. (BA Hons). Teacher, 1949-66 (latterly Head, Eng. Dept, Halstead Sec. Sch.). Mem., Braintree RDC, 1952-61. Contested (Lab) Lowestoft, 1964; MP (Lab) Preston North, 1966-70. Pres., Coggeshall Local Labour Pty; Tutor and Lectr, Nat. Coun. of Labour Colls. *Recreations:* jazz, dancing, walking. *Address:* 6 Buttermere Close, Fulwood, Preston; 5 Kelvedon Road, Coggleshall, Essex. *Clubs:* Preston North End Supporters (Vice-Pres.); various Labour.

**ATKINS, William Sydney Albert,** CBE 1966; Chairman: W. S. Atkins & Partners, since 1951 Mount Diston Ltd; *b* 6 Feb. 1902; 2nd *s* of Robert Edward and Martha Atkins; *m* 1928, Elsie Jessie, *d* of Edward and Hilda Barrow, Hockley, Essex; two *d*. *Educ:* Coopers' Sch.; London Univ. Chief Engr, Smith Walker Ltd, 1928; Man. Dir, London Ferro-Concrete Co. Ltd, 1935, Chm. 1937; Founder and Sen. Partner, W. S. Atkins & Partners, 1938. Director: W. S. Atkins & Partners (Ethiopia) Ltd, 1963; W. S. Atkins Private Ltd, India, 1964; W. S. Atkins International Ltd. Mem. Council, London Chamber of Commerce. Fellow, University Coll., London. *Publications:* many technical papers. *Recreations:* gardening and horticultural research. *Address:* Chobham Place, Chobham, near Woking, Surrey. *T:* Chobham 8867. *Club:* Royal Automobile.

**ATKINSON, Brooks;** *see* Atkinson, J. B.

**ATKINSON, Colin Ronald Michael;** Acting Headmaster, Millfield School, Somerset, 1969-70 (Headmaster from Sept. 1971); *b* 23 July 1931; *s* of R. and E. Atkinson; *m* 1957, Shirley Angus; two *s* one *d*. *Educ:* Hummersknott, Darlington, Co. Durham; Durham Univ. (BA); Queen's Univ., Belfast (BA, MA); Nottingham Univ. (Teaching Certif.); Loughborough Coll. of Educn (Physical Educn Dip.); Postgrad. work in Psychology. Served 5th Fusiliers (Northumberland) in Kenya (Mau Mau) and in N Ireland, National Service, 1954-56. The Friends' School, Great Ayton, 1956-58; Haughton School, Darlington, 1958-60; Millfield, 1960-. West of England Hockey and Chief Divl coach; Founder Mem.: Nat. Hockey Coaching Cttee; Nat. Cricket Coaching Cttee. *Publications:* (manual) Hockey Coaching, 1967; An Experiment in Closed Circuit TV at Millfield School, 1970; Somerset in the Sixties, 1971. *Recreations:* County Representation in five sports; former Captain Somerset CCC XI and County Hockey XI. *Address:* Millfield School, Street, Somerset. *T:* Street 2291. *Clubs:* MCC, Free Foresters, I Zingari.

**ATKINSON, Rt. Hon. Sir Fenton,** PC 1968; Kt 1960; **Rt. Hon. Lord Justice Atkinson;** a Lord Justice of Appeal since 1968; *b* 6 Jan. 1906; *s* of late Hon. Sir Cyril Atkinson; *m* 1929, Margaret Mary, *d* of James Edward and Mary Roy, Scotscraig, Radlett; one *s* two *d*. *Educ:* Winchester; New Coll., Oxford (MA). Called to Bar, 1928; Bencher of Lincoln's Inn, 1958. Joined Northern Circuit and practised in Manchester, 1928-39. Served War of 1939-45: 2/Lieut Royal Norfolk Regt, 1939; Staff Captain and DAAG Madras District, 1940-42; AAG Southern Army, India, 1943; AAG, GHQ, India, 1944; Pres. Military Govt Court, Germany, 1945; released with rank of Colonel, 1945. QC 1953; Judge of the Salford Hundred Court of Record, 1953-60; Deputy Chm., Hertfordshire Quarter Sessions, 1958-60; Judge of High Court, Queen's Bench Div., 1960-68. Member, Royal Commn on Assizes and Quarter Sessions, 1966-67. *Recreations:* gardening, golf and reading. *Address:* Royal Courts of Justice, Strand, WC2; Dalbeathie House, Dunkeld, Perthshire. *T:* 230.

**ATKINSON, Frank Stuart,** MEng, MInstCE, MIMinE; Professor of Mining, Sheffield University, 1954-65, retired; Emeritus Professor, 1965; Dean of the Faculty of Engineering, 1963-65; *b* 3 Oct. 1899; *s* of Thomas Henry and Ettie Atkinson; *m* 1925, Winifred Sarah Routledge; two *s* one *d*. *Educ:* Chesterfield Grammar Sch.; Sheffield Univ. Articled pupil to Dr J. H. W. Laverick, JP; Asst Manager of Frickley Colliery, 1924-27; Manager of the Hatfield Main Colliery of the Carlton Main Group, 1927-35; Professor of Mining, Univ. of Leeds, 1936-41; Gen. Manager Upton Colliery of Dorman, Long & Co. Ltd, 1941-46; Shaw, Wallace & Co. Ltd, India, 1946-49; Asst Production Dir, NE Div. Nat. Coal Bd, 1949-54. *Publications:* contributed many papers to technical press. *Address:* 15 Blenheim Chase, Leigh-on-Sea, Essex.

**ATKINSON, Frederick John;** Controller (Economics and Statistics), Ministry of Technology, since 1970; *b* 7 Dec. 1919; *s* of George Edward Atkinson and of late Elizabeth Sabina Cooper; *m* 1947, Margaret Grace Gibson; two *d*. *Educ:* Dulwich Coll.; Jesus Coll., Oxford. Lectr, Jesus and Trinity Colls, Oxford, 1947-49; Economic Section, Cabinet Office, 1949-51; British Embassy, Washington, 1952-54; HM Treasury, 1955-62; Economic Adviser, Foreign Office, 1962-63; HM Treasury, 1963-69 (Dep. Dir, Economic Section, Treasury, 1965-69). *Recreation:* reading. *Address:* 26 Lee Terrace, Blackheath, SE3. *T:* 01-852 1040; Tickner Cottage, Aldington, Kent. *T:* Aldington 514.

**ATKINSON, Professor James;** Professor of Biblical Studies, University of Sheffield, since 1967; *b* 27 April 1914; *s* of Nicholas Ridley Atkinson and Margaret (*née* Hindhaugh); *m* 1939, Laura Jean Nutley (decd); one *s* one *d*. *Educ:* Tynemouth High Sch.; Univ. of Durham. MA 1939, MLitt 1950 Durham; DrTheol, Münster, Germany, 1955. Curate, Newcastle upon Tyne, 1937; Precentor, Sheffield Cath., 1941; Vicar, Sheffield, 1944; Fellow, Univ. of Sheffield, 1951; Canon Theologian, Leicester, 1954; Reader in Theology, Univ. of Hull, 1956; Vis. Prof., Chicago, 1966. Mem., Anglican-Roman Catholic Preparatory Commission, 1967-. *Publications:* Library of Christian Classics, Vol. XVI, 1962; Rome and Reformation, 1965; Luther's Works, Vol. 44, 1966; Luther and the Birth of Protestantism, 1968; The Reformation, Paternoster Church History, Vol. 4, 1968; The Trial of Luther, 1970; contribs to learned jls, also essays and parts of books. *Recreations:* gardening, music. *Address:* Leach House, Hathersage, Derbyshire. *T:* Hathersage 570.

**ATKINSON, John Alexander,** DFC 1943; Assistant Under-Secretary of State, Department of Health and Social Security, since 1968 (Ministry of Social Security, 1966-68); *b* 9 June 1919; *yr s* of late Rev. R. F.

Atkinson and late Harriet Harrold Atkinson, BSc (*née* Lowdon); *m* 1945, Marguerite Louise Pearson; one *d. Educ:* Kingswood Sch.; Queen's Coll., Oxford. Served in RAF, 1939-45. Asst Prin., 1946, Prin., 1949. Min. of Nat. Insce; Cabinet Office, 1950-52; Prin. Private Sec. to Minister of Pensions and Nat. Insce, 1957-58; Asst Sec., 1958. *Address:* Bleak House, The Drive, Belmont, Sutton, Surrey. *T:* 01-642 6479. *Club:* Oxford and Cambridge University.

**ATKINSON, Sir (John) Kenneth,** Kt 1953; retired as Chief Valuer, Valuation Office, Board of Inland Revenue (1951-66); *b* 21 May 1905; 2nd *s* of late James Oswald and Jane Atkinson, Liverpool; *m* 1930, Ellen Elsie Godwin Dod; one *d. Educ:* The Leys, Cambridge. Joined Valuation Office, 1928; Deputy Chief Valuer, 1950. Fellow of the Royal Institution of Chartered Surveyors; Fellow of the Chartered Auctioneers and Estate Agents Institute. *Recreation:* Rugby football. *Address:* Clouds, High Park Avenue, East Horsley, Surrey. *T:* East Horsley 3103.

**ATKINSON, (Justin) Brooks;** US journalist and writer; retired as Staff Writer, New York Times; *b* Melrose, Massachusetts, USA, 28 Nov. 1894; *s* of Jonathan H. Atkinson and Garafelia Taylor; *m* 1926, Oriana Torrey MacIlveen; one step *s. Educ:* Harvard Univ. (AB). Reporter, Springfield Daily News, 1917; Teacher of English, Dartmouth Coll., 1917-18; Boston Evening Transcript, Reporter and Asst Drama Critic, 1919-22; New York Times, 1922-65: Editor Book Review, 1922-25; Drama Critic, 1925-42; War Correspondent, China, 1942-44; Correspondent in Russia, 1945-46; Drama Critic, 1946-60; retd, 1965. Pulitzer Prize for Journalism, 1947. Hon. LHD Williams College, Mass, 1941; Hon. LLD: Adelphi Coll., NY; Pace Coll., NY, 1961; Franklin and Marshall Coll., 1962; Brandeis Univ. 1965; Clark Univ., 1966; Washington Coll., 1966. *Publications:* Skyline Promenades, 1925; Henry Thoreau, the Cosmic Yankee, 1927; East of the Hudson, 1931; Cingalese Prince, 1935; Once Around the Sun, 1951; Tuesdays and Fridays, 1963; Brief Chronicles, 1966; Broadway, 1970; (ed) Walden and other writings of Henry David Thoreau, 1937; (ed) Complete Essays and other writings of Ralph Waldo Emerson, 1940; (ed) Sean O'Casey Reader, 1968. *Address:* Durham, NY 12422, USA.

**ATKINSON, Sir Kenneth;** *see* Atkinson, Sir J. K.

**ATKINSON, Leonard Allan,** CMG 1963; *b* 6 Dec. 1906; *s* of L. Atkinson; *m* 1933, Annie R., *d* of A. E. Wells; one *s* two *d. Educ:* Wellington Coll. and Victoria Univ. of Wellington, New Zealand. Joined Customs Dept, 1924; Inspector, Public Service Commission, 1941-44; Sec., 1944-47; Asst Comr, 1947-54; Commission Member, 1954-58; Chm., 1958-62; Chm., State Services Commission, NZ, 1963-66. *Recreation:* bowls. *Address:* 181 The Parade, Island Bay, Wellington, NZ. *Club:* Wellington (NZ).

**ATKINSON, Maj.-Gen. Sir Leonard Henry,** KBE 1966 (OBE 1945); *b* 4 Dec. 1910; *s* of A. H. Atkinson; *m* 1939, Jean Eileen, *d* of C. A. Atchley, OBE; one *s* three *d. Educ:* Wellington Coll., Berks; University Coll., London. BSc (Eng) 1932; commnd in RAOC, 1933; transf. to REME, 1942; Comdr REME (Lieut-Col) Guards Armd Div. (NW Europe), 1943-45; DDEME (Col) Brit. Airborne Corps, India, 1945; Staff Coll., Quetta, 1945-46; served in Far East, UK and WO, 1946-50; JSSC, 1950-51; GSO1, REME Trg Centre, 1951-53; DDEME (Col) HQ 1st Corps (Germany), 1953-55; DDEME (Brig.). WO, 1956-58; Comdt (Brig.) REME Training Centre and Commander Berkshire Dist, 1958-63; Dir, Electrical and Mechanical Engineering, Army, 1963-66; Col Comdt, REME, 1967-. Man. Dir, Harland Simon, 1970-; Director: Harland Engineering, 1966-69; Simon Equipment, 1966-69; Weir Engineering Industries, 1970-. FIMechE; FIEE; FIERE (past Pres.). *Address:* Pound Cottage, Silchester, near Reading, Berks. *T:* Bramley Green 220. *Club:* Naval and Military.

**ATKINSON, Leslie,** CMG 1965; OBE 1961; Managing Director, Leslie Atkinson Pty. Ltd, since 1960; Member of Export Development Council, Sydney, since 1959; *b* 11 Jan. 1913; *s* of J. Atkinson; *m* 1935, Ellen, *d* of J. Kinsey; one *s* one *d. Educ:* Wollongong Technical Sch. Controller, Nock and Kirby Ltd, 1943-49, Associate Dir, 1949-53; Dir and General Manager, Carr and Elliott, 1953-59. Pres., Sydney Junior Chamber of Commerce, 1946-47; Vice-Pres. and Hon. Treasurer, Sydney Chamber of Commerce, 1949-53, Pres., 1953-54, 1957-58; Vice-Pres., Associated Chambers of Commerce of the Commonwealth of Australia (Pres., 1964-65). Mem. of Standing Cttee, NSW Methodist Conference, 1957-62. *Address:* 28 Castlereagh Crescent, Sylvania Waters, New South Wales, Australia.

**ATKINSON, Norman;** MP (Lab) Tottenham since 1964; *b* 25 March 1923; *s* of George Atkinson, Manchester; *m* 1948, Irene Parry. *Educ:* elementary and technical schs. Member of Manchester City Council, 1945-49. Chief Design Engineer, Manchester University, 1957-64. Contested (Lab) Wythenshawe, 1955, Altrincham and Sale, 1959. *Recreations:* walking, cricket, football. *Address:* House of Commons, SW1; 4 Willow Court, Willow Place, SW1.

**ATKINSON, Prof. Richard John Copland,** MA; FSA 1946; Professor of Archaeology, University College, Cardiff, since 1958; Deputy Principal, University College, Cardiff, since 1970; *b* 22 Jan. 1920; *e s* of Roland Cecil Atkinson and Alice Noel Herbert Atkinson (*née* Wright); *m* 1942, Hester Renée Marguerite Cobb; three *s. Educ:* Sherborne School; Magdalen College, Oxford. Asst Keeper, Department of Antiquities, Ashmolean Museum, Oxford, 1944-49; Lectr in Prehistoric Archæology, Univ. of Edinburgh, 1949-58. Member: Ancient Monuments Board for Wales, 1959-; Cttee of Enquiry into Arrangement for Protection of Field Monuments, 1966-68; Royal Commission: on Ancient Monuments (Wales) 1963-; on Historical Monuments (England), 1968-. Vice-President: Prehistoric Society, 1963-67; Council for British Archæology, 1970- (Hon. Sec., 1964-70); Dir, BBC Silbury Hill project, 1967-69. *Publications:* Field Archæology, 1946; Stonehenge, 1956; Stonehenge and Avebury, 1959; Archæology, History and Science, 1960. Articles in archæological journals. *Recreations:* archæology, wood-work and wine. *Address:* The Old Rectory, Wenvoe, Glamorgan CF5 6AN. *Club:* United University.

**ATKINSON, William Christopher;** Stevenson Professor of Hispanic Studies in University of Glasgow since 1932; Director, Institute of Latin-American Studies, since 1966; *b* Belfast, 9 Aug. 1902; *s* of Robert Joseph Atkinson; *m* 1928, Evelyn Lucy, *d* of C. F. Wakefield, Hampstead; one *s* three *d. Educ:* Univs of Belfast and Madrid. Lectr in Spanish at Armstrong Coll., Newcastle upon Tyne, 1926-32; Hon. Sec., Modern Humanities Research Assoc., 1929-36; Head of Spanish and

Portuguese sections, Foreign Research and Press Service of Royal Institute of International Affairs, 1939-43; Visiting British Council Lecturer to Latin America, 1946, 1960; Hon. Prof. National Univ. of Colombia, 1946; Chm. 1st Scottish cultural delegation to USSR, 1954; Carnegie Research Fellow visiting US Univs, 1955; Member, Hispanic Society of America, 1955 (Corres. Mem., 1937); Rockefeller Fellow visiting LatinAmerican Univs, 1957; Visiting Prof. of Portuguese Studies, University Coll. of Rhodesia and Nyasaland, 1963. *Publications:* Spain, A Brief History, 1934; The Lusiads of Camoens, 1952; The Remarkable Life of Don Diego, 1958; A History of Spain and Portugal, 1960; The Conquest of New Granada, 1961. Contributions to Encyclopædia Britannica, learned periodicals and reviews, and to composite works on Spanish and Portuguese studies. *Recreations:* travel and tramping. *Address:* Andorra, Bearsden, Glasgow. *T:* 041-942 0368.

**ATTENBOROUGH, David Frederick;** Director of Programmes, Television, BBC, since 1969; *b* 8 May 1926; *s* of Frederick Levi Attenborough, *qv*; *m* 1950, Jane Elizabeth Ebsworth Oriel; one *s* one *d*. *Educ:* Wyggeston Gram. Sch. for Boys, Leicester; Clare Coll., Cambridge. Served in Royal Navy, 1947-49. Editorial Asst in an educational publishing house, 1949-52; joined BBC Television Service as trainee producer, 1952; undertook zoological and filming expeditions to: Sierra Leone, 1954; British Guiana, 1955; Indonesia, 1956; New Guinea, 1957; Paraguay and Argentina, 1958; South West Pacific, 1959; Madagascar, 1960; Northern Territory of Australia, 1962; the Zambesi, 1964; Controller, BBC-2, BBC Television Service, 1965-68. Silver Medal, Zool Soc. of London, 1966. *Publications:* Zoo Quest to Guiana, 1956; Zoo Quest for a Dragon, 1957; Zoo Quest in Paraguay, 1959; Quest in Paradise, 1960; Zoo Quest to Madagascar, 1961; Quest under Capricorn, 1963. *Recreations:* music, books, and natural history. *Address:* 5 Park Road, Richmond, Surrey. *T:* 01-940 5055.

**ATTENBOROUGH, Frederick L.,** MA; Principal of University College, Leicester, 1932-51; *b* 4 April 1887; *s* of Frederick and Mary Attenborough, Stapleford, Notts; *m* 1922, Mary (*d* 1961), *d* of Samuel and Mary Clegg, New Sawley, Notts; three *s*. *Educ:* County Schs, Long Eaton; Emmanuel Coll., Cambridge. Entered Normal Coll., Bangor, 1906; Schoolmaster in Liverpool and Long Eaton, 1908-15; entered Emmanuel Coll., 1915: Foundation Scholar and Choral Exhibitioner; First Class Hons Modern and Medieval Languages Triposes; Research Student, 1918-20; Fellow, 1920-25; Principal, Borough Road Training Coll., Isleworth, 1925-32. *Publication:* The Laws of the Earliest English Kings, 1922. *Recreations:* photography, music. *Address:* 22 Marchmont Road, Richmond, Surrey. *T:* 01-940 0237.

*See also David F. Attenborough, Richard S. Attenborough.*

**ATTENBOROUGH, James,** CMG 1915; TD; Colonel (retired) TF; Solicitor; *b* 7 Aug. 1884; *e s* of Stanley J. Attenborough, 30 Clarges Street, Piccadilly; *m* 1915, Phyllis, *d* of late Edwin J. Layton. *Educ:* Rugby. Served European War, 1914-18 (CMG) and War of 1939-45; commanded 9th Batt. Royal Fusiliers (TF) and Halton Camp RAF. *Recreations:* shooting and golf. *Address:* The Old Rectory, Great Mongeham, near Deal, Kent. *Clubs:* Devonshire; Royal St George's (Sandwich).

**ATTENBOROUGH, John Philip,** CMG 1958; CBE 1953 (OBE 1946); retired; *b* 6 Nov. 1901; *s* of late Frederick Samuel and Edith Attenborough; *m* 1947, Lucie Blanche Woods, *y d* of late Rev. J. R. and Mrs Prenter and *widow* of late Dr P. P. Murphy; one *step s*. *Educ:* Manchester Grammar Sch.; Corpus Christi Coll., Oxford (MA). Superintendent of Education, Northern Nigeria, 1924-30; Lecturer and Senior Inspector, Education Dept, Palestine, 1930-37; Dir of Education, Aden, 1937-46; Deputy Dir of Education, Palestine, 1946-48; Asst Educational Adviser, Colonial Office, 1948; Dir of Education, Tanganyika, 1948-55; Mem. for Social Services, Tanganyika, 1955-57; Min. for Social Services, Tanganyika, 1957-58; Consultant: UNICEF, 1963-65; UNESCO, 1967; Devon, CC, 1961-68; Mem. SW Regional Hospital Board; Pres. Torbay Conservative Assoc. *Address:* Fellside, Oxlea Road, Torquay, Devon. *T:* Torquay 27291. *Club:* East India and Sports.

**ATTENBOROUGH, Richard (Samuel),** CBE 1967; actor, producer and director; *b* 29 Aug. 1923; *s* of Frederick L. Attenborough, *qv*; *m* 1945, Sheila Beryl Grant Sim; one *s* two *d*. *Educ:* Wyggeston Grammar Sch., Leicester. Leverhulme Schol. to Royal Acad. of Dramatic Art, 1941 (Bancroft Medal). First stage appearance as Richard Miller in Ah Wilderness, Intimate Theatre, Palmers Green, 1941. West End début as Ralph Berger in Awake and Sing, Arts Theatre, 1942. First film appearance in In Which We Serve, 1942. In The Little Foxes, Piccadilly Theatre, 1942; Brighton Rock, Garrick, 1943. Joined RAF 1943; seconded to RAF Film Unit, 1944, and appeared in Journey Together; demobilised, 1946. Returned to Stage, Jan. 1949, in The Way Back (Home of the Brave), Westminster; To Dorothy, a Son, Savoy, 1950 (transf. to Garrick, 1951); Sweet Madness, Vaudeville, 1952; The Mousetrap, Ambassadors, 1952-54; Double Image, Savoy, 1956-57, St James', 1957; The Rape of the Belt, Piccadilly, 1957-58. Films include: School for Secrets, The Man Within, Dancing With Crime, Brighton Rock, London Belongs to Me, The Guinea Pig, The Lost People, Boys in Brown, Morning Departure, Hell is Sold Out, The Magic Box, Gift Horse, Father's Doing Fine, Eight O'Clock Walk, The Ship That Died of Shame, Private's Progress, The Baby and the Battleship, Brothers in Law, The Scamp, Dunkirk, The Man Upstairs, Sea of Sand, Danger Within, I'm All Right Jack, Jet Storm, SOS Pacific. Formed Beaver Films with Bryan Forbes and appeared in, and co-prod, The Angry Silence, 1959; formed Allied Film Makers and appeared in their first film The League of Gentlemen, 1960; prod Whistle Down the Wind, also appeared in Only Two Can Play and All Night Long, 1961; appeared in The Dock Brief, prod The L-Shaped Room and appeared in The Great Escape, 1962; appeared in and prod Séance On a Wet Afternoon, and appeared in The Third Secret, 1963; appeared in: Guns at Batasi, 1964; The Flight of the Phœnix, 1965; The Sand Pebbles, Dr Dolittle, 1966; The Bliss of Mrs Blossom, 1967; Only When I Larf, 1968; directed Oh! What a Lovely War, 1968 (15 Internat. Awards inc. Hollywood Golden Globe and Soc. of Film & Television Arts UN Award); appeared in: The Last Grenade, A Severed Head, David Copperfield, Loot, 1969; 10 Rillington Place, 1970. Best Actor Award, San Sebastian Film Festival, 1964; Best Actor, British Film Academy, 1964; Hollywood Golden Globe, 1966; First of Annual Awards by Cinematograph Exhibitors' Assoc. for distinguished service to British Cinema, 1967; Hollywood Golden Globe, 1967. Chairman:

RADA, 1970- (Mem. Council, 1963-); Sussex Univ. Arts Centre Board, 1969-; Member: Arts Council of Great Britain, 1970-; Cinematograph Films Council, 1967-; British Actors' Equity Assoc. Council, 1949-; Governor, Nat. Film Sch., 1970-. Dir, Chelsea Football Club, 1969-. Hon. DLitt Leicester, 1970. *Recreations:* listening to music, collecting paintings, watching football. *Address:* Old Friars, Richmond Green, Surrey. *Clubs:* Garrick, Beefsteak, Green Room.

**ATTEWELL, Humphrey Cooper;** National Organiser, National Union of Boot and Shoe Operatives, 1950-59, retired; *b* 1894; *m* 1915, Rose, *d* of David Brazier; one *s*. European War, 1914-18, served overseas (Meritorious Service Medal). Mem. Middlesex County Council, 1940-49; MP (Lab) Harborough Div. of Leicestershire, 1945-50. *Address:* 32 Cornbrook Road, Selly Oak, Birmingham 29.

**ATTLEE,** family name of **Earl Attlee.**

**ATTLEE,** 2nd Earl, *cr* 1955; **Martin Richard Attlee;** Viscount Prestwood, 1955; Assistant Publicity Officer, Southern Region, British Rail, since 1970; Owner of Prestwood Publicity; *b* 10 Aug. 1927; *o s* of 1st Earl Attlee, KG, PC, OM, CH, FRS, and Violet Helen (*d* 1964), *d* of H. E. Millar; *S* father, 1967; *m* 1955, Anne Barbara, *er d* of James Henderson, Bath, Somerset; one *s* one *d*. *Educ:* Millfield Coll.; Southampton University Coll. (now Southampton Univ.). Served in Merchant Navy, 1945-50. Active Mem. Hon. Artillery Company, 1951-55. MIPR 1964. *Recreations:* cars, carpentry, small boats. *Heir: s* Viscount Prestwood, *qv*. *Address:* 125 Hendon Lane, N3. *Club:* Press.

**ATTYGALLE, Sir Nicholas,** Kt 1953; Emeritus Professor of Obstetrics and Gynaecology, Ceylon University; Vice-Chancellor, 1955; Consulting Obstetrician and Gynaecologist, General Hospital, Colombo, Ceylon; *b* 14 July 1894; *m* 1925, Conyta Attygalle; one *s* one *d*. *Educ:* Royal College, Ceylon. Medical Officer Government Medical Service, 1919; Surgeon, 1929; Gynaecologist, Gen. Hosp., Colombo, 1934; Prof. of Obst. and Gynaec., Univ. of Ceylon, 1943; Dean of Faculty of Medicine of Univ. of Ceylon, 1944-53; Senator (Upper House), 1951, President of the Senate of Ceylon, 1952-55. *Recreation:* horticulture. *Address:* 108 Horton Place, Colombo, Ceylon. *T:* 9334. *Club:* Sinhalese Sports (Colombo).

**ATWELL, John William,** CBE 1970; CEng; FIMechE, FRSE; Chairman of Engineering Division, The Weir Group Ltd, since 1968; Director, The Weir Group Ltd, since 1961; *b* 24 Nov. 1911; *s* of William Atwell and Sarah Workman; *m* 1945, Dorothy Hendry Baxter, *d* of J. H. Baxter and Janet Muir; no *c*. *Educ:* Hyndland Secondary Sch., Glasgow; Royal Technical Coll., Glasgow (ARTC); Cambridge Univ. (MSc). General Management, Stewards and Lloyds Ltd, 1939-54; Dir 1955-61, Man. Dir 1961-68, G. & J. Weir Ltd. Member: University Grants Commn, 1965-69; NEL Adv. Board, 1969-; NEDC Mech. Eng Commn, 1969-; Court, Strathclyde Univ., 1967-; Vice-Pres., IMechE, 1966-. *Recreation:* golf. *Address:* Elmfield, Buchanan Drive, Rutherglen, Glasgow. *T:* 041-647 1824. *Clubs:* Caledonian, Royal Automobile; Western (Glasgow).

**AUBIN, Charles Walter Duret,** CBE 1945; *b* St Helier, Jersey, 22 May 1894; *o s* of late Walter Duret Aubin, MB, CM Edinburgh, and of Catherine Francesca Murrow; *m* 1919, Isabel Mary, 2nd *d* of George Touzel; two *d*. *Educ:* Victoria Coll., Jersey, and privately. Called to Jersey Bar, 1920; English Bar (Middle Temple), 1923; Solicitor-Gen. for Jersey, 1931; Attorney-Gen. for Jersey, 1936-48; retired 1948. *Address:* Belfontaine, La Rocque, Jersey. *T:* Jersey, Eastern 449.

**AUBREY, Henry M. W.;** *see* Windsor-Aubrey.

**AUBREY-FLETCHER, Sir John (Henry Lancelot),** 7th Bt *cr* 1782; Metropolitan Magistrate since 1959; *b* 22 Aug. 1912; *s* of Major Sir Henry Aubrey-Fletcher, 6th Bt, CVO, DSO, and Mary Augusta (*d* 1963), *e d* of Rev. R. W. Chilton; *S* father, 1969; *m* 1939, Diana Fynvola, *d* of late Lieut-Col Arthur Egerton, Coldstream Guards, and late Mrs Robert Bruce; one *s* one *d*. *Educ:* Eton; New Coll., Oxford. Called to Bar, 1937. Served War of 1939-45, Grenadier Guards, reaching rank of temp. Lieut-Col and leaving Army with rank of Hon. Major. Dep. Chm., Bucks Quarter Sessions, 1959-. High Sheriff, Bucks, 1961. *Heir: s* Henry Egerton Aubrey-Fletcher, *b* 27 Nov. 1945. *Address:* The Gate House, Chilton, Aylesbury, Bucks. *T:* Long Crendon 347.
*See also Hon. R. O. Stanley.*

**AUCHINCLOSS, Louis Stanton;** author; Partner, Hawkins Delafield and Wood, NYC, since 1957 (Associate, 1954-57); *b* NY, 27 Sept. 1917; *s* of J. H. Auchincloss and P. Stanton; *m* 1957, Adèle Lawrence; three *s*. *Educ:* Groton Sch.; Yale Univ.; Univ. of Virginia (LLB). Lieut USNR; served, 1941-45. Admitted to NY Bar, 1941; Associate Sullivan and Cromwell, 1941-51. Pres., Museum of City of NY, 1967. *Publications:* The Indifferent Children, 1947; The Injustice Collectors, 1950; Sybil, 1952; A Law for the Lion, 1953; The Romantic Egoists, 1954; The Great World and Timothy Colt, 1956; Venus in Sparta, 1958; Pursuit of the Prodigal, 1959; The House of Five Talents, 1960; Reflections of a Jacobite, 1961; Portrait in Brownstone, 1962; Powers of Attorney, 1963; The Rector of Justin, 1964; Pioneers and Caretakers, 1966; The Embezzler, 1966; Tales of Manhattan, 1967; A World of Profit, 1969; pamphlets on American writers. *Address:* 1111 Park Avenue, New York, NY 10028, USA; (office) 67 Wall Street, New York, NY 10005. *Club:* Century Association (NY).

**AUCHINLECK, Field-Marshal Sir Claude John Eyre,** GCB 1945 (CB 1934); GCIE 1940; CSI 1936; DSO 1917; OBE 1919; Hon. LLD (Aberdeen), 1948; Hon. LLD (St Andrews), 1948; *b* 21 June 1884; *s* of late Col John Claude Auchinleck, RA; *m* 1921, Jessie (from whom he obtained a divorce, 1946), *d* of late Alexander Stewart, of Innerhadden, Kinloch-Rannoch, Perthshire. *Educ:* Wellington Coll.; RMC Sandhurst. 2nd Lieut, Indian Army Unattached List, 1903; joined 62nd Punjabis 1904; served Egypt, 1914-15; Aden, 1915; Mesopotamia, 1916-19; Kurdistan, 1919 (despatches, DSO, Croix de Guerre, OBE, Brevet Lieut-Col); operations against Upper Mohmands, 1933 (despatches, CB); Mohmand Operations, 1935 (despatches, CSI); Imperial Defence Coll., 1927; commanded 1st Batt. 1st Punjab Regt, 1929-30; Instructor Staff Coll., Quetta, 1930-33; Comdr Peshawar Brigade, India, 1933-36; Dep. Chief of General Staff Army Headquarters, India, 1936-38; Comdr Meerut District, India, 1938; Mem., Expert Cttee on the Defence of India, 1938; GOC-in-C, Northern Norway, 1940; GOC-in-C, Southern Command, 1940; C-in-C in India, 1941 and 1943-47; C-in-C Middle East, 1941-42; ADC Gen. to the King, 1941-46; War Mem. of the Viceroy's Executive Council, 1943-46; Field-Marshal, 1946; Supreme Comdr in India and Pakistan, 1947, under Joint Defence Council; Col of 1st Punjab Regt; Col of the

Indian Grenadiers, 1939-47, of the Royal Inniskilling Fusiliers, 1941-47: a Governor of Wellington Coll., 1946-59; Pres., London Federation of Boys' Clubs, 1949-55; Pres. National Small-bore Rifle Association, 1956; a Vice-Pres. Forces Help Soc. and Lord Roberts Workshops; Chm., Armed Forces Art Soc., 1950-67. Virtuti Militari (Poland), 1942; War Cross (Czecho-Slovakia), 1944; Order of Chief Comdr, Legion of Merit (USA), 1945; Order of the Star of Nepal, 1st Class, 1945; Grand Cross of Order of St Olaf (Norway), 1947; 1st Class Order of Cloud and Banner (China), 1947; Grand Officer Legion of Honour; Croix-de-Guerre (France), 1918, 1949. *Recreations:* walking, fishing, sketching. *Address:* Villa Rikichou, rue Hafid Ibrahim, Marrakech, Morocco. c/o National & Grindlays Bank, 13 St James's Square, SW1. *Clubs:* United Service, East India and Sports, Naval and Military, Cavalry, Norwegian; Karachi Yacht. Service,

**AUCHMUTY, Prof. James Johnston,** PhD; Vice-Chancellor and Principal, University of Newcastle, New South Wales, since 1965; Professor of History since 1955; *b* Portadown, N Ireland, 29 Nov. 1909; *s* of Canon J. W. Auchmuty, MA; *m* 1934, Margaret, BA (Vassar) Phi Beta Kappa, *d* of R. F. Walters, Detroit, USA; one *s* one *d* (and one *s* decd). *Educ:* Armagh Royal Sch.; Trinity Coll., Dublin (Scholar). First Cl. Moderator and Gold Medallist in Hist. and Polit. Science, 1931 (Gold Medallist in Hist., 1930, and Auditor, 1931-32, of College Hist. Soc.); MA 1934, PhD 1935. Lectr in Sch. of Educn, Dublin Univ., 1936-46; Head of Dept of Mod. Hist., Farouk Univ., Alexandria, 1946-52; joined Univ. of NSW, 1952; Dean of Faculty of Humanities and Social Sciences, 1956-59 and Mem. Council, 1959-61; Head of Dept of Arts at Newcastle Univ. Coll., 1954; Warden of the College, 1960-64. First Chm. of Irish Cttee of Historical Sciences, 1938-44; Mem., Internat. Commn on the Teaching of History, 1938. Chm., Aust. Humanities Research Council, 1962-65; Mem., Aust. Nat. Cttee for UNESCO (Chm. of Letters Cttee), 1962-; Mem., Aust. Delegn to Fourth Commonwealth Educn Conf., Lagos, 1968; Chm., Aust. Commonwealth Adv. Cttee on the Teaching of Asian Languages and Cultures, 1969; Chm., Aust. Vice-Chancellors' Cttee, 1969-70; Mem. Council, Assoc. of Commonwealth Univs, 1967-70. FRHistS 1938; MRIA 1941; Foundn Fellow, Aust. Acad. of the Humanities, 1970. *Publications:* US Government and Latin American Independence 1810-1830, 1937; Irish Education: a historical survey, 1937; Sir Thomas Wyse, 1791-1862, 1939; The Teaching of History, 1940; Lecky, 1946; (ed) The Voyage of Governor Phillip to Botany Bay, 1970; contrib. to The Australian Dictionary of Biography; many papers in historical and other jls. *Recreations:* golf, swimming. *Address:* University of Newcastle, NSW 2308, Australia. *T:* 685360; (home) 12 High Street, Newcastle, NSW 2300, Australia. *T:* 23790. *Clubs:* Athenæum; Pioneers (Sydney); Newcastle (NSW).

**AUCKLAND,** 9th Baron (*cr* Irish Barony, 1789; British 1793); **Ian George Eden;** Associate Director, Cargill, Attwood & Thomas Ltd, Management Consultants; *b* 23 June 1926; *s* of 8th Baron Auckland; *S* father 1957; *m* 1954, Dorothy Margaret, *d* of H. J. Manser, Eastbourne; one *s* two *d*. *Educ:* Blundell's Sch. Royal Signals, 1945-48; 3/4 County of London Yeomanry (Sharpshooters) (TA), 1948-53. Underwriting Mem. of Lloyd's, 1956-64. Vice-Pres., Royal Society for Prevention of Accidents. *Recreations:* music, shooting, tennis and walking. *Heir:* *s* Hon. Robert Ian Burnard Eden, *b* 25 July 1962. *Address:* Tudor Rose House, 30 Links Road, Ashtead, Surrey. *T:* Ashtead 74393. *Clubs:* City Livery, Constitutional; Epsom.

**AUCKLAND, (NZ), Bishop of,** since 1960; **Rt. Rev. Eric Austin Gowing;** *b* 11 March 1913; *s* of Frederic Lanchester and Beryl Moselle Gowing; *m* 1940, Muriel Sherwood Jones; two *s*. *Educ:* North Sydney High Sch.; Sydney Univ.; Oxford Univ. BA Sydney, 1934; BA Oxon, 1938; MA Oxon, 1943; Curate: St Mary, Deane, 1938-42; St Andrew, Plymouth, 1942-45; Vicar of St Peter, Norbiton, 1945-50; Dean of Nelson, NZ, 1950-56; Archdeacon of Christchurch and Vicar of St Mary's, Merivale, NZ, 1956-60. *Recreations:* tennis, cricket. *Address:* Bishopscourt, Auckland, NZ. *T:* 41-177.

**AUCKLAND (NZ), Bishop of, (RC),** since 1929; **Most Rev. James Michael Liston,** CMG 1968; *b* New Zealand, 1881. *Educ:* Holy Cross Coll., Dublin; Irish Coll., Rome. Priest 1904; Rector of Holy Cross Coll., Mosgiel, NZ, 1910-20; Co-adjutor to Bishop Cleary of Auckland, 1920-29. Asst at the Papal Throne, 1950; appointed to personal title of Archbishop, 1953. Chevalier Legion of Honour, 1939. *Address:* Bishop's House, Auckland W1, NZ.

**AUCKLAND (NZ), Assistant Bishop and Dean of;** *see* Monteith, Rt Rev. G. R.

**AUDEN, Wystan Hugh;** poet; *b* 21 Feb. 1907; 3rd *s* of George Augustus Auden, MD. *Educ:* Gresham's Sch., Holt; Christ Church, Oxford (exhibitioner). Associate Prof. of English Literature, Ann Arbor Univ., Michigan; Guggenheim Research Fellowship, 1942; Prof. of Poetry, Univ. of Oxford, 1956-61. Hon. Student of Christ Church, Oxford, 1962. King George's Gold Medal for Poetry, 1937; Pulitzer Prize, 1948; Feltrinelli Prize, 1957; National Medal for Literature, USA, 1967. Resident in USA. Mem., American Acad. of Arts and Letters, 1954; Hon. Pres., Associated Socs of Edinburgh Univ. *Publications:* Poems, 1930; The Orators, 1932; The Dance of Death, 1933; (with Christopher Isherwood) The Dog Beneath the Skin, 1935; (with John Garrett) The Poet's Tongue, 1935; (with Christopher Isherwood) The Ascent of F6, 1936; Look Stranger, 1936; (with Louis MacNeice) Letters from Iceland, 1937; Oxford Book of Light Verse (ed), 1938; (with Christopher Isherwood) On the Frontier, 1938, and, Journey to a War, 1939; Selected Poems, 1940; Another Time, 1940; New Year Letter, 1941; For the Time Being, 1944; Tennyson, 1946; Nones, 1951; (with Chester Kallman) Libretto of the Rake's Progress (music by Igor Stravinsky), 1951; ed (with Norman Holmes Pearson) Poets of the English Language, 5 vols, 1952; 50 Selections from Kierkegaard, 1952; The Knights of the Round Table (from French Play of Jean Cocteau), 1954; Kierkegaard (selections and introduction), 1955; The Shield of Achilles, 1956; ed The Faber Book of Modern American Verse, 1956; ed (with Chester Kallman) An Elizabethan Song Book, 1957; trans. (with Chester Kallman) The Magic Flute, 1957; ed The Selected Writings of Sydney Smith, 1957; Homage to Clio, 1960; (with Chester Kallman) Libretto of Elegy for Young Lovers (Music by Hans Werne Henze), 1961; The Dyer's Hand, 1963; ed (with L. Kronenberger) The Faber Book of Aphorisms, 1964; trans. (with Leif Sjöberg) Markings (by Dag Hammerskjöld), 1964; About the House, 1966; Collected Shorter Poems, 1927-57, 1966; ed Nineteenth-Century Minor Poets, 1967; Collected Longer Poems, 1968; Secondary Worlds (T. S. Eliot

Lectures), 1968; City without Walls, 1969; G. K. Chesterton: a selection from his non-fictional prose, 1969. *Address:* c/o Random House, Madison Avenue, New York City.

**AUDLAND, Christopher John;** Counsellor (Head of Chancery), British Embassy, Bonn, since 1970; *b* 7 July 1926; *s* of Brig. Edward Gordon Audland, *qv*; *m* 1955, Maura Daphne Sullivan; two *s* one *d*. *Educ:* Winchester Coll. RA, 1944-48 (Temp. Capt.). Entered Foreign (subseq. Diplomatic) Service, 1948; has served in: Bonn; British Representation to Council of Europe; Washington; UK Delegn to Common Market negotiations, Brussels, 1961-63; Buenos Aires; FCO, 1968-70. *Address:* British Embassy, Bonn, BFPO 19. *T:* (office) Bonn 222021, (home) Bad Godesberg 64174. *Club:* Oxford and Cambridge University.

**AUDLAND, Brigadier Edward Gordon,** CB 1950; CBE 1943; MC 1917; DL; JP; late RA; *b* 30 Dec. 1896; *s* of William Edward Audland, MBE, KStJ, Wellingborough; *m* 1923, Violet Mary, *d* of late Herbert Shepherd-Cross, MP, JP, Hamels Park, Herts; two *s* one *d*. *Educ:* Winchester. Served European War, 1914-19, France, Belgium (despatches, MC); Brevet Major, 1935; DAQMG Southern Command, 1936; Brevet Lieut-Col, 1939; Col, 1942; Brig., 1942. War of 1939-45 (despatches thrice, CBE); France, 1939-40; North Africa, 1942-43; Italy, 1943-44; Greece, 1944-46; late Cmdr Cyrenaica District Middle East Land Forces; retired. Hon. Col 653 HAA Regt RA (TA), 1948-50. DL Westmorland, 1957. Cmdr: Order of St John of Jerusalem; Order of George I with Swords (Greece). *Address:* Ackenthwaite, Milnthorpe, Westmorland. *Club:* Army and Navy.

*See also C. J. Audland.*

**AUDLEY, Baroness** (24th in line), *cr* 1312-13; **Rosina Lois Veronica Macnamee;** *b* 10 July 1911; *o d* of Thomas Touchet Tuchet-Jesson (*d* 1939), and *sister* of 23rd Baron Audley; granted title, rank and precedence as *d* of a baron, 1946; *S* brother, 1963; *m* 1943, John Archibald Joseph Macnamee, MA, journalist, *yr s* of late Bernard Macnamee, Glasgow; no *c*. *Heir: kinsman* Richard Michael Thomas Souter [*b* 31 May 1914; *m* 1941, Lily Pauline, *d* of D. L. Eskell; three *d*]. *Address:* House of Lords, SW1.

**AUDSLEY, Matthew Thomas,** CMG 1949; retired from Civil Service 1956; *b* 15 Oct. 1891; *s* of late Matthew Robert Audsley, 54 Spur Road, Orpington, Kent; *m* 1919, Florence (*d* 1948), *d* of late Henry Moody, 44 Broadwood Avenue, Ruislip; one *s* two *d*; *m* 1952, Hilda Margaret, *d* of late John Fairless, Blythe, Northumberland. *Educ:* privately. Entered Civil Service, 1912. Min. of Labour: Asst Regional Controller, 1941; Dep. Regional Controller, 1947; Counsellor (Labour), British Embassy, Cairo and Labour Adviser to Middle East Development Div., 1945-56. *Recreations:* motoring and music. *Address:* 8 Nevill Park, Tunbridge Wells, Kent. *T:* Tunbridge Wells 21749.

**AUDU, Dr Ishaya Shu'aibu;** Vice-Chancellor of Ahmadu Bello University since 1966; *b* 1 March 1927; *s* of Malam Bulus Audu and Malama Rakiya Audu; *m* 1958, Victoria Abosede Ohiorhenuan; one *s* five *d*. *Educ:* Ibadan and London Univs. House Officer, Sen. House Officer, Registrar in Surgery, Medicine, Obstetrics and Gynæcology and Pædiatrics, King's Coll. Hosp., London and Univ. Coll. Hosp., Ibadan, 1954-58; postgrad. studies, UK, 1959-60; Specialist Physician, Pædiatrician to Govt of Northern Nigeria and Personal Physician to Premier of North Region Govt, 1960-62; Lectr to Associate Professorship in Pæds, Univ. of Lagos Med. Sch., 1962-66; Vis. Res. Associate Prof., Univ. of Rochester Med. Sch., NY, 1964-65; Dep. Chm., Lagos Univ. Teaching Hosp. Man. Bd and Mem. Council, Univ. Lagos Med. Coll., 1962-66; Mem. Senate, Lagos Univ., 1963-66. Hon. LHD Ohio; FMC (Pæd) Nigerian Med. Council; FRSocMed. *Publications:* contribs to learned jls. *Recreations:* walking, table tennis. *Address:* Ahmadu Bello University, Zaria, Nigeria. *T:* Zaria 03255.

**AUDUS, Professor Leslie John,** MA, PhD, ScD Cantab; FLS, FInstBiol; Hildred Carlile Professor of Botany, Bedford College, University of London, since 1948; *b* 9 Dec. 1911; English; *m* 1938, Rowena Mabel Ferguson; two *d*. *Educ:* Downing Coll., Cambridge Univ. Downing Coll. Exhibitioner, 1929-31; Frank Smart Research Student (Cambridge Univ.), 1934-35; Lecturer in Botany, University Coll., Cardiff, 1935-40. Served War of 1939-45: RAFVR (Technical, Radar, Officer), 1940-46; PoW South Pacific, 1942-45. Scientific Officer, Agricultural Research Council, Unit of Soil Metabolism, Cardiff, 1946-47; Monsanto Lecturer in Plant Physiology, University Coll., Cardiff, 1948. Recorder, 1961-65, Pres., 1967-68, Section K, British Assoc. for the Advancement of Science. Vis. Prof. of Botony: Univ. of California, Berkeley, 1958; Univ. of Minnesota, Minneapolis, 1965; Vice-Pres. Linnean Soc. of London, 1959-60; Life Mem. New York Academy of Sciences, 1961. Editor, Journal Exp. Botany, 1965-. *Publications:* Plant Growth Substances, 1953, 2nd edn 1959; The Physiology and Biochemistry of Herbicides (ed), 1964; original research on plant respiration, hormones, growth inhibitors, soil micro-biology, etc in Annals of Botany, New Phytologist, Nature, Journal of Experimental Botany, etc. *Recreations:* music, photography. *Address:* Botany Department, Bedford College, Regent's Park, NW1. *T:* 01-486 4400.

**AUERBACH, Charlotte,** FRS 1957; PhD, DSc; FRSE; Professor of Animal Genetics in the University of Edinburgh (Institute of Animal Genetics), 1967, Emeritus 1969 (Lecturer, 1947-57; Reader, 1957-67). Has done pioneering work on the chemical induction of mutations. Hon. Mem., Genetics Soc., Japan, 1966; Foreign Mem., Kongelige Danske Videnskabernes Selskab, 1968; Foreign Associate, Nat. Acad. of Sciences, USA, 1970. *Publications:* Genetics in the Atomic Age, 1956; The Science of Genetics, 1961; Mutation Pt 1Methods, 1962; Heredity, 1965. Papers in various genetical journals. *Address:* Institute of Animal Genetics, The University, West Mains Road, Edinburgh 9.

**AUERBACH, Frank Helmuth;** painter, draughtsman; *b* 29 April 1931; *s* of Max Auerbach, lawyer, and Charlotte Norah Auerbach. *Educ:* privately; St Martin's Sch. of Art; Royal Coll. of Art. *One-man exhibitions:* Beaux Arts Gallery, 1956, 1959, 1961, 1962, 1963; Marlborough Fine Art, 1965, 1967; Marlborough-Gerson, New York, 1969. *Mixed exhibitions:* Carnegie International, Pittsburgh, 1958, 1962; Dunn International, Fredericton, 1963; Gulbenkian International, Tate Gallery, 1964, etc. *Public collections:* Tate Gallery, London; National Gallery of Victoria, Melbourne; Chrysler Museum, Provincetown, Mass; Hull, Leeds, Manchester, Nottingham, Oldham Galls; Arts Council, Contemporary Art Soc., etc. *Address:* c/o Marlborough Fine Art, 39 Old Bond Street, W1.

**AUGER, Pierre Victor,** Grand Officer, Legion of Honour; retired as Director-General European Space Research Organisation (ESRO); Professor, Faculty of Sciences, University of Paris, since 1937; *b* 14 May 1899; *s* of Victor E. Auger, Prof., Univ. of Paris, and Eugénie Blanchet; *m* 1921, Suzanne Motteau; two *d*. *Educ:* Ecole Normale Supérieure, Paris; Univ. of Paris. Université de Paris (Faculté des Sciences): Asst 1927; Chef de Travaux, 1932; Maître de Conférences, 1937. Research Associate, Univ. of Chicago, 1941-43; Head of Physics Div., joint Anglo-Canadian research project on atomic energy, 1942-44; Dir of Higher Education, Min. of Education, France, 1945-48; Mem. exec. Board of UNESCO, 1946-48; Membre du comité de l'Energie Atomique, France, 1946-48; Dir, Natural Sciences Dept, UNESCO, 1948-59; Special Consultant, UNO and UNESCO, 1959-60; Chm., French Cttee on Space Research, 1960-62. Feltrinelli International Prize, 1961. *Publications:* Rayons cosmiques, 1941; L'Homme microscopique, 1952; Current Trends in Scientific Research, 1961; scientific papers on physics (X-rays, neutrons, cosmic rays), 1923-; papers on philosophy of science, 1949-. *Address:* 12 rue Emile Faguet, Paris XIV. *T:* Gobelins 331 96 34.

**AURIC, Georges,** Officer, Legion of Honour; Commander, Order of Academic Palms; French composer; General Administrator, Paris Opéra and Opéra Comique, 1962-68; *b* Lodève, 15 Feb. 1899; *m* 1938, Nora Smith. *Educ:* Paris Conservatoire; Schola Cantorum, Paris. *Publications include:* Trois Interludes; Chandelles Romaines; Trio pour Hautbois; *ballet music:* Le Peintre et son Modèle, 1949; Phèdre, 1950; Chemin de Lumière, 1952; Coup de Feu, 1952; *opera:* Sous le Masque; *music for films:* Le Sang d'un Poète; A Nous la Liberté; Entrée des Artistes; L'Eternel Retour; La Belle et la Bête; La Symphonie Pastorale; Torrents; Ruy Blas; L'Aigle à Deux Têtes; Les Parents Terribles; Maya; Orphée: Caroline Chérie; La P . . . Respectueuse; La Fête à Henriette, etc.

**AUSTEN, Harold Cholmley Mansfield,** CBE 1935; MInstCE; *b* 21 Nov. 1878; 4th *s* of Rev. George Austen, late Chancellor of York Minster; *m* 1st, Annie Alice Mary, *d* of Henry Maclean of Kingairloch; two *d*; 2nd, 1966, Helena Frances Kerslake. *Educ:* Repton; King's Coll., London. Pupil in grandfather's firm (James Abernethy, FRSE, Past Pres. InstCE), Westminster; Asst Engineer Midland Railway, 1898-1901; Asst and Resident Engineer Bristol Docks, 1901-07; Dover Harbour, 1908; Engineer and Agent for Perry & Co. (Bow) Ltd, Contractors, 1909-15; served during European War as Supt Engineer, Ministry of Munitions, Yorkshire (OBE); Harbour Engineer, Mauritius, 1923-31; Gen. Manager of Railways and Harbour Engineer, Mauritius; designed, constructed, and supervised traffic of new deep-water quay; dredged harbour and constructed Granary to contain whole rice supply of Colony; Retired 1940; Dep. Area Officer Ministry of Supply, Bristol, 1940; Dep. Regional Controller, 1942; Regional Controller, 1943; retired 1945. *Publications:* Modern Development of British Fishery Harbours; Sea Fights and Corsairs of the Indian Ocean (The Naval History of Mauritius from 1715-1810). *Recreation:* walking. *Address:* Delabole Cottage, Minehead, Som.

**AUSTERBERRY, Ven. Sidney Denham;** Archdeacon of Salop and Vicar of Great Ness, since 1959; *b* 28 Oct. 1908; *s* of late Mr and Mrs H. Austerberry; *m* 1934, Eleanor Jane Naylor; two *s* two *d*. *Educ:* Hanley High Sch.; Egerton Hall, Manchester. Curate, Newcastle-under-Lyme Parish Church, 1931-38; Vicar of S Alkmund, Shrewsbury, 1938-52; Vicar of Brewood, 1952-59; Hon. Clerical Sec., Lichfield Diocesan Conf., 1954-70; Rural Dean of Penkridge, 1958-59. *Address:* Great Ness Vicarage, Shrewsbury. *T:* Nesscliffe 240.

**AUSTIN, Professor Colin Russell;** Charles Darwin Professor of Animal Embryology, University of Cambridge, since 1967; *b* 12 Sept. 1914; *s* of Ernest Russell Austin and Linda Mabel King; *m* 1941, Patricia Constance Jack; two *s*. *Educ:* Univ. of Sydney, Australia (BVSc 1936; DSc 1954). Mem. Research Staff, CSIRO, Australia, 1938-54; Mem. Scientific Staff of MRC, UK, 1954-64; Ed., Jl of Reproduction and Fertility, 1959-64; Head of Genetic and Developmental Disorders Research Program, Delta Regional Primate Research Center, and Prof. of Embryology, Tulane Univ., New Orleans, 1964-67. *Publications:* The Mammalian Egg, 1961; Fertilization, 1965; Ultrastructure of Fertilization, 1968; numerous research papers. *Recreations:* tennis, swimming, sailing. *Address:* Manor Farm House, Toft, Cambridge. *T:* Comberton 2101.

**AUSTIN, George Wesley,** OBE 1935; MA, MSc; FIM; Goldsmiths' Professor of Metallurgy, University of Cambridge, 1945-58; sometime Fellow of Trinity Hall, Cambridge; *b* 1 March 1891; *s* of Edwin and Marie Austin; *m* 1933, Isabella Mary Murray; one *s*. *Educ:* Friends Sch., Sibford; Queens Coll., Taunton. Metallurgical training Univ. of Birmingham (1851 Exhibitioner) and Royal Technical High Sch., Aachen. Successively Metallurgist, Principal Scientific Officer and Superintending Scientist RN Torpedo Factory and Torpedo Experimental Establishment, Greenock. Vice-Pres. Institute of Metals and Institution of Metallurgists; Chm. Home Office Cttee on Gas Cylinders and Containers; Research Supervisor, Metallurgy Div., BISRA; Chm. ISMRC; OECD Consultant. *Publications:* trans. Modern Open Hearth Steelworks, 1924; Effect of Molten Solder on some Stressed Materials, Burnt Alloy Steels (in technical journals), 1936. *Recreations:* art and travel. *Address:* New Barn House, Lindsell, Essex. *T:* Great Easton 242; Cove Castle, Cove, Dunbartonshire. *T:* Kilcreggan 2311. *Clubs:* Savage, National Liberal; Royal Scottish Automobile (Glasgow).

**AUSTIN, Sir John (Byron Fraser),** 3rd Bt, *cr* 1894; *b* 14 July 1897: *s* of Sir William Austin, 2nd Bt, and Violet Irene (*d* 1962), *d* of Alex. Fraser, Westerfield House, near Ipswich; *S* father, 1940; *m* 1st, 1953, Sheila McNaught (marr. diss., 1958); 2nd, 1960, Rhoda Noreen Rose, *widow* of Col C. V. D. Rose. *Educ:* Downside; Royal Military Coll., Sandhurst. Late Lieut 7th Hussars; Major Indian Army; retired, 1935; served with Somaliland Camel Corps and King's African Rifles, Tanganyika; European War, 1915-18, as Flight-Comdr RFC and RAF; served War of 1939-45, Lieut-Col Comdg Bn (despatches). Director: Baronetcy Properties; St Anthonys Properties Ltd; Solid State Nutronics Ltd. *Heir: b* William Ronald Austin [*b* 20 July 1900; *m* 1st, 1926, Dorothy Mary (*d* 1957), *d* of late L. A. Bidwell, FRCS; two *s*; 2nd, 1958, Mary Helen Farrell]. *Address:* Treeps Manor House, Hurstpierpoint, Sussex. *Clubs:* Royal Air Force; Royal Dart Yacht.

**AUSTIN, Prof. Lloyd James;** FBA 1968; Fellow of Jesus College, Cambridge, since 1961; Drapers' Professor of French since 1967; *b* 4 Nov. 1915; *s* of late J. W. A. Austin and late Mrs J. E. Austin (*née* Tymms), Melbourne,

Australia; *m* 1939, Jeanne Françoise Guerin, Rouen, France; three *s* one *d*. *Educ:* Melbourne Church of England Grammar Sch.; Univ. of Melbourne; Univ. of Paris. French Government Scholar, Paris, 1937-40; Lecturer in French, Univ. of Melbourne, 1940-42. Active Service as Lieut (Special Branch) RANVR, SW Pacific area, 1942-45. Lecturer in French, Univ. of Melbourne, 1945-47; Lecturer in French, Univ. of St Andrews, 1947-51; Research work in Paris, 1951-55; Fellow of Jesus Coll., Cambridge, 1955-56; Professor of Modern French Literature, Univ. of Manchester, 1956-61; Lecturer in French, Univ. of Cambridge, 1961-66, Reader, 1966-67; Librarian, Jesus Coll., Cambridge, 1965-68. Herbert F. Johnson Visiting Prof., Inst. for Research in the Humanities, Univ. of Wisconsin, 1962-63; Mem., Editorial Bd, French Studies, 1964-, Gen. Editor, 1967-; Pres., Assoc. Internat. des Etudes Françaises, 1969- (Vice-Pres., 1966-69). *Publications:* Paul Bourget, 1940; Paul Valéry: Le Cimetière marin, 1954; L'Univers poétique de Baudelaire, 1956; ed (with E. Vinaver and G. Rees) Studies in Modern French Literature, presented to P. Mansell-Jones, 1961; (with H. Mondor) Les Gossips de Mallarmé, 1962; ed (with H. Mondor) Stéphane Mallarmé: Correspondance (1871-1885), 1965, (1886-1889), 1969, (1890-1892), 1971. Contrib. to French Studies, Modern Languages, Modern Language Review, Forum for Modern Language Studies, Bulletin of the John Rylands Library, Mercure de France, Revue des Sciences Humaines, Revue d'Histoire littéraire de la France, Revue de littérature comparée, Romanic Review, Synthèses, L'Esprit créateur, Comparative Literature Studies, Wingspread Lectures in the Humanities, Encyclopædia Britannica, Yale French Studies, Meanjin Quarterly, Australian Jl for French Studies, AUMLA, etc. *Recreations:* cricket, tennis, travel. *Address:* 14 Park Terrace, Cambridge. *T:* 59630; Jesus College, Cambridge.

**AUSTIN, Richard,** FRCM; Professor since 1946, Director of Opera since 1955, Royal College of Music; *b* 26 Dec. 1903; *s* of Frederic and Amy Austin; *m* 1935, Leily, *y d* of Col Wilfred Howell, CBE, DSO. *Educ:* Gresham's Sch., Holt; RCM; Munich. Conductor, Carl Rosa Opera Co., 1929; Musical Dir of the Bournemouth Corporation, 1934-40; Music Advisor Northern Command, 1941-45; Music Dir, New Era Concert Soc., 1947-57. Guest Conductor: Sadler's Wells, London and Provincial Orchestras, Holland, Belgium, Germany, Spain, Sweden, Switzerland, Finland, Yugoslavia, Czechoslovakia, Cuba, Mexico, South Africa, South America and USA. *Recreations:* squash, tennis. *Address:* Stubbles, Ashampstead, Berks. *T:* Yattendon 265. *Club:* Savage.

**AUSTIN, Robert Sargent,** RA 1949 (ARA 1939); RWS 1934 (ARWS, 1930); RE 1928 (ARE 1921); Professor of Engraving, Royal College of Art; President: Royal Society of Painters in Water Colours, since 1956; Royal Society of Painter-Etchers and Engravers, since 1962; *b* Leicester, 23 June 1895; *s* of Robert Austin and Elizabeth Smith, both of Leicester; *m* 1924, Ada (*d* 1958), *d* of Henry Harrison; one *s* two *d*. *Educ:* Sch. of Art, Leicester; Royal College of Art, South Kensington. Active Service, 1915-19; Rome Scholar, 1922. *Recreation:* bird-watching. *Address:* Lingard House, Chiswick Mall, W4. *T:* 01-994 4852.

**AUSTIN, Roland Gregory,** MA; Professor of Latin, University of Liverpool, 1954-68, now Emeritus; *b* Gloucester, 19 Feb. 1901; *s* of late Roland Austin; *m* 1931, Violet Margerie, *y d* of late Robert Wilson Dron, Prof. of Mining, Univ. of Glasgow. *Educ:* Crypt Sch., Gloucester; Balliol Coll, Oxford (Exhibitioner in Classics). First Class, Classical Hon. Moderations, 1921; 2nd Class, Literae Humaniores, 1923; *prox acc.*, Gaisford prize for Greek verse, 1923; Asst to Prof. of Humanity (Prof. J. S. Phillimore), Univ. of Glasgow, 1923-26; Lecturer in Humanity, 1926-37; Prof. of Latin, University Coll. of South Wales and Monmouthshire, 1937-54. Leverhulme Research Fellow, 1960-61; Public Orator, Liverpool Univ., 1965-68. A Vice-President: Soc. for the Promotion of Roman Studies, 1964; Classical Assoc., 1966. Mem. Classical Journals Bd, 1947-68. Hon. DLitt, Glasgow, 1960; Dr *hc* Besançon, 1961. *Publications:* Arma, in Glossaria Latina, vol. II, 1926 (with W. M. Lindsay); Cicero, pro M. Cælio (ed), 1933, new edn, 1960; (ed) Quintilian Inst. Or. XII, 1948; (ed) Virgil, Aeneid IV, 1955; (ed) Virgil, Aeneid II, 1964; articles and reviews in classical and archæological periodicals. *Address:* Utica, Stanton, Broadway, Worcs. *T:* Stanton (Glos) 350.

**AUSTIN, Sumner Francis,** MA Oxon; Hon. FGSM; late Technical Director, Sadler's Wells Opera, London; late Captain Intelligence Corps; *b* Anerley, Kent, *s* of late Ware Plumtre Austin, ICS, and Frances Laura Greenaway; *m* Dorothy Stirling (*née* Blackwell). *Educ:* Bexhill; Magdalen Coll. Sch.; St John's Coll., Oxford. Studied for Indian Forest Service; studied singing and music, Dresden, Germany, 1910-14; first engagement, Royal Theatre, Potsdam; interned Prisoner of War, Ruhleben, 1914-18; Carl Rosa Opera Co., 1919; Surrey Theatre, 1920; Old Vic and later Sadler's Wells, 1919-; recitals in Holland, Berlin, London, and provinces, BBC, and various Choral Societies; Scarborough Open Air Production, 1935; Covent Garden, 1952, 1955, etc; numerous productions. *Publications:* translations from the Italian, French and German. *Address:* 10 Launceston Place, Kensington, W8. *T:* 01-937 2280.

**AUSTIN, Sir Thomas,** KCIE, *cr* 1945 (CIE 1941); *b* 20 July 1887; *e s* of Rev. T. Austin, RN; *m* 1915, Christina Wilson, MB (*d* 1960) ; *m* 1961, Mrs Cecile Rosemary Macann (*née* Stallard). *Educ:* Plymouth Coll.; Jesus Coll., Cambridge. Entered ICS, 1910, and posted to Madras, 1911; Asst Resident in Travancore and Cochin, 1915-17; military duty, 1918-19; Collector, C and M Station, Bangalore, 1922-24; Chm., Assam Labour Board, 1924-28; called to Bar, Gray's Inn, 1931; Dewan of Travancore, 1932-34; Registrar of Co-operative Societies, Madras, 1934-38; Mem., Board of Revenue, 1938-40; Chief Sec. to Government of Madras, 1940; Adviser to Governor of Madras, 1941-46; retired from ICS 1946; Prime Minister of Kolhapur State, 1946-47. *Recreations:* reading, fishing. *Address:* 29 Chivelston, Wimbledon Parkside, SW19. *T:* 01-788 3240.

**AUSTIN, Thomas Aitken,** CMG 1949; LRCP, LRCS, LM (Ireland); DTM and H (Liverpool); DPH (Dublin); late Public Health Officer for East and Central Africa, UN World Health Organisation; *b* 1895. *Educ:* Derry Church Sch.; Royal Coll. of Surgeons, Dublin. Storey Memorial Gold Medal (Anatomy), De Renzy Centenary Prize, 1st place 1st class honours DPH, Royal Coll. of Surgeons, Dublin. Served War of 1939-45, 1939-40; Major. Appointed Zanzibar Protectorate, 1924; Nyasa, 1930; SMO, Tanganyika Territory, 1939; DMS: Nyasa, 1943; Uganda, 1946; PMO, Colonial Office, 1949. *Address:* 38 Sycamore Road, Mount Merrion, Blackrock, Co. Dublin.

**AUSTRALIA, North-West, Bishop of,** since 1965; **Rt. Rev. Howell Arthur John Witt;** *b* 12 July 1920; *s* of Thomas Leyshon Witt and Harriet Jane Witt; *m* 1949, Gertrude Doreen Edwards; three *s* two *d*. *Educ:* Newport Sec. Sch.; Leeds Univ.; Coll. of the Resurrection, Mirfield. Deacon 1944; Priest 1945. Asst Curate of: Usk, Mon, 1944-47; St George's, Camberwell, 1948-49; Chaplain, Woomera, S Australia, 1949-54; Rector, St Mary Magdalene's, Adelaide, 1954-57; Priest in charge of Elizabeth, 1957-65; Missioner of St Peter's Coll. Mission, 1954-65. *Recreations:* Rugby football coaching; script writing. *Address:* Bishop's House, Bluff Point, Geraldton, Western Australia 6530. *T:* Geraldton 231202. *Club:* Public Schools (Adelaide).

**AUTY, Prof. Robert,** MA (Cantab and Oxon); DrPhil (Münster); Professor of Comparative Slavonic Philology, University of Oxford, and Fellow of Brasenose College since October 1965; *b* Rotherham, 10 Oct. 1914; 2nd *s* of George Auty, schoolmaster and Martha Louise Richards; *m* 1944, Kathleen Marjorie Milnes-Smith; one *s* one *d*. *Educ:* Rotherham Grammar School; (Scholar) Gonville and Caius Coll., Cambridge; Münster Univ. Tiarks German Schol., Cambridge Univ., 1935; Faculty Asst Lectr in German, 1937; Univ. Lectr (in German), 1945, (in German and Czech), 1948, (in Slavonic Studies), 1957-62; Head of Dept of Other Languages, 1948-56; Sen. Proctor, 1949-50; Fellow and Coll. Lectr in Modern Langs, Selwyn Coll., 1950-62; Dean of Selwyn Coll., 1953-56; Professor of Comparative Philology of the Slavonic Languages, Univ. of London, and Head of Dept of Languages and Literature, Sch. of Slavonic and East European Studies, 1962-65. War work with Czechoslovak authorities in London, 1939-43, attached to the Foreign Office, 1944-45. Visiting Prof. Slavic Languages, Univ. of California, Los Angeles, 1968. Sec. Assoc. Internationale des Langues et Littératures Slaves, 1957-60, Vice-Pres., 1963, Pres. 1966; Sec., British Univs Assoc. of Slavists, 1957-63, Pres., 1964-67, Vice-Pres., 1967; Treas., Philological Society, 1962-65; Vice-Pres., Fédération Internationale des Langues et Littératures Modernes, 1966; Pres., Assoc. of Teachers of Russian, 1967-69; Chm., Modern Humanities Research Assoc., 1968; Member: International Cttee of Slavists, 1965 (Vice-Pres., 1966); Governing Body, GB-E Europe Centre, 1970; Editorial Board of Slavonic and East European Review (Chm., 1963-65); Ed. Board, International Journal of Slavic Linguistics and Poetics, 1965; Slavonic Editor, Modern Language Review, 1966. Josef Dobrovský Gold Medal, Czechoslovak Acad. of Sciences, 1968. *Publications:* Old Church Slavonic Texts and Glossary, 1960. Articles in Brit. and foreign learned jls and encyclopædias. *Recreation:* travel, especially in Central and South-Eastern Europe. *Address:* Brasenose College, Oxford. *T:* Oxford 48641. *Club:* United University.

**AVEBURY,** 3rd Baron, *cr* 1900; **John Lubbock,** Bt *cr* 1806; *b* 13 May 1915; *o s* of late Capt. Harold Fox Pitt Lubbock, 4th *s* of 1st Baron Avebury, and Dorothy Charlotte, *d* of 1st Baron Forster (she *m* 2nd, Lord Wardington, *qv*); *S* uncle, 1929; *m* 1st, 1938, Cecily Kathleen (who obtained a divorce 1945), *d* of late Dr N. A. K. Sparrow and of Mrs M. H. Ormsby, Bosworth House, Woodbridge; 2nd, 1946, Diana Mary Margaret (marr. diss. 1955), *d* of late Capt. Edward Westcott King, RA: one *d*; 3rd, 1956, Betty Gay, *d* of late William Oscar Ingham, Poulton-le-Fylde. *Educ:* Eton. *Heir: cousin* Eric Reginald Lubbock, *qv*. *Address:* Yacht Kailva, Royal Gibraltar Yacht Club, Gibraltar. *Club:* Royal Yacht Squadron.

**AVERILL, Leslie Cecil Lloyd,** CMG 1961; MC 1918; MD; FRCSEd; FRCOG; Specialist in Obstetrics and Gynaecology, Christchurch, NZ, since 1934; Chairman, North Canterbury Hospital Board, NZ, since 1956; *b* 25 March 1897; 2nd *s* of late Most Rev. A. W. Averill, CMG, DD (Oxon) (Archbp of NZ, 1925-40); *m* 1925, Isabel Mary Wilkie Roberton, *o d* of Ernest Roberton, MD, Auckland; two *s* two *d*. *Educ:* Christ's Coll., Christchurch, NZ; Univ. of Edinburgh (medical). War Service with NZ Rifle Brigade: Lieut, France (MC), 1917-19. General medical practice, Christchurch, NZ, 1925-34. Pres. BMA (NZ), 1951-52. Chm. NZ Regional Council, Royal Coll. of Obstetricians and Gynaecologists, 1951-55. Citoyen d'Honneur, Le Quesnoy, France, 1968. *Publications:* articles in medical journals. *Recreations:* golf, horticulture. *Address:* 41 Wairarapa Terrace, Christchurch 1, New Zealand. *T:* 557751. *Club:* Christchurch (NZ).

**AVERY JONES, Sir Francis;** *see* Jones, Sir F. A.

**AVES, Geraldine Maitland,** CBE 1963 (OBE 1946); *b* 22 Aug. 1898; *er d* of Ernest Aves, MA, FSS, and Eva Mary (*née* Maitland). *Educ:* Frognal Sch., Hampstead; Newnham Coll., Cambridge (MA). Education Dept, LCC: Sch. Care Organiser, 1924-38; assisting planning and develt of war-time evacuation services, 1938-41; Ministry of Health, Chief Welfare Officer and Head of Welfare Divn, 1941-62. Seconded: to UNRRA as Chief Child Care Consultant (Europe), 1945-46; to Home Office, to initiate child care training, 1947-48; various assignments to UN Headqrs, in field of family and child welfare and to direct UN Seminars for European Region, 1949-69. Governor, Nat. Inst. for Social Work Training, 1961-; Mem. Council for Training in Social Work, 1962-; Associate Fellow, Newnham Coll., 1962-65 and 1966-69; Chm., Adv. Council of Nat. Corp. for the Care of Old People, 1965-; Chm., Cttee of Enquiry into Voluntary Workers in the Social Services, 1966-69 (Report: The Voluntary Worker in the Social Services, 1969). Pres., Newnham College Roll, 1969-. *Recreation:* birdwatching. *Address:* 24 North Grove, Highgate Village, N6. *T:* 01-340 1685. *Clubs:* University Women's, United University.

**AVON,** 1st Earl of, *cr* 1961; **Robert Anthony Eden,** KG 1954; PC 1934; MC 1917; Viscount Eden, *cr* 1961; Hon. DCL, Oxford and Durham; Hon. LLD: Birmingham, Bristol, Cambridge, Leeds, Sheffield, Belfast, Toronto, California, McGill, Columbia, Denver; *b* 12 June 1897; 2nd *surv s* of Sir William Eden, 7th and 5th Bt; *m* 1st, 1923, Beatrice Helen (marr. diss. 1950; she *d* 1957), *d* of Hon. Sir Gervase Beckett, 1st Bt; one *s* (and *er s*, Pilot Officer Simon Eden, RAF, killed in Burma, 1945); 2nd, 1952, Clarissa Anne, *d* of late Major John Spencer Churchill and Lady Gwendeline Spencer Churchill. *Educ:* Eton; Christ Church, Oxford. BA First Cl. Hons (Oriental langs), 1922. Formerly Capt. KRRC; served European War, 1915-19, with his regt and as GSO3, also as Bde Major (MC). Contested Spennymoor Division of Durham, 1922; MP (C) Warwick and Leamington, 1923-57. Attended Imperial Press Conference, Melbourne, 1925; Parliamentary Private Sec. to Sec. of State for Foreign Affairs (Sir Austen Chamberlain, KG), 1926-29; Parliamentary Under-Sec., Foreign Office, 1931-33; Lord Privy Seal, 1934-35; Minister without Portfolio for League of Nations Affairs, 1935; Sec. of State: for Foregn Affairs, 1935-38; for Dominion Affairs, 1939-40; for War, 1940; for Foreign Affairs, 1940-45, also Leader of House of Commons, 1942-45; Dep. Leader of the Opposition, 1945-51; Sec. of State for Foreign

Affairs and Deputy Prime Minister, 1951-April 1955; Prime Minister and First Lord of the Treasury, April 1955-Jan. 1957. Chm. of OEEC, 1952-54. Hon. Mem. Salters' Company, 1946, and of Fishmongers' Company, 1955. Trustee of National Gallery, 1935-49; Chancellor of Univ. of Birmingham, 1945; Elder Brother of Trinity House, 1953; Wateler Peace Prize, Carnegie Foundation, 1954. Pres. of Royal Shakespeare Theatre, Stratford-on-Avon, 1958-66. JP (Hon.) Co. Durham; Freeman of Durham, Leamington Spa, Warwick, Perth, Athens. Hon. Col Queen's Westminsters, KRRC, 1952-60, Queen's Royal Rifles, 1960-62; Hon. Air Cdre No 500 (Co. Kent) Squadron, RAF, 1943-. Hon. Life Patron, Young Cons. Organisation; Pres., Anglo-Ethiopian Soc., 1966-; Patron, Hereford Herd Book Soc., 1968-. *Publications:* Places in the Sun; Foreign Affairs, 1939; Freedom and Order; Days for Decision (selected speeches), 1949; The Eden Memoirs: Full Circle, 1960; Facing the Dictators, 1962; The Reckoning, 1965; Towards Peace in Indo-China, 1966. *Heir:* *s* Viscount Eden, *qv*. *Address:* Manor House, Alvediston, Salisbury, Wilts; Villa Nova, St John, Barbados. *Clubs:* Carlton, Buck's.

**AVONSIDE, Rt. Hon. Lord; Ian Hamilton Shearer,** PC 1962; a Senator of the College of Justice in Scotland since 1964; *b* 6 Nov. 1914; *s* of Andrew Shearer, OBE, and Jessie Macdonald; *m* 1st, 1942; one *s* one *d*; 2nd, 1954, Janet Sutherland Murray (OBE 1958). *Educ:* Dunfermline High Sch.; Glasgow Univ.; Edinburgh Univ. MA Glasgow, 1934; LLB Edinburgh, 1937. Admitted to Faculty of Advocates, 1938; QC (Scotland) 1952. Served War of 1939-45: RA (Fd), 1939; Capt. 1941; Major 1943; released 1946, Emerg. R of O. Standing Counsel: to Customs and Excise, Bd of Trade and Min. of Labour, 1947-49; to Inland Revenue, 1949-51; to City of Edinburgh Assessor, 1949-51; Junior Legal Assessor to City of Edinburgh, 1951; Sheriff of Renfrew and Argyll, 1960-62; Lord Advocate, 1962-64. Chm. Nat. Health Service Tribunal, Scotland, 1954-62; Mem. Scottish Cttee of Coun. on Tribunals, 1958-62; Chm. Scottish Valuation Advisory Coun., 1965-68. *Publications:* Purves on Licensing Laws, 1947; Acta Dominorum Concilli et Sessionis, 1951. *Recreation:* golf. *Address:* 10 Mortonhall Road, Edinburgh. *T:* 031-667 8784. *Clubs:* Garrick; New (Edinburgh).

**AWDRY, Daniel (Edmund),** TD; MP (C) Chippenham Division of Wiltshire, since November 1962; *b* 10 Sept. 1924; *s* of Col Edmund Portman Awdry, MC, TD, DL, Coters, Chippenham, Wilts, and Mrs Evelyn Daphne Alexandra Awdry, JP (formerly French); *m* 1950, Elizabeth Cattley; three *d*. *Educ:* Winchester Coll. RAC, OCTU, Sandhurst, 1943-44 (Belt of Honour). Served with 10th Hussars as Lieut, Italy, 1944-45; ADC to GOC 56th London Div., Italy, 1945. Qualified Solicitor, 1950. Mayor of Chippenham, 1958-59; Pres., Southern Boroughs Assoc., 1959-60. PPS to Minister of State, Board of Trade, Jan.-Oct. 1964. Served in Royal Wilts Yeo., 1947-62, and commanded Sqdn as Major, 1955-62. Director: BET Omnibus Services, 1966-; Sheepbridge Engineering, 1968-. *Recreations:* cricket (mem. Free Foresters and Butterflies), chess. *Address:* Old Manor, Beanacre, near Melksham, Wilts. *T:* Melksham 2315. *Club:* Cavalry.

**AXISA, John Francis,** MBE 1950; High Commissioner for Malta in the United Kingdom, 1964-69; also Ambassador of Malta to: France, 1966-69; Federal Republic of Germany, 1967-69; *b* 20 Nov. 1906; *s* of late Emmanuel Axisa and Vincenzina (*née* Micallef); *m* 1939, Ariadne Cachia; three *s* one *d*. *Educ:* St Paul's Sch., Malta and privately. Joined Malta Civil Service, 1927; Dir of Emigration, 1947-56; Dir of Technical Education, 1956-59; Dir of Emigration, Labour and Social Welfare, 1959-60; Under-Sec., 1960-61; Commissioner-Gen. for Malta in London, 1961-64; Malta's first High Commissioner on Malta's Independence, 1964-; Ambassador of Malta to: Libya, 1966-68; Belgium, 1967-68; Netherlands, 1968-69. *Recreations:* carpentry, fishing, reading. *Address:* 59 Stella Maris Street, Sliema, Malta, GC. *Clubs:* Royal Commonwealth Society, Royal Over-Seas League, Naval and Military, Travellers'.

**AXON, Sir Albert (Edwin),** KBE 1959; consulting engineer in private practice, Australia, since 1929; Chairman: Queensland Cement & Lime Co. Ltd; Central Queensland Cement Pty Ltd; Director: Walkers Ltd; South Brisbane Gas & Light Co. Ltd; North Australian Cement Ltd; *b* 21 Dec. 1898; *s* of Herbert Fisher Axon, Lancashire, England and Florence Emily (*née* Parker), Galway, Ire.; *m* 1926, Hilda Harris Withecombe; one *s* one *d*. *Educ:* Brisbane Grammar Sch.; Univ. of Queensland. Master of Engrg, Qld, 1928; Dr of Engrg, Melbourne Univ., 1961; Dr of Science, Univ. of New England, 1962. Consulting engineer in private practice, 1929-; Mem. Royal Commn on Electricity, Qld, 1936; part-time Mem. State Electricity Commn of Qld, 1938-47. Mem. of Senate, Univ. of Qld, 1935-66; Chancellor of Univ. of Qld, 1957-66; Mem., Commonwealth Banking Corp. Bd, 1959-64. Peter Nicol Russell Memorial Medal of Instn of Engrs, Aust., 1960. *Recreations:* fishing, gardening, conchology. *Address:* 25 Stafford Street, Clayfield, Brisbane, Australia. *T:* 6-2729. *Clubs:* Queensland, Brisbane, Johnsonian, United Service (all in Brisbane).

**AXWORTHY, Geoffrey (John);** Artistic Director of Sherman Theatre, University College, Cardiff, since 1970; *b* Plymouth, England, 10 Aug. 1923; *s* of William Henry Axworthy and Gladys Elizabeth Kingcombe; *m* 1951, Irene Dickinson; two *s* one *d*. *Educ:* Exeter Coll., Oxford (MA). On staff of: Univ. of Baghdad 1951-56; Univ. of Ibadan, Nigeria, 1956-67. First Director, Univ. of Ibadan Sch. of Drama, 1962-67. Principal, Central School of Speech and Drama, London, 1967-70. Founded Univ. of Ibadan Travelling Theatre, 1961. *Address:* Monkton House, Marine Parade, Penarth, Glamorgan, S Wales. *T:* Penarth 707889.

**AYER, Sir Alfred (Jules),** Kt 1970; FBA 1952; Wykeham Professor of Logic in the University of Oxford, since 1959; Fellow of New College, Oxford; Hon. Fellow of Wadham College, Oxford, since 1957; *b* 29 Oct. 1910; *s* of late Jules Louis Cyprien Ayer; *m* 1932, Grace Isabel Renée Lees; one *s* one *d*; *m* 1960, Alberta Constance Chapman (Dee Wells); one *s*. *Educ:* Eton Coll. (scholar); Christ Church, Oxford (scholar). 1st class Lit. Hum. 1932; MA 1936; Lecturer in Philosophy at Christ Church, 1932-35; Research Student, 1935-44; Fellow of Wadham Coll., Oxford, 1944-46; Dean, 1945-46; Grote Professor of the Philosophy of Mind and Logic in the Univ. of London, 1946-59; Visiting Prof. at: NY Univ., 1948-49; City Coll., New York. 1961-62; William James Lectr, Harvard, 1970; John Dewey Lectr, Columbia, 1970. Mem., Central Advisory Council for Education, 1963-66; President: Humanist Assoc., 1965-70; Modern Languages Assoc., 1966-67. Hon. Mem. Amer. Acad. of Arts and Sciences 1963. Dr hc Univ. of

Brussels, 1962. Enlisted in Welsh Guards, 1940; commissioned, 1940; Capt. 1943. Attaché at HM Embassy, Paris, 1945. *Publications:* Language, Truth and Logic, 1936 (revised edn 1946); The Foundations of Empirical Knowledge, 1940; Thinking and Meaning (Inaugural Lecture), 1947; (ed with Raymond Winch) British Empirical Philosophers, 1952; Philosophical Essays, 1954; The Problem of Knowledge, 1956; (ed) Logical Positivism, 1959; Privacy (British Academy lecture), 1960; Philosophy and Language (Inaugural lecture), 1960; The Concept of a Person and Other Essays, 1963; Man as a Subject for Science (Auguste Comte Lecture), 1964; The Origins of Pragmatism, 1968; (ed) The Humanist Outlook, 1968; Metaphysics and Common Sense, 1969; articles in philos. and lit. jls. *Address:* New College, Oxford; 10 Regent's Park Terrace, NW1. *T:* 01-485 4855. *Club:* Garrick.

**AYKROYD, Sir Cecil William,** 2nd Bt, *cr* 1929; Chairman of F. A. Aykroyd & Co. Ltd and Midland Combing Co. Ltd; Director National Provincial Bank Ltd (also Bradford & District Local Board); *b* 23 April 1905; *e s* of Sir Frederic Alfred Aykroyd, 1st Bt and late Lily May, *e d* of Sir James Roberts, 1st Bt, LLD, of Strathallan Castle, Perthshire, and Fairlight Hall, near Hastings; *S* father 1949; unmarried. *Educ:* Charterhouse; Jesus Coll., Cambridge. BA 1926. *Recreations:* fishing and shooting. *Heir: b* Frederic Howard Aykroyd [*b* 10 Oct. 1907; *m* 1932, Ruth Joan, *d* of Carlton Oldfield, Moor Hill, Harewood, Yorks; three *d. Educ:* Rugby; Jesus Coll., Cambridge, BA 1928]. *Address:* Birstwith Hall, near Harrogate, Yorks. *T:* Birstwith 250.

**AYKROYD, Wallace Ruddell,** CBE 1943; MD, ScD; *b* 30 July 1899; *e s* of Alfred Constantine Aykroyd, Bradford and Dublin; *m* 1931, Freda Kathleen Buttery; one *s* two *d. Educ:* The Leys Sch., Cambridge; Trinity Coll., Dublin (Vice-Chancellor's Prizeman in English Prose). MB, BCh 1924; MD 1928; ScD 1938; after various hospital appts Beit Memorial Research Fellow, 1928; Mem. of Health Section, League of Nations, 1931-35; Dir, Nutrition Research Laboratories, Coonoor, S India, 1935-45; Delegate of Govt of India to League of Nations Inter-governmental Conference on Rural Hygiene, Bandoeng, 1937; Far Eastern Representative, 1938, of League of Nations Technical Commission on Nutrition; Delegate to United Nations Conference on Food and Agriculture, Hot Springs, Virginia 1943; Dir, Nutrition Div., FAO, 1946-60; Senior Lectr, Dept of Human Nutrition, London Sch. of Hygiene and Tropical Medicine, 1960-66. Hon. Fellow, Amer. Public Health Assoc., 1954; Hon. Mem. American Nutrition Soc., 1960. *Publications:* Vitamins and other Dietary Essentials, 1933; Three Philosophers, 1935; Nutrition and Public Health, 1935 (with Et. Burnet); Sweet Malefactor: Sugar, Slavery and Human Society, 1967; numerous scientific papers on various aspects of nutrition. *Recreations:* reading, walking, gardening. *Address:* Queen Anne House, Charlbury, Oxon.

**AYKROYD, Sir William Miles,** 3rd Bt *cr* 1920; MC 1944; *b* 24 Aug. 1923; *s* of Sir Alfred Hammond Aykroyd, 2nd Bt, and Sylvia Ambler Aykroyd (*née* Walker), *widow* of Lieut-Col Foster Newton Thorne; *S* father, 1965. *Educ:* Charterhouse. Served in 5th Royal Inniskilling Dragoon Guards, Lieut, 1943-47. Dir, Hardy Amies Ltd, 1950-. *Heir: u* Lieut-Col Harold Hammond Aykroyd, OBE, MC, TD, *b* 7 April 1896. *Address:* 69 Eaton Place, SW1. *T:* 01-235 4176. *Club:* Boodle's.

**AYLEN, Rt. Rev. Charles Arthur William;** Assistant Bishop in Diocese of Peterborough, 1950-63; *b* 12 Mar 1882; *s* of late John Robert Aylen, Lieut RN; *m* 1932, Elisabeth Margaret Anna, *er d* of late Judge Eustace Hills; two *s* one *d. Educ:* Bradfield; Keble Coll., Oxford; Cuddesdon Theol. Coll. BA, 3rd Cl. Mod. History, 1904; MA. Curate, Henley-on-Thames, 1905-12; Vicar of Shiplake, Oxon, 1913-25; Chaplain, HMS St Vincent, Grand Fleet, 1916-19; Mission Priest, Empangeni District, Zululand, 1926-30; Bishop of Zululand, 1930-35; Bishop of St Helena, 1935-39; Rector of Aston Tirrold, Berkshire, 1939-45; Vicar of Flore, Northants, 1945-58. Non-residentiary Canon, Peterborough, 1946-61; Rural Dean of Weedon, 1947-51. *Recreation:* scoutmaster since 1913 (District Commissioner for Zululand, 1927). *Address:* 40 Latimer Road, Oxford. *T:* 61911.

**AYLEN, Rear-Adm. Ian Gerald,** CB 1962; OBE 1946; DSC 1942; CEng; FIMechE; Assistant Secretary, Council of Engineering Institutions, since 1966; *b* 12 Oct. 1910; *s* of late Commander A. E. Aylen, RN and Mrs S. C. M. Aylen; *m* 1937, Alice Brough Maltby; one *s* two *d. Educ:* Blundell's, Tiverton. RNE Coll., Keyham, 1929-33; served in HMS Rodney; Curacoa; Galatea, 1939-40; Kelvin, 1940-42; Cossack; 30 Assault Unit, 1945; Fleet Engineer Officer, Home Fleet, 1957-58; CO HMS Thunderer, RNE Coll., 1958-60; Rear-Admiral, 1960; Admiral Superintendent, HM Dockyard, Rosyth, 1960-63; retd 1963. Formerly Dep. Sec., Inst. Mechanical Engineers. Mem. Council, Soc. for Underwater Technology. *Recreations:* fishing, golf, gardening. *Address:* Sisters' Cottage, Wargrave, Berks; 21 Ovington Square, SW3. *Club:* St Stephen's.

**AYLESFORD,** 11th Earl of; **Charles Ian Finch-Knightley,** JP; Vice-Lieutenant of Warwickshire since 1964; Baron Guernsey, 1703; *b* 2 Nov. 1918; *er s* of 10th Earl of Aylesford; *m* 1946, Margaret Rosemary Tyer; one *s* two *d. Educ:* Oundle. Lieut RSF, 1939; Capt. Black Watch, 1947. JP 1948, DL 1954, Warwicks. County Commissioner for Scouts. *Recreations:* wild life and nature conservation. *Heir: s* Lord Guernsey, *qv. Address:* Packington Hall, Coventry, Warwicks. *T:* Meriden 274.

**AYLESTONE,** Baron *cr* 1967 (Life Peer), of Aylestone; **Herbert William Bowden;** PC 1962; CBE 1953; Chairman, Independent Television Authority, since 1967; *b* 20 Jan. 1905; *m* 1928, Louisa Grace, *d* of William Brown, Cardiff; one *d.* RAF, 1941-45. MP (Lab) S Leicester, 1945-50, S-W Div. of Leicester, 1950-67. PPS to Postmaster-Gen., 1947-49; Asst Govt Whip, 1949-50; a Lord Comr of the Treasury, 1950-51; Dep. Chief Oppn Whip, 1951-55; Chief Oppn Whip, 1955-64; Lord Pres. of the Council and Leader of the House of Commons, 1964-66; Secretary of State for Commonwealth Affairs, 1966-67. *Address:* ITA, 70 Brompton Road, SW3.

**AYLING, Air Vice-Marshal Richard Cecil,** CB 1965; CBE 1961 (OBE 1948); Adjudicator, Immigration Appeals, since 1970; *b* 7 June 1916; *s* of A. C. Ayling, LDS, Norwood, London; *m* 1941, Patricia Doreen Wright (*d* 1966); one *s* one *d. Educ:* Dulwich Coll. No 3(F) Sqdn, 1936-39. Served RNZAF, 1940-43; Comd No 51 Sqdn (Bomber Comd), 1944; Station Comdr, Bombay Comd, 1944-45; Staff Coll., 1945. Staff of Central Bomber Estabt, 1946-48; Air Staff (Plans) Far East, 1948-50; Air Min. (OR1 and Dep. Dir Policy Air Staff), 1951-54; Station Comdr, Bomber Comd, 1954-58; Asst Chief of Defence Staff, Min. of

Defence, 1958-59; Dir of Organisation (Estabts), Air Min., 1960-61; SASO, Flying Training Command, 1962-65; Min. of Defence, 1965-66; AOA, RAF Air Support (formerly Transport) Comd, 1966-69; retd, 1969. *Recreations:* ski-ing, sailing, gardening. *Address:* 24 River Green, Hamble, Hants. *T:* Hamble 3033. *Clubs:* Royal Ocean Racing; various yacht clubs and sailing associations.

**AYLMER,** family name of **Baron Aylmer.**

**AYLMER,** 9th Baron *cr* 1718; **John Frederick Whitworth Aylmer;** Bt 1662; *b* 1880; *e s* of 8th Baron and Amy Gertrude, *d* of Hon. John Young; *S* father, 1923; *m* 1928, Gertrude Emma, *d* of late Colin Black, CE, Victoria, BC. *Heir: b* Hon. Kenneth Athalmar Aylmer [*b* 1883; *m* 1924, Eleanor Katharine (*d* 1970), 3rd *d* of late John F. Rogers, of Swanington, Norfolk]. *Address:* Willow Point, RR1 Nelson, BC, Canada.

**AYLMER, Sir Felix, (Sir Felix E. Aylmer-Jones),** Kt 1965; OBE 1950; Actor; *b* 21 Feb. 1889; *s* of Lieut-Col T. E. Aylmer-Jones, RE, and Lilian Cookworthy *m* Cecily Byrne; one *d* (and two *s* decd). *Educ:* Magdalen Coll. Sch.; Exeter Coll., Oxford. First stage appearance, Coliseum, with Seymour Hicks, 1911; Birmingham Rep. Theatre, 1913. Served European War, 1914-18, RNVR. Pres., British Actors' Equity Assoc., 1949-69. *Principal London appearances:* R. E. Lee, 1923; The Terror, 1927; Bird in Hand, 1928; The Nelson Touch, 1931; The Voysey Inheritance, St Joan, 1934; Heroes Don't Care, Waste, 1936; Yes and No, 1937; The Flashing Stream, 1938; Scandal at Barchester, 1944; Daphne Laureola, 1949; Spider's Web, 1955; The Chalk Garden, 1956. New York: 1922, 1925, 1939; The Prescott Proposals, 1953-54. Numerous films and broadcasts. *Principal films:* Tudor Rose, Victoria the Great, The Demi-Paradise, Henry V, Mr Emmanuel, The Ghosts of Berkeley Square, Hamlet, Prince of Foxes, Quo Vadis, The Lady With a Lamp, Ivanhoe, The Knights of the Round Table, The Angel Who Pawned Her Harp, St Joan, Separate Tables, The Doctor's Dilemma, The Mummy, Never Take Sweets from a Stranger, From the Terrace, Exodus, The Chalk Garden. *Publications:* Dickens Incognito, 1959; The Drood Case, 1964. *Address:* 6 Painshill House, Cobham, Surrey. *Clubs:* Garrick, Green Room, Beefsteak.

**AYLMER, Sir Fenton Gerald,** 15th Bt, *cr* 1622; *b* 12 March 1901; *s* of Sir Gerald Evans-Freke Aylmer, 14th Bt, and Mabel Howard, *d* of late Hon. J. K. Ward, MLC, Province of Quebec; *S* father, 1939; *m* 1928, Rosalind Boultbee, *d* of J. Percival Bell, Hamilton, Ont; one *s* one *d*. *Educ:* Lower Canada Coll., Montreal; Bishop's Coll. Sch., Lennoxville. *Heir: s* Richard John Aylmer [*b* 23 April 1937; *m* 1962, Lise Demers; one *s* one *d*]. *Address:* 29 Church Hill, Westmount, Quebec, Canada.

**AYLMER-JONES, Sir Felix E.;** *see* Aylmer, Sir Felix.

**AYNSLEY, George Ayton,** CMG 1956; CBE 1949; *b* 2 May 1896; *e s* of George Morrison Thomas Aynsley and Annie Sarah Jones Aynsley (*née* Ayton); *m* 1920, Margaret Studdy Oliver; one *d*. *Educ:* Rutherford Coll., Newcastle upon Tyne. Colonial Office, 1912-13; Crown Agents for Colonies, 1913-15; joined London Scottish, 1915; served France, Balkans, Egypt and Palestine, 1916-19; Min. of Pensions, 1919-20; Mercantile Marine Dept, Bd of Trade, 1920-23; Customs and Excise, 1923-39; Establishment Officer, Min. of Information, 1939-44; recruited personnel for Allied Commission in Austria, and Control Commission for Germany, 1944-45; administration of Commissions under War Office, 1945, Control Office for Germany and Austria, 1946-47, and Foreign Office, 1947. Head of Personnel Dept, Foreign Office (German Section), 1947-56; Establishment Officer, British Council for Aid to Refugees (Hungarian Dept), 1956-57 (reception and administration of refugees from Hungary). Coronation Medal, 1953. *Recreations:* golf, bowls. *Address:* 9 The Grove, St Margarets, Twickenham, Middlesex. *T:* 01-892 8556.

**AYOUB, John Edward Moussa,** FRCS; Surgeon, Moorfields Eye Hospital, since 1950; Ophthalmic Surgeon, London Hospital, since 1947; Consultant Ophthalmic Surgeon, Royal Masonic Hospital, since 1967; Consulting Ophthalmic Surgeon, Royal Navy; *b* 7 Sept. 1908; British; *m* 1939, Madeleine Marion Coniston Martin; one *s* one *d*. *Educ:* St Paul's Sch.; Lincoln Coll., Oxford; St Thomas' Hospital. BM, BCh Oxon 1933; FRCS 1935. Fellow and Vice-President, Royal Society of Medicine (Mem. Ophth. Cttee); Past Mem. Council, Faculty of Ophthalmologists (Vice-Pres., 1959-). Served War of 1939-45, Surg. Lieut-Comdr RNVR, specialist in ophthalmology. *Publications:* contributions to medical journals. *Recreations:* rowing, sailing. *Address:* 11 Wimpole Street, W1. *T:* 01-580 1251; Cromwell Lodge, 8 The Terrace, Barnes, SW13. *Clubs:* Leander; Royal Solent Yacht; Royal Cruising.

**AYRE, Captain Leslie Charles Edward,** CBE 1941 (OBE 1919); RN, retired; *b* 30 May 1886; *er s* of late Rev. H. E. Ayre, Rector of Brendon, North Devon; *m* 1911, Dorothy Beatrice Agnes, *e d* of late Rev. J. F. Vallings, Vicar of Sopley, Hants; (one *s* killed on active service, Dec. 1941) one *d*. *Educ:* St John's Sch., Leatherhead. Entered Royal Navy, 1904; Paymaster of Royal Yacht Alexandra, 1913-14; HMS Agincourt (Grand Fleet), 1914-15; Secretary to: Admiral Commanding Coastguard, 1917-21; to Rear-Admiral Commanding Destroyer Flotillas, 1922-23; to Asst Chief of Naval Staff, 1923-24; to Rear-Admiral Commanding First Cruiser Squadron, 1924-26; to Commander-in-Chief, China Station, 1928-31; to Commander-in-Chief, Portsmouth, 1931-34; Deputy-Paymaster-Dir-Gen., 1935-37; Command Accountant Officer, Plymouth Command, 1939-43; Polonia Restituta, 1942. *Recreations:* gardening; played football (association) for Navy. *Address:* 38 Chapel Street, Ely, Cambs. *T:* Ely 2704.

**AYRE, Sir Wilfrid,** Kt 1945; JP Fife; *b* 12 April 1890; *s* of late Amos Lowery Ayre, JP South Shields; *m* 1914, Mary Johnson; one *d*. *Educ:* S Shields; King's Coll., Newcastle upon Tyne (Hons Final Degree in Naval Architecture). First place in Final Exam. Naval Architecture, Co. of Shipwrights; Apprenticeship, Wood, Skinner & Co. Ltd, Newcastle; subseq. served in exec. capacity with Jos. T. Eltringham & Co. Ltd, Newcastle, John Lewis & Sons Ltd, Aberdeen; then, with (brother) late Sir Amos L. Ayre, KBE, DSc, founded The Burntisland Shipbuilding Co. Ltd, 1918; Dir, Allen Lithographic Co. Ltd. Past President: The Shipbuilding Conference and The Shipbuilding Employers Federation; Past Chairman, British Shipbuilding Research Assoc.; Underwriting Mem. of Lloyd's; Chm., Fife Emergency Reconstruction Panel, Min. of Aircraft Production and Admiralty, 1940-45; Leader of Admiralty Shipbuilding Mission to USA and Canada, 1942, and of Government Shipbuilding Trade Mission to S American countries, 1946; Chm., Scottish Cttee of Board of Trade Wool Working Party, 1946;

Member: Special Cttee of Advisory Council on Technical Education in Scotland, 1943-46; Census of Production Cttee, 1945-51; Iron and Steel Bd, 1946-48 and of Railway Executive, 1947-50; Pres. Inst. of Engineers and Shipbuilders in Scotland, 1939-41. Mem. Royal Inst. of Naval Architects; Mem. NE Coast Inst. Engineers and Shipbuilders; Mem. Inst. Marine Engineers; Freeman and Liveryman of City of London; Past Prime Warden of Worshipful Co. of Shipwrights. *Recreations:* shooting, angling. *Address:* Priory House, Aberdour, Fife, Scotland. *T:* Aberdour 396.

**AYRTON, Michael;** painter, sculptor, author, theatre designer and illustrator; *b* 20 Feb. 1921; *s* of late Gerald Gould, poet and critic, and late Barbara Ayrton Gould; *m* 1951, Elisabeth (*née* Walshe). *Educ:* London, Vienna and Paris. Exhibitions: Leicester Galls 1942, Redfern Gallery 1943, 1945, 1947, 1949, 1951, 1952, 1953 and 1959, Arts Council 1946 and 1952, Hanover Gallery, 1948, Wakefield City Art Gallery (retrospective), 1949, Milan 1950, Rome, 1950, Zürich 1951, Paris, 1952, Whitechapel Gall. (retrospective), 1955, Leicester Galls. 1957, 1959 (sculpture), Chicago (sculpture), 1960, 1967, 1969, Matthiesen Gall., 1961, Grosvenor Gall., 1964, 1966, 1967, Athens (Greece), 1966, Buffalo (USA), Toronto, 1966, Santa Barbara, 1968, Hamet Gall., 1969, Reading Museum (retrospective), 1969, etc. Décor for theatrical productions: John Gielgud's revival of Macbeth, 1942; Sadler's Wells Ballet Le Festin de l'Araignée, 1944; Covent Garden revival of Purcell's Fairy Queen, 1946 and 1951. Constructions: Arkville Maze, 1969. Art critic of The Spectator, 1944-46. Documentary Films: The Drawings of Leonardo da Vinci, 1953; Greek Sculpture, 1960. *Publications:* British Drawings, 1946; Hogarth's Drawings, 1948; Tittivulus, 1953; Golden Sections, 1957; The Testament of Daedalus, 1962; Drawings and Sculpture, 1962; The Maze Maker, 1967 (Heinemann Award for Literature, 1968); Berlioz, a Singular Obsession, 1969; Giovanni Pisano, 1970, etc. Illustrator of: Poems of Death, 1945; The Duchess of Malfi, 1945; Summers Last Will and Testament, 1946; The Unfortunate Traveller, 1948; Macbeth, 1951; The Human Age, 1956, The Golden Ass, 1961; The Oresteia, 1961; Three Plays of Euripides, 1967, etc. *Recreation:* conversation. *Address:* Bradfields, Toppesfield, near Halstead, Essex. *T:* Gt Yeldham 228. *Club:* Savile.

**AYUB KHAN, Field-Marshal Mohammad;** *see* Khan, M. A.

**AZCARATE y FLOREZ, Pablo de,** MA, DCL; Spanish diplomat; *b* Madrid (Spain), 30 July 1890; *s* of Cayo de Azcarate, Colonel of Military Engineers, and Delfina Florez; *m* 1915, Amelia Diz (*d* 1944); two *s* two *d*; *m* 1948, Frida Herter. *Educ:* Institución Libre de Enseñanza, Madrid; Univs of Madrid, Zaragoza, and Paris. Professor of Administrative Law, Univ. Santiago de Compostela, 1913; Prof. Administrative Law, Univ. Granada, 1915; Mem. of Spanish Parliament, 1918-19; Mem. of Secretariat of League of Nations, 1922; Dir of its Minorities Section, 1929-33; Deputy Sec.-Gen. of League of Nations, 1933-36; Spanish Ambassador in London, 1936-39; Chm. of Servicio para la Emigración de Republicanos Españoles, Paris, 1939-40; Hon. Sec. Juan Luis Vives Scholarship Trust, 1942-43; Dir and Founder Instituto Español, London; Vice-Sec. UNO Palestine Commission and Head of its advance Mission in Palestine, 1948; Sec. of Consular Truce Cttee, Jerusalem; Principal Sec. United Nations Palestine Conciliation Commission, 1949-52. *Publications:* El Regimen Parroquial en Inglaterra, 1912; La Intervención Administrativa del Estado en los Ferrocarriles, 1917; La Guerra y los Servicios Públicos de Caracter Industrial (vols I and II), 1921; Report on Minorities in Encyclopædia Britannica; League of Nations and National Minorities: an Experiment (Carnegie Endowment for International Peace, Washington, 1944); Memoria sobre los Vaughan papers; Boletin de la Real Academia de la Historia (Vol. CXLI), Madrid, 1957; La Nota de la Junta Suprema de Sevilla al Zar Alejandro I de Rusia; Boletin de la Real Academia de la Historia (Vol. CXLIV), Madrid, 1959; La Guerra Hispano-Americana: Estudio de Historia Diplomatica, 1960; Wellington y España, 1961; Apunte biográfico de D. Patricio de Azcárate (Boletin de la Real Academia de la Historia (Vol. CLI, 1962)); Mission to Palestine 1948-1952, 1966; Protection of National Minorities, NY, 1967; La guerra del 98, Madrid, 1969; Gumersindo de Azcárate: estudio biográfico-documental, Madrid, 1969; Protection de Minorités, Genève, 1969; I Sanz del Rio, 1969. *Recreation:* walking. *Address:* 19 Rue Ferdinand Hodler, Geneva, Switzerland. *T:* 36.98.81.

**AZIKIWE, Rt. Hon. Nnamdi,** PC 1960; LLD, DLitt, MA, MSc; (First) President of the Federal Republic of Nigeria, 1963-66; Governor-General and Commander-in-Chief of Nigeria, 1960-63; *b* Zungeru, Northern Nigeria, 16 Nov. 1904; *s* of Obededom Chukwuemeka and Rachel Chinwe Azikiwe; *m* 1936, Flora Ogbenyeanu Ogoegbunam, *d* of Chief Ogoegbunam, the Adazia of Onitsha (Ndichie Chief); three *s* one *d*. *Educ:* CMS Central Sch., Onitsha; Methodist Boys' High Sch., Lagos; Storer Coll., Harpers Ferry, W Va, USA; Howard Univ., Washington, DC; Lincoln Univ., Pa; Univ. of Pennsylvania. Overseas Mem., Inst. Journalists, London, 1933-. Editor-in-Chief, African Morning Post, Accra, 1934-37; Editor-in-Chief, West African Pilot, 1937-45; Correspondent for Associated Negro Press, 1944-47; Gen. Sec., Nat. Council of Nigeria and the Cameroons, 1944-46 (Pres., 1946-60); Correspondent for Reuter's, 1944-46; Chm. African Continental Bank Ltd, 1944-53. MLC Nigeria, 1947-51; Mem. Foot Commission for Nigerianisation of Civil Service, 1948. Leader of Opposition in the Western House of Assembly, 1952-53; Mem. Eastern House of Assembly, 1954-59; MHR 1954; Minister, Eastern Nigeria, 1954-57; Leader, Educational Missions to UK and USA, for establishment of Univ. of Nigeria, 1955 and 1959; Premier of Eastern Nigeria, 1954-59; President of Senate of Federation, Jan.-Nov. 1960. Chm., Provisional Council of Univ. of Nigeria, 1960-61; Chancellor of Univ. of Nigeria, 1961-66. (Life) FREconS; (Life) FRAI; (Life) Mem. British Association for Advancement of Science; Member: American Soc. of International Law; American Anthropological Assoc. KStJ 1961. *Publications:* Renascent Africa; Political Blueprint of Nigeria; Economic Reconstruction of Nigeria; Meditations: A Collection of Poems; Treasury of West African Poetry, etc. *Recreations:* athletics, boxing, cricket, soccer, swimming, tennis, reading.

# B

**BABCOCK, Horace Welcome;** Director, Hale Observatories, since 1964; *b* 13 Sept. 1912; *s* of Harold D. Babcock and Mary G. Henderson; *m* 1st, 1940; one *s* one *d*; 2nd, 1958, Elizabeth M. Aubrey; one *s* (one step *s* one step *d*). *Educ:* California Institute of Technology (BS); Univ. of California (PhD). Instructor, Yerkes and McDonald Observatories, 1939-41; Radiation Laboratory, Mass Inst. of Tech., 1941-42; Calif Inst. of Tech., 1942-45; Staff Mem., Mount Wilson Observatory, 1946-51; Astronomer, Mount Wilson and Palomar Observatories, 1951-57, Asst Dir, 1957-63, Associate Dir, 1963-64, Dir, 1964. Elected to: National Acad. of Sciences, 1954; American Acad. of Arts and Sciences, 1959; American Philosophical Soc., 1966; Corres. Mem., Société Royale des Sciences de Liège, 1968; Associate, Royal Astronomical Soc., 1969; Member: American Astronomical Soc.; Astronomical Soc. of the Pacific; Internat. Astronomical Union. Hon. DSc Univ. of Newcastle upon Tyne, 1965. Eddington Gold Medal, RAS, 1958; Henry Draper Medal of the National Acad. of Sciences, 1957; Bruce Medal, Astronomical Soc. of the Pacific, 1969; Gold Medal, RAS, 1970. *Publications:* scientific papers in Astrophysical Jl, Publications of the Astronomical Soc. of the Pacific, Jl of Optical Soc. of America, etc, primarily on magnetic fields of the stars and sun, astrophysics, and astronomical instruments. *Address:* Hale Observatories, 813 Santa Barbara Street, Pasadena, California 91106, USA. *T:* (213) 577-1122.

**BABINGTON, Rt. Hon. Sir Anthony Brutus,** PC (N Ire.) 1926; Kt, *cr* 1937; QC 1917; *b* 1877; *e s* of Hume Babington Londonderry; *m* 1907, Ethel Vaughan Hart; one *s* two *d*. *Educ:* Glenalmond; Trinity Coll., Dublin. Called to the Bar, 1900; MP South Belfast in Northern Parliament, 1925-29, Cromac, 1929-37; Attorney-Gen. for Northern Ireland, 1925-37; Lord Justice of Appeal for Northern Ireland, 1937-49; retired 1949. *Recreations:* golf and fishing. *Address:* Creevagh, Portrush, Co. Antrim. *T:* Portrush 2738. *Club:* Northern Counties (Londonderry).

**BABINGTON, Anthony Patrick;** Metropolitan Stipendiary Magistrate since 1964; *b* 4 April 1920; 2nd *s* of late Oscar John Gilmore Babington, MAI, AMICE, Monkstown, Co. Cork. *Educ:* Reading Sch. Served with Royal Ulster Rifles and Dorset Regt, 1939-45 (wounded twice); Croix de Guerre with Gold Star (France), 1944. Called to the Bar, Middle Temple, 1948; Central Criminal Court, London Sessions, Middlesex and Kent Bar Messes, South Eastern Circuit; Prosecuting Counsel to Post Office, SE Circuit (South), 1959-64. *Publications:* No Memorial, 1954; The Power to Silence, 1968; A House in Bow Street, 1969; Great Ideas in Law-Making, 1970. *Address:* 3 Gledhow Gardens, South Kensington, SW5. *T:* 01-373 4014. *Clubs:* Garrick; Kildare Street (Dublin).

**BABINGTON, Air Marshal Sir John T.;** *see* Tremayne, Air Marshal Sir J. T.

**BABINGTON, Ven. Richard Hamilton;** Archdeacon of Exeter and Canon Residentiary of Exeter Cathedral, 1958-70; Treasurer of Exeter Cathedral, 1962-70; retired; *b* 30 Nov. 1901; *s* of Very Rev. R. Babington; *m* 1926, Evelyn Ruth Montgomery; two *s* two *d*. *Educ:* Malvern; Keble Coll., Oxford. Curate of Banstead, 1925; Vicar of West End, Southampton, 1929; Vicar of St Mary-le-Tower, Ipswich, 1942; Hon. Canon of St Edmundsbury, 1947. *Recreations:* gardening, trout fishing. *Address:* Thatch End, Whimple, Exeter. *T:* Whimple 479.

**BABINGTON SMITH, Michael James,** CBE 1945; Director: Glyn, Mills & Co. (late Deputy Chairman); Bank for International Settlements, and other companies; Brigadier R of O (TA); *b* 20 March 1901; *e s* of Sir Henry Babington Smith, GBE, KCB, CH, and Lady Elisabeth Mary Bruce; *m* 1943, Jean Mary Meade, *yr d* of late Admiral Hon. Sir Herbert Meade-Fetherstonhaugh, GCVO, CB, DSO; one *s* two *d*. *Educ:* Eton; Trinity Coll., Cambridge. Dir, Bank of England, 1949-69. Sheriff of London, 1953 and 1962. *Recreations:* fishing, shooting, etc. *Address:* 10 Chester Row, SW1. *T:* 01-730 4776; 67 Lombard Street, EC3. *Club:* Brooks's.

**BACHAUER, Gina, (Mrs Alec Sherman);** concert pianist; *b* Athens, Greece, 21 May 1913; *d* of John and Ersilia Bachauer; *m* 1st, 1937, John Christodoulo; 2nd, 1951, Alec Sherman, British conductor. *Educ:* Athens Conservatoire (studied with Woldemar Freeman); Ecole Normale, Paris (studied with Alfred Cortot); worked later with Sergei Rachmaninoff; Gold Medal of Athens Conservatoire, 1929; Prix d'Honneur, Internat. Music Competition, Vienna, 1933. Début in Athens with Nat. Symphony Orchestra of Athens, 1935; toured Europe, 1937, 1938 and 1939; resided in Egypt during War, 1940-45, giving more than 600 concerts for Allied Forces in Base Camps and Hospitals. Début in London, Royal Albert Hall, with the London Orchestra, 1947, in New York, Carnegie Hall, with the New York Philharmonic Symphony Orchestra, 1950. Visited USA annually, 1951- for coast to coast concert tours; has also made concert tours in Canada, S America, Australia, New Zealand, South, East and West Africa, France, Holland, Germany, Austria, Italy, Greece, Israel, Norway, Sweden, Portugal, Cuba, Puerto Rica, Honolulu, Belgium, Hong Kong, Yugoslavia, Finland, Roumania, Poland, Spain, and Czechoslovakia. Comdr, Order of Golden Phœnix (Greece), 1948; Comdr of Order of Welfare (Greece), 1951. *Recreations:* swimming, cooking, reading. *Address:* 6 Cumberland Terrace, Regents Park, NW1. *T:* 01-935 0182. *Club:* Cosmopolitan (New York City, USA).

**BACK, Mrs J. H.;** *see* Harrison, Kathleen.

**BACK, Patrick,** QC 1970; *b* 23 Aug. 1917; *s* of Ivor Back, FRCS, and Barbara Back (*née* Nash). *Educ:* Marlborough; Trinity Hall, Cambridge. Captain, 14th Punjab Regt, 1941-46. Called to Bar, 1940; commenced practice, Western Circuit, 1948; Dep. Chm., Devon QS, 1968. *Recreation:* dinghy racing. *Address:* 30 Seymour Walk, SW10. *T:* 01-352 9870.

**BACKETT, Prof. Edward Maurice;** Professor of Community Health, University of Nottingham, since 1969; *b* 12 Jan. 1916; *o s* of Frederick and Louisa Backett, Cheapside, Ascot; *m* 1940, Shirley Paul-Thompson; one *s* two *d*. *Educ:* Univ. Coll., London; Westminster Hospital. Operational Research with RAF, 1944; Nuffield Fellow in Social Medicine, 1948; Research Worker, Medical Research Council, 1950; Lecturer, Queen's Univ., Belfast, 1953; Senior Lecturer, Guy's Hospital and London Sch. of Hygiene and Tropical Medicine, 1956; Prof. and Head of Dept of Public Health and Social Medicine, Univ. of Aberdeen, 1958-69. *Publications:* papers in scientific journals. *Recreations:* tennis, swimming, walking, sailing. *Address:* Department of Community Health, The Medical School, University of Nottingham, Nottingham. *T:* 56101.

**BACKHOUSE, Col (Hon. Brig.) Edward Henry Walford,** CBE 1961; Vice-Lieutenant of Suffolk since 1965; *b* 7 Feb. 1895; *er s* of Rev. E. B. Backhouse, Northwood, Middx; *m* 1920, Eileen Noël Newby Jenks, Colchester; one *s* one *d*. *Educ:* St Lawrence Coll.; RMC Sandhurst. Commnd into Suffolk Regt, 1914; wounded and POW, Le Cateau, Aug. 1914. Staff Coll., Camberley, 1927-28; Staff Capt. and Bde Major, 1929-33; comd Depot Suffolk Regt, 1934-35; War Office, 1936-38; comd 1st Bn Suffolk Regt, 1938-39; comd 54 Inf. Bde, 1939-42; POW, Singapore, 1942. Bt Major 1932; Bt Lieut-Col 1937; Brig. 1948, retired. Col Suffolk Regt, 1947-57; Chm. Suffolk TA Assoc., 1953-59. DL Suffolk, 1949; Mem. W Suffolk CC, 1958-70. *Recreations:* shooting, fishing. *Address:* Rowen House, Stonebridge Avenue, Bury St Edmunds, Suffolk. *T:* 4028. *Club:* Army and Navy.

**BACKHOUSE, Jonathan;** Director, J. Henry Schroder, Wagg & Co. Ltd; director of other companies; *b* 16 March 1907; 2nd *s* of late Lieut-Col M. R. C. Backhouse, DSO, TD, and of Olive Backhouse; *m* 1934, Alice Joan Woodroffe; two *s* one *d*. *Educ:* RNC Dartmouth. Merchant Bank, 1924-28; Stock Exchange, 1928-50; Merchant Bank, 1950. Served War of 1939-45, Royal Artillery. *Recreations:* sailing, shooting, etc. *Address:* Breewood Hall, Great Horkesley, Colchester, Essex. *T:* Great Horkesley 260. *Clubs:* Royal Thames Yacht; Bembridge Sailing.

**BACKHOUSE, Sir Jonathan Roger,** 4th Bt, *cr* 1901; Director, W. H. Freeman & Co. Ltd, Publishers; *b* 30 Dec. 1939; *s* of Major Sir John Edmund Backhouse, 3rd Bt, MC, and Jean Marie Frances (who *m* 1953, W. N. Gray), *d* of Lieut-Col G. R. V. Hume-Gore, MC, The Gordon Highlanders; *S* father, 1944. *Educ:* Oxford. *Heir: b* Oliver Richard Backhouse, *b* 18 July 1941. *Address:* c/o Lloyds Bank, 39 Piccadilly, W1.

**BACON,** family name of **Baroness Bacon.**

**BACON,** Baroness *cr* 1970 (Life Peeress), of Leeds and Normanton; **Alice Martha Bacon,** PC 1966; CBE 1953; *d* of late County Councillor B. Bacon, miner. *Educ:* Elementary Schs, Normanton, Yorks; Normanton Girls' High Sch.; Stockwell Training Coll.; external student of London Univ. Subsequently schoolmistress. MP (Lab) NE Leeds, 1945-55, SE Leeds, 1955-70; Minister of State: Home Office, 1964-67; Dept of Educn and Science, 1967-70. Mem. National Executive Cttee of Labour Party, 1941-70; Chm., Labour Party, 1950-51. *Address:* 53 Snydale Road, Normanton, Yorks. *T:* Normanton 3229.

**BACON, Sir Edmund (Castell),** 13th Bt of Redgrave, *cr* 1611, and 14th Bt of Mildenhall, *cr* 1627; KG 1970; KBE 1965 (OBE 1945); TD; JP; Premier Baronet of England; HM Lieutenant of Norfolk since 1949; Pro-Chancellor, University of East Anglia, since 1964; Church Commissioner, 1955-63; Director of Lloyds Bank Ltd; Chairman, Agricultural EDC since 1966; *b* 18 March 1903; *s* of Sir Nicholas Henry Bacon, 12th and 13th Bt, and Constance Alice, CBE (*d* 1962), *y d* of late A. S. Leslie Melville; *S* father 1947; *m* 1936, Priscilla Dora, *d* of Col Sir Charles Ponsonby, Bt, *qv*; one *s* four *d*. *Educ:* Eton Coll.; Trinity Coll., Cambridge. Served War of 1939-45, Lieut-Col commanding 55 (Suffolk Yeomanry) Anti-tank Regt RA, 1940-44, Normandy and Belgium 1944 (despatches, OBE). Hon. Col, RA (TA), 1947-67. Chm. British Sugar Corp., Ltd, 1957-68. High Steward: of Norwich Cathedral, 1956; of Great Yarmouth, 1968-. JP Norfolk. Hon. DCL East Anglia, 1969. *Heir: s* Nicholas Hickman Bacon, *b* 17 May 1953. *Address:* Raveningham Hall, Norwich. *T:* Raveningham 206; Ash Villa, Morton Terrace, Gainsborough, Lincs. *T:* Gainsborough 2898. *Clubs:* Carlton, Pratt's.

*See also Sir C. B. Barrington.*

**BACON, Francis;** artist; *b* Dublin 1909. One-man exhibitions: Hanover Gall., London, 1949, 1950, 1951, 1952 (after travelling in S Africa and Kenya), 1954, 1957; Durlacher Gall., New York, 1953; Galerie Rive Droite, Paris, 1957; Galleria D'Arte Galatea, Turin; Galleria Dell' Ariete, Milan; Galleria Obelisco, Rome, 1958; Marlborough Fine Art Gall., London, 1960; Tate Gall., 1962. Exhibitions etc: Beaux Arts Gall., London, 1953; (rep. Great Britain, with Ben Nicholson and Lucien Freud) 27th Venice Biennale, 1954; Hanover Gall., and in New York, 1954; Inst. of Contemporary Arts, London, 1955 (retrospective); New Decade Show, Museum of Modern Art, New York, 1955; New London Gall., 1963, 1965; Solomon Guggenheim Museum, New York, 1963; Gallerie Maeght, Paris, 1966; Marlborough Fine Art, 1967; Marlborough-Gerson Gall., New York, 1968. Travelling exhibitions: Mannheim, Turin, Zürich, Amsterdam, 1962; Hamburg, Stockholm, Dublin, 1965. Paintings acquired by: Tate Gall., 1950-, Arts Council of Great Britain, Contemporary Arts Soc.; works also shown in: Museum of Modern Art, New York, Art Inst. of Chicago, National Gall. of Victoria, Melbourne, etc. Rubens Prize, 1966; Prize, Carnegie Inst., Pittsburgh, 1967. *Address:* c/o Marlborough Fine Art, 39 Old Bond Street, W1.

**BACON, Francis Thomas,** OBE 1967; Consultant on fuel cells to Energy Conversion Ltd, Basingstoke, since 1962; *b* 21 Dec. 1904; 2nd *s* of T. W. Bacon, Ramsden Hall, Billericay; *m* 1934, Barbara Winifred, *y d* of G. K. Papillon, Manor House, Barrasford; one *s* one *d* (and one *s* decd). *Educ:* Eton Coll.; Trinity Coll., Cambridge. With C. A. Parsons & Co. Ltd, Newcastle-on-Tyne, 1925-40 (i/c production of silvered glass reflectors, 1935-39); experimental work on hydrogen/oxygen fuel cell at King's Coll., London, for Merz & McLellan, 1940-41; Temp. Exper. Off. at HM Anti-Submarine Experimental Estbt, Fairlie, 1941-46; exper. work on hydrogen/oxygen fuel cell at Cambridge Univ., 1946-56 (for ERA); Cons. to NRDC on fuel cells at Marshall of Cambridge Ltd, 1956-62. S. G. Brown Award and Medal (Royal Soc.), 1965; British Silver Medal (RAeS), 1969. *Publications:* chapter 5 in Fuel Cells (ed G. J. Young), 1960; chapter 4 in Fuel Cells (ed W. Mitchell), 1963; papers on fuel cells for World Power Conf., Royal Instn, Nature, two UN Confs, Amer. Inst. of Chem. Eng., Inst. of Fuel, Electrochimica Acta. *Recreations:* hill walking, music, photography. *Address:* Westfield, Little Shelford, Cambridge CB2 5ES. *T:* Shelford 2244.

**BACON, Professor George Edward,** MA, DSc Cantab, PhD London; Professor of Physics, University of Sheffield, since 1963; *b* 5 Dec. 1917; *s* of late George H. Bacon and of Lilian A. Bacon, Derby; *m* 1945, Enid Trigg; one *s* one *d*. *Educ:* Derby Sch.; Emmanuel Coll., Cambridge (Open and Sen. Schol.). Air Ministry, Telecommunications Research Estabt, 1939-46. Dep. Chief Scientific Officer, AERE, Harwell, 1946-63. FInstP. *Publications:* Neutron Diffraction, 1955; Applications of Neutron Diffraction in Chemistry, 1963; X-ray and Neutron Diffraction, 1966; Neutron Physics, 1969; many scientific pubns on X-ray and neutron crystallographic studies in Proc. Royal Society, Acta Cryst., etc. *Recreations:* gardening, photography, travel. *Address:* Carr

House, Edale Road, Hope, Sheffield S30 2RF. *T:* Edale 279.

**BACON, Sir Ranulph Robert Maunsell,** Kt 1966; King's Police Medal, 1953; Director: Securicor Ltd, since 1966; International Intelligence Inc., USA, since 1970; Member, Gaming Board for Great Britain, since 1968; *b* 6 Aug. 1906; *s* of late Arthur Ranulph and Hester Mary (*née* Ayles), Westgate-on-Sea; *m* 1932, Alfreda Violet (*née* Annett); one *d* decd. *Educ:* Tonbridge Sch; Queens' Coll., Cambridge (BA). Joined Metropolitan Police, 1928; Metropolitan Police Coll., 1935 (Baton of Honour); seconded to Provost Service, 1940; Capt. 1940, Major 1941, Lieut-Col 1941; all service was in Middle East; Dep. Provost Marshal, Ninth Army, 1942; seconded to Colonial Police Service, 1943; Dep. Inspector-Gen., 1943, Inspector-Gen., 1944-47, Ceylon Police; Chief Constable of Devon, 1947-61; Asst Comr, Met. Police, 1961-66; Dep. Comr New Scotland Yard, 1966. CStJ 1964. *Address:* Two Toonagh, Maidens Green, Winkfield, Berks. *T:* Winkfield Row 2624. *Club:* United University.

**BACON, Sidney Charles,** BSc(Eng); CEng, FIMechE, FIProdE; Controller of Royal Ordnance Factories since 1969; *b* 11 Feb. 1919; *s* of Charles and Alice Bacon. *Educ:* Woolwich Polytechnic; London Univ. Military Service, 1943-48, Capt. REME. Min. of Supply, 1948-60; Asst Dir, ROF, Nottingham, 1960-61; Supt, ROF: Leeds, 1961-62; Woolwich, 1962-63; Birtley, 1965; idc, 1964; Dir of Ordnance Factories, Weapons and Fighting Vehicles, 1965-66; Dep. Controller, ROFs, 1966-69. *Recreation:* golf. *Address:* 228 Erith Road, Bexleyheath, Kent. *Clubs:* Oxford and Cambridge University; Royal Blackheath Golf.

**BADDELEY, Angela;** *see* Clinton-Baddeley, Madeline A.

**BADDELEY, Hermione;** actress; *b* Broseley, Shropshire, 13 Nov. 1908; *d* of late W. H. Clinton-Baddeley and Louise Bourdin; *m* 1st, 1928, Hon. David Tennant (marr. diss., 1937); one *s*; 2nd, Capt. J. H. Willis, MC. *Educ:* privately. Appeared on London stage in La Boîte à Joujoux, Court Theatre, 1918; 1919-23: West End parts; early success as Florrie Small in The Likes of Her, St Martin's, 1923; joined the Co-Optimists, London Pavilion, 1925; continuous appearances in West End theatres in varied plays, including The Greeks had a Word for It; Nine Sharp; Rise Above It; Sky High; Brighton Rock; one and a half years entertaining the troops; A La Carte; Grand National Night; Fallen Angels; Far East and Middle East tour in Cabaret, 1955-56; A Taste of Honey, US tour, 1961-62; The Milk Train Doesn't Stop Here Any More, (New York) 1963; The Killing of Sister George, St Martin's, 1966. Debut in Commercial Television, 1956; constant appearances in films and TV, 1957-61. *Films include:* Caste; Kipps; It Always Rains on Sunday; Brighton Rock; No Room at the Inn; Quartet; Passport to Pimlico; Scrooge; The Belles of St Trinian's; Midnight Lace; Room at the Top (Oscar nomination). *Address:* Round Corner House, 2881 Coldwater Canyon Drive, Beverley Hills, California, USA.

**BADDELEY, Sir John Beresford,** 3rd Bt, *cr* 1922; Managing Director of Baddeley Bros (London) Ltd since 1929; *b* 23 Nov. 1899; *er s* of Sir William Baddeley, 2nd Bt, and Kate (*d* 1956), *d* of Matthew Shaw, Clapton; *S* father, 1951; *m* 1929, Nancy Winifred, *d* of Thomas Wolsey; one *s* two *d*. *Educ:* Lancing Coll. *Heir: s* John Wolsey Beresford Baddeley [*b* 27 Jan. 1938; *m* 1962, Sara Rosalind, *o d* of Colin Crofts, Scarborough, and Mrs John Holman, Ferring, Sussex; two *d*]. *Address:* Street Cottage, Bury, Sussex. *T:* Bury 442. *Club:* Royal Automobile.

**BADDELEY, Rev. William Pye,** BA; Rector of St James's, Piccadilly, since 1967; *b* 20 March 1914; *s* of W. H. Clinton and Louise Rosalie Baddeley, Shropshire; *m* 1947, Mary Frances Shirley, *d* of Col E. R. C. Wyatt, CBE, DSO; one *d*. *Educ:* Durham Univ.; St Chad's Coll., Durham; Cuddesdon Coll., Oxford. Deacon, 1941; Priest, 1942; Curate of St Luke, Camberwell, 1941-44; St Anne, Wandsworth, 1944-46; St Stephen, Bournemouth, 1946-49; Vicar of St Pancras (with St James and Christ Church from 1954), 1949-58; Dean of Brisbane, 1958-67; Commissary to Archbishop of Brisbane, 1967-. Chaplain: Elizabeth Garrett Anderson Hospital, London, 1949-59; St Luke's Hostel, 1952-54; Qld Univ. Anglican Soc., 1960-64; St Martin's Hosp., Brisbane, 1960; Lord Mayor of Westminster. Actors' Church Union Chaplain to Criterion Theatre; Chaplain, Royal Acad. of Arts, 1968-. Hon. Chaplain to Archbishop of Brisbane and Diocesan Chaplain, 1963-67. President: Brisbane Repertory Theatre, 1961-64; Qld Ballet Co., 1962-67; Qld Rep. Elizabethan Theatre Trust, 1963-67; Dir, Australian Elizabethan Theatre Trust, 1965-67; Chairman: Diocesan Radio and Television Coun., 1961-67; weekly television Panel "Round Table", 1962-66; monthly television Panel "What Do YOU Think", 1960-67. Chm. Governors, Burlington Sch., 1967-; Governor, Archbishop Tennison's Sch., 1967-; Member: Assoc. for Promoting Retreats, 1968-; Trustees, Malcolm Sargent Cancer Fund for Children, 1968-. Life Governor of Thomas Coram Foundation, 1955-. SBStJ 1959. *Recreations:* theatre, music, photography. *Address:* St James's Rectory, 197 Piccadilly, W1. *T:* 01-734 0956. *Club:* East India and Sports'.

**BADDILEY, Professor James,** FRS 1961; PhD, DSc; Professor of Organic Chemistry, University of Newcastle upon Tyne, (formerly King's College, University of Durham) since 1955, and Head of School of Chemistry, since 1968; Hon. Director, Microbiological Chemistry Research Laboratory; *b* 15 May 1918; *s* of late James Baddiley; *m* 1944, Hazel Mary (*née* Townsend); one *s*. *Educ:* Manchester Grammar Sch.; Manchester University (BSc 1941, PhD 1944, DSc 1953). Imperial Chemical Industries Fellow, University of Cambridge, 1945-49; Swedish Medical Research Council Fellow, Wenner-Grens Institute, Stockholm, 1947-49; Mem. of Staff, Lister Institute of Preventive Medicine, London, 1949-55; Rockefeller Fellowship, 1954. Member: Council, Chemical Soc., 1962-65; Cttee, Biochemical Soc., 1964-67. Tilden Lectr, Chem. Soc., 1959; Karl Folkers Lectr, Illinois Univ., 1962; Leeuwenhoek Lectr, Royal Society, 1967. Meldola Medal (Royal Institute of Chemistry), 1947; Corday-Morgan Medal (Chemical Society), 1952. *Publications:* numerous in Journal of the Chemical Society, Nature, Biochemical Journal, etc; articles in various chemical and biochemical reviews. *Address:* Department of Organic Chemistry, The University, Newcastle upon Tyne NE1 7RU. *T:* Newcastle 28511.

**BADEL, Alan;** actor; *b* 11 Sept. 1923; *s* of Auguste Firman Joseph Badel and Elizabeth Olive Durose; *m* Yvonne Owen. *Educ:* Burnage High Sch., Manchester; Royal Acad. of Dramatic Art (Bancroft Gold Medallist). First London appearance as Pierrot in L'Enfant

Prodigue, Mercury, 1941; Lennox and 1st Murderer in Macbeth, Piccadilly, 1941. Served with 6th Airborne Div., 1942-47 (appearing with Army Play Unit in Egypt, ME, and Germany). Stevie in Peace in Our Time, Lyric, 1947; Sandman in Frenzy, St Martins (and tour), 1948; Stratford-on-Avon, 1950: Claudio in Measure for Measure, Octavius in Julius Caesar, the Fool in King Lear, and others; Stratford Fest. Season, 1951: parts incl.: The Dauphin in Henry V, Ariel in The Tempest, Justice Shallow and Poins in Henry IV Parts I and II; Old Vic Seasons, 1951-53: Quince in A Midsummer Night's Dream; Romeo; François Villon in The Other Heart; Berowne in Love's Labour's Lost; Lucio in Measure for Measure, and others. Hamlet, Stratford, 1956. Played in and directed The Public Prosecutor, Arts, 1957. First NY appearance, as Hero, in The Rehearsal, 1963 (same prod. Globe, 1961); John Tanner in Man and Superman, New Arts, 1965. Entered management (with Lord Furness), 1957, as Furndel Productions Ltd, and presented: Ulysses Nighttown (played Stephen Dedalus), Arts 1959 (again, in Paris and Holland); The Ark, 1959; Visit to a Small Planet, and others, 1960. Numerous film and television appearances. *Address:* 1a St Martin's Square, Chichester, Sussex.

**BADEN-POWELL,** family name of **Baron Baden-Powell.**

**BADEN-POWELL,** 3rd Baron, *cr* 1929, of Gilwell; **Robert Crause Baden-Powell;** Bt, *cr* 1922; *b* 15 Oct. 1936; *s* of 2nd Baron and Carine Crause Baden-Powell (*née* Boardman); *S* father, 1962; *m* 1963, Patience Hélène Mary, *d* of Major D. M. Batty, S Rhodesia. *Educ:* Bryanston (Blandford). *Recreations:* fishing, camping, scouting. *Heir:* *b* Hon. David Michael Baden-Powell [*b* 11 Dec. 1940; *m* 1966, Joan Phillips, *d* of H. W. Berryman, Melbourne, Australia]. *Address:* Chapel Farm, Ripley, Surrey. *T:* Ripley 2262.

**BADEN-POWELL, Olave, Lady; (Olave St Clair),** GBE, *cr* 1932; World Chief Guide since 1930; *b* 22 Feb. 1889; *yr d* of Harold Soames, Lilliput, Dorset; *m* 1912, 1st Baron Baden-Powell, OM, GCMG, GCVO, KCB; two *d* (one *s*, 2nd Baron Baden-Powell, *d* 1962). County Commissioner for Girl Guides of Sussex, 1916; Chief Commissioner for the Girl Guides of Great Britain and Empire; elected World Chief Guide, 1930. 1914-18 War Medal. Order of Merit (Poland), 1933; Order of White Rose (Finland) 1934; Order of Silver Phœnix (Greece), 1949; Order of Honour and Merit (Haiti), 1951; Order of St Bernard (Chile), 1959; Order of the Sun (Peru), 1959; Order of Vasco de Balboa (Panama), 1959; Order of Cedars of Lebanon, 1960; Order of the Sacred Treasure (Japan), 1963. *Address:* Hampton Court Palace, East Molesey, Surrey. *T:* 01-977 2100. *Club:* Guide.

**BADENOCH, Alec William,** MA, MD, ChM, FRCS; *b* 23 June 1903; *s* of late John Alexander Badenoch, accountant, Banff; *m* 1942, Jean McKinnell, MB, ChB (Edinburgh), *d* of late Alexander Brunton; three *s*. *Educ:* Banff Academy; Aberdeen Univ. Pres. Student Representation Council of Scotland, 1926. Served RAFVR, 1937-45, as Temp. Wing Comdr, i/c Surgical Divs, RAF Hosps Rauceby, Wroughton and St Athan; Surgeon: Royal Hosp. of St Bartholomew, 1947-68; St Peter's Hosp. for Stone and other Urological Diseases, 1946-68; Visiting Urologist: Royal Masonic Hosp.; King Edward VII's Hosp. for Officers; Civilian Consultant in Urology to RAF, 1968-. Prof., RCS, 1948; FRSocMed (Past Pres. Section of Urology); Fellow and Trustee, Hunterian Soc. (Pres. 1949, Vice-Pres. and Orator, 1957); Chm., Editorial Bd, British Jl of Urology (Treasurer, 1961-67); Member: BMA (Vice-Pres. Section of Urology, 1955); Internat. Soc. of Urology (Treas. London Congress, 1964, British Delegate, 1966); Council, Royal College of Surgeons, 1963; GMC, 1966-; GDC, 1969-. Hon. Mem. Peruvian and American Urological Assocs; Corresp. Mem. French and Mexican Urological Assocs. *Publications:* Manual of Urology, 1953; contrib. to British Surgery, Modern Operative Surgery, and Modern Trends in Urology. Articles in scientific jls. *Recreations:* golf, music, swimming. *Address:* 149 Harley Street, W1. *T:* 01-935 4444. *Club:* Royal Automobile.

**BADENOCH, Sir (Alexander) Cameron,** KCIE 1944 (CIE 1931); Kt 1941; CSI 1937; KStJ 1941; *b* Torphins, Aberdeenshire, 2 July 1889; *s* of Rev. Alexander Badenoch; *m* 1914, Jess Greg, *d* of P. Fraser Mackenna, Procurator-Fiscal, Ayrshire; two *s* one *d*. *Educ:* Dunfermline High Sch.; Edinburgh Univ.; Balliol Coll., Oxford. Entered Indian Civil Service, 1912; various posts in Punjab, 1912-19; Accountant Gen., Central Provinces, 1919-21; Accountant Gen., Posts and Telegraphs, 1923-28; various posts, 1928-32 (including Mem. Frontier Defence Cttee, 1931); Dep. Auditor-Gen. of India, 1932-40; Auditor-Gen. of India, 1940-45, retired, 1945; Controller, Finance Div., British Council, 1947-49. *Address:* Pedlar's Way, Gifford, East Lothian. *T:* Gifford 209.

**BADER, Group Captain Douglas Robert Steuart,** CBE 1956; DSO 1940; DFC 1940; Air Adviser: TO Hunting Light Industries, since 1970; to Cunard, since 1970; *b* 21 Feb. 1910; *s* of Frederick Roberts Bader and Jessie Scott-Mackenzie; *m* 1933, Olive Thelma Exley Edwards; no *c*. *Educ:* St Edward's Sch., Oxford; RAF Coll., Cranwell. Commissioned 1930. Lost both legs in flying accident, Dec 1931; invalided out of RAF, May 1933; joined Asiatic Petroleum Co. Ltd; re-joined RAF as Flying Officer, Nov. 1939; Flight Lieut April 1940; fought first action during evacuation of BEF from Dunkirk May-June 1940: Squadron Leader, June 1940, commanding first RAF Canadian Fighter Squadron (242); Wing Comdr, March 1941; captured 9 Aug. 1941, after collision with enemy aircraft over Bethune; released 15 April 1945 by American 1st Army from prison near Leipzig (despatches thrice, DSO and Bar, DFC and Bar, Légion d'Honneur, Croix de Guerre); Group Capt. June 1945; retired 1946; rejoined Shell Petroleum Co. (late Asiatic Petroleum Co.); Man. Dir, Shell Aircraft Ltd, 1958-69, retd. Led first post-war Battle of Britain fly-past, 15 Sept. 1945. *Relevant publication:* biography, Reach for the Sky, by Paul Brickhill. *Recreation:* golf. *Address:* 5 Petersham Mews, Gloucester Road, SW7. *T:* 01-584 0902. *Clubs:* Buck's, Royal Air Force.

**BADGER, Geoffrey Malcolm,** PhD, DSc, FRIC, FRACI, FAA; Emeritus Professor; Vice-Chancellor, University of Adelaide, since 1967 (Deputy Vice-Chancellor, 1966-67); *b* 10 Oct. 1916; *s* of J. McD. Badger; *m* 1941, Edith Maud, *d* of Henry Chevis. *Educ:* Geelong Coll.; Gordon Inst. of Technology; Univs of Melbourne, London, Glasgow. Instructor Lieut, RN, 1943-46. Finney-Howell Research Fellow, London, 1940-41; Research Chemist, ICI, 1941-43; Research Fellow, Glasgow, 1946-49. Univ. of Adelaide: Sen. Lectr, 1949-51; Reader, 1951-54; Prof. of Organic Chemistry, 1955-64. Mem. Executive, CSIRO, 1964-65. *Publications:* Structures and Reactions of Aromatic Compounds, 1954; Chemistry of Heterocyclic Compounds, 1961;

The Chemical Basis of Carcinogenic Activity, 1962; numerous papers in Jl Chem. Soc., etc. *Address:* 7 Rectory Walk, Springfield, South Australia. *T:* 79-4071. *Club:* Adelaide (Adelaide).

**BADHAM, Rev. Leslie (Stephen Ronald)**; Vicar of Windsor since 1958; Chaplain to the Queen since 1964; *b* 1908; *s* of late Stephen Badham and Elizabeth (*née* Lewis); *m* 1938, Effie Garratt, BSc, *y d* of David and Nellie Garratt; two *s* two *d. Educ:* St David's Coll., Lampeter; Jesus Coll., Oxford. BA(Eng), Senior Scholar, St David's Coll., 1931; BA (Theol) Oxon. 1931; MA Oxon. 1935. Curate of: Pembroke Dock, 1933-37; Tenby, 1937-39; Rector of Walton West, with Talbenny, 1939; Chaplain, RAFVR, 1940-46 (despatches; 1939-45 Star; France and Germany Star); Rector of Rotherfield Peppard, 1946-58. Chaplain, Edward VII Hospital, 1958, Surrogate, 1960-. *Publications:* These Greatest Things, 1942; Verdict on Jesus, 1950; Love Speaks from the Cross, 1956. *Recreations:* motoring, writing. *Address:* The Vicarage, Windsor, Berks. *T:* 64572.

**BADIAN, Ernst,** FBA 1965; Professor of Classics and History, State University of New York at Buffalo, since 1969; *b* 8 Aug. 1925; *s* of Joseph Badian and Sally (*née* Horinger), Vienna (later Christchurch, NZ); *m* 1950, Nathlie Anne (*née* Wimsett); one *s* one *d. Educ:* Christchurch Boys' High Sch.; Canterbury Univ. Coll., Christchurch, NZ; University Coll., Oxford (Chancellor's Prize for Latin Prose, 1950; Craven Fellow, 1950; Conington Prize, 1959). MA (1st cl. hons), NZ, 1946; LitD, Victoria, NZ, 1962. BA (1st cl. hons Lit. Hum. Oxon, 1950; MA 1954; DPhil 1956. Asst Lectr in Classics, Victoria University Coll., Wellington, 1947-48; Rome Scholar in Classics, British Sch. at Rome, 1950-52; Asst Lectr in Classics and Ancient History, Univ. of Sheffield, 1952-54; Lectr in Classics, Univ. of Durham, 1954-65; Prof. of Ancient History, Univ. of Leeds, 1965-69. Vis. Professor: Univs of Oregon, Washington and California (Los Angeles), 1961; Univ. of S Africa, 1965; Harvard, 1967; State Univ. of NY (Buffalo), 1967-68. Lecturing visits to Australia, Canada, Germany, Holland, NZ, and S Africa. *Publications:* Foreign Clientelae (264-70 BC), 1958; Studies in Greek and Roman History, 1964; Polybius (The Great Histories Series), 1966; Roman Imperialism in the Late Republic, 1967 (2nd edn 1968); contribs to Artemis-Lexikon, Encyc. Britannica, Oxf. Class. Dictionary and to classical and historical journals. *Recreations:* travelling, reading (especially newspapers and political magazines). *Address:* 82 Allenhurst Road, Buffalo, NY 14214, USA.

**BADMIN, Stanley Roy,** RE 1935 (ARE 1931); (Hon. retired 1965); RWS 1939 (ARWS 1932); ARCA 1927; FSIA 1959; *b* Sydenham, 18 April 1906; 2nd *s* of Charles James and Margaret Badmin, Somersetshire; *m* 1st, 1929; one *s* one *d*; 2nd, 1950, Mrs Rosaline Flew, *widow* of Dr R. Flew; one *d* one step-*d. Educ:* private tutor; Royal College of Art. One man exhibns London, New York, Worthing; works bought by Liverpool, Huddersfield, Bradford, Birmingham, V & A Museum, Chicago Inst. of Art, South London Galleries, Newport, Ashmolean, Worthing, Boston Museum, London Museum, etc. *Publications:* Etched Plates; Autolithoed Educational books; Village and Town, Trees in Britain and Farm Crops in Britain; colour prints; illustrations to: British Countryside in Colour; Trees for Town & Country and Famous Trees; Shell Guide to Trees and Shrubs; The Seasons (by Ralph Wightman); Trees of Britain (Sunday Times); Ladybird Book of Trees; Readers' Digest Publications. *Recreations:* painting and gardening. *Address:* Streamfield House, Bignor, Pulborough, Sussex. *T:* Sutton (Sussex) 229.

**BAERLEIN, Edgar M.,** BA (Cantab); MICE; *b* Manchester, 13 Dec. 1879; 2nd *s* of M. Baerlein, The Grange, Withington, Manchester; *m* 1909, Dorothy, *d* of R. A. Dixon, Cottingham, E Yorks; one *s* (*yr s* killed in action, RAF 1941), two *d. Educ:* Eton; Cambridge. Open Rackets Champion of Great Britain, 1910; open Tennis Champion, 1931; won amateur Rackets Championships (singles) first in 1903, and 9 times in all; won amateur Tennis Championship first in 1912, and 13 times in all; won many other prizes at tennis, including MCC Gold Racket (9 years in succession); French amateur Championship (4 times); Olympic Games Tennis (1924) and at rackets, golf, lawn tennis, etc. *Publications:* in Lonsdale Library, Rackets, Squash Rackets, Tennis, Fives, and Badminton. *Recreations:* shooting, fishing, and various games. *Address:* The White House, Whytings, Sedgwick Lane, Horsham, Sussex. *T:* Horsham 62446. *Clubs:* Queen's, Royal Automobile, MCC, Oxford and Cambridge Golfing Society.

**BAGENAL, (Philip) Hope (Edward),** OBE 1956; DCM; FRIBA; architect and writer on architectural subjects; consultant in the acoustics of buildings; *b* 11 Feb. 1888; *s* of Philip Henry Bagenal; *m* 1914, Alison Mary, *d* of Stuart Hogg; two *s* one *d. Educ:* Uppingham Sch.; Leeds Univ.; Architectural Assoc. Sch. Articled to Niven & Wigglesworth, FFRIBA. War Service, France, RAMC 27th F. Ambulance. RIBA Prize Essay and Silver Medal; holder of Athens Bursary, etc. Acoustic Consultant for: Free Trade Hall, Manchester; Guild Hall, Portsmouth; Coventry Hippodrome; Fairfield Halls, Croydon; Royal Festival Hall, etc. *Publications:* Fields and Battlefields, 1918; Sonnets in War and Peace, 1940; Practical Acoustics and Planning against Noise; (With Robert Atkinson) Theory and Elements of Architecture, 1926; (with late Dr Alex. Wood) Planning for Good Acoustics, 1931. *Address:* Leaside, Hertingfordbury, Hertford.

**BAGGALEY, Ernest James;** Bursar of Chichester Theological College, since 1968; *b* 2 June 1900; *er s* of A. H. Baggaley, Wokefield, Mortimer, Berks; *m* 1929, Sylvia Austen Bell, LRAM; one *s* one *d. Educ:* University Coll., Reading (BSc London). Asst Master (later Second Master), Bembridge Sch., IOW, 1923-41; Asst Master (later Second Master) Queen Elizabeth Grammar Sch., Wakefield, 1941-56, Headmaster, 1956-64. Mem. of Selection Board, Voluntary Service Overseas. *Publication:* A Geography of New Zealand, 1967. *Recreations:* walking, gardening, lecturing for the Commonwealth Institute. *Address:* 57 Cedar Drive, Chichester, Sussex. *T:* Chichester 82624.

**BAGGALLAY, Lt-Col Richard Romer Claude,** DSO 1919; MC 1917; *b* 4 May 1884; *s* of late Claude Baggallay, KC, 20 Elvaston Place, SW, and Wilderwick, East Grinstead; *g s* of Rt Hon. Sir Richard Baggallay, PC; *m* 1st, 1910, Kathleen Constance Charlotte Murphy; one *s*; 2nd, 1922, Phyllis Legge. *Educ:* Marlborough Coll.; RMC Sandhurst. Lieut-Col (retired) Irish Guards; served European War, 1914-19, commanded 1st Bn Irish Guards France and Germany, 1918-19 (wounded, despatches twice, DSO, MC, 1914 Star); Military Sec. to Lord Lieut of Ireland, April-July 1919. Asst Military Sec. to Viscount Allenby and Egyptian Expeditionary Force, Aug. 1919-

May 1920; Asst District Commissioner Sudan, 1920-22; served in Constantinople, 1922-23; commanded Men's Alien Internment Camps, Isle of Man, 1940-42; Capt. Derbyshire County Cricket, 1913-14 and 1919. *Recreations:* cricket, riding, ski-ing, all games. *Club:* Guards.

**BAGGE, Sir John (Alfred Picton),** 6th Bt *cr* 1867; ED; *b* 27 Oct. 1914; *e s* of Sir Picton Bagge, 5th Bt, CMG, and Olive Muriel Mary (*d* 1965), *d* of late Samuel Mendel; *S* father, 1967; *m* 1939, Elizabeth Helena (Lena), *d* of late Daniel James Davies, CBE, Comr for Newfoundland in London; three *s* three *d*. *Educ:* Eton and abroad. Served Inns of Court Regt, 1936-39; commnd into Cheshire Yeo., 1939; served War of 1939-45, Palestine, Sudan, Liberation Campaign of Ethiopia; Major 1941; GSO 2, Brit. Mil. Mission to Ethiopia, 1941-44; GSO 2, HQ, E Africa Comd Liaison with French, 1944; Mil. Asst to Brit. Comdr Allied Control Commn for Bulgaria, 1944-45; GSO 2, War Office, 1945. CStJ 1964; Chm. Council of St John in Norfolk, 1969. *Recreations:* hunting, shooting, ski-ing and water ski-ing. *Heir: s* (John) Jeremy (Picton) Bagge [*b* 21 June 1945; Chartered Accountant, 1968]. *Address:* Stradsett Hall, Kings Lynn, Norfolk. *T:* Fincham 215. *Clubs:* Boodle's; Allsorts (Norfolk).

**BAGGLEY, Charles David Aubrey,** MA; Headmaster of Bolton School since 1966; *b* 1 Feb. 1923; *s* of A. C. and M. Baggley, Bradford, Yorks; *m* 1949, Marjorie Asquith Wood, *d* of M. H. Wood, Harrogate; one *s* one *d*. *Educ:* Bradford Grammar Sch.; King's Coll., Cambridge (1942 and 1945-47) (Exhibitioner in Classics, Scholar in History; Class I, Part II of Historical Tripos, 1947; BA 1947, MA 1952). Temp. Sub. Lieut, RNVR, 1942-45. History Master, Clifton Coll., 1947-50; Head of History Side, Dulwich Coll., 1950-57; Headmaster, King Edward VII Sch., Lytham, 1957-66. Sec., Operational Research Cttee, Div. XII, IAHM, 1960-63; Sec, Div. XII IAHM, 1963-67. Pres., Bolton branch, Historical Assoc., 1966-. Member: Council, IAHM, 1963-65; Cttee of Headmasters' Conf., 1968-; Educational Adv. Council, ITA, 1970-; Bolton Civic Trust; Bolton Commonwealth Friendship Council. *Recreations:* walking, gardening, reading. *Address:* Leverhouse, Greenmount Lane, Bolton, Lancs. *T:* Bolton 40202 (School), Bolton 40607 (Home).

**BAGIER, Gordon Alexander;** MP (Lab) Sunderland South since 1964; *b* July 1924; *m* 1949, Violet Sinclair; two *s* two *d*. *Educ:* Pendower Secondary Technical Sch., Newcastle upon Tyne. Signals Inspector, British Railways; Pres., Yorks District Council, NUR, 1962-64. Mem. of Keighley Borough Council, 1956-60; Mem. of Sowerby Bridge Urban Council, 1962-65. PPS to Home Secretary, 1968-. *Address:* House of Commons, SW1; Rahana, Whickham Highway, Dunston, Gateshead, Durham.

**BAGNALL, Frank Colin,** CBE 1950; Commercial Director, Imperial Chemical Industries Ltd, 1965-70, also Finance Director, 1967-68; African Explosives and Chemical Industries Ltd, 1965-70; *b* 6 Nov. 1909; *s* of late Francis Edward Bagnall, OBE and of Edith Bagnall; *m* 1st, 1933, Ethel Hope Robertson (*d* 1941), *d* of late Dr and Mrs F. W. Robertson, Blechingley; 2nd, 1941, Rona Rooker Roberts, *d* of late Arthur Rooker Roberts, Belmont, Mill Hill, and Pattie Rooker Roberts; one *s* one *d*. *Educ:* Repton; Brasenose Coll., Oxford (MA); Dept of Business Administration, London Sch. of Economics. ICI Ltd, 1932-38; Urwick, Orr and Partners, 1938-40. War Office, 1940-42. Mem., Oxford Univ. Appts Cttee, 1948-69; Governor, Ashridge Coll., 1958-70; Chm. Regular Forces Resettlement Cttee for Wales, 1958-68. Pres., Univ. Coll. of S Wales and Monmouthshire, 1963-68. Dir and Gen. Man., British Nylon Spinners, 1944-45, Man. Dir, 1945-64; Finance Dir, ICI, 1967-68; Chm. Wales Business Training Cttee, 1946-49; Mem. Council Brit. Inst. of Management, 1949-52; Dir Oxford Univ. Business Summer Sch., 1954; Mem. Govt Cttee of Enquiry into Electricity Supply Industry, 1954-55; Chm. SW Reg. Council, FBI, 1956-57; Mem. Air Transport Licensing Bd, 1960-64; Chm. Man-Made Fibres Producers Cttee, 1961-65; Vice-Pres. British Man-Made Fibres Fedn, 1965-70 (Chm. 1963-65); Pres. Textile Inst., 1964-65. Hon. LLD, Wales, 1969. OStJ. *Address:* Wyck Rissington, near Bourton-on-the-Water, Glos. *T:* Bourton-on-the-Water 268. *Clubs:* Boodle's, Farmers'.

**BAGNALL, Rt Rev. Walter Edward;** *see* Niagara, Bishop of.

**BAGNALL, Hon. Sir (William) Arthur,** Kt 1970; MBE 1945; **Hon. Mr Justice Bagnall;** a Judge of the High Court of Justice, Probate, Divorce and Admiralty Division, since 1970; *b* 24 March 1917; *s* of late William Brookes Bagnall and Mary Bagnall (*née* Wood), Wolverhampton; *m* 1955, Margaret Jean, *er d* of John Robert Kerr Tyre and late Dora Tyre (*née* Smyth); one *s* one *d*. *Educ:* Wolverhampton Grammar Sch.; Univ. Coll., Oxford (MA). Served in War of 1939-45: RA in Malta, 1940-44; DAAG Land Forces, Adriatic (despatches), 1944-45. Called to Bar, Lincoln's Inn, 1946; QC 1961; Bencher, 1968. Junior Counsel to Registrar of Restrictive Trading Agreements, 1959-61. Mem. Review Body on Doctors' and Dentists' Remuneration, 1964-70. *Recreation:* golf. *Address:* Yew Tree House, Rotherfield, Sussex. *T:* Rotherfield 408. *Clubs:* Garrick, Beefsteak, MCC.

**BAGNOLD, Enid, (Lady Jones);** writer; *d* of late Colonel A. H. Bagnold, CB, CMG; *m* 1920, Sir Roderick Jones, KBE (*d* 1962), for 25 years Chairman of Reuters; three *s* one *d*. *Educ:* Prior's Field, Godalming; Paris; Marburg. *Publications:* A Diary Without Dates, 1916; Sailing Ships (poems), 1917; Enid Bagnold's Autobiography, 1969; *novels:* The Happy Foreigner, 1920; Serena Blandish (or the Difficulty of Getting Married), 1924; Alice and Thomas and Jane, 1930; National Velvet, 1935 (filmed and TV); The Squire (US, The Door of Life), 1938; The Loved and Envied, 1951; The Girl's Journey, 1956; *plays:* Lottie Dundass, (perf. Vaudeville, 1943); National Velvet, (perf. Embassy, 1945); Poor Judas, (perf. Arts, 1951; Arts Theatre Prize, with John Whiting, 1951); Gertie, (perf. New York, 1952; perf. London as Little Idiot); The Chalk Garden, 1956 (perf. New York and London, 1956; Award of Merit Medal, Amer. Acad. of Arts and Letters); The Last Joke, (perf. Phoenix, 1960); The Chinese Prime Minister, (perf. New York, 1964, London, 1965); Call me Jacky, (perf. Oxford, 1967); Four Plays, 1970; *translation:* Alexander of Asia (from Princess Marthe Bibesco, Alexandre Asiatique), 1955. *Recreations:* "as above." *Address:* North End House, Rottingdean, Sussex, BN2 7HA. *T:* Brighton 32337.

**BAGNOLD, Brig. Ralph Alger,** OBE 1941; FRS 1944; Consultant on movement of sediments by wind and water, since 1956; *b* 3 April 1896; *s* of late Col A. H. Bagnold, CB, CMG: *m* 1946, Dorothy Alice, *d* of late A. E. Plank; one *s* one *d*. *Educ:* Malvern College; Royal Military Academy, Woolwich; Gonville and Caius Coll.,

Cambridge. Commission RE, 1915; Capt, 1918; transferred Royal Corps of Signals, 1920; Major, 1927; retired, 1939. Served European War, Western Front, 1915-18 (despatches); North-West Frontier of India, 1930 (despatches). Organised and led numerous explorations on Libyan Desert and elsewhere, 1925-32; Founder's Medal of Royal Geographical Soc., 1935. Called up, 1939. Raised and commanded Long Range Desert Group in Middle East, 1940-41 (despatches); Deputy Signal-Officer-in-Chief, Middle East, 1943-44; released from Army Service, 1944. G. K. Warren Prize, US Acad. of Sciences, 1969. *publications:* Libyan Sands, 1935; Physics of Blown Sand and Desert Dunes, 1941; papers, etc, on deserts, hydraulics, and beach formation. *Recreations:* exploration, research. *Address:* Rickwoods, Mark Beech, near Edenbridge, Kent. *T:* Cowden 516. *Club:* Athenæum.

**BAGOT,** family name of **Baron Bagot.**

**BAGOT,** 7th Baron, *cr* 1780; **Harry Eric Bagot;** Bt 1627; *b* 4 Feb. 1894; *s* of late Charles Frederick Heneage Bagot (4th *s* of *g s* of 1st Baron) and late Florence Eleanor (*née* Bagot); *S* kinsman, 1961; *m* 1951, Kathleen Elizabeth Saddler, *widow* of Noel Murray Puckle, Melbourne, Australia. *Educ:* Marlborough. Served European War, 1914-19, as Captain RFA, also RFC (severely wounded). *Heir: b* Reginald Walter Bagot, Major (retired) Royal Marines [*b* 24 Aug. 1897; *m* 1st, 1922, Winifred Gwyneth Bowen (marr. diss., 1934); 2nd, 1934, Millicent Brenda Bowden]. *Address:* 103 Caroline Street, South Yarra, Victoria, Australia.

**BAGRIT, Sir Leon,** Kt 1962; Chairman, Elliot-Automation Ltd since 1963 (Deputy Chairman from its formation, 1957, until 1962); Deputy Chairman, English Electric Co. Ltd since 1967; Director: Electronic Trust Ltd since 1963; Technology Investments Ltd, since 1963; *b* 13 March 1902; *s* of Manuel and Rachel Bagrit; *m* 1926, Stella Feldman; two *d. Educ:* St Olave's; London Univ. After various posts in Engineering Industry, organised the first company in Europe devoted to automation. Mem., Council for Scientific and Industrial Research, 1963-65; Mem., Advisory Council on Technology, 1964-. Dir, Royal Opera House, Covent Garden, 1962-70; Founder, Friends of Covent Garden, Chm., 1962-69. Reith Lecturer, 1964. RSA Albert Medal, 1965. D. Univ. Surrey, 1966; DSc Univ. Reading, 1968. *Publication:* The Age of Automation, 1966. *Recreations:* music and visual arts. *Address:* Upper Terrace House, Hampstead, NW3. *Club:* Devonshire.

**BAGSHAWE, Thomas Wyatt,** FSA, FRHistS; *b* 18 April 1901; *yr s* of late Arthur Bagshawe, The Grove House, Dunstable, Beds; *m* Grace Geering; two *s. Educ:* Rugby School; Gonville and Caius Coll., Cambridge. Geologist, Expedition to Graham Land (Antarctica), 1920-22. Dir, Bagshawe & Co., Ltd, Dunstable, 1925-47. Hon. Curator, later Hon. Dir, Luton Museum, 1928-47. Liveryman, Curriers' Company, 1936, also Past-Master. Served War of 1939-45, RAFVR and Combined Operations, 1940-45. High Sheriff of Beds, 1949; Hon. Adviser, The Moot Hall, Elstow, Bedford, 1952-58; Vice-Pres., Royal Anthropological Institute, 1952-55. Name given to Bagshawe Glacier, Danco Coast, Antarctica, 1958. *Publications:* Notes on the Habits of the Gentoo and Ringed or Antarctic Penguins, 1938; Two Men in the Antarctic, 1939; Pompey was a Penguin, 1940; numerous articles and notes in jls relating to antiquarian matters, folk life, early furniture, sculpture, etc. *Recreations:* the study of the history of trades; collecting antiques. *Address:* 95 Orchard Avenue, Worthing, Sussex. *Club:* Antarctic.

**BAHADUR SHAMSHER JANG BAHADUR RANA, Commanding-General,** (retired); GBE (Hon.), 1934; and Mil., 1938; KCB (Hon.), 1945; Nepalese Army, retired: Hon. Colonel British Army, 1942; *b* 1892; *e surv s* of H. H. Maharaja Joodha Shamsher Jang Bahadur Rana of Nepal, GCB, GCSI, GCIE; *m* 1st, 1906, Chandra Rajya Lakshmi (*d* 1934); one *s* three *d*; 2nd, 1937, Lakshmi Kumari Devi; one *s* two *d*. In command Patan Bde, 1910-29; led 1st Nepalese Contingent to India, 1915-16 (British War Medal); present during Prince of Wales's visit to Nepal, 1921; Rotary Judge of Supreme Court of Appeal, Nepal, 1922-29; Dir-Gen. of Public Instruction, Nepal, 1924-29; Pres. of Development Bd, 1935-40; Dir-Gen., Nepal Bank Ltd, 1937-40; First Nepalese Minister at the Court of St James, 1934-35; head of First Special Nepalese Missions to present Decorations to King George V and others; visited India and concluded agreement between India and Nepal Govts in connection with Nepalese Contingent for India on outbreak of War, 1939; GOC-in-C Nepalese Contingent in India, 1940-43; Chief Justice Supreme Court of Nepal, 1943-45 (KCB). In charge of 8 provinces of Nepal Terai, 1946-47; Dir-Gen. of Foreign Aff., 1937-40, and again from 1943; Pres. Cttee to negotiate with Goodwill Mission of USA, 1947; Pres. Constitutional Reforms Cttee set up in Kathmandu under order of Maharaja of Nepal, 1947; Eastern Comg Gen. and Act. Senior Gen., 1948; has Order of Star of Nepal 1st Class (with title of Supradipta Manyabara), and Nepalese Orders of Gorkha Dashina Bahu 1st Class (with title of Prasidha Pravala Gorkha Dakshina Bahu), 1935, and of Trishakti Patta, 1st Class (with the title of Subikhyat-Trishakti-Patta), 1939; Om Rama Patta, 1948. Hon. Grand Cross, Crown of Italy, 1934, and Legion of Honour (France), 1939. *Recreations:* riding, shikar, lawn tennis. *Address:* Bahadur Bhavan, Nepal, *via* India.

**BAILEY,** family name of **Baron Glanusk.**

**BAILEY, Arthur,** OBE 1945; FRIBA 1946; Architect; *s* of Charles Hill and Winnifred Bailey; *m* 1930, Phyllis, *d* of William and Harriet Martin; one *s*. Consulting Architect to: King George's Fields Foundn; London Dio.; Rochester Dio.; Min. of Transport (Bridges); GLC (Housing); Worshipful Co. of Vintners; London Electricity Bd; Nat. Council of Social Service; Church Pastoral-Aid Soc; Lloyds Bank Ltd; Hambros Bank Ltd; Nat. Deposit Friendly Soc.; ICAA Commissions include: remodelling and extensions, Sheffield Cath. (Civic Trust Award, 1969); rebuilding St Nicholas Cole Abbey (Wren) London (Civic Trust Award, 1967); re-building and remodelling St George-in-the-East (Hawksmoor), Stepney (Civic Trust Award, 1967); Churches: New Dutch, Austin Friars, EC2; St James-the-Less, Bethnal Green; St Mary's, Shortlands, Kent; Holy Trinity, Gillingham (Civic Trust Award, 1969); Baptist, Norwood and Paddington; London Electricity Bd: Divl Offices, Ilford and Bexleyheath; Meter Test Stn and Labs, Bexleyheath, also Stores; Offices: Austin Friars; Holborn Circus; St Peter's Square, Manchester; Church Pastoral-Aid Soc., Fleet Street; Divl Offices for Nat. Deposit Friendly Soc. in various cities; new HQ, CMS, SE1; Bridges: Stratford-upon-Avon; Ross-on-Wye; Maidstone By-Pass; M4, Maidenhead; M6, Cheshire and Westmorland; Housing for:

LCC, Mortimer Crescent, Tower Hamlets, Hawgood Street; West Ham Corp.; Sevenoaks RDC; Brit. Drug Houses Ltd; Tower Court Flats, Bournemouth; Convalescent Home, Portal House, Bournemouth; Arts Block, Highgate Sch.; Pilgrims Sch., Seaford, and Edith Edwards House Sch., Banstead, ICAA; Highgate Sch. Swimming Bath; many private commissions. Min. of Lab. and Nat. Service, 1940-45; Chief Inspector, Building Labour Supply, and Advisor on War Building Programme. Prize Winner of Open Architectural Competitions: Swansea City Hall, Coun. Offices and Law Cts; Wimbledon Town Hall; Wiggeston Gram. Sch., Leicester; Bradford Civic Centre Improvement Scheme; Wolverhampton Town Hall; Overhead Motorway; Liverpool RC Cathedral. Member: Architects' Registration Coun. (RIBA Rep.); and Finance Cttee (Vice-Chm.); RIBA Practice Cttee (Vice-Chm. and Past Chm.); Councillor, Artists General Benevolent Instn; Hon. Architect to: ICAA; Nat. Council of Social Service; Queen Alexandra's House; Exhibitor, Royal Academy (Water Colours and Architecture). Officer, Order of Orange Nassau, 1954. *Publications:* papers in learned jls. *Recreations:* water colours, sailing, fly-fishing, ice-skating. *Address:* 2 & 12 Gray's Inn Square, WC1. *T:* 01-242 5691, 6244-5; 48 Tower Court, West Cliff Road, Bournemouth, Hants. *T:* 23991. *Clubs:* Athenæum, Reform; Royal Motor Yacht, Poole Parkstone Yacht, Bar Yacht.

**BAILEY, D(avid) R(oy) Shackleton,** LittD; FBA 1958; Professor of Latin, University of Michigan, since 1968; *b* 10 Dec. 1917; *y s* of late Rev. J. H. Shackleton Bailey, DD, and Rosamund Maud (*née* Giles); *m* 1967, Hilary Ann, *d* of Leonard Sidney and Margery Bardwell. *Educ:* Lancaster Royal Grammar Sch.; Gonville and Caius Coll., Cambridge. Fellow of Gonville and Caius Coll., 1944-55, Praelector, 1954-55; Fellow and Dir of Studies in Classics, Jesus Coll., Cambridge, 1955-64; Visiting Lecturer in Classics, Harvard Coll., 1963; Fellow and Dep. Bursar, Gonville and Caius Coll., 1964; Senior Bursar 1965-68; Univ. Lectr in Tibetan, 1948-68. *Publications:* The Satapañcāśatka of Mātrceta, 1951; Propertiana, 1956; Towards a Text of Cicero, *ad Atticum,* 1960; Ciceronis Epistulae ad Atticum IX-XVI, 1961; Cicero's Letters to Atticus, Vols I and II, 1965; Vol. V, 1966, Vol. VI, 1967, Vols III and IV, 1968, Vol. VII, 1970; articles in Classical and Orientalist periodicals. *Recreation:* cats. *Address:* Department of Classical Studies, University of Michigan, Ann Arbor, Mich 48104, USA.

**BAILEY, Rev. Dr (Derrick) Sherwin;** Canon Residentiary of Wells Cathedral, since 1962; Precentor and Prebendary of Whitchurch, since 1968; *b* 30 June 1910; *s* of William Thomas and Ellen Mary Bailey, Alcester, Warwks; *m* 1st, 1939, Philippa Eleanor (*d* 1964), *d* of Capt. Philip James and Eleanor Frances Vandeleur Green; one *s* two *d*; 2nd, 1966, Morag Stuart Macdonald, MD. *Educ:* The Grammar Sch., Alcester, Warwks; Lincoln Theological Coll.; Edinburgh Univ. In business, 1928-40; ACII 1934; Linc. Theol Coll., 1940-42; Univ. of Edin., PhD 1947; DLitt, 1962; Fellow of Eugenics Soc., 1957. Deacon, 1942; Priest, 1943; Curate, Mablethorpe St Mary and Theddlethorpe St Helen with Theddlethorpe All Saints, 1942-44; Chaplain to Anglican students at Univ. and Colls of Edinburgh, and Curate of St John Evang., Edin., 1944-51; Anglican Lectr in Divinity, Moray House Trg Coll., Edin., 1948-51; Central Lectr, C of E Moral Welfare Counc., 1951-55; Actg Educ. Sec., 1954-55; Study Sec., 1955-59; Permission to officiate in Dio. B'ham, 1951-59; Rector of Lyndon with Manton, Martinsthorpe and Gunthorpe, 1959-62; Chancellor of Wells Cathedral, and Prebendary of Litton, 1962-69. Select Preacher, Univ. of Camb., 1963. Examining Chaplain to Bishop of Bath and Wells, 1963-. *Publications:* Sponsors at Baptism and Confirmation, 1952; Thomas Becon and the Reformation of the Church in England, 1952; The Mystery of Love and Marriage, 1952; Homosexuality and the Western Christian Tradition, 1955; Sexual Offenders and Social Punishment, 1956; The Man-Woman Relation in Christian Thought, 1959; Common Sense about Sexual Ethics, 1962; (Joint-Author) Celibacy and Marriage, 1944. Contributor: They Stand Apart, 1955; The Human Sum, 1957; Die Religion in Geschichte und Gegenwart, 1959; Westminster Dict. of Christian Educ., 1961; Dictionary of Christian Ethics, 1967; Sexual Ethics and Christian Responsibility, 1970; also to: Theology; Journal of Ecclesiastical History; Church Quarterly Review; Scottish Jl of Theol.; London Quarterly and Holborn Review; The Churchman, etc. *Recreations:* railways and railway modelling, photography. *Address:* 4 The Liberty, Wells, Somerset BA5 2SU. *T:* Wells 3188.

**BAILEY, Sir Derrick Thomas Louis,** 3rd Bt, *cr* 1919; DFC; *b* 15 Aug. 1918; 2nd *s* of Sir Abe Bailey, 1st Bt, KCMG; *S* half-brother, 1946; *m* 1946, Katharine Nancy Stormonth Darling; four *s* one *d*. *Educ:* Winchester. Engaged in farming. *Recreations:* all sports, all games. *Heir:* *s* John Richard Bailey, *b* 11 June 1947. *Address:* de Poort, Colesberg, Cape, South Africa;Brinsop Court, Hereford. *Club:* Rand (Johannesburg).

**BAILEY, Desmond Patrick; His Honour Judge Bailey;** a Judge of the County Courts, Circuit No 8 (Manchester), since 1970; *b* 6 May 1907; 3rd *s* of Alfred John Bailey, Bowden, Cheshire, and of Ethel Ellis Johnson; unmarried. *Educ:* Brighton Coll.; Queens' Coll., Cambridge (BA, LLB). Called to Bar, Inner Temple, 1931. Northern Circuit. Served War of 1939-45: Rifle Brigade, Lancashire Fusiliers, Special Operations Executive, North Africa, Italy (Major). Recorder of Carlisle, 1963-65; a Judge of Co. Courts, Circuit No 6, 1965-70. *Recreations:* cricket, fishing, gardening. *Address:* Chaseley, Bowdon, Cheshire. *T:* Altrincham 0059. *Clubs:* St James's (Manchester); Athenæum (Liverpool).

**BAILEY, Sir Donald Coleman,** Kt 1946; OBE 1944; JP; Dean of the Royal Military College of Science, 1962-66; *b* 15 Sept. 1901; *s* of J. H. Bailey, Rotherham, Yorkshire; *m* Phyllis, *d* of Charles Frederick Andrew, Wick, Bournemouth; one *s*. *Educ:* The Leys, Cambridge; Univ. of Sheffield (BEng). Posts: Rowntree & Co. Ltd, York, Efficiency Dept; London Midland & Scottish Rly, Civil Engineers Dept; City Engineer's Dept, Sheffield; Dir, Military Engineering Experimental Estabt. Hon. Fellow, Inst. of Welding; Fellow, Instn of Structural Engineers; MICE; Hon. Member: Instn of Royal Engrs; Inst. of Engrg Designers. Hon. DEng Sheffield. JP 1946. Commander of the Order of Orange-Nassau, 1947. *Recreation:* golf. *Address:* 14 Viking Close, Southbourne, Bournemouth. *T:* Bournemouth 49181.

**BAILEY, Air Cdre George Cyril,** CB 1944; DSO 1917; BSc; MICE; RAF, retired; *b* 15 July 1890; *s* of Dr Bailey; *m* 1st, 1918, Phyllis (*d* 1927), *y d* of late Sir John Foster Stevens; one *s*; 2nd, 1944, Mary Ellen Goldney (*d* 1970), *o d* of late Dr Frederick St John Kemm and Mrs Kemm, Bristol. *Educ:* King Edward VI Sch.,

Stratford-on-Avon; Manchester Univ. Served European War, 1914-18 (despatches, DSO). Joined Royal Flying Corps, 1916; psa 1925; Group Capt., 1935; Air Commodore, 1939; retired from Royal Air Force, 1944. *Address:* BM/DNIF, London, WC1.

**BAILEY, George Leo,** CBE 1952; MSc, FIM; Director, British Non-Ferrous Metals Research Association, 1944-66; *b* 1 July 1901; *s* of late Charles and Annie Bailey; *m* 1925, Blanche Joy, *d* of late J. A. Pearce; one *s* one *d.* *Educ:* King Edward VI Grammar Sch., Birmingham; Birmingham Univ. Metallurgist, Research Dept, Woolwich, 1922; Chief Development Officer, BNFMRA, 1930-44. Past-Pres. Inst. of Metals and of Instn of Metallurgists. Hon. DMet (Sheffield). *Publications:* The Casting of Brass Ingots (with R. Genders). Papers on metallurgical and related subjects in Jl of Inst. of Metals and other scientific instns. *Recreations:* walking and bridge. *Address:* Broomfield, Box Lane, Hemel Hempstead, Herts. *T:* Hemel Hempstead 52488.

**BAILEY, Harold,** CMG 1960; Under-Secretary, Board of Trade, 1958; *b* 26 Feb. 1914; *yr s* of late John Bailey and Elizabeth Watson, Preston, Lancashire; *m* 1946, Rosemary Margaret, *d* of Harold and Irene Brown, Shotesham St Mary, Norfolk; two *s* one *d.* *Educ:* Preston Grammar Sch.; Christ Church, Oxford. Asst Principal Air Ministry, 1937; Principal, Min. of Aircraft Production, 1942; Served, Royal Air Force, 1942-45; Private Sec. to Minister of Supply and Aircraft Production, 1945-47; Asst Sec., 1947; Min. of Supply Rep. and Adviser (Defence Supplies) to UK High Comr, Ottawa, 1953-55; Under-Sec., Ministry of Supply, 1957; British Senior Trade Comr in India, and Economic Adviser to the British High Comr, 1958-63. *Address:* 83 Redington Road, NW3. *T:* 01-435 8916.

**BAILEY, Sir Harold (Walter),** Kt 1960; FBA 1944; MA, W Aust.; MA, DPhil Oxon; Professor of Sanskrit, Cambridge Univ., 1936-67, Professor Emeritus, 1967; *b* Devizes, Wilts, 16 Dec. 1899. Was Lecturer in Iranian Studies at Sch. of Oriental Studies. Member of: Danish Academy, 1946; Norwegian Academy, 1947; Kungl. Vitterhets Historie och Antikvitets Akademien, Stockholm, 1948; Governing Body, Sch. of Oriental and African Studies, Univ. of London, 1946-; L'Institut de France; Associé étranger, Académie des Inscriptions et Belles-Lettres, 1968. Pres., Philological Soc., 1948-52; Pres. Royal Asiatic Society, 1964-67. Hon. Fellow Sch. of Oriental and African Studies, London Univ., 1963-; Hon. Fellow, Queens' Coll., Cambridge, 1967. Hon. DLitt, W Aust., 1963. *Publications:* in Bulletin of Sch. of Oriental Studies, Journal of Royal Asiatic Soc., Zeitschrift der Deutschen Morgenländischen Gesellschaft, etc. Codices Khotanenses, 1938; Zoroastrian Problems in the Ninth Century Books, 1943; Khotanese Texts I, 1945; Khotanese Buddhist Texts, 1951; Indoscythian Studies, Khotanese Texts II, 1953; III, 1956; IV, 1961; V, 1963; VI, 1967; Corpus inscriptionum iranicarum, Saka Documents, Portfolios I-IV, 1960-67; Saka Documents, text volume, 1968. *Address:* Queens' College, Cambridge.

**BAILEY, James Vincent;** Executive Director, Bank of England, 1964-69; *b* 26 July 1908; *s* of R. H. Bailey; *m* 1946, Ida Hope Weigall; no *c.* *Educ:* Malvern; Pembroke Coll., Oxford. Entered Bank of England, 1928; Deputy Chief Cashier, 1959-62; Chief Accountant, 1962-64. *Address:* Common Barn, Remenham, Henley-on-Thames, Berks. *T:* Henley 2480.

**BAILEY, John Everett Creighton,** CBE 1947; Chairman and Managing Director, Baird & Tatlock Group of Cos, since 1941; Director, Tarmac Derby Ltd, also of other Cos; Special Member, Prices and Incomes Board; *b* 2 Nov. 1905; *s* of late John Edred Bailey and late Violet Constance Masters; *m* 1928, Hilda Anne Jones; one *s* four *d.* *Educ:* Brentwood Sch. Mem. Admlty Chemical Advisory Panel, 1940-50; Pres. Scientific Instrument Manufacturers Assoc., 1945-50; Chm. Brit. Laboratory Ware Assoc., 1950-52; Chm. Brit. Sci. Instr. Research Assoc., 1952- (Pres. 1962-); Mem. Grand Council FBI, 1945-58; Mem. Bd of Trade Exhibns Adv. Cttee, 1957-, and Census of Production Adv. Cttee, 1960-. Second Master, Co. of Scientific Instrument Makers, 1957-58; Liveryman, Worshipful Co. of Needlemakers; Freeman of City of London. Mem. Inst. of Export; MRI; FBIM. *Recreation:* golf. *Address:* 72 Melton Court, Kensington, SW7. *Clubs:* Athenæum, Royal Aero.

**BAILEY, Sir Kenneth (Hamilton),** Kt 1958; CBE 1953; QC; Special Adviser in International Law to the Departments of the Attorney General and of External Affairs, Canberra, since 1969; *b* 1898; *e s* of late E. T. Bailey, Melbourne; *m* 1925 (Editha Olga) Yseult (OBE 1961), *d* of late Frank S. Donnison of Blewbury, Berks; three *s.* *Educ:* Wesley Coll., Melbourne; Queen's Coll., Univ. of Melbourne; Corpus Christi Coll., Oxford. 2nd Divn Australian Field Artillery, 1918-19; Victorian Rhodes Scholar for 1918; BA Oxon (Mod. Hist.), 1921; MA 1927; Bachelor of Civil Law, Oxon, 1923; called to Bar, Gray's Inn, 1924; Bencher, 1961. Prof. of Jurisprudence, 1928-30, of Public Law, 1931-46, Univ. of Melbourne; consultant, Commonwealth Attorney-Gen.'s Dept, 1943-46. Solicitor-Gen. and Sec. of the Attorney-Gen.'s Department of the Commonwealth of Australia, 1946-64; Australian High Comr in Canada, 1964-69. Mem. of Australian Delegations, League of Nations Assembly, 1937 and 1946, United Nations Conference on Internat. Organisation, San Francisco, 1945, United Nations Preparatory Commn and Gen. Assembly, 1945-46, and many later years; Leader of Australian Delegation and Chm. First Cttee, United Nations Conf. on Law of the Sea, 1958. Hon. Fellow, Corpus Christi Coll., Oxford. Hon. LLD, Dalhousie, 1966; ANU, 1970. *Publications:* articles on constitutional and international matters. *Address:* c/o Department of External Affairs, Canberra, ACT 2600, Australia.

**BAILEY, Reginald Bertram;** Director, South-Eastern Postal Region, since 1970; *b* 15 July 1916; *s* of George Bertram Bailey and Elizabeth Bailey, Ilford; *m* 1942, Phyllis Joan Firman; one *s* one *d.* *Educ:* Owen's School. Served War of 1939-45: RAPC, 1940-42; RE, 1942-46. Entered Post Office as Exec. Officer, 1935; Higher Exec. Officer, 1947; Sen. Exec. Officer, 1948; Principal, 1950; Instructor, Management Trng Centre, 1957; Staff Controller, SW Region, 1958; Comdt, Management Trng Centre, 1962; Asst Sec., 1965; Dir, Wales and the Marches Postal Region, 1967. *Recreations:* walking, gardening, philately, old railway timetables. *Address:* c/o South-Eastern Postal Region HQ, Russell House, 84 Churchill Square, Brighton BN1 2EQ. *T:* 0273-201555.

**BAILEY, Ronald William,** CMG 1961; Ambassador to Bolivia since 1967; *b* 14 June 1917; *o s* of William Staveley and May Eveline Bailey, Southampton; *m* 1946, Joan Hassall, *d* of late A. E. Gray, JP, Stoke-on-Trent; one *s* one *d.* *Educ:* King Edward VI Sch.,

Southampton; Trinity Hall, Cambridge (Wootton Isaacson Scholar in Spanish). Probationer Vice-Consul, Beirut, 1939-41; HM Vice-Consul, Alexandria, 1941-45; Asst Oriental Sec., British Embassy, Cairo, 1945-48; Foreign Office, 1948-49; 1st Sec., British Legation, Beirut, 1949-52 (acted as Chargé d'Affaires, 1949, 1950 and 1951); 1st Sec., British Embassy, Washington, 1952-55; Counsellor, Washington, 1955-57; Khartoum, 1957-60 (acted as Chargé d'Affaires in each of these years); Chargé d'Affaires, Taiz, 1960-62; Consul-Gen., Gothenburg, 1963-65; Minister, British Embassy, Baghdad, 1965-67. *Recreations:* walking, photography, gardening. *Address:* Redwood, Tennyson's Lane, Haslemere, Surrey. *T:* Haslemere 2800; c/o Foreign and Commonwealth Office, King Charles Street, SW1. *Clubs:* Athenæum, Oriental.

**BAILEY, Reverend Dr Sherwin;** *see* Bailey, Reverend Dr D. S.

**BAILEY, Sidney Alfred,** CB 1946; MBE 1918; *b* 16 Sept. 1886; *m* 1912, Ethel Alice Towse; three *s* one *d.* Entered Civil Service, Board of Education, 1906; Insurance Commission, 1912; Ministry of Health, 1919, Principal, 1931, Senior Deputy Chief Inspector, 1937; Ministry of Transport, Asst Sec., 1937, Principal Asst Sec., 1941, Under-Sec., 1946; Dir of Studies, Administrative Staff Coll., 1950-51. *Address:* Milestone, The Fair Mile, Henley on Thames, Oxon. *T:* Henley 5170.

**BAILEY, Prof. Stanley John,** LLD; Rouse Ball Professor of English Law in the University of Cambridge, 1950-68; Fellow of St John's College, Cambridge, since 1931; Barrister-at-Law, Inner Temple, 1924; *b* 19 June 1901; *o s* of John Bailey and Evelyn Mary Bailey (*née* Campkin); *m* 1st, 1926, Kathleen Aimée (*d* 1949), *d* of late Rev. F. J. Hamilton, DD; 2nd, 1952, Wilhelmina, *d* of late Dr H. W. Leeksma, The Hague, Holland; one *s. Educ:* Queen's Coll., Taunton; St John's Coll., Cambridge. Lecturer in Univ. Coll. of Wales, Aberystwyth, 1926; Reader in English Law in Univ. of Birmingham, 1930; Coll. Lecturer at St John's Coll., Cambridge, 1931-50; Lecturer in Univ. of Cambridge, 1934, Senior Proctor, 1936-37; Tutor of St John's Coll., 1939-46; Reader in Law, Cambridge, 1946-50. *Publications:* Law of Wills, 1935 (6th edn, 1967); contrib. to Law Quarterly Review, Cambridge Law Journal, The Conveyancer; Ed. of Cambridge Law Journal, 1948-54. *Address:* St John's College, Cambridge. *T:* Cambridge 61621.

**BAILEY, Thomas Aubrey,** MBE 1959; Director, Peter Cox Ltd, Building Restoration Specialists (Member of SGB Group of Cos), since 1970; *b* 20 Jan. 1912; *o s* of late Thomas Edward Bailey and Emma Bailey; *m* 1944, Joan Woodman, *d* of late John Woodman Hooper; one *s. Educ:* Adams' Grammar Sch., Newport, Shropshire; Regent Street Polytechnic Sch. of Architecture. Entered HM Office of Works, Ancient Monuments Br., 1935; Asst Architect, 1945-49; Architect, London and E Anglia, 1949-54; Sen. Architect in charge Ancient Monuments Br., Eng., Wales and Overseas, Min. of Public Building and Works, 1954-69; Architectural Adv. to Oxford Historic Bldgs Fund, 1963-69. Served on various cttees on stone decay and preservation; seconded to Sir Giles G. Scott, OM, RA, for Rebuilding of House of Commons, 1944-49. *Principal works:* Direction of MPBW Survey for Oxford Historic Bldg Appeal, 1957-62 and Cambridge Appeal, 1963; re-erection of fallen Trilithons at Stonehenge, 1958-64; Conservation of Claudian Aqueduct and Aurelian Wall, Brit. Embassy at Rome, 1957-69; etc. Resigned professional membership of RIBA and ARCUK, to enter specialised Bldg Industry, 1969. Mem. Conservation Cttee, for Council for the Care of Churches, 1968; Mem. Cttee, Ancient Monuments Soc., 1970. FSA 1957; FRSA 1969; Fellow of Faculty of Bldg, 1969. Hon. MA Oxon 1963; Freeman of City of London, 1967. *Publications:* (jointly) The Claudian Aqueduct in the Grounds of the British Embassy, Rome, 1966; many technical reports on conservation of Historic Monuments. *Recreations:* music, photography, travel, motoring. *Address:* (home) 32 Anne Boleyn's Walk, Cheam, Sutton, Surrey. *T:* 01-642 3185; (office) 11 Wates Way, Mitcham, Surrey. *T:* 01-640 1151.

**BAILEY, Wilfrid;** Chairman, Southern Gas Board, since 1969; Chartered Accountant; *b* 9 March 1910; *s* of late Harry Bailey and Martha Bailey (*née* Pighills); *m* 1934, Vera (*née* Manchester); two *s* one *d. Educ:* Keighley Grammar Sch. Borough Treasurer, Bexley BC, 1945-47; Chief Financial Officer, Crawley Development Corp., 1947-49; Gas Council: Chief Accountant, 1949-58; Secretary, 1958-61; Dep. Chm., Southern Gas Bd, 1961-69. FCA 1935; FBIM 1959. *Recreations:* cricket, motoring, music, photography, gardening. *Address:* (home) Bramble Way, Clease Way, Compton Down, near Winchester. *T:* Twyford 3382.

**BAILLIE,** family name of **Baron Burton.**

**BAILLIE, Sir Gawaine George Hope,** 7th Bt of Polkemmet, *cr* 1823; *b* 8 March 1934; *s* of Sir Adrian Baillie, 6th Bt, and Hon. Olive Cecilia, *d* of 1st Baron Queenborough, GBE; *S* father, 1947; *m* 1966, Mrs Margot Gardner, *d* of Senator Louis Beaubien, Montreal; one *d. Address:* 33 Wilton Crescent, SW1.

**BAILLIE, George Henry;** Director: Canadian Pacific Railway Company, Montreal; Soo Line Railroad Co.; Consolidated Mining and Smelting Co. of Canada Ltd; Chairman, Metro Centre Land Co., Toronto, since 1969; *b* 1 July 1901; *s* of William James Baillie and Caroline Cross; *m* 1930, Madeleine Hyland; no *c. Educ:* High Sch., St Lambert, Quebec; Sir George Williams Coll., Montreal. Canadian Pacific Railway: Clerk, Montreal, 1918-28; Chief Clerk, Winnipeg, 1928-30; Superintendent of Railway, various places Western Canada, 1930-42; Gen. Supt Rly, Calgary and Vancouver, 1942-45; Gen. Man., Western Lines, CPR, Winnipeg, 1945-47; Vice-Pres., CPR: Vancouver, BC, 1947-50; Toronto, 1950-58; in charge all rail operations for system, Montreal, 1958-63; elected to Bd of Dirs, CPR Co., March 1963; apptd Managing Dir, Europe, April 1963-66; Vice-Pres. and Dir, CPR Co., 1966-68. *Recreation:* golf. *Address:* 561 Avenue Road, Toronto, Ont, Canada. *Clubs:* Royal Automobile Club (London); Mount Royal, St James's, Mount Bruno Golf (Montreal); York, Toronto, Toronto Golf (Toronto); Manitoba (Winnipeg); Ranchmen's (Calgary); Vancouver, Shaughnessy Heights Golf and Country, Capilano Golf and Country (Van.); Swinley Forest Golf (Ascot, Eng.).

**BAILLIE, Ian Fowler,** CMG 1966; OBE 1962; Assistant Secretary, The Thistle Foundation, Edinburgh, since 1970; *b* 16 Feb. 1921; *s* of late Very Rev. Principal John Baillie, CH, DLitt, DD, LLD and Florence Jewel (*née* Fowler); *m* 1951, Sheila Barbour (*née* Mathewson); two *s* one *d. Educ:* Edinburgh Acad.; Corpus Christi Coll., Oxford (MA). War service, British and Indian Armies, 1941-46. HM Overseas Civil

Service (formerly Colonial Service), 1946-66: Admin. Officer (District Comr), Gold Coast, 1946-54; Registrar of Co-operative Socs and Chief Marketing Officer, Aden, 1955; Protectorate Financial Sec., Aden, 1959; Dep. British Agent, Aden, 1962; Brit. Agent and Asst High Comr, Aden, 1963; Dir, Aden Airways 1959-66; Sen. Research Associate and Administrative Officer, Agricultural Adjustment Unit, Dept of Agricultural Economics, Univ. of Newcastle upon Tyne, 1966-69. *Recreation:* angling. *Address:* 4 Grange Loan Gardens, Edinburgh EH9 2EB. *T:* 031-667 2647.

**BAILLIE, Isobel,** CBE 1951; Hon. MA (Manchester Univ.), 1950; Singer; *b* Hawick, Scotland; *m* 1918, H. L. Wrigley; one *d. Educ:* Dover Street High Sch. for Girls, Manchester. Appeared at all leading Festivals, including Three Choirs, Edinburgh, London, etc.; only British singer to appear with Toscanini on three occasions. Concerts with Sir Malcolm Sargent, Sir Adrian Boult, Sir Hamilton Harty, Sir Henry Wood, Bruno Walter, De Sabata, etc. Sang at Covent Garden in Orphée, and in Hollywood Bowl. Toured New Zealand twice; concerts in Malaya, 1948, South Africa, 1952, etc. Professor of Singing: Cornell Univ., USA, 1960-61; Royal Coll. of Music, London. *Address:* 3 Langford Close, St John's Wood, NW8. *T:* 01-624 7508. *Club:* Cowdray.

**BAILLIE, John Strachan,** CBE 1965; *b* 1896; *s* of William T. Baillie, Belfast; *m* 1926, Eileen Mary, *d* of Saxon J. Payne. *Educ:* Queen's Univ., Belfast (BComSc). Joined Harland and Wolff, Belfast, 1913, and (apart from service in RN, 1914-18) was with Co. throughout his career; transf. to Co.'s London Office, 1924; Asst Sec., Harland & Wolff, Belfast, 1937; London Manager, 1945; Dir 1947; Dep. Chm. 1958; Chm. 1962-65; Dir, Short Brothers & Harland Ltd, 1948-67; Dep. Chm. Brown Bros & Co. Ltd, 1962-67. Liveryman, Worshipful Co. of Shipwrights. Mem., Br. Cttee, Det Norske Veritas. Commander: Order of St Olav (Norway), 1960; Dannebrog (Denmark) 1964. *Address:* Merrydown, 12 Aldersey Road, Guildford, Surrey.

**BAILLIE, Lady Maud L. E.,** CBE 1945; JP; *b* 20 April 1896; *e d* of 9th Duke of Devonshire; *m* 1st, 1917, Captain Angus Alexander Mackintosh, RHG (*d* 1918); one *d*; 2nd, 1928, Brig. Hon. G. E. M Baillie, MC (*d* on active service, 1941); two *s* one *d. Educ:* privately. Master High Peak Harriers, 1922-47. Served ATS, 1938-45. *Address:* Ballindarroch, Inverness. *T:* Scaniport 208.

**BAILLIE-GROHMAN, Vice-Admiral Harold Tom,** CB 1941; DSO 1917; OBE 1922; RN retired; *b* Victoria, British Columbia, 16 Jan. 1888; *o s* of late W. A. Baillie-Grohman, Kootenay pioneer, author and sportsman; *m* 1915, Evelyn, *e d* of Arthur S. Taylor, MD, FRCS; two *s.* Joined HMS Britannia, 1903; Lieut 1909; Lt-Com. 1917; Captain 1930; Rear-Adm. 1941; Vice-Admiral, 1943 (retd). Served European War, 1914-18, with Grand Fleet, in Dover Patrol in destroyers and minesweepers (DSO, OBE, Chevalier of Order of Leopold, Star of Ethiopia, Order of the Brilliant Jade); in Persian Gulf and Red Sea, 1922-23; as SO 1st Minesweeping Flotilla, 1923-24; and as ACNS and DNI in Navy Office, Melbourne, 1925-27; Military Staff Coll., Camberley, 1928; Head of British Naval Mission to China, 1931-33; in command First Destroyer Flotilla, Mediterranean, 1934-36; in command HMS St Vincent and in charge Boys' Training Establishment, 1936-38; commanded HMS Ramillies, 1st Battle Squadron, Mediterranean, 1939-40; attached to Staff of GOC Mid. East, 1941; Rear-Admiral Combined Operations, 1942; FOIC, Harwich, 1944, Kiel and Schleswig-Holstein, 1945-46, to eliminate the remains of the German naval forces. *Publication:* (with A. Heckstall-Smith) Greek Tragedy, 1941. *Address:* 6 St Martin's Square, Chichester, Sussex. *T:* Chichester 82753. *Clubs:* United Service; Alpine Ski; (Naval Member) Royal Yacht Squadron; RN Sailing Assoc.

**BAILLIE-HAMILTON,** family name of **Earl of Haddington.**

**BAILLIEU,** family name of **Baron Baillieu.**

**BAILLIEU,** 2nd Baron, *cr* 1953, of Sefton, Australia, and Parkwood, Co. Surrey; **William Latham Baillieu;** Assistant Master, St Peter's Sch., Seaford, Sussex; *b* 10 Dec. 1915; *s* of 1st Baron Baillieu, KBE, CMG and Ruby (*d* 1962), *d* of late William Clark; *S* father 1967; *m* 1st, 1945, Anne Bayliss (marriage dissolved, 1961) *d* of Leslie William Page, Southport, Queensland; two *s*; 2nd, 1962, Mrs Delia Muriel Champion. *Educ:* Winchester; Magdalen Coll., Oxford (MA). *Recreations:* gardening, and fishing. *Heir:* *s* Hon. James William Latham Baillieu, *b* 16 Nov. 1950. *Address:* The Oast House, Park Farm, Chiddingly, Lewes, Sussex. *T:* Chiddingly 319. *Clubs:* Bath; Leander (Henley-on-Thames); Melbourne (Melb.).

**BAILY, Robert Edward Hartwell,** CBE 1932; retired from Sudan Political Service; Chairman, Herefordshire Scout Council since October 1960 (County Commissioner, Herefordshire Boy Scouts, 1939-60); *b* 6 June 1885; *s* of E. P, Baily, Hazelwood, Limpsfield; *m* 1920, Brenda (*d* 1962), *d* of H. A. Wadworth and *widow* of Captain G. E. Lea, Worcestershire Regt. *Educ:* Harrow; Cambridge. Captain Harrow Cricket XI, 1903-4; Cambridge Cricket XI, 1908. Sudan Political Service, 1909-32; Governor Kassala Province, 1926-32. Secretary, Roy. Empire Soc., 1935-38. *Address:* Castle Pool Hotel, Hereford. *T:* Hereford 3551. *Clubs:* Travellers', Royal Commonwealth Society, Chatham House, MCC, Free Foresters.

**BAIN, Prof. Andrew David;** Esmee Fairbairn Professor of the Economics of Finance and Investment since 1970, Director of Institute of Finance and Investment since 1969 and Head of Department of Economics since 1967, University of Stirling; *b* 21 March 1936; *s* of Hugh Bain and Kathleen Eadie; *m* 1960, Anneliese Minna Frieda Kroggel; three *s. Educ:* Glasgow Academy; Christ's Coll., Cambridge. PhD Cantab 1963. Junior Res. Officer, Dept of Applied Econs, Cambridge Univ., 1958-60; Res. Fellow, Christ's Coll., Cambridge, 1960; Instructor, Cowles Foundn, Yale Univ., 1960-61; Lectr, Cambridge, 1961-66; Fellow, Corpus Christi Coll., Cambridge, 1962; on secondment to Bank of England, 1965-67; Prof. of Econs, Univ. of Stirling, 1967-70. *Publications:* The Growth of Television Ownership in the United Kingdom (monograph), 1964; The Control of the Money Supply, 1970; articles on demand analysis, monetary policy and other subjects. *Recreation:* golf. *Address:* 7 Pathfoot Avenue, Bridge of Allan, Stirlingshire. *T:* Bridge of Allan 2433. *Club:* Oxford and Cambridge University.

**BAIN, Cyril William Curtis,** MC; DM Oxford; FRCP; Hon. Consulting Physician, Harrogate General Hospital; Past President BMA; *b* Thornfield, Heaton Mersey, near Manchester, 5 June 1895; *e s* of late William Bain, MD, FRCP, and Ellen, *d* of late John Curtis, Rose

Leigh, Heaton Chapel, near Manchester; *m* 1930, Diana Alice, *y d* of late Lt-Col H. R. Pease, and *ggd* of late Joseph Robinson Pease, Hesslewood, near Hull; three *s* one *d*. *Educ:* Bilton Grange, near Rugby; Wellington Coll.; Christ Church, Oxford; St Thomas's Hospital, London. Served European War, 1914-18; gazetted to the Duke of Wellington's Regt 29 August 1914; Captain, 1916; Major, 1918; served in Machine Gun Corps (despatches, MC); active service in France and Flanders, 1915-17; retired, 1918; Extra-ordinary member of the Cardiac Society. *Publications:* Recent Advances in Cardiology (with C. F. T. East), 5th edition, 1959; Incomplete Bundle Branch Block; Bilateral Bundle Branch Block; The Oesophageal Lead; Clinical Value of Unipolar Chest and Limb Leads, etc. *Recreations:* fishing, sailing. *Address:* Red Willows, The Belyars, St Ives, Cornwall. *T:* St Ives 6298. *Club:* Royal Cornwall Yacht.

**BAIN, William Alexander;** formerly Professor of Pharmacology, University of Leeds; *b* Dunbar, 20 Aug. 1905; *o s* of late Rev. Alex. Wright Bain and late Grace Martin, *e d* of James Brough, JP, Inveresk; *m* 1st, 1929, Bessie Beveridge Smith (*d* 1961), Uphall; one *s* one *d*; 2nd, 1962, Freda Dratman, Philadelphia, Pa, USA. *Educ:* Broxburn High Sch.; Bathgate Academy (John Newland Bursar); Univ. of Edinburgh. BSc, 1st Cl. Hons Physiol., and Wellcome Gold Medallist, History of Medicine, 1928; Ellis Prizeman, 1930; Crichton Research Scholar, 1930 and 1931; FRSE, 1931; PhD, Faculty of Medicine, 1932; DSc, 1953. Asst to Sir E. Sharpey Schafer, FRS, 1928; Lecturer in Experimental Physiology, Univ. of Edin., 1931; Lecturer in Physiol., Univ. of Leeds, 1934; Reader in Pharmacology, Univ. of Leeds, 1935; Professor of Pharmacology, Univ. of Leeds, 1946-59; Dir, Smith Kline and French Research Inst., Welwyn Garden City, Herts, 1959-66. Academic Sub-Dean, Faculty of Medicine, Leeds, 1943-48; Hon. Treas., Brit. Pharmacological Soc., 1947-64; Mem. Brit. Nat. Cttee for Physiological Sciences, 1955-60, 1967-; Assessor Univ. Grants Cttee, 1958-69; Member: Physiolog. Soc.; Soc. for Experimental Biol.; Biometric Soc.; Royal Med. Soc. (Edin.); Royal Soc. Med.; Institute of Biology (Fellow). Sometime Examiner in Pharmacology, Univs of Cambridge, Aberdeen, Durham and London and for the Pharmaceutical Society of Great Britain. Press Editor, British Journal of Pharmacology and Chemotherapy, 1953-57. Hon. ScD (TCD), 1967, Hon. Mem. Brit. Pharmacol. Soc., 1967 (Mem. 1939-67). *Publications:* articles in medical and scientific journals on autonomic nerves, adrenaline, histamine antagonists, quantitative human pharmacology etc. *Recreations:* music, gardening, reading dictionaries. *Address:* Oakdene, Digswell, Welwyn, Herts. *T:* Welwyn 4119. *Club:* Royal Societies.

**BAINBRIDGE, Maj.-Gen. Henry,** CB 1948; CBE 1944; psc; retired; late Corps of Royal Engineers; *b* 1903. 2nd Lieut Royal Engineers, 1923. Served War of 1939-45, 1939-44 (despatches twice, CBE). Dir of Man-power Planning, War Office, 1949-52; Dep. QMG, War Office, 1952-55, retired 1955. *Address:* Brizlee, Hoe Lane, Peaslake, Surrey. *Club:* United Service.

**BAINES, Rt. Rev. Henry W.;** *see* Wellington (NZ), Bishop of.

**BAIRAMIAN, Sir Vahe (Robert),** Kt 1959; *b* 30 Nov. 1900; 2nd *s* of Dr Bairamian, Cyprus; *m* 1934, Eileen Elsie Connelly; one *s*. *Educ:* English Sch., Nicosia, Cyprus; University Coll., London. Barrister-at-Law, Middle Temple, 1923. Served in the Courts and Land Registry, Cyprus, 1926-44; Legal Asst, Lands and Survey, Nigeria, 1944; Chief Registrar, Supreme Court, Nigeria, 1944; Magistrate, 1946; Puisne Judge, 1949; Senior Puisne Judge, High Court, Northern Region of Nigeria, 1955; Chief Justice, Sierra Leone, 1957-60; Justice, Supreme Court of Nigeria, 1960-68. Ed, All Nigeria Law Reports of 1963, 1964, 1965 and 1966 (Supreme Court Judgments). Fellow UCL, 1963. Jubilee Medal, 1935; Coronation Medal, 1953. *Address:* 17 The Crescent, Sandgate, Folkestone, Kent. *T:* Folkestone 38240. *Club:* Royal Commonwealth Society.

**BAIRD,** family name of **Viscount Stonehaven.**

**BAIRD, Sir David Charles,** 5th Bart of Newbyth, *cr* 1809; *b* 6 July 1912; *s* of late William Arthur Baird, of Lennoxlove, and Lady Hersey Baird; *S* uncle, 1941. *Educ:* Eton; Cambridge. *Heir: b* Robert Walter Stuart Baird [*b* 1914; *m* 1st, 1938, Maxine Christine (marriage dissolved, 1960), *o c* of Rupert Darrell, New York; one *s*; 2nd, 1960, Maria Florine Viscart; one *d*]. *Address:* Senwick, Borgue, Kirkcudbright.

**BAIRD, Sir Dugald,** Kt 1959; MD, FRCOG, BSc, DPH; Regius Professor of Midwifery in the University of Aberdeen, 1937-65, retired; formerly Obstetrician-in-Chief, Aberdeen Maternity Hospital and Visiting Gynæcologist, Aberdeen Royal Infirmary; *b* 16 Nov. 1899; *er s* of David Baird, MA, Gourock, Renfrewshire; *m* 1928, May Tennent (*see* Lady Baird); two *s* two *d*. *Educ:* Greenock Acad.; University of Glasgow; University of Strasbourg. Formerly Sen. Asst to the Muirhead Chair of Obstetrics and Gynæcology, University of Glasgow; Visiting Obstetrician, Glasgow Royal Maternity and Women's Hospital; Asst Gynæcologist, Glasgow Royal Infirmary; Consulting Gynæcologist, Glasgow Royal Cancer Hospital. Pres., Childbirth Research Centre, 1968-. Hon. LLD: Glasgow, 1959; Aberdeen, 1966; Hon. DSc: Manchester, 1962; Wales, 1966; Hon. DCL, Newcastle. *Publications:* various papers on obstetrical and gynæcological subjects. *Recreation:* golf. *Address:* Fae-me-well, Dyce, Aberdeenshire.

**BAIRD, James Craig,** CB 1967; retired Civil Servant, now farming; *b* 4 Nov. 1906; *s* of John Jackson and Martha Baird; *m* 1934, Janet Gentiles McFarlane; two *d* (two *s* decd). *Educ:* Methodist Coll., Belfast; Queen's Univ., Belfast (BSc, BAgr). Agricl Chem. Dept, QUB, 1927-38; Min. of Agric., NI, 1927-66; Chief Inspector, 1948; Asst Sec., 1955; Perm. Sec., 1963; retired, 1966. *Recreation:* Rugby football. *Address:* Holestone, Doagh, Co. Antrim, N Ireland. *T:* Doagh 232.

**BAIRD, Maj.-Gen. James Parlane,** QHP, MD, FRCP, FRCPEd; Director of Medicine and Consulting Physician to the Army since 1969; *b* 12 May 1915; *s* of Rev. David Baird and Sara Kathleen Black; *m* 1948, Anne Patricia Anderson; one *s* one *d*. *Educ:* Bathgate Academy; Univ. of Edinburgh. FRCPEd 1952, MD 1958, FRCP 1959. Commissioned, RAMC, 1939; Lt-Col 1956; Prof. of Military Medicine, Royal Army Medicial Coll., 1965; Cons. Physician, BAOR, 1967. QHP 1969. *Publication:* Tropical Diseases Supplement to Principles and Practice of Medicine, 1968. *Recreation:* golf. *Address:* Ministry of Defence (Army), Lansdowne House, Berkeley Square, SW1. *T:* 01-499 8040. *Club:* Army and Navy.

**BAIRD, Sir James Richard Gardiner,** 10th Bt *cr* 1695; MC 1945; *b* 12 July 1913; *er s* of Captain William Frank Gardiner Baird (killed in action

1914) (2nd *s* of 8th Bt) and Violet Mary (*d* 1947), *d* of late Richard Benyon Croft; *S* uncle, Sir James Hozier Gardiner Baird, 9th Bt, 1966; *m* 1941, Mabel Ann (Gay), *d* of A. Algernon Gill, Toronto, Canada; two *s* one *d*. *Educ:* Eton. Served War of 1939-45. Lieut, Royal Artillery, 1940; Captain, Kent Yeomanry, 1944. *Recreation:* shooting. *Heir:* *s* James Andrew Gardiner Baird [*b* 2 May 1946. *Educ:* Eton]. *Address:* Wareside, Ware, Herts. *T:* Ware 3695. *Club:* Bath.

**BAIRD, Lady, (May Deans),** CBE 1962; National Governor of the BBC in Scotland since Nov. 1965; *b* 14 May 1901; *er d* of Matthew Tennent, Newton, Lanarks; *m* 1928, Sir Dugald Baird, *qv*; two *s* two *d*. *Educ:* Glasoow High Sch. for Girls; Glasgow Univ. BSc 1922; MB, ChB 1924. Hospital appts until marriage; social and local govt work, 1938-54; Chm. of Public Health Cttee, Aberdeen Town Council; Chm. NE Regional Hosp. Bd (Scotland), 1947-66. Hon. LLD, Aberdeen Univ., 1958. *Address:* Fae-me-well, Dyce, Aberdeenshire. *T:* Dyce 251. *Club:* Ladies' Town and County (Aberdeen).

**BAIRD, William George,** CMG 1949; JP; MA, LLB; Transport Licensing Authority, Otago Province, 1950-60; *b* East Taieri, 1889; *s* of Robert Baird, farmer. *Educ:* Allanton; Mosgiel; Victoria Coll. Entered Public Trustee Office as clerical cadet, 1906; Asst District Public Trustee, Christchurch; Controller of Estates Div., Head Office; Asst Public Trustee, 1931, Public Trustee, 1942, Wellington, NZ; retired, 1949. JP, Wellington, 1932-. *Address:* 101 Highgate, Dunedin, NZ. *Clubs:* Wellington, Wellesley (Wellington); University (Dunedin).

**BAKER, Alex Anthony,** MD, DPM; Director, National Health Service, Hospital Advisory Service, since 1969; *b* 22 March 1922; *m* 1944; two *s* two *d*. *Educ:* St Mary's Hosp. Med. Sch. Consultant Psychiatrist: Banstead Hosp., 1955; Mother and Baby Unit, Downview Hosp., 1958; St Mary Abbotts Hosp., 1967; Medical Administrator, Banstead Hosp., 1964; sometime Consultant to WHO; Sen. Principal Medical Officer, Dept of Health, 1968. *Publications:* (jtly) Psychiatric Services and Architecture, 1958; (jtly) Social Psychiatry; Psychiatric Disorders in Obstetrics, 1967; chapters in sundry books; papers in numerous jls on research, psychiatric treatment, organisation of psychiatric services, etc. *Address:* 33 Colcokes Road, Banstead, Surrey.

**BAKER, Alfreda Helen,** MD; FRCS; Consulting Surgeon: to Elizabeth Garrett Anderson Hospital, since 1937; to Hounslow Hospital, since 1930; to Marie Curie Hospital, since 1937; *b* 2 Oct. 1897; *d* of Alfred Rawlings and Hannah Mary Baker. *Educ:* Queen's Univ., Belfast. MB, BCh, QU Belfast, 1921 (hons); MD 1926 (Commendation); FRCS, Eng. 1927. Demonstrator of Anatomy, QU Belfast, 1922-24; House Surgeon, Royal Cancer Hosp., 1926; Riddel Research Fellow, Royal Free Hosp., 1924-26; Surgical Registrar, Elizabeth Garrett Anderson Hosp., 1930-33; Surgeon, EMS, 1939-45. Fellow Assoc. of Surgeons of Gt Brit. and Ire., 1950. *Publications:* original work published in: British Journal of Surgery; Lancet; British Journal of Obstetrics and Gynæcology, etc. *Recreations:* water colour painting, photography, foreign travel. *Address:* Arkesden, Saffron Walden, Essex. *T:* Clavering 370.

**BAKER, Allan;** *see* Baker, J. F. A.

**BAKER, Allan Ivor,** CBE 1944; JP; Chairman, Baker Perkins Holdings Ltd, since 1944; Director of various subsidiary and other companies; *b* 2 June 1908; *s* of late Allan Richard Baker; *m* 1935, Josephine, *d* of late A. M. Harley, KC; three *s* one *d*. *Educ:* Bootham, York; King's Coll., Cambridge; Harvard, USA. Baker Perkins: Student apprentice, 1931; Director, 1935-; Jt Man. Dir., 1942-67; Chm., 1944-. British Engineers' Assoc.: Mem. Council, 1943-68; Pres., 1960-61; Regional Dir, Lloyds Bank Ltd, 1953-; Dir, Mitchell Construction Holdings Ltd, 1963-; Member: Economic Planning Council for East Anglia, 1965-69; Peterborough Development Corp., 1968-. JP 1954; High Sheriff, Huntingdon and Peterborough, 1968-69. *Recreations:* golf, gardening. *Address:* 29 Westwood Park Road, Peterborough. *T:* Peterborough 3301.

**BAKER, Prof. Arthur Lemprière Lancey,** DSc (Eng), FICE, FIStructE, Hon. ACGI; Professor of Concrete Structures and Technology, University of London (Imperial College), since 1945; *b* 16 Dec. 1905; *s* of late W. L. Baker, Exeter; *m* 1930, Lillian Hollings; two *d*. *Educ:* Queen Elizabeth's Sch., Crediton; University of Manchester. Asst Engineer, Mersey Tunnel, Edmund Nuttall, Sons & Co. Ltd, 1926-28; Dist Engineer, PWD, Nigeria, 1928-30; Asst Engineer, Christiani & Nielsen Ltd, 1930-33; Senior Design Engineer, Reinforcing Steel Co., Johannesburg, 1933-36; Senior Civil Engineer, Trinidad Leaseholds Ltd, 1936-45; Consultant to HM Govt, Marine Structures, floating port equipment, underground oil storage, pre-cast concrete multi-storey buildings; Mem., Nuclear Safety Advisory Cttee, 1963-. *Publications:* Raft Foundations, 1937; Reinforced Concrete, 1949; The Ultimate Load Theory Applied to the Design of Reinforced and Pre-stressed Concrete Frames, 1956; The Inelastic Space Frame, 1967. *Address:* Department of Civil Engineering, Imperial College of Science and Technology, SW7. *T:* 01-589 5111.

**BAKER, Air Marshal Sir Brian Edmund,** KBE, *cr* 1944; CB 1943; DSO 1918; MC; AFC; *b* 31 Aug. 1896; *m* 1926, Jaimsie Derby Robinson; two *d*. *Educ:* Haileybury. Served European War, 1914-18 (despatches, MC, DSO, AFC); Chief Flying Instructor, RAF Training Base, Leuchars, 1932-34; HMS Eagle, 1934; HMS Courageous, 1936; commanded RAF Station, Gosport, 1937-38; RAF Station, Leuchars, 1938; No. 51 Group, 1940-41; RAF Iceland, 1941; No. 16 Group, 1941-42; No. 19 Group, 1943-44; AOC East Africa, 1945; Senior Air Staff Officer, HQ, Middle East, 1945; AOC-in-C, Transport Command, 1947-50; retd 1950. *Address:* 3 Howard Place, St Andrews, Fife.

**BAKER, Charles E. S.;** *see* Smalley-Baker.

**BAKER, Doris Manning,** MD, FRCP; Physician Elizabeth Garrett Anderson Hospital and South London Hospital; Physician, Arthur Stanley Institute, Middlesex Hospital, retired. *Educ:* London Univ. MRCS; LRCP 1924; MB, BS 1925; DOMS 1927; MD London 1927; MRCP 1927; FRCP 1952; late Major RAMC. FRSocMed. *Publications:* Cardiac Symptoms in the Neuroses, 1942; articles in medical journals. *Address:* 132 Richmond Hill, Richmond, Surrey. *T:* 01-940 0412.

**BAKER, Rev. Dr Eric Wilfred,** MA; Secretary of the Methodist Conference, 1951-71; *b* 17 Feb. 1899; *s* of Alfred and Eliza Baker, Birmingham; *m* 1934, Winifred Mary, *o d* of Thomas Laban and Mary Thorne, Ilfracombe; one *s* one *d*. *Educ:* King Edward's Sch., Birmingham; Christ's Coll., Cambridge; Wesley House, Cambridge. Served European War, 1914-18; Second Lieut, Norfolk Regt, 1917; Egypt,

1918-19. Classical and Theological Triposes, Carus Greek Testament Prize, Cambridge; MA (Cantab.), 1925; PhD (Edin.), 1941. Minister: Hall Green Methodist Church, Birmingham, 1923-27; King Street Methodist Church, Derby, 1927-31; Harrow-on-the-Hill Methodist Church, 1931-35; Edinburgh Central Hall, 1935-44; Bowes Park Methodist Church, London, 1944-46; Chm., London North Dist Methodist Church, 1945-51; Sec., Methodist Education Cttee, 1946-51; Pres. of the Methodist Conference, 1959-60; Moderator, Free Church Federal Council, 1964-65. Delegate to: Second Assembly, World Council of Churches, Chicago, 1954; Third Assembly, New Delhi, 1961; Mem. World Council of Churches Central Cttee, 1954-68; Vice-Pres., World Methodist Council (Mem., 1947-); Vice-Pres., British Council of Churches, 1962-65; Vice-Pres. British and Foreign Bible Soc.; Hon. Vice-Pres., The Boys' Brigade; Gov. of The Leys Sch., Cambridge; Chm. of Govs, Farringtons Sch., Chislehurst, 1960-65; Gov. of Kingswood Sch., Bath; Gov. of Queenswood Sch.; Willson Lecturer, Southwestern Univ., Texas, 1950; Fernley-Hartley Lecturer, 1958; Cambridge Univ. Select Preacher, 1960; Fondren Lectr, Southern Methodist Univ., Texas, 1963; Brown Lectr, Randolph-Macon Coll., Ashland, Virginia, 1963; Willson Lectr, Nashville, Tenn, 1963; Cato Lectr, Australia, 1963. Hon. DD Randolph-Macon, Virginia, 1956; Hon. LLD Mount Union, Ohio. *Publications:* He Shall Suffice Me, 1947; A Herald of the Evangelical Revival, 1948; From the Church in the Orchard, 1949; Belief and Behaviour, 1950; Preaching Theology, 1954; John Scott Lidgett (part author), 1957; The Faith of a Methodist, 1958; The Neglected Factor, 1963. *Recreations:* tennis, golf. *Address:* (office) 1 Central Buildings, Westminster, SW1. *T:* 01-930 7608; (residence) The Mearns, Hall Road, Wallington, Surrey. *T:* 01-647 8487. *Club:* Athenæum.

**BAKER, Brig. Euston Edward Francis,** CB 1957; CBE 1936; DSO 1919; MC 1917 and Bar 1918; TD; DL Middlesex; JP Bucks; Chairman, Amersham Bench, 1954-69; Hon. Colonel 5th Battalion Middlesex Regiment, 1961-63; Chairman: Middlesex T & AFA, 1951-59; Middlesex County Cadet Committee, 1944-51; National Association of Bolt and Nut Stockholders, 1948-59; *b* 5 April 1895; *s* of H. R. Baker; *m* 1920, Mary Helena, *d* of T. Sampson; two *s* one *d* (and *y s* decd). *Educ:* Sherborne (captain of football and shooting, 1913-14). Winner of Spencer Cup, Bisley, 1914. Gazetted to 5th Middlesex Regt, 15 Aug. 1914; served in France, 1914-19, continuously; commanded 2nd Bn Middlesex Regt 1918-19 (DSO, MC and bar, despatches thrice); commanded 8th Bn Middlesex Regt 1923-30 and 1936-37; Brevet Col, 1927; commanded 7th City of London Regt, 1931-36; Col, 1927; Comdr Infantry Bde, TA, 1939-42; ADC to the King, 1941-51; retd (ill-health), 1945; Hon. Col, 2/8th Batt. Middlesex Regt, 1939-47; Hon. Col 11th Bn Parachute Regt, 1948-56; Hon Col 8th Bn Middlesex Regt, 1956-61. Citoyen d'Honneur of Douai, France, 1947-. *Address:* Stanbridge House, Amersham, Bucks. *T:* 6230 *Club:* United Service.

**BAKER, Francis E. N.;** *see* Noel-Baker.

**BAKER, Geoffrey,** QC 1970; Recorder of Pontefract since 1967; *b* 5 April 1925; *er s* of late Sidney and Cecilia Baker, Bradford; *m* 1948, Sheila (*née* Hill); two *s* one *d*. *Educ:* Bradford Grammar Sch.; Leeds Univ. (LLB). Called to Bar, Inner Temple, 1947. *Recreations:* gardening, painting, photography. *Address:* 7 Bentcliffe Lane, Leeds 17, Yorks. *T:* Leeds 685181. *Club:* Sheffield (Sheffield).

**BAKER, Gen. Sir Geoffrey Harding,** GCB 1968 (KCB 1964; CB 1955); CMG 1957; CBE 1946; MC 1941; Chief of the General Staff, 1968-71; *b* 20 June 1912; *s* of late Col Cecil Norris Baker, CIE, IA, and late Ella Mary Baker; *m* 1946, Valerie, *d* of Major J. L. Lockhart and late Mrs Lockhart; two *s* one *d*. *Educ:* Wellington Coll.; RMA Woolwich (Sword of Honour). Commnd RA, 1932; India, with 11th Field Bde, RA, 1935; "F" (Sphinx) Battery, RHA, 1937 (Egypt, 1939); Middle East Staff Coll., 1940; Bde Major RA, 4th Indian Div., Western Desert and Eritrea, 1940, 1941; Instructor ME Staff Coll., 1942; GSO1, HQ Eighth Army, 1942-43; CO 127th Field Regt, 51st Highland Div., Sicily, 1943. BGS, HQ 21st Army Gp, North West Europe, 1944; Dep. Dir, War Office, 1947; Commanding Officer 3rd Regt RHA, 1950-52; Dir War Office, 1952-54; Dir of Operations and Chief of Staff to Governor of Cyprus, Nov. 1955-Feb. 1957; CRA, 7th Armd and 5 Divs, BAOR, 1957-59; Asst C of S, HQ, Northern Army Gp, Germany, 1959; Chief of Staff, HQ Southern Command, 1960-61; Chief of Staff, Contingencies Planning, Supreme HQ, Allied Powers Europe, 1961-63. Colonel Commandant: RA, 1964-; RMP, 1968-. Vice-Chief of the General Staff, 1963-66; GOC-in-C, Southern Command, 1966-68. ADC General to the Queen, Freeman: Haberdashers' Co.; City of London. US Legion of Merit (Comdr), 1946. *Address:* c/o National and Grindlay's Bank, 26 Bishopsgate, EC2. *Club:* Army and Navy.

**BAKER, Geoffrey Hunter,** CMG 1962; HM Consul-General, Munich, since 1966; HM Diplomatic (formerly Foreign) Service; *b* 4 Aug. 1916; *s* of late Thomas Evelyn Baker, and of Gladys Beatrice Baker (*née* Marsh); *m* 1963, Anita Wägeler; one *d*. *Educ:* Haberdashers' Aske's Hampstead Sch.; Royal Masonic Sch., Bushey, Herts; Gonville and Caius Coll., Cambridge (Scholar). Joined Consular Service, 1938; Vice-Consul at Hamburg, 1938, Danzig, 1939, Bergen, 1939; captured by German forces there, April 1940; Vice-Consul, Basra, 1942, Jedda, 1942; Foreign Office, 1945-47; First Sec., Rangoon, 1947-51, Tehran, 1951-52; FO, 1953-54; NATO Def. Coll., Paris, 1954; Consul-Gen., Hanoi, 1954-56; UK Delegation, UN, Nov. 1956-March 1957; Cabinet Office, 1957-60; UK Delegation to the European Free Trade Association, Geneva, 1960-66. *Recreations:* tennis, sailing, reading, and listening to music. *Address:* c/o Foreign and Commonwealth Office, SW1. *Clubs:* Oxford and Cambridge University; Cambridge University Cruising (Cambridge).

**BAKER, George,** FRCM; Hon. RAM; baritone singer, adjudicator, lecturer and journalist; *b* 10 Feb. 1885; *e s* of Walter and Elizabeth Baker, Birkenhead; *m* 1st, Kathlyn Hilliard (*d* 1933); 2nd, 1936, Olive Groves. *Educ:* privately; Birkenhead Inst.; Royal College of Music. Organist Woodchurch Parish Church, Cheshire, at the age of 16; subsequently held similar appointments at St Matthew's and St Michael's Churches, Birkenhead; won open scholarship for singing at the Royal College of Music, 1908; studied in Milan with Thomas Blackburn, 1914; has sung at all the principal concerts in Great Britain; played in opera and musical comedy; toured Australia, 1922-23; The Beggar's Opera in USA and Canada, 1927-28, and played in New York, 1928; toured South Africa, 1937; Holland, 1937 and 1947; USA 1939-40; Overseas Music Dir, BBC, 1944-47; Hon. Mem. and Hon. Treas. Royal

Philharmonic Society; Mem. Incorporated Soc. of Musicians; Vice-Pres., Catholic Stage Guild. *Publications:* This Singing Business, 1947; The Common Sense of Singing, 1963; musical and miscellaneous journalism. *Address:* 15 St John's Wood Court, NW8. *T:* 01-286 5898. *Clubs:* Savage (Trustee); Salmagundi (New York).

**BAKER, Hon. Sir George (Gillespie),** Kt 1961; OBE 1945; **Hon. Mr Justice Baker;** Judge of the High Court of Justice, Probate, Divorce and Admiralty Division, since 1961; Presiding Judge, Wales and Chester Circuit, since 1970; *b* 25 April 1910; *s* of late Captain John Kilgour Baker, Stirling; *m* 1935, Jessie McCall Findlay; three *s*. *Educ:* Glasgow Academy; Strathallan Sch., Perthshire; Brasenose Coll., Oxford (Hon. Schol.; Sen. Hulme Schol.). Called to the Bar, Middle Temple, 1932 (Harmsworth Schol.). Army, 1939-45; Queen's Own RWK 1939-40; Commnd The Cameronians (Scottish Rifles), 1940; DAAG War Office, 1941-42; AAG Allied Force HQ, 1942-44; Col. 'A' 15 Army Gp, 1945: AAG British War Crimes Executive, Nuremberg, 1945. Contested (C) Southall (Middlesex), 1945. Recorder of Bridgnorth, 1946-51; of Smethwick, 1951-52, of Wolverhampton, 1952-61. Dep. Chm. of Court of QS, Shropshire, 1954-. QC 1952, Leader of Oxford Circuit, 1954-61. Governor, Strathallan Sch., 1947-57; Governor, Epsom Coll., 1958-, Hon. Governor 1968-. Commissioner holding Government enquiry, Feb.-April 1956 into objections to proposed British Egg Marketing Scheme and for Kenya Government into pyrethrum industry, 1960; First Chm. of the General Optical Council, 1959-61. Chm., Departmental Cttee on Mechanical Recording of Court Proceedings, 1964-70. Hon. Fellow, Brasenose Coll., Oxford, 1966. *Recreations:* golf, fishing. *Address:* Camrie, Overstream, Londwater, Rickmansworth, Herts. *T:* Rickmansworth 77296. *Club:* Denham Golf (Captain 1967-68).

**BAKER, Henry,** PhD, MSc, CEng, MICE, MIMechE; Principal Nottingham and District Technical College, 1946-55; *b* 22 June 1893; *s* of Alfred Baker; *m* 1918, Constance Mary Lightbown; one *s*. *Educ:* The Fielden Sch.; University of Manchester. MSc Manchester, PhD Birmingham. Experience in Industry, subsequently Lecturer, University of Birmingham, 1920-23, and Armstrong (now King's) Coll., University of Durham, 1923-29; Head of Dept of Civil and Mechanical Engineering, Sunderland Tech. Coll., 1929-34; Principal, Tech. Colls of Norwich, 1934-36, West Ham, 1936-46. *Address:* 7 Cissbury Drive, Findon Valley, Worthing, Sussex. *T:* Findon 2241.

**BAKER, Sir Humphrey D. B. S.;** *see* Sherston-Baker.

**BAKER, Janet Abbott,** CBE 1970; professional singer; *b* 21 Aug. 1933; *d* of Robert Abbott Baker and May (*née* Pollard); *m* 1957, James Keith Shelley. *Educ:* The College for Girls, York; Wintringham, Grimsby. Daily Mail Kathleen Ferrier Award, 1956; Queen's Prize, Royal College of Music, 1959. Hon. DMus, Birmingham, 1968. *Recreations:* reading, tennis, walking. *Address:* Bamford Cottage, South Hill Avenue, Harrow, Middlesex.

**BAKER, John B.;** *see* Brayne-Baker.

**BAKER, Sir John (Fleetwood),** Kt 1961; OBE 1941; FRS 1956; MA, ScD Cantab; DSc Wales; Hon. LLD Glasgow; Hon. DSc Leeds, Manchester, Edinburgh, Aston, Leicester; Hon. DEng Liverpool; Hon. DS Ghent; Hon. FIMechE; Hon. ARIBA; FICE; FIStructE; Associate MASCE; Chairman, School of the Physical Sciences, Cambridge University, since 1968; Fellow of Clare College, Cambridge, 1943; *b* 19 March 1901; *s* of J. W. Baker, Wallasey, and Emily C. Fleetwood; *m* 1928, Fiona Mary MacAlister, *d* of late John Walker; two *d*. *Educ:* Rossall; Clare Coll., Cambridge (Scholar). Technical Asst, Design Dept, Royal Airship Works, 1925; Asst Lecturer, University Coll., Cardiff, 1926; Scientific Asst, Building Research Station, 1928; Prof. of Civil Engineering, Bristol Univ., 1933-43. Prof. of Mechanical Sciences and Head of Dept of Engineering, Cambridge Univ., 1943-68. Technical Officer to the Steel Structures Research Cttee, 1931-36; Telford Gold Medal, 1932, Telford Premium, 1936 and 1953; Howard Quinquennial Medal and Prize, 1937; Ewing Medal, 1952; Inst. Lecture to Students, 1936-37. Unwin Memorial Lecture, 1961. Mem. of Council Inst. of Civil Engineers, 1947-56, 1958-63, 1964-66, Vice-Pres., 1968-70; Research Medal 1951, Instn Silver Medal 1951, Gold Medal 1953, Mem. of Council, 1936-39, Institution of Structural Engineers; Member: Civil Defence Research Cttee, 1939-48; Scientific Advisory Com., Ministry of Works, 1945-46; Advisory Council to Military Coll. of Science, 1947-52; Univ. Grants Cttee, 1953-63; Council, British Welding Res. Assoc.; Chm., Naval Educn Advisory Cttee, 1958-64; Consultant, Naval Constructional Research Establishment, Rosyth, 1948-63; Dep. Chm., Industrial Develt Consultants Ltd; Director: Technical Development Capital Ltd; John Brown & Co. Ltd; IDC Group Ltd; Cambridge Fender & Engineering Co. Ltd. Scientific Adviser, and in charge of Design and Development Section, Ministry of Home Security, ARP Dept, 1939-43; designer of Morrison indoor shelter, 1940. Officier du Mérite pour la Recherche et l'Invention, Paris. *Publications:* Differential Equations of Engineering Science, 1929; Analysis of Engineering Structures, 1936, 1943, 1957, 1968; The Steel Skeleton, Vol. 1, 1954, Vol. 2, 1956; Plastic design of frames, Vol. 1, 1969; numerous scientific and technical papers on Theory of Structures and Strength of Materials, etc. *Address:* 100 Long Road, Cambridge. *T:* Trumpington 2152. *Club:* Athenæum.

**BAKER, (John Frederic) Allan,** CB 1957; CEng, FICE (former Member Council); Ministry of Transport, retired; *b* 5 Oct. 1903; *s* of late H. J. Baker; *m* 1927, Nancy Elizabeth Wells; one *s* one *d*. *Educ:* St Paul's Sch. After Local Authority experience in Middlesex, 1922-, joined Ministry of Transport, 1929, serving in Exeter, Bedford, Nottingham and London; apptd Divisional Road Engineer for Wales and Mon, at Cardiff, 1947, and Dep. Chief Engineer at Headquarters, 1953; Chief Engineer and Dir of Highway Engineering, 1954-65. Member: Road Research Board, 1954-65; London Roads Cttee, 1959; Traffic Signs Cttee, 1963; Cons. Adviser to Automobile Assoc., 1965-69. Mem. (Past Chm.), Road Engrg Industry Cttee of BSI; Vice-Pres., Internat. Exec. Cttee of Permanent Internat. Assoc. of Road Congresses and Chm. Brit. Nat. Cttee; Mem. (Past-Pres.); Jt Cttee of World Touring & Automobile Organisation, and Permanent Internat. Assoc. of Road Congresses; Vice-Pres. Institute of Asphalt Technology and Public Works and Municipal Services Congress and Exhibn Council. Hon. FIMunE; Hon. MInstHE. Viva Shield and Gold Medal, Worshipful Co. of Carmen, 1968. *Address:* 36 Imber Close, Ember Lane, Esher, Surrey. *T:* 01-398 3331. *Club:* Royal Automobile.

**BAKER, Rt. Rev. John Gilbert Hindley;** *see* Hong Kong and Macao, Bishop of.

**BAKER, John Randal,** MA, DPhil, DSc Oxon; FRS 1958; Emeritus Reader in Cytology, Oxford University (Reader, 1955-67); *b* 23 Oct. 1900; *y s* of Rear-Adm. Julian A. Baker, RN; *m* 1st, 1923, Inezita Davis; one *s* one *d*; 2nd, 1939, Mrs Helen Savage. *Educ:* New Coll., Oxford (1st Class in Honour Sch. of Natural Science). Scientific expeditions to New Hebrides, 1922-23, 1927, 1933-34; Joint editor Quarterly Journal of Microscopical Science, 1946-64; Professorial Fellow, New Coll., Oxford, 1964-67; Pres. Royal Microscopical Society, 1964-65, Hon. Fellow, 1968. Oliver Bird Medal for researches on chemical contraception, 1958. *Publications:* Sex in Man and Animals, 1926; Man and Animals in the New Hebrides, 1929; Cytological Technique, 1933 (5th edition, 1966); The Chemical Control of Conception, 1935; The Scientific Life, 1942; Science and the Planned State, 1945; Abraham Trembley of Geneva, 1952; Principles of Biological Microtechnique, 1958. *Address:* The Mill, Kidlington, Oxford OX5 2EG.

**BAKER, Air Chief Marshal Sir John (Wakeling),** GBE 1954; KCB 1949 (CB 1942); MC 1918; DFC 1925; RAF retired; *b* Winnipeg, Canada, 23 Oct. 1897; *er s* of late Rev. F. V. Baker, DD, BA; *m* 1927, Hilary, *o d* of late Lieut-Col H. Bonham-Carter; three *s* one *d*. *Educ:* Eastbourne Coll.; RMA Woolwich. Commissioned RA, 1916; transferred RFC 1917; RAF 1918 (MC); 60 Sqdn, India, NWF, 1923-28 (DFC); RAF Staff Coll., 1931; 33 Sqdn, Middle East, 1935-36; Imperial Defence Coll., 1938; Director of Bomber Operations, Air Ministry, 1942 (CB); SASO Air Command, SE Asia, 1943-44 (despatches); AOC 12 (Fighter) Group, 1945-46; Dir-Gen. of Personnel, Air Ministry, 1946-48; AOC-in-C, Coastal Command, 1948-49 (KCB); C-in-C MEAF, 1950-52; DCAS then VCAS, Air Ministry, 1952-53; Controller of Aircraft, Ministry of Supply, 1953-56 (GBE). Air ADC to the Queen, 1952-56. *Address:* 10 The Glebe, Chislehurst, Kent. *Club:* United Service.

**BAKER, Sir Joseph,** *see* Baker, Sir S. J.

**BAKER, Joshua,** MA, LLB, PhD; Lecturer in Hebrew at University of Dublin; Barrister-at-Law practising at Dublin; *b* 30 Jan. 1907; *e s* of late Philip Baker and Fanny Berman; *m* 1935, Fortunée Yvonne, *d* of Albert Lesbona, formerly of Manchester and now of London. *Educ:* Wesley Coll.; Trinity Coll., University of Dublin (Sizar in Classical Hebrew, Wall Biblical Scholar). Hons LLB 1928; Double Moderatorship in 1928 in (a) Legal and Political Science (b) Oriental Languages (Large Gold Medal and Moderatorship Research Prize); PhD 1930; Lecturer in Hebrew at Trinity Coll., 1932; Called to Bar at Dublin, 1932. Reid Prof. of Law at Trinity Coll., University of Dublin, 1935-40. *Recreations:* golf, chess, tennis. *Address:* 29 St Mary's Road South, Pembroke, Dublin. *Club:* Rathfarnham Golf.

**BAKER, Kenneth Wilfred;** MP (C) St Marylebone since Oct. 1970; Industrial Consultant; *b* 3 Nov. 1934; *s* of late W. M. Baker, OBE and of Mrs Baker (*née* Harries); *m* 1963, Mary Elizabeth Gray-Muir; one *s* two *d*. *Educ:* St Paul's Sch.; Magdalen Coll., Oxford. Nat. Service, 1953-55: Lieut in Gunners, N Africa; Artillery Instructor to Libyan Army. Oxford, 1955-58 (Sec. of Union). Served Twickenham Borough Council, 1960-62. Contested (C): Poplar, 1964; Acton, 1966; MP (C) Acton, March 1968-1970. *Recreation:* collecting books. *Clubs:* Bath, Carlton.

**BAKER, Mrs Noel John Horne;** *see* Scott-Moncrieff, J. C.

**BAKER, Olive Katherine Lloyd L.;** *see* Lloyd-Baker.

**BAKER, Philip J. N.;** *see* Noel-Baker.

**BAKER, Reginald George Gillam,** CBE 1945; retired; *b* 1 Feb. 1887; *s* of John Edward Baker; *m* 1st, 1915, Dora Winifred Withycombe, Kaisar-i-Hind Silver Medal, 1945 (*d* 1947); no *c*; 2nd, 1951, Pamela Mary, *d* of Stanley Johnson; one *s*. British American Tobacco Co., Oct. 1910; landed India, March 1911; retired, 1945. Served India 34 years, 21 years as Dir, last 9 years as Chm. Imperial Tobacco Co. of India. Interested in Agriculture. Pres. Calcutta Club, 1944; British War Savings Cttee in India; Red Cross work for Bengal. *Address:* Rivermeadow, Harlyn Bay, Padstow, Cornwall. *T:* St Merryn 270. *Club:* Oriental.

**BAKER, Richard St Barbe;** FIAL; Forestry Adviser and Silviculturist; Founder of The Men of the Trees; *b* 9 Oct. 1889; *s* of John R. St Barbe Baker and Charlotte Purrott; *m* 1st, 1946, Doreen Whitworth (from whom he obtained a divorce, 1953), *d* of G. H. W. Long, Strensham, Worcs; one *s* one *d*; 2nd, 1959, Catriona Burnett. *Educ:* Dean Close Sch., Cheltenham; Saskatchewan Univ.; Gonville and Caius Coll., Cambridge. Forestry Diploma, Cantab., 1920; Canada, 1909-13; Expeditionary Force, France, King Edward's Horse, Royal Field Artillery and Remounts, 1914-18; Army Sch. of Education, 1919; Asst Conservator of Forests, Kenya, 1920-23; Asst Conservator of Forests, Nigeria, 1924-29; initiated silvicultural experiments in the mahogany forests: delegate to World Forestry Congress, Rome; forest research Oxford and Continent, 1926; lecture tours in USA and Canada, 1930; World Lecture Tour, 1931; founded The Men of the Trees Soc., Kenya, 1922, Great Britain, 1924, Palestine, 1929, and as a world wide society, 1932; Junior Men of the Trees, 1956; travelled 17,000 miles visiting forests of USA and Canada to prepare forestry plan; conferred with Franklin D. Roosevelt on this with view to forestry employment scheme, which developed into Civilian Conservation Corps Camps; addressed delegates at Ottawa Conference on Empire Forestry situation, 1932-33; forest survey in South America, 1936; organised Forestry Summer Sch., Oxford, 1938, and at various places since then. Lectured for Army Sch. of Education to Cadets of Army and Air Force. Supervised forestry training and prepared plan for rehabilitation of returning service men; General Meeting of The Men of the Trees, Chelsea, assumed world leadership in earthwide regeneration, 1947; took New Earth Charter to USA, 1950; convened World Forestry Charter Gatherings, 1945-56; led Sahara Univ. Expedn, surveying 9000 miles of desert and equatorial Africa; revisited New Zealand in interest of Forest and Soil Conservation, 1954; settled in NZ, 1959; Delegate to 5th World Forestry Congress, Seattle; convened 1st Redwood Reunion, Mill Creek, 1960; for UNA covered 1200 miles on horseback in NZ, giving talks to schools on Trees, 1962-63; convened 1st Sahara Reclamation Conf., Rabat; reported to 24 heads of state, 1964; gave broadcasts and lectured to schools in NZ on Conservation and Sahara Reclamation, 1965; Visited forests of Australia to check felling and burning high forest; revisited Kenya, Nat. Tree-Planting Week and Reunion of Men of the Trees; deleg.,

6th World Forestry Congress, Spain, 1966; fact finding mission for Forestry, NZ and Q'land; rep. NZ, S Island at S Pacific Conf. Sydney, 1967; promoted afforestation, India and Pakistan, and inspected progress, Kuwait, Iran, Lebanon, UAR, Tunisia, and Spain; prepared forestry plans, Jamaica and British Honduras, 1968; conferred FAO, Rome, then visited Tunisian Pre-Sahara with group of scientists; inspected Austrian techniques of dune-stabilisation, Libya; addressed students, Univ. of Vienna, to recruit personnel for Sahara Reclamation Programme, 1969; revisited Silvicultural Experimental Area, Mahogany Forests, Nigeria, and explored southern perimeter of Sahara, Nigerian and Niger frontiers, 1970. *Publications:* Tree Lovers Calendar, 1929 and following years; Book of the Seasons, 1940; Africa Drums, 1942; The Redwoods, 1943; I Planted Trees, 1944; Green Glory: Forests of the World, 1947; New Earth Charter, 1949; Famous Trees, 1953; Sahara Challenge, 1954; Land of Tanē, 1956; Dance of the Trees, 1957; Kamiti: A Forester's Dream, 1958; The Redwoods (Famous Trees of the World, 1), 1959; Horse Sense: Story of My Horses in War and Peace, 1961; Trees of the World, 1962; Trees of the Bible Lands, Famous Trees of New Zealand, True Book of Trees, 1963; Sahara Conquest, 1966; Caravan Story and Country Notes 1969; My Life, My Trees, 1970. Founder Trees and Life, Journal of The Men of the Trees; many articles and pamphlets on forestry. *Recreations:* riding, gardening, music and tree photography. *Address:* Mount Cook Station, Box 3, Lake Tekapo, New Zealand. *Club:* Naval and Military.

**BAKER, Sir Rowland,** Kt 1968; OBE 1946; Technical Director, Polaris Executive, Ministry of Defence (Navy), 1963-68, retired; *b* 3 June 1908; *s* of Isaac and Lizzie Baker; *m* 1931, Frances Cornish; one *s* three *d. Educ:* RNC Greenwich. Assistant Constructor, HM Dockyards, 1933-39; Constructor, Admty, 1939-42; Supt of Landing Craft, 1942-46; Naval Constructor-in-Chief, Royal Canadian Navy, 1948-56; Technical Chief Exec., Dreadnought Project, 1958-63. Medal of Freedom with Silver Palm (US), 1946. *Publications:* contribs to jls. *Recreations:* golf, bridge. *Address:* Newfield, Entry Hill, Bath. *T:* Bath 22452.

**BAKER, Sir (Stanislaus) Joseph,** Kt 1958; CB 1947; retired as Receiver for the Metropolitan Police District and Courts (1952-60); *b* 7 March 1898; *s* of Henry G. Baker, Liverpool; *m* 1920, Eleonore White; two *d. Educ:* St Francis Xavier Sch.; Liverpool Univ. BSc 1919, Hons 1920. Served European War, 1914-18, RE 1915-17; Royal Artillery, 1917-18. Local Government Board for Ireland, 1920; Chief Sec.'s Office, Dublin Castle, 1922; Irish Office, 1922; Home Office, 1924; Sec. to Privy Council Cttee on question of contributions to Imperial Funds from the Islands of Jersey, Guernsey and Man, 1925. Asst Under-Sec. of State, Home Office, 1941-52. Chairman: National Police Fund Advisory Council, 1946-52; Police Regional Services Cttee, 1945-48; Police Common Services Cttee, 1948-52; Mem. Board of Governors of Police Coll., 1947-52. Chm., Kenya Police Commission, 1953. *Address:* Grenfields, Grenofen, Tavistock, Devon. *T:* Tavistock 2702.

**BAKER, Prof. Stephen Leonard;** Professor Emeritus, Manchester University; *b* 24 Oct. 1888; *s* of Arthur de Chair Baker and Sophia Baker (*née* Sandes); *m* 1921, Georgina Mary (*née* Barnes); five *s. Educ:* Whitgift Grammar Sch.; London Hospital Medical Sch. Temp. Surgeon Lieut RN, 1915-18; Pathologist to King Edward VII Sanatorium, Midhurst, 1919-21; Chief Asst, Bland-Sutton Institute, Middlesex Hospital, 1922-31; Proctor Prof. of Pathology, Manchester Univ., 1931-50; Professor of Osteo-pathology, Manchester Univ., 1950-55. John Hunter Medal and Triennial Prize, Royal Coll. of Surgeons, 1955. *Publications:* numerous publications in medical journals. *Recreations:* gardening, photography, geology. *Address:* Sea Winds, Orford, Woodbridge, Suffolk.

**BAKER, Rev. Preb. Thomas George Adames,** MA; Principal of Wells Theological College and Prebendary of Combe II in Wells Cathedral since 1960; Recognised Teacher, University of Bristol, since 1969; *b* 22 Dec. 1920; *s* of Walter and Marion Baker, Southampton; unmarried. *Educ:* King Edward VI Sch., Southampton; Exeter Coll., Oxford; Lincoln Theological Coll. Curate of All Saints, King's Heath, Birmingham, 1944-47; Vicar of St James, Edgbaston, 1947-54; Sub-Warden of Lincoln Theological Coll., 1954-60; Canon Theologian of Leicester Cathedral, 1959-66. Select Preacher, Univ. of Cambridge, 1963. *Publication:* What is the New Testament?, 1969. *Recreation:* music. *Address:* The Principal's House, The Theological College, Wells, Somerset. *T:* Wells 3209.

**BAKER, Col Thomas MacDonald,** CBE 1951; TD 1931; DL; retired as Solicitor, Metropolitan Police, (1934-60), also as Solicitor, Central Criminal Court, Court Prosecutions, County of London Sessions and County of Middlesex Sessions; Legal Member, London Rent Assessment Panel, 1966; *b* 1 Aug. 1894; *s* of late Thomas John Baker, Castle Hotel, Lynton, and of Margaret Grant Baker (*née* MacDonald), Forres, Scotland; *m* 1926, Vera Evelyn, *d* of late Philip Smith, Solihull, Warwickshire; one *s* one *d. Educ:* Radley Coll. Inspector of Taxes, Inland Revenue, 1920-24; Asst Solicitor, Inland Revenue, Somerset House, 1924-34; set up new Solicitor's Dept, and became first Solicitor, Met. Police, 1934. 6th Bn, E Surrey Regt, TA, 1911-32, Lt-Col comdg, 1928-32; Col, TA, 1933-54; served European War overseas, with 6th Bn, E Surrey Regt, 1914-19, (Hon. Col, 1949-61); Ft-Lieut, RAFVR, 1941-46; founder and first Comdg Officer, 1349 Woking Sqdn, ATC, and 167 Gliding Sch., 1942-46; mem. of Surrey T&AFA, 1928-63. DL Surrey, 1949. *Publications:* on Taxation and on Criminal Law. *Recreations:* motoring, gardening. *Address:* Netley, Hurst Close, Hook Heath Road, Woking, Surrey.

**BAKER, Willfred Harold Kerton,** TD; MP (C) Banffshire since 1964; *b* 6 Jan. 1920; *o s* of late W. H. Baker; *m* 1945, Kathleen Helen Sloan (*née* Murray Bisset); one *s* two *d* (and one *step d*). *Educ:* Hardye's Sch.; Edinburgh Univ.; Cornell Univ., USA. Joined TA, and served War of 1939-45 (Major). Edinburgh Univ. (BSc Agriculture), 1946-49. Farming, Mayen Home Farm, Banffshire. *Recreations:* fishing, philately. *Address:* Mayen, Rothiemay, by Huntly, Aberdeenshire. *T:* Rothiemay 276.

**BAKER, Rt. Rev. William Scott,** MA; Assistant Bishop, Diocese of Liverpool, since 1968; Lecturer, St Katherine's College; *b* 22 June 1902; *s* of late Rev. Canon William Wing Carew Baker, Vicar of Southill, Beds; unmarried. *Educ:* King's Coll. Choir Sch., Cambridge; Aldenham; King's Coll., Cambridge; Cuddesdon. Deacon, 1925; Priest, 1927; Chaplain of King's Coll., Cambridge, and Asst Curate of St Giles with St Peter's Church, Cambridge, 1925-32; Vicar of St John The Baptist's, Newcastle on Tyne, 1932-43; Examining Chaplain to Bishop of Wakefield,

1928-32; to Bishop of Newcastle, 1941-43; Proctor in Convocation for Diocese of Newcastle, 1943; Bishop of Zanzibar and Dar-es-Salaam, 1943-65, of Zanzibar and Tanga, 1965-68. *Publication:* (contributor) The Parish Communion, 1937. *Address:* 11 Woolacombe Road, Liverpool L16 9JG. *T:* 051-722 5035.

**BAKER, Wilson,** FRS 1946; FRIC; BSc, MSc, PhD, DSc (Manchester); MA (Oxon.); retired; Alfred Capper Pass Professor of Organic Chemistry, University of Bristol, 1945-65 (Dean of the Faculty of Science, 1948-51; Emeritus Professor, University of Bristol, 1965); *b* 24 Jan. 1900; *yr s* of Harry and Mary Baker, Runcorn, Cheshire; *m* 1927, Juliet Elizabeth, *d* of Henry and Julia R. Glaisyer, Birmingham; one *s* two *d*. *Educ:* Liverpool Coll. Upper Sch.; Victoria Univ. of Manchester (Mercer Schol., Baeyer Fellow and Dalton Scholar). Asst Lecturer in Chemistry, Univ. of Manchester, 1924-27; Tutor in Chemistry, Dalton Hall, Manchester, 1926-27; Univ. Lecturer and Demonstrator in Chemistry, Univ. of Oxford, 1927-44; Fellow and Praelector in Chemistry, The Queen's Coll., Oxford, 1937-44. Vice-Pres. of the Chemical Society, 1957-60. *Publications:* numerous original papers on organic chemistry, dealing chiefly with the synthesis of natural products, the development of synthetical processes, compounds of abnormal aromatic type, organic inclusion compounds, and the preparation of large-ring compounds, published mainly in Journal of the Chemical Society; (with T. W. J. Taylor) 2nd Edition of Professor N. V. Sidgwick's The Organic Chemistry of Nitrogen, 1937. *Recreations:* walking, gardening, music. *Address:* School of Chemistry, The University, Bristol, 2; Lane's End, Church Road, Winscombe, Somerset. *T:* Winscombe 3112.

**BAKER-CARR, Air Marshal Sir John (Darcy),** KBE 1962 (CBE 1951); CB 1957; AFC 1944; Controller of Engineering and Equipment, Air Ministry, 1962-64, retired; *b* 13 January 1906; *s* of late Brigadier-General C. D. Baker-Carr, CMG, DSO and Sarah Quinan; *m* 1934, Margery Dallas; no *c*. *Educ:* England and USA. Entered RAF as Pilot Officer, 1929; No. 32 Fighter Sqdn 1930, Flying Officer; Flying Boats at home and overseas, 1931; Armament Specialist Course, 1934; Flight-Lieut; Armament and Air Staff appts, 1935-38; Sqdn Ldr, 1938; Armament Research and Development, 1939-45 (AFC); Wing Comdr, 1940; Gp Captain, 1942; Central Fighter Estab., 1946-47; Dep. Dir Postings, Air Min., 1947-48; Air Cdre, 1948; Dir of Armament Research and Development, Min. of Supply, 1948-51 (CBE); idc 1952; Comdt RAF, St Athan, 1953-56; Senior Technical Staff Officer, HQ Fighter Command, RAF, 1956-59; Air Vice-Marshal, 1957; Air Officer Commanding, No. 41 Group, Maintenance Command, 1959-61; Air Marshal, 1962. *Recreations:* sailing and carpentry. *Address:* Thatchwell Cottage, King's Somborne, Hants. *Club:* Royal Air Force Yacht (Hamble, Hants).

**BAKER WILBRAHAM, Sir R. J.;** *see* Wilbraham.

**BAKEWELL, Robert Donald,** CMG 1952; Chm. Australian Woolgrowers' Council, 1949-54 (Member, 1940-); Member Australian Wool Realization Commission, 1945-59; *b* 9 Sept. 1899; *s* of late E. H. Bakewell, Adelaide; *m* 1929, Ydonea, *d* of Hylton Dale, Toorak; one *d*. *Educ:* Kyre Coll. (now Scotch Coll.), Adelaide. Man. Dir Farnley Grazing Pty. Ltd; Pres., Graziers' Federal Council of Aust., 1948-49 (Mem. 1940-50); Pres., Graziers' Assoc. of Vic., 1943-46 (Mem. Council and Exec., 1937-, Trustee, 1945-); Mem. Exec. Chamber of Agric. of Vic., 1940-50 (Vice-Pres. 1946-48); Graziers Rep., Primary Producers' Council of Aust., 1947-49; Mem. Wool Industry Conference, 1963-. *Recreation:* bowls. *Address:* Farnley, Benalla, Vic., Australia. *T:* Thoona 65-2320. *Clubs:* Australian (Melbourne); Adelaide (S Australia); Benalla (Victoria).

**BALANCHINE, George Melitonovitch;** Choreographer; Artistic director, New York City Ballet Company from 1948; *b* St Petersburg (now Leningrad), Russia, 9 Jan. 1904; *s* of Meliton Balanchivadze, composer, and Maria Vassiliev; became a citizen of the US. *Educ:* Imperial Academy of Dance, Imperial Academy of Music, St Petersburg. Left Russia on a European tour with the Soviet State Dancers, 1924, playing in Germany, England and France. Ballet-Master: for Serge Diaghilev, 1925-29; staged dances for Cole Porter production of Wake up and Dream, London, 1929; Maître de Ballet at Royal Theatre, Copenhagen, 1930; with Boris Kochno organized Ballets de Théâtre de Monte Carlo, under patronage of Princess of Monaco, 1932; presented Les Ballets, 1933; went to US, 1933, and founded School of American Ballet, 1934 (Chm. of Faculty); Artistic director, Ballet Society, New York, 1946; with Lincoln Kirstein as General director and himself as artistic director the New York City Ballet Company was started, 1948; it has subsequently made several tours in US and abroad. Has composed over 80 ballets and his choreography includes ballets in operas, musical comedies and films. Was guest of Grand Opera, Paris, 1947, and Sadler's Wells, London, 1950. *Publication:* Balanchine's Complete Stories of the Great Ballets, 1954. *Address:* c/o School of American Ballet, Inc., 2291 Broadway, New York 24, NY, USA.

**BALCOMBE, Alfred John,** QC 1969; *b* 29 Sept. 1925; *er s* of Edwin Kesteven Balcombe; *m* 1950, Jacqueline Rosemary, *yr d* of late Julian Cowan; two *s* one *d*. *Educ:* Winchester (schol.); New Coll., Oxford (exhibnr). Served, 1943-47: Royal Signals; India and Egypt; 2/Lt 1945, Lt 1946. BA 1949 (1st class Hons Jurisprudence), MA 1950. Called to Bar, Lincoln's Inn, 1950; has practised at Chancery Bar, 1951-; Mem., Gen. Council of the Bar, 1967-. *Publication:* The Law and Practice relating to Exempt Private Companies, 1953. *Address:* 6 Highbury Road, Wimbledon, SW19. *T:* 01-947 0980; 9 Old Square, Lincoln's Inn, WC2. *T:* 01-405 9471. *Club:* Oxford and Cambridge.

**BALCON, Sir Michael,** Kt 1948; Film Producer since 1920; Director of Border Television Ltd; *b* 19 May 1896; *s* of Laura and Louis Balcon, Birmingham; *m* 1924, Aileen, MBE, 1946, *d* of H. Leatherman, Johannesburg; one *s* one *d*. *Educ:* George Dixon Sch., Birmingham. Founder and Dir of Gainsborough Pictures Ltd, 1928; subsequently (1931) Dir of Production for Gaumont-British Picture Corporation Ltd; Dir and Producer Ealing Films Ltd, 1938-59; Chairman: British Lion Films Ltd and of British Lion Films (Holdings) Ltd, 1964-65. Fellow, British Film Academy; Governor, British Film Institute; Chairman: Film Production Board (British Film Institute); Council, London Academy of Music and Dramatic Art. Fellow, British Film Acad.; Hon. Fellow, British Kinematograph Soc.; a Sen. Fellow, Royal Coll. of Art. Hon. DLitt Birmingham, 1967. Knight First Class of Order of St Olav (Norway). *Films* include: (1945-): The Captive Heart; The Overlanders; It Always Rains on Sunday; Scott of the Antarctic; Kind Hearts and Coronets; Whisky

Galore; The Blue Lamp; The Lavender Hill Mob; The Man in the White Suit; Where No Vultures Fly; The Cruel Sea; The Maggie; The Divided Heart; The Ladykillers; The Long Arm; The Man in the Sky; The Shiralee; Dunkirk; The Scapegoat; The Siege of Pinchgut; The Long and the Short and the Tall; Sammy Going South. *Publication:* A Lifetime of Films, 1969. *Recreation:* walking. *Address:* Upper Parrock, Hartfield, Sussex. *T:* Forest Row 2370. *Clubs:* Savile, Garrick.

*See also C. Day Lewis.*

**BALDOCK, John Markham,** VRD 1949; Lieutenant Commander RNVR 1948; Chairman Lenscrete Ltd, 1949; Director CIBA United Kingdom Ltd; *b* 19 Nov. 1915; *s* of late Captain W. P. Baldock, and Mrs H. Chalcraft; *m* 1949, Pauline Ruth Gauntlett; two *s. Educ:* Rugby Sch.; Balliol Coll., Oxford. Agric. degree, 1937. Served War of 1939-45, with Royal Navy, Atlantic, Mediterranean, Indian Ocean; Russian convoys, 1942-43. Lloyds, EC3, 1945. Joined Board of Lenscrete, 1946. MP (C) Harborough Div. of Leics, 1950-Sept. 1959, retd, also as Parl. Private Sec. to Rt Hon. D. Ormsby Gore (Minister of State, Foreign Office). *Recreations:* country life, sailing, steam engines, industrial archæology, theatre. *Address:* Hollycombe House, Liphook, Hants. *T:* Liphook 3233; 17 Aylesford Street, SW1; *T:* 01-834 8759. *Clubs:* Carlton, Farmers', Royal Cruising.

**BALDRY, Prof. Harold Caparne;** Professor of Classics, University of Southampton, since 1954; Dean of the Faculty of Arts, 1959-62; Deputy Vice-Chancellor, 1963-66; Public Orator, 1959-67; *b* 4 March 1907, *s* of William and Gertrude Mary Baldry, Nottingham; *m* 1934, Carina Hetley (*née* Pearson); one *s* two *d. Educ:* Nottingham High Sch.; Trinity Hall, Cambridge (Warr Schol., MA). Editor Cambridge Review, 1931. Educational Staff, Trinity Hall, Cambridge, 1931-34; Asst Lecturer in Classics, University Coll. of Swansea, 1934-35; Univ. of Cape Town: Lecturer in Classics, 1936-43, Prof. of Classics, 1948-54. Chm., Council of University Classical Depts, 1969-; Pres., Orbilian Soc., 1970. *Publications:* The Classics in the Modern World (an Inaugural Lecture), 1949; Greek Literature for the Modern Reader, 1951; Ancient Utopias (an Inaugural Lecture), 1956; The Unity of Mankind in Greek Thought, 1965; Ancient Greek Literature in its Living Context, 1968; The Greek Tragic Theatre, 1970. Articles and reviews in Classical Journals. *Address:* 19 Uplands Way, Highfield, Southampton. *T:* Southampton 55290.

**BALDRY, Jack Thomas;** Director, Purchasing and Supplies, Post Office, since 1969; *b* 5 Oct. 1911; *s* of late John Baldry, Badingham, Suffolk and Mrs Ellen Baldry; *m* 1936, Ruby Berenice (*née* Frost); three *d. Educ:* Framlingham Coll. Post Office: Asst Traffic Supt, 1930; Asst Surveyor, 1935; Asst Princ., 1940; Princ., 1947 (Private Sec. to PMG, 1950-53); Asst Sec., 1953; Dep. Dir, External Telecommunications, 1960; Dir of Personnel, 1967. *Recreations:* tennis, farming, foreign travel. *Address:* 4 Rowben Close, Totteridge, N20. *T:* 01-445 6251.

**BALDWIN,** family name of **Earl Baldwin of Bewdley.**

**BALDWIN OF BEWDLEY,** 3rd Earl, *cr* 1937; Viscount Corvedale, *cr* 1937, of Corvedale; **Arthur Windham Baldwin;** *b* 22 March 1904; 2nd *s* of 1st Earl Baldwin of Bewdley, KG, PC, FRS, and Lucy, GBE 1937, DGStJ (*d* 1945), *e d* of late Edward Lucas J. Ridsdale, The Dene, Rottingdean, Sussex; *S* brother 1958; *m* 1936, Joan Elspeth, *y d* of late C. Alexander Tomes, New York, USA; one *s. Educ:* Eton; Trinity Coll., Cambridge. Served War of 1939-45, in the Royal Air Force, 1941–45. Formerly a Dir of the Great Western Railway Company. Dir, Equitable Life Assurance Society; Dir, Equitable Reversionary Interest Society Limited; Dir, Reversionary Interest Society Limited. *Publications:* My Father: The True Story, 1956; The Macdonald Sisters, 1960; A Flying Start (autobiog.), 1967. *Recreations:* none. *Heir: s* Viscount Corvedale, *qv. Address:* Bushey House, Apperley, Glos. *Clubs:* Reform, MCC.

**BALDWIN, James (Arthur);** Author; *b* Harlem, New York City, 2 Aug. 1924; *s* of David and Berdis Emma Baldwin. *Educ:* DeWitt Clinton High Sch., New York. Various non-literary jobs, 1942-45. Moved to Paris, 1948; lived in Europe until 1956. Active in civil rights movement in USA. Saxton Fellow, 1945; Rosenwald Fellow, 1948; Guggenheim Fellow, 1954; Nat. Inst. of Arts and Letters Award, and Partisan Review Fellow, 1956. Mem. Nat. Inst. of Arts and Letters, 1964. DLitt, Univ. of British Columbia, 1963. *Publications: novels:* Go Tell It on the Mountain, 1953; Giovanni's Room, 1956; Another Country, 1962; Going to Meet the Man, 1965; Tell Me How Long the Train's Been Gone, 1968; *essays:* Notes of a Native Son, 1955; Nobody Knows My Name, 1961; The Fire Next Time, 1963; Nothing Personal (with Richard Avedon), 1964; *plays:* The Amen Corner, 1955 (prod Saville, London, 1965); Blues for Mr Charlie, 1964; essays and short stories in many jls and anthologies, 1946-. *Recreation:* American Negro music. *Address:* 137 West 71st Street, New York, NY, USA. *T:* Trafalgar 7-7773.

**BALDWIN, Air Marshal Sir John Eustace Arthur,** KBE 1943 (CBE 1942; OBE 1919); CB 1938; DSO 1918; DL Lincolnshire; JP Rutland; High Sheriff of Rutland, 1955; Hon. Air Cdre, R Aux. AF; *b* 13 April 1892; *e s* of late J. H. L. Baldwin; *m* Kathleen Betsy, *y d* of T. W. L. Terry, York; one *d. Educ:* Rugby; Sandhurst. Gazetted to 8th (KRI) Hussars, 1911; ADC to the King, 1931-33; Dir of Personal Services, Air Min., 1935-36; Comdt RAF Coll., Cranwell, 1936-39; Dep. AOC-in-C India, 1942-43; commanded No 3 Tactical Air Force 1943-44. Col 8th King's Royal Irish Hussars, 1948-58; Dep. Col, Queen's Royal Irish Hussars, 1959-60. KStJ, 1962. Officer of Crown of Belgium; Belgian Croix de Guerre; White Lion 2nd Class; American Air Medal; Czech War Cross. *Address:* Park Farm, Ketton, Stamford, Lincs. *T:* Ketton 256. *Clubs:* Cavalry, Royal Air Force.

**BALDWIN, Peter Robert;** Under Secretary, HM Treasury, since 1968; *b* 10 Nov. 1922; *s* of Charles Baldwin and Katie Baldwin (*née* Field); *m* 1951, Margaret Helen Moar; two *s. Educ:* City of London Sch.; Corpus Christi Coll., Oxford. Foreign Office, 1942-45; Gen. Register Office, 1948-54; HM Treasury, 1954-62; Cabinet Office, 1962-64; HM Treasury, 1964-; Principal Private Sec. to Chancellor of Exchequer, July 1966-Jan. 1968. Chm., St Catherine's Home, Ventnor. *Recreations:* painting, watching cricket. *Address:* Sanders, 21 Crescent Road, Beckenham, Kent. *T:* 01-658 6956. *Club:* Royal Over-Seas League.

**BALERNO,** Baron *cr* 1963, of Currie (Life Peer); **Alick Drummond Buchanan-Smith;** Kt 1956; CBE 1945 (OBE 1939); TD 1938; MA, DSc; MSA Iowa; FRSE; Lecturer in Animal Genetics, University of Edinburgh, 1925-60, retired; *b* 9 Oct. 1898; *s* of late Very Rev. Sir George Adam Smith, DD, LLD, FBA, Principal of Aberdeen Univ., 1909-35 and of late Lilian, *d* of Sir George Buchanan, LLD, FRS; *m* 1926, Mary Kathleen (*d* 1947), *d* of late Captain George Smith of Pittodrie; four *s* one *d*. *Educ:* Glasgow Acad., Glenalmond; University of Aberdeen; Iowa State Univ. Lt-Col Comdg 5/7th, 5th and 9th Bns The Gordon Highlanders, TA, 1936-42; Brigadier and Dir Selection of Personnel, War Office, 1942-45; Col Comdg Edinburgh Univ. Contingent, OTC, 1945-53; Chm. Edinburgh, Lothians and Peebles TA & AFA, 1953-57. Pres. Scottish Unionist Assoc., 1955-56; Dep. Chm., Unionist Party in Scotland, 1960-63. Vice-Chm., Pigs Industry Develt Authority, 1957-69; Vice-Pres. Brit. Council of Churches, 1967-; Pres., Royal Scottish Geographical Soc., 1968-; Mem., Edinburgh Univ. Court, 1961-68; Chm. Heriot-Watt Univ. Court, 1966-. Pres. Edinburgh Bn The Boys' Brigade, 1955-68. Hon. Col 5/6th Bn The Gordon Highlanders, 1958-61, of 3rd Bn, 1961. Iowa State Univ. Distinguished Achievement Citation, 1967. *Publications:* papers on breeding of farm livestock, in various sci. jls. *Address:* House of Cockburn, Balerno, Midlothian EH14 7JD. *T:* 031-449 3737. *Clubs:* Caledonian, Royal Automobile; New (Edinburgh).

*See also Janet Adam Smith (Mrs John Carleton), A. L. Buchanan-Smith.*

**BALFOUR,** family name of **Earl of Balfour** and **Barons Balfour of Inchrye, Kinross** and **Riverdale.**

**BALFOUR,** 4th Earl of, *cr* 1922; **Gerald Arthur James Balfour;** Viscount Traprain 1922; *b* 23 Dec. 1925; *er s* of 3rd Earl of Balfour and Jean, 4th *d* of late Rev. Canon J. J. Cooke-Yarborough; *S* father, 1968; *m* 1956, Natasha Georgina, *d* of late Captain George Anton. *Educ:* Eton; HMS Conway. Holds Master Mariner's certificate. *Heir: cousin* Eustace Arthur Goschen Balfour [*b* 26 May 1921; *m* 1946, Anne, *d* of late Major Victor Yule; two *s*]. *Address:* The Tower, Whittingehame, Haddington, Scotland. *Club:* RNVR (Glasgow).

**BALFOUR OF BURLEIGH,** Baron *cr* 1607 (*de facto* 8th Baron, 12th but for the Attainder); **Robert Bruce,** CEng, FIEE; Director: Bank of Scotland, since 1968; The British Linen Bank, since 1969; Scottish Investment Trust; Second Scottish Investment Trust; *b* 6 Jan. 1927; *e s* of 11th Baron Balfour of Burleigh and Dorothy, *d* of late R. H. Done; *S* father 1967. Formerly: Asst foreman and Asst superintendent, The English Electric Co. at Stafford and Liverpool, Dir and Gen. Manager, The English Electric Co. of India Ltd, Madras, also Gen. Manager, The English Electric Co. Ltd, Netherton, Liverpool, and later of D. Napier & Son Ltd. *Recreations:* music, climbing, flying, amateur dramatics. *Heir: b* Master of Burleigh, *qv*. *Address:* Brucefield, Clackmannan, Scotland.

**BALFOUR OF INCHRYE,** 1st Baron *cr* 1945, of Shefford; **Harold Harington Balfour,** PC 1941; MC; *b* 1 Nov. 1897; *s* of Col N. H. Balfour, Belton, Camberley, Surrey; *m* 1st, 1921, Diana Blanche (marriage dissolved, 1946), *d* of Sir Robert G. Harvey, 2nd Bt; one *s*; 2nd, 1947, Mary Ainslie Profumo, *d* of late Baron Profumo, KC, and of Baroness Profumo; one *d*. *Educ:* Chilverton Elms, Dover; RN Coll., Osborne. Joined 60th Rifles, 1914; attached RFC 1915; RAF 1918; served European War, 1914-18 (MC and bar); RAF 1918-23; journalism and business since 1923; contested (C) Stratford, West Ham, 1924; MP (C) Isle of Thanet, 1929-45; Parliamentary Under-Sec. of State for Air, 1938-44; Minister Resident in West Africa, 1944-45. President, Federation Chambers of Commerce of the British Empire, 1946-49; President, Commonwealth and Empire Industries Association, 1956-60; Part-time Member, Board of BEA, 1955-66; Chairman, BEA Helicopters Ltd, 1964-66. *Recreations:* fishing, shooting. *Heir: s* Hon. Ian Balfour [*b* 21 Dec. 1924; *m* 1953, Josephine Maria Jane, *d* of Mr and the Hon. Mrs Morogh Bernard, Shankill, Co. Dublin; one *d*]. *Address:* End House, St Mary Abbot's Place, W8. *T:* 01-603 6231; Tressady, Rogart, Sutherland. *Clubs:* Carlton, Pratt's.

*See also J. D. Profumo.*

**BALFOUR, David,** CBE 1960, FIL; retired diplomat; free-lance conference interpreter; *b* London, 20 Jan. 1903; *s* of Reginald Balfour and Charlotte Warre Cornish; *m* 1948, Louise Fitzherbert; one *d*. *Educ:* Oratory Sch., Edgbaston; and at Angers, Prague, Salzburg, Rome, Athens. Graduate of Oriental Institute, Rome, and of Athens Univ. (1940). On staff of the Institute of English Studies, Athens, 1939-41. Served War of 1939-45 in Army, 1941-43, GSO II, GHQ, Middle East Forces (despatches). Entered HM Foreign Service, 1943, established 1946; served Cairo, Athens, Foreign Office, Tel Aviv (Oriental Sec., 1949-50), Smyrna (Consul-Gen., 1951-55), Genoa (Consul-Gen., 1955-60), and Geneva (Consul-Gen., 1960-63); Interpreter and Translator, FO, 1963-68; retd 1968. Mem., Internat. Assoc. of Conf. Interpreters, 1969. *Address:* The Old Mill, Kingsclere, Hants.

**BALFOUR, Rear-Adm. George Ian Mackintosh,** CB 1962; DSC 1943; Chief Appeals Officer, British Empire Cancer Campaign, since 1963; *b* 14 Jan. 1912; *yr s* of late Dr T. Stevenson Balfour, Chard, Som, and late Mrs Balfour; *m* 1939, Pamela Carlyle Forrester, *y d* of late Major Hugh C. C. Forrester, DL, JP, Tullibody House, Cambus, and late Mrs Forrester; two *s* one *d*. *Educ:* Royal Naval Coll., Dartmouth. Served in China, 1930-32; South Africa, 1935-37. Commanded Destroyers for most of War of 1939-45, on various stations. Mediterranean, 1948, Far East, 1949-50, USA 1951-53, Captain (D) 2nd Destroyer Flotilla, 1956-58; Dir of Officer Appointments, 1958-59; Senior Naval Mem., Imperial Defence Coll., 1960-63; retired list, 1963. *Recreations:* general sporting activities. *Address:* Westover, Farnham Lane, Haslemere. *T:* 3876.

**BALFOUR, Sir John,** GCMG, 1954 (KCMG, 1947; CMG, 1941); GBE 1959; *b* 26 May 1894; *s* of Charles Barrington Balfour, CB, Newton Don and Balgonie, and of Lady Nina Balfour; *m* 1933, Frances (CVO 1969; Lady-in-Waiting to Princess Marina, Duchess of Kent, 1961-68), *d* of Prof. Alexander van Millingen, DD. *Educ:* Eton; New Coll., Oxford. Interned in Germany, 1914-18; 3rd Sec. in the Diplomatic Service or Foreign Office, 1919; served in Foreign Office, at HM Legations at Budapest, Sofia and Belgrade, and at HM Embassies at Madrid and Washington; Minister in Lisbon, 1941-43; in Moscow, 1943-45; in Washington, 1945-48; Ambassador to Argentine Republic, 1948-51; Ambassador to Spain, 1951-54; retired from Foreign Service, 1954. UK Commissioner-Gen. to Brussels International Exhibition of 1958. Chairman: British and French Bank, 1959-69; United Bank for Africa, 1961-69. *Address:* 38 Onslow Square, SW7. *T:* 01-584 1970. *Club:* Brooks's.

**BALFOUR, Patrick;** *see* Kinross, Baron.

**BALFOUR, Peter Edward Gerald;** Chairman and Managing Director, Scottish & Newcastle Breweries Ltd; *b* 9 July 1921; *y s* of late Brig. Edward William Sturgis Balfour, CVO, DSO,

OBE, MC and Lady Ruth Balfour, CBE, MB; *m* 1st, 1948, Grizelda Davina Roberta Ogilvy (marr. diss. 1967); two *s* one *d*; 2nd, 1968, Diana Rosemary Wainman; one *d*. *Educ:* Eton College. Regular Officer, Scots Guards, 1950-54. Joined Wm McEwan & Co. Ltd, 1954, Dir, 1956. Director: Scottish & Newcastle Breweries Ltd, 1961; British Assets Trust Ltd; Second British Assets Trust Ltd; Atlantic Assets Trust Ltd. Croix de Guerre (France), 1945. *Recreations:* fishing, shooting, golf. *Address:* Scadlaw House, Humbie, East Lothian. *T:* Humbie 252. *Clubs:* Guards; New (Edinburgh).

**BALFOUR, Lieut-Gen. Sir Philip Maxwell,** KBE, *cr* 1950 (CBE 1944); CB 1946; MC 1917; late RA; *b* 10 March 1898; *s* of late C. F. Balfour, ICS; *m* 1930, Catharine Marjorie, *d* of Lieut-Col Sir Charles Frederick Rugge-Price, Bt. *Educ:* Wellington Coll.; RMA, Woolwich. 2nd Lieut RA 1915; served European War, 1916-18, France and Belgium (MC and Bar); War of 1939-45 (despatches, CBE, CB); Comdr 2nd Infantry Div., 1947-49; Gen. Officer, Commanding-in-Chief, N Command, 1949-53; retired from Army, 1953. Col Commandant RA, 1950-60. *Address:* Broad Oak House, Semley, Shaftesbury, Dorset. *Club:* Naval and Military.

**BALFOUR, Sir Robert George Victor FitzGeorge;** *see* FitzGeorge-Balfour.

**BALFOUR PAUL, Hugh Glencairn,** CMG 1968; Ambassador to Iraq, since 1969; *b* 23 Sept. 1917; *s* of late Lt-Col J. W. Balfour Paul, DSO; *m* 1950, Margaret Clare Ogilvy; one *s* three *d*. *Educ:* Sedbergh; Magdalen Coll., Oxford. Served War of 1939-45, Sudan Defence Force. Sudan Political Service, Blue Nile and Darfur, 1946-54; joined Foreign Office, 1955; Santiago, 1957; Beirut, 1960; Counsellor, Dubai, 1964; Dep. Political Resident, Persian Gulf, 1966; Counsellor, FO, attached St Antony's Coll., Oxford, 1968. *Recreations:* archaeology, fishing, tennis. *Address:* c/o Foreign and Commonwealth Office, SW1. *Club:* Travellers'.

**BALGONIE, Lord; David Alexander Leslie Melville;** *b* 26 Jan. 1954; *s* and *heir* of 14th Earl of Leven and 13th Earl of Melville, *qv*.

**BALKWILL, Bryan Havell;** conductor; *b* 2 July 1922; *s* of Arthur William Balkwill and Dorothy Silver Balkwill (*née* Wright); *m* 1949, Susan Elizabeth Roberts; one *s* one *d*. *Educ:* Merchant Taylors' Sch.; Royal Academy of Music. Asst Conductor, New London Opera Co., 1947-48; Associate Conductor, Internat. Ballet, 1948-49; Musical Director and Principal Conductor, London Festival Ballet, 1950-52; Music staff and subseq. Associate Conductor, Glyndebourne Opera, 1950-58; Musical Dir, Arts Council 'Opera For All', 1953-63; Resident Conductor, Royal Opera House, Covent Garden, 1959-65; Musical Director: Welsh Nat. Opera Company, 1963-67; Sadler's Wells Opera, 1966-69. Guest Conductor: Royal Opera House, Covent Garden, Glyndebourne, Wexford Festival, Aldeburgh, RPO, LPO, Royal Liverpool Ph. Orchestra, Bournemouth Symphony Orch., City of Birmingham Symphony Orch., BBC Promenade Concerts, Festival Ballet; also Montreal, Vancouver, continental engagements. Mem. Royal Philharmonic Society; FRAM. *Recreation:* open air. *Address:* 19 Lingfield Road, Wimbledon Common, SW19. *T:* 01-946 5422.

**BALL, Alan Hugh;** Chairman and Joint Managing Director of Lonrho Ltd, and associated companies; *b* 8 June 1924; *s* of late Sir George Joseph Ball, KBE and Mary Caroline Ball; *m* 1948, Eleanor Katharine Turner; two *s* one *d*. *Educ:* Eton. KRRC, 1943-47. Lonrho Ltd and associated cos, 1947-. *Recreations:* fishing, shooting. *Address:* The Old Mill, Ramsbury, Wilts. *T:* Ramsbury 266. *Clubs:* Carlton, City of London, East India and Sports, Royal Automobile.

**BALL, Air Vice-Marshal Alfred Henry Wynne,** CB 1967; DSO 1943; DFC 1942; idc, jssc, psc, pfc; Assistant Chief of Staff, Automatic Data Processing (ADP) Division, SHAPE, since Dec. 1968; *b* 18 Jan. 1921; *s* of Captain J. A. E. Ball, MC, BA, BE; *m* 1942, Nan McDonald; three *s* one *d*. *Educ:* Campbell Coll., Belfast; RAF Coll., Cranwell. Served War of 1939-45: Pilot Officer, 1939; Flying Officer, 1940; Flight-Lieut 1941; Sqdn-Ldr 1942; Wing Comdr 1944; air operations, Lysanders, Spitfires, Mosquitoes. E Africa, 1947; Bomber Comd, 1952; Gp Captain, Washington, 1959; Air Cdre, Aden, 1964; Imp. Def. Coll., 1967; Dir of Operations, (RAF), MoD, 1967-68. US Air Medal, 1943. *Recreation:* golf. *Address:* c/o SHAPE, Belgium, BFPO 26. *Club:* Royal Air Force.

**BALL, Air Vice-Marshal Sir Ben,** KBE 1969 (CBE 1946; OBE 1943); CB 1963; Air Officer Commanding-in-Chief, RAF Signals Command, 1966-68; retired 1969; *b* 6 Sept. 1912; *s* of late John William Ball, Barrister-at-Law, Kingstown, Co. Dublin; *m* 1938, Pamela, *d* of late Captain W. E. Caldbeck, Beds and Herts Regt; three *s*. *Educ:* Trinity Coll., Dublin. De Havilland Sch. of Flying, 1933-34; BA Dublin, 1934; RAF Coll., Cranwell, 1934-35; No 209 (FB) Sqdn, RAF, 1935-38; Signals Specialist Course, 1938-39; RAF Bircham Newton, 1939; CSO of: Reserve Comd, RAF, 1939-40; No 1 Trg Comd, RCAF, 1940-42; No 2 Trg Comd, RCAF, 1942-43; Gp Captain Ops No 26 Gp, RAF, 1943-46 (despatches); RAF Staff Coll., 1946; CSO, Bomber Comd, RAF, 1946-48; Dir of Signals, Air Force Staff, BJSM, Washington, USA, 1948-51; Comd, RAF Debden, 1951-53; DDOR, Air Min., 1953-56; CSO Bomber Comd, RAF, 1957-60; DCSO, SHAPE, 1960-63; SASO, Technical Training Cmd, RAF, 1963-66. *Recreation:* sport. *Address:* Ripley, Thamesfield Gardens, Marlow, Bucks. *Club:* Royal Air Force.

**BALL, Major Charles James Prior,** DSO 1918; MC 1916; FRAeS 1938; *b* 15 Feb. 1893; *s* of George William Ball, JP; *m* 1920, Eva (*d* 1964), *d* of Herbert Lucas, Shepleigh Court, Devon; two *s* one *d*. *Educ:* Charterhouse; London Univ. Royal Artillery, 1914-23; served European War, 1914-18 (despatches, DSO, MC); Military Inter-Allied Commission of Control (disarming Germany), 1919-23. Fellow of University Coll., London, 1959; Fellow of Institute of Metals, 1960. *Publication:* The Campaign in Gallipoli. *Address:* Manor Farm, Brown Candover, near Alresford, Hants. *T:* Preston Candover 225. *Clubs:* Army and Navy, Royal Thames Yacht.

**BALL, Sir Edmund Lancaster,** Kt 1941; *b* 1883; *s* of William Edmund Ball, LLD, Barrister-at-law; *m* 1911, Harriet Estelle (*d* 1963), *d* of Capt. Hugo Beaumont Burnaby, RN; two *s*. *Educ:* City of London Sch.; Christ Church, Oxford. 1st Class Classical Hon. Mods, 1904; 1st Class Lit. Hum., 1906; MA. Auditor of India Home Accounts, India Audit Office, 1934-43. *Address:* Clavell Edge, 12 Ballard Estate, Swanage, Dorset. *Club:* United University.

**BALL, George T.;** *see* Thalben-Ball.

**BALL, Dr Harold William;** Keeper of Palæontology, British Museum (Natural History), since 1966; *b* 11 July 1926; *s* of Harold Ball and Florence (*née* Harris); *m* 1955, Patricia Mary (*née* Silvester); two *s* two *d*. *Educ:* Yardley Gram. Sch.; Birmingham Univ. BSc 1947, PhD 1949, Birmingham. Geologist, Nyasaland Geological Survey, 1949-51; Asst Lectr in Geology, King's Coll., London, 1951-54; Dept of Palæontology, British Museum (Nat. Hist.), 1954-: Dep. Keeper, 1965; Keeper, 1966. Council, 1960-64, Sec., 1968-, Geological Soc. of London; Wollaston Fund, Geological Soc. of London, 1965. *Publications:* papers on the stratigraphy of the Old Red Sandstone and on the palæontology of the Antarctic in several scientific jls. *Recreations:* music, rhododendron species, collecting early books on natural history and voyages. *Address:* Wilderbrook, Dormans Park, East Grinstead, Sussex. *T:* Dormans Park 426.

**BALL, Prof. John Geoffrey;** Professor of Physical Metallurgy, Imperial College, University of London, since 1956 and Head of Metallurgy Department since Oct. 1957; Dean, Royal School of Mines, Imperial College, 1962-65; Dean, Faculty of Engineering, University of London, since 1970; *b* 27 Sept. 1916; *s* of late I. H. Ball and late Mrs E. M. Ball; *m* 1941, Joan C. M., *d* of Arthur Wiltshire, JP, Bournemouth. *Educ:* Wellington (Salop) High Sch.; University of Birmingham. British Welding Research Association, 1941-49; Senior Metallurgist, 1945-49; Atomic Energy Research Establishment, Harwell, 1949-56; Head of Reactor Metallurgy, 1953-56. Min. of Tech. Visitor to British Non-Ferrous Metals Res. Assoc., 1962-. Chairman: Res. Bd and Mem. of Council Br. Welding Res. Assoc., 1964-; Engrg Physics Sub-Cttee, Aeronautical Res. Council, 1964-68; Metallurgy Bd, Council for Nat. Academic Awards, 1965-; Metallurgy and Materials Cttee and Univ. Science and Technology Bd, Science Res. Council, 1967-70; Engrg Bd, Science Res. Council, 1969-; Manpower Utilisation Working Party, 1967-. Pres., Inst. of Welding, 1965-66. Member: Council, Instn of Metallurgists, 1951-56, 1958-(Pres., 1966-67); Council, Br. Nuclear Forum, 1964-; Manpower Resources Cttee, 1965-; Council, Inst. of Metals, 1965; Council, Iron and Steel Inst., 1965; Council, City Univ., 1966; Brain Drain Cttee, 1966-67; Public Enquiry into loss of "Sea Gem", 1967; Materials and Structures Cttee, 1967-70; Technology Sub-Cttee of UGC, 1968-. Governor, Sir John Cass Foundation. Hon. ARSM 1961. *Recreations:* gardening, furniture design and making. *Address:* 3 Sylvan Close, Limpsfield, Surrey. *T:* Oxted 3511.

**BALL, Rev. Kenneth Vernon James,** MA; Vicar of Leatherhead, Surrey, since 1959; *b* 10 July 1906; *s* of Vernon Arthur and Eveline Ball, Brighton; *m* 1939, Isabella Jane Armstrong, MB, ChB, *d* of Archibald Armstrong, JP, and Eleanor Elsie Armstrong, Strachur, Argyll; one *s* one *d*. *Educ:* The College, Swindon; Jesus Coll., Oxford; Wycliffe Hall, Oxford. Acting Headmaster, Busoga High Sch., Uganda, 1930-32; Curate, St Paul, Bedminster, 1932-35; Curate, Temple or Holy Cross Church, Bristol, 1935-38; Vicar, St Barnabas, Bristol, 1938-42; Vicar, St Leonard, Redfield, Bristol, 1942-47; Bishop of Liverpool's Special Service Staff, 1947-50; Vicar, St Nicholas, and Chap. St Bartholomew's Hosp., Rochester, 1950-59; Oriel Canon of Rochester Cath., 1953-59. *Publication:* Spiritual Approach to Marriage Preparation, 1948. *Recreations:* rowing, walking, camping. *Address:* The Vicarage, Leatherhead, Surrey. *T:* 2313.

**BALL, Sir Nigel Gresley,** 3rd Bt, *cr* 1911; MA, ScD, FLS; *b* 27 Aug. 1892; *s* of late Sir Charles Bent Ball, Bt, MD; *S* brother, 1945; *m* 1922, Florine Isabel, *d* of late Col Herbert Edwardes Irwin; two *s* one *d*. *Educ:* St Columba's Coll., Rathfarnham, Co. Dublin; Trinity Coll., Dublin. Received commission in 8th (S) Bn Royal Dublin Fusiliers, Nov. 1914; demobilised March 1919; Asst to the University Prof. of Botany, Trinity Coll., Dublin, 1920-24; Prof. of Botany, University Coll., Colombo, 1924-43; Lecturer in Botany, University of London, King's Coll., 1944-55, Reader, 1955-57, Special lecturer, 1957-59. *Publications:* chapters on physiology of plant movements in: Vistas in Botany, vol. 3 (ed Turrill), 1963; Plant Physiology, vol. 5A (ed Steward), 1969; Physiology of Plant Growth and Development (ed Wilkins), 1969; various papers on plant physiology in scientific jls. *Heir:* *s* Charles Irwin Ball [*b* 12 Jan. 1924; *m* 1950, Alison Mary, *d* of Lieut-Col P. H. Bentley, MBE, MC, Farnham, Surrey; one *s* one *d*]. *Address:* 4 Ennerdale Road, Kew Gardens, Surrey. *T:* 01-940 3569.

**BALL, Robert Edward,** MBE 1946; Chief Master of the Supreme Court of Judicature (Chancery Division) since 1969 (Master, 1954-68); *b* 8 March 1911; *s* of James Ball, LLB, Purley, Surrey, and Mabel Louise (*née* Laver); *m* 1935, Edith Margaret Barbara, *d* of late Dr Patrick Edward Campbell; two *s* two *d*. *Educ:* Westminster Sch.; Lycée de Vendôme, France; Germany; London Univ. (LLB). Law Soc.'s Studentship, 1929. Admitted Solicitor, 1933; junior partner, James Ball & Son, 1933-46; served War, 1939-46; commissioned in Queen's Royal Regt, 1940; served KORR and in various staff appts, England, France and India; AA & QMG, Madras; released with rank of Lt-Col, 1946; formed practice of Potts and Ball, Chester and London, with Henry Potts, 1946. Formerly: Hon. Sec., Chester and North Wales Incorp. Law Soc.; Chm. Chester Insurance Tribunal, etc. *Recreations:* history, gardening. *Address:* 62 Stanstead Road, Caterham, Surrey. *T:* Caterham 43675.

**BALL, William Antony,** TD; MRCS, LRCP, MB, BS London; Medical Practitioner; late Temporary Lt-Col RAMC, TA (despatches for service in Italy); *b* 9 April 1904; *s* of late Arthur Franklin and Edith Mary Ball; *m* 1933, Barbara Pauline Johnston. *Educ:* King's Coll. Sch., Wimbledon; King's Coll., London; King's Coll. Hospital. House appointments at King's Coll. Hospital, Westminster Hospital, Belgrave Hospital for Children. *Publications:* in Practitioner, Lancet, BMJ, Medical Press and Circular, American Year Book of Surgery for 1940. *Recreations:* tennis, old Sussex maps, touring in France and her vineyards. *Address:* Ivy House, Tillington, Petworth, Sussex. *T:* Petworth 2248, 3258. *Clubs:* Carlton; Royal Tennis (Hampton Court).

**BALLANCE, Rear-Adm. Frank Arthur,** CB 1953; DSO 1944; Royal Navy, retired; *b* 16 Nov. 1902; *s* of Sydney Ballance, Sandon, Herts; *m* 1930, Marie Arundell, *d* of Reavely Maitland, Loughton, Essex; one *s*. *Educ:* Royal Naval Colls Osborne and Dartmouth. Commander, 1939; HMS Phoebe; HMS Gosling; Capt., 1943; took part in Invasion of Normandy; Admiralty, 1944-46; Ordnance Board, 1946-48; HMS Jamaica, 1949-50; Chief of Naval Staff, New Zealand, 1950-53; Flag Officer Flotilla, Indian Fleet, 1953-55; Rear-Admiral, 1953; Admiralty, 1955; retired, 1956. *Recreation:* shooting. *Address:* Malthouse Cottage, Rogate, Petersfield, Hants. *T:* Rogate 338.

**BALLANTYNE, Alexander Hanson,** CVO 1957; CBE 1963; HM Consul-General, Frankfurt-am-Main, 1964-69; *b* 27 Feb. 1911; *s* of late Dr Harold Sherman Ballantyne and of Mrs Gladys Pauline Ballantyne; *m* 1944, Hélène Georgette Contorouissi; one *s* one *d*. *Educ:* Rugby; Christ's Coll., Cambridge. BA (Hons) Cantab. HM Consular Service, 1934. Vice-Consul: Bangkok, 1934-38; Valencia, 1938 and 1939; Tokyo, 1940-42; Antananarivo, 1942-45; Actg Consul-Gen. Antananarivo, 1945 and 1946; Foreign Office, 1946 and 1947; First Sec. (Commercial), Istanbul, 1947-50; Actg Consul-Gen, Istanbul, 1950 and 1951; Foreign Office, 1951 and 1952; First Sec. (Commercial), Bangkok, 1952-55; Counsellor (Commercial) and Consul-General, Copenhagen, 1956-60; Chargé d'Affaires, Ankara, 1962; Counsellor (Commercial), Ankara, 1960-64. Commander of the Danebrog, 1957. *Recreation:* music. *Address:* 2 Avenue Marie-Christine, 06 Nice, France. *Club:* Royal Automobile.

**BALLANTYNE, Archibald Morton,** OBE 1966; TD 1951; FRAeS 1956; Secretary, Royal Aeronautical Society, since 1951; *b* 1908; *o s* of late Archibald Morton Ballantyne and of Janet Ballantyne, Pollokshields, Glasgow; *m* 1941, Catherine Mary, 2nd *d* of J. Warner Crofts, Kilsby Grange, Rugby; one *s* one *d*. *Educ:* Hutchesons' Grammar Sch.; Glasgow Univ. BSc (Eng) 1930; PhD 1936; Diploma in Town Planning; MICE; AMIStructE; ARICS; Hon FCASI; FAIAA. Senior Lecturer in Civil and Municipal Engineering Department, University College, London, 1936-51. Served War of 1939-45, in Royal Artillery, attached to Inspector-Gen. of Armaments; Captain Royal Artillery, TA. *Recreations:* sailing, mountaineering, golf, writing. *Address:* Royal Aeronautical Society, 4 Hamilton Place, W1. *T:* 01-499 3515; 27 Clifton Lawns, Chesham Bois, Bucks. *T:* Amersham 3711.

**BALLANTYNE, Air Vice-Marshal Gordon Arthur,** CBE 1945; DFC 1918; FDS, RCS (Eng.); FDS, RCS (Edin.); Director of Dental Services, RAF, 1943-54; *b* 12 Feb. 1900; *e s* of late John Alexander and Ida Ballantyne; *m* 1st, 1925, Brenda Muriel, *d* of Rev. Bernard Cuzner; one *d*; 2nd, 1945 Rachel Mary, *er d* of late Francis Reid Brown. *Educ:* King's Coll. Sch.; London Hosp. Probationary Flight Officer, Royal Naval Air Service, 1917; Flying Officer RAF 1918. Served in France with No 8 Squadron, RFC (wounded); LDS, RCS 1923; Lieut Army Dental Corps, 1924; Captain, 1927. Transferred to RAF Dental Branch, 1930; Squadron Leader, 1934; Wing Commander, 1937; Acting Group Captain, 1941; Temp. Group Captain, 1942; Group Captain and Acting Air Commodore, 1943; Temp. Air Commodore, 1944; Air Commodore, 1947; Air Vice-Marshal, 1952; Senior Dental Officer, Iraq, 1935; Inspecting Dental Officer, Home Commands, 1938; Training Officer (Dental), 1941; retd 1954; Hon. Dental Surgeon to King George VI, 1945-52. Member Board of Faculty of Dental Surgery of Royal Coll. of Surgeons of England, 1947-53; Hon. member British Dental Association; Hon. Pres. Armed Forces Commn, Federation Dentaire Internationale, 1953; Hon. Dental Surgeon to the Queen, 1952-54. *Publications:* various professional papers. *Recreations:* painting and motoring. *Address:* 3 St Martin's Hill, Canterbury, Kent. *T:* Canterbury 61103.

**BALLANTYNE, Henry,** CBE 1968; DL, JP; Chairman and Managing Director, Scottish Worsteds & Woollens Ltd; *b* 27 Nov. 1912; *er s* of Lieut-Col David Ballantyne, OBE, Barns Kirkton Manor, Peeblesshire; *m* 1938, Barbara Mary, *d* of C. S. Gavin, Worthing; one *s* three *d*. *Educ:* Cheltenham Coll.; Pembroke Coll., Cambridge. Entered family business, D. Ballantyne Bros & Co. Ltd, 1937: Dir, 1937; Chm., 1940, also of subsid. cos; merged nine Border woollen firms to form Scottish Worsteds & Woollens Ltd, 1968; Dir., Bristol Siddeley Whittle Tool Co. Ltd and other cos. Pres., S of Scotland Chamber of Commerce, 1942-44; Pres., Nat. Assoc. of Scottish Woollen Manufrs, 1951-55; Member: BoT Adv. Cttee, 1961-67; Scottish Econ. Planning Cttee, 1965-68; Royal Commn on Local Govt in Scotland, 1967-69; Scottish Constitutional Cttee of Conservative Party, 1969-70. Member of the Royal Company of Archers (Queen's Body Guard for Scotland). DL 1953, JP 1943, Peeblesshire. *Recreations:* shooting, yachting, gardening. *Address:* Caerlee House, Innerleithen, Peeblesshire. *T:* Innerleithen 392. *Clubs:* Caledonian, Lansdowne, Royal Ocean Racing; Leander (Henley-on-Thames).

**BALLARAT, Bishop of,** since 1961; **Rt. Rev. William Auchterlonie Hardie,** MA, BD. *Educ:* Univ. of Queensland. BA 1928, MA 1936, Univ. of Queensland; BD Melbourne Coll. of Divinity, 1931. Deacon, 1930; priest, 1931; Curate of Holy Trinity, Fortitude Valley, Brisbane, 1930-33; Chaplain Southport Sch., 1933-37; Rector of Holy Trinity, Woolloongabba, Brisbane, 1937-46; Warden of St John's Coll., Brisbane, 1946-50; Canon of St John's Cathedral and Examining Chaplain to the Archbishop of Brisbane, 1947-50; Archdeacon of Moreton, 1948-50; Dean of Newcastle, NSW, 1950-61. Served War of 1939-45 as Chaplain, Royal Australian Air Force, 1941-44. *Address:* Bishopscourt, Ballarat, Victoria, Australia.

**BALLARAT, Bishop of, (RC),** since 1942; **Most Rev. James Patrick O'Collins;** *b* Melbourne, Australia, 31 March 1892. *Educ:* St Columba's, Springwood; St Patrick's, Sydney; Urban Coll., Rome. Ordained Priest, Rome, 1922, for the Diocese of Melbourne; RC Bishop of Geraldton, 1930-42. Nominated Asst Bishop at the Papal Throne, 1955. *Address:* Bishop's House, 1444 Sturt Street, Ballarat, Victoria, Australia.

**BALLARD, Ven. Arthur Henry;** Archdeacon of Rochdale since 1966; Rector of All Saints, Stand, Manchester, since 1946; *b* 9 March 1912; 3rd *s* of Alfred and Lillian Ballard; *m* 1943, Phyllis Marion, *d* of Walter East, Theydon Bois, Essex; two *s*. *Educ:* privately; St John's Coll., Univ. of Durham. BA 1938; DipTh. 1939; MA 1941. Deacon 1939; Curate of Walthamstow, 1939-43; Rector of Broughton, Manchester, 1943-46. Rural Dean of Radcliffe and Prestwich, 1952-67. Hon. Canon of Manchester, 1958-66. *Address:* Stand Rectory, Whitefield, Manchester. *T:* 061-766 2619.

**BALLARD, Lieut-Col Basil W.;** *see* Woods-Ballard.

**BALLARD, Bristow Guy,** OBE 1946; President: Canadian Patents and Development Ltd, since 1967; National Research Council of Canada, Ottawa, 1963-67; *b* 19 June 1902; *s* of Charles Ballard and Etta Moffat; *m* 1928, Irene Foreman; no *c*. *Educ:* Queen's Univ., Kingston, Ont. (BSc). Electrical Engineering, Westinghouse Electric & Manufacturing Co., East Pittsburgh, Pa, 1925-30; Div. of Physics, National Research Council of Canada, 1930-46; Asst Dir, Div. of Physics and Elect. Engrg, NRC, 1946-48; Dir, Radio & Electrical Engrg Div., NRC, 1948-63. Vice-Pres. (Scientific), NRC, 1954-63. Fellow Inst. of Electrical and Electronic Engrs, 1955; Hon. Member: Engrg Inst. of Canada, 1960; Instrument Soc., America, 1964. Coronation Medal, 1953.

Fellow, Royal Soc. of Canada, 1963. Hon. DSc: Queen's Univ., 1956; Assumption Univ. of Windsor, 1961; Memorial Univ., Newfoundland, 1964; Hon. DEng, Nova Scotia Tech. Coll., 1964; Hon. LLD, Univ. of Victoria, 1965. *Publications:* articles in technical jls. *Recreations:* nature study, camping. *Address:* 390 Cloverdale Road, Rockcliffe Park, Ottawa 2, Ont., Canada. *T:* 749-9744. *Club:* Rideau (Ottawa).

**BALLARD, Prof. Clifford Frederick;** Professor of Orthodontics, London University, since 1956; Head of Department of Orthodontics, Institute of Dental Surgery, British Post-Graduate Medical Federation, University of London, since 1947; *b* 26 June 1910; *s* of Frederick John Ballard and Eliza Susannah (*née* Wilkinson); *m* 1937, Muriel Mabel Burling; one *s* one *d*. *Educ:* Kilburn Grammar Sch.; Charing Cross Hosp. and Royal Dental Hospital. LDS 1934; MRCS, LRCP 1940. Pres. of Brit. Soc. for the Study of Orthodontics, 1957, Senior Vice-Pres., 1963, 1964; Mem. Council of Odontological Section of Royal Society Med., 1954-56, 1959-62 (Sec., 1957); Mem. Board, Faculty of Dental Surgery. RCS, 1966-. FDS 1949; Diploma in Orthodontics, 1954 (RCS); FFDRCS Ire., 1964. Charles Tomes Lectr, RCS, 1966; Northcroft Memorial Lectr, Brit. Soc. for Study of Orthodontics, 1967. *Publications:* numerous contributions to learned journals, 1948-. *Recreations:* golf, gardening, sailing. *Address:* Lawns, 56 High View, Pinner, Middlesex. *T:* 01-866 4004.

**BALLARD, Brig. (Retd) James Archibald William,** CBE 1957 (MBE 1940); DSO 1943; *b* 31 July 1905; *s* of late Admiral G. A. Ballard, CB and Mrs M. F. H. Ballard (*née* Paterson); *m* 1st, 1939, Helen Mary (*d* 1941), *d* of late F. Longdon; 2nd, 1945, Ursula Mary (*d* 1962), *d* of late Rev. F. Icely, Naval Chaplain. *Educ:* Rugby. Joined Northamptonshire Regiment, 1925; psc 1939; HQ 2 Corps, BEF, 1940; Military mission to S Africa, 1941-42; in command 2nd Bn Northamptonshire Regt, 1942-43 and 1944; USA, 1943-44; SHAEF Mission to Denmark, 1945; BGS British Troops, Egypt, 1946-48; in comd 2nd Bn Northamptonshire Regt, 1948-50; Chief of Staff British Forces, Trieste, 1950-52; in comd 133 Inf. Bde (TA), 1952-54. War Office, 1954-57. *Address:* Laundry Cottage, Hanmer, Whitchurch, Salop. *Club:* Naval and Military.

**BALMAIN, Pierre Alexandre;** Chevalier de la Légion d'Honneur, 1962; Couturier, established in 1945; *b* St-Jean-de-Maurienne (Savoie), 18 May 1914; *s* of Maurice Balmain and Françoise Balmain (*née* Ballinari). *Educ:* Lycée of Chambéry; Ecole des Beaux-Arts, Paris. Dress designer with Molyneux, 1934-39; dress designer with Lelong, 1939-45. Kt Order of Dannebrog (Denmark) 1963. Cavaliere Ufficiale del Merito Italiano, 1966. *Publication:* My Years and Seasons, 1964. *Recreations:* horse-riding, yachting. *Address:* 44 Rue François 1er, Paris 8e, France. *T:* Balzac 6804. *Clubs:* Polo, Maison de l'Amérique Latine (Paris).

**BALME, David Mowbray,** CMG 1955; DSO 1943; DFC 1943; MA; Professor of Classics, Queen Mary College, London University, since 1964; *b* 8 Sept. 1912; *s* of late Harold Balme, OBE, MD, FRCS; *m* 1936, Beatrice Margaret Rice; four *s* one *d*. *Educ:* Marlborough; Clare Coll., Cambridge; Res. Student, Clare Coll. and Univ. of Halle, Germany, 1934-36; Lecturer, Reading Univ., 1936-37; Research Fellow, Clare Coll., Cambridge, 1937-40; Fellow of Jesus Coll., 1940. Served with No 207 (Bomber) Squadron, 1943; Comd No 49 Squadron, 1945. Tutor of Jesus Coll., 1945-47; Senior Tutor, 1947-48; University Lecturer in Classics, 1947-48; Principal, University College of Ghana, 1948-57; Reader in Classics, Queen Mary Coll., London, 1957-64. *Publications:* articles in classical journals on Greek Philosophy. *Recreation:* music. *Address:* Gumley, near Market Harborough, Leics. *T:* Kibworth 2762. *Club:* Athenæum.

**BALMER, Sir Joseph (Reginald),** Kt 1965; JP; Retired Insurance Official; *b* 22 Sept. 1899; *s* of Joseph Balmer; *m* 1927, Dora, *d* of A. Johnson; no *c*. *Educ:* King Edward's Grammar Sch., Birmingham. North British and Mercantile Insurance Co. Ltd, 1916-60; National Chairman Guild of Insurance Officials, 1943-47. Pres. Birmingham Borough Labour Party, 1946-54; elected to Birmingham City Council, 1945, 1949, 1952; Alderman 1952; Chairman Finance Cttee, 1955-64; Lord Mayor of Birmingham, 1954-55; City Magistrate, 1956. Mem. Council, Birmingham Univ.; Governor King Edward VI Schs, Birmingham; Member or ex-member various cttees. Served European War, 1914-18, overseas with RASC and Somerset Light Infantry. *Recreations:* gardening, woodwork and reading. *Address:* 26 Stechford Lane, Ward End, Birmingham 8. *T:* 021-783 3198.

**BALMFORTH, Rev. Canon Henry,** MA; Residentiary Canon and Chancellor in Exeter Cathedral since 1956; Lecturer in Theology, Exeter University, since 1959; *b* 2 Oct. 1890; *s* of William Albert Balmforth and Sarah Crowther; *m* 1916, Helen Haigh; two *d*. *Educ:* Manchester Grammar Sch.; Corpus Christi Coll., Oxford (Open Classical Scholar), 1st Class Honours Classical Moderations, 2nd Class Final Classical Sch. Attached to General Manager's Staff, Parr's Bank, 1913-15; Lower Sixth Form Master, Manchester Grammar Sch., 1916; Sixth Form Master and Librarian of Repton Sch., 1916-32; Headmaster of St Edmund's Sch., Canterbury, 1932-41; Deacon, 1916; Priest, 1917; Asst Priest, St Werburgh's, Derby, 1920-25; Reader in Derby Cathedral, 1929-32; Examining Chaplain to the Bishop of Derby, 1931-32; Select Preacher, Oxford, 1934-35; Cambridge, 1938 and 1949; Examining Chap. to Archbishop of Canterbury, 1936; to Bishop of Bath and Wells, 1946-60; to Bishop of Exeter, 1956; Dir, Archbishop's Examination in Theology, 1947-64; Six-Preacher in Canterbury Cathedral, 1938-41; Canon of Ely and Principal of Ely Theological Coll., 1941-56. *Publications:* Is Christian Experience an Illusion?, 1923; editor, Gospel according to St Luke (Clarendon Bible), 1930; (joint), Introduction to Pastoral Theology, 1937; The Christ of God, 1938; The Christian Religion: A Brief Account, 1945; The Royal Priesthood, 1956; Christian Priesthood, 1963; contributor to Theology and other journals. *Recreations:* walking, painting. *Address:* 6 The Close, Exeter. *Club:* Oxford Union.

**BALNIEL, Lord; Robert Alexander Lindsay;** MP (C) Hertford Division of Hertfordshire since 1955; Minister of State, Ministry of Defence, since 1970; Lieutenant Grenadier Guards; *b* 5 March 1927; *er s* of 28th Earl of Crawford and 11th of Balcarres, *qv*; *m* 1949, Ruth Beatrice, *d* of Leo Meyer-Bechtler, Zürich; two *s* two *d*. *Educ:* Eton; Trinity College, Cambridge. Parliamentary Private Secretary: to Financial Secretary of Treasury, 1955-57; to Minister of Housing and Local Government, 1957-60. President, Rural District Councils Assoc., 1959-65; Chm., National Association for Mental Health, 1963-. *Heir:* *s* Master of

Lindsay, *qv*. *Address:* House of Commons, SW1.

**BALOGH,** family name of **Baron Balogh.**

**BALOGH,** Baron *cr* 1968 (Life Peer), of Hampstead; **Thomas Balogh,** MA, Dr rer. pol. (Budapest); Fellow of Balliol College, Oxford, since 1945; Reader in Economics, Oxford University, since 1960; Economic Adviser to the Cabinet, October 1964-67, Consultant to the Prime Minister, 1968; *b* Budapest, 2 Nov. 1905; *e s* of Emil Balogh; *m* 1945, Penelope (marr. diss. 1970), *widow* of Oliver Gatty, sometime Fellow of Balliol; two *s* one *d* one *step-d*. *Educ:* The Gymnasium of Budapest Univ.; Univs of Budapest, Berlin, Harvard. Fellow of Hungarian Coll., Berlin, 1927; Rockefeller Fellow, 1928-30; League of Nations, 1931; economist in the City, 1931-39; National Institute of Economic Research, 1938-42; Oxford Univ. Institute of Statistics, 1940-55; Special Lecturer, 1955-60. Visiting Prof., Minnesota, Wisconsin, 1951; Delhi and Calcutta, 1955; Member and acting Chairman Minerals Cttee, Min. of Fuel and Power; Consultant: Reserve Bank of Australia; UNRRA Mission to Hungary, 1946; Govt of Malta, 1955-57, of Jamaica, 1956, 1961-62; Food and Agricultural Organisation of UN, 1957-59, 1961-62; UN Economic Commn for Latin America, 1960; Government of India Statistical Inst., 1960; Greece, 1962; Mauritius, 1962-63; UN Special Fund, 1964, 1970; OECD, 1964; Turkey, Peru, 1964. Member, Economic and Financial Cttee of the Labour Party, 1943-64. Chm., Fabian Soc., 1970. Fellow, New York Univ., 1969. *Publications:* Hungarian Reconstruction and the Reparation Question, 1946; Studies in Financial Organisation, 1946; Dollar Crisis, 1949; Planning through the Price Mechanism, 1950; (with D. Seers) The Economic Future of Malta (Valetta), 1955; Planning and Monetary Organisation in Jamaica, 1956; The Economic Problem of Iraq, 1957; The Economic Development of the Mediterranean (as Head of a Research team), 1957; Economic Policy and Price Mechanism, 1961; Development Plans in Africa, 1961; (with M. Bennett) Sugar Industry in Mauritius; Unequal Partners, 2 vols, 1963; Planning for Progress, 1963; Economics of Poverty, 1966; (co-author) Economics of Full Employment, 1945; War Economics, 1947; Foreign Economic Policy for the US; Fabian International and Colonial Essays; The Establishment, 1960; Crisis in the Civil Service, 1968; papers in Economic Journal, Bulletin of Oxford Institute of Statistics, etc. *Address:* Balliol College, Oxford. *T:* Oxford 49601. *Club:* Reform.

**BALSDON, John Percy Vyvian Dacre,** DLitt Oxon; FBA 1967; *b* 4 Nov. 1901; *e s* of late Robert Percy (farmer). *Educ:* Exeter Sch.; Exeter Coll., Oxford (MA). Stapeldon Scholar, Exeter Coll., 1920; Literae Humaniores, 1924. Asst Master, Sedbergh Sch., 1924-26; Tutor, Keble College, Oxford, 1926-27, Junior Proctor, 1940; Fellow, Exeter Coll., Oxford, 1927-69. Ministry of Labour and National Service, 1940-45. Pres., Soc. for the Promotion of Roman Studies; Mem. of Council of the British Sch. at Rome. Hon. LLD Dalhousie. *Publications:* The Emperor Gaius (Caligula), 1934 (reprinted 1965); Oxford Life, 1957 (new edition, 1962); Roman Women: their History and Habits, 1962; Julius Caesar and Rome, 1967 (in USA, Julius Caesar: a Political Biography); Life and Leisure in Ancient Rome, 1969; Oxford Now and Then, 1970, and various novels. Contributor to Cicero, 1964; Editor, The Romans, 1965. Papers and reviews (mainly on Roman History) in Journal of Roman Studies, Classical Review, Gnomon, Historia, etc. *Address:* The Orchard, Great Haseley, Oxford. *T:* Great Milton 275.

**BAMBER, John;** Stipendiary Magistrate, City of Manchester, since 1965; *b* 10 Aug. 1915; *s* of John and Ada Helen Bamber; *m* 1947, Jean Buchanan Love; one *s* one *d*. *Educ:* Manchester Gram. Sch.; Wadham Coll., Oxford. Called to Bar, Gray's Inn, 1938. Practised on Northern Circuit. Served in Manchester Regt in England and in Staff appts, SE Asia Comd, 1939-46. *Recreations:* association football, cricket. *Address:* 108 Radcliffe New Road, Whitefield, Manchester. *T:* 061-766 2572. *Clubs:* National Liberal; Reform (Manchester).

**BAMBERG, Harold Rolf,** CBE 1968; *b* 17 Nov. 1923; *m* 1957, June Winifred Clarke; one *s* two *d* (and one *s* one *d* of a former marriage). *Educ:* Fleet Sch.; William Ellis Sch., Hampstead. *Recreations:* polo, shooting, travel. *Address:* Harewood, Sunninghill, Ascot, Berks. *Club:* Royal Aero.

**BAMBOROUGH, John Bernard;** Principal of Linacre College, Oxford, since 1962; Pro-Vice-Chancellor, Oxford University, since 1966; *b* 3 Jan. 1921; *s* of John George Bamborough; *m* 1947, Anne, *d* of Olav Indrehus, Indrehus, Norway; one *s* one *d*. *Educ:* Haberdashers' Aske's Hampstead Sch. (Scholar); New College, Oxford (Scholar). 1st Class, English Language and Literature, 1941; MA 1946. Service in RN, 1941-46 (in Coastal Forces as Lieut RNVR; afterwards as Educ. Officer with rank of Instructor Lieut, RN). Junior Lectr, New Coll., Oxford, 1946; Fellow and Tutor, Wadham Coll., Oxford, 1947-62 (Dean, 1947-54; Domestic Bursar, 1954-56; Sen. Tutor, 1957-61); Univ. Lectr in English, 1951-62; Mem. Hebdomadal Council, Oxford Univ. Hon. Fellow, New Coll., Oxford, 1967. Editor, Review of English Studies, 1964-. *Publications:* The Little World of Man, 1952; Ben Jonson, 1959; (ed) Pope's Life of Ward, 1961; Jonson's Volpone, 1963; The Alchemist, 1967. *Address:* 40 St Giles', Oxford. *T:* 59886.

**BAMFORD, Prof. Clement Henry,** FRS 1964; MA, PhD, ScD Cantab; FRIC; Campbell Brown Professor of Industrial Chemistry, University of Liverpool, since 1962; *b* 10 Oct. 1912; *s* of Frederic Jesse Bamford and Catherine Mary Bamford (*née* Shelley), Stafford; *m* 1938, Daphne Ailsa Stephan, BSc Sydney, PhD Cantab, of Sydney, Australia; one *s* one *d*. *Educ:* St Patrick's and King Edward VI Schs, Stafford; Trinity Coll., Cambridge (Senior Scholar). Fellow, Trinity Coll., Cambridge, 1937; Dir of Studies in Chemistry, Emmanuel Coll., Cambridge, 1937. Awarded Meldola Medal of Royal Inst. of Chemistry, 1941. Joined Inter-Services Research Bureau, 1941; joined Fundamental Research Laboratory of Messrs Courtaulds Ltd, at Maidenhead, 1945; head of laboratory, 1947-62; Dean, Faculty of Science, Univ. of Liverpool, 1965-68. *Publications:* Synthetic Polypeptides (with A. Elliott and W. E. Hanby), 1956; The Kinetics of Vinyl Polymerization by Radical Mechanisms (with W. G. Barb, A. D. Jenkins and P. F. Onyon), 1958. Papers on physical chemistry and polymer science in learned journals. *Recreations:* music, especially playing violin in string quartets, hill walking, gardening. *Address:* Broom Bank, Tower Road, Prenton, Birkenhead. *T:* 051-608 3979.

**BAMFORD, Joseph Cyril,** CBE 1969; Chairman and Managing Director: J. C. Bamford Excavators Ltd; JCB Farms Ltd; JCB Research Ltd; JCB Service; Chairman, JCB Sales Ltd; *b* 21 June 1916; *m* 1941, Marjorie

Griffin; two *s*. *Educ:* St John's, Alton, Staffs; Stonyhurst Coll. Founded J. C. Bamford Excavators Ltd, 1945; more than fifty per cent of total production now goes to export market. *Recreations:* yachting, landscape gardening. *Address:* Wootton Lodge, Ellastone, near Ashbourne, Derbyshire; 6 Deanery Street, Park Lane, W1. *Club:* Lighthouse.

**BAMPFYLDE,** family name of **Baron Poltimore.**

**BANBURY,** family name of **Baron Banbury of Southam.**

**BANBURY OF SOUTHAM,** 2nd Baron, *cr* 1924, of Southam; **Charles William Banbury;** 2nd Bt, *cr* 1902; late 12th Lancers; *b* 18 May 1915; *s* of Captain Charles William Banbury, *e s* of 1st Baron (killed in action, Sept. 1914), and Josephine, *d* of José Reixach; *S* grandfather, 1936; *m* 1945, Hilda Ruth (marr. diss. 1958), 2nd *d* of late A. H. R. Carr; one *s* two *d*. *Educ:* Stowe. *Heir: s* Hon. Charles William Banbury, *b* 29 July 1953. *Address:* Daglingworth Place, near Cirencester, Glos. *T:* Cirencester 3521.

**BANBURY, (Frederick Harold) Frith;** Theatrical director, producer and actor; *b* 4 May 1912; *s* of Rear-Adm. Frederick Arthur Frith Banbury and Winifred (*née* Fink); unmarried. *Educ:* Stowe Sch.; Hertford Coll., Oxford; Royal Academy of Dramatic Art. First stage appearance in "If I Were You", Shaftesbury Theatre, 1933; for next 14 years appeared both in London and Provinces in every branch of theatre from Shakespeare to revue. Appearances included: Hamlet, New Theatre, 1934; Goodness How Sad, Vaudeville, 1938; (revue) New Faces, Comedy, 1939; Uncle Vanya, Westminster, 1943; Jacobowsky and the Colonel, Piccadilly, 1945; Caste, Duke of York's, 1947. During this time he also appeared in numerous films including The Life and Death of Colonel Blimp and The History of Mr Polly, and also on the television screen. Since 1947 he has devoted his time to production and direction, starting with Dark Summer at Lyric, Hammersmith (later transferred St Martin's), 1947; subseq. many, in both London and New York, including The Holly and the Ivy, Duchess, 1950; Waters of the Moon, Haymarket, 1951; The Deep Blue Sea, Duchess, 1951, and Morosco, New York, 1952; A Question of Fact, Piccadilly, 1953; Marching Song, St Martin's, 1954; Love's Labour Lost, Old Vic, 1954; The Diary of Anne Frank, Phoenix, 1956; A Dead Secret, Piccadilly, 1957; Flowering Cherry, Haymarket, 1957, and Lyceum, New York, 1959; A Touch of the Sun, Saville, 1958; The Ring of Truth, Savoy, 1959; The Tiger and the Horse, Queen's, 1960; The Wings of the Dove, Lyric, 1963; The Right Honourable Gentleman, Billy Rose, New York, 1965; Howards End, New, 1967; Dear Octopus, Haymarket, 1967; Enter A Free Man, St Martin's, 1968; A Day In the Death of Joe Egg, Cameri Theatre, Tel Aviv, 1968; Le Valet, Théâtre de la Renaissance, Paris, 1968; On the Rocks, Dublin Theatre Festival, 1969; My Darling Daisy, Lyric, 1970. *Recreation:* playing the piano. *Address:* 4 St James's Terrace, Prince Albert Road, NW8. *T:* 01-722 8481.

**BANBURY, Frith;** *see* Banbury, Frederick Harold F.

**BANCROFT, Ian Powell;** a Deputy Secretary, Department of the Environment (Director of Organization and Establishments), since Oct. 1970; *b* 23 Dec. 1922; *s* of A. E. and L. Bancroft; *m* 1950, Jean Swaine; two *s* one *d*. *Educ:* Coatham Sch.; Balliol Coll., Oxford. Served Rifle Brigade, 1942-45. Entered Treasury, 1947; Private Secretary: to Sir Henry Wilson Smith, 1948-50; to Chancellor of the Exchequer, 1953-55; to Lord Privy Seal, 1955-57; Cabinet Office, 1957-59; Principal Private Sec. to successive Chancellors of the Exchequer, 1964-66; Under-Sec., HM Treasury, 1966-68, Civil Service Dept, 1968-70. *Address:* 4 Melrose Road, West Hill, SW18. *T:* 01-874 8020.

**BANDA, Hastings Kamuzu,** MD; President of Malawi since 1966; Chancellor, University of Malawi, since 1965; Member, Malawi Congress Party; *b* Nyasaland, 1905. *Educ:* Meharry Medical Coll., Nashville, USA (MD); Universities of Glasgow and Edinburgh. Further degrees: BSc, MB, ChB, LRCSE. Practised medicine in Liverpool and on Tyneside during War of 1939-45 and in London, 1945-53. Returned to Africa, 1953, and practised in Gold Coast. Took over leadership of Nyasaland African Congress in Blantyre, 1958, and became Pres.-Gen.; was imprisoned for political reasons, 1959; unconditionally released, 1960; Minister of Natural Resources and Local Government, Nyasaland, 1961-63; Prime Minister of Malawi (formerly Nyasaland), 1963-66. *Address:* Office of the President, Zomba, Malawi.

**BANDARANAIKE, the Hon. Mrs Sirimavo;** Member of Ceylon Parliament; Prime Minister, 1960-65, and since 1970, also Minister of Defence, of External Affairs, and of Planning and Employment; President, Sri Lanka Freedom Party, since 1960; *b* 17 April 1916; *d* of Barnes Ratwatte, Ratemahatmaya of Ratnapura Dist, Mem. of Ceylon Senate; *m* 1940, Solomon West Ridgeway Dias Bandaranaike (*d* 1959), Prime Minister of Ceylon, 1956-59; one *s* two *d*. *Educ:* Ratnapura Ferguson Sch.; St Bridget's Convent, Colombo. Assisted S.W.R.D. bandaranaike in political career. Campaigned for Sri Lanka Freedom Party in election campaigns, March and July 1960. Formerly Pres. and Treasurer, Lanka Mahila Samiti. Prime Minister of Ceylon, also Minister of Defence and External Affairs, 1960-65; Minister of Information and Broadcasting, 1964-65; Leader of the Opposition, 1965-70. *Address:* 65 Rosmead Place, Colombo, Ceylon.

**BANDON,** 5th Earl of, *cr* 1880; **Percy Ronald Gardner Bernard,** GBE 1961 (KBE 1957); CB 1945; CVO 1953; DSO 1940; Baron Bandon, 1793; Viscount Bandon, 1795; Viscount Bernard, 1800; Air Chief Marshal, Royal Air Force, retired; *b* 30 Aug. 1904; *s* of late Lt-Col Ronald P. H. Bernard and Lettice Mina, *yr d* of late Captain Gerald C. S. Paget (she *m* 2nd, late Hon. Charles C. J. Littleton, DSO); *S* cousin, 1924; *m* 1st, 1933, Elizabeth (marr. diss., 1946; she *m* 1965, Sir Reginald Holcroft, 2nd Bt, *qv*), 2nd *d* of R. W. Playfair; two *d*; 2nd, 1946, Lois White, *d* of Francis Russell, Victoria, Australia. *Educ:* Wellington; RAF Coll., Cranwell. RAF Staff Coll., 1938; served War of 1939-45; commanded No. 82 Squadron, 1939-40; commanded RAF Station, West Raynham, 1941-42; AOC No. 224 Group, South-East Asia, 1945 (despatches thrice, American DFC and Bronze Star); Commandant, ROC, 1945-48; idc 1949; AOC No. 2 Group, BAFO, Germany, 1950-51, No. 11 Group, 1951-53; ACAS (Trg), Air Ministry, 1953-Dec. 1955; C-in-C, 2nd Tactical Air Force, and Comdr, 2nd Allied Tactical Air Force, 1955-57; C-in-C, Far East Air Force, 1957-60; Comdr, Allied Air Forces, Central Europe, 1961-63. Governor Wellington Coll. *Heir: twin b* Hon. Charles Brodrick Amyas Bernard, *qv*. *Address:* Castle Bernard, Bandon, Co. Cork. *Clubs:* Royal Air Force; County (Cork).

**BANERJEA, A. C.,** CIE 1943; DrPH; *b* 5 Feb. 1894; *s* of late A. T. Banerjea; *m* 1917, Prabhabati; one *s* four *d*. *Educ:* India, England and USA. MB, BS 1920; DPH 1922; DrPH 1928; Malariologist, UP Govt for ten years. Dir of Public Health, UP, India, 1939; Dir of Medical and Health Services, 1948; retired, 1950. *Publications:* In official files and records. *Address:* 31 Station Road, Lucknow, UP, India. *T:* 2686.

**BANERJEE, Rabindra Nath,** CSI 1946; CIE 1938; Chairman, Union Public Service Commission, India, 1949-55, retired; *b* 1 Feb 1895; *s* of late Haradhan Banerjee; *m* Manisha (*d* 1953) *d* of late Lieut-Col Upendra Nath Mukerjee, IMS; one *s* one *d*. *Educ:* Calcutta Univ. (MA 1915); Emmanuel Coll., Cambridge (BA 1918). Entered Indian Civil Service, 1920; Registrar Co-operative Societies and Dir Of Industries, Central Provinces and Berar, 1929-33; Vice-Chm. Provincial Banking Enquiry Cttee, 1929; Sec. to Govt, Central Provinces and Berar, Revenue Dept, 1933; Sec. to Govt, CP and Berar, Local Self-Government Dept, 1936; Mem. CP and Berar Legislative Council, 1929-36; Sec. to the Governor, CP and Berar, 1937; Commissioner, 1941; Commissioner of Food Supply, 1943; Sec. to Govt of India, Commonwealth Relations Dept and Min. of Home Affairs, 1944-48. Mem. Council of State (India), 1944, 1945, 1947; MLA (India), 1946. Mem. of Cttee of Experts of International Labour Organisation, 1956-58. *Address:* 17 Friends' Colony, Mathura Road, New Delhi, India. *T:* New Delhi 73998.

**BANERJI, Amiya Charan,** MA (Cantab.), MSc (Cal); FRAS (Lond); IES (Retd); Emeritus Professor of Mathematics, Allahabad University; Conducting research in Astrophysics under CSIR scheme for retired scientists; *b* 23 Sept. 1891; *m* 1921, Probha Niyogi; two *s* one *d*. *Educ:* Bhagalpur Zila Sch.; Presidency Coll., Calcutta; Clare Coll., Cambridge (Foundation Scholar). First Class in Applied Mathematics, Calcutta Univ., 1913; Behar Government Scholar to Cambridge, 1915; First Class in Mathematical Tripos Part I, 1916, and First Class in Mathematical Tripos Pt II, 1918; Prof. of Mathematics, Muir Central Coll. from 1920, and a Mem. of the Indian Educational Service from 1921; services lent to the Teaching Univ. of Allahabad from 1922; Junior Selection Grade of the Indian Educational Service, 1934, Senior Selection Grade, 1943; Pres. UP Secondary Educational Conference, 1933 and 1943; Hon. Sec., Allahabad Public Library, 1926-44; Registrar of Marriages under Act III of 1872, 1930-54; Sec. National Academy of Sciences, 1930-34 (Pres. 1947, 1948); Mem. International Astronomical Union; Fellow and Vice-Pres. National Institute of Science, India, 1947; President: Mathematics Section, Indian Science Congress, 1940; Benares Mathematical Soc., 1942-45; Calcutta Mathematical Soc., 1947-49; Allahabad Univ. Teachers' Assoc., 1947-49; Indian Astronomical Soc.; Indian Interplanetary Soc.; sent on deputation by Indian Government to Europe and America to visit observatories and univs, 1950; Vice-Chancellor, Allahabad Univ., 1952-55; Commonwealth Univs Congress, 1953; Pres. Principal's Conference, UP Intermediate Colls, 1953; Adviser, Jadaypur Univ., 1956-57; Pres.-elect Indian Science Congress, 1969. *Publications:* several research papers in Hydrodynamics, Nuclear Physics, Wave Mechanics, Relativity, Theory of Expanding Universe, Galactic Dynamics, Stellar Energy, Variable Stars, Origin of Solar System, Magnetohydrodynamics. *Address:* Gyan Kutir, New Katra, Allahabad, UP, India.

**BANGOR,** 7th Viscount *cr* 1781; **Edward Henry Harold Ward;** Baron, 1770; free-lance journalist (as Edward Ward); *b* 5 Nov. 1905; *s* of 6th Viscount Bangor, PC (Northern Ireland), OBE and Agnes Elizabeth, 3rd *d* of late Dacre Hamilton of Cornacassa, Monaghan; *S* father, 1950; *m* 1st, 1933, Elizabeth (who obtained a divorce, 1937), *e d* of T. Balfour, Wrockwardine Hall, Wellington, Salop; 2nd, 1937, Mary Kathleen (marriage dissolved, 1947), *d* of W. Middleton, Shanghai; 3rd, 1947, Leila Mary (marriage dissolved, 1951; she died, 1959), *d* of David R. Heaton, Brookfield, Crownhill, S Devon; one *s*; 4th, 1951, Mrs Marjorie Alice Simpson, *d* of late Peter Banks, St Leonards-on-Sea; one *s* one *d*. *Educ:* Harrow; RMA, Woolwich. Formerly Reuter's correspondent in China and the Far East; BBC War Correspondent in Finland, 1939-40, ME, 1940-41, and Foreign Correspondent all over world, 1946-60. *Publications:* 1940 Despatches from Finland, 1946; Give Me Air, 1946; Chinese Crackers, 1957; The New Eldorado, 1957; Oil is Where They Find It, 1959; Sahara Story, 1962; Number One Boy, 1969; I've Lived like a Lord, 1970. With his wife, Marjorie Ward: Europe on Record, 1950; The US and Us 1951; Danger is Our Business, 1955. *Heir: s* Hon. William Maxwell David Ward, *b* 9 Aug. 1948. *Address:* 105 Devonshire Mews South, W1. *T:* 01-935 4854. *Club:* Savile.

**BANGOR, Bishop of,** since 1957; **Rt. Rev. Gwilym Owen Williams,** DD Lambeth 1957; *b* 23 March 1913; *s* of Owen G. Williams; *m* 1941, Megan, *d* of T. D. Jones; one *s*. *Educ:* Llanberis Gram. Sch.; Jesus Coll., Oxford. BA 1st Class Hons English, 1933; 1st Class Hons Theol. 1935; Gladstone Student at St Deiniol's Library, Hawarden, 1935; St Stephen's House, Oxford, 1936; MA 1937. Curate of Denbigh, 1937; Reader in Theology, St David's Coll., Lampeter, 1940; Warden of Church Hostel, Bangor; Lecturer in Theology, University Coll., Bangor; Canon of Bangor Cathedral, 1947. Warden and Headmaster, Llandovery Coll., 1948-56. Chaplain and Sub-Prelate of Order of St John of Jerusalem, 1965. *Publication:* The Church's Work, 1959. *Recreations:* fishing and walking. *Address:* Tŷ'r Esgob, Bangor, Caerns. *Club:* Reform.

**BANGOR, Dean of;** *see* Richards, Very Rev. Gwynfryn.

**BANK-ANTHONY, Sir Mobolaji,** KBE 1963 (OBE 1956); Company Director, Lagos, Nigeria; *b* 11 June 1907; *e s* of Alfred Bank-Anthony and Rabiatu Aleshinloye Williams, Lagos; *m* 1935, Olamide Adeshigbin. *Educ:* Methodist Boys' High Sch., Lagos; CMS Gram. Sch., Lagos; Ijebu-Ode Gram. Sch. Postal Clerk in Nigerian P & T Dept, 1924; course in Palm Oil cultivation methods, in England, 1931-33, when returned Nigeria, and gradually built up extensive business, opening stores in many parts of Lagos; Dir of some leading local companies. Fellow of Royal Commonwealth Society; FRSA, FInstD. Stella della Solidarieta (Italy), 1957. *Recreations:* working, reading, newspapers, dancing. *Address:* Executive House, 2a Oil Mill Street, Lagos, Nigeria. *T:* Lagos 24660, 24669; Fountainpen House, 29 Okotie-Eboh Street, Ikoyi, Lagos, Nigeria. *T:* Lagos 21900 and 21363. *Clubs:* Royal Aero, Royal Automobile (London); Rotary, Metropolitan, Island, Lagos Race, Lagos Motor, Lagos Amateur Cricket, Yoruba Tennis, Skal, Lodge Academic (Lagos).

**BANKES, Henry John Ralph;** Barrister, Inner Temple, 1925; JP Dorset; *b* 14 July 1902; *s* of Walter Ralph Bankes of Corfe Castle and

Kingston Lacy, Dorset; *m* 1935, Hilary (*d* 1966), *d* of late Lieut-Col F. Strickland-Constable, Wassand Hall, Yorks; one *s* one *d*. *Educ:* Eton; Magdalen Coll., Oxford. High Sheriff of Dorset, 1939. RNVR, 1939-45. *Address:* Kingston Lacy, Wimborne, Dorset. *Clubs:* Carlton; Royal Dorset Yacht (Weymouth); Royal Motor Yacht (Sandbanks).

**BANKES, Robert Wynne,** CBE 1929; *b* 23 June 1887; *s* of late Rt Hon. Sir John Bankes, PC, GCB; *m* Mabel Elizabeth, 2nd *d* of Major H. Pelham Burn; two *s* one *d*. *Educ:* Eton; University College, Oxford (BA). Called to Bar, Inner Temple, 1911; on active service European War, 1914; Captain, Montgomeryshire Yeomanry, 1914-17; ADC to Brig.-Gen. C. A. C. Godwin, 6th Mounted Brigade, EEF, 1917-18; ADC FM Lord Allenby, 1918-19 (despatches); Private Sec. to successive Lord Chancellors, 1919-29; Asst Sec., Institute of Chartered Accountants, 1929-35, Sec., 1935-49; High Sheriff, Flintshire, 1945; KStJ, 1960. *Address:* Soughton Hall, Northop, Mold, Flintshire. *Club:* Anglo-Belgian.

**BANKES-WILLIAMS, Ivor Maredydd;** Headmaster, Wellington School, Somerset, 1945-April 1957; *b* 10 June 1896; *s* of late Rev. W. Bankes-Williams, MA, JP; *m* 1924, Winifred Mary Grellier Barnes. *Educ:* Radley Coll.; CCC, Cambridge. BA 1923; MA 1931; served in Gallipoli and France, 1914-19. Capt. RFA. Classical Scholar CCC, Cambridge, 1914; Hons Natural Sciences Tripos, 1922; Asst Master, Harrow Sch., 1923-41. Chm. of Cttee, Science Masters' Assoc., 1931. Dir of Training, St Dunstan's, for Men and Women blinded on war service, 1941-44. *Recreations:* sketching, gardening. *Address:* Greenway Cottage, Kington Magna, Gillingham, Dorset. *TA* and *T:* East Stour 286.

**BANKS, Alan George;** HM Acting Consul-General, Alexandria, since 1967; *b* 7 April 1911; *s* of George Arthur Banks and Sarah Napthen; *m* 1946, Joyce Frances Telford Yates; two *s*. *Educ:* Preston Gram. Sch. Served in HM Forces, 1939-43; at Consulate-Gen., Dakar, 1943-45; Actg Consul, Warsaw, 1945-48; HM Vice-Consul: Bordeaux, 1948-50; Istanbul, 1950-52; Zagreb, 1952-55; FO, 1955-58; HM Consul, Split, 1958-60; 1st Sec. and Consul, Madrid, 1960-62; 1st Sec., FO, 1962-67. *Recreations:* tennis, swimming, classical music, bridge. *Address:* British Consulate-General, 3 Rue de Mina, Rouchdi, Ramleh, Alexandria, UAR. *T:* Alexandria 49458. *Clubs:* Sporting, Yacht, AA (all Alexandria).

**BANKS, A(rthur) Leslie,** MA Cantab; MD Lond.; FRCP; DPH; Barrister-at-Law (Lincoln's Inn); Professor of Human Ecology, Cambridge, since 1949; Professorial Fellow Gonville and Caius College since 1951; *b* 12 Jan. 1904; *o s* of late A. C. and E. M. F. Banks; *m* 1933, Eileen Mary (*d* 1967), *d* of Sidney Barrett, Arkley, Herts; two *s*. *Educ:* Friern Barnet Gram. Sch.; Middlesex Hospital and Medical Sch. Resident hospital appointments, including house-surgeon, resident officer to special depts and acting Registrar, Middlesex Hosp., 1926-28; Locum tenens and asst in general practice, Asst Medical Officer, Gen. Post Office, EC1, 1928-34; Divisional Medical Officer, Public Health Dept, LCC (duties included special public health enquiries and slum clearance), 1934-37; Min. of Health, 1937-49; seconded as Medical Officer of Health to City of Newcastle, 1946. Formerly Principal Medical Officer, Min. of Health. First Viscount Bennett prize, Lincoln's Inn, for essay on the Jurisdiction of the Judicial Cttee of the Privy Council. Member: Gen. Med. Council; Gen. Dental Council; WHO Expert Advisory Panel on Organisation of Med. Care; Med. Advisory Panel, Nuffield Provincial Hosps Trust; Registrar-General's advisory Cttee on Medical Nomenclature and Statistics; Medical Geography Cttee, Royal Geographical Society; Society for Social Medicine; Hon. Society of Lincoln's Inn; Middlesex Hosp. Club. FRSocMed. *Publications:* Social Aspects of Disease, 1953; (Ed.) Development of Tropical and Sub-tropical countries, 1954; (with J. A. Hislop) Health and Hygiene, 1957; (with J. A. Hislop) Art of Administration, 1961; private and official papers on medical and social subjects. *Address:* Department of Human Ecology, Fenner's, Gresham Road, Cambridge. *T:* Cambridge 58217; Harvey Court, West Road, Cambridge. *T:* Cambridge 53275.

**BANKS, Sir Donald,** KCB 1935 (CB 1933); DSO 1918; MC 1917; TD 1942; *b* 31 March 1891; *m* 1921, Dorothy (*d* 1947), *d* of late Dr Norman Webster, Guernsey; one *d*; *m* 1948, Elizabeth, 2nd *d* of Lt-Col R. W. Bradley, DSO, Lymington; one *s* one *d*. *Educ:* Elizabeth Coll., Guernsey. Exchequer and Audit Dept, 1909, Private Sec. to the Sec. GPO, and to four Postmasters-General, 1920-23; Deputy Controller, Post Office Savings Bank, 1924, Controller, 1931; First Dir-Gen. of Post Office, 1934-36; Transatlantic Air Mission to Ottawa and Washington, 1935; Permanent Sec. to the Air Ministry, 1936-38; First Permanent Under Sec. of State for Air, 1938-39; Air Mission to Australia and New Zealand, 1939; Mem. of National Savings Cttee, 1931-39; of Import Duties Advisory Cttee, 1939; JP (London), 1936-42; London Yeomanry, 1910-14; served European War in France, 1915-18; commanded 10th (Service) Bn Essex Regt and 8th (Service) Bn Royal Berkshire Regt (DSO, MC, Fr. Croix de Guerre; despatches twice); commanded Princess Louise's Kensington Regt TA, 1927-31; Asst Adjutant and Quartermaster General 50th (Northumbrian) Div. 1939; Temp. Brig., 1940; Maj.-Gen., 1943; Deputy Adjutant-Gen. GHQ BEF 1940 (despatches); Local Defence Area Commander for Hampshire, 1940; Dir-Gen. Petroleum Warfare Dept (involving operations Pluto, Fido, etc.), 1940-45. (Commander, US Legion of Merit); Chm. Anglo-Chinese Chamber of Commerce, 1946-54; Head of UK delegation to first Assembly International Civil Aviation Organisation, Montreal, 1946; Deputy Chm., Air Transport Advisory Council, 1947-51. *Publications:* With the Tenth Essex in France; Flame over Britain. *Address:* Cadnam Lodge, Hants. *Club:* Reform.

**BANKS, Air Cdre Francis Rodwell,** CB 1946; OBE 1919; RAF (retired); *b* 22 March 1898; *s* of late Bernard Rodwell and Frances Emily Banks; *m* 1925, Christine Constance Grant Langlands; two *d*. *Educ:* Christ's Coll., London, N. Served in two wars, 1914-19 in Navy and 1939-46 in RAF. Between the two wars specialised in the development of aviation engines and their fuels with The Associated Ethyl Co.; responsible in the recent war sucessively for the production, the research and development of aero engines, including gas turbines, at MAP. Principal Dir of Engine Research and Development, Min. of Supply, 1952-53; Dir, The British Aeroplane Co., 1954-59; Dir, Hawker Siddeley Aviation Ltd, 1954-59, now Engrg Consultant. Pres. RAeS, 1969. CEng; Hon. CGIA; Hon. FRAeS; Hon. FAIAA; FIMechE; FInstPet. *Publications:* technical papers on aviation engines and their fuels. *Recreation:* golf. *Address:* 5a Albert Court, SW7. *T:* 01-584 2740. *Clubs:* Royal Air Force, Royal Aero.

**BANKS, James Dallaway,** MA, FHA; House Governor and Secretary to Board of Governors, King's College Hospital, Denmark Hill, since 1960; *b* 3 Jan. 1917; *s* of late Dr Cyril Banks; *m* 1942, Winifred Holt; two *s* one *d*. *Educ:* Nottingham High Sch.; St John's Coll., Cambridge. BA 1938, MA 1943. Indian Civil Service, 1939-47. Dep. House Governor, King's Coll. Hosp., 1947-53; House Governor: Royal Marsden Hospital 1953-59, The Hospital for Sick Children, Great Ormond Street, 1959-60. Fellow of Institute of Hospital Administrators, 1955. *Recreation:* photography. *Address:* 60 Scotts Lane, Bromley, Kent. *T:* 01-650 0063.

**BANKS, Sir John (Garnett),** Kt 1956; CBE 1953; DL; JP; LLD; Property Agent and Surveyor; *b* 9 May 1889; *s* of John Garnett Banks and Elizabeth Forrest Grieve; *m* 1st 1923, Gertrude Rosamond Marshall Symonds (*d* 1941); one *s*; 2nd, 1952, Margaret Wallace Macdonald. *Educ:* Leith Walk Public Sch., Edinburgh. Chairman: Poole's Roxy (Edinburgh) Ltd; several Property Investment Companies. Edinburgh Town Council: Member, 1936; Treasurer, 1950-53; Lord Provost, City of Edinburgh, 1954-57. DL Edinburgh, 1958. Hon. LLD Edinburgh, 1956. OStJ 1958. *Recreations:* music and travel. *Address:* Cairn Lodge, 48 Duddingston Road West, Edinburgh. *T:* 031-661 2146.

**BANKS, Richard Alford,** CBE 1965; JP; Member of the Water Resources Board since 1964; *b* 11 July 1902; *s* of William Hartland Banks, Hergest Croft, Kington, Hereford; *m* 1937, Lilian Jean, *d* of Dr R. R. Walker, Presteigne, Radnorshire; two *s* one *d*. *Educ:* Rugby; Trinity Coll., Cambridge (BA). Dir of Imperial Chemical Industries Ltd, 1952-64; Chm. of the Industrial Training Council, 1962-64. JP, Hereford, 1963-. *Recreations:* arboriculture, gardening and travel. *Address:* Ridgebourne, Kington, Hereford.

**BANKS, Sir Thomas Macdonald;** *see* Banks, Sir Donald.

**BANKS, Captain William Eric,** CBE 1943; DSC; RN retired; *b* 17 July 1900; *er s* of late Walter Banks; *m* 1937, Audrey Steel; two *s*. *Educ:* University Coll. Sch. Joined Navy in 1918; retired list, 1952. *Address:* Villa Fort, Lija, Malta, GC. *Club:* Naval and Military.

**BANNER;** *see* Harmood-Banner.

**BANNER, Mrs Delmar;** *see* Vasconcellos, J. de.

**BANNERMAN, David Armitage,** OBE 1961 (MBE 1918); MA, ScD, FRSE, FZS; *b* 27 November 1886; *o s* of late David Alexander Bannerman; *m* 1911, Muriel (*d* 1945), 2nd *d* of T. R. Morgan of Las Palmas, Grand Canary; twin *d* (one *s* decd); *m* 1952, Winifred Mary (Jane), OBE, *e d* of David Holland, Cardiff. *Educ:* Wellington College; Pembroke College, Cambridge. Graduated 1909; joined temp. Staff Natural History Museum, 1910; travelled extensively West Indies, N, S, and W Africa, S America, Atlantic Isles and Europe; carried out Zoological Survey of Canary Islands, 1908-13. Served with BEF (Europe), first as Ambulance driver, then, as Sen. Officer, on HQ Staff BRCS (France), 1915-18 (MBE); 1914-15 Star, British and French War Medals; after Armistice rejoined staff of Natural History Museum; Leader, British Museum Expedition to Tunisia, 1925. Assistant Editor, Ibis, 1931-41. On outbreak of Second World War, 1939, appointed Deputy Assistant Censor (Liaison Branch) on Staff of Controller of Postal and Telegraph Censorship, War Office; Assistant Censor, IRB Censorship Hqrs, 1940-42; Sgt in Home Guard. Retd from Natural History Museum, 1952, to take up book-writing and stock-breeding in Kirkcudbrightshire. Carried out ornithological surveys of Morocco, 1950-52, Cyprus, 1954, Madeira and Azores, 1960-64, Cape Verde Islands, 1966. Chairman, British Ornithologists' Club, 1932-45; Brit. representative Internat. Council Bird Preservation, Vienna, 1937, Rouen, 1938; MBOU (Vice-Pres., 1943-45); Member Council: RGS, 1935-38; Zoological Soc., 1943-50; RSPB, 1938-52 (Vice-Pres., 1961); Hon. Associate, British Museum (Natural History), 1950; Hon. Pres., Scottish Ornithologists' Club; Hon. Mem., Société Ornithologique de France; Hon. Fellow, Amer. Ornith. Union. Hon. LLD Glasgow, 1964. Gold Medal of British Ornithologists' Union, 1959. OStJ. *Publications:* The Canary Islands, their History, Natural History and Scenery, 1922; Reports on numerous British Museum Expeditions for the Advancement of Ornithological Knowledge; The Birds of Tropical West Africa, by order of the Secretary of State for the Colonies, vols i-viii, 1930-51; The Birds of West and Equatorial Africa (2 vols), 1953; The Birds of the British Isles Vols 1-12 1953-63; The Larger Birds of West Africa, 1958, in Penguin series; (by request of Government) The Birds of Cyprus (in conjunction with W. Mary Bannerman), 1958; Birds of the Atlantic Islands (with W. Mary Bannerman): Vol. 1, Canary Islands, 1963; Vol. 2, Madeira, 1965; Vol. 3, Azores, 1966; Vol. 4, Cape Verde Islands, 1968. *Recreations:* natural history and fly-fishing. *Address:* Bailiff's House, Slindon, by Arundel, Sussex. *Clubs:* Travellers'; New (Edinburgh).

*See also Maj.-Gen. J. H. Gibbon.*

**BANNERMAN, Lieut-Col Sir Donald Arthur Gordon,** 13th Bt, *cr* 1682; *b* 2 July 1899; *s* of Lieut-Col Sir Arthur D'Arcy Gordon Bannerman, KCVO, CIE, 12th Bt and of late Virginia Emilie Bannerman; *S* father 1955; *m* 1932, Barbara Charlotte, *d* of late Lieut-Col A. Cameron, OBE, IMS; two *s* twin *d*. *Educ:* Harrow; Royal Military Coll., Sandhurst; commissioned into Queen's Own Cameron Highlanders, 1918; served in N Russian Campaign, 1919; 1st Class Interpreter (Russian), 1925; served with 1st and 2nd Bns of his Regt in Egypt and India, 1931-34 and 1936-39; served War of 1939-45: with 4th Indian Div. and in MEF, 1940-43; in NW Europe, 1945, attached to US 9th Army, in closing stages of fighting, and then for 3 yrs with Control Commission as Senior Control Officer; retired from Army as Lieut-Col, 1947. On staff of Gordonstoun Sch., 1948-52, of Fettes Coll., 1952-60. *Recreations:* gardening, walking, reading. *Heir:* *s* Alexander Patrick Bannerman, *b* 5 May 1933. *Address:* 11 Learmouth Place, Edinburgh. *T:* 031-332 1076. *Club:* United Service.

**BANNISTER, Prof. Frank Kenneth,** PhD, CEng, FIMechE; Professor of Thermodynamics, Department of Mechanical Engineering, University of Birmingham, since 1952; *b* Colne, Lancs, 29 June 1909; *s* of late Frank Foulds Bannister; *m* 1937, Alice Mary, *d* of late Clement Turner, Halifax, Yorks; one *s* two *d*. *Educ:* Grammar Sch., Colne, Lancs; University of Leeds. BSc Hons Physics Leeds 1930; BSc (Eng) Hons London 1937; PhD Mech Eng Birmingham, 1946. Lecturer in Mechanical Engineering, Municipal Coll., Burnley, 1937-40; Lecturer in Mechanical Engineering, University of Birmingham, 1941-51; Reader in Thermodynamics, University of Birmingham, 1951-52. *Publications:* papers in Proc. Instn Mech. Engineers. *Recreation:*

motor sport. *Address:* 401 Heath Road South, Northfield, Birmingham 31. *T:* 021-475 1081.

**BANNISTER, Dr Roger (Gilbert),** CBE 1955; DM (Oxon); FRCP; Consultant Physician: National Hospital for Nervous Diseases, Queen Square, WC1; Department of Nervous Diseases, St Mary's Hospital, W2; Consultant Neurologist, Western Ophthalmic Hospital, NW1; Hon. Consultant, King Edward VII Convalescent Home for Officers, Osborne; *b* 23 March 1929; *s* of Ralph and Alice Bannister, Harrow; *m* 1955, Moyra Elver, *d* of late Per Jacobsson; two *s* two *d*. *Educ:* City of Bath Boys' Sch.; University Coll. Sch., London; Exeter and Merton Colls, Oxford; St Mary's Hospital Medical Sch., London. Amelia Jackson Studentship, Exeter Coll., Oxford, 1947; BA (hons) Physiology, Junior Demonstrator in Physiology, Harmsworth Senior Scholar, Merton Coll., Oxford, 1950; Open and State Schol., St Mary's Hosp., 1951; BSc Thesis in Physiology, 1952; MRCS, LRCP, 1954; BM, BCh Oxford, 1954; DM Oxford, 1963. William Hyde Award for research relating physical education to medicine; MRCP 1957. Junior Medical Specialist, RAMC, 1958; Resident MO, National Hospital, Queen Square, WC1, 1961; Radcliffe Travelling Fellowship, at Harvard, USA, 1962-63. Pres. of National Fitness Panel, NABC, 1956-59. Mem. Council, King George's Jubilee Trust, 1961-67; Chm. Research Cttee Sports Council, 1964-; Mem., Min. of Health Adv. Cttee on Drug Dependence, 1967-. Winner Oxford *v* Cambridge Mile, 1947-50; Pres. OUAC, 1948; Capt. Oxford & Cambridge Combined American Team, 1949; Finalist, Olympic Games, Helsinki, 1952; British Mile Champion, 1951, 1953, 1954; World Record for One Mile, 1954; British Empire Mile title and record, 1954; European 1500 metres title and record, 1954. *Publications:* First Four Minutes, 1955. Papers on Physiology of exercise, heat illness and neurological subjects. *Recreations:* sailing, golf, orienteering. *Address:* 17 Harley Street, W1. *T:* 01-935 1964; 31 Edwardes Square, W8. *T:* 01-603 9903; Churchfield, Lyminster, Sussex. *Club:* Vincent's (Oxford).

**BANTING, Air Vice-Marshal George Gaywood,** CB 1946; CBE 1943; RAF; retired; *b* 25 Feb. 1898; *s* of G. F. Banting, Roehampton; *m* Helen Margaret Ramsay, MBE 1920. *Educ:* Emanuel Sch.; RMC Sandhurst. Served European War, 1914-18, E Surrey Regt and RFC; RAF, 1918-51; War of 1939-45 (despatches, CBE, CB); Air Officer Commanding Rhodesian Air Training Group, 1946-49; Air Officer Commanding No. 21 Group, Flying Training Command, 1949-51; Wing Cdr 1937; Air Commodore, 1947; retired, 1951, with rank of Air Vice-Marshal. *Address:* Ridgeway, St Margaret's Bay, Dover, Kent. *Club:* Royal Air Force.

**BANTON, Prof. Michael Parker,** PhD, DSc; Professor of Sociology, University of Bristol, since 1965; Director, Social Science Research Council Race Relations Research Unit, since 1970; *b* 8 Sept. 1926; *s* of Francis Clive Banton and Kathleen Blanche (*née* Parkes); *m* 1952, Rut Marianne (*née* Jacobson), Luleå; two *s* two *d*. *Educ:* King Edward's Sch., Birmingham; London Sch. of Economics. BSc Econ. 1950; PhD 1954; DSc 1964. Midn, then Sub-Lieut RNVR, 1945-47. Asst, then Lecturer, then Reader, in Social Anthropology, University of Edinburgh, 1950-65; Visiting Prof., Massachusetts Inst. of Technology, 1962-63. Editor, Sociology, 1966-69. Pres., Section N, British Assoc. for the Advancement of Science, 1970-71; Mem., SW Regl Hosp. Board, 1966-70. JP Bristol, 1966. *Publications:* The Coloured Quarter, 1955; West African City, 1957; White and Coloured, 1959; The Policeman in the Community, 1964; Roles, 1965; Race Relations, 1967. *Address:* 22 Falcondale Road, Bristol BS9 3JU. *T:* 622769.

**BANWELL, Derick Frank;** General Manager, Runcorn Development Corporation, since 1964; *b* 19 July 1919; *s* of Frank Edward Banwell; *m* 1945, Rose Kathleen Worby; two *s* one *d*. *Educ:* Kent Coll., Canterbury. Admitted as Solicitor, 1947; Asst Solicitor, Southend-on-Sea Co. Borough Coun., 1947-48; Sen. Asst Solicitor, Rochdale Co. Borough Coun., 1948-51; Chief Common Law Solicitor, City of Sheffield, 1951-56; Sen. Asst Solicitor, 1956-59, Asst Town Clerk, 1959-60, Southend-on-Sea Co. Borough Coun.; Dep. Town Clerk and Dep. Clerk of the Peace, Swansea Co. Borough Coun., 1960-64. Legal Assoc. MTPI. *Recreations:* history, music, model railways. *Address:* Holly Bank House, Main Street, Halton, Runcorn, Ches. *T:* Runcorn 3902.

**BANWELL, Sir (George) Harold,** Kt 1955; Chairman, National Citizens Advice Bureaux Council, since 1961; Deputy Chairman, Commission for the New Towns; Member: Parliamentary Boundary Commission of England; Local Government Advisory Panel, Ministry of Overseas Development; *b* 11 Dec. 1900; *yr s* of late Edward and Marion Banwell, Whitstable, Kent; *m* 1924, Kate Mary, *d* of late Rev. A. B. Bull, Durham; two *s* three *d*. *Educ:* Tankerton Coll., Kent. Admitted Solicitor, 1922; articled to Town Clerk, Canterbury; Asst Solicitor: West Hartlepool; Cumberland County Council; Sheffield City Council; Dep. Town Clerk, Norwich, 1929-32; Town Clerk, Lincoln, 1932-41; Clerk of the County Council of Lincoln, Parts of Kesteven, 1941-44; Sec., Association of Municipal Corporations, 1944-Oct. 1962. Alderman, Lincoln City Council. Chairman: Cttee on Placing of Management of Contracts for Building and Civil Engineering Work, 1962-64; Congregational Church in England and Wales, 1966-69; Member: Gen. Adv. Council of BBC, 1961-64; Nat. Incomes Commn, 1962-65. *Address:* 2 Vicars' Court, Lincoln. *T:* Lincoln 28869. *Clubs:* National Liberal, Royal Commonwealth Society.

**BANWELL, Godwin Edward,** CBE 1955; MC 1917 and Bar 1918; Chief Constable of Cheshire 1946-63; *b* 1897; *s* of Edward and Rose Banwell, Polegate, Sussex; *m* 1st, 1924, Kathleen Frances Cole (*d* 1939); 2nd, 1940, Gladys Lilian Banwell; three *s* one *d*. *Educ:* Merchant Taylors' Sch., London. Leics Regiment, TA, 1916-19; Indian Police, Burma, 1920-38; Regional Officer, Min. of Home Security, 1939-41; Actg Inspector of Constabulary, 1941-42; Chief Constable of East Riding of Yorks, 1942-46. King's Police Medal, 1931. *Address:* Sunnycroft, Manley, via Warrington, Cheshire. *Club:* National Liberal.

**BANWELL, Sir Harold;** *see* Banwell, Sir G. H.

**BARBADOS, Bishop of,** since 1960; **Rt. Rev. Edward Lewis Evans,** BD, MTh; *b* 11 Dec. 1904; *s* of Edward Foley Evans and Mary (*née* Walker). *Educ:* St Anselm's, Croydon; Tonbridge Sch.; Bishops' Coll., Cheshunt. BD London 1935, MTh 1938. Deacon, 1937; priest 1938; Curate of St Mary's, Prittlewell, Essex, 1937-39; Warden of St Peter's, Theological Coll., Jamaica, 1940-49; Rector, Kingston Parish Church, Jamaica, 1949-52; Rector of Woodford and Craigton, 1952-57; Archdeacon of Surrey, Jamaica, 1950-57; Bishop Suffragan of Kingston, 1957-60. *Address:* Bishopscourt, St Michael 16, Barbados. *T:* 93139.

**BARBER, Alan Theodore,** MA (Oxon); Headmaster of Ludgrove Preparatory School, Wokingham, Berks, since 1937; *b* 17 June 1905; *s* of Harold Priestman Barber, Todwick House, Todwick, Yorks; *m* 1937, Dorothy Shaw; one *s* two *d*. *Educ:* Shrewsbury Sch.; Queen's Coll., Oxford. BA 1929; Triple Blue, captained cricket and football XIs, Oxford; captained Yorks County Cricket XI, 1929 and 1930; played football regularly for Corinthians. Asst master, Ludgrove, 1930. *Recreations:* golf, cricket, Eton Fives. *Address:* Ludgrove, Wokingham, Berks. *T:* Wokingham 126. *Clubs:* Sports, MCC; Berkshire Golf (Bagshot).

**BARBER, Rt. Hon. Anthony Perrinott Lysberg,** PC 1963; TD; MP (C) Altrincham since Feb. 1965; Chancellor of the Exchequer since 1970; *b* 4 July 1920; *s* of John Barber, CBE, Doncaster; *m* 1950, Jean Patricia, *d* of Milton Asquith, Wentbridge, Yorks; two *d*. *Educ:* Retford Grammar Sch.; Oriel Coll., Oxford Univ. (PPE, MA). Served War of 1939-45: commnd in Army (Dunkirk); seconded to RAF as pilot, 1940-45 (despatches; prisoner of war, 1942-45, took Law Degree with 1st Class Hons while POW, escaped from Poland, prisoner of the Russians). Barrister-at-law, Inner Temple, 1948 (Inner Temple Scholarship). MP (C) Doncaster, 1951-64; PPS to the Under-Sec. of State for Air, 1952-55; Asst Whip, 1955-57; a Lord Comr of the Treasury, 1957-58; Parl. Private Sec. to the Prime Minister, 1958-59; Economic Sec. to the Treasury, 1959-62; Financial Sec. to the Treasury, 1962-63; Minister of Health and Mem. of the Cabinet, 1963-64; Chancellor of the Duchy of Lancaster, June-July 1970. Chm., Conservative Party Organisation, 1967-70. *Address:* 15 Montpelier Square, SW7. *T:* 01-589 9517; Wentbridge, near Pontefract, Yorks. *T:* Wentbridge 311. *Club:* Carlton.

**BARBER, Elizabeth;** *see* Barber, M. E.

**BARBER, Sir Herbert (William),** Kt 1952; *b* 8 Nov. 1887; *m* 1912, Annie Nora Heys (*d* 1953); one *s*. *Educ:* Salford Technical Coll. Mem. of Southport County Borough Council, 1931-62; Mayor, 1937-39 and 1943-44; only Freeman of Southport, 1962. *Recreations:* Rugby Union football and cricket. *Address:* 40 Hesketh Road, Southport, Lancs. *T:* Southport 4600.

**BARBER, Prof. Horace Newton,** FAA 1958; FRS 1963; Professor of Botany, University of New South Wales, since 1964; *b* Warburton, Cheshire, 26 May 1914; *s* of H. M. Barber, Bowdon, Cheshire; *m* 1946, Nancy P., *d* of late Mr and Mrs F. J. O'Grady, Sydney, NSW; one *s* one *d*. *Educ:* Manchester Grammar Sch.; Emmanuel Coll., Cambridge. MA Cantab. 1941; PhD London 1942; ScD, Cantab, 1963. Scientific Officer, John Innes Inst., London, 1936-40; Scientific Officer, TRE, 1940-45. Flt-Lieut (Hon.) RAFVR, 1943-45. Lecturer, Univ. of Sydney, 1946-47. Rockefeller Foundation Fellow at California Inst. of Technology, 1953-54; Professor of Botany, Univ. of Tasmania, 1947-63. Royal Society Vis. Prof., Ibadan Univ., Nigeria, 1967. *Publications:* Papers in scientific jls. *Recreations:* wandering around Australia and the rest of the world. *Address:* University of NSW, PO Box 1, Kensington, NSW 2033, Australia. *T:* Sydney 663-0351. *Club:* Tasmanian (Hobart).

**BARBER, Rear-Adm. John L.;** *see* Lee-Barber.

**BARBER, John Norman Romney,** Director, British Leyland Motor Corp. Ltd, since 1968; *b* 22 April 1919; *s* of George Ernest and Gladys Eleanor Barber; *m* 1941, Babette Chalu; one *s*. *Educ:* Westcliff. Served with Army, 1939-46 (Capt.). Min. of Supply, 1946-55 (Princ.). Joined Ford Motor Co. Ltd, 1955, Finance Dir, 1962; Chm., Ford Motor Credit Co. Ltd, 1963; Dir, Henry Ford & Son Ltd, Cork, 1963; Dir Autolite Motor Products Ltd, 1963; Finance Dir, AEI Ltd, 1965; Chm., Telephone Cables Ltd, 1967; Finance Dir, Leyland Motor Corp. Ltd, 1968. Mem., Royal Commn on Medical Educn, 1965-68; Chm., Adv. Cttee to BoT on Investment Grants, 1967-68. FBIM; Mem. Council BIM, 1967-. *Publications:* papers on management subjects in various jls. *Recreations:* motor sport, forestry, photography. *Address:* Copthall Green House, Upshire, Essex. *T:* Waltham Cross 23241. *Clubs:* British Automobile Racing, British Racing and Sports Car.

**BARBER, (Mary) Elizabeth,** OBE 1968; MA; General Secretary, Society of Authors, since 1963; *b* 14 March 1911; *yr d* of Frederic Viccars and Margaret Filmer Barber; unmarried. *Educ:* St Swithun's Sch., Winchester; Somerville Coll., Oxford. Called to the Bar, Gray's Inn, 1935. Asst-Sec., then Sec., Society of Authors, 1936-63. *Publications:* Contrib. on copyright and allied subjects to British and foreign books and periodicals. *Address:* 84 Drayton Gardens, SW10.

**BARBER, Philip Stanley,** CBE 1949; DSO 1919; MC; Director of Edward Barber & Son, Ltd, London, EC4; *b* Ravenscroft, South Norwood, Surrey, 12 June 1895; 2nd *s* of Herbert H. Barber; *m* 1921, Iris, 2nd *d* of late E. C. S. Baker, CIE, OBE; one *s* (and *er s* killed as Pilot Royal Air Force, War of 1939-45). *Educ:* King's Sch., Canterbury. Served European War, 1914-19; Private, HAC 1914; Commission, Dorset Regt, Dec. 1914; General Staff, 1916; Brigade Major, 1917-19 (DSO, MC and bar, despatches five times). *Publication:* History of the 50th Infantry Brigade, 1914-19. *Address:* Brooks House, 48 Upper Thames St, EC4. *Club:* Bath.

**BARBER, Samuel;** Composer; *b* West Chester, Pennsylvania, 9 March 1910; *s* of Samuel Leroy Barber and Marguerite McCleod Beatty; unmarried. *Educ:* Curtis Institute of Music, Philadelphia. Compositions performed by all leading American orchestras and by many European orchestras; Conductors include Toscanini, Koussevitzky, Walter, etc. Has conducted own works in Prague, Vienna, London, Three Choirs Festival (Hereford, 1946), etc. Member: National Institute of Art and Letters, USA; American Society of Composers, Authors and Publishers. *Compositions:* First Symphony, 1936; Violin Concerto, 1941; Second Symphony, 1944; Capricorn Concerto (flute, oboe, trumpet and strings), 1944; Cello Concerto, 1946. Overture to The School for Scandal, 1932; Music for a Scene from Shelley, 1933; Adagio for Strings, 1936; First Essay for Orchestra, 1942; Ballet Suite, Medea, 1946; Knoxville: Summer of 1915 (for soprano and orchestra), 1947; Score for A Blue Rose (ballet), 1957; Vanessa (opera), 1958; also songs, piano pieces, chamber music, choruses. *Address:* Capricorn, Mt Kisco, NY, USA.

**BARBER, Sir William (Francis),** 2nd Bt *cr* 1960; TD; JP; *b* 20 Nov. 1905; *yr* and *o surv. s* of Sir Philip Barber, 1st Bt, DSO, TD, JP, DL, and of Beatrice Mary (*d* 1962), *d* of Lieut-Col W. Ingersoll Merritt; *S* father, 1961; *m* 1936, Diana Constance, *d* of late Lieut-Col Thomas Owen Lloyd, CMG, Minard Castle, Argyll; one *s* one *d*. *Educ:* Eton Coll,. South Nottinghamshire Hussars Yeomanry (Commnd, 1924). Royal Horse Artillery; served in Palestine, Egypt, North Africa, NW

Europe; Lieut-Col 1947, JP Notts, 1952. Hon. Col, South Nottinghamshire Hussars Yeomanry, 1961-66. High Sheriff, Notts., 1964. *Heir: s* Thomas David Barber, *b* 18 Nov. 1937. *Address:* Lamb Close, Eastwood, Notts; Dunmaglass, Aberarder, Invernessshire.

**BARBERTON, Ivan Graham Mitford-;** ARCA (Sculptor); ARBS; CLJ; *b* 1 Feb 1896; *e s* of late Henry Mitford Barberton and Mary, *d* of Thomas H Bowker, MLA; *m* 1st, 1921, Cecile, *d* of late T. T. Hoole, Atherstone, Cape Province; two *s* one *d*; 2nd, 1939, Pamela, *d* of Harold Gibbs, Romford, Essex; one *s* one *d*. *Educ:* St Andrew's Coll., Grahamstown. Emigrated to British East Africa, 1912; served German East African Campaign, 1915-19; presented the Barberton Duiker, a new antelope from Mt Elgon, Kenya, to the British Museum; first studied art in Grahamstown, 1919; entered Royal College of Art, 1923; Diploma, ARCA; studied in Italy, 1926, and later in Paris, returning to Kenya, 1927; settled in Cape Town, 1930; has various sculptural works in leading South African galleries. *Publications:* The Barbers of the Peak; The Bowkers of Tharfield; Ivan Mitford-Barberton, Sculptor; Some Frontier Families. *Address:* Castleton, Hout Bay, Cape, Republic of South Africa.

**BARBOUR, George Brown;** MA, PhD, FRSE, FRGS, FGS, FGSAm; Professor Emeritus of Geology, University of Cincinnati; *b* 22 Aug. 1890; *s* of A. H. F. Barbour, MD, and Margaret Nelson Brown; *m* 1920, Dorothy, *d* of Dr R. L. Dickinson of New York; three *s*. *Educ:* Merchiston; Marburg Univ.; Edinburgh Univ.; St John's Coll., Cambridge; Columbia Univ., NY. Active Service, FAU and RFA, Sep. 1914-Jan. 1919. Prof. of Applied Geology, Peking Univ., 1920-22; Head of Dept of Geology, Pelyang Univ., Tientsin, 1922-23; Prof. of Geology, Yenching Univ., Peiping, 1923-32; Lecturer, Columbia Univ., 1928-29; Univ. of Cincinnati, 1932-33; Visiting Physiographer, Cenozoic Laboratory, Peiping, 1934; Visiting Prof., Stanford Univ., 1935; Hon. Lecturer, London Univ., 1934-37; Dean of McMicken Coll. of Arts and Science, 1938-58. Academic Coordinator US Army Air-Force College Training Programme, 1943-45. Member Royal Society of South Africa; Hon. Member Société belge de Géologie, de Paléontologie et d'Hydrologie, 1937; Corresp. Fellow R. Belgian Geog. Soc., 1946; Corresp. Member, Geological Survey of China; Foreign Member, Geolog. Soc. of Finland; Member Soc. géol. de France; Geologist, Univ. of California African Expedition, 1947; Pres. Ohio Academy of Science, 1948-49; Corresp. Mem. Ital. Inst. of Hum. Paleontology, 1955. RGS Gill Memorial Award, 1937; Viking Fund Award, Wenner-Gren Foundation, 1951, 1954. Visiting Professor, Duke Univ., 1961-62, Univ. of Louisville, Ky, 1964-65. *Publications:* Geology of the Kalgan Area; Physiographic History of the Yangtze; In the Field with Teilhard de Chardin; Geological Reports and papers in scientific jls. *Recreations:* mountaineering, music. *Address:* University of Cincinnati, Cincinnati, Ohio 45221, USA; 3521 Cornell Place, Cincinnati, Ohio 45220. *TA:* University, Cincinnati. *Club:* Athenæum.

**BARBOUR, Walworth;** US Ambassador to Israel since 1961; *b* 4 June 1908; *s* of Samuel Lewis Barbour and Clara Hammond; unmarried. *Educ:* Harvard Coll. USA. Vice Consul, Naples, 1932; Athens, 1933; Baghdad, 1936; Sofia, 1939; Dip. Sec., Cairo, 1941; Athens, 1944; Dept. of State, Washington, 1945-49; Minister, Moscow, 1949-51; Dept. of State, Washington, 1951-55; Deputy Asst Sec. of State for European Affairs, 1954-55; American Minister, London, 1955-61. *Recreation:* golf. *Address:* American Embassy, Tel Aviv, Israel. *Clubs:* White's, Travellers', American; Chevy Chase (Md, USA).

**BARCLAY, Alexander,** CBE 1957; ARCS, FRIC; Keeper, Department of Chemistry and Photography, Science Museum, S Kensington, 1938-59; retired. *b* 25 July 1896; *o s* of late Alexander Barclay; *m* 1921, Irene Margaret, *y d* of late Frank Carrington Falkner, Wisbech. *Educ:* Berkhamsted Sch.; Royal College of Science. Served European War with Special Gas Brigade, RE, 1916-17; invalided, 1917; Postal Censorship Research Dept, 1918; entered Science Museum, 1921; Asst Keeper, 1930; Board of Education, 1940 and 1943; Postal Censorship, 1944-45. Hon. Member Royal Photographic Soc.; Mem. of Nat. Film Library Cttee, British Film Institute, 1938-55. *Publications:* Official Handbooks to the Chemistry Collections, Science Museum, 1927-37; various papers in scientific journals. *Address:* Towers End, Walberswick, Southwold, Suffolk. *T:* Southwold 2146.

**BARCLAY, Christopher Francis Robert,** CMG 1967; Assistant Secretary, Civil Service Department, since 1969; *b* 8 June 1919; *s* of late Captain Robert Barclay, RA (retired) and late Annie Douglas Dowdeswell Barclay (*née* Davidson); *m* 1st, 1950, Clare Justice Troutbeck (marr. diss., 1962); two *s* one *d*; 2nd, 1962, Diana Elizabeth Goodman; one *s* one *d*. *Educ:* Eton Coll.; Magdalen Coll., Oxford. 2nd Lieut The Rifle Bde, 1940; Capt. 1942; Major 1943; served in Egypt; Middle East Centre of Arab Studies, Jerusalem, 1944-45; Political Officer, Northern Iraq, 1945; Asst Information Officer, Brit. Embassy, Baghdad, 1946. Joined Foreign Office, 1946; Second Sec., British Embassy, Cairo, 1947; First Sec., Foreign Office, 1950; Brit. Embassy, Bonn, 1953; FO, 1956; Regional Information Officer, Beirut, 1960; FO, 1961; Counsellor and Head of Information Research Dept, 1962-66; Head of Personnel Dept (Training and General), FCO (formerly DSAO), 1967-69. *Recreations:* fishing; travel. *Address:* 88 Redcliffe Gardens, SW10. *T:* 01-373 1677.

**BARCLAY, Sir Colville Herbert Sanford,** 14th Bt, *cr* 1668; Painter; *b* 7 May 1913; *s* of late Rt Hon. Sir Colville Adrian de Rune Barclay, 3rd *s* of 11th Bt, and Sarita Enriqueta, *d* of late Herbert Ward; *S* uncle, 1930; *m* 1949, Rosamond Grant Renton Elliott; three *s*. *Educ:* Eton, Trinity Coll., Oxford. Third Sec., Diplomatic Service, 1937-41; enlisted in Navy, Nov. 1941; Sub-Lieut RNVR 1942; Lieut 1943; Lieut Commander 1945; demobilised, 1946. Exhibitor: Royal Academy, RBA, London Group, Bradford City and Brighton Art Galleries. Chm. Royal London Homoeopathic Hospital, 1970 (Vice-Chm., 1961-65). *Recreations:* ski-ing, gardening, plant-hunting. *Heir: s* Robert Colraine Barclay, *b* 12 Feb. 1950. *Address:* Pitshill, Petworth, Sussex. *T:* Lodsworth 341. *Club:* St James'.

**BARCLAY, Brig. Cyril Nelson,** CBE 1945; DSO 1940; Cameronians (Scottish Rifles); free-lance writer; Military Adviser and Contributor to the Encyclopædia Britannica; *b* 20 Jan. 1896; *o s* of late E. J. Barclay; *m* 1934, Margaret, *d* of G. Roberts; one *d*. *Educ:* Thanet Coll., St Peter's, Kent; Elstow Sch., Beds. Commissioned in Cameronians (Scottish Rifles), 1915; served European War, 1914-18, France and Mesopotamia; 3rd Afghan War, 1919; War of 1939-45: Dunkirk, Holland, Germany and South-East Asia; retired, 1946. Editor, Army Quarterly, 1950-66; Jt Editor, Brassey's Annual, 1950-69. *Publications:* History The Cameronians (Scottish Rifles),

1933-46; Part-Time Farmer; History of the London Scottish, 1939-45; History of the Royal Northumberland Fusiliers in the Second World War; History of the 3rd QAO Gurkha Rifles, 1927-47; The New Warfare; History of the Duke of Wellington's Regiment, 1919-52; The First Commonwealth Division, Korea, 1950-53; Against Great Odds; History of the 53rd (Welsh) Division in the Second World War; History of the Sherwood Foresters, 1919-57; History of the 16th/5th The Queen's Royal Lancers, 1963; On Their Shoulders, 1964; Battle 1066, 1966; Armistice 1918, 1968. *Recreation:* bridge. *Address:* 44 Painters Field, St Cross, Winchester, Hants. *T:* Winchester 4232. *Club:* Army and Navy.

**BARCLAY, Sir Roderick (Edward),** GCVO 1966 (KCVO 1957; CVO 1953); KCMG 1955 (CMG 1948); Chairman, Barclays Bank SA, since 1970 (Director since 1969); Director, Slough Estates, since 1969; *b* 22 Feb. 1909; *s* of J. Gurney Barclay and the late Mrs Barclay; *m* 1934, Jean Cecil, *d* of late Sir Hugh Gladstone; one *s* three *d. Educ:* Harrow; Trinity Coll., Cambridge. Entered Diplomatic Service, 1932. Served at HM Embassies at Brussels, Paris, Washington and in FO; Counsellor in FO 1946; Principal Private Sec. to Sec. of State for Foreign Affairs, 1949-51; Asst Under-Sec. of State, 1951; Dep. Under-Sec. of State, 1953-56; HM Ambassador to Denmark, 1956-60; Adviser on European Trade Questions, Foreign Office, and Dep. Under-Sec. of State for Foreign Affairs, 1960-63; Ambassador to Belgium, 1963-69. Knight Grand Cross of the Dannebrog (Denmark) and of the Couronne (Belgium). *Recreations:* shooting, fishing. *Address:* Great White End, Latimer, Bucks. *T:* Little Chalfont 2050. *Club:* Brooks's.

**BARCLAY, Theodore David;** banker; *b* 6 Sept. 1906; *e s* of Rev. Canon David Barclay and Loetitia Caroline Rowley, *d* of late Rt Rev. Rowley Hill, Bishop of Sodor and Man; *m* 1934, Anne Millard, *d* of late T. W. M. Bennett, Hatfield; two *s* one *d. Educ:* Harrow; Trinity Coll., Cambridge. Entered Barclays Bank Ltd, 1927; Local Director at 54 Lombard Street, 1934, Director of the Bank, 1948; Director: the British Linen Bank; Sun Alliance and London Insurance Ltd (former Chm.); The Bank of Scotland. High Sheriff of Suffolk, 1959. *Recreations:* shooting and fishing. *Address:* Desnage Lodge, Higham, Bury St Edmunds. *T:* Kentford 254. *Clubs:* Boodle's; New (Edinburgh).

**BARCLAY, Prof. William,** CBE 1969; Professor of Divinity and Biblical Criticism, University of Glasgow, since 1963; *b* Wick, 1907; *m* Barbara Gillespie; one *s* two *d. Educ:* Dalziel High Sch., Motherwell; Univs of Glasgow and Marburg; Trinity Coll., Glasgow. Minister, Trinity Church, Renfrew, 1933-46; Lectr in New Testament Language and Literature, Univ. of Glasgow, 1946-63. External Examiner: Edinburgh, St Andrews, Aberdeen, Leeds. Lectures: Bruce, 1935; Croall, 1955; Kerr, 1956; Baird, 1969-70; Sir David Owen Evans, Aberystwyth, 1969; James Reid Memorial, 1969, 1970. Member: Joint Cttee, New English Bible; Soc. of New Testament Studies; Soc. of Old Testament Studies. Chm., Glasgow YMCA; Hon. Vice-Pres., Boys Bde. *Publications:* Ambassador for Christ, 1950; And Jesus Said, 1953; The Daily Study Bible, 1953-59; And He had Compassion on Them, 1955; A New Testament Word Book, 1955; The Mind of Paul, 1957; Letters to the Seven Churches, 1957; More New Testament Words, 1958; Educational Ideas in the Ancient World, 1959; The Plain Man's Book of Prayers, 1959; The Master's Men, 1959; The Mind of Jesus, 1960; The Promise of the Spirit, 1960; Crucified and Crowned, 1961; Flesh and Spirit, 1962; Jesus as they saw Him, 1962; More Prayers for the Plain Man, 1962; Prayers for the Young People, 1962; Many Witnesses, One Lord, 1963; Turning to God, 1963; The All-Sufficient Christ, 1964; New Testament Words, 1964; The Plain Man Looks at the Lord's Prayer, 1964; Prayers for the Christian Year, 1964; Prayers for Help and Healing, 1968; Translator, The New Testament: vol. I, The Gospels and the Acts of the Apostles, 1968. Contribs to learned journals. *Address:* 8 Berridale Avenue, Cathcart, Glasgow, S4. *T:* 041-637 4917. *Clubs:* Royal Over-Seas League; Royal Scottish Automobile (Glasgow).

**BARCLAY, Mrs William;** *see* Minton, Y. F.

**BARCLAY-SMITH, (Ida) Phyllis,** MBE 1958; Ornithologist; 2nd *d* of late Prof. Edward Barclay-Smith, MD. *Educ:* Church House Sch., Worthing; Blackheath High Sch.; King's Coll., London. Asst Sec. Royal Society for the Protection of Birds, 1924-35; Asst Sec. Internat. Cttee for Bird Preservation, 1935-46; Foreign Office, 1939-42; Sec. to Business Manager, Bristol Aeroplane Shadow Factory, Corsham, 1942-43; Specialist Local Welfare Officer (Transport Workers), SW Region, Min. of Labour, 1943-45; Hon. Sec. British Ornithologists' Union, 1945-51; Member: Home Office Advisory Cttee on Wild Birds, 1948-53; Exec. Bd of Internat. Union for Protection of Nature, 1950-56; Council, Royal Geographical Soc., 1970-. Sec. Internat. Council for Bird Preservation, 1946-; Editor Avicultural Magazine, 1939; Jt Hon. Sec. Internat. Wildfowl Research Bureau, 1948-69, Sec. of Honour, 1969-; Hon. Sec. Advisory Cttee on Oil Pollution of the Sea, 1952-; Organising Sec., Internat. Conferences on Prevention of Oil Pollution of the Sea: London, 1953; Copenhagen, 1959; Rome, 1968; Mem. Home Office Advisory Cttee on Protection of Birds for England and Wales, 1954-; Vice-Pres. Commn on Migratory Gamebirds of Conseil Internat. de la Chasse, 1950-61, Hon. Vice-Pres. 1965-; Vice-President: British Ornithologists Union 1957-60; Agricultural Soc., 1970-. Hon. Member: Avicultural Soc.; British Falconers' Club; Fauna Preservation Soc.; Corresp. Mem. Bavarian, German, Netherlands, S African Ornithological Unions and Hungarian Inst. of Ornithology. Gold Medal, Sveriges Djurskyddsforenigars Riksforbund, 1954; Isidore Geoffroy St Hilaire Gold Medal of Société Nationale de Protection de la Nature et d'Acclimatation de France, 1963. Silver Medals: Soc. d'Acclimatation de France, 1951; Royal Society for the Protection of Birds, 1951; V. v. Heidenstams Fond (Sweden), 1958; President's Medal, Avicultural Soc., 1960. Coronation Medal, 1953. *Publications:* British Birds on Lake, River and Stream, 1939; (with Hugh Pollard) British and American Game Birds, 1939; Garden Birds, 1945; A Book of Ducks, 1951; Woodland Birds, 1945; (trans. from German) The Bird (by Gertrude Hess), 1951; (trans. from French) Birds of the World (by P. Barruel) 1954; (trans. form French) Water Birds with Webbed Feet (by P. Géroudet), 1965. *Recreations:* bird-watching; dancing; travelling. *Address:* 51 Warwick Avenue, W9. *T:* 01-286 3006.

**BARCROFT, Prof. Henry,** FRS 1953; MA; MD; FRCP; Professor of Physiology, St Thomas's Hospital Medical School, London, since 1948; Hon. Consultant, St Thomas' Hospital; a Wellcome Trustee, since 1966; *b* 18 Oct. 1904; *s* of late Sir Joseph Barcroft, CBE, FRS; *m* 1933, Bridget Mary, *d* of late A. S. Ramsey; three *s* one *d. Educ:* Marlborough Coll.; King's Coll. Cambridge; Exhibitioner, 1923. Natural

Science Tripos Class I, Parts I and II; Harold Fry and George Henry Lewis studentships at Cambridge, 1927-29; Gedge Prize, 1930; Harmsworth Scholar, St Mary's Hospital, London, 1929-32; Lectr in Physiology, University Coll., London, 1932-35; Dunville Prof. of Physiology, Queen's Univ., Belfast, 1935-48, Arts and Gale Lectr, RCS, 1945; Louis Bertram Abrahams Lectr, RCP, 1960; Visiting Prof., Univ. of Adelaide, 1964. Chairman: Editorial Bd, Monographs of Physiological Soc., 1957-65; Research Defence Soc., 1968-. Hon. Member: Academic Adv. Cttee, Loughborough Coll. of Technology, 1964-66; Société Française d'Angiologie; Japanese Coll. of Angiology; Czechoslovak Med. Soc. J. E. Purkinje. Hon. DSc Univ. Western Australia, 1963; Hon. MD Leopold-Franzens Univ., Innsbruck, 1969. Pro meritis médaille in silver, Karl Franzens Univ., Graz. *Publications:* (with H. J. C. Swan) Sympathetic Control of Human Blood Vessels, 1953; papers in the Journal of Physiology. *Recreations:* sailing and golf. *Address:* 44 Wood Lane, N6. *T:* 01-340 2338. *Club:* Athenæum.

**BARD, Dr Basil Joseph Asher,** CBE 1968; Member since 1956 and Chief Executive, Department of Applied Science, since 1965, National Research Development Corporation; *b* London, 20 Aug. 1914; *s* of Abram Isaac Bard and Anita Bard; *m* 1942, Ena Dora Birk; three *s*. *Educ:* Owen's Sch.; RCS (Imperial Coll.). BSc(Chem.) 1934, DIC (Chem. Engrg and Fuel Technology) 1935, PhD (Chem. Constitution of Coal) 1936, London; Bar Finals (1st cl. hons) and Studentship, Coun. of Legal Educn, 1937; called to Bar, Gray's Inn (Birkenhead and William Shaw Schol.), 1938. Practised at Bar, 1938-39; Legal Dept, Coal Commn, 1939-41; Explosives Prodn Dept, Min. of Supply, 1941-43; Materials Dept, Min. of Aircraft Production, 1943-45; Depts of Industrial Res., Educn, Design, etc, FBI, 1945-49; NRDC, 1950-; in turn, Commercial Man., Techn. Dir, Exec. Dir, and Chief Exec., Dept of Applied Science; Mem. Bd, 1956. Vice-Pres., UK Br., Licensing Execs Soc.; Chm., Dracone Devts Ltd; Dir, Technograph Printed Circuits Ltd; has served on various Govt Cttees; ARCS; MInstF; FInstD. *Publications:* (ed) Industry and Research, 1947; various articles on science, technology, patents, industry, commerce and their inter-relationships. *Recreations:* music, bridge, chess, social life. *Address:* 24 The Ridgeway, Finchley, N3. *T:* 01-346 1160; NRDC, Kingsgate House, Victoria Street, SW1. *T:* 01-828 3400.

**BARDEEN, Prof. John;** Professor of Physics and Electrical Engineering, University of Illinois, since 1951; *b* Madison, Wisconsin, 23 May 1908; *s* of Dr Charles R. Bardeen and Althea Bardeen (*née* Harmer); *m* 1938, Jane Maxwell; two *s* one *d*. *Educ:* Univ. of Wisconsin; Princeton Univ. BS 1928, MS 1929, Univ. of Wisconsin; PhD 1936, Princeton Univ. Geophysicist, Gulf Research and Development Corp., Pittsburgh, Pa, 1930-33; Junior Fellow, Soc. of Fellows, Harvard Univ., 1935-38; Asst Prof. of Physics, Univ. of Minnesota, 1938-41; Physicist, Naval Ordnance Laboratory, Washington, DC, 1941-45; Research Physicist, Bell Telephone Laboratories, Murray Hill, NJ, 1945-51. Holds hon. doctorates. Nobel Prize for Physics (with W. H. Brattain and W. Shockley), 1956; National Medal of Science, 1965. *Publications:* articles on solid state physics, including semi-conductors, metals, superconductivity in Physical Review and other periodicals and books. *Address:* 55 Greencroft, Champaign, Illinois, USA. *T:* Champaign 352-6497.

**BARDSLEY, Rt. Rev. Cuthbert Killick Norman;** *see* Coventry, Bishop of.

**BARENBOIM, Daniel;** pianist and conductor; *b* Buenos Aires, 15 Nov. 1942; *s* of Enrique Barenboim and Aida Barenboim (*née* Schuster); *m* 1967, Jacqueline du Pré, *qv*. *Educ:* Santa Cecilia Acad., Rome; studied with his father; coached by Edwin Fischer, Nadia Boulanger, and Igor Markevitch. Pianist with: Israel Philharmonic Orchestra, 1953-; Royal Philharmonic Orchestra, 1956; Berlin Philharmonic Orchestra, 1963-65; NY Philharmonic Orchestra, 1964; tours include: Australia, 1958, 1962; South America, 1960; Far East, 1962. Regular appearances at Edinburgh, Lucerne, Prague and Salzburg Festivals. Beethoven Medal, 1958; Paderewski Medal, 1963; subsequently other awards. *Address:* c/o Israel Philharmonic Orchestra, Tel Aviv, Israel; c/o Harold Holt Ltd, 122 Wigmore Street, W1.

**BARFF, Stafford (Edward Douglas),** OBE 1954; HM Diplomatic Service, retired; *b* 26 Dec. 1909; *s* of late Capt. Arthur Douglas Barff, RN, OBE and Ellen Barff; *m* 1937, Hélène Iost, Geneva; no *c*. *Educ:* Highfield Sch., Liphook, Hants; Brentwood Coll., Victoria, BC, Canada. Bank of Montreal and Vancouver Stock Exchange, 1928-30; returned to England, 1931; employed by British Gas Light Co. and Philips Lamps Ltd, 1932-39. Civil Defence forces, 1939-40. Min. of Information, 1940-45. Asst-Dir, British Information Services, Chicago, 1945-46, Dir, 1947-56; UK High Commission, New Delhi, 1956-58; First Sec., British Embassy, Washington, DC, 1958-60; Dir, Press Division, British Information Services, New York, 1960-62; temp. appt, Brussels, 1962; Consul, St Louis, 1962-64; Consul-Gen., New Orleans, 1964-69. *Recreations:* fishing; boating and swimming; reading; gardening. *Address:* 15 Palmeira Avenue, Hove, Sussex. *T:* Brighton 735164. *Clubs:* Travellers'; Pickwick, Plimsoll, (New Orleans).

**BARFOOT, Most Rev. Walter Foster,** DD (Hon.) 1937; DD (Lambeth), 1958; Primate of All Canada, 1951-Dec. 1958; *b* 17 Oct. 1893; *m* 1942. *Educ:* Wycliffe Coll., Toronto, BA 1923; Univ. of Toronto, MA 1930. Deacon, 1922; priest 1923; Tutor at Em. Coll., Saskatoon, 1926-33, Prof., 1933-34; Prof. of St John's Coll., Winnipeg, 1934-35. Warden, 1935-41; Canon of St John's Cathedral, Winnipeg, 1934-41; Bishop of Edmonton 1941-51, Archbishop, 1951-53; Archbishop and Metropolitan of Rupert's Land, 1953-60; retired Dec. 1960. Served European War, 1915-19. Capt. 2nd Royal Sussex Regt (Croix de Guerre). *Address:* 14837 Prospect Avenue, White Rock, British Columbia.

**BARFORD, Edward,** MC 1918; Landowner; *b* 1898; *m* 1st, 1928, Hon. Grace Lowrey Stanley (from whom he obtained a divorce, 1940), *yr d* of 1st and last Baron Ashfield; one *s* two *d*; 2nd, 1944, Mrs June Johnstone (marr. diss. 1963); one *s*; 3rd, 1964, Hon. Mrs Marian Hubbard (separated, 1968), *er d* of 1st and last Baron Ashfield. *Educ:* Rugby. Enlisted, European War, 1915 (wounded twice, despatches twice), Acting Major 1918. Founded Aveling-Barford Ltd, 1933; Chm., 1933-68. Under-writing Member of Lloyd's. *Address:* Rowney Priory, Ware, Herts. *T:* Dane End 222; 48 Grosvenor Square, W1. *T:* 01-629 9560. *Clubs:* Buck's, Boodle's.

**BARFORD, Sir Leonard,** Kt 1967; Chief Inspector of Taxes, Board of Inland Revenue, since 1964; Commissioner of Inland Revenue since 1970; *b* 1 Aug. 1908; *s* of William and Ada

Barford, Finsbury Park; *m* 1939, Betty Edna Crichton, Plymouth; two *s*. *Educ:* Dame Alice Owen's Sch.; St Catharine's Coll., Cambridge Univ. (Exhibitioner in History). Asst Inspector of Taxes, 1930; Administrative Staff Coll., Henley, 1948; President, Assoc. of HM Inspectors of Taxes, 1951-53; Principal Inspector of Taxes, 1953; Senior Principal Inspector of Taxes, 1957; Deputy Chief Inspector, 1960. *Publication:* (jointly) Essay on Management in Tax Offices, 1950. *Recreations:* badminton, tennis, chess, bridge. *Address:* Harley House, 79 Sutton Road, Seaford, Sussex. *T:* Seaford 3364. *Club:* Civil Service.

**BARGE, Lieut-Col Kenneth,** DSO 1918; MC; psc; DL; JP; late 17th Cavalry Indian Army; *b* 1883; *s* of Robert Henry Barge; *m* 1915, Debonnaire Eva Ruth (*d* 1959), *o c* of late Maj.-Gen. Sir Herbert Mansfield, KCB; one *s* two *d* (and one *s* killed in action). *Educ:* Larchfield; Trinity Coll., Glenalmond. Served in S Africa with 3rd Argyll and Sutherland Highlanders, 1901 (Queen's medal two clasps); Cameronians, India, 1903-5; joined 17th Cavalry Indian Army, 1905; served European War, 1914-18 (despatches thrice, MC, DSO); The Order of the Serbian White Eagle while serving in the Balkans at the end of the War; ADC, OC Northern Army, 1909-10; ADC, C-in-C India, 1911-12; Adjutant, Imperial Cadet Corps, 1913-14; GSO3, Brigade Major, GSO2, GSO1, 1914-18; retired, 1922; Mem. of Queen's Body Guard for Scotland, Royal Company of Archers. *Recreation:* active farmer still! *Address:* Armadale, Rhu, Dunbartonshire. *T:* Rhu 202. *TA:* Rhu; Evanachan Farm, Otter Ferry, Argyll. *T:* Kilfinan 214.

**BARHAM, Rt. Rev. E(dward) Lawrence;** an Assistant Bishop of Southwark since 1967; Incumbent of Emmanuel Church, Wimbledon, since 1967; *b* 25 June 1901; *s* of Harold and Florence Barham; *m* 1931, Julia Mary Bazett Leakey; three *s* two *d*. *Educ:* Merchant Taylors' Sch.; Gonville and Caius Coll., Cambridge; Ridley Hall, Cambridge. Deacon, 1925; Priest, 1926. Curate of St James', Hatcham (Southwark), 1925-28; CMS Missionary: Uganda, 1928-38; Ruanda-Urundi, 1938-57; Canon of Uganda, 1939; Archdeacon of Nkore-Kigezi (Uganda), 1957-59; General Sec., Ruanda Mission (CMS), London, 1959-64; Bishop of Rwanda and Burundi, 1964-66; Examining Chaplain to the Bishop of Southwark, 1968-. Médaille D'Or. Ordre Royal du Lion (Belgium), 1955. *Address:* 6 Malcolm Road, Wimbledon, SW19.

**BARING,** family name of **Baron Ashburton,** of **Earl of Cromer,** of **Baron Howick of Glendale,** of **Baron Northbrook,** and of **Baron Revelstoke.**

**BARING, Sir Charles Christian,** 2nd Bt, *cr* 1911; JP; DL; Member of Board of Visitors, HM Prison, Parkhurst; *b* 16 Dec. 1898; *s* of Sir Godfrey Baring, 1st Bt, KBE, DL, and Eva Hermione Mackintosh of Mackintosh (*d* 1934); *S* father 1957; *m* 1948 Jeanette (Jan), *d* of Henry Charles Daykin. *Educ:* Eton. Served European War: Lieut Coldstream Guards, 1917-18 (severely wounded); War of 1939-45: Major Coldstream Guards, 1940-45; Political Warfare Executive, 1943-44; Staff, AFHQ, Italy, War Office, 1944-45. Attaché, HM Legation, Warsaw, 1922-23; Cunard White Star Ltd, 1933-36; HM Prison Service, 1936-38; Probation Officer: West London Magistrates' Court, 1938-40; Central Criminal Court, 1945-46; Inspector, Probation Branch Home Office, 1946-49; Colonial Service: Warden of Prisons, Bermuda, 1949-53. Member, Cttee of Management, RNLI JP, Isle of Wight County, 1956; DL, Co. Southampton, 1962; Chm. of Justices, IW Petty Sessional Div., 1962. *Recreations:* golf, swimming, walking (country). *Heir: nephew* (Charles) Peter Baring [*b* 24 May 1939; *m* 1964, Sarah, *d* of late Col William Gill Withycombe; two *d*]. *Address:* 4 Sandlands, Seaview, Isle of Wight.

**BARING, Hon. John Francis Harcourt;** a Managing Director, Baring Brothers & Co. Ltd, since 1955; *b* 2 Nov. 1928; *er s* and *heir* of 6th Baron Ashburton, *qv*; *m* 1955, Susan Mary Renwick, *e d* of 1st Baron Renwick, *qv*, and Mrs John Ormiston; two *s* two *d*. *Educ:* Eton; Trinity Coll., Oxford (MA). Director: Trafford Park Estates Ltd, 1964-; Royal Insurance Co Ltd, 1964-; Pye Holdings Ltd, 1966-; Cogevam SA, Luxembourg, 1963-; Outwich Ltd, Johannesburg, 1967-; Chm., Outwich Investment Trust Ltd, 1968-; Mem., British Transport Docks Bd, 1966-. Rhodes Trustee, 1970. *Address:* Stratton Park, Micheldever, near Winchester, Hants. *T:* Micheldever 283; Flat 18, 33 Bryanston Square, W1. *Clubs:* Turf, Pratt's.

**BARING, Mark,** CVO 1970; JP; Managing Director, Seccombe Marshall and Campion Ltd, Discount Brokers, since 1950; General Commissioner for Income Tax, since 1966; Executive Chairman, King Edward VII's Hospital for Officers, since 1969; *b* 9th June 1916; *yr s* of late Hon. Windham Baring and Lady Gweneth Cavendish, 3rd *d* of 8th Earl of Bessborough; *m* 1949, Victoria Winifred Russell, *d* of late Col R. E. M. Russell, CVO, CBE, DSO; two *d*. *Educ:* Eton Coll.; Trinity Coll., Cambridge. Served War of 1939-45, Grenadier Guards; in Italy and UK; Mil. Liaison Officer HM Embassy, Rome, 1945-46 (Major 1945); retd 1946. JP, Inner Area of London, 1963. Treasurer, Inst. of Urology; Mem. Bd of Governors, St Peter's Hosps; Chm., Assoc. of Independent Hosps; Pres., St Marylebone Housing Assoc. *Recreations:* tennis, bridge. *Address:* 18 Thurloe Square, SW7. *T:* 01-589 8455. *Clubs:* Brooks's, White's.

**BARING, Lady Rose (Gwendolen Louisa),** CVO 1964; Woman of the Bedchamber to the Queen since 1953; *b* 23 May 1909; *er d* of 12th Earl of Antrim and of Margaret, *y d* of late Rt Hon. J. G. Talbot; *m* 1933, Francis Anthony Baring (killed in action, 1940); two *s* one *d*. *Address:* 43 Pembroke Square, W8.

**BARK, Evelyn (Elizabeth Patricia),** CMG 1967; OBE 1952; retired as Director International Affairs Dept of British Red Cross (1950-66); *b* 26 Dec. 1900; *e d* of Fredk Wm Bark. *Educ:* privately. On staff of Swedish Match Co. (at home and abroad) until 1939, when joined British Red Cross. Served War, 1939-44, VAD (Stars: of 1939-45, of France, and of Germany; Defence Medal, and War Medal, 1939-45). Foreign Relations Officer, 1944-48. Commissioner, NW Europe, 1948-49; Foreign Relations and Relief Adviser, 1950 (title later changed to Dir International Affairs). Serving Sister of St John's, 1953; British Red Cross Certificate First Class, 1966. *Publication:* No Time to Kill, 1960. *Recreations:* reading, music, nordic languages. *Address:* 4 Milton Mansions, Queen's Club Gardens, W14. *T:* 01-385 2181. *Club:* VAD Ladies'.

**BARKE, James Allen;** Director, De La Rue Company Ltd; *b* 16 April 1903; *s* of James E. Barke and Emma Livsey; *m* 1st, 1937, Doris Marian Bayne (*d* 1952); two *s* one *d*; 2nd, 1953, Marguerite Amy Sutcliffe (*née* Williams) (*d* 1968); one *step d*. *Educ:* Birley Street Central Sch.; Manchester Coll. of Technology. Mather & Platt and general engineering experience, 1922-32; joined Ford Motor Co., 1932; Buyer,

Purchase Dept, 1939; Chief Buyer (Tractors), 1947; Manager, Leamington Foundry, 1948; Executive Dir and General Manager, Briggs Motor Bodies Ltd, 1953; Dir, Product Divs, 1959; Asst Man. Dir, 1961; Man. Dir, Dagenham, 1962; Chief Exec. Officer and Man. Dir, 1963; Vice-Chm., Ford Motor Company, 1965-68. *Recreations:* golf, rock climbing, walking, reading. *Address:* Thurlestone, Mill Green, Ingatestone, Essex. *Clubs:* Royal Automobile, Oriental.

**BARKER, Alan;** *see* Barker, William A.

**BARKER, Sir Alwyn (Bowman),** Kt 1969; CMG 1962; BSc, BE; FIEAust; Chairman, Kelvinator Australia Ltd, since 1967 (Managing Director, 1952-67); *b* 5 Aug. 1900; *s* of late A. J. Barker, Mt Barker, South Australia; *m* 1926, Isabel Barron Lucas; one *d* (one *s* decd). *Educ:* St Peter's Coll., Adelaide; Geelong C of E Grammar Sch.; Univ. of Adelaide. British Thomson Houston Co. Ltd, England, 1923-24; Hudson Motor Car Co., Detroit, 1925; Production Manager, Holden's Motor Body Builders Ltd, Adelaide, 1925-30; Works Manager, Kelvinator Aust. Ltd, Adelaide, 1931-40; Gen. Man., Chrysler Aust. Ltd, Adelaide, 1940-52; Chm., Municipal Tramways Trust SA, 1953-67; Dir, several public companies. Mem. Faculty of Engineering, Univ. of Adelaide, 1938-67 (Lectr in Industrial Engineering, 1929-1954). Chm., Industrial Develt Adv. Council; Member: Internat. Acad. of Scientific Management; Manufacturing Industries Adv. Council. Hon. Fellow Australian Institute of Management (Federal Pres., 1952-53, 1959-61; Pres. Adelaide Div., 1952-53). *Recreations:* golf; pastoral. *Address:* 51 Hackney Road, Hackney, South Australia. *T:* 632838. *Clubs:* Adelaide, Royal Adelaide Golf (Adelaide).

**BARKER, Lt-Col Arthur James;** writer; retired from Army; *b* 20 Sept. 1918; *o s* of late John Robert Barker and Caroline Barker, Hull; *m* 1st, 1939, Dorothy Jean (marr. diss. 1968), *o d* of late W. E. Hirst, MBE; one *s*; 2nd, 1969, Alexandra Franziska, *o d* of late Eugen Franz Roderbourg, Berlin. *Educ:* Hymers Coll., Hull; Royal Mil. Coll. of Science. Commissioned E Yorks Regt, 1936; E African campaign with 1st/4th KAR, 1940-41; Ceylon, India, Burma, 1941-46; Staff Coll., Quetta, 1944. Subseq. service as a Staff Officer in Middle East, 1947-48; WO (techn intell.), 1950-52; Far East, 1956-58; a Regtl Officer in Malaya, 1952-53; Mem. Directing Staff, RMCS, 1954-56; retd, 1958, and employed until 1968 by UKAEA; NATO Research Fellowship, 1968. *Publications:* Principles of Small Arms, 1953; The March on Delhi, 1963; Suez: The Seven Day War, 1964; Eritrea 1941, 1966; The Neglected War, 1967; Townshend of Kut, 1967; The Civilising Mission, 1968; German Infantry Weapons of World War 2, 1969; British and US Infantry Weapons of World War 2, 1969; Pearl Harbour, 1969; The War Against Russia, 1970; Midway, 1971. *Recreation:* travel. *Address:* 6325 N Sheridan Road, Chicago, Ill 60626, USA. *Club:* United Service.

**BARKER, Arthur Vincent,** OBE 1955; Scottish Chartered Accountant; Member, British Railways Board, since 1968; Chairman, British Transport Hotels Ltd, since 1968; *b* 10 Nov. 1911; *e s* of late Arthur and Susannah Mary Barker; *m* 1936, Dorothy Drew; one *d*. *Educ:* Whitley and Monkseaton High Sch.; London Sch. of Economics. Qual. as CA, 1934; with Price Waterhouse & Co., 1934-35; with NAAFI in Middle East and UK, 1935-62 (Jt Gen. Man., 1955); Asst Gen. Man., Southern Region, British Railways, and Mem., Southern Railway Bd, 1962; Asst Gen. Man., London Midland Region, British Railways, and Mem., LMR Bd, 1965; Chm., Shipping and Internat. Services Div., British Railways, 1968-69. *Recreation:* fly-fishing. *Address:* Lime Tree Cottage, High Park Avenue, East Horsley, Surrey. *T:* East Horsley 2914.

**BARKER, Cecil;** *see* Barker, H. C. J.

**BARKER, Sir (Charles Frederic) James,** Kt 1970; MBE 1944; Chairman and Chief Executive, Unigate Ltd, since 1970; Director, Cadbury Schweppes Ltd, since 1962; *b* 17 Feb. 1914; *s* of Charles F. J. Barker and Ethel (*née* Brooke), Walton-on-the-Naze; *m* 1940, Thora Daphne, *d* of Amos Perry and Anne (*née* Asplande); two *s*. *Educ:* Royal Grammar Sch., Colchester. Served War of 1939-45, Wilts Regt (Major): Staff Coll., 1943; GSO2, 43rd Wessex Division. L. Rose & Co. Ltd, 1934-39 and 1948: Man. Dir, 1957; Schweppes Ltd, 1958-69: Dir, 1962; Man. Dir, 1969. Fellow Inst. of Management. Pres., Food Manufacturers Fedn, 1967-70. Mem., Potato Marketing Board. Croix de Guerre. *Recreations:* sailing, reading, family. *Address:* Gartness, West Common, Harpenden, Herts. *T:* Harpenden 3063; Cottage Manse, Suffolk Street, Walton-on-the-Naze, Essex. *T:* Frinton-on-Sea 2103. *Clubs:* Carlton, Royal Thames Yacht; Walton and Frinton Yacht.

**BARKER, Air Vice-Marshal Clifford Cockcroft,** CBE 1960; AFC 1944; MB, ChB; Principal Medical Officer, Training Command, 1968-69 (Technical Training Command, 1966-68), retired; *b* 19 Sept. 1909; *s* of Dr A. C. Barker, Hull; *m* 1939, Diana (*née* Coxhead) Exmouth, Devon; one *s* one *d*. *Educ:* Trent Coll.; Edinburgh Univ. Joined RAF, 1936; Iraq, 1937-39; PMO Ferry Comd, Canada, 1943-44 (King's Commendation); India, 1944-45 (despatches); Flying Personnel MO in UK, 1945-50; Aden, 1950-52; CO Headley Court, 1952-54; SHAPE, 1954-57; CO, RAF Hosp., Wroughton, 1957-61; CO, RAF Hosp., Halton, 1961-62; PMO Bomber Comd, 1962-63; Far East Air Force, 1963-65. QHP 1966-69. *Recreations:* golf, croquet; formerly Rugby football (Capt. Edinburgh Univ., 1932-33). *Address:* 34 Greenway Lane, Budleigh Salterton, Devon. *Club:* Royal Air Force.

**BARKER, Prof. David (Faubert),** MA, DPhil (Oxon); Professor of Zoology, University of Durham, since 1962; *b* 18 Feb. 1922; *s* of Faubert and Doreen Barker; *m* 1945, Kathleen Mary Frances Pocock; three *s* two *d*. *Educ:* Bryanston Sch.; Magdalen Coll., Oxford. Senior Demy of Magdalen Coll., 1946; Leverhulme Research Scholar, Royal Coll. of Surgeons, 1946; Demonstrator in Zoology and Comparative Anatomy, Oxford, 1947; DPhil 1948; Rolleston Prizeman, 1948; Prof. of Zoology, Univ. of Hong Kong, 1950-62; led scientific expeditions to Tunisia, 1950, North Borneo, 1952; Dean of Faculty of Science, Hong Kong, 1959-60; Public Orator, Hong Kong, 1961. *Publications:* (Founder) Editor, Hong Kong Univ. Fisheries Journal, 1954-60; Editor, Symposium on Muscle Receptors, 1962; scientific papers, mostly on muscle innervation. *Address:* Department of Zoology, Science Laboratories, South Road, Durham. *T:* Durham 4971.

**BARKER, Denis William Knighton;** a Managing Director, The British Petroleum Co. Ltd, since 1967; *b* 21 Aug. 1908; *m* 1938, Esmee Doris Marsh; two *d*. *Educ:* Holgate Grammar School, Barnsley; Sheffield Univ. (MSc). With the British Petroleum Co. Ltd, 1929-: President, BP (North America) Ltd, 1959; Asst Gen. Manager, Refineries Dept, 1960;

Gen. Manager, Refineries Dept, 1966. Director: BP Trading Ltd, BP Chemicals Ltd, BP Refineries Ltd, Britannic Estates Ltd, The British Petroleum Co. of Canada Ltd, and others. *Recreations:* golf, gardening. *Address:* Stable Cottage, Upper House Lane, Shamley Green, near Guildford, Surrey. *T:* Cranleigh 2726.

**BARKER, Dennis Albert,** QC 1968; Deputy Chairman, Bucks Quarter Sessions, since 1963; *b* 9 June 1926; *s* of J. W. and R. E. Barker; *m* 1949, Daphne (*née* Ruffle); one *s* one *d* (and one *d* decd). *Educ:* Nottingham High Sch.; The Queen's Coll. Oxford (Jodrell Schol.). Flying Officer, RAFVR, 1944-47. 1st cl. hons (Jurisprudence), Oxon, 1949; 1st cl. Certif. of Honour and Studentship, Bar Finals, 1950; Harmsworth Law Schol., 1950; Eldon Law Schol., 1950. Mem. Midland Circuit. Mem., Criminal Injuries Compensation Bd. *Recreations:* golf, flying. *Address:* 1 Harcourt Buildings, Temple, EC4. *T:* 01-353 0375; Heathlands, Great Brickhill, Bletchley, Bucks. *T:* Great Brickhill 251. *Clubs:* Bath; Nottinghamshire (Nottingham).

**BARKER, Douglas William Ashley,** CMG 1966; Secretary to the Treasury, New Zealand, 1965-66; *b* 19 Sept. 1905; *s* of John Joseph and Annie Barker; *m* 1934, Elsie May Owen; one *s* one *d*. *Educ:* Palmerston North Boys' High Sch.; Victoria Univ. Coll., Wellington; LSE. joined NZ Treasury, 1922; seconded NZ High Comr's Office, London, 1934; Treasury, NZ, 1937. Director: Cable Price Downer Ltd, 1967; S. W. Peterson Ltd, 1967. *Recreations:* bowls, golf, gardening. *Address:* 7 Amritsar Street, Wellington, NZ. *T:* 797151. *Clubs:* Wellesley; Civil Service (Wellington, NZ).

**BARKER, Edward,** OBE 1966; QPM 1961; Chief Constable of Sheffield and Rotherham Constabulary since 1967; *b* 1 Nov. 1909; *s* of George and Gertrude Barker; *m* 1935, Clare Garth; one *d*. *Educ:* The Grammar School, Malton. Joined Preston Borough Police, 1931; transf. Lancs Constabulary, 1938; Inspector/Chief Inspector, Comdt of Constabulary Trng Sch., 1946-51; Supt 1954; Vis. Lectr to Bermuda Police, 1955; Chief Supt 1956; Asst Comdt, Police Coll., Bramshill, 1956-57; Chief Constable: Bolton Borough Police, 1957; Sheffield City Police, 1964. Area Vice-Pres., St John Ambulance Assoc.; Vice-Pres., S Yorks Area, British Red Cross Soc.; Hon. Sec., Sheffield Accident Prevention Council; Mem., Home Office Standing Cttee on Crime Prevention. Police Long Service and Good Conduct Medal, 1953. SBStJ. *Recreations:* golf, gardening, watching field sports. *Address:* Knowle Cottage, 201 Carter Knowle Road, Sheffield 7. *T:* Sheffield 55549. *Clubs:* St John House; Sheffield (Sheffield).

**BARKER, Eric Leslie;** Author and Entertainer; *b* 20 Feb. 1912; *s* of Charles and Maude Barker; *m* 1936, Pearl Hackney; one *d*. *Educ:* Whitgift Sch. Character actor Birmingham, Oxford and Croydon Repertory Theatres, 1932-33; Comedian, also sketch and lyric writer, Charlot revues, Windmill, and Prince of Wales Theatre, 1933-38. Author and star of radio series: Howdyfolks, 1939-40; Navy Mixture, 1944-45; Merry-Go-Round, 1945-49; Just Fancy, 1950-62; Passing Parade, 1957; Barker's Folly, 1958; Law and Disorder, 1960. Lieut RNVR, 1940-45. Author and star of television series: Eric Barker Half Hour, 1952-55; Absolutely Barkers, 1963. *Films:* Brothers-in-Law; Clean Sweep; Blue Murder at St Trinians; Happy Is The Bride; Carry on, Sergeant; Eye Spy; Bachelor of Hearts; Right, Left and Centre; Carry on, Constable; Dentist in the Chair; Raising the Wind; The Fast Lady; Those Magnificent Men in their Flying Machines; Doctor in Clover; Maroc 7. *Publications:* Short stories, 3 novels, 1931-33; The Watch Hunt, 1931; Day Gone By, 1932; Steady Barker (Autobiog.), 1956; Golden Gimmick, 1958. *Recreations:* antiques, ski-ing, photography, gardening, history, cricket, swimming, gastronomy. *Address:* c/o Lloyds Bank, Faversham, Kent.

**BARKER, General Sir Evelyn Hugh,** KCB, *cr* 1950 (CB 1944); KBE, *cr* 1945 (CBE 1940); DSO 1918; MC; *b* 22 may 1894; *y s* of late Maj.-Gen. Sir George Barker, KCB, and late Hon. Lady Barker; *m* 1923, Violet Eleanor, *y d* of T. W. Thornton of Brockhall, near Weedon, Northants; one *s*. *Educ:* Wellington Coll.; RM Coll., Sandhurst. Joined Army, 1913; Capt. 1916; Bt-Maj. 1929; Major 1930; Bt Lieut-Col 1934; LieutlCol 1936; Bt-Col 1937; Col 1938; Maj.-Gen., 1941; Lieut-Gen., 1944; General, 1948. Served European War, 1914-18, France, Salonica, and South Russia; GSO3, 1917; Bde-Major, 1917; GSO3 (War Office), 1919 (despatches, DSO, MC); Brigade-Major 8th Infantry Brigade, 1931-33; commanded 2nd Bn KRRC, 1936-38; commanded 10th Infantry Brigade, 1938-40; commanded 54th Div. 1941-42, and 49th (West Riding) Div. 1943-44; commanded 8 Corps, 1944-April 1946; commanded British Troops in Palestine and Transjordan, 1946; ADC General to the King, 1949-50; GOC-in-C Eastern Command, 1947-50; retd 1950. Col Comdt 2nd Bn KRRC, 1946-56; Hon. Col Loyal Suffolk Hussars (Yeomanry), 1946-50; Hon. Col, Beds Yeo., 1951-60; Hon. Col Herts and Beds Yeo., 1961-62. DL, Beds, 1952-67. Cmdr, Legion of Honour; Croix de Guerre (with palm) France; Silver Medal, Italy; O St Stanislas, Russia; Grand Cross of Dannebrog, Denmark. *Address:* Park House, Bromham, Bedford. *Club:* Royal Automobile.

**BARKER, George Granville;** writer; *b* 26 Feb. 1913; *s* of George Barker and Marion Frances Barker (*née* Taaffe); *m* 1964, Elspeth Langlands. *Educ:* Marlborough Road London County Council Sch., Chelsea. Prof. of English Literature at Imperial Tohoku Univ., Japan, 1939; visited America, 1940; returned to England, 1943; lived in Rome, 1960-65. Arts Fellow York Univ., 1966-67. *Publications:* Thirty Preliminary Poems, 1933; Alanna Autumnal, 1933; Poems, 1935; Janus, 1935; Calamiterror, 1937; Lament and Triumph, 1940; Eros in Dogma, 1944; News of the World, 1950; The Dead Seagull, 1950; The True Confession of George Barker, 1950; A Vision of Beasts and Gods, 1954; Collected Poems, 1930-55, 1957; The True Confession of George Barker, 1957; Two Plays, 1958; The View from a Blind I, 1962; Dreams of a Summer Night, 1966; The Golden Chains, 1968; Essays, 1968; Runes & Rhymes & Tunes & Chimes, 1970; To Aylsham Fair, 1970; When I get up at Morning, 1970; Poems of Places and People, 1970. *Address:* Bintry House, Itteringham, Aylsham, Norfolk. *T:* Saxthorpe 240.

**BARKER, (Harold) Cecil (James),** CMG 1949; retired; *b* 27 May 1893; *s* of late Harold Hastings Barker, MBE; *m* 1922, Sylvia Mary Stanford; one *s* one *d*. *Educ:* Woolwich. Farming in S Rhodesia, 1912-14. Served European War, 1914-18, German SW Africa, in Imperial Light Horse, 1914-15; E Africa, in Rhodesian Service Column, attached BSAP, 1915-16; commissioned in 1/1 KAR, 1916-18. Nyasaland Administration (Provincial Commissioner), 1919-52; seconded as Political Liaison Officer, Staff HQ, Nairobi, 1939-40.

*Address:* 47 Westcliff Road, Hermanus, CP, South Africa. *T:* 31.

**BARKER, Hugh Purslove;** Chairman (1956) and Managing Director (1945), Parkinson Cowan Group; Vice-President, British Institute of Management, since Oct. 1962 (Chairman, 1960-62); Member, Royal Commission on Assizes, since 1967; *b* 11 March 1909; *s* of Arthur Henry Barker and Florence Barker (*née* Saich); *m* 1935, Joye Frances Higgs, two *s* one *d*. *Educ:* Oundle Sch. Mech. Engr Apprenticeship (concurrently studied Engineering, Accountancy and (Law), Waygood-Otis Ltd, 1927-31; private mfg business, 1931-35; Cons. Engr, A. H. Barker & Partners, 1935-39. Dir Mfg Cos. Min. of Aircraft Prodn (Dep. Dir Instrument Prodn), 1940-44. Part-time Mem., British Railways Bd, 1962-67 (British Transport Commn, 1951-62); Chm., EDC for the Rubber Industry, 1968-. CEng; FIEE; FIMechE; FInstGasE; MIHVE; MInstT; FBIM. *Publications:* papers and articles to Technical Institutes and press, on engineering subjects, and to financial and econ. press on management science. *Recreations:* fishing, music. *Address:* Terminal House, Grosvenor Gardens, SW1. *T:* 01-730 0111. *Clubs:* Junior Carlton; Union Interalliée (Paris).

**BARKER, Sir James;** *see* Barker, Sir C. F. J.

**BARKER, John,** FRS 1953; MA, PhD (Trinity College, Cambridge); ScD; Emeritus Reader in Plant Physiology in the University of Cambridge. Fellow of Trinity College, Cambridge. *Address:* 67 Grantchester Street, Cambridge; The Botany School, Downing Street, Cambridge.

**BARKER, Air Vice-Marshal John Lindsay,** CB 1963; CBE 1946; DFC 1945; RAF (Retired); *b* 12 Nov. 1910; *s* of Abraham Cockroft Barker and Lilian Alice (*née* Woods); *m* 1948, Eleanor Margaret Hannah; one *s*. *Educ:* Trent Coll., Derbys; Brasenose Coll., Oxford. RAFO, 1930, RAF, 1933. Served War of 1939-45: France, 1939-40; N Africa, 1942-44; Bomber Command, 1944-45; Far East, 1945-48; Egypt, 1950-53; Air Attaché, Rome, 1955-58; Cmdr Royal Ceylon Air Force, 1958-63. Air Vice-Marshal, 1959. Retd, 1963. Order of Merit, Italy, 1958. *Recreations:* golf, photography, sailing. *Address:* Greengates, Loddon Drive, Wargrave, Berks. *T:* Wargrave 2895. *Club:* Royal Air Force.

**BARKER, Lancelot Elliot;** Metropolitan Stipendiary Magistrate since 1960; *b* 29 Feb. 1908; *s* of Elliot Francis Barker and Margaretha Maria (*née* Walker); *m* 1937, Sylvia Marvell Haworth-Booth. *Educ:* Westminster Sch.; Trinity Coll., Cambridge (MA). BA Hons in Law, 1929. Admitted Solicitor of Supreme Court, Dec. 1932. Partner in firm of Wontner & Sons, solicitors, 1935-60. *Recreations:* riding; photography; formerly athletics (University Relay Team *v* Oxford, 1928). *Address:* The Walled House, 87 Christ Church Road, East Sheen, SW14. *T:* 01-876 6956. *Clubs:* Oxford and Cambridge University; MCC.

**BARKER, Brig. Lewis Ernest Stephen,** CBE 1943; DSO 1941; MC 1918; *b* 5 May 1895; *s* of late Richard Barker, Mulgrave, Vic, Australia; *m* 1921, Alice Hope McEachern; two *s*. *Educ:* Brighton Grammar Sch., Vic.; Royal Military Coll., Duntroon. Permanent Army Officer. European War, 1917-18 (MC). Various staff appointments AMF 1919-39. Comd 2/1 Australian Fd Regt in first Libyan campaign, 1940-41 (DSO); Dir of Artillery, LHQ Melbourne, 1941-42; CCRA 1 Australian Corps in New Guinea for the operations to the capture of Buna (CBE); subsequently BRA New Guinea up to the capture of Madang, 1944. BRA LHQ Melbourne, July 1945; Commandant, 4th Military District (S Australia), 1946-Dec. 1948; retired. *Address:* c/o Bank of NSW, University Avenue, Canberra, ACT, Australia.

**BARKER, Paul;** Editor of New Society since 1968; *b* 24 Aug. 1935; *s* of Donald and Marion Barker; *m* 1960, Sally, *e d* of James and Marion Huddleston; two *s* one *d*. *Educ:* Hebden Bridge Grammar Sch.; Calder High Sch.; Brasenose Coll., Oxford (Hulme Exhibr). Intell. Corps (commn), 1953-55; BA 1958; MA 1970; lecteur, Ecole Normale Supérieure, Paris, 1958-59; The Times, 1959-64; New Society, staff writer, 1964; The Economist, 1964; New Society, Assistant Editor, 1965-68. *Publications:* various articles; contrib.: Youth in New Society (ed Timothy Raison), 1966; Your Sunday Paper (ed Richard Hoggart), 1967. *Address:* 26 Patshull Road, NW5. *T:* 01-485 8861.

**BARKER, Ronald Ernest,** OBE 1968; author; Secretary, The Publishers Association; Director: Book Development Council Ltd; Standard Book Numbering Agency Ltd; Publishers' Information Cards Services Ltd; University Mailing Service Ltd; *b* 22 Dec. 1920; *s* of Charles Jacob and Margaret Grace Barker; *m* 1941, Joyce Edith Wynne; one *s* one *d* (and one *s* decd). *Educ:* largely war-time reading. Served War of 1939-45, demobilized as Captain (non-med.) RAMC, 1946. Publishers Assoc.: apptd Asst Sec. (Export), 1947; Dep. Sec., 1950; Secretary, 1958-. Curtis Brown Ltd, Literary Agents, 1956-58. Mem., Crime Writers' Assoc.; Hon. Mem., Soc. of Bookmen. Koninklijke Nederlandsche Uitgeversbond Medal of Honour, 1968. *Publications:* Books for All: a study of international book trade, 1956; Books Are Different: the defence of the Net Book Agreement (Jt Editor), 1966; Photocopying Practices in the United Kingdom, 1970; A Handbook on Copyright for Authors and Publishers, 1971; *novels:* Tendency to Corrupt, 1957; The Days are Long, 1959; *thrillers:* Clue for Murder, 1962; and, as E. B. Ronald (*pseudonym*): Cat and Fiddle Murders, 1954; Death by Proxy, 1956; A Sort of Madness, 1958; contributor to The Bookseller, The Writer, etc. on copyright and other book trade subjects. *Recreations:* cooking, swimming, listening to music. *Address:* Desmond House, Romanhurst Avenue, Bromley, Kent. *T:* 01-464 2885.

**BARKER, Ronald Hugh,** PhD, BSc, CEng, FIEE; Deputy Director, Royal Armament Research and Development Establishment, since 1965; *b* 28 Oct. 1915; *s* of E. W. Barker and L. A. Taylor; *m* 1943, W. E. Hunt; two *s*. *Educ:* University of Hull. Physicist, Standard Telephones and Cables, 1938-41; Ministry of Supply, 1941-59; Dep. Dir, Central Electricity Research Laboratories, 1959-62; Technical Dir, The Pullin Group Ltd, 1962-65. *Publications:* various, on servomechanisms and control systems. *Address:* Linden, Church Way, Hurst Green, Surrey. *T:* Oxted 2108.

**BARKER, Dame Sara Elizabeth,** DBE 1970; National Agent, Labour Party, 1962-69; *b* 15 Feb. 1904; *d* of late George Barker and late Ethel Barker (*née* Brier). *Educ:* Siddal Elementary Sch., Halifax; Halifax Technical Coll. Sec.-Agent to Halifax Labour Party, 1935-42; Woman Organiser of Labour Party for Yorks, 1942-52; Senior Asst National Agent and Chief Woman Officer of the Labour Party, 1960-62 (Asst Nat. Agent, 1952-60).

*Publications:* (pamphlet) How the Labour Party Works, 1946. Editor, Labour Organiser. *Recreations:* reading, music, walking. *Address:* 4 Chevin Edge Crescent, Exley, Halifax, Yorks.

**BARKER, Sir William,** KCMG 1967 (CMG 1958); OBE 1949; Bowes Professor of Russian, University of Liverpool, since 1969; *b* 19 July 1909; *s* of Alfred Barker; *m* 1939, Margaret Beirne; one *s* one *d*. *Educ:* Universities of Liverpool and Prague. Employed in Foreign Office, 1943; First Sec., Prague, 1945; Foreign Service Officer, Grade 7, Senior Branch of Foreign Service, 1946; Chargé d'Affaires, Prague, 1947; transferred Moscow, Aug. 1947; granted rank of Counsellor, Dec. 1948; Grade 6, 1950; Counsellor, Oslo, 1951, also Chargé d'Affaires; Consul-Gen., Boston, Mass, Sept. 1954; Counsellor, Washington, 1955; Minister, Moscow, 1960-63; Fellow, Center for Internat. Affairs, Harvard Univ., 1963-64. Asst Under-Sec. of State, FO, 1965-66; British Ambassador to Czechoslovakia, 1966-68. *Address:* Russian Department, The University, Liverpool 3; 53 Eske Road North, Liverpool L23 8UE.

**BARKER, (William) Alan;** Headmaster of The Leys School since 1958; *b* 1 Oct. 1923; 2nd *s* of late T. L. Barker, Edinburgh and Beaconsfield; *m* 1954, Jean Alys, *d* of late Capt. A. E. Campbell-Harris, MC; one *s*. *Educ:* Rossall Sch.; Jesus Coll., Cambridge (scholar). Lieut Royal Artillery, 69 (WR) Field Regt, NW Europe; wounded, 1944. 1st cl. Hons Hist. Tripos Pt I, 1946, Pt II, 1947; BA 1946, MA 1948. Asst Master, Eton Coll., 1947-53; Commonwealth Fund Fellow, Yale Univ., 1951-52, MA (Yale) 1952. Fellow Queen's Coll., Cambridge, and Dir Studies in History, 1953-55; Asst Master, Eton Coll., 1955-58. Governor: Rossall Sch.; St Felix Sch.; Queenswood Sch.; Cambridgeshire Coll. of Arts and Technology (Chm.). Mem. Eton UDC, 1956-59; Councillor, Cambs and I of Ely, 1959-70, Alderman 1970. Select Preacher, Oxford Univ., 1966. *Publications:* (jt) A General History of England 1688-1950, 2 vols, 1952, 1953; Religion and Politics (1558-1642) 1957; The Civil War in America, 1961; (contrib.) The Rebirth of Britain, 1964. *Recreations:* bridge; American history, golf. *Address:* The Leys School, Cambridge. *T:* 55327; Luckboat House, Sandwich. *T:* 3007. *Clubs:* Pitt (Cambridge); Elizabethan (Yale).

**BARKING, Bishop of,** since 1959; **Rt. Rev. William Frank Percival Chadwick.** *Educ:* Wadham College, Oxford; Harvard Univ. USA (Davison Scholar). Deacon, 1929, Priest, 1930, Diocese Liverpool; Curate, St Helens, 1929-34; Vicar: Widnes, 1934-38; Christ Church, Crouch End, N8, 1938-47; Barking, 1947-59. Proctor, Diocese of London, 1946, Diocese of Chelmsford, 1951; Examining Chaplain to Bishop of Chelmsford, 1951; Asst RD Barking, 1950-53, RD, Barking, 1953; Hon. Canon of Chelmsford, 1954; Pro-Prolocutor, Lower House of Canterbury, 1956; Exchange Preacher, USA, British Council of Churches, 1958; Chm., Church of England's Commn on Roman Catholic Relations, 1968-. *Publication:* The Inner Life. *Recreation:* golf. *Address:* West Dene, Whitehall Lane, Buckhurst Hill, Essex. *T:* 01-504 3754. *Club:* Royal Commonwealth Society.

**BARKLEY, Rev. Prof. John Monteith,** Professor of Ecclesiastical History in the Presbyterian College, Belfast, since 1954; Vice-Principal and Secretary of Faculty, since 1964; *b* 16 Oct. 1910; *s* of Rev. Robert James Barkley, BD, and Mary Monteith; *m* 1936, Irene Graham Anderson; one *d*. *Educ:* Magee Univ. Coll. Derry; Trinity Coll., Dublin; The Presbyterian Coll., Belfast. BA 1934, MA 1941, BD 1944, PhD 1946, DD 1949, Trinity Coll., Dublin; BA 1952, MA 1953, Queen's Univ., Belfast. Thompson Memorial Prizeman in Philosophy, 1934; Larmour Memorial Exhibitioner in Theology, 1944; Paul Memorial Prizeman in History, 1953; Carey Lecturer, 1954-56; Lecturer in Ecclesiastical History, Queen's Univ., Belfast, 1951-54. FRHistS. Ordained, Drumreagh Presbyterian Church, 1935; installed in II Ballybay and Rockcorry, 1939; installed in Cooke Centenary, Belfast, 1949. *Publications:* Handbook on Evangelical Christianity and Romanism, 1949; Presbyterianism, 1951; Westminster Formularies in Irish Presbyterianism, 1956; History of the Presbyterian Church in Ireland, 1959; Weltkirchenlexikon (arts), 1960; History of the Sabbath School Society for Ireland, 1961; The Eldership in Irish Presbyterianism; The Baptism of Infants, 1963; The Presbyterian Orphan Society, 1966; Worship of the Reformed Church, 1966. Articles in Scottish Journal of Theology, Verbum Caro, Biblical Theology, etc. *Recreations:* bowls, golf. *Address:* 55 Cranmore Park, Belfast 9.

**BARKSHIRE, Robert Hugh,** CBE 1968; Consultant to Committee of London Clearing Bankers and British Bankers' Association, since 1970; Hon. Secretary to Meetings of Officers of European Bankers' Associations, since 1959; General Commissioner of Income Tax for the City of London; *b* 24 Oct. 1909; *yr s* of late Lt-Col Charles Robert Barkshire, OBE; *m* 1934, Emily Blunt; one *s*. *Educ:* King's Sch., Bruton. Bank of England, 1927-55: Private Sec. to the Governor (C. F. Cobbold), 1949-53; Asst Chief Cashier, 1953. Sec. to Cttee of London Clearing Bankers, British Bankers' Assoc., Bankers' Clearing House and Foreign Exchange Cttee, and mem. of various inter-bank cttees, 1955-70. Governor, Nat. Inst. of Economic and Social Research, 1970-. FIB 1960. *Recreation:* golf. *Address:* 22 Clareville Court, SW7. *Clubs:* Gresham; Hurlingham; Royal Wimbledon Golf.

**BARLAS, Richard Douglas,** CB 1968; OBE 1943; Second Clerk Assistant and Clerk of Committees, House of Commons, since 1967; *b* 19 May 1916; *s* of E. D. M. Barlas and Elena Barlas (*née* Kenyon); *m* 1940, Ann, *d* of Canon R. W. Porter; three *s*. *Educ:* Westminster; Christ Church, Oxford. War Service, 1939-45, Wing Cmdr, RAF; RAF Staff Coll., 1942. Asst Clerk, House of Commons, 1946; Senior Clerk, 1947. Called to the Bar, Middle Temple, 1949. Fourth Clerk at the Table, House of Commons, 1959; Second Clerk Asst, 1962. *Recreations:* travel; gardening. *Address:* Frogs Hole, Goudhurst, Kent. *T:* Goudhurst 213. *Club:* Athenæum.

**BARLEY, Lieut-Col Leslie John,** DSO 1917; late Royal Engineers and Cameronians; *b* Gosport, 7 July 1890; *s* of Rev. A. G. Barley; *m* 1915, Muriel More, *d* of James Kerr Love, LLD, MD, Glasgow; two *d*. *Educ:* Taunton Sch.; University Coll., Southampton; Kiel Univ.; Queen's Coll., Oxford. MA (Hons Chemistry) Oxon; BSc (London); Commissioned The Cameronians, June 1913; 1st Batt. France, Dec. 1914; when first gas attack occurred made one of first efficient respirators, instituted the gas-proof dugout and other methods of protection and training of troops in anti-gas measures; Army Chemical Adviser, June 1915; Asst Dir and Head, Gas Services, Italy, Nov. 1917; Superintendent Anti-Gas Dept (Ministry of Munitions), 1919 (despatches thrice, DSO; Croix de Guerre, 1918; Cavalier of the Order of St Maurice and St Lazarus of Jerusalem, 1918; brevet majority, 1918;

Officer of the Order of the Crown of Italy, 1919); Head of Development Dept of Nobel Industries Ltd, 1919, and of ICI Ltd, 1926; re-employed with RE, 1939-43, served in most Overseas Commands and USA with Chemical Warfare Liaison Mission, 1942. Pacific Relations Conf., 1947. Overseas Development Controller of ICI Ltd until retirement, 1952. *Publications:* The Riddle of Rationalisation, 1932; (part) A Food Plan for India, 1945. *Address:* West Lodge, West Kingston, Littlehampton, Sussex. *Clubs:* Royal Automobile; Ham Manor Golf.

**BARLOW, Sir Christopher Hilaro,** 7th Bt, *cr* 1803; *b* 1 Dec. 1929; *s* of Sir Richard Barlow, 6th Bt, AFC, and Rosamund Sylvia, *d* of late F. S. Anderton (she *m* 2nd, 1950, Rev. Leonard Haslet Morrison, MA); *S* father, 1946; *m* 1952, J. C. de M. Audley, *e d* of J. E. Audley, Bahamas; one *s* two *d* (and one *s* decd). *Educ:* Eton; McGill Univ., Montreal. *Heir: s* Crispian John Edmund Audley Barlow, *b* 20 April 1958. *Address:* 18 Winter Avenue, St John's, Newfoundland.

**BARLOW, Donald Spiers Monteagle,** MS London; FRCS; Consultant Surgeon, Hospitals for Diseases of the Chest, since 1947; Consultant Surgeon, Southend Group of Hospitals, since 1936, Senior Consultant Surgeon since 1958; Consultant Surgeon, Luton Group of Hospitals, since 1940, Senior Consultant Surgeon since 1955; Honorary Thoracic Surgeon, Italian Hospital, since 1955; Surgical Tutor to the Royal College of Surgeons of England, since 1962; Lecturer, Institute of Diseases of the Chest, University of London, since 1967 (Teacher, 1964-67); *b* 4 July 1905; *s* of late Leonard Barlow, MIEE, and Katharine Barlow; *m* 1934, Violet Elizabeth (*née* Maciver); one *s* three *d* (and one *d* decd). *Educ:* Whitgift Sch.; University Coll. Hospital and Medical Sch. MRCS, LRCP 1927; MB, BS London 1928; MS London 1930; FRCS 1930. Formerly: RMO, Wimbledon Hosp., 1927; Ho. Phys., University Coll. Hosp., 1928; Ho. Surg., University Coll. Hosp., 1929; Ho. Surg., Norfolk and Norwich Hosp., 1930-31; Resident Asst Surg., West London Hosp., 1931-35; Surg. Registrar London Lock Hosp., 1936; Research work at University Coll., London, 1936-37; Hon. Surg., St John's Hosp., Lewisham, 1937-47; Cons. Thoracic Surg., LCC, 1945-48. Coronation Medal, 1953. *Publications:* contribs to: Progress of Clinical Surgery, 1960 (ed Rodney Smith); Operative Surgery, 2nd edn 1969 (ed Rob and Smith). Many publications in learned jls mostly concerning diseases of oesophagus, chest and abdomen. Also 3 reports (Ceylon Govt White Papers), 1952, 1954, 1967. *Recreations:* golf, painting. *Address:* 118 Harley Street, W1. *T:* 01-935 3616; Deacons Field, High Elms, Harpenden, Herts. *T:* Harpenden 3400. *Club:* Carlton. *See also Prof. H. E. M. Barlow.*

**BARLOW, Prof. Frank,** MA, DPhil; FBA 1970; Professor of History and Head of Department, University of Exeter, since 1953; *b* 19 April 1911; *e s* of Percy Hawthorn and Margaret Julia Barlow; *m* 1936, Moira Stella Brigid Garvey; two *s*. *Educ:* Newcastle High Sch.; St John's Coll., Oxford. Open Schol., St John's Coll., Oxford, 1929; 1st Cl. Hons Sch. of Modern History, 1933; Bryce Student, 1933; Oxford Senior Student, 1934.; BLitt, 1934; Fereday Fellow, St John's Coll., Oxford, 1935-38; DPhil 1937. Asst Lecturer, University Coll., London, 1936-40; War service in the Army, 1941-46, commissioned into Intelligence Corps, demobilised as Major; Lecturer 1946, Reader 1949, Dep. Vice-Chancellor, 1961-63, University of Exeter. *Publications:* The Letters of Arnulf of Lisieux, 1939; Durham Annals and Documents of the Thirteenth Century, 1945; Durham Jurisdictional Peculiars, 1950; The Feudal Kingdom of England, 1955; (ed and trans.) The Life of King Edward the Confessor, 1962; The English Church, 1000-1066, 1963; William I and the Norman Conquest, 1966; Edward the Confessor, 1970. *Recreation:* gardening. *Address:* Middle Court Hall, Kenton, Exeter. *T:* Starcross 438.

**BARLOW, George William,** BScTech, CEng, FIMechE, FIEE; Group Chief Executive, Ransome Hoffman Pollard Ltd, since 1969; Director, Dorman Smith Holdings and subsidiaries, since 1969; *b* 8 June 1924; *s* of Albert Edward and Annice Barlow; *m* 1948, Elaine Mary Atherton (*née* Adamson); one *s* one *d*. *Educ:* Manchester Grammar Sch.; Manchester Univ. (Kitchener Schol., Louis Atkinson Schol.). Served as Elec. Lt, RNVR, 1944-47. Various appts, The English Electric Co. Ltd, 1947-48 (in Spain, 1952-55, Canada, 1958-62); Gen. Manager, Liverpool and Netherton, 1964-67; Managing Director: English Electric Domestic Appliance Co. Ltd, 1965-67; English Electric Computers Ltd, 1967-68. Mem., Univ. of Liverpool Appts Bd, 1965-68; Vice-Chm., Merseyside Training Council, 1965-68; Mem. Council, Instn of Electrical Engineers, 1969-. *Recreations:* golf, shooting. *Address:* 2 Neville Drive, N2. *Clubs:* Army and Navy; Highgate Golf, Royal Birkdale Golf.

**BARLOW, Professor Harold Everard Monteagle,** FRS 1961; BSc (Eng.) London, PhD (Sci.), London; FIEEE; FIEE; MIMechE; Emeritius Professor of Electrical Engineering, University College, London (Pender Professor, 1950-67); *b* Highbury, 15 Nov. 1899; *s* of late Leonard Barlow, MIEE, and Katherine Monteagle, Glasgow; *m* 1931, Janet Hastings, *d* of the late Rev. J. Hastings Eastwood, BA; three *s* one *d*. *Educ:* Wallington Grammar School; City & Guilds Engineering College; University College, London. Sub-Lieut. RNVR 1917-19; Student at University College, London, 1919-23; Practical engineering training with East Surrey Ironworks and Barlow & Young Ltd, 1923-25; Member of Academic Staff, Faculty of Engineering, UCL, 1925-67 (absent from University on War Service, Sept. 1939-Oct. 1945). Joined staff of Telecommunications Research Establishment, Air Ministry, to deal with Radar development, Sept. 1939; Superintendent, Radio Dept, RAE, 1943-45. Fellow of University College, 1946. Prof. of Elec. Engineering, 1945-50; Mem. of: Radar and Signals Advisory Bd, Min. of Supply, 1947; Scientific Advisory Council, Min. of Supply, 1949; Radio Research Bd, DSIR, 1948 and 1960; London Regional Advisory Council and of Academic Bd for Higher Technological Educn, 1952-67; Academic Council, Univ. London, 1953-55; BBC Scientific Advisory Committee, 1953-; Dean of Engineering Faculty, and Member of UCL Cttee, 1949, 1961; Gov. Woolwich Polytechnic, 1948; Member of Council of IEE, 1955-58 and 1960-; awarded Kelvin Premium, J. J. Thomson Premium, Oliver Lodge and Fleming Premium of IEE; Faraday Medal, 1967; Fellow, City and Guilds Inst., 1969. For. Mem., Polish Acad. of Science, 1966. Director, Marconi Instruments 1963. Dellinger Gold Medal, Internat. Radio Union, 1969. *Publications:* Micro-waves and Wave-guides, 1947; (with A. L. Cullen) Micro-Wave Measurements, 1950; (with J. Brown) Radio Surface Waves, 1962; many scientific papers. *Recreations:* sailing, walking, reading. *Address:* Penrith, 12 Higher Drive, Banstead, Surrey. *T:* Ewell 5820; University College,

Gower Street, WC1. *T:* 01-387 7050. *Club:* Athenæum.
*See also D. S. M. Barlow.*

**BARLOW, Prof. Horace Basil,** FRS 1969; Professor of Physiological Optics and Physiology, University of California, Berkeley, since 1964; *b* 8 Dec. 1921; *s* of Sir (James) Alan (Noel) Barlow, 2nd Bt, GCB, KBE (*d* 1968), and of Nora Barlow (*née* Darwin); *m* 1954, Ruthala, *d* of Dr M. H. Salaman, *qv*; four *d*. *Educ:* Winchester; Trinity Coll., Cambridge. Research Fellow, Trinity Coll., 1950-54, Lectr, King's Coll., Cambridge, 1954-64. Demonstrator and Asst Dir of Research, Physiological Lab., Cambridge, 1954-64. *Publications:* several, on neurophysiology of vision in Jl of Physiology, and elsewhere. *Address:* Physiology Dept, University of California, Berkeley, Calif 94720, USA. *T:* Calif (415) 642-6440.
*See also Sir T. E. Barlow, Bt.*

**BARLOW, James;** Novelist; *b* 1 Dec. 1921; *s* of late Stanley Barlow and of Gladys Barlow; *m* 1949, Joyce Margaret Everiss, *d* of Alfred and Lily Everiss; three *s* one *d*. *Educ:* schools at Leamington Spa, Potteries, North Wales. Joined City of Birmingham Water Dept, 1939; joined RAF, 1940, invalided out, 1941; returned after illness to City of Birmingham Water Dept; retired 1960, to follow writing career full time. Wrote articles for Aeroplane and Flight, 1944; for Punch, 1948-53 then began writing novels. *Publications:* The Protagonists, 1956; One Half of the World, 1957; The Man with Good Intentions, 1958; The Patriots, 1960; Term of Trial, 1961; The Hour of Maximum Danger, 1962; This Side of the Sky, 1964; One Man in the World, 1966; The Love Chase, 1968; The Burden of Proof, 1968; Goodbye, England, 1969; Liner, 1970. *Recreations:* photography, motoring, collecting beer and wine labels, watching, listening and reading. *Address:* c/o Charles Lavell Ltd, Mowbray House, Norfolk Street, WC2.

**BARLOW, Sir John (Denman),** 2nd Bt, *cr* 1907; JP for Cheshire; Joint Partner of Thomas Barlow and Bro., Manchester and London; Director: Barclay's Bank Ltd. (Manchester Local Board); Manchester Chamber of Commerce; The Calico Printers; The Falkland Islands Co.; Chairman: various Rubber Plantation Companies; *b* 15 June 1898; *er s* of Sir John Barlow, 1st Bt, and Hon. Anna Maria Heywood Denman (*d* 1965), *sister* of 3rd Baron Denman, PC, GCMG, KCVO; *S* father, 1932; *m* 1928, Hon. Diana Helen Kemp, *d* of 1st Baron Rochdale, CB, and *sister* of 1st Viscount Rochdale, *qv*; three *s* one *d*. Contested (L) Northwich Division of Cheshire, 1929; MP (Nat Lib) Eddisbury Division of Cheshire, 1945-50; contested (U and Nat Lib) Walsall Div. of Staffordshire, 1950; MP (C) Middleton and Prestwich Division of Lancashire, 1951-66. Led CPA Mission to Malaya, 1959; led Parl. Mission to new Malaysian Parl., taking gift of Speaker's chair, 1963; Chm., Cons. Trade and Industries Cttee, 1955-60. Vice-Chm., Cotton Bd, 1940. Mem. Council, RASE, 1942-53. *Heir: s* John Kemp Barlow [*b* 22 April 1934; *m* 1962, Susan, *er d* of Col. Sir Andrew Horsburgh-Porter, *qv*; four *s*]. *Address:* Bradwall Manor, Sandbach, Cheshire. *T:* Sandbach 2036. *Club:* Brooks's.

**BARLOW, Ralph Mitford Marriott,** MA Cantab; *b* 3 Jan. 1904; *s* of late H. G. Barlow, late of Clifton College, Bristol; *m* 1934, Agnes Margaret, 2nd *d* of late G. M. Carey, Sherborne; one *s* two *d*. *Educ:* Clifton College; Corpus Christi College, Cambridge (Choral Scholar). Assistant Master and House Master, Sherborne School, Dorset, 1926-48; Warden of Trinity College, Glenalmond, 1948-64. *Recreations:* fishing, walking, gardening; formerly Rugby football (Cambridge University XV, 1925; English Trial Cap, 1926). *Address:* Brook House, Chew Stoke, Bristol. *T:* Chew Magna 488.

**BARLOW, Sir Robert,** Kt 1944; President of the Metal Box Company since 1961 (formerly Chairman); *b* 1 September 1891; *s* of Edward Charles and Annie Eleanor Barlow; *m* 1942, Margaret Rawlings, *qv*; one *d*. *Educ:* Grocer's Company's School. *Address:* Rocketer, Wendover, Bucks. *T:* Wendover 2234.

**BARLOW, Thomas Bradwall;** merchant banker; director of rubber, insurance and other public companies; Joint Senior Partner in Thomas Barlow & Bro., London and Manchester; 2nd *s* of Sir John Emmott Barlow, 1st Bt; *m* 1943, Elizabeth Margaret, *d* of Hon. B. G. Sackville-West; one *s* one *d*. *Educ:* Leighton Park, Reading; Haverford, Pa, USA. Chairman: Br. Assoc. of Straits Merchants, 1937; Rubber Trade Assoc., 1942-43; Rubber Growers' Association, 1945-46; British Association of Malaysia, 1965. *Recreations:* hunting, steeplechasing, and travelling. *Address:* Thornby House, Northampton. *T:* Guilsborough 214. *Clubs:* Brooks's, City of London, Hurlingham.

**BARLOW, Sir Thomas (Erasmus),** 3rd Bt *cr* 1902; DSC 1945; Secretary General, Charles Darwin Foundation for the Galapagos Islands, since 1967; *b* 23 Jan. 1914; *s* of Sir Alan Barlow, 2nd Bt, GCB, KBE, and of Nora, *d* of late Sir Horace Darwin, KBE; *S* father, 1968; *m* 1955, Isabel, *d* of late Dr T. M. Body, Middlesbrough, Yorks; two *s* two *d*. *Educ:* Winchester College. Entered RN as cadet, 1932; qualified Submarines, 1937; served in Submarines in Atlantic, Mediterranean, Indian Ocean and Far East during War of 1939-45; Naval Staff Course, 1946; Joint Services Staff Course, 1947, Commander, 1950. British Joint Services Mission, Washington, 1950-53; Captain 1954; Imperial Defence Coll., 1957; Chief Staff Officer to Flag Officer Submarines, 1960-62; Commodore, HMS Drake, Devonport, 1962-64; retired, 1964. Now farms at Wendover, Bucks. Pres. Chiltern Hills Agricultural Assoc., 1968; actively concerned in Wildlife and Countryside Conservation movements: Soc. for Promotion of Nature Reserves; Berks, Bucks and Oxfordshire Naturalists' Trust; Roy. Soc. for Protection of Birds. *Recreations:* bird watching, the countryside. *Heir: s* James Alan Barlow, *b* 10 July 1956. *Address:* Boswells, Wendover, Bucks. *T:* Wendover 2119. *Clubs:* Athenæum, Savile.
*See also Prof. H. B. Barlow.*

**BARMAN, Christian,** OBE 1963; RDI; Past President, Society of Industrial Artists; *b* 1898. *Educ:* University of Liverpool School of Architecture. Editor, the Architect's Journal and the Architectural Review; Publicity Officer, London Passenger Transport Bd, 1935-41; was generally responsible for the visual presentation of the undertaking to the public; Asst Dir of Post-War Building, Min. of Works, 1941-45; Public Relations Adviser, GWR, 1945-47; Chief Publicity Officer, British Transport Commn, 1947-62; Exec. Mem., BTC Design Panel, 1956-62. *Publications:* Sir John Vanbrugh, 1924; edition of James Gibbs, Rules for Drawing the various Parts of Architecture, 1925; Balbus, or the Future of Architecture, 1926; Architecture: An Introduction for the General Reader, 1927; Public Transport (The Things We See Series), 1949; Early British Railways, 1950;

Introduction to Railway Architecture, 1950. Under psuedonym Christian Mawson: Ramping Cat (a novel), 1941; Portrait of England (an anthology), 1941. *Recreation:* collecting edible fungi. *Address:* 12a Hillbrow, Whitley Wood Road, Reading, Berks.

**BARNA, Prof. Tibor;** Professor of Economics, University of Sussex, since 1962; Member, Monopolies Commission, since 1963; *b* 1919. *Educ:* London School of Economics. Lecturer, London School of Economics, 1944; Official Fellow, Nuffield College, Oxford, 1947; senior posts in UN Economic Commission for Europe, 1949; Assistant Director, National Institute of Economic and Social Research, London, 1955. *Publications:* Redistribution of Income through Public Finance in 1937, 1945; Investment and Growth Policies in British Industrial Firms, 1962. Papers in Jl Royal Statistical Soc. *Address:* Beanacre, Westmeston, Hassocks, Sussex. *T:* Hassocks 2384.

**BARNARD,** 11th Baron, *cr* 1698; **Harry John Neville Vane,** TD 1960; Landowner; Lord Lieutenant of County Durham, since 1970; *b* 21 Sept. 1923; *er s* of 10th Baron and Sylvia Mary, *d* of Herbert Straker; *S* father, 1964; *m* 1952, Lady Davina Mary Cecil, OStJ, *e d* of 6th Marquess of Exeter, *qv*; one *s* four *d*. *Educ:* Eton. Served War of 1939-45, RAFVR, 1942-46 (Flying Officer, 1945). Lieut. Northumberland Hussars, 1948; Captain, 1951; Major, 1957; Lt-Col commanding, 1964. County Councillor, Durham, 1952-61. Chm., Durham Co. AEC, 1970-; President: Farmway Ltd; Durham Co. Br. BRCS, 1969-. DL Durham, 1956, Vice-Lieutenant, 1969-70; JP Durham, 1961. Joint Master of Zetland Hounds, 1963-65. *Heir: s* Hon. Henry Francis Cecil Vane, *b* 11 March 1959. *Address:* (Residence) Selaby, Gainford, Darlington, County Durham. *T:* Gainford 206; (Seat) Raby Castle, Staindrop, Darlington, Co. Durham. *Clubs:* Brooks's, Junior Carlton; Durham County (Durham); Northern Counties (Newcastle upon Tyne).

**BARNARD, Sir (Arthur) Thomas,** Kt 1958; CB 1954; OBE 1946; Director-General of Inspection, Ministry of Supply, 1956-58, retired; *b* 28 Sept. 1893; *s* of late Arthur Barnard; *m* 1921, Grace, *d* of William Magerkorth, Belvedere, Kent. *Educ:* Erith Technical Coll. Is a Chartered Civil Engineer. Chief Superintendent, Royal Ordnance Factories, Woolwich, 1951-55; Dep. Dir-Gen., Royal Ordnance Factories, Adelphi, London, 1955-56. *Address:* Kentmere, Heathfield, Chislehurst, Kent. *Club:* Royal Automobile.

**BARNARD, Beverley Gayer,** CMG 1959; consultant on Middle East Affairs, since 1959; *b* 4 Aug. 1916; *s* of late Frederick William Barnard, Thursley, Surrey; *m* 1945, Joan Anne Mary (*née* Fernandes); three *s*. *Educ:* Imperial Coll. of Science and Technology, London. Television research, Scophony Ltd, 1938-40; Westland Aircraft Ltd, Yeovil, 1940-41; Royal Aircraft Establishment, Farnborough, 1941-44; CCG, Advance Element, 1944-46; Civil Air Attache at Baghdad, Teheran and Persian Gulf, 1947-52; Civil Air Attaché in the Middle East (resident at Cairo and Beirut), 1952-59. *Recreations:* painting, making films, golf. *Address:* Langhurst Manor, Chiddingfold, Surrey. *Clubs:* Royal Aero, royal Air Force Reserves.

**BARNARD, Eric,** CB 1951; CBE 1943; DSO 1917; MA (Oxon); Deputy Secretary, Department of Scientific and Industrial Research, 1945-55; *b* 19 Sept. 1891; *m* 1923; one *s* one *d*. Gloucestershire Regt, 1914-19 (DSO, despatches twice).

**BARNARD, Vice-Adm. (Retd) Sir Geoffrey,** KCB 1957 (CB 1953); CBE 1943; DSO 1941, Bar, 1945; Légion d'Honneur; Croix de Guerre (with Palm); *b* 12 Nov. 1902; *s* of T. H. Barnard, JP, Banker, Bedford and Bertha Mary Lambton; *m* 1926, Julyan Frances Crawley; one *s* two *d*. *Educ:* Cheam Sch.; RNC Dartmouth. Specialised in Gunnery, 1927; Fleet Gunnery Officer, Africa Station; Comdr, 1935; commanded HMS Daring, China Station; Staff Course, 1937; Fleet Gunnery Officer, Mediterranean (HMS Warspite), 1939-41; Capt. 1942; Dep. Chief of Staff to Naval C-in-C for North African landings, 1942, and subsequently to C-in-C Mediterranean, 1942-43; commanded HMS Aurora, Mediterranean 1944-45; Chief Staff Officer to Flag Officer (Air), 1946-47; Dir Royal Naval Tactical Sch., 1948-49. Lent to Indian Navy for command of IN Squadron, 1950-51; Rear-Adm, 1951; Asst Chief of Naval Staff (Warfare), 1952-53; a Lord Commissioner of the Admiralty and Deputy Chief of Naval Staff, 1953-54; Admiral, British Joint Services Mission, Washington, 1954-56; Pres. of the Royal Naval Coll., Greenwich, 1956-Dec. 1958; retired, 1959. *Recreations:* gardening and fishing. *Address:* 109 Sussex Road, Petersfield, Hants. *T:* Petersfield 4327. *Club:* English-Speaking Union.
*See also T. T. Barnard.*

**BARNARD, Prof. George Alfred,** MA, DSc; Professor of Mathematics, University of Essex, since 1966; Statistical consultant to various organisations; Member, University Grants Committee, since 1967; *b* 23 Sept. 1915; *s* of Frederick C. and Ethel C. Barnard; *m* 1st, 1942, Helen J. B. Davies; three *s*; 2nd, 1949, Mary M. L. Jones; one *s*. *Educ:* Sir George Monoux Grammar Sch., Walthamstow; St John's Coll., Cambridge. Math. Trip., Pt III, 1936, Res. Studentship, St John's Coll., spent at Grad. Sch. Princeton, NJ, USA, 1937-39. Plessey Co., Ilford, as Math. Consultant, 1940-42; Ministry of Supply Adv. Unit, 1942-45; Lecturer in Math. Dept, Imperial Coll., 1945-47; Reader in Math. Statistics, Imperial Coll., 1948-54, Professor, 1954-66. Royal Statistical Society: Council Mem. and Vice-Pres., 1952, 1962 (Chm. Res. Sect., 1958); Mem. Internat. Statistical Inst., 1952; Statistical Adviser, Brit. Standards Instn (with Prof. E. S. Pearson), 1954; Chm. Inst. of Statisticians, 1960-; Pres. Inst. of Mathematics and its Applications, 1970-; Fellow, Amer. Statistical Assoc., Inst. of Mathematical Statistics, 1961. *Publications:* Papers in Jl Royal Statistical Society; Technometrics; Biometrika. (Ed.) The Foundations of Statistical Inference, 1962. *Recreations:* viola playing, boating. *Address:* Mill House, Hurst Green, Brightlingsea, Essex. *T:* Brightlingsea 2388.

**BARNARD, Captain Sir George (Edward),** Kt 1968; Deputy Master of Trinity House, since 1961; Director, Royal Exchange Assurance; *b* 11 Aug. 1907; 2nd *s* of Michael and Alice Louise Barnard; *m* 1940, Barbara Emma Hughes; one *s*. Apprenticed at sea, 1922; 1st Command, Blue Star Line, 1945. Elder Brother of Trinity House, 1958-. Trustee, Nat. Maritime Museum, 1967-; Treasurer, Internat. Assoc. of Lighthouse Authorities, 1961-; Hon. Sec., King George's Fund for Sailors, 1967-. FRSA 1969. *Recreation:* gardening. *Address:* The Lodge, Rayleigh Road, Hutton, Essex. *T:* Brentwood 2320.

**BARNARD, Sir Henry William,** Kt 1944; Judge of High Court of Justice (Probate, Divorce and Admiralty Division), 1944-59; *b* 18 April 1891; *s* of late William Tyndal Barnard, KC. *Educ:* Wellington Coll.; Merton Coll., Oxford. Called to Bar, Gray's Inn, 1913; KC 1939. Bencher Gray's Inn, 1939, Treasurer, 1953. Admiralty Judge of the Cinque Ports. Served European War as a Captain in Royal West Kent Regt (5th Bn). *Address:* Boscobel, Hawkshill, Walmer, Kent. *Club:* United University.

**BARNARD, Howard Clive,** MA, BLitt Oxon; MA (Educ), DLitt London, FCP, FTCL. Professor of Education, Reading University, 1937-51; Emeritus since 1951; *b* City of London, 7 June 1884; Freeman of the City and Mem. of the Goldsmiths' Co. by patrimony; *s* of late Howard Barnard, journalist; *m* Edith Gwendolen (*d* 1956), *d* of late John Wish, Civil Servant; one *s* one *d*. *Educ:* University Coll. Sch., London; Brasenose Coll., Oxford (Sen. Hulme Scholar); London Sch. of Economics; King's Coll., London (Advanced Student); also studied in France and Germany. Asst Master at Manchester, Ramsgate, and Bradford; Headmaster, Grammar Sch., Gillingham, Kent; Examiner at various times to Univs of Oxford, Cambridge, London, Durham, Birmingham, Liverpool, Manchester, Leeds, Sheffield, Wales, Nottingham and Hull, the Civil Service Commission, the LCC, the Coll. of Preceptors, etc.; mem. of Corporation of Trinity Coll. of Music, London. *Publications:* The Little Schools of Port-Royal; The Port-Royalists on Education (source-book); The French Tradition in Education; Madame de Maintenon and Saint-Cyr; Fénelon on Education; Girls at School under the Ancien Régime; Education and the French Revolution (also Italian edn); A History of English Education from 1760; Were those the Days?; An Introduction to Teaching; Principles and Practice of Geography and Teaching; Observational Geography and Regional Survey; The Expansion of the Anglo-Saxon Nations (ed); A Handbook of British Educational Terms (with Prof. J. A. Lauwerys); and numerous school books. *Recreations:* walking, organ-playing. *Address:* 54 Grosvenor Road, Caversham, Reading, Berks. *T:* Reading 73001.

**BARNARD, Sir Thomas;** *see* Barnard, Sir A. T.

**BARNARD, Thomas Theodore,** MC; MA Oxon; PhD Cantab; *b* 31 Aug. 1898; *e s* of late T. H. Barnard, banker, Bedford; *m* 1924, Gillian Sarah (*d* 1961), *d* of late Lieut-Col Hon. A. S. Byng, DSO; one *s* two *d*. *Educ:* Eton, Christ Church, Oxford; King's Coll., Cambridge. Lieut, Coldstream Guards, 1917-19; Prof. of Social Anthropology, and Dir of the Sch. of African Life and Languages, University of Cape Town, 1926-34. Rejoined Coldstream Guards, 1940-45, Capt., Guards Depôt. VMH 1965. *Address:* Furzebrook House, Wareham, Dorset. *Club:* Guards.

*See also Vice-Adm. sir Geoffrey Barnard.*

**BARNBY,** 2nd Baron, *cr* 1922; **Francis Vernon Willey;** CMG 1918; CBE 1919; MVO 1918; *b* Bradford, Yorks., 1884; *e s* of 1st Baron and Florence (*d* 1933), *d* of Frederick Chinnock, Dinorbin Court, Hants; *S* father, 1929; *m* 1940, Banning Grange, Bryn Mawr, Pennsylvania. *Educ:* Eton; Magdalen Coll., Oxford. Late Brevet Col Comdg Sherwood Rangers, Notts Yeomanry (TF). Hon. Col 1948; mobilised, 1914; served Egypt and Gallipoli, 1915; recalled as Asst Dir of Ordnance Stores (Clothing); Controller of Wool Supplies under War Dept, June 1916, and organised the purchase and distribution of the British and Colonial Wool Clips on Government and civilian account; MP (Co. U) South Bradford, Dec. 1918-22; MFH Blankney Hunt, Lincolnshire, 1919-33. Past Pres. FBI; Member: Surplus Govt Property Disposals Board, 1918-21; Central Electricity Board, 1927-46; Overseas Settlement Board, 1937-; a former Director: Lloyds Bank Ltd; Commercial Union Assurance Co. Ltd; President: Textile Institute, 1961-62; Aire Wool Co. Ltd; Past Master, Worshipful Company of Woolmen. *Heir:* none. *Address:* Hillthorpe, Ashtead, Surrey; 2 Caxton Street, SW1. *T:* 01-222 3003; 35-37 Grosvenor Square, W1. *T:* 01-499 2112. *Clubs:* Carlton, Cavalry, Bath, Hurlingham.

**BARNELL, Herbert Rex,** MA, PhD (Cantab); BSc (London); Chief Scientific Adviser (Food), Ministry of Agriculture, Fisheries and Food, 1959-68, retired; *b* 8 Nov. 1907; *o s* of Herbert Joseph Barnell, Luton, Beds.; *m* 1933, Elsie Eileen, 3rd *d* of D. McCullough, Capetown. *Educ:* Luton Modern Sch.; Downing Coll., Cambridge. 1st Class Hons Pt II Nat. Sci. Tripos (Botany); Frank Smart Univ. Prize (Botany) and Univ. Studentship (Botany). Research Asst and Lectr in Plant Physiology, Sch. of Agric., Cambridge, 1932-37; Plant Biochemist on staff of Imperial Coll. of Trop. Agric., Trinidad (Low Temperature Research Stn, Research on storage and transport of trop. fruits and vegs), 1937-43. Various scientific posts in Min. of Food and in combined Min. of Agric., Fisheries and Food. FIBiol; Fellow, Institute of Food Science and Technology. *Publications:* papers on plant physiology, plant biochem. and food technology in various scientific jls. *Recreations:* sea fishing; reading. *Address:* 22b Radnor Cliff, Folkestone, Kent. *T:* Folkestone 38484. *Clubs:* Athenæum, Authors', New Arts Theatre, Royal Commonwealth Society.

**BARNES,** family name of **Baron Gorell.**

**BARNES, Rt. Hon. Alfred;** PC 1945; a Designer by trade; *b* North Woolwich, 1887. *Art Educ:* Northampton Institute; LCC Sch. of Arts and Crafts. MP (Lab-Co-op) South East Ham, 1922-31 and 1935-55; Lord Commissioner of the Treasury, 1929-30; Minister of War Transport, 1945-46, Minister of Transport, 1946-51; Chairman of the Co-operative Party, 1924-45. *Address:* Eastcliffe Hotel, Walton-on-the-Naze, Essex.

**BARNES, (Alice) Josephine (Mary Taylor), (Mrs Warren),** FRCP, FRCS, FRCOG; Obstetrician and Gynaecologist, Charing Cross Hospital and Elizabeth Garrett Anderson Hospital; Chairman, Women's National Cancer Control Campaign, since 1969; *b* 18 Aug. 1912; *er d* of late Rev. Walter W. Barnes, MA(Oxon), and Alice Mary Ibbetson, FRCO, ARCM; *m* 1942, Dr Brian Warren (marr. diss. 1964); one *s* two *d*. *Educ:* Oxford High Sch.; Lady Margaret Hall, Oxford University College Hosp. Med. Sch. 1st class Hons Physiology, Oxford, BA 1934, MA, BM, BCh 1937, DM 1941. University College Hospital: Goldschmid Scholar; Aitchison Scholar; Tuke Silver Medal; Fellowes Silver Medal; F. T. Roberts Prize; Suckling Prize. Various appointments at UCH, Samaritan Hosp., Queen Charlotte's Hosp., and Radcliffe Infirmary, Oxford; Dep. Academic Head, Obstetric Unit, UCH, 1947-52; Surgeon, Marie Curie Hosp., 1947-67. Medical Women's Federation: Hon. Sec., 1951-57; Pres., London Assoc., 1958-60; Pres., 1966-67. Royal Society of Medicine: Mem. Council, 1949-50; Hon. Editor, Sect. of Obstetrics. Examiner in Obstetrics and Gynaecology: Univ. of London; RCOG; Examining Bd in

England, Queen's Univ., Belfast. Member: Council, Med. Defence Union; Royal Commn on Med. Educn, 1965-68; Council, RCOG; Med. Res. Council Cttee on Analgesia in Midwifery; Min. of Health Med. Manpower Cttee; Medico-Legal Soc.; Population Investigation Cttee, Eugenics Soc. Pres., W London Medico-Chirurgical Soc., 1969-70. Mem. of Honour, French Gynaecological Soc., 1945; Corresp. Mem., Royal Belgian Soc. of Obstetricians and Gynaecologists, 1949. Governor: Charing Cross Hosp.; Chelsea Coll. of Science and Technology; Mem. Council, Benenden Sch. Fawcett Lectr, Bedford Coll., 1969; Rhys-Williams Lectr, Nat. Birthday Trust, 1970. Commandeur de Bontemps du Médoc et des Graves, 1966. *Publications:* Gynaecological History, 1948; The Care of the Expectant Mother, 1957; Lecture Notes on Gynaecology, 1966. Numerous contribs to med. jls, etc. *Recreations:* music, gastronomy, motoring, foreign travel; formerly hockey (Oxford Univ. Women's Hockey XI, 1932, 1933, 1934). *Address:* 7 Wimpole Street, W1. *T:* 01-580 1584; 8 Aubrey Walk, W8. *T:* 01-727 9832.

*See also F. W. I. Barnes.*

**BARNES, Anthony Charles,** DSO 1916; OBE 1943; Past Director of Barclays Bank DCO (Deputy Chairman, 1947-59), and of Barclays Bank Ltd. (Vice-Chairman, 1951-56); *yr s* of late Sir George Barnes, KCB, KCSI; *b* 13 October 1891; *m* 1920, Honor Dorothea, *d* of late Stanley V. Coote, JP; one *s* two *d. Educ:* Eton; New Coll., Oxford (BA). Served with 9th Batt. Yorkshire Regt, Sept. 1914-April 1918; commanded 4th (Territorial) Batt. Yorkshire Regt, June 1918-Oct. 1918, and 15th Batt. the Durham Light Infantry, Oct. 1918-April 1919 (DSO and bar, despatches thrice). Mem. Joint Anglo-Egyptian Cotton Commn, 1941; a Trustee of the Whiteley Homes; Chm. Guildford Diocesan Bd of Finance, 1961-64. *Recreation:* gardening. *Address:* Foxholm, Cobham, Surrey. *T:* Byfleet 45183. *Club:* Brooks's.

**BARNES, Arthur Chapman,** CMG 1936; FRIC; BSc (Hons); Sugar Consultant; *b* 1891. *Educ:* Deacon's School, Peterborough; Municipal College of Technology and Victoria Univ., Manchester. Entered Survey Dept, East Africa Protectorate, 1914; agricultural chemist, Nigeria, 1923; Asst Director of Agriculture, Zanzibar, 1927; Director of Agriculture, Fiji, 1929; Director of Agriculture and Island Chemist, Jamaica, 1933; General Manager West Indies Sugar Co. Ltd, 1938; seconded for duty as Director of Research for The Sugar Manufacturers' Association (of Jamaica), Ltd, 1947; retired 1951. *Publications:* Agriculture of the Sugar-cane, 1953; The Sugar Cane, 1964. *Address:* PO Box 1278, Durban, Natal, South Africa. *Club:* West Indian.

**BARNES, Sir Denis (Charles),** KCB 1967 (CB 1964); Permanent Under-Secretary of State, Department of Employment and Productivity, since 1968 (Permanent Secretary, Ministry of Labour, 1966, Deputy Secretary 1963); *b* 15 Dec. 1914; *s* of Frederick Charles Barnes; *m* 1938, Patricia Abercrombie. *Educ:* Hulme Gram. Sch., Manchester; Merton Coll., Oxford. Postmaster, Merton Coll., Oxford, 1933-37. BA, 1st Cl. Mod. History, 1936; PPE 1937. Entered Min. of Labour, 1937; Private Sec. to Minister of Labour, 1945-47. Commonwealth Fellowship, 1953. *Address:* 170 Gloucester Place, NW1. *T:* 01-723 0887. *Club:* Savile.

**BARNES, Eric Cecil,** CMG 1954; Colonial Administrative Service; Provincial Commissioner, Nyasaland, 1949-55, retired; *b* 1899; *m* 1950, Isabel Margaret Lesley, *d* of late Mrs Isabel Wauchope; one *s* one *d. Educ:* Bishop Cotton's Sch., Simla; Bedford Sch. and Cadet Coll., Quetta, India. Indian Army, 1917-23; Administrative Service, Nyasaland, 1925. Deputy Provincial Commissioner, 1946. *Address:* Polmear, Frogham, near Fordingbridge, Hants. *T:* Fordingbridge 3357.

**BARNES, (Ernest) John (Ward);** Ambassador to Israel, since 1969; *b* 22 June 1917; *er s* of Rt Rev. Ernest William Barnes, 3rd Bishop of Birmingham, and Adelaide, *d* of Sir Adolphus Ward, Master of Peterhouse, Cambridge; *m* 1948, Cynthia Margaret Ray, *d* of Sir Herbert Stewart, CIE; two *s* three *d. Educ:* Winchester; Trinity Coll., Cambridge. Classical Tripos, Pts I and II, Class I; Porson Scholar, 1939. Royal Artillery, 1939-46 (Lt-Col, MBE, US Bronze Star). HM Foreign Service, 1946; served Washington, Beirut, Bonn and Harvard Univ. (Center for International Affairs). *Address:* British Embassy, Tel Aviv, Israel. *Clubs:* Athenæum, Brooks's.

**BARNES, Francis Walter Ibbetson;** Recorder of Smethwick, Staffordshire, Dec. 1964, Warley, since 1966; Deputy Chairman, Oxfordshire Quarter Sessions, since 1965; *b* 10 May 1914; *s* of late Rev. Walter W. Barnes, MA (Oxon) and Alice Mary Ibbetson, FRCO, ARCM; *m* 1st, 1941, Heather Katherine (marr. diss. 1953), *d* of Frank Tamplin; two *s*; 2nd, 1955, Sonia Nina (Nina Walker, pianist), *d* of Harold Higginbottom; two *s* one *d. Educ:* Dragon Sch., Oxford; Mill Hill Sch.; Balliol Coll., Oxford. BA Jurisprudence (Hons), Oxford, 1937; MA 1967. Called to Bar, Inner Temple, 1938. Profumo Prize, Inner Temple, 1939. Served War, 1939-46 in Army (Middlesex Regt) and Home Office and Military Fire Services; Sen. Company Officer NFS and Capt. comdg military Fire Fighting Co. of BLA; later Staff Capt., JAG (War Crimes Section). Functioned as Judge Advocate and Prosecutor in various trials of war criminals in Germany. Life Governor, Mill Hill Sch., 1939-; Mem., Dame Henrietta Barnett Bd (Educl Trust), 1951-. Elected to Bar Council, 1961. Bar Council's rep. (observer) on cons. cttee of Lawyers of the Common Market countries from 1962; contrib. to Common Market Law Review. Union Internat. des Avocats: Mem. Council, 1964-; Rapporteur Général at Vienna Congress, 1967; Rapporteur National at Paris Congress, 1971. *Recreations:* music, outdoor games, motoring. *Address:* 2 Harcourt Buildings, Temple, EC4. *T:* 01-353 8549; 11 Park Hill, Ealing, W5. *T:* 01-997 5501.

*See also A. J. M. T. Barnes.*

**BARNES, Harold William;** Director, Telecommunications Finance, Telecommunications Headquarters, GPO, since 1968; *b* 7 Nov. 1912; *s* of Edgar and Florence Barnes; *m* 1941, Mary M. Butchart; one *s* one *d. Educ:* Chesterfield Grammar Sch. Entered Civil Service as Exec. Officer, 1931. Served HM Forces, RE Postal Services, 1940-46 (final rank, Major). Asst Accountant Gen., GPO, 1952-55; Dep. Dir, Finance and Accounts, GPO, 1955-64; Controller, Post Office Supplies Dept, 1964-68. *Recreations:* golf, choral music, (City of London Choir). *Address:* 3 Little Court, West Wickham, Kent. *T:* 01-777 6785. *Club:* Langley Park Golf (Beckenham).

**BARNES, Harry Cheetham;** Technical Editor, Thornton Research Centre; *b* 12 April 1898; *s* of James and Ann Barnes; *m* 1921, Doris Brogden; one *s* three *d. Educ:* Hyde Grammar Sch.; Coll. of Technology, Manchester Univ. NCO 181st Brigade, 40th Div. RFA; Lieut

RFA 18th Div., Manchester Univ. BSc Tech. (Hons); London Univ. BCom.; Mem. of Council, Textile Inst.; Editor The Textile Manufacturer until March 1945; Deputy Director, Labour, the Cotton Board until 1948. Technical Editor Thornton Research Centre (Shell). *Publications:* various lectures, papers, articles. *Recreations:* farming. *Address:* Beacon Hurst, Frodsham, Cheshire.

**BARNES, James Edwin;** Under-Secretary (Aerodromes), Board of Trade, since 1966 (Ministry of Aviation, 1964-66); *b* 23 Nov. 1917; *s* of James Barnes and Kate (*née* Davies); *m* 1943, Gloria Parkinson; two *s* one *d*. *Educ:* King Edward VI Sch., Nuneaton. Joined Civil Service as Executive Officer, War Office, 1936; Higher Executive Officer, Min. of Supply, 1942; Sen. Exec. Officer 1945, Principal, 1946, Asst Sec. 1952. Coronation Medal, 1953. *Address:* 117 Lawrie Park Gardens, Sydenham, SE26. *T:* 01-778 2537.

**BARNES, John;** *see* Barnes, E. J. W.

**BARNES, Prof. John Arundel,** DSC 1944; Professor of Sociology, University of Cambridge, since 1969; *b* Reading 9 Sept. 1918; *s* of T. D. and M. G. Barnes, Bath; *m* 1942, Helen Frances, *d* of Charles Bastable; three *s* one *d*. *Educ:* Christ's Hosp.; St John's Coll., Cambridge. Fellow, St John's Coll., Cambridge, 1950-53; Simon Research Fellow, Manchester Univ., 1951-53; Reader in Anthropology, London Univ., 1954-56; Prof. of Anthropology, Sydney Univ., 1956-58; Prof. of Anthropology, Inst. of Advanced Studies, ANU, Canberra, 1958-69; Overseas Fellow, Churchill Coll., Cambridge, 1965-66. *Publications:* Marriage in a Changing Society, 1951; Politics in a Changing Society, 1954; Inquest on the Murngin, 1967. *Address:* Churchill College, Cambridge CB3 0DS. *T:* Cambridge 61200.

**BARNES, Dr John Morrison,** CBE 1962; Director, Toxicology Research Unit, Medical Research Council Laboratories, Carshalton, since 1947; *b* 11 Jan. 1913; *s* of Dr A. E. Barnes, Sheffield; *m* 1941, Ruth Eleanor, *d* of Rev. Edward Joseph Northcote-Green, Oxford; two *s* one *d*. *Educ:* Repton; Trinity Hall, Cambridge. BA 1933; MB, BCh, MRCS, LRCP, 1936. Served War of 1939-45; RAMC, 1942-45 (Lieut-Col). *Recreations:* none. *Address:* 16 Holmwood Gardens, Wallington, Surrey. *T:* 01-647 1388.

**BARNES, Josephine;** *see* Barnes, A. J. M. T.

**BARNES, Kenneth,** CB 1970; Deputy Under-Secretary of State, Department of Employment and Productivity, since 1968; *b* 26 Aug. 1922; *s* of Arthur and Doris Barnes, Accrington, Lancs; *m* 1948, Barbara Ainsworth; one *s* two *d*. *Educ:* Accrington Grammar Sch.; Balliol Coll., Oxford. Entered Ministry of Labour, 1948; Asst Sec., 1963; Under-Sec., Cabinet Office, 1966-68. *Address:* Hill House, 35 Pilgrim's Way, Reigate, Surrey. *T:* Reigate 45237. *Club:* United University.

**BARNES, Michael Cecil John;** MP (Lab) Brentford and Chiswick since 1966; Member, Public Accounts Committee, since 1967; *b* 22 Sept. 1932; *s* of late Major C. H. R. Barnes, OBE and of Katherine Louise (*née* Kennedy); *m* 1962, Anne Mason; one *s* one *d*. *Educ:* Malvern; Corpus Christi Coll., Oxford. Marketing Consultant. Contested (Lab) Wycombe, 1964; Chm., Parly Labour Party Social Security Group, 1969-70; Sec., Labour Cttee for Europe, 1969-70. *Recreations:* lawn tennis, walking, reading. *Address:* 45 Ladbroke Grove, W11. *T:* 01-727 2533.

**BARNES, Richard Cumberland;** retired from HM Diplomatic Service, November 1964; *b* 19 July 1912; *er s* of William Cumberland Barnes and Olive Child Stainsby; *m* 1964, Mrs Yanna Psarra-Athanatos. *Educ:* Heath Grammar Sch., Halifax; Pembroke Coll., Oxford. Served with HM Forces, 1940-46: Major, RA; with guerillas in Crete during German Occupation, 1943-45. Seconded to Embassy, Athens, 1945; apptd Mem. Foreign Service, 1946; trans. to UK Delegn, UNSCOB, 1947; 1st Sec., 1948; Foreign Office, 1950; NATO Defence Coll., Paris, 1953; 1st Sec. at UK Delegation, UN, New York, Sept. 1953; Counsellor, 1959; Counsellor and Consul-General, Djakarta, Oct. 1959; Acting Chargé d'Affaires, 1960 and 1961; seconded for service with Commonwealth Relations Office, October 1961. Counsellor and Consul-General, Athens, Oct. 1962; Acting Chargé d'Affaires, 1962 and 1963. *Address:* Villa Athanatos, Kifissia, Athens, Greece. *T:* Athens 8012614.

**BARNES, Dr Robert Sandford;** Director, Research and Development of the British Steel Corporation, since 1970; *b* 8 July 1924; *s* of William Edward Barnes and Ada Elsie Barnes (*née* Sutherst); *m* 1952, Julia Frances Marriott Grant; one *s* three *d*. *Educ:* Univ. of Manchester. BSc 1948, MSc 1959, DSc 1962. Radar Research, Admiralty Signals Estab., Witley, Surrey, 1944-47; AERE, Harwell: Metallurgical Research, 1948-62; Head of Irradiation Branch, 1962-65; Vis. Scientist, The Science Center, N Amer. Aviation Co., Calif, 1965; Head of Metallurgy Div., AERE, Harwell, 1966-68; Dep. Dir, BISRA, July 1968-Feb. 1969; Dir, BISRA, 1969-70. Member: CBI Research and Technology Cttee, 1968; Council, The Welding Inst., 1970. Governor, Sheffield Polytechnic, 1968; Mem., Court of Univ. of Surrey, 1968. Rosenhain Medallist, Inst. of Metals, 1964. FInstP 1961, FIM 1965. *Publications:* contrib. chapters to several specialist books of science; scientific papers in various learned jls. *Recreation:* family yachting. *Address:* (business) 33 Grosvenor Place, SW1. *T:* 01-235 1212; (home) Pigeon Forge, Daneshill, The Hockering, Woking, Surrey. *T:* Woking 61529. *Club:* Athenæum.

**BARNES, Roland,** CBE 1970; BSc, MB, ChB, FRCS, FRCSE, FRCSGlas; Professor of Orthopaedic Surgery, University of Glasgow, since 1959; Orthopaedic Surgeon, Western Infirmary, Glasgow, and Killearn Hospital, Stirlingshire, since 1943; *b* 21 May 1907; *y s* of Benjamin Barnes and Mary Ann Bridge, Accrington, Lancs.; *m* 1938, Mary Mills Buckley; one *s* two *d*. *Educ:* University of Manchester. BSc 1927; MB, ChB 1930; Medical and Surgical Clinical prizes. Usual resident appointments; Resident Surgical Officer, Manchester Royal Infirmary, 1934-35; Dickinson Travelling Scholar, Univ. of Manchester, 1935-36; visited orthopaedic clinics in USA; Fellow, Hospital for Ruptured and Crippled, New York. Chief Asst to Sir Harry Platt, Bt, Orthopaedic Department, Royal Infirmary, Manchester, 1937-39; Surgeon in Charge of Orthopædic and Peripheral Nerve Injury Centre, EMS Hospital, Winwick, Lancs, 1940-43. Past Pres., British Orthopædic Assoc.; Hon. Mem. French, Finnish, German and S African Orthopædic Assocs; Corresp. Mem. Amer. Orthopædic Assoc. *Publications:* papers on injuries of the peripheral nerves and spine, fractures of neck of femur, and on tumours of bone. *Recreation:* gardening. *Address:* 35 Boclair Road, Bearsden, Glasgow. *T:* 041-942 2699.

**BARNES, Sir William Lethbridge G.;** *see* Gorell Barnes.

**BARNES, Winston Herbert Frederick,** MA (Oxon); Vice-Chancellor, University of Liverpool, 1963-69; *b* 30 May 1909; *er s* of Frederick Charles and Martha Lilley Barnes; *m* 1938, Sarah, *d* of late Thomas David Davies; two *d*. *Educ:* Manchester Grammar Sch.; Corpus Christi Coll., Oxford (Hugh Oldham Scholar, Haigh Scholar). 1st Cl., Classical Hon. Mods. 1930; 1st Cl., Lit. Hum. 1932; John Locke Scholar in Mental Philosophy, Oxford, 1932; Sen. Demy, Magdalen Coll., Oxford, 1933-34; Asst Lecturer in Philosophy, 1936-39. Lecturer 1939-41, Univ. of Liverpool; served in RAFVR, 1941-42; Temporary Principal, Ministry of Supply, 1942-45; Prof. of Philosophy, Univ. of Durham (Durham Colls) 1945-59; Prof. of Moral Philosophy, Univ. of Edinburgh, 1959-63, Gifford Lectr in Natural Theology, 1968-69, 1969-70. Pres., Mind Association, 1948. Mem. Planning Bd, Independent Univ., 1970-. Hon. DCL, Durham, 1964. *Publications:* The Philosophical Predicament, 1950; contributions to Mind, Philosophy, Aristotelian Society Proceedings. *Recreations:* walking, swimming. *Address:* 7 Great Stuart Street, Edinburgh 3. *T:* 031-226 3158. *Club:* Athenæum.

**BARNETSON, Maj.-Gen. James Craw,** CB 1965; OBE 1945; Director of Medical Services, BAOR, December 1964-66, retired; *b* 26 July 1907; *s* of Dr R. B. Barnetson; *m* 1935, Sylvia Joan Milner Moore; three *s*. *Educ:* Edinburgh Academy; Edinburgh Univ. (MB, ChB). Staff Coll., Camberley, 1942; ADMS, AFHQ, 1942-43; ADMS, 6th Armd Div., 1943-46, ADMS, Scot. Comd, 1946-47; Asst DGAMS, War Office, 1947-50; Joint Staff Coll., Latimer, 1950; ADMS, 11th Armd Div., 1951; ADMS, Plans, SHAPE, 1951-53; OC Commonwealth Mil. Hosp., Japan, 1953-54; ADMS, GHQ, E Africa, 1954-57; ADMS, 6 Armd Div., 1958-59; Comdt Field Trg Centre, HQ, AER, RAMC, 1959-60; DDMS, Northern Comd, 1960-61; Dep. DGAMS, 1961-64. QHP 1961. Col Comdt, RAMC, 1968. *Recreations:* golf and fishing. *Address:* The Old Cottage, Wardley Green, Milland, West Sussex. *T:* Milland 371.

**BARNETSON, William Denholm;** Chairman and Managing Director, United Newspapers Ltd, since 1966; Chairman: Reuters Ltd, since 1968; Bradbury Agnew and Co., since 1969; *b* 21 Mar. 1917; *e s* of late William Barnetson and Ella Moir, Edinburgh; *m* 1940, Joan Fairley, *d* of late W. F. Davidson; one *s* three *d*. *Educ:* Royal High Sch., Edinburgh; Edinburgh Univ. (MA). Served War of 1939-45 in AA Comd (Battery Comdr); detached for special duty on reorganisation of newspaper and book publishing in British Zone of Germany, and in launching Die Welt, 1944-47; sucessively Leader Writer, Editor and Gen. Man., Edinburgh Evening News, 1948-61; Dir, Provincial Newspapers Ltd, 1958- and of parent co., 1962-. Extra-mural Lectr., Edinburgh Univ. 1949-57; regular contrib. to BBC radio and TV in Scotland, 1950-61. Pres., Edinburgh Press Club, 1957-59; Dir, Edinburgh Chamber of Commerce, 1957-60; Mem., Press Council, 1958-61; Chm., Nat. Council for Trng of Journalists, 1959-60; Vice-Pres., Scottish Daily Newspaper Soc., 1960-61; Dir, Press Assoc., 1963-70 (Chm., Centenary Year, 1967-68); Mem. Council, Commonwealth Press Union, 1964-70 (UK delegate Quinquennial Conf. in W Indies, 1965; Chm., Public Relations Cttee, 1968-69); Mem., UK Cttee of Internat. Press Inst., 1964-; Mem. Council, Newspaper Soc. 1967-; Hon. Vice-Pres., Press Club, 1969-; Mem., Punch Table, 1969-. *Recreations:* books, gardening. *Address:* (business) 23-27 Tudor Street, EC4. *T:* 01538 9199; (home) Broom, Chillies Lane, Crowborough, Sussex. *T:* Crowborough 5748. *Clubs:* Beefsteak, Reform, Press.

**BARNETT, Sir Ben L(ewis),** KBE 1952; CB 1948; MC 1918; MA Cantab; Hon. Treasurer IEE, 1966-69; Chairman Commonwealth Telecommunications Board, 1956-62; *b* London, 20 July 1894; *s* of Isaac and Eva Barnett. *Educ:* Christ's Hosp.; Trinity Coll., Cambridge. Entered GPO, 1920; Principal, 1930; Telecoms Controller, Scotland, 1935; Asst Sec. (HQ), 1939; Reg. Dir, Home Counties Region, 1945; Dir Inland Telecommunications, 1946; Dep. Dir-Gen., GPO, 1949-56. Served European War, 1914-18. Lieut RE (TA) (despatches twice, MC). OStJ 1959. *Club:* Royal Societies.

**BARNETT, Correlli (Douglas);** author; *b* 28 June 1927; *s* of D. A. Barnett; *m* 1950, Ruth Murby; two *d*. *Educ:* Trinity Sch., Croydon; Exeter Coll., Oxford. Second class hons, Mod. Hist. with Mil. Hist. and the Theory of War as a special subject; MA 1954. Intell. Corps, 1945-48. North Thames Gas Bd, 1952-57; Public Relations, 1957-63. FRSL. *Publications:* The Hump Organisation, 1957; The Channel Tunnel (with Humphrey Slater), 1958; The Desert Generals, 1960; The Swordbearers, 1963; Britain and Her Army, 1970; (historical consultant and writer to) BBC Television series: The Great War, 1963-64; The Lost Peace, 1965-66. Reviews Mil. Hist. for The Sunday Telegraph; contrib. to: Jl of Contemp. Hist.; Horizon Magazine (USA); The Promise of Greatness (a symposium on the Great War), 1968, and to Governing Elites (a symposium), 1969. *Recreations:* gardening, interior decorating, idling, eating. *Address:* Catbridge House, East Carleton, Norwich. *T:* Mulbarton 410. *Club:* Savage.

**BARNETT, Air Chief Marshal Sir Denis Hensley Fulton,** GCB 1964 (KCB 1957; CB 1956); CBE 1945; DFC 1940; RAF, retired; Member for Weapons Research and Development, Atomic Energy Authority, since 1965; *b* 11 Feb. 1906; *y s* of late Sir Louis Edward Barnett; *m* 1939, Pamela, *y d* of late Sir Allan John Grant; one *s* two *d*. *Educ:* Christ's Coll., NZ; Clare Coll., Cambridge (BA 1929, MA 1935). Perm. Commn, RAF, 1929; Flt Lieut, 1934; Sqdn Ldr 1938; comd 84 Sqdn, Shaibah, 1938. Served War of 1939-45; Sqdn Comdr, Stn Comdr and G/C Ops, Bomber Comd, 1939-44; Dep. Dir Bomber Ops, Air Min., 1944; Dep. SASO at HQ Bomber Comd, 1945; Actg Wing Cdr, 1940; Gp Capt., 1941; Air Cdre, 1945; Dir of Ops at Air Min., 1945-46; Air Staff, India, 1946-47; Jt Services Staff Coll., 1948; Comdt Central Bomber Estabt, 1949; Dir of Ops Air Min., 1950-52; idc, 1952; Representative of UK Chiefs of Staff at HQ, UN Command, Tokyo, 1952-54; AOC, No. 205 Group, Middle East Air Force, 1954-56; Commandant, RAF Staff Coll., Bracknell, 1956; Commander Allied Air Task Force, Near East, 1956; Air Secretary, Air Ministry, 1957-59; AOC-in-C, RAF Transport Command, 1959-62; Air Officer Commanding-in-Chief, RAF Near East; Commander, British Forces Cyprus, and Administrator of the Sovereign Base Areas, 1962-64; Subst. Air Commodore, 1950; Air Vice-Marshal, 1953; Air Marshal, 1959; Air Chief Marshal, 1962. Comdr, US Legion of Merit, 1954; French Légion d'Honneur (Commandeur) and Croix de Guerre, 1958. *Recreations:* tennis, shooting. *Address:* The Lodge, Swallowfield, Berks. *Club:* United Service.

**BARNETT, Guy;** *see* Barnett, N. G.

**BARNETT, Dame Henrietta;** *see* Barnett, Dame M. H.

**BARNETT, Joel,** JP; MP (Lab) Heywood and Royton Division of Lancashire since 1964; Member, Public Accounts Committee, since 1965; *b* 14 Oct. 1923; *s* of Louis and Ettie Barnett, both of Manchester; *m* 1949, Lillian Goldstone; one *d*. *Educ:* Derby Street Jewish Sch.; Manchester Central High Sch. Qualified accountant; in private practice in Manchester. Served RASC and British Military Govt in Germany. Mem. of Prestwich, Lancs, Borough Council, 1956-59; JP Lancs 1960; Hon. Treas. Manchester Fabian Society, 1953-65. Contested (Lab) Runcorn Div. of Cheshire, Oct. 1959. Chm. Parly Labour Party Economic and Finance Group, 1967- (Vice-Chm., 1966-67). *Recreations:* walking, conversation and reading; good food. *Address:* Flat 65, 24 John Islip Street, SW1. *T:* 01-828 3620; 10 Park Lane, Whitefield, Lancs. *T:* (home) Whitefield 3634, (office) Central 6938.

**BARNETT, Dame (Mary) Henrietta,** DBE 1958 (CBE 1956; OBE 1950); Director of the Women's Royal Air Force, 1956-60; *d* of Col George Henry Barnett, 60th Rifles, Glympton Park, Woodstock, Oxon. *Educ:* Heathfield, Ascot. Joined Women's Auxiliary Air Force in 1939. *Address:* Hoggrove House, Park Street, Woodstock, Oxon. *T:* Woodstock 502. *Club:* English-Speaking Union.

**BARNETT, Rev. Dr Maurice;** Minister, Westminster Central Hall, London, since 1964; *b* Coppenhall, Crewe, 21 March 1917; *s* of Edward Percy and Beatrice Barnett; *m* 1943, Margaret Brown, Chester; one *s*. *Educ:* Crewe Grammar Sch.; Hartley Victoria Coll., The University, Manchester. BA Manchester, 1939, BD 1941, MA 1946; PhD Sheffield, 1960. Minister, East Ham Central Hall, 1941-43; Eden Grove Methodist Church, Bristol, 1943-46; Tutor, Cliff Coll., Derbyshire, 1946-47; Minister, Eastbrook Hall, Bradford, 1947-64. *Publications:* The Living Flame, 1953; This Concerns You, 1954; What Next?, 1954; articles, etc. *Recreations:* organ and piano. *Address:* Westminster Central Hall, SW1. *T:* 01-930 1801.

**BARNETT, Nicolas Guy;** Chief Education Officer of the Commonwealth Institute, since 1969; *b* 23 Aug. 1928; *s* of B. G. Barnett; *m* 1967, Daphne Anne, *d* of Geoffrey William Hortin, JP; one *s* one *d*. *Educ:* Highgate; St Edmund Hall, Oxford. Teacher: Queen Elizabeth Gram. Sch., 1953-59; Friends Sch., Kamusinga, Kenya, 1960-61. Famine Relief Sec., Christian Council of Kenya, 1962. Contested (Lab) NR Yorks (Scarborough and Whitby Div.), 1959; MP (Lab) S Dorset Div., Nov. 1962-Sept. 1964. *Publication:* By the Lake, 1964. *Recreations:* music, walking. *Address:* 11A Brandram Road, SE13. *Club:* Royal Commonwealth Society.

**BARNETT, Sir Oliver (Charles),** Kt 1968; CBE 1954 (OBE 1946); QC 1956; a Deputy Chairman, Somerset Court of Quarter Sessions, since 1967; *b* 7 Feb. 1907; *er s* of Charles Frederick Robert Barnett, 2nd Lieut Gloucestershire Regt (TA) (killed in action, 1915), and late Cicely Frances Barnett (*née* Cornish); *m* 1945, Joan, *o surv c* of Capt. W. H. Eve, 13th Hussars (killed in action, 1917), *o s* of late Rt Hon. Sir Harry Trelawney Eve, a Judge of the High Court. *Educ:* Eton. Called to Bar, Middle Temple, 1928; Bencher, Middle Temple, 1964, Oxford Circuit; Central Criminal Court Sessions. Dir of Public Prosecutions Office, 1931; Legal Asst, Judge Advocate General's Office, 1934; Second Deputy Judge Advocate, 1937; First Deputy Judge Advocate, 1938, RAF, 1939-47 (OBE); Wing Comdr (RAFVR); Asst Judge Advocate Gen. (RAF), 1942-47; Asst Judge Advocate Gen. (Army and RAF), 1947-54; Deputy Judge Advocate Gen. (Army and RAF) BAOR, BTA and 2nd TAF, 1953-54; Vice Judge Advocate Gen., 1955-62; Judge Advocate Gen., 1963-68. *Address:* Zinch Cottage, Stogumber, near Taunton, Somerset. *T:* Stogumber 264. *Clubs:* Brooks's, Pratt's, United Service.

**BARNETT, Richard David,** MA, DLitt; FBA 1962; FSA; Keeper, Department of Western Asiatic Antiquities, British Museum, since 1955; *b* Acton, 23 Jan. 1909; *o s* of late Lionel David Barnett, CB; *m* 1948 Barbara Joan, *d* of Ralph Pinto; two *s* one *d*. *Educ:* St Paul's Sch., London; Corpus Christi Coll., Cambridge. Student of British Sch. of Archaeology at Athens, 1930-32; Asst Keeper, Dept of Egyptian and Assyrian Antiquities, British Museum, 1932; Dep. Keeper, 1953. Sec., British Sch. of Archaeology at Athens, 1933-35; Pres. Jewish Historical Society of England, 1959-61. Corr. Mem., Greek Archaeological Soc.; Ordinary Fellow, German Archaeological Inst., 1961. Served War of 1939-45: Admiralty 1939-40; Foreign Office, 1940-42; Intelligence Officer, RAF, 1942-46, Egypt, Syria, Libya, Turkey. *Publications:* (ed) Treasures of a London Temple, 1951; (with Sir L. Woolley) British Museum Excavations at Carchemish, Vol. III, 1952; Catalogue of Nimrud Ivories in the British Museum, 1957, 2nd edn 1970; (trans.) The Jewish sect of Qumran and the Essenes (by J. Dupont-Sommer), 1954; Assyrian Palace Reliefs, 1960; (with M. Falkner), The Sculptures of Tiglath-pileser III, 1962; Illustrations of Old Testament History, 1966; The Sculptures of Ashurbanipal, 1970; (ed) The Sephardi Heritage, 1970; articles on archæology and Anglo-Jewish history in various learned jls. *Address:* 14 Eldon Grove, NW3. *T:* 01-794 2066.

**BARNEWALL,** family name of **Baron Trimlestown.**

**BARNEWALL, Sir Reginald Robert,** 13th Bt, *cr* 1622; pastoral interests; Director of Island Airways Pty Ltd, Pialba, Queensland; Director and Vice-Chairman of Directors, J. Roy Stevens Pty Ltd, Printers and Publishers, Melbourne; *b* 1 Oct 1924; *o s* of Sir Reginald J. Barnewall, 12th Bt and of Jessie Ellen, *d* of John Fry; *S* father 1961; *m* 1st, 1946, Elsie Muriel (*d* 1962), *d* of Thomas Matthews-Frederick, Brisbane; *three d* (one *s* decd); 2nd, 1962, Maureen Ellen, *d* of William Joseph Daly, South Caulfield, Vic; one *s*. *Educ:* Xavier Coll., Melbourne. Served War of 1939-45, overseas with Australian Imperial Forces. Served with Citizen Military Forces Unit, Royal Australian Armoured Corps, 1948-56. Managing Dir, Southern Airlines Ltd of Melbourne, 1953-58; Operation Manager, Polynesian Airlines, Apia, Western Samoa, 1958-62. *Heir: s* Peter Joseph Barnewall, *b* 26 Oct. 1963. *Address:* 184 Esplanade, Point Vernon, Queensland, Australia. *Clubs:* Royal Aero; Public Schools (Vic).

**BARNIE, Mrs Donald;** *see* Veitch, Marian.

**BARNS, Rev. Prof. John Wintour Baldwin,** MA, DPhil; (Queen's) Professor of Egyptology, Oxford University, since Oct. 1965; *b* 12 May 1912; *o s* of late William Henry Barns and of Helen Maria (*née* Baldwin), Bristol; *m* 1954, Dorothy Eileen Constance, *e d* of late Col W. E. Sturges, Clevedon. *Educ:* Fairfield Sch., Bristol; Bristol Univ.; Corpus Christi Coll., Oxford. BA Bristol, 1932; Classical Scholar Corpus Christi Coll., Oxford, 1933; BA 1937; MA 1942; DPhil 1947. Foreign Office, 1940-45; Lady Wallis Budge Research Fellow in Egyptology at University Coll., Oxford, 1945-

53; Lecturer in Papyrology in University of Oxford, 1953-65. S Stephen's House, Oxford; deacon, 1955; priest, 1956. British Academy award, 1963. *Publications:* The Ashmolean Ostracon of Sinuhe, 1952; Five Ramesseum Papyri, 1956; Part XXIV of Oxyrhynchus Papyri (with E. Lobel, E. G. Turner, C. H. Roberts), 1957; Merton Papyri, vol. II (with Sir Harold Idris Bell and B. R. Rees), 1959; Part II of Antinoopolis Papyri (with H. Zilliacus), 1960; Part XXXI of Oxyrhynchus Papyri (with P. J. Parsons, J. Rea, E. G. Turner), 1966; Part III of Antinoopolis Papyri (with H. Zilliacus), 1967; articles in Journal of Egyptian Archaeology, Classical Quarterly, Chronique d'Egypte, Journal of Theological Studies, etc. *Recreations:* church music and madrigals; cats. *Address:* 23 Victoria Road, Abingdon, Berks. *T:* Abingdon 711. *Club:* Oxford and Cambridge.

**BARNSLEY, Alan Gabriel;** *see* Fielding, Gabriel.

**BARNSLEY, Edward;** *see* Barnsley, W. E.

**BARNSLEY, (William) Edward,** CBE 1945; Designer and maker of furniture and building woodwork; Adviser in woodwork design, Loughborough Training College, 1938-65; Consultant in Furniture Design to Rural Industries Bureau, 1945-60; *b* 1900; *s* of Sidney Howard Barnsley, Sapperton, Cirencester; *m* 1925, Tatiana, *d* of late Dr Harry Kellgren; one *s* one *d*. *Educ:* Bedales. *Address:* Froxfield, Petersfield, Hants. *T:* Hawkley 233.

**BARNSTAPLE, Archdeacon of;** *see* Herniman, Ven. R. G.

**BARNWELL, Col Ralph Ernest,** CBE 1943; retired; *b* 20 Jan. 1895; *s* of late E. F. Barnwell, Rugby; *m* 1927, Lilian Katharine Oliphant, *d* of late C. R. Bradburne, Official Solicitor to the Supreme Court of Judicature; one *d* (one *s* decd). *Educ:* Rugby Sch. HAC 1914; 2nd Lieut Royal Warwicks Regt 1914; served in France in European War, 1914-18 (despatches); Capt. 1923; Adjutant, 7th Bn Royal Warwicks Regt, 1924-27; Staff Coll., Camberley, 1928-29; Staff Capt., War Office, 1930-32; GSO Weapon Training, Eastern Command, 1932-34; Bt Major 1935; Major, 1938; DAAG Lahore District, 1937-39; Lieut-Col 1939; DAA and QMG (France), 1939; AQMG 2nd Corps (France), 1940; Asst Adjutant-Gen., War Office, 1940-45; Col (temp.) 1941; retd pay 1945; Commandant, Duke of York's Royal Military Sch., 1945-53. *Recreations:* painting; fishing. *Address:* Woodrow, Fifehead Neville, Sturminster Newton, Dorset. *T:* Hazelbury Bryan 297. *Club:* Army and Navy.

**BARON, Alexander;** Writer; *b* 4 Dec. 1917; *s* of Barnet Baron and Fanny Levinson; *m* 1960, Delores Salzedo; one *s*. *Educ:* Hackney Downs Sch., London. Asst Editor, The Tribune, 1938-39. Served War of 1939-45, Army. Editor, New Theatre, 1946-49. *Publications: novels:* From the City, From the Plough, 1948; There's No Home, 1950; Rosie Hogarth, 1951; With Hope, Farewell, 1952; The Human Kind, 1953; The Golden Princess, 1954; Queen of the East, 1956; Seeing Life, 1958; The Lowlife, 1963; Strip Jack Naked, 1966; King Dido, 1969; also film scripts and television plays. *Address:* 31 Medina Villas, Hove, Sussex. *T:* Brighton 773786. *Club:* PEN.

**BARON, Cyril Faudel Joseph,** MRCS, LRCP; Barrister-at-law; HM Coroner for County of Greater London (Western District) since 1965 (Surrey, 1939-64); *b* 22 Jan. 1903; *s* of John and Lily Baron; *m* 1933, Kathleen Julia, *d* of Henry and Hilda Jacob; one *d*. *Educ:* Owen's Sch.; University Coll., London; St Bartholomew's Hospital (Wix Prize, 1923), MRCS, LRCP, 1924; Bar Final (1st Class Criminal Law), 1926. Practised medicine, 1924-36; called to Bar Middle Temple, 1936; practised at Bar (Common Law) from 1936. Pres., Coroners' Soc. of England and Wales; Vice-Pres., Medico-legal Soc.; Hon. Sec., Association of Whole-time Coroners. *Publications:* various articles on medico-legal subjects in learned journals. *Recreations:* tennis, swimming, foreign travel. *Address:* The Spinney, More Lane, Esher, Surrey. *T:* Esher 64240. *Club:* Royal Automobile.

**BARR, Alfred Hamilton, jun.;** Counsellor to the Trustees, Museum of Modern Art, New York; *b* Detroit, Mich, 28 Jan. 1902; *s* of Alfred Hamilton Barr and Annie Elizabeth Wilson; *m* 1930, Margaret Scolari-Fitzmaurice, Rome, Italy; one *d*. *Educ:* Princeton Univ. AB 1922, AM 1923 (University Fellow, 1922-23); Thayer Fellow, 1924-25. PhD 1946, Harvard; Doctor of Letters (hc), Princeton Univ., 1949; PhD (hc), Univ. of Bonn, 1958; DFA (hc): Univ. of Buffalo, 1962; Yale, 1967; Columbia Univ., 1969. Instructor, Vassar Coll., Dept of Art, 1923-24; Asst, Dept of Fine Arts, Harvard, 1924-25; Instr, Dept Art and Archaeology, Princeton, 1925-26; Assoc. Prof., Art Dept, Wellesley, 1926-29; Museum of Modern Art, NY: Dir, 1929-43; Vice-Pres. of Bd, 1939-43; Trustee, 1939-; Dir, Research in Painting and Sculpture, 1944-46; Dir of Museum Collections, 1947-67. Mary Flexner Lectureship, Bryn Mawr Coll., 1946; Overseer, Harvard Coll., 1965-70. Member: Adv. Council, Dept of Art and Archaeology, Princeton, 1946-, Columbia Univ., 1960-; Vis. Cttee on Fine Arts, Fogg Museum, Harvard, 1958-60; Pres., Foundation for Arts, Religion and Culture, 1962-65, Mem. Bd of Dirs, 1965-. Special Merit Award for Notable Creative Achievement, Brandeis Univ., 1964; NY State Award, 1968; Nat. Inst. of Arts and Letters Award for Distinguished Service to the Arts, 1968. Cross of Chevalier, Légion d'Honneur, 1959; Grand Cross, Order of Merit, German Federal Republic, 1959. *Publications:* Author or Editor of: Cézanne, Gauguin, Seurat, van Gogh, 1929; Modern German Painting and Sculpture, 1931; Henri-Matisse, 1931; Edward Hopper, 1933; The Lillie P. Bliss Collection, 1934; Modern Works of Art, 1934; Vincent van Gogh, 1935; Cubism and Abstract Art, 1936; Fantastic Art, Dada and Surrealism, 1936; Trois siècles d'art aux Etats-Unis, Paris, 1938; Art in our Time, 1939; Picasso: Forty Years of his Art, 1939; Italian Masters, 1940; What is Modern Painting?, 1943; Picasso: Fifty Years of his Art, 1946; (with Holger Cahill) Art in America: A Complete Survey, 1935; Painting and Sculpture in the Museum of Modern Art, 1948; Matisse: His Art and His Public, 1951; Masters of Modern Art, 1954; Editor: American Painter series, Penguin Books, London, 1944-46; articles on art, films, architecture in British, Russian, French, German and American periodicals, notably Cézanne d'après les lettres de Marion à Morstatt (Gazette des Beaux-Arts), Jan. 1937. *Recreations:* music, ornithology. *Address:* Museum of Modern Art, 11 West 53 Street, New York; (home) 49 East 96 Street, New York. *TA:* Modernart, New York. *T:* Atwater 9-3936.

**BARR, A. W. Cleeve,** FRIBA; FIOB; Managing Director, National Building Agency, since 1967; *b* 1910; *s* of Albert John Barr and Ellen (*née* Cleeve); *m* 1st, 1935, Edith M. Edwards, BA (*d* 1965); one *s* one *d* (and one *s* decd); 2nd, 1966, Mrs Mary W. Harley (*widow*). *Educ:* Borlase, Marlow; Liverpool Univ. Private offices (Charles Holden and Paul Mauger); Herts CC (schools) and LCC (housing). Dep.

Housing Architect, LCC, 1956-57; Development Architect, Ministry of Education, 1957-58; Chief Architect, Min. of Housing and Local Govt, 1959-64. Dep. Chm. and Chief Architect, Nat. Building Agency 1964-67. Hon. Sec. RIBA, 1963-65. *Publications:* Public Authority Housing, 1958; contributions to technical press and radio. *Recreation:* dinghy sailing. *Address:* 49 Brookland Rise, Hampstead Garden Suburb, NW11. *Club:* Reform.

**BARR, Cleeve;** *see* Barr, A. W. C.

**BARR, Rev. Prof. James,** MA, BD, DD; FBA; Professor of Semitic Languages and Literatures, Manchester University, since 1965; *b* 20 March 1924; *s* of Rev. Prof. Allan Barr, DD; *m* 1950, Jane J. S. Hepburn, MA; two *s* one *d. Educ:* Daniel Stewart's Coll., Edinburgh; Edinburgh Univ. (MA 1948, BD 1951). Served War of 1939-45 as pilot in RNVR (Fleet Air Arm), 1942-45. Minister of Church of Scotland, Tiberias, Israel, 1951-53; Prof. of New Testament Literature and Exegesis, Presbyterian Coll., Montreal, 1953-55; Prof. of Old Testament Literature and Theology, Edinburgh Univ., 1955-61; Prof. of Old Testament Literature and Theology, Princeton Theological Seminary, 1961-65; lectured in Princeton Univ., 1962-63; in Union Theol. Seminary, New York, 1963; Currie Lectr, Austin Theol. Seminary, Texas, 1964; Guggenheim Memorial Fellowship for study in biblical semantics, 1965; Cadbury Lectr, Birmingham Univ., 1969; Croall Lectr, Edinburgh Univ., 1970. Editor, Jl of Semitic Studies, 1965-. FBA 1969; FRAS 1969. Hon. DD, Knox Coll., Toronto, 1964; MA Manchester, 1969. *Publications:* The Semantics of Biblical Language, 1961; Biblical Words for Time, 1962; Old and New in Interpretation, 1966; Comparative Philology and the Text of the Old Testament, 1968; article, Daniel, in Peake's Commentary on the Bible, 1962; translated Ehrlich, Concise History of Israel, 1963; articles, God, Messiah, etc., in Hastings' Dictionary of the Bible, 1963; articles in Semitic and biblical journals. *Recreation:* bird watching. *Address:* Anchor House, 269 Bramhall Lane South, Bramhall, Cheshire SK7 3DW. *T:* 061-439 2050.

**BARRACLOUGH, Frank,** CBE 1951; Secretary for Education, North Riding of Yorkshire, 1934-65; *b* 22 March 1901; *yr s* of George and Eleanor Barraclough, Bradford; *m* 1930, Barbara, *y d* of Samuel and Mary Clegg, New Sawley, Long Eaton; one *s. Educ:* Bradford Grammar Sch.; Queen's Coll., Oxford. Hon. Scholar, Queen's Coll., Oxford, 1919; MA 1926. Tutor, Borough Road Training Coll., Isleworth, 1925-28; Asst Master, Clifton Coll., Bristol, 1928-31; Technical Officer, Leeds Education Cttee, 1931-32; Vice-Principal, Leeds Technical Coll., 1932-34; Asst Sec., North Riding Education Cttee, 1934. Hon. Treasurer, Association of Education Cttees, 1948-65; Member: Burnham Cttees, 1948-65; Loveday Cttee on Agricultural Education, 1944; Cttee on Cadet Entry to Royal Navy, 1952; Pres., Assoc. of Education Officers, 1954. *Address:* 72 Thirsk Road, Northallerton. *T:* Northallerton 2286. *Club:* United University.

**BARRACLOUGH, Prof. Geoffrey,** MA; Chichele Professor of Modern History, University of Oxford, and Fellow of All Souls College, since 1970; *b* 10 May 1908; *e s* of late Walter and Edith M. Barraclough. *Educ:* Bootham Sch., York; Oriel Coll., Oxford; Univ. of Munich. Bryce Research Student, 1931; Rome Scholar, British Sch. at Rome, 1931; Fellow of Merton Coll., Oxford, 1934; Fellow and Lectr, St John's Coll., Cambridge, 1936; Univ. Lectr, Cambridge, 1937; Foreign Office, 1940; RAFVR, 1942-45; Prof. of Mediæval History, University of Liverpool, 1945-56. Research Prof. of Internat. History, University of London, 1956-62; Prof. of History, Univ. of California, 1965-68; Springer Prof. of History, brandeis Univ., 1968-70. Pres., Historical Assoc., 1964-67. Hon. Mem., Austrian Inst. Historical Research. *Publications:* Public Notaries and the Papal Curia, 1934; Papal Provisions, 1935; Mediæval Germany, 1938; The Origins of Modern Germany, 1946; Factors in German History, 1946; The Mediæval Empire, 1950; The Earldom and County Palatine of Chester, 1953; History in a Changing World, 1955; Early Cheshire Charters, 1957; (ed) Social Life in Early England, 1960; European Unity in Thought and Action, 1963; An Introduction to Contemporary History, 1964; The Mediæval Papacy, 1968; (with R. F. Wall) Survey of International Affairs, 1955-56; Survey of International Affairs, 1956-58; Survey of International Affairs, 1958-60. *Address:* All Souls College, Oxford.

**BARRACLOUGH, Henry,** MVO 1958; *b* 10 Aug. 1894; *s* of late Thomas Barraclough, Shipowner, West Hartlepool; *m* 1922, Ethel Mary, *d* of Wilkinson Dix Sunderland; two *s. Educ:* Giggleswick Sch. On leaving school joined staff of Lambert Bros Ltd, Newcastle on Tyne office, 1911. Served European War, 1914-18, Durham LI, retiring as Capt.; served in Mesopotamia and NW Persia, 1916-19. Silver Line Ltd: Treasury Dir, 1940-48; Chm. and Man. Dir, 1948-60. Chairman, Prince of Wales Dry Dock Co., Swansea, Ltd, 1943-65 (Dir of the company, 1931-66); Dir, Dene Shipping Co. Ltd (Chm., 1941-66), and of other cos; Mem. of Lloyd's. Chm. London General Shipowners' Soc., 1946-47; Dep. Chm. and Chm. of Sub-Cttees of Classification of Lloyd's Register of Shipping, 1949-50. Chm. Governors, The "Cutty Sark" Soc.; Hon. Treasurer and Chm. Finance Cttee, King George's Fund for Sailors; Governor, Pangbourne Coll. Liveryman of Worshipful Company of Shipwrights. *Address:* Bix Manor, Henley-on-Thames, Oxon. *T:* Henley-on-Thames 5454; Cotehow, Martindale, Penrith. *Clubs:* Boodle's, City of London; Huntercombe Golf.

**BARRACLOUGH, Air Marshal Sir John,** KCB 1970 (CB 1969); CBE 1961; DFC 1942; AFC 1941; Vice-Chief of the Defence Staff, since March 1970; *b* 2 May 1918; *s* of late Horatio and Marguerite Maude Barraclough; *m* 1946, Maureen (*née* McCormack); one *d. Educ:* Cranbrook Sch. Commissioned RAF, 1938. Air Cdre 1961; Air Vice-Marshal, 1964. Served Near, Middle and Far East; first single-engined jet flight to S Africa, 1952; on staffs of Central Flying Sch. and IDC, 1949-54; Dir of Public Relations, Air Ministry, 1961-64; AOC No 19 Gp Coastal Command, 1964-67; Harvard Business Sch., 1967; AOA, Bomber Command, 1967-68; AO i/c Administration, Strike Comd, 1968-70. Pres., RAF Modern Pentathlon Assoc. *Recreations:* sailing, hunting. *Address:* 14 Trevor Street, Knightsbridge, SW7. *Clubs:* Royal Air Force; United Hunts; Royal Western Yacht.

**BARRACLOUGH, Brig. Sir John (Ashworth),** Kt 1962; CMG 1950; DSO 1941; OBE 1941; MC 1918; DL; Chairman, Engineering Employers' Association, 1950-67. Served European War, 1914-19, with KORR, RFC, and Machine Gun Corps; served in Iraq (severely wounded), 1920, Ireland, 1922, Palestine, 1929, Egypt, 1932, and India, 1934; military commander, Hebron District, Palestine, 1939; War of 1939-

45, comd 1st Bn King's Own Royal Regt, Syria, Lebanon and at Siege of Tobruk, 1941 (despatches five times, wounded); reg. comdr North Rhine Province, 1945-46; dep. reg. cmdr Land North Rhine-Westphalia, 1946-50. Member: Nat. Adv. Council for the Employment of the Disabled; Piercy Cttee on the Rehabilitation of the Disabled, 1953-56. KStJ, 1964. DL Warwicks, 1962. Comdr Order of Orange Nassau with Swords (Netherlands). *Address:* 6 Devonshire Mews South, W1. *T:* 01-935 3680. *Club:* Boodle's.

**BARRACLOUGH, Kenneth James Priestley,** CBE 1967 (OBE 1945); TD; JP; Metropolitan Magistrate since 1954; Chairman of the Poisons Board (Home Office) since 1958; *b* 1907; *s* of Herbert Barraclough, Leeds; *m* 1931, Gladys Evelyn, *d* of Charles Henderson, Liverpool and Rio de Janeiro; two *s* one *d*. *Educ:* Oundle Sch.; Clare Coll., Cambridge. Barrister, Middle Temple, 1929, North Eastern Circuit, Inns of Court Regt, TA, 1938; Col 1945. HQ, 21st Army Group (despatches). Dep. Chm. Appeals Cttee, Hampshire QS, 1957-62; Member: Adv. Cttee on Drug Dependence; Medicines Commn, 1969. JP Hampshire, 1957. *Address:* Elgin, Fitzroy Road, Fleet, Hants. *Club:* Oxford and Cambridge.

**BARRAN, David (Haven);** Chairman, since 1967 and Managing Director, since 1964, Shell Transport and Trading Co. Ltd (Deputy Chairman, 1964-67); Chairman, Shell Oil Co., since 1970; *b* 23 May 1912; *s* of Sir John Barran, 2nd Bt and Alice Margarita (*née* Parks); *m* 1944, Jane Lechmere Macaskie; four *s* three *d*. *Educ:* Winchester; Trinity Coll., Cambridge. BA 1934. Joined Asiatic Petroleum Co., 1934; served in Egypt, Palestine, Sudan, India, 1935-46. Pres., Asiatic Petroleum Corp., New York, 1958; Managing Dir, Royal Dutch/Shell Group, 1961. *Recreations:* gardening, shooting; embroidery. *Address:* 36 Kensington Square, W8. *T:* 01-937 5664; Brent Eleigh Hall, Suffolk. *T:* Lavenham 202. *Clubs:* Garrick; River (New York).

**BARRAN, Sir John (Leighton),** 3rd Bt, *cr* 1895; *b* 24 March 1904; *e s* of Sir John Barran, 2nd Bt and Alice Margarita (*d* 1939), *d* of Rev. Leighton Parks, DD, New York City; *S* father 1952; *m* 1929, Hon. Alison Mary Hore-Ruthven, 3rd *d* of 9th Baron Ruthven, CB, CMG, DSO; one *s*. *Educ:* Winchester Coll.; Trinity Coll., Cambridge. BA (Cambridge), 1925. Served War of 1939-45, Lieut Royal Naval Volunteer Reserve, 1939; Comdr, 1945. CC for Pateley Bridge, West Riding of Yorks, 1952; JP W Riding, Yorks, 1952. *Heir: s* John Napoleon Ruthven Barran [*b* 14 Feb. 1934; *m* 1965, Jane Margaret, *d* of Dr S. G. Hooker, *qv*]. *Address:* The Hermitage, East Bergholt, near Colchester, Essex. *T:* East Bergholt 236. *Club:* Bath.

**BARRATT, Sir Charles,** Kt 1966; LLB; Town Clerk and Clerk of the Peace for the City of Coventry, 1946-70; *b* Huddersfield, 27 May 1910; *s* of late H. T. Barratt; *m* 1938, Kathleen Mary, *d* of late E. M. Johnson; two *d*. *Educ:* Royds Hall Grammar Sch.; Leeds Univ. Articled pupil, Huddersfield County Borough Council; Asst Solicitor, Halifax County Borough Council, 1931-35; Dep. Town Clerk: Rochdale County Borough Council, 1935-41; Coventry City Council, 1941-46. Univ. of Warwick: Sec., Promotion Cttee, 1961-65; Sec., Academic Planning Bd, 1961-65; Mem. Council, 1965-. Council for National Academic Awards: Mem. Legal Studies Board, 1966-; Mem., Public Administration Bd, 1968-. President: Coventry Sch. of Music, 1964- (Chm., Management Cttee, 1950-63); Coventry and Warwicks Council on Alcoholism, 1969-; Soc. of Town Clerks, 1969-70; Chm., Crafts Council of Great Britain, 1969-; Member: Cttee on Local Authority and Allied Personal Social Services (Seebohm Cttee), 1965-68; Exec. Council, Town Clerks' Soc., 1963-70; Local Authorities' Management Services and Computer Cttee, 1966-70 (Chm., Technical Adv. Sub-Cttee, 1966-70); AMC Law Cttee, 1965-70; AMC Management Techniques Gp, 1965-70; Local Govt Training Bd, 1967; Adv. Council, Civil Service Coll., 1970-. *Publications:* Your Local Authority; numerous articles and reviews in technical jls. *Recreations:* travel, music, gardening, sailing (Cdre, Banbury Sailing Club, 1962-64; Chm., Draycote Water Steering Cttee, 1967-69; Cdre, Draycote Water Sailing Club, 1969-). *Address:* Kenilworth Lodge, Kenilworth, Warwicks. *T:* Kenilworth 54317.

**BARRATT, Francis Russell;** Under Secretary, HM Treasury, since 1968; *b* 16 Nov. 1924; *s* of Frederick Russell Barratt; *m* 1949, Janet Mary Sherborne; three *s*. *Educ:* Durban High Sch., SA; Clifton; University Coll., Oxford. Asst Principal, HM Treasury, 1949; Principal, 1953; First Sec., UK High Commission, Karachi, 1956-58; Asst Sec., HM Treasury, 1962. *Recreations:* reading, golf, music. *Address:* 25 Highgate Close, N6. *T:* 01-348 1319.

**BARRATT, Herbert George Harold,** OBE 1966; General Secretary, Confederation of Shipbuilding and Engineering Unions, 1957-70; *b* 12 Jan. 1905; *m* 1926; one *s* three *d*. *Educ:* Vicarage Street Church of England Sch., Nuneaton. Nuneaton Borough Councillor, 1945-47; Mem. Nat. Cttee AEU, 1943-48; Delegate to USSR, 1946. Chm. Nuneaton Labour Party, 1944-46; Coventry Dist. Cttee AEU, 1943-49; Shop Steward Convener, Daimler Motors, 1940-49; Appeals Board Assessor during war years; Nat. Insurance Tribunal Assessor; elected Nat. Organiser AEU, 1949-57. Formerly Member: Gas Adv. Council; Shipbuilding and Ship repairing Council; Nat. Adv. Council for the Motor Manufacturing Industry; Motor Industry Joint Labour Council; British Railways Productivity Council; Econ. Develt Cttee for Mech. Engrg Industry; Econ. Develt Cttee for Electrical Engrg Industry; Econ. Develt Cttee for Motor Manufacturing Industry; Industrial Training Board, Engrg; Industrial Training Board, Shipbuilding; British Productivity team to Swedish Shipyards, 1959; visited German Federal Railways, 1960; Exchange Leader Scheme visitor to USA, 1961; Vice-Chm., Sub-Cttee on Programme and Planning, Metal Trades Cttee, ILO, Geneva, 1965. *Recreation:* gardening. *Address:* (home) 58 The Crescent, West Wickham, Kent. *T:* 01-777 7638.

**BARRATT, Prof. Michael George;** Professor of Pure Mathematics, Manchester University since 1964; *b* 26 Jan. 1927, *e s* of George Bernard Barratt and Marjorie Holloway Barratt (*née* Oldham); *m* 1952, Jenepher Hudson; one *s* four *d*. *Educ:* Stationers' Company's Sch.; Magdalen Coll., Oxford. Junior Lecturer, Oxford Univ., 1950-52; Fellow, Magdalen Coll., Oxford, 1952-56; Lectr, Brasenose Coll., Oxford, 1955-59; Sen. Lectr and Reader, Manchester Univ., 1959-63. Vis. Prof., Chicago Univ., 1963-64. *Publications:* Papers in Mathematical Jls. *Address:* Holmbury, Winton Road, Bowdon, Cheshire. *T:* 061-928 0384.

**BARRATT, Major Stanley George Reeves E;** *see* Elton-Barratt.

**BARRATT, Sir Sydney,** Kt 1961; Chairman, Albright & Wilson Ltd, 1958-67, retired; *b* 11 Aug. 1898; *s* of Peter Barratt; *m* 1927, Isabel Vaughan Lucas; one *s* one *d*. *Educ:* Clifton Coll., Bristol; Balliol Coll., Oxford. BA 1920. Lecturer in Chemistry, University of Leeds, 1922-24, UCL 1924-32; Asst Dir of Research, Albright & Wilson Ltd, 1932; Director: Albright & Wilson Ltd, 1938; Joseph Lucas Ltd, 1959-68. A Pro-Chancellor of Bath Univ. of Technology, 1970-; Chairman: Clifton Coll. Council, 1958-67 (Pres., 1967-); Ramsay Memorial Fellowships Trustees, 1954. Hon. Fellow, University Coll. London, 1960. Pres., Soc. of Chemical Industry, 1963-65. Hon. LLD Manchester, 1964. *Address:* Crowe Hall, Widcombe, Bath.

**BARRAULT, Jean-Louis;** Officer of the Legion of Honour; actor, director, producer; Director: Odéon-Théâtre de France, 1959-68; Théâtre des Nations, Paris, 1965-67; *b* Vésinet, France, 8 Sept. 1910; *m* Madeleine Renaud, *qv*. *Educ:* public sch., Paris; Collège Chaptal. Taught at Collège Chaptal, 1931; Atelier Dramatic Sch. and Theatre (schol.), 1931-35; formed experimental theatrical company. Served War of 1939-40. With Comédie-Française as producer-director, 1940-46. At instigation of French Govt formed company with Madeleine Renaud, Marigny Theatre. Has appeared at Venice; Edinburgh Festival, 1948 and 1957: St James's Theatre, London, 1951; Palace Theatre, London, 1956, etc.; produced Duel of Angels, Apollo, 1958; World Theatre Season, Aldwych, 1965, 1968; toured Western Europe, S America, Canada, and US. Films include: Les Beaux Jours, Hélène, Les Perles de la couronne, La Symphonie fantastique, Les Enfants du Paradis, D'Hommes à hommes, Versailles, Chappaqua. *Publications:* Une Troupe et ses auteurs, 1950; Reflections on the Theatre (autobiography), 1951; articles in theatrical publications. *Address:* 18 avenue du Président Wilson, Paris XVIe, France.

**BARRER, Prof. Richard Maling,** FRS 1956; PhD Cantab; DSc (NZ); ScD Cantab; FRIC 1939; Hon. ARCS, 1959; Professor of Physical Chemistry, Imperial College of Science and Technology, University of London, since 1954, and Head of Department of Chemistry since 1955; Dean of the Royal College of Science, 1964-66; *b* 16 June 1910; *s* of T. R. Barrer, 103 Renall Street, Masterton, New Zealand; *m* 1939, Helen Frances Yule, Invercargill, NZ; one *s* three *d*. *Educ:* Canterbury University Coll., NZ (MSc); Clare Coll., Cambridge (1851 Exhibition Scholar). PhD Cantab, 1935; DSc NZ, 1937; ScD Cantab, 1948. Major Research Student, 1935-37, Research Fellow, 1937-39, Clare Coll.; Head of Chemistry Dept, Technical Coll., Bradford, 1939-46; Reader in Chemistry, London Univ., 1946-49; Prof. of Chemistry, Aberdeen Univ., 1949-54. Member Council: Faraday Soc., 1952-55; Chemical Soc., 1956-59; Royal Institute of Chemistry, 1961-64; Soc. of Chemical Industry, 1965-. Hon. FRSNZ 1965; Hon. DSc Bradford, 1967. *Publications:* Diffusion in and through Solids, 1941. Various research papers in British and foreign scientific journals. *Recreations:* tennis and interest in athletics. Full Blue for cross-country running, 1934. *Address:* 1 London Lane, Bromley, Kent. *Clubs:* Hawks (Cambridge); Achilles.

**BARRÈRE, Prof. Jean-Bertrand Marie;** Croix de Guerre (France), 1940; Légion d'Honneur, 1969; Professor of French Literature, University of Cambridge, since 1954; Fellow of St John's College, Cambridge, 1957; *b* Paris, 15 Dec. 1914; *s* of Alexandre Barrère and Marie-Claire Lavigne; *m* 1941, Micheline, *d* of Henri Cousin and Inès Dumontier; three *s* three *d*. *Educ:* Lycées Buffon and Louis-le-Grand; Ecole Normale Supérieure and Sorbonne, Paris. MA; Agrégé des Lettres; Docteur ès Lettres. Served War: Sous-Lieut, 32e Régiment d'Infanterie, 1939-40; 1re Armée Française, 1945; Lieut 1945; Capitaine de réserve, 1954; Capitaine Honoraire, 1967. Teacher of French and Classics, Lycée d'Amiens, 1940-42; Asst Lectr on French Literature, Sorbonne, 1942-46; Lectr on French Literature, Institut Français, London, 1946-49; Lectr on French Literature, Univ. of Lyons, 1949-50; appointed Prof. of French Literature, Univ. of Lyons, 1950; seconded as Prof. of French Literature, Ibrahim Univ., Cairo, 1950-52; Prof. at Lyons, 1952-54. *Publications:* Explications françaises, 1946; La Fantaisie de Victor Hugo (vol I, 1949: vol. II 1960; vol. III, 1950); Hugo, l'homme et l'œuvre, 1952; Romain Rolland par lui-même, 1955; Le Regard d'Orphée, 1956; La Cure d'amaigrissement du roman, 1964; Critique de chambre, 1964; Un Carnet des Misérables, 1965; Victor Hugo devant Dieu, 1965; Victor Hugo à l'œuvre, 1966; Romain Rolland, l'âme et l'art, 1966. *Recreations:* painting, violin. *Address:* Coleby, 31 Storey's Way, Cambridge.

**BARRETT, Sir Arthur George,** Kt 1942; *b* Geelong, 7 May 1895; *s* of A. O. and F. M. Barrett, Melbourne; *m* 1922, Jean Beatrice, *d* of late E. S. Mair, Melbourne; two *d*. *Educ:* Melbourne Church of England Grammar Sch. Served European War, AIF, 1916-19; Lord Mayor of Adelaide, 1937-41; Alderman, Adelaide City Council, 1941-53; business: maltster. Formerly Wing Comdr Air Training Corps RAAF. *Recreations:* golf, tennis. *Address:* 210 Stanley Street, North Adelaide, South Australia 5006, Australia. *T:* 67.1171. *Club:* Adelaide (Adelaide).

**BARRETT, Rev. Prof. Charles Kingsley,** DD; FBA 1961; Professor of Divinity, Durham University, since 1958; *b* 4 May 1917; *s* of Rev. F. Barrett and Clara (*née* Seed); *m* 1944, Margaret E. Heap, Calverley, Yorks; one *s* one *d*. *Educ:* Shebbear Coll.; Pembroke Coll., Cambridge; Wesley House, Cambridge. DD Cantab, 1956. Asst Tutor, Wesley Coll., Headingley, 1942; Methodist Minister, Darlington, 1943; Lecturer in Theology, Durham Univ., 1945. Hewett Lecturer (USA), 1961; Shaffer Lecturer (Yale), 1965; Delitzsch Lectr, Münster, 1967; Cato Lecturer (Australia), 1969. Vice-Pres., British and Foreign Bible Soc. Hon. DD Hull, 1970. Burkitt Medal for Biblical Studies, 1966. *Publications:* The Holy Spirit and the Gospel Tradition, 1947; The Gospel according to St John, 1955; The New Testament Background: Selected Documents, 1956; Biblical Preaching and Biblical Scholarship, 1957; The Epistle to the Romans, 1957; Westcott as Commentator, 1959; Yesterday, Today and Forever: The New Testament Problem, 1959; Luke the Historian in Recent Study, 1961; From First Adam to Last, 1962; The Pastoral Epistles, 1963; Reading Through Romans, 1963; History and Faith: the Story of the Passion, 1967; Jesus and the Gospel Tradition, 1967; The First Epistle to the Corinthians, 1968; The Signs of an Apostle, 1970; Das Johannesevangelium und das Judentum, 1970; contributions to learned journals and symposia in Britain, the Continent, and USA. *Address:* 8 Princes Street, Durham.

**BARRETT, Denis Everett;** a Special Commissioner of Income Tax since 1967; *b* 7 Jan. 1911; *o s* of late Walter Everett Barrett, London, and Julia Barrett (*née* MacCarthy), Cork; *m* 1947, Eilish, *y d* of late William and

Margaret Phelan, Co. Laois; one *s* two *d*. *Educ:* Wimbledon Coll.; London Univ. Entered Inland Revenue Dept, 1930; Asst Sec., 1948. *Address:* 4 The Linkway, Sutton, Surrey. *T:* 01-642 1520.

**BARRETT, Edwin Cyril Geddes,** CMG 1958; MA; Lecturer in Malay, School of Oriental and African Studies, University of London, since 1957; *b* 15 Feb. 1909; *s* of late Lieut-Col C. C. J. Barrett, CSI, CIE, IA, and late Mrs Mabel Ada Barrett (*née* Geddes); *m* 1936, Eleanor Nelson Raymond (*d* 1970); one *s*. *Educ:* Marlborough Coll.; Jesus Coll., Cambridge. Cadet, Malayan Civil Service, 1931; many appts in Malaya and Borneo, 1931-42. Military Service, 1942-45. Resumed duty in the Malayan CS, 1946; Chief Registration Officer, Fedn of Malaya, 1949; Pres. Municipal Council, Kuala Lumpur, 1951; Comr for Resettlement of Special Constables in Civil Life, Fedn of Malaya, 1952; Acting British Adviser, Perak, 1953; British Adviser, Kedah, 1953; left Malaya on abolition of appt, 1957. *Recreation:* gardening. *Address:* Hillfield, Amlets Lane, Cranleigh, Surrey. *T:* Cranleigh 3533.

**BARRETT, Hugh Tufnell-;** *see* Tufnell-Barrett.

**BARRETT, Col John Cridlan,** VC 1918; TD; DL; FRCS 1928; Emeritus Surgeon, Leicester Royal Infirmary (Senior Surgeon, 1945-62); *b* 10 Aug. 1897; *er s* of late Josephus Teague and Fanny Ada Barrett; *m* 1935, Ernestine Helen, *o c* of late Ernest and Edith Wright, Leics. *Educ:* Merchant Taylors' Sch.; St Thomas' Hosp. LRCP 1924; MB, BS (London) 1925. Joined Army, Jan. 1916; served in France (VC for 24 Sept. 1918; thrice severely wounded). Commanded 5th Bn, Royal Leics Regt, 1937-39 (Hon. Col, 1953-58). Formerly Consulting Surgeon: Leicester Isolation Hosp. and Sanatorium; City Gen. Hosp., Leicester; formerly Surgeon, Hinckley and District Hosp. Pres., Provincial Surgical Club of Great Britain, 1961-63; Dep. Pres., Leics Br. of BRCS, 1967- (Dir, 1962-67); Mem. Council, RCS, 1958-66. DL Leics, 1951. *Recreations:* swimming, philately. *Address:* Selby Lodge, 11 Southernhay Road, Leicester. *T:* 708309. *Club:* Army and Navy.

**BARRETT, Norman Rupert,** CBE 1969; FRCS 1930; Surgeon to King Edward VII Sanatorium, Midhurst, since 1938; Consulting Thoracic Surgeon to Royal Navy and to Ministry of Social Security, since 1944; Lecturer in Surgery, University of London, since 1935; Formerly: Senior Surgeon, St Thomas' Hospital; Surgeon, Brompton Hospital; *b* Adelaide, Australia, 16 May 1903; *o s* of late Alfred Barrett, Sussex; *m* 1931, Elizabeth, *d* of late H. Warington Smyth, CMG; two *d*. *Educ:* Eton Coll., Trinity Coll., Cambridge (1st class Hons Natural Science Tripos, 1925, MA 1930); St Thomas' Hosp. (MB 1928, MChir 1931). Rockefeller Travelling Fellowship, 1935; Vis. Prof. of Surgery, Royal North Shore Hosp., Sydney, 1963. Thomas Vicary Lecturer, 1970; Tudor Edwards Lecturer, 1970. Formerly Examiner in Surgery: Univs of Cambridge, Oxford, Birmingham, London, Khartoum; RCS. Hunterian Prof., RCS, 1955, and Arris and Gale Lectr, RCS, 1957. President: Thoracic Surgeons of Great Britain and Ireland, 1962; The Thoracic Soc., 1963. Fellow, Assoc. of Surgeons of Great Britain and Ireland. Member: Council, RCS; Tuberculosis Assoc. Hon. Mem., Amer. Assoc. for Thoracic Surgery. Editor of Thorax, 1946-. *Publications:* many papers on surgical and historical subjects; contribs to many textbooks of surgery. *Recreation:* yacht cruising. *Address:* Old Palace Place, Richmond Green, Surrey. *T:* 01-940 3834. *Club:* Royal Corinthian Yacht.

**BARRETT, William Spencer,** FBA 1965; Fellow of Keble College, Oxford, since 1952, Sub-Warden since 1968, and Tutor in Classics since 1939; Reader in Greek Literature, University of Oxford, since 1966; *b* 29 May 1914; *o s* of William Barrett and Sarah Jessie Barrett (*née* Robbins); *m* 1939, Georgina Margaret Elizabeth, *e d* of William and Alma Georgina Annie Hill; one *s* one *d*. *Educ:* Derby Sch; Christ Church, Oxford (Scholar). Ireland and Craven Schol. 1933; 1st Class Classical Hon. Mods, 1934; Gaisford Prize for Greek Verse, 1934; de Paravicini Schol., 1934; 1st Class Lit. Hum., 1937; Derby Schol., 1937; Charles Oldham Prize, 1938. Lectr, Christ Church, Oxford, 1938-39; Lectr, Keble Coll. 1939-52; Librarian, 1946-66; Univ. Lectr in Greek Literature, 1947-66. Temp. Civilian Officer, Admty (Naval Intelligence Div.), 1942-45. *Publications:* (Ed) Euripides, Hippolytos, 1964; articles in learned jls. *Address:* Keble College, Oxford. *T:* Oxford 59201; Sumner House, Mill Street, Kidlington, Oxford. *T:* Kidlington 3170.

**BARRETT-LENNARD, Sir (Thomas) Richard F.;** *see* Lennard.

**BARRIE, Derek Stiven Maxwelton,** OBE 1969 (MBE 1945); MInstT; Director: British Transport Advertising, Ltd; Transportation Systems & Market Research Ltd; East Yorkshire Motor Services, Ltd; *b* 8 Aug. 1907; *s* of John Stiven Carruthers Barrie and Dorothea Barrie; *m* 1936, Kathleen Myrra Collins; one *s* one *d*. *Educ:* Apsley House, Clifton; Tonbridge Sch. London and provincial journalism (Daily Graphic, Allied Newspapers, etc.), reporter and sub-editor, 1924-32; joined LMS Railway, 1932; on return from war service, rejoined LMS, 1946; PRO Railway Exec., 1948; Chief PRO British Transport Commn, 1956; Asst Sec.-Gen., BTC, 1958; Asst Gen. Man., York, 1961; Chm., British Railways (Eastern) Bd, and Gen. Man., British Railways Eastern Region, 1968-70. Mem. Council, Inst. of Transport, 1968. Served with Royal Engineers, 1941-46; Hon. Col 74 Movement Control Regt, RE and RCT, 1961-67; Major, Engr. and Rly Staff Corps (T & AVR), 1967, Lt-Col 1968. Bronze Star Medal (US), 1945. OStJ 1968. *Publications:* numerous railway historical books and monographs; contribs Railway Gazette, Railway Magazine, Modern Transport, etc., 1928-. *Recreations:* railways, authorship, country life. *Address:* 23 The Mount, Malton, Yorks. *T:* Malton 2409.

**BARRIE, Sir Walter,** Kt 1958; Chairman of Lloyd's, 1953, 1954, 1957, 1958; Director, Ulster Bank Ltd; Member, Inner London Board, National Westminster Bank Ltd; *b* 31 May 1901; *y s* of late Right Hon. H. T. Barrie, MP, DL, JP, and late Katie Barrie; *m* 1927, Noele Margaret (*d* 1968), *d* of G. J. Furness, JP; two *s*. *Educ:* Coleraine; Merchiston Castle, Edinburgh; Gonville and Caius Coll., Cambridge. Entered Lloyd's, 1926; first served on Cttee of Lloyd's, 1946; Deputy-Chm. of Lloyd's, 1951, 1952. Lloyd's Gold Medal, 1958. Pres., Insurance Inst. of London, 1955-56; Vice-Pres., Chartered Insurance Inst., 1957, 1958, 1959, Dep. Pres. 1961. Pres. 1962-63. Mem., Export Guarantees Advisory Council, 1967-. Governor: Cutty Sark Soc.; Pangbourne Coll. *Recreation:* golf. *Address:* Compton Elms, Pinkneys Green, Berks. *T:* Maidenhead 27151. *Club:* City of London.

**BARRINGTON,** family name of **Viscount Barrington.**

**BARRINGTON,** 11th Viscount *cr* 1720; **Patrick William Daines Barrington;** Baron Barrington, 1720; Baron Shute (UK) 1880 (sits as Baron Shute); *b* 29 Oct. 1908; *s* of Hon. Walter Bernard Louis Barrington (*d* 1959); *S* uncle, 1960. *Educ:* Eton; Magdalen Coll., Oxford (BA). Called to the Bar, Inner Temple, 1940. Late 2nd Lieut, RA. Formerly Hon. Attaché, HBM's Embassy, Berlin, and sometime in Foreign Office. *Heir: uncle* Hon. Rupert Edward Selborne Barrington, *qv. Address:* 8 Addisland Court, Holland Villas Road, W14. *T:* 01-727 2009.

**BARRINGTON, Sir Charles Bacon,** 6th Bt, *cr* 1831; Nurseryman (Orchid grower and Carnation specialist); *b* 6 June 1902; *s* of Sir Charles Burton Barrington, 5th Bt, and Mary Rose (*d* 1943), *d* of Sir Henry Hickman Bacon, 10th and 11th Bt; *S* father 1943; *m* 1930, Constance Doris, *d* of E. J. Elkington; two *d*. *Educ:* Eton. *Recreation:* horticulture. *Heir: b* Capt. Alexander Fitzwilliam Croker Barrington, *b* 19 Nov. 1909. *Address:* Barrihurst, Cranleigh, Surrey.

**BARRINGTON, Prof. Ernest James William,** FRS 1967; Professor of Zoology, Nottingham University since 1949; Deputy Vice-Chancellor, 1956-59; Public Orator, 1964; *b* 17 Feb. 1909; *o s* of late William Benedict and Harriet Barrington; *m* 1943, Muriel Catherine Anne Clinton; one *s* one *d*. *Educ:* Christ's Hosp.; Oriel Coll., Oxford (Organ Scholar). ARCO 1926; LRAM 1927; BA (Oxford), 1931; BSc 1934; MA 1936; Lectr in Zoology, Univ. Coll., Nottingham, 1932, Head of Zoology Dept, 1934, Reader, 1945. Rockefeller Foundation Fellow in Comparative Physiology at McGill Univ., 1939, and Harvard Univ., 1940; Buell Gallagher Visiting Professor, City Coll., New York, 1966. DSc (Oxford), 1948. *Publications:* European Editor General and Comparative Endocrinology, 1960; Introduction to General and Comparative Endocrinology, 1963; Hormones and Evolution, 1964; The Biology of Hemichordata and Protochordata, 1965; Zoological Editor, Contemporary Biology Series, 1966; Invertebrate Structure and Function, 1967; The Chemical Basis of Physiological Regulation, 1968; Perspectives in Endocrinology (Jt Editor with C. B. Jœrgensen), 1968; papers on chordate morphology and physiology in various jls. *Recreation:* music. *Address:* 5 Manor Court, Bramcote, Nottingham NG9 3DR. *T:* Nottingham 255402. *Club:* United University.

**BARRINGTON, His Honour John Harcourt,** TD; County Court Judge, 1955-70, retired; *b* 3 March 1907; *s* of late George Harcourt Barrington, Great Missenden, Bucks; *m* 1st, 1934, Margaretta Rowena Marion Whitfield Hayes (*d* 1962); one *s* one *d*; 2nd, 1963, Virginia Beatrice Cunard, OBE. *Educ:* Clifton; Trinity Coll., Cambridge. Called to the Bar, 1930. Served War of 1939-45 in Royal Artillery (despatches). Staff Coll., Camberley, 1942; Normandy Landing 1944. *Recreation:* fishing. *Address:* 13 The Terrace, Barnes, SW13. *Club:* Athenæum.

**BARRINGTON, Hon. Rupert Edward Selborne,** DSO 1918; *b* 10 Dec. 1877; *y s* of 9th Viscount Barrington, and *heir-presumptive* of 11th Viscount, *qv*; *m* 1903, Mary Georgina, *d* of Lieut-Col G. A. Ferguson; one *s*. *Educ:* Cheam; Charterhouse. Served South African War, 1900-1; South African Constabulary, 1901-7; European War, 1914-18, Gallipoli, Egypt, Salonika and France (wounded, DSO, despatches thrice).

**BARRINGTON-WARD, Sir (Victor) Michael,** KCVO 1952; CBE 1945; DSO 1916; MInstT; CStJ; Colonel, retired, Railway Staff Corps, RE; *b* 17 July 1887; 3rd *s* of late Canon M. J. Barrington-Ward, DD, Rector of Duloe; *m* 1st, 1920, Barbara (marriage dissolved, 1938), *o d* of late J. T. Pilling, Wolverley Court, Worcester; three *d*; 2nd, 1938, Isobel, *er d* of late Dr S. J. Kerfoot, Clifton, Bristol; one *d*. *Educ:* Westminster; Edinburgh. Formerly an Asst Engineer on the staff of W. B. Worthington, MInstCE, Engineer-in-Chief, Midland Railway; an Asst to General Superintendent, Midland Railway; Dir Railway Operations, Ministry of Transport, 1919-21; General Manager's Staff, NER, 1922; District Supt, LNER, Middlesbrough, 1923-27; Supt, LNER (Western Section), 1927-39; Supt, LNER, Southern Area, 1939-42; Asst Gen. Man., LNER, 1942-45; Divisional General Manager, LNER, 1945-47; Mem. of Railway Exec., 1947-53. BSc (Engineering) Edinburgh; Miller Prizeman, Institution of Civil Engineers; Operations Gold Medal, Institute of Transport, 1938; at beginning of 1914-18 war Captain, South Lancashire Regt; transferred and promoted Major in Royal Engineers, 1915, for duty with the Railway Operating Division, and commanded a large group of Railway Operating Companies (despatches four times, DSO, Bt Lt-Col; citation, French Army and Croix de Guerre with Palm); Lieut-Col Comdg Headquarters Railway Operating Group Supp. Reserve RE, 1924-28; Vice-Pres. Inst. Transport, 1945-48; Chm. Operating Cttee, REC, 1938-45; Chm. Rly Clearing House, 1948-53. Medal of Freedom with Silver Palm (USA). *Publications:* contributions Proceedings of Institution of Civil Engineers, Institute of Transport, and several lectures on transport subjects. *Address:* Beverley, Ledborough Lane, Beaconsfield, Bucks. *T:* Beaconsfield 3211.

**BARRITT, Sir David (Thurlow),** Kt 1969; BSc, MIChemE; Chairman: Davy-Ashmore Ltd, since 1970; Twyfords Holdings Ltd; Vice-President, Otto Construction Corporation, USA; Director, Hart-Carter Company, USA; *b* 17 Oct. 1903; *er s* of late David Webster Barritt and Rachel Barritt; *m* 1931, Hilda Marshall Creyke; one *s*. *Educ:* High Sch., Newcastle-under-Lyme, Staffs. Chm., Simon Engineering Ltd, 1963-70. Chm. Govs, The Newcastle-under-Lyme Endowed Schs, Newcastle, Staffs, 1962. FInstF. *Publications:* papers in technical jls. *Recreations:* golf, music, gardening, photography. *Address:* Stone Cottage, Prestbury, Cheshire, SK10 4AH. *T:* Prestbury 89716. *Clubs:* Carlton; Manchester (Manchester).

**BARRON, Donovan Allaway,** CBE 1962; MIEE; Engineer-in-Chief of the Post Office, 1965-67; *b* 1907; *s* of late George Barron; *m* 1941, Margaret Kathleen, *d* of Percival Aylwin Selfe; one *d*. *Educ:* Bristol Grammar Sch.; Bristol Univ. BSc 1927, MSc 1936. General Post Office: Asst Engineer, 1927-35; Area Engineer, 1936-40; Asst Staff Engineer, 1941-48; Staff Engineer, 1949-53; Asst Engineer-in-Chief, 1954-59; Deputy Engineer-in-Chief, 1960-65. Formerly Member of the Council of the Institution of Electrical Engineers. *Publications:* various contributions to learned journals. *Recreations:* music, gardening, philately. *Address:* 18 Reddons Road, Beckenham, Kent. *T:* Sydenham 4162.

**BARRON, Douglas Shield,** CIE 1945; Chairman, Godfrey Phillips, India, Ltd; Director, Godfrey Phillips, Ltd; *b* 18 March 1904; *s* of Thomas Barron; *m* 1934, Doris Katherine (*d* 1970), *o d* of late Henry Deakin; no *c*. *Educ:*

Holgate Grammar Sch.; Corpus Christi Coll., Cambridge. Joined Indian Civil Service, 1926; retired, 1948. *Recreations:* shooting, fishing, golf. *Address:* Eyeworth Lodge, Fritham, Hants. *T:* Cadnam 2256. *Clubs:* Oriental; Bombay Yacht.

**BARRON, Rt. Rev. Patrick Harold Falkiner;** *see* George, Bishop of.

**BARRON, Wilfrid F. S.;** *see* Shepherd-Barron.

**BARROW, Rt. Hon. Errol Walton,** PC 1969; Prime Minister and Minister of Finance, Barbados; *b* 21 Jan. 1920; *s* of Reginald Grant Barrow, LTh, DD (retired), and Ruth Barrow (*née* O'Neal); *m* 1945, Carolyn Plaskett; one *s* one *d. Educ:* Harrison Coll., Barbados; LSE (BSc). Royal Air Force, 1940-47. Barrister, Lincoln's Inn, 1949. Elected Legislature, Barbados, 1951; Premier, 1961; Prime Minister, 1966. Hon. LLD, McGill, 1966. *Recreations:* sailing, flying, diving, tennis. *Address:* Culloden Farm, Barbados, West Indies. *T:* 5172.

**BARROW, Prof. Geoffrey Wallis Steuart;** Professor of Mediaeval History, University of Newcastle upon Tyne (formerly King's College University of Durham), since 1961; *b* Headingley, Leeds, 28 Nov. 1924; *s* of Charles Embleton Barrow and Marjorie, *d* of Donald Stuart; *m* 1951, Heather Elizabeth, *d* of James McLeish Lownie; one *s* one *d. Educ:* St Edward's Sch., Oxford; Inverness Royal Acad.; St Andrews Univ.; Pembroke Coll., Oxford. Lecturer in History, University Coll., London, 1950-61. *Publications:* Feudal Britain, 1956; Acts of Malcolm IV, King of Scots, 1960; Robert Bruce and the Community of the Realm of Scotland, 1965; contrib. Scottish Historical Review, etc. *Recreation:* hill walking. *Address:* The University, Newcastle upon Tyne 1.

**BARROW, Rev. Canon John Harrison,** MA; Vicar of Stansted Mountfitchet, Essex, 1932-54; Honorary Canon of Chelmsford Cathedral since 1935; *b* 11 Oct. 1881; *s* of James and Elizabeth Agnes Barrow; *m* 1917, Mary Irene Debnam; one *s. Educ:* Durham Sch.; Pembroke Coll., Oxford. Curate of St Luke, Victoria Docks, E, 1904-10; St Mary's, Chelmsford, 1911-14; Precentor of St Mary's Cathedral, Chelmsford, 1914-17; Rector of St Andrew, Romford, 1917; Curate of Dalton-in-Furness, 1917-19; Sec. of Bishop of Chelmsford's Crusade Fund, 1919-22; Metropolitan Organising Sec. of SPCK, Dioceses Chelmsford, London, St Albans, and Southwark, 1922-32; Surrogate since 1915; Proctor in Convocation, Diocese of Chelmsford, 1926-50; Vice-Chm., Royal Sch. of Church Music. Hon. Chaplain to Bishop of Chelmsford, 1951-61, 1962; Chaplain to High Sheriff 1955-56, 1962-63; Chapter Clerk, 1957; Priest-in-charge, Margaret Roding, 1955-56, Roxwell, 1957-59. *Recreation:* motoring. *Address:* 14 Cedar Avenue, Chelmsford. *T:* Chelmsford 52160. *Club:* Church House.

**BARROW, Hon. Sir Malcolm (Palliser),** Kt 1953; CBE 1946 (OBE 1942); Deputy Prime Minister, Defence, Economic Affairs and Power, Federation of Rhodesia and Nyasaland, 1962-63; Tea and Tung Planter; *b* 1900; *s* of late Sir Samuel Barrow; *m* 1927, Frances Teresa, *d* of F. E. Richards, Coombe Hall, East Grinstead, Sussex. *Educ:* Malvern Coll., Clare College, Cambridge (BA). Chm., Tea Res. Foundation of Central Africa; Mem., Agricultural Res. Council of Malawi. *Address:* Namingomba Estate, Cholo, Malawi. *Club:* Salisbury (Rhodesia).

**BARROW, Captain Sir Richard John Uniacke,** 6th Bt *cr* 1835; *b* 2 Aug. 1933; *s* of Sir Wilfrid John Wilson Croker Barrow, 5th Bt and (Gwladys) Patricia (*née* Uniacke); *S* father 1960; *m* 1961, Alison Kate, *yr d* of late Capt. Russell Grenfell, RN, and of Mrs Lindsay-Young; one *s* one *d. Educ:* Abbey Sch., Ramsgate; Beaumont Coll., Old Windsor. Commnd. 2nd Lieut Irish Guards, 1952; served: Germany, 1952-53; Egypt, 1953-56; Cyprus, 1958; Germany, 1959-60; retired, 1960; joined International Computers and Tabulators Ltd; now Principal, Senior Executive Education, International Computers Ltd. *Heir: s* Anthony John Grenfell Barrow, *b* 24 May 1962. *Address:* 53 Pymers Mead, Croxted Road, Dulwich, SE21. *T:* 01-670 6471.

**BARROWCLOUGH, Anthony Richard;** Barrister-at-Law, Inner Temple; *b* 24 June 1924; *m* 1949, Mary Agnes Pery-Knox-Gore; one *s* one *d. Educ:* Stowe; New Coll., Oxford. Served RNVR, 1943-46 (Sub-Lieut and later Lieut). Called to the Bar, Inner Temple, 1949. Part-time Member, Monopolies Commn, 1966-69. *Recreation:* country pursuits. *Address:* Spencer Cottage, Spencer Walk, Putney, SW15. *T:* 788-9146; King's Cottage, South Hole, near Hartland, Devon.

**BARROWCLOUGH, Rt. Hon. Sir Harold (Eric),** PC 1954; KCMG 1954; CB 1944; DSO 1919; MC, ED; Chief Justice of New Zealand, 1953-65; *b* 1894; *s* of late A. E. Barrowclough, Dunedin; *m* 1921, Mary Ogilvy (*d* 1964), *d* of James S. Duthie, Dunedin; two *s* one *d. Educ:* Palmerston N High Sch.; Otago Univ., LLB. Served European War, 1914-19, in France, Belgium and Egypt, eventually commanding 4th Bn NZ Rifle Brigade, and as Asst Dir Education for NZ Division (despatches, MC, DSO, French Croix de Guerre); formerly Lecturer on Procedure, Faculty of Law and Commerce, Otago Univ.; commanding 1st Bn Otago Regt NZ Military Forces, 1924-29; commanded 3rd New Zealand Infantry Brigade, 1930-31; Comdr 6th NZ Infantry Brigade, 2nd NZ Expeditionary Force, 1940-42 (despatches, Bar to DSO, Greek Military Cross, Class A); Comdr 1st NZ Div., Apr.-Sept. 1942; commanded 3rd NZ Div. and 2nd NZ Expeditionary Force in the Pacific, 1942-44, as Maj.-Gen. (CB). Comdr Legion of Merit (US). LLD *hc* Otago, 1969. *Address:* 29 Salamanca Road, Kelburn, Wellington, New Zealand. *T:* Wellington 43.377. *Clubs:* Northern; Royal New Zealand Yacht Squadron (Auckland); Wellington (Wellington).

**BARROWS, William Leonard,** JP; formerly Partner, Price Waterhouse & Co., and Howard Smith Thompson & Co., Chartered Accountants, Birmingham and London, retired 1970; Chairman: Averys, Ltd; Duport Ltd; Evered & Co. Holdings Ltd; Director, Needle Industries Group Ltd, and other companies; *b* 13 July 1905; *s* of Rev. F. W. Barrows; *m* 1929, Elizabeth Goodman; two *s* two *d. Educ:* Marlborough. Qualified as Chartered Accountant, 1929; Partner in Howard Smith Thompson & Co., 1931-70. Member: Council of Inst. of Chartered Accountants, 1941-66 (Pres., 1958-59); Excess Profits Tax Advisory Panel, 1947-56; Board of Referees, 1953-; Geddes Cttee on Carriers' Licensing, 1963; Board of United Birmingham Hospitals, 1953-68; Life Governor, Birmingham Univ. Hon. LLD Birmingham, 1958. JP City of Birmingham. *Recreations:* shooting and gardening. *Address:* The Croft, Rowington, near Warwick. *T:* Lapworth 2264. *Clubs:* Reform; Conservative (Birmingham).

**BARRY, Rt. Rev. (Frank) Russell,** MA, DSO 1916; Hon. DD (St Andrews) 1936, Nottingham 1951; DD (Lambeth) 1947; Hon. Fellow of Oriel College, Oxford, 1943; Hon. STD Gen. Theological Seminary, New York, 1952; FKC, London, 1929; *b* 28 Jan. 1890; *e s* of Rev. George Duncan Barry, formerly Rector of Bratton Fleming, Barnstaple; *m* 1929, Lilian Janet, *o d* of late Dr G. Buchanan Gray; one *d*. *Educ:* Bradfield; Oriel Coll., Oxford (Scholar). 1st Class Mods. and Lit. Hum.; Passmore Edwards Prize; Hall Greek Testament Prize; Denyer Johnson Scholarship; Fellow and Lecturer of Oriel, 1913-19; TCF, 1915-19 (DSO, despatches, Montenegrin medal); Hon. CF 2nd Class; Principal of Ordination Test Sch., Knutsford, 1919-23; Archdeacon of Egypt and Chaplain of All Saints, Cairo, 1923; Prof. of New Testament Interpretation at King's Coll., London, 1923-28; Vicar of St Mary the Virgin (the University Church), and Fellow and Tutor of Balliol Coll., Oxford, 1928-33; Canon of Westminster and Rector of St John's, Smith Square, 1933-41; Sub-Dean of Westminster, 1940-41; Bishop of Southwell, 1941-63. Canon Theologian of Liverpool Cathedral, 1932-33; Examining Chaplain to the Bishop of Southwark, 1920-32, of Salisbury, 1928-33, of Winchester, 1932-34; Select Preacher: Cambridge, 1921, 1934, 1936 and 1939; Oxford, 1927-29 and 1938; Chaplain to the King, 1930-41; Moorhouse Lecturer, St Paul's Cathedral, Melbourne, 1934; Lectr, St Michael, Cornhill, EC4, 1967. *Publications:* One Clear Call, 1922; St Paul and Social Psychology, 1923; Christianity and Psychology, 1923; contributor to the Church in the Furnace, 1917; A Philosophy from Prison, 1926; The Relevance of Christianity, 1931; The Relevance of the Church, 1935; What has Christianity to say?, 1937; Contributor, Christianity and the Crisis, 1933; The Christian Faith, 1936; Convictions, 1939; I heard a Voice, 1940; Faith in Dark Ages, 1940; Church and Leadership, 1945; Recovery of Man, 1948; Vocation and Ministry, 1958; Asking The Right Questions, 1960; Mervyn Haigh, 1964; Questioning Faith, 1965; Christian Ethics and Secular Society, 1966; The Atonement, 1968; Weep not for me, 1968; Secular and Supernatural, 1969. *Recreations:* indescribable. *Address:* The Coppice, Manesty, Keswick. *T:* Borrowdale 252; 26 Tufton Court, SW1. *T:* 01-222 2505. *Club:* Athenæum.

**BARRY, Geraldine Mary;** retired; late Senior Surgeon, Royal Free Hospital, and Senior Surgeon, London Homœopathic Hospital; Examiner in Surgery, University of London; *b* 4 Oct. 1897; *d* of Rev. Walter George and Anna Barry. *Educ:* Queen Anne's Sch., Caversham; London (Royal Free Hosp.); Sch. of Medicine for Women, MRCS, LRCP 1921; MB, BS London Univ. Gold Medal, Distinction Medicine and Surgery, 1922; FRCS, 1926; MS London, 1929; Asst Surgeon, London Homœopathic Hospital, 1929; Asst Surgeon, Royal Free Hospital, 1930; EMS, Surgeon to Three Counties Emergency Hospital, Arlesey, Beds, 1940. *Address:* Three Hedges, Dungells Lane, Yateley, near Camberley, Surrey. *T:* Yateley 3187.

**BARRY, Rt. Rev. Hugh Van Lynden O.;** *see* Otter-Barry.

**BARRY, Michael, (James Barry Jackson);** OBE 1956; Head of Speech and Drama, Stanford University, California, since 1969; *b* 15 May 1910; *s* of A. G. and Helen Jackson; *m* 1st, 1934, Judith Gick (marriage dissolved, 1947); one *d*; 2nd, 1948, Rosemary Corbett (*d* 1968); one *d*. Studied farming and horticulture in Glos and Herts. Studied for theatre at RADA and subsequently as actor, stage-manager, designer and producer at the Northampton, Birmingham, Hull and Croydon Repertory Theatres before working in London. Appointed BBC television producer, 1938. Served Royal Marine Brigade, Landing-Craft and as AMS, RM Office, 1939-45. Producer and writer, BBC television drama and documentary, 1946-51 (Programmes included: The Silence of the Sea, I Want to Be a Doctor, Promise of Tomorrow, The Passionate Pilgrim, Shout Aloud Salvation). Head of Drama, BBC Television, 1952-61; Programme Controller, Irish Television, 1961-63. Literary Adviser, Council of Repertory Theatres, 1964-67; Member: Drama Panel, Arts Council, 1955-68; Council, RADA, 1966-69. *Publication:* (selected) The Television Playwright, 1960. *Address:* The Midland Bank, 29 Haymarket, SW1.

**BARRY, Rev. Noel Patrick,** OSB; Headmaster of Ampleforth College since Sept. 1964; *b* 6 Dec. 1917; 2nd *s* of Dr T. St J. Barry, Wallasey, Cheshire. *Educ:* Ampleforth Coll.; St Benet's Hall, Oxford. Housemaster, Ampleforth Coll., 1954-64. *Publication:* Handwriting Sheets, 1954. *Address:* Ampleforth College, York. *T:* Ampleforth 224.

**BARRY, Sir Patrick (Redmond),** Kt 1950; MC; Judge of Queen's Bench Division of the High Court of Justice, 1950-66; Chairman of Advisory Council on the Treatment of Offenders, 1958-66; Deputy Chairman, Wilts Quarter Sessions, since 1964; *b* 4 Sept. 1898; *o s* of late Rt Hon. Redmond Barry, PC, Lord Chancellor of Ireland, 1911-13, and late Mrs Redmond Barry, 6 Bushell Place, Preston; *m* 1933, Ruth Marion, *o d* of late Ernest Agnew and late Mrs Agnew, of Westwood, Alderley Edge, Cheshire; one *d*. *Educ:* Downside; RMC Sandhurst; Balliol Coll., Oxford. Joined Irish Guards, 1917; served with 1st Bn in France and Germany, 1918-19. Lieut, a/Adjutant (MC); transferred to Reserve of Officers, 1919. BA Oxford, 1922; called to Bar, 1923; joined Northern Circuit; contested (L) Bolton, 1928. KC 1938; Bencher, Inner Temple, 1946. Recorder of Oldham, 1942-50; Judge of Appeal, Isle of Man, 1946-50. Mem., Radcliffe Tribunal, 1962-63. Recalled to Irish Guards, Aug. 1939; Capt. and Adjutant, 1939-40; transferred to General Staff, 1940; Lt-Col 1942. *Recreations:* fishing and gardening. *Address:* Apsehill House, Chicksgrove, Tisbury, Wilts. *T:* Fovant 662. *Clubs:* White's, Army and Navy.

**BARRY, Philip Stuart M.;** *see* Milner-Barry.

**BARRY, Maj.-Gen. Richard Hugh,** CB 1962; CBE 1953 (OBE 1943); retired; *b* 9 Nov. 1908; *s* of Lieut-Col Alfred Percival Barry and Helen Charlotte (*née* Stephens); *m* 1940, Rosalind Joyce Evans; one *s* two *d*. *Educ:* Winchester; Sandhurst. 2nd Lieut Somerset LI, 1929; Staff Coll., Camberley, Capt., 1938; served War of 1939-45; BEF, SOE, AFHQ, Algiers. Military Attaché, Stockholm, 1947; Deputy Chief of Staff Western Europe Land Forces, 1948; Dir, Standing Group, NATO, 1952; Chief of Staff, HQ British Troops in Egypt, 1954-56; Imperial Defence Coll., 1957; Standing Group Representative, North Atlantic Council, 1959-62; retired, 1962. Maj.-Gen. 1959. Africa Star, 1943; 1939-45 Star; Defence, Victory Medals, 1945. *Recreation:* hunting. *Address:* Corridor House, Odiham, Hants. *T:* Odiham 97. *Club:* Army and Navy.

**BARRY, Sir Rupert (Rodney Francis Tress),** 4th Bt *cr* 1899; MBE 1945; *b* 6 Dec. 1910; *s* of Sir (Claude) Francis Barry, 3rd Bt and Angela Doris Manners (*d* 1960), *er d* of Herbert

Charles Hume-Spry; *S* father, 1970; *m* 1st, 1936, Diana Madeline (*d* 1948), *o d* of R. O'Brien Thompson; one *s* one *d*; 2nd, 1951, Sheila Georgina Veronica, *o d* of Major George Joseph Francis White, MBE; three *s* two *d*. *Educ:* King's School, Canterbury; RMC. Major, retd, Oxfordshire and Bucks LI; served War, 1939-40. *Heir: s* Lawrence Edward Anthony Tress Barry, *b* 1 Nov. 1939. *Address:* Brisley Rise, Willesborough Lees, Ashford, Kent.

**BARRY, Rt. Rev. Russell;** *see* Barry, Rt. Rev. F. R.

**BARRY, William Whitmore O.;** *see* Otter-Barry.

**BARSTOW, Stan(ley);** professional writer since 1962; *b* 28 June 1928; *s* of Wilfred Barstow and Elsie Gosney; *m* 1951, Constance Mary Kershaw; one *s* one *d*. *Educ:* Ossett Grammar Sch. Employed in Engineering Industry, 1944-62, mainly as Draughtsman. *Publications:* A Kind of Loving, 1960; The Desperadoes, 1961; Ask Me Tomorrow, 1962; Joby, 1964; The Watchers on the Shore, 1966; Through the Green Woods (ed), 1968; A Raging Calm, 1968. *Address:* Goring House, Goring Park Avenue, Ossett, Yorks. *T:* Ossett 3362.

**BART, A. S.;** *see* Schwarz-Bart.

**BART, Lionel;** Composer, Lyricist and Playwright; *b* 1 Aug. 1930. Wrote lyrics for Lock Up Your Daughters, 1959; music and lyrics for Fings Ain't Wot They Used T'be, 1959; music, lyrics and book for Oliver!, 1960; music, lyrics and direction of Blitz!, 1962; music and lyrics of Maggie May, 1964. Has also written several film scores and many individual hit songs. *Films:* Serious Charge; In the Nick; Heart of a Man; Let's Get Married; Light up the Sky; The Tommy Steele Story; The Duke Wore Jeans; Tommy the Toreador; Sparrers Can't Sing; From Russia with Love; Man in the Middle. Ivor Novello Awards as a song writer: three in 1957; four in 1959; two in 1960. Variety Club Silver Heart as Show Business Personality of the Year, 1960. Broadway, USA; Tony (Antoinette Perry) Award, etc (for Oliver!), best composer and lyricist, 1962. *Address:* Neo-Cortic Productions Ltd, 91 Shaftesbury Avenue, W1. *T:* 01-437 3010.

**BARTER, John (Wilfred);** Chartered Secretary; Management Consultant; *b* 6 Oct. 1917; *s* of late W. F. Barter; *m* 1941, Joan Mackay; two *s* one *d*. *Educ:* Royal Pinner Sch. Contested (C) East Ham South, 1951; MP (C) Ealing North, 1955-64; PPS to Minister of Health, 1957; PPS to Parly Sec., Min. of Power, 1958-60. Middlesex County Council: Mem., 1949; Alderman, 1961-65; Leader of Majority Party, 1962-63; Vice-Chm., 1963-64; last Chm., 1964-65. Chm. of the Middlesex Association. *Club:* St Stephen's.

**BARTER, Sir Percy,** Kt 1951; CB 1947; Chairman of the Board of Control and Under Secretary, Ministry of Health, 1945-52, retired; *b* 27 April 1886; *yr s* of late Frank Barter, Plymouth; *m* 1928, Doris Sheriff; one *d*. *Educ:* Dulwich Coll.; Jesus Coll., Oxford. Entered Local Government Board, 1910; Sec. to Depatmental Cttee on the Blind, 1915; Private Sec. to Rt Hon. C. Addison, Minister of Reconstruction and Minister of Health, 1918-21; Secretary, to Cttee on Asylum Administration, 1921-22, to Royal Commission on Lunacy and Mental Disorder, 1924-26, to Royal Commission on Local Government, 1928-29; Sec. of the Board of Control, 1930-39; Principal Officer, SW Region, Civil Defence, 1939-40; Principal Asst Sec., Ministry of Health, 1940-45. *Address:* Trenant, The Highway, Sutton, Surrey.

**BARTINGTON, Dennis Walter,** CB 1950; *b* 12 May 1901; *s* of late Walter Bartington; *m* 1934, Margaret Christina Skinner. *Educ:* Dulwich Coll.; Trinity Coll., Cambridge (Sen. Schol., MA). Inland Revenue, 1923; Department of Scientific and Industrial Research, 1925; War Office, 1926-39; Asst Sec., Ministry of Supply, 1939, Principal Asst Sec., 1942; Under-Sec., 1947-59. Min. of Aviation, 1959-61; retired, 1961. *Address:* Kingsfield, Orchard Way, Esher, Surrey. *T:* Esher 63918. *Club:* United University.

**BARTLETT, Lt-Col Sir Basil Hardington,** 2nd Bt, *cr* 1913; BA; dramatic author; *b* 15 Sept. 1905; *s* of late Hardington Arthur Bartlett, *e s* of 1st Bt and Irene, *d* of Prof. Henry Robinson; *S* grandfather, 1921; *m* 1937, Mary (marr. diss. 1960), *o d* of late Sir Ian Malcolm, KCMG; three *d*. *Educ:* Repton; Corpus Christi Coll., Cambridge. Served War of 1939-45 (wounded, despatches); Lt-Col, Intelligence Corps. Drama script supervisor, BBC, Television, 1952-55. *Publications:* My First War, 1940; Next of Kin, 1944. *Plays:* This Seat of Mars, 1938; The Intruder, 1939; The Jersey Lily, produced Gate Theatre, 1940; Less than Kind, 1947; A Fish in the Family, 1947. *Heir: b* Henry David Hardington Bartlett [*b* 18 March 1912; *m* 1936, Katherine Rosemond, *d* of Lt-Col W. H. Stanbury; three *s*]. *Clubs:* Garrick, Beefsteak.

**BARTLETT, Charles;** *see* Bartlett, Harold Charles.

**BARTLETT, Charles Vernon Oldfeld;** *see* Bartlett, Vernon.

**BARTLETT, Rt. Rev. David Daniel,** DD (Lambeth); *b* 5 Nov. 1900. *Educ:* St David's College, Lampeter; St John's College, Oxford. BA 1920, BD 1930, Lloyd Williams Fellow, 1927, St David's College; late Casberd Scholar, BA (1st Cl. Theology), 1922. MA 1926, St John's Coll. Deacon, 1923; Priest, 1924. Chaplain and Lecturer in Theology, St David's College, Lampeter, 1923-31; Vicar of Pembroke Dock with Nash and Upton, 1931-46; Examining Chaplain to the Bishop of St David's from 1938, to the Bishop of Monmouth from 1947; Professor of Hebrew and Theology, St David's College, Lampeter, and licensed preacher, Diocese of St David's, 1946; Bishop of St Asaph, 1950-70. Chaplain and Sub-Prelate, Order of St John of Jerusalem, 1965. *Publication:* (ed) Book of Numbers in A New Commentary, 1931. *Address:* c/o The Palace, St Asaph, Flintshire.

**BARTLETT, (Harold) Charles,** ARCA 1949; RE 1961 (ARE 1950); RWS 1970 (ARWS 1959); artist and teacher; *b* Grimsby, 23 Sept. 1921; *s* of Charles Henry and Frances Kate Bartlett; *m*; one *s*. *Educ:* Eastbourne Grammar Sch.; Eastbourne Sch. of Art; Royal College of Art. First one man exhibition in London, 1960. *Recreations:* music, sailing. *Address:* 14 Ascott Avenue, Ealing, W5. *T:* 01-567 5584.

**BARTLETT, Henry Francis,** OBE 1964; HM Diplomatic Service; Counsellor (Commercial), Manila, since 1969; *b* 8 March 1916; *s* of F. V. S. and A. G. Bartlett, London; *m* 1940, A. D. Roy. *Educ:* St Paul's Sch.; Queen's Coll., Oxford; Univ. of California (Commonwealth Fellow). Min. of Inf., 1940-45; Paris, 1944-47; Vice-Consul Lyons, 1948-49; FO, 1949-50; Vice-Consul, Szczecin, 1950; Second, later First, Sec., Warsaw, 1951-53; FO, 1953-55; First Sec. (Commercial), Caracas, 1955-60; First Sec. (Inf.), Mexico City, 1960-63;

Consul, Khorramshahr, 1964-67; Dep. High Comr, Brisbane, 1967-69. *Recreation:* painting (one-man shows Paris, London, Caracas, Mexico City, Brisbane). *Address:* c/o Foreign and Commonwealth Office, SW1.

**BARTLETT, Prof. Maurice Stevenson,** FRS 1961; MA Cambridge, DSc London; Professor of Bio-mathematics in the University of Oxford, since 1967; *b* 18 June 1910; *s* of W. S. Bartlett, Scrooby; *m* 1957, Sheila, *d* of late C. E. Chapman. *Educ:* Latymer Upper Sch.; Queens' Coll., Cambridge. Wrangler, 1932; Rayleigh Prize, 1934. Asst Lectr in Statistics, University Coll., London, 1933-34; Statistician, Imperial Chemical Industries, Ltd, 1934-38; Lectr in Mathematics, Univ. of Cambridge, 1938-47. National Service, Min. of Supply, 1940-45. Visiting Prof. of Mathematical Statistics, Univ. of North Carolina, 1946; Prof. of Mathematical Statistics, Univ. of Manchester, 1947-60; Prof. of Statistics, Univ. of London (University Coll.), 1960-67. Mem. Internat. Statistical Institute, 1949; President: Manchester Statistical Soc., 1959-60; Biometric Soc. (Brit. Reg.), 1964-66; Internat. Assoc. Statistics Phys. Sci., 1965-67; Royal Statistical Society, 1966-67. Hon. DSc (Chicago). *Publications:* An Introduction to Stochastic Processes, 1955; Stochastic Population Models in Ecology and Epidemiology, 1960; Essays in Probability and Statistics, 1962; papers on statistical theory and methodology. *Address:* 441 Banbury Road, Oxford.

**BARTLETT, Vernon,** CBE 1956; Publicist and Broadcaster; *b* Westbury, Wilts, 30 April 1894; *s* of late T. O. Bartlett, Swanage; *m* 1st, Marguerite van den Bemden (*d* 1966); two *s*; 2nd, Eleanor Needham Ritchie. *Educ:* Blundell's, Tiverton. Travelled abroad, 1911-14; European War, 1914-15; joined staff of Daily Mail, 1916; Reuter's Agency, 1917; Paris Peace Conference for Reuter's, and later, for Daily Herald; joined staff of The Times, 1919; special correspondent of that paper in Switzerland, Germany, Poland, 1919-20; Correspondent in Rome, 1921-22; London Director of the League of Nations, 1922-32; Broadcast regularly on foreign affairs, 1928-34; Staff of News Chronicle, 1934-54; Political Commentator for the Straits Times, Singapore, 1954-61; SE Asia Correspondent for Manchester Guardian (now The Guardian), 1954-61. MP (Ind Prog) Bridgwater Div. of Som, 1938-50; Mem. of UN Advisory Cttee of Information Experts, 1948. *Publications:* some twenty-five books of which the most recent are: And Now, Tomorrow, 1960; Tuscan Retreat 1964; A Book about Elba, 1965; Introduction to Italy, 1967; The Past of Pastimes, 1969; The Colour of their Skin, 1969. *Recreation:* growing grapes and olives. *Address:* San Ginese Di Compito, 55060 Lucca, Italy. *T:* Capannori 34125. *Clubs:* Garrick, Beefsteak, Special Forces.

**BARTON, Arthur Edward Victor,** CBE 1936 (OBE 1933); *b* 26 Aug. 1892; *s* of Arthur Moore Barton and Margaret (*née* Bourke); *m* 1st, 1919, Megan Lewis (*d* 1960), *d* of Anthony Matthews, Liverpool; one *s* one *d*; 2nd, 1962, Aileen, *widow* of Ronald S. Lonergan, Mexico City and London. *Educ:* Manchester Grammar Sch. Imperial Customs and Excise Service, 1912; Asst to Chief of Customs, Kenya and Uganda, 1919; Comptroller Customs and MLC, Br. Guiana, 1924; Collector General and MLC, Jamaica, 1927; Collector of Customs and Excise and MLC, Trinidad and Tobago, 1929; MEC, 1936; Mem. West Indies Cricket Board of Control, 1938-39; Comptroller of Customs and Mem. of Legislative Council, Nigeria, 1939-44; retired from Colonial Service, 1944; Sec. to the West India Cttee, 1949-61. Mem. Council, Football Assoc., 1952-70. *Address:* 36 Salmons Lane, Whyteleafe, Surrey. *T:* 01-660 4716. *Clubs:* West Indian; Queen's Park Cricket (Port of Spain); West Indian Students' Centre; British Caribbean Association.

**BARTON, Dr Arthur Willoughby;** Schools Liaison Officer, University College, London, since 1965; Member Panel of Referee Instructors and Lecturers of Fédération Internationale de Football Associations; *b* 14 Sept. 1899; *yr s* of late Professor E. H. Barton, FRS, and Mary Ann Barton, Nottingham; *m* 1935, Alison Mary, 2nd *d* of Colin Read Shaw, Bolton, Lancs; no *c*. *Educ:* Nottingham High Sch.; Trinity Coll. Cambridge. Served European War, 1914-18, 2nd Lieut RE, 1918. Research Asst, Cavendish Lab., Cambridge, 1922-25; Chief Physics Master, Repton Sch., 1925-39; Head Master, King Edward VII Sch., Sheffield, 1939-50; Head Master, City of London Sch., 1950-65. *Publications:* Text Book on Heat, 1933; Text Book on Light, 1939. *Recreations:* Refereeing at football and umpiring at cricket; Hon. Member, Repton Pilgrims Cricket Club; lawn tennis, squash, mountaineering. *Address:* 2 Stone Road, Bromley, Kent. *T:* 01-460 2372. *Clubs:* Alpine, MCC.

**BARTON, Cecil James Juxon Talbot,** CMG 1937; OBE 1932; MA 1921; *b* 13 April 1891; *e s* of late Rev. R. C. E. Barton, MA, and Emma Isabella Talbot; *m* 1926, Cicely (*d* 1940), *y d* of Lieut-Col F. E. Bradshaw, DSO; one *s* one *d*; *m* 1945 Sheila Jean, *d* of A. Macgregor, Dannevirke, NZ. *Educ:* Denstone; Downing Coll., Cambridge, BA 1913. Asst District Comr, Kenya, 1914; served in various administrative posts; Asst for Native Affairs, 1923; acted in various Secretariat posts; Senior Asst Colonial Sec. Kenya, 1933; MLC 1934 and 1935; Colonial Sec. Fiji, 1936-41; MLC; Chm. Public Service Reorganisation Cttee, 1936; Administered Government of Fiji and acted as High Commissioner for the Western Pacific and as Consul General for the Western Pacific in 1936, 1938, 1939; Chief Sec. Nyasaland, 1941; MLC; Mem. Central African Council; Chm. Development Cttee; Administered Government of Nyasaland in 1942, 1944; retired 1945. Employed in Colonial Office, 1945-58. *Publications:* various papers on East African tribes and local history. *Recreations:* fishing; bird shooting; gardening. *Address:* The Old Coach House, Rye, Sussex.

**BARTON, Prof. Derek Harold Richard,** FRS 1954; FRSE 1956; Professor of Organic Chemistry, Imperial College of Science and Technology, University of London, since 1957; *b* 8 Sept. 1918; *s* of William Thomas and Maude Henrietta Barton; *m* 1st, 1944, Jeanne Kate Wilkins; one *s*; 2nd, 1969, Christiane Cognet. *Educ:* Tonbridge Sch.; Imperial Coll., Univ. of London. BSc Hons (1st Class) 1940; Hofmann Prizeman; PhD (Organic Chemistry) 1942; DSc London 1949. Research Chemist: on Govt project, 1942-44. Albright and Wilson, Birmingham, 1944-45; Asst Lectr, Dept of Chemistry, Imperial Coll., 1945-46, ICI Research Fellow, 1946-49; Visiting Lectr in Chemistry of Natural Products, Harvard Univ., USA, 1949-50; Reader in Organic Chemistry, Birkbeck Coll., 1950, Prof. of Organic Chemistry, 1953-55; Regius Prof. of Chemistry, Glasgow Univ., 1955-57. Arthur D. Little Visiting Prof., MIT, 1958; Karl Folkers Visiting Prof., Univs of Illinois and Wisconsin, 1959; Lectures: Tilden, Chem. Soc., 1952; Max Tischler, Harvard Univ., 1956; First Simonsen Memorial, Chem. Soc., 1958; Falk-Plaut, Columbia Univ., 1961; Aub,

Harvard Med. Sch., 1962; Renaud, Michigan State Univ., 1962; Inaugural 3 M's, Univ. of Western Ontario, 1962; 3 M's, Univ. of Minnesota, 1963; Hugo Müller, Chem. Soc., 1963; Pedler, Chem. Soc., 1967; Sandin, Univ. of Alberta, 1969; Robert Robinson, Chem. Soc., London, 1970; Bakerian, Royal Society, 1970. President: Section B, British Assoc. for the Advancement of Science, 1969; Organic Chemistry Div., Internat. Union of Pure and Applied Chemistry, 1969. Mem., Council for Scientific Policy, 1965-. Hon. Member: Sociedad Quimica de Mexico, 1969; Belgian Chem. Soc., 1970; Chilean Chem. Soc., 1970; Corresp. Mem., Argentinian Chem. Soc., 1970; Foreign Hon. Mem. American Academy of Arts and Sciences, 1960; Foreign Associate, Nat. Acad. of Sciences, USA, 1970. Harrison Memorial Prize, Chem. Soc., 1948; First Corday-Morgan Medallist, Chemical Soc., 1951; Fritzsche Medal, Amer. Chem. Soc., 1956; First Roger Adams Medal, Amer. Chem. Soc., 1959; Davy Medal, Royal Society, 1961; Nobel Prize for Chemistry (jointly), 1969. Hon. DSc: University of Montpellier, 1962; Univ. of Dublin, 1964; St Andrews, 1970; Columbia Univ., NYC, 1970. Hon. Fellow: Deutsche Akademie der Naturforscher Leopoldina, 1967; Birkbeck Coll., 1970. *Publications:* numerous, in Journal of Chemical Society. *Address:* Department of Chemistry, Imperial College of Science and Technology, Prince Consort Road, SW7.

**BARTON, Maj.-Gen. Francis Christopher,** CB 1966; CBE 1964; *b* 17 Jan. 1916; *s* of Rev. John Bernard Barton, Elphinstone House, Hastings; *m* 1939, Olivia Mary Darroll-Smith; two *d. Educ:* Haileybury Coll. 2nd Lieut, Royal Marines, 1934; Lieut-Col, 1956; Brig., 1961; Maj.-Gen., 1964. Comd 45 Commando, RM, 1958-60; Comd 3 Commando Brigade, RM, 1962-63; Comdt, Joint Warfare Establishment, Old Sarum, 1964-66; retired, 1966. *Address:* c/o National Westminster Bank, 661 Christchurch Road, Boscombe, Bournemouth, Hants.

**BARTON, Guy Trayton,** CMG 1960; OBE 1957; retired from HM Overseas Civil Service; *b* 7 June 1908; *s* of late Canon H. Barton; *m* 1946, Sybil Maud Seddon, *d* of late Canon G. E. W. Holmes; one *s* one *d. Educ:* Weymouth Coll.; Selwyn Coll., Cambridge. Nigerian Administrative Service, 1931-46; Asst Chief Sec., Barbados, 1946-58; Chief Sec., Barbados, 1958-61; was acting Governor of Barbados for periods during 1958 and 1959. *Publication:* The Prehistory of Barbados, 1953 (Barbados). *Recreations:* gardening; golf; archaeology. *Address:* Five Turnings, Rosea Bridge Lane, Combe Martin, Devon.

**BARTON, Rt. Rev. Mgr. John Mackintosh Tilney,** DD; Priest-in-charge, SS Peter and Edward's, Palace Street, SW1, since 1950; *b* 20 May 1898; *o c* of Tilney Wallace Barton and Marian Barton (*née* Jowitt). *Educ:* Harrow (Entrance Scholar); St Edmund's Coll., Ware; Angelico Univ., Rome; École Biblique, Jerusalem. Priest, 1921; DD (magna cum laude), 1922; LSS 1928. Prof. of Holy Scripture, Hebrew and Liturgy, St Edmund's, Ware, 1924-36; Warden of Edmonton House of Studies, 1936-37; Administrator of St Catherine's Parish and House of Studies, West Drayton, 1937-50. Named Consultor of Pontifical Biblical Commn and *ex-officio* examiner for Papal degrees, 1935 (jubilarian, 1960); Privy Chamberlain to HH, 1936; Prelate of Honour to HH, 1952. Pres. Soc. for OT Study, 1952. Chairman: Catholic Biblical Assoc., 1942-57; Soc. of S John Chrysostom, 1959-65 (Vice-Pres., 1965-;) Pro-Synodal Judge, Westminster Metropolitan Tribunal, 1944-46 and 1963-; Promoter of justice and Defender of the Bond, 1946-63; Dir of Diploma Course in Theology, 1943-; a diocesan censor. FSA 1944; FRSA 1945. Mem., Newman Assoc. *Publications:* The Holy Ghost, 1930; Semitic Religions, 1933; The Religion of Israel, 1934; The Phases of the Sacred Passion, 1954; Penance and Absolution, 1961; Our Lord's Last Farewells before His Passion, 1967. Edited: D. Buzy's St John the Baptist, 1933; Cardinal Wiseman's Lectures on the Blessed Eucharist, 1933; Abbot Chapman's Matthew, Mark and Luke, 1937; S Salaville's Introduction to Eastern Liturgies, 1938; J. Bonsirven's Theology of the New Testament; P. Drijvers, On the Psalms Scripture Textbooks for Catholic Schools; Studies in Comparative Religion; articles in Clergy Review, Tablet, Theology, etc. *Recreations:* swimming and criminology. *Address:* SS Peter and Edward's Presbytery, 43 Palace Street, SW1. *T:* 01-834 7635.

**BARTON, Margaret,** LRAM; writer; *b* 1897; *y d* of Thomas Lloyd Barton and Fanny Roberta Isaacs. *Educ:* St Paul's Girls' Sch.; Royal Academy of Music. *Publications:* Tunbridge Wells, 1937; Garrick, 1948; (with Sir Osbert Sitwell) Sober Truth, 1930; Victoriana, 1931; Brighton, 1935. *Address:* 18 Kensington Court Place, W8.

**BARTON, Robert Childers;** *b* 1881; *e s* of Charles William Barton, JP, DL; *m* 1950, Rachel Warren Lothrop, Cambridge, Mass, *d* of late Fiske Warren, Boston, Mass. *Educ:* Rugby; Christ Church, Oxford. Chm. of Wicklow County Council, 1920; a farmer in Co. Wicklow; served European War; MP (S Fein) West Wicklow, Dec. 1918-22; Mem. of Dail Eireann for Cos Kildare and Wicklow, 1921-23; Minister of Agriculture, 1919-21; Sec. for Economic Affairs, 1921-22; an Irish Peace Delegate to London Conference, 1921; Chm. Agricultural Credit Corporation, 1934-59; Chm. Turf Development Board (now Bord Na Mona), 1935-60. *Address:* Glendalough House, Annamoe, Co. Wicklow.

**BARTON, Sidney James;** *b* 5 March 1909; *s* of James George Barton and Emily Hannah Jury; *m* 1933, Lorna Beatrice Mary Williams; one *s* one *d. Educ:* Elliott Sch., Wandsworth. Laboratory Technician, Metropolitan Asylums Board and LCC, 1927-34; appointed a full-time Officer, National Union of Public Employees, 1934, National Officer, 1962. Mem. Exec. Cttee, London Labour Party. Member: General Council, Nurses and Midwives Council; Ancillary Staffs Council; Professional and Technical Staffs Council for the Health Services; TUC Local Govt and Nurses Advisory Cttees; (part-time) London Transport Executive, 1969; Vice-Chm., London Trades Council, 1952. Former Member: Surrey County Council (1945-49); Sutton and Cheam Borough Council (1945-48); Surrey Exec. Council for Health Services (1947-54); Epsom Group Hosp. Management Cttee and Long Grove Hosp. Management Cttee; South West Metropolitan Regional Hosp. Board. JP 1955; Alderman LCC 1953-65 (Chm. Public Control Cttee, 1954-59); Chm., LCC, 1959-60 (Chm., Primary and Secondary Schools Sub-Cttee, 1960-61); Vice-Chm. General Purposes Cttee, 1961-65. Alderman London Borough of Sutton, 1964-68. Vice-Chm. Governors, Garratt Green Comprehensive Sch. (Chm., 1958-67); Member: Met. Regional Exams Bd for Cert. of Secondary Educn, 1964; London and Home Counties Regional Advisory Council for Technological Educn, 1965; Heathrow Airport London Consultative Cttee. Order of Homayoun Class III (Iraq), 1959; Grand Cross of Order Al Merito (Peru), 1960; Comdr Legion of Honour (France), 1960. *Address:* 14 Chatsworth Road, Cheam, Surrey. *T:* 01-644 9222.

**BARTON-CHAPPLE, Mrs Derek;** *see* Tutin, Dorothy.

**BARTOSIK, Rear-Adm. Josef,** CB 1968; DSC 1943; Coordinating Director, Australia Europe Container Service, since 1969; *b* Poland, 20 July 1917; *m* 1st, 1943, Cynthia Pamela (*d* 1965), *d* of late Humphrey Bowman, CMG, CBE; three *s* one *d*; 2nd, 1969, Mrs Jeannine Scott, *d* of late Paul Bridgeman. *Educ:* in Poland. Joined Polish Navy, 1935; served in Polish destroyers under British operational control, 1939-46; transf. to RN as Lieut RN, 1948; served in Admty (Ops Div.) as Comdr, 1953-54 and as Dep. Dir, 1958-59; commanded: HMS Comus, 1955-56; HMS Scarborough and as Capt. (F) 5th FS, 1960-61; RN Air Station Culdrose, 1962-63, HMS London, 1964-65; Rear-Adm. 1966; Asst Chief of Naval Staff (Ops), MoD, 1966-68; retired 1968. *Recreations:* all outdoor. *Address:* 33 Cheval Place, SW7. *Clubs:* Junior Army and Navy, Arts Theatre.

**BARTTELOT, Captain Sir Brian Walter de Stopham,** 5th Bt, *cr* 1875; Assistant Regimental Adjutant, Coldstream Guards; Temporary Equerry to the Queen, since 1970; *b* 17 July 1941; *s* of Lt-Col Sir Walter de Stopham Barttelot, 4th Bt, and Sara Patricia (who *m* 2nd, 1965, Comdr James Barttelot, RN retd), *d* of late Lieut-Col H. V. Ravenscroft; *S* father, 1944; *m* 1969, Hon. Mary Angela Fiona Weld-Forester, *y d* of Col Lord Forester, *qv*. *Educ:* Eton; RMA, Sandhurst. *Heir:* *b* Robin Ravenscroft Barttelot, *b* 15 Dec. 1943. *Address:* Keepers Stopham, Pulborough, Sussex. *T:* Fittleworth 347. *Clubs:* Guards, Buck's.

**BARWELL, Prof. Claud Foster,** MA, MD; Goldsmiths' Company's Professor of Bacteriology, University of London, at London Hospital, since 1952; *b* 12 Nov. 1912; *s* of late Harold Barwell; *m* 1938, Joanna O'Toole; no *c*. *Educ:* Marlborough Coll.; Trinity Hall, Cambridge. Qualified at St George's Hosp., London, 1938; Asst Bacteriologist, London Hosp., 1938; Asst Pathologist, EMS, at Colchester, 1940, and Epping, 1942; Pathologist at Epping, 1943, and Sector Pathologist for Essex Div., 1944; Lecturer in Bacteriology, London Hosp. Medical Coll., 1946; Reader in Bacteriology, 1949. *Publications:* experimental work on viruses of the psittacosis group, in Nature, British Jl of Experimental Pathology, Jl of Clinical Pathology. *Recreations:* gardening, fly fishing. *Address:* 17 Holly Walk, NW3. *T:* 01-435 4747.

**BARWICK, Rt. Hon. Sir Garfield (Edward John),** PC 1964; GCMG 1965; Kt 1953; QC (Australia); Chief Justice of Australia since 1964; *b* 22 June 1903; *s* of late Jabez Edward Barwick and Lilian Grace Ellicott; *m* 1929, Norma Mountier Symons; one *s* one *d*. *Educ:* Fort Street Boys' High Sch., Sydney; University of Sydney, BA 1923; LLB (Hons) 1926. New South Wales Bar, 1927; KC 1941; Victorian Bar, 1945; KC (Vic) 1945; Queensland Bar, 1958; QC Queensland, 1958. Practised extensively in all jurisdictions: Supreme Court, High Court of Australia and Privy Council. Pres. NSW Bar Assoc., 1950-52 and 1954-55; Attorney-Gen. Commonwealth of Australia, Dec. 1958-Feb. 1964; Minister for External Affairs, Dec. 1961-April 1964; Pres. Law Council of Australia, 1952-54. Hon. Bencher, Lincoln's Inn, 1964. Leader: Australian Delegation, SEATO Council, Bangkok, 1961, Paris, 1963; UN Delegation, 1960, 1962-64; Australian Delegation to ECAFE, Manila, 1963; Australian Delegation, ANZUS, Canberra, 1962, Wellington, 1963. Chancellor, Macquarie Univ., 1967. *Recreations:* golf; fishing; yachting. *Address:* Mundroola, 133 George Street, Careel Bay, Sydney, NSW; High Court of Australia, Darlinghurst, NSW. *Clubs:* Australian (Sydney); Melbourne (Melbourne); Royal Sydney Yacht Squadron; Cruising Yacht Club of Australia.

**BARWICK, Sir Richard (Llewellyn),** 3rd Bt, *cr* 1912; *b* 4 Nov. 1916; *o surv. s* of Sir John Storey Barwick, 2nd Bt, and Gwladys Jessie (*d* 1949), 3rd *d* of George William Griffith Thomas, Ystrad Mynach, Co. Glamorgan; *S* father 1953; *m* 1st, 1948, Valerie Maud (Ward) (marr. diss.), *d* of Robert J. Skelton, Nairobi, Kenya Colony; three *d*; 2nd, 1968, Mrs Denise Radcliffe, *widow* of Hugh Christian Radcliffe. *Educ:* Harrow; Christ's Coll., Cambridge. Served Royal Air Force, 1940-46. *Heir:* none. *Address:* Thimbleby Hall, Northallerton, North Riding, Yorks. *T:* Osmotherly 212. *Club:* Northern Counties (Newcastle upon Tyne).

*See also R. A. Cookson.*

**BARZUN, Prof. Jacques;** Professor of History, Columbia University, New York, since 1945; Dean of the Graduate Faculties, 1955-58; Dean of Faculties and Provost, 1958-67; University Professor, 1967; *b* 30 Nov. 1907; *s* of Henri Barzun and Anna-Rose Martin; *m* 1936, Mariana Lowell; two *s* one *d*. *Educ:* Lycée Janson de Sailly; Columbia Univ. Instructor in History, Columbia Univ., 1929; Research Fellow, American Council of Learned Socs, 1933-34: Asst Prof., Columbia Univ., 1938; Associate Prof., 1942. Membre Associé de l'Académie Delphinale, Grenoble, 1952; Member: Nat. Inst. of Arts and Letters, USA; Amer. Acad. of Arts and Sciences; Council on Foreign Relations, USA; American Historical Assoc.; FRSA, USA (Benjamin Franklin Fellow). Seth Low Prof. of History, Columbia Univ., 1960; Extraordinary Fellow, Churchill Coll., Cambridge, 1961-. Chevalier de la Légion d'Honneur. *Publications:* The French Race: Theories of its Origin, 1932; Race: A Study in Superstition, 1937 (revd, 1965); Of Human Freedom, 1939 (revd, 1964); Darwin, Marx, Wagner, 1941 (revd, 1958); Teacher in America, 1945 (revd, 1954); Berlioz and the Romantic Century, 1950 (revd, 1969); Pleasures of Music, 1951; Selected Letters of Byron, 1953; Nouvelles Lettres de Berlioz, 1954; God's Country and Mine, 1954; Music in American Life, 1956; The Energies of Art, 1956; The Modern Researcher (with Henry F. Graff), 1957 (revd, 1970); The House of Intellect, 1959; Classic, Romantic and Modern, 1961; Science: The Glorious Entertainment, 1964; (Ed) Follett's Modern American Usage, 1967; The American University, 1968. Contrib to leading US journals. *Address:* Columbia University, New York 27, NY, USA. *T:* 280-2841. *Clubs:* Athenæum; Authors'; Century (New York).

**BASHFORD, Humphrey John Charles,** MA; Headmaster, Hessle High School, since 1964; *b* 5 Oct. 1920; *s* of late Sir Henry Bashford, MD, FRCP, and late Margaret Eveline Sutton; *m* 1942, Alyson Margaret Liddle; two *s* three *d*. *Educ:* Sherborne Sch.; Clare Coll., Cambridge. MA Cambridge 1950. Served War of 1939-45: commissioned 2nd Bn Oxford Bucks LI, 1941; GSO3 HQ Airborne Corps 1944-46. Senior History Master, Leys Sch., Cambridge, 1947; Part-time Tutor, WEA, 1950; Headmaster, Wellingborough Sch., 1956-64. *Recreations:*

cricket, fly-fishing. *Address:* 27 Marlborough Avenue, Hessle, East Yorks. *Club:* MCC.

**BASING,** 4th Baron *cr* 1887; **George Lutley Sclater-Booth;** *b* 7 Dec. 1903; *s* of Hon. Charles Lutley Sclater-Booth (*d* 1931) (2nd *s* of 1st Baron) and Ellen Geraldine (*d* 1957), *y d* of George Jones, Mitton Manor, Staffs; *S* cousin, 1969; *m* 1st, 1938, Jeannette (marr. diss. 1944; she *d* 1957), *d* of late N. B. MacKelvie, New York; one *s*; 2nd, 1951, Cynthia, *widow* of Carl H. Beal, Los Angeles, and *d* of late Charles W. Hardy, Salt Lake City, Utah. *Educ:* Winchester. *Heir: s* Hon. Neil Lutley Sclater-Booth, *b* 16 Jan. 1939. *Address:* PO Box 301, Pebble Beach, California, USA. *Clubs:* Bel Air Country (Los Angeles); Eldorado Country (Palm Desert, Calif).

**BASINGSTOKE, Archdeacon of;** *see* Rudgard, Ven. Richard Cuthbert.

**BASKETT, Sir Ronald (Gilbert),** Kt 1966; OBE 1947; BSc (London), MSc (Reading); FRIC; Director of the National Institute for Research in Dairying and Research Professor, Reading University, 1959-67, now Professor Emeritus; *b* 30 Oct. 1901; *s* of Charles Henry Baskett, RE, and Florence Maud Baskett; *m* 1927, Joan Shirley Staples Firth; three *s*. *Educ:* King Edward VI Grammar Sch., Chelmsford; University Coll., Reading. Demonstrator in Agricultural Chemistry, University Coll., Reading, 1923-24; Asst to Head of Chemical and Animal Nutrition Div., Ministry of Agriculture, Northern Ireland, 1924, and Asst Agricultural Chemistry Dept, Queen's Univ.; Lecturer in charge of Agricultural Chemistry Dept, 1928; Head of Chemical and Animal Nutrition Div., Ministry of Agriculture for Northern Ireland, 1928; Prof. of Agricultural Chemistry, Queen's Univ. of Belfast, 1935-59. Chief Scientific Officer, Ministry of Agriculture for Northern Ireland, 1947-59; Agricultural Attaché, British Embassy, Washington DC, 1950-52. Hon. DSc (Belfast). *Publications:* Scientific papers to agricultural journals. *Recreations:* sailing; gardening. *Address:* 15 The Brae, Groomsport, Bangor, Co. Down, Northern Ireland. *Club:* Athenæum.

**BASNETT, David;** National Industrial Officer, General and Municipal Workers' Union, since 1960; *b* 9 Feb. 1924; British; *m* 1956, Kathleen Joan Molyneaux; two *s*. *Educ:* Quarry Bank High School, Liverpool. Served War of 1939-45, RAF. Trade Union Official, 1948; TUC General Council, 1966. Numerous committees of enquiry including Royal Commission on Penal Reform and Commission on the Constitution. *Address:* Ruxley Towers, Claygate, Surrey. *T:* Esher 62081.

**BASNYAT, Shri Upendra Bahadur,** Prasiddha Prabal Gorkha Dakshin Bahu; Long Service, War Service, Defence and Coronation Medals (Nepal); Ambassador of Nepal to the Court of St James's since 1969; *b* 1919; *m*; two *s*. *Educ:* Calcutta University. Commnd Lieut, Royal Nepalese Army, 1940; served War of 1939-45 with Nepalese contingent as Adjt. Mil. Attaché (Lt-Col), Royal Nepalese Embassy, New Delhi and Nepalese Liaison Officer to Gorkha Rifles of Indian Army, 1951-56; transf. to Foreign Service of Nepal, 1957; Consul-General in Lhasa, 1958-61; Deputy, Peking, 1961-65; Ambassador to Pakistan, Iran and Turkey, 1965-69. *Address:* Royal Nepalese Embassy, 12a Kensington Palace Gardens, W8.

**BASON, Fred, (Frederick Thomas Bason);** bookseller since 1922; author since 1931; Lecturer on authors, books and collecting books since 1941; *b* Southwark, 29 Aug. 1907; *s* of William Bason and Annie (*née* Blount), Southwark; bachelor. *Educ:* Westmorland Road LCC Sch. Became a bookseller at age of 15; journalist, 1924. Many broadcasts for BBC and appearances on TV; frequent broadcasts to Australia and America; has given over 800 lectures in Gt Britain and abroad. *Publications:* The W. Somerset Maugham Bibliography (introd by Somerset Maugham), 1931 (2 edns); Gallery Unreserved (introd by Somerset Maugham), 1931; The Cigarette Card Hand Book and Guide to Values, 1938; Toys for Nothing, 1941; More Toys for Nothing, 1942; Fred Bason's Diary (introd by N. Bentley), 1951 (2nd edn 1952); Fred Bason's Second Diary (introd by L. A. G. Strong), 1952; The Third Diary of Fred Bason (introd etc by Michael Sadleir), 1955; The Last Bassoon, A Cockney's Diary (ed and introd by Noël Coward), 1960; Fishing, 1960; Fred Bason Has A Picnic, 1961; Spring, 1962 (ltd edn); Summer, 1963 (ltd edn); contribs to The Saturday Book, vols 5-30; contribs to all leading magazines etc. in which there is an interest in authors, books or collecting books; has had over 2,000 articles published all over the world. *Recreations:* meeting people and making them laugh; encouraging writers by lecturing; visitors welcomed any Thursday. *Address:* Four, Broadmayne, Portland Street, Walworth, SE17. *T:* none. *Clubs:* none.

**BASOV, Prof. Nikolai Gennadievich;** Physicist, USSR; Vice-director of the PN Lebedev Physical Institute, Moscow, since 1958, also Head of the Laboratory of Quantum Radiophysics; Professor, Moscow Institute of Physical Engineers; *b* 1922; *s* of Prof. Gennadiy Phedorovitsch Basov and Zinaida Andreevna Basova; *m* 1950, Kseniya Tichonovna Basova; two *s*. *Educ:* secondary; Institute of Physical Engineers, Moscow. Joined the PN Lebedev Physical Institute, 1948. Corresponding Mem. USSR Acad. of Sciences. 1962-; Academician, 1966. Mem. German Acad. of Sciences, 1967. Awarded Lenin Prize, 1959; Nobel Prize for Physics (jointly with Prof. A. M. Prokhorov of the PN Lebedev Physical Institute, Moscow, and prof. C. H. Townes of MIT Cambridge, Mass, USA) 1964. *Address:* PN Lebedev Physical Institute, Academy of Sciences of the USSR, Lenin Prospekt 53, Moscow, USSR.

**BASS, Harry Godfrey Mitchell;** British High Commissioner in Lesotho, since 1970; *b* 26 Aug. 1914; *s* of late Rev. Arthur Edward Bass and Mildred Bass; *m* 1948, Monica Mary, *d* of late Rev. H. F. Burroughs; two *s* one *d*. *Educ:* Marlborough Coll.; Gonville and Caius Coll., Cambridge; St John's Coll., Oxford. British Museum, Dept of Egyptian and Assyrian Antiquities, 1939; Admiralty, 1940; Dominions Office, 1946; Asst Sec., Office of UK High Commissioner, Australia, 1948-51; Mem. of Secretariat, Commonwealth Economic Conference, 1952 and Meeting of Commonwealth Prime Ministers, 1953; Counsellor, Office of UK High Commissioner, Calcutta, 1954-57; Dep. UK High Commissioner, Federation of Rhodesia and Nyasaland, 1959-61; British Minister (Pretoria and Cape Town) in the Republic of S Africa, 1961-62; seconded to Central African Office, 1963-64; British Dep. High Commissioner, Ibadan, 1965-67; Head of Consular Dept, FCO, 1967-70. *Publications:* contrib. to Oxford Review, Journal of Egyptian Archæology. *Recreations:* birdwatching; walking. *Address:* c/o Barclays Bank, 95 Victoria Street, SW1. *Club:* United University.

**BASSET, Ronald Lambart;** Director of: The National Discount Co. Ltd; Gulf Oil (Great

Britain) Ltd; *b* 30 Nov. 1898; *s* of late Arthur Francis Basset; *m* 1931, Lady Elizabeth Legge (Extra Woman of the Bedchamber to Queen Elizabeth the Queen Mother), 2nd *d* of 7th Earl of Dartmouth; one *s* (and one *s* decd). *Educ:* Eton; RMC Sandhurst. 2nd Lieut Royal Scots Greys; served European War, France, 1918; Partner Reeves Whitburn and Co., 1923, Chm., 1932-38; Emergency Commission Welsh Guards, 1940; Temp. Lieut-Col 1942. *Recreations:* shooting; fishing. *Address:* The Lodge House, Hatfield Park, Hatfield, Herts. *T:* 2150. *Clubs:* Turf, White's; Travellers' (Paris).

**BASSETT, George Arthur,** CB 1945; *b* 3 Aug. 1884; *s* of late George Bassett; *m* 1907, Mabel Alice (*d* 1957), *d* of late John Gransden, Luton, Chatham; one *s* three *d*. *Educ:* Mathematical Sch., Rochester; RN Coll., Greenwich. Royal Corps of Naval Constructors, 1907; Asst Constructor Admiralty and Overseeing HM Submarines, Vickers, Barrow, 1911-18; Constructor Commander Naval Armistice Commission and Naval Inter-Allied Commission of Control, Germany, 1919-20; Chief Constructor, HM Dockyard, Gibraltar, 1932-35; Superintendent of Repairs by Contract, Admiralty, 1940; Dep. Dir of Dockyards, Admiralty, 1941-46. *Recreation:* books. *Address:* 115 Farnaby Road, Bromley, Kent. *T:* 01-460 0704.

**BASSETT, His Honour John Harold,** QC 1951; a County Court Judge, Circuit 58, Ilford, etc., 1955-65; called to the Bar, Middle Temple, 1931. South Eastern Circuit; South London Sessions; Central Criminal Court. *Address:* 2 Garden Court, Temple, EC4; Hillcrest, 66 Leopold Road, Wimbledon, SW19.

**BASSETT, Sir Walter (Eric),** KBE 1959; MC; FIEAust; Senior Partner W. E. Bassett & Partners, Consulting Engineers; President, Mt Lyell M. & R. Co., Australia; Director, Renison Ltd, Australia; *b* Melbourne, 19 Dec. 1892; *s* of late Walter and Caroline Bassett, Melbourne; *m* 1923, Flora Marjorie, *d* of late Sir David Orme Masson; one *s* one *d*. *Educ:* Wesley Coll., Melbourne; Melbourne Univ. (MMechE, BEE). Served European War, 1914-18, with AIF; Lieut 5th Field Co. Engineers and Australian Flying Corps. Senior Lecturer, Mechanical Engineering and Aerodynamics, Melbourne Univ., 1919-28. Pres. Instn Engrs Australia, 1942; Dir, Gas and Fuel Corporation, Victoria, etc.; Mem. Council, Monash Univ., Victoria. Kernot Memorial Medal, 1948; Peter Nicol Russell Memorial Medal, 1958. Hon. DrEng Monash, 1970. *Recreations:* fishing, sailing, woodwork. *Address:* 133 Kooyong Road, Armadale, Victoria, Australia; 522 Little Collins Street, Melbourne, Victoria 3000, Australia. *T:* 62-1321. *Clubs:* Melbourne, Naval and Military, Royal Melbourne Golf, Royal Yacht Club of Victoria (all Melbourne); Adelaide (Adelaide).

**BASTEN, Sir Henry (Bolton),** Kt 1966; CMG 1947; MA Oxon and Adelaide; Chairman, Australian Universities Commission, since 1968; University of Adelaide, 1953-67, Vice-Chancellor, 1958-67. Formerly Chairman & General Manager, Singapore & Penang Harbour Boards. Investigated conditions in Australian ports for Commonwealth Government, 1951-52, report published, 1952. Hon. DLitt Flinders Univ. (S Australia), 1967. *Address:* 14 Day Road, Glen Osmond, South Australia 5064, Australia.

**BASTYAN, Lt-Gen. Sir Edric (Montague),** KCMG 1962; KCVO 1963; KBE 1957 (CBE 1943; OBE 1942); CB 1944; Governor of Tasmania, since 1968; *b* 5 April 1903; *s* of late Lt-Col S. J. Bastyan, Ferndown, Dorset; *m* 1944, Victoria Eugénie Helen (*née* Bett), DStJ 1969; one *s*. *Educ:* RMC, Sandhurst. 2nd Lieut Sherwood Foresters, 1923; Capt. West Yorks Regt, 1935; Staff Coll., 1936-37; Royal Irish Fusiliers, 1937; Major, 1940; Temp. Lt-Col 1941; Temp. Brigadier, 1942; Acting Maj.-Gen, 1944; Col, 1945; Maj.-Gen. (with seniority, 1946), 1948. Served Palestine, 1938-39 (despatches); War of 1939-45, Africa, Italy, SEAC (despatches, OBE, CBE, CB). Chief Admin. Officer, Eighth Army, 1943; Maj.-Gen. i/c Administration Allied Land Forces, SE Asia, 1944-45. Imperial Defence Coll., 1946. Maj.-Gen. i/c Administration, British Army of the Rhine, 1946-48; employed in special duties, War Office, 1949; Chief of Staff Eastern Command, 1949-50; Dir of Staff Duties, WO 1950-52; Comdr 53rd (Welsh) Infantry Div. (TA) and Mid-West District, 1952-55; Vice Adjutant Gen., War Office, 1955-57; Lieut-Gen., 1957; Comdr, British Forces, Hongkong, 1957-60; retired, 1960. Governor of South Australia, 1961-68. KStJ, 1961. *Recreations:* golf; tennis; painting. *Address:* Government House, Hobart, Tasmania. *Club:* United Service.

*See also Maj.-Gen. K. C. O. Bastyan.*

**BASTYAN, Maj.-Gen. Kenneth Cecil Orville,** CB 1959; CBE 1953 (OBE 1943); *b* 10 Dec. 1906; *s* of late Lieut-Col S. J. Bastyan, OBE, Ferndown, Dorset; *m* 1934, Patricia, *e d* of Major P. B. Riley, MRCVS; one *s*. *Educ:* Bedford Sch. 2nd Lieut, Royal Signals, 1926; served War of 1939-45 in India, Iraq and Burma (OBE); Malaya, 1951-53; Chief Signal Officer, FARELF, 1953-54; Dep. Signal Officer in Chief at the War Office, 1954-57; Chief Signal Officer, BAOR and Northern Army Group, 1957-60. *Address:* 23 Brownsea View Avenue, Lilliput, Poole, Dorset.

*See also Lieut-Gen. Sir Edric Bastyan.*

**BATCHELOR, Alfred Alexander Meston,** MA; Headmaster, Temple Grove School, Heron's Ghyll, near Uckfield, 1935-57; *b* 8 March 1901; *s* of late Rev. Canon A. W. Batchelor, and late Agnes Lowe; *m* 1949, Thelma Williams. *Educ:* Temple Grove; Charterhouse (Scholar); Christ Church, Oxford (Holford Exhibitioner). Hon. Mods. 1922; Lit. Hum. 1924; Senior Asst Master, The Old Ride, Bournemouth, 1926-30; Joint Headmaster, St Christopher's, near Bath, 1930-35; Private Holiday Tutor to the late Duke of Connaught, 1929-34. *Publications:* Contributor to Punch, The Times, etc. *Recreations:* natural history, music. *Address:* Hundred End, Fairwarp, near Uckfield, Sussex. *T:* Nutley 2151.

**BATCHELOR, G(eorge) F(rederick) Grant,** MB, ChB, LRCP, FRCS; retired as consulting surgeon; *b* 6 April 1902; *s* of Robert and Margaret Grant Batchelor; *m* 1944, Helen Elspeth Mackintosh, *d* of late Lieut-Col C. H. Simpson, Harrogate. *Educ:* Dundee High Sch.; St Andrews Univ. MB, ChB (St Andrews), 1923; MRCS, LRCP, 1925; FRCS, 1926; Asst Surgeon, West London Hospital, 1929; Hounslow Hospital, 1930; Surgeon: Wembley Hospital, 1930; West London Hospital, 1935; EMS, London, 1939-42; Lieut-Col, RAMC, 1942. *Recreations:* golf; shooting. *Address:* 14 Lexham House, 45 Lexham Gardens, W8. *T:* 01-373 9008. *Club:* Constitutional.

**BATCHELOR, George Keith,** FRS 1957; Professor of Applied Mathematics, University of Cambridge, since 1964, and Head of Department of Applied Mathematics and Theoretical Physics, since 1959; *b* Melbourne, 8 March 1920; *s* of George Conybere Batchelor and Ivy Constance Batchelor (*née* Berneye); *m* 1944, Wilma Maud Rätz; three *d*. *Educ:*

Essendon and Melbourne High Schs; University of Melbourne. BSc 1940, MSc 1941, University of Melbourne; PhD 1948, Adams Prize, 1951, University of Cambridge; Research Officer, Aeronautical Research Laboratory, Melbourne, 1940-44; Fellow of Trinity Coll., Cambridge, 1947-; Lecturer, University of Cambridge, 1948-59; Reader in Fluid Dynamics, Univ. of Cambridge, 1959-64; Editor, Cambridge Monographs on Mechanics and Applied Mathematics, 1953-; Editor, Journal of Fluid Mechanics, 1956-. Dr *hc* Univ. of Grenoble, 1959. *Publications:* The Theory of Homogeneous Turbulence, 1953; An Introduction to Fluid Dynamics, 1967; various papers on fluid mechanics in journals devoted to physical science. *Address:* Cobbers, Conduit Head Road, Cambridge. *T:* Cambridge 56387.

**BATCHELOR, John Richard;** Director, McIndoe Research Unit, Queen Victoria Hospital, East Grinstead, since 1967; *b* 4 Oct. 1931; *s* of B. W. Batchelor, CBE and Mrs C. E. Batchelor; *m* 1955, Moira Ann (*née* McLellan); two *s* two *d. Educ:* Marlborough Coll.; Emmanuel Coll., Cambridge; Guy's Hospital, London. MB, BChir Cantab, 1955; MD Cantab 1965. Nat. Service, RAMC, 1957-59; Dept of Pathology, Guy's Hospital: Res. Fellow, 1959-61; Lectr and Sen. Lectr, 1961-67. Prof. of Transplantation Research, RCS, 1967. *Publications:* scientific articles upon tissue transplantation research in various special jls. *Recreations:* sailing; tennis; walking. *Address:* Little Ambrook, Nursery Road, Walton-on-the-Hill, Tadworth, Surrey. *T:* Tadworth 2028. *Club:* Royal Automobile.

**BATCHELOR, John Stanley,** FRCS; Orthopaedic Surgeon, Guy's Hospital, since 1946; *b* 4 Dec. 1905; *s* of Dr Ferdinand Stanley Batchelor and Florence Batchelor; *m* 1934, Marjorie Blanche Elvina Rudkin; two *s* one *d. Educ:* Christ's Coll., Christchurch, NZ; Otago Univ.; Guy's Hospital. MRCS, LRCP 1931; FRCS 1934. Pres., Section of Orthopaedics, RSocMed, 1958-59; British Orthopaedic Assoc.: Hon. Treas. 1960-65; Hon. Sec. 1964; Vice-Pres. 1967-68; Pres. 1970-72. *Publications:* contribs to med. jls. *Recreations:* golf, walking, antiques. *Address:* c/o Bank of New Zealand, 1 Queen Victoria Street, EC4. *T:* 01-248 6401.

**BATE, Ven. Alban F.,** MA; DCnL; Archdeacon of St John, 1949-63, retired; Rector of St Paul's Church, St John, New Brunswick, 1936-63, retired; *b* 12 May 1893; *s* of Rev. William John Bate and Alice C. McMullen; *m* 1919, Norah F. Warburton, Charlottetown, PEI; two *s* five *d. Educ:* Rothesay Collegiate Sch.; Dalhousie, Superior Sch.; University of King's Coll., Nova Scotia, (made Hon. Fellow 1939), BA, 1914; Divinity Testamur, 1916; MA, 1918; Deacon, 1916; Priest, 1917; Curate of Cathedral, Fredericton, 1916-19; Asst at Parish Church, Fredericton, 1919-20; Rector of Fredericton 1920-36 and Archdeacon of Fredericton, 1932-36; Canon of Christ Church Cathedral, Fredericton, 1946; Chaplain of the Legislature of Province of New Brunswick, 1925-35; Chaplain 7th Machine Gun Bn, 1927; 1936; Chaplain, St George's Soc., 1939-42; Pres. Rotary Club of Fredericton, 1928-29; Saint John, 1941-42. DCnL (King's Univ. Halifax) 1955. *Recreation:* gardening. *Address:* Hempton Village, King's County, NB, Canada. *Clubs:* Rotary, Canadian (St John, NB).

**BATE, David Lindsay,** CBE 1968; **Hon. Mr Justice Bate;** Puisne Judge, High Court of Justice, Northern States of Nigeria, since 1957; *b* 3 March 1916; *m* 1948, Thadeen June, *d* of R. F. O'Donnell Peet; two *s. Educ:* Marlborough; Trinity Coll., Cambridge. Called to Bar, Inner Temple, 1938. Commissioned, Royal Artillery, 1939 and served, Royal Artillery, 1939-46. Entered Colonial Legal Service, 1947; Crown Counsel, Nigeria, 1947-52; Senior Crown Counsel, Nigeria, 1952-54; Senior Crown Counsel, Northern Nigeria 1954-56; Solicitor-Gen., Northern Nigeria, 1956. *Recreations:* shooting; fishing; riding. *Address:* Judge's Chambers, High Court, Jos, Northern Nigeria. *Club:* Flyfishers'.

**BATE, Sir Edwin;** *see* Bate, Sir W. E.

**BATE, Sir (Walter) Edwin,** Kt 1969; OBE 1955; Barrister, Solicitor and Notary Public, Hastings, New Zealand, since 1927; *b* 12 March 1901; *s* of Peter and Florence Eleanor Bate; *m* 1925, Louise Jordan; two *s* one *d. Educ:* Victoria Univ., Wellington. LLM (first class hons), 1922. Admitted Barrister and Solicitor, 1922; practised: Taumarunui, NZ, 1923; Hastings, NZ, 1927. Mayor, City of Hastings, NZ, 1953-59; Chm., Hawke Bay Hosp. Bd, 1941-; Pres., Hosp. Bds Assoc. of NZ, 1953-; Pres., Associated Trustee Savings Banks of NZ, 1968 and 1969. OStJ 1961. *Recreations:* fishing, gardening. *Address:* PO Box 749 Hastings, New Zealand. *T:* 89170. *Club:* Wellesley (Wellington, NZ).

**BATE, Prof. Walter Jackson;** Abbott Lawrence Lowell Professor of the Humanities, Harvard University, since 1962; *b* 23 May 1918; *s* of William George Bate. *Educ:* Harvard Univ. AB 1939, PhD 1942. Harvard University: Associate Prof. of English, 1949-55; Prof. of English, 1955-62; Chm., Dept of English, 1955-62. Member: Amer. Acad. of Arts and Sciences; Amer. Philosophical Soc.; Cambridge Scientific Soc. Christian Gauss Award, 1956; Pulitzer Prize for Biography, 1964. *Publications:* Stylistic Development of Keats, 1945; From Classic to Romantic, 1946; Criticism: The Major Texts, 1952; The Achievement of Samuel Johnson, 1955; Prefaces to Criticism, 1959; Yale Edition of Samuel Johnson, Vol. II, 1963; John Keats, 1963; Coleridge, 1968; The Burden of the Past, 1970. *Recreation:* farming. *Address:* 3 Warren House, Cambridge, Mass, USA. *Club:* Saturday (Boston, Mass).

**BATE, Dame Zara (Kate);** *see* Holt, Dame Z. K.

**BATE-SMITH, Dr Edgar Charles,** CBE 1963; FLS 1959; FIFST; ScD; Director, Low Temperature Research Station, Cambridge, 1947-65, retired; *b* 24 Aug. 1900; *s* of Albert Edward Smith and Avis Ellen Jenkinson; *m* 1934, Margaret Elizabeth Bate Hardy; one *s. Educ:* Wellingborough Sch.; Manchester Univ.; Gonville and Caius Coll., Cambridge. Soc. of Chemical Industry Food Group (Cttee 1939-41, 1956-60; Jubilee Memorial Lectr, 1962-63); Inst. of Food Science and Technology; Cambridge Philosophical Soc. (Pres., 1953-55); Phytochemical Soc. (formerly Plant Phenolics Group) (Chm. 1958-60). *Publications:* Food Science (with T. N. Morris), 1952. Papers in scientific jls on post-mortem physiology of muscle, chemistry and taxonomy of plants. *Recreations:* plants and animals; sketching. *Address:* 39 Grange Road, Cambridge. *T:* Cambridge 52591.

**BATEMAN, Rev. Arthur Fitzroy Dobbie-:** *see* Dobbie-Bateman.

**BATEMAN, Sir Cecil (Joseph),** KBE 1967 (MBE 1944); Director: Co-operative Permanent Building Society, since 1970; Provincial Bank of Ireland, since 1970; G. Heyn & Sons Ltd, since 1970; *b* 6 Jan. 1910; *s* of Samuel and Annie

Bateman; *m* 1938, Doris M. Simpson; one *s* one *d*. *Educ:* Queen's Univ., Belfast. Served War of 1939-45, Royal Artillery (Major). Entered NI Civil Service, Nov. 1927. Dir of Establishments, Min. of Finance, 1958-63; Sec. to Cabinet and Clerk of Privy Council of N Ireland, 1963-65; Permanent Sec., Min. of Finance, and Head of Northern Ireland Civil Service, 1965-70, retd. Member: Jt Exchequer Bd, 1966-; Statute Law Cttee for N Ireland, 1967-. *Recreations:* golf, reading. *Address:* 60 Knocklofty Park, Belfast 4, N Ireland. *T:* Belfast 650818. *Clubs:* Royal Commonwealth Society; Shandon Park Golf.

**BATEMAN, Sir Charles Harold,** KCMG, *cr* 1950 (CMG 1937); MC; *b* Portsmouth, 4 Jan. 1892; *s* of late Charles Bateman; *m* 1940, Bridget Mary, *d* of late Michael Kavanagh, Co. Wicklow. *Educ:* London Univ. (BA); Sorbonne, Paris. Served European War, 1914-18, with 2nd London Regt (Royal Fusiliers), Gallipoli and France; Royal Artillery, France and Belgium (MC, twice wounded); entered Diplomatic Service, 1920; Third Sec., Santiago, Chile; Foreign Office, 1924; First Sec., 1929; transferred Bagdad, 1932; Acting Counsellor, 1935; Counsellor, Lisbon, 1937; Minister at Cairo, 1938; transferred Foreign Office, 1940; Minister to Mexico, 1941-44, Ambassador, 1944-47; Asst Under Sec., Foreign Office, 1948-50; British Ambassador to Poland, 1950-52; retired, 1952. *Address:* 30 Longcroft Avenue, Banstead, Surrey.

**BATEMAN, Geoffrey Hirst,** FRCS; Surgeon, Ear, Nose and Throat Department, St Thomas' Hospital, London, since 1939; *b* 24 Oct. 1906; *s* of Dr William Hirst Bateman, JP, Rochdale, Lancs; *m* 1931, Margaret, *d* of Sir Samuel Turner, Rochdale; three *s* one *d*. *Educ:* Epsom Coll.; University Coll., Oxford. Theodore Williams Schol. in Anat., Oxford Univ., 1926; BA Oxon, Hons sch. Physiol., 1927; Epsom schol. to King's Coll. Hosp., 1927; BM, BCh Oxon, 1930; FRCS, 1933; George Herbert Hunt Trav. Schol., Oxford Univ., 1933. RAFVR, Wing Comdr, 1939-45. Mem., Bd Governors, St Thomas' Hosp., 1948; Mem. Collegium Otolaryngologica Amicitiæ Sacrum, 1949; Hon. Corr. Mem. Amer. Laryngological Assoc., 1960; Past Mem. Council, RCS; Editor, Jl of Laryngology and Otology; Hon. Cons. on Oto-rhino-laryngology to the Army; Cons. Adviser in Otolaryngology, Dept of Health and Social Security. Pres., British Assoc. of Otolaryngologists, 1970 (Vice-Pres., 1967). *Publications:* Diseases of the Nose and Throat (Asst. Editor to V. E. Negus, 6th edn.), 1955. Contributor various jls, etc. *Recreations:* tennis, golf, fishing. *Address:* 55 Harley Street, W1. *T:* 01-580 3191. *Club:* Royal Automobile.

*See also R. M. Bateman.*

**BATEMAN, Lt-Col (Hon. Brig.) Harold Henry,** CBE 1945 (OBE 1942); DSO, 1917; MC; *b* 3 July 1888; *s* of late Robert Edward Bateman of Brighton; *m* 1920, Eileen, *d* of late Henry Boyd, CBE; one *s* two *d*. *Educ:* Cheltenham Coll.; RMA Woolwich. Entered Royal Engineers, 1908; Captain, 1914; Bt. Major, 1919; Major, 1925; Bt. Lieut-Col, 1929; Lieut-Col 1933; served European War, 1914-18 (despatches four times, Bt. Major, DSO, MC); retired pay, 1935; rejoined 1939; relegated to unemployment, 1945; Dir of Works, Prison Commission, 1945-53. Croix de Guerre (Belgium), 1919; Legion of Merit (USA), 1945. *Address:* Redwell Mount, Ightham, Kent.

**BATEMAN, Leslie Clifford;** CMG 1965; FRS 1968; Chairman, Malayan Rubber Fund Board and Controller of Rubber Research, since 1962; *b* 21 March 1915; *s* of Charles Samuel Bateman; *m* 1945, Marie Louise Pakes (*d* 1967); two *s*. *Educ:* Bishopshalt Sch., Uxbridge; University Coll., London. BSc, 1st cl. Hons Chem., 1935; PhD and Ramsey Memorial Medal, 1938; DSc 1955. Oriel Coll., 1940-41. Chemist, Natural Rubber Producers Research Assoc., 1941-53; Dir of Research, 1953-62. Hon. DSc Malaya, 1968. Colwyn Medal, Inst. of Rubber Industry, 1963. *Publications:* Ed. and Contrib. to The Chemistry and Physics of Rubber-like Substances, 1963. Numerous scientific papers in Jl Chem. Soc., etc., and articles on technical-economic status of natural rubber and its developments. *Recreations:* cricket (Herts CCC), golf. *Address:* PO Box 508, Kuala Lumpur, Malaysia. *T:* Kuala Lumpur 23451; 3 Palmerston Close, Welwyn Garden City, Herts. *T:* Welwyn Garden 22391. *Club:* Athenæum.

**BATEMAN, Ralph Melton,** MA Oxon; Chairman, Turner & Newall Ltd, since 1967; *b* 15 May 1910; 3rd *s* of William Hirst Bateman, MB, BCh, and of Ethel Jane Bateman, Rochdale, Lancs.; *m* 1935, Barbara Yvonne, 2nd *d* of Herbert Percy Litton and Grace Vera Litton, Heywood Lancs.; two *s* two *d*. *Educ:* Epsom Coll.; University Coll., Oxford. Turner & Newall Ltd: joined as management trainee, 1931; held various directorships in Group, 1942-; Dir, 1957; Dep. Chm., 1959. FCIS, FBIM. Hon. DSc. *Recreations:* family and social affairs; tennis. *Address:* Highfield, Withinlee Road, Prestbury, Cheshire. *T:* Prestbury 89071.

*See also G. H. Bateman.*

**BATES, Alan (Arthur);** actor; *b* 17 Feb. 1934. *Educ:* Herbert Strutt Grammar Sch., Belper, Derbyshire; RADA. *Theatre:* English Stage Co. (Royal Court Theatre, London): The Mulberry Bush; Cards of Identity; Look Back in Anger; The Country Wife; In Celebration; London (West End): Long Day's Journey into Night; The Caretaker; The Four Seasons. Has also appeared on Broadway, New York, in Poor Richard; at Stratford, Ont, in Richard III and The Merry Wives of Windsor; at Bristol Old Vic, in Venice Preserved. *Films:* The Entertainer, Whistle Down the Wind, A Kind of Loving, The Running Man, The Caretaker, Zorba the Greek, Nothing but the Best, Georgie Girl, King of Hearts, Far from the Madding Crowd, The Fixer (Oscar nomination), Women in Love, The Three Sisters (National Theatre Co.), A Day in the Death of Joe Egg. *Television:* various plays. *Recreations:* swimming, squash, driving, riding, water skiing, reading. *Address:* c/o Judy Scott-Fox, William Morris Agency (UK) Ltd, 4 Savile Row, W1.

**BATES, Sir Alfred,** Kt 1952; MC 1918; DL; Solicitor; County Alderman; *b* 3 July 1897; *s* of Alfred Bates (Solicitor) and Agnes Bates; *m* 1925, Margaret, *d* of the Rev. J. H. Clarke, MSc, Heywood; three *s* one *d*. *Educ:* Royal Grammar Sch., Lancaster (Scholar). Member Lancs CC 1931-; Chm., 1949-52, 1955-58 and 1961-64; CA 1949; Chairman; Planning Cttee of County Councils Assoc., 1948-68; Lancs Police Cttee, 1952-; North West Police Training Centre, 1952-; Governor, Police Coll., 1957-. Served on W Lancs. T & AFA, 1949-61. Deputy Pro-Chancellor, Lancaster Univ., 1964-. DL 1951. Hon. MTPI 1959; Hon. LLD (Lancaster), 1964. *Address:* 191 Coleherne Court, SW5. *T:* 01-373 4799. *Club:* Royal Automobile.

**BATES, Allan Frederick,** CMG 1958; *b* 15 July 1911; *s* of John Frederick Lawes and Ethel Hannah Bates; *m* 1937, Ena Edith, *d* of John Ricard Boxall; three *s*. *Educ:* Woolwich

Central Sch.; London Univ. Qualified as Certified Accountant, 1938; practised in London, 1938-44. Joined Colonial Service (now Overseas Civil Service), 1944; Deputy Comptroller Inland Revenue, Cyprus, 1944-48; Comptroller Inland Revenue, Cyprus, 1948-52; Financial Secretary: Cyprus, 1952-60; Mauritius, 1960-64; Man. Dir, Develt Bank of Mauritius, 1964-70. Fellow Inst. of Taxation 1950. *Recreations:* swimming, painting, carving. *Address;* 5 Redford Avenue, Coulsdon, Surrey. *T:* 01-660 7421. *Club:* Royal Commonwealth Society.

**BATES, Sir Darrell;** *see* Bates, Sir J. D.

**BATES, Prof. David Robert,** FRS 1955; MSc; DSc; MRIA; Professor of Theoretical Physics, Queen's University, Belfast, since 1968; *b* Omagh, Co. Tyrone, N Ireland, 18 Nov. 1916; *s* of late Walter Vivian Bates and of Mary Olive Bates; *m* 1956, Barbara Morris; one *s* one *d*. *Educ:* Royal Belfast Academical Institution; Queen's Univ., Belfast; University Coll., London. Engaged at Admiralty Research Laboratory, 1939-41, and at Mine Design Department, 1941-45; Lecturer in Mathematics, University Coll., London, 1945-50; Consultant at US Naval Ordnance Test Station, Inyokern, Calif., 1950; Reader in Physics, University Coll., London, 1951; Prof. of Applied Mathematics, Queen's Univ., Belfast, 1951-68. *Publications:* papers in geophysical and physical journals. Editor-in-Chief, Planetary and Space Science. *Recreations:* reading and watching television. *Address:* 6 Deramore Park, Belfast BT9 5JT. *T:* Belfast 665640.

**BATES, Sir Dawson;** *see* Bates, Sir J. D.

**BATES, Maj.-Gen. Sir (Edward) John (Hunter),** KBE 1969 (OBE 1952); CB 1965; MC 1944; Director, Thomson Regional Newspapers, since 1969; *b* 5 Dec. 1911; *s* of Ernest Bates, FRIBA; *m* 1947, Sheila Ann Norman; two *s* two *d*. *Educ:* Wellington Coll.; Corpus Christi Coll., Cambridge. BA 1933; MA 1963. Commissioned, 1932; Pre-war service in UK and Malaya; War Service in Africa, Middle East, Sicily, Italy and Greece; Senior Army Instructor, JSSC, 1954-57; Student, IDC, 1958; CRA, 2 Div., 1959; CCRA 1 (British) Corps, 1960-61; Dir, RA, War Office, 1961-64; Comdt of RMCS, 1964-67; Dir, Royal Defence Acad., 1967-68. Col Comdt, RA 1966-. Mem. Court of Assistants, Worshipful Co. of Haberdashers. *Recreations:* fishing, shooting. *Address:* Seymours Oast, Leeds, near Maidstone, Kent. *T:* Otham 275. *Club:* Army and Navy.

**BATES, Eric;** Chairman, Midlands Electricity Board, since 1969; *b* 1 Nov. 1908; *s* of late John Boon Bates and late Edith Anne Bates; *m* 1933, Beatrice, *d* of late William Henry Herapath and late Beatrice Herapath; one *s* two *d*. Trained Ilford Elec. Dept.; Asst, County of London Elec. Supply Co., 1929-32; Consumers' Engr: West Kent Electric Co., 1933-36; Isle of Thanet Elec. Supply Co., 1937-42; Elec. Engr, Kennedy & Donkin, 1942-44; Consumers' Engr, Luton Elec. Dept, 1944-48; Sect. Head, Eastern Elec. Bd, 1948-49; Dep. Chief Commercial Officer, Eastern Elec. Bd, 1949-57; North Eastern Electricity Board: Chief Commercial Officer, 1957-62; Dep. Chm., 1962-67; Chm., 1967-69. Mem., Midlands Regional Council of CBI. *Publications:* contribs to Proc. IEE. *Recreation:* golf. *Address:* c/o Midlands Electricity Board, Mucklow Hill, Halesowen, Birmingham.

**BATES, Air Vice-Marshal Eric Cecil,** CB 1958; CBE 1945; AFC 1941; RAF retired; Principal of the College of Air Training, Hamble, Hants, since 1960; *b* 9 June 1906; *s* of late R. J. Bates, Perth, Western Australia; *m* 1938, Kathleen May Norminton; one *s*. *Educ:* Perth Modern Sch.; Univ. of W Australia. Cadetship, RAAF, 1929; Commissioned RAF, 1930; Iraq, 1936-38; Australia, 1939-41; Canada, 1941-43; Bomber Command 1943-45; Pacific, 1945-46; Flying Training Command, 1947-50; Imperial Defence Coll., 1951; Singapore, 1952-53; Dir of Intelligence, Air Ministry, 1953-55; Air Officer i/c Administration, Far East Air Force, 1955-58, retired. *Address:* Hamble House, Hamble, Hants.

**BATES, Sir Geoffrey Voltelin,** 5th Bt, *cr* 1880; MC 1942; *b* 2 Oct. 1921; *s* of Major Cecil Robert Bates, DSO, MC (3rd *s* of 2nd Bt) and Hylda, *d* of Sir James Heath, 1st Bt; *S* uncle, 1946; *m* 1st, 1945, Kitty Kendall Lane (*d* 1956); two *s*; 2nd, 1957, Olivia Gwyneth Zoë (*d* 1969) *d* of Capt. Hon. R. O. FitzRoy (now 2nd Viscount Daventry, *qv*); two *d*. *Educ:* Radley. High Sheriff, Flintshire, 1969. *Recreations:* hunting, shooting, fishing. *Heir:* *s* Edward Robert Bates, *b* 4 July 1946. *Address:* Gyrn Castle, Llanasa, near Holywell, Flintshire. *T:* Prestatyn 3500. *Clubs:* Cavalry; Palatine (Liverpool).

**BATES, Harry Stuart,** CSI 1947; *b* 16 March 1893; *s* of late Albert Bates, Congleton, Cheshire; *m* 1920, *d* of late William Hammond Walker, Congleton, Cheshire; two *s* one *d*. *Educ:* Denstone; St Catherine's Coll., Cambridge (BA). Served in British and Indian Armies 1914-19. Joined Indian Civil Service, 1920; retired, 1949. Employed Colonial Office, 1948-57. *Address:* Rowhurst Cottage, Milford-on-Sea, Hants. *T:* Milford 2906.

**BATES, Herbert Ernest;** author; former Squadron Leader in RAF; *b* 16 May 1905; *s* of Albert Ernest Bates and Lucy Elizabeth Lucas; *m* 1931, Marjorie Helen Cox; two *s* two *d*. *Educ:* The Grammar Sch., Kettering. Worked as a provincial journalist and clerk before publishing first novel at the age of 20; subsequently became known both as a novelist and short story writer in England and America; his stories are widely anthologised; his novels have been translated into sixteen languages; has also written plays and many essays on country life. *Publications: novels:* The Two Sisters; Catherine Foster; Charlotte's Row; The Fallow Land; The Poacher; A House of Women, 1936; Spella Ho, 1938; Fair Stood the Wind for France, 1944; The Purple Plain, 1947; The Jacaranda Tree, 1949; Dear Life, 1950; The Scarlet Sword, 1951; Love for Lydia, 1952; The Feast of July, 1954; The Sleepless Moon, 1956; The Darling Buds of May, 1958 (play: A Breath of French Air, 1959); When the Green Woods Laugh, 1960; The Day of the Tortoise, 1961; A Crown of Wild Myrtle, 1962; Oh! To Be In England, 1963; A Moment in Time, 1964; The Distant Horns of Summer, 1967; The Wild Cherry-Tree, 1968; *short stories:* Day's End, Seven Tales and Alexander; The Black Boxer; The Woman who had Imagination; Cut and Come again; Something Short and Sweet; The Flying Goat; My Uncle Silas; Country Tales; The Beauty of the Dead; The Bride Comes to Evensford; Colonel Julian, 1951; The Nature of Love, 1953; The Daffodil Sky, 1955; Death of a Huntsman, 1957; Sugar for the Horse, 1957; The Watercress Girl, 1959; An Aspidistra in Babylon, 1960; Now Sleeps the Crimson Petal, 1961; The Four Beauties, 1968; A Little of What You Fancy, 1969; *autobiography:* The Vanished World, 1969; *miscellaneous:* Flowers and Faces; Through the Woods; Down the River; The Seasons and the Gardener; The Last Bread; The Modern

Short Story; The Heart of the Country; The Day of Glory (play); The Country of White Clover; as Flying Officer X: The Greatest People in the World, 1942; How Sleep the Brave, 1943; The Face of England, 1952. *Recreations:* gardening and fishing. *Address:* The Granary, Little Chart, Kent. *T:* Pluckley 255.

**BATES, James P. M.;** *see* Martin-Bates.

**BATES, Maj.-Gen. Sir John;** *see* Bates, Maj.-Gen. Sir E. J. H.

**BATES, Sir John (David),** Kt 1969; CBE 1962; VRD; retired; *b* 1 March 1904; *s* of H. W. Bates, Plymouth, Devon; *m* 1930, Phyllis Helen Muller; one *s. Educ:* Plymouth. Joined sea staff of Orient Line, 1925; transf. to shore staff, in Australia, 1929; RANVR, 1932-57, Comdr; Gen. Manager in Australia of Orient Line, 1954-60; Dep. Chm., P & O Lines of Australia, 1960-67; Chm., Hon. Bd of Australian Nat. Travel Assoc., 1956-67; Chm. Australian Tourist Commn, 1967-69. Federal Pres., Navy League of Australia, 1950-56; Trustee Art Gallery of NSW, 1962-; Lay Member, Trade Practices Tribunal, 1968-. *Recreation:* farming. *Address:* Calool, Grose Vale, NSW 2753, Australia. *T:* Grose Vale 72.1233. *Clubs:* Union, Royal Sydney Golf (Sydney).

**BATES, Sir (John) Dawson,** 2nd Bt, *cr* 1937; MC 1943; Area Land Agent for the National Trust; *b* 21 Sept. 1921; *o s* of Sir (Richard) Dawson Bates, 1st Bt, PC, and Muriel, *d* of late Sir Chas. Cleland, KBE, MVO, LLD; *S* father, 1949; *m* 1953, Mary Murray, *o d* of late Lieut-Col Joseph M. Hoult, Norton Place, Lincoln; two *s* one *d. Educ:* Winchester; Balliol. BA 1949. FLAS; FRICS. Served War of 1939-45, Major, Rifle Brigade (MC). *Heir: s* Richard Dawson Hoult Bates, *b* 12 May 1956. *Address:* Eaton Hastings Grange, Faringdon, Berks.

**BATES, Sir (Julian) Darrell,** Kt 1966; CMG 1956; CVO 1954; *b* 10 Nov. 1913; *y s* of late E. Stuart Bates; *m* 1944, Susan Evelyn June Sinclair; two *s* one *d. Educ:* Sevenoaks Sch.; Keble Coll., Oxford. Entered Colonial Service, Tanganyika Territory, 1936; served King's African Rifles (despatches), 1940-43; seconded Colonial Office, 1944-46; Officer Administering the Government, Seychelles, 1950-51; Deputy Chief Secretary, Somaliland Protectorate, 1951-53; Colonial Sec., Gibraltar, 1953-64, Permanent Sec., 1964-68. *Publications:* A Fly Switch from the Sultan; The Shell at My Ear; The Mango and the Palm; A Longing for Quails; Susie. *Address:* Mellinpons, St Buryan, Cornwall. *Club:* Travellers'.

**BATES, Leslie Fleetwood,** CBE 1966; FRS 1950; BSc Bristol, PhD Cambridge, DSc London; FInstP; Emeritus Professor of Physics, Nottingham University (formerly University College, Nottingham), since 1964 (Lancashire-Spencer Professor, 1936-64); Deputy Vice-Chancellor, University of Nottingham, 1953-56; *b* 7 March 1897; *e s* of late W. F. Bates, Kingswood, Bristol; *m* 1925, Winifred Frances Furze Ridler, MSc, (*d* 1965), *o d* of late F. Ridler, Bristol; one *s* one *d. Educ:* Merchant Venturers' Sch., Bristol; University of Bristol; Trinity Coll., Cambridge. Served as radiographer, Capt. Unattached List, i/c X-Ray Laboratory IX Division, Secunderabad, Deccan, India, 1916-20; Research at University of Bristol, 1920-22, and Cavendish Laboratory, 1922-24; Lecturer in Physics, University Coll., London, 1924-30, Reader in Physics, 1930-36; Pres. of Physical Soc., 1950-52; Holweck Prizeman (French and English Physical Socs), 1949; Mem. of Board of Institute of Physics, 1947-49; Pres. Association of University Teachers, 1938-39. Consultant to Inter-Services Research Bureau, 1941-45; Vice-Principal, University Coll. Nottingham, 1944-46; Vice-Pres., Lace Research Association, 1955-63; Senior Scientific Adviser for Civil Defence, North Midland Region (No. 3), 1951-68. May Lecture, Inst. of Metals, 1954; Rippon Lectures University of Calcutta, 1960; Guthrie Lecture, 1963. *Publications:* Modern Magnetism, 1939, 1948, 1951, 1961, 1963; Sir Alfred Ewing, 1946; Recent Advances in Physics, Science Progress, 1928-36; Research publications mainly on electricity and magnetism in various journals. *Address:* Flat 2, Castlethorpe, Newcastle Circus, The Park, Nottingham. *T:* Nottingham 42135. *Club:* Athenæum.

**BATES, Ven. Mansel Harry,** MA; Archdeacon of Lindisfarne and Vicar of Eglingham, Diocese of Newcastle, since 1970; *b* 4 Aug. 1912; *s* of Rev. John Handel Greenhalgh and Alice Bates; *m* 1939, Queenie Mary Fraser Campbell; one *s* three *d. Educ:* Liverpool Institute; Brasenose Coll., Oxford; Wycliffe Hall. BA 1934; Dip. in Theol., 1935; MA 1938. Deacon, 1935, Priest, 1936, Dio. Liverpool. Curate, SS John and James, Litherland, 1935-38; Curate in Charge of Netherton, 1938-41; Vicar: St Saviour, Everton, 1941-47; Jesmond, Newcastle upon Tyne, 1947-59 (Proctor in Convocation, 1950-59); Great Crosby, Liverpool, 1959-70. Hon. Canon of Liverpool Cath., 1964-70. *Address:* Eglingham Vicarage, Alnwick, Northumberland. *T:* Powburn 250.

**BATES, Ralph;** *b* Swindon, Wilts, 3 Nov. 1899; *s* of Henry Roy and Mabel Stevens Bates; *m* 1940, Eve Salzman; one *s. Educ:* Swindon and North Wilts. Secondary Sch. After service in 16th Queen's Royal West Surreys, 1917-19, worked in Great Western Railway Factory at Swindon; in Spain, 1930-37; took active part in Republican politics in Spain; began literary career in 1933 as consequence of unemployment; Capt. in the Spanish Loyalist Army and in the International Brigade, Madrid sector, 1936-37; lecture tour in USA 1937-38; one year resident in Mexico, 1938-39; Adjunct Prof. of Literature, New York Univ. 1948-68, now Professor Emeritus of Literature. *Publications:* Sierra, 1933; Lean Men, 1934, Schubert, 1934, The Olive Field, 1936; Rainbow Fish, 1937; The Miraculous Horde, 1939; The Fields of Paradise, 1941; The Undiscoverables, 1942; The Journey to the Sandalwood Forest, 1947; The Dolphin in the Wood, 1949. *Recreations:* small boating, music. *Address:* 37 Washington Square West, New York, NY 10011, USA. *T:* Yukon 2-5825.

**BATES, Stewart Taverner,** QC 1970; *b* 17 Dec. 1926; *s* of John Bates, Greenock; *m* 1950, Anne Patricia, *d* of David West, Pinner; two *s* four *d. Educ:* Univs of Glasgow and St Andrews; Corpus Christi Coll., Oxford. Called to Bar, Middle Temple, 1954; Mem. Bar Council, 1962-66. *Recreations:* theatre, travel, ski-ing. *Address:* 2 Maids of Honour Row, The Green, Richmond, Surrey. *T:* 01-940 0438.

**BATES, William Stanley;** HM Diplomatic Service; High Commissioner in Guyana, since 1970; *b* 7 Sept. 1920. *Educ:* Christ's Hospital; Corpus Christi Coll., Cambridge. Asst Principal, Colonial Office, 1948; Principal, 1951; Commonwealth Relations Office, 1956; Canberra, 1956-59; Asst Sec., 1962. British Deputy High Commissioner, Northern Nigeria, 1963-65. *Address:* c/o Foreign and Commonwealth Office, SW1. *Club:* Travellers'.

**BATESON;** *see* de Yarburgh-Bateson.

**BATESON, Lieut-Col David Mayhew,** DSO 1944; TD 1941; DL, JP; Partner, Neilson Hornby Crichton & Co., State House, Liverpool; Deputy Chairman, Wrexham & East Denbighshire Water Co.; *b* 3 March 1906; *s* of Ernest Bateson, Pant-y-Ochin Hall, Gresford, N Wales; *m* 1948, Ursula Mary Browne, *d* of Major A. S. C. Browne, *qv*; one *s* one *d*. *Educ:* Eton; University Coll., Oxford. Joined Denbighshire Yeomanry (61 Medium Regt RA), 1925; Comd. 1943-45. Served with BEF, 1939-40, and with BLA, 1944-45 (despatches, DSO). Master of Border Counties (NW) Otter Hounds, 1946-50. JP, 1946, DL, 1947, Denbighshire; High Sheriff of Cheshire, 1961. *Address:* Cherry Hill, Malpas, Cheshire. *T:* Malpas 355. *Clubs:* Cavalry, Army and Navy; Palatine (Liverpool).

**BATESON, Frederick Wilse;** Fellow and tutor in English Literature, Corpus Christi College, Oxford, 1946-69, now Emeritus; *b* 25 Dec. 1901; *s* of Alfred Bateson, Styal, Cheshire; *m* 1931, Jan Cancellor, JP; one *s* one *d*. *Educ:* Charterhouse; Trinity Coll., Oxford. Commonwealth Fellow, Harvard Univ., 1927-29; Editor of Cambridge Bibliography of English Literature, 1930-40; Lecturer WEA, 1935-40; Statistical Officer, Bucks War Agric. Exec. Cttee, 1940-46; Agricultural correspondent, The Observer and The New Statesman, 1944-48; Founder and Editor of Essays in Criticism (Quarterly). 1951-. Visiting Professor: Cornell Univ., USA, 1955, California Univ. (Berkeley), 1958; Pennsylvania State Univ., 1960, 1962 and 1964. *Publications:* English Comic Drama, 1700-1750, 1929; English Poetry and the English Language, 1934; Towards a Socialist Agriculture, 1946; Mixed Farming and Muddled Thinking, 1946; English Poetry; a Critical Introduction, 1950 (rev. 1966); Pope's Epistles to Several Persons, 1951 (rev. 1961); Wordsworth: a Re-interpretation, 1954; Selected Poems of William Blake, 1957; A Guide to English Literature, 1965; Brill: a Short History, 1966. *Recreation:* local history. *Address:* Temple House, Brill, Aylesbury. *T:* Brill 255.

**BATESON, Mrs Gregory;** *see* Mead, Dr M.

**BATESON, Air Vice-Marshal Robert Norman,** CB 1964; DSO 1943 and Bar, 1944; DFC 1940; idc; jssc; psa. *b* 10 June 1912; *s* of late George Rowland Bateson; *m* 1942, Elizabeth Lindsay Davidson. *Educ:* Watford Grammar Sch. Joined RAF 1936. Served War of 1939-45. Asst Chief of Air Staff, Operational Requirements, Air Min., 1959-61; Air Officer Comdg No. 12 Group, Fighter Comd, 1961-62; SASO, Fighter Comd, 1963-67. ADC to the Queen, 1958-60. Air Cdre, 1958; actg Air Vice-Marshal, 1959; Air Vice-Marshal, 1960. Dutch Flight Cross, 1943; Order of Dannebrog, 1944. *Recreations:* squash, tennis, sailing, motor sport. *Address:* Greenways, Parsonage Road, Newton Ferrers, Devon. *T:* Newton Ferrers 476. *Club:* Royal Air Force.

**BATESON, Rear-Adm. Stuart Latham,** CB 1950; CBE 1948; MIEE; retired; *b* 7 July 1898; *twin s* of late Sir Alexander Dingwall Bateson, Judge of the High Court, and Isabel Mary (*née* Latham); *m* 1923, Marie Elphinstone Fleming Cullen; one *s* one *d*. *Educ:* Lockers Park; Rugby; RNC Keyham. Joined Navy, 1916; specialised in Torpedo, 1923; Comdr, 1934; Capt., 1939; Rear-Admiral (L), 1949, the first holder of the rank. Served War of 1939-45; Commanded HMS Latona, 1941; HMS Ajax, 1941-42; HMS London, 1944-46; Dir of Naval Electrical Department, Admiralty, 1946-51; retd, 1951. County Comr for Boy Scouts of Rutland, 1953-66. Chm. and Sec. Rutland Historic Churches Preservation Trust, 1954. Sheriff of Rutland, 1958; Vice-Lieut Co. Rutland, 1957, 1963. *Recreation:* shooting. *Address:* Ridlington, Rutland. *Club:* United Service.

**BATEY, Charles Edward,** OBE 1943; Hon. MA Oxon, 1941 (by Decree, 1946, Lincoln College); JP; *b* 22 Feb. 1893; *e s* of Edward Batey and Christian Allan Morison; *m* 1922, Ethel May, *d* of George Reed; one *d*. *Educ:* Edinburgh Board Schs.; Heriot Watt College (Hon. Fellow 1954). Apprenticed Leith Observer, 1908-15; served European War, 1915-20, RAMC. Hazell, Watson & Viney, Aylesbury, 1920; Works Manager, Univ. Tutorial Press, 1922-28; Asst Printer, University of Oxford, 1929-46; Printer to the University of Oxford, 1946-58. Mem. Council British Federation of Master Printers, 1944-50, and Mem. of Labour Cttee, 1944-49; Chairman: Jt Industrial Council of Printing and Allied Trades, 1948-49; Apprenticeship Authority, 1946-48; City of Oxford Youth Employment Cttee, 1944-54. Pres. Assoc of Teachers of Printing and Allied Subjects, 1953-58. Mem. various industrial education cttees. Hon. Mem. City and Guilds of London Institute, 1959; Hon. Fellow Inst of Printing, 1961; Hon. City and Guilds Insignia Award, 1965. *Publication:* (with T. W. Chaundy and P. R. Barrett) The Printing of Mathematics, 1954. *Recreation:* gardening. *Address:* Carfax, Up Nately, Basingstoke, Hants. *T:* Hook 2170.

**BATH,** 6th Marquess of, *cr* 1789; **Henry Frederick Thynne,** Bt 1641; Viscount Weymouth and Baron Thynne, 1682; Major Royal Wiltshire Yeomanry; JP; *b* 26 Jan. 1905; *o surv. s* of 5th Marquess, KG, PC, CB and Violet Caroline (*d* 1928), *d* of Sir Charles Mordaunt, 10th Bt; *S* father, 1946; *m* 1st, 1927, Hon. Daphne (marr. diss., 1953; she *m* 2nd, 1953, Major A. W. Fielding, DSO), *er d* of 4th Baron Vivian, DSO; three *s* one *d*; 2nd, 1953, Mrs Virginia Penelope Tennant, *d* of late Alan L. R. Parsons; one *d*. *Educ:* Harrow; Christ Church, Oxford. MP (U) Frome Division, Som., 1931-35. Served War of 1939-45 (wounded). *Publication:* (jtly) The Lions of Longleat, 1969. *Heir: s* Viscount Weymouth, *qv*. *Address:* Jobs Mill, Warminster, Wilts. *T:* Warminster 2279; Longleat, Warminster, Wilts. *Club:* White's.

*See also* *Duke of Beaufort, Baron Nunburnholme.*

**BATH and WELLS, Bishop of,** since 1960; **Rt. Rev. Edward Barry Henderson,** DSC 1944; *b* 22 March 1910; 2nd *s* of late Dean of Salisbury the Very Rev. E. L. Henderson; *m* 1935, Hester Borrowdaile Taylor; one *s* two *d*. *Educ:* Radley; Trinity Coll., Cambridge. Curate of St Gabriel's, Pimlico, 1934-36; Priest-in-charge, All Saints, Pimlico, 1936-39; Rector of Holy Trinity, Ayr, 1939-47; Chaplain, RNVR, 1943-44; Vicar of St Paul's, Knightsbridge, 1947-55; Rural Dean of Westminster, 1952-55; Bishop Suffragan of Tewkesbury, 1955-60. Chm., Church of England Youth Council, 1961-69. Chaplain and Sub-Prelate, Order of St John of Jerusalem, 1961. *Recreations:* fishing, golf, and sailing. *Address:* The Palace, Wells, Somerset. *T:* 2341.

**BATH and WELLS, Assistant Bishops of;** *see* Jackson, Rt Rev. F. M. E. and Wilson, Rt Rev. D. J.

**BATH, Archdeacon of;** *see* Hopley, Ven. Arthur.

**BATHER, Elizabeth Constance,** OBE 1946; retired as Chief Superintendent Metropolitan

(Women) Police, (1946-60); *b* 11 Oct. 1904; *d* of late Rev. Arthur George Bather, MA, and Lilian Dundas Firth, Winchester. *Educ:* St Swithuns Sch., Winchester. Mem. Hampshire County Council, 1937-46. Served in WAAF, 1939-45; Rank: Group Officer, 1944-45. JP Winchester, 1937-46. *Address:* Laburnum Cottage, Odiham, Hants.

**BATHO, Edith Clara,** MA, DLit (London); Principal Royal Holloway College, University of London, 1945-62, retired; *b* 21 Sept. 1895; 3rd *d* of late William John Batho and Ellen Clara Hooton. *Educ:* Highbury Hill High Sch.; University Coll., London. BA (Hons English), 1915, MA 1920, DLit 1935; war work, 1916-18; on staff of Roedean Sch., 1918-19; Downe House Sch., 1919-21; Quain Student and Asst in English at University Coll., London, 1921; Fellow of University Coll., London, 1934; Reader in English Literature, University Coll., London, 1935-45. Visiting Prof., Univ. of Wisconsin, 1963. An active mem. British Fedn of Univ. Women. Hon. D de l'U (Poitiers), 1962. *Publications:* The Ettrick Shepherd, 1927; The Later Wordsworth, 1934 (reprinted, 1964); The Poet and the Past (Warton Lecture of the British Acad.), 1937; The Victorians and After (with Bonamy Dobrée), 1938; Chronicles of Scotland by Hector Boece, tr. Bellenden (ed for STS), Vol. I with R. W. Chambers, 1936, Vol. II with H. W. Husbands, 1941; A Wordsworth Selection, 1962; other articles and reviews. *Recreations:* travelling, languages, needlework. *Address:* 130 Wood Street, Barnet, Herts. *Club:* New Arts Theatre, English-Speaking Union.

**BATHO, Sir Maurice Benjamin,** 2nd Bt, *cr* 1928; Chairman and Managing Director, Ridgley (Huntingdon) Ltd and associated companies, *b* 14 Jan. 1910; *o surv. s* of Sir Charles Albert Batho, 1st Bt, and Bessie (*d* 1961), 4th *d* of Benjamin Parker, Oulton Broad, Suffolk; *S* father, 1938; *m* 1934, Antoinette, *o d* of Baron d'Udekem d'Acoz, Ghent; two *s* two *d*. *Educ:* Uppingham; Belgium. Served War of 1939-45: Lt-Col, KRRC. Jt Sub-Dir, Syrian Wheat Collection Scheme of Spears Mission, 1943; Adviser on Cereals Collection, Min. of Finance of Imp. Iranian Govt, 1944; Dep. Dir, Rice Procurement, Bengal, 1945; Managing Dir, Reed Paper & Board Sales Ltd, 1959, resigned 1965; formerly Director: Reed Paper & Board (UK) Ltd; London Paper Mills Co. Ltd; Empire Paper Mills Ltd; Reed Board Mills (Colthorp) Ltd; Reed Brookgate Ltd. *Recreations:* golf. *Heir: s* Peter Ghislain Batho [*b* 9 Dec. 1939; *m* 1966, Lucille Mary, *d* of Wilfrid F. Williamson; two *s*]. *Address:* Carlton Hall, Saxmundham, Suffolk. *T:* 2505. *Clubs:* Naval and Military, Constitutional.

**BATHURST,** family name of **Earl Bathurst** and **Viscount Bledisloe.**

**BATHURST,** 8th Earl, *cr* 1772; **Henry Allen John Bathurst,** DL; Baron Bathurst of Battlesden, Bedfordshire, 1712; Baron Apsley of Apsley, Sussex, 1771; Earl Bathurst of Bathurst, Sussex, 1772; Capt. Royal Gloucestershire Hussars (TA); TARO, 1959; *b* 1 May 1927; *s* of late Lord Apsley, DSO, MC, MP (killed on active service, 1942), and late Lady Apsley, CBE; *gs* of 7th Earl; *S* grandfather, 1943; *m* 1959, Judith Mary, *d* of Mr and Mrs A. C. Nelson, Springfield House, Foulridge, Lancs.; two *s* one *d*. *Educ:* Ridley Coll., Canada; Eton; Christ Church, Oxford, 1948-49. Late Lieut 10th Royal Hussars (PWO). Capt., Royal Glos. Hussars, TA, 1949-57. Hon. Sec. Agricultural Cttee (Conservative), House of Lords, 1957; a Lord-in-Waiting, 1957-61; Joint Parliamentary Under-Sec. of State, Home Office, 1961-July 1962. Governor, Royal Agricultural Coll.; Pres. Glos. Branch CPRE DL County of Gloucester, 1960. Chancellor, Primrose League, 1959-61. Member: CLA Council, 1965; (Chm., Glos Branch of CLA, 1968); Timber Growers' Organisation (TGO) Council, 1966. *Heir: s* Lord Apsley, *qv*. *Address:* Cirencester Park, Cirencester, Glos GL7 2BT. *T:* Cirencester 3112. *Clubs:* White's, Turf.

*See also Lord A. M. Graham.*

**BATHURST, (NSW), Bishop of,** since 1959; **Rt. Rev. Ernest Kenneth Leslie;** *b* 14 May 1911; *s* of Rev. Ernest Thomas Leslie and Margaret Jane Leslie; *m* 1941, Isabel Daisy Wilson; two *s* one *d* (and one *s* decd). *Educ:* Trinity Gram. Sch., Kew, Vict.; Trinity Coll., University of Melbourne (BA). Aust. Coll. of Theology, ThL, 2nd Cl 1933, Th Schol. 1951, 2nd Cl. 1952; Deacon, 1934; Asst Curate, Holy Trinity, Coburg, 1934-37; Priest-in-Charge, Tennant Creek, Dio. Carpentaria, 1937-38; Alice Springs with Tennant Creek, 1938-40; Rector of Christ Church, Darwin, 1940-44; Chaplain, AIF, 1942-45; Rector of Alice Springs with Tennant Creek, 1945-46; Vice-Warden, St John's Coll., Morpeth, NSW, 1947-52; Chap. Geelong Church of Eng. Gram. Sch., Timbertop Branch, 1953-58. *Recreations:* walking, woodwork, cycling. *Address:* Bishopscourt, Bathurst, NSW, Australia. *T:* Bathurst 3501.

**BATHURST, (NSW), Bishop of, (RC),** since 1963; **Rt. Rev. Albert Reuben Edward Thomas;** *b* Farnborough, Hants, 26 Oct. 1908; *s* of Albert Charles Thomas and Esperie Loreto Clarke. *Educ:* St Joseph's College, Hunter's Hill; St Columbia's Coll., St Patrick's Coll., Manly. Diploma of Social Studies, Sydney Univ., 1944. Ordained, 1931. Asst Suburban Parishes, 1931-38; Diocesan Dir, Pontifical Missions, 1938-63, National Dir, 1944-70. Founder of Catholic Welfare Bureau, 1941. Initiated Australian National Pilgrimage, 1950-63; Hon. Chaplain of House of Lourdes, 1960; Foundation Chm. of St Vincent's Hospital Advisory Board, 1955; Chm. of Unity Movement for Christian Christmas, 1956-63. *Publication:* contrib. to Australian Encyclopaedia, on Catholic Missions and Welfare, 1958. *Address:* Bishop's House, Bathurst, Australia.

**BATHURST, Sir Frederick Peter Methuen Hervey-,** 6th Bt, *cr* 1818; *b* 26 Jan. 1903; *s* of Sir Frederick Edward William Hervey-Bathurst, 5th Bt, DSO and Hon. Moira O'Brien, 2nd *d* of 14th Baron Inchiquin; *S* father 1956; *m* 1st, 1933, Maureen (marriage dissolved, 1956), *d* of Charles Gordon, Boveridge Park, Salisbury; one *s* one *d*; 2nd, 1958, Mrs Cornelia Shepard Riker, *widow* of Dr John Lawrence Riker, Rumson, NJ, USA. *Educ:* Eton. Served War of 1939-45, Capt. Grenadier Guards. *Recreations:* sailing, riding, ski-ing, flying. *Heir: s* Frederick John Charles Gordon Hervey-Bathurst [*b* 23 April 1934; *m* 1957, Caroline Myrtle, *d* of Lieut-Col Sir William Starkey, Bt, *qv*; one *s* two *d*]. *Address:* Bellevue Avenue, Rumson, New Jersey, USA. *T:* 842-0791. *Clubs:* Guards, Royal Ocean Racing; New York Yacht.

**BATHURST, Maurice Edward,** CMG 1953; CBE 1947; QC 1964; *b* 2 Dec. 1913; *o s* of Edward James and Annie Mary Bathurst; *m* 1941, Dorothy (marr. diss. 1963), *d* of late W. S. Stevens, LDS, RCS; one *s*; *m* 1968, Joan Caroline Petrie, *qv*. *Educ:* Haberdashers' Aske's, Hatcham; King's Coll., London; Gonville and Caius Coll., Cambridge; Columbia Univ. LLB, First Class Hons. (London), 1937; University Law School, (London); Post-grad. Research Studentship, 1938; Bartle Frere Exhibitioner (Camb.),

1939; Tutorial Fellow (Chicago), 1939; Special Fellow (Columbia), 1940; LLM (Columbia), 1941; Hon. DCL (Sacred Heart, NB), 1946; PhD (Camb.), 1949; LLD (London), 1966. Solicitor of Supreme Court, 1938-56. Called to Bar, Gray's Inn, 1957; Master of the Bench, 1970. Legal Adviser, British Information Services, 1941-43; Legal Adviser, British Embassy, Washington, 1943-46 (First Sec., 1944; Counsellor, 1946); Legal Member, UK Delegation to United Nations, 1946-48; UK Representative, Legal Advisory Cttee, Atomic Energy Commission, 1946-48; Legal Adviser to British Chm., Bipartite control Office, Frankfurt, 1949; Dep. Legal Adviser, CCG, 1949-51; Legal Adviser, UK High Commn, Germany, 1951-55; Judge, Supreme Court, British Zone, Germany, 1953-55; Legal Adviser, British Embassy, Bonn, 1955-57; British Judge, Arbitral Commn, Germany, 1968-69. Mem. UK Delegations to UNRRA; United Nations San Francisco Conference; Bermuda Civil Aviation Conference; PICAO; Washington Financial Talks; UN Gen. Assembly; FAO; WHO; UNICEF; Internat. Tin Study Group; UK-US Double Taxation Treaty Negotiations; London Nine-Power Conf.; Paris Conf. on W Eur. Union; NATO Status of Forces Conf., Bonn. Internat. Vice-Pres. UN League of Lawyers; Vice-Chm. Council, Brit. Inst. of International and Comparative Law. Member: Panel of Arbitrators, Internat. Centre for Settlement of Investment Disputes; Ct of Assistants, Haberdashers' Co.; Editorial Cttee, British Yearbook of International Law; *ad eundem*, Inner Temple. Hon. Vis. Prof. in Internat. Law, King's Coll., London, 1967-; Hon. Fellow, King's Coll., London. Foundation Governor, Haberdashers' Aske's Hatcham Schools. Freeman of the City of London and of the City of Bathurst, NB. *Publications:* Germany and the North Atlantic Community: A Legal Survey (with J. L. Simpson), 1956; notes and articles in legal jls, etc., British and American. *Recreation:* theatre. *Address:* 5 King's Bench Walk, Temple, EC4. *T:* 01-353 2882. *Club:* Garrick.

**BATSFORD, Brian Caldwell Cook;** Chairman of B. T. Batsford Ltd, since 1952; MP (C) for Ealing South since 1958; *b* 18 Dec. 1910; *s* of late Arthur Caldwell Cook, Gerrards Cross, Bucks.; assumed mother's maiden name of Batsford by Deed Poll 1946; *m* 1945, Joan (Wendy), *o d* of late Norman Cunliffe, DSc, of Oxford; two *d*. *Educ:* Repton Sch. Joined B. T. Batsford Ltd, Booksellers and Publishers, 1928. Lectured in Canada under auspices Canadian National Council of Education, 1935, 1937; lectured in Scandinavia and Baltic States under auspices British Council, 1940. Hon. Sec. Empire Youth Sunday Cttee, 1938; Chm. Youth City Cttee of Enquiry, 1939. RAF, 1941-46. Contested Chelmsford Div. of Essex for Nat. Govt, 1945. PPS to Minister of Works, 1959-60; Asst Govt Whip, 1962-64; Opposition Deputy Chief Whip, 1964-67. Alderman, GLC, and Parly Rep. of GLC Majority Party, 1967-70; co-opted Mem., GLC Arts and Recreation Cttee, 1970. Pres., London Appreciation Soc., 1955. FRSA 1955, Mem. Council, 1967. Mem. PMG's Stamp Adv. Cttee, 1967. *Recreations:* painting, gardening. *Address:* 19 Norfolk Road, NW8. *T:* 01-722 0242; Pendower, Polzeath, Cornwall. *T:* Trebetherick 3462. *Clubs:* Carlton, St James', MCC.

**BATSON, Prof. Reginald George,** MEng, FKC, CEng, FICE, FIMechE; Professor of Civil Engineering, University of Liverpool, 1936-50 (Dean, Faculty of Engineering, 1938-48), Emeritus since 1950; *b* 1885; *m* 1914, Nellie Eva Seal; one *s*. *Educ:* Tiffins Boys' Sch., Kingston-on-Thames; King's Coll., Univ. of London. Building Works Department of Woolwich Arsenal, 1904-8; Principal Scientific Officer Engineering Dept. of National Physical Laboratory, 1908-33; Principal Scientific Officer in charge of Road Research Laboratory of Department of Scientific Industrial Research, 1933-36. *Publications:* Mechanical Testing; Roads, 1950; numerous technical papers to Institution of Civil Engineers, Institution of Mechanical Engineers, Iron and Steel Institute, British Association, Soc. of Chemical Industry, etc. *Recreations:* gardening, motoring and cricket. *Address:* Trelawney, Bradshaw Lane, Mawdesley, Ormskirk, Lancs. *T:* Mawdesley 692.

**BATT, Lt-Col William Elliott,** CMG 1918; late RFA, TF; a Metropolitan Magistrate, retired 1956; Stipendiary Magistrate of East Ham, 1939 and West Ham, 1943-46; *b* 6 Dec. 1882; 2nd *s* of late Capt. H. E. Batt, Heavitree, Exeter; *m* 1st, 1912, Gladys Edith (*d* 1918), *o c* of E. E. Hopewell, Rugby; one *d*; 2nd, 1925, Dorothy Anne (marriage dissolved), *e d* of Charles Manville, Northumberland; 3rd, Joan, *d* of Rev. Bruce Mackay, Sutton Courtney, Berks. *Educ:* Heles Sch., Exeter; privately. Articled to R. Tapley, Solicitor, Exeter, 1900; admitted Solicitor, 1905; called to Bar, Gray's Inn, 1920; practised in London; joined 1st Devon Volunteer RGA, 1904; transferred to 1st London Brigade RFA; TF, 1908; served throughout European War (lieut-Col 1916). *Recreations:* cooking, crosswords. *Address:* 27 Strand Court, Topsham, Devon. *T:* Topsham 4247.

**BATTEN, Edith Mary,** OBE 1948; Research Officer, Board for Social Responsibility of the Church Assembly, 1967-70; Principal, William Temple College, 1950-66; *b* 1905, British. *Educ:* High Sch. for Girls, Southport; Liverpool Univ.; London School of Economics; St Anne's Coll., Oxford. BSc Liverpool; BSc (Econ) London; MA Oxon. Asst Industrial Personnel Officer; Sec. North West Ham Branch, Invalid Children's Aid Association; Sub-Warden, St Helen's Settlement, E15; Warden, Birmingham Settlement, 1933-38; JP City of Birmingham, 1937-38; Organising Sec. British Assoc. of Residential Settlements, 1938-42; Mem. Factory and Welfare Advisory Board to Min. of Labour, 1940-42; Min. of Labour and National Service, 1942-47. *Recreations:* reading, listening to music. *Address:* Guillard's Oak House, Midhurst, Sussex. *Club:* Royal Commonwealth Society.

**BATTEN, Jean Gardner,** CBE 1936; *b* 1909; *d* of Capt. F. H. Batten, Dental Surg., Auckland, New Zealand. *Educ:* Cleveland House Coll., Auckland, NZ. Gained Private pilot's licence at London Aeroplane Club, 1930; commercial pilot's licence London, 1932; solo flight England-Australia (women's record) May 1934; solo flight Australia-England (first woman to complete return flight), April 1935; solo flight England-Argentina (first woman to make solo flight across South Atlantic Ocean to South America), Nov. 1935; world records established: England-Brazil 61 hrs 15 mins; fastest crossing of South Atlantic Ocean by air 13 hrs 15 mins; solo flight England-New Zealand 11 days 45 mins, Oct. 1936; first direct flight from England to New Zealand; solo record England-Australia 5 days 21 hrs; record flight across Tasman Sea, Australia-New Zealand, 9hrs 29 mins; record solo flight Australia-England, 5 days 18 hrs 15 mins, Oct. 1937; Officer of the Order of the Southern Cross, Brazil; Chevalier of the Legion of Honour, France; awarded Britannia Trophy,

Royal Aero Club, 1935 and 1936; Harmon Trophy awarded by international vote, 1935, 1936 and 1937; Johnston Memorial Air Navigation Trophy, 1935; Challenge Trophy (USA), Women's International Association of Aeronautics, 1934, 1935 and 1936; Segrave Trophy, 1936; Coupe de Sibour, 1937; gold medals: Fédération Aéronautique Internationale; Royal Aero Club, Aero Club de France, Belgian Royal Aero Club, Académie des Sports, Royal Swedish Aero Club, Ligue International des Aviateurs, Aero Club of Argentine, Royal Danish Aeronautical Society, Royal Norwegian Aero Club, Aero Club of Finland. *Publication:* My Life, 1938. *Recreations:* walking, swimming, music. *Address:* c/o Barclays Bank Ltd, 25 Charing Cross Road, WC2. *Clubs:* Royal Aero, Forum, Royal Commonwealth Society (Hon. Life Fellow); Aero Club de France (Paris).

**BATTEN, John Charles,** MD, FRCP; Physician to HM Royal Household since 1970; Physician: St George's Hospital, since 1958; Brompton Hospital, since 1959; King Edward VII Hospital for Officers, since 1968; King Edward VII Hospital, Midhurst, since 1969; Hon. Physician to St Dunstan's and New Victoria Hospital, Kingston; Deputy Chief Medical Referee, Confederation Life Assoc. of Canada, since 1958; *b* 11 March 1924; *s* of Raymond Wallis Batten, JP and Gladys (*née* Charles); *m* 1950, Anne Mary Margaret, *d* of late John Oriel, CBE, MC; one *s* two *d* (and one *d* decd). *Educ:* Mill Hill School; St Bartholomew's Medical School. MB, BS 1946 London Univ.; MRCP London 1950; MD London 1951; FRCP London 1964. Junior appts, St George's Hosp. and Brompton Hosp., 1946-58. Surgeon Captain, Royal Horse Guards, 1947-49. Dorothy Temple Cross Research Fellow, Cornell Univ. Medical Coll., New York, 1954-55. Examiner in Medicine, London Univ., 1968; Marc Daniels Lectr, RCP, 1969. Member: Board of Governors, Brompton Hosp., 1966-69; St George's Hosp. Medical School Council, 1969; Council of Royal Society of Medicine, 1970. *Publications:* contributions to medical books and journals. *Recreations:* music and sailing. *Address:* 7 Lion Gate Gardens, Richmond, Surrey. *T:* 01-940 3282.

**BATTEN, Mark Wilfrid,** RBA 1962; FRBS 1952 (ARBS 1950); Sculptor, direct carver in stone; *b* 21 July 1905; *s* of Edward Batten; *m* 1933, Elsie May Owston Thorneloe (*d* 1961); one *d*. *Educ:* Beckenham Co. Sch.; Beckenham Sch. of Art; Chelsea Sch. of Art. Commenced to experiment individually with stone carving, 1927; exhibited only drawings and paintings until 1934; combined experiment in sculpture with learning craft of stone carving mainly in granite mason's yards in Cornwall; first exhibited sculpture, 1936; FRSA 1936. Collaborated with Eric Gill, 1939; first exhibited sculpture at Royal Academy, 1939. War service in Life Guards, 1940-45. Exhibited Paris Salon, 1949, and thereafter frequently at RA and most sculpture exhibitions in Paris, London and provincial cities. Many commissions for stone sculptures on public buildings. President, RBS 1956-61; Council, 1953-; Council, RBA 1964-. Société des Artistes Français: Silver Medal for Sculpture, 1952; Associate, 1970. Hon. Mem. National Sculpture Soc. of the USA, 1956; Syracuse Univ., USA, estab. Mark Batten Manuscripts Collection, 1965. *Publications:* Stone Sculpture by Direct Carving, 1957; Direct Carving in Stone, 1966; articles in art magazines. *Recreations:* country life, travel, contemplation of other men's sculptures. *Address:* Christian's River, Dallington, Heathfield, Sussex; 53 Castletown Road, W14. *T:* 01-385 1680. *Club:* Chelsea Arts.

**BATTEN, Maj.-Gen. Richard Hutchison,** CB 1961; CBE 1953 (OBE 1945); DSO 1943; DL; Colonel, Royal Hampshire Regiment; *b* 1908; *s* of Charles Henry Batten; *m* 1931, Betty Mary, *d* of Edward Andrews. *Educ:* Cheltenham; RMC, Sandhurst; Caius Coll., Cambridge. Served in Palestine, 1936-39; War of 1939-45, N Africa, Sicily, Italy, France and Germany (DSO, OBE, North Africa Star with 8th Army, Clasp); Korea, 1953 (CBE), Chief of Staff, HQ, Eastern Command, 1959-60; Chief of Staff, HQ, Northern Army Group, 1960-63; retd, 1964. DL Hants, 1967. *Recreations:* sailing, golf, fishing. *Address:* Godshill Wood, Fordingbridge, Hants. *T:* Fordingbridge 2238. *Clubs:* United Service; Royal Lymington Yacht.

**BATTERBEE, Sir Harry Fagg,** GCMG, *cr* 1946 (KCMG, *cr* 1931; CMG 1918); KCVO, *cr* 1927 (CVO 1918); *b* 1880; *s* of N. S. Batterbee, Faversham; *m* 1909, Eleanor Laura (*d* 1950), *d* of Rev. John Harding. *Educ:* Queen Elizabeth's Grammar Sch., Faversham; Hertford Coll., Oxford; MA; Hon. Fellow, 1956. Entered the Colonial Office in 1905; Private Sec. to Sec. of State for the Colonies (Rt Hon. Walter H. Long, MP), 1916-19; Political Sec. to Vice-Admiral Commanding Special Service Squadron, Empire Cruise, 1923-24; Asst Sec. Dominions Office, 1925-30; Asst Under-Sec. of State, Dominions Office, 1930-38; Political Sec. to Duke of York during Australian and New Zealand Tour, 1927; Registrar of the Order of St Michael and St George, 1930-38; Deputy Sec., Imperial Conferences, 1930 and 1937; High Comr for UK in New Zealand, 1939-45. A Governor: Dominion Students' Hall Trust, London; Queen Elizabeth's Sch. Faversham. A Vice-Pres., Royal Commonwealth Society. *Address:* The Mews, Middle Row Faversham, Kent. *T:* 3287. *Club:* United University.

**BATTERSBY, Alan Rushton,** FRS 1966; PhD (St Andrews); DSc (Bristol); MSc (Manchester); Professor of Organic Chemistry, University of Cambridge, since 1969; Fellow of St Catharine's College, Cambridge; *b* Leigh, 4 March 1925; *s* of William and Hilda Battersby; *m* 1949, Margaret Ruth, *d* of Thomas and Annie Hart, Whaley Bridge, Cheshire; two *s*. *Educ:* Grammar Sch., Leigh; Univ. of Manchester (Mercer and Woodiwis Schol.); Univ. of St Andrews. Asst Lectr in Chemistry, Univ. of St Andrews, 1948-53; Commonwealth Fund Fellow at Rockefeller Inst., NY, 1950-51 and at Univ. of Illinois, 1951-52; Lectr in Chemistry, Univ. of Bristol, 1954-62; Prof. of Organic Chemistry, Univ. of Liverpool, 1962-69. Mem. Deutsche Akademie der Naturforscher Leopoldina, 1967. Chemical Soc. Tilden Lectr, 1963; Treat Johnson Lectr, Yale Univ., 1969; Vis. Prof., Cornell Univ., 1969. Corday-Morgan Medal, 1959. *Publications:* papers in chemical jls, particularly Jl Chem. Soc. *Recreations:* music, camping, sailing and gardening. *Address:* University Chemical Laboratory, Lensfield Road, Cambridge. *T:* Cambridge 56491.

**BATTEY, Mrs E. J.;** *see* White, E. Evelyne McI.

**BATTISCOMBE, Mrs (Esther) Georgina,** BA; FRSL 1964; author; *b* 21 Nov. 1905; *d* of late George Harwood, MP, Master Cotton Spinner, Bolton, Lancs, and Ellen Hopkinson, *d* of Sir Alfred Hopkinson, KC, MP, First Vice-Chancellor of Manchester Univ.; *m* 1932, Lt-Col Christopher Francis Battiscombe, OBE, FSA (*d* 1964), Grenadier Guards; one *d*. *Educ:* St Michael's Sch., Oxford; Lady

Margaret Hall, Oxford. *Publications:* Haphazard, 1932; Charlotte Mary Yonge, 1943; Two on Safari, 1946; English Picnics, 1949; Mrs Gladstone, 1956; John Keble (James Tait Black Memorial Prize for best biography of year), 1963; Christina Rossetti (Writers and their Work), 1965; ed, with M. Laski, A Chaplet for Charlotte Yonge, 1965; Queen Alexandra, 1969. *Recreations:* walking, travel. *Address:* 3 Queen's Acre, King's Road, Windsor, Berks. *T:* Windsor 60460.

**BATTLE, Richard John Vulliamy,** MBE 1945; FRCS; Plastic Surgeon to St Thomas' Hospital since 1946; Hon. Consultant in Plastic Surgery to the Army since 1955; Plastic Surgeon to King Edward VII Hospital for Officers; *b* 21 Jan. 1907; *s* of late William Henry Battle and Anna Marguerite (*née* Vulliamy); *m* 1941, Jessie Margaret King; three *s*. *Educ:* Gresham's Sch.; Trinity Coll., Cambridge. BA 1928, MA 1935, Cantab; MRCS, LRCP, 1931; FRCS, 1933; MChir (Cantab) 1935. Joined Territorial Army; served War of 1939-45 in RAMC, France, 1939-40, Italy, 1943-46; Comd No. 1 Maxillo Facial Unit and 98 General Hospital; Major 1940; Lt-Col 1945. Consultant Plastic Surgeon to Queen Mary's Hospital, Roehampton. Pres., British Assoc. of Plastic Surgs, 1952, 1967; FRSM. *Publications:* Plastic Surgery, 1964; contrib. on plastic surgery to scientific periodicals. *Recreations:* golf, music. *Address:* 61 Wimpole Street, W1. *T:* 01-935 3117. *Clubs:* East India and Sports, Roehampton, MCC.

**BATTY, Mrs Ronald;** *see* Foyle, C. A. S.

**BATTY, William Bradshaw,** TD 1946; Managing Director, Ford Motor Co. Ltd, since 1968; *b* 15 May 1913; *s* of Rowland and Nellie Batty; *m* 1946, Jean Ella Brice; one *s* one *d* (and one *s* decd). *Educ:* Hulme Gram. Sch., Manchester. Served War of 1939-45, RASC (Lt-Col). Apprentice toolmaker, Ford Motor Co. Ltd, Trafford Park, Manchester, 1930; Co. trainee, 1933; Press liaison, Advertising Dept, 1936; Service Dept, 1937; Tractor Sales Dept, 1945; Asst Man, Tractor Dept, 1948; Man., Tractor and Implement Product Planning, 1953; Man., Tractor Div., 1955; Gen. Man., Tractor Gp, 1961; Dir, Tractor Gp, 1963; Dir, Car and Truck Gp, 1964; Exec. Dir, Ford Motor Co. Ltd, 1963. Chairman: Ford Motor Credit Co. Ltd, 1968; Ford Leasing Develt Co. Ltd, 1970; Director: Ford Motor Credit Co. Ltd, 1963; Henry Ford & Son Ltd, Cork, 1965; Ford Motor Co. A/S Denmark, 1970. *Recreations:* golf, sailing, gardening. *Address:* Blackmore House, Hook End, Brentwood, Essex. *T:* Blackmore 352. *Clubs:* Royal Automobile; Thorndon Park Golf.

**BATTYE, Maj.-Gen. (Retd) Stuart Hedley Molesworth,** CB 1960; *b* 21 June 1907; *s* of late Lieut-Col W. R. Battye, DSO, MS, LRCP, Chev. de la Légion d'Honneur, CStJ, and late M. St G. Molesworth; *m* 1940, Evelyn Désirée, *d* of late Capt. G. B. Hartford, DSO and bar, RN; one *s* two *d*. *Educ:* Marlborough Coll.; RMA, Woolwich; Cambridge Univ. (MA). Commissioned 2nd Lieut, RE, 1927; served with Bengal Sappers and Miners, India, 1930-44 (NW Frontier Campaign, 1930-31); Iraq, 1941-42; India, 1942-44; 21 Army Group, BLA, 1945-47; MELF, 1952-55; War Office, 1955; Dir of Movements, the War Office, 1958-61; Dir, Council for Small Industries in Rural Areas (formerly Rural Industries Bureau), 1963-. FRSA 1963. *Publications:* contrib. to Blackwood's and RE Journal. *Recreations:* photography, fishing, shooting, painting. *Address:* Sunninghill, Ascot, Berks. *Club:* Army and Navy.

**BATY, Charles Witcomb;** *e s* of late Wm Baty and late Margarette Ballinger; *m* 1923, Edith Halina, *d* of late Robert Bevan; one *s* two *d*. *Educ:* Westminster Sch. (King's Scholar); Christ Church, Oxford (Scholar). asst Master, later sixth form Master, Bedford Sch. 1923-29; Head Master of the King's Sch., Chester, 1930-46; Dir, Education Div., Allied Commn for Austria, 1946-48; one of Her Majesty's Inspectors of Schools, 1949-62 (Staff Inspector, 1954), retd, 1962. A Vice-Pres., The Classical Assoc., 1966. *Address:* Greenbank, West Street, Mayfield, Sussex. *T:* Mayfield 2273.

**BAUD, Rt. Rev. Joseph A.,** BA; Titular Bishop of Troas; Bishop of Visakhapatnam (RC), 1947-66; *b* Bellevaux (Haute-Savoie, France), 23 July 1890. *Educ:* Evian-les-Bains; Yeovil; Univ. studies at Fribourg (Switzerland). Came to Vizag in 1914; Teacher in St Aloysius' European High-School, Vizagapatam, 1914-30; Principal there, 1930-40; Vicar-General of Diocese of Vizagapatam in 1940; Coadjutor-Bishop of Vizagapatam (British India), 1942-47. *Address:* c/o Bishop's House, Maharanipeta, PO (Visakhapatnam), India. *Club:* Waltair.

**BAUDOUX, Most Rev. Maurice;** *see* St Boniface, Archbishop of, (RC).

**BAUER, Dr Louis Hopewell;** retired as Hon. Secretary and Treasurer, United States Committee of World Medical Association; *b* Boston, Mass., USA, 18 July 1888; *s* of Charles Theodore Bauer and Ada Marian Bauer (*née* Shute); *m* 1st, 1913, Helena Meredith; one *s*; 2nd, 1930, Margaret Louise Macon; one step-*d*. *Educ:* Harvard Univ. AB, 1909; MD *cum laude* 1912. US Army Medical Corps, 1913-26; Medical Reserve Corps, 1927-39; now Col USA retd. Medical Dir, Aeronautics Branch, US Dept of Commerce (now Federal Aviation Agency), 1926-30; in private practice, confined to cardiology, 1930-53. Dipl. Amer. Bd of Internal Medicine (cardiovascular disease); Dipl. Amer. Bd of Preventive Med. (in aviation medicine); Fellow Amer. Coll. of Physicians; Fellow in Aviation Med., Aero-space Medical Assoc. Member: Nassau County Med. Soc. (Pres. 1938-39); Medical Soc. of State of New York (Pres. 1947-48); American Med. Assoc. (Pres. 1952-53); Aero-space Medical Assoc. (Pres. 1929-31); World Medical Assoc. (mem. Council, 1947-48; Sec. Gen., 1948-61), Consultant, 1961-62; New York State Public Health Council, 1946-60. Editor Emeritus (formerly Editor-in-Chief) Jl of Aviation Medicine; Cons. Cardiologist to five hospitals, Nassau County, NY Hon. DSc, Univ. of Sydney. Holds several awards in medicine, science, etc. *Publications:* Aviation Medicine Textbook, 1926; Chapters on Aviation Medicine in Tice's Practice of Medicine and Oxford Medicine, 1943; Private Enterprise or Government in Medicine, 1947; articles in medical journals. *Recreation:* travel. *Address:* (home) 341 Harvard Avenue, Rockville Center, New York; (business) 10 Columbus Circle, New York 19, NY, USA. *Club:* Harvard (NY City).

**BAUER, Prof. Peter Thomas,** MA; Professor of Economics (with special reference to economic development and under-developed Countries) in the University of London, at the London School of Economics, since Oct. 1960; Fellow of Gonville and Caius College, Cambridge, 1946-60, and since 1968; *b* 6 Nov. 1915; unmarried. *Educ:* Scholae Piae, Budapest; Gonville and Caius Coll., Cambridge. Reader in Agricultural Economics, University of London, 1947-48; University Lecturer in Economics, Cambridge

Univ., 1948-56; Smuts Reader in Commonwealth Studies, Cambridge Univ., 1956-60; Woodward Lectr, Yale Univ., 1965; Roush Distinguished Vis. Scholar, Hoover Instn, Stanford, Calif., 1967; Sir William Meyer Lectr, Madras Univ., 1969-70. *Publications:* The Rubber Industry, 1948; West African Trade, 1954; The Economics of Under-developed Countries (with B. S. Yamey), 1957; Economic Analysis and Policy in Under-developed Countries, 1958; Indian Economic Policy and Development, 1961; (with B. S. Yamey) Markets, Market Control and Marketing Reform, 1968. Articles on economic subjects. *Address:* London School of Economics and Political Science, Houghton Street, Aldwych, WC2.

**BAULKWILL, Sir (Reginald) Pridham,** Kt 1960; CBE 1955 (OBE 1950); Solicitor; Public Trustee, 1956-61; *b* 1895. *Educ:* Shebbear College, North Devon. LLB (Hons) 1914. Served with London Rifle Brigade in European War, 1914-18. Qualified as Solicitor, 1918. Previously Asst Public Trustee. mem. of the Egyptian Loans Advisory Board, 1962-; a Governor of Shebbear Coll. *Address:* 5 Derncleugh Gardens, Holcombe, Dawlish, S Devon. *T:* Dawlish 3169.

**BAVERSTOCK, Donald Leighton;** Director of Programmes, Yorkshire Television, since 1967; *b* 18 Jan. 1924; *s* of Thomas Philip Baverstock and Sarah Ann; *m* 1957, Gillian Mary, *d* of late Kenneth Darrell Waters, FRCS, and Enid Blyton; two *s* two *d*. *Educ:* Canton High Sch., Cardiff; Christ Church, Oxford (MA). Served with RAF, 1943-46; completed tour of operations Bomber Command, 1944; Instructor, Navigation, 1944-46. History Master, Wellington Coll., 1949. Producer, BBC General Overseas Service, 1950-54; Producer, BBC Television Service, 1954-57; Editor, Tonight Programme, 1957-61; Asst Controller, Television Programmes, BBC, 1961-63; Chief of Programmes BBC TV (1), 1963-65; Partner, Jay, Baverstock, Milne & Co., 1965-67. *Address:* (Office) Yorkshire Television, Leeds, Yorks.; (Home) Low Hall, Middleton, Ilkley, Yorks. *T:* Ilkley 2693. *Club:* Savile.

**BAVIN, Alfred Robert Walter,** CB 1966; Deputy Under-Secretary of State, Department of Health and Social Security, since 1968 (Ministry of Health, 1966-68); *b* 4 April 1917; *s* of late Alfred and Annie Bavin; *m* 1947, Helen Mansfield; one *s* three *d*. *Educ:* Christ's Hosp.; Balliol Coll., Oxford. 1st cl. Hon. Mods. 1937; 1st cl. Lit. Hum. 1939. Min. of Health, Asst Principal, 1939, Principal, 1946; Cabinet Office, 1948-50; Min. of Health, Principal Private Sec. to Minister, 1951; Asst Sec. 1952; Under-Sec. 1960. Nuffield Home Civil Service Travelling Fellowship, 1956. *Address:* Abbotsleigh, 20 Camborne Road, Sutton, Surrey. *T:* 01-642 1970.

**BAWDEN, Edward,** CBE 1946; RA 1956 (ARA 1947); RDI 1949; Painter and Designer; Draughtsman; a Tutor in the School of Graphic Design, Royal College of Art, since 1932; *b* Braintree, Essex, 1903; *m* 1932, Charlotte (*d* 1970), *d* of Robert Epton, Lincoln; one *s* one *d*. *Educ:* Cambridge Sch. of Art; Royal Coll. of Art. As an Official War Artist he travelled in Middle East, 1940-45; visited Canada during 1949 and 1950 as a guest instructor at Banff Sch. of Fine Arts, Alberta. His work is represented in the Tate Gallery, London, and by water-colour drawings in several London, Dominion and provincial galleries; exhibitions: at Leicester Galleries, 1938, 1949, 1951; at Zwemmer Gallery, 1963 at Fine Art Soc., 1968. Illustrated books include: The Arabs, Life in an English Village, London is London. He has designed and cut blocks for a series of wallpapers printed by Messrs Cole & Son, and has painted mural decorations for the SS Orcades and SS Oronsay, also for Lion and Unicorn Pavilion on South Bank site of Festival of Brtain. Trustee of Tate Gallery, 1951-58. *Relevant publications:* "Edward Bawden" by J. M. Richards (Penguin Modern Painters); "Edward Bawden" by Robert Harling (English Masters of Black and White). *Address:* Royal College of Art, Exhibition Road, SW7; Brick House, Great Bardfield, Braintree, Essex. *T:* Gt Bardfield 491.

**BAWDEN, Sir Frederick (Charles),** Kt 1967; FRS 1949; FRSA 1959; Director of Rothamsted Experimental Station, Harpenden, since 1958; *b* 18 Aug. 1908; *s* of George Bawden and Ellen Balment; *m* 1935, Marjorie Elizabeth Cudmore; two *s*. *Educ:* Emmanuel Coll., Cambridge. Research Asst, Potato Virus Research Station, Cambridge, 1930-36; Virus Physiologist, Rothamsted Experimental Station, 1936-40; Deputy Dir, Rothamsted Experimental Station, 1950-58; Head of Plant Pathology Dept, 1940-58. Leeuwenhoek Lectr, Royal Soc. 1959; Hon. Life Member: New York Academy of Sciences, 1959; Indian Botanical Soc., 1960; Association Applied Biologists, 1966; Indian Phytopathological Soc., 1967; Foreign Mem. Royal Netherlands Academy of Sciences, 1960; President: Society of General Microbiology, 1959-61; Association Applied Biologists, 1965; British Insecticide and Fungicide Council, 1966-68; Internat. Congress of Plant Pathology, 1968; British Crop Protection Council; Inst. of Biology; a Vice-Pres. and Treasurer, Royal Soc., 1968-. Chm., Agricultural Research Council of Central Africa. Mem., Natural Environment Research Council. Hon. DSc: Hull, 1964; Bath, 1969; Reading, 1970; Hon. DTech Brunel, 1967. Research Medal, Royal Agricultural Soc. of England, 1955; Elvin C. Stokman Award, Univ. of Minnesota, 1968. *Publications:* Plant Viruses and Virus Diseases, 1939, 4th edn 1964; Plant Diseases, 1948, 2nd edn 1950; many papers on viruses and virus diseases in scientific journals. *Address:* 1 West Common, Harpenden, Herts. *T:* Harpenden 2264.

**BAWN, Cecil Edwin Henry,** CBE 1956; FRS 1952; BSc, PhD; Brunner Professor of Physical Chemistry in the University of Liverpool, since 1969 (Grant-Brunner Professor of Inorganic and Physical Chemistry, 1948-69); *b* 6 Nov. 1908; British; *m* 1934, Winifred Mabel Jackson; two *s* one *d*. *Educ:* Cotham Grammar Sch., Bristol. Graduated, Univ. of Bristol, 1929; PhD in Chemistry (Bristol), 1932; Asst Lectr in Chemistry, Univ. of Manchester, 1931-34; Lectr in Chemistry, 1934-38; Lectr in Physical Chemistry, Univ. of Bristol, 1938-45; Reader in Physical Chemistry, 1945-49. During War of 1939-45 was in charge of a Physico-Chemical Section in Armament Research Dept, Min. of Supply. Mem., Univ. Grants Cttee, 1965-. Swinburne Gold Medal, 1966. Hon. DSc: Bradford, 1966; Birmingham, 1968. *Publications:* papers in chemical journals; the Chemistry of High Polymers, 1948. *Address:* Department of Inorganic, Physical and Industrial Chemistry, The University, Liverpool. *T:* 051-709 6022. *Club:* Athenæum.

**BAX, Rodney Ian Shirley,** QC 1966; *b* 16 Sept. 1920; *s* of late Rudolph Edward Victor Bax, Barrister-at-Law, and of Shirley Winifred, *d* of Canon G. A. Thompson; *m* 1953, Patricia Anne, *d* of late Martin Stuart Turner, MC; one *s* one *d*. *Educ:* Bryanston Sch. (Scholar); Royal Coll. of Music (Exhibitioner). Served with Royal Fusiliers and Intelligence Corps, 1940-46 (Major GS). Called to Bar, Gray's Inn,

1947; S Eastern Circuit. Mem., General Council of the Bar, 1961-65. Asst Commissioner, Boundary Commn for England, 1965-69. *Recreations:* music, books. *Address:* 1 Harcourt Buildings, Temple, EC4. *T:* 01-353 9631; 4 Jocelyn Road, Richmond, Surrey. *T:* 01-940 3395. *Club:* Reform.

**BAXANDALL, David Kighley,** CBE 1959; Director of National Galleries of Scotland, 1952-70; *b* 11 Oct. 1905; *m* 1931, Isobel, *d* of Canon D. J. Thomas; one *s* twin *d*. *Educ:* King's Coll. Sch., Wimbledon; King's Coll., University of London. Asst Keeper, 1929-39, and Keeper of the Department of Art, 1939-41, National Museum of Wales. Served in RAF, 1941-45. Dir of Manchester City Art Galleries, 1945-52. Fellow, Museums Assoc. of Great Britain. *Publications:* Ben Nicholson, 1962; numerous articles, gallery handbooks, catalogues and broadcast talks. *Address:* 3 Abercromby Place, Edinburgh EH3 6JX. *T:* 031-556 4844.

**BAXTER, Prof. Alexander Duncan,** CEng; Technical Executive, Bristol Engine Division, Rolls Royce Ltd, since 1968 (Bristol Siddeley Engines Ltd, 1963-68); Director, de Havilland Engine Co. Ltd since December 1958; Chief Executive Rocket Division and Nuclear Power Group, de Havilland Engine Co. Ltd, since 1957; *b* 17 June 1908; *e s* of Robert Alexander and Mary Violet Baxter; *m* 1933, Florence Kathleen McClean; one *s* two *d*. *Educ:* Liverpool Institute High Sch.; Liverpool Univ. BEng (1st Cl. Hons MechEng) 1930; MEng 1933. Post-graduate pupil with Daimler Company, 1930-34; commissioned in RAFO, 1930-35; Research Engineer with Instn. of Automobile Engrs, 1934-35; Scientific Officer at RAE, Farnborough, 1935; engaged on aircraft propulsion and gas turbine research until 1947; Supt, Rocket Propulsion, RAE, 1947-50; Prof. of Aircraft Propulsion, Coll. of Aeronautics, Cranfield, 1950-57; Dep. Principal, Cranfield, 1954-57; Mem. Council: InstMechE, 1955-57; RAeS, 1953-70 (Vice-Pres, 1962-66, Pres., 1966-67). Member: RAF Education Advisory Cttee; Aeronautical Board, National Council for Academic Awards; Board of Council of Engineering Institutions, 1962-69; various Govt advisory cttees. Member of Court: Univ. of Bristol; Cranfield Inst. of Technology. FIMechE, FRAeS, FInstPet. *Publications:* various reports in government R & M series; papers in Proc. Instn Mech. Engineers and RAeS. *Recreations:* fell walking, swimming, cine photography. *Address:* Court Farm, Pucklechurch, Glos. *T:* Abson 204. *Club:* Royal Aero.

**BAXTER, Frederick William;** Professor of English Language and Literature in The Queen's University of Belfast, 1949-58, retired (Professor of English Literature, 1930-49); *b* Auckland New Zealand, April 1897; *m* 1925, Marjorie Newsam Coles, Newbury, Berks. *Educ:* Auckland Grammar Sch.; Auckland Univ. Coll.; Worcester Coll., Oxford. Divisional Signal Company, New Zealand Engineers, 1917-19; King's Coll., London, 1921-24; McGill Univ., Montreal, Canada, 1924-26; The University of Leeds, 1926-30. *Address:* 18 Gloucester Road, Painswick, Glos GL6 6RA. *T:* Painswick 2102.

**BAXTER, Herbert James,** OBE 1946; **His Honour Judge Baxter;** County Court Judge since 1955; *b* 6 March 1900; *s* of James Baxter; *m* 1931, Mary Kathleen Young; one *s* two *d*. *Educ:* Bishop Wordsworth Sch., Salisbury; Exeter Coll., Oxford (BA Modern History). Inns of Court OTC, and No. 7 Officers Cadet Bn, 1918; 2nd Lieut 1919. Called to Bar, Inner Temple, 1927 (Certificate of Honour); South Eastern Circuit, Kent Sessions. Civil Asst, War Office, 1939; Major, Intelligence Corps, 1940-43; Lieut-Col, 1943-45. Commander Order of Orange Nassau, 1946. *Recreations:* reading, golf, gardening. *Address:* Many Trees, Packhorse Road, Bessels Green, Sevenoaks, Kent. *T:* Sevenoaks 54512. *Clubs:* Reform; Wildernesse (Sevenoaks).

**BAXTER, James Houston,** MA, BD; FRSE; Regius Professor of Ecclesiastical History, University of St Andrews, 1922-70; *b* Glasgow, 23 Feb. 1894; *y s* of James Baxter and Mary Houston; *m* 1919, Helen, 2nd *d* of A. K. Robertson, Kilmarnock; one *s*. *Educ:* Whitehill Sch., Glasgow Univ. (First Class Hons, Classics; Prize for Essay; Ramsay Memorial Medal; Logan Medal and Prize; Geo. A. Clarke Scholar in Classics; Faulds Fellow in Arts; MA 1918); Aberdeen Univ. (Asst to Prof. of Humanity, 1918-20; BD 1920). Instructor Commander, RN, 1943-45. Ordained to Ministry of Church of Scotland, 1921; Parish Minister of Ballantrae, 1921-22. Excavated Byzantine Imperial Palace, Istanbul, 1933-39. Sec., British Acad. Cttee on New Dictionary of Medieval Latin; Trustee, Scottish National Library, 1927-47. Member: Scottish Records Commission; Scottish Dictionaries Council. Corr. Member: Vereeniging voor de uitgave van Grotius, The Hague; Société de l'Histoire du Protestantisme français. Associate Member, Royal Belgian Acad. Associate: Royal Flemish Acad; Naples Acad.; Hon. Mem., Royal Geographical Soc., Antwerp, 1952. Officier de l'Instruction Publique. Hon. DLitt: St Andrews, 1930; Louvain, 1956; Hon. DD Glasgow, 1932. *Publications:* Contrib. to: Dictionnaire d'Histoire et de Géographie ecclésiastiques (Louvain), Chambers's Encyclopaedia and Bibliotheca Sanctorum; (Ed) A Dictionary of Later Latin, AD 125-750; (Co-Ed) Bulletin Du Cange; Bibliography of St Andrews, 1926; History of the Church, 312-800 (in History of Christianity), 1928; Select Letters of St Augustine, 1930; Copiale Prioratus S Andree, 1930; (Co-Ed) Books printed abroad by Scotsmen to 1700, 1932; Index to Scottish Historical Review, vols 13-25, 1932; A St Andrews Music Manuscript, 1932; (Ed) R. F. Murray, The Scarlet Gown, 1932, 1955; (Co-Ed) Index of British and Irish Latin Writers, 1933, and A Word List of Medieval Latin, 1934 (and later edns); Turkey and the Middle East, 1943; The Reformation in Dundee, 1960. *Address:* 41 South Street, St Andrews. *T:* 1230. *Club:* National Liberal.

**BAXTER, Prof. Sir John Philip,** KBE 1965 (OBE 1945); CMG 1959; PhD; Chairman, Australian Atomic Energy Commission, since 1957; *b* 7 May 1905; *s* of John and Mary Netta Baxter; *m* 1931, Lilian May Baxter (*née* Thatcher); three *s* one *d*. *Educ:* University of Birmingham. BSc 1925, PhD 1928. University of Birmingham. Research Dir, ICI General Chemicals Ltd and Dir, Thorium Ltd, until 1949. Prof. Chem. Eng, NSW University of Technology, 1950; Vice-Chancellor, Univ. of NSW, 1953-69. Fellow Aust. Acad. of Science. FRACI; MIE(Aust). Hon. LLD University of Montreal, 1958. *Address:* 1 Kelso Street, Enfield, NSW, Australia. *T:* UJ 4261. *Clubs:* Royal Automobile of Australia (NSW); University (Sydney).

**BAXTER, Raymond Frederic;** broadcaster and writer; *b* 25 Jan. 1922; *s* of Frederick Garfield Baxter and Rosina Baxter (*née* Rivers); *m* 1945, Sylvia Kathryn (*née* Johnson), Boston, Mass; one *s* one *d*. *Educ:* Ilford County High Sch. Joined RAF, 1940; flew Spitfires with 65, 93 and 602 Sqdns, in UK, Med. and Europe. Entered Forces Broadcasting in Cairo, still as serving officer, 1945; civilian deputy Dir BFN BBC, 1947-49; subseq. short attachment West Region and finally joined Outside Broadcast Dept, London; with BBC until 1966; Dir, Motoring Publicity, BMC, 1967-68. *Publications:* (with James Burke and Michael Latham) Tomorrow's World (based on BBC TV Series); film commentaries, articles and reports on motoring and aviation subjects, etc. *Recreations:* motoring, riding, boating. *Address:* The Old Rectory, Denham, Bucks. *Clubs:* British Racing Drivers, etc.

**BAXTER, Walter;** author; *b* 1915. *Educ:* St Lawrence, Ramsgate; Trinity Hall, Cambridge. Worked in the City, 1936-39; served War of 1939-45, with KOYLI in Burma; afterwards, in India, ADC to General Slim, and on Staff of a Corps HQ during re-conquest of Burma. After completion of first novel, returned to India to work temporarily on a mission. *Publications:* Look Down in Mercy, 1951; The Image and The Search, 1953. *Address:* 119 Old Brompton Road, SW7.

**BAXTER, William;** MP (Lab) West Stirlingshire since 1959; *b* 4 Dec. 1911; *s* of William Baxter, Kilsyth; *m* 1938, Margaret, *d* of Anthony Bassy, Kilsyth; one *s*. *Educ:* Banton Public Sch. County Councillor, Stirlingshire, 1932; Vice-Convener Stirling CC, 1957-; JP 1952; Stirling Representative, County councils Association. *Address:* Gateside Farm, Kilsyth, by Glasgow. *T:* Kilsyth 2167; House of Commons, SW1.

**BAXTER, William T.,** BCom Edinburgh; Professor of Accounting, London School of Economics, since 1947; *b* 27 July 1906; *s* of W. M. Baxter and Margaret Threipland; *m* 1940, Marjorie Allanson; one *s* one *d*. *Educ:* George Watson's Coll.; Univ. of Edinburgh. Chartered Accountant (Edinburgh), 1930; Commonwealth Fund Fellow, 1931, at Harvard Univ.; Lectr in Accounting, Univ. of Edinburgh, 1934; Prof. of Accounting, Univ. of Cape Town, 1937. *Publications:* Income Tax for Professional Students, 1936; The House of Hancock, 1945. *Address:* 1 The Ridgeway, NW11. *T:* 01-455 6810. *Club:* Athenæum.

**BAYHAM, Viscount; James William John Pratt;** *b* 11 Dec. 1965; *s* and *heir* of Earl of Brecknock, *qv*.

**BAYLEY, Gordon Vernon,** FIA, FSS; Director, Manager and Actuary, National Provident Institution for Mutual Life Assurance, since 1964; *b* 25 July 1920; *s* of late Capt. Vernon Bayley, King's Regt, and Mrs Gladys Maud Bayley; *m* 1945, Miriam Allenby, *d* of late Frederick Walter Ellis and Miriam Ellis, Eastbourne; one *s* two *d*. *Educ:* Abingdon. Joined HM Forces, 1940; commissioned Royal Artillery, Major 1945. Asst Actuary, Equitable Life Assurance Soc., 1949; Partner, Duncan C. Fraser and Co. (Actuaries), 1954-57; National Provident Institution: Assistant Sec., 1957, Joint Sec. 1959. Institute of Actuaries: Fellow, 1946; Hon. Sec., 1960-62; Vice-Pres., 1964-67; Chm., Life Offices Assoc., 1969-70 (Dep. Chm., 1967-68). *Publications:* contribs. to Jl Inst. Actuaries, Jl Royal Statistical Soc. *Recreations:* tennis, ski-ing, swimming, water ski-ing. *Address:* the Old Manor, Witley, Surrey. *T:* Wormley 2301. *Clubs:* English Speaking Union, New Arts.

**BAYLEY, Mrs J. O.;** *see* Murdoch, J. I.

**BAYLEY, Lt-Comdr Oscar Stewart Morris,** RN Retd; Clerk of the Fishmongers' Company since 1969; *b* 15 April 1926; *er* surv. *s* of late Rev. J. H. S. Bayley; *m* 1948, Cecilia, *d* of late C. A. Jeffery; one *s* one *d*. *Educ:* St John's Sch., Leatherhead; King James's Grammar Sch., Knaresborough. Called to Bar, Lincoln's Inn, 1959. Entered RN, 1944: Ceylon, 1956-58; Supply Off., HMS Narvik and Sqdn Supply Off., 5th Submarine Div., 1960-62; Sec. to Comdr British Forces Caribbean Area, 1962-65; retd from RN at own request, 1966. Legal Asst (Unfair Competition), The Distillers Co. Ltd, 1966-68. Council of Assoc. of Retired Naval Officers, 1966. Clerk to Governors of Gresham's Sch., Holt; Hon. Sec., Salmon and Trout Assoc. and of Shellfish Assoc. of Great Britain; Vice-Chm., National Anglers' Council; Sec., Atlantic Salmon Research Trust; Joint Hon. Sec., Central Council for Rivers Protection. *Recreations:* fishing, bridge, assistant gardener. *Address:* 51 Montserrat Road, Putney, SW15. *T:* 01-788 9829.

**BAYLEY, Victor,** CIE 1917; CBE 1926; FICE; Indian State Railways, retired; *b* 1880. *Educ:* University Coll. Sch. *Publications:* Permanent Way Through the Khyber, 1934; Carfax of the Khyber, 1935; Liquid Fury, 1936; Nine Fifteen from Victoria, 1937; Frontier Fires, 1937; Pathan Treasure, 1937; Khyber Contraband, 1938; City of Fear, 1938; Indian Artifex, 1939; North-West Mail, 1939; Is India Impregnable?, 1942. *Address:* Steeple Cottage, Westport Road, Wareham, Dorset.

**BAYLIS, Clifford Henry;** Controller of HM Stationery Office and Queen's Printer of Acts of Parliament, since 1969; *b* 20 March 1915; *s* of late Arthur Charles and of Caroline Jane Baylis, Alcester, Warwicks; *m* 1939, Phyllis Mary Clark; two *s*. *Educ:* Alcester Grammar Sch.; Keble Coll., Oxford. Harrods Ltd, 1937-39. Served with HM Forces, 1940-46: Major RASC. Principal, Board of Trade, 1947; Asst Sec., UK Trade Commissioner, Bombay, 1955; Export Credits Guarantee Dept, 1963-66; Under-Sec., Board of Trade, 1966-67; Under-Sec., Min. of Technology, 1967-69. *Recreations:* gardening. *Address:* 19 College Road, Dulwich Village, SE21. *T:* 01-693 5537. *Club:* Royal Automobile.

**BAYLIS, Harry Arnold,** MA, DSc (Oxon.); *b* 1889; *s* of late Rev. F. Baylis and Ellen Husbands; *m* 1915, Edith Baylis; one *d*. *Educ:* Epsom Coll.; Jesus Coll., Oxford. BA (Oxon.) 1912; MA, 1918; DSc (Oxon.) 1921; Asst Keeper, Dept of Zoology, British Museum (Natural History) 1912; Protozoologist, Royal Naval Hospital, Haslar, 1916-18; Deputy Keeper, Dept of Zoology, British Museum (Natural History), 1936-49. *Publications:* A Manual of Helminthology, Medical and Veterinary, 1929; Fauna of British India, Nematoda, Vol. 1, 1936; Vol. 2, 1939; various articles in Encyclopædia Britannica (14th ed.), 1929; A Synopsis of the Families and Genera of Nematoda (with R. Daubney), 1926; many papers on zoological subjects, chiefly systematic helminthology.

**BAYLISS, Edwin,** OBE 1960; Member: the National Assistance Board and Board of Social Security, 1961-67; LCC for East Islington, 1946-65 (Chairman, LCC, 1952-53); GLC for Islington, 1964-67; Chairman, North Thames Gas Consultative Council, 1949-69; *b* 1894; *s* of Edwin Bayliss, Wolverhampton; *m* 1st, 1913, Lily Smithers (*d* 1948), Windsor, Berks.; (two *s* decd); 2nd, 1949, Constance Shipley (*d* 1965), London. *Educ:* Wolverhampton; WEA; Nottingham Coll. Served European War, 1914-18 (wounded, Mons star, war medals). Founder Mem. British Legion, 1921, served Area Councils, etc.; Vice-Pres. and Founder Anglo-Turkish Soc.; Vice-Chm., Northern Polytechnic; served LCC cttees; Chm. Gen. Purposes Cttee, 1948-52; Chm. LCC Parks Cttee, 1955-58. JP 1950, DL 1951, County of

London. KStJ 1966 (CStJ 1959). Vice-Pres. London District St John Ambulance Brigade. *Address:* 48 Biddestone Road, N7. *T:* 01-607 4351.

**BAYLISS, Colonel George Sheldon,** CB 1966; OBE 1945; TD 1941; DL; *b* 26 Dec. 1900; *s* of Francis and E. M. Bayliss, Walsall; *m* 1935, Margaret Muriel Williamson (*d* 1962), *widow* of Dr K. B. Williamson, MC, and *d* of J. S. Harker, Penrith; one *s* and one *step s*. *Educ:* Shrewsbury Sch. Joined TA, 2nd Lieut, 1921; Major 1926-40; Lieut-Col 1940-45 (despatches 4 times, 1941-45). Hon. Col 473 HAA Regt, 1947-53. DL Co. Stafford, 1953; Chm., Staffs. T & AFA, 1959-65. Managing Dir, S B & N Ltd, Walsall, 1930-. Bronze Star (USA). *Address:* Littlefield House, Wall, Lichfield, Staffs. *T:* Shenstone 208.

**BAYLISS, Richard Ian Samuel,** MD, FRCP; Physician to the Queen since 1970; Consultant Physician to Westminster Hospital since 1954; Physician to King Edward VII's Hospital for Officers since 1964; Hon. Consultant Physician, Newspaper Press Fund; Medical Director, Swiss Reinsurance Co.; *b* 2 Jan. 1917; *o s* of late Frederick William Bayliss, Tettenhall, and late Muryel Anne Bayliss; *m* 1st, 1941, Margaret Joan Hardman (marr. diss. 1956); one *s* one *d*; 2nd, 1957, Constance Ellen, *d* of Wilbur J. Frey, Connecticut; two *d*. *Educ:* Rugby; Clare Coll., Cambridge; St Thomas' Hosp., London. MB, BChir Cambridge 1941; MRCS, LRCP 1941; MRCP 1942; MD Cambridge 1946; FRCP 1956. Casualty Office, Ho.-Phys, Registrar, Resident Asst Phys., St Thomas' Hosp.; Off. i/c Med. Div., RAMC, India; Sen. Med. Registrar and Tutor, Hammersmith Hosp.; Rockefeller Fellow in Medicine, Columbia Univ., New York, 1950-51; Lectr in Medicine and Physician, Postgrad. Med. Sch. of London; Dean, Westminster Med. Sch., 1960-64; Physician to HM Household, 1964-70. Hon. Sec., Assoc. of Physicians, 1958-63, Cttee 1965-68; Pres., Section of Endocrinology, RSM 1966-68; Examr in Medicine, Cambridge and London Univs.; Examr, MRCP. Member: Bd of Governors, Westminster Hosp. 1960-64, 1967-; Council, Westminster Med. Sch.; Soc. for Endocrinology (Council, 1956-60); Brit. Cardiac Soc., 1952; Med. Research Soc.; Council, RCP, 1968-71. *Publications:* Practical Procedures in Clinical Medicine, 3rd edn. Various, in med. jls and textbooks, on endocrine, metabolic and cardiac diseases. *Recreations:* ski-ing, music, gardening. *Address:* 9 Park Square West, NW1. *T:* 01-935 2071; Cell Farm Cottage, Loughton, Bucks. *T:* Shenley Church End 272.

**BAYLY, Vice-Adm. Sir Patrick (Uniacke),** KBE 1968; CB 1965; DSC 1944, and 2 bars, 1944, 1951; RN retired; *b* 4 Aug. 1914; *s* of late Lancelot F. S. Bayly, Nenagh, Eire; *m* 1945, Moy Gourlay Jardine, *d* of Robert Gourlay Jardine, Newtonmearns, Scotland; two *d*. *Educ:* Aravon, Bray, Co. Wicklow; RN Coll., Dartmouth. Midshipman, 1932; Sub-Lieut, 1934; Lieut, 1935; South Africa, 1936; China station, 1938; Combined operations, 1941-44, including Sicily and Salerno; Lieut-Comdr 1944; HMS Mauritius, 1946; Comdr 1948, Naval Staff, 1948; Korean War, 1952-53, in HMS Alacrity and Constance; Captain 1954, Naval Staff; Imperial Defence Coll., 1957; Capt. (D) 6th Destroyer Sqdn, 1958; Staff of SACLANT, Norfolk, Va, 1960; Chief of Staff, Mediterranean, 1962; Rear-Admiral, 1963; Flag Officer, Sea Training, 1963; Adm. Pres., RN Coll., Greenwich, 1965-67; Chief of Staff, COMNAVSOUTH, Malta, 1967-70; retd, 1970. Vice-Adm. 1967. US Legion of Merit, 1951. *Recreation:* golf. *Address:* Dunning House, Liphook, Hants. *Club:* United Service.

**BAYNE, John;** Advocate; Sheriff-Substitute of Lanarkshire at Glasgow since 1959. *Address:* Sheriffs' Library, Sheriff Court, Ingram Street, Glasgow C1.

**BAYNE, Rt. Rev. Stephen Fielding, Jr;** Professor of Christian Mission, General Theological Seminary, New York, since 1970; *b* New York, NY, 21 May 1908; *s* of Stephen Fielding Bayne and Edna Mabel (*née* Ashley); *m* 1934, Lucie Culver Gould; four *s* one *d*. *Educ:* Trinity Sch., NY; Amherst Coll. (BA); General Theological Seminary, NY (STM). Fellow and Tutor, Gen. Theological Seminary, 1932-34; Rector, Trinity Church, St Louis, Mo, 1934-39; Rector, St John's Church, Northampton, Mass, 1939-42; Chaplain, Columbia Univ., 1942-47. Chaplain USNR, 1944-45. Bishop of Olympia, 1947-59; Anglican Executive Officer and Bishop-in-charge, Amer. Churches in Europe, 1960-64; Dir, Overseas Dept, Episcopal Church, USA, 1964-68; 1st Vice-Pres. and Deputy for Program, Episcopal Church, USA, 1968-70. Hon. degrees: STD: Gen. Theol. Sem. 1947; Columbia Univ. 1952; DD: Amherst Coll. 1948; Whitman Coll., 1952; Anglican theol. Coll., 1954; St Paul's, Tokyo, 1960; Harvard Univ., 1961; Huron Coll., 1963; Cuttington Coll., 1967; LLD, Mills Coll., 1951; DLitt: Hobart Coll., 1957; Kenyon Coll., 1960; LHD, Univ. Puget Sound, 1959; ThD, Australian Coll. of Theology, 1962. *Publications:* Gifts of the Spirit, 1943; The Optional God, 1953; Christian Living, 1957; In the Sight of the Lord, 1958; Enter with Joy, 1961; Mindful of the Love, 1962; An Anglican Turning-point, 1964. *Address:* Chelsea Square, 175 Ninth Avenue, New York, NY 10011, USA. *Clubs:* Athenæum; Century (New York); University (Seattle).

**BAYNES, Edward Stuart Augustus,** OBE 1950; United Kingdom Trade Commissioner in Dublin, 1946-54; *b* 25 June 1889; *s* of Edward Neil Baynes and Charlotte Augusta Baynes, OBE, *d* of Hon. Augustus Anthony Frederick Irby; *g s* of Sir William J. W. Baynes, 3rd Bart; *m* 1918, Helen Mary, *widow* of J. S. White, and *d* of G. A. Meredith; one *s*. *Educ:* Cheam Sch. and Radley Coll. Served European War, 1914-18, 11th Bn KRRC; Capt. 1916 (wounded twice, 1914-15 Star). Foreign Office 1918; Dept of Overseas Trade, 1919-41; Asst to British Trade Comr in NZ, 1920-22; visited Canada on official business, 1929; Dep. Comr Gen. for UK at British Empire Exhibition, Johannesburg, 1936; Official organizer, British Pavilion, Glasgow Exhibition, 1938; Dep. Comr Gen. for British Pavilion, New York World's Fair, 1939 (Hon. Citizen, New York, 1940). Dominions Office, 1942-45. *Publication:* A Revised Catalogue of Irish Macrolepidoptera. *Recreation:* entomology (FRES 1912). *Address:* Sandford, Adelaide Road, Glenageary, Co. Dublin. *T:* Dublin 805087. *Clubs:* Green Jackets (Winchester); Kildare Street (Dublin); Royal Irish Yacht (Kingstown).

**BAYNES, Keith Stuart;** Artist; *b* 1887; *s* of Rev. M. C. Baynes and Margaretha, *d* of Rev. Canon Arthur Cazenove. *Educ:* Harrow; Trinity Coll., Cambridge; Slade Sch. Held exhibitions at the Independent Gallery, London Artists Association, Lefevre Gallery and Agnew's Gallery; exhibn, 50 Years of Painting, England, France and Portugal, Colchester, 1969; exhibited France, Denmark, Germany, Italy, USA, Canada, Australia. *Publications:* (illustrated) Vineyards of France, 1950; (illustrated) English Channel, 1952. *Address:* 16 Cavendish House, Warrior

Square, St Leonard's-on-Sea, Sussex. *T:* Hastings 2454. *Club:* Athenæum.

**BAYNES, Sir William Edward Colston,** 5th Bt, *cr* 1801; MC; *b* 23 Feb. 1876; *er s* of Sir Christopher W. Baynes, 4th Bt; *S* father, 1936. *Educ:* Harrow; Trinity Coll., Cambridge (MA, LLM). Barrister-at-Law Inner Temple, 1900; Licencié en droit, Paris, 1905; Egyptian Civil Service, 1906-22; Judge, Egyptian Native Courts, 1913; Chief Inspector of Justice, 1919; Coldstream Guards, 1915-19 (Capt., MC). *Heir: c* Rory Malcolm Stuart Baynes [Lt-Col late Cameronians; *b* 16 May 1886; *m* 1925, Audrey (*d* 1947), *d* of late Edward Giles, CIE; one *s*]. *Club:* Brooks's.

**BAYÜLKEN, Ümit Halûk;** Turkish Ambassador to the United Nations, since 1969; *b* 7 July 1921; *s* of Staff Officer H. Hüsnü Bayülken and Mrs Melek Bayülken; *m* 1952, Mrs Valihe Salci; one *s* one *d*. *Educ:* Lycée of Haydarpasa, Istanbul; Faculty of Political Science (Diplomatic Sect.), Univ. of Ankara. Joined Min. of For. Affairs, 1944; 3rd Sec., 2nd Political Dept; served in Private Cabinet of Sec.-Gen.; mil. service as reserve Officer, 1945-47; Vice-Consul, Frankfurt-on-Main, 1947-49; 1st Sec., Bonn, 1950-51; Dir of Middle East Sect., Ankara, 1951-53; Mem. Turkish Delegn to UN 7th Gen. Assembly, 1952; Political Adviser, 1953-56, Counsellor, 1956-59, Turkish Perm. Mission to UN; rep. Turkey at London Jt Cttee on Cyprus, 1959-60; Dir-Gen., Policy Planning Gp, Min. of Foreign Affairs, 1960-63; Minister Plenipotentiary, 1963; Dep. Sec.-Gen. for Polit. Affairs, 1963-64; Sec.-Gen. with rank of Ambassador, 1964-66; Ambassador to London, 1966-69. Mem., Turkish Delegns to 8th-13th, 16th-20th Gen. Assemblies of UN; rep. Turkey at internat. confrs, 1953-66; Leader of Turkish Delegn: at meeting of For. Ministers, 2nd Afro-Asian Conf., Algiers, 1965; on official visit to UAR, 1966. Univ. of Ankara: Mem., Inst. of Internat. Relations; Lectr, Faculty of Polit. Scis, 1963-66. Hon. Gov., Sch. of Oriental and African Studies, London. Isabel la Catolica (Spain), 1964; Grand Cross of Merit (Germany), 1965; Hon. GCVO, 1967. *Publications:* lectures, articles, studies and essays on subject of minorities, Cyprus, principles of foreign policy, internat. relations and disputes. *Recreations:* music, painting, reading. *Address:* Permanent Mission of Turkey to the United Nations, 866 United Nations Plaza, New York, NY 10017, USA. *Clubs:* St James', Hurlingham, Travellers', Royal Automobile.

**BAZELL, Prof. Charles Ernest;** Professor of General Linguistics, School of Oriental and African Studies, University of London, since 1957; *b* 7 Dec. 1909; *s* of Charles Thomas Bazell. *Educ:* Berkhamstead Sch.; Wadham Coll., Oxford; Fellow of Magdalen Coll., Oxford 1934-42; Prof. of English Language and General Linguistics, Univ. of Istanbul, 1942-57. *Publications:* Linguistic Form, 1953; articles and reviews for Archivum Linguisticum, Word, Acta Linguistica, etc. *Address:* School of Oriental and African Studies, University of London, WC1.

**BAZIN, Germain René Michel;** Officier, Légion d'Honneur; Officier des Arts et des Lettres; Conservateur en chef du Musée du Louvre, since 1951; Professeur de muséologie, Ecole du Louvre, since 1942; *b* Paris, 1907; *s* of Charles Bazin, engineer and industrialist, and Laurence Mounier Pouthôt; *m* 1947, Countess Heller de Bielotzerkowka. *Educ:* Ste. Croix de Neuilly; Collège de Pontlevoy; Sorbonne. D ès L; Lic. en Droit; Dipl. Ecole du Louvre. Served French Infantry (Capt.), 1939-40. Prof., Univ. Libre de Bruxelles 1934; joined staff of Louvre, 1937; lecturer and writer; responsible for numerous exhibitions of paintings in France and elsewhere; his books are translated into English, German, Spanish, Italian, Japanese, Portuguese, Yugoslav, Hebrew, Swedish, dutch. Permanent Delegate, Internat. Commn for Care of Cultural Treasures. Corresponding Mem. of many Academies. Holds foreign Orders. Dr *hc:* Univ. of Rio de Janiero; Villanova, Pa, Univ. *Publications:* Mont St Michel, 1933; Le Louvre, 1933; Les primitifs français; La peinture italienne aux XIVe et XVe siècles; De David à Cézanne; Memling; Fra Angelico, 1941; Corot, 1942; Crépuscule des images, 1946; L'Epoque impressioniste, 1947; Les grands maîtres de la peinture hollandaise, 1950; Histoire générale de l'art, 1951; L'Architecture religieuse baroque au Brésil, 1957; Trésors de la peinture au Louvre, 1957; Trésors de l'impressionisme au Louvre, 1958; Musée de l'Hermitage: écoles étrangères, 1959; Gallery of flowers, 1960; The Loom of Art, 1962; Baroque and Rococo, 1964; Aleijadinho, la sculpture baroque au Brésil, 1964; Le Temps des Musées, 1967; Le Monde de la sculpture, 1968; La peinture d'avant garde, 1969; numerous articles in principal art journals of Europe and America. *Recreation:* collecting. *Address:* 29 avenue Georges Mandel, Paris XVIe. *T:* Passy 22-54; Palais du Louvre, Paris, Ier. *Clubs:* Army and Navy, Carlton, Public Schools, National; Cercle de l'Union, Cercle Interallié, Maison de l'Amérique Latine (Paris).

**BAZIRE, Ven. Reginald Victor;** Archdeacon of Southwark, since 1967; *b* 30 Jan. 1900; *s* of Alfred Arsène Bazire and Edith Mary (*née* Reynolds); *m* 1927, Eileen Crewsdon Brown; two *s*. *Educ:* Christ's Hospital. Missionary, China Inland Mission, 1922-45; Vicar, St Barnabas, Clapham Common, 1949-67. Rural Dean of Battersea, 1953-66; Hon. Canon of Southwark, 1959-67. Proctor in convocation, 1959-64. *Address:* 68 Wandsworth Common North Side, SW18. *T:* 01-874 5766.

**BAZLEY, Sir Thomas Stafford,** 3rd Bt, *cr* 1869; *b* 5 Oct. 1907; *s* of Capt Gardner Sebastian Bazley, *o s* of 2nd Bt (*d* 1911) and Ruth Evelyn (*d* 1962), *d* of late Sir E. S. Howard (she *m* 2nd, Comdr. F. C. Cadogan, RN, retd; he *d* 1970); *S* grandfather, 1919; *m* 1945, Carmen, *o d* of J. Tulla, 11 Stanley Gardens, W11; three *s* two *d*. *Educ:* Harrow; Magdalen Coll., Oxford. *Heir: s* Thomas John Sebastian Bazley, *b* 31 Aug. 1948. *Address:* Eastleach Folly, near Hatherop, Cirencester, Glos. *T:* Southrop 252.

**BEACH;** *see* Hicks-Beach.

**BEACH, Surgeon Rear-Adm. William Vincent,** CB 1962; OBE 1949; MRCS; LRCP; FRCSE; Retd; *b* 22 Nov. 1903; *yr s* of late William Henry Beach; *m* 1931, Daphne Muriel, *yr d* of late Eustace Ackworth Joseph, ICS; two *d*. *Educ:* Seaford Coll.; Guy's Hospital, London. Joined RN Medical Service, 1928. Served War of 1939-45 as Surgical specialist in Hospital ships, Atlantic and Pacific Fleets. Surgical Registrar, Royal Victoria Infirmary, Newcastle upon Tyne; Senior Specialist in Surgery, RN Hospitals, Chatham, Haslar, Malta, Portland; Senior Medical Officer, RN Hospital, Malta; Medical Officer i/c RN Hospital, Portland; Sen. Medical Officer, Surgical Division, RN Hospital, Haslar; Medical Officer in charge of Royal Naval Hospital, Chatham, and Command MO on staff of C-in-C the Nore Command, 1960-61; MO i/c RN Hospital, Malta, and on staff of C-in-C, Mediterranean and as Medical Adviser to C-in-C, Allied Forces, Mediterranean, 1961-

63. Surg. Rear-Admiral, 1960. QHS 1960. Fellow, Assoc. of Surgeons of Great Britain and Ireland, 1947, Senior Fellow, 1963. *Publications:* Urgent Surgery of the Hand, 1940; Inguinal Hernia–a new operation, 1946; The Treatment of Burns, 1950. *Recreations:* ski-ing, shooting, fishing. *Address:* Cherrytree Cottage, Easton, Winchester. *T:* Itchen Abbas 222. *Club:* Naval and Military.

**BEACHAM, Arthur,** OBE 1961; MA, PhD; Gonner Professor of Applied Economics, University of Liverpool, since 1966; *b* 27 July 1913; *s* of William Walter and Maud Elizabeth Beacham; *m* 1938, Margaret Doreen Moseley; one *s* one *d*. *Educ:* Pontywaun Grammar Sch.; University Coll. of Wales and Univ. of Liverpool. BA Wales 1935, MA Liverpool, 1937, PhD Belfast 1941. Jevons Res. Student, University of Liverpool, 1935-36; Leon Res. Fellow, University of London, 1942-43; Lectr in Economics, Queen's Univ. of Belfast, 1938-45; Sen. Lectr, University Coll. of Wales, 1945-47; Prof. of Indust. Relations, University Coll., Cardiff, 1947-51; Prof. of Economics, University Coll. of Wales, Aberystwyth, 1951-63; Vice-Chancellor, Univ. of Otago, Dunedin, New Zealand, 1964-66. Chm., Mid-Wales Industrial Develt Assoc., 1957-63; Member: Advisory Council for Education (Wales), 1949-52; Transp. Consultative Cttee for Wales, 1948-63 (Chm. 1961-63); Central Transp. Consultative Cttee, 1961-63; Economics Cttee of DSIR, 1961-63; North West Economic Planning Council, 1966-; Merseyside Passenger Transport Authority, 1969-; Council, Royal Economic Soc., 1970-. Hon. LLD Otago, 1969. *Publications:* Economics of Industrial Organisation, 1948 (5th edn 1970); Industries in Welsh Country Towns, 1950. Articles in Econ. Jl, Quarterly Jl of Economics, Oxford Econ. Papers, etc. *Recreations:* golf, gardening. *Address:* 2 Davenport Close, Barton Hey Drive, Caldy, Wirral, Ches. *T:* 051-625 7390.

**BEACHCOMBER;** *see* Morton, J. C. A. B. M.

**BEACHCROFT, Thomas Owen;** Author; Chief Overseas Publicity Officer, BBC, 1941-61; *b* 3 Sept. 1902; *s* of Dr R. O. Beachcroft, Dir of Music at Clifton Coll., and Nina Cooke, Beckley Grove, Oxfordshire; *m* 1926, Marjorie Evelyn Taylor; one *d*. *Educ:* Clifton Coll.; Balliol Coll., Oxford. Scholarship, Balliol. Joined BBC 1924; subsequently in Messrs. Unilevers Advertising Service; rejoined BBC 1941. *Publications: fiction:* A Young Man in a Hurry, 1934; You Must Break Out Sometimes, 1936; The Man Who Started Clean, 1937; The Parents Left Alone, 1940; Collected Stories, 1946; Asking for Trouble, 1948; Malice Bites Back, 1948; A Thorn in The Heart, 1952; Goodbye Aunt Hesther, 1955; (with Lowes Luard) Just Cats, 1936; Calling All Nations, 1942; British Broadcasting, 1946 (booklets about BBC); The English Short Story, 1964; The Modest Art, 1968; contributor of short stories and literary criticism to numerous publications throughout world, and to BBC Gen. Editor British Council series Writers and their Work, 1949-54. *Recreations:* the arts in general; formerly track and cross-country running (represented Oxford against Cambridge at mile and half-mile). *Address:* The White Cottage, Datchworth Green, Herts. *Club:* Oxford and Cambridge.

**BEADLE, Prof. George Wells;** President Emeritus, Professor of Biology, University of Chicago; *b* Wahoo, Nebraska, 22 Oct. 1903; *s* of Chauncey E. Beadle and Hattie Albro; *m* 1st, 1928, Marion Cecile Hill (marr. diss., 1953); one *s*; 2nd, 1953, Muriel McClure Barnett; one *step s*. *Educ:* Univ. of Nebraska; Cornell Univ. BS 1926, MS 1927, Nebraska; MA Oxford, 1958; PhD Cornell, 1931. Teaching Asst, Cornell, 1926-27; Experimentalist, 1927-31; National Research Fellow, Calif. Institute of Technology, 1931-33; Research Fellow and Instructor, Calif. Institute of Technology, 1933-35; Guest Investigator, Institut de Biologie Physico-Chimique, Paris, 1935; Asst Prof. of Genetics, Harvard Univ., 1936-37; Prof. of Biology, Stanford Univ., 1937-46; Prof. of Biology and Chm. of the Division of Biology, California Institute of Technology, 1946-60, Acting Dean of Faculty, 1960-61; Univ. of Chicago: Pres., 1961-68, Emeritus, 1969. Trustee and Prof. of Biology, 1961-68; William E. Wrather Distinguished Service Prof., 1969-. Hon. DSc: Yale, 1947; Nebraska, 1949; Northwestern, 1952; Rutgers, 1954; Kenyon Coll., 1955; Wesleyan Univ., 1956; Oxford Univ., 1959; Birmingham Univ., 1959; Pomona Coll., 1961; Lake Forest Coll., 1962; Univ. of Rochester, Univ. of Illinois, 1963; Brown Univ., Kansas State Univ., Univ. of Pennsylvania, 1964; Wabash Coll., 1966; Syracuse, 1967; Loyola, 1970; Hon. LLD: Univ. of California at Los Angeles, 1962; Univ. of Miami, Brandeis Univ., 1963; Johns Hopkins Univ., Beloit Coll., 1966; Michigan, 1969; Hon. DHL: Jewish Theological Seminary of America, 1966; DePaul Univ., 1969; Univ. of Chicago, 1969; Canisius Coll., 1969; Knox Coll., 1969. Pres., Chicago Horticultural Soc., 1968-; Trustee: Museum of Sci. and Industry, Chicago, 1967-; Nutrition Foundn, 1969-. Member: Twelfth Internat. Congress of Genetics (Hon. Pres.,), 1968; Member: National Academy of Sciences (Mem. Council, 1969-); American Philosophical Soc.; Amer. Assoc. of Adv. Sci. (Pres., 1946). Amer. Acad. of Arts and Sciences; Genetics Soc. of America (Pres., 1955); President's Sci. Adv. Cttee, 1960; Genetics Soc. (Gt Britain); Indian Soc. of Genetics and Plant Breeding; Inst. Lombardo di Scienze E Lettre; Sigma Xi. Hon. Member: Japan Acad.; Phi Beta Kappa. Royal Danish Academy of Sciences; Foreign Member, Royal Society, 1960. Laskar Award, American Public Health Association, 1950; Emil Christian Hansen Prize (Denmark), 1953; Albert Einstein Commemorative Award in Science, 1958; Nobel Prize for Medicine (jointly), 1958; National Award, American Cancer Soc., 1959; Kimber Genetics Award, National Acadmy of Sciences, 1959; Priestley Memorial Award, 1967; (with Muriel B. Beadle) Edison Award for Best science book for youth, 1967. George Eastman Visiting Professor, University of Oxford, 1958-59. Trustee Pomona Coll., 1958-61. *Publications:* An Introduction to Genetics (with A. H. Sturtevant), 1939; Genetics and Modern Biology, 1963; The Language of Life (with Muriel Beadle), 1966. Technical articles in Cytology and Genetics. *Address:* 5533 Dorchester Avenue, Chicago, Illinois 60637, USA. *T:* 493-2119. *Clubs:* Chicago; Cosmos (Washington, DC); Tavern, University (New York).

**BEADLE, Sir Gerald (Clayton),** Kt 1961; CBE 1951; retired from BBC in 1961 after 38 years' service in broadcasting; Member Councils of: Bath and West Society; Imperial Society of Knights Bachelor; *b* 17 April 1899; *e s* of late Clayton Beadle; *m* Jocelyn Corinne, *d* of late Hugh Rae; two *s*. *Educ:* Tonbridge Sch.; Pembroke Coll., Cambridge. Subaltern RA, 1917-19. With BBC 1923-61 during which period held office as: Dir of Broadcasting, Durban, S Africa; Controller N Ireland; Asst Director of Programmes, London; Head of Staff Training, London; Controller, West Region; wartime Dir of Administration and Principal Asst to Jt Dirs Gen., London; Dir of

BBC Television, London. Trustee, Bath Municipal Charities. *Publication:* Television: a Critical Review, 1963. *Recreations:* fishing, golf. *Address:* Little Priory, Bathwick Hill, Bath, Somerset. *TA* and *T:* Bath 5388. *Clubs:* Savile; Bath and County.

**BEADLE, Rt. Hon. Sir Hugh;** *see* Beadle, Rt Hon. Sir T. H. W.

**BEADLE, Rt. Hon. Sir (Thomas) Hugh (William),** PC 1964; Kt 1961; CMG 1957; OBE 1946; QC 1946; Chief Justice, Rhodesia, since 1961 (Judge of the High Court, Rhodesia, 1950); *b* 6 Feb. 1905; *s* of late A. W. Beadle, OBE, Sec. to Southern Rhodesia Treasury; *m* 1st, 1934, Leonie Barry (*d* 1953); two *d*; 2nd, 1954, Olive Staley Jackson. *Educ:* Salisbury Boys' High Sch.; Diocesan Coll., Rondebosch; University of Cape Town (BA, LLB); Queen's Coll., Oxford (BCL). Advocate, Bulawayo, 1930-39; Seconded Royal WAfFF, Gold Coast, 1939-40; Deputy Judge Advocate-Gen., S Rhodesia Forces, and Parliamentary Sec. to Prime Minister, 1940-46; MP Bulawayo North (United Party), 1939-50; Southern Rhodesia, 1946-50; Minister of Justice; of Internal Affairs; of Health; of Education. Cross of the Grand Commander of Royal Hellenic Order of the Phœnix (Greece), 1950. Hon. Fellow Queen's Coll., Oxford, 1966. *Recreations:* shooting, fishing, tennis. *Address:* Chief Justice's Chambers, High Court, Bulawayo, Rhodesia. *T:* Bulawayo 88594. *Clubs:* Bulawayo, Salisbury (Rhodesia).

**BEAGLEHOLE, John Cawte,** OM 1970; CMG 1958; FRSNZ 1967; Professor of British Commonwealth History, Victoria University of Wellington, New Zealand, 1963-66, Emeritus 1967; *b* 13 June 1901; *s* of David Ernest Beaglehole and Jane Butler; *m* 1930, Elsie Mary Holmes; three *s*. *Educ:* Wellington Coll., NZ; Victoria Univ. Coll.; University of London. MA (New Zealand), 1924; PhD (London), 1929. Asst in History Department, Victoria Univ. Coll., 1924-26; Post-graduate travelling scholarship, 1926-29; WEA Tutor-organiser, 1930-31; lecturer in history, Auckland Univ. Coll., 1932; odd jobs, 1933-35; Lecturer in History, Victoria Univ. Coll., 1936-47, senior lecturer, 1947-48; Senior Research Fellow and Lecturer in Colonial History, 1949-63; Historical Adviser, NZ Department of Internal Affairs, 1938-52. Chm. of Board of Management, NZ University Press, 1947-61. Pres., NZ Council for Civil Liberties, 1952-; Member: NZ Historic Places Trust, 1955-; NZ Arts Advisory Council, 1960-64. Hon. Fellow, Australian Acad. of the Humanities, 1969. Univ. Canterbury Condliffe Memorial Award, 1952; Royal Geographical Society's Gill Memorial Award for contributions to biography of Capt. Cook, 1957; University of Melbourne Ernest Scott Prize, 1962. Hon. DLitt: Oxford, 1966; Sydney, 1970; Hon. LitD Wellington, 1968; Hon. LittD Otago, 1969; *Publications:* Captain Hobson and the New Zealand Company, 1928; The Exploration of the Pacific, 1934, 3rd edn 1966; New Zealand, A Short History, 1936; The University of New Zealand, 1937; The Discovery of New Zealand, 1939, 2nd edn 1961; Victoria University College, an Essay towards a History, 1949; (Ed.) Abel Janszoon Tasman and the Discovery of New Zealand, 1942; New Zealand and the Statute of Westminster, 1944; The Journals of Captain James Cook on his Voyages of Discovery, 3 Vols, 1955-67; The *Endeavour* Journal of Joseph Banks, 1962; articles and reviews. *Recreations:* books, typography, music. *Address:* 6 Messines Road, Wellington, W3, New Zealand.

**BEALE, Dame Doris Winifred,** DBE, *cr* 1944; RRC 1941 (and Bar 1944); OStJ, *b* 9 Aug. 1889; *o d* of late George Beale, Forest Hill. *Educ:* Prendergast Sch., Lewisham. Trained at London Hospital; joined QARNNS, 1917; served at Royal Naval Establishments at Chatham, Haslar, Dartmouth, Malta, Gibraltar and Plymouth; Superintending Sister, 1933; Matron, 1937; Matron-in-Chief, Queen Alexandra's Royal Naval Nursing Service, 1941-44; Deputy-Matron-in-Chief, Joint War Organization of the Red Cross Soc. and Order of St John, 1944-46. A Governor of Lewisham Prendergast Sch., 1945-64. Florence Nightingale Medal by ICRC, 1951. *Recreations:* travel and gardening. *Address:* Trinity Lodge, London Road, Forest Hill, SE23. *Club:* United Nursing Services.

**BEALE, Prof. Geoffrey Herbert,** MBE 1947; FRS 1959; PhD; Royal Society Research Professor, Edinburgh University, since 1963; *b* 11 June 1913; *s* of Herbert Walter and Elsie Beale; *m* 1949, Betty Brydon McCallum; three *s*. *Educ:* Sutton County Sch.; Imperial Coll. of Science, London. Scientific Research Worker, John Innes Horticultural Institution, London, 1935-40. Served in HM Forces (1941-46). Research worker, department of Genetics, Carnegie Institute, Cold Spring Harbor, New York, 1947; Rockefeller Fellow, Indiana Univ., 1947-48; Lecturer, Dept of Animal Genetics, 1948-59, Reader in Animal Genetics, 1959-63, Edinburgh Univ. *Publications:* The Genetics of Paramecium aurelia, 1954. *Address:* 12 Middleby Street, Edinburgh 9. *T:* Edinburgh Newington 4496.

**BEALE, Hon. Sir Howard;** *see* Beale, Hon. Sir O. H.

**BEALE, Josiah Edward Michael;** British Government Shipping Representative for Far East, Singapore, since 1968; *b* 29 Sept. 1928; *s* of late J. E. Beale and of Mrs P. A. Beale, Upminster, Essex; *m* 1958, Jean Margaret McDonald; two *d* (and one *d* decd). *Educ:* Brentwood Sch.; Jesus Coll., Cambridge. Entered Civil Service, 1950; Principal, Min. of Transport, 1956; Asst Sec., Bd of Trade, 1968. *Address:* 1 Braddell Rise, Singapore 20. *Club:* Tanglin (Singapore).

**BEALE, Sir Louis,** KCMG 1937; CBE 1929; *b* 28 Nov. 1879; *s* of Louis S. and Mary A. Beale; *m* 1902, May A., *d* of T. N. and Mary Marr; two *s*. *Educ:* Skinners' Sch., Tunbridge Wells. HM Trade Comr: Canada, 1919-25; New Zealand, 1926-28; on special mission to British Malaya, 1928-29; Trade Comr Overseas Trade Development Council, Dept of Overseas Trade; Commercial Counsellor British Embassy, Shanghai, 1932-37; Commissioner-Gen. for HM Govt in the UK, New York World's Fair, 1939-40; Mem. of Anglo-French Purchasing Board, New York, 1940. *Address:* 1 Wall Street, New York, USA. *Clubs:* Devonshire; Union (Victoria, BC); Vancouver (Vancouver).

**BEALE, Hon. Sir (Oliver) Howard,** KBE 1961; QC; Australian Ambassador to United States, 1958-64; formerly Barrister-at-Law, Member of Commonwealth Parliament and Cabinet Minister; *b* 1898; *s* of late Rev. Joseph Beale; *m* 1927, Margery Ellen Wood; one *s*. *Educ:* Sydney High Sch.; University of Sydney. BA 1921; LLB 1925. Called to NSW Bar and High Court of Australia, 1925; served War of 1939-45, RANVR, 1942-45. Elected MHR (L) Parramatta, 1946, re-elected, 1949, 1951, 1954, 1955; Mem. Commonwealth Parly. Public Works Cttee, 1947-49; Austr. Deleg., Internat. Bar Congress at The Hague, 1948; apptd KC 1950. Minister for Information and

Minister for Transport (Menzies Govt), 1949-50; Chm., Austr. Transp. Adv. Council, 1949-50; Minister for Supply, 1950-58, including control of guided missiles research and Woomera Rocket Range, and atomic weapons research and Maralinga atomic testing ground; Minister i/c Austr. Aluminium Prod. Commn, 1950-58; Minister i/c Austr Atomic Energy Commn and Rum Jungle uranium project, 1950-56; Minister for Defence Prod., 1956-58, responsible for govt ordnance ammunition, explosives, chemicals, aircraft and engine factories; Actg Minister; For Immigration, 1951-52, 1953 and 1954; for Nat. Development, 1952-53; for Air, 1952; for Defence, 1957; Mem. Austr. Defence Council, 1950-58; Mem. Cabinet Defence Preparations Cttee and Cabinet Cttee on Uranium and Atomic Energy, 1950-58. Austr. rep., Anzus Council, Washington, 1958, 1959, Canberra, 1962; Leader, Austr. Delegn, Colombo Plan Conf., Seattle, 1958; Dep. Leader, Austr. Delegn to UN, New York, 1959; Dep. Leader, later Leader Austr. Delegn to Antarctic Conf., Washington, 1959; Austr. Deleg. SEATO Conf., Washington, 1959, 1960; Alt. Gov., Internat. Monetary Fund, 1960, 1962, 1963; Leader, Austr. Delegn, World Food Congress, Washington, 1963; Woodward Lectr, Yale Univ., 1960; Dean of British Commonwealth Diplomatic Corps, Washington, 1961-64; Pres., Arts Council of Australia, 1964-68. Dir of various corporations. Regents' Visiting Prof., Univ. of Calif., 1966; Marquette Univ., Wisconsin, 1967. Holds Hon. degrees. *Address:* 21 Cranbrook Lane, Bellevue Hill, Sydney, NSW 2023, *Clubs:* Union, Australasian Pioneers' (Sydney); American National; Elanora Country.

**BEALE, Percival Spencer;** *b* 14 Sept. 1906; *m* 1938, Rachel M. H. (*née* Wilson); two *s. Educ:* St Paul's Sch. Entered Bank of England Oct. 1924; Chief Cashier, Bank of England, 1949-Jan. 1955; General Manager, Industrial Credit and Investment Corporation of India, 1955-58. Director: Samuel Montagu & Co. Ltd, 1960-65; The British Oxygen Co. Ltd, 1958-69; Carpet Manufacturing Co. Ltd, 1958-69. *Address:* Villa Aurore, Route de Genève, 1299 Commugny, Vaud, Switzerland.

**BEALE, Thomas Edward,** CBE 1966; JP; Chairman, Inner London (EC) Bench; Chairman, Beale's Ltd; *b* 5 March 1904; *s* of late Thomas Henderson Beale, London; *m* Beatrice May, *d* of William Steele McLaughlin, JP, Enniskillen; one *s. Educ:* City of London Sch. Mem. Bd, British Travel Assoc., 1950-70, Dep. Chm. 1965-70. Vice-Pres. and Fellow, Hotel and Catering Inst., 1949-; Chm., Caterers' Assoc. of Gt Britain, 1949-52; Pres., Internat. Ho-Re-Ca (Union of Nat. Hotel, Restaurant & Caterers Assocs), 1954-64. Chm., Treasury Cttee of Enquiry, House of Commons Refreshment Dept, 1951. Master, Worshipful Co. of Bakers, 1955. Mem., Islington Borough Council, 1931-34; JP Inner London, 1950. FRSH 1957; FRSA 1968. Médaille d'Argent de Paris, 1960. *Recreation:* arboriculture. *Address:* West Lodge Park, Hadley Wood, Herts; Shoreacres, Banks Road, Sandbanks, Poole, Dorset. *Club:* Carlton.

**BEALE, Sir William (Francis),** Kt 1956; OBE 1945; Director: Melbray Group Ltd; National Cash Register Co. Ltd; Maple & Co.; Randalls Group Ltd; Fir View Furniture Holdings Ltd; Commercial Union Group (local director); Bewac Motor Corp. Ltd; *b* 27 Jan. 1908; *y s* of late George and Elizabeth Beale, Potterspury Lodge, Northants; *m* 1934, Dēva Zaloudek; one *s* one *d. Educ:* Downside Sch., Pembroke Coll., Cambridge. Joined Green's Stores (Ilford) Ltd, Dir, 1929-63 (Chm., 1950-63). Navy, Army and Air Force Institutes, UK, 1940-41, Dir, 1949-61 (Chm. 1953-61). EFI, GHQ West Africa, 1942-43; EFI, 21st Army Gp, 1944-46. *Recreations:* hunting, shooting; formerly Rugby football (Eastern Counties Cap, 1932). *Address:* 16-20 Catherine Place, SW1. *Club:* Bath.

**BEALES, Arthur Charles Frederick,** MA, DLit (London); Professor of History of Education, King's College, University of London, since 1965; Fellow of King's College, London, 1966; *b* 24 Jan. 1905; *er s* of Arthur Beales and Elizabeth (*née* Matthews), Kensington; *m* 1936, Freda, *er d* of Augustine Coleman Morris, Enniskillen; no *c. Educ:* Latymer Upper Sch.; King's Coll., University of London. BA, 1st cl. Hons, Hist., 1925; MA (dist.) 1927; University of London Teacher's Dipl., 1928; DLit 1964. Asst Master, Haberdashers' Askes' Hampstead Sch., 1928-31; Lectr in History, University Coll., Swansea, 1931-32; Lectr in Education, 1933-34; Lectr in Education, King's Coll. University of London, 1935-53; Reader, 1953-64. Talks Producer, Religious Broadcasting Dept, BBC, 1941-45. Received into Catholic Church, 1935; Cross, Pro Ecclesia et Pontifice, 1960. Mem. Council Historical Association, 1939-50; Chm. Editorial Bd Catholic Record Soc., 1948-55; Hon. Sec., Sword of the Spirit Movement, intermittently, 1941-47 (Chm. 1949). On British Delegation to 1st World Congress of UNESCO, Paris, 1947; Brit. deleg. internat. Educ. Conf., Santander, 1949; Mem. Catholic Educ. Council; Editor, Brit. Jl of Educational Studies, 1952-. *Publications:* The History of Peace: a Short Account of the Movements for International Order, 1931; A Guide to the Teaching of History in Schools, 1937; The Catholic Church and International Order, 1941 (Penguin); Education under Penalty: the Education of English Catholics, 1547-1689, 1963. Articles in Journal of Education, Dublin Review, The Tablet, and foreign educl jls. *Address:* 18 Grosvenor Court, Rayners Road, SW15. *T:* 01-788 5343.

**BEALES, Hugh Lancelot;** Reader in Economic History in University of London, 1931-56; *b* 18 Feb. 1889; 3rd *s* of Rev. W. Beales; *m*; two *s* one *d. Educ:* Kingswood Sch., Bath; University of Manchester. Lecturer in Economic History, University of Sheffield, 1919-26; Lecturer in Economic History, University of London (London Sch. of Economics), 1926-31. Visiting Prof., Columbia Univ., 1954-55, Harvard Univ., 1956, University of Washington, 1959, USA. Editorial Adviser, Penguin and Pelican Books, to 1945; Ed. of Agenda, a journal of reconstruction issued by London Sch. of Economics to 1945; mem. of Editorial Bd of Political Quarterly; Editor, Kingswood Books on Social History. Mem. of CS Arbitration Tribunal, 1955-65. Hon. DLitt Exeter, 1969. *Publications:* Industrial Revolution, 1929; Early English Socialists, 1932; Making of Social Policy (Hobhouse Lecture), 1945, etc. Contributor to Economic History Review and various periodicals. *Address:* 16 Denman Drive, London, NW11. *T:* 01-455 4091.

**BEALES, Reginald Edwin,** CBE 1961; Deputy Director, Central Statistical Office, Cabinet Office, since 1957; *b* 16 Sept. 1909; *s* of Charles Neslen Beales, Norwich; *m* 1938, Margaret Alice Poulton (*d* 1964); one *s* one *d. Educ:* City of Norwich Sch. Norwich Union Life Ins. Soc., 1926; Northern Assce Co., 1931; Central Statistical Office, 1943; Chief Statistician, Inland Revenue, 1949; Dir of Statistics and Intell., Inland Revenue, 1952-57. FIA 1934, FSS 1947 (Mem. Coun., 1965-69; Vice-Pres., 1967-68). *Publications:* articles in: Jl of Royal

Statistical Soc.; Review of Income and Wealth. *Recreations:* tennis, badminton, gardening. *Address:* Barnet Wood, Barnet Wood Road, Bromley, Kent, BR2 8HJ. *T:* 01-462 2813. *Club:* Royal Automobile.

**BEALEY, Prof. Frank William;** Professor of Politics, University of Aberdeen, since 1964; *b* Bilston, Staffs, 31 Aug. 1922; *er s* of Ernest Bealey and Norah (*née* Hampton), both of Netherton, Dudley; *m* 1960, Sheila Hurst; one *s* two *d*. *Educ:* Hill Street Elem. Sch.; King Edward VI Grammar Sch., Stourbridge; London Sch. of Economics. Seaman in RN, 1941-46; Student, LSE, 1946-48; Finnish Govt Scholar, 1948-49; Research Asst for Passfield Trust, 1950-51; Extra-Mural Lectr, University of Manchester (Burnley Area), 1951-52; Lectr, University of Keele, 1952-64. *Publications:* (with Henry Pelling) Labour and Politics, 1958; (with J. Blondel and W. P. McCann) Constituency Politics, 1965; The Social and Political Thought of the British Labour Party, 1970; articles in academic jls. *Recreations:* reading poetry, eating and drinking, watching football and cricket, darts, squash, playing with the children. *Address:* 355 Clifton Road, Aberdeen. *T:* Aberdeen 44689. *Club:* Economicals Association Football and Cricket.

**BEALS, Carlyle Smith,** SM (Canada) 1970; FRS 1951; FRSC 1933; Private Scientific Consultant in Celestial and Earth Sciences, since 1964; *b* 29 June 1899; *s* of Rev. F. H. Beals, Inglisville, NS, and Annie F. N. Smith, Albert, NB; *m* 1931, Miriam White Bancroft; one *d*. *Educ:* Acadia Univ., NS (BA 1919); Toronto Univ. (MA (Physics), 1923); honDSc Acadia Univ., 1951; Imperial Coll. of Science and Technology (DIC 1925); London Univ. (PhD 1926, DSc 1934); DSc hon.: University of New Brunswick, 1956; Queen's Univ., 1960; Pittsburgh Univ., 1963. Tory Medal, RSC 1957; Gold Medal of Professional Inst. of the Public Service of Canada, 1958; F. C. Leonard Medal of Meteoritical Soc., 1966. Asst Prof. of Physics, Acadia Univ., 1926-27; Astronomer, Dominion Astrophysical Observatory, Victoria, BC, 1927-40; Asst Dir, 1940-46; Dominion Astronomer, Ottawa, 1946-64. *Publications:* about seventy papers in astronomical and physical journals on emission line stars, interstellar matter, meteorite craters, and the development of scientific instruments, also analysis of line spectra. *Recreations:* print collecting, amateur photography and geology. *Address:* Manotick, Ont, Canada. *T:* Manotick 692-3247.

**BEAM, Jacob D.;** US Ambassador to USSR since 1969; *b* Princeton, NJ, 24 March 1908; *s* of Jacob Newton Beam and Mary Prince; *m* 1952, Margaret Glassford; one *s*. *Educ:* Kent Sch., USA; Princeton Univ. (BA); Cambridge Univ., England (1929-30). Vice-Consul, Geneva, 1931-34; Third Sec., Berlin, 1934-40; Second Sec., London, 1941-45; Asst Political Adviser, HQ, US Forces, Germany, 1945-47; Chief of Central European Div., Dept of State, 1947-49; Counsellor and Consul-Gen., US Embassy, Djakarta, 1949-51; Actg US Rep., UN Commn for Indonesia, 1951; Counsellor, Belgrade, 1951-52; Minister-Counsellor, US Embassy, Moscow, 1952-53 (actg head); Dep. Asst Sec. of State, 1953-57; US Ambassador to Poland, 1957-61; Asst Dir, Internat. Relations Bureau, Arms Control and Disarmament Agency, USA, 1962-66; US Ambassador to Czechoslovakia, 1966-68. *Address:* US Embassy, Moscow, USSR. *Club:* Metropolitan (Washington, DC).

**BEAMENT, James William Longman,** FRS 1964; ScD; Drapers' Professor of Agriculture and Head of the Department of Agricultural Science and Applied Biology, University of Cambridge, since 1969; *b* 17 Nov. 1921; *o c* of T. Beament, Crewkerne, Somerset; *m* 1962, Juliet, *o d* of late Prof. Sir Ernest Barker and Lady Barker, Cambridge; two *s*. *Educ:* Crewkerne Grammar Sch.; Queens' Coll., Cambridge; London Sch. of Tropical Medicine. Exhibitioner, Queens' Coll., 1941; BA 1943; MA 1946; PhD London 1945; ScD Cantab 1960. Research Officer with Agricultural Research Council, Cambridge, 1946; Univ. Lectr, and Fellow and Tutor of Queens' Coll., Cambridge, 1961; Reader in Insect Physiology, 1966. Member: Composers' Guild of Great Britain, 1967; Natural Environment Research Council, 1970. Scientific Medal of Zoological Soc., 1963. *Publications:* many papers on insect physiology in scientific journals; Editor of several review volumes. *Recreations:* acoustics, playing the double-bass. *Address:* 19 Sedley Taylor Road, Cambridge CB2 2PW. *T:* 46045; Queens' College, Cambridge CB3 9ET. *T:* 50425.

**BEAMISH, Air Vice-Marshal Cecil Howard,** CB 1970; QHDS; Director of Dental Services, Royal Air Force, since 1969; *b* 31 March 1915; *s* of Frank George Beamish, Coleraine; *m* 1955, Frances Elizabeth Sarah Goucher; two *s*. *Educ:* Coleraine Acad.; Queen's Univ., Belfast. Joined Royal Air Force, 1936; Group Capt., 1958; Air Cdre, 1968; Air Vice-Marshal, 1969. QHDS 1969. *Recreations:* Rugby football, golf, squash. *Address:* 15 Birch Crescent, RAF, Uxbridge, Middlesex. *T:* Uxbridge 32801. *Club:* Royal Air Force.

**BEAMISH, Col Sir Tufton (Victor Hamilton),** Kt 1961; MC 1940; DL; MP (C) Lewes Division of East Sussex since 1945; *b* 27 Jan. 1917; *o surv s* of late Rear-Admiral T. P. H. Beamish, CB, DL; *m* 1950, Janet McMillan, *yr d* of Andrew Stevenson, New York; two *d*. *Educ:* Stowe Sch.; RMC, Sandhurst. 2nd Lieut Royal Northumberland Fusiliers, 1937; Active Service, Palestine, 1938-39; War of 1939-45 (wounded twice, despatches, MC); served in France, Belgium, 1940; Malaya, 1942; India and Burma front, 1942-43; North Africa and Italy, 1943-44; Staff Coll., Camberley, 1945 (psc). Hon. Col 411 (Sussex) Coast Regt RA (TA), 1951-57. Mem. Church of England Council on Inter-Church Relations, 1950-60; Delegate to Council of Europe and Chm. Assembly Cttee, 1951-54; Vice-Chairman: British Group Inter-Parly Union, 1952-54; Conservative and Unionist Members Cttee, 1958-64, 1966-; Chm. Conservative For. Affairs Cttee, 1960-64; an Opposition defence spokesman, 1965-67; Council Mem. Royal Society for Protection of Birds, 1948-61, Pres., 1967-70; Salmon and Trout Assoc. Governor, Stowe Sch. Dir of companies. DL Sussex, 1970-. Hon. Freeman, Borough of Lewes, 1970. Golden Cross of Merit, Poland, 1944; Comdr, Order of the Phoenix, Greece, 1949. Mem. of the Soc. of Authors. *Publications:* Must Night Fall?, an analysis of Marxism in Eastern Europe, 1950; Battle Royal, a new account for the 700th Anniversary of Simon de Montfort's struggle against Henry III, 1965; contribs to newspapers and periodicals. *Recreations:* shooting, fishing, ornithology, photography, music. *Address:* 5 Eaton Mansions, SW1; Chelworth House, Chelwood Gate, Sussex. *Clubs:* Brooks's, Buck's, White's, MCC.

**BEAMONT, Wing Comdr Roland Prosper,** CBE 1969 (OBE 1953); DSO 1943, Bar 1944; DFC 1941, Bar 1943; DFC (US) 1946; FRAeS; Director and Manager, Flight Operations, British Aircraft Corporation, Preston, since 1965; *b* 10 Aug. 1920; *s* of Lieut-Col E. C.

Beamont and Dorothy Mary (*née* Haynes); *m* 1946, Patricia Raworth; three *d. Educ:* Eastbourne Coll. Commissioned in RAF, 1939; served War of 1939-45, Fighter Command, RAF, BEF, Battle of Britain (despatches), Battle of France and Germany. Attached as Test Pilot to Hawker Aircraft Ltd during rest periods, in 1941-42 and 1943-44; Experimental Test Pilot, Gloster Aircraft Co. Ltd, 1946; Chief Test Pilot, English Electric Co., 1947-61; Special Dir and Dep. Chief Test Pilot, BAC, 1961-64. Events while Chief Test Pilot, English Electric Co. Ltd; 1st British pilot to fly at speed of sound (in USA), May 1948; 1st Flight of Britain's 1st jet bomber (the Canberra), May 1949; holder of Atlantic Record, Belfast-Gander, 4 hours 18 mins. Aug. 1951 and 1st two-way Atlantic Record, Belfast-Gander-Belfast, 10 hrs 4 mins Aug. 1952 (in a Canberra); first flight of P1, 1954 (Britain's first fully supersonic fighter); first British pilot in British aircraft to fly faster than sound in level flight, 1954, and first to fly at twice the speed of sound, Nov. 1958; first flight of Lightning supersonic all-weather fighter, 1957; first flight of TSR2, Sept. 1964 (Britain's first supersonic bomber). Britannia Trophy for 1953; Derry and Richards Memorial Medal, 1955; R. P. Alston Memorial Medal, RAeS, 1960; British Silver Medal for Aeronautics, 1965. Master Pilot and Liveryman, Guild of Air Pilots. *Publication:* Phoenix into Ashes, 1968. *Recreations:* sailing, fishing. *Address:* Samlesbury Hall Cottage, Samlesbury, Preston, Lancs. *Club:* Royal Air Force.

**BEAN, Ven. Arthur Selwyn,** MBE 1939; Chaplain to the Queen, 1952-69, Extra Chaplain, since 1969; *b* 23 April 1886; *s* of Charles and Ellen Annie Bean; *m* 1912, Nellie Lingard Hackwood; two *d* (one *s* decd). *Educ:* Christ's Coll., Christchurch, NZ; Keble Coll., Oxford (MA); University of Manchester (BD). Curate of Rugby, 1910-17; Vicar of Ribby with Wrea, 1917-22; Vicar of Weaste, 1922-27; Vicar of Astley, 1927-34; Archdeacon of Manchester and Canon Residentiary of Manchester Cathedral, 1934-66. Church Comr, 1948-68. Dir, Ecclesiastical Insurance Office Ltd, 1949-66; Chm., C. of E. Pensions Board, 1959-65. Prolocutor, Lower House, York Convocation, 1955-66. Archdeacon Emeritus, 1966. *Address:* 2 The Brae, Longdown Road, Lower Bourne, Farnham, Surrey. *T:* Farnham 5348.

**BEAN, Sir Edgar Layton,** Kt 1955; CMG 1937; MA (Oxon), LLB; Parliamentary Draftsman, State of South Australia, 1926-58; *b* Melbourne, 15 Oct. 1893; *m* Constance Mary, *d* of William James Greenlees, Adelaide; two *s*. *Educ:* Scotch Coll., Western Australia; Adelaide Univ.; Merton Coll., Oxford. BA 1st Class Hons Classics, Adelaide, 1913; Exhibitioner Merton Coll., Oxford, 1914; served BEF France, 1916-19; BA Oxford, 1919; MA Oxford, 1922; LLB Adelaide, 1922; twice awarded Stow Prize for Law; admitted to Bar of South Australia, 1922; Chm., Local Government Commission, 1929-34; Editor, South Australian Statutes, 1934; Mem. SA Public Service Board, 1942-51; Chm., Education Enquiry Cttee, 1943-45; Chm., Teachers' Salaries Bd, 1946-64. *Publications:* South Australian Statutes, with notes, etc (8 vols). *Recreations:* fishing, history, literature. *Address:* 51 Godfrey Terrace, Leabrook, South Australia 5068. *Clubs:* Naval Military and Air Force; Royal South Australia Yacht Squadron (Adelaide).

**BEAN, Hon. Sir George (Joseph),** Kt 1970; OBE 1945; **Hon. Mr Justice Bean;** a Judge of the High Court, Queen's Bench Division, since 1969; *b* 19 Sept. 1915; *s* of late George and Phoebe Bean; *m* 1953, Zdenka White; one *s*. *Educ:* Liverpool Institute; Liverpool Univ. Pres. Liverpool Univ. Union, 1937-38. Served in Army, 1939-46 (despatches). Col RASC. Called to Bar, Middle Temple, 1940; Bencher, 1969. QC 1963; Recorder of Carlisle, 1965-69. *Recreations:* gardening, reading. *Address:* 27 Seymour Road, SW19. *T:* 01-947 1706.

**BEAN, Hugh (Cecil),** CBE 1970; violinist (freelance); Professor of Violin, Royal College of Music, since 1954; *b* 22 Sept. 1929; *s* of Cecil Walter Claude Bean and Gertrude Alice Chapman; *m* 1963, Mary Dorothy Harrow; one *d*. *Educ:* Beckenham Grammar Sch. Studied privately, and at RCM, London (principal prize for violin) with Albert Sammons, 1938-57; Boise Trav. Schol., 1952; at Brussels Conservatoire with André Gertler (double premier prix for solo and chamber music playing), 1952-53. National Service, Gren. Gds, 1949-51. Formerly Leader of Harvey Phillips String Orch. and Dennis Brain Chamber Orch.; Leader of Philharmonia and New Philharmonia Orch., 1957-67; Associate Leader, BBC Symph. Orch., 1967-69. Member: Boise Trio; Bean-Parkhouse Duo; Alan Civil Horn Trio; Music Gp of London. Has made solo commercial records, and has performed as soloist with many major orchestras. Hon. ARCM 1961, FRCM 1968. *Recreations:* design and construction of flying model aircraft; steam-driven passenger hauling model railways; gramophone record collection. *Address:* Rosemary Cottage, 30 Stone Park Avenue, Beckenham, Kent. *T:* 01-650 8774.

**BEAN, Leonard,** CMG 1964; MBE 1945; MA; Secretary, since 1966, and Director of Personnel, since 1969, Southern Gas Board; *b* 19 Sept. 1914; *s* of late Harry Bean, Bradford, Yorks, and late Agnes Sherwood Beattie, Worcester; *m* 1938, Nancy Winifred, *d* of Robert John Neilson, Dunedin, NZ; one *d*. *Educ:* Canterbury Coll., NZ; Queens' Coll., Cambridge. Served War of 1939-45: Major, 2nd NZ Div. (despatches, MBE). Entered Colonial Service, N Rhodesia, 1945; Provincial Comr, 1959; Perm. Sec. (Native Affairs), 1961; acted as Minister for Native Affairs and Natural Resources in periods, 1961-64; Permanent Secretary: to Prime Minister, 1964; also to President, 1964. Adviser to President, Zambia, 1964-66. *Recreations:* cricket, golf, gardening. *Address:* Amcotts, Bassett Green Road, Southampton, Hampshire. *T:* Southampton 68293. *Clubs:* Oxford and Cambridge University; MCC; Stoneham Golf.

**BEAN, Thomas Ernest,** CBE 1957; Secretary, London Orchestral Concert Board; *b* 11 Feb. 1900; *s* of Arthur Charles Bean; *m* 1929, Eleanor Child; one *d*. Asst Circulation Manager, Manchester Guardian, 1928-44; General Manager, Hallé Concerts Soc., Manchester, 1944-51; General Manager, Royal Festival Hall, London, 1951-65. Austrian Order of Merit (Officer's Class), 1959. *Recreation:* gardening. *Address:* 5 Pixholme Court, Dorking, Surrey. *T:* Dorking 2900.

**BEANEY, Alan;** MP (Lab) Hemsworth Division of West Riding of Yorkshire since 1959; *b* 3 March 1905; *s* of John Beaney, New Silksworth, Co. Durham; *m* 1926, Mary Elizabeth, *d* of William Wass, new Silksworth, Co. Durham; one *s* two *d*. *Educ:* Elementary Sch.; NCLC. Mem. Dearne Urban District Council, 1938-; County Councillor, WR Yorks, 1949; Mem., Yorks Executive Cttee, National Union of Mineworkers. *Recreations:* hiking, fishing, reading. *Address:* 364 Romford Road, Forest Gate, E7; 190 Houghton Road,

Thurnscoe, Rotherham, W R Yorks. *T:* Goldthorpe 3304. *Club:* Royal Automobile.

**BEAR, Leslie William;** Editor of Official Report (Hansard), House of Commons, since 1954; *b* 16 June 1911; *s* of William Herbert Bear, Falkenham, Suffolk; *m* 1st, 1932, Betsy Sobels (*d* 1934), Lisse, Holland; 2nd, 1936, Annelise Gross, Trier, Germany; two *s*. *Educ:* Gregg Sch., Ipswich. Served War, 1943-44, Royal Air Force. Mem. of Official Reporting Staff, League of Nations, Geneva, 1930-36; joined Official Report (Hansard), House of Commons, 1936; Asst Ed., 1951. *Recreations:* ski-ing, sailing, gardening, chess. *Address:* Medleys, Ufford, Woodbridge, Suffolk. *T:* Eyke 358.

**BEARD, Allan Geoffrey;** Assistant Under-Secretary of State, Department of Health and Social Security, since 1968 (Ministry of Social Security 1966-68); *b* 18 Oct. 1919; *s* of late Major Henry Thomas Beard and Florence Mercy Beard; *m* 1945, Helen McDonagh; one *d*. *Educ:* Ormskirk Grammar Sch. Clerical Officer, Air Min., 1936; Exec. Off., Higher Exec. Off., Asst Principal, Assistance Board, 1938-47; Army Service, 1940-46 (Capt., RE); Principal, Nat. Assistance Board, 1950; Asst Sec., 1962. *Recreations:* gardening, photography, reading. *Address:* 3 Chalgrove Road, Sutton, Surrey. *T:* 01-642 6735. *Club:* Royal Automobile.

**BEARD, Maj.-Gen. (Hon.) Edmund Charles,** CB 1947; CBE 1940; MC; *b* 21 April 1894; *s* of late C. T. Beard, CB, ISO, and *y d* of late E. J. Figgis, JP, Dublin; *m* 1922, Helen Beatrice Beryl (*d* 1968), *yr d* of late Percy Barlow, JP, Acton, W3; one *s* two *d* (and *er s* killed in Malaya, Dec. 1952). *Educ:* Marlborough; Brasenose Coll., Oxford (BA). Commissioned The Royal Irish Regiment, 1914; served European War in Gallipoli, Salonika, Palestine and France (despatches, wounded, MC); transferred to South Lancs Regt, 1922; SSO and Staff Capt. India, 1922-26; Staff Coll., Camberley, 1927-28; Gen. Staff, S Command, 1929-30; Bde Major 9th Inf. Bde, 1930-33; Brevet Major 1930; GSO 2, War Office, 1933-38; Brevet Lieut-Col 1935; transferred to Duke of Wellington's Regt, 1937, and commanded 1st Bn 1939. AA and QMG 44 Div., France and Belgium, 1940; commanded 133 Inf. Bde, 1940-42; Brig. GS Home Forces, 1942-43; Area commd (Maj.-Gen.) India, 1943-46. ADC to the King, 1946; retired pay, 1946. Col S Lancs Regt, 1948-57. *Recreation:* golf. *Address:* Nutcombe Height, Hindhead, Surrey. *Clubs:* Golfers'; MCC.

**BEARD, John Stanley Coombe,** JP; retired; Founder of J. Stanley Beard, Bennett & Wilkins, Chartered Architects, London; *b* 17 July 1890; *e s* of Percy Edward Beard, Rayleigh, Essex; *m* 1st, 1914, Amelia Cheer; one *s* (and one *s* killed on active service, 1942; two *d* decd); 2nd, 1935, Mildred Evelyn, *d* of Aubrey Bertram Drayton, Montevideo; one *s* one *d*. *Educ:* King Alfred's Sch., Wantage. FRIBA 1927, resigned; FIArb 1935. Served European War in Royal Artillery (wounded in France, 1918). Commenced practising in London in 1910. Has specialised in the designing of theatres, music-halls and cinemas, and has been responsible for the design of a large number of commercial buildings, including factories, offices, and flats. On St Marylebone Borough Council, 1932-37; commanded Grayshott contingent of Home Guard, 1940-42; Hon. District Representative of Royal Air Force Benevolent Fund in the Counties of Hants, Surrey, and Sussex, 1942; General Commissioner of Income Tax for Hants; Council of the London Soc., 1943. Council of Architects Benevolent Soc., 1944; Chm. several Property Cos. Formerly of Grayshott Hall, near Hindhead. Purchased Compton Acres, Dorset, 1950, reconstructed the 7 famous gardens and opened these to the public, 1952. *Address:* Colliston House, Canford Cliffs, Dorset. *T:* Canford Cliffs 77411. *Clubs:* MCC; Royal Motor Yacht.

**BEARD, Paul,** OBE 1952; FRAM; FGSM; Professor of Violin, Guildhall School of Music; *b* 4 Aug. 1901; *m* 1925, Joyce Cass-Smith; one *s* one *d*. *Educ:* Birmingham Oratory and St Philip's. Began violin playing at 4, being taught by father; first public appearance at 6; studied as Scholarship holder at RAM; appointed ARAM, 1921, and FRAM 1939; Principal 1st Violin of following Orchestras: City of Birmingham and Spa, Scarborough, 1920-32; National of Wales, 1929; London Philharmonic, 1932-36; BBC Symphony Orchestra, 1936-62. *Recreations:* golf, gardening. *Address:* 84 Downs Wood, Epsom Downs, Surrey. *T:* Burgh Heath 50759.

**BEARDS, Paul Francis Richmond;** *b* 1 Dec. 1916; *s* of late Dr Clifford Beards and Dorothy (*née* Richmond); *m* 1950, Margaret Elizabeth, *y d* of late V. R. Aronson, CBE, KC; one *s* one *d*. *Educ:* Marlborough; Queen's Coll., Oxford (Open Scholar; 1st cl. hons Mod. Hist.). Entered Admin. Class of Home Civil Service, 1938; Asst Princ., War Office; served in Army, 1940-44; Principal War Office, 1945; Asst Private Sec. to successive Prime Ministers, 1945-48; Princ. Private Sec. to successive Secs of State for War, 1951-54; Asst Sec., 1954; Imp. Def. Coll., 1961; Asst Under-Sec. of State, MoD, 1964-69; Comr for Administration and Finance, Forestry Commn, 1969; retd, 1970. Coronation Medal, 1953. *Recreations:* fishing, gardening, archæology. *Address:* Seaforth, Woodfield Lane, Ashtead, Surrey. *T:* Ashtead 3535. *Club:* Royal Commonwealth Society.

**BEARDS, Samuel Arthur,** MS; Hon. Surgeon Royal National Ear, Nose and Throat Hospital; Consulting Laryngologist St Mary Abbots Hospital, W8. MRCS, LRCP 1924; MB, BS, 1926; MS London 1929. Late Surgical Registrar and Senior House Surgeon, Hospital for Diseases of the Throat, Golden Square; Hon. Assistant, Bacteriological Department, London Hospital; House Surgeon, West London Hospital. *Address:* 48 Wimpole Street, W1. *T:* 01-935 8825.

**BEARE, Robin Lyell Blin,** MB, BS; FRCS; Consultant Plastic Surgeon, St Mary's Hospital, London, since 1959; Plastic Surgery Centre, East Grinstead, since 1960; Brighton General Hospital and Brighton and Lewes Group of Hospitals, since 1960; *b* 31 July 1922; *s* of Stanley Samuel Beare, OBE, FRCS, and Cecil Mary Guise Beare (*née* Lyell); *m* 1947, Iris Bick; two *s* two *d*. *Educ:* Radley (scholar). Middlesex Hosp. Medical Sch. MB, BS (Hons) 1952 (dist. Surg.); FRCS (Eng) 1955. Served with RAF Bomber Command (Aircrew) 1940-46. Formerly Ho. Surg., Casualty Officer, Asst Pathologist and Surgical Registrar, The Middlesex Hosp., 1952-56. Surg. Registrar, Plastic Surgery and Jaw Injuries Centre, Queen Victoria Hosp., East Grinstead, 1957-60. Fellow Assoc. of Surgeons of Gt Britain and Ireland; Fellow Royal Society Med.; Mem. Brit. Assoc, of Plastic Surgeons; Mem. of Bd of Trustees, McIndoe Memorial Research Unit, E Grinstead; Hon. Mem. Societé Française de Chirurgie Plastique et Reconstructive. *Publications:* various on surgical problems in BMJ, Amer. Jl of Surgery, etc. *Recreations:* fishing, shooting. *Address:* 149 Harley Street, W1N 2DE. *T:* 01-935 4444;

Scraggs Farm, Cowden, Kent. *T:* Cowden 386. *Club:* MCC.

**BEARN, Prof. Alexander Gordon,** MD; FRCP, FRCPEd, FACP; Professor of Medicine, Cornell University Medical College, Physician-in-Chief, The New York Hospital, since 1966; *b* 29 March 1923; *s* of E. G. Bearn, CB, CBE; *m* 1952, Margaret, *d* of Clarence Slocum, Fanwood, NJ, USA; one *s* one *d*. *Educ:* Epsom Coll.; Guy's Hosp., London. Postgraduate Medical Sch. of London, 1949-51. Rockefeller Univ., 1951-64; Hon. Research Asst, University Coll. (Galton Laboratory), 1959-60; Prof. and Sen. Physician, Rockefeller Univ., 1964-66, Vis. and Adjunct Prof. 1966-. Mem. Editorial Bd, several scientific and med. jls. Lowell Lecture, Harvard, 1958; Lecture, Medical Research Soc., 1969. *Publications:* articles on Human Genetics and Liver Disease, 1950-; (Co-Editor) Progress in Medical Genetics; (Associate Editor) Cecil and Loeb: Textbook of Medicine. *Recreations:* biography, travel. *Address:* 1225 Park Avenue, New York, NY 10028, USA. *T:* Templeton 1-0133. *Clubs:* Bath; Century, Grolier (NY).

**BEARN, Frederic Arnot,** CBE 1945; DSO 1917; MC; MB, ChB Manchester; MD Manchester 1920; Dauntesey, Turner, and Bradley Scholar, Platt Scholar, University of Manchester; Hon. Assistant Physician Devonshire Hospital, Buxton; *b* 1890; *m* Alice (*d* 1968), *d* of James Bell, JP, Colinton, Edinburgh. Late House Physician and Senior House Surg., Manchester Royal Infirmary; served European War, 1914-19 (despatches, DSO, MC); also in Mesopotamia, 1918; and in India, 1919; war of 1939-45, Col AMS (Bar to DSO, CBE, King Haakon VII Liberty Cross) County Commissioner, SJAB, Derbys.; KStJ. *Address:* Brooklands, Temple Road, Buxton, Derbyshire. *T:* Buxton 3587.

**BEARNE, Air Vice-Marshal Guy,** CB 1956; *b* 5 Nov. 1908; *y s* of late Lieut-Col L. C. Bearne, DSO, and of Mrs V. Bearne, Chart Sutton, Kent; *m* 1933, Aileen Cartwright, *e d* of late H. J. Randall, Hove; one *s* two *d*. Commissioned RAF, 1929; served in various Bomber Sqdns, 1930-33; specialist armament course, 1933; armament duties, 1934-44; Bomber Command, 1944-45 (despatches twice); Staff Officer i/c Administration, RAF Malaya, 1946; Joint Services Staff Coll., 1947; Dep. Dir Organisation (Projects), 1947-49; Command of Central Gunnery Sch., 1949-51; SASO, Rhodesian Air Training Gp, 1951-52; AOC Rhodesian Air Training Gp, 1953; Dir of Organisation (Establishments), Air Ministry, 1954-56; Air Officer in Charge of Administration, Technical Training Command, 1956-61; retd, 1961. *Recreation:* golf. *Address:* Fagus, Elmhurst Road, Goring-on-Thames, Reading, Berks.

**BEARSTED,** 3rd Viscount, *cr* 1925, of Maidstone; **Marcus Richard Samuel, TD 1945; DL;** Baron, *cr* 1921; Bt *cr* 1903; Director: Hill Samuel Group Ltd; The 1928 Investment Trust Ltd; Lloyds Bank Ltd; Samuel Properties Ltd; Sun Alliance & London Insurance Group, and other Companies; *b* 1 June 1909; *e s* of 2nd Viscount and Dorothea (*d* 1949), *e d* of late E. Montefiore Micholls; *S* father 1948; *m* 1st, 1947, Elizabeth Heather (marr. diss. 1966), *er d* of G. Firmston-Williams; one *d* (and one *d* decd); 2nd, 1968, Mrs Jean Agnew Somerville, *d* of R. A. Wallace. *Educ:* Eton; New Coll., Oxford. Served War of 1939-45, Warwicks Yeomanry (Major), Middle East, Italy (wounded); DL Warwicks. Chm., Warwicks Hunt, 1960-. Trustee and Chm. of Whitechapel Art Gallery; Governor, St Mary's Hosp., Paddington; Chm., Bearsted Memorial Hosp.; Pres., Jewish Home and Hospital at Tottenham. *Recreations:* hunting, shooting. *Heir: b* Hon. Peter Montefiore Samuel, *qv*. *Address:* 1 Eaton Close, SW1. *T:* 01-730 4040; Upton House, Banbury, Oxon. *T:* Edgehill 242. *Clubs:* White's; Cavalry.

**BEASLEY, Prof. William Gerald,** BA, PhD; FRHistS; FBA 1967; Professor of the History of the Far East, University of London, since 1954; *b* 1919; *m* 1955, Hazel Polwin; one *s*. *Educ:* Magdalen Coll. Sch., Brackley; University Coll., London. Served War, 1940-46, RNVR. Lecturer, Sch. of Oriental and African Studies, University of London, 1947. *Publications:* Great Britain and the opening of Japan, 1951; Select Documents on Japanese foreign policy, 1853-1868, 1955; The Modern History of Japan, 1963. *Address:* School of Oriental and African Studies, University of London, WC1. *T:* 01-580 9021.

**BEASLEY-MURRAY, George Raymond,** DD, PhD; Principal, Spurgeon's College, London, since 1958; *b* 10 Oct. 1916; *s* of George Alfred Beasley; *m* 1942, Ruth Weston; three *s* one *d*. *Educ:* City of Leicester Boys' Sch.; Spurgeon's Coll. and King's Coll., London; Jesus Coll., Cambridge (MA). BD 1941, MTh 1945, PhD 1952, DD 1964, London. Baptist Minister, Ilford, Essex, 1941-48; Cambridge, 1948-50; New Testament Lectr, Spurgeon's Coll., 1950-56; New Testament Prof., Baptist Theological Coll., Rüschlikon, Zürich, 1956-58. Pres., Baptist Union of Great Britain and Ireland, 1968-69. *Publications:* Christ is Alive, 1967; Jesus and the Future, 1956; Preaching the Gospel from the Gospels, 1956; A Commentary on Mark Thirteen, 1957; Baptism in the New Testament, 1962; The Resurrection of Jesus Christ, 1964; Baptism Today and Tomorrow, 1966. *Recreation:* music. *Address:* Spurgeon's College, South Norwood Hill, SE25. *T:* 01-653 1235.

**BEATON, Arthur Charles,** CMG 1954; Assistant Area General Manager, North Staffs Area, West Midlands Division, National Coal Board, 1955-61; National Coal Board Civil Defence Organiser, 1961, retired 1967; *b* 22 Aug. 1904; *s* of Samuel and Alice Ellen Beaton; *m* 1935, Jessie, *d* of Albert and Sarah Burrow; one *s* one *d*. *Educ:* Leeds Grammar Sch.; Keble Coll., Oxford. BA Litt. Hum. (Oxon), 1927; MA (Oxon), 1935. Sudan Political Service, 1927; District Comr, 1937; Dep. Gov., Equatoria, 1947; Dir, Local Govt Branch, 1950; Dep. Civil Sec., 1952; Actg Civil Sec., 1953; Permanent Under Sec. Ministry of the Interior, Sudan Government, 1954-55. 4th Class, Order of the Nile, 1941. *Publications:* Handbook, Equatoria Province, 1952. Articles in Sudan Notes and Records on anthropological subjects. *Recreations:* tennis, squash, cricket, golf. *Address:* 50 Chiltern Road, Sutton, Surrey. *T:* 01-642 2022.

**BEATON, Cecil Walter Hardy,** CBE 1957; photographer and designer; *b* London, 14 Jan. 1904; *s* of late Ernest Walter Hardy Beaton and Etty Sisson. *Educ:* Harrow; Cambridge. Exhibitions of photographs: Cooling Gallery, 1930; Nat. Portrait Gallery, 1968. Exhibitions of painting and stage designs: Redfern Gallery, 1936, 1958, 1965; Lefevre Gallery, 1966; Wright Hepburn Gallery, 1968. Writer; Photographer for Min. of Information; Designer of scenery and costumes for ballet and opera, and for many theatrical productions (London and New York stage); including sets and costumes for Lady Windermere's Fan, Quadrille, The Grass Harp; The School for Scandal (Comédie Française); costumes for: My Fair Lady (New

York, London); *films:* Gigi, The Doctor's Dilemma, My Fair Lady. Legion d'Honneur, 1960. *Publications:* The Book of Beauty, 1930; Cecil Beaton's Scrapbook, 1937; Cecil Beaton's New York, 1939; My Royal Past, 1939 (rev. 1960); (with P. Quennell) Time Exposure, 1941; Air of Glory, 1941; Winged Squadrons, 1942; Near East, 1943; British Photographers, 1944; Far East, 1945; Time Exposure, 1946; Portrait of New York, 1949; Ashcombe, 1949; Ballet, 1951; Photobiography, 1951; (with Kenneth Tynan) Persona Grata, 1953; The Glass of Fashion, 1954; It Gives me Great Pleasure, 1955; The Face of the World, 1957; Japanese, 1959; The Wandering Years, 1961; Quail in Aspic, 1962; Royal Portraits, 1963; Images, 1963; Cecil Beaton's Fair Lady 1964; The Years Between, 1965; The Best of Beaton, 1968. Photograph illustrations and drawings for many books including: History Under Fire (James Pope Hennessy), Bomber Command, The Importance of Being Earnest (Folio Society) 1960; author of play The Gainsborough Girls. *Recreations:* diaries, scrap-books, decoration, travel. *Address:* 8 Pelham Place, SW7. *T:* 01-589 4351; Reddish House, Broadchalke, near Salisbury. *T:* Broadchalke 211.

**BEATON, Surg. Rear-Adm. Douglas Murdo,** CB 1960; OBE 1940; retired as Medical Officer in Charge, RN Hospital, Plymouth, and Command Medical Officer, Plymouth Command (1957-60); *b* 27 May 1901; *s* of late Murdo Duncan Beaton, Kishorn, Ross-shire; *m* 1929, Violet, 2nd *d* of late David R. Oswald, MD, Kinross, Scotland; one *s* one *d*. *Educ:* Bristol Grammar Sch.; Edinburgh, Royal Colleges LDS 1923; LRCPE, LRCSE, LRFPS (Glas), 1924; Surg. Lieut Royal Navy, 1924; Surg. Comdr, 1936; Surg. Capt., 1948; Surg. Rear-Adm., 1957. Asst to Medical Dir-Gen., 1944-46; Medical Officer in Charge, HMHS Maine, 1947-48; MO i/c RN Sick Quarters, Shotley, 1949-51; Senior Medical Officer, Medical Section, RN Hospital, Plymouth, 1951-54; Asst to Medical Dir-Gen., Admiralty, 1954-57. QHP 1956-60; CStJ 1958. *Recreations:* golf, gardening, sailing. *Address:* Ardarroch, Auchterarder, Perthshire. *T:* Auchterarder 2329.

**BEATON, John Angus;** Principal Assistant Solicitor, Scottish Office, since 1966; *b* 24 July 1909; *s* of Murdoch Beaton, TD, ISO, Inverness, and Barbara Mackenzie Beaton (*née* Rose); *m* 1942, Margaret Florence McWilliam; two *s* one *d*. *Educ:* Inverness Royal Acad.; Edinburgh Univ. Admitted Solicitor and Asst with Macandrew, Wright & Murray, WS, Edinburgh, 1933; Legal Asst, Dept of health for Scotland, 1938; Sen. Legal Asst, Scottish Office, 1947; Asst Solicitor, Scottish Office, 1960. Vice-Pres., 1960-63 and Hon. Mem., 1963, Instn of Professional Civil Servants. *Publications:* articles in Encycl. of Scots Law and in legal jls. *Recreations:* curling, golf, fishing, etc. *Address:* 2 Dryden Place, Edinburgh EH9 1RP. *T:* 031-667 3198. *Clubs:* Civil Service; Royal Scots (Edinburgh).

**BEATTIE, Prof. Arthur James,** FRSE 1957; Professor of Greek at Edinburgh University, since 1951; Dean of the Faculty of Arts, 1963-65; *b* 28 June 1914, *e s* of Arthur John Rait Beattie. *Educ:* Montrose Academy; Aberdeen Univ.; Sidney Sussex Coll., Cambridge. 1st Cl. Hons Classics, Aberdeen, 1935; 1st Cl Classical Tripos, Cambridge, Part I, 1936, Part II, 1938; Wilson Travelling Fellowship, Aberdeen, 1938-40. Served War, 1940-45; RA, 1940-41; Intelligence Corps, 1941-45; Major GSO2; despatches, 1945; Staff Officer, Military Government, Germany, 1945; Fellow and Coll. Lectr, Sidney Sussex Coll., 1946-51; Faculty Asst Lectr and Univ. Lectr in Classics, Cambridge, 1946-51. Comdr, Royal Order of the Phœnix (Greece), 1966. *Publications:* articles contributed to classical jls. *Recreations:* walking, bird-watching. *Clubs:* New, Scottish Arts (Edinburgh).

**BEATTIE, Charles Noel,** QC 1962; *b* 4 Nov. 1912; *s* of Michael William Beattie and Edith Beattie (*née* Lickfold); *m* 1947, Maria Luisa, *d* of Cesare Paparini; one *s* two *d*. *Educ:* Lewes Grammar Sch. LLB (London). Admitted a solicitor, 1938. Served War of 1939-45 (despatches), Capt. RASC. Called to the Bar, 1946. *Publications:* Beattie's Elements of Income Tax, 1951; Beattie's Elements of Estate Duty, 1952; Beattie's Corporation Tax, 1965. *Address:* 24 Old Buildings, Lincoln's Inn, WC2A 3UJ. *T:* 01-242 2744.

**BEATTIE, Colin Panton,** MA, MB, ChB, DPH; FCPath; Professor of Bacteriology, University of Sheffield, 1946-67; now Emeritus Professor; *b* 11 Sept. 1902; *s* of James Beattie, MA, and Eleanor Anne Beattie; *m* 1937, May Hamilton Christison, BA, PhD; no *c*. *Educ:* Fettes Coll., Edinburgh; University of Edinburgh. House appointments in Royal Infirmary, Edinburgh, and Royal Northern Infirmary, Inverness, 1928-30; Asst in Bacteriology Dept., University of Edinburgh, 1930-32; Rockefeller Travelling Fellow, 1932-33; Lecturer in Bacteriology Dept, University of Edinburgh, 1933-37; Prof. of Bacteriology in The Royal Faculty of medicine of Iraq and Dir of Govt Bacteriology Laboratory, Baghdad, 1937-46. *Publications:* various papers on bacteriological and parasitological subjects. *Recreation:* gardening. *Address:* 39 Stumperlowe Crescent Road, Sheffield 10. *T:* 302158.

**BEATTIE, John,** MD; Consultant, Asbestosis Research Council and Institute of Occupational and Environmental Health, Montreal, Canada, since 1966; *b* 30 June 1899; *s* of James and M. Beattie, Dunmurry, Co. Antrim, N Ireland; *m* 1926, Elizabeth Hall Price, MB; two *s* one *d*. *Educ:* Royal Academical Institute, Belfast; Queen's Univ., Belfast; University Coll., London. Demonstrator of Embryology, Queen's Univ., Belfast, 1923-24; Research Associate and Demonstrator of Anatomy, University Coll., London, 1924-27; Anatomist to Zoological Soc. of London, 1926-27; Asst Prof. of Anatomy, 1927-30, Assoc. Prof. of Anatomy, 1930-33, McGill Univ., Canada; Conservator of Museum and Dir of Research, Royal College of Surgeons, 1933-42; Prof. of Experimental Surgery, Royal College of Surgeons, 1938-42; Bernhard Baron Research Prof., Royal College of Surgeons, 1942-50; Col AMS, Dir Army Blood Transfusion Service, 1939-40; Consultant, Surg.-Gen. US Army, 1948-50; Arris and Gale Lecturer, Royal College of Surgeons, 1935-42; Henderson Trust Lecturer, University of Edinburgh, 1936; Banting Memorial Lecturer, University of Toronto, 1949; Research Associate Physiology Dept and Low Temperature Research Station, Cambridge, 1950-58; Visiting Prof., University of Calif, 1963, 1964; Physiologist, Houghton Poultry Research Station, Houghton, Hunts, 1958-66. *Publications:* articles in scientific journals. *Address:* Queens' College, Cambridge. *T:* Swavesey 284, Cambridgeshire.

**BEATTIE, Brigadier Joseph Hamilton,** CBE 1945; DSO 1944; *b* 29 Sept. 1903; *s* of Malcolm Hamilton Beattie and Maria Isabel Beattie, Burntwood, Eastbourne, Sussex; *m* 1938, Margaret Antonia, *er d* of J. R. Makeig-Jones, CBE, Budleigh Salterton, Devon; three *s* (and one *s* decd), three *d*. *Educ:* Rugby; RMA Woolwich, 2nd Lieut RA, 1924; ADC to Viceroy of India, 1933-34; served Mohmand Campaign, NWF, India, 1935; served War of 1939-45; France, Belgium, Holland, Germany and Burma (despatches twice); Lieut-Col 1942, Brig. 1945; retd, 1956. *Recreations:* shooting, fishing. *Address:* San Anard, Zabbar, Malta.

**BEATTIE, Captain Stephen Halden,** VC 1942; Royal Navy, retired; *b* 29 March 1908; *s* of Rev. Prebendary E. H. Beattie, MC; *m* 1933, Philippa Mary Blanchflower; four *s*. *Educ:* Abberley Hall; Rugby. Joined Royal Navy, 1926; Captain, 1951. Senior Officer, 1st Australian Frigate Squadron, 1952-54. Senior Naval Officer, Persian Gulf, 1956-58; in command HMS Birmingham, 1958; retd 1960. Naval Adviser to Ethiopian Govt, 1965. Chevalier Légion d'Honneur, 1947; Croix de guerre with palms, 1947; Officer, Order of Menelik, 1969. *Address:* Salt House, Mullion, Cornwall. *Club:* Army and Navy.

**BEATTIE, William,** CBE 1963; Librarian, National Library of Scotland, 1953-70; *b* 27 Aug. 1903; *s* of William Beattie and Elizabeth Vallance; *m* 1932, Agnes Howie, *d* of Henry Wood; three *d*. *Educ:* Jedburgh Grammar Sch.; George Watson's Coll.; University of Edinburgh. Asst Librarian, University of Edinburgh, 1926-30; Keeper of Printed Books, National Library of Scotland, 1931-53. Visiting Fellow, Folger Library, 1957. Lyell Reader in Bibliography, University of Oxford, 1964-65. Chm., Standing Conference of National and University Libraries, 1964-67. Vice-Pres., Bibliographical Soc. Hon. LLD St Andrews, 1957; Hon. LittD, Trinity Coll., Dublin, 1967; Hon. Prof., Univ. of Edinburgh, 1967. *Publications:* The Chepman and Myllar Prints; The Taill of Rauf Coilyear (facsimiles, with introductions), 1950, 1966; articles in Edinburgh Bibliographical Soc. Transactions. *Address:* 7 South Gillsland Road, Edinburgh 10.

**BEATTIE, William John Hunt Montgomery,** MA Cantab; MD, FRCS, FRCOG; Consultant Gynæcologist and Obstetric Surgeon, St Bartholomew's Hospital; Gynæcologist: Leatherhead Hospital; Florence Nightingale Hospital; retired. *Educ:* Cambridge Univ.; London Univ. MRCS; LRCP 1927; BCh (Cantab) 1928; FRCS 1929; MB 1930; MD 1933; FRCOG 1942; Examiner: Central Midwives' Board; Univs. of Oxford, Cambridge and London (Obst. and Gynæcol.); Conjoint Board (Midwifery and Gynæcol.). FRSocMed. *Publications:* (jt) Diseases of Women by Ten Teachers, 1941; articles in medical journals. *Address:* Ivy Cottage, Reigate Heath, Surrey.

**BEATTY,** 2nd Earl, *cr* 1919, of the North Sea and of Brooksby, **David Field Beatty,** DSC 1942; Commander RN (retired); *b* 22 Feb. 1905; *er s* of 1st Earl and Ethel (*d* 1932), *o d* of Marshall Field, sen., of Chicago; *S* father 1936; *m* 1st, 1937, Dorothy Power Sands (marriage dissolved, 1945; she *m* 1954, 6th Baron Brownlow, *qv*); 2nd 1946, Mrs Dorothy Rita Bragg (marriage dissolved, 1950; she *m* 1951, Abram Stevens Hewitt, New York); one *s*; 3rd, 1951, Mrs Adelle O'Connor (marriage dissolved, 1958), New York; one *d*; 4th, 1959, Diane, *d* of Mrs Duncan Kirk and step *d* of Capt. Duncan Kirk, Sheaves Farm, Loxwood, Sussex; one *s* one *d*. MP (U) Peckham Div. of Camberwell, 1931-36; PPS to Financial Secretary to the Admiralty, 1931-36; Joint Parliamentary Sec., Air Ministry, 1945; Mem. LCC for Peckham, 1937-46; Chm. of Navy League, 1937-41, Pres., 1941-44; served War of 1939-45 with Royal Navy; commanded: HMS Puffin, Buxton and Boreas, 1940-41; Combined Operations Dieppe and Sicily, 1942-43; Dep. Dir Combined Operations Dept, Admiralty, 1944-45. Chm., British Empire Games (England), 1950-. Chm., Home Oil of Canada Limited, 1966-. *Heir: s* Viscount Borodale, *qv*. *Recreations:* shooting and fishing. *Address:* Regency Cottage, 5 Rutland Gardens, SW7. *T:* 01-589 5093; Chicheley Hall, Newport Pagnell, Bucks. *T:* North Crawley 252. *Clubs:* White's; Royal Yacht Squadron (Cowes).

*See also Ronald Tree.*

**BEATTY, (Alfred) Chester;** Chairman: Selection Trust Ltd; Auselex Investment Holding (Pty) Ltd; Australian Selection (Pty) Ltd; CAST Holdings Ltd; Consolidated African Selection Trust Ltd; North Sea Selection Co. Ltd; RST Group London Advisory Committee; Selcast Holdings (Pty) Ltd; Sierra Leone Selection Trust Ltd; also Chairman or Director of many other companies; *b* 1907; *o s* of late Sir (Alfred) Chester Beatty and late Grace Madeline, *d* of Alfred Rickard, Denver, USA; *m* 1st, 1933, Pamela (marr. diss. 1936; she *d* 1957), *o d* of Captain George Belas; one *d*; 2nd, 1937, Enid (marr. diss. 1950), *d* of S. H. Groome, Golfe Juan, France; 3rd, 1953, Helen Gertrude, *widow* of Roger Casalis de Pury. *Educ:* Eton; Trinity Coll., Cambridge. Past-Pres., Overseas Mining Assoc.; Jt Master, Ashford Valley Foxhounds, 1927-31, Master, 1931-53. FID. *Address:* Owley, Wittersham, Kent; 76 Park Street, W1. *Club:* Royal Yacht Squadron.

**BEATTY, Chester;** *see* Beatty, A. C.

**BEAUBIEN, De Gaspé,** CBE 1944; Consulting Engineer; De Gaspé Beaubien & Co., 462 St Catherine Road, Outremont, Montreal; Past National Joint Chairman War Savings Committee; President Beaubien Limitée; Director, Dominion Tar Co. Ltd, and other companies; *b* Outrement, 18 May 1881; *s* of Hon. Louis Beaubien, Montreal, and Lauretta Stuart, Quebec; *m* 1st, Gabrielle (*decd*), *d* of Rt Hon. Senator Raoul Dandurand, KC, LLD, PC; one *s* two *d*; 2nd, Angéline Rodier. *Educ:* St Mary's and Montreal Colls; McGill Univ. (BSc 1906). With Montreal Light, Heat & Power, 1903; Demonstrator, McGill Univ., 1907; Westinghouse Electric & Manufacturing Company, at East Pittsburg, 1908; Consulting Engineer under own name, 1908-22; consulting engineering under the name of Beaubien, Busfield & Company, 1922-27. Past-Pres., Engineering Institute of Canada, Hon. DSc University of Manitoba. *Address:* 462 St Catherine Road, Outremont, Quebec. *T:* CR6-3136. *Clubs:* (PP) Canadian, (PP) Royal Automobile of Canada, University, (PP) Cercle Universitaire, (PP) Rotary, Mount Royal, Montreal.

**BEAUCHAMP,** 8th Earl, *cr* 1815, **William Lygon,** Baron Beauchamp, 1806; Viscount Elmley, 1815; *b* 3 July 1903; *e s* of 7th Earl and Lady Lettice Grosvenor (*d* 1936), *d* of late Earl Grosvenor and *sister* of 2nd Duke of Westminster, GCVO, DSO; *S* father, 1938; *m* 1936, Else Doronville de la Cour, MBE 1944, Order of the Dannebrog (RDI) 1964, Kt of Dannebrog 1970, DStJ, *widow* of Director C. de la Cour. *Educ:* Eton; Magdalen Coll., Oxford. MP (L) Norfolk E, 1929-31 (LNat), 1931-38. Parliamentary Private Sec. to late Lord Hore-Belisha, in four Government Departments, 1931-38; DL 1948; JP 1941, CC 1940-52, Worcs. Pres., Three Counties Show, 1964. Served in RAOC Aug. 1941-45 at home and in Italy. *Heir: cousin* Reginald Arthur Lygon [*b* 28 July 1904; *m* 1930, Agnes Mary Louise, *o d* of late Rev. Canon George

Fancourt Bell; three *d*]. *Address:* Madresfield Court, Great Malvern, Worcs. *T:* Malvern 3024. *Club:* St James'.

*See also Baron Ampthill, Sir Richard Cotterell.*

**BEAUCHAMP, Sir Brograve (Campbell),** 2nd Bt, *cr* 1911; *b* 5 May 1897; *s* of 1st Bt and Betty Campbell, *d* of late Archibald Woods, Columbus, Ohio, USA; *S* father, 1925; *m* 1923, Lady Evelyn Leonora Alima Herbert, *e d* of 5th Earl of Carnarvon; one *d*. MP (U) Walthamstow East, 1931-45. *Heir:* none. *Address:* 19 Kingston House, Princes Gate, SW7. *Club:* White's.

**BEAUCHAMP, Sir Douglas Clifford** (commonly known as **Sir Peter**), 2nd Bt, *cr* 1918; *b* 11 March 1903; *s* of Sir Frank Beauchamp, 1st Bt, and Mabel Constance (*d* 1957), *e d* of James Norman Bannon, Kent; *S* father 1950; *m* 1st, 1926, Nancy (who obtained a divorce, 1933), *o d* of Laurence E. Moss, Sydney, NSW; 2nd, 1933, Pamela Dorothy May Chandor. *Educ:* Eton. *Heir:* none. *Address:* 2 Lion House, Fore Street Hill, Budleigh Salterton, Devon. *T:* Budleigh Salterton 2960.

**BEAUCHAMP, Rev. Sir Ivor Cuthbert Proctor-,** 8th Bt, *cr* 1744; MA; MB, BCh; late Medical Missionary of the China Inland Mission; *b* 19 Aug. 1900; *s* of Rev. Sir Montagu Proctor-Beauchamp, 7th Bt and Florence (*d* 1955), *d* of Robert Barclay of Reigate; *S* father 1939; *m* 1933, Caroline Muriel (of the same Mission), *d* of Frank Densham, Stoneygate, Leicester; two *s* one *d*. *Educ:* Marlborough; King's Coll., Cambridge. *Heir:* *s* Christopher Radstock Proctor-Beauchamp [*b* 30 Jan. 1935; *m* 1965, Rosalind Emily Margot, 3rd *d* of G. P. Wainwright, St Leonards-on-Sea; one *s* one *d*. *Educ:* Rugby; Trinity College, Cambridge (MA)]. *Address:* 335 Springfield Road, Chelmsford, Essex. *T:* Chelmsford 58216.

**BEAUCHAMP, Sir Peter;** *see* Beauchamp, Sir D. C.

**BEAUCLERK,** family name of **Duke of St Albans.**

**BEAUFORT,** 10th Duke of, *cr* 1682; **Henry Hugh Arthur FitzRoy Somerset,** KG 1937; PC 1936; GCVO 1930; JP; Royal Victorian Chain, 1953; Baron Botetourt, 1305, confirmed, 1803; Baron Herbert of Raglan, Chepstow, and Gower, 1506; Earl of Worcester, 1514; Marquess of Worcester, 1642; late Royal Horse Guards; Master of the Horse since 1936; Lord Lieutenant of County of Gloucester and Bristol since 1931; Hon. Colonel of Royal Gloucestershire Hussars, TA, 1925-69, T&AVR since 1969; *b* 4 April 1900; *o s* of 9th Duke and Louise Emily (*d* 1945), *d* of William H. Harford of Oldown, Almondsbury, Glos, and *widow* of Baron Carlo de Tuyll; *S* father, 1924; *m* 1923, Lady Mary Cambridge, *er d* of 1st Marquess of Cambridge. *Educ:* Eton; Sandhurst. Chancellor, Univ. of Bristol, 1966-70. Received Freedom of City of Gloucester 1945. KStJ 1935. *Heir: cousin* David Robert Somerset [*b* 23 Feb. 1928; *m* 1950, Lady Caroline Jane Thynne, *o d* of 6th Marquess of Bath, *qv.*; three *s* one *d*]. *Address:* Badminton, Glos. *TA:* Badminton. *Club:* Turf.

*See also Sir Robert A. Sheffield.*

**BEAUMAN, Brigadier-General Archibald Bentley,** CBE 1937; DSO 1916; *e s* of Bentley Martin Beauman; *m* 1923, Eva Dorothy (*d* 1949), *d* of Albert E. Pullar Durn, Perth; one *d* (one *s* decd); *m* 1952, Barbara Arnold. *Educ:* Malvern Coll.; Sandhurst. Joined 2nd South Staffs. Regt, 1908; served South Africa and England prior to War; landed in France, Aug. 1914, with original Expeditionary Force; invalided home Nov. 1914; rejoined in France, Jan. 1915; served as Staff Capt., DAA and QMG, and acting Lieut-Col 1st battalion S Staffs. Regt; Brig.-Gen., 26 May 1918, and commanded 69th Infantry Brigade in Italy until 6 April 1919; Bt Lieut-Col Jan. 1919 (DSO and bar, Bt Major, despatches six times, Italian Silver Medal for Valour and Italian Croce di Guerra); Staff Coll., Camberley, 1920; Gen. Staff Officer, 2nd Grade, Baluchistan District, India, 1921-25; Chief Instructor RMA Woolwich, 1926-27; commanded 1st Battalion The York and Lancaster Regiment 1928-32; Asst Commandant, and Chief Instructor, Netheravon Wing, Small Arms School, 1932-34; Comdr 15th Infantry Bde 1934-38; ADC to the King, 1938; retired pay, 1938; commanded a Division, 1940 (despatches twice); Commander North Riding District, 1943; reverted to retired pay, 1944. Vice-Chm., Racehorse Owners' Assoc., 1959. *Publications:* Common Mistakes in the Solution of Tactical Problems; A Short Outline of Modern Tactics, 1939; Then a Soldier, 1960. *Recreations:* fishing, shooting, racing. *Address:* The Flat, Orwell, Walton-on-the-Hill, Surrey.

**BEAUMAN, Wing Commander Eric Bentley;** Librarian, Royal United Service Institution, 1952-57; *b* 7 Feb. 1891; *yr s* of late Bentley Martin Beauman; *m* 1940, Katharine Burgoyne, MA, *yr d* of late F. W. Jones; one *s*. *Educ:* Malvern Coll.; Geneva Univ.; Royal Aero Flying Certificate, 1913; served European war, 1914-18: commnd RNAS Aug. 1914; Anti-Submarine patrols, Home and Aegean; Home Defence and flying instruction: comd seaplane stations at Dundee and Newhaven (despatches). Major, RAF 1918; psa 1922-23; psc 1929-30; instructor at RAF Staff Coll., 1932-33; retd, 1938; Air Ministry, 1938-51. War of 1939-45; RAF liaison officer with BBC. Expeditions: Mount Kamet, 1931; Coast Range of British Columbia, 1934; climbed the Matterhorn 5 times. Pres. Alpine Ski Club, 1933-35; Hon. Librarian, Alpine Club, 1947-58. Vice-Pres. RAF Mountaineering Assoc. 1951-; Chm., Touring and Mountaineering Cttee of Ski Club of Gt Britain, 1952-54. Broadcasts on many occassions. *Publications:* compiled: Winged Words, 1941 (Book Soc. Choice); The Airmen Speak, 1941; (with Cecil Day Lewis) compiled: We Speak from the Air, 1942; Over to You, 1943; chapters in: Living Dangerously, 1936; Travellers' Tales, 1945; The Boys' Country Book, 1955. Contributor to The Times, The Field, The Listener, National Review, The Geographical Magazine, Dictionary of National Biography, Encyclopædia Britannica. *Recreations:* mountaineering, exploring, ski-ing, fishing. *Address:* 59 Chester Row SW1. *T:* 01-730 9038. *Clubs:* Alpine, Royal Air Force, Army and Navy, Society of Authors.

**BEAUMONT,** family name of **Viscount Allendale** and **Baron Beaumont of Whitley.**

**BEAUMONT,** Baroness, 11th in line, *cr* 1309; **Mona Josephine Tempest Fitzalan-Howard,** *née* **Stapleton;** OBE 1946; *b* Broughton Hall, Skipton, 1 Aug. 1894; *e d* of 10th Baron and late Ethel Mary, *d* of Sir Charles H. Tempest, 1st and last Bt of Heaton; *s* father, 1896; *m* 1914, 3rd Baron Howard of Glossop, *qv*; four *s* four *d*. Roman Catholic. *Heir:* *s* Maj.-Gen. Hon. Miles Francis Fitzalan-Howard, *qv*. *Address:* 23 Lennox Gardens, SW1. *T:* 01-589 2824; Carlton Towers, York.

*See also Maj.-Gen. Hon. Michael Fitzalan-Howard.*

**BEAUMONT OF WHITLEY,** Baron *cr* 1967 (Life Peer), of Child's Hill; **Rev. Timothy Wentworth Beaumont,** MA (Oxon); *b* 22 Nov.

1928; *o s* of Major and Hon. Mrs M. W. Beaumont; *m* 1955, Mary Rose Wauchope; two *s* two *d*. *Educ:* Gordonstoun; Christ Church, Oxford; Westcott House, Cambridge. Asst Chaplain, St John's Cathedral, Hong Kong, 1955-57; Vicar, Christ Church Kowloon Tong, Hong Kong, 1957-59; Hon. Curate, St Stephen's Rochester Row, London, 1960-63. Editor: Prism, 1960-63 and 1964; New Outlook, 1964; Chm., Studio Vista Books Ltd, 1963-68; Proprietor of New Christian, 1965-70. Liberal Party Organisation: Jt Hon. Treas., 1962-63; Chm., Liberal Publications Dept., 1963-64; Head of Org., 1965-66; Chm., Liberal Party's Org. Cttee, 1966; Chm., Liberal Party, 1967-68; Pres., Liberal Party, 1969-70; Liberal Spokesman on Educn, House of Lords. Chm., Albany Trust, 1969-. *Publication:* (ed) Modern Religious Verse, 1965. *Recreation:* collecting pictures. *Address:* 59 West Heath Road, NW3. *Clubs:* Buck's, Pratt's, National Liberal, Boodle's.

**BEAUMONT, Cyril William,** OBE 1962; FRSL; FRSA; bookseller, publisher, writer on Theatre and Dance, particularly the Classical Ballet; Hon. Fellow, Imperial Society of Teachers of Dancing (Chairman, 1958-70); Editor of Dance Journal since 1924; *b* 1 Nov. 1891; *e s* of Frederick John Beaumont (inventor, mechanical and electrical engineer) and Mary Henrietta Balchin; *m* 1914, Alice Mari Beha; no *c*. *Educ:* Stationers' Company's Sch.; privately. Antiquarian bookseller, 1910-65; in 1910 saw the dancing of Pavlova and Mordkin and developed interest in Ballet, intensified by visits to the Diaghilev Ballet in 1912; founded the Beaumont Press, 1917; codified Cecchetti's method of training in Classical Ballet for benefit of future dancers, 1918-22; Ballet Critic to Dancing World, 1921-24; Sunday Times, 1950-59; initiated foundation of Cecchetti Soc., 1922, which amalgamated with Imperial Soc. of Teachers of Dancing, 1924. Pres., Critics' Circle, 1957. Gold Medal, Inst. Historique et Héraldique de France, 1934; Officier d'Académie, 1934; Gold Medal, Renaissance Française, 1938; Chevalier de la Légion d'Honneur, 1950; Imperial Society's Imperial Award, 1961; Royal Academy of Dancing's Queen Elizabeth II Coronation Award, 1962; Kt Officer, Order of Merit (Italy), 1962. *Publications:* as Author: Impressions of the Russian Ballet, 12 parts, 1914-21; The Art of Lydia Lopokova, 1920; The Art of Lubov Tchernicheva, 1921; A Manual of the Theory and Practice of Classical Theatrical Dancing (with Stanislas Idzikowsky), 1922; The Mysterious Toyshop, 1924; A Burmese Pwe at Wembley, 1925; The Art of Stanislas Idzikowsky, 1926; The Strange Adventures of a Toy Soldier, 1926; The History of Harlequin, 1926; The First Score, an Account of the Beaumont Press, 1927; The Wonderful Journey, 1927; Sea Magic, 1928; Serge Lifar, 1928; Enrico Cecchetti, a Memoir, 1929; A Bibliography of Dancing, 1929; The Theory and Practice of Allegro in Classical Ballet (with Margaret Craske), 1930; Toys, 1930; A History of Ballet in Russia (1613-1881), 1930; Flash-back, 1931; A French-English Dictionary of Technical Terms used in Classical Ballet, 1931; Fanny Elssler, 1931; Anna Pavlova, 1932; Vaslav Nijinsky, 1932; A Short History of Ballet, 1933; Serge Diaghilev, 1933; A Miscellany for Dancers, 1934; Three French Dancers of the 18th Century, 1934; The Monte Carlo Russian Ballet, 1934; Three French Dancers of the 19th Century, 1935; Alicia Markova, 1935; The Vic-Wells Ballet, 1935; Michel Fokine and his Ballets, 1935; A Primer of Classical Ballet for Children, 1935; A Second Primer of Classical Ballet for Children, 1935; Design for the Ballet, 1937; The Complete Book of Ballets, 1937; The Romantic Ballet in Lithographs of the Time (with Sacheverell Sitwell), 1938; Puppets and the Puppet Stage, 1938; Five Centuries of Ballet Design, 1939; The Diaghilev Ballet in London, 1940; A Third Primer of Classical Ballet for Children, 1941; Supplement to the Complete Book of Ballets, 1942: The Ballet called Giselle, 1944; The Sadler's Wells Ballet, 1946; The Sleeping Beauty, 1946; Margot Fonteyn, 1948; Dancers under my Lens, 1949; The Swan Lake, 1949; The Ballet called Swan Lake, 1952; Antonio, 1952; Ballets of Today, 1954; Ballets Past and Present, 1955; Puppets and Puppetry, 1958; has translated and edited classic French and other works on the technique and history of the dance, etc. Contributions to specialist jls. *Recreations:* Research work in British Museum Library, reading, music, searching for material relative to the history of Ballet. *Address:* 68 Bedford Court Mansions, Bedford Avenue, WC1. *T:* 01-636 6487.

**BEAUMONT, George Ernest,** MA, DM (Oxon), FRCP; DPH London; Consulting Physician, Middlesex Hospital and Hospital for Consumption, Brompton; Physician, Royal Masonic Hospital, 1925-43; *b* 16 July 1888; *s* of late E. T. Beaumont, JP, Oxford; *m* 1917, Norah (*d* 1969), *y d* of late Philip Hamill; one *d*. *Educ:* Magdalen Coll. Sch., Oxford; University Coll., Oxford (scholar). 1st cl. Final Hon. Sch. of Physiology, Oxford, 1910; University scholar, Middlesex Hospital, 1910; Theodore Williams Pathology scholar, 1912; Temp. Capt. RAMC, 1914 (Mons Star); Radcliffe Travelling Fellow, 1916; Fellow of Royal College of Physicians, 1920; Fellow of the Royal Soc. of Medicine, 1925; Examiner in Medicine, University of Oxford; Censor, Royal College of Physicians, London, 1938-40. President, Section of Medicine: BMA, 1954; Royal Soc. of Medicine, 1955-57. *Publications:* Applied Medicine, 1950, reprinted 1950 and 1951; The Clinical Approach in Medical Practice, 1956; Medicine: Essentials for Practitioners and Students, 9th edn; Recent Advances in Medicine (jointly), 13th edn; A Pocket Medicine, 5th edn; Scientific and Clinical Medicine of Today, 1968; articles, Diseases of the Lungs; Price's Text-Book of Medicine (10th edn); Diseases of the Adrenals and Pituitary, Dictionary of Medicine; Haemoglobinuria, and Ascites, British Encyclopædia of Medical Practice; Bronchiectasis, Current Therapy, 1969; various articles in the medical journals. *Address:* 1 Hamilton Terrace, NW8. *T:* 01-286 6973.

**BEAUMONT, Sir George Howland Francis,** 12th Bt, *cr* 1661; late Lieutenant 60th Rifles; *b* 24 Sept. 1924; *s* of 11th Bt and Renée Muriel, 2nd *d* of late Maj.-Gen. Sir Edward Northey, GCMG, CB; *S* father 1933; *m* 1949, Barbara Singleton (marr. annulled, 1951); *m* 1963, Henrietta Anne, *d* of late Dr A. Waymouth and of Mrs J. Rodwell, Ladywell House, Speen, Berks; twin *d*. *Educ:* Stowe Sch. *Address:* Duntrune Nurseries, Deddington Mill, Deddington, Oxfordshire. *T:* Deddington 277. *Club:* Lansdowne.

**BEAUMONT, Herbert Christopher,** MBE 1948; Metropolitan Magistrate since 1962; *b* 3 June 1912; *s* of late Gerald Beaumont, MC, and Gwendolene Beaumont (*née* Haworth); *m* 1940, Helen Margaret Gordon Smail, *d* of William Mitchell Smail; one *s* two *d*. *Educ:* Uppingham Sch.; Worcester Coll., Oxford. Indian Civil and Political Services, 1936-48; Foreign Office, 1948-52. Called to the Bar, Inner Temple, 1951; Asst Recorder, Hull, 1960; Chm. of the London Juvenile Courts, 1964; Dep. Chm., North Riding QS, 1966.

*Recreations:* foreign travel and bridge. *Address:* 13 Kings Bench Walk, Temple, EC4. *T:* Central 5115; Minskip Lodge, Boroughbridge, Yorks. *T:* Boroughbridge 365. *Club:* Brooks's.

**BEAUMONT, Hugh;** Managing Director HM Tennent Ltd and of Tennent Productions Ltd; Director, London Pavilion; Governor, Shakespeare Memorial Theatre since 1950; Member, National Theatre Board, 1962-68; *b* 27 March 1908. *Educ:* privately. *Recreation:* gardening. *Address:* 14 Lord North Street, SW1. *T:* 01-222 5216. *Club:* Crockford's.

**BEAUMONT, James Buchan;** Under-Secretary, Scottish Development Department, since 1968; *b* 29 Sept. 1925; *s* of late James Beaumont and Jessie Bruce, Edinburgh; *m* 1952, Irene Alexandria Dow; one *s* one *d.* *Educ:* Royal High Sch., Edinburgh; Glasgow Univ.; Edinburgh Univ. Asst Lecturer Glasgow Univ., 1949; Scottish Education Dept, 1950; Under-Sec., Scottish Development Dept, 1968. *Recreations:* golf, music. *Address:* 183 Craigcrook Road, Edinburgh 4. *T:* 031-336 3237.

**BEAUMONT, Rt. Hon. Sir John William Fisher,** PC 1944; Kt 1931; QC 1930; a Member of the Judicial Committee of the Privy Council since 1944; *b* 4 Sept. 1877; *s* of late Edward Beaumont of the Chancery Bar and Elizabeth Helen Beaumont; *m* 1904, Mabel Edith (*d* 1958), *d* of late William Wallace; one *s* decd. *Educ:* Winchester Coll.; Pembroke Coll., Cambridge; 1st Cl. History Tripos, 1899; Hon. Fellow of Pembroke Coll., 1946; Called to Bar, Lincoln's Inn, 1901; practised at Chancery Bar; Lieut RGA, 1916-19; Chief Justice of Bombay, 1930-43; acting Judge of Federal Court of India, 1942-43; Bencher of Lincoln's Inn, 1943 (Treasurer 1963). Master Cutlers' Co., 1951-52. *Address:* 52 Dorset House, Gloucester Place, NW1. *Clubs:* Athenæum, Alpine.

**BEAUMONT, Hon. Ralph Edward Blackett,** CBE 1967; TD; JP; Vice-Lieutenant of Montgomeryshire since 1962; *b* 12 Feb. 1901; 2nd *s* of 1st Viscount Allendale; *m* 1926, Helena Mary Christine (*d* 1962), *yr d* of late Brig.-Gen. Cecil Wray, CB, CMG, CVO; two *s* one *d.* *Educ:* Eton; Christ Church, Oxford (MA). MP (U) Portsmouth Central, 1931-45; Parliamentary Private Sec.: To Postmaster-Gen., 1935-40; To Sec. of State for War, 1942-45; Chm. of Montgomeryshire County Agricultural Executive Cttee, 1948-69. Lieut-Col 636 Lt AA Regt RA (RWF) TA, 1947-51. A Development Commissioner, 1952-69. Member: Council on Tribunals, 1958-; Welsh Economic Council, 1965-68; Welsh Council, 1968; Council of Management, Council for Small Industries in Rural Areas. JP 1932, High Sheriff, 1957, DL 1961, Montgomeryshire. *Recreations:* shooting, fishing, gardening. *Address:* Plas Llwyngwern, Machynlleth, Montgomeryshire. *T:* Machynlleth 2355. *Club:* Carlton.

**BEAUMONT, Sir Richard Ashton,** KCMG 1965 (CMG 1955); OBE 1949; Ambassador to the United Arab Republic, since 1969; *b* 29 Dec. 1912; *s* of A. R. Beaumont, FRCS, Uppingham, and Evelyn Frances (*née* Rendle); *m* 1942, Alou, *d* of M. Camran, Istanbul; one *d.* *Educ:* Repton; Oriel Coll., Oxford. Joined HM Consular Service, 1936; posted Beirut, 1936; Damascus, 1938. Served War, 1941-44. Foreign Office, 1945; Mosul, 1946; Jerusalem, 1948; Foreign Office, 1949; Caracas, Venezuela, 1950; Baghdad, 1953; Imperial Defence Coll., 1958; Head of Arabian Department, Foreign Office, 1959; Ambassador: to Morocco, 1961-65; to Iraq, 1965-67; Dep. Under-Sec. of State, FO, 1967-69. *Recreations:* riding, shooting, golf. *Address:* c/o Foreign and Commonwealth Office, SW1; 25 Tite Street, SW3. *Club:* Oxford and Cambridge University.

**BEAUMONT-NESBITT, Maj.-Gen. Frederick George,** CVO 1938; CBE 1945; MC; retired; *b* 26 March 1893; *s* of late E. J. Beaumont-Nesbitt, JP, Lord Lieutenant of King's Co. and late of Tubberdaly, Edenderry, King's Co., and Helen Thomas, *sister* of 1st Marquis of Willingdon; *m* 1st, Lavinia (*d* 1920), *d* of Maj.-Gen. Hon. Sir C. Bingham, GCVO, KCMG, CB; one *d* (and one *s* decd); 2nd, 1928, Hon. Ruby Hardinge, *d* of 3rd Visc. Hardinge; two *s* one *d.* *Educ:* Eton Coll.; RMC Sandhurst. Joined Grenadier Guards 1912; served European War; Commanding 2nd Bn Grenadier Guards, 1932-35; Military Attaché, Paris, 1936-38; Dep. Dir Military Intelligence, 1938-39; Dir of Military Intelligence, War Office, 1939-40; Military Attaché, Washington, 1941; Maj.-Gen., Gen. Staff, 1941-45; ADC to King George VI 1944-45; retd pay, 1945. Gentleman Usher to the Queen, 1959-67; Extra Gentleman Usher, 1967. *Address:* 53 Melton Court, SW7. *Club:* Turf.

*See also Maj.-Gen. J. E. Cordingley.*

**BEAUREPAIRE, Ian Francis,** CMG 1967; Chairman and Managing Director, Olympic Consolidated Industries Ltd, since 1959; *b* 14 Sept. 1922; *s* of late Sir Frank and Lady Beaurepaire; *m* 1946, Beryl Edith Bedggood; two *s.* *Educ:* Carey Grammar Sch., Scotch Coll., Melbourne; Royal Melbourne Inst. of Technology. Served RAAF (Flying Officer), 1942-44. Man. Dir, Beaurepaire Tyre Service Pty Ltd, 1953-55; Gen. Man., The Olympic Tyre & Rubber Co. Pty Ltd, 1955-61; Member, Melbourne City Council, 1956- (Lord Mayor of Melbourne, 1965-67); Adv. Cttee to Dept of Management, Royal Melbourne Inst. of Technology, 1966-; Management Cttee of Royal Victorian Eye and Ear Hosp., 1966-; Exhibition Trustees, 1967-; Chm., Rubber Industry Adv. Cttee, 1965-. *Recreations:* golf, fishing, sailing. *Address:* PO Box 1, West Footscray, Victoria 3012, Australia. *Clubs:* Athenæum, Kelvin, Naval and Military, Melbourne (Melbourne); Peninsula Country Golf (Frankston).

**BEAUVOIR, Simone de;** French author; *b* Paris, 9 Jan. 1908. *Educ:* Univ. of Paris. Taught, 1931-43. Prix Goncourt, France, 1954. *Publications:* L'Invitée, 1943 (trans. She Came to Stay, 1949); Pyrrhus et Cinéas (essay), 1944; Le Sang des autres, 1944 (trans. The Blood of Others, 1948); Les Bouches Inutiles (play), 1945; Tous les hommes sont mortels, 1947; Pour une morale de l'ambiguité (essay), 1947; L'Amérique au jour le jour, 1948 (trans. America Day by Day, 1952); L'Existentialisme et la sagesse des nations (essay), 1948; Le Deuxième Sexe, 1949: vol. I, Les Faits et les myths; vol. II, L'Expérience vécue; Faut-il Brûler Sade?, 1951 (trans. Must We Burn Sade?, 1963); Les Mandarins, 1954 (Prix Goncourt; trans. The Mandarins, 1957); Privilèges (essay), 1955; La Longue marche (essay on China), 1957 (trans. The Long March, 1958); Mémoires d'une jeune fille rangée, 1958 (trans. The Memoirs of a Dutiful Daughter, 1959); La Force de L'âge, 1960 (trans. The Prime of Life, 1963); Brigitte Bardot, 1960; (with G. Halimi) Djamila Boupacha, 1963; La Force des choses, 1963 (trans. Force of Circumstance, 1965); Une mort très douce, 1964 (trans. A Very Easy Death, 1966); Les Belles Images, 1966; La Femme Rompue, 1968 (trans. The Woman

Destroyed, 1969); La Vieillesse, 1970. *Address:* 11 bis rue Schoelcher, Paris 14e, France.

**BEAVAN,** family name of **Baron Ardwick.**

**BEAVERBROOK,** Barony of (*cr* 1917, of Beaverbrook, New Brunswick and Cherkley, Surrey); title disclaimed by 2nd Baron; *see under* Aitken, Sir (John William) Max, 2nd Bt.

**BEAVIS, David;** Chairman, West Midlands Gas Board, since 1968; *b* 12 Dec. 1913; *s* of David Beavis; *m* 1946, Vera, *d* of F. C. Todd; one *s* one *d*. *Educ:* Whitehill Secondary Sch.; Royal Technical Coll., Glasgow (now Strathclyde Univ.). Dep. Engineer and Manager, Helensburgh Town Council Gas Dept, 1935-41; Asst Engineer, Camb. Univ. and Town Gas Light Co., 1942-47; Dep. Engineer and Manager, Edin. Corp. Gas Dept, 1947-49; Divisional Gen. Man. Edin. and SE Div., and subseq. Area Manager, Scottish Gas Bd, 1949-64; Mem. Scottish Gas Bd, 1962-64; Dep. Chm., Eastern Gas Bd, 1964-68. Member: Gas Industry Training Bd; Bd, Council of Engineering Instns; W Midlands Economic Planning Council. *Publications:* technical papers presented to Engineering Instns. *Recreations:* technological education, golf. *Address:* 1 Sandal Rise, Solihull, Warwickshire. *T:* 021-705 0455. *Club:* Anglo-Belgian.

**BEAVIS, Maj.-Gen. Leslie Ellis,** CB 1952; CBE 1942; DSO 1918; Australian Staff Corps; *b* 1895; *s* of late H. C. Beavis, Bathurst, New South Wales; *m* Ethel, *d* of L. Blumer, Hunter's Hill, NSW; one *s* one *d*. Served European War, 1915-18 (despatches twice, DSO); psc, pac; War of 1939-45, DOS, AIF, Middle East, 1940-42 (CBE); Master General of the Ordnance HQ, AMF, 1942-46; Defence Dept, 1946-52; High Commissioner for Australia in Pakistan, 1952-54. *Address:* Rothesay, 131 Warrandyte Road, Ringwood, Melbourne, Victoria. *T:* Melbourne 870-6282. *Club:* Naval and Military (Melbourne).

**BEBBINGTON, Bernard Nicolas,** CBE 1969 (OBE 1955); Adviser to Home Office Community Development Project, since 1970; *b* 23 Nov. 1910; *yr s* of Canon John Henry and Mabel Edith Bebbington; *m* 1936, Daphne Frizelle Drury; two *s*. *Educ:* Sutton Valence Sch.; Jesus Coll., Cambridge. Joined Metropolitan Police, 1932; attended Hendon Police Coll., 1935-36; apptd Chief Constable of Cambridge, 1944; Sec. of Assoc. of Chief Police Officers, 1961-63; HM Inspector of Constabulary, 1963-70; Dir, Home Office Police Research and Develt Branch, 1965-69; Home Office Adviser on Police Management Services, 1969-70; retd, 1970. Hon. MA Cantab 1963. OStJ 1959; Queen's Police Medal, 1962. *Publications:* articles and broadcasts on Police. Several children's books including The Policeman, 1952. *Recreations:* painting, writing. *Address:* Shornbrook, Steel Cross, Crowborough, Sussex. *Club:* Pitt (Cambridge).

**BECH, Joseph;** Grande Croix, Ordre de la Couronne de Chêne (Luxembourg); Président d'Honneur de la Chambre des Députés du Luxembourg (Président, 1959-64); Ministre d'état honoraire; *b* 17 Feb. 1887; *m* 1918, Georgette Delahaye; one *s* one *d*. *Educ:* Universities of Fribourg and Paris. Mem. (PSC) Chamber of Deputies, 1914; Minister Interior and Education, 1921-25; Minister of State, President of the Government and Minister of Foreign Affairs, 1926-37; leading Luxembourg Delegate to League of Nations, 1926-39; Vice-Pres., League of Nations, 1929; Chief of Luxembourg Deleg. to San Francisco Conf., 1945; Pres., Political and General Affairs Cttee, UNO, 1946; Minister of Foreign Affairs, 1926-58 (Minister of State, President of the Government, 1954-57). Dr (*hc*) University Louvain, 1954. Knight Grand Cross British Empire (Hon. GBE 1959); Grand' Croix de la Légion d'Honneur, Grand' Croix Ordre de Léopold (Belgium), Grand Cross, Order of Netherlands Lion, etc. *Publication:* Statut International du Luxembourg. *Address:* 34 Avenue Monterey, Luxembourg. *T:* 242-24.

**BECHER, Rear-Adm. Otto Humphrey,** CBE 1961; DSO 1950; DSC 1940, and Bar, 1944; retd; Director-General of Recruiting; *b* 13 Sept. 1908; *m* 1935, Valerie Chisholm Baird; three *s*. *Educ:* Harvey State Sch.; RAN Coll. Served War of 1939-45 (DSC and Bar): in Norwegian waters, Atlantic, Mediterranean, Indian and Pacific Oceans. Capt. of HMAS: Quickmatch, 1944-45; Warramunga, 1950-51; Vengeance, 1954-55; idc 1956; Capt. of HMAS Melbourne, 1957-58; Deputy Chief of Naval Staff, Australia, 1959-61; Head of Australian Joint Services Staff, London, 1962-63; Flag Officer Comdg Australian Fleet, 1964; Flag Officer in Charge, East Australian Area, 1965. Officer, Legion of Merit (USA), 1950. *Recreations:* gardening, golf, tennis. *Clubs:* Naval and Military (Melbourne); Australian (Sydney).

**BECHER, Major Sir William Fane Wrixon-,** 5th Bt, *cr* 1831; MC 1943; Temp. Major, Rifle Brigade (SRO); *b* 7 Sept. 1915; *o s* of Sir Eustace W. W. W. Becher, 4th Bt, and Hon. Constance Gough-Calthorpe, *d* of 6th Baron Calthorpe; *S* father, 1934; *m* 1st, 1946, Vanda (marriage dissolved, 1960; she *m* 1962, Rear-Adm. Viscount Kelburn, now 9th Earl of Glasgow, *qv*), *d* of 4th Baron Vivian; one *s* one *d*; 2nd, 1960, Hon. Mrs Yvonne Mostyn. *Educ:* Harrow; Magdalene Coll., Cambridge. Served War of 1939-45, Western Desert and Tunisian Campaigns, 1940-43 (MC, wounded twice); Italian Campaign, 1944. *Recreations:* golf and cricket. *Heir:* *s* John William Michael Wrixon-Becher, *b* 29 Sept. 1950. *Address:* 16 Wilton Place, SW1. *Clubs:* MCC, White's.

**BECK, Prof. Arnold Hugh William,** BSc (Eng.), MA; Professor of Engineering, University of Cambridge, since 1966; Fellow of Corpus Christi College, Cambridge, since 1962; *y s* of Major Hugh Beck and Diana L. Beck; *m* 1947, Katharine Monica, *y d* of S. K. Ratcliffe; no *c*. *Educ:* Gresham's Sch., Holt; University Coll., London. Research Engr, Henry Hughes & Sons, 1937-41; seconded to Admty Signal Estab., 1941-45; Standard Telephones & Cables, 1947-58; Lectr, Cambridge Univ., 1958-64; Reader in Electrical Engrg, 1964-66. FIEEE 1959. *Publications:* Velocity Modulated Thermionic Tubes, 1948; Thermionic Valves, 1953; Space-charge Waves, 1958; Words and Waves, 1967; (with H. Ahmed) Introduction to Physical Electonics, 1968; Handbook of Vacuum Physics, Vol. 2, Parts 5 and 6, 1968. papers in Jl IEE, Inst. Radio Engrs, etc. *Address:* 12 Rutherford Road, Cambridge. *T:* Trumpington 3324.

**BECK, Edgar Charles,** CBE 1967; Chairman: John Mowlem & Company Ltd; SGB Group Ltd; *b* 11 May 1911; *s* of Edgar Bee Beck and Nellie Stollard Beck (*née* Osborne); *m* 1933, Mary Agnes Sorapure; three *s* two *d*. *Educ:* Lancing Coll.; Jesus Coll., Cambridge (MA). Joined John Mowlem & Co. Ltd as Engineer, 1933: Dir 1940; Man. Dir 1958; Chm. 1961. Scaffolding Great Britain Ltd: Dir 1942; Chm. 1958, Dir, Building & Civil Engineering Holidays Scheme Management Ltd, 1959-; Dir, Builders' Accident Insce Ltd, 1959, Dep. Chm., 1969; Mem., ECGD Adv. Coun., 1964-

69; Chairman: Fedn of Civil Engrg Contractors, 1958-59; Export Gp for the Constructional Industries, 1959-63; Brit. Hosps, Export Council, 1964. pres., Builders' Clerks' Benevolent Instn, 1966; Fellow of Building Centre, 1957-; Under-writing Mem. of Lloyd's, 1955-. FICE. *Recreations:* golf, salmon fishing. *Address:* 13 Eaton Place, SW1. *T:* 01-235 7455. *Clubs:* Bath, East India and Sports; Royal and Ancient Golf (St Andrews); Swinley Forest Golf, Berkshire Golf.

**BECK, Maj.-Gen. Edward Archibald,** CB 1938; DSO 1916; *b* 16 March 1880; *o s* of Col. C. E. Beck; *m* 1912, Mary, *o d* of late Rt Rev. H. R. Wakefield, late Bishop of Birmingham; two *d*. *Educ:* Wellington; Sandhurst. Joined RS Fusiliers, 1900; served S Africa with 2nd Bn and with 12th Bn Mounted Infantry (Queen's Medal 3 clasps, King's Medal 2 clasps); with Egyptian Army, 1909-12; Capt., 1910; Major, 1915; served European War, 1914-18, (despatches, 6 times, DSO Brevet Lieut-Col); Lieut-Col King's Own Yorkshire Light Infantry, 1929; Col, 1923; Chief Instructor, Small Arms Sch., Hythe, 1925-29; Operations NW Frontier, India, 1930-31; Instructor, Senior Officers' Sch., Sheerness, 1932-33; Gen. Staff Officer, 1st Grade, Scottish Command, 1933-34; Commander 2nd Infantry Brig. Aldershot, 1935-36; ADC to the King, 1935-36; Maj.-Gen., 1936; Dir of Personal Services, War Office, 1938-40; Comdr 9th (High.) Div., 1940; retd pay, 1940. Comdr Perthshire Home Guard, 1940-45; Country Comdt Perthshire Cadets, 1943-50; Hon. Col 4/5th Bn Royal Scots Fusiliers, 1942-49. Order of SS Maurice and Lazarus (Italy), 1918; Croix de Guerre (France), 1918; Croix de Guerre (Belgium), 1918. *Recreations:* shooting, fishing. *Club:* Army and Navy.

*See also Sir Robert H. Bruce Lockhart.*

**BECK, Most Rev. George Andrew;** *see* Liverpool, Archbishop of, (RC).

**BECK, John Melliar Adams;** Clerk and Solicitor of the Worshipful Company of Ironmongers since 1946; *b* 9 April 1909; *s* of late James Francis Adams Beck and Elsie (*née* Foster-Melliar); *m* 1st, 1939, Doris Elsie Neep (*d* 1966); two *s*; 2nd, 1968, Mrs Mary Elizabeth Helen Coates, *widow* of Captain Patrick Coates and *e d* of Comdr Sir John Best-Shaw, *qv*. *Educ:* Shrewsbury Sch. Admitted Solicitor, 1932, Consultant with firm of Solicitors. Served War of 1939-45; joined Hon. Artillery Co., 1939; commissioned RA, 1940; India and Ceylon, 1942; demobilised with rank of Major 1945. Governor of the City and Diocese of London Voluntary Schs Fund, 1947; Trustee, City and Metropolitan Welfare Charity, 1968. *Recreations:* shooting, golf. *Address:* Kells, Maltman's Hill, Smarden, Kent. *T:* Smarden 257; Ironmongers Hall, Shaftesbury Place, Aldersgate, EC2. *T:* 01-606 2725.

**BECK, (Richard) Theodore,** FRIBA, FSA, AMTPI; architect; *b* 11 March 1905; *s* of Alfred Charles Beck and Grace Sophia Beck (*née* Reading); *m* 1950, Margaret Beryl Page; one *s* one *d*. *Educ:* Haileybury; Architectural Association Sch. Past Mem. Council, Royal Archaeological Inst.; Past Master of Broderers Company; Master, Barber-Surgeons Company; Mem. Court of Common Council, Corporation of London; Sheriff, City of London, 1969-70. *Recreations:* golf, archaeology. *Address:* Great House, Hambledon, Godalming, Surrey. *T:* Wormley 2662. *Club:* East India and Sports.

**BECK, Theodore;** *see* Beck, R. T.

**BECKE, Mrs Shirley Cameron;** Woman Commander, Metropolitan Police, since 1969; *b* 29 April 1917; *er d* of late George L. Jennings, AMIGasE and Marion Jennings; *m* 1954, Rev. Justice Becke, MBE, TD, FCA; no *c*. *Educ:* privately; Ealing Co. Gram. Sch. Trained in Gas Engineering, 1935-40. Joined Metropolitan Police as Constable, 1941; served in various ranks; now in charge of Women Police. *Recreations:* philately, reading, keeping cats. *Address:* 12 Frewin Road, SW18. *T:* 01-874 9053.

**BECKE, Lt-Col William Hugh Adamson,** CMG 1964; DSO 1945; Private Secretary/Comptroller to the Governor of Victoria, Melbourne; *b* 24 Sept. 1916; *er s* of late Brig.-Gen. J. H. W. Becke, CMG, DSO, AFC, and late Mrs A. P. Becke (*née* Adamson); *m* 1945, Mary Catherine, 3rd *d* of late Major G. M. Richmond, Kincairney, Murthly, Perthshire. *Educ:* Chaterhouse; RMC Sandhurst. Commissioned in The Sherwood Foresters, 1937. British Military Mission to Greece, 1949-52; Asst Military Adviser to the High Commissioner for the UK in Pakistan, 1957-59; Military Attaché, Djakarta, 1962-64; retd 1966. *Recreation:* shooting. *Address:* Priestoun, Edzell, Angus, Scotland. *Clubs:* Army and Navy, MCC.

**BECKER, Sir Ellerton;** *see* Becker, Sir J. E.

**BECKER, Harry (Thomas Alfred);** Publishers' Representative for: Gondolier; Electrical Construction Design; Test Engineering; Buyers Purchasing Digest; Society of Plastic Engineers, SPE Journal; Midwest Electrical News; Master Plumber & Heating Contractor; Heating and Plumbing Merchandiser; The Sciences; Medical Research Engineering; *b* Wandsworth, 16 June 1892; *e s* of late Sir Frederick Becker; *m* 1st, 1912; one *d*; 2nd, 1926; one *s* one *d*; 3rd, 1939 (marriage dissolved, Reno, Nevada, USA, 1952), *d* of John Henry and Elizabeth Newman; one *d*; 4th, 1952, in USA, Mary Beth, *d* of Clyde and Mae Browder, Tenn, USA. *Educ:* Colet Court; Uppingham; Bristol Univ. Served European War, 1914-18; was invalided from the Service through wounds; retd with rank of 2nd Lieut Suffolk Regt, 1918 (medals, 1914-15 Star, etc.); many years spent in newspaper production in Fleet Street; MP Richmond (Ind) 1922-23, (Ind C) 1923-24; contested W Bermondsey, 1918, as ex-Servicemen's candidate. *Recreations:* swimming, cricket. *Address:* 68b Broad Street, Charleston, SC 29401, USA.

**BECKER, Sir (Jack) Ellerton,** Kt 1962; FAA; pastoralist; Chairman of Directors of private pastoral companies since 1929; *b* 4 Oct. 1904; *s* of Percy Harold and Mabel Martha Becker, Adelaide, S Australia; *m* 1928, Gladys Sarah, *d* of Percival John and Mary Elizabeth Duggan, Adelaide, S Australia. *Educ:* Unley High Sch.; Adelaide Sch. of Technology and Univ. Manufacturing jeweller, 1920; commenced teaching music, 1926. Founded Adelaide Coll. of Music and, as Principal, built it up; three world tours; organised Music League of S Australia and directed for charity, theatrical productions. Retired from music 1943, to farm scientifically in S Australia. FAA, 1961 (only the seventh Australian non-scientist ever elected) between Sir R. Menzies, 1958 and Lord Casey, 1966; Academy Building Auditorium named Becker Hall in 1962. Mem. Council of Australian Academy of Science, 1965-68. Acquired important stud cattle and sheep properties, Hereford, England, and NSW, Australia, 1962 and 1964. *Recreations:* overseas travel, antique collecting. *Address:* Winslow Gardens, Darling Point Road,

Darling Point, Sydney, NSW. *T:* 32-2368. *Clubs:* Royal Sydney Yacht Squadron (Sydney); Stock Exchange (Adelaide).

**BECKERMAN, Prof. Wilfred;** Professor of Political Economy, University of London, since 1969; Head of Department of Political Economy, University College London, since 1969; Member, Royal Commission on Environmental Pollution, since 1970; *b* 19 May 1925; *s* of Morris and Mathilda Beckerman; *m* 1952, Nicole Geneviève Ritter; one *s* two *d*. *Educ:* Ealing County Sch.; Trinity Coll., Cambridge. RNVR, 1943-46. Trinity Coll., Cambridge, 1946-50; Lecturer in Economics, Univ. of Nottingham, 1950-52; OEEC and OECD, Paris, 1952-61; National Inst. of Economic and Social Research, 1962-63. Fellow of Balliol Coll., Oxford, 1964-69; The Economic Adviser to the Board of Trade (leave of absence from Balliol), 1967-69. *Publications:* (with Associates) The British Economy in 1975, 1965; International Comparisons of Real Incomes, 1966; An Introduction to National Income Analysis, 1968. Articles in Economic Jl, Economica, Econometrica, Review of Economic Studies, Review of Economics and Statistics, etc. *Recreations:* swimming, tennis. *Address:* 12 Chadlington Road, Oxford. *T:* Oxford 54384. *Club:* Reform.

**BECKETT,** family name of **Baron Grimthorpe.**

**BECKETT, Prof. Arnold Heyworth;** Professor of Pharmaceutical Chemistry and Head, Dept of Pharmacy, Chelsea College (University of London); *b* 12 Feb. 1920; *m* 1942, Miriam Eunice Webster; one *s* one *d*. *Educ:* Baines Grammar Sch., Poulton-le-Fylde; Sch. of Pharmacy and Birkbeck Coll., University of London, FPS 1942; BSc 1947; PhD 1950; DSc London, 1959. Prof. of Pharmaceutical Chemistry and Head, Dept of Pharmacy, Chelsea Coll. of Sci. and Technology, 1959-. Member: Council, Pharmaceutical Soc. of Gt Brit., 1965- (Chm. Educn Cttee); Steering Cttee of Scientific Sect., Fédération Internat. Pharmaceutique, 1960-; Standing Jt Cttee on Classification of Proprietary Preparations, 1964-; Olympic Games Medical Commn, 1968. Vis. Prof. to Univs, USA and Canada. Examr in Pharmaceut. Chem., Univs in UK, Nigeria, Ghana, Singapore, and for Pharmaceut. Soc. of Gt Brit. Pereira Medal, 1942; STAS Medal, Belg. Chem. Soc., 1962. *Publications:* (co-author) Practical Pharmaceutical Chemistry, 1962; founder Co-editor, Jl of Medicinal Chemistry; research contribs to jls. *Recreations:* travel, sport, photography. *Address:* 5 Blyth Road, Bromley, Kent. *T:* 01-460 0231.

**BECKETT, Bruce Probart,** FRIBA; Chief Architect, Scottish Development Department, since 1967; *b* 7 June 1924; *s* of J. D. L. Beckett and Florence Theresa (*née* Probart); *m* 1957, Jean McDonald; two *s* three *d*. *Educ:* Rondebosch Boys' High Sch., Cape Town; Univ. of Cape Town (BArch with distinction, 1950); University Coll. London (Diploma in Town Planning, 1963). Active Service SA Navy, 1943; Midshipman, 1943; Sub-Lieut, 1944; seconded RN, 1944; Lieut, 1946. ARIBA 1950, FRIBA 1968; FRIAS 1968. Mem. Inst. S African Architects, 1950; AMTPI 1966. Private practice in S Africa, 1952-59, London, 1960. Sen. Architect, War Office, 1961; Superintending Grade Arch., Directorate-Gen. of Res. and Development, 1963-67. Dep. Leader, Timber Trade Mission to Canada, 1964. *Publications:* papers on industrialised building, contract procedure, etc, in various jls. *Recreations:* sailing, golf, walking. *Address:* 71 Ravelston Dykes Road, Edinburgh EH4 3NU. *T:* 031-337 7301. *Clubs:* New (Edinburgh); Western Province Sports (Kelvin Grove, Cape Town).

**BECKETT, Maj.-Gen. Clifford Thomason,** CB 1945; CBE 1943; MC; Chevalier Légion d'Honneur, 1951; *b* 9 Nov. 1891; *e s* of late Brig.-Gen. W. T. C. Beckett, CBE, DSO; *m* Winifred Mary Ackerley (*d* 1960), *d* of late C. A. W. Chichester; one *s* two *d*. *Educ:* Tonbridge; RMA, Woolwich. 2nd Lieut RA 1911; served European War, 1914-18, Gallipoli, France, Salonika, Palestine (wounded MC); Iraq Rebellion, 1919-21; Persia, Egypt, Turkey, 1922; Staff Capt., War Office, 1926-30. Special Award War Office Cttee on Awards to Inventors, 1929; Major, 1928; travelled in Afghanistan and Australia. Employed on Strategic Reconnaissances in Western Europe, 1929, 1931; served in Lahore, 1935-36 (suppressed riots; organised Military Jubilee Tattoo). Gold Staff Officer at Coronation 1937; served frequently with French Army and in 1937 with German Army; Lieut-Col, 1938; Comd 12th Field Regt, RA, 1938-39, 1st Survey Regt, RA, 1939-40; CRA 15th Scottish Div., 1940-41; Flanders campaign, 1939-40 (despatches); Col, 1941; commanded the Artillery of the Fortress of Malta, 1941-43; Acting GOC Troops, Malta, July-Aug. 1942; Maj.-Gen. RA 1942; commanded 4th and 5th AA Groups, 1943-46; retired pay with hon. rank of Maj.-Gen., 1946; DL for Somerset, 1952-67. Hon. Fellow and Pres. Emeritus, Huguenot Soc. of London (Pres. 1949-52 and subseq., a Vice-Pres.). Dir, French Hospital of La Providence; Pres. SSAFA, Somerset, 1949-58; Executive Cttee, Squash Rackets Assocn, 1928-31. Judged at Rhône and Delhi Horse Shows. Hereditary Keeper, Inchgaw Castle, Fife. *Publications:* The Yeomanry of Devon (with Comdr W. Benson Freeman); numerous contributions to military jls and Jl of Huguenot Soc. of London. *Recreations:* the study of history, travel; formerly: rackets, squash rackets, polo, hunting, fencing, fishing. *Address:* 36 Belvedere Court, Upper Richmond Road, Putney, SW15. *Clubs:* Athenæum, Army and Navy; Jesters.

**BECKETT, Maj.-Gen. Denis Arthur,** DSO 1944; OBE 1960; Director of Personal Services (Army), since 1968; *b* 19 May 1917; *o s* of Archibald Beckett, Woodford Green, Essex; *m* 1946, Elizabeth, *er d* of late Col Guy Edwards, Upper Slaughter, Glos; one *s*. *Educ:* Forest Sch.; Chard Sch. Joined Hon. Artillery Co., 1939; commnd into Essex Regt, 1940; served in W. Africa, Middle East, Italy and Greece, 1940-45; DAA & QMG and Bde Major, Parachute Bdes, 1948-50; Instructor, RMA Sandhurst, 1951-53; Staff Coll., Camberley, 1953-56; Second in Comd 3rd Bn Para. Regt, 1956-58; comd 2nd Bn Para. Regt, 1958-60; jssc 1960-61; comd 19 Bde, 1961-63; idc 1964; DAG, BAOR, 1965-66; Chief of Staff, Far East Land Forces, 1966-68. *Address:* Shipton Lodge, Shipton-under-Wychwood, Oxon. *T:* Shipton-under-Wychwood, 473. *Club:* Army and Navy.

**BECKETT, Sir Eric (Frederick),** Kt 1964; CBE 1956, FRCVS; *b* Nov. 1895; *s* of late F. L. and Jane Louise Beckett; *m* 1932, Margaret Patricia, *d* of late John J. Jones, The Teak House, Bournemouth; no *c*. *Educ:* Liverpool Coll.; Liverpool Univ. MRCVS 1924. Served European War, 1914-18: BEF, RFA, France, 1915-18 (wounded). Chm. of the North Dorset Conservative Assoc., 1947-67. MFH The Portman Hounds, 1944 (Master or Joint Master for 12 seasons). *Recreations:* foxhunting, shooting. *Address:* Berkeley

Lodge, Blandford, Dorset. *T:* Blandford 2494. *Club:* British Legion (Blandford).

**BECKETT, Prof. James Camlin,** MA; Professor of Irish History, Queen's University of Belfast, since 1958; *b* 8 Feb. 1912; 3rd *s* of Alfred Beckett and Frances Lucy Bushell. *Educ:* Royal Belfast Academical Instn; Queen's Univ., Belfast. History Master, Belfast Royal Academy, 1934; Lectr in Modern History, Queen's Univ., Belfast, 1945, Reader in Modern History, 1952. Fellow Commoner, Peterhouse, Cambridge, 1955-56; Member: Irish Manuscripts Commn, 1959; Royal Commission on Historical Manuscripts, 1960; FRHistS; MRIA. *Publications:* Protestant Dissent in Ireland, 1687-1780, 1948; Short History of Ireland, 1952; (Ed., with T. W. Moody) Ulster since 1800: a Political and Economic Survey, 1954; (Ed., with T. W. Moody) Ulster since 1800: a Social Survey, 1957; (with T. W. Moody) Queen's Belfast, 1845-1949, 1959; The Making of Modern Ireland 1603-1923, 1966; (Ed., with R. E. Glasscock) Belfast: the Origin and Growth of an Industrial City, 1966; articles, reviews, etc., in English Hist. Rev., History, Irish Hist. Studies and other jls. *Recreations:* chess, walking. *Address:* 19 Wellington Park Terrace, Belfast 9, N Ireland. *Club:* Ulster (Belfast).

**BECKETT, John Angus,** CB 1965; CMG 1956; MA; Under Secretary, Petroleum Division, Ministry of Technology (formerly Ministry of Power), since 1963; *b* 6 July 1909; *s* of late John Beckett, BA; *m* 1935, Una Joan, *yr d* of late George Henry Wright; one *s* two *d*. *Educ:* privately; Sidney Sussex Coll., Cambridge. BA 2nd Cl. Hons (Geog. Tripos); Mem., Cambridge Iceland Expedition, 1932. Schoolmaster, 1933-40; entered Civil Service, 1940; Principal Private Sec. to Minister of Fuel and Power, 1946-47; Asst Sec., Min. of Fuel and Power, 1947-59; Chm., Petroleum Cttee of OEEC, 1948-50 and 1955-59; Petroleum Attaché, British Embassy, Washington, 1950-53. *Publication:* Iceland Adventure, 1934. *Recreations:* rowing, Rugby football. *Address:* The Timber House, Aldercombe Lane, Caterham, Surrey. *T:* Caterham 44054.

**BECKETT, Sir Martyn Gervase,** 2nd Bt, *cr* 1921; MC 1945; ARIBA; Architect; Lieutenant (temp. Captain) Welsh Guards; *b* 6 Nov. 1918; *s* of Hon. Sir Gervase Beckett, 1st Bt, and Lady Marjorie Beckett (*d* 1964); *S* father, 1937; *m* 1941, Hon. Priscilla Brett, *y d* of 3rd Visc. Esher, GBE; two *s* one *d*. *Educ:* Eton; Trinity Coll., Cambridge. Served War of 1939-45 (MC). Renovations and alterations to E end of King's College, Cambridge; private houses and council estates. *Recreations:* fishing, painting, piano. *Heir:* *s* Richard Gervase Beckett, *b* 27 March 1944. *Address:* 3 St Albans Grove, W8. *T:* 01-937 7834; Kirkdale Farm, Nawton, Yorks. *Club:* Brooks's, Garrick.

*See also Vice-Adm. H. J. Egerton.*

**BECKETT, Richard Henry,** CSI 1934; CIE 1928; *b* 1882; *s* of Richard Beckett; *m* 1928, Doris May, *d* of W. T. Sutcliffe and *widow* of Capt. Cedric F. Horsfall. *Educ:* Imperial Coll. of Science. Entered Indian Educational Service, 1906; Principal, Coll. of Science, Nagpur, 1908; Officiating Dir of Public Instruction and Sec. for Education to the Govt of the Central Provinces India, 1924; Dir of Public Instruction, Bombay Presidency, 1930-34. *Recreations:* tennis, golf. *Address:* c/o Lloyds Bank (Cox's and King's Branch), 6 Pall Mall, SW1. *Club:* East India and Sports.

**BECKETT, Ronald Brymer;** Art Historian; *b* 17 Jan. 1891; *s* of James Robertson Beckett and Annie Bertha Murray; *m* 1918, Norah Ford Anderson; two *d*. *Educ:* Woodbridge Sch.; Lincoln Coll., Oxford; University Coll., London; Middle Temple. Entered Indian Civil Service, 1913; Guardian to the Nawab of Mamdot; Under-Sec. to Govt, Punjab, 1921-22; Sec. to Municipal Cttee, Lahore; Dep. Comr, Montgomery, and Colonization Officer, Lower Bari Doab Canal; Registrar, High Court, Lahore, 1927-30; Legal Remembrancer to Govt, Punjab, 1937-40; Acting or Additional Judge, High Court, Lahore, 1934-41; Puisne Judge, 1941-46. British Academy award, 1963. *Publications:* Hogarth, 1949; Lely, 1951; annotated vols, Constable's correspondence, 1953-68; (under name of John Anthony) The Story of Hassan, 1928; The Story of Maryam, 1930. *Address:* Chanonry, Northmoor, Oxon. *Clubs:* Athenæum, Royal Automobile.

**BECKETT, Samuel;** author and playwright; *b* Dublin, 1906. *Educ:* Portora Royal School; Trinity Coll., Dublin (MA). Lectr in English, Ecole Normale Supérieure, Paris, 1928-30; Lectr in French, Trinity Coll., Dublin, 1930-32; from 1932 has lived mostly in France, in Paris since 1937. Nobel Prize for Literature, 1969. *Publications: verse:* Whoroscope, 1930; Echo's Bones, 1935: *novels:* Murphy, 1938; Watt, 1944; Molloy, 1951 (Eng. trans. 1956); Malone meurt, 1952 (Eng. trans. Malone Dies, 1956); L'Innommable, 1953 (Eng. trans. 1960); Comment C'est, 1961 (Eng. trans. 1964); Imagination Dead Imagine, 1966 (trans. from French by author). *Short Stories:* More Pricks than Kicks, 1934; Nouvelles et textes pour rien, 1955; *plays:* En attendant Godot, 1952 (Eng. trans. Waiting for Godot, 1954); Fin de Partie, 1957 (Eng. trans. End Game); Krapp's Last Tape, 1959; La Dernière Bande, 1961; Happy Days, 1961; Play 1963; *radio plays:* All that Fall, 1957; Embers, 1959; Cascando, 1964. *Address:* c/o Faber & Faber Ltd, 24 Russell Square, WC1.

**BECKINGHAM, Charles Fraser;** Professor of Islamic Studies, University of London, since 1965; *b* 18 Feb. 1914; *o c* of Arthur Beckingham, ARBA and Alice Beckingham, Houghton, Hunts; *m* 1946, Margery (*d* 1966), *o d* of John Ansell; one *d*. *Educ:* Grammar Sch., Huntingdon; Queens' Coll., Cambridge (scholar, Members' English prizeman, 1934). Dept of Printed Books, British Museum, 1936-46. Seconded for service with military and naval Intelligence, 1942-46. Foreign Office, 1946-51; Lectr in Islamic History, Manchester Univ., 1951-55; Sen. Lectr, 1955-58. Prof. of Islamic Studies, 1958-65. Mem. Council, Hakluyt Soc., 1958-62, 1964-69, Pres. 1969-; Treas., Royal Asiatic Society, 1964-67, Pres., 1967-70. Jt Editor, 1961-64, Editor, 1965, Jl of Semitic Studies. *Publications:* contribs to Admiralty Handbook of Western Arabia, 1946; (with G. W. B. Huntingford) Some Records of Ethiopia, 1954; Introduction to Atlas of the Arab World and Middle East, 1960; (with G. W. B. Huntingford) A True Relation of the Prester John of the Indies, 1961; Bruce's Travels (ed. and selected), 1964; The Achievements of Prester John, 1966; (ed) Islam, in, Religion in the Middle East (ed A. J. Arberry), 1969; articles in learned jls. *Address:* Flat 2, 74 Cornwall Gardens, SW7. *T:* 01-937 9570.

**BECKWITH, Air Vice-Marshal William Flint,** CBE 1954; RAF retired; Director, Seaglider Ltd, since 1970; *b* 21 April 1913; *s* of Harold Beckwith, MIChemE, Leeds and Ilminster, and Lillie Hewitt Beckwith; *m* 1938, Helen Zina Yeo; one *d*. *Educ:* Bishops Stortford Coll.; Univ. of London. BSc (Eng) 1933. Entered RAF, 1934. Served War of 1939-45 in UK, West Africa and Air Ministry. Command

Engineer Officer, Far East AF, 1951-54; Asst Commandant, RAF Technical Coll., 1954-57; Senior British Rep., Cape Canaveral, 1957-60; Dir of Weapons Engineering, Air Min., 1960-63; Student IDC, 1963-64; Dir-Gen., Ground Training, Air Min., 1964-66; Vice-Pres., Ordnance Board, 1966-68, Pres., 1968-69. *Recreations:* water ski-ing, building, shooting, olive growing. *Address:* Benchmark, Little Hatherden, Andover, Hants. *T:* Hatherden 262; La Bergerie Sclos de Contes, AM, France. *Club:* Royal Air Force.

**BECTIVE, Earl of; Thomas Michael Ronald Christopher Taylour;** *b* 10 Feb. 1959; *s* and *heir* of 6th Marquis of Headfort, *qv.*

**BEDDALL, Maj.-Gen. Walter Samuel,** CB 1954; OBE 1941; Director of Army Education, 1952-57, retired; HM Commissioner, Duke of York's Royal Military School, Dover, 1952; Governor of British Society for International Understanding, 1952; *b* 7 Feb. 1894; *s* of late W. Beddall; *m* 1937, Alice May, *d* of Henry Greaves, London; one *d. Educ:* Kelham Coll., Notts; Cambridge Univ. Served European War, 1916-18, in France, with MGC; AEC 1920; Instructor, WO Sch. of Educ., 1920-24 (Capt.); Dist. Educ. Officer, NWFP, India, 1924-30; Officer, RMC Sandhurst, 1930-37; Chief Educ. Officer, E Comd, India, 1937-45; Comdt, Army Schs of Educ., 1945-49; Chief Educ. Officer, GHQ, Far East Land Forces, Singapore, 1949-52; Dir Army Educ., WO, 1952. Lieut-Col, 1949; Col, 1949; Brig., 1952; Maj.-Gen., 1954. *Publications:* articles on educn in Times Educnl Supp., Army Educ. *Recreations:* golf, tennis. *Address:* Crown Villa, Halstead, Sevenoaks, Kent. *Club:* Army and Navy.

**BEDDINGTON, Charles Richard;** Metropolitan Magistrate since 1963; *b* 22 Aug. 1911; *s* of late Charles Beddington, Inner Temple, and Stella (*née* de Goldschmidt); *m* 1939, Debbie, *d* of Frederick Appleby Holt; two *s* one *d. Educ:* Eton (scholar); Balliol Coll., Oxford. Barrister, Inner Temple, 1934. Joined TA, 1939; served RA, 1939-45, Major. Practised at the Bar in London and on SE Circuit. Mem. Mental Health Review Tribunal (SE Metropolitan Area), 1960-63. *Recreations:* golf, cricket, lawn tennis. *Address:* Rosehill, Cuckfield, Sussex. *T:* Haywards Heath 4063; 1 Temple Gardens, Temple, EC4. *Club:* Royal Ashdown Forest Golf.

**BEDDINGTON, Maj.-Gen. William Richard,** CBE 1941; Major-General, retired; *b* 8 Oct. 1893; *s* of late Gerald Ernest Beddington, CBE; *m* 1946, Elizabeth Rees, *d* of Sir Guy Fison, 3rd Bt, MC; one *s* (and one *s* decd). *Educ:* Eton; New Coll., Oxford. Served European War, 2nd Lieut 2nd Co. of London Yeomanry, Egypt, Gallipoli, Macedonia, 1914-16; The Queen's Bays, France, 1916-18 (wounded); Staff Coll., 1927-28; Staff Capt., 1930-32; Bde Major, 1932-34; GSO2 Southern Command, 1936-38; commanded the Queen's Bays, 1939; GSO1 Palestine, 1940; Brig., Middle East, Persia-Iraq, Mediterranean, France, and Germany, 1941-45; Acting Maj.-Gen. 1945; temp. Maj.-Gen., 1945-47; retired pay, 1947. Comdr, Legion of Merit (US) and Chevalier, Légion d'Honneur, 1945. *Recreation:* hunting. *Address:* The Old Rectory, Winterbourne Stickland, Blandford, Dorset. *Clubs:* Cavalry, Shikar, MCC.
*See also Sir R. G. Fison, Bt.*

**BEDDOE, Jack Eglinton;** Under-Secretary, Ministry of Housing and Local Government (again) 1966; *b* 6 June 1914; *s* of Percy Beddoe and Mabel Ellen Hook; *m* 1st, 1940, Audrey Alison Emelie (*d* 1954); two *s* one *d*; 2nd, 1957, Edith Rosina Gillanders. *Educ:* Hitchin Grammar Sch.; Magdalen Coll., Cambridge. Entered Ministry of Health, 1936; Principal Private Sec. to Minister of Health, 1948-51; to Minister of Housing and Local Government, 1951-53; Asst Sec., 1953; Under-Sec., Ministry of Housing and Local Government, 1961-65; Asst Under-Sec. of State, Dept of Economic Affairs, 1965-66; Chm., SE Planning Board, during 1966. *Address:* 75 St Andrews Road, Henley, Oxon.

**BEDDY, James Patrick,** DEconSc; MRIA; Chairman, The Industrial Credit Company Ltd, since 1952; Member, Executive Board, Economic and Social Research Institute, since 1960; *b* Cobh, County Cork, 1900. *Educ:* O'Connell Schs, Dublin; National Univ. of Ireland, University Coll., Dublin. Inspector of Taxes, 1927-33; Sec., Industrial Credit Co. Ltd, 1933-49; Dir, The Industrial Credit Co. Ltd, 1949-52, Man. Dir 1952-69; Lectr in Commerce, University Coll., Dublin, 1936-51. Pres., Statistical and Social Inquiry Soc. of Ireland, 1954-56. Chairman: Commn on Emigration and Other Population Problems, 1948-54; Cttee of Inquiry into Internal Transport, 1956-57; An Foras Tionscail, 1952-65; The Industrial Development Authority, 1949-65. Member: Tribunal of Inquiry into Public Transport, 1939; Industrial Res. Cttee of Inst. for Industrial Res. and Standards, 1946-60. LLD (*hc* Dublin). *Publications:* Profits, Theoretical and Practical Aspects, 1940. Various articles on matters of economic interest. *Address:* 15 Spencer Villas, Glenageary, County Dublin. *T:* Dublin 801542. *Clubs:* Stephen's Green (Dublin); Royal Irish Yacht (Dun Laoghaire).

**BEDFORD,** 13th Duke of, *cr* 1694; **John Robert Russell;** Marquess of Tavistock, 1694; Earl of Bedford, 1550; Baron Russell of Chenies, 1540; Baron Russell of Thornhaugh, 1603; Baron Howland of Streatham, 1695; *b* 24 May 1917; *er s* of 12th Duke and Louisa Crommelin Roberta (*d* 1960), *y d* of Robert Jowitt Whitwell; *S* father 1953; *m* 1st, 1939, Clare Gwendolen Hollway, *née* Bridgman (*d* 1945); two *s*; 2nd, Lydia (marr. diss., 1960), *widow* of Capt. Ian de Hoghton Lyle, 3rd *d* of 3rd Baron Churston and late Duchess of Leinster; one *s*; 3rd, 1960, Mme Nicole Milinaire, *d* of Paul Schneider. Coldstream Guards, 1939; invalided out, 1940. *Publications:* A Silver-Plated Spoon, 1959; (with G. Mikes) Book of Snobs, 1965; The Flying Duchess, 1968. *Heir: s* Marquess of Tavistock, *qv. Address:* (seat) Woburn Abbey, Beds. *T:* Woburn 666; 42 Chester Terrace, NW1. *T:* 01-486 3646. *Clubs:* Brooks's, Pratt's.

**BEDFORD, Bishop Suffragan of,** since 1968; **Rt. Rev. John Tyrrell Holmes Hare;** Archdeacon of Bedford since 1962; *b* 24 Nov. 1912; *s* of Henry and Beatrice Hare, Tamworth, Staffs; *m* 1944, Mary Eirene Sumner Wetherall, *d* of late Rev. A. S. Wetherall; two *s. Educ:* Brighton Coll.; Corpus Christi Coll., Oxford (MA); Cuddesdon Theological Coll. Ordained, 1937; Curate: St Francis of Assisi, West Bromwich, 1937-39; Epping, 1939-40; St Mary, Hendon, 1940-46; Vicar: St Matthias, Colindale, 1946-51; St Andrew, Bedford, 1951-62; Rural Dean of Bedford, 1958-62; Hon. Canon of St Albans, 1961-62. Proctor in Convocation of Canterbury, 1960-. *Recreation:* doing it yourself. *Address:* 168 Kimbolton Road, Bedford. *T:* Bedford 57551.

**BEDFORD, Archdeacon of;** *see* Bedford, Bishop Suffragan of.

**BEDFORD, Alfred William, (Bill),** OBE 1961; AFC 1945; FRAeS; Sales Manager, Harrier,

Hawker Siddeley Aviation, since 1968; *b* 18 Nov. 1920; *m* 1941, Mary Averill; one *s* one *d*. *Educ:* Loughborough College School, Leics. Electrical engineering apprenticeship, Blackburn Starling & Co. Ltd. RAF 1940-51: served Fighter Sqdns, 605 (County of Warwick) Sqdn, 1941; 135 Sqdn, 1941-44; 65 Sqdn, 1945. Qualified Flying Instructor, Upavon, 1945, and Instructor, Instrument Rating Examiner, until 1949; Graduate Empire Flying School all-weather course. Awarded King's Commendation, 1949; Graduate and Tutor, Empire Test Pilots' School, 1949-50; Test Pilot, RAE Farnborough, 1950-51; Experimental Test Pilot, Hawker Aircraft Ltd, 1951-56; Chief Test Pilot, Hawker Aircraft Ltd, 1956-63; Chief Test Pilot (Dunsfold); Hawker Siddeley Aviation Ltd, 1963-67. London-Rome and return world speed records, 1956. Made initial flight, Oct. 1960, on the Hawker P1127 (the World's first VTOL strike fighter), followed by first jet V/STOL operations of such an aircraft from an Aircraft Carrier (HMS Ark Royal) on 8 Feb. 1963; Harrier first flight, Aug. 1966. Holder Gliding Internat. Gold 'C' with two diamonds; held British and UK national gliding records of 257 miles and altitude of 21,340 ft (19,120 ft gain of height); awarded BGA trophies: de Havilland (twice), Manio, and Wakefield, 1950-51. Approved Air Registration Bd glider test pilot. Chm. and founder Mem., Test Pilots' Group, RAeS, 1964-66. Member SBAC Test Pilots' Soc., 1956-67. Member Society of Experimental Test Pilots. RAeS Alston Memorial Medal, 1959; Guild of Air Pilots and Air Navigators Derry Richards Memorial Medal, 1959-60; Segrave Trophy, 1963; Britannia Trophy, 1964; Air League Founders Medal, 1967. *Recreations:* squash, sail-plane flying. *Address:* The Chequers, West End Lane, Esher, Surrey. *T:* Esher 62285. *Club:* Woking and Esher Squash.

**BEDFORD, D(avis) Evan,** CBE 1963; MD, FRCP, London; FACP (corresp); MD (Hon) Cairo; Hon. Consultant Physician, Middlesex, National Heart and Connaught Hospitals; late Consultant in Cardiology to the Army; Hon. Civil Consultant in Cardiology, RAF; Chairman Council, British Heart Foundation; *b* 1898; *s* of William Bedford, JP, Boston, Lincs; *m* 1935, Audrey Selina North, *e d* of Milton Ely, CBE; two *s*. *Educ:* Epsom Coll.; Middlesex Hospital. Medical Registrar, Middlesex Hospital, 1923-25; Paterson Research Scholar, London Hospital Cardiographic Dept, 1926-27; Medical Officer in Charge Cardiac Wards, Ministry of Pensions Hospital, Orpington, 1922; studied in Paris and Lyons, 1926; Surg.-Sub-Lieut RNVR, 1918, 20th Destroyer Flotilla. Served in RAMC, 1939-45, Brig. Cons. Physician, MEF (despatches). Late Pres. British Cardiac Soc.; Corresp. mem., Soc. Française de Cardiologie, Soc. Belge de Cardiologie, Soc. Suisse de Cardiologie; Hon. Member: Cardiac Soc. of Australia and NZ, Brazilian Soc. of Cardiology and Egyptian Cardiological Soc.; Hon. Pres., European Soc. of Cardiology; late Vice-Pres. International Soc. of Cardiology; Corresp. Acad. of Med., Rome. Carey Coombs Lectr, 1963. *Publications:* articles on Diseases of Coronary Arteries, Angina Pectoris and Congenital Heart Disease, in Lancet, Heart, etc, and other papers and addresses on Diseases of the Heart; Strickland Goodall Memorial Lecture, 1939; Bradshaw Lecture, RCP, 1946; St Cyres' Lecture, 1947; Lumleian Lectures, RCP 1960; Harveian Oration, RCP 1968. *Recreation:* golf. *Address:* 62 Wimpole Street, W1. *T:* 01-935 4740. *Club:* Oriental.

**BEDFORD, Eric,** CB 1959; CVO 1953; ARIBA 1933; Chief Architect, Ministry of Works, 1952-70 (Chief Architect, Directorate General of Works, Ministry of Public Building and Works, 1963-70). Grissell Gold Medal of Royal Institute of British Architects, 1934. Was responsible for Ministry of Works decorations for the Coronation, 1953. *Address:* Ministry of Public Building and Works, Lambeth Bridge House, SE1. *T:* 01-735 7611, Ext. 1836.

**BEDFORD, John,** OBE 1948 (MBE 1944); Chairman, 1956-71 and Managing Director, 1956-70, Debenhams Ltd; Director: North British & Mercantile Insurance Co. Ltd; Commercial Union Assurance Co. Ltd; *b* 16 Jan. 1903; *o s* of John and Rosalind Bedford; *m* 1930, Florence Mary Oddy; one *d*. Mem., Banwell Cttee to look at Contractual matters in the Construction Industries for Ministry of Public Bldg and Works, 1962; Mem., Board of Nat. Bldg Agency, 1964- (Dep. Chm. of Bd and Chm. Finance Cttee, 1967-); Part-time Mem., London Transport Bd, 1962-68. Chm., Central Finance Bd of Methodist Church, 1966-. Governor, The Leys Sch., Cambridge; Trustee, The Cottage Homes for Old People. *Recreations:* golf, reading, walking. *Address:* North Gate, Regent's Park, NW8.

**BEDFORD, Leslie Herbert,** CBE 1956 (OBE 1942); retired as Director of Engineering, Guided Weapons Division, British Aircraft Corporation Ltd, 1968; *b* 23 June 1900; *s* of Herbert Bedford; *m* 1928, Lesley Florence Keitley Duff; three *s*. *Educ:* City and Guilds Engineering Coll., London (BSc); King's Coll., Cambridge (MA). Standard Telephones & Cables Ltd, 1924-31; Dir Research, A. C. Cossor Ltd, 1931-47; Chief TV Engr, Marconi's Wireless Telegraph Co. Ltd, 1947-48. Chief Engineer, GW Div., The English Electric Aviation Ltd, 1948-59; Dir, 1959-60. Mem., Council for Scientific and Industrial Research, 1961-. CEng, FCGI, FIEEE, MBritIRE, FIEE, FRAeS. Silver Medal (RAeS), 1963; Gold Medal, Société d'Encouragement pour la Recherche et l'Invention, 1967; Faraday Medal, 1968. *Publications:* Articles in: Proc. Phys. Soc., Jl BritIRE, Jl RSA, Jl RAeS, Jl IEE, Wireless Engineer, Electronic and Radio Engineer, Electronic Technology. *Recreations:* music, sailing. *Address:* 82a Hendon Lane, N3. *T:* 01-346 1558.

**BEDINGFELD, Sir Edmund;** *see* Paston-Bedingfeld.

**BEDNALL, Maj.-Gen. Sir (Cecil Norbury) Peter,** KBE 1953; CB 1949; OBE 1941; MC 1917; director of companies; *b* 1895; *s* of late Peter Bednall, Endon, Staffs; *m* 1937, Eileen Margaret, *d* of late Col C. M. Lewin, Cowfold, Sussex; one *s* one *d*. *Educ:* Hanley; privately. Army Officer since 1915; Chartered Accountant since 1920. Commissioned 1915, RFA; served European War, 1916-19, France and Belgium. Palestine, 1936-37; War of 1939-45 in France, Abyssinia, and East Africa. Maj.-Gen., 1948. Paymaster-in-Chief, the War Office, 1948-55. Col Comdt RAPC, 1955-60. *Recreation:* golf. *Address:* PO Box 454, Blantyre, Malawi; Effingham Golf Club, Effingham, Surrey; Sandapple House, Ruwa. *Clubs:* Army and Navy; New, Ruwa Country (Salisbury).

**BEDNALL, Maj.-Gen. Sir Peter;** *see* Bednall, Maj.-Gen. Sir (C. N.) P.

**BEDOYERE, Count Michael de la;** *see* de la Bedoyere.

**BEEBY, Clarence Edward,** CMG 1956; PhD; *b* 16 June 1902; *s* of Anthony and Alice Beeby; *m* 1926, Beatrice Eleanor, *d* of Charles Newnham; one *s* one *d*. *Educ:* Christchurch Boys' High Sch.; Canterbury Coll., University of NZ (MA); University Coll., London; University of Manchester (PhD). Lectr in Philosophy and Education, Canterbury Univ. Coll., University of NZ, 1923-34; Dir, NZ Council for Educational Research, 1934-38; Asst Dir of Education, Education Dept, NZ, 1938-40; Dir of Education, NZ, 1940-60 (leave of absence to act as Asst Dir-Gen. of UNESCO, Paris, 1948-49); NZ Ambassador to France, 1960-63; Research Fellow, Harvard Univ., 1963-67; Commonwealth Visiting Prof., Univ. of London, 1967-68; Consultant on Educn in Developing Countries, 1969-; Consultant: to Australian Govt in Papua and New Guinea, 1969; to Ford Foundn in Indonesia, 1970. Leader of NZ Delegs, to Gen. Confs of UNESCO, 1946, 1947, 1950, 1953, 1954, 1956, 1958, 1960, 1962. Hon. Counsellor of UNESCO, 1950; Mem., Exec. Bd, UNESCO, 1960-63 (Chm., Exec. Bd, 1962-63). Hon. LLD Otago, 1969; Hon. LittD Wellington, 1970. Order of St Gregory (1st cl.), 1964. *Publications:* The Intermediate Schools of New Zealand, 1938; (with W. Thomas and M. H. Oram) Entrance to the University, 1939; The Quality of Education in Developing Countries, 1966; (ed) Qualitative Aspects of Educational Planning, 1969; articles in educational periodicals. *Recreations:* gardening, fishing, cabinet-making. *Address:* 73 Barnard Street, Wellington N2, New Zealand.

**BEEBY, George Harry,** PhD, BSc, CEng, FRIC, President, Society of Chemical Industry, since 1970; *b* 9 Sept. 1902; *s* of George Beeby and Lucy Beeby (*née* Monk); *m* 1929, Helen Elizabeth Edwards; one *d*. *Educ:* Loughborough Grammar Sch.; Loughborough Coll. BSc Hons 1922; PhD 1924, London Univ. Various appts in rubber and chemical industries, 1924-; Divisional Chm., ICI, 1954-57; Chm., British Titan Products Co. Ltd, 1957-69. Chairman: EDC for Chemical Industry, 1964-67; Nat. Sulphuric Acid Assoc., 1963-65; British Standards Instn, 1967-70. Vice-President: Soc. of Chemical Industry, 1966-69; RoSPA, 1968; Mem. Council, Chemical Industries Assoc. FIChemE; FBIM 1965; FRSA 1969. Hon. DTech Loughborough Univ. of Technology, 1969. *Publications:* contribs to various jls on industrial safety, industrial economics and business administration. *Recreations:* golf, travel, racing, collection of antique glass paperweights. *Address:* The Laurels, Sandy Drive, Cobham, Surrey. *T:* Oxshott 2346. *Clubs:* Savile, Royal Automobile; Metropolitan (New York).

**BEECH, Patrick Mervyn,** CBE 1970; Controller, English Regions, BBC, since 1969; *b* 31 Oct. 1912; *s* of Howard Worcester Mervyn Beech and Stella Patrick Campbell; *m* 1st, 1935, Sigrid Gunnel Christenson (*d* 1959); two *d*; 2nd, 1960, Merle-Mary Barnes; one *d*. *Educ:* Stowe; Exeter Coll., Oxford. Joined BBC as Producer, West Region, 1935; News Editor, West Region, 1945; Asst Head of programmes, West Region, 1954; Controller, Midland Region, 1964-69. *Recreations:* riding, photography, music, theatre. *Address:* Mill Bank, Cradley, near Malvern, Worcs. *T:* Ridgway Cross 234.

**BEECHAM, Sir Adrian (Welles),** 3rd Bt *cr* 1914; *b* 4 Sept. 1904; *er s* of Sir Thomas Beecham, 2nd Bt, CH (Kt 1916) and of Utica, *d* of Dr Charles S. Welles, New York; *S* father, 1961; *m* 1939, Barbara Joyce Cairn; two *s* one *d*. *Educ:* privately. MusBac Durham, 1926. *Publications:* Four Songs, 1950; Little Ballet Suite, 1951; Traditional Irish Tunes, 1953; Three part-songs, 1955; Ruth (sacred cantata), 1957; Sonnet cxlvi (Shakespeare), 1962. *Recreation:* hunting. *Heir: er s* John Stratford Roland Beecham, *b* 21 April 1940. *Address:* Compton Scorpion Manor, Shipston-on-Stour, Warwicks. *T:* Shipston 482. *Club:* Savage.

**BEECHER, Rt. Rev. Leonard James,** CMG 1961; ARCS, MA, DD; *b* 21 May 1906; *er s* of Robert Paul and Charlotte Beecher; *m* 1930, Gladys Sybil Bazett, *yr d* of late Canon Harry and Mrs Mary Leakey; two *s* one *d*. *Educ:* St Olave's Grammar Sch., Southwark; Imperial Coll. and London Day Trg Coll., University of London. ARCS 1926; BSc 1927; MA (London) 1937. DD Lambeth, 1962. Asst Master, Alliance High Sch., Kikuyu, Kenya, 1927-30; Missionary, Church Missionary Soc., Diocese of Mombasa, 1930-57; Unofficial Mem. of Legislative Council, Colony of Kenya, representing African interests, 1943-47; MEC of the Colony of Kenya, 1947-52; Asst Bishop of Mombasa, Kenya Colony, 1950-53; Archdeacon and Canon of the Diocese, 1945-53; Bishop of Mombasa, 1953-64; Archbishop of East Africa, 1960-70; Bishop of Nairobi, 1964-70. *Publications:* (with G. S. Beecher) A Kikuyu-English Dictionary, 1933; translator of parts of the Kikuyu Old Testament, 1939-49; Ed. of Kenya Church Review, 1941-50. *Recreations:* recorded music, bird-watching, photography. *Address:* PO Box 21066, Nairobi, Kenya. *T:* Nairobi 67485.

**BEECHING,** family name of **Baron Beeching.**

**BEECHING,** Baron, *cr* 1965 (Life Peer); **Richard Beeching,** PhD; Chairman, Redland Ltd, since 1970; Director: Lloyds Bank Ltd, since 1965; Rolls-Royce Ltd, since 1970; *b* 21 April 1913; *s* of Hubert J. Beeching; *m* 1938, Ella Margaret Tiley. *Educ:* Maidstone Grammar Sch.; Imperial Coll. of Science and Technology, London. ARCS, BSc, 1st Cl. Hons; DIC; PhD London. Fuel Research Station, 1936; Mond Nickel Co. Ltd 1937; Armaments Design Dept, Min. of Supply, 1943; Dep. Chief Engineer of Armaments Design, 1946. Joined Imperial Chemical Industries, 1948, Dir, 1957-61 and 1965, Dep. Chm. 1966-68. Vice-Pres. ICI of Canada Ltd, 1953; Chm., Metals Div., ICI, 1955. Member: Special Adv. Gp on BTC, 1960; NEDC, 1962-64; Chairman: British Railways Bd, 1963-65; BTC, 1961-63; Royal Commn on Assizes and QS, 1966. First Pres., Inst. of Work Study Practitioners, 1967; Pres., RoSPA, 1968-. Fellow, Imperial Coll.; CIMechE, FBIM, FInstP, MInstT; Hon. LLD London; Hon. DSc NUI. *Publication:* Electron Diffraction, 1936. *Address:* Little Manor, East Grinstead, Sussex. *Club:* Athenæum.

**BEELEY, Sir Harold,** KCMG 1961 (CMG 1953); CBE, 1946; *b* 15 Feb. 1909; *s* of Frank Arthur Beeley; *m* 1st, 1933, Millicent Mary Chinn (marr. diss., 1953); two *d*; 2nd, 1958, Mrs Patricia Karen Brett-Smith; one *d*. *Educ:* Highgate; Queen's Coll., Oxford. 1st Cl. in Modern History, 1930. Asst Lectr in Modern History, Sheffield Univ., 1930-31; University Coll., London, 1931-35; Junior Research Fellow and Lecturer, Queen's Coll., Oxford, 1935-38; Lecturer in Charge of History Dept, University Coll., Leicester, 1938-39. Mem. of wartime organisation of Royal Institute of International Affairs, and subsequently of Foreign Office Research Dept, 1939-45. Mem. of Secretariat of San Francisco Conf. and of Preparatory Commission of UN, 1945; Sec. of Anglo-American Cttee of Enquiry on

Palestine, 1946. Entered Foreign Service, 1946; Counsellor of Embassy, Copenhagen, 1949-50; Baghdad, 1950-53; Washington, 1953-55; Ambassador to Saudi Arabia, during 1955; Asst Under-Sec., Foreign Office, 1956-58; Dep. UK Representative to UN, New York, 1958-61; UK Representative, Disarmament Conf., Geneva, 1964-67; Ambassador to the United Arab Republic, 1961-64, 1967-69. *Publications:* Disraeli, 1936; contrib. to Survey of International Affairs, 1936-38. *Address:* 2 Ormond Road, Richmond, Surrey. *Club:* Reform.

**BEER, Ian David Stafford,** MA; JP; Head Master, Lancing College, Sussex, since 1969; *b* 28 April 1931; *s* of William Beer, Lloyd's Register of Shipping; *m* 1960, Angela Felce, *d* of Col E. S. G. Howard, MC, RA; two *s* one *d*. *Educ:* Whitgift Sch.; (Exhibitioner) St Catharine's Coll., Cambridge. Second Lieut in 1st Bn Royal Fusiliers, 1950. House Master, Marlborough Coll., Wilts, 1957-61; Head Master, Ellesmere Coll., Salop, 1961-69. *Recreations:* coaching Rugby football (formerly: played Rugby for England; CURFC (Capt.), Harlequins, Old Whitgiftians), swimming, golf, reading, zoology, meeting people. *Address:* Lancing College, Sussex. *T:* Shoreham-by-Sea 2213. *Clubs:* Public Schools; Hawks (Cambridge).

**BEER, Prof. János Miklós,** DSc, PhD, Dipl-Ing; Newton Drew Professor of Chemical Engineering and Fuel Technology and Head of Department, University of Sheffield, since 1965; *b* Budapest, 27 Feb. 1923; *s* of Sándor Beér and Gizella Trismai; *m* 1944, Marta Gabriella Csató. *Educ:* Berzsenyi Dániel Gymnasium, Budapest; Univ. of Budapest. PhD (Sheffield), 1960. Heat Research Inst., Budapest: Research Officer, 1949-52; Head, Combustion Dept, 1952-56; Princ. Lectr (part-time), University of Budapest, 1953-56; Research Engr, Babcock & Wilcox Ltd, Renfrew, 1957; Research Bursar, University of Sheffield, 1957-60; Head, Research Stn, Internat. Flame Research Foundn, Ijmuiden, Holland, 1960-63; Prof., Dept of Fuel Science, Pa State Univ., 1963-65. DSc (Tech) Sheffield, 1967. *Publications:* (Ed.) Fuel and Energy Science Monograph Series; contribs to Nature, Combustion and Flame, Basic Engrg. Jl, Amer. Soc. Mech. Engrg, Jl Inst. F, ZVDI, Internat. Gas Wärme, Proc. Internat. Symposia on Combustion, etc. *Recreations:* swimming, rowing, reading, music. *Address:* Dept of Chemical Engineering and Fuel Technology, University of Sheffield, Mappin Street, Sheffield S1 3JD. *T:* 78555.

**BEER, Nellie, (Mrs Robert Beer),** OBE 1957; JP; DL; Member of Manchester City Council since 1937 (Alderman since 1964; Lord Mayor of Manchester, 1966); *b* 22 April 1900; *d* of Arthur Robinson and Nelly Laurie Robinson (*née* Hewitt); *m* 1927, Robert Beer; one *d*. *Educ:* Ardwick Higher Grade Sch. JP Manchester, 1942; DL Lancs, 1970. *Address:* (home) 6 Princes Avenue, Didsbury, Manchester. *T:* 061-445 6237.

**BEESLEY, Mrs Alec M.;** *see* Smith, Dodie.

**BEESLY, Lewis Rowland,** CB 1966; CEng, FIMechE, FIProdE; Head of Engineering Staff, 1962, and Director-General of Aircraft Production, Ministry of Aviation, 1960; *b* 1 May 1912; *s* of Edward Rowland Beesly, Derby; *m* 1936, Kathleen Lilian, *d* of late Rev. S. Ivan Bell, Glasgow; four *d*. *Educ:* Bemrose Sch., Derby. Various managerial positions in Royal Ordnance Factories, 1935-49; Asst Dir, Longterm Production Planning (Air), Ministry of Supply, 1950; Dir, Engine Production, Ministry of Supply, 1951-59; Superintendent-Dir, Royal Small Arms Factory, Enfield, 1959-60. Chairman: Greenwich Council of Social Service; London Derbyshire Soc. *Address:* 50 West Park, Mottingham, SE9. *T:* 01-857 8426.

**BEESON, Cyril Frederick Cherrington,** CIE 1941; *b* 10 Feb. 1889; *s* of Walter Thomas Beeson, Oxford, and Rose Eliza Clacy; *m* 1922, Marion Cossentine Fitze (*d* 1946); one *d*. *Educ:* City of Oxford Sch.; St John's Coll., Oxford. BA (Oxon.) Geology; DSc (Oxon.) Entomology; Indian Forest Service, 1911-42, Conservator of Forests and Forest Entomologist; Dir, Imperial Forestry Bureau, Oxford, 1945-47. Medals: General Service, Victory, Jubilee, Coronation. *Publications:* The Ecology and Control of the Forest Insects of India and the neighbouring countries, 1941; Clockmaking in Oxfordshire, 1400 to 1850; from 1910 many publications in various journals, or separately, on taxonomy, ecology, and control of insect pests, on forest protection, and on horology. *Recreation:* horology. *Address:* Westway Cottage, Adderbury, Banbury, Oxon. *T:* Adderbury 272.

**BEESON, Prof. Paul Bruce,** FRCP; Nuffield Professor of Clinical Medicine, Oxford University, since 1965; Fellow of Magdalen College; *b* 18 Oct. 1908; *s* of John Bradley Beeson, Livingston, Mont; *m* 1942, Barbara Neal, *d* of Ray C. Neal, Buffalo, NY; two *s* one *d*. *Educ:* Univ. of Washington, McGill Univ. Med. Sch. MD, CM, 1933. Intern, Hosp. of Univ. of Pa, 1933-35; Gen. practice of medicine, Wooster, Ohio, 1935-37; Asst Rockefeller Inst., 1937-39; Chief Med. Resident, Peter Bent Brigham Hosp., 1939-40; Instructor in Med., Havard Med. Sch., and Chief Phys., American Red Cross-Harvard Field Hosp. Unit, Salisbury, 1940-42; Asst and Assoc. Prof. of Med., Emory Med. Sch., 1942-46; Prof. of Med. Emory Med. Sch., 1946-52; Prof. of Med. and Chm. Dep. of Med., Yale Univ., 1952-65; Vis. Investigator, Wright-Fleming Inst., St Mary's Hosp., 1958-59. Pres., Assoc. Amer. Physicians, 1967; Master, Amer. Coll. of Physicians, 1970. *Alumnus Summa Laude Dignatus,* Univ. of Washington, 1968; Hon. DSc Emory Univ., 1968. *Publications:* Edited: Cecil-Loeb Textbook of Medicine; Yale Journal Biology and Medicine, 1959-65; numerous scientific publications relating to infectious disease, pathogenesis of fever and pyelonephritis. *Address:* Radcliffe Infirmary, Oxford. *Club:* Athenæum.

**BEESTON, Prof. Alfred Felix Landon,** MA, DPhil, FBA 1965; Laudian Professor of Arabic, Oxford, since 1956; *b* 1911; *o s* of Herbert Arthur Beeston and Edith Mary Landon. *Educ:* Westminster Sch.; Christ Church, Oxford. James Mew Arabic Scholarship, Oxford, 1934; MA (Oxford), 1936; DPhil (Oxford), 1937. Asst in Dept of Oriental Books, Bodleian Library, Oxford, 1935-40; Sub-Librarian and Keeper of Oriental Books, Bodleian Library, 1946-55. *Publications:* Descriptive Grammar of Epigraphic South Arabian, 1962; Written Arabic, 1968; The Arabic Language Today, 1970. *Address:* St John's College, Oxford.

**BEETHAM, Sir Edward (Betham),** KCMG 1955 (CMG 1950); CVO 1947; OBE 1946; retired as Governor and Commander-in-Chief, Trinidad and Tobago (1955-60); *b* 19 Feb. 1905; *s* of late Dr Beetham, Red House, Knaresborough; *m* 1933, Eileen Joy Parkinson, CStJ; one *d*. *Educ:* Charterhouse; Lincoln Coll., Oxford. District Officer, Kenya, 1928-38; seconded to Colonial Office, 1938; District Commissioner, Sierra Leone, 1938-40; Chief Asst Colonial Sec.,

Sierra Leone, 1940-46; acted as Colonial Sec. and Governor's Deputy, Sierra Leone, on many occasions; Resident Commissioner of Swaziland, 1946-50; of the Bechuanaland Protectorate, 1950-53; Governor and C-in-C, Windward Is, 1953-55. Chairman, Norbury Insulation Group Ltd; Director: Barclays Overseas Development Corp. Ltd; Denys Robinson Ltd. KStJ 1953. *Recreation:* golf. *Address:* 21 Eresby House, Rutland Gate, SW7; Millstream, Mill End, Hambleden, Henley-on-Thames, Oxon. *Club:* Army and Navy.

**BEETON, William Hugh,** CMG 1954; *b* 14 Oct. 1903; *s* of late E. H. and late Mrs F. E. Beeton, Oulton Broad, Suffolk; *m* 1932, Mary Alice (*d* 1959), *d* of late F. H. and A. C. Wagstaff, Croydon, Surrey; one *s*; *m* 1962, Margaret Rachel Frances Crowley. *Educ:* Strathallan Sch.; London Sch. of Economics, University of London. Colonial Administrative Service, Gold Coast, 1926-54; Asst District Comr, 1926-32; District Comr, 1932-43; Dep. Provincial Comr, 1943-46; Asst Chief Comr, 1946-50; Chief Comr Ashanti, 1950; title changed to Chief Regional Officer, 1952; retd, 1954. Training Officer, Oversea Service, 1954-68. *Recreation:* golf. *Address:* 17 Harewood Road, South Croydon, Surrey. *T:* 01-688 2002. *Clubs:* Travellers', Royal Commonwealth Society; Croham Hurst Golf (Croydon).

**BEEVOR, John Grosvenor,** OBE 1945; Chairman: The Lafarge Organisation Ltd; Doulton & Co.; Director: Williams & Glyns Bank Ltd; Glaxo Group Ltd; Tilbury Contracting Group; Ciments Lafarge SA; Member Councils: The Officers' Association; Overseas Development Institute; *b* 1 March 1905; *s* of Henry Beevor, Newark-on-Trent, Notts; *m* 1st, 1933, Carinthia Jane (marr. diss., 1956), *d* of Aubrey and Caroline Waterfield, Aulla, Italy; three *s*; 2nd, 1957, Mary Christine Grepe. *Educ:* Winchester; New Coll., Oxford. Solicitor, 1931-53, Slaughter and May, London, EC2. Served HM Army, 1939-45, RA and Gen. Staff. Adviser to British Delegation to Marshall Plan Conf., Paris, 1947; Mem. Lord Chancellor's Cttee on Private Internat. Law, 1952-53; Man. Dir, Commonwealth Development Finance Co. Ltd, 1954-56; Vice-Pres., Internat. Finance Corp., Washington, DC, 1956-64. *Recreations:* golf, travel. *Address:* 51 Eaton Square, SW1. *T:* Belgravia 7987. *Clubs:* Brooks's; Royal St George's (Sandwich); Sunningdale Golf.

**BEEVOR, Miles;** Solicitor and Director of Companies; *b* 8 March 1900; 2nd *s* of Rowland Beevor; *m* 1st, 1924, Margaret Florence Platt (*d* 1934); one *s* (and one *d* decd); 2nd, 1935, Sybil Gilliat; two *s* one *d*. *Educ:* Winchester (Scholar); New Coll., Oxford (Scholar), BA 1921. Admitted a Solicitor, 1925. Served European War, 1914-18, in Army (RE Officer Cadet Battalion), 1918; War of 1939-45, RAFVR (Flt-Lieut Admin. and Special Duties Br.), 1941-43. Chief Legal Adviser, LNER, 1943-47; Actg Chief General Manager, LNER, 1947; Chief Sec. and Legal Adviser, British Transport Commission, 1947-51; Managing Dir, Brush Electrical Engineering Co. Ltd (which became The Brush Group Ltd), 1952-56; Deputy Chm. and Joint Managing Dir, 1956-57. *Recreations:* fishing, shooting. *Address:* Parkside, Welwyn, Herts. *T:* Welwyn 4087. *Club:* Junior Carlton.

**BEEVOR, Sir Thomas Agnew,** 7th Bt, *cr* 1784; *b* 6 Jan. 1929; *s* of Comdr Sir Thomas Beevor, 6th Bt, and of Edith Margaret Agnew (who *m* 2nd, 1944, Rear-Adm. R. A. Currie, *qv*); *S* father 1943; *m* 1st, 1957, Barbara Clare (marriage dissolved, 1965), *y d* of Capt. R. L. B. Cunliffe, RN (retd); one *s* two *d*; 2nd, 1966, Carola, *d* of Judge J. B. Herbert, *qv*. *Heir:* *s* Thomas Hugh Cunliffe Beevor, *b* 1 Oct. 1962. *Address:* Hargham Hall, Norwich.

*See also Col Sir E. C. H. Warner, Bt.*

**BEGBIE, Rt. Rev. Herbert Gordon Smirnoff;** Bishop Coadjutor of Sydney since 1967, and Bishop resident in Parramatta since 1969; *b* 28 Oct. 1905; *s* of Herbert Smirnoff Begbie and Emily Augusta (*née* Miller); *m* 1932, Gwendoline Dean; one *s* one *d*. *Educ:* Trinity Gram. Sch. and C of E Gram. Sch., Sydney; University of Sydney; Mooore Theol Coll. BA (Sydney) 1927. Deacon 1928; Priest, 1929. Curate: Eastwood, Dio. of Sydney, 1929-31; St George's, Hobart, Dio. of Tasmania, 1931-34; Rector: Narrabeen, 1934-37; Moss Vale, 1937-47; Campsie, 1947-49; Wollongong, 1949-60; Archdeacon of: Camden, 1949-54; Wollongong, 1954-62; Cumberland, 1962-67 (all Dio. of Sydney); Registrar, Diocese of Sydney, 1960-69; *Recreation:* gardening. *Address:* 5 Keith Place, Baulkham Hills, NSW 2153, Australia. *T:* 639-4752.

**BEGG, Very Rev. Ian Forbes,** MA; Priest-in-Charge of St Ninian's Episcopal Church, Seaton, Aberdeen since 1935; Dean of the United Diocese of Aberdeen and Orkney since 1969; Canon of St Andrew's Cathedral, Aberdeen; *b* 12 Feb. 1910; *e s* of Rev. John Smith Begg and Elizabeth Macintyre; *m* 1949, Lillie Taylor Paterson. *Educ:* Aberdeen Grammar Sch.; Aberdeen Univ.; Westcott House, Cambridge. Deacon 1933; Priest 1934. Curate, St Paul's, Prince's Park, Liverpool, 1933-35. Vice-Chm., Aberdeen Telephone Samaritans, 1960-; Chm., Church Guest Houses' Assoc., 1969-. *Recreations:* fishing, gardening. *Address:* St Ninian's House, 696 King Street, Aberdeen.

**BEGG, Jean,** CBE 1948 (OBE 1946; MBE 1943); *b* 7 Oct. 1887; *d* of John Begg, Dunedin, NZ. *Educ:* Girls' High Sch.; Teachers' Training Coll.; Otago Univ., Dunedin, NZ. Teacher, London Missionary Soc., Tutuila, Samoa, 1910-19; graduate, Sch. of Social Work, New York, and executive sec. of Inwood House for Delinquent Girls, New York City, 1919-23; Investigator, Child Welfare Dept, Govt of NZ, Organizer, Women's Section, NZ and South Seas Exhibition, NZ, 1924-26; Gen. Sec., YWCA, Auckland, NZ; Leader NZ deleg. to Pan Pacific Conf., Honolulu, 1926-31; Nat. Gen. Sec., YWCA of India, Burma and Ceylon, 1931-40; Dir, YWCA Welfare, with British and Allied Servicewomen of the Forces, Middle East, Central Mediterranean, India, SE Asia, Japan, 1940-48 (despatches); Head Warden, YWCA Residence, Helen Graham House, London, 1948-51; Pres. YWCA, Dunedin, 1957; Organiser, Council of Organisations for Relief Services Overseas, Wellington, NZ; Pres. United Nations Assoc. (Otago), 1960; Field Vice-Pres., YWCA of NZ. *Address:* 3 Queen's Drive, Dunedin, C2, NZ.

**BEGG, Admiral of the Fleet Sir Varyl (Cargill),** GCB 1965 (KCB 1962; CB 1959); DSO 1952; DSC 1941; Governor and Commander-in-Chief of Gibraltar, since 1969; *b* 1 Oct. 1908; *s* of Francis Cargill Begg and Muriel Clare Robinson; *m* 1943, Rosemary Cowan, CStJ; two *s*. *Educ:* St Andrews Sch., Eastbourne; Malvern Coll. Entered RN, special entry, 1926; Qualified Gunnery Officer, 1933; HMS Glasgow, 1939-40; HMS Warspite, 1940-43; Comdr Dec. 1942; Capt. 1947; commanded HM Gunnery Sch., Chatham, 1948-50; 8th Destroyer Flotilla, 1950-52; HMS Excellent, 1952-54; HMS Triumph, 1955-56; idc 1954; Rear-Adm. 1957; Chief of Staff to C-in-C Portsmouth 1957-58; Flag Officer

Commanding Fifth Cruiser Squadron and Flag Officer Second-in-Command, Far East Station, 1958-60; Vice-Adm. 1960; a Lord Commissioner of the Admiralty and Vice-Chief of Naval Staff, 1961-63; Admiral, 1963; C-in-C, British Forces in the Far East, and UK Military Adviser to SEATO, 1963-65; C-in-C, Portsmouth, and Allied C-in-C, Channel, 1965-66; Chief of Naval Staff and First Sea Lord, 1966-68. KStJ 1969. PMN 1966. *Recreations:* cricket, tennis, gardening. *Address:* The Convent, Gibraltar; The Cottage, Harpsden, Henley-on-Thames, Oxon. *Clubs:* United Service, MCC.

**BEHAN, Harold Garfield,** CMG 1967; MBE 1958; JP; Grazier; *b* 22 Feb. 1901; *s* of Thomas and Mary Behan, Jericho; *m* 1942, Kathleen, *d* of John Costello; two *s* four *d*. *Educ:* Nudgee Coll.; Brisbane Gram. Sch. Member: Jericho Shire Coun., 1922-25; Isisford Shire Coun., 1926-67 (Chm. 1945-67); Executive Member: Queensland Local Govt Assoc., 1945-67 (Pres. 1952-67); Australian Coun. of Local Govt. Assocs, 1945-67 (Pres. 1967); Graziers' Assoc. of Central and N Queensland, 1942-67 (Pres. 1962-67); Mem. Coun. and Exec. Coun., United Graziers' Assoc. of Queensland, 1939-67. *Address:* Bilbah Downs, Isisford, Queensland, Australia. *Clubs:* Longreach, Blackall (Qld).

**BEHARRELL, Sir (George) Edward,** Kt 1961; Chairman, The Dunlop Co. Ltd, 1957-67; President since 1968; *b* 26 May 1899; *e s* of late Sir George Beharrell; *m* 1921, Barbara (*d* 1970), *yr d* of late Walter Waddington, York; two *s* two *d*. *Educ:* Wellingborough. Served European War, 1914-18, in Inns of Court Regt and RE. Early training in Shipping business. Joined Dunlop Rubber Co. Ltd, 1928; various executive appointments; Dir, 1942; Joint-Managing Dir, 1943; Managing Dir, 1945; Deputy Chm., 1949; Chm., 1957. Chm., Internat. Synthetic Rubber Co. Ltd, 1955. Member: Pres. of Board of Trade's Informal Advisory Group on Exports, 1955-59; Iron & Steel Bd, 1953-58; President: Federation of British Rubber Manufacturers Assocns, 1948-50; Tyre Manufacturers' Conference, 1947-56; Soc. of Motor Manufacturers and Traders, 1951-52; Instn of the Rubber Industry, 1962-64. *Recreations:* golf, literature. *Address:* Carinya, Priory Road, Sunningdale, Berks. *T:* Ascot 23278.

**BEHRENS, Edgar Charles,** CBE 1951 (OBE 1919); JP West Riding Yorks; FRSA; Chairman, Craig Convalescent Home for Children, Morecambe, 1927-67; Director (previously Chairman): Sir Jacob Behrens & Sons Ltd, Bradford, Manchester and Hong Kong; Francis Willey (British Wools, 1935) Ltd; J. E. Pickles & Co. Ltd, Fisher, Fox & Co. Ltd, all of Bradford, and other textile companies in Manchester; *b* 13 May 1885; 3rd *s* of late Gustav and Fanny Behrens, Manchester; *m* 1926, Winifred, *o d* of late Charles Luckhurst, Coneysthorpe, near York; one *s* one *d*. *Educ:* Rugby Sch. Served European War, RASC (Capt.), and on Staff (despatches twice, OBE). Chm. National Wool Textile Export Group, 1942-58 (Vice-Chm. 1958-65); President, Bradford Chamber of Commerce, 1938-40; mem. of NE Tribunal for Conscientious Objectors, 1939-57. *Address:* Norwood House, Ilkley, Yorks. *T:* Ilkley 3518. *Club:* English-Speaking Union.

**BEHRENS, Sir Leonard (Frederick),** Kt 1970; CBE 1956; JP; MCom; Vice-President, Liberal Party Organisation; Vice-Chairman and Hon. Member, Royal Manchester College of Music; Member of Council, Manchester University; Vice-President, UN Association; Hon. President, World Federation of UN Associations and acting President, Stockholm, 1951; New York, 1963; *b* 15 Oct. 1890; *y s* of late Gustav Behrens; *m* 1920, Beatrice Mary, *y d* of late Dr W. Sandham Symes, Maryborough, Queen's Co. and Chesterfield; two *d*. *Educ:* Ladybarn House Sch.; Manchester Grammar Sch.; Rugby Sch.; Manchester Univ. Partner Sir Jacob Behrens and Sons, 1920-48; Dir Sir Jacob Behrens and Sons Ltd. 1948-54, Dep.-Chm. Cotton and Rayon Merchants' Assoc., 1939-42 and 1954. Chm. Manchester Information Cttee, and Lecturer to HM Forces, 1940-45; Royal Observer Corps. 1941-52 (now Hon. Mem.). Pres., Manchester Statistical Soc., 1942-44; Dir, Manchester Chamber of Commerce, 1923-67, now Emeritus. Liberal Candidate, Withington, 1945 and 1950; Pres. Liberal Party Org., 1955-57; Chm. of Exec., 1959-61. Pres. Manchester Reform Club, 1956-57; Pres. Manchester Liberal Fedn, 1947-49; Chm. Hallé Concerts Soc., 1952-59. Order of St Sava (Jugoslavia), 1919; Brilliant Star with Ribbon (China), 1949. *Publications:* pamphlets, articles and letters to the Press. *Recreations:* music and crossword puzzles. *Address:* Netherby, 119 Barlow Moor Road, Didsbury, Manchester M20 8TS. *T:* 061-445 3600. *Clubs:* National Liberal, English-Speaking Union; Manchester (Manchester).

*See also Sir B. H. Flowers.*

**BEHRMAN, Simon,** FRCP; Physician, Moorfields, Eye Hospital; Consulting Neurologist; Regional Neurosurgical Centre, Brook Hospital; Lewisham, Dulwich, St Olave's, St Giles', St Francis', St Leonard's, Bromley and Farnborough Hospitals; *s* of late Leopold Behrman; *m* 1940, Dorothy, *d* of late Charles Engelbert; two *s* two *d*. *Educ:* University Coll. and St Bartholomew's Hosp., London. BSc (Hons) London. 1925; MRCS Eng. 1928; MRCP London 1932. Member: Assoc. of British Neurologists; Ophthalmological Soc. of UK; Academic Bd of Inst of Ophthalmology, University of London; FRSocMed. House Physician and Registrar, Hosp. for Nervous Diseases, Maida Vale, 1930-33; Registrar: Nat. Hosp., Queen Square, 1934-38; Dept of Nervous Diseases, Guy's Hosp., 1935-45. *Publications:* articles on neurology and neuro-ophthalmology. *Address:* 33 Harley Street, W1. *T:* 01-580 3388; The Dover House, Oxney, St Margaret's-at-Cliffe, Kent. *T:* St Margaret's Bay 2161.

**BEHRMAN, S. N.;** Playwright; *b* 9 June 1893; *s* of Joseph Behrman and Zelda Feingold; *m* 1936, Eliza Heifetz; one *s*. *Educ:* Harvard Coll., AB 1916; Columbia Univ., MA 1918. Brandeis Univ. Creative Arts Award, Theatre Medal, 1962. First play, The Second Man, Prod. in New York, 1927 with Alfred Lunt and Lynn Fontanne, prod. London, 1928, with Noel Coward. Subsequent productions: Serena Blandish, 1928; Meteor, 1929; Brief Moment, 1932; Biography, 1933; Love Story, 1934; Rain from Heaven, 1935; End of Summer, 1936; Amphitryon (adapted from French), 1937; Wine of Choice, 1938; No Time for Comedy, 1939; The Talley Method, 1941; The Pirate, 1942; Jacobowsky and the Colonel (with Franz Werfel), 1944; Dunnigan's Daughter, 1945; Jane (from Somerset Maugham), 1946; I Know my Love (from Achard), 1949; Fanny (with Joshua Logan), 1954; The Cold Wind and the Warm, 1959; Lord Pengo, 1962; But for Whom Charlie, 1964. *Publications:* Duveen, 1952; The Worcester Account, 1954; Portrait of Max (USA edn, 1960), Conversation with Max (GB, 1960); The Suspended Drawing Room, 1965; The Burning Glass, 1968; also plays. *Address:* 1185 Park Avenue, New York, NY 10028, USA.

**BEIT, Sir Alfred Lane,** 2nd Bt, *cr* 1924; Trustee of the Beit Trust; Trustee of Beit Fellowships for scientific research; *b* London, 19 Jan. 1903; *o surv s* of 1st Bt and Lilian (*d* 1946), *d* of late T. L. Carter, New Orleans, USA; *S* father, 1930; *m* 1939, Clementine, 2nd *d* of late Major the Hon. Clement Mitford, DSO and Lady Helen Nutting. *Educ:* Eton; Christ Church, Oxford. Contested West Islington in LCC election 1928; South-East St Pancras (C) in general election, 1929; MP (U) St Pancras South-East, 1931-45. Trustee, Beit Memorial Fellowships for Medical Research, 1930-49. Mem. Adv. Cttee, Tanganyika Concessions Ltd. *Heir:* none. *Address:* Russborough, Blessington, Co Wicklow, Eire; Gordon's Bay, CP, S Africa. *Clubs:* Buck's, Carlton; Kildare Street (Dublin); Civil Service (Cape Town); Muthaiga (Nairobi).

**BEITH, Sir John,** KCMG 1969 (CMG 1959); HM Diplomatic Service; Ambassador to Belgium, since 1969; *b* 4 April 1914; *s* of late William Beith and Margaret Stanley, Toowoomba, Qld; *m* 1949, Diana Gregory-Hood, *d* of Sir John Gilmour, 2nd Bt, *qv*; one *s* one *d* (and one *d* decd), (one step *s* one step *d*). *Educ:* Eton; King's Coll., Cambridge. Entered Diplomatic Service, 1937, and served in FO until 1940; 3rd Sec., Athens, 1940-41; 2nd Sec., Buenos Aires, 1941-45; served Foreign Office, 1945-49; Head of UK Permanent Delegation to the UN at Geneva, 1950-53; Head of Chancery at Prague, 1953-54; Counsellor, 1954; Counsellor and Head of Chancery, British Embassy, Paris, 1954-59; Head of Levant Dept, FO, 1959-61; Head of North and East African Dept, Foreign Office, 1961-63; Ambassador to Israel, 1963-65; an Asst Sec.-Gen., NATO, 1966-67; Asst Under-Sec. of State, FO, 1967-69. *Recreations:* music, racing, tennis. *Address:* c/o The Foreign and Commonwealth Office, SW1; 4 Cadogan Square, SW1. *T:* Belgravia 4458. *Clubs:* White's, Royal Automobile; Jockey (Paris).

**BÉKÉSY, Dr Georg von;** Professor of Sensory Sciences, University of Hawaii, since 1966; *b* 3 June 1899; *s* of Alexander von Békésy and Paula (*née* Mazaly). *Educ:* University of Berne; University of Budapest (PhD). Research Laboratory, Hungarian Telephone System, 1923-26; Central Lab., Siemens & Halske, Berlin, 1926-27. University of Budapest: Privatdozent, 1932-39, Ausserordentlicher Prof., 1939-40, Ordentlicher Prof., 1940-46; Karolinski Inst, Stockholm, 1946-47, Research Prof., 1947-49; Research Lectr, Harvard, 1947-49; Sen. Research Fellow in Psychophysics, Harvard, 1949-66. Member: Nat. Acad. of Science; Amer. Acad. of Science; Akad. Leopoldina; Corres. Mem., Akad. der Wissenschaften, Mainz; Hon. Mem. of various assocs. Hon. MD: Wilhelm Univ., Münster, 1955; Univs Berne, 1959, Padua, 1962, Budapest, 1969; Hon. DSc: Gustavus Adolphus Coll. 1963; Pennsylvania 1965; Cordoba 1968; Buenos Aires 1968; Hawaii, 1969. Nobel Prize in Medicine and Physiology, 1961. *Publications:* Experiments in Hearing, 1960; Sensory Inhibition, 1967; articles in scientific publications. *Address:* Laboratory of Sensory Sciences, 1993 East-West Road, University of Hawaii, Honolulu, Hawaii 96822, USA.

**BELCHEM, Maj.-Gen. Ronald Frederick King,** CB 1946; CBE 1944; DSO 1943; Chairman and Managing Director, GUS Export Corporation Ltd, and Director of Exports, GUS Industrial Division; *b* 21 Jan. 1911; *s* of O. K. Belchem and Louise Morris; *m* 1947 (marr. diss. 1954); *m* 1958, Ellen, *d* of late William Cameron, Ross-shire. *Educ:* Guildford; Sandhurst. 2nd Lieut Royal Tank Regt, 1931, Interpreter, Russian, Italian and French. Served Egypt and Palestine, 1936-39 (despatches); War of 1939-45 (despatches seven times); Greece; with Eighth Army; Western Desert (commanded 1st Royal Tank Regiment, 1943); Sicily and Italy, BGS (Ops) North-West Europe (BGS (Ops) 21 Army Group). Comd. 6 Highland Bde BAOR, 1948; Chief of Staff to Field Marshal Viscount Montgomery, 1948-50; retd, 1953; Chairman's Staff, Tube Investments Ltd, 1954-59; Chairman's Staff, BSA. Group, 1959-61; Managing Dir Metal Components Div. of the BSA Group 1961. Chm., BNEC Hotel and Public Buildings Equipment Group, 1968-69. Freeman, City of London, 1956. Mem., Worshipful Co. of Barbers, 1956. Legion of Merit (US), Order of White Lion and MC (Czech), 1946; Order of Orange-Nassau (Dutch), 1947. *Publication:* A Guide to Nuclear Energy. *Recreation:* language study. *Address:* 35 South Grove House, Highgate Village, N6. *T:* 01-340 5700. *Club:* United Service.

**BELCHER, John Rashleigh,** MS 1946; FRCS 1942; Consultant Thoracic Surgeon, NW Metropolitan Regional Hospital Board, since 1950; Surgeon, London Chest Hospital, since 1951; Thoracic Surgeon, Middlesex Hospital, since 1955; *b* 11 Jan. 1917; *s* of late Dr Ormonde Rashleigh Belcher, Liverpool; *m* 1940, Jacqueline Mary, *d* of late C. P. Phillips; two *s* one *d*. *Educ:* Epsom Coll.; St Thomas' Hosp. MB 1939; FRCS 1942; MS 1946; Resident appointments at St Thomas' Hospital, 1939-40. RAF, 1940-46: Medical Service; general duties and surgical specialist; Squadron Leader. Resident and Asst posts at St Thomas', Brompton, London Chest, and Middlesex Hosps; followed by consultant appointments; co-editor, Brit. Jl of Diseases of the Chest. Member: Assoc. of Thoracic Surgeons; Thoracic Soc.; Cardiac Soc. Toured Far East for British Council, 1969. *Publications:* Thoracic Surgical Management, 1953; chapters in Standard Text-books; papers in British and foreign medical journals. *Recreations:* golf, ski-ing, photography. *Address:* 26 Albert Hall Mansions, SW7. *T:* 01-589 4373.

**BELCHER, Ronald Harry,** CMG 1958; Under-Secretary, Ministry of Overseas Development, since 1965; *b* 5 Jan 1916; *s* of Harry Albert Belcher; *m* 1948, Hildegarde (*née* Hellyer-Jones); one *s*. *Educ:* Christ's Hosp., Horsham; Jesus Coll., Cambridge; Brasenose Coll., Oxford. BA (Hons Classics) Cantab 1937; Dipl. Class. Arch. Cantab 1938; BA Oxon 1938. Indian Civil Service, Punjab, 1939-48; Commonwealth Relations Office, 1948-65; seconded to Foreign Office for service in British Embassy, Washington, 1951-53; Private Sec., 1953-54; Asst Sec., 1954; Deputy High Commissioner for the UK in S Africa, 1956-59; Asst Under Sec. of State, CRO, 1960-61; British Dep. High Comr, Delhi, 1961-65. *Address:* Ministry of Overseas Development, Eland House, Stag Place, SW1; Kenilworth, 3 St Mary's Close, Fetcham, Surrey. *Club:* Oxford and Cambridge.

**BELDAM, Alexander Roy Asplan,** QC 1969; *b* 29 March 1925; *s* of George William Beldam and Margaret Frew Shettle (formerly Beldam, *née* Underwood); *m* 1953, Elisabeth Bryant Farr; two *s* one *d*. *Educ:* Oundle Sch.; Brasenose Coll., Oxford. Sub-Lt, RNVR Air Branch, 1943-46. Called to Bar, Inner Temple, 1950. *Recreations:* sailing, cricket, naval history. *Address:* Ivy Cottage, 66 Station Road, Barnes, SW13. *T:* 01-876 4843. *Club:* Naval.

**BELFRAGE, Leif Axel Lorentz,** GBE (Hon.), 1956; Swedish Ambassador to the Court of St

James's since 1967; *b* 1 Feb. 1910; *s* of J. K. E. Belfrage and G. U. E. Löfgren; *m* 1937, Greta Jering; one *s* three *d*. *Educ:* Stockholm University. Law degree, 1933. Practised law at Stockholm Magistrates Court; joined Min. of Commerce, 1937; Dir, Swedish Clearing Office, 1940; Dir, war-time Swedish Trade Commn, 1943-45; entered Swedish Diplomatic Service, as Head of Section in Commercial Dept, 1945; Commercial Counsellor, Swedish Embassy, Washington, 1946; Head of Commercial Dept, FO, Stockholm, 1949-53; Dep. Under-Sec. of State, FO, 1953; Perm. Under-Sec. of State FO, 1956. Grand Cross, Order of North Star (Sweden). *Address:* Royal Swedish Embassy, 23 North Row, W1. *T:* 01-499 9500. *Clubs:* Athenæum, Turf.

**BELGION, (Harold) Montgomery;** author; *b* Paris, 28 Sept. 1892, British subject by birth; *m* 1945, Gladys Helen, *e d* of late J. R. Mattock, Headington. Editor-in-charge, New York Herald (European edition), Paris, 1915-16; private, HAC, 1916-18; commissioned July 1918 to The Dorsetshire Regt; BEF, France, 1916 and 1918-19; foreign sub-editor, London Daily Mail, 1919-21 and 1922-24; editorial staff of the New York World, New York, 1921-22; chief sub-editor. Westminster Gazette, 1924-25; with Harcourt, Brace and Co., publishers, New York, 1925-28; Daily Mirror, 1935-37; Daily Sketch, 1939. Capt. Royal Engineers, 1940-45; BEF France, 1940; Greece, 1941 (prisoner of war). Sec. of Westwood House Sch. Trust, 1950-61. *Publications:* Our Present Philosophy of Life, 1929 (translated into French as Notre Foi Contemporaine, 1934); The Human Parrot, 1931; News of the French, 1938 (translated into German as Neues aus Frankreich, 1939); Reading for Profit, 1945 (translated into French, 1947, expanded version, USA, 1950, Britain, 1951); Introduction to Cresset Press Moby Dick, 1947; Epitaph on Nuremberg, 1947; (new and exp. version, Victors' Justice, USA, 1949); Lydgate and Dorothea in New Road No. 6, 1949; A Selection of Poe's Poems with Introduction, 1948; A Man After My Own Heart (USA), 1949; H. G. Wells, 1953 and David Hume, 1965 (British Council booklets); Contrib. to Promise of Greatness, 1968; The Worship of Quantity: a Study of Megalopolitics, 1969; André Malraux in the Politics of the 20th Century Novelists, 1970; contributions to numerous reviews and other periodicals. *Address:* Highfield, Titchmarsh, Kettering, Northants. *Club:* Athenæum.

**BELHAVEN and STENTON,** 13th Baron, *cr* 1647; **Robert Anthony Carmichael Hamilton;** farming; *b* 27 Feb. 1927; *o s* of 12th Baron; *S* father, 1961; *m* 1952, Elizabeth Ann, *d* of late Col A. H. Moseley, Warrawee, NSW; one *s* one *d*. *Educ:* Eton. Commissioned, The Cameronians, 1947. *Heir: s* Master of Belhaven, *qv*. *Address:* The Mark Twynholm, Kirkcudbrightshire, Scotland. *T:* Twynholm 209.

**BELHAVEN, Master of; Hon. Frederick Carmichael Arthur Hamilton;** *b* 27 Sept. 1953; *s* of 13th Baron Belhaven and Stenton, *qv*.

**BELISARIO, Dr John Colquhoun,** CMG 1968; CBE 1945 (OBE 1942); ED 1946; *b* Sydney, 30 April 1900; *s* of Guy Alexander Fernandez Belisario and Isobel Colquhoun Fraser; *m* 1930, Freda Adele Sauber; two *d*. *Educ:* King's Sch., Parramatta; University of Sydney. MB, ChM 1926; DDM Sydney 1947; MD Sydney. 1950; FRACP 1959; MACD 1966. Post-grad. study in dermatology, London, Edinburgh, Paris and Breslau. Served War of 1939-45, AAMC, commanding 2/3 CCS, 1940-41 (Lt-Col) and 2/5 AGH, 1941-44 (Col). Royal Prince Alfred Hosp., Sydney: RMO 1926; Registrar, 1927-28; Hon. MO Venereal Dept, 1929-41; Hon. Asst Physician, Diseases of the Skin, 1932-44, Hon. Physician, 1944-60, Hon. Cons. Physician, 1960-; Mem., Board of Dirs, 1955-. Holds hon. consultancies in many other hosps. Charter Mem., Bd of Dirs, Internat. Soc. of Tropical Dermat., 1962, Vice-Pres. 1964, Pres., 1969; 1st President: Dermatological Assoc. of Australia, 1949-50; Australasian Coll. of Dermatologists, 1967-68. Hon. Mem. and Corres. Mem. of Dermatological Societies throughout the world; Mem. Editorial Bd, 6 overseas dermat. jls. *Publications:* Cancer of the Skin, 1959; many contribs to symposia and journals. *Recreations:* surfing, gardening. *Address:* Harley, 143 Macquarie Street, Sydney, New South Wales 2000, Australia. *T:* 27-1981 or 36-6536. *Clubs:* Union, American National, Tattersall's, Royal Sydney Golf (Sydney).

**BELL, Adrian Hanbury;** Author; *b* 4 Oct. 1901; *e s* of Robert Bell and Frances Hanbury; *m* 1931, Marjorie Gibson; one *s* two *d*. *Educ:* Uppingham. After leaving school went as pupil on a Suffolk farm, and has farmed in West and East Suffolk. *Publications:* Corduroy; Silver Ley; The Cherry Tree; Folly Field; The Balcony; By-Road; The Shepherd's Farm; Men and the Fields; Poems; Apple Acre; Sunrise to Sunset; The Budding Morrow; The Flower and the Wheel; The Black Donkey; The Path by the Window; Music in the Morning; A Young Man's Fancy; A Suffolk Harvest; The Mill House; My Own Master; A Street in Suffolk.

**BELL, Archibald Angus,** QC (Scot.) 1961; in practice at Scottish Bar since 1949; *b* 13 April 1923; *o s* of James Dunlop Bell, Solicitor, Ayrshire, and Katherine Rachel Gordon Miller; *m* 1949, Dorothy, *d* of Dr Pollok Donald, Edinburgh, and Mrs Dorothy Donald; two *s*. *Educ:* The Leys Sch., Cambridge; University of St Andrews; University of Glasgow. Served War, Royal Navy, 1941-45. Sub-Lieut RNVR MA, St Andrews, 1947; LLB, Glasgow, 1949; admitted to Faculty of Advocates, 1949; Reporter, Court of Session Cases, 1952-55. Contested (C and U) Maryhill Div. of Glasgow, Gen. Elec., 1955. Standing Junior Counsel in Scotland: to Board of Trade, 1955-57; to War Dept, 1957-61. *Recreations:* watching the sun rise, getting fun out of games. Formerly: hockey and cricket blue, St Andrews, and Pres. UAU and Dramatic Soc. *Address:* 1, Heriot Row, Edinburgh 3. *T:* Waverley 4940. *Clubs:* Royal and Ancient (St Andrews); RNVR (Scotland).

**BELL, Sir Arthur (Capel Herbert),** Kt 1963; FRCS, FRCOG; Past President of the Royal College of Obstetricians and Gynæcologists; Consultant Gynæcological Surgeon: Westminster Hospital; Chelsea Hospital for Women; Consultant Surgeon, Queen Charlotte's Maternity Hospital; Consulting Gynæcological Surgeon, Thames Ditton Cottage Hospital and Edenbridge Memorial Hospital; *b* 18 Sept. 1904; *o s* of late J. H. Bell; *m* 1933, Hilda, *d* of late H. M. F. Faure; three *s* two *d*. *Educ:* Marlborough Coll.; St Bartholomew's Hosp. MRCS Eng, LRCP London 1927; MB, BS London 1930; FRCS Eng 1930; FRCOG 1946; Hon. MMSA; Hon. FRCPSG. Formerly: House Surgeon to Surg. Prof. Unit, and Obstetric House Surg., St Bartholomew's Hosp.; Obstetric House Surg., Liverpool Royal Infirmary; Obstetric and Gynæcological Registrar and Tutor, Charing Cross Hosp. and Westminster Hosp.; Obstetric Surgeon, Westminster Hosp.; Gynæcological Surgeon, Chelsea Hosp. for Women. Hon. Adviser on Obstetrics and Gynæcology to the Army, 1963-70. Sometime

Examr to the Univs of London, Glasgow, Belfast, Durham, Birmingham, Oxford, Conjoint Board of RCP and RCS, RCOG, Soc. of Apothecaries, Central Midwives Board. *Publications:* A Pocket Obstetrics; (jointly) Queen Charlotte's Practice of Obstetrics; Hysterectomy; Total and Subtotal (Jl of Obst. and Gynec. of Br. Empire). *Recreations:* gardening, shooting, fishing, tennis and golf. *Address:* Manor House, Claygate, Surrey. *T:* Esher 62455. *Club:* Boodle's.

**BELL, Arthur Doyne Courtenay,** MA, DM (Oxford); FRCP; Consulting Physician (lately Physician in Charge of Children's Department), Charing Cross Hospital; Physician Belgrave Children's Hospital; Hon. Physician, Children's Department, Queen Mary's Hospital for the East End of London; Member of Board of Governors and Chairman of Planning Committee, Charing Cross Hospital; Examiner in Medicine and Child Health, Royal College of Physicians; Examiner in Pediatrics, University of Birmingham; *b* 15 June 1900; *s* of Robert Arthur Bell and Evelyn Maud (*née* Richardson). *Educ:* Gresham's Sch.; St John's Coll., Oxford (open Scholar and Adrian Graves Memorial Exhibitioner); St Thomas's Hosp. Perkins' Travelling Fellowship, Vienna, 1931. Chief Asst, Children's Dept, St Thomas' Hosp., 1932; Examiner for Diploma in Child Health, RCS, 1947. Mem. of Worshipful Soc. of Apothecaries: Freeman of City of London; FRSocMed. Past Pres. pædiatric Section, RSM; Past Pres. W London Med. Chirurgical Soc. *Publications:* communications to Med. Jls. *Recreations:* angling and deipnosophism. *Address:* (residence) 14a Compton Road, Canonbury, N1. *T:* 01-226 8731; 144 Harley Street, W1. *T:* 01-935 9770. *Clubs:* Savile, United University; Wilton Fly-fishing.

**BELL, Captain Charles Leigh de Hauteville,** DSC 1943; RD 1938; Commodore Captain, Canadian Pacific Steamships Ltd, 1961-63, retired; *b* 24 March 1903; *s* of Commander Charles de H. Bell, RNR, and Ethel Maud Bell (*née* Leigh); *m* 1938, Hilda Olga Ottilie Kohn Speyer; one *s* two *d*. *Educ:* St Bees; HMS Conway. Joined Canadian Pacific Steamships as cadet, 1918; commissioned as Sub-Lieut, RNR, 1925. Served Comdr, RNR, in comd of destroyers, 1940-43; Commodore of convoys, 1944; Capt. RNR, 1945; HMS Palomares, 1946; subsequently rejoined CPS in command. Mem. Hon. Company of Master Mariners. *Recreations:* golf, philately. *Address:* Mogador Point, Lower Kingswood, Surrey. *T:* Reigate 42909.

**BELL, Charles William,** CBE 1968; Chairman of Coats Patons Ltd, since 1967; *b* 4 June 1907; *s* of Herbert James Bell and Bertha Alice Bell (*née* Jones), Pen-y-Ffordd, Flintshire; *m* 1931, Eileen, *d* of Edwin James Hannaford, Eastham, Cheshire; three *s*. *Educ:* Chester City Gram. Sch.; Selwyn Coll., Cambridge (Open Exhibr). Joined Coats Patons Ltd, 1930; Dir, Central Agency Ltd (subsid. co.), 1934; Dir, J. & P. Coats Ltd, (Subsid. Co.), 1947; Man. Dir, J. & P. Coats Ltd, 1961; Dir, Coats Patons Ltd, 1961. *Recreations:* shooting, fishing, golf. *Address:* The White Cottage, 19 Lennox Drive East, Helensburgh, Dunbartonshire. *T:* Helensburgh 4973. *Clubs:* Conservative (Glasgow); Royal and Ancient (St Andrews); Royal Northern Yacht; Helensburgh Golf.

**BELL, Donald Munro;** International Concert and Opera Artist; Freelance; *b* 19 June 1934; *m* 1968, Ingrid von Krannhals; one *s* (by former marr.). *Educ:* South Burnaby High Sch., BC, Canada, Made Wigmore Hall Debut, 1958, since when has sung at Bayreuth Wagner Festival, 1958, 1959, 1960; Lucerne and Berlin Festivals, 1959; PHiladelphia and New York Debuts with Eugene Ormandy, 1959; Israel, 1962; Russia Recital Tour, 1963; Glyndebourne Festival, 1963; with Deutsche Oper am Rhein, Düsseldorf, 1964-66. Has made recordings. Arnold Bax Medal, 1955. *Address:* c/o Ibbs & Tillett, Ltd, 124 Wigmore Street, W1.

**BELL, Sir Douglas (James),** Kt 1966; CBE 1962; *b* 16 June 1904; *s* of William and Helen Bell, Glasgow; *m* 1936, Phyllis Maude Jones; one *s* one *d*. *Educ:* Allan Glen's Sch., Glasgow. Resident Dir in India, Indian Steelworks Construction Co., 1958-62; Gen. Man., Hindustan Steel Ltd, Durgapur Steel Plant, Bengal, 1962-65; Chairman: British Steelworks Equipment Ltd, 1965-67; Davy-Ashmore Ltd, 1969-70. *Address:* Casa Nova Esperança, Cerro, São Miguel, Silves, Algarve, Portugal. *Clubs:* Oriental; Bengal, Calcutta (Calcutta).

**BELL, Douglas Maurice;** Chief Executive of ICI (Europa) Ltd since Oct. 1965; *b* Shanghai, China, 15 April 1914; *s* of Alexander Dunlop Bell; *m* 1947, Elizabeth Mary Edelsten; one *s* two *d*. *Educ:* The Edinburgh Academy; St Andrews Univ. War Dept, Chemist, Woolwich Arsenal, 1936. Imperial Chemical Industries: Dyestuffs Div., 1937-42; Regional Sales Manager, 1946-53; Billingham Dir, 1953; Billingham Man. Dir, 1955-57; Heavy Organic Chemicals Managing Dir, 1958-61; Chm. of European Council, Imperial Chemical Industries Ltd, 1960-65. Director: British Titan Products Ltd; Dyestuffs Division, ICI. Comendador de Numero de la Orden de Merito Civil, 1967. *Recreations:* sports and gardens. *Address:* 14 Drève des Rhododendrons, Boitsfort, Brussels, Belgium. *T:* Brussels 73. 46. 71. *Clubs:* Anglo-Belgian; Cercle Royal Gaulois (Brussels); Royal Waterloo and Tandridge Golf.

**BELL, Prof. Frank,** DSc, PhD; FRIC; FRSE; FSAScot; Professor of Chemistry, Heriot-Watt University (formerly College), Edinburgh, 1950-66 (now Emeritus); *b* 24 Dec. 1904; *o s* of Thomas Bell, Derby; *m* 1930, May Perryman; one *s* one *d*. *Educ:* Crypt Grammar Sch., Glos; Queen Mary Coll., University of London. Head of Science Dept, Blackburn Tech. Coll. 1935-41; Principal Lancaster Tech. Coll., 1941-46; Prof. of Chemistry, Belfast Coll. of Tech., 1947-50. *Publications:* original papers mainly in Journal of Chemical Soc. *Recreations:* numismatics, walking and field-club activities. *Address:* Hilcot, Finchcroft Lane, Prestbury, Cheltenham, Glos.

**BELL, Sir Frederick (Archibald),** Kt 1947; OBE 1943; MC 1918; Farmer; Chairman of Herring Industry Board, 1944-61, retired; *b* 19 Sept. 1891; *s* of Robert King Bell, Paisley; *m* 1917, Lilian Hunter Wilson (*d* 1948); two *s* three *d*; *m* 1950, Marjory Helen, MB, ChB, DPH, *widow* of Charles G. Kennaway, WS, Auchterarder. *Educ:* Loretto. Royal Engineers (TF), European War, 1914-18, Capt. (MC); commanded 3rd Perthshire Battalion Home Guard, War of 1939-45, Lieut-Col (OBE). Vice-Chm., Scottish Milk Marketing Board, 1935-38; Mem. of Herring Industry Board, 1938, Chm., 1944. *Address:* Chapelbank, Auchterarder, Perthshire. *T:* Gask 221. *Clubs:* Farmers'; Royal (Perth).

**BELL, Col Frederick Charles,** CMG 1919; retired; late Canadian Army Medical Corps; *b* 1883; *s* of Charles Napier Bell, LLD, Winnipeg; *m* 1957, Marcella Ellen, *d* of late Lieut-Col W. H. Moodie, Kelowna, BC,

Canada. BA Queen's Univ., Kingston, Ont., 1905; MD University of Manitoba, 1909. Served European War, 1914-19 (despatches, CMG). *Address:* Tyndrum, 6015 Eagle Ridge Drive, West Vancouver, British Columbia. *Club:* Alpine of Canada.

**BELL, Capt. Frederick Secker,** CB 1939; RN retired; *b* 17 Aug. 1897; *y s* of late Col F. B. Bell, HAC; *m* Dulcie, *d* of Nahun Barnet, FRIBA, Melbourne, Australia. *Educ:* Matfield Grange, Kent; RN Colls, Osborne and Dartmouth. Served in HMS Cumberland in Cameroons campaign, 1914-15; HMS Canada (Grand Fleet and Jutland); Submarines, 1916-23; lent to RAN, 1930-32; Comdr, 1931; RN Staff Coll., 1933; Executive Officer, HMS Repulse, 1935-38; Capt., 1938; Exeter in command, 1939; served in battle with Graf Spee, 1939 (CB). Retired list, 1948; ADC to the King, 1947-48.

**BELL, Sir Gawain (Westray),** KCMG 1957; CBE 1955 (MBE 1942); Secretary-General, South Pacific Commission, 1966-70; *b* 21 Jan. 1909; *s* of late William Westray Bell; *m* 1945, Silvia, *d* of Major Adrian Cornwell-Clyne; three *d*. *Educ:* Winchester; Hertford Coll., Oxford. Sudan Political Service, 1931; seconded to the Government of Palestine, 1938. Military Service in Middle East, 1941-45; Lieut-Col Arab Legion, 1942-45. District Comr, Sudan Political Service, 1945-49; Dep. Sudan Agent, Cairo, 1949-51; Dep. Civil Sec., Sudan Government, 1953-54; Permanent Under-Sec., Ministry of the Interior, 1954-55; Governor, Northern Nigeria, 1957-62; Sec Gen., Council for Middle East Trade, 1963-64; engaged, with Sir Ralph Hone, as Constitutional Adviser to Govt of Fedn of S Arabia, 1965-66. Mem. Chapter Gen., Order of St John, 1964-66; KStJ 1958, Order of Independence 3rd Class (Trans Jordan), 1944. *Recreations:* walking, riding, skiing, shooting, rifle shooting (Capt. Oxford Univ., 1931; shot for Sudan). *Address:* Hidcote Bartrim Manor, Chipping Campden, Glos. *T:* Mickleton 305. *Clubs:* Athenæum, Bath.

**BELL, Geoffrey Foxall,** MC; MA; *b* 16 April 1896; *s* of late F. R. Bell, Burton-on-Trent; *m* 1926, Margaret, *d* of late R. Austin-Carewe, Montreal, Canada; three *s*. *Educ:* Repton; Balliol Coll., Oxford. Served in RFA, 1915-19; Asst Master, Upper Canada Coll. and Christ's Hospital; Headmaster, Trent Coll., Derbs, 1927-36; Headmaster, Highgate Sch., 1936-54; Oxford Univ. Cricket XI, 1919. *Publications:* Establishing a Fruit Garden, 1963; Seven Old Testament Figures (Bishop of London's Lent Book), 1968. *Address:* Widford, Haslemere, Surrey.

**BELL, George Douglas Hutton,** CBE 1965; FRS 1965; PhD; Director, Plant Breeding Institute, Cambridge, 1947-70; *b* 18 Oct. 1905; *er s* of George Henry and Lilian Mary Matilda Bell; *m* 1934, Eileen Gertrude Wright; two *d*. *Educ:* Bishop Gore's Grammar Sch., Swansea; Univ. Coll. of North Wales, Bangor; University of Cambridge. BSc 1928; PhD 1931. Research Officer, Plant Breeding Inst., 1931; University Demonstrator, Cambridge, 1933, Lectr, 1944; Fellow of Selwyn Coll., Cambridge, 1944-54, Hon. Fellow, 1965. Research Medal, Royal Agricultural Soc. of England, 1956; Royal Society Mullard Medal, 1967. Hon. DSc: Reading Univ., 1968; University of Wales, 1968. *Publications:* Cultivated Plants of the Farm, 1948; The Breeding of Barley Varieties in Barley and Malt, 1962; Cereal Breeding in Vistas in Botany, Vol. II, 1963; Phylogeny of Temperate Cereals in Crop Plant Evolution, 1965; papers on barley and breeding in Jl of Agricultural Science, etc. *Recreations:* outdoor games, tennis, swimming; natural history; theatre and concert going. *Address:* 6 Worts Causeway, Cambridge. *T:* Cambridge 47449.

**BELL, Prof. George Howard,** MD; FRCPGlas 1946; FRSE 1947; FIBiol 1968; Symers Professor of Physiology in the University of Dundee (formerly Queen's Coll., Dundee), since 1947; Dean of The Faculty of Medicine, 1954-56 and 1963; *b* 24 Jan. 1905; *m* 1934, Isabella Margaret Thomson, MB, ChB; two *s*. *Educ:* Ayr Academy; Glasgow Univ. BSc 1929; MB (Hons) 1930; MD (Hons) 1943. House Physician, Royal Hosp. for Sick Children, 1930; Asst Lecturer in Physiology Dept, University of Glasgow, 1931-34; Lecturer in Physiology: Univ. of Bristol, 1934-35; Univ. of Glasgow, 1935-47. Mem. Physiological Soc., 1934-, and Sec., 1949-54; Mem. Inter-University Council for Higher Education Overseas, 1957-; Mem. Eastern Regional Hospital Board, 1957-67 (Vice-Chm., 1966-67); Gen. Dental Council Visitor, 1960-62; Comr, Royal University of Malta, 1962-. Hon. Fellow, Accademia Anatomico-Chirurgica, Perugia, 1959. *Publications:* Experimental Physiology for Medical Students, 6th Edition, 1959; (with J. N. Davidson and H. Scarborough) Textbook of Physiology and Biochemistry, 7th Edition, 1968; papers in Journal of Physiology, Journal of Endocrinology, Lancet, etc. *Address:* Duntulm, 80 Grove Road, Broughty Ferry, Dundee DD5 1LB. *T:* Dundee 78724.

**BELL, George Raymond,** CB 1967; Third Secretary, HM Treasury, since 1966; *b* 13 March 1916; *e s* of late William Bell and Christabel Bell (*née* Appleton); *m* 1944, Joan Elizabeth, *o d* of late W. G. Coltham and of Christina Coltham; two *s* two *d*. *Educ:* Bradford Grammar Sch.; St John's Coll., Cambridge (Scholar). Entered Civil Service, Assistant Principal, 1938; Min. of Health, 1938; transf. Treasury, 1939; served War 1941-44, Royal Navy (Lieut RNVR). Principal, Civil Service, 1945; Asst Sec., 1951; Under-Sec., 1960; Sec. (Finance), Office of HM High Commissioner for the UK in Canada, 1945-48; Counsellor, UK Permanent Delegn to OEEC/NATO, Paris, 1953-56; Principal Private Sec. to Chancellor of Exchequer, 1958-60. Mem. UK Delegation to Brussels Conference, 1961-62. *Recreations:* music, reading, travel. *Address:* Devoncroft, Twickenham, Mddx. *T:* 01-892 2884.

**BELL, George Trafford,** CMG 1961; OBE 1952; retired; now Secretary to Architects; *b* 9 March 1913; 2nd *s* of late George H. Bell and of Veronica Jessie Bell, Alderley Edge, Ches; *m* 1944, Eileen Patricia, *d* of late A. Geoffrey Southern, Wilmslow, Ches; two *s* one *d*. *Educ:* Sedbergh; St John's Coll., Cambridge. Apptd Admin. Offr, Tanganyika, 1936; Sen. Admin. Offr, 1954; Provincial Comr, 1958-62. *Recreations:* golf, fishing. *Address:* Dukenfield Grange, Mobberley, Knutsford, Cheshire.

**BELL, Grace Effingham Laughton,** CBE 1946; *y d* of late Sir John Knox Laughton, RN; *m* 1st, 1915, John Russell Little (killed in action May 1917); 2nd, 1918, Harry Graham Bell (*d* 1950); two *s*. *Educ:* Convent Schs; King's Coll., London Univ. Women's Forestry Corps (Travelling Officer for Wales and West of England), 1915-19; Women's Royal Naval Service, Sept. 1939-Jan. 1946; Superintendent, WRNS: The Nore, 1942; Western Approaches, 1944. *Recreations:* painting, gardening. *Address:* Apart: Yuca 12, Fuengirola, Spain. *Clubs:* Service Women's; Royal Burnham Yacht (Burnham-on-Crouch).

**BELL, Harry,** OBE 1945; MA; MEd; *b* 11 April 1899; *s* of late John Nicol Bell, Aberdeen, and late Isabella Georgina Reith; *m* 1933, Sophia McDonald, *d* of late Alexander B. Fulton, Kilkerran, Newlands, Glasgow; two *s* one *d*. *Educ:* Robert Gordon's Coll.; Aberdeen Univ. (Kay Prize and Dey Scholarship); Clare Coll., Cambridge (Foundation Scholar); Glasgow Univ. (EdB). Asst Master, Glasgow Academy, 1927-33; Rector of Elgin Academy, 1933-36; Rector of Dollar Academy, 1936-60. Scottish Educational Adviser Air Training Corps, 1941-45; Mem. of Scottish Youth Advisory Cttee, 1942-45; Pres. of Scottish Association of Headmasters, 1948. Adviser with UNESCO Delegation, Florence, 1950; Mem. of Advisory Council on Scottish Education, 1957-61. Fellow Internat. Inst. of Arts and Letters, 1960. Research Scholar, University of St Andrews, 1967. *Publications:* English for Air Cadets; Stevenson's Travels and Essays; Thirteen Short Stories; Selected English Prose; Approach to English Literature; General Editor of Oxford Comprehension Course; articles on literary, historical and educational subjects. *Recreations:* walking, reading, golf. *Address:* Viewpark, Lawhead Road, St Andrews, Fife. *T:* St Andrews 2867. *Clubs:* Scottish Mountaineering; Royal and Ancient.

**BELL, Mrs Harry Graham;** *see* Bell, G. E. L.

**BELL, Ian Wright,** CBE 1964; HM Consul-General, Stuttgart, since 1969; *b* Radlett, Herts, 21 Aug. 1913; *s* of late T. H. D. Bell, Hohenort, Constantia, S Africa; *m* 1940, Winifred Mary Ruth Waterfield, *y d* of late E. H. Waterfield, ICS; three *s*. *Educ:* Canford Sch.; St Peter's Hall, Oxford. Entered Consular Service, 1938; Vice-Consul: Valparaiso, 1938; Montevideo, 1940; Foreign Office, 1946; First Sec., 1947; First Sec., Addis Ababa, 1949, Chargé d'Affaires, 1949, 1950, 1952 and 1953; Consul, Innsbruck, 1953; First Sec., Prague, 1954, Chargé d'Affaires, 1954 and 1956; Counsellor and Consul-Gen., Jedda, 1956; Counsellor and Official Sec., Office of UK High Commissioner, Canberra, 1957; HM Consul-Gen., Lyons, France, 1960-65; Ambassador, Santo Domingo, Dominican Republic, 1965-69. *Publication:* The Scarlet Flower (Poems), 1947. *Recreations:* painting, drama, music, riding, walking. *Address:* Liveras House, Broadford, Skye; British Consulate-General, Königstrasse 45, Stuttgart, Germany. *Clubs:* Athenæum, Garrick, Royal Geographical Society, PEN.

**BELL, Very Rev. John,** MM 1917; Dean Emeritus of Perth, WA; Dean, 1953-59, retired; *b* 11 Nov. 1898; *s* of Thomas and Isabella McCracken Bell; unmarried. *Educ:* Gair Sch., Dumfriesshire; privately; St John's Coll., Perth, WA. Deacon, 1926, Priest, 1928; Curate of Christ Church, Claremont, 1926-29; Rector of S Perth, 1929-32; Priest-in-Charge of Claremont, 1933, Rector, 1933-43; Canon of St George's Cathedral, Perth, 1938-44; Org. Sec. (for NSW) Austr. Bd of Missions, 1943-46; Dean of Armidale, 1946-48; Exam. Chap. to Bp of Armidale, 1946-48; Rector of Oddington with Adlestrop, Dio. Gloucester, 1948-52. *Publications:* This Way Peace, 1939; Many Coloured Glass, 1943; Facing the Week, 1947; For Comfort and Courage, 1958. *Recreation:* travel. *Address:* 22/8 Darley Street, South Perth, Western Australia. *T:* 67-4434. *Club:* Weld (Perth, WA).

**BELL, John Elliot;** *b* 6 Nov. 1886; *e s* of late David Bell and Elizabeth Elliot; *m* 1924, Olga, *er d* of late Henry Banks and Elizabeth Ritchie, Edinburgh; one *s* one *d*. *Educ:* George Watson's Coll.; Edinburgh Univ. Vice-Consul at Paris, 1911; Boston, USA 1912; Leopoldville, Belgian Congo, 1913-14; Magallanes, Chile, 1915-19; Santo Domingo, 1920; Consul at Galveston, USA 1920-23; Portland, Ore., 1923-29; Bahia, Brazil, 1930-32; Basle, 1932-34; Consul Gen. at Cologne, 1934-39; at Zurich, 1939-42; at Strasbourg, 1945-46; retired, 1947. *Recreations:* golf, riding. *Address:* 3175 Point Grey Road, Vancouver 8, BC, Canada. *T:* 731-3490.

**BELL, John Geoffrey Y.;** *see* Yates-Bell.

**BELL, Sir John Lowthian,** 5th Bt *cr* 1885; *b* 14 June 1960; *s* of Sir Hugh Francis Bell, 4th Bt and of Lady Bell (Mary Howson, MB, ChB, *d* of late George Howson, The Hyde, Hambledon); *S* father, 1970. *Heir:* *b* David Hugh Bell, *b* 8 Oct. 1961. *Address:* Arncliffe Hall, Ingleby Cross, Northallerton, Yorks.

**BELL, Joseph,** CBE 1953; Chief Constable, City of Manchester, 1943-58, retired; *b* 15 July 1899; *s* of late Joseph Bell; *m* 1926, Edith, *d* of late Matthew Adamson; one *s* (one *d* decd). *Educ:* Alderman Wood Sch., Stanley, Co. Durham. Royal Naval Volunteer Reserve, 1917-19. Newcastle on Tyne City Police, 1919-33; Chief Constable, Hastings, 1933-41; Asst Chief Constable, Manchester, 1941-43. *Address:* Norwood, 246 Windlehurst Road, Marple, Cheshire.

**BELL, Julia,** MA; FRCP; retired; *b* 28 Jan. 1879; unmarried. *Educ:* Nottingham Girls' High Sch.; Girton Coll., Cambridge; London Sch. of Medicine for Women; St Mary's Hospital. Mathematical Tripos, Cambridge. Hon. aegrotat degree, 1901; MA granted by Trinity Coll. Dublin (Cambridge degree not then given to women). Research into Solar Parallax, Cambridge Observatory, 1902-08; Statistical Asst, UC London, 1908-14; medical student and research (with Karl Pearson, FRS), 1914-20; MRCS, LRCP; research asst under Med. Res. Council (during much of time on permanent Acad. Staff), working in Galton Lab., University Coll., 1920-65; Hon. Research Associate at University Coll., London, 1944-65; MRCP (on basis of research work), Galton Research Fellow, 1926; FRCP 1938. Weldon Medal and Prize, Oxford Univ., 1941. *Publications:* in Treasury of Human Inheritance, Vol. II, 6 Monographs on Hered. Diseases of the Eye, 1922-33; Vol. IV, 6 monographs on Nerv. Disease and Muscular Dystrophies, 1934-48; Vol. V, Pts 1 and 2, monographs on Digital Anomalies, 1951-53; Pt 3, on the Lawrence-Moon Syndrome, 1958. A number of papers in Biometrika and Annals of Eugenics, etc. *Recreations:* music, plays, reading, delights of friendship; chief interests Applied Statistics and Historical side of Medicine and Science. *Address:* 35 Circus Lodge, Circus Road, NW8. *T:* 01-286 4648.

**BELL, P(hilip) Ingress,** TD 1950; **His Honour Judge Ingress Bell;** Judge of the County Courts (Circuit 4) since 1962; *b* 10 Jan. 1900; *s* of Geoffrey Vincent and Mary Ellen Bell; *m* 1933, Agnes Mary Eastwood; two *s* one *d*. *Educ:* Stonyhurst, Blackburn; Royal Naval College, Keyham; Queen's Coll., Oxford (BA Jurisprudence, BCL). Called to the Bar, Inner Temple, 1925; QC 1952. Cadet RN, 1918; Midshipman RN, 1918-20. Lieut TA, 1939; JAG Dept, 1941, Temp. Major, 1944. MP (C) Bolton East, 1951-60. Judge of the County Courts (Circuit 40, Bow) 1960-62. *Publication:* Idols and Idylls, 1918. *Recreations:* golf; Capt., Oxford University Boxing Club, 1923. *Address:* Blackmoss House, Longridge, Lancs.

**BELL, Prof. Quentin (Claudian Stephen);** Professor of the History and Theory of Art, Sussex University, since Oct. 1967; painter, sculptor, potter, author, art critic; *b* 19 Aug.

1910; 2nd *s* of late Clive Bell; *m* 1952, Anne Olivier Popham; one *s* two *d*. *Educ:* Leighton Park. Exhibitions, 1935, 1947, 1949. Political warfare executive, 1941-43. Lectr in Art Education, King's Coll., Newcastle, 1952; Senior Lecturer, 1956; Prof. of Fine Art, University of Leeds, 1962-67 (Head of Dept of Fine Art, 1959); Slade Professor of Fine Art, Oxford Univ., 1964-65; Ferens Prof. of Fine Art, University of Hull, 1965-66. MA Dunelm, 1957. Regular contributor to Listener, 1951-. *Publications:* On Human Finery, 1947; Those impossible English (with Helmut Gernsheim), 1951; Roger Montané, 1961; The Schools of Design, 1963; Ruskin, 1963; Victorian Artists, 1967; Bloomsbury, 1968. Articles in Burlington Magazine, Jl of Warburg and Courtauld Insts, History Today, Durham Research Review. *Recreations:* none worth speaking of. *Address:* Cobbe Place, Beddingham, Sussex. *T:* Glynde 201. *Club:* Reform.

**BELL, Robert Donald Murray,** CB 1966; Under-Secretary, Scottish Development Department, 1959-69 and since 1970; *b* 8 Oct. 1916; *s* of Robert William and Mary Caroline Bell; *m* 1941, Karin Anna Smith; one *s* one *d*. *Educ:* Christ's Hosp.; Clare Coll., Cambridge. First Class Honours, Natural Sciences Tripos (Physics), 1938. Joined Scottish Office, 1938. War of 1939-45: Royal Artillery, 1940-45 (Mil. Coll. of Science, Bury, 1943). Principal, Scottish Home Dept, 1946; Private Sec. to Sec. of State for Scotland, 1947-50; Asst Sec., Scottish Home Dept, 1950; Under-Sec., Scottish Educn Dept, 1969-70. *Address:* Smeaton House, Inveresk, Musselburgh, Midlothian. *T:* Musselburgh 2940. *Club:* Royal Scottish Automobile (Glasgow).

**BELL, Prof. Robert Edward,** FRS 1965; FRSC 1955; Rutherford Professor of Physics, McGill University, Montreal, since 1960; Principal and Vice-Chancellor, McGill University, since 1970; Director of the Foster Radiation Laboratory, 1960-69; Dean of the Faculty of Graduate Studies and Research, 1969-70; *b* 29 Nov. 1918; *s* of Edward Richardson Bell and Edith E. Rich, British Columbia; *m* 1947, Jeanne Atkinson; one *d*. *Educ:* Univ. of British Columbia (BA 1939, MA 1941); McGill Univ. (PhD 1948). Wartime Radar development, Nat. Research Council, Ottawa, 1941-45; Sen. Research Officer, Chalk River Nuclear Laboratories, 1946-56; seconded to Foster Radiation Lab., McGill Univ., 1952-56; Assoc. Prof. of Physics, 1956-60; visiting scientist, Copenhagen Univ. Inst. for Theoretical Physics, under Niels Bohr, 1958-59. Vice-Dean for Physical Sciences, 1964-67. Sec., Sect. III (Science), Royal Society of Canada, 1962-64; Pres. Cdn Assoc. of Physicists, 1965-66. Fellow, American Physical Soc. *Publications:* contribs to books: Annual Reviews of Nuclear Science, 1954; Beta and Gamma Ray Spectroscopy, 1955; Alpha, Beta and Gamma Ray Spectroscopy, 1964; papers on nuclear physics and allied topics in scientific jls. *Address:* 363 Olivier Avenue, Westmount, Montreal 215, Canada. *T:* 935-3769.

**BELL, Ronald McMillan,** QC 1966; MP (C) South Buckinghamshire since 1950; *b* 14 April 1914; *yr s* of late John Bell, Cardiff; *m* 1954, Elizabeth Audrey, *e d* of late Kenneth Gossell, MC, Burwash, Sussex; two *s* two *d*. *Educ:* Cardiff High Sch.; Magdalen Coll., Oxford (Demy). BA 1936; MA 1941; Sec. and Treas., Oxford Union Soc., 1935; Pres., Oxford Univ. Conservative Assoc., 1935. MP (C) for Newport (Monmouth), May-July 1945. Contested Caerphilly Div. of Glamorgan at by-election 1939, Newport, Monmouth, July 1945. Served RNVR, 1939-46. Called to Bar, Gray's Inn, 1938; practises in London and on South-Eastern circuit. Mem. Paddington Borough Council, 1947-49. *Publication:* Crown Proceedings, 1948. *Recreation:* athletics. *Address:* 2 Mitre Court Buildings, Temple, EC4. *T:* 01-353 6981; First House, West Witheridge, Knotty Green, Beaconsfield, Bucks. *T:* Beaconsfield 4606.

**BELL, Ronald Percy,** MA; FRS 1944; FRSE 1968; FRIC; Professor of Chemistry, University of Stirling, since 1967; *b* 1907; *e s* of E. A. Bell, Maidenhead; *m* 1931, Margery Mary West; one *s*. *Educ:* County Boys' Sch., Maidenhead; Balliol Coll., Oxford. Bedford Lecturer in Physical Chemistry, Balliol Coll., 1932; Fellow of Balliol Coll., 1933 (Vice-Master, 1966); Hon. Fellow, 1967; Univ. Lecturer and Demonstrator, Oxford Univ., 1938; Univ. Reader, Oxford Univ., 1955. President: Faraday Soc., 1956; Chemistry Section, British Assoc. Meeting, Durham, 1970; Vice-Pres. Chemical Soc., 1958; George Fisher Baker Lectr, Cornell Univ., 1958; National Science Foundation Fellow, Brown Univ., 1964. Foreign Mem. Royal Danish Acad. of Arts and Sciences, 1962; Hon. LLD Illinois Inst. of Techn., 1965; Hon. DTech, Tech. Univ. of Denmark, 1969. Meldola Medal, Inst. of Chemistry, 1936. *Publications:* Acid-Base Catalysis, 1941; Acids and Bases, 1952; The Proton in Chemistry, 1959; papers in scientific journals. *Address:* 6 Victoria Square, Stirling, Scotland. *T:* Stirling 3502; University of Stirling. *T:* Stirling 3171; Bowderbeck, Buttermere, Cumberland. *Club:* Athenæum.

**BELL, Sir Stanley,** Kt 1954; OBE 1943; JP; DL; Chairman, Astley Industrial Trust Ltd, Manchester; *b* 30 Oct. 1899; *s* of Thomas George Bell, Wigan, Lancs; *m* 1923, Margaret Frances, *d* of James Slevin, Wigan; one *d*. Served European War, 1914-19, with RASC and RAF; 2nd Lieut 1918. Col 1944. Director of Companies; Pres. N-W Provincial Area Council, Conservative Party, 1956-60; Chm., National Union of Conservative Associations, 1958. Contested Westhoughton and West Salford divs, 1945 and 1950. JP Lancs, 1942; DL, Co. Palatine of Lancaster, 1967. *Recreations:* golf, shooting. *Address:* Euxton Hall, Euxton, near Chorley, Lancs. *T:* Chorley 3359. *Clubs:* Carlton; St James's (Manchester).

**BELL, Stewart Edward;** Advocate; Sheriff-Substitute of Lanarkshire at Glasgow since 1961; *b* 4 Aug. 1919; *yr s* of late Charles Edward Bell, Shipowner, and late Rosalind Stewart; *m* 1948, Isla, 2nd *d* of James Spencer and late Adeline Kelly; three *d*. *Educ:* Kelvinside Academy, Glasgow; Trinity Hall, Cambridge; Glasgow Univ. Trinity Hall, 1937-39 and 1946 (MA Cantab), Glasgow Univ., 1946-48 (LLB). Commissioned, Loyal Regt, 1939; served with 2nd Bn in Singapore and Malaya, 1940-42 (wounded, POW in Singapore and Korea, 1942-45). Admitted Advocate, 1948; practised: in Malacca, Malaya as Advocate and Solicitor, 1949-51; at Scottish Bar, 1951-61. *Recreation:* Highland bagpipe. *Address:* 23 Cleveden Drive, Glasgow, W2. *T:* 041-339 3481. *Clubs:* Western (Glasgow); Caledonian (Edinburgh).

**BELL, Rev. Vicars,** MBE 1964; author; Vicar of Clawton; Rector of Tetcott; lecturer and broadcaster; *b* 24 Jan. 1904; *s* of W. A. Bell, Edinburgh; *m* 1926, Dorothy Carley. *Educ:* Radnor Sch., Redhill; Reigate Grammar Sch.; Goldsmiths' Coll., King's Coll., University of London. Asst master at Horley Boys' Council Sch., 1925; Headmaster: Spaldwick Council Sch., 1926; Little Gaddesden C of E Sch., 1929-63. *Publications:* Little Gaddesden, The

Story of an English Parish, 1949; Death Under the Stars, 1949; The Dodo, 1950; Two by Day and One by Night, 1950; Death has Two Doors, 1950; This Way Home, 1951; Death Darkens Council, 1952; On Learning the English Tongue, 1953; Death and the Night Watches, 1954; To Meet Mr Ellis, 1956; Death Walks by the River, 1959; That Night, a play for the Nativity, 1959; Orlando and Rosalind, three tales, 1960; Steep Ways and Narrow, 1963; The Flying Cat, 1964; Prayers for Every Day (edited), 1965. *Recreations:* walking, village activities past and present. *Address:* Clawton Vicarage, Holsworthy, Devon.

**BELL, Walter (Fancourt),** CMG 1967; *b* 7 Nov. 1909; *s* of Canon George Fancourt Bell; *m* 1948, Katharine Spaatz, Washington, DC, USA; no *c. Educ:* Tonbridge Sch., Schoolmaster, 1927-32; Barrister, Inner Temple, 1932-34. Vice-Consul (Acting): New York, 1935-40; Mexico City, 1940-41; New York, 1941-42; Foreign Office, London, 1942-45; 1st Sec., Brit. Embassy, Washington, DC, 1946-48; attached E Africa High Commn, Nairobi, Kenya, 1949-52; 1st Sec., Brit. High Commn, New Delhi, 1952-55; attached War Office, London, 1956-57; Adviser, Federal Govt, W Indies, 1957-60; attached Govt of Kenya, 1961-63; Counsellor, British High Commn, Nairobi, Kenya, 1963-67. US Medal of Freedom with Bronze Palm, 1946. *Recreations:* tennis, walking. *Address:* 6 Onslow Square, SW7. *Clubs:* Travellers'; Nairobi (Nairobi).

**BELL, Sir William H. D. M.;** *see* Morrison-Bell.

**BELL, William Lewis,** CMG 1970; MBE 1945; Head of British Development Division in the Caribbean, Ministry of Overseas Development, since 1966; *b* 31 Dec. 1919; *s* of Frederick Robinson Bell and Kate Harper Bell (*née* Lewis); *m* 1943, Margaret Giles; one *s* one *d. Educ:* Hymers Coll., Hull; Oriel Coll., Oxford. Served The Gloucestershire Regt (Major), 1940-46. Colonial Administrative Service, Uganda, 1946-63: Dep. Sec. to the Treasury, 1956-58; Perm. Sec., Min. of Social Services, 1958-63; Fellow, Economic Develt Inst., World Bank, 1958; Chm., Uganda National Parks, 1962; Pres., Uganda Sports Union, 1961-62. Director, Cox & Danks Ltd (Metal Industries Group), 1963-64. Sec. to the Governors, Westfield Coll., Univ. of London, 1964-65; seconded to ODM as Head of British Develt Div. in the Caribbean, 1965. *Recreations:* cricket, writing, Caribbeana. *Address:* Top Rock House, Graeme Hall, Barbados; Oakgate, Windsor Road, Gerrards Cross, Bucks. *Clubs:* MCC; Bridgetown (Barbados).

**BELL, William Rupert Graham;** Under-Secretary, Ministry of Technology (formerly Ministry of Power), since 1966; *b* 29 May 1920; *m* 1950, Molly Bolton; two *d. Educ:* Bradford Grammar Sch.; St John's Coll., Cambridge (Scholar). Served Royal Artillery, 1940-45 (despatches). Asst Principal, Min. of Fuel and Power, 1948; Principal, 1949; Asst Sec., 1959. Imperial Defence Coll., 1965. *Address:* 46 Kidbrooke Grove, Blackheath, SE3. *T:* 01-858 2103.

**BELL-KINGSLEY, Brig. H. E. W.;** *see* Kingsley.

**BELLAMY, Instr Rear-Adm. Albert John,** CB 1968; OBE 1956; Academic Registrar, Borough Polytechnic, SE1, since 1970; *b* Upton-on-Severn, 26 Feb. 1915; *s* of late A. E. Bellamy and late Mrs A. E. Bellamy; *m* 1942, Dorothy Joan Lawson; one *s* one *d. Educ:* Hanley Castle Grammar Sch.; Downing Coll., Cambridge (Buchanan Exhibitioner). 1st cl. hons Pts I and II, Math. tripos. Asst master, Berkhamsted Sch., 1936-39. Joined RN, 1939, as Instructor Lieut; Fleet Instr and Meteorological Officer, America and WI, 1948-50 (HMS Glasgow); Instr Comdr, 1950; Headmaster, RN Schs, Malta, 1951-54; HMS Ark Royal, 1955-56; Dean of the College, RN Engineering Coll., Manadon, Plymouth, 1956-60; Instr Capt., 1958; Staff of Dir, Naval Educn Service, 1960-63; Dir of Studies, RN Electrical, Weapons and Radio Engineering Sch., HMS Collingwood, 1963-65; Instr Rear-Adm., 1965; Dir, Naval Educn Service, MoD, 1965-70. *Recreations:* golf, amateur drama, gardening; hockey umpire. *Address:* Coombdale, Barns Green, Horsham, Sussex. *T:* Southwater 246.

**BELLAMY, Alexander (William);** Senior Legal Assistant, Council on Tribunals, since 1967 (temporary Legal Assistant, 1963-67); *b* Aug. 1909; *m* 1931, Lena Marie Lauga Massy. *Educ:* Mill Hill Sch.; Clare Coll., Cambridge. Called to Bar, Gray's Inn, 1934; practised at Bar, London, 1934-38; Magistrate, Straits Settlements and FMS, 1938; seconded as District Magistrate, Gold Coast, 1942; legal staff, Malaya Planning Unit, WO, 1944; Crown Counsel, Singapore, 1946; District Judge (Civil), Singapore, 1948; District Judge and 1st Magistrate, Singapore, 1952; actg Puisne Judge, Fed. of Malaya, 1953-54; Puisne Judge, Supreme Court, Nigeria, 1955; Actg Chief Justice, High Court of Lagos and Southern Cameroons, 1959, 1960; Actg Chief Justice, High Court of Lagos, 1961; a Judge of High Court of Lagos and Southern Cameroons, 1955-62. *Address:* 505 Frobisher House, Dolphin Square, SW1.

**BELLAMY, Basil Edmund;** Under-Secretary, Board of Trade, since 1965; *b* 9 Feb. 1914; *s* of William Henry and Mary Bellamy; *m* 1943, Sheila Mary Dolan; one *d. Educ:* Whitgift Sch. Joined Board of Trade, 1932; Asst Dir, Min. of War Transport, 1943; Asst Sec., Min. of Transport, 1951; Under-Sec., 1963-65; Imperial Defence Coll., 1957. *Address:* 127 Hamilton Terrace, St John's Wood, NW8. *T:* 01-624 1440.

**BELLAMY, Prof. Edmund Henry,** MA, PhD; Professor of Physics in the University of London, Westfield College, since 1960; *b* 8 April 1923; *s* of Herbert Bellamy and Nellie (*née* Ablett); *m* 1946, Joan Roberts; three *s. Educ:* Quarry Bank Sch., Liverpool; King's Coll., Cambridge. Lectr in Natural Philosophy, Univ. of Glasgow, 1951-59, Sen. Lectr, 1959-60. Mem., Nuclear Physics Board of Science Research Council, 1965-66. Visiting Prof., Univ. of Stanford, 1966-67. *Publications:* numerous scientific papers in Proc. Phys. Soc. and other journals. *Address:* 7 Homefield Road, Radlett, Herts. *T:* Radlett 4677.

**BELLAMY, Dr Lionel John,** CBE 1970; Director, Explosives Research and Development Establishment, Ministry of Technology (formerly Ministry of Aviation), since 1964; *b* 23 Sept. 1916; *m* Jill Stanley; one *s* one *d* (and one *s* decd). *Educ:* Clapham Coll.; London Univ. BSc Lond 1st cl. 1937; PhD Lond 1939. Scientific Civil Service: Chemical Inspectorate, Min. of Supply, 1939-59; Explosives Research and Development Establishment, 1954-. Adrian Visiting Fellow, Dept of Chemistry, Univ. of Leicester, 1967-; Hon. Prof., Univ. of East Anglia, 1968-. *Publications:* The Infra-Red Spectra of Complex Molecules, 1954 (2nd edn 1958); Advances in IR Group Frequencies, 1968; contribs to Jl Chem. Soc., Spectrochimica Acta, Transactions Faraday Soc., etc.

*Recreation:* spectroscopy. *Address:* The Lodge, Powdermill Lane, Waltham Abbey, Essex. *T:* Waltham Cross 26597.

**BELLAMY, Brig. Robert Hugh,** CBE 1956; DSO 1944 (and Bar 1945); with Hawker Siddeley Group since 1959; *b* 8 Dec. 1910; *yr s* of late Lieut-Col Robert Bellamy, DSO, St Leonards-on-Sea, and late Mrs Constance Gwendoline Stephenson Clarke, Knightsbridge Court, Sloane Street, SW1; *m* 1940, Kathleen Louisa Isabel (marriage dissolved, 1953), *d* of late Sir Alfred Lascelles, Terrington, Yorks; one *s* one *d*. *Educ:* Sherborne; RMC, Sandhurst. 2nd Lieut DCLI, 1930; Lieut-Col 1943; Brig. 1945. Served in France, 1940 (despatches), Adjt DCLI; NW Europe, 1944-45; Palestine, 1945-46 (despatches); comd Air Landing Brigade, 1945; comd Parachute Brigade, 1946-48; Dep. Dir of Weapons Development, 1950-52; Imperial Defence Coll., 1953; Dep. Comdr, Hong Kong, and Comdr 40 Infantry Div., 1954-56; Chief of Staff, 1 Corps, 1956-58; retired, 1958. psc; idc. *Recreations:* yachting, shooting. *Address:* 7 Eaton Place, SW1. *T:* 01-235 7187. *Clubs:* Bath, Royal Ocean Racing; Royal Yacht Squadron.

**BELLERBY, Rev. Alfred Courthope Benson,** MA Cantab; Headmaster, King Edward School, Witley, Surrey, 1926-51; retired, 1951; *b* 26 Jan. 1888; *s* of late E. J. Bellerby, MusDoc Oxon., LRAM, and Charlotte Bellerby; *m* 1922, Enid Florence Apperly. *Educ:* St Lawrence Coll., Ramsgate; Emmanuel Coll., Cambridge; Ridley Hall, Cambridge. Cambridge Univ. Athletic Blue, 1907, 1908, 1909, 1910; Pres. Cambridge Univ. Athletic Club, 1910; Holder of Univ. Gold Medal for 3 wins in succession against Oxford; Cambridge Univ. Hockey Blue, 1909-10; International Hockey Trials, 1909-10; represented United Kingdom in Olympic Games, 1908 (High Jump). Deacon, 1911; Priest, 1913; Chaplain, Games Master and Senior House Master, St Lawrence Coll., 1911-26. *Publication:* The Lonely Dog. *Recreations:* gardening, lecturing. *Address:* Gatesbury, Wonersh, near Guildford, Surrey. *T:* Bramley 3367.

**BELLERBY, Major John Rotherford,** MC; author; *b* 25 May 1896; *e s* of George A. Bellerby, York; *m* 1st, 1929, Mary Eirene Frances (marriage dissolved, 1949), *o d* of Rev. F. Talbot Parker, Winchester; 2nd, 1961, Rosalind Winifred, *e d* of late Frederick Arthur James, Olton, Warwicks. *Educ:* Archbishop Holgate's Grammar Sch., York; Leeds Univ.; Harvard Univ. Served in 8 W York R and Machine Gun Corps, 1914-19; Leeds Univ., BCom 1920; MA 1924; ILO, League of Nations, 1921-27; Commonwealth Fund Fellow, Harvard, 1925-26; Technical adviser, British Delegation to the International Economic Conference, Geneva, 1927; Fellow of Gonville and Caius Coll., Cambridge, 1927-30; Brunner Prof. of Economic Science, University of Liverpool, 1930-32; Leverhulme Research Fellow, 1940-42; Lecturer, University of Glasgow, 1942; Ministry of Food, 1943-47; Oxford Institute of Agricultural Economics Research, 1947-61; University Demonstrator, 1951-61; Dir, Hunter and Smallpage Ltd, York, 1965-69. *Publications:* Control of Credit as a Remedy for Unemployment; Monetary Stability; Stabilisation of Employment in the United States; Coalmining, a European Remedy; A Contributive Society; The Conflict of Values; (with others): Industrial Survey of Merseyside; Economic Reconstruction; Agriculture and Industry, Relative Income; Agricultural Economic Theory and the Indian Economy. *Address:* 19 Norham Road, Oxford.

**BELLEW,** family name of **Baron Bellew.**

**BELLEW,** 5th Baron, *cr* 1848; **Edward Henry Bellew,** Bt 1683; MBE 1919; late Captain RAF; *b* 6 Feb. 1889; *e s* of late Hon. R. E. Bellew, 4th *s* of 2nd Baron; *S* uncle 1935; *m* 1912, Barbara Helen Mary (*d* 1967), *d* of late Sir Henry Farnham Burke, KCVO. *Heir: b* Hon. Bryan Bertram Bellew, MC [*b* 1890; *m* 1918, Jeanie Ellen Agnes, *d* of late James O. Jameson; one *s*]. *Address:* Barmeath Castle, Co. Louth. *Clubs:* Turf, Pratt's; Kildare Street (Dublin).

**BELLEW, Sir Arthur John G.;** *see* Grattan-Bellew.

**BELLEW, Hon. Sir George (Rothe),** KCB 1961; KCVO 1953 (CVO 1950; MVO 1935); Kt 1950; FSA 1948; Secretary of the Order of the Garter since 1961, Garter Principal King of Arms, 1950-61; Genealogist of the Order of the Bath, 1950-61; Genealogist Order of St John, 1951-61; Knight Principal of Imperial Society of Knights Bachelor, 1957-62 (Deputy Knight Principal, 1962); Inspector of Regimental Colours, 1957-61; *b* 13 Dec. 1899; *s* of late Hon. Richard Bellew and Gwendoline, *d* of William R. J. Fitzherbert Herbert-Huddleston of Clytha; *m* 1935, Ursula Kennard, *e d* of Anders Eric Knös Cull, Warfield House, Bracknell; one *s*. *Educ:* Wellington Coll.; Christ Church, Oxford. Served War of 1939-45: Squadron Leader RAFVR, 1940-45 (despatches). Formerly Portcullis Pursuivant of Arms; Somerset Herald, 1926-50, and Registrar of the Coll. of Arms, 1935-46. KStJ 1951. *Address:* Little Dower House, Old Windsor, Berks. *Club:* Turf.

**BELLEW, Sir Henry Charles G.;** *see* Grattan-Bellew.

**BELLINGER, Sir Robert (Ian),** GBE 1967; Kt 1964; Chairman: Kinloch (Provision Merchants) Ltd, N15; Charles Arkcoll Ltd, Maidstone, Kent; Ivens Kellets and Childs Ltd, London, Worthing and Fareham; Sheppey Trust Ltd; National Savings Committee since 1970; *b* Tetbury Glos, 10 March 1910; *s* of David Morgan Bellinger, Cardiganshire, and Jane Ballantine Deans, Edinburgh; *m* 1962, Christiane Marie Louise Janssens, Brussels; one *s* one *d*. *Educ:* Church of England sch. Elected Court of Common Council, 1953; Chm. City of London Freemen's Sch., 1957; Alderman for Ward of Cheap, 1958; Sheriff, City of London, 1962-63; Lord Mayor of London, 1966-67. Chairman: Panel for Civil Service Manpower Review, 1968-; Adv. Cttee on Magistracy, City of London, 1968-; Licensing Cttee, City of London; Finance Cttee, BBC; Governor: BBC; United Westminster Schs; King Edward's Sch., Witley; Dir, Arsenal Football Club. Past Master, Broderers' Company; Liveryman, Fletchers' Company. Hon. DSc City Univ., 1966. Gentleman Usher of the Purple Rod, Order of the British Empire, 1969-. KStJ 1966; Commandeur, Ordre de Léopold, cl. III (Belgium), 1963; Comdr, Royal Order of the Phoenix (Greece), 1963; Officier, Ordre de la Valeur Camerounaise (Cameroons), 1963. *Recreations:* tennis, football, music, motoring. *Address:* 30 Cumberland Terrace, Regent's Park, NW1. *T:* 01-486 3300; Penn Wood, Fulmer, Bucks. *T:* Fulmer 2029. *Club:* City Livery.

**BELLINGHAM, Sir Roger Carroll Patrick Stephen,** 6th Bt (2nd creation), *cr* 1796; Physician; *b* 23 April 1911; *s* of Capt. Roger Charles Noel Bellingham, RFA, 2nd *s* of 4th Bt (*d* 1915), and Alice Ann Naish (*d* 1949); *S* uncle, Brig.-Gen. Sir Edward Henry Charles

Patrick Bellingham, 5th Bt, CMG, DSO, 1956; *m* 1941, Mary, *d* of late William Norman; two *s*. *Educ:* France; Edinburgh Univ. MB, ChB Edinburgh 1936; DA England 1956. Served as Flight-Lieut RAFVR, 1941-46. Knight of the Sovereign Order of Malta. *Recreation:* travel. *Heir:* *s* Noel Peter Roger Bellingham, *b* 4 Sept. 1943. *Address:* 1 Adswood Lane West, Stockport, Cheshire. *T:* Stockport 2564; Castle Bellingham, Co. Louth, Ireland.

**BELLOW, Saul;** American writer; *b* 10 June 1915; *s* of Abraham and Liza Gordon Bellow; *m* 1961, Susan Alexandra Glassman; three *s*. *Educ:* Univ. of Chicago: Northwestern Univ. Three one-act plays: Out From Under, Orange Soufflé, and The Wen, prod. London, 1966. Hon. DLitt, Northwestern Univ., 1962. *Publications:* Dangling Man, 1944; The Victim, 1947; The Adventures of Augie March, 1953; Seize the Day, 1956; Henderson the Rain King, 1959; Herzog, 1964; Mosby's Memoirs and Other Stories, 1969; Mr Sammler's Planet, 1970. Play: The Last Analysis, 1967. *Address:* University of Chicago, Chicago, Ill 60637, USA.

**BELLOWS, James Gilbert;** Journalist, US; *b* 12 Nov. 1922; *s* of Lyman Hubbard Bellows and Dorothy Gilbert Bellows; *m* 1964, Maggie Savoy. *Educ:* Kenyon Coll. (BA, LLB). Columbus (Ga) Ledger, 1947; News Editor Atlanta (Ga) Jl, 1950-57; Asst Editor, Detroit (Mich.) Free press, 1957-58; Managing Editor Miami (Fla) News, 1958-61; Exec. Editor (News Ops), NY Herald Tribune, 1961-62; Managing Editor, 1962-63; Editor, associate Editor, Los Angeles Times, 1966-. *Address:* 2270 Betty Lane, Beverly Hills, Calif, USA.

**BELMONT, Abbot of;** *see* Martin, Rt Rev. D. M. L.

**BELMORE,** 8th Earl of, *cr* 1797; **John Armar Lowry-Corry;** Baron Belmore, 1781; Viscount Belmore, 1789; *b* 4 Sept. 1951; *s* of 7th Earl of Belmore and Gloria Anthea, *d* of late Herbert Bryant Harker, Melbourne Australia (she *m* 1963, Lieut-Col R. J. T. Irwin, the Royal Inniskilling Fusiliers); *S* father 1960. *Educ:* Lancing. *Heir:* *kinsman* Lt-Col Sir Henry Lowry-Corry, *qv*. *Address:* Castlecoole, Enniskillen, Co. Fermanagh, N Ireland. *T:* Enniskillen 2368.

**BELOE, Robert,** CBE 1960; Secretary to the Archbishop of Canterbury, 1959-69; *b* 12 May 1905; *s* of late Rev. R. D. Beloe, Headmaster of Bradfield Coll., and of Clarissa, *d* of Rev. Prebendary J. T. Bramston, Winchester Coll.; *m* 1933, Amy, *d* of Capt. Sir Frank Rose, 2nd Bt (killed in action, 1914) and of late Daphne, Lady Rose; one *s* two *d*. *Educ:* Winchester; Hertford Coll., Oxford. Asst Master: Bradfield, 1927-28; Eton, 1928-30; Reading elementary sch., 1930-31. Kent Education Office, 1931-34; Asst Education Officer, Surrey, 1934-39; Dep. Education Officer, 1939-40; Chief Education Officer, 1940-59. Mem. of various commissions and departmental cttees, including Royal Commission on Marriage and Divorce, 1951-55; Mauritius Electoral Boundary Commission, 1957; Higher Agricultural Education Cttee, 1944-46; Secondary Sch. Examinations Council, 1947-64 (Chm. Cttee on Exams other than GCE, 1958-60, leading to establishment of Cert. of Secondary Educn); Hon. Consultant, CSE Sub-Cttee of Schools Council, 1964-; Home Office Central Training Council for Child Care, 1947-53. Hon. Sec. County Education Officers Soc., 1958-59; Governor of Commonwealth Inst., 1949-67. Trustee of Duke of Edinburgh's Award Scheme, 1960-66. Secretary: Monckton Cttee on Admin of Church Commn, 1963; Archbishop's Advisers on Needs and Resources, 1963-69. *Recreations:* gardening, travel. *Address:* The Hill House, Queen's Road, Richmond, Surrey. *Club:* United University.

*See also Sir Julian Rose, Bt.*

**BELOFF, Prof. Max,** BLitt, MA (Oxon); FRHistS; Gladstone Professor of Government and Public Administration, University of Oxford, and Fellow of All Souls College, since 1957; *b* 2 July 1913; *er s* of late Simon and Mary Beloff; *m* 1938, Helen Dobrin; two *s*. *Educ:* St Paul's Sch.; Corpus Christi Coll., Oxford (Scholar). Gibbs Schol. in Mod. Hist., 1934; 1st Cl. Hons, School of Modern History, 1935; Senior Demy, Magdalen Coll., Oxford, 1935. Junior Research Fellow, Corpus Christi Coll., 1937; Asst Lecturer in History, Manchester Univ., 1939-46; Nuffield Reader in Comparative Study of Institutions, Oxford Univ., 1946-56; Fellow of Nuffield Coll., 1947-58. War of 1939-45, Royal Corps of Signals, 1940-41. Hon. LLD Pittsburgh, USA. Gov., St Paul's Schs; Pres., South Oxfordshire Liberal Assoc. Trustee and Ex-Librarian, Oxford Union Soc. *Publications:* Public Order and Popular Disturbances, 1660-1714, 1938; The Foreign Policy of Soviet Russia, Vol. 1, 1947, Vol. 2, 1949; Thomas Jefferson and American Democracy, 1948; ed, The Federalist, 1948; Mankind and his Story, 1948; The Debate on the American Revolution, 1949; Soviet Policy in the Far East, 1944-51, 1953; The Age of Absolutism, 1660-1815, 1954; Foreign Policy and the Democratic Process, 1955; Europe and the Europeans, 1957; The Great Powers, 1959; (ed) On the Track of Tyranny, 1959; The American Federal Government, 1959; (ed) L'Europe du XIXe et XXe siècle, 1960-67; New Dimensions in Foreign Policy, 1961; The United States and the Unity of Europe, 1963; The Balance of Power, 1967; The Future of British Foreign Policy, 1969; Imperial Sunset, vol. 1, 1969; The Intellectual in Politics, 1970; articles in English, French, Italian and American journals. *Recreation:* watching cricket. *Address;* All Souls College, Oxford. *T:* Oxford 49641. *Club:* Reform.

**BELPER,** 4th Baron *cr* 1856; **Alexander Ronald George Strutt;** formerly Major, Coldstream Guards; *b* 23 April 1912; *s* of 3rd Baron and Hon. Eva Isabel Mary Bruce, 2nd *d* of 2nd Baron Aberdare (she *m* 2nd, 6th Earl of Rosebery); *S* father 1956; *m* 1940, Zara Sophie Kathleen Mary (marr. diss. 1949), *y d* of Sir Harry Mainwaring, 5th Bt; one *s*. *Educ:* Harrow. Served War with Coldstream Guards, 1939-44 (wounded). *Heir:* *s* Hon. Richard Henry Strutt [*b* 24 Oct. 1941; *m* 1966, Jennifer Vivian, *d* of late Capt. Peter Winser and of Mrs James Whitaker; one *s*]. *Address:* Kingston Hall, Nottingham.

*See also Duke of Norfolk.*

**BELSTEAD,** 2nd Baron, *cr* 1938; **John Julian Ganzoni;** Bt 1929; JP; Parliamentary Under-Secretary of State, Department of Education and Science, since 1970; *b* 30 Sept. 1932; *o s* of 1st Baron Belstead and Gwendolen Gertrude Turner (*d* 1962); *S* father, 1958. *Educ:* Eton; Christ Church, Oxford. MA 1961. JP Borough of Ipswich, 1962. *Heir:* none. *Address:* The Old Rectory, Great Bealings, near Woodbridge, Suffolk. *T:* Grundisburgh 278. *Clubs:* Bath; All England Lawn Tennis (Wimbledon); MCC.

**BEMROSE, Sir Max, (John Maxwell),** Kt 1960; DL; Chairman, Universal Printers Ltd, since 1952 (Director, 1938); *b* 1 July 1904; *y s* of late Dr Henry Howe Bemrose and late Mrs Bemrose; *m* 1933, Margaret Le Mare; one adopted *s* and one adopted *d*. *Educ:* Derby

Sch.; Brighton Coll.; Clare Coll., Cambridge. MA (Economics). Joined family firm, 1926. Prospective Conservative Candidate for Derby, 1938; fought Gen. Election, 1945; contested Watford Div., 1950; Chm. East Midlands Provincial Area, Conservative & Unionist Assoc., 1957-61; Mem. Exec. and Gen. Purposes Cttee of Conservative Assoc.; Chm. Nat. Union of Conservative & Unionist Associations, 1964-65; Pres., British Fedn of Master Printers, 1967-68. DL Derbyshire, 1967, High Sheriff of Derbyshire, 1969-70. *Recreations:* swimming, music, gardening. *Address:* Hazelbrow, Duffield, Derbyshire. *T:* Duffield 2388. *Clubs:* Carlton, Lansdowne.

**BEN-GURION, David;** Israeli statesman; past Prime Minister and Minister of Defence, Government of Israel; *b* Plonsk, 16 Oct. 1886; *m* 1917, Paula Mounvas (*d* 1968); one *s* two *d. Educ:* privately; Constantinople Univ. (Faculty of Law). Active in Zionist Labour Movement from early youth; settled in Israel, 1906; exiled as Zionist by Turkish admin., 1915; went to USA; founded Hechalutz organization there; helped raise Jewish Legion and served in its ranks under Gen. Allenby; Mem. Gen. Council, Zionist Organization, 1920; co-organizer, Jewish Labour Party (Mapai) and Gen. Fedn of Jewish Labour (Histadruth); Sec.-Gen. of Fedn, 1921-35; political missions abroad; Mem. Exec. Jewish Agency for Palestine, 1933; Chm., Jewish Agency for Palestine, 1935-48; following UN Partition Resolution, 1947, elected Chm. Nat. Council (in charge of security and defence); proclaimed Independence of State of Israel, May 1948; Prime Minister and Minister of Defence: (Provisional Govt), 1948-49; also 1949-53; resigned, 1953; Minister of Defence, 1955; Prime Minister and Minister of Defence, Nov. 1955-June 1963. Dr *hc* of Hebrew Letters, Jewish Theological Seminary of America; Bialik Literary Prize for Judaica, 1952; Dr *hc* of Philosophy, Hebrew Univ., Jerusalem, 1957; Hon. LLD: Brandeis Univ., Boston, 1960; Rangoon Univ., 1961. *Publications:* (in Hebrew) Self-Government of Villayets, 1914; Eretz Israel, 1918; We and Our Neighbours, 1920; The Labour Movement and Revisionism, 1933; From Class to Nation, 1933 (new edn 1955); Mishmarot (essays on Labour Zionism), 1935; The Struggle (5 vols), 1947-50; Israel at War, 1950 (in Yiddish, NY, 1951); Vision and Implementation (5 vols), 1951-57; Mima-amed Leam, 1955; Rebirth and Destiny of Israel, 1954; Nezach Israel (in Yiddish), 1953 (Buenos Aires); En la Patria Libre (Buenos Aires), 1954; The Sinai Campaign (Hebrew), 1959; Israel: Years of Challenge (in English), 1963; Ben-Gurion looks back, 1965; Dvarim Kehavayatam; (ed) The Jews in their Land, 1966; Talks with Arabs; Michtavim LePaula, 1969; The Restored State of Israel (2 vols), 1969; Iyunim Batanach, 1969; essays and articles. *Address:* Sdeh-Boker, Israel.

**BENCE, Cyril Raymond;** *b* 26 Nov. 1902; *s* of Harris Bryant Bence; *m* 1926, Florence Maud Bowler; one *s* one *d. Educ:* Pontywaen Sch.; Newport High Sch., Mon. Apprenticed to Ashworth Son & Co. Ltd of Dock Street, Newport, Mon, Weighing Machine Manufacturers; moved to Birmingham, 1937. Member of National Union of Scalemakers; Mem. of AEU; Mem. of Birmingham Trades Council, 1942-45; Pres. Witton Branch AEU. Contested (Lab) Handsworth Div. of Birmingham, at Gen. Elections of 1945 and 1950, and Bye-election Nov. 1950; MP (Lab) Dunbartonshire East, 1951-70. *Address:* Leda, Sweethay Close, Staplehay, Taunton, Som.

**BENCE-JONES, Col Philip Reginald,** MC; MA Hons (Cantab.), MInstCE, MICEI, MIMechE; Director Irish Wire Products, Ltd; *b* 12 Jan. 1897; *s* of late Reginald Bence-Jones, DL, JP, Lisselane, Co. Cork, and late Ethel Da Costa; *m* 1925, Victoria May, *d* of William Thomas, Alexandria, Egypt; one *s. Educ:* Rugby; Pembroke Coll., Cambridge; Bonn; Paris. Served with Royal Engineers in France, Belgium and Germany, 1914-19; Pembroke Coll., Cambridge, 1919-22, taking 1st Cl. Hons Mechanical Sciences Tripos and post-graduate Engineering Scholarship; Construction of Blue Nile Dam and Gezira Irrigation Project for Sudan Govt, 1922-26; Principal Asst to Chief Engineer to the London County Council, and other engineering work in UK, 1926-34; Punjab Govt service, 1934-46; Col Comdt, Punjab Univ. OTC, Indian Territorial Force, 1936-45; Staff Officer RE First Grade, GHQ, India, 1941-44. *Recreations:* country life. *Address:* Glenville Park, Glenville, Co. Cork. Ireland. *T:* Glenville 3. *Clubs:* Leander; Cork and County (Cork).

**BENDALL, David Vere,** CMG 1967; MBE 1945; HM Diplomatic Service; Asistant Under-Secretary of State, Foreign and Commonwealth Office, since 1969; *b* 27 Feb. 1920; *s* of John Manley Bendall; *m* 1941, Eve Stephanie Merrilees Galpin; one *d. Educ:* Winchester; King's Coll., Cambridge. Served Grenadier Guards, 1940-46. Third Sec., Allied Force HQ, Caserta, 1946; Rome, 1947; FO, 1949; First Sec., Santiago, 1952; FO, 1955; seconded to NATO Secretariat, Paris, 1957; FO, 1960; NATO Secretariat, Paris, 1962; Counsellor, 1962; Counsellor, Washington, 1965-69. *Recreations:* golf, tennis, languages. *Address:* 16 Chapel Street, SW1. *T:* 01-235 7633. *Clubs:* Boodle's, Hurlingham.

**BENDIGO, Victoria, Bishop of,** since 1957; **Rt. Rev. Ronald Edwin Richards,** MA, ThD (*jure dig.*); *b* Ballarat, Vic., 25 Oct. 1908; *s* of Edward and Margaret Elizabeth Richards, Ballarat; *m* 1937, Nancy, *d* of W. E. Lloyd Green; one *d. Educ:* Ballarat High Sch.; Trinity Coll., Melbourne Univ. BA 2nd Cl. Hons Phil., 1932, MA 1937; Asst Master, Ballarat C of E Gram. Sch., 1926, Malvern C of E Gram. Sch., 1927-28; deacon, 1932; priest, 1933; Curate of Rokewood, 1932-33, Priest-in-charge, 1934; Priest-in-charge, Lismore, 1934-41 and 1945-46; Chaplain AIF, 1941-45; Vicar of Warrnambool, 1946-50; Archdeacon of Ballarat, and Examining Chapl. to Bp of Ballarat, 1950-57; Vicar-Gen., 1952-57. *Address:* Bishopscourt, Bendigo, Victoria 3550, Australia. *Club:* Naval and Military (Melbourne).

**BENDIT, Gladys;** *see* Presland, John.

**BENEY, Frederick William,** CBE 1962; QC 1943; *s* of late William Augustus Beney, JP, Beckenham, Kent; *m* Irene Constance, *e d* of Henry Ward-Meyer, Weybridge; two *s. Educ:* Mill Hill Sch.; New Coll., Oxford (MA). Called to Bar, Inner Temple, 1909, Bencher 1948. Legal Asst, War Office, 1914-20; Recorder of Norwich, 1944-59; Mem., Deptl Ctte on Alternative Remedies, 1944-46; Chm. Deptl Cttee on Nat. Insurance against Industrial Diseases, 1953-54; Commissioner, Central Criminal Court, 1959-64; Commissioner of Assize, SE Circuit, 1959; Western Circuit, 1961; retd from practice, 1961. BBC Braodcasting, 1961-. *Publications:* contributions to legal journals. *Address:* Longmynd, Burwood Park, Walton-on-Thames, Surrey. *T:* Walton-on-Thames 21295.

**BENIN, Oba of; Akenzua II; Godfrey Okoro,** CMG 1946; *b* 1899; *e s* of Oba Eweka II and *o s* of Queen Ariowa (titled Queen Ezon); *S* father 1933; first marriage, 1922; over 50 *s* and *d*. *Educ:* Government Sch., Benin City; King's Coll., Lagos. Transport Clerk, 1922; Private Sec. and Clerk to Oba Eweka II and to Benin Judicial Council, 1924-25; Administrative Training, Abeokuta, 1926-27; District Head, Ekiadolor District in Benin Div., 1928-33. Minister Without Portfolio, Western Nigeria, 1955-60. JP 1960. Jubilee medal, 1935; Coronation medal, 1937; Medal for African Chiefs. *Recreations:* snooker, etc. *Heir: s* Solomon Igbinoghodua Aisiokuoba Akenzua, *b* 22 June 1923. *Address:* PO Box 12, Benin City, Western Nigeria. *T:* 1 Benin City.

**BENJAMIN, Bernard;** Director of Statistical Studies, Civil Service College, since 1970; *b* 8 March 1910; *s* of Joseph and Lucy Benjamin, London; *m* 1937, Mary Pate, Horham, Suffolk; two *d*. *Educ:* Colfe Grammar Sch.; Sir John Cass Coll. (London University). BSc (Hons); PhD London. LCC, 1928; statistician Public Health Dept, 1940; served War, 1943-46, RAF; statistician, General Register Office, 1952; Chief Statistician, 1954; Dir of Statistics, Ministry of Health, 1963-65; Dir of Research and Intelligence, GLC, 1965-70; Hon. Cons. in Med. Stats to Army, 1966. Mem. Statistics Cttee, Soc. Sci. Res. Coun. Fellow, Institute of Actuaries (A Vice-Pres. 1963; Pres., 1966-68). *Publications:* (with F. J. Bentley and S. Grzybowski) Tuberculosis in Childhood and Adolescence, 1954; Social and Economic Factors in Mortality, 1965; Health and Vital Statistics, 1968; Demographic Analysis, 1969; numerous medical and population statistical papers and contribs to Jl of Royal Statistical Society and Jl of Inst. of Actuaries. *Recreations:* gardening, painting (both kinds). *Address:* 39 Dale Wood Road, Orpington, Kent. *T:* Orpington 24092. *Club:* Athenæum.

**BENJAMIN, Brooke;** *see* Benjamin, T. B.

**BENJAMIN, Dr Ralph,** PhD, BSc, ACGI, CEng, FIEE; Director and Chief Scientist, Admiralty Underwater Weapons Establishment, since 1964, and Director, Underwater Weapons Research and Development (Navy), since 1965; *b* 17 Nov. 1922; *s* of Charles Benjamin and Claire Benjamin (*née* Stern); *m* 1951, Kathleen Ruth Bull, BA; two *s*. *Educ:* in Germany and Switzerland; St Oswald's Coll., Ellesmere; Imperial Coll. of Science and Technology, London. Joined Royal Naval Scientific Service, 1944; Senior Scientific Officer, 1949; Principal Scientific Officer, 1952; Senior Principal Scientific Officer (Special Merit), 1955; Deputy Chief Scientific Officer (Special Merit), 1960; Head of Research and Deputy Chief Scientist, Admiralty Surface Weapons Establishment, 1961. Hon. consultant to Univ. of Illinois and to US Office of Naval Research, 1956. *Publications:* Modulation, Resolution and Signal Processing for Radar Sonar and Related Systems, 1966; contribs to various advisory cttees, working parties, symposia, etc; articles in Jls of Instn of Electrical Engineers and Inst. of Electronic and Radio Engineers. *Recreations:* work, mountaineering, ski-ing, swimming, sailing, sub-aqua judo. *Address:* Admiralty Underwater Weapons Establishment, Portland, Dorset. *Club:* Athenæum.

**BENJAMIN, Prof. (Thomas) Brooke,** MEng, PhD; FRS 1966; Professor and Augustine Courtauld Fellow in Oceanography, University of Essex, since 1970; *b* 15 April 1929; *s* of Thomas Joseph Benjamin and Ethel Mary Benjamin (*née* Brooke); *m* 1956, Helen Gilda-Marie Rakower Ginsburg; one *s* two *d*. *Educ:* Wallasey Grammar Sch.; University of Liverpool; Yale Univ. (USA); University of Cambridge. BEng (Liverpool) 1950; MEng. (Yale) 1952; PhD (Camb.) 1955. Fellow of King's Coll., Cambridge, 1955-64; Asst Dir of Research, University of Cambridge, 1958-67; Reader in Hydrodynamics, Univ. of Cambridge, 1967-70. Editor, Journal of Fluid Mechanics, 1960-65; Consultant to English Electric Co., 1956-67. William Hopkins Prize, Cambridge Philosophical Soc., 1969. *Publications:* various papers on theoretical and experimental fluid mechanics. *Recreation:* music. *Address:* Department of Mathematics, University of Essex, Wivenhoe Park, Colchester, Essex. *T:* Colchester 5141. *Club:* Oxford and Cambridge University.

**BENN, Anthony,** OBE 1945; Chairman, Price & Pierce (Holding Company) Ltd, since 1956; *b* 7 Oct. 1912; *s* of late Francis Hamilton Benn and late Arta Clara Benn (*née* Boal); *m* 1943, Maureen Lillian Kathleen Benn (*née* Denbigh); two *s* four *d*. *Educ:* Harrow; Christ Church, Oxford. Scholar; 1st cl. Hon. Mods; 2nd cl. Greats. Price & Pierce Ltd, 1935 (Director, 1947). Joined Surrey and Sussex Yeomanry, 1936. Served War of 1939-45 (OBE): Staff Coll., 1942; Instructor, Middle East Staff Coll., 1943; GSO1, GHQ, Middle East, 1943; GSO1, AFHQ, Italy, 1945. Comdr, Order of the Lion of Finland, 1958. *Recreations:* golf, shooting, travel; Oxford Univ. Cricket XI, 1935. *Address:* Rock House, Runfold, Farnham, Surrey. *T:* Farnham 5750. *Club:* City of London.

**BENN, Rt. Hon. Anthony (Neil Wedgwood),** PC 1964; MP (Lab) Bristol South-East since Aug. 1963; *b* 3 April 1925; *er surv. s* of Rt Hon. William Wedgwood Benn, DSO, DFC, PC, MP, Viscount Stansgate (*d* 1960) (whose title he finally disclaimed, July 1963, after unsuccessful attempts to renounce, 1955 and 1960; never used title or took his seat in the House of Lords); *m* 1949, Caroline Middleton De Camp, MA, *e d* of late James Milton De Camp, Cincinnati, Ohio, USA; three *s* one *d*. *Educ:* MA Oxford, 1949. Joined Labour Party, 1943. Pilot Officer, RAFVR, 1943-45; Sub-Lieut (A) RNVR, 1945-46. Pres. Oxford Union, 1947. Producer, BBC North American Service, 1949-50. MP (Lab) Bristol (South-East), Nov. 1950-Nov. 1960; re-elected, May 1961, but debarred from sitting by judgment of Election Court, July 1961; re-elected, Aug. 1963; Postmaster-Gen. Oct. 1964-July 1966; recommended establishment of GPO as a public corporation and founded GIRO; Minister of Technology, 1966-70; assumed responsibility for Min. of Aviation, 1967, and Min. of Power, 1969. Chairman: Fabian Soc., 1964; Labour Party's Broadcasting Advisory Cttee, 1957-64; Member: Exec. Cttee, British-Amer. Parly Group, 1953; Exec., H-Bomb National Campaign, 1954; Select Cttee on Procedure, 1958; National Executive Cttee of Labour Party, 1959-60, and again, 1962-; NUJ; Founder Mem., Movement for Colonial Freedom, 1954. Hon. LLD Strathclyde, 1969; Hon. DTech Bradford, 1969. FRSA 1970. *Publications:* The Privy Council as a Second Chamber, 1957; The Regeneration of Britain, 1964. *Recreations:* family and politics. *Address:* House of Commons, SW1.

**BENN, Edward Glanvill;** Chairman, Benn Brothers, Ltd, Publishers, since 1945; Chairman, Exchange Telegraph Co., Ltd; *b* 1905; 2nd *s* of late Sir Ernest Benn, 2nd Bt, CBE; *m* 1931, Beatrice Catherine, MBE, *d* of Claude Newbald; one *s* one *d*. *Educ:* Harrow; Clare Coll., Cambridge. Served War of 1939-45, East Surrey Regt, 1940-45; Brigade Major, 138 Infantry Brigade, Italy, 1944 (despatches). Trustee Nat. Advertising Benevolent Soc., and

Pres., 1961-62; Chm., Readers' Pension Cttee, 1950; Vice-Pres., Newspaper Press Fund; Hon. Treasurer, Commonwealth Press Union. *Address:* 27 Lennox Gardens, SW1; Bouverie House, Fleet Street, EC4. *T:* 01-353 3212.
*See also Sir J. A. Benn.*

**BENN, Sir John Andrews,** 3rd Bt, *cr* 1914; Chairman: English-Speaking Union of the Commonwealth; Cincinnati Milacron Ltd; Vice-Chairman, Technical Development Capital Ltd; Director, Benn Brothers Ltd and Ernest Benn Ltd; *b* 28 Jan. 1904; *e s* of Sir Ernest Benn, 2nd Bt, CBE and Gwendolen, *d* of F. M. Andrews, Edgbaston; *S* father, 1954; *m* 1929, Hon. Ursula Helen Alers Hankey, *o d* of 1st Baron Hankey, PC, GCB, GCMG, GCVO, FRS; two *s* three *d*. *Educ:* Harrow; Princeton Univ., USA; Gonville and Caius Coll., Cambridge. Toured Latin America, founding Industria Britanica to promote British export trade, 1931. Helped to get new industries to Crook, South-West Durham, depressed area, 1936-38. Served War of 1939-45, KOYLI. Chm. and Man. Dir, UK Provident Instn, 1949-69. Contested Bradford N (Nat. C), General Election, 1945. Chm., John Benn Boys Hostels Assoc., 1946-; Vice-Chm. Stockwell (formerly King George's) House, YMCA, 1957-; Mem. London Adv. Bd, Salvation Army, 1965; Associate, Princeton Univ. Press, 1965; Pres., Princeton Club of London, 1970. *Publications:* Columbus-Undergraduate, 1928; A Merchant Adventurer in South America, 1931; Tradesman's Entrance, 1935; I Say Rejoice, 1942; Something in the City, 1959. *Recreation:* painting. *Heir: s* James Jonathan Benn [*b* 27 July 1933; *m* 1960, Jennifer, *e d* of Dr Wilfred Howells; one *s* one *d*. *Educ:* Harrow]. *Address:* High Field, Limpsfield, Surrey. *Club:* Nassau (Princeton, NJ).
*See also E. G. Benn.*

**BENN, John Meriton,** CB 1969; Northern Ireland Commissioner for Complaints, since 1969; *b* 16 July 1908; *s* of late Ernest and late Emily Louise Benn, Burnley; *m* 1933, Valentine Rosemary, *d* of late William Seward, Hanwell; two *d*. *Educ:* Burnley Gram. Sch.; Christ's Coll., Cambridge (Scholar; Modern Languages Tripos, 1st Cl. Hons French, 2nd Cl. Hons German). Asst Master, Exeter Sch., 1931-34; Lektor, Halle Univ., Germany, 1934; Asst Master, Regent Street Polytechnic Secondary Sch., 1935; Inspector of Schs., Ministry of Education for Northern Ireland, 1935-44; Principal Officer, 1944-51; Asst Sec., 1951-59; Senior Asst Sec., 1959-64; Permanent Sec., 1964-69. *Publication:* Practical French Proses, 1935. *Recreations:* gardening, bell-ringing. *Address:* 13 Knockmarloch Park, Belfast BT4 2LD. *T:* 63320. *Club:* Royal Over-Seas League.

**BENN, Captain Sir Patrick (Ion Hamilton),** 2nd Bt *cr* 1920; Captain, Reserve of Officers, late Duke of Cornwall's Light Infantry; Major, Norfolk Army Cadet Force, 1960; *b* 26 Feb. 1922; *o s* of late Col Ion Bridges Hamilton Benn, JP (*o s* of 1st Bt), Broad Farm, Rollesby, Gt. Yarmouth, and of Theresa Dorothy, *d* of late Major F. H. Blacker, Johnstown, Co. Kildare; *S* grandfather, 1961; *m* 1959, Edel Jærgine, *d* of late Col W. S. Læback, formerly of The Royal Norwegian Army, Andenes, Vesteraalen; one *s* one *d* (both adopted). *Educ:* Rugby. Served War of 1939-45 (despatches); North Africa, Italy, Greece, 1941-45; Capt. 1943; served Korea, 1951-52; retd, 1955. *Recreations:* shooting, fishing. *Address:* Rollesby Hall, Great Yarmouth, Norfolk. *T:* Marham 313. *Club:* Norfolk (Norwich).

**BENNER, Patrick;** Assistant Under-Secretary of State, Department of Health and Social Security, since 1968 (Ministry of Health, 1967-68); *b* 26 May 1923; *s* of Henry Grey and Gwendolen Benner; *m* 1952, Joan Christabel Draper; two *d*. *Educ:* Ipswich Sch.; University Coll., Oxford. Entered Min. of Health as Asst Princ., 1949; Princ., 1951; Princ. Private Sec. to Minister, 1955; Asst Sec., 1958; Under-Sec., 1967. *Address:* 44 Ormond Crescent, Hampton, Middx. *T:* 01-979 1099.

**BENNET,** family name of **Earl of Tankerville.**

**BENNET, Edward Armstrong,** MC; MD; Consultant Physician Emeritus, Bethlem Royal and Maudsley Hospital; occasional Lecturer, Institute of Psychiatry, University of London; Patron C. G. Jung-Inst. Zürich; *s* of late William Boyd Bennet and Marion McCaldin; *m* 1st, 1926, Flora (*d* 1952), *d* of late Rev. Alex Wylie, Edinburgh; two *s*; 2nd, 1958, Frances Eveline, *d* of late Rev. R. F. R. Routh. *Educ:* Campbell Coll., Belfast; Trinity Coll., Dublin. Stewart Sch. in Mental Disease, Moderator Mental and Moral Science; MB, BCh, BAO, 1925; DPM England 1926; MA, MD 1930; ScD 1939. Fellow Royal Society of Medicine; Fellow Brit. Psychological Soc. (Past Chm. Med. Sect.). War of 1939-45: Major RAMC, 1940; Command Psychiatrist Aldershot Command, 1940-42; Brigadier, RAMC, 1942; Consultant in Psychiatry, India Command, and 11th Army Group, 1942-45. Formerly Consulting Psychiatrist, India and Burma Office. *Publications:* C. G. Jung, 1961; The Freud-Janet controversy: an unpublished letter, British Medical Journal, 1965; What Jung Really Said, 1966; etc. *Address:* 99 Harley Street, W1. *T:* 01-935 6400; 2 St Katharine's Precinct, Regent's Park, NW1. *T:* 01-935 6252; Underwood Cottage, Langrish, Hants. *T:* Petersfield 3972. *Club:* Oriental.

**BENNET, Maj.-Gen. John;** *b* 12 Feb. 1893; *s* of late John R. and Elizabeth S. Bennet, Hillwood, Ratho; *m* 1926, Margaret Scott, *d* of late Samuel S. Tanner, Hillwood Mains, Ratho; two *s*. *Educ:* George Heriot's Sch.; Edinburgh Univ. MB, ChB (Hons) University of Edinburgh, 1916; DPM London, 1926; MD Edinburgh, 1935; DTM&H London, 1938; FRCP 1948 (Member 1937). joined RAMC 1916; regular commission, 1920; served Salonika, Egypt, China, India, Malaya; Medical Specialist, 1928. Consulting Physician, Malaya Command, 1941-42; despatches (Malaya), 1946; Dir of Medicine and Consulting Physician to the Army, Jan. 1947-51. Col 1947; Brig. 1947; Maj.-Gen., 1950; KHP, 1947-51. Medical Superintendent, East Fife Hospital Group, 1951-59, retd. *Publications:* contribution to Medical History of World War II; Nutrition POW Camps Far East (MRC). *Recreation:* golf. *Address:* 21 Esslemont Road, Edinburgh 9. *T:* 031-667 2407.

**BENNET-CLARK, Thomas Archibald,** CBE 1966; FRS 1950; BA, PhD (Cantab.), MA (Dublin); Professor Emeritus of Biology, University of East Anglia, Norwich, since 1967 (Professor of Biology and Dean of School of Biological Sciences, 1962-67); Fellow of King's College, University of London; *b* 13 Jan. 1903; *s* of Thomas Bennet-Clark, CA, JP, and Anne Chalmers (*née* Hanna), 32 Buckingham Terrace, Edinburgh; *m* 1926, Elizabeth Constance, *d* of Rev. James Haythornthwaite, Dublin; one *s* one *d*. *Educ:* Marlborough Coll., Wilts; Trinity Coll., Cambridge (Sen. Scholar). Natural Sciences Tripos, 1923; Frank Smart Prize; Asst to Prof. of Botany in Trinity Coll., Dublin, 1924-30; Lectr, Univ. of Manchester, 1930-36; Prof. of

Botany, University Coll., Nottingham, 1936-44; Prof. of Botany, King's Coll., University of London, 1944-62. Mem., ARC, 1957-67. Formerly Editor, Jl of Experimental Botany. FRSA, 1959; Hon. FRSE, 1969. Hon. ScD, E Anglia, 1968; Hon. DSc, Leicester, 1968. *Publications:* papers in scientific journals. *Address:* 242/2 Canongate, Edinburgh EH8 8AB.

**BENNETT, Sir Albert (Edward),** Kt 1965; Member Midlands Electricity Board, since 1948; *b* 1 Oct 1900; *s* of Wm Bennett, coalminer; *m* 1923, Minnie Smith; one *s* two *d*. *Educ:* Elem. Sch. Colliery Blacksmith, until 1926; Labour Party Agent, 1929-35; full-time Trade Union Officer, 1935-48; Councillor (Leader) and Alderman, Stoke on Trent City Council, 1944-. *Recreations:* bowls, horticulture. *Address:* 35 Harpfield Road, Trent Vale, Stoke on Trent. *T:* Stoke on Trent 44715.

**BENNETT, Engr-Rear-Adm. Cecil Reginald Percival,** CBE 1952 (OBE 1943); retired; *b* Morchard Bishop, Devon, 29 July 1896; *s* of Albert Webber Bennett; *m* 1923, Ethel Elizabeth (*née* Bartlett); two *d*. *Educ:* Crediton Grammar Sch., Devon. Boy Artificer, HMS Indus, Devonport, 1912-16; served European War in HMS Iron Duke, Grand Fleet, 1916-18; HMS Courageous, 1918-19; HMS Calcutta, 1919-20; commissioned as Mate (E), 1921; RN Colls Greenwich and Keyham, 1921-22; Eng.-Lieut, 1923; Eng.-Lieut-Comdr, 1931; Eng.-Comdr, 1935; served in HMS Formidable, War of 1939-45, 1939-42 (despatches, OBE); Eng.-Capt, 1944; served with Royal Canadian Navy, 1944-45; Chief Engineer, Sheerness Yard, 1945-47; Manager, Engineering Dept: Malta, 1947-50; HM Dockyard, Devonport, 1950-54; retd 1954. AMIMechE, 1930; MIMechE, 1947. *Recreations:* tennis, golf. *Address:* The Maples, Goats Hill, Northam, North Devon.

**BENNETT, Charles John Michael,** FCA; Partner in Barton, Mayhew & Co., Chartered Accountants; *b* 29 June 1906; *m* 1931, Audrey Thompson; two *d*. *Educ:* Clifton Coll.; Trinity Coll., Cambridge. Served with HM Forces, 1939-45. Member: Electricity Supply Companies Commn, 1959, in Hong Kong; Fiji Sugar Inquiry Commn, 1961; Commn of Inquiry (Sugar Industry) 1962, in Mauritius; Commn of Inquiry into Banana Industry of St Lucia, 1963; Commn of Inquiry (Chm.) into Sugar Industry and Agriculture of Antigua, 1965; Commn of Enquiry into Sugar Industry of Guyana, 1967; Cttee of Enquiry into the pricing of certain contracts for the overhaul of aero-engines by Bristol Siddeley Engines Ltd. Mem. of Council, Institute of Chartered Accountants, 1963-69. Part-time Mem., Commonwealth Development Corp., 1965, Dep. Chm. 1970-; Independent Mem., NEDC for Chemical Industry, and Chm., Pharmaceuticals Working Party, 1969. Dir, British Field Products Ltd. *Recreations:* golf, fishing and shooting. *Address:* 15 St Olave's Court, St Petersburgh Place, W2. *T:* 01-229 9554; The Ship House, Burnham Market, Norfolk.

**BENNETT, Air Vice-Marshal Donald Clifford Tyndale,** CB 1944; CBE 1943; DSO 1942; late Royal Air Force; Chairman and Managing Director: Fairthorpe Ltd; Dart Aircraft Ltd (operating Blackbushe Airport); Fairtravel Ltd; consultant, director, etc.; *b* 14 Sept. 1910; *s* of G. T. Bennett, Brisbane, Queensland; *m* 1935, Elsa Gubler, Zürich; one *s* one *d*. Royal Australian Air Force; Royal Air Force; AOC the Pathfinder Force of RAF Bomber Command, war of 1939-45; resigned commission, 1945; Imperial Airways; Empire and Atlantic Air Route Development; holder of the world's long-distance seaplane record (Dundee, Scotland, to Alexandra Bay, South Africa); a founder as Flying Superintendent of the Atlantic Ferry organisation (later Ferry Command); MP (L) Middlesbrough West, 1945; Managing Director and Chief Exec., British South American Airways, 1945-48. Chairman: Exec. Cttee United Nations Assoc. of Gt Britain and N Ireland, 1946-49; Political Freedom Movement; Pres. Radar Assoc., 1952-55; Patron Pathfinder Assoc. FRAeS. Oswald Watt Medallist, 1938, 1946; Johnston Memorial Trophy, 1937-38. Order of Alexander Nevsky, 1944. *Publications:* Complete Air Navigator, 1935, 7th edn. 1967; Air Mariner, 1937, 2nd edn 1943; Freedom from War, 1945; Pathfinder, 1958; Let us try Democracy, 1970. *Recreations:* tennis, ski-ing, car racing. *Address:* Blackbushe Airport, Camberley, Surrey; Monte Carlo. *Club:* Royal Aero.

**BENNETT, Sir Frederick (Mackarness),** Kt 1964; MP (C) Torquay since Dec. 1955 (Reading N, 1951-55). *b* 2 Dec. 1918; 2nd *s* of late Sir Ernest Bennett and of Lady (Marguerite) Bennett; *m* 1945, Marion Patricia, *e d* of Cecil Burnham, OBE, FRCSE. *Educ:* Westminster. Served War of 1939-45, enlisted Middx Yeo., 1939; commissioned RA, 1940; Military Experimental Officer in Petroleum Warfare Dept, 1943-46, when released to reserve with rank of Major. Called to English Bar, Lincoln's Inn, 1946, Southern Rhodesian Bar, 1947. Visited Greece as guest of Greek Govt, 1947 and 1949, to observe Communist war there and children's refugee camps. Retained as diplomatic correspondent, Birmingham Post, Jan. 1950 until election to Parliament. Contested (C) Burslem, 1945, Ladywood Div. of Birmingham, 1950. PPS: to Under-Sec. of State, Home Office, 1953-55, to Minister of Supply, 1956-57, to Paymaster-Gen, 1957-59, and to Pres. of Bd of Trade, 1959-61. Director: Kleinwort Benson Europe SA; Sir Lindsay Parkinson Ltd; Arawak Trust Co. Bahamas Ltd; Harlech Television Ltd; Squibb A/S; Commercial Union Assurance Co. Ltd, West End and Exeter Bds; Marine Midland International, NY, Adv. Bd; Gibraltar Building Soc. Lord of the Manor of Mawddwy. Comdr, Order of Phœnix, Greece, 1963; (Sithari) Star of Pakistan, 1st cl., 1964. *Recreations:* shooting, fishing, ski-ing. *Address:* Cwmllecoediog, Aberangell, Montgomeryshire. *T:* Aberangell 230; Kingswear Castle, South Devon; 2 Stone Buildings, Lincoln's Inn, WC2. *Club:* Carlton.

**BENNETT, Captain Geoffrey Martin,** DSC 1944; RN retired; Secretary to the Lord Mayor of Westminster, and Hon. Secretary to The London Mayors Association, since 1960; *b* 7 June 1909; *s* of Martin Gilbert Bennett, Rear-Adm., and Esme Geraldine Bennett (*née* Hicks), both of Deepdene, Emsworth, Hants; *m* 1932, Rosemary Alys (*née* Béchervaise); two *s*. *Educ:* Royal Naval Coll., Dartmouth, 1923-26; specialized in Signals, 1935; Flag Lieut, Second Cruiser Squadron, Home Fleet, 1938-40; Fleet Signal Officer, S Atlantic, 1940-42; Signal Officer to Adm. Comdg Force H, for ops against Sicily and Salerno, 1943; Sig. Off. to Flag Officer Levant and E Med., 1943-44; Admlty, Radio Equipment Dept, 1945-56; HMS Ajax, Executive Officer, 1947; HMS St Bride's Bay, in command, 1948; CSO, Combined Ops HQ, 1949-50; Admiralty, Naval Equipment Dept, 1951-53; Capt. 1953; Naval Attaché, Moscow, Warsaw and Helsinki, 1953-55; CSO (Plans) to C-in-C, Channel and UK Home Stn, 1956-57; City Marshal (London), 1958-59. Common Cryer and Serjeant-at-Arms

(London), 1959-60. Gold Medal and Trench-Gascoigne Prize of RUSI, 1934, 1942 and 1943. FRHistS, 1963. *Publications:* By Human Error, 1961; Coronel and the Falklands, 1962; Cowans' War, 1964; The Battle of Jutland, 1964; Charlie B: a biography of Admiral Lord Beresford, 1968; Naval Battles of First World War, 1968; contrib. to A History of the Royal Navy (ed Peter Kemp), 1969; *novels:* (under Pseudonym "Sea-Lion"): Phantom Fleet, 1946; Sink Me the Ship, 1947; Sea of Troubles, 1947; Cargo for Crooks, 1948; When Danger Threatens, 1949; The Invisible Ships, 1950; This Creeping Evil, 1950; The Quest of John Clare, 1951; The Diamond Rock, 1952; Meet Desmond Drake, 1952; Damn Desmond Drake!, 1953; Desmond Drake Goes West, 1956; Death in Russian Habit, 1958; Operation Fireball, 1959; Down Among the Dead Men, 1961; Death in the Dog Watches, 1962; also several books for children; *radio plays:* Phantom Fleet; The Fair Quaker of Deal; The Quest of John Clare, etc. *Address:* Westminster City Hall, SW1. *T:* 01-828 8070; 33 Argyll Road, W8. *T:* 01-937 8943.

**BENNETT, Harry Graham,** QC 1968; Recorder of York, since 1968; Chairman, Agricultural Land Tribunal (Northern Area), since 1967; Deputy Chairman, East Riding Quarter Sessions, since 1964; *b* 19 Sept. 1921; *s* of Ernest and Alice Mary Bennett, Cleckheaton, Yorks. *Educ:* Whitcliffe Mount Grammar Sch., Cleckheaton; King's Coll., London. Royal Artillery, 1943-47. Called to Bar, Gray's Inn, 1948. Recorder of Doncaster, 1967-68. *Recreation:* music. *Address:* 39 Park Square, Leeds, Yorks. *T:* Leeds 26633; 5 King's Bench Walk, Temple, EC4. *Club:* Leeds (Leeds).

**BENNETT, Henry Stanley,** FBA; Life Fellow, Emmanuel College, Cambridge (Librarian, 1934-59); Emeritus University Reader in English; Vice-President of The British Academy, 1959-60; *b* 15 Jan. 1889; *e s* of William Henry Bennett, Hastings; *m* 1920, Joan (*see* Joan Bennett, MA), *d* of Julia Frankau (Frank Danby); one *s* three *d*. *Educ:* Emmanuel Coll., Cambridge. Entered S Mark's Coll., Chelsea, 1907; Elementary Schoolmaster in London, 1909-15; invalided from Army, 1918; entered Emmanuel Coll., 1918. Mem. of Council of the Senate, Cambridge, 1943-50; Mem., of Bd of Advisers in English in University of London, 1942-50; Pres. 1958-60, and Trustee, 1965-, Bibliographical Soc. Chm. Cambridge Univ. Press Syndicate, 1952-64; Visiting Prof. University of Chicago, 1931, 1948, 1952, 1955, and 1958-; Leverhulme Research Fellow, 1947-49; Sandars Reader in Bibliography, 1951; Gregynog Lectr, University Coll. of Wales, Aberystwyth, 1953. Fellow, Folger Library, 1958 and 1961. Hon. DHL (Chicago), 1955. *Publications:* The Pastons and their England, 1922; England from Chaucer to Caxton, 1928; Marlowe's Jew of Malta and The Massacre at Paris, edited for the definitive edition of the Works and Life of Christopher Marlowe, 1931; Life on the English Manor, 1937; Quia Amore Langueo (edition of), 1937; The Author and his Public in the Fourteenth and Fifteenth Centuries, and Medieval Literature and the Modern Reader (Essays and Studies of English Assoc.), 1938 and 1945; Vol. II Part I, The Oxford History of English Literature, 1947; English Books and Readers: Vol. I, 1475 to 1557, 1952; Six Medieval Men and Women, 1955; English Books and Readers: Vol. II, 1558-1603, 1965; Vol. III, 1603-1640, 1970. *Recreation:* travel in Austria and Switzerland. *Address:* Church Rate Corner, Cambridge. *T:* Cambridge 53571. *Club:* Athenæum.

**BENNETT, Sir Hubert,** Kt 1970; FRIBA; FSIA; Architect to the Greater London Council (formerly London County Council) and Superintending Architect of Metropolitan Buildings, 1956-71; *b* 4 Sept. 1909; *s* of late Arthur Bennett and Eleanor Bennett; *m* 1939, Louise F. C. Aldred; three *d*. *Educ:* Victoria University, Manchester, School of Architecture. Asst Lecturer, Leeds School of Architecture, 1933-35; Asst Lecturer, Regent Street Polytechnic Sch. of Architecture, 1935-40; Superintending Architect (Lands), War Dept, 1940-43; Borough Architect, Southampton, 1943-45; County Architect, W Riding of Yorks, 1945-56. Mem. of Council, RIBA, 1952-55, 1957-62, 1965-66, 1967-69; Hon. Treas. RIBA, 1959-62; Pres., W Yorks Soc. of Architects, 1954-66; Member, Building Research Bd, 1959-66; Technical Panel, Standing Conference on London Regional Planning, 1962-64; Timber Res. and Devl. Ass. Adv. Panel, 1965-68; Housing Study Mission from Britain to Canada, 1968. Architect for the Hyde Park Corner-Marble Arch Improvement Scheme, Crystal Palace Recreational Centre and South Bank Arts Centre. RIBA: Silver Medallist for Measured Drawings (Hon. Mention), 1932; Arthur Cates Prize, 1933; Sir John Soane Medallist, 1934; Neale Bursar, 1936; Godwin and Wimperis Bursar, 1948; RIBA London Architecture Bronze Medal, 1959; RIBA Bronze Medal, 1968. Royal Society of Arts Medal, 1934; Rome Scholarship Special Award, 1936; Min. of Housing and Local Govt Housing Medal, 1954, 1963, 1964, 1966, 1968; Civic Trust Awards; Sir Patrick Abercrombie Award (for planning project Thamesmead), Internat. Union of Architects, 1969. Hon. Mem., Soc. of Architects of Venezuela. *Address:* Linton House, Bramley, Surrey. *T:* Bramley 3460.

**BENNETT, Prof. Jack Arthur Walter,** MA, DPhil; Professor of Medieval and Renaissance English, Cambridge University, since 1964; Fellow of Magdalene College, Cambridge, since 1964; Keeper of the Old Library, Magdalene College, since 1968; *b* Auckland, New Zealand, 28 Feb. 1911; *s* of Ernest and Alexandra Bennett; *m* 1951, Gwyneth Mary Nicholas; two *s*. *Educ:* Mt Albert Grammar Sch.; Auckland Univ. Coll.; Merton Coll., Oxford. MA (NZ) 1933; BA Oxon 1st Cl. Eng. Lang. and Lit., 1935; Harmsworth Scholar, Merton Coll., 1935-38; MA, DPhil, 1938, Res. Fellow, The Queen's Coll., Oxford, 1938-47; Head of Research Dept, later Dir, British Information Services, New York, 1940-45; Fellow and Tutor, Magdalen Coll., Oxford, 1947-64. Editor of Medium Ævum, 1957-; Mem. of Council, Early English Text Soc.; Editor, Clarendon Medieval and Tudor Series. *Publications:* The Knight's Tale, 1954; (with H. R. Trevor-Roper) The Poems of Richard Corbett, 1955; Devotional Pieces in Verse and Prose, 1957; The Parlement of Foules, 1957; (ed.) Essays on Malory, 1963; The Humane Medievalist, 1965; (jointly) Early Middle English Verse and Prose, 1966; Chaucer's Book of Fame, 1968; Selections from John Gower, 1968. Articles and reviews in Listener, TLS, Review of English Studies, Landfall (NZ), etc. *Recreation:* collecting books on Oxford and Cambridge. *Address:* 10 Adams Road, Cambridge. *T:* Cambridge 55322.

**BENNETT, James;** MP (Lab) Bridgeton Division of Glasgow since Nov. 1961; Parliamentary Private Secretary to Secretary of State for Scotland, 1964-67; *b* 18 Dec. 1912; *s* of Samuel and Elizabeth Bennett; *m* 1936, Dorothy Maclaren; one *s* one *d*. *Educ:* Grove Street Primary and North Kelvinside Secondary Schs., Glasgow. Elected Councillor, Glasgow, Nov. 1947. JP, Glasgow,

1950-52. *Recreations:* reading, bowls, gardening. *Address:* 105 Boreland Drive, Glasgow W3. *T:* 041-959 2393.

**BENNETT, Prof. James Allan Jamieson,** DSc, PhD; Hon. FRAeS, FAIAA; Professor Emeritus, Cranfield Institute of Technology, since 1969; Visiting Professor, United States Naval Postgraduate School, Monterey, Calif, 1969-71; helicopter consultant; *b* 1 July 1903; *m* Elizabeth Roxburgh Hodge; one *s* one *d*. *Educ:* Universities of Glasgow, London and Göttingen. The College of Aeronautics: Prof. of Aerodynamics, 1954-69; Deputy Principal, 1960-61 and 1965-68. Vis. Prof., US Naval Postgraduate Sch., Monterey, Calif, 1967. Engaged in development of rotary-wing aircraft since 1930; designed first production direct take-off aircraft (C40 Autogiro) and first compound helicopter (Gyrodyne); originator of helicopter which established International Speed Record for helicopters, 1948; originator of rotorcraft which established Internat. Speed Record for rotorcraft, 1959; originator of numerous patents relating to rotary-wing aircraft. Royal Aeronautical Society: Vice-Pres., 1966-69; Pres., 1969-70; Hon. Fellow 1968. Hon. Fellow American Helicopter Soc., 1968. Hon. LLD Glasgow, 1970. American Helicopter Soc. Award, 1947; Louis Breguet Memorial Trophy, 1959. *Publications:* many papers published in technical journals (mainly on rotary-wing aircraft). *Address:* Box 2473, Carmel-by-the-Sea, Calif 93921, USA. *T:* 408-624-0732.

**BENNETT, Jill;** actress; *b* Penang, SS, 24 Dec. 1931; *d* of Randle and Nora Bennett; *m* 1st, 1962, Willis Hall, *qv* (marr. diss., 1965); 2nd, 1968, John Osborne, *qv*. *Educ:* Tortington Park; Priors Field. Stratford-upon-Avon, 1949-50. First London appearance in Captain Carvallo, St James's Theatre, 1950; Iras in Anthony and Cleopatra, and Caesar and Cleopatra (Olivier Season), St James's, 1951; Helen Elliot in Night of the Ball, New, 1955; Masha in The Seagull, Saville, 1956; Sarah Stanham in The Touch of Fear, Aldwych, 1956; Isabelle in Dinner with the Family, New, 1957; Penelope in Last Day in Dream Land, Lyric, Hammersmith, 1959; Feemy Evans and Lavinia in Shaw double bill, Mermaid, 1961; Estelle in In Camera, Oxford Playhouse, 1962; Ophelia in Castle in Sweden, Piccadilly, 1962; Hilary and Elizabeth in double bill of Squat Betty and The Sponge Room, Royal Court, 1962; The Countess in A Patriot for Me, Royal Court, 1965; Anna Bowers in A Lily of Little India, St Martin's, 1965; Katrina in The Storm, and Imogen Parrott in Trelawney of the Wells, National, 1966; Pamela in Time Present, Royal Court (and later) Duke of York's, 1968 (won Evening Standard Award and Variety Club's Best Actress Award); Anna in Three Months Gone, Royal Court and Duchess, 1970. *Films include:* Lust for Life; The Nanny; The Criminal; The Charge of the Light Brigade; Inadmissible Evidence; Julius Caesar (Calpurnia). Numerous TV appearances in classical works, etc. *Recreations:* riding, water ski-ing, ski-ing, having holidays, collecting paintings. *Address:* 30 Chelsea Square, SW3.

**BENNETT, Joan,** MA; Life Fellow of Girton College, Cambridge; Lecturer in English, Cambridge University, 1936-64; *b* 26 June 1896; *d* of Arthur Frankau and of Julia Frankau (Frank Danby); *m* 1920, Henry Stanley Bennett, *qv*; one *s* three *d*. *Educ:* Wycombe Abbey; Girton Coll., Cambridge. Visiting Lectr in the University of Chicago, 1952, 1955, and 1958. Warton Lecturer (Brit. Acad.), 1958; Rose Mary Crawshay Prize (Brit. Acad.), 1963. Fellow, Folger Library, 1961. *Publications:* Five Metaphysical Poets, 1965 (formerly Four Metaphysical Poets, 1934); Virginia Woolf; Her Art as a Novelist, 1945, 2nd edn enl. 1964; George Eliot: Her Mind and her Art, 1948; Sir Thomas Browne, 1962; The Love Poetry of John Donne (chapter in Seventeenth Century Studies), 1938. *Address:* Church Rate Corner, Cambridge. *T:* Cambridge 53571.

**BENNETT, Joan;** Actress (films and plays); *b* 27 Feb. 1910; *d* of Richard Bennett and Adrienne Morrison; *m* 1st, 1926, John Fox (marr. diss., 1928); one *d*; 2nd, 1932, Gene Markey (marr. diss., 1936); one *d*; 3rd, 1940, Walter Wanger (marr. diss., at Juarez, Mexico, 1965; he *d* 1968); two *d*. *Educ:* St Margaret's Sch., Waterbury, Conn.; Mlle Lataple's, Versailles, France. *Films include:* (first film) Bulldog Drummond, 1929; Three Live Ghosts; Disraeli; Little Women; Pursuit of Happiness; Private Worlds; The Man in the Iron Mask; Margin for Error; Woman on the Beach; Father of the Bride; Love that Brute; Desire in the Dust. *Plays include:* (first play) Jarnegan, 1928; Bell, Book and Candle; We're no Angels; Love Me Little; Never too Late, Prince of Wales Theatre, London, 1963. Has appeared on Television: (series) Too Young to go Steady; Dark Shadows. *Recreations:* interior decorating, swimming, tennis; particularly likes Shakespeare's works and classical literature. *Address:* 150 East 72nd Street, New York City, NY 10021, USA.

**BENNETT, John; Hon. Mr Justice Bennett;** Justice of Appeal, Courts of Appeal for the Seychelles, St Helena, The Falkland Islands Colony and Dependencies, and The British Antarctic Territory, since 1965; Chief Adjudicator, Immigration Appeals Act 1969, since 1970; *b* 20 July 1909; 2nd *s* of late John and Mary Bennett, Armagh, NI; *m* 1953, Rachael Kathleen, *o d* of late Major John Watson Laidlay, the Royal Scots, and late Hilda Eleanor Laidlay, Edinburgh. *Educ:* Royal School, Armagh; Queen's Univ., Belfast. Solicitor, Supreme Court of N Ireland, 1932; Asst Administrator-Gen. and Dep. Public Trustee, Zanzibar, 1934; Land Officer, Zanzibar, 1938; Registrar, Supreme Court and Registrar-Gen., Fiji Islands, 1940; Resident Magistrate, 1943, Chief Magistrate, 1945; Chm., Commission on Juvenile Delinquency, Fiji, 1944; Chm., European Civil Servants Assoc., Fiji and W Pacific, 1946; Magistrate, Nigeria, 1949, Chief Magistrate, Nigeria, 1951; Judge of the High Court of Lagos and the Southern Cameroons, 1956-62. Called to Bar, Gray's Inn, 1952. Chairman: S Mddx Rent Tribunal, 1964-70; Industrial Tribunals, England and Wales, 1966-70. Served Fiji Infantry Regt, 1940-43, Capt. 3 Bn. *Recreations:* polo, fishing, shooting, travel. *Address:* 153a Old Church Street, SW3. *T:* 01-352 2506. *Club:* Chelsea Arts.

**BENNETT, John,** MBE 1945; HM Senior Chief Inspector of Schools for Scotland, since 1969; *b* 14 Nov. 1912; *m* 1940, Johanne R. McAlpine, MA; two *s* one *d*. *Educ:* Edinburgh Univ. MA (first class hons) 1934. Schoolmaster until 1951. Served War of 1939-45: Capt. REME, 79 Armd Div., 1940-46. HM Inspector of Schools, 1951. *Recreations:* mathematics, golf, bridge. *Address:* 35 Cadzow Drive, Cambuslang, Glasgow. *T:* 041-641 1058.

**BENNETT, John Reginald William,** MA (Oxon.); late ICS; *b* 18 Oct. 1888; *s* of John Bennett and Elizabeth Mary Balfour; *m* 1922, Margaret Winifred Seabrook; two *s* one *d*. *Educ:* Warwick Sch.; Worcester Coll., Oxford (Hons Classical Moderations and History). Entered

Indian Civil Service after 1911 examination; Judge, Chief Court of Oudh, 1940-44; Judge, High Court of Allahabad, 1945-47; retired, 1947. *Recreation:* reading. *Address:* Beechurst, Shaftesbury Road, Woking. *T:* Woking 60216.

**BENNETT, John Sloman,** CMG 1955; Foreign and Commonwealth Office, Gibraltar and South Atlantic Department, since 1968; *b* 1914. Assistant Principal 1936, Principal, 1940, Colonial Office; Min. of Information tour of Middle East posts, 1940; seconded to Office of Minister of State in Middle East, 1941-45; Middle East Supply Centre, 1943-45; Asst Sec., 1946; seconded Imperial Defence Coll., 1955; Colonial Office, 1954-66; Commonwealth Office, Dependent Territories Div., 1966-68. *Address:* Foreign and Commonwealth Office, SW1.

**BENNETT, John Still,** CVO 1961; CBE 1964 (OBE 1959); High Commissioner in Barbados, since 1966; *b* 22 March 1911; *m* 1943, Danica (*née* Ribnikar) (*d* 1967); no *c*. *Educ:* Clifton Coll.; Peterhouse, Cambridge. Called to Bar, 1936. Served with HM Forces, 1939-43. Dir, British Information Services, Istanbul, 1943-46; Information Officer: Bucharest, 1946-48; Stockholm, 1949-52; Consul: Houston, Texas, 1952-54; Khorramshahr, Iran, 1955-59; Regional Information Officer, Singapore and Bangkok, 1959-63; Ambassador to Burundi and Rwanda, 1964-66. *Recreations:* golf, shooting, riding. *Address:* PO 95, Bridgetown, Barbados. *Club:* United Hunts.

**BENNETT, Sir John W. W.;** *see* Wheeler-Bennett.

**BENNETT, Kenneth Geoffrey,** CMG 1966; Puisne Judge, Kenya, 1968; *b* 15 Jan. 1911; *er s* of late Wallace Bennett and Beatrice Norman Jeffery; unmarried. *Educ:* Clifton Coll. and privately. Called to the Bar (Middle Temple), 1932; Western Circuit; Resident Magistrate, Tanganyika, 1938; Crown Counsel, Tanganyika, 1946; Solicitor-Gen., Nyasaland, 1948. Acting Attorney-Gen., various occasions, 1949-53; Puisne Judge, Uganda, 1953; Acting Chief Justice, various occasions, 1955-65. Chairman: Uganda Immigration Appeals Tribunal, 1954-60; Commn of Inquiry into disturbances in Eastern Province of Uganda, 1960. *Recreation:* fishing. *Address:* PO Box 30041, Nairobi, Kenya. *Club:* East India and Sports.

**BENNETT, Rt. Rev. Manu Augustus;** *see* Aotearoa, Bishop of.

**BENNETT, Mrs Mary Letitia Somerville,** MA; Principal, St Hilda's College, Oxford, since 1965; *b* 9 Jan. 1913; *o c* of Rt Hon. H. A. L. Fisher, OM, and Lettice Ilbert; *m* 1955, John Sloman Bennett, CMG. *Educ:* Oxford High Sch.; Somerville Coll. (Schol.). 2nd Cl. Mods, 1st Cl. Lit. Hum. Mary Ewart Travelling Schol., 1936-37; Jt Broadcasting Cttee, 1940-41; Transcription Service of BBC, 1941-45; Colonial Office, 1945-56. Hon. Sec., Society for the Promotion of Roman Studies, 1960-. *Address:* St Hilda's College, Oxford. *T:* Oxford 41821. *Club:* University Women's.

**BENNETT, Patrick,** QC 1969; Deputy Chairman of Lindsey Quarter Sessions since 1970; *b* 12 Jan. 1924; *s* of Michael Bennett; *m* 1951, Lyle Reta Pope; two *d*. *Educ:* Bablake Sch., Coventry; Magdalen Coll., Oxford. State Scholar, 1941, MA, BCL 1949. Served RNVR, 1943-46, Sub Lt. Called to Bar, 1949; Asst Recorder, Coventry, 1969. *Recreations:* food, flying (Pres., English Section, Anglo-German Flying Club, 1968). *Address:* (home) 22 Wynnstay Gardens, W8. *T:* 01-937 2110; (professional) 2 Crown Office Row, Temple, EC4. *T:* 01-236 9337. *Clubs:* Hurlingham; Spartan Flying (Denham).

**BENNETT, Ralph Featherstone;** Member, London Transport Executive (formerly London Transport Board), since 1968; *b* 3 Dec. 1923; *o s* of late Ralph J. P. Bennett and of Mrs E. M. Bennett, Whitchurch, Tavistock, Devon; *m* 1948, Delia Marie, *o d* of late J. E. Baxter and of Mrs D. D. Baxter, Hartley, Plymouth; two *s* two *d*. *Educ:* Plympton Grammar Sch.; Plymouth Technical Coll. Articled pupil to City of Plymouth Transport Manager, 1940-43; Techn. Asst, Plymouth City Transp., 1943-54; Michelin Tyre Co., 1954-55; Dep. Gen. Man., City of Plymouth Transp. Dept, 1955-58; Gen. Manager: Gt Yarmouth Transp. Dept, 1958-60; Bolton Transp. Dept, 1960-65; Manchester City Transp., 1965-68. CEng; MIMechE; MInstT. *Recreations:* music, gardening, tennis. *Address:* Fuller's Farm Oast House, Smarden, near Ashford, Kent. *T:* Smarden 580. *Club:* National Liberal.

**BENNETT, Dr Reginald Frederick Brittain,** VRD 1944; MA Oxon; BM, BCh, 1942; LMSSA 1937; DPM 1948; MP (C) Gosport and Fareham since 1950; Chairman, Advanced Metal Techniques Ltd; Director: Bowmaker Ltd; British Car Auctions Ltd; Comprehensive Designers International Ltd; industrial and commercial consultant; formerly psychiatrist; *b* 22 July 1911; *e s* of late Samuel Robert Bennett, MA, and of Gertrude (*née* Brittain); *m* 1947, Henrietta, *d* of Capt. H. B. Crane, CBE, RN (retd); one *s* three *d*. *Educ:* Winchester Coll.; New College, Oxford. Junior Demonstrator of Anatomy, Oxford, 1933-34; Specialised in psychiatry, 1945; Maudsley Hospital, 1946-49; Institute for Study and Treatment of Delinquency, 1950-54. RNVR, 1934-46; Fleet Air Arm, Medical Officer and Pilot; torpedoed twice. Parly Private Secretary: to Rt Hon. Iain Macleod, MP, 1956-63; to the Home Sec., 1951-54; to Minister of Fuel and Power, 1954-55; Mem. Executive Franco-British Parly Relations Cttee, 1959-; Hon. Sec., Anglo-Italian Parly Gp, 1961-; Parly and Scientific Cttee: Hon. Sec., 1955-58; Dep. Chm., 1958-59; Chm., 1959-62; Vice-Pres., 1962-65; Member: Exec. Inter-Parly Union (Brit. Gp), 1962-; SW Metrop. Regional Hosp. Bd, 1953-58; Council, Research Defence Soc., 1959-70; President: Brit. Launderers' Research Association, 1960-; Southern Boroughs Assoc., 1950-; Swanwick and District Fruit Growers' Assoc., 1950-. International yacht races in Germany, 1934, USA, 1935; Shamrock V, 1934-35; Evaine, 1936-38; Olympic Games (reserve), 1936; in British-American Cup Team, 1949 and 1953 in USA; various trophies since. Hon. Lieut-Col, Georgia Militia, 1960; Commandeur de l'Ordre du Bontemps-Médoc; Galant de la Verte Marennes. Hon. Citizen of Atlanta, Ga, 1960. *Publications:* articles on psychological medicine and criminology; on yachting and aviation. *Recreations:* sailing, shooting, foreign travel, basking in the sun, avoiding exercise. *Address:* Rosemullion, Bembridge, Isle of Wight. *Clubs:* White's; Imperial Poona Yacht (Cdre); Wykehamist Sailing (Cdre); House of Commons Yacht (Vice-Cdre); House of Commons Motor (Vice-Chm.); Royal Cork Yacht; Royal St George Yacht; Royal Alfred Yacht; Royal Colombo Yacht; Yacht Club de Monaco; Clube Naval de Cascais; Bembridge Sailing, etc.

**BENNETT, Rex George,** CB 1946; *b* 11 April 1885; *s* of Rex Bennett and Charlotte Heath, Hildenborough, Kent; *m* 1909, Maud Louise Emmoney; one *s* one *d*. *Educ:* Bancroft's Sch.,

Woodford Green. Entered GPO, 1904; Asst Controller, Stores Dept, 1935; Vice-Controller, 1939; Controller, 1940; Dir of Contracts, 1941-46; Mem. Forests Products Research Board, Dept of Scientific and Industrial Research, 1947-52, Chm., 1952-58. Seconded to Federated Malay States Post Office, 1920-24, and to Ministry of Home Security, 1939. *Publications:* various papers on Wood Preservation to British Wood Preserving Association and Soc. of Chemical Engineering, 1935-52. *Recreations:* philately, local history. *Address:* 70 Hervey Road, Blackheath, SE3. *T:* 01-856 0055.

**BENNETT, Richard Rodney;** composer; *b* 29 March 1936; *s* of H. Rodney and Joan Esther Bennett. *Educ:* Leighton Park Sch., Reading; Royal Academy of Music. Works performed, 1953-, at Festivals of Aldeburgh, Cheltenham, and City of London; also in Europe, S Africa, USA, Vancouver, Australia, etc. Has written music for numerous films including: Indiscreet; The Devil's Disciple; Only Two Can Play; The Wrong Arm of the Law; Heavens Above; Billy Liar; One Way Pendulum; The Nanny; Far from the Madding Crowd; Billion Dollar Brain; Secret Ceremony; The Buttercup Chain; Figures in a Landscape; also the music for Television series, Hereward the Wake. Commissioned to write 2 full-length operas for Sadler's Wells: The Mines of Sulphur, 1965, A Penny for a Song, 1968; commnd to write opera for Covent Garden: Victory, 1970; (children's opera) All the King's Men, 1969. *Publications include:* two symphonies, Epithalamion, chamber music, orchestral music, educational music, song cycles, etc; articles for periodicals, about music. *Recreations:* cinema, modern jazz. *Address:* c/o Mrs Keys, London Management, Regent House, 235 Regent Street, W1.

**BENNETT, Maj.-Gen. Roland Anthony,** CB 1959; MD, FRCPE; Physician, Royal Hospital, Chelsea, 1959-69; *b* 10 April 1899; *s* of late Roland Ponsonby Bennett and of Johanna Morrison; *m* 1937, Constance Elizabeth Nanette Stokes; two *d. Educ:* Stornoway; Edinburgh Univ. MD (Edin) 1936; FRCP (Edin) 1947. Joined Seaforth Highlanders, 1917; served France, 1918 (wounded). Graduated, Edinburgh Univ., 1924; joined RAMC, 1925. Medical Officer, Houston Mount Everest Expedition, 1933. Served in France, Egypt, Palestine, India, Burma, 1939-45; Consulting Physician: Far East Land Forces, 1946-49; BAOR, 1950-55; Hon. Physician to the Queen, 1955-59; Dir of Medicine and Consulting Physician to the Army, 1955-59, retired. *Publications:* articles in RAMC Jl and BMJ. *Address:* c/o Glyn Mills & Co., Kirkland House, Whitehall, SW1.

**BENNETT, Ronald Alistair,** QC (Scotland) 1959; Hon. Sheriff-Substitute of Lanarkshire, Ayrshire and Dunbartonshire; *b* 11 Dec. 1922; *s* of Arthur George Bennett, MC and Edythe Sutherland; *m* 1950, Margret Magnusson, *d* of Sigursteinn Magnusson, Icelandic Consul-Gen. for Scotland; three *s* three *d. Educ:* Edinburgh Academy; Edinburgh Univ.; Balliol Coll., Oxford. MA, LLB Univ. of Edinburgh, 1942; Muirhead and Dalgety Prizes for Civil Law, 1942. Lieut, 79th (Scottish Horse) Medium Regt RA, 1943-45; Capt. attached RAOC, India and Japan, 1945-46. Called to Scottish Bar, 1947; Vans Dunlop Schol. in Scots Law and Conveyancing, 1948; Standing Counsel to Min. of Labour and National Service, 1957-59. Lectr in Mercantile Law, Edinburgh Univ., 1956-68. *Publications:* Bennett's Company Law, 2nd edn, 1950; Fraser's Rent Acts in Scotland, 2nd edn 1952; Editor: Scottish Current Law and Scots Law Times Sheriff Court Reports. *Recreations:* shooting, swimming, badminton, reading, music. *Address:* Laxamyri, Cammo Road, Barnton, Edinburgh 4. *T:* 031-336 1337.

**BENNETT, Rev. Canon Ronald D. G.;** *see* Grange-Bennett.

**BENNETT, Sir Ronald (Wilfred Murdoch),** 3rd Bt, *cr* 1929; *b* 25 March 1930; *o s* of Sir Wilfred Bennett, 2nd Bt, and Marion Agnes (OBE 1953), *d* of late James Somervell, Sorn Castle, Ayrshire, and step *d* of late Edwin Sandys Dawes; *S* father 1952; *m* 1953, Rose-Marie Audrey Patricia, *o d* of Major A. L. J. H. Aubépin, France and Co. Mayo, Ireland; two *d. Educ:* Wellington Coll.; Trinity Coll., Oxford. *Heir: uncle* Frank Carleton Bennett, Lieut RN (retd) [*b* 28 Sept. 1900; *m* 1923, Mariella, *d* of late Algernon Douglas-Pennant; two *s*]. *Address:* PO Box 15148, Kampala, Uganda. *Clubs:* Kampala, Uganda (Kampala).

**BENNETT, Sir Thomas (Penberthy),** KBE, *cr* 1954 (CBE 1942); Kt, *cr* 1946; FRSA; FRIBA; Hon. FIOB; Hon. FIBD; Chairman: New Town of Crawley, 1947-60; Stevenage Development Corporation, 1951-53; *b* 14 Aug. 1887; *s* of Thomas William Bennett and Anne Frances Penberthy; *m* 1916, Mary Langdon Edis; one *s. Educ:* Royal Academy Schs; Heatherleys, etc. Architectural Staff of LNWR; Staff of HM Office of Works; Head of Northern Polytechnic Sch. of Architecture, Surveying and Building, 1920-28; Dir of Bricks, 1940, Dir of Works, 1941-44, and Controller of Temporary Housing, Min. of Works, 1944-45; Chm., Bd of Trade Boot and Shoe Working Party, 1945; Lecturer Board of Education; Private Practice as Architect: *theatres:* including Saville; *cinemas:* including several Odeons; *offices:* incl. Diamond Corp.; Rank Organisation; Anglo-American: Metal Box; Marks & Spencer; Pearl Assurance; Portman Building Soc.; Esso House, Iraq Petroleum Company; Ford Motor Co.; Rugby Portland Cement; Norwich Union Insurance Co.; South Bank Estates; Hill, Samuel & Co. Ltd; *flats:* incl. Eyre Court; Westminster Gardens; Marsham Court; Caroline House; Campbell Court; Queensmead, St John's Wood; *factories:* for Smiths (Eng.); Kodak; *department stores:* Hammonds, Hull; Harrods (Rackhams); Bentalls; Fenwicks; Grants; stores in Africa for United Africa Co.; *hospital work at;* King Edward VII Hosp. for Officers; London Hosp.; Middlesex Hosp.; Westminster Hosp.; *air terminal and offices:* for BOAC; *chapel at:* Hyde Park; *synagogues:* St John's Wood; Great Cumberland Pl.; *banks:* for Westminster; Barclay's; Bank of Ireland; *hotel:* The Royal Lancaster. *Publications:* The Relation of Sculpture and Architecture; Architectural Design in Concrete; articles in Architectural Press, etc. *Recreations:* architecture, golf. *Address:* The Sycamores, 19 North Road, Highgate Village, N6. *T:* 01-340 6081. *Club:* Reform.

**BENNETT, Sir William Gordon,** Kt 1955; Member of Glasgow Royal Exchange; Member of the Glasgow Chamber of Commerce; Member of the Glasgow Trades House. Formerly a Magistrate and Member of Glasgow Corporation. Past President of the Scottish Unionist Association. Contested (C) Shettleston Division of Glasgow, July 1945. MP (C) Woodside Division of Glasgow, 1950-55. Served European War, 1914-18 (wounded); Officer in the Tank Corps. *Address:* 229 Nithsdale Road, Glasgow, S1.

**BENNETT, Sir William James,** Kt 1966; CBE 1953; DL; JP; CA; Member Eastern Electricity Board since 1948 and Chairman Eastern

Electricity Consultative Council; Railway Clerk (consecutively LNWR, LMS, LMR) since 1912; *b* 30 March 1896; *s* of James William Cator Bennett and Marion Blanche Pearson; *m* 1916, Juliet Emily, *d* of John William Watkins, engraver; one *s* one *d*. *Educ:* elementary sch.; Mr Fegan's Orphanage; London Sch. of Economics. Chm. Tilbury Electricity Undertaking, 1929-49. Formerly Tilbury (subseq. Thurrock) UDC (Chm. 1931-32, 1932-33); CC Essex, 1934-, CA 1946- (Vice-Chm. CC, 1948-49, Chm. 1952-55, 1958-60). DL County of Essex, 1962-; JP Essex 1937-. FRSA 1950. *Recreations:* music, operatics (amateur), astronomy, chess. *Address:* 26 Ruskin Road, Chadwell St Mary, Grays, Essex. *T:* Tilbury 2911.

**BENNETT, William John,** OBE 1946; President and Director: Iron Ore Company of Canada, Montreal (Vice-President, 1960-65); Quebec North Shore and Labrador Railway Co.; St Mary's Hospital; Vice-President and Director, Gulf Power Co.; Chairman of Board, BNA Holdings Ltd; Director: Canadian British Aluminium Co. Ltd (President, 1958-60); The Investors Group; Eldorado Nuclear Ltd; Twin Falls Power Corporation Ltd; Labrador Mining and Exploration Co. Ltd; Hollinger North Shore Exploration Co. Ltd; Canron Ltd; Cominco Ltd; Canadian Pacific Railway; Member, Economic Council of Canada; *b* 3 Nov. 1911; *s* of Carl Edward Bennett and Mary Agnes Downey; *m* 1936, Elizabeth Josephine Palleck; three *s* four *d*. *Educ:* University of Toronto (BA Hons). Chief Exec. Asst to Minister of Munitions and Supply, 1940-45; President: Atomic Energy of Canada Ltd, 1946-58; Eldorado Mining & Refining Ltd, 1946-58. Hon. LLD, Toronto Univ., 1955; Hon. Dr of Science, St Francis Xavier Univ., Antigonish, NS, 1956; Hon Dr of Laws, University of Ottawa, 1957. *Recreations:* ski-ing, music. *Address:* 4304 Montrose Avenue, Montreal 218, Quebec, Canada. *Club:* Mount Royal, Canadian (Montreal); Rideau (Ottawa, Ontario); Union (Cleveland, Ohio).

**BENNION, Claud,** Director British United Shoe Machinery Co. Ltd; *b* 12 June 1886; *s* of late Charles Bennion, The Grange, Thurnby, Leics; *m* 1912, Nora Grace (*d* 1967), *d* of late W. G. Jarvis, Leicester; two *s* one *d*. *Educ:* Uppingham; Pembroke Coll., Cambridge. BA, LLB (Cantab.), 1907; Solicitor, 1910; High Sheriff, Leics, 1938-39. *Recreations:* reading, walking, golf. *Address:* Billesdon Coplow, Leics. *T:* Billesdon 208.

**BENNION, Francis Alan Roscoe;** Chairman, World of Property Housing Trust; *b* 2 Jan. 1923; *o s* of Thomas Roscoe Bennion, Liverpool; *m* 1951, Barbara Elisabeth Braendle; three *d*. *Educ:* John Lyon's, Harrow; Balliol Coll., Oxford. Pilot, RAF, 1941-46. Gibbs Law Scholar, Oxford, 1948. Called to Bar, Middle Temple, 1951 (Harmsworth Scholar). Lectr and Tutor in Law, St Edmund Hall, Oxford, 1951-53; joined Office of Parly Counsel to HM Treasury, 1953; Dep. Parly Counsel, 1964; seconded to Govt of Pakistan to advise on drafting of new Constitution, 1956; seconded to Govt of Ghana to advise on legislation and drafting Constitution converting the country into a Republic, 1959-61. Sec., RICS, 1965-68; Governor, College of Estate Management, 1965-68. Member: Cttee, Help the Aged Housing Assoc. (1968) Ltd; Estate Agents Registration Council; Council, Statute Law Soc.; Law Reform Cttee, Bar Assoc. for Commerce, Finance and Industry. *Publications:* Constitutional Law of Ghana, 1962; Professional Ethics: The Consultant Professions and their Code, 1969; Tangling with the Law, 1969; Registration of Estate Agents, 1970. *Address:* 16 Lincoln's Inn Fields, WC2. *T:* 01-405 0785; The Old Rectory, Farleigh, Warlingham, Surrey. *T:* Upper Warlingham 3038. *Clubs:* Oxford and Cambridge University, Royal Commonwealth Society.

**BENNITT, Mortimer Wilmot;** Deputy Director, Land Commission, since 1967; *b* 28 Aug. 1910; *s* of Rev. F. W. and Honoria Bennitt. *Educ:* Charterhouse; Trinity Coll., Oxford. Entered Office of Works, 1934; Private Sec. to Sir Philip Sassoon, 1937-38. Served War of 1939-45: RAF, marine craft section, 1943-45. Regional Dir, Newcastle upon Tyne, 1949-51; Under Sec., 1951-63; Asst Sec., 1963-67. Chm., Little Theatre Guild of Gt Britain, 1959-60. *Address:* 8 Alwyne Villas, N1. *T:* 01-226 5937; 200a Osborne Road, Newcastle upon Tyne NE2 3LD. *Clubs:* Oxford and Cambridge University, Tower Theatre; People's Theatre Arts Group (Newcastle upon Tyne).

**BENOY, Brig. James Francis,** CMG 1951; CBE 1944; Brigadier (retired) late South Staffordshire Regiment; *b* 10 July 1896; *s* of late Rev. J. Benoy, Asst Chaplain-Gen. to the Forces; *m* 1923, Margery Frances Stewart (*d* 1969), *d* of late H. C. Stewart, Jersey; one *s*. *Educ:* St John's Coll., Cambridge. Served European War, 1914-19, France, Belgium (wounded, despatches, 1914-15 star, 2 medals). GSO, Aldershot Comd, 1932-35; DAAG, China Comd, 1936-40; AQMG, BEF, 1940; AQMG, Home Forces, 1941; Brig. i/c Admin West Africa, 1942-43; DA & QMG SE Asia Comd, 1944-45; Head of Lord Mountbatten's Liaison Staff in Australia, 1945-46; Dep.-Dir of Civil Affairs, War Office, 1947-49; Dep. Dir-Gen., Foreign Office Administration of African Territories, 1949-52. Comdr Legion of Merit (USA), 1946. *Address:* Inholmes Lodge, Woodlands St Mary, near Newbury, Berks. *Club:* Army and Navy.

**BENOY, Maj.-Gen. John Meredith,** CBE 1943 (OBE 1931); Major-General Retired; *b* 13 July 1896; *s* of late Rev. J. Benoy; *m* 1920, Ursula Hulme Cox; one *s* one *d*. *Educ:* Denstone Coll., Staffs; Felsted Sch., Essex; RMC, Sandhurst. 2nd Lieut, South Staffs Regt, 1914; served European War, 1914-18, in France and Belgium with South Staffs and Royal Warwicks Regts (wounded twice); GSO3 Supreme War Council, Versailles and Peace Conference, Paris, 1918-20; Internal Security, S Ireland, 1920-21. Palestine Riots, 1929-30 (OBE); Staff Coll., Camberley, 1932-33; GSO3 War Office, 1934-36; Brigade Major, Aldershot, Palestine, and Transjordan, 1936-39; Bt Lieut-Col, 1940; AA & QMG, BEF, France and Belgium, 1940; Dep. Dir, War Office, 1941-42; Col, 1942; Brig., DA & QMG. First Army, BNAF, 1942-43; DA & QMG Second Army, 1943-44; Maj.-Gen. i/c Administration, Anti-Aircraft Command, 1944-45; Chief Administrator, Eritrea, 1945-46. Mem. Council of Industrial Design, 1949-66; Controller, Association of Socs of Art and Design, 1966-70. *Address:* c/o National Westminster Bank, 208 Piccadilly, W1. *Club:* United Service.

**BENSKIN, Gladys (Mrs Joseph Benskin),** CBE 1918; *d* of Michael Paul Grace, 40 Belgrave Square, SW; *m* 1st, 1912, Major Raymond Sheffield Hamilton-Grace (*d* 1915); 2nd, 1919, Col Joseph Benskin, DSO, OBE (*d* 1953). Was Sec. to Mesopotamian Relief Fund. *Address:* Knowle, Frant, near Tunbridge Wells, Kent.

**BENSON, Sir Arthur (Edward Trevor),** GCMG 1959 (KCMG 1954; CMG 1952); *b* 21 Dec. 1907; *s* of late Rev. Arthur H. Trevor Benson,

Vicar of Ilam, Staffs, formerly of Castle Connell, Co. Limerick and of St Saviour's, Johannesburg, and Emily Maud Malcolmson, Woodlock, Portlaw, Co. Waterford, late of Hanson Mount, Ashbourne, Derbyshire; *m* 1933, Daphne Mary Joyce, *d* of E. H. M. Fynn, Serui, near Hartley, S Rhodesia; two *d*. *Educ:* Wolverhampton Sch.; Exeter Coll., Oxford. Colonial Administrative Service; Cadet, N Rhodesia, 1932; seconded to Colonial Office, 1939; to War Cabinet Office, 1940-43; to Colonial Office, 1943-44; Northern Rhodesia, 1944-46; Administrative Sec., Uganda, 1946-49; Chief Sec., Central African Council, 1949-51; Chief Sec. to Govt of Nigeria, 1951-54; Governor of Northern Rhodesia, 1954-59. Hon. Fellow, Exeter Coll., Oxford, 1963. JP Devon, 1962-66. KStJ 1954. *Recreations:* fishing, and shooting. *Address:* Combe Hill, Combe Raleigh, near Honiton, Devon. *Clubs:* Leander, Royal Societies.

**BENSON, Rev. Sir (Clarence) Irving,** Kt 1963; CBE 1960 (OBE 1951); DD; Superintendent of the Wesley Church Central Mission, Melbourne, 1926-67; *b* 1 Dec. 1897; *s* of Walter Benson; *m* 1st, 1919, Agnes Lyell (*d* 1947); three *d*; 2nd, 1967, Marjorie Featonby. *Educ:* Hull Technical Coll.; DD 1939. Minister, Hamilton (Victoria) Circuit, 1916-17; Toorak, 1918-23; Brunswick, 1923-26. Pres., Methodist Conf., 1943. Pres., Australian Reading Union; Vice-Pres., Library Association of Victoria; Pres. of Trustees, State Library of Victoria; Chm., Free Library Service Board. *Publications:* The Man with the Donkey; A Century of Victorian Methodism; The Craft of Prayer; The Craft of Finding God. *Recreations:* swimming, book collecting. *Address:* 25 Hoddle Street, Elsternwick, Victoria 3185, Australia. *Clubs:* Melbourne, Savage (Melbourne).

**BENSON, Rear-Adm. Cyril Herbert Gordon,** DSO 1918; RN, retired; *b* 17 Feb. 1884; *s* of late James Bourne Benson; *m* 1919, May (*d* 1951), *d* of late James Boyd. *Educ:* Winchester; HMS Britannia. Lieut, 1906; Shadwell Testimonial Prize, 1910; Comdr, 1917; Capt. 1924; Rear-Adm., 1936; served European War, 1914-18 (despatches, DSO and bar); commanded 4th Destroyer Flotilla, 1926-28; commanded Royal Australian Naval Coll. at Captain's Point, Jervis Bay, 1929-31; Capt.-Superintendent of Training at Flinders Naval Depôt, Vic.; 2nd Naval Mem. Royal Australian Naval Board, 1930-32; HMS Cumberland, 1933-35; retired list, 1936; Hon. Wing Comdr RAFVR, 1937-39; Commodore M/S, 1940; HMS Cochrane, 1940-43; Commodore of Convoys, 1943-45; HMS Valkyrie, 1945-47. Royal Humane Society's bronze medal, 1915. *Recreations:* golf and fishing. *Address:* Granny's Cottage, 348 Sea Front, Hayling Island. *Clubs:* Royal and Ancient Golf (St Andrews), Hon. Co. of Edinburgh Golfers.

**BENSON, Maj.-Gen. Edward Riou,** CB 1952; CMG 1950; CBE 1945; *b* 4 April 1903; *yr s* of late Brig.-Gen. Riou Philip Benson, CB, CMG, Guildford, Surrey; *m* 1931, Isolda Mary Stuart, *d* of late Gen. Sir John Stuart Mackenzie Shea, GCB, KCMG, DSO; one *s* (one *d* decd). *Educ:* Cheltenham Coll.; RMA Woolwich, 2nd Lieut, Royal Field Artillery, 1923; Lieut, RA, 1925; Capt. 1936; Major 1940; Temp. Lieut-Col 1941; Temp. Brig. 1942; Col 1946; Maj.-Gen. 1951. Served War of 1939-45, North-West Europe, 1944-46. Dep. Dir Mil. Govt (BE), Berlin, 1948-50; Comdr 4 Anti-Aircraft Group, 1951-53; Chief of Staff, GHQ, Middle East Land Forces, 1954-57, retired. Col. Commandant, Royal Artillery, 1960-65. *Address:* Well House, Aldermaston, Berks. *T:* Woolhampton 3347. *Club:* Army and Navy.

**BENSON, Prof. Frank Atkinson,** BEng, MEng (Liverpool); PhD, DEng (Sheffield); FIEE, Sen. Mem. IEEE, FIES; Professor and Head of Department of Electronic and Electrical Engineering, University of Sheffield, since 1967; *b* 21 Nov. 1921; *s* of late John and Selina Benson; *m* 1950, Kathleen May Paskell; two *s*. *Educ:* Ulverston Grammar Sch.; Univ. of Liverpool. Mem. research staff, Admty Signal Estab., Witley, 1943-46; Asst Lectr in Electrical Engrg, University of Liverpool, 1946-49; Lectr 1949-59, Sen. Lectr 1959-61, in Electrical Engrg, University of Sheffield; Reader in Electronics, University of Sheffield, 1961-67. *Publications:* Voltage Stabilizers, 1950; Electrical Engineering Problems with Solutions, 1954; Voltage Stabilized Supplies, 1957; Problems in Electronics with Solutions, 1958; Electric Circuit Theory, 1959; Voltage Stabilization, 1965; Electric Circuit Problems with Solutions, 1967; Millimetre and Submillimetre Waves, 1969; many papers on microwaves, gas discharges and voltage stabilization in learned jls. *Address:* 64 Grove Road, Sheffield S7 2GZ. *T:* Sheffield 363493.

**BENSON, Sir George,** Kt 1958; estate agent and valuer; *b* 3 May 1889; *s* of Thomas Duckworth Benson; *m* 1919, Marjorie Lodge; one *s* one *d*. *Educ:* Manchester Grammar Sch. MP (Lab) Chesterfield Div., 1929-31 and 1935-50, Chesterfield, 1950-64. *Publication:* History of Socialism. *Address:* c/o G. M. Russell, Grove House, 140 Salmons Lane, Whyteleafe, Surrey.

**BENSON, Guy Holford;** Partner and Director, Robert Benson & Co., 1913-60; Director of London Assurance, 1927-60; *b* 1888; *e s* of late R. H. Benson; *m* 1921, Lady Violet, 2nd *d* of 8th Duke of Rutland, *widow* of Lord Elcho; three *s*. Served in Gallipoli and France. *Educ:* Eton; Balliol Coll., Oxford. *Address:* Stanway, Winchcomb, Glos. *T:* Stanton 208; Walpole House, Chiswick Mall, W4. *T:* 01-994 2297. *Clubs:* Brooks's, Bath.

**BENSON, Sir Henry (Alexander),** Kt 1964; CBE 1946; FCA; Partner, Cooper Brothers & Co., Chartered Accountants, since 1934; *b* 2 Aug. 1909; *s* of Alexander Stanley Benson and Florence Mary (*née* Cooper); *m* 1939, Anne Virginia Macleod; two *s* one *d*. *Educ:* Johannesburg, South Africa. ACA (Hons) 1932; FCA 1939. Commissioned Grenadier Guards, 1940-45; seconded from Army to Min. of Supply to advise on reorganisation of accounts of Royal Ordnance Factories, 1943-44, and in Dec. 1943 apptd Dir Ordnance Factories, to carry out reorganisation; apptd Controller of Building Materials, Min. of Works, 1945; Special appt to advise Minister of Health on housing production, 1945, and subseq. other appts, also Mem. Cttee (Wilson Cttee) to review work done on, and to make recommendations for further research into, processes for transformation of coal into oil, chemicals and gas, 1959-60. Mem. Crawley Development Corp., 1947-50; Mem. Royal Ordnance Factories Board, 1952-56; Dep. Chm. Advisory Cttee (Fleck Cttee) to consider organisation of National Coal Board, 1953-55. Dir Hudson's Bay Co., 1953-62 (Dep. Governor 1955-62); Dir Finance Corporation for Industry Ltd, 1953-; Council, Institute of Chartered Accountants, 1956- (Pres., 1966); Mem. Advisory Cttee on Legal Aid, 1956-60; Mem. Tribunal under Prevention of Fraud (Investments) Act 1939, 1957-; Mem. Special Advisory Cttee to examine structure, finance and working of organisations controlled by British Transport Commission, 1960; apptd by Minister of Commerce, N Ireland, to investigate position of railways; to make recommendations about their future, and to report on effect which recommendations will have on transport system of Ulster Transport Authority, 1961; apptd Chm. of a Cttee to examine possible economies in the shipping and ancillary services engaged in meat, dairy products and fruit trades of New Zealand, 1962. Mem. Cttee apptd by Chancellor of the Exchequer to investigate practical effects of introduction of a turnover tax, 1963. Joint Comr to advise on integration of Nat. Assoc. of Brit. Manufrs, FBI, Brit. Employers' Confed., and on formation of a Nat. Industrial Organisation, 1963; Joint Inspector, Bd of Trade, to investigate affairs of Rolls Razor Ltd, 1964; Indep. Chm. of British Iron & Steel Fedn Development Co-ordinating Cttee, 1966. A Trustee, The Times Trust, 1967-; Indep. Mem., Permanent Jt Hops Cttee, 1967-. Apptd by Nat. Trust as Chm. of adv. cttee to review management, organisation and responsibilities of Nat. Trust, 1967; apptd by Jt Turf Authorities as chm. of The Racing Industry Cttee of Inquiry to make detailed study of financial structure and requirements of racing industry, 1967; Vice-Pres., Union Européene des Experts Comptables économiques et financiers (UEC), 1969; Mem. Cttee to enquire into admin. and organisation of MoD. *Recreations:* shooting, golf, sailing. *Address:* The Red House, Merstham, Surrey. *T:* Merstham 2247. *Clubs:* Brooks's, Jockey; Royal Yacht Squadron.

**BENSON, Horace Burford;** *b* 3 April 1904; *s* of Augustus W. Benson and Lucy M. (*née* Jarrett); *m* 1930, Marthe Lanier; one *s* one *d.* Called to Bar, Gray's Inn, 1936; practised as Barrister, Seychelles Islands, 1936-46; District Magistrate, Ghana, 1946; Puisne Judge, Ghana, 1952-57; retired, 1957. Temp. Magistrate, Basutoland, 1958-60; Puisne Judge, Basutoland, Bechuanaland Protectorate and Swaziland, 1960-61; Chief Justice, Basutoland (now Lesotho), 1965; Puisne Judge, Malawi, 1967-69. *Recreations:* bowls, bridge. *Address:* c/o Barclays Bank Ltd, Tulse Hill, SE27.

**BENSON, Rev. Sir Irving;** *see* Benson, Rev. Sir C. I.

**BENSON, Rev. Niale Shane Trevor,** AFC 1942; MA; Vicar of Broadchalke with Bowerchalke, since 1970; *b* Johannesburg, SA, 14 Dec. 1911; *s* of late Rev. A. H. T. Benson, Vicar of Ilam, Staffs, formerly of Castle Connell, Co. Limerick and of St Saviour's, Johannesburg, and late Emily Maud Malcolmson, Woodlock, Portlaw, Co. Waterford; *m* 1939, Helen Marjorie, *d* of late Air Chief Marshal Sir John Miles Steel, GCB, kbe, CMG; two *s* one *d.* *Educ:* Wolverhampton Grammar Sch.; St John's Coll., Oxford (Open Classical Scholar). BA 1934; MA 1945. Asst Master, Shrewsbury Sch., 1934; Giggleswick Sch. (Housemaster, Officer Comdg OTC), 1935-39. Served War of 1939-45, RAF (AFC); Sqdn-Ldr, 1941; Dep. Chief-Instructor, Empire Central Flying Sch., 1942-43. Giggleswick Sch., 1945-47; Headmaster: Queen Elizabeth's Grammar Sch., Blackburn, 1948-56; Giggleswick Sch., 1956-60; The Cathedral Sch., Salisbury, 1963-70. Deacon, 1968; priest, 1969. *Address:* Broadchalke Vicarage, near Salisbury, Wilts.

**BENSON, Preston;** journalist, retired; *b* Kendal, Westmorland, 4 April 1896; *s* of W. P. Benson, journalist; *m* 1932, Winifred Frances Gadd; two *s.* *Educ:* village sch., Orton, Westmorland; King Edward VII Sch., Sheffield. Middlesex and Bucks Advertiser, 1912-16; Navy, 1916-19; Daily News, 1919-23; Daily Chronicle, 1923-30; Star, 1930-60. *Publications:* Unknown Country, 1941; various pamphlets. *Recreations:* playing piano and recorder; painting, gardening, bee-keeping. *Address:* 7 Groveland Avenue, SW16. *T:* 01-679 3017.

**BENSTEAD, Sir John,** Kt 1953; CBE 1946; DL; Member British Transport Commission, 1947-61 (Deputy Chairman); *b* 10 Jan. 1897; *m* 1922, Gladys Mary Palmer (*d* 1965); one *d*; *m* 1967, Catherine Ferguson McCabe. *Educ:* King's Sch., Peterborough. Gen. Sec., National Union of Railwaymen, 1943-47; Pres., International Transport Workers' Federation, 1946; Member: Advisory Council for Scientific and Industrial Research, 1943-48; Colonial and Economic Development Council, 1947-48; Royal Commission on Press, 1946; Mem. Institute of Transport. DL Huntingdon and Peterborough, 1967. *Address:* 98a Lincoln Road, Peterborough. *T:* Peterborough 62072.

**BENTALL, Gerald Chalmers,** CBE 1950; *b* 17 Feb. 1903; *s* of late Leonard Hugh Bentall and Winifred Ivy Bentall; *m* 1959, Sybil Brett; one *s* (by a former marriage). *Educ:* Tonbridge. *Recreation:* agriculture. *Address:* Witley Park, Brook, Godalming, Surrey.

**BENTALL, Hugh Henry,** MB; FRCS; Professor of Cardiac Surgery, Postgraduate Medical School of London, since 1965; Consultant Thoracic Surgeon, Hammersmith Hospital, since 1955; *b* 28 April 1920; *s* of Henry Bentall and Lilian Alice Greeno; *m* 1944, Jean, *d* of late Hugh Cameron Wilson, MD, FRCS; three *s* one *d.* *Educ:* Seaford Coll., Sussex; Medical Sch. of St Bartholomew's Hospital, London. RNVR, Surg Lieut, 1945-47. Lecturer in Thoracic Surgery, Postgraduate Medical Sch., London, 1959; Reader 1962-65. *Publications:* books and papers on surgical subjects. *Recreation:* sailing. *Address:* Postgraduate Medical School of London, Ducane Road, W12. *T:* 01-743 2030. *Clubs:* Royal Naval Volunteer Reserve; Royal Naval Sailing Association (Portsmouth).

**BENTHALL, Sir (Arthur) Paul,** KBE, *cr* 1950; FLS; Chairman: Amalgamated Metal Corporation Ltd; Bird & Co. (London) Ltd; Director: Chartered Bank; Royal Insurance Co. Ltd and associated companies; *b* 25 Jan. 1902; *s* of Rev. Charles Francis Benthall and Annie Theodosia Benthall; *m* 1932, Mary Lucy, *d* of John A. Pringle, Horam, Sussex; four *s.* *Educ:* Eton; Christ Church, Oxford. Joined Bird & Co. and F. W. Heilgers & Co., Calcutta, 1924; partner in both firms, 1934; Vice-Pres. Bengal Chamber of Commerce, 1947; Pres. 1948 and 1950; Pres. of Assoc. Chambers of Commerce of India, 1948 and 1950; Member: Calcutta Local Board, Imperial Bank of India, 1946-48 and 1950-53; Central Board, 1948 and 1950-53; Chm. All India Board of Technical Studies in Commerce and Business Administration, 1950-53; Pres. Royal Agri-Horticultural Society of India, 1945-47; Vice-Pres. UK Citizens' Assoc., 1951; Pres. 1952. *Publication:* The Trees of Calcutta and its Neighbourhood, 1946. *Recreations:* botany, sailing. *Address:* Benthall Hall, Broseley, Salop. *T:* Ironbridge 3380. *Clubs:* Oriental, City of London, Lansdowne.

**BENTHALL, Michael Pickersgill,** CBE 1960; Theatrical Producer and Company Director; *b* 8 Feb 1919; *s* of late Sir Edward Charles Benthall, KCSI. *Educ:* Eton; Christ Church, Oxford. Actor, 1938-39. Joined RA, Oct. 1939; served War of 1939-45 (despatches); demobilised with rank of Major (Royal Artillery), May 1946. Co-produced with Tyrone Guthrie, Hamlet, for Old Vic Company, New Theatre, 1944. Wrote scenarios for two Sadler's Wells Ballets,

Miracle in the Gorbals, 1944, Adam Zero, 1946. *Produced operas:* Don Pasquale, Cambridge Theatre, 1946; Turandot, Covent Garden, 1947; Aida, Covent Garden, 1948; Queen of Spades, Covent Garden, 1950; Macbeth, Royal Opera House, 1960. *Produced plays:* The White Devil, Duchess, 1947; The Wild Duck, St Martin's, 1948; Master of Arts, Strand, 1949; She Stoops to Conquer, Old Vic Co., New, 1949; (at Stratford-on-Avon) Merchant of Venice, 1947, King John, Merchant of Venice (revival), Hamlet, Taming of the Shrew, 1948, A Midsummer Night's Dream, Cymbeline, 1949; As You Like It, Cort Theatre, New York, 1950; Golden City, Adelphi, 1950; Cæsar and Cleopatra, Antony and Cleopatra, St James's, 1951, and Ziegfeld Theatre, New York, 1951; The Tempest, Stratford-on-Avon, 1951 and 1952; The Millionairess, New, London and Shubert Theatre, New York, 1952; A Woman of No Importance, Savoy, 1953; Hamlet, Edinburgh Festival and Old Vic, 1953; All's Well that Ends Well, Old Vic, 1953; Coriolanus, Old Vic, 1954; Macbeth, Edinburgh Festival and Old Vic, 1954; A Midsummer Night's Dream, Edinburgh Festival and Metropolitan Opera House, New York, 1954; Richard II, 1955; The Merchant of Venice, Measure for Measure, The Taming of the Shrew, Old Vic Australian Tour, 1955; Julius Caesar, Edinburgh Festival and Old Vic, 1955; A Winter's Tale, Henry V, Old Vic, 1955; Othello, Old Vic, 1956; Revival of Richard II and Macbeth for Old Vic American Tour, 1956; Timon of Athens, Cymbeline, Merchant of Venice, Old Vic, 1956; Hamlet, A Midsummer Night's Dream, Old Vic, 1957; Twelfth Night, Henry VIII, Old Vic, 1958; Revival of Hamlet, Henry V, Twelfth Night, for Old Vic American Tour, 1958; The Cenci, Old Vic, 1959; The Double Dealer, Edinburgh Festival and Old Vic, 1959; The Importance of Being Earnest, Old Vic, 1959; Macbeth (Verdi), Covent Garden, 1960; Revival of Macbeth, and the Importance of Being Earnest, for Russian tour, 1961; Doctor Faustus, Edinburgh Festival and Old Vic, 1961; Man and Boy, Queen's 1963, and Brooks Atkinson Theatre, New York, 1963; Macbeth, Lisbon, 1964 (and Chichester, 1966); Romeo and Juliet, Tokyo, 1965; Katharine Hepburn in Coco, New York, 1969. Director of Old Vic Theatre, 1953-62. *Address:* 72 Eaton Square, SW1.

**BENTHALL, Sir Paul;** *see* Benthall, Sir A. P.

**BENTINCK;** *see* Cavendish-Bentinck.

**BENTLEY, Rt. Rev. David Williams Bentley,** CBE 1938. *Educ:* Univ. of Durham. Deacon, 1906; Priest, 1907; Curate, St John's Barrow-in-Furness, 1906-10; St James-the-less, 1910-14; Vicar of St Mary's, Plaistow, 1914-16; Warden of St Peter's Coll., Jamaica, 1917-27; Examining Chaplain to Bishop of Jamaica, 1918; Asst Bishop of Jamaica, 1919; Bishop of Barbados, 1927-45. *Address:* Fenshaw, Rectory Hill, St George, Barbados, West Indies.

**BENTLEY, Frederick Herbert,** OBE 1944; Resident Lecturer and Surgeon, Sommer Memorial Trust, Portland, Oregon; *b* Bolton, Lancs 1905; *e s* of Fred Bentley, JP, and Laura Evelyn Bentley; *m* 1946, Radmila Novakovic, of Belgrade. *Educ:* Church Institute Sch., Bolton; University of Manchester. BScManch. 1926; MB, ChB, 1929; FRCS 1932; MD Manchester, 1946; Bradley Memorial Schol. Clinical Surgery, Manchester Royal Infirmary, 1928. Formerly House Surgeon, Asst RSO; First Asst and Tutor, Manchester Royal Infirmary; formerly House Surg. and Res. Surg. Off., St Mark's Hospital, London; formerly Hon. Surgeon various hospitals in Manchester area. Hunterian Prof., Royal College of Surgeons, England, 1936 and 1937; Prof. of Surgery, the University of Durham, 1945-52; formerly Mackenzie Mackinnon Research Fellow, RCP London and RCS England; Bernhard Baron Scholar RCS Eng; Dickinson Scholar and Demonst. Anatomy, University of Manchester. On Active Service with RAMC 1942-45, rank Lieut-Col. First as Officer in charge a Surgical Division and later OC Penicillin Control Team in Mediterranean area; separate mission to Russian Army in Rumania, and Partisan Army in Yugoslavia. *Publications:* various contributions to Medical and Physiological Journals since 1936. *Recreations:* tennis, angling, music. *Clubs:* Waverley, Portland, Arlington (Portland); Reform (London, England).

**BENTLEY, Rev. Canon Geoffrey Bryan;** Canon of Windsor since 1957; *b* 16 July 1909; *s* of late Henry Bentley; *m* 1938, Nina Mary, *d* of late George Coombe Williams, Clerk; two *s* two *d*. *Educ:* Uppingham Sch.; King's Coll., Cambridge (Scholar); Cuddesdon Coll., Oxford. BA and Carus Greek Testament Prize, 1932; MA 1935. Ordained, 1933; Asst Curate, St Cuthbert's, Copnor, 1933-35; Tutor of Scholae Cancellarii, Lincoln, 1935-38; Lecturer, 1938-52; Priest Vicar of Lincoln Cathedral and Chaplain of Lincoln County Hosp., 1938-52; Proctor in Convocation, 1945-55; Rector of Milton Abbot with Dunterton, Dio. Exeter, 1952-57; Examg Chap. to Bp of Exeter, 1952; Commissary to Bp of SW Tanganyika, 1952-61; Canon of Windsor, 1957, Precentor, 1958-69, President and Proctor for Chapter, May-Dec. 1962, Steward 1969; Mem., Archbp's Group on Reform of Divorce Law, 1964; William Jones Golden Lectr., 1965; Scott Holland Lectr., 1966. *Publications:* The Resurrection of the Bible, 1940; Catholic Design for Living, 1940; Reform of the Ecclesiastical Law, 1944; God and Venus, 1964; Dominance or Dialogue?, 1965. *Address:* 8 The Cloisters, Windsor Castle, Berks. *T:* Windsor 63001. *Club:* National Liberal.

**BENTLEY, Nicolas Clerihew,** FSIA; Publisher, Artist, and Author; *b* Highgate, London, 14 June 1907; *yr s* of late Edmund Clerihew Bentley; *m* 1934, Barbara, *e d* of late Sir Patrick Hastings, QC; one *d*. *Educ:* University Coll. Sch., London; Heatherley Sch. of Art. Dir, André Deutsch Ltd; Editor, Thos. Nelson Ltd. *Publications:* Ballet-Hoo; The Tongue-Tied Canary; The Floating Dutchman; Third Party Risk; A Choice of Ornaments; A Version of the Truth; The Victorian Scene; Golden Sovereigns, etc. *Address:* 7 Hobury Street, SW10. *Club:* Garrick.

**BENTLEY, Phyllis Eleanor,** OBE 1970; BA; Hon. LittD Leeds, 1949; FRSL 1958; Author; *b* Halifax, Yorks, 19 Nov. 1894; *d* of Joseph Edwin and Eleanor Bentley; unmarried. *Educ:* Halifax; Cheltenham Ladies' Coll. *Publications:* The World's Bane, 1918; Pedagomania, 1918; Environment, 1922; Cat-in-the-Manger, 1923; The Spinner of the Years, 1928; The Partnership, 1928; Carr, 1929; Trio, 1930; Inheritance, 1932; A Modern Tragedy, 1934; The Whole of the Story, 1935; Freedom, Farewell!, 1936; Sleep in Peace, 1938; Take Courage, 1940; Manhold, 1941; Here is America, 1941; The English Regional Novel, 1942; The Rise of Henry Morcar, 1946; Some Observations on the Art of Narrative, 1946; Colne Valley Cloth, 1947; The Brontës, 1947; Life Story, 1948; Quorum, 1950; Panorama, 1952; The House of Moreys, 1953; Noble in Reason, 1955; Love and Money, 1957; Crescendo, 1958; Kith and Kin, 1960; The Young Brontës, 1960; O Dreams, O

Destinations (autobiography), 1962; Committees, 1964; Public Speaking, 1964; The Adventures of Tom Leigh, 1964; Tales of the West Riding, 1965; A Man of His Time, 1966; Ned Carver in Danger, 1967; Gold Pieces, 1968; The Brontës and their World, 1969; Ring in the New, 1969; (Ed) Heather Edition of the Works of the Brontës, 1949. *Recreation:* reading. *Address:* The Grange, Warley, Halifax, Yorks. *T:* Halifax 31624. *Clubs:* PEN, English-Speaking Union.

**BENTLEY, Walter Owen,** MBE 1919; retired; MIME; *b* 16 Sept. 1888; *s* of Alfred Bentley and Emily, *d* of Thomas Waterhouse; *m* 1934, Margaret Roberts Hutton, *d* of Thomas Roberts and Ann Murray; no *c. Educ:* Lambrook; Clifton Coll. Premium Apprentice, Great Northern Railway Loco. Works, Doncaster, 1905-10; Served in RNVR, attached RNAS, 1915-18. Originated use of aluminium for pistons in internal combustion engines, 1913. Responsible for design of: BR1 and BR2 rotary aero engines; all Bentley cars, 1919-31; 12 cylinder 4½ litre and 2½ litre Lagondas, 1935-46; 2½ litre Lagonda engine used later in Aston Martin. *Publications:* "W.O.", 1958; Cars in My Life, 1961; Illustrated History of the Bentley Car, 1964; My Life and my Cars, 1967. *Address:* Little Garden Cottage, Shamley Green, near Guildford, Surrey. *T:* Bramley 2136.

**BENTON, Gordon William,** CIE 1946; *b* 25 March 1893; *s* of William Benton, Cannock, Staffs; *m* 1922, Ethel Beatrice, *d* of George Mark Robinson; no *c. Educ:* Merchant Taylors' Sch. Joined Indian Police, 1912; Deputy Inspector-General; retd, 1947. Indian Police Medal, 1940; King's Police Medal, 1945. *Address:* South Lodge, Hill Head, Hants. *Club:* East India and Sports.

**BENTON, Kenneth Carter,** CMG 1966; *b* 4 March 1909; *s* of William Alfred Benton and Amy Adeline Benton (*née* Kirton); *m* 1938, Peggie, *d* of Maj.-Gen. C. E. Pollock, CB, CBE, DSO; one *s* (and two step *s*). *Educ:* Wolverhampton Sch.; London Univ. Teaching and studying languages in Florence and Vienna, 1930-37; employed British Legation, Vienna, 1937-38; Vice-Consul, Riga, 1938-40; 2nd Sec., British Embassy, Madrid, 1941-43; 2nd, later 1st Sec., Rome, 1944-48; FO, 1948-50; 1st Sec., Rome, 1950-53; 1st Sec., Madrid, 1953-56; FO, 1956-62; 1st Sec. and Consul, Lima, 1963-64; FO, 1964-66; Counsellor, Rio de Janeiro, 1966-68; retd from Diplomatic Service, 1968. *Publications:* Twenty-fourth Level, 1969; Sole Agent, 1970. *Recreations:* writing, carpentry. *Address:* Vine House, Appledore, near Ashford, Kent. *T:* Appledore 260. *Club:* Travellers'.

**BENTON, William;** Chairman and Publisher, Encyclopædia Britannica, Inc., since 1943; *b* Minneapolis, Minn., 1 April 1900; *s* of Charles William Benton and Elma Caroline Hixson; *m* 1928, Helen Hemingway; two *s* two *d. Educ:* Shattuck Sch., Faribault, Minn.; Carleton Coll. BA Yale Univ., 1921. Hon. Degrees: LLD: Louisville Univ., 1948, Bard Coll., 1951, Montana State Coll., 1957; Knox Coll., 1960; Carleton Coll. 1961. With advertising agencies, 1922-36; founder Benton & Bowles. University of Chicago: Vice-Pres., 1937-45; Asst Chancellor, 1945, Trustee, 1946-. Asst Sec. of State of US, Washington, DC, 1945-47; US Senator from Connecticut, 1949-53. Chm. Encyclopædia Britannica Ltd (London), 1942-; Chm. Encyclopædia Britannica Films, 1943-; Founding Vice-Chm., Bd Trustees, Cttee for Economic Development, 1942-45, Mem. Exec. Cttee, Bd Trustees, 1958-63; Vice-Chm. US Commn of Inter-Amer. Devel., 1943-45; Mem. Adv. Cttee. Coordinator of Inter-Amer. Affairs, 1939-45; Mem. US Delegs: Inter-Amer. Conf. on War and Peace, Mexico City, 1945; Constitutional Convention, Unesco, London, 1945; Consultative Assembly, Council of Europe, Strasbourg, 1951. Chm. US Delegs: Unesco Gen. Confs at Paris, 1946, Mexico City, 1947. UN Conf. on Freedom of Press, Geneva, 1948; US Mem., Executive Board of Unesco, 1963, with rank of Ambassador; Chm., US Observer Delegn to 1st Sess. of Conf. of Ministers of Educn of African Countries, Abidjan, 1964. Trustee: Univs Chicago; Connecticut; Bridgeport; Brandeis Univ., etc. Contributor to magazines. Dist. Service Medal, Sch. of Journalism, Syracuse Univ., 1960. *Publications:* This Is the Challenge, 1958; The Voice of Latin America, 1961. *Address:* (home) Fairfield, Connecticut; (office) 342 Madison Avenue, New York.

**BENTWICH, Helen Caroline, (Mrs Norman Bentwich),** CBE 1965; *b* 6 Jan. 1892; *yr d* of Arthur and Caroline Franklin; *m* 1915, Norman Bentwich, *qv. Educ:* St Paul's Girls' Sch.; Bedford Coll., London. Hon. Secretary: Palestine Council of Women, 1921-30; Movement of Children from Germany, 1939-40; Parliamentary Candidate, 1932 and 1935; co-opted LCC Education Cttee, 1934 (Chm. 1947-50); LCC Mem. for N Kensington, 1937-46, for NE Bethnal Green, 1946-49, for Stoke Newington and N Hackney, 1955-58; Vice-chm. LCC, 1950-51; Chm. of the Council, 1956-57. Alderman of LCC, 1949-55 and 1958-65. Governor: Bedford Coll.; Haberdashers' Aske's Schs; NW Polytechnic; Dartford Physical Training Coll.; Central Sch. of Arts and Crafts; King Edward's Sch., Witney; Almoner, Christs's Hosp.; Chm., RoSPA House Panel. *Publications:* Our Councils, 1962; The Vale of Health on Hampstead Heath, 1777-1967, 1968; (with Norman Bentwich), Mandate Memories, 1965. *Recreations:* gardening, travel. *Address:* Hollycot, Vale of Health, Hampstead, NW3. *T:* 01-435 2881; 17 Upper Strand Street, Sandwich. *Club:* Royal Commonwealth Society.

**BENTWICH, Norman,** OBE; MC; LLD (Hon.) Aberdeen and Melbourne; PhD (Hon.) Jerusalem; Barrister-at-law, Lincoln's Inn, 1908; *b* 1883; *e s* of late Herbert Bentwich; *m* 1915, Helen (*see* H. C. Bentwich), *y d* of Arthur E. Franklin. *Educ:* St Paul's Sch.; Trinity Coll., Cambridge. Members' Essay Prize, Whewell Scholarship for International Law, and Yorke Prize. Called to Bar, 1908: Co-editor of the Jewish Review, 1910-13 and 1932-34; Ministry of Justice, Cairo, 1912-15; Major, Camel Transport, 1916-18. Lectr at Hague Academy of International Law, 1929, 1934 and 1955. Dir of High Commission for Refugees from Germany, 1933-35; Attorney-General, Government of Palestine, 1920-31; Prof. of International Relations, Jerusalem Univ. 1932-51; Vice-Pres. Jewish Cttee for Relief Abroad; Chm. National Peace Council, 1944-46; Chm. United Restitution Office, 1948-; Foreign Office Cttee on Restitution in British Zone of Germany, 1951; Pres., Jewish Historical Soc., 1960-62; Chm., Friends of Hebrew Univ., Jerusalem. *Publications:* Philo-Judæus; Josephus; Hellenism; The Declaration of London; Domicile and Succession; The Practice of the Privy Council; The Mandates System, 1930; England in Palestine, 1932; A Wanderer in the Promised Land, 1932; The Religious Foundations of Internationalism, 1933; Palestine, 1934; The Jews, 1934; The Refugees from Germany, 1936; Wanderer Between Two Worlds, 1941; Judea Lives Again, 1943; Jewish Youth Comes Home, 1944; Wanderer in War, 1946; From Geneva to

San Francisco, 1946; I Understand the Risks, 1950; (with A. Martin) A Commentary on the Charter, 1950; Israel, 1952; The Rescue and Achievement of Refugee Scholars, 1953; Life of Judah Magnes, 1954; Israel and Her Neighbours, 1955; They Found Refuge, 1956; The Jews in Our Time, 1960; Israel Resurgent, 1960; The New-Old Land of Israel, 1960; The Hebrew University, 1961; My 77 Years, 1962; (with Helen Bentwich) Mandate Memories, 1965; (with Michael Kisch) Biography of Brigadier Fred Kisch, 1966; Israel: Two Fateful Years 1967-69, 1970. *Recreations:* music, travel. *Address:* Hollycot, Vale of Health, NW3. *T:* 01-435 2881; University, Jerusalem. *Clubs:* Reform, Maccabæans.

**BENYON, William Richard,** JP; DL; MP (C) Buckingham since 1970; *b* 17 Jan. 1930; *e s* of late Vice-Adm. R. Benyon, CB, CBE, and of Mrs. Benyon, The Lambdens, Beenham, Berkshire; *m* Elizabeth Ann Hallifax; two *s* three *d*. *Educ:* Royal Naval Coll., Dartmouth. Royal Navy, 1947-56; Courtaulds Ltd, 1956-64; Farmer, 1964-. Mem., Berks CC, 1964-; JP 1962, DL 1970, Berks. *Address:* Englefield House, Englefield, Theale, Berkshire. *T:* Theale 221.

**BEOVICH, Most Rev. Matthew;** *see* Adelaide, Archbishop of, (RC).

**BERAR, State of; Gen. HH the Prince of, Sir Mir Himayat Ali Khan, Walashan Nawab Azam Jah Bahadur,** GCIE 1946; GBE 1943; *b* 1907; *s* of Nizam of Hyderabad, GCSI, GBE; *m* 1931, Princess Durru Shehvar, *d* of Ex-Sultan Abdul Mejid; two *s*. Sometime Gen. and Commander-in-Chief of Hyderabad-Deccan State Forces. *Address:* Bella Vista Palace, Hyderabad, Deccan, India.

**BERE, Rennie Montague,** CMG 1957; Retired; *b* 28 Nov. 1907; *s* of late Rev. M. A. Bere; *m* 1936, Anne Maree Barber; no *c*. *Educ:* Marlborough Coll.; Selwyn Coll., Cambridge (MA). Colonial Administrative Service, Uganda, 1930-55; Asst District Officer, 1930; District Officer, 1942; Provincial Commissioner, 1951-55. Commandant, Polish Refugee Settlements, 1943-44; Dir and Chief Warden, Uganda National Parks 1955-60; Pres., Cornwall Naturalists-Trust, 1967. *Publications:* The Wild Mammals of Uganda, 1961; The African Elephant, 1966; Wild Animals in an African National Park, 1966; The Way to the Mountains of the Moon, 1966; Birds in an African National Park, 1969; Antelopes, 1970; articles (chiefly of mountaineering and wild life and anthropological interest) in Alpine Jl, Uganda Jl, Oryx, Animals, etc. *Recreations:* mountaineering; game and bird watching; cricket. *Address:* West Cottage, Bude, N Cornwall. *T:* Bude 2082. *Clubs:* Alpine, Royal Commonwealth Society; Uganda Kobs (past Pres.).

**BERENDSEN, Sir Carl August,** KCMG 1946 (CMG 1936); LLM; *s* of Ferdinand and Fannie Berendsen; *m* 1917, Nellie Ellis Brown; two *s*. *Educ:* Gore District High Sch.; Victoria Univ. Coll., Wellington. Civil Service, 1906; Chief Clerk Labour Department and Deputy Registrar of Industrial Unions, 1916. Permanent Head, Prime Minister's Department, Wellington, NZ, 1932-43; Sec. of External Affairs, 1928-43; New Zealand High Commissioner in Australia, 1943-44; Minister of New Zealand in the USA, 1944-48, Ambassador, 1948-52. *Address:* 16 Waiteata Road, Kelburn, Wellington, NZ.

**BERENS, Herbert Cecil Benyon,** MC 1942; Chairman, International Distillers and Vintners Ltd; Director, Hambros Bank; *b* 16 Oct. 1908; *s* of Cecil Berens, JP, St Mary Cray, Kent; *m* 1931, Moyra Nancy Mellard; three *s* one *d*. *Educ:* Wellington Coll.; Christ Church, Oxford. Hambro's Bank, 1931-39. Served War of 1939-45; Major, 4th County of London Yeomanry (MC); POW, 1941-43. Managing Dir, Anglo Foreign Securities Ltd, 1944-51; Managing Dir, The Bentworth Trust Ltd, 1951-; Chm. (non-exec.) International Distillers and Vintners Ltd. (formerly United Wine Traders Ltd), Nov. 1961. *Recreations:* cricket, golf, racing, shooting. *Address:* Bentworth Hall, Alton, Hants. *T:* Medstead 2140. *Clubs:* Turf, Royal Automobile, MCC, I Zingari.

**BERESFORD,** family name of **Baron Decies** and **Marquess of Waterford.**

**BERESFORD, Eric George Harold; His Honour Judge Beresford;** Judge of County Courts, since 1959, Circuit 46, Willesden, since 1967; *b* 19 Nov. 1901; *s* of Henry Beresford, Sutton Coldfield; *m* 1930, Barbara Muriel, *d* of Wallace Edwin Marley, Sutton Coldfield; one *s* one *d*. *Educ:* King Edward's Sch., Birmingham; Emanuel Coll., Cambridge (MA, LLB). Called to Bar, Lincoln's Inn, 1926; practised on Midland Circuit. Chm., Licensed Premises Cttee, New Town of Redditch, 1965. *Recreations:* history and literature. *Address:* The Mound, Long Crendon, Bucks. *T:* Long Crendon 235; The Mill House, Farway, Colyton, Devon. *T:* Farway 323.

**BERESFORD, Jack,** CBE 1960; Member, British Olympic Council, since 1936; Member, Council for England, British Empire and Commonwealth Games (BE & CG) since 1931; Director, Lightweight Laminates Ltd; *b* 1 Jan. 1899; *s* of Julius and Ethel Mary Beresford; *m* 1st, 1940, Mary Leaning (marr. diss.); one *s* one *d*; 2nd, 1958, Stroma Jean Margaret Morrison; two *d*. *Educ:* Bedford Sch. Served, European War of 1914-18: enlisted Artists' Rifles, 1917; commissioned. Liverpool Scottish Regiment; served 1917-19, Northern France; wounded, 1918. Champion Sculler of Great Britain, 1920-26; winner of Diamond Sculls, 1920, 1924, 1925, 1926; only winner of all five principal events, Henley Royal Regatta; Grand (twice), Stewards, Silver Goblets (twice), Diamonds (four times), Double Sculls; Olympic Games: (Brussels) 1920 silver medal Olympic Sculls, (Paris) 1924 gold medal Olympic Sculls, (Amsterdam) 1928 silver medal Olympic Eights, (Los Angeles) 1932 gold medal Olympic Fours, (Berlin) 1936 gold medal Olympic Double Sculls; 1930 British Empire Games silver medal Empire Sculls. Philadelphia Gold Cup, World Amateur Sculling Championship, 1924-25; leader of British Olympic team, Berlin, 1936; coach and manager, English oarsmen in Argentina and Uruguay, 1947; awarded gold medal of honour of the Fédération Internationale des Sociétés d'Aviron (FISA), Lucerne, 1947; Organising Cttee, Olympic Games, London, 1948; Olympic diploma of merit, Amsterdam, 1949; coach and manager, English crews to New Zealand and Australia, British Empire and Commonwealth Games, 1950; coach and manager, British rowing team, Olympic Games, Finland, 1952; Founder Mem. of the Furniture Makers' Guild; Liveryman of Painter Stainers' Company; Member: Council, National Playing Fields Assoc., British Field Sports Assoc.; Greater London and South East Sports Council; Council, Amateur Rowing Assoc., 1932-67; Selection Cttee for British crews, 1938-64; Court of Worshipful Co. of Furniture Makers. Rowing correspondent of The Field, 1966-. Played Umpire in film "Half a Sixpence". Freeman of

City of London, 1952. *Recreations:* family life, beagling, rowing, and swimming. *Address:* Highlands House, Shiplake-on-Thames, Oxon. *T:* Wargrave 2346. *Clubs:* Thames Rowing; Leander; British Sportsman's; Farley Hill Beagles.

**BERESFORD, Prof. Maurice Warwick;** Professor of Economic History, University of Leeds, since 1959; *b* 6 Feb. 1920; *s* of late H. B. Beresford and Mrs N. E. Beresford. *Educ:* Boldmere and Green Lane Elementary Schs; Bishop Vesey's Grammar Sch., Sutton Coldfield; Jesus Coll., Cambridge. Historical Tripos, Pt I class I, 1940, Pt II class I, 1941; MA 1945. On Staff of Birmingham Univ. Settlement, 1941-42; Sub-warden, Percival Guildhouse, Rugby, 1942-43; Warden, 1943-48; University of Leeds: Lecturer, 1948-55; Reader, 1955-59; Prof., 1959-; Dean, 1958-60; Chm., Sch. of Economic Studies, 1965-68; Chm. of Faculty Bd, 1968-70. Chm., Yorks Citizens' Advice Bureaux Cttee, 1963-69. Minister's nominee, Yorkshire Dales National Park Cttee, 1964-; Member: Consumer Council, 1966-; Hearing Aids Council, 1969-. *Publications:* The Leeds Chambers of Commerce, 1951; The Lost Villages of England, 1954; History on the Ground, 1957; (with J. K. S. St Joseph) Medieval England: an Aerial Survey, 1958; Time and Place, 1962; New Towns of the Middle Ages, 1967; (Ed. with G. R. J. Jones) Leeds and Its Region, 1967. Contributions to Economic History Review, Agricultural History Review, Medieval Archaeology, etc. *Recreations:* music, theatre, maps. *Address:* 10 Holt Close, Leeds 16. *T:* Leeds 674015.

**BERESFORD-PEIRSE, Sir Henry (Campbell de la Poer),** 5th Bt, *cr* 1814; CB 1957; BA; Director-General of the Forestry Commission, 1962-68, and Deputy Chairman 1965-68 (seconded for 1960-62, as Deputy Director of Forestry Division of Food and Agriculture Organisation of UN, Rome); *b* 24 April 1905; *er s* of Sir Henry Beresford-Peirse, 4th Bt, DSO, and Lady Mabel M. Campbell (*d* 1966), *d* of 3rd Earl Cawdor; *S* father, 1949; *m* 1932, Margaret, *d* of F. M. S. Grant, Knockie, Inverness-shire; one *s* (and one *s* decd); one adopted *d*. *Educ:* Eton; Magdalen Coll., Oxford. (BA). Served War of 1939-45, with Lovat Scouts, 1939-40. Gold Medal, Royal Forestry Society, 1963. Hon. Mem., Soc. of American Foresters, 1967. *Heir: s* Henry Grant de la Poer Beresford-Peirse [*b* 7 Feb. 1933; *m* 1966, Jadranka Njers, Zagreb, Yugoslavia; one *s*]. *Address:* Bedall Manor, Bedale, Yorks. *T:* Bedale 2811.

**BERESFORD-STOOKE, Sir George;** *see* Stooke.

**BERGANZA, Teresa;** singer (mezzo-soprano); *b* Madrid, Spain, 1936; *d* of Guillermo and Maria Ascension Berganza; *m* 1957, Felix Lavilla; one *s* one *d*. Début in Madrid, 1955; début in England, Glyndebourne, 1958; appeared at Glyndebourne, 1959; Royal Opera House, Covent Garden, 1959, 1960, 1963, 1964; Royal Festival Hall, 1960, 1961, 1962, 1967; has also sung in Vienna, Milan, Aix-en-Provence, Holland, Edinburgh, Israel, America. *Recreations:* fishing, hunting. *Address:* c/o Miss Lies Askonas, 19a Air Street, Regent Street, W1. *T:* 01-734 5459.

**BERGEL, Prof. Franz,** FRS 1959; DPhil. Nat. (Freiburg), PhD (London), DSc (London), FRIC, FIBiol; Professor Emeritus of Chemistry, University of London; Member, Institute of Cancer Research: Royal Cancer Hospital; *b* Vienna, 13 Feb. 1900; *s* of Moritz Martin Bergel and Barbara Betty Spitz; *m* 1939, Phyllis Thomas. *Educ:* Universities of Vienna and Freiburg im Breisgau. Head of Dept of Medical Chemistry, Inst. Chem., 1927-33, and Privatdoz., Univ. of Freiburg, 1929-33; research worker: Med. Chem. Dept, Univ. of Edinburgh, 1933-36; Lister Inst. of Preventive Med., Dept of Biochemistry, 1936-38; Dir of Research, Roche Products Ltd, Welwyn Garden City, 1938-52; Head, Chemistry Dept, Chester Beatty Res. Inst., 1952-66; Dean, Inst. Cancer Research, 1963-66. Hon. Lectr, Pharmacology Dept, Faculty of Medical Sciences. University Coll., London 1946-; Consultant, Harvard Med. Sch. and Children's Cancer Research Foundn, Boston, Mass, 1959-60, 1967-; FChemSoc; FRSM; Member: Soc. Chem. Ind.; Biochem. Soc.; Amer. Assoc. Adv. Sci.; Brit. Pharm. Soc.; NY Acad. Sci.; Royal Soc. of Health. *Publications:* Chemistry of Enzymes in Cancer, 1961; All about Drugs, 1970; papers and reviews in chemical, biochemical and pharmacological journals. *Recreation:* sketching. *Address:* Magnolia Cottage, Bel Royal, Jersey, CI. *T:* Central 33688. *Club:* Athenæum.

**BERGIN, John Alexander;** Under-Secretary, Board of Trade, since 1968; *b* 25 May 1920; *s* of B. A. G. and L. L. Bergin; *m* 1953, Pierrette Marguerite Wack. *Educ:* Varndean Sch., Brighton; St Catharine's Coll., Cambridge. BA Hons (Natural Science) 1947. REME, 1940-46: Italy, Greece (T/Major, despatches). Asst Principal, Bd of Trade, 1948; HM Customs and Excise, 1954-56; HM Treasury, Office of Chancellor of the Duchy of Lancaster, as Asst Sec., 1960; Dept of Economic Affairs, 1964; IDC, 1966. *Address:* 15 Granard Avenue, SW15.

**BERGIN, Kenneth Glenny,** MA, MD Cantab; DPH London; FRAeS; JP; Physician; *b* 10 June 1911; *er s* of Dr F. Gower Bergin, Clifton, Bristol; *m* 1938, Joan Mary, *o d* of G. H. Sinnott, Clifton, Bristol and *gd* of Maj.-Gen. N. F. J. Sampson-Way, CB, Henbury, Glos; two *s* one *d*. *Educ:* Clifton Coll.; Queens' Coll., Cambridge; St Bartholomew's Hospital, London. Served with RAF Med. Br., 1939-46 (despatches twice); Flying Trng Bomber (Pathfinder) and Fighter Comds (Wing Comdr, qual. service pilot). BOAC, 1946-64: Dir Personnel and Medical Services, 1959-63; Dir Medical Services, 1963-64. Pres. Airline Med. Directors' Assoc., 1965; Vice-Chm., Air League, 1960-64; Mem. Council: Brit. Soc. for Internat. Understanding; Internat. Acad. of Aviation Med. (Vice-Chm.); Aerospace Med. Assoc.; Member: Airline Personnel Directors' Assoc., 1959-64; Nat. Jt Council for Civil Air Transport, 1959-64; Nat. Jt Adv. Council to Minister of Labour, 1959-64; Bd of Govs, Clifton Coll.; Assoc. of Industrial Med. Officers; WHO Cttee on INternat. Quarantine; Nat. Aviation Council; Econ. Research Council; Adv. Council, Coll. of Aeronautical and Automobile Engineering; Vice-Chm., Bd of Govs, Coll. of Air Trng., 1962-64; Chm., Air Centre Trust; Master, Guild of Air Pilots and Air Navigators, 1959-61; Custodian, Guild of Air Pilots Benevolent Fund; Freeman and Liveryman, City of London. Hon. Steward of Westminster Abbey. Invitation Lectr., Oxford, Cambridge and Bristol Univs., Brit. Assoc., Royal Soc. of Health, BMA, etc. Director, Cunard Line, 1969-; FRSocMed.; OStJ 1959. *Publications:* Aviation Medicine, 1948; numerous others on Aviation Medicine and allied subjects. *Recreations:* fishing, shooting, riding, sailing, flying. *Address:* 23 Wilton Row, SW1. *T:* 01-235 8440; 99 Harley Street, W1. *T:* 01-935 7501. *Clubs:* Athenæum, Boodle's, Royal Air Force; Pitt (Cambridge).

**BERGMAN, (Ernst) Ingmar;** Swedish film producer, and Head of Royal Dramatic Theatre, Stockholm, 1963-66 (also Director from 1959); director of productions on television; *b* Uppsala, 14 July 1918; *s* of a Chaplain to the Royal Court at Stockholm; *m* Käbi Laretei, concert pianist; one *s* (and six *c* by previous marriages). *Educ:*Stockholm Univ. Producer, Royal Theatre, Stockholm, 1940-42; Producer and script-writer, Swedish Film Co., 1940-44; Theatre Director: Helsingborg, 1944-46; Gothenburg, 1946-49; Malmo, 1952-1959. Produced Hedda Gabler, Cambridge, 1970. Films (British titles) produced include: Torment, 1943; Crisis, 1945; Port of Call, 1948; Summer Interlude, 1950; Waiting Women, 1952; Summer with Monika, 1952; Sawdust and Tinsel, 1953; A Lesson in Love, 1953; Journey into Autumn, 1954; Smiles of a Summer Night, 1955; The Seventh Seal, 1956-57; Wild Strawberries, 1957; So Close to Life, 1957; The Face, 1958; The Virgin Spring, 1960 (shown Edinburgh Fest., 1960); The Devil's Eye, 1961 (shown Edinburgh Fest., 1961); Through a Glass Darkly, 1961; Winter Light, 1962; The Silence, 1963; Now About all these Women, 1964 (first film in colour); Persona, 1967; Hour of the Wolf, 1968; Shame, 1968; The Rite, 1969; The Passion, 1970. Has gained several international awards and prizes for films. *Address:* Svensk Filmindustri, Kungsgatan 36, Stockholm, Sweden.

**BERGMAN, Ingmar;** *see* Bergman, E. I.

**BERGMAN, Ingrid;** actress; *d* of Justus and Friedel Bergman; *m* 1937, Petter Lindstrom (marriage dissolved, 1950, Los Angeles; dissolution ruled not valid by a Rome court, 1960); one *d*; *m* 1950 (by proxy, Mexico), Roberto Rossellini (marriage ruled not valid by a Rome court, 1960); one *s* twin *d*; *m* 1958, (in London), Lars Schmidt. *Educ:* Lyceum for Flickor and Sch. of Royal Dramatic Theatre, Stockholm. Has played in following stage plays: Liliom, 1940; Anna Christie, 1941; Joan of Lorraine, 1947; Tea and Sympathy (Paris), 1956; Hedda Gabler (Paris), 1962; A Month in the Country, Guildford (Yvonne Arnaud), 1965, and Cambridge Theatre, London; More Stately Mansions, New York, 1967-68. *Films:* Intermezzo, 1939; Adam Had Four Sons, 1940; Rage in Heaven, 1941; Dr Jekyll and Mr Hyde, 1941; Casablanca, 1942; For Whom the Bell Tolls, 1943; Gaslight, 1944; Saratoga Trunk, 1945; Spellbound, 1945; The Bells of St Mary's, 1946; Notorious, 1946; Arch of Triumph, 1947; Joan of Arc, 1948; Under Capricorn, 1948; Stomboli, 1950; Anastasia, 1957; Elena et les Hommes; The Inn of the Sixth Happiness; Indiscreet, 1958; Goodbye Again, 1961; The Visit, 1963; The Yellow Rolls-Royce, 1964; Cactus Flower, 1970; A Walk in the Spring Rain, 1970. *Opera:* Joan of Arc at the Stake, 1954. Awarded two Oscars. Has appeared on Television. *Address:* 3 Avenue Vélasquez, Paris 8e, France.

**BERGNER, Elisabeth;** *b* Austria; naturalised British subject, 1938; *m* Dr Paul Czinner. Appeared in St Joan, The Constant Nymph, Escape Me Never, The Last of Mrs Cheyney, Nju, Impetuous Youth, The Boy David, The Two Mrs Carrolls, The Duchess of Malfi (New York, 1946), The Gay Invalid, Garrick, 1951. *Films:* Ariane, Dreaming Lips, Catherine the Great, Stolen Life. *Address:* 14 East 75th Street, New York City, NY, USA.

**BERIOZOVA, Svetlana;** Ballerina, The Royal Ballet; *b* 24 Sept. 1932; *d* of Nicolas and Maria Beriozoff (Russian); *m* 1959, Mohammed Masud Khan. *Educ:* New York, USA. Joined Grand Ballet de Monte Carlo, 1947; Metropolitan Ballet, 1948-49; Sadler's Wells Theatre Ballet, 1950-52; Sadler's Wells Ballet (now The Royal Ballet), 1952-. Has created leading rôles in Designs for Strings (Taras), Fanciulla delle Rose (Staff), Trumpet Concerto (Balanchine), Pastorale (Cranko), The Shadow (Cranko), Rinaldo and Armida (Ashton), The Prince of the Pagodas (Cranko), Antigone (Cranko), Baiser de la Fee (MacMillan), Diversions (MacMillan), Persephone (Ashton), Images of Love (MacMillan). Classical Roles: Le Lac des Cygnes, The Sleeping Beauty, Giselle, Coppēlia, Sylvia, Cinderella. Other rôles currently danced: Les Sylphides, The Firebird, The Lady and Fool, Checkmate, Fête Etrange, Ondine, Nutcracker. Has danced with The Royal Ballet in USA, France, Italy, Australia, S Africa, Russia, and as guest ballerina in Belgrade, Granada, Milan (La Scala), Stuttgart, Bombay, Nervi, Helsinki, Paris, Vienna, New Zealand, Zurich. Played the Princess in The Soldier's Tale (film), 1966. Has frequently appeared on television. *Relevant publications:* Svetlana Beriosova (by C. Swinson), 1956, Svetlana Beriosova (by A. H. Franks), 1958. *Recreation:* the arts. *Address:* Royal Opera House, Covent Garden, WC2. *T:* 01-240 1200.

**BERKELEY, Baroness** (17th in line); (*cr* 1421; called out of abeyance, 1967); **Mary Lalle Foley-Berkeley;** *b* 9 Oct. 1905; *e d* of Col Frank Wigram Foley, CBE, DSO (*d* 1949), Royal Berks Regt, and Eva Mary Fitzhardinge, Baroness Berkeley; *S* mother, Baroness Berkeley (16th in line) (*d* 1964). *Address:* Pickade Cottage, Great Kimble, Aylesbury, Bucks. *T:* Princes Risborough 3051.

**BERKELEY, (Augustus Fitzhardinge) Maurice,** MA; Chief Registrar of The High Court in Bankruptcy since 1966, also Registrar of The Companies Court since 1957 and Clerk of the Restrictive Practices Court since 1965; *b* 26 Feb. 1903; *s* of late Dr Augustus Frederic Millard Berkeley and Anna Louisa Berkeley; *m* 1931, Elaine Emily, *d* of Adin Simmonds; no *c*. *Educ:* Aldenham Sch.; Pembroke Coll., Cambridge. Called to the Bar, Inner Temple, 1927. Served War of 1939-45, in The Welch Regiment, 1940-45; Temp. Lieut-Col; AAG, AG3d, War Office. Junior Counsel in Chancery Matters to Ministry of Agriculture, Fisheries and Food, The Commissioners of Crown Lands and the Forestry Commissioners, 1956-57. Bar Council, 1955-57. *Recreations:* lawn tennis, watching cricket, ski-ing, travel, theatre, reading. *Address:* 3 Dr Johnson's Buildings, Inner Temple, EC4. *T:* 01-353 2448; Freshwell Cottage, Litte Sampford, near Saffron Walden, Essex. *T:* Great Sampford 244. *Club:* Garrick.

**BERKELEY, Humphry John;** writer and broadcaster; Joint Managing Director of Investeco (Investment Development and Technical Services Ltd); Director: John Howard & Co. (Africa) Ltd; Fosse Construction Co. Ltd; *b* 21 Feb. 1926; *s* of late Reginald Berkeley, author and playwright, former MP (L), and of Mrs Hildegarde Tinne. *Educ:* Dragon Sch., Oxford; Malvern; Pembroke Coll., Cambridge (exhibnr). BA 1947; MA 1963. President, Cambridge Union, 1948; Chm. Cambridge Univ. Conservative Association, 1948; at Conservative Political Centre, 1949-57; Chm., Coningsby Club, 1952-55; MP (C) Lancaster, 1959-66. Member: Prince Philip's Cttee on Overseas Volunteers, 1966-70; British Parly. Delegn to Council of Europe and to Council of WEU, 1963-66. Hon. Secretary: Conservative Parliamentary West Africa Cttee, 1959-64; UN Parly Gp, 1962-64. Chm., United Nations Assoc. of GB and NI, 1966-70; Vice-Chm., Nat. Co-ordinating Cttee for 25th Anniversary of United Nations, 1970; Mem., UK Nat. Commn for UNESCO, 1966-; Hon. Treas, Howard League for Penal Reform. *Publication:* The Power of the Prime Minister, 1968. *Address:* 3 Lowndes Street, SW1. *Club:* Hurlingham.

**BERKELEY, Lennox Randal Francis,** CBE 1957; Composer; *b* 12 May 1903; *o s* of Capt. Hastings George Fitzhardinge Berkeley, RN, and Aline Caria (*née* Harris); *m* 1946, Elizabeth Freda Bernstein; three *s*. *Educ:* Gresham's Sch., Holt; Merton Coll., Oxford. BA Oxford, 1926; Hon. DMus Oxford, 1970. Studied music in Paris under Nadia Boulanger, 1927-32. Returned to London, 1935; on staff of BBC Music Dept, 1942-45. Composition Professor, Royal Acad. of Music, 1946-68. Awarded Collard Fellowship in Music, 1946; Cobbett Medal 1962; Ordre de Mérite Culturel, Monaco, 1967. *Compositions include: orchestra:* Divertimento; Serenade; two symphonies; Concertos for Piano and Orch.; 2 Pianos and Orch.; Flute and Orch.; Violin and Chamber Orch.; Five Pieces for Violin and Orchestra; Winter's Tale Suite; Partita for Chamber Orchestra. *chamber music:* String Trio; Trio for Horn, Violin and String Quartet; Sextet for Clarinet, Horn and String Quartet; Oboe Quartet; *voice and orchestra:* Three Poems of St Teresa for Contralto and Strings; Stabat Mater for Soloists and Chamber Orchestra; Four Ronsard Sonnets for Tenor and Orchestra; Batter My Heart Three-person'd God (Cantata); Signs in the dark (poems by Laurie Lee) for choir and strings; Magnificat for choir and orchestra; *piano:* Sonata; Six Preludes; Three Mazurkas; *opera:* Nelson (3 Acts); A Dinner Engagement (1 Act); Ruth (1 Act); Castaway (1 Act). *Recreation:* reading. *Address:* 8 Warwick Avenue, W2. *T:* 01-262 3922.

**BERKELEY, Maurice;** *see* Berkeley, A. F. M.

**BERKIN, John Phillip,** CBE 1952; Director: "Shell" Transport & Trading Co. since 1957; Shell Petroleum Co. since 1953; National & Grindlays Bank, since 1966; National & Grindlays Holdings Ltd, since 1969; The Nuclear Power Group Ltd, since 1969; *b* 23 Oct. 1905; *s* of John Berkin and Leila Louise (*née* Doolittle); *m* 1st, 1934, Elizabeth Mary Joseph Arnold (*d* 1967); one *s*; 2nd, 1968, Mrs Lilian Ivy Beatrice Chisholm, *widow* of Lieut W. B. Chisholm, RNVR. Educ: Taunton Sch.; Sidney Sussex Coll., Cambridge. BA 1927, MA 1956. Joined Royal Dutch/Shell Group of Cos, 1927 and served in Far East, US and London; a Man. Dir, Royal Dutch/Shell Group, 1957-66; Chairman: Shell Internat. Marine, 1963-66; Shell Co. of the UK, 1961-66; Shell Chemicals UK Ltd, 1962-66; Dir, Shell Petroleum NV (formerly Bataafse Petroleum Maatschappij), 1957-68. Part-time Mem., IRC, 1966-68. *Address:* Shell Centre, SE1; Oriel, Fairfield Road, Southdown, Shawford, Winchester, Hants. *T:* Twyford (Hants) 2331. *Club:* Junior Carlton.

**BERKSHIRE, Archdeacon of;** *see* Wild, Ven. Eric.

**BERLE, Adolf Augustus;** Senior Partner of Berle & Berle, USA; *b* Boston, Mass, 29 Jan. 1895; *s* of Rev. A. A. Berle and Mary Augusta, *d* of Prof. G. Frederick Wright; *m* 1927, Beatrice Bend Bishop; one *s* two *d*. *Educ:* Harvard (AB 1913, AM 1914, LLB 1916). Lawyer; Prof. Emer. of Law, Columbia University; US Govt, Asst Secretary of State, 1938-44; US Ambassador to Brazil, 1945-46. Holds hon. doctorates. Commander, Order of Southern Cross (Brazil), 1948; Ordine "Al Merito della Repubblica Italiana", 1969. *Publications:* Studies in the Law of Corporation Finance, 1928; Cases and Materials in the Law of Corporation Finance, 1930; The Modern Corporation and Private Property (with Dr G. C. Means), 1932; Liquid Claims and National Wealth (with V. J. Pederson), 1934; New Directions in the New World, 1940; Business Organizations: (with Prof. Wm C. Warren) Corporations, 1948; The Twentieth Century Capitalist Revolution, 1955; Tides of Crisis, 1957; Power without Property, 1959; Latin America: Diplomacy and Reality, 1962; The American Economic Republic, 1963; Power, 1969. *Address:* 70 Pine Street, New York, USA. *Clubs:* Century, Harvard, Players (NY); Army and Navy (Washington).

**BERLIN, Irving;** author and composer; *b* Russia, 11 May 1888; *s* of Moses Baline and Leah Lipkin; brought to USA, 1893; *m* 1st, 1913, Dorothy Goetz (*d* 1913); 2nd, 1926, Ellin, *d* of Clarence H. Mackay, NY; three *d*. *Educ:* public schools, NY City, for two years only. First song published, Marie From Sunny Italy, 1907; first complete Broadway score, Watch Your Step, 1914; Music Box Revue, 1921-24; Ziegfeld Follies, 1919, 1920, 1927. Pres. Irving Berlin Music Corp. Served as Sergt Infantry at Camp Upton, LI. Hon. Degrees, Bucknell, Temple, and Fordham Univs; Medal of Merit for This Is The Army; awarded a special Gold Medal by Congress for God Bless America; Legion of Honour, France. Has composed about 800 songs, including: Alexander's Ragtime Band; Oh, How I Hate To Get Up In the Morning; When I Lost You; A Pretty Girl Is Like A Melody; Say It With Music; Always; Remember; Blue Skies; Easter Parade; Heat Wave; Isn't This A Lovely Day; Top Hat, White Tie and Tails; I've Got My Love To Keep Me Warm; White Christmas; This Is The Army, Mr Jones; Anything You Can Do; Doin' What Comes Natur'lly; The Girl That I Marry; There's No Business Like Show Business. Musicals (several of which have been filmed) include: Face The Music; Louisiana Purchase; Annie Get Your Gun; Call Me Madam. *Address:* Irving Berlin Music Corp., 1290 Avenue of the Americas, New York City, USA. *Clubs:* Lambs, Friars.

**BERLIN, Sir Isaiah,** Kt 1957; CBE 1946; FBA 1957; MA; President of Wolfson College, Oxford, since 1966; Chichele Professor of Social and Political Theory, 1957-67; Fellow of All Souls, 1932-38 and 1950-66; *b* 6 June 1909; *s* of Mendel and Marie Berlin; *m* 1956, Aline, *d* of late Pierre de Gunzbourg. *Educ:* St Paul's Sch.; Corpus Christi Coll., Oxford. Lectr in Philosophy, New Coll., 1932; Fellow of New Coll., 1938-50. War service with Min. of Information, in New York, 1941-42, at HM Embassy in Washington, 1942-45, HM Embassy, Moscow, Sept. 1945-Jan. 1946; Mem. Cttee of Award, Commonwealth (Harkness) Fellowships, 1960-64. Vice-Pres., British Academy, 1959-61; Pres. Aristotelian Soc., 1963-64. Mem., Academic Adv. Cttee., Univ. of Sussex, 1963-66. Visiting Professor: Harvard Univ., 1949, 1951, 1953, 1962; Bryn Mawr Coll., 1952; Chicago Univ., 1955. Princeton Univ., 1965; Prof. of Humanities, city Univ. of NY, 1966-. Northcliffe Lectr, University Coll., London, 1953; Mellon Lectr, Nat. Gall. of Art, Washington, DC, 1965. Foreign Member: American Academy of Arts and Sciences; American Academy-Institute of Arts and Letters. Member, Board of Directors, Royal Opera House, Covent Garden, 1954-65. Governor, Univ. of Jerusalem, Jewish Theol. Seminary, NY. Hon. DLitt: Hull, 1965; Glasgow, 1967; Brandeis (USA), 1967; Cambridge, 1970; Hon. LD: E Anglia, 1967; Columbia, 1968. Hon. Fellow, Corpus Christi Coll., Oxford. *Publications:*

Karl Marx, 1939, 1963; Translation of First Love by I. S. Turgenev, 1950; The Hedgehog and the Fox, 1953; Historical Inevitability, 1954; The Age of Enlightenment, 1956; Moses Hess, 1958; Two Concepts of Liberty, 1959; Mr Churchill in 1940, 1964; Four Essays on Liberty, 1969. *Address:* Wolfson College, Oxford. *Clubs:* Athenæum, Brooks's; Century (New York).

**BERMAN, Lawrence Sam;** Assistant Director, Central Statistical Office, since 1968; *b* 15 May 1928; *yr s* of Jack and Violet Berman; *m* 1954, Kathleen D. Lewis; one *s* one *d*. *Educ:* St Clement Danes Grammar Sch.; London Sch. of Economics. BSc (Econ) 1st cl. hons 1947; MSc (Econ) 1950. Res. Asst, LSE, 1947; Nuffield Coll., Oxford, 1948; Econ. Commn for Europe, 1949; Central Statistical Office: Asst Statistician 1952; Statistician 1955; Chief Statistician 1964. Editor, National Income Blue Book, 1954-60; Mem. Council, Royal Statistical Soc., 1970-; Mem., Atlas Computer Cttee, 1969-. *Publications:* articles and papers in Jl of Royal Statistical Soc., Economica, Economic Trends, Statistical News, etc. *Recreations:* travel, theatre, gardening and other do-it-yourself activities. *Address:* 10 Carlton Close, Edgware, Mddx. *T:* 01-985 6938. *Club:* Reform.

**BERMUDA, Bishop of,** since 1970; **Rt. Rev. Eric Joseph Trapp;** *b* 17 July 1910; *s* of late Archibald Edward Trapp and Agnes Trapp, Leicester and Coventry; *m* 1937, Edna Noreen Thornton, SRN; two *d*. *Educ:* Alderman Newton's Sch., Leicester; Leeds Univ.; College of the Resurrection, Mirfield. BA 1st Class, philosophy. Asst Curate, St Olave's, Mitcham, Surrey, 1934-37; Director, Masite Mission, Basutoland, 1937-40; Rector, St Augustine's Bethlehem, Orange Free State, 1940-43; Rector, St John's, Maseru and Director of Maseru Mission, Basutoland, 1943-47; Canon of Bloemfontein Cathedral, 1944-47; Bishop of Zululand, 1947-57; Secretary, Society for the Propogation of the Gospel, 1957-64, United Soc. for the Propogation of the Gospel, 1965-70. Hon. DD, Trinity College, Toronto, 1967. *Address:* Bishop's Lodge, PO Box 769, Bermuda.

**BERNACCHI, Michael Louis,** CMG 1955; OBE 1952; *b* 5 May 1911; *s* of late Louis Charles Bernacchi, Physicist and Antarctic explorer, and Winifred Edith Harris; *m* 1943, Elaine Chapman; one *s* one *d*. *Educ:* RN Colls Dartmouth and Greenwich; Magdalene Coll., Cambridge. Royal Navy, 1925-34; entered Colonial Service as Cadet, Fiji, 1936; District Commissioner, 1937; acting ADC to Governor of Fiji, 1939; served Royal Navy, 1940-44; Lieut Comdr RN (retd); transferred Malayan Civil Service, 1944; special duty, N Borneo, 1944; Military Administration N Borneo (Col), 1945-46; acting Chief Sec., N Borneo, 1946, Malaya, 1947-52; Class Ic Malayan Civil Service, 1951; (Perak Meritorious Service Medal, 1951); Resident Commissioner, Gilbert and Ellice Islands Colony, 1952-61, retd 1962. *Recreation:* swimming. *Address:* 61 Leinster Road, Christchurch 1, New Zealand. *Club:* Athenæum.

**BERNAL, John Desmond,** FRS, 1937; MA Cantab; Professor of Crystallography, Birkbeck College, University of London, 1963-68, now Emeritus Professor; Hon. Fellow, Emmanuel College, Cambridge, 1965; Fellow, Birkbeck College, 1969; *b* Nenagh, Ireland, 10 May 1901; *m* 1922; two *s*. *Educ:* Stonyhurst Coll.; Bedford Sch.; Emmanuel Coll., Cambridge (Scholar). Research at Davy Faraday Laboratory, 1923-27; Lectr and later Asst Dir of Research in Crystallography, Cambridge, 1934-37; Prof. of Physics, Birkbeck Coll., 1937-63. Royal Medal, Royal Society, 1945; Mem. Hungarian Academy of Sciences, 1954; Mem. Polish Acad. of Sciences, 1954. Hon. Prof. Moscow Univ., 1956; Mem. Rumanian Acad. of Sciences, 1957; Mem. Bulgarian Acad. of Sciences, 1958; For. Mem. Acad. of Sciences, USSR, 1958; Regular Mem. Czechoslovak Acad. of Sciences, 1960; Corresponding Mem. German Acad. of Sciences, Berlin, 1962; Mem. Acad. of Sciences, Norway, 1966. Lenin Peace Prize, 1953; Grotius Medal, 1959. *Publications:* The World, The Flesh, and the Devil, 1929 (repr. 1969); The Social Function of Science, 1939 (repr. 1967); The Freedom of Necessity, 1949; The Physical Basis of Life, 1951; Marx and Science, 1952; Science and Industry in the Nineteenth Century, 1953 (repr. 1969); Science in History, 1954 (revised edns 1957, 1965; illus. edn 1969); World without War, 1958 (revised edn, 1960); The Origin of Life, 1967; various scientific papers on crystallographical, physical and biochemical subjects; contributions on scientific, philosophical and social questions. *Address:* Department of Crystallography, Birkbeck College, Malet Street, WC1. *T:* 01-580 6622.

**BERNARD,** family name of **Earl of Bandon.**

**BERNARD, Hon. Charles Brodrick Amyas,** CBE 1962; Chairman, East Suffolk County Council, since 1968 (Vice-Chairman 1964-68); *b* 30 Aug. 1904, *twin s* of late Lt-Col Ronald P. H. Bernard and Lettice Mina, *yr d* of late Capt. Gerald C. S. Paget; *twin b* and *heir-pres.* of 5th Earl of Bandon, *qv*; granted rank and precedence of an earl's son, 1925; *m* 1937, Hon. Ursula Margaret Vivian (*d* 1963), *d* of 3rd Baron Swansea, DSO, MVO, TD. *Educ:* Wellington Coll., RMC. Lieut, Oxford and Bucks LI 1926, ADC to Comdr 2nd Div., 1937-39, Major 1940 (despatches). Chm., Eye Div., Conservative Assoc., 1957-66. County Councillor, East Suffolk, 1952-. *Recreations:* hunting, shooting. *Address:* By the Crossways, Kelsale, Saxmundham, Suffolk. *T:* Saxmundham 2044.

**BERNARD, Sir Dallas (Gerald Mercer),** 1st Bt, *cr* 1954; Lieutenant of the City of London; *b* 22 March 1888; *s* of late Edmund Bowen Bernard, JP, of Snakemoor, Botley, Hants; *m* 1922, Betty, *e d* of late Sir Charles Addis, KCMG; one *s* two *d*. *Educ:* Stubbington House, Fareham, Hants; HMS Britannia. Left the Navy as a midshipman, 1906; Man. Dir of Jardine Matheson & Co. Ltd (Hong-Kong, China and Japan), 1922-28; mem. of Exec. Council of Hong-Kong, 1927-28, and Legislative Council, 1926-28; Chm., Hong-Kong General Chamber of Commerce, 1923, 1926-27; Chm., Court of Directors Hong-Kong and Shanghai Banking Corporation, 1924, 1926-27; Dir, Matheson & Co. Ltd, 1928-42; Alliance Assurance Co. Ltd, 1931-42; Mem. of London Consultative Cttee of Hong-Kong and Shanghai Banking Corporation, 1929-42, and 1960-64. Dir, Bank of England, 1936-49; Dep. Governor, Bank of England, 1949-54; Chairman: Courtaulds Ltd, 1962-64; British Bank of the Middle East, 1954-65 (Dir, 1965-67). Dir, The Proprietors of Hay's Wharf Ltd, 1961-69. Sheriff of County of London, 1942. *Heir: s* Dallas Edmund Bernard [*b* 14 Dec. 1926; *m* 1959, Sheila Mary, *er d* of Arthur Gordon Robey, Hadley Wood, Herts; three *d*]. *Address:* Sandylands, Englefield Green, Surrey.

**BERNARD, Rt. Rev. Canon Eustace A. M.;** *see* Morrogh Bernard.

**BERNARD, Jean-Jacques;** auteur dramatique et homme de lettres; *b* 30 juillet 1888; *s* of late Tristan Bernard and Suzanne Bomsel; *m* 1911, Georgette Fray; two *s* one *d*. *Educ:* Paris. *Théâtre:* Le Voyage à deux; la Joie du Sacrifice; la Maison Epargnée; le Feu qui reprend mal; Martine; le Printemps des autres; l'Invitation au Voyage; Denise Marette; l'Ame en peine; le Secret d'Arvers; le Roy de Malousie; la Louise; A la Recherche des Cœurs; les Sœurs Guédonec; Jeanne de Pantin; Nationale 6; le Jardinier d'Ispahan; Louise de la Vallière; Marie Stuart Reine d'Ecosse; la Librairie Jalin; Notre-Dame d'en haut; la Route de France; Mon grand ami; De Tarse, en Cilicie. *Pièces jouées à Londres* (tr J. Leslie Frith): The Springtime of others; The Sulky Fire (Le Feu qui reprend mal); The Unquiet Spirit (l'Ame en peine); Martine; l'Invitation au Voyage; le Secret d'Arvers; Nationale 6; Madeleine (Le Jardinier d'Ispahan); The Clay and the Flame (Notre Dame d'en haut). *Romans, contes, nouvelles, récits:* l'Epicier, nouvelles; les Enfants jouent . . . récits de guerre; les Tendresses menacées, contes; le Roman de Martine; Madeleine Landier; New Chicago, nouvelle; Le Camp de la Mort Lente, souvenirs de captivité Compiègne, 1941-42; Le Pain rouge, récits de l'occupation; Marie et le vagabond, roman; Mon Père Tristan Bernard; Mon Ami le théâtre; Saint Paul ou la Fidélité. *Address:* 22 rue Eugène Flachat, Paris 17e. *T:* Etoile 29-00; Loguivy-de-la-Mer (Côtes-du-Nord), France.

**BERNARD, Madame R. K.;** *see* Delysia, A.

**BERNAYS, Lewis Edward,** OBE 1929; *b* 27 May 1886; *s* of late Henry Arthur Bernays, of Rochester and Chatham and later of Moscow, and Alice Mary Hardy; *m* 1st, 1915, Alida Winona (*d* 1940), *d* of late Andrew McDermid, AM, MD, Winnipeg and Chicago; three *s*; 2nd, 1953, Jeanne Françoise Foss (*née* Beurton) (marr. diss.). Passed a competitive examination and appointed a Vice-Consul in the Consular Service, 1910; Vice-Consul, New Orleans, 1911-12; Portland, Oregon, 1913; Lobito, San Thomé, and Fernando Po, 1913; Chicago, 1914-18; Philadelphia, 1919-20; Consul, New York, 1920-29; Danzig, 1930; Liège, 1931; Consul-Gen., Chicago, 1932-42; retired from the Career Service, 1944; Consul-Gen. in charge of the Vice-Consulate at Dallas, Texas, 1945-50. Since retirement has lectured in Political Science at Northwestern Univ., Evanston; at MacMurray Coll., Jacksonville, Ill; at Rockford Coll., Rockford, Ill; and at Univ. of Plano, Plano, Texas. *Recreations:* fishing, walking, cycling. *Address:* c/o Richard Bernays, Attorney-at-Law, 2500 Fidelity Union Tower, Dallas, Texas 75201, USA.

**BERNERS, Baroness** (15th in line) *cr* 1455; **Vera Ruby Williams;** *b* 25 Dec. 1901; *d* of late Hon. Rupert Tyrwhitt, Major RA (5th *s* of Emma Harriet, Baroness Berners) and of Louise I. F. (*née* Wells); *S* cousin, 1950; *m* 1927, Harold Williams, Colonial Civil Service; two *d*. *Educ:* Ladies' Coll., Eastbourne; St Agnes' Sch., East Grinstead. *Co-heiresses: d* [Hon. Mrs Michael Kirkham, *b* (Pamela Vivian Williams) 30 Sept. 1929; *m* 1952; two *s* one *d*] and *d* [Hon. Mrs Kelvin Pollock, *b* (Rosemary Tyrwhitt Williams) 20 July 1931; *m* 1959; two *s*]. *Address:* Ashwellthorpe, Charlton Lane, Cheltenham, Glos. *T:* Cheltenham 59595.

**BERNEY, Captain Sir Thomas Reedham,** 10th Bt, *cr* 1620; MC; late Royal Norfolk Regiment; *e s* of Captain Thomas Hugh Berney and Fridzwede Katherine, *d* of Lieut-Col F. W. Bell, of Fermoy; *b* 6 July 1893; *S* grandfather, 1907; *m* 1st, 1921, Estelle Irene (who obtained a divorce, 1927), *yr d* of R. Norton Dawson, Remony, Watford; one *d*; 2nd, 1927, Marjorie Agnew Erskine Gill; one *s* two *d*; 3rd, 1947, Peggie, *yr d* of late Howard M. Page, The Elms, Ewell, Surrey. *Educ:* Wellington Coll.; Trinity Hall, Cambridge. ADC to Governor of Southern Rhodesia, 1925-26. *Heir: gs* Julian Reedham Stuart Berney, [*b* 26 Sept. 1952 (posthumous); *s* of Lieut John Reedham Erskine Berney, Royal Norfolk Regt (killed on active service in Korea, 1952) and Jean Davina, *o d* of Viscount Stuart of Findhorn, *qv*]. *Address:* St George's Cottage, Downton, Wilts.

**BERNSTEIN,** family name of **Baron Bernstein.**

**BERNSTEIN,** Baron *cr* 1969 (Life Peer), of Leigh; **Sidney Lewis Bernstein,** LLD; Chairman: Granada Group Ltd; Granada Television Ltd; Granada Theatres Ltd; Granada Publishing Ltd; *b* 30 Jan. 1899; *s* of Alexander and Jane Bernstein; *m* Sandra, *d* of Charles and Charlotte Malone, Toronto; one *s* two *d*. A founder, Film Society, 1924; introduced Saturday morning matinées for children, 1927. Films Adviser, Min. of Inf., 1940-45; Liaison, British Embassy, Washington, 1942; Chief Film Section, AFHQ N Africa, 1942-43; Chief, Film Section, SHAEF, 1943-45. Lectr on Film and Internat. Affairs: New York Univ., 1946; Yale, 1947. *Address:* 36 Golden Square, W1; Coppings Farm, Leigh, Kent. *Club:* Garrick.

**BERNSTEIN, Cecil (George);** Deputy Chairman, Granada Group Ltd; *b* 28 July 1904; *s* of Alexander and Jane Bernstein; *m* 1929, Myra Ella, *d* of Rachel and Lesser Lesser; one *s* one *d*. *Educ:* Haberdashers' Aske's. Member, Cinematograph Films Council, 1948-; Pres., Cinema and Television Benevolent Fund. *Address:* 7 Grosvenor Square, W1; Five Trees, Craigweil-on-Sea, Sussex.

**BERNSTEIN, Leonard;** conductor, composer, pianist, lecturer; *b* Lawrence, Mass, 25 Aug. 1918; *s* of Samuel J. and Jennie (Resnick) Bernstein; *m* 1951, Felicia Montealegre Cohn; one *s* two *d*. *Educ:* Boston Latin Sch.; Harvard Univ.; Curtis Inst. of Music. Asst to Koussevitzky, Berkshire Music Center, 1942, Head of Conducting Dept, 1951-56; Asst Conductor, NY Philharmonic Orch., 1943-44; Conductor, NYC Symphony, 1945-48; Musical Adviser, Israel Philharmonic Orch., 1948-49; Prof. of Music, Brandeis Univ., 1951-56; co-conductor (with Dimitri Mitropoulos), NY Philharmonic Orch., 1957-58; Music Dir, NY Philharmonic Orch., 1958-69, now Laureate Conductor. Has conducted all major orchestras of US and Europe in annual tours, 1944-; has toured N and S America, Europe, Near East, USSR and Japan with NY Philharmonic Orch. *Works include:* Clarinet Sonata, 1942; Symphony, No 1, Jeremiah, 1942; Song cycle (I Hate Music), 1943; Seven Anniversaries for Piano, 1943; Fancy Free, 1944; Hashkivenu, 1945; Facsimile, 1946; Five Pieces for Brass Instruments, 1947; Four Anniversaries for Piano, 1948; Symphony, No 2, The Age of Anxiety, 1949; Song Cycle (La Bonne Cuisine), 1949; songs, Afterthought and Silhouette, 1951; Trouble in Tahiti (one-act opera), 1952; Serenade for violin solo, with string orch. and percussion, 1954; Symphony, No 3, Kaddish, 1963; Five Anniversaries for Piano, 1964; Chichester Psalms (a choral work with orchestra), 1965; Scores for Broadway musicals including: On the Town, 1944, Wonderful Town, 1953, Candide, 1956, West Side Story, 1957; Score for Film, On the Waterfront, 1954. Has received Hon. Degrees from universities and colleges. *Publications:* The Joy of Music, 1959; Leonard Bernstein's Young People's Concerts; for Reading and Listening, 1962; The Infinite Variety of Music,

1966. *Address:* 205 West 57th Street, New York, NY 10019, USA.

**BERNSTEIN, Ronald Harold,** DFC 1944; QC 1969; *b* 18 Aug. 1918; *s* of Mark and Fanny Bernstein; *m* 1955, Judy, *d* of David Levi, MS, and Vera Levi; three *s* one *d. Educ:* Swansea Grammar Sch.; Balliol Coll., Oxford. BA (Jurisprudence) 1939. Served in RA, 1939-46, and in 654 Air OP Sqdn, RAF, 1942-46. Commanded 661 Air OP Sqdn, RAuxAF, 1954-56. Mem., Gen. Council of the Bar, 1965-69; Mem., Law Commn Working Party on the Law of Landlord and Tenant, 1966-. Mem., Highgate Soc. (which he founded, 1966). *Publications:* (jointly) The Restrictive Trade Practices Act, 1956; (Ed. jointly) Foa, Landlord and Tenant, 8th edn, 1957. *Address:* (professional) 11 King's Bench Walk, Temple, EC4. *T:* 01-353 2484; (home) Church House, South Grove, Highgate, N6.

**BERRIDGE, Reginald John;** Director, F. W. Woolworth and Co. Ltd, 1953-62 (Chairman, 1955-61); retired; *b* 30 Dec. 1900; *s* of late Arthur Edwin and Emma Berridge; *m* 1925, Sybil Edith Weller; one *d. Educ:* South Western Polytechnic. Business career almost entirely with F. W. Woolworth and Co. Ltd. *Recreations:* fishing, golf, music, etc. *Address:* Carlton Cottage, Angmering, Sussex.

**BERRILL, Kenneth,** BSc, MA; Chairman, University Grants Committee, since 1969; *b* 28 Aug. 1920; *m* 1950, June Phillips; one *s* one *d. Educ:* London Sch. of Economics; Trinity Coll., Cambridge. BSc London; MA Cantab, 1949. Economic Adviser to Turkey, British Guiana, Cameroons, OECD, and IBRD. Univ. Lectr in Economics, Cambridge, 1949-69; Fellow and Bursar, St Catharine's Coll., Cambridge, 1949-62; Fellow and First Bursar, King's Coll., Cambridge, 1962-69; HM Treasury Special Adviser, 1967-69. *Recreation:* ski-ing. *Address:* University Grants Committee, 14 Park Crescent, W1; 11 Chester Place, NW1. *T:* 01-935 9742.

**BERRILL, Prof. Norman John,** FRS 1952; FRS (Canada); PhD, DSc; Lecturer in Biology, Swarthmore College, Pennsylvania; lately Strathcona Professor of Zoology, McGill University, Montreal *b* 28 April 1903. *Educ:* Bristol Gram. Sch., Somerset, England; Bristol Univ.; London Univ. BSc Bristol; PhD, DSc London. *Publications:* The Tunicata 1951; The Living Tide, 1951; Journey into Wonder, 1953; Sex and the Nature of Things, 1954; The Origin of Vertebrates, 1955; Man's Emerging Mind, 1955; You and the Universe, 1958; Growth, Development and Pattern, 1962; Biology in Action, 1966; Worlds Apart, 1966; Life of the Oceans, 1967; The Person in the Womb, 1968. *Address:* 410 Swarthmore Avenue, Swarthmore, Pa 19081, USA.

**BERRY,** family name of **Viscount Camrose, Baron Hartwell** and **Viscount Kemsley.**

**BERRY, Hon. Anthony George;** MP (C) Southgate since 1964; *b* 12 Feb. 1925; *y s* of 1st Viscount Kemsley, GBE; *m* 1st, 1954, Hon. Mary Cynthia Burke Roche (from whom he obtained a divorce, 1966), *er d* of 4th Baron Fermoy; one *s* three *d*; 2nd, 1966, Sarah Anne, *d* of Raymond Clifford-Turner, *qv*; one *s* one *d. Educ:* Eton; Christ Church, Oxford (MA). Served as Lieut, Welsh Guards, 1943-47. Asst Editor, Sunday Times, 1952-54; Editor, Sunday Chronicle, 1954; Dir, Kemsley Newspapers, 1954-59; Managing Dir, Western Mail and Echo Ltd, 1955-59. Dep. Chm., Leopold Joseph & Sons Ltd; Dir of other companies. Pres., Welsh Games Council, 1959- . JP Cardiff. High Sheriff, Glamorgan, 1962. CStJ. *Publication:* (jt Editor) Conservative Oxford, 1949. *Address:* 91 Eaton Place, SW1. *T:* Belgravia 3801; Warbrook House, Eversley Hants. *T:* Eversley 2174. *Clubs:* Carlton, White's, Pratt's; Cardiff and County (Cardiff).

**BERRY, Prof. Francis;** Professor of English Language and Literature, Royal Holloway College, University of London, since 1970; *b* 23 March 1915; *s* of James Berry and Mary Augusta Jane Berry (*née* Ivens); *m* 1st, 1947, Nancy Melloney (*d* 1967), *d* of Cecil Newton Graham; one *s* one *d*; 2nd, 1970, Patricia, *d* of John Gordon Thomson. *Educ:* Hereford Cathedral Sch.; Dean Close Sch.; University Coll., Exeter. BA London; MA Exeter. Solicitor's articled clerk, 1931; University Coll., Exeter, 1937. War Service, 1939-46. University Coll., Exeter, 1946; successively Asst Lectr, Lectr, Sen. Lectr, Reader in English Literature, and Prof. of English Literature, Univ. of Sheffield, 1947-70. Visiting Lectr: Carleton Coll., Minn, USA, 1951-52; University Coll. of the West Indies, Jamaica, 1957; Lectr for British Council, in India, 1966-67. FRSL 1968. *Publications:* Gospel of Fire, 1933; Snake in the Moon, 1936; The Iron Christ, 1938; Fall of a Tower, 1942; Murdock and Other Poems, 1947; The Galloping Centaur, 1952; Herbert Read, 1953; An Anthology of Medieval Poems (ed), 1954; Poets' Grammar, 1958; Morant Bay and other poems, 1961; Poetry and the Physical Voice, 1962; The Shakespeare Inset, 1965; Ghosts of Greenland, 1967; John Masefield: the Narrative Poet, 1968; (ed) Essays and Studies for the English Association, 1969. Contributor: Essays in Criticism; BBC Third Programme, etc. *Recreations:* boating, walking, watching cricket. *Address:* 38 Doughty Street, WC1. *T:* 01-837 7287.

**BERRY, Prof. Harry,** BSc London; FPS; FRIC; Dip. Bact. London; ACT Birmingham; retired; Dean, School of Pharmacy, University of London, 1949-56; Professor of Pharmaceutics, 1944-56; Professor Emeritus, 1956; *b* 6 Oct. 1890; *s* of late William Berry and Lois Robinson Blood; *m* 1918, Agnes May, *d* of late Robert Boardman; two *s* one *d. Educ:* Nantwich and Acton Grammar Sch. Served European War, 1914-19, Royal Fusiliers, RE, RGA (Lieut). Lecturer in Pharmacy, Robert Gordon Colls, Aberdeen, 1919; Head, Dept of Pharmacy, Tech. Coll., Birmingham, 1919-33; Vice-Dean, 1933, Dean, 1937, College of the Pharmaceutical Soc.; Reader in Pharmaceutics, University of London, 1933. Hon. Fellow, School of Pharmacy, Univ. of London, 1956; Mem. Royal Free Hosp. Sch. of Medicine; Hon. Assoc., Coll. of Technology, Birmingham, 1956; Hon. Mem. Guild of Public Pharmacists 1965. Mem. of the British Pharmacopoeia Commission. Examiner for the Universities of London, Glasgow, Manchester, Wales, and the Pharmaceutical Soc.; Member: British Pharmaceutical Codex Revision Cttee; Central Health Services Council Standing Pharmaceutical Advisory Cttee, and Jt Sub-Cttee of Ministry of Health on Definition of Drugs; Cttee of Management of University of London Inst. of Educ.; Chm. Brit. Pharm. Conf., 1951. *Publications:* (jt) Whitla's Pharmacy, Materia Medica and Therapeutics, 12th edn, 1933; (jt) Penicillin, Fleming, 1st and 2nd edn, 1949; original contributions to Journal of Pharmacy and Pharmacol., Lancet. *Address:* 5 Walnut Tree Walk, Willingdon, Eastbourne. *T:* Eastbourne 52537.

**BERRY, Sir (Henry) Vaughan,** Kt 1949; *b* 28 March 1891; *s* of late John Henry Berry; *m* 1st, 1921, Dorothy Loveday (*d* 1959), *d* of late

Charles Baldwin, Bath, Somerset; (two *s* decd); 2nd, 1960, Mrs Joan Ogilvie Kirke, *d* of Percy Lachlan, Wadhurst, Sussex. *Educ:* City of London Sch.; Caius Coll., Cambridge. Somerset Light Infantry and Intelligence Corps, 1914-18; on staff of Inter-Allied Rhineland High Commission, 1919-25; Mem. Union Discount Company of London Ltd, 1925-45; Chm. Southern Region Manpower Board, 1941-44; Mem. Capital Issues Cttee, 1946; Regional Commissioner Hamburg, CCG, 1946-49; British delegate to the Internat. Authority for the Ruhr, 1949-50; Full-time Mem., Iron and Steel Corporation of Great Britain, 1950-53. Hon. Senator, University of Hamburg. *Recreations:* gardening, walking. *Address:* Dutch House, College Road, Bath, Somerset. *T:* Bath 61879. *Club:* Reform.

**BERRY, Very Rev. Hugh Frederick,** BD; Dean of Cloyne, 1934-52; retired 1952. *Educ:* Trinity College, Dublin. BA (Resp.) and Div. Test 1st Cl. 1896, BD 1899. Deacon, 1897; priest, 1898. Curate of Fermoy, 1897-1903; Rector of Kanturk, 1903-05; of Timoleague with Abbeymahan, 1905-08; Incumbent of Templebreedy, 1908-34. *Publication:* The Cathedral Church of St Colman's Cloyne, 2nd Edn, 1951. *Address:* North Esk Castle, Glanmire, Cork.

**BERRY, Prof. Jack,** Professor and Chairman, Department of Linguistics, Northwestern University, Evanston, Ill, USA, since 1964; *b* 13 Dec. 1918; *s* of H. and N. Berry; *m* 1942, Winifred Mary; one *s*. *Educ:* Univ. of Leeds (BA). Formerly Reader in West African Languages and subsequently Professor of West African Languages, Oct. 1960-Sept. 1963, at the Sch. of Oriental and African Studies; Prof. of West African Languages at Michigan State Univ., USA, 1963-64. Editor, Journal of African Languages, 1962-64. *Address:* Northwestern University, Evanston, Ill, USA.

**BERRY, John,** CBE 1968; MA (Cantab); PhD (St Andrews); FRSE 1936; DL; Consultant on Freshwater Fisheries and Impoundment Biology; UK member, Executive Board, International Wildfowl Research Bureau; Vice-President, Royal Zoological Society of Scotland; a Vice-President: Wildfowlers Association of Great Britain and Ireland; Wildfowl Trust; *b* Edinburgh, 5 Aug. 1907; *o s* of late William Berry, OBE, DL, Tayfield, Newport, Fife; *m* 1936, Hon. Bride Fremantle, MA (Cantab), 3rd *d* of 3rd Baron Cottesloe, CB; two *s* one *d*. *Educ:* Eton; Trinity Coll., Cambridge. BA 1929 (Zoo. Chem. Phys. Pt I and Law Pt II); MA 1933; PhD 1935; Salmon research, Fishery Bd for Scotland, 1930-31; Bological Research Station, University Coll., Southampton, Research Officer, 1932-36 and Dir, 1937-39. Press Censor for Scotland, 1940-44; Biologist and Information Officer, North of Scotland Hydro-Electric Bd, 1944-49 (Consultant and Fisheries Adviser to the Board, 1968-); Dir of Nature Conservation in Scotland, 1949-67. Pres. 1954-56, Vice-Pres. 1956-60, and Mem., 1966-, Commn on Ecology, Internat. Union for Conservation of Natural Resources. Hon. LLD Dundee, 1970. DL Fifeshire, 1969. *Publications:* The Status and Distribution of Wild Geese and Wild Duck in Scotland, 1939; various papers and articles on fresh-water fisheries, hydro-electric development and ornithology. *Recreations:* wild geese, photography, music. *Address:* Tayfield, Newport-on-Tay, Fife DD6 8HA. *T:* Newport-on-Tay 3118.

**BERRY, John Hatton,** CMG 1946; OBE 1943; retired; *b* 24 Sept. 1898, English; *m* 1925, Joyce Henderson; one *d*. *Educ:* Wallasey, Cheshire. Engineer; European War, Royal Naval Air Service; General Motors Export Corporation in London and Japan; Vauxhall Motors, Ltd, Luton. War of 1939-45; Canadian Government Service; Mem., Joint War Production Cttee (Canada-United States); Vice-Chm., Production Board (Canada); Motor Vehicle Controller; Dir-Gen., Automotive and Tank Production Branch of Dept of Munitions and Supply. Pres., War Assets Corporation, Canada; Chm., Crown Assets Allocation Cttee; Dir-Gen. Import Control Branch, Dept of Trade and Commerce. Dir of Manufacturing, A. V. Roe Canada Ltd, 1950-52; Gen. Manager, Canadian Arsenals Ltd, 1953-63. *Recreations:* cricket, tennis, gardening. *Address:* c/o 317 Lyndeview Drive, Whitby, Ont., Canada.

**BERRY, John William Edward,** CBE 1943; FRSA; AMInstT; Partner, Kilburn & Co., Ltd, Calcutta, 1945; Senior Managing Director, Kilburn & Co. (Pakistan) Ltd, Agents, India General Navigation & Railway Co. Ltd; *b* 27 Sept. 1901; *s* of late Rev. P. E. FitzPatrick Berry, Mallow, Co. Cork, and Hayle, Cornwall; *m* 1932, Marie Griffin, *d* of late W. E. Ranson, Needham Market, Suffolk, and *widow* of R. H. Read, The Beeches Hayle; no *c*. *Educ:* St John's Sch., Leatherhead. George Henderson & Co., Ltd, Calcutta, 1920-32; India General Navigation & Railway Co. Ltd, Calcutta, 1933-45 (Sen. Exec. Officer, 1939-45). Chm. East Bengal Branch European Assoc., 1935-38; Adviser on Inland Water Transport to Govt of India Defence Dept since 1941; Mem. Calcutta Traffic Advisory Bd and E Bengal Labour Advisory Bd; Lieut Calcutta Scottish Emergency Reserve Co. AF (1), 1941. Mem. Calcutta Diocesan Council, 1939-; Bengal Provincial Bd of Communications, 1940-; Pilots "A" Licence, 1929; Gliding "B" Cert., 1949. *Publication:* Report on Inland Water Transport in Iraq, 1941. *Recreations:* fishing, flying, sailing, swimming, golf. *Address:* 5 Peter Road, Narayanganj, Bengal; Parc Sparbles, Carbis Bay, Cornwall. *TA:* Mindaros. *T:* Calcutta 5502, St Ives 516. *Clubs:* Oriental, Royal Automobile; Bengal (Calcutta); West Cornwall Golf (Lelant).

**BERRY, Michael Francis;** Director of Robert Fleming & Co. Ltd, Merchant Bankers, since 1937; *b* 17 Oct. 1906; *e s* of C. Seager Berry and Constance, *d* of Rev. D. C. Cochrane; *m* 1939, Prudence *d* of C. G. Atha, Haverbrack House, Milnthorpe; one *d*. *Educ:* Eton; Hertford Coll., Oxford. Entered City, 1929; served War of 1939-45, Royal Artillery. Director: National Westminster Bank Ltd, 1968; Chairman, Sterling Trust Ltd, 1951-; a Crown Estate Commissioner, 1956-65. *Publications:* A History of the Puckeridge Hunt, 1950; (with C. M. Floyd) A History of the Eton College Hunt 1857-1968, 1969. *Recreations:* hunting, farming. *Address:* Benefield House, near Peterborough. *T:* Benefield 219. *Club:* Boodle's.

**BERRY, Lady Pamela;** *see* Hartwell, Lady.

**BERRY, Air Cdre Ronald,** CBE 1965 (OBE 1946); DSO 1943; DFC 1940 and Bar, 1943; RAF retired; Director of Control Operations, Board of Trade, 1965-68; *b* 3 May 1917; *s* of W. Berry, Hull; *m* 1940, Nancy Watson, Hessle, near Hull; one *d*. *Educ:* Hull Technical Coll. VR Pilot, Brough Flying Sch., 1937-39; 603 F Sqdn, Turnhouse/Hornchurch, 1939-41 (Battle of Britain); Sqdn Ldr, and CO 81 F Sqdn, North Africa, 1942; Wing Comdr, and CO 322 F Wing, North Africa, 1942-43; Camberley Army Staff Coll., 1944; CO, RAF

Acklington, 1945-46; jssc 1955; various operational appts in Fighter and Bomber Comd; V Sqdn, 1957-59; Group Capt., Air Min. and HQ Bomber Comd, 1959. *Recreations:* motoring, gardening, flying. *Address:* Aldrian, Mereview Avenue, Hornsea, Yorks.

**BERRY, Sir Vaughan;** *see* Berry, Sir H. V.

**BERRYMAN, Lieut-Gen. Sir Frank Horton,** KCVO *cr* 1954; CB 1944; CBE 1941; DSO 1919; Company Director since 1961; Director and Chief Executive Officer, Royal Agricultural Society, Sydney, 1954-61; *b* 11 April 1894; *s* of William Berryman; *m* 1925, Muriel Whipp; one *s* one *d. Educ:* Melbourne High Sch.; Sydney Univ.; RMC, Duntroon; Staff Coll., Camberley (psc); Artillery Coll., Woolwich (pac). Served European War, 1915-19 (DSO, despatches twice, wounded); served as regimental officer, battery commander in field artillery, and infantry brigade-major. Army Representative High Commissioner's Office, London, 1931; Brigade-Major 14 Infantry Brigade, Sydney, 1932-34; GSO Operations and Asst Dir Military Operations, Army HQ, Melbourne, 1934-37; GSO1 3 Aust. Div., 1938-39; War of 1939-45; GSO1, 6 Australian Div. at capture of Bardia and Tobruk in 1941 (CBE); CRA 7 Aust. Div. and Comdr Berryforce in Syrian Campaign, 1941 (despatches); Brig. Gen. Staff, 1 Aust. Corps, Aug. 1941, and served in Middle East and Java; Maj.-Gen. General Staff, 1st Australian Army, 1942; Dep. Chief of Gen. Staff, Sept. 1942; DCGS and mCGS on New Guinea Force, Dec. 1942-Oct. 1943; Admin Comd, 2 Aust. Corps, Nov. 1943; Lieut-Gen. GOC 2 Aust. Corps, Finchhaven, Huon Peninsula, New Guinea, Jan. 1944 (CB); GOC 1 Aust. Corps, April 1944; Chief of Staff, Advanced Land Force HQ, South-West Pacific Area, July 1944; served with GHQ SWPA in Hollandia, Leyte, and Manila; present on USS Missouri, Tokyo Bay, at official Japanese surrender ceremony as representative of Australian Army, 2 Sept. 1945; Chief of Staff Adv. HQ, AMF, Oct.-Dec. 1945; Chief of Staff HQ Morotai Force, Dec. 1945-March 1946; GOC Eastern Command, Australia, 1946-50, and 1952-53. Awarded Medal of Freedom with Silver Palm by US Govt 1946; Commonwealth Dir Royal Tour (1949), 1948; seconded to Prime Minister's Dept as Dir-Gen. Commonwealth Jubilee Celebrations (1951), and Dir-Gen. Royal Visit (1952), 1951-52; seconded to Prime Minister's Dept as Dir-Gen. Royal Visit (1954), 1953-54; retd list, 1954. Col Comdt, Royal Australian Artillery, 1956-61. *Recreation:* golf. *Address:* 17 Wentworth Street, Point Piper, Sydney, NSW, Australia. *Clubs:* Union, Australian, Royal Sydney Golf (Sydney); Naval and Military (Melbourne).

**BERRYMAN, Montague Levander,** QC 1945; JP; **His Honour Judge Berryman;** Chairman, Kent County Quarter Sessions since Oct. 1962; *b* 21 July 1899; *er s* of late Frederic John Berryman, LLB, Great Chesterford, Essex; *m* Marjorie Myhill; one *s* two *d. Educ:* Westminster Sch. Called to Bar, Middle Temple, 1921; Mem. of Middle and Inner Temple, South Eastern Circuit; Bencher, Middle Temple, 1953-66; Bencher Emeritus, 1966. Served Royal Sussex Regt and attached RAF, 1917-18. Contested (C) Romford, 1945; Recorder of Gravesend, 1945-47, Dover, 1947-62; Dep. Chm., 1950-59, Chm., 1959-63, Herts QS. JP Herts and Kent. Admitted to Hon. Freedom of Borough of Dover, 1963. *Recreations:* anything connected with the theatre and ships; books and print collecting. *Address:* 1020 Kings House, St James Court, Buckingham Gate, SW1. *T:* 01-828 8278; Fairycroft, Great Chesterford, Essex. *T:* Great Chesterford 237. *Club:* Garrick.

**BERTHOUD, Sir Eric Alfred,** KCMG 1954 (CMG 1945); MA; DL; retired from HM Foreign Service, 1960; Member of Board, BP associated companies in Switzerland and Belgium; Member of Council: Essex University; School of Slavonic and East European Studies, London University; United World Colleges; *b* 10 Dec. 1900; 2nd *s* of late Alfred E. Berthoud; *m* 1927, Ruth Tilston, *d* of Sir Charles Bright, FRSE; two *s* two *d. Educ:* Gresham's Sch., Holt; Magdalen Coll., Oxford; MA. Demy; Hons in Natural Science. Anglo-Austrian Bank Ltd, London, 1922-26; Anglo-Iranian Oil Co. (BP) Ltd, 1926-39. Served in France and Germany. Commercial Sec. to HM Legation, Bucharest, 1939-41; Asst Sec., Min. of Fuel and Power (Petroleum Div.), 1942-44; Dir Economic Div., Allied Commission for Austria (British Element), 1944-46; Under-Sec., Petroleum Div., Min. of Fuel and Power, 1946-48; Asst Under-Sec., FO, 1948-52; HM Ambassador to Denmark, 1952-56, to Poland, 1956-60. Member of Board: Chelmsford Prison; Sue Ryder Foundn. DL Essex, 1969. Knight Comdr's Cross with star, Order of Polonia Restituta, 1965. *Recreations:* country recreations. *Address:* Holts, Little Horkesley, near Colchester, Essex. *T:* Great Horkesley 262. *Clubs:* St James', Sesame Pioneer and Lyceum, MCC.

*See also R. G. Pentney.*

**BERTIE,** family name of **Earl of Lindsey and Abingdon.**

**BERTRAM, Anthony,** MA; author and lecturer; Editor, History of Art, for Visual Publications; *b* London, 19 Nov. 1897; *s* of Ernest Bertram; *m* 1929, Barbara Randolph; two *s. Educ:* Douai Abbey; Pembroke Coll., Oxford. Served in Army, 1915-19 (wounded) and 1940-45 (Legion of Honour and Croix de Guerre); Art Critic to Spectator, 1922-24; to Saturday Review, 1924-27; Lectr to National Portrait Gallery, 1922-24; Stipendiary Lectr to Extramural Delegacy, Oxford, 1927-68; Ed., Design for To-day, 1934; Lectr in Fine Arts, Queen's Univ. Belfast, 1938-39; Dep.-Dir of British Council in France, 1945-46. Vis. Prof., Elmira Coll., NY, USA, 1958. *Publications:* English Portraiture in National Portrait Gallery, 1924; The Pool, 1926; Here We Ride, 1927; Life of Rubens, 1928; The Sword Falls, 1929; To the Mountains, 1929; The Man who made Gottlieb, 1930; They Came to the Castle, 1931; Three Meet, 1932; Pavements and Peaks, 1933; Men Adrift, 1935; The House, 1935; The King Sees Red, 1936; Design in Daily Life, 1937; Design, 1938; Contemporary Painting, 1939; Bright Defiler, 1940; Pleasures of Poverty, 1950; A Century of British Painting, 1951; Paul Nash, 1955; Michelangelo, 1964; 1000 Years of Drawing, 1966; Florentine Sculpture, 1969; various small monographs on artists. *Recreations:* gardening, reading. *Address:* Coates Castle, Fittleworth, Sussex. *T:* Fittleworth 213. *Club:* Savile.

**BERTRAM, Prof. Douglas Somerville;** Professor of Medical Entomology and Director of Department of Entomology, London School of Hygiene and Tropical Medicine, since 1956; *b* 21 Dec. 1913; *s* of William R. J. Bertram and Katherine Arathoon Macaskill, Glasgow, Scotland; *m* 1947, Louisa Menzies MacKellar (*d* 1956); two *d. Educ:* Hillhead High Sch., Glasgow; Univ. of Glasgow. 1st cl. hons BSc (Zoology), 1935, PhD 1940, DSc 1964, Glasgow Univ.; Strang-Steel Scholar, Glasgow Univ., 1935-36. Demonstrator, Dept of

Zoology, Glasgow Univ., 1936-38; Lectr, Liverpool Sch. of Tropical Medicine, 1938-40, and 1946-48; Reader in Entomology, London Sch. of Hygiene and Tropical Medicine, 1948-56. Overseas work in East and West Africa, India and Ceylon, Central America periodically. Served War of 1939-45: Lieut to Major, Royal Army Medical Corps, Middle East, POW Germany, Army Sch. of Health Staff, 1945-46. *publications:* scientific papers in Annals of Trop. Medicine and Parasitology, Transactions Royal Society Tropical Medicine and Hygiene, Adv. Parasitology, Bulletin WHO, etc. *Recreations:* gardening, painting, travel. *Address:* London School of Hygiene and Tropical Medicine, Keppel Street, WC1.

**BERTRAM, Neville Rennie,** CMG 1960; MBE 1941; director of companies since 1959; *b* 13 March 1909; *s* of late C. F. Bertram, 1890 Rhodesian Pioneer; *m* 1935, Eve Cook; one *s* one *d*. *Educ:* Chaplin High Sch., Gwelo; Univ. of Witwatersrand. Southern Rhodesia Civil Service: Treasury, 1926; Under-Sec., Treasury, 1943; Under-Sec., Internal Affairs, 1946; Asst Sec., Treasury, 1947; Sec. for Trade and Industrial Development, 1948; Federal Govt of Rhodesia and Nyasaland: Sec. for Commerce and Industry, 1953-59, retired. Central African Air Transport Authority, 1949-53; Rhodesian Iron and Steel Commn, 1952-54; Tobacco Export Promotion Council of Rhodesia, 1959-60; represented S Rhodesia and subsequently the Federation at numerous international and Commonwealth conferences, 1948-58. Pres., Automobile Assoc. of Rhodesia; Prov. Pres., Boy Scouts' Assoc; Past Pres., Rhodesian Economic Soc. City Councillor, 1961-62. *Publications:* Strange Instrument, 1948; various economic and commercial publications. *Recreations:* fishing, bridge, Africana and Rhodesiana. *Address:* 20 Chelmscote Mansions, Baines Avenue, Salisbury, Rhodesia. *T:* 23586; PO Box 8244, Causeway, Salisbury, Rhodesia. *Clubs:* Royal Commonwealth Society; Salisbury, Enterprise Country (Salisbury); Automobile Association of Rhodesia.

**BERTRAND, Cavalier Léon;** Professor at the London Fencing Club; British; father of French extraction; *b* 10 July 1897; unmarried. *Educ:* St George's Coll., Wimbledon; Grenoble Univ. Diplomé L'Accademia Nazionale di Scherma, Naples; studied fencing under Profs Georges and Adolphe Rouleau, Paris, and Maestro Commendatore Guiseppe Nadi, Leghorn; served European War, Artists' Rifles; active service, commnd in RFC and RAF; War of 1939-45: commnd in RAFVR, 1939, and served until Nov. 1945 in France, Middle East, Italy, home stations (African Star with clasp, etc). Past Pres., British Academy of Fencing. awarded (twice) Gold Medal of the Amateur Fencing Assoc. Order of the Crown of Italy, 1938. *Publications:* Cut and Thrust: The Subtlety of the Sabre; The Fencer's Companion, 1935. *Recreations:* billiards and snooker. *Address:* 3 Cutcombe Villas, Cutcombe Road, SE5. *T:* 01-274 8168; London Fencing Club, 83 Perham Road, West Kensington, W14. *T:* 01-385 7454. *Club:* London Sketch.

**BESLEY, Christopher;** a Metropolitan Magistrate since 1964; *b* 18 April 1916; *s* of late C. A. Besley, Tiverton; *m* 1947, Pamela, *d* of Dr W. E. David, Sydney, Australia; four *s* two *d*. *Educ:* King's Coll., Wimbledon; King's Coll., London. Barrister, Gray's Inn, 1938. Served War of 1939-45, Devon Regt. *Address:* Queen Elizabeth Building, Temple, EC4; 15 Belvedere Avenue, SW19. *T:* 01-946 2184.

**BESSBOROUGH,** 10th Earl of, *cr* 1739, Earl (UK), *cr* 1937; **Frederick Edward Neuflize Ponsonby;** Baron of Bessborough; Viscount Duncannon, 1723; Baron Ponsonby, 1749; Baron Duncannon (UK), 1834; Chairman of Governors, British Society for International Understanding (Governor since 1939); President: British Drama League; Men of the Trees; Chichester Festival Theatre Trust; Member Council, Zoological Society of London; *b* 29 March 1913; *s* of 9th Earl of Bessborough, PC, GCMG, and Roberte de Neuflize, GCStJ, *d* of late Baron Jean de Neuflize; *S* father, 1956; *m* 1948, Mary, *d* of Charles A. Munn, USA; one *d*. *Educ:* Eton; Trinity Coll., Cambridge (MA). Contested W Div. Islington (Nat. Govt), 1935. Joined Sussex Yeomanry (TA), 1936; Sec., League of Nations High Commission for Refugees, 1936-39. Served War of 1939-45, France, Flanders and Dunkirk; ADC to Comdr, Canadian Corps; Experimental Officer (Capt.) Tank Gunnery; GSO2 (liaison) in West and North Africa; Second and subsequently First Sec., British Embassy, Paris, 1944-49. With Robert Benson, Lonsdale and Co. Ltd and Dir High Definition Films, Associated Broadcasting Development Co. Ltd, ATV, Glyndebourne Arts Trust; English Stage Co. Ltd, etc, 1950-63. Chairman: International Atlantic Cttee, 1952-55; European Atlantic Group, 1954-61. Mem. of UK Parly Delegn to USSR, 1960. Parly Sec. for Science, Oct. 1963; Jt Parly Under-Sec. of State for Educn and Science, 1964; Minister of State, Min. of Technology, June-Oct. 1970. Dep. Chm., Metrication Board, 1969-70. OStJ; Chevalier Legion of Honour; MRI. *Plays and publications:* Nebuchadnezzar (with Muriel Jenkins), 1939; The Four Men (after H. Belloc), 1951; Like Stars Appearing, 1953; The Noon is Night, 1954; Darker the Sky, 1955; Triptych, 1957; A Place in the Forest, 1958; Return to the Forest, 1962; articles, reviews. *Heir pres.: c* Arthur Mountifort Longfield Ponsonby [*b* 11 Dec. 1912; *m* 1939, Patricia (*d* 1952), *d* of Col Fitzhugh Lee Minnigerode, Va, USA; one *s* one *d*; *m* 1956, Princess Anne Marie Galitzine (marr. diss., 1963), *d* of late Baron Sir Rudolph Slatin Pasha; *m* 1963, Madeleine, *d* of Maj.-Gen. Laurence Grand, *qv*; two *s*]. *Address:* 6 Hyde Park Gardens, W2. *T:* 01-262 9201; Stansted Park, Rowland's Castle, Hants. *Clubs:* Turf, Garrick; Grolier (New York).

**BESSELL, Peter Joseph;** *b* 24 Aug. 1921; *o s* of Joseph Edgar Bessell, Ludlow, and Olive Simons Hawkins, Bath; *m* 1942, Joyce Margaret Thomas (*d* 1947), Bath; *m* 1948, Pauline Colledge, Saltford, Bristol; one *s* one *d*. *Educ:* Lynwyd Sch., Bath. Ministry of Information Lecturer to HM Forces, 1943-45. Contested (L): Torquay, Gen. Election, 1955, and bye-election, Dec. 1955; Bodmin, 1959; MP (L) Bodmin, 1964-70, retd. Member: Estimates Cttee, 1964-66, 1966-67; Parly Commn to S Vietnam, 1967; Select Cttee on Agriculture, 1967; Select Cttee on Procedure, 1964-65; Select Cttee on Vehicle Excise Duty (Allegations), 1969; Liberal Executive and Council, 1956-60; Nat. Pres., Brotherhood Movement, 1967-68. Property Finance Broker; Director: Peter Bessell Ltd; 20th Century Securities Ltd; Cornish Developments Ltd, etc. *Recreations:* music, history, travel. *Address:* Polrean, Sandplace, Looe, Cornwall. *T:* Looe 2596; 41 Pall Mall, SW1. *T:* 01-839 2157; 1 East 57th Street, New York, NY 10022, USA. *T:* (212)355-0606. *Clubs:* Reform, National Liberal.

**BESSEY, Gordon Scott,** CBE 1968; Director of Education, Cumberland, since 1949; *b* 20 Oct. 1910; *s* of late Edward Emerson and Mabel Bessey, Great Yarmouth; *m* 1937, Cynthia (JP

1966), *d* of late William and Mary Bird, Oxford; one *s* three *d. Educ:* Heath Sch., Halifax; St Edmund Hall, Oxford. BA 1932, Dip Ed 1933, MA 1937. Teaching: Keighley and Cheltenham, 1933-37; Admin. Asst, Surrey, 1937-39; Asst, later Dep. Educn Officer, Norfolk, 1939-45; Dep. Educn Officer, Somerset, 1945-49. Mem., Youth Service Development Council, 1960-67; Chm., Working Party on part-time training of Youth Leaders, 1961-62; Pres., Assoc. of Chief Educn Officers, 1963 (Treas., 1964-); Chairman: Schools Cttee of ITA, 1968-; Educnl Adv. Council of ITA, 1970-; County Educn Officers' Soc., 1969-70. Governor, Centre for Educl Development Overseas, 1969-; Mem., Educn Advisory Cttee of UK Nat. Cttee for UNESCO 1969-. Hon. DCL Newcastle upon Tyne, 1970. *Recreations:* fishing, golf, fell-walking, ornithology. *Address:* 8 St George's Crescent, Carlisle. *T:* Carlisle 22253. *Clubs:* United University; Border (Carlisle).

**BEST,** family name of **Baron Wynford.**

**BEST, Alfred Charles,** CBE 1962 (OBE 1953); DSc (Wales); Director of Services, Meteorological Office, 1960-66; *b* 7 March 1904; *s* of late Charles William Best, Barry, Glam; *m* 1932, Renée Margaret, *d* of late John Laughton Parry, Blaina, Mon; two *s. Educ:* Barry Grammar Sch.; University Coll., Cardiff. Professional Asst, Meteorological Office, 1926; appointments: Shoeburyness, 1926; Porton, 1928; Air Min., 1933; Malta, 1936; Larkhill, 1939; Air Min., 1940; Wing Comdr RAFVR, ACSEA, 1945; Air Min., 1945; Research, 1945-54; Meteorological Office Services, 1955-66. *Publications:* Physics in Meteorology, 1957; meteorological papers in jls. *Recreation:* photography. *Address:* Blaina, 10 Flintgrove, Bracknell, Berks. *T:* Bracknell 21772.

**BEST, Charles Herbert,** CC (Canada) 1967; CBE 1944; FRS 1938; MA, MD, DSc; FRSC, FRCP(C); Professor of Physiology and Head of Department, University of Toronto, 1929-65, Director Emeritus, 1966; Director of Banting-Best Department of Medical Research, University of Toronto, 1941-67, Director Emeritus, 1967; *b* West Pembroke, Maine, USA, 27 Feb. 1899 (parents both Canadian); *s* of Herbert Huestis Best, MD, and Luella May Best; *m* 1924, Margaret Hooper Mahon; two *s. Educ:* Univ. of Toronto; Univ. of London. BA 1921, MA 1922, MD 1925, Toronto; DSc 1928, London. FRCP 1961. Went overseas with 70th Battery (2nd Canadian Tanks Corps section), serving as Driver and Sergeant, 1918-19; Surg. Lt-Comdr, RCNVR, 1941; Surg.-Comdr 1942; Surg.-Capt. 1943. co-discoverer of insulin with late Sir Frederick Banting in 1921; in charge of production of insulin, Connaught Laboratories, Univ. of Toronto, 1922-41. Hon. Mem., American Diabetes Assoc., 1940 (Past Pres., 1948-49; Hon. Pres., 1960); Vice-Pres., British Diabetic Assoc., 1934; Hon. Pres., Internat. Diabetes Fedn, 1949; Hon. Dir, Muscular Dystrophy Assoc. of Canada, 1964; Hon. Mem., European Assoc. for the Study of Diabetes, 1965. Initiated Canadian Serum Project for securing dried human serum for military use, 1939; Dir, RCN Med. Res. Unit 1941-; Scientific Dir, Internat. Health Div., Rockefeller Foundn, 1941-43, re-appointed 1946; Consultant to Nat. Inst. of Health, US Public Health Service, 1946; Member: Research Defence Board, Dept Nat. Defence, Canada, 1946-65; Nat. Research Council of Canada, 1947; Interim Cttee, Nat. Cancer Inst. of Canada, 1947. Mem., Paris Acad. of Medicine, 1945; Hon. Mem., Royal Acad. of Sciences, Amsterdam, 1946; For. Corresp., Académie Royale de Medécine de Belgique, 1946; Corresp. Fellow, NY Acad. of Medicine, 1947; Hon. Life Mem., NY Acad. of Sciences, 1950; For. Assoc., Nat. Acad. of Sciences, 1950; Mem., Amer. Philosophical Soc., 1950; Hon. FRSocMed, 1951; Hon. FRCPE, 1953; First Pres., Internat. Union of Physiological Sciences, 1953; Mem., Pontifical Acad. of Sciences, 1955; Mem., Royal Danish Acad. of Sciences and Letters, 1956. Hon. Mem., Ont. Med. Assoc., 1959; For. Mem., Royal Swedish Acad. of Science, 1961; Adv. Vice-Pres., Pan American Med. Assoc., 1961; Adv. Cttee on Medical Research, WHO, 1963. Hon. DSc: Chicago, 1941; Laval, 1952; Maine 1955; Oxford, 1947; Northwestern, 1959; Hon. ScD Cambridge, 1946; Hon. Doctor of Medicine: Amsterdam, 1947; Louvain, 1947; Liège, 1947; Freie Univ. of Berlin, 1966; Hon. LLD: Dalhousie, 1949; Queen's, 1950; Melbourne, 1952; Edinburgh, 1959; Hon. Degrees, Univs of Chile, Uruguay, San Marcos (Peru), 1951; Hon. Doctorate: Paris, 1945; Central Univ. of Venezuela, 1958; Aristotelian Univ. of Thessaloniki, 1963. Holds many medals from Canadian, American and European instns. Legion of Merit, US, 1947; King Haakon VI Liberty Cross, Norway, 1947; Comdr of Order of the Crown, Belgium, 1948. *Publications:* (with F. G. Banting) original publication on insulin, 1922; Co-author books: The Human Body, 1932; Physiological Basis of Medical Practice, 1937 (7th edn, 1961); Selected Papers of Charles H. Best, 1963; numerous articles on insulin, carbohydrate and fat metabolism, muscular exercise, heparin, histamine, etc. *Recreations:* riding, golf. *Address:* The Charles H. Best Institute, University of Toronto, Toronto, Canada. *T:* 928-2586. *Clubs:* Athenæum; University; (Hon. Life) Canadian (Toronto); York Downs Golf.

**BEST, Edna;** actress, stage and films; *d* of Leonard William Best and Claire Romaire; *m* 1st, 1920, Seymour Beard (marr. diss., 1928); twin *s*; 2nd, 1928, Herbert Marshall (*d* 1966); one *d*; 3rd, 1940, Nat Wolff. First appeared on stage at Grand Theatre, Southampton, 1917; Peter in Peter Pan, 1920; Teresa Sanger in The Constant Nymph, 1926; Leonora Perrycoste in There's Always Juliet, 1931; many subsequent appearances in London; also Played in US where appearances include: Mary Adams in Yankee Point, 1942; Millie Crocker-Harris in The Browning Version, 1949; Edna Selby in Harlequinade, 1949; Lady Cicely Waynflete in Captain Brassbound's Conversion, 1950; Jane, 1952; Mme Alexandra in Mademoiselle Colombe, 1954. *Films:* began career, 1929; successes in South Riding, Prison Without Bars, etc. *Address:* c/o Actors' Equity Association, 45 West 47th Street, New York 36, USA.

**BEST, Sir John Victor Hall,** Kt 1956; BDS, DMD, FDSRCS, FACD; President of the Australian Dental Association, 1940-44 and 1950-54 (Vice-President, 1948-50); *s* of Rev. John Hall Best, MA, Greenwich, NSW; *m* 1927, Marion E., *d* of Dr E. H. Burkitt; one *s* one *d.* Pres., NSW Branch of Australian Dental Association, 1935-37; Lt-Col AA Dental Corps, Consulting Dental Surg. LHQ, 1942-44; Chm. Central Dental Advisory Cttee, Directorate of Manpower, 1943-45. Pres., 12th Australian Dental Congress, 1950. Foundn Fellow, Aust. Coll. of Dental Surgeons. *Address:* BMA House, 135 Macquarie Street, Sydney, NSW 2000, Australia. *Club:* Australian.

**BEST, Ven. Joseph;** Archdeacon of Ballarat, 1926-50, now Archdeacon Emeritus; *b* 1880; 3rd *s* of Henry Best, JP, one of Australia's pioneer settlers; *m* 1910, Marjorie Jean

Wallace; three *s* two *d*. *Educ:* Stawell TS; St Aidan's Coll., Ballarat. Curate of Berringa, 1905-07; Vicar of Nhill, 1907-12; Linton, 1912-14; St John's Ballarat, 1915-21; Rural Dean of Ballarat North, 1919; Archdeacon of Maryborough, 1921-26; served European War; Chaplain, 39th Battalion AIF in France, 1916-17; Chaplain, 11th Regt Australian Light Horse, Palestine, 1918; Senior Chaplain, Australian Mounted Division, 1918; Examining Chaplain to the Bishop of Ballarat, 1934-50; Vicar Gen. of Diocese of Ballarat, 1947-50. Editor, Ballarat Chronicle, 1926-37. *Publications:* The Apostolic Ministry; Big Business in Religion; What Every Anglican Should Know. *Recreations:* angling, geology, chess.

**BEST, Rear-Adm. Thomas William,** CB 1966; *b* Hoshangabad, India, 1 Sept. 1915; *s* of late Hon. James William Best, OBE, and Florence Mary Bernarda (*née* Lees); *m* 1942, Brenda Joan, *d* of late F. A. Hellaby, MC, Auckland, New Zealand; two *s* one *d*. *Educ:* Farnborough Sch.; Royal Naval Coll., Dartmouth. Served in NZ Div. of RN (HMS Leander, 1937-41); War of 1939-45 (despatches); Qualified Gunnery Specialist, 1942. Korean War, 1951-52 (despatches); i/c HMS Barrosa, 1952-54; Dep. Dir Naval Ordnance, 1955-58; i/c HMS Ausonia, 1958-60; Capt. Supt, Admiralty Surface Weapons Establishment, 1961-64. ADC to the Queen, 1964; Flag Officer Gibraltar, 1964-66; retd 1967. *Recreations:* fishing, shooting. *Address:* Hincknowle, Melplash, Bridport, Dorset. *T:* Netherbury 221. *Club:* United Service.

**BEST-SHAW, Sir John (James Kenward),** 9th Bt *cr* 1665; Commander (E) RN, retired; *b* 11 June 1895; *s* of Rev. Sir Charles J. M. Shaw, 8th Bt, and Louisa (*d* 1961), *d* of J. W. Bosanquet; *S* father, 1922; assumed the name and arms of Best by Royal Licence, 1956; *m* 1921, Elizabeth Mary Theodora, *e d* of Sir Robert Hughes, 12th Bt; three *s* four *d*. *Educ:* Cheam Sch., Sutton, Surrey; Royal Naval Colls, Osborne and Dartmouth. A lay guardian of the Sanctuary of Our Lady of Walsingham, 1931. Served with Royal Navy, War of 1939-45. High Sheriff, Kent, 1961. Pres., Church Union, 1969. OStJ. *Heir:* *s* John Michael Robert Best-Shaw [*b* 28 Sept. 1924; *m* 1960, Jane Gordon, *d* of A. G. Guthrie, Hampton Court House, Farningham, Kent; two *s* one *d*]. *Address:* Boxley Abbey, Maidstone, Kent. *T:* Maidstone 52910. *Club:* Royal Societies.
*See also J. M. A. Beck.*

**BESTERMAN, Edwin Melville Mack,** MD, MA, Cantab; FRCP; Consultant Cardiologist, St Mary's Hospital, W2 and Princess Louise Kensington Hospital for Children, W10 since 1962; *b* 4 May 1924; *s* of T. D. N. Besterman, *qv*; *m* 1955, Eleanor Mary Rymer Till, *d* of T. Till, Caerleon; four *s*. *Educ:* Stowe Sch.; Trinity Coll., Cambridge; Guy's Hospital. BA (Cantab) 1943 (1st cl. hons Physiology); MB, BChir 1947; MRCP 1949; MD 1955 (Raymond Horton Smith Prize); FRCP 1967. Out-patient Officer, Guy's Hosp., 1947; House Physician, Post-graduate Medical Sch., Hammersmith, 1948; Registrar, Special Unit for Juvenile Rheumatism, Canadian Red Cross Memorial Hosp., Taplow, Berks, 1949-52; First Asst (Lectr), Inst of Cardiology and Nat. Heart Hosp., 1953-56; Sen. Registrar, Middlesex Hosp., 1956-62. Member: Brit. Cardiac Soc.; Med. Research Soc.; Harveian Soc.; Faculty of History of Medicine and Pharmacy; Osler Club; Scientific Fellow, Zoological Soc. *Publications:* articles on phonocardiography, pulmonary hypertension and atherosclerosis in Brit. Heart Jl, Brit. Med. Jl, Lancet, Circulation, etc. *Recreations:* photography, gardening, fishing, tennis, dogs. *Address:* 29 Harley Street, W1N 1DA. *T:* 01-580 9347; 24 Meadway, NW11. *T:* 01-458 1930.

**BESTERMAN, Theodore Deodatus Nathaniel,** Hon. DLitt Oxford, Hon. LLD St Andrews, DèsL *hc* Geneva; Director, Institut et Musée Voltaire, Geneva, Switzerland; *b* 18 Nov. 1904; *y s* of B. J. N. Besterman, Bradford, and Augusta (*née* Cringle); *m* 1st, Evelyn, *y d* of Arthur Mack, New York; one *s*; 2nd, Marie-Louise van Muyden. *Educ:* privately; Lycée de Londres; Oxford (extra-mural). Chm., British Federation of Youth Movements, 1925-26; Investigation Officer, etc of Soc. for Psychical Research, 1927-35; Special Lectr in Univ. of London Sch. of Librarianship, 1931-38. Served 1939-45 in CD, RA (Field), and Army Bureau of Current Affairs. Joint Editor, Oxford Books on Bibliography; Gen. Editor, Assoc. of Special Libraries and Information Bureaux, 1942-46; Ed. and Exec. Officer, British Union Catalogue of Periodicals, 1944-46; founded and ed. Journal of Documentation, 1945-47; Chm., St Martin's Sch. of Art, 1946; Head, Dept for the Exchange of Information, UNESCO, 1946-49; President: Internat. Congress on the Enlightenment, 1963-71; Internat. Soc. for 18th century studies, 1967-. Corresp. Member: Académies de Dijon, de Lyons, de Marseille; Institut de France; Hon. FLA; FRSL. Hon. Mem., Soc. for French Studies, Société d'Histoire littéraire de la France. Hon. DLitt Case Western Reserve. Chevalier de la Légion d'Honneur. *Publications:* A Bibliography of Annie Besant, 1924; Crystal-Gazing: a Study in the History, etc, of Scrying, 1924; The Divining-Rod: an Experimental and Psychological Investigation (with Sir William Barrett, FRS), 1926; Library Catalogue of the Society for Psychical Research, 1927; supplements, 1928, 1929, 1931, 1934; The Mind of Annie Besant, 1928; Some Modern Mediums, 1930; Men against Women; a Study of Sexual Relations, 1934; A Bibliography of Sir James George Frazer, OM, 1934; Mrs Annie Besant: a Modern Prophet, 1934; ed. and contributor to Inquiry into the Unknown (BBC Talks), 1934; The Druce-Portland Case, 1935; A Bibliography of Sir Oliver Lodge, FRS, 1935; The Beginnings of Systematic Bibliography, 1935; 1935; 3rd edn (in French, Les Débuts de la Bibliographie Méthodique), 1950; The Publishing Firm of Cadell and Davis, 1793-1836, 1938; Water-Divining, 1938; The Travellings and Sufferings of Father Jean de Brébeuf among the Hurons of Canada, 1938; The Pilgrim Fathers, 1939; A World Bibliography of Bibliographies, two vols, 1939-40; 2nd edn, three vols, 1947-49; 3rd edn, four vols, 1955-56; 4th edn, five vols, 1965-66; Early Printed Books to the End of the Sixteenth Century, 1940, 2nd edn 1961; British Sources of Reference and Information, 1948; Unesco: Peace in the Minds of Men, 1951; Index Bibliographicus, two vols, 1952; Voltaire's Notebooks, two vols, 1952, 2nd edn 1968; Voltaire's Correspondence, 107 vols, 1953-65, definitive edn 1968-; founded and edited Studies on Voltaire and the eighteenth century, Vols I-LXX, 1955-; Le Goût des manuscrits, 1956; Lettres de la Marquise Du Châtelet, two vols, 1958; Lettres d'amour de Voltaire à sa nièce, 1958; Voltaire Essays and another, 1962; Select Letters of Voltaire, 1963; Flaubert's Théâtre de Voltaire, two vols, 1967; Voltaire on Shakespeare, 1967; Collected Papers on the Paranormal, 1968; editor of the Complete Works of Voltaire, 1968-; Voltaire (biography), 1969; edited several works by E. Crawley, translations of Hans Driesch, etc; also numerous papers and miscellaneous writings. *Recreations:* The Guyon House Press, for the printing and binding of fine books (until completely

destroyed by enemy action, Dec. 1940); collecting English drawings, etc. *Address:* 68 Pall Mall, SW1; Les Délices, Geneva, Switzerland. *Clubs:* Reform; Century (new York).
*See also E. M. M. Besterman.*

**BESTOR, Arthur (Eugene);** Professor of History, University of Washington since 1962; *b* 20 Sept. 1908; *s* of Arthur Eugene and Jeanette Louise Lemon Bestor; *m* 1st, 1939, Anne Carr (*d* 1948); two *s*; 2nd, 1949, Dorothy Alden Koch; one *s*. *Educ:* Yale Univ. PhB 1930; PhD 1938. Yale University: Instructor in English, 1930-31; Instructor in History, 1934-36; Teachers Coll., Columbia University: Associate in History, 1936-37; Asst Prof. of History, 1937-42; Stanford University: Asst Prof. of Humanities, 1942-45; Associate Prof. of History, 1945-46; Lectr in American History, Univ. of Wisconsin, 1947; University of Illinois: Associate Prof. of History, 1947-51; Prof. of History, 1951-62. Harold Vyvyan Harmsworth Prof. of American History, Oxford, 1956-57; Fulbright Vis. Prof., University of Tokyo, 1967. Editor-in-chief, Chautauquan Daily, Chautauqua, NY, 1931-33. Fellow, Newberry Library, Chicago, Ill., 1946; John Simon Guggenheim Memorial Fellow, 1953-54, 1961-62; Pres., Ill. State Historical Soc., 1954-55; Pres., Council for Basic Education, 1956-57. MA (Oxon) by decree, 1956; LLD Lincoln Univ. (Pa), 1959. *Publications:* Chautauqua Publications, 1934; David Jacks of Monterey, 1945; Education and Reform at New Harmony, 1948; Backwoods Utopias, 1950; Educational Wastelands, 1953; The Restoration of Learning, 1955; jointly: Problems in American History, 1952, 3rd edn 1966; Three Presidents and Their Books, 1955; The Heritage of the Middle West, 1958; Education in the Age of Science, 1959; Interpreting and Teaching American History, 1961; Habeas Corpus and American Constitutionalism, 1969; contribs to Amer. Hist. Review, Jl of Hist. of Ideas, William and Mary Quarterly, American Scholar, Daedalus, New England Quarterly, Jl of Southern History, Harvard Educational Review, New Republic, Scientific Monthly, School and Society. *Recreations:* photography, walking. *Address:* Department of History, 312-B Smith Hall, University of Washington, Seattle, Washington 98105, USA; (home) 4553 55th Avenue NE, Seattle, Washington, 98105, USA. *Club:* Elizabethan (New Haven).

**BESWICK,** Baron, *cr* 1964 (Life Peer); **Frank Beswick,** PC 1968; JP; Chief Opposition Whip, House of Lords, since 1970; *b* 1912; *m* Dora, *d* of Edward Plumb; one *s* one *d*. Joined RAF, 1940; Transport Command (despatches). MP (Lab Co-op.) Uxbridge Div. of Middlesex, 1945-Oct. 1959. PPS to Under-Sec. of State for Air, 1946-49; Parly Sec., Min. of Civil Aviation, 1950-Oct. 1951. UK Govt Observer, Bikini Tests, 1946; Delegate UN General Assembly, 1946. Formerly: Chm., Parly Labour Party Civil Aviation Sub-Cttee; Chm., Co-operative Party Parly Group; a Lord-in-Waiting, 1965; Parly Under-Sec. of State in CO, 1965-67; Captain, Hon. Corps of Gentlemen at Arms, and Govt Chief Whip, House of Lords, 1967-70. Vice-Pres., British Air Line Pilots Assoc., 1965. JP Co. of London, 1963. *Address:* 28 Skeena Hill, SW18.

**BETHE, Prof. Hans Albrecht,** PhD; John Wendell Anderson Professor of Physics, Cornell University, USA; Professor of Theoretical Physics since 1937; *b* Strassburg, Germany, 2 July 1906; *m* 1939, Rose Ewald; one *s* one *d*. *Educ:* Goethe Gymnasium, Frankfurt on Main; Univs of Frankfurt and Munich. PhD Munich, 1928. Instructor in Theoretical Physics, Univs of Frankfurt, Stuttgart, Munich and Tübingen, 1928-33; Lectr, Univs of Manchester and Bristol, England, 1933-35; Asst Prof., Cornell Univ., Ithaca, 1935-37. Dir, Theoretical Physics Div. of Los Alamos Atomic Scientific Laboratory, 1943-46. Sabbatic leave to Cambridge Univ., academic year, 1955-56. Mem., President's Science Adv. Cttee, 1956-59. Member: Nat. Acad. Science; Amer. Physical Soc.; Amer. Astron. Soc.; For. Mem., Royal Society. Holds hon. Doctorates in Science. US Medal of Merit, 1946; Planck Medal, German Physical Soc., 1955; Eddington Medal, Royal Astronomical Soc., 1961; Enrico Fermi Award, US Atomic Energy Commn, 1961; Nobel Prize for Physics, 1967. *Publications:* (jt author) Elementary Nuclear Theory, 1947; Mesons and Fields, 1955; Contributions to: Handbuch der Physik, 1933, 1954; Reviews of Mod. Physics, 1936-37; Physical Review. *Address:* Laboratory of Nuclear Studies, Cornell University, Ithaca, NY, USA.

**BETHELL,** family name of **Barons Bethell** and **Westbury.**

**BETHELL,** 4th Baron *cr* 1922, of Romford; **Nicholas William Bethell;** Bt 1911; a Lord in Waiting (Government Whip, House of Lords), since 1970; freelance writer; *b* 19 July 1938; *s* of Hon. William Gladstone Bethell (*d* 1964) (3rd *s* of 1st Baron), and of Ann Margaret Bethell (*née* Barlow, now Thornycroft); *S* kinsman, 1967; *m* 1964, Cecilia Mary, *er d* of Prof. A. M. Honeyman, *qv*; two *s*. *Educ:* Harrow; Pembroke Coll., Cambridge. On editorial staff of Times Literary Suplement, 1962-64; a Script Editor in BBC Radio Drama, 1964-67. *Publications:* Gomulka: his Poland and his Communism, 1969; (trans.) Six Plays by Slawomir Mrozek, 1967; (trans.) Elegy to John Donne by Joseph Brodsky, 1967; (trans., with David Burg) Cancer Ward, 1968, and The Love-Girl and the Innocent, 1969, by Alexander Solzhenitsyn, 1968; dramatic works for radio and TV; occasional reviews for Times Literary Supplement. *Recreation:* poker. *Heir:* *s* Hon. James Nicholas Bethell, *b* 1 Oct. 1967. *Address:* Cranbourne Court, Windsor Forest, Berkshire. *T:* Winkfield Row 2921; Villa Domino, Tangier, Morocco. *Club:* Garrick.

**BETHUNE, Sir Alexander Maitland Sharp,** 10th Bt (NS), *cr* 1683; *b* 28 March 1909; *o s* of late Alexander Bethune, JP, DL, of Blebo, Cupar, 9th Bt of Scotscraig, and Elisabeth Constance Carnegie (*d* 1935), 3rd *d* of Frederick Lewis Maitland Heriot, of Ramonie, Fife; *S* father, 1917; *m* 1955, Ruth Mary, *d* of J. H. Hayes; one *d*. *Educ:* Eton; Magdalene Coll., Cambridge. *Address:* 21 Victoria Grove, W8.

**BETJEMAN, Sir John,** Kt 1969; CBE 1960; CLit 1968; poet and author; *b* 1906; *s* of late E. E. Betjeman; *m* 1933, Penelope Valentine Hester (author, as Penelope Chetwode, of Two Middle-aged Ladies in Andalusia, 1963), *d* of Field-Marshal Lord Chetwode, GCB, OM, GCSI; one *s* one *d*. *Educ:* Marlborough; Oxford. UK Press Attaché, Dublin, 1941-42; Admiralty, 1943. A Royal Fine Art Commissioner; Mem. Roy. Commn on Historical Monuments (England) 1969-. A Governor of Pusey House, Church of England. Hon. LLD (Aberdeen); Hon. DLitt (Reading, Birmingham); Hon. ARIBA. *Publications:* Mount Zion; Ghastly Good Taste, 1933; Continual Dew; An Oxford University Chest; Shell Guides to Cornwall and Devon, and (with John Piper) Shropshire; Antiquarian Prejudice; Old Lights for New Chancels; Selected Poems, 1948 (Heinemann Award); First and Last Loves, 1952; A Few Late Chrysanthemums, 1954 (Foyle Poetry Prize);

Collected Poems, 1958 (Duff Cooper Prize; Foyle Poetry Prize; Queen's Gold Medal for Poetry, 1960): Summoned By Bells (verse autobiography), 1960; High and Low (poems), 1966; (ed with John Piper): Buckinghamshire Guide, 1948; Berkshire Guide, 1949; (ed with late Geoffrey Taylor): An Anthology of Landscape Verse; English Love Poems; English Churches (with Basil Clarke), 1964; (ed) Pocket Guide to English Parish Churches, 1968; Victorian and Edwardian London, 1969. *Address:* The Mead, Wantage, Berks. *Clubs:* Beefsteak; Kildare Street (Dublin).

**BETTLEY, F(rancis) Ray,** TD 1945; FRCP; Physician for Diseases of the Skin, Middlesex Hospital, London, since 1946; Physician, St John's Hospital for Diseases of the Skin, London, since 1947; formerly Dean, Institute of Dermatology, British Postgraduate Medical Federation; Lieutenant-Colonel RAMC, TARO; *b* 18 Aug. 1909; 2nd *s* of late Francis James Bettley; *m* 1951, Jean Rogers, 2nd *d* of late Archibald Barnet McIntyre; one *s* one *d*(and one adopted *d*). *Educ:* Whitgift Sch., Croydon; University Coll., London; University Coll. Hosp. Medically qualified, 1932; MD 1935; FRCP 1948. Gazetted RAMC TA, 1932; Resident House-appointments, 1932-33; Radcliffe-Crocker Student (Vienna, Strasbourg), 1936; Hon. Dermatologist to Cardiff Royal Infirmary, 1937; various military hosps in UK and Middle East, 1939-44; Dermatologist and Venereologist, E Africa Comd, 1944-45. Malcolm Morris Lectr, 1959 and 1970; Watson Smith Lectr (RCP), 1960; Hon. or Corresp. Mem. of dermatological assocs of: Belgium, Denmark, France, Holland, India, Israel, Poland, USA, Venezuela. *Publications:* Skin Diseases in General Practice, 1949; Editor, British Jl of Dermatology, 1949-59; medical papers in various medical jls. *Recreation:* painting. *Address:* 19 Harley Street, W1. *T:* 01-580 1851; Manor Cottage, Newton Valence, Alton, Hants. *Clubs:* Athenæum. MCC.

**BETTS, Alan Osborn,** PhD, MA, BSc, MRCVS; Principal and Dean, The Royal Veterinary College, since Oct. 1970; *b* 11 March 1927; *s* of A. O. and D. S. A. Betts; *m* 1952, Joan M. Battersby; one *s* one *d*. *Educ:* Royal Veterinary Coll.; Magdalene Coll., Cambridge. Asst in Gen. Practice, 1949; Animal Health Trust Research Scholar, 1950-52; Demonstrator, Univ. of Cambridge, 1952-56; Commonwealth Fund Fellow, Cornell Univ. of Cambridge, 1952-56; Commonwealth Fund Fellow, Cornell Univ., USA, 1955-56; University Lectr, Cambridge, 1956-64; Prof. of Veterinary Microbiology and Parasitology, Univ. of London, 1964-70. Treasurer, British Veterinary Assocn, 1967-70. *Publications:* Viral and Rickettsial Infections of Animals, 1967; papers in microbiological and veterinary jls. *Recreations:* travel, gardening. *Address:* Redwall, Shenley Hill, Radlett, Hertfordshire. *T:* Radlett 5541.

**BETTS, Edward William;** journalist and critic; *b* London, 27 March 1881; *e s* of late Edward Betts, London and Tunbridge Wells; *m* 1904, Elizabeth Annie (*d* 1945), 2nd *d* of late William West, Tunbridge Wells. *Educ:* privately. Began journalistic career on Kent and Sussex Courier; afterwards on editorial staff of Sussex Daily News; Actg Ed., Malton Gazette, 1904-12; Asst Ed. and Dramatic Critic, Birmingham Gazette, 1912-19; Asst London Editor and Dramatic Critic, Birmingham Gazette and associated papers, 1919-21; Dramatic and Film Critic, Westminster Gazette, 1921-28; Editor, The Era, to 1939; Associate Editor, Daily Film Renter, retd 1951. Mem. of Council, Critics' Circle; contributor to Daily Telegraph, Stage, Weekly Westminster, Theatre and Stage, and other periodicals on theatrical and kinema subjects. *Recreations:* music, seeing and reading plays. *Address:* 6 Watford Road, Northwood, Middx. *T:* Northwood 25410. *Club:* National Liberal.

**BETTS, Prof. James Anthony;** Professor of Fine Art, University of Reading, 1934-63; Emeritus since 1963; *b* 28 Dec. 1897; *s* of James and Ellen Betts; *m* 1925, Nellie Serena Flexen; one *s*. *Educ:* St Stephens, Skipton; Bradford Coll. of Art; Royal College of Art. Head, Sch. of Painting, Sheffield Coll. of Art, 1926-30; Principal, Kingston-on-Thames Sch. of Art, 1930-34. *Address:* Norfolk House, 28 Kidmore Road, Caversham, Reading, Berks. *T:* Reading 71600. *Club:* Athenæum.

**BETTS, Rt. Rev. Stanley Woodley,** CBE 1967; Dean of Rochester, since Oct. 1966; *b* 23 March 1912; *yr s* of Hubert Woodley and Lillian Esther Betts. *Educ:* Perse Sch.; Jesus Coll., Cambridge. MA 1937. Curate of St Paul's Cheltenham, 1935-38; Chaplain, RAF, 1938-47 (despatches); Sen. Chaplain of BAFO, Germany, 1946-47; Comdt, RAF Chaplains' Sch., Dowdeswell Court, 1947; Chaplain, Clare Coll., Cambridge, 1947-49; Chaplain, Cambridge Pastorate, 1947-56; Proctor in Convocation, 1952-59; Vicar of Holy Trinity Cambridge, 1949-56; Exam. Chaplain to Bishop of Southwell, 1947-56; Select Preacher to University of Cambridge, 1955; Suffragan Bishop of Maidstone, 1956-66; Archbishop of Canterbury's Episcopal Representative with the three Armed Forces, 1956-66. Chm. Governors, King's Sch., Rochester; Vice-Chm., Lee Abbey Council; Member: Archbishops' Council of Evangelism; Council, Christ Church Coll., Canterbury; Council, Wadhurst Coll. *Address:* The Deanery, Rochester, Kent. *T:* Medway 44023; 2 Kings' Houses, Old Pevensey, Sussex. *Club:* National.

**BETUEL, Herbert William Norman;** Assistant Legal Officer, Foreign Compensation Commission, since 1965; *b* Johannesburg, 9 July 1908; *s* of Leon Louis Betuel, solicitor and advocate of self-governing Colony of the Transvaal (as it was then known), and Christina Ferran, *d* of a planter, both of Port Louis, Mauritius; *m* 1938, Kathleen Harriette Meredith Welsh, Dublin. *Educ:* Ecole Publique St Julien, Marseilles; Wandsworth Technical Coll., University Tutorial Coll., University Coll., London; Gray's Inn, London. Lee Prizeman, Gray's Inn, 1932; Barrister, 1933; LLB, London, 1934. Magistrate, 1939, Chief Magistrate, 1953, Nigeria; Judge of the High Court of Eastern Nigeria, 1958-65, retd. Chm. Arbitral Tribunal (arrears of overtime among Maritime Workers), 1941. Fellow, Royal Commonwealth Soc. (formerly Royal Empire Soc.), 1939; FRSA 1969. *Recreations:* walking, travelling, literature, history and Contract Bridge. *Address:* 28 Ashfield Road, W3. *T:* 01-743 7439. *Clubs:* Gray's Inn, Royal Commonwealth Society.

**BEVAN, Rt. Hon. Mrs Aneurin;** *see* Lee, Rt Hon. Jennie.

**BEVAN, Cecil Wilfrid Luscombe,** CBE 1965; Principal, University College, Cardiff, since 1966; *b* 2 April 1920; *s* of Benjamin Cecil Bevan and Maud Luscombe; *m* 1944, Elizabeth Bondfield, *d* of Henry Dale Bondfield; four *s*. *Educ:* University Coll. of Wales, Aberystwyth; University Coll., London. BSc Wales 1940; PhD London 1949; FRIC 1957. Served Royal Welch Fusiliers and Nigeria Regt, 1940-46 (despatches). Univ. of Exeter, 1949-53; Prof. and Head of Dept of Chemistry, Univ. of Ibadan, 1953-66, Vice Principal and Dep. Vice-

Chancellor, 1960-64. Chm., Conciliation Cttee for Wales and the South West, Race Relations Board. Member: Welsh Council; Council, University Coll., Cape Coast, Ghana. Fellow UCL, 1969. *Publications:* papers, mainly in Jl of Chemical Soc., 1951-. *Recreation:* fishing. *Address:* University College, Cathays Park, Cardiff. *Clubs:* Athenæum, Oxford and Cambridge University; Cardiff and County.

**BEVAN, Sir David Martyn E.;** *see* Evans Bevan.

**BEVAN, John Henry,** CB 1945; MC 1917; company director; *b* 5 April 1894; *y s* of late David Augustus Bevan and late Hon. Dame Maud Bevan, DBE; *m* 1927, Lady Barbara Bingham (*d* 1963), *d* of 5th Earl of Lucan, PC, GCVO, KBE, CB; one *s* two *d*. *Educ:* Eton Coll.; Christ Church, Oxford. Served European War, 1914-19, with the Herts Regt; Capt., 1916; Major, 1918; TARO General List, recalled, 1939. *Address:* 92 Arlington House, Arlington Street, SW1. *T:* 01-629 2656. *Club:* Brooks's.

**BEVAN, John Sage;** Managing Director, The Union-Castle Mail Steamship Co. Ltd, 1956-65; *b* 29 Nov. 1900; *er s* of E. H. Bevan, Southampton; *m* 1953, Lilian Ellen, *d* of C. Channing, Exeter; no *c*. *Educ:* King Edward VI Sch., Southampton. Joined Union-Castle Co., 1917; Chairman's Private Sec., 1932; Asst Head, Freight Dept, 1934; Asst Manager, 1946; Asst Man. Dir, 1953; Dep. Man. Dir, 1955. Ministry of Shipping and War Transport, 1939-46. Chairman: South and East African Confs, 1954-66; London General Shipowners Soc. Cttee, 1958-60; Member: Port of London Authority 1958-67 (Chm., Docks and Warehouse Cttee, 1964-67); Old Edwardians Assoc. (Pres., 1959-60, and Chm., London Br.); Governor, King Edward VI Sch., Southampton. Mem., House Cttee, Royal Devon and Exeter Hosp. Hon. Mem., Baltic Mercantile and Shipping Exchange. FCIS. *Recreations:* gardening, walking, reading. *Address:* Redlands, Rewe, Exeter, Devon. *T:* Stoke Canon 329. *Club:* Royal Commonwealth Society.

**BEVAN, Rt. Rev. Kenneth Graham;** Warden of Readers, and Assistant Bishop of Wakefield, since 1968; *b* 27 Sept. 1898; *s* of late Rev. James Alfred Bevan, MA; *m* 1927, Jocelyn Duncan Barber; three *d*. *Educ:* The Grammar Sch., Great Yarmouth; London Coll. of Divinity. Deacon, 1923; Priest, 1924; Curate of Holy Trinity, Tunbridge Wells, 1923-25; Missionary, Diocese of Western China, 1925-36, Diocese of Eastern Szechwan, 1936-40; Bishop of Eastern Szechwan, 1940-50; Vicar of Woolhope, 1951-66; Rural Dean, Hereford (South) 1955-66; Prebendary de Moreton et Whaddon, Hereford Cathedral, 1956-66; Master of Archbishop Holgate's Hosp., Wakefield, 1966-68. *Address:* Archbishop Holgate's Hospital, Hemsworth, Yorks. *T:* Hemsworth 610434.

**BEVAN, Lawrence Emlyn Douglas,** CBE 1960; banker; *b* 7 Jan. 1903; *o s* of late Herbert Spencer Bevan and late Jennie Douglas, *d* of Gen. J. R. Williams; unmarried. *Educ:* Lancing. Entered Barclays Bank Ltd as junior clerk, 1922, and after serving various capacities apptd a local Dir at 54 Lombard Street, 1929; Director, 1938; Vice-Chm., 1961-68. director: Barclays Bank SA; Barclays Bank (London & International) Ltd; National Provident Instn (Chm., 1953-67); Banque de Bruxelles; Credit Congolais; Courage, Barclay & Simonds Ltd; Yorkshire Bank Ltd; and other Companies. Pres., St Peter's, St Paul's and St Philip's Hospitals Board; Treas., British Post-graduate Medical Federation and Queen's Inst. of District Nursing. Officers' Emergency Reserve, 1938; commissioned Scots Guards, 1940; Staff Capt., London District, 1941. Officier de la Couronne (Belgium), 1966. *Recreations:* fishing, gardening. *Address:* Troston Cottage, Bury St Edmunds, Suffolk. *Clubs:* Carlton, Guards, White's, Pratt's.

**BEVAN, Percy Archibald Thomas,** CBE 1958; BSc, CEng, FIEE, FIEEE; The Chief Consultant Engineer, Independent Television Authority, 1966-68 (Chief Engineer, 1954-66); retired 1968; now independent broadcasting and telecommunications consultant; *b* 8 Jan. 1909; *s* of late Albert James Bevan, Abertillery, and Florence Violet Perkins, Worcester. *Educ:* Newport Grammar Sch.; University Coll. and Welsh Coll. of Advanced Technology, Cardiff. Graduate Apprentice, British Thomson-Houston Company, Rugby, 1930-34; Senior Engineer, Transmitter Development, BBC, 1934-46; Consultant, Cambridge Cavendish Laboratory Cyclotron, 1940-43; Senior Television Engineer, Planning and Construction, BBC, 1946-50; The Senior Planning Engineer, BBC, 1950-54. Member: PMG's Television Advisory Cttee (Techn. Sub-Cttee); PMG's Frequency Advisory Cttee; PMG's Advisory Cttee on Wireless Interference, 1955-68; UK Rep., Internat. Radio Consultative Cttee, 1955-68; Member: UK Space and Radio Research Station Adv. Cttee, 1960-68; European Broadcasting Union Techn. Cttee, 1955-68; Internat. Colour Television Cttee, 1963-68. Mem. of Council and Chm. Electronics Bd, IEE, 1967-68; Chm., Prof. Group for Sound and Television Broadcasting, 1962-66. Awarded Duddell Premium of IEE, 1951. Fellow, Royal Television Soc.; Hon. Fellow, British Kinematograph and Television Soc., 1967. *Publications:* many technical and scientific papers in the radio and television broadcasting field. *Recreations:* motor sport, photography, country life. *Address:* 40 Roehampton Close, Roehampton Lane, SW15. *T:* 01-876 4302; Little Thatch, Thorn Common, Toat, near Pulborough, W Sussex. *T:* Pulborough 2700.

**BEVAN, Rear-Adm. Sir Richard Hugh Loraine,** KBE 1946; CB 1942; DSO 1916; MVO 1923; DL Glos., 1946; *b* 10 July 1885; *s* of late Capt. Eustace B. L. Bevan, Royal West Kent Regt, and Mary, *d* of late Rev. Dr G. W. Hill, for many years Vicar of Halifax, NS, and *g s* of late Richard Lee Bevan, Brixworth Hall, Northampton; *m* 1934, Frances Anne Beckford, *o* surv. *d* of late Algernon Beckford Bevan, JP, Bury St Edmunds. *Educ:* Foster's, Stubbington House; Britannia. Midshipman in Implacable, 1901-04; Sub-Lieut in Drake, 1905-06; Lieut in Aboukir, 1907-09; Signal Sch., and in command of TBD Express, 1911; Lieut of HMS Medina when their Majesties went to Bombay for Durbar; Flag-Lieut to Vice-Adm. Sir Rosslyn Wemyss in Orion, 1912-13, and on his staff during the European War; promoted Commander, 1918; Capt., 1923; landed at Cape Helles in charge of signal stations during occupation of Gallipoli; present at evacuation of Suvla and Anzac (DSO); Comdr HM Yacht Victoria and Albert, 1921-23; Flag Capt. Africa Station, 1923-26; Naval Attaché to HM Missions in Italy, Greece, etc, 1928-31; commanded HMS York, 1932-33; comdg HM Signal Sch., Portsmouth, 1934-35; Rear-Adm. and retired list, 1935; rejoined Navy, 1939; Naval Attaché, Rome, Feb.-June 1940; Senior British Naval Officer, North Russia, 1941-42; Flag Officer, in charge Northern Ireland, 1942-45. County Councillor, Glos, 1949; County Alderman, 1952. Order of the Nile, 4th Class, 1917; Legion of Honour, Chevalier, 1918; Officer of Legion of Merit (USA), 1946. *Address:*

Greylands, Minchinhampton, Glos. *T:* Brimscombe 3215.

**BEVAN, Robert Alexander Polhill,** CBE 1963 (OBE 1941); Chairman, S. H. Benson Ltd, 1954-64; *b* 15 March 1901; *s* of late Robert Polhill Bevan and late Stanislawa, *d* of Alexander de Karlowski; *m* 1946, Natalie, *d* of Court Denny. *Educ:* Westminster (King's Scholar); Christ Church, Oxford (Scholar). Joined S. H. Benson Ltd, 1923. Dir of General Production, Ministry of Information, 1940; RNVR 1940-45; Dep. Chief of Naval Information, Washington, 1944-45; UK representative on UN Cttee on Public Information, 1958. Member: Advisory Council on Middle East Trade, 1958-63; Export Publicity Council, 1959-63; National Advisory Council on Art Education, 1960-64; Advertising Standards Authority, 1962-66. FIPA (Pres., 1961). *Recreations:* sailing, travel. *Address:* Boxted House, Colchester, Essex. *T:* Boxted 254. *Clubs:* Garrick, Royal Ocean Racing.

**BEVAN, Timothy Hugh;** Vice-Chairman, Barclays Bank Ltd, since 1968; *b* 24 May 1927; *y s* of Hugh Bevan and Pleasance (*née* Scrutton); *m* 1952, Pamela, *e d* of Norman Smith and late Margaret Smith; two *s* two *d*. *Educ:* Eton. Lieut Welsh Guards. Called to Bar, 1950. Joined Barclays Bank Ltd, 1950: Local Dir 1957; Dir 1957; Dir 1966. Mem., Council of Foreign Bondholders; Dir, London Adv. Board, Bank of New South Wales; Governor, St Peter's, St Paul's and St Philip's Hosps, 1961-70; Mem., Institut International d'Etudes Bancaires. *Recreations:* sailing, gardening. *Address:* Tyes Place, Staplefield, Haywards Heath, Sussex. *T:* Handcross 367. *Clubs:* Guards, Royal Ocean Racing; Royal Yacht Squadron.

**BEVERIDGE, William Ian Beardmore,** MA Cantab; DVSc Sydney; Professor of Animal Pathology, Cambridge, since 1947; Fellow of Jesus College; *b* 1908; *s* of J. W. C. and Ada Beveridge; *m* 1935, Patricia, *d* of Rev. E. C. Thompson; one *s*. *Educ:* Cranbrook Sch., Sydney; St Paul's Coll., University of Sydney. Research bacteriologist, McMaster Animal Health Laboratory, Sydney, 1930-37; Commonwealth Fund Service Fellow at Rockefeller Inst. and at Washington, 1938-39; Walter and Eliza Hall Inst. for Medical Research, Melbourne, 1941-46; Visiting Worker, Pasteur Inst., Paris, 1946-47; Vis. Prof., Ohio State Univ., 1953; Guest Lectr, Norwegian Veterinary Sch., 1955. Consultant, WHO, Geneva, 1964-70. Chm. Permanent Cttee of the World Veterinary Assoc., 1957-. DVM (*hc*) Hanover, 1963; Hon. Assoc. RCVS, 1963; Hon. Foreign Mem., Académie Royale de Médicine de Belgique, 1970. *Publications:* The Art of Scientific Investigation, 1950; articles on infectious diseases of man and domestic animals and comparative medicine, in scientific jls. *Address:* Jesus College, Cambridge; 15 Montpelier Place, SW7. *T:* 01-589 3344. *Club:* Athenæum.

**BEVERLEY, Frank;** Barrister-at-law, North-Eastern Circuit; Recorder of Bradford, 1926-55; *o s* of late Walter Beverley, Barrister-at-law, Bramley, Leeds; *m* 1934, Lucy, *d* of late Norman McDougall, Winnipeg, *widow* of Allan J. Kerr, Quebec. *Educ:* Shrewsbury; LLB London Univ. Called to Bar, 1908; served European War, Capt. RGA, France, Flanders, Italy (MC, Italian Croce di Guerra). *Recreations:* fly-fishing, motoring, empire travel. *Address:* Low Hall, Travers Farm Road, St Brelade, Jersey, CI.

**BEVERLEY, Vice-Adm. Sir (William) York (La Roche),** KBE 1952 (CBE 1947); CB 1949; *b* 14 Dec. 1895; *s* of Major W. H. Beverley; *m* 1931, Maria Teresa Matilde (*d* 1957), *d* of Enrico Palazio, Santa-Margherita-Ligure, Italy; one *s* one *d* (and one *s* decd). *Educ:* Royal Naval Colls, Osborne and Dartmouth. Served throughout European War, 1914-18, and War of 1939-45; ADC to the King, 1947-48; Admiral Supt, Portsmouth, 1949-51; Vice-Adm., 1950; Dir of Dockyards, 1951-54, retired Dec. 1954. *Address:* c/o National and Grindlays Bank Ltd, 13 St James's Square, SW1. *Club:* Bath.

**BEVERLEY, Vice-Adm. Sir York;** *see* Beverley, Vice-Adm. Sir W. Y. La R.

**BEVINGTON, Eric Raymond,** CMG 1961; Appeals Inspector, Ministry of Housing and Local Government, since 1967; *b* 23 Jan. 1914; *s* of late R. Bevington and N. E. Bevington (*née* Sutton); *m* 1939, Enid Mary Selina (*née* Homer); one *d*. *Educ:* Monkton Combe Sch.; Loughborough Coll.; Queens' Coll., Cambridge. CEng, MIMechE. Cadet, HM Overseas Service, Gilbert and Ellice Islands, 1937; District Officer, Fiji, 1942; Sec., Commn of Enquiry into Cost of Living Allowances, Nigeria, 1945-46; Admin. Officer Cl I, Fiji, 1950; Asst Col Sec. (Devel.), Fiji, 1951; Devel. Comr, Brunei, 1954; Financial Sec., Fiji, 1958-61, Development Commissioner, 1962-63; Mem., Executive Council, Fiji, 1958-63. *Recreations:* golf, sailing. *Address:* Holmans, Bisterne Close, Burley, Hants. *T:* Burley 3316. *Club:* National Liberal.

**BEVINS, Rt. Hon. John Reginald,** PC 1959; *b* 20 Aug. 1908; *e s* of John Milton and Grace Eveline Bevins, Liverpool; *m* 1933, Mary Leonora Jones; three *s*. *Educ:* Dovedale Road and Liverpool Collegiate Schs. Served War of 1939-45; gunner, 1940; Major, RASC, 1944; MEF and Europe. Mem. Liverpool City Council, 1935-50. Contested West Toxteth Div., 1945, and Edge Hill (bye-election), 1947; MP (C) Toxteth Div. of Liverpool, 1950-64; PPS to the Minister of Housing and Local Government, 1951-53; Parliamentary Sec., Ministry of Works, 1953-57, Ministry of Housing and Local Govt, 1957-59; Postmaster-General, 1959-64. *Publication:* The Greasy Pole, 1965. *Address:* 37 Queen's Drive, Liverpool 18.

*See also K. M. Bevins.*

**BEVINS, Kenneth Milton,** TD 1951; Chief General Manager (and Director), Royal Insurance Co. Ltd; Director: British Aviation Insurance Co. Ltd; Fire Protection Assoc. (Past Chm.); Mutual & Federal Insurance Holdings Ltd; Trade Indemnity Co. Ltd; Watling Street Properties Ltd; *b* 2 Nov. 1918; *yr s* of late John Milton Bevins and late Grace Eveline Bevins, Liverpool; *m* 1940, Joan Harding (*d* 1969); two *d*. *Educ:* Liverpool Collegiate Sch. Joined Royal Insurance Co. Ltd, 1937. Served War, 1939-46: 136 Field Regt, RA, incl. with 14th Army in Burma, 1943-46 (Major). Sec., Royal Ins. Co. Ltd, 1957; Gen. Manager, 1963; Dep. Chief Gen. Manager 1966; Chief Gen. Manager and Dir, 1970. Member: Jt Fire Research Organisation Steering Cttee, 1966-68; Home Secretary's Standing Cttee on Crime Prevention, 1967-; Dep. Chm., British Insurance Assoc., 1967-. *Address:* St Patrick's, Bessels Green, near Sevenoaks, Kent. *T:* Sevenoaks 54065; 136 Whitehall Court, Whitehall Place, SW1. *T:* 01-930 3160.

*See also Rt Hon. J. R. Bevins.*

**BEVIR, Sir Anthony,** KCVO 1952 (CVO 1946); CBE 1944; *b* 7 Nov. 1895; 4th *s* of late Ernest

Bevir, Hendon; *m* 1935, Noël Sidney, *d* of late Dominick Sidney Browne, Breaghwy, Co. Mayo. *Educ:* Eton; Hertford Coll., Oxford. Served European War, 1915-18, 7th Bn King's Liverpool Regt (despatches twice); Colonial Office, 1921-39; Private Sec. to Rt Hon. W. G. A. Ormsby Gore, Parly Under-Sec. of State for the Colonies, 1926-29; Sec. to Colonial Office Conference, 1930; Asst Sec., War Cabinet Office, 1939; Private Sec. to Rt Hon. Neville Chamberlain, 1940, Rt Hon. Winston Churchill, 1940-45, Rt Hon. C. R. Attlee, 1945-51, Rt Hon. Winston Churchill, 1951-55, Rt Hon. Anthony Eden, 1955-56; Sec. for Appointments to the Prime Minister, 1947-Feb. 1956. *Recreation:* reading. *Address:* Blenaskill Lodge, Achill Sound, Co. Mayo. *Clubs:* United University; Kildare Street (Dublin).

**BEWICK, Herbert;** barrister-at-law; *b* 4 April 1911; *s* of late James Dicker and Elizabeth Jane Bewick. *Educ:* Whitehill Secondary Sch., Glasgow; Royal Grammar Sch., Newcastle upon Tyne; St Catharine's Coll., Cambridge. Called to Bar, Gray's Inn, Nov. 1935. Recorder of Pontefract, 1961-67. Chm. of Industrial Tribunal (Newcastle upon Tyne), 1967-. *Address:* 81 St Mary's Place, Newcastle upon Tyne 1. *T:* Newcastle 24519; 27 Mitchell Avenue, Jesmond, Newcastle upon Tyne NE2 3JY. *T:* Newcastle 811138.

**BEWICKE-COPLEY;** family name of Baron Cromwell.

**BEWLEY, William Fleming,** CBE 1935; DSc; VMH; Scientific Horticultural Consultant since 1956; *b* Newcastle upon Tyne, 1891; *s* of late William Bewley, Maryport, Cumberland; *m* Olive Mary, *d* of late Richard Price, MBE, Woolwich; one *d*. *Educ:* Univ. of Durham. Served overseas in Royal Field Artillery during European War. Dir of Experimental and Research Station, Cheshunt, 1921; Dir of Glasshouse Crops Research Inst., Littlehampton, from its inception, 1954-56, retired. Veitch Memorial Gold Medal, RHS, 1956. *Publications:* Diseases of Glasshouse Plants; The Cultivation of Mushrooms; Commercial Glasshouse Crops; Science has Green Fingers; various publications on horticulture and related sciences in scientific journals and the Press. *Recreations:* local government (RD and Parish Councils), golf, fishing. *Address:* Brayton, The Thatchway, Angmering, Sussex. *T:* Rustington 3836.

**BEYEN, Dr Johan Willem;** banker and diplomat, Netherlands; Chairman, Wm H. Müller & Co., Rotterdam; *b* 2 May 1897; *m* 1922; two *s* one *d*; *m* 1945, Margaretha Antonia Lubinka. *Educ:* Utrecht, Holland. Treasury of the Netherlands, 1918-23; Legal Adviser, Phillips Incandescent Lamp Works, Eindhoven, Holland, 1924-25; representative at Amsterdam of Javasche Bank, Batavia, Dutch East Indies, 1925-27; Man. Dir, Rotterdamsche Bankvereeniging, 1927-35. Alternate Pres. of Bank for International Settlements, Basle, 1935-37, Pres., 1937-40; Director: Lever Bros and Unilever Ltd, 1940-46; Flag Investment Co; Irish Investment Co.; formerly Executive Dir, International Bank for Reconstruction and Development; Executive Dir, Internat. Monetary Fund, Washington, DC. Minister of Foreign Affairs, Netherlands, 1952-56; Netherlands Ambassador in Paris, 1958-63. *Publications:* Money in a Maelstrom (New York) 1949, (London) 1950; Helspel en de Knikkus (Rotterdam), 1968. *Address:* Ridderlaan 14, Wassenaar, Holland. *Club:* Witte Societeit (The Hague).

**BEYNON, Albert Gwyn;** Chief Veterinary Officer, Ministry of Agriculture, Fisheries and Food, since 1970; *b* 11 Feb. 1908; *s* of Daniel and Jane Beynon; *m* 1935, Margaret Markillie, Diss, Norfolk; one *s* one *d*. *Educ:* Llanelli Gram. Sch.; Royal Veterinary College, London; Manchester Univ. Joined Animal Health staff of Min. of Agric., Fisheries and Food, 1932; Divisional Veterinary Officer, 1938-52; Regional Vet. Off. for Wales, 1952-60; Dep. Chief Vet. Off., 1960-64; Director of Vet. Field Service, 1965-70. Pres., Brit. Vet. Assoc., 1961-62. Dalrymple-Champneys Award, for services to animal welfare and health both nationally and internationally, 1967. *Publications:* several contribs to veterinary jls on animal disease and control. *Recreations:* travel, golf, gardening. *Address:* Oaks Cottage, 6 Oaks Way, Tattenham Corner, Epsom, Surrey. *T:* Burgh Heath 50461. *Club:* Royal Automobile Country (Epsom).

**BEYNON, Ven. James Royston;** Archdeacon of Winchester since 1962; *b* 16 Sept. 1907; *s* of James Samuel and Catherine Beynon; *m* 1933, Mildred Maud Fromings; four *d*. *Educ:* St Augustine's Coll., Canterbury. LTh Durham. Ordained, 1931; Chaplain, Indian Eccl. Estabt, 1933; Senior Chaplain: Peshawar, 1941; Quetta, 1943; Archdeacon of Lahore, 1946-48; Vicar of Twyford, Winchester, 1948; Rural Dean of Winchester, 1958-62. Hon. CF 1945. *Address:* Twyford Vicarage, Winchester, Hants. *T:* Twyford 2208.

**BEYNON, Prof. William John Granville,** CBE 1959; PhD, DSc; Professor of Physics, University College of Wales, Aberystwyth, since 1958; *b* 24 May 1914; *s* of William and Mary Beynon; *m* 1942, Megan Medi, *d* of Arthur and Margaret James; two *s* one *d*. *Educ:* Gowerton Grammar Sch.; University Coll., Swansea. Scientific Officer, later Senior Scientific Officer, National Physical Laboratory, 1938-46; Lecturer, later Senior Lecturer in Physics, University Coll. of Swansea, 1946-58. *Publications:* (ed) Solar Eclipses and the Ionosphere, 1956; (ed) Proceedings Mixed Commission on the Ionosphere, 1948-58; numerous publications in scientific jls. *Recreations:* music, cricket, tennis, Rugby. *Address:* Bryn Eithin, Brynhir, Dunvant, Swansea. *T:* 23585.

**BHAGAT, Maj.-Gen. Premindra Singh,** VC 1941; psc 1945; Divisional Commander, Indian Army; *b* 14 Oct. 1918; *s* of S. S. Bhagat, ISE; *m* 1942, Mohini, *d* of Col M. G. Bhandari; one *s* one *d*. *Educ:* Royal Indian Mil. Coll. and Indian Mil. Acad., Dehra Dun. Under Officer in 1939. Joined Royal Bombay Sappers and Miners as Company Officer and proceeded overseas, 1940; served with Indian Divs in Abyssinia, Eritrea and North Africa (VC). Has held staff appts including: Commandant, Royal Bombay Sappers and Miners; Dep. Commandant and Chief Instructor, Staff Coll., Wellington; Brigade Comdr; Dir of Military Intelligence; Commandant, Indian Military Academy; Chief of Staff. *Publications:* Forging the Shield, 1965; contributions to The Statesman (Indian newspaper). *Recreations:* tennis, squash, golf, shooting. *Address:* c/o Indian Military Academy, Dehra Dun, India.

**BHUTTO, Zulfikar Ali,** HPk; politician and lawyer, Pakistan; Founder and Chairman, Pakistan People's Party, since 1967; *b* Larkana, Jan. 1928; *s* of late Sir Shahnawaz Khan Bhutto; *m*; two *s* two *d*. *Educ:* Univ. of California, Berkeley (grad. Hons Pol. Sci.); Christ Church, Oxford (MA with dist. Jurisprudence). Called to Bar, Lincoln's Inn, 1953. Lectr in Internat. Law, Univ. of

Southampton, 1952; Legal Practice, West Pakistan High Court, Karachi, 1953-58; taught Constitutional Law, Sind Muslim Law Coll., Karachi, 1956-58. Minister for Commerce, Pakistan, 1958-60; Minister of Minority Affairs and Nat. Reconstruction and Information, 1960-62, also of Fuel, Power and Nat. Resources and of Kashmir Affairs, April 1960-62; and of Industries and Natural Resources, 1962-63; Minister for Foreign Affairs and Atomic Energy, 1963-66; returned to legal profession, 1966. Mem. Pakistan Delegn to Gen. Assembly, UN, 1957; Leader of various Delegns and Special Missions, including UN Conf. on Law of the Sea, Geneva, 1958, and UN General Assembly, 1959, 1960 and 1963. Hilal-i-Pakistan, 1964; holds foreign orders. *Publication:* The Myth of Independence, 1969. *Recreations:* studies and big game. *Address:* Al-Murtaza, Larkana, Pakistan.

**BIANCHI, Rt. Rev. Lorenzo;** Bishop of Hong Kong, (RC), 1951-69; Pontifical Foreign Mission Institute (PIME) of Milan; *b* Corteno (Prov. Brescia, Italy), 1 April 1899. Ordained, 1922; consecrated Coadjutor Bishop of Hong Kong, 1949. *Address:* c/o Bishop's House, 16 Caine Road, Hong Kong.

**BIBBY, Major Sir (Arthur) Harold,** 1st Bt *cr* 1959; Kt 1956; DSO 1917; DL; LLD (Hon.) Liverpool; President, Bibby Line Ltd; *b* 18 Feb. 1889; *s* of late Arthur Wilson Bibby; *m* 1920, Marjorie, *d* of late Charles J. Williamson and The Lady Royden; one *s* three *d* (and one *s* decd). Educ: Rugby. Served in RFA (TF), 1908-19; in France and Flanders, 1915-18 (despatches twice, DSO awarded on field of Cambrai). Senior Partner, Bibby Bros & Co., Shipowners and Bankers; Chm., Bibby Line Ltd, 1935-69; Director: Sea Insurance Co. Ltd, 1922-68 (Chm., 1930-56); Liverpool & London Steamship Protection & Indemnity Association, 1921-68; Martins Bank Ltd, 1929-67 (Chm., 1947-62); Suez Canal Co., 1939-57; Member: Mersey Docks & Harbour Board, 1931-65; Governing Body of Rugby Sch., 1932-67; Chairman: Liverpool Steam Ship Owners' Association, 1927 and 1958 (Centenary Year); Employers' Association of Port of Liverpool, 1938-47; Vice-Chm., National Assoc. of Port Employers, 1941-47; Jt Vice-Chm., General Council of British Shipping, 1958-59; President: Training Ship Indefatigable (Chm., 1931-60); Liverpool Sailors' Home (Chm., 1921-51); Liverpool Conservative Assoc., 1959-66; Northwich Conservative Association. DL, Chester, 1937; High Sheriff of Cheshire, 1934-35. Hon. Freeman, City of Liverpool, 1970. *Recreation:* shooting. *Heir:* *s* Derek James Bibby, MC [*b* 29 June 1922; *m* 1961, Christine Maud, *d* of late Rev. F. J. Okell; four *s* one *d*]. *Address:* Tilstone Lodge, Tarporley, Cheshire. *Clubs:* Bath; Palatine (Liverpool).

**BIBBY, Dr Cyril;** Principal of Kingston upon Hull College of Education since 1959; *b* 1914; *s* of William and Elizabeth Jane Bibby, Liverpool; *m* 1936, Frances (Florence Mabel) Hirst, Mddx; two *s* two *d*. *Educ:* Liverpool Collegiate Sch.; Queens' Coll., Cambridge. Open Major Scholar in natural sciences, 1932; Coll. Prizeman, 1933; Icelandic expedn, 1934; BACantab, 1935. Physics and Chemistry Master, Oulton Sch., Liverpool, 1935-38; Scientific research, Univ. of Liverpool, 1935-40; MACantab, 1939; Sen. Biology Master, Chesterfield Grammar Sch., 1938-40; MSc Liverpool, 1940. Educn Officer to Brit. Social Hygiene Council and then Central Council for Health Educn, 1941-46; Tutor in Biol. (becoming Co-ordinator of Sciences and Sec. to Academic Bd), Coll. of S Mark and S John, London, 1946-59; educl, etc, research, 1947-59. Visiting Prof., Univ. of Illinois, 1950; PhD London, 1955; Silver Medal of RSA, 1956. Visiting Lecturer at several Univs in USA (also investigatory visits for US Nat. Science Foundn, 1962). Delegate to many internat. congresses, etc., 1947-64. At various periods, Mem. Executive of: Internat. Union of Family Organisations; Fraternité Mondiale; Assoc. of Teachers in Colls and Depts of Educn; Council of Christians and Jews; Eugenics Soc., Nat. Foundn for Educl Research; Soc. for Research into Higher Educn; School Broadcasting Council of UK, etc. Many political activities. FLS, 1942; FRSA, 1954. *Publications:* Evolution of Man and His Culture, 1938; Heredity, Eugenics and Social Progress, 1939; Experimental Human Biology, 1942; Simple Experiments in Biology, 1943; Sex Education, 1944; How Life is Handed On, 1946; Healthy and Happy, 1948; Healthy Day, 1949; Active Human Biology, 1950; Health Education, 1951; Healthy People, 1954; Human Body, 1955; T. H. Huxley, 1959; Race, Prejudice and Education, 1959; Essence of T. H. Huxley, 1968; Biology of Mankind, 1968; Scientist Extraordinary, 1970. Papers in various scientific, health, educl, political, sociological and gen. lit. jls. *Recreations:* reading, writing, walking, sun-bathing, film, theatre, travel. *Address:* 246 Cottingham Road, Hull. *T:* Hull 407815; (College) Hull 41451. *Club:* Westfield Country (Cottingham, E Yorks).

**BIBBY, Samuel Leslie,** CBE 1947 (OBE 1945); DL; *b* 19 Jan. 1897; *s* of Samuel Gawith Bibby, Sutton, Surrey; *m* 1923, Eva Margaret Wood, *d* of Dr G. Benington Wood, Sandown, IoW; one *s* one *d* (and one *s* decd). *Educ:* Malvern. Served European War, 1915-18, Capt. RA(TA) (despatches). Col TA, 1943; Comd 6th (Leatherhead) Bn Surrey Home Guard, 1940-43; Comdt Surrey Army Cadet Force, 1943-49; Chm. Army Cadet Force Sports Council, 1940-49; Military Mem. Surrey T&AFA, 1940-49. DL 1955; High Sheriff of Surrey, 1959. *Address:* Villans Wyk, Headley, Surrey. *T:* Headley 252; Lairg Lodge, Sutherland. *T:* Lairg 4. *Clubs:* Bath, Gresham, MCC.

**BICESTER,** 3rd Baron *cr* 1938, of Tusmore; **Angus Edward Vivian Smith;** *b* 20 Feb. 1932; *s* of Lt-Col Hon. Stephen Edward Vivian Smith (*d* 1952) (2nd *s* of 1st Baron) and Elenor Anderson, *d* of Edward S. Hewitt, New York City; *S* uncle, 1968. *Educ:* Eton. *Heir:* *b* Hugh Charles Vivian Smith, *b* 8 Nov. 1934.

**BICKERSTETH, Rev. Edward Monier,** OBE 1962; MA; *b* 20 Nov. 1882; *e s* of late Rev. Samuel Bickersteth, DD; *m* 1911, Inez Katharine (*d* 1936), 3rd *d* of late Rev. Dr G. E. Jelf; two *s* two *d*. *Educ:* Rugby; Christ Church, Oxford; Wells Theological Coll. Deacon, 1907; Priest, 1908; Curate, Lambeth Parish Church, 1907-09; Bedale, 1909-10; Leeds Parish Church, 1910; Rector, Castle Bromwich, 1911-15; Sec. of Jerusalem and the East Mission, 1915-35; Rector, Chiddingstone, 1935-50; Hon. Canon Rochester, 1946-50; Rector of The Orchestons, Salisbury, 1950-59; Commissary to Archbishop in Jerusalem, Bishop in Egypt and Bishop in the Sudan; Ed. of Bible Lands, 1930-63; Hon. Canon, St George's Collegiate Church, Jerusalem, from 1953. *Address:* Ivy House, Worton, Devizes, Wilts. *T:* Devizes 3727.

*See also Bishop of Warrington.*

**BICKERSTETH, Geoffrey Langdale;** Emeritus Professor in the University of Aberdeen; *b* 1884; 2nd *s* of late Rev. Samuel Bickersteth, DD; *m* 1918, Jean, *d* of late Prof. W. R. Sorley; one *s* two *d* (and two *s* decd). *Educ:* Charterhouse (scholar); Christ Church,

Oxford, BA (2nd class Lit Hum), 1907; MA 1910. Asst master, Marlborough Coll., 1909-13; studied philology, Munich and Heidelberg universities, 1913-14; on staff of War Trade Intelligence Dept, 1915-18; Naval Staff, ID, 1918-19; Senior Lecturer in English Language and Literature, Glasgow Univ., 1919-38; Regius (Chalmers) Prof. of English Literature, Aberdeen Univ., 1938-54; Taylorian Lectr, Oxford Univ., 1933; W. P. Ker Lectr, Glasgow Univ., 1950. Hon. LLD (Aberdeen), 1955. Commenda. Ord. al Merito della Repub. Ital., 1960. *Publications:* Carducci, a selection of his poems, with verse translations and three introductory essays, 1913; The Poems of Leopardi, edited with introduction and notes and verse translation in the metres of the original, 1923; Leopardi and Wordsworth, 1927; The Paradiso of Dante Alighieri, with a translation into English triple rhyme, 1933; Form, Tone and Rhythm in Italian Poetry, 1934; The Golden World of King Lear, 1947; Dante's Virgil, 1951; Dante's Divine Comedy trans. into English triple rhyme, 1955; the same, facing Ital. text, 1965. *Address:* 2 St Martin's Square, Chichester. *T:* Chichester 82520.

**BICKERSTETH, John Burgon,** MC, 1918; MA; FSA; *b* 1888; 4th *s* of late Rev. Samuel Bickersteth, DD. *Educ:* Charterhouse; Christ Church, Oxford; University of Paris. Gained Blue for Association football, 1908 (Capt., Oxford Univ. AFC 1910-11); in Western Canada as mem. of the Archbishop's Mission, 1911-13; served European War with The Royal Dragoons, 1914-19 (MC and Bar); on staff of University of Alberta, 1919-21; Warden of Hart House, University of Toronto, 1921-47; served War of 1939-45; Personal Asst and Adviser (Educn) to GOC Canadian Corps and then to GOC-in-C First Canadian Army, 1940-42; Dir of Army Education, War Office, 1942-44. Hon. LLD Toronto. *Publications:* The Land of Open Doors (Letters from Western Canada); The History of the 6th Cavalry Brigade. *Address:* 11a The Precincts, Canterbury, Kent. *Club:* Travellers'.

**BICKERSTETH, Rt. Rev. John Monier;** *see* Warrington, Suffragan Bishop of.

**BICKERTON, John Myles;** Wing Commander RAFVR (retired); late Surgeon Lieutenant RN; late Ophthalmic Surgeon, King's College Hospital; London Specialist; Ophthalmic Surgeon, Denham; Chairman, Bickerton's Aerodromes Ltd; *b* 1894; *y s* of Thomas Herbert and Mary Jessie Bickerton, Liverpool; *m* 1st, 1926, Margaret Alsager, *d* of Col Hawdon; one *s* four *d*; 2nd, 1936, Eva Griffiths; one *d*. *Educ:* Leas Sch., Hoylake; Leighton Park, Reading; Pembroke Coll., Cambridge; King's Coll. Hosp. (Burney Yeo Scholar). MRCS, LRCP, 1919; BA (Hons), BCh Cantab, 1919; FRCS 1923; MA Cantab, 1924. Late Ophthalmic Surg., King's Coll. Hosp.; late Ophthalmic Consultant, LCC, Board of Education; Ophthalmic Surg., Royal Eye, St Olave's and Lewisham Hosps and Dean Royal Eye Hosp.; Surg. Prob. RNVR, 1916-17, HMS Lawford and Sybille; Surg. Lieut RN, HMS Royal Oak, 1918-19; Surgical Specialist to Sir R. Houston Bt Yacht Cruise, 1921. *Publications:* Clinical Ophthalmology, 1933; A Modern Treatment of Squint, 1934; Welfare of the Blind and National Economy, BMJ, 1932; The Inheritance of Blindness, Eugenics Review 1932 and 1933; Eye Diseases in General Practice, Med. Press, 1935; The Bespectacled Pilot and the Air Forces, Aeroplane, 1937. *Recreations:* ski-ing, flying. *Address:* Owls Oak, Denham, Bucks. *T:* Denham 2060. *Clubs:* Denham Golf, Denham Aero (Denham).

**BICKFORD SMITH, John Roger,** TD 1950; Master of Supreme Court, Queen's Bench Division, since 1967; *b* 31 Oct. 1915; *er s* of late Leonard W. Bickford Smith, Camborne, Cornwall, For. Man., ICI, and of Anny Grete (*née* Huth); *m* 1939, Cecilia Judge Heath, *er d* of W. W. Heath, Leicester; two *s*. *Educ:* Eton (King's Schol.); Hertford Coll., Oxford (Schol.). BA 1937; MA 1952. Commnd in Duke of Cornwall's LI (TA), 1939; served 1939-46: UK, India, Burma and Germany; Dept of JAG, India, 1940-44; AJAG (Major), 1942; Lieut-Col 1944; Legal Div., Control Commn for Germany, 1945-46; SO1 (Lieut-Col). Called to Bar, Inner Temple, 1942. Practised at Common Law Bar in London and on Midland Circuit, 1946-67. *Publications:* The Crown Proceedings Act 1947, 1948; various articles in legal jls. *Recreation:* foreign travel. *Address:* Royal Courts of Justice, WC2. *Clubs:* United Service, Bath.

**BICKLEY, Francis (Lawrance);** author; *b* London, 11 June 1885; *o s* of Francis Bridges Bickley, late Asst Keeper of MSS, Brit. Mus.; *m* Nora Magdalen, MBE (*d* 1962), *y d* of Comdr Edward Phillips Statham, RN. *Educ:* Merchant Taylors' Sch. Sub-editor, Victoria County Histories, 1905-08; Editor under Historical MSS. Commission from 1910; War Trade Intelligence Dept, 1915-19; Postal Censorship Dept, 1939-45 (Bermuda, 1940-44). *Publications:* Kings' Favourites, 1910; The Cavendish Family, 1911; Matthew Arnold and his Poetry, 1911; The Story of Marie Antoinette, 1911; Where Dorset Meets Devon, 1911; John Millington Synge and the Irish Dramatic Movement, 1912; The Life of Matthew Prior, 1914; The Adventures of Harlequin, 1923; Lord Maida Vale, 1932; The Pre-Raphaelite Comedy, 1932; The Leiths of Harthill, 1937; (Ed) An English Letter Book, 1925; True Dialogues of the Dead, 1925; Diaries of Sylvester Douglas, Lord Glenbervie, 1928; various reports for Historical MSS. Commission; contributions to the Quarterly, Punch, etc, dictionary of National Biography, Encyclopædia Britannica, etc. *Address:* Charterhouse, EC1.

**BICKNELL, Claud,** OBE 1946; a Law Commissioner since 1970; *b* Rowlands Gill, near Newcastle upon Tyne, 15 June 1910; 2nd *s* of Raymond Bicknell and Phillis Bicknell (*née* Lovibond); *m* 1st, 1934, Esther Irene (*d* 1958), *e d* of Kenneth Bell; one *s* three *d*; 2nd, 1960, Christine Betty Reynolds. *Educ:* Corchester Prep. Sch., Corbridge on Tyne; Oundle Sch.; Queens' Coll., Cambridge (Scholar). Law Tripos, Pts I and II; BA 1931, MA 1936. Articled to A. L. Bird, Solicitor, Newcastle upon Tyne, 1931-34; admitted as a solicitor, 1934; Asst Solicitor, 1934-39, and partner, 1939-70, in firm of Stanton, Atkinson & Bird, Newcastle upon Tyne. Dir, Northern Corporation Ltd, 1939-53. Auxiliary Fire Service, Newcastle upon Tyne, 1939-41; Nat. Fire Service, 1941-45; Sen. Fire Staff Officer, Home Office, 1943-45. Mem. Planning Bd, Lake District Nat. Park, 1951-70 (Chm., Development Control Cttee, 1957-70); Mem. Lord Jellicoe's Cttee on water resources in the North-West, 1964; Newcastle upon Tyne Incorporated Law Society: Hon. Sec., 1966-70; Vice-Pres., 1967; Pres., 1969; Chm., Newcastle upon Tyne Housing Improvement Trust Ltd, 1966-70. *Recreation:* mountains. *Address:* 20 Millers Court, Chiswick Mall, W4. *Clubs:* United University, Alpine; Achilles.

**BICKNELL, Mrs T. W.;** *see* Tushingham, Rita.

**BIDAULT, Georges;** *b* 1899. Before war of 1939-45 was a professor of history and edited L'Aube, the journal of the Christian

Democrats; served in the ranks, was taken prisoner but freed after 18 months; became chm. of the resistance council inside France; Minister for Foreign Affairs in Provisional Govts of 1944 and 1945; Premier and Foreign Minister, France, 1946; Minister of Foreign Affairs, 1947-48; Premier, 1949-50; Vice-Premier of France, 1950 and 1951, and Minister of National Defence, 1951-52; Minister of Foreign Affairs, Jan.-July 1954. Delegate to Council of Europe, 1949. *Publications:* D'une Résistance à l'autre, 1965 (Resistance: the political autobiography of Georges Bidault, 1967); Le Point, 1968. *Address:* 21 rue du Colonel Moll, Paris 17e, France.

**BIDDULPH,** family name of **Baron Biddulph.**

**BIDDULPH,** 3rd Baron *cr* 1903; **Michael William John Biddulph;** *b* 6 March 1898; *e s* of 2nd Baron and Marjorie Caroline Susan (*d* 1961), *d* of Col W. Mure, Caldwell; *S* father, 1949; *m* 1925, Lady Amy Agar, *d* of 4th Earl of Normanton; two *s* two *d*. *Educ:* Eton; RMC Sandhurst. Late Lieut Coldstream Guards. *Recreations:* fishing, golf, shooting, tennis. *Heir:* *s* Hon. Robert Michael Christian Biddulph [*b* 6 Jan. 1931; *m* 1958, Lady Mary Maitland, *e d* of late Viscount Maitland (*o s* of 15th Earl of Lauderdale), and of Viscountess Maitland, Chelsea; two *s* one *d*]. *Address:* Under Down, Ledbury, Herefordshire. *TA:* Ledbury. *T:* Ledbury 2669. *Club:* Kennel.

**BIDDULPH, Sir Francis (Henry),** 9th Bt *cr* 1664; Grazier, Queensland; *b* Mount Playfair, 8 June 1882; *s* of late Walter John Biddulph and Harriette Sophia Biddulph (*née* Foot); *S* kinsman, Sir Theophilus George Biddulph, 8th Bt, who died 1948 (the title became dormant in that year; succ. proved, 1956); *m* 1907, Janet (*d* 1956), *d* of late Walter Bain Hannah, Brisbane; two *s* (one *d* decd). *Educ:* Mount Playfair. *Heir:* *er s* Stuart Royden Biddulph [*b* 24 June 1908; *m* 1939, Muriel Margaret, 3rd *d* of Angus Harkness, Hamley Bridge, S Australia; one *s* two *d*]. *Address:* Mount Playfair, Tambo, Queensland, Australia. *T:* 4.9U Tambo.

**BIDGOOD, John Claude;** Chairman: Anglo-Dominion Finance Co. Ltd; Anglo-Dominion Construction Co. Ltd; Anglo-Dominion Trading Co. Ltd; *b* 12 May 1914; *s* of late Edward Charles Bidgood, Leeds; *m* 1945, Sheila Nancy Walker-Wood; one *s* two *d*. *Educ:* London Choir Sch.; Woodhouse Technical Sch. Served early part of War of 1939-45 as Pilot RAF. Mem. Leeds City Council, 1947-55 (late Chm. Works Cttee and City Architects Cttee); contested (C) N E Leeds, 1950, 1951; MP (C) Bury and Radcliffe, 1955-64; PPS to Joint Parly Secs, Min. of Pensions and Nat. Insurance, 1957-58; Mem. Parly Select Cttee on Estimates, 1958-64. Director: Bidgood Holdings Ltd; Edward Bidgood & Co. Ltd; Bidgood Larsson Ltd; Wright & Summerhill Ltd; R. Horsfield & Co. Ltd; Constructional Erection Ltd; Leeds & County Conservative Club House Co. Ltd; Bidgood Larsson (Iraq) Ltd; Chm., Yorks Assoc. for the Disabled, 1950-58; Member: Inst. of Export; Leeds and Bradford Joint Aerodrome Cttee, 1951-55; W Riding Rating Valuation Court, 1955. Governor, Bury Grammar Schs, 1955. Freeman, City of London; Liveryman, Worshipful Co. of Horners; Mem., Hon. Soc. of Knights of Round Table. *Recreations:* music, travel. *Address:* Linton, Wetherby, Yorks. *T:* Wetherby 2791. *Clubs:* City Livery, Junior Carlton, Royal Aero, Pathfinder; Leeds and County Conservative (Leeds).

**BIDWELL, Sydney James;** MP (Lab) Southall since 1966; *b* Southall, 14 Jan. 1917; *s* of late Herbert Emmett Bidwell; *m* 1941; one *s* one *d*. *Educ:* Elementary sch., evening classes. Railway worker; Tutor and Organiser, Nat. Coun. of Labour Colls. Mem., Southall Bor. Council, 1951-55. Contested (Lab): E Herts, 1959; Herts SW, 1964. Lectr, including for London Co-op. Social Educn Dept. Mem., Parly Select Cttee on Race Relations and Immigration. *Publications:* articles on TU and Labour history. *Recreations:* watching soccer, sketching, water-colours. *Address:* House of Commons, SW1. *Club:* Southall Labour.

**BIERER, Joshua,** MD, DEcon and Soc Sc (Vienna), Dipl Indiv Psych; Medical Director, Institute of Social Psychiatry since 1946; Consultant Psychiatrist, Runwell Hospital, since 1948; Founder and Medical Director, Marlborough Day-Hospital, since 1946; Editor-in-Chief, International Journal of Social Psychiatry and British Journal of Social Psychiatry; *b* 1 July 1901; *s* of Dr Josef Bierer, X-Ray specialist. *Educ:* Vienna Univ. Training in Individual Psychology by Prof. Alfred Adler and Dr A. Neuer (Vienna), 1926-28; Training-Analysis by Dr A. Neuer; private practice as Psychotherapist, 1927-; Lectr, Teaching Inst. of Individual Psychology, Berlin, 1928-29; Research: at Inst. of Physiology, Vienna Univ., 1933; in Psychotherapy and Psychiatry at Mental Hosp., Vienna Univ., 1934-36; at Runwell Hosp., Essex, 1938-40. Psychotherapist, Southend Gen. Hosp. and East Ham Memorial Hosp., 1939-43; Clinical Asst, Guy's Hosp., 1942-44; Visiting Psychotherapist, Runwell Mental Hosp., 1942-44 and 1946-48. Served as Specialist Psychiatrist, Major RAMC, 1944-46. Originated idea of Self-Governed Therapeutic Social Clubs, Day Hosps, Night and Week-end Hosps, and Therapeutic Community Hostels; Founder mem. and Pres. of NN (Neurotics *nomine*). Co-Founder, Kibbutz Mishmar Haemek, Israel. *Publications:* (jt) Innovation in Social Psychiatry; The Day-Hospital, 1951; (ed) Therapeutic Social Clubs; pioneer research work in problems of social psychiatry, social psychotherapy, group psychotherapy, treatment of psychotics in mental hosps and in out-patient depts by psychotherapy in Jl of Mental Science, Lancet, Brit. Med. Jl, etc. *Recreations:* golf, swimming, tennis, table tennis, chess, bridge. *Address:* 140 Harley Street, W1. *T:* 01-935 2440; (home) 7 Hollycroft Avenue, NW3. *T:* 01-435 3144. *Club:* Garrick.

**BIFFEN, William John;** MP (C) Oswestry Division of Shropshire since Nov. 1961; *b* 3 Nov. 1930; *s* of Victor W. Biffen; unmarried. *Educ:* Dr Morgan's Grammar Sch., Bridgwater; Jesus Coll., Cambridge (BA). Worked in Tube Investments Ltd, 1953-60; Economist Intelligence Unit, 1960-61. *Address:* Middle Farm, Kinton, Nesscliffe, Salop.

**BIGG, Wilfred Joseph,** CMG 1948; *b* 20 July 1897; 2nd *s* of late Joseph Henry Bigg; *m* 1925, Ivy Lillian Daniel; three *d*. *Educ:* Bournemouth Sch. Entered GPO 1912. Served European War, 1914-19. Entered Colonial Office, 1919; Private Sec. to Permanent Under Sec., Dominions Office, 1930-31; returned to Colonial Office, June 1931; Asst Sec., 1943; retired 1957. Member: Commonwealth Shipping Cttee, 1952-57; Bd of Governors, Coll. of Aeronautics, 1955-58; Commonwealth Telecommunications Board, 1955-62. *Recreations:* gardening, motoring. *Address:* Headley, 35 Manwell Road, Swanage, Dorset. *T:* Swanage 2603. *Club:* Civil Service.

**BIGGART, Sir John Henry,** Kt 1967; CBE 1948; DSc, MD; FRCP, FRCPath; Director of

Institute of Pathology, Queen's University, Belfast, since 1948; also Dean of Faculty of Medicine since 1943, Professor of Pathology since 1937, Pro-Vice-Chancellor since 1968; *b* 17 Nov. 1905; *s* of John Henry Biggart and Mary Gault; *m* 1934, Mary Isobel Gibson, Knock, Belfast; one *s* one *d*. *Educ:* Royal Belfast Academical Instn; Queen's Univ., Belfast; Johns Hopkins Medical Sch. MB (Hons) 1928; MD (Gold Medal), 1931; DSc 1937; MRCP 1952; FRCP 1957; FCPath 1964; Hon. FRCPI 1969. Commonwealth Fellowship, Johns Hopkins, 1931-33; Pathologist to Scottish Asylums Board, 1933-37; Lecturer in Neuropathology, Edinburgh Univ., 1933-37; Regional Dir, Blood Transfusion Service, 1939-46. Robert Campbell Orator, 1948; Mem., University Senate, 1948; Chm., Laboratory Services Cttee, Hospitals Authority, 1948-54; Chm., Medical Education and Research Cttee, Hospitals Authority, 1950-64; Gen. Med. Coun., 1951; Gen. Dental Coun., 1959; Chm., Standing Med. Adv. Cttee, Min. of Health, NI, 1967-; Council, Brit. Empire Cancer Campaign, 1968; Council, Coll. of Pathologists, 1968. MD (*hc*) Dublin, 1957. *Publications:* Text Book of Neuropathology, 1936; papers on general and nervous pathology in Brain, Jl Pathology and Bacteriology, Ulster Med. Jl, and Johns Hopkins Bulletin. *Recreations:* reading, writing, gardening, music. *Address:* 64 King's Road, Belfast. *T:* Belfast 653107.

**BIGGE, Sir John Amherst S.;** *see* Selby-Bigge.

**BIGGS, Christopher Thomas Ewart E.;** *see* Ewart-Biggs.

**BIGGS, Vice-Adm. Sir Hilary Worthington,** KBE 1958; CB 1955; DSO 1940 (Bar 1941); RN retired; *b* 15 Jan. 1905; *s* of late Lieut-Col C. W. Biggs; *m* 1934, Florence, *d* of late Adm. of the Fleet Sir Roger Backhouse, GCB, and of Lady Backhouse, MBE; two *s* two *d*. *Educ:* RNC Osborne and Dartmouth. Midshipman, 1923; Sub-Lieut 1925; Lieut 1926; Lieut-Comdr 1934; Comdr 1938; Capt. 1943; Rear-Adm. 1952; Vice-Adm. 1956. War Service: HMS Revenge (Exec. Officer), 1939-40; HMS Hero (in command), 1940-42, Norwegian Campaign and Mediterranean; Admiralty, 1942-44; Capt.(D) 11th Destroyer Flotilla, Eastern Fleet, 1944-45; Deputy Chief of Naval Personnel (Personal Services), 1953-55; Flag Officer, Home Fleet Training Squadron, 1955-56; Comdr-in-Chief, East Indies Station, 1956-58. *Address:* Hill House, Meonstoke, Southampton SO3 1NH. *T:* Droxford 409.

*See also Brig. M. W. Biggs.*

**BIGGS, Sir Lionel (William),** Kt 1964; JP; solicitor and notary public; *b* 28 May 1906; *s* of William Henry Moore Biggs and Lilian (*née* Bush); *m* 1934, Doris Rose, *d* of late William Davies; one *s*. *Educ:* Manchester Gram. Sch. Admitted Solicitor, 1929; Notary Public, 1934. Served Royal Air Force, 1940-45 (despatches). Mem., Manchester City Council, 1936- (served as Chm., Development, Airport and Watch Cttees); JP 1949; Alderman, 1958; Lord Mayor of Manchester, 1961-62. Chm., Aerodrome Owners' Assoc. of Gt Brit., 1955; Director, Caledonian Insurance Co. (Manchester Bd). *Recreations:* gardening, swimming. *Address:* Eagle Cottage, Alderley Park, via Macclesfield, Ches. *T:* Alderley Edge 3135. *Club:* St James's (Manchester).

**BIGGS, Brig. Michael Worthington,** CBE 1962 (OBE 1944); MICE; Manager, Hatfield and Welwyn Garden City, Commission for New Towns, since 1967; *b* 16 Sept. 1911; *s* of late Lt-Col Charles William Biggs, OBE, Cheltenham and late Winifred Jesse Bell Biggs (*née* Dickinson); *m* 1940, Katharine Mary, *d* of late Sir Walter Harragin, CMG, QC, Colonial Legal Service, and of Lady Harragin; two *d*. *Educ:* Cheltenham Coll.; RMA Woolwich; Pembroke Coll., Cambridge. MA (Cantab) 1966; AMICE 1967. 2nd Lieut RE, 1931; served War of 1939-45, E Africa, Abyssinia (Bde Major), and Burma (GSO1 and CRE); Lt-Col 1942; Col 1954; Mil. Adviser to High Comr, Australia, 1954-57; Brig. 1960; Chief of Staff, E Africa Comd, 1960-62; Dir of Quartering (Army), MoD, 1963-66; retd, 1966. Group Building Exec., Forte's (Holdings) Ltd, 1966-67. *Publications:* contribs to RE Jl and Army Quarterly (winner Bertram Stewart Prize Essay twice). *Recreations:* lawn tennis, golf, gardening. *Address:* Bylands House, Redbourn, Herts. *T:* Redbourn 2532. *Club:* Army and Navy.

*See also Vice-Adm. Sir H. W. Biggs.*

**BIGGS, Norman Parris;** Chairman, Esso Petroleum Company, Ltd, since 1968; Director: Esso Europe Inc.; Esso Africa Inc.; The National Bank Ltd; Gillett Bros Discount Co. Ltd; *b* 23 Dec. 1907; *s* of John Gordon Biggs and Mary Sharpe Dickson; *m* 1936, Peggy Helena Stammwitz; two *s* one *d*. *Educ:* John Watson's Sch., Edinburgh. Bank of England, 1927-46; Dir, Kleinwort Sons & Co. Ltd, 1946-52; Dir, Esso Petroleum Company, Ltd, 1952-66; Vice-Pres., Finance, Esso Europe Inc., 1966-67. Late Chm. Council, Hansard Soc. for Parly Govt. *Recreations:* enjoyment of the arts and landscapes. *Address:* 8 Sussex Square, W2. *T:* 01-723 0141. *Club:* American.

**BIGGS-DAVISON, John Alec;** MP (C) Chigwell Division of Essex since 1955 (Ind C 1957-58); *b* 7 June 1918; *s* of Major John Norman Biggs-Davison, RGA, retd; *m* 1948, Pamela Mary, 2nd *d* of late Ralph Hodder-Williams, MC; two *s* four *d*. *Educ:* Clifton (scholar); Magdalen Coll., Oxford (exhibitioner, MA). Royal Marines, 1939, Lieut 1940; served in RM Brigade and RM Division. Indian Civil Service: Asst Comr, 1942; Forward Liaison Officer, Cox's Bazar, 1943-44; Sub-Divisional Officer, Pindi Gheb, 1946; Political Asst and Comdt, Border Military Police, subsequently Dep. Comr, Dera Ghazi Khan, during and after transfer of Power to Dominion of Pakistan, 1947; retired from Pakistan Administrative Service, 1948. Conservative Research Dept, 1950-55; Sec., Brit. Conservative Delegn to Council of Europe, 1952, 1953. Contested (C) Coventry South, 1951. co-founder Pakistan Soc., 1951. Indep. observer of Malta Referendum, 1956. Mem. Parly Delegations: West Africa, 1956; Guernsey, 1961; Austria, 1964; France, 1965; Canada (Inter-Parly Union Conf.), 1965; Malawi, 1968; Tunisia, Gibraltar, 1969. Chm., Brit. Commonwealth Union; Vice-Pres., Pan-European Union. *Publications:* George Wyndham, 1951; Tory Lives, 1952; The Uncertain Ally, 1957; The Walls of Europe, 1962; Portuguese Guinea: Nailing a Lie, 1970; contribs to Royal Central Asian Jl and many other periodicals. *Recreations:* reading, riding, tennis, walking (Gold Medal London-Brighton Pacesetters' Walk, 1963). *Address:* 35 Hereford Square, SW7. *T:* 01-373 2924; Green Farm Cottage, Stapleford Tawney, Essex.

**BIGHAM,** family name of **Viscount Mersey** and of **Baroness Nairne.**

**BIGNALL, John Reginald,** FRCP; Physician, Brompton Hospital, since 1957; Hon. Consultant in Diseases of the Chest, Royal Marsden Hospital, since 1958; *b* 14 Oct. 1913; *s* of Walter and Nellie Bignall; *m* 1939, Ruth Thirtle; one *s* three *d*. *Educ:* Nottingham High Sch.; St John's Coll. Cambridge; London hospital. MA 1938; MD 1947; FRCP 1961. Served in RAMC, 1941-46, Middle East and Mediterranean (Major). Editor of Tubercle, 1956-. *Publications:* various articles on diseases of the chest. *Address:* Berry Barton, 8 Engliff Lane, Pyrford, Woking, Surrey. *T:* Byfleet 42603. *Club:* Athenæum.

**BIGNOLD, Sir (Charles) Robert,** Kt 1938; DL Norfolk; JP Norwich; *b* 22 Aug. 1892; *s* of Charles Arthur Bathurst-Bignold, DL, JP; *m* 1919, Ethel, *d* of late W. H. Dale, Kensington. *Educ:* Charterhouse. Capt. 4th Bn Norfolk Regt; Lord Mayor of Norwich, 1925-26; sometime Leader and Chm. of Norwich Conservative Association; Hon. Life Governor, Norwich Union Insurance Socs; Past President: Norwich Union Life Insurance Society; Norwich Union Fire Insurance Soc.; Scottish Union and Nat. Insurance Co.; Chm., Securicor (Southern) Ltd; Dir, Anglia Television Ltd. *Address:* Flat 1, Gwydyr Mansions, Holland Road, Hove 2, Sussex. *Clubs:* Constitutional; Norfolk County (Norwich); Royal Thames Yacht.

**BIKANER, Maharaja of; HH Maharaja (Dr Karni Singhji Bahadur);** MP Indian Parliament; *b* 21 April 1924; *e s* of late Lt-Gen. HH Maharaja Sri Sadul Singhji Bahadur of Bikaner, GCSI, GCIE, CVO; *S* father, 1950; *m* 1944, Princess Sushila Kumari, *d* of the Maharawal of Dungapur, *qv*; one *s* two *d*. *Educ:* St Stephen's Coll., Delhi; St Xavier's Coll., Bombay. BA (Hons) (History and Politics); PhD (thesis) Bombay Univ., 1964. Visited Middle East War Front in Nov. 1941 with his grandfather, Maharaja Sri Ganga Singhji Bahadur. Insignia Grand Commander: Order of Vikram Star (Bikaner), Order of Sadul Star (Bikaner), Order of Star of Honour (Bikaner); Africa Star; War Medal; India Service Medal; Arjun Award for Shooting, 1961. Has travelled extensively in Europe, Egypt, USA, Mexico, Honolulu and Far East, etc. Elected to House of People (Parliament of India) as an Independent, 1952; re-elected for 2nd and 3rd terms; elected 4th time, 1967, with largest margin (193816) in the country, serving on various consultative cttees of different ministries. Mem., Asiatic Soc. of India; Mem., Bombay Natural History Soc. *Recreations:* tennis; shooting (National Champion in clay pigeon traps and skeet; rep. India, clay pigeon shooting, Olympic Games: Rome, 1960, Tokyo, 1964, Mexico, 1968; World Shooting Championships: Oslo, 1961, Cairo (Capt.), 1962, Wiesbaden, 1966, Japan (1st Asian), 1967, Bologna, 1967; Mexico, 1968, San Sebastian, Spain, 1969; golf; flying (qualified for private pilot's licence); cricket; mechanics; photography; social service. *Address:* Lallgargh Palace, Bikaner, Rajasthan (India). *Clubs:* Willingdon Sports, Cricket Club of India, Bombay Flying, Bombay Presidency Golf, Western India Automobile Association (Bombay); Roshanara, Delhi Flying, Delhi Gymkhana, Delhi Golf (Delhi); Rajputana (Abu), etc.

**BILAINKIN, George;** diplomatic correspondent; author; lecturer; *b* 12 Feb. 1903; *m* 1940, Dr Lilian Rivlin (marr. diss., 1949); one *d*. *Educ:* Haberdashers' Aske's Sch., NW; Athenée Royal, Belgium. Joint News Ed., Jamaica Daily Gleaner, 1924-25; Special Writer, Leicester Mail, 1925-27; Sub-Ed., Press Association, 1927-29; Ed., Straits Daily Echo, Penang, 1929-30, and Times Correspondent in N Malaya; Asst Literary Ed., Daily Mail, 1934-36; Editorial Staff, News-Chronicle, 1936-38; Diplomatic Correspondent, Allied Newspapers, 1938-40; Special Correspondent, Russia, 1942, for The Star, London, and American newspapers. Special mission to Paris, Berlin, Prague, and Belgrade for Daily Mail, 1945. Delivered 120 lectures in British Univs, clubs, prisons, schools, on Europe, early in 1946. Since then has visited various personalities and countries every year, from Petsamo to Tierra del Fuego. Contributed since 1920 to Encyclopædia Britannica and leading newspapers and reviews. *Publications:* Lim Seng Hooi, 1930; Hail Penang, 1932; Within Two Years, 1934; Front Page News–Once, 1937; Changing Opinions, 1938: Poland's Destiny, 1939; Diary of a Diplomatic Correspondent, 1942; Maisky (a biography), 1944; Second Diary of a Diplomatic Correspondent, 1947; Four Weeks in Yugoslavia, 1948; Tito (a biography), 1949; Cairo to Riyadh Diary, 1950; Destination Tokyo, 1965; Four Guilty Britons, 1971; Kennedy's Fateful Embassy, 1971. *Recreations:* listening; playing with chow-chow and bull-terrier puppies; major diplomatic receptions; reforming the world. Aversions: cats, chain-smokers, solicitors, interrupters, trains. *Address:* 12 Regency Close, Sheerness, Kent. *T:* Sheerness 4808. *Club:* Royal Commonwealth Society.

**BILL, Commander Robert,** DSO 1940; FRICS; FRGS; RN, retired 1955; Principal Officer (Hydrographic), Nigerian Ports Authority; *b* 1 April 1910; *s* of late R. W. Bill, Penn, Staffs; *m* 1st, 1933, Peggy Shaw (marr. diss. 1952), *d* of late Comdr A. R. S. Warden, AM, RN (retd), Paignton, Devon; 2nd, 1952, Wendy Jean (*d* 1962), *d* of late C. P. Booth, Hampstead, NW2; one *s* one *d*; 3rd, 1965, Mrs Nancy Johnson, *d* of late Major Arthur Edward Phillips, DSO, MFH, Mompesson House, Salisbury. *Educ:* RNC, Dartmouth and Greenwich. Specialised in Hydrographic Surveying, 1931. Comdr in charge of Survey, 1945. *Address:* c/o Westminster Bank, 1 St James's Square, SW1. *Club:* Royal Automobile.

**BILLING, Melvin George,** CMG 1961; retired as Provincial Commissioner, Provincial Administration, Northern Rhodesia (1951-62); *b* 24 June 1906; *s* of Stuart Morrison Billing and Gertrude Roswell Billing; *m* 1934; no *c*. *Educ:* Dulwich Coll.; Worcester Coll., Oxford. Provincial Administration, Northern Rhodesia: Cadet, 1930; District Officer, 1932; Grade II, 1942; Grade I, 1946; Senior, 1950. *Recreations:* bowls, photography. *Address:* c/o Mrs A. B. Emery, Box 33, Bryanston, Transvaal, S Africa. *Club:* Royal Commonwealth Society.

**BILLINGHAM, Prof. Rupert Everett,** FRS 1961; MA, DPhil, DSc Oxon; Professor and Chairman, Department of Medical Genetics, University of Pennsylvania Medical School, Philadelphia, Pa, USA, since 1965; *b* 15 Oct. 1921; *o s* of Albert Everett and Helen Louise Billingham, Oxford; *m* 1951, Jean Mary Morpeth; two *s* one *d*. *Educ:* City of Oxford High Sch.; Oriel Coll., Oxford. Served 1942-46, as Lieut RNVR. Asst Lectr, later Lectr in Zoology, University of Birmingham, 1947; Junior Research Fellow, British Empire Cancer Campaign, 1950; Intermediate Research Fellow, Brit. Emp. Cancer Campaign, 1953; Hon. Res. Asst, later Res. Associate, Dept of Zoology, University Coll., London, 1951; Wistar Prof. of Zoology, Univ. of Pennsylvania, USA, and Mem. of Wistar Institute of Anatomy and Biology, Philadelphia, 1957. Member: Allergy and Immunology Study Section, Nat. Insts of Health, US Public Health Service, 1958-62; Transplantation and Immunology Cttee, Nat. Insts of Health, 1968-70. Fellow, New York

Acad. of Sciences, 1962; Fellow, Amer. Acad. of Arts and Sciences, 1965; Alvarenga Prize, Coll. Physicians, Philadelphia, 1963; Herman Beerman Lecture, Soc. for Investigative Dermatology, 1963; Hon. Award Medal, American Assoc. of Plastic Surgeons, 1964; I. S. Ravdin Lecture, Amer. College of Surgeons, 1964; *Sigma Xi* Lecture, Yale, 1965; National Institutes of Health Lecture, 1965; J. W. Jenkinson Memorial Lecturer, Oxford, 1965-66; Harvey Lectr, New York, 1966. Adair Award, Amer. Gynecological Soc., 1971. Hon. DSc, Trinity Coll., Hartford, Conn, USA. *Publications:* The Immunology of Transplantation (with W. K. Silvers), 1971; contribs to scien. jls on biology of skin, and immunology of tissue transplantation. *Recreations:* woodwork, gardening. *Address:* Department of Medical Genetics, University of Pennsylvania Medical School, Philadelphia, Pa 19104, USA; (home) 102 Anton Road, Wynnewood, Pa 19096, USA.

**BILLINGS, Rear-Adm. Frederick Stewart,** CBE 1953; CEng; FIMechE; *b* 11 Aug. 1900; *s* of F. W. Billings, Cheltenham; *m* 1933, Mary Sheila (*née* Howell); two *s* two *d*. *Educ:* Royal Naval Coll., Dartmouth. As Capt. (E): Fleet Engineer Officer on staff of C-in-C, Mediterranean, 1945-47; Asst Engineer-in-Chief (Personnel) at Admiralty, 1947-48; Fleet Engineer Officer (Submarines), 1948-50; Manager, Engineering Dept, HM Dockyard, Portsmouth, 1950-54; retd list, 1954. Local Dir and Chief Engineer, the Consett Iron Co., County Durham, 1956-62. Chilean Order Al Merito, 1932. *Address:* Southover Lodge, Frampton, Dorchester, Dorset. *T:* Maiden Newton 370.

**BILLINGTON, Prof. Ray Allen;** Senior Research Associate, Huntington Library, San Marino, California, since 1963; *b* Bay City, Michigan, USA, 28 Sept. 1903; *s* of Cecil Billington and Nina Allen Billington; *m* 1928, Mabel Ruth Crotty; one *s* one *d*. *Educ:* University of Wisconsin (PhB); University of Michigan (MA); Harvard University (PhD). Instructor and Asst Prof. of History, Clark Univ., Worcester, Mass, 1931-37; Asst Prof., Associate Prof., Prof., Smith Coll., Northampton, Mass, 1937-44; William Smith Mason Prof. of History, Northwestern Univ., 1944-63. Visiting Professor: Western Reserve Univ., 1939; Ohio State Univ., 1942; Harvard Univ., 1948. Dir, Massachusetts Federal Writers' Project, 1936-37; Guggenheim Memorial Fellow, 1943-44; History Editor, The Dryden Press, 1949-56; History Editor, Rinehart & Co., 1956-60; Board of Trustees, The Newberry Library, 1952-63; Dir., Social Science Research Council, 1952. Harold Vyvyan Harmsworth Prof. of American History, Oxford Univ., 1953-54. Hon. MA Oxford, 1953; Hon. LittD: Bowling Green Univ., 1958; Redlands Univ., 1965; Hon. LLD: Park Coll., 1961; Occidental Coll., 1969; Univ. of Toledo, 1970. *Publications:* The Protestant Crusade, 1938 (reissued 1953); The United States, American Democracy in World Perspective, 1947; Westward Expansion, 1949 (3rd edn 1966); The Making of American Democracy, 1950; American History after 1865, 1950; American History before 1877, 1951; The Journal of Charlotte L. Forten, 1953; The Far Western Frontier, 1830-1860, 1956; The Westward Movement in the United States, 1959; Frontier and Section, 1961; The Historian's Contribution to Anglo-American Misunderstanding, 1966; The Frontier Thesis, 1966; America's Frontier Heritage, 1966; America's Frontier Story, 1969; contribs to historical jls. *Address:* 2375 Lombardy Road, San Marino, Calif, USA. *Club:* Wayfarers (Chicago).

**BILNEY, Air Vice-Marshal Christopher Neil Hope,** CB 1949; CBE 1946 (OBE 1940); RAF, retired; *b* 26 Oct. 1898; *s* of late William A. and late Maud H. Bilney, Fir Grange, Weybridge, Surrey; *m* 1926, Nellie G. Perren; two *d*. *Educ:* Tonbridge Sch. Joined RNAS, 1917; commissioned 1917; served European War, 1914-18, N Sea and Middle East; Flt-Lieut RAF, 1926; India, 1925-30 (despatches); Sqdn Leader, 1935, serving at Air Ministry; Wing Comdr, 1939; served War of 1939-45: Boscombe Down, 1939; MAP, 1940-41; Group Capt, 1941; Air Cdre, Vice-Pres. Ordnance Board, 1942; HQ Bomber Comd as Comd Armament Officer, 1944; AOC No. 25 Group, 1945; Air Ministry, Dir Technical Training, 1947; Air Officer i/c Administration, HQ Maintenance Comd, 1949-51; Dir-Gen. of Technical Services (1), Air Ministry, 1951-52; retd 1954. Pres. Ordnance Board, Ministry of Supply, 1953-54 (Vice-Pres., 1952-53). *Recreations:* shooting, gardening. *Address:* Middle Acre, Wildhern, Andover, Hants.

**BILSLAND,** family name of **Baron Bilsland.**

**BILSLAND,** 1st Baron, *cr* 1950, of Kinrara, Inverness-shire; **Alexander Steven Bilsland,** 1907; KT 1955; MC; DL, JP; Past Chairman: Glasgow Stockholders Trust Ltd; Scottish National Trust Co. Ltd; Past Director: Colvilles Ltd; Burmah Oil Co. Ltd; John Brown & Co. Ltd; Past Governor of the Bank of Scotland; Past President, Scottish Amicable Life Assurance Society; Hon. Fellow, St John's College, Cambridge; Hon. Member, American Academy of Arts and Sciences; Member, Royal Company of Archers (Queen's Body Guard for Scotland); late Captain, 8th Scottish Rifles and Staff; *b* Glasgow, 13 Sept. 1892; *s* of Sir William Bilsland, LLD, 1st Bt and Agnes Anne (*d* 1935), 3rd *d* of Alexander Steven, Provanside, Glasgow; *S* to father's baronetcy, 1921; *m* 1922, Amy, *d* of late David Colville, Jerviston House, Motherwell. *Educ:* Glasgow; St John's Coll., Cambridge. Pres., Glasgow Chamber of Commerce, 1933-35; District Commissioner for Western District of Scotland under Civil Defence Regional Organisation, 1940-44. Freeman of Aberdeen, 1956. Hon. LLD: Glasgow, 1948; Aberdeen, 1956. Hon. ARIBA. US Medal of Freedom. *Heir:* none. *Recreations:* fishing and shooting. *Address:* Garden, Buchlyvie, Stirlingshire; Kinrara, Aviemore, Inverness-shire. *Clubs:* Brooks's, Caledonian; New (Edinburgh); Western (Glasgow); Northern (Inverness).

**BILTON, Percy;** Chairman and Managing Director, Percy Bilton Ltd, London, W5, and other companies; *b* 28 Nov. 1896; *s* of Christopher G. Bilton, Ormskirk, Lancs, and Hannah Dunlop, Edinburgh; three *s* two *d*. Founder: Vigzol Oil Co. Ltd, 1919; Percy Bilton Ltd, 1927; and various other property companies. Past Master, Worshipful Co. of Fan Makers, 1959. *Recreations:* yachting, golf, farming (pedigree Jerseys at 5000 acre farm, De Hoek, CP, and Ayrshire pedigree herd at Barnes Farm, King's Langley). *Address:* Barnes Farm, King's Langley, Herts. *T:* King's Langley 62839. *Clubs:* Royal Thames Yacht; Civil Service (Cape Town).

**BINCHY, Daniel A.;** Senior Professor, Dublin Institute for Advanced Studies; *b* 3 June 1900. *Educ:* Clongowes Wood Coll.; University Coll., Dublin; Munich, Berlin, Paris and the Hague. MA (NUI), Dr Phil (Munich). Prof. of Jurisprudence and Legal History, University Coll., Dublin, 1925-45; Senior Research Fellow, Corpus Christi Coll., Oxford, 1945-50. Envoy Extraordinary and Minister Plenipotentiary for the Irish Free State to Germany, 1929-32. Mem. Council, Royal Irish

Academy, 1926, Vice-Pres., 1945. Rhys Lectr, British Academy, 1943; Lowell Lectr, Boston, 1954; Visiting Prof. of Celtic, Harvard Univ., 1962-63; Gregynog Lectr, Univ. of Wales, 1966; O'Donnell Lectr, Oxford, 1967-68. DLitt (*hc*) Dublin, 1956, Wales, 1963. Corresp. Mem., Norwegian Instituttet for Sammenlignende Kulturforsking, 1960; For. Mem., Amer. Acad. of Arts and Sciences, 1962. *Publications:* Church and State in Fascist Italy, 1941, repr. 1970; Crith gablach, An Early Irish Legal Tract, 1940; Celtic and Anglo-Saxon Kingship, 1970; papers on Old Irish law; various articles in Irish, English, and German reviews. *Address:* Lisnagree, Castleknock, Co. Dublin. *Club:* United Service (Dublin).

**BINDOFF, Prof. Stanley Thomas;** Professor of History, Queen Mary College, University of London, since 1951; *b* 8 April 1908; 2nd *s* of late Thomas Henry and Mary Bindoff, Brighton; *m* 1936, Marjorie, *d* of William George and Helen Blatcher, New Malden; one *s* one *d*. *Educ:* Brighton Grammar Sch.; University Coll., London. BA (History Hons), 1929; MA (with mark of distinction), 1933; Alexander Medallist of the RHistS, 1935. Research Asst, Inst. of Historical Research, 1930-33; Sec., Netherlands Information Bureau, 1933-34; successively Asst Lectr and Lectr in History, University Coll., London, 1935-45; service in Naval Intelligence Div., Admty, 1942-45; Reader in Modern History, University Coll., London, 1945-51. Visiting Prof. in History: Columbia Univ., NY, 1960; Claremont Graduate Sch., Calif., 1966; Wellesley Coll., Mass., Harvard Univ., 1968. FRHistS, 1946; Vice-Pres., 1967. Fellow of University Coll., London, 1958. Member: Utrecht Historical Soc., 1947; Royal Dutch Soc. of Literature, 1950; Senate, Univ. of London, 1966. *Publications:* (with E. F. Malcolm Smith and C. K. Webster) British Diplomatic Representatives, 1789-1852, 1934; The Scheldt Question to 1839, 1945; Ket's Rebellion (Hist. Assoc. Pamphlet), 1949; Tudor England, 1950; (ed jtly) Elizabethan Government and Society, 1961; articles and reviews in historical journals. *Recreations:* walking and climbing; watching games which he has grown too old to play. *Address:* 5 Carlton Road, New Malden, Surrey. *T:* 01-942 0259. *Club:* Reform.

**BING, Geoffrey Henry Cecil,** CMG 1960; QC 1950; Barrister; Consultant to the Irish University Press, since 1970; *b* 24 July 1909; *s* Down; *m* 1956, Eileen Mary, *d* of late Alderman Frederick Cullen; one *s* (adopted) (and two *s* by former marriage). *Educ:* Tonbridge Sch.; Lincoln Coll., Oxford. Jane Eliza Proctor Visiting Fellow, Princeton Univ., USA, 1932-33. Called to Bar, Inner Temple, 1934, Gibraltar, 1937, Gold Coast, 1950, Nigeria, 1954. Joined Royal Signals, 1941; commissioned, 1943; GSO2 Airborne Forces Development Centre, 1943; British North Africa Forces, 1943; Major, BLA, 1944-45 (despatches). MP (Lab) Hornchurch Div. of Essex, 1945-50, Hornchurch, 1950-55; Asst Govt Whip, 1945-46. Constitutional Adviser to Prime Minister of Ghana, 1956-57; Attorney-Gen. of Ghana, 1957-61; Adviser to Pres. Nkrumah, 1961-66. Fellow, Ghana Academy of Sciences. *Publications:* (as Henry Blythe) Spain over Britain, 1937; John Bull's Other Ireland, 1950, new edn 1970; Reap the Whirlwind–an account of Kwame Nkrumah's Ghana, 1950-66, 1967; (editor) The Family Lawyer, new rev. edn, 1970. *Address:* 11 Clarendon Gardens, Maida Vale, W9.

**BING, Rudolf F. J.,** CBE 1956; General Manager, Metropolitan Opera, New York, since 1950; *b* Vienna, 9 Jan. 1902; *m* 1929, Nina (*née* Schelemskaja). *Educ:* Vienna. Hessian State Theatre, Darmstadt, 1928-30; Civic Opera, Berlin-Charlottenburg, 1930-33. Gen. Manager, Glyndebourne Opera, 1935-49; Artistic Director, Edinburgh Festival, 1947-49. Holds hon. doctorates in music and in letters, from the US. Légion d'Honneur, 1958; Comdr's Cross of Order of Merit, Federal Republic of Germany, 1958; Grand Silver Medal of Honour, Republic of Austria, 1959; Comdr, Order of Merit, Republic of Italy, 1959, Grand Officer, 1970. *Address:* Metropolitan Opera, New York, USA.

**BINGEN, Sir Eric Albert,** Kt 1966; *b* 12 April 1898; *yr s* of late Max and Leily Bingen; *m* 1st, 1928, Peggy Ida (*d* 1964), *d* of late Arthur M. Lawrence; one *d*; 2nd, 1967, Eileen Peel, *widow* of T. Ainslie Robertson. *Educ:* Cheltenham Coll.; St John's Coll., Oxford (Classical Scholar). Served European War, France and Flanders, Lieut, Royal Sussex Regt and RAF (wounded), 1917-18. MA (Oxon) 1st class Final Honours Sch. of Jurisprudence, 1921; Solicitor, 1924 (Law Society's Prizeman); Imperial Chemical Industries Ltd: Legal Dept, 1927-51; Dir, 1951-63; Deputy Chm., 1959-63; retd, 31 March 1963. Chm., Remploy Ltd, 1963-69. Member: Advisory Cttee on Commercial Information Overseas, 1957-59; Departmental (Jenkins) Cttee on Company Law, 1959-62; Restrictive Practices Court, 1963-. Pres., Cheltonian Soc., 1965-66. Leader, UK Delegation to UN Industrial Develt Organisation Symposium, Athens, Dec. 1967. *Address:* Flat 1, 25 Princes Gate, Kensington, SW7. *T:* 01-584 4499. *Club:* Royal Air Force.

**BINGHAM,** family name of **Baron Clanmorris** and of **Earl of Lucan.**

**BINGHAM, Lord; George Charles Bingham;** *b* 21 Sept. 1967; *s* and *heir* of 7th Earl of Lucan, *qv.*

**BINGHAM, John;** *see* Clanmorris, 7th Baron.

**BINGHAM, Lieut-Col Ralph Charles,** CVO 1953; DSO 1917; *b* 1885; *m* 1913, Dorothy Louisa (*d* 1967), *d* of late Edward Roger Murray Pratt; one *s* one *d*. *Educ:* Eton. Served European War, 1914-18 (DSO, Italian Silver Medal, despatches thrice); commanded 4th Bn City of London Regt (The Royal Fusilliers), 1934-37; Sec. The Order of St John of Jerusalem, 1927-37; Exon in the Yeoman of the Guard, 1938; Clerk of the Cheque and Adjutant of the Yeoman of the Guard, 1950-55. *Recreations:* sailing (passed Board of Trade Yacht Master (Coastal) Exam., 1945); bookbinding and calligraphy. *Address:* 10 Evelyn Gardens, SW7. *T:* 01-373 5543.

*See also Baron Alport.*

**BINGHAM, Richard Martin,** TD 1949; QC 1958; Recorder of Oldham since 1960; Judge of Appeal, Isle of Man, since 1965; *b* 26 Oct. 1915; *s* of John and Dorothy Ann Bingham; *m* 1949, Elinor Stephenson; one *d*. *Educ:* Harrow; Clare Coll., Cambridge. Called to Bar, Inner Temple, 1940; Bencher, 1964; joined Northern Circuit, 1946. Served with 59th Med. Regt, RA (TA), 1937-46 and 1947-49: Major from 1945; Campaigns, Dunkirk and NW Europe (despatches, 1944). Mem. of Liverpool City Council, 1946-49. MP (C) Garston Division of Liverpool, Dec. 1957-March 1966. Member: HO Departmental Cttee on Coroners, 1965; Royal Commn Assizes and Quarter Sessions, 1966. *Publication:* Cases on Negligence, 1st edn 1961, 2nd edn 1964. *Address:* Lane End, Croft Drive, Caldy, Wirral, Ches. *T:* 051-625 6830. 2 Pump Court, Temple, EC4. *T:* 01-353 3106. *Clubs:* Royal Automobile; Liverpool Racquet, Royal Liverpool Golf.

**BINGHAM, Robert Porter,** CMG 1956; JP; Malayan Civil Service, retired; *b* 3 Jan. 1903; *s* of late Robert William Bingham, Dungannon, Co. Tyrone; *m* 1936, Elizabeth Walker, *d* of late Vincent Andrew Acheson, Castlecaulfield, Co. Tyrone; one *s* one *d*. *Educ:* Royal School, Dungannon; Trinity Coll., Dublin. Entered Malayan Civil Service, 1926; in China, studying Chinese, 1926-28; Protector of Chinese, various parts of Malaya, 1928-41; interned, Singapore, 1942-45; Commr for Labour, Singapore, 1946-50; Sec. for Chinese Affairs, Federation of Malaya, 1950-51; Resident Commissioner, Penang, 1951-57. JP, Tyrone, 1962. *Address:* Rookwood, Benburb, Co. Tyrone, Northern Ireland. *T:* Benburb 219.

**BINGLEY, Adm. Sir Alexander Noel Campbell,** GCB 1962 (KCB 1959; CB 1956); OBE 1943; Rear-Admiral of the United Kingdom and of the Admiralty, 1966-68; *b* 15 Feb. 1905; *s* of R. N. G. Bingley; *m* 1948, Juliet Martin, *d* of R. M. Vick, *qv*; one *s* two *d*. *Educ:* RN Colls Osborne, Dartmouth and Greenwich. Naval Observer, 1929; commanded HM Ships: Slinger, 1943: Biter, 1944; Nabaron, 1945; Eagle, 1952-53; Fifth Sea Lord and Deputy Chief of Naval Staff (Air), 1954-57; Flag Officer, Aircraft Carriers, 1958-59; Commander-in-Chief, Mediterranean, 1959-61; Commander-in-Chief, Portsmouth, and Allied Commander-in-Chief, Channel, 1961-63; retd list 1963. Rear-Adm. 1954; Vice-Adm. 1957; Actg Adm. 1959; Adm. 1960. Pres. Royal Naval Benevolent Trust, 1963-; Sec., SEMBAL Trust, 1964-. *Recreation:* farm work. *Address:* Hoddesdonbury Farm, Hoddesdon, Herts. *T:* Hoddesdon 63238. *Club:* Naval and Military.

**BINGLEY, Col Robert Albert Glanville,** CVO 1954; DSO 1944; OBE 1946; retired; *b* 15 Nov. 1902; *s* of R. Noel G. Bingley, OBE, and Mrs Bingley, Notley Abbey, Thame, Oxon, Braiseworth, Suffolk; *m* 1st, 1933, Sybil Gladys Rodney Duff; one *s* one *d*; 2nd, 1941, May Olivia Lenox-Conyngham; one *d*. *Educ:* Charterhouse; RMC Sandhurst. Joined 11th Hussars, 1923; ADC to GOC-in-C, Aldershot, 1930-31; Adjt, 11th Hussars, 1933-35; Adjt Inns of Court Regt, 1936-40; served War of 1939-45; raised and commanded Inns of Court Armoured Car Regt, 1940-45 (DSO); Asst Mil. Sec. to Field-Marshal Viscount Montgomery, 21 Army Group and BAOR, 1945-46 (OBE); Head of Brit. Mil. Mission, Luxembourg, 1946-47; Military Attaché, Brit. Embassy, The Hague, 1947-51; Asst Mil. Sec. to: Gen. Sir Gerald Templer, 1951-52; Gen. Sir George Erskine, 1952-53; Lt-Gen. G. K. Bourne, 1953-54. Dir, St John Ambulance Assoc., Glos. Landowner and farmer. Commander Order of Orange Nassau, 1950. CStJ. *Address:* Higher Eggbeer, Cheriton Bishop, Exeter, Devon. *Club:* Cheltenham Steeplechase.
*See also Earl of Gowrie.*

**BINNALL, Rev. Canon Peter Blannin Gibbons,** FSA; Canon Residentiary, Sub-Dean and Treasurer of Lincoln Cathedral, since 1961; *b* 5 Jan. 1907; *s* of late Rev. R. G. Binnall and Geraldine (*née* Pearson); *m* 1936, Stephanie, *d* of late Rev. W. Goss; one *s*. *Educ:* Worksop Coll.; Lichfield Theological Coll. Deacon, Grantham for Lincoln, 1932; priest, Lincoln, 1933. Curate of Caistor with Holton le Moor and Clixby, 1932-36; Vicar of Holland Fen with Amber Hill, 1936-45; Rector of East and West Barkwith with S. Willingham, 1945-61; Hon. Canon of Lincoln, 1956. Hon. Sec., Lincs Old Churches Trust, 1952-68; Chm., Lincoln Dio. Adv. Cttee; Vice-Chm., Lincs Association. Pres., N Lincs Branch, English Folk Dance and Song Soc.; Vice-Pres., Tennyson Soc.; Mem., British Soc. of Master Glass-Painters. FSA 1944; MA (Lambeth) 1962. *Publications:* contribs to: Collins' Guide to English Parish Churches; Antiquaries Jl, Jl Brit. Soc. Master Glass Painters, Hibbert Jl, various archæological transactions etc, Folklore. *Recreations:* history, folklore, ornithology. *Address:* The Subdeanery, Lincoln. *T:* Lincoln 25435.

**BINNEY, Anthony Lockhart,** CSI 1945; CIE 1939; *b* 1890; 5th *s* of T. G. Binney, late of Guisnes Court, Tolleshunt D'Arcy, Essex; *m* 1919, Dorothy Margery, *d* of late J. H. Cox, CIE, CBE, ICS; one *s* two *d*. *Educ:* Rugby. Entered ICS, 1914; served European war, 1915-19 (RFA (T) and RHA in Mesopotamia and Afghanistan, Capt., 1918); on deputation in Hyderabad, Dir Gen. Revenue, Controller to the Princes, 1928-34; Financial Sec. to Govt, CP, 1935; Chief Sec. (offg) 1936; Financial Commissioner, 1940; Adviser to Governor, 1944-46. *Address:* Crossland, Copthorne, Sussex.

**BINNEY, Sir George,** Kt 1941; DSO 1944; MA; FRGS; *b* 23 Sept. 1900; *s* of late Rev. M. F. B. Binney and late Emily Blinkhorn; *m* 1946, Evelyn Mary (marr. diss., 1955), *er d* of T. G. Marriott; *m* 1955, Sonia, *widow* of Lt-Col F. Simms and *d* of late Paymaster Rear-Adm. Sir William Beresford-Whyte, KCB, CMG. *Educ:* Eton Coll. (scholar); Merton Coll., Oxford (Chambers Postmastership). Ed. of Isis, 1920; Organiser and Sec., Oxford Univ. Spitzbergen Expedition, 1921; Leader, Merton Coll. Arctic Expedition, 1923; Leader, Oxford Univ. Arctic Expedition, 1924; received Back Award of RGS and Gold Medal de la Roquette of Geographical Society of Paris for his journey across North East Land; Founder's Gold Medal, Royal Geographical Society, 1957. Served Hudson's Bay Company, 1926-31, spending much time in Canadian Arctic. Joined United Steel Companies Ltd, 1931; seconded from United Steel Cos for service with Iron and Steel Control, Min. of Supply, 1939; Asst Commercial Attaché, Stockholm, 1940-42; Comdr RNVR, 1942-45 (retired, 1945). Led United Kingdom Trade and Industrial Mission to Ghana, 1959. *Publications:* With Seaplane and Sledge in the Arctic, 1925; The Eskimo Book of Knowledge, 1931. *Recreations:* shooting, antique collecting, travel. *Address:* Domaine des Vaux, St Lawrence, Jersey, CI. *T:* Jersey North 52. *Clubs:* White's, Garrick.

**BINNEY, H(arry) A(ugustus) Roy,** CB 1950; Director-General (formerly Director and Secretary), British Standards Institution, 1951-70; *b* 18 May 1907; *s* of Harry Augustus Binney, Churston, Devon; *m* 1944, Barbara Poole; three *s* one *d* (and one *d* decd). *Educ:* Royal Dockyard Sch., Devonport; London Univ. BSc(Eng). Entered Board of Trade, 1929; Under-Sec. of the Board of Trade, 1947-51. Member: Council, Queen Elizabeth Coll., 1952-68; Council, Internat. Standards Organization (Vice-Pres., 1964-69); Gen. Bd, and Exec. Cttee, Nat. Physical Laboratory, 1957-63. Hon. Life Fellow, Standards Engineers Soc. of America; Hon. Life Mem., American Soc. for Testing and Materials. *Recreations:* gardening, golf. *Address:* 38 Parkside, Wimbledon, SW19. *T:* 01-946 5800. *Clubs:* Reform, Canning.

**BINNIE, Alfred Maurice,** FRS 1960; Fellow of Trinity College (1944) and University Reader Emeritus in Engineering, Cambridge; *b* 6 Feb. 1901; *s* of late David Carr Binnie. *Educ:* Weymouth Coll.; Queens' Coll., Cambridge. Jun. Research Engineer, Bridge Stress Cttee, 1923-25; Demonstrator and Lectr, Engrg

Lab., Oxford, 1925-44; Rhodes Travelling Fellow, 1932-33; Lectr, New Coll., Oxford, 1933-44; Univ. Lectr, Engrg Lab., Cambridge, 1944-54; Sen. Research Fellow, California Inst. of Technology, 1951-52; Scott Visiting Fellow, Ormond Coll., Univ. of Melbourne, 1966; Vis. Scholar, Univ. of California, Berkeley, 1967-68. FIMechE 1937; FICE 1947. *Publications:* articles in scientific and engrg jls. *Recreation:* mountaineering. *Address:* Trinity College, Cambridge. *T:* 58201. *Clubs:* Alpine, Oxford and Cambridge University.

**BINNING, Lord; John George Baillie-Hamilton;** *b* 21 Dec. 1941; *o s* of 12th Earl of Haddington, *qv. Educ:* Ampleforth. *Address:* Mellerstain, Gordon, Berwickshire; Tyninghame, Dunbar, East Lothian.

**BINNS, Sir Arthur (Lennon),** Kt 1954; CBE 1945; MC 1916; *b* 31 March 1891; *er s* of John Binns, Grimsby; *m* 1915, Florence Gertrude Coggon; two *d. Educ:* Wintringham Grammar Sch.; St John's Coll., Cambridge. Lincolnshire Regt and Gen. Staff, 1914-19. Chief Education Officer: West Riding of Yorks, 1936-45; Lancs, 1945-47. Mem. Fleming Cttee on Public Schs, 1944; Mem. Colonial Office Advisory Cttee, 1945-53; Special Commissioner in Sierra Leone, 1949; Mem. Beveridge Cttee on BBC, 1940; Chm. Colonial Office Mission to East and Central Africa, 1951-52; Pres. Section L, British Association, 1952; Governor: Welbeck Coll., 1953-57; Sedbergh Sch., 1954-62; Royal Lancaster Grammar Sch., 1958-62; King Edward Sch., Lytham, 1958-62; Chm. Standing Conference of Regional Examining Unions, 1957-60; Visiting Lecturer, University of British Columbia, 1958; Pres. North of England Educational Conference, 1962; Mem. of several other Govt Departmental Cttees. *Address:* The Firs, Woodville Terrace, Lytham, Lancs. *T:* Lytham 7310. *Club:* Lytham Yacht.

**BINNS, Edward Ussher Elliott E.;** *see* Elliott-Binns.

**BINNS, Professor Howard Reed,** CMG 1958; OBE 1948; MA (Cantab), BSc (Edin), MRCVS; Chairman, Centre for International Programs, and Professor of Veterinary Bacteriology, University of Guelph, since 1969; *b* 3 Aug. 1909; *s* of Cuthbert Evelyn Binns and Edith Mildred Edwards; *m* 1935, Katharine Vroom Lawson; one *s* one *d. Educ:* Bootham Sch., York; St John's Coll., Cambridge; Royal (Dick) Veterinary Coll.; Edinburgh Univ. Veterinary Officer, Nyasaland, 1935-39; Veterinary Research Officer, Palestine, 1940-41; Senior Veterinary Research Officer, Palestine, 1941-47; Dep. Dir of Veterinary Services, Palestine, 1947-48; Director, East African Veterinary Research Organization, 1950-67 (Principal Scientific Officer, EAVRO, 1948-50). Scientific missions to: USA and Canada, 1939; Syria and the Lebanon, 1945; India, 1946; USA, 1947; South Africa, 1949; Australia, 1960; Carnegie Travel Grant for scientific visits in USA and Canada, 1956. Consultant to US Nat. Acad. of Sciences, on animal science in tropical Africa, 1959. Mem. Scientific Council for Africa, 1961-65 (Assoc. Mem., 1955-61). Hon. Prof. of Vet. Science in Univ. of East Africa. *Publications:* contribs to scientific jls. *Recreations:* travel, photography. *Address:* Centre for International Programs, University of Guelph, Guelph, Ont, Canada.

**BINNS, John;** *b* June 1914; *m*; one *s. Educ:* Holycroft Sec. Sch., Keighley. Mem., Keighley Borough Council, 1945-; Alderman, 1954-; Mayor, 1958-59. Joined Labour Party, 1944; MP (Lab) Keighley, 1964-70. Mem. Amalgamated Engineering Union; former Trades Union Officer. *Address:* 43 Prospect Mount, Fell Lane, Keighley, Yorks.

**BINNS, Joseph,** CBE 1961; Consulting Engineer; Chairman of Public Works Loans Board, since 1970 (Deputy Chairman, 1958-70); *b* 19 March 1900; *s* of Alderman Joseph Binns (a former Lord Mayor of Manchester); *m* 1924, Daisy Graham; two *s. Educ:* Primary and Secondary Sch., Manchester; Manchester Coll. of Technology. MP (Lab) Gillingham Div. of Rochester, 1945-50; PPS to Minister of Supply, 1946-47; Chm. Metropolitan Boroughs Standing Joint Cttee, 1945-49. *Address:* 39 Stade Street, Hythe, Kent. *T:* Hythe (Kent) 67274. *Club:* Reform.

**BINNS, Kenneth Johnstone,** CMG 1960; Under-Treasurer and Commissioner of State Taxes, Government of Tasmania, since 1952; Director, Comalco Aluminium (Bell Bay) Ltd; *b* New South Wales, Australia, 3 June 1912; *s* of late Kenneth Binns, CBE; *m* 1940, Nancy H. Mackenzie; no *c. Educ:* Melbourne Church of England Grammar Sch.; Univ. of Melbourne (MA, BCom); Harvard Univ., USA. Tasmanian Treasury, 1942-. Fellow, Commonwealth Fund of New York, 1950; Fiscal Review Comr to Federal Republic of Nigeria, 1964; with IMF as Adviser to Minister of Finance, Indonesia, 1969. *Publications:* Federal-State Financial Relations, Canada and Australia, 1948; Social Credit in Alberta, 1947; articles in Economic Record. *Recreation:* tennis. *Address:* c/o Tasmanian Treasury, Murray Street, Hobart, Tasmania. *T:* 30-3474; 3 Ellington Road, Sandy Bay, Tasmania. *T:* 5 1863. *Clubs:* Athenæum, Tasmanian, Hobart.

**BINNY, John Anthony Francis;** Chairman and Managing Director, The Law Debenture Corporation Ltd; *b* 13 Dec. 1911; *s* of late Lieut-Col S. S. Binny, DSO, and Bertha Marjorie, *d* of late Henry Champion; *m* 1950, Diana Heather, *er d* of late John Buchanan Muir, Kiftsgate Court, Campden, Glos; two *d. Educ:* Wellington Coll. Supplementary Reserve of Officers, 15th/19th The King's Royal Hussars, 1936. Served War of 1939-45, France and Burma (despatches). Vice-Chm., Associated Portland Cement Manufacturers Ltd; Dep. Chm., Mercantile Investment Trust Ltd; Dir of National Westminster Bank Ltd (Chm., W Midlands and Wales Regional Office); Dir of other companies. A Governor of Wellington Coll., 1968-. *Address:* Kiftsgate Court, Campden, Glos. *Clubs:* Cavalry, White's.

**BINYON, Basil,** OBE; MA; CEng, FIEE, FIEEE, AFRAeS; *b* 1885; *s* of Brightwen Binyon; *m* Gladys (*d* 1960), *o d* of late J. Howard Keep; one *s* (and one killed in action, Arnhem, 24 Sept. 1944) one *d*; *m* 1962, V. M. Hibbert. *Educ:* Leighton Park Sch.; Trinity Coll., Cambridge. War Service, Flight-Comdr RNAS; Major RAF, 1914-18; Group Comdt No. 19 Group Royal Observer Corps, rank Observer Comdr, 1939-47; retired 1947. Past Chm. Electronics Section, IEE; Dir, British Broadcasting Co., 1922-26. *Address:* Longridge, The Glen, Farnborough Park, Kent. *T:* Farnborough 54371. *Club:* Royal Air Force.

**BIOBAKU, Dr Saburi Oladeni,** CMG 1961; MA, PhD; Vice-Chancellor, University of Lagos; *b* 16 June 1918; *s* of late Chief S. O. Biobaku, Are of Iddo, Abeokuta; *m* 1949, Muhabat Folasade, *d* of Alhaji L. B. Agusto, barrister-at-law, Lagos; one *s. Educ:* Govt Coll., Ibadan; Higher Coll., Yaba; University Coll., Exeter;

Trinity Coll., Cambridge. BA London, 1945; BA Cantab, 1947, MA. 1951; PhD London, 1951. Education Officer, Nigeria, 1947-53; Registrar, University Coll., Ibadan, 1953-57; Dir, Yoruba Historical Research Scheme, 1956-; Sec. to Premier and Executive Council, Western Nigeria, 1957-61; Pro-Vice-Chancellor, Univ. of Ife, Nigeria, 1961-65. Created Arẽ of Iddo, Abeokuta, 1958. *Publications:* The Origin of the Yoruba, 1955; The Egba and Their Neighbours, 1842-1872, 1957; contribs to Africa, jl of Nigerian Historical Soc., Odu (Joint Ed.), etc. *Recreations:* soccer, tennis, badminton, swimming, walking. *Address:* University of Lagos, Lagos, Nigeria. *T:* (home) 21860. *Clubs:* Metropolitan (Lagos); Dining (Ibadan).

**BION, Arnold Eustace,** CIE 1942; *b* 2 Feb. 1890; *s* of W. R. Bion; *m* 1925, Eileen Evelyn Byrne (*d* 1968); two *s*. *Educ:* Blackheath. Joined Indian (Imperial) Police, 1910; war service, 1916-17, in Indian Army (Cavalry) R of O on NW Frontier of India and in Iraq, rank Capt.; Iraq Police Force, 1917-21; returned to Indian Police, 1921; Inspector-Gen. of Police, Bihar, 1939-45; retired. *Address:* c/o National & Grindlays Bank Ltd, 13 St James's Square, SW1.

**BIRCH,** family name of **Baron Rhyl.**

**BIRCH, Alexander Hope,** CMG 1970; OBE 1961; Deputy High Commissioner, British High Commission, Perth (Western Australia), since 1970; *b* 19 Jan. 1913; *s* of Denys Goldney and Lucy Helen Booth Birch; *m* 1st, 1940, Honor Pengelley (marr. diss., 1948); 2nd, 1953, Joan Hastings-Hungerford; no *c*. *Educ:* St Catherine's and St Mark's Colls, Alexandria, and privately. Appointed to: HM Embassy, Cairo, 1937; Addis Ababa, 1942; Moscow, 1946; Budapest, 1947; Tel-Aviv, 1949; Second Sec. (Inf.), Baghdad, 1950, First Sec. and Consul, Seoul, 1951, and Djakarta, 1954; First Sec. (Commercial), Khartoum, 1956, and Paris, 1961; Counsellor (Commercial), Paris, 1962, and Baghdad, 1965; Counsellor (Economic and Commercial), Accra, 1967-70. *Recreations:* reading, walking. *Address:* c/o FCO, King Charles Street, SW1. *Club:* Oriental.

**BIRCH, Prof. Anthony Harold,** PhD; Professor of Political Science, University of Exeter, since 1970; *b* 17 Feb. 1924; *o s* of late Frederick Harold Birch and of Rosalind Dorothy Birch; *m* 1953, Dorothy Madeleine Overton, Bayport, New York; one *s* one *d*. *Educ:* The William Ellis Sch.; University Coll., Nottingham; London Sch. of Economics. BSc (Econ) London, with 1st cl. hons, 1945; PhD London, 1951. Asst Principal, Board of Trade, 1945-47; University of Manchester: Asst Lectr in Govt, 1947-51; Lectr, 1951-58; Senior Lectr in Government, 1958-61; Prof. of Political Studies, Univ. of Hull, 1961-70. Commonwealth Fund Fellow at Harvard Univ. and University of Chicago, 1951-52. Consultant to Government of Western Region of Nigeria, 1956-58. Vis. Prof. Tufts Univ., 1968. *Publications:* Federalism, Finance and Social Legislation, 1955; Small-Town Politics, 1959; Representative and Responsible Government, 1964; The British System of Government, 1967; articles in various journals. *Recreations:* sailing and bridge. *Address:* University of Exeter, Exeter, Devon. *T:* Exeter 77911.

**BIRCH, Prof. Arthur John,** DPhil (Oxon), MSc; FRS 1958; FAA, FRIC, FRACI; Professor of Organic Chemistry, Australian National University, Canberra, since 1970; *b* 3 Aug. 1915; *s* of Arthur Spencer and Lily Birch; *m* 1948, Jessie Williams; three *s* two *d*. *Educ:* Sydney Technical High Sch.; Sydney Univ. Scholar of the Royal Commission for the Exhibition of 1851, Oxford, 1938-41; Research Fellow, Oxford, 1941-45; ICI Research Fellow, Oxford, 1945-48; Smithson Fellow of the Royal Society, Cambridge, 1949-52; Prof. of Organic Chemistry, University of Sydney, 1952-55; Prof. of Organic Chemistry, Manchester Univ., 1955-67; Dean, Research Sch. of Chemistry, ANU, Canberra, 1967-70. *Publications:* How Chemistry Works, 1950; about 300 original scientific communications, chiefly in Journal of Chemical Soc. and Australian Journal of Chemistry. *Address:* 3 Arkana Street, Yarralumla, Canberra, ACT 2600, Australia; Research School of Chemistry, Australian National University, Box 4, PO, Canberra, ACT 2600, Australia.

**BIRCH, John Anthony,** FRCO(CHM), LRAM, ARCM; Organist and Master of the Choristers, Chichester Cathedral, since 1958; University Organist, University of Sussex, since 1967; Organist since 1966 to the Royal Choral Society; Professor, Royal College of Music, since 1959; Examiner to Associated Board, Royal Schools of Music; Musical Adviser, Chichester Festival Theatre; *b* 9 July 1929; *s* of late Charles Aylmer Birch, Leek, Staffs; unmarried. *Educ:* Trent Coll.; Royal Coll. of Music. Organist and Choirmaster, St Thomas's Church, Regent Street, London, 1950-53; Accompanist to St Michael's Singers, 1952-58; Organist and Choirmaster, All Saints Church, Margaret Street, London, 1953-58; Sub-Organist, HM Chapels Royal, 1957-58; Choirmaster, Bishop Otter Coll., Chichester, 1963-69. Accompanist, Royal Choral Soc., 1965-70. Special Comr, Royal Sch. of Church Music; Mem. Council, Royal Coll. of Organists. Has made concert appearances in France, Germany and Switzerland; recital tours: Canada and US, 1966 and Australia and NZ, 1969. *Address:* 2 St Richard's Walk, Cathedral Close, Chichester, Sussex. *T:* Chichester 84790. *Clubs:* Athenæum, Public Schools.

**BIRCH-REYNARDSON, Lieut-Col H. T.;** *see* Reynardson.

**BIRCHENOUGH, Charles,** MA; FCP; *b* 8 Aug. 1882; *s* of late Samuel Birchenough, Stockport; *m* 1910, Gertrude Mary Elizabeth Angel (*d* 1947), *d* of late James Thomas, Cardiff; one *d* (one *s* decd); *m* 1964, Rhoda Mary, *d* of late Philip Taylor, Street. *Educ:* Balliol Coll., Oxford. Asst Lecturer in Education, University Coll. of South Wales, Cardiff, 1905-09; Lecturer in Education and Master of Method, Sheffield Univ., 1909-19; County Inspector of Education, Kent Education Cttee, 1919-27; Asst for Further Education, 1925-27; Chief Inspector of Education, 1927-47; Commissioned RGA 1916; served with 105 Siege Battery, RGA, France, Belgium, 1917, Italy, 1917-18 (despatches); Chief Educn Officer, Heavy Artillery, Italy, 1918-19. Examiner in Educn for Univ. of Wales, etc; advised on the reorganisation of education, Borough of Chesterfield; Vice-Pres., Coll. of Preceptors, 1952-65; Asst Ed., Journal of Education, 1947-55. *Publications:* A Primer of Teaching Practice (with J. A. Green), 1911; History of Elementary Education in England and Wales since 1800, 1914 (enlarged, 1925, 1939); Report on Elementary Education in the Borough of Chesterfield, 1927; Articles in the Encyclopædia and Dictionary of Education, Journal of Education, etc. *Address:* Montrose, 1 Brooks Road, Street, Somerset.

**BIRCHENOUGH, (John) Michael,** BSc, PhD, FRIC, FIBiol; Chief Inspector of Schools,

Department of Education and Science, since 1968; *b* 17 Jan. 1923; *s* of John Buckley Birchenough and Elsie Birchenough; *m* 1945, Enid Humphries; two *s*. *Educ:* Ashford Grammar Sch.; Chiswick Grammar Sch.; London Univ. Chemist, May & Baker Ltd, 1943-45; teaching posts, 1946-60; HM Inspector of Schools, 1960; Staff Inspector, 1966. *Publications:* contribs to Jl Chem. Soc. and other scientific jls. *Address:* 43 Watford Road, Radlett, Herts. *T:* Radlett 5176. *Club:* English-Speaking Union.

**BIRCHENOUGH, Michael;** *see* Birchenough, J. M.

**BIRD, Lt-Gen. Sir Clarence August,** KCIE 1943; CB 1940; DSO 1917; late RE; *b* 5 Feb. 1885; *m* 1919, Dorothea Marian, MBE 1918, K-i-H 1932, *d* of late Major W. E. Nichols; one *s*. *Educ:* Cheltenham Coll. Joined Royal Engineers, 1904; served in India, 1907-13, 1917-25, 1930-33, 1939-44; with Indian Expeditionary Force in France, 1914-15; with BEF in France, 1916-17 (Bt Maj.); psc 1921; AHQ India, 1922-25; Army Course, London Sch. of Economics, 1925; Chief Instructor in Fortification, SME, Chatham, 1926-29; Commandant, KGVO Bengal Sappers and Miners, 1930-33; Bt Lieut-Col, 1926; Lieut-Col, 1929; Col, 1933; AQMG Aldershot Command, 1933-35; Chief Engineer, Aldershot Command, 1935-39; Maj.-Gen. 1939; Engineer-in-Chief, Army Headquarters, India, 1939-42; Lieut-Gen. 1941; Master Gen. of Ordnance, India, 1942-44; retd 1944. Col Comdt RE, 1942-52; Col Comdt Indian Electrical and Mechanical Engineers, 1944-48. Dept of Food, Govt of India; Regional Commissioner, NW Region, 1944-45; Special Commissioner, 1945-47; Min. of Food: Divisional Food Officer, North Midland Div., 1947-48; Chm., Rhodesia Railways, 1948-53. FRSA. *Address:* Polesden Lacey, Dorking, Surrey. *Club:* United Service.

**BIRD, Sir Cyril (Pangbourne),** Kt 1968; Company Director, Perth, Western Australia; *b* 5 April 1906; *s* of late Walter Pangbourne Bird and late Alice Emma Bird; *m* 1934, Margery Isabel; two *s* three *d*. *Educ:* Perth, W Australia. FASA. *Recreations:* fishing, music. *Address:* 4 Riverside Drive, Mosman Park, Western Australia. *T:* 33884. *Clubs:* Royal Freshwater Bay Yacht; Royal King's Park Tennis.

**BIRD, Sir F. Hugh W. S.;** *see* Stonehewer Bird.

**BIRD, Air Vice-Marshal Frank Ronald,** DSO 1945; DFC 1944; AFC 1958; FRAeS; 1968. Director General of Organisation (RAF), since 1968; *b* 18 Nov. 1918; *s* of Frank Bird and Minnie (*née* Robinson); *m* 1943, Joan Dodson, WAAF; two *s*. *Educ:* Chesterfield Sch., Halton; RAF Coll., Cranwell. Commnd RAF, 1939; Flying Instruction and Experimental Flying, 1940-43; 105 Sqdn Bomber Comd (Pathfinder Force), 1943-45; Empire Test Pilots Sch. and A & AEE, 1945-46; RAF Coll., Cranwell (Cadet Wing), 1946-48; Perm. Commng Bds, Air Min., 1948-50; RAF Staff Coll., Andover, 1950-51; Brit. Jt Services Mission, Washington, USA, 1951-54; A & AEE, Boscombe Down, 1954-57; HQ Bomber Comd (Plans), 1957; CO, RAF Gaydon, 1957-60; Bomber Ops Staff, Air Min., 1960-63; Canadian Nat. Def. Coll., Kingston, Ont., 1963-64; Comdt, A & AEE, Boscombe Down, 1964-68. FRAeS 1968. *Recreations:* fell walking, golf, music, photography. *Address:* 11 Capella Road, Northwood, Middx. *T:* Northwood 23334. *Club:* Royal Air Force.

**BIRD, James Gurth,** MBE 1945; TD 1951; Head Master, William Hulme's Grammar School, Manchester, since 1947; *b* 30 Jan. 1909; *s* of Charles Harold Bird and Alice Jane Bird (*née* Kirtland); *m* 1940, Phyllis Ellis Pownall; one *s* two *d*. *Educ:* King William's Coll., Isle of Man (Scholar); St Catharine's Coll., Cambridge (exhibnr). Classical Tripos Pts I and II, BA 1931, MA 1933. Asst Master, Rossal Sch., 1931-33; Asst Master and House Master, Denstone Coll., 1933-47 (interrupted by War Service). FRSA 1969. *Recreations:* sailing, caravanning, gardening. *Address:* 254 Wilbraham Road, Manchester M16 8GN. *T:* 061-226 2058.

**BIRD, Sir Richard (Geoffrey Chapman),** 4th Bt *cr* 1922; *b* 3 Nov. 1935; *er surv. s* of Sir Donald Bird, 3rd Bt, and of Anne Rowena (*d* 1969), *d* of late Charles Chapman; *S* father, 1963; *m* 1st, 1957, Gillian Frances (*d* 1966), *d* of Bernard Haggett, Solihull; two *s* four *d*; 2nd, 1968, Helen Patricia, *d* of Frank Beaumont, Pontefract; one *d*. *Educ:* Beaumont. *Heir: s* John Andrew Bird, *b* 19 Jan. 1964. *Address:* 12 Hampton Lane, Solihull, Warwicks.

**BIRD, Terence Frederick,** CB 1954; Executive Director, P. & O., since 1965; Chairman, Committee of European Shipowners, since 1968; *b* 29 Sept. 1906; *s* of F. J. Bird and G. M. Bird (*née* Caulfield); *m* 1939, Prudence Ann Hutton Moss; one *s* one *d*. *Educ:* Southern Rhodesia; Balliol Coll., Oxford; Harvard Univ. Zoologist and Surveyor to Oxford Univ. Expedition to New Hebrides, 1933-34; Sec., Aerodromes Advisory Board, 1934-35. Entered Civil Service, 1935; Home Civil Service Commonwealth Fellow, 1947-48; Under-Sec., Min. of Transport, 1951-65; Under-Sec., BoT, 1965. *Address:* The Old Rectory, Little Bromley, Manningtree, Essex. *Club:* Athenæum.

**BIRD-WILSON, Air Vice-Marshal Harold Arthur Cooper,** CBE 1962; DSO 1945; DFC 1940 and Bar 1943; AFC 1946 and Bar 1955; AOC No 23 Group, since 1970; *b* 20 Nov. 1919; *m* 1942, Audrey Wallace; one *s* one *d*. *Educ:* Liverpool Coll. Joined RAF, Nov. 1937; No 17 Fighter Sqdn, Kenley, 1938. Served War of 1939-45 (Dunkirk, Battle of Britain): Sqdn Comdr Nos 152 and 66, 1942 (despatches); Wing Comdr (flying first Spitfire Wing in No 83 Gp), 1943; Comd and Gen. Staff Sch., Fort Leavenworth, Kansas, USA, 1944; Wing Comdr Flying Harrowbeer, Spitfire Wing and then Bentwater Mustang Wing, 1944-45. CO, Air Fighting Development Sqdn, CFE, 1946-47; Op. Staff, HQ, MEAF, 1948; RAF Staff Coll., Bracknell, 1949; Personal Staff Officer to C-in-C, MEAF, 1949-50; RAF Flying Coll., Manby, 1951; OC Tactics, CFE, 1952-54; Staff, BJSM, Washington, USA, 1954-57; Staff, Air Sec. Dept., Air Min., 1957-59; CO, RAF Coltishall, 1959-61; Staff Intell., Air Min., 1961-63; AOC and Comdt, CFS, 1963-65; AOC Hong Kong, 1965-67; Dir of Flying (Research and Develt), Min. of Technology, 1967-70. Czechoslovak Medal of Merit 1st class, 1945; Dutch DFC, 1945. *Address:* Rufforth Hall, Rufforth, York. *T:* Rufforth 329. *Club:* Royal Air Force.

**BIRDWOOD,** family name of **Baron Birdwood.**

**BIRDWOOD,** 3rd Baron, *cr* 1938, of Anzac and of Totnes; **Mark William Ogilvie Birdwood;** Bt 1919; *b* 23 Nov. 1938; *s* of 2nd Baron Birdwood, MVO, and of Vere Lady Birdwood, MVO; *S* father, 1962; *m* 1963, Judith Helen, *e d* of R. Seymour Roberts, Newton Aycliffe, Darlington, Co. Durham; one *d*. *Educ:* Radley Coll.; Trinity Coll., Cambridge. *Address:* 7 Bloomfield Terrace, SW1. *T:* 01-730 8700.

**BIRGI, Muharrem Nuri;** Permanent Turkish Delegate to NATO since 1960; *b* Istanbul, 4 Feb. 1908; *o s* of late Ziya Nuri Birgi Pasha, Prof., Faculty of Med., Univ. of Istanbul, later Mem. Grand Nat. Assembly, Turkey, and of Mme Husniye Birgi, *d* of Hassan Rami Pasha, Minister of Marine; *m* (marr. diss.). *Educ:* Lycée Galata Saray, Istanbul; Sch. of Pol. Sciences, Paris (Grad. 1929); Faculty of Law, Geneva (LLB 1931). Entered Turkish For. Min., 1932; 3rd, 2nd and then 1st Sec., Turkish Embassy, Warsaw, 1935-39; Min. for For. Affairs, 1939-41; 1st Sec., Turkish Embassy, Paris-Vichy, 1941; transferred to Madrid, 1942, later promoted Counsellor there. Min. for For. Affairs, Ankara: Co-Dir-Gen. 1st Political Dept, 1944; Dir-General: Dept of Internat. Affairs, 1945; Dept of Co-ordination, 1946; Dept of Consular Affairs, 1946; 2nd Political Dept, 1950; Dep. Sec.-Gen., 1951; Under-Sec. of State, 1952; Sec.-Gen., 1954-57; Turkish Ambassador to Court of St James's, 1957-60. Has rep. Turkey at Internat. confs, inc. UN, 1946, 1949, 1950; Suez Confs, 1956, and Cyprus Conf., 1955. One-man exhibn of paintings, Trafford Gall., London, 1964. Grand Cross, Order of Phœnix, Greece, 1953; Grand Cross with Star and Schulterband, Verdienst Order, Fed. Germany, 1954; Grand Officer, Order of Star of Yugoslavia, 1954; Grand Cordon, Order of Merit, Spain, 1956; Order of Taj, Iran, 1956; Grand Officer, Order of Cedar, Lebanon, 1956; Grand Cordon, Order of Brilliant Star, China, 1957. *Address:* Turkish Delegation, NATO, 1110 Bruxelles, Belgium.

**BIRK,** family name of **Baroness Birk.**

**BIRK,** Baroness *cr* 1967 (Life Peeress), of Regent's Park in Greater London; **Alma Birk,** JP; Chairman, Health Education Council, since 1969; Associate Editor of Nova since 1965; *d* of late Barnett and Alice Wilson; *m* Ellis Birk; one *s* one *d*. *Educ:* South Hampstead High Sch.; LSE. BSc Econ (Hons) London, 1939. Leader of Labour Group, Finchley Borough Council, 1950-53; contested (Lab): Ruislip-Northwood, 1950; Portsmouth West, 1951, 1955. Formerly lectr and Prison Visitor, Holloway Prison. Mem., Youth Service Develt Coun., 1967-; Vice-President: Coun. for Children's Welfare, 1968-; H. G. Wells Soc., 1967-; Stamford Hill Associated Clubs, 1967-; Member: Fabian Soc., 1946- (Sec., Fabian Soc. Res. Cttee on Marriage and Divorce, 1951-52); Howard League for Penal Reform, 1948-; Hendon Group Hosp. Management Cttee, 1951-59; Panel, London Pregnancy Adv. Service, 1968-; Hon. Cttee, Albany Trust. JP Highgate, 1952. *Publications:* pamphlets, articles. *Recreations:* travelling, theatre, reading, talking, especially to men. *Address:* 13 Hanover Terrace, NW1.

**BIRKBECK, Harold Edward;** Secretary of the Headmasters' Conference and Incorporated Association of Headmasters, 1965-69; *b* 1902. *Educ:* Bradford Grammar Sch.; Queen's Coll., Oxford. Asst Master, Edinburgh Academy, 1925-35; Headmaster of Barnard Castle School, 1935-64. *Address:* 65 Parkside Drive, Watford, Herts.

**BIRKBECK, Maj.-Gen. Theodore Henry,** CB 1963; CBE 1958; DSO 1945 and Bar, 1948; JP; *b* 17 Nov. 1911; *s* of late Maj.-Gen. Sir William Henry Birkbeck, KCB, CMG, Settle, Yorks and Lady Mabel (*née* Shaw), New York, USA; *m* 1939, Rozanne Elizabeth Wyatt (*née* Metcalfe) (marr. diss., 1961); two *s*; *m* 1962, Moyra L. M. Hewitt. *Educ:* Oundle Sch. 2nd Lieut, Border Regt, 1932; seconded to King's African Rifles, 1935-46; ADC to Governor and C-in-C, Nyasaland, 1937-39. Served War of 1939-45 (despatches thrice) with KAR in Ethiopia, Eritrea, Somaliland, Ceylon and Burma; commanded 11 KAR, 1944-46; seconded to Parachute Regt, 1947-50; OC 3rd Bn, Palestine, 1947-48; GSO1 (Trg) Eastern Comd, 1950-51; GSO1 (SD) Northern Comd, 1951-52; commanded New Coll., RMA, Sandhurst, 1952-55; commanded 70th Inf. Bde (KAR), Kenya, 1955-58; Dep. Military Sec. (A), War Office, 1958-60; GOC North Midland Area and 49th Div., TA, 1960-62; Dir, TA Cadets, War Office, 1962-66; Dir of Civil Defence, NE Region, 1966-68. JP W Riding of Yorks, 1967. *Address:* Anley, Settle, Yorks. *Club:* Army and Navy.

**BIRKENHEAD,** 2nd Earl of, *cr* 1922; **Frederick Winston Furneaux Smith;** Viscount Furneaux, 1921; Baron Birkenhead, 1919; Bt 1919; TD; High Steward of HM Manor of the Savoy, London, since 1942; *b* 7 Dec. 1907; *o s* of 1st Earl and Margaret Eleanor, 2nd *d* of late Rev. H. Furneaux, Fellow of Corpus Christi Coll., Oxford; *S* father, 1930; *m* 1935, Hon. Sheila Berry (author of Against Oblivion, 1943, Peace in Piccadilly, 1958, Illustrious Friends, 1965) (temporary Lady-in-Waiting to the Duchess of Kent, 1949-53), 2nd *d* of 1st Viscount Camrose; one *s* one *d*. *Educ:* Eton; Christ Church, Oxford. Parliamentary Private Sec. to Sec. of State for Foreign Affairs, 1938-39. A Lord-in-Waiting to King George VI, 1938-40 and 1951-52, to the Queen, 1952-55. Joined 53 (Oxfordshire Yeomanry) Anti-Tank Regt, 1938; served War of 1939-45, Capt. 1940, Staff Coll., 1941, Major, 1942; attd Pol. Intelligence Dept, Foreign Office, 1942; attd Brit. Mil. Mission to Yugoslav Partisans, 1944-45. *Publications:* Frederick Edwin, 1st Earl of Birkenhead: 2 vols, 1933, 1935; Strafford, 1938; Lady Eleanor Smith–a Memoir, 1953; FE, 1959; The Prof. in Two Worlds, 1961; Halifax, 1965; Walter Monckton, 1969. *Recreations:* lawn tennis, golf. *Heir: s* Viscount Furneaux, *qv*. *Address:* Charlton, Banbury, Oxon; 24 Wilton Street, SW1. *Clubs:* Beefsteak, Buck's, White's; Royal Yacht Squadron (Cowes).

*See also Baron Hartwell.*

**BIRKENHEAD, Suffragan Bishop of,** since 1965; **Rt. Rev. Eric Arthur John Mercer;** *b* 6 Dec. 1917; *s* of Ambrose John Mercer, Kent; *m* 1951, Rosemary Wilma, *d* of John William Denby, Lincs; one *s* one *d*. *Educ:* Dover Gram. Sch.; Kelham Theol. Coll. Enlisted Sherwood Foresters, 1940, commd 1940; Capt. and Adjt, 14th Foresters, 1943; served Italy (despatches), 1944; Staff Coll., Haifa, 1944; DAA&QMG, 66 Inf. Bde, Palestine, 1945; GSO2 (SD), HQ, MEF, 1945. Returned Kelham Theol. Coll., 1946-47. Ordained, Chester, 1947; Curate, Coppenhall, Crewe, 1947-51; Priest in charge, Heald Green, 1951-53; Rector, St Thomas', Stockport, 1953-59; Chester Diocesan Missioner, 1959-65; Rector, Chester St Bridget, 1959-65; Hon. Canon of Chester Cathedral, 1964. *Publication:* (contrib.) Worship in a Changing Church, 1965. *Address:* Trafford House, Queen's Park, Chester. *T:* Chester 25677.

**BIRKETT,** family name of **Baron Birkett.**

**BIRKETT,** 2nd Baron *cr* 1958, of Ulverston; **Michael Birkett;** film producer since 1961; *b* 22 Oct. 1929; *s* of 1st Baron Birkett, PC and Ruth Birkett (*née* Nilsson, she *d* 1969); *S* father, 1962; *m* 1960, Junia Crawford. *Educ:* Stowe; Trinity Coll., Cambridge. Asst Dir at Ealing Studios and Ealing Films, 1953-59; Asst Dir, 1959-61, on films including: The Mark; The Innocents; Billy Budd; Associate Producer: Some People, 1961-62; Modesty Blaise, 1965; Producer: The Caretaker, 1962; Marat/Sade, 1966; A Midsummer Night's Dream, 1967;

King Lear, 1968-69; Director: The Launching and The Soldier's Tale, 1963; Overture and Beginners, the More Man Understands, 1964. *Recreations:* music, reading, ballet, theatre. *Address:* Challens Green, Chalfont St Giles, Bucks.

**BIRKETT, George William Alfred,** CBE 1960; CEng, FIEE, FIMechE; Director of Weapons Production, Ministry of Defence (Naval), 1965-70; *b* 16 June 1908; *m* 1939, Doris Lillian Prince; one *s*. *Educ:* Portsmouth Municipal College. Portsmouth Dockyard, 1929; Techn. Officer, HM Signal Sch., 1938; Prin. Scientific Officer, RNSS, 1946; Sen. Prin. Production Engr, Admty Production Pool, 1953; Supt of Production Pool, Admty, 1956. *Recreation:* sailing. *Address:* 81 Ferndale, Inhurst Wood, Waterlooville, Portsmouth, Hants. *T:* Waterlooville 52695.

**BIRKIN, Sir Charles (Lloyd),** 5th Bt *cr* 1905; *b* 24 Sept. 1907; *s* of late Col Charles Wilfrid Birkin, CMG (4th *s* of 1st Bt); *S* uncle, 1942; *m* 1940, Janet Johnson; one *s* two *d*. *Educ:* Eton. Served War of 1939-45, with 112th Regt, 9th Sherwood Foresters. *Publications:* collections of short stories: The Kiss of Death, 1964; The Smell of Evil, 1965; Where Terror Stalks, 1966; My Name is Death, 1966; Dark Menace, 1968; So Cold . . . So Fair, 1970. *Heir: s* John Christian William Birkin, *b* 2 July 1953. *Club:* Carlton.

**BIRKIN, Group Capt. James Michael,** CB 1956; DSO 1944; OBE 1951; DFC 1944; AFC 1942; Director, Birkin & Company Limited, New Basford, Nottingham (Lace Manufacturers); *b* 23 April 1912; *s* of late Major H. L. Birkin, Lincoln House, The Park, Nottingham, and late Olive Isobel, *d* of late Rev. H. C. Russell, Wollaton, Notts; *m* 1956, Antonia Edith, *d* of late Lt-Col A. F. Stanley Clarke and Mrs Charles Graves; one *s* one *d*. *Educ:* Harrow; Trinity Coll., Cambridge (MA). London Stock Exchange until 1939; Birkin & Co. Ltd, 1945-. RAFVR, 1938-47; RAuxAF, 1947-63 (Inspector, 1952-62); Hon. Air Commodore, 1956. ADC to the Queen, 1957-63. *Address:* c/o Birkin & Co. Ltd, New Basford, Nottingham. *T:* Nottingham 79351. *Clubs:* Royal Automobile, MCC, Pathfinder; Nottinghamshire (Nottingham); Royal Yacht Squadron, Royal Victoria Yacht, Royal Air Force Yacht.

**BIRKINSHAW, Air Commodore George William,** CB 1946; *b* 17 June 1896. *Educ:* Downing Coll., Cambridge (BA 1927). RFC and RAF from 1915; served European War, 1914-18, France; India and Iraq, 1920-24; Egypt and Palestine, 1933-38; Dir, Repair and Maintenance, Ministry of Supply, 1943-46; Senior Technical Staff Officer, RAF HQ, India, 1946-47; retired, 1947. Freeman of York, Freeman of London. *Club:* Pathfinder.

**BIRKINSHAW, Prof. John Howard,** DSc; FRIC; retired as Professor of Biochemistry and Head of Department of Biochemistry, London School of Hygiene and Tropical Medicine, University of London (1956-62), now Emeritus; *b* 8 Oct. 1894; *s* of John Thomas and Madeline Birkinshaw, Garforth, near Leeds; *m* 1929, Elizabeth Goodwin Guthrie, Ardrossan, Ayrshire; one *s* one *d*. *Educ:* Leeds Modern Sch.; Leeds Univ. War service, 1915, West Yorks Regt and Machine Gun Corps (POW); demobilised, 1919. BSc Hons 1920, MSc 1921, DSc 1929, Leeds. Research Biochemist to Nobel's Explosives Co. (later ICI), 1920-30; Research Asst to Prof. Raistrick, London Sch. of Hygiene and Tropical Medicine, 1931; Senior Lecturer, 1938; Reader, 1945. *Publications:* about 60 scientific papers in Biochemical Journal, Philos. Trans. Royal Society, etc. *Recreation:* photography. *Address:* 87 Barrow Point Avenue, Pinner, Middlesex. *T:* 01-866 4784.

**BIRKMYRE, Sir Henry,** 2nd Bt *cr* 1921, of Dalmunzie; Director: Assam Consolidated Tea Estates Ltd; Malaya General Co. Ltd; *b* 24 March 1898; *er s* of Sir Archibald Birkmyre, 1st Bt and Anne, *e d* of Capt. James Black; *S* father, 1935; *m* 1922, Doris Gertrude, *er d* of late Col H. Austen Smith, CIE; one *s* one *d*. *Educ:* Wellington. War Service in France with RFA, 1917. *Heir: s* Archibald Birkmyre [*b* 12 Feb. 1923; *m* 1953, Gillian Mary, *o d* of Eric Downes, OBE; one *s* two *d*]. *Recreation:* golf. *Address:* Springbank, Cooden, Bexhill-on-Sea, Sussex. *T:* Cooden 2214. *Club:* Bath.

**BIRKS, Maj.-Gen. (retired) Horace Leslie,** CB 1945; DSO 1941; *b* 7 May 1897; *m* 1920, Gladys Hester (*d* 1957), MBE, *d* of Lieut-Col Hugh Harry Haworth Aspinall, OBE; one *s*. *Educ:* University College Sch. Enlisted London Rifle Brigade, 1915; 2nd Lieut Machine Gun Corps Heavy Branch, 1917, later Tank Corps; served France, 1915-16 and again 1917 (twice wounded); Instructor RTC Schools, 1919-24; Staff Coll., Quetta, 1927, 1928; General Staff, Western Command and War Office, 1930-37; Instructor Staff Coll., Quetta, 1937-39; India, 1924-29 and 1937-39; GSO1, 7th Armoured Division, Army of the Nile, 1939-40; 2nd in Command 4th Armoured Bde, 1940-41 (DSO, despatches twice); Commander 11th Armoured Brigade, 1941; Commander 10th Armoured Division, 1942; MG, RAC, CMF, 1944 (CB); retired pay, 1946. Secretary, University College Hospital Medical Sch., 1946-63, retired. *Recreations:* travel, golf, squash, swimming in warm water. *Address:* 506 Frobisher House, Dolphin Square, SW1. *Clubs:* Army and Navy, Roehampton, Pilgrims.

**BIRLEY, Prof. Eric,** MBE 1943; FSA 1931; FBA 1969; Professor of Roman-British History and Archæology, University of Durham, since 1956; *b* 12 Jan. 1906; *y s* of J. Harold Birley; *m* 1934, Margaret Isabel, *d* of Rev. James Goodlet; two *s*. *Educ:* Clifton Coll.; Brasenose Coll., Oxford. Lecturer, University of Durham, 1931; Reader, 1943. Served War of 1939-45: Military Intelligence, Lt-Col, GSO1 Military Intelligence Research Section; Chief of German Military Document Section, War Dept. Vice-Master, Hatfield Coll., Durham, 1947-49, Master, 1949-56; first Dean of Faculty of Social Sciences, Univ. of Durham, 1968-70. President: Soc. of Antiquaries of Newcastle upon Tyne, 1957-59; Cumberland and Westmorland Antiquarian and Archaeological Soc., 1957-60; Architectural and Archæological Soc. of Durham and Northumberland, 1959-63; Member: German Archæological Inst.; Ancient Monuments Board for England, 1966-; Hon. Member, Gesellschaft Pro Vindonissa (Switzerland). Polonia Restituta, 1944; Legion of Merit, 1947. *Publications:* Roman Britain and the Roman Army, 1953; (ed) The Congress of Roman Frontier Studies, 1949, 1952; Research on Hadrian's Wall, 1961; numerous papers on Roman Britain and on the Roman army, excavation reports, etc. *Recreation:* archæology. *Address:* Observatory House, Durham City. *T:* Durham 2218.

**BIRLEY, Michael Pellew,** MA (Oxon); Housemaster at Marlborough College, since 1970; *b* 7 Nov. 1920; *s* of Norman Pellew Birley, *qv*; *m* 1949, Ann Grover (*née* Street); two *s* two *d*. *Educ:* Marlborough Coll.; Wadham Coll., Oxford. 1st class Classical Honour Moderations, 1940; 1st class *Litterae*

*Humaniores,* 1947; MA 1946. Served War of 1939-45 with the Royal Fusiliers; joined up, Sept. 1940; commissioned, April 1941; abroad, 1942-45 (despatches); demobilised, Jan. 1946. Taught Classics: Shrewsbury Sch., 1948-50; Eton Coll., 1950-56; Headmaster, Eastbourne College, 1956-70. *Recreations:* sailing, playing the flute. *Address:* Preshute House, Marlborough, Wilts. *T:* Marlborough 2291.

**BIRLEY, Norman Pellew,** DSO 1918; MC 1916; *b* Pelton Vicarage, Co. Durham, 29 April 1891; *s* of Rev. Hugh Hornby Birley and Florence Lydia Birley; *m* 1919, Eileen Alice Morgan, Underwood, Mumbles, Glamorgan; two *s*. *Educ:* Repton Sch.; New Coll., Oxford. Served European War, 1914-19. History Master, Gresham's Sch., Holt, 1919; Asst Master, Marlborough Coll., 1922-27; Headmaster, King's Sch., Canterbury, 1927-35; Headmaster, Merchant Taylors' Sch., 1935-46; retired, 1946; Mem., Wiltshire Education Cttee, 1948-66. *Recreations:* fishing and gardening. *Address:* Hyde Leaze, Hyde Lane, Marlborough, Wilts.

*See also M. P. Birley.*

**BIRLEY, Sir Robert,** KCMG 1967 (CMG 1950); MA; FSA; Chairman, Central Council of the Selly Oak Colleges, since 1969; *b* 14 July 1903; *s* of late Leonard Birley, CSI, CIE; *m* 1930, Elinor Margaret, *d* of Eustace Corrie Frere, FRIBA; two *d*. *Educ:* Rugby Sch.; Balliol Coll., Oxford (Brackenbury Scholar; Hon. Fellow, 1969). Gladstone Memorial Prize, 1924, 1st Class Hons History. Asst Master, Eton Coll., 1926-35; Headmaster, Charterhouse, 1935-47; Educational Adviser to the Military Governor, CCG, 1947-49; Head Master, Eton Coll., 1949-63; Vis. Prof. of Education, Univ. of the Witwatersrand, 1964-67; Prof. and Head of Dept of Social Science and Humanities, City Univ., London, 1967-70. Mem., Fleming Cttee on Public Schools, 1944; Burge Memorial Lecture, 1948; Reith Lectures, 1949; Clark Lectures, 1961; Chancellor's Lecture, University of Witwatersrand, 1965; Chichele Lectures, All Souls Coll., Oxford, Michaelmas Term, 1967. Gresham Lecturer in Rhetoric, 1967-70. Hon. Doc. Ing., Technical Univ., Berlin, 1949; Hon. LLD: Edinburgh, 1950; Leeds, 1950; Liverpool, 1953; Witwatersrand, 1965; Hon. DPhil, Frankfurt Univ., 1959. Grosse Verdienstkreuz (Germany), 1955. *Publications:* The English Jacobins, 1925; Speeches and Documents in American History (selected and edited), 1944; Sunk Without Trace (Clark Lectures), 1962. *Address:* Lomans, West End, Somerton, Somerset. *T:* Somerton 640. *Club:* Travellers'.

*See also B. Rees.*

**BIRMINGHAM, Archbishop of, (RC),** since 1965; **Most Rev. George Patrick Dwyer,** DD, PhD; *b* 25 Sept. 1908; *s* of John William and Ima Dwyer. *Educ:* St Bede's Coll., Manchester; Ven. English Coll., Rome; Christ's Coll., Cambridge. PhD 1929, DD 1934, Gregorian Univ., Rome; ordained Priest, 1932; BA Mod. and Med. Lang. Trip. Cambridge (Lady Margaret Scholar, Christ's Coll.). Teaching, St Bede's, Manchester, 1937-47; Catholic Missionary Society, 1947; Editor of Catholic Gazette, 1947-51; Superior, Catholic Missionary Society, 1951-57; Bishop of Leeds, 1957-65. Lecture and Mission Tour in New Zealand, 1956. *Publications:* The Catholic Faith, 1954; Mary–Doctrine for Everyman (with Rev. T. Holland, DD), 1956; articles in the Press; booklets. *Address:* Archbishop's House, St Chad's Ringway, Birmingham 4.

**BIRMINGHAM, Bishop of,** since 1969; **Rt. Rev. Laurence Ambrose Brown,** MA; *b* 1 Nov. 1907; 2nd *s* of Frederick John Brown; *m* 1935, Florence Blanche, *d* of late William Gordon Marshall; three *d*. *Educ:* Queens' College, Cambridge (MA); Cuddesdon Theological College, Oxford. Asst Curate, St John-the-Divine, Kennington, 1932-35; Curate-in-Charge, St Peter, Luton, Beds, 1935-40; Vicar, Hatfield Hyde, Welwyn Garden City, 1940-46; Sec. Southwark Dio. Reorganisation Cttee, 1946-60; Sec. S London Church Fund and Southwark Dio. Bd of Finance, 1952-60; Canon Residentiary, Southwark, 1950-60; Archdeacon of Lewisham and Vice-Provost of Southwark, 1955-60; Suffragan Bishop of Warrington, 1960-67. Mem. Church Assembly and Proctor in Convocation, 1954-; Chm., Advisory Council for Church's Ministry, 1966-. *Publications:* pamphlets on church building in post-war period. *Recreation:* Scout movement. *Address:* Bishop's Croft, Harborne, Birmingham 17. *T:* 021-427 0163. *Club:* Royal Commonwealth Society.

**BIRMINGHAM, Assistant Bishop of and Provost of;** *see* Sinker, Rt Rev. George.

**BIRMINGHAM, Auxiliary Bishops of, (RC);** *see* Cleary, Rt Rev. Joseph, Emery, Rt Rev. A. J.

**BIRMINGHAM, Archdeacon of;** *see* Nicholls, Ven. V. S.

**BIRNIE, Col Eugene St John,** OBE 1965; FRGS; The Guides Cavalry (QVOFF); *b* 18 March 1900; *s* of Cyril Montague Birnie and Margaret Dannatt; *m* 1933, Lady Marguerite Kathleen Courtenay, 3rd *d* of Rev. 16th Earl of Devon; two *d*. *Educ:* Charterhouse. Commissioned to 25th Cavalry (Frontier Force) now Sam Browne's Cavalry (12th FF), 1919; transferred to Guides Cavalry, 1937; served 3rd Afghan War, 1919; Capt., 1925; Major, 1937; ADC to Governor of Bengal, 1929-30; Adjutant to Governor of Bengal's Body Guard, 1930-32; AMS, AHQ India, 1939-41; DAMS, GHQ Middle East, 1941 (despatches); Private Secretary to C-in-C India, 1941-42; AAG, MEF, 1942; AAG Paiforce, 1942-43; Commandant Hyderabad Lancers, 1943-44; HQ CMF, Italy, 1944-45; Director AWS Alfsea, SEAC, 1946; Military Secretary to Governor-General of Pakistan, 1947-48; Secretary, Church of England Children's Soc., 1949-65. "A" Pilot's Certificate, 1930; Kamet Expedition, 1931; MacGregor Memorial Medal for 1932 by the C-in-C and Council of the United Services Institution of India for Reconnaissances in Tehri Garhwal during 1931; Everest Expedition, 1933. *Address:* The Cottage, Longparish, Hants.

**BIRSAY, Hon. Lord; Harald Robert Leslie,** CBE 1963 (MBE 1945); TD 1944; MA 1927, LLB (Glas.) 1930; QC (Scot.), 1949; Chairman, Scottish Land Court, since 1965; *b* 8 May 1905; *s* of Robert Leslie, Master Mariner, Stromness, Orkney, and Margaret Mowat Cochrane, Stromness; *m* 1945, Robina Margaret Marwick, MB, ChB (Edin.), *o d* of ex-Provost J. G. Marwick, FSA (Scot.), Stromness, Orkney; one *s* one *d*. *Educ:* Earlston Public Sch.; Berwickshire High Sch.; Glasgow High Sch.; Glasgow Univ. Served in Glasgow High Sch. (1918-23) and Glasgow Univ. (1923-30) OTCs. Extracted as Solicitor, 1930; called to Scottish Bar, 1937. War of 1939-45 (MBE; despatches); served in the Royal Scots and on HQs 15 (S) Div.; 8 Corps and 21 Army Group; released, 1945, to TARO, as (Hon.) Lieut-Col. Standing Counsel to Dept of Agriculture; Junior Assessor to City of Edinburgh Assessor and Dean of Guild and Burgh Courts, 1949; Senior Assessor, 1960; Advocate-Depute, Scottish Bar, 1947-51; Sheriff of Roxburgh, Berwick and Selkirk,

1956-61; Sheriff of Caithness, Sutherland, Orkney and Zetland, 1961-65. Candidate (Lab) for Orkney and Shetland Constituency, 1950; Chairman: Scottish Advisory Council on the Treatment of Offenders, 1959; Scottish Cttee of British Council, 1963-70; Scottish Joint Council for Teachers' Salaries, 1964; Executive Edinburgh Council of Social Service, 1956-69; Cttee on Gen. Med. Services in the Highlands and Islands, 1964-67; Nat. Savings Cttee for Scotland, 1965-; Board of Governors, St Hilary's Sch., Edinburgh, 1959; Hon. President: Glasgow, Orkney and Shetland Association also Edinburgh, Orkney and Zetland Association, 1962; Scottish Council for National Parks until 1965; Hon. Vice-President, Boys' Brigade, 1966- (Hon. Pres., Leith Bn, 1963-); Scottish Council of Boys' Clubs and Youth Clubs, 1962; Shipwrecked Fishermen and Mariners' Royal Benevolent Society (Scotland), 1966; Orkney Council of Social Service, 1966. Lord High Commissioner to the General Assembly of the Church of Scotland, 1965 and 1966. Hon. Air Cdre, No. 2 (City of Edinburgh) Maritime HQ Unit, RAuxAF, 1967-. DL Orkney, 1965. Hon. LLD: Strathclyde, 1966; Glasgow, 1966. Hon. FEIS, 1966. *Address:* 27 Queensferry Road, Edinburgh EH4 3HB. *T:* 031-332 3315; Queenafiold, Birsay, Orkney. *T:* (Orkney) Birsay 286. *Clubs:* Royal Scots, Caledonian, Arts (Edinburgh).

**BIRT, Guy Capper,** CVO 1935; MRCS, LRCP, LDS; retired; Extra Surgeon-Dentist to Queen Mary, 1949; *b* 6 Aug. 1884; *s* of Daniel Birt and Mary Ella Capper; *m* 1913, Roberta Ross; two *s. Educ:* Wellington Coll.; St Thomas's and Royal Dental Hospitals. Practised dentistry in Cavendish Square, 1910; Asst in Dental Dept, St Thomas's Hospital, 1910-14; Surgeon Dentist to King George V, 1925-36; to Queen Mary, 1925-49; Dental Surgeon to Metropolitan Police, 1910-34; Capt. (Plastic Surgeon) in RAMC, European War, 1914-18; member Board of Governors of and Hon. Consulting Dental Surgeon to St Thomas's Hospital. *Recreations:* Caravanning and yachting. *Address:* Merlebank, Moulsford, Wallingford, Berks. *T:* Cholesey 347. *Club:* Lansdowne House.

**BIRT, Rev. Roderick Harold Capper,** MA Oxon; Canon Emeritus of St George's Cathedral, Cape Town; *b* 24 Oct. 1882; *s* of Daniel and M. E. Birt; *m* 1st, 1909, Sophie (*d* 1942), *o d* of Walter Kidd, MD, formerly of Blackheath; no *c*; 2nd, 1944, Mary, *widow* of Frank Goch, SAAF, and *er d* of Canon T. Gerald Le Mesurier, Cape Town. *Educ:* Wellington Coll.; New Coll., Oxford. Deacon, 1907; Priest, 1908; Asst Master, Radley Coll., 1906-18; Principal of the Diocesan Coll., Rondebosch, Cape Town, 1919-43; Canon of St George's Cathedral, Cape Town, 1940-51; Honorary Canon, 1951; Asst Priest, St Saviour's, Claremont, Cape, 1944-60. *Recreation:* gardening. *Address:* 4 Glebe Road, Rondebosch, near Cape Town, S. Africa. *Club:* Leander.

**BIRTWISTLE, Ivor Treharne,** OBE 1951; literary editor and cadet counsellor, The West Australian, Perth, WA, 1945-57; *b* Beaumaris, Victoria, Australia, 8 April 1892; *s* of James Birtwistle, architect, Perth, and Emily, *d* of David Davies, Daylesford, Victoria; *m* 1925, Kathleen Winifred, *d* of late James Herbert Broadley, North Perth, WA, formerly of Bath, England; one *s* one *d. Educ:* State Sch., Claremont, WA. Studied for Presbyterian ministry, but joined literary staff Melbourne Age, 1913; enlisted AIF 1915, serving Egypt, Gallipoli and France; Publicity Officer, National Cttee Australian YMCA, 1918; Peace Loan Campaign (Victoria), 1919; National Campaign Council, Federal elections (Victoria), 1920; Vice-Chairman, State Repatriation Board (Victoria), 1919-20; joined literary staff The West Australian, Perth, 1920; Editor, The Western Mail, 1924-45; State President Boy Scouts' Assoc., 1938-50; State President Surf Life Saving Assoc., 1929-37; Dir, Studies in Journalism, University of W. Australia, 1930-40; President: Royal WA Historical Soc., 1945-65; WA Regional YMCA Council, 1964-67; Perth YMCA, 1951-63; Gallipoli Legion of Anzacs of WA. Mem., Armadale-Kelmscott Shire Council, 1964-69. *Recreations:* swimming, walking, gardening, historical research. *Address:* Greenway, Peet Road, Roleystone, West Australia. *T:* Roleystone 976333. *Club:* Legacy (Perth, WA).

**BISAT, William S.,** FRS 1947; DSc, MSc, FGS; retired civil engineer and surveyor, lately engaged on construction of large civil engineering works and gravel and sand quarries for H. Arnold & Son Ltd, Public Works Contractors, Doncaster and Leeds 1903; *b* 19 Oct. 1886; *s* of Charles Edward Bisat, bookseller, Doncaster; *m* 1st, 1915, Enid Alice, *d* of Rev. T. Powell, MA; 2nd, 1940, Mary St Agnes, *d* of Rev. W. H. Stansfield; one *d* (and two *s* one *d* decd). *Educ:* Grammar Sch., Doncaster. Hon. MSc Leeds, 1938; Hon. DSc Durham, 1963. Lyell Medal, Geol. Soc. London, 1942; Silver Medal, Liverpool Geol. Soc., 1954; Clough Medal, Edinburgh Geol. Soc., 1960; Sorby Medal, Yorkshire Geol. Soc., 1961. Hon. Member: Belgian Geol. Soc.; Yorkshire Geol. Soc.; Doncaster Sci. Soc. *Publications:* many geological treatises on fauna of carboniferous rocks and their stratigraphical succession; also the drift deposits (gravels and boulder-clays) of Yorkshire. *Recreation:* geological research. *Address:* Leighton, Crabtree Hill, Collingham, Wetherby, Yorkshire. *T:* Collingham Bridge 2365.

**BISCOE, Rear-Adm. Alec Julian;** *see* Tyndale-Biscoe.

**BISHOP, Maj.-Gen. Sir Alec, (Alexander);** *see* Bishop, Maj.-Gen. Sir W. H. A.

**BISHOP, Ann,** FRS 1959; ScD; *b* 19 Dec. 1899; *o d* of late James Kimberly and Ellen Bishop. *Educ:* Manchester High Sch. for Girls; Manchester Univ.; Cambridge Univ. BSc 1921, DSc 1932, Manchester; PhD 1926, ScD 1941, Cambridge. Hon. Research Fellow, Manchester Univ., 1925-26; Research Asst, Medical Research Council, 1926-29; Beit Memorial Research Fellow, 1929-32; Yarrow Fellow of Girton Coll., Cambridge, 1932-37; Research Fellow of Girton Coll., Cambridge, 1937-66, Life Fellow, 1966; Director, MRC Chemotherapy Research Unit at the Molteno Inst., Univ. of Cambridge, 1942-64. *Publications:* articles on the biology of Protozoa, and Chemotherapy, published in Scientific Journals. *Address:* 47 Sherlock Close, Cambridge.

**BISHOP, Rt. Rev. Clifford Leofric Purdy;** *see* Malmesbury, Suffragan Bishop of.

**BISHOP, Edward Stanley,** AMIED, ARAeS; JP; MP (Lab) for Newark, Notts, since 1964; *b* 3 Oct. 1920; *e s* of Frank Stanley Bishop and Constance Camilla Bishop (*née* Dawbney); *m* 1945, Winifred Mary Bryant, JP, *o c* of Frank and Elizabeth Bryant; four *d. Educ:* S. Bristol Central Sch.; Merchant Venturers' Technical Coll.; Bristol Univ. (extra mural studies); William Temple Coll., Rugby. Apprenticed: Aeronautical Engineering, Bristol Aeroplane

Co., 1937-43; Flight Test Engineer, 1943-45; Aeronautical Design Engineer, 1945-64 (British Aircraft Corp.). Member Bristol City Council, 1946-59, 1963-66 (Dep. Leader and Chm. Finance and General Purposes Cttee, 1956-59). JP, City and County of Bristol, 1957; Visiting Magistrate, HM Bristol Prison, 1959-. Contested (Lab): Bristol West, 1950; Exeter, 1951; S Gloucester, 1955. Chm., SW Reg. Council, Labour Party, 1953-54; Past Member, various Cttees. Member: House of Commons Estimates Cttee, 1965-66; Ecclesiastical Cttee, 1966-; Asst Govt Whip, 1966-67. Lecturer in Local Government and Social Studies for WEA; Vice-President RDC Assoc., 1965-; Member, Draughtsmen and Allied Technicians' Assoc.; Member: Archbishop of Canterbury's Commn on Organisation of Church by Dioceses in London and SE England, 1965-67; Redundant Churches Fund, 1970. A Church Commissioner, 1968-. FAMS. *Recreations:* archæology, genealogy; National Trust visits; being with family. *Address:* 31 Wick Crescent, Brislington, Bristol 4. *T:* Bristol 75112; House of Commons, SW1.

**BISHOP, Sir (Frank) Patrick,** Kt 1964; MBE 1945; Barrister-at-Law; Director, Rediffusion Ltd; *b* 7 March 1900; *m* 1st, Vera (*d* 1953), *d* of late Arthur Drew, Coulsdon, Surrey; one *s* two *d*; 2nd, 1955, Ella Mary Hunt. *Educ:* Tottenham Grammar Sch.; King's Coll., London. Called to the Bar, Gray's Inn, 1923; practised as a barrister-at-law, 1924-29; joined the staff of The Times, Asst Manager, 1937-45; Gen. Man. Newsprint Supply Co., 1947-57. MP (C) Harrow Central, 1950-64. Formerly Chairman: Advertisement Cttee, Newspaper Proprietors' Assoc.; Advertisement Cttee, Internat. Chamber of Commerce; Exec. Cttee, Advertising Assoc. Served European War, 1914-18, in RAF, 1918; War of 1939-45, Second in Command, 5th City of London (Press Battalion) of the Home Guard. *Publications:* Advertising and the Law, 1928; The Economics of Advertising, 1944; The Ethics of Advertising, 1949. *Address:* Scotland Street, Stoke-by-Nayland, Suffolk. *Clubs:* Carlton, Devonshire.

**BISHOP, Frederick Arthur,** CB 1960; CVO 1957; Director-General of the National Trust, since 1971; *b* 4 Dec. 1915; *o s* of A. J. Bishop, Bristol; *m* 1940, Elizabeth Finlay Stevenson; two *s* one *d*. *Educ:* Colston's Hospital, Bristol. LLB (London). Inland Revenue, 1934. Served in RAF and Air Transport Auxiliary, 1942-46. Ministry of Food, 1947, where Principal Private Secretary to Ministers, 1949-52; Asst Secretary, Cabinet Office, 1953-55; Principal Private Secretary to the Prime Minister, 1956-59; Deputy Secretary: of the Cabinet, 1959-61; Min. of Agriculture, Fisheries and Food, 1961-64; Perm. Sec., Min. of Lands and Natural Resources, 1964-65, resigned. Chairman, Home Grown Timber Advisory Cttee, 1966-. Director: Pearson Longman; Air Holdings Ltd. *Address:* Gainsford House, Cowden, Kent. *T:* Cowden 587. *Club:* Reform.

**BISHOP, George Sidney,** CB 1958; OBE 1947; Chairman: Bookers Agricultural Holdings Ltd, since 1964; Booker McConnell Ltd, since 1970, Director since 1961; Director, Nigerian Sugar Co. Ltd, since 1966; *b* 15 Oct. 1913; *o s* of late J. and M. Bishop; *m* 1940, Marjorie Woodruff (marr. diss. 1961); one *d*; *m* 1961, Una Padel. *Educ:* Ashton-in-Makerfield Grammar Sch.; London Sch. of Economics. Social service work in distressed areas, 1935-38; SW Durham Survey, 1939; Ministry of Food, 1940; Private Secretary to Minister of Food, 1945-49; Under-Secretary, Ministry of Agriculture, Fisheries and Food, 1949-59, Dep. Secretary, 1959-61. Chairman Internat. Sugar Council, 1957; Vice-Chairman Internat. Wheat Council, 1959; Chairman, West India Cttee, 1969-. Mem. Panel for Civil Service Manpower Review, 1968-70; Governor, Nat. Inst. for Economic and Social Research, 1968-. *Recreations:* mountaineering, motoring, photography. *Address:* Brenva, Egham's Wood Road, Beaconsfield, Bucks. *T:* Beaconsfield 3096. *Clubs:* Reform, National Liberal, West India; Club Alpin Français.

**BISHOP, Sir Harold,** Kt, *cr* 1955; CBE 1938; FCGI; BSc (Engineering) London; Hon. FIEE, FIMechE; FIEEE; Director, Automatic Light Controlling Co. Ltd; *b* 29 Oct. 1900; 3rd *s* of Henry Thomas Bishop; *m* 1925, Madge Adeline, *d* of Frank Harry Vaus; two *d* (one *s* decd). *Educ:* Alleyn's Sch., Dulwich; City and Guilds Coll. Engineer, HM Office of Works, 1920-22; Engineer, Marconi's Wireless Telegraph Co. Ltd, 1922-23; Senior Supt BBC, 1923-29; Asst Chief Engineer, BBC, 1929-43; Chief Engineer, 1943-52; Dir of Engineering, 1952-63. Hon. FIEE (Pres. 1953-54, Vice-Pres. 1948-53); President: Electrical Industries Benevolent Assoc., 1955-56; Association of Supervising Electrical Engineers, 1956-58; Institution of Electrical and Electronic Techn. Engineers, 1965-69; Royal Television Soc., 1960-62; Fellow, Imperial Coll. of Science and Technology; Mem., Science Museum Advisory Council (Chm. 1965-). *Address:* Carbis, Harborough Hill, Pulborough, Sussex. *T:* West Chiltington 3325. *Club:* Athenæum.

**BISHOP, Rev. Hugh (William Fletcher Bishop);** Father Superior of the Community of the Resurrection, Mirfield, Yorkshire, since 1965 (Principal of the College, 1956-65); *b* 17 May 1907; *e s* of John and Mary Bishop, Haughton House, Shifnal, Shropshire. *Educ:* Malvern Coll.; Keble Coll., Oxford (MA). Cuddesdon Coll., Oxford, 1932-33; Deacon, 1933; Priest, 1934. Curate of St Michael's, Workington, 1933-35; Curate of Cuddesdon and Lectr, Cuddesdon 1935-37. Professed in Community of the Resurrection, Mirfield, 1940 (taking name of Hugh); Chaplain to the Forces (EC), 1940-45 (POW, 1942-45); Warden, Hostel of the Resurrection, Leeds, 1946-49; Guardian of Novices, Mirfield, 1949-52. *Publications:* The Passion Drama, 1955; The Easter Drama, 1958; Life is for Loving, 1961; (contrib. to) Mirfield Essays in Christian Belief, 1962; The Man for Us, 1968. *Address:* House of the Resurrection, Mirfield, Yorkshire. *T:* Mirfield 3272.

**BISHOP, Dame Joyce;** *see* Bishop, Dame M. J.

**BISHOP, Dame (Margaret) Joyce,** DBE 1963 (CBE 1953); MA Oxon; Head Mistress of The Godolphin and Latymer School, Hammersmith, W6, 1935-63, retired; *b* 28 July 1896; 2nd *d* of Charles Benjamin and Amy Bishop. *Educ:* Edgbaston High Sch., Birmingham; Lady Margaret Hall, Oxford. English Mistress, Hertfordshire and Essex High Sch., 1918-24; Head Mistress, Holly Lodge High Sch., Smethwick, Staffs, 1924-35. Member Working Party set up by Minister of Education to enquire into Recruitment of Women to Teaching Profession, 1947. President, Association of Head Mistresses, 1950-52. Member: Secondary School Examinations Council, 1950-62; University Grants Cttee, 1961-63; Council for Professions Supplementary to Medicine, 1961-; TV Research Cttee set up by Home Secretary, 1963-69. Chairman, Joint Cttee of the Four Secondary Associations, 1956-58. *Recreations:* reading, the theatre. *Address:* 22

Malbrook Road, Putney, SW15. *T:* 01-788 5862. *Club:* English-Speaking Union.

**BISHOP, Sir Patrick;** *see* Bishop, Sir F. P.

**BISHOP, Peter Maxwell Farrow,** DM (Oxon); FRCP (Lond); FRCOG; Medical Consultant, Family Planning Association, since 1968; Master, Society of Apothecaries, 1969-70; Endocrinologist Emeritus, Guy's Hospital and Chelsea Hospital for Women, 1969; *b* 14 Aug. 1904; *o s* of late Dr T. H. Bishop; *m* 1937, Winifred Phyllis, *o d* of Lt-Col E. O. Thurston, IMS; one *s* two *d. Educ:* Berlin; Charterhouse; Trinity Coll., Oxford. Guy's Hosp. Medical Sch.: Senior Demonstrator in Physiology, 1930-33; Lectr in Physiological Chemistry, 1933-38; Lectr in Applied Physiology and Pharmacology, 1938; Warden of the College, 1938-47; Dep. Supt, 1938-45; MO in charge (EMS), Guy's Hosp., 1939-45. First Treas., Member Editorial Board and one of founders of Journal of Endocrinology, 1939; Member Council of Management, Soc. for Endocrinology, 1947; one of first two Hon. Co-Secretaries Section of Endocrinology, Royal Society Medicine, 1946 (Pres. 1955); Member Cttee, Soc. for Study of Fertility, 1958 (Hon. Sec. 1959, Chm. 1960-63); Hon. Dipl. Acad. of Med., Barcelona, 1949; Chm. Coun. of Management, Jl of Reproduction and Fertility, 1960-66; Ayerst Lectr, 1958, and Hon. Mem., American Soc. for Study of Sterility; Hon. Librarian, Royal Soc. Med., 1963-69. Sir Arthur Sims Commonwealth Travelling Prof., 1964. Hon. Mem., Endocrine Soc., Madrid, 1965; H. D. Rolleston Lecturer, Royal Coll. Physicians, 1965; Litchfield Lecturer, Oxford Univ., 1967. *Publications:* Gynæcological Endocrinology, Recent Advances in Endocrinology; Chemistry of the Sex Hormones; various articles on endocrine subjects. *Address:* 32 Connaught Square, W2. *T:* 01-262 4211; 56 Wimpole Street, W1. *T:* 01-935 8737. *Clubs:* Hurlingham; Hanstown.

**BISHOP, Prof. Richard E. D.,** PhD Stanford, DSc (Eng) London, ScD Cantab, FIMechE, AFRAeS; Kennedy Professor of Mechanical Engineering in the University of London since 1957; Fellow of University College, London, since 1964; *b* London, 1 Jan. 1925; *s* of Rev. Dr N. R. Bishop; *m* 1949, Jean Paterson, London; one *s* one *d. Educ:* The Roan Sch., Greenwich. RNVR, 1943-46. University Coll., London, 1946-49; Commonwealth Fund Fellow in Stanford Univ., California, 1949-51; Sen. Scientific Officer, Ministry of Supply, 1951-52; Cambridge Univ.: Demonstrator, 1952; Fellow of Pembroke Coll., 1954; University Lecturer in Engineering, 1955; Visiting Prof.: Massachusetts Institute of Technology, Summer, 1959; Visiting Lecturer, National Science Foundation, USA, Spring, 1961; Member of Council, Instn of Mechanical Engineers, 1961-64, 1969-70; President, British Acoustical Soc., 1966-68; Hon. Member Royal Corps of Naval Constructors, 1968; George Stephenson Res. Prize, IMechE, 1959; Thomas Hawksley Gold Medal, IMechE, 1965; Silver Medal of Skoda Works, 1967; Křižík Gold Medal, Acad. Sci. CSSR, 1969. *Publications:* (with D. C. Johnson) Vibration Analysis Tables, 1956; (with D. C. Johnson) The Mechanics of Vibration, 1960; (with G. M. L. Gladwell and S. Michaelson) The Matrix Analysis of Vibration, 1965; Vibration, 1965; many scientific papers. *Recreations:* motoring, sailing. *Address:* University College, WC1. *T:* 01-387 7050.

**BISHOP, Ronald Eric,** CBE 1946; FRAeS; Deputy Managing Director, de Havilland Aircraft Co. Ltd, 1958-64; Design Director, de Havilland Aircraft Co. Ltd, Hatfield, since 1946; *b* 1903. Joined de Havilland Aircraft Co. Ltd, as an apprentice, 1921; entered Drawing Office; appointed in charge, 1936. Responsible for following designs: Flamingo, Mosquito, Hornet, Vampire, Dove, Venom, Heron, DH 108, DH 110, Comet Jet Airliner. Gold Medal, RAeS, 1964. *Address:* de Havilland Aircraft Co. Ltd, Hatfield, Herts. *T:* Hatfield 2345.

**BISHOP, Stanley Victor,** MC 1944; Director, British Printing Corporation Ltd, since 1966, latterly Deputy Chairman and Managing Director, and Chairman International Learning Systems Corporation; *b* 11 May 1916; *s* of George Stanley Bishop, MA; *m* 1946, Dorothy Primrose Dodds, Berwick-upon-Tweed; two *s* one *d. Educ:* Leeds. Articled to Beevers & Adgie, Leeds; CA 1937. Served War of 1939-45: enlisted London Scottish (TA), 1938; commissioned, West Yorkshire Regt, 1940; served overseas, 1940-45, Middle East, India and Burma (MC) (Hon. Major). Joined Albert E. Reed and Co. Ltd, 1946; Brush Group, 1951; Massey Ferguson Ltd, 1959; Perkins Diesel Engine Group, 1963. Has lectured to British Institute of Management, Institute of Chartered Accountants, Oxford Business Summer School, etc. *Publication:* Business Planning and Control, 1966. *Recreations:* golf, swimming, pottering. *Address:* 44 Great Queen Street, WC2. *Clubs:* Army and Navy, Royal Automobile.

**BISHOP, Instructor Rear-Adm. Sir William (Alfred),** KBE 1955 (OBE 1941); CB 1950; MA; Director of Naval Education Service, 1948-56, retired; *b* 29 May 1899; *s* of late Alfred Bishop, Purley, Surrey; *m* 1929, Stella Margaret Macfarlane, MBE; no *c. Educ:* Whitgift Sch.; Corpus Christi, Cambridge. 2nd Lieut, RE Signals, 1918; Cambridge 1919. Entered RN as Instructor Lieut, 1922; Instructor Lieut-Comdr, 1928; Instructor Comdr, 1936; Instructor Captain, 1945; Instructor Rear-Adm., 1951. Chief Naval Meteorological Officer, South Atlantic Station, 1939; Asst Director of Naval Meteorological Service, 1944; Dep. Director of Education Dept, 1947. Naval ADC to the King, 1950. Retired Sept. 1956. *Recreation:* yachting. *Address:* Myrtle Cottage, Burlawn, Wadebridge, Cornwall. *T:* Wadebridge 2773.

**BISHOP, William Fletcher;** *see* Bishop, Rev. Hugh.

**BISHOP, Maj.-Gen. Sir (William Henry) Alexander (Alec),** KCMG 1964 (CMG 1961); CB 1946; CVO 1961; OBE 1941; psc; psa; *b* 20 June 1897; *s* of Walter Edward and Elizabeth Bishop; *m* 1926, Mary Patricia, *d* of Henry Corbett, Physician, Plymouth; one *s. Educ:* Plymouth Coll.; RMC Sandhurst. Served European War, 1914-19, Mesopotamia and Palestine; with Dorset Regt; Bt Lt-Col 1938; Col 1941; Brig. 1941; Maj.-Gen. 1944. Served in India, 1919-25, War Office, 1933-35 and Colonial Office, 1937-39; served in East Africa, North Africa, and West Africa during War, 1939-44; Director of Quartering, War Office, 1944-45; Chief of Information Services and Public Relations, CCG, 1945-46; Deputy Chief of Staff, CCG, 1946-48; Regional Commissioner, Land North Rhine/Westphalia, 1948-50; Asst Secretary, Commonwealth Relations Office, 1951; Principal Staff Officer to Secretary of State for Commonwealth Relations, 1953-57; British Dep. High Commissioner in Calcutta, 1957-62; Director of Information Services and Cultural Relations, Commonwealth Relations Office, 1962-64; British High Commissioner, Cyprus, 1964-65, retired. CStJ 1951. Ehren-Nadel, Johanniter Orden, 1951. *Address:* Combe House, Beckley, Sussex. *T:* Beckley

221. *Clubs:* Army and Navy, Royal Commonwealth Society; Bengal (Calcutta).

**BISHOP, Sir William (Poole),** Kt 1961; CMG 1947; AASA; Auditor-General, State of South Australia, 1946-59, retired; *b* 8 Aug. 1894; *s* of Henry Bishop, Adelaide, South Australia; *m* 1922, Leira Viola (*d* 1967); one *s* two *d*; *m* 1968, Daphne Rhea, *widow* of Walter Richard Birks. *Educ:* Adelaide High Sch. Official appts: Comr of Taxes for State of South Australia and Federal Dep. Comr of Taxation, 1935-46; Trustee Savings Bank of S Australia, 1946-; Director: Adelaide Cement Co. Ltd (Chm. 1965); Johnson & Sons (S Australia) Ltd; Santos Ltd; Chairman City Bricks (Holdings) Ltd. Charitable organisations: Member Exec. and Chairman Finance Cttee, Fighting Forces Comforts Fund (S Australia Div. of Australian Fund), 1939-46; Member Board of Management and Chairman of Finance Cttee, Legacy Club of Adelaide, 1944-56; Member AIF Cemetery Trust, 1928-67 (Chm. 1958-67); Member Exec. War Veterans' Home, Myrtle Bank Inc., 1933-67; Mem. Board of Governors, Burnside War Memorial Hosp., 1959-63; Dir, Nat. Heart Foundn of Australia (and the SA Div.), 1961-70. Served European War, 1914-18, AIF, 1915-19; War of 1939-45, Volunteer Defence Corps, 1942-45. *Address:* 67 Tusmore Avenue, Tusmore, South Australia 5065, Australia. *Clubs:* Naval, Military and Air Force (S Australia); Glenelg Golf.

**BISS, Godfrey Charles D'Arcy;** Senior Partner of Ashurst, Morris, Crisp & Co., Solicitors; *b* 2 Sept. 1909; *s* of Gerald Biss and Sarah Ann Coutts Allan; *m* 1946, Margaret Jean Ellis; two *s*. *Educ:* St Paul's Sch. (Scholar); Worcester Coll., Oxford (Exhibitioner). 1st Class Jurisprudence, 1932. Solicitor, 1935; Partner in Ashurst, Morris, Crisp & Co., 1947. Royal Artillery, 1940-46; Staff Capt. RA, 23rd Indian Div. Chairman: The Fairey Company Ltd; Fairey Surveys Ltd; UK Optical & Industrial Holdings Ltd; Siebe Gorman & Co. Ltd; Scribbans-Kemp Ltd. Director: Aspro-Nicholas Ltd; International Harvester Co. of Great Britain Ltd. *Recreations:* gardening, racing. *Address:* Bucksbridge House, Wendover, Bucks. *T:* Wendover 2131; 17 Throgmorton Avenue, EC2. *T:* 01-283 1070. *Club:* Oriental.

**BISSELL, Claude Thomas,** MA, PhD; FRSC 1957; President of the University of Toronto since 1958; *b* 10 Feb. 1916; *m* 1945, Christina Flora Gray; one *d*. *Educ:* University of Toronto; Cornell Univ. BA 1936, MA 1937, Toronto; PhD Cornell, 1940. Instructor in English, Cornell, 1938-41; Lecturer in English, Cornell, 1938-41; Lecturer in English, Toronto, 1941-42. Canadian Army, 1942-46; demobilised as Capt. University of Toronto: Asst Prof. of English, 1947-51; Assoc. Prof. of English, 1951-56; Prof. of English, 1962; Asst to Pres., 1948-52; Vice-Pres., 1952-56; Dean in Residence, University Coll., 1946-56; Pres., Carleton Univ., Ottawa, 1956-58; Chm., The Canada Council, 1960-62. President, Nat. Conference of Canadian Universities and Colleges, 1962-; Chairman, Canadian Universities Foundation, 1962-; President, World University Service of Canada, 1962-63. Visiting Prof. of Canadian Studies, Harvard, 1967-68. Hon. DLitt, Manitoba, 1958; Hon LLD: McGill, 1958; Queen's, 1959; New Brunswick, 1959; Carleton, 1960; Montreal, 1960; The St Lawrence, 1962; British Columbia, 1962; Michigan, 1963; Columbia, 1965; Laval, 1966; Prince of Wales Coll., 1967; Windsor, 1968. *Publications:* (ed) University College, A Portrait, 1853-1953, 1953; (ed) Canada's Crisis in Higher Education, 1957; (ed) Our Living Tradition, 1957; number of articles on literary subjects in Canadian and American jls. *Address:* 93 Highland Avenue, Toronto 5, Ontario, Canada. *Clubs:* Arts and Letters, University, York (Toronto); Rideau, Cercle Universitaire (Ottawa).

**BJÖRNSSON, Henrik Sveinsson,** KBE (Hon.) 1963; Icelandic Ambassador to France, Luxembourg, and Yugoslavia, and concurrently Permanent Representative to OECD, and UNESCO, since 1965, and to the Council of Europe, 1968-70; *b* 2 Sept. 1914; *s* of Sveinn Björnsson (late President of Iceland) and Georgia Hoff-Hansen; *m* 1941, Gróa Torfhildur Jónsdóttir; one *s* two *d*. *Educ:* Reykjavik Grammar Sch.; Univ. of Iceland. Graduated in Law, 1939. Entered Foreign Service, 1939; served in Copenhagen, Washington, DC, Oslo, Paris and Revkjavik; Secretary to President of Iceland, 1952-56; Secretary-General of Min. of Foreign Affairs, Iceland, 1956-61; Ambassador to the Court of St James's, 1961-65, also to Royal Netherlands Court, and Minister to Spain and Portugal, 1961-65; Ambassador to Belgium and Permanent Representative to NATO, 1965-67. Comdr (with Star) of the Order of the Icelandic Falcon, 1963. Holds various foreign decorations. *Address:* 124 Blvd. Haussmann, Paris 8e, France.

**BLACHE, Jules Adolphe Lucien;** Officier de la Légion d'Honneur, Croix de Guerre, etc.; retired as Rector, University of Aix-Marseille; *b* 28 Jan. 1893; *m* 1920, Lucile Bout; two *s*. *Educ:* Faculté des Lettres, Grenoble. Teacher at the Lycée de Grenoble; subsequently Lecturer, Faculté des Lettres, Grenoble, and Prof., Faculté des Lettres, Nancy; Préfet of Meurthe-et-Moselle, 1944-46. Agrégé de l'Université; Docteur ès Lettres. Hon. DLitt Oxford Univ., 1957. *Publications:* various geographical books on the Alps, North Africa and Scandinavia. *Address:* 125 rue de France, Nice, France. *T:* 87-49-21.

**BLACHE-FRASER, Louis Nathaniel,** CMG 1959; Secretary, Alstons Ltd; Chairman, Guyana and Trinidad Mutual Fire Insurance Co.; Director: Central Bank of Trinidad and Tobago; Trinidad Building and Loan Association; *b* 19 Feb. 1904; *s* of late Winford and Emma Blache-Fraser, Trinidad; *m* 1941, Gwenyth, *d* of George Kent, Grenada; two *s* one *d* (and one *d* decd). *Educ:* Queen's Royal Coll., Trinidad. Joined Trinidad and Tobago Government Service, 1924; Dep. Accountant-General, 1947; Accountant-General, 1948; Dep. Financial Secretary, 1952; Financial Secretary, 1953; Financial Secretary, The West Indies, 1956-60; Chairman, Public Service Commission of The West Indies, 1961-62. President, Trinidad Chamber of Commerce, 1965. *Address:* 14 Coblentz Gardens, St Ann's, Trinidad. *Clubs:* Queen's Park Cricket, Harvard Sports (Trinidad).

**BLACK,** family name of **Baron Black.**

**BLACK,** Baron *cr* 1968 (Life Peer), of Barrow in Furness; **William Rushton Black;** Kt 1958; Chairman and Managing Director, Associated Commercial Vehicles Ltd; Chairman, Park Royal Vehicles Ltd; Director of other companies; *b* 12 Jan. 1893; *s* of J. W. and F. M. Black; *m* 1916, Patricia Margaret Dallas; one *d* (one *s* decd). *Educ:* Barrow Secondary Sch.; Barrow Technical Coll. Apprenticed Vickers Ltd (Engineer), 1908; Works Manager, Vickers Crayford, 1924; General Manager, Weymanns Motor Bodies, 1928; Director and General Manager, Park Royal Vehicles Ltd, 1934, Man. Dir 1939, Chairman 1962; Director, Associated Commercial Vehicles

Ltd, 1949, Managing Dir 1957. President, Society of Motor Manufacturers and Traders Ltd, 1953; Chairman: National Research Development Corporation, 1957-69; Leyland Motor Corporation, 1963-67. *Recreations:* golf, gardening. *Address:* Birchwood Grange, Ruxley Crescent, Claygate, Surrey. *T:* Esher 62823. *Club:* Royal Automobile.

**BLACK, Archibald Niel;** Professor of Engineering, University of Southampton, since 1968; *b* 10 June 1912; *s* of late Steuart Gladstone Black, Glenormiston, Victoria, Australia, and Isabella McCance (*née* Moat); *m* 1940, Cynthia Mary Stradling; one *s* two *d*. *Educ:* Farnborough Sch.; Eton Coll.; Trinity Coll., Cambridge. 1st cl. hons with distinction in Applied Mechanics in Mech. Sciences Tripos, Cambridge, 1934; MA 1938. Lectr and Demonstrator in Engrg Science, Oxford Univ., 1935; Donald Pollock Reader in Engrg Science, Oxford Univ., 1945-50; Prof. of Mech. Engrg, Southampton Univ., 1950-67. Dep. Chm., Universities Central Council on Admissions, 1964-. *Publications:* (with K. Adlard Coles) North Biscay Pilot, 1970; papers in Proc. Royal Soc. and technical jls. *Recreation:* sailing. *Address:* 11 Pine Road, Chandler's Ford, Eastleigh, Hampshire, SO5 1LQ. *T:* Chandler's Ford 2898. *Club:* Royal Ocean Racing.

**BLACK, Sir Cyril (Wilson),** Kt 1959; DL, JP; *b* 1902; *s* of Robert Wilson Black, JP, and Annie Louise Black (*née* North); *m* 1930, Dorothy Joyce, *d* of Thomas Birkett, Wigston Hall, Leicester; one *s* two *d*. *Educ:* King's College Sch. Chartered Surveyor, FRICS, FAI; Senior Partner in Knight & Co., 180 Brompton Road, SW3. Chairman of Temperance Permanent Building Soc. and other Companies. JP County of London, 1942; Member Wimbledon Borough Council, 1942-65; Mayor, 1945-46, 1946-47; Alderman, 1942-65; Member, London Borough of Merton Council, 1965-; Mayor, 1965-66; Member Surrey County Council, 1943-65; County Alderman, 1952-65, and Chm., 1956-59; MP (C) Wimbledon, 1950-70. DL Surrey, 1957-66; DL Greater London, 1966. Governor of King's College Sch., Wimbledon Coll., Ursuline Convent Sch., Wimbledon, and other Schools. Freedom of City of London, 1943; Freedom of Wimbledon, 1957. Chairman: Moral Law Defence Assoc.; Houses of Parliament Christian Fellowship; Houses of Parliament Temperance Group; Patron, Wimbledon Youth Cttee; Chairman, Wimbledon Community Assoc.; Member: SW Metrop. Regional Hospital Board, 1959-62; Baptist Union Council (Pres., 1970-71); Free Church Federal Council; Vice-President: Council of Christians and Jews; Girls' Bde, 1969- (Hon. Treasurer, 1939-69); Hon. Vice-Pres., Boys' Bde, 1970- (Hon. Treasurer, 1962-69). Pres., United Nations Association (London Region), 1964-65. *Recreations:* public work, music, reading. *Address:* Rosewall, Calonne Road, Wimbledon, SW19. *T:* 01-946 2588. *Clubs:* Carlton, City Livery, London Magistrates, St Stephen's.

**BLACK, Donald Harrison,** CMG 1956; PhD, MSc, FInstP; *b* 18 June 1899; *s* of Robert Black, Nelson, NZ; *m* 1927, Winifred Maida Robertson; two *s* one *d*. *Educ:* Nelson Coll., New Zealand; Canterbury University Coll., New Zealand; Emmanuel Coll. and Cavendish Laboratory, Cambridge. Standard Telephones and Cables Ltd (and associates), 1925-39; Supt of Research, Radar Research and Development Establishment, Min. Supply, 1939-43 and 1945-47; Admiralty Liaison Officer in USA, 1943-45; Asst Director Telecommunication Research and Development, Ministry of Supply, 1947-49; Director, Electronics Research and Development, Ministry of Supply, 1949-53; Head of UK Ministry of Supply Staff, Australia, 1953-56; Director-General of Electronics Research and Development, Ministry of Supply, 1956-58; Director, Royal Armament Research and Development Establishment, WO, Fort Halstead, Sevenoaks, Kent, 1958-62; Electronics Adviser to Chief Scientist, WO, 1962-66. *Publications:* contributions to Proc. Royal Society, Phil. Mag., Proc. Cambridge Phil. Soc., Jl Sci. Inst. *Recreations:* gardening, woodworking. *Address:* 5 Prince Consort Drive, King's Ride, Ascot, Berks.

**BLACK, Douglas Andrew Kilgour,** MD, FRCP; Professor of Medicine, Manchester University and Physician, Manchester Royal Infirmary, since 1959; *b* 29 May 1913; *s* of Walter Kilgour Black and Mary Jane Crichton; *m* 1948, Mollie Thorn; one *s* two *d*. *Educ:* Forfar Academy; St Andrews Univ. BSc 1933; MB, ChB 1936; MD 1940; MRCP 1939; FRCP 1952. MRC Research Fellow, 1938-40; Beit Memorial Research Fellow, 1940-42. Major RAMC, 1942-46. Lecturer, then Reader, in Medicine, Manchester Univ., 1946-58. Horder Travelling Fellow, 1967; Sir Arthur Sims Commonwealth Travelling Prof., 1971. Lectures: Goulstonian, RCP, 1953; Bradshaw, RCP, 1965; Lumleian, RCP, 1970. Secretary, Manchester Medical Soc., 1957-59. Member: Medical Research Council, 1966-70; GMC; Assoc. of Physicians; Medical Research Soc.; Renal Assoc., etc. *Publications:* Sodium Metabolism in Health and Disease, 1952; Essentials of Fluid Balance (4th edn), 1967; (ed) Renal Disease (2nd edn), 1967; The Logic of Medicine, 1968; contributions to various medical journals. *Recreations:* reading and writing. *Address:* Department of Medicine, Manchester Royal Infirmary, Oxford Road, Manchester. *T:* 061-273 3300. *Club:* Athenæum.

**BLACK, Eugene R(obert);** Banker, United States; Special Financial Consultant to Secretary-General of United Nations (U Thant); Special Adviser to President Johnson on SE Asia Development, 1965-69; Consultant Director, American Express Co.; Director: Chase International Investment Corporation; International Telephone and Telegraph Co.; New York Times; Trust Company of Georgia; Chairman and Director, howmet Corporation; Trustee: Bowery Savings Bank; Cummins Engine Co., etc; *b* Atlanta, Ga, USA, 1 May 1898; *s* of Eugene R. Black and Gussie Grady; *m* 1st, 1918, Elizabeth Blalock (decd); one *s* one *d*; 2nd, 1930, Susette Heath; one *s*. *Educ:* Univ. of Georgia. Atlanta Office, Harris, Forbes & Co. (NY Investment Bankers), 1919; Manager, Atlanta Office, Chase-Harris, Forbes Corp., in charge of Atlanta, New Orleans, Houston and Dallas offices, 1933; Chase National Bank of the City of NY: 2nd Vice-Pres., 1933; Vice-Pres., 1937; Senior Vice-Pres., 1949, resigned. US Executive Director, Internat. Bank for Reconstruction and Development, 1947-49, President, 1949-63. Has various financial trusteeships. Medal of Freedom (US), 1969. Holds numerous hon. doctorates and has been decorated by many countries. *Publication:* The Diplomacy of Economic Development (trans. other languages); Alternative in Southeast Asia. *Recreations:* golf, fishing; student of William Shakespeare. *Address:* (office) American Express Company, 65 Broadway, New York, NY 10006, USA. *T:* 212-944-2000; (home) 178 Columbia Heights, Brooklyn, New York 11201. *Clubs:* Athenæum (London, England); Lotus, River, Century, Recess (New York); International (Washington, DC); National

Golf Links of America (Southampton, NY), etc.

**BLACK, Prof. Gordon;** Professor of Computation, Faculty of Technology, University of Manchester, since 1964; Director, University of Manchester Regional Computing Centre, since 1969; Member: National Electronics Council, since 1967; Computer Board for Universities and Research Councils, since 1966; International Council of Scientific Unions Committee on data in Science and Technology; *b* 30 July 1923; *s* of Martin Black and Gladys (*née* Lee), Whitehaven, Cumberland; *m* 1953, Brenda Janette, *y d* of H. Josiah Balsom, London; two *s* two *d*. *Educ:* Workington Grammar Sch.; Hatfield Coll., Durham Univ.; Imperial Coll., London Univ. BSc Durham, 1945; MSc Manchester, 1968; PhD, DIC London, 1954; FInstP 1952; FBCS 1968. Physicist, British Scientific Instrument Research Assoc., 1946-56. UK AEA, 1956-66; Principal Sci. Officer, 1956-58; Senior Principal Sci. Officer, 1958-60; Dep. Chief Sci. Officer, 1960-64. Dir, Nat. Computing Centre, 1965-69. *Publications:* scientific papers in learned jls (physics and computers). *Recreations:* piano playing; listening to piano players; old clocks. *Address:* Manchester University Institute of Science and Technology, Sackville Street, Manchester. *T:* 061-236 3311; Highlawn, Alan Drive, Hale, Cheshire. *T:* 061-980 4644. *Club:* Oxford and Cambridge University.

**BLACK, Sir Harold,** Kt 1970; Secretary to the Cabinet and Clerk of the Privy Council, Northern Ireland, since 1965; *b* 9 April 1914; *s* of Alexander and Adelaide Black, Belfast; *m* 1940, Margaret Saxton; one *s* one *d*. *Educ:* Royal Belfast Academical Institution. Joined Northern Ireland Civil Service, 1934; Asst Sec., NI Cabinet, 1959-63; Dir of Establishments, Min. of Finance, NI, 1963-65. *Recreations:* photography, sailing. *Address:* 19 Rosepark, Belfast BT5 7RG, Northern Ireland. *T:* Dundonald 2151. *Clubs:* Royal Commonwealth Society; Strangford Lough Yacht, Quoile Yacht (Co. Down).

**BLACK, Hugo LaFayette;** Associate Justice, United States Supreme Court, since 1937; *b* Harlan, Clay County, Alabama, 27 Feb. 1886; *s* of William LaFayette Black and Martha Ardellah Toland; *m* 1st, 1921, Josephine Foster (*d* 1952); two *s* one *d*; 2nd, 1957, Elizabeth Seay. *Educ:* Public Sch., Ashland, Alabama. LLB University of Alabama, 1906; began practice at Ashland, Ala, 1906; moved to Birmingham, Ala, and began practice there, 1907; Police Judge, 1910-11; Solicitor (Prosecuting Attorney) Jefferson County, Alabama, 1915-17; in general practice, Birmingham, 1919-27; US Senator from Alabama 2 terms, 1927-37. Entered 2nd OTC, Fort Oglethorpe, Ga, 1917; Comd Capt. FA; served European War, 1917-18; 81st FA and Adjt 19th Army Bde. *Recreation:* tennis. *Address:* Supreme Court Building, Washington, DC, USA.

**BLACK, Kenneth Oscar,** MA, MD Cantab, FRCP, BChir, MRCS; Physician, St Bartholomew's Hospital, since 1946; Examiner in Medicine for the MRCP London since 1967; *b* 10 Nov. 1910; *s* of late George Barnard Black, Scarborough; *m* 1959, Virginia, *d* of Herbert Lees, Petersham, Surrey; two *d*. *Educ:* Bootham Sch., York; King's Coll., Cambridge (1st Class Nat. Science Tripos part 1, Senior Exhibitioner); St Bartholomew's Hospital, London. BA (Cantab) 1932; MRCS, LRCP 1935. House appointments, Demonstrator of Physiology and Medical Chief Asst, St Bartholomew's Hospital. MB, BChir 1937; MRCP 1937; MD 1942; FRCP 1946. War service temp. Lt-Col RAMC; served W. Africa and India as Medical Specialist and OC Medical Div. Mem., Assoc. of Physicians; Fellow Royal Society Medicine (Councillor Med. Sect. 1952); Fellow, Med. Soc. of London (Councillor 1953). Examiner in Medicine to University of London, 1953, to Soc. of Apothecaries, 1957. Dir, Clerical, Medical & General Life Assurance Soc., 1964-. *Publications:* contributions to journals and textbooks on diabetes and other medical topics. *Recreation:* natural history. *Address:* 149 Harley Street, W1. *T:* 01-935 4444; (home) 12 Brookfield Park, NW5. *Club:* Bath.

**BLACK, Margaret McLeod;** Head Mistress, Bradford Girls' Grammar school, since 1955; *b* 1 May 1912; *d* of James Black and Elizabeth Malcolm. *Educ:* Kelso High Sch.; Edinburgh Univ. (MA). Classics Mistress, Lancaster Girls' grammar Sch., 1936-44, and Manchester High Sch. for Girls, 1944-50; Head Mistress, Great Yarmouth Girls' High Sch., 1950-55. President: Leeds Branch of Classical Assoc., 1963-65; Joint Assoc. of Classical Teachers, 1967-69; Yorkshire Divl Union of Soroptimist Clubs, 1968-69. *Recreation:* music. *Address:* Bradford Girls' Grammar School, Bradford 9. *T:* Bradford 45395. *Club:* Royal Over-Seas League.

**BLACK, Very Rev. Matthew,** DD, DLitt, DTheol; FBA 1955; Professor of Divinity and Biblical Criticism, and Principal of St Mary's College, University of St Andrews, since 1954; Dean of the Faculty of Divinity, 1963-67; *b* 3 Sept. 1908; *s* of James and Helen Black, Kilmarnock, Ayrshire; *m* 1938, Ethel M., *d* of late Lt-Comdr A. H. Hall, Royal Indian Navy; one *s* one *d*. *Educ:* Kilmarnock Academy; Glasgow Univ. Glasgow: 1st cl. hons MA Classics, 1930; 2nd cl. hons Mental Philosophy, 1931; BD with distinction in Old Testament, 1934; DLitt 1944. PhD Bonn, 1937; DTheol Münster. Hon. DD: Glasgow, 1954; Cambridge, 1965. Buchanan Prize, Moral Philosophy, 1929; Caird Scholar, Classics, 1930; Crombie Scholar, Biblical Criticism, 1933 (St Andrews award); Brown Downie Fellow, 1934; Maxwell Forsyth Fellow and Kerr Travelling Scholarship, Trinity Coll., Glasgow, 1934. Asst to Prof. of Hebrew, Glasgow, 1935-37; Warden of Church of Scotland Students' Residence, 1936-37; Asst Lecturer in Semitic Languages and Literatures, University of Manchester, 1937-39; Bruce Lectr, Trinity Coll., Glasgow, 1940; Lectr in Hebrew and Biblical Criticism, Univ. of Aberdeen, 1939-42; Minister of Dunbarney, Church of Scotland, 1942-47; Officiating CF, Bridge of Earn, 1943-47; Lecturer in New Testament Language and Literature, Leeds Univ., 1947-52; Prof. of Biblical Criticism and Biblical Antiquities, University of Edinburgh, 1952-54. Chm., Adv. Cttee of Peshitta Project of Univ. of Leiden, 1968-. Morse Lectr, 1956 and De Hoyt Lectr, 1963, Union Theological Seminary, NY; Thomas Burns Lectr, Otago, 1967. President, Soc. for Old Testament Study, 1968; Corresponding Member, Göttingen Akademie der Wissenschaften, 1957. Hon. Member: American Soc. of Biblical Exegesis, 1958; American Bible Soc., 1966. British Academy Burkitt Medal for Biblical Studies, 1962. *Publications:* Rituale Melchitarum (Stuttgart), 1938; An Aramaic Approach to the Gospels and Acts, 3rd edn, 1967; A Christian Palestinian Syriac Horologion, Texts and Studies, Contributions to Patristic Literature, New Series, Vol. I, 1954; The Scrolls and Christian Origins, 1961; General and New Testament Editor, Peake's Commentary on the Bible (revised edn, 1962); Bible Societies' edn of the Greek New

Testament (Stuttgart), 1966; (Jt Editor) In Memoriam Paul Kahle (Berlin), 1968; (Editor and contributor) The Scrolls and Christianity, 1968; Editor, New Testament Studies; articles in learned journals. *Address:* St Mary's College, St Andrews, Fife. *Club:* Royal and Ancient.

**BLACK, Prof. Misha,** OBE 1946; RDI 1957; FSIA, MInstRA, Hon. DRCA; Architect and Industrial Designer; Senior Partner, Design Research Unit, since 1946; Partner, Black, Bayes & Gibson, Architects, since 1963; Professor of Industrial Design (Engineering), Royal College of Art, since 1959; Director of research programme into design of hospital and industrial equipment at Royal College of Art, since 1962; Industrial Design Consultant to: London Transport Board, since 1964; Mather & Platt Ltd, since 1966; Vickers Ltd, since 1968; Turner & Newall Ltd, since 1969; *b* 16 Oct. 1910; *m* 1935, Helen Lillian Evans (marr. diss., 1952); one *s* one *d*; *m* 1955, Edna Joan Fairbrother; one *s*. Coordinating Architect, Mars Exhibition, 1938; Designer, interior British Pavilion, World's Fair, NY, 1939; Principal Exhibition Architect to Ministry of Information, 1940-45; Industrial Design Consultant to Gas Light and Coke Co., 1946-48; Exhibition Consultant to UNESCO, 1947 and 1953; Co-ordinating Architect to South Bank Exhibition, Festival of Britain, 1951 and Co-Architect for Regatta Restaurant; Industrial Design Consultant to BOAC for Headquarters Bldg, London Airport, 1951-56; Consultant to Govt of Ceylon for Colombo Exhibition, 1952 and also Architect United Kingdom Pavilion there; Architect United Kingdom Pavilion, Rhodes Centenary Exhibition, Bulawayo, 1953; Design Consultant to British Transport Commn for Diesel and Electric Locomotive programme, 1956-66; Joint Interior Architect architect to Orient Line, 1957-61. Architect to Civic Trust for Norwich and Burslem Projects, 1959-60; Design Consultant Beagle Aircraft, 1961-65; Architect to Zoological Society for small Mammal House, 1967; Member: Advisory Council Inst. of Contemporary Art, 1951-67; Council Soc. of Industrial Artists, 1933-52, 1954-57 (Pres. 1954-56); Council of Industrial Design, 1955-64; Nat. Advisory Council on Art Education, 1959-; Advisory Council to the Science Museum, 1966-; Vice-President Internat. Council of Societies of Industrial Design, 1957-59, President 1959-61; Vice-President Modular Soc., 1965-; Hon. Vice-President Nat. Union of Students, 1967-; Member, Internat. Jury for: Compasso d'Oro, 1957 and 1964; Signe d'Or, 1958; Triennale, 1960; Trustee, British Museum, 1968-. Gold Medal of Soc. of Industrial Artists and Designers, 1965. *Publications:* Public Interiors, 1959; (ed) Exhibition Design, 1950; contributions to: Physical Planning, 1945; Architects' Year Book, 1945; The Practice of Design, 1946; Group Practice in Design, 1968; and architectural press. *Address:* 32 Aybrook Street, W1; 160 Gloucester Road, SW7. *Club:* Reform.

**BLACK, Sir Robert Andrew Stransham,** 2nd Bt *cr* 1922; JP; *b* 17 Jan. 1902; *s* of 1st Bt and Ellen Cecilia, 2nd *d* of late Gen. W. P. La Touche, IA; *S* father, 1925; *m* 1927, Ivy, *o d* of late Brig.-Gen. Sir Samuel Wilson, GCMG, KCB, KBE; one *s*. *Educ:* Eton; Cambridge Univ. Sheriff of Berks, 1934. *Heir: s* Robert David Black [*b* 29 March 1929; *m* 1953, Rosemary Diana, *d* of Sir Rupert Hardy, 4th Bt, *qv*; three *d*]. *Address:* Elvendon Priory, Goring, near Reading, Berks. *T:* Goring 160. *Club:* Bath.

**BLACK, Sir Robert (Brown),** GCMG 1962 (KCMG 1955; CMG 1953); OBE 1949 (MBE 1948); *b* 3 June 1906; *s* of late Robert and Catherine Black, formerly of Blair Lodge, Polmont, Stirlingshire; *m* 1937, (Elsie) Anne Stevenson, CStJ; two *d*. *Educ:* George Watson's Coll.; Edinburgh Univ. Colonial Administrative Service, 1930; served in Malaya, Trinidad, N Borneo, Hong Kong. Served War of 1939-45, commissioned in Intelligence Corps, 1942; 43 Special Military Mission; POW Japan, 1942-45. Colonial Secretary, Hong Kong, 1952-55; Governor and C-in-C: Singapore, 1955-57; Hong Kong, 1958-64. Chancellor: Hong Kong Univ., 1958-64; Chinese University of Hong Kong, 1963-64. Commonwealth War Graves Commn. Director: Clerical, Medical and General Life Assurance Soc. (Dep. Chm.); General Reversionary and Investment Co. Ltd (Dep. Chm.); Haleybridge Investment Trust Ltd; British Tourist Authority. LLD (*hc*): Univ. of Hong Kong; Chinese Univ. of Hong Kong. KStJ. Grand Cross Order of Merit, Peru. *Recreations:* golf, walking, fishing. *Address:* Mapletons House, Ashampstead Common, near Reading, Berks. *Clubs:* East India and Sports, Royal Commonwealth Society.

**BLACK, Sheila (Psyche);** Woman's Editor, The Financial Times, since 1959; *b* 6 May 1920; *d* of Clement Johnston Black, CA, and Mildred Beryl Black; *m* 1st, 1939, Geoffrey Davien, Sculptor (marr. diss. 1951); one *d* (one *s* decd); 2nd, 1951, L. A. Lee Howard, *qv*. *Educ:* Dorset; Switzerland; RADA. Actress, until outbreak of War of 1939-45, she became Asst to production manager of an electrical engineering factory. Post-war, in advertising; then in journalism, from the mid-fifties; joined The Financial Times, 1959. *Recreations:* mini-horticulture in London mews patio; grandchildren; do-it-yourself. *Address:* c/o The Financial Times Ltd, Bracken House, Cannon Street, EC4.

**BLACK, Stanley Matthew;** HM Consul-General, Lille, since 1969; *b* 10 Jan. 1924; *s* of late David Thomas Black and Jean McKail Gourlay Black; *m* 1950, Pamela Margaret, *d* of Alfred Herbert Vincent; one *s* two *d*. *Educ:* Allan Glen's Sch.; Glasgow Univ. Commissioned, RA, 1942; served, 1942-46. Third Sec., HM Foreign Service, 1949. Has served in: Formosa, 1951; West Berlin, 1954; Lebanon, 1959; Kuwait, 1960; Iran, 1964. *Recreations:* Lawn tennis, golf. *Address:* c/o Foreign and Commonwealth Office, SW1.

**BLACK-HAWKINS, Clive David,** MA (Cantab); Head Master, University College School, Hampstead, since 1956; *b* 2 July 1915; *o c* of late Capt. C. C. R. Black-Hawkins, Hants Regt, and Stella Black-Hawkins (*née* Stein); *m* 1941, Ruth Eleanor, 3rd *d* of late H. Crichton-Miller, MA, MD, FRCP; one *s* one *d*. *Educ:* Wellington Coll.; Corpus Christi Coll., Cambridge. Asst Master, University College Sch., 1938; Vice-Master, 1953. Intelligence Corps, Capt., 1940-46; GHQ Middle East, 1942-44. *Recreations:* travel, reading memoirs, gardening. *Address:* 5 Redington Road, Hampstead, NW3.

**BLACKALL, Sir Henry (William Butler),** Kt 1945; QC (Cyprus); Hon. LLD (*jd*) (Dublin); Vice-President, Irish Genealogical Research Society; *b* 19 June 1889; *s* of Henry Blackall, Garden Hill, Co. Limerick, and Isabella, *d* of William Butler, JP, Bunnahow, Co. Clare (descended from Hon. Piers Butler, *yr s* of 10th Baron Dunboyne); *m* 1934, Maria, *o d* of D. Severis, Chairman, Bank of Cyprus. *Educ:* Stonyhurst; Trinity Coll., Dublin. BA (Senior Mod., Gold Medallist); LLB (1st place); 1st of

1st Class Hons Mod. Hist.; 1st Prizeman Roman Law; 1st Prizeman International Law and Jurisprudence (TCD); John Brooke Scholar and Victoria Prizeman (King's Inn); called to Irish Bar, 1912; served European War, 1914-18; Crown Counsel, Kenya, 1919; Member Legislative Council, 1920; Crown Counsel, Nigeria, 1923; Acting Solicitor-General, various periods, 1923-31; Attorney-General, Cyprus, 1932-36; Attorney-General, Gold Coast, 1936-43; MEC, MLC; Governor's Deputy, 1940; Chairman, Cttee of Enquiry into Native Tribunals, 1942; Chief Justice of Trinidad and Tobago, and President of the West Indian Court of Appeal, 1943-46; Chief Justice of Hong Kong, 1946-48; President of the West African Court of Appeal, 1948-51; retired, 1951. *Publications:* The Butlers of Co. Clare; The Galweys of Munster; articles in various historical and genealogical journals. *Recreation:* genealogy. *Address:* PO Box 14, Kyrenia, Cyprus. *T:* Kyrenia 308. *Clubs:* Travellers'; Kildare Street (Dublin).

**BLACKBURN, Bishop of,** since 1960; **Rt. Rev. Charles Robert Claxton,** MA, DD; *b* 16 Nov. 1903; *s* of Herbert Bailey and Frances Ann Claxton; *m* 1930, Agnes Jane Stevenson; two *s* two *d. Educ:* Monkton Combe Sch.; Weymouth Coll.; Queens' Coll., Cambridge. Deacon, 1927; Priest, 1928; Curate, St John's, Stratford, E15, 1927-29; St John, Redhill, 1929-33; St Martin-in-the-Fields, 1944-46; Vicar, Holy Trinity, Bristol, 1933-38; Hon. Canon of Bristol Cathedral, 1942-46; Hon. Chaplain to Bishop of Bristol, 1938-46; Hon. Chaplain to Bishop of Rochester, 1943-46; Rector of Halsall, near Ormskirk, Lancs, 1948-59; Suffragan Bishop of Warrington, 1946-60. *Recreations:* golf, squash, tennis. *Address:* Bishop's House, Clayton-le-Dale, Blackburn, Lancs. *Club:* United University.

**BLACKBURN, Archdeacon of;** *see* Hodd, Ven. Henry Norman.

**BLACKBURN, Provost of;** *see* Robinson, Very Rev. N.

**BLACKBURN, Lt-Col Sir Charles Bickerton,** KCMG 1960; Kt, 1936; OBE 1919; BA, MD, ChM; FRCP, FRCPE (Hon.), FRACP, FRSM; Hon. LLD, Melbourne and Western Australia; Hon. DSc, Tasmania, Queensland and NSW; Physician engaged in consulting practice; Hon. Consulting Physician, Royal Prince Alfred Hospital, Sydney; Consulting Physician, Commonwealth Repatriation Department, New South Wales; Chancellor, Sydney University, 1941-64; Member of Council of New South Wales Branch of BMA, 1910-58; Vice-President, AMA, 1967; *b* Greenhithe, Kent, England, 1874; *s* of Rev. Thomas Blackburn and Jessie Anne Wood; *m* 1910, Vera Louise Le Patourel (*d* 1936); one *s* one *d. Educ:* St Peters Collegiate Sch., Adelaide; Adelaide Univ.; Univ. of Sydney. Engaged in practice of medicine since qualification in 1898 (retired); Member of Hon. Staff, Royal Prince Alfred Hosp., 1904-; Australian Army Medical Corps, 1916; Lieut-Col 14th Australian General Hospital, 1916-19 (despatches twice, OBE); AAMC, 1941, Lieut-Col (Home Service). *Publications:* various medical papers including Lister Oration, Adelaide, Bancroft Memorial Oration, Brisbane, Sir Richard Stawell Oration, Melbourne. *Recreations:* golf, trout, and game fishing. *Address:* 152/177 Bellevue Road, Double Bay, NSW 2028, Australia. *Clubs:* Union, University, Royal Sydney Golf (Sydney).

**BLACKBURN, (Evelyn) Barbara;** novelist and playwright; *b* Brampton Brien, Hereford, July 1898; *d* of late E. M. Blackburn, Fairway Cottage, Henley-on-Thames; *m* 1927, Claude Leader; two *s* one *d. Educ:* Eversley, Folkstone. *Publications: novels:* Return to Bondage, 1926; Season Made for Joy, 1927; Sober Feast, 1929; Courage for Martha, 1930; Marriage and Money, 1931; The Club, 1932; The Long Journey, 1933; Lover be Wise, 1934; Good Times, 1935; Abbots Bank, 1948; Georgina Goes Home, 1951; Star Spangled Heavens, 1953; The Briary Bush, 1954; Summer at Sorrelhurst, 1954; The Buds of May, 1955; The Blackbird's Tune, 1957; Spinners Hall (as Barbara Leader), 1957; Green for Lovers, 1958; Story of Alix, 1959; The Little Cousin, 1960; Love Story of Mary Britton, 1961; Doctor and Debutante, 1961; Lovers' Meeting, 1962; Learn Her by Heart, 1962; City of Forever, 1963; Come Back My Love, 1963; (as Frances Castle, with Peggy Mundy Castle) The Sisters' Tale, 1968; (as Frances Castle) Tara's Daughter, 1970; *play:* (with Mundy Whitehouse) Poor Man's Castle; *biography:* Noble Lord, 1949. *Address:* Anchor Cottage, Latchingdon, Chelmsford, Essex. *T:* Latchingdon 367.

**BLACKBURN, Fred;** *b* 29 July 1902; *s* of Richley and Mary Blackburn, Mellor; *m* 1930, Marion, *d* of Walter W. and Hannah Fildes, Manchester; two *s. Educ:* Queen Elizabeth's Grammar Sch., Blackburn; St John's Coll., Battersea; Manchester Univ. Teacher. MP (Lab) Stalybridge and Hyde Div. of Cheshire, 1951-70. *Publications:* The Regional Council; Local Government Reform; George Tomlinson. *Address:* 114 Knutsford Road, Wilmslow, Cheshire. *T:* Wilmslow 23142.

**BLACKBURN, Guy,** MBE 1944; MChir, FRCS; Surgeon, Guy's Hospital, Putney Hospital, St Andrew's Hospital, Dollis Hill, etc; *b* 20 Nov. 1911; *s* of Dr A. E. Blackburn, Beckenham; *m* 1953, Joan, *d* of Arthur Bowen, Pontycymmer, Wales; one *d. Educ:* Rugby; Clare Coll., Cambridge (MA). MRCS, LRCP 1935; MB, BChir 1935; FRCS 1937; MChir 1941. House appointments, St Bartholomew's Hospital, 1935-37; Brackenbury Scholar in Surgery, 1935; Demonstrator of Anatomy and Chief Asst in Surgery, 1938-39; Military Service, 1942-46; Lt-Col i/c Surgical Div., 1945-46; served in N Africa and Italy. Hunterian Prof., RCS, 1946; Examiner in Surgery: London Univ., 1947-48; Cambridge Univ., 1961; Member Court of Examiners, RCS, 1962-. Hon. Visiting Surgeon, Johns Hopkins Hospital, Baltimore, USA, 1957; President, Medical Society of London, 1964-65. Hon. Consulting Surgeon, British Army at Home, 1967-. *Publications:* various publications in medical journals and books; (co-ed) A Textbook of Surgery, 1958. *Recreation:* tennis. *Address:* 107 Harley Street, W1. *T:* 01-935 2255. *Club:* Garrick.

**BLACKBURN, Sir Thomas,** Kt 1968; Director: Beaverbrook Newspapers Ltd (Chairman, 1955-68); British Printing Ink Co. Ltd; Evening Citizen Ltd; Joseph Batchelor and Sons Ltd. *Educ:* University College, Nottingham. Served European War, 1914-18: Seaforth Highlanders. *Recreations:* cattle breeding, motor racing. *Address:* Beaverbrook Newspapers Ltd, 121 Fleet Street, EC4.

**BLACKBURNE, Rev. Canon Hugh Charles;** Rector of Hilborough Group of Parishes, Norfolk, since 1961; Chaplain to the Queen since 1962; Hon. Canon of Norwich, since 1965; *b* 4 June 1912; *s* of late Very Rev. Harry William Blackburne; *m* 1944, Doris Freda, *widow* of Pilot Officer H. L. N. Davis; two *s* one *d. Educ:* Marlborough; Clare Coll., Cambridge (MA); Westcott House, Cambridge. Deacon,

1937; Priest, 1938; Curate of Almondbury, Yorks, 1937-39. Chaplain to the Forces, 1939-47; served with 1st Guards Bde, 11th Armoured Div., HQ Anti-Aircraft Comd, and as Chaplain, RMC, Sandhurst. Rector, Milton, Hants, 1947-53; Vicar, St Mary's, Harrow, 1953-61. Commissary for Bishop of Jamaica, 1959-. *Recreations:* sailing, bird-watching. *Address:* Cockley Cley Rectory, Swaffham, Norfolk. *T:* Swaffham 297. *See also Sir Kenneth Blackburne.*

**BLACKBURNE, Sir Kenneth (William),** GCMG 1962 (KCMG 1952; CMG 1946); GBE 1962 (OBE 1939); *b* 12 Dec. 1907; *er s* of late Very Rev. H. W. Blackburne; *m* 1935, Bridget Senhouse Constant, *d* of James Mackay Wilson, DL, Currygrane, Co. Longford; one *s* one *d*. *Educ:* Marlborough; Clare Coll., Cambridge. Asst District Officer, Nigeria, 1930; Asst District Comr, Nazareth, Palestine, 1935; Actg District Comr, Galilee District, Palestine, May-Sept. 1938; Actg Asst Princ. and Princ., CO, 1938; Colonial Sec., The Gambia, 1941; Administrative Sec. to the Comptroller for Development and Welfare in the West Indies, 1943-47 (Actg Comptroller, 1944 and 1946); Dir of Information Services, CO, 1947-50; Governor and C-in-C of the Leeward Islands, 1950-56; Capt.-General and Governor-in-Chief, Jamaica, 1957-62; Governor-General of Jamaica, 1962; retd 1963; Chm., Sussex Church Campaign. KStJ, 1952. *Recreations:* sailing, gardening. *Address:* Gratwicks, Steyning, Sussex. *TA* and *T:* Partridge Green 217. *Club:* Athenæum. *See also Rev. Canon H. C. Blackburne.*

**BLACKER, Carlos Paton,** MC, GM; MA, MD (Oxford); FRCP; Hon. Secretary, Population Investigation Committee; Consultant, Ex-Services Mental Welfare Society; Hon. Consultant, Royal Bethlem Hospital and The Maudsley Hospital; *b* 8 Dec. 1895; *e s* of Carlos Blacker and Caroline Frost; *m* 1923, Helen Maud, *d* of Major A. J. Pilkington; one *s* two *d*. *Educ:* Eton. Coldstream Guards, 1915-19 (Captain, MC, despatches twice, wounded); Balliol, Oxford, 1919-22 (Distinction shortened course Natural Science, Zoology); Capt. OU Boxing Club, 1920 and 1922; represented University foil, 1920; Registrar, Dept Psychological Medicine, Guy's Hosp., 1927-36; Regimental MO 2nd Bn Coldstream Guards, 1940-42. Galton Medal 1959. *Publications:* Neurosis and the Mental Health Services; Eugenics: Galton and After; The Chances of Morbid Inheritance; Human Values in Psychological Medicine; Voluntary Sterilization; papers on psychological medicine, birth control, eugenics, and population. *Address:* Pasturewood, Shamley Green, Surrey. *T:* Bramley 3081. *Clubs:* United University; Vincent's (Oxford).

**BLACKER, Lt-Gen. Sir Cecil (Hugh),** KCB 1969 (CB 1967); OBE 1960; MC 1944; Vice-Chief of the General Staff since 1970; *b* 4 June 1916; *s* of Col Norman Valentine Blacker and Olive Georgina (*née* Hope); *m* 1947, Felicity Mary, *widow* of Major J. Rew and *d* of Major I. Buxton, DSO; two *s*. *Educ:* Wellington Coll. Joined 5th Royal Inniskilling Dragoon Guards, 1936; Commanded 23rd Hussars, 1945; Instructor, Staff Coll., Camberley, 1951-54; Commanded 5th Royal Inniskilling Dragoon Guards, 1955-57; Military Asst to CIGS, 1958-60; Asst Commandant, RMA, Sandhurst, 1960-62; Commander, 39 Infantry Brigade Group, 1962-64; GOC 3rd Div., 1964-66; Dir, Army Staff Duties, MoD, 1966-69; GOC-in-C Northern Command, 1969-70. *Publications:* The Story of Workboy, 1960; Soldier in the Saddle, 1963. *Recreations:* riding, painting, fishing and reading. Amateur Steeplechase rider, 1947-54; represented GB in World Modern Pentathlon Championships, 1951; represented GB in Showjumping, 1959-61. *Address:* c/o Lloyds Bank, 6 Pall Mall, SW1. *Club:* Cavalry.

**BLACKER, Maj.-Gen. George Patrick Demaine,** CB 1957; CBE 1944; *b* 21 Feb. 1906; *s* of late Sir George Blacker, CBE, MD, FRCS, FRCP; *m* 1939, Marion, *d* of H. Kinahan, Belfast; one *s* one *d*. *Educ:* Cheltenham Coll.; RMA Woolwich. 2nd Lieut RA, 1926; NW Frontier of India, 1930-31; psc 1938; served BEF, France, 1939-40; Sicily and Italy, 1943-44; NW Europe, 1944-45; HQ SACSEA, 1945; DAG BAOR, 1947; Student US National War Coll., 1949-50; Chief of Staff, AA Command, 1952-54; Director, Mobile Defence Corps, 1955; Chief of Staff, HQ, UK Land Forces, 1956-59; retired 1959. Officer Legion of Merit (USA), 1945. *Recreation:* gardening. *Address:* Sandheys, Tekels Avenue, Camberley, Surrey. *T:* Camberley 3752. *Club:* Army and Navy.

**BLACKETT,** family name of **Baron Blackett.**

**BLACKETT,** Baron *cr* 1969 (Life Peer), of Chelsea; **Patrick Maynard Stuart Blackett,** OM 1967; CH 1965; FRS 1933; MA; Professor Emeritus and Senior Research Fellow, Imperial College of Science and Technology, since 1965, Fellow since 1967; Scientific Adviser (part-time), Ministry of Technology, since Nov. 1964 (on leave of absence from Imperial College); President of the Royal Society since 1965 (Member of Council, 1963); *b* 18 Nov. 1897; *s* of Arthur Stuart Blackett; *m* 1924, Costanza Bayon; one *s* one *d*. *Educ:* RNC, Osborne and Dartmouth; Magdalene Coll., Cambridge. Served with RN, 1914-19. Fellow, King's Coll., Cambridge, 1923-33, Hon. Fellow, 1949. Prof. of Physics, Birkbeck Coll., 1933-37; Langworthy Prof. of Physics, Univ. of Manchester, 1937-53; Pro-Vice-Chancellor, Univ. of Manchester, 1950-52; Prof. of Physics, Imperial Coll. of Science and Technology, 1953-65; Dean, RCS, Imperial Coll., 1955-60; Pro-Rector, Imperial Coll., 1961-64. Member: Bd of National Res. Development Corp., 1949-64; Scientific Policy Cttee, European Organisation for Nuclear Res., 1954-58; Governing Bd, National Inst. for Res. in Nuclear Science, 1957-60; Council, DSIR, 1955-60 (Chm., Res. Grants Cttee, 1956-60); Council, Overseas Development Inst., 1960-; Council for Scientific Policy, 1965-. Pres., British Assoc. for the Advancement of Science, 1957-58; Trustee, British Museum, 1963-65. Member: Berlin Acad. of Science, 1950; Soviet Acad. of Sciences, 1966. Corr. Mem., Acad. of Sciences, Inst. of France. Foreign Mem., Accademia Nazionale dei Lincei, Rome, 1965. Rede Lectr, Cambridge Univ., 1969. Hon. Fellow: Magdalene Coll., Cambridge, 1948; Indian Acad. of Sciences, 1949; Weizmann Inst. of Science, Israel, 1954; Inst. of Physics, 1962; Manchester Coll. of Technology, 1966; Fellow, Birkbeck Coll., University of London, 1970. Foreign Associate, Nat. Acad. of Sciences, Washington, 1966. Hon. DSc: New Delhi, Strasbourg, 1947; Reading, 1948; QUB, 1953; Leeds, Durham, Manchester, 1962; Oxon, 1963; Exeter, Bristol, York, Hull, Sussex, 1966; Chicago, 1969; Hon. ScD Cantab, 1954; Hon. LLD: Glasgow, 1955; Dalhousie (Halifax), 1960; St Andrews, 1962. Royal Medal of Royal Soc., 1940, Copley Medal, 1956; Nobel Prize for Physics, 1948. American Medal for Merit, 1946. *Publications:* scientific papers on nuclear and atomic physics, cosmic rays and rock magnetism; Rayons Cosmiques, 1934; Military and Political Consequences of Atomic Energy, 1948; Lectures on Rock Magnetism, 1956;

Atomic Weapons and East-West Relations, 1956; Studies of War, 1962. *Address:* 806 Nelson House, Dolphin Square, SW1. *Club:* Athenæum.

**BLACKETT, Sir George (William),** 10th Bt *cr* 1673; *b* 26 April 1906; *s* of Sir Hugh Douglas Blackett, 8th Bt, and Helen Katherine (*d* 1943), *d* of late George Lowther; *S* brother, 1968; *m* 1st, 1933, Euphemia Cicely (*d* 1960), *d* of late Major Nicholas Robinson; 2nd, 1964, Daphne Laing, *d* of late Major Guy Laing Bradley, TD, Hexham, Northumberland. Served with Shropshire Yeomanry and CMP, 1939-45. *Recreations:* hunting, forestry, farming. *Heir: b* Major Francis Hugh Blackett [*b* 16 Oct. 1907; *m* Mrs Elizabeth Eily Barrie, 2nd *d* of late Howard Dennison; two *s* two *d*]. *Address:* Colwyn, Corbridge, Northumberland. *T:* Corbridge 2252. *Club:* English-Speaking Union.

**BLACKFORD,** 2nd Baron *cr* 1935, of Compton Pauncefoot; **Col. Glyn Keith Murray Mason,** Bt 1918; CBE 1962; DSO 1916 and Bar, 1918; JP; late 14th (King's) Hussars; a Deputy Speaker, House of Lords, 1949-66; Deputy Chairman, Midland Bank, 1960-67 (Director, 1932-67); Chairman, Guardian Assurance Co., 1950-67 (Hon. President, 1967-); a Lieutenant of the City of London; *b* 29 May 1887; *s* of 1st Baron Blackford and Edith (*d* 1958), *d* of late Alexander Murray Affleck of Dumfries; *S* father, 1947; *m* 1918, Grace Ellinor, 2nd *d* of N. Keen; one *s* (and one killed on Active Service). *Educ:* Eton; Sandhurst. Served in India until 1914; France, 1914-15 (wounded); Salonika, 1915-17 (DSO); Comd Dorset Yeo. in Palestine, 1917-18 (wounded, bar to DSO); Sector Comdr London Home Guard, 1940-44. MP (C) North Croydon, 1922-40. JP Somerset, 1946. *Heir: s* Hon. Keith Alexander Henry Mason, DFC [*b* 3 Feb. 1923; *m* 1957, Sarah Worthington-Evans, *er d* of Sir (William) Shirley (Worthington) Worthington-Evans, *qv*; one *s* one *d*]. *Address:* 17 Ennismore Gardens, SW7. *Clubs:* Brooks's, Hurlingham.

**BLACKHAM, Rear-Adm. Joseph Leslie,** CB 1965; DL; *b* 29 Feb. 1912; *s* of Dr Walter Charles Blackham, Birmingham, and Margaret Eva Blackham (*née* Bavin); *m* 1938, Coreen Shelford Skinner, *er d* of Paym. Captain W. S. Skinner, CBE, RN; one *s* one *d*. *Educ:* West House Sch., Edgbaston; RNC Dartmouth. Specialised in Navigation; served war of 1939-45; JSSC 1950; Comdr, RNC Greenwich, 1953-54; Captain 1954; Admty, 1955-57; Sen. Officer, Reserve Fleet at Plymouth, 1957-59; Admty Naval Staff, 1959-61; Cdre. Supt, HM Dockyard, Singapore, 1962-63; Rear-Adm. 1963; Admiral Supt, HM Dockyard, Portsmouth, 1964-66; retired. Member: IoW Hosp. Management Cttee, 1968-; Bd of Visitors, HM Prison, Parkhurst, 1968-. CC Isle of Wight, 1967-; DL Hants and IoW, 1970-. Mentioned in despatches for service in Korea, 1951. *Address:* Downedge, The Mall, Brading, Isle of Wight. *T:* Brading 218.

**BLACKIE, John Ernest Haldane,** CB 1959; retired as Chief Inspector of the Department of Education (1951-66); *b* 6 June 1904; *e s* of late Rt Rev. E. M. Blackie, sometime Bishop of Grimsby and Dean of Rochester and late Caroline, *d* of Rev. J. Haldane Stewart of Ardsheal; *m* 1st, 1933, Kathleen Mary (*d* 1941), *d* of F. S. Creswell; no *c*; 2nd, 1942, Pamela Althea Vernon, *d* of A. J. Margetson, HMI; two *s* two *d*. *Educ:* Bradfield; Magdalene Coll., Cambridge (MA). Asst Master: Lawrenceville Sch., NJ, USA, 1926-27; Bradfield, 1928-33; Asst Director, Public Schools Empire Tour to NZ, 1932-33; HM Inspector of Schools, 1933; District Inspector, Manchester, 1936-47; Divisional Inspector, Eastern Divn, 1947-51; Chief Inspector of: Further Educn, 1951-58; Primary Educn, 1958-66; Secretary of State's Assessor on Central Advisory Council (Plowden), 1963-66. Lectr (part-time), Homerton Coll. of Educn, Cambridge, 1966-70. Mem. Directorate, Anglo-American Primary Project, 1969. 47th County of Lancaster Home Guard, 1940-44. FRES. *Publications:* Family Holidays Abroad (with Pamela Blackie), 1961; Good Enough for the Children?, 1963; Inside the Primary School, 1967; English Teaching for Non-Specialists, 1969; Inspecting and the Inspectorate, 1970; various books and articles on education, travel and entomology. *Recreations:* travel, gardening, natural history. *Address:* The Bell House, Alconbury, Huntingdon. *T:* Woolley 270. *Club:* Pitt (Cambridge).

**BLACKIE, Dr Margery Grace;** Physician to the Queen since 1969; Hon. Consulting Physician to the Royal London Homœopathic Hospital since 1966; Dean of the Faculty of Homœopathy since 1965; *y d* of Robert and Elizabeth Blackie, Trafalgar House, Downham Market, Norfolk. *Educ:* Royal Free Hosp. and Medical School. MRCS, LRCP 1923; MB, BS 1926; MD London 1928. Asst Phys., Children's Dept, Royal London Homœopathic Hosp., 1929-36; Asst Phys., Royal London Homœopathic Hosp., 1937-57; Sen. Consultant Phys., 1957-66. Pres., Internat. Homœopathic Congress, 1965. *Publications:* The Place of Homœopathy in Modern Medicine (Presidential address), 1950; The Richards Hughes Memorial Lecture 1959. *Address:* 18 Thurloe Street, SW7. *T:* 01-589 2776; Hedingham Castle, Halstead, Essex. *T:* Hedingham 261.

**BLACKLEY, Travers Robert,** CMG 1952; CBE 1949 (OBE 1946); farmer; *b* 10 March 1899; *o s* of late Travers R. Blackley, Drumbar, Cavan, and of Ethel, *d* of Col E. W. Cuming, Crover, Mount Nugent, Co. Cavan; *m* 1932, Elizabeth, *o d* of late Major A. Deane, Royal Warwickshire Regt, and *g d* of Lieut-Col Charles Deane, Gurrane, Fermoy; four *s* two *d*. *Educ:* Charterhouse (Scholar); Worcester Coll., Oxford (Senior Exhibitioner). Served European War, 1914-18, in Royal Artillery; joined Sudan Political Service 1922, and served in Blue Nile, Kordofan and Kassala Provinces; seconded for service in Occupied Territory Administrations, 1940. Lieut-Col 1940-41; Col 1942; Brig. 1943. Served in Ethiopia and Tripolitania. Chief Administrator, Tripolitania, 1943-51; British Resident in Tripolitania, 1951. Order of the Nile (4th Class), 1936. *Recreations:* farming, shooting, fishing. *Address:* Gurrane, Fermoy, Co. Cork, Eire. *T:* Fermoy 89. *Club:* Friendly Brothers (Dublin).

**BLACKLOCK, Prof. John William Stewart,** MD; FRCPGlas; retired as Professor of Pathology, University of London, at St Bartholomew's Hospital Medical College, 1962, now Emeritus. *Educ:* University of Glasgow. MB, ChB (Hons) 1920, MD (Hons) 1937, FRCPGlas 1933. Formerly: Prof. of Pathology, University of Glasgow; Pathologist, Royal Infirmary, and Royal Hospital for Sick Children, Glasgow. Member Path. Soc. Gt Britain; FRSM. *Publications:* contribs to medical jls, etc. *Address:* 18 Hill Head Road, Hill Head, Fareham, Hants. *T:* Stubbington 3063.

**BLACKLOCK, Captain Ronald William,** CBE 1944; DSC 1917; RN (retired); *b* 21 June 1889; *s* of late J. H. Blacklock, JP, Overthorpe,

Banbury; *m* 1920, Aline Frances Astell; one *s*. *Educ:* Preparatory Sch.; HMS Britannia. Midshipman, 1906. Specialised in Submarines in 1910. Served European War in Submarines (despatches twice, DSC); Captain 1931; retired owing to ill-health, 1938; War of 1939-45, Director of Welfare Services, Admiralty. *Address:* Dolphin Cottage, Carron Lane, Midhurst, Sussex. *Club:* United Service.

**BLACKMAN, Rear-Adm. Charles Maurice,** DSO 1919; *b* 7 March 1890; 2nd *surv s* of late Charles W. Blackman; *m* 1917, Brenda Olive (*d* 1969), *y d* of late Lawrence Hargrave; two *d*. *Educ:* Stubbington House, Fareham; HMS Britannia. Lieut 1910; Lieut-Commander, 1918; Commander, 1924; Captain 1931; retired list, 1941; promoted to Rear-Adm. for war services, 1946; a Younger Brother of Trinity House; served European War, 1914-18 (DSO); Baltic Operations, 1919-20; lent for service League of Nations, 1925-28; Disarmament Conference, 1932-33; War of 1939-45. *Address:* Ripa, Shore Lane, Bishops Waltham, Hants S03 1EA. *T:* Bishops Waltham 2329. *Club:* Army and Navy.

**BLACKMAN, Geoffrey Emett,** FRS 1959; Sibthorpian Professor of Rural Economy, University of Oxford, 1945-70, and Director of Agricultural Research Council Unit of Experimental Agronomy until 1970; *b* 17 April 1903; *er s* of late Prof. V. H. Blackman, FRS, and Edith Delta Emett; *m* 1931, Audrey Babette, *o d* of Richard Seligman and Hilda McDowell; no *c*. *Educ:* King's College Sch.; St John's Coll., Cambridge. Head of Botany Section, Jealott's Hill Agricultural Research Station, Warfield, Berks, 1927-35; Lecturer in Ecology, Imperial Coll. of Science and Technology, London, 1935-45; since 1941 directed research under the aegis of Agricultural Research Council on introduction of new crops, principles of selective toxicity and development of selective herbicides. Delegate of the Clarendon Press since 1950; Secretary of the Biology War Cttee, 1942-46. Chairman Advisory Cttee enquiring into Production Development and Consumption Research, in Natural Rubber Industry, 1956. Member, Sub-Cttees, UGC: Technology, 1960-68, Biological Sciences, 1968-70. President, Institute of Biology, 1963-64; Vice-President, Royal Society, 1967-68; Fellow, Imperial Coll. of Science and Technology, 1968-. *Publications:* papers in scientific jls on agricultural, ecological, physiological and statistical investigations. *Recreations:* ski-ing, gardening with the Ericaceae, collecting water-colours. *Address:* Woodcroft, Foxcombe Lane, Boars Hill, Oxford. *Club:* Athenæum.

**BLACKMAN, Dr Lionel Cyril Francis;** Director General, BCURA Industrial Laboratories, since 1968; *b* 12 Sept. 1930; *s* of Ernest Albert Cecil Blackman and Amy McBain; *m* 1955, Susan Hazel Peachey; one *s* one *d*. *Educ:* Wanstead High Sch.; Queen Mary Coll., London. BSc 1952; PhD 1955. Scientific Officer, then Senior Research Fellow, RN Scientific Service, 1954-57; ICI Research Fellow, then Lectr in Chemical Physics of Solids, Imperial Coll., London, 1957-60; Asst Dir (London), then Dir, Chemical Research Div., BR, 1961-64; Dir of Basic Research, then Dir Gen., British Coal Utilisation Research Assoc. (now BCURA Industrial Laboratories), 1964-. FRIC; DIC; FInstF; AICeram. *Publications:* (ed) Modern Aspects of Graphite Technology, 1970; papers in various scientific and technical jls on dropwise condesation of steam, ferrites, sintering of oxides, graphite and its crystal compounds, glass surface coatings. *Recreations:* oenology, antique glass, gardening. *Address:* Brookleigh, Fairmile Lane, Cobham, Surrey. *T:* Cobham 3157.

**BLACKMAN, Prof. Moses,** FRS 1962; Professor of Physics, Imperial College of Science and Technology, London, since 1959; *b* 6 Dec. 1908; *e s* of late Rev. Joseph Blackman and Esther Oshry; *m* 1959, Anne Olivia, *d* of late Arthur L. Court, Sydney, Australia. *Educ:* Victoria Boys' High Sch., Grahamstown, SA; Rhodes University Coll., Grahamstown; Universities of Göttingen, London and Cambridge. MSc (SA) 1930; DPhil (Göttingen) 1933; PhD (London) 1936; PhD (Cantab) 1938. Queen Victoria Scholar (University of SA) 1931; Beit Scholar (Imperial Coll.) 1933; DSIR Sen. Res. Scholar, 1935; Member staff Physics Dept, Imperial Coll., 1937-. Mem. British Cttee on Atomic Energy, 1940-41; scientific work for Min. of Home Security, 1942-45. Member Internat. Commn on Electron Diffraction, 1957-66. Member Safety in Mines Research Advisory Board, Min. of Power, 1963-. *Publications:* scientific papers on the physics of crystals. *Address:* 48 Garden Royal, Kersfield Road, SW15. *T:* 01-789 1706.

**BLACKMAN, Raymond Victor Bernard,** MBE 1970; CEng, MIMarE, MRINA; Editor of Jane's Fighting Ships since Feb. 1949; Author and Journalist; *b* 29 June 1910; *e s* of late Leo Albert Martin Blackman and late Laura Gertrude, *e d* of Albert Thomas; *m* 1935, Alma Theresa Joyce, *y d* of late Francis Richard Hannah; one *s* one *d*. *Educ:* Southern Grammar Sch., Portsmouth. Contrib. to general and technical press, and associated with Jane's Fighting Ships since 1930; Naval Correspondent, Hampshire Telegraph and Post, 1936-46, Sunday Times, 1946-56. Served War of 1939-45, HMS Vernon, Mine Design Dept, Admiralty. Member of The Press Gang. Broadcaster on naval topics. *Publications:* Modern World Book of Ships; Ships of the Royal Navy; The World's Warships. Contributor to The Statesman's Year Book, The Diplomatist, Encyclopædia Britannica Book of the Year, The Engineer, Navy, Lloyd's List, etc. *Recreations:* seagoing, foreign travel, philately. *Address:* St Johns, The Brow, Widley, Portsmouth, Hants. *T:* Cosham 76837. *Clubs:* Anchorites; Press; Royal Naval (Portsmouth).

**BLACKMORE, Col Lindsay William Saul,** CB 1960; TD 1935; DL; Chairman, Territorial and Auxiliary Forces Association of Hampshire and the Isle of Wight, 1956-61; Member of T. & AFA since 1930; *b* 24 May 1896; *s* of Major Charles Nelson Lindsay Blackmore, MBE, and Lucy Blackmore; *m* 1921, Katherine May Lacey; one *s* one *d* (and one *s* decd). *Educ:* Eastmans Naval Acad., Southsea; Churchers Coll., Petersfield. Gazetted 2nd Lieut 6th (DCO) Bn, The Hampshire Regt (TA), 1915; Bn and Machine-Gun Corps, 1915-19; Lt-Col i/c Bn, 1932-39; Bt-Col 1936; Southampton Home Guard, 1939-45. Lloyds Bank Ltd, 1912-56, Manager: Portswood, Southampton Branch, 1938-47; Albert Road, Southsea Branch, 1947-50; Kings Road and Clarendon Road, Southsea Branches, 1950-56. DL Hampshire, 1952. *Address:* Seafield, Lennox Road South, Southsea, Hampshire. *T:* Portsmouth 23908. *Club:* Nuffield United Service Officers (Portsmouth).

**BLACKSHAW, James William,** CMG 1951; MBE 1920; Assistant Secretary, Ministry of Supply, 1946-55, retired; *b* 8 June 1895; *s* of Arthur Joseph Blackshaw; *m* 1927, Edith Violet, *d* of George Hansford. *Educ:* Doncaster Grammar Sch. Civil Service from

1911. *Address:* 70 Victoria Avenue, Shanklin, Isle of Wight. *T:* Shanklin 2336.

**BLACKSHAW, Maurice Bantock,** CBE 1953; MA Cantab; ARIBA; retired Civil Servant, formerly Deputy Chief Architect, Ministry of Housing and Local Government; UK Technical Representative to Housing Committee of Economic Commission for Europe, 1947-62; Chairman, Association of Civil Service Art Clubs, 1947-64; *b* 1903; *s* of Rev. William Blackshaw; *m* 1929, Elena Mary, *d* of A. E. Pater. *Educ:* Rossall; Corpus Christi Coll., Cambridge. *Address:* The Coach House, Grovehurst, Pembury Road, Tunbridge Wells, Kent.

**BLACKWELL, Sir Basil Henry,** Kt 1956; JP; Chairman of B. H. Blackwell Ltd, 1924-69, Basil Blackwell and Mott Ltd, 1922-69, and The Shakespeare Head Press, 1921-69; *b* 29 May 1889; *s* of late Benjamin Henry and late Lydia Blackwell; *m* 1914, Marion Christine, *d* of late John Soans; two *s* three *d*. *Educ:* Magdalen College Sch.; Merton Coll., Oxford. 2nd Class Lit. Hum; studied publishing at the Oxford Press, Amen Corner; joined father in Oxford, 1913; started publishing independently, 1919; formed the Shakespeare Head Press Ltd to carry on and develop the work of the late A. H. Bullen, 1921; formed Basil Blackwell and Mott Ltd (publishers), 1922; succeeded father (the founder of the firm) as Chairman of B. H. Blackwell Ltd (booksellers), 1924; President: International Association of Antiquarian Booksellers, 1925 and 1926; Associated Booksellers of Great Britain and Ireland, 1934 and 1935; The Classical Assoc., 1964-65; William Morris Soc., 1968-; English Assoc., 1969-70. Hon. Freeman of Oxford City. Hon. Fellow, Merton Coll., Oxford; Hon. LLD Manchester Univ., 1965. Officier d'Académie, France. *Recreations:* boating, perennial outdoor swimming, reading. *Address:* Osse Field, Appleton, Berks. *T:* Cumnor 2436. *Clubs:* Athenæum; Leander.

**BLACKWELL, Prof. Donald Eustace,** MA, PhD; Savilian Professor of Astronomy, University of Oxford, and Fellow of New College, Oxford, since Oct. 1960; *b* 27 May 1921; *s* of John Blackwell and Ethel Bowe; *m* 1951, Nora Louise Carlton; two *s* two *d*. *Educ:* Merchant Taylors' Sch.; Sandy Lodge; Sidney Sussex Coll., Cambridge. Isaac Newton Student, University of Cambridge, 1947; Stokes Student, Pembroke Coll., Cambridge, 1948; Asst Director, Solar Physics Observatory, Cambridge, 1950-60. Various Astronomical Expeditions: Sudan, 1952; Fiji, 1955; Bolivia, 1958 and 1961; Canada, 1963; Manuae Island, 1965. *Publications:* papers in astronomical journals. *Address:* Department of Astrophysics, South Parks Road, Oxford.

**BLACKWELL, John Humphrey,** CBE 1937; MC; *b* 25 April 1895; *e s* of John Thomas Blackwell, Architect, Kettering, Northants; *m* 1922, Jessie Pauline Luard Pears; one *s* two *d*. *Educ:* Bedford Sch. Served European War (France), Bedfordshire Regt, 1914-18 (despatches, MC and Bar); Beds and Herts Regt, India, 1919-20; joined staff of Asiatic Petroleum Co. (India) Ltd, 1920; MLA (Central), 1935; Chairman, Karachi Chamber of Commerce, 1939-40 and 1943-44; Trustee, Karachi Port Trust. Director, Burmah-Shell (India) Ltd (Pakistan) Ltd, 1946-50; Resident Manager, Shell Training Centre, Teddington, Middlesex, 1951-54. *Address:* 17 Chancellor House, Mount Ephraim, Tunbridge Wells, Kent. *T:* 21620.

**BLACKWELL, John Kenneth,** CBE 1965; Senior British Trade Commissioner, Hong Kong, since 1969; *b* 8 May 1914; *s* of late J. W. Blackwell; *m* 1951, Joan Hilary, *d* of late D. W. Field; two *s* one *d*. *Educ:* Downing Coll., Cambridge (MA). HM Foreign Service, 1938; Vice-consular posts, in China and Mozambique, 1938-42; Second Secretary, British Embassy, Copenhagen, 1946; Consul, Canton, 1947; served in FO, 1950; Consul: Recife, 1952; Basle, 1956; First Secretary and Head of Chancery, British Embassy, Seoul, 1957; served in FO, 1959; First Secretary with UK Delegn to the European Communities in Brussels, 1961; Consul-General: Hanoi, 1962; Lille, 1965. *Recreations:* linguistics and entomology; walking. *Address:* c/o Foreign and Commonwealth Office, SW1. *Club:* Royal Commonwealth Society.

**BLACKWOOD, HAMILTON-TEMPLE-;** family name of **Marquess of Dufferin.**

**BLACKWOOD, Rt. Rev. Donald Burns,** MC; VD; MA, ThD; Bishop of Gippsland, 1942-55; authority to officiate, Tasmania, since 1955; *b* 3 Nov. 1884; *s* of Archibald Charles Blackwood and Emma Elizabeth Macbeth; *m* 1910, Ida Maria Pitt; two *s* two *d*. *Educ:* State Sch., New Norfolk; Queen's Coll. and Univ. of Tasmania, Hobart; Australian Coll. of Theology. Scholar, BA Hons 1906, MA 1908, Tasmania; ThL (1st Class) 1908, Th Schol 1920, Th Soc (now ThD), 1938, Australian Coll. of Theology. Deacon, 1907; Priest, 1908; Chaplain of AMF from 1912; VD 1932; now Chaplain First Class; Chaplain, AIF, 1915-19 (despatches, MC); Rector of Latrobe, 1920; Rector of Cressy and Warden, St Wilfrid's Coll., Tasmania, 1921-24; Rector of Holy Trinity, Hobart, 1924-42; Canon of St David's Cathedral, Hobart, 1925-42; Archdeacon of Hobart, 1929-42; Diocesan Inspector, 1920-42; Chairman and Founder of St John's Hosp. (C of E), Hobart, 1931-42. Nat. Vice-Pres., CEMS of Australia, 1947-60. *Publication:* (ed) Our Greatest Asset (Handbook of Australian Sunday Schools), 1934. *Recreation:* gardening. *Address:* Eldersyde, Deloraine, Tasmania.

**BLACKWOOD, Sir Francis Elliot Temple,** 6th Bt, *cr* 1814; Assistant Vice-President, retired, Crocker-Citizens National Bank, San Francisco; *b* 11 March 1901; *s* of late Henry Robert Temple Blackwood (*e s* of 4th Bt) and Rebecca Paffard (she *m* 2nd, 1930, Walter G. C. Stevenson), *d* of J. Scullard; *S* brother, 1948; *m* 1921, Lily M. *d* of H. F. MacGougan. *Heir: cousin,* Francis Blackwood [*b* 10 May 1916; *m* 1941, Margaret, *d* of Hector Kirkpatrick, Lindfield, NSW; two *s* one *d*]. *Address:* 114-1050 West Capitol Avenue, West Sacramento, Calif 95691, USA.

**BLACKWOOD, Wing Comdr George Douglas;** Editor of Blackwood's Magazine, and Managing Director of William Blackwood & Sons Ltd, publishers, since 1948; *b* 11 Oct. 1909; *e s* of late James H. Blackwood and *g g g s* of Wm Blackwood, founder of Blackwood's Magazine; *m* 1936, Phyllis Marion, *y d* of late Sir John Caulcutt, KCMG; one *s* one *d*. *Educ:* Eton; Clare Coll., Cambridge. Short Service Commission in RAF, 1932-38; re-joined 1939. Formed first Czech Fighter Squadron, 1940-41; Battle of Britain (despatches); commanded Czech Wing of Royal Air Force 2nd TAF, 1944 (despatches); retired 1945. Czech War Cross, 1940; Czech Military Medal 1st class, 1944. *Recreations:* hunting, golf, etc. *Address:* Bonnytoun House, Linlithgow, West Lothian. *T:* Linlithgow 2165; 45 George Street, Edinburgh. *T:* 031-225 5835. *Club:* New (Edinburgh).

**BLACKWOOD, Sir Robert (Rutherford),** Kt 1961; Director: Dunlop Rubber, Australia, Ltd (General Manager, 1948-66); Humes Ltd;

*b* Melbourne, 3 June 1906; *s* of Robert Leslie Blackwood and Muriel Pearl (*née* Henry); *m* 1932, Hazel Lavinia McLeod; one *s* one *d*. *Educ:* Melbourne C of E Grammar Sch.; Univ. of Melbourne. BEE 1929, MCE 1932, Melbourne. Senior Demonstrator and Res. Scholar, University of Melbourne, 1928-30; Lecturer in Agric. Engineering, 1931-33; Res. Engineer Dunlop Rubber, Australia, Ltd, 1933-35; Tech. Man., 1936-46; Prof. of Mech. Engineering, University of Melbourne, 1947. Chm. Interim Council, Monash Univ., 1958-61; Chancellor, Monash Univ., 1961-68. Member Cttee on Medical Education, Victoria, 1960. MIE Aust. 1948. Trustee, National Museum of Victoria, 1964-. *Publications:* Monash University: the first ten years, 1968; Beautiful Bali, 1970; papers in Engrg jls. *Recreations:* marine biology, painting. *Address:* 8 Huntingfield Road, Melbourne, Victoria 3186, Australia. *T:* 92-5925. *Clubs:* Melbourne, Athenæum (Melbourne).

**BLACKWOOD, Prof. William;** Professor of Neuropathology, University of London, at The Institute of Neurology, The National Hospital, Queen Square, since 1958; *b* 13 March 1911; *m* 1940, Cynthia Manlove Talboys Gledstone; one *s* one *d*. *Educ:* Cheltenham Coll.; Edinburgh Univ. MB, ChB Edinburgh 1934; FRCSEd 1938; FRCPEd 1961; FRCPath (FCPath 1963). Pathologist, Scottish Mental Hospitals Laboratory; Neuropathologist, Edinburgh Royal Infirmary, and Municipal Hospitals, 1939; Senior Lecturer in Neuropathology, University of Edinburgh, 1945; Asst Pathologist, 1947, Pathologist, 1949, The National Hospital, Queen Square, London. *Publication:* Atlas of Neuropathology, 1949. *Address:* Hilders Field, Seal Hollow Road, Sevenoaks, Kent. *T:* Sevenoaks 54345. *Club:* Scottish Mountaineering (Edinburgh).

**BLADES,** family name of **Baron Ebbisham.**

**BLADIN, Air Vice-Marshal Francis Masson,** CB 1950; CBE 1943; *b* 26 Aug. 1898; *s* of F. W. Bladin, Melbourne, Victoria; *m* 1927, Patricia Mary (decd), *d* of P. J. Magennis, Jeir Station, Yass, NSW; one *s* two *d*. *Educ:* Melbourne; RMC, Duntroon. Attached Royal Field Artillery, 1920-22; joined Royal Australian Air Force, 1923; served War of 1939-45, in Pacific and North-West Europe (despatches, CBE, American Silver Star); AOC North Australia, 1942; SASO, 38 Group, Royal Air Force, 1943-44; Chief of Staff, British Commonwealth Occupation Forces, Japan, 1946-47; Air Member for Personnel, RAAF, 1949-53, retired 1953. Hon. National Treasurer, Returned Servicemen's League of Australia. *Address:* 13 Acheron Avenue, Camberwell, Victoria, Australia.

**BLAGDEN, Sir John (Ramsay),** Kt 1970; OBE 1944; TD 1943; Regional Chairman of Industrial Tribunals for East Anglia, since 1969; *b* Davos, Switzerland, 25 July 1908; *s* of John William Blagden, PhD, MA, and Johanna Alberta (*née* Martin); *m* 1937, Pauline Catherine Robinson; three *d*. *Educ:* Hawtreys; Marlborough; Emmanuel Coll., Cambridge (MA). Joined 7th Bn The Essex Regt TA, 2nd Lieut, 1928; Capt. 1935; Major 1938; called to Bar, Lincoln's Inn, 1934; Practised at Bar, 1934-39; War Service, 1939-45; Lt-Col, CO 64th HAA Regt, RA, 1943; BNAF, 1943; CMF and Land Forces Adriatic, 1944-45; BLA, 1945 (OBE, despatches twice, TD two clasps). Col 1945, Perm. Pres., Mil. Govt Courts, BAOR, Nov. 1945; Judge of Control Commn Courts, Germany, 1947; Sen. Magistrate, Sarawak, 1950; Actg Puisne Judge and Sen. Magistrate, Sarawak, 1951-56; Co-Ed. Sarawak Gazette, 1955; Puisne Judge, Trinidad, 1956-60; Trinidad Ed., West Indian Reports, 1959-60; Puisne Judge, Northern Rhodesia, 1960-64; Justice of Appeal, Northern Rhodesia and Zambia, 1964-65; Chief Justice, Zambia, 1965-69. Grand Cordon of Order of Star of Honour of Ethiopia, 1965. *Recreations:* photography, ski-ing, riding, walking, tennis, alpinism; watching cricket and motor racing. *Address:* c/o Barclays Bank Ltd, 207 High Road, Loughton, Essex; The White House, Finningham, Stowmarket, Suffolk. *T:* Bacton 302. *Clubs:* Ski Club of Great Britain; Special Forces.

**BLAIKLEY, John Barnard,** CBE 1967; FRCS, FRCOG; Obstetric and Gynæcological Surgeon since 1941, and Medical Superintendent, 1958-67, Guy's Hospital; Surgeon, Chelsea Hospital for Women, since 1936; Gynæcological Surgeon, Royal Marsden Hospital, since 1944; Hon. Consultant: in Gynæcology, to Queen Alexandra Military Hospital, Millbank, since 1954; in Obstetrics and Gynæcology, to the Army, since 1969; *b* 21 Sept. 1906; *s* of late Alex. J. Blaikley; *m* 1932, Vivien Maude Johnson; two *s*. *Educ:* Christ's Coll., Finchley; Guy's Hospital. LRCP, MRCS 1928; MB, BS, London, 1932; FRCS 1931; MRCOG 1933; FRCOG 1944. Sometime Examiner in Obstetrics and Gynæcology for Universities of Oxford, London, Birmingham, Bristol, and for RCOG (Vice-Pres., 1964-67); Member Council and Chairman of Examination Cttee, RCOG, 1955-58; Sims-Black Travelling Prof., RCOG, 1958. Joseph Price Orator, American Assoc. Obstetricians and Gynæcologists, 1964. Member Gynæcological Visiting Soc. of Great Britain. Hon. Member: American Gynæcological Club; American Assoc. of Obstetricians and Gynæcologists; Pres., Section of Obstetrics and Gynæcology, Royal Soc. of Medicine, 1964-65. Various appts at Guy's Hosp.; Pathologist, Chelsea Hosp. for Women, 1933. Mem. Scientific Adv. and Pathology Cttees, RCOG, 1959-67. Governor: Guy's Hosp. Med. Sch., 1963-; Guy's Hosp., 1969-. *Publications:* contributor to British Gynæcological Practice (3rd Edn), 1963; various articles in Medical Jls. *Recreations:* golf, gardening, etc. *Address:* Keats' House, Guy's Hospital, London Bridge, SE1. *T:* 01-407 3351. *Clubs:* Garrick, Royal Automobile.

**BLAIKLEY, Robert Marcel;** Counsellor, British High Commission, Jamaica, since 1968; *b* 1 Oct. 1916; *s* of late Alexander John Blaikley and late Adelaide Blaikley (*née* Miller); *m* 1942, Alice Mary Duncan; one *s* one *d*. *Educ:* Christ's Coll., Finchley; St John's Coll., Cambridge. Served HM Forces, 1940-46. Inland Revenue, 1946-48; General Register Office, 1948-65, Asst Secretary, 1958; transferred to Diplomatic Service as Counsellor, 1965; on loan to Colonial Office, 1965-66; Head of Aviation and Telecommunications Dept, CO, 1966-68. *Recreations:* walking, choral singing. *Address:* c/o Foreign and Commonwealth Office, SW1. *Club:* Athenæum.

**BLAIR, Sir Alastair Campbell,** KCVO 1969 (CVO 1953); TD 1950; WS; JP; *b* 16 Jan. 1908; 2nd *s* of late William Blair, WS, and late Emelia Mylne Campbell; *m* 1933, Catriona Hatchard, *o d* of late Dr William Basil Orr; four *s*. *Educ:* Cargilfield; Charterhouse; Clare Coll., Cambridge (BA); Edinburgh Univ. (LLB). Writer to the Signet, 1932; Partner, Davidson & Syme, WS, Edinburgh. Director: Bank of Scotland; Scottish Widows Fund & Life Assurance Society; British Assets Trust Ltd (Chm.) and other Companies. RA (TA) 1939; served 1939-45 (despatches); Secretary,

Queen's Body Guard for Scotland, Royal Company of Archers, 1946-59; appointed Brig., 1961; Purse Bearer to The Lord High Commissioner to the General Assembly of the Church of Scotland, 1961-69. JP Edinburgh, 1954. *Recreations:* archery, curling, golf, shooting. *Address:* 14 Ainslie Place, Edinburgh 3. *T:* 031-225 3081. *Club:* New (Edinburgh).

**BLAIR, Rev. Andrew Hamish;** Member of the Community of the Resurrection, Mirfield, Yorks, since 1935; *b* 19 June 1901; *s* of Andrew Buchanan Blair, Edinburgh, and Banwell, Somerset, and Constance Elizabeth Blair; unmarried. *Educ:* Merchiston Castle; Exeter Coll., Oxford. BA 1923, MA 1926. Deacon, 1924; Priest, 1925; Curate of St Mark, Swindon, 1924; CR Missionary in Borneo, 1936; Subwarden, Hostel of the Resurrection, Leeds Univ., 1937, Warden, 1940; Prior of Mirfield, 1943-49 and 1951-61; Principal, College of the Resurrection, Mirfield, 1949-55; Proctor in Convocation, Wakefield, 1958-61; Prior, St Paul's Priory, Holland Park, W11, 1963-66. *Publication:* The Why and Wherefore of the Church, 1946. *Recreations:* various. *Address:* House of the Resurrection, Mirfield, Yorks. *T:* Mirfield 4318.

**BLAIR, Maj.-Gen. Chandos,** MBE 1961; MC 1941 and bar, 1944; Defence Services Secretary, Ministry of Defence, since 1970; *b* 25 Feb. 1919; *s* of Brig.-Gen. Arthur Blair and Elizabeth Mary (*née* Hoskyns); *m* 1947, Audrey Mary Travers; one *s* one *d. Educ:* Harrow; Sandhurst. Commnd into Seaforth Highlanders, 1939; comd 4 KAR, Uganda, 1959-61; comd 39 Bde, Radfan and N. Ireland. GOC 2nd Division, BAOR, 1968-70. *Recreations:* golf, tennis, fishing, shooting, hunting. *Address:* c/o Royal Bank of Scotland, 64 Brompton Road, SW3. *Club:* Naval and Military.

**BLAIR, Charles Neil Molesworth,** CMG 1962; OBE 1948; Lt-Col; *b* 22 Oct. 1910; *o s* of late Col J. M. Blair, CMG, CBE, DSO, Glenfoot, Tillicoultry, Scotland; *m* 1938, Elizabeth Dorothea, *d* of late Lord Justice Luxmoore, PC; one *d* (one *s* decd). *Educ:* Stowe; RMC Sandhurst. 2nd Lieut The Black Watch, 1930. Served War of 1939-45 in Europe, North Africa and Sicily; DA & QMG, 4 Infantry Div., 1940; Bde Major, 122 Infantry Bde, 1941; Instructor, Army Staff Coll., 1941 and 1944; commanded 1st Black Watch, 1943. Retired from Army on account of war wounds, 1951. *Recreations:* fishing, model engineering, writing, philately. *Address:* Portbane, Kenmore, Perthshire. *T:* Kenmore 229. *Club:* Army and Navy.

**BLAIR, David,** CBE 1964; Premier Dancer, Royal Ballet at Covent Garden, since Sept. 1955; *b* 27 July 1932; *m* 1957, Maryon Lane; twin *d. Educ:* Trinity Sch., Halifax; Royal Ballet Sch. Joined Sadler's Wells Theatre Ballet, 1948, and became principal dancer of that company, 1950; toured USA, Canada, Holland, Belgium, Germany and Rhodesia; created rôle of Capt. Belaye in Pineapple Poll and Harlequin in Harlequin in April; danced all leading classical and character rôles in repertoire. Joined Royal Ballet at Covent Garden, 1953. Has danced all classical and many leading character rôles; created rôles include: the Prince in The Prince of the Pagodas; Colas in Frederick Ashton's production of La Fille Mal Gardée. Danced as guest artist at La Scala, Milan, May 1957. Has appeared on TV in USA and England. Toured Australia with Royal Ballet, 1958; danced in: Turkey and Spain, 1959; Leningrad, Moscow, USA and Canada, 1961; Australia, New Zealand, Manila and Hong Kong, 1962; USA, 1963. Principal Productions for Amer. Ballet Theatre, Metropolitan Opera House, NY: Swan Lake, 1967; Giselle, 1968. Directed film, Giselle, 1968-69. *Address:* 19 Holland Park Road, Kensington, W14.

**BLAIR, G. W. S.;** *see* Scott Blair.

**BLAIR, Rev. Canon Harold Arthur,** MA, BD; Canon Residentiary and Chancellor of Truro Cathedral since 1960; *b* 22 Sept. 1902; *s* of Rev. A. A. Blair, SPG Mission, India, some time rector of Saxlingham, Holt, Norfolk; *m* 1933, Honor MacAdam, *d* of Col W. MacAdam, CB, RE; two *s* one *d. Educ:* Lancing Coll.; St Edmund Hall, Oxford. BA (2nd cl. Hons Theol.) 1925; MA 1937; BD (Oxon) 1945. Classical Tutor, Dorchester Missionary Coll., 1925-27; Gold Coast Administrative Service, 1927; Asst District Comr, 1928; District Comr, 1935, retd 1939. Ordained Deacon, 1939, Priest, 1940; Asst Curate, Sherborne, 1939-41; Vicar of: Horningsham, Wilts, 1941-45; Winterbourne Earls with Winterbourne Dauntsey and Winterbourne Gunner, 1945-54; St James, Southbroom, Devizes, 1954-60. Hon. Canon of Salisbury, 1953 (prebend of Alton Australis); Examining Chaplain: to Bishop of Salisbury, 1952-60; to Bishop of Truro, 1960-. *Publications:* A Creed before the Creeds, 1954; The Ladder of Temptations, 1960; A Stranger in the House, 1963; essay in Agreed Syllabus of Religious Education (Cornwall), 1964; two essays in Teilhard Reassessed (symposium), 1970; various articles in Church Quarterly Review. *Recreations:* gardening, cycling, story-telling. *Address:* Lynn Allen, Truro, Cornwall. *T:* Truro 3290.

**BLAIR, Rt. Rev. James Douglas;** *see* Dacca, Bishop of.

**BLAIR, Sir James H.;** *see* Hunter-Blair.

**BLAIR, Col Sir Patrick James,** KBE 1958 (CBE 1943); DSO 1919; TD; DL; *b* 1891; 2nd *s* of Hugh Blair, CA Edinburgh; *m* 1930, Dorothy Leslie, OBE (*d* 1966), *er d* of late Lt-Col J. Leslie Findlay. *Educ:* Edinburgh Acad.; Balliol Coll., Oxford (MA). Served European War, 1914-19 (France and Belgium, 1915-19), with 9th (Highrs) Bn The Royal Scots, as Bde Major 44th Inf. Bde, and temp. Lieut-Col commanding 13th (Scottish Horse) Bn the Black Watch, 1918; Lieut-Col comdg 9th Bn (Highrs) The Royal Scots, 1920-27 (DSO, French Croix de Guerre, despatches twice); Bt Col 1924; Col (TA), 1924; Hon. Col 7th/9th (Highrs) Bn The Royal Scots, 1945-55. Mem. of Queen's Body Guard for Scotland, Royal Company of Archers. Admitted to Faculty of Advocates, 1921; Political Sec. to Chm. of Unionist Party in Scotland, 1922-60. *Address:* 9 Magdala Crescent, Edinburgh. *Club:* New (Edinburgh).

**BLAIR-CUNYNGHAME, James Ogilvy,** OBE 1945 (MBE 1943); Chairman: National & Commercial Banking Group Ltd, since 1968; Royal Bank of Scotland, since 1971; Director: Provincial Ince Co.; Williams Deacon's Bank; Culter Guard Bridge Holdings; Glyn, Mills & Co.; Associated Securities Ltd, Australia; Scottish Mortgage and Trust Co.; The National Bank Ltd; Member, Scottish Economic Planning Council, since 1965; *b* 28 Feb. 1913; 2nd *s* of late Edwin Blair Cunynghame and Anne Tod, both of Edinburgh. *Educ:* Sedbergh Sch.; King's Coll., Cambridge (MA). Elected Fellow, St Catharine's Coll., 1939. Served War of 1939-45 (MBE, OBE); RA and Intelligence, Mediterranean and Europe, Lt-Col 1944. FO, 1946-47; Chief Personnel Officer, BOAC, 1947-55; Dir-Gen. of Staff, National Coal

Board, 1955-57; Mem. for Staff of Nat. Coal Bd, 1957-59. Mem., Queen's Body Guard for Scotland. Hon. LLD St Andrews, 1965; Hon. DSc (Soc. Sci.) Edinburgh, 1969. *Publications:* various articles on aspects of personnel management. *Recreation:* fishing. *Address:* Broomfield, Moniaive, Thornhill, Dumfriesshire. *T:* Moniaive 217. *Clubs:* Savile; New, Scottish Arts (Edinburgh).

**BLAIR-KERR, William Alexander; Hon. Mr Justice Blair-Kerr**; Puisne Judge, Supreme Court, Hong Kong, since 1961; *b* 1 Dec. 1911; *s* of William Alexander Milne Kerr and Annie Kerr (*née* Blair), Dunblane, Perthshire, Scotland; *m* 1942, Esther Margaret Fowler Wright; one *s* one *d*. *Educ:* McLaren High Sch., Callander; Edinburgh Univ. (MA, LLB). Solicitor in Scotland, 1939; Advocate (Scots Bar), 1951. Advocate and Solicitor, Singapore, 1939-41; Straits Settlements Volunteer Force, 1941-42; escaped from Singapore, 1942; Indian Army: Staff Capt. "A" Bombay Dist. HQ, 1942-43; DAAG 107 Line of Communicaton area HQ, Poona, 1943-44; British Army: GSO2, War Office, 1944-45; SO1 Judicial, BMA Malaya, 1945-46. Colonial Legal Service (HM Overseas Service): Hong Kong: Magistrate, 1946-48; Crown Counsel, 1949; Pres. Tenancy Tribunal, 1950; Crown Counsel, 1951-53; Sen. Crown Counsel, 1953-59; District Judge, 1959-61. *Recreations:* golf, walking, music. *Address:* Supreme Court, Hong Kong; (private) The Albany, Hong Kong. *T:* 227642. *Clubs:* Royal Over-Seas League; Royal Hong Kong Golf; United Services Recreation (Hong Kong).

**BLAIR-OLIPHANT, Air Vice-Marshal David Nigel Kington,** CB 1966; OBE 1945; *b* 22 Dec. 1911; *y s* of Col P. L. K. Blair-Oliphant, DSO, Ardblair Castle, Blairgowrie, Perthshire, and Laura Geraldine Bodenham; *m* 1942, Helen Nathalie Donald, *yr d* of Sir John Donald, KCIE; two *s* one *d*. *Educ:* Harrow; Trinity Hall, Cambridge (BA). Joined RAF, 1934; Middle East and European Campaigns, 1939-45; RAF Staff Coll., 1945-48; Group Capt. 1949; Air Cdre 1958; Director, Weapons Engineering, Air Ministry, 1958-60; British Defence Staffs, Washington, 1960-63; Acting Air Vice-Marshal, 1963; Pres., Ordnance Board, 1965-66; Air Vice-Marshal, 1966. *Recreations:* sailing, shooting. *Address:* c/o Lloyds Bank Ltd, Cox's & King's Branch, 6 Pall Mall, SW1. *Club:* Royal Air Force.

**BLAKE, Alfred (Lapthorn),** MC 1945; Director, The Duke of Edinburgh's Award Scheme, since 1967; Partner in Blake, Lapthorn & Co., Solicitors, Portsmouth and area; *b* 6 Oct. 1915; *s* of late Leonard Nicholson Blake and Nora Woodfall Blake (*née* Lapthorn); *m* 1st, 1940, Beatrice Grace Nellthorp (*d* 1967); two *s*; 2nd, 1969, Mrs Alison Kelsey Dick, Boston, Mass, USA. *Educ:* Dauntsey's Sch. LLB (London), 1938. Qual. Solicitor and Notary Public, 1938. Royal Marines Officer, 1939-45: Bde Major 2 Commando Bde, 1944; Lieut-Col comdg 45 (RM) Commando and Holding Operational Commando, 1945 (despatches). Mem., Portsmouth CC, 1950-67 (Past Chm., Portsmouth Educn Cttee); Lord Mayor of Portsmouth, 1958-59. Mem., Youth Service Development Coun., 1960-66; Pres., Portsmouth Youth Organisations Cttee and Portsmouth Youth Action. Lay Canon, Portsmouth Cathedral. *Recreations:* golf (playing), football (non-playing), youth work. *Address:* 2 Cresta Court, Eastern Parade, Portsmouth, Hants. *T:* Portsmouth 29851. *Clubs:* Army and Navy; Royal Naval (Portsmouth).

**BLAKE, Lieut-Col Arthur O'Brien ffrench,** TD; DL; *b* 22 Feb. 1879; *e s* of late Rev. Robert ffrench Blake of Staple Rectory, Canterbury, Kent and Kilnock, Co. Mayo; *m* 1910, Laura Iris, *d* of late C. H. Walker of Muckridge, Co. Cork; one *s* three *d*. *Educ:* Eton; Christ Church, Oxford. Master of West Street Harriers, 1905-10 (Jt Master, 1902-03); Jt master of Wilton Hounds, 1922-26; Jt Master of the Grove Hounds, 1926-30; Master of the East Kent Hounds, 1930-32 (Jt Master, 1932-33); Master of South Shropshire Hounds, 1938-46. Served European War in Gallipoli, Egypt, Palestine, Syria, 1914-19. DL Kent, 1955. *Recreations:* hunting, cricket, shooting. *Address:* 5 South Close, The Precincts, Canterbury, Kent. *T:* Canterbury 62424. *Clubs:* MCC; Free Foresters.

**BLAKE, Charles Henry,** CB 1966; A Commissioner of Customs and Excise; *b* 29 Nov. 1912; *s* of Henry and Lily Blake, Westbury on Trym, Bristol; *m* 1938, M. Jayne McKinney, *d* of James and Ellen McKinney, Castle Finn, Co. Donegal; three *d*. *Educ:* Cotham Grammar Sch.; Jesus Coll., Cambridge (Major Scholar). Administrative Class, Home Civil Service, 1936; HM Customs and Excise: Princ., 1941; Asst Sec., 1948; Comr and Sec., 1957-64; Asst Under-Sec. of State, Air Force Dept, MoD, 1964-68. *Recreation:* gardens. *Address:* Belshade, Shepherds Way, Rickmansworth, Herts. *T:* Rickmansworth 2924. *Clubs:* United University; Moor Park.

**BLAKE, Comdr Sir Cuthbert Patrick,** 6th Bt *cr* 1772, of Langham; DSO 1916; late RN; *b* 2 Jan. 1885; *o s* of 5th Bt and Emma Gertrude (*d* 1924), *o d* of late T. P. Dawson; *S* father, 1930; *m* 1916, Florence Wilhelmina (*d* 1958), *d* of late Engr-Capt. W. R. Apps, MVO; one *d*. Served European War, including Battle of Jutland (despatches, DSO, Russian Order of St Anne); retired list, 1928; recalled, 1939-45. *Heir:* none. *Address:* Poplar House, Beyton, Bury St Edmunds, Suffolk.

**BLAKE, Dr Eugene Carson;** General Secretary, World Council of Churches, since 1966; *b* St Louis, Mo, USA, 7 Nov. 1906; *s* of Orville P. Blake and Lulu (*née* Carson); *m* 1929, Valina Gillespie. *Educ:* Princeton Univ.; New Coll., Edinburgh; Princeton Theological Seminary. Taught at Forman Christian Coll., Lahore, 1928-29; Asst Pastor, St Nicholas, NYC, 1932-35; Pastor: First Presbyterian Church, Albany, 1935-40; Pasadena Presbyterian Church, 1940-51. Stated Clerk, Gen. Assembly: Presbyterian Church of USA, 1951-58; United Presbyterian Church in USA, 1958-66. National Council of Churches of Christ in USA: Pres., 1954-57; subseq. Mem., Gen. Board; Chm., Commn on Religion and Race. Member: Central Cttee, Exec. Cttee, World Council of Churches. Trustee: Princeton Seminary; Occidental Coll.; San Francisco Theol Seminary. Visiting Lectr, Williams Coll., 1938-40. Has many hon. degrees. *Publications:* He is Lord of All, 1956; The Church in the Next Decade, 1966. *Recreation:* golf. *Address:* World Council of Churches, 150 Route de Ferney, Geneva 20, Switzerland.

**BLAKE, Sir Francis Michael,** 3rd Bt *cr* 1907; *b* 11 July 1943; *o s* of Sir F. Edward C. Blake, 2nd Bt and Olive Mary (*d* 1946) *d* of Charles Liddell Simpson; *S* father, 1950; *m* 1968, Joan Ashbridge, *d* of F. C. A. Miller. *Educ:* Rugby. *Heir: cousin* Lt-Comdr Ian Francis Blake, RN [*b* 18 Aug. 1929; *m* 1954, Frances Jillian, *d* of W. T. Barton; one *s* one *d*]. *Address:* The Dower House, Tillmouth Park, Cornhill-on-Tweed, Northumberland. *T:* Coldstream 2443.

**BLAKE, Maj.-Gen. Gilbert Alan,** CB 1944; MB; *b* 9 Jan. 1887; *s* of Edgar Frederick Blake, Grove Park, Lee, SE; *m* 1925, Margaret Brooke, *d* of H. A. Eastwood, Fleet, Hants. *Educ:* Eastbourne Coll.; Guy's Hospital. European War, 1914-18, Indian Frontier, Afghanistan, East Persia. Service: Egypt, Soudan and India; Norway, 1940. Retired, 1946. *Address:* Field House, Hartley Wintney, Hants. *T:* 2512.

**BLAKE, Henry Elliott,** TD 1955; MA; FRCS, FRCSE; Plastic Surgeon, St George's Hospital; Visiting Consultant, St Helier Hospital, Carshalton; Consultant Plastic Surgeon to Westminster Hospital Group (Queen Mary's Hospital, Roehampton); *b* 25 Dec. 1902; *s* of Henry Thomas Blake, JP, of Herefordshire, and Maud Blake; *m* 1945, Mary, Baroness Swaythling, *d* of Hon. Mrs Ionides. *Educ:* Dean Close, Cheltenham; Cambridge Univ.; St Thomas's Hospital, London. MRCS; LRCP 1929; MA, BChir (Cambridge) 1931; FRCS 1941; FRCSE 1941; late Major (surg. specialist), RAMC (TA). Founder Mem. British Assoc. Plastic Surgeons; FRSocMed. Sometime Consultant Plastic Surgeon: Victoria Hosp. for Children, Tite Street; Royal Alexandra Hosp. for Sick Children, Brighton, Royal Sussex County Hosp., Brighton, and Senior Surgeon to the Ministry of Pensions. *Publications:* four chapters in: Operative Surgery (ed. Prof. Charles Robb and Rodney Smith); Butterworths Operative Surgery-Service Vol. 3(b), The Reconstruction of the Penile Urethra in Hypospadias; articles in medical journals. *Address:* 55 Harley Street, W1. *T:* 01-580 6360; 17 Cadogan Square, SW1. *T:* 01-235 5398. *Club:* Boodle's.

**BLAKE, (Henry) Vincent;** General Manager, Indulex Engineering Company Ltd, since Sept. 1966; *b* 7 Dec. 1912; *s* of Arthur Vincent Blake and Alice Mabel (*née* Kerr); *m* 1938, Marie Isobel Todd; one *s*. *Educ:* King Edward's High Sch., Birmingham. Pupil apprentice, Chance Brothers, Lighthouse Engineers, Birmingham, 1931-34; subseq. Asst Sales Manager, 1937 and Sales Manager there, of Austinlite Ltd, 1945; Textile Marketing Manager, Fibreglass Ltd, 1951; Commercial Manager: Glass Yarns and Deeside Fabrics Ltd, 1960; BTR Industries Ltd, Glass and Resin Div., 1962-63, Plastics Group, 1963-66. Mem. Council and Chm., Reinforced Plastics Gp, British Plastics Fedn, 1959. *Publications:* articles in technical jls on reinforced plastics. *Recreations:* sailing, motoring, reading, and talking about reinforced plastics. *Address:* Farthings End, Dukes Ride, Gerrards Cross, Bucks. *T:* Gerrards Cross 82606. *Club:* Royal Aero.

**BLAKE, John Clifford,** CB 1958; *b* 12 July 1901; *s* of late Alfred Harold and Ada Blake, Prestwich, Lancs; *m* 1928, Mary Lilian Rothwell; one *s* two *d*. *Educ:* Manchester Grammar Sch.; Queen's Coll., Oxford (MA). Admitted solicitor, 1927. Ministry of Health Solicitor's Dept, 1929; Solicitor and Legal Adviser to Ministries of Health and Housing and Local Government, and to Registrar Gen., 1957-65; Mem., Treasurer and Jt Exec. Sec., Anglican-Methodist Unity Commn, 1965-69; Vice-Pres., Methodist Conference, 1968. *Recreations:* music, especially organ and choral. *Address:* New Hatch, 24 Gisburn Avenue, Lytham St Anne's FT8 3PB. *T:* St Anne's 24766. *Club:* United University.

**BLAKE, John William;** Vice-Chancellor, University of Botswana, Lesotho and Swaziland (formerly Basutoland, Bechuanaland Protectorate and Swaziland), since 1964; *b* 7 Dec. 1911; *s* of Robert Gay Blake and Beatrice Mary Blake (*née* Tucket); *m* 1938, Eileen Florence Lord; two *s* one *d*. *Educ:* Kilburn Grammar Sch.; King's Coll., London (MA). Inglis Student and Derby Scholar, 1933-34; QUB: Asst Lectr, 1934; Lectr, 1944; Sen. Lectr, 1945; served War of 1939-45 in Civil Defence and as Offical War Historian to NI Govt; Prof. of History, Univ. of Keele (until 1962 University Coll. of N Staffs), 1950-64; Acting Principal of University Coll. of N Staffs, 1954-56; Mem. Staffs Co. Educn Cttee, 1955-61; Mem. Inter-Univ. Council for Higher Educn Overseas, 1955-64; FRHist Soc. *Publications:* European Beginnings in West Africa, 1937; Europeans in West Africa, 2 vols 1942; Offical War History of Northern Ireland, 1956; contribs to historical jls. *Recreations:* hockey, cricket. *Address:* Vice-Chancellor's Lodge, Maseru, Lesotho.

**BLAKE, Nicholas;** *see* Day-Lewis, Cecil.

**BLAKE, Sir Richard;** *see* Blake, Sir T. R. V.

**BLAKE, Robert Norman William,** FBA 1967; JP; Provost of The Queen's College, Oxford, since 1968; *b* 23 Dec. 1916; *er s* of William Joseph Blake and Norah Lindley Daynes, Brundall, Norfolk; *m* 1953, Patricia Mary, *e d* of Thomas Richard Waters, Great Plumstead, Norfolk; three *d*. *Educ:* King Edward VI Sch., Norwich; Magdalen Coll., Oxford (MA). 1st Cl. Final Honour Sch. of Modern Greats, 1938; Eldon Law Scholar, 1938. Served War of 1939-45; Royal Artillery; North African campaign, 1942; POW in Italy, 1942-44; escaped, 1944; despatches, 1944. Lectr in Politics, Christ Church, Oxford, 1946-47; Student and Tutor in Politics, Christ Church, 1947-68, Emeritus Student, 1969; Censor, 1950-55; Senior Proctor, 1959-60; Ford's Lectr in English History for 1967-68. Mem. (Conservative) Oxford City Council, 1957-64. Governor of Norwich Sch., and of Trent, Bradfield and Malvern Colls. *Publications:* The Private Papers of Douglas Haig, 1952; The Unknown Prime Minister (Life of Andrew Bonar Law), 1955; Disraeli, 1966; The Conservative Party from Peel to Churchill, 1970. *Address:* The Queen's College, Oxford; Riverview House, Brundall, Norfolk. *Clubs:* Athenæum, Beefsteak, United University; Vincent's (Oxford); Norfolk County.

**BLAKE, Sir (Thomas) Richard (Valentine),** 17th Bt *cr* 1622, of Menlough; in motor trade since 1959; *b* 7 Jan. 1942; *s* of Sir Ulick Temple Blake, 16th Bt, and Elizabeth Gordon (she *m* 1965, Vice-Adm. E. Longley-Cook, *qv*); *S* father, 1963. *Educ:* Bradfield Coll., Berks. *Recreations:* shooting; Royal Naval Reserve. *Heir: kinsman* Bernard Blake, *b* 1872. *Address:* Court Hill House, East Dean, Chichester, Sussex; 23 Whittingstall Road, SW6. *T:* 01-736 4080; Menlough Castle, Co. Galway, Eire.

**BLAKE, Vincent;** *see* Blake, H. V.

**BLAKE, Mrs William J.;** *see* Stead, Christina E.

**BLAKELEY, Hon. Arthur;** retired; *b* Gilberton, S Australia, 3 July 1886; *s* of Simeon Blakeley; *m* 1914, Ruby Pauline McCarroll; two *s* two *d*. *Educ:* North Broken Hill Convent Sch. Organiser, Sec., Gen. Pres., Australian Workers' Union, 1910-21; Federal mem. for Darling, 1917-34; Sec. to Federal Parliamentary Labour Party, 1920-28 and 1932-34; Dep. Leader of Federal Parliamentary Labour Party, 1928-29; Minister for Home Affairs, Commonwealth of Australia, 1929-31; Commonwealth Arbitration Inspector, 1935-40; Senior Commonwealth Arbitration Inspector, 1940-47; Conciliation Comr, 1941-52, retired. Mem. Cttee Public Works, 1922-

25. *Recreations:* fishing, billiards, reading. *Address:* Millewa, Wanda Road, Caulfield, SE7, Melbourne, Australia. *T:* WY4717. *Club:* Commercial Travellers of Australia.

**BLAKELOCK, Denys (Martin)**; actor, writer, poet; *b* 22 June 1901; *s* of Rev. Martin Ogle Blakelock and Constance Rose (*née* Pike). *Educ:* Aldenham. Trained RADA. First appearance Philip in You Never Can Tell, 1920; Hugo in The World of Light, 1931; Aristophanes in Acropolis, 1933; Aguecheek in Twelfth Night, 1942; Bob Acres in The Rivals, 1943; Androcles in Androcles and the Lion, 1943; title role in The Magistrate, 1943; title role in The Bread-Winner, 1944; Cecil Graham in Lady Windermere's Fan, 1945; The Dean in Dandy Dick, 1948; Mr Goldfinch in A Pair of Spectacles, 1948; Lamprett Bellboys in A Penny for a Song, 1951. Teacher of Audition Technique and Diction, Royal Academy of Dramatic Art, 1947-62. Has appeared in numerous films and on television; also broadcasts. *Publications:* The Waters (collected poems), 1955; The Chastening (collected poems), 1957; Advice to a Player (letters to a young actor), 1957; Finding My Way (A Spiritual Journey), 1958; Choosing Your Piece (auditions anthology), 1960; Acting My Way (further letters to a young actor), 1964; Making the Stage Your Career, 1965; Eleanor: Portrait of a Farjeon, 1966; Round the Next Corner (autobiography), 1967. *Recreations:* walking, antique-collecting. *Address:* 42 Lancaster Close, St Petersburgh Place, W2. *T:* 01-229 4695. *Clubs:* Garrick, BBC.

**BLAKEMAN, Joan, (Mrs L. T. Blakeman)**; *see* Woodward, Joan.

**BLAKEMAN, Leslie Thompson,** CBE 1968; Member of Commission on Industrial Relations since 1969; *b* 11 July 1904; *m* 1951, (Dorothy) Joan Woodward, *qv*. *Educ:* Wallasey Grammar School. Senior Labour Manager, Min. of Supply, 1941-52; Director of Labour Relations, Ford Motor Co, 1952-69. Fellow, Inst. of Personnel Management; President, 1965-67. Member: SE Economic Planning Council, 1966-69; Race Relations Bd, 1969-. Governor, SE Essex Technical Coll., 1959-69. *Recreations:* music, photography. *Address:* Fishponds Farm, Brook, Ashford, Kent. *T:* Wye 514; 71 Roebuck House, Stag Place, SW1. *T:* 01-828 6203.

**BLAKENEY, Frederick Joseph,** CBE 1968; Australian Ambassador to USSR since 1968; *b* Sydney, NSW, 2 July 1913; *s* of Frederick Joseph Blakeney, Sydney; *m* 1943, Marjorie, *d* of John Martin, NSW; one *d*. *Educ:* Marist Darlinghurst and Mittagong; Univ. of Sydney. AMF, 1940-41; RAAF Flt Lieut (Navigator), 1942-45. Teaching Fellow, Univ. of Sydney, 1946; Dept of External Affairs, Canberra, 1946; 2nd Sec. and 1st Sec., Austr. Embassy, Paris, 1947; 1st Sec., then Chargé d'Affaires, Austr. Embassy, Moscow, 1949-51; Dept of Ext. Affairs, Canberra, 1952-53; Counsellor, Austr. Embassy, Washington, 1953-56; Minister to Vietnam and Laos, 1957-59, and to Cambodia, 1957; Asst Sec. (S and SE Asia), Dept of Ext. Affairs, Canberra, 1959-62; Australian Ambassador to Federal Republic of Germany, 1962-68. *Address:* Australian Embassy, Moscow, USSR; c/o Department of External Affairs, Canberra, ACT 2600, Australia.

**BLAKENHAM,** 1st Viscount *cr* 1963, of Little Blakenham; **John Hugh Hare,** PC 1955; OBE 1945 (MBE 1943); DL; *b* 22 Jan. 1911; *s* of 4th Earl of Listowel; *m* 1934, Hon. Beryl Nancy Pearson, *d* of 2nd Viscount Cowdray; one *s* two *d*. *Educ:* Eton Coll. Business, London County Council, Territorial Army, Suffolk Yeomanry, then served during War of 1939-45 in England, North Africa and Italy (despatches, MBE, OBE, Legion of Merit, USA). Alderman LCC, 1937-52; Chm. of London Municipal Soc., 1947-52. MP (C) Woodbridge Div. of Suffolk, 1945-50, Sudbury and Woodbridge Div. of Suffolk, 1950-63. A Vice-Chm. Conservative Party Organisation, (Dec.) 1951-55; Minister of State for Colonial Affairs, Dec. 1955-Oct. 1956; Sec. of State for War, Oct. 1956-Jan. 1958; Minister of Agriculture, Fisheries and Food, Jan. 1958-60; Minister of Labour, 1960-63; Chancellor of the Duchy of Lancaster, also Dep. Leader of the House of Lords, 1963-64; Chairman: Conservative Party Organisation, 1963-65; Council, Toynbee Hall, 1966-; Governing Body, Peabody Trust. DL, Suffolk, 1968. *Recreations:* golf, gardening. *Heir:* *s* Hon. Michael John Hare [*b* 25 Jan. 1938; *m* 1965, Marcia, *o d* of Hon. Alan Hare; two *d*]. *Address:* 10 Holland Park, W11; Cottage Farm, Little Blakenham, near Ipswich, Suffolk. *T:* Claydon 344. *Clubs:* White's, Buck's.

**BLAKER, George Blaker,** CMG 1963; Under-Secretary, Department of Education and Science, since 1964; *b* Simla, India, 30 Sept. 1912; *s* of Col William Frederick Blaker and Helen Elizabeth Blaker; *m* 1938, Richenda Dorothy Buxton; one *d*. *Educ:* Eton; Trinity Coll., Cambridge. Entered Civil Service, 1938. Private Sec. to Ministers of State in the Middle East, 1941-43; Cabinet Office, 1943; Private Sec. to Sec. of War Cabinet, 1944; Principal Private Sec. to Minister of Production and Presidents of the Board of Trade, 1945-47; accompanied Cabinet Mission to India, 1946; Sec. of UK Trade Mission to China, 1946; HM Treasury, 1947; UK Treasury Representative in South Asia, also Financial Adviser to UK High Commissioners in India and Ceylon and to HM Ambassador in Burma, 1957-63. Pres., Surrey Naturalists' Trust, 1969-. Gold Medal, Royal Soc. for the Protection of Birds, 1934. *Recreation:* ornithology. *Address:* Lake House, Ockley, Surrey.

**BLAKER, Peter Allan Renshaw,** MA; MP (C) Blackpool South, since 1964; *b* Hong Kong, 4 Oct. 1922; *s* of late Cedric Blaker, CBE, MC; *m* 1953, Jennifer, *d* of late Sir Pierson Dixon, GCMG, CB; one *s* two *d*. *Educ:* Shrewsbury; Trinity Coll., Toronto (BA, 1st class, Classics); New Coll., Oxford (MA). Served 1942-46: Argyll and Sutherland Highlanders of Canada (Capt., wounded). Admitted a Solicitor, 1948. New Coll., Oxford, 1949-52; 1st Class, Jurisprudence, Pass degree in PPE. pres. Oxford Union. Called to Bar, Lincoln's Inn, 1952. Admitted to HM Foreign Service, 1953; HM Embassy, Phnom Penh, 1955-57; UK High Commn, Ottawa, 1957-60; FO, 1960-62; Private Sec. to Minister of State for Foreign Affairs, 1962-64. Attended Disarmament Conf., Geneva; UN Gen. Assembly, 1962 and 1963; signing of Nuclear Test Ban Treaty, Moscow, 1963. An Opposition Whip, 1966-67; Joint Secretary: Conservative Party Foreign Affairs Cttee, 1965-66; Trade Cttee, 1967-70; PPS to Chancellor of Duchy of Lancaster, 1970-. *Address:* Woodsland Farm, Lindfield, Sussex. *T:* Lindfield 2381. *Clubs:* Brooks's, Travellers'.

**BLAKER, Sir Reginald,** 2nd Bt *cr* 1919; TD 1942; *b* 27 April 1900; *s* of 1st Bt and Lily (she *m* 2nd, 1928, Lieut Arthur D. Cutts), *d* of Sam. Cowell; *S* father, 1926; *m* 1930, Sheila Kellas, 3rd *d* of Dr Alexander Cran, Little Court, Merrow; one *s* one *d*. *Educ:* Charterhouse. MP

(U) Spelthorne Div. of Middx, 1931-45. *Heir:* s John Blaker [*b* 22 March 1935; *m* 1st, 1960, Catherine Ann (marr. diss. 1965), *o d* of late F. J. Thorold, Tye Farm, Hartfield, Sussex; 2nd, 1968, Elizabeth Katherine, *d* of late Col John Tinsley Russell, DSO]. *Address:* Knowles, Ardingly, Sussex. *T:* Ardingly 217.

**BLAKISTON, Sir Arthur Frederick,** 7th Bt *cr* 1763; MC; farmer; *b* 16 June 1892; *s* of late F. T. Blakiston, *y b* of 5th Bt, and Mrs Blakiston, Aspley Guise, Bucks; *S* uncle, 1941; *m* 1915, May Walton (marr. diss. 1954), *d* of Frederick Walton Fuller, West Didsbury, Manchester; *m* 1954, Ann Hope, *yr d* of Purcell Jeans, Cortington Grange, Warminster, Wilts. *Educ:* Bedford Sch.; Trent Coll.; Emmanuel Coll., Cambridge. Served European War, 1914-18, King Edward's Horse and RFA (MC). *Recreation:* fox-hunting. *Heir: kinsman,* Arthur Norman Hunter Blakiston [*b* 26 April 1899; *m* 1962, Mary Ferguson, *d* of late A. E. Gillingham, NZ; two *s*]. Address: Saracen's Head, Corton, Warminster, Wilts.

**BLAMEY, Norman Charles,** ARA 1970; ROI 1952; Senior Lecturer, Chelsea School of Art, London, since 1963; *b* 16 Dec. 1914; *s* of Charles H. Blamey and Ada Blamey (*née* Beacham); *m* 1948, Margaret (*née* Kelly); one *s*. *Educ:* Holloway Sch., London; Sch. of Art, The Polytechnic, Regent Street, London. Exhibited at: RA, RHA, ROI, RBA, NEAC, and provincial galleries; *mural decorations in:* Anglican Church of St Luke, Leagrave, Beds, 1956; Lutheran Church of St Andrew, Ruislip Manor, Middx, 1964; *works in permanent collections:* Municipal Gall., Port Elizabeth, S Africa; Beaverbrook Gall., Fredericton, NB; Beecroft Art Gall., Southend-on-Sea; Towner Art Gall., Eastbourne; Preston Art Gall.; works in private collections in UK and USA. *Recreation:* walking. *Address:* 39 Lyncroft Gardens, NW6. *T:* 01-435 9250.

**BLANCH, Mrs Lesley;** author; *b* 1907; *m* 2nd, 1945, Romain Gary Kacew (*see* Romain Gary). *Educ:* by reading, and listening to conversation of elders and betters. *Publications:* The Wilder Shores of Love (biog.), 1954; Round the World in Eighty Dishes (cookery), 1956; The Game of Hearts (biog.), 1956; The Sabres of Paradise (biog.), 1960; Under a Lilac Bleeding Star (travels), 1963; The Nine Tiger Man (fict.), 1965; Journey into the Mind's Eye (autobiog.), 1968. *Recreations:* travel, opera, acquiring useless objects, animal welfare, gardening. *Address:* Roquebrune Village, Cap Martin, AM, France. *Club:* Taharir (formerly Mahommed Ali) (Cairo).

**BLANCH, Rt. Rev. Stuart Yarworth;** *see* Liverpool, Bishop of.

**BLANCO WHITE, Amber,** OBE; *b* 1 July 1887; *d* of William Pember Reeves and Magdalen Stuart Robison; *m* George Rivers Blanco White; one *s* two *d*. *Educ:* Kensington High School; Newnham College, Cambridge. Director of Women's Wages, Ministry of Munitions, 1916-19; Member National Whitley Council for Civil Service, 1919-20; University Tutorial Lectr on Moral Science, Morley Coll.; retired 1965. Editor, The Townswoman, 1933; contested Hendon Division, 1931 and 1935. *Publications:* The Reward of Virtue; A Lady and Her Husband; Helen in Love; Give and Take; The Nationalisation of Banking; articles on literature and finance; collaborated H. G. Wells in The Work, Wealth, and Happiness of Mankind; The New Propaganda; Worry in Women; Ethics for Unbelievers. *Address:* 44 Downshire Hill, Hampstead, NW3. *See also T. A. Blanco White.*

**BLANCO WHITE, Thomas Anthony,** QC 1969; *b* 19 Jan. 1915; *s* of late G. R. Blanco White, QC, and of Amber Blanco White (*see* A. B. White); *m* 1950, Anne Katherine Ironside Smith; two *s* one *d*. *Educ:* Gresham's Sch.; Trinity Coll., Cambridge. Called to Bar, Lincoln's Inn, 1937. Served RAFVR, 1940-46. *Publications:* Patents for Inventions, 1950, 1955, 1962, etc. *Recreations:* gardening, photography. *Address:* Francis Taylor Building, EC4.

**BLAND, Sir (George) Nevile (Maltby),** KCMG 1947 (CMG 1927); KCVO 1937; Comdr Order of Leopold, 1930; Kt Grand Cross Order of Orange-Nassau, 1950; King of Arms, Order of St Michael and St George, 1952-61; *b* 6 Dec. 1886; *y s* of late Francis Maltby Bland, DL, JP, Inglethorpe Manor, Wisbech, Cambs; *m* 1919, Portia (*d* 1968), *y d* of late Canon Edward Bickersteth Ottley; one *s* (and one *s* killed in action, 1943, one *d* decd). *Educ:* Eton; King's Coll., Cambridge. Rowed in Eton eight, 1905. Entered FO, 1911; served on Peace Delegation in Paris, 1919; Private Sec. to Lord Hardinge of Penshurst, Under-Sec. of State for Foreign Affairs, 1919; to Sir Eyre Crowe, 1920; to Sir William Tyrrell, 1925; to Sir Ronald Lindsay, 1928; t0 Sir Robert Vansittart, 1930; Counsellor of Embassy, Brussels, 1930-35; Counsellor in 1935-38; Envoy Extraordinary and Minister Plenipotentiary to Netherlands, 1938-42, Ambassador, 1942-48; Special Ambassador to Pres. of Malagasy Republic, July 1960; reapptd to Foreign Service, as Special Representative of Sec. of State, Nov. 1960-69. Chairman: Anglo-Netherlands Soc., 1949-63; Children's Aid Soc., 1952-67; Royal Surgical Aid Society, 1959-69. Consultant, Abbott Laboratories (England). Vice-Pres., Amateur Orchestral Soc. *Publication:* (ed) 4th edn of Satow's Guide to Diplomatic Practice. *Address:* 164 Ebury Street, SW1. *Clubs:* Oxford and Cambridge; Leander; Royal Fowey Yacht.

**BLAND, Sir Henry (Armand),** Kt 1965; CBE 1957; Chairman, United Bearing Corporation Pty Ltd; Director: Associated Portland Cement Manufacturers (Aust.) Ltd; Westinghouse Brake A/asia Pty Ltd; McKenzie & Holland (Aust.) Pty Ltd. *b* 28 Dec. 1909; *s* of Emeritus Prof. F. A. Bland, CMG, and Elizabeth Bates Jacobs; *m* 1933, Rosamund, *d* of John Nickal; two *d* (and one *d* decd). *Educ:* Sydney High Sch.; Univ. of Sydney. LLB (Hons) 1932. Admitted Solicitor Supreme Court of NSW, 1935. Entered NSW Public Service, 1927; Alderman, Ryde (NSW) Municipal Council, 1937-39; Acting Agent-Gen. for NSW in London, 1940-41; Adviser on Civil Defence to NSW and Commonwealth Govts, 1941; Princ. Asst to Dir-Gen. of Manpower, 1941-45; Asst Sec., First Asst Sec., 1946-51, Sec. 1952-68, Dept of Labour and National Service; Sec., Dept of Defence, Australia, 1968-70. Leader, Austr. Govt Delegns to Confs: 1948, 1953, 1957, 1960, 1962, 1963, 1964, 1966; Austr. Govt Rep. on the Governing Body of ILO, 1963-67; Adviser on industrial relations to Singapore Govt. 1958. *Address:* 1 Russell Street, Camberwell, Victoria. *T:* 82.6093. *Clubs:* Athenæum (Melbourne); University (Sydney); Commonwealth (Canberra).

**BLAND, Lieut-Col (retd) John Edward Michael,** OBE 1945; DL; JP; late Scots Guards; *b* 25 Oct. 1899; *s* of late Francis Lawrence Bland, JP, Copdock, near Ipswich, and Mabel Barbara Gooch, Bracknell; *m* 1933, Nancy Mary, *d* of late Major H. Bull, RHA; two *s* one *d* (and one *s* decd). Educ: Cheam Sch.; Eton Coll. Scots Guards, 1918-47: Adjt 2nd Bn (China), 1927-29; Regimental Adjt, 1932-35; Comd Holding Bn, 1942-43. Served War, 1939-45, in UK, 1939-43, in Italy, 1944-45; retired

1947. Asst Sec., Suffolk Territorial Assoc., 1948-52; Comdt, Suffolk Army Cadet Force, 1952-55; Area Comr, St John Ambulance Brigade, 1954-60. Member: East Suffolk CC, 1951-67; Samford RDC. High Sheriff of Suffolk, 1958; DL, Suffolk, 1958; JP, 1949. OStJ. *Recreations:* shooting, boating, tennis. *Address:* Little Hall, Stutton, near Ipswich. *T:* Holbrook 357. *Clubs:* Guards; County (Ipswich).

**BLAND, Sir Nevile;** *see* Bland, Sir G. N. M.

**BLANDFORD, Marquess of; John George Vanderbilt Henry Spencer-Churchill;** JP; late Captain Life Guards; *b* 13 April 1926; *s* of 10th Duke of Marlborough, *qv*; *m* 1st, 1951, Susan Mary (marr. diss., 1960; she *m* 1962, Alan Cyril Heber-Percy), *d* of Michael Hornby, *qv*; one *s* one *d* (and one *s* decd); 2nd, 1961, Mrs Athina Livanos (who *m* 1946, Aristotle Socrates Onassis, *qv*), *d* of late Stavros G. Livanos, Paris. *Educ:* Eton. Lieut Life Guards, 1946; Capt., 1953; resigned commission, 1953. CC 1961, JP 1962, Oxon. *Heir:* *s* Earl of Sunderland, *qv*. *Address:* Lee Place, Charlbury, Oxon. *T:* Charlbury 244. *Clubs:* Buck's; White's.

**BLANDFORD, Eric George,** CBE 1967; **Hon. Mr Justice Blandford;** Deputy Assistant Registrar of Criminal Appeals, Royal Courts of Justice, since 1968; *b* 10 March 1916; *s* of George and Eva Blanche Blandford; *m* 1940, Marjorie Georgina Crane; one *s*. *Educ:* Bristol Gram. Sch. Admitted Solicitor Supreme Court, England, 1939; LLB (London) 1939. War Service, 1939-46 (despatches): India, Burma, Malaya; rank on release Temp. Major RA. Solicitor in London, 1946-51; Asst Comr of Lands, Gold Coast, 1951; Dist Magistrate, Gold Coast, 1952; called to the Bar, Inner Temple, 1955; Chief Registrar, Supreme Court, Gold Coast, 1956; Registrar of High Court of Northern Rhodesia, 1958; Judge, Supreme Court of Aden, 1961-68. Chm. Aden Municipality Inquiry Commn, 1962. *Publication:* Civil Procedure Rules of Court, Aden, 1967. *Recreations:* photography, travel. *Address:* 72 Gloucester Terrace, W2. *T:* 01-402 6284. *Clubs:* Royal Commonwealth Society; Royal Over-Seas League.

**BLANDY, John Peter,** MA, DM, MCh, FRCS; Consultant Surgeon: The London Hospital, since 1964; St Peter's Hospital for the Stone, since 1969; Professor of Urology, University of London, since 1969; *b* 11 Sept. 1927; *s* of late Sir E. Nicolas Blandy, KCIE, CSI, ICS and Dorothy Kathleen (*née* Marshall); *m* 1953, Anne, *d* of Hugh Mathias, FRCS, Tenby; four *d*. *Educ:* Clifton Coll.; Balliol Coll., Oxford; London Hosp. Med. Coll. BM, BCh 1951; MA 1953; FRCS 1956; DM 1963; MCh 1963. House Phys. and House Surg., London Hosp., 1952; RAMC, 1953-55; Surgical Registrar and Lectr in Surgery, London Hosp., 1956-60; exchange Fellow, Presbyterian St Luke's Hosp., Chicago, 1960-61; Sen. Lectr, London Hosp., 1961; Resident Surgical Officer, St Paul's Hosp., 1963-64. Member: BMA; RSM; Internat. Soc. Pædiatric Urol. Surg.; Internat. Soc. of Urological Surgeons; British Assoc. Urological Surgeons; Fellow, Assoc. of Surgeons. Hunterian Prof., Royal College of Surgeons, 1964. *Publications:* (with A. D. Dayan and H. F. Hope-Stone) Tumours of the Testicle, 1970; papers in surgical and urological jls. *Recreation:* painting. *Address:* The London Hospital, Whitechapel, E1. *T:* 01-247 5454.

**BLANKENHORN, Herbert,** GCVO (Hon.) 1965; German Ambassador to the Court of St James's, 1965-70; *b* 15 Dec. 1904; *s* of Erich Blankenhorn; *m* 1944, Gisela Krug; two *s* two *d*. *Educ:* Gymnasiums in Strasbourg, Berlin, and Karlsruhe; Universities of Munich, London, Heidelberg and Paris. Entered Foreign Service, 1929; served in: Athens, 1932-35; Washington, 1935-39; Helsinki, 1940; Berne, 1940-43; Foreign Office, Berlin (Protocol Section), 1943-45; Dep. Sec.-Gen., Zonal Advisory Council, Hamburg, 1946-48; Sec.-Gen. Christian Democratic Party (British Zone), 1948; Private Sec. to President of Parliamentary Council, Bonn (Dr Adenauer), 1948-49; Political Dir, Foreign Office, 1950-55; German Ambassador: to NATO, 1955-58; to France, 1958-63; to Italy, 1963-65. *Address:* 7847 Badenweiler, Hintere Au 2, Germany.

**BLANTYRE, Archbishop of, (RC),** since 1968; **Most Rev. James Ciona;** *b* 1924. *Educ:* Nankhunda Minor Seminary, Malawi; Kachebere Major Seminary, Malawi. Priest, 1954; Asst Parish Priest, 1954-57; Prof., Nankhunda Minor Seminary, 1957-60; study of Pastoral Sociology, Rome, 1961-62; Asst Parish Priest, 1962-65; Auxiliary Bishop of Blantyre and Titular Bishop of Bacanaria, 1965; Vicar Capitular of Archdiocese of Blantyre, 1967. *Recreation:* music. *Address:* Archbishop's House, PO Box 385, Blantyre, Malawi. *T:* 8537.

**BLASCHKO, Hermann Karl Felix,** MD, FRS 1962; Emeritus Reader in Bio-chemical Pharmacology, Oxford University, and Emeritus Fellow, Linacre College, Oxford, since 1967; Hon. Professor, Faculty of Medicine, Heidelberg, since 1966; *b* Berlin, 4 Jan. 1900; *o s* of late Prof. Alfred Blaschko, MD and late Johanna Litthauer; *m* 1944, Mary Douglas Black, *d* of late John Robert Black, Yelverton, S Devon; no *c*. *Educ:* Universities of Berlin, Freiburg im Breisgau and Göttingen. MD Freiburg; PhD Cambridge; MA Oxon. Research Asst to late Prof. O. Meyerhof at Berlin-Dahlem and Heidelberg at various periods, 1925-32; University Asst in Physiology, Univ. of Jena, 1928-29; worked at UCL, 1929-30 and 1933-34; Physiological Lab., Cambridge Univ., 1934-44; came to Oxford, 1944. Visiting Professor: Yale Univ., 1967-68; Upstate Medical Center, Syracuse, NY, 1968; RCS, 1968-; Univ. of Bergen, Norway, 1969-70. Member of Editorial Board of: Pharmacological Reviews, 1957-64; British Journal of Pharmacology and Chemotherapy, 1959-65; Journal of Physiology, 1965; Neuropharmacology, 1962; Naunyn-Schmiedebergs Arch. Exp. Path. Pharmak, 1966; Molecular Pharmacol., 1966. Mem. Neuropharmacology Panel, International Brain Research Organisation (IBRO); Corresp. Mem., German Pharmacolog. Soc. Hon. MD Berlin (Free Univ.), 1966. *Publications:* numerous papers in scientific publications. *Address:* Department of Pharmacology, South Parks Road, Oxford OX1 3QT; 24 Park Town, Oxford OX2 6SH.

**BLAXTER, Dr Kenneth Lyon,** FRS 1967; FRSE 1965; Director, Rowett Research Institute, Bucksburn, Aberdeen, and Consultant Director, Commonwealth Bureau of Animal Nutrition since 1965; *b* 19 June 1919; *s* of Gaspard Culling Blaxter and Charlotte Ellen Blaxter; *m* 1957, Mildred Lillington Hall; two *s* one *d*. *Educ:* City of Norwich Sch.; University of Reading; University of Illinois. BSc(Agric.), PhD, DSc, NDA (Hons). Scientific Officer, Nat. Inst. for Research in Dairying, 1939-40 and 1941-44. Served RA, 1940-41. Research Officer, Ministry of Agriculture Veterinary Laboratory, 1944-46; Commonwealth Fellow, University of Ill, 1946-47; Head of Dept of Nutrition, Hannah Inst., Ayr, Scotland, 1948-65. Thomas Baxter Prize and Gold Medal,

1960; Gold Medallist, RASE 1964. *Publications:* Energy Metabolism of Ruminants, 1962; Energy Metabolism, 1965. Scientific papers in Jl Endocrinology, Jl Agricultural Science, British Jl Nutrition, Research in Veterinary Science, etc. *Recreation:* painting. *Address:* Wardenhill, Bucksburn, Aberdeen. *T:* Bucksburn 2751.

**BLEANEY, Prof. Brebis,** CBE 1965; FRS 1950; MA, DPhil; Dr Lee's Professor of Experimental Philosophy, University of Oxford, since 1957; Fellow of Wadham College, Oxford, since 1957; *b* 6 June 1915; *m* 1949, Betty Isabelle Plumpton; one *s* one *d*. *Educ:* Westminster City Sch.; St John's Coll., Oxford. Lecturer in Physics at Balliol Coll., Oxford, 1947-50. Research Fellow, Harvard Univ. and Mass Institute of Technology, 1949. University Demonstrator and Lectr in Physics, Univ. of Oxford, 1945-57; Fellow and Lectr in Physics, St John's Coll., Oxford, 1947-57; Tutor, 1950-57; Hon. Fellow, 1968. Visiting Prof. in Physics in Columbia Univ., 1956-57; Harkins Lectr, Chicago Univ., 1957; Kelvin Lectr, Instn Electrical Engineers, 1962; Andrew Mellon Visiting Prof., Univ. of Pittsburgh, 1962-63. Mem. Council for Scientific and Industrial Res., 1960-62. Charles Vernon Boys Prize, Physical Soc., 1952; Hughes Medal, Royal Society, 1962. *Publications:* (with B. I. Bleaney) Electricity and Magnetism, 1957; (with A. Abragam) Electron Paramagnetic Resonance, 1970; various papers in Proceedings of the Royal Society and Proceedings of the Physical Society, etc. *Recreations:* music and amusing one *s* and one *d*. *Address:* Clarendon Laboratory, Oxford. *Club:* Athenæum.

**BLECH, Harry,** OBE 1962; Conductor; Hon. Member of the Royal Academy of Music; *b* 2 March 1910; British; *m* 1935, Enid Marion Lessing; one *s* two *d*; *m* 1957, Marion Manley, pianist; one *s* three *d*. *Educ:* Central London Foundation; Trinity Coll. of Music (Fellow); Manchester Coll. of Music (Fellow). Violin soloist, 1928-30; joined BBC Symphony Orchestra, 1930-36. Responsible for formation of: Blech Quartet, 1933-50; London Wind Players, 1942 (conductor); London Mozart Players, 1949; Haydn-Mozart Soc., 1949; London Mozart Choir, 1952. Dir of Chamber Orchestra, RAM, 1961-65. FRSA. *Address:* The Owls, 70 Leopold Road, Wimbledon, SW19.

**BLEDISLOE,** 2nd Viscount, *cr* 1935; **Benjamin Ludlow Bathurst,** QC 1952; *b* 2 Oct. 1899; *er s* of 1st Viscount Bledisloe, PC, GCMG, KBE, and Hon. Bertha Susan Lopes (*d* 1926), *y d* of 1st Baron Ludlow, PC; *S* father 1958; *m* 1933, Joan Isobel Krishaber; two *s*. *Educ:* Eton; Magdalen Coll., Oxford (BA). Served European War, 1914-18, 2nd Lieut RA. Called to Bar, Inner Temple, 1927. War of 1939-45: Squadron Leader, RAF, 1939-40; Senior Comdr, ATA, 1940-45. Bencher, Lincoln's Inn, 1956. Late Chm., Plant Variety Rights Tribunal; Vice-President: Gen. Council and Register of Osteopaths; West London Flying Club. Past-Pres., St Moritz Tobogganing Club; Verderer of Forest of Dean. *Recreations:* mountaineering, ski-ing, tobogganing, shooting, flying, rowing, gardening, photography. *Heir:* *s* Hon. Christopher Hiley Ludlow Bathurst, 11th Hussars [*b* 24 June 1934; *m* 1962, Elizabeth Mary, 2nd *d* of Sir Edward Thompson, *qv*; one *s* one *d*. *Educ:* Eton. Barrister-at-Law]. *Address:* 14 Mulberry Walk, SW3. *T:* 01-352 7533; 4 Stone Buildings, Lincoln's Inn, WC2. *T:* 01-405 0695; Lydney Park, Glos. *T:* Lydney 2538. *Clubs:* Garrick, Portland, Alpine; Leander (Henley-on-Thames).

**BLEE, David,** CBE 1955; MInstT; *b* 7 Aug. 1899; *m* 1926, Catharine Rosetta Vaughan; one *s*. Served European War, 1917-19, France, Belgium, Germany. Apptd Chief Goods Manager, GWR, 1946; Mem. of Railway Executive, 1947-53; Chief of Commercial Services, British Transport Commission, 1953-55; becoming Traffic Adviser, 1955; Gen. Manager of the London Midland Region of British Railways, 1956-61. Col, Eng. & Rly Staff Corps RE (TA). Former Mem. Council and Vice-Pres., Institute of Transport. Dir, Atlantic Steam Navigation Co.; Member: Permanent Commn of Internat. Rly Congress Assoc.; Internat. Chamber of Commerce. *Publications:* papers and lectures on transport subjects. *Recreations:* walking, travel. *Address:* Crindle, The Gore, Burnham, Bucks. *T:* Burnham (Bucks) 358. *Club:* Athenæum.

**BLEGEN, Carl William;** Professor of Classical Archæology, University of Cincinnati, from 1927 (and Head of Department of Classics, 1950-57), Emeritus, since 1957, Distinguished Service Professor Emeritus, 1969; Fellow of Graduate School of Arts and Sciences; *b* 27 Jan. 1887; *s* of Prof. John H. Blegen and Anna B. (*née* Olsen); *m* 1924, Elizabeth Denny (*d* 1966), *d* of William L. and Flora McKnight Pierce, Englewood, NJ. *Educ:* Augsburg Seminary; University of Minn; Yale Univ.; Amer. Sch. of Classical Studies, Athens. Sec., Amer. Sch. of Classical Studies, Athens, 1913-20; Asst Dir, 1920-26; Actg Dir, 1926-27; Dir, 1948-49; Field Dir, Archeol Expedn of University of Cincinnati, 1932-; Excavations at Troy, 1932-38, at ancient PYlos, 1939, 1952- . With office of Strategic Services, Washington, 1942-45; Cultural Relations Attaché, Amer. Embassy, Athens, 1945-46. Hon. Degrees: MA Yale, 1927; PhD Oslo, 1951; Thessaloniki, 1951; DLitt Oxford, 1957; LLD Cincinnati, 1958; DHL, Hebrew Union Coll., Jewish Inst. of Religion, 1963; LittD Cambridge, 1963; Doctorate, Univ. of Athens, 1963. Fellow Amer. Academy of Arts and Sciences; Corr. Fellow British Acad.; Member: Royal Society of Letters of Lund; Swedish Royal Acad. of Letters, History and Antiquities (Stockholm); Acad. of Science and Letters, Oslo; Arch. Soc. of Athens; Amer. Philosoph. Soc.; Hon. Mem. Soc. for Promotion of Hellenic Studies. Kenyon Medal, British Academy, 1963. First Gold Medal of Archæological Inst. of America, 1965; Gold Medal of the Soc. of Antiquaries of London. 1966; Gold Medal, Cincinnati Univ., 1969. *Publications:* Korakou, 1921; Zygouries, 1927; Acrocorinth (with others), 1934; Prosymna (with Elizabeth Blegen), 1937; Troy, Vols I-IV (with others), 1950, 1951, 1953, 1958; Troy and the Trojans, 1963; The Palace of Nestor at Pylos, Vol. I (with Marion Rawson), 1966. *Recreations:* travel and reading. *Address:* 9 Plutarch Street, Athens 139, Greece; Department of Classics, University of Cincinnati, Cincinnati 21, Ohio, USA. *Clubs:* University; Literary (Cincinnati); Yale (NY); Cosmos (Washington).

**BLELLOCH, Ian William,** CMG 1955; retired; *b* 2 Aug. 1901; *s* of late John Stobie Blelloch and late Christina Macdonald; *m* 1st, 1929, Leila Mary Henderson (*d* 1936); one *s* (and one *s* decd); 2nd, 1946, Margaret Rachel Stevenson. *Educ:* Dunfermline High Sch.; Edinburgh University. MA 1st Class Hons, 1924. Cadet, Federated Malay States, 1926; Class V, 1929; District Officer, Raub, Class IV, 1933; Legal Adviser and Deputy Public Prosecutor, Perak, 1935-37; Sec. to Resident, Negri Sembilan, Class III, 1938; Legal Adviser, Public Prosecutor, Kedah, 1939-41; interned by Japanese, 1942-45; Class II, 1943; Class IB, 1946; Secretary, Resident Commissioner,

Perak, 1946-47; Acting British Adviser, Trengganu, 1948-50; British Adviser, Perak, Federation of Malaya, 1951; retired 1957. Perak Meritorious Service Medal, 1953; created Datoh Kurnia Bakti, Perak, 1956; CStJ 1964 (OStJ 1956). *Recreation:* golf. *Address:* The Garth, Blairgowrie, Perthshire. *T:* Blairgowrie 567. *Club:* East India and Sports.

**BLENKINSOP, Arthur,** FCIS; MP (Lab) South Shields since 1964; *b* 30 June 1911; *s* of John Matthewson Blenkinsop and Anne Douglas Rowell; *m* 1939, Mary Norman Harrold; two *s* one *d*. *Educ:* Newcastle Royal Grammar Sch. MP (Lab) for Newcastle upon Tyne East, 1949-51. Chm. Housing and Local Govt Parliamentary Labour Group. Vice-President, Health Inspectors Assoc.; Delegate to Council of Europe, 1966-70 (Pres. Social Commission, 1968-70). Member, Exec. Cttee: National Trust; Town and Country Planning Assoc.; Mem., Adv. Cttee on Drug Dependence. *Recreations:* walking and reading. *Address:* 233 Wingrove Road, Newcastle upon Tyne 4. *T:* Newcastle 35187.

**BLENNERHASSETT, Francis Alfred,** QC 1965; Recorder of New Windsor since 1965; Deputy Chairman, Staffordshire Quarter Sessions, since 1963; *b* 7 July 1916; 2nd *s* of John and Annie Elizabeth Blennerhassett; *m* 1948, Betty Muriel Bray; two *d*. *Educ:* Solihull Sch. Served War of 1939-45 RA and Royal Warwicks Regt, Britain and East Africa (Captain). Called to Bar, Middle Temple, 1946; Oxford Circuit. *Recreation:* golf. *Address:* Broome Cottage, Old Station Road, Hampton in Arden, Warwickshire. *T:* Hampton in Arden 2660; Lamb Building, Temple, EC4. *T:* 01-583 6094. *Clubs:* Conservative; Midland (Birmingham); Copt Heath Golf.

**BLENNERHASSETT, Sir Marmaduke Adrian Francis William,** 7th Bt, *cr* 1809; *b* 25 May 1940; *s* of Lieut Sir Marmaduke Blennerhassett, 6th Bt, RNVR (killed in action, 1940), and Gwenfra (*d* 1956), *d* of Judge Harrington-Morgan, Churchtown, Co. Kerry, and of Mrs Douglas Campbell; *S* father 1940. *Heir: kinsman* Major (retired) Rowland Paul Francis Casimir Blennerhassett [*b* 1911; *m* 1945, Elizabeth Charlotte Josephine (*née* Stapleton), *widow* of Major F. J. A. Skeet; one *s* one *d*]. *Address:* 17 Campden Hill Road, W8.

**BLIGH,** family name of **Earl of Darnley.**

**BLIGH, Sir Edward Clare,** Kt 1949; Chief Officer of Welfare Department, London County Council, 1932-51; *b* 1887; *s* of James Blight, Doncaster; *m* 1915, Patricia Greville (*d* 1941); one *s* (and two *s* decd). *Educ:* Doncaster; Balliol Coll., Oxford. Resident, Toynbee Hall; served in 8th Bn London Regt (Captain); Assistant General Inspector, Ministry of Health. *Address:* Holmesdale, Horton Kirby, Dartford, Kent.

**BLISS, Sir Arthur,** KCVO 1969; Kt 1950; composer; Master of the Queen's Musick since 1953; *b* London, 2 Aug. 1891; *m* 1925, Gertrude Hoffmann, Santa Barbara, California; two *d*. *Educ:* Rugby; Pembroke Coll., Cambridge (BA, MusBac). Served European War (wounded), despatches; Prof. of Music, University of California, 1940; Asst Overseas Music Director, BBC, 1941-42; Director of Music, BBC, 1942-44; Chairman Music Cttee, British Council, 1946-50; President: Western Orchestral Soc. Ltd, 1954-; Performing Right Soc., 1954-; Internat. Confederation of Authors' and Composers' Societies, 1964-; Hon. President, London Symphony Orchestra, 1956-. Hon. MusD: Edinburgh; London; Cambridge; Lancaster; Hon. DMus Bristol; Hon. LLD Glasgow; Hon. DFA Westminster Coll., Princeton, USA. Hon. FRCM, Hon. RAM; Hon. FTCL; FRCO; Hon. Fellow, Pembroke Coll., Cambridge, 1953; Hon. Freeman Worshipful Company of Musicians, 1954. Gold Medal, Royal Philharmonic Society, 1963. Commander of the Order of Leopold II. *Compositions:* Madam Noy, 1918; Rhapsody, 1919; Rout, 1920; Conversations, 1920; Concerto, 1920; Two Studies for Orchestra, 1920; Mêlée Fantasque for Orchestra, 1920; Two Nursery Rhymes, 1920; Music to the Tempest, 1921; A Colour Symphony, 1922; Introduction and Allegro for Orchestra, 1926; Hymn to Apollo, 1927; Pastoral; Oboe Quintet; Morning Heroes, 1930; Clarinet Quintet, 1932; Viola Sonata, 1933; Film Music to Things to Come, 1935; Music for Strings, 1935; Ballet, Checkmate, 1937; Film Music to Conquest of the Air; Piano Concerto, 1939; String Quartet, 1941; Ballet, Miracle in the Gorbals, 1944; Film Music to Men of Two Worlds, 1945; Ballet, Adam Zero, 1946; Opera, The Olympians, 1948; Film Music to Christopher Columbus, 1949; 2nd String Quartet, 1950; Scena, The Enchantress; Piano Sonata, 1951; Film Music to The Beggar's Opera, 1953; Song of Welcome, 1954; Violin Concerto, 1955; Meditations on a Theme of John Blow, 1955; Overture 'Edinburgh', 1956; Discourse for Orchestra, 1957; Ballet, The Lady of Shalott, 1958; Television Opera, Tobias and the Angel, 1960; Cantata, The Beatitudes, 1962; A Knot of Riddles, 1963; Golden Cantata, 1964; (song cycle) Angels of the Mind, 1969; (cantata) The World is Charged, 1969; Cello Concertino, 1970. *Publication:* As I Remember, 1970. *Address:* 8 The Lane, Marlborough Place, NW8. *Clubs:* Athenæum (elected under rule 2), Garrick.

**BLISS, John Cordeux;** Deputy Assistant Commissioner, Metropolitan Police; seconded as National Co-ordinator of Regional Crime Squads of England and Wales since inception in Dec. 1964; *b* 16 March 1914; *s* of late Herbert Francis Bliss and Ida Muriel (*née* Hays); *m* 1947, Elizabeth Mary, *d* of Charles Gordon Howard; one *s* two *d*. *Educ:* Haileybury Coll. Joined Metropolitan Police, 1936; Metropolitan Police Coll., Hendon, 1936-37. Served in RAF, 1941-45, Flt Lt, 227 Sqdn, MEF. Various ranks of Criminal Investigation Dept of Metropolitan Police, 1946-62; seconded as Dir of Criminal Law at Police Coll., Bramshill, 1962-63; Dep. Comdr, 1963-64. Barrister, Middle Temple, 1954. Liveryman, Merchant Taylors' Company. Churchill Memorial Trust Fellowship, 1967; Queen's Police Medal, 1969. *Recreations:* squash rackets, hillwalking; but mostly gardening; formerly: Rugby football, tennis. *Address:* Foxhanger Down, Hurtmore, Godalming, Surrey. *T:* Godalming 22487. *Club:* Royal Air Force.

**BLISS, Kathleen Mary, (Mrs Rupert Bliss),** MA Cantab 1934; Lecturer in Religious Studies, University of Sussex, since 1967; *b* 5 July 1908; *née* Moore; *m* 1932, Rev. Rupert Bliss; three *d*. *Educ:* Girton Coll., Cambridge. Educational work in India, 1932-39; Editor, the Christian Newsletter, 1945-49; organized Christian-humanist debate, BBC, 1951-55; Studies of education in industry, 1956-57; General Sec., Church of England Board of Education, 1958-66. Member of Public Schools Commn, 1967-70. Hon. DD (Aberdeen), 1949. Select Preacher before the Univ. of Cambridge, 1967. *Publications:* The Service and Status of Women in the Churches, 1951; We the People, 1963; The Future of Religion, 1969. *Address:* 9 Pratt Walk, Lambeth, SE11. *T:* 01-735 6073.

**BLISS, Mrs Rupert;** *see* Bliss, K. M.

**BLIVEN, Bruce;** editor and author; *b* Emmetsburg, Iowa, 27 July 1889; *s* of Charles F. and Lilla C. Bliven; *m* 1913, Rose F. Emery; one *s*. *Educ:* public schools in Emmetsburg; Stanford Univ. Editorial staff, San Francisco Bulletin, 1909-12; magazine contributor and advertising writer, 1912-14; Director, Dept of Journalism, University of Southern California, 1914-16; editorial staff, Printer's Ink Magazine, 1916-18; Member: Editorial Board, New York Globe, 1919-23; Editorial Board, New Republic, 1923-54; New York correspondent Manchester Guardian, 1927-47; Lecturer in Communication and Journalism, Stanford Univ., 1957-; Trustee, Twentieth Century Fund, 1922-57. *Publications:* The Men Who Make the Future, 1942; Preview for Tomorrow: The Unfinished Business of Science, 1953; The World Changers, 1965; Five Million Words Later (autobiog.), 1970. Edited: What the Informed Citizen Needs to Know, 1945; Twentieth Century Unlimited, 1950. Contributor to about 20 American magazines. *Recreations:* reading, music, the theatre. *Address:* Kingscote Gardens, Lagunita Drive, Stanford, California 94305, USA.

**BLOCH, Prof. Felix,** PhD; Professor of Physics, Stanford University, USA, since 1934, *b* 23 Oct. 1905; *s* of Gustav Bloch and Agnes Mayer; *m* 1940, Lore Misch; three *s* one *d*. *Educ:* Zurich, Switzerland. PhD Leipzig, 1928. Asst Zurich, 1928-29; Lorentz Fellow, Holland, 1929-30; Asst Leipzig, 1930-31; Oersted Fellow, Copenhagen, 1931-32; Lecturer, Leipzig, 1932-33; Rockefeller Fellow, Rome, 1933-34; Director-General European Council for Nuclear Research, Geneva, 1954-55. Hon. DSc: Grenoble, 1959; Oxon, 1960; Jerusalem, 1962; Hon. DPhil Zurich, 1966. Fellow American Phys. Society; Member Nat. Academy of Sciences, 1948; Hon. Fellow, Weizmann Inst., 1958. (jointly) Nobel Prize for Physics, 1952. *Publications:* about 50 articles on atomic and nuclear physics in various European and American scientific journals. *Recreations:* ski-ing, mountaineering, piano. *Address:* 1551 Emerson Street. Palo Alto, California, USA. *T:* 327-8156.

**BLOCH, Prof. Konrad E.;** Higgins Professor of Biochemistry, Harvard University, since 1954; *b* 21 Jan. 1912; *s* of Frederick D. Bloch and Hedwig (*née* Striemer); *m* 1941, Lore Teutsch; one *s* one *d*. *Educ:* Technische Hochschule, Munich; Columbia Univ., New York. Instructor and Research Associate, Columbia Univ., 1939-46; University of Chicago: Asst Prof., 1946-48; Associate Prof., 1948-50; Prof., 1950-54. Nobel Prize for Medicine (jointly), 1964. *Publications:* Lipide Metabolism, 1961; numerous papers in biochemical journals. *Address:* 16 Moon Hill Road, Lexington, Mass., USA. *T:* Volunteer 2-9076.

**BLOCK, Maj.-Gen. (retired) Adam Johnstone Cheyne,** CB 1962; CBE 1959 (OBE 1951); DSO 1945; Chief Information Officer to the General Synod (formerly Church Assembly), since 1965; *b* 13 June 1908; *s* of late Col Arthur Hugh Block, RA; *m* 1945, Pauline Bingham, *d* of late Col Norman Kennedy, CBE, DSO, TD, DL, Doonholm, Ayr; three *d*. *Educ:* Blundell's; RMA Woolwich. 2nd Lieut RA 1928; served War of 1939-45 (France, UK, N Africa and Italy); CO 24th Field Regt, RA, 1943-45. GSO1, RA and AMS, GHQ, 1945-47; AQMG and GSO1 Trg AA Comd, 1947-50; Lieut-Col, 1950; Senior Directing Staff (Army). Joint Services Staff College, 1950-53; Col, 1953; CRA 6 Armd Div., 1953; Comdt, School of Artillery, Larkhill, 1956; Maj.-Gen. 1959; GOC Troops, Malta, 1959-62; retd. Col Comdt, Royal Regt of Artillery, 1965-. *Recreations:* all country pursuits. *Address:* Twinley Manor, Whitchurch, Hampshire. *T:* Whitchurch 2717. *Club:* Army and Navy.

**BLOCK, Brig. Allen Prichard,** CB 1945; CBE 1944; DSO 1943; retired; *b* 13 Jan. 1899, British; *m* 1924, Loveday Glasgow; one *s* one *d*. *Educ:* Repton; Royal Military College, Sandhurst. Served European War, France, May-Nov. 1918; India, 1919-27 and 1938-39; Service NWFP, India, 1920-21; Home Service, 1927-38; War of 1939-45, CO Queen's Bn, 1940-43; Brig., 139 Infantry Bde, 1943-45; Service North Africa with 8th Army, Italy and Greece (DSO, CBE, CB); retired May 1953. *Address:* Creek Cottage, 41 Beach Road, Emsworth, Hants. *T:* Emsworth 2599. *Club:* Army and Navy.

**BLOCK, Brig. David Arthur Kennedy William,** CBE 1961; DSO 1945; MC 1943; retired; *b* 13 June 1908; *s* of late Col Arthur Hugh Block; *m* 1949, Elizabeth Grace, *e d* of Lieut-Col E. G. Troyte-Bullock, Zeals House, Wiltshire, and *widow* of Major G. E. Sebag-Montefiore, D'Anvers House, Culworth, near Banbury; no *c*. *Educ:* Blundell's; RMA, Woolwich. Served War of 1939-45 (despatches, MC, DSO); CO 152nd (Ayrshire Yeomanry) Field Regt, RA, 1943-45. CO 2nd Regt RHA, 1950-53; CRA, 7th Armoured Div., 1954-57; Comd 18th Trg Bde, RA, 1958-61; retired, 1961. ADC to the Queen, 1959. *Recreations:* hunting, shooting, golf. *Address:* Benville Manor, Evershot, Dorset. *T:* Corscombe 354. *Club:* Army and Navy.

**BLOCK, His Honour Commander Leslie Kenneth Allen,** DSC 1945; DL; Assistant Judge of the Mayor's and City of London Court, 1954-69; Commissioner, Central Criminal Court, since 1955; Chairman, West Sussex Quarter Sessions, since 1967 (Deputy Chairman, 1955-67); *b* 9 Aug. 1906; *s* of Harry Allen Block, Esher; *m* 1930, Maud Marion (*née* Hicks); two *s* one *d*. *Educ:* RN Colleges Osborne and Dartmouth. Joined Royal Navy, 1920; Emergency List, RN, 1933; called to Bar, Inner Temple, 1936; served War of 1939-45; Navigating Officer, HMS Hermes, 1939-42; Rosyth Escort Force, 1942-43; HMS Duke of York, 1943-44; Fleet Navigating Officer, Home Fleet, 1944-45; Commander, 1945. Chairman Agricultural Land Tribunal, SE Area, 1948-54. JP 1947, DL 1960, Sussex. *Address:* Shiprods, Henfield, Sussex. *T:* Henfield 2004. *Clubs:* United Service; MCC; Royal Yacht Squadron.

**BLODGET, Mrs A. S.;** *see* Skinner, Cornelia O.

**BLOEMFONTEIN, Bishop of,** since 1967; **Rt. Rev. Frederick Andrew Amoore;** *b* 6 June 1913; *s* of Harold Frederick Newnham Amoore and Emily Clara Amoore, Worthing; *m* 1948, Mary Dobson; three *s*. *Educ:* Worthing Boys' High Sch.; University of Leeds. BA (Hons Hist) Leeds, 1934. Curate of: Clapham, London, 1936; St Mary's, Port Elizabeth, S Africa, 1939; Rector of St Saviour's, E London, S Africa, 1945; Dean of St Albans Cathedral, Pretoria, 1950; Exec. Officer for Church of Province of S Africa, 1962. *Recreations:* music, italic script. *Address:* Bishop's House, 16 York Road, Bloemfontein, South Africa. *T:* 7-3861. *Club:* Bloemfontein.

**BLOFIELD, Edgar Glanville,** DSO 1940; Lieutenant (E) RN, retired; *b* 1 June 1899; *s* of Shipwright Lieut-Comdr C. Blofield, RN; *m* 1926, Gladys Enid Learmouth; one *d*. *Educ:* Esplanade House Sch., Portsmouth. Joined

Royal Navy, 1915; served in various ships in Home Fleet, Mediterranean and China Stations; was serving in HM Yacht Victoria and Albert on outbreak of war; retired list, 1949. *Recreations:* those connected with country and sea. *Address:* 91 Festing Grove, Southsea, Hants.

**BLOIS, Sir Charles (Nicholas Gervase),** 11th Bt, *cr* 1686; farming since 1965; *b* 25 Dec. 1939; *s* of Sir Gervase Ralph Edmund Blois, 10th Bt and Mrs Audrey Winifred Blois (*née* Johnson); *S* father, 1968; *m* 1967, Celia Helen Mary Pritchett. *Educ:* Harrow; Trinity Coll., Dublin; Royal Agricultural Coll., Cirencester. Australia, 1963-65. *Recreations:* yachting, shooting. *Heir: b* Rodney John Derek Blois [*b* 12 Nov. 1941; *m* 1968, Lady Caroline Giffard, *er d* of Earl of Halsbury, *qv*]. *Address:* Red House, Westleton, Saxmundham, Suffolk. *T:* Westleton 200. *Club:* Cruising Association.

**BLOM-COOPER, Louis Jacques,** QC 1970; JP; Joint Director of Legal Research Unit, Dept of Sociology, Bedford College, University of London, since 1967; *b* 27 March 1926; *s* of Alfred Blom-Cooper and Ella Flesseman, Rotterdam; *m* 1952, Miriam (marr. diss. 1970), *er d* of Daniel Swift; two *s* one *d*; *m* 1970, Jane Elizabeth, *e d* of Maurice and Helen Smither, Woodbridge, Suffolk. *Educ:* Port Regis Prep. Sch.; Seaford Coll.; King's Coll., London; Municipal Univ. of Amsterdam; Fitzwilliam Coll., Cambridge. LLB London, 1952; Dr Juris Amsterdam, 1954. HM Army, 1944-47: Capt., E Yorks Regt. Called to Bar, Middle Temple, 1952; Vis. Lectr in Criminology, Bedford Coll., 1961. Mem., Home Secretary's Adv. Coun. on the Penal System, 1966-. Chm., London Local Radio Council, 1970-. Joint Editor, Common Market Law Reports. JP Inner London, 1966 (transf. City of London, 1969). *Publications:* Bankruptcy in Private International Law, 1954; The Law as Literature, 1962; The A6 Murder (A Semblance of Truth), 1963; (with T. P. Morris) A Calendar of Murder, 1964; Language of the Law, 1965; (with O. R. McGregor and Colin Gibson) Separated Spouses, 1970; contrib. to Modern Law Review, Brit. Jl of Criminology, Brit. Jl of Sociology. *Recreations:* watching and reporting on Association football, reading, music, writing, broadcasting. *Address:* 25 Andrewes House, Barbican, EC2. *T:* 01-638 9076. *Club:* MCC.

**BLOMEFIELD, Peregrine Maitland; His Honour Judge Blomefield;** a Judge of County Courts since 1970; Deputy Chairman, Berkshire Quarter Sessions, since 1967; *b* 25 Oct. 1917; 2nd *s* of Lt-Col Wilmot Blomefield, OBE; *m* 1941, Angela Catherine, *d* of Major Geoffrey Hugh Shenley Crofton, Heytesbury, Wilts; one *s*. *Educ:* Repton Sch.; Trinity Coll., Oxford (MA). Royal Signals, 1940-46 (Captain). Called to the Bar, Middle Temple, 1947, Bencher, 1967; Oxford Circuit; Recorder of Burton-on-Trent, 1969-70. *Address:* Dorndon House, Hurst, Berkshire. *T:* Hurst 44.

**BLOMEFIELD, Sir Thomas Edward Peregrine,** 5th Bt, *cr* 1807; Director, Whitehall Securities Corporation, Ltd; *b* 31 May 1907; *s* of late Commander T. C. A. Blomefield, *e s* of 4th Bt and Margaret, *e d* of E. P. Landon; *S* grandfather, 1928; *m* 1947, Ginette Massart, Paris; one *s*. *Educ:* Wellington; Trinity Coll., Oxford. Temp. Lieut-Comdt RNVR, 1939-46. *Heir: s* Thomas Charles Peregrine Blomefield, *b* 24 July 1948. *Address:* 16 Campden House, Sheffield Terrace, W8. *T:* 01-229 8729. *Club:* Turf.

**BLOMFIELD, Douglas John,** CIE 1941; ACGI; Regional Technical Adviser, Home Office, 1941-52; *b* 20 Dec. 1885; *s* of Charles Edward Blomfield; *m* 1915, Coralie (*d* 1967), *d* of F. H. Tucker, Indian Police; one *s* one *d*. *Educ:* St Dunstan's Coll.; City and Guilds Central Technical Coll. Joined Indian Service of Engineers, 1908; retired as Chief Engineer (Communications and Works Branch), Bengal, 1940. *Address:* c/o National and Grindlay's Bank Ltd, 13 St James's Square, SW1.

*See also J. R. Blomfield.*

**BLOMFIELD, Brig. John Reginald,** OBE 1957; MC 1944; New Towns Commission Manager for Hemel Hempstead since 1969; *b* 10 Jan. 1916; *s* of Douglas John Blomfield, *qv*; *m* 1939, Patricia Mary McKim; two *d*. *Educ:* Clifton Coll.; RMA, Woolwich; Peterhouse, Cambridge (MA). Commissioned Royal Engineers, 1936; Lt-Col 1955; Col 1961; Brig. 1965. Retired as Dep. Director, Military Engineering Experimental Establishment, 1969. MBIM 1966. *Recreations:* cruising, ocean racing. *Address:* c/o Lloyds Bank Ltd, Cox & King's Branch, 6 Pall Mall, SW1. *Club:* Royal Ocean Racing.

**BLOMFIELD, Maj.-Gen. Valentine,** CB 1947; DSO 1944; *b* 29 March 1898; *e s* of late Frederick Charles Blomfield; *m* 1925, Gladys Edith, *d* of late Col A. M. Lang, CB, RE; three *s*. *Educ:* Rugby; RMC, Sandhurst. Commissioned Border Regt, 1916; served in France, 1916-18 (despatches); NWF India, 1922-23; graduated Staff Coll., Camberley; served in France, 1939-40 (despatches) and 1944 (DSO). Director of Prisoners of War, Aug. 1945-47; Director of Personal Services, War Office, 1947-50; Commander, North-West District and 42nd (Lancs) Div., TA, 1950-53; retired pay, 1954. Col The Border Regt, 1952-59; Col The King's Own Royal Border Regt, 1959-61. *Address:* c/o Lloyds Bank Ltd, 6 Pall Mall, SW1. *Club:* Naval and Military.

**BLOOD, Brig. William Edmund Robarts,** CBE 1943; MC 1918; late RE; *b* 20 Feb. 1897; *s* of late Col William Persse Blood, Shankill, Co. Dublin, and Marienne Frances Robarts; *m* 1st, 1919, Eva Gwendoline Harrison; one *s*; 2nd, 1945, Janet, *d* of Col W. W. Edwards, US Army. *Educ:* Imperial Service Coll.; RMA, Woolwich. 2nd Lieut, RE, 1915; Capt., 1917; retired 1925; Director, William Blood Ltd, Building and Civil Engineering Contractors; recalled to military service, Sept. 1939-45. Croix de Guerre (France), 1917; Legion of Merit (USA), 1945. *Address:* 39 Hans Place, SW1. *T:* 01-584 0170.

**BLOOD, Brig. William Holcroft,** MVO 1922; Indian Army (retired); *b* 29 May 1887; *s* of late John Blood, Ballykilty, Quin, Co. Clare, Ireland; *m* 1st, 1920, Ierne Cecilia (against whom he obtained a divorce, 1935), *d* of late Capt. H. Montgomery Hawkins, Holme Lodge, Dorchester, Dorset; one *s* one *d*; 2nd, 1936, Helen, *widow* of Col J. D. Crawford, Indian Army. *Educ:* Clifton Coll. Indian Army, 1905; NW Frontier, India, 1915; European War, Mesopotamia (despatches); Afghan War, 1919; Bt Major, 1920; Bt Lieut-Col 1931; Commandant QVO Corps of Guides (Cavalry), 1932-36. Re-employed 1940-42, Administrative Comdt Delhi Area; Chief Administrative Officer, GHQ, India, 1942-44; Dep. Secretary, Defence Dept, Govt of India, 1944-45. *Recreations:* shooting, fishing. *Address:* Pear Tree Cottage, near Burwash, Sussex.

**BLOOM, André Borisovich;** *see* Anthony, Archbishop.

**BLOOM, Claire;** *b* 15 Feb, 1931; *d* of late Edward Bloom and of Elizabeth Bloom; *m* 1st, 1959, Rod Steiger (marr. diss. 1969); one *d*; 2nd, 1969, Hillard Elkins. *Educ:* Badminton, Bristol; America and privately. First work in England, BBC, 1946. Stratford: Ophelia, Lady Blanche (King John), Perdita, 1948; The Damask Cheek, Lyric, Hammersmith, 1949; The Lady's Not For Burning, Globe, 1949; Ring Round the Moon, Globe, 1949-50. Old Vic: 1952-53: Romeo and Juliet; 1953: Merchant of Venice; 1954: Hamlet, All's Well, Coriolanus, Twelfth Night, Tempest; 1956: Romeo and Juliet (London, and N American tour). Cordelia, in Stratford Festival Company, 1955 (London, provinces and continental tour); Duel of Angels, Apollo, 1958; Rashomon (New York), 1959; Altona, Royal Court, 1961; Ivanov, Phoenix, 1965. First film, Blind Goddess, 1947. *Films include:* Limelight; The Man Between; Richard III; Alexander the Great; The Brothers Karamazov; The Buccaneers; Look Back in Anger; Three Moves to Freedom; The Brothers Grimm; The Chapman Report; The Haunting; 80,000 Suspects; Alta Infedelta; Il Maestro di Vigevano; The Outrage; The Spy Who Came in From The Cold; Charly; Three into Two won't go. First appearance on television programmes, 1952, since when she has had frequent successes on TV in the US; appeared on BBC TV, 1962. *Recreations:* ballet, skating, reading.

**BLOOM, G(eorge) Cromarty;** General Manager, The Press Association Ltd, since 1961; Member Council of Commonwealth Press Union since 1962; *b* 8 June 1910; *s* of late George Highfield Bloom and Jessie Bloom (*née* Cromarty); *m* 1st, 1940, Patricia Suzanne Ramplin (*d* 1957); two *s*; 2nd, 1961, Sheila Louise Curran; one *s*. *Educ:* Australia and China, privately; Keble Coll., Oxford. With Reuters, 1933-60; Commercial Services Manager (Far East), 1938; Latin American Manager, 1945; Asst General Manager, 1958. Vice-Pres., Alliance Européenne des Agences de Presse, 1969-. *Recreations:* travel, theatre. *Address:* 45 Duchess of Bedford House, W8. *T:* 01-937 6682.

**BLOOM, Ursula, (Mrs Gower Robinson);** authoress; *b* Chelmsford, Essex; *o d* of late Rev. J. Harvey Bloom, MA; *m* 1st, 1916, Capt. Arthur Brownlow Denham-Cookes, 24th London Regt (Queen's) (*d* 1918); one *s*; 2nd, 1925, Paymaster Comdr Charles Gower Robinson, RN (retired). *Educ:* privately. First book, Tiger, published privately when seven years old. *Publications:* The Great Beginning, 1924; Vagabond Harvest, 1925; The Driving of Destiny, 1925; Our Lady of Marble, 1926; The Judge of Jerusalem, 1926; Candleshades, 1927; Spilled Salt, 1927; Base Metal, 1928; An April After, 1928; Tarnish, 1929; To-morrow for Apricots, 1929; The Passionate Heart, 1930; The Secret Lover, 1930; Lamp in the Darkness: a volume of Religious Essays, 1930; Fruit on the Bough, 1931; Packmule, 1931; The Pilgrim Soul, 1932; The Cypresses Grow Dark, 1932; The Log of an NO's Wife, 1932; Wonder Cruise, 1933; Mistress of None, 1933; Rose Sweetman, 1933; Pastoral, 1934; Holiday Mood, 1934; The Questing Trout, 1934; The Gypsy Vans Come Through, 1935; Harvest of a House, 1935; The Laughing Lady, 1936; Laughter on Cheyne Walk, 1936; Three Cedars, 1937; Leaves Before the Storm, 1937; The Golden Venture, 1938; Without Makeup, 1938; The ABC of Authorship, 1938; A Cad's Guide to Cruising, 1938; Lily of the Valley, 1938; Beloved Creditor, 1939; These Roots Go Deep, 1939; The Woman Who Was To-morrow, 1940; Log of No Lady, 1940; The Flying Swans, 1940; Dinah's Husband, 1941; The Virgin Thorn, 1941; Lovely Shadow, 1942; Time, Tide and I, 1942; Age Cannot Wither, 1942; No Lady Buys a Cot, 1943; Robin in a Cage, 1943; The Fourth Cedar, 1943; The Faithless Dove, 1944; No Lady in Bed, 1944; The Painted Lady, 1945; The Changed Village, 1945; Rude Forefathers, 1945; No Lady With a Pen, 1946; Four Sons, 1946; Adam's Daughter, 1947; Three Sisters, 1948; Façade, 1948; No Lady Meets No Gentleman, 1948; Next Tuesday, 1949; Elinor Jowitt, Antiques; No Lady in the Cart; Song of Philomel, 1950; The King's Wife, 1950; Mum's Girl was no Lady, 1950; Pavilion, 1951; Nine Lives, 1951; How Dark, My Lady!, 1951; The Sentimental Family, 1951; As Bends the Bough, 1952; Twilight of a Tudor, 1952; Sea Fret, 1952; The Gracious Lady, 1953; The First Elizabeth, 1953; Hitler's Eva, 1954; Trilogy, 1954; Curtain Call for the Guvnor, 1954; Matthew, Mark, Luke and John, 1954; Daughters of the Rectory, 1955; The Silver Ring, 1955; The Tides of Spring Flow Fast, 1955; Victorian Vinaigrette, 1956; No Lady Has a Dog's Day, 1956; Brief Springtime, 1957; The Elegant Edwardian, 1957; Monkey Tree in a Flower Pot, 1957; He Lit the Lamp, 1958; The Abiding City, 1958; Down to the Sea in Ships, 1958; The Inspired Needle, 1959; Youth at the Gate, 1959; Undarkening Green, 1959; Sixty Years of Home, 1960; The Thieving Magpie, 1960; Prelude to Yesterday, 1961; The Cactus has Courage, 1961; War Isn't Wonderful, 1961; Ship in a Bottle, 1962; Harvest Home Come Sunday, 1962; Parson Extraordinary. 1963; The Gated Road, 1963; Mrs Bunthorpe's Respects, 1963; The House That Died Alone, 1964; The Rose of Norfolk, 1964; The Ring Tree, 1964; The Ugly Head, 1965; The Quiet Village, 1965; Rosemary for Stratford-on-Avon, 1965; Price Above Rubies, 1965; The Dandelion Clock, 1966; The Mightier Sword, 1966; The Old Adam, 1967; A Roof and Four Walls, 1967; Two Pools in a Field, 1967; The Dragon Fly, 1968; Yesterday is To-morrow, 1968; Flight of the Peregrine, 1969; The House of Kent, 1969; The Hunter's Moon, 1970; Rosemary for Frinton, 1970; Unborn Tomorrow, 1970; The Tune of Time, 1970. *Address:* 191 Cranmer Court, SW3. *T:* 01-589 8966.

**BLOOMER, Rt. Rev. Thomas,** DD 1946 (TCD); *b* 14 July 1894; *s* of Thomas and Mary Bloomer; *m* 1935, Marjorie Grace (*d* 1969), *d* of late Rev. David Hutchison; one *s* two *d*. *Educ:* Royal Sch., Dungannon, N Ireland; Trinity Coll., Dublin. Ordained to curacy of Carrickfergus, N Ireland, 1918; Curate of: Castleton, Lancs, 1922; Cheltenham, Glos, 1923; Vicar of St Mark's, Bath, 1928; Vicar of Barking, 1935-46; Rural Dean of Barking and Canon of Chelmsford Cathedral, 1943-46; Bishop of Carlisle, 1946-66. Chaplain to: the King, 1944-47; House of Lords, 1953-66. Proctor in Convocation of Canterbury, 1945. Freedom of City of Carlisle, 1966. *Publications:* A Fact and a Faith, 1943; A Fact and an Experience, 1944. *Recreations:* golf, gardening. *Address:* Hwiccanstede, North Road, Bath, Somerset. *Clubs:* Bath and County; County (Carlisle).

**BLOOMFIELD, Hon. Sir John (Stoughton),** Kt 1967; QC (Victoria) 1965; LLB; Member for Malvern, Legislative Assembly, Victoria, 1953-70, retired; *b* 9 Oct. 1901; *s* of Arthur Stoughton Bloomfield, Chartered Accountant, Melbourne, and Ada Victoria Bloomfield; *m* 1931, Beatrice Madge, *d* of W. H. Taylor, Overnewton, Sydenham, Victoria; one *s* one *d*. *Educ:* Geelong Grammar Sch.; Trinity Coll., Melbourne Univ. Served AIF, 1940-45; Lieut-Col. retired. Solicitor, 1927-45; called to Victorian Bar, 1945. Government of Victoria: Minister of Labour and Industry and of Electrical Undertakings, 1955-56; Minister of Education, 1956-67. Member: Council, University of Melbourne, 1956-70; Board of Management, Royal Victorian Eye and Ear Hospital. *Publications:* Company Law Amendments, 1939; Screens and Gowns: Some Aspects of University Education Overseas, 1963; articles in professional journals. *Recreations:* painting, golf. *Address:* 25 Mercer Road, Armadale, Victoria 3143, Australia. *T:* 20-2947. *Clubs:* Melbourne, Naval and Military (Melbourne).

**BLOSSE, Sir David Edward;** *see* Lynch-Blosse.

**BLOUGH, Roger M.;** Partner, White & Case, since 1969; former Chairman of the Board of Directors, United States Steel Corporation; *b* 19 Jan. 1904; *s* of Christian E. Blough and Viola (*née* Hoffman); *m* 1928, Helen Martha Decker; twin *d. Educ:* Susquehanna Univ. (AB); Yale Law Sch. (LLB). General practice of law with White & Case, New York City, 1931-42; General Solicitor, US Steel Corp. of Delaware, 1942-51; Exec. Vice-President law and Secretary, US Steel Corp., 1951; Vice-Chairman, Director and Member Finance Cttee, US Steel Corp., 1952; General Counsel, 1953-55; Chairman, Chief Exec. Officer and Member Exec. Cttee, 1955. Holds numerous hon. degrees. *Publication:* Free Man and the Corporation, 1959. *Address:* (business) 14 Wall Street, New York, NY 10005, USA; (home) Blooming Grove, Hawley, Pennsylvania 18428. *Clubs:* Blooming Grove Hunting and Fishing (Pa); Links (NYC); Duquesne (Pittsburgh); Links Golf; Pine Valley Golf.

**BLOUNT, Bertie Kennedy,** CB 1957; DrPhilNat; *b* 1 April 1907; *s* of late Col G. P. C. Blount, DSO, and late Bridget Constance, *d* of Maj.-Gen. J. F. Bally, CVO; unmarried. *Educ:* Malvern Coll.; Trinity Coll., Oxford (MA 1932, BSc 1929); Univ. of Frankfurt (DrPhilNat 1931). Ramsay Memorial Fellow, 1931; 1851 Senior Student, 1933; Dean of St Peter's Hall, Oxford, 1933-37; Messrs Glaxo Laboratories Ltd: Head of Chemical Research Laboratory, 1937; Principal Technical Executive, 1938-40. Served Army (Intelligence Corps), War of 1939-45; Capt. 1940; Major 1942; Col 1945. Asst Director of Research, The Wellcome Foundation, 1947; Director of Research Branch, Control Commission for Germany, 1948, and subsequently also Chief of Research Div. of Military Security Board; Director of Scientific Intelligence, Min. of Defence, 1950-52; Dep. Secretary, DSIR, 1952; Min. of Technology, 1964; retired 1966. Chairman Steering Cttees: Torry Res. Station and Forest Products Res. Lab., 1958-66; Lab. of the Govt Chemist, 1962-66; Building Res. Station, Joint Fire Res. Organisation, Hydraulics Res. Stat., Water Pollution Res. Lab., Warren Spring Lab., 1965-66. Member Exec. Cttee, British Council, 1957-66. Royal Society of Arts: Armstrong Lecturer, 1955; Cantor Lecturer, 1963. Member Parry Cttee to review Latin American Studies in British Universities, 1962; President Exec. Cttee, International Institute of Refrigeration, 1963. FRIC. *Publications:* papers in scientific and other journals. *Address:* Tarrant Rushton House, Blandford, Dorset. *T:* Blandford 256. *Club:* Athenæum.

**BLOUNT, Sir Edward Robert,** 11th Bt, *cr* 1642; retired; *b* 2 Dec. 1884; *s* of Sir Walter Blount, 9th Bt; *S* brother (Sir Walter Blount, 10th Bt) 1958; *m* 1914, Violet Ellen (*d* 1969), *d* of Alpin Grant Fowler; one *s* one *d. Educ:* Convent, Bath; Wimbledon Coll. (RC). Lieut RAF, 1914-18. British Sugar Corporation Ltd, 1924-50. *Recreation:* sailing. *Heir: s* Walter Edward Blount, DSC, MA [*b* 31 Oct. 1917; *m* 1954, Eileen Audrey, *o d* of late Hugh B. Carritt; one *d*]. *Address:* St Leonard's, Seaview, IOW. *Clubs:* Island Sailing (Cowes); Seaview Yacht.

**BLOW, Sandra;** Tutor, Painting School, Royal College of Art, since 1960; *b* 1925; *d* of Jack and Lily Blow. *Educ:* St Martin's School of Art; Royal Academy Sch.; Accademia di Belle Arti, Rome. *One-man Exhibitions:* Gimpel Fils, 1952, 1954, 1960, 1962; Saidenburg Gallery, NY, 1957; New Art Centre, London, 1966, 1968. Represented in group exhibitions in Britain, USA, Italy, Denmark, France. Won British Section of Internat. Guggenheim Award, 1960; 2nd prize, John Moore's Liverpool Exhibition, 1961; Arts Council Purchase Award, 1965-66. *Official Purchases:* Peter Stuyvesant Foundation; Nuffield Foundation; Arts Council of Great Britain; Arts Council of N Ireland; Walker Art Gallery, Liverpool; Allbright Knox Art Gallery, Buffalo, NY; Museum of Modern Art, NY; Tate Gallery; Gulbenkian Foundation; Min. of Public Building and Works; Contemp. Art Society; silk screen prints: Victoria and Albert Museum; Fitzwilliam Museum, Cambridge; City of Leeds Art Gall.; Graves Art Gall., Sheffield; painting purchased for liner Queen Elizabeth II. *Address:* 12 Sydney Close, SW3. *T:* 01-589 8610.

**BLOY, Rt. Rev. F. Eric;** *see* Los Angeles, Bishop of.

**BLUCKE, Air Vice-Marshal Robert Stewart,** CB 1946; CBE 1945; DSO 1943; AFC 1936, Bar 1941; RAF, retired; *b* 22 June 1897; *s* of late Rev. R. S. K. Blucke, Monxton Rectory, Andover, Hants; *m* 1926, Nancy, *d* of late Frank Wilson, Auckland, NZ; one *s* one *d. Educ:* Malvern Coll. Dorset Regt and RFC, 1915-18; Mesopotamia, 1916-18; Royal Air Force, 1922; India, 1927-32; Test Pilot Royal Aircraft Establishment, Farnborough, 1933-37; served in Bomber Comd, 1942-46; AOC No 1 Group RAF, 1945; SASO, AHQ, India, 1947; AOA, Technical Trg Comd, 1947-49; AOA, Far East Air Force, 1949-50; AOC Malaya, 1951; AOC-in-C Transport Comd, 1952; retired 1952. General Manager, National Assoc. for Employment of Regular Sailors, Soldiers and Airmen, 1952-65. *Recreation:* golf. *Address:* 9 Royal Chase, Tunbridge Wells, Kent. *T:* Tunbridge Wells 20912. *Club:* RAF.

**BLUETT, Maj.-Gen. Douglas,** CB 1958; OBE 1942; MA, MB; *b* 23 Aug. 1897; *s* of Rev. R. D. Bluett, BD, The Rectory, Delgany, Co. Wicklow, Ireland; *m* 1940, Johanna Catharine (*d* 1960), *d* of Mr Simpson-Smith, Huddersfield, Yorks; no *c*; *m* 1964, Noeline, *widow* of Col C. Day. *Educ:* St Andrews Coll., and Trinity Coll., Dublin. Served European War, 1914-18, in Greek Macedonia, Bulgaria, Serbia, European Turkey and Islands of the Aegean Sea; War of 1939-45, with RAMC, ADMS 10th and 11th Armoured Divs, Western Desert, France and Germany; Lieut-Col, 1943; Col, 1945; Brig., 1953; Maj.-Gen., 1956; QHP 1956-58; retired, 1958. Col Comdt, RAMC, 1958-63. CStJ. Officer, Order of Leopold II avec Palme and Croix de Guerre avec Palme (Belgium), 1945. *Recreation:* golf. *Address:* c/o Glyn, Mills & Co., Kirkland House, Whitehall, SW1; Galtymore, 111 Rochester Road, Aylesford, Kent. *Club:* United Service.

**BLUNDELL, Commandant Daphne Mary;** Director, WRNS, since 1970; *b* 19 Aug. 1916. *Educ:* St Helen's Sch., Northwood; Bedford Coll., London. Worked for LCC as Child Care Organiser. Joined WRNS, Nov. 1942; commnd 1943; served in Orkneys, Ceylon, E Africa; Malta, 1954-56; Staff of Flag Officer Naval Air

Comd, 1964-67; Staff of C-in-C Portsmouth, 1967-69; Supt WRNS Training and Drafting, 1969-70. Supt 1967; Comdt 1970. Hon. ADC to the Queen, 1970-. *Address:* 47 Wolsey Road, Moor Park, Northwood, Middx. *T:* Northwood 21546. *Club:* Service Women's.

**BLUNDELL, Sir Denis;** *see* Blundell, Sir E. D.

**BLUNDELL, Sir (Edward) Denis,** KBE 1967 (OBE 1944); High Commissioner for New Zealand in London, since 1968; Barrister and Solicitor of the Supreme Court of New Zealand; Senior Partner of Bell, Gully & Co., Barristers and Solicitors, Wellington, New Zealand; *b* 29 May 1907; British; *m* 1945; one *s* one *d*. *Educ:* Waitaki High Sch. (NZ); Trinity Hall, Cambridge Univ. Called to Bar, Gray's Inn, 1929; admitted as Barrister and Solicitor of the Supreme Court of New Zealand at end of 1929. President of the New Zealand Law Society, 1962-68. *Recreations:* cricket, golf, swimming, tennis. *Address:* New Zealand High Commission, Haymarket, SW1; 25 Upland Road, Wellington, New Zealand. *T:* 26-417 (private) and 49-760 (business). *Clubs:* Wellington; Wellesley (New Zealand).

**BLUNDELL, Lionel Alleyne,** QC 1959; *b* 30 Dec. 1910; *s* of John Joseph and Florence Blundell; *m* 1935, Muriel Theresa Timson. *Educ:* King's Norton and George Dixon Grammar Schools; Birmingham Univ.; Gray's Inn. Certificate of Honour, Bar Final Examinations, 1932; Arden Scholar and Sen. Holker Scholar, Gray's Inn. Called to the Bar, Gray's Inn, 1933; LLM, Birmingham Univ., 1934. Royal Air Force, 1940-45. Bencher, Gray's Inn, 1965. Practice, specialising in: landlord and tenant, town planning, compensation and other branches of law affecting property. *Publications:* Rent Restrictions Guide, four editions, 1943-56; Rent Restrictions Cases, three editions, 1944-55; (with V. G. Wellings): The Landlord and Tenant Acts 1927 and 1954, two editions; The Complete Guide to the Rent Acts, 1958; (with G. Dobry) Town and Country Planning, 1963. Editor, Woodfall, Law of Landlord and Tenant, 24th edition 1939, 25th edition 1954, 26th and 27th editions (with V. G. Wellings), 1960, 1968; Joint Contributor Landlord and Tenant Title, Encyclopædia of Forms and Precedents, 4th edition, 1966. *Recreations:* cycling (Pres. Cyclists' Touring Club, 1963), walking, photography, hi-fi. *Address:* 11 King's Bench Walk, The Temple, EC4. *T:* 01-353 2484.

**BLUNDELL, Sir Michael,** KBE 1962 (MBE 1943); *b* 7 April 1907; *s* of Alfred Herbert Blundell and Amelia Woodward Blundell (*née* Richardson); *m* 1946, Geraldine Lötte Robarts; one *d*. *Educ:* Wellington Coll. Settled in Kenya as farmer, 1925. 2nd Lieut, RE, 1940; Major, 1940; Lieut-Col, 1941; Col, 1944; served Abyssinian campaign and SEAC. Commissioner, European Settlement, 1946-47; MLC, Rift Valley Constituency, Kenya, 1948-62; Leader European Members, 1952; Minister on Emergency War Council, Kenya, 1954; Minister of Agriculture, Kenya, 1955-59 and April 1961-June 1962; Leader of New Kenya Group, 1959-63. Chairman: Pyrethrum Board of Kenya, 1949-54; Egerton Agricultural Coll., 1962-; EA Breweries Ltd, 1964-; Uganda Breweries Ltd, 1965-; Dir, Barclays Bank DCO Ltd (Kenya), 1968-. *Publication:* So Rough a Wind, 1964. *Recreations:* gardening, music, 18th century English porcelain. *Address:* Box 100, Nakuru, Kenya. *T:* Bahati 219. *Clubs:* Brooks's, Farmers'; Muthaiga (Nairobi).

**BLUNDEN, Edmund Charles,** CBE 1951; MC; MA; CLit; LittD (Leeds, Leicester); FRSL; Professor of Poetry, University of Oxford, 1966-68; Hon. Member of the Japan Academy; *b* 1 Nov. 1896; *m* 1945, Claire Margaret Poynting; four *d*. *Educ:* Christ's Hospital; Queen's Coll., Oxford. Prof. of English Literature, Tokyo Univ., 1924-27; served in France and Belgium, 1916-19, with the Royal Sussex Regt. Awarded the Hawthornden Prize, 1922. Fellow and Tutor in English Literature, Merton Coll., Oxford, 1931-43; on staff of Oxford Univ. Senior Training Corps, 1940-44; with UK Liaison Mission, Tokyo, 1948-50; Emeritus Prof. at the University of Hong Kong. Queen's Gold Medal for Poetry, 1956; Benson Medallist, RSL; Midsummer Prize, Corporation of London, 1970. Order of the Rising Sun, 3rd Class (Japan), 1963. *Publications: poetry:* Poems, 1914-1930; second series, 1930-1940; Shells by a Stream, 1944; After the Bombing, 1948; Poems of Many Years, 1957; A Hong Kong House, 1962; Eleven Poems, 1966; (with Bernard Mellor) Wayside Poems of the Seventeenth Century (anthology), 1963; *prose:* The Bonadventure, 1922; On the Poems of Henry Vaughan, 1927; Undertones of War, 1928, new editions, 1956, 1964; Nature in English Literature, 1929; Life of Leigh Hunt, 1930; The Face of England, 1932; Charles Lamb and His Contemporaries, 1934; The Mind's Eye, 1934; Keats's Publisher, 1936; English Villages, 1941; Thomas Hardy, 1942; Cricket Country, 1944; Shelley, a Life-Story, 1946. *Editorship:* has edited Clare, Collins, Smart, Keats, Shelley, Wilfred Owen, Ivor Gurney. *Address:* Hall Mill, Long Melford, Sudbury, Suffolk.

**BLUNDEN, Sir William,** 6th Bt, *cr* 1776; RN, retired; *b* 26 April 1919; *s* of 5th Bt and Phyllis, *d* of P. C. Creaghe; *S* father, 1923; *m* 1945, 2nd Officer Pamela Mary Purser, WRNS; five *d*. *Educ:* Repton. Lieut-Comdr, RN, 1949; retired 1958. *Heir:* *b* Philip Overington Blunden [*b* 27 Jan. 1922; *m* 1945, Jeanette Francesca (WRNS), *e d* of Captain D. Macdonald, RNR, Portree, Isle of Skye; two *s*]. *Address:* Castle Blunden, Kilkenny. *T:* Kilkenny 128.

**BLUNT, Sir Anthony Frederick,** KCVO 1956 (CVO 1947); FBA 1950; FSA 1960; Professor of History of Art, University of London, and Director, Courtauld Institute of Art, since 1947; Surveyor of the Queen's Pictures, since 1952 (of the Pictures of King George VI, 1945-52); *b* 26 Sept. 1907; *y s* of late Rev. A. S. V. Blunt, Vicar of St John's, Paddington. *Educ:* Marlborough Coll.; Trinity Coll., Cambridge. Served War of 1939-45: France, 1939-40; WO, 1940-45. Fellow, Trinity Coll., Cambridge, 1932-36; on staff of Warburg Inst., London, 1937-39; Reader in History of Art, London Univ., and Dep. Dir, Courtauld Inst. of Art, 1939-47. Slade Prof. of Fine Art, Cambridge, 1965-66. Hon. Fellow, Trinity Coll., Cambridge, 1967. Hon. DLitt: Bristol, 1961; Durham, 1963; DèsL hc Paris, 1966. Commander: Order of Orange Nassau (Holland), 1948; Legion of Honour (France), 1958. *Publications:* (with Walter Friedlaender), The Drawings of Nicolas Poussin, 1939-; Artistic Theory in Italy, 1940; François Mansart, 1941; French Drawings at Windsor Castle, 1945; (with Margaret Whinney) The Nation's Pictures, 1951; Rouault's Miserere, 1951; Poussin's Golden Calf, 1951; Art and Architecture in France, 1500-1700, 1953, rev. edn 1970; The Drawings of G. B. Castiglione and Stefano della Bella at Windsor Castle, 1954; Venetian Drawings at Windsor Castle, 1957; Philibert de l'Orme, 1958; The Art of William Blake, 1960; (with H. L. Cooke) The Roman Drawings at Windsor Castle, 1960; (with Phoebe Pool) Picasso: The Formative Years, 1962; Nicolas Poussin:

Catalogue raissoné, 1966; Nicolas Poussin (2 vols), 1967; Sicilian Baroque, 1968; Picasso's Guernica, 1969; articles in Burlington Magazine, Jl of Warburg and Courtauld Insts, Spectator, etc. *Address:* 20 Portman Square, W1. *T:* 01-935 9392. *Club:* Travellers'.

**BLUNT, Christopher Evelyn,** OBE 1945; FBA 1965; retired; *b* 16 July 1904; 2nd *s* of Rev. A. S. V. Blunt and Hilda Violet Blunt; *m* 1930, Elisabeth Rachel Bazley; one *s* two *d. Educ:* Marlborough (Foundation Scholar). Entered merchant banking firm of Higginson & Co., 1924; partner, 1947; executive director of successor companies, 1950-64. Served War, 1939-46; 52 AA (TA) Regt; GHQ (Gen. Staff), BEF (despatches), Home Forces, 21 Army Group; SHAEF; retired 1946 (Col). FSA 1936; President British Numismatic Soc., 1946-50; President Royal Numismatic Soc., 1956-61. Officer Legion of Merit (USA), 1945. *Publications:* contributions to Numismatic Chronicle, British Numismatic Journal, Archæologia, etc. *Recreations:* travel and archæology. *Address:* Ramsbury Hill, Ramsbury, Marlborough, Wilts. *T:* Ramsbury 358; H4 Albany, Piccadilly, W1. *T:* 01-734 5320. *Clubs:* Travellers', Pratt's.

**BLUNT, Sir Richard David Harvey,** 11th Bt *cr* 1720; *b* 22 Oct. 1912; *s* of Sir John Blunt, 9th Bt, and Maud Julia (*d* 1935), *e d* of late Sir David Lionel Goldsmid-Stern-Salomons, 2nd Bt; *S* brother, 1969; *m* 1st, 1936, Elisabeth Malvine Ernestine, *er d* of Comdr F. M. Fransen Van de Putte, Royal Netherlands Navy (retd); one *s*; 2nd, 1943, Margaret, *e d* of John Dean, Nutbeam, Cirencester; two *d. Recreations:* racing, shooting, stud management. *Heir:* *s* David Richard Reginald Blunt, *b* 8 Nov. 1938. *Address:* Diana Lodge Stud, Purton, Wilts.

**BLUNT, Wilfrid Jasper Walter;** Curator of the Watts Gallery, Compton, since 1959; *b* 19 July 1901; *s* of late Rev. Arthur Stanley Vaughan Blunt and Hilda Violet Master. *Educ:* Marlborough Coll.; Worcester Coll., Oxford; Royal College of Art. Art Master, Haileybury Coll., 1923-38; Drawing Master, Eton Coll., 1938-59. ARCA (London) 1923. Introduced into the Public Schs the craft of pottery (Haileybury, 1927) and Italic handwriting (Eton, 1940). *Publications:* The Haileybury Buildings, 1936; Desert Hawk, 1947; The Art of Botanical Illustration, 1950; Tulipomania, 1950; Black Sunrise, 1951; Sweet Roman Hand, 1952; Japanese Colour Prints, 1952; Georg Dionysius Ehret, 1953; Pietro's Pilgrimage, 1953; Sebastiano, 1956; Great Flower Books (with Sacheverell Sitwell and Patrick Synge), 1956; A Persian Spring, 1957; Lady Muriel, 1962; Of Flowers and a Village, 1963; Cockerell, 1964; Omar, 1966; Isfahan, 1966; John Christie of Glyndebourne, 1968; The Dream King, 1970. *Recreations:* writing, singing and travel. *Address:* The Watts Gallery, Compton, near Guildford, Surrey. *T:* Puttenham 235.

**BLYDE, Sir Henry (Ernest),** KBE 1969 (CBE 1952); Chairman, Taranaki Harbours Board, since 1953; Chairman Lepperton Dairy Co. since 1942; *b* 25 Oct. 1896; *s* of James Blyde; *m* 1929, Mary, *d* of W. J. McCormick; two *s* two *d. Educ:* St Paul's School, St Leonards-on-Sea, Sussex. Formerly Chairman, Taranaki Hospital Bd. JP. *Recreations:* bowling, billiards. *Address:* 233 Carrington Street, New Plymouth, New Zealand. *T:* 88928 New Plymouth. *Club:* Taranaki (New Plymouth).

**BLYTH,** family name of **Baron Blyth.**

**BLYTH,** 3rd Baron, *cr* 1907; **Ian Audley James Blyth;** Bt, *cr* 1895; *s* of late Hon. James Audley Blyth (2nd *s* of 1st Baron); *b* 28 Oct. 1905; *S* uncle, 1943; *m* 1928, Edna Myrtle, *d* of Ernest Lewis, Wellington, NZ; two *s* three *d. Heir:* *s* Hon. Anthony Audley Rupert Blyth [*b* 3 June 1931; *m* 1954, Elizabeth Dorothea (marr. diss. 1962), *d* of R. T. Sparrow, Vancouver, BC; one *s* one *d*]. *Address:* Rockfield House, Athenry, Co. Galway.

**BLYTH, Robert Henderson,** RSA 1958 (ARSA 1949); RSW 1950; Head of Drawing and Painting, Gray's School of Art, Aberdeen, since 1954; *b* 21 May 1919; *s* of William Blyth and Susan McGowan; *m* 1948, Isabel Mary Izatt; one *d. Educ:* Glasgow Sch. of Art; Hospitalfield Art Coll. On staff of Edinburgh Coll. of Art, 1945-54. *Address:* 106 Desswood Place, Aberdeen AB2 4DQ. *T:* 21735. *Clubs:* Royal Northern (Aberdeen); Scottish Arts (Edinburgh).

**BLYTHE, Ernest;** Director of Abbey Theatre, Dublin (Managing Director, 1943-67); Member of Royal Irish Academy; *b* 13 April 1889; *s* of James Blyth, Magheragall, Lisburn, Co. Antrim; *m* 1919, Annie McHugh; one *s.* MP (S Fein) N Monaghan 1918-21; Mem. of Dail Eireann for Co. Monaghan, 1921-33; Mem. of Seanad Eireann, 1934-36. Minister: for Trade and Commerce in Provisional Government, 1921-22; for Local Government, 1922-23; Minister of Finance, 1923-32, and Minister of Posts and Telegraphs, 1927-32; Vice-Pres. of Executive Council, 1927-32; Mem. of Radio Eireann Authority, 1961-65; sometime Editor of the Southern Star Skibbereen; Mem. of Church of Ireland. *Publications:* Fraoch is Fothannāin, a volume of Gaelic verse, 1938; Briseadh Na Teorann, a study in Gaelic of Irish Partition, 1955; Trasna na Bōinne (Across the Boyne), vol. i of autobiography in Gaelic, 1957; Slān le Ultaibh (Good-bye to Ulster), vol. II of autobiography, 1970. *Address:* 50 Kenilworth Square, Rathmines, Dublin.

**BLYTHE, Wilfred Lawson,** CMG 1953; *b* 9 Nov. 1896; *s* of late Joseph Blythe; *m* 1925, Muriel Gertrude Woodward (*d* 1969); one *d. Educ:* Universities of Liverpool and Grenoble. Served European War, 1915-19, Capt. RFA (despatches). Malayan Civil Service, 1921; studied Chinese at Canton, 1922-24; Protector of Chinese, various parts of Malaya, 1924-36; Dep. Pres., Municipality, Penang, 1936-37 and 1939-40; Dep. Controller of Labour (Chinese), 1941-42; served with Army in Malaya, 1942; interned, 1942-45; Sec. for Chinese Affairs, Federation of Malaya, 1946-48; Pres. Municipal Commission, Singapore, 1948-50; Colonial Sec., Singapore, 1950-53. *Publications:* The Impact of Chinese Secret Societies in Malaya, 1969; articles on Chinese Secret Societies and Chinese Labour. *Address:* Le Grand Pré, Grouville, Jersey, Channel Islands. *T:* Jersey East 962. *Club:* Royal Commonwealth Society.

**BLYTON,** family name of **Baron Blyton.**

**BLYTON,** Baron, *cr* 1964 (Life Peer); **William Reid Blyton;** Miners' Secretary Harton Lodge, Durham Miners' Association, since 1941 (Chairman, 1928-41); Councillor South Shields Borough Council since 1936; *b* 2 May 1899; *s* of Charles H. Blyton, retired labourer, and late Hannah A. Blyton; *m* 1919, Jane B. Ord; three *d. Educ:* Elementary Education Holy Trinity Sch. and Dean Road Sch., South Shields. Chm. South Shields Labour Party, 1928-29, 1931-32; Mem. Durham Miners' Executive Cttee, 1930-32, 1942-43; Chm. of South Shields Education Cttee, 1943, and of South Shields Electrical

Cttee, 1937-40; MP (Lab) Houghton-le-Spring Div. of County Durham, 1945-64; late PPS to Ministry of Civil Aviation; resigned, 1949. Chm. High Sch. Governors and Chm. Secondary and Technical Cttee of South Shields. Served in HM Submarines in European War, 1914-18. *Address:* 139 Brockley Avenue, South Shields, Durham.

**BOAG, Prof. John Wilson;** Professor of Physics as Applied to Medicine, University of London, Institute of Cancer Research, since 1965; *b* Elgin, Scotland, 20 June 1911; *s* of John and Margaret A. Boag; *m* 1938, Isabel Petrie; no *c*. *Educ:* Universities of Glasgow, Cambridge and Braunschweig. Engineer, British Thomson Houston Co., Rugby, 1936-41; Physicist, Medical Research Council, 1941-52; Visiting Scientist, National Bureau of Standards, Washington, DC, 1953-54; Physicist, British Empire Cancer Campaign, Mount Vernon Hospital, 1954-64; Royal Society (Leverhulme) Visiting Prof. to Poland, 1964. *Publications:* papers on radiation dosimetry, statistics, and radiation chemistry. *Address:* 40 Overton Road, Sutton, Surrey.

**BOARD, Air Commodore Andrew George,** CMG 1919; DSO 1918; *b* 1878; 3rd *s* of late Major John Board, JP, of Farley, Westerham, Kent; *m* 1932, Phyllis, *widow* of Capt. V. C. W. Agnew, 2nd *d* of late Claude Baggallay, KC. *Educ:* Charterhouse. Formerly Major and Temporary Lieut-Col South Wales Borderers; served in India and South Africa; Aviators Royal Aero Club Certificate No. 36, Nov. 1910; Seconded to RFC, 1912; served European War, 1914-18 (despatches, DSO, CMG); Major S Wales Borderers, 1915; Col RFC, 1917; Wing Comdr RAF, 1919; Group Capt., 1923; Air Commodore, 1928; Dep. Dir Personnel, Air Ministry, 1922-23; served in Iraq, 1923-26; Chief Staff Officer, HQ RAF Middle East, Cairo, 1927-31; retired list, 1931; Dir of Egyptian Military Aviation, 1931-32; re-employed Air Min., 1939-45. DL (Caerns) 1943. *Clubs:* Army and Navy, Royal Air Force, Royal Aero; Royal Welsh Yacht (Caernarvon).

**BOARD, Sir (Archibald) Vyvyan,** Kt 1941; DSO 1918; MC 1916; *b* Bristol 5 Feb. 1884; *s* of Alderman Joseph Thomas Board; *m* 1908, Isobel Phyllis (*d* 1968), *er d* of Dr G. G. Willett, Keynsham, Somerset; one *s* one *d*. *Educ:* Clifton Coll. Served European War in 3rd Bn Essex Regt, Machine Gun Corps and Gen. Staff; War of 1939-45, at Ministry of Supply: Controller, Industrial Alcohol Molasses, 1939, Plastics, 1941, Rubber, 1944; Dir of Economy, 1942; Chm. Salvage Bd. Dir, Distillers Co. Ltd, 1924, retd 1946. Late Dir, Hector Whaling Ltd. Retired, 1965. *Address:* Clevedon House, Hillhead, near Fareham, Hants.

**BOARD, Sir Vyvyan;** *see* Board, Sir A. V.

**BOARDMAN, Harold;** MP (Lab) Leigh since 1945; Trade Union Official; *m* 1936; one *d*. Parliamentary Private Sec. to Ministry of Labour, 1947-51. *Address:* 18 Norris Road, Brooklands, Sale, Manchester.

**BOARDMAN, John,** FBA; Reader in Classical Archaeology, University of Oxford, since 1959; Fellow of Merton College, Oxford, since 1963; *b* 20 Aug. 1927; *s* of Frederick Archibald Boardman; *m* 1952, Sheila Joan Lyndon Stanford; one *s* one *d*. *Educ:* Chigwell Sch.; Magdalene Coll., Cambridge. BA 1948, MA 1951, Walston Student, 1948-50; Cromer Greek Prize, 1959. 2nd Lt, Intell. Corps, 1950-52. Asst Dir, British Sch. at Athens, 1952-55; Asst Keeper, Ashmolean Museum, Oxford, 1955-59. Editor, Journal of Hellenic Studies, 1958-65. Conducted excavations on Chios, 1953-55, and at Tocra, in Libya, 1964-65. Mem. Managing Cttee of: British Sch. at Athens; Hellenic Soc. Coun.; Libya Exploration Soc. Coun.; FSA 1957; FBA 1969. *Publications:* Cretan Collection in Oxford, 1961; Date of the Knossos Tablets, 1963; Island Gems, 1963; Greek Overseas, 1964; Greek Art, 1964; Excavations at Tocra, 1966; Pre-Classical, 1967; Greek Emporio, 1967; Engraved Gems, 1968; Archaic Greek Gems, 1968; Greek Gems and Finger Rings, 1970; articles in jls. *Address:* House of Winds, Harcourt Hill, North Hinksey, Oxford. *T:* Oxford 43758.

**BOARDMAN, Thomas Gray,** MC 1944; TD 1952; MP (C) Leicester South-West, since Nov. 1967; solicitor and company director; *b* 12 Jan. 1919; *s* of John Clayton Boardman, late of Daventry, and Janet Boardman, formerly Houston; *m* 1948, Norah Mary Deirdre, *widow* of John Henry Chaworth-Musters, Annesley Park, Nottingham, and *d* of Hubert Vincent Gough; two *s* one *d*. *Educ:* Bromsgrove. Served Northants Yeomanry, 1939-45 and subsequently; Commanding Northants Yeomanry, 1956. Qualified as a Solicitor, 1947. Chm. Chamberlain Phipps Ltd; Director: Allied Breweries Ltd; British Chrome Tanning Co. Ltd. *Recreation:* riding. *Address:* 9 Tufton Court, SW1. *T:* 01-222 6793; The Manor House, Welford, Rugby. *T:* Welford 235. *Clubs:* Cavalry, St Stephens; Northampton and County (Northampton); Leicester Constitutional (Leicester).

**BOAS, Leslie,** OBE 1961; HM Ambassador to Santo Domingo, since June 1969; *b* Buenos Aires, Argentine, 25 Feb. 1912; *s* of late Gustavus Thomas Boas and late Flora Shield McDonald; *m* 1st, 1944, Margaret Ann Jackson (marr. diss. 1951); one *s*; 2nd, 1951, Patricia Faye Fenning; no *c*. *Educ:* Spain; Gibraltar; Grenada Univ. In business, 1933-39. Joined Coldstream Guards, 1940; commissioned in Royal Ulster Rifles, 1940; invalided out of Army as result of injuries, 1944. Joined Latin American Section of BBC, 1944. Apptd Temp. Press Attaché, Panama, 1946; Temp. First Sec. (Inf.), Bogotá, 1948; Temp. First Sec. (Inf.), Caracas, 1952; estab. as a Permanent First Sec., 1959; Regional Inf. Counsellor, Caracas, 1962-69; Chargé d'Affaires, Panama, April-May 1964. *Recreations:* golf, chess, Latin American studies. *Address:* c/o FCO, King Charles Street, SW1. *Clubs:* United Service; Jockey (Bogotá, Colombia).

**BOASE, Alan Martin,** MA, PhD; Officier de la Légion d'Honneur; *b* 1902; *s* of late W. Norman Boase, CBE, St Andrews; *m* 1931, Elizabeth Grizelle, *e d* of late Prof. E. S. Forster; four *s*. *Educ:* Eton Coll.; New College, Oxford; Trinity Coll., Cambridge; Univ. of Paris. Lectr in French, Univ. of Sheffield, 1929-36; Prof. of French, University Coll., Southampton, 1936-37; Marshall Prof. of French, Univ. of Glasgow, 1937-65. Ex-Chm. of Assoc. of Heads of French Depts. Visiting Professor: Univ. of Calif (Berkeley), 1962; Monash Univ., Australia, 1969. *Publications:* Montaigne, Selected Essays (with Arthur Tilley), 1934; The Fortunes of Montaigne, 1935; Contemporary French Literature (in France: A Companion to French Studies, ed R. L. G. Ritchie), 1937; Les Poëmes de Jean de Sponde, 1950; The Poetry of France, Part III, 1952, Part I, 1964, Part IV, 1969; Les Méditations de Jean de Sponde, 1954; articles and reviews in periodicals. *Recreation:* gardening. *Address:* 39 Inverleith Place, Edinburgh. *T:* 031-552 3005.

**BOASE, Arthur Joseph,** CMG 1968; OBE 1951; Warden, Ophthalmic Hospital of the Order of St John, Jerusalem, 1956, retired; *b* 23 June 1901; 2nd *s* of William George Boase, medical practitioner; *m* 1929, Alice Mary, *d* of Sir Charles Griffin, QC; five *s* five *d*. *Educ:* Mount St Mary's Coll., Derbyshire; St Thomas' Hosp., London. MRCS, LRCP 1923; DOMS 1933; FRCS 1952. Uganda Med. Service, 1924; Sen. Med. Off., 1937; Specialist (Ophthalmologist), 1945; Sen. Specialist, 1954; retd from Uganda, 1956. Past Pres., E African Assoc. of Surgs. Coronation Medal, 1953. Kt, Order of St Gregory (Papal), 1951; KStJ 1961; Kt, Order of Holy Sepulchre (Greek Orthodox), 1965; Kt, Order of Holy Sepulchre (Armenian), 1969. Istiqlal (Independence) Order, 2nd cl. (Jordan), 1967. *Recreation:* woodworking. *Address:* Kilworth, Maresfield, Uckfield, Sussex.

*See also Sir J. B. Griffin.*

**BOASE, Thomas Sherrer Ross,** MC; MA; FBA 1961; Chairman, British School at Rome, since 1965; *b* 31 Aug. 1898; *s* of late Charles Millet Boase and Anne Malcolm Ross. *Educ:* Rugby Sch.; Magdalen Coll., Oxford. Served European War, 1914-18: Oxford and Bucks Lt Infantry, France, 1917-19 (MC). Fellow and Tutor, Hertford Coll., Oxford, 1922-37; Prof. of History of Art, Univ. of London, and Dir, Courtauld Inst. of Art, 1937-47. Temp. Civil Servant, Air Min., Cairo and UK, 1939-43; Chief Representative, British Council, Middle East, 1943-45. Pres., Magdalen Coll., Oxford, 1947-68; Vice-Chancellor, Oxford Univ., 1958-60. Trustee: National Gall., 1947-53 (Chm., 1951-53); Shakespeare Birthplace Trust, 1949-; British Museum, 1950-69. Member: Adv. Council of V & A Museum, 1947-; Council, Royal Albert Hall, 1968-. Governor: Rugby Sch., 1951-65; Royal Shakespeare Theatre, 1952-. Comr for Exhibition of 1851, 1956-. Hon. Fellow: Hertford Coll., 1947; St Mark's Coll., Adelaide, 1956; Magdalen Coll., Oxford, 1968. Foreign Member, Amer. Philosophical Soc. Hon. DCL Oxon; Hon. LLD: St Andrews; Melbourne; Rockefeller Inst.; Hon. DLitt: Durham; Reading. Grosses Verdienstkreuz der Bundesrepublik Deutschland, 1958. *Publications:* Boniface VIII, 1933; St Francis of Assisi, 1936 (new edn, 1968); English Art, 1100-1216, 1953; English Art, 1800-70, 1959; The York Psalter, 1962; Castles and Churches of the Crusading Kingdom, 1967; articles in the Jl of the Warburg and Courtauld Insts; (ed) Oxford History of English Art. *Address:* 6 Atherton Drive, Wimbledon Common, SW19. *T:* 01-946 1131. *Club:* Oxford and Cambridge University.

**BOATENG, Prof. Ernest Amano,** GM 1968; Principal, University College of Cape Coast, Ghana, since 1969; Professor of Geography, University of Ghana, since 1961; *b* 30 Nov. 1920; 2nd *s* of Rev. Christian Robert Boateng and Adelaide Akonobea, Aburi, Ghana; *m* 1955, Evelyn Kensema Danso, *e d* of Rev. Robert Opong Danso, Aburi; three *d*. *Educ:* Achimota Coll.; St Peter's Hall, Oxford (Gold Coast Govt Schol.). Henry Oliver Beckit Meml Prize, 1949; BA (Geog.) 1949, MA 1953, BLitt 1954. UC Ghana: Lectr in Geography, 1950-57; Sen. Lectr, 1958-61; Vis. Asst Prof., Univ. of Pittsburgh and UCLA, 1960-61; Dean, Faculty of Social Studies, 1962-69. Pres., Ghana Geographical Assoc., 1959-69; Foundn Fellow, Ghana Acad. of Sciences (Sec. 1959-62); Mem., Unesco Internat. Adv. Cttee on Humid Tropics Research, 1961-63; Mem., Scientific Council for Africa, 1963-; Mem., Nat. Planning Commn of Ghana, 1961-64; Smuts Vis. Fellow, Univ. of Cambridge, 1965-66; Vis. Prof., Univ. of Pittsburgh, 1966; Deleg., UN Conf. on geographical names, Geneva, 1967; Mem., Council for Scientific and Industrial Research, Ghana, 1967-; Dir, Ghana Nat. Atlas Project; Chm., Geographical Cttee, Ghana 1970 population census. *Publications:* A Geography of Ghana, 1959; (contrib.) Developing Countries of the World, 1968; various pamphlets, encyclopaedia articles and articles in geographical and other jls. *Recreations:* photography, gardening. *Address:* Principal's Lodge, University College of Cape Coast, Cape Coast, Ghana. *T:* Cape Coast 2095.

**BOCKETT, Herbert Leslie,** CMG 1961; Chairman, Workers' Compensation Board, New Zealand, since 1960; Professional Accountant, and Member New Zealand Society of Accountants; *b* 29 June 1905; *s* of C. F. Bockett and L. M. Bockett (*née* Bridger); *m* 1932, Constance Olive Ramsay; two *d*. *Educ:* Dilworth Sch.; Seddon Memorial Technical Coll. Joined NZ Public Service, 1921; Accountant, Unemployment Board, 1934; Asst Director: Social Security Dept, 1939; National Service Dept, 1940; Controller of Man-power, 1942; Dir of National Service, 1944; Sec. of Labour, New Zealand, 1947-64; retd Dec. 1964. *Recreation:* bowls. *Address:* 189 The Parade, Island Bay, Wellington, NZ. *T:* 838-549.

**BODDIE, George Frederick,** BSc Edinburgh; FRCVS; FRSE; William Dick Chair of Veterinary Medicine, Edinburgh University (in the Royal Dick School of Veterinary Studies), since 1953; *b* 23 Jan. 1900; *m* 1926; one *s* two *d*. *Educ:* Merchiston Castle Sch.; Edinburgh Univ.; Royal (Dick) Veterinary College, Edinburgh. Clinical Asst Royal (Dick) Veterinary College, 1924; gen. veterinary practice, 1924-30; veterinary inspector local authority; Prof. of Medicine and Pharmacology Royal (Dick) Veterinary College, Edinburgh, 1930. Pres., RCVS, 1964-65, Vice-Pres., 1959-60, 1963-64 and 1965-66. director: Hill Farm Research Organisation, 1957-66; Scottish Soc. for Prevention of Cruelty to Animals; Chm. of Cttee, Edinburgh Dog and Cat Home; formerly Hon. Advisory Officer, Highlands and Islands Veterinary Services Scheme. *Publications:* Diagnostic Methods in Veterinary Medicine, 1944, sixth edn, 1969; An Introduction to Veterinary Therapeutics, 1952; Editor Hoare's Veterinary Materia Medica and Therapeutics (6th edn), 1942 (jointly); many articles in veterinary and scientific jls. *Address:* Royal (Dick) Veterinary College, Edinburgh. *Club:* Caledonian.

**BODDINGTON, Lewis,** CBE 1956; Director, Westland Aircraft Ltd, since 1961; *b* 13 Nov. 1907; *s* of James and Anne Boddington; *m* 1936, Morfydd, *d* of William Murray; no *c*. *Educ:* Lewis' Sch., Pengam; City of Cardiff Technical Coll.; University Coll. of S Wales and Monmouthshire. Pupil Engineer, Fraser & Chalmers Engineering Works, Erith, 1928-31; Asst to Major H. N. Wylie, 1931-36; Royal Aircraft Establishment, 1936; Head of Catapult Section, 1938; Supt of Design Offices, 1942-45; Head of Naval Aircraft Dept, 1945-51; Asst Dir (R & D) Naval, Min. of Supply, 1951-53; Dir Aircraft R & D (RN), 1953-59; Dir-Gen., Aircraft R & D, 1959-60. Medal of Freedom of USA (Bronze Palm), 1958. *Address:* 7 Pine House, Lingwood Close, Southampton.

**BODILLY, Hon. Sir Jocelyn,** Kt 1969; VRD; **Hon. Mr Justice Bodilly;** Chief Justice of the Western Pacific since 1965; *b* 1913. *Educ:* Munro Coll., Jamaica; Schloss Schule, Baden; Wadham Coll., Oxford. Called to Bar, Inner Temple, 1937; engaged in private practice until War; Royal Navy until 1946; RNVR, 1937-56

(Lt-Comdr (S)). High Court Judge, Sudan, 1946-55; Crown Counsel, Hong Kong, 1955, Principal Crown Counsel, 1961-65. *Address:* The Judiciary Department, Honiara, British Solomon Islands. *Club:* Royal Ocean Racing.

**BODLEY SCOTT, Sir Ronald,** KCVO 1964; DM; FRCP; Physician to: the Queen since 1952; St Bartholomew's Hospital, since 1946, Senior Physician, since 1965; Memorial Hospital, SE18, since 1936; Florence Nightingale Hospital, since 1958; King Edward VII Hospital for Officers since 1963; King Edward VII Hospital, Midhurst, since 1965; Member of Board of Governors, St Bartholomew's Hospital, since 1966; Principal Medical Officer, Equity and Law Life Assurance Society, since 1952; Consultant Physician to: British Railways (Eastern Region), since 1957; Royal Navy since 1963; Hon. Consultant Physician, Ministry of Defence (Army) since 1965; Examiner in Medicine, University of Edinburgh; *b* 10 Sept. 1906; *s* of late Maitland Bodley Scott, OBE, FRCSE, and Alice Hilda Durancé George; *m* 1931, Edith Daphne, *d* of late Lt-Col E. McCarthy, RMA; two *d. Educ:* Marlborough Coll.; Brasenose Coll., Oxford. BA Oxon, Hons Sch. of Nat. Sci., 1928; MA, BM, BCh, Oxon, 1931; MRCP, 1933; DM Oxon, 1937; FRCP 1943. Chief Asst to Medical Unit, St Bartholomew's Hospital, 1934. Served in Middle East, 1941-45, Lt-Col RAMC; Officer i/c Medical Div. in No 63 and No 43 Gen. Hospitals; Physician to the Household of King George VI, 1949; Hon. Consultant to the Army at Home, 1957-65. Lectures: Langdon Brown, RCP, 1957; Lettsomian, Medical Soc. of London, 1957; Thom Bequest Lectr, RCPE, 1965; Croonian, RCP, 1970. president: Med. Soc. of London, 1965-66; British Soc. for Hæmatology, 1966-67; Section of Medicine, Royal Society Med., 1967-68. Member: Council, RCP, 1963-66; Court of Assistants, Soc. of Apothecaries of London, 1964-. Formerly Examiner in Medicine, Universities of Oxford, London, Glasgow, Cairo, to the RCP, London and Edinburgh, and to the Conjoint Board. Editor: The Medical Annual, 1959; Price's Textbook of the Practice of Medicine. *Publications:* various papers in medical jls. *Address:* 76 Harley House, Marylebone Road, NW1. *T:* 01-935 7877. *Club:* Athenæum.

**BODMER, Prof. Walter Fred;** Professor of Genetics, University of Oxford, since 1970; *b* 10 Jan. 1936; *s* of Dr Ernest Julius and Sylvia Emily Bodmer; *m* 1956, Julia Gwynaeth Pilkington; two *s* one *d. Educ:* Manchester Grammar Sch.; Clare Coll., Cambridge. BA 1956, MA, PhD 1959, Cambridge. Research Fellow 1958-61, Official Fellow 1961, Clare Coll., Cambridge; Demonstrator in Genetics, Univ. of Cambridge, 1960-62; Asst Prof. 1962-66, Assoc. Prof. 1966-68, Prof. 1968-70, Dept of Genetics, Stanford Univ. *Publications:* research papers in genetical, statistical and mathematical jls, etc. *Recreations:* playing the piano, swimming. *Address:* 2 St John's Street, Oxford.

**BODMIN, Archdeacon of;** *see* Meyer, Ven. C. J. E.

**BODY, Maj.-Gen. Kenneth Marten,** CB 1942; CMG 1918; OBE 1919; *b* 9 June 1883; *s* of H. M. Body, Crediton, Devon; *m* 1907, Isabel, *d* of W. Fell-Smith, Deer Park, Honiton, Devon; four *d. Educ:* Blundell's Sch., Tiverton. Royal Military Academy, Woolwich. Commission in Royal Field Artillery, 1900; Instructor RAOC Sch. of Instruction, 1931-34; Dir of Army Ordnance Services, War Office, 1939; retired pay, 1942; Capt. 1913; Major, 1915; Bt Lieut-Col 1916; Lieut-Col 1928; Col 1934; Maj.-Gen. 1939. Col Comdt RAOC, 1942-51. Ordre de la Couronne (Belgium), 1919. *Recreations:* Capt. of Coventry Rugby FC, 1907-08; played hockey for Midlands, 1904-05. *Address:* Normanswood, Telford, Farnham, Surrey. *See also J. D. Fergusson, Lieut-Col J. K. La T. Mardon.*

**BODY, Richard Bernard;** Barrister-at-law; MP (C) Holland with Boston, since 1966; *b* 18 May 1927; *s* of Lieut-Col Bernard Richard Body, formerly of Hyde End, Shinfield, Berks; *m* 1959, Marion, *d* of late Major H. Graham, OBE; one *s* one *d.* Called to the Bar, Middle Temple, 1949. Contested (C) Rotherham, 1950; Abertillery bye-election, 1950; Leek, 1951; MP (C) Billericary Div., Essex, 1955-Sept. 1959. *Publication:* The Architect and the Law, 1954. *Address:* Jewell's House, Stanford Dingley, Berks. *T:* Bradfield 295. *Club:* Carlton.

**BOEGNER, Marc,** DTheol; Grand Officier, Légion d'Honneur; French ecclesiastic; *b* Epinal, 21 Feb. 1881; *m* 1st, Jeanne Bargeton (*d* 1933); three *s* one *d*; 2nd, Mary Thurneyssen (*d* 1951). *Educ:* Orléans; Paris. Ordained Pastor, Reformed Church of France, 1905; Pastor, Aouste, 1905-11; Prof. of Theology, Coll. of Soc. of Evangelical Missions, Paris, 1911-18; Pastor of Church of Passy, 1918-53. President: French Fedn of Student Christian Assocs, 1922-39; Fedn of French Protestant Churches, 1929-61; Nat. Coun. of Reformed Church of France, 1938-50; World Coun. of Churches, 1948-54. Mem. French Inst., 1946; Mem. French Acad., 1962. Hon. DD: Edinburgh, Toronto, North Western, Aberdeen; Hon. DTheol: Prague, Bonn, Geneva. *Publications:* La Vie et la Pensée de T. Fallot, vol. 1, 1914, vol. 2, 1926; Dieu, l'éternel tourment des hommes, 1929; Jésus-Christ, 1930; Qu'est-ce que l'Eglise, 1931; L'Eglise et les questions du temps présent, 1932; La Vie chrétienne, 1933; Le Christ devant la souffrance et la joie, 1935; Le Problème de l'Unité chrétienne, 1947; La Prière de l'Eglise universelle, 1951; La Vie Triomphante, 1954; Le Chrétien et la Souffrance, 1955; Les Sept Paroles de la Croix, 1957; Notre Vocation à la Sainteté, 1958; The Long Road to Unity, 1968. *Recreation:* travelling. *Address:* 34 Avenue d'Eylau, Paris 16e, France.

**BOERMA, Addeke Hendrik;** Director-General, Food and Agriculture Organisation of the United Nations, since 1968; *b* 3 April 1912. *Educ:* Agricultural Univ., Wageningen. Netherlands Farmers' Organisation, 1935-38; Ministry of Agriculture of the Netherlands, 1938-45; Commissioner for Foreign Agricultural Relations, 1946; FAO positions: Regional Representative for Europe, 1948-51; Dir, Economics Div., 1951-58; Head of Programme and Budgetary Service, 1958-62; Asst Dir-Gen., 1960; Exec. Dir, World Food Programme, 1962-67. Knight, Netherlands Order of Lion; Commander, Order of Leopold II, Belgium; Officer, Ordre Mérite Agricole, France. *Address:* Food and Agriculture Organisation of the United Nations, Via delle Terme di Caracalla. Rome, Italy.

**BOEVEY, Sir Thomas (Michael Blake) C.;** *see* Crawley-Boevey.

**BOGARDE, Dirk;** *see* Van den Bogaerde, D. N.

**BOGGIS-ROLFE, Hume,** CBE 1962; Deputy Clerk of the Crown in Chancery, since 1968, and Deputy Secretary, Lord Chancellor's Office, since 1970; *b* 20 Oct. 1911; *s* of Douglass Horace Boggis-Rolfe and Maria Maud (*née* Bailey); *m* 1941, Anne Dorothea, *e d* of Capt.

Eric Noble, Henley-on-Thames; two *s* one *d*. *Educ:* Westminster Sch.; Freiburg Univ.; Trinity Coll., Cambridge. Called to Bar, Middle Temple, 1935. Army, Intelligence Corps, 1939-46 (Lieut-Col). Private Sec. to Lord Chancellor, 1949-50; Asst Solicitor in Lord Chancellor's Office, 1951-65; Sec. to Law Commn, 1965-68. *Recreations:* farming, gardening, travelling. *Address:* 22 Victoria Square, SW1. *T:* 01-834 2676; The Grange, Wormingford, Colchester, Essex. *T:* Bures 303. *Club:* Athenæum.

**BOGGON, Roland Hodgson,** MS, MB London; FRCS, LRCP; *b* 11 Aug. 1903; *s* of late Richard Octavius Boggon, OBE, Civil Servant; *m* 1932, Mollie Daphne, *d* of T. H. Newall; one *s* one *d*. *Educ:* St Paul's Sch. Retired as Consulting Surg. to St Thomas' Hospital, London. Mem. Court of Examiners of the Royal College of Surgeons; Examiner in Surgery, Univ. of London. *Publications:* Numerous Medical. *Recreation:* gardening. *Address:* 74 Woodland Drive, Hove 4, Sussex.

**BOGLE, David Blyth,** CBE 1967; Senior Partner, Lindsays, WS, Edinburgh; Member of Council on Tribunals since 1958 and Chairman of Scottish Committee since 1962; *b* 22 Jan. 1903; *s* of late Very Rev. Andrew Nisbet Bogle, DD and late Helen Milne Bogle; *m* 1955, Ruth Agnes Thorley. *Educ:* George Watson's Coll., Edinburgh; Edinburgh Univ. (LLB). Writer to the Signet, 1927. Commissioned in the Queen's Own Cameron Highlanders, 1940, and served in UK and Middle East, 1942-45; demobilised, with rank of Major, 1945. *Recreations:* golf, curling, stalking. *Address:* (home) Hartwood House, West Calder, Midlothian. *T:* West Calder 248; (office) 32 Charlotte Square, Edinburgh. *T:* 031-225 1300. *Clubs:* United Service; New (Edinburgh).

**BOHEMAN, Erik,** KBE (hon.) 1948; Swedish diplomat; *b* 19 Jan. 1895; *s* of Carl Boheman and Ellen Abramson; *m* 1932, Margaret Mattsson; two *s* two *d*. *Educ:* Stockholm Univ. Lieut 4th Hussars, 1915; entered Foreign Service, 1918, served at legations in Paris and London, 1918-19; Sec., Councillor and Director. Political Dept, Foreign Office, Stockholm, 1919-31; Minister to Ankara and Athens, 1931-34, to Warsaw, 1934-37; Sec. Gen., Foreign Office, 1938-45; Minister to Paris, 1945-47, to London, 1947; Ambassador to London, 1947-48; Ambassador to Washington, 1948-58. Attended council meetings and assemblies, League of Nations, as Sec. and Deleg., 1920-32. Conducted negotiations for commercial treaties with several countries. Headed Swedish Delegation for War Trade Agreements with Gt Britain during War of 1939-45; Deleg. to Gen. Assembly of UN, 1949-50, 1960-62. Mem. of Swedish Parliament (First Chamber) for City of Gothenburg, 1959-; Speaker of First Chamber, 1965. Dir Stockholms Enskilda Bank and a number of other Swedish companies. *Recreations:* travelling, farming, golf. *Address:* Anneberg, Orserumsbrunn, Sweden. *Club:* Travellers'.

**BOHLEN, Charles Eustis;** Deputy Under-Secretary of State for Political Affairs, USA, 1968-Jan. 1969, retired; *b* 30 Aug. 1904; *m* Avis Howard Thayer; one *s* two *d*. *Educ:* Harvard Univ. AB 1927. Entered Foreign Service, 1929; Vice-Consul, Prague, 1929-31; Paris, 1931-34; Moscow, 1934; Dept of State, 1935; Second Sec., Moscow, 1937, Consul, 1938; Second Sec., Tokyo, 1941-42; Dept of State 1942; Asst Chief, Div. of European Affairs, 1943; First Sec., Moscow, 1943-44; Chief, Div. of Eastern European Affairs, 1944; Asst to Sec. of State for White House Liaison, 1944; Special Asst to Sec. of State, 1946; Counsellor, Dept of State, 1947; Minister, US Embassy, Paris, 1949; Counsellor, Dept of State, 1951-53; US Ambassador to the USSR, 1953-57; to the Philippines, 1957-59. Asst to Sec. of State of the United States, in the field of Soviet Affairs, 1959-62; US Ambassador to France, 1962-68. Has attended many internat. confs, etc. *Address:* (home) 2811 Dumbarton Avenue NW, Washington, DC, USA. *T:* 338-3051; (office) 3029 M Street NW, Washington, DC 20007. *T:* 337 1993.

**BOHM, Prof. David (Joseph),** PhD; Professor of Theoretical Physics, Birkbeck College, University of London, since Oct. 1961; *b* 20 Dec. 1917; *s* of Samuel and Freda Bohm; *m* 1956, Sarah Woolfson; no *c*. *Educ:* Pa State Coll. (BS); University of Calif (PhD). Research Physicist, University of Calif, Radiation Laboratory, 1943-47; Asst Prof., Princeton Univ., 1947-51; Prof., University de São Paulo, Brazil, 1951-55; Prof., Technion, Haifa, Israel, 1955-57; Research Fellow, Bristol Univ., 1957-61. *Publications:* Quantum Theory, 1951; Causality and Chance in Modern Physics, 1957. One Chapter in Observation and Interpretation, 1957; Special Theory of Relativity, 1965. Various papers in Physical Review, Nuovo Cimento, Progress of Theoretical Physics, British Jl for Philosophy of Science, etc. *Recreations:* walking, conversation, music (listener), art (viewer). *Address:* Physics Department, Birkbeck College, Malet Street, WC1.

**BOILEAU, Sir Gilbert George Benson,** 6th Bt, *cr* 1838; MOH for Shire of Dandenong; *b* 13 Feb. 1898; *e s* of Sir Francis James Boileau, 5th Bt; *S* father 1945; *m* 1st, 1924, Chica Patricia, *d* of late J. L. Edgeworth-Somers; two *d*; 2nd, 1941, Mary Catherine, *d* of late Lawrence Riordan; three *d*. *Educ:* Xavier Coll., Kew, Vic; Newman Coll., University of Melbourne. MB, BS, Melbourne 1923. Service with rank of Major, 1940-44, AAMC Australian Military Forces, now on Reserve. *Recreation:* Turf. *Heir:* *b* Edmond Charles Boileau, Capt. AIF [*b* 1903; *m* 1934, Marjorie, *d* of C. M. D'Arcy, Launceston, Tasmania; two *s*]. *Address:* Minto Lodge, Dandenong, Vic, Australia. *T:* Dandenong 353. *Clubs:* Athenæum, Naval and Military, Savage (Melbourne).

**BOLAND, Bridget;** author; *b* 13 March 1913; *d* of late John Boland. *Educ:* Sacred Heart Convent, Roehampton; Oxford Univ. (BA 1935). Screenwriter 1937-; numerous films. Served War, 1941-46, in ATS; Senior Comdr. Stage plays: Abca Play Unit productions, 1946; Cockpit, 1948; The Damascus Blade, 1950; Temple Folly, 1952; The Return, 1953; The Prisoner, 1954 (adapted film version, 1955); Gordon, 1961; The Zodiac in the Establishment, 1963. *Publications: novels:* The Wild Geese, 1938; Portrait of a Lady in Love, 1942. *Address:* 1 Long Acre, WC2.

**BOLAND, Sir (Edward) Rowan,** Kt 1964; CBE 1945 (OBE 1941); MD; FRCP; Physician Emeritus, Guy's Hospital, SE1; Consulting Physician, Hospital of St John and St Elizabeth; Hon. Consulting Physician to the Army since 1945; *b* 9 March 1898; *s* of John Patrick and Margaret Boland, Broughty Ferry, Scotland; *m* 1931, Barbara Scott; no *c*. *Educ:* Stonyhurst; Wimbledon Coll.; Caen, France, 2nd Lieut London Rifle Brigade, France and Flanders, 1916-18, discharged owing to wounds. Entered Guy's, 1915. MRCS, LRCP 1921; MRCP 1925; DPH 1928; FRCP 1934. Asst Physician Guy's Hospital, 1934. Lt-Col RAMC 1940; Egypt, 1940-42; Brig., Consulting Physician Allied Force

Headquarters, 1942-45, North Africa, Sicily, Italy and Greece (despatches); Dean of Faculty of Medicine, University of London, 1948-52; Dean of Medical and Dental Sch., Guy's Hospital, 1945-65; late Mem. of Senate, University of London; Mem. Gen. Med. Council (Treas.); Chm., Army Medical Advisory Board; Chm., Central Medical Recruitment Cttee. MD (*hc*): University Algiers, 1944; TCD, 1956. Officier Legion of Merit. *Recreation:* gardening. *Address:* Guy's Hospital, SE1. *T:* 01-407 0082; Hill House, Stowting, Kent. *T:* Lyminge 87329.

**BOLAND, Frederick Henry;** former Irish diplomat; Director: Bank of Ireland; Arthur Guinness Son & Co. and other companies; Chancellor, Dublin University; *b* 1904; 2nd *s* of Henry Patrick Boland and Charlotte (*née* Nolan), Dublin; *m* 1935, Frances Kelly, Drogheda; one *s* four *d. Educ:* Clongowes Wood Coll.; Trinity Coll., Dublin; King's Inns, Dublin. BA; LLB 1925; LLD (jure dignitatis), 1950. University Studentship in Classics, TCD, 1925; Rockefeller Research Fellowship in Social Sciences (Harvard and University of Chicago), 1926-28; 3rd Sec., Dept of External Affairs, 1929; 1st Sec., Paris, 1932; Principal Officer Dept of Industry and Commerce, 1936; Dept of External Affairs: Asst Sec., 1938; Permanent Sec., 1946; Irish rep., Cttee on European Economic Co-operation, Paris, 1947; Irish Ambassador to the Court of St James's, 1950-56; Permanent Representative of Eire at UN, 1956-63 (Pres., 1960); Irish Representative UN Security Council, 1962-63. Member: Cttee on Seasonal Migration, 1936; Cttee on Design in Industry, 1938; Nat. Industrial Economic Council; Royal Irish Acad. Pres., Coll. Historical Soc., TCD. Knight Comdr, Order of St Gregory the Great, 1948; Grand Cross, Order of the North Star of Sweden, 1950. *Recreations:* reading, piano, fishing. *Address:* 60 Ailesbury Road, Dublin, Eire. *T:* Dublin 693599. *Clubs:* Athenæum; Stephens Green, Kildare Street (Dublin).

**BOLAND, Sir Rowan;** *see* Boland, Sir E. R.

**BOLES, Sir Jeremy John Fortescue,** 3rd Bt, *cr* 1922; *b* 9 Jan. 1932; *s* of Sir Gerald Fortescue Boles, 2nd Bt, and Violet Blanche, *er d* of late Major Hall Parlby, Manadon, Crown Hill, S Devon; *S* father 1945; *m* 1955, Dorothy Jane, *yr d* of James Alexander Worswick; two *s* one *d. Heir: s* Richard Fortescue Boles, *b* 12 Dec. 1958. *Address:* Lydeard House, Bishops Lydeard, Taunton, Somerset. *T:* Bishops Lydeard 209.

*See also D. D. Carver.*

**BOLINGBROKE, and ST JOHN,** 6th Viscount *cr* 1712; **Vernon Henry St John;** Bt 1611; Baron St John of Lydiard Tregoze, 1712; Viscount St John and Baron St John of Battersea, 1716; *b* 15 March 1896; *s* of 5th Viscount and Mary Emily Elizabeth Howard (*d* 1940); *S* father, 1899. Owns about 4000 acres. *Heir: cousin* Geoffrey Robert St John, *qv. Address:* Moorhayes, Crow Hill, Ringwood, Hants.

**BOLITHO, (Henry) Hector;** author; *b* Auckland, New Zealand, 1898; *s* of Henry and Ethelred Frances Bolitho. Travelled in South Sea Islands, 1919; through New Zealand with the Prince of Wales, 1920; came to England, 1922; travelled in Africa, Australia, Canada, America, and Germany, 1923-24; lecture tours, USA, 1938-39, 1947, 1948, and 1949. Served War of 1939-45, Sqdn Ldr RAFVR; Editor RAF Journal. *Publications:* With the Prince in New Zealand, 1920; The Islands of Wonder, 1920; Solemn Boy, a novel, 1927; The Letters of Lady Augusta Stanley, 1927; Thistledown and Thunder, 1928; The New Zealanders, 1928; Judith Silver, a novel, 1929; The New Countries, 1929; The Later Letters of Lady Augusta Stanley, 1929; The Glorious Oyster, 1929; (with Very Rev. A. V. Baillie) A Victorian Dean: A Memoir of Arthur Stanley, 1930; The Flame on Ethirdova, 1930; Albert the Good, a Life of the Prince Consort, 1932; Alfred Mond: First Baron Melchett, a biography, 1933; Beside Galilee: a diary in Palestine, 1933; The Prince Consort and his Brother, 1934; Victoria, the Widow and her Son, 1934; Older People, 1935; The House in Half Moon Street, 1936; James Lyle MacKay, First Earl of Inchcape, 1936; Marie Tempest, a biography, 1936; Edward VIII, his life and reign, 1937; Royal Progress, 1937; George VI, 1937; Victoria and Albert, 1938; (ed) Further Letters of Queen Victoria, 1938; Victoria and Disraeli, a play for the radio, performed 1938; (with John Mulgan) The Emigrants, 1939; Roumania under King Carol, 1939; America Expects, 1940; War in the Strand, 1942; Combat Report, 1943; No Humour in My Love, 1946; Task for Coastal Command, 1946; The Romance of Windsor Castle, 1947; The Reign of Queen Victoria, 1949; A Biographer's Notebook, 1950; A Century of British Monarchy, 1951; Their Majesties, 1951; (with Derek Peel) Without the City Wall, 1952; Jinnah, Creator of Pakistan, 1954; A Penguin in the Eyrie, 1955; The Wine of the Douro, 1956; The Angry Neighbours, 1957; No 10, Downing Street, 1957; My Restless Years, 1962; The Galloping Third, 1963; Albert, Prince Consort, 1964; (with Derek Peel) The Drummonds of Charing Cross, 1967. *Address:* 1 St Nicholas Road, Brighton, Sussex.

**BOLITHO, Major Simon Edward,** MC 1945; DL; JP; Director: Barclays Bank, 1959 (Local Director, Penzance, 1953); English China Clays; Vice-Lieutenant of Cornwall, since 1970; *b* 13 March 1916; *s* of late Lieut-Col Sir Edward Bolitho, KBE, CB, DSO; *m* 1953, Elizabeth Margaret, *d* of late Rear-Adm. G. H. Creswell, CB, DSO, DSC; two *s* two *d. Educ:* Royal Naval Coll., Dartmouth; RMC Sandhurst. Grenadier Guards, 1936-49; Lt-Col, DCLI, 1957-60. DL Cornwall, 1964; High Sheriff of Cornwall, 1956-57; JP 1959; CC 1953-67. *Recreations:* shooting, fishing, hunting, sailing. *Address:* Trengwainton, Penzance, Cornwall. *T:* Penzance 3097. *Clubs:* Guards, Pratt's, MCC, Royal Yacht Squadron.

**BOLLAND, Edwin;** Counsellor, British Embassy, Washington, since 1967; *b* 20 Oct. 1922; *m* 1948, Winifred Mellor; one *s* three *d* (and one *s* decd). *Educ:* Morley Grammar Sch.; University Coll., Oxford. Served in Armed Forces, 1942-45. Foreign Office, 1947; Head of Far Eastern Dept, FO, 1965-67. *Recreation:* gardening. *Address:* Lord's Spring Cottage, Godden Green, Sevenoaks, Kent. *T:* Sevenoaks 61105.

**BOLLAND, Group Captain Guy Alfred,** CBE 1943; Chief Intelligence Officer, BJSM (AFS), Washington, USA, 1956-59, retired; *b* 5 Nov. 1909; 3rd *s* of late Capt. L. W. Bolland; *m* 1935, Sylvia Marguerite, 2nd *d* of late Oswald Duke, Cambridge; one *s* three *d. Educ:* Gilbert Hannam Sch., Sussex. Commissioned RAF, 1930. Served in Iraq and Home Squadrons. Served War of 1939-45: commanded 217 Squadron during attacks on French ports, 1940; North African Operations, 1943 (despatches, CBE). *Recreation:* golf. *Address:* Woodland Croft, Shaftesbury Road, Woking, Surrey. *T:* Woking 60548.

**BOLLERS, Hon. Sir Harold (Brodie Smith),** Kt 1969; Chief Justice of Guyana, since 1966; *b* 5

Feb. 1915; *s* of late John Bollers; *m* 1st, 1951, Irene Mahadeo (*d* 1965); two *s* one *d*; 2nd, 1968, Eileen Hanoman; one *s*. *Educ:* Queen's Coll., Guyana; King's Coll., London; Middle Temple. Called to the Bar, Feb. 1938; Magistrate, Guyana, 1946, Senior Magistrate, 1959; Puisne Judge, Guyana, 1960. *Recreations:* reading, walking. *Address:* Chief Justice's Residence, 245 Vlissengen Road, Georgetown, Guyana. *T:* 5204. *Club:* West Indian (London).

**BOLS, Hon. Maj.-Gen. Eric Louis,** CB 1945; DSO 1944, and bar 1945; *b* 8 June 1904; *s* of Lt-Gen. Sir Louis Bols, KCB, KCMG, DSO; *m* 1st, 1930, Rosa Vaux (marr. diss., 1947); one *s*; 2nd, 1948, Marion du Plessis (marr. diss., 1965); 3rd, 1967, Barbara Brown. *Educ:* Wellington Coll.; Royal Military Coll., Sandhurst. 2nd Lieut Devonshire Regt 1924; Capt The King's Regt 1935; Major, 1940; Temp. Lieut-Col 1941; Temp Col 1944; Temp. Brig. 1944; Temp. Maj.-Gen. and War Subs. Col 1945; Comdr 6th Airborne Div., 1945; retd pay, 1948. War Service in Ceylon, UK, and NW Europe. *Address:* Newlands Farm, Pounsley, Blackboys, near Uckfield, Sussex.

**BOLSOVER, George Henry,** CBE 1970 (OBE 1947); Director, School of Slavonic and East European Studies, University of London, since 1947; *b* 18 Nov. 1910; *yr s* of Ernest and Mary Bolsover; *m* 1939, Stephanie Kállai; one *d*. *Educ:* Leigh Grammar Sch.; Univ. of Liverpool; Univ. of London. BA 1931, MA (Liverpool), PhD (London), 1933. Univ. of Birmingham, Resident Tutor in Adult Education in Worcs, 1937-38; Asst Lectr in Modern European History, Univ. of Manchester, 1938-43; Attaché and First Sec., HM Embassy, Moscow, 1943-47; Mem. of Editorial Board, Slavonic and East European Review, 1947-63, and Chm., 1958-63; Member: UGC Sub-Cttee on Oriental, African, Slavonic and East European Studies, 1961-; Treasury Cttee for Studentships in Foreign Languages and Cultures, 1948-58; Inst. of Historical Res. Cttee, 1948-; Adv. Cttee on Educn of Poles in Gt Britain, 1948-67; Ct of Govs of London Sch. of Economics and Political Science, 1955-; Council and Exec. Cttee of St Bartholomew's Med. Coll., 1962-; Council of Royal Dental Hosp., London Sch. of Dental Surgery, 1966-; Min. of Educn Cttee on Teaching of Russian, 1960-62; Senior Treasurer of University of London Union, 1958-; Chm., Tutorial Classes Cttee of Council for Extra-Mural Studies of Univ. of London, 1965-; Chm., Council for Extra-Mural Studies, 1968-; Treas., British Nat. Historical Cttee, 1966-; Mem. Governing Body and Gen. Purposes Cttee, GB/East Europe Centre. *Publications:* essays in: Essays presented to Sir Lewis Namier, 1956, Transactions of Royal Historical Society, 1957; articles in English Historical Review, Journal of Modern History, Slavonic and East European Review, International Affairs, etc. *Recreations:* music, travel. *Address:* School of Slavonic and East European Studies, University of London, Malet Street, WC1. *T:* 01-636 9782; 7 Devonshire Road, Hatch End, Middx. *T:* 01-428 4282.

**BOLT, Rear-Adm. Arthur Seymour,** CB 1958; DSO 1951; DSC 1940 and bar 1941; Director, Newmark Instruments Ltd; *b* 26 Nov. 1907; *s* of Charles W. Bolt, Alverstoke, Hants; *m* 1933, Evelyn Mary June, *d* of Robert Ellis, Wakefield, Yorks; four *d*. *Educ:* Nautical Coll., Pangbourne; RN Coll., Dartmouth. Joined RN, 1923. Served War of 1939-45; HMS Glorious and Warspite (DSC and Bar), and at Admiralty. Capt. HMS Theseus (Korea), 1949-51; Dir Naval Air Warfare, Admty, 1951-53; Chief of Staff to Flag Officer Air (Home), 1954-56; Dep. Controller of Military Aircraft, Min. of Supply, 1957-60; retd. Capt. 1947; Rear-Adm. 1956. *Recreations:* tennis, squash, sailing. *Address:* Dolphins, Derby Road, Haslemere, Surrey. *T:* Haslemere 4410. *Clubs:* Junior Carlton, Royal Naval; Bosham Sailing.

**BOLT, George Thomas,** CMG 1955; Chairman, Public Service Commission, New Zealand, 1953-58; *b* 16 June 1900; *s* of late George Henry and Emma Sarah Bolt; *m* 1925, Linda May, *d* of late S. Roberts; one *s*. *Educ:* Wellington Coll., New Zealand. Joined NZ Public Service, 1917; Sec., Public Service Commissioner's Office, 1936; Asst Public Service Comr, 1944; Mem. and Dep. Chm., Public Service Commission, 1946. *Address:* 305 The Parade, Island Bay, Wellington 2, New Zealand.

**BOLT, Robert Oxton;** playwright; *b* 15 Aug. 1924; *s* of Ralph Bolt and Leah Binnion; *m* 1st, 1949, Celia Ann Roberts (marr. diss., 1967); one *s* two *d*; 2nd, 1967, Sarah Miles; one *s*. *Educ:* Manchester Grammar Sch. Left sch., 1941; Sun Life Assurance Office, Manchester, 1942; Manchester Univ., 1943; RAF and Army, 1943-46; Manchester Univ., 1946-49; Exeter Univ., 1949-50; teaching, 1950-58; English teacher, Millfield Sch., 1952-58. Author of plays: Flowering Cherry, produced Haymarket, 1958; A Man for All Seasons, prod Globe, 1960 (filmed 1967); The Tiger and The Horse, prod Queen's, 1960; Gentle Jack, prod Queen's, 1963. Has also had produced: The Critic and the Heart, Oxford Playhouse, 1957; several radio plays and one play on TV; wrote screen play for Lawrence of Arabia (British Film Academy Award, 1962) and for Dr Zhivago, 1965. *Club:* The Spares (Somerset) (Hon. Life Mem.).

**BOLTE, Hon. Sir Henry (Edward),** KCMG 1966; MLA; Premier and Treasurer of the State of Victoria, Australia, since 1955; *b* Skipton, Victoria, 20 May 1908; *s* of J. H. Bolte; *m* 1934, Edith L., *d* of late D. F. M. Elder. *Educ:* Skipton State Sch.; Ballarat C of E Grammar Sch. Grazier, with sheep property near Meredith in western district of Victoria. Entered Parliament as MLA for Hampden, 1947; Minister of: Water Supply and Mines, 1948-50; Soil Conservation, 1949-50; Water Supply and Soil Conservation, 1950; Leader of Liberal Party (formerly Liberal and Country Party), 1953- (Dep. Leader, Nov. 1950-53). Hon. LLD: Melbourne Univ., 1965; Monash Univ., 1967. *Recreations:* golf, shooting, turf. *Address:* Kialla, Meredith, Victoria 3333, Australia. *Clubs:* Australian, Athenæum (Melbourne).

**BOLTON,** 7th Baron, *cr* 1797; **Richard William Algar Orde-Powlett,** JP; *b* 11 July 1929; *s* of 6th Baron Bolton; *S* father, 1963; *m* 1951, Hon. Christine Helena Weld-Forester, *e d* of 7th Baron Forester, *qv*; two *s* one *d*. *Educ:* Eton; Trinity Coll., Cambridge (BA). Chairman, Richmond Div., Conservative Assoc., 1957-60; Chairman Yorkshire Div., Royal Forestry Soc., 1962-64; Member Council, Timber Growers' Organization. Chm., Waterers Group; Director, Yorkshire Insurance Company; Vice-Chairman, Farm Records Ltd. JP, North Riding of Yorkshire, 1957. FLAS. *Recreations:* shooting, fishing. *Heir:* *s* Hon. Harry Algar Nigel Orde-Powlett, *b* 14 Feb. 1954. *Address:* Bolton Hall, Leyburn, Yorkshire. *T:* Leyburn 2303. *Clubs:* Turf; Central African Deep Sea Fishing.

**BOLTON, Lt-Col Edward Frederick,** DSO 1940; The Queen's Royal Regiment (retired); *b* 27 Aug. 1897; 2nd *s* of late E. C. Bolton, Bibbenluke Estate, Mysore, India; *m* 1926, Alice Joy Tillie; no *c*. *Educ:* Haileybury Coll.;

RMC, Sandhurst. Commissioned 1915; served European War, 1914-18, Mesopotamia, 1917-18; in Ireland, 1920-23; Nigeria Regt, Royal West African Frontier Force, 1924-30; India, 1937-39; commanded 2/6th Bn, Queen's Royal Regt, 1940-42 (in BEF, France, April-June 1940); OC 70th Bn Queen's Royal Regt, Aug.-Nov. 1942; Instructor Senior Officers School, Nov. 1942; GSO1 Aldershot District, 1944-45. *Publication:* Horse Management in West Africa. *Recreations:* cricket (Haileybury XI, Member of MCC, Free Foresters CC and Grasshoppers CC), racquets (Captain of Haileybury), fives (Haileybury team). *Address:* 94b Lexham Gardens, W8. *Club:* Army and Navy.

**BOLTON, Col Geoffrey George Hargreaves,** CBE 1960 (MBE 1946); MC 1916; Chairman, North Western Division, National Coal Board, 1951-60 (Marketing Director, 1946-49, Deputy Chairman, 1950-51); *b* 5 Aug. 1894; 4th and *o surv. s* of late Henry Hargreaves Bolton, MBE, Newchurch-in-Rossendale, Lancs; *m* 1st, 1919, Ethel (*d* 1942), 2nd *d* of late Rev. James Robinson, Broughton, Preston; one *s* one *d* (and one *s* decd); 2nd, 1943, Margaret, *y d* of late Rev. James Robinson. *Educ:* Clifton Coll., Bristol. Served European War, 1914-18, East Lancs Regt (Gallipoli, Sinai, France); Comd East Lancs Regt TA, 1920-28 (retired 1928). Associated with Coal Industry, 1912-; Dir, hargreaves Collieries Ltd, 1932-46; Exec. Officer, Lancashire Associated Collieries, 1935-46. DL 1935, JP 1935, Lancaster; High Sheriff, Lancashire, 1962-63. KStJ 1969. *Address:* Fairfield House, Chatburn, Clitheroe, Lancs BB7 4BB. *T:* Chatburn 335.
*See also Baron Hacking.*

**BOLTON, Sir George (Lewis French),** KCMG 1950; Director: Bank of London and South America (Chairman, 1957-70; President, since 1970); Bank of London and Montreal (Chairman); Commonwealth Development Finance Co. (Chairman, since 1968); Intercontinental Banking Services (Chairman, since 1968); Balfour Williamson Investment Co. Ltd; Sun Life Assurance Co. of Canada; Canadian Pacific Railway Co.; Canadian Pacific Air Services Ltd; Canadian Pacific Steamships Ltd; Canadian Pacific Oil & Gas of Canada Ltd; *b* 16 Oct. 1900; *s* of William and Beatrice Bolton; *m* 1928, May, *er d* of Charles and Amelia Howcroft; one *s* two *d.* Helbert, Wagg & Co. Ltd, 1920; Bank of England to assist in management of Exchange Equalisation Funds, 1933; Tripartite Monetary Agreement, 1936; Adviser to Bank of England, 1941-48; Exec. Director, 1948-57; Director, Bank for Internat. Settlements, 1949-57; UK Alternate Governor of Internat. Monetary Fund, 1952-57 (UK Exec. Director, 1946-52). Director, Bank of England, 1948-68. Member Court of Governors, London School of Economics and Political Science; Member Council, Benenden School. Sheriff of the County of London, 1952 and 1961. Gran Oficial de la Orden de Mayo (Argentina), 1960; Orden del Merito (Chile), 1965. *Recreation:* reading. *Address:* Pollards Cross, Hempstead, near Saffron Walden, Essex. *T:* Radwinter 270.

**BOLTON, Guy;** Playwright; *b* Broxbourne, Herts, 23 Nov. 1884; *o s* of Reginald Pelham Bolton and Katherine Behenna; *m* 1st, Julia Currie; one *s* one *d*; 2nd, Marguerite Namara; one *s* one *d*; *m* Virginia De Lanty. *Educ:* Private tutors; Ecole des Beaux Arts. Started life as an architect practising in NY City; engaged by War Dept for special work on the rebuilding of West Point; concurrently wrote magazine stories, the first being published when the writer was 19; in 1913, started career as a playwright and is the author of more than fifty plays and musical comedies; among these are: Polly-with-a-Past, Sally, Kissing-Time, The Dark Angel, Tiptoes, Lady Be Good, Polly Preferred, Oh Joy, Song of the Drum, Anything Goes, Who's Who, Seeing Stars, Swing Along, This'll Make You Whistle, Going Greek, The Fleet's Lit Up, Magyar Melody, Hold On To Your Hats, Follow the Girls, Don't Listen Ladies, Larger than Life (adapted from W. Somerset Maugham's Theatre), The Shelley Story, Music at Midnight, Anastasia, Child of Fortune, Guardian Angel, Fireworks in the Sun. Author of films: Transatlantic, The Love Parade, Words and Music, 'Til the Clouds Roll By, Weekend at the Waldorf. *Publications:* (joint autobiography with P. G. Wodehouse) Bring on the Girls, 1954; The Olympians (novel); 1961; The Enchantress (novel); Gracious Living (novel), 1965; Anya (musical play), 1965; A Man and his Wife, 1970; Jeeves, a musical (with P. G. Wodehouse). *Recreation:* travelling. *Address:* Remsenburg, Long Island, USA.

**BOLTON, Captain Sir Ian Frederick Cheney,** 2nd Bt *cr* 1927; KBE 1957 (OBE 1946); DL; late 3rd Bn Argyll and Sutherland Highlanders; chartered accountant, Arthur Young, McClelland, Moores and Co., Glasgow and London; *b* 29 Jan. 1889; *s* of Sir Edwin Bolton, 1st Bart, and Elinor, *d* of Sir John H. N. Graham, 1st Bt; *S* father, 1931. *Educ:* Eton. Served European War, 1914-19 (despatches). Past President Institute of Accountants and Actuaries in Glasgow; Past President Institute of Chartered Accountants of Scotland; Member (part-time) British Transport Commission, 1947-59; Chairman Scottish Area Board, British Transport Commission, 1955-59; President, Scottish Boy Scout Assoc., 1945-58; Lord Dean of Guild, Glasgow, 1957-59. DL Stirling, 1965 (re-appointed, with seniority 1939); HM Lieut of Stirlingshire, 1949-64. Hon. LLD Glasgow Univ., 1955. *Recreation:* Boy Scouts. *Heir:* none. *Address:* West Plean, Stirling. *TA* and *T:* Bannockburn 2208. *Clubs:* Western (Glasgow); County (Stirling).

**BOLTON, John;** Chief Engineer, Department of Health and Social Security, since 1969; *b* 30 Dec. 1925; *s* of John and Elizabeth Ann Bolton, Great Harwood, Lancs; *m* 1950, Nell Hartley Mount, *d* of John and Kathleen Mount; three *d. Educ:* Blackburn Techn. College. Mech. Engrg Apprentice, Bristol Aeroplane Co. Ltd; Civil Engrg Pupil, Courtaulds Ltd; subseq. with English Electric Co. Ltd and NW Gas Board. Entered Health Service as Group Engr, W Manchester HMC, 1954; subseq. Chief Engr to Board of Govs of United Liverpool Hosps, Dep. Regional Engr to Leeds Regional Hosp. Board and Regional Engr to E Anglian Regional Hosp. Board. Part-time lectr in building and engrg subjects for many years and Principal, 1955-59, Irlam Evening Inst., Manchester. *Publications:* technical articles in various jls. *Recreations:* theatre, music, reading, gardening, swimming. *Address:* Allsprings House, High Street, Little Shelford, Cambs. *T:* Shelford 2591.

**BOLTON, John Eveleigh,** DSC 1945; Chairman, Committee of Inquiry on Small Firms, since 1969; Chairman and Managing Director, Growth Capital Ltd, since 1968; chairman or director many companies; *b* 17 Oct. 1920; *s* of late Ernest and Edith Mary Bolton; *m* 1948, Gabrielle Healey Hall, *d* of late Joseph and Minnie Hall; one *s* one *d. Educ:* Ilkley Sch.; Wolverhampton Sch.; Trinity Coll., Cambridge; Harvard, USA. Articled pupil to Chartered Acct, 1937-40; intermed. exam. of Inst. of Chartered Accts, 1940. Served War of

1939-45 (DSC): Destroyers, Lt RNVR, 1940-46. Cambridge, Hons Economics, MA; Cassel Travelling Schol., 1948; Harvard Business Sch., 1948-50; Baker Scholar, 1949; Master in Business Admin. (with Dist.), 1950. Research for Harvard in British Industry, 1950-51; Finance Dir, Solartron Laboratory Instruments Ltd, Kingston-upon-Thames, 1951-53 (Chm., 1953); Chm. and Man. Dir: Solartron Engineering Ltd, 1952; The Solartron Electronic Group Ltd, Thames Ditton and subseq. Farnborough, Hants, 1954-63 (Dep. Chm., 1963-65). Life Vice-Pres. (Chm. Council, 1964-66) Brit. Inst. of Management; FBIM; Chm. and Founder Subscriber: Advanced Management Programmes Internat. Trust; Foundn for Management Educn; Chm., Management Publications Ltd; Mem. Exec. Cttee, Automobile Assoc.; Governor and Dir: Cranborne Chase Sch. Ltd; Knighton House Sch. Ltd; Port Regis Sch. Ltd; Chm. Council, Surrey Univ.; Mem. Adv. Panel on Business Management Studies, Univ. Grants Cttee; Mem. Org. Cttee, World Research Hospital. Member: UK Automation Council, 1964-65; Adv. Cttee for Management Efficiency in Nat. Health Service, 1964-65; Cttee for Exports to New Zealand, 1965-68; Chm., Economic Develt Cttee for the Rubber Industry, 1965-68; Vice-Chm., Royal Commn on Local Govt in England, 1966-69. *Publications:* articles in: Scope; Control; The Listener; Christian Science Monitor; various radio and TV broadcasts on industrial topics. *Recreations:* shooting, swimming, tennis, gardening, opera, antiques. *Address:* Brook Place, Chobham, Woking, Surrey. *T:* Chobham 8157. *Clubs:* Oxford and Cambridge University, Harvard Business School Club of London, Harvard Club of London; Philippics, Wentworth (Surrey).

**BOLTON, Percy,** MA Cantab; *b* 1889; *s* of James Bolton, Blackburn; *m* Florence Madeleine, 2nd *d* of late Rev. D. L. Scott, MA, LLD Cantab.; one *s* one *d*. *Educ:* Blackburn Grammar Sch.; King's Coll., Cambridge (Scholar). Mathematical Tripos, Wrangler, 1911; Natural Science Tripos, Part II, 1912. Asst Master, Cheltenham Coll.; eleven years Head of Physics and Engineering Dept of Oundle Sch.; Headmaster of Dean Close Sch., Cheltenham, 1924-38; Headmaster of Watford Grammar Sch., 1938-51; retired 1951. *Address:* Brabourne, Kimpton, near Hitchin, Hertfordshire. *T:* Kimpton 362.

**BOMBAY, Cardinal Archbishop of; His Eminence Valerian Cardinal Gracias;** Archbishop of Bombay since Dec. 1950; Cardinal since Jan. 1953; *b* 23 Oct. 1900; *s* of José Antonio and Charlotte. *Educ:* St Patrick's High Sch., Karachi; St Joseph's Seminary, Mangalore; Papal Seminary, Kandy; Gregorian Univ., Rome. Secretary to Archbishop of Bombay, 1929-36; Chancellor of Archdiocese, 1929; Rector of Pro-Cathedral, Dec. 1941; Titular Bishop of Tannis and Auxiliary to Archbishop of Bombay, 1946-50; Consultor to Sacred Congregation for the Oriental Churches, Sacred Congregation of the Sacraments and Sacred Congregation for the Propagation of the Faith; Member: Council for the Implementation of the Constitution on the Sacred Liturgy; Commission for the Revision of the Code of Canon Law; Pontifical Commission for the Study of Family and Population Problems; President, Catholic Bishops' Conference of India. Awarded Padma Vibhushan (India), 1966. *Publications:* Features of Christian Life; Heaven and Home; The Vatican and International Policy; The Decline of Public Morals; The Chief Duties of Christians as Citizens. *Address:* Archbishop's House, Bombay 1, India. *T:* 213131 and 213132.

**BOMBAY, Bishop of,** since 1962; **Rt. Rev. Christopher James Gossage Robinson,** MA; *b* 10 June 1903; *s* of late Canon Albert Gossage Robinson; unmarried. *Educ:* Marlborough; Christ's Coll., Cambridge. Lecturer at St Stephen's Coll., Delhi, 1926-29; Deacon, 1929; Priest, 1930; Curate St Mary's, Portsea, 1929-31; Asst Priest, St James, Delhi, 1931-32; Vicar of St James, and Chaplain of Delhi, 1932-42; Vicar of St Thomas, New Delhi, 1942-45; Hon. Canon of Lahore Cathedral, 1944-47; Bishop of Lucknow, 1947-62. Member Cambridge Brotherhood of the Ascension, Delhi, since 1931. *Address:* St John's House, Colaba, Bombay 5, India. *Club:* Royal Commonwealth Society.

*See also E. A. G. Robinson.*

**BOMFORD, Richard Raymond,** CBE 1964; DM Oxon; FRCP; formerly Physician to London Hospital; Treasurer, Royal College of Physicians; Member of the Association of Physicians; *b* 15 May 1907; *s* of Raymond Bomford, Evesham, and Evelyn Mary Perkins; unmarried. *Educ:* Bromsgrove Sch.; Wadham Coll., Oxford; London Hospital. Hon. Colonel; late Consultant Physician, 14th Army. *Publications:* contributions to medical journals and text-books. *Recreation:* gardening. *Address:* Reza Shah Kabir Hospital, Shahr-e-Rey, Tehran, Iran; Woodways, Colam Lane, Little Baddow, Chelmsford, Essex. *T:* Danbury 2100. *Club:* Oriental.

**BOMPAS, Donald George,** CMG 1966; Secretary, Guy's Hospital Medical and Dental Schools, since 1969 (Deputy Secretary, 1966-69); *b* 20 Nov. 1920; *yr s* of Rev. E. Anstie Bompas; *m* 1946, Freda Vice, *y d* of F. M. Smithyman, Malawi; one *s* one *d*. *Educ:* Merchant Taylors' Sch., Northwood; Oriel Coll., Oxford. MA Oxon, 1947. Overseas Audit Service, 1942-66, retired; Nyasaland, 1942-47; Singapore, 1947-48; Malaya (now Malaysia), 1948-66; Deputy Auditor-General, 1957-60; Auditor-General, Malaysia (formerly Malaya), 1960-66. JMN (Hon.) Malaya, 1961. *Address:* 8 Birchwood Road, Petts Wood, Kent. *T:* Orpington 21661.

**BONALLACK, Michael Francis;** Sales Director, Bonallack Group of Companies, since 1962; *b* 31 Dec. 1934; *s* of Sir Richard (Frank) Bonallack, *qv*; *m* 1958, Angela Ward; one *s* three *d*. *Educ:* Chigwell; Haileybury ISC. National Service, 1953-55 (1st Lieut, RASC). Joined family business, 1955; Director, 1962. *Recreation:* golf (British Amateur Champion, 1961, 1965, 1968, 1969, 1970; English Amateur Champion, 1962-63, 1965-67 and 1968). *Address:* Whitecroft, 112 Burgess Road, Thorpe Bay, Essex. *T:* Southend-on-Sea 88901. *Clubs:* Eccentric, Golfers'.

**BONALLACK, Sir Richard (Frank),** Kt 1963; CBE 1955 (OBE 1944); MIMechE; Chairman, Bonallack & Sons, Ltd, since 1953; *b* 2 June 1904; *s* of Francis and Ada Bonallack; *m* 1930, Winifred Evelyn Mary Esplen; two *s* one *d*. *Educ:* Haileybury. War service in TA; transferred to TA Reserve, 1946, with rank of Colonel. Chm., Freight Container Section, SMMT; Vice-Pres., European Container Manufacturers Cttee. Member, Basildon Development Corporation, 1962. *Recreation:* golf. *Address:* 65 Thorpe Bay Gardens, Thorpe Bay, Essex. *T:* Southend 88180.

*See also M. F. Bonallack.*

**BONAR, Sir Herbert (Vernon),** CBE 1946; Chairman and Managing Director, The Low & Bonar Group Ltd; *b* 26 Feb. 1907; *s* of George

Bonar and Julia (*née* Seehusen); *m* 1935, Marjory (*née* East); two *s*. *Educ:* Fettes Coll.; Brasenose Coll., Oxford (BA). Joined Low & Bonar Ltd, 1929; Director, 1934; Managing Director, 1938; Chairman and Managing Director, 1949. Jute Control, 1939-46; Jute Controller, 1942-46. Hon. LLD, St Andrews Univ., 1955. *Recreations:* golf, fishing, photography, wild life preservation. *Address:* St Kitts, Albany Road, Broughty Ferry, Dundee, Angus. *T:* Dundee 79947. *Clubs:* Eastern (Dundee); Blairgowrie Golf; Panmure Golf.

**BONCOUR, J. P.;** *see* Paul-Boncour.

**BOND, Arthur;** Chairman, Yorkshire Electricity Board, since 1962; *b* 19 July 1907; *s* of Rev. A. and Mrs Anne Bond, Darwen, Lancs; *m* 1935, Nora Wadsworth; one *s* one *d*. *Educ:* Darwen Grammar Sch. Solicitor to Cleethorpes Corporation, 1930; Dep. Town Clerk, Luton, 1935; Town Clerk: Macclesfield, 1938; Stockport, 1944; Secretary, Eastern Electricity Board, 1948; Dep. Chairman, Yorkshire Electricity Board, 1952. Solicitor, Legal Member, TPI; Comp. IEE; FBIM. *Address:* 5 Linton Road, Wetherby, Yorks. *T:* Wetherby 2847; Yorkshire Electricity Board, Scarcroft, near Leeds. *T:* Leeds 658271.

**BOND, Maj.-Gen. George Alexander,** CB 1956; CBE 1953 (OBE 1942); Director of Supplies and Transport, War Office, since 1957; late RASC; *b* 1901; *s* of late Alexander Maxwell Bond, Dover; *m* 1929, Dora Margaret, *d* of late H. A. Gray; two *s*. *Educ:* Dover Grammar Sch.; RMC. Served War of 1939-45 (despatches, OBE); Brig. 1948; Director of Supplies and Transport, BAOR, 1950-53; DDST, Southern Command, 1953-54; Maj.-Gen. 1955; Inspector RASC, War Office, 1954-57; retd. Col Comdt, RASC, 1960-65; Col Comdt, Royal Corps of Transport, 1965-66. *Address:* Three Horseshoes, Kirdford, Billingshurst, Sussex. *T:* Kirdford 340. *Club:* Airborne.

**BOND, Ralph Norman,** CMG 1953; OBE 1950; *b* 31 Aug. 1900; *s* of Ralph Bond, Morecambe, Lancs; *m* 1929, Dorothy Ward; three *d*. *Educ:* Royal Grammar Sch., Lancaster; St John's Coll., Cambridge. BA Classical Tripos, 1922; MA 1929. Eastern Cadetship in Colonial Service, Dec. 1923; arrived in Ceylon, Jan. 1924; Revenue and judicial posts, 1924-36; Customs (Landing Surveyor and Deputy Collector), 1936-39; Import, Export and Exchange Control, 1939-42; Assistant Chief Secretary, 1942-45; Secretary to C-in-C, Ceylon, 1945-46; Permanent Secretary to Ministry of Posts and Broadcasting, Ceylon, 1947-55; retired, 1955. *Recreations:* formerly Rugby, soccer, hockey, cricket, tennis and swimming; now gardening. *Address:* 48 Stuart Avenue, Morecambe, Lancs. *T:* Morecambe 3237.

**BOND, Maj.-Gen. Richard Lawrence,** CB 1943; CBE 1937; DSO 1915; MC 1918; Hon. FRAM 1954; *s* of late Maj.-Gen. Sir F. G. Bond, KBE; *b* 10 June 1890; *m* Isabelle Helewise (*d* 1943), *y d* of late Col T. J. R. Mallock; one *d* (one *s* killed in action, 1941); *m* 1949, Dorothy Mary, *d* of late Sydney How. Entered Army, 1910; Major, 1926; Bt Lieut-Col, 1931; Lieut-Col, 1934; Col, 1937; Maj.-Gen., 1941; served European War, 1914-19 (despatches, DSO for gallantry in the successful attack on the Railway Embankment at Cuinchy); Waziristan Operations, 1936-37 (CBE); GSO 2nd Grade, War Office, 1930-31; Imperial Defence Coll., 1933; CRE India, 1934-37; AQMG, War Office, 1937-39; Chief Engineer, Aldershot Command, 1939; Chief Engineer, 1 Corps BEF, 1939-40, Maj.-Gen. i/c Administration, 1940; Deputy Quartermaster-General in India, 1941-42; Engineer-in-Chief in India, 1942-43; Commander, 1943 and 1944-46; retired pay, 1946. Vice-Pres., Royal Acad. of Music, 1967. *Address:* The Dykeries, Compton, Guildford, Surrey. *Club:* United Service.

**BOND, Walter Fitzgerald;** *see* Fitzgerald, Walter.

**BONDI, Hermann,** FRS 1959; FRAS; Professor of Mathematics, King's College, London, since 1954 (on leave of absence); Director-General, European Space Research Organisation, since 1967; *b* Vienna, 1 Nov. 1919; *s* of late Samuel and Helene Bondi, New York; *m* 1947, Christine M. Stockman, *d* of H. W. Stockman, *qv*; two *s* three *d*. *Educ:* Realgymnasium, Vienna; Trinity Coll., Cambridge (MA). Temporary Experimental Officer, Admiralty, 1942-45; Fellow Trinity Coll., Cambridge, 1943-49, and 1952-54; Asst Lecturer, Mathematics, Cambridge, 1945-48; University Lecturer, Mathematics, Cambridge, 1948-54; Research Associate, Cornell Univ., 1951; Lecturer, Harvard Coll. Observatory, 1953; Lowell Lecturer, Boston, Mass, 1953; Visiting Prof. Cornell Univ., 1960; Halley Lecturer, Oxford, 1962; Tarner Lectr, Cambridge, 1965. Chairman: Space Cttee, MoD, 1964-65; Nat. Cttee for Astronomy, 1963-67; Secretary, Royal Astronomical Soc., 1956-64; Member Rationalist Press Assoc. Ltd; Member Board and Hon. Vice-President Advisory Centre for Education (ACE); Mem., Ct, London Univ., 1963-67. Governor: Birkbeck Coll.; several Surrey Schools. Fellow, King's Coll., London, 1968. *Publications:* Cosmology, 1952 (2nd edn, 1960); The Universe at Large, 1961; Relativity and Commonsense, 1964; Assumption and Myth in Physical Theory, 1968; papers on astrophysics, etc, in Proc. Royal Society, Monthly Notices, Royal Astronomical Society, Proc. Cam. Phil. Society, etc. *Recreation:* travelling. *Address:* East House, Buckland Corner, Reigate Heath, Surrey. *T:* Reigate 45945; European Space Research Organisation, 114 Avenue de Neuilly, Neuilly sur Seine, France.

**BONE, Captain Howard Francis,** CBE 1957; DSO 1940, and Bar 1941; DSC 1940 and Bar, 1942; RN (retired); *b* 20 Oct. 1908; *s* of late Engineer Rear-Adm. H. Bone, CB, and late Mrs A. S. Bone; *m* 1932, Heather Maud Marion Fletcher; one *d*. *Educ:* Felsted; RNC, Dartmouth. Entered RN, 1922; served in submarines, 1930-50. Comdr 1941; Captain, 1947; Dep. Director of Naval Equipment, 1952-54; Captain-in-Charge, Simonstown, and Captain Superintendent, Simonstown Dockyard, 1954-57. ADC to the Queen, Jan. 1956-May 1957. Retired, 1957. *Address:* Inner Meadow, Combe Hay, near Bath, Somerset. *T:* Combe Down 3363. *Clubs:* Western Province Sports, Kelvin Grove (Newlands, Cape Town).

**BONE, Phyllis Mary,** RSA 1944 (ARSA, 1939); animal sculptor; *b* Hornby, Lancs; *d* of Dr Douglas John Mayhew Bone. *Educ:* St George's High Sch. for Girls, Edinburgh. Studied sculpture at the Edinburgh College of Art (Sculpture Diploma), Paris and Italy; exhibited in Royal Scottish Academy, Edinburgh; Paris Salon, Royal Academy, Walker Art Gallery, Liverpool, and Royal Glasgow Institute; Aberdeen Art Gallery purchased two bronzes, 1930, and Glasgow Corporation one, 1942; executed all the animal sculpture on the Scottish National War Memorial; the animal sculpture in the New Zoology Buildings, Edinburgh Univ.; sculpture on New Government Buildings, Edinburgh; other work: in St Peter's RC

Church, Edinburgh; St John's Church, Perth; Stowe Chapel, Buckinghamshire; St Winifred's Church, Welbeck; Preening and Drying (bronze group) 1952 (bought by Min. of Works for a scheme for decorating British Embassies throughout the World). Shere Khan, bronze, and Shelties, bronze (diploma work at Royal Scottish Academy) to private collection, NSW. *Publication:* Deer Talk, 1962. *Address:* Hillview, Barrhill Road, Kirkcudbright. *Club:* Ladies' Caledonian (Edinburgh).

**BONE, Group Captain Reginald John,** CB 1934; CBE 1919; DSO 1916; *b* Dorking, Surrey, 2 Oct. 1888; *m* Sylvia Joan Mary (*née* Fitzpatrick), *widow* of Douglas A. Payne. *Educ:* Ripley Court, Ripley, Surrey. Service in Royal Navy in destroyers and in submarines. Learned to fly at Eastbourne Aviation Company Sch., 1912, and at Central Flying Sch., Upavon, 1913. Served in Naval Wing, RFC, RNAS and RAF, 1913-34. Director-General of Civil Aviation under Egyptian Government, 1936-39; commanded RAF base, Pembroke Dock, 1939-41; Civil Air Attaché, Far East, 1948-51. *Address:* 25 Pitmaston Court, Moseley, Birmingham 13. *Club:* United Service.

**BONE, Mrs Stephen;** *see* Adshead, Mary.

**BONHAM, Major Sir Antony Lionel Thomas,** 4th Bt, *cr* 1852; late Royal Scots Greys; *b* 21 Oct. 1916; *o s* of Maj. Sir Eric H. Bonham, 3rd Bt, and Ethel (*d* 1962), *y d* of Col Leopold Seymour; *S* father 1937; *m* 1944, Felicity, *o d* of late Col. Frank L. Pardoe, DSO, Bartonbury, Cirencester; three *s*. *Educ:* Eton; RMC. Served Royal Scots Greys, 1937-49; retired with rank of Major, 1949. *Recreation:* hunting. *Heir: s* George Martin Antony Bonham, *b* 18 Feb. 1945. *Address:* St Joseph's, Herongate, Essex. *T:* Herongate 355. *Club:* Cavalry.

**BONHAM-CARTER, Sir Arthur Desmond,** Kt 1969; TD 1942; Director, Unilever Ltd, 1953-68, retired; *b* 15 Feb. 1908; 2nd *s* of Gen. Sir Charles Bonham-Carter, GCB, CMG, DSO, and Beryl, *née* Codrington; *m* 1933, Ann Parker Hazelwood; one *s*. *Educ:* Winchester; Magdalene Coll., Cambridge. Served with Royal Tank Regt, 1938-45. Joined J. Crosfield & Sons Ltd, 1929; Director, Crosfield, Watson & Gossage, 1938; Chairman, J. Knight Ltd, 1948; Member: Royal Commission to consider Pay of Doctors and Dentists, 1957-60; Advisory Cttee, Recruitment for the Forces, 1958; Plowden Cttee on Representational Services Overseas, 1962-64; Central Health Services Council, 1965. Trustee, Nightingale Fund, 1961; Chairman: Board of Governors, University College Hospital, 1963-; S-W Metropolitan Regional Hospital Board, 1968-. *Recreations:* cricket, golf. *Address:* Harkaway, Hillgrove, Lurgashall, Petworth, Sussex. *T:* Northchapel 217. *Club:* Travellers'.

**BONHAM CARTER, Rear-Adm. Sir Christopher Douglas,** KCVO 1968 (CVO 1962); CB 1959; Treasurer to the Duke of Edinburgh, 1959-70, Treasurer and Private Secretary 1970; *b* 3 Nov. 1907; *e s* of Captain A. E. Bonham Carter, 60th Rifles, and Margaret (*née* Malcolm of Poltalloch); *m* 1931, Maryanne M. H. Taylor, Glasgow, and Ardgarten, Argyll; one *s*. *Educ:* Elstree Sch.; RNC Dartmouth. Served War of 1939-45 (despatches, 1943); Captain RN 1948; Commanded Second Frigate Flotilla, 1949-51; Naval Attaché, Rome, 1951-53; Admiralty, 1953-55; Commanded HMS Glasgow, 1955-56; Rear-Adm. 1957; Chief of Staff, Mediterannean, 1957-59. Comdr, Legion of Honour. *Recreations:* shooting and fishing. *Address:* Nottingham Cottage, Kensington Palace, W8. *Club:* White's.

**BONHAM-CARTER, Air Commodore David William Frederick,** CB 1950; DFC 1945; psa 1933; *b* 22 Feb. 1901; *s* of late Walter Henry Bonham-Carter, Solicitor, and late Anita Bonham-Carter (*née* Heuer); *m* 1927, Joyce Angela Palmer; three *s* one *d*. *Educ:* Winchester Coll.; RAF Coll., Cranwell (first term). Seconded to RCAF, 1940-43; with No 5 (Bomber) Group, 1943-45 (despatches); Officer Commanding No 45 Wing, RAF Dorval, PQ, Canada, 1946; seconded to Ministry of Civil Aviation, 1947-49; AOC, RAF Hong Kong, 1951-53; retired 1953. Member of Council, Nightingale Fund, 1947-; Vice-President: East Anglian Flying Club; Anglo-Belgian Union, 1967. *Recreation:* photography. *Address:* Mariner's Cottage, Felixstowe Ferry, Suffolk. *T:* Felixstowe 3511. *Clubs:* Royal Aero; Royal Channel Islands Yacht.

**BONHAM-CARTER, John Arkwright,** DSO 1942; OBE 1967; ERD 1952; Chairman and General Manager, British Railways Western Region, since 1968; *b* 27 March 1915; *s* of late Capt. Guy Bonham-Carter, 19th Hussars, and Kathleen Rebecca (*née* Arkwright); *m* 1939, Anne Louisa Charteris; two *s*. *Educ:* Winchester Coll.; King's Coll., Cambridge (Exhibitioner). 1st class hons Mech. Scis, Cantab, 1936; MA. Joined LNER Co. as Traffic Apprentice, 1936; served in Royal Tank Regt, 1939-46 (despatches, 1940 and 1942); subsequently rejoined LNER; held various appointments; Asst General Manager, BR London Midland Region, 1963-65; Chief Operating Officer, British Railways Board, 1966-68. Lieut-Col, Engr and Rly Staff Corps RE (T&AVR IV), 1966-. SBStJ 1962. *Recreations:* theatre, foreign travel, cabinet making and carpentry. *Address:* c/o Lloyds Bank, Alton, Hants. *Club:* United Service.

**BONHAM CARTER, Hon. Mark Raymond;** (first) Chairman, Race Relations Board, since 1966; a Director, Royal Opera House, Covent Garden, since 1958; Governor, The Royal Ballet; Member Council: Consumers' Association, since 1966; Institute of Race Relations, since 1966; *b* 11 Feb. 1922; *e s* of late Sir Maurice Bonham Carter, KCB, KCVO, and Violet, *d* of 1st Earl of Oxford and Asquith, KG, PC (Baroness Asquith of Yarnbury, DBE); *m* 1955, Leslie, *d* of Condé Nast, NY; three *d*. *Educ:* Winchester; Balliol Coll., Oxford (Scholar); University of Chicago (Commonwealth Fund Fellowship). Served Grenadier Guards, 1941-45; 8th Army (Africa) and 21st Army Group (NW Europe); captured, 1943; escaped; (despatches). Contested (L) Barnstaple, 1945; MP (L), Torrington Div. of Devonshire, March 1958-59; Mem., UK Delegn to the Council of Europe, 1958-59; contested (L) Torrington, 1964. Director, Wm Collins & Co. Ltd, 1955-58. *Publications:* (ed) The Autobiography of Margot Asquith, 1962; contributor to: Radical Alternative (essays), 1962. *Address:* 49 Victoria Road, W8. *T:* 01-937 4142. *Clubs:* Brooks's, MCC.

**BONHAM CARTER, Richard Erskine;** Physician to the Hospital for Sick Children, Great Ormond Street, since 1947, to University College Hospital, 1948-66; *b* 27 Aug. 1910; *s* of late Capt. A. E. Bonham-Carter and late M. E. Bonham-Carter (*née* Malcolm); *m* 1946, Margaret (*née* Stace); three *d*. *Educ:* Clifton Coll.; Peterhouse, Cambridge; St Thomas's Hospital. Resident Asst Physician, Hospital for Sick Children, Great Ormond Street, 1938.

Served War of 1939-45 in RAMC; DADMS 1 Airborne Div., 1942-45; despatches, 1944. *Publications:* contributions to Text-Books of Pædiatrics and to medical journals. *Recreations:* gardening, fishing. *Address:* 167 Torrington Park, N12. *T:* 01-368 6722; Castle Sweyn Cottage, Achnamara, Argyll.

**BONHAM-CARTER, Adm. Sir Stuart Sumner,** KCB 1943 (CB 1941); CVO 1934; DSO 1918; RN; *b* 1889; *yr s* of late Lothian George Bonham-Carter, Buriton House, Petersfield, and Emily Maud, *d* of Rev. J. M. Sumner; *m* 1933, Eve, *widow* of Brig. C. R. Lloyd, Indian Army, and *d* of late Donald Shaw; one *d.* Served European War, 1914-18 (despatches, DSO, Legion of Honour, French Croix de Guerre, with Palm, Italian Silver Cross for Valour, Belgian Croix de Guerre); commanded HMS Intrepid at Zeebrugge. Asst Director of Naval Equipment, 1932-34; Commodore Royal Naval Barracks, Chatham, 1937-39; Naval Secretary to first Lord of the Admiralty, 1939; RA 3rd BS 1940; Rear-Adm. 18th Cruiser Squadron, 1944; Vice-Adm. Malta, 1943; retired 1944; Commodore of Convoys, 1944-45. *Address:* Ardmoy, 76 Heath Road, Petersfield, Hants. *T:* Petersfield 4154.

**BONHOTE, Rev. Edward Frederic,** MA; Canon of Rochester, 1953 (Emeritus, 1961); *b* 13 Oct. 1888; *s* of late Thomas T. and late Marie Rose Bonhote; unmarried. *Educ:* Merchant Taylors' Sch.; Clare Coll., Cambridge (Scholar). 1st Class Hons in Mathematics, 10th Wrangler, 1909; Deacon, 1912; Priest, 1913; Asst Master at Rugby Sch., 1911-14 and 1919-34; CMS Missionary at St John's Coll., Agra, 1914-17; served in ranks with 58th and 59th Divisions, MGC, 1917-19; Housemaster at Rugby Sch., 1925-34; Master of Haileybury Coll. (now Haileybury and Imperial Service Coll.), 1934-48; Hon. Canon of St Albans, 1935-48; Vicar of St Thomas', Southborough, 1949-61. *Address:* 27 Sondes Place Drive, Dorking, Surrey.

**BONINGTON, Christian John Storey;** writer and photographer; *b* 6 Aug. 1934; *s* of Charles Bonington, journalist, and Helen Anne Bonington (*née* Storey); *m* 1962, Muriel Wendy Marchant; two *s* (and one *s* decd). *Educ:* University Coll. Sch., London. RMA Sandhurst, 1955-56; commnd Royal Tank Regt, 1956-61. Unilever Management Trainee, 1961-62; writer and photographer, 1962-. Climbs: Annapurna II, 26,041 ft (1st ascent) 1960; Central Pillar Freney, Mont Blanc (1st ascent), 1961; Nuptse, 25,850 ft (1st ascent), 1961; North Wall of Eiger (1st British ascent), 1962; Central Tower of Paine, Patagonia (1st ascent), 1963; Leader of successful Annapurna South Face Expedition, 1970. Member of team that made first descent of Blue Nile, 1968. *Publications:* I Chose to Climb, 1966; Annapurna South Face, 1971. *Recreation:* mountaineering. *Address:* Newcroft, West Road, Bowdon, Cheshire. *T:* 061-928 3450. *Clubs:* Alpine, Army and Navy, Climbers.

**BONNER, Frederick Ernest;** Member, Central Electricity Generating Board, since 1969; *b* 16 Sept. 1923; *s* of George Frederick Bonner and late Mrs Bonner, Hammersmith; *m* 1957, Mrs P. Oliver, *widow* of W. A. Oliver. *Educ:* St Clement Danes Holborn Estate Grammar Sch. BSc(Econ) London; DPA, JDipMA. Local Govt (Fulham and Ealing Borough Councils), 1940-49. Central Electricity Authority: Sen. Accountant, 1949-50; Asst Finance Officer, 1950-58; Central Electricity Generating Board: Asst Chief Financial Officer, 1958-61; Dep. Chief Financial Officer, 1961-65; Chief Financial Officer, 1965-69. FCA, FIMTA. *Recreations:* music, gardening, reading. *Address:* 12 Tanners Dean, Leatherhead, Surrey.

**BONNET, C. M.;** *see* Melchior-Bonnet.

**BONNET, Georges,** Hon. GCMG 1938; Deputy for Dordogne, France, 1924-40, 1956-68; Conseiller-Général de la Dordogne, 1951-68; *b* 1889. *Educ:* Ecole des Hautes Etudes; Ecole des Sciences Politiques. Held Cabinet rank from 1925; President French delegation to London Economic and Monetary Conference, 1934; Ambassador to USA, 1937; Minister of Foreign Affairs, Daladier Cabinet, 1938-39; Minister of Justice, 1939-40. Président, Union Mondiale des Intellectuels. *Publications:* Défense de la paix; De Washington au Quai d'Orsay; Le Quai d'Orsay sous Trois Républiques; Miracle de la France; De Munich à la Guerre. *Address:* 94 Boulevard Flandrin, Paris 16e.

**BONNEY, George Louis William,** MS, FRCS; Consultant Orthopædic Surgeon to St Mary's Hospital, London; Consulting Orthopædic Surgeon to the Florence Nightingale Hospital; *b* 10 Jan. 1920; *s* of late Dr Ernest Bonney and Gertrude Mary Williams; *m* 1950, Margaret Morgan; two *d. Educ:* Eton (Scholar); St Mary's Hospital Medical Sch. MB, BS, MRCS, LRCP 1943; FRCS 1945; MS (London) 1947. Formerly: Surg.-Lieut RNVR; Research Assistant and Senior Registrar, Royal National Orthopædic Hospital; Consultant Orthopædic Surgeon, Southend Group of Hospitals. Travelling Fellowship of British Postgraduate Med. Fedn, Univ. of London, 1950; Fellow British Orthopædic Assoc. Mem. Council, Medical Defence Union. Associate Editor, Journal of Bone and Joint Surgery. *Publications:* Chapters in Operative Surgery, 1957; papers in medical journals on visceral pain, circulatory mechanisms, nerve injuries and on various aspects of orthopædic surgery. *Recreations:* fishing, photography, music. *Address:* 71 Porchester Terrace, W2. *T:* 01-262 4236; 107 Harley Street, W1; Wyeside Cottages, Much Fawley, Hereford. *Club:* Leander.

**BONSALL, Prof. Frank Featherstone,** FRS 1970; Professor of Mathematics, University of Edinburgh, since 1965; *b* 1920; *m* 1947, Gillian Patrick. *Educ:* Bishop's Stortford Coll.; Merton Coll., Oxford. *Recreations:* walking, climbing. *Address:* Mathematical Institute, 20 Chambers Street, Edinburgh EH1 1HZ.

**BONSER, Air Vice-Marshal Stanley Haslam,** CB 1969; MBE 1942; CEng, FRAeS; Deputy Controller of Equipment, Ministry of Technology, since 1969; *b* 17 May 1916; *s* of late Sam Bonser and late Phoebe Ellen Bonser; *m* 1941, Margaret Betty Howard; two *s. Educ:* Sheffield University. BSc 1938; DipEd 1939. Armament Officer, Appts, 1939-44; British Air Commn, Washington, DC, 1944-46; Coll. of Aeronautics, 1946-47; RAE, Guided Weapons, 1947-51; Chief Instr (Armament Wing) RAF Techn. Coll., 1951-52; Staff Coll., Bracknell, 1953, psa 1953; Project Officer, Blue Streak, Min. of Technology, 1954-57; Asst Dir, GW Engineering, 1957-60; Senior RAF Officer, Skybolt Development Team, USA, 1960-62; Dir, Aircraft Mechanical Engineering, 1963-64; Dir, RAF Aircraft Development (mainly NIMROD), 1964-69. *Recreations:* scout movement, gardening. *Address:* Chalfont, Waverley Avenue, Fleet, Aldershot, Hants. *T:* Fleet 5835. *Club:* Royal Air Force.

**BONSER, Wilfrid;** Librarian, University of Birmingham, 1929-52; *b* 1887; *s* of A. E. Bonser; *m* Madoline Carrie, *d* of Henry Davis,

Beckenham. *Educ:* Highgate Sch.; University Coll., London. BA London, 1914; PhD London, 1927; Fellow, Library Assoc.; Sub-Librarian of University College, London, till 1928; Member of Council of Folklore Society till 1928 and 1953-; Hon. Secretary, Birmingham Library, 1939-40, 1944-45; President 1941. *Publications:* Catalogue of the Geological Books in the Library of University College, London, 1927; Proverb Literature (General Editor), 1930; Union Catalogue of Periodical Publications in University Libraries of British Isles (Co-Editor), 1937; An Anglo-Saxon and Celtic Bibliography (450-1087), 1957; A Bibliography of Folklore, 1961; The Medical Background of Anglo-Saxon England, 1963; A Romano-British Bibliography, 1964; articles and reviews in Folklore, Antiquity, The Library, Library Association Record, Man, Nature, etc. *Recreations:* folklore and archæology. *Address:* 1 Parkwood, Beckenham, Kent BR3 1TR. *T:* 01-650 2476.

**BONSOR, Sir Bryan Cosmo,** 3rd Bt, *cr* 1925; MC 1945; TD; Director of Watney Mann, 1958-69 (Watney's, 1947-58), retired; *b* 26 Aug. 1916; *er s* of Major Sir Reginald Bonsor, Bt; *S* father 1959; *m* 1942, Elizabeth Hambro; two *s. Educ:* Eton. Served War of 1939-45 with Bucks Yeomanry (despatches, MC). Major RA. *Recreations:* shooting, fishing, sailing. *Heir: s* Nicholas Cosmo Bonsor, *b* 9 Dec. 1942. *Address:* Liscombe, Leighton Buzzard, Bedfordshire. *Clubs:* White's, Pratt's.

**BONY, Prof. Jean V.;** Professor of the History of Art, University of California at Berkeley, since 1962; *b* Le Mans, France, 1 Nov. 1908; *s* of Henri Bony and Marie Normand; *m* 1st, 1936, Clotilde Roure (*d* 1942); one *d*; 2nd, 1953, Mary England, BA. *Educ:* Lycée Louis-le-Grand, Paris; Sorbonne. Agrégé d'Histoire; MA Cantab. Bulteau-Lavisse Research Scholarship, 1935-37; Asst Master, Eton Coll., 1937-39 and 1945-46. Served War of 1939-45; 1st Lieut, French Infantry, 1939-44; POW, Germany, June 1940-Dec. 1943. Research Scholar, Centre Nat. de la Recherche Scientifique, 1944-45; Lecturer in History of Art at the French Inst. in London, 1946-61. Focillon Fellow and Vis. Lectr, Yale Univ., 1949; Slade Prof. of Fine Art, University of Cambridge, and Fellow of St John's Coll., Cambridge, 1958-61; Visiting Prof., Columbia Univ., 1961; Mathews Lecturer, 1961; Lecturer in History of Art at the University of Lille, France, 1961-62; Wrightsman Lectr, New York Univ., 1969. *Publications:* Notre-Dame de Mantes, 1946; French Cathedrals (with Dr Martin Hürlimann), 1951 (revised edn, 1967); articles in Bulletin Monumental, Congrès Archéologiques de France, Journal of Warburg and Courtauld Institutes, Journal of British Archæological Assoc., etc. *Address:* Department of Art, University of California, Berkeley, California 94720, USA.

**BONYNGE, Mrs Richard;** *see* Sutherland, Joan.

**BOORD, Sir Richard (William),** 3rd Bt, *cr* 1896; late RAFVR; *b* 9 Nov. 1907; *o s* of late Alexander Edgar Boord, 3rd *s* of 1st Bt, and Coralie Mary, *y d* of late Herman Hoskier; *S* uncle, 1928; *m* 1st, 1933, Yvonne Swingler (from whom he obtained a divorce, 1944), *o d* of J. A. Hubert Bird; two *s*; 2nd, 1944, Ethel El Marie, *d* of Herman Moline, Duluth, Minnesota, USA. *Educ:* Marlborough; Lincoln Coll., Oxford. *Heir: s* Nicolas John Charles Boord [*b* 10 June 1936; *m* 1st, 1960, Françoise (marr. diss. 1965), *d* of Guiseppe Tempra, Pas de Calais; 2nd, 1965, Françoise Renée, *d* of M. C. Mouret, Marseilles]. *Address:* 4 Trumpeters House, Old Palace Yard, Richmond, Surrey.

**BOOS, Sir Werner (James),** Kt 1965; CBE 1961; Chairman, Public Service and Police Service Commissions and Member, Judicial and Legal Service Commission of Trinidad and Tobago, since 1960 (relinquished positions temporarily to act as Governor-General of Trinidad and Tobago, 15 May-15 Sept. 1964 and April-July 1967); *b* 25 July 1911; *s* of late Julius Edward Boos, and late Audrey (*née* Hobson); *m* 1932, Alisa (*née* Pasea); two *s* two *d. Educ:* St Mary's Coll., Trinidad; Oxford Univ. Various appointments Trinidad and Tobago Civil Service, 1928-60; retired, 1960, as Dep. Chief Sec.; acted on various occasions as Chief Sec., Financial Sec., Governor's Deputy. *Recreations:* gardening, fishing, swimming, reading. *Address:* (home) 7 Fondes Amandes, St Ann's, Trinidad. *T:* 42692; Service Commissions' Offices, Red House, Port of Spain, Trinidad. *T:* 38916 or 32971. *Club:* Trinidad Country (Maraval).

**BOOSEY, Leslie Arthur;** Hon. President: International Confederation of Societies of Authors and Composers; Performing Right Society; President, Boosey & Hawkes Ltd; Chairman, Hammond Organ UK Ltd; *b* 26 July 1887; *s* of Arthur and Lucy Ashton Boosey; *m* 1921, Ethel Torfrida, *d* of Frank Marchant; three *s* one *d. Educ:* Malvern Coll.; abroad. Served with 22nd London Regt The Queens, 1908-19; France, 1915-18. Chevalier, Légion d'Honneur. *Address:* Bourne Orchard, Hertford. *T:* Bayford 250. *Clubs:* Savile, Oriental.

**BOOT, Dr Henry Albert Howard,** Senior Principal Scientific Officer, Royal Naval Scientific Service, 1954 (Principal Scientific Officer, 1948-54); *b* 29 July 1917; *s* of late Henry James and late Ruby May Boot; *m* 1948, Penelope May Herrington; two *s. Educ:* King Edward's High Sch., Birmingham (Scholar); Univ. of Birmingham. BSc 1938; PhD 1941. Invention of the cavity magnetron (with Prof. J. T. Randall, FRS), 1939; research on the cavity magnetron at Univ. of Birmingham, 1939-45; Nuffield Research Fellow in Physics at Univ. of Birmingham, 1945-48. Royal Society of Arts Thomas Gray Memorial Prize (with J. T. Randall), 1943; Award by Royal Commission on Awards to Inventors, 1949; John Price Wetherill Medal of the Franklin Institute, 1958; John Scott Award, 1959 (with Prof. J. Randall). *Publications:* various papers on the production of high power ultra high frequency oscillation and controlled thermonuclear fusion, also optical masers. *Recreation:* sailing. *Address:* The Old Mill Cottage, Rushden, near Buntingford, Herts. *T:* Broadfield 231. *Club:* Athenæum.

**BOOTE, Col Charles Geoffrey Michael,** MBE 1945; TD 1943; Vice-Lieutenant of Staffordshire since 1969; *b* 29 Sept. 1909; *s* of Lt-Col Charles Edmund Boote, TD, The North Staffordshire Regt (killed in action, 1916); *m* 1937, Elizabeth Gertrude, *er d* of Evan Richard Davies, Market Drayton, Salop; three *s. Educ:* Bedford Sch. 2nd Lt 5th Bn North Staffordshire Regt, 1927. Served 1939-45, UK and NW Europe; despatches, 1945; Lt-Col, 1947. Director, T. & R. Boote Ltd, Stoke-on-Trent, 1931, Man. Dir 1946, Chm. and Man. Dir, 1955 (taken over by Richards Tiles Ltd, 1963); Dir, Richards Tiles Ltd, 1963 (taken over by H. & R. Johnson Ltd 1968); retired Oct. 1969; Dir, h. Clarkson (Midlands) Ltd, 1969-. Director, Brit. Pottery Manufacturers' Fedn (Trustee) Ltd, 1955, retd Dec. 1969; Pres., Brit. Pottery Manufacturers' Fedn, 1957-58; Vice-Chm., Glazed and Floor Tile Manufacturers' Assoc., 1953-57. Hon. Col 5/6 Bn North Staffordshire Regt, 1963-67; Mem. Staffs TAVR Cttee. JP,

Stoke-on-Trent, 1955-65; DL, 1958, JP 1959, High Sheriff, 1967-68, Staffordshire. Dep. Chm., Eccleshall PS Div., 1966-; Mem. Court of Governors, Keele Univ., 1957. *Recreations:* salmon fishing; British Racing Drivers' Club (Life Mem.); North Staffordshire Hunt (Hon. Sec. 1948-59). *Address:* Croxtonbank House, near Eccleshall, Stafford. *T:* Wetwood 230.

**BOOTH;** *see* Gore-Booth and Sclater-Booth.

**BOOTH, Albert Edward;** MP (Lab), Barrow-in-Furness since 1966; *b* 28 May 1928; *e s* of Albert Henry Booth and Janet Mathieson; *m* 1957, Joan Amis; three *s*. *Educ:* St Thomas's Sch., Winchester; S Shields Marine Sch.; Rutherford Coll. of Technology. Engineering Draughtsman. Election Agent, 1951 and 1955. County Borough Councillor, 1962-65. Contested (Lab) Tynemouth, 1964. *Address:* 145 Woodwarde Road, SE22. *T:* 01-693 7456.

**BOOTH, Catherine B.;** *see* Bramwell-Booth.

**BOOTH, Charles Leonard,** MVO 1961; Deputy High Commissioner, British High Commission, Kampala, since 1969; *b* 9 March 1925; *s* of Charles Leonard and Marion Booth; *m* 1958, Mary Gillian Emms, two *s* two *d*. *Educ:* Pembroke Coll., Oxford. Oxford Univ., 1942-43 and 1947-50. Served RA (Capt.), 1943-47. Joined HM Foreign Service, 1950; Foreign Office, 1950-51; Third and Second Secretary, Rangoon, 1951-55; FO, 1955-60 (Private Sec. to Parly Under-Sec. of State, 1958-60); First Sec., Rome, 1960-63; Head of Chancery, Rangoon, 1963-64, and Bangkok, 1964-67; FO, 1967-69. Counsellor, 1968. Officer of Order of Merit of Italian Republic, 1961. *Recreations:* Italian opera, gardening, walking, tennis. *Address:* British High Commission, PO Box 7070, Kampala, Uganda. *T:* Kampala 57054. *Club:* Travellers'.

**BOOTH, Prof. Christopher Charles;** Professor of Medicine and Director of Department of Medicine, Postgraduate Medical School of London; *b* 22 June 1924; *s* of Lionel Barton Booth and Phyllis Petley Duncan; *m* 1959, Lavinia Loughridge, Belfast; one *s* one *d*. *Educ:* Sedbergh Sch., Yorks; University of St Andrews. Junior appointments at Dundee Royal Infirmary, Hammersmith Hosp. and Addenbrooke's Hosp., Cambridge; successively Medical Tutor, Lecturer in Medicine and Senior Lecturer, Postgraduate Medical School of London. FRCP 1964. *Publications:* papers in med. jls on relationship of nutritional disorders to disease of the alimentary tract, and on medical history. *Recreations:* fishing, history. *Address:* 13 The Green, Twickenham, Mddx. *T:* 01-894 5746.

**BOOTH, Ven. David Herbert,** MBE 1944; Archdeacon of Lewes since 1959; Chaplain to the Queen since 1957; *b* 26 Jan. 1907; *s* of Robert and Clara Booth; *m* 1942, Diana Mary Chard; two *s* one *d*. *Educ:* Bedford Sch.; Pembroke Coll., Cambridge; Ely Theological Coll. BA (3rd cl. Hist. Trip. part II), 1931; MA 1936; deacon, 1932; priest, 1933; Curate, All Saints', Hampton, 1932-34; Chaplain, Tonbridge Sch., 1935-40; Chaplain, RNVR, 1940-45; Rector of Stepney, 1945-53; Vicar of Brighton, 1953-59; Prebendary of Waltham in Chichester Cathedral, 1953-59. Select Preacher, University of Cambridge, 1947. Mem. of Archbishop's Commission on South East, 1965. *Recreations:* horses, gardening and family life. *Address:* 45 Tongdean Road, Hove, Sussex BN3 6QE. *T:* Brighton 501557.

**BOOTH, Sir Douglas Allen,** 3rd Bt, *cr* 1916; student; *b* 2 Dec. 1949; *s* of Sir Philip Booth, 2nd Bt, and Ethel, *d* of Joseph Greenfield, NY, USA; *S* father 1960. *Educ:* Beverly Hills High Sch.; Harvard Univ. (Harvard Nat. Scholarship, Nat. Merit Scholarship, 1967). *Recreations:* football, baseball. *Heir: b* Derek Blake Booth, *b* 7 April 1953. *Address:* 9955 Durant Drive, Beverly Hills, Calif, USA.

**BOOTH, Dame Edith;** *see* Evans, Dame Edith.

**BOOTH, Eric Stuart,** FRS 1967; Member Central Electricity Generating Board since 1959; Member UK Atomic Energy Authority (part-time), since 1965; *b* 14 Oct. 1914; *s* of Henry and Annie Booth; *m* 1945, Mary Elizabeth Melton; two *d*. *Educ:* Batley Grammar Sch.; Liverpool Univ. Apprentice, Metropolitan Vickers Electrical Co. Ltd, 1936-38; Technical Engineer, Yorks Electric Power Co., 1938-46; Dep., later City Electrical Engineer and Manager, Salford Corporation, 1946-48; various posts associated with construction of Power Stations with British, later Central, Electricity Authority, 1948-57, Dep. Chief Engineer (Generation Design and Construction), 1957; Chief Design and Construction Engineer, Central Electricity Generating Bd, 1958-59. *Address:* Oakcroft, Ashley Park Avenue, Walton-on-Thames, Surrey. *T:* Walton-on-Thames 25584. *Club:* Royal Automobile.

**BOOTH, Sir (G.) Arthur (W.),** KBE *cr* 1935; *b* 28 Oct. 1879; *e s* of Frank H. A. Booth, of Sydenhurst, Chiddingfold, Surrey, and Florence Eliza, *d* of E. Giffard, late of the Admiralty; *m* 1925, Claire, *d* of John Sibley. *Educ:* Bradfield; New Coll., Oxford. Called to the Bar, Middle Temple, 1905; practised in London and at Alexandria, Egypt; Legal Adviser to Custodian of Enemy Property in Egypt, 1916-18; Judge of the Mixed Tribunal, Cairo, 1918; Royal Counsellor Egyptian State Legal Dept, 1926; Judicial Adviser to the Egyptian Government, 1928-37; Grand Cordon, Order of the Nile, Egypt, 1936. *Address:* Little Shalwyn, Three Gates Lane, Haslemere, Surrey. *T:* Haslemere 2885.

**BOOTH, George Macaulay;** *b* 22 Sept. 1877; 2nd *s* of late Rt Hon. Charles Booth and Mary Catherine, *o d* of Charles Zachary Macaulay; *m* 1906, Margaret (*d* 1959), 2nd *d* of late Daniel Meinertzhagen; three *s* three *d*. *Educ:* Harrow; Trinity Coll., Cambridge. Served War of 1914-18. Past Director: White Drummond & Co.; Municipal and General Securities Co. Ltd; Manaos Harbour Ltd; Manaos Tramway and Light Co. Ltd; CAC Ltd. Dep. Dir-Gen., Min. of Munitions, 1914-19; Dir Bank of England, 1915-47; first Chm. Brazilian Chamber of Commerce and Economic Affairs in Great Britain, 1942-45. One of HM Lieuts of the City of London; High Sheriff, City of London. The Order of Stanislov, 1st Class (Russia); Cross of Chevalier of Legion of Honour (France), 1919; Order of the Southern Cross (Brazil), 1947. *Relevant Publication:* A Man of Push and Go: George Macaulay Booth, by Duncan Crow, 1965. *Address:* Funtington Lodge, Chichester, Sussex. *T:* West Ashling 205. *Club:* Reform.

**BOOTH, Gordon,** CMG 1969; Director, Coordination of Export Services, Board of Trade, since 1969; *b* 22 Nov. 1921; *s* of Walter and Grace Booth, Bolton, Lancs; *m* 1944, Jeanne Mary Kirkham; one *s* one *d*. *Educ:* Canon Slade Sch.; London Univ. (BCom). Served War of 1939-45: Capt. RAC and 13/18th Royal Hussars, 1941-46. Min. of Labour and Bd of Trade, 1946-55; Trade Comr, Canada and West Indies, 1955-65; Mem. HM Diplomatic Service, 1965-; Counsellor (Commercial), British Embassy in Copenhagen, 1966-69. *Recreations:* golf, bridge. *Address:* c/o Foreign and Commonwealth Office, SW1.

**BOOTH, James; His Honour Judge Booth;** a County Court Judge since 1969; *b* 3 May 1914; *s* of James and Agnes Booth; *m* 1954, Joyce Doreen Mather; two *s* one *d*. *Educ:* Bolton Sch.; Manchester Univ. Called to Bar, Gray's Inn, 1936 (Arden Scholar, Gray's Inn). Town Clerk, Ossett, Yorks, 1939-41. RAFVR, 1941-46 (Flt-Lieut). Contested (L): West Leeds, 1945; Darwen, 1950. Recorder of Barrow-in-Furness, 1967-69. *Recreation:* fell walking. *Address:* Spinney End, Worsley, Lancs. *T:* 061-790 2003. *Club:* Manchester (Manchester).

**BOOTH, John Wells;** Chairman, Alfred Booth & Co. Ltd.; Director: Phoenix Assurance Co. Ltd.; Unit Construction Co. Ltd.; *b* 19 May 1903; *s* of late Charles and Grace Wells Booth, Liverpool; *m* 1929, Margaret, *d* of late S. J. Lawry, Plympton, Devon, and of Mrs Susan Lawry; two *s* one *d*. *Educ:* Royal Naval Colls Osborne and Dartmouth. Royal Navy, 1917-25 (Lieut Comdr). Booth Steamship Co. Ltd., 1926-45 (Chm., 1939-45). Civil Aviation, 1945-50. Chm., British South American Airways Corporation, 1946-49; Dep. Chm., BOAC, 1949-50; Bd Mem., BOAC, 1950-65. Former Chairman: Liverpool Seamens' Welfare Cttee (Mem. Seamens' Welfare Bd); Liverpool Steamship Owners' Assoc.; former JP for Co. of Cheshire. *Address:* Park House, Easebourne, Midhurst, Sussex. *T:* Midhurst 3285. *Clubs:* Royal Automobile, Reform; Nairobi (Nairobi).

**BOOTH, Sir Michael Savile Gore-,** 7th Bt, *cr* 1760; *b* 24 July 1908; *s* of 6th Bt and Mary (*d* 1968), *d* of Rev. S. L'Estrage-Malone; *S* father, 1944. *Educ:* Rugby; Trinity Coll., Cambridge. *Heir: b* Angus Josslyn Gore-Booth [*b* 25 June 1920; *m* 1948, Hon. Rosemary Vane (marr. diss., 1954), *o d* of 10th Baron Barnard; one *s* one *d*]. *Address:* Lissadell, Sligo.

**BOOTH, W. S.;** retired as Headmaster of the Borlase School, Marlow, Bucks (1927-56); *b* 1896. *Educ:* Manchester Grammar Sch.; Manchester Univ. Former Senior Classical Master Blackburn Grammar Sch. *Address:* 24 Burford Road, Stratford-on-Avon.

**BOOTH-GRAVELY, Sir Walter,** KCMG, *cr* 1939; CSI 1936; CIE 1931; late ICS; *b* 22 May 1882; *m* 1939, Dorothy Faickney. *Educ:* Daniel Stewart's Coll. and Univ., Edinburgh; Trinity Coll., Oxford. Entered Indian Civil Service, 1906; Chief Sec. to Government, Burma, 1932; Governor's Counsellor, Burma, 1937-40. *Address:* 11 Elliot Place, Edinburgh 11. *T:* 031-441 3215.

**BOOTHBY,** family name of **Baron Boothby.**

**BOOTHBY,** Baron *cr* 1958, of Buchan and Rattray Head (Life Peer); **Robert John Graham Boothby,** KBE 1953; President, Anglo-Israel Association; *b* 1900; *o s* of late Sir Robert Tuite Boothby, KBE, Beechwood, Edinburgh, and Mabel, *d* of late H. H. Lancaster; *m* 1st, 1935, Diana (marr. diss. 1937), *d* of late Lord Richard Cavendish, PC, CB, CMG; 2nd, 1967, Wanda, *d* of Giuseppe Sanna, Sardinia. *Educ:* Eton; Magdalen Coll., Oxford. ba 1921, MA 1959. Contested Orkney and Shetland, 1923; MP (U) East Aberdeenshire, 1924-58; Parliamentary Private Sec. to the Chancellor of the Exchequer (Rt Hon. Winston S. Churchill, MP), 1926-29; Parliamentary Sec., Ministry of Food, 1940-41; a British delegate to the Consultative Assembly of the Council of Europe, 1949-57; Vice-Chm. Cttee on Economic Affairs, 1952-56; Hon. Pres., Scottish Chamber of Agriculture, 1934. Rector, University of St Andrews, 1958-61. Chairman, Royal Philharmonic Orchestra, 1961-63; Founder Mem., Royal Philharmonic Orchestra Assoc. Radner Lectr, Columbia Univ., NY, 1960. Hon. LLD St Andrews, 1959. Hon. Burgess of the Burghs of Peterhead, Fraserburgh, Turriff and Rosehearty. Officer of the Legion of Honour, 1950. *Publications:* The New Economy, 1943; I Fight to Live, 1947; My Yesterday, Your Tomorrow, 1962. *Address:* 1 Eaton Square, SW1. *Clubs:* White's; Royal and Ancient (St Andrews).

**BOOTHBY, Basil;** *see* Boothby, E. B.

**BOOTHBY, (Evelyn) Basil,** CMG 1958; HM Diplomatic Service, retired; Lecturer, Morley College, since 1969; *b* 9 Sept. 1910; *s* of Basil T. B. Boothby and Katherine Knox; *m* 1946, Susan Asquith; three *s* one *d*. *Educ:* Winchester; CCC, Cambridge. Student Interpreter, China Consular Service, 1933; appointed a Vice-Consul in China, 1936; served at Shanghai and Hankow (periods Acting Consul); Vice-Consul, Boston, 1940; employed at New York, Dec. 1941-June 1942, when reappointed a Vice-Consul in China and transf. to Chungking; seconded to Govt of India for service in Chinese Relations Office, Calcutta, Oct. 1943-July 1944; Actg Consul Kweilin and Kunming, also Athens, successively, 1944-45; promoted Consul, Sept. 1945; apptd Foreign Service Officer, Grade 7, in Foreign Office, Nov. 1946; promoted Counsellor, Foreign Service Officer, Grade 6, and became Head of UN (Economic and Social) Dept, Sept. 1949; seconded to Commonwealth Relations Office for service in Ontario and attached to Canadian National Defence Coll., Sept. 1950; apptd Counsellor, Rangoon, Nov. 1951 (Chargé d'Affaires, 1952); Counsellor, British Embassy, Brussels, 1954; Head of African Dept, Foreign Office, 1959; British Ambassador to Iceland, 1962-65; Permanent British Rep. to Council of Europe, 1965-69. *Address:* 23 Holland Park Avenue, W11.

**BOOTHBY, Sir Hugo (Robert Brooke),** 15th Bt, *cr* 1660; JP; Vice-Lieutenant, Glamorgan, since 1957; *b* 10 Aug. 1907; *s* of Sir Seymour William Brooke Boothby, 14th Bt, and Clara Margaret (*d* 1969), *d* of late Robert Valpy; *S* father 1951; *m* 1938, Evelyn Ann, *o d* of H. C. R. Homfray; one *s* two *d*. *Educ:* Lancing; Hertford Coll., Oxford. Served War of 1939-45, Capt. RA 53 (Welsh) Div., 1942-44. Capt. RA (TA). Dir, Wales Tourist Bd, 1965. S Wales Regional Dir, Lloyds Bank, 1963; Member: Cardiff Rural Dist Council, 1936-58 (Chm. 1948-49 and 1949-50); Representative Body, Church in Wales, 1955; National Broadcasting Council for Wales, 1953-56; Glamorgan County Agricultural Executive Cttee, 1953-62. Fellow, Woodard Corporation, 1961-. JP 1950, DL 1953, Glamorgan; High Sheriff, Glamorgan, 1953. *Heir: s* Brooke Charles Boothby, *b* 6 April 1949. *Address:* Fonmon Castle, Barry, Glamorgan CF6 9ZN. *T:* Rhoose 206. *Club:* Cardiff and County (Cardiff).

**BOOTHE, Clare;** *see* Luce, Mrs Henry R.

**BOOTHROYD, Edith Hester, (Mrs Francis Boothroyd);** Under-Secretary, Treasury, since 1969; *b* 11 Jan. 1915; *d* of late Stanley John Benham; *m* 1940, Francis Boothroyd; two *d*. *Educ:* St Felix Sch., Southwold; Newnham Coll., Cambridge. Min. of Economic Warfare, 1939-44; BoT, 1945-49; Statistician and Prin., Treasury, 1949-64; Asst Sec., DEA, 1965-67, Asst Under-Sec. of State, 1967-69. *Recreations:* gardening, music, travel. *Address:*

82 Elm Park Road, SW3. *T:* 01-352 3278; Adwell Cottage, Postcombe, Oxon.

**BOOTHROYD, (John) Basil;** an Assistant Editor, Punch; *b* 4 March 1910; *m* 1939, Phyllis Barbara Youngman; one *s*. *Educ:* Lincoln Cathedral Choir Sch.; Lincoln Sch. Bank Clerk, 1927. Served with RAF Police, 1941-45; Personal Asst to Provost-Marshal from 1943. Punch contributor continuously from 1938; joined Punch staff, 1952, Mem. Punch Table, 1955. Much broadcasting and miscellaneous frivolous journalism; some television, lecturing and public speaking. *Publications:* Home Guard Goings-On, 1941; Adastral Bodies, 1942; Are Sergeants Human? 1945; Are Officers Necessary?, 1946; Lost, A Double-Fronted Shop, 1947; The House About a Man, 1959; Motor If You Must, 1960; To My Embarrassment, 1961; The Whole Thing's Laughable, 1964; A Word in Public, 1965; You Can't be Serious, 1966; Let's Stay Married, 1967 (and US, 1967); Stay Married Abroad, 1968. Boothroyd at Bay (radio talks), 1970. *Recreations:* playing the piano, working. *Address:* Green Ridges, Cuckfield, Sussex. *T:* Haywards Heath 4340. *Clubs:* Savage, New Arts, BBC, Cowdray.

**BOOTLE-WILBRAHAM,** family name of **Baron Skelmersdale.**

**BOR, Max;** *see under* Adrian, Max.

**BOR, Norman Loftus,** CIE 1945; OBE 1957; MA; DSc; FNI; FLS; FRSE; Assistant Director, Royal Gardens, Kew, retired; formerly Indian Forest Service (Conservator of Forests), retired; *b* 2 May 1893; 2nd *s* of late E. N. C. Bor and Mabel Thornton, Kilcoran House, Callan, County Kilkenny, Eire (of Dutch descent); *m* 1931, Eleanor Constance (*d* 1957), *d* of late Rev. J. W. Rundall, St Ninian's, Moffat; no *c*. *Educ:* Kilkenny Coll.; Mountjoy Sch., Dublin; Dublin and Edinburgh Univs. Served European War, 1914-18, in Connaught Rangers, Capt. (wounded). Indian Forest Service, 1921, Assam; Forest Botanist, Forest Research Institute, Dehra Dun, UP, 1937-42. Chief Refugee Administrator, Assam, 1943-46; in charge rehabilitation, Naga Hills and Manipur State, 1944-46. Pres., Botany Sect., Indian Science Congress, 1942; Pres., Indian Botanical Soc., 1945. Paul Johannes Brühl Medal, Royal Asiatic Society of Bengal, 1945; Linnean Gold Medal, 1962. *Publications:* Manual of Indian Forest Botany; Beautiful Indian Shrubs and Climbers (with M. B. Raizada); Grasses of Burma, Ceylon, India and Pakistan, 1960; over 100 papers on botanical subjects. *Recreations:* botany and walking. *Address:* 20 Royston Court, Lichfield Road, Kew, Richmond, Surrey. *T:* 01-940 5838; Lloyds Bank, Cox's and King's Branch, 6 Pall Mall, SW1.

*See also Max Adrian.*

**BORDEN, Henry,** CMG 1943; QC 1938; LLD 1960; DCL 1960; Canadian Lawyer; Chairman: Canadian Board, Norwich Union Life Insurance Society; Norwich Union Fire Insurance Society; Canada Security Assurance Co.; Director: British Newfoundland Corporation Ltd; Bell, Canada; Canadian Imperial Bank of Commerce; Canadian Investment Fund Ltd; Canadian Fund Incorporated; Churchill Falls (Labrador) Corporation Ltd; Huron and Erie Mortgage Corporation; International Business Machines Co. Ltd; Massey-Ferguson; Tinto Holdings Canada Ltd; Rio Algom Mines Ltd; Brascan Ltd; Maple Leaf Gardens Ltd; *b* Halifax, NS, 25 Sept. 1901; *s* of Henry Clifford and Mabel (Ashmere) Barnstead Borden, both of Halifax, NS; *m* 1929, Jean Creelman, *d* of late Dr D. A. MacRae, Toronto, Ont; three *s* two *d*. *Educ:* King's Coll. Sch., Windsor, NS; McGill Univ.; Dalhousie Law Sch.; Exeter Coll., Oxford (Rhodes Schol.). BA Political Science and Economics, McGill, 1921; BA Oxon, 1926. With Royal Bank of Canada, 1921-22. Called to Bar, Lincoln's Inn, 1927; to Bar of Nova Scotia, 1927; to Bar of Ont, 1927. Senior Mem., Borden, Elliot, Kelley, Palmer, 1936-46; Gen. Counsel, Dept of Munitions and Supply, Ottawa, 1939-42; Chairman: Wartime Industries Control Bd, Ottawa, and Co-ordinator of Controls, Dept of Munitions and Supply, Sept. 1942; Royal Commission on Energy, 1957-59; Mem. Advisory Bd, Industrial Estates Ltd. Hon. Pres., Royal Agric. Winter Fair. Formerly Lectr, Corp. Law, Osgoode Hall Law Sch.; Past Pres. Canadian Club of Toronto. Hon. Chm., Bd of Governors, Univ. of Toronto. Is an Anglican. Grand Officer, Nat. Order of the Southern Cross (Brazil), 1962. *Publications:* (jtly) Fraser & Borden, Hand Book of Canadian Companies, 1931; ed Robert Laird Borden: His Memoirs. *Recreations:* farming, fishing. *Address:* Tannery Hill Farm, RR No 2, King, Ont., Canada. *Clubs:* York, Toronto (Toronto).

**BORDER, Hugh William;** *b* 26 Nov. 1890; *s* of William Border and Mary Abbott; *m* 1917, Mabel Evelyn Watts; one *d*. *Educ:* Latymer Upper Sch., Hammersmith. Employed in the Ministry of Labour, 1912-14; Consulate-Gen., Rotterdam 1914-20; Probationer Vice-Consul at Colon, July 1920; Acting Consul, 1921 and 1923; Acting Vice-Consul at Constantsa and Braila, 1924; Vice-Consul at Braila, 1924; Acting Consul-Gen., Galatz, 1925 and 1926; Vice-Consul, 1926; Acting Consul-General, Galatz, 1927, 1928 and 1929; Chargé d'Affaires a.i., Managua, 1930; HM Consul, Managua, July 1930; HM Consul-Gen. (local rank) Havana, 1932; Chargé d'Affaires, Havana, Feb.-June 1933; HM Consul, Havre, 1934-37; HM Consul, Bordeaux, 1937; HM Consul Nantes, 1939-40; HM Consul-Gen. at Seville, 1945-50; retired, 1950. *Address:* 36 Bonfields Avenue, Swanage, Dorset. *T:* Swanage 2508.

**BOREEL, Sir Francis (David),** 13th Bt, *cr* 1645; Counsellor, Netherlands Foreign Service, since 1966 (Attaché, 1956); *b* 14 June 1926; *s* of Sir Alfred Boreel, 12th Bt and Countess Reiniera Adriana (*d* 1957), *d* of Count Francis David Schimmelpenninck; *S* father 1964; *m* 1964, Suzanne Campagne; two *d*. *Educ:* Utrecht Univ. *Recreations:* tennis, sailing. *Heir: kinsman* Gerard Lucas Boreel [*b* 23 July 1913; *m* 1943, Virginia Bright; two *s* one *d*]. *Address:* Netherlands Embassy, Untere Donanstrasse 13/15, Vienna II, Austria.

**BOREHAM, Arthur John;** Head of Economic and Statistical Analysis Division, Ministry of Technology, since 1967; *b* 30 July 1925; 3rd *s* of late Ven. Frederick Boreham, Archdeacon of Cornwall and Chaplain to the Queen, and late Caroline Mildred Boreham; *m* 1948, Heather, *o d* of Harold Edwin Horth, FRIBA, and Muriel Horth; three *s* one *d*. *Educ:* Marlborough; Trinity Coll., Oxford. Agricultural Economics Research Inst., Oxford, 1950; Min. of Food, 1951; Min. of Agric., 1952; Gen. Register Office, 1955; Central Statistical Office, 1958; Chief Statistician, Gen. Register Office, 1963. *Recreation:* music. *Address:* Piperscroft, Brittain's Lane, Sevenoaks, Kent. *T:* Sevenoaks 54678.

**BOREHAM, Leslie Kenneth Edward,** QC 1965; Barrister-at-law; Recorder of Margate since 1968; Chairman of East Suffolk Quarter Sessions since 1965 (Deputy Chairman, 1962-65); Deputy Chairman, Agricultural Lands

Tribunal; *m*; one *s* one *d*. Served War of 1939-45, RAF. Called to the Bar at Lincoln's Inn, Nov. 1947. Joined South-Eastern Circuit. *Recreations:* gardening, golf. *Address:* 1 Paper Buildings, Temple, EC4.

**BORG COSTANZI, Prof. Edwin J.;** Vice-Chancellor and Rector Magnificus, Royal University of Malta, since 1964; *b* 8 Sept. 1925; 2nd *s* of late Michael Borg Costanzi and M. Stella (*née* Camilleri); *m* 1948, Lucy Valentino; two *s* one *d*. *Educ:* Lyceum, Malta; Royal University of Malta; Balliol College, Oxford. Malta Rhodes Scholar, 1945. Appointed Professor of Mathematics, Royal University of Malta, 1950. *Recreations:* fishing, photography. *Address:* 35 Don Rua Street, Sliema, Malta. *T:* 32958. *Club:* Casino Maltese (Valletta, Malta).

**BORG OLIVIER, George,** LLD; Prime Minister and Minister of Commonwealth and Foreign Affairs, Malta, since 1965; Leader of the Nationalist Party, Malta, since 1950; *b* 5 July 1911; *s* of Oliviero Borg Olivier, Architect and Civil Engineer; *m* 1943, Alexandra (*née* Mattei); two *s* one *d*. *Educ:* Lyceum and Royal University of Malta. Mem. of Council of Government, Malta, 1939-45; Mem. of Legislative Assembly, 1947; Minister of Works and Reconstruction, 1950-55; Minister of Education, and of Justice, 1950-51; Prime Minister, 1950-55; Leader of the Opposition, 1955-58; Minister of Economic Planning and Finance, 1962-65. Hon. DLitt, Royal University Malta, 1964. Kt Grand Cross: Order of St Sylvester, 1962; Order of Pope Pius IX, 1964. *Address:* Auberge d'Aragon, Valetta, Malta. *T:* 25231.

**BORINGDON, Viscount; Mark Lionel Parker;** *b* 22 Aug. 1956; *s* and *heir* of 6th Earl of Morley, *qv*.

**BORLAND, David Morton;** Chairman, Cadbury Ltd; Director, Cadbury Schweppes Ltd; *b* 17 Jan. 1911; *s* of David and Annie J. Borland; *m* 1947, Nessa Claire Helwig; one *s* one *d*. *Educ:* Glasgow Academy; Brasenose Coll., Oxford (BA). Management Trainee, etc., Cadbury Bros Ltd, Bournville, Birmingham, 1933. War service, Royal Marines (Lieut-Col), 1940-46. Sales Manager, J. S. Fry & Sons Ltd, Somerdale, Bristol, 1946; Sales Dir and a Man. Dir, J. S. Fry & Sons Ltd, 1948; a Man. Dir, British Cocoa & Chocolate Co. Ltd, 1959, and of Cadbury Bros Ltd, 1963. Mem. Council of Bristol Univ. and of Univ. Appts Bd, 1962; Mem. Govt Cttee of Inquiry into Fatstock and Meat Marketing and Distribution, 1962. *Recreations:* golf, sailing. *Address:* 130 Bournville Lane, Birmingham 30. *T:* 021-458 4544. *Clubs:* Bath; Achilles; Vincent's (Oxford).

**BORN, Gustav Victor Rudolf;** Vandervell Professor of Pharmacology in the Royal College of Surgeons of England, and in the University of London, since 1960; Hon. Director, MRC Thrombosis Research Group; *b* 29 July 1921; *s* of late Prof. Max Born, FRS; *m* 1st, 1950, Wilfrida Ann Plowden-Wardlaw (marr. diss., 1961); two *s* one *d*; 2nd, 1962, Dr Faith Elizabeth Maurice-Williams; one *s* one *d*. *Educ:* Oberrealschule, Göttingen; Perse Sch., Cambridge; Edinburgh Academy; University of Edinburgh. Vans Dunlop Scholarship and Pattison Prize; MB, ChB, 1943; DPhil (Oxford), 1951, MA 1956. Med. Officer, RAMC, 1943-47; MRC Studentship, 1949-52; Mem. Scientific Staff, MRC, 1952-53; Grad. Asst, later Research Officer (Sen. Grade), Nuffield Inst. for Med. Research, University of Oxford, 1953-60; Deptl Demonstrator in Dept of Pharmacology, 1956-60, and Lectr in Med. Subjects, St Peter's Hall, University of Oxford, 1959-60. Member: Cttee, Brit. Pharmacological Soc., 1961-63; Ed. Board, Pharmacological Reviews; Cttee of Enquiry into Relationship of Pharmaceut. Industry with Nat. Health Service (Sainsbury Cttee), 1965-67. Corresp. Mem., German Pharmacological Soc. *Publications:* chapters in books on general pathology, smooth muscle and Blood Platelets; papers in Jl of Physiology and Brit. Jl of Pharmacology and Chemotherapy. *Recreations:* music, walking. *Address:* Department of Pharmacology, Royal College of Surgeons, Lincoln's Inn Fields, WC2. *T:* 01-405 3474; 58B Redington Road, NW3. *T:* 01-435 7202.

**BORNEMAN, Roy Ernest,** QC 1952; *b* 1904; *s* of Ernest Borneman, London; *m* 1932, Winifred Dixon, *d* of Dr William Hunter, Aberdeen; two *s*. *Educ:* University Coll., Reading; University Coll., London. BA 1924. Called to the Bar, Gray's Inn, 1929; Bencher, 1956. Chm., Board of Referees and Finance Act 1960 Tribunal, 1960. Served War of 1939-45, Wing Comdr, Royal Air Force. *Recreation:* golf. *Address:* 11 New Square, Lincoln's Inn, WC2. *T:* 01-242 4017; Hazelwood, South Ridge, St George's Hill, Weybridge, Surrey; *T:* Weybridge 42414.

**BORODALE, Viscount; David Beatty;** *b* 21 Nov. 1946; *s* of 2nd Earl Beatty, *qv*. *Educ:* Eton. *Address:* Regency Cottage, 5 Rutland Gardens, SW7; Chicheley Hall, Newport Pagnell, Bucks.

**BORRADAILE, Maj.-Gen. Hugh Alastair,** CB 1959; DSO 1946; Vice Adjutant-General, War Office, 1960-63, retired; *b* 22 June 1907; *s* of Lieut-Col B. Borradaile, RE, Walnut Cottage, Wylye, Wilts; *m* 1936, Elizabeth Barbara, *d* of late R. Powell-Williams, Woodcroft, Yelverton, Devon; one *s* one *d*. *Educ:* Wellington Coll.; RMC Sandhurst. Commissioned Devon Regt, 1926; King's African Rifles, 1931-37; Staff Coll., Camberley, 1939; GSO1, GHQ West Africa, 1942-43; CO 5, E Lancs Regt, 1944; Co 7 Somerset LI, 1944-45; GSO1, 30 Corps, 1945; Asst Chief of Staff (Exec.), CCG, 1945-46; CO 1 Devon, 1946-48; Dep. Chief Intelligence Div., CCG, 1948-50; National Defence Coll., Canada, 1950-51; Brig. A/Q AA Command, 1951-53; Comd 24 Inf. Bde, 1953-55; Dept. Military Sec. (A), War Office, 1955-57; Gen. Officer Commanding South-West District and 43rd (Wessex) Infantry Div., TA, 1957-60. Col, Devon and Dorset Regt, 1962-67. *Recreations:* golf, shooting, fishing. *Address:* Almora, Park Avenue, Camberley, Surrey. *T:* Camberley 21827. *Club:* Army and Navy.

**BORRIE, Peter Forbes,** MD, FRCP; Physician in charge of the Skin Department, St Bartholomew's Hospital, since 1968; Consultant Dermatologist to Moorfields, Westminster and Central Eye Hospitals, since 1950, and to Barnet General Hospital since 1954; *b* 26 March 1918; *s* of late Dr David Forbes Borrie and Martha Ruth Downing; *m* 1942, Helen Patricia, *e d* of Major H. G. Chesney; two *s* two *d*. *Educ:* Rugby Sch.; Clare Coll., Cambridge; St Bartholomew's Hospital. BA (Nat. Sci. Tripos) 1939; MB, BChir Cantab 1942; MRCP 1948; FRCP 1960; MA Cantab 1950; MD Cantab 1951. House Physician, St Bartholomew's Hospital, 1942; Senior Registrar, Skin Dept, St Mary's Hospital, Paddington, 1948; Chief Asst, Skin Dept, St Bartholomew's Hospital, 1950. Fellow Royal Society of Medicine; Mem. British Association of Dermatology; Lecturer at the Institute of Dermatology. *Publications:* Editor, Roxburgh's Common Skin Diseases (11th edn, 1959, 12th edn, 1961; 13th edn, 1967); many articles in medical journals. *Address:* 115a Harley Street, W1. *T:* 01-935 6465.

**BORTHWICK, Brig.-Gen. Francis Henry,** CMG 1919; DSO 1918; *b* 1883; *s* of Alexander Borthwick; *m* 1929, Gertrude Anne Frances, *o d* of Milne Keay, Edinburgh. Served European War, 1914-19 (despatches four times, DSO with bar, CMG). *Address:* Broad Close, Rossett Green, Harrogate, Yorks.

**BORTHWICK, Sir John Thomas,** 3rd Bt *cr* 1908; MBE 1945; *b* 5 Dec. 1917; *s* of Hon. James Alexander Borthwick (*d* 1961), and Irene, *d* of late George Wise, Sydney, Australia; *S* to Btcy of uncle (1st and last Baron Whitburgh), 1967; *m* 1st, 1939, Irene (marriage dissolved, 1961), *o c* of Joseph Heller; three *s*; 2nd, 1962, Irene, *d* of Leo Fink; two *s*. *Educ:* Eton; Trinity Coll., Oxford. Formerly Major, Rifle Brigade, TA. Served War of 1939-45 (MBE). *Heir: s* Antony Thomas Borthwick [*b* 12 Feb. 1941; *m* 1966, Gillian Deirdre Broke, *d* of late Lieut Nigel Vere Broke Thurston, RN; one *s* one *d*]. *Address:* Fox Hills, Long Cross, Surrey; 10 Cheyne Gardens, SW3.

**BORWICK,** family name of **Baron Borwick.**

**BORWICK,** 4th Baron, *cr* 1922; **James Hugh Myles Borwick;** Bt *cr* 1916; MC 1945; Major HLI retired; *b* 12 Dec. 1917; *s* of 3rd Baron and Irene Phyllis, *d* of late Thomas Main Paterson, Littlebourne, Canterbury; *S* father 1961; *m* 1954, Hyllarie Adalia Mary, *y d* of late Lieut-Col William Hamilton Hall Johnston, DSO, MC, DL, Bryn-y-Groes, Bala, N Wales; four *d*. *Educ:* Eton; RMC, Sandhurst. Commissioned as 2nd Lieut HLI, 1937; Capt. 1939; Major 1941; retired, 1947. *Recreations:* field sports, sailing and ocean racing. *Heir: half b* Hon. George Sandbach Borwick, *b* 18 Oct. 1922. *Address:* Pentwyn, Clyro, Hereford. *T:* Hay-on-Wye 380. *Clubs:* Caledonian, Royal Automobile, Royal Ocean Racing.

**BORWICK, Lt-Col Sir Thomas Faulkner,** Kt 1946; CIE 1941; DSO 1917; late AIF; MIMechE; BMechE; *b* 1890; *s* of Harry Barton Borwick, Melbourne; *m* 1918, Elsa, *y d* of Eduardo and Fanny de Ambrosis, Florence; one *s* one *d*. *Educ:* Scotch Coll. and University, Melbourne. Served European War, 1914-18 (twice wounded, despatches twice, DSO, Croix de Guerre). Worshipful Master, Kitchener Lodge, Simla, 1939. Chm., Indian Advisory Cttee, Institution of Mechanical Engineers, 1950; Dir-Gen. Ordnance Factories, India, 1943-47; Gen. Manager, National Machinery Manufacturers, Ltd, Bombay, 1947-52; joined The Plessey Co., Ilford, 1952; Divisional Manager, 1957; Group Gen. Manager, 1958; Gen. Manager, Swindon Region, 1959-60. Director: The Amar Tool & Gauge Co., 1958-60; Hawley Products Ltd, 1959-60. Chm. of Governors, Farmor's Sch., Fairford, 1967. *Address:* The New Vicarage, Fairford, Glos. *T:* Fairford 467.

**BOSANQUET, Charles Ion Carr,** MA; Hon DCL (Durham); Hon. LLD (Cincinnati); Vice-Chancellor of University of Newcastle upon Tyne, 1963-68 (Rector of King's College, Newcastle upon Tyne, 1952-63); *b* 19 April 1903; *s* of late Robert Carr Bosanquet and Ellen S. Bosanquet; *m* 1931, Barbara, *d* of late William Jay Schieffelin, New York; one *s* three *d*. *Educ:* Winchester; Trinity Coll., Cambridge (Scholar). Asst Gen. Manager, Friends Provident and Century Life Office, 1933-39; Principal Asst Sec., Ministry of Agriculture and Fisheries, 1941-45; Treasurer of Christ Church, Oxford, 1945-52. High Sheriff of Northumberland, 1948-49; Fellow of Winchester Coll., 1951; Chm., Reorganisation Commission for Pigs and Bacon, 1955-56; Development Comr, 1956-70; Chm. Min. of Agric. Cttee of Enquiry into Demand for Agricultural Graduates. Chm., Carliol Investment Trust. FRSA. Comdr, Order of St Olav. *Address:* Rock Moor, Alnwick, Northumberland. *T:* Charlton Mires 24. *Clubs:* Brooks's; Northern Counties (Newcastle).

**BOSCAWEN,** family name of **Viscount Falmouth.**

**BOSCAWEN, Hon. Robert Thomas,** MC 1944; MP (C) Wells since 1970; *b* 17 March 1923; 4th *s* of 8th Viscount Falmouth and of Dowager Viscountess Falmouth, CBE; *m* 1949, Mary Alice, JP London 1961, *e d* of Col Sir Geoffrey Ronald Codrington, *qv*; one *s* two *d*. *Educ:* Eton; Trinity College, Cambridge. 2nd Lieut, Coldstream Guards, 1942, Captain 1945; served in NW Europe. Mem., London Exec. Council, Nat. Health Service, 1954-65; Underwriting Mem. of Lloyds, 1952-. Contested Falmouth and Camborne (C), 1964, 1966. *Recreation:* sailing. *Address:* 14 Tite Street, SW3. *Clubs:* Pratt's, Royal Yacht Squadron.

**BOSCH, Baron Jean van den;** Belgian Ambassador to the Court of St James's and Belgian Permanent Representative to the Council of Western European Union since 1966; *b* 27 Jan. 1910; *s* of Baron Firmin van den Bosch and Anne de Volder; *m* 1944, Hélène Cloquet; two *d*. *Educ:* Ecole Abbatiale, Maredsous; Notre-Dame de la Paix, Namur; Université Catholique de Louvain. Docteur en droit; licencié en sciences historiques; licencié en sciences politiques et diplomatiques. Entered Belgian Diplomatic Service, 1934; Attaché, London and Paris, 1934; Sec., Pekin, 1937; 1st Sec., Ottawa, 1940; Chargé d'Affaires to Luxembourg Govt in London, 1943; Counsellor, Prince Regent's Household, 1944; Counsellor and Chargé d'Affaires, Cairo, 1948; Counsellor, Chargé d'Affaires, Paris, 1949; Minister, consul-Gen., Hong Kong, Singapore and Saigon, 1954; Ambassador, Cairo, 1955; accredited Minister, Libya, 1956; Sec.-Gen. of Min. of For. Aff. and For. Trade, 1959-June 1960, and again, Sept. 1960; Ambassador, Congo, July-Aug. 1960. Grand Officier, Ordres Léopold, Couronne, Léopold II. Médaille Civique (1st cl.). Holds foreign decorations including GCVO (Hon.), 1966. *Recreations:* golf, sight-seeing. *Address:* 36 Belgrave Square, SW1. *T:* 01-235 1752. *Clubs:* Anglo-Belgian, Beefsteak, St James', Travellers', Turf, White's.

**BOSE, Prof. Satyendranath,** FRS 1958; Emeritus Professor of Physics in the University of Calcutta; National Professor, 1958; *b* 1894. *Educ:* Calcutta Univ. (MSc). Came to Europe, 1924; collaborated with Einstein in discovery of Bose-Einstein law of quantum mechanics. Reader in Physics, later Prof. and Head of Dept, Dacca Univ., 1927-46; Khaira Prof. of Physics, Calcutta Univ., 1946-56. Formerly Vice-Chancellor, Visa-Bharati Univ., India. Chm. Nat. Inst. of Sciences of India, 1948-50; Mem. Governing Body, CSIR, India, 1948-. *Publications:* numerous scientific papers. *Address:* 92 Upper Circular Road, Calcutta 9, India.

**BOSE, Vivian;** *b* Ahmedabad, India, 9 June 1891; *s* of late Lalit Mohun Bose and *g s* of late Sir Bipin Krishna Bose; *m* 1930, Irene, *d* of late Dr John R. Mott (winner of Nobel Prize, 1946); one *s* one *d*. *Educ:* Dulwich Coll.; Pembroke Coll., Cambridge. (BA, LLB). Called to Bar, Middle Temple, 1913; practised at the Nagpur Bar; Principal, University Coll. of Law, Nagpur, 1924-30; Govt Advocate and Standing

Counsel to the Govt of the Central Provinces and Berar, 1930-36; Additional Judicial Commissioner, Nagpur, for short periods, 1931-34; Puisne Judge, Nagpur High Court, 1936-49; Chief Justice, High Court of Judicature, Nagpur, 1949-51; Puisne Judge, Supreme Court of India, New Delhi, 1951-56, retd; recalled as *ad hoc* Judge, Supreme Court, Sept. 1958-Aug. 1959; Chm., two Government Commissions of Inquiry, 1958-62. Member International Commission of Jurists, 1958-; Pres., 1959-66 (Actg Sec.Gen. March-Oct. 1963); Hon. Pres. 1966 (toured, on Commission's behalf: Europe, Asia Minor, Australia, Indonesia, Malaya, Burma, East and West Africa, UK, Ireland, Eire, USA, Brazil, 1961 and 1962-63). Hon. Provincial Sec., Boy Scouts Assoc. Central Provinces and Berar, 1921-34; Provincial Commissioner, 1934-37; Chief Commissioner for India, 1948; National Commissioner, 1959-62; Silver Wolf, 1942; Capt. the Nagpur Regt, Indian Auxiliary Force. Volunteer Long Service Medal, 1929; King's Silver Jubilee Medal, 1935; Kaisar-i-Hind Silver Medal, 1936. *Recreations:* photography, wireless, motoring (from and to India, etc), travel; amateur magic, mainly stage illusions. *Address:* Henessy Road, Nagpur, Mha, India. *Club:* Gondwana (Nagpur).

**BOSSOM, Major Hon. Sir Clive,** 2nd Bt, *cr* 1953; MP (C) Leominster Division of Herefordshire since 1959; *b* 4 Feb. 1918; *s* of late Baron Bossom (Life Peer); *S* to father's Baronetcy, 1965; *m* 1951, Lady Barbara North, *sister* of 9th Earl of Guildford, *qv*; three *s* one *d*. *Educ:* Eton. Regular Army, The Buffs, 1939-48; served Europe and Far East. Kent County Council, 1949-52; Chm. Council Order of St John for Kent, 1951-56; Mem. Jt Cttee, Order of St John and British Red Cross Soc. Contested (C) Faversham Div., 1951 and 1955. Parliamentary Private Secretary: to Jt Parly Secs, Min. of Pensions and Nat. Insce, 1960-62; to Sec. of State for Air, 1962-64; to Minister of Defence for RAF, 1964. President: Anglo-Belgian Union, 1970- (Chm., 1967-70); Industrial Fire Protection Assoc. Liveryman of Worshipful Companies of Grocers, Paviors, Needlemakers. FRSA; KStJ 1961; Comdr, Order of Leopold II. *Recreation:* travel. *Heir: s* Bruce Charles Bossom, *b* 22 Aug. 1952. *Address:* Parsons Orchard, Eastnor, near Ledbury, Herefordshire. *T:* Ledbury 2318; 3 Eaton Mansions, Cliveden Place, SW1. *T:* 01-730 1108. *Clubs:* Carlton, Royal Automobile, MCC; Farmers' (Hereford).

**BOSTOCK, James Edward,** RE 1961 (ARE 1947); ARCA London; Academic Development Officer, Bristol Polytechnic, since 1970; *b* Hanley, Staffs, 11 June 1917; *s* of William George Bostock, pottery and glass-worker, and Amy (*née* Titley); *m* 1939, Gwladys Irene (*née* Griffiths); three *s*. *Educ:* Borden Grammar Sch., Sittingbourne; Royal College of Art. War Service as Sgt in Durham LI and Royal Corps of Signals. Full-time Teacher, 1946-; Vice-Principal, West of England Coll. of Art, 1965-70. Elected Mem. of Soc. of Wood Engravers, 1950. Mem. Council. Soc. of Staffs Artists, 1963. Exhibited water-colours, etchings, wood engravings and drawings at RA, NEAC, RBA, and other group exhibitions and in travelling exhibitions to Poland, Czechoslovakia, South Africa, Far East, New Zealand, USA, and the provinces. Works bought by V & A Museum, British Museum, British Council, Hull, Swindon, Stoke-on-Trent and Bristol Education Cttees and private collectors. Commissioned work for: ICI Ltd, British Museum (Nat. Hist.), Odhams Press, and other firms and public authorities. *Publications:* Roman Lettering for Students, 1959; articles in: Times, Guardian, Staffordshire Sentinel, Studio, Artist. *Address:* 16 Claremont Road, Bishopston, Bristol 7. *T:* Bristol 47376.

**BOSTOCK, Canon Peter Geoffrey,** MA; Assistant Secretary, Missionary and Ecumenical Council of Church Assembly, since 1967; Canon Emeritus, Diocese of Mombasa, 1958; *b* 24 Dec. 1911; *s* of Geoffrey Bostock; *m* 1937, Elizabeth Rose; two *s* two *d*. *Educ:* Charterhouse; The Queen's Coll., Oxon; Wycliffe Hall, Oxon. Deacon, 1935; Priest, 1937; CMS Kenya, 1935-58; became Canon of Diocese of Mombasa, 1952; Archdeacon, 1953-58; Vicar-Gen., 1955-58. Examining Chaplain to Bishop of Mombasa, 1950-58; Chm., Christian Council of Kenya, 1957-58; Archdeacon of Doncaster and Vicar, High Melton, 1959-67. *Recreations:* home and photography. *Address:* 10 Moreton Road, Oxford. *T:* Oxford 55460. *Clubs:* Royal Commonwealth Society; Vincent's (Oxford).

**BOSTON,** 8th Baron *cr* 1761; Bt 1704; **Cecil Eustace Irby,** MC 1917; DL; *b* 14 July 1897; *yr s* of Hon. Cecil Saumares Irby (*s* of 5th Baron); *S* brother 1958. *Educ:* Eton; RMC Service European War (MC). Grenadier Guards, 1916-35; R of O, 1935-39; Gren. Gds, 1939-48. Major (Retd). DL Anglesey, 1960. *Heir: cousin* Gerald Howard Boteler Irby, MBE [*b* 29 Aug. 1897; *m* 1st, 1926 (marr. diss.); one *d*; 2nd, 1936, Erica Hill; one *s*]. *Address:* Cae'r Borth, Moelfre, Anglesey. *T:* Moelfre 249. *Clubs:* Guards, Royal Automobile.

**BOSTON, David Merrick,** MA; Curator, Horniman Museum and Library, London, since 1965; *b* 15 May 1931; *s* of Dr H. M. Boston, Salisbury; *m* 1961, Catharine, *d* of Rev. Dr E. G. Parrinder; one *s* two *d*. *Educ:* Rondesbosch, Cape Town; Bishop Wordsworth's, Salisbury; Selwyn Coll., Cambridge; Univ. of Cape Town. BA History Cantab 1954; MA 1958. RAF, 1950-51; Adjt, Marine Craft Trng School. Field survey, S African Inst. of Race Relations, 1955; Keeper of Ethnology, Liverpool Museums, 1956-62; Asst Keeper, British Museum, New World archaeology and ethnography, 1962-65. Mem. Council: Museums Assoc., 1969; Royal Anthropological Inst., 1969. Vis. Scientist, National Museum of Man, Ottawa, 1970. FRAS; FRGS. *Publications:* contribs to learned jls and encyclopaedias and on Pre-European America, in World Ceramics (ed R. J. Charleston). *Address:* 10 Oakleigh Park Avenue, Chislehurst, Kent. *T:* 01-467 1049.

**BOSTON, Terence George;** *b* 21 March 1930; *yr surv s* of George T. Boston and Kate (*née* Bellati); *m* 1962, Margaret Joyce, *er d* of late R. H. J. Head and of Mrs H. F. Winters, and step *d* of late H. F. Winters, Melbourne, Australia. *Educ:* Woolwich Polytechnic Sch.; King's Coll., University of London. Dep. President (for a time Acting Pres.), University of London Union, 1955-56. Commnd in RAF during Nat. Service, 1950-52; later trained as pilot with University of London Air Sqdn. Called to the Bar, Inner Temple, 1960. BBC News Sub-Editor, External Services, 1957-60; Senior BBC Producer (Current Affairs), 1960-64; also Producer of Law in Action series (Third Programme), 1962-64. Joined Labour Party, 1946; contested (Lab) Wokingham, 1955 and 1959; MP (Lab) Faversham, Kent, June 1964-70; PPS to: Minister of Public Building and Works, 1964-66; Minister of Power, 1966-68; Minister of Transport, 1968-69; Asst Govt Whip, 1969-70. Member: Executive Cttee, International Union of Socialist Youth, 1950; Nat. Cttee, Council for

Education in World Citizenship (UNA), 1950-51; Standing Joint Cttee on New Towns, 1954-59; Fabian Soc.; Soc. of Labour Lawyers; Nat. Union of Journalists; Nat. Union of General and Municipal Workers; Select Cttee on Broadcasting Proceedings of Parliament, 1966; Select Cttee on Armed Forces Bill, 1966; Speaker's Conference on Electoral Law, 1965-67. Founder Vice-Chm., Great Britain-East Europe Centre, 1967-69. *Recreations:* flying, opera (going, not singing). *Address:* 3 Manwood Close, Sittingbourne, Kent. *T:* Sittingbourne 72303.

**BOSVILLE MACDONALD OF Sleat, Sir Ian Godfrey,** 17th Bt, *cr* 1625; 25th Chief of Sleat; *b* 18 July 1947; *er s* of Sir (Alexander) Somerled Angus Bosville Macdonald of Sleat, 16th Bt, MC, 24th Chief of Sleat and of Mary, Lady Bosville Macdonald of Sleat; *S* father 1958; *m* 1970, Juliet Fleury, *o d* of Maj.-Gen. J. M. D. Ward-Harrison, *qv*. *Educ:* Pinewood Sch.; Eton Coll. *Heir:* *b* James Alexander Bosville Macdonald of Sleat, *b* 11 April 1949. *Recreations:* ornithology, riding. *Address:* Thorpe Hall, Rudston, Driffield, Yorkshire. *T:* Kilham 239.

*See also Miss C. V. B. Macdonald of Sleat.*

**BOSWALL, Sir Thomas;** *see* Houstoun-Boswall.

**BOSWELL, Captain Lennox Albert Knox,** DSO 1940; RN (retired); fruit farmer since 1950; *b* 18 May 1898; 3rd *s* of William Albert Boswell and Florence Helen Rotch; *m* 1942, Diana de Lacy Bacon; three *s* (and one *d* decd). *Educ:* RN Colleges, Osborne and Dartmouth. Cadet and Midshipman HMS Irresistible, 1914-15, Belgian Coast and Dardanelles; Midshipman and Sub-Lieut HMS Queen Elizabeth, 1915-19, Flagship of Admiral Sir D. Beatty; surrender of High Sea Fleet, Nov. 1918; Trinity Coll., Cambridge, 1919, First Trinity VIII Henley; qualified in Gunnery, 1923; Comdr 1933; Comdr "G" HMS Excellent, 1933-35; Fleet Gunnery Officer, Home Fleet, 1936-37; RN Staff Coll., 1935; RAF Staff Coll., 1938; War of 1939-45, commanded HMS Pelican, 1939-41; Captain 1940; Ordnance Board and Gunnery Div. Admiralty, 1941-43; Hedgehog and VT Fuse Trials; commanded aircraft carriers HMS Dasher and HMS Biter, 1943-44; Chief of Staff to Flag Officer Western Mediterranean and BNLO, Algiers, 1944-45; commanded RN Air Station Halesworth (HMS Sparrowhawk), 1945-46; commanded HMS Kenya (A and WI Station), 1946-48; Chief of Staff to C-in-C, The Nore, 1948-49; retired 1950. *Recreations:* gardening, music, colour cinematography. *Address:* Holts, Bosham, Chichester, Sussex. *T:* Bosham 3092. *Clubs:* United Service, Ski Club of Great Britain.

**BOSWORTH, George Herbert;** retired; *b* 17 May 1896; *s* of John Henry Bosworth. *Educ:* Peter Symonds, Winchester; University of Southampton. Served European War: RNAS and RAF; Air Ministry, 1919; Private Secretary to Marshal of RAF Sir Cyril (later Lord) Newall, 1932; Asst Secretary, 1939; Dir of Housing, Ministry of Aircraft Production, 1940; Asst Secretary Min. of Works, 1944; Under Secretary, 1952-59. *Publications:* How To Be Happy in France, 1930; Prelude (novel), 1932; Where Shall We Go?, 1939. *Recreations:* music, salmon fishing. *Address:* 31 Church Street, Willingdon, Eastbourne, Sussex. *Club:* National Liberal.

**BOSWORTH, John Michael Worthington,** FCA; Vice-Chairman, British Railways Board, since 1968; Chairman, British Rail Engineering Ltd; *b* 22 June 1921; *s* of Humphrey Worthington Bosworth and Vera Hope Bosworth; *m* 1955, Patricia Mary Edith Wheelock; one *s* one *d*. *Educ:* Bishop's Stortford Coll. Served Royal Artillery, 1939-46. Peat, Marwick, Mitchell & Co., 1949-68; Partner, 1960. *Recreations:* skiing and vintage cars. *Address:* The Folly, Blindley Heath, Lingfield, Surrey. *Club:* Royal Automobile.

**BOSWORTH, Neville Bruce Alfred;** Director: Dares Estates Ltd; National Exhibition Centre Ltd; Senior Partner, Bosworth, Bailey Cox & Co., Solicitors, Birmingham; *b* 18 April 1918; *s* of W. C. N. Bosworth; *m* 1945, Charlotte Marian Davis; one *s* two *d*. *Educ:* King Edward's Sch., Birmingham; Birmingham Univ. LLB. Admitted Solicitor, 1941. Birmingham City Council, 1950-: Councillor (Erdington Ward), 1950-61; Alderman, 1961-; Chm., Gen. Purposes Cttee, 1966-69; Lord Mayor of Birmingham, 1969-70; Dep. Mayor, 1970-71. Trustee, several charitable trusts; Mem. Council, Birmingham Univ.; Governor King Edward VI Schools, Birmingham, Chm., Sutton Coldfield Conservative and Unionist Assoc., 1963-66; Vice-Pres., Birmingham and Dist Property Owners Assoc. *Recreations:* politics, football (Dir, Birmingham City Football Club Ltd). *Address:* Hollington, Luttrell Road, Four Oaks, Sutton Coldfield, Warwickshire. *T:* 021-308 0647; 54 Newhall Street, Birmingham 3. *T:* 021-236 8091. *Club:* St Paul's (Birmingham).

**BOTHA, Colin Graham,** MA, LLD; FSA; FRHistS; VD; Lieut-Col retired list; formerly Chief Archivist for Union of South Africa; *b* Knysna, Cape Colony, 15 Aug. 1883; *y s* of late Rev. Michiel Christiaan Botha and Elizabeth Mary Young; *m*; two *s* one *d*. *Educ:* Cape Town. Entered Civil Service of the Cape Colony, 1901; Keeper of Archives of Cape Province, 1912; first Chief Archivist, 1919; retired, 1944; Member of the Archives Commn, 1922-; President: SA National Soc. for preservation of hist. objects; The Heraldry Soc. of Southern Africa; Member War Histories Cttee Union; Past President SA Assoc. for Advancement of Science; Fellow Huguenot Soc., London; Fellow Genealogical Soc., London; Member of various South African and Dutch literary societies, etc; sent by Union Government of South Africa to Europe, USA, and Canada, 1920-21, to examine into system of keeping Archives; visited Europe, USA and Canada again in 1938 to examine into archival systems; was at first Assembly League of Nations, 1920; was OC Duke of Edinburgh's Own Rifles; served South African War, 1901; 1914-18; Chief Recruiting Officer, Cape Fortress Command, War of 1939-45; over 42 years service with Volunteers and Active Citizen Force. KJStJ; awarded Carnegie Visitors' Grant, 1938. Hon. LLD: Cape Town, 1943; Witwatersrand, 1952. *Publications:* Place Names in Cape District, 1917; A Brief Guide to the Documents in the Cape Archives, 1652-1806, 1918; The French Refugees at the Cape, 1919 (second edition, 1921, Afrikaans translation, 1939); Report of a Tour to various Archives in Europe, Canada and USA, 1921; Social Life in the Cape Colony in the 18th Century, 1927; Place Names in the Cape Province, 1927; The Public Archives of South Africa, 1652-1910, 1928; The Romance of Our Roads for Two Centuries, 1937; Our South Africa, Past and Present, 1938; Collected Writings (from 1912, 3 vols), 1962; edited 5th vol. of van Riebeeck Society Publications; articles in SA Law Journal and Science Journal; contributor to various magazines, and newspapers. *Recreations:* reading, writing. *Address:* Nairn, Isobel Avenue, Newlands, CP, S Africa. *Clubs:* Authors' (London); Civil Service (Cape Town).

**BOTTOMLEY, Rt. Hon. Arthur George,** PC 1951; OBE 1941; MP (Lab) East Division of Middlesbrough since 1962; *b* 7 Feb. 1907; *s* of George Howard Bottomley and his late wife Alice; *m* 1936, Bessie Ellen Wiles (see Dame Bessie Bottomley); no *c. Educ:* Gamuel Road Council Sch.; Extension Classes at Toynbee Hall. London Organiser of National Union of Public Employees, 1935-45, 1959-62. Walthamstow Borough Council, 1929-49; Mayor of Walthamstow, 1945-46; Chairman of Emergency Cttee and ARP Controller, 1939-41. Dep. Regional Commissioner for S-E England, 1941-45. MP (Lab) Chatham Division of Rochester, 1945-50, Rochester and Chatham 1950-59. Parliamentary Under-Secretary of State for Dominions, 1946-47; Sec. for Overseas Trade, Board of Trade, 1947-51; Sec. of State for Commonwealth Affairs, 1964-66; Minister of Overseas Develt, 1966-67. Land Tax Comr, Becontree Div. of Essex; Member: Parliamentary Mission to India, 1946; Special Govt Mission to Burma, 1947; Deleg. to UN, New York, 1946, 1947 and 1949; Leader: UK delegation to World Trade and Employment Conference, Havana, 1947; UK Delegn to Commonwealth Conference, Delhi, 1949; Trade Mission to Pakistan, 1950; Special Mission to West Indies, 1951; Member: Consultative Assembly, Council of Europe, 1952, 1953 and 1954; Special Parliamentary Mission to Kenya, 1954; Parliamentary Mission to Ghana, 1959; Leader: Parliamentary Labour Party Mission to Burma, 1962, to Malaysia, 1963; UK Delegation to CPA Conference, Ottawa, 1966; Member: Parliamentary Mission to Cyprus, 1963; Special Mission to Hong Kong, 1964. Chairman: Commonwealth Relations and Colonies Group, Parly Labour Party, 1963; Select Parly Cttee on Race Relations and Immigration, 1969; Vice Chm., Commonwealth Parly Assoc., 1968. Governor, Commonwealth Inst., 1968. Hon. Freeman of Chatham, 1959. *Publications:* The Use and Abuse of Trade Unions; Two Roads to Colonialism; Why Britain should Join the Common Market. *Recreations:* walking and theatre-going. *Address:* 19 Lichfield Road, Woodford Green, Essex.

**BOTTOMLEY, Dame Bessie (Ellen),** DBE 1970; JP; *b* 28 Nov. 1906; *d* of Edward Charles Wiles and Ellen (*née* Estall); *m* 1936, Rt Hon. Arthur George Bottomley, *qv*; no *c. Educ:* Maynard Road Girls' Sch.; North Walthamstow Central Sch. On staff of NUT, 1925-36. Member: Walthamstow Borough Council, 1945-48; Essex CC, 1962-65; Chm., E Walthamstow Labour Party Women's Section, 1946-. Mem., Forest Group Hosp. Man. Cttee, 1949-. Chm., Walthamstow Nat. Savings Cttee, 1949-65. Mayoress of Walthamstow, 1945-46. Mem., WVS Regional Staff (SE England), 1941-45. Past Mem., Home Office Adv. Cttee on Child Care. Chm. of Govs of two Secondary Modern Schools, 1948-68, also group of Primary and Infant Schools. JP 1955 and on Juvenile Bench. *Recreations:* theatre, gardening. *Address:* 19 Lichfield Road, Woodford Green, Essex.

**BOTTOMLEY, James Reginald Alfred,** CMG 1965; Deputy Under Secretary of State, Foreign and Commonwealth Office; *b* 12 Jan. 1920; *s* of Sir (William) Cecil Bottomley, KCMG, and Alice Thistle Bottomley (*née* Robinson), JP; *m* 1941, Barbara Evelyn (Vardon); two *s* two *d* (and one *s* decd). *Educ:* King's College Sch., Wimbledon; Trinity Coll., Cambridge. Served with Inns of Court Regt, RAC, 1940-46. Dominions Office, 1946; Pretoria, 1948-50; Karachi, 1953-55; Washington, 1955-59; UK Mission to United Nations, 1959; Dep. High Commissioner, Kuala Lumpur 1963-67. *Recreation:* golf. *Address:* Chiltern Rise, Aldbury, Tring, Herts. *T:* Aldbury Common 304. *Club:* East India and Sports.

**BOTTRALL, (Francis James) Ronald,** OBE 1949; MA; FRSL; *b* Camborne, Cornwall, 2 Sept. 1906; *o s* of Francis John and Clara Jane Bottrall; *m* 1st, 1934, Margaret Florence (marr. diss., 1954), *o d* of Rev. H. Saumarez Smith; one *s*; 2nd, 1954, Margot Pamela Samuel. *Educ:* Redruth County Sch.; Pembroke Coll., Cambridge. Foundress' Scholar; First Class English Tripos, Parts I and II (with distinction); Charles Oldham Shakespeare Scholarship, 1927. Lector in English, University of Helsingfors, Finland, 1929-31; Commonwealth Fund Fellowship, Princeton Univ., USA, 1931-33; Johore Prof. of English Language and Literature, Raffles Coll., Singapore, 1933-37; Asst Director amd Prof. of English, British Institute, Florence, 1937-38; Secretary, School of Oriental and African Studies, London Univ., 1939-45; Temp. Administrative Officer, Air Ministry, 1940; Priority Officer, Air Ministry, 1941; British Council Representative: in Sweden, 1941; in Italy, 1945; in Brazil, 1954; in Greece, 1957; in Japan (and Cultural Attaché HM Embassy, Tokyo), 1959; Controller of Education, 1950-54. Chief, Fellowships and Training Br., Food and Agriculture Org. of the United Nations, 1963-65. Syracuse International Poetry Prize, 1954. FRSL 1955. *Publications:* The Loosening and other Poems, 1931; Festivals of Fire, 1934; The Turning Path, 1939; (with Gunnar Ekelöf) T. S. Eliot: Dikter i Urval, 1942; Farewell and Welcome, 1945; (with Margaret Bottrall) The Zephyr Book of English Verse, 1945; Selected Poems, 1946; The Palisades of Fear, 1949; Adam Unparadised, 1954; Collected Poems, 1961; Rome (Art Centres of the World), 1968. *Recreations:* music, travel, tennis (lawn, table and deck). *Address:* Villa Cornubia, Via Miramare 11/12, Albano Laziale, Rome, Italy. *T:* 931417. *Club:* Athenæum.

**BOTVINNIK, Mikhail;** Order of Lenin, 1957; Order of the Badge of Honour, 1936 and 1945; Order of the Red Banner of Labour, 1961; Senior Scientist, USSR Research Institute for Electro-energetics, since 1955; *b* Petersburg, 17 Aug. 1911; *s* of a dental technician; *m* 1935, Gayane Annova; one *d. Educ:* Leningrad Polytechnical Institute (Grad.). Thesis for degree of: Candidate of Technical Sciences, 1937; Doctor of Technical Sciences, 1952. Chess master title, 1927; Chess grandmaster title, 1935. Won Soviet chess championship in 1931, 1933, 1939, 1941, 1944, 1945, 1952; World chess title, 1948-57, 1958 and 1961. Honoured Master of Sport of the USSR, 1945. *Publications:* Flohr-Botvinnik Match, 1934; Alekhin-Euwe Return Match, 1938; Selected Games, 1937, 1945, 1960; Tournament Match for the Absolute Champion Title, 1945; Botvinnik-Smyslov Match, 1955; Eleventh Soviet Chess Championship, 1939; Smyslov-Botvinnik Return Match, 1960; Regulation of Excitation and Static Stability of Synchronous Machines, 1950; Asynchronized Synchronous Machines, 1960; Algorithm Play of Chess, 1968; Controlled AC Machines (with Y. Shakarian), 1969. *Address:* 3 Frunsenskaja 7 (flat 154), Moscow. *T:* 242.15.86. *Club:* Central Chess Club of the USSR (Moscow).

**BOUCHIER, Air Vice-Marshal Sir Cecil Arthur,** KBE 1953 (CBE 1941; OBE 1936); CB 1945; DFC 1918; *b* 14 Oct. 1895, British; *m* 1st, 1927, Gladys Dorothy Sherwood (*d* 1964); one *s*; 2nd, 1968, Isabella Dorothy Guyver, *d* of Frank Guyver Britton, Yokohama. *Educ:* Chichester. Served in "A" Battery HAC, 1915-17, in Palestine; commissioned RFC

1918; served with RAF in Middle East and N Russia, 1918-19; India and Iraq, 1920-21; RAE Experimental Pilot, Farnborough, 1922-25; No 41 (F) Squadron, 1926-28; Test Pilot, egypt, 1929; graduated RAF Staff Coll., Andover, 1930; HQ RAF India, 1931-32; formed and commanded Indian Air Force, 1932-35; commanded: No 54 (F) Sqdn, 1936-37; No 11 Group, 1938-39; commanded RAF Sector, Hornchurch (Battle of Britain), 1940 (despatches); No 11 Group and RAF Station, Kenley, 1941 (CBE, despatches); Air Ministry, 1942; No 11 (F) Group, 1943-45 (in control Fighter umbrella at Normandy Beach landings); AOC No 221 Group in Burma, 1945; AOC, British Commonwealth Air Forces of Occupation, Japan, 1945-48; AOC No 21 Group, Swinderby, Lincs, 1948-49; retired list, 1949; re-instated on active list, 1950; Personal Representative of British Chiefs of Staff to Generals MacArthur, Ridgway and Mark Clark throughout Korean War, 1950-53; retired list 1953. Order of St Anne (Russia), 1919; Legion of Merit (Commander), USA, 1945. *Recreations:* golf, chess. *Address:* 2275 Isshiki, Hayama, Kanagawa-ken, Japan. *T:* 0468-75-1217.

**BOUGHEY, John Fenton C.;** *see* Coplestone-Boughey.

**BOUGHEY, Sir Richard (James),** 10th Bt, *cr* 1798; JP; DL; *b* 30 July 1925; *s* of Sir George Menteth Boughey, 9th Bt; *m* 1950, Davina Julia, 2nd *d* of Fitzherbert Wright; two *s* three *d*. *Educ:* Eton. Served with Coldstream Guards, 1943-46, in France and Germany, Lieut. Chairman, Apple and Pear Development Council, 1967-; Liaison Officer to Minister of Agriculture, Fisheries and Food, 1965-; Chairman, East Sussex Agricultural Exec. Cttee, 1958-67; Pres., Nat. Fedn of Young Farmers Clubs, 1970. High Sheriff of Sussex, 1964; DL, Sussex, 1970-. OStJ. *Heir: s* John George Fletcher Boughey, *b* 12 Aug. 1959. *Address:* Ringmer Park, Lewes, Sussex. *T:* Ringmer 310. *Clubs:* Boodle's, Guards.

**BOULANGER, Nadia (Juliette);** Commandeur de la Légion d'Honneur; teacher of composition; conductor; lecturer; *b* Paris, 16 Sept. 1887; *d* of Ernest and Raïssa (Princess Mychetsky) Boulanger. Studied at Paris Nat. Conservatory. Formerly head of theory dept, Ecole Normale de Musique, Paris. Went to US in 1924, 1935, 1940, 1958, 1962; was faculty member in many American Schools. Now Conservatory of Music, Paris (Hon. Prof.); Prof. and Director, Conservatoire Americain, Fontainebleau; Guest Conductor: Boston Symphony Orchestra; Royal Philharmonic, London; NY Philharmonic; Philadelphia Orchestra; Washington Symphony. Maître de Chapelle to the Prince of Monaco. Has lectured and conducted in many European countries and in US. Has made numerous recordings. FRCM. Dr *hc:* Oxford; Harvard; holds several other hon. doctorates. Commander, Arts et Lettres (France); Commander, Order of Polonia Restituta (Poland); Commander of St Charles (Monaco). *Address:* 36 rue Ballu, Paris IX, France.

**BOULEZ, Pierre;** composer of music, and orchestral conductor; *b* Montbrison, Loire, France, 26 March 1925. *Educ:* Saint-Etienne and Lyon (music and higher mathematics); Paris Conservatoire. Studied with Messiaen and René Leibowitz. Theatre conductor, Jean-Louis Barrault Company, Paris, 1948; visited USA with French Ballet Company, 1952. Has conducted major orchestras in his own and standard classical works in Great Britain, Europe and USA, including Edinburgh Festival, 1965; also conducted Wozzeck in Paris and Frankfurt; Parsifal at Bayreuth, 1966. Interested in poetry and aesthetics of Baudelaire, Mallarmé and René Char. *Compositions include:* Trois Psalmodies (Piano solo), 1945; Sonatine for flute and piano, 1946; Polyphonie X for 18 solo instruments, 1951; Visage nuptial (2nd version), 1951; Structures for 2 pianos, 1952; Le Marteau sans Maître (voice and 6 instruments), 1954; Sonata No 3 (piano), 1956; Deux Improvisations sur Mallarmé for voice and 9 instruments, 1957; Doubles for orchestra, 1958; Poésie pour Pouvoir for voices and orchestra, 1958; Soleil des Eaux (text by René Char) for chorus and orchestra, 1958; Pli selon Pli: Hommage à Mallarmé, for voices and orchestra, 1960; Eclat (in progress), 1964; Domaines for solo clarinet, 1968. *Publications:* Penser la musique d'aujourd'hui, 1966 (Boulez on Music Today, 1970); Relevés d'apprenti, 1967. *Address:* Kapuzinerstrasse 9, Baden-Baden.

**BOULT, Sir Adrian,** CH 1969; Kt 1937; MA, DMus, Oxon; Vice-President, Council of Royal College of Music, since 1963; *b* Chester, 8 April 1889; *o s* of late Cedric R. Boult, JP, formerly of Liverpool, and Katharine Florence Barman; *m* 1933, Ann, *yr d* of late Capt. F. A. Bowles, RN, JP, Dully, Sittingbourne, Kent. *Educ:* Westminster Sch.; Christ Church, Oxford; Leipzig Conservatorium. President, Oxford Univ. Musical Club, 1910. Musical Staff, Royal Opera, 1914; Asst Director of Music, 1926. During European War, served in War Office and Commission Internationale de Ravitaillement. Teaching staff of Royal College of Music, 1919-30 and 1962-66; Conductor of Patron's Fund, 1919-29; Musical Director, Birmingham City Orchestra, 1924-30 and 1959-60; Vice-President, City of Birmingham Symphony Orchestra, 1960-; Director of Music, BBC, 1930-42; Conductor, BBC Symphony Orchestra, 1930-50; Conductor, London Philharmonic Orchestra, 1950-57, President, 1966-. Since 1922, has conducted all over Europe, in Canada, USA and USSR, introducing British music; has conducted all permanent orchestras in England, Scotland and Wales and directed many schools for conductors, recently for Schools' Music Assoc. and Surrey CC. Has also conducted: Bach Choir, 1928-33; Promenade Concerts, 1942-50; Petersfield Festival, 1920-39; Three Choirs Festivals, Worcester, Gloucester and Hereford, and many amateur festivals. Assisted at Coronation Services, 1937, 1953, and took part in concerts and services during Westminster Abbey 900th Anniversary Year, 1966. President: Incorp. Society of Musicians, 1928-29; Nat. Youth Orchestra, 1947-57; Schools' Music Assoc., 1947-; Leith Hill Musical Festival, 1959-; Royal Scottish Academy of Music, 1959-. Hon. LLD (Birmingham, Liverpool); Hon. MusDoc (Edinburgh, Cambridge); Hon. RAM: Hon. Student, Christ Church, Oxon; Hon. Fellow, Manchester Coll., Oxford; Hon. Member Royal Academy of Music, Sweden; Hon. GSM; Hon. TCL; Gold Medal, Royal Philharmonic Soc., 1944; Harvard Medal, with Dr Vaughan Williams, 1956. OStJ. *Publications:* A Handbook on The Technique of Conducting, 1920, rev. edn 1968; (joint) Bach's Matthew Passion, 1949; Thoughts on Conducting, 1963; contribs on musical subjects to various journals. *Address:* 38 Wigmore Street, W1. *T:* 01-935 1387. *Club:* Athenæum.

**BOULTER, Robert,** CMG 1923; OBE 1947; *b* 6 April 1885; *s* of H. J. Boulter, Brook Vale, Rattlesden, Bury St Edmunds; *m* 1914, Ethel Marie Brazier; one *s*. *Educ:* Framlingham Coll.

Entered British Consular Service in Japan, 1907; Commercial Secretary, British Embassy, Tokio, 1925-29; Trade Commissioner, Singapore, 1929-34; Trade Commissioner, Wellington, 1934-49; Economic Adviser to High Commissioner for the United Kingdom in New Zealand, 1944-49; given title of Senior Trade Commissioner, 1946; retired, 1949. *Recreations:* walking, bridge. *Address:* Carey's Manor Hotel, Brockenhurst, Hants. *Clubs:* East India and Sports; Lymington (Lymington).

**BOULTING, John Edward;** Producer-Director: Charter Film Productions Ltd; BLC Films Ltd; British Lion Films Ltd (Managing Director, since 1968); *b* 21 Nov. 1913; *s* of Arthur Boulting and Rose Bennett. *Educ:* Reading Sch. Office boy in Wardour Street, 1933. Spent eighteen months selling bad films to reluctant exhibitors; joined independent producer as general factotum on production, 1935; served hard but educative apprenticeship, in small studios. Went to Spain, served in International Brigade, front line ambulance driver, 1937; returned to England. Nov. 1937 formed independent film production company with twin brother Roy. Served War of 1939-45; joined RAF as AC2, 1940; retired Flt-Lieut, 1946. Continued film production; since War has produced Fame is the Spur, The Guinea Pig, Seagulls over Sorrento, Josephine and Men, Brothers in Law; has directed Brighton Rock, Seven Days to Noon, The Magic Box, Lucky Jim (Edinburgh Festival 1957); directed, and co-author of, screen-play Private's Progress, 1955; produced Carlton-Browne of the FO, 1958; directed and co-author screenplay, I'm All Right Jack, 1959; produced The Risk and The French Mistress, 1960; co-author novel and screen-play and director, Heavens Above!, 1962; produced the film The Family Way, 1966. *Recreations:* cricket, tennis, reading, film making, horse riding and irritating the conservative minded in all stratas. *Address:* Charter Film Productions, Broadwick House, Broadwick Street, W1. *T:* 01-437 8676.

**BOULTING, Roy;** Producer-Director, Charter Film Productions Ltd; Director, British Lion Films Ltd; *b* 21 Nov. 1913; *s* of Arthur Boulting and Rose Bennett. *Educ:*HMS Worcester; Reading Sch. Formed independent film production company with twin brother John, 1937. Served War of 1939-45, RAC, finishing as Capt.; films for Army included Desert Victory and Burma Victory. Producer: Brighton Rock, 1947; Seven Days to Noon, 1950; Private's Progress, 1955; Lucky Jim (Edinburgh Festival), 1957; I'm All Right Jack, 1959; Heavens Above!, 1962. Director: Pastor Hall, 1939; Thunder Rock, 1942; Fame is the Spur, 1947; The Guinea Pig, 1948; High Treason, 1951; Singlehanded, 1952; Seagulls over Sorrento, Crest of the Wave, 1953; Josephine and Men, 1955; Run for the Sun, 1955; Brothers in Law, 1956; Happy is the Bride, 1958; Carlton-Browne of the FO, 1958-59; I'm All Right Jack, 1959; The Risk, 1960; The French Mistress, 1960; Suspect, 1960; The Family Way, 1966; Twisted Nerve, 1968. *Address:* Charter Film Productions Ltd, Broadwick House, Broadwick Street, W1. *T:* 01-437 8676. *Club:* Lord's Taverners.

**BOULTING, S. A.;** *see* Cotes, Peter.

**BOULTON, Edward Henry Brooke,** MC; MA; Timber and Forestry Consultant; Forestry and Timber Counsellor to Marquess of Bath; *b* 1897; *s* of Joseph Henry and Florence Helena Boulton; *m*; one *s*. *Educ:* Portora Royal Inniskillen; St Catharine's Coll., Cambridge. Served with Royal Naval Division, 1915-16, Gallipoli and France; Royal Field Artillery, Capt., 1917-19; School of Forestry, Cambridge, 1920-22; Degree in Forestry and Post-grad. Diploma with Distinction in Timber Technology; University Lecturer in Forestry, 1922-34; Manager Timber Development Assoc. Ltd, 1934; Technical Dir, Timber Development Assoc., Ltd, 1936-48; Past President and Fellow, Inst. of Wood Science; President, British Wood Preserving Assoc. *Publications:* A Pocket Book of British Trees; A Dictionary of Wood; Timber Houses; Timber Buildings for the Country; British Timbers; many papers on Forestry and Identification of Timbers. *Recreations:* riding, golf, fishing. *Address:* The Island, Horningsham, Warminster, Wilts. *Clubs:* British Empire, Farmers'.

**BOULTON, Major Sir Edward (John),** 2nd Bt, *cr* 1944; *b* 11 April 1907; *s* of Sir William Boulton, 1st Bt and Rosalind Mary (*d* 1969), *d* of Sir John D. Milburn, 1st Bt of Guyzance, Northumberland; *S* father, 1949; unmarried. *Educ:* Eton; Trinity Coll., Cambridge (BA). Joined Staffordshire Yeomanry, 1939. Served War of 1939-45, Middle East, Italy, 1940-44 (despatches); North West Europe (HQ 21 Army Group), 1944-45, Major 1944. Contested Southern Division of Ilford (C), 1945. Retired from membership of London Stock Exchange, 1970. *Heir: b* William Whytehead Boulton, *qv*. *Address:* Ouaisné Lodge, Portelet, Jersey, CI. *T:* Jersey Central 42935. *Clubs:* Cavalry, City of London.

**BOULTON, Sir (Harold Hugh) Christian,** 4th Bt *cr* 1905; *b* 29 Oct. 1918; *s* of Sir (Denis Duncan) Harold (Owen) Boulton, 3rd Bt, and Louise McGowan, USA; *S* father, 1968. *Educ:* Ampleforth College, Yorks. Late Captain, Irish Guards (Supplementary Reserve). *Address:* c/o Bank of Montreal, City View Branch, 1481 Merivale Road, Ottawa 5, Ontario, Canada.

**BOULTON, Prof. Norman Savage,** DSc, FICE; Emeritus Professor of Civil Engineering, University of Sheffield, since 1964 (Professor, 1955-64); *b* 8 May 1899; *s* of late Professor William Savage Boulton; *m* 1929, Constance (*d* 1968), *d* of late H. Deakin; one *d*. *Educ:* King Edward's Sch., Birmingham; University of Birmingham. RGA, 1918; BSc (Birmingham), First Class Hons and Bowen Research Schol., 1922; MSc and Dudley Docker Res. Schol., 1923; DSc (Civil Engineering), 1966. Engineering Asst, Public Works Dept, City of Birmingham, 1924-29; University Lecturer in Civil Engineering, King's Coll., Newcastle upon Tyne, 1929-36; Sen. Lecturer in charge of Dept of Civil Engineering, University of Sheffield, 1936-55. Chairman, Yorkshire Assoc. Inst. Civil Engineers, 1947-48 and 1961-62. AMICE, 1927; MICE, 1950. *Publications:* various technical papers in Proc. Instns Civil and Mechanical Engineers, Philosophical Magazine, etc. *Recreation:* music. *Address:* 68 Endcliffe Vale Road, Sheffield S10 3EW. *T:* Sheffield 61049.

**BOULTON, Very Rev. Walter,** MA Oxon; Rector of Market Overton with Thistleton since 1961; *s* of Walter and Clara Elizabeth Boulton, Smallthorne, Staffs.; *m* 1932, Kathleen Lorna York Batley; one *s* four *d*. *Educ:* Balliol Coll., Oxford. Exhibitioner of Balliol, 2nd Class Modern History, 1922, BA 1923, MA 1930. Cuddesdon Coll., 1923. Deacon, 1924; Priest, 1925; Curate of St Mark, Woodhouse, Leeds, 1924-27; Asst Chaplain of the Cathedral Church, Calcutta, 1927-34; Chaplain of Lebong, 1934-35. Furlough, 1937. Chaplain, Shillong, 1935-39; St Paul's Cathedral, Calcutta, 1939-45; Canon of

Calcutta, 1940-48. Furlough, 1945. Chaplain, Shillong, 1945-47; Vicar of Fleet, Hampshire, 1948-52; Provost of Guildford and Rector of Holy Trinity with St Mary, Guildford, 1952-61. *Address:* Market Overton Rectory, Oakham, Rutland.

**BOULTON, William Whytehead,** CBE 1958; TD 1949; Secretary, General Council of the Bar, since 1950; *b* 21 June 1912; *s* of Sir William Boulton, 1st Bt, and *b* and *heir* of Sir Edward Boulton, 2nd Bt, *qv; m* 1944, Margaret Elizabeth, *o d* of late Brig. H. N. A. Hunter, DSO; one *s* two *d. Educ:* Eton; Trinity Coll., Cambridge. Called to Bar, Inner Temple, 1936; practised at the Bar, 1937-39. Served War of 1939-45: with 104th Regt RHA (Essex Yeo.) and 14th Regt RHA, in the Middle East, 1940-44; Staff Coll., Camberley, 1944. Control Commission for Germany (Legal Div.), 1945-50. Gazetted 2nd Lieut TA (Essex Yeo.), 1934; retired with rank of Hon. Lieut-Col. *Publications:* A Guide to Conduct and Etiquette at the Bar of England and Wales, 1st edn 1953, 2nd edn, 1957, 3rd edn 1961, 4th edn 1965. *Address:* Garth End, Wickham Bishops, Essex. *T:* Wickham Bishops 417.

**BOUQUET, Rev. Alan Coates,** DD; Honorary CF; *b* 26 May 1884; *o c* of late Robert Coates Bouquet of The Laurel House, Padbury, Buckingham, and Elizabeth, *d* of John Stow, Sepham Court, Shoreham, Kent; *m* 1910, Edith Gertrude (*d* 1952), *d* of late G. W. Sayer of London; no *c. Educ:* St Dunstan's Coll., London; Trinity Coll., Cambridge (Scholar); Jesus Coll., Cambridge (Scholar); Westcott House, Cambridge. Bowen Prize for Modern History, 1903; Corrie Prize for Greek Testament, 1907; Winchester Reading Prize, 1907; 1st Class Theological Tripos, Part I, 1907; BA 1905; MA 1910; BD 1918; DD 1922. asst Curate of Putney, 1907-12; Lecturer in Church History, Deaconesses' Institution, 1911-12; Senior Curate, St Margaret's, Altrincham, 1912-14; Army Chaplain, 1914-1919 (despatches); Member Archbishop's No 1 Cttee of Reform, 1917; Central Organising Secretary SPCK, 1919-22; Hon Asst Curate St Martin-in-the-Fields, 1920-22; Vicar of All Saints, Cambridge, 1922-45. Recognised Lecturer in Theology in University of Cambridge, 1914-36, and in the History and Comparative Study of Religions, 1934-44; Select Preacher, University of Cambridge, 1917, 1923, 1931, and 1942; Hulsean Lecturer, Cambridge Univ., 1924-25; Stanton Lecturer in the Philosophy of Religion, Cambridge Univ., 1931-34; OCF Anti-Aircraft Troops, Cambridge Area, 1942-45; Lectr in the History and Comparative Study of Religion, Univ. of Cambridge, 1945-54; Lecturer on Upton Foundation, Michaelmas Term, Oxford, 1946. Has given lectures at Harvard, Princeton, New York, University of California, Delhi and Andhra Universities, 1955-65. *Publications:* A Point of View, 1913; Christian Reunion, 1914; A Man's Pocket-Book of Religion, 1916; When He is Come, 1917; The Greatest Relationship, 1919; Is Christianity the Final Religion?, 1921; The Christian Religion and its Competitors Today (Hulsean Lectures, 1924-25), 1925; The Real Presence, 1928; Modern Handbooks of Religion, vols 1-4, 1932-33; Man and Deity, 1933; Jesus (A New Outline and Estimate), 1933; The Doctrine of God, 1934; Translation of Przywara's Philosophy of Religion (Polarity), 1935; A Lectionary of Christian Prose, 1939 (3rd edn enlarged, 1965); Comparative Religion (in Pelican Books), 1941, 7th edn 1968; Hinduism (University Series), 1949, 4th edn 1969; Everyday Life in New Testament Times, 1953, 2nd edn, 1956 (and numerous foreign edns); Sacred Books of the World, 1953, 4th edn, 1967; contrib. to Encyclopædia Britannica (new edn); Chambers's Encyclopædia (new edn); Oxford Encyclopædia for Schools, 1948; Old Monumental Brasses in Great Britain, 1956; Christianity and Non-Christian Faiths (in Library of Constructive Theology), 1958; contrib. to Telugu Encyclopædia, 1960, to Encyclopædia Americana, 1963; Studies in The Problems of Peace (with Prof. K. S. Murty), 1960; European Brasses (with Dr M. J. Waring), 1967; Religious Experience: Its nature, types, and validity, 2nd edn 1969. *Recreations:* bird-watching; Hon. Vice-President Cambridge Univ. Judo Club. *Address:* Gilling House, Cambridge. *T:* 53119.

**BOURDILLON, Henry Townsend,** CMG 1952; Assistant Under-Secretary of State, Department of Education and Science, since 1964; *b* 19 Aug. 1913; 2nd *s* of late Sir Bernard Henry Bourdillon, GCMG, KBE, and of Lady (Violet Grace) Bourdillon; *m* 1942, Margareta d'Almaine (*née* Tham); one *s* two *d. Educ:* Rugby Sch.; Corpus Christi Coll., Oxford. Asst Principal, Colonial Office, 1937; Acting Principal, Colonial Office, 1940; lent to: Foreign Office, 1942; Cabinet Office, 1943; Ministry of Production, 1944; returned to Colonial Office, 1944; Asst Secretary, 1947-54; Asst Under-Secretary of State, Colonial Office, 1954-59; Deputy UK Commissioner for Singapore, 1959-61; returned to Colonial Office, 1961; Under-Secretary, Ministry of Education, 1962-64. *Recreations:* gardening, writing, music. *Address:* Orchard House, Horsenden Lane, Princes Risborough, Bucks. *T:* Princes Risborough 5416. *Club:* Athenæum.

**BOURDILLON, Robert Benedict,** CBE 1946; MC 1917; AFC 1918; retired; *b* 8 Sept. 1889; *s* of Francis William Bourdillon, Buddington, Midhurst, Sussex; *m* 1922, Harriet Ada, *d* of Henry Broughton Barnes, Henley, Sussex; one *s* (and one *s* decd). *Educ:* Balliol Coll., Oxford; St Mary's Hospital, London. BA (Nat. Science) 1912 Oxon.; MA 1919; BM, BCh, 1925; DM, 1935; Lecturer in Chemistry Balliol Coll., Oxford, 1912-14; Fellow and Praelector in Chemistry, University Coll., Oxford, 1913-21; Dean, University Coll., Oxford, 1920-21; Ho. Physician and later Asst Medical Unit, St Mary's Hospital, London, 1925-26; National Institute for Medical Research, Hampstead, 1926-46; Director, Electro-medical Research Unit, Stoke Mandeville Hospital (Ministry of Health and Medical Research Council, 1946-54). War Service, 1914-19, Intelligence Corps, RFC and RAF. *Publications:* various papers in scientific journals. *Recreations:* mountaineering and walking. *Address:* Ganges, British Columbia, Canada. *Club:* Athenæum.

**BOURKE,** family name of **Earl of Mayo.**

**BOURKE, Major Sir (Edward Alexander) Henry L.;** *see* Legge-Bourke.

**BOURKE, Sir Paget John,** Kt 1957; Judge of the Court of Appeal, Bahamas and Bermuda, since 1965, British Honduras, since 1968; President of Court, since 1970; Judge of Court of Appeal, Gibraltar, since 1970; *b* 1906; *s* of H. C. Bourke, Amana, Ballina, Co. Mayo, Ireland; *m* 1936, Susan Dorothy (*née* Killeen); three *s* one *d. Educ:* Mount St Mary's Coll., Chesterfield; Trinity Coll., Dublin (Mod. BA, LLB). Barrister-at-law, King's Inn, 1928, Gray's Inn, 1957. Legal Adviser and Crown Prosecutor, Seychelles, 1933; MEC and MLC; Chief Magistrate, Palestine, 1936; Relieving President, District Court, 1941; President, 1945; Judge of Supreme Court of Kenya, 1946; Chief Justice, Sierra Leone, 1955-57; Cyprus, 1957-60. Senior Counsel, Irish Bar, 1961. Acting Chief Justice, Gibraltar, Oct.-Dec.,

1965. *Publication:* Ed. Digest of Cases, Seychelles, 1870-1933. *Recreation:* golf. *Address:* 10 Herbert Park, Ballsbridge, Dublin. *Club:* Royal Irish Yacht (Dun Laoghaire).

**BOURKE-WHITE, Margaret;** on staff of Life Magazine since 1936; *b* 14 June 1906; *d* of Joseph White and Minnie Elizabeth Bourke; *m* 1st, 1925, Everett Chapman; 2nd, 1939, Erskine Caldwell (marr. diss., 1942); no *c*. *Educ:* Universities of Columbia, Michigan and Cornell. Industrial photographer, 1927-. Has taken photographs in various countries. Associate editor: Fortune Magazine, 1929-33; Life Magazine, 1936- (UN War corresp. in Korea, 1952; accredited War corresp.-photographer to US Air Forces in Great Britain, N. Africa and Europe, 1942-45). Has executed photo-murals for firms. Is represented in Library of Congress and in notable museums. Holds numerous awards. AFD (hon.) Michigan, 1951; LittD (hon.) Rutgers, 1949. *Publications:* Eyes on Russia, 1931; USSR, A Portfolio of Photographs, 1934; You Have Seen Their Faces (with Erskine Caldwell), 1937; North of the Danube (with Erskine Caldwell), 1939; Say! Is This The USA? (with Erskine Caldwell), 1941; Shooting the Russian War (text and photographs), 1942; Purple Heart Valley, 1944; Dear Fatherland, Rest Quietly, 1946; Halfway to Freedom, A Study of the New India, 1949; A Report on the American Jesuits (with Father John LaFarge, SJ), 1956; Portrait of Myself, 1963. *Recreation:* gardening. *Address:* Life Magazine, Time and Life Building, Rockefeller Center, New York, NY 10020, USA. *T:* Judson 6-1212. *Club:* Overseas Press (New York).

**BOURN, James;** HM Ambassador to Somalia, since 1970; *b* 30 Aug. 1917; *s* of James and Sarah Gertrude Bourn; *m* 1944, Isobel Mackenzie; one *s*. *Educ:* Queen Elizabeth's Grammar Sch., Darlington. Executive Officer, Ministry of Health, 1936. War of 1939-45; served (Royal Signals), in India, North Africa and Italy; POW; Captain. Higher Exec. Officer, Ministry of National Insurance, 1947; Asst Principal, Colonial Office, 1947; Principal, 1949; Secretary to the Salaries Commission, Bahamas, 1948-49; seconded to Tanganyika, 1953-55; UK Liaison Officer to Commn for Technical Co-operation in Africa (CCTA), 1955-57; Commonwealth Relations Office, 1961; seconded to Central African Office, 1962; Dar es Salaam, 1963; Deputy High Commissioner in Zanzibar, Tanzania, 1964-65; Counsellor and Dep. High Comr, Malawi, 1966-70. *Address:* c/o Foreign and Commonwealth Office, SW1.

**BOURNE,** Baron *cr* 1964 (Life Peer), of Atherstone; **Geoffrey Kemp Bourne,** GCB 1960; KBE 1954; CMG 1952; Chairman (part-time), National Building Agency, since 1967; *b* 5 Oct. 1902; *s* of Col. W. K. Bourne, Sway, Hants; *m* 1928, Agnes Evelyn, *d* of late Sir Ernest Thompson, Prestbury, Cheshire; one *s* one *d*. *Educ:* Rugby; RMA Woolwich. Commissioned into RA, 1923; served in Hong Kong, 1930-32; Gibraltar, 1933-34; Staff Coll., Camberley, 1935-36; Colchester, 1937; War Office, 1938-41. Served War of 1939-45; Comdr 5th Indian Div., May-Sept. 1946 (Java and India); idc 1947; Head of British Services Mission to Burma, 1948; GOC Berlin (British Sector), 1949-51; GOC 16th Airborne Div. (TA), 1951-52; GOC-in-C, Eastern Command, 1953; GOC Malaya Command, and Director of Operations, 1954-56; C-in-C Middle East Land Forces, 1957; Commandant, Imperial Defence Coll., 1958-59; ADC General to the Queen, 1959-60. Col. Commandant RA, 1954-67; Hon. Col 10th Bn The Parachute Regt, TA., 1960-65. Retired April 1960. Director-General, Aluminium Federation, 1960-63. US Silver Star and Legion of Merit (degree of officer); Duncan Essay Gold Medal, 1935 (RA Institution). *Recreations:* golf, shooting. *Address:* Drove House, Cranborne, Wimborne, Dorset. *T:* Cranborne 321. *Club:* Army and Navy.

**BOURNE, Aleck William,** MA, MB, BCh Cantab, FRCS, FRCOG; retired; formerly Consulting Obstetrical Surgeon, Queen Charlotte's Hospital, St Mary's Hospital; Consulting Surgeon, Samaritan Hospital; *b* 4 June 1886; *o s* of Rev. W. C. Bourne, formerly of Barnet; *m* 1912, Bessie, *e d* of G. W. Hayward, Barnet; three *d*. *Educ:* Rydal Sch., Colwyn Bay; Downing Coll., Cambridge (open scholar). 1st Class Nat. Science Tripos, 1908; Senior Univ. Scholar, St Mary's Hosp., 1908; War Service as Surgical Specialist, Egypt and France, 1914-17; filled resident and other appointments at St Mary's, Queen Charlotte's, and Samaritan Hospitals, 1910-14; former Examiner, University of Cambridge; former Mem. of Central Health Services Council (1948); Pres. Obstetrical and Gynæcological Section, Royal Society of Medicine, 1938-39. *Publications:* Recent Advances in Obstetrics and Gynæcology, 12th edn, 1962; Synopsis of Midwifery and Gynæcology, 13th edn, 1965; A Doctor's Creed, 1962; (Jt Ed.) British Practice of Obstetrics and Gynæcology, 3rd edn, 1963, and various papers in periodical medical journals. *Address:* Mead House, Woodfield Lane, Ashtead, Surrey.

**BOURNE, Prof. Edward John,** FRIC; PhD, DSc Birmingham; Professor of Chemistry in the University of London, Royal Holloway College, since 1956; *b* 1 Jan. 1922; *s* of Arthur John and Florence Grace Bourne, Cannock, Staffs; *m* 1947, Kathleen Joyce, *d* of James and Ellen Cryer; one *s*. *Educ:* Rugeley Grammar Sch., Staffs; University of Birmingham. Lecturer in Chemistry, University of Birmingham, 1944-50; Senior Lecturer, 1950-55; Reader in Organic Chemistry, 1955-56; Vice-Principal, Royal Holloway Coll., Univ. of London, 1967-69. Council of Chemical Soc., 1954-56. Joint Library Cttee, 1959-63. Chairman: Board of Studies in Chemistry, University of London, 1959-63; Downland Section, Royal Institute of Chemistry, 1966-67. *Publications:* scientific papers mainly in Journal of Chemical Society. *Address:* Royal Holloway College, Englefield Green, Surrey. *T:* Egham 4455. *Club:* Wentworth (Virginia Water, Surrey).

**BOURNE, Sir Frederick Chalmers,** KCSI 1946 (CSI 1944); CIE 1941; late ICS; *b* 12 Aug. 1891; *s* of late Sir Frederick Bourne, CMG, Mayfield, Sussex; *m* 1918, Heather Frances, *d* of late Lieut-Col F. W. Burbury. *Educ:* Rugby; Christ Church, Oxford, MA. Served in 4th Bn Queen's Own (RW Kent Regt), 1910-20. Entered Indian Civil Service, 1920; Sec. to Government, Punjab, Electricity and Industries Dept, 1934-37; Dep. Commissioner, Lahore, 1937-40; Sec. to Government of Punjab, Home Dept, 1940-41; Chief Sec. to Govt, Punjab, 1941-45; Acting Governor Central Provinces and Berar, May-Oct, 1945; Acting Governor of Assam, 1946; Governor of Central Provinces and Berar, 1946-47; Governor of East Bengal, Aug. 1947-50. Appointed as Adviser, Gold Coast, 1955. *Address:* Eachen Hill, Buxted, Sussex. *T:* Buxted 3108.

**BOURNE, Geoffrey,** MD, FRCP; Consulting Physician and Consulting Cardiologist to St Bartholomew's Hospital; Consulting

Cardiologist to British Air Corporations Joint Medical Service and to The Artists General Benevolent Institution, etc.; *b* 1893; *s* of late James Bourne and Ethel Ellen Bourne; *m* 1st, Margherita Cotonio (*d* 1952), New Orleans; 2nd, 1953, Patricia Mary, *d* of late Rev. W. F. H. McCready, and of Mrs. McCready. *Educ:* Highgate Sch.; St Bartholomew's. MD (London), 1920; FRCP 1929; Lawrence Research Scholar and Gold Medallist, 1919; Rockefeller Travelling Fellow, 1926-27, etc. *Publications:* Return to Reason, 1942; We met at Barts', 1963; articles on Cardiac subjects in Quarterly Journal of Medicine, British Heart Journal, Lancet, British Medical Journal, etc. *Recreations:* fishing, painting. *Address:* 73 Harley Street, W1. *T:* 01-935 9942; (private) 61 Farley Court, Allsop Place, NW1. *T:* 01-935 2138. *Club:* English-Speaking Union.

**BOURNE, Lt-Col Geoffrey (H.),** FRSM, FZS; DPhil, DSc; *b* West Perth, Western Australia, 17 Nov. 1909; *s* of Walter Howard Bourne and Mary Ann Mellon; *m* 1935, Gwenllian Myfanwy Jones, BA; two *s*; *m* 1965, Maria Nelly Golarz, PhD. *Educ:* Perth Modern Sch., W Australia; University of Western Australia (BSc 1930, BSc Hons 1931; MSc 1932, DSc 1935); University of Melbourne. DPhil (Oxford), 1943; Hackett Research Student, University of W Australia, 1931-33; Biologist and in charge of Experimental Work, Australian Institute of Anatomy, Canberra, 1933-35; Biochemist Commonwealth of Austr. Advisory Council on Nutrition, 1935-37; Beit Memorial Fellow for Medical Research, Oxford, 1938-41; Mackenzie-Mackinnon Research Fellow of Royal College of Physicians of London and Royal College of Surgeons of England, 1941-44; Demonstrator in Physiology, Oxford, 1941-44, 1946, 1947; in charge of research and development (rations and physiological matters) for Special Forces in South-East Asia, 1944-45; Nutritional Adviser to British Military Administration, Malaya, 1945-46; Reader in Histology, University of London, at the London Hospital Medical Coll., 1947-57; Prof. and Chm. of Anatomy, Emory Univ., Atlanta, Ga, USA, 1957-63; Dir, Yerkes Regional Primate Research Center of Emory Univ., 1962-. Member: Soc. Experimental Biology; Nutrition Soc. (foundation Mem.); Anatomical Soc. of Gt Brit. and N Ireland, Internat. Soc. for Cell Biology; Aerospace Med. Soc., etc. *Publications:* Nutrition and the War, 1940; Wartime Food for Mother and Child, 1942; Cytology and Cell Physiology (ed and part author), 1942, 2nd edn 1951; Starvation in Europe, 1943; How Your Body Works, 1949; The Mammalion Adrenal Gland, 1949; Aids to Histology, 1950; (ed jtly) International Review of Cytology, 1952; (ed jtly) Biochemistry and Physiology of Nutrition, Vols 1, 2; Introduction to Functional Histology; Biochemistry and Physiology of Bone; (ed jtly) The Biology of Ageing; Structure and function of Muscle; The Division of Labour in Cells; (ed jtly) Muscular Dystrophy in Man and Animals; World Review of Nutrition and Dietetics, 1962; Atherosclerosis and its origins; Structure and Function of Nervous Tissue; contributor on Famine to Encyclopædia Britannica; contributions to scientific and medical journals. *Recreations:* water ski-ing, tennis, ballet and running (State Mile Championship and Record Holder, Australia). *Address:* Yerkes Regional Primate Research Center, Emory University, Atlanta, Ga 30322, USA.

**BOURNE, James Gerald,** MA, MD (Cantab), FFARCS; Formerly Senior Anæsthetist, St Thomas' Hospital, London; Consultant Anæsthetist, Salisbury Hospital Group; *b* 6 March 1906; *y s* of late W. W. Bourne, Garston Manor, Herts and of late Clara (*née* Hollingsworth); *m* 1957, Jenny Liddell (*d* 1967); one *s*; *m* 1968, Susan Clarke; two *s*. *Educ:* Rugby; Corpus Christi Coll., Cambridge; St Thomas' Hospital. 1st class Geographical Tripos Part I, 1925; 1st class Geographical Tripos Part II, 1926; Exhibition and Prizes; MRCS, LRCP 1937; MB, BChir Cantab 1939; DA England 1945; FFARCS 1953; MD (Cantab), 1960. Major RAMC, 1939-45. *Publications:* Nitrous Oxide in Dentistry: Its Danger and Alternatives, 1960; Studies in Anæsthetics, 1967; contributions to medical literature. *Recreations:* ski-ing, riding, fishing. *Address:* Melstock, Nunton, Salisbury, Wilts. *T:* Bodenham (Wilts) 234.

**BOURNE, Stafford,** MA Cantab; Chairman since 1938, and life Governing Director of Bourne & Hollingsworth Ltd; *b* 20 Feb. 1900; *e s* of late Walter William and Clara Louisa Bourne (*née* Hollingsworth), Garston Manor, Herts; *m* 1940, Magdalene Jane, *d* of Frederick and Anne Leeson; one *s* one *d* (and one *s* decd). *Educ:* Rugby; Corpus Christi, Cambridge; in France. War of 1939-45, Admiralty Ferry Crews. Entire career with Bourne & Hollingsworth Ltd. Co-Founder and First Pres., Oxford Street Assoc., 1958-68. Freeman, City of London, in Livery of Weavers' Co. Is actively interested in interchange of young people between UK and W Europe for business and cultural purposes. *Recreations:* yacht cruising, ski-ing, painting, chess. *Address:* Drokes, Beaulieu, near Brockenhurst, Hants SO4 7XE. *T:* Bucklers Hard 252; 58 Gower Street, WC1. *T:* 01-636 6962. *Clubs:* Garrick, Royal Automobile, Royal Thames Yacht, Royal Cruising.

**BOURNE-ARTON, Major Anthony Temple,** MBE 1944; JP; *b* 1 March 1913; 2nd *s* of W. R. Temple Bourne, Walker Hall, Winston, Co. Durham, and Evelyn Rose, 3rd *d* of Sir Frank Wills, Bristol; assumed surname of Bourne-Arton, 1950; *m* 1938, Margaret Elaine, *er d* of W. Denby Arton, Sleningford Park, Ripon, Yorks; two *s* two *d*. *Educ:* Clifton. Served Royal Artillery, 1935-48; active service, 1936, Palestine; 1939-45: France, N Africa, Sicily and Italy (despatches, MBE); Malaya, 1947-48. Gen. Commissioner Income Tax; has served on Bedale RDC, and N Riding County Agric. Cttee; County Councillor, N Riding of Yorks, 1949-61; CC, W Riding of Yorks, 1967-. MP (C) Darlington, 1959-64; PPS to the Home Sec., 1962-64. JP N Riding of Yorks, 1950-. *Recreations:* fishing and shooting. *Address:* Tanfield Lodge, Ripon, Yorks. *T:* Well 333. *Clubs:* Army and Navy, Carlton; Yorkshire (York).

**BOURTON, Cyril Leonard;** Assistant Under-Secretary of State for Finance and Accountant-General, Department of Health and Social Security, since 1968 (Ministry of Health, 1967-68); *b* 28 Dec. 1916; *s* of late Leonard Victor Bourton; *m* 1940, Elizabeth Iris Savage; two *s* one *d*. *Educ:* St Dunstan's Coll., Catford. Entered Nat. Debt Office, 1933; transf. Min. of Health, 1937; Dep. Accountant-Gen., 1958; Asst Sec., Exec. Councils Div., 1964. *Recreations:* fishing, photography. *Address:* 58 Manor Way, Beckenham, Kent BR3 3LJ. *T:* 01-658 6121.

**BOUSFIELD, Guy William John,** MD, BS London; *b* 20 Oct. 1893; *s* of Edward Collins Bousfield, MRCS, LRCP, DPH Cantab.; *m* 1923, Phyllis Doyle; one *s*. *Educ:* St Olaves; St Thomas's Hospital. Formerly Dir of Public Health Laboratory (MRC) Denmark Hill, and of Camberwell Laboratories; Immunological Specialist to LCC and Middx. CC; Ho.

Physician, Ho. Surg. and Clinical Asst. of Electrocardiograph Dept, St Thomas's Hosp. (publ. first tracings ever recorded of changes during and after an attack of Angina pectoris, Lancet 1918); Pathologist to St Giles and Dulwich Hosp., LCC; Dep. Principal MO, St John Amb. Assoc., and County Surg., St John Amb. Bde; Supt (Surg.) City of London Special Constabulary. Commissioned Infantry, Oct. 1914; served with Oxon and Bucks Light Infantry; Commissioned Royal Air Force Medical Service, 1918; Capt. 1919; Awarded Pilot's Certificate of Fédération Aéronautique Internationale, 1918. Major (Medical Officer) 44th Co. of London Bn Home Guard. OStJ. *Publications:* A Practical Guide to the Schick Test and Diphtheria and Scarlet Fever Immunisation, 1929; A Preliminary Course of Hygiene, 1953; numerous technical articles. Children's book: In Search of Alice, 1949. *Recreations:* yachting, amateur cinema film production, engineering, winter sports, bowls, etc. *Address:* Well Cottage, Goose Green, Warnham, Sussex. *T:* Horsham 5324. *Clubs:* Savage, Chelsea Arts.

**BOUSSAC, Marcel;** French industrialist; *b* Châteauroux, Indre, 17 April 1889; *s* of Louis-Alexandre Boussac and Primitive Jeanne (*née* Mette); *m* 1939, Margarita Decenninck (Fanny Heldy), Chevalier de la Légion d'Honneur. Since 1917 has been Dir, Managing Dir, Chm., and Dir-Gen. of many companies (dealing in textiles, chemicals, dyes, printing, sizing, etc.). Chm. and Dir-Gen. of the Comptoir de l'Industrie Cotonnière. Is a leading racehorse owner and his horses have won numerous international trophies. *Address:* (business) 21 rue Poissonnière, Paris 2e.

**BOUSTEAD, Col Sir (John Edmund) Hugh,** KBE 1965 (OBE 1934); CMG 1954; DSO 1941; MC and Bar; Vladimir with cross swords; St George's Military Medal with one Palm (Ethiopia); FRGS; late Gordon Highlanders; British Political Agent, Abu Dhabi, Nov. 1961-May 1965, retired; Development Secretary to Sultanate of Muscat and Oman, Oct. 1958-Oct. 1961; Resident Adviser, Hadhramaut States and British Agent, East Aden Protectorate, Southern Arabia, Oct. 1949-Oct. 1958; *b* 14 April 1895; *s* of Lawrence Twentyman Boustead and Ethel Margaret Alers-Hankey; unmarried. *Educ:* RNC Osborne and Dartmouth; HMS Cornwall; Oxford Univ. Midshipman and acting Sub Lieut, 1913-15; Royal Navy, German East and German South West Africa and Cape Station; S African Bde, Egypt, Western Desert and France, 1915-19; Capt. S African Brigade attached General Denikin's Army in South Russia, 1919; Worcester Coll., Oxford (while still serving in South African Brigade), 1920; appointed Gordon Highlanders, Malta, Constantinople, Chanak and Eastern Thrace, 1921-24; Sudan Camel Corps, 1924-29; Gen. Staff SDF, Khartoum, 1930; commanded Sudan Camel Corps, 1931; retired from Army 1935 to Sudan Political Service; District Commissioner Western District, Darfur, 1935-40; recalled to service with temp. rank of Lieut-Col 1940, raised and trained Sudan Frontier Bn SDF and commanded it, Jan.-July 1941, in operations in Central Abyssinia against the Italians (despatches, DSO); 2nd in command SDF Bde, Eritrea, 1943, with temp. rank of Col; Commanded 2nd SDF Brigade, April 1945; recalled to Political Service, Aug. 1945; late District Commissioner Sudan Political Service; Hon. rank of Col on ceasing to belong to R of O. Captained British Olympic Team Modern Pentathlon, Antwerp, and winner Army Lightweight Championships, 1920; Mem. of Fourth Everest Expedition, 1933. Awarded Lawrence of Arabia Memorial Medal by Royal Central Asian Society, 1966. *Publication:* The Wind of Morning, 1971. *Recreations:* riding, shooting, mountaineering, and ski-ing. *Clubs:* United Service, Athenæum.

**BOUTWOOD, Rear-Adm. Laurence Arthur,** CB 1955; OBE 1940; DL; *b* 7 Sept. 1898; *yr s* of W. A. Boutwood, Luton; *m* 1925, Audrey Winifred, *d* of H. Dale Morris, Polperro; one *s* two *d*. *Educ:* Bedford Sch. Royal Navy, 1916; served European War, 1916-18; Cambridge Univ., 1919-21; HM Ships, in E Indies, Home Fleet, etc., 1921-31; Sec. to Rear-Adm., Aircraft Carriers, 1931-33; Sec. to Third Sea Lord and Controller, 1934-39; HMS Glasgow (despatches), 1939-42; Base Supply Officer, Greenock, 1942-43; Sec. to Fourth Sea Lord, 1943-44; Base Supply Officer, Kilindini, 1944; Fleet Supply Officer, Brit. Pacific Fleet, 1945-46; Asst Dir of Plans, Admty, 1946-48; RN Barracks, Lee-on-Solent, 1948-50; Fleet Supply Officer, Mediterranean Stn, 1950-53; Comd Supply Officer, Portsmouth, 1953-56; retired, 1956. County Comr St John Ambulance Brigade, Cornwall, 1958. DL Cornwall, 1965. KStJ 1966. *Address:* Golden Gap, Tideford, Saltash, Cornwall. *T:* Landrake 237.

**BOUVERIE, Pleydell-;** *see* Pleydell-Bouverie.

**BOVELL, Sir (Conrad Swire) Kerr,** Kt 1961; CMG 1958; Bursar, Radley College, since 1968; *b* St Leonards-on-Sea, Sussex, 9 Sept. 1913; *s* of late C. W. K. Bovell, MBE, Colonial Police Service, and of Edith Margaret Bovell (*née* Haughton); *m* 1941, Ethne Jane, *d* of late A. V. Perrin; two *d*. *Educ:* Bradfield Coll., Berks. Appointed to Colonial Police Service as a Probationary Asst Supt of Police. Federated Malay States, 1934; served in Malaya until outbreak of Pacific War; interned in Singapore, 1942-45; returned to Malaya; served until 1956; apptd Inspector-Gen. of Police, Federation of Nigeria, 1956; served until retirement in 1962. Bursar, Worksop Coll., 1963-68. Colonial Police Medal, 1951; Queen's Police Medal, 1954; OStJ 1957. *Recreations:* golf, cricket, tennis. *Address:* Radley College, Abingdon, Berkshire. *T:* Abingdon 1272. *Clubs:* East India and Sports; MCC.

**BOVENIZER, Vernon Gordon Fitzell,** CMG 1948; Assistant Under-Secretary of State, Ministry of Defence, 1964-68, retired; *b* 22 July 1908; *s* of Rev. Michael Fitzell Bovenizer and Mary Gordon; *m* 1937, Lillian Cherry (*d* 1970), *d* of John Henry Rowe, Cork; two *s* two *d*. *Educ:* Liverpool Coll.; Sidney Sussex Coll., Cambridge (Scholar). War Office, 1931-45; Control Commission for Germany, 1945, until return to War Office, 1948; Asst Private Sec. to Secretaries of State for War, 1936, and 1940-42; Resident Clerk, 1934-37; Asst Sec., 1942, civilian liaison with US Armies in the UK; Establishment Officer and Dir of Organisation, CCG, 1945-47; Asst Sec. and Dep. Comptroller of Claims, War Office, 1948-58; Counsellor, UK Delegation to NATO, 1958-60; Asst Under-Sec. of State, War Office, 1960-64. us medal of Freedom, 1945. *Recreations:* tennis and squash. *Address:* 6 Cambanks, Union Lane, Cambridge; The Harbour, Annalong, Co. Down. *Club:* Reform.

**BOVENSCHEN, Sir Frederick Carl,** KCB 1943 (CB 1927); KBE 1938; *s* of late C. and Mrs Bovenschen; *m* Mabel Alice, *o d* of the late Right Hon. Sir A. H. D. Acland, 13th Bart; one *d*. *Educ:* King's Sch., Canterbury; Corpus Christi Coll., Oxford (Scholar). 1st Class Classical Mods, 1905; 1st Class Lit. Hum., 1907. Asst Private Sec. to Viscount Haldane,

Sec. of State for War, 1908-12; Private Sec. to Sir Charles Harris, KCB, 1912-15; Principal, War Office, 1920; Asst Sec., 1921; lent to Government of India to serve on Army Retrenchment Cttee, 1931; Dir of Army Contracts, 1932; Dir of Finance, 1936; Dep. Under-Sec. of State for War, 1936-42; Joint Permanent Under-Sec. of State for War, and Mem. of the Army Council, 1942-45. Chevalier Légion d'Honneur, 1920. A Governor of Westminster Hospital and Chm. of its Finance Cttee, 1948-60; a Governor of King's Sch., Canterbury; Mem. Kent County Council, 1949-55; Alderman Hythe Borough Council; Baron of the Cinque Ports, 1953. *Address:* Dunkery, Church Road, Hythe, Kent. *T:* Hythe 67854. *Club:* Athenæum.

**BOVET, Prof. Daniel;** Nobel Prize for Physiology and Medicine, 1957; Professor of Pharmacology, Faculty of Medicine, University of Sassari, Italy, since 1964; Director, Laboratorio di Psicobiologia e Psicofarmacologia of Consiglio Nazionale delle Ricerche, Rome, since 1969; *b* Neuchatel, Switzerland, 23 March 1907; *s* of Pierre Bovet and Amy Babut; *m* Filomena Nitti; three *s*. Institut Pasteur, Paris, 1929-47 (first as an asst and afterwards Chief of the Laboratory of Therapeutic Chemistry); Chief of the Laboratory of Therapeutic Chemistry, Instituto Superiore di Sanitã, Rome, 1947-64. Mem. of the Accademia Nazionale dei XL, 1949; Mem. of Accademia naz. dei Lincei, 1958; Foreign Mem., Royal Soc., 1962. Chevalier de la Légion d'Honneur, 1946; Grande Ufficiale Dell' Ordine della Repubblica Italiana, 1959. *Publications:* (in collaboration with F. Bovet-Nitti) Structure chimique et activité pharmacodynamique du systéme nerveux végétatif, 1948 (Bale, Switzerland); (in collaboration with F. Bovet-Nitti and G. B. Marini-Bettolo) Curare and Curare-like Agents, 1957 (Amsterdam, Holland). *Recreation:* wandering in Amazonia. *Address:* 30 Via Giovanni Battista de Rossi, Rome, Italy. *T:* 865055; Laboratorio di Psicobiologia e Psicofarmacologia CNR, 1 via Reno, 00198 Rome, Italy.

**BOWATER, Sir Dudley;** *see* Bowater, Sir T. D. B.

**BOWATER, Sir Ian (Frank),** GBE 1970; Kt 1967; DSO 1945; TD 1953; Alderman, Coleman Street Ward, since 1960; one of HM's Lieutenants for the City of London since 1960; *b* 1904; *y s* of late Major Sir Frank Henry Bowater, 1st Bt, TD; *m* 1927, Hon. Ursula Margaret, *d* of late Viscount Dawson of Penn, PC, GCVO, KCB, KCMG, MD; one *s* two *d*. *Educ:* Eton; Magdalen Coll., Oxford. Territorial Commission Berks & Bucks Yeo., 1926-27; rejoined TA, 1938. Served War of 1939-45; Staff Capt. 1st AA Div., London, 1940; E Africa, Madagascar, 1942; CRA Islands area, 1942; CMF Sicily and Italy; Comd 53rd LAA (KOYLI) Regt, 1943-45. Comd 490 (M) HAA Regt (TA), 1947-48; Hon. Col 553 LAA Regt (KOYLI), 1953. Joined family Business, W. V. Bowater & Sons, 1926; later Dir Bowater Sales Co. and subseq. of Bowater Paper Corp. until resignation, 1953; Director, Spicers Ltd, 1953-58; Chm., Bowaters Hotels, 1937-; Dir, GKN Birfield Industries, 1968 retired 1969. Dep. Chm., Country Gentlemen's Assoc., 1957; First Pres., City and Metropolitan Bldg Soc., 1965 (Dir 1963-65). Junior Warden, Haberdashers' Company, 1955 and 1961; Master, 1967; Sheriff, City of London, 1965-66; Lord Mayor of London, 1969-70. Chancellor, The City Univ., 1969-70. Hon. DSc The City Univ., 1970.KStJ 1970. *Recreations:* painting, travel, art. *Address:* Calverton Place, Stony Stratford, Bucks. *T:* Stony Stratford 2143; Dashwood House, 69 Old Broad Street, EC2. *T:* 01-283 7431. *Clubs:* White's, City Livery, Coleman Street Ward, United Wards.

**BOWATER, Sir Noël Vansittart,** 2nd Bt, *cr* 1939; GBE 1954; MC 1917; *b* 25 Dec. 1892; *s* of Sir Frank H. Bowater, 1st Bt and Ethel Anita (*d* 1943), *d* of late Mark Fryar, Burmah; *S* father 1947; *m* 1921, Constance Heiton Bett; one *s* two *d*. *Educ:* Rugby. Commnd Territorial Force RA, 1913; served in France, 1915-19 (MC). Sheriff of City of London, 1948, Lord Mayor, 1953-54; Master, Company of Vintners, 1954-55. KStJ; Kt Comdr Royal Order of the North Star; Kt Comdr Order of Menelik the Second. *Heir: s* Euan David Vansittart Bowater [*b* 9 Sept. 1935; *m* 1964, Susan Mary Humphrey, *d* of A. R. O. Slater, FCA, and Mrs N. M. Slater; one *s* two *d*]. *Address:* Conifers, St George's Hill, Weybridge, Surrey. *T:* Weybridge 42744; Riscombe, Exford, Somerset. *T:* Exford 280. *Clubs:* City Livery, United Wards, St James', Guildhall.

**BOWATER, Sir (Thomas) Dudley (Blennerhassett),** 3rd Bt, *cr* 1914; *b* 29 Sept. 1889; 2nd *s* of Sir T. Vansittart Bowater, 1st Bt, MP; *S* brother 1945; *m* 1916, Kathleen Mary (*d* 1921), *o d* of A. A. Frost, Rugby; one *d*; *m* 1948, Mrs Jessie F. Bowater. *Educ:* Whitgift; Maison-de-Melle, Belgium. Liveryman of the Gardeners Company. Capt. 2/2nd County of London (Westminster Dragoons) Yeomanry, 1914-18. Capt. TF Reserve; Chief Observer, Royal Observer Corps, 1940-44. *Recreations:* tennis, golf and the garden. *Heir: nephew* John Vansittart Bowater [*b* 6 June 1918; *m* 1943, Joan Kathleen, *d* of late W. E. H. Scullard; one *s* one *d*]. *Address:* 15 Encombe, Sandgate, Kent.

**BOWDEN,** family name of **Baron Aylestone** and **Baron Bowden.**

**BOWDEN,** Baron, *cr* 1963, of Chesterfield (Life Peer); **Bertram Vivian Bowden,** MA, PhD, FIEE, FIEEE, MScTech; Principal, The University of Manchester Institute of Science and Technology (called Manchester College of Science and Technology until May 1966) since 1964; *b* 18 Jan. 1910; *s* of B. C. Bowden, Chesterfield; *m* 1939, Marjorie Browne (marr. diss., 1954; she *d* 1957); one *s* two *d*; *m* 1967, Mary Maltby. *Educ:* Chesterfield Grammar Sch.; Emmanuel Coll., Cambridge. Worked with late Lord Rutherford, 1931-34; PhD 1934; University of Amsterdam, 1934-35. Physics Master, Liverpool Collegiate Sch., 1935-37; Chief Physics Master, Oundle Sch., 1937-40; Radar Research in England, 1940-43; Radar Research in USA, 1943-46; Sir Robert Watson Watt and Partners, 1947-50; Ferranti Ltd, Manchester (Digital Computers), 1950-53; Dean of the Faculty of Technology, Manchester Univ., and Principal, Manchester Coll. of Science and Technology, 1953-64. Chm. Electronics Research Council of Ministry of Aviation, 1960-64; Minister of State, Dept of Education and Science, 1964-65 (on leave of absence as Principal of Manchester Coll. of Science and Technology). Pres. The Science Masters Assoc., 1962. *Publications:* Faster Than Thought, 1953; The Development of Manchester College of Science and Technology; numerous papers on education. *Recreations:* listening to music, exercising gigantic Alsatian. *Address:* Pine Croft, Stanhope Road, Bowden, Altrincham, Cheshire. *T:* 061-928 4005. *Club:* Athenæum.

**BOWDEN, Andrew,** MBE 1961; MP (C) Kemp Town Division of Brighton since 1970; *b* 8 April 1930; *s* of William Victor Bowden,

Solicitor, and Francesca Wilson; *m* 1970, Benita Napier. *Educ:* Ardingly College. Paint industry, 1955-68; Man. Dir, Personnel Assessments Ltd, 1969-; Man. Dir, Haymarket Personnel Selection Ltd, 1970-; Dir, Sales Education & Leadership Ltd, 1970-. Contested (C): North Hammersmith, 1955; North Kensington, 1964; Kemp Town, Brighton, 1966. Nat. Chm., Young Conservatives, 1960-61; Mem., Wandsworth Borough Council, 1956-62. *Recreations:* fishing, chess, golf. *Address:* House of Commons, SW1. *Club:* Junior Carlton.

**BOWDEN, Major Aubrey Henry,** DSO 1918; Chairman, Bowden Bros Ltd, Grand Buildings, Trafalgar Square, WC2; *e s* of Henry White Bowden, MICE, Great Missenden; *m* 1st, 1918, Helen (*d* 1939), *o d* of late R. G. Modera, Wilbury Lodge, Hove; one *s* one *d*; 2nd, 1941, Andrée Marguerite July; one *s* two *d*. *Educ:* Oundle. Electrical Engineer. Training: Brompton and Kensington Electricity Supply Co.; London Underground Railway; Metropolitan Railway; Oerlikon Co.; from here commissioned: to 11th Service Batt. Royal Warwicks Regt, to Capt. and Brigade Machine Gun Officer, to Machine Gun Corps. *Address:* Danesfort, Gong Hill Drive, Farnham, Surrey. *T:* Frensham 2709.

**BOWDEN, Sir Frank,** 3rd Bt *cr* 1915; MA Oxon; industrialist and landowner; *b* 10 Aug. 1909; *o s* of Sir Harold Bowden, 2nd Bt, GBE, and of Vera, *d* of Joseph Whitaker, JP, FZS; *S* father 1960; *m* 1st, 1935; one *s*; 2nd, 1937, Lydia Eveline, *d* of Jean Manolovici, Bucharest; three *s*. *Educ:* Rugby; Merton Coll., Oxford. Served with RNVR, 1939-44. Pres., University Hall, Buckland, 1967-70. Pres., British Kendo Association, 1969. *Recreations:* collecting weapons and armour, particularly Japanese (Vice-Chm. Japan Soc. of London, 1970; Member: Soc. for Preservation of Art Swords of Japan, Tokyo; Japanese Sword Soc. of US; To-Ken Soc. of GB); shooting, archery, cricket. *Heir:* *s* Nicholas Richard Bowden, *b* 13 Aug. 1935. *Address:* Thame Park, Oxon. *Clubs:* White's, Bath, Royal Thames Yacht, United and Cecil.

**BOWDEN, Rev. Guy Arthur George;** Vicar of All Saints, Highbrook in Diocese of Chichester; *b* 19 April 1909; *s* of Arthur Ashfordby and Ellen Louisa Bowden; *m* 1942, Jessie Margaret Guild; two *s* one *d*. *Educ:* Haileybury Coll.; Magdalene Coll., Cambridge; Westcott House, Cambridge. Cambridge Mission to Delhi, 1931-34; Westcott House, 1934-36; Curate, St Mary and St John's, Birmingham, 1936-39; Curate, Hatfield, Herts, 1939-40; Instructor and officiating Chaplain, RAF, 1940-43; Chaplain, RAF, 1943-46; Chaplain and Lecturer in Divinity, King Alfred's Coll., Winchester, 1946-51; Canon and Chancellor, Truro Cathedral, 1951-60, and Diocesan Dir of Religious Education; Warden of the SPG Coll. of the Ascension, Selly Oak, Birmingham, 1960-64. *Publication:* The Dazzling Darkness, 1950. *Recreation:* golf. *Address:* Lucaslands, Highbrook, Ardingly, Sussex.

**BOWDEN, Prof. Kenneth Frank,** DSc, FInstP; Professor of Oceanography in the University of Liverpool since 1954; Pro-Vice-Chancellor, since 1968; *b* 23 Dec. 1916; *s* of Frank and Margaret N. Bowden; *m* 1946, Lilias T. M. Nicol; one *d*. *Educ:* Itchen Secondary Sch.; University Coll., Southampton. Scientific Officer, Anti-Submarine Experimental Establishment (Admiralty), 1939-45; Lecturer in Oceanography, University of Liverpool, 1945-52; Principal Scientific Officer, Nat. Inst. of Oceanography, 1952-54; Dean, Faculty of Science, Univ. of Liverpool, 1959-62. *Publications:* papers on physical oceanography in various scientific journals. *Address:* 100 Meols Parade, Hoylake, Wirral, Cheshire. *T:* 051-632 4083.

**BOWDEN, Dr Richard Charles,** OBE 1941; PhD, MSc, FRIC, FCS; Consultant, Ministry of Aviation (formerly Ministry of Supply), 1952-60; *b* 31 Aug. 1887; *s* of Richard Charles Bowden, Bristol, and Minnie Clara Thatcher; *m* 1913, Nina Adeline, *er d* of Thomas Fisher, Bristol; no *c*. *Educ:* Merchant Venturers Sch., Bristol; Merchant Venturers Technical Coll., Bristol; Bristol Univ. (Hons, Physical Chemistry). Asst Chemist, Research Dept, Royal Arsenal, Woolwich, 1911; Chemist, Royal Gunpowder Factory, 1912; Chemist 2nd Class, 1915; Chemist in Charge, 1923; Technical Asst (temp.) under Dir of Ordnance Factories, War Office, 1930; Technical Asst, 1932; Chemical Engineer, 1934; Superintendent, Royal Ordnance Factories, 1934-41; Asst Dir of Ordnance Factories (X); Dep Dir of Ordnance Factories (X), 1941; Dir, of Ordnance Factories (X), 1942-52. Patentee or Joint Patentee of various patents relating to chemical processes and chemical plant. Medals: Silver Jubilee, 1935; Coronation, 1937 and 1953. *Publications:* Author or Joint Author of publications in Journal of Chemical Society, 1911, 1912, 1923. *Address:* The Mount, 77 Cheam Road, Sutton, Surrey. *T:* 01-642 7834.

**BOWDEN, Prof. Ruth Elizabeth Mary,** DSc London, MB, BS, MRCS, LRCP; Professor of Anatomy, Royal Free Hospital School of Medicine, University of London, since 1951; *b* 21 Feb. 1915; *o c* of late Frank Harold and of Louise Ellen Bowden. *Educ:* Westlands Sch.; St Paul's Girls' Sch.; London (Royal Free Hospital) Sch. of Medicine for Women, University of London. House Surg. and later House Physician, Elizabeth Garrett Anderson Hosp. (Oster House branch), 1940-42; House Surg., Royal Cancer Hosp., 1942; Grad. Asst in Nuffield Dept of Orthopædic Surgery, Peripheral Nerve Injury Unit, Oxford, 1942-45; Asst Lecturer in Anatomy, Royal Free Hospital Sch. of Medicine, 1945; later Lecturer, then University Reader in Human Anatomy, 1949; Rockefeller Travelling Fellowship, 1949-50; Hunterian Prof., RCS, 1950. Pres., Anat. Soc. of Gt Brit. and Ireland, 1970; Fellow, Brit. Orthopædic Assoc.; Fellow Royal Society Med.; Chm. Council of Chartered Soc. of Physiotherapy, 1960-; Pres. of Inst. of Science Technology, 1960-65. *Publications:* contribs to Peripheral Nerve Injuries Report of Medical Research Council; Peripheral Nerve Injuries; contribs to medical and scientific jls. *Recreations:* reading, music, painting, walking, gardening, carpentry. *Address:* 6 Hartham Close, Hartham Road, N7. *T:* 01-607 3464.

**BOWEN, Catherine Drinker;** author; *b* Haverford, Pa; *d* of Henry Sturgis Drinker and Aimée Ernesta (*née* Beaux); *m* 1st, Ezra Bowen; one *s* one *d*; 2nd, 1939, Thomas McKean Downs. *Educ:* Peabody Institute; Juilliard Music Conservatory. Fellow: Royal Society of Literature; Royal Society of Arts; World Acad. of Art and Science; Mem. Amer. Philosophical Soc. Holds hon. degrees from Amer. Univs, and several Amer. awards. *Publications:* numerous books, including: Friends and Fiddlers (essays), 1935; (with Barbara Von Meck) Beloved Friend, biography of Tchaikowsky, 1937; Free Artist, biography of Anton and Nicolas Rubinstein, 1939; Yankee from Olympus, biography of Justice Holmes, 1944; John Adams and the American Revolution, 1950; The Lion and the Throne, biography of Sir Edward Coke, 1957;

Adventures of a Biographer, 1960; Francis Bacon, The Temper of a Man, 1963; Miracle at Philadelphia, 1966; Biography: the craft and the calling, 1968; Family Portrait, 1970. *Address:* 260 Booth Lane, Haverford, Pa 19041, USA. *T:* Midway 9-4975.

**BOWEN, Edmund John,** FRS 1935; MA, DSc Oxon; Hon. Fellow of University College, Oxford; lately Aldrichian Praelector in Chemistry; *b* 29 April 1898; *s* of Edmund Riley Bowen and Lilias Kamester; *m* 1924, Edith Moule; one *s* one *d*. *Educ:* Royal Grammar Sch., Worcester; Balliol Coll., Oxford (Brackenbury Scholar). BA, 1920; MA, 1922; Fellow of University Coll., Oxford, 1922; Junior Proctor, 1935-36; Lieut 13th Siege Battery, RGA (France), 1917-18. Davy Medal, Royal Society, 1963; Niels Finsen Medal, 1968. *Publications:* The Chemical Aspects of Light, 1942; papers on physical chemical subjects in scientific journals. *Address:* 10 Park Town, Oxford. *T:* Oxford 57631.

**BOWEN, Elizabeth (Dorothea Cole),** CBE 1948; Hon. DLitt: TCD 1949; Oxon 1956; CLit 1965; *o c* of Henry Cole Bowen, Bowen's Court, Co. Cork, and Florence Isabella Pomeroy Colley; *m* 1923, Alan Charles Cameron (*d* 1952). *Educ:* Downe House, Downe, Kent. *Publications:* Encounters (short stories), 1923; Ann Lee's (short stories), 1926, The Hotel, 1927; The Last September, 1929; Joining Charles (short stories), 1929; Friends and Relations, 1931; To the North, 1932; The Cat Jumps (short stories), 1934; The House in Paris, 1935; The Death of the Heart, 1938; Look at All those Roses (short stories), 1941; Bowen's Court, 1942; Seven Winters, 1943; The Demon Lover (short stories), 1945; The Heat of the Day, 1949; Collected Impression (essays), 1950; The Shelbourne, 1951; A World of Love, 1955; A Time in Rome, 1960; After-thought (essays), 1962; The Little Girls, 1964; A Day in the Dark, 1965; Eva Trout, 1969. *Address:* Carbery, Church Hill, Hythe, Kent.

**BOWEN, (Evan) Roderic,** QC 1952; MA, LLB; Bencher of the Middle Temple; National Insurance Commissioner for Wales, since 1967; Chairman, Montgomeryshire Quarter Sessions, since 1959; *b* 6 Aug. 1913; 2nd *s* of late Evan Bowen, JP, and late Margaret Ellen Twiss, The Elms, Cardigan. *Educ:* Cardigan Schs; University Coll., Aberystwyth; St John's Coll., Cambridge. Practised at the bar with chambers in Cardiff until 1940; served in HM Forces, 1940-45, in the ranks and subsequently as an officer on staff of Judge Advocate-Gen. MP (L), County of Cardigan, 1945-66; Dep. Chm. of Ways and Means, House of Commons, 1965-66. Recorder of: Carmarthen, 1950; Merthyr Tydfil, 1953-60; Swansea, 1960-64; Cardiff, 1964-67. Chm. Welsh Parliamentary Party, 1955. *Address:* 7 Park Place, Cardiff. *T:* Cardiff 32623; Pencartws, Aberporth, Cardigan. *T:* Aberporth 273. *Clubs:* National Liberal; County (Cardiff).

**BOWEN, Gordon,** CB 1962; CMG 1956; Director, Metrication Board, since 1969; *b* 17 June 1910; *e s* of late Arthur Thomas Bowen and Dora Drinkwater; *m* 1938, Elsa Catriona, *y d* of late Rev. Dr Alexander Grieve, MA, PhD; two *s*. *Educ:* Birkenhead Institute Sch.; University of Liverpool. Asst Lecturer in Geography, University of Glasgow, 1933-36; Commonwealth Fund Fellow, University of Calif., 1936-38; Lecturer in Geography, University of Glasgow, 1938-41; Principal, Board of Trade, 1941-44; Asst Sec., Board of Trade, 1944-53; United Kingdom Senior Trade Commissioner in Canada, 1953-58; Under Secretary: Board of Trade, 1958-66; Min. of Technology, 1966-69. *Address:* 17 Somerset Lodge, Briar Walk, SW15. *T:* 01-788 5311. *Clubs:* Athenæum, Civil Service.

**BOWEN, Ian;** *see* Bowen, Ivor I.

**BOWEN, Ira Sprague;** astrophysicist; Staff Member, Mount Wilson Observatory, Pasadena, California (Director, 1946-64) and of Palomar Observatory (Director, 1948-64); (Observatories maintained jointly by Carnegie Institution and California Institute of Technology since 1948); *b* New York, 21 Dec. 1898; *s* of James Henry Bowen and Philinda May Sprague; *m* 1929, Mary Jane Howard. *Educ:* Oberlin Coll., Oberlin, Ohio (BA). Asst in physics, University of Chicago, further study, 1919-21; Calif. Institute of Technology, Pasadena: Instructor, 1921; PhD 1926; Hon. PhD University of Lund, 1950; Hon. ScD: Oberlin Coll., 1948; Princeton Univ., 1953. Asst Prof., 1926; Associate Prof., 1928; Prof., 1931-45; Morrison Research Associate at Lick Observatory, Mount Hamilton, Calif, 1938-39; associated with Office of Scientific Research and Development during War of 1939-45, specialising in rockets and in new types of cameras, etc. Mem. National Academy of Sciences, and of several scientific societies. Medals for work on nebulæ, 1942, 1946, 1949, 1957, 1966. *Address:* Mt Wilson and Palomar Observatories, Pasadena, Calif 91106, USA; 2388 North Altadena Drive, Altadena, Calif 91001.

**BOWEN, Ivor,** CMG 1954; MSc, FRAeS, MIEE; Consultant in Aeronautical Engineering; *b* 21 Feb. 1902; *o s* of James and Barbara Bowen, Oxton, Ches; *m* 1941, Hilda, *o d* of Arthur and Florence Mary Fakes, Cambridge; one *s* one *d*. *Educ:* Birkenhead Institute; University of Liverpool; Trinity Coll., Cambridge. Oliver Lodge Fellow, University of Liverpool, 1923-24; Research Asst to Sir J. J. Thomson, OM, FRS, 1924-26; Demonstrator in Physics, Cavendish Laboratory, Cambridge, 1925-26; Founder Mem. of Cambridge Univ. Air Squadron, 1925. Lecturer in Air Navigation and Aircraft Instruments, Imperial Coll. of Science, 1938-40; Hon. Sec. Instn of Professional Civil Servants, 1938-40; Dep. Dir of Armament Research, Min. of Aircraft Production, 1940; Dir of Instrument Research and Development, Min. of Supply, 1941-47; Chm. Air Photography Research Cttee, 1945-47; Mem. of Council, British Scientific Instrument Research Assoc., 1945-47; Chief Superintendent, Aeroplane and Armament Experimental Establishment, Boscombe Down, 1947-50; Scientific Adviser to UK High Comr to Australia, and Head of UK Min. of Supply Staff, Australia, 1951-53; Principal Dir of Aircraft Equipment Research and Development, Ministry of Supply, 1953-54; Chm. Air Navigation Cttee of Aeronautical Research Council, 1958-61; Mem. Council, Air League of the British Empire; Mem. Air Traffic Control and Navigation Cttee of Electronics Research Council, 1961-68. Liveryman of Worshipful Company of Carpenters, 1959 (Freeman 1954), and of Worshipful Company of Scientific Instrument Makers. Freeman of City of London, 1955. *Publications:* numerous scientific papers on Physics and Aeronautics. *Recreations:* archæology, arboriculture, shooting. *Address:* Stancote, Kippington Road, Sevenoaks, Kent. *T:* Sevenoaks 52495. *Clubs:* Athenæum, Savage, City Livery, Royal Air Force.

**BOWEN, Prof. (Ivor) Ian,** MA Oxon; Professor of Economics, University of Western Australia, since 1958; *b* Cardiff, 3 Dec. 1908; *s* of Ivor Bowen, KC, later County Court Judge, and Edith May (*née* Dummett); *m* 1st,

1935, Erica Baillie (marr. diss., 1950); one *s* one *d*; 2nd, 1951, Isobel Margaret Lindsay Smith; one *s* one *d*. *Educ:* Westminster Sch.; Christ Church, Oxford. Fellow, All Souls Coll., 1930-37, and 1968; Lecturer, Brasenose Coll., 1931-40; Chief Statistical Officer, Ministry of Works, 1940-45; Lectr, Hertford Coll., 1946-47; Prof. of Economics and Commerce, Hull Univ., 1947-58. *Publications:* Cobden (Great Lives Series), 1934; Britain's Industrial Survival, 1947; Population (Cambridge Economic Handbooks), 1954. *Recreation:* golf. *Address:* 7 Circe Circle, Dalkeith, Western Australia. *Clubs:* Reform; Royal Bangkok Sports; Cottesloe Golf (Western Australia).

**BOWEN, John Griffith;** Playwright and Novelist; *b* 5 Nov. 1924; *s* of Hugh Griffith Bowen and Ethel May Cook; unmarried. *Educ:* Queen Elizabeth's Grammar Sch., Crediton; Pembroke Coll., Oxford; St Antony's Coll., Oxford. Frere Exhibition for Indian Studies, Oxford, 1951-52 and 1952-53. Asst Editor, The Sketch, 1954-57; Advertising Copywriter and Copy Chief, 1957-60; Consultant on TV Drama, Associated TV, 1960-67. *Publications:* The Truth Will Not Help Us, 1956; After the Rain, 1958; The Centre of the Green, 1959; Storyboard, 1960; The Birdcage, 1962; A World Elsewhere, 1965; The Essay Prize, 1965; *plays:* I Love You, Mrs Patterson, 1964; After the Rain, 1967; Fall and Redemption, 1967; Little Boxes, 1968; The Disorderly Women, 1968; The Corsican Brothers, 1970; The Waiting Room, 1970; criticism for London Magazine, Sunday Times and New York Times. *Recreations:* science fiction, cooking. *Address:* 7 Sydney Place, SW7. *T:* 01-584 5812. *Club:* PEN.

**BOWEN, Rt. Rev. Michael George;** Titular Bishop of Lamsorti; Coadjutor Bishop with right of succession to See of Arundel and Brighton (RC) since 1970; *b* 23 April 1930; *s* of late Major C. L. J. Bowen and of Lady Makins (who *m* 1945, Sir Paul Makins, Bt, *qv*). *Educ:* Downside; Trinity Coll., Cambridge; Gregorian Univ., Rome. Army, 1948-49, 2nd Lieut Irish Guards; Wine Trade, 1951-52; English Coll., Rome, 1952-59; ordained 1958; Curate at Earlsfield and at Walworth, South London, 1959-63; taught theology, Beda Coll., Rome, 1963-66; Chancellor of Diocese of Arundel and Brighton, 1966-70. *Recreations:* golf, tennis. *Address:* c/o St Joseph's Hall, Storrington, Sussex. *T:* Storrington 2172.

**BOWEN, Roderic;** *see* Bowen, (Evan) Roderic.

**BOWEN, Sir Thomas Frederic Charles,** 4th Bt *cr* 1921; *b* 11 Oct. 1921; *s* of 2nd Bt and May Isobel, *d* of John Frederick Roberts; *S* brother, 1939; *m* 1947, Jill, *d* of Lloyd Evans, Gold Coast; one *s* two *d*. Lieut, Wiltshire Regt, 1944, Captain 1945. *Heir: s* Mark Edward Mortimer Bowen, *b* 17 Oct. 1958. *Address:* Beechcroft, St George's Avenue, Weybridge, Surrey.

**BOWEN-DAVIES, Alan,** FRCS; Senior Consulting Surgeon, Ear, Nose and Throat Department, The London Hospital, since 1946; *b* 26 July 1907; *s* of Dr W. L. Bowen-Davies and Mrs H. A. Bowen-Davies (*née* Burton); *m* 1944, Irenée Maude Atkinson; one *s* two *d*. *Educ:* Harrow Sch.; Pembroke Coll., Cambridge; Guy's Hospital. MA, MB, BChir Cantab 1933; FRCS 1936. Wing Comdr, RAFVR (retired), 1942-46. *Publications:* contributions to Scott-Brown's Diseases of the Ear, Nose and Throat, Proc. Royal Society Med., Lancet, Guy's Hospital reports. *Recreations:* tennis, shooting, fishing. *Address:* 69 Harley Street, W1. *T:* 01-935 9721. *Clubs:* East India and Sports, MCC.

**BOWER;** *see* Dykes Bower.

**BOWER;** *see* Nott-Bower.

**BOWER, Sir Frank,** Kt 1960; CBE 1948; *b* 25 Aug. 1894; *s* of Herbert Austin Bower; *m* 1920, Ethel Shaw (*d* 1970); one *s* two *d*. *Educ:* Lancaster Royal Grammar Sch.; St Catharine's Coll., Cambridge. Served European War of 1914-18; 2/5th King's Own Royal Lancaster Regt, 2/5 Prince Albert Victoria Rajputs, IARO. BA (Classics), 1920; MA 1924. HM Inspector of Taxes, 1920-24; Taxation Officer, Unilever Group, 1924-59. Late Chairman of Tax Cttees of Business Groups; late Director of industrial companies. Member of Court of Lancaster Univ. Past President, Association of British Chambers of Commerce. *Publication:* United Kingdom Volume, World Tax Series, Harvard Law School; contribs to professional journals on tax subjects. *Recreation:* gardening. *Address:* 31 Traps Hill, Loughton, Essex. *T:* 01-508 3030.

**BOWER, Air Marshal Sir Leslie William Clement,** KCB 1962 (CB 1954); DSO 1945; DFC 1944; *b* 11 July 1909; *s* of William Clarke Bower, Co. Cork, Eire; *m* 1963, Clare, *widow* of Commander Jasper Abbott, RN, Uppaton, Yelverton, S. Devon, and *d* of H. W. Etkins, OBE, Curlews, Constantine Bay, N. Cornwall. *Educ:* Harvey Grammar Sch., Folkestone; Cranwell. Royal Air Force 1929; served War of 1939-45 (despatches twice, DFC, DSO), in Europe and Canada; OC 217 (TB) Sqdn, 1941-42; Dir Op. Trg, HQ, RCAF, Ottawa, 1942-43; Group Capt., 1942; Air Cdre, 1952; Air Vice-Marshal, 1954; OC 138 Wing 2nd TAF, 1943-45; AOC 81 (Fighter) Group, 1952-54; Senior Air Staff Officer, HQ Fighter Command, 1954-57; Senior Air Staff Officer, MEAF, 1957-58; Dep. Commander-in-Chief, Middle East Air Force, 1958-59; Air Officer Commanding No 19 Group, RAF Coastal Command, 1959-61; UK Representative in Ankara on Permanent Military Deputies Group of Central Treaty Organisation (Cento), 1962-65; retired. Air Marshal, 1962. *Address:* Coppicetown Lodge, Yelverton, Devon. *T:* Yelverton 3500. *Club:* Royal Air Force.

**BOWER, Norman;** *b* 18 May 1907. *Educ:* Rugby; Wadham Coll., Oxford. Called to Bar, Inner Temple, 1935; contested West Bermondsey, 1931, North Hammersmith, 1935; MP (C) Harrow West, 1941-51; Member Westminster City Council, 1937-45. *Recreations:* golf, cricket, theatre. *Club:* Carlton.

**BOWER, Commander Robert Tatton;** *b* 9 June 1894; *o s* of late Sir Robert Lister Bower, KBE, CMG, and Annette Norah, *d* of late Henry Head, Thornhill, Bray, Co. Wicklow; *m* 1922, Henrietta, 4th *d* of 1st Baron Strickland, GCMG; one *s* seven *d*. *Educ:* Cheam Sch.; RN Colleges Osborne and Dartmouth. Joined RN 1907; served throughout European War; present at Battle of Jutland in HMS Inconstant; in submarines, 1916-18; Flag-Lieut to C-in-C, Portsmouth (Hon. Sir S. C. Colville), 1918-19; in HMS Iron Duke (Turkey and South Russia), 1919-21; psc (RN), 1925; attached RAF Staff Coll., 1928, retired, 1931; returned to service at the outbreak of War of 1939-45, with RAF Coastal Command and at sea escorting convoys; MP (U) Cleveland, Yorks, 1931-45. Chairman Exec. Cttee Society for Individual Freedom, 1950-53; Vice-President Cleveland Bay Horse Society. *Publications:* memoirs and occasional contributions to Reviews and Press. *Recreations:* racing, sailing. *Address:* Gatto-Murina Palace, Mdina, Malta. *T:* 74370. *Clubs:*

Royal Yacht Squadron (Cowes); Union (Malta).

*See also Viscount Monckton of Brenchley.*

**BOWER, Lt-Gen. Sir Roger (Herbert),** KCB 1959 (CB 1950); KBE 1957 (CBE 1944); *b* 13 Feb. 1903; *s* of Herbert Morris Bower and Eileen Francis Fitzgerald Bower, Ripon; *m* 1939, Hon. Catherine Muriel Hotham, *d* of late Capt. H. E. Hotham, and *y sister* of 7th Baron Hotham, CBE; (one adopted *s*) one *d* (and one *s* decd). *Educ:* Repton; RMC, Sandhurst. Served in India with KOYLI, 1923-30; Staff Coll., Camberley, 1935-36; Bde Major, Hong Kong, 1937-38. Served War of 1939-45; NW Europe with HQ Airborne Corps, 1944; Norway, 1945; Comd 1 and 6 Air Landing Bdes; Palestine, 1945-46 (despatches); Comd Hamburg District, 1948-49, with rank of Maj.-Gen.; Director Land/Air Warfare, War Office, 1950-51; Director of Military Training and Director of Land/Air Warfare, 1951-52; Commander East Anglian District, 1952-55; Chief of Staff, Allied Forces, Northern Europe, 1955-56; GOC and Director of Operations, Malaya, 1956-57; Commander-in-Chief, Middle East Land Forces, 1958-60, retired. Col The KOYLI, 1960-66. Treasurer to The Princess Margaret, Nov. 1960-Feb. 1962; Lieut HM Tower of London, 1960-63. US Bronze Star, 1944; King Haakon VII Liberty Cross, 1945. *Recreations:* sailing, shooting, fishing. *Address:* Hill House, St Mary Bourne, Andover, Hants. *T:* St Mary Bourne 263. *Clubs:* Army and Navy, Royal Cruising.

**BOWERING, John;** *b* 29 Oct. 1894; *s* of late Thomas Bowering, Axbridge, Somerset; *m* 1931, Sylvia Elizabeth, *d* of Ernest Hobbs, Santiago, Chile; one *s* one *d*. *Educ:* Clifton; abroad. Served European War, 1914-18 (despatches). During career in the Foreign Service has been stationed at Berlin, Stuttgart, New York, Santo Domingo, Magallanes, Brussels, Antofogasta, Reykjavik and Monrovia; Envoy Extraordinary and Minister Plenipotentiary to the Republic of Liberia, 1946-49; Consul-General at Nice, France, 1949-52; retired 1952. *Recreations:* country pursuits and fishing. *Address:* Ringmere, Town Hill, Lingfield, Surrey. *T:* 307.

**BOWERMAN, David Alexander;** Director, Jamaica Producers Marketing Co. Ltd, and Subsidiaries; Director and Chairman, Linden Hall Hotel, Bournemouth; *b* 19 April 1903; *s* of Frederick and Millicent Bowerman; *m* 1925, Constance Lilian Hosegood (*d* 1959); four *s* one *d*; *m* 1962, June Patricia Ruth Day. *Educ:* Queen's Coll., Taunton. Farmer, 1923-36; Wholesale Fruit and Potato Merchant (Director), 1936-60. Chairman, Horticultural Marketing Council, 1960-63. *Recreations:* sailing, golf, gardens. *Address:* The Spinney, Brenchley, Kent. *T:* Brenchley 2149; Godlingston Manor, Swanage. *T:* Swanage 2083. *Clubs:* Farmers'; Parkstone Yacht (Dorset); Lamberhurst Golf; Swanage Golf.

**BOWERMAN, Brig. John Francis,** CBE 1946; Indian Army (retired); *b* 28 Nov. 1893; *s* of John Bowerman, Cullompton, Devon; *m* 1931, Mary Monica Faed Macmillan; one *d*. *Educ:* Queen Elizabeth's Sch., Crediton. Commissioned West Yorks Regt, 1915; served European War, 1914-18, Mesopotamia, Marri Field Force, 1914-18 (wounded); transferred 129th Duke of Connaught's Own Baluchis, Nov. 1918; active service Afghanistan, 1919, Zhob, 1919-21, Waziristan, 1921-23 and NW Frontier, 1930; Burma Rebellion, 1931-32. Served War of 1939-45, Burma; Chief Liaison Officer, 6th Chinese Army, 1942; Brigadier 1942, as Inspector General Burma Frontier Force; with Chinese-American Forces, Burma, 1943-45; despatches, 1946; retired 1946. King's Police Medal, 1928; American Bronze Star, 1945. FRGS, FRSA. *Publications:* Report on exploration, China, Burma, Tibet Border (MacGregor Memorial Medal of United Services Institution, India, 1928); paper on Frontier Areas of Burma (Silver Medal of RSA, 1947). *Recreations:* golf, fishing. *Address:* Arlington, Woodcock Hill, East Grinstead, Sussex. *T:* East Grinstead 111.

**BOWERS, Mrs Faubion;** *see* Rau, Santha Rama.

**BOWERS, Prof. Fredson Thayer;** Linden Kent Professor of English, University of Virginia, USA; *b* 25 April 1905; *s* of Fredson Eugene Bowers and Hattie May Quigley; *m* 1st, 1924, Hyacinth Sutphen; three *s* one *d*; 2nd, 1942, Nancy Hale. *Educ:* Brown Univ. (PhB); Harvard Univ. (PhD). Instructor in English: Harvard Univ., 1926-36; Princeton Univ., 1936-38; Asst Prof., Univ. of Virginia, 1938-46. USNR, Comdr, 1942-46. Associate Prof., Univ. of Virginia, 1946-48, Prof., 1948-, Alumni Prof., 1959-68, Linden Kent Prof., 1968- (Dean of the Faculty, 1968-69). Fulbright Fellow for Research in UK, 1953; Guggenheim Fellow, 1959; Sandars Reader in Bibliography, Cambridge, 1958; Lyell Reader in Bibliography, Oxford, 1959; Exec. Council, Mod. Lang. Assoc. of Amer., 1964-68 (Pres., S Atlantic MLA, 1969); Corresp. FBA, 1968; Gold Medal, Bibliographical Soc., 1969. Hon. DLitt: Brown, 1970; Clark, 1970. *Publications:* Elizabethan Revenge Tragedy, 1940; Randolph's Fairy Knight (ed), 1942; Principles of Bibliographical Description, 1949; George Sandys: A Bibliographical Catalogue, 1950; Dramatic Works of Thomas Dekker (ed, 4 vols), 1953-61; On Editing Shakespeare and the Elizabethan Dramatists, 1955; Whitman's Manuscripts, 1955; Textual and Literary Criticism, 1959; Bibliography and Textual Criticism, 1964; Dramatic Works in the Beaumont and Fletcher Canon (ed), 1966-; Works of Stephen Crane (ed), 1969-. *Recreations:* philately, music, dogs. *Address:* Woodburn, Route 5, Charlottesville, Virginia, USA. *T:* 703-973-3629. *Club:* Grolier (NYC).

**BOWES, Sir (Harold) Leslie,** KCMG 1968; CBE 1943; Chairman, The Pacific Steam Navigation Company, 1960-65, Managing Director, 1952-65 (Deputy Chairman 1959-60); Chairman, Royal Mail Lines Ltd, 1960-65, Managing Director, 1958-65 (Deputy Chairman 1959-60); *b* 18 Nov. 1893; *m* 1st, 1921; two *s* one *d*; 2nd 1950; one *d*. Served European War, RFC and RAF. The Pacific Steam Navigation Company: Manager for Chile, 1921-48; Director and General Manager, 1949-51. Director: Rea Bros Ltd; Wilson Sons & Co. Ltd; C. R. Harper & Co. Ltd; Ocean Wilsons (Holdings) Ltd; Member: General Purposes Cttee of Shipping Federation, 1958-61; Central Transport Consultative Cttee, 1959-61; Chairman Liverpool Steam Ship Owners' Assoc., 1954; Chairman General Council of British Shipping, 1954; Chairman Liverpool Port Welfare Cttee, 1955-58; Chairman Liverpool Marine Engineers' and Naval Architects Guild, 1955-56; Chairman Govt Cttee of Inquiry into Canals and Inland Waterways, 1956-58; Member General Cttee of Lloyd's Register of Shipping, 1956-; Director, "Indefatigable" and Nat. Sea Training Sch. for Boys, 1954-58; Chairman Liverpool Chamber of Commerce, 1957-58; Governor, City of Liverpool College of Commerce, 1958-60; President: Institute of Shipping and Forwarding Agents, 1957-58; Chairman British Ship Adoption Society, 1958-68; Vice-President Institute of

Transport, 1958-59, Member Council, 1959-; Chairman Shipping Advisory Cttee, Institute of Transport, 1959-65; Member Mersey Docks and Harbour Board, 1956-58; Member Shipping Advisory Council of BTC, 1960-62; Member Shipping and International Services Cttee of British Railways Board, 1963; Chairman, BNEC Cttee for Exports to Latin America, 1966-67 (Dep. Chm. 1964-66). Member Exec. Cttee: Anglo-Chilean Society, 1960-; Anglo-Peruvian Society; Hispanic and Luso-Brazilian Councils, 1960- (Chm. 1963-64 and 1965-66); Member: Cttee of Management, Canning Club; Exec. Cttee, Anglo-Portuguese Society. Liveryman Worshipful Company of Shipwrights (Member Court of Assistants, 1963); Comdr of Chilean Order of Merit, 1942, Grand Officer, 1952; Comdr, Ecuadorian Order of Merit, 1956; Comdr, Peruvian Order of Merit, 1957, Grand Cross, 1959; Order of Vasco Nuñez de Balboa, 1963; Grand Officer, Orden de Mayo, Argentina, 1964; Grand Cross, Order of San Carlos (Colombia), 1966. *Recreations:* golf, gardening. *Address:* Woodside, Kingwood Common, Henley-on-Thames, Oxon. *T:* Rotherfield Greys 230. *Clubs:* Reform, Canning, City Livery.

**BOWES-LYON,** family name of **Earl of Strathmore.**

**BOWES-LYON, Maj.-Gen. Francis James Cecil,** CB 1970; OBE 1962; MC and Bar, 1944; GOC Berlin (British Sector), 1968-70; *b* 19 Sept. 1917; *o s* of Capt. Geoffrey Bowes-Lyon; *m* 1941, Mary, 2nd *d* of Sir Humphrey de Trafford, 4th Bart, *qv*; two *s* one *d*. *Educ:* Eton; Royal Military Coll., Sandhurst. Commissioned into Grenadier Guards, 1938; served War of 1939-45, Guards Armoured Division; Commandant, Guards Depot, 1955-57; comd 2nd Bn Grenadier Guards, 1957-59; Mil. Assistant (GSO1) to CIGS, 1960-62; comd 157 Lowland Bde (Scotland), 1963; GOC 52nd Lowland Division District, 1966-68. *Recreations:* shooting, gardening, racing. *Address:* Highfield House, Slindon, Sussex. *Clubs:* White's, Guards, Pratt's.

**BOWEY, Olwyn,** ARA 1970; practising artist (painter); *b* 10 Feb. 1936; *o d* of James and Olive Bowey. *Educ:* William Newton Sch., Stockton; West Hartlepool Sch. of Art; Royal Coll. of Art. One-man shows: Zwemmer Gall., 1961; New Grafton Gall., 1969; also exhibited at Leicester Gall., Royal Academy; work purchased through Chantrey Bequest for Tate Gall., Royal Academy, Min. of Works, etc. *Recreations:* natural history, music, antique collecting. *Address:* 8 Winthorpe Road, Putney, SW15. *T:* 01-789 2943.

**BOWKER, Sir James;** *see* Bowker, Sir R. J.

**BOWKER, Sir (Reginald) James,** GBE 1961; KCMG 1952 (CMG 1945); Member, London Committee of Ottoman Bank, since 1961; *b* 2 July 1901; *yr s* of Lieut-Col F. J. Bowker, Hampshire Regt, and Edith Sophie Mary Elliott; *m* 1947, Elsa, *d* of Michel Gued and Mme Gued Vidal. *Educ:* Charterhouse; Oriel Coll., Oxford. 3rd Secretary, Foreign Office and Diplomatic Service, 1925. Served in Paris, Berlin, Ankara, Oslo and Madrid. British Minister in Cairo, 1945-47; High Commissioner in Burma, 1947-48; Ambassador to Burma, 1948-50; an Asst Under-Secretary of State, FO, 1950-53; Ambassador to Turkey, 1954-58; Ambassador to Austria, 1958-61; retired from Foreign Service, 1961. *Address:* 3 West Eaton Place, SW1. *T:* 01-235 3852. *Club:* Brooks's.

**BOWLBY, Sir Anthony Hugh Mostyn,** 2nd Bt, *cr* 1923; *b* 13 Jan. 1906; *e s* of Sir Anthony Bowlby, 1st Bt and Maria Bridget (*d* 1957), *d* of Rev. Canon Hon. Hugh W. Mostyn; *S* father, 1929; *m* 1930, Dora Evelyn, *d* of John Charles Allen; two *d*. *Educ:* Wellington Coll.; New Coll., Oxford. *Heir: b* Edward John Mostyn Bowlby [*b* 26 Feb. 1907; *m* 1938, Ursula, 3rd *d* of Mrs Dora Longstaff; two *s* two *d*]. *Address:* The Old Rectory, Ozleworth, near Wotton-under-Edge, Glos.

*See also E. H. P. Brown.*

**BOWLBY, Hon. Mrs Geoffrey,** CVO 1937; Extra Woman of the Bedchamber to Queen Elizabeth, the Queen Mother; 4th *d* of 11th Viscount Valentia, Bletchington Park, Oxford; *m* 1911, Capt. Geoffrey Vaux Salvin Bowlby, Royal Horse Guards (killed in action, 1915); one *s* one *d*. Commandant of Auxiliary Hospital, 1916-19 (despatches twice); a Lady-in-Waiting to Duchess of York, 1932; Woman of the Bedchamber to the Queen, 1937-45. *Address:* Middleton Stoney, Bicester, Oxon. *T:* Middleton Stoney 237.

*See also Earl of Meath.*

**BOWLE, Horace Edgar;** Consul-General in HM's Foreign Service (retired); *b* 13 Aug. 1886; *y s* of late Edward Bowle, Salisbury, Wilts; *m* 1917, Letitia Constance, *y d* of late Charles Penruddocke, Compton Park, Wilts. *Educ:* Pembroke Coll., Cambridge (BA 1908); abroad. Served in USA, Colombia (Chargé d'Affaires, 1914), France, Belgium, Argentina and Portuguese E Africa; retired on pension, Nov. 1944. *Address:* 23 Merrywood Park, Reigate, Surrey. *T:* Reigate 46103.

**BOWLE, John Edward;** historian; *b* 19 Dec. 1905; *o s* of Edward Francis Bowle, Salisbury, and Edith Beatrice, *y d* of late Silas Taunton, Fugglestone, Wilton, Wilts. *Educ:* The Old Malthouse, Langton Matravers; Marlborough Coll. (Council and Keith Rae Exhibitioner); Balliol Coll., Oxford (Brackenbury Scholar, 1924; BA 1927; MA 1932). Senior History Master, Westminster Sch., 1932-40; History Master, Eton, 1940-41. Air Ministry and Foreign Office, 1941-45. Lecturer in Modern History, Wadham Coll., Oxford, 1947-49; Leverhulme Research Fellow, 1949-50; Prof. of Political Theory, Oxford, 1950-67. Visiting Prof., Columbia Univ., NY, 1949; Dir, Preparatory Session, College of Europe, Bruges, 1949; Visiting Professor: Grinnel Coll., Iowa, 1961; Occidental Coll., Los Angeles, 1965; Indiana Univ., 1966; Lecturer, Smith Coll., Northampton, Mass, 1967. Editor, The World To-day, for RIIA, 1949-51. *Publications:* Western Political Thought, 1947 (Arts Council Prize, 1966); The Unity of European History, 1948; Hobbes and his Critics, 1951; Politics and Opinion in the Nineteenth Century, 1954; Minos or Minotaur?, 1956; Viscount Samuel, a biography, 1957; Ed. The Concise Encyclopædia of World History, 1958; A New Outline of World History, 1963; Henry VIII, a biography, 1964; England, a portrait, 1966; Survey of English History, 1971; contrib. to Punch and various periodicals. *Recreations:* travel, painting. *Address:* 24 Woodstock Close, Oxford. *T:* 58379. *Club:* Travellers'.

**BOWLER, Air Vice-Marshal Thomas Geoffrey,** CB 1951; CBE 1944; RAF, retired; *b* 1 March 1895; 2nd *s* of Thomas William Bowler; *m* 1924, Evelyn Mary, *o d* of Charles Luxon, MVO; one *s* one *d*. *Educ:* Bloxham Coll. Commissioned Dorset Regt, 1914; served European War, 1914-18, Captain, 1915; Suvla Bay landing, Gallipoli, 1915 (wounded); transferred to RFC and RAF, 1918; Sqdn Ldr, 1924; RAF Staff Coll., psa, 1930; Wing Comdr, 1938; Group Capt., 1940; Air Commodore, 1942; Air Vice-Marshal, 1947; retired 1951. *Address:*

Two Guns, Kingswear, Devon. *Clubs:* Royal Air Force; Veteran Car; Royal Dart Yacht.

**BOWLES,** family name of **Baron Bowles.**

**BOWLES,** Baron *cr* 1964 (Life Peer); **Francis George Bowles;** *b* 2 May 1902; *s* of late Horace Edgar Bowles, Freshwater, IoW; *m* 1950, Kay, *e d* of late E. H. Musgrove, and *widow* of Air Commodore E. D. M. Hopkins. *Educ:* Highgate Sch.; London Univ. LLB Lond.; BSc (Econ.). Admitted a solicitor, 1925. Contested (Lab) Hackney North, 1929, 1931 and 1935, and Preston, 1936; MP (Lab) Nuneaton Division of Warwickshire, 1942-64; Vice-Chairman Parliamentary Labour Party, 1946-48; Deputy Chairman of Ways and Means, 1948-50; Captain of the Queen's Bodyguard of the Yeomen of the Guard, 1965-70. Freeman, City of London. Adm., Port of Brixham Trawler Racing Assoc. *Address:* 88 St James's Street, SW1. *T:* 01-930 9134; House of Lords, SW1; Redwells, Southdown Hill, Brixham, Devon. *T:* Brixham 2181.

**BOWLES, Mrs Ann P.;** *see* Parker Bowles.

**BOWLES, Chester;** United States Ambassador to India, 1963-69; *b* Springfield, Mass, 5 April 1901; *s* of Allen Bowles and Nellie Harris; *g s* of Samuel Bowles, Founder of the Springfield Republican; *m* 1934, Dorothy Stebbins Bowles; two *s* three *d. Educ:* Choate Sch., Wallingford, Conn.; Yale Univ., New Haven, Conn. Founded advertising and marketing research agency in NY City with William Benton, 1929; Chm. Board of this agency (Benton & Bowles, Inc.), 1936-41, when sold out interests. Administrator of Office of Price Administration, 1943-46, appointed by President Roosevelt; Mem. of War Production Bd, 1943-46; appointed Dir of Economic Stabilization by President Truman, 1946, and resigned from that post, 1946; Special Asst to UN Sec.-Gen., 1946-48; Governor of Connecticut, 1949-51; American Ambassador to India, and first American Ambassador to Nepal, 1951-53; Mem., 86th Congress, House of Representatives, 1959-60 (2nd Dist. Conn); Under-Sec. of State, USA, Jan.-Nov. 1961; President's Special Representative and Adviser on African, Asian and Latin American Affairs with rank of Ambassador, Nov. 1961-May 1963; Mem. of Congress, US (2nd Dist Conn). Member: Democratic Advisory Council on Foreign Policy; Institute of International Education; American African Soc.; American National Commission for United Nations Economic, Scientific and Cultural Organizations Conference in Paris, 1946; (Internat. Chm.) UN Appeal for Children, 1947; Board of Advisers, Fletcher Sch. of Law and Diplomacy, Medford, Mass; Delivered The Anna Howard Shaw Memorial Lectures at Bryn Mawr Coll., 1953-54; Godkin Lectr, Harvard Univ., 1956; Berkeley Lectr, University of Calif, 1956; Chubb Lectr, Yale Univ., 1957; Rosenfeld Lectr, Grinnell Coll., 1959. Conn Delegate to Democratic Nat. Convention, 1940, 1944, 1948, 1956, 1960; Chm., Platform Cttee, Democratic National Convention, July 1960. Franklin Delano Roosevelt Award for fight against racial discrimination, 1950; Roosevelt Coll. Award for outstanding public service, 1953. Associate Fellow Silliman Coll., Yale Univ.; Hon. LLD Amer. Univ., Washington, DC; Hon. DSc The New Sch. for Social Research, New York; Hon. Dr of Laws, Howard Univ., Washington, DC, Hon. Dr of Law: Oberlin Coll., 1957; Bard Coll., 1957; Hon. LLD: University of Rhode Island, 1958; Yale, 1968. *Publications:* Tomorrow Without Fear, 1946; Ambassador's Report, 1954; The New Dimensions of Peace, 1955; American Politics in a Revolutionary World, 1956; Africa's Challenge to America, 1956; Ideas, People and Peace, 1958; The Coming Political Breakthrough, 1959; Conscience of a Liberal, 1962; Makings of a Just Society, 1963; A View from New Delhi, 1969; My Years in Public Life, 1941-1969, 1971; and many articles on economic problems and foreign policy. *Recreation:* sailing. *Address:* Hayden's Point, Essex, Conn 06426, USA. *TA:* Essex, Conn. *Clubs:* Essex Yachting (Essex, Conn); Cruising Club of America, Yale (New York).

**BOWLES, Rt. Rev. Cyril William Johnston;** *see* Derby, Bishop of.

**BOWLING, Air Vice-Marshal Victor Swanton,** CB 1958; CBE 1948; DL; *b* 3 July 1908; *s* of Lieut-Col William Henry Bowling, TD, Pembroke Dock, South Wales; *m* 1936, Margaret Jennette, *d* of late Rev. R. T. Jones, Hope, Wrexham, Denbighshire; one *s* two *d. Educ:* Haverfordwest Grammar Sch.; St Lawrence Coll., Ramsgate. Entered RAF, 1927; served War of 1939-45 in Egypt, Iraq, North Africa, Norway (despatches); Senior Air Staff Officer, 11 Group, 1946-48; Group Capt., Operations Central Fighter Establishment, 1948-50; OC 323 Wing Canal Zone, 1950-51; Senior Air Staff Officer, Air Headquarters Iraq, 1951-52; Air Officer Commanding, Cyprus, 1952-54; Sector Comdr, Northern Fighter Sector, 1954-56; Air Officer Commanding 11 Group, 1956-59; Asst Chief of Staff (Air Defence), Supreme Headquarters, Allied Powers, Europe, Paris, 1959-61; Group-Capt. 1947; Air Commodore, 1952; Air Vice-Marshal, 1956; Retired, 1961. DL Pembrokeshire, 1967. Freedom Cross of King Haakon VII, Norway. *Recreations:* ski-ing, sailing. *Address:* Old Chimneys, St Florence, Tenby, Pembrokeshire. *T:* Manorbier 205. *Clubs:* Royal Air Force, Ski Club of Great Britain.

**BOWMAN, Sir James,** 1st Bt *cr* 1961; KBE 1957 (CBE 1952); JP; DCL; *b* 8 March 1898; *m* 1922, Jean, *d* of Henry Brook, Ashington, Northumberland; one *s* one *d.* Served European War, 1914-18, Royal Marines. Gen. Sec., Northumberland Miners' Association (later National Union of Mineworkers, Northumberland Area), 1935-49; Vice-Pres., National Union of Mineworkers, 1938-49; Mem. of Gen. Council of TUC, 1945-49; Chm., National Coal Board Northern (N & C) Div., 1950-55; Dep. Chm., National Coal Board, 1955-56; Chm., National Coal Board, 1956-61. JP, Northumberland, 1935. Mem., Court of Governors of Administrative Staff Coll., 1957-. Former member: National Miners' Welfare Joint Council; DSIR; Royal Commission on the Press. *Heir: s* George Bowman [*b* 2 July 1923; *m* 1960, Olive (*nee* Case); three *d*]. *Address:* Woodlands, Killingworth Station, Forest Hall, Newcastle upon Tyne. *T:* Newcastle 661252. *Club:* Reform.

**BOWMAN, Sir John Paget,** 4th Bt, *cr* 1884; *b* 12 Feb. 1904; *s* of Rev. Sir Paget Mervyn Bowman, 3rd Bt, and Rachel Katherine (*d* 1936), *d* of late James Hanning, Kilcrone, Co. Cork; *S* father 1955; *m* 1st, 1931, Countess Cajetana Hoyos (*d* 1948), *d* of Count Edgar Hoyos, Schloss Soss, Lower Austria; one *s* one *d*; 2nd, 1948, Frances Edith Marian, *d* of Sir Beethom Whitehead, KCMG (*d* 1928), Efford Park, Lymington. *Educ:* Eton. Formerly 2nd Lieut 98th (Surrey and Sussex Yeomanry) Field Brigade RA. *Heir: s* David Anthony Paget Bowman [*b* 16 Oct. 1935; *m* 1968, Valerie Winifred, *o d* of R. C. Tatham, N Ferriby, Yorks]. *Address:* Bishops Green House, Newbury, Berks.

**BOWMAN, Robert Ritchie,** CBE 1945; Chairman, Northern Ireland Paper Box Wages Council; Chairman, Joint Advisory Councils for Local Authority Services, 1954-64; *b* Belfast, 1883; 2nd *s* of late Alexander and Rose Bowman; *m* 1913, Margaret, *yr d* of Henry Page; no *c. Educ:* Belfast and Oxford. Entered service of Labour Dept, Board of Trade, 1911; Sec. Irish Trade Boards, 1919-21; Asst Sec., Ministry of Labour (Northern Ireland), 1922-39; Permanent Sec., Ministry of Labour and National Insurance, Northern Ireland, 1939-49; Mem. of N Ireland National Assistance Board, 1949-52. Sec. and later mem. of Commission on the Natural and Industrial Resources of Northern Ireland, 1923-26. Represented Govt of Northern Ireland at Int. Labour Organisation Conferences, 1934-48. *Address:* 8 Garranard Park, Belfast 4. *T:* Belfast 653712.

**BOWMAN, Thomas Patrick;** Chairman, P A Management Consultants Ltd, since 1966; President, European Federation of Management Consultants, since 1967; Governor, Sundridge Park Management Centre, since 1955; Member, Monopolies Commission, since 1969; *b* 25 Sept. 1915; *s* of Thomas Marshall Bowman and Louisa Hetherington Macfarlane; *m* 1950, Norma Elizabeth Deravin; one *s. Educ:* Oundle Sch.; Hertford Coll., Oxford. Joined Industrial Engineering Div. of Thomas Hedley & Co. (now Proctor & Gamble Ltd), 1937; P A Management Consultants Ltd, 1945 (Dir, 1955; Managing Dir, 1961). Chairman, UK Management Consultants Assoc., 1966; Founder Member and Fellow of Inst. of Management Consultants; FBIM 1959. *Address:* 9 Clement Road, Wimbledon, SW19. *T:* 01-946 3828. *Club:* Royal Thames Yacht.

**BOWMAN-SHAW, George Neville;** Chairman: Lancer Boss Group Ltd, 1966; Lancer Boss Ltd, 1967; Boss Trucks & Equipment, 1959; Lancer Boss International SA Geneva, 1962; Boss Engineers Ltd, 1961; *b* 4 Oct. 1930; *s* of George Bowman-Shaw and Hazel Bowman-Shaw (*née* Smyth); *m* 1962, Georgina Mary Blundell; three *s* one *d. Educ:* Caldicott Preparatory Sch.; then private tutor. Farming Trainee, 1947; Management Trainee in Engineering Co., 1948. Commissioned in 5th Royal Inniskilling Dragoon Guards, 1950. Sales Manager: Matling Ltd, Wolverhampton, 1953; Materials Handling Equipment (GB) Ltd, London, and Matbro Ltd, London, 1955. Mem., Development Commn, 1970-. *Recreations:* shooting, skiing, wildfowl collection. *Address:* Toddington Park, Toddington, Bedfordshire. *T:* Toddington 2576. *Clubs:* Constitutional, Cavalry, Hurlingham.

**BOWMONT and CESSFORD, Marquis of; Guy David Innes-Ker;** *b* 18 Nov. 1954; *s* and *heir* of 9th Duke of Roxburghe, *qv*.

**BOWRA, Sir (Cecil) Maurice,** Kt 1951; FBA 1938; Warden of Wadham College, University of Oxford, 1938-70; *b* 8 April 1898; *y s* of late Cecil A. V. Bowra, Chinese Customs Service. *Educ:* Cheltenham Coll. (Scholar); New Coll., Oxford (Scholar). 1st class Hons Mods, 1920; 1st class Literae Humaniores, 1922; MA 1923; DLitt 1937. Joined RFA, 1917; served in France, 1917-18. University of Oxford: Fellow and Tutor, Wadham Coll., 1922-38; Prof. of Poetry, 1946-51; Vice-Chancellor, 1951-54; Romanes Lectr, 1966. Pres., British Acad., 1958-62. Hon. Fellow, New Coll., Oxford, 1946. Hon. Member: Amer. Acad. of Arts and Letters; Royal Irish Acad. Hon. LittD: Dublin; Hull; Wales; Harvard; Columbia; Hon. LLD St Andrews; Hon. DCL Oxford; Docteur hc: Paris; Aix. Conington Prize, Univ. of Oxford, 1930; Kenyon Medal for Classical Studies, 1966. Commandeur de la Légion d'Honneur; Kt-Comdr, Royal Order of Phoenix (Greece); Pour le Mérite (W Germany). *Publications:* (trans. with H. T. Wade-Gery) Pindar's Pythian Odes, 1928; (co-Ed.) Oxford Book of Greek Verse, 1930; Tradition and Design in the Iliad, 1930; Ancient Greek Literature; Pindari Carmina, 1935; Greek Lyric Poetry, 1936; rev. edn 1961; (co-Ed.) Oxford Book of Greek Verse in Translation, 1937; Early Greek Elegists, 1938; The Heritage of Symbolism, 1943; A Book of Russian Verse, 1943; Sophoclean Tragedy, 1944; From Virgil to Milton, 1945; The Creative Experiment, 1949; The Romantic Imagination, 1950; Heroic Poetry, 1952; Problems in Greek Poetry, 1954; Inspiration and Poetry, 1955; The Greek Experience, 1957; Primitive Song, 1962; In General and Particular, 1964; Pindar, 1964; Landmarks in Greek Literature, 1966; Poetry and Politics, 1900-1960, 1966; Memories, 1898-1939, 1966; (trans.) The Odes of Pindar, 1969; On Greek Margins, 1970; articles in learned jls. *Recreations:* none. *Address:* Wadham College, Oxford. *T:* Oxford 44045.

**BOWRING, Edgar Rennie;** *b* 8 Feb. 1899; *yr s* of Henry A. Bowring, St John's, NF, and Liverpool; *m* 1929, Jean Douglas, *d* of C. A. C. Bruce. *Educ:* Shrewsbury Sch. Formerly Director: C. T. Bowring & Co. Ltd. and assoc. companies; Martins Bank Ltd (a former Dep. Chm. and Chm. of London Bd); Royal Insurance Company Ltd (a former Dep. Chm.) The Liverpool and London and Globe Insurance Co. Ltd; The London and Lancs Insurance Co. Ltd; Cunard Steam-Ship Co. Ltd. Served European War, 1914-18, Lieut RFA. High Sheriff of Cheshire, 1948-49. *Address:* 116 Grosvenor House, Park Lane, W1.

**BOWRING, Maj.-Gen. John Humphrey Stephen,** CB 1968; OBE 1958; MC 1941; FICE; Colonel, The Gurkha Engineers, since 1966; Colonel Commandant, Corps of Royal Engineers, since 1968; *b* 13 Feb. 1913; *s* of late Major Francis Stephen Bowring and late Mrs Maurice Stonor; *m* 1956, Iona Margaret (*née* Murray); two *s* two *d. Educ:* Downside; RMA Woolwich; Trinity Coll., Cambridge. MA 1936. Commissioned, 1933; Palestine, 1936; India, 1937-40; Middle East, 1940-42; India and Burma, 1942-46; British Military Mission to Greece, 1947-50; UK, 1951-55; CRE, 17 Gurkha Div., Malaya, 1955-58; Col GS, War Office, 1958-61; Brig., Chief Engineer, Far East, 1961-64; Brig. GS, Ministry of Defence, 1964-65; Engineer-in-Chief, 1965-68. Dir, Consolidated Gold Fields. *Recreations:* sailing, flying. *Address:* The Upper House, Chedglow, Crudwell, near Malmesbury, Wilts. *T:* Crudwell 238. *Clubs:* Army and Navy, Royal Ocean Racing.

**BOWSER, Ernest William;** *b* 21 April 1887; 2nd *s* of late Charles Henry Bowser, Spalding, Lincs; *m* 1909, Margaret, *yr d* of late Robert King, Moulton, Lincs; one *s. Educ:* Louth Grammar Sch. Agriculturist and Landowner. High Sheriff of Lincs, 1943. *Recreations:* shooting and ornithology. *Address:* 79 Spilsby Road, Boston, Lincs. *T:* Boston 4316.

**BOWYER,** family name of **Baron Denham.**

**BOWYER, John Francis,** CB 1966; Lieutenant-Commander RN; lately Chief Registrar of the High Court in Bankruptcy; *b* 11 Jan. 1893; *s* of Col W. G. Bowyer, RE, and Eva Mary (formerly Lane); *m* 1919, Violet Wright (widow; *née* Shakespeare); four *s* one *d. Educ:* Royal Naval Colls, Osborne and Dartmouth.

Served in Royal Navy as Midshipman, Sub-Lieut, Lieut, 1910-19, and as Capt of HM Destroyer Nonsuch, 1918-19; Lieut-Cmdr (Emergency List), 1922. Called to Bar, Inner Temple, 1928; joined Lincoln's Inn, 1934; Bencher, Lincoln's Inn, 1952. Apptd Registrar of the High Court in Bankruptcy, Dec. 1953; Chief Registrar, 1957. *Recreations:* golf, painting. *Address:* Avenue Lodge, Avenue Road, NW8. *Clubs:* United Service; Seaford Golf.

**BOWYER-SMYTH, Sir P. W.;** *see* Smyth.

**BOX, Betty Evelyn, (Mrs P. E. Rogers),** OBE 1958; Film Producer; *b* 25 Sept. 1915; *m* 1949, Peter Edward Rogers; no *c. Educ:* home. *Films include:* (producer) Doctor in the House; Doctor at Sea; The Wind Cannot Read; A Tale of Two Cities; The 39 Steps; Doctor in Love; No Love for Johnnie. *Address:* Pinewood Studios, Iver, Bucks.

**BOX, Donald Stewart;** Member Midlands & Western Stock Exchange and Partner, Lyddon, Thomas Freeguard & Co., Stockbrokers; *b* 22 Nov. 1917; *s* of late Stanley Carter Box and Elizabeth Mary Stewart Box; *m* 1st, 1940, Margaret Kennington Bates (marr. diss., 1947); 2nd, 1948, Peggy Farr (*née* Gooding); no *c. Educ:* Llandaff Cathedral Sch.; St John's Sch., Pinner; County Sch., Harrow. RAF ranks, 1939, commissioned, 1941; overseas service Egypt, Palestine, Transjordan, 1941-44; demobbed with rank of Flt-Lieut, 1945. MP (C) Cardiff North, 1959-66. *Recreations:* reading, photography. *Address:* Laburnum Cottage, Sully Road, Penarth, Glam. *T:* Penarth 707966. *Clubs:* Junior Carlton; County, Exchange (Cardiff).

**BOX, Sydney;** Author and Film Producer; *b* 29 April 1907; *m* 1st, 1929, Katherine Knight (marr. diss. 1934); 2nd, 1935, Muriel Baker (marr. diss. 1969); one *d.* In 1939 founded Verity Films Ltd, which produced more than 100 documentary and training films for War Office, Ministry of Information, etc; Producer, Two Cities Films, Denham Studios, 1941-42; Producer, Riverside Studios, 1943-45; Man. Dir and Executive Producer, Gainsborough Pictures, 1946-50. Films include: The Seventh Veil (Academy award for best original screen play, 1946); Quartet; Trio; Holiday Camp; Portrait from Life; The Years Between; The Man Within; The Passionate Stranger, and The Truth About Women (both with Muriel Box). Author (often in collaboration with Muriel Box) of more than 50 one-act plays, including Not This Man, winner of British Drama League National Festival at Old Vic, 1937. In charge of production London Independent Producers, 1951. Dir, Tyne Tees Television (ITA), 1958-65; Chairman: London Independent Television Producers Ltd, 1963; National Film Corp. Ltd, 1965; Triton Publishing Co. Ltd. *Publication:* Diary of a Drop Out, 1969. *Address:* 42 Welbeck Street, W1.

**BOXALL, Bernard,** CBE 1963; Chairman, British United Trawlers Ltd, since 1969; Director, Lindustries Ltd (Deputy Chairman, 1960-70), and Chairman of its associated engineering companies; Director: Export Packing Service Ltd; A. J. Mills (Holdings) Ltd; Member: Scottish Economic Planning Council; Scottish Advisory Committee for Civil Aviation; Monopolies Commission; *b* 17 Aug. 1906; *s* of late Arthur Boxall and of Mrs Maud Mary Boxall (*née* Mills); *m* 1931, Marjorie Lilian, *d* of late William George Emery and Mrs Emery; one *s* one *d. Educ:* King's Coll. Sch., Wimbledon; Imperial Coll., London Univ. (BSc (Hons), FCGI). James Howden & Co. Ltd, 1928-33; J. A. King & Co. Ltd, 1934-42; Production-Engineering Ltd, 1942-59; Management Consultant, 1959-. Mem., Company of Coachmakers and Coach Harness Makers. FIMechE, FIProdE., Associate Inst. T. *Recreations:* golf, sailing. *Address:* Gilridge, Sandy Lane, Kingswood, Surrey. *T:* Mogador 2125. *Clubs:* Royal Automobile, Royal Thames Yacht; Walton Health Golf, Cryptics Cricket.

**BOXALL, Mrs Lewis;** *see* Buss, Barbara Ann.

**BOXER, Air Vice-Marshal Sir Alan (Hunter Cachemaille),** KCVO 1970; CB 1968; DSO 1944; DFC 1943; Defence Services Secretary, Ministry of Defence, Nov. 1967-70; *b* 1 Dec. 1916; *s* of late Dr E. A. Boxer, CMG, Hastings, Hawkes Bay, NZ; *m* 1941, Pamela Sword; two *s* one *d. Educ:* Nelson Coll., New Zealand. Commissioned in RAF, 1939. Served War of 1939-45; Trng Comd until 1942; flying and staff appts, Bomber Comd, 1942-45. RAF Staff Coll., 1945; Jt Staff, Cabinet Offices, 1946-47; Staff Coll., Camberley, 1948; Strategic Air Comd, USAF and Korea, 1949-51; Central Fighter Estabt, 1952-53; Mem. Directing Staff, RAF Staff Coll., 1954-56; CO No 7 Sqdn, RAF, 1957; Group Capt. and CO, RAF Wittering, 1958-59; Plans, HQ Bomber Comd, 1960-61; Air Cdre, idc, 1962; SASO: HQ No 1 Gp, RAF, 1963-65; HQ Bomber Comd, 1965-67; Virtuti Militari (Polish), Bronze Star (US), Air Medal (US). *Recreations:* fishing and sailing. *Address:* 19 Queen's Gate Place, SW7. *Club:* Royal Air Force.

**BOXER, Prof. Charles Ralph,** FBA 1957; Professor of the History of the Expansion of Europe Overseas, Yale University, since 1969; Emeritus Professor of Portuguese, University of London, since 1968; Fellow, King's Coll., 1967; *b* 8 March 1904; *s* of Col Hugh Boxer and Jane Boxer (*née* Patterson); *m* 1945, Emily Hahn; two *d. Educ:* Wellington Coll.; Royal Military Coll., Sandhurst. Commissioned Lincs Regt, 1923. Served War of 1939-45 (wounded, POW in Japanese hands, 1941-45). Retired with rank of Major, 1947. Camoens Prof. of Portuguese, London Univ., 1947-51; Prof. of the History of the Far East, London Univ., 1951-53; resigned latter post and re-apptd Camoens Prof., 1953-67. Visiting Research Prof., Indiana Univ., 1967-. A Trustee of National Maritime Museum, 1961-68. Dr *hc* Universities of Utrecht (1950), Lisbon (1952), Bahia (1959) and Liverpool (1966); Order of Santiago da Espada (Portugal); Grand Cross of the Order of the Infante Dom Henrique (Portugal); Kt Order of St Gregory the Great, 1969. *Publications:* The Commentaries of Ruy Freyre de Andrade, 1929; The Journal of M. H. Tromp, *Anno* 1639, 1930; Jan Compagnie in Japan, 1600-1817, 1936 (2nd edn 1950); Fidalgos in the Far East, 1550-1770, 1948; The Christian Century in Japan, 1549-1640, 1951, 2nd edn 1967; Salvador de Sá and the Struggle for Brazil and Angola, 1952; South China in the 16th Century, 1953; The Dutch in Brazil, 1624-1654, 1957; The Tragic History of the Sea, 1589-1622, 1959; The Great Ship from Amacon, 1959; Fort Jesus and the Portuguese in Mombasa, 1960; The Golden Age of Brazil, 1695-1750, 1962; Race Relations in the Portuguese Colonial Empire, 1415-1825, 1963; The Dutch Seaborne Empire, 1600-1800, 1965; Portuguese Society in the Tropics, 1966; Further Selections from the Tragic History of the Sea, 1969; The Portuguese Seaborne Empire, 1415-1825, 1969; numerous articles in learned periodicals. *Address:* Ringshall End, Little Gaddesden, Herts. *Club:* United Service.

**BOXER, Air Cdre Henry Everard Crichton,** CB 1965; OBE 1948; psa, ndc, idc; Counsellor (Defence Equipment), British High Commission, Canada, since 1968; *b* 28 July 1914; *s* of late Rear-Adm. Henry P. Boxer; *m* 1938, Enid Anne Louise, *d* of late Dr John Moore Collyns; two *s* two *d*. *Educ:* Shrewsbury Sch.; RAF Coll., Cranwell. Commissioned RAF, 1935; No 1 Fighter Squadron, 1935-37; No 1 Flying Training Sch. (Chief Instructor), 1937-39; Specialist Navigator, 1939. Served War of 1939-45, in UK, S Africa and Europe. BJSM, Washington, DC, 1945-48; directing Staff, RAF Staff Coll., 1949-50; Coastal Command, 1951-52; Nat. Defence Coll., Canada, 1952-53; Air Ministry, 1953-56; OC, RAF Thorney Island, 1956-58. ADC to the Queen, 1956-59; IDC, 1959; Sen. Air Liaison Officer and Air Adviser to British High Comr in Canada, 1960-62; AO i/c Admin, HQ Coastal Comd, 1962-65; Dir of Personnel (Air), MoD (RAF), 1965-67; retd, 1967. *Address:* British High Commission, 80 Elgin Street, Ottawa 4, Canada. *Club:* Royal Air Force.

**BOYCE, Air Vice-Marshal Clayton Descou Clement,** CB 1946; CBE 1944; Assistant Controller of Aircraft, Ministry of Supply, since 1957; *b* 19 Sept. 1907; *er s* of Col C. J. Boyce, CBE, late IA; *m* 1928, Winifred, *d* of late J. E. Mead, Castletown, Isle of Man; one *s*. *Educ:* Bedford Sch.; Cranwell. Sec.-Gen., Allied Air Forces, Central Europe, 1953; AOC, Cyprus, 1954-56. *Address:* c/o Lloyds Bank, Cox's and King's Branch, 6 Pall Mall, SW1.

**BOYCE, Air Cdre George Harold,** CB 1945; AFC; late RAF; *b* 1894; *s* of late John Boyce, Ottawa; *m* 1921, Constance Browning, Carnoustie, Scotland. Served European War, 1914-19; Senior Air Staff Officer, No. 15 Group, 1939; Air Commodore, 1941; retired list, 1946. *Address:* 22 Swaylands Drive, Brooklands, Sale, Manchester.

**BOYCE, Sir Robert (Charles) Leslie,** 3rd Bt *cr* 1952; *b* 2 May 1962; *s* of Sir Richard (Leslie) Boyce, 2nd Bt, and of Jacqueline Anne, *o d* of Roland A. Hill; *S* father, 1968. *Heir: uncle* John Leslie Boyce [*b* 16 Nov. 1934; *m* 1957, Finola Mary, *d* of late James Patrick Maxwell; one *s* three *d*]. *Address:* 6 Court Close, Shipton-under-Wychwood, Oxfordshire.

**BOYCOTT, Rev. D. M.;** *see* Morse-Boycott.

**BOYD,** family name of **Baron Kilmarnock.**

**BOYD OF MERTON,** 1st Viscount *cr* 1960; **Alan Tindal Lennox-Boyd,** PC 1951; CH 1960; DL; Joint Vice-Chairman of Arthur Guinness, Son & Co. Ltd, since 1967 (Managing Director, 1960-67); Director: Tate & Lyle, since 1966; Imperial Chemical Industries, since 1967; *b* 18 Nov. 1904; 2nd *s* of Alan Walter Lennox-Boyd, and Florence, *d* of James Warburton Begbie; *m* 1938, Lady Patricia Guinness, 2nd *d* of 2nd Earl of Iveagh, KG, CB, CMG, FRS; three *s*. *Educ:* Sherborne; Christ Church, Oxford (Scholar; MA; Beit Prizeman; Hon. Student, 1968). Pres. of the Oxford Union, 1926. Contested Gower Div. of Glamorgan, 1929; MP (C) Mid-Beds, 1931-60; Parliamentary Sec., Ministry of Labour, 1938-39; Parliamentary Sec., Ministry of Home Security, 1939; Parliamentary Sec., Ministry of Food, 1939-40; Called to the Bar, Inner Temple, 1941; Parliamentary Sec., Ministry of Aircraft Production, 1943-45; Minister of State for Colonial Affairs, 1951-52; Minister of Transport and Civil Aviation, 1952-54; Sec. of State for the Colonies, 1954-Oct. 1959. Lieut RNVR, 1940-43. DL Beds, 1954-61, Cornwall, 1965. President: The Save the Children Fund, 1960-; British Leprosy Relief Assoc., 1960-; RNVR Officers' Assoc., 1964-; Royal Commonwealth Soc., 1965- (Chm., 1961-64); Chairman: Voluntary Service Overseas, 1962-64; Brewers Soc., 1965; Trustee, BM, 1962-; Trustee, Natural History Museum, 1963-; Governor, Sherborne Sch., 1962-, Chm. of Governors, 1968; Mem. Council, Institute of Directors, 1962-; Mem. Court of Directors, Royal Exchange, 1962-; Pres. Overseas Employers Federation, 1962-; Prime Warden, Goldsmiths' Co., 1964-65. Messel Medal, Soc. of Chemical Industry, 1966. *Heir: s* Hon. Simon Donald Rupert Neville Lennox-Boyd [*b* 7 Dec. 1939; *m* 1962, Alice, *d* of late Major Meysey Clive, Whitfield, Hereford and of Lady Mary Clive; two *s* two *d*]. *Address:* 6 Iveagh House, Ormond Yard, SW1. *T:* 01-839 4296; Ince Castle, Saltash, Cornwall. *T:* Saltash 2274. *Clubs:* Carlton, Pratt's, Buck's, RNVR; Royal Yacht Squadron; Kildare St (Dublin).

**BOYD, Prof. Alexander Michael,** FRCS; Professor of Surgery, University of Manchester, since 1947; *b* 5 March 1905; *s* of Henry Strene Boyd and Beatrice Kate Boyd (*née* Tatham). *Educ:* Haileybury. MRCS, LRCP, MB, BS London, 1929; FRCS 1931. Senior Demonstrator of Anatomy, St Bartholomew's Hosp., 1933; 1st Asst Surg. Professional Unit, Bart's, 1934-39. War Service RAMC, 1940-45, principally in Egypt; Lieut-Col; O/C Surgical Div., 63rd Gen. Hospital, Cairo, Hon. Asst Surg. and Asst Dir Surgical Professional Unit, Bart's, 1946; MSc (Hon.) University of Manchester, 1950. Comdr Order of the Phœnix, Greece, 1942. *Publications:* numerous, upon surgery of peripheral vascular disease in all Med. Jls. *Recreations:* fishing, shooting. *Address:* 64 Platt Lane, Rusholme, Manchester. *T:* 061-224 4180.

**BOYD, Sir Alexander Walter,** 3rd Bt, *cr* 1916; *b* 1934; *s* of late Cecil Anderson Boyd, MC, MD, and Marjorie Catharine, *e d* of late Francis Kinloch, JP, Shipka Lodge, North Berwick; *S* uncle, 1948; *m* 1958, Molly Madeline, *d* of late Ernest Arthur Rendell; two *s* three *d*. *Heir: s* Ian Walter Rendell Boyd, *b* 14 March 1964. *Address:* RR 3, Vernon, British Columbia, Canada.

**BOYD, Arthur Merric Bloomfield,** OBE 1970; painter, sculptor, designer (stage, ballet); *b* 24 July 1920; *s* of William Merric Boyd and Doris Lucy Eleanor Gough; *m* 1945, Yvonne Hartland Lennie; one *s* two *d*. *Educ:* State Sch., Murrumbeena, Vic., Australia. Was taught painting and sculpture by parents and grandfather, Arthur Merric Boyd; first exhibited painting in Melbourne, 1937; served in Australian Army, 1940-43; painted and exhibited, 1944-59, also sculptured and exhibited ceramics, 1953-56, in Australia; designed for theatre in Melbourne, 1955-57; rep. Australia at Venice Biennale, 1958. First visited Europe, 1959; first one-man exhibn painting, London, 1960; designed for Ballet at Edinburgh Festival and Sadler's Wells Theatre, 1961, and at Covent Garden Royal Opera House, 1963; retrospective exhibn of painting at Whitechapel Gallery, 1962; exhibn Zwemmer's Gallery, 1963; retrospective exhibitions: Nat. Gallery of S Australia, Adelaide, 1964; Edinburgh; Exhibn, Tooth's Gall., 1969. *Address:* c/o The Commercial Bank of Australia Ltd, 34 Piccadilly, W1. *Club:* Savile.

**BOYD, Christopher;** *see* Boyd, T. C.

**BOYD, Maj.-Gen. Ian Herbert Fitzgerald,** CB 1962; CBE 1957 (OBE 1950); *b* 21 Dec. 1907; *s* of late Sir Donald James Boyd, KCIE, Indian Civil Service, Punjab, and late Laura Caroline (*née* Hope); *m* 1931, Dorothy Margaret, *d* of Lewis French, CIE, CBE, ICS; two *s* one *d*. *Educ:* Fettes; RMA, Woolwich; Christ's Coll., Cambridge (BA). Commissioned RE 1927; served Mohmand, 1933; Waziristan, 1936 (despatches); Instr Staff Coll., Quetta, 1943-44; served Burma and Malaya, 1944-45 (despatches 4 times). Chief Instr SME, 1946-47; AA and QMG, War Office, 1948-50 (OBE); Col, Q (Movements), Far ELF, 1950-53; DQMG, BAOR, 1954-57; Chief Engineer, Far ELF, 1957-59; Chief Engineer, Northern Army Group and BAOR, 1959-62; retd, 1963. Col Comdt, Corps of Royal Engineers, 1966-. *Recreations:* sailing, shooting, fishing, horology. *Address:* Primrose Hill, Barcombe, Lewes, Sussex. *T:* Barcombe 203; c/o Coutts & Co., 440 Strand, WC2. *Club:* United Service.

**BOYD, Brig. Sir John (Smith Knox),** Kt 1958; OBE 1942; FRS 1951; MD, FRCP, DPH; *b* 18 Sept. 1891; *s* of J. K. Boyd, Largs, Ayrshire; *m* 1st, 1918, Elizabeth Edgar (*d* 1956); 2nd, 1957, Mary Bennett (*d* 1968), *d* of late Denis Harvey Murphy, Northwood. *Educ:* Largs Sch.; Glasgow Univ. (MB, ChB, 1913; MD, 1948). Entered RAMC 1914; Lieut-Col 1938; Col 1944; Brig. 1945. Served European War, 1914-18; France and Belgium, 1914-15, Salonika, 1916-18. War of 1939-45, Middle East Force, 1940-43, North-West Europe, 1944-45; Dir of Pathology, War Office, 1945-46. KHP 1944-46; retired, 1946. Dir, Wellcome Laboratories of Tropical Medicine, 1946-55. Wellcome Trustee, 1956-66; Scientific Consultant to Wellcome Trust, 1966-68. Mem. of Colonial Medical Research Cttee, 1945-60; Member: Tropical Medicine Research Board, 1961-63; Army Pathology Advisory Cttee, 1946-; Managing Cttee, Bureau of Hygiene and Trop. Diseases, 1956-. Chairman: Research Defence Soc., 1956-68; Medical Research Council Malaria Cttee and Leprosy Cttee, 1961-63; Royal Society Trop. Diseases Cttee, 1956-64. Hon. Sec., Royal Society of Trop. Medicine and Hygiene, 1946-57, Pres., 1957-59. Hon. FRCPE 1960; Hon. FRCPath; Hon. LLD Glasgow 1957; Hon. DSc Salford, 1969. Manson Medal, 1968. *Publications:* scientific papers on the pathology of tropical diseases and on bacterial viruses. *Recreation:* golf. *Address:* Mossbank, 6 The Covert, Northwood, Middx. *Clubs:* Athenæum; Royal and Ancient (St Andrews).

**BOYD, Lachlan Macpherson,** CMG 1955; *b* 29 Sept. 1904; *s* of late Hugh Boyd, S Uist; *m* 1936, Betty Pinkerton, MBE 1958, *d* of late Dr Robert Scott, Exeter. *Educ:* Portree Secondary Sch.; Edinburgh Univ. Colonial Administrative Service, Uganda, 1930-46; Resident, Buganda, 1947-51; Sec. for African Affairs, 1951-55; Minister of Local Government, Uganda, 1955-60; retired, 1960. *Address:* Devoran, 33 Granary Lane, Budleigh Salterton, Devon. *T:* Budleigh Salterton 2452. *Clubs:* Royal Commonwealth Society, Royal Over-Seas League, East Africa House.

**BOYD, Leslie Balfour;** Clerk of the Court, Central Criminal Court, Old Bailey, since 1955, and Clerk of the Peace of the City of London and Town and Borough of Southwark, since 1955; *b* 25 Nov. 1914; *e s* of late Henry Leslie Boyd, Mem. of Lloyds, of Crowborough, Sussex, and Beatrix Boyd, *d* of Henry Chapman, for many years British Consul at Dieppe; *m* 1936, Wendy Marie, *d* of George and Nancy Blake, Oswestry, Salop; one *s* one *d*. *Educ:* Evelyn's; Royal Naval College, Dartmouth. Invalided out of Royal Navy, 1931. Called to the Bar, Gray's Inn, 1939; joined staff of Central Criminal Court, 1941; Dep. Clerk of Court, 1948; Dep. Clerk of Peace, City of London and Town and Borough of Southwark, 1949-55. Master, Worshipful Company of Gold and Silver Wyre Drawers, 1969. *Publications:* contributor to Criminal Law and Juries titles of Halsbury's Laws of England, 3rd edn. *Recreations:* gardening and travel. *Address:* Stone Cross Farm, Crowborough, Sussex. *Club:* Bar Yacht.

**BOYD, Martin à Beckett;** Author; *b* Lucerne, Switzerland, 10 June 1893; *s* of late Arthur M. Boyd and Emma, *d* of Hon. William à Beckett, Penleigh, Wilts, and Melbourne, Vic. Served European War as Lieut The Buffs, Observer, RFC and Pilot, RAF. Trained as architect. Began to write, 1925. Reviewed for Times Literary Supplement, 1930-40. *Publications:* Fourteen novels, including: The Lemon Farm, 1935; Lucinda Brayford, 1946; The Cardboard Crown, 1952; A Difficult Young Man, 1954; Outbreak of Love, 1957; When Blackbirds Sing, 1962; The Tea-Time of Love, 1969. Autobiography, Day of my Delight, 1965. Travel book, Much Else in Italy, 1958. *Address:* c/o Australia and New Zealand Bank, Ltd, 71 Cornhill, EC3.

**BOYD, Prof. Maurice James;** Professor of Latin since 1939 and University Adviser on Schools, Queen's University, Belfast; Chairman, N Ireland GCE Examinations Board; *b* 7 Jan. 1911; *s* of James Boyd, MA, LLB, Londonderry and Belfast; *m* 1936, Constance Eveline, *d* of Harry Marlow, JP, Croydon; two *s* one *d*. *Educ:* Royal Academical Institute, Belfast; Queen's Univ., Belfast (BA 1931); Trinity Coll., Oxford (MA). Asst and Junior Lecturer in Latin, Queen's Univ., Belfast, 1933-39; Dean of the Faculty of Arts, 1944-47 and 1956-57; Dean of the Faculty of Theology, 1962-68; Editor of Annual Record of QUB, 1940-49, 1959-; Pres. QU Assoc., 1954; Chm. of Convocation, QUB, 1956-65. *Publications:* articles in Classical Periodicals. *Address:* 8 Maryville Park, Belfast BT9 6LN. *T:* Belfast 665610.

**BOYD, Prof. Robert Lewis Fullarton,** FRS 1969; Professor of Physics in the University of London since 1962; Head, Mullard Space Science Laboratory of Department of Physics of University College, London, since 1965; *b* 1922; *s* of late William John Boyd, PhD, BSc; *M* 1949, Mary, *d* of late John Higgins; two *s* one *d*. *Educ:* Whitgift Sch.; Imperial Coll., London. Exp. Officer at Admty Mining Estabt, 1943-46; DSIR Res. Asst, 1946-49; ICI Res. Fellow, 1949-50, Maths Dept, UCL; ICI Res. Fellow, Physics Dept, UCL, 1950-52; Lectr in Physics, UCL, 1952-58, Reader in Physics, UCL, 1959-62. Prof. of Astronomy (part-time), Royal Institution, 1963-69. *Publication:* The Upper Atmosphere (with H. S. W. Massey), 1958. *Recreation:* vintage Rolls Royce motor cars. *Address:* 48 Mitchley Hill, Sanderstead, South Croydon CR2 9HB. *T:* 01-657 7568.

**BOYD, (Thomas) Christopher;** farmer; *b* 1916; *m*; one *s* two *d*. Army, 1940-44; civil servant, 1939 and 1944-48; MP (Lab) Bristol NW, 1955-59; Chelsea Borough Councillor, 1953-59. *Address:* Middlegill, Moffat, Dumfriesshire. *T:* Beattock 415.

**BOYD, Thomas J. L. Stirling;** Barrister-at-law; *b* Edinburgh, 23 Oct. 1886; *o c* of late P. J. Stirling Boyd, DL, *y s* of late Sir Thomas Boyd, Lord Provost of Edinburgh, and late Beatrice Rachel, OBE, *d* of late Prof. Thomas Laycock, MD, Edinburgh. *Educ:* Edinburgh Academy; Trinity Coll., Oxford (MA 1915;

Hon. Fellow, 1969). Asst Paymaster, RNVR, 1914; Lieut, RAF, 1918; Barrister, Inner Temple, 1919. Chief Justice, Sarawak, 1930-39. Air Ministry, 1939-43. Mem. Westminster City Council, 1945-65. Mem. Special Cttee for Province of Canterbury, constituted under Reorganisation Areas Measure, 1944, 1947-60. Chairman: Works and Traffic Cttee, Westminster CC, 1952-55; Westminster Health Soc., 1956-59. *Publications:* The Web (play), 1925; The Laws of Sarawak, 1936. *Address:* 16/17 Pall Mall, SW1. *T:* 01-839 5332; 11 King's Bench Walk, Temple, EC4. *Clubs:* Athenæum, MCC.

**BOYD, William,** CMG 1943; CBE 1919; *b* 1876; *s* of Robert F. Boyd; *m* Helen (*d* 1954), *d* of William Bow, JP; three *d.* Was Dep. Dir-Gen., British Ministry of Shipping, New York, 1916-18; Dep. Rep. Min. of War Transport in USA, 1939-45, Representative, 1945. *Address:* 1143 Fifth Avenue, New York City.

**BOYD, William;** *b* 21 June 1885; *s* of Dugald Cameron and Eliza M. Boyd; *m* Enid G. Christie. *Educ:* Trent Coll., Derbyshire; Edinburgh Univ. MB, ChB 1908; MD Edinburgh (Gold Medal), 1911; Diploma in Psychiatry, Edinburgh, 1912; MRCPE 1912; FRCP 1932; LLD Saskatchewan, 1937; MD Oslo, 1945; DSc Manitoba, 1948; FRCS Canada, 1949; FRCPE 1955; FRCSEd 1966; LLD Queen's, 1956. MO, Derby Borough Asylum, Derby, England, 1909-12; Pathologist, Winwick Asylum, Warrington, England, 1912-13; Pathologist, Royal Wolverhampton Hosp., Wolverhampton, 1913-14; Prof. of Pathology, University of Manitoba, Winnipeg, 1915-37; Prof. of Pathology and Bacteriology, University of Toronto, 1937-51, Prof. of Pathology, University of British Columbia, 1951-53. Capt. 3rd Field Ambulance, 46th Div. Imperial Forces, France, 1914-15. *Publications:* With a Field Ambulance at Ypres, 1917; The Physiology and Pathology of the Cerebrospinal Fluid, 1920; Pathology for the Surgeon, 7th edn, 1955; Pathology for the Physician, 7th edn, 1965; Text-Book of Pathology, 7th edn, 1961; Introduction to the Study of Disease, 5th edn, 1962. *Recreations:* mountaineering, golf, gardening. *Address:* 40 Arjay Crescent, Toronto, Ont, Canada.

**BOYD-CARPENTER, Rt. Hon. John Archibald,** PC 1954; MP (C) for Kingston-upon-Thames since 1945; Chairman, Public Accounts Committee, since 1964; Barrister-at-law; *b* 2 June 1908; *s* of late Sir Archibald Boyd-Carpenter, MP; *m* 1937, Margaret, *e d* of Lieut-Col G. L. Hall, OBE; one *s* two *d. Educ:* Stowe; Balliol Coll., Oxford. Pres. Oxford Union, 1930; BA (History, 1930); Diploma Economics, 1931; toured USA with Oxford Univ. Debating Team, 1931; Harmsworth Law Scholar, Middle Temple, 1933; Council of Legal Education's Prize for Constitutional Law, 1934; called to Bar, Middle Temple, 1934, and practised in London and SE Circuit. Contested (MR) Limehouse for LCC, 1934. Joined Scots Guards, 1940; held various staff appointments and served with AMG in Italy; Financial Sec., to the Treasury, 1951-54; Minister of Transport and Civil Aviation, 1954-Dec. 1955; Minister of Pensions and National Insurance, Dec. 1955-July 1962; Chief Sec. to the Treasury and Paymaster-Gen., 1962-64; Front Bench Spokesman on Housing, Local Government and Land, 1964-66. Chm., Greater London Area Local Govt Cttee, Conservative Party, 1968. Chairman: Orion Insurance Co., 1969-; CLRP, 1970-. *Publications:* The Conservative Case, 1950; essays and newspaper articles on political subjects. *Recreations:* tennis and swimming. *Address:* 12 Eaton Terrace, SW1. *T:* 01-730 7765. *Club:* Carlton.

*See also Baron Hailsham of Saint Marylebone.*

**BOYD GRAHAM, Lieut-Col Howard;** *see* Graham.

**BOYD ORR,** 1st Baron, *cr* 1949, of Brechin Mearns in the County of Angus; **John Boyd Orr,** CH 1968; Kt 1935; DSO 1917; MC; FRS 1932; LLD; Director of several cos; Rector of Glasgow University, 1945, Chancellor, 1946; *b* Kilmaurs, Ayrshire, 23 Sept. 1880; *s* of late R. C. Orr of Holland Green, Kilmaurs; *m* Elizabeth Pearson, *d* of late John Callum, West Kilbride; two *d* (and one *s* killed in action). *Educ:* University, Glasgow; MA, MD, DSc; Bellahouston Gold Medallist. Hon. Graduate St Andrews, Edinburgh, Glasgow, Aberdeen, Princeton USA, Santiago Chile, Brazil, Groeningen Holland, Manchester, Vollebach Norway, Delhi India, Uppsala Sweden; Hon. Fellow New York Academy of Medicine; Harben Medal, Royal Inst. of Public Health, 1949; Borden Medal (USA), 1958; Gold Medal, NFU of USA; Gold Medal, Internat. League of Agric. Producers. Hon. FRCS Dublin. Served European War 1914-18, RAMC (MC, DSO, despatches); Member: Reorganisation Commission for Fat Stock Industry, 1932; Reorganisation Commission for Milk, 1935-36; Cattle Cttee (Ministry of Agriculture); Colonial Advisory Council of Agriculture and Animal Health; Advisory Cttee on Nutrition (Ministry of Health); Technical Commission on Nutrition, League of Nations; Chm. Scottish Scientific Advisory Cttee; Prof. of Agriculture, University of Aberdeen, 1942-45; MP (Ind.) Scottish Universities, 1945-46; late Dir of Rowett Research Inst., Aberdeen; formerly Dir of Imperial Bureau of Animal Nutrition; Joint Editor Nutrition Abstracts and Reviews; Dir-Gen. United Nations Food and Agricultural Organisation, 1945-48; Nobel Peace Prize, 1949. Comdr Légion d'Honneur; Comdr and Cross with Star, Polonia Restituta. *Publications:* History of Scotch Church Crisis of 1904; Minerals in Pastures and their relation to Animal Nutrition, 1928; Food, Health and Income, 1936; Fighting for What, 1943; Food and the People, 1944; The White Man's Dilemma, 1952; Feast and Famine, 1960; As I Recall, 1966; several papers on physiological subjects in scientific journals. *Recreation:* farming. *Heir:* none. *Address:* Newton, by Brechin, Angus. *T:* Edzell 294. *Clubs:* Athenæum, Farmers'; Strathcona (Aberdeen).

**BOYD-ROCHFORT, Sir Cecil (Charles),** KCVO 1968 (CVO 1952); Trainer Racehorses, Newmarket, retired 1968; *b* 16 April 1887; 3rd *s* of late Major R. H. Boyd-Rochfort, 15th Hussars, Middleton Park, Westmeath; *m* 1944, Hon. Mrs Henry Cecil, *d* of Sir James Burnett, of Leys, 13th Bt, CB, CMG, DSO; one *s. Educ:* Eton. Late Capt. Scots Guards (SR); served European War, 1914-18 (wounded, Croix de Guerre). Kilnahard Castle, Ballyheelan, Co. Cavan, Eire. *T:* Ballyheelan 112. *Clubs:* Turf, White's; Kildare Street (Dublin).

**BOYD-WILSON, Edwin John,** MA, BSc (NZ), BA (Cantab.); Professor of Modern Languages, Victoria University College, Wellington, NZ, 1920-54, retired; *b* 1886; *m* 1910, Helen Walker, Hobart; two *s* two *d. Educ:* Nelson Coll., NZ; Canterbury Univ. Coll., NZ; Emmanuel Coll., Cambridge. *Recreations:* Rugby football, tramping, shooting. *Address:* 44 Pukatea Street, Eastbourne, Wellington, NZ.

**BOYDELL, (The Worshipful Chancellor) Peter Thomas Sherrington,** QC 1965; Chancellor of

Dioceses of Truro since 1957, Oxford since 1958 and Worcester since 1959; *b* 20 Sept. 1920; *s* of late Frank Richard Boydell, JP, and late Frances Barton Boydell, Blenheim Lodge, Whitegate Drive, Blackpool; unmarried. *Educ:* Arnold Sch., Blackpool; Manchester Univ. LLB Manchester 1940. Served War of 1939-45; Adjt, 17th Field Regt, RA, 1943; Bde Major, 1st Armoured Div., RA, 1944; Bde Major, RA, 10th Indian Div., 1945. Qualified as Solicitor, 1947. Called to Bar, Middle Temple, 1948. Mem., Legal Board of Church Assembly, 1958- . Contested (C) Carlisle, 1964. *Recreations:* mountaineering, swimming, squash, music, opera, ballet, theatre, travel. *Address:* 45 Wilton Crescent, SW1. *T:* 01-235 5505; 2 Harcourt Buildings, Temple, EC4. *T:* 01-353 8415. *Clubs:* Garrick, Royal Automobile; Climbers.

**BOYDEN, (Harold) James;** MP (Lab) Bishop Auckland since Oct. 1959; *b* 19 Oct. 1910; *s* of late Claude James and late Frances Mary Boyden; *m* 1935, Emily Pemberton. *Educ:* Elementary Sch., Tiffin Boys, Kingston; King's Coll., London. BA (History), 1932; BSc (Econ), London External, 1943; Barrister-at-law, Lincoln's Inn, 1947. Pres., King's Coll. Union Soc., 1931-32. Master: Henry Mellish Grammar Sch., 1933-35; Tiffin Boys Sch., 1935-40; Lectr, Extra-Mural Depts of London, Nottingham and Southampton Univs, 1934-47. RAF, 1940-45; Sqdn-Ldr, 1944-45; Chief Training Officer, Admiralty, 1945-47; Dir Extra-Mural Studies, Durham Univ., 1947-59. Durham City and County Magistrate since 1951; CC for Durham City, 1952-59; Chm. Durham County Education Cttee, 1959. Vice-Chm. 1957-59; Chm., Exec. Cttee Nat. Inst. for Adult Education, 1958-61; Mem. Newcastle Regional Hospital Board, 1958-64; Fabian Soc. Executive, 1961-. Jt Parly Under-Sec. of State, Dept of Education and Science, 1964-65; Parliamentary Sec., Ministry of Public Building and Works, 1965-67; Parly Under-Sec. (Army), MoD, 1967-69. Overseas Lecture Tours: for Foreign Office, Germany, 1955 and 1957; for British Council, Ghana, Sierra Leone, 1956; Sierra Leone, 1961; for Admiralty, Malta, 1959. Member: WEA; Fabian Soc.; Nat. Union of General and Municipal Workers; National Trust; Council of Europe, 1970-. FKC 1969. *Recreations:* walking, gardening, foreign travel, swimming, local government. *Address:* Appledown, The Avenue, Kingston, near Lewes, Sussex. *T:* Lewes 3724. *Clubs:* South Church Workman's, Eldon Lane Workman's (Bishop Auckland).

**BOYDEN, James;** *see* Boyden, H. J.

**BOYES, James Ashley;** Headmaster of City of London School since 1965; *b* 27 Aug. 1924; *s* of late Alfred Simeon Boyes and of Edith May Boyes; *m* 1949, Diana Fay (*née* Rothera), MA Cantab; two *d*. *Educ:* Rugby Sch.; Clare Coll., Cambridge. Lieut RNVR; N Russian convoys and Brit. Pacific Fleet, 1942-46. Cambridge Univ., 1942, 1946-48; 1st class Hons Mod. Hist., 1948; Mellon Fellowship, Yale Univ., 1948-50; MA Yale, 1950. Asst Master, Rugby Sch., 1950-55; Headmaster, Kendal Grammar Sch., Westmorland, 1955-60; Dir of Studies, Royal Air Force Coll., Cranwell, 1960-65. *Recreations:* squash racquets, sailing. *Address:* City of London School, EC4. *Clubs:* Harlequins RUFC (Hon. Mem.); Hawks (Cambridge); Royal Windermere Yacht.

**BOYES, Prof. John,** FRCSE, FDS England, FDS Edinburgh; Professor of Dental Surgery, Edinburgh, since 1958; Hon. Dental Surgeon, Royal Victoria Infirmary, Newcastle; *b* 23 June 1912; *o s* of John and Helen Boyes; *m* 1946, Jean Wood; one *s*. *Educ:* George Watson's Coll., Edinburgh; Dental Sch. and Sch. of Medicine of the Royal Colleges, Edinburgh. House Surg. and Clinical Asst, Edinburgh Dental Hosp.; House Surg., Middx Hosp.; Res. Surgical Officer and Dental Surg., Plastic and Jaw Unit, Bangour EMS Hosp.; Br. Corresp. of Amer. Dental Assoc.; Mem. of Dental Advisory Cttee of RCSE; Nuffield Prof. of Oral Medicine, University of Durham; Sub-Dean of King's Coll., at Dental Sch.; Dir Newcastle upon Tyne Dental Hospital. *Publications:* Dental Analgesia in A Textbook of Anaesthetics, by Minnitt & Gillies. *Recreations:* book and picture collecting; hill walking. *Address:* University of Edinburgh, Edinburgh 8. *Clubs:* Oral Surgery; Scottish Arts (Edinburgh); Cairngorm (Aberdeen).

**BOYLAND, Prof. Eric,** PhD London, DSc Manchester; Professor of Biochemistry, University of London, at Chester Beatty Research Institute, Institute of Cancer Research, Royal Marsden Hospital (Free), Fulham Road, SW3, 1948-70; Visiting Professor in Industrial Toxicology, London School of Hygiene and Tropical Medicine, since 1970; Consultant to International Agency for Research on Cancer, Lyon, since 1970; *b* Manchester, 24 Feb. 1905; *s* of Alfred E. and Helen Boyland; *m* 1931, Margaret Esther, *d* of late Maj.-Gen. Sir Frederick Maurice, KCMG, CB; two *s* one *d*. *Educ:* Manchester Central High Sch.; Manchester Univ. BSc Tech. 1926; MSc 1928; DSc 1936. Research Asst in Physiology, Manchester Univ., 1926-28; Grocers' Company Scholar and Beit Memorial Fellow for Med. Research at Lister Institute for Preventive Medicine, 1928-30, and Kaiser Wilhelm Institut für Medizinische Forschung, Heidelberg, 1930-31; Physiological Chemist to Royal Cancer Hosp., London, 1931; Reader in Biochemistry, University of London, 1935-47. Research Officer in Ministry of Supply, 1941-44; Ministry of Agriculture, 1944-45. Consultant to Internat. Agency for Research on Cancer, Lyon, 1970; Member WHO Panel on Food Additives. Judd Award for Cancer Research, New York, 1948. *Publications:* scientific papers in biochemistry and pharmacology. *Recreations:* walking, looking at paintings. *Address:* 42 Bramerton Street, SW3. *T:* 01-352 2601; Maltmayes, Warnham, W Sussex. *T:* Oakwood Hill 428. *Clubs:* Athenæum; Chelsea Arts; Rucksack (Manchester).

**BOYLE,** family name of **Earls of Cork, Glasgow,** and **Shannon** and of **Baron Boyle of Handsworth.**

**BOYLE, Viscount; Richard Henry John Boyle;** *b* 19 Jan. 1960; *s* and *heir* of 9th Earl of Shannon, *qv*.

**BOYLE OF HANDSWORTH,** Baron *cr* 1970 (Life Peer), of Salehurst, Sussex; **Edward Charles Gurney Boyle;** Bt 1904; PC 1962; Vice-Chancellor of Leeds University, since 1970; Director, Penguin Books Ltd, since 1966; Pro-Chancellor of Sussex University, since 1965; *b* 31 Aug. 1923; *s* of 2nd, Bt, and Beatrice (*d* 1961), *er d* of Henry Greig, Belvedere House, Kent; *S* father, 1945. *Educ:* Eton; Christ Church Oxford (Schol.). Temp. Junior Admin. Officer, FO, 1942-45; Mem., Oxford Union Debating Team, USA, Oct. 1947-Feb. 1948; Pres., Oxford Union Soc., Summer 1948; Parliamentary Candidate (U) Birmingham (Perry Bar), 1950; MP (C) Handsworth Div. of Birmingham, (Nov.) 1950-70; Parliamentary Private Sec. to the Under-Sec. for Air, 1951-52 and to the Parliamentary Sec. to the Ministry of Defence, 1952-53; Parliamentary Sec., Ministry of Supply, 1954-April 1955; Economic Sec. to the Treasury, 1955-56; Parliamentary Sec., Ministry of Education,

1957-59; Financial Sec. to the Treasury, Oct. 1959-July 1962; Minister of Education, 1962-64; Minister of State, Dept of Education and Science, April-Oct. 1964. Chm., Youth Service Development Council, 1962-64; Dep. Chm., Nat. Book League, 1967-. President: Soc. of British Gas Industries, 1965-66; Johnson Soc., 1965-66; Incorporated Soc. of Preparatory Schools, 1970-. Member: Court of Governors, Birmingham Univ.; IBRD Commn on Internat. Devel t, 1968-. Trustee: British Museum; Winston Churchill Memorial Trust; Rhodes Trust; Glyndebourne Arts Trust; Acton Soc. Trust; Allen Lane Foundation; Pilgrim Trust; a Governor: Ditchley Foundation; Brit. Inst. of Recorded Sound. Richard Feetham Memorial Lectr on Academic Freedom, Univ. of Witwatersrand, 1965; Earl Grey Lectr, Univ. of Newcastle, 1966; Sidney Ball Meml Lectr, Oxford, 1967. Hon. LLD: Leeds and Southampton, 1965; Hon. DSc, University of Aston in Birmingham, 1966. *Heir* (to Baronetcy only): *b* Richard Gurney Boyle [*b* 14 May 1930; *m* 1961, Elizabeth Anne, *yr d* of Norman Dennes]. *Address:* The Vice-Chancellor's Lodge, Grosvenor Road, Leeds 6. *Clubs:* Carlton, Pratt's.

**BOYLE, Archibald Cabbourn,** MD; FRCP; DPhysMed; Director, Department of Rheumatology and Physical Medicine, Middlesex Hospital; Senior Consultant Rheumatologist, Charterhouse Rheumatism Clinic; Consultant to BOAC; *b* 14 March 1918; *s* of late Arthur Hislop Boyle and of Flora Ellen Boyle; *m* 1st, Patricia Evelyn Tallack (*d* 1944); one *d*; 2nd, Dorothy Evelyn, *widow* of Lieut G. B. Jones; one *s*. *Educ:* Dulwich Coll.; St Bartholomew's Hospital. House Physician, St Bartholomew's Hosp., 1941-42. Served War of 1939-45 in Far East, and later as Command Specialist in Physical Medicine. Registrar and Sen. Asst, 1946-49, and Asst Physician, 1949-54, Mddx Hosp.; Consultant in Physical Medicine, Bromley Gp of Hosps, 1950-54; Physician, Arthur Stanley Inst. for Rheumatic Diseases, 1950-65. Chm., Med. Cttee, Mddx Hosp., 1970-71; Member: Bd of Governors, Mddx Hosp.; Bd of Governors, Charterhouse Rheumatism Clinic; Bd of Studies in Medicine, Univ. of London; British Assoc. of Physical Medicine and Rheumatology (Vice-Pres., 1965-68; Mem. Council, 1949-); Section of Physical Medicine, RSM (Pres., 1956-58; Mem. Council, 1950-); Heberden Soc. Formerly: Examnr in Physical Medicine, RCP; Examnr to Chartered Soc. of Physiotherapy; Editor, Annals of Physical Medicine, 1956-63; Sec., Internat. Fedn of Physical Medicine, 1960-64; Chm., Physical Medicine Gp, BMA, 1956-58; Pres., London Br., Chartered Soc. of Physiotherapy. Former Member: Cttee on Chronic Rheumatic Diseases, BMA; Regional Scientific, and Educn, Sub-Cttees, Arthritis and Rheumatism Council; Physiotherapists Bd, Council for Professions supplementary to Medicine; Central Consultants and Specialists Cttee, BMA; Med. Adv. Cttee, British Rheumatism and Arthritis Assoc. *Publications:* contribs to medical jls, mainly on rheumatic disease. *Recreation:* gardening. *Address:* 103 Harley Street, W1. *T:* 01-935 6111; Stall House, North Heath, Pulborough, Sussex. *T:* Pulborough 2137.

**BOYLE, Marshal of the Royal Air Force Sir Dermot (Alexander),** GCB 1957 (CB 1946); KCVO 1953; KBE 1953 (CBE 1945); AFC 1939; *b* 2 Oct. 1904; 2nd and *e surv s* of A. F. Boyle, Belmont House, Queen's Co., Ire.; *m* 1931, Una Carey; two *s* one *d* (and one *s* decd). *Educ:* St Columba's Coll., Ireland; RAF (Cadet) Coll., Cranwell. Commissioned RAF 1924; Air ADC to the King, 1943; Air Commodore, 1944; Air Vice-Marshal, 1949; Air Marshal, 1954; Air Chief Marshal, 1956; Marshal of the Royal Air Force, 1958; Dir-Gen. of Personnel, Air Ministry, 1948-49; Dir-Gen. of Manning, Air Ministry, 1949-51; AOC No. 1 Group Bomber Command, 1951-53; AOC-in-C, Fighter Command, 1953-55; Chief of Air Staff, 1956-59. Dir, British Aircraft Corp. Ltd (Vice-Chm.). Master, Guild of Air Pilots and Air Navigators, 1965-66. Chairman: Bd of Trustees, RAF Museum, 1965-; Ct of Governors, Mill Hill Sch., 1969-. *Address:* Pauls Place, Sway, Lymington, Hants. *Club:* Royal Air Force.

**BOYLE, Rev. Desmond;** *see* Boyle, Rev. J. D.

**BOYLE, Air Commodore Hon. John David,** CBE 1919; DSO 1917; late RAF; *b* 8 July 1884; 4th *s* of 7th Earl of Glasgow; *m* 1st, 1913, Ethel (*d* 1932), *d* of Sir Henry A. Hodges, Judge of the Supreme Court, Victoria, Australia; *er s* Major, The Black Watch, killed in action, 1945; *yr s* Sqdn-Ldr, RAF, killed on flying duty, 1960; 2nd, 1935, Marie (JP, Co. Councillor for Wigtownshire), *d* of John Gibb, Chillesford, Orford, Suffolk. *Educ:* Winchester. Gazetted 2nd Lieut Rifle Brigade, 1906; Lieut 1910; Seconded to Royal Flying Corps, 1912; Wing-Comdr in Royal Air Force on formation, 1918; Group-Capt., 1922; Air Commodore, 1929. Served European War, 1914-18 (despatches twice, Brevet-Major, Italian Order of St Maurice and St Lazarus); Chief Air Staff Officer, Air Defence of Great Britain, 1929-30; Air Officer Commanding Fighting Area, 1930-31; retired list, 1932; Aerodrome Board, Air Ministry, 1934-36; Commandant, RAFVR, Glasgow, 1936-39; re-employed active list Sept. 1939; retired list, 1941. Formerly JP Counties of Ayr and Kirkcudbright. *Address:* Dinvin, Portpatrick, Wigtownshire. *Clubs:* United Service; Royal Scottish Automobile (Glasgow).

**BOYLE, Rev. (John) Desmond,** SJ; Chaplain at St John's, Beaumont, since 1967; *b* 29 Aug. 1897; 2nd *s* of late Patrick J. Boyle, Donamon, County Roscommon, Ireland, and Ellen Mary Ryan. *Educ:* Wimbledon Coll.; St Francis Xavier's Coll., Liverpool; Campion Hall, Oxford. Entered Soc. of Jesus, 1913; ordained Priest, 1929; Prefect of Studies, Beaumont Coll., 1931-50; Rector of: Beaumont Coll., 1947-50; Heythrop Coll., 1950-52; Provincial of Eng. Prov. of Soc. of Jesus, 1952-58; Rector of Stonyhurst Coll., 1958-64; Chaplain, Beaumont Coll., 1964-67. *Address:* St John's, Beaumont, Old Windsor, Berks. *T:* Egham 2428.

**BOYLE, Kay, (Baroness Joseph von Franckenstein);** writer; Professor in English Department, San Francisco State College; *b* St Paul, Minn, USA, 19 Feb. 1903; *d* of Howard Peterson Boyle; *m* 1921, 1931 and 1943; one *s* five *d*. Mem. National Institute of Arts and Letters, 1958. O Henry Memorial Prize for best short story of the year, 1936, 1941; Guggenheim Fellowship, 1934, 1961; Center for Advanced Studies Wesleyan Univ. Fellowship, 1963; Radcliffe Inst. for Independent Study, 1965. *Publications: novels:* Plagued by the Nightingale; Year Before Last; Gentlemen, I Address You Privately; My Next Bride; Death of a Man; Monday Night; Primer for Combat; Avalanche; A Frenchman Must Die; "1939"; His Human Majesty; The Seagull on the Step, 1955; Three Short Novels, 1958; Generation Without Farewell, 1959; *volumes of short stories:* Wedding Day; The First Lover; The White Horses of Vienna; The Crazy Hunter; Thirty Short Stories; The Smoking Mountain; Nothing Ever Breaks Except the Heart, 1966; The Autobiography of Emanuel

Carnevali, 1967; Being Geniuses Together, 1968; The Long Walk at San Francisco State and other essays, 1970. A Glad Day (poems); American Citizen (poem); Collected Poems, 1962; Testament for my Students and other poems, 1970. *For Children:* The Youngest Camel; Pinky, the Cat Who Liked to Sleep, 1966; Pinky in Persia, 1968. *Recreations:* skiing, mountain climbing. *Address:* c/o Ann Watkins Inc., 77 Park Avenue, New York, NY 10016, USA.

**BOYNE,** 10th Viscount *cr* 1717; **Gustavus Michael George Hamilton-Russell,** DL; JP; Baron Hamilton, 1715; Baron Brancepeth, 1866; *b* 10 Dec. 1931; *s* of late Hon. Gustavus Lascelles Hamilton-Russell and *g s* of 9th Viscount; *S* grandfather, 1942; *m* 1956, Rosemary Anne, 2nd *d* of Major Sir Dennis Stucley, *qv*; one *s* three *d*. *Educ:* Eton; Sandhurst. Commissioned Grenadier Guards, 1952. JP 1961, DL 1965, Salop. Mem. Telford (formerly Dawley) New Town Development Corporation, 1963. Pres., St John Ambulance Brigade, Salop. OStJ. *Heir: s* Hon. Michael Gustavus Stucley Hamilton-Russell, *b* 27 May 1965. *Address:* Burwarton House, Bridgnorth, Salop. *T:* Burwarton 263. *Clubs:* Turf; Shropshire.

*See also Baron Forbes.*

**BOYNE, Henry Brian,** CBE 1969; Political Correspondent, The Daily Telegraph, London, since 1956; *b* 29 July 1910; 2nd *s* of late Lockhart Alexander Boyne, Journalist, Inverness, and late Elizabeth Jane Mactavish; *m* 1935, Margaret Little Templeton, Dundee; one *d*. *Educ:* High Sch. and Royal Academy, Inverness. Reporter, Inverness Courier, 1927; Dundee Courier and Advertiser, 1929. On active service, 1939-45, retiring with rank of Major, The Black Watch (RHR). Staff Correspondent, Glasgow Herald, at Dundee, 1945, and Edinburgh, 1949; Political Correspondent, Glasgow Herald, 1950. Chairman: Parly Lobby Journalists, 1958-59 (Hon. Sec., 1968-); Parly Press Gallery, 1961-62. *Recreations:* reading, playgoing, cycling. *Address:* 11 Marsham Court, Westminster, SW1. *T:* 01-834 8863. *Clubs:* Press, Victory, Arts Theatre; Western (Dundee).

**BOYS, Rt. Rev. John,** MA, LTh; Provincial Commissary to the Archibishop of Cape Town, since 1961; Assistant Bishop of Southwark, since 1968; *b* 17 Jan. 1900; *s* of Walter and Frances Boys. *Educ:* S Olave's Grammar Sch., Southwark; Hatfield Coll., Durham; S Boniface Theological Coll., Warminster. Service with BRCS in France, 1916-19. In business in Athens (Greece), 1919-21; in business in London, 1921-28; Sec., Guildford YMCA, 1929-30; Reader in Diocese of Salisbury, 1930-31; Deacon, 1935; priest, 1936; Asst Curate at S Paul's, Egham Hythe (Guildford), 1935-36; Personal Chaplain to Bishop of Gibraltar, 1936-38; Missionary in Diocese of Lebombo, 1938-47; Archdeacon of Lebombo, 1947; Bishop of Lebombo, 1948-51; Bishop of Kimberley and Kuruman, 1951-60; Asst Bp and Canon of St Albans, 1961-68; Dir of S African Church Inst., London, 1961-69. *Recreations:* chess, travelling. *Address:* 41 Elm Bank Gardens, SW13. *T:* 01-878 0770.

**BOYS-SMITH, Captain Humphry Gilbert,** DSO 1940; DSC 1943; RD; RNR, retired; *b* 20 Dec. 1904; *s* of late Rev. Edward Percy Boys Smith, MA, Rural Dean of Lyndhurst, Hants, and Charlotte Cecilia, *d* of late Thomas Backhouse Sandwith, CB, HM Consular Service; *m* 1935, Marjorie Helen, *d* of Capt. Matthew John Miles Vicars-Miles, JP; no *c*. *Educ:* Pangbourne Nautical Coll. Joined Royal Naval Reserve, 1921; Merchant Navy, 1922-35; Extra Master's Certificate, 1930; HM Colonial Service, 1935-40 (Palestine) and 1946-50 (Western Pacific High Commission as Marine Supt); Addnl Mem. RNR Advisory Cttee, 1949-51; War Course, Royal Naval Coll., Greenwich, 1950-51. Courtaulds Ltd, Central Staff Dept, 1951-68. Placed on Retired List of RNR, 1952; Younger Brother of Trinity House, 1944; Mem. of Hon Company of Master Mariners, 1946; Assoc. Instn Naval Architects, 1948; served War of 1939-45 (DSO and Bar, DSC, despatches and American despatches). *Address:* Mark Beacon, Mockbeggar, Ringwood, Hants. *T:* Ringwood 3469.

**BOYS SMITH, Rev. John Sandwith,** MA; Master of St John's College, Cambridge, 1959-69 (Fellow, 1927-59 and since 1969; Senior Bursar, 1944-59); Vice-Chancellor, University of Cambridge, 1963-65; Canon Emeritus of Ely Cathedral since 1948; *b* 8 Jan. 1901; *e s* of late Rev. E. P. Boys Smith, formerly Vicar of Hordle, Hants, and Charlotte Cecilia, *e d* of late T. B. Sandwith, CB; *m* 1942, Gwendolen Sara, *o d* of late W. J. Wynn; two *s*. *Educ:* Sherborne Sch.; St John's Coll., Cambridge. Economics Tripos Part I, Class II, division 2, 1921; BA, Theological Tripos, Part I, Sec. B, Class I, 1922; Scholar and Naden Student in Divinity, St John's Coll., 1922; Theological Tripos Part II, Sec. V, Class 1, 1924; Burney Student, 1924; Marburg University, 1924-25; Deacon, 1926; Curate of Sutton Coldfield, Birmingham, 1926-27; Priest, 1927; Chaplain of St John's Coll., Cambridge, 1927-34, and Director of Theological Studies, 1927-40, and 1944-52; Assistant Tutor, 1931-34; Tutor, 1934-39; Junior Bursar, 1939-40; University Lecturer in Divinity, Cambridge, 1931-40; Stanton Lecturer in the Philosophy of Religion, Cambridge Univ., 1934-37; Ely Professor of Divinity in the University of Cambridge and Canon of Ely Cathedral, 1940-43. Hon. Fellow: Trinity Coll., Dublin, 1968; Darwin Coll., Cambridge, 1969. Hon. LLD, Cambridge, 1970. *Publication:* (with late J. M. Creed) Religious Thought in the Eighteenth Century, 1934. *Address:* Brookside, Clare, Sudbury, Suffolk. *T:* Clare 200; St John's College, Cambridge. *Club:* United University.

**BOZMAN, Geoffrey Stephen,** CSI 1946; CIE 1938; ICS (retired); *b* 1896; *s* of late Samuel Bozman; *m* 1927, Kathleen Hilary (marr. diss.), *d* of late Sir Percy Rothera; one *s*. *Educ:* Whitgift Sch.; Brasenose Coll., Oxford. Served European War, 1914-18, 2nd Lieut, 4th Queens Royal West Surrey Regt, 1915; transferred to RFC, 1916; joined ICS Madras, 1922; Settlement Officer, 1924; Under Secretary, Govt of Madras, 1927; Secretary, Indian Tariff Board, 1930; Secretary Agent General for India in S. Africa, 1932; Commissioner of Coorg, 1935; Dep. Secretary and Joint Secretary, Govt of India, Education, Health and Lands Dept, 1936; Secretary, Govt of India, Indians Overseas Dept, 1941; Secretary, Govt of India, Information and Broadcasting Dept, 1943-47. *Address:* Shawside, Hosey Hill, Westerham, Kent. *T:* Westerham 3377. *Club:* Oriental.

**BRAADLAND, Erik;** diplomat, retired; *b* 21 Nov. 1910; *m* 1940, Aase Rydtun; one *s* two *d*. *Educ:* Oslo Univ. (Degree in Economics). Served in Hamburg, Marseille, Stockholm, Berlin; various periods Ministry of Foreign Affairs, Oslo; Acting Head of Military Mission in Berlin, 1949; Chargé d'Affaires at Bonn, 1951; Minister in Belgrade, 1952; Ambassador in Moscow, 1954-58, in London, 1959-61, for Norway; Mem. of Storting, 1961-69. Knight Commander, Order of St Olav; Order of the Yugoslav Flag, 1st Class. *Address:* Oer,

Halden, Norway. *Clubs:* Norwegian, London; Norske Selskab (Oslo).

**BRABANT, Rev. Frank Herbert,** DD; Curate of Ferreira's Town, City and Diocese of Johannesburg, since 1956; *b* 22 May 1892; *s* of Frederick and Augusta Brabant, Oxford. *Educ:* Winchester; Balliol Coll., Oxford (MA, DD). BD and DD by accumulation, 1952. Ordained, 1920; Chaplain of Wadham Coll., 1920-31; Diocese of Zululand, 1931-37; Canon Residentiary of Winchester Cathedral, 1938-42; Asst Master, Winchester Coll., 1942-46; Principal, St Patrick's Coll., Gwelo, Southern Rhodesia, 1946; Principal of St Bede's Coll., Umtata, 1948; Lecturer in Philosophy at Fort Hare African Coll., 1949-56. Examining Chaplain to Bishop of Kimberley and Kuruman, 1952-. *Publications:* Faith and Truth (with Rev. P. Hartill); Prayer; Religion and the Mysterious; Time and Eternity in Christian Thought (Bampton Lecture for 1936); The Beginning of the Third Republic in France; Neville Stuart Talbot, 1879-1943, A Memoir, 1949. *Address:* S Alban's Mission House, Ridout Street, Ferreiras Town, Johannesburg, S Africa.

**BRABAZON,** family name of **Earl of Meath.**

**BRABAZON OF TARA,** 2nd Baron, *cr* 1942, of Sandwich; **Derek Charles Moore-Brabazon,** CBE 1960; Member of the Stock Exchange, London; Partner, Read, Hurst-Brown & Co.; *b* 24 Dec. 1910; *er* and *o surv s* of 1st Baron Brabazon of Tara, PC, GBE, MC, and Hilda Mary Krabbé, Buenos Aires; *S* father 1964; *m* 1939, Mrs Henriette Mary Krabbé, *d* of late Sir Rowland Clegg; one *s*. *Educ:* Harrow; Trinity Coll., Cambridge. BA 1931. National Fire Service, 1939-45. Member, Kensington Borough Council, 1948-52. Chairman: South Kensington Conservative Assoc., 1952-54; London Conservative Union, 1957-58. President: North Kensington Conservative Assoc., 1966-; St Moritz Tobogganing Club, 1964-68. *Heir: s* Hon. Ivon Anthony Moore-Brabazon [*b* 20 Dec. 1946. *Educ:* Harrow]. *Address:* 28 Lansdowne Road, W11. *T:* 01-727 5638; The Watch House, Bembridge, Isle of Wight. *T:* Bembridge 2258. *Clubs:* White's, City of London; Royal Yacht Squadron.

**BRABHAM, John Arthur, (Jack Brabham);** OBE 1966; retired, 1970, as Professional Racing Driver; Managing Director: Jack Brabham (Motors) Ltd; Brabham Racing Organisation Ltd; Engine Developments Ltd; *b* Sydney, Australia, 2 April 1926; *m* 1951, Betty Evelyn; three *s*. *Educ:* Hurstville Technical Coll., Sydney. Served in RAAF, 1944-46. Started own engineering business, 1946; Midget Speedway racing, 1946-52; several championships (Australian, NSW, South Australian); numerous wins driving a Cooper-Bristol, Australia, 1953-54; to Europe, 1955; Australian Grand Prix, 1955 and 1963 (debut of Repco Brabham); World Champion Formula II, 1958, also many firsts including Casablanca, Goodwood, Brands Hatch, NZ Grand Prix, Belgian Grand Prix; Formula II Champion of France, 1964. World Champion Driver: (after first full Formula I Season with 2½-litre car), 1959-60, 1960-61. First in Monaco and British Grandes Epreuves, 1959; won Grand Prix of: Holland, Belgium, France, Britain, Portugal, Denmark, 1960; Belgium, 1961. Elected Driver of the Year by Guild of Motoring Writers, 1959, Sportsman of the Year by Australian Broadcasting Co., 1959; left Cooper to take up building own Grand Prix cars, 1961; debut, 1962; first ever constructor/driver to score world championship points, 1963; cars finished first: French GP; Mexican GP, 1964; Formula II and Formula III cars world-wide success, 1963; awarded Ferodo Trophy, 1964 and again, 1966; won French Grand Prix and British Grand Prix, 1966; won French Grand Prix, 1967. RAC Gold Medal, 1966; BARC Gold Medal, 1959, 1966, 1967; World Champion Driver, 1966; Formula I Manufacturers' Championship, 1966, 1967. *Publications:* Jack Brabham's Book of Motor Racing, etc.; contribs to British journals. *Recreations:* photography, water ski-ing, under-water swimming, flying. *Address:* c/o 248 Hook Road, Chessington, Surrey. *T:* Lower Hook 4343; 11 Laycock Road, Penshurst, NSW 2222, Australia. *Clubs:* Lord's Taverners', Royal Automobile, British Racing and Sports Car, British Racing Drivers'; Australian Racing Drivers'; Grand Prix Drivers' Association.

**BRABIN, Hon. Sir Daniel James,** Kt 1962; MC 1945; **Hon. Mr Justice Brabin;** Judge of High Court, Queen's Bench Division, since 1962; *b* 14 Aug. 1913; *yr s* of late William Henry and Sarah Brabin; *m* 1949, Mary, *y d* of late John McParland and Mrs McParland. *Educ:* Douai Sch.; Trinity Hall, Cambridge. Called to the Bar, Inner Temple, 1936; Master of the Bench, 1960. Joined Northern Circuit, 1937. Served War of 1939-45, in RA. QC 1951; Recorder of Bolton, 1953-62; Judge of Appeal, Isle of Man, 1960-62. *Address:* Royal Courts of Justice, WC2; 4 Kidderpore Avenue, NW3. *T:* 01-435 1081. *Club:* Liver.

**BRABOURNE,** 7th Baron, *cr* 1880; **John Ulick Knatchbull,** 16th Bt, *cr* 1641; film and television producer; *b* 9 Nov. 1924; *s* of 5th Baron and Lady Doreen Geraldine Browne (Order of the Crown of India; DStJ), *y d* of 6th Marquess of Sligo; *S* brother, 1943; *m* 1946, Lady Patricia Edwina Victoria Mountbatten, *er d* of Earl Mountbatten of Burma, *qv*; five *s* (including twin *s*) two *d*. *Educ:* Eton; Oxford. Films Produced: Harry Black, 1958; Sink the Bismark!, 1959; HMS Defiant, 1961; Othello, 1965; The Mikado, 1966; Romeo and Juliet; Up the Junction, 1967; Dance of Death, 1968. Pres., Kent Trust for Nature Conservation; Vice-Pres., RSA; Chairman: Council, Caldecott Community; Governors, Ashford Grammar Sch.; Governor: Wye Coll.; Gordonstoun Sch.; Mem. Council, Univ. of Kent. *Heir: s* Hon. Norton Louis Philip Knatchbull, *b* 8 Oct. 1947. *Address:* Newhouse, Mersham, Ashford, Kent. *T:* Ashford 23466; GW Films Ltd, 41 Montpelier Walk, SW7. *T:* 01-589 8829.

**BRABY, Frederick Cyrus,** CBE 1962; MC 1918; DL; CEng, FIMechE; Hon. Major; retired, from Frederick Braby and Co. Ltd, etc.; *b* 1 May 1897; *e s* of late Cyrus and Mabel Braby (*née* Weddell), of Sutton, Surrey, and High Hurstwood, Sussex; *m* 1931, Margaret Isabel, *e d* of late F. H. Marshall, Sutton and Hove; no *c*. *Educ:* Charterhouse; Manchester Univ. (BSc (Eng.)). Served 1915-19 with Lancashire Fusiliers (wounded twice, despatches, MC), and 1921-23 in TA. Apprenticeship with Metropolitan-Vickers Electrical Co. Ltd, Manchester, 1922-24; joined Frederick Braby & Co. Ltd (estab. 1839), 1925, and held various appointments; Director, 1929; Chairman, 1942-65. President: Engineering and Allied Employers' London & District Assoc., 1941-43; Nat. Council, Building Material Producers, 1960-65; Chairman: Industrial Coal Consumers' Council, 1958-65; British Non-Ferrous Metals Res. Assoc., 1958-64. Member of UK Employer/Trade Union Mission to USA, 1941; Vice-President, Engineering and Allied Employers' National Federation, 1952-56; President, 1956-58. County Commissioner (Kent), Boy Scouts

Assoc., 1952-67; Member, Sevenoaks RDC, 1963-70; a Governor, Star and Garter Home for Disabled Sailors, Soldiers and Airmen, 1963-; Master, Carpenters' Company, 1968-69 (Warden, 1965-68). DL (Kent), 1955. *Recreations:* fishing, photography. *Address:* Great Maythan Hall, Rolvenden, Cranbrook, Kent. *Club:* Junior Carlton.

**BRACEGIRDLE, Rear-Adm. Sir Leighton Seymour,** KCVO, *cr* 1947; CMG 1935; DSO 1916; *b* Balmain, Sydney, 31 May 1881; 4th *s* of late Captain Frederick Bracegirdle of Kaikoura, East Balmain; *m* 1910, Lilian Anne (*d* 1966), 2nd *d* of late Paterson Saunders, The Hill, Newcastle, New South Wales; two *s*. *Educ:* Sydney High Sch. Joined New South Wales Naval Forces as Naval Cadet, 1898; Midshipman, 1900; Midshipman with Naval Brigade in China (Boxer War Tientsin and Peking), 1900-1 (China Medal); Attached British Forces S. African War 1901-2 (Queen's Medal with 3 clasps); Sub-Lieut, 1902; Lieut, 1911; Naval Staff Officer with Naval Brigade landed to attack German New Guinea, Sept. 1914, and later succeeded to command (prom. Acting Lieut-Comdr); commanded 1st Royal Australian Naval Bridging Train, abroad 1915-17; present at first landing Suvla Bay, Gallipoli, and evacuation (despatches thrice, DSO), also at defence of Suez Canal and advance on Palestine; Commander, 1917; Captain, 1924; Rear-Admiral, retired list, Royal Australian Navy, 1945; Military and Official Secretary to the Governor-General of Australia, 1931-45; Official Secretary to the Duke of Gloucester, Governor-General of Australia, 1945-47; Personal Assistant to Governor of Victoria (late Lord Dugan), 1948. President Commonwealth Coal Board in Queensland, 1918, and in S. Australia, during coal shortage, 1919-20; Director of Naval Reserves and Mobilisation, Navy Office, Melbourne, 1922-31; Director: Peter Lloyd Ltd; Consultant to Internat. Combustion Australia Ltd, Sydney, and Taubmans Industries Ltd, Sydney; Vice-President Royal NSW Institution for Deaf and Blind Children. *Recreations:* fishing and gardening. *Address:* Green Hills, Forest Way, French's Forest, NSW, Australia. *Club:* Union (Sydney).

**BRACEWELL SMITH, Sir G.;** *see* Smith, Sir G. B.

**BRADBROOK, Prof. Muriel Clara,** MA, PhD, 1933; LittD Cantab 1955; Professor of English, Cambridge University, since 1965 (Reader 1962-65); Mistress of Girton College, since 1968 (Vice-Mistress, 1962-66; Fellow, 1932-35 and since 1936); *b* 27 April 1909; *d* of Samuel Bradbrook, Supt HM Waterguard at Liverpool and Glasgow. *Educ:* Hutchesons' Sch., Glasgow; Oldershaw Sch., Wallasey; Girton Coll., Cambridge. English Tripos, Class I, 1929, 1930; Harness Prize, 1931, Allen Scholar, 1935-36; in residence, Somerville Coll., Oxford, 1935-36. University Lecturer, Cambridge, 1945-62. Board of Trade, Industries and Manufacturers Depts 2 and 3, 1941-45; in residence at Folger Library, Washington, and Huntington Library, California, 1958-59; Tour of the Far East for Shakespeare's Fourth Centenary, 1964; Trustee, Shakespeare's Birthplace, 1967; Freedom of the City of Hiroshima; Visiting Professor: Santa Cruz, California, 1966; Kuwait, 1969; Clark Lecturer, Trinity Coll., Cambridge, 1968. FRSL 1947. Hon. LittD Liverpool, 1964; Hon. LLD Smith Coll., USA, 1965. Foreign Member Norwegian Acad. of Arts and Sciences, 1966. FRSA 1968. *Publications:* Elizabethan Stage Conditions, 1932; Themes and Conventions of Elizabethan Tragedy, 1934; The School of Night, 1936; Andrew Marvell (with M. G. Lloyd Thomas), 1940; Joseph Conrad, 1941; Ibsen the Norwegian, 1947; T. S. Eliot, 1950; Shakespeare and Elizabethan Poetry, 1951; The Queen's Garland, 1953; The Growth and Structure of Elizabethan Comedy, 1955; Sir Thomas Malory, 1957; The Rise of the Common Player, 1962; English Dramatic Form, 1965; That Infidel Place, 1969; Shakespeare the Craftsman, 1969; numerous articles and reviews. *Recreations:* travel, theatre. *Address:* Girton College, Cambridge. *T:* Cambridge 76219. *Clubs:* University Women's; ADC (Cambridge).

**BRADBURY,** family name of **Baron Bradbury.**

**BRADBURY,** 2nd Baron, *cr* 1925, of Winsford; **John Bradbury;** *b* 7 Jan. 1914; *s* of 1st Baron Bradbury, GCB, and Hilda (*d* 1949), 2nd *d* of W. A. Kirby; *S* father 1950; *m* 1st, 1939, Joan, *o d* of W. D. Knight, Darley, Addlestone, Surrey; one *s* one *d*; 2nd, 1946, Gwerfyl, *d* of late E. S. Roberts, Gellifor, Ruthin; one *d*. *Educ:* Westminster; Brasenose Coll., Oxford. *Heir: s* Hon. John Bradbury [*b* 17 March 1940; *m* 1968, Susan, *d* of late W. Liddiard, East Shefford, Berks]. *Address:* Sunridge, Downsway, Merrow, Guildford, Surrey. *T:* Guildford 66204.

**BRADBURY, Surgeon Vice-Adm. Eric Blackburn,** CB 1968; QHP 1966; Medical Director-General of the Navy, since 1969; *b* 2 March 1911; *s* of late A. B. Bradbury, Maze, Co. Antrim; *m* 1939, Elizabeth Constance Austin; three *d*. *Educ:* Royal Belfast Academical Instn; Queen's Univ., Belfast. MB, BCh 1934; DMR(D) 1949. Joined RN (Medical Service), 1934; served at sea in HMS Barham, HMS Endeavour, HMS Cumberland, 1935-38 and in HMS Charybdis and HMHS Oxfordshire, 1942-45; served in RN Hospitals: Haslar, Chatham, Plymouth and Malta; Med. Officer-in-Charge, RN Hosp., Haslar, and Comd MO, Portsmouth, 1966-69. *Recreation:* tennis. *Address:* The Gate House, Nevill Park, Tunbridge Wells, Kent. *T:* 27661. *Clubs:* Army and Navy; Royal Naval (Portsmouth).

**BRADBURY, Ray Douglas;** author; *b* Waukegan, Ill, USA, 22 Aug. 1920; *s* of Leonard S. Bradbury and Esther Moberg; *m* 1947, Marguerite Susan McClure; four *d*. *Educ:* Los Angeles High Sch. First Science-Fiction stories, 1941-44; stories sold to Harpers', Mademoiselle, The New Yorker, etc., 1945-56. Stories selected for: Best American Short Stories, 1946, 1948, 1952, 1958; O. Henry Prize Stories, 1947, 1948; and for inclusion in numerous anthologies. Benjamin Franklin Award for Best Story Published in an American Magazine of General Circulation, 1954; 1000 dollar Grant from Institute of Arts and Letters, 1954. *Publications:* Dark Carnival, 1947; The Martian Chronicles, 1950; The Illustrated Man, 1951; The Golden Apples of the Sun, 1953; Fahrenheit 451, 1953; Switch on the Night, 1955; The October Country, 1955; Dandelion Wine (novel), 1957; A Medicine for Melancholy (English publication as The Day It Rained Forever), 1959; Something Wicked This Way Comes (novel), 1962; R Is For Rocket (short stories), 1962; The Anthem Sprinters (one-act plays), 1963; The Machineries of Joy (short stories), 1964; The World of Ray Bradbury (one-act plays), 1964; The Wonderful Ice Cream Suit and The Day It Rained Forever (one-act plays), 1965; The Vintage Bradbury (stories), 1965; I Sing the Body Electric (short stories), 1970; *screenplays for:* Moby Dick; The Dreamers; And The Rock Cried Out. *Recreations:* oil painting, ceramics, collecting native masks.

*Address:* 10265 Cheviot Drive, Los Angeles 64, California, USA.

**BRADBY, Edward Lawrence;** Principal, St Paul's College, Cheltenham, since 1949; *b* 15 March 1907; *y s* of late H. C. Bradby, Ringshall End, near Berkhamsted, Herts; *m* 1939, Bertha Woodall, *y d* of late Henry Woodall, Yotes Court, Mereworth, Maidstone; three *s* one *d*. *Educ:* Rugby Sch.; New College, Oxford. Asst Master, Merchant Taylors' Sch., 1930-34; International Student Service, 1934-39; Secretary to Cttee for England and Wales, 1934-36; Asst General Secretary, Geneva, 1936-37; General Secretary, Geneva, 1937-39; Principal, Royal Coll., Colombo, Ceylon, 1939-46; late Principal, Eastbourne Emergency Training Coll. *Publications:* Editor, The University Outside Europe, a collection of essays on university institutions in 14 countries, 1939. *Address:* St Paul's College, Cheltenham. *T:* Cheltenham 28114. *Club:* Royal Commonwealth Society.

**BRADDELL, Dorothy Adelaide;** decorative-artist; *b* London; *d* of J. L. Bussé; *m* 1914, Darcy Braddell (*d* 1970); one *s* one *d*. *Educ:* Miss Manville's Sch.; King's Coll., London. Studied art at Regent Street Polytechnic and at Byam Shaw School of Art; won National Gold Medal for decorative design; is chiefly known as a designer of interior decoration and a domestic planner and has been associated largely with all kinds of exhibition work, being responsible for rooms at the Royal Academy Exhibition of Industrial Art, the British Pavilion, Paris Exhibition, 1938, Dorland Hall Exhibitions of British Industrial Art, Ideal Home Exhibitions, the Empire Exhibition, Glasgow, 1938, and Britain Can Make It Exhibition, 1946. *Address:* 8 Lansdowne Road, Holland Park, W11. *T:* 01-727 5487.
*See also John Gilbert N. Brown.*

**BRADDOCK, Mrs Elizabeth Margaret,** JP; Member Liverpool City Council, 1930-61, Alderman, 1955-61; *b* 1899; *d* of late Mary Bamber, JP, National Organiser, NUDAW, and Hugh Bamber; *m* 1922, John Braddock (*d* 1963), Alderman, Leader Liverpool City Council; no *c*. *Educ:* Liverpool Elementary. President Liverpool Trades and Labour Council, 1944. MP (Lab) Exchange Div. of Liverpool, 1945-70; Vice-Chm., Labour Party, 1968-. Director, Securicor North-West, 1967-. Freeman of Liverpool, 1970. *Publication:* (with Jack Braddock) The Braddocks. *Recreations:* reading, housekeeping. *Address:* 2 Zigzag Road, Liverpool 12. *T:* 051-228 1247.

**BRADDOCK, Thomas,** FRIBA; *b* 1887; British; *s* of Henry William Braddock, Bolton, Lancs; *m* 1910, Betty Dolleri, *d* of Henry Parker Houghton; one *s*. *Educ:* Rutlish Sch., Merton, Surrey. Member: Surrey County Council, 1934-46; Wimbledon Borough Council, 1936-45; LCC 1958-61. Contested: Wimbledon, 1929, 1931, 1935, 1966; Kingston-upon-Thames, 1964. MP (Lab) Mitcham, 1945-50. *Address:* 5 Lingfield Road, Wimbledon, SW19. *T:* 01-946 0810.

**BRADDON, Russell Reading;** author; *b* 25 Jan. 1921; *s* of Henry Russell Braddon and Thelma Doris Braddon (*née* Reading). *Educ:* Sydney Church of England Grammar Sch.; Sydney Univ. Failed Law finals; began writing, by chance, 1949; writing ever since then. *Publications:* The Piddingtons, 1950; The Naked Island, 1951; Those in Peril, 1954; Cheshire, V.C., 1954; Out of the Storm, 1956; Nancy Wake, 1956; End of a Hate, 1958; Gabriel Comes to 24, 1958; Proud American Boy, 1960; Joan Sutherland, 1962; The Year of the Angry Rabbit, 1964; Roy Thomson of Fleet Street, 1965; Committal Chamber, 1966; When the Enemy is Tired, 1968; The Inseparables, 1968; Will You Walk a Little Faster, 1969; The Siege, 1969; Prelude and Fugue for Lovers, 1970. *Recreation:* not writing. *Address:* c/o John Farquarson Ltd, 15 Red Lion Square, WC1.

**BRADEN, Bernard;** Free-lance actor and dabbler; *b* 16 May 1916; *s* of Rev. Dr Edwin Donald Braden and Mary Evelyn Chastey; *m* 1942, Barbara Kelly; one *s* two *d*. *Educ:* Maple Grove Public Sch., Point Grey Junior High Sch., Magee High Sch., Vancouver, Canada. Radio engineer, announcer, singer, actor in Vancouver, Canada, 1937-40; wrote and performed in plays for Canadian Broadcasting Corporation, 1940-43; went to Toronto, 1943; wrote and produced plays for Canadian Broadcasting Corporation, 1943-49; came to England, 1949. London plays include: Street-Car Named Desire; Biggest Thief in Town; The Man; No News From Father; Anniversary Waltz; The Gimmick; Period of Adjustment; Spoon River Anthology. Also performs for radio, television and films. Hon. Chancellor, London School of Economics, 1955. *Publication:* These English (Canada), 1948. *Recreations:* family, tennis, swimming.

**BRADFORD,** 6th Earl of, *cr* 1815; **Gerald Michael Orlando Bridgeman,** TD; JP, Shropshire; Bt 1600; Baron Bradford, 1794; Viscount Newport, 1815; Captain Shropshire Yeomanry, TARO (retired); Vice-Lieutenant of Shropshire since 1970; *b* 29 Sept. 1911; *o s* of 5th Earl of Bradford and Hon. Margaret Cecilia Bruce (*d* 1949), *e d* of 2nd Baron Aberdare; *S* father, 1957; *m* 1946, Mary Willoughby, *er d* of Lt-Col T. H. Montgomery, DSO, Cadogan House, Shrewsbury; two *s* two *d*. *Educ:* Harrow; Trinity Coll., Cambridge (MA). Served War of 1939-45 (despatches). President, Country Landowners' Assoc., 1955-57; Crown Estate Commissioner, 1956-67. President Timber Growers' Organisation, 1962-64; Chairman Forestry Cttee of Great Britain, 1964-66; President, Soil Assoc.; Chairman of Governors, Harper Adams Agricultural Coll. JP 1949, DL 1951, Salop. *Heir: s* Viscount Newport, *qv*. *Address:* Weston Park, Shifnal, Salop. *T:* Weston-under-Lizard 218; 61d Eaton Square, SW1. *T:* 01-235 4942. *Clubs:* Turf, Farmers', Ski, MCC.
*See also Sir Robert Abdy, Bt, Lieut-Col Hon. Henry G. O. Bridgeman.*

**BRADFORD, Bishop of,** since 1961; **Rt. Rev. Clement George St Michael Parker;** *b* 29 Sept. 1900; *s* of late Rev. W. H. Parker, Vicar of S Peter, Birmingham. *Educ:* Christ Church, Oxford. Ordained, 1923; Asst Curate, S Bartholomew and S Jude, Birmingham; Vicar of King's Heath, 1939-61; Rural Dean, King's Norton, 1943-61; Hon. Canon of Birmingham, 1944-61; Archdeacon of Aston, 1946-54; Bishop Suffragan of Aston, 1954-61. *Address:* Bishopscroft, Heaton, Bradford 9.

**BRADFORD, Provost of;** *see* Cooper, Very Rev. William Hugh Alan.

**BRADFORD, Archdeacon of;** *see* Johnston, Ven. William.

**BRADFORD, Sir Edward Alexander Slade,** 5th Bt, *cr* 1902; *b* 18 June 1952; *s* of Major Sir Edward Montagu Andrew Bradford, 3rd Bt (*d* 1952) and his 2nd wife, Marjorie Edith (*née* Bere); *S* half-brother, Sir John Ridley Evelyn Bradford, 4th Bt, 1954. *Heir: uncle* Donald Clifton Bradford [*b* 22 May 1914; *m* 1949, Constance Mary Morgan; three *d*]. *Address:* c/o Lady Bradford, Faith Cottage, Pett, near Hastings, Sussex.

**BRADFORD, Prof. Eric Watts,** MDS (Sheffield); DDSc (St Andrews); Professor of Dental Surgery, University of Bristol, since 1959; *b* 4 Nov. 1919; *e s* of E. J. G. and C. M. Bradford; *m* 1946, Norah Mary Longmuir; two *s* three *d. Educ:* King Edward VII Sch., Sheffield; High Storrs Grammar Sch., Sheffield; University of Sheffield (Robert Styring Scholar). LDS, Sheffield, 1943; BDS, Sheffield, 1944; MDS, Sheffield, 1950; DDSc St Andrews, 1954. Lieut, Army Dental Corps, Nov. 1944; Capt. Nov. 1945. Lecturer, University of Sheffield, 1947-52; Senior Lecturer, University of St Andrews, 1952-59. *Publications:* many papers on dental anatomy in British and other journals. *Address:* 11 Grove Road, Coombe Dingle, Bristol 9. *T:* 681849.

**BRADFORD, Rt. Hon. Roy Hamilton,** PC (NI) 1969; Minister of Commerce, Government of Northern Ireland, since 1969; MP (U) for Victoria, Parliament of Northern Ireland, since 1965; *b* 7 July 1920; *s* of Joseph Hamilton Bradford, Rockcorry, Co. Monaghan, and Isabel Mary (*née* McNamee), Donemana, Co. Tyrone; *m* 1946, Hazel Elizabeth, *d* of Capt. W. Lindsay, Belfast; two *s. Educ:* Royal Belfast Academical Institution; Trinity Coll., Dublin. Foundation Schol. 1940; First Class Hons (BA) German and French (with Gold Medal) 1942 (TCD). Army Intelligence, 1943-47 (France, Belgium, Germany). BBC and ITV Producer and Writer, 1950-. Dir, Geoffrey Sharp Ltd, 1962-. Asst Whip (Unionist Party), 1966; Parly Sec., Min. of Educn, 1967; Chief Whip, Sept. 1968-April 1969. *Publication:* Excelsior (novel), 1960. *Recreations:* golf, architecture. *Address:* Ardkeen, Carnalea, Bangor, Co. Down, N Ireland. *T:* Bangor 5012. *Club:* Ulster (Belfast).

**BRADFORD, William Vincent,** CB 1942; until 1943 a Commissioner of Inland Revenue and a Secretary to the Board; *b* 14 May 1883; *s* of William Masters Bradford; *m* 1st, 1914, Lizzie (*d* 1962), 4th *d* of James Bowman; 2nd, 1962, Kathleen Winifred Peacock. *Educ:* Christ's Hospital; Oxford. *Address:* Ringmore, The Street, Washington, Pulborough, Sussex. *Club:* United University.

**BRADFORD HILL, Sir Austin;** *see* Hill.

**BRADING, Brig. Norman Baldwin,** CMG 1958; CBE 1945; retired; *b* 25 May 1896; *s* of late Rev. F. C. Brading, Ditton, Kent; *m* Helen Margaret, *d* of G. Gatey, Windermere; one *s* one *d. Educ:* Whitgift; Royal Military College, Sandhurst. 2nd Lieut East Surrey Regt, 1915; served European War, 1914-19 (wounded); War of 1939-45; France, Holland, Germany; despatches, 1945; Lieut-Col 1940, Col 1943, Brig. 1944. Lent to UNO as Dep. Dir for Ops in Brit. Zone of Germany; National Health Services, 1949; lent to Nigerian Govt as House Governor, University Coll. Hospital, Ibadan, Nigeria, 1952. FHA. Knight Comdr Order of Orange Nassau, with swords (Netherlands), 1945. *Recreations:* polo, swimming. *Address:* 2 Royal Crescent, Bath. *T:* Bath 25322; Casita Alison, Basetes, Calpe, Alicante, Spain. *Club:* Royal Over-Seas League.

**BRADLAW, Prof. Sir Robert (Vivian),** Kt 1965; CBE 1950; President, General Dental Council, since 1964; Hon. Professor of Oral Pathology, Royal College of Surgeons of England; Emeritus Professor of Oral Medicine, University of London; Consultant: Royal Navy; World Health Organisation; *b* 14 April 1905; *s* of Philip Archibald Bradlaw, Blackrock, Co. Dublin; unmarried. *Educ:* Cranleigh; Guy's Hosp.; University of London. Hilton Prize, etc., Guy's Hosp.; holds degrees of the Univs of Belfast, Durham, Malta, Melbourne, Meshed, Montreal and Newcastle upon Tyne, and diplomas of the Royal Colleges of Surgeons of England, Edinburgh, Glasgow and Ireland. Tomes Prize for Research, RCS 1939-41; Howard Mummery Prize for Research, BDA, 1948-53; Colyer Gold Medal, RCS; Hunterian Prof., RCS 1955; Chevalier de la Santé Publique (France), 1950; Knight, Order of St Olaf, Norway; Commander, Order of Homayoun, Iran. *Recreations:* fishing, shooting, orchids, oriental ceramics. *Address:* The Manse, Stoke Goldington, Newport Pagnell, Bucks. *Clubs:* Athenæum, Savage.

**BRADLEY, Albert James,** FRS 1939; MA, DSc; *b* 5 Jan. 1899; *s* of Thomas Henry and Amy Bradley; *m* 1929, Marjorie Dinnis; one *s. Educ:* Chesterfield Grammar Sch.; Manchester Univ. 1851 Senior Exhibitioner, 1926-28; Royal Society Warren Research Fellow, 1932-38; formerly Asst Dir of Research in Crystallography, Cavendish Laboratory, Cambridge. Associate Mem. Royal Aubomobile Club. *Publications:* various publications on x-ray crystallography. *Address:* 169 Ashgate Road, Chesterfield, Derbyshire. *T:* Chesterfield 2081.

**BRADLEY, Edgar Leonard;** Metropolitan Stipendiary Magistrate, since 1967; *b* 17 Nov. 1917; 2nd *s* of Ernest Henry and Letitia Bradley, W. Felton, Oswestry; *m* 1942, Elsa, *o d* of Colin and Elizabeth Matheson, Edinburgh; two *s* three *d. Educ:* Malvern Coll.; Trinity Hall, Cambridge. BA 1939; MA 1944. Called to Bar, Middle Temple, 1940. Served 1940-46, RA; Capt. and Adjt, 1943-45; Major, GSO2, Mil. Govt of Germany, 1946. Practised at Bar, 1946-51, SE Circuit, Central Criminal Ct, S London and Surrey Sessions. Legal Dept of Home Office, 1951-54. Sec., Departmental Cttee on Magistrates' Courts Bill, 1952; Sec. of Magistrates' Courts Rule Cttee, 1952-54; Clerk to Justices: Wrexham and Bromfield, 1954-57; Poole, 1957-67. Justices' Clerks Society: Mem. Coun., 1957-67; Hon. Sec., 1963-67. Mem., Nat. Adv. Coun. on Trng of Magistrates, 1965-67; Mem. Coun., Magistrates' Assoc., 1968. Adv. tour of Magistrates' Courts in Ghana, 1970. *Recreations:* gardening, golf. *Address:* Shallows, Hurst Drive, Walton-on-the-Hill, Tadworth, Surrey. *T:* Tadworth 3655. *Club:* Kingswood Golf.

**BRADLEY, Gladys Lilian;** Head Mistress, Fairfield High School for Girls, Droylsden, Manchester, 1941-60; *d* of late T. R. Bradley. *Educ:* The Cowley Sch. for Girls, St Helens; Chester City and County High Sch. for Girls (now City High Sch. for Girls, Chester); Manchester Univ. (Scholar). BA (Hons Eng.). Asst Mistress: Withington Girls' Sch., Manchester; Havergal Coll., Toronto; Miss Edgar's and Miss Cramp's Sch., Incorp., Montreal; Gunnerside Sch., Plymouth; Head of English Dept, Cowley Sch. for Girls, St Helens; Head Mistress, Farringtons Sch., Chislehurst, Kent (at Trecarn, Babbacombe, S Devon) Sept. 1939-Dec. 1940 (closed for duration of War). *Publications:* Punctuation Hints and Exercises, 1934; sundry articles on youth and Girl Guide work, 1925-30. *Recreations:* walking, boating, swimming, riding, travelling. *Address:* Belvedere Court, Mooragh Promenade, Ramsey, Isle of Man. *T:* Ramsey 3066. *Club:* University Women's.

**BRADLEY, Harry,** CBE 1951; (First) Director, British Boot, Shoe and Allied Trades Research Association (SATRA), 1922-63, retired; President, British Boot and Shoe Institution, since 1962; *b* 1897; *s* of late George Craven Bradley, Silsden, Yorks; *m* 1921, Bertha

Ceridwen, *d* of late Rev. T. Henry Jones, USA and North Wales; one *s* two *d*. *Educ:* Keighley Grammar Sch.; Royal College of Science; Imperial Coll. of Science and Technology. Served European War, 1914-18, RFC and RNVR Anti-submarine Div. On demobilisation completed ARCS (hons), BSc (1st cl. hons); 1 yr research for Admiralty; 1 yr Lectr/Demonstrator, 3rd yr Physics, Royal College of Science. John Arthur Wilson Memorial Lectures, Amer. Leather Chemists' Assoc., 1966. Mem., Royal Institution. *Publications:* many research reports, scientific papers and articles in various jls. *Recreations:* music, gardening, reading; fond of dogs and horses. *Address:* Volta, 38 Piper's Hill Road, Kettering, Northants. *T:* Kettering 3210.

**BRADLEY, Air Marshal Sir John Stanley Travers,** KCB, *cr* 1942; CBE 1941 (OBE 1919); RAF retired. Director of Equipment, Air Ministry, 1935-38; Air Commodore, 1935; Air Vice-Marshal, 1938; Air Officer Commanding, Maintenance Command, 1938; Temp. Air Marshal, 1942; Deputy Air Member for Supply and Organisation, Air Ministry, 1942-45; Air Marshal, 1944; retired, 1945. *Club:* United Service.

**BRADLEY, Sir Kenneth (Granville),** Kt 1963; CMG 1946; Director of the Commonwealth Institute, 1953-69; *b* 5 Jan. 1904; *s* of Major H. V. Bradley, 9th Gurkha Rifles and Norah Foster; *gs* of Very Rev. G. G. Bradley, sometime Dean of Westminster; *m* 1926, Emily Guyon Rea, Cleveland, Ohio; two *s*. *Educ:* Wellington Coll., Berks; University Coll., Oxford. District Officer Northern Rhodesia, 1926-39; Information Officer Northern Rhodesia, 1939-42; Colonial and Financial Sec., Falklands Islands, 1942-46; Under-Sec., Gold Coast, 1946-49, actg Colonial Sec., 1946 and 1947; retd, 1949; first Editor, Corona, Colonial Service Journal, 1948-53. Chm., League for the Exchange of Commonwealth Teachers, 1962-; a Vice-Pres., Royal African Society. *Publications:* Africa Notwithstanding, 1928; Hawks Alighting, 1930; Lusaka, 1936; Story of Northern Rhodesia, 1942; Native Courts and Authorities in Northern Rhodesia, 1942; Diary of a District Officer, 1942; The Colonial Service as a Career, 1950; Copper Venture, 1952; Britain's Purpose in Africa, 1955; Once a District Officer, 1966; (Ed.) The Living Commonwealth, 1961. *Recreations:* writing, golf. *Address:* 10 Benson Place, Norham Road, Oxford. *T:* 54581. *Club:* Royal Commonwealth Society.

**BRADLEY, General of the Army Omar Nelson,** KCB (Hon.) 1944 (CB (Hon.) 1944); DSM (US) 1943 (with 3 oak leaf clusters); DSM (US Navy); Legion of Merit, etc; Chairman Bulova Watch Company Inc., Flushing, NY, since 1958; assigned no active military duties since Aug. 1953; *b* 12 Feb. 1893; *s* of John S. and Sarah Elizabeth Hubbard Bradley; *m* 1st, 1916, Mary Quayle (*d* 1965); one *d*; 2nd, 1966, Esther Dora Buhler. *Educ:* United States Military Academy, West Point. 2nd Lieut US Army, 1915; Lieut-Col, 1936; Brig.-Gen. (temp.), 1941, (perm.) 1943; Maj.-Gen. (temp.), 1942, (perm.) 1944; Lieut-Gen. (temp.), 1943; Gen. (temp.), 1945, (Perm.) 1949; General of the Army (perm.), 1950. Commanded II United States Corps in Northern Tunisia and in Sicily, April-Sept. 1943; commanded US troops in invasion of France, June 1944; commanded Twelfth Army Group (American First, Third, Ninth and Fifteenth Armies), 1944; Administrator of Veterans Affairs, 1945-47; Chief of Staff US Army, 1948-49; Chm. of Joint Chiefs of Staff, 1949-53. Grand Officer, French Legion of Honour, and many other foreign decorations. *Publication:* A Soldier's Story, 1951. *Recreations:* shooting, golf, fishing. *Address:* 630 Fifth Avenue, New York, NY 10020, USA. *Clubs:* Army Navy Country, Burning Tree Country (Washington, DC).

**BRADLEY, Prof. Peter Colley S.;** *see* Sylvester-Bradley.

**BRADLEY, Maj.-Gen. Peter Edward Moore,** CB 1968; CBE 1964 (OBE 1955); DSO 1946; Chief of Staff to C-in-C Allied Forces Northern Europe, Oslo, 1968-70, retired; *b* 12 Dec. 1914; *s* of late Col Edward de Winton Herbert Bradley, CBE, DSO, MC, DL; *m* Margaret, *d* of Norman Wardhaugh of Stakeford, Northumberland; three *s*. *Educ:* Marlborough; Royal Military Academy, Woolwich. 2nd Lieut, Royal Signals, 1934. Served War of 1939-45; India, Middle East, Italy and North West Europe (DSO 6th Airborne Div.). Lieut-Col 1954; Col 1957; Brig. 1962; Maj.-Gen. 1965; Signal Officer in Chief (Army), Ministry of Defence, 1965-67. Col Comdt, Royal Signals, 1967-, Master of Signals, 1970-; Col, Gurkha Signals, 1967-. CEng, FIEE, 1966. *Address:* Hill House, Haydon Bridge, near Hexham, Northumberland. *Club:* Army and Navy.

**BRADLEY, Reginald Livingstone,** CBE 1955; MC 1916; Commissioner of Prisons, 1949-57, retired; *b* 9 Aug. 1894; *s* of Frederick L. and Florence Bradley; *m* 1920, Phyllis Mary Richardson; one *s* three *d*. *Educ:* Repton; Oriel Coll., Oxford (MA). Oxford, 1913-14 and 1919-20. Served European War, 1914-18 (despatches, MC); 22nd London Regt, The Queen's; Capt. Sec., Oxford and Bermondsey Club, SE1, 1920-21; Prison Service: Dep. Governor, 1922-26, HM Borstal, Portland; Dep. Governor, 1926-29, Governor, 1929-36, HM Borstal, Rochester; Governor Cl. II, 1936-38, HM Prison, Wormwood Scrubs; Asst Commissioner, Prison Commission, 1938-52; Dir of Borstal Administration, 1948-57; Commissioner and Dir of Borstal Administration, 1952-57. Coronation Medal, 1953. *Recreations:* walking, reading, chores. *Address:* 43 Wildcroft Manor, Putney Heath, SW15. *T:* 01-788 0434. *Clubs:* United University; Vincent's (Oxford); Surrey County Cricket.

*See also R. A. Bradley.*

**BRADLEY, Richard Alan;** Warden of St Edward's School, Oxford, since 1966; *b* 6 Oct. 1925; *s* of Reginald Livingstone Bradley, *qv*; *m* 1950, Meryll J. Braddy; one *s* two *d*. *Educ:* Marlborough Coll.; Trinity Coll., Oxford (Scholar). 2nd cl. hons Mod. History. Royal Marines, 1944-46; Oxford, 1946-48; Club Manager, Oxford and Bermondsey Club, 1949. Asst Master: Dulwich Coll., 1949-50; Tonbridge Sch., 1950-66 (Head of History Dept, 1957-66; Housemaster of Ferox Hall, 1961-66). *Recreations:* games, dramatics, mountains. *Address:* The Warden's House, St Edward's School, Oxford. *T:* Oxford 55241. *Club:* Vincent's (Oxford).

**BRADLEY, Thomas George;** MP (Lab) Leicester North-East since July 1962; Parliamentary Private Secretary to Chancellor of the Exchequer, since 1967 (to Minister of Aviation, 1964-65; to Home Secretary, 1966-67); President, Transport Salaried Staffs' Association since 1964 (Branch Officer, 1946-58; Member Exec. Cttee, 1958-; Treas., 1961-64); Member, Labour Party National Executive, 1966-; *b* 13 April 1926; *s* of George Henry Bradley, Kettering; *m* 1953, Joy, *d* of George Starmer, Kettering; two *s*. *Educ:* Kettering Central Sch., Northants. Elected to Northants County Council, 1952, County

Alderman, 1961; Mem., Kettering Borough Council, 1957-61. Contested (Lab.) Rutland and Stamford, 1950, 1951 and 1955, Preston South, 1959. *Address:* 50 Greenfield Avenue, Kettering, Northants. *T:* Kettering 3019.

**BRADLEY, Prof. William,** PhD, DSc (Manchester); FRIC; Professor of Colour Chemistry and Dyeing, University of Leeds, 1948-63; Emeritus Professor, since 1963; *b* 24 July 1903; *s* of John T. and Mary A. Bradley, Leigh, Lancs; *m* 1932, Charlotte, *d* of J. E. Dolman, Brightwell, Berks; one *s*. *Educ:* Leigh Grammar Sch.; Manchester Univ. University Awards: Woodiwis Exhib. in Chemistry, 1922, Dalton Chemical Scholarship, 1925, Darbishire Fellowship, 1925, Beyer Fellowship, 1926, Sir Clement Royds Mem. Scholarship in Chemistry, 1927. Research Asst, University Coll., London, 1927-29; Research Asst, Dyson Perrins Lab., Oxford, 1929-31; Lecturer in Tinctorial Chemistry and Dyestuffs, Coll. of Technology, Manchester, 1931-42; Research in industry, 1942-48. DSIR Visitor to The British Hat and Allied Feltmakers' Research Association, 1956-62; Gold Medal for services to Soc. of Dyers and Colourists, 1959; Mem. of Council Royal Inst. of Chemistry, 1959-63; Mem. Bd of Studies, Nat. Council for Technological Awards, 1961-63. *Publications:* papers on organic chemistry mainly in Journal of Chem. Soc. *Address:* Rosedale, Broadsands Park Road, Paignton, Devon. *T:* Churston 2440.

**BRADLEY, William Ewart;** Special Commissioner of Income Tax since 1950; *b* 5 Sept. 1910; *s* of W. E. Bradley, Durham City; *m* 1949, Mary Campbell Tyre; two *s*. *Educ:* Johnston Sch., Durham; London Univ. *Address:* Bourne Cottage, Bourne Lane, Tonbridge, Kent. *T:* Tonbridge 2880.

**BRADLEY-WILLIAMS, Col William Picton,** DSO 1919; *b* 9 Oct. 1890; *s* of late Herbert Edward Bradley, The Grange, Bitton, Glos (took name of Williams from late Capt. William Williams, Pontypridd, Glamorgan); *m* 1918, Frances Mary, *y d* of late John Selwin Calverley of Oulton, near Leeds; two *s* two *d*; *m* 1947, Sylvia Mary Maxwell Jackson, Ferriby, East Yorks (*d* 1969); one *d*. *Educ:* Haileybury. Served European War, 1914-19 (despatches, DSO); Mesopotamia, 1920-21; North West Frontier, India, 1930; Chief Instructor Army Sch. of PT, Aldershot, 1927-30. Commanded 1st Bn The King's Own Yorks Light Infantry, 1936-39; Garrison Comdr, Hull, 1940-41; Commandant Army Physical Training Corps, 1941-44; Comdr No. 1 War Material Reconnaissance Team BAOR, Dec. 1944-June 1945; Army Welfare Officer, HQ Colchester, 1946-54. *Address:* Burstall House, Burstall, near Ipswich, Suffolk. *T:* Hintlesham 277. *Club:* Naval and Military.

**BRADMAN, Sir Donald (George),** Kt, *cr* 1949; Vice-President of South Australian Cricket Association; Member Australian Board of Control; *b* Cootamundra, NSW, 27 Aug. 1908; *s* of George and Emily Bradman; *m* 1932, Jessie, *d* of James Menzies, Mittagong, NSW; one *s* one *d*. *Educ:* Bowral Intermediate High Sch. Played for NSW 1927-34; for S Australia, 1935-49; for Australia 1928-48, Capt. 1936-48; records include: 452 not out, NSW *v* Queensland, 1929-30, world record in first-class cricket; highest aggregate and greatest number of centuries in England *v* Australia test matches; highest score for Australia *v* England in test matches (334 at Leeds, 1930). Formerly stock and share broker and Mem. Stock Exchange of Adelaide Ltd. *Publications:* Don Bradman's Book, 1930; How to Play Cricket, 1935; My Cricketing Life, 1938; Farewell to Cricket, 1950; The Art of Cricket, 1958. *Recreations:* cricket, golf, tennis, billiards, squash. *Address:* 23 Grenfell Street, Adelaide, South Australia. *Clubs:* MCC (Hon. Life Mem.); Stock Exchange (Adelaide).

**BRADNACK, Brian Oswald,** MC; MA; Headmaster, College for the Blind, Worcester, 1938-59, retired; *b* 3 March 1898; *s* of Oswald H. Bradnack, Combe Down, Bath; *m* 1929, Doris (*d* 1945), *d* of D. M. Milne, JP, of Gosforth, Newcastle upon Tyne; two *s*; *m* 1947, Margaret, *d* of H. E. Tringham, Great Crosby, Lancs. *Educ:* Repton Sch.; Brasenose Coll., Oxford. Served European War, France, with RGA 1917-18; Intercollegiate Sec. of Student Christian Movement in Northumberland and Durham, 1921-23; Asst Master at Dean Close Sch., Cheltenham, 1923-38. *Recreations:* various. *Address:* Merry Mead, 90 Bowes Hill, Rowlands Castle, Hants. *T:* 431.

**BRADSHAW, Brig. George Rowley,** CB 1953; CBE 1946; *b* 1 July 1898; *s* of Surg.-Comdr F. Bradshaw, OBE, RN, and Mrs Bradshaw, Malahide, County Dublin; *m* 1928, Mary Constance, *d* of W. T. Ford, Malpas, Mon; one *s* two *d*. *Educ:* King's Sch., Rochester; RMA, Woolwich. Commissioned into Royal Artillery, 1917; Served European War, 1917-18; Iraq, 1921-22; Staff Coll., 1934-35; Served War of 1939-45, NW Europe, 1944-45; Col 1944; Brig. 1946. Dep. District Comdr, 1950-53; retired, 1953. Kt Comdr Order of Orange Nassau, 1946. *Recreations:* tennis, cricket, riding. *Address:* Kingswood, St George's Hill, Weybridge, Surrey. *T:* Weybridge 42876. *Club:* United Service.

**BRADSHAW-ISHERWOOD, C. W.;** *see* Isherwood.

**BRADWELL, Bishop Suffragan of,** since 1968; **Rt. Rev. William Neville Welch,** MA; Archdeacon of Southend since 1953; *b* 30 April 1906; *s* of Thomas William and Agnes Maud Welch; *m* 1935, Kathleen Margaret Beattie; two *s* two *d*. *Educ:* Dean Close Sch., Cheltenham; Keble Coll., Oxford; Wycliffe Hall, Oxford. Asst Curate: Kidderminster, 1929-32; St Michael's, St Albans, 1932-34. Organising Sec., Missions to Seamen, 1934-39; Vicar of Grays, 1939-43; Officiating Chaplain, Training Ship Exmouth, 1939-40; Proctor in Convocation, 1945 and 1950; Vicar of Ilford, 1943-53; Rural Dean of Barking, 1948-53; Vicar of Great Burstead, 1953-56. Hon. Canon of Chelmsford, 1951-53. *Address:* 222 Springfield Road, Chelmsford, Essex. *T:* 55856.

**BRAGG, Sir (William) Lawrence,** CH 1967; Kt 1941; OBE 1918; MC 1918; FRS 1921; MA Cantab; Hon. DSc Dublin, Leeds, Manchester, Lisbon, Paris, Brussels, Liège, Durham; Hon. PhD Cologne, Cantab; Hon. LLD St Andrews; Fullerian Professor of Chemistry, Royal Institution, 1953-66, and Director of the Royal Institution, 1964-66; *b* Adelaide, South Australia, 31 March 1890; *s* of late Sir William Henry Bragg, OM, KBE, FRS; *m* 1921, Alice Grace Jenny, *er d* of the late Albert Hopkinson; two *s* two *d*. *Educ:* St Peter's Coll., Adelaide; Adelaide Univ.; Trinity Coll., Cambridge (Allen Scholar). Fellow and Lecturer in Natural Sciences, Trinity Coll. Cambridge, 1914; awarded Barnard Medal, 1914, and Nobel Prize for Physics, 1915, for work on X-Rays and Crystal Structure done with Sir W. H. Bragg; Hughes Medal of Royal Society, 1931; Royal Medal of Royal Society, 1946; Copley Medal of Royal Society, 1966; Roebling Medal of Min. Soc. of America, 1948; Technical Adviser on Sound Ranging to Map

Section, GHQ, France, 1915-19; Langworthy Prof. of Physics, Victoria Univ. of Manchester, 1919-37; Dir of National Physical Laboratory, 1937-38; Cavendish Prof. of Experimental Physics, Cambridge, 1938-53; Chm., Frequency Advisory Cttee, 1958-60. Hon. FInstP; Hon. FRIC; Hon. FRSE; Hon. MRIA; Hon. MInstMet; Foreign Associate, Acad. Sciences, Paris; Hon. Mem., Swedish Acad. of Sciences; Mem. American Philosophical Soc.: Hon. Mem., New York Mineralogical Club; Chinese Phys Soc.; For. Hon. Mem. Amer. Acad. of Arts and Sciences; For. Associate, Nat. Acad. Sci. Washington; For. Mem., Dutch Acad. Sci.; Associate, Royal Acad. Belgium; Membre d'Honneur de la Soc. française de Minéralogie et Cristallographie. Comdr of the Order of Leopold of Belgium. *Publications:* various scientific papers on Crystal Structure; (with Sir W. H. Bragg), X-Rays and Crystal Structure, 1915; The Crystalline State, 1934; Electricity, 1936; Atomic Structure of Minerals, 1937; Crystal Structures of Minerals (with W. F. Claringbull), 1965. *Recreations:* painting, bird-watching. *Address:* 6 The Boltons, SW10. *T:* 01-370 5189; Quietways, Waldringfield, near Woodbridge, Suffolk. *T:* Waldringfield 220. *Club:* Athenæum.

**BRAHAM, Harold,** CBE 1960; HM Diplomatic Service (Retired); *b* Constantinople, 11 Oct. 1907; *er s* of late D. D. Braham, of The Times; *m* 1941, Cicely Edith Norton Webber; one *s* one *d. Educ:* St Peter's Coll., Adelaide; New College, Oxford. Entered HM Consular Service, China, 1931. Retired as HM Consul-Gen., Paris, 1966. *Recreations:* gardening, carpentry. *Address:* Torret 19, San Luis, Menorca, Balearic Islands, Spain. *Club:* Athenæum.

**BRAHMS, Caryl;** critic and novelist; journalist specialising in criticism of the theatre arts; ballet critic; writer of film, broadcast and television scripts; *b* Surrey. *Educ:* privately and at Royal Academy of Music. *Publications:* Footnotes To The Ballet, 1936; Robert Helpmann, Choreographer, 1943; A Seat at the Ballet, 1951; Away went Polly, 1952; No Castanets, 1963; A Seat at the Ballet, 1964; (with S. J. Simon) A Bullet in the Ballet, 1937; Casino for Sale, 1938; The Elephant is White, 1939; Envoy on Excursion, 1940; Don't Mr Disraeli, 1940; No Bed for Bacon, 1941; No Nightingales, 1944; Titania Has a Mother, 1944; Six Curtains for Stroganova, 1945; Trottie True, 1946; To Hell with Hedda, 1947; You Were There, 1950; The Rest of the Evening's My Own, 1964; (with Ned Sherrin): Cindy-Ella or I gotta Shoe, 1962; Rappel 1910, 1964; Benbow was his name, 1966; Co-adapter of stage version: A Bullet in the Ballet; No Bed for Bacon; Cindy-Ella or I gotta Shoe; No Castanets, 1963. *Address:* 3 Cambridge Gate, Regent's Park, NW1. *T:* 01-935 6439.

**BRAILSFORD, Prof. Frederick,** PhD; FIEE; Professor of Electrical Engineering, University College, London, since 1951; *b* 22 Sept. 1903; *s* of John James and Frances Ann Brailsford; *m* 1934, Sarah Remington Smyth, Knock, County Down; one *d. Educ:* University Coll., Swansea. Whitworth Scholar, 1923; BSc(Eng) London (1st Class Hons), 1927; PhD, London, 1939. Apprentice in HM Dockyard, Pembroke, 1919-23; Electrical Engineer with Metropolitan-Vickers Electrical Co., Manchester, 1926-50. *Publications:* Magnetic Materials, 1960; Physical Principles of Magnetism, 1966; Introduction to the Magnetic Properties of Materials, 1968; various papers to Institution of Electrical Engineers and elsewhere. *Address:* Locks Green, 244 Brooklands Road, Weybridge, Surrey. *T:* Weybridge 47548.

**BRAILSFORD, John William;** Keeper, Department of Prehistoric and Romano-British Antiquities, British Museum, since 1969; *b* 14 July 1918; *o s* of Alfred and Dorothy H. M. Brailsford; *m* 1945, Mary Freeman Boaden; one *s* one *d. Educ:* Bedales; Emmanuel College, Cambridge. Sen. Exhibnr and Scholar, BA, MA 1943. Royal Artillery (Survey), 1939-45; Intell. (Air Photo Interpretation), 1945-46. Asst Keeper, Dept of British and Medieval Antiquities, Brit. Mus., 1946; Dep. Keeper, 1963. FMA; FSA 1949; Fellow, German Archaeolog. Inst., 1967. *Publications:* Museum Handbooks to Mildenhall Treasure, 1947; Antiquities of Roman Britain, 1951; Later Prehistoric Antiquities of the British Isles, 1953; Antiquities from Hod Hill in the Durden Collection, 1962; Hod Hill: Excavations, 1951-58 (ed), 1968. Papers in learned jls. *Recreations:* various. *Address:* 205 Ashley Gardens, SW1. *T:* 01-828 5045. *Clubs:* Athenæum, United University.

**BRAIN,** family name of **Baron Brain.**

**BRAIN,** 2nd Baron *cr* 1962, of Eynsham; **Christopher Langdon Brain;** Bt 1954; *b* 30 Aug. 1926; *s* of 1st Baron Brain, MA, DM, FRS, FRCP and Stella, *er d* of late Reginald L. Langdon-Down; *S* father 1966; *m* 1953, Susan Mary, *d* of George P. and Ethelbertha Morris; three *d. Educ:* Leighton Park Sch., Reading; New College, Oxford. MA 1956. Royal Navy, 1946-48. Liveryman, Worshipful Company of Weavers, 1955. Chm., Rhone-Alps Regional Council, British Chamber of Commerce, France, 1967. *Recreations:* bird watching, sailing, ski-ing. *Heir: b* Hon. Michael Cottrell Brain, MA, DM, FRCP [*b* 6 Aug. 1928; *m* 1960, Dr The Hon. Elizabeth Ann Herbert, *e d* of Baron Tangley, *qv*; one *s* two *d.*]. *Address:* 12 Kingsley Place, Highgate, N6. *Clubs:* Savile; Oxford University Yacht; Oxford and Cambridge Sailing Society.

**BRAIN, Sir (Henry) Norman,** KBE 1963 (OBE 1947); CMG 1953; *b* 19 July 1907; *s* of late B. Brain, Rushall, Staffs; *m* 1939, Nuala Mary, *d* of late Capt. A. W. Butterworth; one *s* (and one *s* decd). *Educ:* King Edward's Sch., Birmingham; The Queen's Coll., Oxford (MA). Entered the Consular Service, 1930, and served at Tokyo, Kobe, Osaka, Tamsui, Manila, Mukden, Shanghai and Dairen; interned by Japanese, 1941-42; repatriated and served in Foreign Office, 1943; appointed to Staff of Supreme Allied Comdr, South-East Asia, 1944-46; Political Adviser to Saigon Control Commission, 1945; served with Special Commissioner in South-East Asia, at Singapore, 1946-48; Counsellor in Foreign Office, 1949; Inspector of HM Foreign Service Estabts, 1950-53; Minister, Tokyo, 1953-55; Ambassador to Cambodia, 1956-58; Asst Under-Sec. of State, FO, 1958-61; Ambassador to Uruguay, 1961-66, retired, 1966. Chairman: Royal Central Asian Soc., 1970-; Japan Soc. of London, 1970-. *Recreations:* music, golf. *Address:* St Andrews, Abney Court, Bourne End, Bucks. *Club:* Athenæum.

**BRAIN, Sir Norman;** *see* Brain, Sir H. N.

**BRAIN, Dr Reginald T.,** MD, BS, FRCP; Hon. Consulting Physician: Royal Free Hospital; The Hospital for Sick Children, Great Ormond Street; St John's Hospital for Diseases of the Skin; Corresponding Member: American Dermatological Association; La Société Dermatologique Danoise; La Société

Française de Dermatologie et de Syphiligraphie; Australasian College of Dermatologists; Hon. Member, Sociedad Venezolana de Dermatologia, Venereologia e Leprologia; *b* 6 June 1894; *s* of Robert Brain and Mary Elizabeth Kimberlin; *m* 1928, Hallie Frances Weir; two *s* one *d*. *Educ:* Queen Elizabeth's Grammar Sch., Tamworth; London Hospital Medical Coll. Served European War BEF, RAMC, 1914-19; past appointments at The London Hospital, the British Post-Graduate Medical Sch., The Evelina Hospital for Sick Children. Prosser White Orator, 1961. Past. Pres. Section Derm., RSM and BMA. Retired. *Publications:* Sequeira's Diseases of the Skin (Ingram & Brain), 1957, Skin Diseases (Modern Health Series), 1955; papers on Biochemistry, Pathology (Virus Diseases), and Skin Diseases. *Recreations:* electrical engineering, fishing, gardening. *Address:* Home Wood, Loudwater, Herts.

**BRAIN, Ronald,** CB 1967; Deputy Secretary, Ministry of Housing and Local Government, since 1966; *b* 1 March 1914; *s* of T. T. G. Brain, RN, and E. C. Brain (*née* Fruin); *m* 1943, Lilian Rose (*née* Ravenhill); one *s* one *d*. *Educ:* Trowbridge High Sch. Audit Asst, Min. of Health, 1932; Principal, Min. of Health, 1946; Asst Sec., Min. of Housing and Local Govt, 1952; Under-Sec., 1959. *Recreations:* music, chess. *Address:* 267 Surbiton Hill Park, Surbiton, Surrey. *T:* 01-399 8263.

**BRAINE, Bernard Richard;** MP (C) South-East Division of Essex since 1955 (Billericay Division of Essex, 1950-55); Director, Purle Brothers Holdings Ltd; *b* Ealing, Middx, 24 June 1914; *s* of Arthur Ernest Braine; *m* 1935, Kathleen Mary Faun; three *s*. *Educ:* Hendon County Grammar Sch. Served North Staffs Regt in War of 1939-45: West Africa, SE Asia, NW Europe; Staff Coll., Camberley, 1944 (sc); Lt-Col. Chm., British Commonwealth Producers' Organisation, 1958-60; Founder and Chm., Anglo-Ethiopian Parly Group; Parly Sec., Min. of Pensions and National Insurance, 1960-61; Parly Under-Sec. of State for Commonwealth Relations, 1961-62; Parly Sec., Min. of Health, 1962-64; Conservative front bench spokesman on Commonwealth Affairs and Overseas Aid, 1967-70; Dep. Chm., UK Branch of Commonwealth Parly Assoc., 1964, Treasurer, 1965-68. A Governor of the Commonwealth Institute. CStJ. *Address:* King's Wood, Rayleigh, Essex. *Club:* Carlton.

**BRAINE, John (Gerard);** Author; *b* 13 April 1922; *s* of Fred and Katherine Braine; *m* 1955, Helen Patricia Wood; one *s* three *d*. *Educ:* St Bede's Grammar Sch., Bradford. Furniture-shop asst, bookshop asst, laboratory asst, progress chaser, in rapid succession, 1938-40; Asst, Bingley Public Library, 1940-49; HM Navy, 1942-43; Chief Asst, Bingley Public Library, 1949-51; free-lance writer, London and Yorks, with interval in hospital, 1951-54; Branch Librarian, Northumberland County Library, 1954-56; Branch Librarian, West Riding of Yorks County Library, 1956-57. ALA 1950. *Publications:* Room at the Top, 1957 (filmed 1958); The Vodi, 1959; Life at the Top, 1962 (filmed 1965); The Jealous God, 1964; The Crying Game, 1968; Stay with Me till Morning, 1970. *Recreations:* walking, talking, Victoriana, and dieting. *Address:* The Holt, Pyrford Heath, Pyrford, Woking, Surrey. *T:* Byfleet 43155. *Clubs:* Authors', Arts Theatre, PEN, Savage.

**BRAINE, Rear-Adm. Richard Allix,** CB 1956; Retired; *b* 18 Nov. 1900; *m* 1922; one *s*. *Educ:* Dean Close Memorial Sch., Cheltenham. Joined RN as asst clerk, 1918; Comdr (S), Dec. 1938; Capt. (S), Dec. 1948; Rear-Adm. 1954. Command Supply Officer, Staff of Flag Officer Air (Home), 1954-56, Portsmouth, 1956-57. *Recreation:* fishing. *Address:* The Old Cottage, Littlewick Green, near Maidenhead, Berks. *T:* Littlewick Green 2760.

**BRAIS, F. Philippe,** CBE 1943; QC (Quebec) 1927; Hon. LLD: University of Montreal 1945, Laval University, Quebec, 1953; MLC Quebec since 1940; Senior Partner, Brais, Campbell, Pepper & Durand, Place Ville Marie, Dorchester Blvd W, Montreal, Quebec; *b* Montreal, Que., 18 Oct. 1894; *s* of N. E. Brais and Blanche (*née* Brunet); *m* 1925, Louise, *d* of J. E. Doré; one *s* five *d*. *Educ:* Montreal High Sch.; Ste Marie de Monnoir Coll., St John's Que.; McGill Univ., Montreal. Pres. Canadian Bar Association, 1944-45; mem. of Provincial Cabinet, Quebec, and Government Leader in Legislative Council, 1940-42; Sec. Montreal Bar Association, 1920-21; Bâtonnier, Montreal Bar Assoc., 1949; Bâtonnier Gen., Quebec Bar Assoc., 1949-1950; Director: Sun Life Assurance Co. of Canada, Montreal Trust Company, Canadian Pacific Railway; Canadian Investment Fund Ltd; Canadian Fund Inc.; Woods Manufacturing Co.; Chm., Board of Banque Canadienne Nationale; Pres., Les Cinémas Odéon Ltée; Canada Iron Foundries Ltd; Wabasso Cotton Co. Ltd; Golden Eagle Refining Co. of Canada Ltd; Seigniory Club Community Assoc., Ltd; Chm. Rediffusion Inc.; Mem. Canadian Advisory Bd, Sun Alliance and London Insurance Group, of London, England; Vice-Chm., Canadian Disaster Relief Fund, Inc.; Pres., Donor's Cttee, University of Montreal; Hon. Life Member: Montreal Board of Trade; American Bar Association; Governor: Montreal Children's Hospital; Children's Memorial Hospital; Royal Edward Laurentian Hospital; mem. of Dominion executive and Joint Chm., Quebec Div., National War Finance Cttee, 1941-45; Vice-Chm. Wartime Information Board, 1941-45. Mem. Nat. Board, Canadian Council of Christians and Jews; Roman Catholic. *Recreations:* riding and hunting. *Address:* 21 Roskilde Avenue, Outremont, PQ. *Clubs:* Mount Royal, St Denis, Montreal Reform; Seigniory, Quebec Reform, Garrison (Quebec).

**BRAITHWAITE, Eustace Adolph;** Ambassador of Guyana to Venezuela, 1968-69; *b* 27 June 1912. *Educ:* New York Univ.; Cambridge Univ. Served War of 1939-45, RAF. Schoolteacher, London, 1950-57; Welfare Officer, LCC, 1958-60; Human Rights Officer, World Veterans Foundation, Paris, 1960-63; Lecturer and Education Consultant, Unesco, Paris, 1963-66; Permanent Rep. of Guyana to UN, 1967-68. Ainsfield-Wolff Literary Award, 1961; Franklin Prize. *Publications:* To Sir With Love, 1959; Paid Servant, 1962; A Kind of Homecoming, 1962; Choice of Straws, 1965. *Recreations:* dancing and tennis. *Address:* c/o The Bodley Head Ltd, 9 Bow Street, WC2.

**BRAITHWAITE, Sir John (Bevan),** Kt 1953; *b* 22 Nov. 1884; *s* of late Joseph Bevan Braithwaite and Anna Sophia (*née* Gillett); *m* 1908, Martha Janette, *d* of late Joseph Allen Baker, MP and Elizabeth B. Baker; two *s* one *d*. *Educ:* Leighton Park Sch., Reading; Owens Coll., Manchester (now Manchester Univ.). Mem. of Stock Exchange, 1907; Mem. of Cttee, 1937; Joint Chm. Cttee on Quotations, 1946-49; Dep. Chm. of Council, 1946-49. Chm. City of Montreal British Stockholders' Cttee, 1942-44; Director: City of London Electric Lighting Co., 1934-48 (Chm. 1943-48); Victoria Falls and Transvaal Power Co., 1937-49; County of London Electric Supply Co., 1939-48; South London Elec. Supply Corp. Ltd, 1943-48.

Chm., Council of the Stock Exchange, 1949-59. Governor of LSE, 1953-64. *Recreations:* English literature, music, photography. *Address:* 85 Hampstead Way, NW11. *T:* 01-455 3570. *Club:* Garrick.

**BRAITHWAITE, Prof. Richard Bevan,** FBA 1957; Emeritus Knightbridge Professor of Moral Philosophy in the University of Cambridge; *b* 15 Jan. 1900; *s* of William Charles Braithwaite, Banbury; *m* 1st, 1925, Dorothea Cotter (*d* 1928), *d* of Sir Theodore Morison; 2nd, 1932, Margaret Mary, *d* of Rt Hon. C. F. G. Masterman; one *s* one *d*. *Educ:* Sidcot Sch., Somerset; Bootham Sch., York; King's Coll., Cambridge (Scholar, Prizeman, Research Student). MA Camb. 1926; Fellow of King's Coll., Camb. 1924-; University Lectr in Moral Science, 1928-34; Sidgwick Lectr in Moral Science, 1934-53; Knightbridge Prof. of Moral Philosophy, 1953-67; Tarner Lectr at Trinity Coll., Camb., 1945-46; Pres. Mind Assoc., 1946; Pres. Aristotelian Soc., 1946-47; Annual Philosophical Lectr to British Academy, 1950; Pres. Brit. Soc. for the Philosophy of Science, 1961-63; Deems Lectr, New York Univ., 1962; Forwood Lectr, Liverpool Univ., 1968; Visiting Prof. of Philosophy: Johns Hopkins Univ., 1968; Univ. of Western Ontario, 1969; City Univ. of New York, 1970. Syndic Cambridge Univ. Press, 1943-62; Mem. Gen. Bd of Faculties, 1945-48; Mem. Council Senate, 1959-64. Hon. DLitt Bristol, 1963. *Publications:* Moral Principles and Inductive Policies (British Acad. Lecture, 1950); Scientific Explanation, 1953; Theory of Games as a tool for the Moral Philosopher (Inaugural Lecture), 1955; An Empiricist's view of the nature of Religious Belief (Eddington Lecture), 1955; Introd. to trans. of Gödel, 1962. Articles in Mind, Proc. Aristotelian Soc., etc. *Recreations:* walking, reading novels. *Address:* King's College, Cambridge. *T:* Cambridge 50411; 11 Millington Road, Cambridge. *T:* Cambridge 50822. *Club:* Union Society (Cambridge).

**BRAITHWAITE, Warwick,** FRAM; Conductor, Australian National Opera Co.; *b* 9 Jan. 1896; *s* of Joseph and Mary Braithwaite, Dunedin, NZ; *m* 1931, Lorna, *d* of Ewart Davies, Dinas Powis, Cardiff; two *s* one *d*. *Educ:* Selwyn Coll., Dunedin, NZ; Royal Academy of Music, London. Conductor O'Mara Opera Co., 1919; Repetiteur BNOC, 1921; Asst Musical Dir, BBC, 1922; Musical Dir, BBC Western Regional, 1922; Conductor Cardiff Musical Soc. and National Orchestra of Wales till 1930; Conductor Sadler's Wells Opera Co., 1932-40; Conductor Robert Mayer Children's Concerts, season, 1934; Conductor Opera at RAM, 1937-38; Conductor all important orchestras in Great Britain, recording HMV, Decca, Columbia; Conductor of Scottish Orchestra, 1940-46; Principal Conductor of Sadler's Wells Ballet, 1948; Conductor, Opera, Covent Garden, 1949-53; Conductor National Orchestra of New Zealand, 1953-54; Artistic Director, National Opera of Australia, 1954-55; Musical Dir, Welsh National Opera Co.; Conductor, Sadler's Wells Opera, 1960-68. *Publications:* The Conductor's Art. *Recreations:* drama, literature, composition. *Address:* 23 Linden Lea, N2. *T:* 01-455 9570.

**BRAMALL, (Ernest) Ashley;** Leader of the Inner London Education Authority, since 1970; *b* 6 Jan. 1916; *er s* of Major E. H. Bramall; *m*; three *s*. *Educ:* Westminster and Canford Schs; Magdalen Coll., Oxford. Served in Army, 1940-46; Major; psc 1945. Contested Fareham Div. of Hants, 1945; MP (Lab) for Bexley, 1946-50; contested Bexley, 1950, 1951, 1959; Watford, 1955. Barrister-at-Law, Inner Temple. Member: LCC (Lab) Bethnal Green, 1961; Greater London Council (Lab) Tower Hamlets, 1964; Westminster City Council, 1959-68; Chm., Inner London Education Authority, 1965-67. *Address:* 21 Hugh Street, SW1. *T:* 01-828 0973.

**BRAMBLE, Courtenay Parker,** CIE 1946; Managing Director Abercrombie, Bramble & Co. Ltd, Liverpool; *b* 10 June 1900; *s* of Frank and Violet Bramble, Portsmouth; *m* 1st, 1928, Margaret Louise Lawrence, MBE, 1943, *d* of late Sir Henry Lawrence, KCSI; two *s* one *d*: 2nd, 1958, Doreen, *d* of C. E. Cornish, Lytham St Annes, Lancs. *Educ:* St Paul's Cathedral Choir Sch.; Cranleigh Sch.; King's Coll., Cambridge (MA, LLB). Barrister-at-law, Middle Temple; with The Bombay Co. Ltd, India, 1922-33; Senior partner Drennan & Co., Bombay, 1933-52; Dir, East India Cotton Assoc., Bombay, 1925-33; Mem., Indian Central Cotton Cttee, 1935-50. Mem. of Legislature, Bombay, 1935-50 (Leader, Progress Party); JP and Hon. Magistrate, Bombay; Chm., Children's Aid Soc., Bombay, 1931-39; Pres. Bombay Chamber of Commerce, 1940, 1945-46; Dep. Pres. Associated Chambers of Commerce, India, 1945; Chm. European Assoc., Bombay Branch, 1942-44; Mem., Bombay Presidency War Cttee, 1941-45; Trustee of Port of Bombay, 1949; Chairman: All India Quadrangular Cricket Cttee, 1935-39; UK Citizens Assoc. (Bombay), 1948-50; National Service Advisory Cttee, 1940-45; Bombay European Hospital Trust, 1943-50; Hon. Lieut, RINVR, 1940-47. Dir (Pres. 1962), Liverpool Cotton Association; Mem., Council, Cotton Research Corp., 1960-. *Address:* Lyndhurst, Childer Thornton, Cheshire. *T:* 051-339 3545. *Clubs:* United University; Royal Yacht (Bombay).

**BRAMMER, Leonard Griffith,** RE 1956 (ARE 1932); painter and etcher; Supervisor of Art and Crafts, Stoke-on-Trent Education Authority, 1952-69; *b* 4 July 1906; *s* of Frederick William Brammer and Minnie Griffith; *m* 1934, Florence May, *d* of William and Mary Barnett, Hanley; one *d*. *Educ:* Burslem Sch. of Art; Royal College of Art (Diploma Associate); awarded Travelling Scholarship, School of Engraving, Royal College of Art, 1930; represented in Tate Gallery, Victoria & Albert Museum, City of Stoke-on-Trent Art Gallery, City of Carlisle Art Gallery, Wedgwood Museum, Barlaston, Keele Univ., Collection of Contemporary Art Soc., The Collections of The British Council, etc.; exhibitor at Royal Academy and all leading English and American exhibitions. *Recreation:* golf. *Address:* Wayside, 22 The Greenway, May Bank, Newcastle, Staffs.

**BRAMWELL, John Crighton,** MA Camb; MD, Manchester; FRCP, London; Hon. FRCP Ed; Professor Emeritus, University of Manchester; Consulting Physician, Manchester Royal Infirmary; *b* 4 March 1889; *y s* of late Sir Byrom Bramwell, MD, LLD, DCL, FRCP; *m* 1929, Elsa, 2nd *d* of James Risk, Gogarbank House, Midlothian; two *s* one *d*. *Educ:* Cheltenham Coll.; Trinity Coll., Cambridge (Exhibitioner, 1st Class Natural Science Tripos); Manchester Univ. (Entrance Scholar, MD, Gold Medal). Rockefeller Fellow, Medical Research Council, 1923; Lumleian Lecturer Royal College of Physicians of London, 1937; Gibson Lectr, Royal College of Physicians of Edinburgh, 1939; Finlayson Memorial Lecture, Royal Fac. of Physicians and Surgeons of Glasgow, 1941; St Cyres Lecturer, 1945; Carey Coombs Memorial Lecture, University of Bristol, 1954; First John Hay Memorial Lecture, University of Liverpool, 1965; Harveian Orator, Royal College of Physicians, 1956;

Ramsden Memorial Lecture, Manchester Literary and Philosophical Society, 1949; Professor of Systematic Medicine, Manchester Univ., 1942-46; Professor of Cardiology, Manchester Univ., 1946-54; Senior Editor, Quarterly Journal of Medicine; Member of Editorial Board, British Heart Journal; President Assoc. Physicians of Great Britain and Ireland, 1955-56. Hon. Member of British Cardiac Society, 1956; Senior Censor, 1949, Councillor, 1945-48, and Member of Science Cttee, Royal College of Physicians; President Manchester Medical Soc., 1952-53; Member Physiological Soc.; Member of Medical Priority Cttee of Ministry of Health, 1941-48; Member of Grading Cttee, Central Medical War Cttee, 1941. Late Examiner in Medicine, Universities of Cambridge, Aberdeen, Sheffield, Edinburgh, Durham and St Andrews. Served European War, 1914-19, in Egypt, France, Italy. Temp. Capt. RAMC; DADMS, GHQ, Italy, 1918. *Publications:* Heart Disease, Diagnosis and Treatment, 1932; Heart Disease and Pregnancy (jointly), 1938; Principles and Practice of Cardiology (jointly), 1941; The Approach to Cardiology, 1951; A Clinical Introduction to Heart Disease, 1959; numerous papers to Medical and Scientific Journals. *Recreations:* fishing and gardening. *Address:* Orchard Cottage, Outgate, near Ambleside, Westmorland. *T:* Hawkshead 233.

**BRAMWELL-BOOTH, Catherine;** a Commissioner of the Salvation Army; *b* London, 1883; *e c* of late General Bramwell Booth. Entered Salvation Army as an Officer, 1903; engaged in training Cadets at International Training Coll., 1907-17; International Sec. for Salvation Army in Europe, 1917; command of Women's Social Work in Great Britain and Ireland, 1926; International Sec. for Europe, 1946-48; retired 1948. *Publications:* Messages to the Messengers; A Few Lines; Bramwell Booth, 1933; (compiler) Bramwell Booth Speaks, 1947; Verse, 1947; Catherine Booth, the story of her loves, 1970. *Address:* North Court, Finchampstead, Berks.

**BRAMWELL DAVIS, Maj.-Gen. Ronald Albert,** CB 1957; DSO and bar, 1945; GOC Aldershot District, 1957-60, retired; *b* 8 Oct. 1905; *s* of late Capt. P. Bramwell Davis, The Highland Light Infantry, and of late Mrs E. M. Bramwell Davis, Crookham House, Newbury; *m* 1942, Lorna Winifred Hobling; one *s* one *d. Educ:* Wellington Coll.; RMC, Sandhurst. Joined HLI, 1925, as 2nd Lieut; Instructor, RMC Sandhurst, 1937-39; Company Comdr, OCTU, 1939-40; Staff Coll., student, 1940; Bde Major, 1940-41; Joint Staff Mission, Washington (Lieut-Col), 1941-42; CO 5th HLI (UK) (Lieut-Col), 1943; Joint Staff Mission, Washington (Col), 1943-44; CO 10th HLI (NW Europe) (Lieut-Col), and BAOR Training Centre, 1945; Bde Comdr, 146 Infantry Bde (49 WR Div.), 1945-46; BGS (Training) GHQ, MELF, 1946-49; Lieut-Col, Black Watch, 1948; Col, 1949; Bde Comdr 153 Infantry Bde (51st Highland Div.), 1950-51; Canadian National Defence Coll., student, 1951-52; Chief of Staff, Scottish Command, 1953-54; Brig. 1953; Maj.-Gen. 1955; Chief of Staff, Southern Command, 1955-56. Col, The Highland Light Infantry, 1957-59; Col, The Royal Highland Fusiliers, 1959-63. Pres., Modern Pentathlon Assoc. of Great Britain (Chm., 1963). USA Legion of Merit (Degree of Officer), 1944. *Recreations:* field sports. *Address:* Hamilton House, Downton, near Salisbury, Wilts. *T:* Downton 510. *Clubs:* Army and Navy, MCC; I Zingari, Free Foresters.

**BRANCKER, Sir (John Eustace) Theodore,** Kt 1969; Speaker, House of Assembly, Barbados, since 1961; *b* 9 Feb. 1909; *s* of Jabel Eustace and Myra Enid Vivienne Brancker; *m* 1967, Esme Gwendolyn Walcott. *Educ:* Harrison Coll., Barbados. Called to Bar, Middle Temple, 1933; in private practice as Barrister; QC (Barbados) 1961. Coronation Medal, 1953. *Recreations:* classical music, chess, drama. *Address:* Valencia, St James's, Barbados. *T:* 04138. *Clubs:* Challoner (London); Empire (Barbados); Rotary International.

**BRANCKER, Sir Theodore;** *see* Brancker, Sir J. E. T.

**BRAND,** family name of **Viscount Hampden.**

**BRAND, Sir Alfred;** *see* Brand, Sir W. A.

**BRAND, Prof. Charles Peter;** Professor of Italian, University of Edinburgh, since 1966; *b* 7 Feb. 1923; *er s* of Charles Frank Brand and Dorothy (*née* Tapping); *m* 1948, Gunvor, *yr d* of Col I. Hellgren, Stockholm; one *s* three *d. Educ:* Cambridge High Sch.; Trinity Hall, Cambridge. War Service, Intelligence Corps, 1943-46. Open Maj. Scholar, Trinity Hall, 1940; 1st Class Hons. Mod. Languages, Cantab., 1948; PhD, Cantab., 1951. Asst Lecturer, Edinburgh Univ., 1952; Asst Lecturer, subsequently Lecturer, Cambridge Univ., 1952-66. *Publications:* Italy and the English Romantics, 1957; (Joint Ed.) Italian Studies presented to E. R. Vincent, 1962; Torquato Tasso, 1965; contributions to learned journals. *Recreations:* sport, travel, gardening. *Address:* 21 Succoth Park, Edinburgh 12. *T:* 031-337 1980.

**BRAND, Hon. Sir David,** KCMG 1969; MLA (WA); Premier of Western Australia since 1959; also Treasurer and Minister for Tourists; *b* Dongara, WA, 1 Aug. 1912; *s* of late Albert John Brand and late Hilda (*née* Mitchell), Dongara, WA; *m* 1944, Doris Elspeth, *d* of H. McNeill, Arrino, WA; two *s* one *d. Educ:* Mullawa Sch., WA. Joined AIF, 1939; served in Middle East and Greece (wounded, 1941, and discharged on med. grounds, 1942); joined Volunteer Defence Force, 1942, and apptd Chief Instr, Geraldton Area, WA. Elected to WA Legislative Assembly (for Greenough), Oct. 1945; Junior Minister, 1949; Minister for Works and Water Supplies, 1950-53; Leader of Opposition, 1957-59. Hon. LLD (Univ. of WA). *Recreations:* golf, tennis. *Address:* Parliament House, Perth, Western Australia. *T:* Perth (WA) 21.8711. *Club:* West Australian (Perth).

**BRAND, David William Robert,** QC Scotland, 1959; Solicitor-General for Scotland, since 1970; *b* 21 Oct. 1923; *s* of late James Gordon Brand, Huntingdon, Dumfries, and Frances (*née* Bull); *m* 1st, 1948, Rose Josephine Devlin (*d* 1968); four *d*; 2nd, Bridget Veronica Lynch (*née* Russell), *widow* of Thomas Patrick Lynch, Beechmount, Mallow, Co. Cork. *Educ:* Stonyhurst Coll.; Edinburgh Univ. Served War of 1939-45; Commissioned Argyll and Sutherland Highlanders, 1942; Capt. 1945. Admitted to Faculty of Advocates, 1948; Standing Junior Counsel to Dept of Education for Scotland, 1951; Advocate-Depute for Sheriff Court, 1953; Extra Advocate-Depute for Glasgow Circuit, 1955; Advocate-Depute, 1957-59; Senior Advocate-Depute, 1964; Sheriff of Dumfries and Galloway, 1968; Sheriff of Roxburgh, Berwick and Selkirk, 1970. *Publications:* Joint Editor, Scottish Edn of Current Law, 1948-61; Scottish Editor, Encyclopedia of Road Traffic Law and Practice, 1960-64; contributor to Scots Law Times. *Recreation:* golf. *Address:* 38 Moray

Place, Edinburgh EH3 6BT. *T:* 031-225 8102. *Clubs:* New (Edinburgh); Honourable Company of Edinburgh Golfers.

**BRAND, Sir (William) Alfred,** Kt 1965; CBE 1958; *b* 22 Aug. 1888; *m* 1913, Myrtle M. Kingston; one *s* two *d* (and one *d* decd). *Educ:* Childers and Appletree Creek State Schools. Canefarmer. MLA for Burrum, Qld, 1920-32, for Isis, 1932-50; MP for Wide Bay, Qld, 1954-58. *Recreations:* cricket and bowls. *Address:* North Street, Childers, Queensland, Australia. *T:* Childers 33. *Clubs:* Childers, Isis (Queensland).

**BRANDER, George Maconachie,** CIE 1946; ICS retired; *b* 12 Oct. 1906; *s* of late J. P. Brander, ICS; *m* 1936, Joan (*née* Darley); three *d. Educ:* Edinburgh Academy; Exeter Coll., Oxford. Entered Indian Civil Service, 1930; Secretary to HE the Governor of Punjab, 1942; Additional Commissioner, Lahore, 1947; retired 1947. *Address:* 13a Porchester Terrace, W2. *T:* 01-262 6012.

**BRANDER, Maj.-Gen. Maxwell Spieker,** CB 1937; OBE 1925; MIMechE; Col Comdt RASC, 1942-49; *b* 11 Oct. 1884; *s* of late Lt-Col William Maxwell Brander; *m* 1919, Mary Frances Alice, *d* of late Campbell Fortescue Stapleton Sanctuary, Bridport, Dorset; one *s. Educ:* Bedford Sch.; RMC, Sandhurst. Commissioned ASC 1906; served European War, 1914-18 (despatches, Bt Maj. and Bt Lieut-Col); Capt. 1914; Maj. 1925; Lieut-Col 1933; Col 1933; Maj.-Gen. 1936; Inspector, RASC, 1936-37; Director of Supplies and Transport, War Office, 1937-40; Maj.-Gen., i/c Administration, Eastern Command, 1940-41; Deputy Director-Gen. of Mechanization, Ministry of Supply, 1941-47. *Address:* Vincent Lodge, Bishopsteignton, Devon. *T:* Bishopsteignton 200. *Clubs:* United Service, Royal Automobile.

**BRANDO, Marlon;** American actor, stage and screen; *b* Omaha, Nebraska, 3 April 1924; *s* of Marlon Brando; *m* 1957, Anna Kashfi (marr. dissolved, 1959); one *s. Educ:* Libertyville High Sch., Illinois; Shattuck Military Academy, Minnesota. Entered Dramatic Workshop of New School for Social Research, New York, 1943; has studied with Elia Kazan and Stella Adler. *Plays include:* I Remember Mama, Broadway, 1944; Truckline Café, 1946; Candida, 1946; A Flag is Born, 1946; The Eagle Has Two Heads, 1946; A Streetcar Named Desire, 1947. *Films include:* The Men; A Streetcar Named Desire; Viva Zapata!; Julius Cæsar; The Wild One; Desirée; On the Waterfront; Guys and Dolls; Tea House of the August Moon; Sayonara; The Young Lions; The Fugitive Kind; Mutiny on the Bounty; The Ugly American; The Saboteur, Code Name–Morituri; The Chase; Southwest to Sonora; A Countess from Hong Kong; Reflections in a Golden Eye; The Night of the Following Day; Candy. Directed, produced and appeared in One-Eyed Jacks, 1959. Academy Award, best actor of year, 1954. *Address:* Hawley Road, Mundelein, Illinois, USA; c/o Paramount Studios, 5451 Marathon, Hollywood, California, USA.

**BRANDON, Henry;** *see* Brandon, O. H.

**BRANDON, Hon. Sir Henry (Vivian),** Kt 1966; MC 1942; **Hon. Mr Justice Brandon;** Judge of the High Court of Justice (Probate, Divorce and Admiralty Division), since 1966; *b* 3 June 1920; *y s* of late Captain V. R. Brandon, CBE, RN, and Joan Elizabeth Maud Simpson; *m* 1955, Jeanette Rosemary, *e d* of J. V. B. Janvrin; three *s* one *d. Educ:* Winchester Coll. (Scholar); King's Coll., Cambridge (Scholar 1938, Stewart of Rannoch Scholar 1939). Commnd 2nd Lieut RA 1939; Major 1944; served Madagascar, 1942, India and Burma, 1942-45. BA 1946. Barrister, Inner Temple, 1946 (Entrance and Yarborough Anderson Scholar); Member Bar Council, 1951-53; QC 1961. Member panel of Lloyd's arbitrators in salvage cases, 1961-66; Member panel from which Wreck Commissioners chosen, 1963-66. *Recreation:* cricket. *Address:* 18 Regent's Park Terrace, NW1. *T:* 01-485 3033; Royal Courts of Justice, Strand, WC2.

**BRANDON, (Oscar) Henry;** Associate Editor and Chief American correspondent of the Sunday Times; *b* 9 March 1916; *m* 1970, Mabel Hobart Wentworth. *Educ:* Univ. of Prague and Lausanne. Joined Sunday Times, 1939; War Correspondent, N Africa and W Europe, 1943-45; Paris Correspondent, 1945-46; Roving Diplomatic Correspondent, 1947-49; Washington Correspondent, 1950-. Foreign corresp. award, Univ. of California, Los Angeles, 1957; award, Lincoln Univ., Jefferson City, Missouri, 1962; Hannen Swaffer award, 1964. *Publications:* As We Are, 1961; In The Red, 1966; Conversations with Henry Brandon, 1966; The Anatomy of Error, 1970. *Recreations:* ski-ing, tennis, swimming, photography. *Address:* 3067 Whitehaven Street, NW, Washington, DC 20008, USA. *T:* 628-4310. *Clubs:* Federal City, National Press, Overseas Writers (Washington, DC).

**BRANDON, Rev. Prof. Samuel George Frederick,** MA, DD Leeds; MA Manchester 1955; Hon. CF; Professor of Comparative Religion in the University of Manchester since 1951, and Pro-Vice-Chancellor of the University, 1967-70; *b* 2 Oct. 1907; *s.* of Samuel James and Lilian Emily Brandon; *m* 1934, Ivy Ada Miles; one *s* (and one *s* decd). *Educ:* College of the Resurrection, Mirfield; University of Leeds. Curate of St Mark's, Ford, Devonport, 1932-36; Curate-in-Charge of Westward Ho!, N. Devon, 1936-39; Chaplain to the Forces: Aldershot, 1939; BEF, 1939-40; Home Forces, 1940-42; Senior Chaplain to the Forces: North Africa, 1942-44; Italy, 1944-45 (despatches); Catterick, 1945-47; Austria, 1947-51. Wilde Lecturer in Natural and Comparative Religion, Oxford Univ., 1954-57; Forwood Lecturer in Philosophy and History of Religion, Liverpool Univ., 1964. Examiner in History and Philosophy of Religion, University of Wales, 1957-59; Dean of Faculty of Theology, University of Manchester, 1959-60, 1967-69. *Publications:* Time and Mankind, 1951; The Fall of Jerusalem and the Christian Church, 1951; The Formation of Christian Dogma (trans. from the German of M. Werner), 1957; Man and his Destiny in the Great Religions, 1962; Creation Legends of the Ancient Near East, 1963; The Saviour God (ed. and contrib.), 1963; History, Time and Deity, 1965; Jesus and the Zealots, 1967; The Judgement of the Dead, 1967; The Trial of Jesus of Nazareth, 1968; Religion in Ancient History, 1969; (ed and contrib.) Dictionary of Comparative Religion, 1970; contributions to: Myth, Ritual and Kingship, 1958; The Voices of Time, 1965; The Hibbert Journal, Folklore, The Modern Churchman, Numen, History Today, Encyclopædia Judaica, Dictionary of the History of Ideas, Encyclopædia Britannica, etc. *Address:* Ewen, 18 Woodvale Road, Knutsford, Cheshire. *T:* 2370.

**BRANDT, Willy;** Grosskreuz des Verdienstordens der Bundesrepublik Deutschland, 1959; Chairman Social Democratic Party (SPD), since 1964; Chancellor, Federal Republic of Germany, since 1969; *b* 18 Dec. 1913; *m* 1948, Rut Hansen; three *s* one *d. Educ:* Johanneum,

Lübeck; University of Oslo. Fled from Lübeck to Norway, 1933; journalistic work of various kinds in Norway and Sweden; Chief Editor, Berliner Stadtblatt, 1950-51. Rep. Federal Board of SPD (German Social Democratic Party) in Berlin, 1948-49, Deputy Chairman of SPD, 1962-64. Member German Federal Parliament, 1949-57; President Berlin House of Representatives, 1955-57; Vice-Chancellor and Foreign Minister, Federal Republic of Germany, Dec. 1966-69. Governing Mayor of W Berlin, 1957-66; President German Conference of Mayors, 1958-63; President German Federal Council, 1957-58. Chairman: Governing Bodies, Free University and Technical University, Berlin; Board of Directors, Berliner Bank. Hon. Chairman, German Red Cross, Berlin; Senator, Max Planck Society. Dr (*hc*): Pennsylvania Univ., 1959; Maryland Univ., 1960; Harvard Univ., 1963; Hon. DCL, Oxford Univ., 1969. Holds foreign decorations from Jordan, Norway, Greece, Austria. *Publications:* Krigen i Norge, 1945; Forbrytere og andre tyskere, 1946; (with Richard Löwenthal) Ernst Reuter: Ein Leben für die Freiheit, 1957; Von Bonn nach Berlin, 1957; Mein Weg nach Berlin (recorded by Leo Lania), 1960; Plädoyer für die Zukunft, 1961; The Ordeal of Co-existence, 1963; Begegnungen mit Kennedy, 1964; (with Günter Struve) Draüssen, 1966 (GB 1970); Friedenspolitik in Europa, 1968; many publications on topical questions in Sweden and Norway; articles in home and foreign journals. *Address:* (office) Bundeskanzleramt, Adenauerallee 139, Bonn, Germany. *T:* 1051.

**BRANIGAN, Sir Patrick (Francis),** Kt 1954; QC; JP; Deputy Chairman, Devon Quarter Sessions; Chairman: Agricultural Land Tribunal for South West Area of England; Mental Health Review Tribunal for SW Region of England; National Insurance Medical Appeal Tribunal for SW Region; Pensions Appeal Tribunal; *b* 30 Aug. 1906; *e s* of late D. Branigan and Teresa, *d* of Thomas Clinton, Annagassan, Co. Louth; *m* 1935, Prudence, *yr d* of late Dr A. Avent, Seaton, Devon; one *s* one *d*. *Educ:* Newbridge Coll., Co. Kildare; Trinity Coll., Dublin. BA 1st Class Hons in Law and Political Science and gold medallist, 1928; called to Irish Bar, Certificate of Honour, 1928 (1st Victoria Prize, 1927); called to Bar, Gray's Inn, 1935. Practised at Irish Bar, 1928-30; Downing Coll., Cambridge, 1930-31; Colonial Administrative Service, Kenya, 1931; Crown Counsel, Tanganyika, 1934; Solicitor-General, N. Rhodesia, 1938; Chairman NR Man-power Cttee, 1939-41; Chairman Conciliation Board, Copperbelt Strike, 1940; Member NR Nat. Arbitration Tribunal, 1940-46; Member Strauss Arbitration Tribunal, Bulawayo, 1944; Chairman, Road Transport Services Board and Electricity Board of N. Rhodesia, 1939-46; Legal Secretary to Govt of Malta and Chairman Malta War Damage Commission, 1946-48; periodically acting Lieut-Governor of Malta, 1947-48. Minister of Justice and Attorney-General, Gold Coast, 1948-55; QC Gold Coast, 1949; retired, 1955. Chairman of Commission of inquiry into Copperbelt industrial unrest, 1956; Member Industrial Disputes Tribunal, 1955-59. JP Devon 1955. Knight Commander of Order of St Gregory, 1956. *Recreations:* golf, fishing. *Address:* Willhayne, Colyton, Devon. *T:* Colyton 435.

**BRANNAN, Charles Franklin;** lawyer; *b* 23 Aug. 1903; *s* of John Brannan and Ella Louise Street; *m* 1932, Eda Seltzer; no *c*. *Educ:* Regis Coll., and University of Denver Law Sch., Denver, Colorado, USA. Private law practice, Denver, Colorado, 1929-35; Asst Regional Attorney: Resettlement Administration, Denver, 1935-37; Regional Attorney, Office of the Solicitor, US Dept of Agriculture, Denver, 1937-41; Regional Director of Farm Security Administration, US Dept of Agriculture, Denver, 1941-44; Asst Administrator, Farm Security Administration, US Dept of Agriculture, Washington, DC, April-June 1944; Asst Secretary of Agriculture, Washington, DC, June 1944-48; Secretary of Agriculture, USA, 1948-Jan. 1953. Hon. Degrees: Doctor of Laws from the University of Denver and Doctor of Science from the Colorado Agricultural and Mechanical Coll. *Address:* (home) 3131 East Alameda, Denver, Colorado 80209, USA; (office) 12025 E 45th Avenue, Denver, Colo 80239. *Club:* Denver Athletic (Denver, Colorado).

**BRANNIGAN, Owen,** OBE 1964; Bass Singer; *b* 10 March 1908; *s* of Owen Brannigan and Sarah (*née* Connelly); *m* 1933, Mary Ashley; one *s*. *Educ:* privately; Guildhall School of Music. Studied with Walter Hyde and George Baker; Principal Bass: Glyndebourne, Covent Garden, Sadler's Wells Opera; first performance of Britten's Peter Grimes (later at Covent Garden), at 1958 Centenary Gala Performance before the Queen, Paris Opera, La Monnaie Brussels; and in Vienna, Prague, Hamburg and Geneva Opera Houses, 1965; created Collatinus in Rape of Lucretia, Glyndebourne, afterwards in Amsterdam, The Hague, etc.; original Dr Coutras in Moon and Sixpence, Sadler's Wells, 1957; created rôle of Noah in Britten's Noyes Fludde at Aldeburgh Festival, 1958, and of Bottom in Britten's Midsummer Night's Dream, Aldeburgh Festival, 1960 (re-created at Montreal Expo '67); Hasselbacher in Our Man in Havana, Sadler's Wells, 1963. Edinburgh International Festival, 1947, 1948, 1951, 1954; Lucerne and Brussels Festivals, 1969; leading Festivals in Great Britain, including Three Choirs, Leeds Triennial, Bath, Canterbury, Malvern; soloist with Royal Philharmonic, Royal Choral and Hallé Societies, and regular appearances at Promenade Concerts, BBC recitals and Television. Films include: The Gilbert and Sullivan Story, The Tales of Hoffmann. President Northumberland and Durham Association in London. Repr. Incorp. Society of Musicians, Catholic Stage Guild; Vice-Pres., Northern Arts Assoc. (formerly N Eastern Assoc. of the Arts). FGSM; Hon. RAM 1967; FIAL. Hon. MA Newcastle upon Tyne, 1969. Worshipful Company of Musicians' Award, Oct. 1943, and Liveryman, 1963; Sir Charles Santley Memorial Award, 1969. Papal Cross, Pro Ecclesia Pontifice, 1958. *Recreations:* golf and joinery. *Address:* 9 Lauradale Road, E Finchley, N2. *T:* 01-883 6368. *Club:* Savage.

**BRANSON, Col Sir Douglas (Stephenson),** KBE 1954; CB 1950; DSO 1918, and 2 bars; MC 1917; TD; MA; *b* 25 July 1893; *s* of Col George Ernest Branson, JP, Broomgrove, Sheffield; *m* 1st, 1930, Edith Eileen (*d* 1959), *d* of Joseph Bradbury, Sheffield; 2nd, 1961, Ailie (*widow* of Brig. John Malcolm Fisher), *d* of late Sir William Bell. *Educ:* Marlborough; New Coll., Oxford. Admitted a Solicitor, 1920 and practised until 1970. Served European War, 1914-18, The Hallamshire Bn York and Lancaster Regt. Col, 1924; Commander 148 Infantry Brigade (TA), 1925-29; Additional ADC to the King, 1927. DL West Riding of Yorks, 1934. High Sheriff of Hallamshire, 1963. *Address:* 6 Paradise Square, Sheffield, Yorks. *T:* 24181; 23 Ranmoor Park Road, Sheffield 10, Yorks. *T:* 302149.

**BRANSON, William Rainforth,** CBE 1969; Director, Woodall-Duckham Group Ltd, since 1969; *b* 2 Jan. 1905; *s* of late A. W. Branson, JP;

*m* 1932, Dorothy Iris Green; no *c*. *Educ:* Rydal Sch.; University of Leeds. BSc, 1st Class Hons (Fuel and Gas Engrg), 1927; MSc 1930. Asst Engineer, Gas Light & Coke Co., London, 1927-37; Asst Engineer, later Dep. Engineer, Cardiff Gas Light & Coke Co., 1937-45; Dep. Controller, later Controller, Public Utilities Br., Control Commn for Germany, 1945-49; Planning Engineer, Wales Gas Board, 1949-51; Technical Officer, E. Midlands Gas Board, 1952-54; Dep. Chairman, W. Midlands Gas Board, 1954-65; Chm., Scottish Gas Bd, 1965-68. President, Instn of Gas Engineers, 1964-65. Director, Scottish Tar Distillers, 1965. *Recreation:* music. *Address:* 32 Poolfield Drive, Solihull, Warwickshire. *T:* 021-705 9240. *Club:* Anglo-Belgian.

**BRASH, Rev. Alan Anderson,** OBE 1962; Associate General-Secretary, World Council of Churches, Geneva, since 1970; *b* 5 June 1913; *s* of Thomas C. Brash, CBE, New Zealand, and Margaret Brash (*née* Allan); *m* 1938, Eljean Ivory Hill; one *s* one *d*. *Educ:* Dunedin Univ., NZ (MA); Edinburgh Univ. (BD). Parish Minister in NZ, 1938-46 and 1952-56; Gen. Sec., NZ Nat. Council of Churches, 1947-52 and 1957-64, East Asia Christian Conf., 1958-68. Dir, Christian Aid, London, 1968-70. *Address:* c/o World Council of Churches, 150 Route de Ferney, Geneva, Switzerland. *Club:* Royal Commonwealth.

**BRASH, Robert;** Canadian Defence College, since Aug. 1970; *b* 30 May 1924; *s* of Frank and Ida Brash; *m* 1954, Barbara Enid Clarke; three *s* one *d*. *Educ:* Trinity Coll., Cambridge. War Service, 1943-46. Entered Foreign Service, 1949; Djakarta, 1951-55; FO, 1955-58; First Sec., 1956; Jerusalem, 1958-61; Bonn, 1961-64; Bucharest, 1964-66; FCO, 1966-70; Counsellor, 1968. *Recreations:* walking, gardening, some golf. *Address:* c/o Foreign and Commonwealth Office, SW1. *Club:* Royal Automobile.

**BRASHER, William Kenneth,** CBE 1951; MA, FIEE; Secretary, The Institution of Electrical Engineers, 1939-62 (Hon. Secretary, 1962-63); *b* 31 March 1897; *e s* of late Dr C. W. J. Brasher, Clifton, and late Mabel M. Westlake, Bristol; *m* 1922, Katie Howe Howe; two *s* two *d*. *Educ:* Clifton Coll.; St John's Coll., Cambridge. Served European War, 1914-18, commission in Royal Engineers (TF) Signals, France, 1915-18. Asst Engineer, Marconi's Wireless Telegraph Co., 1921; Asst Engineer, Post Office, British Guiana, 1922, Chief Engineer, 1927; Senior Executive Engineer Posts and Telegraphs, Iraq 1929; Engineer-in-Chief, Posts and Telegraphs, Palestine, 1933. Hon. Associate, College of Technology, Aston, 1959. Chairman, Advisory Cttee, Conference of Engineering Societies of Western Europe and the USA (EUSEC), 1960-63; Secretary Exec. Cttee, Conference of Engineering Institutions of the Commonwealth, 1950-62. Al Rafidain, 5th Class, 1937; Commander Order of King Leopold II, 1963. *Recreations:* motoring and gardening. *Address:* 10 Kensington Mansions, SW5. *T:* 01-373 9999. *Club:* Athenæum.

**BRASNETT, Rev. Dr Bertrand Rippington,** DD Oxon, 1935; *b* 22 Jan. 1893; *e s* of Stanley Brasnett, The Manor House, Marham, Norfolk, *gs* of Edward Rowing Brasnett, West Bilney House, Norfolk; unmarried. *Educ:* Oxford High Sch.; private tutor; Keble Coll., Oxford; Cuddesdon Theological Coll. Squire Scholar of the University of Oxford, 1911-15, 2nd class Classical Moderations, 2nd class Literæ Humaniores, BA, MA, Diploma in Theology with Distinction, BD; Deacon, 1916; Priest, 1918; Chaplain and Asst Master, Bradfield Coll., Berks, 1916-18; Priest-in-charge, Coleshill, Bucks, 1918-22; Chaplain and Lecturer, Bishops' Coll., Cheshunt, 1922-25; Vice-Principal, 1925-29, Principal and Pantonian Prof., 1930-42, of the Theological Coll. of the Scottish Episcopal Church, Edinburgh; Hon. Chaplain of St Mary's Cathedral, Edinburgh, 1926-29; Canon, 1930-42, and Chancellor, 1940-42, of St Mary's Cathedral, Edinburgh; Examining Chaplain to the Bishop of Edinburgh, 1930-42; Select Preacher, University of Oxford, 1941-43. *Publications:* The Suffering of the Impassible God, 1928; The Infinity of God, 1933; God the Worshipful, 1935. *Address:* Pleasant View, 15 Jack Straw's Lane, Headington, Oxford.

**BRASS, John,** CBE 1968; BSc, CEng, FIME, MICE; FRSA; Regional Chairman, Yorkshire and North-Western Areas, National Coal Board, since April 1967; *b* 22 Oct. 1908; 2nd *s* of late John Brass, Mining Engineer, and late Mary Brass (*née* Swainston); *m* 1934, Jocelyn Constance Cape, Stroud, Glos.; three *s* one *d*. *Educ:* Oundle Sch.; Birmingham Univ. (BSc Hons). Various appointments, all in mining; Chairman W. Midlands Division, NCB, 1961-67. *Address:* The Old Granary, Linton, near Wetherby, Yorks.

**BRASSEY,** family name of **Baron Brassey of Apethorpe.**

**BRASSEY OF APETHORPE,** 3rd Baron, *cr* 1938, of Apethorpe; **David Henry Brassey;** Bt 1922; *b* 16 Sept. 1932; *er s* of 2nd Baron Brassey of Apethorpe, MC, TD, and late Lady Brassey of Apethorpe; *S* father, 1967; *m* 1958, Myrna Elizabeth, *o d* of Lieut-Col John Baskervyle-Glegg; one *s*. Commissioned, Grenadier Guards, 1951; Major, 1966, retired, 1967. *Heir: s* Hon. Edward Brassey, *b* 9 March 1964. *Address:* The Manor House, Apethorpe, Peterborough. *T:* Kingscliffe 231. *Club:* White's.

**BRASSEY, Brevet-Col Hugh Trefusis,** OBE 1959; MC 1944; Vice-Lieutenant of Wiltshire, since 1968; *b* 5 Oct. 1915; *s* of Lieut-Col Edgar Hugh Brassey, MVO, and Margaret Harriet (*née* Trefusis); *m* 1939, Joyce Patricia, *d* of Captain Maurice Kingscote; two *s* two *d* (and one *d* decd). *Educ:* Eton; Sandhurst. Regular Commission, The Royal Scots Greys, 1935-46; served Palestine, Africa, Italy and NW Europe, Lieut-Col Comdg Royal Wilts Yeomanry, 1955-58. ADC (TA) to the Queen, 1964-69; Exon, Queen's Bodyguard, Yeoman of the Guard, 1964-70, Ensign, 1970-. Chairman, Chippenham Conservative Assoc., 1951-53, 1966-68 (pres. 1968). Pres., Wilts Assoc. of Boys Clubs, 1968. JP 1951, DL 1955, High Sheriff 1959, Wilts. Croix de Guerre (France), 1944. *Recreation:* country. *Address:* Manor Farm, Little Somerford, Chippenham, Wilts. *T:* Malmesbury 2255. *Club:* Cavalry.

**BRASSEY, Lt-Col Hon. Peter (Esmé);** Vice-Lieutenant, County of Huntingdon and Peterborough, since 1966; *b* 5 Dec. 1907; *o surv s* of 1st Baron Brassey of Apethorpe; *m* 1944, Lady Romayne Cecil, 2nd *d* of 5th Marquess of Exeter, KG, CMG; two *s* one *d*. *Educ:* Eton; Magdalene Coll., Cambridge. Barrister-at-Law, Inner Temple, Midland Circuit, 1931. Northamptonshire Yeomanry, Lieut-Col, 1945; served NW Europe (wounded). Dir, The Essex Water Co. Ltd; Member: Welland & Nene River Authority; Water Resources Bd. Alderman, Huntingdon and Peterborough CC; DL, 1961, High Sheriff, 1966, County of Huntingdon and Peterborough. *Recreations:* shooting, fishing. *Address:* The Close House, Barnack, Stamford. *T:* Bainton 238. *Clubs:*

Carlton, Farmers'
*See also Baron Brassey of Apethorpe.*

**BRATBY, Jean Esme Oregon;** *see* Cooke, Jean E. O.

**BRATBY, John Randall,** ARA 1959; ARCA; FIAL; RBA; Painter and Writer; Member of London Group; Editorial Adviser for Art Quarterly; *b* 19 July 1928; *s* of George Alfred Bratby and Lily Beryl Randall; *m* 1953, Jean Esme Oregon Cooke, ARA (*see* Jean E. Cooke); three *s* one *d*. *Educ:* Tiffin Boys' Sch.; Kingston School of Art; Royal College of Art. Teacher: Carlisle College of Art, 1956; Royal College of Art, 1957-58. Gained prizes and scholarships, 1954-57. Numerous one-man exhibitions at Beaux Arts Gallery from 1954; Zwemmer Gallery from 1959; also in galleries abroad. Exhibited: Royal Academy (yearly) from 1955; has also shown pictures in various international exhibitions and festivals. Guggenheim Award for Great Britain, 1956 and 1958; Paintings for film The Horse's Mouth, 1958. Works in public collections: Tate Gallery; Arts Council of Great Britain; British Council; Contemporary Arts Society. National Galleries: Canada; New Zealand; NSW and Victoria; galleries in many cities and towns of Great Britain; Victoria and Albert Museum; Ashmolean Museum; Museum of Modern Art, New York; also in many other public and private art collections, in Great Britain, the Commonwealth and USA. Has made television appearances and sound broadcasts. *Publications:* fiction: Breakdown, 1960; Breakfast and Elevenses, 1961; Break-Pedal Down, 1962 (also TV play); Break 50 Kill, 1963; non-fiction: studio publication of colour reproductions of own work, 1961; contrib., illustrations, Oxford Illustrated Old Testament, 1968; Stanley Spencer, 1969. *Recreations:* family life, television, snooker, squash, gardening, tennis, swimming, walking, dialectics, 17th Century English furniture. *Address:* 7 Hardy Road, Blackheath, SE3. *T:* 01-858 6288.

**BRATTAIN, Dr Walter H(ouser);** Research Physicist, Bell Telephone Laboratories, Inc., 1929-67; *b* Amoy, China, 10 Feb. 1902; *s* of Ross R. Brattain and Ottilie Brattain (*née* House); *m* 1st, 1935, Keren Gilmore (*d* 1957); one *s*; 2nd, 1958, Emma Jane Miller (*née* Kirsch). *Educ:* Whitman Coll., Walla Walla, Washington; University of Oregon, Eugene, Oregon; University of Minnesota, Minneapolis, Minn. BS 1924, Whitman Coll.; MA 1926, University of Oregon; PhD 1929, University of Minnesota. Asst Physicist, Bureau of Standards, 1928-29; Technical Staff, Bell Telephone Labs, Inc., 1929-. Division of War Research, Columbia Univ., 1942-44. Visiting Lecturer, Harvard Univ., 1952-53; Visiting Prof. of Physics (part-time) Whitman Coll., 1963-. Hon. Dr of Science: Portland Univ., 1952; Union Coll., 1955; Whitman Coll., 1955; University of Minnesota, 1957; Gustavus Adolphus Coll. Stuart Ballantine Medal, Franklin Institute, 1952; John Scott Medal, City of Philadelphia, 1955; Nobel Prize for Physics (with J. Bardeen and W. Shockley), 1956. Fellow: American Academy of Arts and Sciences, 1956; National Academy of Sciences, 1959. Hon. LHD, Hartwick Coll., 1964. *Publications:* many scientific papers on Thermionics and Semiconductors in various physics journals. *Recreation:* golf. *Address:* Whitman College, Walla Walla, Washington, 99362, USA. *T:* JA 9-5100.

**BRAY, Frederick,** CB 1949; MA Oxon; Consultant to the City and Guilds of London Institute; *b* 1895; *y s* of late Herbert James Bray; *m* 1926, Emily Lloyd, *d* of Richard Poole; two *s*. *Educ:* Queen Elizabeth's, Tamworth; Pembroke Coll., Oxford. War Service, 1914-18. Master, Clifton Coll., 1922-25; Asst Director of Education, Leeds, 1925-28; Board of Education: HM Inspector of Schools, 1928-38; Staff Inspector, 1938-40; Divisional Inspector, 1940-45; Ministry of Education; Principal Asst Secretary, 1945-46, Under-Secretary, 1946-56. Technical Adviser to City and Guilds of London Institute; Educational Adviser to the British Assoc. for Commercial and Industrial Education, 1956; Dean of College of Preceptors, 1957; Adviser on Technical Education to the Federal Govt of Rhodesia and Nyasaland and to the Govt of Southern Rhodesia, 1957-63. *Publications:* Light, 1927; General Science, 1928. *Recreation:* golf. *Address:* 8 Pall Mall, 97 Third Street, Salisbury, Rhodesia. *Clubs:* Civil Service, (Hon.) Chelsea Arts; Royal Salisbury Golf.

**BRAY, Jeremy William;** Director, Mullard Ltd, since 1970; *b* 29 June 1930; *s* of Rev. Arthur Henry Bray and Mrs Edith Muriel Bray; *m* 1953, Elizabeth (*née* Trowell); four *d*. *Educ:* Aberystwyth Grammar Sch.; Kingswood Sch.; Jesus Coll., Cambridge. Researched in pure mathematics at Cambridge, 1953-55; Choate Fellow, Harvard Univ., USA, 1955-56; Technical Officer, Wilton Works of ICI. Contested (Lab) Thirsk and Malton, General Election, 1959; MP (Lab) Middlesbrough West, 1962-70. Member, Select Cttee on Nationalised Industries, 1962-64; Chairman: Labour, Science and Technology Group, 1964-66; Economic Affairs Estimates Sub-Cttee, 1964-66; Parliamentary Secretary, Min. of Power, 1966-67; Jt Parly Sec., Min. of Technology, 1967-69; formerly PPS to First Secretary of State. *Publications:* The New Economy, 1965; Decision in Government, 1970. *Recreations:* arts, sailing. *Address:* 11 Luttrell Avenue, Putney, SW15.

**BRAY, Gen. Sir Robert (Napier Hubert Campbell),** GBE 1966 (CBE 1952); KCB 1962 (CB 1957); DSO 1944, and Bar 1945; Deputy Supreme Commander Allied Powers Europe, 1967-70; late Duke of Wellington's Regiment (Colonel of the Regiment, 1965); *b* 1908; *s* of late Brig.-Gen. Robert Napier Bray, CMG, DSO; *m* 1936, Nora, *d* of G. C. G. Gee, Rothley, Leics.; three *s*. *Educ:* Gresham's Sch., Holt; Royal Military Coll. 2nd Lieut, Duke of Wellington's Regt, 1928. Served War of 1939-45 Norway, Middle East and North Western Europe (despatches, DSO and Bar); Lieut-Col 1941; Brig., 1945; Brig. General Staff British Army of the Rhine, 1950-52; Korea, 1954; Director of Land-Air Warfare, and Director of North Atlantic Treaty Organisation Standardisation, War Office, 1954-57; Maj.-Gen., 1954; General Officer Commanding 56 Infantry Div. (TA), 1957-59; Commander, Land Forces, Arabian Peninsula, 1959; GOC, MELF, 1961; Lieut-Gen. 1961; General Officer Commanding-in-Chief, Southern Command, 1961-63; Commander-in-Chief, Allied Forces, Northern Europe, 1963-67; General 1965; ADC General to the Queen, 1965-68. *Recreations:* sailing, shooting. *Clubs:* Army and Navy, Royal Cruising.

**BRAY, Ronald William Thomas;** MP (C) Rossendale since 1970; mechanical engineer; farmer; Underwriting Member of Lloyds; *b* 5 Jan. 1922; *s* of William Ernest Bray, mech. engr and co. dir, Earls Court, and Ada Bray, Killington, Westmorland; *m* 1944, Margaret Florence, *d* of James B. Parker, St Margarets-on-Thames; no *c*. *Educ:* Latymer Upper School. Joined family business, 1938; Man. Dir 1946; pioneered develt of British construction equipment incl. heavy earthmoving equipment, four-wheel-drive tractor shovels; travelled extensively, Europe, N and S Africa, America, Canada, Caribbean and Middle East, developing exports; served on numerous professional and British Standards cttees; resigned 1959. Mem., Woking UDC, 1959-62; Chm./Vice-Chm. of various cttees. Commenced farming activities, 1962, specialising in beef and hill sheep production, large breeder of Fell Ponies. Contested (C) Stockton-on-Tees, 1964. *Recreations:* swimming, riding, walking. *Address:* Greenfield, Buckden, Skipton, Yorks. *T:* Kettlewell 832. *Clubs:* Constitutional, Royal Automobile; Royal Automobile Country (Epsom).

**BRAY, William John;** Director of Research, Post Office, since 1966 (Dep. Director, 1965); *b* 10 Sept. 1911; British; *m* 1936, Margaret Earp; one *d* (and one *d* decd). *Educ:* Imperial Coll., London Univ. Electrical engineering apprenticeship, Portsmouth Naval Dockyard, 1928-32; Royal and Kitchener Scholarships, Imperial Coll., 1932-34; entered PO Engineering Dept as Asst Engineer, 1934; Commonwealth Fund Fellowship (Harkness Foundation) for study in USA, 1956-57; Staff Engineer, Inland Radio Br., PO Engineering Dept, 1958. Participation in work of International Radio Consultative Cttee of International Telecommunication Union and European Postal and Telecommunication Conferences. MSc(Eng), FCGI, DIC, CEng, FIEE. *Publications:* papers in Proc. IEE (IEE Ambrose Fleming Radio Sect. and Electronics Div. Premium Awards). *Recreations:* sailing, travel. *Address:* Post Office Research Station, Dollis Hill, NW2. *T:* 01-452 3376 ext. 489; 17 The Crossways, Wembley Park, Middx. *T:* 01-904 7966.

**BRAYBROOKE,** 9th Baron *cr* 1788; **Henry Seymour Neville;** DL; JP; Hon. MA Camb. 1948; Hereditary Visitor of Magdalene Coll., Cambridge; Patron of three livings; *b* 5 Feb. 1897; *er s* of late Rev. Hon. Grey Neville (2nd *s* of 6th Baron) and late Mary Peele, *e d* of late Canon Francis Slater; *S* cousin, 1943; *m* 1st, 1930, Muriel Evelyn (*d* 1962), *d* of late William C. Manning and *widow* of E. C. Cartwright; one *s*; 2nd, 1963, Angela Mary, *d* of late William H. Hollis and *widow* of John Ree. *Educ:* Shrewsbury Sch. (Scholar); Magdalene Coll., Cambridge. Served European War, 1914-18, in RNA Service and RAF; later held various appointments with Anglo-Iranian and Shell Groups of oil companies. *Heir: s* Hon. Robin Henry Charles Neville [*b* 29 Jan. 1932; *m* 1955, Robin Helen, *d* of late T. A. Brockhoff, Sydney, Australia; three *d*]. *Address:* Mutlow Hall, Wendens Ambo, Saffron Walden, Essex. *T:* Newport (Essex) 200.

**BRAYE,** 7th Baron *cr* 1529; **Thomas Adrian Verney-Cave;** JP; DL; Major, late 13/18th Royal Hussars; *b* 26 July 1902; *er s* of 6th Baron Braye and Ethel Mary (*d* 1955), *d* of Capt. Edward Bouverie Pusey, RN; *S* father, 1952; *m* 1934, Dorothea, *yr d* of late Daniel C. Donoghue, Philadelphia; one *d*. *Educ:* Eton. Was Flying Officer, RAF; re-employed 13/18th Royal Hussars, 1939; Major, 1942; served on personal staff of The Prince of the Netherlands, 1945-46 (Order of Orange Nassau). Director, George Spencer Ltd. JP Leicestershire, 1953, DL, 1954. *Heir: d* Hon. Penelope Mary Verney-Cave, *b* 30 Sept. 1941. *Address:* Stanford Park, Rugby. *T:* Swinford 250. *Club:* Cavalry.

**BRAYLEY, Sir (John) Desmond,** Kt 1970; MC; DL, JP; Chairman, Canning Town Glass Works Group, since 1961; Director, General & Engineering Industries Group; *b* 29 Jan. 1917; *s* of Frederick and Jennie Brayley. *Educ:* privately; grammar sch.; military. FICA 1958. Regular Army, 1934-45 (MC, despatches; Lt-Col). Joined Phoenix Glass Co. Ltd, 1946. Hon. Col Comdt, Royal Regt of Artillery; Mem. Bd of Management, and Chm. Finance and Gen. Purposes Cttee, RA Assoc. Mem., Sports Council; Pres., Boys' Amateur Boxing Club. Patron, Masonic Hosp.; Vice-Patron, Masonic Schs. Companion, Grand Order of Water Rats. Freeman, City of London, 1961; Freeman, Worshipful Co. of Barber-Surgeons. DL Greater London, 1970; JP Middlesex Area of Greater London, 1968. *Recreations:* politics, books and letters, charities, flying (holds private pilot's licence); boxing (pre-war International, ISBA, and Army representative); yachting, shooting, fishing, horse-racing. *Address:* Arlington House, St James's, SW1; Hailey House, Ipsden, Oxon. *Clubs:* Eccentric, Saints and Sinners (past Chm. and Trustee), House of Commons Terrace; Bristol, University (Bristol).

**BRAYNE-BAKER, John,** CMG 1957; Colonial Administrative Service, Nigeria (retired); *b* 13 Aug. 1905; *s* of Francis Brayne-Baker and Dorothea Mary Brayne-Baker (*née* Porcher); *m* 1947, Ruth Hancock; no *c*. *Educ:* Marlborough Coll.; Worcester Coll., Oxford. Nigeria: Asst District Officer, 1928; District Officer, 1938; Senior District Officer, 1948; Resident, 1953. Senior Resident and Deputy Commissioner of the Cameroons, 1954-56; retired 1956. Member, Tiverton RDC, 1959-. *Recreations:* gardening and golf. *Address:* Culmside, Uffculme, Cullompton, Devon. *T:* Craddock 236. *Club:* Tiverton Golf (Tiverton).

**BRAYNE-NICHOLLS, Rear-Adm. Francis Brian Price,** CB 1965; DSC 1942; General Secretary, Officers Pensions Society; *b* 1 Dec. 1914; *s* of late Dr G. E. E. Brayne-Nicholls and *gs* of Sir Francis W. T. Brain; *m* 1939, Wendy (*née* Donnelly); one *d*. *Educ:* RNC, Dartmouth. Sub-Lieut and Lieut, HMS Bee on Yangtse River, 1936-39; specialised in Navigation, 1939; Navigating Officer of: HM Ships Nelson, Rodney, Cardiff, 1939-41, Manxman (during many mining ops, Malta convoys and Madagascar op.), 1941-42; Combined Ops, taking part in Sicily (despatches), Salerno, and Normandy landings. Navigating Officer: HMS Glory, 1944-46; HMS Vanguard, 1948; Comdr 1948; Comdg Officer: HMS Gravelines, 1952-53; HMS St Kitts, 1953-54; Capt 1954; Naval Asst to First Sea Lord, 1954-55; Comdg Officer, HMS Apollo, 1955-57; NATO Standing Group, Washington, 1957-59; Captain of Navigation Direction Sch., HMS Dryad, 1959-61; Admiralty, 1961-63; Rear-Adm. 1963; Chief of Staff to Commander, Far East Fleet, 1963-65. *Recreation:* golf. *Address:* 3 Tedworth Square, SW3. *T:* 01-352 1681. *Club:* Naval and Military.

**BRAZENDALE, George William,** CMG 1958; FCA; *b* 1909; *s* of late Percy Ridout Brazendale, and late Edith Mary Brazendale (*née* Maystre); *m* 1938, Madeleine, *o d* of Thomas and Betty Wroe; two *d*. *Educ:* Arnold Sch., Blackpool, Lancs. Chief Accountant, Colclough China Ltd, Stoke-on-Trent, 1936-41; Asst Area Officer, MAP, 1941-42; Chief Progress Officer, ROF Swynnerton, 1942-43; Secretary, Midland Regional Board, 1943-45; Regional Controller Board of Trade; Northern Region, 1945-46; North-Western Region, 1946-50; Asst Secretary, Board of Trade, 1946; Trade Commissioner for the UK in charge Calcutta, 1950-60. Principal British Trade Commissioner: in the Federation of Rhodesia and Nyasaland, 1961-63; also Economic Adviser to British High Commissioner in Rhodesia, 1964-65; Economic Adviser to

Special British Representative in East and Central Africa, 1966-67; retired from HM Diplomatic Service, 1967. ACA 1931. *Recreations:* golf, fishing, gardening. *Address:* Slydles Close, Forest Lane, Hightown, Ringwood, Hants. *Clubs:* Oriental; Barton-on-Sea Golf, Brokenhurst Manor Golf.

**BRAZIER, Rt. Rev. Percy James;** *b* 3 Aug. 1903; *m* 1933, Joan Cooper, MB, BS; one *s* four *d*. *Educ:* Weymouth Coll., Dorset; Emmanuel Coll., Cambridge. 2nd class Hist. Trip., Part I, 1924, 2nd class, Part II, and BA, 1925; MA 1939. Ridley Hall, Cambridge, 1925-27, Deacon, 1927; Priest, 1928; Curate of St John the Evangelist, Blackheath, 1927-29; CMS (Ruanda Mission), 1930; Kabale, 1930-34; Kigeme, Diocese of Uganda, 1934-50; Archdeacon of Ruanda-Urundi, 1946-51; Asst Bishop of Uganda for Ruanda-Urundi, 1951-60; Bishop of Rwanda and Burundi, 1960-64 (name of diocese changed when Ruanda-Urundi was granted independence, 1962); retired 1964. Rector of Padworth and Vicar of Mortimer West End, Diocese of Oxford, 1964. Chevalier de l'Ordre Royal du Lion (Belgium), 1955. *Recreations:* photography, gardening and golf. *Address:* Lark Rise, Peasemore, Newbury, Berks.

**BRAZIER-CREAGH, Maj.-Gen. Sir (Kilner) Rupert,** KBE 1962 (CBE 1947); CB 1954; DSO 1944; Secretary of the Horse Race Betting Levy Board, 1961-65; Director of Staff Duties, War Office, 1959-61, retired; *b* 12 Dec. 1909; 2nd *s* of late Lt-Col K. C. Brazier-Creagh; *m* 1st, 1938, Elizabeth Mary (*d* 1967), *d* of late E. M. Magor; one *s* two *d*; 2nd, 1968, Mrs Marie Nelson. *Educ:* Rugby; RMA, Woolwich. 2nd Lieut, 1929; served War of 1939-45 (despatches, DSO); Bde Major, 9th Armoured Div., 1941; GSO1 12th Corps, 1943; Commanded 25th Field Regt, 1944; BGS 21st Army Group and BAOR, 1945-48 (CBE); idc 1949; DDRA, War Office, 1950; CRA 11th Armoured Div., 1951-52; Chief of Staff Malaya Command, 1952-55 (despatches, CB); Asst Comdt, Staff Coll., 1955-57; Chief of Staff, Eastern Command, 1957-59. Officer, American Legion of Merit, 1945. *Recreation:* racing. *Address:* Tarbrook, Croom, Co. Limerick, Eire. *T:* Croom 32263; Travis Corners Road, Garrison, New York, USA.

**BREADALBANE and HOLLAND,** 10th Earl of, *cr* 1677; **John Romer Boreland Campbell;** Viscount of Tay and Paintland; Lord Glenorchy, Benederaloch, Ormelie and Weik, 1677; Bt of Glenorchy; Bt of Nova Scotia, 1625; *b* 28 April 1919; *o s* of 9th Earl of Breadalbane and Holland, MC, and Armorer Romer, *d* of Romer Williams, DL, JP, and *widow* of Capt. Eric Nicholson, 12th Royal Lancers; *S* father, 1959; *m* 1949, Coralie, *o d* of Charles Archer. *Educ:* Eton; RMC, Sandhurst. Entered Black Watch (Royal Highlanders), 1939; served France, 1939 (despatches); invalided, 1942. *Heir:* none. *Address:* c/o National Bank Ltd, 15 Whitehall, SW1.

**BREAM, Julian,** OBE 1964; guitarist and lutenist; *b* 15 July 1933; *e s* of Henry G. Bream. *Educ:* Royal College of Music (Junior Exhibition Award, 1945 and Scholarship, 1948). Began professional career at Cheltenham, 1946; London début, Wigmore Hall, 1950; subsequently has appeared in leading world festivals, and regularly tours Europe, USA, Australia and Far East. A leader in revival of interest in Elizabethan Lute music, on which he has done much research; has encouraged contemporary English compositions for the guitar. *Recreations:* playing the guitar; cricket. *Address:* c/o Basil Douglas Ltd, 8 St George's Terrace, NW1.

**BREBNER, Sir Alexander,** Kt 1938; CIE 1920; BSc Edinburgh; Indian Service of Engineers, retired; Member of Council and Executive of National Trust for Scotland, retired 1961; Board of Scottish Special Housing Association (appointed by Secretary of State for Scotland), 1954-61; Acting Secretary, Royal Scottish Academy, Edinburgh, 1954-55, retired; *b* 19 Aug. 1883; *s* of R. C. Brebner, Edinburgh; *m* 1911, Margaret Patricia, *d* of W. Cunningham, Edinburgh; one *s* two *d*. *Educ:* George Watson's Coll., Edinburgh; Edinburgh Univ. Asst Engineer, PWD, 1906; Executive Engineer, 1912; Under-Secretary, Bihar and Orissa, 1919; Under-Secretary to Govt of India, 1919-23; Superintending Engineer, 1923. Consulting Engineer to Govt of India, 1927 and 1929; Chief Engineer, Govt of India, 1931-38, retired, 1938; one-time Member Council of State; employed in Chief Divisional Food Office for Scotland, Ministry of Food, 1940-42; Ministry of Works (Licensing Officer, Scotland), 1942-54. *Recreation:* golf. *Address:* 4 Ainslie Place, Edinburgh. *T:* 031-225 1991. *Clubs:* New (Edinburgh); Hon. Co. Edinburgh Golfers; Royal and Ancient (St Andrews).

**BRECHIN, Bishop of,** since 1959; **Rt. Rev. John Chappell Sprott,** MA; DD St Andrews 1965; *b* 16 Oct. 1903; *s* of Thomas Sprott, Master Mariner, and Catherine Chappell; *m* 1932, Winifred Helen Cameron, *d* of late Sir David W. Bone, CBE, LLD; two *s* one *d*. *Educ:* Castle Hill Sch., Ealing; Glasgow Univ.; Edinburgh Theological Coll. Deacon, 1927; Priest, 1928; Chaplain and Succentor, St Mary's Cathedral, Edinburgh, 1927-29; Lecturer in Music, Edinburgh Theological College, 1928-29; Curate, All Saints, Glasgow, 1929-33; St George the Martyr, Holborn, 1933-37; Rector, West Hackney, 1937-40; Provost of St Paul's Cathedral, Dundee, 1940-59. *Recreation:* Music. *Address:* Forbes Court, Farington Terrace, Dundee, Angus.

**BRECHIN, Dean of;** *see* Gibson, Very Rev. Matthew Sayer.

**BRECHIN, Sir Herbert Archbold,** Kt 1968; CBE 1961 (OBE 1952); DL; Lord Provost of the City of Edinburgh, 1966-69; Lord Lieutenant, County of the City of Edinburgh, 1966-69; Chartered Quantity Surveyor; *b* 3 Nov. 1903; *s* of late David Brechin and Katharine Mary (*née* O'Brien); *m* 1934, Jane Richmond Cameron; two *s*. *Educ:* Edinburgh; Heriot-Watt Coll., Edinburgh. Senior Partner, H. A. Brechin & Co., FRICS, Chartered Quantity Surveyors, Edinburgh and Kelso. Chm. 9th British Commonwealth Games (1970). Dist. Comr, Scout Assoc.; Holder of Scout Wood Badge, 1944; Silver Wolf, 1969; Scout Medal of Merit; and awarded Scout Silver Acorn by Chief Scout (1962); retired from Movement 1962 after 45 years' service. Member Edinburgh Town Council, 1949-69; City Treasurer, 1962-65. Chm. Bd of Governors, Heriot-Watt Coll., 1966. FRSE 1969; FRICS; FH-WC (*hc*) 1962. Hon. DLitt, Heriot-Watt, 1967. DL Edinburgh, 1970. Grand Officer, Order of Al-Kawkab Al-Urduni, Jordan, 1966; Grand Ufficiale dell' Ordine al Merito della Repubblica Italiana, 1969. *Address:* The Garth, Colinton, Edinburgh EH13 0DN. *T:* 031-441 2226; 13 Great King Street, Edinburgh EH3 6QP. *T:* 031-556 5441.

**BRECKNOCK, Earl of; David George Edward Henry Pratt;** late Lieutenant, Scots Guards; *b* 13 Aug. 1930; *o s* of 5th Marquess Camden, *qv*, and Marjorie, Countess of Brecknock, *qv*; *m* 1961, Virginia Ann, *o d* of late F. H. H. Finlaison, Arklow Cottage, Windsor, Berks; two *s* one *d*. *Educ:* Eton. Dir, Clive Discount

Co. Ltd, 1958-69. *Heir: s* Viscount Bayham, *qv*. *Address:* Lodsworth House, Lodsworth, near Petworth, Sussex. *T:* Lodsworth 224.

**BRECKNOCK, Marjorie Countess of,** DBE 1967; Superintendent-in-Chief, St John Ambulance Brigade, 1960-70, retired; *b* 28 Mar. 1900; *o c* of late Col A. E. Jenkins and of late Mrs Anna Jenkins, Wherwell Priory, Andover, Hants; *m* 1920, Earl of Brecknock (now Marquess Camden; from whom she obtained a divorce, 1941); one *s* one *d*. *Educ:* at home and Heathfield, Ascot. A Lady-in-waiting to Princess Marina, Duchess of Kent, 1937-39. War of 1939-45: Company Asst, ATS, 1940; Junior Commander, 1941; Senior Commander, 1942 (Senior ATS Officer SHAEF, 1944-45); despatches 1945; Bronze Star (USA), 1945. Commanded 310 (Southern Command) Bn WRAC (TA), 1948-54. Joined St John Ambulance Brigade HQ, 1947; appointed Controller Overseas Dept, 1950. DStJ 1958. Mem. Order of Mercy. *Publication:* Edwina Mountbatten–her life in pictures, 1961. *Recreations:* gardening, shooting, travelling, fishing. *Address:* 23 South Audley St, W1. *T:* 01-499 1305; Wherwell Priory, Andover, Hampshire. *T:* Chilbolton 388.

**BRECON,** 1st Baron, *cr* 1957; **David Vivian Penrose Lewis,** PC 1960; JP; Director: Powell Duffryn Ltd; A. B. Electronic Components Ltd (Chairman); Andrews Weatherfoil Ltd (Chairman); Stothert & Pitt Ltd (Chairman); Aberthaw & Bristol Channel Portland Cement Co.; United Capitals Investment Trust; formerly a Proprietor of Quarries; *b* 14 Aug. 1905; *s* of late Alfred William and Elizabeth Mary Lewis, Craiglas, Talybont-on-Usk; *m* 1933, Mabel Helen (CBE 1964; JP), 2nd *d* of late John McColville and late Mrs McColville, Abergavenny; two *d*. *Educ:* Monmouth Sch. Governor: Christ Coll., Brecon; Monmouth Schools. Held various political offices in Wales including: Chairman, Conservative Party in Wales and Monmouthshire, 1956-58; Mem., Brecon CC, 1946-58; Mem. Brecon RDC, 1938-49; Chm., Breconshire County Planning Cttee (4 yrs); ex-Chm., Jt Industrial Council for Quarrying Industry; President, Brecknock Agricultural Soc., 1957. Minister of State for Welsh Affairs, 1957-64. *Recreations:* trout fishing; Pres., Newport Athletic Club; formerly Rugby football (G. Crawshay's Welsh XV, etc.) and cricket (Capt. of Crickhowell CC 16 yrs). *Address:* (private) Greenhill, Cross Oak, Brecon. *T:* Talybont-on-Usk 247. *Clubs:* Carlton, Royal Automobile; MCC; Cardiff and County (Cardiff).

*See also A. L. Price.*

**BRECON, Dean of;** *see* Jacob, Very Rev. W. U.

**BREDIN, George Richard Frederick,** CBE 1947; MA; Sudan Political Service (retired); Supernumerary Fellow of Pembroke College, Oxford; *b* 8 June 1899; *s* of late Dr Richard Bredin, Valparaiso, Chile; *m* 1932, Dorothy Wall, *d* of late T. R. Ellison, West Kirby, Cheshire; one *s* one *d*. *Educ:* Clifton College; Oriel College, Oxford. MA (Oxon) 1925; served European War, 1914-18, Lieut RE (64th Field Company) (despatches). Oriel College, Oxford, 1919-21; Hons Degree in Lit. Hum. (Distinction), 1921. Asst District Comr, Sudan Political Service, 1921; District Comr, 1930; Dep. Governor, 1935; Dep. Civil Secretary, 1939; Governor Blue Nile Province, Sudan, 1941-48; member, Governor-General's Council, 1945-48; Chairman, Governing Body of Gordon Memorial Univ. Coll., Khartoum, 1945-48; retired, 1948. Asst Registrar, University of Liverpool, 1948-49; Fell. and Bursar, Pembroke College, Oxford, 1950-66; a Church Comr, 1951-; Chm., Oxford Diocesan Board of Finance, 1956-58; Chm., Oxford Diocesan Trusts Corporation; a Curator of the Oxford Univ. Chest, 1957-69. Chairman of Governors of Abingdon School; Vice-Chairman, Dorset House School of Occupational Therapy, Oxford; Treas., Gordon Boys School, Woking; Oxford City Councillor, 1965-67. Order of the Nile (3rd Cl.), 1937. *Recreations:* golf, bridge. *Address:* Rough Lea, Boar's Hill, Oxford. *T:* Oxford 35375.

**BREDIN, Maj.-Gen. Humphrey Edgar Nicholson,** CB 1969; DSO 1944 (and bars, 1945 and 1957); MC 1938 (and bar, 1939); Director, Volunteers, Territorials and Cadets, since 1968; *b* 28 March 1916; *s* of Lieut-Colonel A. Bredin, late Indian Army, and Ethel Bredin (*née* Homan); *m* 1st, 1947, Jacqueline Geare (marriage dissolved, 1961); one *d*; 2nd, 1965, Anne Hardie; two *d*. *Educ:* King's School, Canterbury; RMC, Sandhurst. Commissioned Royal Ulster Rifles, 1936; Commanded: 6th Royal Inniskilling Fusiliers, 1944; 2nd London Irish Rifles, 1945; Eastern Arab Corps, Sudan Defence Force, 1949-53; 2nd Parachute Regt, 1956-57; 99th Gurkha Infty Bde Group, 1959-62. Campaigns: Dunkirk, 1940; N Africa, 1943; Italy, 1943-45; Palestine, 1937-39 and 1946-47; Suez, 1956; Cyprus, 1956-57; Singapore-Malaya Internal Security, 1959-62; Chief of British Commander-in-Chief's Mission to Soviet Forces in Germany, 1963-65; Commanded 42nd Div. (TA), 1965-68. Brig. 1964; Maj.-Gen. 1965. Col. Comdt, The King's Division, 1968-. *Recreations:* shooting, travelling, entertaining. *Address:* Bovills Hall, Ardleigh, Essex. *T:* Ardleigh 217. *Clubs:* Army and Navy, Airborne, United Hunts.

**BREDIN, James John;** Managing Director, Border Television Ltd, since 1964; *b* 18 Feb. 1924; *s* of John Francis and late Margaret Bredin; *m* 1958, Virginia Meddowes, *d* of John Meddowes and Mrs K. Thomas; one *s* two *d*. *Educ:* Finchley Catholic Grammar Sch.; London University. Scriptwriter, This Modern Age Film Unit, 1946-50; Producer, current affairs programmes, BBC TV, 1950-55; Sen. Producer, Independent Television News, 1955-59; Smith-Mundt Fellowship, USA, 1957; Producer of Documentaries, Associated Television, 1959-64. Chm., Guild of Television Producers and Directors, 1961-64. Director: Independent Television News Ltd; James Archibald & Associates. Mem., Exec. Cttee, Northern Arts Assoc. *Address:* The Gatehouse, Naworth Castle, Brampton, Cumberland. *T:* Brampton 2460. *Clubs:* Reform; County (Carlisle).

**BREECH, Ernest Robert;** Chairman Trans World Airlines Inc., 1961-69; Director: Ford Motor Co.; Rexall Drug & Chemical Co.; The Lehman Corporation; One William Street Fund Inc.; *b* Lebanon, Missouri, 24 Feb. 1897; *s* of Joseph F. E. Breech; *m* 1917, Thelma Rowden; two *s*. *Educ:* Drury Coll., Springfield, Mo; Walton Sch. of Commerce; Univ. of Ill. Accountant, Fairbanks, Morse & Co., 1917-20; auditor, Adams & Westlake, 1920-22; Comptroller, Yellow Cab Mfg Co., 1923-29; Dir Yellow Truck & Coach Mfg Co., Chicago, 1927-33; Dir Pan-American Airways, 1933-35; Gen. Asst Treas., Gen. Motors Corp., NYC, 1929-33, Vice-Pres. i/c household appliance div. and aviation subsids, also Mem. administration cttee, 1939-42; Dir N Amer. Aviation Inc., 1933-1946 (Chm., 1933-42); Pres., and Dir Bendix Aviation Corp., 1942-46; Exec. Vice-Pres. and Dir Ford Motor Co., 1946-55; Chairman, 1955-60; Chm. Finance Cttee, 1960-61. *Address:* c/o Trans World

Airlines Inc., 10 Richards Road, Kansas City, Mo, USA.

**BREENE, Very Rev. Richard Simmons,** MA, LLD; Rector, St Peter's, Belfast, from 1926, Dean of Connor, 1956-63, retd from active ministry, 1963; *b* Co. Clare, 25 June 1886; 2nd *s* of late T. J. Breene, formerly HMCS, Belfast; *m* 1st, 1913, Louise (*d* 1957), *e d* of late Robert Denison, Belfast; one *s* one *d*; 2nd, 1958, Mrs Vera Elizabeth Capper, *d* of late David Clugston Hutchinson, Belfast. *Educ:* Privately; Royal Univ.; and Queen's Univ. of Belfast. BA Hons 1910; MA Hon. School of Modern History, 1914; LLB 1918; LLD 1919; Universities Theological Examination, 1911; Deacon, 1911; Priest, 1912; Curate of Ballynure, Co. Antrim, till 1913; Glenavy, 1913-15; Chaplain to the Forces, 1915-19 (despatches); served in Mediterranean, Egypt, etc (1914-15 Star, King's and Victory medals); Hon. Chaplain to the Forces, 1920; Rector, Killinchy Union, 1920-26; Editor, The Irish Churchman, 1920-34; Member of General Synod, 1924-63; Rural Dean, North Belfast, 1931-47; Domestic Chaplain to the Bishop of Down, 1935; Examining Chaplain to the Bishop of Down, 1938; Examining Chaplain and Domestic Chaplain to the Bishop of Connor, 1945; Chancellor of Connor Cathedral, 1941-56, and Diocesan Registrar, 1941-63. Select Preacher (Trinity College, Dublin), 1941. Member of Faculty of Theology, QUB, 1944. Pres., Belfast Nat. History and Philosophical Soc., 1969. *Publications:* numerous short stories, literary sketches, theological articles, reviews, and essays. *Recreations:* antiquities, archæology, literature. *Address:* 2 Mount Pleasant, Belfast 9. *T:* Belfast 660494.

**BRENAN, (Edward Fitz-) Gerald,** MC 1918; Author; *b* 7 April 1894; English; *m* 1931, Elisabeth Gamel Woolsey; one *d*. *Educ:* self-educated. Served War: Croix de Guerre, 1918. *Publications:* The Spanish Labyrinth, 1943; The Face of Spain, 1950; The Literature of the Spanish People, 1953; South from Granada, 1957; A Holiday by the Sea, 1961; A Life of One's Own, 1962; The Lighthouse Always Says Yes, 1966; and other books. *Recreations:* walking and talking. *Address:* c/o Hamish Hamilton Ltd, 90 Gt Russell Street, WC1.

**BRENAN, Gerald;** *see* Brenan, Edward Fitz-Gerald.

**BRENAN, John Patrick Micklethwait,** MA, BSc Oxon; FLS; Deputy Director and Keeper of the Herbarium and Library, Royal Botanic Gardens, Kew, since 1965; *b* 19 June 1917; *s* of Alexander Richard Micklethwait Brenan, MD, and Jill Fraser Brenan (*née* Parker); *m* 1950, Jean Helen Edwardes; one *s* two *d*. *Educ:* Tonbridge; Brasenose Coll., Oxford. At Imperial Forestry Inst., Oxford, 1940-48; Mem. Cambridge Botanical Expedn to Nigeria and Cameroons, 1948; apptd Sen. Scientific Officer in the Herbarium, Royal Botanic Gardens, Kew, 1948; Princ. Sci. Off., 1954; i/c of Tropical African Section, 1959-65. Botanical Sec., Linnean Soc. of London, 1965. *Publications:* Check List of the Forest Trees and Shrubs of Tanganyika Territory, 1949 (with Dr P. J. Greenway); contrib. various accounts to Flora of Tropical East Africa, etc.; numerous papers on flowering plants of Europe and Africa in scientific jls. *Recreations:* reading, fishing, natural history, walking. *Address:* Herbarium House, 55 The Green, Kew, Richmond, Surrey. *T:* 01-948 1530. *Club:* Athenæum.

**BRENAN, Terence Vincent,** CBE 1948 (OBE 1921); *b* 29 Nov. 1887; *s* of late Edward Vincent Brenan and Rose Peyton; *m* 1925, Marjorie Winifrede, *d* of late Thomas Draper Harrison; no *c*. *Educ:* King William's College, Isle of Man; Switzerland and Germany. Business; HM Land Forces, 1915-18, as an Officer; Vice-Consul at Birjand, Persia, 1917; Acting Consul at Sistan, Persia, 1920; Vice-Consul, Levant Consular Service, 1921; Vice-Consul, Resht, 1921-23, Teheran, 1924-32; Consul at Teheran, 1932-35; in FO, 1936-38; attached to Representative of Iran at Coronation of King George VI, May 1937; Consul to Sofia, 1938; in charge of Consulate at Mersin, Turkey, May-Oct. 1941; Consul, Shiraz, Nov. 1941-Oct. 1943 when transferred to Damascus as Consul and Political Officer to Spears Military Mission; Consul-General at Tunis, 1944-46; at Rabat, 1946-47; retired, 1947; Director of Middle East Centre for Arab Studies, Beirut, 1948-53. *Address:* Champlins, Ewhurst, Robertsbridge, Sussex.

**BRENCHLEY, Thomas Frank,** CMG 1964; MA (Oxon); Ambassador to Norway, since 1968; *b* 9 April 1918; *m* 1946, Edith Helen Helfand; three *d*. Served with Royal Corps of Signals, 1939-46; Major on Staff of Military Attaché, Ankara, 1943-45; Director, Telecommunications Liaison Directorate, Syria and Lebanon, 1945-46. Civil Servant, 1947; transferred to Foreign Office, 1949; First Secretary: Singapore, 1950-53; Cairo, 1953-56; Counsellor, Khartoum, 1960-63; Chargé d'Affaires, Jedda, 1963; Head of Arabian Department, Foreign Office, 1963-67; Assistant Under-Secretary of State, Foreign Office, 1967-68. *Recreations:* skiing, sailing; collecting (and sometimes reading) books. *Address:* British Embassy, Oslo, Norway. *Club:* Travellers'.

**BRENDEL, Alfred;** concert pianist since 1948; *b* 5 Jan. 1931; *s* of Albert Brendel and Ida Brendel (*née* Wieltschnig); *m* 1960, Iris Heymann-Gonzala; one *d*. Studied piano with: S. Deželić, 1937-43; L. V. Kaan, 1943-47; also under Edwin Fischer, P. Baumgartner and E. Steuermann; composition with Artur Michl. Vienna State Diploma, 1947; Premio Bolzano Concorso Busoni, 1949. Concerts: most European countries, North and Latin America, Australia and New Zealand, also N and S Africa. Many appearances Vienna and Salzburg Festivals, 1960-. Other Festivals: Athens, Granada, Bregenz, Würzburg, Aldeburgh, York, Cheltenham, Edinburgh (1970). Many long playing records (Haydn to Schoenberg) incl. first complete recording of Beethoven's piano works (Grand Prix du Disque, 1965). Cycle of Beethoven Sonatas: London, 1962; Copenhagen, 1964; Vienna, 1965; Puerto Rico, 1968; BBC, also Rome, 1970. *Publications:* essays on music, in: Phono, Fono Forum, Osterreichische Musikzeitschrift, etc. *Recreations:* literature, art galleries, zoos, unconscious humour, "kitsch". *Address:* Ungargasse 11, 1030 Vienna, Austria. *T:* 72 13 58.

**BRENNAN, Charles John,** OBE 1949; MA (*hc*), QUB; MusB, FRCO, LRAM; Organist and Director of Choir, Belfast Cathedral, 1904-64; City Organist; Examiner in Music to Ministry of Education, and other examining authorities; *b* Gosport, 25 Oct. 1876; *m* 1903; three *s*. *Educ:* privately. Organist and Choirmaster, Clifton, Beds, 1892; Fellowship of Royal College of Organists, 1897; Organist and Choirmaster, Parish Church, Strabane, Co. Tyrone, 1897; Elmwood Church, Belfast, 1901. Conductor of the Ulster Male Choir, the Queen's Island Operatic Society and the Belfast City Amateur Operatic Society; Conductor of the Belfast Professional Orchestra; PPGO of Masonic Province of

Down; President, Ulster Society Organists and Choirmasters; Past President, Society of Professional Musicians of Ulster; ex-Captain Royal Irish Fusiliers. *Publications:* Four Traditional Irish Songs; Words in Singing, a Handbook on Pronunciation for Singers. *Address:* Belgravia Hotel, Belfast, BT9 7AP.

**BRENNAN, Joseph;** *b* 1887; *e s* of late Joseph Brennan, Kilbrogan House, Bandon, Co. Cork; *m* 1918, Evelyn, *d* of late James Simcox, Cork; one *s* two *d*. *Educ:* Clongowes Wood Coll., Co. Kildare; Univ. College, Dublin; Christ's College, Cambridge. Hon. LLD National University of Ireland; Board of Customs and Excise, London, 1911; Chief Secretary's Office, Dublin Castle, 1912; Comptroller and Auditor-General of the Provisional Government, Irish Free State, 1922; Secretary of the Department of Finance, 1923-27; Chairman of the Irish Currency Commission, 1927-43; Chairman, Commission of Inquiry into Civil Service, 1932-34; Chairman, Investments Advisory Committee, 1933; Chairman, Commission of Inquiry into Banking, Currency and Credit, 1934-38; President, Statistical and Social Inquiry Society of Ireland, 1934-38; President, Institute of Bankers in Ireland, 1946; Governor of Central Bank of Ireland, 1943-53. *Recreations:* golf, travel. *Address:* Clancool, Shrewsbury Road, Dublin. *T:* 691540.

**BRENNAN, Lieut-General Michael;** retired as Chief Superintendent of Divisions, Office of Public Works, Dublin. Chief of Staff, Irish Army, 1931-40. *Address:* South Hill, Killiney, Co. Dublin.

**BRENNAN, Maj.-Gen. William Brian Francis,** CB 1966; RAMC; retired; *b* 23 May 1907; *s* of Captain C. J. Brennan, OBE, MA, Belfast; *m* 1943, Margaret Patricia, *d* of late A. B. Miners, MC, Essex; two *d*. *Educ:* Campbell College; Queen's University, Belfast. MB, BCh, BAO, Belfast, 1930. Lieut RAMC, 1930. Served NW Frontier, India, 1932-37 (Mohmand, Loë Agra and Waziristan campaigns). Served War of 1939-45, Middle East and Europe. Deputy DMS: Scottish Command, 1960; 17 Gurkha Division, and Overseas Commonwealth Land Forces, 1962-63; Southern Command, 1963-67. QHP 1962-67. Lieut-Col. 1942; Col. 1952; Brig. 1960; Maj.-Gen. 1963. Officer, Legion of Merit (US), 1946. *Address:* Clifton Cottage, Broughton, Hants. *T:* Broughton 294.

**BRENNAN, William Joseph, Jr;** Legion of Merit, 1945; Associate Justice, Supreme Court of the US since 1956; *b* 25 April 1906; *s* of William J. Brennan and Agnes McDermott; *m* 1928, Marjorie Leonard; two *s* one *d*. *Educ:* University of Pennsylvania; Harvard. BS Univ. of Pennsylvania, 1928; LLB Harvard, 1931. Admitted to New Jersey Bar, 1931; practised in Newark, New Jersey, 1931-49, member Pitney, Hardin, Ward & Brennan; Superior Court Judge, 1949-50; Appellate Division judge, 1950-52; Supreme Court of New Jersey justice, 1952-56; served War of 1939-45 as Colonel, General Staff Corps, United States Army. Hon. LLD; Univ. of Pennsylvania, 1957; Wesleyan, 1957; St John's, 1957; Rutgers, 1958; Notre Dame, 1968; Harvard, 1968. Hon. DCL, New York Univ., 1957; Colgate, 1957. Hon. SJD Suffolk Univ., 1956. *Address:* 3037 Dumbarton Avenue, Washington 7, DC, USA. *Club:* University (Washington, DC).

**BRENNER, Sydney,** FRS 1965; DPhil Oxon; Member of Scientific Staff of Medical Research Council at the Medical Research Council Laboratory of Molecular Biology, Cambridge, since 1957; Fellow of King's College, Cambridge, since 1959; *b* Germiston, South Africa, 13 Jan. 1927; *s* of Morris Brenner and Lena (*née* Blacher); *m* 1952, May Woolf Balkind; one *s* two *d* (and one step *s*). *Educ:* Germiston High School; University of the Witwatersrand, S Africa; Oxford University. MSc 1947, MB, BCh 1951, Univ. of the Witwatersrand; DPhil Oxon., 1954. Warren Triennial Prize, 1968. Foreign Hon. Member, American Academy of Arts and Sciences, 1965. Hon. DSc, Dublin, 1967. William Bate Hardy Prize, Cambridge Philosophical Soc., 1969. *Publications:* papers in scientific journals. *Recreation:* conversation. *Address:* 7 Long Road, Cambridge. *T:* 47258.

**BRENTFORD,** 3rd Viscount, *cr* 1929; Bt, *cr* 1919 and 1955; **Lancelot William Joynson-Hicks;** solicitor; formerly Senior Partner of Joynson-Hicks & Co.; elected Member, Church Assembly, since 1934; *b* 10 April 1902; 2nd *s* of 1st Viscount Brentford, PC, DL, and Grace Lynn (*d* 1952), *o c* of Richard Hampson Joynson, JP, Bowdon, Cheshire; *S* brother, 1958; *m* 1931, Phyllis, *o d* of late Major Herbert Allfrey, Newnton House, Tetbury, Gloucestershire; one *s*. *Educ:* Winchester College; Trinity College, Oxford (MA). Admitted a Solicitor, 1926. Served War of 1939-45 as acting Lt-Comdr, RNVR. MP (C) Chichester Division of West Sussex, 1942-58; Parliamentary Secretary, Ministry of Fuel and Power, Nov. 1951-Dec. 1955. Chairman, Automobile Association, 1956-. *Heir:* *s* Hon. Crispin William Joynson-Hicks [*b* 7 April 1933; *m* 1964, Gillian Evelyn, *er d* of G. E. Schluter, OBE, Valehyrst, Sevenoaks; two *d*. *Educ:* Eton; New College, Oxford]. *Address:* Newick Park, Sussex; 5 Astell House, Astell Street, SW3.

**BRENTWOOD, Bishop of, (RC),** since 1969; **Rt. Rev. Patrick Joseph Casey;** *b* 20 Nov. 1913; *s* of Patrick Casey and Bridget Casey (*née* Norris). *Educ:* St Joseph's Parochial Sch., Kingsland; St Edmund's Coll., Ware. Ordained priest, 1939; Asst, St James's, Spanish Place, 1939-61; Parish Priest of Hendon, 1961-63; Vicar Gen. of Westminster, 1963; Domestic Prelate, and Canon of Westminster Cathedral, 1964; Provost of Westminster Cathedral Chapter, 1967; Auxiliary Bishop of Westminster and Titular Bishop of Sufar, 1966-69. *Address:* Bishop's House, 38 The Drive, South Woodford, E18. *T:* 01-989 1347.

**BRESSON, Robert;** film producer since 1934; *b* 25 Sept. 1907; *s* of Léon Bresson and Marie-Elisabeth Clausels; *m* 1926, Leidia Van der Zee. *Educ:* Lycée Lakanal, Sceaux. Started as painter; then producer of short films, Affaires Publiques. Full-length films produced include: Les Anges du Péché, 1943; Les Dames du Bois de Boulogne, 1948; Journal d'un Curé de Campagne, 1951 (Internat. Grand Prix, Venice); Un Condamné à Mort s'est Echappé, 1956; Pickpocket, 1960; Le Procès de Jeanne d'Arc, 1962 (Jury's special prize, Cannes); Au Hasard Balthazar, 1966; Mouchette, 1967; Une Femme Douce, 1970. *Address:* 49 quai de Bourbon, Paris 4e, France.

**BRETHERTON, Russell Frederick,** CB 1951; Under-Secretary, the Treasury, 1961-68; *b* 3 Feb. 1906; *s* of F. H. Bretherton, Solicitor, Gloucester; *m* 1930, Jocelyn Nina Mathews; three *s* one *d*. *Educ:* Clifton College; Wadham College, Oxford. Fellow of Wadham College, 1928-45, Lecturer and Tutor in Economics and Modern History; University Research Lecturer, 1936-39. Temporary Civil Servant, Ministry of Supply and Board of Trade, 1939-45; Under-Secretary, Raw Materials Dept, Board of Trade, 1946-48; Cabinet Office (Economic Section), 1949-51; Under-

Secretary: Min. of Materials, 1951-54; Board of Trade, 1954-61; Treasury, 1961-68. *Publications:* (with R. L. Lennard and others) Englishmen at Rest and Play (17th Century Studies), 1932; (with Burchardt and Rutherford) Public Investment and the Trade Cycle, 1941; articles in Social Survey of Oxford, Economic Journal, Econometrica, and in various entomological journals, etc. *Recreations:* walking, mountaineering, entomology. *Address:* Folly Hill, Birtley Green, Bramley, Surrey. *T:* Bramley 3377. *Club:* Oxford and Cambridge University.

**BRETSCHER, Egon,** CBE 1966; PhD; retired as Head of Nuclear Physics Division, AERE (1948-66), now Consultant; *b* 23 May 1901; 2nd *s* of Julius Bretscher and Anna Martin; *m* 1931, Hanna Greminger; three *s* two *d.* *Educ:* Gymnasium Zürich; Federal Inst. of Technology (ETH). Dipl. in Chem. Engineering, 1925; PhD (Edinburgh Univ.), 1927. Asst and Privat Dozent für Physik, Eidgenössisch Technische Hochschule, 1929-36; Fellow, Rockefeller Foundn, 1934-35; Clerk Maxwell School, Cavendish Lab., Cambridge, 1936-39; Lectr in Nuclear Physics, Cambridge Univ., 1939-44; Mem., Maud Cttee; Mem., Brit. Mission to Los Alamos Lab., New Mexico, 1944-46; Head of Chemistry Div., AERE, 1947-48. *Publications:* papers in various scientific jls. *Recreations:* maltreating piano, climbing mountains. *Address:* Salix, Conduit Head Road, Cambridge. *T:* Cambridge 59529.

**BRETT,** family name of **Viscount Esher.**

**BRETT, George P., jun.;** retired from The Macmillan Company, 60 Fifth Avenue, New York 11, NY, 1961; *b* Darien, Conn., 9 Dec. 1898; *s* of George Platt and Marie Louise (Tostevan) Brett; *m* 1917, Isabel Yeomans; two *s.* *Educ:* Collegiate School, New York City; Salisbury School, Salisbury, Conn. Joined staff of The Macmillan Company, Sept. 1913; six months training with competing publishing house, Doubleday, 1915. Served European War, 1914-18, with US Army, private 1916, 2nd Lieut 1917, 1st Lieut Jan. 1918, Capt. July 1918, 16 months service in France, 1918-19; Maj. Reserve Corps until 1940; Lieut-Col, Asst Chief of Staff, NY Guard, 1940-43; Adviser to War Production Board, State Dept, 1943-45. Returned to Macmillan, 1919; Dir and Sales Manager, 1920; Treas., 1920-31; General Manager, 1928-34; Pres., 1931-58; Chairman of the Board, 1959-61. Trustee: Union Square Savings Bank, New York City, 1926-61; Southport (Connecticut) Savings Bank, 1954-58. President: Sasquanaug Assoc. for Southport Improvement, 1954-56; Pequot Library, Southport, Connecticut, 1955-56. *Publications:* occasional contributor to trade journals. *Recreations:* walking, sailing, fishing. *Address:* (home) 648 Harbor Road, Southport, Connecticut 06490, USA. *Clubs:* Century, Players, Union, Cruising of America (New York); Lake Placid, Pequot Yacht (Cdre, 1955-56).

**BRETT, John Alfred,** MA; Headmaster, Durham School, Durham, 1958-67; *b* 26 Oct. 1915; *s* of Alfred Brett, Harrogate, Yorks; *m* 1939, Margaret Coode; one *s* three *d.* *Educ:* Durham School; St Edmund Hall, Oxford. MA (Hons Modern History). Temp. teacher, Stowe School, 1938; Teacher of History and English, Diocesan College, Rondebosch, South Africa, 1939; restarted Silver Tree Youth Club for non-Europeans, Cape Town. Served in Army, Gunner to Major, RA, 1940-44; Instructor 123 OCTU Catterick; wounded in invasion of Normandy, 1944, and lost right eye; Military testing officer, War Office Selection Boards, finally Senior Military Testing Officer, War Office Selection Centre. Returned to post at Diocesan College, Rondebosch, 1946; Housemaster, 1948; Temp. teacher, Canford School, Wimborne, Dorset, 1954; Headmaster, Shaftesbury Grammar School, 1954. Diocesan Lay Reader. Mem. Council, Brathay Hall Centre. Governor, Bernard Gilpin Society. *Recreations:* sport (Captain Oxford University Rugby Football Club, 1937, and Member British Touring XV to Argentina, 1936); travel; reading. *Address:* 2A Buckland Crescent, Hampstead, NW3. *Club:* Royal Commonwealth Society.

**BRETT, Sir Lionel,** Kt 1961; *b* 19 Aug. 1911; 3rd *s* of late Very Rev. H. R. Brett, Dean of Belfast, and Constance Brett (*née* White). *Educ:* Marlborough; Magdalen College, Oxford. BA 1934; MA 1946. Called to bar, Inner Temple, 1937. War service, 1939-46, released as Major. Joined Colonial Legal Service as Crown Counsel, Nigeria, 1946; Senior Crown Counsel, 1950; Legal Secretary, Northern Region, 1951; Solicitor-General, Nigeria, 1952, Federation of Nigeria, 1954; Justice, Supreme Court of Nigeria, 1958-68. *Recreations:* reading, walking. *Address:* The Cottage, Puckington, Nr Ilminster, Somerset. *Club:* United University.

**BRETT, Professor Raymond Laurence;** G. F. Grant Professor of English, University of Hull, since 1952; *b* 10 January 1917; *s* of Leonard and late Ellen Brett, Clevedon, Somerset; *m* 1947, Kathleen Tegwen, *d* of late Rev. C. D. Cranmer; two *s.* *Educ:* Bristol Cathedral School; University of Bristol; University College, Oxford (Plumptre Exhibitioner). 1st Class Hons BA, English and Philosophy, Bristol, 1937; Taylor Prizeman, Hannam-Clark Prizeman, Haldane of Cloan Post-Grad. Studentship; BLitt, Oxf., 1940. Service in Admiralty, 1940-46; on Staff of First Lord; Lecturer in English, University of Bristol, 1946-52. Visiting Professor, University of Rochester, USA, 1958-59; Dean of Faculty of Arts, University of Hull, 1960-62. *Publications:* The Third Earl of Shaftesbury: A Study in 18th Century Literary Theory, 1951; Coleridge's Theory of Imagination (English Essays), 1949; George Crabbe, 1956; Reason and Imagination, 1961; (with A. R. Jones) a critical edition of Lyrical Ballads by Wordsworth and Coleridge, 1963; Thomas Hobbes (The English Mind), 1964; Poems of Faith and Doubt (ed), 1965; An Introduction to English Studies, 1965; Fancy and Imagination, 1969. Articles in: The Times, Time and Tide, Essays and Studies, Review of English Studies, Modern Language Review, Philosophy, English, South Atlantic Quarterly, etc. *Address:* The Gables, Station Walk, Cottingham, E Yorks. *T:* 847115.

**BRETT-JAMES, (Eliot) Antony;** author (Military History); Head of War Studies Department, Royal Military Academy Sandhurst, since 1970 (Deputy Head, 1968-69); *b* 4 April 1920; *er surv. s* of late Norman George Brett-James, MA, BLitt, FSA, Mill Hill, and Gladys Brett-James. *Educ:* Mill Hill Sch.; Paris; Sidney Sussex Coll., Cambridge. 2nd cl. Mod. Langs Tripos, 1947; MA. Served War of 1939-45: Royal Signals, 2nd Lt, 1941; 2nd Air Formation Signals; Lebanon, Syria; 5th Indian Divl Signals, in Alamein Line, 1942; Iraq, India; Capt., 1943; commanded 9th Indian Inf. Bde Signals, Arakan, Imphal, Burma (despatches), 1944; Burma, 1945. Entered publishing: George G. Harrap (mod. langs editor), 1947-52; Chatto & Windus (reader and publicity manager, 1952-58; Cassell, 1958-61 (educl manager, 1960-61). Lectr, then Sen. Lectr, in Mil. Hist., RMA

Sandhurst, 1961-67. Member: RUSI; Military Commentators' Circle; FRHistS 1970. *Publications:* Report My Signals, 1948; Ball of Fire: the 5th Indian Division in the Second World War, 1951; The Triple Stream, 1953; General Graham, Lord Lynedoch, 1959; Wellington at War, 1794-1815, 1961; (with Lt-Gen. Sir G. Evans) Imphal, 1962; The Hundred Days, 1964; 1812, 1966; The British Soldier 1793-1815, 1970; Europe against Napoleon, 1970; Daily Life in Wellington's Army, 1971; articles in: History Today, Purnell's History of the Second World War, etc. *Recreations:* meeting people, cricket, browsing in antiquarian bookshops, gardening, music. *Address:* RMA Sandhurst, Camberley, Surrey. *T:* Camberley 63344. *Club:* The Sette of Odd Volumes.

**BRETTON**; *see* Monk Bretton.

**BRETTON, Very Rev. William Frederick**; Dean of Nelson, New Zealand, 1956-70, Dean Emeritus 1970; Vicar of Christ Church Cathedral, 1956-70; *b* 2 May 1909; *s* of William and Alice Bretton; *m* 1934, Mary Hope Rokeby Robinson; two *s* two *d. Educ:* Downing College, Cambridge; Ridley Hall, Cambridge. BA, 1931; MA, 1935. Deacon 1933; Priest, 1935; Curate: St Andrew's, Watford, 1933-35; St John's, Sparkhill, 1936-39; Vicar: St Cuthbert's, Birmingham, 1939-42; St John the Evangelist, Sandown, 1942-46; Johnsonville, NZ, 1946-50; Lower Hutt, NZ, 1950-56. Hon. Canon, Wellington, NZ, 1953-57. Examining Chaplain to Bishop of Nelson, 1965-. Coronation Medal, 1953. *Publication:* ABC of Our Religion. *Address:* 1 Marybank Road, Atawhai, Nelson, New Zealand.

**BREWER, Frank,** CMG 1960; OBE 1953; *b* 1915; *s* of late Lewis Arthur Brewer; *m* 1950, Eileen Marian, *d* of A. J. Shepherd. *Educ:* Swindon Commonweal School; Pembroke College, Oxford (MA). Malayan Civil Service, 1937-59: Chinese Secretariat, Labour Dept; Secretary for Chinese Affairs and Dep. Chief Sec., Fed. of Malaya, 1955-57; Sec. for Defence, 1957-59; FCO (formerly FO), 1960-. War Service, 1941-45, Special Forces (POW Sumatra). *Address:* Osborne House, 4 Dry Hill Park Crescent, Tonbridge, Kent. *T:* Tonbridge 3811. *Clubs:* Royal Commonwealth Society, Special Forces.

**BREWIN, Elizabeth Maud (Mrs P. K. Brewin)**; *see* Pepperell, E. M.

**BREWIS, Henry John**; MP (C) for Galloway since April 1959; DL; Managing Director Ardwell Estates, Stranraer; farming; *b* 8 April 1920; *s* of Lt-Col F. B. Brewis, Norton Grove, Malton, Yorks; *m* 1949, Faith A. D. MacTaggart-Stewart, Ardwell, Wigtownshire; three *s* one *d. Educ:* Eton; New College, Oxford. Served Royal Artillery, 1940-46 (despatches twice); on active service, North Africa and Italy; demobilized with rank of Major. Barrister-at-law, 1946. Wigtownshire County Council, 1955; Convener, Finance Committee, 1958. Parliamentary Private Sec. to The Lord Advocate, 1960-61. Speaker's Panel of Chairmen, 1965. Mem., British Deleg. to Council of Europe, 1966-69. DL Wigtownshire, 1966. *Recreations:* golf, tennis, shooting. *Address:* Ardwell House, Stranraer. *T:* Ardwell 227; Norton Grove, Malton, Yorks. *Clubs:* Carlton, Caledonian.

**BREWIS, John Fenwick,** CMG 1962; CVO 1957; Tourist and Publicity Officer, Winchester Corporation; HM Diplomatic Service (retired); *b* 26 April 1910; *s* of late Arthur Brewis and of Mary Brewis; *m* 1948, Rachel Mary, *d* of late Hilary G. Gardner; one *s* one *d. Educ:* Repton; CCC, Camb. Entered China Consular Service in 1933 and served in China till 1944; First Secretary, Baghdad, 1946-49; Consul, Bordeaux, 1950-52; Foreign Office, 1945-46, 1954-55 and 1959-65; Counsellor, Lisbon, 1955-59; Consul-General, Lyons, 1965-67. *Recreations:* gardening and country pursuits; historical reading. *Address:* 49 St Cross Road, Winchester. *T:* Winchester 4187.

**BREWIS, Rev. John Salusbury,** MA; Rector of St James's, Piccadilly, 1954-67; *m* 1935, Lady Anne Beatrice Mary Palmer, *e d* of 3rd Earl of Selborne, *qv*; two *s* two *d. Educ:* Eton; Hertford College, Oxford (Scholar), 1st Class Final Honour School of Modern History; Princeton Univ. (Henry P. Davison Scholar); Cuddesdon College. Assistant Master at Eton, 1927-29; Examining Chaplain to the Bishop of Carlisle, 1929-46; Vice-Principal and Tutor of St Edmund Hall, Oxford, 1929-37 (Fellow Emeritus, 1956); Examining Chaplain to the Bishop of Durham, 1937-47; Principal, St Chad's Coll., Durham, 1937-47; Vicar, Melton-on-the-Hill, Yorks, 1947-54. Hon. Canon of Durham, 1947. Archdeacon, 1947-54, and Rural Dean, 1947-54, of Doncaster. Examining Chaplain to the Bishop of London, 1956. *Address:* Benhams House, Benhams Lane, Blackmoor, Liss, Hants.

**BREWSTER, George,** CVO 1969; MD; practitioner of medicine; formerly Surgeon Apothecary to HM Household at Holyrood Palace, Edinburgh, resigned 1970; Medical Officer to French Consulate-General in Scotland; *b* 27 Sept. 1899; *m* 1930; two *s. Educ:* High School, Stirling; Edinburgh Univ. MB, ChB, Edin., 1921; DPH Edin., 1924; MD (with distinction) Edin., 1926. House Surgeon, Edin. Royal Infirmary. Chevalier de la Légion d'Honneur (France), 1957. *Address:* (home and consulting room) 53 Bruntsfield Place, Edinburgh. *T:* 031-229 2301.

**BREWSTER, Kingman, Jr**; President, Yale University, New Haven, Connecticut, since 1963; *b* Longmeadow, Massachusetts, 17 June 1919; *s* of Kingman Brewster and Florence Besse; *m* 1942, Mary Louise Phillips; three *s* two *d. Educ:* Yale University; Harvard University. AB Yale, 1941; LLB Harvard, 1948. Military Service: Lieut (Aviation) USNR, 1942-46. Special Asst Coordinator Inter-American Affairs, 1941; Research Assoc., Dept Economics, Massachusetts Inst. of Technology, 1949-50; Asst. General Counsel, Office US Special Representative in Europe, 1948-49; Cons., Pres. Materials Policy Commission, 1951, Mut. Security Agency, 1952; Asst Prof. of Law, Harvard, 1950-58; Prof. of Law, Harvard, 1953-60; Provost, Yale, 1961-63. Chm., Nat. Policy Panel of UN; Mem. Bd of Dirs: Amer. Council of Learned Socs; Amer. Council on Educn; Nat. Educn Television. Hon. LLD: American Internat. College, 1961; Butler Univ. (Indiana), Univ. of Bridgeport, Columbia Univ., Trinity College, Harvard Univ., Princeton Univ. (all in 1964); Univ. of Pennsylvania; St Lawrence Univ.; Case Institute of Technology; Williams College (all in 1965); Amherst College, 1967; Brown Univ., 1967; George Washington Univ., 1968; Boston College, 1968; Dartmouth Coll., Dickinson, Johns Hopkins, Michigan State, all in 1969; Carlton Coll., Massachusetts, 1970. *Publications:* Antitrust and American Business Abroad, 1959; (with M. Katz) Law of International Transactions and Relations, 1960. *Recreation:* sailing. *Address:* (office) Yale University, New Haven, Connecticut; (home) 43 Hillhouse Avenue, New Haven, Connecticut. *T:* 203:432-4180. *Clubs:* Yale, Century Association (New York); Tavern (Boston, Mass.); Vineyard Haven

Yacht (Vineyard Haven, Mass.); Yale Sailing Associates, Graduates (New Haven, Conn).

**BREZHNEV, Leonid Ilyich;** Hero of the Soviet Union; Orders of Lenin (3); Orders of the Red Banner (2); Order of Bogdan Khmelnitsky (2nd cl.); Order of the Patriotic War (1st cl.); Order of the Red Star; Hero of Socialist Labour; First Secretary of Central Cttee, CPSU, since Oct. 1964; Member, Presidium of Supreme Soviet (President, 1960-64); *b* Kamenskoye (now Dnieprodzerzhinsk), Ukraine, 19 Dec. 1906. *Educ:* Institute of Metallurgy, Dnieprodzerzhinsk (graduate). Began career as engineer and was active in social work. Joined Communist Party, 1931; 1st Secretary, Central Cttee, Communist Party of Moldavia, 1950. Elected to Supreme Soviet of USSR, 1950, 1954, 1958, 1962. Member, Central Cttee, CPSU, 1952-; Alternate Member Presidium of Central Cttee, CPSU, 1952-57; Secretary, Central Cttee, Communist Party, Kazakhstan, 1954-56; Member Presidium of Central Cttee, CPSU, 1957-; Member Party Secretariat, Central Cttee, 1952-53, 1956-57, 1963-. Maj.-Gen. 1943; Lieut-Gen. 1953. *Address:* Central Committee, CPSU, Kremlin, Moscow, USSR.

**BRIAN, Percy Wragg,** FRS 1958; Professor of Botany, University of Cambridge, and Fellow of Queens' College, Cambridge, since Oct. 1968; *b* 5 Sept. 1910; *s* of Percy Brian, Macclesfield, and Adelaide Wragg, Shirley, nr Birmingham; *m* 1st, 1935, Iris Neville Hunt (marr. diss. 1947); one *s* two *d*; 2nd, 1948, Margaret Audrey Gilling. *Educ:* King Edward's School, Birmingham; King's College, Cambridge. Univ. of Cambridge. Frank Smart Univ. Student in Botany, 1933-34; PhD 1936; ScD 1951. Assistant Mycologist, Long Ashton Research Station, 1934; Mycologist, Jealott's Hill Research Station, ICI Ltd, 1936; Head of Dept of Microbiology, Akers Research Labs ICI Ltd, Welwyn, 1946; Associate Research Manager, Pharmaceuticals Div., 1961-62; Regius Prof. of Botany, Glasgow Univ., 1962-68; Clive Behrens Lectr in Agric., Leeds Univ., 1964-65. President: British Mycological Society, 1959, 1965; Assoc. of Applied Biologists, 1961; Society for General Microbiology, 1965; Leeuwenhoek Lectr, Royal Soc., 1966; Mem. Council, Royal Soc., 1968-70. *Publications:* many in learned journals on subjects concerned with plant pathology, microbiology and plant physiology. *Recreation:* gardening. *Address:* Walkers Field, Kingston, Cambridge. *T:* Comberton 2200.

**BRIANCE, John Albert,** CMG 1960; HM Diplomatic Service; Foreign and Commonwealth Office (formerly Foreign Office), since 1964; *b* 19 Oct. 1915; *s* of late Albert Perceval and Louise Florence Briance; *m* 1950, Prunella Mary, *d* of Col. E. Haldane Chapman; one *s* one *d*. *Educ:* King Edward VII School. Colonial Police, Palestine, 1936-48; Foreign Office, 1949; British Embassy, Tehran, 1950-52; British Middle East Office, 1953; Foreign Office, 1954-57; Counsellor, British Embassy, Washington, 1958-60; Counsellor, Office of UK Commissioner for SE Asia Singapore, 1961-63. *Address:* c/o Barclays Bank DCO, 1 Cockspur Street, SW1. *Clubs:* Bath; Metropolitan (Washington).

**BRIAULT, Dr Eric William Henry;** Deputy Education Officer, Inner London Education Authority, since 1956; *b* 24 Dec. 1911; *s* of H. G. Briault; *m* 1935, Marie Alice (*née* Knight); two *s* one *d*. *Educ:* Brighton, Hove and Sussex Grammar Sch.; Peterhouse, Cambridge (Robert Slade Schol.). 1st cl. hons Geography, 1933; MA Cantab 1937; PhD London 1939. School teaching, 1933-47; Inspector of Schools, LCC, 1948-56. *Publications:* Sussex, East and West (Land Utilisation Survey report), 1942; (jtly) Introduction to Advanced Geography, 1957; (jtly) Geography In and Out of School, 1960. *Recreations:* travel, gardening, music, theatre and ballet; formerly athletics (Cambridge blue) and cross-country running (Cambridge half-blue). *Address:* 5 Mulgrave Road, Harrow, Middx. *T:* 01-422 5761. *Club:* Athenæum.

**BRICKER, John William,** LLB; Lawyer, USA; Republican; *b* 6 Sept. 1893; *s* of Lemuel Spencer Bricker and Laura (*née* King) *m* 1920, Harriet Day; one *s*. *Educ:* State Univ., Ohio. AB 1916; admitted to Bar, Ohio, 1917; LLB 1920. Solicitor, Grandview Heights, 1920-28; Assistant Attorney-General of Ohio, 1923-27; Attorney-General, 1933-37. Governor of Ohio, 1939-41, 1941-43, 1943-45. Candidate (Republican) for US Vice-Presidency, 1944; Senator from Ohio, 1947-58. Member firm of Bricker, Evatt, Barton & Eckler. Member Public Utilities Commission, Ohio. LLD Ohio State University, 1940. Served European War, 1917-18, 1st Lieut. Holds various trusteeships. *Address:* 2407 Tremont Road, Columbus, Ohio, USA; 100 East Broad Street, Columbus, Ohio, USA.

**BRICKHILL, Paul Chester Jerome;** author; *b* 20 Dec. 1916; 3rd *s* of G. R. Brickhill, Sydney, Aust.; *m* 1950, Margaret Olive Slater, Sydney (marr. diss., 1964); one *s* one *d*. *Educ:* North Sydney High School; Sydney University. Journalist in Sydney, 1935-40; joined RAAF 1940; service in United Kingdom and Middle East as fighter pilot; shot down in Tunisia, 1943; POW Germany; Flight Lieut; Foreign Correspondent in Europe and USA, 1945-47; left journalism to concentrate on books, 1949. *Publications:* Escape to Danger (with Conrad Norton), 1946; The Great Escape, 1951; The Dam Busters, 1951; Escape or Die, 1952; Reach for the Sky, 1954; The Deadline, 1962. *Recreations:* golf, squash. *Address:* c/o John Farquharson Ltd, 15 Red Lion Square, WC1. *T:* 01-242 4843. *Club:* Royal Air Force.

**BRICKMAN, Brig. Ivan Pringle,** CB 1949; CBE 1942 (OBE 1929); Regular Army retired; *b* 14 May 1891; *s* of Francis Brickman, Edinburgh, and Eliza Macdonald; *m* 1920, Mildred Ducker; one *d*. *Educ:* Edinburgh Academy; Bowdon College. Served European War, 1914-18, France (despatches); War of 1939-45; ME, 1941 (despatches); BNAF, 1943; CMF, 1944 (despatches), Bronze Star (USA), 1946. *Recreations:* fishing, golf. *Address:* Sunnydale, Meliden, Flints. *T:* Prestatyn 3442.

**BRICKWOOD, Sir Rupert Redvers,** 2nd Bt, *cr* 1927; Director of Brickwoods Ltd, brewers, Portsmouth; *b* 18 Feb. 1900; *e s* of Sir John Brickwood, 1st Bt, and Jessie (*d* 1917), *d* of John Cooper of Burghfield, Berks; *S* father 1932; *m* 1932, Rachel Neale, *o d* of late Dr M. W. Shutte, Newnham, Oatlands Chase, Weybridge; two *d*. *Educ:* Twyford School; Cheltenham College; RMC Sandhurst. *Address:* Little Boarhunt, Liphook, Hants. *Club:* Royal Automobile.

**BRIDGE, Ann, (Lady O'Malley);** author; *b* 1891; *d* of James Harris Sanders and Marie Louise, *d* of James Ingersoll Day; *m* 1913, Sir Owen St Clair O'Malley, *qv*; one *s* two *d*. *Educ:* Home; London School of Economics. *Publications:* Peking Picnic, 1932 (Atlantic Monthly Prize); The Ginger Griffin, 1934 (Book Society Choice); Illyrian Spring, 1935 (Book Society Choice); The Song in the House (short stories), 1936; Enchanter's Nightshade, 1937 (Book Society Choice); Four-Part Setting,

1939; Frontier Passage, 1942; Singing Waters, 1945 (Book Society Choice and Choice of the Literary Guild of America); And Then You Came, 1948; (with Susan Lowndes) The Selective Traveller in Portugal, 1949; The House at Kilmartin (for children), 1951; The Dark Moment 1952 (Choice of the Literary Guild of America); A Place to Stand, 1953; Portrait of my Mother, 1955; The Light-Hearted Quest, 1956; The Portuguese Escape, 1958 (Choice of the Literary Guild of America); The Numbered Account, 1960; The Tightening String, 1962; The Dangerous Islands, 1964; Emergency in the Pyrenees, 1965; The Episode at Toledo, 1966; Facts and Fictions, 1968; The Malady in Madeira, 1969; Moments of Knowing, 1970. *Recreations:* sailing, botany, archæology. *Address:* c/o A. D. Peters, 10 Buckingham Street, Adelphi, WC2.

**BRIDGE, Very Rev. Antony Cyprian;** Dean of Guildford since 1968; *b* 5 Sept. 1914; *s* of late Comdr C. D. C. Bridge, RN; *m* 1937, Brenda Lois Streatfeild; one *s* two *d. Educ:* Marlborough College. Scholarship to Royal Academy School of Art, 1932. Professional painter thereafter. War of 1939-45: joined Army, Sept. 1939; commissioned Buffs, 1940; demobilised as Major, 1945. Ordained, 1955; Curate, Hythe Parish Church till 1958; Vicar of Christ Church, Lancaster Gate, London, 1958-68. *Publication:* Images of God, 1960. *Recreations:* bird-watching, fishing, reading. *Address:* The Deanery, 1 Cathedral Close, Guildford, Surrey. *T:* Guildford 60328.
*See also Hon. Sir Nigel Bridge.*

**BRIDGE, Admiral Sir (Arthur) Robin (Moore),** KBE, 1950 (CBE 1940); CB 1948; *b* 15 Feb. 1894; *s* of late Robert Moore and Mary Frances Bridge; *m* 1933, Ida Nancy, *e d* of George Tulk Shepherdson, Santiago, Chile; one *s* one *d. Educ:* RN Colleges, Osborne and Dartmouth. Comd. HMS Eagle, 1939-41; Dir, Naval Air Div., Admiralty, 1941-43; Chief of Staff to Flag Officer, Carrier Training, 1943-44 Commodore 1st Class, Comdg Northern Naval Air Stations, 1944-45; Rear-Adm., 1945; Flag Officer (Air) East Indies, 1945-46; Flag Officer (Air) British Pacific Fleet and East Indies, 1946-47. Senior Naval Representative, British Element of Joint Chiefs of Staff Cttee, Australia, 1947-48; Vice-Adm., 1948; Flag Officer Commanding Reserve Fleet, 1948-50; retired list, 1951; Adm., retired list, 1952. *Address:* Greengates, Emsworth, Hants. *T:* Emsworth 2752.

**BRIDGE, George Wilfred;** Deputy Chairman, Legal and General Assurance Society Ltd and associated societies; *b* 1 Jan. 1894; *s* of Josiah and Mary Bridge; *m* 1st, 1920, Minna (*d* 1962); one *s* one *d*; 2nd, Neta Margaret, *widow* of Alec Aldridge. *Educ:* Westoe Road Secondary School, South Shields. Joined Legal and General Assurance Soc. Ltd, 1919; General Manager, 1946-58; Executive Vice-Chairman, 1958-59. President, Insurance Institute of London, 1951-52; President, Chartered Insurance Institute, 1954-55. Governor, Stowe School and Queenswood School. FCII. *Recreation:* golf. *Address:* 8 Heath Rise, Kersfield Road, Putney, SW15. *T:* 01-788 1703. *Club:* Reform.

**BRIDGE, John,** GC 1944; GM 1940 and Bar 1941; Director of Education for Sunderland County Borough Council since Oct. 1963; *b* 5 Feb. 1915; *s* of late Joseph Edward Bridge, Culcheth, Warrington; *m* 1945, F. J. Patterson; three *d. Educ:* London Univ. BSc Gen. Hons, 1936 and BSc Special Hons (Physics), 1937; Teacher's Dip., 1938. Schoolmaster: Lancs CC, Sept.-Dec. 1938; Leighton Park, Reading, Jan.-Aug. 1939; Firth Park Grammar Sch., Sheffield, Sept. 1939-Aug. 1946 (interrupted by war service). Served War: RNVR June 1940-Feb. 1946, engaged on bomb and mine disposal; demobilised as Lt Comdr RNVR. *Address:* 37 Park Avenue, Roker, Sunderland. *T:* Sunderland 72963.

**BRIDGE, Hon. Sir Nigel (Cyprian),** Kt 1968; **Hon. Mr Justice Bridge;** Judge of High Court, Queen's Bench Division, since 1968; *b* 26 Feb. 1917; *s* of late Comdr C. D. C. Bridge, RN; *m* 1944, Margaret Swinbank; one *s* two *d. Educ;* Marlborough College. Army Service, 1940-46; commnd into KRRC, 1941. Called to the Bar, 1947; Junior Counsel to Treasury (Common Law), 1964-68. *Address:* The Old Rectory, Dowdeswell, near Cheltenham, Glos. *T:* Andoversford 249.
*See also Very Rev. A. C. Bridge.*

**BRIDGE, Adm. Sir Robin;** *see* Bridge, Adm. Sir A. R. M.

**BRIDGE, Roy Arthur Odell,** CMG 1967; Adviser to the Chairman, Mellon National Bank & Trust Co., Pittsburgh, since 1970; Director (since 1970): Julius Baer International Ltd, London; Bär Holdings A. G. Zürich; Baer Securities Corporation, New York; Baer Credit Corporation, New York; Scandinavian Bank Ltd, London; *b* 27 June 1911; *s* of late A. S. W. Bridge and late Mary E. Bridge; *m* 1938, Mary Ethel, *d* of late E. N. Ruddock; two *s* three *d. Educ:* Dulwich College. Bank of England, 1929-69: UK Alternate on Managing Bd of European Payments Union, Paris, 1950-52; Dep. Chief Cashier, Bank of England, 1957-63; Adviser to the Governors, 1963-65; Asst to the Governors, 1965-69. Pres., Assoc. Cambiste Internationale, Paris, 1962-67 (Hon. Pres., 1967–). *Recreations:* people, music, eating and drinking. *Address:* Crofton House, Kew Gardens Road, Richmond, Surrey. *T:* 01-940 3536. *Clubs:* Bath, Overseas Bankers; Forex (Paris).

**BRIDGEFORD, Lt-Gen. Sir William,** KBE 1956 (CBE 1941); CB 1945; MC; Australian Military Forces, retired; *b* 28 July 1894; *s* of George Bridgeford; *m* 1922, Phyllis W., *d* of Walter Frederico; one *s. Educ:* High School, Ballarat; Duntroon Royal Military College. Served European War, 1914-18 (MC); Instructor, Duntroon, 1925; Staff College, Quetta, 1926-27; Bde Major, 6th Cavalry Bde, Adelaide, 1928-31; Training Directorate, Army HQ, 1932-34; GSO 1, 2nd Cavalry Div., Victoria, 1934-38; Instructor Army Command and Staff School, 1938; Imperial Defence College, London, 1939; War of 1939-45 (despatches, CBE, CB). Formerly GOC Eastern Command, Australia; C-in-C British Commonwealth Forces in Korea; retired, 1953. *Address:* c/o Navy and Military Club, Alfred Place, Melbourne, Australia.

**BRIDGEMAN,** family name of **Earl of Bradford** and **Viscount Bridgeman.**

**BRIDGEMAN,** 2nd Viscount, *cr* 1929, of Leigh; **Robert Clive Bridgeman,** KBE 1954; CB 1944; DSO 1940; MC; psc; JP; HM Lieutenant of County of Salop, 1951-Dec. 1969; Alderman, Salop County Council since 1951; *b* April 1896; *e s* of 1st Viscount and Caroline Beatrix, DBE (*d* 1961), *er d* of Hon. Cecil Parker; *S* father, 1935; *m* 1930, Mary Kathleen, 2nd *d* of Baron Bingley, PC; three *d. Educ:* Eton College. 2nd Lieut, The Rifle Bde, 1914; Lieut, 1916; Captain, 1921; Bt Major, 1932; Bt. Lieut-Col, 1935, acting Maj.-Gen., 1941; Col and Temp. Maj.-Gen., 1942; served European War (France), 1915-18; Private Secretary to his father when Parliamentary Secretary to Minister of Labour, 1918; Brigade Major, 7th

Infantry Brigade, 1932-34; GSO2 War Office, 1935-37; retired pay, 1937; served War of 1939-45 (DSO); Deputy Director, Home Guard, 1941; Director-General, Home Guard and Territorial Army, 1941-44; Deputy Adjt-General, 1944-45. Pres. West Midland TA&VRA, 1968-69. JP Salop, 1951. *Heir: b* Hon. Geoffrey John Orlando Bridgeman, *qv. Address:* Leigh Manor, Minsterley, Salop. *T:* Worthen 210. *Clubs:* Beefsteak, Naval and Military.

*See also Hon. Sir Maurice Bridgeman.*

**BRIDGEMAN, Hon. Geoffrey John Orlando,** MC; MB, FRCS; *heir-pres.* to 2nd Viscount Bridgeman, *qv; b* 3 July 1898; 2nd son of 1st Viscount Bridgeman; *m* 1929, Mary Talbot; one *s* two *d. Educ:* Eton; Trinity College, Cambridge. Served European War, RFA, 1917-19; and as Brig. RAMC, 1940-45. Consulting Surgeon, Western Ophthalmic Hospital; Consulting Ophthalmic Surgeon, St George's Hospital; formerly: Classical Exhibitioner, Trinity College, Cambridge; Hon. Consultant Ophthalmologist to India and Burma Offices. Fellow of Royal Society of Medicine; Member of British Medical Association. *Recreations:* cricket, shooting, ski-ing. *Address:* Watley House, Sparsholt, Winchester, Hants. *T:* Sparsholt 297. *Club:* Travellers'.

**BRIDGEMAN, Col Hon. Henry George Orlando,** DSO, 1918; MC; JP and DL Northumberland; Late RFA; 3rd *s* of 4th Earl of Bradford; *b* 15 Aug. 1882; *m* 1930, Joan, *y d* of late Hon. Bernard Constable Maxwell; two *s* two *d. Educ:* Harrow; Royal Military Academy, Woolwich. Entered Royal Field Artillery, 1901; ADC to Field-Marshal Lord Grenfell, then Commander of the Forces in Ireland, 1905-8; for six months to Gen. Hon. Sir N. G. Lyttelton, in the same office; served in India in Royal Horse Artillery, 1908-14; Captain, 1914; Major, 1915; Lt-Col 1918; Commanded a Battery of Field Artillery in France, Sept. 1914-Jan. 1917, when posted as Brigade Major, 47th Divisional Artillery; Commanded Brigade RFA, Oct. 1918 to end of War (DSO, MC, Order of Danilo of Montenegro, despatches five times); retired, June 1919. *Recreations:* shooting, fishing, big-game shooting, and travel. *Address:* Fallodon Hall, Embleton, Alnwick, Northumberland. *T:* Embleton 252. *Club:* Turf.

**BRIDGEMAN, John Wilfred,** CBE 1960; BSc London, AKC; retired as Principal, Loughborough Training College, 1950-63; Principal, Loughborough Summer School, 1931-63; *b* 25 Jan. 1895; *s* of late John Edward Bridgeman and Alice Bridgeman, Bournemouth; *m* 1st, 1928, Mary Jane Wallace (*d* 1961); one *s*; 2nd, 1963, Helen Ida Mary Wallace. *Educ:* King's College, University of London; London Day Training College. Industry, 1910-15; taught at technical colleges, Bournemouth, Bath and Weymouth, 1915-20; Asst Master, Lyme Regis Grammar School, 1923; Senior Maths. Master, Wolverhampton Secondary Gram. Sch., 1926; Head of Dept for Training of Teachers, Loughborough Coll., 1930. Chm., Assoc. of Teachers in Colls and Depts of Education, 1952; Leader of Staff Panel, Pelham Cttee., 1955-63. Governor, Eastbourne Coll. of Education. Hon. MA Nottingham, 1961. *Recreations:* chess and walking. *Address:* c/o National Westminster Bank, Eastbourne, Sussex.

**BRIDGEMAN, Hon. Sir Maurice (Richard),** KBE 1964 (CBE 1946); Chairman of British Petroleum Company, 1960-69; Member, Industrial Reorganisation Corporation, 1969-71; *b* 26 Jan. 1904; 3rd *s* of 1st Viscount Bridgeman; *m* 1933, Diana Mary Erica Wilson; four *d. Educ:* Eton; Trinity Coll., Cambridge. Joined Anglo-Persian Oil Co., 1926; Petroleum Adviser Ministry of Economic Warfare, 1939; Asst Secretary Petroleum Dept and Joint Secretary Oil Control Board, 1940; temporarily loaned as Petroleum Adviser Govt of India, 1942; Principal Assistant Secretary Petroleum Division, Ministry of Fuel and Power, 1944-46; Mem. Advisory Council on Middle East Trade, 1958-63; Pres., Middle East Assoc. Hon. Fellow, Fitzwilliam Coll., Cambridge, 1967. Hon. LLD Leeds Univ., 1969. Cadman Memorial Medal, 1969. KStJ 1961 (CStJ 1957). Knight Grand Cross of the Italian Republic, 1966; Grand Officer, Order of Orange Nassau, 1968; Order of Homayun (Iran), 2nd Class, 1968. *Address:* The Glebe House, Selham, Petworth, Sussex. *T:* Lodsworth 205; 10 Kylestrome House, Ebury Street, SW1. *T:* 01-730 1700. *Club:* White's.

*See also J. L. Harman.*

**BRIDGER, Pearl,** MBE 1947; Director, Central Personnel, General Post Office, since 1968; *b* 9 Dec. 1912; *d* of Samuel and Lottie Bridger. *Educ:* Godolphin and Latymer Girls' Sch., London, W6. Entered Post Office as Executive Officer, 1931; Asst Telecommunications Controller, 1938; Principal, 1947; Asst Sec., 1954; Director, 1968. MIPM. *Recreations:* theatre-going, soroptimism. *Address:* 95 Deanhill Court, SW14. *T:* 01-876 8877. *Clubs:* Over-Seas League, Civil Service, Soroptimist.

**BRIDGES,** family name of **Baron Bridges.**

**BRIDGES,** 2nd Baron *cr* 1957; **Thomas Edward Bridges;** HM Diplomatic Service; Counsellor at British Embassy, Moscow; *b* 27 Nov. 1927; *s* of 1st Baron Bridges, KG, PC, GCB, GCVO, MC, FRS, and Hon. Katharine Dianthe, *d* of 2nd Baron Farrer; *S* father, 1969; *m* 1953, Rachel Mary, *y d* of late Sir Henry Bunbury, KCB; two *s* one *d. Educ:* Eton; New Coll., Oxford. Entered Foreign Service, 1951; served in Bonn, Berlin, Rio de Janeiro, Athens and at FO (Asst Private Sec. to Foreign Secretary, 1963-66). *Heir: s* Hon. Mark Thomas Bridges, *b* 25 July 1954. *Address:* British Embassy, Moscow 72, USSR.

**BRIDGES, Daisy Caroline,** CBE 1954; RRC 1943; General Secretary, International Council of Nurses, 1948-61; *b* 7 April 1894; *d* of late John Henry Bridges, JP and late Edith Isabella Bridges. *Educ:* Heathfield School, Ascot; Ladies' College, Cheltenham. British Red Cross Society, 1914-19 (despatches 1918); Nightingale School, St Thomas' Hosp., 1919-23; Staff, St Thomas' Hosp., 1925-36; Rockefeller Fellowship, US and Canada, 1937-38. TANS. Served War of 1939-45: France, Egypt and India; retired with rank of Prin. Matron; Min. of Health Working Party on Recruitment and Training of Nurses, 1946-47; Fellow Royal Soc. of Health, 1959. Florence Nightingale Medal (awarded by Internat. Red Cross Cttee), 1953; Coronation Medal, 1953. *Publication:* A History of the International Council of Nurses, 1967. *Recreations:* reading, chess. *Address:* 60 Burton Court, Chelsea, SW3. *T:* 01-730 7622. *Club:* Royal Commonwealth Society.

**BRIDGES, John Gourlay,** OBE 1954 (MBE 1944); Consultant: Tourism Promotion, Travel and Capital Development; Supervisor, Press, Publicity and Information to Church of Scotland; Director-General, British Travel and Holidays Association, 1945-63, retd; *b* 5 Dec. 1901; *e s* of late David McKay Bridges and late Margaret Gourlay Bridges, Glasgow; *m* 1931, Marion, *d* of late Andrew Bell, MBE, JP,

Glasgow; one *s* one *d*. *Educ:* elementary and secondary schools, Glasgow; Glasgow and West of Scotland Commercial College and School of Accountancy. Secretary, and latterly Director-Secretary, of private Ltd. Co., Glasgow and London, 1922-24; Accountant, Straits Trading Co. Ltd., Singapore and FM States, 1924-30; Sec. at Edinburgh, and later Gen. Sec. for Scotland, of The Overseas League, 1931-35; then Development Sec. of the movement; Development Sec., Overseas League and Gen. Sec., Overseas League in Canada, 1935-38; Gen. Tours Manager, Donaldson Atlantic Line, Great Britain, Canada and USA, 1939. Served in RAF as Embarkation Officer (Personnel) Liverpool, 1940-45; demobilized with rank of Squadron Leader, 1945. International Union of Official Travel Organizations (with consultative status UN) (Pres., 1960). Director of Studies and Professor of Tourism, Hawaii Univ., 1964-65. FRGS; FRSA; FInstD; Associate Institute of Transport. Member: Association of Scientific Tourism Experts; Council, British Travel and Holidays Association; Exec. Cttee, Scottish Council. *Publications;* numerous articles on Travel and allied subjects. *Recreations:* motoring, golf, fishing, gardening. *Address:* 35A Cluny Drive, Edinburgh 10. *T:* 031-447 4966. *Club:* Royal Over-Seas League.

**BRIDGES, Phillip Rodney,** CMG 1967; **Hon. Mr Justice Bridges;** Chief Justice of The Gambia, since 1968; *b* 9 July 1922; *e s* of late Captain Sir Ernest Bridges, and of Lady Bridges, Bedford; *m* 1st, 1951, Rosemary Ann Streeten (marriage dissolved, 1961); two *s* one *d*; 2nd, 1962, Angela Mary (*née* Dearden), *widow* of James Huyton. *Educ:* Bedford School. Military Service (Capt., RA) with Royal W. African Frontier Force in W. Africa, India and Burma, 1941-47. Admitted Solicitor (England), 1951; Colonial Legal Service, 1954; Barrister and Solicitor, Supreme Court of The Gambia, 1954; Solicitor-General of The Gambia, 1963; QC (Gambia) 1964; Attorney-General of The Gambia, 1964-68. *Recreations:* squash, reading. *Address:* Weavers, Coney Weston, Bury St Edmunds, Suffolk; Supreme Court, Bathurst, The Gambia. *Club:* Travellers'.

**BRIDGEWATER, Bentley Powell Conyers;** Secretary of the British Museum; *b* 6 Sept. 1911; *s* of late Conyers Bridgewater, OBE, Clerk to Commissioners of Taxes for City of London, and Violet Irene, *d* of late Dr I. W. Powell, Victoria, BC. *Educ:* Westminster School (King's Schol.); Christ Church, Oxford (Schol., BA 1933, MA 1965). Asst Keeper, British Museum, 1937; Asst Sec., 1940. Seconded to Dominions Office, 1941-42, and to Foreign Office, 1942-45; Returned to British Museum, 1946; Deputy Keeper, 1950; Keeper, 1961. *Recreation:* music. *Address:* c/o British Museum, WC1. *Club:* Athenæum.

**BRIDGMAN, Leonard;** ARAeS; *b* 15 Feb. 1895; *o s* of late A. H. Bridgman, ISO; unmarried. *Educ:* Cambridge House; Strand School; King's Coll., London. Hon. Artillery Company, 1915-18 and 1921-; Royal Air Force, 1918-19; Editorial Staff, The Aeroplane, 1919-34; Joint Editor and Compiler, All the World's Aircraft, 1923-40, Editor, 1941-60; International Aviation Associates, 1939-47; Esso Export Ltd, 1047-60; Executive Editor, Esso Air World, 1939-60, Advisory Editor, 1960-66. FAI Paul Tissandier Diploma, 1956, in recognition of 35 years' work on All the World's Aircraft. *Publications:* Aircraft of the British Empire, 1935-1939; The Clouds Remember, 1935; also illustrated several air historical books. *Recreations:* gardening, golf, drawing, and painting. *Address:* 35 Bancroft Avenue, N2. *T:* 01-340 3962. *Clubs:* Royal Aero, Pathfinder.

**BRIDPORT,** 4th Viscount, *cr* 1868; **Alexander Nelson Hood;** Baron Bridport, 1794; 7th Duke of Bronte in Sicily (*cr* 1799); *b* 17 March 1948; *s* of 3rd Viscount Bridport and Sheila Jeanne Agatha, *d* of Johann van Meurs; *S* father, 1969. *Educ:* Eton; Sorbonne. With Merchant Bank. *Address:* 45 Cadogan Square, SW1. *T:* 01-235 7798; Castello di Maniace, 95030 Maniace di Bronte, Catania, Sicily. *Club:* Brooks's.

**BRIERCLIFFE, Sir Rupert,** Kt 1939; CMG 1936; OBE 1919; MD, FRCP, DPH, etc; *b* January 1889. *Educ:* Bolton Grammar School; University of Manchester. Resident Medical Officer Manchester Children's Hospital, 1910; House Physician Manchester Royal Infirmary, 1911; Assistant Manchester Public Health Laboratories, 1912; Assistant MOH Manchester, 1913; RAMC (TF), 1914-20; served Egypt, Gallipoli, Palestine (despatches); demobilized with rank of Major; Principal Medical Officer, Haifa, 1919; DADMS Occupied Enemy Territory (South), 1920; Deputy Director of Health, Palestine, 1920-1930; Director of Medical and Sanitary Services, Ceylon, and Principal, Ceylon Medical College, 1930-36; Director of Medical Services, Nigeria, 1936-40; OC 1st WA Bde Field Amb., The Nigeria Regt, 1939-40; Medical Adviser to Comptroller for Development and Welfare in West Indies, 1940-46, and Medical Adviser, British Section, Anglo-American Caribbean Commission, 1942-46. Hon. Col Trinidad Local Forces, 1944. Esquire, Order of St John of Jerusalem, 1926. *Recreation:* sailing. *Address:* Pasea Estate, Tortola, British Virgin Islands. *Club:* Royal Thames Yacht.

**BRIERLEY, Captain Henry,** CBE 1960 (OBE 1942); MC 1917; House Governor, The London Hospital, 1939-62, retired; *b* 10 Aug. 1897; *s* of James William and Zoe Brierley, Rochdale; *m* 1931, Bettine Ariana (*d* 1969), *d* of Sir William Curtis, 4th Baronet, Caynham, Ludlow, Salop; one *d*. *Educ:* Shrewsbury. Commissioned Rifle Bde, 1916; served European War, 1914-18, Iraq, 1919-20; Adjt 1st Bn, 1921-24; Adjt London Rifle Brigade, 1925-29; retired 1929. The London Hospital, 1929; Secretary, 1938. Joint Master Eridge Foxhounds, 1962-68. *Recreation:* foxhunting. *Address:* Stile House, Mark Cross, Crowborough, Sussex. *T:* Rotherfield 283.

**BRIERLEY, John David;** Under-Secretary, Department of Education and Science; Principal Finance Officer and Joint Head of Planning Branch; *b* 16 March 1918; *s* of late Walter George Brierley and late Doris Brierley (*née* Paterson); *m* 1956, Frances Elizabeth Davis; one (adopted) *s* one (adopted) *d*. *Educ:* elementary schools, London and Croydon; Whitgift Sch., Croydon; Lincoln Coll., Oxford. *Lit. Hum.*, BA Hons, 1940. Served War: Army, RASC, 1940-46. Ministry of Education: Asst Principal, 1946; Principal, 1949; Dept of Education and Science: Asst Sec., 1960; Under-Sec., 1969. *Recreations:* fell-walking, cycling, photography, music. *Address:* 98 Arundel Avenue, Sanderstead, Surrey. *T:* 01-657 7508. *Club:* English-Speaking Union.

**BRIERS, Richard;** actor since 1955; *b* 14 Jan. 1934; *s* of Joseph Briers and Morna Richardson; *m* 1956, Ann Davies; two *d*. *Educ:* Rokeby Prep. Sch., Wimbledon; private tuition. RADA, 1954-56 (silver medal). First appearance in London in Gilt and Gingerbread, Duke of York's, 1959. *Plays:* (major parts in): Arsenic and Old Lace, 1965;

Relatively Speaking, 1966; The Real Inspector Hound, 1968; Cat Among the Pigeons, 1969; The Two of Us, 1970. *Television series:* Brothers-in-Law; Marriage Lines. *Recreations:* reading, golf. *Address:* 6 The Orchard, Bedford Park, W4. *T:* 01-994 0547. *Club:* Green Room.

**BRIGDEN, Wallace,** MA, MD, FRCP; Physician, London Hospital, and Physician, Cardiac Department, London Hospital; Physician, National Heart Hospital; Consulting Cardiologist to the Royal Navy; Hugh Morgan Visiting Professor, Vanderbilt University, USA, 1963; *b* 8 June 1916; *s* of Wallis Brigden and Louise Brigden (*née* Clarke); *m* 1940, Joan (marr. diss. 1966), *d* of late Frederick Mack; two *s* one *d*; *m* 1966, Everel, *d* of late Geoffrey Sankey; one *s*. *Educ:* Latymer School; University of Cambridge; King's College Hospital; Yale University. Senior Scholar, King's College, Cambridge; First Class Natural Sciences Tripos, Parts I and II, 1936, 1937; Henry Fund Fellowship, Yale University, USA, 1937-38; Burney Yeo Sch., King's College Hospital, 1938. RAMC, 1943-47, Med. Specialist and O/C Medical Division. Lecturer in Medicine, Post-Grad. Med. School of London; Physician, Hammersmith Hospital, 1948-49; Asst Physician, London Hospital and Asst Physician, Cardiac Dept, 1949; Asst Physician, National Heart Hospital, 1949; Cons. Cardiologist, Special Unit for Juvenile Rheumatism, Taplow, 1955-59; Director Inst. of Cardiology, 1962-66. St Cyres Lectr, 1956; R.T. Hall Lectr, Australia and New Zealand, 1961. Late Assistant Editor, British Heart Journal. Mem. British Cardiac Society and Assoc. of Physicians. *Publications:* Section on Cardio-vascular disease in Price's textbook of Medicine; Cardio-vascular disease in Medical Annual; contributor to the Lancet, British Heart Journal, and Clinical Science. *Recreation:* painting. *Address:* 45 Wimpole Street, W1. *T:* 01-935 1201; Willow House, Totteridge Common, N20. *T:* 01-959 6616. *Club:* Athenæum.

**BRIGGS, Alderman Albert William;** Chairman, South East Metropolitan Regional Hospital Board, since 1968; *b* 30 Dec. 1900; *s* of John Henry Briggs and Lydia Briggs; *m* 1930, Anne Counter; two *s* one *d*. *Educ:* West Ham Central Secondary School. Chairman: Briggs & Son Ltd (trading as Kensington Press), 1924-; Raystede Centre for Animal Welfare, 1965-; Dir, Channel Fairs Ltd, 1965-. Brighton CB Council, 1936-; Mem. Court, Sussex Univ., 1965-. Contested (Lab) Lewes, 1950 and 1951. Lessee, Brighton Racecourse. *Address:* 186 Bevendean Crescent, Brighton, Sussex. *T:* Brighton 66913.

**BRIGGS, Sir (Alfred) George (Ernest),** Kt 1953; Chairman: John Scott and Partners; Unit Trusts Information and Broking Service; Director: Hepworth Ceramic Holdings Ltd; Court Line Ltd; Gulf Development Co. Ltd; *b* 12 Feb. 1900; *s* of Alfred Briggs, Nottingham; *m* 1924, Kathlene Margaret, *d* of Peter MacGregor, JP, Sheffield; one *s*. *Educ:* Oundle. Served European War, Royal Naval Air Service, 1918. Deputy-Controller Iron and Steel Supplies, Ministry of Supply, 1942-45; Deputy-Controller of Supplies (Munitions Production) Ministry of Supply, March 1951-Dec. 1952. Member: Royal Ordnance Factories Board, 1952-59; European Purchasing Commission, 1951-52; Government Cttee on Steel and Tinplate Redundancies, West South Wales, 1953-55; London Electricity Board, 1959-. AMIMechE. *Recreation:* shooting. *Address:* Courtyard House, Lavershot Hall, London Road, Windlesham, Surrey. *T:* Ascot 20144. *Club:* Ends of the Earth.

**BRIGGS, Professor Asa,** MA, BSc (Econ); Professor of History; Vice-Chancellor, University of Sussex, since 1967; *b* 7 May 1921; *o s* of William Walker Briggs and Jane Briggs, Keighley, Yorks; *m* 1955, Susan Anne Banwell, *o d* of Donald I. Banwell, Keevil, Wiltshire; two *s* two *d*. *Educ:* Keighley Grammar School; Sidney Sussex College, Cambridge (1st cl. History Tripos, Pts I and II, 1940, 1941; 1st cl. BSc (Econ.), Lond., 1941). Gerstenberg studentship in Economics, London, 1941. Served in Intelligence Corps, 1942-45. Fellow of Worcester College, Oxford, 1945-55; Reader in Recent Social and Economic History, Oxford, 1950-55; Member, Institute for Advanced Study, Princeton, USA, 1953-54; Faculty Fellow of Nuffield College, Oxford, 1953-55; Professor of Modern History, Leeds Univ., 1955-61; Dean, School of Social Studies, Sussex Univ., 1961-65; Pro Vice-Chancellor, 1961-67. Visiting Professor: Australian National Univ., 1960; Chicago Univ., 1966. Dep. Pres., WEA, 1954-58, Pres., 1958-67. Mem., UGC, 1959-67. Trustee, Glyndebourne Arts Trust, 1966-; Chairman: Standing Conf. for Study of Local History, 1969-; National Selection Panel for Film Festivals; Governor, British Film Institute, 1970. Mem., Amer. Acad. of Arts and Sciences, 1970. Hon. Fellow: Sidney Sussex Coll., Cambridge, 1968; Worcester Coll., Oxford, 1969. Hon. DLitt East Anglia, 1966; Hon. DSc Florida Presbyterian, 1966; Hon. LLD York, Canada, 1968. *Publications:* Patterns of Peace-making (with D. Thomson and E. Meyer), 1945; History of Birmingham (1865-1938), 1952; Victorian People, 1954; Friends of the People, 1956; The Age of Improvement, 1959; Ed. Chartist Studies, 1959; Co-Ed. with John Saville, Essays in Labour History, 1960; Ed. They Saw it Happen, 1897-1940, 1961; A Study of the Work of Seebohm Rowntree, 1871-1954, 1961; The Birth of Broadcasting, 1961; Victorian Cities, 1963; The Golden Age of Wireless, 1965; William Cobbett, 1967; How They Lived, 1700-1815, 1969; The War of Words, 1970. *Recreation:* travelling. *Address:* Ashcombe House, Lewes, Sussex. *Clubs:* Oxford and Cambridge, Savile.

**BRIGGS, D. H. Currer,** MBE 1944; retired; *b* 28 April 1893; *s* of Arthur Currer Briggs; *m* 1917, Elizabeth, *d* of Dr James Denniston, MD, Dunoon and Altrincham; one *s* three *d*. *Educ:* Charterhouse School; Trinity College, Oxford. Mining Engineer in charge of Collieries in the Wakefield and Castleford district of Yorkshire, 1920-47. *Recreations:* shooting, fishing. *Address:* 7 North Hill Road, Headingley, Leeds 6, Yorks. *T:* Leeds 52727.

**BRIGGS, Hon. Sir Francis Arthur,** Kt 1961; a Federal Justice of Supreme Court, Federation of Rhodesia and Nyasaland, 1958-63, retired; *b* 9 July 1902; *yr s* of late William Francis Briggs, Preston, Lancs, and late Jane Greig, *yr d* of late Thomas Macmillan, Glasgow; *m* 1953, Edna Dorothy, *d* of late William Thomas Keylock and Mrs Emily Shillingford Keylock; no *c*. *Educ:* Charterhouse (Schol.); Trinity College, Oxford (Open Classical Schol.). Called to Bar, Inner Temple (Cert. of Honour and Jardine Studentship), 1927. Advocate and Solicitor, FMS, SS and Johore, 1928-40. Served in RAFVR, 1940-46 (despatches), Wing Commander. Colonial Legal Service, 1947; Registrar, Supreme Court, Federation of Malaya, 1948; Puisne Judge, Malaya, 1949; Justice of Appeal, E. African Court of Appeal, 1953, Vice-President, 1957. *Address:* Apartment 5a-F, Maestranza 15, Málaga, Spain. *T:* Málaga 210343.

**BRIGGS, Geoffrey Gould; Hon. Mr Justice Briggs;** a Puisne Judge, Hong Kong, since

1964; *b* 6 May 1914; 2nd *s* of late Reverend C. E. and Mrs Briggs, Amersham, Buckinghamshire; unmarried. *Educ:* Sherborne; Christ Church, Oxford (BA, BCL). Called to Bar (Gray's Inn), 1938; served War of 1939-45, county of London Yeomanry (Major). Attorney-General, E Region, Nigeria, 1954-58; QC (Nigeria), 1955; Puisne Judge, Sarawak, N Borneo and Brunei, 1958-62; Chief Justice of the Western Pacific, 1962-64. *Address:* The Courts of Justice, Hong Kong.

**BRIGGS, Sir George;** *see* Briggs, Sir A. G. E.

**BRIGGS, Professor George Edward,** FRS 1935; MA; Fellow of St John's College, Cambridge (President, 1952-63, retired); Professor Emeritus of Botany, Cambridge University; Professor of Botany, 1948-60; Professor of Plant Physiology, 1946-48, Cambridge University; *b* 25 June 1893; *m* 1920, Nora Burman; one *s* one *d. Educ:* Wintringham Grammar School; St John's College, Cambridge. *Publications:* Electrolytes and Plant Cells (with A. B. Hope and R. N. Robertson), 1961; Movement of Water in Plants, 1967. *Address:* 10 Luard Road, Cambridge CB2 2PJ. *T:* Cambridge 47181.

**BRIGGS, George Henry,** DSc Sydney; PhD Cantab; FInstP; retired, 1958, as Chief CSIRO Division of Physics, then Hon. Research Fellow, Australian National Standards Laboratory, to 1969; *b* Sydney, 1893; *o s* of William and Hannah Briggs; *m* 1923, Edna Dorothy Sayce; two *d. Educ:* Fort Street High School, Sydney; Sydney University. Lecturer in Physics, Sydney University 1916, research at Cavendish Laboratory, Cambridge (Emmanuel College), 1925-26 and 1936. Asst Professor of Physics, University of Sydney, 1928-39. Lyle medal of Australian National Research Council, 1941. Scientific adviser to Australian delegate, Atomic Energy Commission of United Nations, 1946-47. President, Australian Branch, Institute of Physics, 1950-51; Chairman Australian Unesco Committee for Natural Sciences, 1953-55; Member Australian National Advisory Committee for Unesco, 1953-61. Hon. Fellow Australian Institute of Physics, 1964. *Publications:* papers on physical subjects in Proceedings of Royal Society, Philosophical Magazine and other journals. *Address:* Findlay Avenue, Roseville, Sydney, Australia.

**BRIGGS, Martin Shaw,** FRIBA; *b* Otley, 1882; *e s* of late Rev. G. S. Briggs, Congregational minister; *m* 1910, Constance (*d* 1954), *d* of Prof. J. Holland Rose, of Cambridge; one *s* one *d. Educ:* Mill Hill School; Leeds University. Practised as an architect in London. *Principal works:* Keyston Manor; Surbiton Housing Scheme; Golderbrock House (Gt Titchfield Street); Otford Vicarage; the McClure Music School and Winterstoke House, Mill Hill School; houses at Mill Hill and elsewhere. Served in Egypt and Palestine, 1916-19; lecturer in London University School of Architecture, 1919-23, 1947-57; HM Inspector of Technical Schools, Board of Education, 1923-45; Member of RIBA Council, 1929-31, 1933-35, 1948-53; Vice-President 1952-53. *Publications:* In the Heel of Italy, 1910 (Italian translation, 1913); Baroque Architecture, 1913 (German translation, 1914); Through Egypt in Wartime, 1919; Muhammadan Architecture in Egypt and Palestine, 1924; A Short History of the Building Crafts, 1925; Rusticus, 1927; The Architect in History, 1927; English Architecture: an Outline, 1928; The Homes of the Pilgrim Fathers in England and America, 1932; Middlesex, Old and New, 1934; Freiburg and the Black Forest, 1936; How to Plan Your House, 1937; Building To-Day, 1944; Round the Shires, 1945; Puritan Architecture, 1946; Men of Taste, 1947; Architecture (Home University Library), 1947; The Approach to Architecture, 1948; Town and Country Planning, 1948; Down the Thames, 1949; Christopher Wren, 1951; Goths and Vandals, 1952; Wren the Incomparable, 1953; The English Farmhouse, 1953; Everyman's Concise Encyclopædia of Architecture, 1959; Architecture in Italy, 1961; contributions to many other books; numerous illustrated articles and reviews. *Address:* The Orchard, High Street, Mill Hill, NW7. *T:* 01-959 1488.

**BRIGGS, Percy,** CBE 1966; Member Electricity Council, 1962-66; Member (part-time), London Electricity Board, since 1968; *b* 4 Sept. 1903; *s* of late Alfred and late Caroline Briggs; *m* 1927, Annie M. Folker; one *s. Educ:* Deacon's School, Peterborough; Northampton Polytechnic. Held posts at Islington and Fulham Power Stations, becoming Superintendent at Fulham, 1945; Chief Generation Engineer of SE Division, British Electricity Authority, 1948-53; Divisional Controller, Merseyside and N Wales Division, 1953; Deputy Controller NW Merseyside and N Wales Division, Central Electricity Authority, 1954-56; Divisional Controller, Yorks Division, 1957; Regional Director, NE Reg. of Central Electricity Generating Board, 1958-61. Ceng, MIMechE; MInstF. *Recreations:* gardening, fishing. *Address:* Oak Tree Cottage, Echo Barn Lane, Farnham, Surrey. *T:* Farnham 3358.

**BRIGGS, Major-General Raymond,** CB 1943; DSO 1942; psc †; President, Metropolitan Area, British Legion; *b* 19 Jan. 1895; *yr s* of late James Burnett Briggs, Claughton, Cheshire; *m* 1927, Helen Wainwright, *d* of Charles Edward Kenworthy, Liverpool and New Orleans; one *d.* Served European War, 1914-18, France, Belgium, and Mesopotamia, Liverpool Scottish, King's Own Regt, and MGC, 2nd Lieut, 1915; Lieut 1917 (wounded twice); Royal Tank Corps, 1920; Captain, 1926; Bt. Major, 1933; Bt. Lt-Col, 1938; Colonel, 1941; Acting Brig., 1940; Major-General, 1944. Served War of 1939-45, France and Belgium, 1940 (GSO 1), Middle East and North Africa, 1941-43 (Comd 2 Armd Bde, GOC 1 Armd Division); Director, Royal Armoured Corps, War Office, 1943-47. Member Tank Board, 1943-46 (wounded, despatches twice, DSO, CB, Commander Legion of Merit, USA); retired, 1947. *Address:* 1 Linden Gardens, W2. *T:* 01-229 3711. *Clubs:* Army and Navy, Royal Automobile.

**BRIGGS, Rear-Admiral Thomas Vallack,** CB 1958; OBE 1945; DL; *b* 6 April 1906; *e s* of late Admiral Sir Charles John Briggs, and Lady Briggs (*née* Wilson); *m* 1947, Estelle Burland Willing, Boston, USA; one *step s. Educ:* The Grange, Stevenage, Herts; Imperial Service College, Windsor. Joined Royal Navy 1924; Rear-Admiral 1956. Advanced Gunnery Specialist. Served War of 1939-45: HMS Ark Royal, 1939-40; HMS Newcastle, 1943-44; staff of Flag Officer 2nd in Command, Eastern Fleet, 1944-45 (despatches twice). US Naval War Coll., Newport, RI, 1947-48; commanded 5th Destroyer Flotilla, HMS Solebay, 1949-50, and HMS Cumberland, 1954-55; IDC, 1951; Chief of Staff, Home Fleet and Eastern Atlantic, 1956-57; Asst Controller of the Navy, 1958, retired. Director: Hugh Stevenson & Sons Ltd, 1958; Hugh Stevenson & Sons (North East) Ltd, 1964; Bowater-Stevenson Containers Ltd, 1969. Vice-Chm., City of Westminster Soc. for Mentally Handicapped

Children, 1969; Member: European Atlantic Group, 1964; British Atlantic Cttee, 1969; Management Cttee, Haileybury and ISC Junior Sch., Windsor; Life Governor and Mem. Council, Haileybury and Imperial Service College, 1959. DL Greater London, 1970-. *Address:* 145 Marsham Court, Marsham Street, SW1. *Clubs:* White's, United Service; Wentworth (Virginia Water, Surrey); RN Sailing Association; RN Ski.

**BRIGHTMAN, Hon. Sir John (Anson),** Kt 1970; **Hon. Mr Justice Brightman;** Judge of the High Court of Justice, Chancery Division, since 1970; *b* 20 June 1911; 2nd *s* of William Henry Brightman, St Albans, Herts; *m* 1945, Roxane Ambatielo; one *s. Educ:* Marlborough College; St John's College, Cambridge. Called to the Bar, 1932; QC 1961. RNVR (Lieut-Commander), 1940-46; Assistant Naval Attaché, Ankara, 1944. Attorney-General of the Duchy of Lancaster, and Attorney and Serjeant within the County Palatine of Lancaster, 1969-70. Member, General Council of the Bar, 1956-60, 1966-70; Bencher, Lincoln's Inn, 1966. *Recreations:* sailing, ski-ing, travel. *Address:* 45 Parkside, Knightsbridge, SW1. *T:* 01-235 1125; Hurstbourne Tarrant, Andover, Hants. *T:* Hurstbourne Tarrant 280.

**BRIGINSHAW, Richard William;** General Secretary, National Society of Operative Printers and Assistants since 1951, and subsequently Joint General Secretary since 1966 of Society of Graphical and Allied Trades (as a result of amalgamation of Nat. Society of Operative Printers and Assistants with Nat. Union of Printing, Bookbinding and Paper Workers); Vice-President, Printing and Kindred Trades Federation since 1961 (Mem. Exec. Council, 1951-); Mem. General Council of TUC since 1965; *b* Lambeth; married. *Educ:* Stuart School, London. Later studied economics, trade union and industrial law. Elected Asst. Secretary, London Machine Branch of Union, 1938. Joined Services, 1940; subseq. in Army, saw service overseas in India, Iraq, Persia, Palestine, Egypt, France, etc.; left Army, 1946. Returned to printing trade; re-elected to full-time trade union position, 1949. Pres. of two London Confs on World Trade Development, 1963. Member: Joint Committee on Manpower, 1965-; Bd of Govs, Dulwich Coll., 1967-; Court, Cranfield Inst. of Technology. Hon. LLD New Brunswick, 1968. *Publications:* (two booklets): Britain's World Rating; Britain and the World Trade Conference. *Recreations:* swimming, painting, music. *Address:* SOGAT House, 13/16 Borough Road, SE1. *T:* 01-928 1481.

**BRIGSTOCKE, Geoffrey Reginald William;** Under-Secretary, Board of Trade, since 1970; *b* 4 Aug. 1917; *s* of late C. R. Brigstocke, CB, and late Dora Constance Bowen-Davies; *m* 1952, Heather Renwick Brown; three *s* one *d. Educ:* Charterhouse School; Magdalene College, Cambridge. Served Army, 1939-47. Secretary, Transport Directorate, Berlin, CCG, 1946-48; Asst Principal, Foreign Office (German Section), 1948-50; Principal, Ministry of Transport, 1950-60; Assistant Secretary, 1960; Shipping Attaché, Washington, 1960-64; Board of Trade, 1964-67; Under-Sec., Min. of Transport, 1967-70. *Address:* 35 Warwick Gardens, W14. *T:* 01-603 2335.

**BRIGSTOCKE, George Edward;** *m* 1942, Mary Sandford; two *s. Educ:* Marlborough; Keble College, Oxford; Wells Theological College. BA 1913; MA 1923. Deacon, 1914; Priest, 1915; Provost of St Nicholas Cathedral and Vicar of Newcastle upon Tyne, 1938-47; Principal, College of the Venerable Bede, Durham, 1947-59; Canon Residentiary, Durham Cathedral, 1959-61. Examining Chaplain to the Archbishop of Canterbury, 1961-65. Received into the Roman Catholic Church, 1965. *Address:* The Barn House, Elofts, Thorner, Leeds.

**BRILLANT, Jules-André;** CBE 1944; ED; Hon. Colonel, St Lawrence Fusiliers; MLC, Province Quebec 1942-68; *b* St Octave de Métis, 30 June 1888; *s* of Joseph Brillant and Rose Raiche; *m* 1st, 1923, Rose Coulombe (*d* 1933); three *s* two *d*; 2nd, 1940, Agnes Villeneuve. *Educ:* University of St Joseph, NB. President: The Canada & Gulf Terminal Railway Co. Ltd, 1947; The Bonaventure and Gaspe Telephone Co., 1953; Chairman, Les Prévoyants du Canada, 1965-70; Hon. President and Director, Québec-Téléphone, 1967; Hon. President, Administration and Trust Company (Société d'Administration et de Fiducie); Vice-President and Founder, Rimouski Technical and Marine Schools, 1936; Director, Canada Wire & Cable Co. Ltd, 1961-69. Prominent in industrial and commercial affairs for many years; Co-ordinator in Committee of Reconstruction at Ottawa; Director of Communications for defence of Country (War of 1939-45); President Conseil d'Orientation Economique du Québec, 1943-46; Hon. Member Red Cross Society (Quebec Provincial Division); Member, Newcomen Society of England. Bachelor in Commercial Sciences (*hc*), St Joseph University, Memramcook, NB, 1939; LLD (*hc*), St Joseph University, 1942; Doctor in Commercial Sciences (*hc*); Montreal Univ., 1943; Univ. of Moncton, NB, 1967; Dr in Social Sciences (*hc*), St Louis Univ., Edmundston, NB; Dr of The University, Montreal University, 1959. Liberal. Roman Catholic; Commander Order of St Grégoire le Grand, 1949; Knight of Honor, and Devotion, Sovereign Military Order of Malta (Canada Assoc.). *Address:*Rimouski, PQ, Canada. *Clubs:* Garrison (Quebec); Newcomen Society of England (Montreal).

**BRIMELOW, Sir Thomas,** KCMG 1968 (CMG 1959); OBE 1954; Deputy Under-Secretary of State, Foreign and Commonwealth Office, since 1969; *b* 25 Oct. 1915; *s* of late William Brimelow and Hannah Smith; *m* 1945, Jean E. Cull; two *d. Educ:* New Mills Grammar School; Oriel College, Oxford. Laming Travelling Fellow of the Queen's College, Oxford, 1937. Probationer Vice-Consul, Danzig, 1938; served in Consulate, Riga, 1939 Acting Consul, 1940; served in Consulate-Gen., New York, 1940; in charge of Consular Section of Embassy, Moscow, 1942-45; Foreign Office, 1945; Foreign Service Officer, Grade 7, 1946; First Sec. (Commercial), and Consul, Havana, 1948, Chargé d'Affaires, 1948, 1949 and 1951; trans. to Moscow, 1951; Counsellor (Commercial), Ankara, 1954; Head of Northern Department of the Foreign Office, 1956; Counsellor, Washington, 1960-63; Minister, British Embassy, Moscow, 1963-66; Ambassador to Poland, 1966-69. *Address:* 12 West Hill Court, Millfield Lane, N6. *Club:* Athenæum.

**BRINCKMAN, Colonel Sir Roderick (Napoleon);** 5th Bt, *cr* 1831; DSO 1940; MC 1941; *b* 27 Dec. 1902; 2nd *s* of Colonel Sir Theodore Brinckman, 3rd Bt, CB; *S* brother 1954; *m* 1st, 1931, Margaret Southam, Ottawa, Canada; two *s*; 2nd, 1942, Rosemary Marguerite Gilbey, *yr d* of late Lt-Col J. C. Hope Vere, Blackwood, Lanarkshire; one *d. Educ:* Osborne; Dartmouth. Served in Royal Navy two years (HMS Temeraire, Barham); joined Grenadier Guards in 1922; ADC to Lord

Somers (Governor of Victoria), 1926-27; ADC to Lord Willingdon (Governor-General of Canada), 1930-31; served in Egypt, 1931-32, and France, 1940 (DSO, MC, despatches); commanded 2nd (Armoured) Bn Grenadier Guards, 1943; Chief of Staff Military Mission in Moscow, 1944-45; head of British Military Mission to the Netherlands Government in London, 1945-46. *Heir: s* Theodore George Roderick Brinckman [*b* 20 March 1932; *m* 1958, Helen Mary Anne, *d* of A. E. Cook, Toronto; two *s* one *d*]. *Address:* Mornington House, Parkside, Wimbledon Common. *T:* 01-946 2124; Crosskeys, Sandwich, Kent; St Helena, Barbados, BWI. *Clubs:* White's, Turf.

**BRIND, Maj.-Gen. Peter Holmes Walter;** CBE 1962 (OBE 1948); DSO 1945; DL; Director, Surrey Branch, British Red Cross Society, since 1968; *b* 16 Feb. 1912; *yr s* of late General Sir John Brind, KCB, KBE, CMG, DSO; *m* 1942, Patricia Stewart Walker, *er d* of late Comdr S. M. Walker, DSC, RN, Horsalls, Harrietsham, Kent; three *s*. *Educ:* Wellington College; RMC, Sandhurst. Commissioned Dorset Regt, 1932. ADC to Governor of Bengal, 1936-39; Adjt, NW Europe, 1940; GSO 3 War Office, 1940-41; DAAG, HQ 12 Corps and Canadian Corps, 1941-42; Bde Major 1942; GSO 2 (MO) War Office, 1942; Comdt, Battle School, 1944, Comdg 2 Devons, NW Europe, 1944-45, GSO 1 (MT) War Office, 1946; GSO 1 (Ops), Palestine, 1948; GSO 1 (Plans), Egypt, 1949; GSO 1 (SD), War Office, 1950-54; Bt Lt-Col, 1952; Comdg 5th KAR (Kenya), 1954; Lt-Col, 1954; Col, 1955; Comdg 5 Inf. Bde Gp (BAOR), 1956; IDC 1959; Brig., 1960; Brig., AQ Middle East, 1960; BGS Eastern Comd, 1962; ADC to the Queen, 1964; Maj.-Gen., 1965; Ch. of Staff, Northern Comd, 1965-67; Member, BIM 1967. Governor, St Catherine's School, 1968. DL Surrey, 1970. *Recreations:* sailing, ski-ng. *Address:* Pine Ridge, Hill Road, Haslemere, Surrey. *Club:* United Service.

**BRINDLE, Professor Harry;** Professor of Pharmacy, Manchester University, 1946-55; Professor Emeritus, 1955; *m* Ellen Warburton; no *c*. *Educ:* Accrington Secondary School; King's College, London. Served European War, 1916-19, RAMC and RE. Principal, Manchester School of Pharmacy, 1920-28; Lecturer in Pharmaceutical Chemistry, Manchester University, 1928. Chairman British Pharmaceutical Conference, 1944, 1945. Examiner to Pharmaceutical Society of Gt Britain and a number of Universities, from 1925. *Publications:* many papers in Jl of Pharmacy and Pharmacology, Pharmaceutical Jl, Lancet, Analyst, British Medical Jl, etc. *Recreations:* golf, gardening. *Address:* Tintagel, Park Hill Road, Hale, Cheshire. *T:* 061-980 3461.

**BRINDLEY, Giles Skey,** MA, MD; FRS 1965; Professor of Physiology in the University of London at the Institute of Psychiatry, since 1968; Hon. Director, Medical Research Council Neurological Prostheses Research Unit, since 1968; *b* 30 April 1926; *s* of Arthur James Benet Skey and Dr Margaret Beatrice Marion Skey (*née* Dewhurst), later Brindley; *m* 1st, 1959, Lucy Dunk Bennell (marr. diss.); 2nd, 1964, Dr Hilary Richards; one *s* one *d*. *Educ:* Leyton County High School; Downing College, Cambridge; London Hospital Medical College. Fellow of King's College, Cambridge, 1959-62; Fellow of Trinity College, Cambridge, 1963-68; Hon. Fellow of Downing Coll., Cambridge, 1969-. Chm. of Editorial Board, Journal of Physiology, 1964-66 (Member 1959-64). Visiting Prof., Univ. of California, Berkeley, 1968. *Publications:* Physiology of the Retina and Visual Pathway, 1960, 2nd edn 1970; papers in scientific, musicological and medical journals. *Recreations:* climbing, ski-ing, playing various musical instruments, studying obscure languages. *Address:* 102 Ferndene Road, SE24. *T:* 01-274 2598.

**BRINK, Professor Charles Oscar,** FBA 1964; MA Oxford, MA Cambridge, PhD Berlin; Kennedy Professor of Latin in the University of Cambridge since 1954, and Fellow of Gonville and Caius College, since 1955; *b* 13 March 1907; *m* 1942, Daphne Hope Harvey; three *s*. *Educ:* School and University, Berlin; Travelling Scholarship, Oxford. Member of editorial staff, Thesaurus linguæ Latinæ, 1933-38; Member of editorial staff, Oxford Latin Dictionary, 1938-41; Acting Classical Tutor, Magdalen College, Oxford, 1941-45; Member of Faculty of Literæ Humaniores, Oxford, 1941-48; Senior Classics Master, Magdalen College School, Oxford, 1943-48; Senior Lecturer in Humanity, University of St Andrews, 1948-51; Professor of Latin, University of Liverpool, 1951-54. Member Inst. for Advanced Study, Princeton, US, 1960-61, 1966. De Carle Lecturer, University of Otago, NZ, 1965. Hon. Member, Jt Assoc. of Classical Teachers (Pres. 1969-). Chm., Classics Committee, Schools Council, 1965-69. *Publications:* Imagination and Imitation (Inaug. Lect., Liverpool, 1952), 1953; Latin Studies and the Humanities (Inaug. Lect., Cambridge, 1956), 1957; Horace on Poetry: vol. I, Prolegomena, 1963; vol. II, The Ars Poetica, 1970; On reading a Horatian Satire, 1965; papers on Latin and Greek subjects. *Address:* Gonville and Caius College, Cambridge.

**BRINK, Lt-Gen. George Edwin,** CB 1941; CBE 1942; DSO 1917; South African Permanent Force (retired list); *b* Jagersfontein, OFS, 27 Sept. 1889; *m* 1919, Lilian Alice de Villiers; three *d*. *Educ:* Grey College, Bloemfontein. Served European War, 1914-18 in German South-West Africa and in German East Africa (despatches thrice, DSO, French Croix de Guerre); War of 1939-45, served Abyssinia, Egypt, and Cyrenaica as GOC, 1st SA Division (CB, CBE); GOC Inland Area, South Africa, 1942-43; Director-General of Demobilisation, South Africa, 1944-48. Chm., SA Ex-Services National Council; Mem., SA War Histories Adv. Cttee. KStJ 1944. *Address:* PO Box 101, St Michaels-on-Sea, South Coast, Natal, South Africa.

**BRINKWORTH, George Harold,** CBE 1960; Principal Assistant Solicitor, Department of Health and Social Security (formerly Ministry of Social Security) since 1965; *b* 16 Nov. 1906; *yr s* of George Alban Brinkworth and Hana Mary Brinkworth; *m* 1935, Dorothy Betty Suffield; one *s* one *d*. *Educ:* Wimbledon College; University College, London. LLB (Lond.) 1927. Admitted Solicitor, 1931. Entered Solicitor's Dept, Ministry of Labour, 1935; transf. to Ministry of Nat. Insce, 1945; Asst Solicitor, Min. of Pensions and Nat. Insce, 1948. *Address:* The Coach House, Doods Road, Reigate, Surrey. *T:* Reigate 46121.

**BRINSON, Derek Neilson,** MC 1944; HM Diplomatic Service; Head of Guidance Department since 1969 and Information Policy Department since 1970, Foreign and Commonwealth Office; *b* 23 June 1921; 2nd *s* of late H. N. Brinson, DSO, OBE and of Mrs V. M. Brinson; *m* 1st, 1954, Muna Samy; 2nd, 1958, Prudence Elizabeth Wheeler. *Educ:* Bradfield; Hertford Coll., Oxford. Welsh Guards, 1941-46. FO, 1949; 2nd Sec., Rome, 1951; FO, 1953; 1st Sec., 1954; 1st Sec. and Head of Chancery, Saigon, 1957 (acted as Chargé d'Affaires, 1958 and 1959); 1st Sec., later Head of Chancery, UK Delegns Nuclear Tests, Laos and Disarmament Confs, Geneva, 1960-64; FO, 1964; Counsellor, 1964; Counsellor and Head of Chancery, Caracas, 1965 (acted as Chargé d'Affaires, 1968). *Address:* 1 Sloane Square, SW1. *T:* 01-730 5689. *Clubs:* Guards, Pratt's.

**BRINTON, Denis Hubert,** DM Oxon; FRCP; retired; *b* 9 Dec. 1902; *er s* of Hubert Brinton, Eton College; *m* 1928, Joan Violet, *d* of James A. Hood; one *s* (and one *s* decd). *Educ:* Eton; New College, Oxford University; St Mary's Hospital, London University. MRCS, LRCP 1927; BM, BCh, 1928; MRCP 1929; DM Oxon 1937; FRCP 1938. Served War of 1939-45 (despatches), Air Commodore, RAF, Consultant in Neuropsychiatry. Member Internat. Neurological Congress, London, 1935; Physician-in-charge, Department of Nervous Diseases, St Mary's Hospital, 1935-63; Dean, St Mary's Hospital Medical School, 1946-51; Physician, National Hospital for Nervous Diseases, 1935-65; Council RCP, 1956-59. Member Assoc. British Neurologists; Member Assoc. Physicians Great Britain; Ed. Quart. Jl Med., 1954-68. *Publications:* Cerebrospinal Fever, 1941; articles in medical jls. *Address:* 35 Bryanston Square, W1. *T:* 01-262 8687; Bromfields, Vereley Lane, Burley, Hants. *T:* Burley 2319. *Clubs:* Athenæum, Garrick.

**BRINTON, Major Sir (Esme) Tatton (Cecil),** Kt 1964; DL; MP (C) Kidderminster since 1964; Chairman, Brintons Ltd, Kidderminster, since 1968 (Joint Managing Director, since 1952); *b* 4 Jan. 1916; *o s* of Colonel Cecil Charles Brinton, JP, and Cathleen Cecil Brinton (*née* Maude); *m* 1st, 1938, Mary Elizabeth Fahnestock (*d* 1960); four *s* one *d*; 2nd, 1961, Mrs Irene Sophie Borthwick. *Educ:* Eton; Caius College, Cambridge; and in Vienna and Paris. Served with XIIth R. Lancers, France, Desert, Italy, 1939-45. Technical Intelligence, Germany, 1945-46. Contested (C) Dudley, 1945; Mayor of Kidderminster, 1953-54; High Sheriff of Worcestershire, 1961-62; Chm., Kidderminster Conservative Assoc., 1955-56 and 1958-61. Joint Treasurer of the Conservative Party, 1966-. Chm., Home Exec. Cttee., Federation of British Carpet Manfrs, 1960-64; Chm. British Carpets Promotion Council, 1960-66. DL Worcs., 1968. OStJ 1962. *Address:* Kyrewood House, Tenbury Wells, Worcs. *T:* Tenbury Wells 736; 34 de Vere Gardens, W8. *T:* 01-937 5727. *Clubs:* Carlton, Bath; Worcestershire (Worcester).

**BRINTON, Sir Tatton;** *see* Brinton, Sir E. T. C.

**BRISBANE, Archbishop of,** since 1970 (Metropolitan of Queensland); **Most Rev. Felix Raymond Arnott,** MA (Oxon); ThD; MACE; *b* Ipswich, Suffolk, 8 March 1911; *s* of late Richard Girling Arnott, Ipswich; *m* 1938, Anne Caroline, *d* of W. A. P. Lane, Kingston Gorse, Sussex; two *s* two *d*. *Educ:* Ipswich Sch.; Keble Coll., Oxford; Cuddesdon Theol Coll. Curate, Elland, Yorks, 1934-38; Exam. Chaplain, Bp of Wakefield, 1936-39; Vice-Princ., Cheshunt, 1938; Warden, St John's Coll., Brisbane, 1939-46; Warden, St Paul's Coll., Univ. of Sydney, 1946-63; Lectr i/c of Ecclesiastical History, Univ. of Sydney, 1951-63; a Co-Adjutor Bishop of Melbourne, 1963-70. Mem., Monash Univ. Council, 1964-. A Founder of Blake Prize for Religious Art, 1951. *Publications:* The Anglican Via Media in the Seventeenth Century, 1948; contribs to learned jls. *Recreations:* walking, music, golf. *Address:* Bishopsbourne, Hamilton, Queensland 4007, Australia. *Clubs:* Melbourne, Royal Automobile (Victoria); Australian (Sydney); Royal Sydney Golf.

**BRISBANE, Archbishop of, (RC),** since 1965; **Most Rev. Patrick Mary O'Donnell;** *b* Fethard, Co. Tipperary, 2 Feb. 1897; *y s* of Thomas O'Donnell and Johanna Sheehan. *Educ:* Mungret College, Limerick; Pontificio Collegio Urbano, Rome. Priest, 1922; staff of St Mary's Cathedral, Sale, Victoria; Administrator of St Mary's Cathedral, Sale, 1928-37; Pastor, Leongatha, 1937-46; Pastor, Warragul, 1946-49; Vicar General of Sale Dio., 1941; Domestic Prelate to the Pope, 1944; Titular Archbishop of Pelusium and Coadjutor Archbishop of Brisbane, 1949-65. Member Senate, University of Queensland, 1965-. *Recreations:* walking, reading. *Address:* Glengariff, Derby Street, Hendra, Brisbane, Australia. *T:* Brisbane 682327.

**BRISBANE, Coadjutor Bishop of;** *see* Hudson, Rt Rev. Wilfrid John.

**BRISBANE, Dean of;** *see* Muschamp, Rt Rev. Cecil Emerson Barron.

**BRISCO, Sir Donald Gilfrid,** 8th Bt *cr* 1782; JP; *b* 15 Sept. 1920; *s* of Sir Hylton (Musgrave Campbell) Brisco, 7th Bt and Kathleen, *d* of W. Fenwick McAllum, New Zealand; *S* father, 1968; *m* 1945, Irene, *o d* of Henry John Gage, Ermine Park, Brockworth, Gloucestershire; three *d*. Served War of 1939-45 with Royal New Zealand Air Force and Royal Air Force (prisoner of war in Germany and Italy). Retired Farmer. JP Hawke's Bay, 1967. *Heir: uncle* Oriel Arthur Brisco [*b* 6 June 1892; *m* 1921, Lilian Frederica, *d* of E. E. D. Saunderson, Linwood, Christchurch, New Zealand]. *Address:* Longworth, Havelock North, Hawke's Bay, New Zealand.

**BRISCOE, Capt. Henry Villiers,** CIE 1945; OBE 1943; RN (retd); *b* 9 Nov. 1896; *s* of late Maj. A. V. Briscoe, late RA, and G. M. Briscoe; *m* 1925, Lily Miller, *widow* (*decd*); one *s*; *m* 1948, Adaline Mary, *d* of Adam McIntosh, South Bantaskine, Falkirk, Stirling. *Educ:* Yarlet Hall, Staffs; RN Colleges, Osborne and Dartmouth. Royal Navy, 1909-22: Commercial Employment, 1922-31. Colonial Civil Servant, 1931-51; recalled to RN 1941-45; retd from Colonial Service, 1951. *Address:* Flat 3, Balmoral House, Bugibba, St Paul's Bay, Malta, GC.

**BRISCOE, Sir John (Leigh Charlton),** 4th Bt *cr* 1910; DFC 1945; Director of Operations, British Airports Authority, since 1966; *b* 3 Dec. 1911; *er s* of Sir Charlton Briscoe, 3rd Bt, MD, FRCP, and Grace Maud, *d* of late Rev. W. S. Stagg; *S* father 1960; *m* 1948, Teresa Mary Violet, *d* of late Brig.-Gen. Sir Archibald Home, KCVO, CB, CMG, DSO; two *s* one *d*. *Educ:* Harrow; Magdalen College, Oxford, BA 1933; ACA 1937; MA 1951. Served War of 1939-45 (DFC); RAFVR, 1942-46; Director of Aerodromes, Ministry of Aviation, 1961-66. *Recreations:* old cars, castles, and carpets. *Heir: s* John James Briscoe, *b* 15 July 1951. *Address:* Little Acres, Grays Park Road, Stoke Poges, Bucks. *T:* Farnham Common 2394.

**BRISE, Sir John A. R.;** *see* Ruggles-Brise.

**BRISSON, Mrs F.;** *see* Russell, Rosalind.

**BRISTOL,** 6th Marquess of, *cr* 1826; **Victor Frederick Cochrane Hervey;** Baron Hervey, 1703; Earl of Bristol, 1714; Earl Jermyn, 1826; *b* 6 Oct. 1915; *s* of 5th Marquess of Bristol; *S* father 1960; *m* 1st, 1949, Pauline Mary (marr. diss., 1959), *d* of late Herbert Coxon Bolton; one *s*; 2nd, 1960, Lady Anne Juliet Wentworth Fitzwilliam, *o c* of 8th Earl Fitzwilliam, DSC, and of Olive Countess Fitzwilliam, Co. Wicklow; one *s*. *Educ:* Eton; Royal Military

College. The Hereditary High Steward of the Liberty of St Edmund; Patron of 30 Livings; has estates in W. and E. Suffolk, Lincs, Essex. President: Nat. Yacht Harbour Assoc.; Bristol Soc.; Vice Pres., Income Tax Payers' Union; Member: West India Cttee; Monday Club; Grand Council, Monarchist League. Chairman: Ickworth Forestry Contractors Ltd; Estate Associates Ltd; Sleaford Investments Ltd; Eastern Caravan Parks Ltd; The Bristol Publishing Company; Ickworth Automatic Sales Ltd; Radio Marina; British International Airways Ltd; British Powersport Co.; Dominica Paradise Ltd; Marquis of Bristol & Co.; VLC Associates Ltd. Owner of the Ickworth Stud. *Recreations:* yachting, shooting and antiques. *Heir: s* Earl Jermyn, *qv. Address:* 15 Chapel Street, Belgrave Square, SW1; (seat) Ickworth, Bury St Edmunds, Suffolk. *Clubs:* United Hunts, Hurlingham, Eccentric, Royal Worlington Golf, House of Lords Yacht; East Hill (Nassau).

**BRISTOL, Bishop of,** since 1959; **Rt. Rev. Oliver Stratford Tomkins,** MA, DD; *b* 9 June 1908; *s* of Rev. Leopold Charles Fellows Tomkins and Mary Katie (*née* Stratford); *m* 1939, Ursula Mary Dunn; one *s* three *d. Educ:* Trent Coll; Christ's Coll, Cambridge; Westcott House, Cambridge. Asst Gen. Sec., Student Christian Movement, 1933-40, and Editor Student Movement Magazine, 1937-40. Deacon, 1935; Priest, 1936; Vicar of Holy Trinity, Millhouses, Sheffield, 1940-45; an Associate Gen. Sec. World Council of Churches and Sec. of its Commission on Faith and Order, 1945-52; Warden of Lincoln Theological College (Scholæ Cancellarii) and Canon and Prebend, Lincoln Cathedral, 1953-59. Mem., Central and Exec. Cttees, World Council of Churches, 1968-. DD (*hon. causa*) Edinburgh University, 1953. *Publications:* The Wholeness of the Church, 1949; The Church in the Purpose of God, 1950. Editor and contributor The Universal Church in God's Design, 1948; Intercommunion, 1951; (Ed.) Faith and Order (Lund Conference Report), 1953: Life of E. S. Woods, Bishop of Lichfield, 1957; A Time for Unity, 1964. *Recreations:* family life and frivolous reading. *Address:* Bishop's House, Bristol BS8 1BW. *T:* 30222. *Club:* Athenæum.

**BRISTOL, Dean of;** *see* Harrison, Very Rev. D. E. W.

**BRISTOL, Archdeacon of;** *see* Williams, Ven. Leslie Arthur.

**BRISTOL, Major Everett,** CMG 1918; QC (Ont), 1928; *b* Hamilton, Ontario, 21 Oct. 1888; *s* of late George Everett Bristol and Margaret White; *m* 1919, Helen Francis, *o d* of late F. H. and Mrs Mathewson, Montreal; two *d. Educ:* Royal Military College of Canada; University of Toronto (BA); Osgoode Hall Law School, Toronto. On Reserve of Officers, Canada, 1908; called to Bar, Ontario, 1914, and practised till outbreak of war; 2nd Lieut 13th Hussars (Imperials), 7 Sept. 1914; Lieut, 15th Batt. 48th Highlanders (Canadian Infantry) June 1915; Capt. Aug. 1915; wounded, Dec. 1915; Major, Dec. 1916; retired from Canadian Forces, Aug. 1919, and practised as barrister in Toronto until 1970; was Military Secretary to Minister of Overseas Military Forces of Canada. *Recreations:* golf, riding. *Address:* University Club, 380 University Avenue, Toronto, Ontario. *Clubs:* University, Toronto, Toronto Golf (Toronto).

**BRISTOW, Alan Edgar,** OBE 1966; Chairman, Bristow Helicopters Ltd, since 1967; *b* 3 Sept. 1923; *m* 1945; one *s* one *d. Educ:* Portsmouth Grammar School. Cadet, British India Steam Navigation Co., 1939-43; Pilot, Fleet Air Arm, 1943-46; Test Pilot, Westland Aircraft Ltd, 1946-49; Helicopair, Paris/Indo-China, 1949-51; Man. Dir, Air Whaling Ltd (Antarctic Whaling Expedns), 1951-54; Man. Dir, Bristow Helicopters Ltd, 1954-68; Dir, British United Airways Ltd, 1960-70, Man. Dir 1967-70. Cierva Memorial Lectr, RAeS, 1967. FRAeS 1967. Croix de Guerre (France), 1950. *Publications:* papers to RAeS. *Recreations:* flying, golf, shooting, sailing, farming. *Address:* Baynards Park Estate, Cranleigh, Surrey. *T:* Cranleigh 2091. *Clubs:* Royal Aero, Lansdowne.

**BRISTOW, Hon. Sir Peter (Henry Rowley),** Kt 1970; **Hon. Mr Justice Bristow;** a judge of the High Court, Queen's Bench Division, since 1970; *b* 1 June 1913; *s* of Walter Rowley Bristow and Florence (*née* White); *m* 1940, Josephine Noel Leney (*d* 1969); one *s* one *d. Educ:* Eton; Trinity College, Cambridge. Served with RAFVR, 1939-45. Called to the Bar, 1936; Bencher, Middle Temple, 1961; QC 1964; Mem., inns of Court Senate, 1966-70 (Hon. Treas., 1967-70); Judge, Court of Appeal, Guernsey, and Court of Appeal, Jersey, 1965-; Dep. Chm., Hants QS, 1964-. Mem., home Secretary's Cttee on Privacy, 1970-. *Recreation:* sailing. *Address:* Queen Elizabeth Building, Temple, EC4; 13 Pelham Crescent, SW7. *Clubs:* Brooks's, Royal Ocean Racing.

**BRISTOWE, William Syer,** MA, ScD Cantab; *b* 1 Sept. 1901; *s* of Bertram Arthur Bristowe and Mary Rosa (*née* Johnston), Stoke d'Abernon, Surrey; *m* 1934, Helen Mary Harper (marr. diss., 1962); three *d* (and one *d* decd). *Educ:* Wellington Coll; Cambridge. Cambridge Scientific Expeditions to Jan Mayen, 1921, and Brazil, 1923. Joined Brunner Mond, 1925, subsequently merged in ICI 1926; Head of Far East Department, 1936, and Director of Eastern subsidiary companies; Head of Central Staff Department, 1948-62. Member ECA special productivity mission to USA studying education and the employment of graduates, 1950; Member FBI cttee studying shortage of science teachers, 1954. Pres. Ray Society, 1959-62; Master of Armourers and Braziers, 1965-66; Member, Court of City University. Stamford Raffles Award for Zoology, 1961. *Publications:* The Comity of Spiders, 2 vols, 1939-41; Spiders, 1947; The World of Spiders, 1958; Victorian China Fairings, 1964; Natural History of the Garden of Buckingham Palace (pt author), 1964; Queen Emma, Harbinger of the Norman Conquest, 1966; A Book of Islands, 1969; occasional papers on athletics, explorations, early naturalists, giants, Sherlock Holmes and staff management. *Recreations:* lawn tennis, visiting small islands, studies of Viking and Saxon history, Siamese history, Arctic Exploration, genealogy, folklore and curios, biological research; formerly athletics (Camb. Blue, 1922-24; Pres. CUAC, 1924; Capt. Jt Oxf. and Camb. Team to USA, 1924), Rugby football (Harlequins and Sale). *Address:* Mill House, Whatlington, Battle, Sussex.

**BRITISH COLUMBIA, Bishop of,** and **(Hon.) Assistant Bishop of;** *see* Columbia, British.

**BRITISH HONDURAS, Bishop of;** *see* Honduras.

**BRITTAIN, Sir Harry E.,** KBE 1918; CMG 1924; DL, LLD, MA; Barrister-at-Law; *b* 24 Dec. 1873; *e s* of late W. H. Brittain, Storth Oaks, Sheffield; *m* 1st 1905, Alida Luisa, DBE (*d* 1943), *o d* of Sir Robert Harvey; one *s* one *d*; 2nd, 1961, Muriel Leslie, *d* of H. Leslie Dixon, *Educ:* Repton; Worcester Coll, Oxford, BA

1896 (hons in Law), MA 1898. Went through business trng in Sheffield; late Lieut 4th W. York Volunteer Artillery; called to Bar, Inner Temple, 1897, practised successfully for one week, then retd from the Law; former Dir numerous daily and weekly newspapers and other business concerns; First MP (U), Acton, 1918-29; since foundn in 1902, active head of The Pilgrims' Club for 17 years; resigned Chairmanship, 1918; now senr Vice-Pres.; Co-Chm. with US Chm., Internat. Cttee to commemorate 100 yrs of Peace between Gt Britain and the USA, 1912-14; Member Sulgrave Manor Board; Vice-President ESU, 1918; joined Sir C. Arthur Pearson and worked with him in formation of Tariff Reform League, and creation of Tariff Commn, also joining staff of Standard and Evening Standard, 1902; Chm. Political Cttee Constitutional Club, 1920-21; Chm. Middx. Div. of Conservative Assoc., 1926; Vice-Pres. 1927 and Hon. Mem., 1961, Royal Commonwealth Soc.; a founder and Mem. Coun., Oxford Soc., 1932; originated and organised first Imperial Press Conf., 1909; presentation portrait by Sir Wm Orpen from UK Press; Founder and Hon. Life Mem. Empire (now Commonwealth) Press Union. Opened Golden Jubilee Conf., 1959. Hon. LLD McGill for Service to Empire. In Rio on Mission to Brazilian Government, Dec. 1912 to Feb. 1913. Member Canadian and Australian War Contingent Committees, and Chairman Belgium Finance Committee, 1914; British Representative on Amer. Citizens Emergency Cttee, Aug. 1914; on special mission throughout the USA, 1915; Capt. Co. of London Vol. Regt, 1916, on staff Gen. Lloyd; Dir Intell. Nat. Service Dept; Founder and Chm. Amer. Officers' Club in London, 1917-19; Originator, and Hon. Life Mem., Assoc. of Amer. Correspondents in London, 1919; Coun. Brit. Olympic Assoc., British Rep. and British Ski Club Rep. at Chamonix, 1924; President, Anglo-Amer. delegation to Holland for celebrations of Pilgrim Fathers Tercentenary 1920; Pres., British Internat. Association of Journalists, 1920-22, and took delegates to Czecho-Slovakia, Holland, Belgium, and Roumania as guests of respective States; Pres., Press Golfing Soc., 1953; Patron, Soc. of Women Writers and Journalists, 1925-; Mem. Exec. and Publicity Coun., Brit. Empire Exhibn, representing House of Commons, and Chm. Press Hospitality Cttee, 1924; originator and Chm. Reception Cttee, 1st Conf. Students of Univs of the Empire, 1924; Mem. Exec., Empire Parly Assoc., 1919-29, Mem., Commonwealth Parly Assoc., 1929-. For protection of British Birds, steered through Parliament the Brittain Act, passed May, 1925; subseq. (with Prime Minister Baldwin), unveiled Hudson Memorial in Bird Sanctuary, Hyde Park. A Founder and Mem. Coun., British Travel Assoc., and Chm. Publicity Cttee, 1929-31, Travel Cttee, 1939-45, Membership Cttee, 1947; London Chamber of Commerce; Mem. Coun., 1930-51; 1st Chm. Civil Aviation Sect., 1929. Deleg. of Brit. Nat. Cttee, on subject of Air Transport at Congress of Internat. Chambers of Commerce, Washington, 1931, and Vienna, 1933; Co-founder and Hon. Pres., McGill Soc. of GB, 1936-50; Hon. Pres., Friends of Italy, 1936-39; Pres., Schoolboys' Exhibn, 1936-62; President Incorporated Sales Managers' Association (now Institute of Marketing), 1938-44; Vice Pres., Inst. of Export, Chm. Bd St George's School, Harpenden, 1938-47; Chm., Open Air Theatres Cttee, 1939; Mem., Central Council of Welfare, ATC, 1941-62; Mem., Inter-Parly Union, 1942-; Hon. Life Mem., Canadian Legion, 1958, for Service to Canada; Hon. Mem. Soc. of Americans in London; Trustee, Westminster Fund (responsible for Churchill Club, Dean's Yard, and weekly courses for Overseas Service personnel at Balliol Coll., Oxford, 1943-48); Mem., Anglo-Amer. Brains Trust, 1942-44; Chm. Appeal Cttee to save Gilbert White's home at Selborne, 1953. Frequent Broadcaster in GB, US and Commonwealth; awarded Silver Medal of Merit and Diploma, by Poor Richard Club of Philadelphia for his lifelong services to Anglo-American fellowship and understanding, 1958; Mem. Council Economic League, 1946-; President, Old Reptonian Soc. 1950-51; Pres. Yorkshire Soc., and Soc. of Yorkshiremen in London, 1956-57; Hon. Member Inst. of Journalists, 1963-; Hon. Member Foreign Press Assoc., 1963-; admitted to Barbados Bar, 1969. Gold Staff Officer at Coronation, 1937; Freeman, City of London, 1938; Cross of Officer, Order of the Crown, for Services to Belgium during War of 1914-18; Comdr, White Lion of Czecho-Slovakia; Comdr, Star of Roumania. *Publications:* Canada: There and Back, 1908; To Verdun from the Somme, 1916; America and the German Menace, 1917; The ABC of the BBC, Romance of British Wireless, 1932; By Air, 1933; Wings of Speed, 1934; Austria Invites, 1936; Come the Three Corners, 1940; Pilgrim Partners, Forty Years of British American Fellowship, 1942; Pilgrims and Pioneers, an Autobiography, 1945; Happy Pilgrimage, Autobiography, 2nd vol., 1949; articles in London and other periodicals. *Recreations:* travel, gardening, golf, shooting. *Address:* 88 St James's Street, SW1. *T:* 01-839 3222; Headley, Hants *T:* Headley Down 2145. *Clubs:* Carlton, Bath, Pilgrims, Queen's; Hon. Member: American, Wig and Pen, Clambake (Newport, RI), 1900, Royal Commonwealth Society, English-Speaking Union.

**BRITTAIN, Rear-Admiral Wilfred Geoffrey,** CB 1956; CBE 1945; *b* 19 June 1903; *m* 1st, 1935, May Russell Shorto (*d* 1964); two *d*; 2nd, 1968, Mrs Mary Clifton, *d* of late Dennis Hughes. *Educ:* RNC Osborne and Dartmouth. Joined Royal Navy, 1917; Comdr 1939; Captain 1944; Rear-Adm. 1954; Retired 1957. Last appointment Flag Officer, Malta, and Admiral Superintendent, HM Dockyard, Malta, 1954-57. Officer, Legion of Merit, 1946. *Address:* 1 Little Stodham House, Liss, Hants. *T:* 3189.

**BRITTAIN, William James;** Chairman: Brittain Press Ltd; Brittain Publishing Co. (London) Ltd; Brittain Publishing Co. (Canada) Ltd; Editor, Time & Tide; Chairman: Time & Tide Ltd; London and Local Newspapers Ltd; Brittain Newspapers Ltd; Latin-American Trade Ltd; World Trade Publishing Co. Ltd; World Trade Magazines Ltd; Indicator Newspapers Ltd; West London Chronicle Ltd; Practical Banking Ltd; *b* 22 July 1905; *s* of late William James and Eliza Brittain; *m* 1929, Janet Carrick; one *d*. Hull Daily Mail; Liverpool Daily Courier; Night News Editor, Daily Mail, Manchester; Montreal Daily Star; Asst City Ed., Toronto Daily Star; Science Dir, Pall Mall Magazine; Evening News, London; Asst Ed., Sunday Express; Editor, Sunday Dispatch. *Publications:* This Man Beaverbrook; articles television and photo-telegraphy, Universal Encyclopædia; papers in scientific and other journals. *Address:* 5 Brocket Hall, Welwyn, Herts. *T:* Welwyn Garden 26440; 15 Byron Court, Mecklenburgh Square, WC1. *T:* 01-837 6007.

**BRITTAN, Samuel;** Economics Editor, Financial Times, since 1966; *b* 29 Dec. 1933; *s* of Joseph Brittan, MD, and Riva Brittan (*née* Lipetz). *Educ:* Kilburn Grammar Sch.; Jesus Coll., Cambridge. 1st Class in Economics, 1955; MA Cantab. Various posts in Financial Times, 1955-61; Economics Editor, Observer,

1961-64; Adviser, Dept of Economic Affairs, 1965. *Publications:* The Treasury under the Tories, 1964; Left or Right: The Bogus Dilemma, 1968; Steering the Economy, 1969 (rev. edn 1971); The Price of Economic Freedom, 1970; articles in various jls. *Address:* Flat 9, 58 Rutland Gate, SW7. *T:* 01-584 5509.

**BRITTEN, Benjamin;** *see* Britten, E. B.

**BRITTEN, Brigadier Charles Richard,** OBE 1966; MC 1916; DL, JP; Extra Gentleman Usher to the Queen, since 1955; *b* 25 June 1894; 2nd *s* of late Rear-Admiral R. F. Britten and Hon. Blanche Cecile Colville, *o d* of 11th Baron Colville of Culross; *m* 1915, Dorothy (*d* 1970), *d* of late Hon. P. Allsopp; one *s. Educ:* Eton; RMC Sandhurst. Served European War, 1914-19, and War of 1939-45; Grenadier Guards, 1914; Capt. 1917; Lieut-Col 1935; Bt. Col 1937; Col 1938; Brig. 1939; Comdg Grenadier Guards, 1937-39, and 1st (London) Infantry Bde, 1937-41; attached RAF, 1942; retired, 1946. Mem., Worcs CC, 1946 (CA 1963); Mem., Martley RDC, 1948. DL Worcs, 1947; High Sheriff of Worcs, 1952. *Recreations:* shooting, hunting and fishing. *Address:* Kenswick Manor, Worcester. *T:* Hallow 210. *Clubs:* Guards; Union and County (Worcester).

**BRITTEN, (Edward) Benjamin,** OM 1965; CH 1953; *b* Lowestoft, England, 22 Nov. 1913; *s* of Robert Victor and Edith Rhoda Britten. *Educ:* South Lodge Preparatory School; Gresham's School, Holt; Royal Coll. of Music, London; privately with Frank Bridge, Harold Samuel. Composer; pianist (recitals with Peter Pears); occasional conductor; Artist Dir, Aldeburgh Festival; Dir, English Opera Group. Worked with GPO film unit, 1935-37. Worked in America, 1939-42; Coolidge medal, 1941; founded, 1948, Aldeburgh Festival, with Peter Pears and Eric Crozier. Pres., National Youth Orchestra, 1968-. Freedom of: Borough of Lowestoft, 1953; Borough of Aldeburgh, 1962; Worshipful Co. of Musicians, 1965; Hon. Fellow, Magdalene Coll., Camb., 1965; Hon. Member: Accademia Nazionale di Santa Cecilia, Rome; Academie Royale des Sciences, des Lettres et des Beaux-Arts de Belgique; Royal Academy of Music, London; Akademie der Künste in Hamburg; Svenska Musicaliska Academiens, Vagnar; Amer. Acad. of Arts and Letters. National Instiute of Arts and Letters. Mus.Doc (*hc*): Univs of: Belfast 1954; Cambridge, 1959; Nottingham, 1961; Hull, 1962; Oxford, 1963; Manchester, 1964; London, 1964; Leicester, 1965. Awarded Hanseatic Goethe Prize, for 1961; Aspen Award, Colorado, USA, 1964; Royal Philharmonic Society's Gold Medal, 1964; Sibelius Prize, 1965; Mahler Medal of Honour (Bruckner and Mahler Soc. of America), 1967; Leonie Sonning Prize (Denmark), 1968. Commander of Royal Order of the Pole Star (Sweden), 1962. *Publications include:* On Receiving the First Aspen Award, 1964; *Operas:* Peter Grimes, The Rape of Lucretia, Albert Herring, The Beggar's Opera (new version), Let's make an Opera, Billy Budd, Gloriana, The Turn of the Screw, Noye's Fludde, A Midsummer Night's Dream, Curlew River, The Burning Fiery Furnace, The Golden Vanity, The Prodigal Son; *Choral works:* A Boy was Born, Ballad of Heroes, Hymn to St Cecilia, Ceremony of Carols, Rejoice in the Lamb, Saint Nicolas, Spring Symphony, Cantata Academica, Missa Brevis, War Requiem, Psalm 150, Cantata Misericordium, Voices for Today, The Building of the House, Children's Crusade; *Orchestral Works:* Simple Symphony, Sinfonietta, Soirées Musicales, Variations on a Theme of Frank Bridge, Mont Juic (with Lennox Berkeley), Piano Concerto No. 1, Violin Concerto No. 1, Matinées Musicales, Sinfonia da Requiem, Kermesse Canadienne, Diversions, Scottish Ballad, Young Person's Guide to the Orchestra, Prelude and Fugue, Prince of the Pagodas (ballet), Cello Symphony, Hankin Booby (Wind and Drums); *Chamber music:* Phantasy (Oboe Quartet), Violin Suite, 2 String Quartets, Lachrymae (Viola and Piano), Ovid Metamorphoses (Oboe Solo), Cello Sonata, Nocturnal after Dowland (for Guitar), 2 Suites for Cello, Gemini Variations, Harp Suite; *Song Cycles, etc:* Friday Afternoons, Our Hunting Fathers, On this Island, Holy Sonnets of John Donne, Les Illuminations, Seven Sonnets of Michelangelo, Serenade, 3 Canticles, Charm of Lullabies, Winter Words, Sechs Hölderlin Fragmente, Songs from the Chinese, Nocturne, Songs and Proverbs of William Blake, Poet's Echo; Anthems; Part-songs; Incidental music to plays and films; folk song arrangements; Purcell realisations, etc. *Recreations:* tennis, swimming, walking, bird-watching. *Address:* The Red House, Aldeburgh, Suffolk. *Club:* Aldeburgh Festival.

**BRITTEN, Brig. George Vallette,** CBE 1947 (OBE 1942, MBE 1940); retd from Army; Head of Chancery, British Embassy, Berne, since 1967; *b* 3 March 1909; *s* of John Britten, Bozeat Manor, Northamptonshire, and Elizabeth Franziska Britten (*née* Vallette); *m* 1937, Shirley Jean Stewart Wink; three *s. Educ:* Wellingborough; RMC Sandhurst. Regtl duty in UK, 1929-38; Staff Coll., Camberley, 1938-39. Served War: HQ 2 Corps, France and Belgium, 1939-40; Staff appts in UK, 1940-41; with 1st Airborne Div. in UK, N Africa and Sicily, 1942-43; DCS, 5(US) Army, N Africa and Italy, 1943-44; HQ, 21st Army Gp, NW Europe, 1944-45. DCS, Brit. Military Govt, Germany, 1945-47. Regtl Duty, Berlin and Austria, 1947-49; WO, 1949-51; Comdt, Sch. of Infty, Hythe, 1952-54; Instr, US Army Staff Coll., Kansas, 1954-56; Planning Staff, NATO, Fontainebleau, 1956-58; Mil. Attaché, Brit. Embassy, Bonn, 1958-61; Ghana Desk, Commonwealth Office, 1961-62; with British High Commissions, Enugu, Kaduna, and Bathurst, 1962-66. American Legion of Merit, 1946; W German Crosses Verdienst Kreuz, 1959. *Recreations:* riding, tennis, squash, rifle shooting, philately. *Address:* British Embassy, Thunstrasse 50, Berne. *T:* (031).44.50.21. *Club:* Army and Navy.

**BRITTEN, Rae Gordon;** HM Diplomatic Service; Head of Trade Policy Department, Foreign and Commonwealth Office, since 1968; *b* 27 Sept. 1920; *s* of Leonard Arthur Britten and Elizabeth Percival Taylor; *m* 1952, Valentine Alms; one *s* three *d. Educ:* Liverpool Institute High School; Magdalen College, Oxford. Served War 1941-45 (artillery and infantry). Research Assistant with Common Ground Ltd, 1947; apptd Commonwealth Relations Office, 1948; 2nd Sec., Brit. High Commn in India (Calcutta, 1948-49, Delhi, 1949-50): Brit. Deleg. to GATT Review Session, 1954-55; 1st Sec. Brit. High Commn., Bombay, 1955-58, Karachi, 1961-62; Deputy High Commissioner: Peshawar, March 1962; Lahore, June 1962-July 1964; Kingston, Jamaica, Oct. 1964-July 1968. *Address:* Foreign and Commonwealth Office, Great George Street, SW1. *Club:* Royal Commonwealth Society.

**BRITTENDEN, (Charles) Arthur;** Editor, Daily Mail, since Dec. 1966; Director Harmsworth Publications Ltd, since 1967; *b* 23 Oct. 1924; *o s* of late Tom Edwin Brittenden and Caroline (*née* Scrivener); *m* 1st, 1953, Sylvia Penelope Cadman (marr. diss., 1960); 2nd, 1966, Ann Patricia Kenny. *Educ:* Leeds Grammar School.

Served in Reconnaissance Corps, 1943-46. Yorkshire Post, 1940-43, 1946-49; News Chronicle, 1949-55; joined Sunday Express, 1955: Foreign Editor, 1959-62; Northern Editor, Daily Express, 1962-63; Dep. Editor, Sunday Express, 1963-64; Exec. Editor, Daily Mail, 1964-66. *Address:* Northcliffe House, Tudor Street, EC4. *T:* 01-353 6000.

**BRITTON, Prof. Denis King;** Professor of Agricultural Economics at Wye College, since 1970; Member: Economic Development Committee for Agriculture, since 1966; Home Grown Cereals Authority, since 1969; *b* 25 March 1920; *s* of Rev. George Charles Britton and Harriet Rosa (*née* Swinstead); *m* 1942, Margaret Alice Smith; one *s* two *d. Educ:* Caterham School; London School of Economics, London University (BSc (Econ.)). Asst Statistician, Ministry of Agriculture and Fisheries, 1943-47; Lecturing and Research at University of Oxford, Agricultural Economics Res. Inst., 1947-52; MA Oxon 1948 (by decree); Economist, United Nations Food and Agriculture Organisation, Geneva, 1952-59; Gen. Manager, Marketing and Economic Res., Massey-Ferguson (UK) Ltd, 1959-61; Prof. of Agricultural Economics, Univ. of Nottingham, 1961-70; Dean, Faculty of Agriculture and Horticulture, Univ. of Nottingham, 1967-70. Farmers' Club Cup, 1966. FSS 1943. *Publications:* Cereals in the United Kingdom, 1969; articles in Jl of Royal Statistical Society, Jl of Agricultural Economics, Farm Economist, Incorporated Statistician, etc. *Recreations:* music, photography. *Address:* 29 Chequers Park, Wye, Ashford, Kent. *Club:* Farmers'.

**BRITTON, Edward Louis,** CBE 1967; General Secretary, National Union of Teachers, since 1970; *b* 4 Dec. 1909; *s* of George Charles Edwin and Ellen Alice Britton; *m* 1936, Nora Arnald; no *c. Educ:* Bromley Grammar School, Kent; Trinity College, Cambridge. Teacher in various Surrey schools until 1951; Headmaster, Warlingham County Secondary School, Surrey, 1951-60; General Secretary, Association of Teachers in Technical Institutions, 1960-68. President, National Union of Teachers, 1956-57. Mem., TUC General Council, 1970-. Fellow College of Preceptors, 1967. Hon. DEd CNAA, 1969. *Publications:* many articles in educational journals. *Recreation:* amateur photography. *Address:* 40 Nightingale Road, Guildford, Surrey.

**BRITTON, Professor Karl William;** Professor of Philosophy, University of Newcastle upon Tyne, since 1951; *b* Scarborough, Yorks, 12 Oct. 1909; *s* of Rev. J. Nimmo Britton and Elsie Clare Britton (*née* Slater); *m* 1936, Sheila Margaret Christie; one *s* two *d* (and one *s* one *d* decd). *Educ:* Southend High School; Clare College, Cambridge. Pres. Cambridge Union Society, 1931. Choate Fellow at Harvard University, USA, 1932-34; Lecturer in Philosophy: University College of Wales, 1934-37; University College of Swansea, 1937-51. War of 1939-45, Regional Commissioner's Office, Reading, 1941-45. Public Orator, Durham University, 1959-62; Dean of the Faculty of Arts, Newcastle upon Tyne, 1961-63 and 1966-69. Examiner, Moral Sciences Tripos: 1949, 1954, 1955, 1964, 1966. Sec., Mind Assoc., 1948-60, Pres. 1963. *Publications:* Communication: A Philosophical Study of Language, 1939; John Stuart Mill, 1953, 1969; Philosophy and the Meaning of Life, 1969; contrib. to: The Times, Proc. Aristotelian Society, Mind, Philosophy, Analysis, Jl of Philosophy, Cambridge Review, etc. *Address:* Harthope, Millfield Road, Riding Mill, Northumberland. *T:* Riding Mill 354.

**BRITTOROUS, Brig. Francis Gerard Russell,** CBE 1964; DSO 1940; MC 1917; late Manchester Regiment; *b* 1 Feb. 1896; *s* of Francis Patrick Brittorous, of Barna, Co. Galway, and Mary Josephine, *d* of John Russell, Londonderry; *m* 1925, Ilynne, *d* of Ernest Chambers Hitchmough, of Co. Cork; two *d. Educ:* Ushaw. 2nd Lieut Manchester Regt, 1915; Captain, 1926; Major, 1938; Lt-Colonel 1940; Brigadier, 1940; Staff Captain, India, 1922-26; Staff Captain, Egypt, 1937-38; served European War, 1915-19, France and Belgium (despatches twice, British War Medal, Victory Medal, MC); Iraq, 1919-20 (Medal and Clasp); Palestine, 1938 (Medal and Clasp); France, 1940 (DSO); commanded Lancashire Fusiliers, 1940-41; Maj.-General GOC Agean, 1943. Retired pay, 1946. Chm., North West Hants Conservative Assoc., 1952-68, Pres. 1968-. *Recreations:* hunting, cricket, golf. *Address:* Longhouse Farm, St Mary Bourne, Hants. *T:* St Mary Bourne 224. *Clubs:* Army and Navy, MCC.

**BROACKES, Nigel;** Chairman, Trafalgar House Investments Ltd; *b* Wakefield, 21 July 1934; *s* of late Donald Broackes and Nan Alford; *m* 1956, Joyce Edith Horne; two *s* one *d. Educ:* Stowe. Nat. Service, commnd 3rd Hussars, 1953-54. Stewart & Hughman Ltd, Lloyds Underwriting agents, 1952-55; various property developments, etc, 1955-57; Trafalgar House Investments Ltd (named Eastern International Property Investments until 1961): Man. Dir 1958; Dep. Chm. and Jt Man. Dir 1968; Chm. 1969. *Address:* Wargrave Manor, Wargrave, Berks. *T:* Wargrave 2725.

**BROAD, Lieut-General Sir Charles (Noel Frank),** KCB, *cr* 1941 (CB 1938); DSO 1917; *b* 29 Dec. 1882; *s* of Major C. H. Broad, 5th Fusiliers, and Ann Paul; *m* 1st, 1915, Lillian Mary (*d* 1942), *d* of Edwin Mackintosh; one *d*; 2nd, 1944, Diana Myrtle, *yr d* of Col. Philip R. Bald; two *s* one *d* (and one *s* decd). *Educ:* Wellington College; Pembroke College, Cambridge. Entered RA 1905; Staff College, 1914; Captain, 1914; Major, 1916; Bt.-Lieut-Colonel, 1919; Colonel, 1923; Maj.-General, 1936; Lieut-General, 1940; served S. African War, 1902; European War, 1914-18 (1914 Star, Legion of Honour, Belgian Croix de Guerre); War service, 1939-42; Maj.-General in charge of Administration, Aldershot Command, 1937-39; GOC-in-C Aldershot Command, 1939-40; GOC-in-C, Eastern Army, India, 1940-42; retired pay, 1942; Col Comdt Rl T. R., 1939-47. *Address:* The Old Flax Mill, Beaminster, Dorset. *Club:* United Service.

**BROAD, Charlie Dunbar,** MA, LittD Cantab; Hon. LLD Aberdeen, Bristol, Dublin; Hon. ScD Cantab; Hon. Doctor of Philosophy Uppsala; FBA; Fellow of Royal Swedish Academy of Science; Hon. Member of Stockholms Nation (Uppsala); Fellow, Societas Scientiarum Fennica; Fellow, Amer. Acad. of Arts and Sciences; Knightbridge Professor of Moral Philosophy, Cambridge University, 1933-53; *b* London, 30 Dec. 1887; *o c* of late Charles Stephen Broad and Emily Gomme; unmarried. *Educ:* Dulwich College; Trinity College, Cambridge (Major Scholar in Natural Science); first class Nat. Sci. Trip. Part I; first class, with special distinction in metaphysical and ethical philosophy, Moral Sci. Trip. Part II; Arnold Gerstenberg Studentship in philosophy; Burney Prizeman; Fellow of Trinity College, Cambridge. Assistant to Professor of Logic, University of St Andrews; Lecturer on Logic, University College, Dundee; Professor of Philosophy, University of Bristol; Fellow and Lecturer in Moral Science, Trinity College, Cambridge; Sidgwick Lecturer in Moral Science,

University of Cambridge; Tarner Lecturer in the Philosophy of Science, 1923-24; Donnellan Lecturer, Trinity College, Dublin, 1929; President of the Society for Psychical Research, 1935-36 and 1959-60; Pres. of the Aristotelian Society, 1927-28, 1954-55. Visiting Professor in Philosophy, University of Michigan, 1953-54; Flint Professor of Philosophy, University of Calif., in Los Angeles, 1954. Nicholas Murray Butler gold medal, Columbia University, 1960. *Publications:* Perception, Physics, and Reality; Scientific Thought; Mind and its Place in Nature; The Philosophy of Francis Bacon; Five Types of Ethical Theory; Examination of McTaggart's Philosophy; Ethics and the History of Philosophy (Selected Essays); Psychical Research, Religion and Philosophy (Selected Essays); Lectures on Psychical Research; numerous contributions on philosophical subjects to Mind, the Hibbert Journal, Proceedings of the Aristotelian Society, Philosophy, and the International Journal of Ethics. *Recreation:* model engineering. *Address:* Trinity College, Cambridge. *Club:* United University.

**BROADBENT, Donald Eric,** FRS 1968; MA, ScD; Director, Applied Psychology Unit, Medical Research Council, since 1958; *b* 6 May 1926; *m* 1949, Margaret Elizabeth Wright; two *d*. *Educ:* Winchester College; Pembroke College, Cambridge. RAF Engrg short course, 1st cl., 1944; Moral Science Tripos (Psychology), 1st cl., 1949. Scientific Staff, Applied Psychology Res. Unit, 1949-58. Fellow, Pembroke College, 1965. Pres., British Psychol. Society, 1965; Pres., Sect. J. Brit. Assoc. for Advancement of Science, 1967; Vis. Fell., All Souls College, Oxford, 1967-68. Chm., St Dunstan's Sci. Cttee.; Chm., Psychology Sub-Cttee., Flying Personnel Res. Cttee, RAF; Member, Biol. Res. Bd, MRC; Fell., Acoustical Soc. of Amer.; past or present Council Member: British Acoustical Society; British Psychol. Soc.; Ergonomics Res. Soc.; Experimental Psychology Soc.; Fellow, Human Factors Soc.; Lectr: Lister (Brit. Assoc.); Gregynog (Aberystwyth); Pillsbury (Cornell); Fitts (Michigan). *Publications:* Perception and Communication, 1958; Behaviour, 1961; many papers in jls of above societies and of Amer. Psychol Assoc. *Recreations:* reading, camping, photography. *Address:* 15 Chaucer Road, Cambridge. *T:* 55294.

**BROADBENT, Ewen,** CMG 1965; Assistant Under Secretary of State, Ministry of Defence, since 1969; *b* 9 Aug. 1924; *s* of late Rev. W. Broadbent and of Mrs Mary Broadbent; *m* 1951, Squadron Officer Barbara David, *d* of F. L. David, Weston-super-Mare; one *s*. *Educ:* King Edward VI School, Nuneaton; St John's College, Cambridge. Served with Gordon Highlanders, 1943-47 (Captain); Cambridge, 1942-43 and 1947-49; Air Ministry, 1949; Private Sec. to Secretary of State for Air, 1955-59; Asst Secretary, 1959; Dep. Chief Officer, Sovereign Base Areas, Cyprus, 1961, Chief Officer, 1964; MoD 1965-; Private Sec. to Sec. of State for Defence, 1967-68. *Address:* 18 Park Hill, Ealing, W5. *T:* 01-997 1978. *Club:* Royal Commonwealth Society.

**BROADBENT, Sir William Francis,** 3rd Bt, *cr* 1898; Solicitor; *b* 29 Nov. 1904; *s* of Sir John Francis Harpin Broadbent, MD, FRCP, Bt and Margaret Elizabeth Field (*d* 1958); *S* father 1946; *m* 1935, Veronica Pearl Eustace (*d* 1951); no *c*. *Educ:* Winchester College; Trinity College, Oxford (MA). Solicitor, 1933. *Heir:* cousin George Walter Broadbent [*b* 23 April 1935; *m* 1962, Valerie Anne, *o d* of C. F. Ward; one *s* one *d*]. *Address:* 21 Porchester Terrace, W2. *Clubs:* MCC, United University.

**BROADBRIDGE,** family name of **Baron Broadbridge.**

**BROADBRIDGE,** 2nd Baron, *cr* 1945, of Brighton; **Eric Wilberforce Broadbridge,** Bt, *cr* 1937; Company Director; *b* 22 Dec. 1895; *e s* of 1st Baron Broadbridge, KCVO, and Fanny Kathleen (*d* 1928), *d* of late Richard Brigden; *S* father 1952; *m* 1924, Mabel Daisy (*d* 1966), *o d* of Arthur E. Clarke, Carshalton, Surrey; one *s*. *Educ:* Hurstpierpoint College. Commissioned in Machine Gun Corps, 1914; served European War, 1914-18, in France, Salonika, Egypt and Palestine (despatches). After end of war studied and became fully qualified mechanical engineer; Director of several Trust Companies; acquired business of A. J. Barton and Co. (Timber Brokers) and is now Managing Director. Liveryman of Worshipful Company of Woolmen. *Recreations:* shooting, golf. *Heir:* *s* Hon. Peter Hewett Broadbridge, BA, BSc (Oxon.) [*b* 19 Aug. 1938; *m* 1967, Mary, *o d* of W. O. Busch, Germany; one *d*]. *Address:* Beach Rise, Westgate-on-Sea, Kent; St Stephen's House, Westminster, SW1. *Club:* City Livery.

**BROADHURST, Air Chief Marshal (retd) Sir Harry,** GCB 1960 (KCB 1955; CB 1944); KBE 1945; DSO and Bar, 1941; DFC 1940, and Bar, 1942; AFC 1937; Director since 1961, Deputy Managing Director since 1965, Hawker Siddeley Aviation Ltd; Director: The de Havilland Aircraft of Canada Ltd, since 1968; Hawker Siddeley Group Ltd, since 1968; Hawker Siddeley Dynamics Ltd, since 1970; *b* 1905; *m* 1st, 1929, Doris Kathleen French; one *d*; 2nd, 1946, Jean Elizabeth Townley; one *d*. SASO to AOC Western Desert, 1942; AOC Allied Air Forces, W. Desert, 1943; 83 Group Commander Allied Expeditionary Air Force, 1944-45; AO i/c Admin. Fighter Command, 1945-46; AOC 61 Group, 1947-48; idc 1949; SASO, BAFO (now 2nd TAF), Germany, 1950-51; ACAS (Ops), 1952-53; C-in-C 2nd Tactical Air Force, Germany, 1954-56; Air Officer Commanding-in-Chief, Bomber Command, Jan. 1956-May 1959; Cmdr Allied Air Forces, Central Europe, 1959-61. Member Air League Council, 1966-. Kt Grand Cross of Order of Orange Nassau, 1948; Legion of Merit (US). *Address:* Lock's End House, Birdham, Chichester, Sussex. *T:* Birdham 717. *Clubs:* Royal Air Force; Royal Thames Yacht.

**BROADLEY, Sir Herbert,** KBE 1947 (CBE 1943); Representative in Britain of United Nations Children's Fund since 1958; *b* 23 Nov. 1892; *s* of late Stephenson S. Broadley, Louth, Lincs; *m* 1927, Kathleen May, *d* of late Alfred J. Moore, Camden Square, London; no *c*. *Educ:* King Edward VI Grammar School, Louth; Birkbeck College, University of London. Civil Service, 1912; served in India Office (Military Department), 1912-1920; promoted to First Division, 1920; served in Board of Trade, 1920-26; Secretary of Imperial Customs Conference, 1921, German (Reparations) Act Committee, 1921, and Imperial Economic Committee, 1925-26. Resigned from Civil Service, 1926, and joined firm of W. S. Crawford Ltd (Advertising Agents), 1927; Director of W. S. Crawford Ltd and Managing Director of their Berlin Branch, 1927-32; in charge of the Distribution and Research Department, W. S. Crawford Ltd, London, 1932-39; Fellow and Member of Council of Institute of Incorporated Practitioners in Advertising and Chairman of its Research Committee, 1936-39; joined Ministry of Food at outbreak of War, 1939; Asst Secretary, Nov. 1939; Principal Asst

Secretary 1940; Deputy Secretary, 1941; Second Secretary, 1945-48; Leader, UK Delegation to Internat. Wheat Conferences, 1947 and 1948; UK repr. at UNFAO Conferences: Quebec, 1945; Copenhagen, 1946; Dep. Director-General, UN Food and Agriculture Organization, 1948-58 (Acting Dir-Gen., 1955-56), retd. Member UK Nat. Freedom from Hunger Campaign Cttee., 1960-. Hon. Freeman of Louth (Lincs) 1961. Hon. Fellow, Birkbeck College, University of London, 1963; a Governor, Birkbeck College, 1965-. Haldane Memorial Lecture on Food and People, University of London, 1964. Commander of the Order of the Crown of Belgium, 1948. *Publication:* The People's Food (with Sir William Crawford), 1938. *Address:* United Nations Children's Fund, 14-15 Stratford Place, London, W1. *T:* 01-629 1880. *Club:* United Service.

**BROADMEAD, Sir Philip Mainwaring,** KCMG, *cr* 1952 (CMG 1944); MC; retd; *b* 3 Dec. 1893; *s* of late Colonel Henry Broadmead. *Educ:* Wellington College; Christ Church, Oxford. Served European War, 1914-19, with KRRC; Staff Capt. 1918. Third Secretary in Diplomatic Service, 1920; 2nd Secretary 1923; 1st Secretary 1929; Counsellor of Embassy, 1940. Ambassador to Colombia, 1945-47; Minister at Damascus, 1947-50; Ambassador to Czechoslovakia, 1950-53. *Club:* St James'.

**BROADWAY, Leonard Marsham;** *b* 29 Nov. 1903; *m* 1928, Edith Emily Ayckbourn; one *s* two *d*. *Educ:* privately. Joined Castrol Ltd (then C. C. Wakefield & Co. Ltd), 1920; apptd Company Secretary, 1938; Director, 1947; Asst Managing Director, 1951; Deputy Chairman, 1957-62 and Managing Director, 1954-62, Castrol World Gp of Companies. Member Port of London Authority, 1955-58; Member Petroleum Industry Advisory Cttee; Patron, College of Aeronautical and Automobile Engineering. *Recreations:* tennis, swimming, gardening, clay pigeon shooting. *Address:* Long Meadow, Cokes Lane, Chalfont St Giles, Bucks. *T:* Little Chalfont 2815.

**BROADWOOD, Capt. Evelyn Henry Tschudi,** MC 1915; Chairman: John Broadwood & Sons Ltd; John P. Gray & Son Ltd; Senior Governor of Old Vic and of Sadler's Wells, 1938; *b* 17 March 1889; *o s* of late James Henry Tschudi Broadwood, and late Margaret Evelyn, *d* of T. F. Maitland, JP, Garth, Breconshire. *Educ:* Wellington. Captain Norfolk Regt, 1909; served European War, 1914-19 (MC, Mons Star, despatches twice). Past Master of Worshipful Co. of Musicians. JP 1949; Chm., Dorking and Horley District Council, 1949-50; 1951-52. CC Surrey, 1944; High Sheriff, 1957; CA 1959. Royal Warrant Holder to the Queen; Royal Warrant Holder to Queen Elizabeth the Queen Mother. Governor, Royal Normal College for the Blind; Mem. Exec. Council of London Society; Vice-Pres. Royal Hospital and Home for Incurables, Putney, 1960-; Vice-Pres. Institute of Music Instrument Technology, 1961-. Rep. Great Britain on Internat. Congress for Standardisation of Concert Pitch, 1939-. FIMIT. *Address:* Lyne, Capel, Surrey; 9 Hanover Street, W1. *Clubs:* Athenæum, Army and Navy.

**BROATCH, James,** CBE 1961; Deputy Chairman of the Cotton Board, 1963; Deputy Chairman, Textile Council, 1967-68; *b* 13 May 1900; *s* of Alfred and Mary Broatch; *m* 1927, Mary Booth. *Educ:* Manchester Grammar School; University College, Oxford. Editor, Manchester Guardian Commercial, 1930-39; Assistant Secretary, The Cotton Board, 1939-43; Secretary 1943-53; Director-General, 1953-62. *Address:* 5 Lynton Drive, Hillside, Southport, Lancs. *T:* Southport 67976.

**BROCAS, Viscount; Patrick John Bernard Jellicoe;** *b* 29 Aug. 1950; *s* and *heir* of 2nd Earl Jellicoe, *qv*. *Educ:* Eton. *Address:* 20 Chapel Street, Belgrave Square, SW1.

**BROCK,** family name of **Baron Brock.**

**BROCK;** *see* Clutton-Brock.

**BROCK,** Baron, *cr* 1965 (Life Peer), of Wimbledon; **Russell Claude Brock,** Kt 1954; Director, Department of Surgical Sciences, Royal College of Surgeons, since 1968; Surgeon to: Guy's Hospital, 1936-68; Brompton Hospital, 1936-68; *b* 24 Oct. 1903; *s* of Herbert and Elvina Brock; *m* 1927, Germaine Louise Ladevèze; three *d*. *Educ:* Christ's Hospital; Guy's Hospital (Schol.). MB, BS London, Hons med. surg. and anat., 1927; MS London 1932. Rockefeller Travelling Fellow, 1929-30; Demonstrator in Pathology and Anatomy, Surgical Registrar and Tutor, Guy's Hospital, 1932; Research Fell., Assoc. Surg. of Great Britain, 1932; Hunterian Prof., RCS, 1938; Cons. Thoracic Surgeon, LCC, 1935-46; Surgeon, Min. of Pensions (Queen Mary's, Roehampton), 1936-45; Thoracic Surgeon and Regional Adviser in Thoracic Surgery, EMS, 1939-46; Exchange Prof. of Surgery, Johns Hopkins Hospital, Baltimore, 1949. MRCS 1926; FRCS 1928; Member Council RCS, 1949-67; a Vice-Pres., RCS, 1956-58; Pres., 1963-66. President, Thoracic Society of Great Britain and Ireland, 1952; Med. Society London, 1968. LRCP 1926; FRCP 1965; FACS 1949; Hon. FRACS 1957; Hon. ScD Cantab., 1968; Hon. LLD Leeds, 1965; Hon. MD Hamburg, 1962. Hon. Fellow: Surgical section of RSM, 1951; Brazilian College of Surgeons, 1952; RCSEd 1966; RCSI, 1966; RCSCan. 1966. Lettsomian Lecturer, Med. Soc. London, 1952; Bradshaw Lectr, RCS, 1957; Tudor Edwards Memorial Lecture, 1963; Hunterian Orator, RCS, 1961; Lister Orator, 1967; BMA Prize Essay, 1926; Jacksonian Prize Essay, RCS, 1935; Julius Mickle Prize, London University, 1950-51; Cameron Prize, Edinburgh University, 1954; Gairdner Award, 1960-61. Treasurer's Gold Medal for Clin. med. and Clin. Surg., 1926; Golding Bird Gold Medal for Pathology, 1926; Fothergillian Gold Medal, Med. Soc. London, 1953; Leriche Medal, Internat. Soc. Surg., 1953; Gold Medal, Soc. Apoth., 1955; Gold Medal, W. London Med.-Chir. Soc., 1955; Lannelongue Medal, Acad. de Chirurgie, 1963; Bronze Medal of City of NY, 1965; Lister Medal, RCS, 1966. KStJ. *Publications:* Anatomy of the bronchial tree, 1946; Life and Work of Astley Cooper, 1952; Lung Abscess, 1952; Anatomy of Pulmonary Stenosis, 1957; numerous articles in surgical and medical journals. *Recreations:* writing, reading, antiquities and topography of London. *Address:* The Old Rectory House, 84 Church Road, Wimbledon, SW19; 2 Harley Street, W1. *T:* 01-580 1441. *Club:* Athenæum.

**BROCK, Rear-Admiral Patrick Willet,** CB 1956; DSO 1951; RN retd; Chairman, The Naval Review, since 1967; *b* 30 Dec. 1902; *e s* of R. W. and M. B. Brock, Kingston, Ontario; *m* 1931, M. D. Collinson. *Educ:* Royal Naval College of Canada. Transferred from Royal Canadian Navy to RN, 1921; Commander 1938; Exec. Officer, HMS Mauritius, 1942-44 (despatches); Captain 1944; Senior Naval Officer, Schleswig-Holstein, 1946; commanded HMS Kenya, Far East, 1949-51 (despatches, DSO); Director Operations Div., 1951-53; Rear-Admiral, 1954; Flag Officer, Middle East, 1954-56; Admiralty Material

Requirements Committee, 1956-58, retired. Trustee, National Maritime Museum; a Vice-Pres., Soc. for Nautical Research, 1970-. Croix de Guerre (France), 1945; Bronze Star Medal (US), 1951. *Publication:* RUSI Eardley-Wilmot Gold Medal Essay, 1935. *Recreations:* walking, swimming, tennis, naval history. *Address:* Kiln Cottage, Critchmere, Haslemere, Surrey. *T:* Haslemere 2542. *Club:* United Hunts.

**BROCKBANK, Russell Partridge;** Free-lance artist; *b* Niagara Falls, Canada, 15 April 1913; *s* of Clarence and Caroline Brockbank; *m* 1933, Eileen Hames; one *s* one *d*. *Educ:* Ridley College, Ontario; Chelsea School of Art, London. Came to England, 1929, and studied Art; forsook Art for Industry, 1932; forsook Industry for Art, 1936; Free-lance until 1941. Served War of 1939-45, Lieut RNVR, Northern Convoys, British Pacific Fleet; demobilised, 1946. Free-lanced until 1949; Art Editor of Punch, 1949-60. *Publications:* Round the Bend, 1948; Up the Straight, 1953; Over the Line, 1955; The Brockbank Omnibus, 1957; Manifold Pressures, 1958; Move Over, 1963; The Penguin Brockbank, 1963. *Recreation:* motoring, sport. *Address:* Badgers, Thursley, Surrey. *T:* Elstead 2293. *Club:* Savage.

**BROCKBANK, William,** TD 1946; MA, MD Cambridge; FRCP; Consulting Physician, Royal Infirmary, Manchester, since 1965; Hon. Medical Archivist Manchester University, since 1965; *b* Manchester, 28 Jan. 1900; *s* of Edward Mansfield and Mary Ellwood Brockbank; unmarried. *Educ:* Bootham School, York; Caius College, Cambridge; Manchester University. Medical Officer, Manchester Grammar School, 1929-46; Physician, Manchester Royal Infirmary, 1932-65. Lecturer in Medicine, Manchester University, 1933-65; Dean of Clinical Studies, Manchester University, 1939-65. RAMC, Major, 1939-41; Lieut-Colonel, 1941-46. Director, Asthma Clinic, Manchester Royal Infirmary, 1946-65. Fitzpatrick Lecturer, Royal College of Physicians, 1950-51; Chairman Manchester University Medical Library Cttee, 1951-54; Member Council, Royal College of Physicians, 1955-58; President Manchester Medical Society, 1955-56; Vicary Lecturer, Royal College of Surgeons, 1956; Member Hinchliffe Cttee (Cost of Prescribing), 1957-59; Gideon de Laune Lectr, Soc. of Apothecaries, 1963. Dist Comr (now Hon.) Boy Scouts Assoc.; awarded Silver Acorn, 1950. Vice-President, Lancashire CC Club, 1967-. *Publications:* Portrait of a Hospital, 1952; Ancient Therapeutic Arts, 1954; The Honorary Medical Staff of the Manchester Royal Infirmary 1830-1948, 1965; The Diary of Richard Kay, 1716-51, 1968; The History of Nursing at the MRI 1752-1929, 1970; numerous papers to the Lancet, mostly on asthma, and to Medical History. *Recreations:* Medical History, archaeology; collecting cricket literature and water colours. *Address:* 51 Palatine Road, Manchester 20. *T:* 061-445 3259. *Clubs:* National Liberal; Manchester.

**BROCKET,** 3rd Baron, *cr* 1933; **Charles Ronald George Nall-Cain,** Bt 1921; *b* 12 Feb. 1952; *s* of Hon. Ronald Charles Manus Nall-Cain (*d* 1961), and of Elizabeth Mary (who *m* 2nd, 1964, Colin John Richard Trotter), *d* of R. J. Stallard; *S* grandfather, 1967. *Educ:* Eton. *Heir: b* Hon. Richard Philip Christopher Nall-Cain, *b* 5 April 1953. *Address:* Mells Park, Frome, Somerset.

**BROCKHOUSE, Dr Bertram Neville,** FRS 1965; Professor of Physics, McMaster University, Canada, since 1962; *b* 15 July 1918; *s* of Israel Bertram Brockhouse and Mable Emily Brockhouse (*née* Neville); *m* 1948, Doris Isobel Mary (*née* Miller); four *s* two *d*. *Educ:* University of British Columbia (BA); University of Toronto (PhD). Served War of 1939-45 with Royal Canadian Navy. Lectr, University of Toronto, 1949-50; Research Officer, Atomic Energy of Canada Ltd, 1950-59; Branch Head, Neutron Physics Br., 1960-62. *Publications:* some 75 papers in learned journals. *Address:* Department of Physics, McMaster University, Hamilton, Ontario, Canada. *T:* (416) 648-6329.

**BROCKHURST, Gerald L.,** RA 1937 (ARA 1928, now Hon. Retired Senior Member of Royal Academy; *m* 1947, Kathleen Nancy Woodward; no *c*. painter, chiefly of portraits; Exhibited at the Royal Academy, 1915-49; portrait of Bishop Fulton J. Sheen exhibited 1949. Has been living in the United States since 1939. *Address:* 239 Woodside Avenue, Franklin Lakes, NJ 07417, USA.

**BROCKIE, Thomas,** CVO 1967; Under Secretary, Min. of Public Building and Works, 1956-66 (Under Sec. for Scotland, 1962-66); *b* 9 June 1906; *o s* of Thomas Brockie, Peebles, Scotland; *m* 1936, Phyllis, *e d* of Austin Godson, Edinburgh; no *c*. *Educ:* Ayr Academy; Glasgow University (MA). Entered Civil Service, 1928; Ministry of Labour, 1928-33; Assistance Board, 1934-41 (Principal 1939); HM Treasury, 1942-43; Ministry of Public Building and Works, 1944; Asst Secretary, 1944; Under Secretary, 1956. *Recreations:* reading, motoring. *Address:* 19 Gayton Court, Gayton Road, Harrow, Middx. *T:* 01-427 3944. *Club:* Devonshire.

**BROCKINGTON, Prof. Colin Fraser;** Professor of Social and Preventive Medicine, Manchester University, 1951-64, Emeritus, 1964; *b* 8 Jan. 1903; *s* of late Sir William Brockington; *m* 1933, Dr Joyce Margaret Furze; three *s* one *d*. *Educ:* Oakham School; Gonville and Caius College, Cambridge University; Guy's Hospital, London. MD, MA, DPH, MSc Manchester, BChir Cantab, MRCS, MRCP; barrister-at-law, Middle Temple. Medical Superintendent, Brighton Infectious Diseases Hospital and Sanatorium, 1929; Asst County Medical Officer, Worcestershire CC, 1930-33; general medical practice, Kingsbridge, Devon, 1933-36; Medical Officer of Health, Horsham and Petworth, 1936-38; Deputy County Medical Officer of Health, Warwickshire CC, 1938-42; County Medical Officer of Health: Warwickshire CC, 1942-46; West Riding CC, 1946-51. Member: Central Advisory Council for Education (Eng.), 1945-56; Central Training Council in Child Care (Home Office), 1947-53; Advisory Council for Welfare of Handicapped (Ministry of Health), 1949-54; Nursing Cttee of Central Health Services Council (Ministry of Health), 1949-51; Council of Society of Med. Officers of Health, 1944-66; Public Health Cttee of County Councils Assoc., 1945-49. Chairman: WHO Expert Cttee on School Health, 1950; Symposium on "Mental Health-Public Health Partnership," 5th Internat. Congress on Mental Health, Toronto, 1954; WHO Research Study Group on Juvenile Epilepsy, 1955; UK Committee of WHO, 1958-61. Took part as Expert in Technical Discussions on Rural Health at World Health Assembly, 1954, Far Eastern Lecture Tour for British Council, 1956-57; visited India, 1959, 1962, S America 1960, Jordan 1966-67, Spain 1967, Arabia 1968, Turkey 1969, Greece 1970, for WHO. Lecture Tour: S Africa and Middle East, 1964. *Publications:* Principles of Nutrition, 1952;

The People's Health, 1955; A Short History of Public Health, 1956 (2nd edn 1966); World Health, 1958 (2nd edn 1967); The Health of the Community, 1955, 1960, 1965; Public Health in the Nineteenth Century, 1965; The Social Needs of the Over-Eighties, 1966; wide range of contribs to learned jls. *Recreations:* golf, travel. *Address:* Werneth, Silverburn, Ballasalla, Isle of Man. *T:* Castletown (Isle of Man) 3465.

**BROCKLEBANK, Sir John Montague,** 5th Bt, *cr* 1885; TD; *b* 3 Sept. 1915; *s* of 3rd Bt and Hon. Grace Mary Jackson (*d* 1940), *y d* of 1st Baron Allerton; *S* brother 1953; *m* 1950, Pamela Sue, *d* of W. H. Pierce, OBE, JP; one *s*. *Educ:* Eton; Cambridge. *Heir:* *s* Aubrey Thomas Brocklebank, *b* 29 Jan. 1952. *Address:* Il Palazz, Zejtun, Malta GC.

**BROCKLEBANK-FOWLER, Christopher;** MP (C) King's Lynn since 1970; Managing Director, Creative Consultants Ltd, since 1967; *b* 13 Jan. 1934; 2nd *s* of Sidney Stratton Brocklebank Fowler, MA, LLB; *m* 1957, Joan Nowland; two *s*. *Educ:* Perse Sch., Cambridge. Farm pupil and improver; farms in Suffolk, Cambridgeshire and Norfolk, 1950-55. National service (submarines), Sub-Lt, RNVR, 1952-54. Farm Manager, Kenya, 1955-57; Lever Bros Ltd (Unilever Cos Management Trainee), 1957-59; advertising and marketing consultant with various advertising agencies, 1959-66; started own consultancy, 1966. Mem. Bow Group, 1961- (Research Cttee, 1965-69; Council, 1965-70; Sec., 1966-68; Chm., 1968-69; Dir, Bow Publications, 1968-). Mem. London Conciliation Cttee, 1966-67; Vice-Chm. Information Panel, Nat. Cttee for Commonwealth Immigrants, 1966-67. Contested (C) West Ham (North), Gen. Elec., 1964. *Publications:* pamphlets and articles on immigration and race relations. *Recreations:* painting, shooting, swimming. *Address:* 2 Ponsonby Place, SW1. *T:* 01-834 1976; 2 Parkhill, Middleton, King's Lynn, Norfolk. *T:* Middleton 401. *Club:* Junior Carlton (Political Cttee, 1964-68; General Cttee, 1970-).

**BROCKLEHURST, Major-General Arthur Evers,** CB 1956; DSO 1945; late RA; *b* 20 July 1905; *m* 1940, Joan Beryl Parry-Crooke; twin *d*. *Educ:* King's School, Canterbury; RMA Woolwich. 2nd Lieut, RA, 1925; CRA 6th Armoured Div., 1951; IDC 1954; DDPS (B) 1955; Chief of Staff, Malaya Comd, 1956-57; GOC, Rhine Dist., BAOR, 1958-59; Dep. Comdr BAOR, 1959-61; Retired 1961. *Recreations:* fishing, shooting, gardening. *Address:* Woodborough Manor, Pewsey, Wilts. *Club:* Army and Navy.

**BROCKLEHURST, Charles Douglas, F. P.;** *see* Phillips Brocklehurst.

**BROCKLEHURST, Mrs Mary D.;** *see* Dent-Brocklehurst.

**BROCKLEHURST, Sir Philip Lee,** 2nd Bt, *cr* 1903; *b* 7 March, 1887; *s* of 1st Bt and Annie (*d* 1951), *d* of Samuel Dewhurst; *S* father, 1904; *m* 1st, 1913, Gwladys, MBE 1946 (who obtained a divorce, 1947), *d* of late Colonel Gostling Murray of Whitten Park, Hounslow; two *d*; 2nd, 1952, Mrs Audrey Evelyn Mackenzie, *e d* of Hugh Miller Macmillan, Ferniegair, Helensburgh, Dunbartonshire. *Educ:* Eton; Trinity Hall, Cambridge. Accompanied British Antarctic Expedition, 1907; received medal from Royal Geographical Society, 1909; Derbyshire IY, 1904; Bt Lt-Col 1924; served European War with 1st Life Guards, 1914-17 (wounded); Egyptian Army, 1918-20; commanded 2nd Regt Arab Legion Desert Mechanised Bde, 1941-42; British Council, Palestine-Trans-Jordan, 1943-44; is Lord of Manor of Heaton, Swythamley. *Heir:* *n* John Ogilvy Brocklehurst, *b* 1926. *Address:* Swythamley Park, near Macclesfield, Cheshire.

**BROCKLEHURST, Robert James,** DM; Emeritus Professor of Physiology, University of Bristol, since 1965; *b* Liverpool, 16 Sept. 1899; *e s* of George and Sarah Huger Brocklehurst, Liverpool; *m* 1st, 1928, Sybille (*d* 1968), *y d* of Captain R. H. L. Risk, CBE, RN; two *s* one *d*; 2nd, 1970, Dora Millicent, *y d* of late Alexander Watts. *Educ:* Harrow; University College, Oxford (Scholar; 1st Class Honours in Physiology); St Bartholomew's Hospital. BA 1921; MA, BM, BCh, 1924; DM, 1928; MRCS, LRCP, 1925; Demonstrator of Physiology, St Bartholomew's Medical Coll., 1925-26; Radcliffe Travelling Fellow, 1926-28; Lecturer, 1928-29, and Senior Lecturer, 1929-30, in Dept of Physiology and Biochemistry, Univ. Coll., London; Prof. of Physiology, 1930-65, and Dean of Med. Fac., 1934-47, Univ. of Bristol, and Univ. Rep. on GMC, 1935-65 (Jt Treas., 1962-65); Mem. Interdepartmental Cttee on Dentistry, 1943; Mem. Dental Bd of UK, 1945-56; Additional Mem., GDC, 1956-65; Pres., Bath, Bristol and Somerset Branch, BMA 1959-60; Fellow BMA, 1967; Pres. Bristol Medico-Chirurgical Society, 1960-61; Member Council, 1958-63, and President Sect. I (Physiology), 1950, British Association; Mem., S-W Regional Hosp. Bd, and Bd of Govs of United Bristol Hosps, 1947-66; Chm, Moorhaven Hosp. Management Cttee; a representative of Diocese of Bristol in the Church Assembly, 1945-65; Member, Central Board of Finance, 1957-65; Chm., Bristol Diocesan Bd of Finance, 1951-65. Chm., Council Westonbirt School, 1956-68; Member Council, Christ Church College, Canterbury; Churchwarden, Stoke Bishop, 1939-60; a Vice-President Gloucester and Bristol Diocesan Association of Church Bell Ringers. Youth Hostels Assoc.: Chm., Glos., Somerset and N. Devon Regional Group, 1934-45; Pres. Glos., Somerset and Exmoor Regional Group, 1945-65; Vice-Pres., South-West Regional Group, 1966-. Served in Tank Corps, 1918-19. *Publications:* Papers on physiological, biochemical and educational subjects in Journal of Physiology, American Journal of Physiology, Journal of Biological Chemistry, Medical Press, etc. *Recreations:* mountaineering, music, gardening. *Address:* Cleeve, Court Road, Newton Ferrers, Plymouth, Devon PL8 1DE. *T:* Newton Ferrers 397. *Clubs:* Alpine, Royal Commonwealth Society, Royal Over-Seas League.

**BROCKMAN, Edward Phillimore,** MChir Cantab; FRCS; Retired; Hon. Consulting Orthopædic Surgeon to: Westminster Hosp.; Royal National Orthopædic Hosp. and St Vincent's Orthopædic Hosp., Northwood Hills. *Educ:* Cambridge University; St Thomas's Hospital, London University. BA Cantab; MRCS, LRCP 1919; MB, BCh 1921; FRCS 1924; MChir Cantab 1925. Fellow British Orthopædic Association. *Address:* Hook Cottage, Askett, Nr Aylesbury, Bucks.

**BROCKMAN, Ralph St Leger,** MA, MChir Cantab, FRCS; formerly Professor of Surgery, Sheffield University; Hon. Surgeon, Royal Infirmary, Sheffield; Consulting Surgeon, City General Hospital, Sheffield; Member of Court of Examiners, Royal College of Surgeons; Examiner to Gen. Nursing Council; *b* 3 June 1889; *s* of Ralph Thomas Brockman and Anna Sheldrake; *m* 1915, Estelle Wilson (*d* 1964); one *s* one *d*; *m* 1965, Elizabeth Ritchie, *widow* of Dr Alexander

Ritchie. *Educ:* Liverpool Coll.; Gonville and Caius Coll., Camb. (Nat. Science Tripos); St Bartholomew's Hosp. Brackenbury Surgical Scholarship. Willett Medal for Operative Surgery, Walsham Prize for Surgical Pathology; Temp. Surgeon, RN; Hunterian Professor, Royal Coll. of Surgeons: Arris and Gale Lecturer, Royal Coll. of Surgeons; Erasmus Wilson Lecturer, Royal College of Surgeons; late Surgeon to Children's Hospital, Sheffield. *Publications:* various scientific. *Recreations:* shooting and fishing. *Address:* West Way, West Street, Mayfield, Sussex.

**BROCKMAN, Vice-Admiral Sir Ronald,** KCB 1965; CSI 1947; CIE 1946; CBE 1943; DL; Gentleman Usher to the Queen since 1967; Comptroller to the Governor of the IoW since 1965; *b* 8 March 1909; *er s* of late Rear-Adm. H. S. Brockman, CB; *m* 1932, Marjorie Jean Butt; one *s* three *d*. *Educ:* Weymouth Coll., Dorset. Entered Navy, 1927; Assistant Secretary to First Sea Lord, Admiral of the Fleet Sir Roger Backhouse, 1938-39; Lieut-Commander 1939; Admiral's Secretary to First Sea Lord, Admiral of the Fleet Sir Dudley Pound, 1939-43; Commander 1943; Admiral's Secretary to Admiral of the Fleet Lord Mountbatten in all appointments, 1943-59; Private Secretary to Governor-General of India, 1947-48. Principal Staff Officer to the Chief of Defence Staff, Min. of Defence, 1959-65. Captain, 1953; Rear-Admiral, 1960; Vice-Admiral, 1963; retired list, 1965. Mem., Rugby Football Union Cttee; Exec. Dir, Variety Club of Great Britain's Children's Charity. DL Devon, 1969. Special Rosette of Cloud and Banner (China), 1946; Chevalier Legion of Honour and Croix de Guerre, 1946; Bronze Star Medal (USA), 1947. *Address:* 3 Court House, Basil Street, SW3. *T:* 01-584 1023; The Chance, Coastguard Road, Budleigh Salterton, Devon. *T:* Budleigh Salterton 2687. *Clubs:* Army and Navy; MCC; Royal Western Yacht Club of England; Liverpool Racquet Club.

**BROCKWAY,** family name of **Baron Brockway.**

**BROCKWAY,** Baron *cr* 1964 (Life Peer); **Archibald Fenner Brockway;** *b* Calcutta, 1888; *s* of Rev. W. G. Brockway and Frances Elizabeth Abbey; *m* 1914, Lilla, *d* of Rev. W. Harvey-Smith; four *d*; *m* 1946, Edith Violet, *d* of Archibald Herbert King; one *s*. *Educ:* Eltham College. Joined staff Examiner, 1907; sub-editor Christian Commonwealth, 1909; Labour Leader, 1911; editor, 1912-17; secretary No Conscription Fellowship, 1917; sentenced to one month's imprisonment under DORA Aug. 1916, and to three months, six months, and two years hard labour under Military Service Act, Dec. 1916, Feb. 1917, and July 1917; Joint Secretary British Committee of Indian National Congress and editor India, 1919; Joint Secretary Prison System Enquiry Cttee, 1920: Organising Secretary ILP 1922; General Secretary ILP, 1928 and 1933-39; Editor of New Leader, 1926-29, and 1931-46; Labour candidate Lancaster, 1922; Chairman No More War Movement and War Resister's International, 1923-28; Labour candidate Westminster 1924; Exec. Labour and Socialist International, 1926-31; Fraternal Delegate Indian Trade Union Congress and Indian National Congress, 1927; MP (Lab) East Leyton, 1929-31; Chairman ILP, 1931-33; took part in last public Socialist campaign against Hitler in Germany, 1932; Political Secretary ILP, 1939-46; Chairman British Centre for Colonial Freedom, 1942-47; ILP candidate, Upton Division of West Ham, 1934, Norwich, 1935, Lancaster, 1941, and Cardiff East, 1942; ILP Fraternal Delegate Hamburg Trade Union May Day Demonstrations and German Social Democratic Party Conference, Hanover, 1946. Resigned from ILP, 1946, and rejoined Labour Party; MP (Lab) Eton and Slough, 1950-64. Member Internat. Cttee of Socialist Movement for United Europe, 1947-52; first Chairman of Congress of Peoples against Imperialism, 1948-; Fraternal Delegate, Tunisian Trade Union Conf., 1951; Mem. unofficial Fact-finding mission, Kenya, 1952; Chairman: Movement for Colonial Freedom, 1954-67 (President, 1967-); British Asian and Overseas Socialist Fellowship, 1959-66; Peace in Nigeria Cttee, 1967-70; Peace Mission to Biafra and Nigeria, 1968; Brit. Council for Peace in Vietnam, 1965-69; Pres., British Campaign for Peace in Vietnam, 1970-. *Publications:* Labour and Liberalism, 1913; The Devil's Business, 1915 (proscribed during the war); Socialism and Pacifism, 1917; The Recruit, 1919; Non-Co-operation, 1919; The Government of India, 1920; English Prisons To-day (with Stephen Hobhouse), 1921; A Week in India, 1928; A New Way with Crime, 1928; The Indian Crisis, 1930; Hungry England, 1932; The Bloody Traffic, 1933; Will Roosevelt Succeed?, 1934; Purple Plague (a novel), 1935; Workers' Front, 1938; Inside the Left: a Political Autobiography, 1942; Death pays a Dividend (with Frederic Mullally), 1944; German Diary, 1946; Socialism Over Sixty Years; The Life of Jowett of Bradford, 1946; Bermondsey Story: Life of Alfred Salter, 1949; Why Mau Mau?, 1953; African Journeys, 1955; 1960—Africa's Year of Destiny, 1960; Red Liner (novel in dialogue), 1961; Outside the Right, 1963; African Socialism, 1964; Commonwealth Immigrants: What is the Answer? (with Norman Pannell), 1965; Woman Against the Desert (with Miss Campbell-Purdie) 1967; This Shrinking Explosive World, 1968; numerous ILP and Movement for Colonial Freedom pamphlets. *Address:* 67 Southway, N20. *T:* 01-445 3054.

**BRODERICK, Brigadier Ralph Alexander,** DSO 1919; MC 1916; TD 1934; DL; Hon. Consulting Dental Surgeon, Children's Hospital and Ear and Throat Hosp., Birmingham; Consulting Dental Surgeon to Ministry of Health; Consulting Dental Surgeon to Birmingham Hospital Regional Board; Director Post Graduate Bureau of General Dental Council; *b* Dorking, Surrey, 17 March 1888; *y s* of George Alexander and Annie Elizabeth Broderick; *m* 1914, Dulcie, 4th *d* of Richard Lunt, Edgbaston; one *s* two *d*. *Educ:* King Edward's School, Birmingham; Berkhamsted School; Birmingham University. LDS, RCS, 1911; MB, ChB Birmingham, 1912; MDS, Birmingham, 1924; FDS RCS, 1947. Commenced practice as Dental Surgeon, 1913; joined RAMC, TF, Aug. 1914; Lieut-Col, 1917; commanded 2nd South Midland Field Ambulance till 1922; ADMS 48th South Midland Div., 1935; Col 1935; Mobilised Aug. 1939 as ADMS 48th Div.; Cons. Dental Surg. to Army, 1944-52; KHDS, 1948; Councillor, Lawn Tennis Assoc. of Great Britain. Vice-Dean, Faculty of Dental Surgery, RCS, 1959-. *Publications:* Dental Bacteriology; various articles in British Dental Journal and Lancet. *Recreations:* shooting, lawn tennis. *Address:* 33 Mackenzie Road, Birmingham 11. *T:* 021-449 0636. *Clubs:* United Service; Union, Edgbaston Lawn Tennis (Birmingham); All England Lawn Tennis.

**BRODEUR, Rear-Admiral Victor Gabriel,** CB 1946; CBE 1943; Rear-Adm. (retd), Royal Canadian Navy; Commanding Officer Pacific Coast, Canada, 1938-40 and 1943-46; *b* 17 Sept. 1892; *s* of Hon. L. P. Brodeur, PC, KC, LLD; *m* 1st, 1915, Doris Fages (decd); two *s*; 2nd, 1938, Dorothy Whitfield Kennard. *Educ:* Montreal. Entered RCN 1909; Sub-Lieut 1913; Lieut 1915; Lieut-Cdr 1923; Qualified

Gunnery at Whale Island, 1921; Comdr 1927; Capt. 1936; Rear-Adm. 1942. Imperial Defence College, 1936; Canadian Naval Attaché, Washington, 1940-42; Naval Member Canadian Joint Staff, US, 1942-43; 16 years on loan to RN. *Recreations:* golf, fishing, shooting, gardening. *Address:* 702-1025 Gilford Street, Vancouver 5, BC, Canada.

**BRODIE, Captain Sir Benjamin Collins,** 4th Bt, *cr* 1834; *b* 6 March 1888; *o s* of Sir Benjamin Vincent Sellon Brodie, 3rd Bt, DL, JP; *S* father, 1938; *m* 1924, Mary Charlotte (*d* 1940), *e d* of R. E. Palmer, Ballyheigue, Co. Kerry; two *s* one *d*. *Educ:* Eton College; Magdalen College, Oxford. BA, 1911, Honour School of Modern History; served European War, Lieut Surrey Yeomanry, MEF (Gallipoli) 29th Division; Captain and Adjutant, 4th Bn The Gordon Highlanders, 51st (Highland) Division, BEF; Staff Captain, 1st Highland Bde British Army of the Rhine (despatches twice, MC and Bar); Officer of Company GCs; Royal Military College, Sandhurst, 1922-27; Headmaster (with L. T. Prosser Evans) Holyrood School, Bognor Regis, 1927-40; Governor of Tonbridge School, 1939- (Chm. of Governors, 1944-45 and 1950-51); Governor Reigate Grammar School, 1938-49, and Chairman Judd School, Tonbridge, 1945-60; Master of the Skinners' Company, 1944-45 and 1950-51; Assistant Commandant, Special Constabulary, 1940-46. *Recreations:* formerly shooting, fishing, riding, photography. *Heir: s* Benjamin David Ross Brodie, *b* 29 May 1925. *Address:* Betchworth Lodge, Betchworth, Surrey. *T:* Betchworth 3265. *Club:* Athenæum.

**BRODIE, Rabbi Sir Israel,** KBE 1969; BA, BLitt, Hon. DD; Hon. DCL; Chief Rabbi of the United Hebrew Congregations of the British Commonwealth of Nations, 1948-65, now Emeritus Chief Rabbi; *b* 10 May 1895; *s* of Aaron Brodie, Newcastle upon Tyne; *m* 1946, F. Levine. *Educ:* Rutherford Coll., Newcastle upon Tyne; Jews' Coll., London; Univ. Coll., London; Balliol Coll., Oxford. CF, 1917-19; Social Service, East End, London, 1921-23; Rabbi, Melbourne, Australia, 1923-37; Lecturer and Tutor, Jews' Coll., 1939-48; Pres., Jews' Coll.; CF, Army and RAF, 1940-44; Senior Jewish Chaplain, 1944-48; Fellow, University College, London; Hon. officer of several public bodies. *Publications:* A Word in Season, 1958; (ed.) The Etz Hayyim by Rabbi Jacob ben Jehuda Hazan of London, Vols 1, 2, 3, 1962, 1964, 1967. *Address:* Flat 15, Edinburgh House, 9b Portland Place, W1.

**BRODIE, Peter Ewen,** OBE 1954; QPM 1963; an Assistant Commissioner, Metropolitan Police, since 1966; *b* 6 May 1914; 2nd *s* of late Captain E. J. Brodie, Lethen, Nairn; *m* 1940, Betty Eve Middlebrook Horsfall; one *s*. *Educ:* Harrow School. Metropolitan Police, 1934-49 (Seconded to Ceylon Police, 1943-47); Chief Constable, Stirling and Clackmannan Police force, 1949-58; Chief Constable, Warwicks Constabulary, 1958-64; HM Inspector of Constabulary for England and Wales, 1964-66. Member: Adv. Cttee on Drug Dependence, 1967-; Exec. Cttee, Internat. Criminal Police Organisation–Interpol, 1967-. OStJ 1960. *Address:* 28 Clare Lawn Avenue, East Sheen, SW14.

**BRODIE, Major-General Thomas,** CB 1954; CBE 1949; DSO 1951; late The Cheshire Regt; *b* 20 Oct. 1903; *s* of Thomas Brodie, Bellingham, Northumberland; *m* 1938, Jane Margaret Chapman-Walker; three *s* one *d*. Commanded: 2 Manchester Regt, 1942-43; 14th Infantry Brigade in Wingate Expedition, 1944; 1 Cheshire Regt, 1946-47; Palestine, 1947-48 (CBE and despatches); commanded 29 Inf. Bde, Korea, 1951 (DSO, US Silver Star Medal, US Legion of Merit); GOC 1 Infantry Div., MELF, 1952-55; Colonel The Cheshire Regiment 1955-61; retired 1957. *Address:* Chapmore End House, Chapmore End, Ware, Herts.

**BRODIE, Thomas Vernor Alexander;** Attorney-General, Federation of Malaya, Nov. 1955-Nov. 1959; *b* 9 Oct. 1907; *s* of late Norman Somerville Brodie, formerly ICS; *m* 1947, Mollie Frances (*née* Chubb); one *d*. *Educ:* Marlborough College; Brasenose College, Oxford. Called to Bar, Middle Temple, 1931; Assistant Legal Adviser, FMS, 1938; Federated Malay States Volunteer Force, 1941-45 (POW, 1942-45). Solicitor-General, Federation of Malaya, 1950: QC (Federation of Malaya), 1952. *Recreations:* golf and tennis. *Address:* Lychett Glade, Upton, Poole, Dorset. *T:* Lychett Minster 348.

**BRODNEY, Spencer;** Writer; *b* Melbourne, Australia, 29 Aug. 1883; *m* 1918, Edith Siebel, New York; two *s*. *Educ:* Scotch College, Melbourne; Universities of Melbourne and London. Has been on staffs of, or written for, Australian, English, and American Newspapers and magazines; editor, Current History, 1931-36 and 1941-43; editor Events, 1937-41; author of a play produced in London in 1912, and Rebel Smith (a play for the Australian theatre), 1925. *Address:* 298 Emerson Lane, Berkeley Heights, New Jersey, 07922, USA.

**BRODRICK,** family name of **Earl of Midleton.**

**BRODRICK, Alan Houghton;** *b* Kensington; *o c* of Alan Brodrick of Wooder Manor, South Devon, and Katherine, *d* of Thomas Houghton and Elizabeth, *g d* of George Moore of Moore Hall; *m* 1923, Hon. Hester Astley, *d* of 20th Lord Hastings; one *s*. *Educ:* privately and abroad. Member of British Military Mission to the French Government, 1917-20; Joint Secretary-General of the International Congress of Anthropological and Ethnological Sciences, 1934-38; has orders of the Legion of Honour, Black Star, Dragon of Annam, Croix de Guerre, Crown of Roumania, White Eagle; Nichan Iftikhar, etc. *Publications:* Little China, 1942; North Africa, 1942; Parts of Barbary, 1944; Beyond the Burma Road, 1945; Cross Channel, 1946; Early Man–a Survey, 1948 (Spanish Edition 1955); Prehistoric Painting, 1948 (Spanish Edition 1950); Lascaux, 1949; Little Vehicle, 1949; Chinese Painting, 1949 (Spanish Edition 1954); Pillars of Hercules, 1950; Danger Spot of Europe, 1951; The Tree of Human History, 1951; Prospect of France, Breuil, mirage of Africa, 1953; Persona, 1955; Casual Change, 1961; Man and his Ancestry, 1961 (American Edn, 1964); The Abbé Breuil, 1963; The Father of Prehistory, 1963; Near to Greatness, 1965; Man and His Ancestors, 1970; Editor, The People's France Series: Normandy, 1947; Touraine, 1948; Paris, 1949; Brittany, 1950; Provence, 1952; Greater Paris and the Ile-de-France, 1953. *Translations:* Life the Great Adventure, 1955; On the Track of Prehistoric Man, 1955; The Rock-Pictures of Europe, 1956; The Prehistory of Africa, 1956: The Inhabited Planet, 1957; Man and Mammoth, 1957; We Come from the Sea, 1958; The Galapagos, 1960; The Mandala, 1961, and other works from French, German, Spanish, Italian, Swedish, Dutch, etc. *Address:* 9 Weymouth Street, Portland Place, W1; 24 rue Barbet-de-Jouy, Paris VIIe.

**BRODRICK, Norman John Lee,** QC 1960; JP; MA; **His Honour Judge Brodrick;** A Judge of the Central Criminal Court since 1967; Deputy Chairman of Isle of Wight Quarter Sessions since 1967; Chairman of Departmental Committee on Death Certification and Coroners, 1964; *b* 4 Feb. 1912; 4th *s* of late William John Henry Brodrick, OBE; *m* 1940, Ruth Severn, *d* of late Sir Stanley Unwin, KCMG; three *s* one *d*. *Educ:* Charterhouse; Merton College, Oxford. Called to Bar, Lincoln's Inn, 1935, Bencher, 1965; Western Circuit, 1935. Temporary civil servant (Ministry of Economic Warfare and Admiralty), 1939-45. Bar Council, 1950-54 and 1962-66. Recorder: of Penzance, 1957-59; of Bridgwater, 1959-62; of Plymouth, 1962-64. Chairman, Mental Health Review Tribunal, Wessex Region, 1960-63; Deputy Chairman, Middlesex Quarter Sessions, 1961-65; Recorder of Portsmouth, 1964-67; Chm., IoW QS, 1964-67. JP Hants, 1967. *Recreations:* gardening, model railways. *Address:* 19 Old Buildings, Lincoln's Inn, WC2. *T:* 01-405 2980; Packhurst Farm House, Clanfield, Hants. *T:* Horndean 3150. *Clubs:* Athenæum; Hampshire (Winchester).

**BRODRICK, Brigadier William Le Couteur,** CIE 1940; Indian Army, retired; *b* 27 Jan. 1888; *m* 1st, 1915, Ora Maxwell; two *d*; 2nd, 1934, Evelyn Ballantyne Wishart. *Educ:* Blundell's School, Tiverton. Joined Indian Army, 1908; in 27th Light Cavalry till 1914, then was in Royal Indian Army Service Corps till 1931; joined Contracts Directorate Army Headquarters and from 1936 to 1940 was Director of Contracts, Army Headquarters, India; served Aden, 1915-16; Sistan, 1916-17; Malabar, 1921-22; Waziristan, 1921-24. *Address:* 18 Grange Terrace, Edinburgh 9. *T:* 031-667 1169.

**BROGAN, Colm,** MA Glasgow; journalist; *b* 20 Oct. 1902; *s* of Denis Brogan and Elizabeth Toner, Glasgow; *m* Helena Rogers, MA (*d* 1967); two *d*. *Educ:* St Columcille's School, Rutherglen; St Aloysius College, Glasgow; Glasgow University. Engaged in teaching and journalism in Glasgow till 1946; from then journalism and political study in London. Editor of monthly magazine, Round the World, 1945-46. *Publications:* Who Are the People? 1943; The Democrat at the Supper Table, 1945; Our New Masters, 1947; Patriots My Foot, 1949; Fifty Years On, 1949; Glasgow Story, 1952; The Educational Revolution, 1955; The Nature of Education, 1962. *Address:* 28 Ridgmount Gardens, WC1. *T:* 01-580 7804; 18 Ailsa Street, Prestwick, Ayrshire.

*See also Sir Denis Brogan.*

**BROGAN, Sir Denis (William),** Kt 1963; MA; Professor of Political Science, Cambridge, 1939-68, now Emeritus Professor, and Fellow of Peterhouse (Hon. Fellow, 1967); Director, Hamish Hamilton Ltd; *b* 11 Aug. 1900; *e s* of Denis Brogan and Elizabeth Toner, Glasgow; *m* Olwen Phillis Frances Kendall, MA, FSA; three *s* one *d*. *Educ:* St Columcille's School; Rutherglen Acad.; Glasgow University; Balliol College, Oxford; Harvard. Lectr, University Coll., London, and at the London School of Economics; Hon. Fellow, Corpus Christi College, Oxford, formerly Fellow and Tutor. FBA; Foreign Member: Mass Historical Society; Institut de France; Amer. Acad. of Arts and Sciences. Hon. DèsL: Algiers, 1943; Clermont, 1947; Besançon, 1950; Hon. LLD: Glasgow, 1946; British Columbia, 1952; Lehigh, 1966; Hon. DLitt Oxon 1969. Benjamin Franklin Medal, Royal Society of Arts, 1966. Chevalier de la Légion d'Honneur; Comdr, Order of Orange-Nassau. *Publications:* The American Political System, 1933; Proudhon, 1934; Abraham Lincoln, 1935; The Development of Modern France, 1870-1939, 1940; USA: An Outline; Is Innocence Enough?; Politics and Law in the United States, 1941; The English People, 1943; The American Problem, 1944; The Free State, 1945; French Personalities and Problems, 1946; American Themes, 1948; Stop on the Green Light, 1950; The Price of Revolution, 1951; The Era of Franklin D. Roosevelt (Eng. edn Roosevelt and the New Deal), 1952; Introduction to American Politics, 1955; The French Nation, 1957; America in The Modern World, 1961; (with Douglas Verney) Political Patterns in Today's World, 1963; American Aspects, 1964; Worlds in Conflict, 1967; numerous articles in British, French, and American journals. *Address:* 1 Hedgerley Close, Cambridge CB3 0EW. *Clubs:* Reform; Lotos (New York); National Press (Washington).

*See also Colm Brogan.*

**BROGAN, Maj.-Gen. Mervyn Francis,** CB 1970; CBE 1964 (OBE 1944); GOC Eastern Command Australia, since 1968; *b* 10 Jan. 1915; *s* of Bernard Brogan, Dubbo, NSW; *m* 1941, Sheila, *d* of David Jones, Canberra; two *s*. *Educ:* RMC Duntroon; Wesley Coll., Univ. of Sydney. Commnd 1935; BEng Sydney, 1938. Served War of 1939-45: New Guinea, 1942-45 (despatches 1943); trng UK and BAOR, 1946-47; Chief Instructor, Sch. of Mil. Engrg, 1947-49; trng UK and USA, 1950-52; jssc 1952; Chief Engr, Southern Comd, 1954-55; Dir of Mil. Trng, 1954-55; BGS: Army HQ, 1956; FARELF, 1956-58; idc 1959; Comdt Australian Staff Coll., 1960-62; GOC Northern Comd, 1962-64; Dir Jt Service Plans, Dept of Defence, 1965-66; QMG 1966-68. *Recreations:* surfing, tennis. *Address:* HQ Eastern Command, Victoria Barracks, Paddington, NSW 2021, Australia. *T:* 31-0455. *Clubs:* Imperial Service, University (Sydney).

**BROINOWSKI, John Herbert,** CMG 1969; Deputy Chairman and Chief Executive, Darling & Co. (Investment Bankers), Australia; Chairman, Consolidated Metal Products Ltd; Director: Peko-Wallsend Ltd; Electrical Equipment of Australia Ltd; United Insurance Co. Ltd; South British United Life Assurance Ltd; *b* 19 May 1911; *s* of late Dr G. H. Broinowski and late Mrs Ethel Broinowski (*née* Hungerford); *m* 1939, Jean Gaerloch Broinowski (*née* Kater); one *s* two step *s*. *Educ:* Sydney Church of England Grammar Sch. Served Australian Imperial Forces (Captain), 1940-44, New Guinea. J. H. Broinowski and Storey, Chartered Accountants, 1944-54; Founder and Managing Dir, Consolidated Metal Products Ltd, 1954-62. Pres., Aust. Council for Rehabilitation of the Disabled, 1964-68; Vice-Pres., Internat. Soc. for Rehabilitation of the Disabled, 1966-. *Recreation:* cattle breeding. *Address:* 1c Wentworth Place, Point Piper, Sydney, Australia. *T:* 362057. *Clubs:* Union, Australian, Royal Sydney Golf (all in Sydney).

**BROGLIE, Louis V. de;** *see* de Broglie.

**BROKE;** *see* Willoughby de Broke.

**BROKE, Maj.-Gen. Robert Straton,** CB 1967; OBE 1946; MC 1940; Director, Wellman Engineering Corporation; *b* 15 March 1913; *s* of Rev. Horatio George Broke and Mary Campbell Broke (*née* Adlington); *m* 1939, Ernine Susan Margaret Bonsey; two *s*. *Educ:* Eton College; Magdalene College, Cambridge (BA). Commissioned Royal Artillery, 1933. Commander Royal Artillery: 5th Division, 1959; 1st Division, 1960; 1st (British) Corps 1961; Northern Army Group, 1964-66, retired. Col Comdt, RA, 1968-. *Recreations:* country sports. *Address:* Holme Hale Hall, Thetford, Norfolk. *T:* Holme Hale 225. *Clubs:* Army and Navy, MCC.

**BROME, Vincent;** author; *s* of Nathaniel Gregory and Emily Brome. *Educ:* Streatham Grammar School; Elleston School; privately. Formerly Feature Writer, Daily Chronicle, 1935-36; Editor, Menu Magazines, 1937-40; Min. of Information, 1941-44; Asst Editor, Medical World, 1945-47. Since then author biographies, novels, plays and essays. Play, The Sleepless One (prod. Edin), 1962. BBC plays and general broadcasting. *Publications:* Anthology, 1936; Clement Attlee, 1947; H. G. Wells, 1951; Aneurin Bevan, 1953; The Last Surrender, 1954; The Way Back, 1956; Six Studies in Quarrelling, 1958; Sometimes at Night, 1959; Frank Harris, 1959; Acquaintance With Grief, 1961; We Have Come a Long Way, 1962; The Problem of Progress, 1963; Love in Our Time, 1964; Four Realist Novelists, 1964; The International Brigades, 1965; The World of Luke Jympson, 1966; Freud and His Early Circle, 1967; The Surgeon, 1967; Diary of A Revolution, 1968; The Revolution, 1969; The Imaginary Crime, 1969; Confessions of a Writer, 1970; The Brain Operators, 1970; Private Prosecutions, 1971. *Recreations:* writing plays and talking. *Address:* 45 Great Ormond Street, WC1. *T:* 01-405 2509. *Clubs:* Savage, PEN.

**BROMET, Air Vice-Marshal Sir Geoffrey R.,** KBE 1945 (CBE 1941; OBE 1919), CB 1943; DSO 1917; DL; *b* 28 Aug. 1891; *e s* of late G. A. Bromet, Tadcaster; *m* 1917, Margaret (*d* 1961), *e d* of late Maj. Ratliffe, Hardingstone, Northampton; one *d*; *m* 1965, Jean Conan Doyle (*see* Air Commandant Dame Jean Bromet). *Educ:* Bradfield; Royal Naval Colls, Osborne and Dartmouth. Royal Navy, 1904-14; RNAS, 1914-18; RAF, 1918-38; retired list, 1938; re-employed Sept. 1939; SASO HQ Coastal Command, 1940-41; AOC 19 Group Plymouth, 1941-43; Senior British Officer Azores Force, 1943-45; reverted to retired list, Oct. 1945; Lieutenant-Governor, Isle of Man, 1945-52; a Vice-President: Royal Air Force Association; RNLI. dl kent, 1958. *Address:* Home Green, Littlestone-on-Sea, Kent; 72 Cadogan Square, SW1. *Club:* Royal Air Force.

**BROMET, Air Comdt Dame Jean (Lena Annette),** DBE 1963 (OBE 1948); Director of the Women's Royal Air Force, 1963-66, retired; *b* 21 Dec. 1912; *d* of late Sir Arthur Conan Doyle and Lady Conan Doyle (*née* Jean Leckie); *m* 1965, Air Vice-Marshal Sir Geoffrey Bromet, *qv*. *Educ:* Granville House, Eastbourne. Joined No. 46 (Co. of Sussex) ATS, RAF Company, Sept. 1938; commnd in WAAF, 1940; served in UK, 1939-45; commnd in RAF, 1949; Comd WRAF Admin Officer: BAFO, Germany, 1947-50; HQ Tech. Trg. Comd, 1950-52 and 1962-63; Dep. Dir, 1952-54 and 1960-62; OC, RAF Hawkinge, 1956-59; Inspector of the WRAF, 1954-56 and 1959-60. Hon. ADC to the Queen, 1963-66. A Governor, Star and Garter Home, 1968-. *Address:* 72 Cadogan Square, SW1. *T:* 01-589 6157; Home Green, Littlestone-on-Sea, New Romney, Kent. *Clubs;* Naval and Military, Royal Air Force.

**BROMHEAD, Sir Benjamin (Denis Gonville),** 5th Bt, *cr* 1806; OBE 1943; Lieut-Col (Retd) Frontier Force Regt (Indian Army): *b* 7 May 1900; *s* of late Maj. E. G. Bromhead (*er s* of 4th Bt); *S* grandfather, Colonel Sir Benjamin Parnell Bromhead, 4th Bt, CB, 1935; *m* 1938, Nancy Mary, *o d* of late T. S. Lough, Buenos Aires; one *s* two *d*. *Educ:* Wellington College; RMC Sandhurst. Entered Indian Army, 1919; Iraq, 1920 (medal with clasp); Waziristan, 1922-24 (Wounded, medal with clasp); NW Frontier of India, 1930 (despatches, medal with clasp); Waziristan, 1937 (despatches); Political Agent, N. Waziristan, NW Frontier Province, 1945-47; retd, 1949. *Heir: s* John Desmond Gonville Bromhead, *b* 21 Dec. 1943. *Address;* Thurlby Hall, Aubourn, Lincoln. *Club:* Naval and Military.

**BROMLEY, Archdeacon of;** *see* Cragg, Ven. H. W.

**BROMLEY, Lance Lee,** MA; MChir; FRCS; Surgeon in charge, Thoracic Department, St Mary's Hospital, W2; Consulting Surgeon, Teddington Hospital; Thoracic Surgeon, St Mary's Hospital, Harrow Road, W9; *b* 16 Feb. 1920; *s* of late Lancelot Bromley, MChir FRCS, of London and Seaford, Sussex, and Dora Ridgway Bromley, Dewsbury, Yorks; *m* 1952, Rosemary Anne Holbrook; three *d*. *Educ:* St Paul's School; Caius Coll., Cambridge. Late Capt. RAMC. Late Travelling Fell. Amer. Assoc. for Thoracic Surgery. *Publications:* various contributions to medical journals. *Recreations:* sailing, golf. *Address:* 2 Hyde Park Crescent, W2. *T:* 01-262 7175. *Club:* Royal Ocean Racing.

**BROMLEY, Sir Rupert Charles,** 10th Bt, *cr* 1757; *b* 2 April 1936; *s* of Major Sir Rupert Howe Bromley, MC, 9th Bt, and Dorothy Vera, *d* of late Sir Walford Selby, KCMG, CB, CVO; *S* father, 1966; *m* 1962, Priscilla Hazel, *d* of late Maj. Howard Bourne, HAC; three *s*. *Educ:* Michaelhouse, Natal; Rhodes Univ.; Christ Church, Oxford. *Recreations:* equestrian. *Heir: s* Charles Howard Bromley, *b* 31 July 1963. *Address:* 44 Main Street, Johannesburg, SA.

**BROMLEY, Sir Thomas Eardley,** KCMG 1964 (CMG 1955); HM Diplomatic Service, retired; Secretary, Churches Main Committee, since Dec. 1970; *b* 14 Dec. 1911; *s* of late Thomas Edward Bromley, ICS; *m* 1944, Diana Marion, *d* of Sir John Pratt, KBE, CMG; *m* 1966, Mrs Alison Toulmin. *Educ:* Rugby; Magdalen College, Oxford. Entered Consular Service, 1935; Vice-Consul, Japan, 1938; Asst Private Sec. to the Permanent Under-Secretary of State, 1943, and Private Secretary, 1945; Grade 7, 1945; served in Washington, 1946; Bagdad, 1949; Counsellor, 1953; Head of African Department, Foreign Office, March 1954-Jan. 1956; Imperial Defence College, 1956; Foreign Office Inspectorate, 1957; seconded to Cabinet Office, Oct. 1957; Consul-General at Mogadishu, 1960; Ambassador: to Somali Republic, 1960-61; to Syrian Arab Republic, 1962-64; to Algeria, 1964-65; FO, 1966; Ambassador to Ethiopia, 1966-69. *Address:* Pusey Furze, Buckland, near Faringdon, Bucks. *Club:* Travellers'.

**BROMLEY-DAVENPORT, Dame Lilian (Emily Isabel Jane),** DBE, *cr* 1954; JP; *d* of late Lieut-Colonel John Henry Bagot Lane, King's Bromley, Staffordshire; *m* 1902, Walter Arthur Bromley-Davenport (*d* 1942); three *s* (and one *s* died of wounds, in Holland, 1944). Alderman and JP Cheshire. *Address:* The Kennels, Capesthorne, Macclesfield, Ches.

**BROMLEY-DAVENPORT, Lt-Col Sir Walter Henry,** Kt 1961; TD; DL; *b* 1903; *s* of late Walter A. Bromley-Davenport, Capesthorne, Macclesfield, Cheshire, and of Lilian Emily Isabel Jane (*née* Lane) (*see* Dame Lilian Bromley-Davenport); *m* 1933, Lenette F., *d* of Joseph Y. Jeanes, Philadelphia, USA; one *s* one *d*. *Educ:* Malvern. Joined Grenadier Guards, 1922; raised and comd 5 Bn Cheshire Regt, Lt-Col 1939. MP (C) Knutsford Div. 1945-70; Conservative Whip, 1948-51. DL Cheshire, 1949. British Boxing Board of Control, 1953. *Address:* 39 Westminster Gardens, Marsham Street, SW1. *T:* 01-834 2929; Capesthorne Hall, Macclesfield, Cheshire. *T:* Chelford 221; Fiva, Romsdalshorn, Norway. *Clubs:* Guards, White's.

**BROMMAGE, Joseph Charles,** CIE 1947; OBE 1945 (MBE 1921); *b* 4 Feb. 1897; *m* 1926, Edith Marie Neilson, MB, ChB, DPH. Served European War, 1914-18, operations France and Belgium; operations Waziristan, Tochi and Derajat columns. 1919-20 (Mahsud Clasp, MBE). Entered service of Govt of India, 1923; various appts in Govt of India, Fin. Dept, until 1940; Joint Financial Adviser, Munitions Production, India, 1940-44 (OBE); Additional Financial Adviser, Military Finance, and ex-officio Joint Secretary to Govt of India Finance Dept, 1944-47; Military Accountant General, India, 1947 (CIE); Chief Bipartite Finance Group, Frankfurt/Main, Germany, 1947-50. *Address:* Les Champignons, Alderney, CI. *Clubs:* Oriental; Royal Calcutta Turf.

**BROMMELLE, Norman Spencer;** Keeper, Department of Conservation, Victoria and Albert Museum, since 1960; *b* 9 June 1915; *s* of James Valentine Brommelle and Ada Louisa Brommelle (*née* Bastin); *m* 1959, Rosa Joyce Plesters. *Educ:* High Pavement School, Nottingham; University College, Oxford. Scientific research in industry on Metallography and Spectroscopy, 1937-48; Picture Conservation, National Gallery, 1949-60. Secretary-General, International Institute for Conservation of Historic and Artistic Works, 1957-64, 1966- (Vice-President, 1964-66). *Publications:* contributions to: Journal of the Institute of Metals; Studies in Conservation; Museums Journal. *Recreation:* gardening. *Address:* 5 Lyndhurst Square, SE15. *T:* 01-701 0607.

**BRONK, Detlev Wulf,** OBE 1947 (Hon.); Foreign Member Royal Society 1948; AB, MS, PhD; President: Johns Hopkins University, 1940-53; Rockefeller University, 1953-68; National Academy of Sciences, 1950-62; Chairman: National Research Council, 1946-50; New York State Science and Technology Foundation; Fell. American Assoc. for the Advancement of Science (President, 1952); *b* 13 Aug. 1897; *s* of Mitchell Bronk and Marie Wulf; *m* 1921, Helen Ramsey; three *s*. *Educ:* Swarthmore College; University of Michigan. Ensign US Naval Aviation Corps, 1918-19; Instructor in Physics, University of Pennsylvania, 1921; University of Michigan, 1921-24; Instructor in Physiology, 1924-26; Assistant Professor of Physiology, 1926; Assistant Professor of Physiology and Biophysics, Swarthmore College, 1926-27; Associate Professor of Physiology and Biophysics, 1927-28; Professor of Physiology and Biophysics, 1928-29; Dean of Men, Swarthmore College, 1927-29; Professor of Physiology, Cornell, 1940-41; Director, Johnson Research Foundation and Professor of Biophysics, also Director Inst. of Neurology, University of Pennsylvania, 1929-49; Fellow in Medicine of the National Research Council at Cambridge and London, 1928-29; Weir Mitchell Lecturer, Philadelphia College of Physicians, 1938; Hughlings Jackson Lecturer, McGill, 1938; Vanuxem Lecturer, Princeton, 1939; Priestley Lecturer, Penna State College, 1941; Herter Lecturer, New York University Medical College, 1943; Colver Lecturer, Brown University, 1946; A. D. Little Lecturer, Mass. Inst. Tech., 1949; Louis H. Bauer Lecturer, 1960; Gideon Seymour Lecturer, 1960; Robert Kennedy Duncan Memorial Lecturer, 1960. Managing Editor, Journal of Cellular and Comparative Physiology and Associate Editor of several specialist journals; Member of: Amer. Acad. Arts and Sciences; French Acad. of Sciences; Roy. Danish Acad. of Sciences and Letters; Roy. Swedish Acad. of Science; Acad. of Sciences, USSR; Brazilian Acad. of Sciences; Swiss Acad. of Sciences; American Philosophical Society; Hon. Member: British Physiological Society, Royal Institution and of numerous scientific societies; Advisory Committee for Biology and Medicine, US Atomic Energy Commission, 1946-50; US National Commission for UNESCO; Sci. Advisory Board, Army Air Forces; National Advisory Committee for Aeronautics; National Science Foundation Board; President's Science Advisory Committee. Trustee: Johns Hopkins University, University of Pennsylvania, Bucknell University, Rockefeller Fund, Rockefeller University, Rensselaer Polytechnic Inst.; Rockefeller Brothers Fund, Sloan Kettering Inst., etc. Presidential Medal of Freedom, 1964; Benjamin Franklin Medal (RSA), 1967; Nat. Medal of Science, 1968. Holds 55 Hon. degrees in Law, Science, etc., from Cambridge, London, Harvard, etc. *Publications:* articles in Astrophysical Journal, Journal of the Optical Society, Journal of Physiology, American Journal of Physiology, etc. *Recreation:* sailing. *Address:* The Rockefeller University, New York, NY 10021, USA. *T:* 360-1000. *Clubs:* Athenæum (London); Century, University, New York Yacht (New York); Rittenhouse (Philadelphia); Cosmos (Washington); Maryland (Baltimore).

**BRONOWSKI, Jacob,** MA, PhD; Senior Fellow, Trustee, and Director of the Council for Biology in Human Affairs, Salk Institute for Biological Studies, since 1964; *b* 18 Jan. 1908; *e s* of Abram and Celia Bronowski; *m* 1941, Rita Coblentz; four *d*. *Educ:* Central Foundation School; Jesus College, Cambridge (Hon. Fellow, 1967). Sr Lecturer at University College, Hull, 1934-42; seconded to Govt service, 1942; Joint Target Group, Washington, and Chiefs of Staff Mission to Japan, 1945; statistical research into economics of building and other industries, Ministry of Works, 1946-50; seconded to UNESCO as Head of Projects, 1948; Carnegie Visiting Professor, Massachusetts Institute of Technology, 1953; Director of Coal Research Establishment, National Coal Board, 1950-59; Director-General of Process Development Department of National Coal Board, 1959-64. Lectures: inaugural Man and Nature, Amer. Mus. Nat. History, 1965; Blashfield, Amer. Acad. Arts and Letters, 1966; Condon, Univ. Oregon, 1967; Silliman, Yale, 1967; Mellon, Nat. Gallery of Art, Washington, DC, 1969; Bampton, Columbia Univ., 1969. Member Society for Visiting Scientists; FRSL; Foreign Hon. Member, American Acad. of Arts and Sciences, 1960; Fellow Member, World Acad. of Art and Science. *Publications:* The Poet's Defence, 1939 and 1966; William Blake, a Man without a Mask, 1944; The Common Sense of Science, 1951; radio plays, including The Journey to Japan, 1948, and The Face of Violence (Italia Prize, 1951), 1954 and 1967; Science and Human Values, 1958; Selection of William Blake's Poems, 1958; The Western Intellectual Tradition, 1960; Insight, 1964; The Abacus and the Rose: A New Dialogue on Two World Systems, 1965; William Blake and the Age of Revolution, 1965; The Identity of Man, 1965; Nature and Knowledge, 1969; numerous papers in mathematics. *Recreations:* squash rackets and chess. *Address:* PO Box 1809, San Diego, California 92112, USA. *Club:* Athenæum.

**BROOK, Caspar;** Director, The Family Planning Association, since 1968; *b* 24 Aug. 1920; *m* 1948, Dinah Fine; one *s* one *d*. *Educ:* UCW, Cardiff. Royal Tank Regt, Glider Pilot Regt, 1940-46. British Export Trade Research Organisation, 1947; Machine Tool and

Electrical Engrs, 1947-53; Publications Ed., Economist Intelligence Unit Ltd, 1953-58; Dir, Consumers' Assoc., 1958-64; Man. Dir, Equipment Comparison Ltd, 1964-67; Man. Dir, Industrial Training and Publishing Div., Pergamon Press, 1966-67. *Recreations:* talking, sailing. *Address:* 39 Fairhazel Gardens, NW6. *T:* 01-624 8582.

**BROOK, Clive;** Actor; *b* 1 June, 1887; *s* of George Alfred and Charlotte Mary Brook; *m* 1920, Charlotte Elizabeth Mildred (*née* Evelyn); one *s* one *d*. *Educ:* privately. Served European War, 1914-18; Artists Rifles, 1914-15; Machine Gun Corps A, 1915-18. Stage plays, 1919-23: Over Sunday, Harbury Points, James the Less, Just Like Judy, Clothes and the Woman; *Films in England,* 1920-24: Trent's Last Case, Kissing Cup's Race, Sportsman's Wife, Daniel Deronda, Loudwater Mystery, Her Penalty, Christine Johnson, Married to a Mormon, Reverse of the Medal, Through Fire and Water, Sonia, Out to Win, Shirley, This Freedom, Woman to Woman; *Films in America,* 1924-34 (Silent): Christine of the Hungry Heart, Enticement, The Mirage, Playing with Souls, Declasse, If Marriage Fails, Human Desires, Woman Hater, The Homemaker, Pleasure Buyers, Seven Sinners, Compromise, Three Faces East, When Love Grows Cold, Why Girls Go Back Home, You Never Know Women, For Alimony Only, Popular Sin, Barbed Wire, Afraid to Love, Underworld, Hula, Devil Dancer, French Dressing, Midnight Madness, Yellow Lily, Perfect Crime, Heliotrope; (Talking): Interference, Four Feathers, Dangerous Woman, Charming Sinners, Sherlock Holmes, Laughing Lady, Slightly Scarlet, Sweethearts and Wives, Anybody's Woman, Scandal Sheet, East Lynne, Tarnished Lady, Lawyer's Secret, Silence, Twenty-four Hours, Husband's Holiday, Shanghai Express, Man from Yesterday, The Night of June 13th, Return of Sherlock Holmes, Cavalcade, Midnight Club, If I Were Free, Gallant Lady, Dover Road, Let's Try Again; The Dictator (England), 1934; Dressmaker of Luneville (America), 1935; *Films in England,* 1935-43: Love in Exile, Lonely Road, Action for Slander, The Ware Case, Return to Yesterday, Convoy, Freedom Radio, The Shipbuilders, Flemish Farm, Breach of Promise, On Approval (also produced, adapted and directed). Returned to stage in England, 1944; appeared in: The Years Between, Play's The Thing, Gioconda Smile, Stratton; Second Threshold, New York, 1950-51; Vaudeville, London, 1952; A Woman of No Importance, London, 1953; The Count of Clérambard, London, 1955; One Bright Day, London, 1956; Judge's Story, 1963. *Film in Hollywood,* 1962: List of Adrian Messenger. Has appeared on television from 1956. Wrote stage play, That's What Victor Hugo Said, prod 1968. *Address:* 95 Eaton Square, SW1. *T:* 01-235 7110. *Club:* Garrick.

**BROOK, Donald Charles;** Chartered Accountant, qualified 1922; Company Director; *b* 31 May 1894; *e s* of late Walter Henry Brook and of Emily Brook. *Educ:* High School and Technical College, Newport. Served European War 1914-18, France and Egypt; War of 1939-45 Upper Thames Patrol, 1941-44. Assisted in formation in 1926 and subseq. development of Perak River Hydro-Electric Co. Ltd, Malaya (now Vice-Chairman); Vice-Chairman Nigerian Electricity Corp., 1944-66; Exec. Member London Boards of: E. African Power & Lighting Co. Ltd, 1942-66; Kenya Power Co. Ltd (1954-66); Dir, Balfour, Beatty & Co. Ltd, 1944-66; Dir and Vice-Chairman, Jerusalem Electric & Public Service Corp., 1942-57; Dir and Chm. British Central Africa Co. Ltd, 1943-63. Executive Member Council, Joint African Board, 1942- (Vice-Chm. 1963-66); Member Council, Exec. Cttee. and Finance and General Purposes Committee, Organisation of Employers' Federations and Employers in Developing Countries, 1958-68. Member Nyasaland Tea Assoc. London Cttee., 1950-63; Member Cttee, E. Africa Dinner Club, 1963-. FRSA; FCA. *Recreations:* fishing, gardening; Cdre. British Motor Yacht Club, 1947 and 1948. *Address:* Creek House, Broom Water, Teddington, Middx. *Clubs:* East India and Sports, Royal Automobile, East Africa House, Royal Commonwealth Society; Muthaiga Country (Nairobi).

**BROOK, Sir Dryden,** Kt 1965; wool merchant; Member Halifax County Borough Council; *b* 25 Aug. 1884; *s* of James Brook. MP (Lab) Halifax, 1945-55. Freeman of County Borough of Halifax, 1964. *Address:* Flat 15, Old Well Head, Halifax, Yorks. *T:*Halifax 52166.

**BROOK, Professor George Leslie,** MA, PhD; Professor of English Language since 1945, and of Medieval English Literature since 1951, University of Manchester; Dean of the Faculty of Arts, 1956-57; Pro-Vice-Chancellor, 1962-65; Presenter of Honorary Graduands, 1964-65; *b* 6 March 1910; 3rd *s* of late Willie Brook, Shepley, Huddersfield; *m* 1949, Stella, *d* of Thomas Maguire, Salford. *Educ:* University of Leeds; Ripon English Literature Prize, 1931. Visiting Professor, University of California, Los Angeles, 1951; Governor, John Rylands Library; Member of Court, University of Leeds, and of Court and Council, University of Keele. *Publications:* An English Phonetic Reader, 1935; English Sound-Changes, 1935; Glossary to the Works of Sir Thomas Malory, 1947; An Introduction to Old English, 1955; A History of the English Language, 1958; English Dialects, 1963; The Modern University, 1965; The Language of Dickens, 1970; (edited) The Harley Lyrics, 1948; The Journal of the Lancashire Dialect Society, 1951-54; (with R. F. Leslie) Layamon's Brut, Vol. I, 1963; (with C. S. Lewis) Selections from Layamon's Brut, 1963. *Address:* 26 Chandos Road South, Manchester 21. *T:* 061-840 3659.

**BROOK, Mrs Helen;** Chairman, Brook Advisory Centre for Young People, since 1963; *b* 12 Oct. 1907; *d* of John and Helen Knewstub; *m* 1937, (Ralph Ellis) Robin Brook, *qv*; two *d* (and one *d* of previous marriage). *Educ:* Convent of Holy Child Jesus, Mark Cross, Sussex. Voluntary Worker, Family Planning Association, 1949-. *Recreations:* painting, gardening. *Address:* 33 Bryanston Square, W1. *T:* 01-262 1607; Claydene Garden Cottage, Cowden, Kent.

**BROOK, Commodore James Kenneth,** CBE 1942; DSO 1918; RD; RNR; retired; Master in the Mercantile Marine; *b* 1889; *s* of late James Alfred Brook, Barnsley Farm, Isle of Wight; *m* 1942, Betty, *d* of late H. L. Brook, AMIEE; one *d* . *Educ:* Isle of Wight College, Ryde; HMS Worcester (Training Ship). Served in square-rigged sailing ships Ladye Doris and Marian Woodside, 1906-11; in Tramp steamers, 1912-14; in HM ships on active service, 1914-19; served in Armed Merchant cruisers, in Grand Fleet (HMS Conqueror) and later in Q and Mystery ships (despatches, DSO for sinking U34 when in command of HMS Privet, Q19); after demobilising joined Andrew Weir & Co. as Chief Officer and 2 years later in command of various Company's Ships until retirement; 1939-44, served as Commodore in various convoys (despatches, CBE); ADC to the King, 1942-43. *Recreations:* stroked Worcester-Conway boat-race, 1905; walking, swimming; music lover (amateur).

*Address:* West Hill, Seaview, Isle of Wight. *T:* Seaview 3294.

**BROOK, Leopold,** BSc, FICE, FIMechE; Chairman, Simon Engineering Ltd, 1970 (Deputy Chairman and Chief Executive 1967-70); *b* 2 Jan. 1912; *s* of Albert and Kate Brook, Hampstead; *m* 1940, Susan, *d* of David Rose, Hampstead; two *s*. *Educ:* Central Foundation School, London; University College, London. L. G. Mouchel & Partners, Cons. Engineers, 1935-44; Simon Engineering Ltd, 1944-; Dir of many wholly owned and associated companies. Fellow, UCL, 1970-. *Recreations:* music, theatre, golf. *Address:* 10 Lindfield Gardens, NW3. *T:* 01-435 3130. *Clubs:* Royal Automobile; Manchester (Manchester).

**BROOK, Peter Stephen Paul,** CBE 1965; Producer; Co-Director, The Royal Shakespeare Theatre; *b* 21 March 1925; 2nd *s* of Simon Brook; *m* 1951, Natasha Parry, stage and film star; one *s* one *d*. *Educ:* Westminster, Greshams and Magdalen College, Oxford. Productions include: The Tragedy of Dr Faustus, 1942; The Infernal Machine, 1945; Birmingham Repertory Theatre: Man and Superman, King John, The Lady from the Sea, 1945-46; Stratford: Romeo and Juliet, Love's Labour Lost, 1947; London: Vicious Circle, Men Without Shadows, Respectable Prostitute, The Brothers Karamazov, 1946; Director of Productions, Royal Opera House, Covent Garden, 1947-50: Boris Godunov, La Bohème, 1948; Marriage of Figaro, The Olympians, Salome, 1949. Dark of the Moon, 1949; Ring Round the Moon, 1950; Measure for Measure, Stratford, 1950; The Little Hut, 1950; The Winter's Tale, 1951; Venice Preserved, 1953; The Little Hut, New York, Faust, Metropolitan Opera House, 1953; The Dark is Light Enough; Both Ends Meet, 1954; House of Flowers, New York, 1954; The Lark, 1955; Titus Andronicus, Stratford, 1955; Hamlet, 1955; The Power and the Glory, 1956; Family Reunion, 1956; The Tempest, Stratford, 1957; Cat on a Hot Tin Roof, Paris, 1957; View from the Bridge, Paris, 1958; Irma la Douce, London, 1958; The Fighting Cock, New York, 1959; Le Balcon, Paris, 1960; The Visit, Royalty, 1960; King Lear, Stratford and Aldwych, 1962; The Physicists, Aldwych, 1963; Sergeant Musgrave's Dance, Paris, 1963; The Persecution and Assassination of Marat . . ., Aldwych, 1964 (New York, 1966); The Investigation, Aldwych, 1965; US, Aldwych, 1966; Oedipus, National Theatre, 1968; A Midsummer Night's Dream, Stratford, 1970. *Directed films:* The Beggar's Opera, 1952; Moderato Cantabile, 1960; Lord of the Flies, 1962; The Marat/Sade, 1967; Tell Me Lies, 1968; King Lear, 1969. Hon. DLitt Birmingham. Chevalier de l'Ordre des Arts et des Lettres, 1965. *Publication:* The Empty Space, 1968. *Recreations:* painting, piano playing and travelling by air. *Address:* c/o P. L. Representation Ltd, 33 Sloane Street, SW1.

**BROOK, Ralph Ellis;** *see* Brook, Robin.

**BROOK, Robin, (Ralph Ellis Brook),** CMG 1954; OBE 1945; Chairman: Gordon Woodroffe & Co.; Ionian Bank; Truscon Ltd; Leda Investment Trust Ltd; Bardolin Ltd; Director: Northern Dairies Group; Hellenic & General Trust Ltd; Dimplex Ltd, etc; HM Government Director, British Petroleum Co. Ltd, since 1970; President, London Chamber of Commerce (Chairman, 1966-68); Hon. Treasurer, Family Planning Association; *b* 19 June 1908; *s* of Francis Brook, FRCS, Harley Street, and Mrs E. I. Brook; *m* 1937, Helen (*see* Helen Brook), *e d* of John Knewstub; two *d*. *Educ:* Eton; King's College, Cambridge. Served 1941-46; Brig., 1945 (OBE, despatches, Legion of Merit (Commander), Legion of Honour, Croix de Guerre and Bar, Order of Leopold (Officer), Belgian Croix de Guerre). Director, Bank of England, 1946-49. Deputy Chairman: British Tourist and Holidays Board, 1946-50; Colonial Development Corp., 1949-53. Mem., Cttee on Invisible Exports, 1969-. High Sheriff of County of London, 1950; Mem. coun. of Festival of Britain. Treasurer, St Bartholomew's Hosp.; Governor, Royal Free Hosp. Past Master, Haberdashers' Co. *Recreation:* British Sabre Champion, 1936; Olympic Games, 1936, 1948; Capt. British Team, 1933, etc. *Address:* 33 Bryanston Square, W1. *T:* 01-723 5342.

**BROOK, Rev. Victor John Knight,** MA; Chaplain of All Souls College, 1935; Fellow, 1938-59; *b* 22 June 1887; *s* of Richard Brook and Emma Knight; *m* 1st, 1914, Marie (*d* 1963), *d* of W. Groux; one *s* one *d*; 2nd, 1965, Janet, *d* of George Swift. *Educ:* Bradford Grammar School; Queen's College, Oxford (Exhibitioner). 1st class Lit. Hum.; 1st class Theology. Curate, Wakefield Cathedral, 1912-15; St James's, Piccadilly, 1915-16; Assistant Master, Charterhouse, 1916-21; Fellow and Chaplain, Lincoln College, Oxford, 1921-30; Prebendary of Lincoln, 1927-33; Senior Proctor, University of Oxford, 1922; Select Preacher, University of Oxford, 1928-30; University of Cambridge, 1938; University Lecturer in Reformation Theology, 1929-34; Member of Hebdomadal Council, 1926-49; Censor St Catherine's Society, Oxford, 1930-52. Hon. Fellow, St Catherine's College, 1963. *Publications:* The Claims of Duty; Divine Justice; John Whitgift and the English Church; A Life of Archbishop Parker. *Recreation:* walking. *Address:* Stonefield, Burford, Oxford.

**BROOKE,** family name of **Viscount Alanbrooke,** of **Baron Brooke of Cumnor,** of **Baroness Brooke of Ystradfellte** and of **Viscount Brookeborough.**

**BROOKE OF CUMNOR,** Baron (Life Peer), *cr* 1966; **Henry Brooke,** PC 1955; CH 1964; *b* 9 April 1903; *y s* of L. Leslie Brooke and Sybil Diana, *d* of Rev. Stopford Brooke; *m* 1933, Barbara (*see* Baroness Brooke of Ystradfellte), *y d* of Canon A. A. Mathews; two *s* two *d*. *Educ:* Marlborough; Balliol College, Oxford. MP (C) West Lewisham, 1938-45, Hampstead, 1950-66. Deputy Chairman, Southern Railway Company, 1946-48. Member of Central Housing Advisory Committee, 1944-54; Member of London County Council, 1945-55, and of Hampstead Borough Council, 1936-57. Financial Secretary to the Treasury, 1954-57; Minister of Housing and Local Government and Minister for Welsh Affairs, 1957-61; Chief Secretary to the Treasury and Paymaster-General, 1961-62; Home Secretary, 1962-64. Member of Governing Bodies of Marlborough College and Charterhouse School. *Address:* The Glebe House, Mildenhall, Marlborough, Wilts.

**BROOKE OF YSTRADFELLTE,** Baroness *cr* 1964 (Life Peeress); **Barbara Brooke,** DBE 1960; *b* 14 Jan. 1908; *y d* of late Canon A. A. Mathews; *m* 1933, Henry Brooke (*see* Baron Brooke of Cumnor); two *s* two *d*. *Educ:* Queen Anne's School, Caversham. Joint Vice-Chm., Conservative Party Organisation, 1954-64. Member: Hampstead Borough Council, 1948-65; North-West Metropolitan Regional Hospital Board, 1954-66; Management Cttee, King Edward's Hospital Fund for London; Board of Governors, Hospital for Sick Children, Great Ormond Street; Chm. Exec. Cttee Queen's Institute of District Nursing. Member Council, Bedford College; Chairman, Governing Body of Godolphin and Latymer

School, Hammersmith. Hon. Fellow, Westfield College. *Address:* The Glebe House, Mildenhall, Marlborough, Wilts.
*See also Rev. A. K. Mathews.*

**BROOKE, Lord; David Robin Francis Guy Greville;** *b* 15 May 1934; *s* and *heir* of 7th Earl of Warwick, *qv*; *m* 1956, Sarah Anne (marr. diss. 1967), *d* of Alfred Chester Beatty and Mrs Pamela Neilson; one *s* one *d*. *Educ:* Eton. Life Guards, 1952; Warwicks. Yeo. (TA), 1954. *Address:* Warwick Castle, Warwick. *T:* Warwick 42917. *Club:* White's.

**BROOKE, Vice-Admiral (Retd) Basil Charles Barrington,** CB 1949; CBE 1947; *b* 6 April 1895; *s* of John C. E. H. Brooke and Hon. Violet M. Barrington; *m* 1925, Nora Evelyn Toppin; two *s* two *d*. *Educ:* Malvern College. Royal Navy, 1913; Captain, 1938; Rear-Admiral, 1947; retired, 1949. Vice-Admiral (Retd), 1950. *Address:* Dingle Hill, Hollybush, Ledbury, Herefordshire. *T:* Bromesberrow 288.

**BROOKE, Professor Bryan Nicholas,** MD, MChir, FRCS; Professor of Surgery, University of London, at St George's Hospital since 1963; *b* 21 Feb. 1915; *s* of George Cyril Brooke, LitD, FSA (numismatist) and Margaret Florence Brooke; *m* 1940, Naomi Winefride Mills; three *d*. *Educ:* Bradfield College, Berkshire; Corpus Christi College, Cambridge; St Bartholomew's Hospital, London. FRCSEng 1942; MChir (Cantab.) 1944; MD (Birm.) with hons 1954. Lieut-Colonel, RAMC, 1945-46. Lecturer in Surgery, Aberdeen University, 1946-47; Reader in Surgery, Birmingham University, 1947-63; Hunterian Prof. RCS, 1951. Examiner in Surgery: Birmingham University, 1951-63; Cambridge University, 1958-; Bristol University, 1961-; London University, 1962-. Member, Medical Appeals Tribunal, 1948-. Copeman Medal for Scientific Research, 1960; Graham Award (Amer. Proctologic Soc.), 1961; Award of NY Soc., Colon and Rectal Surgeons, 1967. *Publications:* Ulcerative Colitis and its Surgical Treatment, 1954; You and Your Operation, 1957; United Birmingham Cancer Reports, 1953, 1954, 1957; (co-editor) Recent Advances in Gastroenterology, 1965; (co-author) Metabolic Derangements in Gastrointestinal Surgery. Contributor to various surgical works. Numerous articles on large bowel disorder, medical education, steroid therapy. *Recreations:* painting, pottery. *Address:* Flat 86, 24 John Islip Street, SW1. *T:* 01-824 2502.

**BROOKE, Prof. Christopher Nugent Lawrence,** MA; FRHistS; FSA, FBA 1970; Professor of History, Westfield College, University of London, since 1967; *b* 1927; *y s* of late Professor Zachary Nugent Brooke and Rosa Grace Brooke; *m* 1951, Rosalind Beckford, *d* of Dr and Mrs L. H. S. Clark; three *s*. *Educ:* Winchester College (Scholar); Gonville and Caius College, Cambridge (Major Scholar). BA 1948; MA 1952. Army service in RAEC, Temp. Captain 1949. Fellow of Gonville and Caius College, 1949-56; College Lecturer in History, 1953-56; Praelector Rhetoricus, 1955-56; Assistant Lecturer in History, Cambridge University, 1953-54; Lecturer, 1954-56; Prof. of Mediæval History, University of Liverpool, 1956-67. *Publications:*(part Editor) The Book of William Morton, 1954; The Letters of John of Salisbury, vol. 1, 1955; Carte Nativorum, 1960; The Dullness of the Past, 1957; From Alfred to Henry III, 1961; The Saxon and Norman Kings, 1963; Europe in the Central Middle Ages, 1964; Time the Archsatirist, 1968; The Twelfth Century Renaissance, 1970; (with A. Morey) Gilbert Foliot and his letters, 1965 and (ed jtly) The Letters and Charters of Gilbert Foliot, 1967; contributed to A History of St Paul's Cathedral, 1957; Studies in the Early British Church, 1958; Celt and Saxon, 1963; Studies in Church History, Vol. I, 1964; general editor: Oxford (formerly Nelson's) Medieval Texts, Nelson's History of England; articles and reviews in English Historical Review, Cambridge Historical Journal, Bulletin of Inst. of Historical Research, Downside Review, Traditio, Bulletin of John Rylands Library; Jl of Soc. of Archivists, etc. *Address:* 28 Wood Lane, Highgate, N6. *T:* 01-340 2650.

**BROOKE, Maj.-Gen. Frank Hastings,** CB 1958; CBE 1954; DSO 1945; Chief Army Instructor, Imperial Defence College, 1960-62, retd; *b* 1909; *s* of Lt-Col G. F. Brooke, DSO; *m* 1935, Helen Mary, *d* of late Major R. Berkeley; two *s*. *Educ:* RMC Sandhurst. 2nd Lieut, The Welch Regt., 1929; Captain 1938. Served NWF, India (Medal and clasp), 1935; staff and regtl appts, 1939-45; Instr Staff College, Camberley, 1945-47; Dep. Comd. (Brig.) Burma Mission, 1948-49; WO, 1950-52; Comdr 1st Malay Inf. Bde, 1953-54 (despatches); GOC Federation Army, Malaya, 1956-59. Col, The Welch Regt, 1965-69. Bronze Star Medal, USA, 1945. *Publications:* contrib. on military subjects to Chambers's Encyclopædia. *Recreation:* sailing. *Club:* Army and Navy.

**BROOKE, Sir George (Cecil Francis),** 3rd Bt, *cr* 1903; MBE 1949; Major, 17/21 Lancers, retired; *b* 30 March 1916; *s* of Sir Francis Brooke, 2nd Bt, and Mabel, *d* of Sir John Arnott, 1st Bt; *S* father 1954; *m* 1959, Lady Melissa Wyndham-Quin, *er d* of 6th Earl of Dunraven, CB, CBE, MC; one *s* one *d*. *Educ:* Stowe. Served War of 1939-45 (wounded, despatches twice), in North Africa and Italy. *Heir: s.* Francis George Wyndham Brooke, *b* 15 Oct. 1963. *Address:* Glenbevan, Croom, Co. Limerick. *Clubs:* Cavalry, Pratt's, White's; Kildare Street (Dublin).

**BROOKE, Humphrey;** *see* Brooke, T. H.

**BROOKE, John;** Chairman, Brooke Bond Liebig Ltd; *b* 7 March 1912; *m* 1936, Bridget (*née* May); two *s* one *d*. *Educ:* Bedales, Petersfield, Hants. Joined Brooke Bond & Co. Ltd, Oct. 1930, as Trainee Salesman. *Address:* Rowmore, Leigh Hill Road, Cobham, Surrey. *T:* Cobham 3361.

**BROOKE, Major Sir John Weston,** 3rd Bt, *cr* 1919; TD; DL; JP; Lovat Scouts; *b* 26 Sept. 1911; *s* of Major Sir Robert Weston Brooke, 2nd Bt, DSO, MC, DL, and Margery Jean, MBE, *d* of Alex. Geddes of Blairmore, Aberdeenshire; *S* father, 1942; *m* 1st, 1945, Rosemary (marr. diss. 1963), *d* of late Percy Nevill, Birling House, West Malling, Kent; two *s*.; 2nd, 1966, Lady Macdonald (*née* Phoebe Napier Harvey), *widow* of Sir Peter Macdonald, Newport, IoW. *Educ:* Repton; Trinity College, Cambridge. Apprenticed in engineering trade with Crompton Parkinsons, Electrical Engineers, Chelmsford; employed previous to hostilities as Constructional Engineer with Associated Portland Cement Manufacturers. DL, Ross and Cromarty, 1964; JP Ross-shire, 1960. *Recreations:* shooting, sailing, ski-ing, farming. *Heir: s* Alistair Weston Brooke, *b* 12 Sept. 1947. *Address:* Midfearn, Ardgay, Ross-shire. *T:* Ardgay 250. *Club:* Royal Ocean Racing.

**BROOKE, Sir (Norman) Richard (Rowley),** Kt 1964; CBE 1958; FCA; *b* 23 June 1910; *s* of William Brooke, JP, Scunthorpe, Lincs; *m* 1st, 1948, Julia Dean (marr. diss. 1957); one *s* one *d*; 2nd, 1958, Nina Mari Dolan. *Educ:*

Charterhouse School. Joined Guest, Keen & Nettlefolds Ltd, 1935; Dir, Guest, Keen & Nettlefolds Ltd, 1961-67; Dir and/or Chm. of several GKN subsidiary cos until retirement in 1967; Director: Richard Brooke Ltd (Chm.); Eagle Star Insurance Co. (S Wales Bd); a Founder Dir, Develt Corp. for Wales, until 1967, now Hon. Vice-Pres. Founder Mem. and Dep. Chm., British Independent Steel Producers Assoc., 1967-. Hon. Life President, Wales and Monmouthshire Conservative and Unionist Council, 1966; President, Cardiff Chamber of Commerce, 1960-61; Member Exec. Cttee and Council, British Iron and Steel Federation (Joint Vice-Pres., 1966-67); Vice-Pres., University College of S. Wales and Monmouthshire, 1965; Member Governing Body, Welsh College of Advanced Technology; Member Territorial Aux. Forces Assoc. of Co. of Glamorgan. JP Glamorgan, 1952-64. *Recreations:* golf and fishing. *Address:* New Sarum, Pwllmelin Lane, Llandaff, Cardiff. *T:* Cardiff 563692. *Clubs:* Constitutional; Cardiff and County (Cardiff); Royal Porthcawl Golf.

**BROOKE, Lieut-Colonel Ralph,** OBE, 1940; PhD, MS, FRCS, MB, LRCP; late RAMC, TA; Hon. Consulting Orthopædic Surgeon, Royal Sussex County Hospital; late: Hon. Surgeon and Hon. Orthopædic Surgeon, Hove Hospital; Hon. Surgeon and Hon. Orthopædic Surgeon, Royal West Sussex Hospital; Hon. Orthopædic Surgeon, Royal Sussex County Hospital; Hon. Surgeon, Worthing Hospital; Consulting Surgeon Bognor War Memorial Hospital; Consulting Surgeon, Midhurst Hospital; also Barrister-at-law, Inner Temple; *b* Bexhill-on-Sea, 2 April 1900; *s* of Herbert Brooke and E. Bones; *m* Marjorie, *d* of H. W. Lee, Managing Director, Messrs Stones, Ltd, Engineers; one *s* three *d*. *Educ:* Christ's College; Guy's Hospital. Late Demonstrator, Anatomy, Physiology, Operative Surgery, Guy's Hospital; late Medical Officer Hackney Hospital. *Publications:* A Shorter Orthopædics; papers in the professional journals. *Address:* Flat 15, Shoreacres, Sandbanks, Poole, Dorset; 36 Mill Road, Worthing. *T:* Worthing 1983.

**BROOKE, Sir Richard;** *see* Brooke, Sir N. R. R.

**BROOKE, Sir Richard Christopher,** 9th Bt, *cr* 1662; *b* 8 Aug. 1888; *s* of 8th Bt and Alice, *d* of J. S. Crawley, Stockwood Park, Luton; *S* father, 1920; *m* 1st, 1912, Marian Dorothea (*d* 1965) *o d* of late Arthur Charles Innes, MP, of Dromantine, Co. Down; one *s* one *d*; 2nd, 1967, Kathleen Enda Gildea, Dun Laoghaire, Dublin. *Educ:* Eton; Christ Church, Oxford. MA. Late Scots Guards. High Sheriff of Worcestershire, 1931; Worcestershire CC, 1928-46; Vice-Chairman Worcestershire War Emergency Cttee for Civil Defence, 1939; Chairman Bewdley Division, Conservative Association, 1945-46. Late JP and DL Worcestershire. *Recreations:* racing, horse breeding, fishing. *Heir: s* Richard Neville Brooke, late Scots Guards; Chartered Accountant [*b* 1 May 1915; *m* 1st, 1937, Lady Mabel Kathleen Jocelyn (marr. diss., 1959), *yr d* of 8th Earl of Roden; two *s*; 2nd, 1960, Jean Evison, *d* of Lt-Col A. C. Corfe, DSO]. *Address:* Oaklands, St Saviour, Jersey, Channel Islands. *T:* Jersey East 805. *Clubs:* Guards; Kildare Street (Dublin).

**BROOKE, (Thomas) Humphrey,** CVO 1969 (MVO 1958); Secretary, Royal Academy of Arts, Piccadilly, W1, 1952-68; *b* 31 Jan. 1914; *y s* of late Major Thomas Brooke, Grimston Manor, York, and late B. Gundreda, *d* of Sir Hildred Carlile, 1st and last Bt; *m* 1946, Countess Nathalie Benckendorff, *o d* of Count Benckendorff, DSO; one *d* (one *s* one *d* decd). *Educ:* Wellington Coll; Magdalen Coll., Oxford. 1st Cl. Hons Mod. History Oxon, 1935; BLitt 1937. Asst Keeper, Public Record Office, 1937. Served War of 1939-45; commissioned KRRC, 1943. Controller, Monuments and Fine Arts Branch, Allied Commission for Austria, 1946; Dep. Keeper, Tate Gallery, 1948; Ministry of Town and Country Planning, 1949; Resigned from Civil Service on appointment to Royal Acad., 1951. Member Order of Santiago (Portugal), 1955; Commander Ordine al Merito della Republica Italiana, 1956; Officier de l'Ordre de l'Etoile Noire (France), 1958. *Recreations:* shooting, fishing. *Address:* 8 Pelham Crescent, SW7. *T:* 01-589 5690; Lime Kiln, Claydon, Suffolk. *T:* Claydon 334. *Club:* Garrick.

**BROOKE, Brigadier Walter Headfort,** CBE 1938; MC; DL; *b* 13 Jan. 1887; *s* of late John Monck Brooke; *m* 1st, 1920, Mary S. G., *d* of late Henry Dawson-Greene, Whittington Hall, Kirkby Lonsdale; (one *s* decd); 2nd, 1923, Lady Edith Mary Stopford, *d* of 6th Earl of Courtown; one *d*. *Educ:* Haileybury Coll. Served European War 1914-19, in France and Belgium (despatches four times, Brevet Major, MC, 4th Class Order of Crown of Roumania). *Publication:* Gladeye the War Horse, 1939. *Recreations:* polo, hunting, shooting, fishing. *Address:* 12 Roborough Lane, Ashburton, Devon. *T:* Ashburton 367.

**BROOKE-LITTLE, John Philip Brooke,** MVO 1969; Richmond Herald since 1967; *b* 6 April 1927; *s* of late Raymond Brooke-Little, Unicorns House, Swalcliffe, and Mrs C. Brooke-Little; *m* 1960, Mary Lee, *o c* of late John Raymond Pierce and Mrs E. G. Pierce, Coleshill, Wimborne Minster; three *s* one *d*. *Educ:* Clayesmore Sch; New Coll., Oxford (MA). Earl Marshal's staff, 1952-53; Gold Staff Officer, Coronation, 1953; Bluemantle Pursuivant of Arms, 1956. Founder of Heraldry Soc. and Chm., 1947; Hon. Editor-in-Chief, The Coat of Arms, 1950; Fellow, Soc. of Genealogists, 1969. Freeman and Liveryman, Scriveners' Co. of London. FSA 1961. OStJ 1964; Knight of Malta, 1955; Comdr Cross of Merit of Order of Malta, 1964; Cruz Distinguida (1st cl.) de San Raimundo de Peñafort, 1955. *Publications:* Royal London, 1953; Pictorial History of Oxford, 1954; Boutell's Heraldry, 1970 (1963 and 1966 edns with C. W. Scott-Giles); Knights of the Middle Ages, 1966; Prince of Wales, 1969; Fox-Davies' Complete Guide to Heraldry, annotated edn, 1969; genealogical and heraldic articles. *Recreations:* cooking, painting. *Address:* Heyford House, Lower Heyford, Nr Oxford. *T:* Steeple Aston 337; 82A Queens Gate, SW7. *T:* 01-373 4105; College of Arms, EC4. *T:* 01-248 1310. *Clubs:* Carlton, City Livery.

**BROOKE-ROSE, Dr Christine, (Mrs Jerzy Peterkiewicz);** novelist and critic; Lecturer in English Language and Literature, University of Paris, since 1969; *m* 1953, Jerzy Peterkiewicz, novelist. *Educ:* Oxford and London Univs. MA Oxon 1953, PhD London 1954. Research and criticism, 1957-. Reviewer for: The Times Literary Supplement, The Times, The Observer, The Sunday Times, The Listener, The Spectator, and The London Magazine, 1956-68; took up post at Experimental Univ. Centre of Vincennes, Univ. of Paris, 1969. Has broadcast in book programmes on BBC, and on 'The Critics', and ABC Television. Travelling Prize of Society of Authors, 1964; James Tait Black Memorial Prize, 1966; Arts Council Translation Prize, 1969. *Publications: novels:* The Languages of Love, 1957; The Sycamore Tree, 1958; The Dear Deceit, 1960; The Middlemen, 1961; Out, 1964; Such, 1965;

Between, 1968; *criticism:* A Grammar of Metaphor, 1958; A ZBC of Ezra Pound, 1971; *short stories:* Go when you see the Green Man Walking, 1970; Short stories and essays in various magazines, etc. *Recreations:* people, travel. *Address:* c/o Michael Joseph Ltd, 52 Bedford Square, WC1.

**BROOKEBOROUGH,** 1st Viscount, *cr* 1952 of Colebrooke; **Basil Stanlake Brooke,** 5th Bt, *cr* 1882; KG 1965; PC Northern Ireland, 1933; CBE 1921; MC 1916; 10th Hussars; Prime Minister of Northern Ireland, 1943-63, resigned; MP (U) Lisnaskea Division, Parliament of Northern Ireland, 1929-68; Vice-Admiral of Province of Ulster since 1961; HM Lieutenant of Fermanagh, 1963-69; *b* 9 June 1888; *s* of 4th Bt and Gertrude Isabella, *o d* of S. R. Batson; *S* father, 1907; *m* 1919, Cynthia (Mary) (*d* 1970) DBE 1959, *d* of late Captain and Hon. Mrs Sergison of Cuckfield Park, Sussex; one *s* (and two killed in action). *Educ:* Winchester; RMC, Sandhurst. Served European War, 1914-19 (Dardanelles) (despatches, MC, Croix de Guerre with Palm); Minister of Agriculture, Northern Ireland, 1933-41; Minister of Commerce, 1941-45 (jointly with Premiership from 1943). Chairman, Carreras of Northern Ireland Ltd; Director, Devenish Trade; President Institute of Directors, Northern Ireland. Hon. Capt. RNVR; Hon. Air Commodore, RAuxAF. KStJ; LLD, Queen's Univ., Belfast. *Recreation:* fishing. *Heir: s.* Hon. John Warden Brooke, Captain 10th Hussars; MP (U) Lisnaskea Div., Parlt of NI [*b* 9 April 1922; *m* 1949, Rosemary-Hilda, *e d* of Col A. O'N. C. Chichester, Galgorm Castle, Ballymena; two *s* three *d*]. *Address:* Colebrooke, Brookeboro', Northern Ireland. *T:* Brookeboro' 204. *Clubs:* (Hon.) Junior Carlton, (Hon.) Constitutional, (Hon.) Cavalry, (Hon.) Buck's; Ulster, (Hon.) Ulster Reform (Belfast).

*See also Rt. Hon. Sir Henry Mulholland.*

**BROOKES, Hon. Edgar Harry,** MA, DLitt; Hon. LLD; Author; late Senator representing the natives of Natal and Zululand in the Union of South Africa Parliament; late Prof. of Public Administration and Political Science, University of Pretoria, and Principal, Adams College, Natal; *b* Smethwick, England, 4 Feb. 1897; *s* of J. H. Brookes and E. E. Thomas; *m* 1925, Heidi Genevieve, *d* of Rev. C. Bourquin, Mission Suisse, Pretoria; three *s* two *d*. *Educ:* Pietermaritzburg College; University of South Africa; London School of Economics. Professor of Public Administration and Political Science, Transvaal University College (later University of Pretoria), 1924; SA Delegate to the League of Nations Assembly, 1927; Observer for Union Government at World Population Conference, 1927; President of SA Institute of Race Relations, 1932 and 1946; Member of Union Social and Economic Planning Council, 1942-52; Member, Native Affairs Commission, 1945-50; Professor of History and Political Science, University of Natal, 1959-62. *Publications:* History of Native Policy in South Africa, 1923; Native Education in South Africa, 1929; A Retrospect and a Forecast; History of the Swiss Mission in South Africa, 1875-1925, 1926; The Colour Problems of South Africa, 1934; South Africa in a Changing World, 1954; The Native Reserves of Natal, 1957; The Commonwealth, 1959, 1959; The City of God and the Politics of Crisis, 1959; Power, Law, Right, and Love: A Study in Political Values, 1963; The History of Natal, 1965; Freedom, Faith and the Twenty-First Century, 1966; A History of the University of Natal, 1967; Apartheid: a Documentary Study of Modern South Africa, 1968. Collaborated in Coming of Age; Studies in South African Citizenship and Politics, 1930, in Western Civilisation and the Bantu of South Africa, 1934; Civil Liberty in South Africa, 1958. *Address:* 15 Elgarth, St Patrick's Road, Pietermaritzburg, South Africa.

**BROOKES, Ernest Roy,** CB 1954; *b* 25 Aug. 1904; *m* 1938, Margaret, *d* of J. T. Reeve; no *c*. *Educ:* Heath Grammar School, Halifax; Magdalene College, Cambridge. Lecturer at St David's College Lampeter, 1926-28; entered Inland Revenue Department, 1929; Sec., Committee on Taxation of Trading Profits, 1949-51; Secretary, Royal Commission on Taxation of Profits and Income, 1951-52; Commissioner of Inland Revenue, 1952-65; Deputy Chairman, Board of Inland Revenue, 1965-67. Mem. E. Africa Commn of Enquiry on Income Tax, 1956. *Recreation:* music. *Address:* 9 Netherhall Gardens, NW3. *T:* 01-435 7254. *Clubs:* Reform, Oxford and Cambridge Musical.

**BROOKES, Air Vice-Marshal Hugh Hamilton,** CB 1954; CBE 1951; DFC 1944; RAF retd; *b* 14 Oct. 1904; *s* of late W. H. Brookes and of Evelyn, *d* of J. Forster Hamilton (she married 2nd Sir John Simpson, KBE, CIE); *m* 1932, Elsie Viola Henry; one *d*. *Educ:* Bedford School; Cranwell. Bomber Command, 1924; 84 Sqdn Iraq, 1929; Staff College, 1933; Sqdn Bomber Command, 1937; Iraq, 1938; Western Desert, 1939; Aden, 1941; Station Bomber Command, 1943; Iraq, 1946; Director of Flying Training, 1949; AOC Rhodesia, 1951; AOC Iraq, 1954; AOC No 25 Group, Flying Training Command, 1956-58, retd. *Address:* c/o National Westminster Bank Ltd, Colchester, Essex. *Club:* Royal Air Force.

**BROOKES, Lady; Mabel Balcombe,** DBE, *cr* 1955 (CBE 1933); Chevalier de la Légion d'Honneur; Hon. LLD; *d* of late Harry Emmerton, solicitor, South Yarra, and Alice Mabel Maud Emmerton, CBE; *m* 1911, Sir Norman Everard Brookes (*d* 1968). *Publications:* St Helena Story, 1960; Riders of Time, 1967. *Address:* 233 Domain Road, South Yarra, Victoria, Australia; Brookwood, Mount Eliza, Victoria, Australia.

**BROOKES, Raymond Percival;** Chairman and Chief Executive, Guest, Keen & Nettlefolds Ltd; *b* 10 April 1909; *s* of William and Ursula Brookes; *m* 1937, Florence Edna Sharman; one *s*. Part-time Mem., BSC, 1967-68. First Pres., British Mechanical Engrg Confedn, 1968-69; a Vice-Pres., Engrg Employers' Fedn, 1967-. Member: Council, UK S Africa Trade Assoc. Ltd, 1967-; Council, CBI, 1968-; BNEC, 1969-; Council, Soc. of Motor Manufacturers & Traders Ltd, 1969-; Court of Governors, Univ. of Birmingham, 1966-; Council, Univ. of Birmingham, 1968-. *Recreations:* golf, fly-fishing. *Address:* Guest, Keen & Nettlefolds Ltd, Group Head Office, Smethwick, Warley, Worcs; (private) Avonside, Bidford-on-Avon, Warwicks.

**BROOKFIELD, G. Piers,** Mem. AIA, FRIBA; Practicing Architect, 1929-42, and since 1946; *b* Halifax, NS, 9 Jan. 1894; *s* of late Walter G. Brookfield and Edith Harrington Piers; *m* 1924, Martha Johnstone Balfour Forgie, *d* of late James Forgie, MICE, Cons. Eng., NYC; one *d*. *Educ:* Dalhousie Univ. (BSc); MIT (SB); Oxford Univ. (BLitt); Atelier Gromort, Ecole des Beaux Arts, Paris. Officer, Canadian Artillery, 1916-18. Architectural draftsman, 1920-28; Bellows and Aldrich, Strickland, Blodget and Law, Boston; Sir Aston Webb & Son, London; Sir Alfred Bossom and Th. Engelhardt, New York; Lend Lease Procurement, British Min. of Supply, Washington, 1942-46; Principal, own office,

NYC. Delegate Fine Arts Federation of New York, 1941-42, 1955-57, 1957-61. Trustee: Kew-Forest School; Theodore Roosevelt Associaton. *Recreations:* tennis, golf, ski-ing. *Address:* 724 Burns Street, Forest Hills Gardens, LI, NY, USA. *T:* BO 8-3578; (office) 10 West 33rd Street, New York, NY 10001, USA. *T:* PE 6-1759. *Clubs:* West Side Tennis (Forest Hills, LI); British Schools and Universities (NYC) (Past Pres.).

**BROOKNER, Prof. Anita;** Lecturer, Courtauld Institute of Art, since 1964; *b* 16 July 1928; *o c* of Newson and Maude Brookner. *Educ:* James Allen's Girls' Sch.; King's Coll., Univ. of London; Courtauld Inst.; Paris. Vis. Lectr, Univ. of Reading, 1959-64; Slade Professor, Univ. of Cambridge, 1967-68. Fellow, New Hall, Cambridge. *Publications:* Watteau, 1968; The Genius of the Future, 1970; articles in Burlington Magazine, etc. *Address:* 68 Elm Park Gardens, SW10. *T:* 01-352 6894.

**BROOKS,** family name of **Baron Crawshaw.**

**BROOKS, Prof. Cleanth;** Gray Professor of Rhetoric, Yale University, USA; *b* 16 Oct. 1906; *s* of Rev. Cleanth and Bessie Lee Witherspoon Brooks; *m* 1934, Edith Amy Blanchard; no *c*. *Educ:* The McTyeire School; Vanderbilt, Tulane and Oxford Universities. Rhodes Scholar, Louisiana and Exeter, 1929; Lecturer, later Prof., Louisiana State Univ., 1932-47; Prof. of English, later Gray Prof. of Rhetoric, Yale Univ., 1947-. Visiting Professor: Univ. of Texas; Univ. of Michigan; Univ. of Chicago; Univ. of Southern California; Bread Loaf School of English. Cultural Attaché at the American Embassy, London, 1964-66. Managing Editor and Editor (with Robert Penn Warren), The Southern Review, 1935-42. Fellow, Library of Congress, 1953-63; Guggenheim Fellow, 1953 and 1960. Hon. DLitt: Upsala Coll., 1963; Kentucky, 1963; Exeter, 1966; Washington and Lee, 1968; Hon. LHD: St Louis, 1968; Tulane, 1969. *Publications:* Modern Poetry and the Tradition, 1939; The Well Wrought Urn, 1947; (with R. P. Warren) Understanding Poetry, 1938; (with R. P. Warren) Modern Rhetoric, 1950; (with W. K. Wimsatt, Jr) Literary Criticism: A Short History, 1957; The Hidden God, 1963; William Faulkner: The Yoknapatawpha Country, 1963; (Gen. Ed., with David N. Smith) The Percy Letters; contrib. articles, reviews to literary magazines, journals. *Address:* (office) 1315 Yale Station, New Haven, Conn, USA; (home) Forest Road, Northford, Conn, USA. *Clubs:* Athenæum, Savile; Yale (New York).

**BROOKS, Edwin;** *b* Barry, Glamorgan, 1 Dec. 1929; *s* of Edwin Brooks and Agnes Elizabeth (*née* Campbell); *m* 1956, Winifred Hazel Soundie; four *s* one *d*. *Educ:* Barry Grammar Sch.; St John's Coll., Cambridge. PhD (Camb) 1958. National Service, Singapore, 1948-49. Lectr, Dept of Geography, Univ. of Liverpool, 1954-66. MP (Lab) Bebington, 1966-70. Councillor, Birkenhead, 1958-67. *Recreations:* gardening, do-it-yourself. *Address:* 39 Waterpark Road, Prenton, Birkenhead, Cheshire. *T:* 051-608 3584.

**BROOKS, Eric Arthur Swatton;** Head of Claims Department, Foreign Office, 1960 until retirement, 1967; *b* 9 Oct. 1907; *yr s* of late A. E. Brooks, MA, Maidenhead; *m* 1947, Daphne Joyce, *yr d* of late George McMullan, FRCSE, Wallingford; one *s* one *d*. *Educ:* Reading Sch.; New Coll., Oxford (MA). 2nd cl. hons Jurisprudence, 1929. Solicitor, 1932; practised in London, 1932-39. Mem. Law Soc., 1934- (Mem. Overseas Relations Cttee, 1949-). Served War of 1939-45 in Admty and Min. of Aircraft Production, and in Operational Research as Hon. Ft-Lieut RAFVR until 1944; Disposal of Govt Factories of Min. of Aircraft Production, 1944-Dec. 1945. Foreign Office, 1946-. Served on Brit. Delegns in negotiations with: Polish and Hungarian Governments, 1953, 1954; Bulgarian Government, 1955; Rumanian Government, 1955, 1956, 1960; USSR, 1964, 1965, 1966, 1967. British Representative on Anglo-Italian Conciliation Commission. *Publications:* articles, on Compensation in International Law, and Distribution of Compensation, in legal jls. *Recreations:* golf (Oxford Univ. team *v* Cambridge Univ., 1929; various later Amateur European Championships); ski-ing; skating; gardening. *Address:* Kitoha, 116b Grenfell Road, Maidenhead, Berks. *T:* Maidenhead 21621. *Club:* Ski Club of Great Britain.

**BROOKS, Rt. Rev. Gerald Henry;** Vicar of St Thomas, New Groombridge, Sussex, since 1967; *b* 11 Feb. 1905; *s* of Capt. Percy Wilmot Brooks and Florence Maud Haward. *Educ:* Tonbridge School, Kent; Keble College, Oxford; Ely Theological College, Deacon, 1930; Priest, 1931; Assistant Priest, St Saviour's, Poplar, 1930-32; Domestic Chaplain to Bishop of Nassau and Priest-in-Charge of St Barnabas, Nassau, Bahamas, 1932-34; Priest-in-Charge of All Saints, Andros, Bahamas, 1934-40; Priest-in-Charge of St Stephen's, Grand Bahama, 1940-45; General Missionary and Diocesan Treasurer of Diocese of Nassau, 1945-46; Archdeacon of Nassau, 1946-50; Bishop of British Honduras, 1950-66. *Address:* St Thomas' Vicarage, New Groombridge, Sussex. *Club:* United University.

**BROOKS, I. M.,** MA Cantab; Lecturer and Member of the Guild of Drama Adjudicators since 1954. *Educ:* Bromley High School (GPDST); Girton College, Cambridge. Headmistress, Malvern Girls' College, Worcs, 1928-54, retired 1954. *Address:* 10 Greenacres, The Avenue, Branksome Park, Dorset. *Club:* English-Speaking Union.

**BROOKS, Mrs Richard;** *see* Simmons, Jean.

**BROOKS, Ronald Clifton,** OBE 1944; MC 1918; Chairman, Commercial Union Assurance Co. Ltd, since 1959; Director: Dalgety & Co. Ltd; London Trust Co. Ltd; Yeoman Investment Trust Ltd; United Planters (Holdings) Ltd; Ceylon Tea Plantations Holdings Ltd; *b* 3 March 1899; 2nd *s* of Robert Brooks; *m* 1928, Iris Winifred, *er d* of M. W. Payne; two *s* one *d*. *Educ:* Haileybury College; Trinity College, Cambridge. Joined The Queen's (Royal West Surrey) Regt, with rank 2nd Lieut, 1917 (MC). Cambridge (BA), 1919-20. Partner, Robert Brooks & Co., Merchants, 1924-68. DAG, SHAEF, 1945. Legion of Merit, USA, 1945; Chevalier, Légion d'Honneur, 1945. *Recreations:* fishing, shooting, golf. *Address:* 14 Whitelands House, Chelsea, SW3. *T:* 01-730 1950. *Clubs:* Bath, City of London.

**BROOKS, William Donald Wykeham,** CBE 1956; MA, DM (Oxon); FRCP; Physician: St Mary's Hospital; Brompton Hospital; Consulting Physician: to the Royal Navy; to the King Edward VII Convalescent Home for Officers, Osborne; Chief Medical Officer, Eagle Star Insurance Co.; *b* 3 Aug. 1905; *er s* of A. E. Brooks MA (Oxon), Maidenhead, Berks; *m* 1934, Phyllis Kathleen, *e d* of late F. A. Juler, CVO; two *s* two *d*. *Educ:* Reading School; St John's College, Oxford (White Scholar); St Mary's Hospital, London (University Scholar); Strong Memorial Hospital, Rochester, New York. First Class Honours, Final Honour School of Physiology, 1928; Cheadle Gold Medallist, 1931; Fereday

Fellow St John's College, Oxford, 1931-34; Rockefeller Travelling Fellow, 1932-33; Goulstonian Lecturer, 1940; Marc Daniels Lecturer, RCP, 1957. Asst Registrar, 1946-50, RCP; Censor, RCP, 1961- (Council, 1959-61, Senior Vice-President and Senior Censor, 1965); Examiner in Medicine, University of Oxford and to RCP; Member Association of Physicians of Great Britain and Ireland. *Publications:* numerous articles on general medical topics and on chest diseases in various medical journals; Sections on Chest Wounds, Respiratory Diseases and Tuberculosis, Conybeare's Textbook of Medicine; Respiratory Diseases section in the Offical Naval Medical History of the War. *Recreations:* golf, shooting, gardening, bridge. *Address:* two Acres, Fryern Road, Storrington, Sussex. *T:* Storrington 2159.

**BROOKS GRUNDY, Rupert Francis;** *see* Grundy, R. F. B.

**BROOKSBANK, Colonel Sir (Edward) William,** 2nd Bt, *cr* 1919; TD 1953; DL Yorkshire Hussars; *b* 15 June 1915; *e s* of late Col Edward York Brooksbank and Hazel, *d* of late H. F. Brockholes Thomas; *S* grandfather, 1943; *m* 1943, Ann, 2nd *d* of Col T. Clitherow; one *s*. *Educ:* Eton. Colonel, Comdg Queen's Own Yorkshire Yeomanry, 1957. Hon. Col, Queen's Own Yorkshire Yeomanry (TA), 1963-69, T&AVR, 1969-. DL East Riding of Yorks, and City and County of Kingston upon Hull, 1959. *Heir: s* Edward Nicholas Brooksbank, 2nd Lieut, 1st Royal Dragoons, *b* 4 Oct. 1944. *Address:* Menethorpe Hall, Malton, Yorks. *Clubs:* Turf, Yorkshire.

**BROOKSBANK, Kenneth,** DSC and Bar, 1944; Chief Education Officer, Birmingham, since 1968; *b* 27 July 1915; *s* of Ambrose and Ethel Brooksbank; *m* 1939, Violet Anne Woodrow; two *d*. *Educ:* High Storrs Gram. Sch., Sheffield; St Edmund Hall, Oxford; Manchester University. Asst Master, Hulme Gram. Sch., Oldham, 1937-41; Royal Navy, 1941-46; Dep. Educn Off., York, 1946-49; Sen. Admin. Asst, Birmingham, 1949-52; Asst Sec. for Educn, NR Yorks CC, 1952-56; Dep. Educn Off., Birmingham, 1956-68. Leader, Unesco Educn Planning Mission to Bechuanaland, Basutoland and Swaziland, 1964. *Address:* 29 Wycome Road, Hall Green, Birmingham, 28. *T:* 021-777 4407.

**BROOKSBY, John Burns;** Director, Animal Virus Research Institute, Pirbright, since 1964; *b* 25 Dec. 1914; *s* of George B. Brooksby, Glasgow; *m* 1940, Muriel Weir; one *s* one *d*. *Educ:* Hyndland Sch., Glasgow; Glasgow Veterinary Coll.; London University. MRCVS 1935; BSc (VetSc) 1936; PhD 1947; DSc 1957; FRSE 1968. Research Officer, Pirbright, 1939; Dep. Dir, 1957; Dir, 1964. *Publications:* papers on virus diseases of animals in scientific jls. *Address:* Heatherdale House, Compton Way, Farnham, Surrey. *T:* Runfold 2164. *Club:* Farmers'.

**BROOM, Air Vice-Marshal Ivor Gordon,** CBE 1969; DSO 1945; DFC 1942 (Bar to DFC 1944, 2nd Bar 1945); AFC 1956; AOC No 11 (Fighter) Group, Strike Command, since 1970; *b* Cardiff, 2 June 1920; *s* of Alfred Godfrey Broom and Janet Broom; *m* 1942, Jess Irene Broom (*née* Cooper); two *s* one *d*. *Educ:* West Monmouth Grammar Sch.; Pontypridd County Sch., Glam. Joined RAF, 1940; commissioned, 1941; 114 Sqdn, 107 Sqdn, 1941; CFS Course, 1942; Instr on: 1655 Mosquito Trg Unit; 571 Sqdn, 128 Sqdn, and 163 Sqdn, 1943-45; HQ, ACSEA, 1945-46. Commanded 28 (FR) Sqdn, 1946-48; RAF Staff Coll. Course, Bracknell, 1949; Sqdn Comdr, No 1 ITS, 1950-52; No 3 Flying Coll. Course, Manby, 1952-53; commanded 57 Sqdn, 1953-54; Syndicate Leader, Flying Coll., Manby, 1954-56; commanded Bomber Command Development Unit, Wittering, 1956-59; Air Secretary's Dept, 1959-62; commanded RAF Bruggen, 1962-64; IDC, 1965-66; Dir of Organisation (Establishments), 1966-68; Commandant, Central Flying School, 1968-70. *Recreations:* golf, skiing. *Address:* c/o 172 Valley Road, Ipswich, Suffolk. *Club:* Royal Air Force.

**BROOME, F. N.;** retired, 1961, as Judge-President, Natal Provincial Division, Supreme Court of South Africa; *b* 1891; *s* of late William Broome, formerly Judge of Supreme Court of S. Africa; *m* 1918, Mary Caroline Jervois; one *s* one *d*. *Educ:* Hilton College, Natal; Oriel College, Oxford (Rhodes Scholar). BA(Oxon) 1912; Barrister-at-law, Inner Temple, 1913; Advocate of Supreme Court of S Africa, 1914; Natal Carbineers and Royal Field Artillery, 1914-19, SW Africa and France, Captain (MC); KC 1931; MP for Pietermaritzburg District, 1938; Chairman, Natal Education Commisiion, 1936-38; Chairman, Indian Penetration Commission, 1940; Chairman, Natal Indian Judicial Commission, 1944; Chairman, Durban Native Enquiry Commission, 1947; Chm. Natal Town Planning Appeals Board; Chm., Stock Exchange Enquiry Commission, 1962; Dep. Chm. Council of Univ. of Natal. Hon. LLD Natal, 1968. *Publication:* Not the Whole Truth, 1962. *Address:* 16 Montgomery Drive, Pietermaritzburg, South Africa. *Club:* Victoria (Pietermaritzburg).

**BROOMHALL, Maj.-Gen. William Maurice,** CB 1950; DSO 1945; OBE 1932; Chairman and Managing Director Cellulose Development Corporation, London; *b* 16 July 1897; *o s* of late Alfred Edward Broomhall, London. *Educ:* St Paul's School; Royal Military Academy, Woolwich. Commissioned Royal Engineers, 1915; France and Belgium, 1914-21 (wounded twice); Waziristan, 1921-24 (medal and clasp); NW Frontier of India, 1929-31 (despatches, clasp, OBE); Staff College, Camberley, 1932-33. Served North-West Europe, 1939-45 (Despatches, DSO); Chief Engineer, Allied Forces, Italy, 1946; Chief Engineer, British Army of the Rhine, 1947-48; Chief Engineer, Middle East Land Forces, 1948-51; retired, 1951. *Recreations:* sailing and shooting. *Address:* 91 Whitehall Court, SW1. *T:* 01-839 4014. *Club:* Army and Navy.

**BROPHY, Brigid (Antonia);** author and playwright; *b* 12 June 1929; *o c* of late John Brophy; *m* 1954, Michael Levey, *qv*; one *d*. *Educ:* St Paul's Girls' Sch.; St Hugh's Coll., Oxford. Awarded Jubilee Scholarship at St Hugh's Coll., Oxford, 1947 and read classics. Awarded Cheltenham Literary Festival First Prize for a first novel, 1954; London Magazine Prize for Prose, 1962. *Publications:* Hackenfeller's Ape, 1953; The King of a Rainy Country, 1956; Black Ship to Hell, 1962; Flesh, 1962; The Finishing Touch, 1963; The Snow Ball, 1964; Mozart the Dramatist, 1964; Don't Never Forget, 1966; (in collaboration with Michael Levey and Charles Osborne) Fifty Works of English Literature We Could Do Without, 1967; Black and White: a portrait of Aubrey Beardsley, 1968; In Transit, 1969. *Play:* The Burglar, Vaudeville, 1967 (published with preface, 1968). Regular contribs to Listener and Sunday Times. *Address:* Flat 3, 185 Old Brompton Road, SW5. *T:* 01-373 9335.

**BROSIO, Manlio;** Secretary-General of NATO since 1964; *b* 10 July 1897; *s* of late Edoardo Brosio and Fortunata Curadelli; *m* 1936,

Clotilde Brosio. *Educ:* Turin University (graduated in Law), Officer in Alpine Troops, European War, 1915-18 (Silver Medal and Cross for Valour). Young political leader, Member of Liberal Party, Central Secretary of "Rivoluzione Liberale" movement, Turin, 1922-25; retired from politics after Fascism took power. Barrister in Turin, in continuous contact with anti-fascist groups, 1926-43; Member of Nat. Liberation Cttee in Rome under German occupation, 1943-44; General Sec. of Liberal Party, 1944-45. Minister without portfolio in Bonomi Cabinet, 1944; Vice-President of Cabinet in De Gasperi Govt, 1945; Minister of War in De Gasperi Govt, 1945-46; Ambassador: in Moscow, Jan. 1947-Dec. 1951; in London, 1952-54; in Washington, 1955-61; in Paris, 1961-64. *Publications:* juridical and political articles. *Recreations:* tennis, swimming, mountaineering. *Address:* (home) 43 Avenue Franklin-Roosevelt, Brussels, Belgium.

**BROTHERHOOD, Air Cdre William Rowland,** CBE 1952; retired as Director, Guided Weapons (Trials), Ministry of Aviation (formerly Supply), (1959-61); *b* 22 Jan. 1912; *s* of late James Brotherhood, Tintern, Mon.; *m* 1939, Margaret, *d* of late Ernest Sutcliffe, Louth, Lincs; one *s* one *d*. *Educ:* Monmouth School; RAF College, Cranwell. Joined RAF, 1930; Group Captain, 1943; Air Commodore, 1955; Director, Operational Requirements, Air Ministry, 1955-58. *Address:* Inglewood, Llandogo, Monmouthshire. *T:* St Briavels 333. *Club:* Royal Air Force.

**BROTHERS, Air Cdre Peter Malam,** CBE 1964; DSO 1944; DFC 1940, and Bar, 1943; Director of Public Relations (RAF), Ministry of Defence (Air), since 1968; *b* 30 Sept. 1917; *s* of late John Malam Brothers; *m* 1939, Annette, *d* of late James Wilson; three *d*. *Educ:* N. Manchester Sch. (Br. of Manchester Grammar). Joined RAF, 1936; Flt-Lieut 1939; RAF Biggin Hill, Battle of Britain, 1940; Sqdn-Ldr 1941; Wing Comdr 1942; Tangmere Fighter Wing Ldr, 1942-43; Staff HQ No. 10 Gp, 1943; Exeter Wing Ldr, 1944; US Comd and Gen. Staff Sch., 1944-45; Central Fighter Estab., 1945-46; Colonial Service, Kenya, 1947–49; RAF Bomber Sqdn, 1949-52; HQ No. 3 Gp, 1952-54; RAF Staff Coll., 1954; HQ Fighter Comd, 1955-57; Bomber Stn, 1957-59; Gp Capt., and Staff Officer, SHAPE, 1959-62; Dir of Ops (Overseas), 1962-65; Air Cdre, and AOC Mil. Air Traffic Ops, 1965-68. Freeman, Guild Air Pilots and Air Navigators, 1966 (Liveryman, 1968); Freeman, City of London, 1967. *Recreations:* golf, sailing, fishing, swimming, flying. *Address:* c/o National Westminster Bank Ltd, Swaythling, Southampton, Hants. *Clubs:* Royal Air Force, Royal Air Force (Reserves); RAF Yacht.

**BROTHERSTON, John Howie Flint;** Chief Medical Officer, Scottish Home and Health Department, since 1964; Hon. Physician to the Queen, 1965-68; *b* Edinburgh, 9 March 1915; *s* of late William Brotherston, WS, Edinburgh, and of Dr Margaret M. Brotherston, MBE, Edinburgh; *m* 1939, Elizabeth Irene Low; two *s* two *d*. *Educ:* George Watson's College, Edinburgh; University of Edinburgh. Graduated: MA 1935, MB, ChB 1940, MD 1950, Edinburgh Univ.; FRSE 1950; FRCPE 1958; FRCPGlas 1964; DrPH Johns Hopkins University 1952. DPH London University, 1947. Served War of 1939-45 with RAMC, 1941-46. Rockefeller Fellow in Preventive Medicine, 1946-48; Lecturer in Social and Preventive Medicine at Guy's Hospital Medical School and London School of Hygiene and Tropical Medicine, 1948-51; Senior Lecturer, subsequently Reader, Public Health, London School of Hygiene and Tropical Medicine, 1951-55; Prof. of Public Health and Social Medicine, University of Edinburgh, 1955-64; Dean of the Faculty of Medicine, University of Edinburgh, 1958-63. *Publications:* Observations on the early Public Health Movement in Scotland, 1952; various contribs to medical and other jls on social medicine and medical education. *Address:* 26 Mortonhall Road, Edinburgh 9. *T:* 031-667 2849.

**BROTHERTON, Harry George,** CBE 1949; President of the Confederation of Shipbuilding and Engineering Unions, 1948-58; General Secretary of the National Union of Sheet Metal Workers and Braziers; 1941-55; *b* 3 Dec. 1890; *s* of Henry William Brotherton; *m* 1915, Daisy Beatrice (*d* 1953), *d* of Walter Henry King. *Recreation:* reading. *Address:* 18 Cornwallis Gardens, Broadstairs, Kent.

**BROUGH, Edward;** Director of Unilever Ltd and Unilever NV, and Head of Marketing Division, since 1968; *b* 28 May 1918; *s* of late Hugh and Jane Brough; *m* 1941, Peggy Jennings; two *s*. *Educ:* Berwick Grammar School; Edinburgh University (MA). Joined Unilever Ltd, 1938. War service, KOSB, 1939-46 (Captain). Rejoined Unilever, 1946; Commercial Dir, 1951, Man. Dir, 1954, Lever's Cattle Foods Ltd; Chairman, Crosfields (CWG) Ltd, 1957; Lever Bros & Associates Ltd: Development Dir, 1960; Marketing Dir, 1962; Chairman, 1965. Mem., NBPI, 1967-70. FBIM 1967. *Recreations:* flyfishing, golf. *Address:* Far End, The Great Quarry, Guildford, Surrey. *T:* Guildford 4064; St John's, Chagford, Devon. *Club:* Farmers'.

**BROUGH, Prof. John,** MA, DLitt; FBA 1961; Professor of Sanskrit, University of Cambridge, since 1967; Fellow of St John's College; *b* 1917; *er s* of Charles and Elizabeth Brough, Maryfield, Dundee; *m* 1939, Marjorie Allan, *d* of Dr W. A. Robertson; one *d*. *Educ:* High School, Dundee; University of Edinburgh; St John's College, Cambridge. First Class Hons in Classics, Edinburgh, 1939; First Class in Classical Tripos, Part II, 1940; First Class in Oriental Langs Tripos, Parts I and II, 1941 and 1942; Fellow St John's College, Cambridge, 1945-48. DLitt Edinburgh, 1945. Worked in agriculture, 1940-43, and as asst in agricultural research, 1943-44. Asst Keeper, Dept of Oriental Printed Books and MSS, British Museum, 1944-46; Lecturer in Sanskrit, School of Oriental and African Studies, University of London, 1946-48; Prof. of Sanskrit in the University of London, 1948-67. *Publications:* Selections from Classical Sanskrit Literature, 1951; The Early Brahmanical System of Gotra and Pravara, 1953; The Gāndhārī Dharmapada, 1962; Poems from the Sanskrit, 1968; articles in Chambers's Encyclopædia and Encyclopædia Britannica; and in specialist journals. *Recreations:* music, gardening. *Address:* 5 Thorn Grove, Bishop's Stortford, Herts. *T:* Bishop's Stortford 51407.

**BROUGHAM,** family name of **Baron Brougham and Vaux.**

**BROUGHAM AND VAUX,** 5th Baron *cr* 1860; **Michael John Brougham;** *b* 2 Aug. 1938; *s* of 4th Baron and Jean, *d* of late Brig.-Gen. G. B. S. Follett, DSO, MVO; *S* father, 1967; *m* 1963, Olivia Susan (marr. diss. 1968), *d* of Rear-Admiral Gordon Thomas Seccombe Gray; one *d*; *m* 1969, Catherine Gulliver. *Educ:* Lycée Jaccard, Lausanne; Millfield School. *Heir:* *b* Hon. David Peter Brougham [*b* 22 Aug. 1940; *m* 1969, Moussie Christina Margareta

Hallström]. *Address:* 52 Wellesley Court, W9. *Club:* Turf.

**BROUGHSHANE,** 2nd Baron (UK), *cr* 1945; **Patrick Owen Alexander Davison;** *b* 18 June 1903; *er s* of 1st Baron and Beatrice Mary, *d* of Sir Owen Roberts; *S* father 1953; *m* 1929, Bettine, *d* of Sir Arthur Russell, 6th Bt; one *s*. *Educ:* Winchester; Magdalen College, Oxford. Barrister, Inner Temple, 1926. Served War of 1939-45: with Irish Guards, 1939-41; Assistant Secretary (Military), War Cabinet, 1942-45. Has US Legion of Merit. Director: Greencoat Properties Ltd (Chairman); Costa Rica Railway Co. Ltd. *Heir: s* Hon. Alexander Davison, *b* 1936. *Address:* 21 Eaton Square, SW1; 28 Fisher Street, Sandwich. *Clubs:* White's, Garrick.

**BROUGHTON,** family name of **Baron Fairhaven.**

**BROUGHTON, Sir Alfred Davies Devonsher,** Kt 1969; MP (Lab) for Batley and Morley, Yorkshire, since Feb. 1949; Consultant Psychiatrist; *b* 18 Oct. 1902; *s* of A. G. S. Broughton, MB, JP; *m* 1st, 1930, Dorothy, MA, PhD (marr. diss. 1967), *d* of late Commander W. D. Parry Jones, RD, RNR; one *s* one *d*; 2nd, 1967, Joyce Diana, *d* of H. S. Denton, Leeds. *Educ:* Rossall School; Cambridge University; London Hospital. MRCS (Eng.), LRCP (Lond.), 1929; MA, MB, BChir (Cantab.), 1936; DPM (Leeds), 1936; DPH (Leeds), 1937; Casualty Officer at Poplar Hospital, 1929-30. Receiving Room Officer at London Hospital, 1930; Resident MO at Rossall School, 1930-32; Medical Practitioner in Batley, 1932-40 and 1945-50. Served War of 1939-45, RAFVR (Squadron Leader), 1940-45. Member of Batley Borough Council, 1946-49. Opposition Whip, 1960-64. UK delegate to Council of Europe and to Assembly of WEU, 1956-58. Member of Speaker's Panel of Chairmen, 1964-. Serving Brother, 1946, Officer, 1951, Order of St John of Jerusalem. *Publication:* Clean Handling of Food, 1953. *Address:* Stockwell Shay Farm, Batley, Yorkshire. *T:* 4321.

**BROUGHTON, Air Marshal Sir Charles,** KBE 1965 (CBE 1952); CB 1961; RAF retired; Air Member for Supply and Organization, Ministry of Defence, 1966-68; *b* 27 April 1911; *s* of Charles and Florence Gertrude Broughton; *m* 1939, Sylvia Dorothy Mary Bunbury; two *d*. *Educ:* New Zealand; RAF College, Cranwell. Commissioned, 1932; India, 1933-37; Flying Instructor, 1937-40. Served War of 1939-45 in Coastal Command and Middle East (despatches four times). Flying Training Command, 1947-49; Air Ministry, 1949-51; Imperial Defence College, 1952; NATO, Washington DC, 1953-55; Far East, 1955-58; Transport Command, 1958-61; Dir-General of Organization, Air Min. (subseq. Min. of Defence), 1961-64; UK Representative in Ankara on Permanent Military Deputies Group of Central Treaty Organization (Cento), 1965-66. *Address:* c/o Flat 20, 25 Cheyne Place, SW3. *Club:* Royal Air Force.

**BROUGHTON, Major Sir Evelyn Delves,** 12th Bt, *cr* 1660; *b* 2 Oct. 1915; *s* of Major Sir Henry Delves Broughton, 11th Bt, and Vera Edyth Boscawen (*d* 1968); *S* father, 1942; *m* 1st, 1947, Hon. Elizabeth Florence Marion Cholmondeley (marr. diss., 1953), *er d* of 4th Baron Delamere, *qv.*; 2nd, 1955, Helen Mary, *d* of J. Shore, Wilmslow, Cheshire; three *d* (one *s* decd). *Educ:* Eton; Trinity Coll., Cambridge. Formerly 2nd Lieut Irish Guards and Major RASC. *Heir: kinsman* David Delves Broughton, *b* 7 May 1942. *Address:* 17 Cadogan Square, SW1. *T:* 01-235 1581; Doddington, Nantwich, Cheshire. *T:* Bridgmere 240. *Club:* St James'.

*See also Baron Lovat.*

**BROUN, Sir Lionel John Law,** 12th Bt, *cr* 1686; *b* 25 April 1927; *s* of 11th Bt and Georgie, *y d* of late Henry Law, Sydney, NSW; *S* father 1962. *Heir: c* William Windsor Broun [*b* 1917; *m* 1952, D'Hrie King, NSW; two *d*.]. *Address:* Coonimbia, Coonamble, NSW 2829, Australia.

**BROWDER, Earl (Russell);** Author, Lecturer, American representative of Soviet publishing houses (OGIZ, *et alia*); *b* Wichita, Kansas, 20 May 1891; *s* of William and Martha (Hankins) Browder; *m* 1926, Raissa Berkmann (*d* 1955); three *s*. *Educ:* self-educated. Candidate for Pres. Communist Party, 1936 and 1940; Sec., 1930-45; Member Exec. Cttee Communist International, 1935-40; Director of Pan-Pacific Trade Union Secretariat, Shanghai, 1926-29; Member Exec. Cttee Red International of Labor Unions, 1921-30. Served prison terms 1917-20 and 1941-42 in connection with conflicts over war policy. Expelled from Communist Party, 1946, for upholding policies of President Roosevelt. No present organisational activities or connections. *Publications:* Communism in US, 1935; What is Communism?, 1936; People's Front, 1938; Fighting for Peace, 1939; Second Imperialist War, 1940; Way Out, 1941; Victory and After, 1942; Teheran, 1944; American Marxists and War, 1945; War or Peace with Russia, 1947; Marx and America, 1959. Author over 100 pamphlets, circulation 8,000,000 copies. *Recreation:* music. *Address:* (Office) 55 W 42nd Street, Room 702, New York 18, NY; (Home) 7 Highland Place, Yonkers 5, NY.

**BROWN;** *see* Clifton-Brown.

**BROWN,** Baron *cr* 1964 (Life Peer); **Wilfred Banks Duncan Brown,** PC 1970; MBE 1944; lately Chairman, The Glacier Metal Co. Ltd (1939-65), and Director, Associated Engineering Ltd; *b* 29 Nov. 1908; British; *m* 1939, Marjorie Hershell Skinner; three *s*. *Educ:* Rossall Sch. Joined The Glacier Metal Co. Ltd, 1931; Sales Manager, 1935; Director, 1936; Joint Managing Director, 1937; Managing Director and Chairman, 1939-65. A Minister of State, Board of Trade, 1965-70. Pro-Chancellor, Brunel University, 1966. Hon. Degrees: BTech., Brunel, 1966; Doctor of Laws, Illinois, 1967. *Publications:* (with Mrs W. Raphael) Managers, Men and Morale, 1947; Exploration in Management, 1960; Piecework Abandoned, 1962; (with Elliott Jacques) Product Analysis Pricing, 1964; Glacier Project Papers, 1965. *Recreation:* golf. *Address:* Flat 13, 23 Prince Albert Road, NW1. *T:* 01-722 8040. *Club:* Reform.

**BROWN, Alan Grahame;** *b* Wood Green, N22, 23 Oct. 1913; *o s* of late Alexander Harris Brown, Bedford, and Blanche Louise Brown, Whitehill, Hitchin, Herts; *m* 1937, Joan Emily Maxey, Bedford; two *s*. *Educ:* Bedford School; College of the Pharmaceutical Society, University of London. Served with Beds & Herts Regt, 5th Bn 1932-37, 4th Bn 1940-44, rank Lieut. Member Socialist Party, 1937-62; Chm. S Tottenham Co-op. Party, 1957-60; Mem. Exec. Cttee Tottenham Trades Council, 1958-; MP Tottenham: (Lab) 1959-61; (Ind) 1961-62; (C) 1962-64; resigned Labour Party March 1962, following differences opinion on fundamental policies; rejoined Labour Party April 1966. Member, Middlesex County Council, 1956-65. Specialises in Welfare of Children and Young Persons, in Juvenile Delinquency and in Prison, Borstal and Approved School Administration; formerly

Member County of Middlesex Approved Schools Sub-cttee and of Children's Cttee; introduced Restriction of Imprisonment of Children Bill, in House of Commons, 1960; introduced Nursing Homes Act in House of Commons, 1963. PhC, FCS, MPS. *Recreations:* motoring, and sailing (Yachting). *Address:* 77 Fitzjohn's Avenue, Hampstead, NW3.

**BROWN, Alan James;** Deputy British High Commissioner in Malta since 1966; *b* 28 Aug. 1921; *s* of W. Y. Brown and Mrs E. I. Brown; *m* 1966, Joy Aileen Key Stone (*née* McIntyre); one *s*, and two step *d*. *Educ:* Magdalene College, Cambridge (MA). Served with HM Forces, 1941-47; CRO 1948; 2nd Sec., Calcutta, 1948-50; CRO, 1951; Private Sec. to Parly Under-Secretary of State, 1951-52; 1st Secretary, Dacca, Karachi, 1952-55; CRO, 1955-57; Kuala Lumpur, 1957-62; CRO, 1962-63; Head of Information Policy Dept, 1963-64; Dep. High Comr, Nicosia, 1964; Head of Far East and Pacific Dept, CRO, 1964-66. *Recreation:* sailing. *Address:* British High Commission, Valletta, Malta, GC. *Club:* Oxford and Cambridge University.

**BROWN, Brig. Alan Ward,** CBE 1955; DSO 1943; MC 1935; retired; *b* 8 July 1909; *s* of Hugh Ward Brown, Dublin, and Gertrude Corisande Brown (*née* Bean, now Stephens); *m* 1936, Pamela Margaret (*née* Preston); one *s*. *Educ:* Bromsgrove Sch., Worcs. Commissioned Royal Tank Corps, 1930; posted 5 RTR, 1931; 2nd Armoured Car Company (India/Pakistan), 1931-35; 2nd Bn RTC, 1936-38; Staff College, 1940; Comd 147 RAC and 3 RTR in NW Europe, 1943-44; Comd 31 Armoured Bde, 1944-45; GSO1 79 Armoured Div., 1942-43; Comd Specialised Armour Estabishment, 1948-49; idc 1949-50; Comd 25 Armoured Bde, 1953-56. Croix de Guerre, Chevalier of the Order of Leopold (Belgium). *Address:* Medleys Farm, High Hurstwood, Sussex.

**BROWN, Albert Peter Graeme;** Director of Information, Department of Health and Social Security, and Adviser to the Secretary of State for Social Services, since 1968; *b* 5 April 1913; *s* of William Edward Graeme Brown, accountant, and Amy Powell Brown; unmarried. *Educ:* Queen Elizabeth's Sch., Darlington. Reporter, Sub-Editor, Dep.-Chief Sub-Editor, Westminster Press, 1932-40. Served War of 1939-45: Royal Navy, Officer, Western Approaches; Normandy; Far East; destroyers and assault ships. Information Divs, Ministries of Health, Local Govt and Planning, also Housing and Local Govt, 1946; Chief Press and Inf. Officer, Min. of Housing and Local Govt, 1958. *Recreations:* cricket, opera (Mem. Friends of Covent Garden), classical music. *Address:* 107 Hamilton Terrace, St John's Wood, NW8. *T:* 01-286 9192. *Club:* MCC.

**BROWN, Sir Allen (Stanley),** Kt 1956; CBE 1953; MA; LLM; Australian Ambassador to Japan, since 1965; *b* 3 July 1911; *m* 1936, Hilda May Wilke; one *s* two *d*. Director-General of Post-War Reconstruction, 1948. Sec., PM's Dept and Sec. to Cabinet, Commonwealth Govt, 1949-58; Deputy Australian High Commissioner to UK, 1959-65. *Address:* Australian Embassy, Tokyo, Japan. *Clubs:* Brooks's, Beefsteak; Savage (Melbourne); Commonwealth (Canberra).

**BROWN, Anthony Geoffrey Hopwood G.;** *see* Gardner-Brown.

**BROWN, Arthur Godfrey Kilner,** MA; Headmaster, Worcester Royal Grammar School, since 1950; *b* 21 Feb. 1915; *s* of Rev. Arthur E. Brown, CIE, MA, BSc, and Mrs Brown, formerly of Bankura, India; *m* 1939, Mary Denholm Armstrong; one *s* three *d*. *Educ:* Warwick School; Peterhouse, Cambridge. BA Cantab. 1938; MA 1950. Assistant Master, Bedford School, 1938-39; King's School, Rochester, 1939-43; Cheltenham College, 1943-50. Elected to Headmasters' Conference, 1950. *Recreations:* athletics (Olympic Games, 1936); music, gardening. *Address:* Whiteladies, The Tything, Worcester. *T:* Worcester 23753. *Clubs:* Achilles; Hawks (Cambridge); Rotary (Worcester).

**BROWN, A(rthur) I(vor) Parry,** FFARCS; Anæsthetist: London Hospital, since 1936; London Chest Hospital, since 1946; Harefield Hospital, since 1940; Royal Masonic Hospital, since 1950; *b* 23 July 1908; *s* of A. T. J. Brown; *m* Joyce Marion Bash. *Educ:* Tollington Sch., London; London Hospital. MRCS, LRCP, 1931; MB, BS London, 1933; DA, 1935; FFARCS, 1951. Member of the Board of the Faculty of Anæsthetists, RCS; Fellow, Assoc. of Anæsthetists; Member, Thoracic Soc. *Publications:* chapter in Diseases of the Chest, 1952; contributions to: Thorax, Anæsthesia. *Address:* The Old Orchard, 32 Albion Hill, Loughton, Essex. *T:* 01-508 4562.

**BROWN, Sir (Arthur James) Stephen,** KBE 1967; CEng, MIMechE; Chairman, Stone-Platt Industries Ltd, since 1968 (Deputy Chairman, 1965-67); Deputy Chairman (Non-Executive), Chloride Electrical Storage Co. Ltd, since 1965; *b* 15 Feb. 1906; *s* of Arthur Mogg Brown, and Ada Kelk (*née* Upton); *m* 1935, Margaret Alexandra McArthur; one *s* one *d*. *Educ:* Taunton School; Bristol University (BSc(Eng.)). Apprenticed British Thomson-Houston Co. Ltd, 1928-32; joined J. Stone & Co. Ltd, 1932, Dir, 1945; Man. Dir J. Stone & Co. (Deptford) Ltd (on formation), 1951; Divisional Dir, Stone-Platt Industries Ltd (on formation), 1958. Pres., Engineering Employers' Fedn, 1964-65; Vice-Pres., Confedn of British Industry, 1969- (Pres., 1966-68); Founder Mem., Export Council for Europe, 1960 (Dep. Chm. 1962-63); Mem., NEDC, 1968-; Chm., Adv. Cttee for Shipbuilding and Shipping, 1969-. Hon. DSc, Aston Univ., 1967. *Recreations:* shooting, fishing, golf. *Address:* Coombe House, Bolney, Sussex. *T:* Bolney 202. *Clubs:* Brooks's, Junior Carlton.

**BROWN, Prof. Arthur Joseph;** Professor of Economics, University of Leeds, since 1947; *b* 8 Aug. 1914; *s* of J. Brown, Alderley Edge, Cheshire; *m* 1938, Joan H. M., *d* of Rev. Canon B. E. Taylor, Holy Trinity, Walton Breck, Liverpool; two *s* (and one *s* decd). *Educ:* Bradford Grammar School; Queen's College, Oxford. First Class Hons in Philosophy, Politics and Economics, 1936. Fellow of All Souls College, Oxford, 1937-46; Lectr in Economics, Hertford College, Oxford, 1937-40; on staff of: Foreign Research and Press Service, 1940-43; Foreign Office Research Dept, 1943-45; Economic Section, Offices of the Cabinet, 1945-47. Head of Dept of Economics and Commerce, University of Leeds, 1947-65. Visiting Professor of Economics, Columbia University, City of New York, Jan.-June 1950. President Section F, British Assoc. for the Advancement of Science, 1958; Member: East African Economic and Fiscal Commn, 1960; UN Consultative Group on Economic and Social Consequences of Disarmament, 1961-62; First Secretary of State's Advisory Group on Central Africa, 1962; Hunt Cttee on Intermediate Areas, 1967-69; Council, Royal

Economic Society, 1950-68; UGC, 1969-. Chairman, Adv. Panel on Student Maintenance Grants, 1967-68. Visiting Prof. ANU, 1963; directing Regional Economics project, National Institute of Economic and Social Research, 1966-. *Publications:* Industrialisation and Trade, 1943; Applied Economics–Aspects of the World Economy in War and Peace, 1948; The Great Inflation, 1939-51, 1955; Introduction to the World Economy, 1959; articles in various journals. *Recreation:* gardening and walking. *Address:* 24 Moor Drive, Leeds 6. *T:* Leeds 55799.

**BROWN, Brig. Athol Earle McDonald,** CMG 1964; OBE 1956; *b* 2 Jan. 1905; *s* of W. J. C. G. and Alice Catherine Brown, Armidale, NSW; *m* 1929, Millicent Alice Heesh, Sydney; two *s* one *d*. *Educ:* The Armidale Sch., NSW; Royal Australian Naval Coll.; Sydney Univ. Served War of 1939-45: Royal Australian Artillery, AIF, Middle East and New Guinea; Director, War Graves Services, AIF, 1944-46; Lt-Col, 1944; Brigadier, 1946. Secretary-General: Imperial War Graves Commn, 1946-60; Commonwealth-Japanese Jt Cttee, 1956-69; Dir and Sec.-Gen., Commonwealth War Graves Commn, Pacific Region, 1960-69. *Recreations:* bowls, motoring. *Address:* 10/6 Rockley Road, South Yarra, Victoria 3141, Australia. *T:* 24.8329. *Club:* Royal Automobile (Victoria).

**BROWN, Dame Beryl P.;** *see* Paston Brown.

**BROWN, Lt-Col Sir Charles Frederick Richmond,** 4th Bt, *cr* 1863; TD; DL; *b* 6 Dec. 1902; *er s* of Frederick Richmond Brown (*d* 1933; 2nd *s* of 2nd Bt); *S* uncle, 1944; *m* 1st, 1933, Audrey (marr. diss., 1948), 2nd *d* of late Col Hon. Everard Baring, CVO, CBE, and late Lady Ulrica Baring; one *s* two *d*; 2nd, 1951, Hon. Gwendolen Carlis Meysey-Thomson (marr. diss. 1969), *y d* of 1st (and last) Baron Knaresborough; 3rd, 1969, Mrs Pauline Hildyard. *Educ:* Eton. Joined Welsh Guards, 1921; Captain 1932; retired with a gratuity, 1936; joined 5th Bn Green Howards, Territorial Army, as a Major, March 1939; Lieut-Colonel comdg 7th Bn Green Howards, July 1939, and proceeded to France with 7th Bn, April 1940. DL, North Riding of County of York, 1962. *Heir: s* George Francis Richmond Brown, *b* 1938. *Address:* Stonely Woods, Fadmoor, York. *T:* Kirby Moorside 293. *Clubs:* Guards, Pratt's; Yorkshire (York).

**BROWN, Sir (Charles) James Officer,** Kt 1969; Consultant Thoracic Surgeon: Alfred Hosp.; St Vincent's Hosp.; Queen Victoria Memorial Hosp.; Austin Hosp. (all in Melbourne); *b* 24 Sept. 1897; *s* of David Brown; *m* 1932, Esme Mai Frankenberg; two *d*. *Educ:* Scotch Coll., Melbourne; Melbourne Univ. MB BS 1920, MD 1922, FRCS 1924, FRACS 1928. Surgeon, Alfred Hosp., 1929-57; Surgeon, Austin Hosp., 1926-67. Mem. Council, Royal Australian Coll. of Surgeons, 1956-68; Pres., National Heart Foundation (Victorian Division), 1966-70. *Publications:* papers in surgical journals. *Recreation:* golf. *Address:* 28 Sargood Street, Toorak, Victoria 3142, Australia. *T.* 24 1888. *Clubs:* Melbourne, Royal Melbourne Golf (Melbourne); Victorian Racing.

**BROWN, Admiral Charles Randall,** Bronze Star 1943; Legion of Merit 1944; Presidential Unit Citation, 1945; DSM 1960; United States Navy, retired, 1962; *b* Tuscaloosa, Alabama, USA, 13 Dec. 1899; *s* of Robison Brown and Stella Seed Brown; *m* 1921, Eleanor Green, Annapolis, Maryland; two *s*. *Educ:* US Naval Academy; US Air University; US Naval War College. Graduated from US Naval Academy, 1921. During War served on original US Joint Chiefs of Staff and US-British Combined Chiefs of Staff organisations; later, Captain of USS Kalinin Bay and USS Hornet and Chief of Staff of a Fast Carrier Task Force. Commander, US Sixth Fleet, Mediterranean, 1956; C-in-C, Allied Forces Southern Europe, 1959-61. Vice-President for European Affairs, McDonnell Aircraft Corps of St Louis, Mo., 1962-. *Recreation:* gardening. *Clubs:* Army and Navy, Army and Navy Country (Washington, DC); The Brook, New York Yacht (NY).

**BROWN, Rev. Cyril James,** OBE 1956; Rector of Warbleton, since 1970; Chaplain to the Queen, since 1956; *b* 12 Jan. 1904; *s* of late James Brown, Clifton, Bristol; *m* 1931, Myrtle Aufrère, *d* of late Mark Montague Ford, London; no *c*. *Educ:* Westminster Abbey Choir School; Clifton College; Keble College, Oxford; St Stephen's House, Oxford. Curate of St Gabriel's, Warwick Square, 1927-31; Chaplain, Missions to Seamen, Singapore, 1931-34, Hong Kong, 1934-41; Chaplain, Hong Kong RNVR, 1941-46; Youth Secretary, Missions to Seamen, 1946-47; Superintendent, 1947-51, General Superintendent, 1951-59; General Secretary, 1959-69; Prebendary of St Paul's, 1958-69. *Publications:* contributions to East and West Review, World Dominion, etc. *Recreation:* choral music. *Address:* Warbleton Rectory, Heathfield, Sussex. *T:* Rushlake Green 421. *Club:* United Service.

**BROWN, Sir (Cyril) Maxwell Palmer, (Sir Max),** KCB 1969 (CB 1965); CMG 1957; Secretary, Department of Trade and Industry, since Oct. 1970; *b* 30 June 1914; *s* of late Cyril Palmer Brown; *m* 1940, Margaret May Gillhespy; three *s* one *d*. *Educ:* Wanganui College; Victoria University College, NZ; Clare College, Cambridge. Princ. Private Secretary to Pres. Board of Trade, 1946-49; Monopolies Commn, 1951-55; Counsellor (Commercial) Washington, 1955-57; Board of Trade: Under-Secretary, 1961-64; Second Secretary, 1964-67; Second Permanent Secretary, 1968-70. *Address:* 20 Cottenham Park Road, Wimbledon, SW20. *T:* 01-946 7237.

**BROWN, Sir David,** Kt 1968; Chairman of The David Brown Corporation Ltd, since 1951; *b* 10 May 1904; *s* of Francis Edwin (Frank) and Caroline Brown; *m* 1st, 1926, Daisie Muriel Firth (marr. diss. 1955); one *s* one *d*; 2nd, 1955, Marjorie Deans. *Educ:* Rossall School; Private Tutor in Engineering; Huddersfield Technical Coll.; MIAE; MIMechE; AFRAeS. David Brown and Sons (Hudd.), Ltd, 1921; Dir, 1929; Man. Dir, 1932. Founded David Brown Tractors Ltd (first company to manufacture an all-British tractor in England), 1935; formed, 1951, The David Brown Corp. Ltd embracing amongst other products, gears, machine tools, tractors, cars (Aston Martin and Lagonda), castings, etc. Chairman: Helicopter Services Ltd; Vosper Ltd; John I. Thornycroft & Co. Ltd; Radyne Ltd; Director, Sonnerdale, Richardson, David Brown Ltd, Australia. Underwriting Member of Lloyd's; Past Member: Board of Governors of Huddersfield Royal Infirmary; Council of Huddersfield Chamber of Commerce. First Englishman to open Canadian Farm and Industrial Equipment Trade Show, Toronto, 1959; inaugurated Chief Flying Sun of Iroquois Tribe of Mohawk Nation, Toronto, 1959. Owner of 1550 acres in Bucks, most of which he farms, and 2000 acres in NSW. *Recreations:* hunting, polo, yachting. *Address:* Chequers Manor, Cadmore End, Nr High Wycombe, Bucks. *T:* Lane End 282; 96/97 Piccadilly, W1. *T:* 01-629 7373. *Clubs:* Royal Thames Yacht, Royal Automobile, British Racing Drivers, Royal Aero; Household Brigade Polo, Ham Polo.

**BROWN, Denise Lebreton,** RE 1959 (ARE 1941); Artist; *d* of Jeanne Lebreton and Frederick Peter Brown; *m* 1938, Frank William Eric Waters; one *s*. *Educ:* Lyzeum Nonnenwerth im Rhein; Royal College of Art. British Instn Schol. in Engraving, 1932; ARCA 1935; Royal College of Art Travelling Schol, 1936. Has exhibited at: Royal Academy; Royal Society of Painter-Etchers and Engravers; also in Canada, USA and S. Africa. *Publications:* books illustrated include: several on gardening; children's books, etc. *Recreations:* music, gardening. *Address:* Casula, Sarratt Lane, Loudwater, Rickmansworth, Herts. *T:* Rickmansworth 75505.

**BROWN, Denys Downing,** CMG 1966; MM 1945; Minister (Economic), British Embassy, Bonn, since 1970; *b* 16 Dec. 1918; *s* of A. W. Brown, Belfast, and Marjorie Downing; *m* 1954, Patricia Marjorie, *e d* of late Sir Charles Bartley; one *s* one *d*. *Educ:* Hereford Cathedral School; Brasenose College, Oxford (Scholar). Served with HM Forces, 1939-45 (prisoner-of-war, 1940; escaped, 1945). Entered Foreign Service, 1946; has served in Poland, Germany, Egypt, Yugoslavia, and Sweden; Chargé d'Affaires, Belgrade, July-Aug. 1963; Head of General Dept, FO, 1963-67; Counsellor, Stockholm, 1967-69. *Recreations:* reading, winter sports. *Address:* c/o Foreign and Commonwealth Office, SW1.

**BROWN, Derek Ernest D.;** *see* Denny-Brown.

**BROWN, Sir Edward (Joseph),** Kt 1961; MBE 1958; JP; MP (C) Bath since 1964; Laboratory Technician (non-ferrous metals); company director; *b* 15 April 1913; *s* of Edward Brown; *m* 1940, Rosa, *d* of Samuel Feldman; one *s* one *d*. *Educ:* Greencoat Elementary; Morley College (Day Continuation). Leading Aircraftsman, RAF, 1942-46. Formerly Mem. Assoc. Supervisory Staffs Executives and Technicians (Chm., Enfield Branch, 1953-63); Dist Councillor for Union. Member Tottenham Borough Council, 1956-64. Chm., National Union of Conservative and Unionist Associations, 1959, 1960; Chm. Conservative Party Conference, 1960; Vice-Chm., Assoc. of Conservative Clubs. Contested Stalybridge and Hyde (C), 1959. JP (Middlesex) 1963. *Recreation:* campanology. *Address:* 71 Holly Walk, Enfield, Middlesex. *T:* 01-363 3450; The Gate House, Bathwick Hill, Bath. *Clubs:* Tottenham Conservative; Harringay-West Green Constitutional; Bath and County.

**BROWN, Edward Percy;** Chief Inspector, HM Customs and Excise, since Sept. 1969; *b* 20 Dec. 1911; *s* of Percy Brown and Lilian Brown (*née* Gibbs), Wanstead, Essex; *m* 1938, Kathleen Julia Gale (*d* 1967); one *s*. *Educ:* Loughton Sch., Loughton, Essex. Career Civil Servant, Oct. 1931-; in Customs and Excise Dept, successively as Officer, Surveyor, Inspector, Collector, and Chief Inspector. *Recreations:* hockey, tennis, ale-conning. *Address:* Barrowfield, Chestnuts, Hutton, Essex.

**BROWN, Captain Eric Melrose,** CBE 1970 (OBE 1945; MBE 1944); DSC 1942; AFC 1947; RN; Chief Executive, British Helicopter Advisory Board, since 1970; *b* 21 Jan. 1919; *s* of Robert John Brown and Euphemia (*née* Melrose); *m* 1942, Evelyn Jean Margaret Macrory; one *s*. *Educ:* Royal High Sch., Edinburgh; Edinburgh University. MA 1947. Joined Fleet Air Arm as Pilot, 1939; Chief Naval Test Pilot, 1944-49; Resident British Test Pilot at USN Air Test Center, Patuxent River, 1951-52; CO No 804 Sqdn, 1953-54; Comdr (Air), RN Air Stn, Brawdy, 1954-56; Head of British Naval Air Mission to Germany, 1958-60; Dep. Dir (Air), Gunnery Div., Admty, 1961; Dep. Dir, Naval Air Warfare and Adviser on Aircraft Accidents, Admty, 1962-64; Naval Attaché, Bonn, 1965-67; CO, RN Air Stn, Lossiemouth, 1967-70. FRAeS 1964. British Silver Medal for Practical Achievement in Aeronautics, 1949. *Publications:* Wings on My Sleeve, 1961; (jtly) Aircraft Carriers, 1969; contribs to aviation and naval jls. *Recreations:* tennis, golf, ski-ing, bridge. *Address:* Carousel, Heron Close, New Domewood, Copthorne, Sussex. *T:* Copthorne 2610. *Club:* Naval and Military.

**BROWN, Ernest Henry Phelps,** MBE 1945; FBA 1960; Professor of Economics of Labour, University of London, 1947-68, now Emeritus Professor; *b* 10 Feb. 1906; *s* of E. W. Brown, Calne, Wiltshire; *m* 1932, Dorothy Evelyn Mostyn, *d* of Sir Anthony Bowlby, 1st Bt, KCB; two *s* one *d*. *Educ:* Taunton School; Wadham College, Oxford (Scholar). Secretary of Oxford Union, 1928; 1st Class Hons Modern History, 1927; Philosophy, Politics and Economics, 1929. Fellow of New College, Oxford, 1930-47; Hon. Fellow, Wadham College, Oxford, 1969-; Rockefeller Travelling Fellow in USA, 1930-31. Served War of 1939-45, with Royal Artillery; BEF; ADGB; First Army; Eighth Army (MBE). Member of Council on Prices, Productivity and Incomes, 1959; Member, Nat. Economic Development Council, 1962. Chairman, Tavistock Inst. of Human Relations, 1966. *Publications:* The Framework of the Pricing System, 1936; A Course in Applied Economics, 1951; The Balloon (novel), 1953; The Growth of British Industrial Relations, 1959; The Economics of Labor, 1963; A Century of Pay, 1968. *Recreations:* walking; represented Oxford *v* Cambridge cross-country running, 1926. *Address:* 16 Bradmore Road, Oxford. *T:* Oxford 56320. *Club:* Athenæum.

**BROWN, Frank Leslie,** CMG 1945; OBE 1938; MC 1916 (and Bar, 1919); *b* 15 Dec. 1896; *s* of late W. F. Brown; *m* 1927, Edith Mary, *yr d* of late S. J. Sandle, Alderman and DL of City of London; one *s* one *d*. *Educ:* Wilson's Grammar School. Sizarship, St John's College, Cambridge, 1915; served European War, 1915-19, KRRC, Captain (MC and bar, despatches); District Administration, Northern Rhodesia, 1919-35; Asst Colonial Secretary, Jamaica, 1935; Deputy Colonial Secretary, Jamaica, 1942-45; Chief Secretary, Nyasaland, 1945-51; retired 1951. *Address:* 1 Church Lane, Hellingly, Sussex.

**BROWN, Sir (Frederick Herbert) Stanley,** Kt 1967; CBE 1959; BSc; CEng, FIMechE, FIEE; Chairman, Central Electricity Generating Board, since 1965 (Deputy-Chairman, 1959-64); *b* 9 Dec. 1910; *s* of Clement and Annie S. Brown; *m* 1937, Marjorie Nancy Brown; two *d*. *Educ:* King Edward's School, Birmingham; Birminhgham University. Corp. of Birmingham Electric Supply Dept, 1932-46; West Midlands Joint Electricity Authority, 1946-47; Liverpool Corporation Electricity Supply Department, 1947-48; Merseyside and N. Wales Division of British Electricity Authority; Generation Engineer (Construction), 1948-49; Chief Generation Engineer (Construction), 1949-51; Deputy Generation Design Engineer of British Electricity Authority, 1951-54; Generation Design Engineer, 1954-57, Chief Engineer, 1957, of Central Electricity Authority; Member for Engineering, Central Elec. Generating Board, 1957-59. President: Instn. of Electrical Engineers, 1967-68; EEIBA, 1969-70. Member: Council, City and Guilds of London Inst., 1969-; Court of Govs, Univ. of Birmingham, 1969-. *Publications:* Various papers to technical institutions. *Recreations:* gardening, motoring. *Address:* 46 Purley Bury Close, Purley, Surrey. *Club:* Royal Automobile.

**BROWN, Hon. Geoffrey E.;** *see* Ellman-Brown.

**BROWN, Rt. Hon. George Alfred G.-;** *see* George-Brown.

**BROWN, Hon. George Arthur,** CMG; Economic Adviser to Government of Jamaica, since 1967; Governor, Bank of Jamaica, since 1967; *b* 25 July 1922; *s* of Samuel Austin Brown and Gertrude Brown; *m* 1964, Leila Leonie Gill; two *d* (and one *s* one *d* by previous marriage). *Educ:* St Simon's College, Jamaica; London School of Economics. Jamaica Civil Service: Income Tax Dept, 1941; Colonial Secretary's Office, 1951; Asst Secretary, Min. of Finance, 1954; Director, General Planning Unit, 1957; Financial Secretary, 1962. *Publications:* contrib. Social and Economic Studies (University College of the West Indies). *Recreations:* hiking, boating, fishing. *Address:* 9 Norbrook Road, Constant Spring, Jamaica. *T:* 41104. *Clubs:* Jamaica, Kingston Cricket (Jamaica).

**BROWN, Rear-Admiral George Herbert Hempson,** CBE 1948; *b* 23 July 1893; *s* of H. S. Brown, Commander RNR, Madras Port Department, and Anna Brown (*née* Hempson); *m* 1919, Ida Mary, *d* of George Hempson, Bradfield, Essex; one *s* three *d*. *Educ:* RN Colleges Osborne and Dartmouth. Midshipman HM Ships Bellerophon, Defence, Indomitable, 1910-12; Acting Sub-Lieut and Sub-Lieut HMS Indomitable, Ajax, Arab, 1912-14; promoted Lieut RN, HMS Adventure, 1914, in command HMS Iris, 1915; appointed Lieut (E) HMS Hercules, 1915; HMS Liverpool, 1917; RN Engineering College, Keyham, 1919-20; Advanced Engineering Course, RN College, Greenwich, 1920-22; Lieut-Comdr (E), Engineer-in-Chief Dept, Admiralty, 1922-25; HMS Warspite, 1925-27; Comdr (E) Engineer-in-Chief Dept, Admiralty, 1927-31; HMS Sussex, 1931-33; HM Dockyard, Portsmouth, 1934-38; HMS Furious, 1938; Captain (E), Engineer-in-Chief Dept, Admiralty, 1939-45. Rear-Admiral (E) 1945; Deputy Engineer-in-Chief of the Fleet, 1947-50; retired 1950. *Recreation:* gardening. *Address:* Robin Hill, 112 Coombe Lane, Westbury-on-Trym, Bristol. *T:* Bristol 683250.

**BROWN, Sir (George) Lindor,** Kt 1957; CBE 1947; FRS 1946; FRCP 1958; Principal, Hertford College, Oxford, since 1967; Waynflete Professor of Physiology, Oxford University, and Fellow of Magdalen College, 1960-67; Biological Secretary, Royal Society, 1955-63 (Vice-President, 1957-63); *b* 9 Feb. 1903; *o s* of late G. W. A. Brown and Helen Brown, Warrington, Lancs; *m* 1930, Jane Rosamond, *d* of late Prof. C. H. Lees, FRS, and late Mrs E. M. Lees, Tonbridge; three *s* one *d*. *Educ:* Boteler Grammar Sch., Warrington. Univ. of Manchester, 1921-28; BSc (Hons Physiology) 1924; Platt Physiological Scholar, 1924; MSc, 1925; MB, ChB, 1928; Bradley Surgical Prize, Medal in Operative Surgery, 1928. Lectr in Physiology, Univ. of Leeds, 1928; Mem. Scientific Staff of MRC, National Institute for Medical Research, 1934-49; Jodrell Prof. of Physiology, University Coll., London, 1949-60. Medical Research Council: Secretary RN Personnel Research Cttee, 1942-49, Chm., 1949-69; Mem. Council, 1951-55; Assessor, 1961-63. Hon. Sec. Physiological Soc., 1941-49, Foreign Sec., 1949-61; Mem. Editorial Board of Journal of Physiology, 1940-47; President, Internat. Union of Physiological Sciences, 1962-68. Mem. Council for Scientific and Industrial Research, 1963-65; Chm., Lister Inst., 1968-. Pres. ASLIB, 1961-63. Feldberg Prize Lectr, Heidelberg, 1961. Mem., Royal Danish Acad. of Science. Officer of Order of Southern Cross of Brazil; Foreign Member Brazilian Academy of Sciences. Hon. LLD St Andrews; Hon. DSc: Leicester; Monash; Hon. D de l'Univ. Liège; Hon. Dr Univ. do Brasil. *Publications:* Papers in Journal of Physiology, and Proc. Royal Soc. *Recreations:* gardening, engraving. *Address:* Hertford College, Oxford. *T:* Oxford 41434. *Club:* Athenæum.

**BROWN, Gilbert Alexander M.;** *see* Murray-Brown.

**BROWN, Gillian Gerda;** HM Diplomatic Service; Counsellor, British Embassy, Berne; *b* 10 Aug. 1923; *er d* of late Walter Brown and late Gerda Brown (*née* Grenside). *Educ:* The Spinney, Gt Bookham; Stoatley Hall, Haslemere; Somerville Coll., Oxford. FO, 1944-52; 2nd Sec., Budapest, 1952-54; FO, 1954-59; 1st Sec., Washington, 1959-62; 1st Sec., UK Delegn to OECD, Paris, 1962-65; FO, 1965-66; Counsellor and Head of Gen. Dept, FO, subseq. Head of Aviation, Marine and Telecommunications Dept, FCO, 1967-70. *Address:* c/o Foreign and Commonwealth Office, SW1.

**BROWN, Harold Arthur Neville,** CMG 1963; CVO 1961; HM Diplomatic Service; Consul-General, Johannesburg, since 1970; *b* 13 Dec. 1914; *s* of Stanley Raymond and Gladys Maud Brown; *m* 1939, Mary McBeath Urquhart; one *s* one *d*. *Educ:* Cardiff High School; University College, Cardiff. Entered Ministry of Labour as 3rd Class Officer, 1939; Asst Principal, 1943; Private Sec. to Permanent Sec. of Min. of Labour and Nat. Service, 1944-46; Principal, 1946; Labour Attaché, Mexico City (and other countries in Central America and the Caribbean), 1950-54; transferred to Foreign Office, 1955; Head of Chancery, Rangoon, 1958 and 1959; British Ambassador in Liberia, 1960-63; Corps of Inspectors, Foreign Office, 1963-66; Ambassador to Cambodia, 1966-70. Knight Great Band of the Humane Order of African Redemption, 1962. *Address:* c/o Foreign and Commonwealth Office, SW1.

**BROWN, Harold James,** BSc, ME; FIE(Australia); FIREE; Technical Director, Philips Industries Ltd, Sydney, since 1961; director of several companies; *b* 10 July 1911; *s* of Allison James and Hilda Emmy Brown; *m* 1936, Hazel Merlyn Dahl Helm; two *s* two *d*. *Educ:* Fort St. Boys' High Sch. and Univ. of Sydney, NSW, Australia. BSc 1933; BE (Univ. Medal) 1935; ME (Univ. Medal) 1945. Research Engineer, Amalgamated Wireless Australasia Ltd, 1935-37; Electrical Engineer, Hydro-electric Commission of Tasmania, 1937-39; Research Officer and Principal Research Officer, Council for Scientific and Industrial Research, 1939-45; Chief Communications Engineer, Australian Nat. Airways Pty Ltd, 1945-47; Prof. of Electrical Engineering, Dean of Faculty of Engineering and Asst Director, NSW Univ. of Technology, 1947-52; Controller, Research and Development Dept of Supply, Melbourne, 1952-54; Controller, Weapons Research Establishment, Department of Supply, Commonwealth Government of Australia, 1955-58; Technical Director, Rola Co. Pty Ltd, Melbourne, 1958-61. Member Council: Canberra Coll. of Advanced Educn; Australian Telecommunications Develt Assoc. *Publications:* numerous technical articles in scientific journals. *Recreations:* gardening, tennis, swimming. *Address:* 2a Casa Blanca, 139 Avenue Road, Mosman, Sydney, NSW 2088, Australia. *Club:* University (Sydney).

**BROWN, Harold John,** MC; **His Honour Judge Harold John Brown;** Judge of County Courts, Circuit No. 50 (Sussex), since 1959; *s* of Charles Edward Brown; *m* 1929, Isabel Margaret Sefton; one *s* two *d. Educ:* Chesterfield; Corpus Christi College, Cambridge. Barrister, Middle Temple, 1930; QC 1955. Recorder of King's Lynn, 1958-59, Norwich, 1959. Dep. Chm. W Sussex QS, 1955-60. *Address:* Fairlawn, Warden Court, Cuckfield, Sussex. *T:* Haywards Heath 4268.

**BROWN, Henry Thomas C.;** *see* Cadbury-Brown.

**BROWN, Herbert Macauley Sandes;** a Judge of the High Court of Nigeria, 1945-58, retd; *b* Dublin, Feb. 1897; *o s* of late William Herbert Brown, KC, sometime County Court Judge, of Glenfern, Blackrock, Co. Dublin, and Elizabeth Rose (*née* Sandes); *m* 1928, Catherine Mary (*née* Hutchinson); one *d. Educ:* The Abbey Tipperary; Trinity College, Dublin. Served War of 1914-18 in Royal Marines. Called to the Irish Bar, 1921. Entered Administrative Service, Nigeria, 1924; Magistrate, 1934; Assistant Judge, 1943; Puisne Judge, 1945. *Address:* 9 Astra House, King's Road, Brighton BN1 2HJ.

**BROWN, Hugh Dunbar;** MP (Lab) Provan Division of Glasgow since 1964; *b* 18 May 1919; *s* of Neil Brown and Grace (*née* Hargrave); *m* 1947, Mary Glen Carmichael; one *d. Educ:* Allan Glen's School and Whitehill Secondary School, Glasgow. Formerly Civil Servant, Ministry of Pensions and National Insurance. Member of Glasgow Corporation, 1954; Magistrate, Glasgow, 1961. *Recreation:* golf. *Address:* 29 Blackwood Road, Milngavie, Glasgow.

**BROWN, Ivor John Carnegie,** CBE 1957; hon. LLD; FRSL; author and Journalist; *b* Penang, 25 April 1891; 2nd *s* of late Dr W. Carnegie Brown; *m* Irene, *e d* of Carl Hentschel; no *c. Educ:* Cheltenham College; Balliol College, Oxford. Entered Home Civil Service, 1913, but resigned to take up literary work; London dramatic critic and leader-writer for the Manchester Guardian, 1919-35; dramatic critic to Saturday Review, 1923-30; Observer, 1929-54; Week End Review, 1930-34; Sketch, 1935-39; Punch, 1940-42. Shute Lecturer in the Art of the Theatre at Liverpool Univ., 1926; Prof. of Drama, Royal Soc. of Literature, 1939; Director of Drama, Council for Encouragement of Music and the Arts, 1940-42; Editor of the Observer, 1942-48 Associate Editor and hon. director, 1948-54. Chm., The British Drama League, 1954-65; Governor: Old Vic; Royal Shakespeare Theatre. Hon. LLD: St Andrews, Aberdeen, 1950; Fell. Inst. of Journalists, 1951. Knight of Dannebrog, Denmark, 1949. *Publications:* (novels) Years of Plenty, 1915; Security, 1916; Lighting-up Time, 1920; Marine Parade, 1932; (politics) The Meaning of Democracy, 1919; English Political Theory, 1920; (essays) H. G. Wells, 1922; Masques and Phases, 1926; First Player, 1927; Parties of the Play, 1928; Now on View, 1929; Brown Studies, 1930; I Commit to the Flames, 1934; Master Sanguine, 1934; The Heart of England, 1935; The Great and the Goods, 1937; Life Within Reason, 1939; Amazing Monument (part author), 1939; A Word in Your Ear, 1942; Just Another Word, 1943; I Give You My Word, 1945; Say the Word, 1947; No Idle Words, 1948; Shakespeare, 1949; Having the Last Word, 1950; Winter in London, 1951; I Break My Word, 1951; Summer in Scotland, 1952; A Word in Edgeways, 1953; The Way of My World, 1954; Balmoral, 1955; Chosen Words, 1955; Theatre (1955), 1956; Theatre (1956), 1957; Dark Ladies, 1957; Words in Our Time, 1958; London 1960; Shakespeare in His Time, 1960; Words in Season, 1961; Mind Your Language, 1962; How Shakespeare Spent the Day, 1963; Dickens in His Time, 1963; (Ed.) A Book of Marriage, 1963; Shakespeare and His World, 1964; What is a Play?, 1964; Bernard Shaw in His Time, 1965; Dr Johnson and His World, 1965; A History of London (illustrated) 1965; A Ring of Words, 1967; The Women in Shakespeare's Life, 1968; A Rhapsody of Words, 1969; Shakespeare and the Actors, 1970; Somerset Maugham: a Profile, 1970; Dickens and His World, 1970. *Address:* 20 Christchurch Hill, NW3. *Clubs:* Garrick, Savile.

*See also C. C. Hentschel.*

**BROWN, Dr James Arthur Kinnear,** CMG 1967; Senior Consultant, Uganda, since 1951; Grantee, Medical Research Council, since 1963; *b* 2 Sept. 1902; *s* of Arthur Kinnear Brown and Ethel (*née* Payling); *m* 1929, Hilda Kirkland, SRN, SCM; one *s* one *d. Educ:* Hymers Coll., Hull; Manchester and Liverpool Universities. BSc Hons Chem., Manchester, 1924; MRCS England, LRCP London, 1929; MB, ChB, Manchester, 1929; DTM&H, Liverpool, 1930; MD, Manchester, 1934. Actg Supt, Itu Leprosy Settlement, Nigeria, 1930; Founder, Uzuakoli Leprosy Settlement, Nigeria, 1930, Supt 1930-36; clinical practice, Altrincham, Ches., 1937-51; Sen. Specialist Leprosy, Uganda, 1951; Mem. WHO Expert Cttee, 1957; Hon. Life Mem., Brit. Red Cr., 1946. FRSTM&H, 1930. *Publications:* chapter in Diseases of Children in Tropics and Subtropics (by Trowell and Jelliffe), 1957; Leprosy (Techn. Information Series, Uganda), 1962; about 60 papers in Internat. Jl Leprosy, Leprosy Review, Central Afr. Jl Medicine, E. African Med. Jl, Lancet, BMJ. *Recreations:* golf, bridge. *Address:* Sonning, Leicester Road, Hale, Ches. *T:* Altrincham 4470. *Club:* (Life Mem.) Manchester University Union.

**BROWN, J. Hullah;** *see* Hullah-Brown.

**BROWN, Sir James Officer;** *see* Brown, Sir (Charles) James Officer.

**BROWN, Sir James (Raitt),** Kt 1948; Third Church Estates Commissioner, 1954-62, retired; a Vice-President, SPCK, 1958; Trustee of Toc H, 1963; *b* 9 May 1892; *s* of James Brown and Margaret Laing, 2nd *d* of David Raitt; *m* 1926, Joanna Martin, *d* of late Lewis Bennett. *Educ:* Merchant Taylors' School, London. Junior Clerk, Ecclesiastical Commission, 1912; Secretary, 1937; Steward of the Manors, 1937; Financial Adviser, 1944; Secretary of Church Comrs for England, 1948-54. Member, Church Assembly (co-opted), 1955-65. Chm., Ecclesiastical Insurance Office Ltd, 1961-71. A Governor, Westfield Coll., Univ. of London, 1954-69; Trustee, City Parochial Foundn, 1963-69; Pres. and Trustee, Highgate Literary and Scientific Instn, and Trustee of other local educnl trusts. Served European War, 1914-19, First Surrey Rifles (TA) and Oxford and Buckinghamshire LI (despatches twice). LLD (Lambeth), 1962. *Publication:* Number One, Millbank, 1944. *Address:* 20 Southwood Lawn Road, Highgate, N6. *T:* 01-340 6147. *Clubs:* Athenæum; Highgate Golf (Highgate).

**BROWN, Joe;** Freelance Guide and Climber; *b* 26 Sept. 1930; *s* of J. Brown, Longsight, Manchester; *m* 1957, Valerie Gray; two *d. Educ:* Stanley Grove, Manchester. Started climbing while working as plumber in Manchester; pioneered new climbs in Wales in early 1950's; gained internat. reputation after climbing West Face of Petit Dru, 1954; climbed Kanchenjunga, 1955; Mustagh Tower, 1956; Mt Communism, USSR, 1962; Climbing Instructor, Whitehall, Derbs, 1961-65; opened climbing equipment shop, Llanberis, 1965; Leader of United Newspapers Andean Expedn, 1970. *Publication:* (autobiog.) The Hard Years, 1967. *Recreations:* mountaineering, ski-ing, canoeing. *Address:* Menai Hall, Llanberis, Caerns, N Wales. *T:* Llanberis 327. *Club:* Climbers'.

**BROWN, John,** CBE 1955 (MBE 1918); MC 1917; retired; *b* 29 March 1890; *s* of Hugh Brown and Maggie Gibb; *m* 1919. *Educ:* Universities of Glasgow and Göttingen MA, BSc 1911; LLD (Glasgow) 1953. Assistant to the Professor of Natural Philosophy, Glasgow University, 1912; Assistant Master, Bellahouston Academy, Glasgow, 1913-19; District Inspector, LCC, 1919-25; Assistant Education Officer, LCC, 1925-36; Chief Inspector, LCC, 1936-47; Deputy Education Officer, LCC, 1947-51; Education Officer, LCC, 1951-Sept. 1956. Served European War, 1915-19 (despatches twice); in Royal Flying Corps and Royal Air Force, in France, Egypt and Palestine. *Publication:* Teaching Science in Schools, 1926. *Recreations:* golf, bowls, gardening. *Address:* 74 Ryecroft Road, SW16. *T:* 01-670 4542. *Club:* Royal Commonwealth Society.

**BROWN, John;** Professor of Light Electrical Engineering, and Head of Electrical Engineering Department, Imperial College of Science and Technology, since Oct. 1967; *b* 17 July 1923; *s* of George Brown and Margaret Ditchburn Brown; *m* 1947, Maureen Dorothy Moore; one *d. Educ:* Edinburgh University. Radar Research and Development Estab., 1944-51; Lectr, Imperial Coll., 1951-54; Univ. Coll., London: Lectr, 1954-56; Reader, 1956-64; Prof., 1964-67; seconded to Indian Inst. of Technology as Prof. of Electrical Engrg, 1962-65. *Publications:* Microwave Lenses, 1953; (with H. M. Barlow) Radio Surface Waves, 1962; Telecommunications, 1964; papers in Proc. IEE, etc. *Recreations:* photography, gardening. *Address:* 34 Wetherby Mansions, Earls Court Square, SW5.

**BROWN, Sir John (Douglas Keith),** Kt 1960; Director, McLeod Russel & Co., Ltd, London, since 1963; Chairman: Robb Caledon Shipbuilders Ltd; Metal Traders Ltd; Titaghur Jute Factory Co. Ltd; Director of other companies; *b* 8 Sept. 1913; *s* of Ralph Douglas Brown and Rhoda Miller Keith; *m* 1940, Margaret Eleanor, *d* of late William Alexander Burnet; two *s. Educ:* Glasgow Acad. CA 1937. Joined Messrs. Lovelock & Lewes, Chartered Accountants, Calcutta, October 1937 (Partnership, 1946; retired 1948); joined Jardine Henderson, Ltd, as a Managing Director, 1949; Chairman, 1957-63. Pres. Bengal Chamber of Commerce and Industry and Associated Chambers of Commerce of India, 1958-60; Pres. UK Citizens' Assoc. (India), 1961. Mem. Eastern Area Local Bd, Reserve Bank of India, 1959-63; Mem. Advisory Cttee on Capital Issues, 1958-63; Mem. Technical Advisory Cttee on Company Law, 1958-63; Mem. Companies Act Amendment Cttee, 1957; Mem. Central Excise Reorganisation Cttee, 1960. *Recreation:* golf. *Address:* Windover, Whitmore Vale Road, Hindhead, Surrey. *T:* Hindhead 173. *Clubs:* Oriental, City of London.

**BROWN, John Gilbert Newton,** CBE 1966; MA; Publisher, Oxford University Press since Oct. 1956; *b* 7 July 1916; *s* of John and Molly Brown, Chilham, Kent; *m* 1946, Virginia, *d* of late Darcy Braddell and of Dorothy Braddell, *qv*; one *s* two *d. Educ:* Lancing Coll.; Hertford Coll., Oxford (MA Zoology). Bombay Branch Oxford University Press, 1937-40; commissioned Royal Artillery, 1941; served with 5th Field Regiment, 1941-46; captured by the Japanese at Fall of Singapore, 1942; prisoner of war, Malaya, Formosa and Japan, 1942-45; returned Oxford University Press, 1946; Sales Manager, 1949. President, Publishers' Association, 1963-65. Mem. Executive, British Council. FRSA 1964. *Address:* 3 Alma Terrace, Allen Street, W8. *T:* 01-937 3779. *Club:* Athenæum.

**BROWN, Prof. John Russell;** Head of Department of Drama and Theatre Arts, University of Birmingham, since 1964; *b* 15 Sept. 1923; *yr s* of Russell Alan and Olive Helen Brown, Coombe Wood, Somerset; *m* 1961, Hilary Sue Baker; one *s* two *d. Educ:* Monkton Combe Sch.; Keble Coll., Oxford. Sub-Lieut (AE) RNVR, 1944-46. Fell., Shakespeare Inst., Stratford-upon-Avon, 1951-55; Lectr and Sen. Lectr, Dept of English, Birmingham Univ., 1955-63; Reynolds Lectr, Colorado Univ., 1957; Vis. Prof. Graduate Sch., New York Univ., 1959; Mellon Prof. of Drama, Carnegie Inst., Pittsburgh, 1964; Vis. Prof., Zürich Univ., 1969-70; Univ. Lectr in Drama, Univ. of Toronto, 1970. Theatre productions include: Twelfth Night, Playhouse, Pittsburgh, 1964; Macbeth, Everyman, Liverpool, 1965; The White Devil, Everyman, 1969. Gen. Editor: Stratford-upon-Avon Studies, 1960-67; Stratford-upon-Avon Library, 1964-. *Publications:* (ed) The Merchant of Venice, 1955; Shakespeare and his Comedies, 1957; (ed) The White Devil, 1960; Shakespeare: The Tragedy of Macbeth, 1963; (ed) The Duchess of Malfi, 1965; (ed) Henry V, 1965; Shakespeare's Plays in Performance, 1966; Effective Theatre, 1969; Shakespeare's The Tempest, 1969; Shakespeare's Dramatic Style, 1970; articles in Shakespeare Survey, Critical Quarterly, Tulane Drama Review, Studies in Bibliography, etc. *Recreations:* gardening, travel. *Address:* Churchill Old Farm, Churchill, near Kidderminster, Worcs. *T:* Blakedown 225.

**BROWN, Sir Kenneth (Alfred Leader),** Kt 1963; *b* 26 Jan. 1906; *s* of late Henry Robert Brown; *m* 1931, Emily Agnes (*d* 1967), *d* of W. J. Pugsley; two *s* one *d. Educ:* Worcester Cathedral King's School. Marine Engineer and Surveyor; Company Director. *Recreations:* shooting, fishing. *Address:* Fairholm, Wellsway, Keynsham, Somerset. *T:* Keynsham 2180. *Clubs:* Constitutional, Bristol, University (all Bristol).

**BROWN, Kenneth Vincent,** CMG 1954; retired Senior Judge, Supreme Court, Trinidad, 1952; *b* 1 Nov. 1890; *m* 1942, Vere Alice Edghill; one *s. Educ:* St George's Coll., Weybridge, Surrey. Barrister, Gray's Inn; Judge, Supreme Court. Coronation Medals, 1937, 1953. *Recreations:* cricket, racing. *Address:* 1 Taylor Street, Woodbrook, Port-of-Spain, Trinidad. *Clubs:* Union, Trinidad Turf, Queen's Park Cricket (Port-of-Spain).

**BROWN, Rt. Rev. Laurence Ambrose;** *see* Birmingham, Bishop of.

**BROWN, Leslie;** Deputy Chairman, Prudential Assurance Co. Ltd, since 1970 (a Director, since 1965); Chairman, Prudential Unit Trust Managers Ltd, since 1968; *b* 29 Oct. 1902; *s* of late W. H. Brown and late Eliza J. Fiveash; *m* 1930, Frances V., *d* of T. B. Lever; two *s* one *d. Educ:* Selhurst Grammar School. Joined

Prudential Assurance Co. Ltd, 1919; Secretary and Chief Investment Manager, Prudential Assurance Co. Ltd, 1955-64 (Joint Secretary 1942). Member, Jenkins Committee on Company Law Amendment, 1960. Deputy-Chairman, Insurance Export Finance Co. Ltd, 1962-65. Inst. of Actuaries: FIA 1929; Vice-Pres., 1949-51. *Recreation:* golf. *Address:* 12 Fitzjames Avenue, Croydon CR0 5DH. *T:* 01-654 3862. *Club:* Royal Automobile.

**BROWN, Leslie F.**; *see* Farrer-Brown.

**BROWN, Air Vice-Marshal Sir Leslie Oswald,** KCB, *cr* 1948 (CB 1945); CBE 1941; DSC 1916; AFC 1918; *b* Durban, 11 June 1893; *m* 1926, P. M. Widowson (whom he divorced); one *s*; *m* 1945, Irene, *widow* of H. F. Seymour, MD, FRCS, FRCOG. *Educ:* Hilton College, Natal, South Africa. South African Defence Force (Artillery) commencement of 1914-18 war; served in German West Africa, 1914-15; commissioned Royal Naval Air Service, Oct. 1915; served in France and East Africa (DSC, despatches, AFC); RAF Staff College, 1929; served in India commanding 20 Squadron and at Karachi, 1930-35; commanded first Reconnaissance Wing at Odiham, 1936-38; Group Captain, 1939; served Middle East, Western Desert, Sept. 1939-April 1941 (despatches); Air Commodore, 1941; AOC Levant, 1941, 1942 (despatches twice, Commander Greek Order of George I with cross swords); Acting Air Vice-Marshal, 1943; AOC No. 84 Group AEAF, 1943-44; Air Vice-Marshal, 1944; Commandant School of Land/Air Warfare, RAF, Old Sarum, 1944-49; retired, 1949. King Haakon VII Liberty Medal. *Address:* 149 North Ridge Road, Durban, S. Africa. *T:* 882794. *Clubs:* RAF; Durban (Durban).

**BROWN, Rt. Rev. Leslie Wilfrid;** *see* St Edmundsbury and Ipswich, Bishop of.

**BROWN, Sir Lindor;** *see* Brown, Sir G. L.

**BROWN, Sir Max;** *see* Brown, Sir C. M. P.

**BROWN, Mervyn,** OBE 1963; Inspector, Foreign and Commonwealth Office, since 1970; *b* 24 Sept., 1923; *m* 1949, Elizabeth Gittings. *Educ:* Ryhope Gram. Sch., Sunderland; St John's Coll., Oxford. Served in RA, 1942-45. Entered HM Foreign Service, 1949; Third Secretary, Buenos Aires, 1950; Second Secretary, UK Mission to UN, New York, 1953; First Secretary, Foreign Office, 1956; Singapore, 1959; Vientiane, 1960; again in Foreign Office, 1963-67; Ambassador to Madagascar, 1967-70. *Recreations:* music, tennis, bridge. *Address:* c/o Foreign and Commonwealth Office, SW1. *Clubs:* Travellers', Hurlingham.

**BROWN, Ven. Michael Rene Warneford;** Archdeacon of Nottingham since 1960; *b* 7 June 1915; *s* of George and Irene Brown. *Educ:* King's School, Rochester; St Peter's College, Oxford; St Stephen's House, Oxford (MA). Deacon 1941; priest, 1942; Asst Master, Christ's Hospital, 1939-43; Curate of West Grinstead, 1941-43. Chap. RNVR, 1943-46; chaplain and Dean of St Peter's College and Curate of St Mary the Virgin, Oxford, 1946; Lecturer, RN College, Greenwich, 1946-47; Librarian, 1948-50 and Fellow, 1948-52, of St Augustine's Coll., Canterbury; Priest-in-charge of Bekesbourne, 1948-50; Asst Secretary, CACTM, 1950-60. Examining Chaplain: to Bishop of Southwell, 1954-; to Archbishop of Canterbury, 1959-60; Commissary to Bishop of Waikato, 1958-. Mem., Church of England, Pensions Board, 1966-; Church Commissioner, 1968-. *Recreations:* antiquarian and aesthetic, especially marine paintings and Eastern carpets. *Address:* 8 Lenton Road, The Park, Nottingham NG7 1DQ. *T:* Nottingham 47177. *Clubs:* United University; Union Soc. (Oxford); The Nottinghamshire.

**BROWN, Lieut-Col Sir Norman S. S.;** *see* Seddon-Brown.

**BROWN, Rev. Oscar Henry,** CIE 1947; OBE 1938; BA, LLB; Barrister-at-Law; *b* 4 July 1896; *s* of Frank and Winifred Brown; *m* 1918, Daisy Cormac; two *s* three *d*. *Educ:* Cathedral High School, St Xavier's Coll., and Govt Law Coll., Bombay; Gray's Inn, London. Barrister-at-Law, and Advocate of High Court of Bombay; Presidency Magistrate, 1929; Chief Presidency Magistrate, and Revenue Judge, Bombay, 1941-51. Ordained Priest, 1969. *Recreations:* yachting, golf, Freemasonry and philosophy. *Address:* Heliopolis, Colaba, Bombay 5, India.

**BROWN, Pamela Mary;** actress; *b* 8 July 1917; *d* of George Edward Brown and Helen Blanche Ellerton; *m* 1941, Peter Copley. *Educ:* St Mary's Convent, Ascot; Royal Academy of Dramatic Art. First appearance Stratford Memorial Theatre (Juliet, Cressida, Jessica), then London, in The King and Mistress Shore, Little Theatre, 1936; toured S Africa, then at Open Air Theatre (Hermia), 1937; Rep. Oxford Playhouse, and Perranporth Summer Theatre, then in The Heart was not Burned (Fanny Brawne), Gate Theatre, 1938; joined Old Vic. (Constance Neville in She Stoops to Conquer, Bianca in The Taming of the Shrew); then Perranporth, 1939; Oxford Playhouse (Hedda Gabler, Nina in The Seagull, Ann Pedersdotter in The Witch, Lady Teazle, Juliet), 1940-41; toured in Golden Boy, then Claudia in Claudia, St Martin's, 1942; Ophelia in Hamlet, New, then Madeleine in Madeleine, Lyric, Hammersmith, 1944; Theatre Royal, Bristol, (Lady Macbeth), 1946; Goneril in King Lear, New, 1946; toured America with John Gielgud, 1947; Janet Spence in The Gioconda Smile, New, 1948; Jennet in The Lady's Not for Burning, Globe, and Royale (New York), 1949-51; Marie Chassaigne in The River Line, Edinburgh Festival, 1952; Rachel Gardiner in A Question of Fact, Piccadilly, 1953; Miss Madrigal in The Chalk Garden, Haymarket, 1956; Heartbreak House, 1959; This Year, Next Year, Vaudeville, 1960. *Films include:* One of Our Aircraft is Missing, 1941; I Know Where I'm Going, 1943; Tales of Hoffmann, 1950; Personal Affair, 1953; Richard III, 1955; Now and Forever, 1956; Lust for Life, 1957; Cleopatra, 1963; Becket, 1964; A Funny Thing Happened on The Way to the Forum, 1966; Secret Ceremony, 1969.

**BROWN, Philip Anthony Russell;** Under-Secretary, Board of Trade, since 1969; *b* 18 May 1924; *e s* of late Sir William Brown, KCB, KCMG, CBE; *m* 1954, Eileen, *d* of late J. Brennan. *Educ:* Malvern; King's Coll., Cambridge. Entered Home Civil Service, Board of Trade, 1947; Private Sec. to Perm. Sec., 1949; Principal, 1952; Private Sec. to Minister of State, 1953; Observer, Civil Service Selection Board, 1957; returned to BoT, 1959; Head of Overseas Information Co-ordination Office (Asst Sec.), 1963; returned to BoT, 1964; Under-Sec., Establishments Div. 1, 1969. *Recreations:* reading, gardening, music. *Address:* Ruthwell, Oak Hill Road, Sevenoaks, Kent. *T:* Sevenoaks 55074. *Club:* United University.

**BROWN, Ralph,** ARA 1968; ARCA 1955; sculptor; Visiting Tutor at Royal College of Art since 1958; Teacher at West of England

College of Art since 1965; *b* 24 April 1928; *s* of W. W. Brown and M. Brown; *m* 1st, 1952, Margaret Elizabeth Taylor (marr. diss., 1963); one *s* one *d*; 2nd, 1964, Caroline Ann Clifton-Trigg; one *s*. *Educ:* Leeds Grammar School. ARCA 1955. Studied Leeds, Hammersmith, Royal College of Art, 1948-56; in Paris with Zadkine, 1954; travel scholarships to Greece 1955, Italy 1957; Work exhibited: John Moore's, Liverpool (prizewinner 1957 and 1959), Tate Gallery; Religious Theme 1958, British Sculpture in the Sixties 1965; Arnhem Open Air Sculpture, 1958; Middelheim Open Air Sculpture, 1959; Battersea Park Open Air Sculpture, 1960, 1963; Japan Internat. Art (British Council), 1963. One man Shows: Leicester Galls, 1961, 1963; Bangor Univ. and Forum Gall., 1964. Work in Collections: Tate Gallery, Arts Council, Contemp. Art Society, Kröller-Müller, Gallery of NSW, Peter Stuyvesant Foundation, Nat. Gallery of Wales and at Leeds, Manchester, Bristol, Norwich, etc. Public Sculpture: at Hatfield, Harlow, LCC Tulse Hill, Loughborough Coll. of Advanced Technology, Newnham Coll., Liverpool Univ. *Address:* The Taut, Oakridge Lynch, near Stroud, Glos. *T:* Frampton Mansell 363.

**BROWN, Hon. Sir Ralph Kilner,** Kt 1970; OBE 1945; TD 1952; DL; **Hon. Mr Justice Kilner Brown;** a Judge of the High Court, Queen's Bench Division, since 1970; Presiding Judge, Northern Circuit, since 1970; *b* 28 Aug. 1909; *s* of Rev. A. E. Brown, CIE, MA, BSc; *m* 1943, Cynthia Rosemary Breffit; one *s* two *d*. *Educ:* Kingswood School; Trinity Hall, Cambridge. Barrister, Middle Temple; Midland Circuit, 1934 (Harmsworth Scholar). TA 1938; War Service, 1939-46; Brig. Q Staff HQ 21 Army Group (despatches, OBE). QC 1958; Recorder of Lincoln, 1960-64; Recorder of Birmingham, 1964-65. Master of the Bench, Middle Temple, 1964; Chairman, Warwicks QS, 1964-67; a Judge of the Central Criminal Court, 1965-67; Recorder of Liverpool, and Judge of the Crown Court at Liverpool, 1967-69. Chairman, Mental Health Review Tribunal, Birmingham RHB Area, 1962-65. Contested (L) Oldbury and Halesowen, 1945 and 1950; South Bucks, 1959 and 1964; Pres., Birmingham Liberal Organisation, 1946-56; Pres., and Chm., W Midland Liberal Fedn, 1950-56; Mem., Liberal Party Exec., 1950-56. Pres., Birmingham Bn, Boys Bde, 1946-56; Mem., Exec., Boys Bde, 1950-55. DL Warwickshire, 1956. *Recreations:* athletics (Cambridge University; Great Britain; British AAA Champion 440 yds hurdles, 1934); cricket. *Address:* Buffbeards, Hindhead Road, Haslemere, Surrey. *Clubs:* Junior Army and Navy; Hawks (Cambridge).

**BROWN, Sir Raymond (Frederick),** Kt 1969; OBE; CompIEE; CompIERE; President, Racal Electronics Ltd; *b* 19 July 1920; *s* of Frederick and Susan Evelyn Brown; *m* 1953, Carol Jacquelin Elizabeth, *d* of H. R. Sprinks, Paris; two *s* two *d*. *Educ:* Morden Terrace LCC School; SE London Technical College; Morley College. Joined Redifon as engineering apprentice, 1934; Sales Man., Communications Div., Plessey Ltd, 1949-50; formerly Chm. and Man. Dir, Racal Electronics Ltd (Joint Founder, 1950), and subsidiary companies. Head of Defence Sales, MoD, 1966-69; Consultant Adviser on commercial policy and exports to Dept of Health and Social Security, 1970. Governor, Wycombe Abbey School; Director, Girls' Educn Co. Ltd. Liveryman, Scriveners' Co. *Recreations:* golf, stud farming, farming, shooting. *Address:* Beech Grove, Church Lane, Sunninghill, Berks. *Clubs:* Royal Aero, City Livery, Royal Air Force; Sunningdale Golf.

**BROWN, Professor Reginald Francis,** PhD; (First) Cowdray Professor of Spanish Language and Literature in the University of Leeds since 1953; *b* 23 April 1910; *m* 1939, Rica Eleanor Jones; one *s* one *d*. *Educ:* Lancaster Royal Grammar School; Liverpool University. BA First Class Hons. Spanish, 1932; PhD, 1939; University Fellowship, Liverpool, 1934. On Staff of Spanish Departments in Universities of Liverpool, Columbia, and New York, NYC, and Dartmouth College, NH, USA, 1937-43. War of 1939-45; service in RAF Intelligence (FO). Head of Dept of Spanish, University of Leeds, 1945-53. Vis. Prof. of Spanish, Princeton Univ., 1958-59. Pres., Modern Language Assoc., 1970. *Publications:* Bibliografía de la Novela Española, 1700-1850, (Madrid) 1953; Spanish-English, English-Spanish Pocket Dictionary, (Glasgow) 1954, 2nd edn, 1956; Spain, A Companion to Spanish Studies (ed. E. Allison Peers), 5th edn revised and enlarged, 1956; D. F. Sarmiento, Facundo, ed. Boston, 1960. Articles in Bulletin of Hispanic Studies, Hispania, Hispanic Review, Modern Languages, Year's Work in Modern Language Studies. *Address:* Rivington House, Clarence Road, Horsforth, nr Leeds. *T:* Horsforth 2443.

**BROWN, Maj.-Gen. Reginald Llewellyn,** CB 1950; CBE 1941; MA; FRICS (Council 1950-53); late RE; Hon. Colonel 135 Survey Engineer Regt TA, 1954-60; Consultant Surveyor; *b* 23 July 1895; *m* 1928, Nancy Katharine Coleridge, one *s*. *Educ:* Wellington College; Royal Military Acad. European War, pow, 1914-18. Served in Middle East, North Africa, Italy, 1939-45. Director of Military Survey, War Office, 1946; Director-General, Ordnance Survey, 1949-53. MA Oxon by decree, 1954 (Member of New College). Senior Lecturer in Surveying, 1954-55. FRGS (Hon. Vice-President, 1969). Consultant to: the Times Atlas, 1955-59; Spartan Air Services of Ottawa. Chm. Meridian Airmaps Ltd. President Photogrammetric Society, 1957-59; President International Society for Photogrammetry, 1956-60 (Vice-President, 1960-64). Legion of Honour (USA), 1945. *Recreation:* golf. *Address:* Cricket Hill Cottage, Yateley, Hants. *T:* Yateley 2130. *Club:* Naval and Military.

**BROWN, Prof. Robert,** DSc London; FRS 1956; Professor of Botany, Edinburgh University, since 1958; *b* 29 July 1908; *s* of Thomas William and Ethel Minnie Brown; *m* 1940, Morna Doris Mactaggart. *Educ:* English School, Cairo; University of London. Assistant Lecturer in Botany, Manchester University, 1940-44; Lecturer in Botany, Bedford College, London, 1944-46; Reader in Plant Physiology, Leeds University, 1946-52; Professor of Botany, Cornell University, 1952-53; Director, Agricultural Research Council Unit of Plant Cell Physiology, 1953-58. *Publications:* various papers on plant physiology in the Annals of Botany, Proceedings of Royal Society and Journal of Experimental Botany. *Recreation:* gardening. *Address:* 15a Corrennie Drive, Edinburgh EH10 6EG.

**BROWN, Robert Crofton;** MP (Lab) Newcastle upon Tyne West since 1966; *b* 16 May 1921; *m* 1945, Marjorie Hogg, Slaithwaite, Yorks.; one *s* one *d*. *Educ:* Denton Road Elementary School; Atkinson Road Technical School. Apprenticed plumber and gasfitter, Newcastle & Gateshead Gas Co., 1937. War Service, 1942-46. Plumber from 1946; Inspector, 1949; in service of Northern Gas Board until 1966. Secretary of Constituency Labour Party and Agent to MP for 16 years. Parly Sec., Ministry of Transport, 1968-70. Member Newcastle Co. Borough Council (Chief Whip, Lab. Gp), retd

1968. *Recreations:* walking, reading, gardening. *Address:* 10 Fawdon Close, Newcastle upon Tyne NE3 2AH. *T:* 55792.

**BROWN, Professor Robert Hanbury,** FRS 1960; Professor of Physics (Astronomy), in the University of Sydney since 1964; *b* 31 Aug. 1916; *s* of Colonel Basil Hanbury Brown and Joyce Blaker; *m* 1952, Hilda Heather Chesterman; two *s* one *d. Educ:* Tonbridge School; Brighton Technical College; City and Guilds College, London. Air Ministry, Bawdsey Research Station, working on radar, 1936-42; British Air Commission, Washington, DC, 1942-45; Principal Scientific Officer, Ministry of Supply, 1945-47; ICI Research Fellow of Manchester University, 1949; Professor of Radio-Astronomy in the University of Manchester, 1960-63. Holweck Prize, 1959; Eddington Medal, 1968. FAA 1967. *Publications:* The Exploration of Space by Radio, 1957; publications in Physical and Astronomical Journals. *Address:* School of Physics, Sydney University, Sydney, NSW 2006, Australia.

**BROWN, Prof. Robert J.;** *see* Jardine-Brown.

**BROWN, Robert Ross Buchanan,** CBE 1968; Chairman Southern Electricity Board since 1954; *b* 15 July 1909; 2nd *s* of Robert and Rhoda Brown, Sydney, Australia; *m* 1940, Ruth Sarah Aird; one *s* two *d. Educ:* The King's School, Sydney; Sydney University; Cambridge University. BA (Cantab.), BSc. Deputy Gen. Manager, Wessex Electricity Co., 1938. Captain 4th County of London Yeomanry, 1940-45. Gen. Manager, Wessex Electricity Co., 1945; Deputy Chairman, Southern Electricity Board, 1948. *Recreations:* tennis, golf. *Address:* Wargrave Court, Wargrave, Reading, Berks. *Club:* Caledonian.

**BROWN, Robson Christie,** MB, MS, FRCS, FRCOG; retired from practice; Hon. Consulting Gynæcologist: St Mary's Group of Hospitals, W2; Samaritan Hospital, W1; City of London Maternity Hospital, N7; Trustee, C. B. Medical Research Fund; *b* 13 July 1898; *o s* of late Robson Brown and Ann H. Christie; *m* Mildred (*d* 1970), *d* of late J. E. Warrington, Redbourn; one *s. Educ:* Royal Kepier Grammar School; Durham University. MB, BS (Hons.) 1920, Goyder Scholar, Phillipson Scholar, Gibson Prize; MS, FRCS 1926. Formerly: Obstetric Tutor: Leeds University; London Hospital Medical School; Demonstrator in Pharmacology, London Hospital Medical School; late Cons. Gynæcologist, West End Hospital for Nervous Diseases; Examiner to Central Midwives Board; Examiner to Royal College of Obstetricians and Gynæcologists. Foundation Member of College Obstetricians and Gynæcologists. *Publications:* Textbook on Midwifery (jointly); Common Gynæcological Conditions and Their Treatment, 1935; Reproduction and Survival, 1948; articles in professional journals. *Recreations:* photography and entomology. *Address:* 15 Rothesay Drive, Highcliffe-on-Sea, Christchurch, Hants. *T:* Highcliffe 3540.

**BROWN, Roland George MacCormack;** Attorney-General, Tanganyika (now Tanzania), since 1961; *b* 27 Dec. 1924; 2nd *s* of late Oliver and of Mona Brown; *m* 1964, Irene Constance, *d* of Rev. Claude Coltman; two *s* one *d. Educ:* Ampleforth College; Trinity College, Cambridge. Called to the Bar, Gray's Inn, Nov. 1949. Practised at the Bar, Nov. 1949-May 1961. *Publication:* (with Richard O'Sullivan, QC) The Law of Defamation. *Recreation:* swimming. *Address:* Attorney-General's Chambers, PO Box 9050, Dar es Salaam, Tanzania. *Club:* Travellers'.

**BROWN, Ronald William;** MP (Lab) Shoreditch and Finsbury since 1964; Assistant Government Whip, 1966-67; JP; *b* 7 Sept. 1921; *s* of George Brown; *m* 1944, Mary Munn; one *s* two *d. Educ:* Elementary School, South London; Borough Polytechnic. Leader, Camberwell Borough Council, 1956; Alderman and Leader, London Bor. of Southwark, 1964. JP Co. London, 1961. *Address:* House of Commons, SW1; 76 Beauval Road, Dulwich, SE22.

*See also Baron George-Brown.*

**BROWN, Rear-Admiral Roy S. F.;** *see* Foster-Brown.

**BROWN, Rt. Rev. Russel Featherstone;** *see* Quebec, Bishop of.

**BROWN, Spencer C.;** *see* Curtis Brown.

**BROWN, Sir Stanley;** *see* Brown, Sir F. H. S.

**BROWN, Sir Stephen;** *see* Brown, Sir A. J. S.

**BROWN, Stephen,** QC 1966; Recorder of West Bromwich since 1965; *b* 3 Oct. 1924; *s* of Wilfrid Brown and Nora Elizabeth Brown, Longdon Green, Staffordshire; *m* 1951, Patricia Ann, *d* of Richard Good, Tenbury Wells, Worcs; two *s* (twins) three *d. Educ:* Malvern College; Queens' College, Cambridge. Served RNVR (Lieut), 1943-46. Barrister, Inner Temple, 1949. Dep. Chairman, Staffs QS, 1963. Member, Parole Board, England and Wales. *Recreation:* sailing. *Address:* 78 Hamilton Avenue, Harborne, Birmingham 17. *T:* Harborne 1313. *Clubs:* RNVR; Union, Conservative (Birmingham).

**BROWN, Thomas James;** *see* Brown, Tom.

**BROWN, Prof. Thomas Julian,** MA, FSA; Professor of Palæography, University of London, since 1961; *b* 24 Feb. 1923; *s* of Tom Brown, land agent, Penrith, Cumberland, and Helen Wright Brown, MBE; *m* 1959, Alison Macmillan Dyson; two *d. Educ:* Westminster School (KS); Christ Church, Oxford. 2nd class, Class. Hon. Mods, 1942, and Lit.Hum, 1948. The Border Regt, 1942-45, mostly attached Inf. Heavy Weapons School, Netheravon. Asst Keeper Dept of MSS, British Museum, 1950-60. FSA 1956. Member, Inst. for Advanced Study, Princeton, NJ, 1966-67. *Publications:* contrib. (with R. L. S. Bruce-Mitford, A. S. C. Ross, E. G. Stanley and others) to Codex Lindisfarnensis, vol. ii, 1960; Latin Palæography since Traube (inaugural lecture), Trans. Camb. Bibliographical Society, 1963; The Stonyhurst Gospel (Roxburghe Club), 1969. *Address:* 12 Chislehurst Road, Richmond, Surrey. *T:* 01-940 5761; King's College, Strand, WC2R 2LS. *T:* 01-836 5454.

**BROWN, Thomas Walter Falconer,** CBE 1958; Consultant in Marine Engineering; *b* 10 May 1901; *s* of Walter Falconer Brown, MB, ChB, DPH, and Catherine Edith (*née* McGhie); *m* 1947, Lucy Mason (*née* Dickie); one *s* one *d. Educ:* Ayr Academy; Glasgow University; Harvard University. BSc (special dist. in Nat. Philos.), 1921; DSc (Glas.), 1927; SM (Harvard), 1928; Assoc. of Royal Technical College, Glasgow, 1922. Asst General Manager, Alex Stephen & Sons Ltd, Linthouse, 1928-35; Technical Manager, R. & W. Hawthorn Leslie & Co. Ltd, Newcastle upon Tyne, 1935-44; Director of Parsons and Marine Engineering Turbine Research and Development Assoc., Wallsend, 1944-62;

Director of Marine Engineering Research (BSRA), Wallsend Research Station, 1962-66. Alderman, City of Newcastle upon Tyne; Councillor: Northumberland CC; Hexham RDC. Liveryman, Worshipful Co. of Shipwrights, Freedom City of London, 1946. Eng Lieut, and Eng Lt-Comdr RNVR, Clyde Div., 1924-36. De Laval Gold Medal, Sweden, 1957. *Publications:* various technical papers in: Trans. Instn Mech. Engineers, Inst. Marine Engineers, NE Coast Instn of Engineers & Shipbuilders, etc. *Recreations:* model-making and gardening. *Address:* Dumbreck, Wylam, Northumberland. *T:* Wylam 2228. *Club:* Union (Newcastle upon Tyne).

*See also Robert Jardine-Brown.*

**BROWN, Tom; (Thomas James);** *b* 12 Aug. 1886; *m* 1912; one *s* one *d. Educ:* Brunswick Schools, Hindley Green. Started work at the pits at the age of 12; at the age of 17 member Branch Committee, later became its President, and then Secretary; Exec. Committee Miners' Federation of Great Britain, 1922 and 1938, rep. this at French Miners' Congress at Alès in 1938; Miners' Agent, 1937. Formerly: JP Lancs; Member Hindley UDC etc.; MP (Lab) Ince-in-Makerfield Division of Lancs, 1942-64. *Address:* 393 Leigh Road, Hindley Green, nr Wigan. *T:* Wigan 55832.

**BROWN, Air Commodore Sir Vernon,** Kt, *cr* 1952; CB 1944; OBE 1937; Fellow Royal Aeronautical Society; Director of the Graviner Manufacturing Co. Ltd; *b* 10 Jan. 1889; *s* of Ernest J. Brown and H. M. Messent, Blackheath; *m* 1914, Constance Mary (*d* 1967), *d* of late F. E. Duckham (Port of London Authority) and Maud McDougall, Blackheath; one *d. Educ:* Eastbourne College; Jesus College, Cambridge (MA). Gas Engineering prior to 1915, then RFC (French Croix de Guerre). Served in UK, France, and after war in Iraq and Egypt. Retired 1937 and became Chief Inspector of Accidents, Air Ministry and later Ministry of Civil Aviation; retired as Permanent Civil Servant, 1952. *Recreation:* music. *Address:* 21 Shrewsbury House, Cheyne Walk, SW3. *T:* 01-352 5002. *Clubs:* Royal Aero, Royal Automobile.

**BROWN, Walter Graham S.;** *see* Scott-Brown.

**BROWN, William,** FRS 1938; MA (Edinburgh), DSc (London); Emeritus Professor of Plant Pathology, University of London since 1953; *b* Dumfriesshire, 1888; *s* of Gavin and Margaret Brown; *m* Lucy Doris Allen (*d* 1966); one *s* three *d. Educ:* Annan Academy; Edinburgh University. After graduation, did research at Imperial College of Science. Subsequently carried on investigations for Department of Scientific and Industrial Research and for Ministry of Agriculture; Assistant Professor at Imperial College, 1923; Professor, 1928-53, and Head of Botanical Dept, 1938-53. *Publications:* Papers in various scientific journals; article, Plant Pathology, in Encyclopædia Britannica. *Recreation:* gardening. *Address:* 93 Church Road, Hanwell, W7.

**BROWN, William;** Managing Director, Scottish Television Ltd, since 1966; *b* 24 June 1929; *s* of Robert C. Brown, Ayr; *m* 1955, Nancy Jennifer, 3rd *d* of Prof. George Hunter, Edmonton, Alta; one *s* three *d. Educ:* Ayr Academy; Edinburgh University. Scottish Television Ltd: London Sales Manager, 1958; Sales Dir, 1961; Dep. Man. Dir, 1963. *Recreations:* gardening, golf, music, chess. *Address:* Ardencraig, 90 Drymen Road, Bearsden, Glasgow. *T:* 041-942 0115. *Club:* Royal Scottish Automobile (Glasgow).

**BROWN, Sir William B. P.;** *see* Pigott-Brown.

**BROWN, Maj.-Gen. William Douglas Elmes,** CB 1967; CBE 1962; DSO 1945; Secretary, The Dulverton Trust; *b* 8 Dec. 1913; *s* of late Joseph William Brown, Manor House, Knaresborough, Yorks; *m* 1947, Nancy Ursula, *d* of Colonel W. F. Basset, Netherton, nr Andover. *Educ:* Sherborne; RMA, Woolwich. 2nd Lieut, RA, 1934. Served War of 1939-45, RA 50 (Northumbrian) Division, E. Africa and N. Africa. Seconded to Royal Iraqi Army, 1947-50; Chief of Staff, Northern Ireland, 1961-62; Commandant, School of Artillery, 1962-64; ADC to the Queen, 1963-64; Director of Army Equipment Policy, 1964-66; Dep. Master-Gen. of the Ordnance, 1966-69. Lt-Col 1955; Brigadier, 1961; Major-General, 1964. Col Comdt, RA, 1970-. *Recreations:* shooting, fishing, golf. *Address:* Gunner's Cottage, Littlewick Green, Maidenhead, Berks. *T:* Littlewick Green 2083. *Clubs:* Army and Navy; Hon. Co. of Edinburgh Golfers.

**BROWN, William Eden T.;** *see* Tatton Brown.

**BROWN, W(illiam) Glanville,** TD; Barrister-at-Law; Lecturer in Germany on behalf of HM Embassy, Bonn, since 1965; Member, Mental Health Review Tribunal for North Eastern Metropolitan Regional Hospital Board Area; *b* 19 July 1907; *s* of late Cecil George Brown, formerly Town Clerk of Cardiff, and late Edith Tyndale Brown; *m* 1st, 1935, Theresa Margaret Mary Harrison (whom he divorced 1946); one *s*; 2nd, 1948, Margaret Isabel Dilks, JP, *o d* of late Thomas Bruce Dilks, Bridgwater. *Educ:* Llandaff Cathedral School; Magdalen College School and Magdalen College, Oxford; in France, Germany and Italy. Called to Bar, Middle Temple, 1932. Contested (L) Cardiff Central, 1935, St Albans, 1964. Served War of 1939-45, in Army (TA), Aug. 1939-Dec. 1945; attached to Intelligence Corps; served overseas 3½ years in E. Africa Command, Middle East and North-West Europe. Junior Prosecutor for UK Internat. Military Tribunal for the Far East, Tokyo, 1946-48; Member: the National Arbitration Tribunal, 1949-51; Industrial Disputes Tribunal, 1959; Deputy-Chairman of Various Wages Councils, 1950-64; Joint Legal Editor of English Translation to Common Market Documents for Foreign Office, 1962-63. *Publication:* Translation of Brunschweig's French Colonialism, 1871-1914, Myths and Realities. *Recreations:* walking, squash, travel. *Address:* 1 Brick Court, Temple, EC4. *T:* Central 1857. *Club:* National Liberal.

**BROWN, William Martyn;** Headmaster, Bedford School, since Sept. 1955; *b* 12 July 1914; *s* of Edward Brown, artist; *m* 1939, Elizabeth Lucy Hill; one adopted *s. Educ:* Bedford School; Pembroke College, Cambridge (Scholar). 1st Class Honours in Modern Languages, 1936, MA 1947. Assistant Master, Wellington College, 1936-47; Housemaster 1943-47; Headmaster, The King's School, Ely, 1947-55. Commissioner of the Peace, 1954. *Recreation:* watercolour painting. *Address:* School House, Bedford. *T:* Bedford 52919.

**BROWN, Sir William R.;** *see* Robson Brown.

**BROWNE,** family name of **Baron Craigton, Baron Kilmaine, Baron Oranmore, Marquess of Sligo.**

**BROWNE, Major Alexander Simon Cadogan;** DL, JP; *b* 22 July 1895; *e s* of Alexander Browne of Callaly Castle, Northumberland; *m* 1918, Dorothy Mary, *d* of late Major F. J. C.

Howard, 8th Hussars of Moorefield, Newbridge, Co. Kildare and Baytown, Co. Meath; one *d*. *Educ:* Eton; RMC Sandhurst. Major 12th Royal Lancers; served European War, 1914-18; retired, 1925; re-employed, 1939-45; served with BEF 1940 (despatches) and with BLA 1945. Secretary to the Duke of Beaufort's Fox Hounds, 1928-38; Joint Master, Percy Hounds, 1938-46. Pres., Berwick-upon-Tweed Conservative Assoc., 1970. Chairman, Rothbury RDC, 1950-55; CC, 1950-67, CA, 1967, Northumberland; High Sheriff of Northumberland, 1958-59; JP 1946, DL 1961, Northumberland. *Address:* Callaly Castle, Alnwick, Northumberland. *T:* Callaly 23. *Clubs:* Cavalry; Northern Counties (Newcastle upon Tyne).

*See also Lt-Col D. M. Bateson.*

**BROWNE, Anthony Arthur Duncan M.;** *see* Montague Browne.

**BROWNE, Air Cdre Charles Duncan Alfred,** DFC 1944; MBIM; Commandant, Aeroplane and Armament Experimental Establishment, Ministry of Technology, Boscombe Down, since 1968; *b* 8 July 1922; *s* of Alfred Browne and Catherine MacKinnon; *m* 1946, Una Felicité Leader; one *s*. *Educ:* City of Oxford School. Joined RAFVR, 1940; served Western Desert, Italy, Corsica and S. France in 274 (Hurricane) and 43 (Spitfire) Sqdns, 1941-44; Perm. Commn, 1945; Staff of Central Gunnery School, 1945-46; Adjt 611 Sqdn RAuxAF, 1946-48; CO 45 Reserve Centre, 1948-51; Flying Instructor and Sqdn Comdr 203 Meteor AFS, 1952-54; Sqdn Comdr Central Flying School, 1954-55; Staff Coll., Andover, 1956-57; Personal Staff Officer to AOC-in-C Bomber Comd, 1957-59; Chief Instructor 231 Canberra Operational Conversion Unit, 1959-61; Jun. Directing Staff, Imp. Def. Coll., 1961-63; Admin. Staff Coll., Henley, 1964; Dep. Dir Air Staff Plans MoD (Air), 1964-66; CO, RAF Brüggen, Germany, 1966-68. *Recreations:* golf, music. *Address:* c/o Midland Bank, Summertown, Oxford. *Club:* Royal Air Force.

**BROWNE, Coral (Edith);** actress; *b* Melbourne, Australia, 23 July 1913; *d* of Leslie Clarence Brown and Victoria Elizabeth (*née* Bennett); *m* 1950, Philip Westrope Pearman (*d* 1964). *Educ:* Claremont Ladies' Coll., Melb. Studied painting in Melbourne. First stage appearance, in Loyalties, Comedy Theatre, Melb., 1931; acted in 28 plays in Australia, 1931-34. First London appearance in Lover's Leap, Vaudeville, 1934, and then continued for some years playing in the West End. From 1940, successes include: The Man Who Came to Dinner, 1941; My Sister Eileen, 1943; The Last of Mrs Cheyney, 1944; Lady Frederick, 1946; Canaries Sometimes Sing, 1947; Jonathan, 1948; Castle in the Air, 1949; Othello, 1951; King Lear, 1952; Affairs of State, 1952; Simon and Laura, 1954; Nina, 1955; Macbeth, 1956; Troilus and Cressida, 1956; (Old Vic season) Hamlet, A Midsummer Night's Dream and King Lear, 1957-58; The Pleasure of His Company, 1959; Toys in the Attic, 1960; Bonne Soupe, 1961-62; The Rehearsal, 1963; The Right Honourable Gentleman, 1964-66; Lady Windermere's Fan, 1966; What the Butler Saw, 1969; My Darling Daisy, 1970. Has also appeared in United States and Moscow. *Films:* Auntie Mame; The Roman Spring of Mrs Stone; Dr Crippen; The Night of the Generals; The Legend of Lylah Clare; The Killing of Sister George, 1969. *Recreation:* needlepoint. *Address:* 16 Eaton Place, SW1.

**BROWNE, Brig. Dominick Andrew Sidney,** CBE 1945 (OBE 1943); *b* 29 Feb. 1904; *s* of Major Dominick S. Browne, DL, JP, and Naomi, *d* of Hon. R. Dobell, Quebec; *m* 1930, Iris, *d* of Major G. H. Deane, Littleton House, Winchester; one *s* three *d*. *Educ:* Eton; RMC Sandhurst. 1st Bn Royal Scots Fusiliers, 1924; retired 1929; Jt Master Co. Galway Hounds, 1933-36. Served War of 1939-45 (CBE). *Recreations:* hunting, shooting, fishing. *Address:* Aghade Lodge, Kilbride, Carlow, Ireland. *Clubs:* Boodle's, Kildare Street (Dublin).

**BROWNE, Sir (Edward) Humphrey,** Kt 1964; CBE 1952; Chairman, John Thompson Group of Companies since 1967; Deputy Chairman, Woodall Duckham Group, since 1967; Director, Bestobell Ltd, since 1969; Member, Commonwealth Development Corporation, since 1969; *b* 7 April 1911; *m* 1934, Barbara Stone (*d* 1970); two *s*. *Educ:* Repton; Magdalene College, Cambridge (BA 1931, MA 1943); Birmingham University (Joint Mining Degree). Manager, Chanters Colliery; Director and Chief Mining Engineer, Manchester Collieries Ltd, 1943-46; Production Director, North-Western Divisional Coal Board, 1947-48; Director-General of Production, National Coal Board, 1947-55; Chairman, West Midlands Division, National Coal Board, 1955-60; Deputy Chairman, National Coal Board, 1960-67; President, The British Coal Utilisation Research Assoc., 1963-68. Director, National Industrial Fuel Efficiency Service, 1960-69; Pres., Institution of Mining Engineers, 1957. *Address:* Beckbury Hall, near Shifnal, Shropshire. *T:* Ryton 207; 31 Dorset House, Gloucester Place, NW1. *T:* 01-935 8958. *Club:* Brooks's.

**BROWNE, (Edward) Michael (Andrew);** QC 1970; *b* 29 Nov. 1910; *yr s* of Edward Granville Browne, Fellow of Pembroke Coll., Cambridge, and Alice Caroline Browne (*née* Blackburne Daniell); *m* 1937, Anna Florence Augusta, *d* of James Little Luddington; two *d*. *Educ:* Eton; Pembroke Coll., Cambridge (Scholar); 1st class History Tripos, 1932; MA. Barrister, Inner Temple, 1934, *ad eundem* Lincoln's Inn. Bencher, Inner Temple, 1964. Served War of 1939-45: RA (anti aircraft) and GS, War Office (finally GSO3, Capt.). *Address:* 29 Pembroke Road, W8. *T:* 01-937 5941; Wiveton Cottage, Wiveton, near Holt, Norfolk. *T:* Cley 203. *Club:* Athenæum.

**BROWNE, E(lliott) Martin,** CBE 1952; FRSL 1955; *b* 29 Jan. 1900; *s* of Lieut-Col Percy J. Browne, CB, and Bernarda Gracia (*née* Lees); *m* 1924, Henzie Raeburn; two *s*. *Educ:* Eton; Christ Church, Oxford. Warden of Educational Settlement, Doncaster, 1924-26; Assistant Professor of Drama, Carnegie Institute of Technology, Pittsburgh, Pa., 1927-30; first Director of Religious Drama, Diocese of Chichester, 1930-34; Producer (London and New York), including all the plays of T. S. Eliot and many of Christopher Fry, since 1934; Director, the Pilgrim Players, including three seasons of New Plays by Poets at Mercury Theatre, 1939-48; Director, British Drama League, 1948-57; revived York Cycle of Mystery Plays at York, 1951-54-57-66; Visiting Professor in Religious Drama, Union Theological Seminary, New York, 1956-62; Hon. Drama Adviser to Coventry Cathedral, 1962-65. Danforth Visiting Lecturer to American Colleges, 1962-65. President, RADIUS (The Religious Drama Society of Great Britain). *Publication:* The Making of T. S. Eliot's Plays, 1969. *Address:* 20 Lancaster Grove, NW3. *T:* 01-794 4322. *Club:* Garrick.

**BROWNE, Hablot Robert Edgar,** CMG 1955; OBE 1942; HM Diplomatic Service, retired;

employed in Commonwealth Office (formerly CRO), 1959-67; *b* 11 Aug. 1905; *s* of Dr Hablot J. M. Browne, Hoylake, Cheshire; *m* 1933, Petra Elsie, *d* of Peter Tainsh, OBE; one *d*. *Educ:* St George's, Harpenden; Christ's College, Cambridge. Colonial Administrative Service, Nigeria, 1928; Assistant Colonial Secretary, Barbados, 1939; Asst. Secretary, Jamaica, 1943; Deputy Colonial Secretary, Jamaica, 1945; acted as Colonial Secretary on various occasions, 1945-49; Admin. Officer, Class I, Nigeria, 1950; Civil Secretary, Northern Region, Nigeria, 1951-55; Actg Lieut Governor, Northern Region, Nigeria, Sept. 1954; Actg Governor, Northern Region, Nigeria, Oct. 1954; retired from Colonial Administrative Service, 1955. Assistant Adviser to the Government of Qatar, Persian Gulf, 1956-57. *Recreation:* watching cricket. *Address:* Flat 3, 51 Abbey Road, NW8. *T:* 01-328 2745. *Clubs:* Travellers', MCC; Royal Barbados Yacht (Barbados).

**BROWNE, Sir Humphrey;** *see* Browne, Sir E. H.

**BROWNE, Professor John Campbell McClure,** FRCOG, FRCS (Ed); Professor of Obstetrics and Gynaecology, University of London, since 1952, at Royal Post-graduate Medical School and Institute of Obstetrics and Gynæcology; Consultant Obstetrician and Gynæcologist, Hammersmith Hospital, since 1948; *b* 7 Feb. 1912; *s* of late Prof. F. J. Browne; *m* 1940, Veronica Evelyn Partridge; one *s* one *d*. *Educ:* Edinburgh Academy; University College, London University (BSc Hons 1934; MB, BS 1938). MRCOG 1948; FRCOG 1954; FRCSEd 1948. Qualified 1937; served War of 1939-45. RAFVR, 1939-46 (despatches twice). Asst Lectr, 1950. Mem. Council, Professions Supplementary to Medicine; Chm., Ministry of Health Cttee on Gynæcological Cytology; Hon. Fellow: American Assoc. of Obstetricians and Gynæcologists (Joseph Price Orator, 1962); Finnish Gynæcological Assoc.; Hon. Mem. Ankara Gynæcological Assoc.; Hon. For. Mem., Royal Belgian Soc. of Obstetricians and Gynæcologists. *Publications:* Co-author Antenatal and Postnatal Care, 10th edn 1969; Co-author Postgraduate Obstetrics and Gynæcology, 3rd edn 1964; numerous articles in medical jls. *Address:* 15 Queens Drive, W3. *Club:* Anglo-Belgian.

**BROWNE, John Edward Stevenson,** CBE 1969; QPM 1959; Chief Constable, Nottinghamshire Combined Constabulary, 1968-70, retired; *b* 27 June 1910; *s* of late Edward Dennis Browne, OBE; *m* 1st, 1936, Muriel May (*d* 1966), *d* of late William Ashcroft Lambert, Sheffield; two *s*; 2nd, 1966, Mrs Sylvia Millicent Goodhew. *Educ:* Imperial Service Coll., Windsor. Joined Sheffield Police, 1930; Chief Constable, Scarborough, 1943-47; Asst Chief Constable, North Riding of Yorks, 1947-49; Chief Constable, Nottinghamshire, 1949-68 (seconded as Chief Constable, Cyprus, 1958-59). *Recreations:* gardening, shooting. *Address:* Wheathill, Goathland, near Whitby, Yorks. *T:* Goathland 303. *Clubs:* Royal Automobile, Forty.

**BROWNE, Rev. Laurence Edward,** DD (Cantab); MA (Manchester); Emeritus Professor, University of Leeds, since 1952; Vicar of Highbrook, Sussex, 1957-64; *b* 17 April 1887; *s* of late E. Montague Browne, Solicitor, Northampton; *m* 1st, 1920, Gladys May Dearden; one *s* two *d*; 2nd, 1938, Margaret Theresa Wingate Carpenter; two *d*. *Educ:* Magdalen College School, Brackley; Sidney Sussex College, Cambridge. Lecturer and Fellow of St Augustine's College, Canterbury, 1913-20; Lecturer at Bishops' College, Calcutta, 1921-25; studying Islam in Cairo, Constantinople and Cambridge, 1926-29; Lecturer at the Henry Martyn School of Islamic Studies, Lahore, 1930-34; Rector of Gayton, Northants, 1935-46; Prof. of Comparative Religion at the University of Manchester, 1941-46; Professor of Theology, University of Leeds, 1946-52; Vicar of Shadwell, near Leeds, 1952-57. Examining Chaplain to Bp of Peterborough, 1937-50, to Bp of Ripon, 1946-57. Hulsean Lecturer, Cambridge, 1954; Godfrey Day Lectr, Trin. Coll., Dublin, 1956. *Publications:* Parables of the Gospel, 1913; Early Judaism, 1920 and 1929; Acts, in Indian Church Commentaries, 1925; From Babylon to Bethlehem, 1926, 1936 and 1951 (Telugn translation, 1932, Chinese translation 1935); The Eclipse of Christianity in Asia, 1933, New York, 1967; Christianity and the Malays, 1936; Prospects of Islam, 1944; Where Science and Religion Meet, 1951; The Quickening Word (Hulsean Lectures), 1955; Contrib. to New Peake's Commentary, 1962. *Address:* 5 Chichester Drive West, Saltdean, Brighton, Sussex. *T:* Brighton 34315.

**BROWNE, Most Rev. Michael;** *see* Galway and Kilmacduagh, Bishop of, (RC).

**BROWNE, Michael;** *see* Browne, E. M. A.

**BROWNE, Cardinal, His Eminence Michael (David),** DD; LLD; OP; *b* Grangemockler, Co. Tipperary, 6 May 1887; *s* of Maurice Browne and Catherine Browne (*née* Fitzgerald). *Educ:* Rockwell College, Cashel, Ireland; St Mary's, Tallaght, Ireland; Collegio S. Tommaso, Rome; the Angelicum, Rome; University of Fribourg, Switzerland. Master of Novices, St Mary's, Tallaght, 1915-19; Professor of Philosophy, the Angelicum, Rome, 1919-32; Rector of the Angelicum, 1932-41; Professor of Theology, the Angelicum, Rome, 1932-51; Master of the Sacred Palace, Vatican City, Rome, 1951-55; Master General of Order of Preachers, 1955-62. Grand Chancellor, the Angelicum, Rome, 1955-62; Cardinal, 1962; consecrated as titular Archbishop of Idelbesso, 1962. Hon. LLD; National University of Ireland, 1954; Univ. of Ottawa, 1955; of Lauras Coll., Dubuque, 1955; Hon. DD, Santo Tomás, Manila, 1958. *Publications:* Contributions to Revue Thomiste, Angelicum, Sapienza, on questions of philosophy and theology. *Address:* Piazza del S. Uffizio 11, Rome (Borghi), Italy.

**BROWNE, Hon. Sir Patrick (Reginald Evelyn),** Kt 1965; OBE 1945; TD 1945; **Hon. Mr Justice Browne;** Judge of the High Court of Justice, Queen's Bench Division, since 1965; *b* 28 May 1907; *er s* of Edward Granville Browne, Sir Thomas Adams's Prof. of Arabic, Fellow of Pembroke Coll., Cambridge, and Alice Caroline (*née* Blackburne-Daniell); *m* 1931, Evelyn Sophie Alexandra (*d* 1966), *o d* of Sir Charles and Lady Walston; two *d*. *Educ:* Eton; Pembroke Coll., Cambridge. Barrister-at-law, Inner Temple, 1931; QC 1960; Bencher, 1962. Deputy Chairman of Quarter Sessions, Essex, Co. Cambridge and Isle of Ely, 1963-66, 1963-65; Served 1939-45; RA (Anti-Aircraft), and General Staff, War Office, ultimately as GSO1. *Publications:* Joint Editor: The Law of Libel and Slander (by W. V. Ball), 2nd edition, 1936; Air Law (by C. N. Shawcross, QC, and K. M. Beaumont). 2nd edn, 1951. *Address:* 7 Campden Hill Square, W8. *T:* 01-727 4972; Thriplow Bury, Thriplow, Cambs. *T:* Fowlmere 234. *Clubs:* Garrick; Cambridge, County.

**BROWNE, Percy Basil;** *b* 2 May 1923; *s* of Lieut-Colonel W. P. Browne, *qv*; *m* 1953, Jenefer Mary, *d* of late Major George Gerald

Petherick and of The Lady Jeane Petherick (*née* Pleydell-Bouverie), 57a The Close, Salisbury. *Educ:* The Downs, Colwall; Eton College. Served War of 1939-45 (commnd in Royal Dragoons): in Sicily, Italy and NW Europe. Farmer and road haulier. Formerly Chm. local party organization. Rode in Grand National, 1953. MP (C) Torrington Division of Devon, 1959-64. *Address:* Torr House, Westleigh, near Bideford, Devon.

**BROWNE, Prof. Richard Charles,** MA, DM, FRCP; Nuffield Professor of Industrial Health, University of Newcastle upon Tyne, since 1946; Chairman, Division of Social Medicine, University of Newcastle upon Tyne, 1970; Consultant Physician, Department of Industrial Health, Royal Victoria Infirmary, Newcastle upon Tyne; *b* 6 July 1911; *s* of Dr Frederick William and Edith Maud Darvel Browne; *m* 1941, Barbara, *o d* of E. Cunningham, *qv*; one *s* three *d*. *Educ:* Clifton; Wadham College, Oxford; Oxford and Bristol Medical Schools. BA honours in human physiology, 1934; Theodore Williams Scholar in Pathology, 1935-36; BM and MA 1937; House Appts, Depts of Medicine, Univs of Oxford and Bristol; MRCP 1940; FRCP 1964; DM Oxon, 1946. Research Asst and Registrar, Dept of Medicine, Oxford; MRC Grant, 1940; Sqdn Ldr (Research Specialist), RAF Medical Br. Nuffield Visitor in Industrial Health to East and Central Africa, 1949 and 1952. Dir, N of England Industrial Health Service, 1960. Council of Europe Fellow in Medicine, 1961. Ernestine Henry Lecturer, Royal College of Physicians, 1964; WHO Consultant, 1965; John Holmes Memorial Lectr, Univ. of Newcastle upon Tyne, 1969; Pres., Sect. of Occupational Medicine, RSM, 1970. *Publications:* Health in Industry, 1961; Chemistry and Therapy of Industrial Pulmonary Disease, 1965; articles in British Medical Jl, Lancet and British Journal of Industrial Medicine. *Recreations:* walking, gardening, photography. *Address:* Sele House, Dunkirk Terrace, Corbridge on Tyne; Department of Industrial Health, Medical School, University of Newcastle upon Tyne, Newcastle upon Tyne 2.

**BROWNE, Stanley George,** OBE 1965; MD, FRCP, FRCS, DTM, AKC; Director, Leprosy Study Centre, London, since 1966; Consultant Adviser in Leprosy, Department of Health and Social Security; Hon. Consultant in Leprosy, UCH; Secretary-Treasurer, International Leprosy Association; Medical Secretary, British Leprosy Relief Association; Medical Consultant, Leprosy Mission; Consultant Leprologist to: St Giles' Homes; Order of Charity; Association of European Leprosy Associations; All-Africa Leprosy Training and Rehabilitation Centre, Addis Ababa; *b* 8 Dec. 1907; *s* of Arthur Browne and Edith Lillywhite; *m* 1940, Ethel Marion Williamson, MA (Oxon.); three *s*. *Educ:* King's Coll. and KCH, London Univ.; Inst. de Méd. Tropicale Prince Léopold, Antwerp. MRCS, LRCP, MB, BS (London) (Hons, Dist. in Surg., Forensic Med., Hygiene), AKC, 1933; MRCP 1934 (Murchison Schol. RCP); FRCS 1935; DTM (Antwerp), 1936; MD (London), 1954; FRCP 1961. Leverhulme Res. Grant for investigating trng of African med. auxiliaries, 1954; Consultant, WHO Expert Cttee on Trng of Med. Auxiliaries; WHO Travel Grant to visit Leprosy Res. Instns, 1963. Med. Missionary, Baptist Miss. Soc., Yakusu, Belg. Congo, 1936-59; Médecin Directeur, Ecole agree d'Infirmiers, Yakusu, 1936-59; Léproserie de Yalisombo, 1950-59; Mem. several Govt Commns concerned with health in Belgian Congo; Sen. Specialist Leprologist and Dir of Leprosy Res. Unit, Uzuakoli, E Nigeria, 1959-66; Associate Lectr in Leprosy, Ibadan Univ., 1960-65, 1968-; Vis. Lectr in leprosy in univs and med. schs in many countries. Sec.-Gen., 9th Internat. Leprosy Congress, London, 1968. Associate Editor and Dir, Internat. Jl of Leprosy of Internat. Leprosy Assoc., Inc. FRSocMed; Mem. Council and Fellow, Royal Soc. Trop. Med. Hygiene. Pres, Christian Med. Fellowship; Co-founder and first Chm., Christian Med. Fellowship of Nigeria; Chm., Editorial Board of Leprosy Review; Founder Member: Internat. Filariasis Assoc.; Assoc. of Tropical Dermatology. Member: Leprosy Expert Cttee, WHO; Assoc. de Léprologues de langue Française (Conseiller technique); Sections Dermatology, Med. Educn, RSM; Medical Policy Cttee, Methodist Missionary Soc.; Medical Adv. Cttee, Baptist Missionary Soc.; British Council, Dr Schweitzer's Hosp. Fund; Medical Commn, European Co-ordinating Cttee of Anti-Leprosy Assocs; Med. Cttee, Hosp. for Tropical Diseases, London; Editorial Bd, Tropical Doctor; Inst. of Religion and Medicine; Soc. for Health Educn; Anglo-Ethiopian Soc.; Acid-Fast Club. Sir Charlton Briscoe Prize for Research, 1934-. A. B. Mitchell Memorial Lectr, Queen's Univ., Belfast 1967. Medal, Royal Africa Soc., 1970. Holds foreign orders incl.: Chevalier de l'Ordre Royal du Lion, 1948; Officier de l'Ordre de Léopold II. 1958. *Publications:* As the Doctor sees it–in Congo, 1950; Leprosy: New Hope and Continuing Challenge, 1967; numerous articles on trop. diseases, esp. leprosy and onchocerciasis, and on med. educn in learned jls; booklets on med. missionary work, med. ethics, etc. *Relevant publication:* Bonganga: the story of a missionary doctor, by Sylvia and Peter Duncan, 1958. *Recreations:* photography, reading, writing. *Address:* 57a Wimpole Street, W1. *T:* 01-935 5848; (home) 16 Bridgefield Road, Sutton, Surrey. *T:* 01-642 1656.

**BROWNE, Ven. Thomas Robert;** Archdeacon of Ipswich, 1946-63, now Archdeacon Emeritus; *b* 15 June 1889; *s* of Horace Browne, London, and Jessie Drury; *m* 1915, Ellen Gertrude Fowler. *Educ:* King's College, University of London. Captain 3rd Battalion Dorsetshire Regt, 1914-19; Deacon, 1919; Priest, 1920; Curate of Christ Church, West Green, Tottenham, 1919-23; Vicar of Edwardstone, Suffolk, 1923-28; Rector of Earl Soham, Suffolk, 1928-36; Vicar of All Saints, Newmarket, Suffolk, 1936-46; Rector of Elmsett and Aldham, Suffolk, 1946-56. Canon of St Edmundsbury, Ipswich, 1936-46; Rural Dean of Hadleigh, 1946-49; Rector of Shotley, Suffolk, 1956-64. Fellow of King's College, University of London, 1957. *Recreations:* tennis and bowls. *Address:* Ellesborough Manor, Aylesbury, Bucks. *T:* Wendover 2175.

**BROWNE, Lieut-Col William Percy,** MC; DL; *b* 22 March 1893; *s* of Col Percy Browne, CB, Fifehead Magdalen, Dorset; *m* 1st, 1921, Richenda Margaret (*d* 1953), 2nd *d* of Basil Hoare, Sutton Veny, Wilts, and 6 Lowndes Street, SW; three *s*; 2nd, 1954, Sheelagh, *d* of John McClintock, Willey Place, Farnham, Surrey. *Educ:* Eton; Sandhurst. Joined The Royals, 1913; served European War with the Regiment (wounded at Ypres, 1914, despatches, MC); MFH The Portman, 1920-30 and 1932-39; MFH Stevenstone, 1946-49. DL Dorset, 1957. *Recreation:* fox-hunting. *Address:* Higher Houghton, Blandford, Dorset. *TA* and *T:* Milton-Abbas 256.

*See also P. B. Browne.*

**BROWNE-CAVE;** *see* Cave-Brown-Cave.

**BROWNING, Amy Katherine,** RP, ROI, ARCA; 2nd *d* of J. D. Browning; *m* 1916, T. C. Dugdale, RA, RP (*d* 1952). *Educ:* Privately. Studied painting, Royal College of Art and Paris; exhibits regularly in Royal Academy, New English Art Club, and other London Exhibitions; one-man show Fine Art Society, 1925; Smiths Gallery, Manchester, 1935; leading provincial exhibitions; Pittsburgh; Salon des Artistes Français, Silver Medal, Gold Medal, HC, two pictures purchased by Luxembourg Gallery; represented in permanent collections, Glasgow, Southport, Manchester, Wolverhampton, National Gallery, Wellington, NZ, Luton; figure subjects, plein air, portraits, flowers. *Recreations:* gardening and open air. *Address:* 58 Glebe Place, SW3. *T:* 01-352 9969.

**BROWNING, Professor Andrew,** MA Glasgow and Oxon, DLitt Glasgow, FBA 1955; Professor of History, Glasgow University, 1931-Sept. 1957, retired; *b* 28 March 1889. *Educ:* Glasgow Univ. and Balliol College, Oxon. *Publications:* Thomas Osborne, Earl of Danby and Duke of Leeds, 1944-51, etc. Editor of Memoirs of Sir John Reresby, 1936; English Historical Documents, Vol. VIII (1660-1714), 1953. *Address:* Durie House, Helensburgh, Dunbartonshire.

**BROWNING, Prof. Carl Hamilton,** FRS 1928; MD; LLD; FRCP (Glas.); FRCPath; *b* 1881. *Educ:* Glasgow Academy and University. MB, ChB with honours, 1903; Carnegie Travelling Fellowship in Pathology, 1904; MD with honours (Bellahouston gold medal for Thesis), 1907 (Glasgow); DPH (Oxon), 1913, LLD, 1935 (St Andrews), 1952 (Glasgow). Official Asst to Prof. Ehrlich, Frankfurt-am-Main, 1906-07; Director of the Bland-Sutton Institute of Pathology, the Middlesex Hosp., 1914-19; Prof. of Bacteriology, Univ. of London; Gardiner Professor of Bacteriology, Glasgow University and Western Infirmary, 1919-51; Cameron prize, Edinburgh University, 1936. *Publications:* Chemotherapy in Trypanosome Infections, 1908; Studies in Immunity (jointly), 1909; Recent Advances in the Diagnosis and Treatment of Syphilis (jointly), 1924; Applied Bacteriology, 1918; Immunochemical Studies, 1925; Textbook of Bacteriology (11 edn. of Muir and Ritchie's Manual) (jointly), 1949; Chemotherapy with Antibacterial Dyestuffs in Experimental Chemotherapy, vol. 2, 1964; studies on chemotherapy, etc., in various scientific journals, etc. *Address:* c/o Bacteriological Laboratory, Shelley Road, Glasgow, W2.

**BROWNING, Colonel George William,** OBE 1946; DL; Welsh Guards, retired; *b* 1 Sept. 1901; *e s* of Rev. B. A. Browning; *g s* of Col M. C. Browning, Brantham Court, Suffolk; *m* 1937, Rosemary Sybil, *y d* of Hubert Edgar Hughes, Flempton, Bury St Edmunds, Suffolk, *g d* of Sir Alfred Collingwood Hughes, Bt, East Bergholt, Suffolk; one *s* two *d. Educ:* Repton; RMC, Sandhurst. Commissioned Suffolk Regt, 1922; transf. Grenadier Guards, 1924; transf. Welsh Guards, 1939. Served War of 1939-45 (wounded); Comd 3rd Bn Welsh Guards, 1941; psc 1942; Comd 1st Bn Welsh Guards, 1944. AQMG, London District, 1945-48; Comd Welsh Guards, 1948-51; retired, 1951. DL Pembrokeshire, 1955. *Recreations:* fishing, shooting, yachting. *Address:* Weatherhill Farm, Icklingham, Bury St Edmunds, Suffolk. *T:* Culford 258. *Clubs:* Guards, Pratt's; Royal Yacht Squadron.

**BROWNING, Maj.-Gen. Langley,** CB 1944; OBE 1919; MC 1915; psc; *b* 28 July 1891; *s* of late Lieut-Col W. B. Browning, CIE, IMS, Cregg, Fermoy, Co. Cork; *m* 1915, Violet, *d* of Alan Thomas Cairnes, The Glen, Drogheda, Co. Meath; one *s* one *d. Educ:* Tonbridge (scholar); RMA Woolwich. Joined RA 1911; served European War, 1914-19 (despatches, Croce di Guerra); NW Frontier Campaign, 1930; Brevet Lieut-Col 1933; Instructor Staff College, 1933-35; Colonel, 1936; GSO1, 1938-39; Acting Maj.-Gen., Inspector of the Royal Artillery, 1939-40; Maj.-Gen. 1941; GOC 10 AA Div., 1940-42; GOC RA Training Establishments and MGRA Training, 1942-44; GOC military mission to the Italian Army, 1944-46; retired pay, 1946. Hon. Citizen of Texas, 1946; USA Legion of Merit (Commander), 1946; Knight Grand Cross of the Crown of Italy, 1946; Cross of Merit, 1st Cl., Sovereign Military Order of Malta, 1946; despatches. *Recreations:* fishing, shooting, golf. *Address:* c/o Bank of Ireland, Ballsbridge, Dublin 4.

**BROWNING, Robert,** CBE 1961; President, Institute of Chartered Accountants of Scotland, 1965-66 (Vice-President 1964-65); Partner John E. Watson & Co., CA, Glasgow, 1927-69, retired; *b* 26 Aug. 1902; *s* of George Browning and Helen Macmillan; *m* 1932, Christina Wallace Freebairn; one *s* one *d. Educ:* Glasgow High Sch.; Univ. of Glasgow. MA (1923) LLB (1925), CA (1926). Mem. Chartered Accountants of Scotland General Examining Board, 1938-44. Member Council of Institute of Chartered Accountants of Scotland, 1952-56; Member Cumbernauld Development Corporation, 1956-58; Chairman, East Kilbride Development Corporation, 1958-69; Director: Clydesdale Bank Ltd, 1957-69; Malcolm Campbell Ltd, 1940-69. Chairman: Glasgow Univ. Graduates Assoc., 1947-52; Glasgow County Scout Council, 1947-52 (and Pres., 1965-69); Member, Royal Commission on the Press, 1961-62; Professor of Accountancy, University of Glasgow, 1950-64. *Publication:* Legal Notes for CA Students, 1931. *Recreations:* golf, fishing. *Address:* 16 West Chapelton Avenue, Bearsden, Dunbartonshire. *T:* 01-942 0108.

**BROWNJOHN, General Sir Nevil (Charles Dowell),** GBE 1957 (OBE 1941); KCB 1951 (CB 1944); CMG 1949; MC 1917; *b* 25 July 1897; *s* of Arthur Dowell Brownjohn, Richmond, Surrey, and Repton; *m* 1929, Isabelle White; one *s. Educ:* Malvern Coll.; RMA, Woolwich. Commissioned in RE, 1915. Served European War, 1916-18, with RE Signals (MC); Palestine, 1938; Dep. Military Governor, Control Commission for Germany (British Element), 1947-49; Vice-Quarter-Master-General, War office, 1949-50; Vice-Chief of the Imperial General Staff, War Office, 1950-52; Chief Staff Officer, Ministry of Defence, Dec. 1952-55; QMG, WO, 1956-58, retd; ADC Gen. to the Queen, 1957-58; Chm. Crawley Development Corp., 1960-62; Member, Commission for the New Towns, 1962-65; President, Malvernian Society, 1964-67; Council, Trust Houses Group Ltd; Chm. Housing Assoc. for Officers' Families. Col Commandant, RE, 1955-62. US Legion of Merit (Comdr) and Medal of Freedom. *Club:* Naval and Military.

**BROWNLEE, Prof. George;** Professor of Pharmacology, King's College, University of London, since 1958; *b* 1911; *s* of late George R. Brownlee and of Mary C. C. Gow, Edinburgh; *m* 1940, Margaret P. M. Cochrane (*d* 1970), 2nd *d* of Thomas W. P. Cochrane and Margaret P. M. S. Milne, Bo'ness, Scotland; three *s. Educ:* Tynecastle Sch.; Heriot Watt Coll., Edinburgh, BSc 1936, DSc 1950, Glasgow; PhD 1939, London. Rammell Schol., Biological Standardization Labs of

Pharmaceutical Soc., London; subseq. Head of Chemotherapeutic Div., Wellcome Res. Labs, Beckenham; Reader in Pharmacology, King's Coll., Univ. of London, 1949. Ed, Jl of Pharmacy and Pharmacology, 1955-. *Publications:* (with Prof. J. P. Quilliam) Experimental Pharmacology, 1952; papers on: chemotherapy of tuberculosis and leprosy; structure and pharmacology of the polymyxins; endocrinology; toxicity of drugs; neurohumoral transmitters in smooth muscle, etc., in: Brit. Jl Pharmacology; Jl Physiology; Biochem. Jl; Nature; Lancet; Annals NY Acad. of Science; Pharmacological Reviews, etc. *Recreations:* collecting books, making things. *Address:* 602 Gilbert House, Barbican, EC2. *T:* 01-638 9543. *Club:* Athenæum.

**BROWNLOW,** family name of **Baron Lurgan.**

**BROWNLOW,** 6th Baron, *cr* 1776; **Peregrine Francis Adelbert Cust;** Bt 1677; *b* 27 April 1899; *o s* of 5th Baron and Maud, *d* of Capt. S. Buckle, RE; *S* father, 1927; *m* 1st, 1927, Katherine Hariot (*d* 1952), *y d* of Brig.-Gen. Sir David Kinloch, 11th Bt; one *s* one *d*; 2nd 1954, Mrs Dorothy Power Beatty (*d* 1966), Broomfield House, Ashford, Co. Wicklow; 3rd, 1969, Leila Lady Manton. *Educ:* Eton; Royal Military College, Sandhurst. Served European War, 1918; entered Grenadier Guards 1918; Adjutant of the 3rd Battalion, 1923-26; sometime ADC to the GOC London District; resigned, 1926; joined Royal Air Force VR as Flight Lieut, 1939; Parliamentary Private Secretary to Lord Beaverbrook, Minister of Aircraft Production, 1940; attached Bomber Command, 1941; Staff Officer to Air Vice-Marshal J. Slessor, Assistant Chief of Air Staff, 1942, and to Deputy Chief of Staff 8th US Air Force, 1943; resigned comm. with rank of Sqn Leader, 1944. Personal Lord in Waiting to King Edward VIII, 1936; Director, British Manufacture and Research Co.; Lord Lieut and Custos Rotulorum of Lincolnshire, 1936-50; JP and DL for Lincs; Mayor of Grantham, 1934-35. *Heir:* s Hon. Edward John Peregrine Cust [*b* 25 March 1936; *m* 1964, Shirlie, *d* of John Yeomans, Upton-on-Severn, Worcs]. *Address:* Belton House, Grantham, Lincs. *T:* Grantham 3278; The Great House, Roaring River, Jamaica, West Indies; Sagesse Estates, St Davids, Grenada, West Indies. *Clubs:* White's; Travellers' (Paris).

**BROWNRIGG, Sir Nicholas (Gawen),** 5th Bt, *cr* 1816; *b* 22 Dec. 1932; *s* of late Gawen Egremont Brownrigg and Baroness Lucia von Borosini, *o d* of Baron Victor von Borosini, California; *S* grandfather, 1939; *m* 1959, Linda Louise Lovelace (marriage dissolved 1965), Beverly Hills, California; one *s* one *d*. *Heir:* *s* Michael Gawen Brownrigg, *b* Oct. 1961. *Address:* 13040 Alta Tierra Road, Los Altos Hills, California, USA.

**BROWNRIGG, Philip Henry Akerman,** CMG 1964; DSO 1945; OBE 1953; TD 1945; Director (appointed by Government of Zambia): Nchanga Consolidated Copper Mines Ltd; Roan Consolidated Mines Ltd; Mindeco Ltd; *b* 3 June 1911; *s* of late Charles E. Brownrigg, Headmaster of Magdalen Coll. Sch., Oxford. *m* 1936, Marguerite Doreen Ottley; three *d*. *Educ:* Eton; Magdalen Coll., Oxford (BA). Journalist, 1934-52; Editor, Sunday Graphic, 1952. Joined Anglo American Corp. of S Africa, 1953: London Agent, 1956; Dir in Rhodesia, 1961-63; Dir in Zambia, 1964-65; retd, 1969. Joined TA, 1938; served War of 1939-45 with 6 R Berks, and 61st Reconnaissance Regt (RAC); Lieut-Col 1944; CO 4/6 R Berks (TA) 1949-52. *Recreations:* golf, sport on TV. *Address:* Wheeler's, Checkendon, Nr Reading, Berks. *T:* Checkendon 328.

**BRUBECK, David Warren;** musician, USA; composer of songs; *b* Concord, Calif, 6 Dec. 1920; *s* of Howard Brubeck and Elizabeth Ivey; *m* 1942, Iola Whitlock; five *s* one *d*. *Educ:* Pacific Univ. (BA); Mills Coll. (postgrad.). Pianist with dance bands and jazz trio, 1946-49; own trio, touring USA, 1950; formed Dave Brubeck Quartet, 1951; tours to festivals and colls, incl. tour of Europe and Middle East (for US State Dept); Europe and Australia, 1960; Quartet at Festival Hall, London, 1961, etc. Fellow, Internat. Inst. of Arts and Sciences. Exponent of progressive Jazz; many awards from trade magazines; numerous recordings. Has composed: over 250 songs; Points of Jazz (ballet); Elementals (orch.); The Light in the Wilderness (oratorio; perf. Cincinnati Symph. Orch. and mixed chorus of 100 voices, 1968). *Address:* c/o Associated Booking Corporation, 445 Park Avenue, New York, NY, USA.

**BRUCE,** family name of **Barons Aberdare** and **Balfour of Burleigh,** and of **Earl of Elgin.**

**BRUCE;** *see* Cumming-Bruce and Hovell-Thurlow-Cumming-Bruce.

**BRUCE, Lord; Charles Edward Bruce;** *b* 19 Oct. 1961; *s* and *heir* of 11th Earl of Elgin, *qv*.

**BRUCE, Alastair Henry,** CBE 1951; DL; Chairman and Managing Director, The Inveresk Paper Company Ltd, 1964-68; Member, Monopolies Commission, 1964-68; Chairman, Paper and Paper Products Industry Training Board, since 1968; *b* 14 April 1900; *s* of Patrick Chalmers Bruce and Lucy Walmsley Hodgson; *m* 1921, Jean Newton Callender; one *s*. *Educ:* Cargilfield, Midlothian; Uppingham. President British Paper and Board Makers Association, 1938-42 and 1948-51; President British Paper and Board Research Association, 1948-51. DL Midlothian, 1943-. *Recreations:* shooting, and fishing. *Address:* Torduff, Juniper Green, Midlothian. *T:* 031-441 2274. *Club:* Bath.

**BRUCE, Alexander Robson,** CMG 1961; OBE 1948; Assistant Secretary, Board of Trade, 1963-67, retired; *b* 17 April 1907; *m* 1936, Isobel Mary Goldie; four *d*. *Educ:* Rutherford Coll., Newcastle upon Tyne; Durham Univ. Asst Trade Comr, 1933-42, Trade Commissioner, 1942-43, Montreal; Commercial Sec., British Embassy, Madrid, 1943-46; Trade Comr, Ottawa, 1946-50; Asst Sec., Bd of Trade, 1950-54 and 1963-; Principal British Trade Commissioner in NSW, 1955-63. *Recreation:* golf. *Address:* 37 North Road, Highgate, N6. *Club:* Highgate Golf.

**BRUCE, Sir Arthur Atkinson,** KBE *cr* 1943; MC 1917; Director: Wallace Brothers & Co. Ltd, 1947-65; Chartered Bank of India, 1949-70; *b* 26 March 1895; *s* of late John Davidson Bruce, Jarrow-on-Tyne; *m* 1928, Kathleen Frances (*d* 1952), *d* of John Emeris Houldey, ICS (retd), Penn, Bucks; three *d*. *Educ:* Cambridge. Director Reserve Bank of India, 1935-46; Chairman Burma Chamber of Commerce, 1936, 1942, 1946. Member of Council, London Chamber of Commerce, 1960-65. *Address:* Little Tylers, Warwicks Bench, Guildford, Surrey. *Club:* Oriental.

**BRUCE, David (Kirkpatrick Este);** retired; Ambassador of the United States of America to the Court of St James's, 1961-69; United States Representative at Vietnam Peace Talks, Paris, since Aug. 1970; *b* 12 Feb. 1898; *s* of William Cabell Bruce and Louise Este Bruce (*née* Fisher); *m* 1st, 1926, Ailsa Mellon (*d*

1969); one *d* (decd); 2nd, 1945, Evangeline Bell; two *s* one *d*. *Educ:* Princeton Univ.; Univ. of Virginia; Univ. of Maryland. Served in US Army, 1917-19 and 1942-45. Admitted to Maryland Bar, 1921; Member Maryland House of Delegates, 1924-26; practised law in Baltimore, Md, 1921-25; Amer. Vice-Consul, Rome, 1926-28; engaged in business and farming, 1928-40; Mem. Virginia House of Delegates, 1939-42; Chief Rep. in Gt Brit. for Amer. Red Cross, 1940; with Office of Strategic Services, 1941-45 (Dir European Theater of Ops, 1943-45); Asst Sec. of Commerce, 1947-48; Chief, Econ. Co-op. Admin, to France, 1948-49; US Ambassador to France, 1949-52; Under Secretary of State, 1952-53; apptd Special US Observer at interim cttee of European Defense Community, 1953; Special Amer. Rep. to European High Authority for Coal and Steel, 1953-54; US Ambassador to Federal Republic of Germany, 1957-59. Hon. CBE (Mil.) 1945. *Publication:* Sixteen American Presidents, 1938. *Address:* 1405 34th Street NW, Washington, DC 20007, USA. *Clubs:* Buck's; Jockey, Travellers' (Paris); various (USA).

**BRUCE, Donald William Trevor;** Economist; Chartered Accountant; Writer; *b* 3 Oct. 1912; *s* of late W. T. Bruce, Norbury, Surrey; *m* 1939, Joan Letitia Butcher; one *s* three *d*. *Educ:* Grammar School, Donington, Lincs; FCA 1947. Re-joined Territorial Army, March 1939; commissioned, Nov. 1939; Major, 1942; served at home and in France until May 1945 (despatches). MP (Lab) for North Portsmouth, 1945-50; Parliamentary Private Sec. to Minister of Health, 1945-50; Member Min. of Health delegn to Sweden and Denmark, 1946, and of House of Commons Select Cttee on Public Accounts, 1948-50. *Publications:* miscellaneous contributions on political science and economics to newspapers and periodicals. *Address:* Pinecroft, Heronsgate, Rickmansworth, Herts. *T:* Chorleywood 2382. *Club:* Reform.

**BRUCE, Sir (Francis) Michael Ian;** *see* Bruce, Sir Michael Ian.

**BRUCE, Prof. Frederick Fyvie,** MA Aberdeen, Cantab, Manchester, DD Aberdeen; Rylands Professor of Biblical Criticism and Exegesis, University of Manchester, since Oct. 1959; *b* 12 Oct. 1910; *e s* of late P. F. Bruce, Elgin, Morayshire; *m* 1936, Betty, *er d* of late A. B. Davidson, Aberdeen; one *s* one *d*. *Educ:* Elgin Acad.; Univs of Aberdeen, Cambridge, Vienna. Gold Medallist in Greek and Latin; Fullerton Schol. in Classics, 1932; Croom Robertson Fellow, 1933; Aberdeen Univ.; Scholar of Gonville and Caius Coll., Camb., 1932; Sandys Student. Camb., 1934; Ferguson Schol. in Classics, 1933, and Crombie Scholar in Biblical Criticism, 1939, Scottish Univs; Diploma in Hebrew, Leeds Univ., 1943. Asst in Greek, Edinburgh Univ., 1935-38; Lectr in Greek, Leeds Univ., 1938-47: Professor of Biblical History and Literature, University of Sheffield, 1955-59 (Head of Dept, 1947-59). Lectures: John A. McElwain, Gordon Divinity School, Beverly Farms, Massachusetts, 1958; Calvin Foundation, Calvin Coll. and Seminary, Grand Rapids, Michigan, 1958; Payton, Fuller Theolog. Seminary, Pasadena, Calif, 1968; Norton, Southern Baptist Theolog. Seminary, Louisville, Kentucky, 1968; Smyth, Columbia Theological Seminary, Decatur, Ga, 1970; Earle, Nazarene Theological Seminary, Kansas City, Mo, 1970; N. W. Lund, N Park Theological Seminary, Chicago, 1970. Examr in Biblical Studies: Leeds University, 1943-47, 1957-60, 1967-69; Edinburgh University, 1949-52, 1958-60; Bristol University, 1958-60; Aberdeen University, 1959-61; London University, 1959-60; St Andrews University, 1961-64; Cambridge University, 1961-62; University of Wales, 1965-68; Sheffield University, 1968-70; Newcastle University, 1969-; Dean of Faculty of Theology, University of Manchester, 1963-64; President: Yorkshire Soc. for Celtic Studies, 1948-50; Sheffield Branch of Classical Association, 1955-58; Victoria Inst., 1958-65; Manchester Egyptian and Oriental Society, 1963-65; Soc. for Old Testament Study, 1965. Editor: Yorkshire Celtic Studies, 1945-57; The Evangelical Quarterly, 1949-; Palestine Exploration Quarterly, 1957-. *Publications:* Are the NT Documents Reliable? 1943; The Hittites and the OT, 1948; The Books and the Parchments, 1950; The Acts of the Apostles, Greek Text with Commentary, 1951; The Book of the Acts, Commentary on English Text, 1954; Second Thoughts on the Dead Sea Scrolls, 1956; The Teacher of Righteousness in the Qumran Texts, 1957; Biblical Exegesis in the Qumran Texts, 1959; The Spreading Flame, 1958; Commentary on the Epistle to the Colossians, 1958; The Defence of the Gospel in the New Testament, 1959; The English Bible, 1961; The Epistle to the Ephesians, 1961; Paul and his Converts, 1962; The Epistle of Paul to the Romans, 1963; Israel and the Nations, 1963; Commentary on the Epistle to the Hebrews, 1964; Expanded Paraphrase of the Epistles of Paul, 1965; New Testament History, 1969; This is That, 1969; Tradition Old and New, 1970; St Matthew, 1970; The Epistles of John, 1970; First and Second Corinthians (Century Bible), 1971; contribs to classical and theological journals. *Recreation:* walking. *Address:* The University, Manchester; The Crossways, Temple Road, Buxton, Derbyshire. *T:* Buxton 3250.

**BRUCE, George Gordon,** MB, ChB Aberdeen, LRCP, FRCS; FRCSE; Extra Surgeon to the Queen in Scotland since 1961 (formerly Surgeon to King George VI, and to the Queen, 1952-61, in Scotland); Surgeon, EMS; retd as Surgeon Aberdeen Royal Infirmary, 1957; *b* 25 Aug. 1891; *s* of George Bruce, Tochineal, Cullen; *m* 1st, 1917; one *d*; 2nd, 1947, Jane Ann Gill, Glenlea, Hopeman, Morayshire. *Educ:* Fordyce Academy; Aberdeen University; St Mary's and St Bartholomew's Hospitals, London. MB, ChB, with Distinction and Keith Gold Medallist in Surgery in 1915; House Surgeon, Aberdeen Royal Infirmary: Active Service, 1915-19 (despatches); FRCS (Eng.), 1921; University Assistant in Surgery, 1929-33; Surgeon to Royal Aberdeen Hospital for Sick Children until 1950; Lecturer and Examiner in Clinical Surgery, University of Aberdeen. *Publications:* numerous papers on surgical subjects. *Recreations:* shooting, fishing. *Address:* 5 Rubislaw Place, Aberdeen AB1 1XN. *T:* Aberdeen 23028. *Club:* University (Aberdeen).

**BRUCE, Hon. George John Done;** *see* Burleigh, Master of.

**BRUCE, Captain Sir Hervey John William,** 6th Bt, *cr* 1804; late Royal Scots Greys; *b* 29 June 1919; *s* of 5th Bt and Margaret Florence (she *m* 2nd, 1925, Lieut-Col C. O. Morris), *d* of Rev. Robert Jackson, Rector of Little Thurlow, Newmarket; *S* father, 1924; *m* 1949, Mrs Innes Ker; one *s* one *d*. *Educ:* Eton; RMC. *Heir: s* Hervey James Hugh Bruce, *b* 4 Sept. 1952. *Address:* Swinstead Hall, Grantham, Lincs.

**BRUCE, Mrs H. J.;** *see* Karsavina, Tamara.

**BRUCE, Sir John,** Kt 1963; CBE 1945; TD 1946; FRSE 1963; FRCSE 1931; Honorary Surgeon to the Queen in Scotland, since 1960; Regius Professor of Clinical Surgery, Edinburgh

University, 1956-70; Surgeon-in-Charge, Royal Infirmary, Edinburgh, since 1956; *b* 6 March 1905; *m* 1935, Mary Whyte Craig. *Educ:* Edinburgh Univ. (MB, ChB Hons 1928). Served War of 1939-45 with RAMC: Norway, 1940 (despatches); Brig.-Consulting Surgeon, 14th Army, SEAC, 1943; Burma, 1945 (despatches). Asst Surgeon, Royal Infirmary, Edinburgh, 1935-46; Lectr on Surgery, Edinburgh Univ., and Surgeon, Western Gen. Hosp., 1946-56. Consulting Surgeon, Scottish Comd; Member: Army Med. Adv. Bd; RAF Med. Adv. Bd. Editor, Jl of RCSE. President: RCSE, 1957-62; Assoc. of Surgeons of Great Britain and Ireland, 1965; (also Archivist) James IV Assoc. of Surgeons, 1966-69; British Cancer Council, 1968-; Eastern Surgical Soc. of America, 1966-67; Internat. Fedn of Surgical Colls. Visiting Professor: (Naffziger) Univ. of California, San Francisco, 1961; Univ. of Copenhagen, 1961; Univ. of Ohio, 1963; (Gunderson) Univ. of Wisconsin, 1964; Univ. of Cincinnati, 1964; (Sir Arthur Sims Commonwealth) Australasia, 1966. Lectures: Francis Shepherd, Montreal, 1951; Donald Balfour, Toronto, 1957; Mayo Foundn, Rochester, 1957; McMurray, Liverpool, 1960; Colles', RCSI, 1960; Phemister, Chicago, 1963; Sir John Marnoch, Aberdeen, 1964; Willis, Richmond, Va, 1964; Sir Gordon Gordon-Taylor, Edinburgh, 1965. External Examiner in Surgery: NUI; Univs of Wales, Glasgow, Liverpool, Oxford, St Andrews, Hong Kong; formerly: RCSI; Coll. of Surgeons in Africa. Hon. Col: 205 Army Gen. Hosp.; formerly 21 Gen. Hosp. AER. Fellow, Assoc. of Surgeons of Great Britain and Ireland; FRSM. Hon. FACS 1957; Hon. FRCS 1960; Hon. FRACS; Hon. FRCPS; Hon. FRCSI; Hon. FCPSO(So. Af.); Hon. FRCS Canada; Hon. Fellow, Royal Coll. of Univ. Surgeons of Denmark. Hon. Member: Acad. of Medicine, Malaya, 1960 (AM Malaya); Amer. Surgical Assoc., 1961; Eastern Surgical Assoc., USA, 1964. Hon. DSc Pa. *Publications:* Manual of Surgical Anatomy, 2nd edn, 1964. contribs to surgical literature. *Recreation:* fishing. *Address:* St Bernard's Cottage, 11 Mackenzie Place Edinburgh. *T:* 031-225 1426. *Clubs:* Athenæum, Royal Commonwealth Society; New (Edinburgh).

**BRUCE, Major-General (retired) John Geoffrey,** CB 1944; DSO 1938; MC 1923; *b* 4 Dec. 1896; *s* of late Colonel Sir Gerald Bruce, KCB, CMG, DSO; *m* 1932, Marjorie Isabel Crump; two *d*. *Educ:* Rugby School. 2nd Lieut Glamorgan Yeomanry, Aug. 1914; served in Egypt and Palestine to 1918. Transferred to 6th Gurkha Rifles; served 3rd Afghan War, 1919; NW Frontier expeditions, 1920-23 and 1937-38; passed Staff College course, Quetta, 1927-28, RAF Staff College course, Andover, 1932, and Imperial Defence College, London, 1939. Instructor at Staff College, 1933-36; commanded 2nd Bn 6th Gurkha Rifles, 1937-38; Brig. General Staff, Norwegian Exped. Force and in France, 1940; commanded Infantry Brigade in India, 1940-41; Deputy Director of Military Operations, India, 1941-42; Maj.-General i/c British Military Mission to China, 1942; Maj.-General's command in India, 1942-44; Deputy Chief General Staff, Indian Army, 1944-46; GOC Lahore District, 1946-47; retired 1948. Commandant Civil Defence Staff College, 1952-56. Member of Mount Everest Expeditions of 1922 and 1924 (MacGregor Memorial Medal and Olympic Gold Medal). Order of Star of Nepal (2nd class), 1946. *Recreations:* riding, shooting, tennis, mountaineering, and travel. *Address:* Queen's Haye, Colyton, Devon. *T:* Colyton 554. *Club:* United Service.

**BRUCE, Sir Michael (Ian),** 12th Bt, *cr* 1629; partner, Gossard-Bruce Co., from 1953; owner, The Eye Witness (legal photo service), from 1956; *b* 3 April 1926; *s* of Sir Michael William Selby Bruce, 11th Bt and Doreen Dalziel, *d* of late W. F. Greenwell; *S* father 1957; is an American citizen; has discontinued first forename, Francis; *m* 1st, 1947, Barbara Stevens (marr. diss., 1957), *d* of Frank J. Lynch; two *s*; 2nd, 1961, Frances Keegan (marr. diss., 1963); 3rd, 1966, Marilyn Ann, *d* of Carter Mallaby. *Educ:* Forman School, Litchfield, Conn; Pomfret, Conn. Served United States Marine Corps, 1943-46 (Letter of Commendation); S Pacific area two years, Bismarck Archipelago, Bougainville, Philippines. *Recreations:* sailing, spear-fishing. *Heir:* *s* Michael Ian Richard Bruce, *b* 10 Dec. 1950. *Clubs:* Rockaway Hunt; Lawrence Beach.

**BRUCE, Robert Elton Spencer;** Editor, Woman's Own, since 1968; *b* 8 Feb. 1936; *s* of F. S. Bruce and A. B. Bruce (*née* Clarke); *m* 1961, Frances Ann Rosemary (*née* Marshall); two *s* one *d*. *Educ:* Christ's Hospital. Editor, Literary Quarterly, New Chapter, 1957-58. *Publications:* Escape and Surrender (poems) 1956; Permissive Paradise (with F. Habicht and H. Cremonesi), 1969. Contributor Contemporary Review. *Recreation:* philately. *Address:* Tauntons, 2 Whyteleafe Road, Caterham, Surrey. *T:* Caterham 45202.

**BRUCE of Sumburgh, Robert Hunter Wingate,** CBE 1967; Lord Lieutenant for the County of Zetland since 1963; *b* 11 Oct. 1907; *s* of John Bruce of Sumburgh and Isobel Abel; *m* 1935, Valmai Muriel, *d* of Charles Frederick Chamberlain and Lillian Muriel Smith; no *c*. *Educ:* Rugby School; Balliol College, Oxford. LMS Railway, 1930-46; on loan to Min. of Economic Warfare, 1941-43. Retired from LMS to manage Shetland property, 1946. Rep. Rio Tinto Co. in N. and S. Rhodesia and S. Africa, 1952-57. Member Zetland CC, 1948-52, 1958-61. Member: Advisory Panel on Highlands and Islands, 1948-52, 1957-65; Crofters Commn, 1960; Board Trustees, Nat. Mus. of Antiquities of Scotland, 1962. Chairman, Highland Transport Board, 1963-66. Medal of Freedom with Silver Palm, USA, 1948. *Recreations:* farming, reading history, tennis, golf, convivial argument. *Address:* Sand Lodge, Sandwick, Shetland. *T:* Sandwick 209. *Clubs:* United University; New (Edinburgh); Highland (Inverness).

**BRUCE, Robert Nigel (Beresford Dalrymple),** OBE 1946; TD; CEng, FIGasE; Chairman, South Eastern Gas Board, since 1960; *b* 21 May 1907; *s* of Major R. N. D. Bruce, late of Hampstead; *m* 1945, Elizabeth Brogden; *d* of J. G. Moore; twin *s* two *d*. *Educ:* Harrow School (Entrance and Leaving Scholar); Magdalen College, Oxford (Exhibitioner). BA (Hons. Chem.) and BSc. Joined Gas Light and Coke Co., 1929. Research Chemist; Assistant to General Manager, 1937; Controller of Industrial Relations, 1946; North Thames Gas Board; Staff Controller 1949; Deputy Chairman 1956. Joined Territorial Army Rangers (KRRC), 1931; Major, 1939; served Greece, Egypt, Western Desert, 1940-42; Lieut-Colonel Comdg Regt, 1942; GHQ, MEF, Middle East Supply Centre, 1943-45; Colonel, Dir. of Materials, 1944. President: British Road Tar Assoc., 1964 and 1965; Coal Tar Research Assoc., 1966; Institution of Gas Engineers, 1968. Chm. Governing Body, Westminster Technical College; Member Inst. Personnel Management, FRSA. *Publications:* Chronicles of the 1st Battalion the Rangers (KRRC), 1939-45; contribs to Proc. Royal Society, Jl Soc. Chemical Industry, Jl

Chemical Society. *Recreations:* tennis and lawn tennis; unconventional holidays. *Address:* Fairwater, Orchid Gate, Esher, Surrey. *Clubs:* Oxford and Cambridge University; Royal Tennis Court.

**BRUCE, Hon. Mrs Victor,** FRGS; Mildred Mary, *d* of Lawrence Joseph Petre, Coptfold Hall, Essex; *m* 1926, Hon. Victor Bruce (marr. diss., 1941), *y s* of 2nd Baron Aberdare. *Educ:* Convent of Sion. Travelled furthest north into Lapland by motor car; holds record for Double Channel Crossing, Dover to Calais, by motor boat; holder of 17 World Records, motoring, and of 24-hour record; single-handed drive, covered longest distance for man or woman, 2164 miles, in 24 hours; Coupe des Dames, Monte Carlo Rally, 1927. Flying records: first solo flight from England to Japan, 1930; longest solo flight, 1930; record solo flight, India to French Indo-China, 1930; British Air refuelling endurance flight, 1933. Managing Director, Bridge Engineering Ltd. Holds 24 hour record by motor boat, covering 674 nautical miles, single handed, 1929; first crossing of Yellow Sea. Show Jumping, 1st Royal Windsor Horse Show, 1939. Order of the Million Elephants and White Umbrella (French Indo-China). Fellow, Ancient Monuments Society. *Publications:* The Peregrinations of Penelope; 9000 Miles in Eight Weeks; The Woman Owner Driver; The Bluebird's Flight. *Address:* Priory Steps, Bradford-on-Avon, Wiltshire. *T:* Bradford-on-Avon 2230; 18 Cumberland Terrace, Regents Park, NW1. *T:* 01-935 3568. *Clubs:* Royal Motor Yacht, British Racing Drivers, Bentley Drivers.

**BRUCE-GARDNER, Sir Douglas (Bruce),** 2nd Bt, *cr* 1945; Chairman: G. K. N. Rolled & Bright Steel Ltd, since 1968; G. K. N. (South Wales) Ltd; Exors of James Mills Ltd; Parson Ltd; Director, Henry Gardner & Co. Ltd, 1952-68; *b* 27 Jan. 1917; *s* of Sir Charles Bruce-Gardner, 1st Bt; *S* father, 1960; *m* 1st, 1940, Monica Flumerfelt (marr. diss. 1964), *d* of late Sir Geoffrey Jefferson, CBE, FRS; one *s* two *d*; 2nd, 1964, Sheila Jane, *d* of Roger and late Barbara Stilliard, Seer Green, Bucks; one *s* one *d*. *Educ:* Uppingham; Trinity College, Cambridge. Dep. Chairman, G. K. N. Steel Co. Ltd, 1962, Gen. Man. Director, 1963-65, Chairman, 1965-67. Director, Guest, Keen & Nettlefolds Ltd, 1960. President, Iron and Steel Inst., 1966-67. *Recreations:* fishing, photography. *Heir:* *s* Robert Henry Bruce-Gardner, *b* 10 June 1943. *Address:* Bishopswood Grange, Nr Ross-on-Wye, Herefordshire. *T:* Lydbrook 444. *Club:* Junior Carlton.

**BRUCE-GARDYNE, John;** MP (U) South Angus since 1964; *b* 12 April 1930; 2nd *s* of late Capt. E. Bruce-Gardyne, DSO, RN, Middleton, by Arbroath, Angus and Joan (*née* McLaren); *m* 1959, Sarah Louisa Mary, *o d* of Comdr Sir John Maitland, *qv*; two *s* one *d*. *Educ:* Winchester; Magdalen College, Oxford. HM Foreign Service, 1953-56; served in London and Sofia; Paris correspondent, Financial Times, 1956-60; Foreign Editor, Statist, 1961-64. PPS to Secretary of State for Scotland, 1970-. *Address:* House of Commons, SW1; 13 Kelso Place, W8; South Eskhill, by Forfar, Angus.

**BRUCE LOCKHART, John Macgregor,** CB 1966; CMG 1951; OBE 1944; Head of Central Staff Department, Courtaulds Ltd; *b* 9 May 1914; *e s* of late John Harold Bruce Lockhart, and Mona Alwine Brougham; *m* 1939, Margaret Evelyn, *d* of late Rt Rev. C. R. Hone; two *s* one *d*. *Educ:* Rugby School; St Andrews University. Harkness Scholarship to St Andrews University, 1933; MA 2nd Class Hons. Modern Languages, 1937. Asst Master, Rugby School, 1937-39; TA Commission, Seaforth Highlanders, 1938; served War of 1939-45, in UK, Middle East, North Africa, Italy; Assistant Military Attaché, British Embassy, Paris, 1946-47; Control Commission Germany, 1948-51; First Secretary, British Embassy, Washington, 1951-53; later employed by the Foreign Office in London; resigned from the Diplomatic Service, 1965; in charge of Development, University of Warwick, 1965-67. *Recreations:* music, real tennis, fishing, golf; formerly Rugby football. *Address:* Hillcrest House, Flecknoe, Nr Rugby, Warwicks. *Clubs:* Reform, Boodle's; Rye Dormy.

**BRUCE LOCKHART, Logie,** MA; Headmaster of Gresham's School, Holt, since 1955; *b* 12 Oct. 1921; *s* of late John Harold Bruce Lockhart; *m* 1944, Josephine Agnew; two *s* two *d* (and one *d* decd). *Educ:* Sedbergh School; St John's College, Cambridge (Schol. and Choral Studentship). RMC Sandhurst, 1941; served War of 1939-45; 9th Sherwood Foresters, 1942; 2nd Household Cavalry (Life Guards), 1944-45. Larmor Award, 1947; Asst Master, Tonbridge School, 1947-55. RAF Educn Cttee. *Recreations:* fishing, writing, natural history, games. Blue for Rugby football, 1945, 1946, Scottish International, 1948, 1950, 1953. *Address:* Howson's, Holt, Norfolk. *T:* Holt 2137. *Club:* Public Schools.

**BRUCE LOCKHART, Rab Brougham,** MA Cantab; Headmaster, Loretto School, Musselburgh, Edinburgh, since Sept. 1960; *b* 1 Dec. 1916; *s* of late J. H. Bruce Lockhart; *m* 1941, Helen Priscilla Lawrence Crump; two *s* one *d*. *Educ:* Edinburgh Academy; Corpus Christi College, Cambridge. BA (Mod. Lang.) 1939; MA 1946. Assistant Master, Harrow, 1939. Served War of 1939-45: Commissioned RA, 1940; Middle East, 1942-44; Major RA 1944; Intelligence, Italy and Austria, 1945. Assistant Master, Harrow, 1946-50; Housemaster, Appleby College, Oakville, Ont, Canada, 1950-54; Headmaster, Wanganui Collegiate School, Wanganui, New Zealand, 1954-60. *Recreations:* squash, tennis, golf and photography; formerly: a Scotland cricket XI, 1935; Scotland XV, 1937, 1939; Rugby "Blue" 1937, 1938. *Address:* Loretto School, Musselburgh, Edinburgh.

**BRUCE-MITFORD, Rupert Leo Scott;** Keeper of Mediæval and Later Antiquities in the British Museum, since 1969 (Keeper of British and Mediæval Antiquities, 1954-69); *b* 14 June 1914; 4th *s* of C. E. Bruce-Mitford, Madras, and Beatrice (*née* Allison), British Columbia; *m* 1941; one *s* two *d*. *Educ:* Christ's Hospital; Hertford College, Oxford. Temp. Asst Keeper, Ashmolean Museum, 1937; Asst Keeper, Dept of British and Mediæval Antiquities, British Museum, 1938; Royal Signals, 1939-45. Deputy Keeper, British Museum, 1954. FSA, 1947. Hon. Litt.D (Dublin) 1966. Secretary of the Society of Antiquaries, 1950-54. Member, German Archæological Inst.; Member, Italian Inst. of Prehistory and Protohistory; Corres. Member, Jutland Archæological Society; Member of Ancient Monuments Board, England; Member, Permanent Council, Internat. Congress of Prehistoric and Protohistoric Sciences, 1957-; President, Society for Mediæval Archæology, 1957-59; Dalrymple Lecturer, Glasgow, 1961; Jarrow Lecturer, 1967. *Publications:* The Sutton-Hoo Ship-burial, 1947; The Society of Antiquaries of London; Notes on its History and Possessions (with others), 1952; Editor and contributor, Recent Archæological

Excavations in Britain, 1956; (with T. J. Brown, A. S. C. Ross and others), Codex Lindisfarnensis (Swiss facsimile edn), 1957-61; The Sutton Hoo Ship-burial, a handbook, 1968; (trans. from Danish) The Bog People, by P. V. Glob, 1969; papers, etc in learned journals. *Address:* 7 Pensioners Court, Charterhouse, EC1; The British Museum, WC1. *Clubs:* Athenæum, MCC.

**BRÜCK, Prof. Hermann Alexander,** CBE 1966; DPhil (Munich); PhD (Cantab); Astronomer Royal for Scotland and Regius Professor of Astronomy in the University of Edinburgh since 1957; Dean of the Faculty of Science since 1968; *b* 15 Aug. 1905; *s* of late H. H. Brück; *m* 1st, 1936, Irma Waitzfelder (*d* 1950); one *s* one *d*; 2nd, 1951, Dr Mary T. Conway; one *s* two *d*. *Educ:* Augusta Gymnasium, Charlottenburg; Universities of Bonn, Kiel, Munich, and Cambridge. Astronomer, Potsdam Astrophysical Observatory, 1928; Habilitation, Berlin University, 1935; Research Associate, Vatican Observatory, Castel Gandolfo, 1936; Asst Observer, Solar Physics Observatory, Cambridge, 1937; John Couch Adams Astronomer, Cambridge University, 1943; Asst Director, Cambridge Observatory, 1946; Director, Dunsink Observatory and Professor of Astronomy, Dublin Institute for Advanced Studies, 1947-57. MRIA, 1948; FRSE, 1958; Member Pontif. Academy of Sciences, Rome, 1955; Corr. Member Academy of Sciences, Mainz, 1955; Vice-President Royal Astronomical Society, 1959-61. *Publications:* scientific papers in journals and observatory publications. *Recreation:* music. *Address:* Royal Observatory, Edinburgh EH9 3HF.

**BRUDENELL-BRUCE,** family name of **Marquess of Ailesbury.**

**BRUFORD, Walter Horace,** MA; FBA 1963; President, English Goethe Society, 1965; *b* Manchester, 1894; *s* of Francis J. and Annie Bruford; *m* 1925, Gerda, *d* of late Professor James Hendrick; one *s* two *d*. *Educ:* Manchester Grammar School; St John's College, Cambridge; University of Zürich. BA Cambridge, 1915 (1st Class Hons. Med. and Mod. Langs). Bendall Sanskrit Exhibitioner; Master Manchester Grammar School; served Intelligence Division, Admiralty, with rank of Lieut RNVR. On demobilisation, research in University of Zürich; Lecturer in German, University of Aberdeen, 1920, Reader, 1923; Professor of German, University of Edinburgh, 1929-51. Seconded to Foreign Office, 1939-43. Schröder Professor of German, University of Cambridge, 1951-61. Corresponding member Deutsche Akademie für Sprache und Dichtung, 1957; Goethe-Medal in Gold, of Goethe-Institut, Munich, 1958; President, Mod. Lang. Assoc., 1959; President, Mod. Humanities Research Assoc., 1965; Corresponding Member, Sächsische Akademie der Wissenschaften, Leipzig, 1965. Hon. LLD Aberdeen, 1958; Hon. DLitt Newcastle, 1969. *Publications:* Sound and Symbol (with Professor J. J. Findlay); Germany in the eighteenth century; Die gesellschaftlichen Grundlagen der Goethezeit; Chekhov and His Russia; two chapters in Essays on Goethe (ed. by W. Rose); Theatre, Drama and Audience in Goethe's Germany; Literary Interpretation in Germany; Goethe's Faust (introd., revised and annotated, Everyman's Library); Chekhov (Studies in Modern European Literature and Thought); The Organisation and Rise of Prussia and German Constitutional and Social Development, 1795-1830 (in Cambridge Modern History, New Series, Vols VII and IX); Culture and Society in Classical Weimar; Deutsche Kultur der Goethezeit; Annotated edition and interpretation of Goethe's Faust, Part I. Articles and reviews in modern language periodicals. *Address:* Moorhouse, Abbey-St-Bathans, Duns, Berwickshire.

**BRUHN, Erik Belton Evers;** Danish Ballet Dancer; Ballet-director, Royal Opera, Stockholm, since 1967; *b* Copenhagen, Denmark, 3 Oct. 1928; *s* of Ernst Emil Bruhn, CE, and Ellen (*née* Evers); unmarried. *Educ:* Royal Danish Theatre, Copenhagen. Started at Royal Danish Ballet School, 1937. Principal rôles include those in: Giselle, Swan Lake, Carmen, La Sylphide, Les Sylphides, The Sleeping Beauty, Miss Julie, Night Shadow, Spectre de la Rose, A Folk Tale; also classical pas de deux and various abstract ballets. *Publication:* Bournonville and Ballet Tecnic. *Address:* Violvej, 16 Gent, Copenhagen, Denmark. *T:* Gentofte 4456.

**BRULLER, Jean;** *see* Vercors.

**BRUNDAGE, Avery;** Engineer; Executive; amateur sportsman; President Comité International Olympique since 1952; Chairman, President and Director of various corporations; *b* 28 Sept. 1887; *s* of Charles and Amelia Lloyd Brundage; *m* 1927, Elizabeth Dunlap, no *c*. *Educ:* University of Illinois. Founder and President, Avery Brundage Company, 1915-47; President: US Olympic Association, 1929-53; Amateur Athletic Union of the US, 1928-37; Comité Deportivo Panamericano, 1940-52. Holds various awards from US organizations and many foreign decorations. *Publications:* numerous articles on Amateur Sport and the Olympic Movement, *Recreations:* Amateur All-around Champion of America, 1914-16-18; US Olympic Team, 1912. Collector of Oriental Art (Trustee, Art Institute of Chicago). *Address:* 10 North La Salle Street, Chicago 2, Illinois, USA. *T:* State 2-6168. *Clubs:* Chicago Athletic Association, Chicago Engineers; Montecito Country (Santa Barbara, Cal.).

**BRUNDRETT, Sir Frederick,** KCB 1956 (CB 1946); KBE 1950; MA; retired as Scientific Adviser to Ministry of Defence and Chairman Defence Research Policy Committee (1954-Dec. 1959); Chairman, Air Traffic Control Board, since Nov. 1959; a Civil Service Commissioner, 1960-67; Chairman Naval Aircraft Research Committee, Aeronautical Research Council, 1960-66; *b* 25 Nov. 1894; *s* of Walter Brundrett, lately of Hinxhill, Kent, and Ada, *d* of James Richardson, Chorlton-cum-Hardy; *m* 1920, Enid, *d* of late George R. James, Cambridge; (only son killed in Italy 1944). *Educ:* Rossall School; Sidney Sussex College, Cambridge. Served in RNVR in European War, 1914-18. Joined Scientific Staff of Admiralty in 1919 and served in HM Signal School, Portsmouth, until 1937 when transferred to Headquarters. Chief of Royal Naval Scientific Service, 1947-50; Dep. Scientific Adviser, Ministry of Defence, 1950-54. Hon. Scientific Adviser to Ministry of Civil Aviation, 1953-59; Chairman, Civil Aviation Radio Advisory Cttee, 1958-60. Hon. Fellow, Sidney Sussex College, Cambridge, 1955. Governor: Rossall School, 1957-66; Prebendal School, Chichester, 1960; Navy League, 1960; Chairman of Trustees, Rural Industries Bureau, 1961-66; Member, White Fish Authority, 1961-; Chm. Board of Governors, Houghton Poultry Research Station, 1962-68; President, Agricultural Co-operative Assoc.; Chm., Council of Red and White Friesian Cattle Soc., 1967-; Director, Thames Valley Egg Ltd. Hon. DSc Manchester, 1967. *Recreations:* games of all kinds. Captain Hampshire County Hockey for many years.

Captain British CS Hockey before the war and also played for Civil Service at cricket; farming and particularly animal breeding–Red and White Friesian cattle; Agricultural Co-operation; philately. *Address:* Thalassa Farm, Prinsted, Emsworth, Hants. *T:* and *TA:* Emsworth 2227. *Club:* United University.

**BRUNE, Sir Humphrey I. P.;** *see* Prideaux-Brune.

**BRUNNER, Sir Felix (John Morgan),** 3rd Bt, *cr* 1895; Director of various Companies; *b* 13 Oct. 1897; *o s* of Sir John Brunner, 2nd Bt, and Lucy Marianne Vaughan (*d* 1941), *d* of late Octavius Vaughan Morgan, MP; *S* father 1929; *m* 1926, Dorothea Elizabeth, OBE 1965, JP, *d* of late Henry Brodribb Irving and late Dorothea Baird; four *s*. *Educ:* Cheltenham; Trinity College, Oxford (MA). Served European War, 1916-18, as Lieut RFA; contested (L) Hulme Division Manchester, 1924, Chippenham, Wilts, 1929, and Northwich, Cheshire, 1945. Chairman, Henley Rural District Council, 1954-57. Chairman, Commons, Open Spaces and Footpaths Preservation Society. President, Liberal Party Organisation, 1962-63. *Heir: s* John Henry Kilian Brunner [*b* 1927; *m* 1955, Jasmine Cecily, *d* of late John Wardrop-Moore; two *s* one *d*]. *Address:* Greys Court, Henley-on-Thames, Oxon. *T:* Rotherfield Greys 296. *Clubs:* Bath, Reform.
*See also Laurence Irving, Sir W. A. Worsley.*

**BRUNSKILL, Catherine Lavinia Bennett,** CBE 1919; *d* of Robert Bennett, Eastbourne; *m* 1918, Brig. George Stephen Brunskill, *qv* (from whom she obtained a divorce, 1946); one *d*. Private Secretary to Adjutant-General to the Forces, War Office, 1916-18; and to Commissioner of Metropolitan Police, New Scotland Yard, 1918-19. Defence Medal London Ambulance Service, 1945. *Address:* Room C, 126 Sloane Street, SW1.

**BRUNSKILL, Brig. George Stephen,** CBE 1941; MC 1914; *b* 26 Aug. 1891; *s* of late Major Arthur Stephen Brunskill, The King's Own Regt and West India Regt, of Buckland Tout Saints, S Devon, and Annie Louisa Churchward; *m* Moira Wallace (*née* Wares); one *s* one *d*. *Educ:* Eastbourne College; Royal Military College, Sandhurst; Staff College, Camberley (psc). Commissioned into Indian Army, 1911, and joined 47th Sikhs; served European War, 1914-18 (MC, Corona d'Italia and Order of St Maurice and Lazarus, Brevet Major); transferred to King's Shropshire Light Infantry, 1918; commanded First Battalion, 1934; Colonel 1937, and served on the staff as Temp. Brigadier in Palestine (CBE), in the Greece and Crete campaigns of 1941 (despatches twice, Greek MC, 1939-43 Star, N. African Star, Defence Medal, Czecho Slovak Order of White Lion, 3rd class); and on the Congo-Cairo War Supply Route, 1942-43; retired, 1945. Agent, Slingsby Estate, 1948-66. Councillor, Nidderdale RDC, 1950-66. *Address:* Cob Cottage, Woolstone, Faringdon, Berks. *T:* Uffington 283.

**BRUNSKILL, Muriel;** contralto; *b* 18 Dec. 1899; *d* of Edmund Capstick Brunskill; *m* 1925, Robert Ainsworth (*d* 1947), conductor, pianist; two *s*. *Educ:* Kendal High School. Studied in London and Germany, pupil of Blanche Marchesi; debut, Aeolian Hall, 1920; sang with British National Opera Company at Covent Garden, His Majesty's Theatre, and provincial theatres, 1922-27; has sung regularly at Three Choirs, Handel, Norwich, and Leeds Festivals, etc., Royal Choral, Royal Philharmonic, Liverpool Philharmonic, and Hallé Societies, etc.; Toronto Symphony Orchestra and Canadian Tour, 1930; Cincinatti May Festival, 1931; Canadian Recitals, Chicago Symphony Orchestra and New York, 1932; Opera Seasons in Melbourne and Sydney and Concert Tour in Australia and New Zealand, 1934-35; frequent appearances in Holland; sang Tanta in Golden City, Adelphi Theatre, 1950. Gilbert and Sullivan Film, 1952; Gilbert and Sullivan Tour in Australia and New Zealand, 1956-57. *Address:* Downrew House, Bishops Tawton, Devon. *T:* Barnstaple 2497.

**BRUNT, Peter Astbury,** FBA 1969; Camden Professor of Ancient History, Oxford University, since 1970; *b* 23 June 1917; *s* of Rev. Samuel Brunt, Methodist Minister, and Gladys Eileen Brunt. *Educ:* Ipswich Sch.; Oriel Coll., Oxford. Open Schol. in History, Oriel Coll., Oxford, 1935; first classes in Class. Mods, 1937, and Lit. Hum., 1939; Craven Fellowship, 1939. Temp. Asst Principal and (later) Temp. Principal, Min. of Shipping (later War Transport), 1940-45. Sen. Demy, Magdalen Coll., Oxford, 1946; Lectr in Ancient History, St Andrews Univ., 1947-51; Fellow and Tutor of Oriel Coll., Oxford, 1951-67, Dean, 1959-64; Fellow and Sen. Bursar, Gonville and Caius Coll., Cambridge, 1968-70. Editor of Oxford Magazine, 1963-64; Chm., Cttee on Ashmolean Museum, 1967. *Publications:* Thucydides (selections in trans. with introd.), 1963; Res Gestae Divi Augusti (with Dr J. M. Moore), 1967; Social Conflicts in the Roman Republic, 1970; articles in classical and historical jls. *Address:* Brasenose College, Oxford.

**BRUNT, Robert Nigel Bright,** CBE 1947; *b* 13 April 1902; *s* of Henry Robert and Mary Madeline Brunt, Leek, Staffs, afterwards of Belle Isle, Co. Fermanagh; *m* 1943, Joan, *er d* of Sir Richard Pierce Butler, 11th Bt, Ballin Temple, Co. Carlow; two *s* one *d*. *Educ:* Repton; King's College, Cambridge. Served in India and Pakistan with Burmah-Shell Oil Companies and Associates, 1922-50; a Director in London, 1951-55. Chairman, Punjab Chamber of Commerce, 1940-41; Chairman, National Service Advisory Cttee, Delhi Area, 1939-42; Adviser to Government of India for Petroleum Products, 1941-45; Member, Advisory Cttee for Development of New Delhi, 1940-45; a Trustee of Port of Karachi, 1949-50. A Governor of Queen Charlotte's and Chelsea Hospitals, 1962-65. *Address:* Old Red House, Weston Green, Esher, Surrey.
*See also Col Sir Thomas Pierce Butler, Bt.*

**BRUNTISFIELD,** 1st Baron, *cr* 1942, of Boroughmuir; **Victor Alexander George Anthony Warrender,** MC 1918; 8th Bt of Lochend, East Lothian, *cr* 1715; late Grenadier Guards; *b* 23 June 1899; *s* of 7th Bt and Lady Maud Warrender (*d* 1945), *y d* of 8th Earl of Shaftesbury; *S* to father's Baronetcy, 1917; *m* 1920, Dorothy (marr. diss., 1945), *y d* of late Colonel R. H. Rawson, MP, and Lady Beatrice Rawson; three *s*; *m* 1948, Tania, *yr d* of Dr Kolin, St Jacob, Dubrovnik, Jugoslavia; one *s* one *d*. *Educ:* Eton. Served European War, 1917-18 (MC, Russian Order of St Stanislas, Star of Roumania, St Ann of Russia with sword); MP (U) Grantham Division of Kesteven and Rutland, 1923-42; an assistant Whip, 1928-31; Junior Lord of the Treasury, 1931-32; Vice-Chamberlain of HM Household, 1932-35; Comptroller of HM Household, 1935; Parliamentary and Financial Secretary to Admiralty, 1935; Financial Secretary, War Office, 1935-40; Parliamentary and Financial Secretary, Admiralty, 1940-42; Parliamentary Secretary, Admiralty, 1942-45. *Heir: s* Colonel Hon. John Robert Warrender, OBE 1963; MC 1943; TD 1967 [*b* 7 Feb. 1921; *m* 1948, Ann

Moireen, 2nd *d* of Sir Walter Campbell, *qv*; two *s* two *d*]. *Address:* 43 Egerton Crescent, SW3. *T:* 01-584 3863; Hillbarn House, Great Bedwyn, Marlborough, Wilts. *T:* Great Bedwyn 207. *Clubs:* Buck's, Turf; Royal Yacht Squadron.

**BRUNTON, Sir (Edward Francis) Lauder,** 3rd Bt, *cr* 1908; Physician; Associate Physician, Royal Victoria Hospital, Montreal; Assistant Professor of Medicine, McGill University; Consultant in Haematology, Queen Mary Veterans' Hospital, Montreal; *b* 10 Nov. 1916; *s* of Sir Stopford Brunton, 2nd Bt, and Elizabeth, *o d* of late Professor J. Bonsall Porter; *S* father 1943; *m* 1946, Marjorie, *o d* of David Sclater Lewis, MSc, MD, CM, FRCP (C) (Pres.), Professor of Therapeutics, McGill University; one *s* one *d*. *Educ:* Trinity College School, Port Hope; Bryanston School; McGill Univ. BSc 1940; MD, CM 1942; served as Captain, RCAMC. Fellow; American Coll. of Physicians; Internat. Soc. of Hematology; Member American Society of Hematology. *Heir:* *s* James Lauder Brunton, *b* 24 Sept. 1947. *Address:* 3182 The Boulevard, Westmount, Montreal 217, Quebec, Canada. *Clubs:* Royal Automobile of Canada (Montreal); Royal Nova Scotia Yacht Squadron.

**BRUNTON, Gordon Charles;** Managing Director, The Thomson Organisation Ltd, since 1968; *b* 27 Dec. 1921; *s* of late Charles Arthur Brunton and Hylda Pritchard; *m* 1st, 1946, Nadine Lucile Paula Sohr (marr. diss. 1965); one *s* two *d* (and one *s* decd); 2nd, 1966, Gillian Agnes Kirk. *Educ:* Cranleigh Sch.; London Sch. of Economics. Commnd into RA, 1942; served Indian Army, Far East; Mil. Govt, Germany, 1946. Joined Tothill Press, 1947; Exec. Dir, Tothill, 1956; Man. Dir, Tower Press Gp of Cos, 1958; Exec. Dir, Odhams Press, 1961; joined Thomson Organisation, 1961; Man. Dir, Thomson Publications, 1961; Dir, Thomson Organisation, 1963; Chm., Thomson Travel, 1965-68; Dir, Times Newspapers Ltd, 1967; Dir of other printing and publishing cos. *Recreations:* boats, books. *Address:* North Munstead, Godalming, Surrey. *T:* Godalming 6313. *Club:* Garrick.

**BRUNTON, John Stirling,** CB 1960; *b* 8 May 1903; *s* of John Brunton, Glasgow; *m* 1934, Mary G. Cameron, Bo'ness; one *s* one *d*. *Educ:* Albert Road Academy, Glasgow; Glasgow University. Appointed HM Inspector of Schools, 1932; seconded to Dept of Health for Scotland, for work on Emergency Hospital Scheme, 1939-42; HM Inspector in charge of counties of Stirling, Perth and Kinross, 1942-48; HM Inspector in charge of Glasgow, 1948-50; Assistant Secretary, Scottish Education Department, 1951-55; HM Senior Chief Inspector of Schools, Scottish Education Department, 1955-66, retd. *Recreations:* golf, motoring. *Address:* 1/12 Pentland Drive, Edinburgh 10. *T:* 031-445 2848.

**BRUSH, Lt-Col Edward James Augustus Howard,** CB 1966; DSO 1945; OBE 1946; DL, JP; *b* 5 March 1901; *s* of Major George Howard Brush, Drumnabreeze, Co. Down; *m* 1937, Susan Mary, *d* of Major F. H. E. Torbett, Britford, Salisbury; one *d*. *Educ:* Clifton Coll.; RMC. Commnd Rifle Brigade, 1920. Served War of 1939-45 (France; wounded; prisoner of war); retired 1946. Chairman, T&AFA, Co. Down, 1954-65. DL Co. Down, 1953; Vice-Lieutenant, 1957-64; High Sheriff, 1953. Member, Irish Nat. Hunt Steeplechase Cttee. *Publication:* The Hunter Chaser, 1947. *Address:* Drumnabreeze, Maralin, Co. Down, N Ireland. *T:* Moira 284. *Club:* Kildare Street (Dublin).

**BRUTINEL, Brig.-Gen. Raymond,** CB 1919; CMG 1918; DSO 1916; late Canadian Machine Gun Corps; *b* 1882. Served European War, 1914-18 (despatches, CB, CMG, DSO, Order of SS. Maurice and Lazarus of Italy, Croix de Guerre, Commander of Legion of Honour). Médaille de Vermeil de la Reconnaissance Française. *Address:* Le Couloumé, Couloume-Mondebat, Gers, France.

**BRUXNER, Lt-Col Hon. Sir Michael (Frederick),** KBE 1962; DSO, 1919; Chevalier Légion d'Honneur; Member Legislative Assembly, NSW, Australia, for Tenterfield, 1920-62; Leader of the Country Party in State Parliament, 1932-58; *b* Sandilands, Clarence River, NSW, 25 March 1882; *s* of C. A. Bruxner; *m* Winifred Hay Caird of Kiama, NSW; two *s* one *d*. *Educ:* The Armidale School, Armidale, NSW (Head Boy); Sydney University. Returned to follow grazing pursuits until enlisting with 6th LH Regt, 1914; served Gallipoli (wounded severely), Sinai, Palestine, Syria, finishing as AA and QMG of Anzac Mounted Div.; returned Australia, July 1919; Leader of Progressive Party, 1922; Minister for Local Government, NSW, 1927-30; Minister for Transport and Deputy Premier, New South Wales, 1932-41. *Address:* Silchester, 4 Trahlee Road, Bellevue Hill, Sydney, NSW, Australia. *T:* FM 4136.

**BRYAN, Sir Andrew (Meikle),** Kt, *cr* 1950; DSc; Hon. LLD (Glasgow); CEng, MIMinE, MICE, FRSE; Cons. Mining Engineer; Member of National Coal Board, 1951-57; *b* 1 March 1893; 2nd *s* of John Bryan, Burnbank, Hamilton, Lanarkshire; *m* 1922, Henrietta Paterson, *y d* of George S. Begg, Allanshaw, Hamilton; one *s*. *Educ:* Greenfield Public School; Hamilton Acad.; Glasgow University, graduated 1919 with Special Distinction. Served in University OTC and HM Forces, 1915-18. Obtained practical mining experience in the Lanarkshire Coalfield; HM Junior Inspector of Mines in the Northern Division, 1920; Senior rank, 1926; Dixon Professor of Mining, University of Glasgow, Professor of Mining, Royal College of Science and Technology, Glasgow, 1932-40; Gen. Manager, 1940, Dir, 1942, Managing Director, 1944, Shotts Iron Co. Ltd; also Director Associated Lothian Coal Owners Ltd; Deputy-Director of Mining Supplies, Mines Department, 1939-40; Chief Inspector of Mines, 1947-51; Member of Council: Mining Institute of Scotland (Past Pres.); Institution of Mining Engineers (Pres. 1950 and 1951); and National Assoc. of Colliery Managers (Past Pres.); Hon. Member: Inst. of Mining and Metallurgy, 1951; National Assoc. of Colliery Managers, 1957; Institution of Mining Engineers, 1957; Geological Society of Edinburgh; Futers Gold Medal of National Association of Colliery Managers, 1937; Medal of Institution of Mining Engineers, 1954; Chm. Mining Qualifications Bd, 1962-70. fellow, Imperial College of Science and Technology. *Publications:* St George's Coalfield, Newfoundland. Contributions to technical journals. *Recreation:* golf. *Address:* 4 Riverdale Gardens, East Twickenham, Middlesex.

**BRYAN, Arthur;** Chairman, Wedgwood Ltd, Barlaston, Staffs, since 1968, and Managing Director since 1963; Lord Lieutenant of Staffordshire, since 1968; *b* 4 March 1923; *s* of William Woodall Bryan and Isobel Alan (*née* Tweedie); *m* 1947, Betty Ratford; one *s* one *d*. *Educ:* Longton High Sch., Stoke-on-Trent. Trainee, Barclays Bank. Served with RAFVR, 1941-45. Business training scheme in industry, Josiah Wedgwood & Sons Ltd, 1947-49; London Man., 1953-57; General Sales Man.,

1959-60; Director and President, Josiah Wedgwood & Sons Inc. of America, 1960-62; Director : Josiah Wedgwood & Sons Ltd, Barlaston, 1962; Josiah Wedgwood & Sons (Canada) Ltd; Josiah Wedgwood & Sons (Australia) Pty Ltd. Pres., British Pottery Manufacturers' Fedn, 1970-; Chm., Stoke-on-Trent local Employment Cttee, 1967; Governor, Stoke-on-Trent Coll. of Art, 1967. FRSA 1964; Fellow, Inst. of Marketing (grad. 1950); FBIM 1968. Member Council of Industrial Design, 1966. *Recreations:* walking, tennis, swimming and reading. *Address:* Parkfields Cottage, Tittensor, Stoke-on-Trent, Staffs. *T:* Barlaston 2686. *Clubs:* Royal Automobile, English-Speaking Union.

**BRYAN, Denzil Arnold,** CMG 1960; OBE 1947; HM Diplomatic Service, retired; *b* 15 Oct. 1909; *s* of James Edward Bryan; *m* 1965, Hope Ross, (*née* Meyer). *Educ:* in India; Selwyn Coll., Cambridge. Appointed to Indian Civil Service in 1933 and posted to Punjab. Dep. Commissioner, Hissar, 1938; Registrar, Lahore High Court, 1939-41; Dep. Comr, Dera Ghazi Khan, 1941-44; Sec. to Prime Minister, Punjab, 1944-47; and to Governor of Punjab, 1947; retired from ICS, 1947. Appointed to UK Civil Service, Bd of Trade, as Principal, 1947; Asst Sec., 1950; Under Secretary, 1961; served as a Trade Comr in India, 1947-55; UK Senior Trade Comr: in New Zealand, 1955-58; in Pakistan, 1958-61; in South Africa, 1961; Minister (Commercial, later Economic), S Africa, 1962-69. *Recreation:* golf. *Address:* c/o Lloyds Bank Ltd, 6 Pall Mall, SW1. *Club:* United University.

**BRYAN, Dora, (Mrs William Lawton);** actress; *b* 7 Feb. 1924; *d* of Albert Broadbent and Georgina (*née* Hill); *m* 1954, William Lawton; one *s* (and one *s* one *d* adopted). *Educ:* Hathershaw Council Sch., Lancs. Pantomimes: London Hippodrome, 1936; Manchester Palace, 1937; Alhambra, Glasgow, 1938; Oldham Repertory, 1939-44; followed by Peterborough, Colchester, Westcliff-on-Sea. ENSA, Italy, during War of 1939-45. Came to London, 1945, and appeared in West End Theatres: Peace in our Time; Travellers' Joy; Accolade; Lyric Revue; Globe Revue; Simon and Laura; The Water Gypsies; Gentlemen Prefer Blondes; Six of One; Too True to be Good; Hello, Dolly!; They Don't Grow on Trees. Has also taken parts in farces televised from Whitehall Theatre. *Films include:* The Fallen Idol, 1949; A Taste of Honey, 1961; Two a Penny, 1968. TV appearances on A to Z, and Sunday Night at the London Palladium; TV series, According to Dora, 1968. *Recreation:* mothercraft. *Address:* 111 Marine Parade, Brighton, Sussex. *T:* 63235. *Club:* Players.

**BRYAN, Gerald Jackson,** CMG 1964; CVO 1966; OBE 1960; MC 1941; General Manager of the Londonderry Development Commission, Northern Ireland, since 1969; *b* 2 April 1921; *yr s* of late George Bryan, OBE, LLD, and of Ruby Elizabeth (*née* Jackson), Belfast; *m* 1947, Georgiana Wendy Cockburn, OStJ, *d* of late William Baraud and Winnifred Hull; one *s* two *d. Educ:* Wrekin Coll.; RMA, Woolwich; New Coll., Oxford. Regular Commn, RE, 1940; served Middle East with No. 11 (Scottish) Commando, 1941; retd 1944, Capt. (temp. Maj.). Apptd Colonial Service, 1944; Asst District Comr, Swaziland, 1944; Asst Colonial Sec., Barbados, 1950; Estabt. Sec., Mauritius, 1954; Administrator, Brit. Virgin Is, 1959; Administrator of St Lucia, 1962-67; Govt Sec. and Head of Isle of Man Civil Service, 1967-69. CStJ. *Recreations:* riding, swimming, sailing. *Address:* c/o The Guildhall, Londonderry, N Ireland; 30 Queen Street, Castletown, Isle of Man. *Clubs:* Royal Commonwealth Society.

**BRYAN, Paul Elmore Oliver,** DSO 1943; MC 1943; MP (C) Howden Division of Yorkshire (East Riding), since 1955; Minister of State, Department of Employment, since 1970; *b* 3 Aug. 1913; *s* of Reverend Dr J. I. Bryan, PhD; *m* 1939, Betty Mary (*née* Hoyle) (*d* 1968); three *d. Educ:* St John's School, Leatherhead (Scholar); Caius College, Cambridge (MA). War of 1939-45; 6th Royal West Kent Regt; enlisted, 1939; commissioned, 1940; Lieut-Col, 1943; served in France, N Africa, Sicily, Italy; Comdt 164th Inf. OCTU (Eaton Hall), 1944. Sowerby Bridge UDC, 1947; contested Sowerby, By-Election, 1948, and General Elections, 1950 and 1951. Member Parliamentary Delegation: to Peru, 1955, to Algeria, 1956, to Germany, 1960, to USA and Canada, 1961, to India, 1966, to Uganda and Kenya, 1967, to Hong Kong, 1969, to Japan and Indonesia, 1969. Assistant Government Whip, 1956-58; Parliamentary Private Secretary to Minister of Defence, 1956; a Lord Commissioner of the Treasury, 1958-61; Vice-Chairman, Conservative Party Organisation, 1961-65; Conservative Front Bench Spokesman on Post Office and broadcasting, 1965. Director, Granada TV Rental Ltd, 1966-70. *Address:* Park Farm, Sawdon, near Scarborough, Yorks. *T:* Snainton 370; 36 Marsham Court, SW1. *T:* 01-834 2050. *Clubs:* Carlton, Junior Carlton.

**BRYAN, Willoughby Guy,** TD 1945; Vice-Chairman, Barclays Bank Ltd, since 1964 (Director, 1957); Chairman, Barclays Bank Trust Co., since 1970; Director: Barclays Bank, DCO since 1963; Barclays Union Ltd, since 1970; Dillon Walker and Co., since 1970; Barclays Griffin Life Assurance Co., since 1970; *b* 16 Jan. 1911; *e s* of late C. R. W. Bryan; *m* 1936, Esther Victoria Loveday, *d* of late Major T. L. Ingram, DSO, MC; one *d. Educ:* Winchester; Hertford College, Oxford. Barclays Bank Ltd, 1932; various appointments including: Local Director, Oxford, 1946; Local Director, Reading, 1947; Local Director, Birmingham, 1955; Chm. Local Bd, Birmingham, 1957-64. Served War of 1939-45, Queen's Own Oxfordshire Hussars. *Recreation:* golf. *Address:* 31 Boundary Road, St John's Wood, NW8. *T:* 01-624 0949. *Club:* Brooks's.

**BRYANS, Dame Anne (Margaret),** DBE 1957 (CBE 1945); OStJ; Vice-Chairman, British Red Cross Society Executive Committee since 1964 (Deputy Chairman, 1953-64); Chairman: Order of St John of Jerusalem and BRCS Service Hospitals Welfare and VAD Committee, since 1960; Royal Free Hospital; Member, Board of Trustees, Queen Mary's Hospital, Roehampton; Member Council, Florence Nightingale Hospital; Vice-President, Royal College of Nursing; *b* 29 Oct. 1909; *e d* of Col Rt Hon. Sir John Gilmour, 2nd Bt, GCVO, DSO, MP of Montrave and late Mary Louise Lambert; *m* 1932, Lieut-Comdr J. R. Bryans, RN, retired; one *s. Educ:* privately. Joined HQ Staff British Red Cross Society, 1938; Deputy Commissioner British Red Cross and St John War Organisation, Middle East Commission, 1943; Commissioner Jan.-June 1945. *Address:* 7 Harriet Walk, SW1. *T:* 01-235 3535. *Clubs:* VAD Ladies; Royal Lymington Yacht.

**BRYANT, Sir Arthur,** Kt 1954; CH 1967; CBE 1949; Hon. LLD: Edinburgh; St Andrews; New Brunswick; MA (Oxon); FRHistS; FRSL; Chairman St John and Red Cross Hospital Library since 1945; Council, Society of Authors; Royal Literary Fund; Trustee:

Historic Churches Preservation Trust; National Folk Music Fund; *b* 18 Feb. 1899; *e s* of late Sir Francis Bryant, CB, CVO, CBE, ISO, JP, The Pavilion, Hampton Court; *m* 1st, 1924, Sylvia Mary (marr. diss. 1939; she *m* 2nd, F. D. Chew, and *d* 1950), *d* of Sir Walter Shakerley, Bt, Somerford Park, Cheshire; 2nd, 1941, Anne Elaine, *y d* of Bertram Brooke (HH Tuan Muda of Sarawak). *Educ:* Harrow; BEF France; Queen's Coll., Oxford. Barrister-at-law, Inner Temple. Principal, Cambridge School of Arts, Crafts and Technology, 1923-25; Lectr in History to Oxford Univ. Delegacy for Extra-Mural Studies, 1925-36; Watson Chair in American History, London Univ., 1935; Corres. Member of La Real Academia de la Historia of Madrid; succeeded G. K. Chesterton as writer of Our Note Book, Illustrated London News, 1936. President: English Association, 1946; Common Market Safeguards Campaign; Friends of the Vale of Aylesbury. Chairman: Ashridge Council, 1946-49; Soc. of Authors, 1949-51. Chesney Gold Medal, RUSI, 1955. Hon. Freedom and Livery, Leathersellers' Company; Hon. Mem. Southampton Chamber of Commerce. KGStJ. *Publications:* King Charles II, 1931; Macaulay, 1932; Samuel Pepys, the Man in the Making, 1933; The National Character, 1934; The England of Charles II, 1934; The Letters and Speeches of Charles II, 1935; Samuel Pepys, the Years of Peril, 1935; George V, 1936; The American Ideal, 1936; Postman's Horn, 1936; Stanley Baldwin, 1937; Humanity in Politics, 1938; Samuel Pepys, the Saviour of the Navy, 1938; Unfinished Victory, 1940; English Saga, 1940; The Years of Endurance, 1942; Dunkirk, 1943; Years of Victory, 1944; Historian's Holiday, 1947; The Age of Elegance, 1950 (Sunday Times Gold Medal and Award for Literature); The Turn of the Tide, 1957; Triumph in the West, 1959; Jimmy, 1960; The Story of England: Makers of the Realm, 1953; The Age of Chivalry, 1963; The Fire and the Rose, 1965; The Medieval Foundation, 1966; Protestant Island, 1967; The Lion and the Unicorn, 1970. *Address:* Wotton Underwood, Bucks. *Clubs:* Athenæum, Beefsteak, Grillions, Pratt's, MCC.

**BRYANT, Rear-Adm. Benjamin,** CB 1956; DSO 1942 (two bars, 1943); DSC 1940; *b* 16 Sept. 1905; *s* of J. F. Bryant, MA, FRGS, ICS (retd); *m* 1929 Marjorie Dagmar Mynors (*née* Symonds) (*d* 1965); one *s* one *d*; *m* 1966, Heather Elizabeth Williams (*née* Hance). *Educ:* Oundle; RN Colls Osborne and Dartmouth. Entered submarine branch of RN, 1927; Commanded: HMS/M Sea Lion, 1939-41; HMS/M Safari, 1941-43; comd 7th and 3rd Submarine Flotillas, 1943-44; comd 4th s/m Flotilla, British Pacific Fleet, 1945-47; comd HMS Dolphin Submarine School, and 5th Submarine Flotilla, 1947-49; Commodore (submarines), 1948; idc 1950; Commodore, RN Barracks, Devonport, 1951-53; Flag Captain to C-in-C Mediterranean, 1953-54; Rear-Admiral, 1954. Deputy Chief of Naval Personnel (Training and Manning), 1954-57; retired, 1957. Staff Personnel Manager, Rolls Royce Scottish Factories, 1957-68. *Recreations:* fishing, golf, shooting. *Address:* Pines, Symington, Biggar, Lanarkshire. *Club:* RNVR (Scotland).

**BRYANT, Rt. Rev. Denis William;** *see* Kalgoorlie, Bishop of.

**BRYANT, Richard Charles,** CB 1960; Under-Secretary, Board of Trade, 1955-68; *b* 20 Aug. 1908; *s* of Charles James and Constance Byron Bryant, The Bounds, Faversham, Kent; *m* 1938, Elisabeth Ellington, *d* of Dr. A. E. Stansfeld, FRCP; two *s* two *d*. *Educ:* Rugby; Oriel College, Oxford. Entered Board of Trade, 1932; Ministry of Supply, 1939-44. *Address:* Spinners Cottage, Southwold, Suffolk. *T:* Southwold 3226. *Club:* Travellers'.

**BRYCE, Gabe Robb,** OBE 1959; Sales Manager (Operations) British Aircraft Corporation, since 1965; *b* 27 April 1921; *m* 1943, Agnes Lindsay; one *s* one *d*. *Educ:* Glasgow High School. Served in RAF, 1939-46. Vickers-Armstrongs (Aircraft) Ltd, 1946-60 (Chief Test Pilot, 1951-60). Participated as First or Second Pilot, in Maiden Flights of following British Aircraft: Varsity; Nene Viking; Viscount 630, 700 and 800; Tay Viscount; Valiant; Pathfinder; Vanguard; VC-10; BAC 1-11; Chief Test Pilot, British Aircraft Corporation, 1960-64. Associated Fellow Soc. of Experimental Test Pilots (USA). *Recreations:* squash, tennis. *Address:* Skerrols, East Road, St George's Hill, Weybridge, Surrey.

**BRYCE, Dame Isabel G.;** *see* Graham Bryce.

**BRYDEN, William James,** CBE 1970; Sheriff-Substitute of Lanarkshire at Glasgow since 1953; Member, Departmental Committee on the Adoption of Children, since 1969; *b* 2 Oct. 1909; *y s* of late James George Bryden, JP and late Elizabeth Brown Tyrie; *m* 1937, Christina Mary, *e d* of late Thomas Bannatyne Marshall, CBE, JP; two *s* one *d*. *Educ:* Perth Academy; Brasenose College, Oxford; Edinburgh University. Barrister-at-Law, Inner Temple, 1933; Advocate of the Scottish Bar, 1935; External Examiner in English Law, Edinburgh University, 1937-40; served in RNVR, 1940-45; Hon. Sheriff-Substitute of Dumfries and Galloway, 1946; Sheriff-Substitute of Lanarkshire at Hamilton, 1946-53. Member: Law Reform Cttee for Scotland, 1957-61; Scottish Adv. Council on the Treatment of Offenders, 1959-63. Hon. Sec. Assoc. of Sheriffs-Substitute, 1950-53. *Address:* Sheriff's Chambers, Sheriff Court House, Glasgow; Ashdene, Abington, Lanarkshire.

**BRYHER, (Annie) Winifred;** Author; *d* of Sir John Reeves Ellerman, 1st Bt, CH, and late Hannah Ellerman (*née* Glover); *m* 1st, 1921, Robert McAlmon (marr. diss., 1926); 2nd, 1927, Kenneth Macpherson (marr. diss., 1947); no *c*. *Educ:* Queenwood, Eastbourne. *Publications:* Development, 1920, etc; The Fourteenth of October, 1952; The Player's Boy, 1953; Roman Wall, 1954; Beowulf, 1956; Gate to the Sea, 1958; Ruan, 1960; The Heart of Artemis, 1963; The Coin of Carthage, 1964; Visa for Avalon, 1965; This January Tale, 1966; The Colors of Vaud, 1970. *Recreations:* travel, the sea, archæology. *Address:* Kenwin, Burier, Vaud, Switzerland.

**BRYMER, Jack,** OBE 1960; Principal Clarinettist, BBC Symphony Orchestra, since 1963; *b* 27 Jan. 1915; *s* of J. and Mrs M. Brymer, South Shields, Co. Durham; *m* 1939, Joan Richardson, Lancaster; one *s*. *Educ:* Goldsmiths' College, London University. Schoolmaster, Croydon, general subjects, 1935-40. Physical Training and Parachute Instructor, RAF, 1940-45. Principal Clarinettist, Royal Philharmonic Orchestra, 1946-63; Prof., Royal Acad. of Music, 1950-58; Member of Wigmore, Prometheus and London Baroque ensembles; Director of London Wind Soloists. Has directed recordings of the complete wind chamber music of Mozart, Beethoven, Haydn and J. C. Bach. Hon. RAM 1955. *Recreations:* golf, tennis, swimming, carpentry, gardening, music. *Address:* Underwood, Ballards Farm Road, South Croydon, Surrey. *T:* 01-657 1698. *Club:* Croham Hurst Golf.

**BRYNNER, Yul;** actor, films and stage. Began acting career in France; radio commentator and announcer for US Government, 1942-45. First stage appearance, 1946, in Lute Song, on Broadway. *Plays include:* Dark Eyes; The King and I. *Films include:* The Ten Commandments; The King and I; Anastasia; The Journey; The Brothers Karamazov; The Sound and the Fury; Once More, With Feeling; Solomon and Sheba; Surprise Package; The Magnificent Seven; Escape to Zahrain; Taras Bulba; Kings of the Sun; Flight from Ashiya; Invitation to a Gunfighter; The Saboteur, Code NameMorituri; Return of the Seven; The Long Duel; The Double Man; Triple Cross; Villa Rides; The Magic Christian. *Publication:* (with Inge Morath) Bring Forth the Children, 1961.

**BRYSON, George Murray,** BL; SSC; Sheriff Substitute of Stirling, Dunbarton and Clackmannan, at Dumbarton, 1966-69; *b* 12 March 1904; *s* of James Guthrie Bryson, Solicitor, Edinburgh, and Ellen Scott Murray; *m* 1933, Marjorie Una Catharine Hayter; one *s* two *d*. *Educ:* Daniel Stewart's College, and University of Edinburgh. Practised as Solicitor in Edinburgh, 1929-56; Senior Partner of Bryson & Davie, WS, Edinburgh; Vice-President, Society of Solicitors in Supreme Courts of Scotland, 1956; Mem. of Council of Law Soc. of Scotland, 1954-56; Sheriff-Substitute of Renfrew and Argyll at Dunoon, 1956-66. *Recreations:* sailing, fishing, golf. *Address:* Sea Bourne, Innellan, Argyll. *T:* Innellan 205. *Club:* Royal Scottish Automobile.

**BUCCLEUCH,** 8th Duke of, *cr* 1663, 10th Duke of **QUEENSBERRY** (*cr* 1684); **Walter John Montagu-Douglas-Scott,** PC 1937; KT 1949; GCVO, *cr* 1935; Baron Scott of Buccleuch, 1606; Earl of Buccleuch, Baron Scott of Whitchester and Eskdaill, 1619; Earl of Doncaster and Baron Tynedale (Eng.), 1662; Earl of Dalkeith, 1663; Marquis of Dumfriesshire, Earl of Drumlanrig and Sanquhar, Viscount of Nith, Torthorwold, and Ross, Baron Douglas, 1684; Lord Clerk Register of Scotland and Keeper of the Signet since 1956; HM Lieutenant of County of Roxburgh since 1932; Chancellor, Order of the Thistle, since 1966; DL Dumfriesshire; DL Selkirkshire. JP Roxburghshire and Dumfriesshire; Captain-General Royal Company of Archers; President: St Andrew's Ambulance Association; Scottish Landowners' Federation; Animal Diseases Research Association; Royal Scottish Agricultural Benevolent Institution; Commonwealth Forestry Association; Scottish Woodland Owners' Association; *b* 30 Dec. 1894; *e s* of 7th Duke and late Lady Margaret Alice Bridgeman, 2nd *d* of 4th Earl of Bradford; *m* 1921, Vreda Esther Mary, *er d* of late Major W. F. Lascelles and Lady Sybil Lascelles, *d* of 10th Duke of St Albans; one *s* two *d*; *S* father, 1935. *Educ:* Eton; Christ Church, Oxford. European War, 1914-18; Royal Scots, 1914; Grenadier Guards, 1914-21; ADC to Governor-General of Canada, 1920; Reserve of Officers, 1921; Colonel late commanding 4th KOSB's, 1923-29; MP (U) Roxburgh and Selkirk, 1923-35; Lord Steward of HM Household, 1937-40. Ex-Governor, Royal Bank of Scotland; Ex-President: Royal Scottish Forestry Society; Dock & Harbour Authorities' Association; The Earl Haig Fund (Scottish Branch); Nat. Playing Fields Association (Scottish Branch); Freeman of Hawick and Selkirk. Hon. LLD Edin. and St Andr. *Heir: s* Earl of Dalkeith, *qv*. *Recreations:* farming, forestry, shooting. *Address:* Bowhill, Selkirk. *T:* Selkirk 2732; Drumlanrig Castle, Thornhill, Dumfriesshire. *T:* Thornhill 248; 15 Grosvenor Square, W1. *T:* 01-629 6985; Boughton House, Geddington, Kettering, Northants. *T:* Kettering 82248. *Clubs:* Turf, White's; New (Edinburgh).

*See also Vice-Adm. Sir Peter Dawnay, Lord Eskdaill, Marquess of Exeter, I. H. J. Gilmour, Viscount Hampden, Admiral Sir G. A. B. Hawkins, Duke of Northumberland.*

**BUCHAN,** family name of **Baron Tweedsmuir** and **Baroness Tweedsmuir of Belhelvie.**

**BUCHAN,** 16th Earl of, *cr* 1469; **Donald Cardross Flower Erskine;** Lord Auchterhouse, 1469; Lord Cardross, 1606; Baron Erskine, 1806; *b* 3 June 1899; *s* of 6th Baron Erskine and Florence (*d* 1936), *y d* of Edgar Flower; *S* father, 1957 (as Baron Erskine); and kinsman, 1960 (as Earl of Buchan); *m* 1927, Christina, adopted *d* of Lloyd Baxendale, Greenham Lodge, Newbury; one *s* two *d*. *Educ:* Charterhouse; Royal Military College, Sandhurst. Lieut 9th Lancers, 1918; Captain, 1928; retired, 1930; re-employed, 1939; Lieut-Colonel 1943. *Heir: s* Lord Cardross, *qv*. *Address:* The Manor, Bourton-on-the-Water, Gloucestershire. *T:* 383.

*See also Air Commodore H. A. Hewat.*

**BUCHAN, Hon. Alastair Francis,** CBE 1968 (MBE 1944); MA Oxon; Commandant, Royal College of Defence Studies (formerly Imperial Defence College), since 1970; *b* 9 Sept. 1918; 3rd *s* of 1st Baron Tweedsmuir, and of Susan Charlotte Grosvenor (*see* Susan, Lady Tweedsmuir); *m* 1942, Hope Gordon Gilmour, Ottawa, Canada; two *s* one *d*. *Educ:* Eton College; Christ Church, Oxford. Junior Fellow, University of Virginia, 1939. Commissioned Canadian Army, 1939; Dieppe Raid, 1942; Staff College, 1943; Major, 14th Canadian Hussars, 1944; North-west Europe Campaign, 1944-45 (MBE). Asst Editor, The Economist, 1948-51; Washington Correspondent, The Observer, 1951-55; Diplomatic and Defence Correspondent, The Observer, 1955-58; Dir, Inst. for Strategic Studies, 1958-69. *Publications:* The Spare Chancellor: the Life of Walter Bagehot, 1959; NATO in the 1960's, 1960 (rev. edn, 1963); The United States, 1963; (part-author) Arms and Stability in Europe, 1963; (ed) China and the Peace of Asia, 1965; War in Modern Society, 1966; (ed) A World of Nuclear Powers?, 1966; (ed) Europe's Futures; Europe's Choices, 1969; articles in: Foreign Affairs, etc. *Recreations:* gardening, fishing. *Address:* Waterloo House, Brill, Bucks. *T:* Brill 212. *Clubs:* Garrick, Beefsteak.

**BUCHAN of Auchmacoy, Captain David William Sinclair;** *b* 18 Sept. 1929; *o s* of late Captain S. L. Trevor, late of Lathbury Park, Bucks, and of Lady Olivia Trevor, *e d* of 18th Earl of Caithness; *m* 1961, Susan Blanche Fionodbhar Scott-Ellis, *d* of 9th Baron Howard de Walden, *qv*; four *s* one *d*. *Educ:* Eton; RMA Sandhurst. Commissioned 1949 into Gordon Highlanders; served Berlin, BAOR and Malaya; ADC to GOC, Singapore, 1951-53; retired 1955. Member of London Stock Exchange. Changed name from Trevor through Court of Lord Lyon King of Arms, 1949, succeeding 18th Earl of Caithness as Chief of Buchan Clan. Member: Queen's Bodyguard for Scotland; The Pilgrims; Friends of Malta GC. *Recreations:* cricket, tennis, squash. *Address:* Auchmacoy House, Aberdeenshire. *T:* Ellon 229; 28 The Little Boltons, SW10. *T:* 01-373 0654; c/o P.O. Box 111, Nakuru, Kenya. *Clubs:* United Service, Royal Automobile, Turf, MCC; Puffins (Edinburgh).

**BUCHAN, Ven. Eric Ancrum;** Archdeacon of Coventry since 1965; *b* 6 Nov. 1907; *s* of late

Frederick Samuel and Florence Buchan. *Educ:* Bristol Grammar School; St Chad's College, University of Durham (BA). Curate of Holy Nativity, Knowle, Bristol, 1933-40. Chaplain RAFVR, 1940-45. Vicar of St Mark's with St Barnabas, Coventry, 1945-59; Hon. Canon of Coventry Cathedral, 1953; Chaplain Coventry and Warwickshire Hospital, 1945-59; Sec. Laymen's Appeal, Dio. of Coventry, 1951-53; Rural Dean of Coventry, 1954-63; Rector of Baginton, 1963-70. Member Central Board of Finance, 1953-; Schools Council, 1958-65; Chm. Dio. Board of Finance, 1958-; Organiser of Bishop's Appeal, 1958-61; Dio. Director of Christian Stewardship, 1959-65; Domestic Chaplain to Bishop of Coventry, 1961-65; Church Commissioner, 1964-; Member, Governing Body, St Chad's College, Durham University, 1966-. *Address:* Baginton Rectory, Coventry. *T:* Coventry 302508. *Club:* National Liberal.

**BUCHAN, John (Thomas Johnston Buchan),** CMG 1961; Chairman and Managing Director, Buchan, Laird and Buchan, Architects and Engineers, since 1957; *b* 3 June 1912; *s* of Thomas Johnston Buchan; *m* 1948, Virginia, *d* of William Ashley Anderson, Penn., USA; one *s* two *d*. *Educ:* Geelong Grammar School. Served Royal Aust. Engineers (AIF), 1940-44 (Capt.). Member Melbourne City Council, 1954-60. Member Federal Exec., Liberal Party, 1959-62; President, Liberal Party, Victorian Division, Australia, 1959-62, Treasurer, 1963-67; Pres., Australian American Assoc., Victoria, 1964-68, Federal Pres., Australian American Assoc., 1968-70. Member: Council, Latrobe University, 1964-; Cttee of Management, Royal Melbourne Hosp., 1968-. Co-Founder Apex Association of Australia. *Recreations:* golf, reading. *Address:* Fairlie Court, South Yarra, Victoria, Australia. *Clubs:* Melbourne, Athenæum, Metropolitan (Melbourne).

**BUCHAN, Norman Findlay;** MP (Lab) Renfrewshire West since 1964; *b* Helmsdale, Sutherlandshire, 27 Oct. 1922; *s* of John Buchan, Fraserburgh, Aberdeenshire; *m* 1945, Janey, *d* of Joseph Kent, Glasgow; one *s*. *Educ:* Kirkwall Grammar School; Glasgow University. Royal Tank Regt (N. Africa, Sicily and Italy, 1942-45). Teacher (English and History); president, Rutherglen District Educational Institute of Scotland; member, Scottish Association of Labour Teachers. Parly Under-Sec., Scottish Office, 1967-70. *Publications:* 101 Scottish Songs (ed.); contributions to New Statesman, Tribune and other journals. *Address:* 72 Peel Street, Glasgow, W1. *T:* 041-339 2583.

**BUCHAN, Thomas Johnston;** *see* Buchan, John.

**BUCHAN-HEPBURN,** family name of **Baron Hailes.**

**BUCHAN-HEPBURN, Sir Ninian (Buchan Archibald John),** 6th Bt, *cr* 1815; *b* 8 Oct. 1922; *s* of Sir John Buchan-Hepburn, 5th Bt; *S* father 1961; *m* 1958, Bridget, *er d* of late Sir Louis Greig, KBE, CVO. *Educ:* St Aubyn's, Rottingdean, Sussex; Canford School, Wimbourne, Dorset. Served QO Cameron Hldrs, India and Burma, 1939-45. *Heir: u* 1st Baron Hailes, *qv*. *Address:* Logan, by Stranraer, Wigtownshire. *T:* Ardwell 221.

**BUCHANAN, Most Rev. Alan Alexander;** *see* Dublin, Archbishop of.

**BUCHANAN, Major Sir Charles James,** 4th Bt, *cr* 1878; HLI; retired; *b* 16 April 1899; *s* of 3rd Bt and Constance (*d* 1914), *d* of late Commander Tennant, RN; *S* father, 1928; *m* 1932, Barbara Helen, *o d* of late Lieut-Colonel Rt Hon. Sir George Stanley, PC, GCSI, GCIE; two *s* two *d*. *Educ:* Harrow; Sandhurst. Served in North Russian Relief Force, 1919; with BEF France, 1939-40 and with AMG in Italy, 1943-44; retired 1945. ADC to Governor of Madras, 1928-32. A member of the Queen's Body Guard for Scotland (Royal Company of Archers); County Commissioner Nottinghamshire. Boy Scouts Association, 1949-62. JP 1952; DL 1954, Notts; High Sheriff of Nottinghamshire, 1962. *Recreations:* fishing and gardening. *Heir: s* Andrew George Buchanan [*b* 21 July 1937; *m* 1966, Mrs Belinda Vaughan, *widow* of Gresham Vaughan; one *d*]. *Address:* St Anne's Manor, Sutton Bonington, Loughborough. *Club:* Lansdowne.

**BUCHANAN, Prof. Colin Douglas;** CBE 1964; Lieut-Colonel; Professor of Transport at Imperial College, London, since Oct. 1963; *b* 22 Aug. 1907; *s* of William Ernest and Laura Kate Buchanan; *m* 1933, Elsie Alice Mitchell; two *s* one *d*. *Educ:* Berkhamsted School; Imperial College, London. Sudan Govt Public Works Dept, 1930-32; Regional planning studies with F. Longstreth Thompson, 1932-35; Ministry of Transport, 1935-39. War Service in Royal Engineers, 1939-46. Ministry of Town and Country Planning (later Ministry of Housing and Local Govt), 1946-61; Urban Planning Adviser, Ministry of Transport, 1961-63. *Publications:* Mixed Blessing, The Motor in Britain, 1958; Traffic in Towns (Ministry of Transport report), 1963; (paperback edn), 1964; Bath: a study in conservation, 1969. Numerous papers on town planning and allied subjects. *Recreations:* photography, carpentry, caravan touring. *Address:* 32 Rectory Road, Wokingham, Berks. *T:* Wokingham 90. *Clubs:* Royal Automobile; Architectural Association.

**BUCHANAN, Brigadier Edgar James Bernard,** DSO 1918; retired; *b* 1892; *s* of Robert Eccles Buchanan, of Templemore Park, Londonderry; *m* 1923, Evelyn Constance (*d* 1970), *d* of Richard Charles Holland, of Glanty House, Egham, Surrey; one *s*. Served European War, 1914-18; commanded 1st Bn RE, 1918 (wounded, DSO); Bt. Lt-Col 1935. Served War of 1939-45; Senior Royal Engineer, Allied Force HQ, 1943; Director of Fortification and Works, War Office, 1945 (despatches); retired 1946. Officer of Legion of Merit, USA. *Address:* Bridge Meadow, Harting, Petersfield, Hants. *Club:* United Service.

**BUCHANAN, Sir George H. M. Leith;** *see* Leith-Buchanan.

**BUCHANAN, George (Henry Perrott);** writer; *b* 9 Jan. 1904; 2nd *s* of Rev. C. H. L. Buchanan, Kilwaughter, Co. Antrim, and Florence Moore; *m* 1st, 1938, Winifred Mary (marr. diss. 1945), *y d* of late A. H. Corn; 2nd, 1949, Noel Pulleyne (*d* 1951), *y d* of late W. G. Beasley and *widow* of Major J. A. Ritter, RA; 3rd, 1952, Hon. Janet Hampden Margesson (*d* 1968), *e d* of 1st Viscount Margesson, PC, MC, and of Mrs F. H. Leggett, New York; two *d*. *Educ:* Campbell College; Queen's University, Belfast. On editorial staff of The Times, 1930-35; News Chronicle, 1935-38; dramatic critic, 1936-37; Operations Officer, RAF Coastal Command, 1940-45; Chm. Town and Country Development Cttee, N. Ireland, 1949-53; Member, Exec. Council, European Soc. of Culture, 1954-. *Publications:* Passage Through the Present, 1932; A London Story, 1935; Words for To-Night, 1936; Entanglement, 1938; The Soldier and the Girl, 1940; Rose Forbes, 1950; A Place to Live, 1952; Bodily Responses (poetry), 1958; Green

Seacoast, 1959; Conversation with Strangers (poetry), 1961; Morning Papers, 1965; Annotations, 1970; Naked Reason, 1971; *plays:* A Trip to the Castle, 1960; Tresper Revolution, 1961; War Song, 1965. *Address:* 27 Ashley Gardens, Westminster, SW1. *T:* 01-834 5722. *Clubs:* Athenæum, Savile.

**BUCHANAN, Sir John (Cecil Rankin),** KCMG 1961 (CMG 1948); MD, FRCP(E), FRACP, DTM&H; Chief Medical Officer, Colonial Office, 1960 (Department of Technical Co-operation, 1961-62), retired; *b* 18 June 1896; *s* of late John Buchanan, CMG, Blantyre, Nyasaland; *m* 1931, Eileen, *e d* of late J. D. Robertson, JP, Redhurst, Ravelston, Dykes, Edinburgh; no *c*. *Educ:* Stewart's College; Edinburgh University. Colonial Medical Service, 1925; Medical Officer Tanganyika and British Somaliland, 1925-35; Senior Medical Officer, British Somaliland, 1935; Aden, 1936; DDMS, Uganda, 1943; Inspector-General, South Pacific Health Service, 1945. Served European War, 1914-18, The Black Watch, 1915-19 (despatches); War of 1939-45, RAMC (rank of Colonel), 1940-43 (despatches). Scottish Rugby XV, 1921-25 (Captain Scottish XV, 1924). KStJ. *Publications:* Guide to Pacific Island Dietaries, 1948; many contributions to scientific journals. *Address:* Broomwood, Woodland Rise, Sevenoaks, Kent. *Club:* East India and Sports.

**BUCHANAN, John David,** MBE 1944; Headmaster of Oakham School, Rutland, since 1958; *b* 26 Oct. 1916; *e s* of late John Nevile Buchanan, and Nancy Isabel (*née* Bevan); *m* 1946, Janet Marjorie, *d* of late Brig. J. A. C. Pennycuick, DSO; three *s* four *d* (and one *s* decd). *Educ:* Stowe; Trinity College, Cambridge. Served with Grenadier Guards, 1939-46; Adjutant, 3rd Bn Grenadier Guards, 1941-43; Brigade Major, 1st Guards Bde, 1944-45; Private Secretary to Sir Alexander Cadogan, Security Council for the UN, 1946. Assistant Master, Westminster Under School, 1948; Assistant Master, Sherborne School, 1948-57. *Recreations:* golf, painting and decorating; trombone playing; gardening. *Address:* Deanscroft, Oakham, Rutland. *T:* (Office) 2487; (Home) 2179.

**BUCHANAN, Maj.-Gen. Sir Kenneth Gray,** Kt, *cr* 1946; CB 1934; CMG 1919; DSO 1916; Seaforth Highlanders; *b* 1880; *m* 1911, Muriel-Kate (*d* 1948), *d* of T. F. Cumming, Melbourne; two *d*; *m* 1952, Mrs A. G. Marr, *widow* of Capt. A. M. Marr, MBE, DCM, The Seaforth Highlanders. *Educ:* Harrow; RMC, Sandhurst. Entered Army, 1900; Major, 1915; Lieut-Colonel, 1923; Colonel, 1927; Maj.-General, 1932; served NW Frontier of India, 1908 (despatches, medal and clasp); European War, 1914-18 (wounded thrice, despatches, DSO, Bt. Lieut-Colonel); GSO 1 Northern Command, 1928-30; Commanded 2nd Infantry Brigade, Aldershot, 1930-32; Commander, 42nd (East Lancashire) Division, TA, 1934-38; retired, pay, 1938. *Club:* Army and Navy.

**BUCHANAN, Major Sir Reginald Narcissus M.;** *see* Macdonald-Buchanan.

**BUCHANAN, Richard,** JP; MP (Lab) Springburn Div. of Glasgow since 1964; *b* 3 May 1912; *s* of late Richard Buchanan and late Helen Henderson; *m* 1938, Margaret McManus (*d* 1963); six *s* two *d*. *Educ:* St Mungo's Boys' School; St Mungo's Academy. Councillor, City of Glasgow, 1949-64 (Past Chm. Libraries, Schools and Standing Orders Cttees); Hon. City Treasurer, 1960-63; Chm., West Day School Management, 1958-64; Governor, Notre Dame College of Education, 1959-64, etc. Chm., Belvidere Hospital; Member Board of Managers, Glasgow Royal Infirmary; President, Scottish Library Assoc., 1963; Chm., Scottish Central Library; Chm. Cttee on Burrell Collection; Director, Glasgow Citizens Theatre. JP Glasgow, 1954. *Recreations:* theatre, golf, snooker, walking, reading. *Address:* 10 Tudor Road, Glasgow, W4. *Club:* St Mungo's Centenary.

**BUCHANAN, Professor Robert Ogilvie;** Emeritus Professor, University of London; *b* 12 Sept. 1894; *s* of Duncan and Janet Buchanan; *m* 1931, Kathleen Mary Parnell; one *s* two *d*. *Educ:* University of Otago, New Zealand; University of London. Served European War, 1914-18, NZEF (Otago Regt), 1915-19, in France. Mount Albert Grammar School, Auckland, NZ, 1922-25; student at London School of Economics, 1925-28. University College, University of London; Asst Lecturer in Geography, 1928. Lecturer, 1930. Reader in Economic Geography, 1938-49; Prof. of Geography, London School of Economics, 1949-61. War of 1939-45, RAF, maps organisation, Air Ministry and War Office. Member Senate, University of London, 1951-67; President: Section E (Geography) British Assoc. for the Advancement of Science, 1952; Inst. of British Geographers, 1953; Geographical Association, 1958. Member Nature Conservancy, 1965-. *Publications:* Pastoral Industries of New Zealand, 1935; An Economic Geography of the British Empire, 1936; articles on various topics in economic geography in geographical periodicals in UK, USA, NZ and India. *Address:* 45 Westminster Palace Gardens, Artillery Row, SW1. *T:* 01-799 4625.

**BUCHANAN-DUNLOP, Commodore David Kennedy,** DSC 1945; RN retired; *b* 30 June 1911; *s* of Colonel Archibald Buchanan-Dunlop, OBE and Mary (*née* Kennedy); *m* 1945, Marguerite, *d* of William Macfarlane; no *c*. *Educ:* Loretto; RNC, Dartmouth. Served as young officer in submarines in Mediterranean and Far East, then Specialist in Fleet Air Arm. Served War of 1939-45 (despatches) in aircraft-carriers world-wide. Asst Naval Attaché, Paris, 1949-52; Dep. Director Nav. Air Org. Naval Staff, 1954-56; Staff of NATO Defence College, Paris, 1957-59; Naval and Military Attaché, Santiago, Lima, Quito, Bogotá and Panama, 1960-62; Captain, Royal Naval College, Greenwich, 1962-64. President, 1964. *Recreation:* fishing. *Address:* Les Nereides, 20 Propriano, Corsica. *Clubs:* Flyfishers', United Hunts.

**BUCHANAN-DUNLOP, Richard,** QC 1966; *b* 19 April 1919; *s* of late Canon W. R. Buchanan-Dunlop and Mrs R. E. Buchanan-Dunlop (*née* Mead); *m* 1948, Helen Murray Dunlop; three *d*. *Educ:* Marlborough College; Magdalene College, Cambridge. Served in Royal Corps of Signals, 1939-46 (Hon. Major). BA (Hons.) Law, Cambridge, 1949; Harmsworth Scholar, 1950. Called to the Bar, 1951. *Recreations:* painting, travel. *Address:* Skiathos, Greece.

**BUCHANAN-JARDINE, Sir A. R. J.;** *see* Jardine.

**BUCHANAN-RIDDELL, Sir J. C.;** *see* Riddell.

**BUCHANAN-SMITH,** family name of **Baron Balerno.**

**BUCHANAN-SMITH, Alick Laidlaw;** MP (U) North Angus and Mearns since 1964; Parliamentary Under-Secretary of State, Scottish Office, since 1970; *b* 8 April 1932; 2nd *s* of Baron Balerno, *qv* and late Mrs Buchanan-Smith; *m* 1956, Janet, *d* of late Thomas Lawrie, CBE; one *s* three *d*. *Educ:* Edinburgh Academy;

Trinity College, Glenalmond; Pembroke College, Cambridge; Edinburgh University. Commissioned Gordon Highlanders, National Service, 1951; subseq. Captain, TA (5th/6th Gordon Highlanders). *Address:* House of Cockburn, Balerno, Midlothian. *T:* 031-449 4242; Bogindollo, Fettercairn, Laurencekirk, Kincardineshire. *T:* Fettercairn 273. *Clubs:* Caledonian; New (Edinburgh).

**BUCHANAN-WOLLASTON, Vice-Admiral H. A.;** *see* Wollaston.

**BUCHER, Gen. Sir Francis Robert Roy;** *see* Bucher, Gen. Sir Roy.

**BUCHER, General Sir Roy,** KBE 1948 (OBE 1943); CB 1945; MC 1919; DL; psc; *b* 1895; *m* 1922, Edith Margaret Reid (*d* 1944); one *d*; *m* 1946, Maureen, OBE, *e d* of late Captain Thomas George Gibson, DL, Welham Hall, Malton, Yorks. *Educ:* Edinburgh Academy; RMC Sandhurst. Served European War, 1914-19, with 1st Bn The Cameronians (wounded 1915, France); India, 1915, attached 55th Coke's Rifles (FF); transferred 31st Duke of Connaught's Own Lancers, 1916; Mahsud, 1917; Afghanistan, Waziristan, 1919-20; Bt. Lieut-Colonel 13 Duke of Connaught's Own Lancers, 1937; Comdt Sam Browne's Cav., Nov. 1939-Feb. 1940; Colonel, 1940; Comdt No. 2 ACTC, Lucknow, 1940; AAG, GHQ, Jan.-June 1941; AQMG, Iraq, 1941; Major-General in charge Administration, Southern Army, India, 1942-45; GOC Bengal and Assam Area, 1946; officiating GOC-in-C Eastern Command, 1946-Jan. 1947; Chief of Staff, AHQ, India, Aug.-Dec. 1947; C-in-C, Army of India, 1948-49; Officer on special duty, Indian Defence Ministry, 1949; retired, 1949. Chairman Transport Users' Consultative Cttee, Yorkshire Area; DL, NR Yorks, 1962-. Past National Chairman, The British Legion (Life Member, Nat. Exec. Council and Chm. Finance and Appeals Cttees); Member of Council of Officers' Association; Vice-President Not-Forgotten Association; Past Chm. and Member of Council of Royal Society of St George. President, York and Derwent Division, BRCS; Chairman, Anglo Polish Society; Chm., Administering Cttee., Govt Grant for Polish Ex-Services Personnel. Order of Star of Nepal Class I. *Address:* Normanby House, Sinnington, York Y06 6RH. *T:* Kirby Moorside 483. *Clubs:* Cavalry, Army and Navy.

**BUCHTHAL, Hugo,** FBA 1959; FRAS; PhD; Professor of Fine Arts, New York University Institute of Fine Arts, since 1965; *b* Berlin, 11 Aug. 1909; *m* 1939, Amalia Serkin; one *d*. *Educ:* Universities of Berlin, Heidelberg, Paris and Hamburg. PhD, Hamburg, 1933; Resident in London from 1934; Lord Plumer Fellowship, Hebrew University, 1938; Librarian, Warburg Institute, 1941; Lecturer in History of Art, University of London, 1944; Reader in the History of Art, with special reference to the Near East, 1949; Professor of the History of Byzantine Art in the University of London, 1960. Visiting Scholarship, Dumbarton Oaks, Harvard University 1950-51, 1965; Temp. Member Inst. for Advanced Study, Princeton, NJ, 1959-60, 1968; Visiting Professor Columbia University, New York, 1963. Prix Schlumberger, Académie des Inscriptions et Belles Lettres, 1958. *Publications:* The Miniatures of the Paris Psalter, 1938; (with Otto Kurz) A Handlist of illuminated Oriental Christian Manuscripts, 1942; The Western Aspects of Gandhara Sculpture, 1944; Miniature Painting in the Latin Kingdom of Jerusalem, 1957; numerous articles in learned journals. *Address:* Institute of Fine Arts, 1 East 78th Street, New York, NY 10021, USA.

**BUCHWALD, Art, (Arthur);** American journalist, author, lecturer and columnist; *b* Mount Vernon, New York, 20 Oct. 1925; *s* of Joseph Buchwald and Helen (*née* Kleinberger); *m* 1952, Ann McGarry, Warren, Pa; one *s* two *d*. *Educ:* University of Southern California. Sergeant, US Marine Corps, 1942-45. Columnist, New York Herald Tribune: in Paris, 1949-62; in Washington, 1962-. Syndicated columnist whose articles appear in numerous newspapers throughout the world. *Publications:* (mostly published later in England) Paris After Dark, 1950; Art Buchwald's Paris, 1954; The Brave Coward, 1957; I Chose Caviar, 1957; More Caviar, 1958; A Gift from the Boys, 1958; Don't Forget to Write, 1960; Art Buchwald's Secret List to Paris, 1961; How Much is That in Dollars?, 1961; Is it Safe to Drink the Water?, 1962; I Chose Capitol Punishment, 1963; ... and Then I told the President, 1965; Son of the Great Society, 1966; Have I Ever Lied to You?, 1968; The Establishment is Alive and Well in Washington, 1969; Sheep on the Runway (Play), 1970. *Recreations:* chess, squash. *Address:* 1750 Pennsylvania Avenue NW, Washington, DC 20006, USA. *T:* Washington 298-7990. *Clubs:* National Press (Washington); Overseas Press (NY).

**BUCK, Antony;** *see* Buck, P. A. F.

**BUCK, Mrs Leonard;** *see* Harper, Heather.

**BUCK, Pearl S.;** *b* Hillsboro, W Va, USA; *d* of American missionaries; *m* 1st, a teacher of Nanking University; two *d*; 2nd, 1935, Richard J. Walsh (*d* 1960). Awarded 1938 Nobel Prize for Literature. *Publications:* The Good Earth; East Wind–West Wind; Sons; The First Wife and other Stories, 1933; All Men are Brothers, a translation of the Old Chinese Classic Shui hu Chuan; The Mother, 1934; A House Divided, 1935; The Exile, 1936; Fighting Angel, 1936; This Proud Heart, 1938; The Patriot, 1939; Other Gods, 1940; Dragon Seed, 1942; The Promise, 1943; What America Means to Me, 1944; Portrait of a Marriage, 1945; Pavilion of Women, 1946; Peony, 1948; Kinfolk, 1949; Far and Near, 1949; God's Men, 1951; The Hidden Flower, 1952; Come My Beloved, 1953; My Several Worlds, 1955; Imperial Woman, 1956; Letter from Peking, 1958; American Triptych, 1958; (with Carlos P. Romulo), Friend to Friend, 1958; Command the Morning, 1959; Fourteen Stories, 1961; A Bridge for Passing, 1962; With a Delicate Air (short stories), 1962; The Living Reed, 1963; Welcome Child, 1964; Joy of Children, 1965; The Gifts They Bring, 1965; Death in the Castle, 1965; The Time is Noon, 1967; The New Year, 1968; The People of Japan, 1968; The Good Deed and Other Stories of Asia, Past and Present, 1969; The Three Daughters of Madame Liang, 1969; The Kennedy Women, 1970; China as I See It, 1970. Also books for children and collections of essays. *Address:* Route 1, Box 164, Perkasie, Pa, USA.

**BUCK, (Philip) Antony (Fyson);** MP (C) Colchester since 1961; Barrister-at-Law; *b* 19 Dec. 1928; *yr s* of late A. F. Buck, Ely, Cambs; *m* 1955, Judy Elaine, *o d* of Dr C. A. Grant, Cottesloe, Perth, W Australia, and late Mrs Grant; one *d*. *Educ:* King's School, Ely; Trinity Hall, Cambridge. BA History and Law, 1951, MA 1954. Chm. Cambridge Univ. Cons. Assoc. and Chm. Fedn of Univ. Conservative and Unionist Associations, 1951-52. Called to the Bar, Inner Temple, 1954; Legal Adviser, Nat. Association of Parish Councils, 1957-59; sponsored and piloted through the Limitation Act, 1963. PPS to Attorney-General, 1963-64. Sec., Conservative Party Home Affairs Cttee,

1964-. *Recreations:* most sports, reading. *Address:* Pete Hall, Abberton, Nr Colchester, Essex. *T:* Peldon 230; 4 Paper Buildings, Temple, EC4. *T:* 01-353 8408/0196. *Club:* Oxford and Cambridge University.

**BUCKEE, Henry Thomas,** DSO 1942; **His Honour Judge Buckee;** Judge of County Courts since 1961 (Circuit 62, Southend, etc. since Oct. 1962); *b* 14 June 1913; *s* of Henry Buckee; *m* 1939, Margaret Frances Chapman; two *d.* *Educ:* King Edward VI School, Chelmsford. Called to Bar, Middle Temple, 1939. Served RNVR, 1940-46; Lieut-Comdr 1944. *Recreation:* sailing. *Address:* Rough Hill House, East Hanningfield, Chelmsford, Essex. *T:* Hanningfield 226. *Clubs:* Royal Ocean Racing, Bar Yacht.

**BUCKHURST, Lord; William Herbrand Sackville;** b 16 Oct. 1921; *e s* of 9th Earl De La Warr, *qv*; *m* 1946, Anne Rachel, *o d* of Geoffrey Devas, Hunton Court, Maidstone; two *s* one *d.* *Educ:* Eton. Lieut Royal Sussex Regt, 1941-43; Lieut Parachute Regt, 1943; Capt. 1945-46. Contested (C) NE Bethnal Green, 1945; Chm. London Young Conservatives, 1946, Pres. 1947-49. *Heir:* *s* Hon. William Herbrand Sackville, *b* 10 April 1948. *Address:* Buckhurst Park, Withyham, Sussex. *T:* Hartfield 346. *Club:* White's.

**BUCKINGHAM, Suffragan Bishop of,** since 1964; **Rt. Rev. George Christopher Cutts Pepys;** *b* 29 June 1914; *s* of late Rev. Charles Sidney Pepys and Adelaide Mary Elizabeth (*née* Cutts); *m* 1947, Elizabeth Margaret Ekin; one *s* four *d.* *Educ:* Winchester; Oriel College, Oxford; Cuddesdon Theological College, Oxford. Assistant Curate, St John the Divine, Kennington, 1939-46; Chaplain, RNVR, 1941-46; Rector of Hartfield, Sussex, 1946-51; Vicar of St Mark, Portsea, 1951-58; Hon. Canon of Portsmouth, 1956; Rector of Liverpool and Rural Dean of Liverpool, 1958-64; Hon. Canon of Liverpool, 1959. *Recreation:* rowing. *Address:* Sheridan, Great Missenden, Bucks. *T:* Gt Missenden 2173. *Club:* Leander (Henley-on-Thames).

**BUCKINGHAM, Archdeacon of;** *see* Eastman, Ven. D. I. T.

**BUCKINGHAM, Amyand David;** Professor of Chemistry, University of Cambridge, since 1969; *b* 28 Jan. 1930; 2nd *s* of late Reginald Joslin Buckingham and of Florence Grace Buckingham (formerly Elliot); *m* 1965, Jillian Bowles; one *s* one *d.* *Educ:* Barker Coll., Hornsby, NSW; Univ. of Sydney; Corpus Christi Coll., Cambridge (Shell Postgraduate Schol.), Univ. Medal 1952, MSc 1953, Sydney; PhD Cantab 1956. 1851 Exhibn Sen. Studentship, 1955-57; Lectr and subseq. Student, Tutor, and Censor of Christ Church, Oxford, 1955-65; Univ. Lectr in Inorganic Chem. Lab., Oxford, 1958-65; Prof. of Theoretical Chem., Univ. of Bristol, 1965-69. Vis. Lectr, Harvard, 1961; Vis. Prof., Princeton, 1965; short vis. appts at Univs of Wisconsin, British Columbia, California (Berkeley), Toronto, Pennsylvania State, Poznań and Hanover, and at Nat. Research Coun. of Canada in Ottawa. FRACI 1961 (Masson Meml Schol. 1952; Rennie Meml Medal, 1958); FCS (Harrison Meml Prize, 1959; Tilden Lectr 1964); Member: Faraday Soc. (Coun., 1965-67); Physical Soc.; Amer. Chem. Soc.; Amer. Physical Soc.; Optical Soc. of America. Assoc. Ed., Jl of Chemical Physics, 1964-66; Editor, Molecular Physics, 1968-. Mem., Chemistry Cttee, SRC, 1967-70. Sen. Treas., Oxford Univ. Cricket Club, 1960-64. *Publications:* The Laws and Applications of Thermodynamics, 1964; papers in various scientific jls. *Recreations:* walking, talking, cricket, tennis, travel. *Address:* Tunwells House, Great Shelford, Cambridge, CB2 5EG. *T:* Shelford 2484. *Club:* English-Speaking Union.

**BUCKINGHAM, George Somerset;** Director and Consultant, Electric Construction Co. Ltd, Wolverhampton; *b* 11 May 1903; *s* of Horace Clifford Buckingham, Norwich; *m* 1927, Marjorie Lanaway Bateson; one *s* (one *d* decd). *Educ:* Norwich Sch.; Faraday House Electrical Engrg Coll. (Gold Medallist; Dipl.). BSc (Eng); CEng; FIEE; FBIM. asst Engr, Yorks Electric Power Co., Leeds, 1924-26; District Engr and Br. Man., Birmingham, for Pirelli-General Cable Works Ltd of Southampton, 1928-48; Midlands Electricity Board: Chief Purchasing Officer, 1948-57; Chief Engr, 1957-62; Dep. Chm., 1962-64; Chm., 1964-69. Member: Electricity Council, 1964-69; Electricity Supply Industry Trng Bd, 1965-69; W Midlands Sports Council, 1966-.; Mem. Convocation, Univ. of Aston in Birmingham; Mem. Council, Electrical Research Assoc.; various sci. and profl Instns and Cttees; Pres. Birmingham Branch, Institute of Marketing, 1967-68. Chairman: South Midland Centre, IEE, 1966-67; Midland Centre, Council of Engineering Instns, 1968-70; Past President, Council of Birmingham Electric Club, 1965; Past President, Faraday House Old Students' Assoc., 1962; Vice-President, Outward Bound Schs. Assoc. (Birm. and Dist), 1964-. *Publications:* papers, articles and reviews in scientific and electrical engrg jls and works of professional engrg bodies. *Recreations:* walking, bridge. *Address:* Parklands, Blossomfield Road, Solihull, Warwicks. *T:* 021-705 2066.

**BUCKINGHAM, John,** CB 1953; Director of Research Programmes and Planning, Admiralty, 1946-Dec. 1959, retired; *b* 23 Dec. 1894; *e s* of late John Mortimer Buckingham, South Molton, N Devon; unmarried. *Educ:* Berkhamsted Sch.; St John's Coll., Cambridge (MA). Joined Admiralty scientific staff for anti-submarine duties under Lord Fisher, 1917, and has been engaged continuously upon scientific work for the Admiralty since that date. Deputy Director of Scientific Research, 1932; Apptd Chief Scientific Officer in RN Scientific Service on its formation in 1946. *Publications:* Matter and Radiation, 1930. Various publications in scientific journals. *Address:* 25 Cliveden Place, SW1. *T:* 01-730 1154. *Clubs:* Brooks's, Travellers', United University.

**BUCKINGHAM, Professor Richard Arthur;** Director, University of London Institute of Computer Science (called University of London Computer Unit, 1957-64) since 1967, and Professor of Computing Science since 1963; *b* 17 July 1911; *s* of George Herbert Buckingham and Alice Mary Watson (*née* King); *m* 1939 Christina O'Brien; one *s* two *d.* *Educ:* Gresham's Sch., Holt; St John's Coll., Cambridge. Asst Lecturer in Mathematical Physics, Queen's University, Belfast, 1935-38; Senior 1851 Exhibitioner, University College, London and MIT, 1938-40. At Admiralty Research Laboratory, Teddington, and Mine Design Dept, Havant, 1940-45. University Coll., London: Lecturer in Mathematics, 1945-50; Lecturer in Physics, 1950-51; Reader in Physics, 1951-57. FBCS; FRSA. *Publications:* Numerical Methods, 1957; papers in Proc. Royal Soc., Proc. Phys. Soc., London, Jl Chem. Physics, Trans. Faraday Soc., Computer Journal, etc. *Recreation:* travel. *Address:* Lordings Cottage, Lordings Lane, West Chiltington, Sussex. *T:* West Chiltington 3294.

**BUCKINGHAMSHIRE,** 9th Earl of, *cr* 1746; **Vere Frederick Cecil Hobart-Hampden;** Bt 1611; Baron Hobart, 1728; *b* 17 May 1901; *s* of Arthur Ernest and Henrietta Louisa Hobart-Hampden; *S kinsman,* 1963; unmarried. *Educ:* St Lawrence College, Ramsgate; Switzerland. Left England for Australia via Canada, 1919; sheep farming and wool business. Served in Royal Australian Air Force, 1942-46. Queensland Railways, 1946-49; returned to England, 1949; employed by Southend-on-Sea Corporation, 1951. *Heir: kinsman* Cyril Langel Hobart-Hampden [*b* 31 Oct. 1902; *m* 1936, Margaret Moncrieff Hilborne, *o d* of George Hilborne Joliffe; one *s* one *d*]. *Address:* 24 Acacia Drive, Thorpe Bay, Essex. *T:* Southend 87765.

**BUCKLAND, Maj.-Gen. Ronald John Denys Eden,** MBE 1956; Chief of Staff, HQ Strategic Command, since 1970; *b* 27 July 1920; *s* of late Geoffrey Ronald Aubert Buckland and Lelgarde Edith Eleanor (*née* Eden); *m* 1968, Judith Margaret Coxhead; one *d. Educ:* Winchester; New College, Oxford (MA). Commissioned into Coldstream Gds, Dec. 1940. Served War of 1939-45: NW Europe, with 4th Coldstream Gds, 1944-45 (wounded twice). GSO3, Gds Div., BAOR, 1946; Adjt, 1st Bn Coldstream Gds, Palestine and Libya, 1948; DAA&QMG, 2nd Gds Bde, Malaya, 1950; DAAG, 3rd Div., Egypt, 1954; Bde Major, 1st Gds Bde, Cyprus, 1958; commanded 1st Bn, Coldstream Gds, 1961, British Guiana, 1962; GSO1, 4th Div., BAOR, 1963; Comdr, 133 Inf. Bde (TA), 1966; ACOS, Joint Exercises Div., HQ AFCENT, Holland, 1967; idc 1968; DA&QMG, 1st British Corps, BAOR, 1969. *Recreations:* cricket, travel, philately. *Address:* c/o Coutts and Co., 440 Strand, WC2; HQ Army Strategic Command, Erskine Barracks, Wilton, near Salisbury, Wilts. *Clubs:* Guards, Pratt's, Leander.

**BUCKLE, (Christopher) Richard (Sandford);** writer; critic; exhibition designer; Acting Secretary, Friends of the Museum of Performing Arts; *b* 6 Aug. 1916; *s* of late Lieut-Col C. G. Buckle, DSO, MC, Northamptonshire Regt, and of Mrs R. E. Buckle (*née* Sandford). *Educ:* Marlborough; Balliol. Founded "Ballet", 1939. Served Scots Guards, 1940-46; in action in Italy (despatches, 1944). Started "Ballet" again, 1946; it continued for seven years. Ballet critic of the Observer, 1948-55; ballet critic of the Sunday Times, 1959; advised Canada Council on state of ballet in Canada, 1962; advised Sotheby & Co. on their sales of Diaghilev Ballet material, 1967-69. First play, Gossip Column, prod Q Theatre, 1953; Family Tree (comedy), prod Connaught Theatre, Worthing, 1956. Organised: Diaghilev Exhibition, Edinburgh Festival, 1954, and Forbes House, London, 1954-55; The Observer Film Exhibition, London, 1956; Telford Bicentenary Exhibition, 1957; Epstein Memorial Exhibition, Edinburgh Festival, 1961; Shakespeare Exhibition, Stratford-upon-Avon, 1964-65; a smaller version of Shakespeare Exhibition, Edinburgh, 1964; Treasures from the Shakespeare Exhibition, National Portrait Gallery, London, 1964-65; The Communities on the March area in the Man in the Community theme pavilion, Universal and Internat. Exhibition of 1967, Montreal; Exhibition of Beaton Portraits, 1928-68, National Portrait Gallery, 1968; presented Kama Dev in recital of Indian dancing, St Paul's Church, Covent Garden, 1970; designed: (temporary) Haldane Library for Imperial College, South Kensington; new Exhibition Rooms, Harewood House, Yorks, 1959; redesigned interior of Dundee Repertory Theatre, 1963 (burnt down 3 months later). *Publications:* John Innocent at Oxford (novel), 1939; The Adventures of a Ballet Critic, 1953; In Search of Diaghilev, 1955; Modern Ballet Design, 1955; The Prettiest Girl in England, 1958; Harewood (a guide-book), 1959 and (re-written and re-designed), 1966; Dancing for Diaghilev (the memoirs of Lydia Sokolova), 1960; Epstein Drawings (introd. only), 1962; Epstein: An Autobiography (introd. to new edn only), 1963; Jacob Epstein: Sculptor, 1963; Monsters at Midnight: the French Romantic Movement as a background to the ballet Giselle (limited edn), 1966; The Message, a Gothick Tale of the A1 (limited edn), 1969. *Recreations:* caricature, light verse. *Address:* 34 Henrietta Street, Covent Garden, WC2.

**BUCKLE, Col Cuthbert,** CB 1931; CBE 1919; TD 1931; retired; *s* of Henry Rogers Buckle and Emily Hotine; *m* 1st, 1909, Edith Marion (*d* 1949), *d* of John Kennedy Barlow; one *s*; 2nd, 1950, Letty Iris, *d* of J. R. T. Nind. *Educ:* Univ. Coll., London; City and Guilds of London Institute. Air Defence Commander Sheppey and Grain, 1916; Air Defence Commander, London Air Defences, 1917-18; raised and commanded 53rd (City of London) Anti-Aircraft Brigade, RA, TA, 1921-27; commanded 27th (London) Air Defence Brigade, TA, 1927-31; elected to Lloyd's, 1920, and is Chartered Adjuster to the Fire Offices and Underwriters. *Publications:* several papers on technical matters connected with insurance. *Recreation:* yachting. *Address:* Galiots, West Mersea, Essex. *T:* West Mersea 2897. *Club:* Royal Artillery Yacht.

**BUCKLE, Maj.-Gen. (Retd) Denys Herbert Vintcent,** CB 1955; CBE 1948 (OBE 1945); Trustee, South Africa Foundation, since 1969; Member Council, South Africa-Britain Trade Association, since 1969; Director, Prince Vintcent & Co. (Pty) Ltd, Mossel Bay, George, and Ondtshoorn; *b* Cape Town, South Africa, 16 July 1902; *s* of Major H. S. Buckle, RMLI and ASC and of Agnes Buckle (*née* Vincent), Cape Town; *m* 1928, Frances Margaret Butterworth; one *d. Educ:* Boxgrove School, Guildford; Charterhouse, Godalming; RMC Sandhurst. 2nd Lieut, E Surrey Regt, 1923; transf. to RASC, 1926; Shanghai Def. Force, 1927-28; Asst Adjt, RASC Trg Centre, 1929-32; Adjt 44th (Home Counties) Divnl RASC, TA, 1932-36; Student Staff Coll., Camberley, 1936-37; Adjt Ceylon ASC, 1938; Bde Maj., Malaya Inf Bde, 1938-40; GSO 2, Trg Directorate, WO, 1940; AA & QMG, 8th Armd Div., 1940-41; GSO 1, Staff Coll., Camberley, 1941-42; Brig. Admin. Plans, GHQ Home Forces, "Cossac" and SHAEF, 1952-44; Brig. Q Ops, WO, 1944; DDST and Brig. Q, 21 Army Gp and BAOR, 1945-46; DQMG, FARELF, 1946-48; DDST, S Comd, 1948-49; Spec. Appts (Brig.), USA, 1949-50; Dir of Equipment, WO, 1950-51, and special appt, Paris, 1951; Comdt RASC Trg Centre, 1952-53; DST, MELF, 1953-56; Maj.-Gen. i/c Admin, GHQ, MELF, 1956-58; despatches, 1956 (Suez); retd 1958; ADC to King George VI 1951, to the Queen, 1952-54. MInstT 1955. Bursar, Church of England Training Colleges, Cheltenham, 1958-59. Divisional Manager SE Division, British Waterways, 1961-63; Director of Reorganisation, British Waterways, 1963-65. Dir, UK-S Africa Trade Assoc., 1965-68; Administrative Mem., Southern Africa Cttee, BNEC, 1967-68. Col Comdt RASC, 1959-64; Representative Col Comdt, RASC, 1961; Hon. Col 44th (Home Counties), RASC 1962-65, Regt, RCT, 1965-67, when Regt disbanded. Legion of Merit (USA), 1944. *Publication:* History of 44th Division, RASC, TA, 1932. *Recreations:* reading, walking, swimming, travel. *Address:* 2 Chelsea Cloisters, Durban Road, Wynberg,

Cape, South Africa. *Clubs:* Army and Navy; Civil Service (Cape Town).

**BUCKLE, Richard;** *see* Buckle, C. R. S.

**BUCKLEY,** family name of **Baron Wrenbury.**

**BUCKLEY, Rt. Hon. Sir Denys (Burton),** PC 1970; Kt 1960; MBE 1945; **Rt. Hon. Lord Justice Buckley;** Lord Justice of Appeal, since 1970; *b* 6 Feb. 1906; 4th *s* of 1st Baron Wrenbury; *m* 1932, Gwendolen Jane, *yr d* of late Sir Robert Armstrong-Jones, CBE, FRCS, FRCP; three *d. Educ:* Eton; Trinity College, Oxford. Called to the Bar, Lincoln's Inn, 1928, Bencher, 1949, Pro-Treasurer, 1967, Treasurer, 1969. Served War of 1939-45, in RAOC, 1940-45; Temporary Major; GSO II (Sigs Directorate), War Office. Treasury Junior Counsel (Chancery), 1949-60; Judge of High Court of Justice, Chancery Div., 1960-70. Member, Restrictive Practices Ct, 1962-70, President, 1968-70; Member: Law Reform Cttee, 1963–; Cttee on Departmental Records, 1952-54; Advisory Council on Public Records, 1958-. Hon. Fellow, Trinity Coll., Oxford, 1969. Pres. St John Ambulance Assoc. for County of London, 1962-. CStJ 1966. Medal of Freedom (USA), 1945. *Address:* 11 Selwood Place, SW7. *T:* 01-373 4752; Stream Farm, Dallington, Sussex. *T:* Rushlake Green 223; Plâs Dinas, Caernarvon. *T:* Llanwnda 274. *Clubs:* United University, Beefsteak; Royal Welsh Yacht.

**BUCKLEY, James Arthur;** Member, Gas Council, since 1968; *b* 3 April 1917; *s* of late James Buckley and of Elizabeth Buckley; *m* 1939, Irene May Hicks; two *s. Educ:* Christ's Hosp., Horsham, Sussex; Westminster Technical Coll.; Bradford Technical Coll. RAFVR, 1940-46. Gas Light & Coke Co.; Gas Supply Pupil, 1934; Actg Service Supervisor, 1939; Service Supervisor, 1946; North Thames Gas Board: Divisional Man., 1954; Commercial Man., 1962; Commercial Man. and Bd Mem., 1964; East Midlands Gas Board: Dep. Chm., 1966-67; Chm., 1967-68.

**BUCKLEY, Professor John Joseph Cronin,** DSc (NUI); Professor Emeritus of Helminthology in the University of London at the London School of Hygiene and Tropical Medicine, since 1967; *b* Dublin, 29 May 1904; *s* of late John Joseph Buckley and late Ellen Mary Cronin, Dublin; unmarried. *Educ:* Catholic University Sch., Dublin; National Univ. of Ireland. Wandsworth Research Scholar, 1931-34; Milner Research Fellow, 1934-38; Lecturer in Helminthology, 1938-40; William Julian Courtauld Professor of Helminthology, University of London, 1947-67. Research expeditions to: British West Indies, 1931; Assam, 1933; Malaya, 1935, 1955, 1956; Kenya, 1941, 1957, 1958; Northern Rhodesia, 1944; Ceylon, 1956; Uganda, 1959. Mem., (Expert) panel of Parasitic Diseases of WHO; Reference Expert in Helminthology to Public Health Laboratory Service; Examiner for higher degrees in Science at London and other British and foreign Universities. FIBiol. *Publications:* Editor, Jl of Helminthology, 1947-; numerous papers on Parasitology in various scientific jls. *Recreation:* proof reading. *Address:* London School of Hygiene and Tropical Medicine, Keppel Street, WC1. *T:* 01-636 8636.

**BUCKLEY, Rear-Adm. Sir Kenneth (Robertson),** KBE 1961; FIEE, MBritIRE; *b* 24 May 1904; 2nd *s* of late L. E. Buckley, CSI, TD; *m* 1937, Bettie Helen Radclyffe Dugmore, one *s* two *d. Educ:* RN Colleges Osborne and Dartmouth. Joined Navy Jan. 1918. Served War of 1939-45 (despatches). Comdr 1942; Capt. 1949; Rear-Adm. 1958. ADC to the Queen, 1956-58. Director of Engineering and Electrical Training of the Navy, and Senior Naval Electrical Officer, 1959-61. *Recreations:* golf, gardening. *Address:* Meadow Cottage, Chark Lane, Lee-on-Solent, Hants. *T:* Lee 79646. *Club:* United Service.

**BUCKLEY, Rear-Adm. Peter Noel,** CB 1964; DSO 1945; retd; Head of Naval Historical Branch, Ministry of Defence, since 1968; *b* 26 Dec. 1909; *s* of late Frank and Constance Buckley, Hooton, Cheshire; *m* 1945, Norah Elizabeth Astley St Clair-Ford, *widow* of Lt-Comdr Drummond St Clair-Ford; one *d* (and two step *s* one step *d*). *Educ:* Holmwood School, Formby, Lancs; RNC, Dartmouth. Midshipman, HMS Tiger, 1927, HMS Cornwall, 1928-30; Lieut: qual. 1931. Submarine Service, 1931-38, in submarines; Lieut-Comdr, CO of HMS Shark, 1938. War of 1939-45 (despatches): POW Germany, 1940-45. Comdr 1945; HMS: Rajah and Formidable, 1946; Siskin, 1947; Glory, 1949; RN Barracks, Portsmouth, 1951; Capt. 1952; Capt. D, Plymouth, 1953; Capt. of Dockyard, Rosyth, 1954; Chief Staff Officer to Flag Officer Comdg Reserve Fleet, 1957; Capt of Fleet, Med. Fleet, 1959; Rear-Adm. 1962; Dir-Gen., Manpower, 1962-64; retd 1965. *Address:* Forest Cottage, Sway, Lymington, Hants. *T:* Sway 442. *Clubs:* United Service, United Hunts.

**BUCKLEY, Hon. Dame Ruth (Burton),** DBE 1959; JP; *b* 12 July 1898; 4th *d* of 1st Baron Wrenbury, PC. *Educ:* Cheltenham Ladies' College. E Sussex County Council: elected member of Council, 1936; Alderman, 1946-; Vice-Chm. 1949-52; Chm. 1952-55. Member of South Eastern Metropolitan Regional Hospital Board, 1948-69; Part-time member of Local Govt Boundary Commn for England, 1958-66. JP Sussex, 1935-. *Address:* Tollwood, Netherfield, Battle, Sussex. *T:* Brightling 222.

**BUCKLEY, Lt-Col William Howell,** DL; Master, Carmarthenshire Fox Hounds, since 1931; Landed Proprietor; Chairman Buckleys Brewery Ltd, Llanelly; *b* 7 Feb. 1896; *s* of William Joseph Buckley and Muriel Howell; *m* 1st, 1920, Karolie Kathleen Kemmis; one *s* one *d*; 2nd, 1952, Helen Josephine, *yr d* of Montagu Turner, Naval and Military Club, and of late Josephine Warton Turner; one *d. Educ:* Radley. 2nd Lieut Glamorgan Imperial Yeomanry, 1914; Lieut The Inniskillings (6th Dragoons), 1915; Capt. 5th Inniskilling Dragoon Guards, 1926; Capt. 1930; served War of 1939-45, 6th Cavalry Bde, Palestine, 1939; Deputy Provost Marshal S Area, Palestine, Malta, Western Command. High Sheriff of Carmarthenshire, 1950-51. DL Carmarthen, 1955. *Recreation:* Hunting. *Address:* Castell Gorfod, St Clears, Carms. *TA:* St Clears. *T:* 10 St Clears. *Clubs:* Cavalry, Buck's, Leander.

*See also Major W. K. Buckley.*

**BUCKLEY, Major William Kemmis,** MBE 1959; Vice-Chairman, Buckleys Brewery Ltd, since 1963; *b* 18 Oct. 1921; *o s* of Lt-Col William Howell Buckley, *qv. Educ:* Radley Coll.; New Coll., Oxford (MA). Commnd into Welsh Guards, 1941; served N Africa, Italy (despatches, 1945); ADC, 1946-47, Mil. Sec., 1948, to Governor of Madras; Staff Coll., Camberley, 1950; GSO2, HQ London Dist, 1952-53; OC Guards Indep. Para. Co., 1954-57; Cyprus, 1956; Suez, 1956; War Office, 1957; Mil. Asst to Vice-Chief of Imp. Gen. Staff, 1958-59; US Armed Forces Staff Coll., Norfolk, Va., 1959-60. Director: Buckleys Brewery Ltd, 1960; Rhymney Breweries Ltd, 1962; Whitbread (Wales) Ltd, 1969; Guardian

Assurance Co. (S Wales), 1966 (Dep. Chm., 1967-). Mem. Council, Brewers' Soc., 1967; Dep. Chm. and Treas., Nat. Trade Develt Assoc., 1966 (Chm., S Wales Panel, 1965); Lay Mem., Press Council, 1967. Chairman: Council of St John of Jerusalem for Carms, 1966; Carms Antiquarian Soc., 1968; Mem., Nat. Trust Cttee for Wales, 1962; Mem., T & AFA (Carms), 1962 and T & AFA (S Wales and Mon.), 1967; Jt Master and Hon. Sec., Pembrokeshire and Carms Otter Hounds, 1962. High Sheriff of Carms, 1967-68, DL Carms 1969. CStJ 1966. *Recreations:* gardening, bee-keeping. *Address:* Briar Cottage, Ferryside, Carms. *T:* Ferryside 359. *Clubs:* St James'; Cardiff and County (Cardiff).

**BUCKMASTER,** family name of **Viscount Buckmaster.**

**BUCKMASTER,** 2nd Viscount, *cr* 1933; **Owen Stanley Buckmaster,** Baron of Cheddington, *cr* 1915; an Underwriting Member of Lloyd's; Vice-Chairman, London County Freehold and Leasehold Properties Ltd, 1952-68; *b* 24 Sept. 1890; *o s* of 1st Viscount and Edith Augusta (*d* 1935), *d* of Spencer Robert Lewin of Widford, Ware; *S* father 1934; *m* 1st, 1916, Joan (marr. diss., 1944), 2nd *d* of Dr Garry Simpson, 89 Lancaster Gate, W2; two *s*; 2nd, 1961, Mrs D. C. Vane-Tempest (*née* Seth-Smith). *Educ:* Winchester; Christ Church, Oxford, BA (Law). Called to Bar, Inner Temple, 1913; served European War, 1914-18, Captain Duke of Cornwall's Light Infantry (wounded, 1914-15 Star). Member of Committee of London Stock Exchange, 1938-42; Member of House of Lords Cttee on Gas, Electricity and Water Holding Cos, 1939; Pres. Assoc. of Land and Property Owners, 1946-57; Pres. Nat. Fed. of Property Owners, 1947-50; Chairman, Friends of Stowe Trust, 1939-59; Pres., Arundel and Shoreham Div. Conservative Assoc., 1951-61. Major, 16th Sussex Home Guard, 1941-44. Resigned from Liberal Party to join Conservative Party, 1947. *Publication:* Roundabout (memoirs), 1970. *Heir: s* Hon. Martin Stanley Buckmaster [*b* 11 April 1921; Capt. Royal Sussex Regt, 1939-46; HM Diplomatic Service, 1946-]. *Address:* Furzefield House, Wineham, Henfield, Sussex. *T:* Partridge Green 380.

**BUCKMASTER, Rev. Cuthbert Harold Septimus;** Rector of Chagford since 1959; *b* 15 July 1903; *s* of Charles John and Evelyn Jean Buckmaster; *m* 1942, Katharine Mary Zoë, 3rd *d* of Reverend Canon T. N. R. Prentice, Stratford-on-Avon; two *d. Educ:* RN Colleges, Osborne and Dartmouth. Asst Curate St John's, Middlesbrough, 1927-30; Curate of Wigan, 1930-33; Chaplain of Denstone College, 1933-35; Warden of St Michael's College, Tenbury, Worcs, 1935-46; Rector of Ashprington, with Cornworthy, 1957-59. Chaplain RNVR, 1940; RN 1947. *Address:* The Rectory, Chagford, Devon.

**BUCKNALL, Lt-Gen. Gerard Corfield,** CB 1943; MC; DL; psc; ns; lately Colonel, The Middlesex Regiment; Assistant Lieutenant for Greater London, since 1965; *b* 14 Sept. 1894; *s* of Harry Corfield Bucknall and Alice Oakshott; *m* 1925, Kathleen Josephine Moore-Burt; two *s* one *d. Educ:* Repton; Sandhurst. Commissioned 1st Battalion Middlesex Regiment, 1914; served throughout European War, 1914-18, France and Flanders, latterly on General Staff (wounded, MC and Bar, despatches, Bt Major); in Sudan with Egyptian Army, 1920-21; Brevet Lieut-Colonel 1936; General Staff Canadian Forces, 1937-38; commanded 2nd Bn Middx, 1939; Colonel on Staff, War Office, 1939; commanded 5th Div. in Sicily and Italy, and 30th Corps in Army of Invasion, 1944; GOC N Ireland, 1945-47; Lord Lieut of Middlesex, 1963-65. *Address:* 25 Belvedere Avenue, Wimbledon, SW19. *Clubs:* Army and Navy, MCC; Royal Wimbledon Golf.

**BUCKNILL, Peter Thomas,** QC 1961; *b* 4 Nov. 1910: *o s* of late Rt Hon. Sir Alfred Bucknill, PC, OBE; *m* 1935, Elizabeth Mary Stark; three *s* three *d. Educ:* Gresham's Sch., Holt; Trinity Coll., Oxford (MA). Called to the Bar, Inner Temple, 1935. Appointed Junior Counsel to the Treasury (Admiralty), 1958; resigned on becoming QC; Bencher, 1967-. On rota for Lloyd's Salvage Arbitrators, and for Wreck Commissioners, 1962. *Publications:* contributed to Halsbury's Laws of England, shipping vol., 2nd and 3rd Edns. *Recreation:* gardening. *Address:* High Corner, The Warren, Ashtead, Surrey; Queen Elizabeth Building, Temple, EC4. *T:* 01-353 5728, 0132.

**BUCKTON,** Baron *cr* 1966 (Life Peer), of Settrington; **Samuel Storey;** Bt, *cr* 1960; *b* 1896; *er s* of late Frederick George Storey, JP; *m* 1929, Elisabeth (*d* 1951) *d* of late Brig.-Gen. W. J. Woodcock, DSO; one *s* one *d. Educ:* Haileybury Coll.; Trinity Coll., Cambridge, MA. Barrister, Inner Temple, 1919; MP (C) Sunderland, 1931-45 and Stretford, 1950-66; Chairman of Ways and Means, and Dep. Speaker, House of Commons, 1965-66; (Dep. Chm. of Ways and Means, 1964-65); Member Chairman's Panel, House of Commons, 1957-64. E Riding CC, 1946-64. *Heir* (to Baronetcy only): *s* Hon. Richard Storey [*b* 23 Jan. 1937; *m* 1961, Virginia Anne, 3rd *d* of Sir Kenelm Cayley, 10th Bt; one *s* two *d*]. *Address:* Settrington House, Settrington Malton, Yorks. *T:* North Grimston 200; 37 St James's Place, SW1. *T:* 01-493 9835. *Clubs:* Carlton; Hon. Company Edinburgh Golfers (Muirfield).

**BUCKTON, Ernest James,** BSc Eng (Lond.); MICE; MIMechE; Fellow of Queen Mary College; retired: *b* 1 July 1883; *m* 1920, Joyce Ethel Pym (*d* 1933), *y d* of Captain Riall Sankey, CB, RE; one *d. Educ:* Drapers' Company School and College (now Queen Mary College), London; Whitworth Exhibitioner. Engineering pupil, London & India Docks Company, 1904; Assistant Engineer, 1907; Assistant Engineer, Port of London Authority, 1909; European War, served 1914-18 in Gibraltar and France; hon. rank of Major on relinquishing Commission; Resident Engineer, New Works, Port of London Authority, 1918; Deputy Resident Engineer, New Port Works, Buenos Aires, Argentine, 1920; Agent and Chief Engineer, Loanda Harbour Works, Portuguese West Africa, 1924; Engineer-in-Charge, Rendel, Palmer & Tritton, Consulting Engineers, 1925, Partner, 1929-47, Consultant, 1947-51, retired, 1951. *Publications:* The Construction of Haifa Harbour, Palestine, 1936; The Demolition of Waterloo Bridge (joint), 1936; The Reconstruction of Chelsea Bridge (joint), 1937; The New Waterloo Bridge (joint), 1943. *Recreations:* riding and golf. *Address:* 11 St Aubin's Court, Sea Lane, Ferring, Sussex. T: Worthing 40434. *Clubs:* Royal Societies, Royal Automobile.

**BUDAY, George,** RE 1953 (ARE 1939); wood engraver; author on graphic arts subjects; *b* Kolozsvar, Transylvania, 7 April 1907; *s* of late Prof. Arpad Buday, Roman archaeologist, and Margaret Buday. *Educ:* Presbyterian Coll., Kolozsvar; Royal Hungarian Francis Joseph Univ., Szeged (Dr). Apptd Lectr in Graphic Arts, Royal Hungarian F. J. Univ., 1935-41; Rome Scholar, 1936-37; won travelling schol.

to England (and has stayed permanently) 1937. Broadcaster, BBC European Service, 1940-42; in a Dept of Foreign Office, 1942-45. Dir, Hungarian Cultural Inst., London, 1947-49, resigned. Illustrated numerous folk-tale and folk-ballad collections, vols of classics and modern authors, publ. in many countries. Since 1938 exhib. Royal Acad., Royal Soc. of Painter-Etchers and Engravers, Soc. of Wood Engravers, and in many countries abroad. Works represented in: Depts of Prints and Drawings, Brit. Mus.; Victoria and Albert Mus.; Glasgow Univ.; New York Public Library; Florence Univ.; Museums of Fine Arts, Budapest, Prague, Warsaw; Phillips Memorial Gall., Washington, DC; etc. Grand Prix, Paris World Exhibn, 1937 (for engravings); subsequently other art and bibliophile prizes. Officer's Cross, Order of Merit (Hungary), 1947. *Publications:* Book of Ballads, 1934; The Story of the Christmas Card, 1951; The History of the Christmas Card, 1954 (1964); (wrote and illustr.): The Dances of Hungary, 1950; George Buday's Little Books, I-XII, incl. The Language of Flowers, 1951; The Cries of London, Ancient and Modern, 1954; Proverbial Cats and Kittens, 1956 (1968). Contrib. articles to periodicals. *Recreations:* bibliophile hand-printing on his 1857 Albion hand-press and collecting old Christmas cards (probably most representative collection of Victorian cards extant). *Address:* Templewood Villa, PO Box 150, Coulsdon, Surrey CR3 1YE. *Club:* Art Workers' Guild.

**BUDD, Bernard Wilfred,** MA; QC 1969; *b* 18 Dec. 1912; *s* of Rev. W. R. A. Budd; *m* 1944, Margaret Alison, *d* of late Rt Hon. E. Leslie Burgin, PC, LLD, MP; two *s*. *Educ:* Cardiff High Sch.; W Leeds High Sch.; Pembroke Coll., Cambridge (schol. in natural sciences). Joined ICS, 1935; various Dist appts incl. Dep. Comr, Upper Sind Frontier, 1942-43; Collector and Dist Magistrate, Karachi, 1945-46; cont. in Pakistan Admin. Service, 1947; Dep. Sec., Min. of Commerce and Works, Govt of Pakistan, 1947; Anti-corruption Officer and Inspector-Gen. of Prisons, Govt of Sind, 1949. Called to Bar, Gray's Inn, 1952. Contested (L), Dover, gen. elec., 1964 and 1966. *Recreations:* squash, birds, hill walking, hedge cutting. *Address:* Highlands, Elham, Canterbury, Kent. *T:* Elham 350; 68 Cliffords Inn, Fetter Lane, EC4. *T:* 01-405 2491; 3 Pump Court, Temple, EC4. *T:* 01-353 4122. *Clubs:* United University; Sind (Karachi).

**BUDD, Hon. Sir Harry Vincent,** Kt 1970; President of the Ligislative Council of New South Wales since 1966 (MLC since 1946); *b* 18 Feb. 1900; *s* of Arthur Eames Budd and Anne (*née* Knight); *m* 1939, Colina Macdonald White, *d* of Alfred White; one *s* two *d* (and one *s* decd). *Educ:* privately. Editor, Tweed Daily, Murwillumbah, 1921-23; Editorial Staff, Sydney Daily Telegraph, 1923-30; Managing Editor, The Land, 1930-. *Recreations:* music, gardening. *Address:* 26 Mistral Avenue, Mosman, Sydney, NSW 2088, Australia. *T:* 969-4810. *Clubs:* Australian, American, Royal Automobile of Australia (Sydney).

**BUDDEN, Kenneth George,** FRS 1966; MA, PhD; Reader in Physics, University of Cambridge, since 1965; Fellow of St John's College, Cambridge, since 1947; *b* 23 June 1915; *s* of late George Easthope Budden and Gertrude Homer Rea; *m* 1947, Nicolette Ann Lydia de Longesdon Longsdon; no *c*. *Educ:* Portsmouth Grammar Sch.; St John's College, Cambridge (MA, PhD). Telecommunications Research Establishment, 1939-41; British Air Commn., Washington, DC, 1941-44; Air Command, SE Asia, 1945. Research at Cambridge, 1936-39 and from 1947. *Publications:* Radio Waves in the Ionosphere, 1961; The Wave-Guide Mode Theory of Wave Propagation, 1961; Lectures on Magnetoionic Theory, 1964; numerous papers in scientific jls, on the propagation of radio waves. *Recreation:* gardening. *Address:* 15 Adams Road, Cambridge. *T:* 54752.

**BUDGE, Rev. Ronald Henderson Gunn;** Minister at Crathie, Aberdeenshire, since 1964; Domestic Chaplain to Her Majesty the Queen in Scotland, since 1964; *b* 4 Oct. 1909; *o s* of late Ex-Provost R. Gunn Budge, Moffat; *m* 1940, Maisie, *o d* of late Very Rev. Prof. Archibald Main, DD, DLitt, LLd. *Educ:* Ashville Coll., Harrogate; Glasgow Univ. (MA). Ordained and inducted to Selkirk West Church, 1938. Served with Church of Scotland Huts and Canteens in France and Scotland, 1939-44. Inducted to Troon Old Church, 1944; inducted to Murrayfield Church, Edinburgh, 1953; Convener of the General Assembly's Stewardship and Budget Committee, 1959-64; Chaplain in attendance to HM the Queen at Gen. Assembly of Church of Scotland, 1969. Guest Preacher in the Scots Church: Sydney, 1951-52; Staunton, Virginia, 1958; Toronto, 1967. Member of the Baird Trust. 1945-. *Recreations:* fishing, gardening. *Address:* The Manse of Crathie, By Ballater, Aberdeenshire. *T:* Crathie 208. *Club:* Conservative (Edinburgh).

**BUFFET, Bernard;** artist, painter; *b* Paris, 10 July 1928; *m* 1958, Annabel May Schwob de Lure; two *d*. Début at Salon des Moins de Trente Ans, 1944. From 1948 has had one-man shows, annually, at Drouant-David and Visconti Galleries. Grand Prix de la Critique, 1948. Solo retrospective exhibition of his works was held at Charpentier Gallery, Paris, 1958. He has exhibited, oils, water colours and drawings and is a lithographer, mural painter and illustrator of books. Work represented in permanent collections: Musée du Petit Palais and Musée National d'Art Moderne, in Paris. Work was shown at Venice Biennale, 1956. Exhibitions: Lefevre Gallery, London, 1961, 1963, 1965. Mem. Salon d'Automne and Salon des Indépendants. *Address:* 11 Boulevard de La Tour, Maubourg, Paris 7e; Château de la Vallée, Saint Cast, Côtes du Nord, France.

**BUFFEY, Brig. William,** DSO 1940; TD 1940; DL Co. London, 1954; *b* 24 Sept. 1899; *s* of late William Buffey, Bromley, Kent; *m* 1926, Dorothy Wensley, *d* of late William Rogers, Nelson, New Zealand; two *d*. *Educ:* St Dunstan's College, Catford. Served War of 1939-45, Cmd 91st Fd Regt RA, France, Belgium (DSO), India, Persia, 1939-43; CRA 5 Div. Middle East, Italy, BLA, 1943-45 (despatches thrice); Hon. Col 291st Airborne Fd Regt RA (TA), 1946-55. Governor, St Dunstan's College. *Recreation:* golf. *Address:* Jenners, Groombridge, Tunbridge Wells, Kent. *T:* Groombridge 309.

**BUFTON, Air Vice-Marshal Sydney Osborne,** CB 1945; DFC 1940; Director: Radionic Products Ltd; Stewart Aeronautical Supply Co. Ltd; *b* 12 Jan. 1908; 2nd *s* of late J. O. Bufton, JP, Llandrindod Wells, Radnor; *m* 1943, Susan Maureen, *d* of Colonel E. M. Browne, DSO, Chelsea; two *d*. *Educ:* Dean Close School, Cheltenham. Commissioned RAF 1927; psa, 1939; idc, 1946. Served War of 1939-45, Bomber Comd, Nos 10 and 76 Sqdns, RAF Station, Pocklington, 1940-41; Dep. Dir Bomber Ops, 1941-43; Dir of Bomber Ops, Air Min., 1943-45; AOC Egypt, 1945-46; Central Bomber Establishment, RAF, Marham, Norfolk, 1947-48; Dep. Chief of Staff (Ops/Plans), Air Forces Western Europe,

1948-51; Dir of Weapons, Air Min., 1951-52; AOA Bomber Command, 1952-53; AOC Brit. Forces, Aden, 1953-55; Senior Air Staff Officer, Bomber Comd, 1955-58; Assistant Chief of Air Staff (Intelligence), 1958-61; retired Oct. 1961. Temp. Gp Capt. 1941; Temp. Air Cdre 1943; Subst. Gp Capt. 1946; Air Cdre 1948; Actg Air Vice-Marshal, 1952; Air Vice-Marshal, 1953. High Sheriff of Radnorshire, 1967. Comdr Legion of Merit (US); Comdr Order of Orange Nassau (with swords), Netherlands. *Recreations:* hockey (Welsh International 1931-37, Combined Services, RAF), golf, squash. *Address:* Norfolk Lodge, London Road, Reigate. *T:* Reigate 43707. *Club:* Royal Air Force.

**BUHLER, Robert,** RA 1956 (ARA 1947); NEAC; painter in oil; Staff Fellow, Royal College of Art; *b* London, 23 Nov. 1916; *s* of Robert Buhler, Journalist; *m* Evelyn Rowell (marriage dissolved, 1951); one *s*; *m* 1962, Prudence Brochocka; two *s*. (one step *d*). *Educ:* Bolt Court; St Martin's School of Art; Royal College of Art. Has exhibited at: Royal Academy, New English Art Club, London Group, London galleries. Work in permanent collections: Stott Bequest; Chantrey Bequest; provincial art galleries. *Address:* Moat House, Hethel, Norwich.

**BUIST, Comdr Colin,** CVO 1961 (MVO 1927); RN (Retired); Extra Equerry to the Queen since 1952 (to King George VI, 1937-52); Chairman Coalite and Chemical Products Ltd; Director: Imperial Continental Gas Association; Phœnix Assurance Co. Ltd; *b* 10 April 1896; *s* of Col Frederick Braid Buist; *m* 1928, Gladys Mary, 4th *d* of late Sir William Nelson, Bt. *Educ:* RN Colleges, Osborne and Dartmouth. Served European War, 1914-18; also 1939-44. *Address:* 9 Cumberland Mansions, George Street, W1. *T:* 01-723 2890; Highmoor Farm, Henley-on-Thames. *T:* Nettlebed 275. *Club:* White's.

**BÜLBRING, Edith,** MA Oxon; MD Bonn; FRS 1958; Professor of Pharmacology, Oxford University, since 1967 (University Reader, 1960-67); *b* 27 Dec. 1903; *d* of Karl Daniel Bülbring, Professor of English, Bonn University, and Hortense Leonore Bülbring (*née* Kann). *Educ:* Bonn, Munich and Freiburg Universities. Postgraduate work in Pharmacology Department of Berlin University, 1929-31; Pediatrics, University of Jena, 1932; Virchow Krankenhaus University of Berlin, 1933; Pharmacological Laboratory of Pharmaceutical Society of Great Britain, University of London, 1933-38; Pharmacological Dept, University of Oxford, 1938-. Research work on: Autonomic transmitters, suprarenals, smooth muscle, peristalsis. Hon. Mem. Pharmaceutical Soc., Torino, Italy, 1957. *Publications:* Mainly in Jl of Physiology and Brit. Jl of Pharmacology. *Recreation:* music. *Address:* 15 Northmoor Road, Oxford. *T:* Oxford 57270; Lady Margaret Hall, Oxford.

**BULGANIN, Marshal Nikolai Alexandrovich;** Hero of Socialist Labour; 2 Orders of Lenin, Order of Red Banner, Order of Suvorov (1st and 2nd class), 2 Orders of Kutuzov, 2 Orders of Red Star; Chairman of the State Bank, USSR, 1958; Chairman, Stavropol Economic Region, 1958-62; *b* Nizhne-Novgorod, 1895. *Educ:* at technical secondary school, Nizhne-Novgorod. Joined Communist Party, 1917; worked in Cheka, 1918-22; held responsible posts in Supreme Economic Council, 1922-27; director Moscow Electrical Works, 1927-30; Chm. Moscow City Soviet, 1931-37; Chm. Council of People's Commissars of RSFSR, 1937-38; Dep. Chm. Council of People's Commissars of USSR, 1938-41; head of board of USSR State Bank, 1938-41; Mem. Military Council, various fronts, 1941-44; Mem. State Cttee of Defence, 1944-45; Dep. People's Commissar of Defence of USSR, 1944-47; Minister of Defence of USSR, 1947-49 and 1953-55; Dep. Chm. USSR Council of Ministers, 1947-49; 1st Dep. Chm. USSR Council of Ministers, 1949-55; Chm. of Council of Ministers of USSR, 1955-58; Mem. Central Cttee, USSR Communist Party, 1934; Mem. Politburo, 1948-52; Mem. Praesidium Central Cttee, Communist Party, 1952; Dep. to Supreme Soviet of USSR, 1937. Marshal of the Soviet Union, 1947. *Address:* c/o Ministry of Social Security of the RSFSR, 14 Shabolovka, Moscow, USSR.

**BULGER, Anthony Clare,** BA, BCL; **His Honour Judge Bulger;** County Court Judge, 1963; Chairman, Gloucestershire Quarter Sessions, since 1970; *b* 1912; *s* of Daniel Bulger; *m* Una Patricia Banks; one *s* one *d*. *Educ:* Rugby; Oriel Coll., Oxford. Called to the Bar, Inner Temple, 1936. Oxford Circuit; Deputy Chairman: Glos QS, 1958-70; Worcs QS, 1962-. Recorder of Abingdon, 1962-63. *Address:* Forthampton, Glos; 1 Dr Johnston's Buildings, Temple, EC4.

**BULKELEY, George Vicary Owen,** CBE 1932; MIMechE; *b* 22 Aug. 1882; *s* of Rev. Owen Tudor Bulkeley, AKC; *m* 1912, Joan Margaret Walker, of Victoria, BC; one *s* one *d*. *Educ:* Victoria Coll., Jersey; Manchester Univ. Served training in Locomotive Department of Great Western Railway of England; Outdoor Engineer to F. W. Horne & Co., Japan and China, 1905-08; on staff of Supt of Motive Power, Canadian Pacific Railway, 1908-10; Marine Engineering in Vancouver and Victoria, BC, 1911-15; Repairs to Army Service Corps lorries, in charge of GWR road motor services and Consultant to Fishery Motor Loan Committee, during War of 1914-18; on Personal staff of Gen. Manager GWR and of Chief Docks Manager GWR, 1918-22; Port Traffic Supt GWR Swansea, 1922-25; Port Manager, Kenya and Uganda Railways and Harbours, 1925-32; General Manager, Nigerian Railways, 1932-36; Director of Transport, Nigeria, and MEC, 1936-39; retired 1939. Temporarily on staff of Mechanical Engineer, SA Railway, Durban, War of 1939-45. *Publications:* Mechanical Appliances for Handling Railway Traffic, 1921; Railway and Seaport Freight Movement, 1930; Transport Administration in Tropical Dependencies, 1947. *Address:* Sydenham Hotel, Randles Road, Durban, Natal, South Africa.

**BULKELEY, Sir Richard H. D. W.;** *see* Williams-Bulkeley.

**BULL, Amy Frances,** CBE 1964; Head Mistress, Wallington County Grammar School for Girls, 1937-64, retired; *b* 27 April 1902; *d* of Herbert Bull, Head Master of Pinewood Preparatory Sch., Farnborough, until 1919, and Ethel Mary Atkinson. *Educ:* Roedean Sch.; Somerville Coll., Oxford. Asst Mistress, Cheltenham Ladies' Coll., 1925-32; Head of History Dept, Portsmouth Northern Secondary Sch., 1932-37; Pres. Head Mistresses' Assoc., 1960-62; Member: National Youth Employment Council, 1959-68; Secondary School Examination Council, 1960-64; Exec. Cttee Central Council for Physical Recreation, 1963-; Fountain and Carshalton Gp Management Cttee, 1964-; Sutton Borough Education Cttee, 1966-; St Helier Hosp. House Cttee; Women's Nat. Commn, 1969. *Recreations:* gardening, walking in mountains, watching games. *Address:*

Firtree Lodge, 16 Broomfield Park, Westcott, Dorking, Surrey. *Clubs:* University Women's, English-Speaking Union.

**BULL, Anthony,** CBE 1968 (OBE 1944); Vice-Chairman, London Transport Executive (formerly London Transport Board), since 1965; *b* 18 July 1908; 3rd *s* of Rt Hon. Sir William Bull, 1st Bt, PC, MP, JP, FSA (*d* 1931), and late Lilian, 2nd *d* of G. S. Brandon, Oakbrook, Ravenscourt Park; *m* 1946, Barbara (*d* 1947), *er d* of late Peter Donovan, Yonder, Rye, Sussex; one *d*. *Educ:* Gresham's Sch., Holt; Magdalene Coll., Cambridge (Exhibitioner; MA). Joined Underground Group of Cos, 1929; served in Staff, Publicity and Public Relations Depts and Chairman's Office. Sec. to Vice-Chm. London Passenger Transport Board, 1936-39. Served War, 1939-45; RE; Transportation Br., War Office, 1939-42; GHQ, Middle East, 1943; Staff of Supreme Allied Comdr, SE Asia (end of 1943); Col. 1944; Transp. Div., CCG, 1945-46. Returned to London Transport as Chief Staff and Welfare Officer, 1946; Member: London Transport Executive, 1955-62; London Transport Board, 1962. Inst. of Transport: served on Council, 1956-59; Vice-Pres., 1964-66; Hon. Librarian, 1966-69; Pres., 1969-70. Mem. Regional Advisory Council for Technological Educ., 1958-62 (Transp. Adv. Cttee, 1950-62; Chm. Cttee, 1953-62). CStJ 1969. Bronze Star (USA), 1946; *Publications:* contrib. to Transport journals. *Recreation:* travel. *Address:* 27 Pelham Place, SW7. *T:* 01-589 1511. *Club:* United University.
*See also Sir George Bull, Bt.*

**BULL, Sir George,** 3rd Bt, *cr* 1922; of Hammersmith; Senior Partner of Bull & Bull, Solicitors, 11 Stone Buildings, Lincoln's Inn; *b* 19 June 1906; 2nd *s* of Rt Hon. Sir William Bull, 1st Bt, and late Lilian, 2nd *d* of G. S. Brandon, Oakbrook, Ravenscourt Park, and Heene, Worthing, Sussex; *S* brother 1942; *m* 1933, Gabrielle, 2nd *d* of late Bramwell Jackson, MC, Bury St Edmunds; one *s* one *d*. *Educ:* RN Colleges, Osborne and Dartmouth; Paris; Vienna. Admitted Solicitor, 1929. Served War of 1939-45 in RNVR; Comdr, 1942. governor: Godolphin and Latymer Sch.; Latymer Foundation; Trustee Hammersmith United Charities; Chm., London Rent Assessment Cttees; Member, Hammersmith Borough Council, 1968; Liveryman Fishmongers' Company; Freeman of City of London; Hon. Solicitor, Royal Society of St George, Royal Life Saving Society. *Recreations:* sailing, travelling. *Heir:* *s* Simeon George Bull [*b* 1 Aug. 1934; *m* 1961, Annick, *y d* of late Louis Bresson and of Mme Bresson, Chandai, France; one *s* one *d*]. *Address:* 3 Hammersmith Terrace, W6. *T:* 01-748 2400; 11 Stone Buildings, Lincoln's Inn. *T:* 01-405 7474. *Clubs:* Carlton, MCC.
*See also A. Bull.*

**BULL, George Lucien,** CBE 1920; Officier de la Légion d'Honneur; Hon. director of the Marey Institute, Paris; *b* Dublin, 5 Jan. 1876; *s* of C. Bull, Bedford, and G. Jouve, Paris; unmarried. *Educ:* Belvedere Coll., Dublin; Faculté des Sciences, Paris Univ. Graduated in Paris Univ. (Zoology, Botany, Geology); retired. Work, principally technical research for new methods of investigation of phenomena in Natural Science, high speed cinematography, sound registering, optical illusions, etc. *Publications:* Various communications to the French Academy of Science and other scientific Societies. *Address:* 14 Rue du Général Delestraint, Paris, 16e. *T:* Jasmin 08.62.

**BULL, Prof. Graham MacGregor;** Director, Medical Research Council, Clinical Research Centre, since 1966; *b* 30 Jan. 1918; *s* of Dr A. B. Bull; *m* 1947, Megan Patricia Jones; three *s* one *d*. *Educ:* Diocesan Coll., Cape Town; Univ. of Cape Town (MD). FRCP. Tutor in Medicine and Asst, Dept of Medicine, Univ. of Cape Town, 1940-46; Lecturer in medicine, Postgraduate Medical Sch. of London, 1947-52; Professor of Medicine, The Queen's Univ., Belfast, 1952-66. Research Fellow, SA Council for Scientific and Industrial Research, 1947; Member, Medical Research Council, 1962-66. Visiting Professor, Middlesex Hosp. Medical Sch., 1966-. *Publications:* contrib. to medical journals. *Address:* Medical Research Council, Clinical Research Centre, Watford Road, Harrow, Mddx HA1 3UJ. *T:* 01-864 5311.

**BULL, James William Douglas,** MA, MD, FRCP, FFR; Consultant radiologist (diagnostic): National Hospital for Nervous Diseases, Queen Square; Maida Vale Hospital for Nervous Diseases; St Andrew's Hospital, Northampton; Honorary Consultant Radiologist, St George's Hospital; Hon. Radiologist, University Hospital, West Indies; Teacher, Institute of Neurology (University of London); Consultant Adviser in Diagnostic Radiology, Department of Health and Social Security; Consultant Neuroradiologist to Royal Navy; *b* 23 March 1911; *o s* of late D. W. A. Bull, MD, JP, Stony Stratford, Bucks; *m* 1941, Edith, *e d* of late Charles Burch, Henley-on-Thames; one *s* one *d*. *Educ:* Repton; Gonville and Caius Coll., Cambridge; St George's Hospital. Entrance schol., 1932. Usual house appts; Asst Curator of Museum, Med. registrar, St George's Hospital, Rockefeller Travelling Schol. (Stockholm), 1938-39. Served War, 1940-46, Temp. Major RAMC (pow Singapore). Dean, Inst. of Neurology, Univ. of London, 1962-68. President: 4th Internat. Symposium Neuroradiologicum, London, 1955; British Inst. of Radiology, 1960; Section of Radiology, RSM, 1968-69; Vice-Pres. Faculty of Radiologists, 1963. Member Assoc. of British Neurologists; Examiner in Diagnostic Radiology: Conjoint Board, 1957; Univ. of Liverpool, 1959; for Fellowship, Faculty of Radiologists, London, 1965. Watson Smith Lecturer, RCP, 1962; Skinner Lecturer, Faculty of Radiologists, 1965; Dyke Memorial Lectr, Columbia Univ., New York, 1969. Member: Council, RCP London, 1964-67; Council, RCS, 1968-. FRSM; Hon. Fellow: American Coll. of Radiologists; Italian Neuroradiological Soc.; Brazilian Radiological Soc. Hon. Mem., Canadian Neurological Soc. *Publications:* Atlas of Positive Contrast Myelography (jointly), 1962. Contrib. to A. Feiling's Modern Trends in Neurology; various papers in medical journals, mostly connected with neuroradiology. *Recreations:* golf, travel. *Address:* 20 Devonshire Place, W1. *T:* 01-935 4444. *Club:* United University.

**BULLARD, Major-General Colin,** CB 1952; CBE 1943; *b* 23 Feb. 1900; *s* of late Canon J. V. Bullard, MA; *m* 1932, Evelyn May Spencer; one *s*. *Educ:* Sedbergh; Ellesmere; Richmond, Yorks; Univ. of Liverpool (BEng). Engineer; apprenticeship, Cammell Laird, Birkenhead. RAOC and REME, 1925-53; retired, 1953. Principal, Royal Technical Coll. of East Africa, 1953-57. ADC to the King during 1950; Maj.-Gen., 1950. CEng; FIMechE; FIEE. *Address:* Went House, East Dean, near Eastbourne, Sussex. *T:* East Dean 3366.

**BULLARD, Denys Gradwell;** *b* 15 Aug. 1912. *Educ:* Wisbech Grammar Sch.; Cambridge Univ. Farmer. Broadcaster on agricultural matters both at home and overseas. MP (C) SW Div. of Norfolk, 1951-55; MP (C) King's Lynn, 1959-64. PPS to Financial Sec.,

Treasury, 1955. *Address:* Elm House, Elm, Wisbech, Cambs. *T:* Wisbech 21. *Club:* Farmers'.

**BULLARD, Sir Edward (Crisp),** Kt 1953; FRS 1941; MA, PhD, ScD; Professor of Geophysics, since 1964, and Fellow of Churchill College, Cambridge, since 1960; Director, IBM United Kingdom; *b* 21 Sept. 1907; *s* of Edward John Bullard and Eleanor Howes Crisp; *m* Margaret Ellen Thomas; four *d. Educ:* Repton; Clare Coll., Cambridge. Research in Physics, 1929-31; Geophysics, 1931-; Demonstrator in Geodesy at Cambridge Univ., 1931-35; Smithson Research Fellow of Royal Society, 1936-43; Experimental Officer HMS Vernon and Admiralty, 1939-45; Asst Dir of Naval Operational Research, 1944-45; Fellow of Clare, 1943-48 and 1956-60; Reader in Experimental Geophysics at Cambridge Univ., 1945-48; Prof. of Physics at Univ. of Toronto, 1948-49; Director National Physical Laboratory, 1950-55; Fellow of Caius Coll., Cambridge, 1956; Asst Dir of Research, Cambridge Univ., 1956-60; Reader in Geophysics, 1960-64. Foreign Corresp. Geol. Soc. Amer., 1952; Foreign Hon. Mem. Amer. Acad. Arts and Sci., 1954; Foreign Assoc. US Nat. Acad. Sci., 1959; Foreign Mem., Amer. Philos. Soc. Segdwick Prize, 1936; Hughes Medal of Royal Soc., 1953; Chree Medal of Physics Soc., 1956; Day Medal of Geol. Soc. Amer., 1959; Gold Medal, Royal Astronomical Soc., 1965; Agassiz Medal, US Nat. Acad. of Sci., 1965; Wollaston Medal of Geol. Soc. of London, 1967; Bakerian Lecturer of the Royal Society, 1967; Vetlesen Prize, 1968. *Publications:* scientific papers. *Address:* Department of Geodesy and Geophysics, Madingley Road, Cambridge. *T:* Cambridge 51686. *Club:* Athenæum.

**BULLARD, Giles Lionel;** Counsellor and Head of Chancery, UK High Commission, Rawalpindi/Islamabad, since 1969; *b* 24 Aug. 1926; 2nd *s* of Sir Reader Bullard, *qv*; *m* 1952, Hilary Chadwick Brooks; two *s* two *d. Educ:* Blundell's Sch.; Balliol Coll., Oxford. Served with Coldstream Guards and Royal Norfolk Regt, W Africa, 1944-48; Oxford Univ., 1948-51 (2nd cl. hons Modern History, Capt. OURFC); H. Clarkson & Co. Ltd, Shipping and Insurance Brokers, 1952-55; HM Foreign (later Diplomatic) Service, 1955; 3rd Sec., Bucharest, 1957; 2nd Sec., Brussels, 1958; 1st Sec., Head of Chancery and Consul, Panama City, 1960; FO, 1964; DSAO, 1965; 1st Sec. and Head of Chancery, Bangkok, 1967. *Address:* The Manor House, West Hendred, Wantage, Berks. *T:* East Hendred 373.
*See also J. L. Bullard.*

**BULLARD, Julian Leonard;** HM Political Agent, Dubai, since 1968; *b* 8 March 1928; *s* of Sir Reader Bullard, *qv*; *m* 1954, Margaret Stephens; two *s* two *d. Educ:* Rugby; Magdalen Coll., Oxford. Fellow of All Souls Coll., Oxford, 1950-57; Army, 1950-52; HM Diplomatic Service, 1953-: served at: FO, 1953-54; Vienna; 1954-56; Amman, 1956-59; FO, 1960-63; Bonn, 1963-66; Moscow, 1966-68. *Address:* 22 Crooms Hill, Greenwich, SE10. *T:* 01-858 3510.
*See also G. L. Bullard.*

**BULLARD, Sir Reader (William),** KCB, *cr* 1944; KCMG *cr* 1936 (CMG 1933); CIE 1916; *b* 5 Dec. 1885; *s* of late Charles Bullard and Mary Bullard, of Walthamstow; *m* 1921, Miriam, 4th *d* of late Arthur Lionel Smith, Master of Balliol Coll., Oxford; four *s* one *d.* Acting Vice-Consul, Beirout, 1909-10; Vice-Consul, Bitlis, 1910-11; 3rd Dragoman, 1911-13; Acting Consul, Trebizond, 1912; Acting Consul, Erzerum, 1913; Acting Consul, Basra, 1914; Civil Adviser to Principal Military Governor, Basra, 1914; Political Officer, Kifri, 1918; Dep. Revenue Sec., Mesopotamia, 1919; Military Governor, Baghdad, 1920; Middle East Dept, Colonial Office, 1921; HBM Agent and Consul, Jedda, 1923-25; Consul at Athens, 1925-28; Consul, Addis Ababa, 1928; Consul-General, Moscow, 1930; Leningrad, 1931-34; Rabat, 1934; Minister, Jedda, 1936-39; Minister (later Ambassador), Tehran, 1939-46; retired, 1946. Director of the Institute of Colonial Studies, Oxford, 1951-56; Member of Governing Body of the School of Oriental and African Studies, Univ. of London, 1953-65. Hon. Fellow: Queens' Coll., Cambridge; Sch. of Oriental and African Studies, Univ. of London. Sir Percy Sykes Memorial Medal, 1962. *Publications:* Britain and the Middle East, 1964; The Camels Must Go (Autobiog.), 1961. *Address:* 46 Plantation Road, Oxford. *T:* Oxford 59259. *Club:* Athenæum.
*See also G. L. Bullard, J. L. Bullard.*

**BULLEN, Keith Edward,** FRS 1949; PhD, ScD; Professor of Applied Mathematics, University of Sydney, since 1946; *b* Auckland, NZ, 29 June 1906; *s* of George S. and Maud H. Bullen; *m* 1935, Florence Mary Pressley, MA, Auckland, NZ; one *s* one *d. Educ:* Auckland Grammar Sch. and Auckland Univ. Coll., NZ; St John's Coll., Cambridge, England. MA 1928, BSc 1930 New Zealand; MA 1945 Melbourne; PhD, ScD 1946 Cambridge; Hon. DSc, Univ. of Auckland, 1963. Premium in pure mathematics, Auckland Univ. Coll., 1923; Senior Scholar in Mathematics, Univ. of NZ, 1925; Strathcona exhibition, St John's Coll., Cambridge, 1932-33. Elected Correspondent of Geol. Soc. of Amer., 1959, Hon. Fellow, 1963; For. Mem. Amer. Acad. of Arts and Sci., 1960; For. Assoc. US Nat. Acad. of Sci., 1961; Fellow Amer. Geophys Union, 1962; Hon. Fellow, Royal Soc. of NZ, 1963; For. and Commonwealth Mem., Geol. Soc. of London, 1967; Pontifical Academician, 1968. Master, Auckland Grammar Sch., New Zealand, 1926-27; Lectr in Mathematics, Auckland Univ. Coll., 1928-31 and 1934-40; Special Lectureship, Hull Univ. Coll., England, 1933; Senior Lecturer in mathematics, Univ. of Melbourne, 1940-45. President Internat. Assoc. of Seismology and Physics of Interior of Earth, 1954-57; Council Member, Australian Acad. of Science, 1955-57; Chm. Australian Nat. Cttee. for Internat. Geophysical Year, 1955-60; Vice-Pres., Scientific Cttee (of Internat. Council of Scientific Unions) on Antarctic Research, 1958-62; Vice-Pres. Internat. Union of Geodesy and Geophys, 1963-67. Lyle Medallist, Aust., 1949; Hector Medallist, NZ, 1952; Walter Burfitt Prize, Royal Soc. of NSW, 1953; Bicentennial Medal, Columbia Univ., NY 1954; William Bowie Medal, Amer. Geophys. Union, 1961; Day Medal, Geol. Soc. of America, 1963; Research Medal, Royal Soc. of Vic., 1965; Flinders Lectr and Medallist, Australian Acad. of Sci., 1969. *Publications:* Introduction to the Theory of Seismology, Cambridge, 1947 (3rd edn, 1963); Introduction to the Theory of Mechanics, Sydney, 1949 (7th edn, 1965); Seismology, 1954; papers in scientific journals. *Recreation:* numismatics. *Address:* 132 Fuller's Road, Chatswood, NSW 2067, Australia. *T:* Sydney; 41 7649.

**BULLER;** *see* Manningham-Buller, and Yarde-Buller.

**BULLEY, Rt. Rev. Sydney Cyril;** *see* Carlisle, Bishop of.

**BULLOCK, Alan Louis Charles,** FBA 1967; Vice-Chancellor, Oxford University, since Oct.

1969; Master of St Catherine's College, Oxford, since 1960; *b* 13 Dec. 1914; *s* of Frank Allen Bullock; *m* 1940, Hilda Yates, *d* of Edwin Handy, Bradford; three *s* one *d* (and one *d* decd). *Educ:* Bradford Grammar Sch.; Wadham Coll., Oxford (Scholar). MA; 1st Class Lit Hum, 1936; 1st Class, Modern Hist., 1938. DLitt Oxon, 1969. Fellow, Dean and Tutor in Modern Hist., New Coll., 1945-52; Censor of St Catherine's Society, Oxford, 1952-62; Chairman: Research Cttee of RIIA; Nat. Advisory Council on the Training and Supply of Teachers, 1963-65; Schools Council, 1966-69; Member: Arts Council of Great Britain, 1961-64; Social Science Research Council, 1966; Advisory Council on Public Records, 1965-. Raleigh Lectr, British Acad., 1967. Hon. Fellow: Merton Coll.; Wadham Coll; Linacre Coll. Hon. Dr Univ. Aix-Marseilles; Hon. DLitt: Bradford; Reading. Chevalier Légion d'Honneur, 1970. *Publications:* Hitler, A Study in Tyranny, 1952 (rev. edn 1964); The Liberal Tradition, 1956; The Life and Times of Ernest Bevin, Vol. I, 1960, Vol. II, 1967. Gen. Editor (with F. W. Deakin) of The Oxford History of Modern Europe. *Address:* Master's Lodgings, St Catherine's College, Oxford. *T:* Oxford 49541.

**BULLOCK, Sir Christopher (Llewellyn),** KCB 1932 (CB 1929); CBE 1926 (OBE 1919); MA; *b* 10 Nov. 1891; 2nd *s* of Rev. Ll. C. W. Bullock, Rector of Great and Little Wigborough, Essex; *m* 1917, Barbara May, *d* of Henry Lupton, Torquay; two *s*. *Educ:* Rugby (Captain of Running Eight); Trinity Coll., Cambridge (Scholar). Abbott and Porson Univ. Scholarships; Charles Oldham Shakespeare Scholarship; Whewell Scholarship in International Law (re-elected, 1921); member's Latin Essay prize; Browne Medals for Latin Ode (twice) and Greek Epigram, etc.; BA 1913; MA 1919; 1st Division 1st Class Classical Tripos; took first place in the open competitive examination for the Home and Indian Civil Services, 1914; selected the ICS and appointed as a probationer to the United Provinces, 1915; Principal, Air Ministry, 1920; late Captain The Rifle Brigade (Special Reserve), and Major, Royal Air Force; served European War, 1915-19 (with 1st Battalion Rifle Brigade in France, 1915; seconded to Royal Flying Corps Oct. 1915, first as Observer and subsequently as Pilot; with RFC in Egypt, 1916; on Air Staff at Air Ministry, 1917-18; (wounded, despatches, OBE); Principal Private Sec. to the Rt Hon. Winston Churchill as Secretary of State for Air, 1919; served in same capacity 1923-30 with successive Secretaries of State, the Rt Hon. Sir Samuel Hoare and the Rt Hon. Lord Thomson, whom he accompanied on tours of inspection by air in Egypt, Palestine, Transjordania and Iraq in 1924 and 1925, to India in 1927, and to the Sudan in 1929; Asst Secretary, Air Ministry, 1929-30; Permanent Secretary, Air Ministry and Member of Air Council, 1931-36; was in 1935 deputed by HM Government to negotiate with the Union of South Africa and other African administrations in connection with the Empire Air Mail Scheme. Subsequently Director, Eagle Star Insurance Co., British Metal Corp., Strong & Co. of Romsey, and other public cos, and Chairman, Beralt Tin & Wolfram, Cox & Wyman, James Norris (Burslem), etc; now retired. *Publication:* The Law of Angary in British Year Book of International Law, 1922. *Recreations:* books, bird-watching, fly-fishing. *Address:* Flat 16, 39 Hyde Park Gate, SW7. *T:* 01-584 6961. *Club:* Oxford and Cambridge.
*See also R. H. W. Bullock.*

**BULLOCK, Sir Ernest,** Kt 1951; CVO 1937; MusD (Dunelm); Hon. LLD (Glasgow, 1955); FRCM; FRCO; Hon. RAM; Director of the Royal College of Music, 1953-60; *b* 15 Sept. 1890; *y s* of late Thos Bullock, Wigan, Lancs; *m* 1919, Margery, *d* of late George H. Newborn, Epworth, Lincolnshire; two *s* one *d*. *Educ:* Wigan Grammar Sch.; privately; musically under Sir E. C. Bairstow, MusD, at Leeds Parish Church; Asst Organist, Leeds Parish Church, and Organist of St Mary, Micklefield and Adel Church, 1906-12; Sub-organist of Manchester Cathedral, 1912-15; served in HM Forces as Captain and Adjutant, 1915-19; Organist of St Michael's Coll., Tenbury, 1919; of Exeter Cathedral, 1919-28; of Westminster Abbey, 1928-41. Joint Musical Director and Conductor of the Coronation Service, 1937. Professor of Music, Glasgow Univ. and Principal Royal Scottish Academy of Music, Glasgow, 1941-52. Pres. Incorporated Assoc. of Organists, 1946-48; Pres. Incorporated Soc. of Musicians, 1947; Pres. Royal Coll. of Organists, 1951-52; Pres. Union of Graduates in Music, 1947-48. *Publications:* Church and organ music, songs, part-songs, etc. *Address:* Welby Cottage, Long Crendon, Aylesbury, Bucks.

**BULLOCK, Hugh,** KBE Hon., 1957 (OBE Hon., 1946); FRSA 1958; Chairman and Chief Executive Officer, Calvin Bullock Ltd, *b* 2 June 1898; *s* of Calvin Bullock and Alice Katherine (*née* Mallory); *m* 1933, Marie Leontine Graves; two *d*. *Educ:* Hotchkiss Sch.; Williams Coll. (BA). Investment banker since 1921; President and Director: Calvin Bullock, Ltd, 1944-66; Bullock Fund, Ltd; Canadian Fund, Inc.; Canadian Investment Fund, Ltd; Dividend Shares, Inc.; Chairman and Director: Carriers & General Corp.; Nation-Wide Securities Co.; US Electric Light & Power Shares, Inc. Civilian Aide to Sec. of the Army, for First Army Area, United States, 1952-53 (US Army Certificate of Appreciation). Trustee: Roosevelt Hospital; Estate and Property of Diocesan Convention of New York; Williams Coll., 1960-68. President: Pilgrims of US; Calvin Bullock Forum. Member Exec. Cttee, Marshall Scholarship Regional Cttee, 1955-58. Member: Amer. Legion; Academy of Political Science; Amer. Museum of Nat. History; Acad. of Amer. Poets (Dir.); Assoc. Ex-mems Squadron A (Gov. 1945-50); Council on Foreign Relations; Ends of the Earth; English-Speaking Union; Foreign Policy Assoc.; Investment Bankers Assoc. of Amer. (Gov. 1953-55); New England Soc.; Nat. Inst. of Social Sciences (Pres. 1950-53); Newcomen Soc.; St George's Soc. Hon. LLD; Hamilton Coll., 1954; Williams Coll., 1957. 2nd Lieut Infantry, European War, 1914-18; Lieut-Col, War of 1939-45 (US Army Commendation Ribbon). Exceptional Service Award, Dept of Air Force, 1961, etc. Assoc. KStJ 1961, and Vice-Pres. Amer. Society. Knight Comdr, Royal Order of George I (Greece), 1964. Is an Episcopalian. *Publication:* The Story of Investment Companies, 1959. *Address:* (office) 1 Wall Street, New York 5. *T:* Bowling Green 9-8800; (home) 1030 Fifth Avenue, New York 28. *T:* Trafalgar 9-5858. *Clubs:* White's (London); Bond, Century, Racquet and Tennis, Recess, River, Union, Williams, Church, New York Yacht (New York); Denver County (Denver, Colo.); Chevy Chase, Metropolitan (Washington); Edgartown Yacht (Mass); West Side Tennis (Forest Hills, NY); Mount Royal (Montreal).

**BULLOCK, Prof. Kenneth,** PhD, MSc, FRIC, MChemA, FPS; Professor of Pharmacy, Manchester University, 1955-70; *b* 27 Dec. 1901; *s* of late James William Bullock, Wigan, Lancashire; *m* 1926, Winifred Mary, *d* of late Rev. F. Ives Cater. *Educ:* Wigan Grammar

Sch.; Manchester Univ. Research and Technical Chemist, 1925-32; joined teaching staff of Pharmacy Dept, Manchester Univ., 1932; Lecturer, 1937; Senior Lecturer, 1946; Reader, 1950. Chairman, British Pharmaceutical Conf., 1956. Formerly Examiner for Univs of Dublin, London, Nottingham, and Manchester and for Pharmaceutical Society of Ireland. *Publications:* original contributions to science, mainly in Journal of Pharmacy and Pharmacology. *Recreations:* gardening and swimming. *Address:* 39 Knutsford Road, Wilmslow, Cheshire SK9 6JB. *T:* Wilmslow 22892.

**BULLOCK, Richard Henry Watson;** Deputy Secretary, Ministry of Technology, since 1970; *b* 12 Nov. 1920; *er s* of Sir Christopher Bullock, *qv*; *m* 1946, Beryl Haddan, *o d* of late Haddan J. Markes, formerly Malay Civil Service; one *s* one *d*. *Educ:* Rugby Sch. (Scholar); Trinity Coll., Cambridge (Scholar). Joined 102 OCTU (Westminster Dragoons), Nov. 1940; Commnd Westminster Dragoons, (2nd County of London Yeo.), 1941; served in England, NW Europe (D-day), Italy, Germany, 1941-45; Instructor, Armoured Corps Officers' Training Sch., India, 1945-46; demobilized 1947, rank of Major. Established in Home Civil Service by Reconstruction Competition; joined Min. of Supply as Asst Principal, 1947; Principal, 1949; Asst Sec., 1956; on loan to War Office, 1960-61; Ministry of Aviation, 1961-64; Under-Secretary, 1963; Min. of Technology, 1964; Head of Space Div., Min. of Technology, 1969-70. *Recreations:* squash, fly-fishing, hockey (Pres. Dulwich Hockey Club, 1962-; Civil Service Hockey Cttee), watching cricket. *Address:* 11 Tregunter Road, SW10. *T:* 01-373 4670. *Clubs:* MCC, Hurlingham; Union (Cambridge).

**BULLOCK-MARSHAM, Brigadier F. W.;** *see* Marsham.

**BULLOUGH, Geoffrey,** MA, FBA 1966; Emeritus Professor, University of London; *b* 27 Jan. 1901; *s* of James Arthur Bullough and Elizabeth Ford; *m* 1928, Doris Margaret Wall; one *s* one *d*. *Educ:* Stand Grammar Sch., Whitefield; Manchester Univ. BA 1922, MA 1923 (Vict.), Teachers' Diploma 1923, Gissing Prize 1921, Withers Prize in Education 1923, John Bright Fellowship in English Literature, 1923-24; studied in Italy. Master, Grammar Sch. of Queen Elizabeth in Tamworth, 1924-26; Asst Lecturer in English Literature, Manchester Univ., 1926-29; Lecturer, Edinburgh Univ., 1929-33; Professor of English Literature, Univ. of Sheffield, 1933-46; Professor of English Language and Literature, KCL, 1946-48. Vice-Chm., Sheffield Repertory Co., 1938-46; Governor of Chelsea Coll. of Science and Technology, 1952-68. FKC 1964. Hon. LittD Manchester, 1969. *Publications:* Philosophical Poems of Henry More, 1931; The Oxford Book of Seventeenth-Century Verse (with Sir H. J. C. Grierson), 1934; The Trend of Modern Poetry, 1934 (revised, 1949); Poems and Dramas of Fulke Greville, 1939; ed (with C. L. Wrenn) English Studies Today, 1951; ed Essays and Studies, 1953; Narrative and Dramatic Sources of Shakespeare, 1957-; Milton's Dramatic Poems (with D. M. B.), 1958; Mirror of Minds, 1962; reviews and articles. *Recreations:* music, theatre, travel. *Address:* 182 Mayfield Road, Edinburgh 9.

**BULLOUGH, Prof. William Sydney,** PhD, DSc Leeds; Professor of Zoology, Birkbeck College, University of London, since 1952; *b* 6 April 1914; *o s* of Rev. Frederick Sydney Bullough and Letitia Anne Cooper, both of Leeds; *m* 1942, Dr Helena F. Gibbs, Wellington, NZ; one *s* one *d*. *Educ:* William Hulme Grammar Sch., Manchester; Grammar Sch., Leeds; Univ. of Leeds. Lecturer in Zoology, Univ. of Leeds, 1937-44, McGill Univ., Montreal, 1944-46; Sorby Fellow of Royal Society of London, 1946-51; Research Fellow of British Empire Cancer Campaign, 1951-52; Hon. Fellow, Soc. for Investigative Dermatology (US). *Publications:* Practical Invertebrate Anatomy, 1950; Vertebrate Sexual Cycles, 1951; (for children) Introducing Animals, 1953; Introducing Animals-with-Backbones, 1954; Introducing Man, 1958; The Evolution of Differentiation, 1967; scientific papers on vertebrate reproductive cycles, hormones, and growth published in a variety of journals. *Recreation:* gardening. *Address:* New Cottage, Uplands Road, Kenley, Surrey. *T:* 01-660 9764.

**BULLUS, Wing Comdr Sir Eric (Edward),** Kt, 1964; MP (C) Wembley North, since 1950; journalist; *b* 20 Nov. 1906; 2nd *s* of Thomas Bullus, Leeds; *m* 1949, Joan Evelyn, *er d* of H. M. Denny; two *d*. *Educ:* Leeds Modern Sch.; Univ. of Leeds. Commnd RAFVR Aug. 1940; served War of 1939-45; Air Min. War Room, 1940-43; joined Lord Louis Mountbatten's staff in SE Asia, 1943; Wing Comdr, 1944; served India, Burma and Ceylon; demobilized, 1945. Journalist Yorkshire Post, Leeds and London, 1923-46. Mem. Leeds City Council, 1930-40; Sec., London Municipal Soc., 1947-50; Mem., Harrow UDC, 1947-50; Vice-Pres. Assoc. of Municipal Corps, 1953. PPS to Secretary for Overseas Trade, and to Minister of State, 1953-56, to Minister of Aviation, 1960-62, to Secretary of State for Defence, 1962-64. FRGS, 1947; Fellow Royal Statistical Society, 1949. Foundation Mem. of Brotherton Collection Cttee of Univ. of Leeds, 1935; Member: Archdeaconry Council of Delhi, 1944; Management Board, Cambridge Mission to Delhi, 1954; House of Laity, Church Assembly, 1960. Ripon Diocesan Reader, 1929; London Diocesan Reader, 1947; St Alban's Diocesan Reader, 1960; Canterbury Diocesan Reader, 1967; Central Readers' Board, 1960; London Readers' Board, 1954; Council Westfield Coll., Univ. of London. Pres., Soc. of Yorkshiremen in London, 1969-70. *Publications:* History of Leeds Modern School, 1931; History of Church in Delhi, 1944; History of Lords and Commons Cricket, 1959. *Recreations:* played Headingley RU Football Club 15 years and Yorkshire Amateurs Assoc. Football Club; cricket and swimming (bronze and silver medallions). *Address:* Westway, Herne Bay, Kent; House of Commons, SW1. *Club:* MCC.

**BULMAN, Oliver Meredith Boone,** FRS 1940; ScD Cambridge; PhD London; ARCSc; FGS; FLS; Woodwardian Professor of Geology, University of Cambridge, 1955-66, now Emeritus; Fellow of Sidney Sussex College; *b* 20 May 1902; *y s* of late Henry H. Bulman, RBA, and Beatrice E. Bulman (*née* Boone); *m* 1938, Marguerite, *e d* of late William George Fearnsides, FRS; one *s* three *d*. *Educ:* Battersea Grammar Sch.; Chelsea Polytechnic; Imperial Coll. of Science and Technology; Sidney Sussex Coll., Cambridge. Beit Scientific Research Fellowship, 1923-25; 1851 Senior Studentship, 1925-28; Huxley Memorial Medal, Imperial Coll., 1928; Demonstrator in Zoology, 1928-29, Demonstrator in Geology, Imperial Coll., 1929-31; Univ. Demonstrator in Geology, 1931-34; Univ. Lecturer in Palæozoology, 1934-44; Reader in Palæozoology, Cambridge, 1944-45. Pres. Sect. C (Geology) British Assoc., 1959. Pres. Geological Society

London, 1962-64, Vice-Pres. 1953-57, 1964-66, 1967-68, Foreign Secretary, 1964-67; Lyell Medallist, 1953; Pres. Palæont. Assoc., 1960-62. Trustee of the British Museum (Natural History), 1963-. Foreign Mem., Royal Physiogr. Soc. Lund; Corresponding Mem., Geol. Soc. Stockholm; Hon. Fellow Pal. Soc. India; Hon. DrPhil (Oslo), 1965; Fellow, Imperial Coll. of Science and Technology, 1961. *Publications:* numerous papers on Lower Palæozoic rocks and fossils. Editor of Geological Magazine. *Address:* The Sedgwick Museum, Cambridge CB2 3EQ.

**BULMER, Dr Gerald;** Rector of Liverpool Polytechnic, since April 1970; *b* 17 Nov. 1920; *s* of Edward and Alice Bulmer; *m* 1943, Greta Lucy Parkes, MA; two *d. Educ:* Nunthorpe Sch., York; Selwyn Coll., Cambridge. BA 1941; PhD 1944; MA 1945; FRIC 1955. Asst Master, King's Sch., Canterbury, 1945-49; Sen. Lecturer, Woolwich Polytechnic, 1949-53; Head of Dept of Science and Metallurgy, Constantine Technical Coll., Middlesbrough, 1954-57; Vice-Principal, Bolton Technical Coll., 1958-59; Principal, West Ham Coll. of Technology, 1959-64; Dir, Robert Gordon's Inst. of Technology, Aberdeen, 1965-70. Mem. Council CNAA, 1967-. Freeman City of York, 1952. *Publications:* papers on organic sulphur compounds in Jl Chem. Soc. and Nature. *Recreation:* organ playing. *Address:* Liverpool Polytechnic, Liverpool; 11 Capilano Park, Winifred Lane, Aughton, Ormskirk, Lancs.

**BULMER-THOMAS, Ivor;** writer; Hon. Secretary, Ancient Monuments Society; Chairman: Faith Press; Redundant Churches Fund; Hon. Director, Friends of Friendless Churches; Vice-President, Church Union; *b* 30 Nov. 1905; *s* of late A. E. Thomas, Cwmbran, Newport, Mon.; *m* 1st, 1932, Dilys (*d* 1938), *d* of late Dr W. Llewelyn Jones, Merthyr Tydfil; one *s*; 2nd, 1940, Margaret Joan, *d* of late E. F. Bulmer, Adam's Hill, Hereford; one *s* two *d.* Assumed additional surname Bulmer by deed poll, 1952. *Educ:* West Monmouth Sch., Pontypool; Scholar of St John's and Senior Demy of Magdalen Coll., Oxford. 1st Class Math. Mods, 1925; 1st Class Lit. Hum., 1928; Liddon Student, 1928; Ellerton Essayist, 1929; Junior Denyer and Johnson Scholar, 1930; MA 1937; represented Oxford against Cambridge at Cross-country Running, 1925-27, and Athletics, 1926-28, winning Three Miles in 1927; Welsh International Cross-country Runner, 1926; Gladstone Research Student at St Deiniol's Library, Hawarden, 1929-30; on editorial staff of Times, 1930-37; chief leader writer to News Chronicle, 1937-39; acting deputy editor, Daily Telegraph, 1953-54. Served War of 1939-45 with Royal Fusiliers (Fusilier), 1939-40, and Royal Norfolk Regt (Captain, 1941), 1940-42, 1945. Contested (Lab) Spen Valley div., 1935; MP Keighley, 1942-50 (Lab 1942-48; C 1949-50); contested Newport, Mon (C), 1950. Parliamentary Secretary, Ministry of Civil Aviation, 1945-46; Parliamentary Under-Sec. of State for the Colonies, 1946-47. Delegate to Gen. Assembly, UN, 1946; first UK Mem., Trusteeship Council, 1947. Mem. of the House of Laity of the Church Assembly, 1950-. Lately Chm., Executive Cttee, Historic Churches Preservation Trust. Stella della Solidarietà Italiana, 1948. *Publications:* Coal in the New Era, 1934; Gladstone of Hawarden, 1936; Top Sawyer, a biography of David Davies of Llandinam, 1938; Greek Mathematics (Loeb Library), 1939-42; Warfare by Words, 1942; The Problem of Italy, 1946; The Socialist Tragedy, 1949; The Party System in Great Britain, 1953; The Growth of the British Party System, 1965; contrib. to Dictionary of Scientific Biography. *Address:* 12 Edwardes Square, W8. *T:* 01-937 1414; Old School House, Farnborough, Berks; Ty'n Mynydd, Rhoscolyn, Anglesey. *Clubs:* Athenæum; Vincent's (Oxford).

**BULPITT, Cecil Arthur Charles;** *b* 6 Feb. 1919; *s* of A. E. Bulpitt; *m* 1943, Joyce Mary Bloomfield; one *s* one *d. Educ:* Spring Grove Sch., London; Regent Street Polytechnic. Territorial Army, to rank of Staff Capt., RA, 1937-45. Carreras Ltd: joined firm, 1935; Gen. Manager, 1960; Asst Managing Dir, 1962; Dep. Chm. and Chief Exec., 1968; Chm. 1969-70. MIPM, 1955; FBIM, 1963. *Recreations:* fishing, climbing, reading, travelling. *Address:* The Rest, Stoke Row, Henley-on-Thames, Oxon. *T:* Checkendon 232. *Club:* Travellers'.

**BULTEEL, Christopher Harris,** MC 1943; Headmaster, Ardingly College, since 1962; *b* 29 July 1921; *er s* of late Major Walter Bulteel and of Constance (*née* Gaunt), Charlestown, Cornwall; *m* 1958, Jennifer Anne, *d* of Col K. E. Previté, OBE and Frances (*née* Capper), Hindgaston, Marnhull, Dorset; one *s* two *d. Educ:* Wellington Coll.; Merton Coll., Oxford. Served War with Coldstream Guards, 1940-46 (MC). Assistant Master at Wellington Coll., 1949-61; Head of history dept, 1959-61. Hon. Sec., Wellington Coll. Mission, 1959-61. *Recreations:* natural history, climbing. *Address:* Ardingly College, Haywards Heath, Sussex. *T:* Ardingly 330.

**BUMBRY, Grace;** *see* Jaeckel-Bumbry, G.

**BUMSTEAD, Kenneth,** CBE 1952; CVO 1958; *b* 28 April 1908; *s* of Ernest and Nellie Bumstead; *m* 1940, Diana, *e d* of Archibald Smollett Campbell; three *s. Educ:* Wallasey Grammar Sch.; Emmanuel Coll., Cambridge. Entered China Consular Service, 1931; served Peking, Tsingtao, Canton, Chungking, Shanghai, 1932-42 (Consul 1939); Madagascar, 1943; London, 1944; Chicago, 1945-48; Shanghai, 1949-52 (Consul-General, 1950); Seattle, 1953-56; Consul-General, Rotterdam, 1957-61; retired, 1961. Commander, Order of Oranje Nassau. *Address:* 63 Cranmore Lane, Aldershot, Hants. *Club:* Officers' (Aldershot).

**BUNBURY;** *see* McClintock-Bunbury.

**BUNBURY, Bishop of,** since 1957; **Rt. Rev. Ralph Gordon Hawkins,** ThD; *b* St John's, Newfoundland, 1911; *s* of late Samuel J. and Alfreda Hawkins; *m* 1938, Mary Edna, *d* of late William James and Grace Leslie, Newport, Mon.; one *s* one *d. Educ:* Univ. Memorial Coll., St John's; St Boniface Coll., Warminster; Durham Univ. (Hatfield Coll.). BA, LTh 1934; deacon, 1935, priest, 1936, Bristol. Curate of St Anne's, Brislington, 1935-38; Rector of Morawa, 1938-43; Rector of Wembley-Floreat Park, 1943-49; Chaplain, RAAF, 1943-45; Rector of St Hilda's, N Perth, 1949-56; Canon of Perth, 1954; Archdeacon of Perth, 1957. *Address:* Bishopscourt, Bunbury, Western Australia. *T:* 2163.

**BUNBURY, Brig. Francis Ramsay St Pierre,** CBE 1958; DSO 1945, Bar 1953; *b* 16 June 1910; *s* of late Lt-Col Gerald Bruce St Pierre Bunbury, Indian Army, and Frances Mary Olivia (*née* Dixon); *m* 1933, Elizabeth Pamela Somers (*née* Liscombe) (*d* 1969) one *s* one *d. Educ:* Rugby and Sandhurst. Commissioned into The Duke of Wellington's Regiment, 1930; Staff Coll., 1941; commanded 1st Bn, The King's Own Royal Regt, Italian Campaign, 1944-45 (despatches, DSO); commanded 1st Bn The Duke of Wellington's Regt, 1951-54, Germany, Korea (Bar to DSO), Gibraltar; AAG, War Office, 1954-56; commanded 50 Independent Infantry Brigade, Cyprus, 1956-

59 (despatches, CBE). Dep. Adjt-Gen., Rhine Army, 1959-61; retired 1962. *Address:* 16 Lancaster Road, Wimbledon, SW19.

**BUNBURY, Sir (John) William Napier,** 12th Bt, *cr* 1681; *b* 3 July 1915; *s* of Sir Charles H. N. Bunbury, 11th Bt, and Katherine (*d* 1965), *d* of H. E. Reid; *S* father, 1963; *m* 1940, Pamela, *er d* of late T. Sutton, Westlecott Manor, Swindon; three *s* (and one *s* decd). *Educ:* Eton; Jesus Coll., Cambridge, 2nd Lieut (TA), 1936. Commissioned, KRRC, 1940; Capt. 1942. *Recreations:* golf, shooting, fishing, motor racing. *Heir: e surv. s* Michael William Bunbury, *b* 29 Dec. 1946. *Address:* Naunton Hall, Rendlesham, Woodbridge, Suffolk. *T:* Eyke 235. *Clubs:* Army and Navy, MCC.

**BUNBURY, Sir Michael;** *see* Bunbury, Sir R. D. M. R.

**BUNBURY, Brigadier Noël Louis St Pierre,** DSO 1937; psc; *b* Woolwich, 25 Dec. 1890; *s* of Lieut-Col William St Pierre Bunbury, S Farnborough; *m* 1923, Iris Graham (*d* 1965), *d* of J. B. Whitelaw, North Berwick; one *s*. *Educ:* Bedford; RMC Sandhurst. Served European War, Mesopotamia and Siberia; Waziristan, 1920-21; NW Frontier, 1930; Waziristan, 1936-37 (DSO); Commandant 6th Royal Bn (Scinde) 13th Frontier Force Rifles, 1934-38; Gen. Staff, India Office, 1938-40; Brigade Comdr in India, 1941-44; ADC to the King, 1943-44; retired, 1944. OC 12th County of London Home Guard Bn, 1952-55. *Address:* 1 Hazelwood Road, Hale, Cheshire.

**BUNBURY, Lt-Comdr Sir (Richard David) Michael (Richardson-),** 5th Bt, *cr* 1787; RN; *b* 27 Oct. 1927; *er s* of Richard Richardson-Bunbury (*d* 1951) and Florence Margaret Gordon, *d* of Col Roger Gordon Thomson, *qv*; *S* kinsman 1953; *m* 1961, Jane Louise, *d* of late Col Alfred William Pulverman, IA; two *s*. *Educ:* Royal Naval College, Dartmouth. Midshipman (S), 1945; Sub-Lieut (S), 1947; Lieut (S), 1948; Lieut-Comdr, 1956; retd 1967. *Heir: s* Roger Michael Richardson-Bunbury, *b* 9 Nov. 1962. *Address:* Woodlands, Mays Hill, Worplesdon, Guildford, Surrey. *T:* Worplesdon 2034.

**BUNCHE, Ralph J.,** PhD; Under Secretary-General, United Nations, since 1968 (Under Secretary for Special Political Affairs, 1954-67); *b* 7 Aug. 1904; *s* of Fred Bunche and Olive Bunche (*née* Johnson); *m* 1930, Ruth Harris; one *s* one *d* (and one *d* decd). *Educ:* Univ. of California, Los Angeles (AB); Harvard Univ., (AM, PhD). Howard Univ., Washington, DC; Chm., Dept of Political Science, 1928-50, Prof. of Political Science, 1937-50; Asst to Pres., 1931-32. Co-Director, Inst. of Race Relations, Swarthmore, Pa., 1936; Staff Member, Carnegie Corp. of New York-Myrdal Survey of Negro in America, 1938-40. Senior Social Science Analyst (Africa and Far East), Office of Co-ordinator of Information, 1941-42; Principal Research Analyst (Africa and the Far East), Office of Strategic Services, 1942-43; Chief, Africa Section, Research and Analysis Branch, Office of Strategic Services, 1943-44; Dept of State, 1944-47: as expert on colonial problems and Africa, held posts of Area Specialist, Associate Chief and Acting Chief of Division, (seconded to UN, May 1946-March 1947); United States Commissioner, Anglo-American Caribbean Commission, Sept. 1945-June 1947 (Presidential Appt); Director, Div. of Trusteeship, UN, 1946-47; Principal Director, Department of Trusteeship, 1947-54; Actg UN Mediator on Palestine, Sept. 1948-Aug. 1949; UN Special Representative in the Congo, 1960; Supervisory responsibilities over UN peacekeeping operations in Kashmir, Near East, Cyprus and Dominican Republic. Prof. of Govt, Harvard, 1950-52. Nobel Prize for Peace, 1950. Grand Cross: of National Order of Honor and Merit, Haiti, 1949; of Order of Merit Carlos Miguel de Cespedes, Cuba, 1951. US Presidential Medal of Freedom, 1963. *Publications:* A World View of Race, 1936; (jointly) An American Dilemma, 1944; Africa: The War and Peace Aims, 1942. Numerous articles in scholarly journals. *Recreations:* baseball, football enthusiast, fishing, theatre, billiards. *Address:* 115-24 Grosvenor Road, Kew Gardens, NY 11418, USA. *T:* Virginia 9-8269.

**BUNDY, McGeorge;** President of the Ford Foundation, USA; *b* 30 March 1919; *s* of Harvey Hollister Bundy and Katharine Lawrence Bundy (*née* Putnam); *m* 1950, Mary Buckminster Lothrop; four *s*. *Educ:* Yale Univ. AB 1940. Political analyst, Council on Foreign Relations, 1948-49. Harvard University: Visiting Lecturer, 1949-51; Associate Prof. of Government, 1951-54; Prof., 1954-61; Dean, Faculty of Arts and Sciences, 1953-61. Special Assistant to the Pres. for National Security Affairs, 1961-66. Member, American Political Science Association. *Publications:* (with H. L. Stimson) On Active Service in Peace and War, 1948; The Strength of Government, 1969; ed Pattern of Responsibility, 1952. *Address:* The Ford Foundation, 320 East 43rd Street, New York, NY 10017, USA.

**BUNFORD, John Farrant,** MA, FIA, FSS; Hon.FFA; Director, National Provident Institution for Mutual Life Assurance, since 1964 (Manager and Actuary 1946-64); *b* 4 June 1901; *s* of late John Henry Bunford and Ethel Farrant Bunford; *m* 1929, Florence Louise, *d* of late John and Annie Pearson, Mayfield, Cork; two *s* one *d*. *Educ:* Christ's Hosp.; St Catharine's Coll., Cambridge. (MA). Scottish Amicable Life Assurance Soc., 1923-29. Royal Exchange Assurance, 1929-32; National Provident Institution: Dep. Asst Actuary, 1932; Asst Sec., 1933; Asst Manager, 1937. Institute of Actuaries: Fellow, 1930; Hon. Sec., 1944-45; Vice-Pres., 1948-50; Treas., 1952-53; Pres., 1954-56. Hon. Fellow the Faculty of Actuaries, 1956. *Recreations:* tennis and gardening. *Address:* 14 Shepherds Way, Liphook, Hants. *T:* Liphook 2594.

**BUNKER, Albert Rowland,** CB 1966; Assistant Under Secretary of State and Principal Establishment and Organisation Officer, Home Office, since 1961; *b* 5 Nov. 1913; *er* and *o surv s* of late Alfred Francis Bunker and late Ethel Trudgian, Lanjeth, St Austell, Cornwall; *m* 1939, Irene Ruth Ella, 2nd *d* of late Walter and late Ella Lacey, Ealing; two *s*. *Educ:* Ealing Gram. Sch. Served in Royal Air Force, 1943-45. Service in Cabinet Office, HM Treasury, Ministry of Home Security and Home Office. *Recreation:* golf. *Address:* 35 Park Avenue, Ruislip. *T:* Ruislip 35331. *Clubs:* Royal Air Force; Denham Golf.

**BUNN, Dr Charles William,** FRS 1967; Dewar Research Fellow of the Royal Institution of Great Britain since 1963; *b* 15 Jan. 1905; *s* of Charles John Bunn and Mary Grace Bunn (*née* Murray); *m* 1931, Elizabeth Mary Mold; one *s* one *d*. *Educ:* Wilson's Grammar Sch., London, SE; Exeter Coll., Oxford. BA, BSc, (Oxon.), 1927; DSc (Oxon.), 1953; FInstP, 1944. Mem. Research Staff, Imperial Chemical Industries, Winnington, Northwich, Cheshire (Now Mond Div.), 1927-46; transf. to ICI Plastics Div., 1946 (Div. Leader of Molecular Structure Div. of Research Dept, and later of Physics Div.); retd 1963. Chm., X-Ray Analysis Group of The Inst. of Physics and The Physical Soc., 1959-62. Amer. Physical

Soc. Award in High Polymer Physics (Ford Prize), 1969. *Publications:* Chemical Crystallography, 1945 (2nd edn 1961); Crystals, Their Role in Nature and in Science, 1964; papers in: Proc. Royal Society; Trans. Faraday Soc.; Acta Crystallographica. *Recreations:* music and horticulture. *Address:* The Royal Institution of Great Britain, 21 Albemarle Street, W1. *T:* 01-493 0669; 6 Pentley Park, Welwyn Garden City, Herts. *T:* Welwyn Garden 23581.

**BUNT, Rev. F(rederick) Darrell,** CB 1958; OBE 1950; retired as Chaplain of the Fleet and Archdeacon of the Royal Navy (1956-60); Hon. Chaplain to the Queen, 1952-60; *b* 3 July 1902; *o s* of F. W. M. Bunt; *m* 1960, Marianne E. Watson; one *d*. *Educ:* City of London Sch.; St Chad's Coll., Durham (BA 1923, DipTh 1924, MA 1926). Deacon, 1926; Priest, 1927, Diocese of Chelmsford; St Luke's, Victoria Docks, 1926; St Augustine's, Wembley Park, 1928; Chaplain, Royal Navy, 1930. Served in Various ships from 1930; HMS President (Asst to Chaplain of the Fleet), 1948-50; HMS Excellent, 1950-51; RN College, Dartmouth, 1951-53; HM Dockyard, Portsmouth, 1953-56. *Recreations:* golf, sailing. *Address:* Ringer's Plat, Lymore, Milford-on-Sea, Hants. *T:* Milford-on-Sea 3213. *Club:* United Service.

**BUNTINE, Martyn Arnold;** retired; *b* 27 Dec. 1898; *s* of Walter Murray Buntine and Bertha Florance Gibbs; *m* 1926, Gladys Selby Spurling, OBE; two *s*. *Educ:* Caulfield Grammar Sch. and Univ., Melbourne; Edinburgh Univ. MA with honours, Melbourne Univ.; PhD Edinburgh Univ.; taught on staff of Heriot's Sch., Edinburgh, Caulfield Grammar Sch., Melbourne, and Scotch Coll., Melbourne; Headmaster, Camberwell Grammar Sch., Melbourne, 1927; Headmaster, Hale Sch., Perth, W Australia, 1931-45; Headmaster, Geelong Coll., 1946-60. Member of Council for Educational Research (WA); Lecturer in History of Education, Univ. of Western Australia, 1935; Pres. of Public Schs Sports Association, 1932 and 1945; Pres. WA Amateur Athletics Association, 1932-45; enlisted for war service overseas with AIF, 1918; enlisted, 1940, 2/28th Bn, and was in Tobruk as Co. Comdr for six months, 1941. Sent back to Australia, 1942, to command 11th Bn with rank of Lt-Col; then returned to civil life. Rotary Club of Perth, 1932-45, Rotary Club of Geelong, 1946-57. Mem. Standing Cttee Headmasters' Conf. of Australia; Chairman Geelong Council of British Commonwealth Youth Sunday Observance; Vice-Pres. Geelong Council for Care of Mentally Handicapped Children. Mem. Australian Coll. of Education. *Publications:* numerous articles. *Recreations:* golf, tennis. *Address:* 70 Boundary Road, Wahroonga, NSW, Australia, *T:* 48-5256.

**BUNTING, Prof. Arthur Hugh;** Professor of Agricultural Botany, Reading University, since 1956; *b* 7 Sept. 1917; *e s* of S. P. and R. Bunting; *m* 1941, Elsie Muriel Reynard; three *s*. *Educ:* Athlone High Sch., Johannesburg, S Africa; Univ. of the Witwatersrand, Johannesburg; Oriel Coll., University of Oxford. BSc 1937. BSc (Hons Botany), MSc 1938. Witwatersrand; Rhodes Scholar for the Transvaal, 1938; DPhil Oxford, 1941; FIBiol. Asst Chemist, Rothamsted Experimental Station, 1941-45; Member Human Nutrition Research Unit, Medical Research Council, 1945-47; Chief Scientific Officer, Overseas Food Corporation, 1947-51; Senior Research Officer, Sudan Min. of Agriculture, 1951-56; Dean, Faculty of Agriculture, Univ. of Reading, 1965-71. pres. Assoc. of Applied Biologists, 1963-64; Jt Editor, Journal of Applied Ecology 1964-68. Found. Trustee, 1968-, and Chm. of Scientific Cttee, 1969-, Internat. Inst. of Tropical Agriculture, Ibadan, Nigeria; Mem., Council for Scientific Policy, 1969-. LLD hc Ahmadu Bello Univ., 1968. *Publications:* (ed) Change in Agriculture, 1969; numerous papers in scientific and agricultural journals. *Recreation:* music. *Address:* 27 The Mount, Caversham, Reading, Berks. *T:* Reading 72487.

**BUNTING, Sir (Edward) John,** Kt 1964; CBE 1960; BA; Secretary to the Australian Cabinet, since 1959 and Secretary, Department of the Cabinet Office, since 1968; *b* Ballarat, Vic, 13 Aug. 1918; *s* of late G. B. Bunting; *m* 1942, (Pauline) Peggy, *d* of late D. C. MacGruer; three *s*. *Educ:* Trinity Grammar School, Melbourne; Trinity Coll., Univ. of Melbourne (BA Hons). official Sec., Office of the High Commissioner for Australia, London, 1953-55; Deputy Sec., Prime Minister's Dept, Canberra, 1955-58; Sec., 1959-68. *Recreations:* tennis and golf. *Address:* 3 Wickham Crescent, Red Hill, Canberra, ACT 2603, Australia. *T:* 92803. *Clubs:* Commonwealth (Canberra); Athenæum (Melbourne); Melbourne Cricket; Royal Canberra Golf.

**BUNTING, Sir John;** *see* Bunting, Sir E. J.

**BUNTON, George Louis,** MChir (Cantab), FRCS; Consultant Surgeon to University College Hospital, London, since 1955, to Metropolitan Hospital since 1957 and to Northwood Hospital since 1958; *b* 23 April 1920; *s* of late Surg. Capt. C. L. W. Bunton, RN, and Marjorie Denman; *m* 1948, Margaret Betty Edwards; one *d*. *Educ:* Epsom; Selwyn Coll., Cambridge; UCH. MB, BChir Cantab 1951; MRCS, LRCP 1944; FRCS 1951; MChir Cantab 1955. Served in RNVR 1944-47. Fellow, Assoc. of Surgeons; Fellow, British Assoc. of Pædiatric Surgeons. *Publications:* contribs. to journals on surgical subjects. *Recreations:* gardening, music, ski-ing. *Address:* Heathersett, West Heath Road, NW3. *T:* 01-794 3078.

**BURBIDGE, (Eleanor) Margaret, (Mrs Geoffrey Burbidge),** FRS 1964; Professor of Astronomy, University of California at San Diego, since 1965; *d* of late Stanley John Peachey, Lectr in Chemistry and Research Chemist, and of Marjorie Peachey; *m* 1948, Geoffrey Burbidge, *qv*; one *d*. *Educ:* Francis Holland Sch., London; University Coll., London (BSc); Univ. of London Observatory (PhD). Asst Director, 1948-50, Actg Director, 1950-51, Univ. of London Observatory; fellowship from Internat. Astron. Union, held at Yerkes Observatory, Univ. of Chicago, 1951-53; Research Fellow, California Inst. of Technology, 1955-57; Shirley Farr Fellow, later Associate Prof., Yerkes Observatory, Univ. of Chicago, 1957-62; Research Astronomer, Univ. of California at San Diego, 1962-65. Abby Rockefeller Manzė Vis. Prof., MIT, 1968. Hon. DSc: Smith Coll., Massachusetts, USA, 1963; Sussex, 1970. Fellow University Coll., London, 1967. *Publications:* Quasi-Stellar Objects (with Geoffrey Burbidge), 1967 (also USA, 1967); contribs to learned jls (mostly USA), Handbuch der Physik, etc. *Recreations:* travel (some done for recreation as well as work!); music (listening–no longer time to play in amateur string orchestra as she used to do). *Address:* Department of Physics, University of California, La Jolla, California 92037, USA. *T:* San Diego 453-2000, Ext. 1632.

**BURBIDGE, Geoffrey (Ronald),** FRS 1968; Professor of Physics, University of California, San Diego, since 1963; *b* 24 Sept. 1925; *s* of

Leslie and Eveline Burbidge, Chipping Norton, Oxon; *m* 1948, Margaret Peachey (*see* E. M. Burbidge); one *d. Educ:* Chipping Norton Grammar Sch.; Bristol University; Univ. Coll., London. BSc (Special Hons Physics) Bristol, 1946; PhD London, 1951. Asst Lectr, UCL, 1950-51; Agassiz Fellow, Harvard Univ., 1951-52; Research Fellow, Univ. of Chicago, 1952-53; Research Fellow, Cavendish Lab., Cambridge, 1953-55; Carnegie Fellow, Mount Wilson and Palomar Observatories, Caltech, 1955-57; Asst Prof., Dept of Astronomy, Univ. of Chicago, 1957-58; Assoc. Prof., 1958-62; Assoc. Prof., Univ. of California, San Diego, 1962-63. Phillips Vis. Prof., Harvard Univ., 1968. Fellow, UCL, 1970-. *Publications:* (with Margaret Burbidge) Quasi-Stellar Objects, 1967; scientific papers in Astrophysical Jl, Nature, Rev. Mod. Phys, Handbuch der Physik, etc. *Address:* Department of Physics, University of California at San Diego, PO Box 109, La Jolla, California 92037, USA.

**BURBIDGE, Mrs Geoffrey;** *see* Burbidge, E. M.

**BURBIDGE, Sir John (Richard Woodman),** 4th Bt, *cr* 1916; Director, Charta Cards Co. Ltd, since 1964; *b* 5 Oct. 1930; *s* of Sir Richard Grant Woodman Burbidge, 3rd Bt, CBE, and Gladys (*d* 1967), *d* of late C. F. Kearley; *S* father, 1966; *m* 1956, Benita Roxane Mosselmans; no *c. Educ:* Rugby Sch. Harrods Ltd, Knightsbridge, 1952-64. *Heir: cousin* Herbert Dudley Burbidge [*b* 13 Nov. 1904; *m* 1933, Ruby, *d* of Charles Ethelbert Taylor, Vancouver I.; one *s*]. *Address:* 41 Old Church Street, SW3. *T:* 01-352 3419. *Clubs:* MCC; Sunningdale Golf.

**BURBIDGE, Mrs Margaret;** *see* Burbidge, E. M.

**BURBIDGE, Prof. Percy William,** CBE 1957; MSc NZ; BARes Cambridge; Professor Emeritus of Physics, University of Auckland; *b* 3 Jan. 1891; *s* of R. W. Burbidge and Agnes Mary Edwards; *m* 1923, Kathleen Black, Wellington; one *s* three *d. Educ:* Wellington Boys' Coll.; Victoria Univ. Coll., Wellington; Trinity Coll., Cambridge. Took 1st class honours in Physics (NZ); gained 1851 Exhibition Research Scholarship, 1913; volunteered NZEF, 1917; took BA Research at Cavendish Laboratory, 1920; Carnegie Corporation Travel Grants, 1933, 1951; Mem. NZ Defence Scientific Advisory Cttee, 1940-47. *Publications:* papers on Fluctuations of Gamma Rays, Absorption of X-Rays, Humidity, Frictional Electricity, Photoconduction in Rock Salt. *Address:* University, Auckland, NZ.

**BURBRIDGE, Rev. Canon (John) Paul,** MA Oxon and Cantab; Precentor since 1969, Canon Residentiary since 1966, and Chamberlain since 1962, of York Minster; *b* 21 May 1932; *e s* of John Henry Gray Burbridge and Dorothy Vera Burbridge; *m* 1956, Olive Denise Grenfell; three *d. Educ:* King's Sch., Canterbury; King's Coll., Cambridge; New Coll., Oxford; Wells Theolog. Coll. Nat. Service Commn in RA, 1957. Jun. Curate, 1959, Sen. Curate, 1961, Eastbourne Parish Church; Chamberlain and Vicar Choral, York Minster, 1962, Succentor Canonicorum, 1966. *Recreations:* reading, railways (modelling and preservation). *Address:* 2 Minster Court, York. *T:* York 24965.

**BURBURY, Hon. Sir Stanley Charles,** KBE 1958; Chief Justice of the Supreme Court of Tasmania, since 1956; *b* 2 Dec. 1909; *s* of Daniel Charles Burbury and Mary Burbury (*née* Cunningham); *m* 1934, Pearl Christine Barren; no *c. Educ:* The Hutchins Sch., Hobart; The Univ., of Tasmania. LLB 1933; admitted to Bar, 1934; QC 1950; Solicitor-Gen. for Tasmania, 1952. Pres., Nat. Heart Foundn of Australia; Dir, Winston Churchill Memorial Trust. *Recreations:* music and theatre. *Address:* Mary's, Hope Road, Rosetta, Tasmania. *T:* 7-7984. *Clubs:* Tasmanian, Athenæum (Hobart); Launceston (Launceston).

**BURCH, Cecil Reginald,** CBE 1958; FRS 1944; BA; DSc; Research Associate, 1936-44 and Fellow, since 1944, of H. H. Wills Physics Laboratory, Bristol University; Warren Research Fellow in Physics, since 1948; *b* 12 May 1901; *s* of late George James Burch, MA, DSc, FRS, and of Constance Emily Jeffries, sometime Principal of Norham Hall, Oxford; *m* 1937, Enid Grace, *o d* of Owen Henry Morice, Ipswich; one *d. Educ:* Oxford Preparatory School; Oundle Sch.; Gonville and Caius Coll., Cambridge. Physicist, Research Dept, Metropolitan Vickers Co., Trafford Park, Manchester, 1923-33; Leverhulme Fellow (in Optics), Imperial Coll. of Science and Technology, 1933-35. Rumford Medal, Royal Society, 1954. *Publications:* A Contribution to the Theory of Eddy Current Heating (with N. Ryland Davis); scientific papers on various subjects in physics and technology in Phil. Mag., Proc. Royal Society, etc. *Recreation:* walking. *Address:* 2 Holmes Grove, Westbury-on-Trym, Clifton, Bristol BS9 4EE. *T:* Bristol 627322.

**BURCH, Maj.-Gen. Frederick Whitmore,** CSI 1946; CIE 1944; MC 1916; DL; Hon. Treasurer, Chelmsford Diocesan Board of Finance, since 1968; late Indian Army; *b* 1 Nov. 1893; 2nd *s* of late Major Frederick Burch, Elvington, York; *m* 1929, Marigold, 2nd *d* of P. U. Allen, late ICS; one *s* one *d. Educ:* Framlingham Coll. Served European War, 1914-19, in Egypt, France, Belgium with E Yorks Regt, and India (wounded, despatches, MC, 1914-15 Star, 2 War Medals, Afghanistan, 1919); Indian Army: 7th Gurka Rifles and Royal Garhwal Rifles; held various staff appointments including AMS (Personal) to C-in-C India, DSD, GHQ, India; War of 1939-45, India and Italy (4 war medals); Bt Major 1930; Bt Lt-Col 1938; Maj.-Gen. 1942; organised India's Victory Celebrations, New Delhi, 1946; Chief of Staff and C-in-C Baroda State Forces, 1946; retired, 1946. Raised and commanded NE Sector Essex Home Guard (5 Bns), 1951; Area Controller, Civil Defence, NE Essex, 1960-64. DL Essex, 1956; Chm., Lexden and Winstree Rural District Council, 1959-63. *Recreations:* golf, tennis, fishing, polo. *Address:* The Well House, Dedham, Essex. *T:* Dedham 2223. *Club:* Army and Navy.

**BURCH, Rt. Rev. William Gerald;** *see* Edmonton, Bishop of.

**BURCHAM, Professor William Ernest,** FRS 1957; Oliver Lodge Professor of Physics, University of Birmingham, since 1951; *b* 1 Aug. 1913; *er s* of Ernest Barnard and Edith Ellen Burcham; *m* 1942, Isabella Mary, *d* of George Richard Todd and of Alice Louisa Todd; two *d. Educ:* City of Norwich Sch.; Trinity Hall, Cambridge. Stokes Student, Pembroke Coll., Cambridge, 1937; Scientific Officer, Ministry of Aircraft Production, 1940, and Directorate of Atomic Energy, 1944; Fellow of Selwyn Coll., Cambridge, 1944; Univ. Demonstrator in Physics, Cambridge, 1945; Univ. Lecturer in Physics, Cambridge, 1946. *Publications:* Nuclear Physics: an Introduction, 1963; papers in Proc. Royal Society, Proc. Physical Soc. and in Philosophical Magazine. *Address:* 95 Witherford Way, Selly Oak, Birmingham 29. *T:* 021-472 1226.

**BURCHNALL, Professor Joseph Langley,** OBE 1956; MC 1918; MA (Oxon); FRSE; Emeritus Professor of Mathematics in University of Durham since 1958; *b* 8 Dec. 1892; *s* of Henry Walter and Ann Newport Burchnall; *m* 1917, Gertrude Frances Rollinson; two *s* one *d.* *Educ:* Boston Gram. Sch.; Christ Church Oxford. Open Exhibn, 1911, Hon. Scholar, 1913, Univ. Jun. Mathematical Exhibn, 1913; BA 1914, MA 1922. Served European War, 1914-18, France and Belgium, officer in RA, 1915-19. Lecturer and Reader in Mathematics in Univ. of Durham, 1919-39, Prof., 1939-58; Sec., Durham Colls Council, 1926-38. *Publications:* papers in mathematical journals. *Address:* 58 Pier Avenue, Southwold, Suffolk.

**BURCKHARDT, Charles James;** Swiss historian, diplomat and author; *b* Basle, Switzerland, 10 Sept. 1891; *s* of Charles Chr. Burckhardt and Hélène Aline (*née* Schazmann von Brugg); *m* 1926, Elizabeth de Reynold; two *d. Educ:* Basle Coll.; Glarisegg Coll.; Univs of Basle, Munich, Göttingen, Zürich and Paris. Attaché Swiss Legation, Vienna, 1918-22; Chief Delegate of International Committee of Red Cross in Turkey, 1923; Prof. of Modern history at the Univ., Zürich, 1923; Prof. Post-graduate Sch. of International Studies, Geneva, 1932; High Commissioner of League of Nations for Free City of Danzig, 1937-39; Pres. of the Mixed Relief Commission of Internat. Red Cross, 1939; Pres. of the Cttee of Internat. Red Cross, 1944-49; Swiss Minister in Paris, 1945-49. Director: ALUSUISSE, Zürich; CIBA, Basle. Associate Member: Acad. of Salamanca, 1945; Institut des Sciences morales et politiques de l'Acad. Française, 1947; Bavarian Acad. of Fine Arts, 1950; Acad. of Arts, Berlin, 1961. Hon. Mem., Austrian Acad. of Science and Art, 1965. Dr hc: Basle, 1939; Lille, 1947; Grenoble, 1947; Rehovot, 1963. Hon. Citizen: Lille, 1947; Lübeck, 1950; Vinzel, 1966. Kt, Pour le Mérite, Germany, 1955; Grand Officier de la Légion d'Honneur, France, 1950. *Publications:* Charles Chr. Burckhardt (biography), 1916; Travel in Asia Minor, 1924; Maria Theresa (biography), 1931; The Cardinal Richelieu, Vol. I, 1934 (trans. as Richelieu and his Age: his rise to power, 1967); Correspondence H. v. Hofmannsthal-C. J. Burckhardt, 1940; My Mission at Danzig, 1937–39; The Cardinal Richelieu, Vols. II and III, 1966; Correspondence C. J. Burckhardt-Max Rychner, 1970; The Cardinal Richelieu, Vol. IV; many other novels, essays and publications. *Address:* Château de Vinzel, La Batie, 1181 VINZEL/VD, Switzerland.

**BURDEN,** family name of **Baron Burden.**

**BURDEN,** 2nd Baron *cr* 1950, of Hazlebarrow, Derby; **Philip William Burden;** *b* 21 June 1916; *s* of 1st Baron Burden, CBE, and of Augusta, *d* of David Sime, Aberdeen; *S* father, 1970; *m* 1951, Audrey Elsworth, *d* of Major W. E. Sykes; three *s* three *d. Educ:* Raines Foundation School. *Heir: s* Hon. Andrew Philip Burden, *b* 20 July 1959. *Address:* Elm Tree Farm, West Wick, Worle, Weston-super-Mare, Somerset.

**BURDEN, Sqn Ldr Frederick Frank Arthur;** MP (C) Gillingham, Kent, since 1950; *b* 27 Dec. 1905; *s* of A. F. Burden, Bracknell, Berks; *m* Marjorie Greenwood; one *d. Educ:* Sloane Sch., Chelsea. Company Director. Served War of 1939-45, RAF: first with a Polish unit, later with Eastern Air Command, and on the staff of Lord Louis Mountbatten. Chm. Parliamentary Animal Welfare Group; Vice-Chm., RSPCA. *Recreation:* fishing. *Address:* 291 Latymer Court, W6. *T:* 01-748 1916; The Knapp, Portesham, Dorset. *T:* Abbots Bury 366.

**BURDEN, Frederick Parker,** BA, BCLS; Consulting Engineer; Partner, Burden, Duffy & Usher, Engineers and Surveyors, since 1958; *b* Queensbury, New Brunswick, 28 Dec. 1874; *s* of Stephen Pharel Burden and Ruth Ann Hagerman; *m* 1908, Jane Burgess Payson; two *s* one *d. Educ:* Common schs; Fredericton High and Normal Schools; Univ. of New Brunswick. Went to British Columbia, 1901; became British Columbia Land Surveyor; practised as such until 1928; elected a member for Fort George Riding in 1928 and became Minister of Lands; resigned 1930; Agent-Gen. for British Columbia, 1930-34; conducted Special Surveys for Canadian Govt on Alaska Highway, 1942-46; special survey of Pacific Great Eastern Railway Right-of-way, 1950-52. *Recreations:* played baseball, football, hockey, and has indulged in horse-racing in an amateur way. *Address:* (Office) 1658 3rd Avenue, Prince George, BC; (Home) 910 Alward Street, Prince George, BC, Canada.

**BURDEN, Major Geoffrey Noel,** CMG 1952; MBE 1938; *b* 9 Dec. 1898; *s* of late A. G. Burden, Exmouth, Devon; *m* 1927, Yolande Nancy, *d* of late G. H. B. Shaddick, Kenilworth, Cape Town; one *s* one *d. Educ:* Exeter Sch.; Royal Military College, Sandhurst. Served European War, 1914-18, Devon Regt, 1915-18; Indian Army, 1918-23. Joined Colonial Administrative Service, Nyasaland, 1925; Director of Publicity, 1936; Nyasaland Labour Officer to S Rhodesia, 1937-38; Nyasaland/N Rhodesian Labour Officer in the Union of South Africa, 1939; Chief Recruiting Officer, Nyasaland, 1940. War of 1939-45: military service in Somaliland, Abyssinia, and N Rhodesia, King's African Rifles, 1941-43. Asst Chief Sec., Nyasaland, 1945-46; Commissioner of Labour, Gold Coast, 1946-50; Chief Commissioner, Northern Territories, Gold Coast, 1950-53. Nyasaland Govt Representative in S Rhodesia, 1954-63. *Address:* The Croft, Hillside Road, Frensham, Surrey. *T:* Frensham 2584.

**BURDER, Sir John Henry,** Kt 1944; ED; Director, Atlas Assurance Co. Ltd, and other Companies; *b* 30 Nov. 1900; *s* of late H. C. Burder; *m* 1928, Constance Aileen Bailey; two *d. Educ:* Eton College. Joined Jardine Skinner & Co., 1920; Chm., Indian Tea Market Expansion Bd, 1939; President: Local Board, Imperial Bank of India, 1943-44; Bengal Chamber of Commerce, 1943-44; Associated Chambers of Commerce of India, 1943-44; Royal Agricultural and Horitcultural Soc. of India, 1938-41; Calcutta Soc. for the Prevention of Cruelty to Animals, 1939-41; Lt-Col Commanding Calcutta Light Horse, 1944; Member of Council of State, 1943-44. *Address:* Swinbrook Manor, near Burford, Oxon; Achaglachgach, Tarbert, Argyll. *Club:* Oriental.

**BURDETT, Sir Savile (Aylmer),** 11th Bt, *cr* 1665; *b* 24 Sept. 1931; *s* of Sir Aylmer Burdett, 10th Bt; *S* father, 1943; *m* 1962, June E. C. Rutherford; one *s* one *d. Educ:* Wellington Coll.; Imperial Coll., London. *Heir: s* Crispin Peter Burdett, *b* 8 Feb. 1967. *Address:* Milton Mill, Hurlford, Kilmarnock, Ayrshire. *T:* Kilmarnock 22990.

**BURDWAN, Maharajadhiraja of;** *see under* Mahtab.

**BURELLI-RIVAS, Dr Miguel Angel,** Grand Cordon, Order of the Liberator; LLB, Dr Pol. Sc.; Lawyer; Venezuelan Ambassador to

London, 1967-69; *b* 8 July 1922. *Educ:* Univ. of Los Andes, Bogotá; Central Univ. of Venezuela; Central Univ. of Ecuador; Nat. Univ. of Bogotá; Univ. of Madrid; Univ. of Florence. Formerly Professor, University of Los Andes, Bogotá. Served in Venezuelan Diplomatic Service: in Colombia, USA, Mexico; as Political Director, Ministry of the Interior; as Director-Gen., Ministry of Foreign Affairs; and as Interim Minister of Foreign Affairs; Mem., Venezuelan Supreme Electoral Council, 1961; Minister of Justice, 1964-65; Ambassador to Colombia, 1965-67. Gen. Sec., Venezuelan Delegn to 4th Session, UN Gen. Assembly. Mem., Commn of Inquiry, British Guiana-Venezuela Boundary. Mem., Ed. Cttee, Meridanian Themes and Collection of Authors, 1964-. Holds foreign decorations. *Address:* Ministry of Foreign Affairs, Caracas, Venezuela.

**BURET, Captain Theobald J. C. P.**; *see* Purcell-Buret.

**BURFORD, Earl of; Murray de Vere Beauclerk**; *b* 19 Jan. 1939; *s* and *heir* of 13th Duke of St Albans, *qv* and 1st wife (now Mrs Nathalie C. Eldrid); *m* 1962, Rosemary Frances Scoones; one *s* one *d*. *Educ:* Tonbridge. Chartered Accountant, 1962. Director: J. A. Peden Ltd; Wine Tasters Ltd; A1 Fund Managers Ltd. *Heir:* *s* Lord Vere of Hanworth, *qv*. *Address:* 100 Campden Hill Road, W8. *T:* 01-727 3347. *Club:* MCC.

**BURFORD, Eleanor**; *see* Hibbert, Eleanor.

**BURGE, James,** QC 1965; *b* 8 Oct. 1906; *s* of George Burge, Masterton, New Zealand; *m* 1958, Elizabeth, *d* of Comdr Scott Williams, RN, Dorset; two *s* one *d*. *Educ:* Cheltenham Coll.; Christ's Coll., Cambridge. Barrister, Inner Temple, 1932; Yarborough Anderson Scholar, Profumo Prizeman, Paul Methuen Prizeman. Pilot Officer RAFVR, 1940; Sqdn Ldr; Dep. Judge Advocate, 1941-44. Formerly Prosecuting Counsel, GPO, at CCC; Deputy Chairman, West Sussex Quarter Sessions, 1963-. *Address:* Queen Elizabeth Building, Temple, EC4. *T:* 01-353 2576; 14 Belgrave Place, Brighton. *T:* Brighton 61850.

**BURGEN, Prof. Arnold Stanley Vincent,** FRS 1964; Sheild Professor of Pharmacology, University of Cambridge, since 1962; Fellow of Downing College, Cambridge; *b* 20 March 1922; *s* of Peter Burgen and Elizabeth Wolfers; *m* 1946, Judith Browne; two *s* one *d*. *Educ:* Christ's Coll., Finchley. Student, Middlesex Hospital Med. Sch., 1939-45; Ho. Phys., Middlesex Hospital, 1945; Demonstrator, 1945-48, Asst Lectr, 1948-49, in Pharmacology, Middlesex Hospital Med. Sch. Prof. of Physiology, McGill Univ., Montreal, 1949-62; Dep. Dir. Univ. Clinic, Montreal Gen. Hospital, 1957-62; Hon. Dir, MRC Molecular Pharmacology Unit. *Publications:* Physiology of Salivary Glands, 1961. Papers in Journals of Physiology and Pharmacology. *Recreation:* sculpture. *Address:* Department of Pharmacology, University of Cambridge Medical School, Hills Road, Cambridge CB2 3EF. *T:* Cambridge 45171.

**BURGER, Warren Earl;** Chief Justice of the United States since 1969; *b* St Paul, Minn, 17 Sept. 1907; *s* of Charles Joseph Burger and Katharine Schnittger; *m* 1933, Elvera Stromberg; one *s* one *d*. *Educ:* Univ. of Minnesota; St Paul Coll. of Law (LLB *magna cum laude*); Mitchell Coll. of Law (LLD). Admitted to Bar of Minnesota, 1931; Mem. Faculty, Mitchell Coll. of Law, 1931-48. Partner in Faricy, Burger, Moore & Costello until 1953. Asst Attorney-Gen. of US, 1953-56; Judge, US Court of Appeals, Washington, DC, 1956-69. Chm., ABA Proj. Standards for Criminal Justice. Past Lectr, Law Schools in US and Europe. Hon. Master of the Bench of the Middle Temple, 1969. Trustee, Mitchell Coll. of Law, St Paul, Minn. *Publications:* articles in legal and professional jls. *Address:* Supreme Court, Washington, DC 20543, USA.

**BURGES, Alan**; *see* Burges, N. A.

**BURGES, (Norman) Alan,** MSc, PhD; Vice-Chancellor, New University of Ulster, Coleraine, Northern Ireland, since June 1966; *b* 5 Aug. 1911; *s* of late Lieut J. C. Burges, East Maitland, NSW; *m* 1940, Florence Evelyn (*née* Moulton); three *d*. *Educ;* Sydney Univ., Australia; Emmanuel Coll., Cambridge. Graduated, Sydney, BSc Hons., 1931; MSc, 1932; PhD Cambridge, 1937. Senior 1851 Scholar, 1937. Research Fellow, Emmanuel Coll., 1938; Prof. of Botany, Sydney Univ., 1947-52; Dean of Faculty of Science and Fellow of Senate, 1949-52; Holbrook Gaskell Prof. of Botany, Univ. of Liverpool, 1952-66, Acting Vice-Chancellor, 1964-65; Pro-Vice-Chancellor, 1965-66. President: British Ecological Soc., 1958, 1959; British Mycological Soc., 1962; Mem. Cttee, Nature Conservancy, England, 1959-66. Served War of 1939-45 (despatches). *Publications:* Micro-organisms in the soil, 1958; (with F. Raw) Soil Biology, 1967; various in scientific journals on plant diseases and fungi. *Address:* Vice-Chancellor's Lodge, Mountsandel Road, Coleraine, Northern Ireland.

**BURGES, Major-General Rodney Lyon Travers,** CBE 1963; DSO 1946; Vice-Quartermaster-General, Ministry of Defence, 1966-67; *b* 19 March 1914; *s* of Richard Burges and Hilda Christine Burges (*née* Lyon); *m* 1946, Sheila Marion Lyster Goldby, *d* of H. L. Goldby; one *s* one *d*. *Educ:* Wellington; RMA, Woolwich. 2nd Lieut RA, 1934; war service in Burma, 1942 and 1944-45; CO The Berkshire Yeomanry (145 Fd Regt, RA), 1945; Comdr, E Battery, RHA, 1949-51; Bt Lt-Col 1953; 2nd in comd, 1 RHA, 1954-55; CO 3 RHA, 1955-57; CRA 3 Div., 1958-59; IDC, 1960; Brig. Q (Ops) WO, 1961-63; CCRA, 1 Corps, BAOR, 1963-64; Major-General 1964; GOC, Cyprus District, 1964-66. Joined Grieveson, Grant & Co., 1968. *Recreations:* racing, tennis, drinking wine in the sun. *Address:* c/o Coutts & Co., 440 Strand, WC2. *Clubs:* United Service, Buck's.

**BURGESS, Anthony,** BA; FRSL; novelist and critic; *b* 25 Feb. 1917; *s* of Joseph Wilson and Elizabeth Burgess; *m* 1942, Llewela Isherwood Jones, BA (*d* 1968); *m* 1968, Liliana Macellari, *d* of Contessa Maria Lucrezia Pasi della Pergola. *Educ:* Xaverian Coll., Manchester; Manchester Univ. Served Army, 1940-46. Lecturer: Birmingham Univ. Extra-Mural Dept., 1946-48; Ministry of Education, 1948-50; English Master, Banbury Grammar Sch., 1950-54; Education Officer, Malaya and Brunei, 1954-59. *Publications:* Time for a Tiger, 1956; The Enemy in the Blanket, 1958; Beds in the East, 1959; The Right to an Answer, 1960; The Doctor is Sick, 1960; The Worm and the Ring, 1961; Devil of a State, 1961; A Clockwork Orange, 1962; The Wanting Seed, 1962; Honey for the Bears, 1963; The Novel Today, 1963; Language Made Plain, 1964; Nothing like the Sun, 1964; The Eve of Saint Venus, 1964; A Vision of Battlements, 1965; Here Comes Everybody–an introduction to James Joyce, 1965; Tremor of Intent, 1966; A Shorter Finnegans Wake, 1966; The Novel Now, 1967; Enderby Outside, 1968; Urgent Copy, 1968; Shakespeare, 1970. As *Joseph Kell:* One Hand Clapping, 1961;

Inside Mr Enderby, 1963. As *John Burgess Wilson:* English Literature: A Survey for Students, 1958. Contributor to Observer, Spectator, Listener, Encounter, Queen, Times Literary Supplement, Hudson Review, Holiday, Playboy, American Scholar, etc. *Recreations:* music composition, piano-playing, painting, language-learning, travel. *Address:* 168 Triq Il-Kbira, Lija, Malta; 1 and 2 Piazza Padella, Bracciano, Italy.

**BURGESS, Lt-Col Charles Roscoe,** CBE 1919; DSO 1917; *b* Dalton-in-Furness, 3 Oct. 1874; *s* of Rev. Henry Martyn Burgess and Edith Bursey; *m* 1905, Letitia, *d* of Charles Henry and Susan Trollip, Umtata, S Africa; two *s* one *d*. *Educ:* Bedford; Barrow-in-Furness. Joined Cape Mounted Riflemen, 1894. Commissioned 1900, Boer War; Adjutant, CM Riflemen, 1907-11; appointed to Staff, Union Defence Forces, 1912; served in S African Rebellion, 1914-15; German West Africa and German East Africa (CBE, DSO, despatches); retired, 1924. *Address:* Private Bag 133K, Bulawayo, Rhodesia; Gladstone Farm, Matopos, Rhodesia. *TA:*Matopos, Rhodesia. *Club:* Bulawayo (Bulawayo).

**BURGESS, Clarkson Leo,** CBE 1951; Clerk of the Peace for the County of London, 1941-68; *b* 7 Sept. 1902; *er s* of late T. C. J. Burgess; *m* 1929, Marie Louise, *d* of late Capt. H. W. Prendergast; one *s* one *d*. *Educ:* Beaumont; Trinity Coll., Cambridge. Called to the Bar, Middle Temple, 1927. Knight of the Holy Sepulchre (KHS), 1963. *Recreations:* following outdoor sports of all kinds. *Address:* 17 Hillview, Cottenham Park Road, SW20. *T:* 01-947 0668. *Clubs:* Public Schools; Essex County Cricket.

**BURGESS, Claude Bramall,** CMG 1958; OBE 1954; Head of Co-ordination and Development Department, European Free Trade Association, Geneva, since 1964; *b* 25 Feb. 1910; *s* of late George Herbert Burgess, Weaverham, Cheshire, and Martha Elizabeth Burgess; *m* 1952, Margaret Joan Webb (marr. diss. 1965); one *s*; *m* 1969, Linda Nettleton, *e d* of William Grothier Beilby, New York. *Educ:* Epworth Coll.; Christ Church, Oxford. Eastern Cadetship in HM Colonial Administrative Service, 1932. Commissioned in RA, 1940; POW, 1941-45; demobilized with rank of Lieut-Col, RA, 1946. Colonial Office, 1946-48. Attended Imperial Defence Coll., London, 1951. Various Government posts in Hong Kong; Colonial Secretary (and Actg Governor on various occasions), Hong Kong, 1958-63, retd. *Recreations:* tennis, golf. *Address:* 17 Avenue de Budé, Geneva, Switzerland. *T:* 34.15.24. *Club:* Junior Carlton.

**BURGESS, Geoffrey,** CMG 1955; CIE 1946; OBE 1942; *b* 29 April 1906; *s* of Charles R. Burgess, Bucknall, Staffs; *m* 1933, Jill Margaret, *d* of John Hope-Almond, Cambridge; one *s* one *d*. *Educ:* Hanley High Sch.; Emmanuel Coll., Cambridge (MA). Served in ICS, 1928-47. Home Office until 1949. Mem. British Board of Film Censors, 1949-51; Dir, Civil Service Academy, Lahore, Pakistan, 1951-59; UN Advisor to Govt of Ghana, 1959-61; to Govt of the Somali Republic, 1961-63; Div. of Public Administration, UN, 1963-68; Advisor to Govt of Iran, 1968-69. *Address:* La Maison des Landes, St Brelade, Jersey, CI. c/o Lloyds Bank Ltd, 6 Pall Mall, SW1.

**BURGESS, John Lawie,** OBE 1944; TD 1945; DL; JP; Chairman and Managing Director, Cumberland Newspapers Ltd, since 1945; Chairman, Border Television Ltd, since 1960; *b* 17 Nov. 1912; *s* of late R. N. Burgess, Carlisle and Jean Hope Lawie, Carlisle; *m* 1948, Alice Elizabeth, *d* of late F. E. Gillieron, Elgin; two *s* one *d*. *Educ:* Trinity Coll., Glenalmond. Served War of 1939-45, Border Regt, France, Middle East, Tobruk, Syria, India and Burma; comd 4th Bn, Chindit Campaign, Burma, 1944 (despatches, OBE); Hon. Col 4th Bn The Border Regt, 1955-68. Chm., Reuters Ltd, 1959-68; Dir, Press Assoc. Ltd, 1950-57 (Chm. 1955); Mem. Council, Newspaper Soc., 1947- (Chm. of Advertising Cttee). Mem. Council, Commonwealth Press Union; Pres., Fedn of Cumberland and Westmorland Societies throughout the world. DL Cumberland, 1955; High Sheriff of Cumberland, 1969; JP City of Carlisle, 1952. *Recreations:* walking; anything to do with Cumberland. *Address:* The Old Hall, Rockliffe, Carlisle, Cumberland. *T:* Rockcliffe 252. *Clubs:* Garrick, Army and Navy; Cumberland County (Carlisle).

**BURGESS, Thomas Arthur Collier, (His Honour Vice-Chancellor Burgess);** Vice-Chancellor, County Palatine of Lancaster, since 1963; *b* 14 April 1906; 3rd *s* of Arthur Henry Burgess, FRCS, and Elspeth Burgess; *m* 1935, Anne Marian Mortimer Hunt, 2nd *d* of Wilfred and Henrietta Hunt. *Educ:* Charterhouse; Lincoln Coll., Oxford (MA). Called to Bar, 1928. RAFVR, 1940-45. Bar Council, 1953-57; Bencher, Lincoln's Inn, 1957. Mem. Council, Duchy of Lancaster, 1966. Legion of Merit (Officer), 1946. *Recreations:* music, travel. *Address:* Tatham Old Rectory, Lancaster. *T:* Hornby 381. *Clubs:* United University; St James's (Manchester).

**BURGH,** 7th Baron, *cr* 1529 (title called out of abeyance, 1916; by some reckonings he is 9th Baron (from a *cr* 1487) and his father was 8th and grandfather 7th); **Alexander Peter Willoughby Leith;** *b* 20 March 1935; *s* of 6th (or 8th) Baron Burgh; *S* father 1959; *m* 1957, Anita Lorna Eldridge; one *s* one *d*. *Educ:* Harrow; Magdalene Coll., Cambridge (BA). *Heir:* *s* Hon. Alexander Gregory Disney Leith, *b* 16 March 1958.

**BURGH, John Charles;** Assistant Under-Secretary of State, Department of Employment and Productivity, since 1968; *b* 9 Dec. 1925; *m* 1957, Ann Sturge; two *d*. *Educ:* Friends' Sch., Sibford; London Sch. of Economics (BSc Econ.). Leverhulme post-intermediate Schol.; Pres. of Union, 1949. Asst Principal, BoT, 1950; Private Sec. to successive Ministers of State, BoT, 1954-57; Colonial Office, 1959-62; Mem., UK Delegation to UN Conf. on Trade Develt, 1964; Asst Sec., DEA, 1964; Principal Private Sec. to successive First Secretaries of State and Secretaries of State for Econ. Affairs, 1965-68. *Recreation:* music. *Address:* 90 Kidbrooke Grove, Blackheath, SE3. *T:* 01-858 4398.

**BURGHARD, Rear-Adm. Geoffrey Frederic,** CB 1954; DSO 1946; retired; *b* 15 Oct. 1900; *m* 1931, Constance Louise Sheppard; one *s* one *d*. *Educ:* RN Colleges, Osborne and Dartmouth. Naval Cadet, 1913; Captain, 1942; Rear-Admiral, 1952; Deputy Controller Electronics, Min. of Supply, 1952-55; retired list, 1955. MIEE 1956-61. *Address:* The Old School, Pebmarsh, Halstead, Essex. *T:* Twinstead 227.

**BURGHERSH, Lord; Henry David Anthony Francis Fane;** *b* 1 Aug. 1951; *s* and *heir* of 15th Earl of Westmorland, *qv*.

**BURGIS, Lawrence Franklin,** CMG 1927; CVO 1938 (MVO 1925); *b* 1892; *e s* of late J. F. Burgis, FCA, and Mary Franklin, Leamington; *m* 1914, Lorna, *d* of late Arthur

Herbert, Whyteleafe, Surrey; one *d. Educ:* King's Sch., Worcester. Private Secretary to Viscount Esher, GCB, 1909-13; Asst Secretary, County of London TF Association, 1913-14; joined 6th Bn The Black Watch, 1913; Captain, 1917; served European War (despatches, Legion of Honour); Asst Secretary, War Cabinet, 1918 and 1939-45; Military Asst Secretary, Cttee of Imperial Defence, 1919-21; late Asst Secretary, Cabinet Office. An Esquire of the Order of St John of Jerusalem. *Address:* The Old Malt House, Steeple Aston, Oxon. *T:* Steeple Aston 353.

**BURHOP, Professor Eric Henry Stoneley,** FRS 1963; MSc, PhD; Professor of Physics, University College, London, since 1960; *b* 31 Jan. 1911; *s* of Henry A. and Bertha Burhop, Melbourne, Australia; *m* 1936, Winifred, *d* of Robert Stevens, Melbourne, Australia; two *s* one *d. Educ:* Ballarat and Melbourne High Schools, Australia; Melbourne Univ.; Trinity Coll., Cambridge. BA 1932, MSc 1933, Melbourne; PhD 1937, Cambridge. Exhibition of 1851 Schol., 1933-35; Research at Cavendish Laboratory, Cambridge, 1933-35; Research Physicist and Lecturer, Univ. of Melbourne, 1935-45; Dep. Dir., Radio Research Laboratory, Melbourne, 1942-44; Technical Officer, DSIR Mission to Berkeley, California, 1944-45; University Coll., London: Lectr in Mathematics, 1945-49; Reader in Mathematics, 1949-50; Reader in Physics, 1950-60. Joliot-Curie medal, 1966. *Publications:* The Challenge of Atomic Energy, 1951; The Auger Effect, 1953; Electronic and Ionic Impact Phenomena (with H. S. W. Massey), 1953; High Energy Physics (ed), Vols I, II, 1967, Vols III, IV, 1969. Various publications on atomic and nuclear physics. *Recreations:* futherance of international scientific co-operation. *Address:* 206 Gilbert House, Barbican, EC2. *T:* 01-638 8816.

**BURKE, Adm. Arleigh Albert;** Navy Cross; DSM (3 Gold Stars); Legion of Merit (with 2 Gold Stars and Army Oak Leaf Cluster). Silver Star Medal, Purple Heart, Presidential Unit Citation Ribbon (with 3 stars), Navy Unit Commendation Ribbon; retired as Chief of Naval Operations, US Navy and Member of Joint Chiefs of Staff (1955-61); Director, Centre for Strategic Studies, Georgetown University; Member of Board of Directors: Texaco, Inc. (and Member Executive Committee); Freeport Sulphur Co.; Thiokol Chemical Corporation; Dukane Corporation; Foster Wheeler Corporation; First National Bank of Washington; NUS Corporation; Oceanarium Inc.; Freedoms Foundation, at Valley Forge; National Capital Area Council, Boy Scouts of America; American Ordnance Association; *b* 19 Oct. 1901; *s* of Oscar A. and Claire Burke; *m* 1923, Roberta Gorsuch; no *c. Educ:* United States Naval Academy; Univ. of Michigan (MSE). Commnd ensign, USN, 1923, advancing through grades to Admiral, 1955. USS Arizona, 1923-28; Gunnery Dept, US Base Force, 1928; Post-graduate course (explosives), 1929-31; USS Chester, 1932; Battle Force Camera Party, 1933-35; Bureau of Ordnance, 1935-37; USS Craven, 1937-39; USS Mugford, Captain, 1939-40; Naval Gun Factory, 1940-43; Destroyer Divs 43 and 44, Squadron 12 Comdg, 1943; Destroyer Squadron 23 Comdg, 1943-44; Chief of Staff to Commander Task Force 58 (Carriers), 1944-45; Head of Research and Development Bureau of Ordnance, 1945-46; Chief of Staff, Comdr Eighth Fleet and Atlantic Fleet, 1947-48; USS Huntington, Captain, 1949; Asst Chief of Naval Ops, 1949-50; Cruiser Div. 5, Comdr, 1951; Dep. Chief of Staff, Commander Naval Forces, Far East, 1951; Director Strategic Plans Div., Office of the Chief of Naval Operations, 1952-53; Cruiser Division 6, Commanding, 1954; Commander Destroyer Force, Atlantic, 1955. Member: American Legion; American Soc. of Naval Engineers and numerous other naval assocs, etc.; National Geographic Society; also foreign societies, etc. Holds several hon. degrees. Ul Chi Medal (Korea), 1954; Korean Presidential Unit Citation, 1954. *Recreations:* reading, gardening. *Address:* (home) 8624 Fenway Drive, Bethesda, Maryland 20034, USA; (office) 810 18th Street NW, Washington, DC 20006, USA. *Clubs:* Army-Navy Town, Chevy Chase, Alfalfa, Admirals, Circus Saints and Sinners, Ends of the Earth, etc. (Washington, DC); Quindecum (Newport, US); The Brook, Lotos, Salmagundi, Inner Wheel, Seawanhaka Corinthian Yacht (New York); Bohemian (San Francisco).

**BURKE, Sir Aubrey (Francis),** Kt 1959; OBE 1941; Vice-Chairman and Deputy Managing Director, The Hawker Siddeley Group, Ltd; Deputy-Chairman and Managing Director, Hawker Siddeley Diesels Ltd; Deputy Chairman: Hawker Siddeley Holdings Ltd; Hawker Siddeley Dynamics Ltd; Hawker Siddeley Electric Ltd; Chairman: Mirrlees National Ltd; Hawker Siddeley Building Supplies Pty Ltd; Hawker Siddeley Brush Pty Ltd; Gloster Saro Ltd; Thomas Green & Son Ltd; Hands Trailers Ltd; Saro Products Ltd; Blackstone & Co. Ltd; Kelvin Construction Ltd; Director: Hawker Aviation Ltd; Hawker Siddeley International Ltd; Hawker Siddeley Australia Pty Ltd; Hawker de Haviland Australia Pty Ltd; Hawker Siddeley Internat. New Zealand Ltd; Hawker Siddeley International Pty Ltd; Hawker Siddeley Brush Ltd; Harrison Lister Engineering Ltd; Racair Ltd; *b* 21 April 1904; *m* 1936, Rosalind Laura, *d* of Rt Hon. Sir Henry Norman, 1st Bt, PC, OBE, and Hon. Lady Norman, CBE, JP; one *s* three *d* (and one *d* decd). Pres., SBAC, 1958-1959-1960. MInstT; FRSA. High Sheriff of Hertfordshire, 1966-67. *Recreations:* shooting, fishing, sailing. *Address:* Rent Street Barns, Bovingdon, Hertfordshire; Ramster, Chiddingfold, Surrey; Clos de la Garoupe, Antibes, AM, France. *Club:* Royal Automobile.

**BURKE, Desmond Peter Meredyth,** MA Oxon; Headmaster, Clayesmore School, 1945-66; *b* 10 May 1912; *yr s* of late Maj. Arthur Meredyth Burke. *Educ:* Cheltenham Coll.; Queen's Coll., Oxford. Honours, Modern Greats, 1933. Housemaster and Senior Modern Language Master, Clayesmore School, 1936-40; served in Army Intelligence Corps at home, Belgium and Germany, 1940-45. *Recreations:* the theatre, travel, tennis, bridge. *Address:* The Old Lodge, 92 Alumhurst Road, Bournemouth West. *T:* Westbourne 71329.

**BURKE, Rt. Rev. Geoffrey;** Titular Bishop of Vagrauta and Auxiliary Bishop of Salford (RC), since 1967; *b* 31 July 1913; *s* of Dr Peter Joseph Burke and Margaret Mary (*née* Coman). *Educ:* St Bede's Coll., Manchester; Stonyhurst Coll.; Oscott Coll., Birmingham; Downing Coll., Cambridge (MA). Taught History, St Bede's Coll., 1940-66; Prefect of Studies, 1950; Rector, 1966. Consecrated Bishop 29 June 1967. *Address:* St John's Cathedral, 250 Chapel Street, Salford 3, Lancs. *T:* 061-834 0333.

**BURKE, Joseph T. A.,** OBE 1946; MA; Professor of Fine Arts, University of Melbourne, since 1946; *b* 14 July 1913; *s* of late R. M. J. Burke; *m* 1940, Agnes, *d* of late Rev. James Middleton, New Brunswick, Canada; one *s. Educ:* Ealing Priory Sch.; King's Coll., Univ. of London; Courtland Institute of Art; Yale Univ., USA.

Entered Victoria and Albert Museum, 1938; lent to Home Office and Min. of Home Security, Sept. 1939; private sec. to successive Lord Presidents of the Council (Rt Hon. Sir John Anderson, Rt Hon. C. R. Attlee, Rt Hon. Lord Woolton), 1942-45; and to the Prime Minister (Rt Hon. C. R. Attlee), 1945-46; Trustee of Felton Bequest; Mem., Australian UNESCO Cttee for Visual Arts. Fellow, Australian Acad. of the Humanities. *Publications:* Hogarth and Reynolds: A Contrast in English Art Theory, 1943; ed William Hogarth's Analysis of Beauty and Autobiographical Notes, 1955; (with Colin Caldwell) Hogarth: The Complete Engravings, 1968; articles in Burlington Magazine, Warburg Journal and elsewhere. *Recreations:* golf, swimming. *Address:* 807 Toorak Road, Melbourne, E3, Victoria, Australia. *Clubs:* Athenæum; Melbourne (Melbourne).

**BURKE, Sir Thomas (Stanley),** 8th Bt, *cr* 1797; *b* 20 July 1916; *s* of Sir Gerald Howe Burke, 7th Bt and Elizabeth Mary (*d* 1918), *d* of late Patrick Mathews, Mount Hanover, Drogheda; *S* father 1954; *m* 1955, Susanne Margaretha, *er d* of Otto Salvisberg, Thun, Switzerland; one *s* one *d*. *Educ:* Harrow; Trinity Coll., Cambridge. *Heir: s* James Stanley Gilbert Burke, *b* 1 July 1956. *Address:* 18 Elmcroft Avenue, NW11. *T:* 01-455 9407.

**BURKE-GAFFNEY, Maj.-Gen. (Hon.) Edward Sebastian,** CBE 1944; RA, retired; *b* 17 Aug. 1900; *s* of Francis Sebastian Burke-Gaffney; *m* 1926, Margot Lawrence; one *s* one *d*. *Educ:* Downside Sch.; RMA, Woolwich. 2nd Lieut RA 1920; Captain, 1933; Major, 1938; Colonel, 1945; Brigadier, 1949; Maj.-General, 1954; Officer Co. Gentleman Cadets, 1933; Staff Coll., Camberley, 1935-36; AHQ, India, 1937; General Officer Commanding, Aldershot District, 1953-54; retired 1954. *Recreations:* cricket, hockey, golf, shooting. *Address:* c/o Lloyds Bank, 6 Pall Mall, SW1.

**BURKILL, John Charles,** FRS 1953; ScD; Master of Peterhouse, Cambridge, since 1968; Emeritus Reader in Mathematical Analysis; *b* 1 Feb. 1900; *m* 1928, Margareta, *d* of Dr A. Braun; one *s* two *d*. *Educ:* St Paul's; Trinity Coll., Cambridge. Smith's Prize, 1923; Professor of Pure Mathematics in the University of Liverpool, 1924-29; Tutor of Peterhouse, 1929-48; Member Institute of Advanced Study, Princeton, 1947; Visiting Professor, Rice Institute, 1956; Tata Institute, Bombay, 1959. Adams Prize, 1949. 2nd Lieut RE 1918; General List TA (Major), 1939-45. *Address:* The Master's Lodge, Peterhouse, Cambridge.

**BURKITT, Miles Crawford,** JP, MA, FSA, FGS; University Lecturer at Cambridge in the Faculty of Archæology and Anthropology, 1926-58; County Councillor, Cambridgeshire, 1939-64 (Vice-Chairman, 1958-61; Chairman, 1961-64); Alderman, 1964-65; Chairman, Town and Country Planning Committee, 1949-56; Chairman, Children's Committee, 1947-60; *b* Cambridge, 27 Dec. 1890; *s* of late Prof. F. C. Burkitt, DD, FBA, and Amy Persis, *d* of Rev. W. Parry, DCL; *m* 1923, Margaret Isobel, *d* of Sir John Fry, 2nd Bt; two *s* one *d*. *Educ:* Eton; Trinity Coll., Cambridge. Has Travelled extensively on archæological work in Spain, N Russia, Africa, Turkey, etc.; Past President of the Prehistoric Soc. of East Anglia, Cambridge Antiquarian Soc., Section H of British Association, 1949. Lieut (Signals Officer) 4th Cambs. Home Guard, 1941-45; Lieut-Colonel Army Cadet Force, 1942-46. JP 1942, High Sheriff of Counties of Cambridge and Huntingdon, 1960-61. *Publications:* Prehistory, 1921, 2nd Edn 1925; Our Forerunners, 1923; Our Early Ancestors, 1926; South Africa's Past in Stone and Paint, 1928; The Old Stone Age, 1933, 3rd Edn 1955, 4th Edn USA paperback, 1963; Rock Paintings of Southern Andalusia (with Professor Breuil); contributed to Man, Antiquaries Journal, Antiquity, Proc. Prehistoric Society, Nature, Scientia, etc. *Recreation:* travel. *Address:* Merton House (South Wing), Grantchester, Cambs. *TA:* Trumpington 2205. *T:* Trumpington 2205.

**BURKITT, Robert William;** Principal Officer, Commercial Policy, UK Atomic Energy Authority, since 1958; *b* 3 March 1908; *s* of late R. F. Burkitt, MC and Alice, *d* of R. Leighton, MA; *m* 1938, Bridget, *d* of Hugh Barber, MD, FRCP; four *s* two *d*. *Educ:* Bedford Sch.; Pembroke Coll., Cambridge. Kitchener Scholar; MA. MIMechE. Employed in industry, 1930-42 and 1943-44; Ministry of Production, 1942-43; Asst Secretary, Board of Trade, 1944-52; Student, Imperial Defence Coll., 1953; Asst Secretary Monopolies and Restrictive Practices Commn, 1954-55; Dep. Comptroller General, Export Credits Guarantee Dept., 1955-58. Reserve of Air Force Officers, 1928-33; Aux. Air Force (600 City of London Sqdn), 1933-35. *Address:* 6 Lower Common South, SW15. *T:* 01-788 9513. *Clubs:* Athenæum, London Rowing, Leander.

**BURLEIGH, Master of; Hon. George John Done Bruce,** RP 1960; painter of portraits, landscapes, still life, ships, flowers, etc.; *b* 28 March 1930; *s* of 11th Baron Balfour of Burleigh and Violet Dorothy Done, Delamere Forest, Tarporley, Cheshire; *b* and *heir-pres.* of 12th Baron Balfour of Burleigh, *qv*. *Educ:* Westminster Sch.; Byam Shaw Sch. of Drawing and Painting. *Recreations:* Mountains, Snow and water ski-ing, carpentry. *Address:* 6 Pembroke Walk, W8. *T:* 01-937 1493. *Club:* Athenæum.

**BURLEIGH, Very Rev. John H. S.,** DD, BLitt; Professor of Ecclesiastical History, Edinburgh University, 1931-64, Emeritus, since 1964; Dean of the Faculty of Divinity, 1956; Moderator of the General Assembly of the Church of Scotland, May 1960-May 1961; *b* Ednam, Kelso, 19 May 1894; *s* of Rev. J. Burleigh; *m* 1926, Mary, *d* of Rev. C. Giles; one *s* one *d*. *Educ:* Kelso High Sch., George Watson's Coll. and Univ., Edinburgh; Strasbourg; Oxford. Parish Minsiter of Fyvie, Aberdeenshire, and St Enoch's, Dundee. Principal, New Coll., Edinburgh, 1956-64. *Publications:* Christianity in the New Testament Epistles; City of God; a Study of St Augustine's Philosophy; St Augustine: Earlier Writings; A Church History of Scotland. *Address:* 4 Braid Avenue, Edinburgh. *T:* 031-447 4195.

**BURLEIGH, Thomas Haydon;** Director, John Brown & Co. Ltd, since 1965; Chairman, Firth Brown Tools Ltd, since 1970; *b* 23 April 1911; *s* of late J. H. W. Burleigh, Great Chesterford; *m* 1933, Kathleen Mary Lenthall, *d* of late Dr Gurth Eager, Hertford; two *s*. *Educ:* Saffron Walden Sch. RAF, short service commission, No 19 (F) Sqdn, 1930-35; Westland Aircraft Ltd, 1936-45; Thos. Firth & John Brown Ltd, 1945-48; Firth Brown Tools Ltd, 1948. Pres., Sheffield Chamber of Commerce, 1963-64; Pres. Nat. Fedn of Engineers' Tool Manufacturers, 1968-70; Master of Company of Cutlers in Hallamshire in the County of York, 1970-71. *Recreations:* golf, gardening. *Address:* Nether House, Storth Lane, Sheffield S10 3HP. *T:* Sheffield 301794. *Clubs:* Royal Air Force; Royal and Ancient Golf (St Andrews).

**BURLINGTON, Earl of; William Cavendish;** *b* 6 June 1969; *s* and *heir* of Marquess of Hartington, *qv.*

**BURMAN, Sir (John) Charles,** Kt 1961; DL; JP; Director: Midland Assurance Ltd (Vice-Chairman); South Staffs Waterworks Co. (Chairman); Tarmac Derby Ltd (Chairman); Birmid-Qualcast Ltd (Deputy Chairman); *b* 30 Aug. 1908; *o s* of Sir John Burman, JP; *m* 1936, Ursula Hesketh-Wright, JP; two *s* two *d*. *Educ:* Rugby Sch. City Council, 1934-66 (Lord Mayor of Birmingham, 1947-49); General Commissioner of Income Tax, 1941-; Indep. Chm., Licensing Planning Cttee, 1949-60; Chm. Birmingham Conservative and Unionist Assoc., 1963-; County Pres. St John Ambulance Brigade, 1950-63; Member, Govt Cttee on Administrative Tribunals, 1955; Member Royal Commission on the Police, 1960. Life Governor, also Trustee, Barber Institute, at University of Birmingham. JP 1942; High Sheriff, Warwickshire, 1958, DL 1967. KStJ, 1961. *Address:* 56 Wellington Road, Edgbaston, Birmingham 15. *T:* 021-440 1715. *Clubs:* Union, Conservative (Birmingham).

**BURMAN, Stephen France,** CBE 1954 (MBE 1943); MA; Chairman, Serck Ltd, Birmingham 1962-70; Director: Averys, Ltd; Duport Ltd; Imperial Chemical Industries Ltd; J. Lucas Industries Ltd; Midland Bank Ltd, and of other industrial companies; *b* 27 Dec. 1904; *s* of Henry Burman; *m* 1931, Joan Margaret Rogers; two *s*. *Educ:* Oundle. Pres. Birmingham Chamber of Commerce, 1950-51 (Vice-Pres. 1949); Chm. United Birmingham Hosps., 1948-53; Dep. Chm. 1953-56. Governor Birmingham Children's Hosp., 1944-48; Dep. Chm. Teaching Hosps. Assoc., 1949-53; Member, Midlands Electricity Board, 1948-65; Chm. Birmingham and District Advisory Cttee for Industry, 1947-49; Member Midland Regional Board for Industry, 1949-65, Vice-Chm. 1951-65; Member of Council and Life Governor, Univ. of Birmingham, 1949-, Pro-Chancellor, 1955-66; General Commissioner for Income Tax, 1950-68. Member Royal Commission on Civil Service, 1953-56. *Recreation:* shooting. *Address:* Cooper's Hill House, Callow Hill, Alvechurch, Worcs. *T:* 021-445 1703.

**BURN, Andrew Robert;** Visiting Professor at A College Year in Athens, Athens, Greece, since 1969; *b* 25 Sept. 1902; *s* of Rev. A. E. Burn and Celia Mary, *d* of Edward Richardson; *m* 1938, Mary, *d* of Wynn Thomas, OBE, Ministry of Agriculture; no *c*. *Educ:* Uppingham Sch.; Christ Church, Oxford. Sen. Classical Master, Uppingham Sch., 1927-40; British Council Rep. in Greece, 1940-41; Intelligence Corps, Middle East, 1941-44; 2nd Sec., British Embassy, Athens, 1944-46; Sen. Lectr and sole Mem. Dept of Ancient History, Univ. of Glasgow, 1946; Reader, 1965; resigned, 1969. Pres. Glasgow Archæological Soc., 1966-69. *Publications:* Minoans, Philistines and Greeks, 1930; The Romans in Britain, 1932; The World of Hesiod, 1936; This Scepter'd Isle: an Anthology, 1940 (Athens); The Modern Greeks, 1942 (Alexandria); Alexander and the Hellenistic World, 1947; Pericles and Athens, 1948; Agricola and Roman Britain, 1953; The Lyric Age of Greece, 1960; Persia and the Greeks, 1962; The Pelican History of Greece, 1966; The Warring States of Greece (illustrated), 1968; Greece and Rome (Hist. of Civilisation Vol. II), 1969 (Chicago); contributions to encyclopædias and historical journals. *Recreation:* travel. *Address:* c/o Midland Bank, Uppingham, Rutland.

**BURN, Duncan (Lyall);** economist, consultant; Visiting Professor of Economics, Manchester University, 1967-69; *b* 10 Aug. 1902; *s* of Archibald William and Margaret Anne Burn; *m* 1930, Mollie White; two *d*. *Educ:* Holloway County Sch.; Christ's Coll. (Scholar), Cambridge. Hist. Tripos, Pts I and II, Cl. I, Wrenbury Schol. 1924, Bachelor Research Schol. 1924, Christ's Coll., Cambridge. Lecturer in Economic History: Univ. of Liverpool, 1925; Univ. of Cambridge, 1927. Min. of Supply (Iron and Steel Control), 1939; Member US-UK Metallurgical Mission, New York and Washington, 1943; leader writer and Industrial Correspondent of the Times, 1946-62. Director of the Economic Development Office set up by AEI, English Electric, GEC, and Parsons, 1962-65. Member: Advisory Cttee on Census of Production, 1955-65; Exec. Cttee, Nat. Inst. of Econ. and Social Research; Econ. Cttee, DSIR, 1963-65. *Publications:* Economic History of Steelmaking, 1867-1939, 1940; The Steel Industry, 1939-59, 1961; ed. and contrib. to: The Structure of British Industry, 2 vols., 1958; The Political Economy of Nuclear Energy, 1967; also contrib. to Journals, Bank Reviews, etc. *Recreations:* walking, gardening. *Address:* 5 Hampstead Hill Gardens, NW3. *T:* 01-435 5344; Upper Falkland Cottages, The Green, Long Melford, Suffolk. *Club:* Oxford and Cambridge.

**BURN, Joshua Harold,** FRS 1942; MA, MD, Cantab; Emeritus Professor of Pharmacology, Oxford University, Emeritus Fellow of Balliol College; *b* 6 March 1892; *s* of J. G. Burn, Barnard Castle; *m* 1st, 1920, Margaret Parkinson; 2nd, 1928, Katharine F. Pemberton; two *s* four *d*. *Educ:* Barnard Castle Sch.; Emmanuel Coll., Cambridge (Scholar); 1st Class Pt 2 Natural Science Tripos; Michael Foster Student and Raymond Horton-Smith Prizeman; temp. Lieut RE, 1914-18; Guy's Hospital, 1918-20; member of staff of Medical Research Council, 1920-25; Director of Pharmaceutical Laboratories of Phamaceutical Soc., 1926-37; Dean of Coll. of Pharmaceutical Soc. and Prof. of Pharmacology, Univ. of London, 1933-37; Prof. of Pharmacology, Oxford Univ., 1937-59. Member of 1932 Pharmacopœia Commn; Hon. Fellow Nat. Institute of Sciences of India; Hon. Member Soc. of Pharmacology and Therapeutics of Argentine Medical Assoc. Abraham Flexner Lecturer, Vanderbilt Univ., 1956; Nathanson Memorial Lecturer Univ. of Southern California, 1956; Dixon Memorial Lecturer Royal Soc. of Medicine, 1956; Visiting Prof. to Washington Univ., St Louis, 1959-68. Hon. DSc Yale, 1957; Hon. MD Johannes Gutenberg Univ., Mainz, 1964; Dr (*hc*), Univ. of Paris, 1965; Hon. Member: Deutsche Pharmakologische Gesellschaft (by whom awarded the Schmiedeberg Plakette); British Pharmacological Society; Deutsche Akademie der Naturforscher (Leopoldina); Czechoslovak Medical Society J. E. Purkyně. Gairdner Foundation Prize, 1959. *Publications:* Methods of Biological Assay, 1928; Recent Advances in Materia Medica, 1931; Biological Standardization, 1937; Background of Therapeutics, 1948; Lecture Notes on Pharmacology, 1948; Practical Pharmacology, 1952; Functions of Autonomic Transmitters, 1956; The Principles of Therapeutics, 1957; Drugs, Medicines and Man, 1962; The Autonomic Nervous System, 1963; Our most interesting Diseases, 1964; A Defence of John Balliol, 1970. *Address:* 3 Squitchey Lane, Oxford. *T:* Oxford 58209.

**BURN, Michael Clive,** MC 1945; Writer; Chairman, Portmadoc Mussels Ltd; *b* 11 Dec. 1912; *s* of late Sir Clive Burn; *m* 1947, Mary Booker (*née* Walter); no *c*. *Educ:* Winchester;

New Coll., Oxford (open scholar). Journalist, The Times, 1936-39; Lieut 1st Bn Queens Westminsters, KRRC, 1939-40; Officer in Independent Companies, Norwegian Campaign, 1940, subseq. Captain No. 2 Commando; taken prisoner in raid on St Nazaire, 1942; prisoner in Germany, 1942-45. Foreign Correspondent for The Times in Vienna, Jugoslavia and Hungary, 1946-49. *Plays:* The Modern Everyman (prod. Birmingham Rep., 1947); The Night of the Ball (prod. New Theatre, 1956). *Publications: novels:* Yes, Farewell, 1946; Childhood at Oriol, 1951; The Midnight Diary, 1952; The Trouble with Jake, 1967; *sociological:* Mr Lyward's Answer, 1956; The Debatable Land, 1970; *poems:* Poems to Mary, 1953; The Flying Castle, 1954; *play:* The Modern Everyman, 1948. *Address:* Beudy Gwyn, Minfordd, Merioneth, North Wales.

**BURN, Rodney Joseph,** RA 1962 (ARA 1954); Artist; *b* Palmers Green, Middlesex, 11 July 1899; *s* of Sir Joseph Burn, KBE, and Emily Harriet Smith; *m* 1923, Dorothy Margaret, *d* of late Edward Sharwood-Smith; one *s* two *d*. *Educ:* Harrow Sch. Studied art at Slade Sch.; Asst Teacher at Royal Coll. of Art, South Kensington, 1929-31 and since 1946; Director of School of the Museum of Fine Arts, Boston, Mass., USA, 1931; returned to England, 1934; Asst Master, City & Guilds of London Art Sch.; Tutor, Royal Coll. of Art, 1947-. Hon. Secretary New English Art Club until 1963; Member Royal West of England Academy, 1963; Pres. St Ives Soc. of Artists, 1963; Hon. Fellow Royal Coll. of Art, 1964; Fellow University Coll. London, 1966. *Address:* 1 The Moorings, Strand on the Green, Chiswick, W4. *T:* 01-994 4190.

**BURNABY, Rev. Prof. John;** Regius Professor of Divinity (Emeritus), Cambridge University; *b* 28 July 1891; 2nd *s* of Rev. J. C. W. Burnaby and Ina, *d* of Maj.-Gen. J. P. Battersby; *m* 1922, Dorothy Helen, *d* of Rev. J. B. Lock, and *widow* of Capt. W. Newton; one *s* one *d* (one step-*d*) (and one *s* decd). *Educ:* Haileybury Coll.; Trinity Coll., Cambridge. Craven Univ. Scholar, 1912; Chancellor's Classical Medalist, 1914. Served European War, 1914-19, 1st Bn The London Regt, Gallipoli and France. Fellow of Trinity Coll., Cambridge, 1915; Junior Dean, 1919; Steward and Prælector, 1921; Junior Bursar, 1921-31; Tutor, 1931-38; Senior Tutor, 1938-45; Dean of Chapel, 1943-58; Hulsean Lecturer, 1938; College Lecturer in Theology, 1939-51; University Lecturer in Divinity, 1945-52; Regius Professor of Divinity, 1952-58. Deacon, 1941; Priest, 1942. *Publications:* Amor Dei: a study in the religion of St Augustine, 1938; Is the Bible Inspired?, 1949; Later Works of St Augustine (trans. and ed) in Library of Christian Classics, 1955; Christian Words and Christian Meanings, 1955; The Belief of Christendom, 1959. *Recreations:* music, reading aloud. *Address:* 6 Hedgerley Close, Cambridge. *T:* 50395.

**BURNE, Sir Lewis (Charles),** Kt 1959; CBE 1955; *b* West Leederville, WA, 14 Jan. 1898; *s* of late William Charles and Sarah Ellen Burne; *m* 1922, Florence Mary Stafford; two *s* two *d*. *Educ:* Xavier Coll., Melbourne. President: Master Builders Assoc. of Victoria, 1941-44; Master Builders' Federation of Australia, 1947; Victorian Employers' Federation, 1948-50 and 1953-61; Australian Council of Employers' Federations, 1957-58. Pres. Royal Melbourne Inst. of Technology, 1961; Chairman: Federation Insurance Ltd, 1956-; VEF Corporate Investments Ltd, 1958. Australian Employers' Deleg. at ILO, 1950-52-55-57-66; Australian Employers' Rep. Asian Advisory Cttee of ILO, 1951-66; Employer Memner at Governing Body meetings of ILO, 1950-66, and elected Member Governing Body, 1957-66. Fellow Australian Inst. of Builders (Foundation Member). Australian Flying Corps, 1918. *Recreations:* golf and bowls. *Address:* 20 Rockingham Street, Kew, Victoria, Australia. *T:* 86-8354. *Clubs:* Victoria Racing, RAC of Victoria (all in Melbourne).

**BURNET, Alastair;** *see* Burnet, J. W. A.

**BURNET, Sir (Frank) Macfarlane,** OM 1958; KBE 1969; Kt 1951; FRS 1942; MD, ScD (Hon.) Cambridge, 1946; DSc (Hon.) Oxford, 1968; FRCP 1953; Past Director, Walter and Eliza Hall Institute for Medical Research, Melbourne, and Professor of Experimental Medicine, Melbourne University, 1944-1965 (Assistant Director, 1928-31 and 1934-44); Emeritus Professor, Melbourne University, 1965; Chairman, Commonwealth Foundation, 1966-69; *b* 3 Sept. 1899; *s* of Frank Burnet, Traralgon, Victoria; *m* 1928, Edith Linda, *d* of F. H. Druce; one *s* two *d*. *Educ:* Geelong Coll., Melbourne Univ. (MD). Resident Pathologist, Melbourne Hosp., 1923-24; Beit Fellow for Medical Research at Lister Institute, London, 1926-27; Visiting worker at National Institute for Medical Research, Hampstead, 1932-33; Dunham Lecturer Harvard Medical Sch., Jan. 1944; Croonian Lecturer, 1950 (Royal Society); Herter Lecturer, 1950 (Johns Hopkins Univ.); Abraham Flexner Lecturer (Vanderbilt Univ.), 1958. Pres., Australian Acad. of Science, 1965-69. Hon. FRCS 1969. Royal Medal of Royal Society, 1947; Galen Medal in Therapeutics, Society of Apothecaries, 1958; Copley Medal, Royal Society, 1959; Nobel Prize for Medicine, 1960. *Publications:* Biological Aspects of Infectious Disease, 1940 (3rd edn Natural History of Infectious Disease, 1962); Virus as Organism, 1945; Viruses and Man (Penguin), 1953; Principles of Animal Virology, 1955; Enzyme Antigen and Virus, 1956; Clonal Selection Theory of Acquired Immunity, 1959; Integrity of the Body, 1962; (with I. R. Mackay) Autoimmune Diseases, 1962; Changing Patterns (autobiography) 1968; Cellular Immunology, 1969, technical papers. *Address:* School of Microbiology, University of Melbourne, Parkville, Victoria 3052; 13 Edward Street, Kew, Victoria 3101, Australia.

**BURNET, James William Alexander, (Alastair Burnet);** Editor of The Economist since 1965; *b* 12 July 1928; *s* of late Alexander and Schonaid Burnet, Edinburgh; *m* 1958, Maureen Campbell Sinclair. *Educ:* The Leys Sch., Cambridge; Worcester Coll., Oxford. Sub-editor and leader writer, Glasgow Herald, 1951-58; Commonwealth Fund Fellow, 1956-57; Leader writer, The Economist, 1958-62; Political editor, Independent Television News, 1963-64. Mem., Cttee of Award, Commonwealth Fund, 1969-. Award winner, Guild of Television Producers and Directors, 1966. *Address:* 43 Hornton Court, Campden Hill Road, W8. *T:* 01-937 7563; 33 Westbourne Gardens, Glasgow, W2. *T:* 041-339 8073. *Club:* Reform.

**BURNETT, of Leys,** Baronetcy of (unclaimed); *see under* Ramsay, Sir Alexander William Burnett, 7th Bt.

**BURNETT, Rt. Rev. Bill Bendyshe;** *see* Grahamstown, Bishop of.

**BURNETT, Air Chief Marshal Sir Brian (Kenyon),** GCB 1970 (KCB 1965; CB 1961); DFC 1942; AFC 1939; Commander-in-Chief, Far East Command, Singapore, since 1970; *b* 10 March 1913; *s* of late Kenneth Burnett and Anita Catherine Burnett (*née* Evans); *m* 1944,

Valerie Mary (*née* St Ludger); two *s. Educ:* Charterhouse; Wadham Coll., Oxford. Joined RAFO 1932; RAF 1934; Long Distance Record Flight of 7,158 miles from Egypt to Australia, Nov. 1938. Served War of 1939-45, in Bomber and Flying Training Commands; RAF Staff Coll. Course, 1944; Directing Staff, RAF Staff Coll., 1945-47; UN Military Staff Cttee, New York, 1947-48; Joint Planning Staff, 1949-50; SASO HQ No. 3 (Bomber) Group, 1951-53; CORAF Gaydon, 1954-55; ADC to the Queen, 1953-57; Director of Bomber and Reconnaissance Ops, Air Ministry, 1956-57; Imperial Defence Coll., 1958; Air Officer Administration, HQ Bomber Command, 1959-61; AOC No 3 Gp, Bomber Command, 1961-64; Vice-Chief of the Air Staff, 1964-67; Air Secretary, MoD, 1967-70. Air ADC to the Queen, 1969-. *Recreations:* tennis, squash rackets, golf, ski-ing. *Address:* (permanent) c/o Westminster Bank Ltd, 40 Market Place, NW11. *Clubs:* RAF; Vincents (Oxford); All England Lawn Tennis; Ski Club of Great Britain; Jesters Squash; International Lawn Tennis Club of Great Britain.

**BURNETT, Sir David Humphery,** 3rd Bt, *cr* 1913; MBE 1945; TD; Chairman, Proprietors of Hay's Wharf Ltd, since 1965; Director, Guardian Royal Exchange Assurance and other companies; Member, Port of London Authority, since 1962; one of HM Lieutenants of the City of London; *b* 27 Jan. 1918; *s* of Sir Leslie Trew Burnett, 2nd Bt, CBE, TD, DL, and Joan, *d* of late Sir John Humphery; *S* father 1955; *m* 1948, Geraldine Elizabeth Mortimer, *d* of Sir Godfrey Arthur Fisher, *qv*; three *s. Educ:* Harrow; St John's Coll., Cambridge, BA 1938, MA 1941. Served War of 1939-45 (despatches, MBE), in France, N Africa, Sicily and Italy; Temp. Lt-Col GSO1, 1945. Chairman: South London Botanical Institute; London Assoc. of Public Wharfingers, 1964-. Master: Company of Watermen and Lightermen of the River Thames, 1964; Girdlers Company, 1970. ARICS 1948; FBIM 1968. *Heir: s* Robert Leslie Fisher Burnett, *b* 24 May 1949. *Address:* Tandridge Hall, near Oxted, Surrey. *Club:* Turf.

**BURNETT, Prof. George Murray;** Professor of Chemistry, University of Aberdeen, since 1955; Vice-Principal 1966-69; *b* 12 July 1921; *s* of G. Burnett, Messina, South Africa; *m* 1946, Anne Edith, *d* of S. M. Bow, Aberdeen; one *s* three *d. Educ:* Robert Gordon's Coll., Aberdeen; Aberdeen Univ. DSIR Senior Fellow, 1947-48. Lectr, Birmingham Univ., 1949-55. FRSE 1960; FRIC 1961 JP 1967. *Publications:* Mechanism of Polymer Reactions, 1964; contrib. to Proc. Royal Society, Trans. Faraday Soc., etc. *Address:* 66 Queens Road, Aberdeen. *T:* Aberdeen 34441.

**BURNETT, Prof. John Harrison;** Sibthorpian Professor of Rural Economy, Oxford, since 1970; *b* 21 Jan. 1922; *s* of Rev. T. Harrison Burnett; *m* 1945, E. Margaret, *er d* of Rev. Dr E. W. Bishop; two *s. Educ:* Kingswood Sch., Bath; Merton Coll., Oxford. Postmaster, Merton Coll., 1940-47, Kitchener Scholar, 1940-47; Honour Sch. Nat. Sci. (Botany) Class I, 1947; BA, MA 1947; DPhil 1953; Christopher Welch Scholar, 1946. Lecturer, Lincoln Coll., 1948-49; Fellow (by Exam.) Magdalen Coll., 1949-53; Univ. Lecturer and Demonstrator, Oxford, 1949-53; Lecturer, Liverpool Univ., 1954-55; Prof. of Botany: Univ. of St Andrews, 1955-60; King's Coll., Newcastle, Univ. of Durham, 1961-63, Univ. of Newcastle, 1963-68; Dean of Faculty of Science, St Andrews, 1958-60, Newcastle, 1966-68; Public Orator, Newcastle, 1966-68; Regius Prof. of Botany, Univ. of Glasgow, 1968-70. Chm. Scottish Horticultural Research Inst., 1959-; Mem., Nature Conservancy (Scottish Cttee), 1961-66; Trustee, The New Phytologist, 1962-; Mem. Academic Adv. Council, Univs of St Andrews and Dundee, 1964-66. Served 1942-46 as Lieut RNVR (despatches). FRSE 1957. *Publications:* The Vegetation of Scotland, ed and contrib., 1964; Fundamentals of Mycology, 1968; papers in various scientific journals. *Address:* Apple Acres, 87 Eynsham Road, Oxford OX1 9BY. *T:* Cumnor 2037.

**BURNETT, Lt-Col Maurice John Brownless,** DSO 1944; *b* 24 Sept. 1904; *o s* of late Ernest Joseph Burnett, MBE, JP, The Red House, Saltburn-by-the-Sea, Yorks, and late Emily Maud Margaret, 2nd *d* of John Brownless, Whorlton Grange, Barnard Castle and Dunsa Manor, East Layton; *m* 1930, Crystal, *d* of late Col H. D. Chamier, The Connaught Rangers; one *s. Educ:* Aysgarth Sch.; Rugby Sch.; RMA, Woolwich; Staff Coll., Camberley. 2nd Lieut RA 1924; psc 1937; Lt-Col 1942; served 1939-45; comd 127th (Highland) Field Regt in 51st Highland Division, Normandy to the Rhine; retd 1948. JP, 1957, DL, 1958, N Riding Yorks. Member: N Riding Yorks Education Cttee, 1956; NR Yorks Standing Joint Cttee, 1958; Richmond, Yorks, RDC 1958 (Chm., 1967-69); Church Assembly, 1955; Ripon Diocesan Bd of Finance, 1953 (Vice-Chm. 1956); Exec. Cttee, N Riding yorks Assoc. of Youth Clubs, 1950 (Chm. 1952 and 1965). Governor, Barnard Castle Sch., 1959-63; District Comr, Scouts Assoc., (formerly Boy Scots Assoc.), NR Yorks, 1950. County-Comr, 1961-69. N Riding CC, 1962 (Chm, Civil Defence Cttee, 1966). Sec., N Riding Yorks Territorial and Auxiliary Forces Assoc., 1950-68. *Recreations:* country sports and pursuits, interest in youth work. *Address:* Dunsa Manor, East Layton, Richmond, Yorks. *T:* East Layton 251. *Clubs:* Army and Navy; Cleveland (Middlesbrough).

**BURNETT, Rev. Canon Philip Stephen;** Church of England Board of Education, since 1970; *b* 8 Jan. 1914; *s* of late Philip Burnett and Mrs Burnett, Salton, York; *m* 1954, Joan Hardy, *e d* of C. F. Hardy, Sheffield; one *s* one *d. Educ:* Scarborough Coll.; Balliol Coll., Oxford; Westcott House, Cambridge. Admitted Solicitor, 1936; Lay Missionary, Dio. Saskatchewan, Canada, 1939-41. Intelligence Corps, 1942-44; Staff Capt., GHQ, New Delhi, 1944-45, Deacon, 1946, Priest, 1948; Curate of St Andrew's, Chesterton, Cambridge, and Staff Sec., Student Christian Movement, 1947-49; Asst Gen. Sec., SCM, 1949-52; Vicar of St Mary, Bramall Lane, Sheffield, 1952-61; Rural Dean of Ecclesall, 1959-65; Canon Residentiary of Sheffield Cathedral, and Educn Secretary, Diocese of Sheffield, 1961-70, Canon Emeritus 1970-. *Address:* 91 Chelverton Road, Putney, SW15. *T:* 01-789 9934.

**BURNETT, Rear-Adm. Philip Whitworth,** CB 1957; DSO 1945; DSC 1943, and Bar, 1944; *b* 10 Sept. 1908; *s* of Henry Ridley Burnett; *m* 1947, Molly, *widow* of Brig. H. C. Partridge, DSO, and *d* of H. M. Trouncer; one *s* two *d. Educ:* Preparatory Sch., Seascale; Royal Naval Coll., Dartmouth. Served War of 1939-45; HMS Kelly, 1939-41; HMS Osprey, 1941-43; Western Approaches Escort Groups, 1943-45. Chief of Staff to Comdr-in-Chief, Portsmouth, 1955-57; retd list 1958. Lieut 1930; Comdr 1940; Capt. 1945; Rear-Adm. 1955. Sec. of the Royal Institution of Chartered Surveyors, 1959-65. *Address:* East Henfold, Beare Green, Dorking, Surrey.

**BURNETT, Lt-Col Robert Richardson,** CMG 1951; CIE 1944; OBE 1932; *b* 22 Oct. 1897; *s* of late Alexander Burnett, JP, Haddington, Scotland; *m* 1927, Dorothy Mary Laetitia, *d* of late Col J. Anderson; one *s* one *d*. *Educ:* George Watson's Coll., Edinburgh. 2nd Lieut Royal Scots (TF), 1915; Lieut Machine-Gun Corps, 1916; served in Belgium, France, and Mesopotamia, 1917-18; Indian Army (27th Punjabis), 1918; Zhob Militia, 1922-25; Indian Political Service, 1925-47; Lt-Col 1944; Resident for Rajputana, 1946-47; Dep. High Commissioner for the UK in Pakistan (Karachi), 1947-52; British Member of Sudanisation Cttee, Khartoum, 1954-55. Gen. Sec. for Scotland, Royal Over-Seas League, 1956-64. *Recreations:* fishing and golf. *Address:* Inverdruie, Gullane, East Lothian. *T:* Gullane 2271.

**BURNETT, William George Esterbrooke,** CB 1946; Commissioner of Inland Revenue and Secretary, Board of Inland Revenue, 1942-49, retired; *b* 1886; *s* of late William Burnett, Belturbet, Co. Cavan; *m* 1918, Dorothea, *y d* of late J. E. Kingsbury, Crawley Down, Sussex; two *s*. *Educ:* Royal School, Cavan; Trinity Coll., Dublin. *Address:* Brookside, 7 Guildford Road, Horsham, Sussex. *T:* 5284.

**BURNEY, Sir Cecil (Denniston),** 3rd Bt *cr* 1921; Managing Director since 1951, and Chairman since 1968, Northern Motors Ltd; Director, Security Building Society, since 1959; *b* 8 Jan. 1923; *s* of Sir Charles Dennistoun Burney, 2nd Bt, CMG, and of Gladys, *d* of George Henry High; *S* father, 1968; *m* 1957, Hazel Marguerite de Hamel, *yr d* of late Thurman Coleman; two *s*. *Educ:* Eton; Trinity Coll., Cambridge. Member of Legislative Council, N Rhodesia, 1959-64; MP Zambia, 1964-68; Chairman, Public Accounts Cttee, Zambia, 1963-67. *Recreations:* tennis, skiing. *Heir:* *s* Nigel Dennistoun Burney, *b* 6 Sept. 1959. *Address:* PO Box 672, Ndola, Zambia; 5 Lyall Street, SW1. *T:* 01-235 4014. *Clubs:* Carlton, Bath, RNVR, Leander; Salisbury, Bulawayo (Rhodesia); Ndola (Zambia).

**BURNHAM,** 5th Baron, *cr* 1903; **William Edward Harry Lawson,** Bt 1892; JP; Lieutenant-Colonel; Scots Guards, retired 1968; *b* 22 Oct. 1920; *er s* of 4th Baron Burnham, CB, DSO, MC, TD, and of (Marie) Enid (*see* Lady Burnham); *S* father, 1963; *m* 1942, Anne, *yr d* of late Major Gerald Petherick, The Mill House, St Cross, Winchester; three *d* (one *s* decd). *Educ:* Eton. Royal Bucks Yeomanry, 1939-41; Scots Guards, 1941-68; commanded 1st Bn, 1959-62. *Recreations:* sailing, shooting, ski-ing. *Heir:* *b* Hon. Hugh John Frederick Lawson [*b* 15 Aug. 1931; *m* 1955, Hilary Mary, *d* of Alan Hunter; one *s* two *d*]. *Address:* Little Hall Barn, Beaconsfield, Bucks. *T:* Beaconsfield 3315. *Clubs:* Turf; Royal Yacht Squadron.

**BURNHAM, Enid,** CBE 1957; JP; (**Enid Lady Burnham**); President, Girl Guides Association for England, since 1961; President, Buckinghamshire Red Cross, 1936-64; *d* of Hugh Scott Robson, Buenos Aires; *m* 1920, 4th Baron Burnham, CB, DSO, MC, TD; two *s* one *d*. *Educ:* Heathfield Sch., Ascot. JP 1943. Pres. Bucks Federation of Women's Institutes, 1947-52; Chief Commissioner for England, Girl Guides, 1951-60. *Publication:* (with Geoffrey Toye) Military Menus. *Recreations:* riding, country life, dogs. *Address:* Wycombe End House, Beaconsfield, Bucks. *Club:* Guide.

**BURNHAM, Forbes;** *see* Burnham, L. F. S.

**BURNHAM, James;** Writer; Editor, National Review, since 1955; *b* 22 Nov. 1905; *s* of Claude George Burnham and Mary May Gillis; *m* 1934, Marcia Lightner; two *s* one *d*. *educ:* Princeton Univ.; Balliol Coll., Oxford Univ. Prof. of Philosophy, New York Univ., 1932-54. *Publications:* The Managerial Revolution, 1941; The Machiavellians, 1943; The Struggle for the World, 1947; The Coming Defeat of Communism, 1950; Containment or Liberation, 1953; The Web of Subversion, 1954; Congress and the American Tradition, 1959; Suicide of the West, 1964; The War We Are In, 1967. (Co-author) A Critical Introduction to Philosophy, 1932; The Case for De Gaulle, 1948. *Address:* Kent, Conn. 06757, USA. *T:* Kent, Conn., 203-927-3117.

**BURNHAM, (Linden) Forbes (Sampson),** QC (British Guiana); Prime Minister of Guyana, since 1966 (of British Guiana, 1964-66); Leader, People's National Congress, since 1957; *b* 20 Feb. 1923; *s* of J. E. Burnham, Headteacher of Kitty Methodist Sch., and Rachel A. Burnham (*née* Sampson); *m* 1st, 1951, Sheila Bernice Lataste; three *d*; 2nd, 1967, Viola Harper; one *d*. *Educ:* Kitty Methodist Sch., Central High Sch., Queen's Coll.; London Univ. British Guiana Scholarship, 1942; BA (London) 1944; Best Speaker's Cup at Univ. of London, 1946; Pres. W Indian Students Union (Brit.); LLB (Hons) 1947. Called to the Bar, 1948. Entered local politics, 1949; Minister of Education, 1953; re-elected to Legislature, 1957 and 1961; Leader of Opposition, 1961-64. Pres. Kitty Brotherhood, 1947-48, 1949-50; Town Councillor, 1952; Mayor of Georgetown, 1959, 1964; Pres. Bar Association, 1959; Pres. British Guiana Labour Union, 1953-54, 1963-65 (Guyana), 1966-. *Recreations:* horse-riding, swimming, reading, listening to all types of music. *Address:* The Residence, Botanical Gardens, Vlissengen Road, Georgetown, Guyana. *Clubs:* Demerara Cricket, Maltenoes Sports, Georgetown Cricket (formerly BGCC); Non Pareil (all in Guyana).

**BURNIE, James,** MC 1918; *b* Bootle, 10 May 1882; *s* of Joseph Burnie; *m* 1910, Ruth E. Thornton (*d* 1939); one *s* one *d*. *Educ:* St John's, Bootle; Merchant Taylors', Crosby. Mobilised as Sergeant at outbreak of war; retired as Major in Bootle Battalion, 7th King's Liverpool Regt (MC). MP (L) Bootle, 1922-24; Mayor of Bootle, 1936-37. *Address:* The Rectory, Pitsford, Northampton. *Club:* National Liberal.

**BURNINGHAM, John Mackintosh;** free-lance author-designer; *b* 27 April 1936; *s* of Charles Burningham and Jessie Mackintosh; *m* 1964, Helen Gillian Oxenbury; one *s* one *d*. *Educ:* Summerhill School, Leiston, Suffolk; Central School of Art, Holborn, 1956-59 (Diploma). Now free-lance: illustration, poster design, exhibition, animated film puppets, and writing for children. Kate Greenaway Medal, 1963. *Publications:* Borka, 1963; Trubloff, 1964; Humbert, 1965; Cannonball Simp, 1966; Harquin, 1967; Seasons, 1969; Mr Gumpy's Outing, 1970. *Address:* 25 Willow Road, Hampstead, NW3. *T:* 01-435 5486.

**BURNLEY, Suffragan Bishop of,** since 1970; **Rt. Rev. Richard Charles Challinor Watson;** Rector of Burnley since 1970; Hon. Canon of Blackburn Cathedral since 1970; *b* 16 Feb. 1923; *o s* of Col Francis W. Watson, CB, MC, DL, The Glebe House, Dinton, Aylesbury, Bucks; *m* 1955, Anna, *er d* of Rt Rev. C. M. Chavasse, OBE, MC, MA, DD, then Bishop of Rochester; one *s* one *d*. *Educ:* Rugby; New Coll., Oxford; Westcott House, Cambridge. Served Indian Artillery, Lt and Capt. RA,

1942-45. Oxford Hon. Sch. Eng. Lang. and Lit., 1948, Theology 1949; Westcott House, Cambridge, 1950-51. Curate of Stratford, London E, 1952-53; Tutor and Chaplain, Wycliffe Hall, Oxford, 1954-57; Chaplain of Wadham Coll. and Chaplain of Oxford Pastorate, 1957-61; Vicar of Hornchurch, 1962-70; Examining Chaplain to Bishop of Rochester, 1956-61, to Bishop of Chelmsford, 1962-70; Asst. Rural Dean of Havering, 1967-70. *Recreations:* reading, gardening. *Address:* Palace House, Burnley, Lancashire. *T:* Burnley 23564. *Club:* Lansdowne.

**BURNS, Sir Alan Cuthbert,** GCMG, *cr* 1946 (KCMG *cr* 1936; CMG 1927); Knight of Order of St John of Jerusalem, 1942; *b* 9 Nov. 1887; *s* of James Burns, Treas. of St Christopher-Nevis; *m* 1914, Kathleen Hardtman, CStJ; two *d. Educ:* St Edmund's Coll., Ware. Colonial Civil Service, Leeward Islands, 1905-12; Nigeria, 1912-24; Colonial Sec., Bahama Islands, 1924-29; administered Govt of Bahamas, May-Oct. 1924, Sept.-Nov. 1925, Sept. 1926-March 1927, June-Sept. 1928; Member Bahamas House of Assembly, 1925-28; Dep. Chief Sec. to Govt of Nigeria, 1929-34; Governor and C-in-C of British Honduras, 1934-40; Assistant Under-Sec. of State for the Colonies, 1940-41; Governor and C-inC, Gold Coast, 1941-47; Acting Governor of Nigeria, 1942; Permanent UK Representative on Trusteeship Council of United Nations, 1947-56. Represented Bahamas at West Indies Conference in London, 1926; served with Cameroons Expeditionary Force, 1914-15, and during Egba rebellion, 1918. Chm., Commission of Enquiry into Land and Population Problems, Fiji, 1959-60. *Publications:* Index to Laws of Leeward Islands (joint compiler); Nigeria Handbook 1917-23; History of Nigeria, 1929; Colour Prejudice, 1948; Colonial Civil Servant, 1949; History of the British West Indies, 1954; In Defence of Colonies, 1957; Fiji, 1963. *Address:* 6 Iverna Gardens, W8. *T:* 01-937 1053. *Club:* Athenæum.

**BURNS, Mrs Anne, (Mrs D. O. Burns)**; British Gliding Champion, 1966; Principal Scientific Officer, Royal Aircraft Establishment, Farnborough, Hants, since 1953; *b* 23 Nov. 1915; *d* of late Major Fleetwood Hugo Pellew, W Yorks Regt, and of late Violet Pellew (*née* Du Pré); *m* 1947, Dennis Owen Burns; no *c. Educ:* The Abbey Sch., Reading; St Hugh's Coll., Oxford (BA). Joined Min. of Supply, 1940. Engaged in aircraft research at RAE, Farnborough, Hants, under various ministries, 1940-. Feminine International Records: 4 gliding records in S Africa, 1961; records, S Africa, 1963, 1965; Colorado USA, 1967. Queen's Commendation for Valuable Services in the Air, 1955 and 1963. Lilienthal Medal, Fédération Aéronautique Internationale, 1966. *Publications:* contrib. scientific jls. *Recreations:* gliding, ski-ing. *Address:* Rapallo, Clumps Road, Lower Bourne, Farnham, Surrey. *T:* Frensham 3343.

**BURNS, Arthur F.**; economist and statistician; Chairman, Board of Governors of the Federal Reserve System in the United States, since 1970; *b* Stanislau, Austria, 27 April 1904; *s* of Nathan Burns and Sarah Juran; *m* 1930, Helen Bernstein; two *s. Educ:* Columbia Univ. AB and AM 1925, PhD 1934. Rutgers Univ.: Instructor in Economics, 1927-30; Asst Prof., 1930-33; Associate Prof., 1933-43; Prof., 1943-44; Columbia Univ.: Vis. Prof., 1941-44; Prof., 1944-59; John Bates Clark Prof., 1959-69. Nat. Bureau of Econ. Research: Res. Associate, 1930-31; Mem. Res. Staff, 1933; Dir of Res., 1945-53; Pres., 1957-67; Chm. of Bureau, 1967-69; Counsellor to the President of the US, 1969-70. Dir and Trustee of various orgs; Member (or Past Mem. or Consultant) of govt and other advisory bds. Chm., President's Coun. of Economic Advisors, 1953-56; Mem., President's Adv. Cttee on Labor-Management Policy, 1961-66, etc. Fellow: Amer. Statistical Assoc.; Econometric Soc.; Philos. Soc.; Amer. Acad. of Arts and Sciences; Amer. Econ. Assoc. (Pres. 1959); Acad. of Polit. Sci. (Pres., 1962-68); Phi Beta Kappa. Many hon. doctorates, 1952-. Alexander Hamilton Medal, Columbia Univ.; Dist. Public Service Award, Tax Foundn. Mugungwha Decoration, S Korea. *Publications:* Production Trends in the United States since 1870, 1934; Economic Research and the Keynesian Thinking of our Times, 1946; Frontiers of Economic Knowledge, 1954; Prosperity Without Inflation, 1957; The Management of Prosperity, 1966; The Business Cycle in a Changing World, 1969; (jointly) Measuring Business Cycles, 1946. *Address:* Federal Reserve Board, Washington, DC 20551, USA; (home) Sheraton-Park Hotel, Washington, DC 20008. *Clubs:* Men's Faculty (Columbia), Century Association (New York); Cosmos (Washington).

**BURNS, Dr B(enedict) Delisle,** FRS 1968; Head, Division of Pharmacology and Physiology, National Institute for Medical Research, London, England, since 1967; *b* 22 Feb. 1915; *s* of C. Delisle Burns and Margaret Hannay; *m* 1st, 1938, Angela Ricardo; four *s*; 2nd, 1954, Monika Kasputis; one *d. Educ:* University Coll. Sch.; Tübingen Univ.; King's Coll., Cambridge; University Coll. Hospital. MRCS, LRCP 1939. Univ. extension lecturing for WEA, 1936-38; operational research, 1939-45; Research Asst, Nat. Inst. for Med. Research, 1945-49; Assoc. Prof of Physiology, McGill Univ., Canada, 1950-58; Scientific Advisor to Dept of Veterans' Affairs, 1950-67; Prof. of Physiology, 1958-67, Chm., Dept of Physiology, 1965-67, McGill Univ., Canada. *Publications:* The Mammalian Cerebral Cortex, 1958; The Uncertain Nervous System, 1968; about 60 articles on neurophysiology in scientific jls. *Recreations:* tennis, ski-ing, painting, interior decoration. *Address:* National Institute for Medical Research, Mill Hill, NW7. *T:* 01-959 3666.

**BURNS, Bryan Hartop;** Hon. Consulting Orthopædic Surgeon, St George's Hospital; St Peter's Hospital, Chertsey; Heatherwood Hospital, Ascot; *b* 14 Dec. 1896; *s* of Hartop Burns, Grendon, Northampton; *m* 1938, Hon. Dorothy Garthwaite, *d* of late Lord Duveen. *Educ:* Wellingborough Sch.; Clare Coll., Cambridge; St George's Hospital Medical Sch. Allingham Scholarship in surgery, St George's Hospital, 1924; served 1914-18, Northants Regt. Orthopædic Surgeon, Royal Masonic Hospital, 1945-61. Ex-Pres. Orthopædic Section, Royal Society Med.; Mem. of Court of Examiners, Royal College of Surgeons, 1943-46; Emer. Fellow, British Orthopædic Association; Member Société Internationale de Chirurgie Orthopédique. *Publications:* Recent Advances in Orthopædic Surgery, 1937 (jointly); articles on orthopædic subjects. *Address;* 6 Chesterfield Hill, W1. *T:* 01-493 3435. *Clubs:* Boodle's, St James'.

**BURNS, Sir Charles (Ritchie),** KBE 1958 (OBE 1947); MD, FRCP; FRACP; Consulting Physician and Consulting Cardiologist, Wellington Hospital, since 1958; Physician to Home of Compassion, Island Bay, NZ, from 1940; *b* Blenheim, Marlborough, NZ, 27 May 1898; *s* of Archibald Douglas Burns, Lands and Survey Dept, NZ; *m* 1st, 1935, Margaret Muriel (decd 1949), *d* of John Laffey, Dunedin, NZ; one *s* one *d*; 2nd, 1963, Doris

Ogilvy, *d* of Keith Ramsay (sen.), Dunedin, New Zealand. *Educ:* St Mary's Sch., Blenheim, NZ; Marlborough and Nelson Colls, NZ. MB, ChB (NZ) 1922 (Batchelor Memorial Medal); MRCP 1925; MD (NZ) 1925; Foundation Fellow RACP 1937; FRCP (Lond.) 1943. Med. Registrar Dunedin Hospital, and Medical Tutor Otago Univ., 1925-27; Asst Phys., Dunedin Hospital, 1927-37; Senior Phys. and Cardiologist, Wellington Hospital, NZ, 1940-58; Mem. Med. Council, NZ, 1943-55; Examr in Medicine, Univ., of NZ, 1947-53, 1959, 1963. Mem. NZ Bd of Censors for RACP, 1954-61; Corresp. Mem. Brit. Cardiac Soc., 1952-; Mem. Cardiac Soc. of Australia and NZ, 1952- (Mem. Council, 1956-58; Chm. 1964-65); Mem. Council and NZ Vice-Pres., RACP, 1956-58; Mem. NZ Lepers' Trust Bd, 1958-; Mem. Advisory Cttee, The Nat. Soc. on Alcoholism (NZ); Patron NZ Haemophilia Soc; Mem. Coun., Wellington Med. Research Foundn, etc. Served War, 1944-47, Military Hospitals, 2nd NZEF, Italy and Japan (OBE). *Publications:* contrib. medical journals and jls of anciliary medical services. *Recreations:* gardening and medical writing, at present; golf and walking, in the past. *Address:* 16 Sefton Street, Wadestown, Wellington, New Zealand. *T:* Wellington 40-355 and 45-870. *Club:* Wellington (Wellington, NZ).

**BURNS, Mrs Denis Owen;** *see* Burns, Mrs Anne.

**BURNS, Lt-Gen. Eedson Louis Millard,** CC (Canada) 1967; DSO 1944; OBE 1935; MC; idc; Research Fellow, Carleton University, since 1970; *b* 17 June 1897; *m* 1927, Eleanor Phelan; one *d. Educ:* Royal Military Coll., Kingston, Canada; Staff Coll., Quetta. Served European War, 1916-18 (France, Belgium) with Royal Canadian Engineers, Signals, Staff; Can. Perm. Force, 1918-39. War of 1939-45; GOC 2nd Can. Div., 1943 (Maj.-Gen.); 5th Can. Div., 1944; 1st Can. Corps, 1944. Dir-Gen. of Rehabilitation, Dept Veteran Affairs, 1945-46, Asst Dep. Minister, 1946-50, Dep. Minister, 1950-54. Chief of Staff, UN Truce Supervision Organisation, Palestine, 1954-56; Comdr UN Emergency Force, 1956-59; Adviser to Govt of Canada on Disarmament, 1960-69, retd; Leader of Canadian Delegation to 18-Nation Disarmament Conference, Geneva, 1962-68. Nat. Pres. UNA, Canada, 1952-53 (Altern. Deleg. to UN, 1949). Officier Légion d'Honneur. *Publications:* Manpower in the Canadian Army, 1939-45, 1955; Between Arab and Israeli, 1962; Mega-murder, 1966. *Address:* 6 Park Road, Ottawa 2, Ont.

**BURNS, George,** CMG 1965; company director; Editor, Christchurch Star, Christchurch, New Zealand, 1945-68; *b* 16 Aug. 1903; *s* of Donald and Marion Sutherland Burns; *m* 1926, Barbara Raeburn Nisbet; (one *s* decd). *Educ:* Oamaru North Sch.; Univ. of Canterbury. Reporter, Oamaru Mail, 1919-23; from 1923 successively: reporter, Parly correspondent, chief sub-editor, asst editor and editor, Christchurch Star, Member, NZ delegn, Imperial Press Conf., Canada, 1950; Smith-Mundt Scholar, Columbia Univ., New York, 1950; leader, NZ press delegn, Korea, 1952; leader, NZ Govt mission, UN Commission on Human Rights, India, 1962. Mem., Bd of Dirs, NZ Press Assoc., 1955-67 (Chm., 1959-60, 1964-65, 1966-67); Chm. NZ Section, Commonwealth Press Union, 1964-69, and leader of delegn to conference, West Indies, 1965. Mem., King George V Memorial Trust Bd, 1956 (Chm. 1964-); Foundation mem., Shirley High Sch. Bd of Govs, 1957- (Chm. 1959-61); Lecturer-in-charge, Sch. of Journalism, Univ. of Canterbury, 1947-58. Mem., Lyttleton Harbour Bd, 1968-; Area Patron, Boy Scouts, 1969-. Major (retd list), Canterbury Regt. *Recreations:* gardening, yachting. *Address:* 34 Glenelg Spur, Murray Aynsley Hill, Christchurch, New Zealand. *T:* 35-553. *Clubs:* Canterbury, Canterbury Officers' (Christchurch); Banks Peninsula Cruising (Lyttelton, NZ).

**BURNS, Maj.-Gen. Sir George;** *see* Burns, Maj.-Gen. Sir W. A. G.

**BURNS, Henry Stuart Mackenzie;** *b* 28 April 1900; *s* of John Stuart Burns and Anne Mackenzie Burns, Aberdeen, Scotland; *m* 1929, Dorcas Jackson, San Francisco, Calif.; two *s. Educ:* Robert Gordon's Coll., Scotland; Aberdeen Univ. (BSc); Cambridge Univ. (BA). Geophysicist, Shell Oil Co., Calif., 1926; transferred to mfg and supplies dept, 1927; asst to div. man., Seattle, 1928-32; asst gen sales mgr, 1932-34, gen. sales mgr, 1934-36; gen. mgr Shell Co. of Colombia, SA, 1936-46; senior vice-pres., Shell Oil Co., Inc., NY, 1946-47, director 1947-60, Pres., 1947-60. Director: American Petroleum Institute; Gen. Dynamics Corporation; Ampex Corporation. Member' St Andrew's Soc.; Metropolitan Opera Assoc. (New York); Burns Soc. hon. LLD Aberdeen Univ., 1956; Hon. Dsc St Louis Univ. 1957. *Recreations:* golf, photography. *Address:* 485 Park Avenue, New York 22, NY, USA. *T:* Eldorado 5-0351. *Clubs:* White's; Pacific Union (San Francisco); Racquet and Tennis, etc (NY); Piping Rock, etc (LI).

**BURNS, James,** CBE 1967; GM 1941; Chairman, Southern Gas Board, 1967-69, retired; *b* 27 Feb. 1902; *s* of William Wilson Burns and Isobella MacDonald; *m* 1934, Kathleen Ida Holt; one *d* (one *s* decd). *Educ:* Inverness Royal Academy; Aberdeen Univ.; Cambridge Univ. BSc 1st cl. Hons 1925, PhD 1928, Aberdeen. Entered Research Dept, Gas Light & Coke Co., 1929; worked as Chem. Engr with Chemical Reactions Ltd, in Germany, 1930-32; Production Engr, Gas Light & Coke Co., 1941, dep. Chief Engr, 1945; Chief Engr, North Thames Gas Board, 1949, Dep-Chm. 1960-62; Chm, Northern Gas Board, 1962-67. President: Instn Gas Engrs, 1957-58; Inst. Fuel, 1961-62, etc. *Publications:* contrib. Jls Instn Gas Engrs, Inst. Fuel, etc. *Recreations:* golf, shooting, country pursuits. *Address:* 4 Corfu, Chaddesley Glen, Canford Cliffs, Dorset. *T:* Canford Cliffs 77370. *Club:* Athenæum.

**BURNS, Sir John (Crawford),** Kt 1957; Director, James Finlay & Co. Ltd, since 1957; *b* 29 Aug. 1903; *s* of William Barr Burns and Elizabeth Crawford; *m* 1941, Eleanor Margaret Haughton James; one *s* three *d. Educ:* Glasgow High Sch. Commissioned 2/16th Punjab Regt (Indian Army), 1940-46 (despatches). *Recreations:* golf, fishing. *Address:* Glenorchard, Dunblane, Perthshire. *Clubs:* Oriental; Western (Glasgow).

**BURNS, Dr Malcolm McRae,** CBE 1959; Principal, Lincoln Agricultural College, New Zealand, since 1952; *b* 19 March 1910; *s* of J. E. Burns and Emily (*née* Jeffrey); *m* 1936, Ruth, *d* of J. D. Waugh, St Louis, USA; one *s* two *d. Educ:* Rangiora High Sch.; Univs of Canterbury (NZ), Aberdeen and Cornell. Plant Physiologist, DSIR, NZ, 1936; Sen. Lectr, Lincoln Agric. Coll., 1937-48; Dir, NZ Fert. Manuf. Res. Assoc., 1948-52. Chm., Physical Environment Commn, 1968-70; Mem., Nat. Develt Council, 1969. FNZIC; FNZIAS; FRSNZ; FAAAS. Chm., DSIR Research Council, 1959-62. NZ Representative, Harkness Fellowships. *Publications:* articles in scientific jls. *Recreations:* golf, fishing, gardening. *Address:* Box 42, Lincoln College, Canterbury, New

Zealand. *Club:* University of Canterbury (NZ).

**BURNS, Robert,** CB 1961; CMG 1952; Second Secretary, Board of Trade, since July 1966; *b* 31 Oct. 1912; *s* of Robert and Jessie V. Burns; *m* Mary, *d* of C. H. Goodland, MBE, TD; three *s* one *d. Educ:* Hamilton Academy; Glasgow Univ. (MA). Asst Principal Dominions Office, 1936; transferred to Colonial Office, 1937; seconded to Ministry of Supply, 1940; Private Sec. to Lord Beaverbrook and Mr Lyttelton, 1941; Asst Sec., Min. of Production, 1944; Board of Trade, 1945; Counsellor Commercial HM Embassy, Washington, 1949-52; Asst Sec., Board of Trade, 1952-53; Under Sec.; Ministry of Supply, 1953-59; Ministry of Aviation, 1959-63 (Dep. Sec. 1963-66). *Address:* 90 Cromwell Avenue, N6. *Club:* Reform.

**BURNS, Thomas Ferrier;** Editor of The Tablet, since 1967; Chairman of Burns & Oates Ltd, 1948-67; Director: BOW Holdings since 1948; The Tablet Publishing Company since 1936; *b* 21 April 1906; *s* of late David Burns and late Clara (*née* Swinburne); *m* 1941, Mabel Marañon; three *s* one *d. Educ:* Stonyhurst. Press Attaché, British Embassy, Madrid, 1940-45. *Recreations:* painting and gardening. *Address:* 14 Ashley Gardens, SW1. *T:* 01-834 1385. *Clubs:* Garrick, Pratt's.

**BURNS, Maj.-Gen. Sir (Walter Arthur) George,** KCVO 1962; CB 1961; DSO 1944; OBE 1953; MC 1940; retired; Lord Lieutenant of Hertfordshire since Dec. 1961; *b* 29 Jan. 1911; *s* of Walter Spencer Morgan and Evelyn Ruth Burns. *Educ:* Eton; Trinity Coll., Cambridge. BA Hons History. Commissioned Coldstream Guards 1932; ADC to Viceroy of India, 1938-40; Adjt 1st Bn, 1940-41 (MC); Brigade Major: 9 Inf. Bde, 1941-42; Sp. Gp Gds Armd Div., 1942; 32 Gds Bde, 1942-43; CO 3rd Bn Coldstream Gds, Italy, 1943-44 (DSO); Staff Coll., Camberley, 1945. Brigade Major, Household Bde, 1945-47; CO 3rd Bn Coldstream Gds, Palestine, 1947-50; AAG, HQ London Dist, 1951, 1952; Regimental Lt-Col Coldstream Gds, 1952-55; Comdg 4th Gds Bde, 1955-59. GOC London District and The Household Brigade, 1959-62; Col, Coldstream Guards, 1966-. Steward, The Jockey Club, 1964-. *Recreations:* shooting and racing. *Address:* North Mymms Park, Hatfield, Herts. *T:* Colney Heath 266. *Clubs:* Guards, Jockey, White's, Pratt's.

**BURNS, Wilfred,** CBE 1967; MEng, PPTPI, MICE; Chief Planner, Ministry of Housing and Local Government, since 1968; *b* 11 April 1923; *m* 1945, Edna Price; one *s* one *d. Educ:* Ulverston Grammar Sch.; Liverpool Univ. Admty, 1944-45; Leeds Corp., 1946-49; Prin. Planning Officer, Coventry Corp., 1949-58; Dep. Planning Officer, Surrey CC, 1958-60; City Planning Officer, Newcastle upon Tyne, 1960-68. Hon. DSc, Univ. of Newcastle upon Tyne, 1966. *Publications:* British Shopping Centres, 1959; New Towns for Old, 1963; Newcastle upon Tyne: A Study in Planning, 1967. *Recreations:* numerous. *Address:* 29a Sydenham Hill, SE26. *T:* 01-670 3525.

**BURNS, Prof. William,** CBE 1966; Professor of Physiology, Charing Cross Hospital Medical School (University of London), since 1947; *b* 15 Oct. 1909; *e s* of late Charles Burns, MB, ChB, JP, and Mary Sillars, lately of Stonehaven, Scotland; *m* 1936, Margaret, *o d* of late W. A. Morgan, Glasgow; one *s* one *d. Educ:* Mackie Acad., Stonehaven; Aberdeen Univ. BSc 1933, MB ChB 1935, DSc 1943 Aberdeen. Asst in Physiology, Aberdeen, 1935; Lectr in Physiology, Aberdeen, 1936; War-time duty with Admiralty, 1942; established in RN Scientific Service, 1946; Supt RN Physiological Laboratory, 1947; Consultant in Acoustic Science to RAF, 1970-. Member: Physiological Soc.; Ergonomics Research Soc.; Council, British Association for the Advancement of Science, 1956-61; British Medical Association; British Acoustical Soc.; British Soc. Audiology. *Publications:* Noise and Man, 1968; (with D. W. Robinson) Hearing and Noise in Industry, 1970; articles on various aspects of hearing, in Journal of the Acoustical Soc. of America, Annals of Occupational Hygiene, Proc. Assoc. of Industrial Med. Officers, etc. *Recreations:* working in wood and metal; interested in engineering in general. *Address:* Ruries, 211 Thames Side, Laleham-on-Thames, Middx. *T:* Staines 53066.

**BURNTWOOD,** Baron *cr* 1970 (Life Peer), of Burntwood, Staffs; **Julian Ward Snow;** *b* 24 Feb. 1910; *s* of late H. M. Snow, CVO, Mottingham, Kent; *m* 1948, Flavia, *d* of late Sir Ralph Blois, 9th Bt, and Lady Blois, Cockfield Hall; one *d. Educ:* Haileybury. Employed by Dunlop Rubber Co. Ltd, in India and East Africa, 1930-37; joined John Lewis Co-Partnership, 1937; Royal Artillery, 1939-45. Amember of the Union of Shop Distributive and Allied Workers. MP (Lab) Portsmouth Central, 1945-50, Lichfield and Tamworth Div. of Staffs, 1950-70; Vice-Chamberlain to the Household, 1945-46; a Lord Comr of HM Treasury, 1946-50; Parliamentary Secretary: Min. of Aviation, 1966-67; Min. of Health, 1967-68; Parly Under-Sec. of State, Dept of Health and Social Security, 1968-69. Vice-Pres., British-Japanese Parly Group. *Address:* 37 Chester Way, SE11.

**BURRA, Edward;** painter; *b* London, 1905. *Educ:* Chelsea Sch. of Art; Royal College of Art. First one-man show, Leicester Galleries, London, 1929; subsequent shows there: May 1932, June 1947, and June 1949; Lefevre Galleries, 1952, 1955, 1957, 1959, 1961, 1963, 1965, 1967, 1969. Has designed scenery and costumes for the ballet and opera. Works bought by Tate Gallery, etc. Travels include: the United States, Mexico, Spain, France. Gaetano Marzotto Prize, 1967. *Address:* c/o Lefevre Galleries, 30 Bruton Street, W1.

**BURRELL, Derek William;** Headmaster, Truro School, since Sept. 1959; *b* 4 Nov. 1925; *s* of late Thomas Richard Burrell and of Flora Frances Burrell (*née* Nash). *Educ:* Tottenham Grammar Sch.; Queens' Coll., Cambridge. Assistant Master at Solihull Sch. (English, History, Religious Instruction, Music Appreciation), 1948-52. Senior English Master, Dollar Academy, 1952-59. *Recreations:* music of any kind, theatre. *Address:* Truro School, Cornwall. *T:* Truro 2763.

**BURRELL, Vice-Adm. Sir Henry Mackay,** KBE 1960 (CBE 1955); CB 1959; RAN retired; *b* 13 Aug. 1904; British (father *b* Dorset; mother *b* Australia, of Scottish parents); *m* 1944, Ada Theresa Weller; one *s* two *d. Educ:* Royal Australian Naval Coll., Jervis Bay, Australia. Cadet-Midshipman, 1918; specialist in navigation, psc Greenwich, 1938; Commands: HMAS Norman, 1941-42 (despatches); Bataan, 1945; Dep. Chief of Naval Staff, Navy Office, Melbourne, 1947-48; HMAS Australia, 1949; idc 1950; HMAS Vengeance, 1953-54; Second Naval Mem., Australian Commonwealth Naval Board, 1956-57; Flag Officer Commanding HM Australian Fleet, 1955 and 1958; Chief of the Australian Naval Staff, 1959-62. *Recreations:* tennis and lawn tennis. *Address:* 87 Endeavour Street, Red Hill, Canberra, ACT 2603, Australia. *Clubs:* Naval and Military (Melbourne); Commonwealth (Canberra, ACT).

**BURRELL, John Glyn,** QC 1961; **His Honour Judge Burrell;** County Court Judge, Circuit 28 (Shropshire and mid-Wales), since 1964; Chairman, Radnorshire County Quarter Sessions, since 1964; *b* 10 Oct. 1912; *o s* of Lewis Morgan Burrell and Amy Isabel Burrell; *m* 1941, Dorothy, 2nd *d* of Prof. T. Stanley Roberts, MA Cantab, Aberystwyth; two *d. Educ:* Friars Sch., Bangor; Univ. Coll. of Wales. Called to Bar, Inner Temple, 1936. Practised Northern Circuit (Liverpool); Recorder of Wigan, 1962-64. Army service, 1940-45. *Address:* Gog Farm, Haddenham, Aylesbury, Bucks. *T:* Haddenham 543.

**BURRELL, John Percy;** Theatrical Producer; Director, Training Academy of American Shakespearean Theatre, since 1955; *b* 6 May 1910; *s* of late Prof. P. S. Burrell, CIE; *m* 1936, Margaret Souttar; two *s. Educ:* Shrewsbury Sch.; Royal Coll. of Art, London. Studied painting, sculpture and stage designing, being at the same time occupied with production, 1928-34; joined Michel St Denis at London Theatre Studio as Producer and Dir of Decor, 1937; War Office, 1939-41; Drama Producer, BBC, 1941-44; programmes included: Marriage of St Francis, Pilgrim's Progress, The Rescue, Don Quixote. Produced Heartbreak House, at Cambridge Theatre, for H. M. Tennent, Ltd, 1942. Chm. of Dirs of the Old Vic Theatre Co., 1944-49. Productions for Old Vic, at New Theatre: Richard III, Arms and the Man, Uncle Vanya, 1944; Henry IV, Part I, Henry IV, Part II, 1945; The Alchemist, 1946; The Taming of the Shrew, 1947; Saint Joan, 1947; The Government Inspector (Gogol), 1948; The Tragical History of Doctor Faustus (Marlowe), 1948; The Way of the World (Congreve), 1948. *Recreations:* drawing, painting, boating. *Address:* 37 Ladbroke Road, W11. *T:* 01-727 7616.

**BURRELL, Peter,** CBE 1957; Director, The National Stud, since 1937; *b* 9 May 1905; *s* of Sir Merrik R. Burrell, 7th Bt; *m* 1929, Pamela Pollen; two *s. Educ:* Eton; Royal Agricultural Coll., Cirencester. *Recreations:* shooting, stalking, hunting. *Address:* Regal Lodge, Exning, Newmarket, Suffolk. *T:* Exning 255. *Clubs:* Boodle's; Kildare Street (Dublin).

**BURRELL, Sir Walter (Raymond),** 8th Bt, *cr* 1774; CBE 1956 (MBE 1945); TD; DL; Trustee Royal Agricultural Society of England, since 1948, President 1964, Chairman of Council, since 1967; *b* 11 Dec. 1903; *er s* of Sir Merrik Burrell, 7th Bt, CBE; *S* father 1957; *m* 1931, Hon. Anne Judith Denman, OBE, *o d* of 3rd Baron Denman, PC, GCMG, KCVO; two *s* two *d. Educ:* Eton. Major 98th Field Regt (Surrey and Sussex Yeo.), Royal Artillery (TA), 1938; Lt-Col (Chief Instructor) 123 OCTU, 1942; Lt-Col BAS (Washington), 1943; Comd 3 Super Heavy Regt, RA 1945 (MBE). Pres. Country Landowners' Assoc., 1952-53. DL Sussex, 1937; County Alderman, 1950; Vice-Chm. West Sussex County Council, 1953. *Heir: s* John Raymond Burrell [*b* 20 Feb. 1934; *m* 1959, Rowena Pearce; one *s* one *d. Educ:* Eton]. *Address:* Knepp Castle, West Grinstead, Horsham, Sussex. *T:* Coolham 247; 43a Reeves Mews, South Audley Street, W1. *T:* 01-499 1318. *Club:* Boodle's.
*See also Peter Burrell.*

**BURRETT, (Frederick) Gordon;** Under-Secretary, Civil Service Department, since 1969; *b* 31 Oct. 1921; *s* of Frederick Burrett and Marion Knowles; *m* 1943, Margaret Joan Giddins; one *s* two *d. Educ:* Emanuel Sch.; St Catharine's Coll., Cambridge. Served in Royal Engrs, 1942-45 (despatches). HM Foreign Service, 1946; 3rd Sec., Budapest, 1946-49; FO, 1949-51; Vice-Consul, New York, 1951-54; FO, 1954-57; 1st Sec., Rome, 1957-60; transf. to HM Treasury, 1960; Private Sec. to Chief Sec., Treasury, 1963-64; Asst Secretary: HM Treasury, 1964; Cabinet Office, 1967-68; Civil Service Dept, 1968. *Recreations:* music, books, walking. *Address:* Trinity Cottage, Church Road, Claygate, Surrey. *T:* Esher 62783.

**BURROUGH, Admiral Sir Harold Martin,** GCB, *cr* 1949 (KCB, *cr* 1944; CB 1939); KBE, *cr* 1942; DSO 1942 (and Bar 1943); DSM (USA), 1943; Legion of Merit (USA), 1946; Knight Grand Cross Orange Nassau (Netherlands), 1947; Grand Officer, Legion of Honour (France), 1949; *b* 4 July 1888; *s* of Rev. Charles Burrough, MA; *m* 1914, Nellie Wills Outhit, Halifax, Nova Scotia; two *s* three *d. Educ:* St Edwards, Oxford; HMS Britannia. Gunnery Officer of HMS Southampton at the Battle of Jutland; Comdr, 1922; Capt., 1928; commanded HMS London, 1930-32; 5th Destroyer Flotilla, 1935-37; HMS Excellent, 1937-38; served War of 1939-45 (DSO and Bar, KBE); Assistant Chief of Naval Staff, Admiralty, 1939-40; commanding Cruiser Squadron, 1940-42; commanding Naval Forces, Algiers, 1942; Flag Officer Commanding, Gibraltar and Mediterranean Approaches, 1943-45; Allied Naval C-in-C. Expeditionary Force, 1945; British Naval C-in-C, Germany, 1945-46; C-in-C The Nore, 1946-48. Rear-Admiral, 1939; Vice-Admiral, 1942; Admiral, 1945; retired list, 1949. *Recreation:* gardening. *Address:* 102 Dorset House, Gloucester Place, NW1. *Club:* Naval and Military.
*See also J. O. H. Burrough and Rear-Adm. A. Davies.*

**BURROUGH, John Outhit Harold,** CBE 1963; an Under-Secretary, Cabinet Office, since Nov. 1967; *b* 31 Jan. 1916; *s* of Adm. Sir Harold M. Burrough, *qv*; *m* 1944, Suzanne Cecile Jourdan; one *s* one *d. Educ:* Manor House, Horsham; RNC Dartmouth. Midshipman, 1934; Sub-Lt 1936; Lieut 1938; Lt-Comdr 1944; retd 1947. Foreign Office, 1946-65; British Embassy, Washington, 1965-67. *Address:* 28 Queens Gate Gardens, SW7. *T:* 01-589 6026. *Club:* Naval and Military (Chm.).

**BURROUGH, Rt. Rev. John Paul;** *see* Mashonaland, Bishop of.

**BURROUGHS, Ronald Arthur,** CMG 1966; Assistant Under-Secretary of State, Foreign and Commonwealth Office, since 1968; *b* 4 June 1917; *s* of Rev. Henry Frederick Burroughs and Ada Burroughs; *m* 1947, Jean Valerie McQuillen; two *d. Educ:* St John's Sch., Leatherhead; Trinity Coll., Cambridge. Fleet Air Arm, 1940-45. FO, 1946; 2nd Sec., HM Embassy, Rio de Janeiro, 1947-49; HM Consul, Marseilles, 1949-50; 1st Sec., HM Embassy, Cairo, 1950-53; FO, 1953-55; Canadian National Defence Coll., 1955-56; 1st Sec., HM Embassy, Vienna, 1956-59; Counsellor, FO, 1959-62; Counsellor and Head of Chancery, Rio de Janeiro, 1962-64; Counsellor, HM Embassy, Lisbon, 1964-67; British Chargé d'Affaires, South Yemen, 1967-68. *Recreations:* reading, shooting, fishing. *Address:* Broc Holt, Abbot Road, Guildford, Surrey. *T:* Guildford 4178. *Club:* Travellers'.

**BURROW, Prof. Harold,** MRCVS, DVSM; Professor of Veterinary Medicine, Royal Veterinary College, University of London,

1944-63; Professor Emeritus since 1963; *b* 24 Aug. 1903; *s* of Henry Wilson and Elizabeth Jane Burrow, Hest Bank Lodge, near Lancaster; *m* 1933, Frances Olivia, *d* of Orlando Atkinson Ducksbury, MRCVS, and Mrs Frances Mary Ducksbury, Lancaster; one *d*. *Educ:* Lancaster Royal Grammar Sch.; Royal (Dick) Veterinary Coll., Edinburgh. Asst Veterinary Officer, City of Birmingham, 1927-30; Chief Veterinary Officer: Birkenhead, 1930-35; Derbyshire CC, 1935-38; Divisional Veterinary Officer, Min. of Agriculture, 1938-42; Private Veterinary Practice, 1942-44. Examiner: to Royal Coll. of Veterinary Surgeons, 1937-44; to Univs. of Liverpool, London, Reading, Edinburgh, Bristol and Ceylon (various dates). Pres. Old Lancastrian Club, 1953; Member of Council, Royal Society Health, 1950- (Chairman, 1956-57, Vice-Pres. 1958-65, Life Vice-Pres., 1965). *Publications:* numerous contributions to veterinary scientific press. *Recreations:* pedigree cattle breeding, gardening. *Address:* Foxfield, Lechlade, Gloucestershire. *T:* Lechlade 232.

**BURROW, Thomas,** MA, PhD; FBA 1970; Boden Professor of Sanskrit in the University of Oxford, and Fellow of Balliol College, since 1944; *b* 29 June 1909; *e s* of Joshua and Frances Eleanor Burrow; *m* 1941, Inez Mary, *d* of Herbert John Haley. *Educ:* Queen Elizabeth's Sch., Kirkby Lonsdale; Christ's Coll., Cambridge. Research Fellow of Christ's Coll., Cambridge, 1935-37; Asst Keeper in Dept of Oriental Printed Books and Manuscripts, British Museum, 1937-44. Leverhulme Research Fellow, 1957-58. *Publications:* The Language of the Kharosthī Documents from Chinese Turkestan, 1937; A Translation of the Kharosthī Documents from Chinese Turkestan, 1940; (with S. Bhattacharya) The Parji Language, 1953; The Sanskrit Language, 1955; (with M. B. Emeneau) A Dravidian Etymological Dictionary, 1961; Supplement, 1968. *Address:* Balliol College, Oxford.

**BURROWES, Edmund Stanley Spencer,** CMG 1959; Financial Secretary, Barbados, 1951-66; *b* 16 Dec. 1906; *m* 1st, 1934, Mildred B. Jackson (decd); one *s* three *d*; 2nd, 1965, Gwen Searson. *Educ:* Queen's Coll., British Guiana. British Guiana Colonial Secretariat, 1924; Inspector of Labour, 1940; Deputy Commissioner, 1945; Labour Commissioner, Barbados, 1947. *Publication:* Occupational Terms on Sugar Estates in British Guiana, 1945. *Recreations:* diving, gardening. *Address:* 66 Meadow Mount, Churchtown, Dublin 14. *T:* 985830.

**BURROWES, His Honour Hugh,** CBE 1965; Magistrate, Antigua, since 1959; *b* 16 Dec. 1909; *m* 1935, Margaret Ethel Lakeman Collins; one *d*. *Educ:* Antigua Grammar Sch. Barrister-at-Law, Lincoln's Inn, 1935; District Officer, Dominica, BWI, 1937; Warden of Nevis, BWI, 1939; Commissioner of Montserrat, BWI, 1946; Administrator of St Kitts-Nevis and Anguilla, BWI, 1949-56. *Address:* c/o Ministry of Overseas Development, Eland House, Stag Place, SW1.

**BURROWS, Albert;** Director-General, Merseyside Passenger Transport Executive, since 1969; *b* 3 Nov. 1919; *s* of John Joseph Burrows and Ada Wainwright; *m* 1944, Blodwen Megan Evans; one *s* one *d*. *Educ:* Warrington Grammar Sch.; Manchester Coll. of Commerce. Armed Forces, 1939-46. Service in transport at: Warrington, 1937-39 and 1948-49; Nottingham, 1949-53; Portsmouth, 1953-56; Gen. Manager, Transport Undertaking: Lancaster, 1956-61; Barrow-in-Furness, 1961-63; Chesterfield, 1963-66; Liverpool City, 1966-69. *Recreation:* golf. *Address:* 24 Hatton Garden, Liverpool, L3 2AN. *T:* 051-236 7411 (Ext. 1). *Clubs:* National Liberal; West Lancashire Golf.

**BURROWS, Sir Bernard (Alexander Brocas),** GCMG 1970 (KCMG 1955; CMG 1950); Permanent British Representative to North Atlantic Council, 1966-70; *b* 3 July 1910; *s* of Edward Henry Burrows and Ione, *d* of Alexander Macdonald; *m* 1944, Ines, *d* of late John Walter; one *s* one *d*. *Educ:* Eton; Trinity Coll., Oxford. Entered HM Foreign Service (later Diplomatic Service), 1934; served at HM Embassy, Cairo, 1938-45; Foreign Office, 1945-50; Counsellor HM Embassy, Washington, 1950-53; Political Resident in the Persian Gulf, 1953-58; Ambassador to Turkey, 1958-62; Dep. Under-Secretary of State, FO, 1963-66. *Address:* Steep Farm, Petersfield, Hants. *T:* Petersfield 2287. *Club:* Travellers'.

**BURROWS, Fred;** Legal Counsellor, HM Diplomatic Service, since 1968; *b* 10 Aug. 1925; *s* of late Charles Burrows; *m* 1955, Jennifer Winsome Munt; two *s*. *Educ:* Altrincham Grammar Sch.; Trinity Hall, Cambridge (MA). Served in RAF, 1944-47. Called to Bar, Gray's Inn, 1950; Asst Legal Adviser, Foreign Office, 1956-65; Legal Adviser, British Embassy, Bonn, 1965-67; returned to FO, 1967; Legal Counsellor, FCO, 1968. *Recreations:* sailing, carpentry. *Address:* 95 Molesey Park Road, East Molesey, Surrey. *T:* 01-979 5488.

**BURROWS, Sir Frederick (John),** GCSI 1947; GCIE 1945; DL, JP; Chairman of Wye River Authority, since 1965; *b* 1887; *s* of John Burrows; *m* 1912, Dora Beatrice (Kaisar-i-Hind Gold Medal) (*d* 1968), *d* of G. Hutchings, Hereford; one *s* one *d*. Served European War, 1914-19, Company Sergeant-Major, Grenadier Guards (Meritorious Service Medal). Pres. Nat. Union of Railwaymen, 1942-44; Member Soulbury Commission on Constitutional Reform, Ceylon, 1945; Governor of Bengal, 1946-47. Chairman of the Agricultural Land Commission, 1948-63 (Commn abolished); Member Governing Body of Sch. of Oriental and African Studies, London Univ., 1951-63; Member Royal Commn on Marriage and Divorce, 1951; formerly a Director Lloyds Bank Ltd until 1958 and of S Wales Local Cttee of Lloyds Bank until Dec. 1962. DL, JP Herefordshire; High Sheriff, Herefordshire, 1955. *Address:* Thrushes Nest, Rope Walk, Ross-on-Wye. *T:* Ross 2693. *Club:* Oriental.

**BURROWS, Harold Jackson,** CBE 1967; MD; FRCS, FRACS; Consulting Orthopaedic Surgeon to Royal Navy, since 1949; Hon. Consultant Orthopaedic Surgeon: St Bartholomew's Hospital; Royal National Orthopaedic Hospital; Star and Garter Home for Disabled Sailors, Soldiers and Airmen; Dean, Institute of Orthopaedics, British Postgraduate Medical Federation, University of London, 1946-64, and since 1967; *b* 9 May 1902; *s* of late Harold Burrows, CBE, and Lucy Mary Elizabeth (*née* Wheeler); unmarried. *Educ:* Cheltenham Coll.; King's Coll., Cambridge (MA); St Bartholomew's Hosp. Served War of 1939-45 as Surgeon Comdr RNVR. Beaverbrook Res. Scholar, RCS, 1930-31; Hunterian Prof., RCS, 1932; Asst Orthopaedic Surgeon, 1937, Orthopaedic Surgeon, 1946 and Surgeon i/c Orthopaedic Dept and Clinical Lectr on Orthopaedic Surgery, St Bartholomew's Hosp., 1958-67; Asst Surgeon, 1946, and Orthopaedic Surgeon, Royal Nat. Orthopaedic Hosp., 1948-67; Orthopaedic Surgeon, Nat. Hosp. for Diseases of the Nervous System, 1937-46; Asst Orthopaedic Surgeon, Miller Gen. Hosp., 1932-46; Consulting Orthopaedic Surgeon,

LCC, 1933-39; Consultant Adviser in Orthopaedics to Min. of Health 1964-; Orthopaedic Surgeon, The Heritage, Chailey, 1937-70. Nuffield Vis. Fellow to British WI on behalf of CO, 1955; Samuel Higby Camp Vis. Prof., Univ. of Calif., San Francisco, 1963. Chairman: Standing Adv. Cttee on Artificial Limbs; British Editorial Bd, Jl of Bone and Joint Surgery. Fellow: RSM (Hon. Mem. and Past Pres., Orthopaedic Section); Assoc. of Surgeons of Great Britain and Ireland; British Orthopaedic Assoc. (Past Pres.). Member: Council, RCS; Soc. Internat. de Chirurgie Orthopédique et de Traumatologie; Corresp. Member: Australian Orthopaedic Assoc.; Amer. Orthopaedic Assoc. Robert Jones Gold Medal, British Orthopaedic Assoc., 1937. *Publications:* papers on surgical subjects. *Address:* 25 Upper Wimpole Street, WIM 7TA.

**BURROWS, Very Reverend Hedley Robert;** Dean Emeritus of Hereford; Dean of Hereford, 1947-61, resigned in Oct. 1961; *b* 15 Oct. 1887; *s* of late Rt Rev. L. H. Burrows; *m* 1921, Joan Lumsden (*d* 1964), *d* of late Rt Rev. E. N. Lovett, CBE; one *s* (*er s* died on active service, 1945), two *d*. *Educ:* Charterhouse; New Coll., Oxford; Wells Theological Coll. Deacon, 1911; Priest, 1912; Curate of Petersfield, Hants, 1911-14; Temp. CF European War, 1914-16, invalided; Hon. CF; Priest in charge St Columba's, Poltalloch, Argyll, 1917-18; Domestic Chaplain to Dr Lang, when Archbishop of York, 1918-19; Curate in charge Dock Street Mission, Southampton, 1919-21; Rector of Stoke Abbott, Dorset, 1921-25; Vicar of St Stephen's, Portsea, 1925-28; Hon. Chaplain to 1st Bishop of Portsmouth, 1927-28. Vicar of Grimsby and Rural Dean of Grimsby and Cleethorpes, 1928-36; Vicar of St Peter's, Bournemouth, 1936-43; Rural Dean of Bournemouth, 1940-43; Prebendary and Canon of Sutton-in-Marisco, Lincoln Cathedral, 1933-43; Archdeacon of Winchester, and Residentiary Canon of the Cathedral, 1943-47. Chm., Midland Region Religious Cttee of the BBC, 1952-57 (*ex-officio*: Member Midland Council of BBC and Member Headquarters Council of BBC Central Religious Cttee of BBC, London). Elected a Church Commissioner for England, and Member Board of Governors, 1952-58. OStJ, 1947. *Address:* Chilland Rise, Itchen Abbas, Winchester.

**BURROWS, Comdr Henry Montagu,** CB 1964; CBE 1956; Royal Navy (retired); Clerk-Assistant of the Parliaments, House of Lords, 1961-63, retired (Reading-Clerk and Clerk of the Journals, 1959-61; Principal Clerk of Public Bills, 1950-59); *b* 24 March 1899; *er s* of late Rev. Montagu John Burrows; *m* 1939, Harriet Elizabeth, *o d* of late Ker George Russell Vaizey, Star Stile, Halstead, Essex; one *s* one *d*. *Educ:* RNC Osborne and Dartmouth. Went to sea at outbreak of European War, 1914-18, as a midshipman in HMS Benbow and served in her at Battle of Jutland. Transferred to RAF, 1923, Flt-Lt in No. 1 (Fighter) Sqdn in Irak. Appointed a Clerk in the House of Lords, 1925. Rejoined Royal Navy as Lieut-Comdr at outbreak of War of 1939-45 and commanded a motor boat at Dunkirk evacuation; later appointed 1st Lieut of HMS Argus (despatches while serving in her in N African landings, 1942); Comdr 1945. Royal Humane Society's bronze medal for life saving, 1920. *Recreation:* golf. *Address:* Little Elfords, Hawkhurst, Kent. *T:* Hawkhurst 2153. *Club:* Travellers'.

**BURROWS, Sir John;** *see* Burrows, Sir R. J. F.

**BURROWS, Lionel John;** Chief Inspector of Schools, Department of Education and Science, since 1966; *b* 9 March 1912; *s* of H. L. Burrows, HM Inspector of Schools, and Mrs C. J. Burrows; *m* 1939, Enid Patricia Carter; one *s* one *d*. *Educ:* King Edward VI Sch., Southampton; Gonville and Caius Coll., Cambridge. BA Cantab (1st cl. hons Mod. Langs Tripos) 1933. West Buckland Sch., Devon, Tiffin Sch., Kingston-upon-Thames and primary schools in London and Surrey, 1934-41; HM Forces (RASC and Intell. Corps), 1941-46; HM Inspector of Schools, 1946; Divisional Inspector, Metropolitan Div., 1960. Commendation from US Army Chief of Staff, 1945. *Recreations:* natural history, fell-walking. *Address:* Department of Education and Science, Curzon Street, W1. *T:* 01-493 7070. *Club:* English-Speaking Union.

**BURROWS, Rev. Millar;** Winkley Professor of Biblical Theology, Yale University, 1934-June 1958; Member of the Standard Bible Committee since 1938, Vice-Chairman, 1954-63; *b* 26 Oct. 1889; *s* of Edwin Jones Burrows and Katharine Millar Burrows; *m* 1915, Irene Bell Gladding (*d* 1967); one *s*. *Educ:* Cornell Univ. (BA 1912), Union Theological Seminary (BD 1915), Yale Univ. (PhD 1925). Rural Pastor in Texas, 1915-19; Rural survey supervisor for Texas, Interchurch World Movement, 1919-20; College pastor and professor of Bible, Tusculum Coll., 1920-23; Asst Professor, Assoc. Professor, and Professor of Biblical Literature and Hist. of Religions, Brown Univ., 1925-34; Visiting Professor of Religion, Amer. Univ. of Beirut, 1930-31; Director, Amer. Sch. of Oriental Research, Jerusalem, 1931-32 and 1947-48; Chm. Dept. of Near Eastern Languages and Literatures, Yale Univ. 1950-58. Pres., Amer. Schools of Oriental Research, 1934-48. Pres., Amer. Middle East Relief, 1954-56. Fellow Amer. Academy of Arts and Sciences, 1949. Hon. DD: Oberlin Coll., 1960; Brown Univ.; Yale Univ., 1961. *Publications:* Founders of Great Religions, 1931; Bible Religion, 1938; Basis of Israelite Marriage, 1938; What Mean These Stones?, 1941; Outline of Biblical Theology, 1946; Palestine is Our Business, 1949; The Dead Sea Scrolls, 1955; More Light on the Dead Sea Scrolls, 1958; Diligently ComparedThe Revised Standard Version and the King James Version of the Old Testament, 1964. Editor, The Dead Sea Scrolls of St Mark's Monastery, 1950-51. Articles in many learned journals. *Address:* 1670 Woodland Avenue, Winter Park, Florida 32789, USA. *T:* 1-305-647-0070. *Club:* University (Winter Park, Florida).

**BURROWS, Reginald Arthur,** CMG 1964; HM Consul-General at Istanbul, 1967-70; *b* 31 Aug. 1918; *s* of late Arthur Richard Burrows; *m* 1952, Jenny Louisa Henriette Campiche; one *s* one *d*. *Educ:* Mill Hill Sch.; St Catharine's Coll., Cambridge. Served with Royal Air Force during War; comd No. 13 (bomber) Sqdn, 1945. Entered the Foreign Service (now the Diplomatic Service), 1947; served in: Paris; Karachi; Tehran; Saigon; The Hague; Foreign Office. *Recreations:* ski-ing, tennis, squash and small boat sailing. *Address:* c/o Foreign and Commonwealth Office, SW1. *Clubs:* United University, Ski Club of Great Britain.

**BURROWS, Sir (Robert) John (Formby),** Kt 1965; MA, LLB; Solicitor; *b* 29 May 1901; *s* of Rev. Canon Francis Henry and Margaret Nelson Burrows; *m* 1926, Mary Hewlett, *y d* of Rev. R. C. Salmon; one *s* one *d*. *Educ:* Eton Coll. (Scholar); Trinity Coll., Cambridge (Scholar); Harvard Law Sch. Governor of the London Sch. of Economics; Pres. of The Law Soc., 1964-65. *Recreation:* planting trees. *Address:* Cronklands, Limpsfield Chart, Surrey. *T:* Limpsfield Chart 3288. *Clubs:*

Oxford and Cambridge, Buck's. *See also W. Hamilton.*

**BURSTALL, Prof. Aubrey Frederic;** Emeritus Professor (Mechanical Engineering), University of Newcastle upon Tyne (formerly King's College, University of Durham); Dean of Faculty of Applied Science, 1955-57; *b* 15 Jan. 1902; *s* of Prof. Frederic William Burstall of Univ. of Birmingham and Lilian Maud Burstall (*née* Adley); *m* 1923, Nora Elizabeth (*née* Boycott); two *s* one *d*. *Educ:* King Edward VI Grammar Sch., Birmingham, Univ. of Birmingham; St John's Coll., Cambridge. BScEng Birmingham, 1922, First Class Hons; MScEng Birmingham, 1923; PhD Cantab 1925; DSc Melbourne; Hon. DSc (NUI), 1959. Research student, St John's Coll., Cambridge, 1923-25. Employed on the staff of Synthetic Ammonia and Nitrates Ltd (later merged into ICI Ltd) as research engineer, asst chief engineer and works engineer at Billingham Factory, 1925-34; Aluminium Plant and Vessel Co., London, as Technical Adviser to the Board responsible for design of chemical plant, 1934-37; Prof. of Engineering and Dean of Faculty of Engineering, Univ. of Melbourne, Australia, 1937-45. Developed mechanical respirators for infantile paralysis epidemic, 1937-38; gas producers for motor vehicles, and built new workshops at the Univ.; part-time Comr of State Electricity Commn of Victoria, 1941-43; leave of absence to work for British Min. of Supply in Armaments Design Dept, Fort Halstead, Kent, 1943-44. Member of Nat. Advisory Cttee on Technical Educ., 1948-; Chm. North Eastern Branch IMechE, 1956; Member Board of Governors, United Newcastle upon Tyne Hospitals, 1964-67; Member Council of Univ. of Durham, 1964-67; Fellow, NEC Inst. Engineers and Shipbuilders; FIMechE. *Publications:* A History of Mechanical Engineering, 1963; Simple Working Models of Historic Machines, 1968; numerous in engineering journals in Britain and Australia. *Address:* The Firs, Kilmington, Axminster, Devon. *T:* Axminster 2385.

**BURSTEIN, Mrs N.;** *see* Heilbron, Rose.

**BURT, Professor Alfred LeRoy;** *b* Listowel, Ont., Canada, 28 Nov. 1888; *e s* of C. K. Burt; *m* 1915, Dorothy, *d* of J. M. M. Duff, Montreal; one *s* three *d*. *Educ:* Toronto Public Schools; Univ. of Toronto, BA 1910; Corpus Christi Coll., Oxford, BA 1912, MA 1916. Rhodes Scholar for Ontario, 1910; divided Beit Prize, Robert Herbert Memorial Prize, 1913, FRHistS. Lecturer, 1913; Asst Prof. of History, Univ. of Alberta, Canada, 1916; Lieut Canadian Tank Batt., CEF, 1918; Associate Prof., 1920; Prof. and Head of History Dept, Univ. of Alberta, 1921; Prof., Univ. of Minnesota, 1930-57, Emeritus Professor of Univ., 1957-. Visiting Professor: Carleton Univ., Canada, 1957-58; Univ. of Chicago, 1959-60; Univ. of Manitoba, 1960-61. Royal Society of Canada Tyrrell Medal, 1946; Canada Centennial Medal, 1967. Hon. Dr Laws, Univ. of Alberta, 1966. *Publications:* Imperial Architects, 1913; A Short History of the League of Nations, 1924; edited vol. 3, Makers of Canada Series, 1926; High School Civics, 1928; Romance of the Prairie Provinces, 1930; The Old Province of Quebec, 1933; The Romance of Canada, 1937; The United States, Great Britain, and British North America from the Revolution to the Establishment of Peace after the War of 1812, 1940; A Short History of Canada for Americans, 1942; (in part) The United States and Its Place in World Affairs, 1943; The Evolution of the British Empire and Commonwealth from the American Revolution, 1956; contributor to various journals and to Cambridge History of the British Empire. *Recreations:* music, gardening, golf. *Address:* 39 Crown Ridge Road, Wellesley, Mass. 02181, USA.

**BURT, C. K. J.;** *see* Johnstone-Burt.

**BURT, Clive Stuart Saxon,** QC 1954; a Metropolitan Magistrate since 1958. Called to the Bar, Gray's Inn, 1925; Western Circuit. Chairman, The Performing Rights Tribunal, 1957-58. *Address:* Flat 6, 83 Vincent Square, SW1; Townley House, Woodbridge, Suffolk.

**BURT, Sir Cyril Lodowic,** Kt, *cr* 1946; MA, DSc Oxon; Hon. LLD Aberdeen; Hon. DLitt Reading; FBA; Hon. Fellow, Jesus College, Oxford; Professor of Psychology, University College, London, 1931-50. Emeritus Professor since 1950; *b* 30 March 1883; *s* of Dr C. Barrow Burt, JP, of Snitterfield, Stratford-on-Avon; *m* Joyce, *d* of late P. F. Woods. *Educ:* Christ's Hospital (Charles Lamb Medallist); Jesus Coll., Oxford (Classical Scholar); Post-graduate Research Scholar; Würzburg Univ. John Locke Scholar in Mental Philosophy in the Univ. of Oxford, 1908; Lecturer in Experimental Psychology and Asst Lecturer in Physiology, Univ. of Liverpool, 1909-13; Asst Lecturer, Psychological Laboratory, Univ. of Cambridge, 1912-13; Psychologist to the London County Council (Education Dept), 1913-32; Professor of Education in the Univ. of London, 1924-31; Pres. Psychological Section, British Assoc., 1923; Pres. British Psychological Soc., 1942; Chm. of the Psychological Cttee of the Industrial Health Board (Medical Research Council); Governor and Almoner of Christ's Hospital; Member of: Nat. Inst. of Industrial Psychology, Industrial Health Research Board; Advisory Cttee to War Office on Personnel Selection; Psychological Consultant to Civil Service Commission. Editor, British Journal of Statistical Psychology. *Publications:* The Distribution of Educational Abilities, 1917; Mental and Scholastic Tests, 1921; Handbook of Tests, 1923; The Young Delinquent, 1925; The Measurement of Mental Capacities, 1927; How the Mind Works, 1933; The Subnormal Mind, 1935; The Backward Child, 1937; Factors of the Mind, 1940; The Causes and Treatment of Backwardness, 1952; A Psychological Study of Typography, 1959; various articles in scientific periodicals. *Address:* 9 Elsworthy Road, Hampstead, NW3. *T:* 01-722 0233.

**BURT, Hugh Armitage,** MA Cantab; FRCP; Director, Department of Physical Medicine, University College Hospital, since 1947; Hon. Consultant in Physical Medicine to Army, since 1954; *b* 16 March 1911; *e s* of late J. Barnes Burt, MD, and Dorothy Armitage; unmarried. *Educ:* Westminster Sch.; Trinity Coll., Cambridge (Westminster Sch. Exhibitioner); UCH. BA Cantab 1932; MB, BCh Cantab 1937; MRCS 1935; FRCP 1952. Late House Physician, House Surgeon and Asst on the Medical Unit, UCH, and Chief Asst, Dept for Chronic Rheumatic Diseases, West London Hosp. War of 1939-45, Lt-Col RAMC and Adviser in Physical Medicine to WO. Examiner in Physical Medicine, RCP. Pres. of the British Assoc. of Physical Medicine, 1959-62 (Member Council 1945-; Vice-President 1956-59); Member Army Health Advisory Cttee; Mem. Council for Professions Supplementary to Medicine; Mem. Bd of Govs, UCH, 1962-. Former Pres. Section of Physical Medicine, Royal Society of Medicine; ex-Member of Executive and Educational Cttees, Empire Rheumatism Council. Former Editor of Annals of Physical Medicine. *Publications:* various articles and chapters in medical journals and textbooks. *Address:* 103 Harley Street, W1. *T:* 01-935 6111. *Club:* Athenæum.

**BURT, Leonard James,** CVO 1954; CBE 1957; Commander of Special Branch, New Scotland Yard, 1946-58, retired; *b* 20 April 1892; *s* of Charles Richard Burt; *m* 1918, Grace Airey; one *s*. *Educ:* Totton High Sch., Hants. CID, 1919-40; Chief Superintendent, CID, 1940; Intelligence Corps (Lieut-Col) 1940-46. Officer Legion of Honour, 1950; Officer Order of Orange Nassau, 1951; Chevalier Order of Danebrog, 1951. *Publication:* Commander Burt of Scotland Yard, 1959. *Address:* Flat 1, Hedley Court, 67/69 Putney Hill, SW15. *T:* 01-788 4598.

**BURT-ANDREWS, Air Commodore Charles Beresford Eaton,** CB 1962; CBE 1959; RAF retired; *b* 21 March 1913; *s* of late Major C. Burt-Andrews, RE; *m* 1941, Elizabeth Alsina Helen, *d* of late Sir Maurice Linford Gwyer, GCIE, KCB, KCSI; one *s* one *d*. *Educ:* Lindisfarne Coll.; Collège des Frères Chrétiens Sophia. Commnd RAF, 1935; served NWF India, 1937-42; S Waziristan ops, 1937; Burma, 1942; comd Army Co-op. Sqdn RAF, 1943; special ops, 1943-44; Air Attaché, British Embassy, Warsaw, 1945-47; Staff Coll., 1948; Sec. Gen. Allied Air Forces Central Europe, Fontainebleau, 1950-52; directing Staff RAF Staff Coll., 1953-55; Head of Far East Defence Secretariat, Singapore, 1955-58; First Comdt, Pakistan Air Force Staff Coll., 1959-61; UK Nat. Mil. Rep., SHAPE, Paris, 1962-65; Asst Comdt, RAF Staff Coll., Bracknell, 1965-68; retd, 1968. *Recreation:* painting. *Address:* Treovis, Upton Cross, Liskeard, Cornwall. *Club:* Royal Air Force.

*See also S. G. Burt-Andrews.*

**BURT-ANDREWS, Stanley George,** CMG 1968; MBE 1948; retired; *b* 1 Feb. 1908; *s* of Major Charles and Menie Celina Burt-Andrews; *m* 1937, Vera Boyadjieva; one *d*. *Educ:* Lindisfarne Coll., Westcliff-on-Sea; St Andrew's Coll., Bloemfontein, S Africa. Vice-Consul, 1946-47, Consul, 2nd Secretary, Sofia, 1948; Consul, Barranquilla, 1949-52; Commercial Secretary, British Embassy, Buenos Aires, 1952-53; Consul: Baltimore, 1953-59; Bilbao, 1959-62; Venice, 1962-64; Consul-General, St Louis, Mo., 1965-67. *Recreations:* golf, fishing. *Address:* Villa Verial, 1 Aldwick Place, Fish Lane, Aldwick, Bognor Regis, Sussex. *Clubs:* Royal Automobile; Bognor Regis Golf.

*See also Air Cdre C. B. E. Burt-Andrews.*

**BURTON,** 3rd Baron, *cr* 1897; **Michael Evan Victor Baillie;** JP; Member of the County Council of Inverness since 1948; *b* 27 June 1924; *er s* of Brig. Hon. George Evan Michael Baillie, MC, TD (*d* 1941) and *g s* of Baroness Burton (2nd in line); *S* grandmother, 1962; *m* 1948, Elizabeth Ursula Forster, *er d* of Capt. A. F. Wise; two *s* four *d*. *Educ:* Eton. Lieut, Scots Guards, 1944. JP 1961, DL 1963-65, Inverness-shire. *Heir:* *s* Hon. Evan Michael Ronald Baillie [*b* 19 March 1949; *m* 1970, Lucinda, *e d* of Robert Law, Newmarket]. *Address:* Dochfour, Inverness. *T:* Dochgarroch 252. *Clubs:* Guards, Brooks's; New (Edinburgh); Highland (Inverness).

**BURTON,** family name of **Baroness Burton of Coventry.**

**BURTON OF COVENTRY,** Baroness, *cr* 1962, of Coventry (Life Peeress); **Elaine Frances Burton;** Consultant to: Courtaulds Ltd, since 1960; The Reader's Digest, since 1969; *b* Scarborough, 2 March 1904; *d* of Leslie and Frances Burton. *Educ:* Leeds Girls' Modern Sch.; City of Leeds Training Coll. Leeds elementary schools and evening institutes, 1924-35; South Wales Council of Social Service and educational settlements, 1935-37; National Fitness Council, 1938-39; John Lewis Partnership, 1940-45. Writer, lecturer, broadcaster, public relations consultant, 1945-50. MP (Lab) Coventry South, 1950-59. Member of parliamentary delegation to Netherlands, 1952 and to Soviet Union, 1954; Siam, 1956; South America, 1958; deleg. to Council of Europe; first woman Chm., Select Cttee on Estimates (sub-Cttee); Chairman: Domestic Coal Consumers' Council, 1962-65; Council on Tribunals, 1967-; Member: Council Industrial Design, 1963-68; ITA, 1964-69; Sports Council, 1965-. Consultant to John Waddington Ltd, 1959-61; Director: Imperial Domestic Appliances Ltd, 1963-66; Consultancy Ltd. *Publications:* What of the Women, 1941; And Your Verdict?, 1943; articles for press, magazines and political journals. *Recreations:* reading, ballet, opera; World's Sprint Champion, 1920; Yorkshire 1st XI (hockey), 1924-32. *Address:* 47 Molyneux Street, W1. *T:* 01-262 0864.

**BURTON, Prof. Alan Chadburn,** MBE 1947; FRS Canada 1952; FRSA (UK) 1954; Professor of Biophysics, University of Western Ontario, Canada, since 1949; *b* 18 April 1904; *s* of Frank Burton, Dental Surgeon, and Annie Grey (*née* Tyrrell), N Ireland; *m* 1933, Clara Ballard, Niagara Falls, Ontario; one *s*. *Educ:* Strand Sch., Streatham Hill; Univ. Coll., London. BSc Physics and Maths, UCL, 1925. Demonstrator in Physics, Univ. Coll., 1925-26; Science Master, Liverpool Collegiate Sch., 1926-27; Demonstrator and lecturer, Univ. of Toronto, Physics Dept., 1927-32; Fellow of Nat. Res. Council, Canada, 1930-32; PhD Physics, Univ. of Toronto, 1932; Research Asst, Dept of Vital Economics, Univ. of Rochester, NY, 1932-34; Rockefeller Gen. Ed. Board Fellow, Univ. of Pennsylvania, 1934-36; Fellow, Johnson Foundation for Medical Physics, 1936-40; Research Assoc., Nat. Research Council of Canada, 1941-46. War Research on Protective Clothing and Equipment for RCAF. Asst Prof., 1946, later Assoc. Prof. of Biophysics, Univ. of W. Ontario. Pres., American Physiological Soc., 1956-57; Pres., Canadian Physical Soc., 1962-63. Hon. LLD, Univ. of Alberta, 1963. Gairnder Internat. Award for Cardiovascular Research, 1961. *Publications:* The Science of Field Testing of Clothing and Equipment (Monograph of Defence Research Board of Canada), 1947; (with O. G. Edholm) Man in a Cold Environment, 1955; about 100 publications in journals of Physiology and Biophysics, 12 in Journals of Physics. *Recreations:* formerly Rugby and tennis, now golf; interested in penal reform and prisoner rehabilitation (John Howard Society). *Address:* 243 Epworth Avenue, London, Ontario, Canada. *T:* GE 4-9938.

**BURTON, Sir Geoffrey Pownall,** KCSI, *cr* 1946; KCIE, *cr* 1937 (CIE 1935); DL; MA; *b* 19 Nov. 1884; *s* of John Albert Burton, JP, and Anne Sophia Hadfield; *m* 1914, Doris Hargreaves Speight; one *s* one *d*. *Educ:* Bradford Grammar Sch.; Queen's Coll., Oxford (Hastings Exhibitioner). Entered Indian Civil Service as Asst Commissioner, 1909; Under Secretary to Government, CP, 1913; Deputy Commissioner, 1918; Excise Commissioner, 1927; Revenue Secretary to Government, CP, 1929; Commissioner, Berar, 1932; Commissioner, Jubbulpore Division, 1933; Revenue and Finance Member of Govt, CP, 1936-37; Financial Commissioner, CP AND

Berar, 1937; Adviser to Governor of Central Provinces, 1939-45. DL Yorkshire, West Riding, 1954. *Address:* 8 Park View Road, Heaton, Bradford 9. *T:* Bradford 44995.

**BURTON, George Vernon Kennedy,** MBE 1945; Senior Vice-Chairman and Chief Executive of the Fison Group of Companies, since 1966; Director, Matthews Holdings Ltd; *b* 21 April 1916; *s* of late George Ernest Earnshaw Burton; *m* 1945, Sarah Katherine Tcherniavsky; two *s*. *Educ:* Charterhouse; Germany. Served RA, 1939-45. A Dep. Chm., Export Council for Europe; Member Council, CBI; Fellow and Mem. Council, British Inst. of Management; Liveryman, Worshipful Co. of Farmers. *Recreations:* music, veteran and vintage cars. *Address:* Fison House, 9 Grosvenor Street, W1. *T:* 01-493 1611.

**BURTON, Air Marshal Harry,** CB 1970; CBE 1963 (MBE 1943); DSO 1941; Air Officer Commanding-in-Chief, Air Support Command, since 1970; *b* 2 May 1919; *s* of Robert Reid Burton, Rutherglen; *m* 1945, Jean, *d* of Tom Dobie; one *s* one *d*. *Educ:* Glasgow High Sch. Joined RAF 1937; served War of 1939-45, Europe, India, and Pacific (POW, 1940, escaped 1941; despatches); CO, RAF Scampton, 1960-62; SASO 3 (Bomber) Group, RAF, 1963-65; Air Executive to Deputy for Nuclear Affairs, SHAPE, 1965-67; AOC 23 Group, RAF, 1967-70. Group Captain 1958; Air Cdre 1963; Air Vice-Marshal 1965. *Address:* c/o Lloyds Bank, 6 Pall Mall, SW1. *Club:* Royal Air Force.

**BURTON, Rev. John Harold Stanley,** MA Oxon; retired as General Secretary, Church Lads' Brigade (1954-64); and Member, Church of England Youth Council (1954-64); *b* 6 Feb. 1913; *o s* of late John Stanley Burton, Grenadier Guards (killed in action 1916), and Lilian Bostock; *m* 1st, 1943, Susan Lella (*d* 1960), *o d* of Sir John Crisp, 3rd Bt; two *d*; 2nd, 1960, Jacqueline Mary Margaret, *o d* of P. L. Forte, Clifton, Bristol; one *d*. *Educ:* Marlborough; University Coll., Oxford; Westcott House, Cambridge. BA 2nd Class Hons. in Theology, Oxford, 1935; MA 1937; Deacon, 1936; Priest, 1938; Curate of Christ Church, Woburn Square, WC1, 1936-39; Cranleigh, Surrey, 1939-40; Head of Cambridge Univ. Settlement, Camberwell, 1940-43; Chaplain RAFVR, 1943; Fighter Command, 1943-44; 2nd Tactical Air Force, 1944; Bomber Command, 1945; Ordination Secretary, Air Command, SE Asia, and Chaplain 9 RAF General Hospital, Calcutta, 1945-46; demobilised Aug. 1946. Chaplain of Middlesex Hospital, W1, 1946-50; Chaplain of the Royal Free Hospital, 1950-54; Chairman of Hospital Chaplains Fellowship, 1953-54. *Publications:* (contrib.) A Priest's Work in Hospital, 1955; (contrib.) Trends in Youth Work, 1967. *Recreations:* Beagling, Fishing, shooting, most games. *Address:* Blair's Cove House, Durrus, near Bantry, Co. Cork. *T:* Durrus 18. *Club:* Cork and County.

**BURTON, Maurice,** DSc; retired 1958; now free-lance author and journalist; *b* 28 March 1898; *s* of William Francis and Jane Burton; *m* 1928, Margaret Rosalie Maclean; two *s* one *d*. *Educ:* Holloway County Sch.; London Univ. Biology Master, Latymer Foundation, Hammersmith, 1924-27; Zoology Dept, British Museum (Natural History), SW7, 1927-58. Science Editor, Illustrated London News, 1946-64; Nature Correspondent, Daily Telegraph, 1949-; Co-editor, Purnell's Encyclopedia of Animal Life, 1968-. FRSA, FZS. *Publications:* The Story of Animal Life, 1949; Animal Courtship, 1953; Living Fossils, 1954; Phœnix Re-born, 1959; Systematic Dictionary of Mammals, 1962, etc.; numerous publications on Sponges in a variety of scientific journals. *Recreation:* gardening. *Address:* Weston House, Albury, Guildford, Surrey. *T:* Shere 2369.

**BURTON, Richard;** stage and film actor, CBE 1970; *b* Pontrhydfen, South Wales, 10 Nov. 1925; *m* 1st, 1949, Sybil Williams (marr. diss., 1963; she *m* 1965, Jordan Christopher); two *d*; 2nd, 1964, Elizabeth Taylor, *qv*. *Educ:* Port Talbot Secondary Sch.; Exeter Coll., Oxford. First appeared on stage as Glan in Druid's Rest, Royal Court Theatre, Liverpool, 1943; played same rôle, St Martin's, London, 1944. Served with Royal Air Force, 1944-47. Returned to stage in Castle Anna, Lyric, Hammersmith, 1948; subsequent stage appearances include: Richard in the Lady's Not For Burning, Globe, 1949, New York, 1950; Cuthman in The Boy With a Cart, Lyric, Hammersmith, 1950. Played Hamlet with Old Vic Company, Edinburgh Festival, 1953, and subsequently; has also appeared with Old Vic Company in King John, The Tempest, Twelfth Night, Coriolanus, etc. Old Vic Season, 1955-56: Othello, Iago, Henry V; Time Remembered, New York, 1957-58; Camelot, New York, 1960; Hamlet, New York, 1964. *Films include:* The Last Days of Dolwyn; My Cousin Rachel; The Desert Rats; The Robe; The Prince of Players; Alexander the Great; The Rains of Ranchipur; Sea Wyf and Biscuit; Bitter Victory; Look Back in Anger; Bramblebush; Ice Palace; Cleopatra; The VIP's; Becket; Hamlet (from Broadway prod.); The Night of the Iguana; The Sandpiper; The Spy Who Came in from the Cold; Who's Afraid of Virginia Woolf; The Taming of the Shrew; Dr Faustus; The Comedians; Boom; Where Eagles Dare; Candy; Staircase; Anne of the Thousand Days. *Address:* c/o John Heyman, 72 Brook Street, W1; c/o Hugh French Agency Inc., 9348 Santa Monica Boulevard, Beverly Hills, California, USA.

**BURTON-CHADWICK, Sir Robert,** 2nd Bt, *cr* 1935; *b* 22 June 1911; *s* of Sir Robert Burton-Chadwick, 1st Bt and Catherine Barbara (*d* 1935), *d* of late Thomas Williams; *S* father 1951; *m* 1st, 1937, Rosalind Mary (marr. diss., 1949), *d* of Harry John Stott; two *d*; 2nd, 1950, Beryl Joan, *d* of Stanley Frederick J. Brailsford; one *s* one *d*. *Educ:* St George's Sch., Harpenden, Herts. Served War of 1939-45, with NZMF, N Africa, Italy, 1942-45. *Heir:* *s* Joshua Kenneth Burton-Chadwick, *b* 1 Feb. 1954. *Address:* 29 Myrtle Street, Lower Hutt, Wellington, NZ. *T:* 64.897.

**BURY, Viscount; Rufus Arnold Alexis Keppel;** *b* 16 July 1965; *s* of Derek William Charles Keppel, Viscount Bury (*d* 1968), and Marina, *yr d* of late Count Serge Orloff-Davidoff; *g s* and *heir* of 9th Earl of Albemarle, *qv*. *Address:* 29 Via del Casone, 50124 Firenze, Italy; Rosa dei Venti, Cala Piccola, Porto S Stefano, Grosseto, Italy.

**BURY, John;** Associate Designer, Royal Shakespeare Theatre, since 1963; free-lance designer for theatre, opera and film; *b* 27 Jan. 1925; *s* of C. R. Bury; *m* 1st, 1947, Margaret Leila Greenwood (marr. diss.); one *s*; 2nd, 1966, Elizabeth Rebecca Blackborrow Duffield; one *s* one *d*. *Educ:* Cathedral Sch., Hereford; University Coll., London. Served with Fleet Air Arm (RN), 1942-46. Theatre Workshop, Stratford, E15, 1946-63; Assoc. Designer, Royal Shakespeare Theatre, 1963-65, Head of Design, 1965-68. FRSA 1970. *Address:* The Vines, Tredington, Shipston-on-Stour, Warwickshire. *T:* Shipston-on-Stour 622.

**BUSBY, Sir Matthew,** Kt 1968; CBE 1958; General Manager, Manchester United Football Club, since 1969 (Manager, 1945-69); *b* 26 May 1909; *m* 1931, Jean Busby; one *s* one *d* (and four *s* decd). *Educ:* St Brides, Bothwell. Footballer: Manchester City, 1929-36; Liverpool, 1936-39. Served Army, 1939-45. Freeman of Manchester, 1967. *Publication:* My Story, 1957. *Recreations:* golf, theatre. *Address:* 210 Kings Road, Manchester 21. *T:* 061-881 3326.

**BUSH, Alan,** MC 1944; Headmaster, Merchiston Castle School, since 1958; *b* 18 July 1914; 5th *s* of Arthur and Sarah Bush, Endmoor, Westmorland; *m* 1946, Kathleen Olivia Guthrie, *e d* of Dr and Mrs Bryson, Dore, Derbyshire; two *s* one *d*. *Educ:* Heversham Grammar Sch.; The Queen's Coll., Oxford (Hons. History). Asst Master, Scarborough Coll., 1935-37; Asst Master, Mill Hill Sch., 1937. Commissioned into Border Regt, 1940; transferred to Parachute Regt. Housemaster of Ridgeway House, Mill Hill Sch., 1950-58. *Recreations:* most games; gardening. *Address:* Castle Gates, Merchiston Castle School, Colinton, Edinburgh 13. *T:* 031-441 3468.

**BUSH, Alan,** FRSA; Composer; Conductor; Pianist; Professor of Composition, Royal Academy of Music, since 1925; *b* 22 Dec. 1900; *s* of Alfred Walter Bush and Alice Maud (*née* Brinsley); *m* 1931, Nancy Rachel Head; two *d* (and one *d* decd). *Educ:* Highgate Sch.; Royal Academy of Music; Univ. of Berlin. ARAM 1922; Carnegie Award 1924; FRAM 1938; BMus London, 1940; DMus London, 1968. Arts Council Opera Award, 1951; Händel Prize, City Council of Halle (Saale), 1962; Corresp. Member, Deutsche Akademie der Künste, 1955. Appeared as piano-recitalist, London, Berlin, etc., 1927-33; played solo part in own Piano Concerto, BBC, 1938, with Sir Adrian Boult conducting. Toured Ceylon, India, Australia as Examiner for Assoc. Board of Royal Schools of Music, London, 1932-33; concert tours as orchestral conductor, introducing British Music and own compositions, to USSR, 1938, 1939, 1963, Czechoslovakia, Yugoslavia, Poland, Bulgaria, 1947, Czechoslovakia and Bulgaria again, 1949, Holland, 1950, Berlin (German Democratic Republic) and Hungary, 1952, and Berlin again, 1958; Première of opera "Wat Tyler" at the Leipzig Opera House, 1953; Première of opera "Men of Blackmoor" at the German National Theatre, Weimar, 1956; Première of opera "The Sugar Reapers" at the Leipzig Opera House, 1966; Première "Joe Hill (The Man Who Never Died)", German State Opera, Berlin, 1970. Musical Adviser, London Labour Choral Union, 1929-40; Chairman Workers' Music Assoc., 1936-41 (President 1941-). Chairman Composers' Guild of Great Britain, 1947-48. *Publications: operas:* Wat Tyler; Men of Blackmoor; and children's operettas. *Choral works:* The Winter Journey, Op. 29; Song of Friendship, Op. 34; The Ballad of Freedom's Soldier, Op. 44 (mixed voices); The Dream of Llewelyn ap Gruffydd, Op. 35 (male voices); The Alps and Andes of the Living World, Op. 66 (mixed chorus); Folksong arrangements, etc. *Songs:* Voices of the Prophets, Cantata for tenor and piano, Op. 41, Seafarers' Songs for baritone and piano, Op. 57; The Freight of Harvest, Song-Cycle for Tenor and Piano, Op. 69, etc. *Orchestral Works:* Dance Overture, Op. 12; Piano Concerto, Op. 18; Symphony No. 1 in C, Op. 21; English Suite for strings, Op. 28; Piers Plowman's Day Suite, Op. 30; Violin Concerto, Op. 32; Symphony No. 2 "The Nottingham," Op. 33; Concert Suite for 'cello and orchestra, Op. 37; Dorian Passacaglia and Fugue, Op. 52; Symphony No. 3 "The Byron Symphony," Op. 53; Variations, Nocturne and Finale on an English Sea Song for piano and orchestra, Op. 60; Partita Concertante, Op. 63; Scherzo for Wind Orchestra with Percussion, Op. 68, etc. *Chamber Music:* String Quartet, Op. 4; Piano Quartet, Op. 5; Five Pieces for Violin, Viola, Cello, Clarinet and Horn, Op. 6; Dialectic for string quartet, Op. 15; Three Concert Studies for piano trio, Op. 31; Suite for Two Pianos, Op. 65; Time Remembered for Chamber Orchestra, Op. 66; Serenade for String Quartet, Op. 70. *Instrumental solos:* Prelude and Fugue for piano, Op. 9; Relinquishment for piano, Op. 11; Concert Piece for 'cello and piano, Op. 17; Meditation on a German song of 1848 for violin and String Orchestra or piano, Op. 22; Lyric Interlude for violin and piano, Op. 26; Le Quatorze Juillet for piano, Op. 38; Trent's Broad Reaches for French horn and piano, Op. 36; Three English Song Preludes for organ, Op. 40; Northumbrian Impressions for oboe and piano, Op. 42a. Autumn Poem for French Horn and piano, Op. 45, Two Ballads of the Sea for piano, Op. 50; Two Melodies for viola with piano accompaniment, Op. 47, Suite for harpsichord or piano, Op. 54; Three African Sketches for flute with piano accompaniment, Op. 55; Two Occasional Pieces for organ, Op. 56; Prelude, Air and Dance for violin with accompaniment for string quartet and percussion, Op. 61; Meditation on the Ballad Geordie for double-bass and piano, Op. 62; Two Dances for Cimbalom, Op. 64; Pianoforte Sonata in A flat, Op. 71, etc. *Textbook:* Strict Counterpoint in Palestrina Style. *Recreations:* walking, foreign travel. *Address:* 25 Christchurch Crescent, Radlett, Herts. *T:* Radlett 6422.

**BUSH, Brian Drex; His Honour Judge Bush;** Judge of County Courts since 1969; *b* 5 Sept. 1925; *s* of William Harry Bush; *m* 1954, Beatrice Marian Lukeman; one *s* one *d*. *Educ:* King Edward's Sch., Birmingham; Birmingham Univ. (LLB). Served, RNVR, 1943-46. Called to the Bar, Gray's Inn, 1947. Dep. Chm., Derbyshire Quarter Sessions, 1966-. Chm., Industrial Tribunal, 1967-69. *Recreations:* sailing, golf. *Address:* 12 Middlepark Close, Weoley Hill, Birmingham 29. *Clubs:* Royal Naval Sailing Association, Bar Yacht.

**BUSH, Captain Eric Wheler,** DSO 1940 (and Bars 1942 and 1944); DSC 1915; RN; psc; *b* 12 Aug. 1899; *s* of late Rev. H. W. Bush, Chaplain to the Forces, and Edith Cornelia (*née* Cardew); *m* 1938, Mollie Noël, *d* of Col B. Watts, DSO; two *s*. *Educ:* Stoke House, Stoke Poges; Royal Naval Colleges, Osborne and Dartmouth. Midshipman in HMS Bacchante, 1941; present at Battle of Heligoland Bight, 28 Aug. 1914; took part in defence of Suez Canal Jan.-March 1915; present at original landing at Anzac, Gallipoli, 25 April 1915, and subsequent operations, also original landing at Suvia Bay 1915 (despatches twice, DSC); Midshipman HMS Revenge 1916 and present at Battle of Jutland, 31 May 1916; Sub-Lieut 1917; Lieut 1920; Qualified Interpreter in Hindustani, 1924; Lt-Comdr 1927; Qualified RN Staff Coll., 1931; Commander, 1933; Captain, 1939; Chief of Staff and afterwards Captain Auxiliary Patrol, Dover Command, 1939-40 (DSO); HMS Euryalus in Command, Mediterranean, 1941-43 (Bar to DSO); Senior Officer Assault Group S3, invasion of Normandy, 1944 (2nd Bar to DSO), afterwards in Command of HMS Malaya; Chief of Staff, Naval Force 'W', SEAC, 1945 (despatches twice); in Command HMS Ganges, Boys' Training Establishment, Shotley, Suffolk, 1946-48; Sec. Sea Cadet

Council, 1948-59. Gen. Manager, Red Ensign Club, Stepney, 1959-64. School Liaison British-India Steam Navigation Co. Ltd, 1965- . Retired list, 1948. *Publications:* How to Become a Naval Officer (Special Entry); Bless our Ship; The Flowers of the Sea; How to Become a Naval Officer (Cadet Entry); Salute the Soldier. *Address:* Hunters, Langton Green, Kent. *T:* Tunbridge Wells 21768. *Club:* United Service.

**BUSH, Prof. Ian (Elcock),** MA; PhD; MB, BChir; Vice-President and Director of Research and Development, Cybertek Inc., New York, and part-time Professor of Physiology, New York University Medical School; *b* 25 May 1928; *s* of Dr Gilbert B. Bush and Jean Margaret Bush; *m* 1st, 1951, Alison Mary Pickard (marr. diss., 1966); one *s* two *d*; 2nd, 1967, Joan Morthland; one *s* one *d*. *Educ:* Bryanston Sch.; Pembroke Coll., Cambridge BA 1949. Natural Sciences Tripos, 1st class I and II; MA, PhD 1953; MB, BChir. 1957. Medical Research Council Scholar (Physiology Lab. Cambridge; National Institute for Medical Research), 1949-52; Commonwealth Fellow 1952 (University of Utah; Mass. General Hospital); Part-time Research Asst, Med. Unit, St Mary's Hosp. London and med. student, 1953-56; Grad. Asst, Dept Regius Prof. of Med., Oxford, 1956-59; Mem. ext. Scientific Staff, Med. Research Council (Oxford), 1959-61. Hon. Dir Med. Research Council Unit for research in chem. pathology of mental disorders, 1960; Bowman Prof. of Physiology and Dir of Dept of Physiology, Univ. of Birmingham, 1960-64; Senior Scientist, The Worcester Foundation for Experimental Biology, 1964-67; Chm. of Dept and Prof. of Physiology, Medical Coll. of Virginia, 1967-70. Fellow, Amer. Acad. of Arts and Sciences, 1966. *Publications:* Chromatography of Steroids, 1961. Contributions to: Jl Physiol.; Biochem. Jl; Jl Endocrinol.; Nature; The Analyst; Jl Biolog. Chem.; Brit. Med. Bulletin; Acta Endocrinologica; Experientia; Biochem. Soc. Symposia, etc. *Recreations:* music, chess, sailing, astronomy, philosophy. *Address:* Cybertek Inc., 200 Express Street, Plainview, NY 11803, USA.

**BUSH, Adm. Sir John (Fitzroy Duyland),** GCB 1970 (KCB 1965; CB 1963); DSC 1941, and Bars, 1941, 1944; Director, Gordan A. Friesen International Inc., Washington, DC, since 1970; *b* 1 Nov. 1914; *s* of late Fitzroy Bush, Beach, Glos.; *m* 1938, Ruth Kennedy Horsey; three *s* two *d*. *Educ:* Clifton Coll. Entered Navy, 1933; served in Destroyers throughout War. Commanded HM Ships: Belvoir, 1942-44; Zephyr, 1944; Chevron, 1945-46. Comdr Dec. 1946; Plans Div., Admiralty, 1946-48; graduated Armed Forces Staff Coll., USA, 1949; Comd, HMS Cadiz, 1950-51; Capt. June 1952; Dep. Sec. Chiefs of Staff Cttee, 1953-55; Capt. (F) Sixth Frigate Sqdn, 1955-56; Cdre, RN Barracks, Chatham, 1957; 1959; Dir. of Plans, Admiralty, 1959-60; Rear-Adm. 1961; Flag Officer Flotillas (mediterranean), 1961-62; Vice-Adm. 1963; Comdr, British Naval Staff and Naval Attaché, Washington, 1963-65; Vice-Chief of the Naval Staff, Ministry of Defence, 1965-67; C-in-C Western Fleet, C-in-C Eastern Atlantic, and C-in-C Channel (NATO), 1967-70; retd, 1970. Admiral 1968. Adm., Texas (USA) Navy. Pres., Old Cliftonians Soc., 1967-69. *Recreations:* fishing, gardening. *Address:* Green Ways, The Avenue, Fareham, Hants. *T:* Fareham 2387. *Club:* Royal Naval Sailing Association.

**BUSH, (John Nash) Douglas;** Professor of English, Harvard University, 1936-66, Gurney Professor, 1957-66; *b* Morrisburg, Ontario, Canada, 21 March 1896; *s* of Dexter C. and Mary E. Bush; *m* 1927, Hazel Cleaver; one *s*. *Educ:* Univ. of Toronto, Canada; Harvard Univ. USA, Sheldon fellow in England 1923-24; Instructor in English, Harvard, 1924-27; Department of English, Univ. of Minnesota, 1927-36; Guggenheim Fellow, in England, 1934-35; member American Philosophical Society; Pres. Modern Humanities Research Association, 1955; Corr. Fellow, British Academy, 1960. Hon. LittD: Tufts Coll., 1952; Princeton Univ., 1958; Toronto Univ., 1958; Oberlin Coll., 1959; Harvard Univ., 1959; Swarthmore Coll., 1960; Boston Coll., 1965; Michigan State Univ., 1968; Merrimack Coll., 1969; LHD Southern Illinois Univ., 1962; LHD, Marlboro Coll., 1966. *Publications:* Mythology and the Renaissance Tradition in English Poetry, 1932 (revised edition, 1963); Mythology and the Romantic Tradition in English Poetry, 1937; The Renaissance and English Humanism, 1939; Paradise Lost in Our Time, 1945; English Literature in the Earlier Seventeenth Century, 1600-1660 (Oxford History of English Literature), 1945 (revised edition 1962); Science and English Poetry, 1950; Classical Influences in Renaissance Literature, 1952; English Poetry; The Main Currents, 1952; Prefaces to Renaissance Literature, 1965; John Milton, 1964; John Keats, 1966; Engaged and Disengaged, 1966. Editor: The Portable Milton, 1949; Tennyson: Selected Poetry, 1951; John Keats: Selected Poems and Letters, 1959; (with A. Harbage), Shakespeare's Sonnets, 1961; Complete Poetical Works of John Milton, 1965. *Address:* 3 Clement Circle, Cambridge, Mass 02138, USA.

**BUSH, Raymond G. W.;** Horticultural consultant and author, retired; *b* 30 Mar. 1885; *s* of Robert Francis Evans Bush and Grace Marion Bush; *m* 1911, Audrey Elizabeth Cobb (*d* 1947); one *s* one *d*. *Educ:* Rugby Sch. Fruitgrower, 1915-38. *Publications:* Soft Fruit Growing, 1942; (with G. H. T. Kimble) The Weather, 1943; Tree Fruit Growing; Frost and the Fruitgrower, 1945; Fruitgrowing Outdoors, 1947; Harvesting and Storing Garden Fruits; A Fruitgrower's Diary; Fruit Salad; Pruning; (with Prof. T. Wallace) Commercial Fruit Growing. *Recreations:* gardening, travelling, photography, swimming and basking in the sun. *Address:* Rock Cottage, Ocho Rios, Jamaica.

**BUSH, Ronald Paul,** CMG 1954; OBE 1946; Colonial Administrative Service, retired; *b* 22 Aug. 1902; *s* of late Admiral Sir Paul Bush; *m* 1938, Anthea Mary Fetherstonhaugh; two *s* one *d*. *Educ:* Marlborough Coll. Appointed to Colonial Administrative Service, 1925; service in Northern Rhodesia: confirmed as District Officer, 1927; promoted Provincial Commissioner, 1947, Sec. for Native Affairs, 1949; retired, 1954; on Commission to enquire into Local Government in Basutoland, 1954. *Address:* Sandbrow, Churt, Near Farnham, Surrey. *T:* Frensham 504. *Club:* Royal Commonwealth Society.

**BUSH, Dr Vannevar,** Hon. KBE 1948; Hon. Chairman of the Corporation, Massachusetts Institute of Technology, since 1959 (Chairman 1957-59); Chairman of Board of Graphic Arts Research Foundation; Trustee, The George Putnam Fund; Trustee, Carnegie Institution of Washington; *b* 11 Mar. 1890; *s* of Richard Perry Bush and Emma Linwood Paine; *m* 1916, Phoebe Davis; two *s*. *Educ:* Tufts Coll. (now Tufts Univ.), Medford, Mass; Harvard, Cambridge, Mass; Massachusetts Inst. of Technology. BS and MS (Tufts Coll.), 1913; EngD Harvard, 1916; EngD Mass Inst. of Tech., 1916; Test Dept, Gen. Electric Co.,

1913; Inspection Dept US Navy 1914; Instr in Maths, Tufts Coll., 1914-15; Asst Prof. of Elec. Eng, Tufts Coll., 1916-17; Research, US Navy, in connection with submarine detection, 1917-18; Mass Inst of Technology: Associate Prof. of Electric Power Transmission, 1919-23, Prof. 1923-32; Vice-Pres. and Dean of Engineering, 1932-38; Hon. Chm. Corp., 1959-; Pres., Carnegie Instn of Washington, 1939-56, Trustee, 1939-; Chm. Nat. Defense Research Cttee, US Govt 1940, 1941; Dir, Office of Scientific Research and Development, US Govt, 1941-46; Chm. Jt Research and Development Board, US Govt, 1946-47; Chairman, Research and Development Board, National Military Establishment, US Government, Washington, DC, 1947-48; Mem. Council on Foreign Relations, 1953; Mem. Nat. Science Foundation Advisory Cttee, on Govt-Univ. Relationships, 1953. Trustee Emeritus, Johns Hopkins Univ. Hon Fellow, American Coll., of Surgeons. Hon. Member: American Society of Mechanical Engineers, American Society of Naval Architects and Marine Engineers; Inst. of Electrical and Electronics Engineers. Holds many medals, awards, and hon. degrees, inc. Atomic Pioneer Medal, awarded by Pres. Nixon, 1970. Officer, Légion d'Honneur, France. *Publications:* (with William H. Timble) Principles of Electrical Engineering (NY and London), 1922; Operational Circuit Analysis (NY and London), 1929; Endless Horizons (Washington), 1946; Modern Arms and Free men, New York, 1949; Science Is Not Enough, 1967. *Address:* Massachusetts Institute of Technology, Cambridge, Mass 02139, USA; 304 Marsh Street, Belmont, Mass, USA. *Club:* St Botolph (Boston, Mass).

**BUSHE-FOX, Patrick Loftus,** CMG 1963; *b* 4 May 1907; *o s* of late Loftus Henry Kendal Bushe-Fox and of Theodora Bushe-Fox (*née* Willoughby). *Educ:* Charterhouse; St John's Coll., Cambridge (MA, LLM). 1st Class Historical Tripos, Pt II, and Whewell Schol. in Internat. Law, 1928. Called to the Bar, Inner Temple, 1932. Ministry of Economic Warfare, 1941-45; HM Embassy, Washington, 1945; Control Office for Germany and Austria, 1945-47; Foreign Office (German Section), 1947-50; Asst Legal Adviser, Foreign Office, 1950-60; Legal Counsellor, Foreign Office, 1960-67; retired, 1967. *Address:* 15 Madingley Road, Cambridge. *T:* 53901. *Club:* Oxford and Cambridge University.

**BUSHELL, John Christopher Wyndowe;** HM Diplomatic Service; Minister and Deputy Commandant, British Military Government, Berlin, since 1970; *b* 27 Sept. 1919; *s* of late Colonel C. W. Bushell, RE, and Mrs Bushell, Netherbury, Dorset; *m* 1964, Mrs Theodora Todd, *d* of late Mr and Mrs Senior; one *s* (and one step *s* one step *d*). *Educ:* Winchester; Clare Coll., Cambridge. Served War of 1939-45. Entered FO, 1945; served in Moscow, Rome, FO; 1st Sec., 1950; NATO Defence Coll., Paris, 1953-54; Deputy Sec.-Gen., CENTO 1957-59; Counsellor, 1961; Political Adviser to the Commander-in-Chief, Middle East, 1961-64; UK Delegn to NATO, Brussels, 1964-68; seconded to Cabinet Office, 1968-70. *Recreations:* varied. *Address:* British Military Government, Berlin, BFPO 45. *Club:* Travellers'.

**BUSHELL, W. F.;** retired; *b* Harrow, 1885; *s* of William Done Bushell, for 50 years assistant master and Hon. chaplain at Harrow School and Lord of the Manor of Caldey Island, Pembrokeshire; unmarried. *Educ:* Charterhouse; King's Coll., Cambridge. Asst Master, Gresham's Sch., Holt, 1907-12; Head of Modern Side and Housemaster, Rossall Sch., 1912-20; Headmaster of Solihull Sch., 1920-27; Rector of Michaelhouse, Natal, 1927-30; Headmaster of Birkenhead Sch., 1930-46. Pres., Mathematical Assoc., 1946-47. Served in the Herefordshire Regiment in European War, 1914-18; saw service in Palestine and France. *Publications:* miscellaneous articles of an educational and archaeological nature; School Sermons, 1950; School memories, 1952. *Recreation:* travelling. *Address:* Colonsay, Talbot Road, Birkenhead, Cheshire. *T:* 051-652 2713. *Clubs:* Royal Automobile, Royal Over-Seas League, Royal Commonwealth Society.

**BUSHNELL, Alexander Lynn,** CBE 1962; County Clerk and Treasurer, Perth and Kinross Joint County Council, since 1946; *b* 13 Aug. 1911; *s* of William and Margaret Bushnell; *m* 1939, Janet Braithwaite Porteous; two *d*. *Educ:* Dalziel High Sch., Motherwell; Glasgow University. Deputy County Clerk and Treasurer, Inverness CC, 1939; County Clerk and Treasurer, Kirkcudbright CC, 1944. *Recreation:* golf. *Address:* 18 Fairies Road, Perth, Scotland. *T:* Perth 22675.

**BUSHNELL, Geoffrey Hext Sutherland,** MA, PhD, FBA 1970; Fellow of Corpus Christi College, Cambridge, since 1963; author; Curator, University Museum of Archaeology and Ethnology, Cambridge, 1948-70, retd; Reader in New World Archaeology, 1966-70, now Emeritus; *b* 31 May 1903; *s* of Rev. G. D. S. Bushnell and Mildred Mary (*née* Earle); *m* 1936, Patricia Louise Egerton Ruck; four *s*. *Educ:* Wellington; Downing Coll., Cambridge. Geologist, Anglo-Ecuadorian Oilfields Ltd, in Ecuador, 1926-38. Served War: Lincolnshire Regt, 1940, RE 1941-46, Major 1946. Asst Curator, Cambridge Univ. Museum of Archaeology and Ethnology, 1947; Curator, 1948; Vice-Pres., Society of Antiquaries of London, 1961-65; FSA 1934. Member: Council for the Care of Churches, 1950-; Cathedrals Advisory Cttee, 1955-; Trustee, Historic Churches Preservation Trust, 1964-. *Publications:* Archaeology of the Santa Elena Peninsula, SW Ecuador, 1951; Ancient American Pottery (with A. Digby), 1955; Peru (Ancient Peoples and Places), 1956, 2nd edn 1963; Ancient Arts of the Americas, 1965; The First Americans, 1968. *Recreations:* gardening, visiting ancient buildings. *Address:* 4 Wordsworth Grove, Cambridge. *T:* Cambridge 59539.

**BUSHNELL, George Herbert;** author; retired as Librarian of the University of St Andrews (1924-61); *b* Wolverhampton, 26 July 1896; 2nd *s* of late George Bushnell and late Bertha Mary Jupp, Moseley, Birmingham; *m* 1922, Elizabeth, *d* of late Thomas Bladon, Birmingham; three *d*. *Educ:* Waverley Sch., Small Heath; Birmingham Sch. of Art; privately. Served in Cavalry; RAMC, 1914-19; Member of League of Interpreters during the European War; Regimental Instructor in French; War Artist. Formerly mem. council, Scottish Library Association. Examiner in Anglo-Saxon, 1955-57. Hon. Corr. mem., Ecole Palatine d'Avignon; D. d'Hon. S. Int. d. Philol.; FLA. *Publications:* Emptyings of my Ashtray (miscellaneous poems), 1917; Library Manual; The Libraries of Shem; The Productions of the Early Presses at St Andrews, 1926; Scottish Entries for Bibl Soc. Dicty of Printers, etc, 1726-76, 1932; University Librarianship, 1930; Diane de Poitiers, 1927; Scottish Bookbindings and Bookbinders, 1450-1800, 1927; The Alexandrian Library translated and published in Japanese, 1932; Life and Work of Edward Raban; Scottish Hist. Research Series, I-VII; The St Andrews Type-Foundry; The World's

Earliest Libraries, 1929, translated and published in Japanese, 1936; Dictionary of Scottish Engravers of Eighteenth Century, 1929, supplement, 1931; Fulke Fitzwarin, 1933; Sindbad the Sailor (in Braille), 1928; The Three Wise Men, 1935; Sir Richard Grenville, 1936; Patrick Bower, 1942; Kosciuszko, 1943; Sir Henry Babington Smith (with Lady Elisabeth Babington Smith), 1943; Ghost Stories, 1945; From Papyrus to Print, 1947; From Bricks to Books, 1949; Scottish Engravers, 1949; contributor to Encyclopædia Britannica; editor of Andrew Lang's History of St Andrews; joint-editor, 1916-18, of The Linseed Lance (trench magazine); contributor to numerous magazines, etc; exhibitor various galleries. *Recreations:* walking, painting. *Address:* The Shielin, Wormit-on-Tay, Fife.

**BUSIA, Dr Kofi Abrefa,** GM; Prime Minister of Ghana since 1969; *b* 11 July 1913; *m* 1950; two *s* two *d.* *Educ:* Mfantsipim Sch., Gold Coast (Methodist Synod Schol., 1927-30); Achimota Coll.; Oxford Univ. (Achimota Council Schol., 1935-36, 1939-41). Carnegie Res. Student, Oxford, 1941-42, 1945-47; Nuffield Coll. Student Oxford, 1946-47. BA London; MA, DPhil Oxon. Mem. Staff: Wesley Coll., Kumasi, 1932-34; Achimota Coll., Accra, 1936-39; Admin. Officer (District Comr), Govt of Gold Coast, 1942-49; Officer i/c Sociological Surveys, 1947-49; UC Gold Coast: Res. Lectr in African Studies, 1949-51; Sen. Lectr in Sociology, 1952-54; Prof. of Sociology, 1954-59; Prof. of Sociology, Inst. of Social Studies, The Hague, 1959-62; Prof. of Sociology and Culture of Africa, Univ. of Leiden, 1960-62; Dir of Studies for World Council of Churches, Birmingham, 1962-64; Prof. of Sociology, St Antony's Coll., Oxford, 1964-. Vis. Professor: Northwestern Univ., Ill., 1954; Nuffield Coll., Oxford, 1955; Agricultural Univ. of Wageningen, Holland, 1956; El Colegie de Mexico, 1962; Univ. of York. Mem., Nat. Assembly of Ghana, 1951-59 (Leader of Parly Opposition, 1956-59). Chairman: Nat. Adv. Cttee, NLC, 1967; Centre for Civic Educn, 1967. Hon. DLitt Ghana, 1970. *Publications:* The Position of the Chief in the Modern Political System of Ashanti, 1951; The Challenge of Africa, 1962; Purposeful Education for Africa, 1964; Urban Churches in Britain, 1966; Africa in Search of Democracy, 1967, etc. *Recreations:* music, walking. *Address:* PO Box 6161, Accra North, Ghana. *T:* 21313.

**BUSK, Sir Douglas Laird,** KCMG 1959 (CMG 1948); *b* 15 July 1906; *s* of late John Laird Busk, Westerham, Kent, and late Eleanor Joy; *m* 1937, Bridget Anne Moyra, *d* of late Brig.-Gen. W. G. Hemsley Thompson, CMG, DSO, Warminster, Wilts; two *d.* *Educ:* Eton; New Coll., Oxford; Princeton Univ., USA (Davison Scholar). Joined Diplomatic Service, 1929; served in Foreign Office and Tehran, Budapest, Union of S Africa (seconded to United Kingdom High Commission), Tokyo, Ankara, Baghdad; Ambassador to Ethiopia, 1952-56; to Finland, 1958-60; to Venezuela, 1961-64. *Publications:* The Delectable Mountains, 1946; The Fountain of the Sun, 1957; The Curse of Tongues, 1965; The Craft of Diplomacy, 1967. *Recreations:* mountaineering and ski-ing. *Address:* Broxton House, Chilbolton, near Stockbridge, Hants. *T:* Chilbolton 272. *Clubs:* Alpine, Travellers', United Service.

**BUSS, Barbara Ann, (Mrs Lewis Boxall);** Editor of Woman magazine since 1964; *b* 14 Aug. 1932; *d* of late Cecil Edward Buss and Victoria Lilian (*née* Vickers); *m* 1966, Lewis Albert Boxall; no *c.* *Educ:* Lady Margaret Sch., London. Sec., Conservative Central Office, 1949-52; Sec./journalist, Good Taste magazine, 1952-56; Journalist: Woman and Beauty, 1956-57; Woman, 1957-59; Asst Editor, Woman's Illustrated, 1959-60; Editor, Woman's Illustrated, 1960-61; Journalist, Daily Herald, 1961; Associate Editor, Woman's Realm, 1961-62; Editor, Woman's Realm, 1962-64. *Recreations:* reading, theatre, cinema. *Address:* Flat 16, 17 Broad Court, WC2. *T:* 01-240 1071.

**BUSTAMANTE, Rt. Hon. Sir (William) Alexander,** PC 1964; GBE 1967; Kt 1955; Prime Minister, and Minister of External Affairs, Jamaica, 1962-67; MHR for Clarendon South since 1944; Leader of Jamaica Labour Party; lately Leader Opposition and Premier, 1962; *b* 1884; *m* 1962, Gladys Maud Longbridge. Organised Bustamante TU; founded Jamaica Labour Party, 1943; Mem. Exec. Council as Min. for Communications, 1944; Chief Minister, 1953. Comr, British Section Caribbean Commn, 1950. *Address:* Kingston, Jamaica.

**BUSVINE, Prof. James Ronald;** Professor of Entomology as applied to Hygiene in the University of London, since 1964; *b* 15 April 1912; *s* of William Robert and Pleasance Dorothy Busvine; *m* 1960, Joan Arnfield; one *s* one *d.* *Educ:* Eastbourne Coll.; Imperial Coll. of Science and Technology, London Univ. BSc Special (1st Class Hons) 1933; PhD 1938; DSc 1948, London. Imperial Chemical Industries, 1936-39; MRC Grants, 1940-42; Entomological Adviser, Min. of Health, 1943-45; London Sch. of Hygiene and Tropical Medicine: Lecturer 1946; Reader 1954; Professor 1964. Member: ODM Cttee on Tropical Pesticides, 1963-; Dept of Educn and Science's Cttee on Pesticides and Other Toxic Chemicals; WHO Expert Cttee on Insecticides, 1956- (Chm. 1959 and 1968). Has travelled professionally in Malaya, Ceylon, Nigeria, USA, India, etc. *Publications:* Insects and Hygiene, 1951 (2nd edn 1966); A Critical Review of the Techniques for Testing Insecticides, 1957, 2nd edn 1970; (with C. B. Symes and R. C. M. Thomson) Insect Control in Public Health, 1962; numerous scientific articles. *Recreations:* painting, golf. *Address:* Musca, 26 Braywick Road, Maidenhead, Berks. *T:* Maidenhead 22888.

**BUTCHART, Brevet Lt-Col Henry Jackson,** DSO 1918; OBE 1951; Hon. LLD Aberdeen 1952; DL, JP County and City of Aberdeen; Secretary to University of Aberdeen, 1919-52; Member: Education Committee of the City of Aberdeen, 1955-66; Valuation Appeal Committee for the City of Aberdeen, 1957-66; President Aberdeen Branch Red Cross Society, 1958-65; Law Agent to University of Aberdeen, 1952-67; *b* 18 April 1882; 4th *s* of James S. Butchart, Advocate in Aberdeen; *m* 1912, Catherine (*d* 1969), 2nd *d* of Alexander Johnston, Aberdeen; four *d.* *Educ:* Aberdeen Grammar Sch.; Univs of Aberdeen and Edinburgh. BL with distinction, Aberdeen Univ., 1905; admitted member of the Society of Advocates in Aberdeen, 1908; commissioned 1st VB Gordon Highlanders, 1907; transferred to Scottish Horse, 1908; Capt. 1913; Major, 1916; served European War, 1914-18 (despatches, DSO); Territorial War Medal for voluntary service overseas, Star of Roumania; held following appointments, 1916-19: A/DAA and QMG, No. 3 Section Canal Defences, EEF; Div. Intelligence Officer, 52nd (Lowland) Division; DAAG Australian and New Zealand Training Centre; DAA and QMG, Imperial Mounted Division; DAA and QMG and DAAG 74th (Yeomanry) Division; transferred to 2nd Highland Scouts (Scottish Horse) Reserve, 1919; Commanded

Aberdeen University contingent OTC, 1925-33; TD 1927; Bt Lieut-Col 1930; in ranks of LDV and Home Guard, 1940-45. Member of City of Aberdeen Territorial Army Assoc., 1919-50, Chm., 1947-50; Hon. Col, Aberdeen Contingent OTC, 1951-52; Pres. North District (Scotland) Rugby Union, 1952-54; Pres. Scottish Ski Club, 1950-56, Hon. Mem., 1956; Pres. Society of Advocates in Aberdeen, 1954-56; Hon. Sheriff-Substitute, County of Aberdeen; County Comr Boy Scouts, Aberdeen, 1937-57; Pres. Aberdeen Grammar Sch. Former Pupils' Club, 1955-56. *Recreations:* walking, ski-ing. *Address:* Willowwood, 626 King Street, Aberdeen. *T:* 43020. *Club:* Caledonian.

**BUTCHER, Rt. Rev. Reginald Albert Claver;** Domestic Prelate to HH Paul VI; Hon. Canon of Westminster (RC) since 1952; *b* 9 Sept. 1905; *e s* of Albert George Butcher and Mary Dore. *Educ:* Downside; Allen Hall, St Edmund's, Ware; Christ's Coll., Cambridge (Scholar). MA History Tripos (1st Class Parts 1 and 2). Headmaster Cardinal Vaughan Sch., Kensington, 1948-52; Pres., St Edmund's Coll., Ware, 1952-64. Mem., Old Brotherhood of English Secular Clergy. *Address:* St Edmund's College, Old Hall, Ware, Herts. *T:* Puckeridge 504. *Club:* Oxford and Cambridge University.

**BUTE,** 6th Marquess of, *cr* 1796; **John Crichton-Stuart,** JP; Viscount Ayr, 1622; Bt 1627; Earl of Dumfries, Lord Crichton of Sanquhar and Cumnock, 1633; Earl of Bute, Viscount Kingarth, Lord Mountstuart, Cumrae, and Inchmarnock, 1703; Baron Mountstuart, 1761; Baron Cardiff, 1776; Earl of Windsor; Viscount Mountjoy, 1796; Hereditary Sheriff of Bute; Hereditary Keeper of Rothesay Castle; Lord Lieutenant of Bute, since 1967; Lieutenant (RARO) Scots Guards, 1953; *b* 27 Feb. 1933; *er s* (twin) of 5th Marquess of Bute and of Eileen, Marchioness of Bute, *yr d* of 8th Earl of Granard; *S* father, 1956; *m* 1955, Nicola, *o d* of late Lt-Comdr W. B. C. Weld-Forester, CBE; two *s* two *d. Educ:* Ampleforth Coll.; Trinity Coll., Cambridge. Pres., Scottish Standing Cttee for Voluntary Internat. Aid, 1968- (Chm., 1964-68); Chairman: Council and Exec. Cttee, National Trust for Scotland, 1969; Scottish Cttee, National Fund for Res. into Crippling Diseases, 1966-; Mem., Countryside Commission for Scotland, 1970-. Hon. Sheriff-Substitute, County of Bute. Fellow, Inst. of Marketing, 1967. Buteshire CC, 1956-; Convener, 1967-70; DL Bute, 1961; JP. Hon. LLD Glasgow, 1970. *Heir: s* Earl of Dumfries, *qv. Address:* 7 Upper Phillimore Gardens, W8; Mount Stuart, Rothesay, Isle of Bute. *T:* Rothesay 30. *Clubs:* Turf, White's; New, Puffin's (Edinburgh); Cardiff and County (Cardiff).

**BUTEMENT, William Alan Stewart,** CBE 1959 (OBE 1945); DSc (Adel.); Chief Scientist Department of Supply, Australia (in exec. charge Australian Defence Scientific Research and Development which includes the Rocket Range at Woomera), 1949-67; a Director of Plessey Pacific (and Director of Research), since 1967; *b* Masterton, NZ, 18 Aug. 1904; *s* of William Butement, Physician and Surgeon, Otago, and Amy Louise Stewart; *m* 1933, Ursula Florence Alberta Parish; two *d. Educ:* Scots Coll., Sydney; University Coll. Sch., Hampstead, London; University Coll., London Univ. (BSc). Scientific Officer at Signals Exptl Estabt, War Office Outstation, Woolwich (now SRDE, Christchurch, Hants), 1928-38; Senior Scientific Officer Bawdsey Research Stn, War Office Outstation; later, under Min. of Supply, Radar Research, 1938-39 (Station moved to Christchurch, Hants, 1939; now RRE, Malvern); Prin. Scientific Officer, Sen. Prin. Scientific Officer, Asst Dir of Scientific Research, Min. of Supply, HQ London, 1940-46; Dep. Chief Scientific Officer of party to Australia under Lt-Gen. Sir John Evetts to set up Rocket Range, 1947; First Chief Supt of Long Range Weapons Estabt (now Weapons Research Establishment), of which Woomera Range is a part, 1947-49. FIEE, CEng, FInstP, FAIP, FIREE (Aust.). *Publications:* Precision Radar, Journal IEE, and other papers in scientific journals. *Address:* 5a Barry Street, Kew, Victoria 3101, Australia. *T:* 86 8375. *Club:* Australian (Melbourne).

**BUTENANDT, Prof. Adolf;** Dr phil., Dr med. hc; Dr med. vet. hc; Dr rer. nat. hc; Dr phil. hc; Dr sci. hc; Dr ing. eh; President, Max Planck Society, since 1960; Director Max Planck Institute for Biochemistry, München (formerly Kaiser Wilhelm Institute for Biochemistry, Berlin-Dahlem), since 1936; Professor Ord. of Physiological Chemistry, München, since 1956; Nobel Prize for Chemistry, 1939; *b* Bremerhaven-Lehe, 24 March 1903; *m* 1931, Erika von Ziegner; two *s* five *d. Educ:* Universities of Marburg and Göttingen. Privatdozent, Univ. of Göttingen, 1931; Prof. Ord. of Organic Chemistry, Technische Hochschule, Danzig, 1933; Honorarprofessor, Univ. Berlin, 1938; Prof. Ord. of Physiological Chemistry, Tübingen, 1945. Foreign Mem., Royal Society, 1968. *Publications:* numerous contribs to Hoppe-Seyler, Liebigs Annalen, Berichte der deutschen chemischen Gesellschaft, Zeitschrift für Naturforschung, etc. *Address:* München 60, Marsop Str. 5, Germany. *T:* 885490.

**BUTLAND, Sir Jack (Richard),** KBE 1966; Founder and Chairman: J. R. Butland Pty Ltd, 1922; NZ Cheese Ltd, 1926; Butland Tobacco Co. Ltd, 1936; Butland Industries Ltd, 1949; Chairman: Greenacres (Morrinsville) Ltd; Blandford Lodge Ltd; Rothmans (NZ) Ltd, 1956; Director: Rothmans Tobacco (Holdings) Ltd (UK); Dairy Industries (Jamaica) Ltd; *s* of late Henry Butland, Westport, NZ; *m* Gretta May Taylor (*d* 1962); two *s* one *d*; *m* Joan Melville Bull. *Educ:* Hokitika High Sch. Chairman: NZ Honey Control Board, 1933-38; NZ Packing Corp., 1953-60. Hon. LLD Auckland, 1967. *Address:* (home) 542 Remuera Road, Remuera, Auckland, NZ; (office) J. R. Butland Pty Ltd, Queen Street, Auckland, NZ. *Club:* Northern (Auckland).

**BUTLER,** family name of **Baron Butler of Saffron Walden,** of **Earl of Carrick,** of **Baron Dunboyne,** of **Earl of Lanesborough,** of **Viscount Mountgarret,** and of **Marquess of Ormonde.**

**BUTLER OF SAFFRON WALDEN,** Baron *cr* 1965 (Life Peer); **Richard Austen Butler,** PC 1939; CH 1954; MA; Master of Trinity College, Cambridge, since 1965; *b* Attock Serai, India, 9 Dec. 1902; *e s* of late Sir Montagu S. D. Butler, KCSI; *m* 1st, 1926, Sydney (*d* 1954), *o c* of late Samuel Courtauld; three *s* one *d;* 2nd, 1959, Mollie, *d* of late F. D. Montgomerie and *widow* of Augustine

Courtauld. *Educ:* Marlborough; Pembroke Coll., Cambridge. President, Union Society, 1924; Fellow, Corpus Christi Coll., Cambridge, 1925-29 (Double First Class; Modern Language Tripos French Section, 1924; Historical Tripos Part II, 1925, First Division First Class). Hon. Fellow: Pembroke Coll., Cambridge, 1941; Corpus Christi Coll., Cambridge, 1952; St Anthony's Coll., Oxford, 1957; Hon. LLD: Cambridge, 1952; Nottingham, 1953; Bristol, 1954; Sheffield, 1955; St Andrews, 1956; Glasgow, 1959; Reading, 1959; Hon. DCL: Oxon., 1952; Durham, 1968; Calgary, 1968; Liverpool, 1968; Witwatersrand, 1969. MP (C) Saffron Walden, 1929-65; Under-Secretary of State, India Office, 1932-37; Parliamentary Secretary, Ministry of Labour, 1937-38; Under-Secretary of State for Foreign Affairs, 1938-41; Minister of Education, 1941-45; Minister of Labour, June-July 1945; Chancellor of the Exchequer, 1951-55; Lord Privy Seal, 1955-59; Leader of the House of Commons, 1955-61; Home Secretary, 1957-62; First Secretary of State, July 1962-Oct. 1963; Deputy Prime Minister, July 1962-Oct. 1963; Minister in Charge of Central African Office, 1962-Oct. 1963; Secretary of State for Foreign Affairs, 1963-64. Chairman: Conservative Party Organisation, 1959-61; Conservative Research Dept, 1945-64; Conservative Party's Advisory Cttee on Policy, 1950-64. Mem., Indian Franchise Cttee, 1932; Chm., Scientific Advisory Cttee and Engineering Advisory Cttee, 1942; Chairman of Council of National Union of Conservative Associations, 1945-56, President, 1956-; Pres., Modern Language Assoc., Chairman of Council Royal India Society, and of Anglo-Netherlands Society, 1946; President National Assoc. of Mental Health, 1946-; President Royal Society of Literature, 1951-; Rector of Glasgow Univ., 1956-59; High Steward, Cambridge Univ., 1958-66; High Steward, City of Cambridge, 1963-; Chancellor of Sheffield Univ., 1960-; Chancellor of Univ. of Essex, 1962-. Azad Memorial Lecture, Delhi, 1970. Freedom of Saffron Walden, 1954. *Recreations:* travel, shooting, agriculture. *Address:* The Master's Lodge, Trinity College, Cambridge. *T:* 58201; Flat 142, Whitehall Court, SW1. *T:* 01-930 0847 and 01-930 3160. *Clubs:* Carlton, Farmers', Beefsteak, Grillions.

*See also Hon. A. C. Butler.*

**BUTLER, Hon. Adam Courtauld,** MP (C) Bosworth since 1970; *b* 11 Oct. 1931; *s* of Baron Butler of Saffron Walden, *qv*; *m* 1955, Felicity Molesworth-St Aubyn; two *s* one *d*. *Educ:* Eton; Pembroke College, Cambridge. National Service, 2nd Lieut KRRC, 1949-51. Cambridge (BA History/Economics), 1951-54. ADC to Governor-General of Canada, 1954-55; Courtaulds Ltd, 1955-; Director, Aristoc Ltd, 1966-; Managing Director, Percy Taylor Ltd, 1969-. Liveryman of Goldsmiths' Co. *Recreations:* field sports, music, pictures. *Address:* The Old Rectory, Lighthorne, near Warwick. *T:* Moreton Morrell 214.

**BUTLER, Colonel Arnold Charles Paul,** CBE 1943; attached General Staff, War Office, 1926-50; *b* 24 March 1890; *e s* of late Col L. W. G. Butler, KRRC, and Adelaide, *d* of late John Bulteel; *m* 1916, Violet Frances Gertrude, *d* of late Col Abel H. Smith and Hon. Mrs Abel Smith; one *s* one *d*. *Educ:* Wellington Coll.; RMC Sandhurst. KRRC, 1909-20; R of O, 1920. *Address:* 11 Manor Court, Grange Road, Cambridge. *T:* Cambridge 62962. *Club:* MCC.

**BUTLER, Rt. Rev. Arthur Hamilton;** *see* Connor, Bishop of.

**BUTLER, Rt. Rev. (Basil) Christopher,** OSB, MA; Auxiliary Bishop to the Cardinal Archbishop of Westminster, since Dec. 1966; President, St Edmund's College, Ware, since 1968, and Chairman of the Board of Governors, since 1969; Titular Bishop of Nova Barbara; Hon. Fellow, St John's College, Oxford; *b* 1902; 2nd *s* of late W. E. Butler, Reading. *Educ:* Reading Sch.; St John's Coll., Oxford (White Schol.; Craven Schol.; Gaisford Greek Prose Prize; prox. acc. Hertford Schol.; 1st Class Classical Mods Greats and Theology). Tutor of Keble Coll., Oxford; Classical Master, Brighton Coll., 1927; Downside Sch., 1928; received into Catholic Church, 1928; entered the noviciate at Downside, 1929; Priest, 1933; Headmaster of Downside Sch., 1940-46; Abbot of Downside, 1946-66. Abbot-President of English Benedictine Congregation, 1961-67. Chairman, Editorial Board, Clergy Review, 1966-. Member: Anglican/Roman Catholic Preparatory Commn, 1967-69; Jt Permanent Commn of Roman Catholic Church and Anglican Communion, 1969-70; Anglican-Roman Catholic Internat. Commn, 1970-. President, Social Morality Council, 1968-. Consultor, Congregation for Catholic Education, 1968-; Member, Congregation for the Doctrine of the Faith, 1968-. Hon. LLD Notre Dame Univ. *Publications:* St Luke's Debt to St Matthew (Harvard Theological Review, 1939); The Originality of St Matthew, 1951; The Church and Infallibility, 1954; Why Christ?, 1960; The Church and the Bible, 1960; Prayer: an adventure in living, 1961; The Idea of the Church, 1962; The Theology of Vatican II, 1967; In the Light of the Council, 1969; articles in Dublin Review, Downside Review, Journal of Theological Studies, Clergy Review. *Address:* St Edmund's College, Old Hall Green, Ware, Herts. *T:* Puckeridge 723. *Club:* Athenæum.

**BUTLER, Prof. Clifford Charles,** FRS 1961; BSc, PhD; Director of the Nuffield Foundation, since 1970; *b* 20 May 1922; *s* of C. H. J. and O. Butler, Earley, Reading; *m* 1947, Kathleen Betty Collins; two *d*. *Educ:* Reading Sch.; Reading Univ. BSc 1942, PhD 1946, Reading. Demonstrator in Physics, Reading Univ., 1942-45; Asst Lecturer in Physics, 1945-47, Lecturer in Physics, 1947-53, Manchester Univ.; Imperial Coll.: Reader in Physics, 1953-57; Professor of Physics, 1957-63; Asst Dir, Physics Dept, 1955-62; Prof. of Physics and Head of Physics Dept, 1963-70; Dean, Royal Coll. of Science, 1966-69. Charles Vernon Boys Prizeman, London Physical Soc., 1956. Member: Academic Planning Board, Univ. of Kent, 1963-; Schools Council, 1965-; Nuclear Physics Board of SRC, 1965-68; University Grants Cttee, 1966-; Council, Charing Cross Hosp. Med. Sch., 1970-. Chm., Standing Education Cttee, Royal Society, 1970-. *Publications:* scientific papers on electron diffraction, cosmic rays and elementary particle physics in Proc. Royal Society and Physical Society, Philosophical Magazine, Nature, and Journal of Scientific Instruments, etc. *Address:* The Gatehouse, Fulmer Road, Gerrards Cross, Bucks. *T:* Gerrards Cross 82871. *Club:* Athenæum.

**BUTLER, Dr Colin Gasking,** OBE 1970; FRS 1970; Head of Bee Department, Rothamsted Experimental Station, Harpenden, since 1943;

*b* 26 Oct. 1913; *s* of Rev. Walter Gasking Butler and Phyllis Pearce; *m* 1937, Jean March Innes; one *s* one *d*. *Educ:* Monkton Combe Sch., Bath; Queen's Coll., Cambridge. MA 1937, PhD 1938, Cantab. Min. of Agric. and Fisheries Research Schol., Cambridge, 1935-37; Supt Cambridge Univ. Entomological Field Stn, 1937-39; Asst Entomologist, Rothamsted Exper. Stn, 1939-43. Hon. Treas., Royal Entomological Soc., 1961-69; Pres., Internat. Union for Study of Social Insects, 1969-. FRPS 1957; FIBiol. Silver Medal, RSA, 1945. *Publications:* The Honeybee: an introduction to her sense physiology and behaviour, 1949; The World of the Honeybee, 1954; (with J. B. Free) Bumblebees, 1959; many scientific papers. *Recreations:* nature photography, sailing. *Address:* 4 Kirkwick Avenue, Harpenden, Herts. *T:* Harpenden 2956.

**BUTLER, David Edgeworth;** Fellow of Nuffield College, Oxford, since 1954; *b* 1924; *yr s* of late Professor Harold Edgeworth Butler and Margaret, *d* of Prof. A. F. Pollard; *m* 1962, Marilyn, *d* of Sir Trevor Evans, *qv*; three *s*. *Educ:* St Paul's; New Coll., Oxford (MA, DPhil). J. E. Procter Visiting Fellow, Princeton Univ., 1947-48; Student, Nuffield Coll., 1949-51; Research Fellow, 1951-54; Dean and Senior Tutor, 1956-64. Served as Personal Assistant to HM Ambassador in Washington, 1955-56. *Publications:* The British General Election of 1951, 1952; The Electoral System in Britain 1918-51, 1953; The British General Election of 1955, 1955; The Study of Political Behaviour, 1958; (ed.) Elections Abroad, 1959; (with R. Rose) The British General Election of 1959, 1960; (with J. Freeman) British Political Facts, 1900-1960, 1963; (with A. King) The British General Election of 1964, 1965; The British General Election of 1966, 1966; (with D. Stokes) Political Change in Britain, 1969. *Address:* Nuffield College, Oxford. *T:* Oxford 48014. *Club:* United University.

**BUTLER, Edward Clive Barber,** FRCS; Surgeon: The London Hospital, E1, 1937-69; Haroldwood Hospital, Essex, 1946-69; retired; *b* 8 April 1904; *s* of Dr Butler, Hereford; *m* 1939, Nancy Hamilton Harrison, Minneapolis, USA; two *s* one *d*. *Educ:* Shrewsbury Sch.; London Hospital. MRCS, LRCP 1928; MB, BS London, 1929; FRCS 1931. Resident posts London Hosp., 1928-32; Surgical Registrar, London Hosp., 1933-36; Surgeon, RMS Queen Mary, Cunard White Star Line, 1936. Hunterian Prof., RCS, 1939; examinerships at various times to London Univ. and Coll. of Surgeons. Pres. section of Proctology, Royal Soc. of Medicine, 1951-52; Member: Medical Soc. London; Royal Soc. Medicine. *Publications:* chapter on bacteraemia, in British Surgical Practice, 1948; on hand infections, in Penicillin (by Fleming), 1950; (jointly) on combined excision of rectum, in Treatment of Cancer and Allied Diseases (New York), 1952; articles on various surgical subjects in Lancet, BMJ, Proc. Royal Soc. Med., British Journal Surgery. *Recreations:* golf, gardening and yachting. *Address:* 5 Stradbroke Drive, Chigwell, Essex. *Clubs:* Devonshire; Royal Corinthian; United Hospitals Sailing.

**BUTLER, Air Vice-Marshal Eric Scott,** CB 1957; OBE 1941; RAF; AOA HQ Fighter Command, 1957-61; *b* 4 Nov. 1907; *s* of Archibald Butler, Maze Hill, St Leonards-on-Sea, Sussex; *m* 1936, Alice Evelyn Tempest Meates; three *s* one *d*. *Educ:* Belfast Academy. Commissioned RAF 1933; Bomber Command European War, 1939-45; idc 1952; Director of Organisation, Air Ministry, 1953-56. *Address:* Camden Cottage, Pevensey, Sussex. *T:* Westham 353. *Club:* Royal Air Force.

**BUTLER, Frank Chatterton,** CBE 1961; MA 1934; retd from HM Diplomatic Service, 1967, and re-employed in Foreign Office Library; *b* 23 June 1907; *s* of late Leonard Butler and late Ada Chatterton Rutter; *m* 1945, Iris, *d* of late Ernest Strater and of Ida Mary Vinall; two *s*. *Educ:* Central Secondary Sch., Sheffield; Gonville and Caius Coll., Cambridge (Scholar); University of Grenoble. 1st Class Hons, Modern and Medieval Langs Tripos; Exhibitioner of the Worshipful Company of Goldsmiths, 1927, German Prize Essayist, 1928 and 1929. Consular Service, 1930 (head of list); Vice-Consul: Paris, 1931; New York, 1932; Mexico City, 1933-36; Panama, 1936-39; Naples, 1939-40; Barcelona, 1940-43; Consul, Barcelona, 1943-45; First Secretary (Commercial), Bogota, 1945-47; Consul General, Düsseldorf, 1948-52; Consul, Bordeaux, 1952-54; Consul General, Dakar, 1955, and Frankfurt, 1956-60; Counsellor at Shanghai, 1960-62; Consul-General at Cape Town, 1962-67. *Recreations:* golf, riding, motoring. *Address:* c/o Foreign and Commonwealth Office, SW1; Wedgwood, Knowl Hill, Woking, Surrey. *Club:* Royal Automobile.

**BUTLER, Maj.-Gen. Geoffrey Ernest,** CB 1957; CBE 1955; *b* Quetta, 1 Jan. 1905; *s* of Major E. G. Butler, W Yorks Regt; *m* 1934, Marjorie Callender (*née* Laine); one *D*. *Educ:* Appleby Grammar Sch.; Leeds Univ. ICI, 1928-30; Lieut, RAOC, 1930; Asst Inspector of Armaments, 1936; Asst Supt of Design, 1937; British Supply Board, N America, 1939-40; British Army Staff, Washington, 1940-43; Asst Chief Supt, Armaments Design, 1943-44; Comdt 3 Base Workshop, REME, 1944-47; Dep. Dir (Production), War Office, 1947-49; Comdt, REME Training Centre, 1949-53; Dir of Mechanical Engineering, Northern Army Group, 1953-56; Inspector, REME, 1956-57; Commandant Base Workshop Group, REME, 1957-60. *Recreations:* golf, gardening, fishing. *Address:* Cornerways, 7 Ashley Road, New Milton, Hants BH25 6BA.

**BUTLER, George,** RWS 1958; RBA; painter, principally in water-colour; *b* 17 Oct. 1904; *s* of John George Butler; *m* 1933, Kcenia Kotliarevskaya; one *s* one *d*. *Educ:* King Edward VII School, Sheffield; Central School of Art. Director and Head of Art Dept, J. Walter Thompson Co. Ltd, 1933-60. Hon. Treasurer: RWS; Artists' General Benevolent Institution. *Address:* Riversdale, Bakewell, Derbyshire. *T:* Bakewell 2204. *Clubs:* Arts, Chelsea Arts; The Sheffield.

**BUTLER, Harold Edwin,** CIE 1944; OBE 1937; OStJ 1947; *b* 1 April 1893; *s* of late Harold Shaw Butler, Newcastle upon Tyne; *m* Winifride Jean, MBE, *d* of late Charles Eglington; two *d*. *Educ:* Worcester Royal Grammar Sch. Joined Indian Police, 1913; IARO 1917-19; District Supt of Police, 1920; Dep. Comr of Police, Bombay, 1928-36; Comr of Police, Bombay, 1928-36; Comr of Police, Bombay, 1942-46; retired 1948. *Recreations:*

golf, shooting. *Address:* Belle Causey, Barnstaple, Devon. *Club:* Royal Bombay Yacht.

**BUTLER, Herbert William;** Member, North-East Regional Hospital Board; *b* 1897; *s* of Frank Butler, London; *m* 1926, Nellie, *d* of H. W. Bingley, London. Served European War, 1914-19, with Royal Navy. Member Hackney Borough Council, 1928-60; Mayor of Hackney, 1936-37. MP (Lab): S Hackney, 1945-55; Hackney Central, 1955-70; PPS to Civil Lord of Admiralty and Parly Sec., Admiralty, 1950-51. JP London, 1929. *Address:* 214 Well Street, Hackney, E9.

**BUTLER, Hugh Montagu,** MA; *b* 24 Jan. 1890; *s* of Rev. Montagu Russell and Mary Elizabeth Butler; *m* 1919, Annie Isabel Wiltshire; two *s* one *d*. *Educ:* Denstone Coll.; Magdalene Coll., Cambridge (Latimer Neville Exhibitioner). 2nd Class Historical Tripos. asst Master, Ardingly Coll., 1911-12; Worksop Coll., 1912-15; Denstone Coll., 1915-20; St George's Sch., Harpenden, 1923; Headmaster, Govt English Sch., Batu Pahat, Malaya, 1920-22; Hexham Grammar Sch., 1923-30; Queen Mary's Grammar Sch., Walsall, 1931-51. Member House of Laity, Church Assembly, 1945-51. Assoc. Guild of Drama Adjudicators, 1952-60. FRHistS, 1923-68. *Publications:* A First Sketch of Empire History; Shakespeare Plays in Schools; articles in many journals; *plays:* Trixie; Sunset at Croxden; The Goose Girl. *Recreations:* travel, painting, play production. *Address:* Meadow Cottage, Station Road, Churchdown, Gloucester. *T:* Churchdown 2755.

**BUTLER, Sir James Ramsay Montagu,** Kt 1958; MVO 1920; OBE 1919; MA; Fellow of Trinity College, Cambridge, since 1913; Chief Historian for the Official Military Histories of War of 1939-45; *b* 1889; *s* of late Rev. Henry Montagu Butler, DD, and late Agnata Frances, *d* of Sir J. H. Ramsay, 10th Bt. *Educ:* Harrow; Trinity Coll., Cambridge. President of the Union, 1910; served in European War, 1914-18, Scottish Horse (despatches twice); MP (Ind) Cambridge Univ., 1922-23; served in War of 1939-45, Intelligence Corps (Chevalier Legion of Honour). Regius Professor of Modern History, Univ. of Cambridge, 1947-54. *Publications:* The Passing of the Great Reform Bill, 1914; Henry Montagu Butler: a Memoir, 1925; History of England, 1815-1918, 1928; Grand Strategy, Vol. II (Sept. 1939-June 1941), in the Official History, 1957; Lord Lothian, 1960; (with J. M. A. Gwyer) Grand Strategy, Vol. III (June 1941-Aug. 1942), 1964. *Address:* Trinity College, Cambridge. *Clubs:* United University, Alpine.

*See also Sir N. M. Butler.*

**BUTLER, James Walter,** ARA 1964; Tutor, Sculpture and Drawing, City and Guilds of London Art School, since 1960; *b* 25 July 1931; *m* 1966, Elizabeth Ann, *d* of Dr and Mrs Reginald Nassim, 6 Addison Crescent, W14; one *d*. *Educ:* Maidstone Grammar Sch.; Maidstone Coll. of Art; St Martin's Art Sch.; Royal Coll. of Art. National Diploma in Sculpture, 1950. Worked as Architectural Carver, 1950-53, 1955-60. Fellow of Digswell House, 1964. *Address:* Old School House, Greenfield, Beds. *T:* Flitwick 2563.

**BUTLER, Prof. John Alfred Valentine,** FRS 1956; DSc; FRIC; Emeritus Professor of Physical Chemistry, University of London; *b* 14 Feb. 1899; *s* of Alfred and Mary Ann Butler; *m* 1929, Margaret Lois Hope; two *s* one *d*. *Educ:* Cheltenham Grammar Sch.; Birmingham Univ. Asst Lecturer, Univ. Coll. of Swansea, 1922-26; Lecturer, Univ. of Edinburgh, 1927-39; Rockefeller Fellow, 1939-41; Exec. Officer, British Commonwealth Scientific Office, Washington, 1941-44; Courtauld Research Fellow (Courtauld Institute of Biochemistry, London), 1946-49; Chester Beatty Research Institute, 1949-66. Editor, Progress in Biophysics and Molecular Biology, 1950-. *Publications:* Chemical Elements and their Compounds, 1927; Chemical Thermodynamics, 1928, 1965; Electrocapillarity, 1940; Electrical Phenomena at Interfaces, 1951; Science and Human Life, 1957; Inside the Living Cell, 1959; The Life of the Cell, 1964; Gene Control in the Living Cell, 1968; The Life Process, 1970; papers in Proc. Royal Soc., Jl Chem. Soc., Trans. Faraday Soc., Biochemical Jl, etc. *Recreations:* gardening, painting. *Address:* Nightingale Corner, Rickmansworth, Herts. *T:* Rickmansworth 72938.

**BUTLER, John Manton,** MSc; Managing Director, Berger J. & N. Paints Ltd, since 1968; Director, Berger, Jenson & Nicholson Ltd and other companies in BJN Group; *b* 9 Oct. 1909; *m* 1940, Marjorie Smith, Melbourne; one *s* one *d*. *Educ:* Southland, NZ; Univ. of Otago (Sen. Schol., NZ Physics; BSc 1929; Smeaton Schol. Chemistry, 1930, John Edmond Fellow, 1930; MSc 1st class Hons). Pres., Students' Union; Graduate Rep. Univ. Council. Joined Shell, NZ, 1934; served various Shell cos in UK, Australia and S Africa until 1957; Man. Dir, Lewis Berger (GB) Ltd, 1957. Chm., BNEC Cttee for Exports to NZ, 1967 (Dep. Chm., 1965). *Recreations:* golf, photography. *Address:* (home) Woodmead House, Hascombe Road, Godalming, Surrey. *T:* Hascombe 344; (office) Berger J. & N. Paints Ltd, Berger House, Berkeley Square, W1. *T:* 01-629 9171. *Clubs:* Royal Automobile, Hurlingham; Royal Mid-Surrey Golf.

**BUTLER, Mrs Joyce Shore;** MP (Lab & Co-op) Wood Green since 1955; *m*; one *s* one *d*. *Educ:* King Edward's High Sch., Birmingham. Member: Wood Green Council, 1947-64 (Leader, 1954-55; Deputy Mayor, 1962-63); First Chm., London Borough of Haringey, 1964-65; First Mayoress, 1965-66. Vice-Chm., Labour Parly Housing and Local Govt Gp, 1959-64; Member: Estimates Cttee, 1959-60; Chairman's Panel, House of Commons; Chm., Co-op. Gp; Convenor, Parly Civil Liberties Gp; Jt Chm., Parly Cttee on Pollution; Parliamentary Private Secretary to Minister for Land and Natural Resources, 1965. A Vice-Chm., Parly Labour Party, 1968-. Dir, Nat. Assoc. for Health; Exec. Mem., Housing and Town Planning Council; Chm., Wood Green Charity Trustees; Founder and First Pres., Women's Nat. Cancer Control Campaign; Pres., London Passenger Action Confedn. *Address:* 25 Maidstone Road, N11.

**BUTLER, Keith Stephenson;** HM Consul-General, Bordeaux, since 1969; *b* 3 Sept. 1917; *s* of Raymond R. Butler and Gertrude Stephenson; *m* 1952, Geraldine Marjorie Clark; no *c*. *Educ:* King Edward's Sch.,

Birmingham; Liverpool Coll.; St Peter's Coll., Oxford (MA). HM Forces, 1939-47 (despatches): served, RA, in Egypt, Greece and Crete; POW, Germany, 1941-45. Foreign Correspondent for Sunday Times and Kemsley Newspapers, 1947-50. Joined HM Foreign Service, 1950; served: First Sec., Ankara and Caracas; Canadian Nat. Defence Coll.; Paris; Montreal. HM Consul-General, Seville, 1968. *Publications:* contrib. historical and political reviews. *Recreation:* historical research. *Address:* British Consulate-General, 15 Cours de Verdun, 33 Bordeaux, France. *T:* Bordeaux 52 28 35 and 52 28 36. *Clubs:* Bath, English-Speaking Union.

**BUTLER, Prof. Lionel Harry,** FRHistS; MA; DPhil; Professor of Mediaeval History in the University of St Andrews since 1955; Dean of the Faculty of Arts, since 1966; a Member of the University Court, since 1968; *b* 17 Dec. 1923; *yr s* of W. H. and late M. G. Butler, Dudley, Worcs; *m* 1949, Gwendoline Williams (author of detective stories), *o d* of A. E. Williams, Blackheath; one *d. Educ:* Dudley Grammar Sch.; Magdalen Coll., Oxford (exhibitioner). Royal Air Force, 1941-43; First Class, Modern History, Oxford, 1945; Sen. Mackinnon Scholar and Junior Lectr, Magdalen Coll., Oxford, 1946; Fellow of All Souls Coll., 1946 (re-elected, 1953); Chatterton Lectr, British Acad., 1955; Leverhulme Lectr, Royal Univ. of Malta, 1962-63; Visiting Prof. of History, Univ. of Pennsylvania, Pa, 1964; Dir, Historical Assoc. Vacation Sch., 1965 and 1966. Convener, Scottish Univs Council on Entrance, 1968-. Librarian, Venerable Order of St John in the British Realm, 1969-; Historical Dir, 13th Council of Europe Exhibn (on Order of St John in Malta), 1970 (introd. and contribs to Catalogue on Exhibn). KStJ 1969. *Publications:* trans. (with R. J. Adam) R. Fawtier, The Capetian Kings of France, 1960; articles in journals and reviews. *Address:* St Salvator's College, St Andrews, Fife. *Club:* Royal and Ancient (St Andrews).

**BUTLER, Lt-Gen. Sir Mervyn (Andrew Haldane),** KCB 1968 (CB 1964); CBE 1957; DSO 1945, and Bar, 1957; MC 1940; General Officer Commanding-in-Chief, Army Strategic Command, from April 1970; *b* 1 July 1913; *s* of Major James Dickson Butler, MBE, Rathgar, Dublin; *m* 1941, Marjorie Millicent, *d* of Frederick G. Dann, Hove, Sussex. *Educ:* St Columba's Coll., Rathfarnham, Eire; RMC Sandhurst. Commissioned South Lancashire Regt, 1933. Served War of 1939-45: BEF, 1939-40, France (MC); N Africa, 1942-43; NW Europe, 1944-45 (DSO); Lt-Col 1944; transferred to Suffolk Regt, 1945. Commanded 16 Independent Parachute Bde, 1955-57; Suez Ops, 1956 (Bar to DSO, French Croix de Guerre); Cyprus, 1957 (CBE); GOC 2 Div., 1962-64; Asst Chief of the Defence Staff (Jt Warfare), MoD, 1964-66; Comdt, Staff Coll., Camberley, 1966-67; GOC 1 (Br) Corps, 1968-70. Col Comdt, The Parachute Regt, 1967-. Brig. 1961; Maj.-Gen. 1961; Lt-Gen. 1968. Chm., Army Rugby Union, 1965-. *Recreations:* climbing, tennis, bird-watching, cricket; assisting in Rugby football. *Address:* c/o Lloyds Bank Ltd, 6 Pall Mall, SW1; Woodmere, Hacketts Lane, Pyrford, Woking, Surrey. *T:* Byfleet 42335; 56 Grosvenor Road, Rathgar, Co. Dublin, Eire. *Club:* Naval and Military.

**BUTLER, Sir Michael;** *see* Butler, Sir R. M. T.

**BUTLER, Michael Dacres;** HM Diplomatic Service; Fellow at Center for International Affairs, Harvard University, 1970-71; *b* 27 Feb. 1927; *s* of T. D. Butler, Almer, Blandford, and Beryl May (*née* Lambert); *m* 1951, Ann, *d* of Rt Hon. Lord Clyde, *qv*; two *s* two *d. Educ:* Winchester; Trinity Coll., Oxford. Joined HM Foreign Service, 1950; served in: UK Mission to UN, New York, 1952-56; Baghdad, 1956-58; FO, 1958-61 and 1965-68; Paris, 1961-65; Counsellor, UK Mission in Geneva, 1968-70. *Recreations:* collecting Chinese porcelain, ski-ing, tennis. *Address:* 11 Carlyle Square, SW3. *T:* 01-352 9360; c/o Foreign and Commonwealth Office, SW1.

**BUTLER, Sir Nevile Montagu,** KCMG 1947 (CMG 1942); CVO 1933; *b* 20 Dec. 1893; *s* of late Very Rev. Henry Montagu Butler, DD, sometime Headmaster of Harrow and Master of Trinity Coll., Cambridge, and late Agnata Frances, *d* of Sir James Henry Ramsay, 10th Bt; *m* 1923, Oonah Rose, *d* of late Col John McNeile, Kippilaw, St Boswells, Roxburgh; two *d. Educ:* Harrow; Trinity Coll., Cambridge. Served European War, 1916-18, Scottish Horse, Household Bn, Intelligence Corps; entered Foreign Office, May 1920; Private Secretary to successive Parliamentary Under-Secretaries of State for Foreign Affairs, Feb. 1924-June 1927; to Viscount Cecil of Chelwood, June-Aug. 1927, and to Lord Cushendun, Oct. 1927-June 1929; a Private Secretary to the Prime Minister, 1930-35; Counsellor at Legation, Tehran, 1936-39; Berne, Sept.-Dec. 1939; Counsellor at Embassy, Washington, 1940, and Minister there, 1940-41; Head of North American Dept in Foreign Office, 1941; an Asst Under-Secretary of State, Foreign Office, 1944-47; Ambassador to Brazil, 1947-51; Ambassador to the Netherlands, 1952-54; Pres., Internat. Inst. of Differing Civilisations, 1956. *Recreations:* walking, lawn tennis, golf. *Address:* North Lodge, Newick, Lewes, Sussex. *T:* Newick 2020. *Clubs:* Travellers', Hurlingham, Royal Commonwealth Society.
*See also Sir J. R. M. Butler.*

**BUTLER, Reg, (Reginald Cotterell Butler);** sculptor; *b* Buntingford, Herts, 1913. *Educ:* privately; Hertford Grammar Sch. ARIBA 1937. Lecturer, Architectural Assoc. School of Architecture, 1937-39; Technical Editor, Architectural Press, 1946-51; Gregory Fellow in Sculpture, Leeds Univ., 1951-53; Associé, Académie Royale des Sciences, des Lettres et des Beaux-Arts de Belgique, 1965. First one-man show, London, 1949. Winner International Competition, The Unknown Political Prisoner, 1953. Retrospective Exhibition: J. B. Speed Art Museum, Louisville, USA, 1963. Galleries: Hanover Gallery, London; Pierre Matisse Gallery, New York. *Publication:* Creative Development, 1962. *Address:* (Studio) Ash, Berkhamsted Place, Berkhamsted, Herts. *T:* Berkhamsted 2933.

**BUTLER, Sir (Reginald) Michael Thomas,** 3rd Bt *cr* 1922; QC (Canada); Barrister and Solicitor; Partner of Farris Co., Vancouver, BC; *b* 22 April 1928; *s* of Sir Reginald Thomas, 2nd Bt, and Marjorie Brown Butler; *S* father, 1959; *m* Marja McLean (marr. diss.); three *s*; *m* 1968, Barbara Anne Chaill; two *s. Educ:* Brentwood Coll., Victoria, BC; Univ. of British Columbia (BA). Called to Bar (Hons) from Osgoode Hall

Sch. of Law, Toronto, Canada, 1954. *Heir: s* (Reginald) Richard Michael Butler, *b* 3 Oct. 1953. *Address:* 2942 W 49th Avenue, Vancouver, BC, Canada. *Club:* University (Toronto).

**BUTLER, Rohan D'Olier,** CMG, MA, FRHistS; Historical Adviser to Secretary of State for Foreign and Commonwealth Affairs (to First Secretary of State and successor), since 1968; Fellow of All Souls since 1938 (a Senior Research Fellow since 1956; Sub-Warden, 1961-63; representative at 12th International Historical Congress at Vienna, 1965); Governor of Felsted School since 1959, representative on GBA since 1964; Trustee of Felsted Almshouse since 1961; on management of Institute of Historical Research, University of London, since 1967; *b* St John's Wood, 21 Jan. 1917; *yr s* of late Sir Harold Butler, KCMG, CB, MA, and Lady Butler, *y c* of late Asst Inspector-General S. A. W. Waters, RIC; *m* 1956, Lucy Rosemary (Lady of the Manor of White Notley, Essex), *y c* of late Eric Byron, Lord of the Manor. *Educ:* Eton; abroad and privately; Balliol Coll., Oxford (Hall Prizeman, 1938). BA (1st Class Hons in History), 1938; on International Propaganda and Broadcasting Enquiry, 1939; on staff of MOI, 1939-41 and 1942-44, of Special Operations Executive, 1941; served with RAPC, 1941-42, with HG, 1942-44 (Defence Medal, War Medal); on staff of FO, 1944-45; Editor of Documents on British Foreign Policy (1919-39), 1945-65 (with Sir Llewellyn Woodward, 1945-54; Senior Editor, 1955-65); Leverhulme Research Fellow, 1955-57; Noel Buxton Trustee, 1961-67. Historical Adviser to Sec. of State for Foreign Affairs (from 14th Earl of Home to last Foreign Sec.), 1963-68. *Publications:* The Roots of National Socialism; Documents on British Foreign Policy, 1st series, vols i-ix, 2nd series, vol. ix; The Peace Settlement of Versailles (in New Cambridge Modern History); Paradiplomacy (in Studies of Diplomatic History in honour of Dr G. P. Gooch, OM, CH, FBA); Introduction to Anglo-Soviet historical exhibition of 1967. *Recreation:* idling. *Address:* All Souls College, Oxford; White Notley Hall, near Witham, Essex. *Club:* Beefsteak.

**BUTLER, Theobald Richard Fitzwalter;** *b* 24 May 1894; *o s* of late Theobald Butler, 28 Molyneux Park, Tunbridge Wells; *m* 1948, Laura Rachel, *d* of late Sir Vincent Nash, DL, Shannon View House, Kilmurry, Co. Limerick. *Educ:* Charterhouse; University Coll., Oxford. Called to the Bar, Inner Temple, 1921; Master of the Bench, 1960. Recorder of Newark, 1945-62, of Derby, 1962-63. Dep. Chm. Notts QS, 1951-54, Chm., 1954-63 (also of Notts Adjourned QS); Dep. Chm., Middlesex QS, 1960-65; Dep. Chm., Kent QS, 1963; Chm., South East Area, Greater London Quarter Sessions, 1965-67. Chancellor, Diocese of Peterborough, 1962-. *Publication:* Senior Editor, Archbold's Criminal Pleading, etc, 37th edn 1969. *Recreations:* walking, swimming, bridge, archæology. *Address:* Flat 1, 70 Shepherds Hill, Highgate, N6. *T:* 01-348 0954. *Club:* Reform.

**BUTLER, Col Sir Thomas Pierce,** 12th Bt *cr* 1682; CVO 1970; DSO 1944; OBE 1954; JP; Resident Governor and Major, HM Tower of London, since 1961, Keeper of the Jewel House since 1968; *b* 18 Sept. 1910; *o s* of Sir Richard Pierce Butler, 11th Bt, OBE, DL, and Alice Dudley (*d* 1965), *d* of Very Rev. Hon. James Wentworth Leigh, DD; *S* father, 1955; *m* 1937, Rosemary Liège Woodgate Davidson-Houston, *d* of late Major J. M. Davidson-Houston, Pembury Hall, Kent; one *s* two *d*. *Educ:* Harrow; Trinity Coll., Cambridge. BA (Hons) Cantab, 1933. Grenadier Guards, 1933; served War of 1939-45 (wounded, POW, escaped); BEF France; 6th Bn, Egypt, Syria, Tripoli, N Africa; Staff Coll., 1944 (psc); Comd Guards Composite Bn, Norway, 1945-46; Comd 2nd Bn Grenadier Guards, BAOR, 1949-52; AQMG, London District, 1952-55; Col, Lt-Col Comdg the Grenadier Guards, 1955-58; Military Adviser to UK High Comr in New Zealand, 1959-61. Pres., London (Prince of Wales's) District, St John Ambulance Brigade. JP Co. of London. FRGS 1954. CStJ. *Recreations:* shooting, under-water exploration, fishing, riding, tennis, travelling. *Heir: s* Richard Pierce Butler [*b* 22 July 1940; *m* 1965, Diana, *yr d* of Col S. J. Borg, London; two *s*]. *Address:* Queen's House, HM Tower of London, EC3; 6 Thurloe Square, SW7. *T:* 01-584 1225; Ballin Temple, Co. Carlow. *Club:* Guards.

*See also R. N. B. Brunt.*

**BUTLIN, Sir William (Edmund),** Kt 1964; MBE 1944; Chairman and Joint Managing Director of Butlin's Ltd and Butlin Properties Ltd, 1935-68; retired, 1968; *b* 29 Sept. 1899; *s* of William Butlin, an engineer, and Bertha; *m* 1959, Norah Faith Butlin (*née* Cheriton); one *s* three *d*. *Educ:* Canada and Bristol. Founder of Butlin's Ltd, holiday camp proprietors. Member, Worshipful Companies of Gardeners and Gold and Silver Wyre Drawers. *Recreations:* President Vaudeville Golfing Society; Companion of the Water Rats; Vice-Pres., Variety Club International. *Address:* c/o 439-441 Oxford Street, W1. *T:* 01-629 6616. *Clubs:* Eccentric, Saints and Sinners, Variety Club of Great Britain; National Sporting; Anglo-American Sporting; World Sporting.

**BUTT, Sir (Alfred) Kenneth (Dudley),** 2nd Bt *cr* 1929; landowner; Underwriting Member of Lloyd's; farmer and bloodstock breeder; *b* 7 July 1908; *o s* of Sir Alfred Butt, 1st Bt and Lady Georgina Mary Butt (*née* Say); *S* father, 1962; *m* 1st, 1938, Kathleen Farmar (marr. diss., 1948); 2nd, 1948, Mrs Ivor Birts (*née* Bain), *widow* of Lt-Col Ivor Birts, RA (killed on active service). *Educ:* Rugby; Brasenose Coll., Oxford. Lloyd's, 1929-39. Royal Artillery, 1939-45, Major RA. Chairman, Parker Wakeling & Co. Ltd, 1946-54. Managing Director, Brook Stud Co., 1962. *Recreations:* tennis, golf, horse-racing, travelling, paintings. *Address:* Wheat Hill, Sandon, Buntingford, Herts. *T:* Kelshall 203; Flat 29, 1 Hyde Park Square, W2. *T:* 01-262 3988. *Clubs:* Junior Carlton, Farmers', etc.

**BUTT, Charles Sinclair,** CMG 1962; Director (formerly Chairman), Olympic Consolidated Industries Ltd and its subsidiary companies; Director, Guthrie & Co. (Aust.) Pty Ltd; *b* Warrnambool, Victoria, 28 July 1900; *s* of late Charles H. S. Butt, Melbourne; *m* 1927, Cicely E. M., *d* of late H. F. Lloyd; two *d*. *Educ:* Melbourne Church of England Grammar Sch. Hon. War-time Controller of Rubber for Commonwealth of Australia, 1942-45. Chm., Commonwealth Serum Laboratories Commn, 1961-67. FAIM. *Recreation:* golf. *Address:* 19 Hamilton Road, Malvern, Victoria 3144, Australia. *T:* 20.3992. *Clubs:* Athenæum, Royal

Automobile of Victoria (Melbourne); Commonwealth (Canberra); Peninsula Country Golf, Royal Melbourne Golf.

**BUTT, Sir Kenneth;** *see* Butt, Sir A. K. D.

**BUTTER, Major David Henry,** MC 1941; JP; landowner and farmer; company director; Vice-Lieutenant of Perth since 1960; *b* 18 March 1920; *s* of late Col Charles Butter, OBE, DL, JP, Pitlochry, and Agnes Marguerite (Madge), *d* of late William Clark, Newark, NJ, USA; *m* 1946, Myra Alice, *d* of Hon. Maj.-Gen. Sir Harold Wernher, Bt, *QV*; one *s* four *d*. *Educ:* Eton; Oxford. Served War of 1939-45: 2nd Lieut Scots Guards, 1940, Western Desert and North Africa, Sicily (Staff), 1941-43; Italy (ADC to GOC 8th Army, Gen. Sir Oliver Leese, 1944); Temp. Major, 1946; retd Army, 1948. County Councillor, Perth, 1955; Member Queen's Body Guard for Scotland (Royal Company of Archers). DL Perthshire, 1956. Governor of Gordonstoun School. *Recreations:* shooting, golf, ski-ing, travel. *Address:* Eastwood, Dunkeld, Perthshire. *T:* Dunkeld 334; 15 Grosvenor Square, W1. *T:* 01-499 1484. *Clubs:* Turf; Royal and Ancient (St Andrews); Mid-Ocean (Bermuda).

**BUTTER, John Henry,** CMG 1962; MBE 1946; Financial Director to Government of Abu Dhabi, since 1970; Dhabi, since 1970; *b* 20 April 1916; *s* of late Captain A. E. Butter, CMG, and of Mrs Baird (now of Gordon, Berwickshire); *m* 1950, Joyce Platt; three *s*. *Educ:* Charterhouse; Christ Church, Oxford. Indian Civil Service, 1939-47; Pakistan Admin. Service, 1947-50 (served in Punjab except for period 1942-46 when was Asst to Political Agent, Imphal, Manipur State). HM Overseas Civil Service, Kenya, 1950-65 (Perm. Sec. to Sec. Treasury, 1959-65); Financial Adviser, Kenya Treasury, 1965-69. *Recreation:* fishing, bridge. *Address:* Government Office, Abu Dhabi, Trucial States, Arabian Gulf. *Club:* East India and Sports.

**BUTTER, Professor Peter Herbert;** Regius Professor of English, Glasgow University, since 1965; *b* 7 April 1921; *s* of late Archibald Butter, Faskally, Perthshire, and of Mrs Baird, Whitehill, Gordon, Berwickshire; *m* 1958, Bridget Younger; one *s* two *d*. *Educ:* Charterhouse; Balliol Coll., Oxford. Served in RA, 1941-46. Assistant, 1948, Lecturer, 1951, in English, Univ. of Edinburgh; Professor of English, Queen's Univ., Belfast, 1958-65. *Publications:* Shelley's Idols of the Cave, 1954; Francis Thompson, 1961; Edwin Muir, 1962; Edwin Muir: Man and Poet, 1966; articles in periodicals. *Address:* Ashfield, Bridge of Weir, Renfrewshire. *T:* Bridge of Weir 3139. *Club:* New (Edinburgh).

*See also J. H. Butter.*

**BUTTERFIELD, Charles Harris,** QC (Singapore) 1952; Assistant Legal Adviser, Foreign and Commonwealth Office, 1966 (temporary Principal, 1959, temporary Senior Legal Assistant, 1961, CRO); *b* 1911; 2nd *s* of William Arthur Butterfield, OBE, and Rebecca Butterfield; *m* 1938, Monica, *d* of Austin Harrison, London; one *d*. *Educ:* Downside; Trinity Coll., Cambridge. Barrister-at-law, Middle Temple, 1934. Entered Colonial Legal Service, 1938; Crown Counsel, Straits Settlements, 1938. Served Singapore RA (Volunteer) and RA, 1941-46; POW, 1942-45. Solicitor-General, Singapore, 1948-55, Attorney-General, 1955-57. *Address:* Lakestreet, Mayfield, E Sussex. *Club:* Royal Thames Yacht.

**BUTTERFIELD, Sir Harry (Durham),** Kt 1963; CBE 1953; MSM 1917; Chairman, Bank of N. T. Butterfield & Son Ltd, since 1966 (Managing Director, 1937-66); *b* 1 Sept. 1898; *s* of Hon. Harry Durham Butterfield and Anna Maria Butterfield; *m* 1925, Florence Blair Heywood; three *s*. *Educ:* Saltus Grammar Sch., Bermuda; McGill Univ., Montreal; University Coll., Oxford. Served as Signal Sgt, 7th Canadian Siege Battery, 1916-18, France and Belgium; Lieut, 2nd Canadian Div. Signals, 1918-19. BA Jurisprudence, Oxford, 1921; Barrister, Middle Temple, 1922. Member, Colonial Parliament, Bermuda, 1937-56; MEC, 1947-56; MLC, 1956-68. Chairman: Hospital Board, 1940-46; Board of Health, 1941-42, 1944-47; Board of Education, 1942; Board of Works, 1947-56. *Recreations:* sailing, golf. *Address:* Sundown, Pembroke, Bermuda. *T:* 1-1315. *Clubs:* Devonshire (London), Royal Thames Yacht; Royal and Ancient (St Andrews); Canadian Club of New York, India House (New York); Royal Bermuda Yacht, Royal Hamilton Dinghy, Mid Ocean Golf, Riddels Bay Golf, Coral Beach (all in Bermuda).

**BUTTERFIELD, Sir Herbert,** Kt 1968; FBA 1965; MA; Hon. LLD, Aberdeen, 1952; Hon. DLitt: UC, Dublin, 1954; Hong Kong, 1961; Sheffield, 1962; Hull, 1963; Warwick, 1967; Bonn, 1968; Hon. DLitt: Belfast, 1955; London, 1968; Hon. LittD: Harvard and Columbia, 1956; Manchester, 1966; Master of Peterhouse, 1955-68; Professor of Modern History, University of Cambridge, 1944-63, Regius Professor, 1963-68 (now Emeritus), and Fellow of Peterhouse, 1923-55 (now an Hon. Fellow); *b* 7 Oct. 1900; *e s* of Albert Butterfield and Ada Mary Buckland; *m* 1929, Edith Joyce (Pamela) Crawshaw; two *s* (and one *s* decd). *Educ:* Trade and Grammar Sch., Keighley; Peterhouse, Cambridge (Scholar). Jane Eliza Procter Visiting-Fellow, Univ. of Princeton, NJ, 1924-25; Lecturer in History, Peterhouse, Cambridge, 1930-44; Editor, Cambridge Historical Journal, 1938-52; President, Historical Assoc., 1955-58; Member, Administrative Board of International Association of Universities, 1960-65; Commn on Higher Education in Ireland, 1960-67; Court of Governors, LSE, 1961-68; Adv. Council on Public Records, 1962-; Inst. of Historical Research Cttee, 1963-. Vice-Chancellor, Univ. of Cambridge, 1959-61; Fellow, Center for Advanced Studies, Wesleyan Univ., Middletown, Conn., 1965. Gifford Lecturer, Glasgow Univ., 1965-67. Foreign Hon. Mem., American Acad. of Arts and Sciences, 1967; Hon. MRIA, 1967; Hon. Mem., American Historical Assoc., 1968. *Publications:* The Historical Novel, 1924; The Peace-tactics of Napoleon, 1806-8, 1929; The Whig Interpretation of History, 1931; (ed.)

Select Documents of European History, Vol. III, 1715-1920, 1931; Napoleon (Great Lives), 1939; The Statecraft of Machiavelli, 1940; The Englishman and his History, 1944; Inaugural Lecture on The Study of Modern History, 1944; George III, Lord North and the People, 1949; The Origins of Modern Science, 1949; Christianity and History, 1949; History and Human Relations, 1951; Christianity in European History, 1951; Christianity, Diplomacy and War, 1953; Man on his Past, 1955; George III and the Historians, 1957; International Conflict in the Twentieth Century, 1960; The University and Education Today, 1962; Inaugural Lecture on The Present State of Historical Scholarship, 1965; (jt ed. with Martin Wight) Diplomatic Investigations, 1966. *Address:* 28 High Street, Sawston, Cambridge CB2 4BG.

**BUTTERFIELD, William John Hughes,** OBE 1953; DM; FRCP; Vice-Chancellor, University of Nottingham, since 1971; *b* 28 March 1920; *s* of late William Hughes Butterfield and of Mrs Doris North; *m* 1st, 1946, Ann Sanders (decd); one *s*; 2nd, 1950, Isabel-Ann Foster Kennedy; two *s* one *d*. *Educ:* Solihull Sch.; Univ. of Oxford; Johns Hopkins Univ. Repr. Oxford Univ.: Rugby football, *v* Cambridge, 1940-41; hockey, 1940-42 (Captain); cricket, 1942 (Captain). Member, Scientific Staff, Medical Research Council, 1946-58: Major RAMC, Army Operational Research Group, 1947-50; Research Fellow, Medical Coll. of Virginia, Richmond, Va, USA, 1950-52; seconded to Min. of Supply, 1952; seconded to AEA, 1956; Prof. of Experimental Medicine, Guy's Hospital, 1958-63; Prof. of Medicine, Guy's Hosp. Med. Sch., and Additional Physician, Guy's Hosp., 1963-70. Chairman: Bedford Diabetic Survey, 1962; Woolwich/Erith New Town Medical Liaison Cttee, 1965-; SE Met. Reg. Hospital Board's Clinical Research Cttee; Scientific Advisory Panel, Army Personnel Research Cttee; Member: UGC Medical Sub-cttee, 1966-; Council, British Diabetic Assoc., 1963- (Chm. 1967-); MRC Cttee on General Epidemiology, 1965-; MRC Clinical Res. Grants Bd, 1969; Anglo-Soviet Consultative Cttee; Minister of Health's Long Term Study Group, 1965-; Council, European Assoc. for Study of Diabetes, 1968- (Vice-Pres.); Consultant, WHO Expert Cttee on Diabetes, 1964-; Visitor, King Edward's Hospital Fund, 1964-; Examiner in Medicine: Oxford Univ., 1960-66; Univ. of E Africa, 1966-; Cambridge Univ., 1967-; Pfizer Vis. Professor, NZ and Australia, 1965; Vis. Professor, Yale, 1966. Oliver-Sherpey Lectr, 1967; Rock Carling Fellow, 1968; Banting Lectr, 1970. Member: Editorial Board, Diabetaloga, 1964-; Jl Chronic Diseases, 1968-. Hon. Fellow, NY Acad. Science, 1962. Patron, Richmond Soc., 1968-. *Publications:* (jointly) On Burns, 1953; Tolbutamide after 10 years, 1967; Priorities in Medicine, 1968; Health Behaviour in an Urban Community, 1971; various contribs to medical jls. *Recreations:* Tennis (not lawn), cricket (village) and talking (too much). *Address:* University of Nottingham, University Park, Nottingham NG7 2RD. *Clubs:* Athenæum, MCC, Queen's.

**BUTTERS, Sir John Henry,** Kt 1927; CMG 1923; MBE 1920; VD; MICE, FIEE, MIE Aust., FASCE; Consultant, Sydney, New South Wales; *b* Alverstoke, Hants, 23 Dec. 1885; *s* of late R. J. Butters; *m* Lilian Gordon, *d* of late T. W. Keele, MICE, Sydney; one *s* three *d*. *Educ:* Tauntons Sch.; University Coll., Southampton. Chief Engineer and General Manager, Hydro-Electric Department, Tasmania, 1912-24; Chief Commissioner, Federal Capital, Canberra, 1924-29; Chairman of Associated Newspapers Ltd, Sydney, 1940-56. Lieut-Colonel Royal Australian Engineers (retired). Hon. Cons. Mil. Engr, AHQ Aust., 1927-43. Pres., Instn of Engineers, Australia, 1927. Director: General Motors Holdings Pty Ltd; Petrochemical Holdings Ltd; Boral Ltd; Chairman: Hadfields Steel Works Ltd; North Shore Gas Co. Ltd; Vumalama Plantations Ltd. *Address:* Alverstoke, Wahroonga, Sydney, NSW, Australia. *TA:* Sydney. *Clubs:* Australian, Royal Automobile (Sydney).

**BUTTERWORTH, George Neville;** Chairman of English Calico Ltd since 1968; *b* 27 Dec. 1911; *s* of Richard Butterworth and Hannah (*née* Wright); *m* 1947, Barbara Mary Briggs; two *s*. *Educ:* Malvern; St John's Coll., Cambridge. Served with Royal Artillery, at home and overseas, 1939-45. Joined English Sewing Cotton Co. Ltd, 1933; Commercial Dir, 1948; Dep. Man. Dir, 1961; Jt Man. Dir, 1964; Man. Dir, 1966; Dep. Chm., 1967; Chm., 1968, on merger with The Calico Printers' Assoc. Ltd. Dir, National Westminster Bank (North Regional Board), 1969. Chm., NW Regional Council of CBI, 1968-70; Mem., Grand Council of CBI; Trustee, Civic Trust for the North-West, 1967; Mem., Textile Council, 1970. FBIM 1968. *Recreation:* farming. *Address:* English Calico Ltd, 56 Oxford Street, Manchester, M60 1HJ; Oak Farm, Ollerton, Knutsford, Cheshire. *T:* 061-567 3150. *Club:* St James's (Manchester).

**BUTTERWORTH, John Blackstock,** MA; DL; JP; Vice-Chancellor, University of Warwick, since 1963; *b* 13 March 1918; *o s* of John William and Florence Butterworth; *m* 1948, Doris Crawford Elder; one *s* two *d*. *Educ:* Queen Elizabeth's Grammar Sch., Mansfield; The Queen's Coll., Oxford. Served in Royal Artillery, 1939-46. MA 1946. Called to Bar, Lincoln's Inn, 1947. New Coll., Oxford: Fellow, 1946-63; Dean, 1952-56; Bursar and Fellow, 1956-63; Sub Warden, 1957-58. Junior Proctor, 1950-51; Faculty Fellow of Nuffield Coll., 1953-58; Member of Hebdomadal Council, Oxford Univ., 1953-63. managing Trustee, Nuffield Foundation, 1964-. Chm., Inter-Univ. Council for Higher Educn Overseas, 1968-. Member: Royal Commn on the Working of the Tribunals of Inquiry (Act), 1921, 1966; Intergovernmental Cttee on Law of Contempt in relation to Tribunals of Inquiry, 1968-; BIM, 1970-. Governor, Royal Shakespeare Theatre, 1964-; Trustee, Shakespeare Birthplace Trust, 1966. DL Warwickshire, 1967; JP City of Oxford, 1962, Coventry, 1963. *Address:* The University of Warwick, Coventry, Warwicks. *T:* Coventry 24011. *Clubs:* Athenæum, Oxford and Cambridge University.

**BUTTERWORTH, Hon. W. Walton;** United States Ambassador to Canada, 1963-68; *b* 7 Sept. 1903; *s* of William W. Butterworth, MD, and Maud Ravencamp Campbell; *m* 1928, Virginia Parker; one *s* one *d*. *Educ:* New Orleans Acad.; Lawrenceville Sch.; Princeton Univ.; Rhodes Scholar, Worcester Coll.,

Oxford Univ., 1925-27. American Foreign Service, 1928; Vice-Consul, Singapore, 1929-31; Dept of State, 1931; Third Secretary of Legation, Ottawa, 1932; Second Secretary of Embassy and Special Rep. Treasury Dept, London, 1934-41; Dept of Commerce, 1941; Member Commn on Trade policy in relation to Lend-Lease Programme, 1942; First Secretary of Embassy, Lisbon and Madrid (in charge of economic and financial affairs) and Dir-General of United States Commercial Corporation, 1942-44; Counselor of Embassy, Madrid, 1944; American Minister, Nanking, 1946; Director, Office of Far Eastern Affairs, 1947; Asst Secretary of State, US, 1949; American Ambassador to Sweden, 1950-53; American Minister, London, 1953-55; United States Representative to the European Communities (US Representative to the European Coal and Steel Community, 1956-63, and to the European Economic and European Atomic Energy Communities) 1958-63, with the rank of Ambassador. *Recreations:* shooting, tennis, golf. *Address:* 30 Battle Road, Princeton, NJ, USA. *Clubs:* White's (London); Metropolitan (Washington, DC); Century (NY); Boston (New Orleans, La); University Cottage, Nassau (Princeton, NJ).

**BUTTFIELD, Archie Montague Carey,** CMG 1959; Chairman, Advisory Board, NSW, National Bank of Australasia Ltd; Director: Mauri Bros & Thomson Ltd; Mount Isa Mines Ltd; Dellingham Corporation of Australia; Member, Principal Board, National Bank of Australasia Ltd; *b* Wagin, WA, 27 Aug. 1898; *s* of late F. Montgomery Buttfield, Wagin; *m* 1930, Ella, *d* of E. Warner; one *s* two *d. Educ:* Perth Modern Sch. Joined Australian Mutual Provident Society, 1914; General Manager, 1948-60. Past Chairman, Life Offices' Assoc. for Australasia; Past Member Council, Aust. Administrative Staff Coll. AAII 1926. *Recreations:* trout fishing, golf, tennis, bowls. *Address:* 146 Middle Harbour Road, Lindfield, NSW, Australia. *Clubs:* Union, Royal Sydney Yacht Squadron (Sydney); Elanora Country; Warrawee Bowling.

**BUTTLE, Gladwin Albert Hurst,** OBE 1942; MA, MB Cantab; FRCP; retired as Wellcome Professor of Pharmacology, School of Pharmacy, London University (1946-66); *b* 11 April 1899; *s* of William and Mary Buttle; *m* 1936, Eva Korella; one *s. Educ:* Whitgift Grammar Sch.; St John's Coll., Cambridge. Qualified University Coll. Hospital, 1924; Pharmacologist Wellcome Physiological Research Laboratories for 14 years. RMA Woolwich, 1917; Lieut RE, 1918. Served War of 1939-45, RAMC (Lt-Col); adviser in Blood Transfusion, MEF and BLA, 1940-45. *Publications:* contribs on chemotherapy and pharmacology to medical jls. *Recreations:* gardening, tennis. *Address:* Park View, Woldingham, Surrey. *T:* Woldingham 2191.

**BUTTON, Henry George;** Under-Secretary, Ministry of Agriculture, Fisheries and Food, since 1960 (Principal Finance Officer since 1965); *b* 11 Aug. 1913; *e s* of late Rev. Frank S. and Bertha B. Button; *m* 1938, Edith Margaret Heslop; two *d. Educ:* Manchester Grammar Sch.; Christ's Coll., Cambridge (Scholar). Mod. and Medieval Langs Tripos, Part II, 1st Class (with dist.) 1934; Tiarks German Scholar (research at Univ. of Bonn), 1934-35; Sen. Studentship of Goldsmiths' Company, 1935-36. Entered Civil Service, 1937; Board of Trade, 1937-57 (served in Min. of Production, 1942; Counsellor, UK Delegn to OEEC, Paris, 1952-55; on staff of Monopolies Commn, 1955-56); transf. Min. of Agriculture, Fisheries and Food, 1957. Mem. Agricultural Research Council, 1960-62. Leader of various UK Delegns to FAO in Rome. BBC Brain of Britain for 1962; rep. Great Britain in radio quiz in Johannesburg, 1966; Bob Dyer's TV show, Sydney, 1967. *Publications:* contribs to various jls both learned and unlearned, and to newspapers. *Recreations:* reading, writing, studying old businesses (hon. review ed., Business Archives Coun.). *Address:* 17 Kent Avenue, Ealing, W13. *T:* 01-997 3241. *Clubs:* Farmers', Civil Service, Royal Commonwealth Society.

**BUTTROSE, Murray;** Puisne Judge, Singapore, 1956-68, retired; a Temporary Deputy Chairman (part time), London Quarter Sessions; *b* 31 July 1903; *s* of William Robert and Frances Buttrose, both British; *m* 1935, Jean Marie Bowering; one *s. Educ:* St Peter's Coll. and Adelaide Univ., South Australia. Admitted and enrolled as a barrister and solicitor of the Supreme Court of S Australia, 1927; apptd to HM Colonial Legal Service, 1946; Crown Counsel, Singapore, 1946, Senior Crown Counsel, 1949, and Solicitor-General, Singapore, 1955. Admitted and enrolled as a solicitor of the Supreme Court of Judicature in England, 1955. Served with Royal Air Force (RAFVR), 1940-45. *Recreations:* reading, tennis, and golf. *Address:* 10 Trevor Square, Knightsbridge, SW7. *Clubs:* Singapore (Singapore); Royal Singapore Golf.

**BUXTON;** *see* Noel-Buxton.

**BUXTON,** family name of **Baron Noel-Buxton.**

**BUXTON, Major Anthony,** DSO 1916; BA; DL, JP Norfolk; *b* 2 Sept. 1881; *y s* of late Edward North Buxton; *m* 1926, Mary (*d* 1953), *e d* of late Hon. Bernard Constable-Maxwell, Farlie House, Inverness; one *s* three *d. Educ:* Harrow; Trinity Coll., Cambridge. Graduated Natural Science Tripos, 1904. Played in the Harrow Eleven, 1900, 1901; served for 11 years in the Essex Yeomanry; served European War with his regiment, 1914-18 (DSO); attached 10th Royal Hussars, 1918-19; Secretariat, Headquarters, League of Nations, 1919-31; travelled in Asia Minor and the Caucasus. High Sheriff of Norfolk, 1945-46. *Publications:* Sport in Peace and War; Sporting Interludes at Geneva, 1932; Fisherman Naturalist, 1946; Travelling Naturalist, 1948; Happy Year, 1950; contributions to reviews and newspapers. *Recreations:* fishing, shooting, hunting, travel, natural history. *Address:* Horsey Hall, near Great Yarmouth, Norfolk. *Club:* Brooks's.

**BUXTON, Aubrey Leland Oakes,** MC 1943; Director of Anglia Television since 1958; *b* 15 July 1918; *s* of Leland Wilberforce Buxton and Mary, *d* of Rev. Thomas Henry Oakes; *m* 1946, Pamela Mary, *d* of Sir Henry Birkin, 3rd Bt; two *s* four *d. Educ:* Ampleforth; Trinity Coll.,

Cambridge. Served 1939-45, RA; combined ops in Arakan, 1942-45 (despatches, 1944). Extra Equerry to Duke of Edinburgh, 1964. A Trustee of the British Museum (Natural History), 1969-. Member: Countryside Commn; Royal Commission on Environmental Pollution; British Trustee, World Wildlife Fund; Vice-President, London Zoological Soc., 1968; Founder, Stansted Wildlife Park. Wildlife Film Producer, Anglia TV; has made more than 60 TV films including: The New Ark; The Enchanted Isles. Golden Awards, Internat. TV Festival, 1963 and 1968; Silver Medal, Zoological Society of London, 1967; Finalist, Internat. Film Festival, NY, 1968; Silver Medal, Royal TV Society, 1968. *Publications:* (with Sir Philip Christison) The Birds of Arakan, 1946; The King in his Country, 1955; numerous articles and papers on wildlife and exloration. *Recreations:* travel, natural history, painting, sport. *Address:* Norman House, Stansted, Essex. *T:* Stansted 2343; Ardvar Lodge, Kylesku, Sutherland. *Club:* White's.

**BUXTON, Major Desmond Gurney,** DL; 60th Rifles, retired; retired as Local Director (Norwich) Barclays Bank, 1958; Member Norfolk County Council, 1958; *b* 4 Jan. 1898; *e s* of late Edward G. Buxton, Catton Hall, Norwich, and of late Mrs Buxton, The Beeches, Old Catton, Norwich; *m* 1930, Rachel Mary, *yr d* of late Colonel A. F. Morse, Coltishall Mead, Norwich; two *s* three *d* (and one *d* decd). *Educ:* Eton; RMC Sandhurst. 60th Rifles, 1917-29; France and Belgium, 1917-18; NW Europe, 1945. Sheriff of Norwich, 1936-37; Lieut-Colonel Royal Norfolk Regt (TA), 1939-40. High Sheriff, Norfolk, 1960; DL Norfolk, 1961. OStJ 1967. *Recreations:* shooting, chess, bridge. *Address:* Hoveton Hall, Wroxham, Norwich.

**BUXTON, Gladys,** CBE 1958; JP; *b* 7 Nov. 1891; *d* of Thomas Edwin and Annie Eliza Stocks; *m* 1919, Frederick Buxton. *Educ:* West Riding Secondary Sch.; Penistone Grammar Sch.; Lincoln Training Coll. for Teachers. Teachers' Certificate, 1913. Mem., Sheffield Regional Hospital Board, 1947-63; Chm., Derby No 3 Hosp. Management Cttee; Member: Council for the Professions Supplementary to Medicine, 1961; Adv. Council for Child Care, 1967. Derbyshire County Council: Mem., 1943; Vice-Chm. 1949; Chm. 1957-62; CA 1952. Chm. Derbyshire Educn Cttee, 1962. Hon. MA Nottingham, 1961. JP County of Derby, 1944. *Recreations:* reading; listening to orchestral music; house and garden. *Address:* The Gables, 17 Quarry Hill Road, Ilkeston, Derbys. *T:* Ilkeston 5536.

**BUXTON, Rt. Rev. Harold Jocelyn;** *b* 1880; 4th *s* of Sir Thomas Fowell Buxton, 3rd Bt, Warlies, Waltham Abbey, Essex; unmarried. *Educ:* Harrow; Trinity Coll., Cambridge. Vicar of Horley with Hornton, Oxon, 1913; Head of Medical Unit (Lord Mayor's Fund) with Russian Army in the Caucasus, 1915-16; temporary Chaplain in France, 1917; British Chaplain at Nicosia, 1927-31; Archdeacon in Cyprus, 1928-33; Bishop of Gibraltar, 1933-47; Rector of Launton, Oxford, 1949-52; Sub-Prelate, Order of St John of Jerusalem; Order of King George I of Greece, 1944; Royal Order of Saint Sava, Yugoslavia, 1945. *Publications:* Travel and Politics in Armenia (part), 1913; Transcaucasia, 1926; Substitution of Law for War, 1925; A Mediterranean Window, 1954. *Address:* 14 Iverna Gardens, W8. *Club:* Royal Commonwealth Society.

**BUXTON, Paul William Jex;** Counsellor, British Embassy, Washington, since 1967; *b* 20 Sept. 1925; *s* of late Denis Buxton and Emily Buxton (*née* Hollins); *m* 1950, Katharine Hull; two *s* one *d*. *Educ:* Rugby Sch.; Balliol Coll., Oxford. Coldstream Guards, 1944-47. HM Foreign Service, 1950-. *Address:* Castle House, Chipping Ongar, Essex. *T:* Ongar 2642. *Clubs:* Brooks's; Federal City (Washington).

**BUXTON, Captain Richard Gurney,** JP Norfolk; *b* 6 May 1887; *s* of S. Gurney Buxton, Catton Hall, Norwich; *m* Mary Primrose, *d* of late Major A. S. Ralli, 12th Lancers; two *d*. *Educ:* Eton; Trinity Coll., Cambridge. *Address:* Wiveton Hall, Holt, Norfolk. *T:* Cley 207. *Club:* Boodle's.

**BUXTON, Dame Rita (Mary),** DBE 1969 (CBE 1955; OBE 1944); *b* 1900; *d* of Charles James Neunhoffer and Alice Neunhoffer (*née* O'Connor), Melbourne, Australia; *m* 1922, Leonard R. Buxton; three *d*. *Educ:* Sacré-Coeur Convent. Interested in philanthropic work. Member of the Victoria League. *Recreations:* golf, tennis, bridge. *Address:* 48 Hampden Road, Armadale, Victoria, Australia. *T:* 50-3333; Glynt, Mount Martha, Victoria, Australia. *T:* Mount Martha 41-216. *Clubs:* English-Speaking Union; Alexandra (Melbourne); Metropolitan Golf, Peninsula County Golf, Frankston Golf.

**BUXTON, Captain Roden Henry Victor,** CBE 1942; RN (retd); Order of Polonia Restituta 3rd class; *b* 17 Dec. 1890; *s* of Sir Victor Buxton, 4th Bt; *heir-pres.* to Sir T. F. V. Buxton, 6th Bt, *qv*; *m* 1st, 1917, Dorothy Alina (*d* 1956), *d* of Col C. W. R. St John, RE; two *s* four *d*; 2nd, 1957, Hilda, MBE, *d* of late Charles Alfred Meadows, Rainham, Kent. *Educ:* Cheam Sch.; RNC Osborne and Dartmouth. Midshipman, 1908; Lieut, 1913; specialised in Signals; Grand Fleet, 1914-18; Flag Lieut and Signal Officer to Vice-Adm. Sir Roger Keyes, 1919-21; Fleet Signal Officer, Mediterranean and Atlantic Fleets, 1921-24; RN Staff Coll., 1925; RAF Staff Coll., 1929; HMS Enterprise East Indies, 1929-31; served at Admiralty Signal Dept; Drafting Comdr, Portsmouth; Admiralty as Director of Manning, 1940-43; Combined Operations HQ and Admiralty, as Director of Combined Operations Personnel, 1943-46; Naval Mission to Greece, 1946-47. JP for Hants, 1948-57. *Recreations:* fishing, gardening. *Address:* Rodwell House, Loddon, Norwich, Norfolk. *T:* Loddon 356. *Club:* United Service.

**BUXTON, Ronald Carlile;** MA Cantab; *b* 20 Aug. 1923; *s* of Murray Barclay Buxton and Janet Mary Muriel Carlile; *m* 1959, Phyllida Dorothy Roden Buxton; two *s* two *d*. *Educ:* Eton; Trinity Coll., Cambridge. Chartered

Structural Engineer (AMIStructE). Director of H. Young & Co., London and associated companies. MP (C) Leyton, 1965-66. *Recreations:* travel, music, riding. *Address:* Kimberley Hall, Wymondham, Norfolk; 67 Ashley Gardens, SW1.

**BUXTON, St John Dudley,** MB, BS (London), FRCS; Hon. Consultant Orthopædic Surgeon to King's College Hospital, and Emeritus Lecturer in Orthopædics to the Medical School; Hon. Consultant Orthopædic Surgeon to the Ministry of Pensions; Member of Council, BRCS; formerly Consultant Orthopædic Surgeon to the Army, Orthopædic Surgeon to Royal Masonic Hospital, Queen Mary's Hospital, Roehampton and Chairman Standing Advisory Committee on Artificial Limbs; *b* 26 Dec. 1891; 2nd *s* of late Dudley W. Buxton, MD; *m* Winifred, 2nd *d* of Picton Warlow; one *s* one *d*. *Educ:* St Peter's Coll., Radley; University Coll. Hospital. Served European War 1914-18 in BEF and Salonika Exp. Force (Croix de Guerre); BEF, 1940 and MEF, 1941-42, Brig. Consultant Orthopædic Surgeon. Regional Adviser to EMS; Formerly Lecturer in Orthopædic Surgery and Examiner in Surgery, Univ. of London; Past Pres. Med. Defence Union; Past Pres. Brit. Orthopædic Assoc.; Examiner for Diploma in Phys. Medicine, RCP and RCS; Hunterian Prof. RCS; Past Pres. Section of Orthopædics, Royal Soc. of Medicine; Mem. Soc. International Chirurg. Orth. Traumatol., Hellenic Surg. Soc. and French and Hellenic Soc. Orth. Surg. and Traumatology. Silver Cross of Royal Order of Phœnix (Greece). *Publications:* Arthroplasty; (jointly) Surgical Pathology; Orthopædics, in Post-Graduate Surgery, ed. by R. Maingot; Two Visits to Greece; Amputations, In Butterworth's British Encycl. Med. Practice; articles in Lancet, Proc. Royal Soc. of Med., etc. *Recreations:* writing, gardening. *Address:* Treetops, Shanklin, IoW. *T:* 2506. *Club:* Royal Commonwealth Society.

**BUXTON, Sir Thomas Fowell Victor,** 6th Bt *cr*1840; *b* 18 Aug. 1925; *s* of Sir Thomas Fowell Buxton, 5th Bt, and Hon. Dorothy Cochrane (*d* 1927), *yr d* of 1st Baron Cochrane of Cults; *S* father, 1945; *m* 1955, Mrs D. M. Chisenhale-Marsh (*d* 1965). *Educ:* Eton; Trinity Coll., Cambridge. *Heir: u* Capt. Roden Henry Victor Buxton, *qv*. *Address:* Woodredon, Waltham Abbey, Essex. *T:* Waltham Cross 22048.

*See also Rt. Rev. H. J. Buxton.*

**BUZZARD, Rear-Adm. Sir Anthony Wass,** 2nd Bt *cr* 1929; CB 1953; DSO 1940; OBE 1941; RN (retired); with International Department, British Council of Churches; *b* 28 April 1902; *er s* of Sir E. Farquhar Buzzard, 1st Bt, KCVO, and May, *d* of late E. Bliss; *S* father, 1945; *m* 1932, Margaret Elfreda, *o d* of late Sir Arthur Knapp, KCIE, CSI, CBE; two *s* one *d*. *Educ:* RN Colls, Osborne and Dartmouth. Director of Naval Intelligence, 1951-54. *Heir: s* Anthony Farquhar Buzzard, *b* 28 June 1935. *Address:* Todd House, West Clandon, Surrey. *T:* Clandon 597.

*See also H. Gardiner-Hill.*

**BUZZARD, John Huxley;** Second Senior Prosecuting Counsel to the Crown since 1964; Recorder of Dover since 1968; *b* 12 Aug. 1912; *s* of late Brig.-Gen. Frank Anstie Buzzard, DSO, and Joan, *d* of late Hon. John Collier; *m* 1946, Hilary Ann Courtney Buzzard (*née* Antrobus); two *s* one *d*. *Educ:* Wellington Coll.; New Coll., Oxford. Open Classical Scholar, New Coll., 1931; commissioned 4th Queen's Own Royal West Kent Regt, TA, 1931; transferred to TA Reserve of Officers, 1935. Called to Bar, 1937 (Master of the Bench, Inner Temple, 1965). Served with RAFVR, in UK, Iceland, and SE Asia, 1940-45 (despatches). Recorder of Great Yarmouth, 1958-68. Mem. National Farmers' Union. *Recreations:* mountaineering, ski-ing, sailing. *Address:* Haxted House, Edenbridge, Kent. *Clubs:* Alpine, Lansdowne, Climbers', Ski Club of Great Britain, Cruising Association.

**BYAM SHAW, Glencairn Alexander,** CBE 1954; a Director, Sadler's Wells, since 1966; *b* 13 Dec. 1904; *s* of Byam Shaw, artist, and Evelyn Pyke-Nott; *m* 1929, Angela Baddeley (*see* M. A. Clinton-Baddeley); one *s* one *d*. *Educ:* Westminster Sch. First stage appearance, Pavilion Theatre, Torquay, 1923; Mem. J. B. Fagan's Company at Oxford Repertory Theatre; played Trophimof, in The Cherry Orchard, New York; Konstantin Treplev, in The Seagull and Baron Tusenbach, in The Three Sisters, London. Was in Max Reinhardt's production of The Miracle. Went to S Africa with Angela Baddeley in repertory of plays. Played Darnley in Queen of Scots and Laertes in John Gielgud's production of Hamlet; was mem. of company for Gieldgud's season at Queen's Theatre. Produced plays in London, New York and Stratford-upon-Avon. A Director of Old Vic Theatre Centre; a Governor, Royal Shakespeare Theatre, 1960-. Co-Dir, with Anthony Quayle, of Shakespeare Memorial Theatre, Stratford-upon-Avon, 1952-56; Director, 1956-59; directed: Ross, Haymarket, 1960; The Lady From the Sea, Queen's, 1961; The Complaisant Lover and Ross, New York, 1961; The Rake's Progress and Idomeneo, Sadler's Wells, 1962; The Tulip Tree, Haymarket, 1962; Cosi fan Tutte, Der Freischütz, Hansel and Gretel, Sadler's Wells, 1963; Where Angels Fear to Tread, St Martin's, 1963; The Right Honourable Gentleman, Her Majesty's, 1964; Faust, Sadler's Wells, 1964; A Masked Ball, Sadler's Wells, 1964; You Never Can Tell, Haymarket, 1966; Die Fledermaus, Sadler's Wells, 1966; The Rivals, Haymarket, 1966; The Dance of Death, National Theatre, 1967; Orpheus and Eurydice, Sadler's Wells, 1967; The Merchant of Venice, Haymarket, 1967; The Mastersingers of Nuremberg (with John Blatchley), 1968; The Valkyrie (with John Blatchley), 1970. In the Royal Scots during War of 1939-45. Hon. DLitt Birmingham, 1959. *Address:* 169 Ashley Gardens, SW1. *Club:* Reform.

*See also J. J. Byam Shaw.*

**BYAM SHAW, (John) James;** Director P. & D. Colnaghi & Co. Ltd, 1937-68; *b* 12 Jan. 1903; *er surv. s* of John Byam Shaw and Evelyn Pyke-Nott; *m* 1st, 1929, Eveline (marr. diss., 1938), *d* of Capt. Arthur Dodgson, RN; 2nd, 1945, Margaret (*d* 1965), *d* of Arthur Saunders, MRCVS; one *s*; 3rd, 1967, Christina, *d* of Francis Ogilvy and *widow* of W. P. Gibson. *Educ:* Westminster; Christ Church, Oxford. Scholar of Westminster and Christ Church; MA 1925. Worked independently in principal museums of Europe, 1925-33; Lecturer and Assistant to the Director, Courtauld Institute of Art, Univ. of London, 1933-34; joined P. & D. Colnaghi & Co., 1934. Served in Royal Scots, UK, India and Burma, 1940-46 (wounded); Major, 1944. Member: Council of the Byam Shaw Sch. of Drawing and Painting; Exec. Cttee, Nat. Art Collections Fund; Council, British Museum Soc. Trustee: Watts Gall.; Paul Mellon foundation for British Art. Lecturer, Christ Church, Oxford, 1964-. FSA; FRSA. Hon. Fellow, Pierpont Morgan Library, NY. *Publications:* The Drawings of Francesco Guardi, 1951; The Drawings of Domenico Tiepolo, 1962; Catalogue of Paintings by Old Masters at Christ Church Oxford, 1968; publications in Old Master Drawings (1926-39), Print Collectors' Quarterly, Burlington Magazine, Master Drawings (New York), Art Quarterly (Detroit), Arte Veneta, Etc. *Address:* 4 Abingdon Villas, Kensington, W8. *T:* 01-937 6944. *Club:* Athenæum.

*See also G. A. Byam Shaw.*

**BYASS, Bt Col Sir Geoffrey Robert Sidney,** 2nd Bt *cr* 1926; TD; DL; *b* Port Talbot, 30 Sept. 1895; *e s* of 1st Bt and Eveline (*d* 1951), *d* of T. L. Stratton, Turweston House, Brackley; *S* father, 1929; *m* 1919, Marian (*d* 1968), *d* of Col Sir Gerald Trevor Bruce, KCB; five *d. Educ:* Winchester. Glamorgan Yeomanry 1914 onwards; served Palestine, Egypt and France (wounded); Major RA (TA) 1922; Lt-Col 1933; commanded 81st (Welsh) Field Brigade RA, TA, 1933-38; Bt Col 1938. Mayor of Port Talbot, 1937-38. *Recreation:* golf. *Address:* The Pump Room, Winkfield, Windsor, Berks. *T:* Winkfield Row 2079.

**BYATT, Ian Charles Rayner;** Director of Economics and Statistics, Ministry of Housing and Local Government, since 1969; *b* 11 March 1932; *s* of Charles Rayner Byatt and Enid Marjorie Annie Byatt (*née* Howat); *m* 1959 (marr. diss. 1969); one *s* one *d. Educ:* Kirkham Grammar Sch.; Oxford University. Commonwealth Fund Fellow, Harvard, 1957-58; Lectr in Economics, Durham Univ., 1958-62; Economic Consultant, HM Treasury, 1962-64; Lectr in Economics, LSE, 1964-67; Sen. Economic Adviser, Dept of Educn and Science, 1967-69. *Publications:* articles on economics in learned jls. *Address:* 33 Ridgmount Gardens, WC1. *T:* 01-636 6533.

**BYERS,** family name of **Baron Byers.**

**BYERS,** Baron *cr* 1964 (Life Peer); **Charles Frank Byers,** OBE 1944; Liberal Leader, House of Lords, since 1967; Chairman of the Liberal Party, 1950-52, 1965-67 (Vice-President, 1954-65); Liberal Chief Whip, 1946-50; MP (L) North Dorset, 1945-50; *b* 24 July 1915; *e s* of late C. C. Byers, Lancing, Sussex; *m* 1939, Joan Elizabeth Oliver; one *s* three *d. Educ:* Westminster; Christ Church, Oxford (MA Hons); Exchange Scholar at Milton Acad., Mass, USA. Chm., British Universities' Sports Federation, 1966-. Blue for Athletics, Oxford, 1937, 220 yds Hurdles; Pres. OU Liberal Club, 1937. Enlisted Sept. 1939, RA; commissioned March 1940; served MEF, CMF, 1940-44; GSO1 Eighth Army, Lt-Col, 1943; served NW Europe, 1944-45, GSO1 HQ, 21 Army Group (despatches thrice); Chevalier Legion of Honour, Croix de Guerre (palmes). FBIM 1965. *Address:* Hunters Hill, Blindley Heath, Lingfield, Surrey.

**BYERS, Joseph Austen;** Judge of the Provincial Court of British Columbia, 1969-70; retired; *b* 1 Oct. 1895; *er s* of Joseph and Sarah Dalton Byers, Newcastle upon Tyne; *m* 1934, Sheila Margaret O'Neill; one *d. Educ:* King's Sch., Chester; Balliol Coll., Oxford. Military Service, 1914-19 with Cheshire Regiment and Army Signal Service in Mediterranean, Egypt, Mesopotamia, and India, NWF; Balliol, 1914-21; MA 1921; Indian Civil Service, 1921. Held various executive posts, 1921-28; joined judicial branch 1928, and served as District and Sessions Judge in various districts in Madras and Orissa, 1930-41; Additional Judge, Madras High Court, Jan. 1942; Puisne Judge, High Court of Judicature, Madras, 1942-47. Called to Bar, Inner Temple, 1936; to Bar of British Columbia, Canada, 1948; Judge of Family Court, Greater Victoria, and Stipendiary Magistrate, BC, 1960-69. *Recreations:* golf and motoring. *Address:* J. A. Byers, Barrister and Solicitor, Post Box 33, Victoria, BC, Canada. *Club:* Union (Victoria, BC).

**BYFORD, Donald,** CBE 1963; Founder and President, D. Byford & Co. Ltd; *b* 11 Jan. 1898; 4th *s* of Charles Watson Byford, JP, Clare, Suffolk; *m* 1922, Marjorie Annie, *d* of Ald. W. K. Billings, JP, Leicester (Lord Mayor, 1933-34); two *s* one *d. Educ:* Bishop's Stortford Coll. 2nd Lieut, Royal Tank Corps, 1917-19. Hosiery Manufacturer, 1919-. Past President: Leicester Hosiery Manufacturers' Assoc.; Nat. Fedn Hosiery Manufacturers. Past Master: Worshipful Co. Framework Knitters; Worshipful Co. Gardeners. Dep. Chm., Cttee for Exports to USA. Mem. Court and Treasurer, Corp. of the Sons of the Clergy; Mem. Council, CBI. *Recreations:* shooting, farming. *Address:* Thurcaston Grange, near Leicester. *T:* Anstey 2544. *Club:* Farmers'.

**BYNG,** family name of **Earl of Strafford,** and of **Viscount Torrington.**

**BYNOE, Dame Hilda Louisa,** DBE 1969; Governor of the Associated State of Grenada, West Indies, since 1968; *b* Grenada, 18 Nov. 1921; *d* of Thomas Joseph Gibbs, JP, Estate Proprietor, and late Louisa Gibbs (*née* La Touche); *m* 1947, Peter Cecil Alexander Bynoe, ARIBA, Dip. Arch., former RAF Flying Officer; two *s. Educ:* St Joseph's Convent, St George's, Grenada; Royal Free Hospital Medical Sch., Univ. of London. MB, BS (London), 1951, MRCS, LRCP, 1951. Teacher, St Joseph's Convents, Trinidad and Grenada, 1939-44; hospital and private practice, London, 1951-53; public service with Govt of Trinidad and Tobago, 1954-55, with Govt of Guyana (then British Guiana), 1955-58, with Govt of Trinidad and Tobago, 1958-65; private practice, Trinidad, 1965-68. *Recreations:* swimming, music, reading. *Address:* Government House, St George's, Grenada. *T:* 2401-2403.

**BYRNE, Sir Clarence (Askew),** Kt 1969; OBE 1964; DSC 1945; Company Director, Mining, Insurance and Construction, Queensland; *b* 17 Jan. 1903; *s* of George Patrick Byrne, Brisbane, Qld, and Elizabeth Emma Askew, Dalby, Qld; *m* 1928, Nellie Ann Millicent Jones; one *s* one *d. Educ:* Brisbane Technical Coll. Mining Develt and Exploration, 1925-30; Oil Exploration, Roma, Qld, 1930-40. Served War, 1940-46 (DSC, Amer. Bronze Star Medal): Lt-Comdr; CO, HMAS Warrego, 1944-45. Dir, Oil Exploration Cos, Roma, Qld; Rep., The Zinc Corp. Ltd; Man. Dir, United Uranium and Associated Oil Gp; Pres., Qld Chamber of Mines, 1961-70; Exec. Dir, Conzinc Riotinto of Australia Ltd (Resident, Qld, 1957-68); Director: Mary Kathleen Uranium Ltd; Interstate Oil Ltd; Qld Alumina Ltd; Coachcraft Ltd; The General Electric Co. of Aust. Ltd; Unity Life Assce Ltd; Thiess Holdings Ltd; Mines Administration Pty Ltd;

Walkers Ltd; Commonwealth Aluminium Corp. Ltd; Mem. Aust. Mining Industries Council, Canberra. *Recreations:* fishing, ocean cruising. *Address:* Pandanus House, Dingle Avenue, Caloundra, Qld 4551, Australia. *T:* Caloundra 91-1228. *Clubs:* Athenæum (Melbourne); Brisbane, United Service, Tattersall's (Brisbane).

**BYRNE, Rt. Rev. Herbert Kevin,** OSB, MA; Abbot of Ampleforth Abbey, 1939-63; *b* 7 Sept. 1884; 3rd *s* of late Andrew Byrne, Croney Byrne, Co. Wicklow. *Educ:* Ampleforth Coll. Joined Benedictine Order, 1902; at the Ampleforth House of Studies, Oxford, 1905-09; Classical Master, Ampleforth Coll., 1909-35; priest, 1911; parish work at St Peter's, Liverpool, 1935-39. *Address:* Ampleforth Abbey, York.

**BYRNE, Muriel St Clare,** OBE 1955; writer and lecturer; engaged in research on the Lisle Letters (1533-41) and preparation of an edition, since 1932; *b* 31 May 1895; *o c* of Harry St Clare Byrne, Hoylake, Ches, and Artemisia Desdemona Burtner, Iowa, USA. *Educ:* Belvedere, Liverpool (GPDST); Somerville Coll., Oxford. English Hons, 1916, BA and MA 1920. Leverhulme Res. Grant, 1945-46; Bedford Coll. Res. Fellowship, 1955-56; Brit. Academy Pilgrim Trust Res. Grants, 1958 and 1959. Teaching: Liverpool Coll., 1916-17; S Hampstead High Sch., 1917-18; English Lectr in Rouen, Army Educn (YMCA), 1918-19; Temp. Asst English Tutor, Somerville, 1919, and English coaching for Final Hons at Oxford, 1920-25; Oxford and London Univ. Extension Lectr, 1920-37; Lectr, Royal Academy of Dramatic Art, London, 1923-55; Eng. Lectr, Bedford Coll., 1941-45; Leverhulme Res. Grant, 1945; Bedford Coll. Research Fellowship, 1955; Examr, London Univ. Dipl. in Dramatic Art, 1951-60; British Acad. Research in the Humanities Grant, 1964, 1965, 1966; Leverhulme Research Fellowship, 1968. Hon. Sec., Malone Soc., 1926-37; Mem. Council, Bibliographical Soc., 1932-39; Mem. Bd, 1952-, Exec., 1959-, Friends of Girls' Public Day Sch. Trust; Mem., Cttee of Soc. for Theatre Research; History Selection Cttee, Nat. Film Archive, 1968. Governor: Royal Shakespeare Theatre, 1960; Bedford Coll., 1968. Mem., Literary Advisory Panel, Shakespeare Exhibn 1564-1964. FSA 1963. *Publications:* History of Somerville College (with C. H. Godfrey), 1921; Elizabethan Life in Town and Country, 1925 (8th revised edn 1961, American edn 1962); The Elizabethan Home, 1925 (3rd rev. edn 1949); The Elizabethan Zoo, 1926; Letters of King Henry VIII, 1936, 2nd edn 1968; Common or Garden Child, 1942; contributed: Shakespeare's Audience, to Shakespeare in the Theatre, 1927; The Social Background, to A Companion to Shakespeare Studies, 1934; Queen Mary I, to Great Tudors, 1935; History of Stage Lighting and History of Make-Up, to Oxford Companion to the Theatre, 1951; The Foundations of Elizabethan Language, to Shakespeare in his own Age, 1964; Elizabethan Life in the Plays, to The Reader's Encyclopedia of Shakespeare, 1966; edited: Anthony Munday's John a Kent (Malone Society), 1923; Massinger's New Way to Pay Old Debts, 1949; The French Littleton of Claudius Holyband, 1953; Essays and Studies, Vol. 13 (Eng. Assoc.), 1960; 4-vol. paper-back illustr. edn of Granville Barker's Prefaces to Shakespeare, with Introd. and Notes, 1963; plays produced: England's Elizabeth, 1928 and 1953; "Well, Gentlemen . . ." (with Gwladys Wheeler), 1933; Busman's Honeymoon (with Dorothy L. Sayers), 1936; No Spring Till Now (Bedford Coll. Centenary Play), 1949; Gen. Ed. Pubns for Soc. for Theatre Research, 1949-59; Eng. edit. rep. of and contrib. to Enciclopedia dello Spettacolo, 1955-58; prep. Arts Council's exhibn and Catalogue, A History of Shakespearian Production in England, 1947 (repr. USA 1970); contributor to: The Times Lit. and Educ. Suppts; The Library; Review of Eng. Studies; Mod. Lang. Review; Shakespeare Survey; Shakespeare Quarterly; Drama; Theatre Notebook; Sunday Times; Theatre Research; Essays and Studies Vol. 18 (Eng. Assoc.), etc. *Recreations:* play-going and all theatrical activities. *Address:* 28 St John's Wood Terrace, NW8. *T:* 01-722 0967.

**BYRNES, James Francis;** lawyer and politician, USA; *b* Charleston, SC, 1879; *m* 1906, Maude Busch. Admitted to Bar, 1903; Editor Journal and Review, Aiken, 1903-07; official Court Reporter, 2nd Circuit, South Carolina, 1900-08; Solicitor, 2nd Circuit, South Carolina, 1908-10; Mem. of Congress, 1911-25; in practice of law, Spartanburg, 1925-31; US Senator, 1931; Associate Justice, US Supreme Court, 1941-42; Director of Economic Stabilisation, 1942-43; Director Office of War Mobilisation, 1943-45; Sec. of State, United States, 1945-47; Governor of State of South Carolina, 1951-55. *Publications:* Speaking Frankly, 1947; All in One Lifetime, 1958. *Address:* Heathwood Circle, Columbia, SC, USA.

**BYRNES, Hon. Sir Percy (Thomas),** Kt 1965; Member of the Legislative Council for North-Western Province, Victoria, Australia, since 1942; Country Party Leader in the Legislative Council since 1952; JP; *b* Eidsvold, Queensland, 28 Jan. 1893; *s* of Thomas Byrnes, Swan Hill, Victoria; *m* 1918, Dorothy, *d* of W. J. Judd; one *s* three *d*. *Educ:* Wesley Coll., Melbourne; Queen's Coll., Univ. of Melbourne. Served European War, 1914-18, with 1st Australian Imperial Forces, in France. Hon. Minister, 1948; Minister for Public Works, Victoria, 1950-52. Director, Woorinen Cooperative Packing Company. *Recreation:* shooting. *Address:* Parliament House, Melbourne, Victoria, Australia; Box 378, Swan Hill, Victoria, Australia. *Club:* Commercial Travellers' Association (Melbourne).

**BYRON,** 11th Baron *cr* 1643; **Rupert Frederick George Byron;** farmer and grazier since 1921; *b* 13 Aug. 1903; *er s* of late Col Wilfrid Byron, Perth, WA, and of Sylvia Mary Byron, 12 College Street, Winchester, England, *o d* of late Rev. C. T. Moore; *S* kinsman, 1949; *m* 1931, Pauline Augusta, *d* of T. J. Cornwall, Wagin, W Australia; one *d*. *Educ:* Gresham's Sch., Holt. Served War of 1939-45, Lieut RANVR, 1941-46. *Heir: kinsman,* Richard Geoffrey Gordon Byron, DSO [*b* 3 Nov. 1899; *m* 1st, 1926, Margaret Mary Steuart (marr. diss. 1946); 2nd, 1946, Dorigen, *o c* of P. Kennedy Esdaile; two *s*. *Educ:* Eton]. *Address:* Field Plains, Donnybrook, W Australia. *Club:* Naval and Military (Perth, WA).

**BYWATER, Thomas Lloyd,** BSc, MS; Emeritus Professor, University of Leeds; *b* 19 Aug. 1905; *m* 1935, Ishobel McL. Millar; two *s* one *d*. *Educ:* Lucton Sch.; University Coll. of North Wales; Univ. of Wisconsin, USA. Lecturer in Agriculture, Univ. of Leeds, 1929-46; Prof. of Agriculture: Aberdeen Univ., 1946-53; Leeds Univ., 1953-69. *Address:* 1 Balmoral Terrace, Shaw Lane, Leeds LS6 4EA.

**BYWATERS, Eric George Lapthorne,** MB (London); FRCP; Professor of Rheumatology, Royal Postgraduate Medical School, University of London, since 1958; Director, Medical Research Council

Rheumatism Research Unit, Taplow; Hon. Consultant Physician, Hammersmith Hospital and Canadian Red Cross Memorial Hospital, Taplow, Bucks; *b* 1 June 1910; *s* of George Ernest Bywaters and Ethel Penney; *m* 1935, Betty Euan-Thomas; three *d*. *Educ:* Sutton Valence Sch., Kent; Middx Hosp. (Sen. Broderip Schol., Lyell Gold Medallist). McKenzie McKinnon Fellow, RCP, 1935; Asst Clin. Pathologist, Bland Sutton Inst., 1936; Rockefeller Travelling Fellow and Harvard Univ. Research Fellow in Med., 1937-39; Beit Memorial Fellow, 1939; Actg Dir, MRC Clin. Res. Unit (Shock), 1943; Lectr in Med., Postgrad. Med. Sch., 1945. Gairdner Foundation Medical Award, 1963; Heberden Orator and Medallist, 1966. Hon. Mem. Dutch, French, Amer., German, Czech and Argentine Rheumatism Assocs. *Address:* Long Acre, 53 Burkes Road, Beaconsfield, Bucks.

# C

**CABLE, James Eric,** CMG 1967; Counsellor, Diplomatic Service; *b* 15 Nov. 1920; *s* of late Eric Grant Cable, CMG; *m* 1954, Viveca Hollmerus; one *s*. *Educ:* Stowe; CCC, Cambridge. Served Royal Signals, 1941-46, Major. Entered Foreign (now Diplomatic) Service, 1947; 2nd Sec., 1948; Vice-Consul, Batavia, 1949; 2nd Sec., Djakarta, 1949; acted as Chargé d'Affaires, 1951 and 1952; Helsinki, 1952; FO, 1953; 1st Sec., 1953; Mem. of British Delegn to Geneva Conf. on Indo-China, 1954; 1st Sec. (Commercial), Budapest, 1956; Head of Chancery and Consul, Quito, 1959; acted as Chargé d'Affaires, 1959 and 1960; FO, 1961 and Head of SE Asia Dept, Dec. 1963; Counsellor, Beirut, 1966; acted as Chargé d'Affaires at Beirut, 1967, 1968 and 1969; Research Associate, Institute for Strategic Studies, 1969-70. *Address:* c/o Foreign and Commonwealth Office, King Charles Street, SW1.

**CABLE-ALEXANDER, Sir Desmond William Lionel,** 7th Bt (1809); *b* 1910; *S* 1956; *m* 1st, Mary Jane (who obtained a divorce), *d* of James O'Brien, JP, Enniskillen; one *s*; 2nd, Margaret Wood, *d* of late John Burnett, Dublin; two *d*. *Educ:* Harrow; Oxford. Assumed addtl name of Cable before that of Alexander, by deed poll, 1931. *Heir: s* Patrick Desmond William Cable-Alexander [*b* 19 April *Address:* Ham House, Toat, Pulborough, Sussex. *T:* Pulborough 3302.

**CABOT, Sir Daniel Alfred Edmond,** Kt 1943; MRCVS; *m* 1949, Anne Le Cornu Blampied, l'Abri, La Rocque. Late Chief Veterinary Officer, Ministry of Agriculture and Fisheries; Veterinary Adviser, 1948. Pres., Office International des Epizooties, 1948-51; Member: Académie Vétérinaire de France; American Veterinary Medical Assoc.; Corresp. Mem., Sociedad veterinaria de zootecnia; late Jurat of Royal Court, Lt Bailiff, Jersey. *Address:* Le Bernage, Longueville, Jersey, CI.

**CACCIA,** family name of **Baron Caccia.**

**CACCIA,** Baron *cr* 1965 (Life Peer), of Abernant; **Harold Anthony Caccia,** GCMG 1959 (KCMG 1950; CMG 1945); GCVO 1961 (KCVO 1957); Provost of Eton since 1965; *B* 21 Dec. 1905; *s* of late Anthony Caccia, CB, MVO; *m* 1932, Anne Catherine, *d* of late Sir George Barstow, KCB; one *s* two *d*. *Educ:* Eton; Trinity Coll., Oxford. Laming Travelling Fellowship, Queen's Coll., Oxford, 1928. Entered HM Foreign Service as 3rd Sec., FO, 1929; transferred to HM Legation, Peking, 1932; 2nd Sec., 1934; FO 1935; Asst Private Sec. to Sec. of State, 1936; HM Legation, Athens, 1939; 1st Sec. 1940; FO 1941; seconded for service with Resident Minister, North Africa, 1943, and appointed Vice-Pres., Political Section, Allied Control Commission, Italy; Political Adviser, GOC-in-C Land Forces, Greece, 1944; Minister local rank, HM Embassy, Athens, 1945; Asst Under-Sec. of State, 1946, Dep. Under-Sec. of State, 1949, Foreign Office; British Ambassador in Austria, 1951-54, and also British High Comr in Austria, 1950-54; Dep. Under-Sec. of State, FO, 1954-56; British Ambassador at Washington, 1956-61; Permanent Under-Sec. of State, FO, 1962-65; Head of HM Diplomatic Service, 1964-65, retired. Hon. Fellow, Trinity Coll., Oxford, 1963. Chm., standard Telephones & Cables, 1968-; Director: National Westminster Bank Ltd; Prudential Assurance Co. Ltd; Foreign & Colonial Investment Trust Co. Ltd. Chm., Gabbitas-Thring Educational Trust, 1967-. Mem., Advisory Council on Public Records, 1968-. Prior of the Order of St John of Jerusalem, 1969-; GCStJ. *Address:* Provost's Lodge, Eton College, Windsor, Berks. *T:* Windsor 66304; 1 Chester Place, Regent's Park, NW1. *T:* 01-935 0302; Abernant, Builth-Wells, Breconshire. *T:* Erwood 233.

**CACOYANNIS, Michael;** director, stage and screen, since 1954; *b* 11 June 1922; *s* of Sir Panayotis Cacoyannis, *qv*. *Educ:* Greek Gymnasium; Gray's Inn and Old Vic Sch., London. Radio Producer, BBC, Greek Service, 1941-50. Actor on English stage, 1946-51; parts included: Herod, in Salome, 1946; Caligula, in Caligula, 1949, etc. Directed films: Windfall in Athens, 1953; Stella, 1954; Girl in Black, 1956; A Matter of Dignity, 1958; Our Last Spring, 1960; The Wastrel, 1961; Electra, 1962; Zorba the Greek, 1964; The Day the Fish Came Out, 1967. Directed plays: produced several of these in Athens for Ellie Lambetti's Company, 1955-61; The Trojan Women, in New York, 1963-65, in Paris, 1965; Things That Go Bump in the Night, and The Devils, New York, 1965; Mourning Becomes Electra, Metropolitan Opera, NY, 1967; Iphigenia in Aulis, New York, 1968. Order of the Phœnix (Greece), 1965. *Recreations:* walking, swimming. *Address:* 96 Boulevard Montparnasse, Paris, France.

**CACOYANNIS, Hon. Sir Panayotis (Loizou),** Kt 1936; LLB; Advocate; Member of Town School Committee, Limassol (Cyprus), since 1925, Chairman, 1946-61; *b* 20 Sept. 1893; *s* of Loizos Cacoyannis, Limassol, Cyprus; *m* 1915, Angeliki, *d* of George M. Efthyvoulos and Zoe Constantinides, Limassol, Cyprus; two *s* two *d*. MLC, Cyprus, 1925-30; MEC, Cyprus, 1929-46; Mem. of Advisory Council, 1933-46; Mem. of Council of Cyprus Anti-Tuberculosis League until 1946. Attended the Coronation Ceremony of King George VI and Queen

Elizabeth as representative of Cyprus, 1937. *Address:* POB 122, Limassol, Cyprus.
*See also M. Cacoyannis.*

**CADBURY, Adrian;** *see* Cadbury, G. A. H.

**CADBURY, (George) Adrian (Hayhurst);** Deputy Chairman of Cadbury Schweppes Ltd, since 1969, Managing Director since 1970; a Director of the Bank of England, since 1970; *b* 15 April 1929; *s* of Laurence John Cadbury, *qv*; *m* 1956, Gillian Mary, *d* of late E. D. Skepper, Neuilly-sur-Seine; two *s* one *d*. *Educ:* Eton Coll.; King's Coll., Cambridge (MA Economics). Coldstream Guards, 1948-49; Cambridge, 1949-52. Olympic Games, 1952. Director: Cadbury Group Ltd, 1962; Cadbury Bros Ltd, 1958; J. S. Fry & Sons, 1964; James Pascall, 1964; R. S. Murray, 1964; Daily News Ltd, 1960; Metal Box Co., 1968. Chm., West Midlands Economic Planning Council, 1967-70. Mem. Council: Univ. of Aston in Birmingham; Graduate Centre management Studies, Birmingham; Industrial Soc.; Governor: William Temple Coll.; Bromsgrove Sch. *Address:* Rising Sun House, near Knowle, Warwicks. *T:* 021-560 2931. *Clubs:* Boodle's; Hawks (Cambridge); Leander (Henley).

**CADBURY, George Woodall;** Chairman, Governing Body of International Planned Parenthood Federation, since 1969 (Vice-Chairman, and Chairman of the Executive, 1963-69, and Special Representative, since 1960); Executive Member, New Democratic Party of Canada, since 1965 (Treasurer, 1965-69, President for Ontario, 1961-66); *b* 19 Jan. 1907; *s* of George Cadbury and Edith Caroline Cadbury (*née* Woodall); *m* 1935, Mary Barbara Pearce; two *d*. *Educ:* Leighton Park Sch., Reading; King's Coll., Cambridge; Univ. of Pennsylvania. Man. Dir, British Canners Ltd, 1929-35; Marketing Controller and Man. Dir, Alfred Bird & Sons Ltd, 1935-45; Dep. Dir Material Production, Min. of Aircraft Production and British Air Commn (USA), 1941-45; Chm. Economic Advisory and Planning Bd, and Chief industrial Executive, Prov. of Saskatchewan, 1945-51; Dir, Technical Assistance Administration, UN, 1951-60 (Dir of Ops, 1951-54; Adviser to Govts of Ceylon, Burma, Indonesia, Jamaica and Barbados, 1954-60). Trustee: Bournville Village Trust, 1928-; Youth Hostels Trust, 1931-; Sponsor and Council Mem., Minority Rights Group, 1967-; Member: Conservation Council of Ontario, 1968-; Bd, Humane Soc. of Ontario, 1969-; Consumers Assoc. of Canada, 1970-. Mem. Meetings Cttee, RIIA, 1931-35; Sec., W Midland Group for Post-War Reconstruction and Planning, 1939-41; Resident, Toynbee Hall, 1929-35, 1941-43. *Publications:* (jointly) When We Build Again, 1940; English County, 1942; Conurbation, 1942. *Address:* 35 Brentwood Road, Oakville, Ont., Canada. *T:* 416-845 3171.

**CADBURY, Henry Joel;** Professor Emeritus, Harvard Divinity School, 1954 (Hollis Professor Divinity, 1934-54); Lecturer, Haverford College, 1954-63; Lecturer, Pendle Hill, since 1954, and Temple University, 1962-66; *b* 1 Dec. 1883; *s* of Joel Cadbury and Anna Kaighn Lowry; *m* 1916, Lydia Caroline Brown; two *s* two *d*. *Educ:* William Penn Charter Sch.; Haverford Coll.; Harvard Univ. Teacher, Haverford Coll., 1910-19; Harvard Divinity Sch., 1919-26; Andover Theological Seminary, 1919-26; Prof., Bryn Mawr Coll., 1926-34. Mem. Translation Cttee of Revised Standard Version of the Bible, 1929-; Dir, Andover-Harvard Theol. Library, 1938-54. Chm., American Friends Service Cttee, 1928-34 and 1944-60, Hon. Chm. 1960-; Chm., Board of Directors of Bryn Mawr Coll., 1956-68. Mem. several learned societies; Mem. Studiorum Novi Testamenti Societas (Pres. 1958); Fellow American Academy of Arts and Sciences. Hon. degrees: LittD Haverford Coll., 1933; DD Glasgow Univ., 1937; LLD Whittier Coll., 1951, Swarthmore Coll., 1954; LHD Howard Univ., 1959, Earlham Coll., 1967. *Publications:* The Style and Literary Method of Luke, 1920; National Ideals in the Old Testament, 1920; The Making of Luke-Acts, 1927 (and 1958); (with K. Lake) Beginnings of Christianity, Vols IV and V, 1933 (and 1966); The Peril of Modernizing Jesus, 1937 (and 1962); Jesus What Manner of Man, 1947 (and 1962); George Fox's Book of Miracles, 1948; The Book of Acts in History, 1955; Quakerism and Early Christianity, 1957; The Eclipse of the Historical Jesus, 1964. *Recreations:* Quaker history, camping. *Address:* 774 Millbrook Lane, Haverford, Pa 19041, USA.

**CADBURY, Kenneth Hotham,** MC 1944; Senior Director, Planning and Purchasing, GPO, since 1969; *b* 25 Feb. 1919; *s* of J. Hotham Cadbury, manufacturer, Birmingham; *m* 1st, Margaret R. King (marr. diss.); one *s* one *d*; 2nd, Marjorie I. Lilley; three *d*. *Educ:* Bootham Sch., York; Univ. of Birmingham. Served in Royal Artillery in Middle East and Italy, 1939-46 (despatches, MC; Major). Joined Foreign Service, 1946. Transferred to GPO, 1947; served in Personnel Dept and Inland Telecommunications Dept; Cabinet Office, 1952-55; PPS to PMG, 1956-57; Dep. Director, 1960, Director, 1962, Wales and Border Counties GPO; Director: Clerical Mechanisation and Buildings, GPO, 1964-65; Inland Telecommunications, GPO, 1965-67; Purchasing and Supply, GPO, 1967-69. Member, EDC for the Post Office, 1966-69. *Recreations:* archæology, gardening. *Address:* Pendle, Burdenshott Hill, Worplesdon, Surrey. *T:* Worplesdon 2084.

**CADBURY, Laurence John,** OBE 1919; *b* 1889; *s* of late George Cadbury; *m* 1925, Joyce, *d* of Lewis O. Matthews, Birmingham; three *s* one *d* (and one *s* one *d* decd). *Educ:* Leighton Park Sch.; Trinity Coll., Cambridge (MA). Economics Tripos. Man. Dir, Cadbury Bros Ltd and associated cos, 1919-59; Chm., Cadbury Bros Ltd, 1944-49 and of J. S. Fry & Sons Ltd, 1952-59; Dir, Bank of England, 1936-61. Director: British Cocoa & Chocolate Co. Ltd, 1920-59; Nation Proprietory Co. Ltd, Tyne Tees Television Ltd, 1958-67; Daily News Ltd; News Chronicle, 1930-60 and Star, 1930-60; Cocoa Investments Ltd, 1937-64; EMB Co. Ltd; Chm., Bournville Village Trust; Treasurer, Population Investigation Cttee, 1936-. Trustee, Historic Churches Preservation Trust (Exec. Cttee); Head, Economic Section, Mission to Moscow, 1941. High Sheriff of County of London, 1947-48 and 1959-60. Mons Medal; 1914 Star; Croix de Guerre. *Publications:* This Question of Population; numerous contribs to the press and periodicals on economics and demographic subjects. *Address:* The Davids, Northfield, Birmingham. *TA:* Birmingham, Priory 1441. *Clubs:* Athenæum, Oxford and Cambridge University, United Service; Leander (Henley); Hawks (Cambridge).
*See also G. A. H. Cadbury.*

**CADBURY, Paul Strangman,** CBE 1948; Chairman, Cadbury Bros Ltd, 1959-65; *b* 3 Nov. 1895; *s* of late Barrow Cadbury; *m* 1919, Rachel E. Wilson; two *s* two *d*. *Educ:* Leighton Park Sch., Reading. Friends' Ambulance Unit, 1915-19; Chm. Friends Ambulance Unit, 1939-48; Bournville Village Trust; Mem., Central Housing Advisory Cttee. *Publication:* Birmingham–Fifty Years On, 1952. *Address:* Low Wood, 32 St Mary's Road, Harborne, Birmingham 17. *T:* 021-427 0636. *Clubs:* Reform; Union (Birmingham).

**CADBURY, Peter (Egbert);** Chairman and Managing Director of: Westward Television Ltd since 1960; Keith Prowse & Co. Ltd since 1954; Chairman: Alfred Hays Ltd since 1955; Ashton & Mitchell Ltd since 1959; TTM Holdings Ltd; *b* Great Yarmouth, Norfolk, 6 Feb. 1918; *s* of late Sir Egbert Cadbury, DSC, DFC; *m* 1st, 1947, Eugenie Benedicta (marr. diss. 1968), *d* of late Major Ewen Bruce, DSO, MC and of Mrs Bruce; one *s* one *d*; 2nd, 1970, Mrs Jennifer Morgan-Jones, *d* of Major Michael Hammond-Maude, Ramsden, Oxon. *Educ:* Leighton Park Sch.; Trinity Coll., Cambridge (BA, MA). Called to Bar, Inner Temple, 1946; practised at Bar, 1946-54. Served Fleet Air Arm, 1940, until released to Ministry of Aircraft Production, 1942, as Research and Experimental Test Pilot; contested (L) Stroud (Glos), 1945. Member, London Travel Cttee, 1958-60; Dir, Willett Investments Ltd. Freeman of City of London, 1948. *Recreations:* theatre, golf and other games, motor cars. *Address:* Cruchfield Manor, near Bracknell, Berkshire. *T:* Winkfield Row 3282. *Clubs:* Garrick, Bath, MCC; Royal Western Yacht (Plymouth), Royal Motor Yacht, RAF Yacht.

**CADBURY-BROWN, Henry Thomas,** OBE 1967; TD; FRIBA; Hon. Fellow RCA; architect; *b* 20 May 1913; *s* of Henry William Cadbury-Brown and Marion Ethel Sewell; *m* 1953, Elizabeth Romeyn, *d* of Prof. A. Elwyn, Croton on Hudson, NY. *Educ:* Westminster Sch.; AA Sch. of Architecture (Hons Diploma). Architect in private practice since winning competition for British Railways Branch Offices, 1937. Work includes pavilions for "The Origins of the People", main concourse and fountain display at Festival of Britain; schools, Housing, display and interiors. Architect for new civic centre at Gravesend and halls for residence for Birmingham Univ. and, with Sir Hugh Casson and Prof. Robert Goodden, for new premises for Royal College of Art; awarded London Architecture Bronze Medal, 1963. Lecture halls for Univ. of Essex. Taught at Architectural Association Sch., 1946-49; Tutor at Royal Coll. of Art, 1952-61. Invited as Visiting Critic to Sch. of Architecture, Harvard Univ., 1956. Member: RIBA Council, 1951-53; British Cttee Internat. Union of Architects, 1951-54; MARS (Modern Architectural Research) group. Pres. Architectural Assoc., 1959-60. TA and military service, 1931-45; Major RA (TD). *Recreations:* numerous, including work. *Address:* 32 Neal Street, WC2. *T:* 01-240 3353; Church Walk, Aldeburgh, Suffolk. *T:* Aldeburgh 2591. *Club:* Naval and Military.

**CADE, Sir Stanford,** KBE 1946; CB 1944; FRCS, FRCP, FRCOG; Hon. DSc (Brit. Columbia); Hon. FRCSE; Hon. FRCSI; Hon. FACS; Hon. FFR; Hon. Consultant Surgeon, Westminster Hospital and Mount Vernon Hospital and Radium Institute; late Civilian Consultant in Surgery RAF; Consultant in Radiotherapeutics to the Army; Past Member: National Radium Commission; Grand Council and Vice-Chairman Executive Committee, British Empire Cancer Campaign; Chairman, Cancer and Radiotherapy Committee and late Member Standing Medical Advisory Committee, Ministry of Health; Member RAF Medical Advisory Board; *b* 22 March 1895; *y s* of Samuel Kadinsky, St Petersburgh, assumed name of Cade by deed poll, 1924; *m* 1920, Margaret Hester (*d* 1951), *e d* of late William Agate, MusB, FRCO, Paisley; three *d*. *Educ:* Bruxelles; King's Coll., London. Westminster Hospital Entrance Scholarship in Anatomy and Physiology, 1916; Bird Prize and Gold Medal and Chadwick Prize, 1917; MRCS, LRCP 1917; held all the resident appts and Surg. Registrar Westminster Hospital; FRCS 1923; MRCP 1941; FRCP 1960; FRCOG 1954. Hunterian Prof., RCS of England, 1925, 1933 and 1954; Arris and Gale Lectr, 1926; Bradshaw Lectr, 1960; Hunterian Orator, 1963; Walker Prize, RCS, 1966; late Mem. Council (Vice-Pres., Mem. Ct of Examiners and Dir of Surgical Studies), RCS. FRSocMed (Mem. Council, Pres. Surgical Section, 1950-51, and United Services Section, 1952-54, Hon. Fellow 1961, Nuffield Lectr 1962); Fellow Medical Soc. of London (Fothergillian Gold Medal, 1959) and Assoc. of Surgeons of Great Britain and Ireland. Formerly Examr in Surgery: Univs of Edinburgh, London, Bristol and Cambridge; Faculty of Radiology. Hon. Member: Assoc. Military Surgeons, USA; American Radium Soc. (Janeway Medal, 1948); New York Cancer Soc. and Soc. Head and Neck Surgeons, USA; Cancer Soc. of Chile; Société de Chir. de Lyon; Skinner Lectr, Faculty of Radiology, 1948; Crookshank Lectr, 1965; Blair-Bell Memorial Lectr, Liverpool, 1950; Mackenzie-Davidson Lectr and Medal, British Inst. Radiology, 1951; Dorothy Platt Lectr, King's College Hosp., London, 1956; Moynihan Lectr, Univ. of Leeds, 1957; Colles' Lectr and Medal, RCSI, 1960; Honeyman Gillespie Lectr, Edinburgh, 1961; Vis. Prof. of Surgery, Sheffield Univ., 1962; Frazer Lectr, Univ. of Edinburgh, 1966; Hon. Gold Medal, RCS, 1968. Pres., 7th Internat. Cancer Congress, London, 1958. Air Vice-Marshal RAFVR; Hon. Air Commodore Central Medical Estabt, RAF. Grand Officier, Order George I (Greece). *Publications:* numerous papers and articles and several books on cancer and various surgical subjects. *Address:* 102 Parkside House, Clarendon Gardens, Southsea, Hants. *T:* Portsmouth 27416.

**CADIEUX, Hon. Leo;** Ambassador of Canada to France, since 1970; *b* 28 May 1908; *s* of Joseph E. Cadieux and Rosa Paquette, both French Canadian; *m* 1962, Monique, *d* of Placide Plante; one *s*. *Educ:* Commercial Coll. of St Jerome and Seminary of Ste Therese de Blainville, Quebec. Editorial staff of La Presse, Montreal, Quebec, 1930-41; Associate Dir of Public Relations, Can. Army, 1941-44; War Corresp. for La Presse, Montreal, 1944; Mayor of St Antoine des Laurentides, Que., 1948. First elected to House of Commons, gen. elec., 1962; re-elected gen. elec., 1963, 1965, 1968; apptd Associate Minister of Nat. Defence, 1965; Minister of National Defence, Canada, 1967-70. *Address:* Ambassade du Canada, Paris, France; 85 Range Road, Ottawa, Canada; St Antoine des Laurentides, Que., Canada.

**CADMAN,** family name of **Baron Cadman.**

**CADMAN,** 3rd Baron *cr* 1937, of Silverdale; **John Anthony Cadman;** farmer since 1964; *b* 3 July 1938; *s* of 2nd Baron Cadman and Marjorie Elizabeth Bunnis; *S* father, 1966. *Educ:* Harrow; Selwyn Coll., Cambridge; Royal Agricultural Coll., Cirencester. *Heir: b* Hon. James Rupert Cadman, *b* 9 June 1944. *Address:* Eakley Manor Farm, Stoke



*

Goldington, Newport Pagnell, Bucks. *T:* Stoke Goldington 249.

**CADOGAN,** family name of **Earl Cadogan.**

**CADOGAN,** 7th Earl, *cr* 1800; **William Gerald Charles Cadogan,** MC 1943; DL; Baron Cadogan, 1718; Viscount Chelsea, 1800; Baron Oakley, 1831; Lieut-Colonel Royal Wiltshire Yeomanry, RAC; Captain Coldstream Guards R of O until 1964 (retaining hon. rank of Lieut-Colonel); *b* 13 Feb. 1914; *s* of 6th Earl and Lilian Eleanora Marie (who *m* 2nd, 1941, Lt-Col H. E. Hambro, CBE), *d* of George Coxon, Craigleith, Cheltenham; *S* father, 1933; *m* 1st, 1936, Hon. Primrose Lillian Yarde-Buller (from whom he obtained a divorce, 1959), *y d* of 3rd Baron Churston; one *s* three *d*; 2nd, 1961, Cecilia, *y d* of Lt-Col H. K. Hamilton-Wedderburn, OBE. *Educ:* Eton; RMC Sandhurst. Served war of 1939-45 (MC); Hereditary Trustee of the British Museum, 1935-63; Mem. Chelsea Borough Council, 1953-59; Mayor of Chelsea, 1964. DL County of London, 1958. *Heir: s* Viscount Chelsea, *qv. Address:* 28 Cadogan Square, SW1. *T:* 01-584 2335; Snaigow, Murthly, Perthshire. *T:* Caputh 223. *Club:* White's.

*See also Baron Lurgan, Baron Rockley.*

**CADOGAN, Prof. John Ivan George,** PhD, DSc London; FRIC, FRSE; Forbes Professor of Organic Chemistry, Edinburgh University, since 1969; *b* Pembrey, Carmarthenshire, 1930; *er s* of Alfred and Dilys Cadogan; *m* 1955, Margaret Jeanne, *d* of late William Evans, iron founder, Swansea; one *s* one *d*. *Educ:* Bishop Gore Grammar Sch., Swansea; King's Coll., London. Research at KCL, 1951-54. Civil Service Research Fellow, 1954-56; Lectr in Chemistry, King's Coll., London, 1956-63; Purdie Prof. of Chemistry and Head of Dept, St Salvator's Coll., Univ. of St Andrews, 1963-69. Samuel Smiles Prize, KCL, 1950; Millar Thomson Medallist, KCL, 1951; Meldola Medallist, Soc. of Maccabaeans and Royal Inst. of Chemistry, 1959; Corday-Morgan Medallist, Chem. Soc., 1965. *Publications:* numerous scientific papers, mainly in Jl Chem. Soc. *Address:* Department of Chemistry, The King's Buildings, West Mains Road, Edinburgh EH9 3JJ. *T:* 031-667 1011.

**CADWALLADER, Sir John,** Kt 1967; Chairman and Managing Director of Allied Mills Ltd since 1949; Chairman, Bushells Investments Ltd; Director, Queensland Insurance Co. Ltd; President, Bank of New South Wales, since 1959; *b* 25 Aug. 1902; *m* 1935, Helen Sheila Moxham; two *s* one *d*. *Educ:* Sydney Church of England Grammar Sch., NSW. *Recreations:* reading, tennis, golf, swimming. *Address:* 27 Marian Street, Killara, NSW, Australia. *T:* 49 1974. *Clubs:* Commonwealth (Canberra, ACT); Australian, Union, Royal Sydney Golf (all Sydney, NSW); Elanora Country (NSW).

**CADZOW, Sir Norman (James Kerr),** Kt 1959; VRD 1943; *s* of late William Cadzow and Jessie, *d* of James Kerr; *b* 21 Dec. 1912. *Educ:* Sedbergh Sch., Yorkshire. President, Unionist Party in Scotland, 1958; contested (U) Bothwell Div. of Lanarkshire, 1950 and 1951. Rector's Assessor, Glasgow Univ., 1959-63. Joined RNVR 1931, active service, 1939-45 (despatches). *Recreations:* golf and bridge. *Address:* Arden, Bothwell, Glasgow. *T:* Bothwell 3164. *Club:* Conservative (Chm. 1955 and 1970) (Glasgow).

**CÆSAR, Irving;** author-lyrist; Past President of Songwriters' Protective Association; Member Board of Directors, American Society of Composers, Authors and Publishers; *b* New York, 4 July 1895; *s* of Rumanian Jews. *Educ:* public school; Chappaqua Quaker Inst.; City Coll. of New York. Protégé of Ella Wheeler Wilcox, who, when he was a boy of nine, became interested in bits of verse he wrote and published at the time; at twenty became attached to the Henry Ford Peace Expedition, and spent nine months travelling through neutral Europe (during the War) as one of the secretaries of the Ford Peace Conference; returned to America, and became interested in writing for the musical comedy stage. *Publications:* most important work up to present time, No, No, Nanette; has written hundreds of songs and collaborated in many other musical comedies; writer and publisher of Sing a Song of Safety, a vol. of children's songs in use throughout the public and parochial schools of USA; also Sing a Song of Friendship, a series of songs based on human rights; in England: The Bamboula, Swanee, Tea for Two, I Want to be Happy, I Was So Young; author of "Peace by Wireless" proposal for freedom of international exchange of radio privilege between governments. *Recreations:* reading, theatre, swimming. *Address:* 1619 Broadway, New York City. *TA:* Cæsaring. *T:* Columbus 5-7868. *Clubs:* Friars, Green Room, City (New York).

**CAFFERY, Jefferson;** diplomat; Honorary Chamberlain to the Pope; *b* Lafayette, La, USA, 1 Dec. 1886; *s* of Charles Duval Caffery and Mary Catherine Parkerson; *m* 1937, Gertrude McCarthy. *Educ:* Tulane Univ., New Orleans (BA 1906; LLD 1968). Studied law privately, 1907-08; Admitted to Bar of Louisiana, 1909. Sec. of Legation, Caracas, 1911; Dept of State, 1913; Sec. of Legation, Stockholm, 1913; Teheran, 1916 (i/c Turkish and German interests, July, British and Italian interests, August); accompanied Special Kerensky Russian Mission to US, 1917; Embassy, Paris, 1917; special rep. of State Dept. on Permanent Inter-allied Commn on treatment and training disabled soldiers and sailors, 1917-22; Head American delegn to Internat. Conf., London, 1918; Sec., American section at Paris, 1919-22; detailed to Dept of State, 1919, for visits of foreign royalty; Counsellor of Embassy, Madrid, 1919; Mem. Board Examiners, Diplomatic Service Exam., Paris, 1919; Chargé d'Affaires *ad interim,* Athens, 1922; helped in assisting Greek refugees from Asia Minor, 1922; Counsellor of Embassy, Tokyo, 1923; Chm. American Red Cross earthquake relief, Japan, 1923-24; Counsellor of Embassy, Berlin, 1925; Minister to El Salvador, 1926; to Columbia, 1928; Rep. of Dept of State, El Salvador, 1931-32; Asst Sec. of State, 1933; Mem. Personnel Board of Foreign Service and Foreign Service Schools Board, 1933; US Ambassador: TO Cuba, 1934; to Brazil, 1937; to France, 1944-49; to Egypt, 1949-55; attended Potsdam Conf., 1945; US Delegn, Paris Peace Conf., 1946; Rep. of US Govt, European Recovery Plan, 1948. acting Dep. US Rep. on UN Security Council, 1948; several times special rep. of President or Govt of US (often with rank of Ambassador); has attended many conferences and has signed various treaties and international agreements; retd from Foreign Service, 1955. Holds several hon. degrees and hon. memberships. has received numerous US awards and medals, also foreign honours, citizenships, and decorations; Catholic Action medal for 1944; State Dept's Distinguished Service Award, 1950. *Recreations:* mountain climbing and riding. *Address:* c/o Fendrich Industries Inc., PO Box 3645, Evansville, Indiana 47701, USA. *Clubs:* Metropolitan, Dacor and Dacor House (Washington, DC); Jockey (Paris); Boston (New Orleans).

**CAFFIN, Albert Edward,** CIE 1947; OBE 1946; Indian Police (retired); *b* 16 June 1902; *s* of Claud Carter and Lilian Edith Caffin, Southsea; *m* 1929, Hilda Elizabeth Wheeler, Bournemouth; no *c. Educ:* Portsmouth. Joined Indian Police as Asst Supt, Bombay Province, 1922; Asst Inspector General, Poona, 1939; Dep. Comr, Bombay, 1944, Comr of Police, Bombay, 1947. *Recreations:* yachting, tennis, etc. *Address:* c/o Standard Bank of South Africa, PO Box 946, Durban, S Africa. *Club:* Royal Bombay Yacht.

**CAFFYN, Brig. Sir Edward (Roy),** KBE 1963 (CBE 1945; OBE 1942); CB 1955; TD 1950; DL; Chairman, County of Sussex Territorial and Auxiliary Forces Association, 1947-67; Vice-Chairman, Council of Territorial and Auxiliary Forces Associations, 1961-66; *b* 27 May 1904; *s* of Percy Thomas Caffyn, Eastbourne; *m* 1st, 1929, Elsa Muriel, *d* of William Henry Nurse, Eastbourne; two *s*; 2nd, 1946, Delphine Angelique, *d* of Major William Chilton-Riggs. *Educ:* Eastbourne and Loughborough Colleges. Commissioned RE (TA), 1930. Raised and commanded an Army Field Workshop, 1939; served with 51st Highland Division in France, 1940; Brigadier, 1941; a Deputy Director, War Office, on formation of REME, 1942; served on Field Marshal Montgomery's staff as Director of Mechanical Engineering (despatches twice), 1943-45. JP Eastbourne, 1948, transferred East Sussex, 1960; Chairman, Hailsham Bench, 1962-; DL Sussex, 1956; Chairman, Sussex Agricultural Wages Board, 1951-. CC for East Sussex, 1958-, Alderman, 1964, Vice-Chairman 1967. *Recreations:* shooting, golf and tennis. *Address:* Norman Norris, Vines Cross, Heathfield, East Sussex. *T:* Horam Road 2674. *Club:* Royal Automobile.

**CAFFYN, Sydney Morris,** CBE 1959; Chairman, 1942, and Joint Managing Director, 1938, Caffyns Ltd; *b* 22 July 1901; *s* of Percy Thomas Caffyn, Hay Tor, Eastbourne; *m* 1925, Annie, *d* of Alex Dawson, Turriff, Aberdeenshire; three *s* one *d. Educ:* Eastbourne Grammar Sch.; Royal Sch. of Mines, Imperial Coll. of Science and Technology, London Univ. Mem., Eastbourne Town Council, 1937-; Alderman, 1944, Mayor, 1956-58. Raised and commanded Sussex Recovery Company, HG, 1940-45, Major. Member: Gen. Purposes Cttee and Coun., British Employers Confedn, 1948-58; Nat. Jt Adv. Coun., Min. of Labour, 1951-59; Nat. Arbitration Tribunal, 1951-59; Civil Service Arbitration Tribunal, 1951-63; Industrial Court, 1959-; many *ad hoc* Tribunals and Courts of Enquiry; EDC for Retail Motor Trade, 1966-. Cttee on Training and Educn of Young Workers, 1956-58; Central Adv. Coun. for Educn (Eng.), 1957-63; Gas Industry Training Coun., 1965-66. Pres., Motor Agents, Assoc., 1948-50; Pres., British Motor Trade Assoc., 1953-54. Chm. of Council and Pro-Chancellor Univ. of Sussex; Chm. Governors: Chelsea Coll. of Physical Education; Eastbourne Coll. of Education. Convener, Finance and Administration Cttee of Presbyterian Church of England, 1966-; Treasurer, Nat. Free Church Federal Council, 1969-. Liveryman, Coachmakers and Coachharness Makers Company. Hon. DSc Sussex, 1963. *Recreations:* book-collecting, reading, concert and theatre going. *Address:* Aymond Grange, 12 Dittons Road, Eastbourne. *T:* Eastbourne 31118. *Clubs:* Athenæum, Royal Automobile.

**CAGE, Edward Edwin Henry;** General Manager, Craigavon Development Commission, since 1966; *b* 15 May 1912; *s* of Edward H. Cage and A. M. Windiate; *m* 1938, Hilda W. M. Barber; no *c. Educ:* Cannock House Sch., Eltham; King's Coll., London. Articles, Chartered Accts, 1929-34; Kent CC, 1935-41; Borough Councils: Dagenham, 1941-42; Willesden, 1942-44; Treas., Eton RDC, and Clerk, Jt Hosp Bd, 1944-47; Local Govt BC, 1947-48; Crawley Development Corp.: Chief Finance Officer, 1948-58, Gen. Manager, 1958-61; Chief Finance and Development Officer, Commn for New Towns, 1961-66. *Publications:* contrib. professional, etc., jls and newspapers. *Recreations:* golf, gardening. *Address:* Charters, Portadown Road, Tandragee, Co. Armagh, N Ireland. *T:* Tandragee 485. *Club:* English-Speaking Union.

**CAHAL, Dr Dennis Abraham;** Senior Principal Medical Officer, Department of Health and Social Security (formerly Ministry of Health), and Medical Assessor, Committee on Safety of Drugs, since 1963; *b* 1 Oct. 1921; *s* of Henry Cahal and Helen Wright; *m* 1948, Joan, *d* of Allan and Laura Grover; one *s. Educ:* Bradford Grammar Sch.; Univ. of Leeds. MB, ChB (Hons) Leeds, 1953; MD (Dist.) Leeds, 1959; MRCP 1968. RA, Indian Artillery and Special Allied Airborne Reconnaissance Force, 1939-46. Hospital appointments and general practice, 1953-55; Lecturer in Pharmacology, Univ. of Leeds, 1955-59; industrial research into drugs, 1959-62. Vis. Prof. of Pharmacology and Therapeutics, St Mary's Hosp. Med. Sch., London. *Publications:* various articles on drugs in scientific jls. *Recreations:* reading, metalwork. *Address:* 207 Merryhill Road, Bushey, Herts.

**CAHILL, Patrick Richard,** CBE 1970 (OBE 1944); Director and Chief Executive Officer, Legal & General Assurance Society Ltd; Managing Director, Gresham Life Assurance Society Ltd and Gresham Fire & Accident Insurance Society Ltd; *b* 21 Feb. 1912; *er s* of late Patrick Francis and Nora Christina Cahill; *m* 1st, 1949, Gladys Lilian May Kemp (*d* 1969); one *s*; 2nd, 1969, Mary Frances Pottinger. *Educ:* Hitchin Grammar Sch. Joined Legal & General Assurance Soc. Ltd, 1929; Pensions Manager, 1948; Agency Manager, 1952; Asst Manager, 1954; Asst General Manager, 1957. Served War with RASC, 1940-45 (despatches, OBE); N Africa, Italy, and N Europe, 1st, 7th and 11th Armd Divs; rank of Lt-Col. Director: Aviation & General Insurance Co. Ltd (Chm.); British Commonwealth Insurance Co. Ltd; Guinea Insurance Co. Ltd; Island (Piccadilly) Developments Ltd (Chm.); Watling Street Properties Ltd. A Vice-Pres., Chartered Insurance Inst., 1961-63, Dep. Pres., 1968, Pres., 1969; Pres., Insurance Charities, 1965-66; Chm., London Salvage Corps, 1964-65; Chm., British Insurance Assoc., 1967-69; Treasurer, Soc. for Protection of Life from Fire. Mem. Council, British Heart Foundation. Governor of Stowe School. *Publications:* various business papers and addresses. *Address:* 56 Northways, NW3. *T:* 01-722 7347; Thorndene, Pluckley, Kent. *T:* Pluckley 306. *Club:* Reform.

**CAHILL, Most Rev. Thomas;** *see* Canberra-Goulburn, Archbishop of, (RC).

**CAHN, Sir Albert Jonas,** 2nd Bt, *cr* 1934; Company Director; *b* 27 June 1924; *s* of Sir Julien Cahn, 1st Bt, and Phyllis Muriel, *d* of A. Wolfe, Bournemouth; *S* father, 1944; *m* 1948, Malka, *d* of late R. Bluestone; two *s* two *d. Educ:* Headmaster's House, Harrow. *Recreations:* cricket, horse riding, photography. *Heir: s* Julien Michael Cahn, *b* 15 Jan. 1951. *Address:* Crossways, 146 Coombe Lane West, Kingston Hill, Surrey. *T:* 01-942 6956.

**CAHN, Charles Montague,** CBE 1956; *b* 27 Dec. 1900; *yr s* of Gottfried Cahn and Lilian Juliet Cahn (*née* Montague); *m* 1939, Kathleen Rose, *d* of Auguste and Kathleen Thoumine; two *d*. *Educ:* Westminster Sch.; Christ Church, Oxford. BA 1923; MA 1968. Called to the Bar, Inner Temple, 1924. Served War of 1939-45 in Army (France and Middle East). Deputy Judge Advocate, 1945; Asst Judge Advocate-General, 1946; Deputy Judge Advocate-General, BAOR and RAF Germany (2 TAF), 1957-60; Vice Judge Advocate-General, 1963-67, retired 1967. Legal Chairman, Pensions Appeal Tribunal. *Recreation:* walking up and down hills. *Address:* Bowhill House, West Stoke, near Chichester, Sussex. *Club:* United University.

**CAIN;** *see* Nall-Cain.

**CAIN, Maj.-Gen. George Robert T.;** *see* Turner Cain.

**CAIN, Major Robert Henry,** VC 1944; late South Staffordshire Regiment; *b* 2 Jan. 1909; *s* of Robert James Cain, Douglas, Isle of Man; *m* 1941, Mary Denise Addison; one *s* three *d*. *Educ:* King William's Coll., Isle of Man. Served War of 1939-45 in N Africa, Sicily, Italy, Arnhem (VC) and Norway. *Address:* Stack House, Oxted, Surrey.

**CAINE, Sir Derwent Hall,** 1st Bt *cr* 1937; Kt 1933; *b* 12 Sept. 1891; *s* of late Sir Hall Caine, CH, KBE. *Educ:* Isle of Man; Eastbourne. Subsequently Chairman, News Letter Ltd; also Argosy and Sundial Libraries Ltd; Founder and late Man. Dir, The Readers' Library Publishing Co. Ltd; contested Parliamentary Divisions of Reading 1922, Clitheroe 1924, and Everton (Nat Lab) 1931; MP (Lab) Everton Division of Liverpool, 1929-31. *Recreations:* motoring, golf, flying. *Address:* Greeba Castle, Isle of Man.

**CAINE, Sir Sydney,** KCMG 1947 (CMG 1945); Governor (new board) of the Reserve Bank of Rhodesia, 1965-67; Director of the London School of Economics and Political Science, 1957-Sept. 1967; *b* 27 June 1902; *s* of Harry Edward Caine; *m* 1st, 1925, Muriel Anne (*d* 1962), *d* of A. H. Harris, MA; one *s*; 2nd, 1965, Doris Winifred Folkard. *Educ:* Harrow County Sch.; London Sch. of Economics. BSc (Econ.) 1st Class Hons 1922. Asst Inspector of Taxes, 1923-26; entered Colonial Office, 1926; Sec., West Indian Sugar Commn, 1929; Sec., UK Sugar Industry Inquiry Cttee, 1934; Fin. Sec., Hong Kong, 1937; Asst Sec., Colonial Office, 1940; Member Anglo-American Caribbean Commission, 1942; Financial Adviser to Sec. of State for the Colonies, 1942; Assistant Under-Secretary of State, Colonial Office, 1944; Deputy Under-Secretary of State, Colonial Office, 1947-48; Third Secretary, Treasury, 1948; Head of UK Treasury and Supply Delegn, Washington, 1949-51; Mem., Financial Mission to Ceylon, 1951; Vice-Chancellor, Univ. of Malaya, 1952-56. Chairman: British Caribbean Federation Fiscal Commission, 1955; Internat. Inst. of Educational Planning, 1963; Planning Bd of Independent Univ., 1969-. Mem., ITA, 1960-67 (Dep. Chm., 1964-67). Hon. LLD, Univ. of Malaya, 1956. *Publications:* The Foundation of the London School of Economics, 1963; British Universities: Purpose and Prospects, 1969. *Recreations:* reading, walking. *Address:* Soke Farm, Silchester, near Reading, Berks. *Club:* Reform.

**CAIRD, Rev. George Bradford,** MA(Cantab), DPhil, DD(Oxon); Principal of Mansfield College, Oxford, since 1970; Reader in Biblical Studies, Oxford University, since 1969; *b* 19 July 1917; *s* of George Caird and Esther Love Caird (*née* Bradford), both of Dundee; *m* 1945, Viola Mary Newport; three *s* one *d*. *Educ:* King Edward's Sch., Birmingham; Peterhouse, Cambridge; Mansfield Coll., Oxford. Minister of Highgate Congregational Church, London, 1943-46; Prof. of OT Lang. and Lit., St Stephen's Coll., Edmonton, Alberta, 1946-50; Prof. of NT Lang. and Lit., McGill Univ., Montreal, 1950-59; Principal, United Theological Coll., Montreal, 1955-59; Sen. Tutor, Mansfield Coll., Oxford, 1959-70. Grinfield Lecturer on the Septuagint, Oxford Univ., 1961-65. Hon. DD: St Stephen's Coll., Edmonton, 1959; Diocesan Coll., Montreal, 1959; Aberdeen Univ., 1966. *Publications:* The Truth of the Gospel, 1950; The Apostolic Age, 1955; Principalities and Powers, 1956; The Gospel according to St Luke, 1963; The Revelation of St John the Divine, 1966; Our Dialogue with Rome, 1967; contribs to: Interpreter's Dictionary of the Bible; Hastings Dictionary of the Bible; Jl of Theological Studies; New Testament Studies; Expository Times. *Recreations:* bird-watching, chess, music. *Address:* Principal's Lodgings, Mansfield College, Oxford. *T:* Oxford 42340.

**CAIRNCROSS, Sir Alexander Kirkland,** (known as Sir Alec Cairncross), KCMG 1967 (CMG 1950); FBA 1961; Master of St Peter's College, Oxford, since 1969; *b* 11 Feb. 1911; 3rd *s* of Alexander Kirkland and Elizabeth Anderson Cairncross, Lesmahagow, Scotland; *m* 1943, Mary Frances Glynn; three *s* two *d*. *Educ:* Hamilton Academy; Glasgow and Cambridge Univs. Univ. Lectr, 1935-39; Civil Servant, 1940-45; Dir of Programmes, Min. of Aircraft Production, 1945; Economic Advisory Panel, Berlin, 1945-46; Mem. of Staff of The Economist, 1946. Mem. of Wool Working Party, 1946; Economic Adviser to Board of Trade, 1946-49; Economic Adviser to Organisation for European Economic Co-operation, 1949-50; Prof. of Applied Economics, Univ. of Glasgow, 1951-61; Dir, Economic Development Inst., Washington DC, 1955-56; Economic Adviser to HM Govt, 1961-64; Head of Govt Economic Service, 1964-69. Chm., Local Development Cttee, 1951-52; Member: Crofting Commn, 1951-54; Phillips Cttee, 1953-54; Anthrax Cttee, 1957-59; Radcliffe Cttee, 1957-59; Coun. of Management, Nat. Inst. of Economic and Social Research; Coun. of Management, PEP; Court of Governors, London Sch. of Economics; Council, Royal Economic Soc. (Pres., 1968-70). President: Scottish Economic Soc., 1969-71; Section F, British Assoc. for Advancement of Science, 1969; British Assoc. for Advancement of Science, 1970-71. Editor, Scottish Journal of Political Economy, 1954-61. Hon. LLD: Mount Allison Univ., 1962; Glasgow Univ., 1966; Exeter Univ., 1969; Hon. DLitt: Reading Univ., 1968; Heriot-Watt Univ., 1969. *Publications:* Introduction to Economics, 1944; Home and Foreign Investment, 1870-1913, 1953; Monetary Policy in a Mixed Economy, 1960; Economic Development and the Atlantic Provinces, 1961; Factors in Economic Development, 1962. *Recreations:* colour photography, travel. *Address:* The Master's Lodgings, St Peter's College, Oxford. *T:* Oxford 40554. *Club:* United University.

**CAIRNCROSS, Neil Francis;** a Deputy Secretary, Cabinet Office, since 1970; *b* 29 July 1920; *s* of late James and Olive Hunter Cairncross; *m* 1947, Eleanor Elizabeth Leisten; two *s* one *d*. *Educ:* Charterhouse; Oriel Coll., Oxford. Royal Sussex Regt, 1940-45. Called to the Bar, 1948. Home Office, 1948; a Private Sec. to the Prime Minister, 1955-58; Sec., Royal Commn on the Press, 1961-62;

Asst Under-Sec. of State, Home Office, 1967-70. *Recreations:* painting, gardening. *Address:* 28 Cassiobury Park Avenue, Watford, Herts. *T:* Watford 23856. *Club:* Oxford and Cambridge University.

**CAIRNS,** family name of **Earl Cairns.**

**CAIRNS,** 5th Earl, *cr* 1878; **David Charles Cairns,** KCVO 1969; CB 1960; Rear-Admiral; Baron Cairns, 1867; Viscount Garmoyle, 1878; Her Majesty's Marshal of the Diplomatic Corps, since 1962; *b* 3 July 1909; *s* of 4th Earl and Olive (*d* 1952), *d* of late J. P. Cobbold, MP; *S* father, 1946; *m* 1936, Barbara Jeanne Harrisson, *y d* of Sydney H. Burgess, Heathfield, Altrincham, Cheshire; two *s* one *d. Educ:* RNC Dartmouth. Served War of 1939-45 (despatches); Dep. Dir, Signal Dept, Admiralty, 1950, comd 7th Frigate Sqdn, 1952; HMS Ganges, 1953-54; Student Imperial Defence Coll., 1955; comd HMS Superb, 1956-57; Baghdad Pact Plans and Training Div., Admiralty, 1958; Pres., RNC Greenwich, 1958-61; retired. Pres., Navy League, 1966. *Heir: s* Viscount Garmoyle, *qv. Address:* St James's Palace, SW1. *T:* 01-930 4749; Clopton Hall, near Woodbridge, Suffolk. *T:* Grundisburgh 248. *Club:* Turf.

**CAIRNS, Rt. Hon. Sir David (Arnold Scott),** PC 1970; Kt 1955; **Rt. Hon. Lord Justice Cairns;** a Lord Justice of Appeal, since 1970; Bencher, Middle Temple, since 1958; *b* 5 March 1902; *s* of late David Cairns, JP, Freeman of Sunderland, and late Sarah Scott Cairns; *m* 1932, Irene Cathery Phillips; one *s* two *d. Educ:* Bede Sch., Sunderland; Pembroke Coll., Cambridge (Scholar); Senior Optime. MA, LLB (Cantab); BSc (London); Certificate of Honour, Bar Final, 1925. called to Bar, Middle Temple, 1926. KC 1947. Liberal Candidate at By-election, Epsom Div., 1947. Mem. of Leatherhead UDC, 1948-54; Chm., Liberal Party Commn on Trade Unions, 1948-49; Mem. of Liberal Party Cttee, 1951-53; Chm., Monopolies and Restrictive Practices Commn, 1954-56; Recorder of Sunderland, 1957-60; Comr of Assize, 1957 (Midland Circuit), May 1959 (Western Circuit), Nov. 1959 (Wales and Chester Circuit); Judge of the High Court, Probate, Divorce and Admiralty Div., 1960-70. Chairman: Statutory Cttee of Pharmaceutical Soc. of Great Britain, 1952-60; Executive of Justice (British Section of International Commn of Jurists), 1959-60; Minister of Aviation's Cttee on Accident Investigation and Licence Control, 1959-60; Govt Adv. Cttee on Rhodesian Travel Restrictions, 1968-69. *Recreations:* swimming, gardening. *Address:* Applecroft, Ashtead, Surrey. *T:* Ashtead 4132; 2 Essex Court, Temple, EC4. *T:* 01-353 3750. *Clubs:* Reform, National Liberal.

**CAIRNS, Julia, (Mrs Paul Davidson);** writer and lecturer; Vice-President: London and Overseas Flower Arrangement Society; Society of Women Writers and Journalists; *o c* of late H. W. Akers, Oxford; *m* 1st, 1915, Frank H. James, The Royal Scots; 2nd, 1925, Capt. Paul Davidson, late 12th Royal Lancers (*d* 1942). *Educ:* Oxford. Entered journalism as a free-lance; Woman Editor of The Ideal Home, 1924; House and Home Director of Woman's Journal, 1927; Editor-in-Chief Weldons Publications, 1929-55; Home Editor, The Queen, 1956-58. President Women's Press Club of London Ltd, 1947 and 1948. *Publications:* Home-Making, 1950; How I Became a Journalist, 1960. *Recreation:* gardening. *Club:* University Women's.

**CAITHNESS,** 20th Earl of, *cr* 1455; **Malcolm Ian Sinclair;** Baron Berriedale, 1455; Bt 1631; *b* 3 Nov. 1948; *s* of 19th Earl of Caithness, CVO, CBE, DSO, DL, JP; *S* father, 1965. *Educ:* Marlborough. *Heir: kinsman* Sir John Sinclair, Bt, *qv. Address:* Hampton Court Palace, East Molesey, Surrey.

**CALCUTTA, Archbishop of, (RC),** since 1969; **Most Rev. Lawrence Trevor Picachy,** SJ; *b* 7 Aug. 1916; Indian. *Educ:* St Joseph's College, Darjeeling and various Indian Seminaries. 1952-60: Headmaster of St Xavier's School, Principal of St Xavier's College, Rector of St Xavier's, Calcutta. Parish Priest of Basanti, large village of West Bengal, 1960-62; (first) Bishop of Jamshedpur, 1962-69, Apostolic Administrator of Jamshedpur, 1969-70. *Address:* Archbishop's House, 32 Park Street, Calcutta 16. *T:* Calcutta 44-4666.

**CALCUTTA, Bishop of,** since 1962; **Most Rev. Hiyanirindu Lakdasa Jacob De Mel,** DD; Metropolitan of the Church of India, Pakistan, Burma and Ceylon since 1962; *b* 24 March 1902; *e s* of late Sir Henry De Mel, Colombo, Ceylon. *Educ:* The Royal Coll., Colombo; Keble Coll.; Cuddesdon Coll., Oxford (MA). Curate, St John the Divine, Kennington, 1926; Curate, St Paul's, Kandy, 1927; Incumbent, Christ Church, Baddegame, 1929; Vicar, St Paul's, Kandy, 1940; Officiating Chaplain, 34 Indian Div., 1942-45; Asst Bishop of Colombo, 1945; Bishop of Kurunagala, 1950. Hon. DD: Univ. of King's Coll., Halifax, 1956; Trinity Coll., Toronto, 1956; Wycliffe Coll., Toronto, 1963. *Publications:* contributor, Sinhalese Encyclopædia. *Recreations:* archaeology, art, music. *Address:* Bishop's House, 51 Chowringhee Road, Calcutta 16, India.

**CALDECOTE,** 2nd Viscount *cr* 1939, of Bristol; **Robert Andrew Inskip;** DSC 1941; Executive Director, Delta Metal Co.; Chairman, Enfield Cables Ltd; *b* 8 Oct. 1917; *o s* of Thomas Walker Hobart Inskip, 1st Viscount Caldecote, PC, CBE, and Lady Augusta Orr Ewing (*d* 1967), *widow* of Charles Orr Ewing, MP for Ayr Burghs and *e d* of 7th Earl of Glasgow; *S* father, 1947; *m* 1942, Jean Hamilla, *d* of late Rear-Adm. H. D. Hamilton; one *s* two *d. Educ:* Eton Coll.; King's Coll., Cambridge. BA Cantab 1939; MA 1944. Served War of 1939-45, with RNVR, 1939-45; RNC Greenwich, 1946-47; an Asst Manager, Vickers-Armstrong Naval Yard, Walker-on-Tyne, 1947-48; Mem., Church Assembly, 1950-55; Fellow, King's Coll., and Lectr, Engineering Dept, Cambridge Univ., 1948-55; Man. Dir, English Electric Aviation, 1960-63; Dep. Man. Dir, British Aircraft Corp., 1961-67 (Dir, 1960-69); Director: English Electric Co., 1953-69; D. Napier & Son Ltd, 1959-69; Dorman Diesels Iran, 1968-69; Cincinnati Milling Machine, 1969-; Consolidated Gold Fields, 1969-. Chairman: EDC Movement of Exports, 1965-; Export Council for Europe, 1970-. President: Soc. of British Aerospace Cos, 1965-66; Internat. Assoc. of Aeronautical and Space Equipment Manufacturers, 1966-68; Parliamentary and Scientific Cttee, 1966-69. Mem. UK Delegn to UN, 1952; Fellow, Eton Coll.; Pres., Dean Close Sch.; Governor, St Lawrence Coll. CEng, FIMechE; FIEE; AMRINA; FRAeS. *Recreations:* sailing, shooting, golf. *Heir: s* Hon. Piers James Hampden Inskip, *b* 20 May 1947. *Address:* Debden Manor, Saffron Walden, Essex. *T:* Saffron Walden 3231. *Clubs:* Pratt's, Boodle's; Royal Ocean Racing, Royal Yacht Squadron.

**CALDER;** *see* Ritchie-Calder.

**CALDER, Alexander;** sculptor; *b* 22 July 1898; *s* of A. Stirling Calder and Nanette Lederer; *m* 1931, Louisa James; two *d. Educ:* Putney Sch., Putney, Vermont, USA. Graduated as Mech.

Engineer, Stevens Inst. of Technology, 1919; various engineering jobs, 1923; Art Students' League, NYC, 1924; lived in Paris, on and off, 1926-33; subsequently domiciled in France. Retrospective exhibn, Gimpel Fils, 1969. Sculpture Award, Venice Biennale, 1952; several architectural medals, etc. *Publications:* Fables d'Æsop, 1931; Three Young Rats, 1944; also Ancient Mariner; Fables de la Fontaine; Bestiary. *Recreations:* swimming, dancing, drinking. *Address:* Roxbury, Conn, USA; Saché, Indre et Loire, France.

**CALDER, James William,** OBE 1957; CEng, FIMinE; HM Chief Inspector of Mines and Quarries since Nov. 1970; *b* Hamilton, Lanarkshire, 20 June 1914; *s* of late Henry Stewart Calder and late Mary McKinlay Calder; *m* 1941, Eileen Elizabeth McLeod; one *d. Educ:* Dunfermline; Edinburgh Univ. BSc Hons, Mining and Metallurgy, 1938; 1st cl. Colliery Manager's Certif., 1939. Served with Fife Coal Co. Ltd and Lochgelly Iron and Coal Co. Ltd, HM Junior Inspector of Mines and Quarries, North Staffordshire, 1941; served in N Wales and Yorkshire; Dist. Inspector, 1946; Sen. Dist. Inspector, 1950; Divisional Inspector: NW Div., 1962; E Midlands Div., 1963; Dep. Chief Inspector of Mines and Quarries, Headquarters, 1967-70. *Publication:* Divisional Inspector's Annual Report, 1963-66 (inclusive). *Recreations:* farming, bird watching, walking, golf. *Address:* 56 Belgravia Court, Ebury Street, SW1. *T:* 01-730 1318; Keith Hills, Fossoway, Kinross, Scotland. *T:* Fossoway 317.

**CALDER, Sir John Alexander,** KCMG 1947 (CMG 1939); MA; *b* 20 Oct. 1889; *s* of Robert Calder, ISO, JP, HM Inspector of Schools, and May Drummond Alexander; *m* 1st, 1915, Phoebe Robertson McCartney Stuart (*d* 1964); no *c*; 2nd, 1966, Mrs Mary E. Saville. *Educ:* Grove and Harris Academies, Dundee; Edinburgh Univ. (MA). 1st Class Hons History, 1911; 1st Class Hons Philosophy, 1912. Appointed to Colonial Office 1912; military service Sept.-Dec. 1918; Sec. to E African Parliamentary Commn, Aug.-Dec. 1924; Asst Sec., Colonial Office, 1933; Principal Asst Sec., Min. of Supply, 1942; Third Crown Agent for the Colonies, 1942-43; Second Crown Agent, 1943; Senior Crown Agent for the Colonies, 1943-53; retired 1953. *Recreations:* golf, chess. *Address:* Gordon House, Ridgemount Road, Sunningdale, Berks. *T:* Ascot 21405. *Club:* Sunningdale Golf.

**CALDER, John Mackenzie;** Managing Director, Calder & Boyars Ltd (originally John Calder (Publishers) Ltd), since 1950; *b* 25 Jan. 1927; *e s* of James Calder, Ardargie, Forgandenny, Perthshire, and Lucianne Wilson, Montreal, Canada; *m* 1st, 1949, Mary Ann Simmonds; one *d*; 2nd, 1960, Bettina Jonic; one *d. Educ:* Gilling Castle, Yorks; Bishops College Sch., Canada; McGill Univ.; Sir George Williams Coll.; Zürich Univ. Studied political economy; subseq. worked in Calders Ltd (timber co.), Director; resigned, 1957, after takeover by Great Universal Stores; founded John Calder (Publishers) Ltd, 1950 (run as a hobby until 1957; name changed to Calder & Boyars Ltd, 1965). Organiser of literary confs for Edinburgh Festival, 1962 and 1963, and Harrogate Festival, 1969. Founded Ledlanet Nights, 1963, in Kinross-shire (four seasons per year, opera, drama, music, etc). Acquired book-selling business of Better Books, London, 1969. Active in fields related to the arts and on many cttees; Sec., Defence of Literature and the Arts Society. Contested (L) Kinross and W Perthshire, 1970. *Publications:* (ed) A Samuel Beckett Reader; (ed) Beckett at 60, etc; articles in many jls. *Recreations:* writing (several plays, stories; criticism, etc; translations); music, theatre, opera, reading; lecturing, conversation; skiing, travelling, promoting good causes, fond of good food and wine. *Address:* c/o Calder & Boyars Ltd, 18 Brewer Street, W1. *Clubs:* Caledonian, Hurlingham; Scottish Arts (Edinburgh).

**CALDER, Air Vice-Marshal Malcolm Frederick,** CB 1957; CBE 1947; Chief of Air Staff, RNZAF, since 1958; Chairman, New Zealand Chiefs of Staff Committee, 1960-62, retired; *b* 1907; *s* of late Andrew Calder; *m* 1935, Margaret Emily, *d* of Henry Mandeno, architect, Dunedin, NZ; one *s* one *d. Educ:* Christ Church Boys' High Sch., NZ; University Coll., Canterbury, NZ (LLB). Joined RAF, 1931; RNZAF, 1939; served War of 1939-45 in NZ and Pacific; Air Member for Personnel, Air Board, NZ, 1945-47, and 1952-53; Air Commodore 1952; NZ Senior Air Liaison Officer, London, 1954-56; served in Malaya, 1957-58. *Recreations:* fishing and golf. *Address:* Herekiekie Street, Turangi, New Zealand. *Club:* United Services (Wellington, NZ).

**CALDER, Nigel David Ritchie,** MA; science writer; *b* 2 Dec. 1931; *e s* of Baron Ritchie-Calder, *qv*; *m* 1954, Elisabeth Palmer; two *s* three *d. Educ:* Merchant Taylors' Sch.; Sidney Sussex Coll., Cambridge. Physicist, Mullard Research Laboratories, 1954-56; Editorial staff, New Scientist, 1956-66; Science Editor, 1960-62; Editor, 1962-66. Science Correspondent, New Statesman, 1959-62 and 1966-; Chairman, Assoc. of British Science Writers, 1962-64. *Publications:* Electricity Grows Up, 1958; Robots, 1958; Radio Astronomy, 1958; (ed) The World in 1984, 1965; The Environment Game, 1967; (ed) Unless Peace Comes, 1968; Technopolis: Social Control of the Uses of Science, 1969; The Violent Universe (TV programme and book), 1970; Living Tomorrow, 1970; The Mind of Man (TV programme and book), 1970. *Recreation:* sailing. *Address:* 8 The Chase, Furnace Green, Crawley, Sussex. *T:* Crawley 26693. *Club:* Athenæum.

**CALDER, Ritchie;** *see* Ritchie-Calder, Baron.

**CALDER-MARSHALL, Arthur;** author; *b* 19 Aug. 1908; *s* of late Arthur Grotjan Calder-Marshall and Alice Poole; *m* 1934, Violet Nancy Sales; two *d. Educ:* St Paul's Sch.; Hertford Coll., Oxford. *Publications: novels:* Two of a Kind; About Levy; At Sea; Dead Centre; Pie in the Sky; The Way to Santiago; A Man Reprieved; Occasion of Glory; The Scarlet Boy; *for children:* The Man from Devil's Island; The Fair to Middling; Lone Wolf; The Story of Jack London; *travel:* Glory Dead; The Watershed; *Biography:* No Earthly Command; Havelock Ellis; The Enthusiast; The Innocent Eye; *art:* Wish You Were Here: the art of Donald McGill; *autobiography:* The Magic of My Youth; *criticism:* Prepare to Shed Them Now: the Ballads of George R. Sims. *Address:* c/o Elaine Greene Ltd, 42 Great Russell Street, WC1. *Clubs:* Savile, National Liberal.

**CALDERBANK, Professor Philip Hugh;** Professor of Chemical Engineering, University of Edinburgh, since 1960; *b* 6 March 1919; *s* of Leonard and Rhoda Elizabeth Calderbank; *m* 1941, Kathleen Mary (*née* Taylor); one *s* one *d. Educ:* Palmer's Sch., Gray's, Essex; King's Coll., London Univ. Research and Development Chemist: Ministry of Supply, 1941-44; Bakelite Ltd, 1944-47. Lecturer in Chemical Engineering Dept,

University Coll., London University, 1947-53; Professor in Chem. Engineering Dept, University of Toronto, 1953-56; Senior Principal Scientific Officer, Dept of Scientific and Industrial Research, 1956-60. *Publications:* contributor: Chemical Engineering Progress; Transactions Instn of Chemical Engineers; Chemical Engineering Science. *Recreations:* reading; experimental research. *Address:* Chemical Engineering Laboratories, University of Edinburgh, Mayfield Road, Edinburgh 9. *T:* 031-667 1011.

**CALDICOTT, Hon. Sir John Moore,** KBE 1963; CMG 1955; *b* 1900; *m* 1945, Evelyn Macarthur; one *s* two step *d*. *Educ:* Shrewsbury School. Joined RAF 1918. Came to Southern Rhodesia, 1925; farmed in Umvukwes District ever since. President: Rhodesia Tobacco Assoc., 1943-45; Rhodesia National Farmers' Union, 1946-48. MP for Mazoe, S Rhodesia Parliament, 1948; Minister of Agriculture and Lands, 1951, of Agriculture, Health and Public Service, 1953, of Economic Affairs, 1958-62, of The Common Market, 1962, and of Finance, until 1963, Federation of Rhodesia and Nyasaland. *Address:* Chigudu, PO Box 37, Umvukwes, Rhodesia. *Club:* Salisbury (Salisbury, Rhodesia).

**CALDWELL, Surgeon Vice-Adm. Sir Dick;** *see* Caldwell, Sir E. D.

**CALDWELL, Surg. Vice-Adm. Sir (Eric) Dick,** KBE 1969; CB 1965; Medical Director-General of the Navy, 1966-69, retired; *b* 6 July 1909; *s* of late Dr John Colin Caldwell; *m* 1942, Margery Lee Abbott. *Educ:* Edinburgh Acad.; Edinburgh Univ. MB, ChB Edinburgh 1933; LRCP, LRCSE, LRFPS(G) 1933; MD Edinburgh 1950; MRCPE 1956; FRCPE 1962; FRCP 1967. Joined Royal Navy, 1934. Served War of 1939-45 in Atlantic, Mediterranean and Pacific. Medical Specialist, RN Hosp., Hong Kong, 1947; Staff MO to Flag Officer, Malta, 1958; Sen. Med. Specialist at RN Hosp., Haslar; MO i/c of RN Hosp., Plymouth, 1963-66. Surg. Capt. 1957; RN Consultant in Medicine, 1962; Surg. Rear-Adm. 1963; Surg. Vice-Adm. 1966. QHP 1963-69. Gilbert Blane Gold Medal, 1962; FRSocMed. CStJ. *Recreations:* golf, tennis, trying to write. *Address:* 9A Holland Park Road, Kensington, W14. *T:* 01-937 7059. *Club:* Army and Navy.

**CALDWELL, Erskine;** author; Editor of American Folkways, 1940-55; Member: Authors' League; American PEN; (Hon.) National Institute of Arts and Letters; *b* 17 Dec. 1903; *s* of Ira Sylvester Caldwell and Caroline Preston Bell; *m* 1st, 1925, Helen Lannigan; two *s* one *d*; 2nd, 1939, Margaret Bourke-White; 3rd, 1942, June Johnson; one *s*; 4th, 1957, Virginia Moffett Fletcher. *Educ:* Erskine Coll.; Univ. of Virginia. Newspaper reporter on Atlanta (Ga) Journal; motion picture screen writer in Hollywood; newspaper and radio correspondent in Russia. *Publications:* The Bastard, 1929; Poor Fool, 1930; American Earth, 1931; Tobacco Road, 1932; God's Little Acre, 1933; We Are the Living, 1933; Journeyman, 1935; Kneel to the Rising Sun, 1935; Some American People, 1935; You Have Seen Their Faces, 1937; Southways, 1938; North of The Danube, 1939; Trouble in July, 1940; Jackpot, 1940; Say! Is This the USA?, 1941; All-Out on the Road to Smolensk, 1942; Moscow Under Fire, 1942; All Night Long, 1942; Georgia Boy, 1943; Tragic Ground, 1944; Stories, 1945; A House in the Uplands, 1946; The Sure Hand of God, 1947; This Very Earth, 1948; Place Called Estherville, 1949; Episode in Palmetto, 1950; Call It Experience, 1951; The Courting of Susie Brown, 1952; A Lamp for Nightfall, 1952; The Complete Stories of Erskine Caldwell, 1953; Love and Money, 1954; Gretta, 1955; Gulf Coast Stories, 1956; Certain Women, 1957; Molly Cottontail, 1958 (juvenile); Claudelle Inglish, 1959; When You Think of Me, 1959; Jenny By Nature, 1961; Close to Home, 1962; The Last Night of Summer, 1963; Around About America, 1964; In Search of Bisco, 1965; The Deer at Our House (juvenile), 1966; In the Shadow of the Steeple, 1966; Miss Mamma Aimee, 1967; Writing In America, 1967; Deep South, 1968; Summertime Island, 1968; The Weather Shelter, 1969. *Address:* c/o McIntosh & Otis Inc., 18 East 41st Street, New York, NY 10017, USA. *T:* New York: MU 9-1050; (home) PO Box 820, Dunedin, Fla 33528, USA. *Clubs:* Overseas Press (New York); Phoenix Press (Phoenix, Arizona); Press and Union League (San Francisco, Calif).

**CALDWELL, Prof. John,** PhD, DSc; Head of Department of Botany, University College and University of Exeter, 1935-69; Director, Hatherly Biological Laboratories 1952-69; Dean of Science, 1938-42 and 1951-54; Deputy Vice-Chancellor, 1957-59; *b* 8 May 1903; *s* of late Peter and Emily Caldwell, Ayr; *m* 1941, Christine Natalie, 2nd *d* of J. H. Hayes, East Harting, Sussex; three *d*. *Educ:* Kilmarnock Acad.; Univ. of Glasgow (Robert Donaldson Student); Univ. of Cambridge. PhD 1929, DSc 1935, Glasgow; PhD Cantab, 1931. Virus Physiologist, Rothamsted Experimental Station, Harpenden, 1929-35; Min. of Agriculture Travelling Fellow, Canada and USA, 1935. Chm., SW Region Careers Advisory Council (Min. of Labour), 1952-; Chm. Management Cttee, Nat. Allotments and Gardens Soc., 1956-62. President: Devonshire Assoc., 1969-70; SW Naturalists' Union, 1969. governor: Long Ashton and National Vegetable Research Stations. *Publications:* numerous papers on plant physiology and virus studies in scientific jls. *Recreations:* gardening, bee-keeping. *Address:* St Germans Lodge, St Germans Road, Exeter. *T:* Exeter 55675.

**CALDWELL, John Foster,** CB 1952; *b* 3 May 1892; *er s* of Charles Sproule Caldwell, Solicitor, Londonderry, and Jeannie Hamilton Foster; *m* 1921, Flora, *yr d* of H. P. Grosse, AMIEE, Belfast and Portrush; one *d*. *Educ:* Foyle Coll., Londonderry; Trinity Coll., Dublin; King's Inns, Dublin. Called to the Bar, 1925; KC (N Ireland) 1946. First Parliamentary Draftsman to the Govt of Northern Ireland, 1945-56; Consolidator of Statute Law, N Ireland, 1956-59; former Member County Court Rules Cttee and Statute Law Cttee, N Ireland; Chief Parliamentary Counsel, Jamaica, 1959-61; Senior Legal Asst, Colonial Office, 1961-62. LLM *hc* Queen's Univ. of Belfast, 1957. *Address:* 40 Marlborough Park South, Belfast 9. *T:* 666917.

**CALDWELL, Taylor, (Janet Miriam Taylor Caldwell),** FIAL; writer; *b* Prestwich, Manchester, England, 7 Sept. 1900; Scots parentage; citizen of USA; *m* 1st, William Fairfax Combs; one *d*; 2nd, Marcus Reback; one *d*. *Educ:* Univ. of Buffalo, Buffalo, NY. Wrote many years before publication. Formerly Sec. of Board of Special Inquiry, US Dept of Immigration and Naturalization, Buffalo, NY. Many awards and citations, national and international, including National Award, Nat. League of American Penwomen (gold medal), 1948, Grande Prix, Prix Chatrain, Paris, 1956, Award of Merit, Daughters of the American Revolution, 1956; McElligott Medal, Marquette Univ., Milwaukee. *Publications:* Dynasty of Death,

1938; The Eagles Gather, 1939; The Earth is the Lord's, 1940; The Strong City, 1941; The Arm and the Darkness, 1942; The Turnbulls, 1943; The Final Hour, 1944; The Wide House, 1945; This Side of Innocence, 1946; There Was a Time, 1947; Melissa, 1948; Let Love Come Last, 1949; The Balance Wheel, 1951; The Devil's Advocate, 1952; Never Victorious, Never Defeated, 1954; Tender Victory, 1956; The Sound of Thunder, 1957; Dear and Glorious Physician, 1959; The Listener, 1960, (Engl. edn) The Man Who Listens, 1961; A Prologue to Love, 1962; To See the Glory, 1963; The Late Clara Beame, 1964; A Pillar of Iron, 1965; Dialogues with the Devil, 1968. *Recreations:* just work; occasionally gardening. *Address:* 34 Audley End, Eggertsville, New York, NY 10021, USA. *Clubs:* American Legion, National League of American Penwomen (Buffalo, NY); League of Women Voters (Amherst Township, Erie County, NY); PEN (New York, NY); Women's National Republican (Washington, DC).

**CALEDON,** 6th Earl of, *cr* 1800; **Denis James Alexander;** Baron Caledon, 1789; Viscount Caledon, 1797; *b* 10 Nov. 1920; *s* of late Lieut-Col Hon. Herbrand Charles Alexander, DSO (*b* of 5th Earl of Caledon), and of Millicent Valla, *d* of Sir Henry Bayly Meredyth, 5th Bt; *S* uncle, 1968; *m* 1st, 1943, Ghislaine Dresselhuys (marr. diss. 1948); one *d*; 2nd, 1952, Baroness Anne de Graevenitz (*d* 1963); one *s* one *d*; 3rd, 1964, Marie Elisabeth Erskine (*née* Allen). *Educ:* Eton; RMC. Major, Irish Guards. *Heir: s* Viscount Alexander, *qv*. *Address:* Caledon Castle, Caledon, Co. Tyrone, Northern Ireland; Tyttenhanger Park, St Albans, Herts. *Club:* Turf.

**CALEDONIA, Bishop of,** since 1969; **Rt. Rev. Douglas Walter Hambidge,** DD; *b* London, England, 6 March 1927; *s* of Douglas Hambidge and Florence (*née* Driscoll); *m* 1956, Denise Colvill Lown; two *s* one *d*. *Educ:* London Univ.; London Coll. of Divinity. BD, ALCD; DD, Anglican Theol. Coll. of BC, 1970. Asst Curate, St Mark's, Dalston, 1953-56; Rector: All Saints, Cassiar, BC, 1956-58; St James, Smithers, BC, 1958-64; Vicar, St Martin, Fort St John, BC, 1964-69. *Address:* Bishop's Lodge, 208 Fourth Avenue-West, Prince Rupert, BC, Canada. *T:* 604-624-6044 or 604-624-6013.

**CALGARY, Bishop of,** since 1968; **Rt. Rev. Morse Lamb Goodman;** *b* Rosedale, Ont, 27 May 1917; *s* of Frederick James Goodman and Mary Mathilda Arkwright; *m* 1943, Patricia May Cunningham; three *s* one *d*. *Educ:* Trinity Coll., Univ. of Toronto. BA Trin., 1940; LTh Trin., 1942. Deacon, 1942, Priest, 1943, Diocese of Algoma; Asst Curate, St Paul's, Ft William, 1942-43; Incumbent, Murillo, Algoma, 1943-46; Rector, St Thomas, Ft William, 1946-53; Rector, St James, Winnipeg, 1953-60; Dean of Brandon, 1960-65; Rector, Christ Church, Edmonton, 1965-67. Conductor of Canadian Broadcasting Corporation Programme, Family Worship, 1954-68. Hon. DD: Trinity, 1961; Emmanuel and St Chad's, 1968. *Recreations:* fishing, walking, photography, ecology. *Address:* Bishop's Court, 1029 Hillcrest Avenue SW, Calgary, Alta, Canada. *T:* 244-4587. *Club:* Ranchmen's (Calgary, Alta).

**CALLAGHAN, Dr Allan Robert,** CMG 1945; Chairman, Australian Wheat Board, 528 Lonsdale Street, Melbourne, since 1965; *b* 24 Nov. 1903; *s* of late Phillip George Callaghan and Late Jane Peacock; *m* 1928, Zillah May Sampson (decd); two *s* one *d*. (and one *s* decd); *m* 1965, Doreen Rhys Draper. *Educ:* Bathurst High Sch., NSW; St Paul's Coll., Univ. of Sydney (BSc Agr. 1924); St John's Coll., Oxford (Rhodes Scholar, BSc 1926, DPhil 1928). Asst Plant Breeder, NSW, Dept of Agriculture, 1928-32; Principal, Roseworthy Agricultural Coll., South Australia, 1932-49; Asst Dir (Rural Industry) in Commonwealth Dept of War Organisation of Industry, 1943; Chm., Land Development Executive in South Australia, 1945-51; Dir of Agriculture, South Australia, 1949-59; Commercial Counsellor, Australian Embassy, Washington, DC, 1959-65. Farrer Medal (for distinguished service to Australian Agriculture), 1954; FAIAS 1959. *Publications:* (with A. J. Millington) The Wheat Industry in Australia, 1956; numerous articles in scientific and agricultural jls on agricultural and animal husbandry matters. *Recreations:* swimming, riding, gardening. *Address:* 10 St Georges, 145 Walsh Street, South Yarra, Victoria 3141, Australia. *T:* 26.6540. *Club:* Naval, Military, and Air Force (Adelaide).

**CALLAGHAN, Rear-Adm. Desmond Noble,** CB 1970; President, Ordnance Board, since 1970 (Senior Naval Member and Vice-President, 1968-70); *b* 24 Nov. 1915; *s* of Edmund Ford Callaghan and Kathleen Louise Callaghan (*née* Noble): *m* 1948, Patricia Munro Geddes; one *s* two *d*. *Educ:* RNC Dartmouth. HMS Frobisher, 1933; RNEC Keyhan, 1934; HM Ships: Royal Oak, 1937; Iron Duke, 1938; Warspite, 1939; Hereward, 1941; Prisoner of War, 1941; HMS Argonaut, 1945; HMS Glory, 1946; RNC Dartmouth, 1947; Admiralty, 1949; C-in-C Med. Staff, 1950; HMS Excellent, 1953; HMS Eagle, 1956; RN Tactical Sch., 1958; Admiralty, 1960; HMS Caledonia, 1962; Admiralty, 1965. CEng, FIMechE. *Recreations:* Rugby, tennis, swimming. *Address:* Willand, Boyn Hill Road, Maidenhead, Berks. *T:* Maidenhead 26840. *Club:* Army and Navy.

**CALLAGHAN, Rt. Hon. (Leonard) James,** PC 1964; MP (Lab) South Cardiff, 1945-50, South-East Cardiff since 1950; *b* 27 March 1912; *s* of James Callaghan, Chief Petty Officer, RN; *m* 1938, Audrey Elizabeth Moulton; one *s* two *d*. *Educ:* Elementary and Portsmouth Northern Secondary Schs. Entered Civil Service as a Tax Officer, 1929; Asst Sec., Inland Revenue Staff Fed., 1936-47 (with an interval during the War of 1939-45, when served in Royal Navy); Parl. Sec., Min. of Transport, 1947-50; Chm. Cttee on Road Safety, 1948-50; Parliamentary and Financial Sec., Admiralty, 1950-51; Chancellor of the Exchequer, 1964-67; Home Secretary, 1967-70. Deleg. to Council of Europe, Strasburg, 1948-50 and 1954. Mem. Nat. Exec. Cttee, Labour Party, 1957-67; Treasurer, Labour Party, 1967-. Consultant to Police Fedn of England and Wales and to Scottish Police Fedn, 1955-64. Pres., United Kingdom Pilots Assoc., 1963-. Visiting Fellow, Nuffield Coll., Oxford, 1959-67; Hon. Fellow, 1967-. *Address:* House of Commons, SW1.

**CALLAGHAN, Morley (Edward);** Canadian novelist; *b* Toronto, 1903; *s* of Thomas Callaghan and Mary (*née* Dewan); *m* 1929, Lorrete Florence, *d* of late Joseph Dee; two *s*. *Educ:* St Michael's Coll., Univ. of Toronto (BA); Osgoode Hall Law School. Holds Hon. Doctorates. *Publications:* Strange Fugitive, 1928; Native Argosy, 1929; It's Never Over, 1930; No Man's Meat, 1931; Broken Journey, 1932; Such Is My Beloved, 1934; They Shall Inherit the Earth, 1935; My Joy in Heaven, 1936; Now That April's Here, 1937; Jake Baldwin's Vow (for children), 1948; The Varsity Story, 1948; The Loved and the Lost, 1951; The Man with the Coat, 1955 (MacLean's Prize, 1955); A Many Coloured

Coat, 1960 (UK 1963); That Summer in Paris, 1963; A Passion in Rome, 1961 (UK 1964); Morley Callaghan, vols 1 and 2, 1964. *Recreation:* sports. *Address:* 20 Dale Avenue, Toronto, Ont., Canada.

**CALLAN, Prof. Harold Garnet,** FRS 1963; FRSE; MA, DSc; Professor of Natural History, St Salvator's College, St Andrews, since 1950; *b* 5 March 1917; *s* of Garnet George Callan and Winifred Edith Brazier; *m* 1944, Amarillis Maria Speranza, *d* of Dr R. Dohrn, Stazione Zoologica, Naples, Italy; one *s* two *d.* *Educ:* King's Coll. Sch., Wimbledon; St John's Coll., Oxford (Exhibitioner). Casberd Scholar, St John's Coll., 1937; Naples Biological Scholar, 1938, 1939; Henry Fellowship, 1939. Served War of 1939-45, Telecommunications Research Establishment, 1940-45, Hon. Commission, RAFVR. Senior Scientific Officer, ARC, Inst. of Animal Genetics, Edinburgh, 1946-50. Mem., Advisory Council on Scientific Policy, 1963-64. Trustee, British Museum (Natural History), 1963-66. Vis. Prof., Univ. of Indiana, Bloomington, USA, 1964-65; Master of United Coll. of St Salvator and St Leonard's, 1967-68. *Publications:* scientific papers, mostly on cytology and cell physiology. *Recreations:* shooting, carpentry. *Address:* The University, St Andrews, Fife.

**CALLANDER, Lt-Gen. Sir Colin (Bishop),** KCB 1955 (CB 1945); KBE 1952; MC; *b* 13 March 1897; *y s* of late W. W. Callander, Ilminster, Som.; *m* 1923, Mary Charteris Stather Dunn; one *s* one *d.* *Educ:* West Buckland Sch.; RMC Sandhurst. 2nd Lieut Royal Munster Fusiliers, 1915; Leicestershire Regt 1922; Capt. 1925; Major 1936; Temp. Lt-Col 1940; Col 1944; Temp. Maj.-Gen. 1944; Maj.-Gen. 1946; Lt-Gen. 1951. Served European War, 1916-17 (wounded thrice, MC); NW Frontier, India, 1938-39 (despatches); War of 1939-45 (CB); GOC 4th Div. (Greece), 1945-46; Dir-Gen. of Military Training, 1948; GOC 2nd Div. (BAOR), 1949-51; Dir-Gen. of Military Training, 1952-54; Military Sec. to the Sec. of State for War, 1954-56; retired 1957. Col Royal Leicestershire Regt, 1954-63. *Address:* Old Way House, Fordwich, Canterbury, Kent. *T:* Sturry 756. *Club:* Army and Navy.

**CALLARD, Eric John,** CEng, FIMechE; Deputy Chairman, Imperial Chemical Industries Ltd, since 1967; *b* 15 March 1913; *s* of late F. Callard and of Mrs A. Callard; *m* 1938, Pauline M. Pengelly; three *d.* *Educ:* Queen's Coll., Taunton; St John's Coll., Cambridge. BA Mech. Scis Tripos, 1935. ICI Ltd Billingham Div., 1936-42; Min. of Aircraft Production, Heysham, 1942-45; ICI Ltd Billingham Div. Research Dept, 1945-47; ICI Ltd Paints Div.: Dep. Chief Engr, 1947-49; Chief Engr, 1949-51; Engrg Dir, 1951-55; Jt Man. Dir, 1955-59; Div. Chm., 1959-64; Director: ICI Ltd, 1964-; Imperial Metal Industries Ltd, 1964-67; Imperial Chemicals Insurance Ltd, 1966-70; Chm., ICI (Europa) Ltd, 1965-67. Mem. Council: Manchester Business Sch., 1964-; Brit. Inst. of Management, 1964-69 (Fellow, 1966); Member: Export Coun. for Europe, 1965-; Coun. of Industry for Management Education, 1967-. Chm., Industrial Co-Partnership Assoc., 1967-. Mem., Univ. of Cambridge Appointments Board, 1968-. *Recreations:* golf, tennis. *Address:* Farthings, Jordans, near Beaconsfield, Bucks. *T:* Chalfont St Giles 4150.

**CALLAS, Maria;** soprano; *b* New York, 2 Dec. 1923; *d* of Greek parents; *m* 1947. *Educ:* New York, USA; Royal Conservatory, Athens. Tour of Italian cities, 1947; South American tour, 1949; Has sung in major rôles at La Scala, Covent Garden, the Metropolitan Opera House, the Vienna State Opera House, Mexico, at Edinburgh Festival, and in other cities in Europe and N and S America. Chief rôles in: Madame Butterfly, Aida, Norma, I Puritani, Pagliacci, Rigoletto, Cavalleria Rusticana, Anna Bolena, Lucia, Medea, Tosca, etc. Has recorded most of main parts. Played Medea in film (from Euripides) directed by Pier Paolo Pasolini, 1969. *Relevant publication:* Callas, by George Jellinek, 1961. *Address:* 36 Avenue Georges Mandel, Paris 16e, France.

**CALLAWAY, Air Vice-Marshal William Bertram,** CBE 1942; AFC; DL; Polonia Restituta (1945); *b* 15 Oct. 1889; *s* of Engineer Capt. R. G. Callaway, RN; *m* 1925, Evelyn Winifred Trim; one *d.* *Educ:* privately. Royal Navy, 1907-16; Royal Naval Air Service, 1916-18 (AFC); Royal Air Force, 1918-45. Air Vice-Marshal, 1942. Commandant, Midland Command, Air Training Corps, 1945-46; Divisional Controller, SW Div., Min. of Civil Aviation, 1947-53. DL Co. Gloucester, 1953. *Address:* Greathed Manor, Lingfield, Surrey. *T:* Lingfield 588. *Club:* Royal Air Force.

**CALLOW, Robert Kenneth,** FRS 1958; MA, DPhil, BSc; Member of Staff, Rothamsted Experimental Station, since 1966; Member of Scientific Staff, Medical Research Council, 1929-66; *b* 15 Feb. 1901; 2nd *s* of late Cecil Burman Callow and Kate Peverell; *m* 1937, Nancy Helen, *d* of J. E. Newman; one *s* one *d.* *Educ:* City of London Sch.; Christ Church, Oxford. Exhibitioner, 1919, and Research Scholar, 1927, of Christ Church. Served in RAF, 1940-45; relief of Datta Khel, 1941 (despatches). Mem. of Editorial Board, Biochemical Journal, 1946-53 (Dep. Chm., 1951-53); Chm., Biological and Medical Abstracts Ltd, 1955-61; Mem. of Council, Bee Research Association, 1962- (Chm., 1963-68); Visitor, Royal Instn of GB, 1970-. *Publications:* papers (many jointly) in jls of learned societies. *Recreations:* gardening, stamp-collecting, natural history. *Address:* 39 Hendon Wood Lane, NW7. *T:* 01-959 2572.

**CALNAN, Prof. Charles Dermot,** MA, MB, BChir Cantab; FRCP; Professor of Dermatology, Institute of Dermatology, since 1960; Hon. Consultant Dermatologist, Royal Free Hospital and St John's Hospital for Diseases of the Skin, London; *b* 14 Dec. 1917; *s* of James Calnan, Eastbourne, Sussex; *m* 1950, Josephine Gerard Keane, *d* of late Lt-Col Michael Keane, RAMC; three *s* one *d.* *Educ:* Stonyhurst Coll.; Corpus Christi Coll., Cambridge; London Hospital. 1st Cl. Hons Nat. Sci. Trip., Cambridge 1939. RAMC Specialist in Dermatology, Major, 1942-46; Marsden Prof., Royal Free Hosp., 1958; Visiting Research Associate, Univ. of Pennsylvania, 1959; Physician i/c Dept of Industrial Dermatoses, Inst. of Dermatology, 1959. Editor, Transactions of the St John's Hosp. Dermatological Soc., 1958. Mem. BMA; Mem. Brit. Assoc. of Dermatology. FRSocMed (Mem. Dermatological Section); Fellow Hunterian Soc. *Publications:* contributor to: Fungus Infections and their Treatment, 1958; Surgical Aspects of Medicine, 1960; various papers in med. and dermatological jls. *Recreations:* squash, books, theatre. *Address:* 132 Harley Street, W1. *T:* 01-935 3678.

**CALNE, Professor Roy Yorke,** MA, MS, FRCS; Professor of Surgery, University of Cambridge, since 1965; Fellow of Trinity Hall, Cambridge, since 1965; Hon. Consulting Surgeon, Addenbrooke's Hospital, Cambridge, since 1965; *b* 30 Dec. 1930; *s* of Joseph Robert and Eileen Calne; *m* 1956,

Patricia Doreen Whelan; one *s* four *d*. *Educ:* Lancing Coll.; Guy's Hosp. Med. Sch. MB, BS London with Hons (Distinction in Medicine), 1953. House Appts, Guy's Hosp., 1953-54; RAMC, 1954-56 (RMO to KEO 2nd Gurkhas); Deptl Anatomy Demonstrator, Oxford Univ., 1957-58; SHO Nuffield Orthopædic Centre, Oxford, 1958; Surg. Registrar, Royal Free Hosp., 1958-60; Harkness Fellow in Surgery, Peter Bent Brigham Hosp., Harvard Med. Sch., 1960-61; Lectr in Surgery, St Mary's Hosp., London, 1961-62; Sen. Lectr and Cons. Surg., Westminster Hosp., 1962-65; Mem., Ct of Examiners, RCS, 1970-. Royal Coll. of Surgeons: Hallet Prize, 1957; Jacksonian Prize, 1961; Hunterian Prof., 1962; Cecil Joll Prize, 1966. Fellow Assoc. of Surgeons of Gt Brit.; Mem. Surgical Research Soc. Prix de la Société Internationale de Chirurgie, 1969. *Publications:* Renal Transplantations, 1963, 2nd edn 1967; (with H. Ellis) Lecture Notes in Surgery, 1965, 3rd edn 1970; A Gift of Life, 1970; papers on tissue transplantation and general surgery; sections in several surgical text-books. *Recreations:* tennis, squash. *Address:* 22 Barrow Road, Cambridge. *T:* Cambridge 59831.

**CALTHORPE;** *see* Anstruther-Gough-Calthorpe, and Gough-Calthorpe.

**CALTHORPE,** 10th Baron *cr* 1796; **Peter Waldo Somerset Gough-Calthorpe;** Bt 1728; *b* 13 July 1927; *s* of late Hon. Frederick Somerset Gough-Calthorpe and Rose Mary Dorothy, *d* of late Leveson William Vernon-Harcourt; *S* brother, 1945; *m* 1956, Saranne, *o d* of James Harold Alexander, Ireland. *Heir:* none. *Address:* Oldfellings, St Lawrence, Jersey, Channel Islands. *T.* North 181.

**CALVERLEY,** 2nd Baron *cr* 1945; **George Raymond Orford Muff;** *b* 1 May 1914; *s* of 1st Baron Calverley, JP, DL and Ellen, *e d* of Charles and Mary Orford; *S* father, 1955; *m* 1940, Mary, *d* of Arthur Farrar, Halifax; two *s*. *Educ:* Bradford Grammar Sch. Formerly Capt., Royal Indian Ordnance Corps. *Heir:* *s* Hon. Charles Rodney Muff, *b* 2 Oct. 1946. *Address:* 77 Cecil Avenue, Great Horton, Bradford 7, Yorks.

**CALVERT, Edwin George Bleakley,** MD, FRCP; Hon. Consultant Physician, Royal Northern Hospital, London; Hon. Consultant Physician to St Paul's Hospital for Genito-Urinary Diseases (Institute of Urology), Samaritan Hospital for Women, City of London Maternity Hospital, National Temperance Hospital, London; *e s* of late James and Annie (*née* Armstrong) Calvert, Lyndhurst, Lurgan, Co. Armagh; *m* 1928, Nancy, *yr d* of late Charles W. Marsden, Sydney, NSW; one *s* two *d*. *Educ:* Methodist Coll., Belfast; Queen's Univ., Belfast; Dublin; St Mary's Hosp., London; Vienna. MD Belfast (Gold Medal), 1920; FRCP 1941; MRCP 1923; DPH 1920; MB, BCh, BAO Belfast (1st Class hons, and Schol. and Special Schol.), 1915; also four other Clinical Schols, Juliet-Symington Gold Medal and two additional 1st Schols in Medicine. Temp. Capt. RAMC, BEF, France, 1915-19; Demonstrator in Physiology, Queen's Univ., Belfast, 1919-20; RMO, Hosp. for Nervous Diseases, Maida Vale, 1920; Asst to Dir of Medical Clinical Unit, St Mary's Hosp., 1920-25; Physician, EMS London, 1939-45. *Publications:* Kidney Function Tests and Examination of the Urine, Pye's Surgical Handicraft, 11th-18th edns, 1939-63; Estimation of Sugar in the Blood, Biochemical Jl, 1923-24; Function Tests in Kidney Disease, BMJ, 1925; various papers in leading med. jls on diabetes, acidosis, kidney disease, diseases of lymphatic glands, endocrine glands, rheumatoid arthritis (lectures given: Internat. Soc. of Internal Med., Philadelphia, and at Harvard Univ.). *Recreation:* golf. *Address:* 132 Harley Street, W1. *T:* 01-935 2296; 1 Solent Drive, Barton-on-Sea, Hants. *T:* New Milton 5153.

**CALVERT, Rt. Rev. George Reginald;** *b* 11 Oct. 1900; *s* of William John Calvert and Mary (*née* Young); *m* 1925, Kate Verona, *d* of William Alexander Moir; one *d*. *Educ:* Univ. of Toronto (BA); Wycliffe Coll., Toronto (LTh). Hon. DD Wycliffe Coll., Toronto, Univ. of King's Coll., Halifax and Univ. of Emmanuel Coll., Saskatoon. Deacon, 1924; Priest, 1925; Incumbent of Snowflake, Manitoba, 1924; Rector: Holland, Man., 1926; Killarney, Man., 1928; St Anne's, West Kildoran, Man., 1932; St Matthew's, Winnipeg, Man., 1933; Hon. Canon, St John's Cathedral, Winnipeg, 1940; Archdeacon of Winnipeg, 1945; Dep. Prolocutor of Gen. Synod of C of E in Canada, 1946, Prolocutor, 1949; Prolocutor of Provincial Synod of Rupert's Land, 1947; Dean and Rector of Christ Church Cathedral, Victoria, British Columbia, 1949-52; Bishop of Calgary, 1952-67, retired. Grand Master, Grand Lodge, Manitoba, Ancient Free and Accepted Masons, 1941. LLD Alberta, 1963. *Address:* 303 Camosack Manor, 1035 Belmont Avenue, Victoria, BC, Canada.

**CALVERT, Henry Reginald,** Dr Phil; Keeper of Department of Astronomy and Geophysics in Science Museum, South Kensington, 1949-67; Keeper Emeritus, 1967-69; *b* 25 Jan. 1904; *e s* of late H. T. Calvert, MBE, DSc, of Min. of Health; *m* 1938, Eileen Mary Frow; two *d*. *Educ:* Bridlington Sch., East Yorks; St John's Coll., Oxford (Scholar, MA); Univ. of Göttingen, Germany (Dr Phil). 1st Cl. Hons BSc (External) London, 1925; Goldsmiths' Company's Exhibitioner, 1925. Research Physicist, ICI, 1928-30; Research Physicist, Callender's Cable & Construction Co., 1932-34. Entered Science Museum, 1934; Dep. Keeper, 1946. Ballistics research for Min. of Supply, 1940-46. Hon. Treas., British Soc. for History of Science, 1952-63. Fellow Royal Astronomical Soc. *Publications:* Astronomy, Globes, Orreries and other Models; papers in learned journals. *Recreations:* chess and gardening. *Address:* North Point, Church Hill, Merstham, Surrey. *T:* Merstham 2362.

**CALVERT, Phyllis;** actress; *b* 18 Feb. 1917; *d* of Frederick and Annie Bickle; *m* 1941, Peter Murray Hill (*d* 1957); one *s* one *d*. *Educ:* Margaret Morris Sch.; Institut Français. Malvern Repertory Company, 1935; York, 1935; Coventry, 1937. First appeared in London in A Woman's Privilege, Kingsway Theatre, 1939; Punch Without Judy, Embassy, 1939; Flare Path, Apollo, 1942; Escapade, St James's, 1953; It's Never Too Late, Strand, 1954; River Breeze, Phoenix, 1956; The Complaisant Lover, Globe, 1959; The Rehearsal, Globe, 1961; Ménage à Trois, Lyric, 1963; Portrait of Murder, Savoy, Vaudeville, 1963; A Scent of Flowers, Duke of York's, 1964; Present Laughter, Queen's, 1965; A Woman of No Importance, Vaudeville, 1967; Blithe Spirit, Globe, 1970. Started films, 1939. *Films include:* Kipps, The Young Mr Pitt, Man in Grey, Fanny by Gaslight, Madonna of the Seven Moons, They were Sisters, Time out of Mind, Broken Journey, My Own True Love, The Golden Madonna, A Woman with No Name, Mr Denning Drives North, Mandy, The Net, It's Never Too Late, Child in the House, Indiscreet, The Young and The Guilty, Oscar Wilde, Twisted Nerve, Oh! What a Lovely War, The Walking Stick. TV series: Kate, 1970. *Recreations:* swimming, gardening, collecting costume books. *Address:* 99 Castelnau, SW13. *T:* 01-748 5365.

**CALVERT-JONES, Major-General Percy George,** CB 1948; CBE 1945; DSO 1943; MC 1917; *b* 24 April 1894; *s* of James George Calvert-Jones and Mary Louisa Saundry; *m* 1936, Jean Stevenson Binning; one *s* one *d*. *Educ:* S Wales Univ. TA Commn, 1915; Regular Commn, 1916; served European War, 1914-18; France, Belgium, Egypt, Palestine, 1915-18; N Russia, 1919; India, 1920-24 and 1930-35. Staff Coll., Camberley, 1928-29; SORA Western Comd, India, 1931-34; Air Staff Officer, HQ Fighter Comd, RAF, 1936-39; served War of 1939-45 (despatches thrice); France, Syria, Western Desert, Italy, 1940-43; France, Belgium, 1944-45; BRA Southern Comd, 1945-46; GOC 4AA Group, Warrington, 1946-49; retired pay, 1949. Comdr American Legion of Merit. Recreations: golf, sailing. *Address:* Little Brooke, Brooke, Isle of Wight. *T:* Brighstone 369. *Clubs:* Naval and Military; Royal Solent Yacht.

**CALVIN, Professor Melvin;** Professor of Chemistry, University of California, since 1947; Professor of Molecular Biology, since 1963; Director, Laboratory of Chemical Biodynamics, since 1960; Associate Director, Lawrence Radiation Laboratory, since 1967; *b* 8 April 1911; *s* of Rose and Elias Calvin; *m* 1942, Marie Genevieve Jemtegaard; one *s* two *d*. *Educ:* Univ. of Minnesota, Minneapolis (PhD). Fellow, Univ. of Manchester, 1935-37. Univ. of California, Berkeley: Instr., 1937; Asst Prof., 1941-45; Assoc. Prof., 1945-47; Prof., 1947-. Foreign Mem., Royal Society, 1959. Member: Nat. Acad. of Sciences (US); Royal Netherlands Acad. of Sciences and Letters; Amer. Philos. Society. Nobel Prize in Chemistry, 1961; Davy Medal, Royal Society, 1964. Hon. Degrees: Michigan Coll. of Mining and Technology, 1955; Univ. of Nottingham, 1958; Oxford Univ., 1959; Northwestern Univ., 1961; Univ. of Notre Dame, 1965; Brooklyn Polytechnic Inst., 1969; Rijksuniversiteit-Gent, 1970. *Publications:* very numerous, including (6 books): Theory of Organic Chemistry (with Branch), 1941; Isotopic Carbon (with Heidelberger, Reid, Tolbert and Yankwich), 1949; Chemistry of Metal Chelate Compounds (with Martell), 1952; Path of Carbon in Photosynthesis (with Bassham), 1957; Chemical Evolution, 1961; Photosynthesis of Carbon Compounds (with Bassham), 1962; Chemical Evolution, 1969. *Address:* University of California, Berkeley, Calif 94720, USA; (home) 2683 Buena Vista Way, Berkeley, Calif 94708, USA. *T:* 848-4036.

**CALVO, Roberto Q.;** *see* Querejazu Calvo.

**CALVOCORESSI, Peter (John Ambrose);** author; Reader (part time) in International Relations, University of Sussex; *b* 17 Nov. 1912; *s* of Pandia Calvocoressi and Irene (Ralli); *m* 1938, Barbara Dorothy Eden, *d* of 6th Baron Henley; two *s*. *Educ:* Eton (King's Scholar); Balliol Coll., Oxford. Called to Bar, 1935. RAF Intelligence, 1940-45; Wing Comdr. Trial of Major War Criminals, Nuremberg, 1945-46. Contested (L) Nuneaton, 1945. Staff of Royal Institute of International Affairs, 1949-54; Mem. Council, Royal Inst. of Internat. Affairs, 1955-; Mem. Council, Inst. for Strategic Studies, 1961-; Mem. UN Sub-Commn on the Prevention of Discrimination and Protection of Minorities, 1962-; Chm., The Africa Bureau, 1963-; Chm., The London Library; Dep. Chm., Greater London Conciliation Cttee; Dir of Chatto & Windus Ltd and The Hogarth Press Ltd, 1954-65. *Publications:* Nuremberg: The Facts, the Law and the Consequences, 1947; Surveys of International Affairs, vol. 1, 1947-48, 1950; vol. 2, 1949-50, 1951; vol. 3, 1951, 1952; vol. 4, 1952, 1953; vol. 5, 1953, 1954; Middle East Crisis (with Guy Wint), 1957; South Africa and World Opinion, 1961; World Order and New States, 1962; World Politics since 1945, 1968. *Recreation:* tennis. *Address:* Guise House, Aspley Guise, Bletchley, Bucks. *T:* Woburn Sands 2156; 42 William IV Street, WC2. *T:* 01-240 1966. *Club:* Garrick.

**CALWELL, Rt. Hon. Arthur Augustus,** PC 1967; Leader of Federal Parliamentary Labour Party, Australia, 1960-67 (Deputy Leader, 1951-60); MHR Melbourne since 1940; *b* 28 Aug. 1896; *s* of A. A. Calwell; *m* 1932, Elizabeth Marren; one *d*. *Educ:* Christian Brothers' Coll., N Melbourne. Dept of Agriculture, Vic., 1913-23; Victorian Treasury, 1923-40. Pres. Vic. Australian Labour Party (ALP), 1931; Vic. Delegate to Fed. Confs of ALP, 1930-51; Mem. Fed. Executive, ALP, 1931-50; Mem. Melbourne City Council, 1939-45; Commissioner, Melbourne and Metropolitan Bd of Works, 1939-45; Mem. Jt Parl. Cttee on Broadcasting, 1941-43; Mem. Central Med. Co-ordination Cttee, 1942-44; Chm. Aliens Classification and Advisory Cttee, 1942-46; Minister for Information, Australia, 1943-49, and for Immigration, 1945-49. Mem. Exec. Cttee of Organising Cttee, 1956 Olympic Games; Chm. Melbourne Cricket Ground Trust, 1952- (Trustee, 1931-). KCSG with Silver Star, 1964. Hon. LLD Melbourne, 1970. *Publication:* Labour's Role in Modern Society, 1963. *Address:* 30 Baroda Street, Flemington, Melbourne, Vic., Australia. *Clubs:* Green Room, Celtic (Melbourne); Tattersall's, Catholic (Sydney); Irish (London); Darwin (Northern Territory).

**CAMACHO, Fabian Joseph;** Puisne Judge, Trinidad and Tobago, 1953-60, retired; *b* 5 Aug. 1898; *s* of late Mr Justice Martin Joseph Camacho and of Mrs Camacho (*née* Craddock); *m* 1927, Beatrice Louise Adamson; one *s* three *d*. *Educ:* The Antigua Grammar Sch.; St Wilfrid's Coll., Oakamoor, N Staffs, England. Served European War, 1914-18, in Army (France), 1917-19. Called to Bar, middle Temple, 1923; practised at Bar, Leeward Islands, 1924-30; Magistrate and Legal Adviser, Montserrat, 1931; Magistrate, Trinidad, 1932; Dep. Chief Magistrate, Trinidad, 1948; Third Puisne Judge, British Guiana, 1952-53. *Recreations:* tennis and fishing. *Address:* c/o The Supreme Court, Trinidad and Tobago, West Indies.

**CAMBELL, Rear-Adm. Dennis Royle Farquharson,** CB 1960; DSC 1940; Chairman, Trans World Helicopters Ltd, since 1965; *b* 13 Nov. 1907; *s* of Dr Archibald Cambell and Edith Cambell, Southsea; *m* 1933, Dorothy Elinor Downes; two *d*. *Educ:* Westminster Sch. Joined RN, 1925, HMS Thunderer Cadet Training; trained as FAA pilot, 1931; served as pilot in various naval fighter squadrons and aircraft carriers, 1932-38; of 803 Squadron, HMS Ark Royal III, 1939-40; HMS Argus, 1942; naval test pilot, 1941, 1943; Comdr, 1943; British Air Commission, USA, 1944-45; HMS Glory, 1947; Capt. of HMS Tintagel Castle, 1948; Capt., 1949; staff appointments, 1950-54; 1st Capt. of HMS Ark Royal IV, 1955-56; Director of Air Warfare, Admiralty, 1957; Rear-Adm., 1958; Flag Officer, Flying Training, 1957-60; retired, 1960. Legion of Merit (US), 1958. *Recreation:* sailing. *Address:* The Old School House, Colemore, Alton, Hants.

**CAMBRIDGE,** family name of **Marquess of Cambridge.**

**CAMBRIDGE,** 2nd Marquess of, *cr* 1917; **George Francis Hugh Cambridge,** GCVO 1933 (KCVO 1927); Earl of Eltham, 1917; Viscount Northallerton, 1917; late Lieut Reserve Regiment 1st Life Guards and Shropshire Yeomanry; Capt. 16th Bn London Regt and RASC, TA; *b* London, 11 Oct. 1895; *er s* of 1st Marquess and Lady Margaret Evelyn Grosvenor (*d* 1929), 3rd *d* of 1st Duke of Westminster; *S* father, 1927; *m* 1923, Dorothy, 2nd *d* of late Hon. Osmond Hastings; one *d*. Royal Trustee, British Museum, 1947-. *Heir:* none. *Address:* The Old House, Little Abington, Cambs.
*See also Duke of Beaufort.*

**CAMDEN,** 5th Marquess *cr* 1812; **John Charles Henry Pratt;** Baron Camden, 1765; Earl Camden, Viscount Bayham, 1786; Earl of Brecknock, 1812; DL, JP; Major R of O; late Scots Guards; *b* 12 April 1899; *er s* of 4th Marquess Camden, GCVO and Lady Joan Marion Nevill, CBE 1920 (*d* 1952), *d* of 3rd Marquess of Abergavenny; *S* father, 1943; *m* 1st, 1920, Marjorie, DStJ 1959 (who obtained a divorce, 1941) (*see* Marjorie, Countess of Brecknock); one *s* one *d*; 2nd, 1942, Averil, *d* of late Col Henry Sidney John Streatfeild, DSO; one *s*. *Educ:* Ludgrove, New Barnet, Herts; Eton Coll.; RMC Sandhurst. ADC to Gen. Lord Jeffreys, GOC London Dist, 1920-24. Raised and formed 45th Battery 16th Light AA Regt RA, 1938, and commanded during early part of war of 1939-45, then rejoined Scots Guards; late Hon. Col 516th LAA Regt, RA; Gold Staff at Coronation of King George VI and Queen Elizabeth, 1937. DL, JP, Kent. Conservative Peer: Younger Brother of Trinity House. Dir, Darracq Motor Engineering Co., Bayard Cars Ltd and late Dir of many cos; Dir, Nat. Sporting Club, 1937-40; Director: RAC Buildings Co. Ltd; RAC Country Club Ltd; RAC Travel Service Ltd; President: Tonbridge Area League of Mercy; Tunbridge Wells Area of RSPCA; SE Counties Agricultural Soc., 1948 (and Mem. Council); Tunbridge Wells Amateur Dramatic and Operatic Soc.; Royal Agricultural Soc. of England; Joint Pres. Royal Tunbridge Wells Civic Assoc.; Chm. Bd of Trustees, Living of King Charles-the-Martyr, Tunbridge Wells; Pres. St Pancras Almshouses; a Vice-Pres. and Mem. Cttee of Management of Royal Nat. Life-Boat Inst.; Mem. Council of Boy Scouts Assoc. for County of Kent. Late President: Women's Lying-in Hosp., Vincent Sq., SW1; Kent and Sussex Hosp., Tunbridge Wells; late Vice-Pres. Royal Northern Hospital, N7; late Trustee Kent Playing Fields association. FIMI. *Recreations:* shooting, boxing, motor-car racing, yachting, motor-boat racing; interests: farming and forestry. *Heir: s* Earl of Brecknock, *qv*. *Address:* Bayham Abbey, Lamberhurst, Kent. *T:* Tunbridge Wells 25009; 42 Belgrave Mews South, Belgrave Place, SW1. *Clubs:* St James', Guards, Pratt's, Turf, Royal Automobile (Senior Vice-Chm., 1952), British Automobile Racing, etc, Royal Aero, MCC, etc; Royal Yacht Squadron (Vice-Cdre); House of Lords Yacht (Vice-Cdre); Royal Motor Yacht (Rear-Adm.); Marine Motoring Assoc. (Vice-Pres.); Royal Naval Sailing Assoc. (Hon. Mem.); Yachtsmen's Assoc. of America (Hon. Mem.), etc.

**CAME, William Gerald,** CIE 1944; BSc (Bristol); retired civil engineer; *b* 8 Dec. 1889; *s* of late John Mathew and Elizabeth Bessie Came, Woodhuish Barton, Brixham, Devon; *m* 1st, 1916, Ada Coombs; one *s* one *d*; 2nd, 1937, Gertrude Marie Farmer; one *s*. Chief Engineer and Sec. to Govt (Roads and Buildings Dept), Bihar, India, 1942-45; retired 1945; re-appointed as Chief Engineer and Secretary of the I and E Depts, 1945-48. Appointed to PWD (B and O) in 1913; previously with T. B. Cooper & Co., Civil Engineers, Bristol. Old Totnesian and an Associate of Univ. Coll., Bristol. *Address:* Somerley View, Ringwood, Hants. *T:* Ringwood 3733.

**CAMERON, Hon. Lord; John Cameron;** Kt 1954; DSC; QC (Scotland) 1936; DL; LLD, Aberdeen and Edinburgh; FRSE; HRSA; a Senator of The College of Justice in Scotland and Lord of Session since 1955; *b* 1900; *m* 1st, 1927, Eileen Dorothea (*d* 1943), *d* of late H. M. Burrell; one *s* two *d*; 2nd, 1944, Iris, *widow* of Lambert C. Shepherd. *Educ:* Edinburgh Acad.; Edinburgh Univ. Served European War, 1918, with RNVR; Advocate, 1924; Advocate-Depute, 1929-36. Served with RNVR, Sept. 1939-44 (despatches, DSC); released to reserve, Dec. 1944. Sheriff of Inverness, Elgin and Nairn, 1945; Sheriff of Inverness, Moray, Nairn and Ross and Cromarty, 1946-48; Dean of Faculty of Advocates, 1948-55. DL Edinburgh, 1953. *Address:* 28 Moray Place, Edinburgh. *T:* 031-225 7585. *Clubs:* New, Scottish Arts (Edinburgh); Highland (Inverness); Royal Forth Yacht.

**CAMERON, Mrs Alan Charles;** *see* Bowen, Elizabeth D. C.

**CAMERON, Lt-Gen. Sir Alexander (Maurice),** KBE 1952; CB 1945; MC; retired; *b* 30 May 1898; *s* of late Major Sir Maurice Alexander Cameron, KCMG; *m* 1922, Loveday (*d* 1965), *d* of Col W. D. Thomson, CMG. *Educ:* Wellington Coll. 2nd Lieut Royal Engineers, 1916. Served European War, France and Belgium (wounded, despatches, MC, 2 medals); S Persia (medal and clasp); Iraq and Kurdistan (two clasps); psc 1929. Brevet Lieut-Col, 1939; RAF Staff Coll., 1939; Brig., 1940; Maj.-Gen. 1943; SHAEF, 1944-45; Dep. QMG, 1945-48; Maj.-Gen. i/c Administration, MELF, 1948-51; GOC East African Comd, 1951-53; retired 1954; Director of Civil Defence South-Eastern Region (Tunbridge Wells), 1955-60. *Club:* Army and Navy.

**CAMERON, Basil;** *see* Cameron, G. B.

**CAMERON, Sir Cornelius,** Kt 1968; CBE 1960; DL, JP, FCA; *b* 21 Nov. 1896; *s* of late John Martin Cameron and Elizabeth Roxburgh Cameron, Lutterworth; *m* 1923, Beatrice M., *d* of George Edward Nicholls, Coventry; two *s*. *Educ:* Trinity Academy, Edinburgh. Served European War, 1914-18, Sub-Lieut, RNVR. CA, 1920. Organised Greek Relief Fund Appeal, Nottingham, during War, 1939-45 (Greek Red Cross Medal, 1946). Jt Man. Dir, William Hollins & Co. Ltd, Nottingham, until retirement in 1961; Mem., East Midlands Gas Board, and Chm., East Midlands Gas Consultative Council, 1961-67. Chm., City of Nottingham Magistrates, 1958-68 (JP 1947); Sheriff of Nottingham, 1960-61, and Lord Mayor, 1963-64; Hon. Alderman. General Commissioner of Income Tax. DL Co. Notts, 1963. Hon. Vice-Pres., Nottingham Chamber of Commerce, 1962; Hon. Treas. and Dep. Chm., City of Nottingham Conservative Assoc., 1958-61 (Hon. Sec., 1950-58), etc. Life Mem., Court of Nottingham Univ. *Address:* Bramble Cottage, Red Lane, Lowdham, Notts. *T:* Lowdham 2691. *Club:* Dorchester (Nottingham).

**CAMERON, Vice-Adm. Cyril St Clair,** CBE 1919; Royal Navy, retired; *b* 22 July 1879; 4th *s* of late Col A. S. Cameron, VC, CB; *m* 1909, Isabel Edith (*d* 1955), *d* of late Peter Hordern, late Director of Public Instruction, Burmah;

two *s* three *d*. *Educ:* private sch. Joined HMS Britannia as Naval Cadet, 1893; Lieut 1901; Comdr 1913; Capt. 1918; served as 2nd in comd HMS Agamemnon during the operations off the Dardanelles, and subsequent operations in the Mediterranean, 1915-17; employed in anti-submarine work in the Mediterranean, 1917 till the Armistice, Oct. 1918; Dir of Torpedo Div. of Naval Staff, 1926-28; Rear-Adm. retired list, 1930; Vice-Adm. retired, 1935. *Recreation:* gardening. *Address:* Whatley Combe House, Whatley, near Frome, Somerset.

**CAMERON of Lochiel, Colonel Donald Hamish,** CVO 1970; TD 1944; JP; Vice-Lieutenant of County of Inverness, 1963; Chartered Accountant; Director since 1954, Deputy Chairman, 1965-69, a Vice-Chairman since 1969, Royal Bank of Scotland; Chairman Scottish Save & Prosper Group, since 1968; Director, Scottish Widows Life Assurance Society, since 1955 (Chairman, 1964-67); *b* 12 Sept. 1910; *s* of Col Sir Donald Walter Cameron of Lochiel, KT, CMG, 25th Chief of the Clan Cameron, and Lady Hermione Emily Graham, 2nd *d* of 5th Duke of Montrose; *S* father, as 26th Chief, 1951; *m* 1939, Margaret, *o d* of Lieut-Col Hon. Nigel Gathorne-Hardy, DSO; two *s* two *d*. *Educ:* Harrow; Balliol Coll., Oxford. Joined Lovat Scouts, 1929; Major 1940; Lieut-Col 1945; Lieut-Col comdg 4/5th Bn (TA) QO Cameron Highlanders, 1955-57; Col 1957 (TARO). Hon. Colonel: 4/5th Bn QO Cameron Highlanders, 1958-67; 3rd (Territorial) Bn Queen's Own Highlanders (Seaforth and Camerons), 1967-69; 51st Highland Volunteers, 1970-. Member (part-time): British Railways Bd, 1962-64; Scottish Bd, BTC, 1964- (Chm., 1963-64, and Chm. Scottish Area Bd, BTC, 1959-62); Transport Holding Co., 1962-65. Crown Estate Comr, 1957-69. DL Inverness-shire, 1952. *Heir: s* Donald Angus, *b* 2 Aug. 1946. *Address:* Achnacarry, Spean Bridge, Inverness-shire. *T:* Gairlochy 208. *Clubs:* Boodle's, Pratt's; New (Edinburgh).

**CAMERON, Francis Ernest,** MA (Oxon), FRCO (CHM); ARAM; Assistant Director, State Conservatorium of Music, Sydney, NSW, since 1969; *b* London, 5 Dec. 1927; *er s* of Ernest and Doris Cameron; *m* 1952, Barbara Minns; three *d*. *Educ:* Mercers' Sch.; Caerphilly Boys' Secondary Sch.; Royal Acad. of Music; University Coll., Oxford. Henry Richards Prizewinner, RAM, 1946. Organist, St Peter's, Fulham, 1943; Pianist, Canadian Legion, 1944; Organist, St Luke's, Holloway, 1945; Sub-organist, St Peter's, Eaton Square, 1945; Organist, St James-the-Less, Westminster, 1946; commissioned RASC, 1948; Organ Scholar, University Coll., Oxford, 1950; Organist: St Anne's, Highgate, 1952; St Barnabas', Pimlico, 1953; St Mark's, Marylebone Road, 1957-58; received into Roman Catholic Church, Holy Week, 1959; Choirmaster, St Aloysius, Somers Town, 1959; Master of Music, Westminster Cathedral, 1959; Visiting Organist, Church of St Thomas of Canterbury, Rainham, Kent, 1961-; Organist and Choirmaster, Church of Our Lady of the Assumption and St Gregory, 1962-68. Travel for UNESCO, 1952-55; Dep. Dir of Music, LCC (subsequently GLC), 1954-68; Asst-Dir of Music, Emanuel Sch., 1954; Music Master, Central Foundation Boys' Grammar Sch., 1956; Prof. of Organ and Composition, RAM, 1959-68; *locum tenens* Dir of Music, St Felix Sch., Southwold, 1963 and 1964; Pres., "Open Score", 1946-68; inaugural Conductor, Witan Operatic Soc., 1957-58; Conductor "I Cantici," 1961-65; British Adjudicator, Fedn of Canadian Music Festivals, 1965; Conductor, Francis Cameron Chorale, 1965-68; Examr Associated Bd of Royal Schools of Music, 1965-68. *Publications:* editor (with John Steele) Musica Britannica vol. xiv (The Keyboard Music of John Bull, part I), 1960; Old Palace Yard, 1963; contributor to: Church Music; Composer; The Conductor; Liturgy; Musical Times. *Address:* 10 Kirkwood Street, Seaforth, NSW 2092, Australia. *T:* 949-3163.

**CAMERON, (George) Basil,** CBE 1957; conductor; *b* Reading, 18 Aug. 1884; unmarried. *Educ:* Grammar Sch., Tiverton; Hochschule für Musik, Berlin. First Conductor of Torquay Municipal Orchestra (Wagner Centenary Festival, 1913, Strauss Festival, 1914); Conductor, Hastings Municipal Orchestra, 1923-30; Harrogate Municipal Orchestra, 1924-30; San Francisco Symphony Orchestra, 1930-32; Seattle Symphony Orchestra, 1932-38. Since 1940 one of principal conductors of Henry Wood Promenade Concerts. Guest conductor BBC Symphony Orchestra, London Symphony Orchestra, Royal Philharmonic, London Philharmonic and Philmarmonia Orchestras; Berlin Philharmonic, Amsterdam Concertgebouw, Budapest Symphony and Belgian National Symphony Orchestra. *Address:* 30 Ingelow House, Holland Street, W8.

**CAMERON, James;** *see* Cameron, M. J. W.

**CAMERON, Prof. James Munro;** Master of Rutherford College and Professor of Philosophy, University of Kent at Canterbury, since 1967; *b* 14 Nov. 1910; *o s* of Alan and Jane Helen Cameron; *m* 1933, Vera Shaw; one *s* one *d*. *Educ:* Central Secondary Sch., Sheffield; Keighley Grammar Sch.; Balliol Coll., Oxford (Scholar). Tutor, Workers' Educational Assoc., 1931-32; Staff Tutor, Univ. Coll., Southampton, 1932-35; Staff Tutor, Vaughan Coll., Leicester (Dept of Adult Education, Univ. Coll., Leicester), 1935-43. Univ. of Leeds: Staff Tutor for Tutorial Classes, 1943-47; Lectr in Philosophy, 1947-60 (Sen. Lectr from 1952); Acting Head of Dept of Philosophy, 1954-55 and 1959-60; Prof. of Philosophy, 1960-67. Vis. Prof., Univ. of Notre Dame, Indiana, 1957-58, 1965; Terry Lectr, Yale Univ., 1964-65. Newman Fellow, Univ. of Melbourne, 1968. *Publications:* Scrutiny of Marxism, 1948; (trans. with Marianne Kuschnitzky) Max Picard, The Flight from God, 1951; John Henry Newman, 1956; The Night Battle, 1962; Images of Authority, 1966; contribs to other books, and articles and papers in many periodicals. *Address:* Rutherford College, The University, Canterbury, Kent.

**CAMERON, Sir John,** DSC, QC (Scot.); *see* Cameron, Hon. Lord.

**CAMERON, Brigadier John S.;** *see* Sorel Cameron.

**CAMERON, (Mark) James (Walter);** journalist and author; *b* 17 June 1911; *s* of William Ernest Cameron, MA, LLB, and Margaret Douglas Robertson; *m* 1st, 1938, Eleanor Mara Murray (decd); one *d*; 2nd, 1944, Elizabeth O'Conor; one *s* (and one step *s*). *Educ:* erratically, at variety of small schools, mostly in France. Began journalism, in Dundee, 1928; after leaving Scotland joined many staffs and wrote for many publications, travelling widely as Foreign Correspt in most parts of the world; finally with (late) News Chronicle. Subseq. prod. numerous TV films, on contemporary subjects. Initiated travel series, Cameron Country, on BBC 2. Hon. Governor, Mermaid Theatre. Granada Award, Journalist of the

Year, 1965; Granada Foreign Correspt of the Decade, 1966; Hannen Swaffer Award for Journalism, 1966. *Publications:* Touch of the Sun, 1950; Mandarin Red, 1955; "1914", 1959; The African Revolution, 1961; "1916", 1962; Witness in Viet Nam, 1966; Point of Departure, 1967; What a Way to Run a Tribe, 1968. *Recreations:* private life, public houses. *Address:* 6 Ashburn Gardens, SW7. *T:* 01-373 0181. *Clubs:* Savile, Chelsea Arts.

**CAMERON, Air Vice-Marshal Neil,** CBE 1967; DSO 1945; DFC 1944; Senior Air Staff Officer, Air Support Command, since 1970; *b* 8 July 1920; *s* of Neil and Isabella Cameron, Perth, Scotland; *m* 1947, Patricia Louise, *d* of Major Edward Asprey; one *s* one *d*. *Educ:* Perth Academy. Fighter and Fighter Bomber Sqdns, 1940-45; Directing Staff, Sch. of Land/Air Warfare, Old Sarum, 1945-48; Student, RAF Staff Coll., 1949; DS, RAF Staff Coll., 1952-55; CO, Univ. of London Air Sqdn, 1955-56; Personal Staff Officer, Chief of Air Staff, 1956-59; CO, RAF Abingdon, 1959-62; Imperial Defence Coll., 1963; Principal Staff Officer, Dep. Supreme Comdr, SHAPE, Paris, 1964; Asst Comdt, RAF Coll., Cranwell, 1965; Programme Evaluation Gp, MoD, 1965-66; Assistant Chief of Defence Staff (Policy), 1968-70. *Publications:* articles in defence jls. *Recreations:* reading, Rugby football, defence affairs. *Address:* 19 Rivermead Court, Ranelagh Gardens, SW6. *T:* 01-736 3483. *Club:* Royal Air Force.

**CAMERON, Major-General (retired) Roderic Duncan,** CB 1952; CBE 1948 (OBE 1945); MC 1918; CStJ 1947; psc; *b* 16 Feb. 1893; *s* of late William Cameron, JP, and Johanna Macdonald, Inverness-shire; *m* 1953, Morva, *d* of late J. H. Nicholson, Loanend, Berwick-upon-Tweed. *Educ:* Glen Urquhart Sch.; George Watson's Coll.; Edinburgh Univ. (MB, ChB). Lieut RAMC, SR, 1914; Lieut RAMC, 1916. Served in Egypt, Greece, Turkey, China, India, UK and North-West Europe (wounded). Major-General, 1950; KHS 1951; QHS 1952-53; DMS, BAOR, 1950-53; Col Comdt RAMC, 1953-58. *Address:* c/o Glyn Mills & Co., Kirkland House, Whitehall, SW1; East Lodge, Woodlands Road, Cobham, Surrey. *T:* Oxshott 2770. *Club:* Army and Navy.

**CAMERON, Thomas Wright Moir,** TD; PhD Edinburgh; HARCVS; MA Edinburgh; DSc Edinburgh; DSc BC; FRSC; Professor Emeritus of Parasitology, McGill University, Montreal; *b* Glasgow, 29 April 1894; *e s* of Hugh Cameron, Edinburgh; *m* Stella Blanche, *y d* of F. H. Hill, Oxford; one *d*. *Educ:* Allan Glen's Sch., Glasgow; Glasgow, Edinburgh, and London Univs; Royal (Dick) Veterinary Coll., Edinburgh. Commission in HLI 1914-16; RAF 1916-19; in Royal (Dick) Vet. Contingent OTC 1921-23; Major RAVC (TA) London (2nd Div.), 1923-35; McGill COTC 1939-42. Res. Schol., Edinburgh Univ., 1921-23; Min. of Agric. Res. Schol., 1921-23; Sen. Res. Asst, Inst. of Agricultural Parasitology, London, 1923-25; Lecturer and Milner Fellow, Dept of Helminthology, London Sch. of Hygiene and Tropical Medicine, 1925-29; Dir. and Founder, Inst. of Parasitology, 1932-64. Sec., Sect. of Tropical Diseases and Parasitology, Vice-President Sect. of Comparative Medicine, RSM, 1926-29; Lecturer in Helminthology, Univ. of Edinburgh and Royal (Dick) Veterinary Coll., 1929-32; Contrib. on Vet. Diseases to Bull. of Hygiene; Sec., Edin. and Can. Brs, Royal Soc. of Tropical Medicine and Hygiene. President: American Society of Parasitologists, 1949; Sect. V, RSC, 1949-50; RSC, 1957-58; Can. Society of Microbiology, 1959; Can. Society of Zoology, 1960; World Federation of Parasitologists, 1965-; Chairman, Can. Cttee, International Biological Programme; Ed., Canadian Jl Zool. *Publications:* Animal Diseases in Relation to Man; Internal Parasites of Domestic Animals; Principles of Parasite Control; Parasites of Man in Temperate Climates; Early History of Caribe Islands; Parasites and Parasitism; numerous papers on parasitic helminths, and on diseases of animals in relation to man. *Address:* PO Box 110, Ste Anne de Bellevue, PQ, Canada.

**CAMERON-RAMSAY-FAIRFAX-LUCY,** Major Sir B. F.; *see* Fairfax-Lucy.

**CAMILLERI, Emanuel,** CMG 1950; OBE 1942; Deputy Chairman, Public Service Commission, Malta, since 1961; Secretary to Maltese Imperial Government, 1947-50, Retired 1950; *b* 29 Dec. 1887; *s* of Dr G. Camilleri, LLD, and Theresa Curmi; *m* 1922, Evelyn Sultana; one *d*. *Educ:* Lyceum, Malta; Royal Malta Univ. Entered Malta Civil Service, 1907; Postmaster General, 1937; Manager, Water, Electricity and Telephones Dept, 1942; Secretary to Government (Malta), 1945; acted as Lieutenant-Governor, March-July 1946. Chairman Advisory and Exec. Board, Medical and Health Dept, 1959-61. *Address:* 56 Rudolphe Street, Sliema, Malta. *T:* 31100. *Club:* Casino Maltese (Malta).

**CAMILLERI, His Honour Sir Luigi A.,** Kt 1954; LLD; Chief Justice and President of the Court of Appeal, Malta, 1952-57, retired; *b* 7 Dec. 1892; *s* of late Notary Giuseppe amd Matilde (*née* Bonello); *m* 1914, Erminia, *d* of Professor G. Cali'; five *s* three *d*. *Educ:* Gozo Seminary; Royal Univ. of Malta (LLD). Called to the Bar, 1913. Consular Agent for France in Gozo, Malta, 1919; Malta Legislative Assembly, 1921; Magistrate, 1924; Visitor of Notarial Acts, Chairman Board of Prison Visitors, Chairman Licensing Board, Magistrate in charge of Electoral Register, 1927-30; Judicial Bench, 1930; Royal Univ. of Malta representative on General Council of the Univ., 1933-36; Chairman Emergency Compensation Board, 1940-41; Court of Appeal, 1940-57; President Medical Council, Malta, 1959; Member Judicial Service Commission, 1959. Examiner in Criminal, Roman and Civil Law, Royal Univ. of Malta. Silver Jubilee Medal, 1935; Coronation Medals, 1937 and 1953. Knight of Sovereign Military Order of Malta, 1952. *Recreation:* walking. *Address:* Victoria Avenue, Sliema, Malta. *T:* Sliema 33532. *Club:* Casino Maltese (Malta).

**CAMOYS,** 6th Baron *cr* 1264 (called out of abeyance, 1839); **Ralph Robert Watts Sherman Stonor,** DL; land manager (independent); company director; Chairman, Chancery Lane Branch Sun Alliance & London Insurance Co.; *b* 5 July 1913; *s* of 5th Baron; *S* father, 1968; *m* 1938, Mary Jeanne Stourton; two *s* three *d*. *Educ:* privately, mostly self taught. Served 4 Bn Oxfordshire and Buckinghamshire LI; 2nd Lieut 1939; Capt. 1940; Major 1941; retired (ill health) 1944. Has served in local government at various levels since 1938; member of many cttees and sub-cttees; Oxfordshire CC; past Chm., County Records Cttee; Past Chm., Henley Area Planning Cttee. DL Oxon, 1953. *Recreations:* the arts, architecture and church crawling; botany especially wild orchids, ornithology, lepidoptera; member CPRE. *Heir:* *s* Hon. Ralph Thomas Campion George Sherman Stonor [*b* 16 April 1940; *m* 1966, Elizabeth Mary Hyde, *d* of late Sir William Stephen Hyde Parker, 11th Bt; two *d*]. *Address:* Stonor Park, Henley-on-Thames, Oxon. *T:* Turville Heath 300. *Clubs:* St James',

Brooks's, Pratt's, British Parachute; Huntercombe Golf.

**CAMPBELL;** *see* Graham-Campbell.

**CAMPBELL,** family name of **Duke of Argyll,** of **Earl of Breadalbane,** of **Earl Cawdor,** and of **Barons Campbell of Eskan, Colgrain, Glenavy** and **Stratheden.**

**CAMPBELL, Earl of; Torquhil Ian Campbell;** *b* 29 May 1968; *s* of Marquess of Lorne, *qv.*

**CAMPBELL OF ESKAN,** Baron *cr* 1966, of Camis Eskan (Life Peer); **John (Jock) Middleton Campbell;** Kt 1957; President, Booker, McConnell Ltd, since 1967 (Chairman 1952-66); Chairman: Statesman & Nation Publishing Co. Ltd; Milton Keynes Development Corporation, since 1967; Deputy Chairman, London Weekend Television, since 1969 (Director since 1967); Director, Commonwealth Development Corporation, since 1968; *b* 8 Aug. 1912; *e s* of late Colin Algernon Campbell, Colgrain, Dunbartonshire and Underriver House, Sevenoaks, Kent; *m* 1st, 1938, Barbara Noel (marr. diss. 1948), *d* of late Leslie Arden Roffey; two *s* two *d*; 2nd, 1949, Phyllis Jacqueline Gilmour Taylor, *d* of Henry Boyd, CBE. *Educ:* Eton; Exeter Coll., Oxford. President: West India Cttee, 1957-; Organisation of Employers' Fedns, 1970-; Vice-Pres., Crafts Council of Gt Britain Ltd; Chm., Commonwealth Sugar Exporters' Group, 1950-; a Dep. Chm., Community Relations Commn, 1968-. Member: Exec. Cttee, Africa Bureau; Council, Overseas Development Inst. Trustee, Runnymede Trust. *Recreations:* reading, hitting balls, painting. *Address:* Crocker End House, Nettlebed, Oxfordshire. *T:* Nettlebed 202; 15 Eaton Square, SW1. *T:* 01-836 2617. *Clubs:* Garrick, Beefsteak, West Indian, MCC, All England Lawn Tennis; Georgetown (Guyana).

**CAMPBELL, Alan Hugh,** CMG 1964; Ambassador to Ethiopia, since 1969; *b* 1 July 1919; *y s* of late Hugh Campbell and Ethel Campbell (*née* Warren); *m* 1947, Margaret Taylor; three *d. Educ:* Sherborne Sch.; Caius Coll., Cambridge. Served in Army, Devonshire Regt, 1940-46. 3rd Sec., HM Foreign (now Diplomatic) Service, 1946; appointed to Lord Killearn's Special Mission to Singapore, 1946; served in Rome, 1952, Peking, 1955; UK Mission to UN, New York, 1961; Head of Western Dept, Foreign Office, 1965; Counsellor, Paris, 1967. *Recreation:* lawn tennis. *Address:* c/o Foreign and Commonwealth Office, SW1. *Clubs:* Oxford and Cambridge University, Hurlingham.

**CAMPBELL, Alan Robertson,** QC 1965; *b* 24 May 1917; *s* of late J. K. Campbell; *m* 1957, Vivien, *y d* of late Comdr A. H. de Kantzow, DSO, RN. *Educ:* Aldenham; Ecole des Sciences Politiques, Paris; Trinity Hall, Cambridge. Called to Bar, Inner Temple, 1939. Commissioned RA (Suppl. Res.), 1939; served France and Belgium, 1939-40; POW, 1940-45. Consultant to: sub-cttee of Legal Cttee of Council of Europe on extra-territorial effect of Anti-Trust Law; sub-cttee on Industrial Espionage. *Publications:* Common Market Law, 1969; Legal Textbooks, works of reference. *Address:* 1 Harcourt Buildings, Temple, EC4. *T:* 01-353 2214. *Club:* Carlton.

**CAMPBELL, Prof. (Alexander) Colin (Patton),** FCPath, FRCPE; Procter Professor of Pathology and Pathological Anatomy, University of Manchester, since 1950; *b* 21 Feb. 1908; *s* of late A. C. Campbell, Londonderry; *m* 1943, Hon. Elisabeth Joan Adderley, 2nd *d* of 6th Baron Norton; two *s* one *d. Educ:* Foyle Coll., Londonderry; Edinburgh Univ. MB, ChB (Hons) Edinburgh 1930; FRCPE 1939. Rockefeller Fellow and Research Fellow in Neuropathology, Harvard Univ., 1935-36; Lectr in Neuropathology, Edinburgh Univ., 1937-39; Lectr in Pathology, Edinburgh Univ., and Pathologist, Royal Infirmary, Edinburgh, 1939-50. War service, 1940-46, RAFVR (Wing-Comdr). *Publications:* papers on pathological subjects in various medical and scientific jls. *Recreations:* carpentry and cabinet-making. *Address:* 7 Stanton Avenue, West Didsbury, Manchester M20 8PT. *T:* 061-445 5821.

**CAMPBELL, Brigadier Alexander Donald Powys,** CB 1945; late Indian Army, 3rd Gurkha Rifles; *b* 6 July 1894; *s* of General A. A. E. Campbell, IA; *m* 1929; one *s. Educ:* Dover Coll.; RMC Sandhurst. 2nd Lieut Indian Army, 1914; Captain 1918; Major 1932; Lieut-Colonel 1936; Colonel 1939; Brigadier 1940; retired 1947. *Address:* Meadowlands, Nutley, Sussex. *Club:* Army and Navy.

**CAMPBELL, Major-General (retired) Sir (Alexander) Douglas,** KBE 1956 (CBE 1945); CB 1949; DSO 1943; MC 1918; MA (Cantab); Colonel Commandant Royal Engineers, 1958-64; *b* 20 June 1899; *s* of late Colonel Alan James Campbell, DSO; *m* 1923, Patience Loveday Carlyon; three *s* one *d* (and one *s* killed in action, 1945). *Educ:* Aravon Sch., Bray; Cheltenham Coll.; RMA Woolwich; Queens' Coll., Cambridge. Served European War, 1914-18, France 1918; DADFW War Office, 1933-39; War of 1939-45 (despatches); France, 1940; Asst Dir, Bomb Disposal, 1940; Chief Engr 9 Corps, N Africa, 1943; Chief Engr 1 Corps, Normandy, June 1944; Chief Engr Second Army, 1944-45; Chief Engr Fourteenth Army, June-Nov. 1945; Dep. Dir Tactical Investigation, 1945-46; Chief Engr MELF, 1947-48. E-in-C War Office, 1948-52; Vice-Adjt General to the Forces, 1952-54; Comdr Aldershot District, 1954-57, retired. Lieut Governor, Royal Hospital, Chelsea, 1957-62. Pres., Instn of Royal Engineers, 1957-61; Pres., Assoc. of Service Newspapers. Vice-Chm., Council of Voluntary Welfare Work, 1956-62; Member: Army Benevolent Fund Control Board, 1958-62; ATS Benevolent Fund Cttee, 1953-57 and 1959-63; Soldiers' and Airmen's Scripture Readers' Assoc. (SASRA). Vice-President: Officers' Christian Union; Sandes Soldiers' Homes; Pres., Cheltonian Soc., 1963-64; Governor and Vice-Chm., Royal Sch. for Daughters of Army Officers; Mem. Exec. Cttee, Gordon Boys' Sch.; Chm., Newells and Desmoor Sch. Dir, Taylor Woodrow Industrial Estates, 1962-65. Hon. Colonel, Queen's Univ., Belfast OTC, 1959-64. Commander USA Legion of Merit, 1946. *Address:* Green Bough Cottage, Shipley, Sussex. *T:* Coolham 291. *Club:* Army and Navy.

**CAMPBELL, Major-General (retired) Alfred Edward,** CB 1957; MD, DPH; late RAMC; *b* 21 May 1901; *s* of Rev. J. W. R. Campbell, MA, Stephen's Green, Dublin; *m* 1938, Hilda, *d* of Dr Henry, Clones, Co. Monaghan; three *d. Educ:* Methodist Coll. and Queen's Univ., Belfast. Lieut, RAMC, 1924; Captain 1928; Major 1934; Lieut-Colonel 1945; Colonel 1949; Brigadier 1953; Maj.-Gen. 1956. Served in general medical and Army Health duties, UK, India, Norway, Iceland, Germany and Malaya. Dep. Dir of Army Health, 1945; Dir of Army Health, 1953; Dep. Director-General of Army Medical Services, 1956-60; Director of Physiological and Biological Research, War Office, 1960-63; Regimental Headquarter Duties, RAMC, 1963-67. QHP 1953-60.

Retired 1960. CStJ 1958. Col Comdt, RAMC, 1961-64. Representative Col Comdt, RAMC, 1962-63. *Address:* 6 West Hill Avenue, Epsom, Surrey. *T:* Epsom 22500.

**CAMPBELL, Alistair;** Rawlinson and Bosworth Professor of Anglo-Saxon, University of Oxford, and Fellow of Pembroke College, Oxford, since Oct. 1963; *b* 12 Dec. 1907; *s* of Lauchlan and Sarah Campbell, Birmingham; *m* 1935, Kathleen Le Pelley Blackmore; three *s*. *Educ:* Malvern Coll.; Birmingham Univ.; Balliol Coll., Oxford. BA Birm. 1929; BLitt 1932, MA 1940, Oxford. Lectr in English Language, Balliol Coll., 1946-53; Univ. Lectr in Mediaeval English, Oxford, 1949-63. Sen. Research Fellow, Balliol Coll., 1953-63. *Publications:* The Battle of Brunanburh, 1938; Gysbert Japicx: The Oxford Text of Four Poems, 1948; Encomium Emmae Reginae, 1949; Frithegodi Monachi Breuiloquium et Wulfstani Cantoris Narratio Metrica, 1950; Thet Freske Riim; Tractatus Alvini, 1952; The Tollemache Orosius, 1953 (Early English Manuscripts in Facsimile, vol. iii); An Old English Grammar, 1959; The Chronicle of Aethelweard, 1962; Aethelwulf: De Abbatibus, 1967; many articles on linguistic and historical subjects. *Address:* 11 Marston Ferry Road, Oxford. *T:* Oxford 55519.

**CAMPBELL, Archibald,** CMG 1966; Assistant Under-Secretary of State, Ministry of Defence, since 1969 (Assistant Secretary, 1967-69); *b* 10 Dec. 1914; *s* of Archibald Campbell and Jessie Sanders Campbell (*née* Halsall); *m* 1939, Peggie Phyllis Hussey; two *s* one *d*. *Educ:* Berkhamsted Sch.; Hertford Coll., Oxford. BA Oxford 1935. Barrister at Law, Middle Temple. Administrative Service, Gold Coast, 1936-46; Colonial Office, 1946; Colonial Attaché, British Embassy, Washington, 1953-56; Asst Secretary, Colonial Office, 1956-59 and 1962-67; Chief Secretary, Malta, 1959-62. *Recreations:* cricket (capped for Bucks in Minor County Competition, 1951); fishing, bird watching, gardening. *Address:* The Gate House, Long Park, Chesham Bois, Bucks. *T:* Amersham 727. *Club:* MCC.

**CAMPBELL, Professor Archibald Duncan;** Professor of Applied Economics, University of Dundee, since 1967; *b* 22 Jan. 1919; *s* of late Duncan Alexander and Catherine Anne Campbell; *m* 1950, Mary Elizabeth McFarlane Wilson; one *s* two *d*. *Educ:* Allan Glen's Sch.; Univ. of Glasgow. Served with Royal Engineers (Major 1945), 1940-45; Lecturer in Political Economy (Senior Lectr from 1952), Univ. of Glasgow, 1945-55; Prof. of Applied Economics, Univ. of St Andrews, 1955-67. Economic Consultant to Sec. of State for Scotland, 1962-; Part-time Mem., Scottish Gas Board, 1966-; Non-exec. Dir, Jute Industries (Holdings) Ltd, 1969-; Chm., Commn on Sugar Industry (St Kitts), 1965-66; Member: Fleck Cttee on the Fishing Industry, 1959-60; Boundary Commn for Scotland, 1961-; Hunter Cttee on Scottish Salmon and Trout Fisheries, 1962-65; Econ. Development Cttee for Building, 1967-; Rochdale Cttee on Shipping, 1967-70; Chm., Arbitration Body on Full-time Further Educn Teachers' Pay in Scotland, 1970-; Joint Dir, Tayside Economic Planning Study, 1967-70. *Publications:* articles in economic and other jls. *Recreation:* golf. *Address:* 23 Strathern Road, West Ferry, Dundee. *T:* Dundee 79030. *Clubs:* Caledonian; Royal and Ancient (St Andrews).

**CAMPBELL, Archibald Hunter,** LLM, BCL, MA, of Lincoln's Inn, Barrister-at-Law; Regius Professor of Public Law, University of Edinburgh, since 1945, and Dean of the Faculty of Law, 1958-64; *b* Edinburgh, 1902; *o c* of late Donald Campbell, MA. *Educ:* George Watson's Coll., Edinburgh (Dux); Univ. of Edinburgh (MA, Mackenzie Class. Schol., Ferguson Class. Schol.; University Coll., Oxford (Class. Exhibitioner). 1st Class in Hon. Mods, Lit. Hum., Jurisprudence and BCL; Sen. Demy of Magdalen Coll., 1927-28; Sen. Student of Oxford Univ., 1928; Fellow of All Souls, 1928-30 and 1936-; Stowell Civil Law Fellow, University Coll., Oxford, 1930-35; Barber Professor of Jurisprudence, Univ. of Birmingham, 1935-45. Vice-President Society of Public Teachers of Law, 1961-62, President 1962-63. President Classical Assoc. of Scotland, 1963-. Hon. LLD Aberdeen, 1963. *Address:* The University, Old College, Edinburgh. *Club:* New (Edinburgh).

**CAMPBELL, Arnold Everitt,** CMG 1966; retired as Director-General of Education, Department of Education, Wellington, New Zealand (1960-66); *b* 13 Aug. 1906; *s* of Fernly Charlwood and Mabel Annie Campbell; *m* 1934, Louise Annie Combs; one *s* two *d*. *Educ:* Palmerston North Boys' High Sch.; Wellington Teachers' Coll., Victoria Univ. of Wellington. Primary school teacher, 1926-28; Lecturer in Education, Victoria Univ. of Wellington, 1929-38; Director, NZ Council for Educational Research, 1939-52; Chief Inspector of Primary Schools, Dept of Education, 1953-58; Asst Director of Education, 1959. *Publication:* Educating New Zealand, 1941. *Address:* 13 Pitt Street, Wellington, New Zealand. *T:* 45-438.

**CAMPBELL, Sir Bruce Colin Patrick,** 3rd Bt UK, *cr* 1913 with precedence from 1804, of Ardnamurchan; *b* 2 July 1904; *s* of Lt-Col Sir John Bruce Campbell, 2nd Bt, DSO, Croix de Guerre, and Jessie Nicholson, 3rd *d* of John Miller, Parkside, S Australia; *S* father, 1943. *Educ:* Edinburgh Academy; Glenalmond; Pangbourne Nautical Coll. *Heir:* none. [*But his name does not, at the time of going to press, appear on the Official Roll of the Baronets.*]

**CAMPBELL, Charles Arthur;** Emeritus Professor since 1961 (Professor of Logic and Rhetoric, Glasgow University, 1938-61); *b* 13 Jan. 1897; *s* of John Munro Campbell and Rose Jane Arthur; *m* 1926, Ruth Stewart, *y d* of Claud Bald; one *s* one *d*. *Educ:* Glasgow Academy; Glasgow Univ.; Balliol Coll., Oxford. Served European War, 2nd Lieut in 10th Border Regt at home and in Egypt, Jan. 1915-Oct. 1917 (invalided out); Asst in Moral Philosophy at Glasgow, 1924; Lecturer, 1925; Professor of Philosophy, University Coll. of North Wales, Bangor, 1932; Gifford Lectr, St Andrews Univ., 1953-54-55. Hon. DLitt, QUB, 1950-. *Publications:* Scepticism and Construction, 1931; Defence of Free Will (Collected Essays), 1967; Moral Intuition and the Principle of Self-realisation (British Academy Lecture), 1948; On Selfhood and Godhood (Gifford Lectures), 1957; papers in Mind, Philosophy, Proc. Aristotelian Soc., etc. *Address:* 11 Lubnaig Drive, Callander, Perthshire.

**CAMPBELL, Charles Douglas,** CB 1961; *b* 8 Oct. 1905; *s* of Charles Edward Campbell; *m* 1932, Margaret Stevenson Miller; no *c*. *Educ:* William Hulme Grammar Sch.; Univ. of Manchester. Asst Lectr in Economics, Manchester Univ., 1927-31; Rockefeller Fellow, USA, 1931-32; Lectr in Commerce, Liverpool Univ., 1932-40; Min. of Supply, 1940-42; British Raw Materials Mission, USA, 1942-47; Board of Trade, 1947-. Under-Sec., 1956-62; Principal Asst Registrar, Office of Restrictive Trading Agreements, 1962-65;

Chm., Timber Trade Fedn of UK, 1966-69. idc 1950. *Publications:* British Railways in Boom and Depression, 1932; (with M. S. Miller) Financial Democracy, 1933; various papers in learned jls, etc. *Recreations:* reading; pottering about. *Address:* 4 Belltrees Grove, SW16. *T:* 01-769 7936. *Club:* Royal Automobile.

**CAMPBELL, Charles Graham;** *er s* of late Colin Campbell of Jura and Frances Monteath Sidey (*d* 1925); *b* 3 June 1880; *m* 1930, Debora Sylvester Fane, *d* of late William Gore Lambarde, Beechmont, Sevenoaks; no *c. Educ:* St Paul's Sch. Served Royal Field Artillery, 1915-19 (despatches); Station owner, NSW, Australia. *Recreations:* hunting, stalking, shooting. *Address:* 2 Campden Hill Gate, Duchess of Bedford's Walk, W8. *T:* 01-937 6795. *Clubs:* Boodle's; New (Edinburgh).

**CAMPBELL, Sir Clifford (Clarence),** GCMG 1962; GCVO 1966; Governor-General of Jamaica since Dec. 1962; *b* 28 June 1892; *s* of late James Campbell, civil servant, and Blanche, *d* of John Ruddock, agriculturist; *m* 1920, Alice Esthephene, *d* of late William Jolly, planter; two *s* two *d. Educ:* Petersfield Sch.; Mico Training Coll., Jamaica. Headmaster: Fullersfield Govt Sch., 1916-18; Friendship Elementary Sch., 1918-28; Grange Hill Govt Sch., 1928-44. Member Jamaica House of Representatives (Jamaica Labour Party) for Westmoreland Western, 1944-49; Chm., House Cttee on Education, 1945-49; 1st Vice-President, Elected Members Assoc., 1945; re-elected 1949; Speaker of the House of Representatives, 1950; Senator and President of the Senate, 1962. KStJ. *Recreations:* agricultural pursuits, reading. *Address:* King's House, Kingston 10, Jamaica. *T:* 76424. *Clubs:* Royal Commonwealth Society; (Hon. Member) Caymanas Golf and Country, Ex-Services, Kingston Cricket, Liguanea, Rotary, St Andrew's, Trelawny (all in Jamaica).

**CAMPBELL, Colin;** *see* Campbell, A. C. P.

**CAMPBELL, Sir Colin,** Kt 1952; OBE 1941; Town Clerk, Plymouth, 1935-53; *b* 1891; *m* 1923, Matilda Hopwood (*d* 1955); two *d. Educ:* Burnley Grammar Sch. Town Clerk, Burnley, 1923-35. ARP Controller of Plymouth, 1939-45. *Recreation:* golf. *Address:* Reedley Hallows, Delgany, Plymouth, Devon. *T:* Plymouth 72115.

**CAMPBELL, Sir Colin Moffat,** 8th Bt *cr* 1667, of Aberuchill and Kilbryde, Dunblane, Perthshire; MC 1945; Senior, Nairobi Branch of James Finlay & Co. Ltd; *b* 4 Aug. 1925; *e s* of Sir John Campbell, 7th Bt and Janet Moffat; *S* father, 1960; *m* 1952, Mary Anne Chichester Bain, *er d* of Brigadier G. A. Bain, Sandy Lodge, Chagford, Devon; two *s* one *d. Educ:* Stowe. Scots Guards, 1943-47, Captain. Employed with James Finlay & Co. Ltd, Calcutta, 1948-58. President Federation of Kenya Employers, 1962-70; Chairman: Tea Board of Kenya, 1961-70; E African Tea Trade Assoc., 1960-61, 1962-63, 1966-67. *Recreations:* racing, cards. *Heir: s* James Alexander Moffat Bain Campbell, *b* 23 Sept. 1956. *Address:* Glenardoch, Doune, Perthshire. *T:* Doune 365; Box 12244, Nairobi. *T:* Nairobi 65045. *Clubs:* Guards; Royal Calcutta Turf, Tollygunge (Calcutta); Nairobi, Muthaiga (E Africa).

**CAMPBELL, Sir David,** Kt 1953; MC; MA, BSc, MD, LLD (Glasgow, Dublin, Liverpool, Aberdeen); DCL (Durham); FRCPG; FRSE; FRCP; Regius Professor of Materia Medica and Therapeutics, University of Aberdeen, 1930-59; Dean of the Faculty of Medicine, 1932-59; President, General Medical Council, 1949-61; *b* 6 May 1889; *m* 1921, Margaret, *o d* of Alexander Lyle of Kerse. *Educ:* Ayr Academy; Univ. of Glasgow; Johns Hopkins Univ. MA (Hons) 1911; BSc 1911; MB, ChB (Hons) 1916; MD (Hons and Bellahouston Gold Medal), 1924; LLD 1950. Captain (a/Major) RAMC (TF), 1916-19; Univ. Asst to Prof. of Materia Medica and Therapeutics, Glasgow Univ., 1919-21; Pollok Lectr in Materia Medica and Pharmacology, 1921-30; Resident Physician, 1915-16; Physician to Out-Patients, 1920-29; Asst Physician to Western Infirmary, Glasgow, 1929-30; Extra-Hon. Physician, Aberdeen Royal Infirmary, 1930-59; Rockefeller Medical Fellow in Pharmacology and Therapeutics, 1925-26. *Publications:* Handbook of Therapeutics; papers on pharmacological and therapeutic subjects in various medical and scientific jls. *Recreations:* golf, motoring. *Address:* Carskeoch, Milltimber, Aberdeenshire. *T:* Culter 3335. *Clubs:* Athenæum; Royal Northern (Aberdeen).

**CAMPBELL, Donald le Strange,** MC; Director: Project Services Overseas Ltd; Macpherson Train & Co. Ltd; *b* 16 June 1919; *s* of late Donald Fraser Campbell and of Caroline Campbell, Heacham, Norfolk; *m* 1952, Hon. Shona Catherine Greig Macpherson, *y d* of 1st Baron Macpherson of Drumochter; one *s* one *d. Educ:* Winchester Coll.; Clare Coll., Cambridge. Served War, 1939-45, Major RA (MC). EFCO Ltd, 1947-55; MEECO Ltd, 1955-61; Davy-Ashmore Ltd, 1961-67. Dep. Chairman, BNEC Latin America, 1967. *Recreations:* farming, sailing, field sports. *Address:* North Dean House, Hughenden, Bucks. *Clubs:* Brooks's; Royal Ocean Racing, Royal London Yacht.

**CAMPBELL, Major-General Sir Douglas;** *see* Campbell, Sir Alexander Douglas.

**CAMPBELL, Douglas Mason,** QC (Scotland) 1953; Sheriff of Inverness, Moray, Nairn, and Ross and Cromarty, since 1958; Chairman, Workmen's Compensation and Pneumoconiosis, Byssinosis and Miscellaneous Diseases Benefit Boards; *b* 14 Nov. 1905; *s* of late David C. Campbell, Glasgow; *m* 1955, Alice Barbara Chalmers, *d* of late W. G. Chalmers Hanna, OBE, MC, CA, Edinburgh. *Educ:* Sedbergh; Worcester Coll., Oxford. BA Oxford, 1928; LLB Glasgow, 1931. Admitted to Scottish Bar, 1931. Served RA, 1940-45. Advocate-Depute, 1951-53 and 1957-58. *Recreations:* fishing, shooting, golf. *Address:* 10 Forres Street, Edinburgh. *T:* 031-225 3150. *Clubs:* United University; New (Edinburgh); Highland (Inverness); Hon. Company of Edinburgh Golfers.

**CAMPBELL, Colonel (Hon. Brigadier, retired) Edmund George,** CBE 1943; *b* 3 April 1893; *e s* of late Brig.-General G. P. Campbell, CBE, CIE; *m* 1918, Esmé, *d* of late H. A. Rose, ICS; no *c. Educ:* Mount St Mary's Coll.; RMA, Woolwich. 2nd Lieut RA 1912. Served European War, 1914-18; passed Staff College, Quetta, and RAF Staff College; Colonel 1939; Temp. Brigadier 1940. Served War of 1939-45 (despatches, CBE); retired 1946. *Recreations:* bridge, and gardening. *Address:* Half Acre, Fleet, Hants. *T:* Fleet 6115.

**CAMPBELL, Evan Roy,** CBE 1958; Chairman: Rhodesia Board, Standard Bank Ltd, since 1965; Albatros Fisons Fertilizers Ltd since 1966; Rhodesia Tea Estates since 1965; Fisons Pest Control (CA) (pvt) Ltd; National Industrial Credit Corp., (Rhod.) Ltd; African Loan and Development Trust Holdings; Central African Branch of Institute of Directors; Director: Manica Trading Co. of

Rhodesia Ltd; Peterhouse School; Fisons (Pty) Ltd (South Africa); Rhodesian Oxygen (Pvt) Ltd; Metal Box Co. of Central Africa Ltd; Discount Co. of Rhodesia Ltd; *b* 2 Sept. 1908; *m* 1934, Norah May Vaughan; one *s* one *d*. *Educ:* St Andrew's Coll., Grahamstown, S Africa; Potchefstroom Agricultural Coll. Started farming in Umvukwes, S Rhodesia, 1931; has farmed in Inyazura since 1935. Enlisted in Rhodesia Regt, 1940; seconded to King's African Rifles (Abyssinia, Burma and India); Staff Coll., Quetta, 1944 (psc); GSO 2, 11 (E Africa) Div.; Bde Major 25 (E Africa) Infantry Bde. Rhodesia Tobacco Assoc.; Mem., 1946; Vice-Pres., 1947; Pres., 1952-58, now Life Vice-Pres.; Chm. Makoni Br., and Mem. Nat. Council, British Empire Service League, 1947; Mem., Tobacco Marketing Board, 1950; Chm., Tobacco Export Promotion Council, 1958; Chm., Gwebi Agric. Coll. Council, 1963; Pres., First Internat. Tobacco Congress; Life Vice-Pres., Manicaland Agricultural Show Society. High Comr in Great Britain for Southern Rhodesia, 1964-65. Farmers' Oscar for outstanding services to agriculture and British Empire Service League meritorious service medal, 1962. *Recreations:* riding, croquet, yachting. *Address:* (business) Standard Bank, Cecil Square, PO Box 373, Salisbury, Rhodesia; (private) P. Bag 9, Inyazura, Rhodesia. *Clubs:* MCC; Salisbury Umtali (Rhodesia); Jockey Club of South Africa; Beira (Mozambique).

**CAMPBELL, Ewen,** CMG 1946; MBE 1926; MC 1917; Member of Council, British Red Cross Society (Chairman, Executive Committee, Scottish Branch, 1962-70); Secretary, South-Eastern Regional Hospital Board, Scotland, 1948-62; Sudan Political Service (retired); Member Queen's Body Guard for Scotland, Royal Company of Archers; *b* 13 Aug. 1897; *er s* of late Colonel Ewen Campbell, VD, JP; *m* 1929, Evelyn Winifred, *o d* of late Philip Robertson, NSW, Australia; three *d*. *Educ:* Edinburgh Academy; Oriel Coll., Oxford. European War, commissioned RFA 1915; served in France (MC) and North Russia; entered Oxford, 1919; played Rugby football for Oxford Univ., 1919, 1920 and captained the XV in 1921; BA Hons 1921; joined Sudan Political Service, 1921; served as Asst District Commissioner in Kassala and Darfur Provinces; Deputy-Governor Kassala Province, 1935-36; Deputy Civil Secretary, Khartoum, 1936-38; Governor of Kordofan Province, Sudan, 1938-47. Order of the Nile 4th Class 1933, 3rd Class 1941; despatches 1943. *Address:* 8 Succoth Gardens, Edinburgh. *Club:* New (Edinburgh).

**CAMPBELL, Engineer Captain George Douglas,** CBE 1944; DSO 1918; Royal Navy, retired; *b* 10 March 1884; *m* 1944, Ruth Evelyn, *d* of F. J. Misselbrook, Southampton. *Educ:* private; abroad. Joined RNE College, 1900; served European War, 1914-18 (despatches, DSO); Engineer Captain, 1931; retired list, 1937. Served War of 1939-45 (CBE). *Club:* Royal Naval (Portsmouth).

**CAMPBELL, Rt. Hon. Gordon Thomas Calthrop,** PC 1970; MC 1944, and Bar, 1945; MP (C) for Moray and Nairn since 1959; Secretary of State for Scotland since 1970; *b* 8 June 1921; *s* of late Maj.-Gen. J. A. Campbell, DSO; *m* 1949, Nicola Elizabeth Gina Madan; two *s* one *d*. *Educ:* Wellington. War of 1939-45: commissioned in Regular Army, 1939; RA, Major, 1942; commanded 320 Field Battery in 15 Scottish Div.; wounded and disabled, 1945. Entered HM Foreign Service, 1946; served, until 1957, in FO, UK Delegn to the UN (New York), Cabinet Office and Vienna. Asst Govt Whip, 1961-62; a Lord Comr of the Treasury, and Scottish Whip, 1962-63; Joint Parly Under-Sec. of State, Scottish Office, 1963-64; formerly Opposition Chief Spokesman on Scottish Affairs. *Recreations:* music, birds. *Address:* Holme Rose, Nairnshire, Scotland. *T:* Croy 223. *Clubs:* Brooks's; Caledonian (Edinburgh).

**CAMPBELL, Sir Guy (Theophilus Halswell),** 5th Bt *cr* 1815; OBE 1954; MC 1941; Colonel, late 60th Rifles, El Kaimakam Bey, Camel Corps, Sudan Defence Force, and Kenya Regiment; *b* 18 Jan. 1910; *s* of Major Sir Guy Colin Campbell, 4th Bt, late 60th Rifles, and Mary Arabella Swinnerton Kemeys-Tynte, *sister* of 8th Lord Wharton; *S* father, 1960; *m* 1956, Lizbeth Webb, Bickenhall Mansions, W1; two *s*. *Educ:* St Aubyn's, Rottingdean; Eton Coll.; St Andrews Univ. War of 1939-45 (wounded); served in KOYLI, 1931-42; seconded to Camel Corps, Sudan Defence Force, 1939-47; Comd 2/7 and 7 Nuba Bns, 1943-47; Shifta Ops, Eritrea, 1946; Acting Brig., 1945, HQ SDF Group (N Africa); Palestine, 1948; Mil. Adviser to Count Folke Bernadotte and Dr Ralph Bunche of United Nations, 1948; attached British Embassy as Civil Affairs Officer, Cairo, 1948; British Mil. Mission to Ethiopia, in Ogaden Province, 1948-51; 2nd i/c 1/60th Rifles, BAOR, 1951; comd Kenya Regt (TF), 1952-56, Mau Mau ops; Head of British Mil. Mission to Libya, 1956-60; retired Aug. 1960. Col R of O, 60th Rifles. C-in-C's (MELF) Commendation, 1945; Gold Medal of Emperor Haile Selassie (non-wearable). *Recreations:* watching cricket, golf, Rugby football, polo, tennis, hockey. *Heir: s* Lachlan Philip Kemeys Campbell, *b* 9 Oct. 1958. *Address:* 30 Bramham Gardens, SW5. *T:* 01-373 1240. *Clubs:* St James', MCC, I Zingari; Puffins (Edinburgh); Royal and Ancient (St Andrews).

**CAMPBELL, Major-General Sir Hamish Manus,** KBE 1963 (CBE 1958); CB 1961; *b* 6 Jan. 1905; *s* of late Major A. C. J. Campbell, Middlesex Regt and Army Pay Dept, and of Alice, *d* of late Comdr Yelverton O'Keeffe, RN; *m* 1929, Marcelle, *d* of late Charles Ortlieb, Neuchâtel, Switzerland; one *s*. *Educ:* Downside School; New Coll., Oxford. Commissioned in Argyll and Sutherland Highlanders, 1927; transferred to Royal Army Pay Corps, 1937; Lieut-Colonel and Staff Paymaster (1st Class), temp. 1945, subs. 1951; Colonel and Chief Paymaster, temp. 1954, subs. 1955; Major-General, 1959. Command Paymaster: Sierra Leone, 1940-42; Burma, 1946-48; Malta, 1953. Deputy Chief, Budget and Finance Division, SHAPE, 1954-56; Commandant, RAPC Training Centre, 1956-59; Paymaster-in-Chief, War Office, 1959-63; retired, 1963. Col Comdt, RAPC, 1963-70. *Address:* 7 Nightingale Close, Storrington, Sussex. *T:* Storrington 3442. *Club:* Army and Navy.

**CAMPBELL, Brigadier Hector,** CB 1933; DSO 1918; MVO 1906; Colonel Queen Victoria's Own Corps of Guides (Cavalry and Infantry), 1935; *b* 24 Oct. 1877; *s* of late Major-General R. B. P. P. Campbell, CB, and Ada, *d* of late L. G. A. Campbell, of Fairfield, Ayrshire. *Educ:* Haileybury Coll.; RMC, Sandhurst. Entered Army, 1897; Captain, 1906; Major, 1915; Lieut-Colonel, 1921; Colonel, 1925; Brigadier, 1931; with 1st Gordon Highlanders during Tirah Expedition, 1897-98, present at action of Dargai (medal and 2 clasps); China Expeditionary Force, 1900 (medal); European War, 1914-18, Egypt, Gallipoli, Egypt and Palestine (despatches twice, 1914-15 Star, two medals, DSO); Military Adviser-in-Chief, Indian States Forces, 1931-34; retired 1934. *Recreations:* polo, riding, shooting; in winning team Indian Championship Polo Tournament,

1909-10. *Address:* c/o National and Grindlay's Bank, 13 St James's Square, SW1. *Club:* United Service.

**CAMPBELL, Rt. Rev. and Rt. Hon. Henry Colville M.;** *see* Montgomery Campbell.

**CAMPBELL, Ian,** CEng, MIMechE, JP; MP (Lab) Dunbartonshire (West) since 1970; *b* 26 April 1926; *s* of William Campbell and Helen Crockett; *m* 1950, Mary Millar; two *s* three *d*. *Educ:* Dumbarton Academy; Royal Technical Coll., Glasgow (now Strathclyde Univ.). Engineer with South of Scotland Electricity Board for 17 years. Councillor, Dumbarton, 1958-70; Provost of Dumbarton, 1962-70. *Address:* 20 McGregor Drive, Dumbarton. *T:* Dumbarton 3612.

**CAMPBELL, Ian George Hallyburton,** TD; QC 1957; Lord Chancellor's Legal Visitor since 1963; *b* 19 July 1909; *s* of late Hon. Kenneth Campbell and Mrs K. Campbell; *m* 1949, Betty Yolande, *d* of late Somerset Maclean and *widow* of Lieut-Col Allan Bruno, MBE; one adopted *s* one adopted *d*. *Educ:* Charterhouse, Trinity Coll., Cambridge. Barrister, Inner Temple and Lincoln's Inn, 1932. Served Artists Rifles and Rifle Brigade, 1939-45; Col 1945. Appts include: GSO2, HQ 1st Army; Chief Judicial Officer, Allied Commission, Italy; Chief Legal Officer, Military Govt, Austria (British zone). *Address:* Greywalls, Liphook, Hants. *T:* Liphook 3344. *Club:* Boodle's.

**CAMPBELL, Ian Macdonald,** BSc; CEng; FICE; MInstT; General Manager, Eastern Region, British Railways, since 1970; *b* 13 July 1922; *s* of late John Isdale Campbell; *m* 1946, Hilda Ann Williams; one *s* three *d*. *Educ:* University Coll., London. BSc(Eng). Asst District Engr, Sheffield, 1953-57; District Engr, Kings Cross, 1957-63; Asst Civil Engr, Scottish Region, 1963-65; Chief Civil Engr, Scottish Region, Asst Gen. Man., LM Region, 1968-70. *Recreations:* golf, music. *Address:* British Railways, York.

**CAMPBELL, Professor Ian McIntyre,** MA; Professor of Humanity, University of Edinburgh, since 1959; *b* 14 Jan. 1915; *s* of late John Campbell and Janet Donaldson; *m* 1945, Julia Margaret Mulgan; two *s* one *d*. *Educ:* Spier's Sch., Beith; Univ. of Glasgow; Balliol Coll., Oxford. First cl. Hons Classics, Glasgow Univ., 1936; First cl., Class. Mods, 1938. Served in Intelligence Corps, Captain, 1939-45; Hon. War Memorial Research Student, Balliol Coll., 1946; Lecturer in Humanity and Comparative Philology, Glasgow Univ., 1947-54; Prof. of Latin, Univ. Coll. of S Wales and Monmouthshire, 1954-59. *Publications:* articles and reviews in learned journals. Jt Editor of Archivum Linguisticum, 1949-. *Recreation:* music. *Address:* 3 McLaren Road, Edinburgh EH9 2BE. *T:* 031-667 4030.

**CAMPBELL, Mrs Ian McIvor;** *see* Corbet, Mrs Freda K.

**CAMPBELL, Vice-Admiral Sir Ian Murray Robertson,** KBE 1955; CB 1951; DSO 1942, Bar 1943; *b* 8 Aug. 1898; 2nd *s* of Brig. A. A. E. Campbell, Indian Army; *m* 1929, Marjorie Mary McCreath, Looseleigh, Tamerton Foliot, Devon; two *s*. Service in N Sea, Adriatic and Eastern Baltic, 1914-19; service in home, Mediterranean and China Stations, 1919-38; specialised in gunnery 1924; Captain in Naval Staff, 1940; Comd 3rd Destroyer Flotilla, HMS Milne, 1942-44; Naval Staff, and Comd HMS Jamaica, E Indies Squadron, 1945-47; Rear-Adm. 1950; Senior British Naval Officer and Flag Officer (Liaison) Middle East, 1950-52; Flag Officer Commanding Reserve Fleet, 1953-54; Commander-in-Chief, South Atlantic Station, 1954-56; retd List, 1956. Vice-Adm., 1953. Hon. Sec. Gloucestershire County Branch, CPRE. *Publication:* (jointly) The Kola Run, 1958. *Address:* Ivy Cottage, Sapperton, Glos.

**CAMPBELL, Air Vice-Marshal Ian Robert,** CBE 1964; AFC 1948; Director of Management and Support Intelligence, Ministry of Defence, since 1970; *b* 5 Oct. 1920; *s* of late Major and of Hon. Mrs D. E. Campbell; *m* 1953, Beryl Evelyn Newbigging; one *s*. *Educ:* Eton; RAF Coll., Cranwell. Anti-Shipping Ops, 1940-42; POW, Italy and Germany, 1942-45; 540 Sqdn, Benson, 1946; psa 1949; PSO to C-in-C Far East, 1950; 124 (F) Wing Oldenburg, 1953; OC, RAF Sandwich, 1956; pfc 1957; OC 213 Sqdn, Bruggen, 1958; ACOS Plans HQ 2ATAF, 1959; OC, RAF Marham, 1961; MoD (Air) DASB, 1964; SASO, HQ No 1 Group, 1965; Air Attaché, Bonn, 1968. *Recreations:* shooting, golf, travel. *Address:* 10 Farley Court, Melbury Road, W14. *T:* 01-602 2399. *Clubs:* Boodle's, Royal Air Force.

**CAMPBELL, Major-General Ian Ross,** CBE 1954; DSO and Bar, 1941; Chairman, NSW Division of Australian Red Cross Society, since 1967; *b* 23 March 1900; *m* 1927, Patience Allison Russell (*d* 1961); one *d*; *m* 1967, Irene Cardamatis. *Educ:* Wesley Coll., Melbourne; Scots Coll., Sydney; Royal Military College, Duntroon, Canberra (Graduate, 1922). Served War of 1939-45, Middle East Campaigns, Libya, Greece and Crete (DSO and bar, Cross of Kt Comdr, Greek Order of Phœnix; pow 1941-45); comd Aust. forces in Korean War, 1951-53 (CBE); Comdt, Australian Staff Coll., 1953-54; Comdt, Royal Mil. Coll. Duntroon, 1954-57; retired, 1957. With James Hardie & Co. Pty Ltd, 1957-67. Pres., Great Public Schs Athletic Assoc., NSW, 1966-. *Recreation:* tennis. *Address:* 15/17 Wylde Street, Potts Point, Sydney, NSW, Australia. *Clubs:* Imperial Service, Royal Sydney Golf (Sydney).

**CAMPBELL, Sir Ian (Vincent Hamilton),** 7th Bt *cr* 1831, of Barcaldine and Glenure; CB 1951; Assistant Under-Secretary of State, Air Ministry, 1945-55, retired 1955; *b* 1895; *e surv s* of Richard Hamilton Campbell, CIE, ICS (retd) (*d* 1923); *S* cousin, Captain Sir (Francis) Eric Dennistoun Campbell, 6th Bt, 1963; *m* 1st, Madeline (*d* 1929), *e d* of late H. Anglin Whitelocke, FRCS, Oxford; one *s*; 2nd, Iris Constance (marriage dissolved, 1942), *d* of late Lt-Col Ronald Charles Gibb, CBE; 3rd, Agnes Louise, *e d* of late William Henry Gerhardi, and *widow* of Vsevolod Victor Watson, MBE. *Educ:* Cheltenham; Corpus Christi Coll., Oxford. Served European War, 1914-18 as Lieut The King's (Liverpool Regt); severely wounded in Battle of the Somme, 1916, and invalided from Army, May 1918. Entered Home Civil Service, 1919, as Asst Principal, Air Ministry; Priv. Sec. to Chief of Air Staff (late Marshal of the RAF Lord Trenchard), 1926-27; Private Sec. to Permanent Sec. of the Air Ministry (late Sir Walter Nicholson), 1927-30; Asst Private Sec. to successive Secs of State for Air (late Lord Thomson, late Lord Amulree, and, late Marquess of Londonderry), 1930-34; Principal, Air Ministry, 1934; Asst Sec. 1939. *Heir:* *s* Niall Alexander Hamilton Campbell [*b* 7 Jan. 1925; *m* 1st, 1949, Patricia Mary (marr. diss., 1956), *d* of R. Turner; 2nd, 1957, Norma Joyce, *d* of W. N. Wiggin; two *s* two *d* (including twin *s* and *d*)]. *Address:* White Rose, Hawkhurst, Kent. *T:* Hawkhurst 2268.

**CAMPBELL, Sir Ilay (Mark),** 7th Bt *cr* 1808, of Succoth, Dunbartonshire; *b* 29 May 1927; only *s* of Sir George Ilay Campbell, 6th Bt; *S* father, 1967; *m* 1961, Margaret Minette Rohais, *o d* of J. Alasdair Anderson; two *d*. *Educ:* Eton; Christ Church, Oxford. BA 1952. Scottish Agent for Messrs Christie, Manson & Woods. *Recreations:* heraldry, horticulture and hunting. *Heir:* none. *Address:* Lennel, Coldstream, Berwickshire. *T:* Coldstream 2254; Crarae Lodge, Inveraray, Argyll. *T:* Minard 204. *Clubs:* Turf; Puffins (Edinburgh).

**CAMPBELL, James Grant,** CMG 1970; President and Chairman of the Board, Demerara Bauxite Co. Ltd, Guyana, since 1970; Director: several subsidiary companies of Alcan Aluminium Ltd and of Guyana Development Corporation; *b* Springville, NS, Canada, 8 June 1914; *s* of John Kay Campbell and Wilna Archibald Campbell (*née* Grant); *m* 1941, Alice Isobel Dougall; one *d*. *Educ:* Mount Allison Univ., Canada. BSc, 1st cl. hons (Chem.). Chemist and Engineer, Aluminium Co. of Canada, Arvida, Que, 1937; various posts, finally Gen. Supt, Demerara Bauxite Co. Ltd, 1941-50; Aluminium Laboratories Ltd, London, England, 1950 (Headqrs for team investigating hydro power, bauxite and aluminium smelting in Asia, Africa and Europe); on staff of Dir of Operations, Aluminium Ltd, Montreal (concerned with world supply of raw materials for Aluminium Ltd), 1951-55; Managing Dir and Chm., 1955-70. Hon. LLD, Mount Allison Univ., 1966. *Recreations:* music, golf, reading. *Address:* 95 Duke Street, Georgetown, Guyana, S America. *T:* 4621. *Clubs:* Royal Automobile; University, Canadian (New York); University Golf, Kanawaki Golf (Montreal); Georgetown, (Georgetown, Guyana).

**CAMPBELL, Mrs John;** *see* Campbell, May Eudora.

**CAMPBELL, Sir John Johnston,** Kt 1957; General Manager, Clydesdale Bank Ltd, 1946-58, retired (Director since 1958); *b* 11 Dec. 1897; *s* of William Campbell, Stewarton, Ayrshire; *m* 1927, Margaret Fullarton (*d* 1967), *d* of John Brown, Dalry, Ayrshire; one *s* one *d*. *Educ:* Stewarton Secondary Sch. Joined service of The Clydesdale Bank at Stewarton, Ayrshire, 1913. Served with Royal Scots Fusiliers in Palestine, France, and Germany, 1916-19. London Manager, Clydesdale Bank, 1944. Pres., Institute of Bankers in Scotland, 1953-55; Chm.: Development Securities Ltd, 1958-67; Cttee of Scottish Bank Gen Managers, 1955-57; Dir of cos. *Recreation:* golf. *Address:* 22 Saffrons Court, Compton Place Road, Eastbourne, Sussex. *T:* 29271. *Club:* Western (Glasgow).

**CAMPBELL of Canna, John Lorne;** owns and farms Isle of Canna, Inner Hebrides; folklorist, editor and author; *b* 1 Oct. 1906; *s* of late Col Duncan Campbell of Inverneill and Ethel Harriet, *e d* of late John I. Waterbury, Morristown, NJ; *m* 1935, Margaret Fay (author of Folksongs and Folklore of South Uist), *y d* of late Henry Clay Shaw, Glenshaw, Pennsylvania (US); no *c*. *Educ:* Cargilfield; Rugby; St John's Coll., Oxford (MA 1933, DLitt, 1965). Hon. LLD, St Francis Xavier Univ., Antigonish, NS, 1953. Hon. DLitt, Glasgow Univ., 1965. *Publications:* Highland Songs of the Forty-Five, 1933; The Book of Barra (with Compton Mackenzie and Carl Hj. Borgstrom), 1936; (Ed.) Orain Ghaidhlig le Seonaidh Caimbeul, 1936; Sia Sgialachdan, Six Gaelic Stories from South Uist and Barra, 1938; Act Now for the Highlands and Islands (with Sir Alexander MacEwen), 1939; Gaelic in Scottish Education and Life, 1945; Gaelic Folksongs from the Isle of Barra (with Annie Johnston and John MacLean), 1950; Fr. Allan McDonald of Eriskay, Priest, Poet and Folklorist, 1954; Gaelic Words from South Uist and Eriskay, collected by Fr. Allan McDonald, 1958; Tales from Barra, told by the Coddy, 1960; Stories from South Uist, 1961; The Furrow Behind Me, the Autobiography of a Hebridean Crofter (trans. from tape recordings), 1962; Edward Lhuyd in the Scottish Highlands (with Prof. Derick Thomson), 1963; A School in South Uist (memoirs of Frederick Rea), 1964; Bardachd Mhgr Ailein, the Gaelic Poems of Fr. Allan McDonald, 1965; Strange Things (with Trevor H. Hall), 1968; Hebridean Folksongs (with F. Collinson), 1969. Contribs to various periodicals, etc. *Recreations:* entomology, sea fishing. *Address:* Isle of Canna, Scotland.

**CAMPBELL, (John) Maurice (Hardman),** OBE; MD Oxon; FRCP; Consulting Physician to Guy's Hospital; Consulting Physician, National Hospital for Diseases of the Heart; Consulting Editor, British Heart Journal; *b* 1891; *s* of J. E. Campbell, FRS; *m* 1924, Ethel Mary, *d* of Captain Chrimes, CBE; two *s* three *d*. *Educ:* Winchester (Scholar); New Coll., Oxford. 1st Class Physiology, Oxford and Senior Demyship, Magdalen Coll.; Captain RAMC (SR), Mesopotamia and North Persia, 1916-19; Beit Memorial Research Fellow, 1923-27; Past Pres., British Cardiac Soc.; Past Chm., British Heart Foundn. *Publications:* various papers on heart disease and goitre in medical journals. *Recreations:* ornithology and Sherlock Holmes. *Address:* 47 Arkwright Road, Hampstead, NW3.

**CAMPBELL, J(ohn) Menzies,** (retired), DDS (cum laude), Toronto University; Hon. FDS (RCS) (1st award to a dentist); FDS (RCS Edin.); LDS (RCDS Ont.); LDS (RFPS Glas.); FRSE; FICD; FACD; FRSM (Council, 1931-34, a Vice-President, 1950-53, Section of Odontology); Dental Historian; a Vice-President of the Ivory Cross; British Correspondent to Journal of Canadian Dental Association; *b* 1887; *s* of John Menzies Campbell; *m* Margaret Williamson, MB, ChB, *d* of James Shirlaw. *Educ:* George Watson's Coll., Edinburgh; Anderson's and St Mungo's Medical Colls, Glasgow; Univ. of Toronto; Royal Coll. of Dental Surgeons of Ontario. LLD (Tor.) was offered, 1952, but unconferred owing to ill-health. Hon. Visiting Dental Surgeon, Woodside and Springburn Red Cross Hospitals, Glasgow (awarded British Red Cross Soc. Medal). Hon. Mem.: Amer. Acad. of History of Dentistry; Pierre Fauchard Academy; Société Française de l'Histoire de l'Art Dentaire; Odonto-Chirurgical Soc. of Scotland; Dental Students' Soc., St Andrews Univ.; The Lindsay (Dental history) Club; Corr. Mem., Svenska Tandläkare-Sällskapet; Mem.: British Dental Association (Pres., 1938, West of Scotland Branch); Odonto-Chirurgical Soc. of Scotland (Pres., 1939-45); Glasgow Odontological Soc.; Secours Dentaire International (Exec.); Scottish Soc. of the History of Medicine (Council, 1950-53); Glasgow Royal Institute of Fine Arts; Soc. of Authors; Foreign Correspondent, Revista da Associacão Paulista de Cirurgiões Dentistas (Brazil). Adviser, Sub-cttee on dental history, International Dental Federation. Delivered John Smith Centenary Oration, RCS Edinburgh, 1956. Menzies Campbell Triennial Lecture on Dental History instituted, RCS Eng., 1958. Collections of early dentistry exhibited in Glasgow Art Galleries and Museum, 1949, and Hunterian Museum, Univ. of Glasgow, 1955. Presented Menzies Campbell collection of dental pictures, instruments, appliances, ornaments, etc. to RCS Edinburgh, 1964. Hon. Lecturer in

History of Dentistry, Edin. Univ., 1960-. *Publications:* Those Teeth of Yours: A Popular Guide to Better Teeth, 1929, rev. and enl. 2nd edn 1931; A Dental Bibliography, British and American, 1682-1880, 1949; Dentistry as practised, 1800-1921, 1955; From a Trade to a Profession: Byways in Dental History, 1958; Dentistry Then and Now, 1963; Foreword to Edward Samson's Men, Manners and Molars, 1963; Catalogue of the Menzies Campbell Collection, RCS Edin., 1966; numerous contributions to dental historical literature. *Recreations:* collecting early dental books and instruments, dental history. *Address:* 70 Great George Street, Glasgow, W2. *T:* 041-339 0011.

**CAMPBELL, Kate Isabel,** CBE 1954; Medical Practitioner; Specialist Pædiatrician since 1937; *b* April 1899; *d* of late Donald Campbell and late Janet Campbell (*née* Mill); unmarried. *Educ:* Hawthorn State Sch.; Methodist Ladies' Coll., Melbourne; Melbourne Univ. MB, BS, 1922; MD 1924; FRCOG 1961; Resident MO: Melbourne Hosp., 1922, Children's Hosp., 1923, Women's Hosp., 1924; Lecturer in Neo-Natal Pædiatrics, Melbourne Univ., 1927-65. Hon. Phys. to Children's Dept, Queen Victoria Hosp., Melbourne, 1926-60; Hon. Pædiatric Consultant in active practice, Queen Victoria Hospital, 1960-66; Hon. Pædiatric Consultant, 1966-; Hon. Neo-Natal Pædiatrician, Women's Hosp., Melbourne, 1945-59; First assistant in Pædiatrics, Professorial Unit, Dept of Obstetrics, Melbourne Univ., 1960-65; Gen. Med. Practice, 1927-37. Consultant to Dept of Infant Welfare, Victoria, 1961-. LLD (Hon.) 1966. *Publications:* (co-author with late Dr Vera Scantlebury Brown) Guide to the care of the young child, 1947 (last edn 1963); Section on Neo-Natal Pædiatrics in L. S. Townsend's Obstetrics for Medical Students. Articles on medical subjects in Medical Journal of Australasia and Lancet. *Recreation:* theatre. *Address:* 1293 Burke Road, Kew, Melbourne, Victoria 3101, Australia. *T:* 80 2536. *Club:* Lyceum (Melbourne).

**CAMPBELL, Keith Bruce,** QC 1964; *b* NZ, 25 Oct. 1916; *yr s* of Walter Henry Pearson Campbell and late Ethel Rose Campbell; *m* 1939, Betty Joan Muffett; two *s* four *d. Educ:* Christchurch Tech. High Sch. and Canterbury Univ. Coll., NZ (LLB); London Univ. (LLB). Served Army, 1939-46: in ranks of 15th/19th Hussars, BEF France, Belgium; evacuated from Dunkirk; commnd into RASC, 1941; with 1st and 8th Armies, N Africa, Italy; comdg squadron of amphibious tanks, 1945. Called to New Zealand Bar, and to English Bar by Inner Temple, 1947. Practised mainly in Probate and Divorce Courts. Gen. Council of the Bar, 1956-60 and 1965-70. Chm. Family Law Assoc. Contested (C) Gorton Div. of Manchester, 1955; Oldham West, 1966; MP (C) Oldham West, June 1968-70. *Recreations:* boating, riding. *Address:* 1 Hare Court, Temple, EC4. *T:* 01-353 3400.

**CAMPBELL of Airds, Brig. Lorne Maclaine,** VC 1943; DSO 1940; OBE 1968; TD 1941; Argyll and Sutherland Highlanders (TA); *b* 22 July 1902; *s* of late Col Ian Maxwell Campbell, CBE; *m* 1935, Amy Muriel Jordan (*d* 1950), *d* of Alastair Magnus Campbell, Auchendarroch, Argyll; two *s. Educ:* Dulwich Coll.; Merton Coll., Oxford (Postmaster, MA). Past Master of Vintners' Company (Hon. Vintner). Served War of 1939-45 (despatches four times, DSO and Bar, VC). Hon. Col 8th Bn Argyll and Sutherland Highlanders, 1954-67. Officer US Legion of Merit. *Address:* 95 Trinity Road, Edinburgh EH5 3JX. *T:* 031-552 6851. *Clubs:* Naval and Military; New (Edinburgh).

**CAMPBELL, Sir Matthew,** KBE 1963; CB 1959; FRSE; Deputy Chairman, White Fish Authority, and Chairman, Authority's Committee for Scotland and Northern Ireland; *b* 23 May 1907; *s* of late Matthew Campbell, High Blantyre; *m* 1939, Isabella, *d* of late John Wilson, Ruthergien; two *s. Educ:* Hamilton Academy; Glasgow Univ. Entered CS, 1928, and after service in Inland Revenue Dept and Admiralty joined staff of Dept of Agriculture for Scotland, 1935; Principal, 1938; Assistant Sec., 1943; Under Sec., 1953; Sec., Dept of Agriculture and Fisheries for Scotland, 1958-68. *Address:* 10 Craigleith View, Edinburgh. *T:* 031-337 5168. *Club:* Royal Commonwealth Society.

**CAMPBELL, Maurice;** *see* Campbell, J. M. H.

**CAMPBELL, May Eudora, (Mrs John Campbell),** CBE 1952 (OBE 1944); JP; *d* of Henry Moncreiff Horsbrugh, CA, Edinburgh; *m* 1st, 1910, Kenneth Mackenzie (*d* 1918), Dolphinton; three *s* one *d*; 2nd, 1922, John Campbell (*d* 1943), WS, Edinburgh; one *d. Educ:* Lansdowne House, Murrayfield. Women's Voluntary Services, 1938-52 (Chm for Scotland, 1946-52); Mem.: Furnished Rents Tribunal for Lothians and Peebles, 1944-68; Royal Commission on Scottish Affairs, 1952; Gen. Advisory Council, BBC 1959-62; Vice-Pres., Women's Advisory Council on Solid Fuel, 1963-70. JP, County of Lanark, 1920. *Address:* Meadowhead, Dolphinton, Lanarkshire. *T:* Dolphinton 210. *Club:* Queen's (Edinburgh).

**CAMPBELL, Mungo,** CBE 1946; MA; retired shipowner; a local director, Barclays Bank Ltd, Newcastle upon Tyne; *b* 5 June 1900; 2nd *s* of late James Campbell, The Manor House, Wormley, Herts; *m* 1944, Esther McCracken, *qv*; one *d* decd. *Educ:* Loretto; Pembroke Coll., Cambridge. Ministry of War Transport, 1939-46 (Dir Ship Repair Div., 1942-46). Comdr Order of Orange Nassau (Netherlands), 1947. *Address:* Rothley Lake House, Morpeth, Northumberland. *Clubs:* Bath; Union (Newcastle upon Tyne).

**CAMPBELL, Mrs Mungo;** *see* McCracken, Esther.

**CAMPBELL, Patrick;** *see* Glenavy, 3rd Baron.

**CAMPBELL, Percy Gerald Cadogan,** MA Oxford; Docteur de l'Université de Paris; Hon. LLD Queen's; Professor Emeritus of French, Queen's University, Canada; *b* 8 Jan. 1878; *e s* of Rev. C. Cadogan Campbell; *m* 1910, Evelyn Amy, *d* of Frank Jessup Rogers; two *s. Educ:* France; Rossall; Balliol Coll., Oxford, Chancellor's Essay, 1902; Univ. of Paris. Went to Queen's Univ. on taking BA at Oxford, 1902; Commandant Fort Henry Internment Station, 1915-16; OC 253rd Bn, CEF, 1916-17; Seconded to Imperial Forces in France, 1917-18; OC Queen's COTC, 1928-32. Treasurer of Diocese of Ontario, 1933-59. *Publication:* L'Epitre d'Othéa de Christine de Pisan. *Address:* 420 Earl Street, Kingston, Ontario, Canada.

**CAMPBELL, Professor Peter Nelson;** Professor of Biochemistry and Head of Department of Biochemistry, University of Leeds, since 1967; *b* 5 Nov. 1921; *s* of Alan A. Campbell and Nora Nelson, Crowborough; *m* 1946, Mollie (*née* Manklow); one *s* one *d. Educ:* Eastbourne Coll.; Univ. Coll., London. BSc, PhD, DSc, London; FIBiol. Research and Production Chemist with Standard Telephones and Cables, Ltd, 1942-46; PhD Student, UCL; 1946-47; Asst Lectr UCL, 1947-49; staff of Nat. Inst. for Med. Research, Hampstead and

Mill Hill, 1949-54; Asst, Courtauld Inst. of Biochem., Middx Hosp. Med. Sch., 1954-57; Sen. Lectr, Middx Hosp. Med. Sch., 1957-64; Reader in Biochem., Univ. of London, 1964-67. Hon. Lectr, Dept of Biochem., UCL, 1954-67. Fellow and Mem. Council, Inst. of Biology; Mem. Exec. Cttee, London Internat. Centre Ltd; Mem. Exec. Cttee and Chm. of Summer Schs Cttee, Fedn of European Biochemical Socs; Sec., Biological Council. *Publications:* Structure and function of Animal Cell Components, 1966. Ed.: Essays in Biochemistry and other vols; many scientific papers in Biochem. Jl. *Recreations:* theatre, travelling, conversation. *Address:* 6 Hall Rise, Bramhope, Leeds LS16 9JG. *T:* Arthington 2335; Dept of Biochemistry, University of Leeds, Leeds LS2 9LS.

**CAMPBELL, Prof. Peter (Walter);** Professor of Politics, Reading University, since 1964; *b* 17 June 1926; *o s* of late W. C. H. Campbell and of L. M. Locke. *Educ:* Bournemouth Sch.; New Coll., Oxford. 2nd class PPE, 1947; MA 1951; Research Student, Nuffield Coll., Oxford, 1947-49. Asst Lecturer in Govt, Manchester Univ., 1949-52; Lectr, 1952-60; Vice-Warden Needham Hall, 1959-60; Visiting Lectr in Political Science, Victoria Univ. Coll., NZ, 1954; Prof. of Political Economy, Reading Univ., 1960-64; Dean, Faculty of Letters, Reading Univ., 1966-69. hon. Sec. Political Studies Assoc., 1955-58; Chm., Inst. of Electoral Research, 1959-65; Editor of Political Studies, 1963-69; Hon. Treas., Joint Univ. Council for Social and Public Administration, 1965-69. *Publications:* (with W. Theimer) Encyclopædia of World Politics, 1950; French Electoral Systems and Elections, 1789-1957, 1958; (with B. Chapman) The Constitution of the Fifth Republic, 1958. Articles in British, French and New Zealand Jls of Political Science. *Recreations:* ambling, idling. *Address:* The University, Reading RG6 2AA. *T:* Reading 85123. *Club:* Reform.

**CAMPBELL, Sir Ralph Abercromby,** Kt 1961; **Hon. Chief Justice Campbell;** Chief Justice of the Bahamas since 1960; *b* 16 March 1906; 2nd *s* of Major W. O. Campbell, MC; *m* 1st, 1936, Joan Childers Blake (marr. diss., 1968); one *s* one *d*; 2nd, 1968, Shelagh Moore. *Educ:* Winchester; Univ. Coll., Oxf. Barrister-at-Law, Lincoln's Inn, 1928; Western Circuit; Avocat à la Cour, Egypt, 1929; Pres. Civil Courts, Baghdad, Iraq, 1931-44; British Military Administration, Eritrea, Pres. British Military Court and Italian Court of Appeal, 1945; Resident Magistrate, Kenya, 1946; Judge of the Supreme Court, Aden, 1952 (redesignated Chief Justice, 1956)-1960. *Publications:* (Ed.) Law Reports of Kenya and East African Court of Appeal, 1950; Aden Law Reports, 1954-55; Bahamas Law Reports, 1968. *Recreations:* polo, golf, fishing. *Address:* Supreme Court, Nassau, Bahamas.

**CAMPBELL, Richard Mitchelson,** CMG 1953; retired as Deputy High Commissioner for New Zealand, London, 1958; *b* Maungatapere, New Zealand, 28 Aug. 1897; *y s* of Norman Campbell; *m* 1935, Mary, *y d* of John Campbell, Glendale, Isle of Skye; one *s* two *d*. *Educ:* Whangarei High Sch.; Victoria Univ., NZ; London Sch. of Economics. LLB NZ 1922; MA Hons NZ 1925; PhD Econ. London, 1929. In NZ Public Service (Educn Dept), 1914-26; Private Sec. to Prime Minister, 1926-27; Travelling Schol. Univ. NZ, 1927-29; Commonwealth Fund Fellow, USA, 1929-31; Sec. to Min. of Finance, 1931-35; NZ Govt in London: Economic Adviser, 1935-40; Official Sec., 1940-46 and 1953-58. Chm. Public Service Commn, NZ, 1946-53. *Address:* 9 Milnthorpe Road, Eastbourne, Sussex. *T:* 24389; 9 Fasach, Glendale, Isle of Skye. *T:* Glendale 219.

**CAMPBELL, Robert Richmond,** CMG 1967; OBE 1958; artist; writer, lecturer and broadcaster on art; Director, National Gallery of South Australia, 1951-67; Member, Commonwealth Art Advisory Board, since 1953; *b* Edinburgh, Scotland, 18 July 1902; *s* of A. R. Campbell, Tynemouth, England; *m* 1933, Jean E., *d* of J. Young; one *s* three *d*. *Educ:* George Watson's Academy, Edinburgh; Wallasey Grammar Sch., Ches. Arrived Australia 1916; first show, Melbourne, 1928; 4 years travelling and painting in Europe; exhibitions in Melbourne, Sydney, Brisbane, Adelaide; represented in all Australian State and Provincial Galleries; Head, Dept of Art, Launceston Technical Coll., 1941-47; Curator of Art Gallery, W Australia, 1947-49; First Dir, Queensland Art Gallery, 1949-51. Mem., Aust. Watercolour Inst.; Past Pres., Perth Soc. of Artists. *Publications:* Paintings of Tom Roberts, 1963; many articles on art subjects. *Recreations:* walking, sketching, reading. *Address:* Innisfail, Gorge Road, Athelstone, South Australia. *T:* 37-4702.

**CAMPBELL, Sir Robin Auchinbreck,** 15th Bt *cr* 1628 (NS); *b* 7 June 1922; *s* of Sir Louis Hamilton Campbell, 14th Bt and Margaret Elizabeth Patricia, *d* of late Patrick Campbell; *S* father, 1970; *m* 1948, Rosemary (Sally), *d* of Ashley Dean, Christchurch, NZ; one *s* two *d*. Formerly Lieut (A) RNVR. *Heir: s* Louis Auchinbreck Campbell, *b* 17 Jan. 1953. *Address:* Glen Dhu, Motunau, North Canterbury, New Zealand.

**CAMPBELL, Ronald Francis Boyd,** MA; Headmaster of the John Lyon School, Harrow, 1951-68; Director of the Public School Appointments Bureau since October 1968; *b* 28 Aug. 1912; *o s* of Major Roy Neil Boyd Campbell, DSO, OBE and Effie Muriel, *y d* of Major Charles Pierce, IMS; *m* 1939, Pamela Muriel Désirée, *o d* of H. L. Wright, OBE, late Indian Forest Service; one *s* two *d*. *Educ:* Berkhamsted Sch.; Peterhouse, Cambridge. Asst Master, Berkhamsted Sch., 1934-39. Walter Hines-Page Travelling Scholarship to USA, 1960. War of 1939-45: Supplementary Reserve, The Duke of Cornwall's Light Infantry, Sept. 1939; served in England and Italy; DAQMG, HQ 3rd Div., 1943; demobilized with hon. rank of Lt-Col, 1945. Housemaster and OC Combined Cadet Force, Berkhamsted Sch., 1945-51. 1939-45 Star, Italy Star, Defence and Victory Medals; Emergency Reserve Decoration (2 clasps). *Recreations:* sailing, fishing. *Address:* Hatch, Thursley, Godalming Surrey. *T:* Elstead 3392. *Clubs:* Royal Cruising, English-Speaking Union, Public Schools; Royal Ocean Racing.

**CAMPBELL, Rt. Hon. Sir Ronald Ian,** PC 1950; GCMG 1947 (KCMG 1941; CMG 1932); CB 1937; Director of Royal Bank of Scotland, 1950-65 (Extra-ordinary Director, 1965-68); *b* 7 June 1890; *s* of Lieut-Col Sir Guy Campbell, 3rd Bt, and Nina, *d* of late Frederick Lehmann, 15 Berkeley Square, W1. *Educ:* Eton Coll.; Magdalen Coll., Oxford. Entered Diplomatic Service, 1914; Third Sec., Washington, 1915-20; Second and First Sec., Paris, 1920-23; Foreign Office, 1923-27; First Sec., Acting Counsellor and Counsellor, Washington, 1927-31; Counsellor, Cairo, 1931-34; Counsellor in Foreign Office, 1934-38; Minister Plenipotentiary, British Embassy, Paris, 1938-39; Minister at Belgrade, 1939-41; Minister in Washington, 1941-45; an Asst Under-Sec. of State in the Foreign Office, 1945-46; Dep. to Sec. of State for Foreign Affairs on Council of Foreign Ministers, 1945-

46; British Ambassador to Egypt, 1946-50; retired, 1950. Mem., Board of Trustees for National Galleries of Scotland, 1956-66. Grand Officer of Legion of Honour. *Address:* 20 Sidegate, Haddington, East Lothian. *Clubs:* Brooks's, MCC; New (Edinburgh).
*See also Sir Guy Campbell.*

**CAMPBELL, Ross,** DSC 1944; Ambassador and Permanent Representative of Canada to NATO since 1967 (Paris, May 1967, transferred Brussels, Oct. 1967); *b* 4 Nov. 1918; *s* of late William Marshall Campbell and of Helen Isabel Harris; *m* 1945, Penelope Grantham-Hill; two *s*. *Educ:* Univ. of Toronto Schs; Trin. Coll., Univ. of Toronto. BA, Faculty of Law, 1940. Served RCN, 1940-45. Joined Dept. of Ext. Affairs, Canada, 1945; Third Sec., Oslo, 1946-47; Second Sec., Copenhagen, 1947-50; European Div., Ottawa, 1950-52; First Sec., Ankara, 1952-56; Head of Middle East Div., Ottawa, 1957-59; Special Asst to Sec. of State for Ext. Aff., 1959-62; Asst Under-Sec. of State for Ext. Aff., 1962-64; Adviser to Canadian Delegns to: UN Gen. Assemblies, 1958-63; North Atlantic Coun., 1959-64; Amb. to Yugoslavia, 1964-67, concurrently accredited Amb. to Algeria, 1965-67. *Recreations:* tennis, skiing, gardening. *Address:* North Atlantic Treaty Organisation, Brussels 39, Belgium. *T:* 15.88.53. *Club:* Royal Leopold (Brussels).

**CAMPBELL, Dr Sidney Scholfield;** Organist, and Master of the Choristers, St George's Chapel, Windsor Castle, since 1961; *b* 7 June 1909. DMus Dunelm, 1945; FRCO 1931; Organist, St Peter's Collegiate Church, Wolverhampton, 1943-47. Sub-Warden, Royal School of Church Music, 1947-49; Organist, Ely Cathedral, 1949-53; Organist and Master of the Music, Southwark Cathedral, 1953-56; Organist, Canterbury Cathedral, 1956-61. Dir of Musical Studies, Royal Sch. of Church Music, 1954-55. *Address:* 23 The Cloisters, Windsor Castle. *T:* Windsor 64529.

**CAMPBELL, Sybil,** OBE 1942; MA; Metropolitan Magistrate, Tower Bridge, 1945-61, retired; *b* 1889; *d* of late Neill Graeme Campbell (Auchendarroch), and Maude Georgiana, *d* of late Sir William Bovill, Chief Justice of Common Pleas. *Educ:* Dunardarigh, North Berwick; Girton Coll., Camb. (Nat. Sciences Tripos Pt I; Economics Tripos Pt II). Inspector under Trade Boards Act, 1914-18; Assistant Enforcement Officer, Min. of Food, Midland Div., 1918-21; Called to Bar, Middle Temple, 1922; a Metropolitan Chm., Courts of Referees, 1930-39; Asst Div. Food Officer (Enforcement), London div., Ministry of Food, 1939-44. *Address:* Drim-na-Vullin, Lochgilphead, Argyllshire.

**CAMPBELL, Thane A.,** MA, LLD; Chief Justice of Prince Edward Island since 1943; Member: Historical Sites and Monuments Board of Canada, 1948-59; Nat. Library Advisory Council, 1949-59; Bd of Govs of: Dalhousie College since 1950; St Dunstan's University, since 1964; Chief War Claims Comr (Canada) since 1952; Adviser on claims under agreement with Bulgaria, 1967; *b* 7 July 1895; *s* of Alexander and Clara Tremaine Campbell; *m* 1930, Cecilia Lillian Bradshaw; two *s* two *d*. *Educ:* Prince of Wales Coll., Charlottetown, PEI; Dalhousie Univ. Halifax, NS; Corpus Christi Coll., Oxford. Admitted to Bar of PEI 1927; Attorney-Gen. of PEI 1930-31 and 1935-43; Mem. of Legislative Assembly, 1931-43; Premier and Provincial Sec.-Treasurer, PEI, 1936-43. Pres., Dominion Curling Assoc., 1942; Vice-Pres., Royal Caledonian Curling Club of Scotland, 1945. Chm., Brier Trustees, 1963-. Holds hon. doctorates. *Address:* Summerside, PEI, Canada. *T:* office 2722, residence 2556.

**CAMPBELL, Sir Thomas Cockburn-,** 6th Bt, *cr* 1821; Retired; *b* 8 Dec. 1918; *e s* of Sir Alexander Thomas Cockburn-Campbell, 5th Bt, and Maude Frances Lorenzo (*d* 1926), *o d* of Alfred Giles, Kent Town, Adelaide; *S* father, 1935; *m* 1944, Josephine Zoi, *e d* of Harold Douglas Forward, Curjardine, WA; one *s*. *Educ:* Melbourne C of E Grammar Sch. *Heir:* *s* Alexander Thomas Cockburn-Campbell [*b* 16 March 1945; *m* 1969, Kerry Ann, *e d* of Sgt K. Johnson]. *Address:* Lot 194, Welshpool Road, Wattle Grove, W Australia 6107.

**CAMPBELL, Maj.-Gen. (retired) Victor David Graham,** CB 1956; DSO 1940; OBE 1946; DL; JP; *b* 9 March 1905; *s* of late Gen. Sir David G. M. Campbell, GCB; *m* 1947, Dulce Beatrix, *d* of late G. B. Collier, and *widow* of Lt-Col J. A. Goodwin. *Educ:* Rugby; RMC Sandhurst. 2nd Lieut The Queen's Own Cameron Highlanders, 1924; AQMG and DA&QMG HQ AFNEI, 1945-46; Lt-Col Comdg 1st Bn The Gordon Highlanders, 1949; Brig. Comdg 31 Lorried Infantry Brigade, 1951; Chief of Staff, HQ Scottish Command, 1954-57; psc 1938; idc 1953. DL and JP, 1962, High Sheriff, 1968, County of Devon. *Address:* Beggars Bush, South Brent, South Devon.

**CAMPBELL, Lt-Col Sir Walter Fendall,** KCIE, *cr* 1946 (CIE 1941); *b* 20 May 1894; 2nd *s* of late Brig-Gen. G. P. Campbell, CIE, CBE, RE; *m* 1920, Ann (*d* 1969), *d* of late T. McLaughlin, Roscommon, Ireland; four *d*. *Educ:* Mount St Mary's Coll., Derbys. Entered Indian Army, 1914; joined Political Dept, 1921; held various posts in Districts and Agencies of Baluchistan and NWFP, 1921-33; Sec. to Agent to Governor-Gen. in states of Western India, 1933; Prime Minister, Alwar, 1935-36; Political Agent, Bundelkhand, 1937; Resident in Waziristan, 1939-40; Adviser to Governor, NWFP, 1941-42; Resident for Central India, 1942-46; Resident in Mysore, 1946-47. *Address:* 2 Clarendon Court, Granville Road, Sevenoaks, Kent. *T:* Sevenoaks 58833.
*See also Baron Bruntisfield.*

**CAMPBELL, William,** CBE 1959; General Secretary, Educational Institute of Scotland, 1952-60, retired; *b* 1 June 1895; *e s* of James Campbell, Auchinleck, Ayrshire; *m* 1925, Agnes Wightman, *d* of Thomas Boyd Stirling, JP, Alexandria, Dunbartonshire; two *s* one *d*. *Educ:* Auchinleck Sch.; Cumnock Academy; Kilmarnock Academy; Glasgow Univ. MA Glasgow 1920; BL Glasgow 1940. Teacher in Glasgow, 1920-45; Asst Sec., Educational Institute of Scotland, 1945-48; Dep. Sec., 1948-52. Fellow of Educational Institute of Scotland (FEIS) 1945. Hon. Mem., Nat. Union of Teachers, 1960. Pres. Educational Institute of Scotland, 1961-62. *Recreations:* bowling, reading. *Address:* 3 Rosebank Road, Edinburgh 5. *T:* 031-552 2664. *Club:* Scottish Liberal (Edinburgh).

**CAMPBELL, William Gordon;** Chartered Accountant; partner in Josolyne Miles & Company, London, Manchester and Paris, 1924-58; *b* Glasgow, 3 Oct. 1891; *er s* of Duncan Macalpine Campbell (BISN Co. Ltd, Calcutta and London); *m* 1919, Ena Clarissa (*d* 1962), *d* of George Henry Castle, Stoke-by-Nayland, Suffolk; one *d*. (one *s* decd). *Educ:* Morrison's Academy, Crieff; Mill Hill Sch.; Trinity Coll., Cambridge. BA, Nat. Sci. Tripos, 1912. Served European War, 1914-18, Lieut, 2/1 Sussex Yeomanry and attached 8th Queens (RWS) Regiment. Mem. of Central Price Regulation Cttee of Board of Trade, 1946-49; Mem.

Council Institute of Chartered Accountants in England and Wales, 1947-58; Mem. of Gen. Nursing Council for England and Wales, 1953-58; Lay mem. of the Restrictive Practices Court, 1958-62. *Recreations:* books, gardening, fishing. *Address:* Hillstead, Cornsland, Brentwood, Essex. *T:* Brentwood 1019.

**CAMPBELL, Major-General William Tait,** CBE 1945 (OBE 1944); Deputy-Quarter-Master-General, M of D (Army Dept), 1964-67, retired; *b* 8 Oct. 1912; *s* of late R. B. Campbell, MD, FRCPE, Edinburgh; *m* 1942, Rhoda Alice, *y d* of late Adm. Algernon Walker-Heneage-Vivian, CB, MVO, Swansea; two *d. Educ:* Cargilfield Sch.; Fettes Coll.; RMC Sandhurst. 2nd Lieut, The Royal Scots (The Royal Regt), 1933; served War of 1939-45: 1st Airborne Div. and 1st Allied Airborne Corps (North Africa, Sicily, Italy and Europe). Lieut-Col Commanding 1st Bn The Royal Scots, in Egypt, Cyprus, UK and Suez Operation (despatches), 1954-57; Col, Royal Naval War Coll., Greenwich, 1958; Brig. i/c Admin. Malaya, 1962; Maj.-Gen., 1964; Col, The Royal Scots (The Royal Regt), 1964. US Bronze Star, 1945. *Recreations:* gardening, golf, shooting, fishing. *Address:* c/o Lloyds Bank Ltd (Cox's & King's Branch), 6 Pall Mall, SW1; Portland House, Ash Vale, near Aldershot, Hants. *T:* Aldershot 24825. *Club:* East India and Sports.

**CAMPBELL GOLDING, F.;** *see* Golding, F. C.

**CAMPBELL-GRAY,** family name of **Baron Gray.**

**CAMPBELL-JOHNSON, Alan,** CIE 1947; OBE 1946; Officer of US Legion of Merit, 1947; MA Oxon; FRSA, MRI; Chairman of: Campbell-Johnson Ltd, Public Relations Consultants; Concord Public Relations Ltd; *b* 16 July 1913; *o c* of late Lieut-Col James Alexander Campbell-Johnson and Gladys Susanne Campbell-Johnson; *m* 1938, Imogen Fay de la Tour Dunlap; one *d* (one *s* decd). *Educ:* Westminster; Christ Church, Oxford (scholar). BA 2nd Cl. Hons Mod. Hist., 1935. Political Sec. to Rt Hon. Sir Archibald Sinclair, Leader of Parl. Lib. Party, 1937-40; served War of 1939-45, RAF; COHQ, 1942-43; HQ SACSEA (Wing Comdr i/c Inter-Allied Records Section), 1943-46. Contested (L) Salisbury and South Wilts. Div., Gen. Elections, 1945 and 1950: Press Attaché to Viceroy and Gov.-Gen. of India (Earl Mountbatten of Burma), 1947-48. Fellow Inst. of Public Relations, Pres. 1956-57. *Publications:* Growing Opinions, 1935; Peace Offering, 1936; Anthony Eden–A Biography, 1938; Viscount Halifax–A Biography, 1941; Mission with Mountbatten, 1951; Sir Anthony Eden–A Biography, 1955. *Recreations:* cricket, mountaineering. *Address:* 21 Ashley Gardens, Ambrosden Avenue, SW1. *T:* 01-834 1532. *Clubs:* St James', National Liberal, MCC.

**CAMPBELL ORDE, Alan Colin,** CBE 1943; AFC 1919; FRAeS; Aviation Consultant since 1958; *b* Lochgilphead, Argyll, NB, 4 Oct. 1898; *s* of Colin Ridley Campbell Orde; *m* 1951, Mrs Beatrice McClure, *e d* of late Rev. Eliott-Drake Briscoe. *Educ:* Sherborne. Served European War, 1916-18, Flight Sub-Lieut, Royal Navy, and Flying Officer, Royal Air Force; Active service in Belgium, 1917; one of original commercial Pilots on London-Paris route with Aircraft Transport & Travel Ltd, 1919-20; Instructur and Adviser to Chinese Govt in Peking, 1921-23; Instructor and latterly Chief Test Pilot to Sir W. G. Armstrong-Whitworth Aircraft, Ltd, Coventry, 1924-36; Operational Manager, British Airways, Ltd, 1936-39; subseq. Operations Manager, Imperial Airways Ltd; was Ops Director BOAC, during first 4 years after its inception in 1939; thereafter responsible for technical development as Development Dir until resignation from BOAC Dec. 1957. *Address:* Smugglers Mead, Stepleton, Blandford, Dorset. *T:* Child Okeford 268. *Clubs:* Boodle's, Royal Automobile.

**CAMPBELL-ORDE, Sir John A.;** *see* Orde.

**CAMPBELL-PRESTON, Hon. Mrs Angela;** Chairman, Westminster Press Provincial Newspapers Ltd, since 1953 (Director since 1945), and of subsidiary companies; *b* 27 Oct. 1910; 3rd *d* of 2nd Viscount Cowdray; *m* 1st, 1930, George Antony Murray (killed in action, 1945); one *s* (*see* Duke of Atholl) (and two *s* decd); 2nd, 1950, Robert Campbell-Preston; one *d. Educ:* home. Chm., S London Hosp. for Women, 1932-48; Chm., Lambeth Gp Hosp. Man. Cttee, 1961-64 (Vice-Chm., 1948-61); Mem., SW London Hosp. Man. Cttee, 1964-70; Sec. of various cttees of King Edward VII Hosp. Fund for London, 1942-50; Past Mem., Glasgow Regional Hosp. Bd; Mem., Oban Hosps Bd of Management. Dir, S Pearson & Son Ltd, 1954-. *Recreation:* renovating houses. *Address:* 31 Marlborough Hill, NW8; Ardchattan Priory, Connel, Argyll, Scotland. *T:* Bonawe 204. *Club:* Cowdray.

**CAMPBELL-PURDIE, Cora Gwendolyn Jean, (Wendy);** Director of Sahara Reafforestation (SR Committee formed in 1965 with Reverend Austen Williams as Chairman); *b* 8 June 1925; *d* of Edmund Hamilton Campbell Purdie and Janie Theodora Williams. *Educ:* Woodford House, New Zealand. Worked with Red Cross Transport Corps in Auckland, 1943-46. English Asst at Lycées in France and Corsica, 1954-56; worked with British timber firm in Corsica, 1957-58; FAO, Rome, on Mediterranean Reafforestation Project, Aug. 1958. Has been planting trees in N Africa, 1959 onwards; now expecting at least 75 per cent success; planted: 1000 trees (given by Moroccan Min. of Agric.) in Tiznit, 1960 and again in 1961; 1000 trees (given by Algerian Min. of Agric. and planted by local Agricl authorities at Bou Saada), 1964; has planted many more thousands of trees (money given by: Men of the Trees; War on Want; St Martin-in-the-Fields; the Bishop of Southwark's Fund; CORSO (New Zealand), etc.). *Publication:* (in collaboration with Fenner Brockway) Woman against the Desert, 1967. *Recreations:* chess, detective novels and science fiction, classical music. *Address:* Bou Saada, Algeria. *T:* Bou Saada 100.

**CAMPBELL SWINTON;** *see* Swinton, Brigadier A. H.

**CAMPBELL-WALTER, Rear-Admiral (retired) Keith McNeil,** CB 1957; *b* 31 Aug. 1904; *s* of Alexander McNeil Walter; *m* 1930, Frances Henriette, FSA Scot., *e d* and senior co-heir of Sir Edward Taswell Campbell of Airds Bay, 1st Bt, MP (*d* 1945); two *s* two *d. Educ:* RN Colls, Osborne and Dartmouth. Comdr, 1938; Captain, 1945; Commodore, 1953; Rear-Adm., 1955. ADC to the Queen 1954; Flag Officer, Germany, and Comdr Allied Naval Forces Northern Area, Central Europe, 1955-58, retd. Legion of Merit, USA, 1946. *Recreation:* fishing. *Address:* 19a Princes Gate Mews, SW7. *T:* 01-589 0897; Clachan Beag, Auchnasaul, by Oban, Scotland. *T:* Balvicar 202. *Clubs:* United Service; Puffins (Edinburgh).

**CAMPDEN, Viscount; Anthony Baptist Noel;** *b* 16 Jan. 1950; *s* and *heir* of 5th Earl of Gainsborough, *qv.*

**CAMPION, Cecil;** *see* Campion, J. C.

**CAMPION, Sir Harry,** Kt 1957; CB 1949; CBE 1945; MA; retired as Director of Central Statistical Office, Cabinet Office, 1967; *b* 20 May 1905; *o s* of John Henry Campion, Worsley, Lancs. *Educ:* Farnworth Grammar Sch.; Univ. of Manchester. Rockefeller Foundation Fellow, United States, 1932; Robert Ottley Reader in Statistics, Univ. of Manchester, 1933-39. Dir. of Statistical Office, UN, 1946-47; Mem. of Statistical Commission, United Nations, 1947-67; Pres.: International Statistical Institute, 1963-67; Royal Statistical Society, 1957-59; Hon. LLD, Manchester, 1967. *Publications:* Distribution of National Capital; Public and Private Property in Great Britain; articles in economic and statistical journals. *Address:* Rima, Priory Close, Stanmore, Middx. *T:* 01-954 3267. *Club:* Reform.

**CAMPION, (John) Cecil;** Magistrate of the Magistrates' Courts of the Metropolis, 1955-70; *b* 8 Aug. 1907; *s* of Bernard Campion and Rose (*née* Lees); *m* 1932, Constance Mary Doggart (*d* 1953); two *d*; *m* 1959, Diana Jacqueline Rodwell; one *d*. *Educ:* Marlborough; Magdalen Coll., Oxf. Called to the Bar, Gray's Inn, 1932; Central Criminal Court, Midland Circuit. Served RASC, 1939-45 (invalided out as Major). *Address:* 111 Crabtree Lane, Harpenden, Herts. *T:* Harpenden 3144.

**CAMPION, Sidney Ronald,** OBE 1953; FRSA; FJI 1950; Author, Barrister, Journalist, Schoolmaster, Lecturer, Sculptor, and from 1940 until retirement in 1957, Head of the Press and Broadcast Division, GPO Headquarters; *b* Coalville, Leics, 30 June 1891; *e s* of Chelsea Pensioner, late Walter Campion and late Martha Robinson, Leicester; *m* 1912, Claire (*d* 1968), *y d* of late Horatio and Elizabeth Armitage, Cotebrook, Tarporley, Cheshire; one *d*. *Educ:* Charnwood Street Elementary Sch., Leicester; Vaughan Working Men's Coll., Leicester; Chester Diocesan Teachers' Training Coll.; Gray's Inn; Morley Coll., London; Wimbledon School of Art; Regent Street Polytechnic School of Art; St Martin's School of Art. Street newspaper seller in Leicester from 11 to 14. Worked in factories, workshops and woodmills in Leicester for three years. Assisted by late Rt Hon. J. Ramsay MacDonald, late Sir Edward Wood (Chm. Freeman Hardy & Willis, Ltd), and late Thomas Adcock, MA, was privately educated and joined editorial staff of Leicester Pioneer. Later worked on Wilmslow Express (Cheshire), Leeds Weekly Citizen, Daily Citizen, Chorley Guardian, Bradford Daily Telegraph, Daily News, London, and served as chief of the Allied (Kemsley) (now Thomson's Allied) Newspapers; Parliamentary Press Gallery staff, 1933-40; Chief Press and Broadcasting Officer to General Post Office, 1940-57. Town Councillor and Poor Law Guardian, Chorley, 1920-23; Parliamentary Labour Candidate, Oswestry, 1923; qualified as schoolmaster with First Class teaching certificate, Liverpool Univ.; admitted Gray's Inn, 1927, honours in Final and called to Bar, 1930; member South-Eastern Circuit; holder bronze medal of Royal Life Saving Society and hon. instructor in life saving; Madden Prizeman, Chester Coll. Life Member: National Union of Journalists, 1957; Newspaper Press Fund; Member: of Francis Bacon Society; Psychical Research Society; Society of Civil Service Authors; Cttee of Post Office Art Club of Great Britain; William Morris Society; League for Abolition of Cruel Sports; Royal National Institute for the Deaf; travelled Scandinavia, Russia (1935 and 1960), Germany, Turkey, etc. European War, 1914-18, served in RFC, RAF, IAF. *Publications:* Sunlight on the Foothills, 1941; Towards the Mountains, 1943; Reaching High Heaven, 1944; Only the Stars Remain, 1946; The World of Colin Wilson: a Biographical Study, 1962; Adventures Under the Sycamore Tree, 1964; contributor to home and overseas newspapers, magazines and periodicals, and to Central Office of Information. *Recreations:* experimenting in literary forms; picture painting, sculpture, modelling (portrait busts, etc., exhibitor in London galleries; Society of British Portrait Sculptors; Paris, 1963-70; Madrid, 1965; one-man exhibitions: London, 1960, Astley Hall, Chorley, Lancs, 1962; Tower Gallery, City of London, 1964); searching for the Shakespeare MSS, chess and golf. *Address:* 22 Erridge Road, Merton Park, Wimbledon, SW19. *T:* 01-542 6766. *Clubs:* Press (became Life Member 1958), Paternosters, English-Speaking Union.

**CAMPLING, Rev. Canon William Charles,** MA; Hon. CF: Canon Emeritus of Southwark, 1960 (Hon. Canon, 1944-60); *b* 13 July 1888; 2nd *s* of late Thomas Campling and Kate Augusta Campling; *m* 1919, Phyllis Russell, 3rd *d* of Francis Henry and Margaret Colet Webb of Backsett, Horsham, Sussex; three *s* one *d*. *Educ:* William Ellis' Sch., Gospel Oak; Trinity Coll., Cambridge; Bishops' Coll., Cheshunt. Curate of St Mary's, Wimbledon, 1914-18; Chaplain to the Forces, BEF, 1918-19 (attached to the 59th Div., France, 1918); Tutor at Ordination Test Sch., Knutsford, 1919; Principal of St Francis' Coll., Nundah, Brisbane, 1919-26; Canon Residentiary of St John's Cathedral, Brisbane, 1919-26; Vicar of St Augustine's, Honor Oak Park, SE, 1926-30; Vicar of St Andrews, Coulsdon, 1930-40; Rector of Charlton, 1940-45; Vicar of Roehampton, 1945-60; Rural Dean of Richmond and Barnes, 1946; Proctor in Convocation, 1944; Priest-in-charge of St Leonard and St James, Rousham, 1960. *Address:* Netherlea, Gig Bridge Lane, Pershore, Worcs.

**CAMPOLI, Alfredo;** violinist; *b* 20 Oct. 1906; *s* of Prof. Romeo Campoli, Prof. of Violin at Accademia di Santa Cecilia, Rome, and Elvira Campoli, dramatic soprano; *m* 1942, Joy Burbridge. Came to London, 1911; gave regular public recitals as a child; Gold Medal, London Musical Festival, 1919; toured British Isles with Melba and with Dame Clara Butt, and was engaged for series of International Celebrity Concerts at age of 15. Has played all over the world. First broadcast from Savoy Hill, 1930; has subsequently made frequent broadcasts and made many gramophone records. *Recreations:* bridge, cine-photography, tennis, table tennis, billiards, croquet. *Address:* 50 Eversley Park Road, Winchmore Hill, N21.

**CAMPS, Francis Edward,** MD, FRCP, FC Path., DMJ; Professor of Forensic Medicine, in the University of London, at the London Hospital Medical College 1963-70 (Reader, 1954-63); Hon. Consultant to the Army in Forensic Medicine since 1964; *b* 28 June 1905; *s* of late P. W. L. Camps, FRCS; *m* 1942, Mary Ross Mackenzie, MB, ChB Aberdeen; one *s* one *d*. *Educ:* Marlborough Coll.; Guy's Hospital Medical Sch.; Sch. of Tropical Medicine, Liverpool; Neuchâtel Univ., Switzerland. Late House Physician, Guy's Hospital; Pathologist, Chelmsford and Essex Hospital; Cons. Pathologist to Essex County Council; Cons. Pathologist to Emergency Med. Service; Travelling Fellowship of the Kellogg Foundation; late Examiner in Forensic Medicine, St Andrews Univ. and

Univs. of Bristol, Durham, Sheffield and London. Member: BMA Special Cttee on the Recognition of Intoxication and the Relation of Alcohol to Road Accidents, 1951; Coroners Rules Cttee, Home Office, 1953; Mortuaries Cttee, Ministry of Housing and Local Govt, 1955; Past President British Assoc. Forensic Medicine; Vice-President Medico-Legal Society; Secretary-General of British Academy of Forensic Sciences; Chairman, Medical Council on Alcoholism, 1967-; Hon. Member: Harvard Associates in Police Science; Pharmaceutical Soc. of GB; Member American Acad. of Forensic Sciences. Swiney Prize for Med. Jurisprudence, 1969. *Publications:* Medical and Scientific Investigations of the Christie Case, 1953; (with Sir Bentley Purchase) Practical Forensic Medicine, 1956; (with Richard Barber) The Investigation of Murder, 1966; (ed) Medicine, Science and Law, 1964; (ed) Gradwohl's Legal Medicine, 2nd edn, 1968; numerous papers on pathological and medico-legal subjects. *Recreation:* fishing. *Address:* 37 Welbeck Street, W1. *T:* 01-935 6373; The Limes, Purleigh, Essex. *Clubs:* Savage, Savile.
*See also W. A. Camps.*

**CAMPS, William Anthony;** Master of Pembroke College, Cambridge, since 1970; *b* 28 Dec. 1910; *s* of P. W. L. Camps, FRCS, and Alice, *d* of Joseph Redfern, Matlock; *m* 1953, Miriam Camp, Washington, DC, *d* of Prof. Burton Camp, Wesleyan Univ., Connecticut. *Educ:* Marlborough Coll.; Pembroke Coll., Cambridge (Schol.). Fellow, Pembroke Coll., 1933; Univ. Lectr in Classics, 1939; Temp. Civil Servant, 1940-45; Asst Tutor, Pembroke Coll., 1945; Senior Tutor, 1947-62; Tutor for Advanced Students, 1963-70; Pres., 1964-70. Mem., Inst. for Advanced Study, Princeton, 1956-57; Vis. Assoc. Prof., UC Toronto, 1966; Vis. Prof., Univ. of North Carolina at Chapel Hill, 1969. *Publications:* edns of Perpertius I, 1961, IV, 1965, III, 1966, II, 1967; An Introduction to Virgil's Aeneid, 1969; sundry notes and reviews in classical periodicals. *Recreations:* unremarkable. *Address:* Pembroke College, Cambridge. *T:* Cambridge 52241. *Club:* Oxford and Cambridge University.
*See also F. E. Camps.*

**CAMROSE,** 2nd Viscount, *cr* 1941, of Hackwood Park; Baron, *cr* 1929, of Long Cross; 2nd Bt, *cr* 1921; **John Seymour Berry,** TD; Deputy Chairman (Past Chairman) of The Daily Telegraph Ltd; *b* 12 July 1909; *e s* of 1st Viscount Camrose and Mary Agnes (*d* 1962), *e d* of late Thomas Corns, 2 Bolton Street, W; *S* father, 1954. *Educ:* Eton; Christ Church, Oxford. Major, City of London Yeomanry. Served War of 1939-45, North African and Italian Campaigns, 1942-45 (despatches). MP (C) for Hitchin Division, Herts, 1941-45. Vice-Chm. Amalgamated Press Ltd, 1942-59. Younger Brother, Trinity House. *Heir: b* Baron Hartwell, *qv. Address:* Hackwood Park, Basingstoke, Hampshire. *T:* Basingstoke 4630. *Clubs:* Buck's, White's, Beefsteak, Marylebone Cricket (MCC); Royal Yacht Squadron (Trustee).
*See also Earl of Birkenhead.*

**CANBERRA and GOULBURN, NSW, Bishop of,** since 1961; **Rt. Rev. Kenneth John Clements;** *b* 21 Dec. 1905; *s* of John Edwin Clements and Ethel Evelyn Clark; *m* 1935, Rosalind Elizabeth Cakebread; one *s* two *d. Educ:* Highgate Sch., London; St Paul's Coll., University of Sydney. BA (Hons) 1933; ThD 1949. Registrar, Diocese of Riverina, 1933-37; Rector of: Narrandera, NSW, 1937-39; Tumbarumba, NSW, 1939-43; Gunning, NSW, 1943-44; Director of Studies, Canberra Grammar Sch., Canberra, ACT, 1945; Registrar Diocese of Canberra and Goulburn, 1946-56; Archdeacon of Goulburn, 1946-56; Asst Bishop of Canberra and Goulburn, 1949-56; Bishop of Grafton, NSW, 1956-61. *Address:* Diocesan Registry, Jamieson House, Constitution Avenue, Reid, ACT 2601, Australia.

**CANBERRA-GOULBURN, Archbishop of, (RC),** since 1967; **Most Rev. Thomas Vincent Cahill,** DD, PhD; *b* 22 Feb. 1913; *s* of Patrick Cahill and Elizabeth Cavagna. *Educ:* Marist Brothers' Coll., Bendigo, Victoria, Australia; Propaganda Coll., Rome. Ordained Priest, Rome, 1935; Asst Priest, Sacred Heart Cathedral, Bendigo, Diocese of Sandhurst, Victoria, Australia, 1936-39; Secretary, Apostolic Delegation, Sydney, 1939-48; Chancellor, Diocese of Sandhurst, 1948; Bishop of Cairns, Queensland, 1948-67. *Address:* Archbishop's House, Commonwealth Avenue, Canberra, ACT, Australia. *T:* Canberra 42247.

**CANDAU, Marcolino Gomes,** MD, DPH; Director-General of the World Health Organization, Geneva, since 1953; *b* Rio de Janeiro, 30 May 1911; *s* of Julio Candau and Augusta Gomes; *m* 1936, Ena de Carvalho; two *s. Educ:* Univ. of Brazil, Rio de Janeiro; Johns Hopkins Univ., USA. Various posts in Health Services of State of Rio de Janeiro, 1934-43; Asst Superintendent, Servico Especial de Saude Publica, Min. of Education and Health, 1944-47, Superintendent 1947-50; World Health Organization: Dir, Div. of Org. of Public Health Services, Geneva, 1950-51; Asst Dir-General, Dept of Advisory Services, Geneva, 1951-52; Asst Dir, Pan-American Sanitary Bureau, Dep. Reg. Dir for the Americas, Washington, 1952-53. Hon. Dr of Laws: Univ. of Michigan; Johns Hopkins Univ.; Univ. of Edinburgh; The Queen's Univ. of Belfast; Seoul Univ., Korea; Hon. Dr of Medicine, Univ. of Geneva; Hon. Dr: Univ. of Brazil; Univ. of Sao Paulo, Brazil; Univ. of Bordeaux; Charles Univ., Prague; Inst. of Medicine and Pharmacy, Bucharest; Univ. of Abidjan; Hon. Dr of Science, Bates Coll., Maine, USA; FRCP, Hon. FRSocMed, and Hon. FRSH (all GB), and various other hon. fellowships in America and Europe; Mem., Royal Soc. of Tropical Medicine and Hygiene, GB; For. Member USSR Acad. of Med. Sciences. Mary Kingsley Medal of Liverpool Sch. of Tropical Medicine; Gold Medal of RSH, London, 1966; also prizes and medals for services to public health. *Publications:* scientific papers. *Address:* World Health Organization, Geneva, Switzerland. *T:* Geneva 34.60.61. *Clubs:* Caicaras, National Press Association (Rio de Janeiro).

**CANDELA OUTERINO, Felix;** Engineer and Architect; President, Cubiertas ALA, SA (building firm), since 1950; Professor, Escuela Nacional de Arquitectura, University of Mexico, since 1953; Chairman, Department of Construction; *b* Madrid, 27 Jan. 1910; *s* of Felix and Julia Candela; *m* 1940, Eladia Martin Galan (*d* 1964); four *d*; *m* 1967, Dorothy H. Davies. *Educ:* Univ. of Madrid, Spain. Architect, Escuela Superior de Arquitectura de Madrid, 1935. Captain of Engineers, Republican Army, Spanish Civil War, 1936-39. Emigrated to Mexico, 1939; Mexican Citizen, 1941. General practice in Mexico as Architect and Contractor. Founded (with brother Antonio) Cubiertas ALA, SA, firm specializing in design and construction of reinforced concrete shell structures. Work includes Sports Palace for Mexico Olympics, 1968. Hon. Member: Sociedad de Arquitectos Colombianos, 1956; Sociedad Venezolana de

Arquitectos, 1961; International Assoc. for Shell Structures, 1962. Charles Elliot Norton Prof. of Poetry, Harvard Univ., for academic year, 1961-62. Gold Medal, Instn Structural Engineers, England, 1961; Auguste Perret Prize of International Union of Architects, 1961. Hon. Fellow American Inst. of Architects, 1963; Hon. Corr. Member Royal Inst. of British Architects, 1963; Plomada de Oro, Soc. de Arquitectos Mexicanos, 1963; Doctor in Fine Arts (*hc*), Univ. of New Mexico, 1964. *Publications:* Candela, the Shell Builder, 1962. Several articles in architectural and engineering magazines all around the world. *Address:* Juarez 14, Tlacopac, Mexico 20, DF. *T:* 482653; Apartado Postal 19149, Mexico 19, DF, Mexico.

**CANDY, Air Vice-Marshal Charles Douglas,** CB 1963; CBE 1957; Air Member for Personnel, RAAF, 1966-69, retired; *b* 17 Sept. 1912; *s* of late C. H. and late Mrs Candy; *m* 1938, Eileen Cathryn Mary (*née* Poole-Ricketts); one *d*. Served War of 1939-45; Command and Staff appointments in Australia, the United Kingdom, West Africa and South-West Pacific Area; AOC North-Eastern Area, RAAF, 1946; Joint Services Staff Coll., 1947; Dept of Defence, Commonwealth of Australia, 1948-50; Director of Organisation and Staff Duties, HQ, RAAF, 1950-52; Imperial Defence Coll., 1953; SASO No. 3 Group Bomber Command, RAF, 1954-56; Deputy Chief of the Air Staff, RAAF, 1956-58 (Air Vice-Marshal, 1957); AOC Home Command, RAAF, 1958-59; Sen. Air Staff Officer, Far East Air Force, Royal Air Force, 1959-62; AOC Support Command, RAAF, 1962-66. *Recreations:* golf, tennis, swimming. *Address:* KT Park, Queanbeyan, NSW, Australia. *Clubs:* Naval and Military (Melbourne); Imperial Service (Sydney); Royal Singapore Golf (Singapore).

**CANDY, Major-General Ronald Herbert,** CIE 1937; IMS, retired; *s* of late Professor Hugh Candy; *m* 1912, Lilian Amy (*d* 1944), *d* of late W. Sutherland; no *c*. *Educ:* City of London Sch.; London Hospital. Hon. Surgeon to the King, 1940-44. *Address:* c/o National and Grindlay's Bank Ltd, 13 St James's Square, SW1.

**CANE, Robert Alexander Gordon,** BSc London; *b* Dulwich, 11 Feb. 1893; *s* of late Robert Coats Cane; *m* 1924, Ida Mary, *d* of Brook Bray, Dulwich and S. Rhodesia; no *c*. *Educ:* Alleyn's Sch., Dulwich; University Coll., London; Bishop's Coll., Cheshunt. House tutor and science master, Saffron Walden Sch., Essex, 1923-24; Headmaster, 1924-29; temp. master, Oratory Sch., Caversham, Oxon, 1929; Headmaster of Kinmel Sch., Abergele, N. Wales, 1929-33; Temp. 2nd Lieut, 11th Batt., KO Yorks LI, 19 Sept. 1914; promoted Captain commanding A Coy 28 Nov. 1914; served with Mediterranean EF (May-Aug. 1915); severely wounded, Gallipoli when attached 1st Royal Dublin Fusiliers; invalided from service, July 1916. *Recreations:* travel, rifle shooting. *Address:* 22 Manscombe Road, Torquay, Devon.

**CANET, Maj.-Gen. Lawrence George,** CB 1964; CBE 1956; Master General of the Ordnance, Australia, 1964-67, retired; *b* 1 Dec. 1910; *s* of late Albert Canet, Melbourne, Victoria; *m* 1940, Mary Elizabeth Clift, *d* of Cecil Clift Jones, Geelong, Victoria; one *s*. *Educ:* RMC Duntroon; Sydney Univ. Served War of 1939-45 with 7th Australian Div. (Middle East and Pacific). GOC Southern Command, 1960-64. Brigadier 1953; Maj.-Gen. 1957.

**CANFIELD, Cass;** Vice-Chairman of the Board, Harper's Magazine, Inc.; Senior Editor, Harper & Row, Publishers; *b* 26 April 1897; *s* of August Cass and Josephone Houghteling; *m* 1st, 1922, Katharine Emmet; two *s*; 2nd, 1938, Jane White Fuller. *Educ:* Groton Sch.; Harvard Univ. (AB); Oxford Univ. Harris, Forbes & Co. 1921-22; NY Evening Post, 1922-23; Foreign Affairs (a quarterly magazine), 1923-24; Manager, London (England) office, Harper & Bros, 1924-27; Harper & Bros, NY City, 1927; President, Harper & Bros, 1931-45; Chairman of the Board, 1945-55; Chairman Exec. Cttee, 1955-67. Served European War, 1917-18, commissioned. President National Assoc. of Book Publishers, 1932-34; Member Board of Directors, Farfield Foundation, Inc.; Trustee, Woodrow Wilson National Fellowship Foundation; Mem. Exec. Cttee, John Fitzgerald Kennedy Library; Chairman, Governing Body, International Planned Parenthood Federation, 1966-69, now Chm. Emeritus. During War of 1939-45 with Board of Economic Warfare, Washington, DC; special advisor to American Ambassador, London, in charge of Economic Warfare Division, 1943; Director, Office of War Information, France, 1945. Albert D. Lasker Award, 1964. Hon. Phi Beta Kappa. *Publication:* The Publishing Experience. *Address:* 49 East 33rd Street, New York, NY 10016, USA. *T:* 889-7500. *Clubs:* Century Association, Harvard (New York).

**CANHAM, Erwin Dain;** Editor in Chief, The Christian Science Monitor, since 1945; President of The Mother Church, The First Church of Christ, Scientist, in Boston, 1966; *b* 13 Feb. 1904; *s* of Vincent Walter Canham and Elizabeth May Gowell; *m* 1st, 1930, Thelma Whitman Hart; two *d*; 2nd, 1968, Patience Mary, *yr d* of Lt-Col Robson Daltry, Bexhill-on-Sea. *Educ:* Bates Coll.; Oxford Univ. (Rhodes Scholar). Reporter, The Christian Science Monitor, 1925; covered League of Nations Assembly, Geneva, 1926-28; Correspondent at League of Nations, Geneva, 1930-32; Chief of Monitor's Washington Bureau, 1932; General News Editor in Boston, 1939; Managing Editor, 1942-45; Editor, 1945-64; Chm. Board of Directors, Federal Reserve Bank of Boston, 1963, 1964, 1965, 1966, 1967. Awarded numerous hon. degrees by universities and colleges in the USA, from 1946 onwards. Officer, Order of Southern Cross (Brazil), 1951; Commander, Order of Orange-Nassau (Netherlands), 1952; Order of George I (Greece), 1954; Officier, Légion d'Honneur (France), 1958 (Chevalier, 1946); Grand Distinguished Service Cross of Order of Merit (German Federal Republic), 1960; Hon. Comdr, Order of British Empire (CBE), 1964. *Publications:* Awakening: The World at Mid-Century, 1951; New Frontiers for Freedom, 1954; Commitment to Freedom: The Story of the Christian Science Monitor, 1958; Man's Great Future, 1959. Co-author, The Christian Science Way of Life, 1962. *Address:* One Norway Street, Boston 15, Massachusetts, USA. *T:* 262-2300; (Home) 6 Acorn Street, Boston 8, Mass., USA. *T:* Lafayette 3-2171. *Clubs:* Gridiron (Washington, DC); Tavern, Harvard, Saturday (Boston).

**CANN, Percy Walter,** Alderman of City of Bristol; *b* 20 June 1884; *m* 1909, Ellen Beatrice Blackburn; no *c*. *Educ:* St Gabriel's Church Sch. and North Street Higher Grade Sch., Bristol. Learning the boot trade, then Commercial Traveller, 1904-22; Director, Haynes & Cann Ltd, Northampton, 1922. Served European War, 1914-18, RASC 1916-18 (Mech. Staff Sergeant); Commandant of Special Constabulary, Bristol, 1939-49 (Special Constab. Police Medal and Bar for long service, 1938-49). Member of Bristol City

Council, 1930; Alderman, 1946; Lord Mayor, 1949-50; served on many Committees of the Council as Chairman or Vice-Chairman, 1959-. Chairman: North Bristol Boy Scouts' Association, 1946-57; North Bristol Nat. Liberal Assoc., 1932-48. President: Rotary Club of Bristol, 1942; Anchor Society, 1951, 1952; National President English Nat. Council of Development Boards, 1947-55; Chairman Bristol Light Opera Co., 1950-; Vice-Chairman, Bristol Branch, Empire Soc., 1952-; Chairman BBC West of England's Appeals Cttee, 1953-; Member BBC UK Appeals Advisory Cttee, 1952-; Chairman and Founder, Bristol Elderly Peoples Assoc. for Permanent Daily Clubs; founded Bristol Branch of Incorp. Sales Managers Assoc. FSMA (Past Sec., Chairman and Pres.). Chm., Bristol Safety First Cttee, 1967-; Vice-Chm., South Western Safety First, 1967-; Mem., Nat. Safety First, RoSPA, 1967-. Free Mason, Methodist. Grand Governor, Loyal Order of Moose, 1929, and Senior Past Governor of GB. Meritorious Service Medal, 1919; Defence Medal, 1939-45. *Recreations:* bowls, golf, gardening and cinematograph photography; music (plays organ and piano; choirmaster and organist). *Address:* Cliftonia, Walsingham Road, Bristol 6. *T:* 44486. *Club:* Royal Commonwealth Society (London and Bristol).

**CANN, Robert John,** MS London, FRCS; Surgeon Ear, Nose and Throat Department, Guy's Hospital; Consulting Ear, Nose and Throat Surgeon Caterham District Hospital and East Surrey Hospital, Redhill. *Educ:* London Univ. MRCS, LRCP 1924; MB, BS 1926; MS (Gold Medal, Lond.) 1930; FRCS 1949. Formerly Aural Surgeon Evelina Hospital for Children. FRSocMed. *Address:* 101 Harley Street, W1. *T:* 01-935 2356; 9 Vineyard Hill Road, Wimbledon, SW19. *T:* 01-946 5040.

**CANNAN, Denis;** Dramatist and screenwriter; *b* 14 May 1919; *s* of late Captain H. J. Pullein-Thompson, MC, and late Joanna Pullein-Thompson (*née* Cannan); *m* 1st, 1946, Joan Ross (marr. dissolved); two *s* one *d*; 2nd, 1965, Rose Evansky; he changed name to Denis Cannan, by deed poll, 1964. *Educ:* Eton. A Repertory actor, 1937-39. Served War of 1939-45, Queen's Royal Regt (despatches). Actor at Citizens' Theatre, Glasgow, 1946-48; first play, Max (prod. Malvern Festival), 1949; Captain Carvallo (Bristol Old Vic and St James's Theatres), 1950; Colombe (trans. from Anouilh), New Theatre, 1951; Misery Me!, Duchess, 1955; You and Your Wife, Bristol Old Vic, 1955; The Power and The Glory (adaptation from Graham Greene), Phoenix Theatre, 1956, and Phœnix Theatre, New York, 1958; Who's Your Father?, Cambridge Theatre, 1958; author of original text, US, Aldwych, 1966; adapted Ibsen's Ghosts, Aldwych, 1966; the screenplays of many feature films. *Recreation:* manual labour. *Address:* Godley's, Rudgwick, Sussex.

**CANNAN, Major-General James Harold,** CB 1915; CMG 1918; DSO 1919; VD; late Manager for NSW, The Insurance Office of Australia, Ltd; *b* Townsville, Queensland, 29 Aug. 1882; *s* of John Kearsey Cannan and Bessie Constance Hodson; *m* Eileen Clair Ranken; no *c*. *Educ:* Brisbane State Sch. and Grammar Sch. Four years in wholesale ironmongers and importers, three years clerk New Zealand Insurance Company, five years manager Patriotic Insurance Company, thirty years manager Insurance Office of Australia in Australia; retired, 1946. Lieut in 1st Queenslanders (Infantry), 1903; merged into 9th Infantry Commonwealth; Adjutant of that batt. for five years; Captain, 1907; Major, 1910; on formation of compulsory service transferred as 2nd in Command of 8th (Oxley) Infantry batt.; Lieut-Colonel, and commanded this batt., 1914; served European War (Dardanelles), 1914-16 (despatches, CB); Colonel and Temp. Brig.-General 30 Aug. 1916; commanded 11th Australian Infantry Brigade (CMG, DSO, despatches 7 times); Command of 2/15th Infantry, Commonwealth Military Forces, 1918-20; commanded 2nd Infantry Brigade, 1920-21 and 11th Infantry Brigade, 1921-25; Inspector-General of Administration under Board of Business Administration, Commonwealth of Australia, Jan.-July 1940; GOC 2nd Australian Div., July-Oct., 1940; Quarter Master General, Army HQ, Australia, 1940-46; Maj.-General 1942; retired list, 1946; Founder and 1st President, Brisbane Legacy, 1924; President, Queensland State Returned Servicemen's League, 1919-20; Director SW Pacific Area (Sydney) of UNRRA, 1946-47. *Recreations:* Inter-State rowing (8 oar), lacrosse, sailing (12-footer and 16-footer), golf, horse racing. *Address:* Flat 7, Craigston, 217 Wickham Terrace, Brisbane, Queensland, Australia. *Clubs:* Pioneers' (Sydney); Queensland (Brisbane).

**CANNING,** family name of **Baron Garvagh.**

**CANNING, Victor;** author; *b* 16 June 1911. Major, RA, 1940-46. *Publications:* Mr Finchley Discovers His England, 1934; The Chasm, 1947; Golden Salamander, 1948; Forest of Eyes, 1949; Venetian Bird, 1951; House of the Seven Flies, 1952; Man from the "Turkish Slave", 1953; Castle Minerva, 1954; His Bones are Coral, 1955; The Hidden Face, 1956; Manasco Road, 1957; The Dragon Tree, 1958; Young Man on a Bicycle and other short stories, 1959; The Burning Eye, 1960; A Delivery of Furies, 1961; Black Flamingo, 1962; The Limbo Line, 1963; The Scorpio Letters, 1964; The Whip Hand, 1965; Doubled in Diamonds, 1966; The Python Project, 1967; The Melting Man, 1968; Queen's Pawn, 1969; The Great Affair, 1970. *Recreations:* fishing, golf. *Address:* c/o Lloyds Bank Ltd, Cranbrook, Kent. *Club:* Bath.

**CANNON, Leslie,** CBE 1968; General President, Electrical, Electronic and Telecommunications Union–Plumbing Trades Union, since 1963; *b* 21 Feb. 1920; *s* of James and Ellen Cannon; *m* 1949, Olga Julinova; two *s*. *Educ:* Wigan and District Technical Coll. Electrical Trades Union: Shop Steward, 1940; District Cttee, 1941; District Secretary, 1942; Area Cttee, 1944; Executive Councillor, 1945; Education Officer, 1954; working electrician, 1957. Student of Inner Temple, 1958, 1959. Chm./Vice-Chm. (alternate years) Nat. Joint Industrial Council for the Electricity Supply Industry, 1967-; Member: Nat. Economic Develt Council, 1968-; Nat. Jt Industry Bd, Electrical Contracting Industry; TUC General Council, 1965-; Industrial Reorganisation Corp. (part-time), 1966-71; Royal Commission on Assizes and Quarter Sessions, 1966-; Cttee of Inquiry into Shipping, 1967. FRSA 1967. *Recreations:* theatre, reading, music. *Address:* 78 Bolton Road, Chessington, Surrey.

**CANNON, Air Vice-Marshal Leslie William,** CB 1952; CBE 1945; retired; *b* 9 April 1904; *s* of late Captain W. E. Cannon, Beds, and Herts Regiment, and of Cathleen Mary Jackson, Bedford; *m* 1930, Beryl (*née* Heyworth). *Educ:* Hertford Grammar Sch.; RAF Coll., Cranwell. RAF Apprentice, 1920-23; Officer Cadet, 1923-25; Pilot Officer, No. 2 (AC) Squadron, 1925-27; Flying Officer: No. 441 Flight Fleet Air Arm, China Station, 1927; No. 2 (AC) Squadron, 1928; Flying Instructor RAF Coll.,

Cranwell, 1929; F/O and Flight-Lt: Officer Engr. Course, RAF Henlow, 1929-31; Flight-Lt: Engr. Officer RAFMT Depôt, Shrewsbury, 1931-32 and RAF Coll., Cranwell, 1932-33; Engr. SO, Air HQ, India, 1933-35; Flight Comdr No. 60 (B) Squdn, Kohat, India, 1935-37 (despatches); Sqdn Ldr: OC No. 5 (AC) Sqdn, India, 1937; Personnel SO, HQ Training Command, 1938; Student RAF Staff Coll., Andover, 1939. Served War of 1939-45 (despatches thrice, CBE, American Silver Star): Staff Officer Directorate of Operations, Air Ministry, 1939-40; Wing Comdr: Engr. SO, HQ Bomber Command, 1940; Chief Technical Officer, No. 21 Operational Training Unit, 1941; Group Captain: Directing SO RAF Staff Coll., 1942; OC Bomber Stations in No. 2 (B) Group, 1942-43. Part of 2nd TAF (England, France, Belgium, Germany); GC and Air Commodore: AO i/c Admin. HQ No. 2 (B) Group, 1943-46; AOC No. 85 Group, Hamburg, 1946; idc, 1947; Asst Comdt and Comdt, RAF Staff Coll., Andover, 1948-49; Director of Organisation (Establishments), 1949-51; Commander-in-Chief, Royal Pakistan Air Force, 1951-55; Director-General of Organisation, Dec. 1955-Nov. 1958, retired. At CRO, 1959. Rolls-Royce Senior Representative, India, 1960-65. *Recreations:* represented RAF at athletics, boxing, pistol shooting. *Address:* Timbered Cottage, Witheridge Lane, Penn, Bucks. *T:* Penn 2181. *Club:* Royal Air Force.

**CANSDALE, George Soper,** BA, BSc, FLS; *b* 29 Nov. 1909; *y s* of G. W. Cansdale, Paignton, Devon; *m* 1940, Margaret Sheila, *o d* of R. M. Williamson, Indian Forest Service; two *s*. *Educ:* Brentwood Sch.; St Edmund Hall, Oxford. Colonial Forest Service, Gold Coast, 1934-48. Superintendent to Zoological Society of London, Regent's Park, 1948-53. *Publications:* The Black Poplars, 1938; Animals of West Africa, 1946; Animals and Man, 1952; George Cansdale's Zoo Book, 1953; Belinda the Bushbaby, 1953; Reptiles of West Africa, 1955; West African Snakes, 1961; Behind the Scenes at a Zoo, 1965; Animals of Bible Lands, 1970; articles in the Field, Geographical Magazine, Zoo Life, Nigerian Field, Natural History, etc. *Recreations:* natural history, photography, sailing. *Address:* Dove Cottage, Great Chesterford, Saffron Walden, Essex. *T:* Great Chesterford 274. *Club:* Royal Commonwealth Society.

**CANT, Rev. Canon Reginald Edward;** Canon and Chancellor of York Minster since 1957; *b* 1 May 1914; 2nd *s* of late Samuel Reginald Cant; unmarried. *Educ:* Sir Joseph Williamson's Sch., Rochester; CCC, Cambridge; Cuddesdon Theological Coll. Asst Curate, St Mary's, Portsea, 1938-41; Vice-Principal, Edinburgh Theological Coll., 1941-46; Lecturer, Univ. of Durham, 1946-52 (Vice-Principal, St Chad's Coll. from 1949); Vicar, St Mary's the Less, Cambridge, 1952-57. *Publication:* Christian Prayer, 1961; part-author, The Churchman's Companion, 1964. *Address:* 3 Minster Court, York YO1 2JJ. *T:* York 25599.

**CANT, Robert (Bowen);** MP (Lab) Stoke-on-Trent Central since 1966; *b* 24 July 1915; *s* of Robert and Catherine Cant; *m* 1940, Rebecca Harris Watt; one *s* two *d*. *Educ:* Middlesbrough High Sch. for Boys; London Sch. of Economics. BSc (Econ.) 1945. Lecturer in Economics, Univ. of Keele, 1962-66. Member, Stoke-on-Trent City Council, 1953-. Contested (Lab.) Shrewsbury, 1950, 1951. *Publication:* American Journey. *Recreations:* bookbinding; Workers' Educational Association. *Address:* House of Commons, SW1; (home) 119 Chell Green Avenue, Stoke-on-Trent, Staffordshire. *Club:* Chell Working Men's.

**CANTERBURY, Archbishop of,** since 1961; **Most Rev. and Rt. Hon. Arthur Michael Ramsey,** PC 1956; MA, BD, Hon. DD; Durham, 1951; Leeds, Edinburgh, Cambridge, Hull, 1957; Manchester, 1961; London, 1962; Hon. DCL: Oxford, 1960; Kent, 1966; Hon. DLitt, Keele, 1967; also has a number of hon. degrees from universities overseas; Hon. Fellow, Magdalene Coll., Cambridge, since 1952 (Fellow, 1950-52); *b* 14 Nov. 1904; *s* of late Arthur Stanley Ramsey, Fellow and sometime President of Magdalene Coll., Cambridge; *m* 1942, Joan, *d* of Lieut-Colonel F. A. C. Hamilton. *Educ:* Repton; Magdalene Coll., Cambridge (Scholar); Cuddesdon. 2nd Class, Classical Tripos, 1925; 1st Class, Theological Tripos, 1927; President of Cambridge Union, 1926; ordained, 1928; curate of Liverpool Parish Church, 1928-30; subwarden of Lincoln Theological Coll., 1930-36; Lecturer of Boston Parish Church, 1936-38; Vicar of S Benedict, Cambridge, 1939-40; Canon of Durham Cathedral and Professor of Divinity in Univ. of Durham, 1940-50; Regius Professor of Divinity, Univ. of Cambridge, 1950-52; Canon and Prebendary in Lincoln Cathedral, 1951-52; Bishop of Durham, 1952-56; Archbishop of York, 1956-61. Examining Chaplain to Bishop of Chester, 1932-39, to Bishop of Durham, 1940-50, and to Bishop of Lincoln, 1951-52; Select Preacher, Cambridge, 1934, 1940, 1948, 1959, 1964, Oxford, 1945-46; Hulsean Preacher, Cambridge, 1969-70. Hon. Master of the Bench, Inner Temple, 1962. A President of World Council of Churches, 1961-68. Trustee, British Museum, 1963-69. *Publications:* The Gospel and the Catholic Church, 1936; The Resurrection of Christ, 1945; The Glory of God and the Transfiguration of Christ, 1949; F. D. Maurice and the Conflicts of Modern Theology, 1951; Durham Essays and Addresses, 1956; From Gore to Temple, 1960; Introducing the Christian Faith, 1961; Canterbury Essays and Addresses, 1964; Sacred and Secular, 1965; God, Christ and the World, 1969. *Recreation:* walking. *Address:* Lambeth Palace, SE1. *T:* 01-928 8282; Old Palace, Canterbury. *T:* 63003.

**CANTERBURY, Assistant Bishops of;** *see* Clarke, Rt Rev. N. H.; Rose, Rt Rev. A. C. W.; Warner, Rt Rev. K. C. H.

**CANTERBURY, Dean of;** *see* White-Thomson, Very Rev. Ian Hugh.

**CANTERBURY, Archdeacon of;** *see* Nott, Ven. M. J.

**CANTLEY, Hon. Sir Joseph (Donaldson),** Kt 1965; OBE 1945; QC 1954; **Hon. Mr Justice Cantley;** Judge of the High Court of Justice, Queen's Bench Division, since 1965; Presiding Judge, Northern Circuit, since 1970; *b* 8 Aug. 1910; *er s* of Dr Joseph Cantley, Crumpsall, Manchester, and Georgina Cantley (*née* Kean); *m* 1966, Lady (Hilda Goodwin) Gerrard, *widow* of Sir Denis Gerrard. *Educ:* Manchester Grammar Sch.; Manchester Univ. Studentship and Certificate of Honour, Council of Legal Education, 1933; Barrister, Middle Temple, 1933 (Bencher 1963). Served throughout War of 1939-45: Royal Artillery and on Staff; 2nd Lieut Royal Artillery 1940; N. Arica and Italy, 1942-45 (despatches twice); Lieut-Colonel and AAG, 1943-45. Recorder of Oldham, 1959-60; Judge of Salford Hundred Court of Record, 1960-65; Judge of Appeal, Isle of Man, 1962-65. Member, General Council of the Bar, 1957-61. Hon. LLD Manchester, 1968. *Recreations:* golf, music. *Address:* Carpmael Building, Temple, EC4. *T:*

01-583 6815; Overhall Cottage, Ashdon, Essex. *T:* Ashdon 398. *Club:* Travellers'.

**CANTLIE, Sir Keith,** Kt 1944; CIE 1939; *s* of Sir James Cantlie, KBE, FRCS; *b* 6 Feb. 1886; *m* May, *d* of James Walker, Lord Provost of Aberdeen; one *s* one *d*. *Educ:* Robert Gordon's Coll. Aberdeen; Universities of Aberdeen and Oxford. Indian Civil Service, 1910; Commissioner, Assam Valley, 1937; Member Revenue Tribunal, 1942, Chairman Public Service Commission, Assam, 1945-47. *Publications:* Notes on Khasi Law; Notes on Revenue Law; Assam in Former Times; entomological papers in Bombay Nat. History Soc. Journal. *Address:* 5 Upper Wimpole Street, W1.

*See also Lt-Gen. Sir Neil Cantlie.*

**CANTLIE, Lt-Gen. Sir Neil,** KCB 1952 (CB 1946); KBE 1949; MC; MB, ChB; FRCS; late RAMC; House Governor and Medical Superintendent, King Edward VII Convalescent Home for Officers, Osborne, IW, 1952-58; *b* 11 Dec. 1892; 3rd *s* of late Sir James Cantlie; *m* 1930, Alice Mary Irene, *d* of Rev. R. H. Lucas; one *s*. *Educ:* Robert Gordon's Coll.; Aberdeen Univ (MB, ChB, 1914 with 2nd class Hons). Entered RAMC July 1914; Captain 1915; European War, 1914-18, France and Flanders; FRCS 1920; Seconded for service, Egyptian Army, 1920-24; Sudan Defence Force, 1924-25; Major, 1924; Lt-Col 1935; War of 1939-45; ADMS 46 Div., DDMS 5 Corps, N. Africa and Italy; Colonel 1941; Maj.-Gen. 1944; DDMS Southern Command, 1946-48; Lt-Gen. 1948; Director-General Army Medical Services, 1948-52; KHS, 1950-52. *Publications:* (joint) Life of Sir James Cantlie, 1939; Diseases of Mongalla (Journal Tropical Medicine and Hygiene, 1921); Treatment of Malaria by Intravenous Quinine (Journal of Tropical Medicine and Hygiene, 1923); Treatment of Injuries of Knee Joint (RAMC Journal, 1939). *Recreation:* sailing. *Address:* Timbers, 25 Manor Road, Milford-on-Sea, Hants. *T:* Milford-on-Sea 3185.

*See also Sir Keith Cantlie.*

**CAPE, Donald Paul Montagu Stewart;** Head of Information Administration Department, Foreign and Commonwealth Office, since 1968; *b* 6 Jan. 1923; *s* of late John Scarvell and Olivia Millicent Cape; *m* 1948, Cathune Johnston; four *s* one *d*. *Educ:* Ampleforth Coll.; Brasenose Coll., Oxford. Scots Guards, 1942-45. Entered Foreign Service, 1946. Served: Belgrade, 1946-49; FO, 1949-51; Lisbon, 1951-55; Singapore, 1955-57; FO, 1957-60; Bogota, 1960-61; Holy See, 1962-67. *Recreations:* riding, tennis, walking, swimming, golf. *Address:* Hilltop, Wonersh, Guildford. *Clubs:* Travellers', Royal Automobile.

**CAPE TOWN, Archbishop of,** since 1964; **Most Rev. Robert Selby Taylor;** *b* 1 March 1909; *s* of late Robert Taylor, Eden Bank, Wetheral, Cumberland; unmarried. *Educ:* Harrow; St Catharine's Coll., Cambridge; Cuddesdon Coll. Ordained deacon, 1932; priest, 1933; served as a curate at St Olave's, York; went out to Diocese of Northern Rhodesia in 1935 as a Mission priest; Principal of Diocesan Theological Coll., 1939; Bishop of Northern Rhodesia, 1941-51; Bishop of Pretoria, 1951-59; Bishop of Grahamstown, 1959-64. Hon. Fellow, St Catharine's Coll., Cambridge, 1964. DD (Hon.) Rhodes Univ., 1966. *Address:* Bishopscourt, Claremont, CP, South Africa. *Clubs:* Royal Commonwealth Society; Civil Service (Cape Town).

**CAPE TOWN, Cardinal Archbishop of; His Eminence Cardinal Owen McCann,** DD, PhD, BCom; Archbishop of Cape Town (RC), since 1951; Assistant at Pontifical Throne, 1960; Cardinal since 1965 (Titular Church, St Praxedes); *b* 26 June 1907. *Educ:* St Joseph's Coll., Rondebosch, CP; Univ. of Cape Town; Collegium Urbanianum de Propaganda Fide, Rome. Priest, 1935. Editor, The Southern Cross, 1940-48; Administrator, St Mary's Cathedral, Cape Town, 1948-50. Hon. DLitt Univ. of Cape Town, 1968. *Address:* 213 Beach Road, Sea Point, CP, South Africa; Chancery Office, Cathedral Place, 12 Bouquet Street, Cape Town. *Club:* Civil Service (Cape Town).

**CAPE TOWN, Dean of;** *see* King, Very Rev. E. L.

**CAPEL, Air Vice-Marshal Arthur John,** CB 1943; DSO 1925; DFC; JP; DL; *b* 1894; *s* of late Arthur Capel, JP, Bulland Lodge, Wiveliscombe, Somerset; *m* 1934, Austin Robina, *y d* of late Charles Austin Horn, and *widow* of Flight Lieut H. M. Moody, MC; one *d*. *Educ:* Marlborough Coll.; Trinity Coll., Oxford; Royal Military Coll., Sandhurst. Was Lieut, Somerset Light Infantry; served European War, RFC and RAF, France, 1914-18 (despatches twice); Waziristan, 1924-25 (DFC, DSO); Commandant School of Army Co-operation, Old Sarum, 1936-38; at Imperial Defence Coll., 1939; War of 1939-45, served France, UK, and Middle East (despatches thrice, CB); retired from RAF Nov. 1945. JP Somerset, 1946; DL Somerset, 1952; High Sheriff of Somerset, 1952. Member Somerset County Council, 1962-64. *Address:* Bulland Lodge, Chipstable, Wiveliscombe, Somerset. *T:* Wiveliscombe 346. *Club:* Royal Air Force.

**CAPEL CURE, (George) Nigel,** TD; JP; Vice-Lieutenant, Essex, since 1958; *b* 28 Sept. 1908; *o s* of late Major George Edward Capel Cure, JP, Blake Hall, Ongar; *m* 1935, Nancy Elizabeth, *d* of late William James Barry, Great Witchingham Hall, Norwich; two *s* one *d*. *Educ:* Eton; Trinity Coll., Cambridge. DL and JP, 1947, High Sheriff, 1951, Essex. *Recreations:* shooting and cricket. *Address:* Blake Hall, Ongar, Essex. *T:* Ongar 2652. *Clubs:* MCC, City University.

**CAPELL,** family name of **Earl of Essex.**

**CAPENER, Norman (Leslie),** CBE 1966; FRCS; Member of Council, Royal College of Surgeons of England, since 1961; Chairman, Board of Examiners for Primary FRCS, 1968; Consultant Adviser (Orthopædics), Ministry of Health, since 1964; Scientific Director, Medical Commission on Accident Prevention, since 1964, Chairman, since 1967; Consultant Orthopædic Surgeon Emeritus, South Western Regional Hospital Board, since 1963; Member of Council, University of Exeter, 1966; *b* 4 May 1898; *s* of Alick Wellstead Capener, Freeman of City of London, and Ada Isabella Tree; *m* 1st, 1922, Marion Constance Vera Clarke (*d* 1970), *d* of Captain J. Stanhope Clarke, RN; one *s* three *d*; 2nd, 1970, Elsa May Batstone. *Educ:* City of London Sch.; The Temple Choir, London; St Bartholomew's Hospital. Surg. Sub-Lt RNVR, 1918. Res. MO, Hospital of St John and St Elizabeth, 1922; House Surg. and Chief Asst, St Bartholomew's Hospital, 1926; Instructor in Anatomy and Asst Prof. of Surgery, Univ. of Michigan, 1926-31; Senior Orthopædic Surg., Princess Elizabeth Orthopædic Hospital, Exeter, 1931-63; Cons. Orthopædic Surg., Royal Devon and Exeter Hospital, and other hospitals in Plymouth and Devon, 1934-63. Hunterian Prof., RCS, 1941; Arris and Gale Lectr, RCS, 1947; Robert Jones Lectr, RCS,

1958; Robert Jones Lectr, NY Hosp. for Joint Diseases, 1947. President: Orthopædic Sect., Royal Society Med., 1951; Devon and Exeter Medico-Chirurg. Society, 1955; British Orthopædic Assoc., 1957-59; Devonshire Assoc., 1965. Vice-Pres., Anatomical Soc. of GB, 1967; Sectional Vice-Pres., British Assoc. for the Advancement of Science, 1969; Chm., Inst. of Sports Medicine, 1967-69. *Publications:* many articles on orthopædics, bio-mechanics, and historical medical subjects; critical reviews, especially relating to surgery. *Recreations:* art and music; a weekend sculptor. *Address:* Webberton Meadows, Dunchideock, Exeter EX2 9TX. *T:* Exeter 83240.

**CAPLAN, Daniel;** Under-Secretary, Ministry of Housing and Local Government, since 1969; *b* 29 July 1915; *y s* of Daniel and Miriam Caplan; *m* 1945, Olive Beatrice Porter; no *c. Educ:* Elem. and Secondary Schools, Blackpool; St Catharine's Coll., Cambridge. Asst Principal, Import Duties Adv. Cttee, 1938; Private Secretary to three Permanent Secretaries, Ministry of Supply, 1940; Principal, 1942; Ministry of Supply Representative and Economic Secretary to British Political Representative in Finland, 1944-45; Asst Secretary, Board of Trade, 1948; Adviser to Chancellor of Duchy of Lancaster, 1957-60; Under-Secretary, Scottish Development Dept, 1963-65; Under-Secretary, National Economic Development Office, 1966; Asst Under-Sec. of State, DEA, 1966-69. *Publications:* numerous papers on religious and economic history in learned journals. *Recreations:* railways, historical research, gardening. *Address:* The Old Cottage, Whitemans Green, Cuckfield, Sussex. *T:* Haywards Heath 4301. *Club:* Royal Automobile.

**CAPLAN, Leonard,** QC 1954; *b* 28 June 1909; *s* of late Henry Caplan, Liverpool; *m* 1942; two *d*. Called to the Bar, Gray's Inn, 1935; Master of the Bench, 1964; joined South Eastern Circuit; Middle Temple, 1949; served War of 1939-45, Royal Artillery (Anti-Tank): Staff Captain, 47th Div.; Staff Captain ("Q" Operations), Southern Command, engaged in D-Day Planning; passed Staff Coll., Camberley; Major, DAAG and Lt-Col, AAG, HQ Allied Land Forces, South East Asia. Conservative candidate, N Kensington, 1950-51. Chm., Coll. Hall (Univ. of London), 1958-67. Chm., Mental Health Review Tribunal, SE Region, 1960-63. *Publication:* (with late Marcus Samuel, MP) The Great Experiment: a critical study of Soviet Five Year Plans, 1935. *Recreation:* yachting. *Address:* 1 Pump Court, Temple, EC4. *T:* 01-353 9332; Skol, Marbella, S Spain. *Clubs:* Savage, Authors', 1900; Marbella Yacht, Bar Yacht.

**CAPLAT, Moran Victor Hingston,** CBE 1968; General Administrator, Glyndebourne Festival Opera, since 1949; Secretary, Glyndebourne Festival Society; Secretary, Glyndebourne Arts Trust; *b* 1 Oct. 1916; *s* of Roger Armand Charles Caplat and Norah Hingston; *m* 1943, Diana Murray Downton; one *s* two *d* (and one *s* decd). *Educ:* privately; Royal Acad. of Dramatic Art. Actor, etc., 1934-39. Royal Navy, 1939-45. Glyndebourne: Asst to Gen. Man., 1945; Gen. Man., 1949 (title subseq. altered to Gen. Administrator). Editor, Glyndebourne Festival Programme Book. FRSA. *Recreations:* ocean racing, gardening, travel. *Address:* The Yew Tree House, Barcombe, near Lewes, Sussex. *T:* Barcombe 202. *Clubs:* Royal Ocean Racing, Garrick; Hanstown, Island Sailing (Cowes).

**CAPON, Norman Brandon,** MD Liverpool; FRCP; FRCOG London; Professor Emeritus of Child Health, University of Liverpool; Hon. Consultant Pædiatrician, Liverpool Regional Hospital Board; and United Liverpool Hospitals; President, Liverpool Pædiatric Club; *b* 14 June 1892; *s* of Robert M. and Agnes Capon; *m* 1924, Dorothy (*d* 1966), *d* of W. H. Packer, MD. *Educ:* Liverpool Coll.; Univ. of Liverpool. MB, ChB with First Class Hons and Distinction in Medicine, Obstetrics and Gynæcology, 1916; MD (Special Merit), 1921; MRCP 1922; FRCP 1931; FRCOG 1957; Dawson Williams Prize, 1955; Lloyd Roberts Lect. (Manchester), 1954. Blackham Memorial Lecturer, 1955. Temp. Lieut and Capt. RAMC 1916-19. Formerly Prof. of Child Health, Univ. of Liverpool, 1944-57. External Examiner in Pædiatrics, Univ. of Birmingham; Examiner for DCH. past-Pres., Liverpool Medical Institution; Original Mem. and Past-Pres. British Pædiatric Association; Charles West Lecturer, Royal Coll. of Physicians; Fellow of the Royal Society of Medicine, and Past-Pres. Section of Pædiatrics; Past-Pres. Section of Child Health, BMA and Section of Maternal and Child Health, Royal Society of Health; Convocation Lecturer, National Children's Home. *Publications:* contribs to British Encyclopædia of Medicine; Diseases of Children, 5th edn (Moncrieff and Evans); Text-Book of Children's Diseases (Parsons & Barling). Various papers on diseases of children in medical journals. *Address:* Gray Gables, Llanbedr, Ruthin, Denbighshire. *T:* Ruthin 2060. *Club:* University (Liverpool).

**CAPOTE, Truman;** author, and painter on glass; *b* New Orleans, USA, 30 Sept. 1924; *s* of Joseph G. Capote and Nina (*née* Fauk). *Educ:* St John's Academy and Greenwich High School (New York). Reader, motion picture scripts for film company. O. Henry Memorial Award for short story, 1946; Creative Writing Award, Nat. Inst. of Arts and Letters, 1959. *Publications:* Other Voices, Other Rooms (novel), 1948; Tree of Night (short stories), 1949; Local Color (travel essays), 1950; The Grass Harp (novel), 1951 (dramatised, 1953); The Muses are Heard (essay), 1956; Breakfast at Tiffany's (short stories), 1958; Selected Writings, 1964; In Cold Blood, 1966; The Thanksgiving Visitor, 1969. Short stories and articles (both fiction and non-fiction) contributed to numerous magazines. *Address:* c/o Random House Inc., 457 Madison Avenue, New York, NY 10022, USA.

**CAPPELL, Daniel Fowler,** CBE 1958; Professor of Pathology, Glasgow University, 1945-67; *b* 28 Feb. 1900; *s* of Robert Cappell and Annabella Fowler; *m* 1927, Isabella Audrey, *yr d* of Charles A. Griffin, Glasgow; no *c. Educ:* Hillhead High Sch.; Glasgow Acad.; Univ. of Glasgow. MB, ChB with Hons, 1921; Struthers Medal and Prize, 1919, McCunn Research Scholar, 1921-23; Asst to Prof. of Pathology, Univ. of Glasgow, 1923-28; Lecturer in Pathological Histology, 1928-31; Prof. of Pathology, Univ. of St Andrews, 1931-45; Dean of the Faculty of Medicine, St Andrews, 1939. Mem., Gen. Med. Council, 1940, re-elected 1960; Adviser, Commonwealth Scholarship and Fellowship Plan, 1962; Mem., Scientific Advisory Cttee, Dept of Health for Scotland, 1944; Mem. Scottish Health Services Advisory Council, 1948; Mem. Scottish Advisory Cttee on Medical Research, Dept of Health for Scotland, 1952; Pathologist, Royal Infirmary, Dundee; Dir, East of Scotland Blood Transfusion Service. MD with Hons, 1929; Bellahouston Gold Medal, 1930; FRCP 1960; FRCPGlas 1962; FRCPE; FRSE; FRSM. Hon. Mem. of Pathological Soc. of Gt Britain and Ireland, 1922; Founder Fellow and former Vice-Pres. Royal Coll. of Pathologists; Past-Pres. Royal Glasgow Medico-Chirurgical Soc.; Past-Pres. Association Clinical Path. and Chm. of Council. LLD (Hon.) St Andrews, 1966. Mem., Angus CC. *Publications:* Intra-vitam Staining, in Journal of Pathology and Bacteriology 1929 et seq.; The Blood Group Rh 1946; Muir's Textbook of Pathology, 8th edn, 1964; Blood Groups, in Chambers's Encyclopædia; and numerous scientific papers in various medical journals. *Recreation:* fishing. *Address:* Heathcote, Edzell, Angus.

**CAPPER, Rt. Rev. Edmund Michael Hubert;** *see* St Helena, Bishop of.

**CAPPER, Sir (William) Derrick,** Kt 1968; Chief Constable of Birmingham, since 1963; *b* 3 Jan. 1912; *s* of James Herman Capper, Upton Magna, Shrewsbury; *m* 1939, Muriel Woodhouse, Shrewsbury; two *d. Educ:* Priory Sch., Shrewsbury; Birmingham Univ. Constable, Metropolitan Police, 1935-37; Police Coll., Hendon, 1937-39; Jun. Station Insp. and Station Insp., Met. Police, 1939-44; Asst Supt, Nigeria Police, 1944-46; Metropolitan Police: Station Insp., 1946-49; Chief Insp., 1949-51; Supt, 1951-57; Chief Supt, 1957-58; Asst Chief Constable, Birmingham, Jan.-April 1959; Dep. Chief Constable, 1959-63. OStJ. *Recreations:* golf, athletics, rugby football. *Address:* 79 Westfield Road, Edgbaston, Birmingham 15. *T:* 021-454 0147.

**CAPRA, Frank;** Writer, Director and Producer of Motion Pictures; President of own producing company, Liberty Films Inc.; *b* 18 May 1897; Italian Parents; *m* 1932, Lucille Rayburn; two *s* one *d. Educ:* California Institute of Technology. Col, Signal Corps, US Army; released from Army, spring of 1945. Produced and directed following pictures: Submarine, The Strong Man, Flight, Dirigible, Ladies of Leisure, Platinum Blonde, American Madness, Lady for a Day, It Happened One Night, Mr Deeds Goes to Town, Broadway Bill, Lost Horizon, You Can't Take It With You, Mr Smith Goes to Washington, Meet John Doe, Arsenic and Old Lace, It's a Wonderful Life, State of the Union, Here Comes the Groom, A Hole in the Head, Pocketful of Miracles. Member of Motion Picture Academy and of Directors' Guild. *Recreations:* Hunting, fishing, music. *Address:* Red Mountain Ranch, Fallbrook, California, USA.

**CARADON,** Baron (Life Peer) *cr* 1964; **Hugh Mackintosh Foot,** PC 1968; GCMG 1957 (KCMG 1951; CMG 1946); KCVO 1953; OBE 1939; *b* 8 Oct. 1907; *s* of late Rt Hon. Isaac Foot, PC; *m* 1936, Florence Sylvia Tod; three *s* one *d. Educ:* Leighton Park Sch., Reading; St John's Coll., Cambridge, Pres. Cambridge Union, 1929; Administrative Officer, Palestine Govt, 1929-37; attached to the Colonial Office, 1938-39; Asst British Resident, Trans-Jordan, 1939-42; British Mil. Administration, Cyrenaica, 1943; Colonial Sec.; Cyprus, 1943-45, Jamaica, 1945-47; Chief Sec., Nigeria, 1947-51. Acting Governor: Cyprus, 1944, Jamaica, Aug. 1945-Jan. 1946, Nigeria, 1949 and 1950. Capt.-Gen. and Gov.-in-Chief of Jamaica, 1951-57; Governor and Comdr-in-Chief, Cyprus, Dec. 1957-60; Ambassador and Adviser in the UK Mission to the UN and Permanent UK representative on Trusteeship Council, 1961-62, resigned; Minister of State for Foreign and Commonwealth Affairs and Perm. UK Rep. at the UN, 1964-70. Consultant, Special Fund of the United Nations, 1963-. Mem. UN Expert Group on South Africa, 1964. Consultant to Internat. Planned Parenthood Fedn, 1970-. KStJ 1952. Hon. Fellow, St John's Coll., Cambridge, 1960. *Publication:* A Start in Freedom, 1964. *Address:* Trematon Castle, Saltash, Cornwall. *T:* Saltash 3778. *Clubs:* Travellers', West Indian.

*See also Baron Foot, Rt Hon. Sir Dingle Foot, Michael Foot.*

**CARBERRY,** family name of **Baron Carbery.**

**CARBERRY, Sir John (Edward Doston),** Kt 1956; Chief Justice, Jamaica, 1954-58, retired; *b* Grenada, BWI, 20 Aug. 1893; *e s* of D. A. and Ruth Carberry; *m* 1920, Georgiana, *y d* of Charles Jackson; one *s* one *d. Educ:* Wesley Hall, Grenada; McGill Univ., Montreal (LLB). Served European War in 1st Bn British West Indies Regt, 1915-19. Called to Bar, Middle Temple, 1925; in practice in Jamaica until 1927, when joined Government Service as Clerk of the Courts; Resident Magistrate, 1932; Puisne Judge, Supreme Court, 1946; Senior Puisne Judge, Jamaica, 1949. *Recreation:* philately. *Address:* 8 East King's House Road, Kingston 6, Jamaica. *Club:* Kingston Cricket.

**CARBERY,** 10th Baron, *cr* 1715; **John Evans Carberry,** Bt 1768; *b* 20 May 1892; *s* of 9th Baron and Mary (who *m* 2nd, Arthur W. Sandford; she *d* 1949), 2nd *d* of Henry J. Toulmin, of The Pré, St Albans; *S* father, 1898. *Educ:* Osborne Naval Coll.; Leipzig. Name changed by deed poll, 1921, Kenya Colony, to John E. Carberry. A Citizen of Republic of S Africa since 1957. *Heir: n* Peter Ralfe Harrington Evans-Freke [*b* 20 March 1920; *m* 1941, Joyzelle Mary, *o c* of late Herbert Binnie; three *s* two *d*]. *Address:* 65 Oxford Road, Saxonwold, Johannesburg, S Africa.

**CARBERY, Dr Thomas Francis;** Senior Lecturer in Government-Business Relations, University of Strathclyde, since 1964; Member of Independent Television Authority, and Chairman of Scottish Committee of ITA, since 1970; *b* 18 Jan. 1925; *o c* of Thomas Albert Carbery and Jane Morrison; *m* 1954, Ellen Donnelly; one *s* two *d. Educ:* St Aloysius Coll., Glasgow; Univ. of Glasgow and Scottish Coll. of Commerce. Cadet Navigator and Meteorologist, RAFVR, 1943-47; Civil Servant, Min. of Labour, 1947-61; Sen. Lectr in Govt and Econs, Scottish College of Commerce, Glasgow, 1961-64. Mem. Court 1968-, Mem. Senate 1964-, Univ. of Strathclyde. *Publication:* Consumers in Politics, 1969. *Recreations:* golf, conversation, spectating at Association football, watching television. *Address:* 32 Crompton Avenue, Glasgow S4. *T:* 041-637 0514. *Clubs:* University of Strathclyde, Glasgow Art, Dalandhui (Glasgow).

**CARBONELL, William Leycester Rouse,** CMG 1956; Commissioner of Police, Federation of Malaya, 1953-58, retired; *b* 14 Aug. 1912; *m* 1937; two *s. Educ:* Shrewsbury Sch.; St Catharine's Coll., Cambridge. Probationary Assistant Commissioner of Police, 1935; (title changed to) Asst Superintendent, 1938; Superintendent, 1949; Asst Commissioner, 1952: Senior, 1952; Commissioner, 1953. King's Police Medal, 1950. Perlawan Mangku Negara (PMN), Malaya, 1958. *Address:* High Poplars, West End, Woking, Surrey.

**CARCANO, Miguel Angel;** Presidente de la Academia Nacional de la Historia; *b* 18 July 1889; *s* of Ramón J. Cárcano, sometime Governor of Cordoba and Ambassador, and of Ana Saenz de Zumarán; *m* Stella, *d* of Marqueses de Morra; one *s* two *d. Educ:*

Faculty of Law, Univ. of Buenos Aires. Prof. of Political Economy and Admin. Law, Univ. of Buenos Aires: National Deputy, 1930-36. Min. in London on special mission for negotiation of Anglo-Argentine Treaty, 1936; Delegate Pan-American Congress, Buenos Aires, 1937; Min. of Agriculture, Industry and Commerce, Argentina, 1936-38; Ambassador of Argentina in France 1938-42, in London, 1942-46; Pres., Argentine Delegn to UN, 1946; Min. of Foreign Affairs and Worship, 1961, 1962; Mem.: Acad. of Letters; Acad. of Economics. Grand Cross of: Legion of Honour; Pius IX; Leopold II. Knight Comdr Order of British Empire (Hon. KBE). Knight Comdr, Order of St Michael and St George (Hon. KCMG), 1933. *Publications:* Evolución Histórica de la Tierra Pública (Premio Nacional en Letras); Organizacion de la Producción; Alberdi, su doctrina Económica, 1934; Dos Años en la Cámara, 1934; Memoria del Ministerio de Agricultura (6 vol.), 1939; Realidad de una Política, 1938; Hommage A Sarmiento, 1938; British Democracy Retains its Prestige, 1942; Victoria Sin Alas, 1949; Fortaleza de Europa, 1951; La Sexta Republica, 1958; Recuerdos del Viejo Congreso, 1960; Travesia Española, 1961; Argentina y Brasil, 1961; Saenz Peña, 1963; Churchill, Kennedy, 1967; La Presidencia de Pellegrini, 1968; Estilo de Vida Argentino, 1969. *Address:* Centeno 3131, Buenos Aires, Argentina. *Clubs:* Athenæum; Circulo de Armas, Jockey (Buenos Aires); Cercle de L'Union (Paris).

*See also Major Hon. J. J. Astor, Viscount Ednam.*

**CARD, Wilfrid Ingram,** MD, FRCP; Physician to the Queen in Scotland, since 1965; Professor of Medicine in relation to Mathematics and Computing, University of Glasgow, since 1966; *b* 13 April 1908; *e s* of Henry Charles Card; *m* 1934, Hilda Margaret Brigstocke Frere; one *s* two *d*. *Educ:* Tonbridge Sch.; St Thomas's Hospital Medical Sch. MB, BS, 1931; MD Lond. 1933; MRCP 1934; FRCP 1944, FRCPE 1953, FRCPGlas 1967. Formerly: Beit Research Fellow; Physician to Out-Patients, St Thomas's Hospital. Physician in Charge, Gastro-intestinal Unit, Western General Hospital, Edinburgh; Reader in Medicine, Edinburgh Univ. Mem.: Association of Physicians of GB; Scottish Soc. of Experimental Medicine. *Publications:* Diseases of the Digestive System; (ed) Modern Trends in Gastro-Enterology, Vols 3 and 4; Contrib. to: Principles and Practice of Medicine; Textbook of Medical Treatment; articles on gastro-enterological subjects in Gut, Gastro-enterology, etc. *Recreation:* sailing. *Address:* Dean House, 5 East Abercromby Street, Helensburgh, Dunbartonshire. *T:* Helensburgh 2023. *Clubs:* Savile; Royal Northern Yacht (Rhu).

**CARDEN, Derrick Charles;** Director, Middle East Centre of Arab Studies, Shemlan, Lebanon, since 1969; *b* 30 Oct. 1921; *s* of Canon Henry Craven Carden and Olive (*née* Gorton); *Heir pres.* to Sir John Craven Carden, 7th Bt, *qv*; *m* 1952, Elizabeth Anne Russell; two *s* two *d*. *Educ:* Marlborough; Christ Church, Oxford. Sudan Political Service, 1942-54. Entered HM Diplomatic Service, 1954; Foreign Office, 1954-55; Political Agent, Doha, 1955-58; 1st Sec., Libya, 1958-62; Foreign Office, 1962-65; Head of Chancery, Cairo, 1965; Consul-General, Muscat, 1965-69. *Recreation:* pleasures of the countryside. *Address:* c/o Lloyds Bank, High Street, Winchester. *Club:* Vincent's (Oxford).

**CARDEN, Sir Henry (Christopher),** 4th Bt *cr* 1887; OBE 1945; Regular Army Officer (17th/21st Lancers), retired; *b* 16 Oct. 1908; *o s* of Sir Frederick Henry Walter Carden, 3rd Bt; *S* father, 1966; *m* 1st, 1943, Jane St C. Daniell (whom he divorced, 1960); one *s* one *d*; 2nd, 1962, Mrs. Gwyneth S. Emerson (*née* Acland), *widow* of Flt-Lt R. Emerson, Argentina. *Educ:* Eton; RMC Sandhurst. 2/Lieut, 17/21 Lancers, 1928; served Egypt and India, 1930-39. Staff Coll., 1941; Comdr, 2 Armoured Delivery Regt, in France, 1944-45. CO 17/21 Lancers, in Greece and Palestine, 1947-48; War Office, 1948-51; Military Attaché in Stockholm, 1951-55; retired 1956. Comdr of the Order of the Sword (Sweden), 1954. *Recreations:* shooting, racing. *Heir:* *s* Christopher Robert Carden, *b* 24 Nov. 1946. *Address:* North Sydmonton House, near Newbury, Berks. *T:* Headley 362. *Club:* Cavalry.

**CARDEN, Sir John Craven,** 7th Bt, *cr* 1787; *b* 11 March 1926; *s* of Capt. Sir John V. Carden, 6th Bt and Dorothy Mary, *d* of Charles Luckrart McKinnon; *S* father, 1935; *m* 1947, Isabel Georgette, *y d* of late Robert de Hart; one *d*. *Educ:* Eton. *Heir:* *cousin* Derrick Charles Carden, *qv*. *Address:* Sulgrave Manor, Cable Beach, Nassau, Bahamas. *Club:* White's.

**CARDEN ROE, Brigadier William,** CB 1950; CBE 1944; MC 1915; retired 1949; *b* 8 Dec. 1894; *s* of Charles Edward Liesching, Tiverton, Devon; assumed surname of Carden Roe in lieu of his patronymic, 1915; *m* 1915, Rosalie (*d* 1967), *d* of David Babington, Londonderry. *Educ:* Blundell's; Royal Military Coll., Sandhurst. 2nd Lieut 1913, Capt. 1917, Royal Irish Fusiliers. Served European War, France and Belgium, 1914-19 (wounded thrice, despatches thrice); Bt Major, Staff Coll., psc 1925-26. Lieut-Col Comdg 2nd Bn Royal Irish Fusiliers, 1937-39; Col, 1939; Brig., 1940; BGS 4th Corps, 1940-41; Bde Comdr 1941-45; Comdr Southern Area, E Africa, 1946; Comdr British Advisory Staff to Polish Resettlement Corps, 1947-49; Home Guard Adviser HQ Western Command, 1951-54. ADC to the King, 1946-49. Chevalier, Légion d'Honneur, 1915. *Recreations:* gardening, fishing. *Address:* Lawnside, Gordon Avenue, Foxrock, Co. Dublin. *T:* Dublin 894301. *Club:* Kildare Street (Dublin).

**CARDIFF, Archbishop of, (RC),** since 1961; **Most Rev. John A. Murphy,** DD; *b* Birkenhead, 21 Dec. 1905; *s* of John and Elizabeth Murphy. *Educ:* The English Coll., Lisbon. Ordained 1931; consecrated as Bishop of Appia and Coadjutor Bishop of Shrewsbury, 1948; Bishop of Shrewsbury, 1949-61. *Address:* Archbishop's House, Westbourne Crescent, Whitchurch, Cardiff. *T:* Cardiff 66063.

**CARDIFF, Auxiliary Bishop in, (RC);** *see* Mullins, Rt Rev. D. J.

**CARDIFF, Brig. Ereld Boteler Wingfield,** CB 1963; CBE 1958 (OBE 1943); *b* 5 March 1909; *m* 1932, Margaret Evelyn, *d* of late Major M. E. W. Pope, Ashwicke Hall, Marshfield; two *d*. *Educ:* Eton, 2nd Lieut, Scots Guards, 1930. Served War of 1939-45: (despatches thrice); 2nd Bn Scots Guards, 201 Guards Bde; 7th Armoured Div., Western Desert. Served Italy, France, Germany, DQMG, Far ELF, 1955-58; SHAPE, 1958-63. Brig. 1958; retired, Nov. 1963. Chevalier, Order of Leopold, and Croix de Guerre, 1944. *Recreations:* shooting, fishing. *Address:* Easton Court, Ludlow, Salop. *T:* Tenbury Wells 475; 1 Fairholt Street, SW7. *T:* 01-589 3287. *Clubs:* Guards, White's, Pratt's.

**CARDIGAN, Archdeacon of;** *see* Evans, Ven. D. E.

**CARDINALE, Most Rev. Hyginus Eugene,** DD, JCD; Papal Nuncio to Belgium, since 1969; Titular Archbishop of Nepte, since 1963; *b* 14 Oct. 1916; *s* of late Gaetano Cardinale and late Uliana Cimino Cardinale. *Educ:* St Agnes Academy, Coll. Point, USA; Pontifical Roman Seminary, Rome; St Louis Theological Faculty, Naples; Pontifical Ecclesiastical Academy, Rome. Sec. of Apostolic Delegation in Egypt, Palestine, Transjordan and Cyprus, 1946-49; Auditor of Apostolic Internunciature to Egypt, 1949-52; Counsellor of Nunciature, 1952-61; Chief of Protocol of the Secretariat of State, 1961-63; Apostolic Delegate to Great Britain, Gibraltar and Bermuda, 1963-69. Under-Sec. of Techn. Organiz. Commn of Ecumenical Vatican Council II; Ecumenical Council Expert. Doctor of Theology, Canon Law; Diplomatic Sciences; Doctor (*hc*) Belles Lettres and Philosophy. Holds Grand Cross and is Knight Comdr in many orders. *Publications:* Le Saint-Siège et la Diplomatie, 1962; Chiesa e Stato negli Stati Uniti, 1958; La Santa Sede e il Diritto Consolare, 1963; Religious Tolerance, Freedom and Inter-Group Relations, 1966; Signs of the Times and Ecumenical Aspirations, 1967; The Unity of the Church, 1968; contrib. to The Vatican and World Peace, 1969. *Address:* 72 Avenue de Tervuren, Brussels, Belgium.

**CARDROSS, Lord; Malcolm Harry Erskine;** *b* 4 July 1930; *s* and *heir* of 16th Earl of Buchan *qv*; *m* 1957, Hilary Diana Cecil, *d* of late Sir Ivan McLannahan Power, 2nd Bt; two *s* two *d*. *Educ:* Eton. Sometime East India merchant. *Recreation:* music. *Heir:* *s* Hon. Henry Thomas Alexander Erskine, *b* 31 May 1960. *Address:* 24 The Little Boltons, SW10. *Club:* Carlton.

**CARDUS, Sir Neville,** Kt 1967; CBE 1964; Music Critic and Cricket Writer; *b* 2 April 1889; *m* 1921, Edith Honorine King (*d* 1968). *Educ:* Manchester; abroad. Music critic to Daily Citizen, 1913, after studying singing with Charles Egan in Manchester; contributed to various musical journals, 1912-14; joined staff of Manchester Guardian, 1917; wrote in most parts of the paper–descriptive articles to leaders; asst to Samuel Langford in music criticism; first contributed cricket articles to that paper, 1919; cricket coach at Shrewsbury Sch., 1912-16; was also sec. to the Headmaster the Rev. C. A. Alington; Music Critic and Cricket Writer: The Manchester Guardian; Sydney Morning Herald, 1941-47; visited Australia to broadcast on music one hour weekly for seven years; on staff of Sunday Times, 1948-49; London music critic of Manchester Guardian, 1951-. Wagner Medal, City of Bayreuth, 1963; Special Press Award, IPC, 1970. *Publications:* A Cricketer's Book, 1921; Days in the Sun, 1924; The Summer Game, 1929; Cricket, 1930; Good Days, 1934; Australian Summer; Ten Composers, 1945; Autobiography, 1947; Tio Tondiktare (Swedish trans. of Ten Composers), 1947; Second Innings: More Autobiography, 1950; Cricket All the Year, 1952; Close of Play, 1955; Ed. Musical Criticisms of Samuel Langford, 1929; Ed. Kathleen Ferrier Memorial Book, 1954; Close of Play, 1956; Talking of Music, 1957; A Composer's XI, 1958 (German trans. 1961); Komponisten und Dirigenten (German trans.), 1959; Sir Thomas Beecham: A Portrait, 1961; The Playfair Cardus, 1963; Gustav Mahler: His Mind and his Music, Vol. I, 1965; The Delights of Music, 1966; (with John Arlott) The Noblest Game, 1969; Full Score, 1970. *Recreations:* conversation, walking, and anything not in the form of a game or sport. *Clubs:* National Liberal, Garrick.

**CARDWELL, David;** Director, Military Vehicles and Engineering Establishment, Ministry of Defence, since 1967; *b* 27 Nov. 1920; *yr s* of George Cardwell; *m* 1948, Eileen Tonkin (*née* Kitt); one *s* one *d*. *Educ:* Dulwich Coll.; City and Guilds Coll., London Univ. BSc (Eng.) London. Royal Aircraft Estab., 1942-51; Min. of Supply Headquarters, 1951-56; Military Vehicles and Engrg Estab. (formerly Fighting Vehicles Research and Development Estab.), 1956-. Imperial Defence Coll., 1965. ACGI, FIMechE, AFRAeS. *Recreation:* gardening. *Address:* Carn Lea, Grove Road, Camberley, Surrey. *T:* Camberley 22636.

**CARE, Henry Clifford,** CB 1948; *b* 1892; *s* of William John Care and Alice Mary Allen; *m* 1923, Helen Ivy May, *d* of late Col James Cameron and Mrs M. I. Cameron, Blackheath. *Educ:* Univ. Coll. Sch., Hampstead; St John's Coll., Cambridge. Higher Div. Clerk, War Office, 1915; Principal, 1923; Asst Sec. 1937; Director of Finance (with rank of Under-Sec.), 1945-54. *Address:* Old Orchard, Little Bedwyn, Marlborough, Wilts. *T:* Great Bedwyn 288.

**CAREW,** 6th Baron (UK) *cr* 1838, **William Francis Conolly-Carew;** Baron Carew (Ireland), 1834; CBE 1966; Bt Major retired, Duke of Cornwall's Light Infantry; *b* 23 April 1905; *e s* of 5th Baron and Catherine (*d* 1947), *o d* of late Thomas Conolly, MP, of Castletown, Co. Kildare; *S* father, 1927; *m* 1937, Lady Sylvia Maitland, CStJ, *o d* of 15th Earl of Lauderdale; two *s* two *d*. *Educ:* Wellington; Sandhurst. Gazetted DCLI 1925; ADC to Governor and Comdr-in-Chief of Bermuda, 1931-36. Chm., British Legion, 1963-66; Pres., Irish Grassland Assn, 1949; Br. Govt Trustee, Irish Sailors' and Soldiers' Land Trust. CStJ. *Heir:* *s* Hon. Patrick Thomas Conolly-Carew, Captain Royal Horse Guards, retd. [*b* 6 March 1938; *m* 1962, Celia, *d* of Col Hon. C. G. Cubitt, *qv*; three *d*]. *Address:* Mount Armstrong, Donadea, Co. Kildare, Ireland. *T:* Naas 68196. *Clubs:* Army and Navy; Kildare Street (Dublin).

**CAREW, Major Robert John Henry,** MC; JP, DL; *b* 7 June 1888; *s* of late Col R. T. Carew, DL, of Ballinamona Park, Waterford, and Constance, *d* of Maj.-Gen. William Creagh; *m* 1st 1915, Leila Vernon (*d* 1934), *d* of late Sir Arthur V. Macan; 2nd, 1936, Dorothea Petrie (*d* 1968), *d* of late Col G. R. Townshend, RA; one *d*. *Educ:* Marlborough Coll.; RMC Sandhurst. Joined Royal Dublin Fus, 1908; served European War as Staff Captain and DAQMG; retired, 1920. *Recreations:* mechanical work; was Hon. Sec. of the Waterford Hunt, 1926-33. *Address:* Ballinamona Park, Waterford. *T:* Waterford 4429. *Club:* Army and Navy.

**CAREW, Sir Thomas Palk,** 10th Bt, *cr* 1661; *b* 1 March 1890; *o s* of Sir Henry Palk Carew, 9th Bt and Frances Gertrude (*d* 1955), *y d* of late Robert Lock-Roe, JP, of the Manor House, Lynmouth, N Devon; *S* father 1934; *m* 1st, 1913, *cousin* Ivy Madeleine Laura (whom he divorced, 1920), *d* of late Col Arthur John Breakey, OBE; one *d*; 2nd, 1927, Phyllis Evelyn, *o c* of late Neville Mayman, Sydney, NSW; one *s* one *d*. *Educ:* Wellington; Pembroke Coll., Oxford. Served European War in IARO. *Recreation:* solitude. *Heir:* *s* Rivers Verain Carew, MA, BAgr(Hort) Dublin [*b* 17 Oct. 1935; *m* 1968, Susan Babington, *yr d* of late H. B. Hill, London; one *d*]. *Address:* Killyon Manor, Hill of Down, Co. Meath, Eire.

**CAREW, William Desmond;** *b* Sligo, Ireland, 19 Nov. 1899; *s* of Dr W. K. Carew, Colonial

Medical Service; unmarried. *Educ:* Clongowes Wood Coll., Ireland; Trinity College, Dublin. 2nd Lieut Duke of Connaught's Own Lancers, Indian Army. Joined Colonial Service, 1921, and served as follows: Fiji, 1921-34; New Hebrides, 1935-40; Malaya, 1941-45 (interned by Japanese at Singapore, 1942-45); Nigeria, 1947; Fiji, 1948. Indian Gen. Service Medal, Bar 1919, Afghanistan Campaign. Puisne Judge, Supreme Court of Fiji, and Chief Justice of Tonga, 1948-55; retired, 1955. Deputy Administrator of Martial Law, Singapore, 1942. Appointed Commissioner to review salaries of Fiji Civil Service and Police Force, 1956; Judge, Court of First Instance, Gibraltar, 1961, retd, 1963. *Recreations:* fishing, golf. *Address:* c/o Bank of New Zealand, 1 Queen Victoria Street, EC4. *Club:* Naval and Military.

**CAREW, William James,** CBE 1937; Retired as Clerk of the Executive Council and Deputy Minister of Provincial Affairs, Newfoundland; *b* 28 Dec. 1890; *s* of late James and Mary Carew; *m* 1920, Mary Florence Channing (decd); one *s* three *d. Educ:* St Patrick's Hall (Christian Brothers), St John's, Newfoundland. Newspaper work, 1908-09; staff of Prime Minister's Office, 1909; Sec., 1914-34; acted as Sec. to Newfoundland Delegate to Peace Conference, 1919; Sec. of Newfoundland Delegation to Imperial Conference, 1923, 1926, 1930; Deputy Min. for External Affairs, 1932; Sec. Newfoundland Delegation to Imperial Economic Conference, Ottawa, 1932; Sec. Cttee for Celebration in Newfoundland of Coronation of King George VI, 1937; Sec. Royal Visit Cttees on occasion of visit of King George VI and Queen Elizabeth to Newfoundland, 1939. *Recreations:* reading, fishing, walking. *Address:* 74 Cochrane Street, St John's, Newfoundland.

**CAREW HUNT, Rear-Adm. Geoffrey Harry,** CB 1967; Director: Atlantic Container Line (Services) Ltd; Joseph Barber & Co. Ltd; *b* 6 April 1917; *s* of late Captain Roland Cecil Carew Hunt, CMG, Royal Navy retd and Mrs Thelma Reay Carew Hunt; *m* 1939, Diana (*d* 1969), *er d* of Rear-Adm. J. F. C. Patterson, *qv*; no *c. Educ:* Winchester Coll. Joined RN, 1934; Midshipman on China Station, 1935-37; served in Submarines, HMS Snapper, Mediterranean and North Sea, 1939-40 (despatches twice); qualified Gunnery Officer, 1941; Home Fleet Destroyers 1942-43; HMS Diadem, Home Station, 1943-45 (despatches three times); HMS Kenya, West Indies, 1947; HMS Vanguard, Mediterranean and Home Station, 1949-50; British Naval Staff, Washington, DC, 1951-53; HMS Theseus, 1953-56; Imperial Defence Coll., 1958; HMS Defender, 1959-60; Admiralty, 1945-47, 1950-51, 1956-57, 1962-65; Admiral Commanding Reserves, 1965-68; retired from Royal Navy, 1968. MBIM; FInstD. *Recreations:* sailing, shooting, golf. *Address:* Itchen Abbas House, Itchen Abbas, Winchester, Hants. *T:* Itchen Abbas 335. *Clubs:* United Service, MCC; Royal Wimbledon Golf; Royal Yacht Squadron (Naval Member), Royal Lymington Yacht, Royal Cruising, Royal Naval Sailing Association.

**CAREW POLE, Sir John G.;** *see* Pole.

**CAREY, Group Captain Alban M.,** CBE 1943; Chairman: Shaw & Sons Ltd, Law Publishers; Shaw & Sons (Bell Yard) Ltd; Gledsdale & Jennings Ltd, Liverpool; Hadden Best Ltd, Ipswich; Chirit Investment Co. Ltd; *b* 18 April 1906; *m* 1934, Enid Morten Bond; one *s. Educ:* Bloxham. Commissioned RAF 1928; left RAF 1946; served War of 1939-45 with RAF Coastal Command both overseas and in the UK. *Recreations:* farming, shooting, fishing, yachting. *Address:* Town Green Farm, Englefield Green, Surrey. *T:* Egham 2135. *Clubs:* Royal Air Force; Royal Air Force yacht.

**CAREY, Cecil William Victor;** retired; formerly Supreme Court Judge, Colonial Service; *b* 6 Oct. 1887; 2nd *s* of late William Percival Carey, Solicitor, Dublin; *m* 1st, Lucy Kathleen (*d* 1922), *d* of late Rev. W. T. Stokes, MA; two *d;* 2nd, Isabella Morrison (*d* 1932), *d* of late John Anderson, Perthshire. *Educ:* Trinity Coll., Dublin Univ. (BA, LLB). Barrister-at-Law (King's Inns, Dublin); practised at Irish Bar, 1910-15; Asst District Officer, Uganda, 1915; Magistrate, 1919; transferred to Nigeria as Crown Counsel, 1921; Judge, Supreme Court, Nigeria, 1930-40; Judge, Supreme Court, SS, 1940-46 (interned in Malaya, 1942-45); acting Chief Justice, Singapore, April-June 1946; Judge, Supreme Court, Malayan Union, 1946-48; retired, 1948. *Address:* Trendle, Bere Alston, Yelverton, Devon.

**CAREY, Chapple G.;** *see* Gill-Carey.

**CAREY, D(avid) M(acbeth) M(oir),** MA Oxon; Legal Secretary to the Archbishop of Canterbury and Principal Registrar to the Province of Canterbury since 1958; Legal Secretary to the Bishops of Ely since 1953 and Gloucester since 1957; Registrar to the Diocese of Canterbury since 1959; *b* 21 Jan. 1917; *s* of Godfrey Mohun Carey, Sherborne, Dorset, and Agnes Charlotte Carey (*née* Milligan); *m* 1949, Margaret Ruth (*née* Mills), Highfield Sch., Liphook, Hants; three *s* one *d. Educ:* Westminster Sch. (King's Scholar); St Edmund Hall, Oxford. Articled Clerk, Messrs Lee, Bolton & Lee, 1938-40. Lt-Cdr (S) RNVR, 1940-46. Qualified Solicitor, 1947; Partnership with Lee, Bolton & Lee, 1948. *Recreations:* rowing, fishing. *Address:* 1 The Sanctuary, SW1. *T:* 01-222 5381; 141 Oakwood Court, W14. *T:* 01-602 2125. *Clubs:* Athenæum, Public Schools; Leander (Henley).

**CAREY, Denis;** producer and actor; *b* London, 3 Aug. 1909; *s* of William Denis Carey and May (*née* Wilkinson); *m* Yvonne Coulette. *Educ:* St Paul's Sch.; Trinity Coll., Dublin. First appearance as Micky in The Great Big World, Royal Court, 1921; subseq. appeared in Dublin, 1929-34, London and New York, 1935-39; Pilgrim Players, 1940-43; Glasgow Citizens' Theatre, 1943-45; Arts Council Theatre, Coventry, 1945-46; in Galway Handicap, Men without Shadows, Lyric Hammersmith, 1947. First production, Happy as Larry, Mercury, later Criterion, 1947; Georgia Story, The Playboy of the Western World, London, 1948; Assoc. Producer, Arts Theatre, Salisbury, 1948; Dir, Bristol Old Vic Company, 1949-54; London and other productions include: Two Gentlemen of Verona (from Bristol), An Italian Straw Hat, Old Vic, 1952; Henry V (from Bristol), Old Vic, 1953; The Merchant of Venice, Stratford-on-Avon, 1953; Twelfth Night, The Taming of the Shrew, Old Vic, 1954; Salad Days (from Bristol), Vaudeville, 1954; Twelfth Night, Théâtre Nat. de Belgique, Brussels, 1954; A Kind of Folly, Duchess, 1955; Follow That Girl, Vaudeville, 1960; Twelfth Night, Regent's Park, 1962. First Director, American Shakespeare Theatre, Stratford, Conn., 1955; prod Julius Cæsar, The Tempest. Director: Bristol Old Vic tour (Brit. Council), India, Pakistan, Ceylon, 1963; The Golden Rivet, Phœnix Theatre, Dublin, 1964; Armstrong's Last Good-Night, Citizen Theatre, Glasgow, 1964; The Saints Go Cycling, Dublin Festival, 1965. *Recreations:* walking, and drinking. *Address:* 5 Eldon Grove, NW3. *T:* 01-435 6110. *Club:* Garrick.

**CAREY, Rt. Rev. Kenneth Moir;** *see* Edinburgh, Bishop of.

**CAREY, Major-General Laurence Francis de Vic,** CB 1959; CBE 1955; Jurat of the Royal Court, Guernsey, 1963; Chairman, British Channel Island Airways; *b* 5 June 1904; *s* of late Sir Victor Carey, and late Adelaide, *d* of late Julius Jeffreys, FRS; *m* 1928, Alicia Frances Liebe, *d* of late Col C. E. Phipps, CB, Blackheath; three *s*. *Educ:* Elizabeth Coll., Guernsey; Royal Naval Coll., Osborne and Dartmouth; Royal Military Academy, Woolwich. Commissioned in Royal Engineeers, 1924; served in RE field units, Madras Sappers and Miners and in various appointments in Ordnance Survey and Military Survey; Director of Military Survey, War Office, 1953; Brig., 1955; Temp. Maj.-Gen. and Maj.-Gen., 1957. Dir-Gen., Ordnance Survey, 1957-61, retd. Mem. Council, RGS, 1957-60; Chm., Joint Advisory Survey Bd, 1957-61; Chm, Field Survey Assoc., 1960-61. *Address:* Courtil Desperques, St Martin, Guernsey. *T:* Guernsey 37565. *Clubs:* Army and Navy; Royal Channel Islands Yacht (Guernsey).

**CAREY, Lionel Mohun,** TD, MA; JP; Headmaster of Bromsgrove School, 1953-July 1971; *b* 27 Jan. 1911; 4th *s* of late G. M. Carey; *m* 1943, Mary Elizabeth Auld, MBE; two *s*. *Educ:* Sherborne Sch.; Corpus Christi Coll., Cambridge. Teaching Diploma Institute of Education, London, 1934. Assistant Master, Bolton Sch., Lancs., 1934-37; Christ's Hospital, 1937-53, Housemaster 1940-53. *Recreations:* walking, reading, golf, people. *Address:* The School House, Bromsgrove, Worcs. *T:* Bromsgrove 72774; (from July 1971) Westbury Cottage, Sherborne, Dorset.

**CAREY, Very Rev. Michael Sausmarez;** Dean of Ely, since 1970; *b* 7 Dec. 1913; *s* of Rev. Christopher Sausmarez and Jane Robinson Carey; *m* 1945, Muriel Anne Gibbs; one *s* one *d*. *Educ:* Haileybury Coll.; Keble Coll., Oxford (MA 1941). Ordained, 1939, Curate St John's Waterloo Rd, SE1; Chaplain Cuddesdon Coll., 1941-43; Mission Priest, Gambia, 1943-44; Rector of Hunsdon, Herts, 1945-51; Rector of Botley, Hants, 1951-62; Archdeacon of Ely, 1962-70, and Rector of St Botolph's, Cambridge, 1965-70. Exam. Chap. to Bp of Portsmouth, 1953-59. Hon. Canon, Portsmouth, 1961-62. MA Cantab Incorp. 1967. *Recreations:* music, painting, golf. *Address:* The Deanery, Ely. *T:* Ely 2432.

**CAREY, Peter Willoughby;** Under-Secretary, Ministry of Technology, since 1969; *b* 26 July 1923; *s* of Jack Delves Carey and Sophie Carey; *m* 1946, Thelma Young; three *d*. *Educ:* Portsmouth Grammar Sch.; Oriel Coll., Oxford; Sch. of Slavonic Studies. Served War of 1939-45: Capt., Gen. List, 1943-45. Information Officer, British Embassy, Belgrade, 1945-46; FO (German Section), 1948-51; Bd of Trade, 1953; Prin. Private Sec. to successive Presidents, 1960-64; IDC, 1965; Asst Sec., Bd of Trade, 1963-67, Under-Sec., 1967-69. *Recreations:* music, theatre, travel. *Address:* 28 London Road, Guildford, Surrey. *T:* Guildford 75109.

**CAREY EVANS, Lady Olwen (Elizabeth),** DBE 1969; *b* 3 April 1892; *d* of 1st Earl Lloyd-George of Dwyfor, PC, OM, and Margaret, GBE, *d* of Richard Owen, Mynydd Ednyfed, Criccieth; *m* 1917, Sir Thomas John Carey Evans, MC, FRCS (*d* 1947); two *s* two *d*. *Address:* Eisteddfa, Criccieth, Caernarvonshire.

**CAREY-FOSTER, George Arthur,** CMG 1952; DFC 1944; AFC 1941; Counsellor, HM Diplomatic (formerly Foreign) Service, 1946-68; *b* 18 Nov. 1907; *s* of George Muir Foster, FRCS, MRCP, and Marie Thérèse Mutin; *m* 1936, Margaret Aloysius Barry Egan ; one *d*. *Educ:* Clifton Coll., Bristol. Royal Air Force, 1929-35; Reserve of Air Force Officers, 1935-39; served War of 1939-45: Royal Air Force, 1939-46 (despatches, AFC, DFC), Group Capt. Served at Foreign Office, Rio de Janeiro, Warsaw, Hanover and The Hague, 1946-68; retired, 1968. *Recreation:* wine. *Address:* Kilkeran, Castle Freke, Co. Cork. *Clubs:* St James'; Haagsche (The Hague).

**CAREY JONES, Norman Stewart,** CMG 1965; Director, Development Administration, Leeds University, since 1965; *b* 11 Dec. 1911; *s* of Samuel Carey Jones and Jessie Isabella Stewart; *m* 1946, Stella Myles; two *s*. *Educ:* Monmouth Sch.; Merton Coll., Oxford. Colonial Audit Service: Gold Coast, 1935; Northern Rhodesia, 1939; British Honduras, 1946; Kenya, 1950; Asst Financial Sec., Treasury, Kenya, 1954; Dep. Sec., Min. of Agric., Kenya, 1956; Perm. Sec., Min. of Lands and Settlement, Kenya, 1962. *Publications:* The Pattern of a Dependent Economy, 1952; The Anatomy of Uhuru, 1966. Articles and reviews for: Journal of Rhodes-Livingstone Inst.; E African Economics Review; Africa Quarterly; Geog. Jl. *Address:* Sandown, Rawdon, near Leeds. *Club:* Royal Commonwealth Society.

**CARIBOO, Bishop of,** since 1957; **Rt. Rev. Ralph Stanley Dean;** Executive Officer of the Anglican Communion, 1964-69; *b* London, 1913; *m* 1939, Irene Florence, *er d* of late Alfred Bezzant Wakefield. *Educ:* Roan Sch., Greenwich; Wembley County Sch.; London Coll. of Divinity, BD Lond. 1938; ALCD 1938; MTh 1944; Deacon 1938; Priest 1939; Curate of St Mary, Islington, 1938-41; Curate-in-charge, St Luke, Watford, 1941-45; Chaplain and Tutor, London Coll. of Divinity, 1945-47, Vice-Principal, 1947-51; Principal, Emmanuel Coll., Saskatoon, Canada, 1951-56; Incumbent of Sutherland and Hon. Canon of Saskatoon, 1955-56. Episcopal Secretary, Lambeth Conference, 1968. Hon. DD: Wycliffe Coll., Toronto, 1953; Emmanuel Coll., Saskatoon, 1957; Anglican Theolog. Coll., Vancouver, 1965; Huron Coll., Ont., 1965; Hon. STD, Hartford Coll., Conn., 1966. *Publication:* In the Light of the Cross, 1961. *Address:* 360 Nicola Street, Kamloops, BC, Canada.

**CARINGTON,** family name of **Baron Carrington.**

**CARLESS, Hugh Michael;** Counsellor, British Embassy, Bonn, since 1970; *b* 22 April 1925; *s* of Henry Alfred Carless and Gwendolen Patullo; *m* 1956, Rosa Maria, *e d* of Martino and Ada Frontini, São Paulo; two *s*. *Educ:* Sherborne; Sch. of Oriental Studies, London; Trinity Hall, Cambridge. Served in Paiforce and BAOR, 1943-47; entered Foreign (subseq. Diplomatic) Service, 1950; 3rd Sec., Kabul, 1951; 2nd Sec., Rio de Janeiro, 1953; Tehran, 1956; 1st Sec., 1957; FO, 1958; Private Sec. to Minister of State, 1961; Budapest, 1963; Civil Service Fellow, Dept of Politics, Glasgow Univ., 1966; Counsellor and Consul-Gen., Luanda, 1967-70. *Recreations:* mountains, history. *Address:* British Embassy, 53 Bonn, Friedrich Ebert Allee 77, Germany; 5 Bryanston Square, W1. *Club:* Travellers'.

**CARLESTON, Hadden Hamilton,** CIE 1947; OBE 1944; Administrative Secretary, School of Veterinary Medicine, University of Cambridge, since Oct. 1952; *b* Pretoria, SA, 25 July 1904; *m* 1946, Eirene Leslie, *d* of Rev. H. L. Stevens, Torquay, S Devon; two *s* one *d*. *Educ:* St Olave's Sch., Southwark; Trinity

Hall, Cambridge (MA). Indian Civil Service, 1927-47; Dist Magistrate of Civil and Military Station, Bangalore, 1939-43, and of various districts in Madras Presidency, including Vizagapatam, 1944-46, and The Nilgiris, 1947. Civil Liaison Officer with 19th and 25th Indian Inf. Divs, 1944. Sec. of St Cuthbert's Soc., Univ. of Durham, 1948-52. *Address:* 32 Storey's Way, Cambridge. *T:* 50983.

**CARLETON, John Dudley;** Headmaster of Westminster School, 1957-70; *b* 29 Aug. 1908; *y s* of late Brig.-Gen. Frederick Montgomerie Carleton, DSO, HM Hon. Corps of Gentlemen-at-Arms, and Emma Gwendoline Priscilla Lloyd; *m* 1965, Janet Adam Smith, *qv*. *Educ:* Westminster; Merton Coll., Oxford. Assistant Master, Westminster Sch., 1932-41 and 1945-49. War Office (attached Special Forces), 1941-45. Under Master and Master of the Queen's Scholars, Westminster, 1949-57. *Publications:* Westminster, 1938; Westminster School: a history, 1965. *Recreations:* travel, sailing. *Address:* 57 Lansdowne Road, W11. *T:* 01-799 9324. *Clubs:* Athenæum, Garrick.

**CARLILE, Rev. Edward Wilson;** Vicar of St Peter's with St Hilda's, Leicester, since 1960; Chief Secretary of The Church Army, 1949-60; *b* 11 June 1915; *s* of Victor Wilson and Elsie Carlile; *m* 1946, Elizabeth (*née* Bryant); two *s* one *d*. *Educ:* Epsom Coll.; King's Coll., London (BD). Chartered Accountant, 1939. Deacon, 1943; priest, 1944; Curate, All Saints, Queensbury, 1943-46; Hon. Asst Sec. of Church Army, 1946-49. *Recreations:* tennis, walking, travel, photography. *Address:* St Peter's Vicarage, Leicester. *T:* Leicester 57726.

**CARLILE, Thomas;** Managing Director, Babcock & Wilcox Ltd, since 1968; *b* 9 Feb. 1924; *s* of late James Love Carlile and Isobel Scott Carlile; *m* 1955, Jessie Davidson Clarkson; three *d*. *Educ:* Minchenden County Sch.; City & Guilds Coll., London. Joined Babcock & Wilcox Ltd, 1944; NY Office Representative, 1950-53; General Works Manager, 1961-66. Director, 1963; Managing Dir., Babcock & Wilcox (Operations) Ltd, 1966. Chm., Shipbuilding Industry Training Board, 1967; First Dep. Pres., Engineering Employers' Federation, 1968. *Address:* 8 Aldenham Grove, Radlett, Herts. *T:* Radlett 6881. *Club:* Caledonian.

**CARLILL, Vice-Admiral Sir Stephen Hope,** KBE 1957; CB 1954; DSO 1942; *b* Orpington, Kent, 23 Dec. 1902; *s* of late Harold Flamank Carlill; *m* 1928, Julie Fredrike Elisabeth Hildegard, *o d* of late Rev. W. Rahlenbeck, Westphalia; two *s*. *Educ:* Royal Naval Colleges, Osborne and Dartmouth. Lieut RN, 1925; qualified as Gunnery Officer, 1929; Commander 1937; Commanded HM Destroyers Hambledon, 1940, and Farndale, 1941-42; Captain 1942; Captain (D), 4th Destoyer Flotilla, HMS Quilliam, 1942-44 (despatches); Admiralty, 1944-46; Chief of Staff to C-in-C British Pacific Fleet, 1946-48; Captain, HMS Excellent, 1949-50; Commanded HMS Illustrious, 1950-51; Rear-Admiral, 1952; Senior Naval Member, Imperial Defence Coll., 1952-54; Vice-Admiral, 1954; Flag Officer, Training Squadron, 1954-55; Chief of Naval Staff, Indian Navy, 1955-58, retired. Representative in Ghana of West Africa Cttee 1960-66; Adviser to W Africa Cttee, 1966-67. *Recreations:* walking and gardening. *Address:* 22 Hamilton Court, Milford-on-Sea, Lymington, Hants. *T:* Milford-on-Sea 2958. *Club:* United Service.

**CARLISLE,** 12th Earl of, *cr* 1661; **Charles James Ruthven Howard,** MC 1945; Viscount Howard of Morpeth, Baron Dacre of Gillesland, 1661; *b* 21 Feb. 1923; *o s* of 11th Earl of Carlisle, and of Lady Ruthven of Freeland, *qv*; *S* father, 1963; is *heir* to mother's barony; *m* 1945, Hon. Ela Beaumont, OStJ, *o d* of 2nd Viscount Allendale, KG, CB, CBE, MC; two *s* two *d*. *Educ:* Eton. Served War of 1939-45 (wounded twice, MC). Lieut late Rifle Brigade, FLAS. *Heir: s* Viscount Morpeth, *qv*. *Address:* Naworth Castle, Brampton, Cumberland. *T:* Brampton 2621.

**CARLISLE, Bishop of,** since 1966; **Rt Rev. Sydney Cyril Bulley;** *b* 12 June 1907; 2nd *s* of late Jethro Bulley, Newton Abbot, Devon; unmarried. *Educ:* Newton Abbot Grammar Sch.; Univ. of Durham, BA 1932; MA 1936; DipTh 1933; Van Mildert Scholar, Univ. of Durham, 1932. Deacon, 1933; priest, 1934; Curate of Newark Parish Church, 1933-42; Director of Religious Education, Diocese of Southwell, 1936-42; Vicar of St Anne's, Worksop, 1942-46; Chaplain to High Sheriff of Notts, 1943; Hon. Canon of Southwell Minster, 1945; Vicar and Rural Dean of Mansfield, 1946-51; Proctor in Convocation of York, 1945-51; Vicar of Ambleside with Rydal, 1951-59; Archdeacon of Westmorland and Dir. Religious Education, Diocese Carlisle, 1951-58; Archdeacon of Westmorland and Furness, 1959-65; Suffragan Bishop of Penrith, 1959-66; Hon. Canon of Carlisle Cathedral, 1951-66; Examining Chaplain to the Bishop of Carlisle, 1952-66. Chairman: Southwell Diocese Education Cttee, 1942-51; Worksop Youth Cttee, 1943-45; Mansfield Youth Cttee, 1947-48; Member: Southwell Diocese Board of Finance, 1942-51; Central Council of the Church for Education, 1951-; Westmorland Education Cttee, 1951-64. Gov. Derby Training Coll., 1938-51, Ripon Training Coll., 1953-58; Lancaster Coll. of Education, 1963; Chm. of Governing Body, Casterton Sch., 1962; Chaplain to the Queen, 1955-59. *Address:* Rose Castle, Dalston, Carlisle.

**CARLISLE, Dean of;** *see* du Toit, Very Rev. L. M. S.

**CARLISLE, Archdeacon of;** *see* Nurse, Ven. Charles Euston.

**CARLISLE, Lt-Col (John Charles) Denton,** DSO 1918; OBE 1944; MC; *b* 15 June 1888; *m* 1922, Elsie Hope (*d* 1970), *d* of Sir C. F. Gill, KC, and *widow* of Hubert Stewart Smiley; one *d*. Served European War, 1914-18 (despatches, DSO, MC); Served War of 1939-45 (OBE). Order of Polonia Restituta (Polish); Order of St Olaf, Knight First Class (Norwegian); Order of the White Lion, Third Class (Czech); Commander Order of Orange Nassau, with Swords (Netherlands); Medal of Military Merit (Brazil). *Address:* Binswood, Kingston Gorse, Angmering-on-Sea, Sussex. *T:* Rustington 3077.

**CARLISLE, Kenneth Ralph Malcolm,** TD; Director: Brooke Bond Liebig Group; Bank of London and South America Ltd; Argentine Southern Land Co. Ltd; Tribune Investment Co. Ltd; *b* 28 March 1908; *s* of late Kenneth Methven Carlisle and Minnie Marie Donner; *m* 1938, Hon. Elizabeth Mary McLaren, *d* of 2nd Baron Aberconway; one *s* three *d*. *Educ:* Harrow; Magdalen Coll., Oxford (BA). Binder, Hamlyn & Co., Chartered Accountants, 1931-32; Liebig's Extract of Meat Co. Ltd, Argentina, Paraguay, Uruguay, 1933-34; Liebig's Companies on Continent of Europe, 1935-37. Major, Rifle Bde, 1939-45. Distinguished Service Medal (Greece); Chevalier de l'Ordre de Leopold (Belgium), 1960. *Recreations:* all sports, including shooting, ski-ing, tennis. *Address:* (private) 18

York House, York House Place, W8. *T:* 01-937 8846; Wyken Hall, Stanton, Bury St Edmunds, Suffolk; (office) Watling House, 35 Cannon Street, EC4. *T:* 01-284 6422. *Clubs:* Boodle's, City of London.

**CARLISLE, Mark;** MP (C) Runcorn since 1964; Parliamentary Under-Secretary of State, Home Office, since 1970; *b* 7 July 1929; 2nd *s* of Philip Edmund and Mary Carlisle; *m* 1959, Sandra Joyce Des Voeux; one *d. Educ:* Radley Coll.; Manchester Univ. LLB (Hons) Manchester, 1952. Called to the Bar, Gray's Inn, 1953; practised throughout on Northern Circuit. Member Home Office Advisory Council on the Penal System; Joint Hon. Secretary, Conservative Home Affairs Cttee, 1965-69; Conservative Front Bench Spokesman on Home Affairs, 1969-70. *Recreations:* golf, tennis. *Address:* 3 King's Bench Walk, Temple, EC4. *T:* 01-353 0431; 43 King Street, Manchester. *T:* 061-834 6875; Newstead, Mobberley, Cheshire. *T:* Mobberley 2275. *Club:* St James's (Manchester).

**CARLOW,** Viscount; **Charles George Yuill Seymour Dawson-Damer;** *b* 6 Oct. 1965; *s* and *heir* of 7th Earl of Portarlington, *qv.*

**CARLYLE, Joan Hildred;** Principal Lyric Soprano, Royal Opera House, Covent Garden, since 1955; *b* 6 April 1931; *d* of Edgar James and Margaret Mary Carlyle; *m* Robert Duray Aiyar; two *d. Educ:* Howell's Sch., Denbigh, N. Wales. Oscar in Ballo in Maschera, 1957-58 season; Sophie in Rosenkavalier, 1958-59; Micaela in Carmen, 1958-59; Nedda in Pagliacci (new Zeffirelli production), Dec. 1959; Mimi in La Bohème, Dec. 1960; Titania in Gielgud Production of Britten's Midsummer Night's Dream, London première, Dec. 1961; Pamina in Klemperer production of The Magic Flute, 1962; Countess in Figaro, 1963; Zdenko in Hartman production of Arabella, 1964; Sœur Angelica (new production), 1965; Desdemona in Otello, 1965, 1967; Sophie in Rosenkavalier (new production), 1966; Pamina in Magic Flute (new production), 1966; Arabella in Arabella, 1967; Marschallin in Rosenkavalier, 1968. Roles sung abroad include: Oscar, Nedda, Mimi, Pamina, Zdenko, Micaela, Desdemona. Début in Salzburg, Lincoln Center, NY, and Buenos Aires, 1968. Has made numerous recordings; appeared BBC, TV (in film). *Recreations:* gardening, cooking, interior decorating. *Address:* 44 Abbey Road, St John's Wood, NW8. *T:* 01-624 4614.

**CARLYON, Thomas Symington,** CMG 1968; OBE 1940; Managing Director, T. S. Carlyon & Co. Pty Ltd, since 1950; *b* Ballarat, 27 April 1902; *s* of late T. S. Carlyon, Melbourne; *m* 1950, Marie Pichoir, *d* of Edward de Launay; one *s* one *d* (by a previous *m*). *Educ:* Geelong Grammar Sch. Hotel Training, Bellevue Stratford Hotel, USA; General Manager, Hotel Australia, Sydney, 1939-40 and 1946. Member Housing and Catering Cttee, 1956 Olympic Games. Served RAAF, 1940-45 (Sqdn Leader). Chm., Victoria Amateur Turf Club. *Recreations:* golf, racing. *Address:* 54 Heyington Place, Toorak, Victoria, Australia. *T:* 20-4215. *Clubs:* Melbourne Cricket, All Racing (Victoria); Metropolitan Golf.

**CARMARTHEN, Archdeacon of;** *see* Jenkins, Ven. J. O.

**CARMICHAEL, Mrs Catherine McIntosh;** Lecturer, University of Glasgow, since 1962; Member, Supplementary Benefits Commission; *b* 22 Nov. 1925; *d* of John D. and Mary Rankin; *m* 1948, Neil George Carmichael, *qv*; one *d. Educ:* Glasgow and Edinburgh. Social worker, 1955-57; psychiatric social work, 1957-60; Dep. Dir, Scottish Probation Training Course, 1960-62. *Recreations:* reading, relaxation. *Address:* 53 Partick Hill Road, Glasgow, W1, Scotland. *T:* 041-334 1718.

**CARMICHAEL, Sir David William G. C.;** *see* Gibson-Craig-Carmichael.

**CARMICHAEL, Edward Arnold;** CBE 1942; FRCP; Hon. Consulting Physician, National Hospital, Queen Square; formerly Director of Neurological Research Unit and Physician National Hospital for Nervous Diseases, Queen Square, London; *b* 25 March 1896; *y s* of late Edward Carmichael, MD, Edinburgh; *m* 1927, Jeanette Marie Montgomerie; two *s. Educ:* Edinburgh Academy; Edinburgh Univ. MB, ChB, Annandale Gold Medal, 1921; FRCPE 1926, FRCP 1932. Served European War, 1914-19. President Royal Medical Society, 1921-22; Morrison Lecturer, RCP Edin., 1938; Oliver Sharpey Lecturer, 1933, Lumleian Lecturer, 1953, RCP (Lond.); Bramwell Memorial Lecturer, Edinburgh, 1963; Wall Memorial Lecturer, Washington, 1963; Visiting Professor of Neurology, Columbia Univ., New York, 1964; Visiting Scientist, Nat. Inst. of Health, Bethesda, USA, 1964-66; Visiting Professor, Montreal Neurological Inst., 1966; Visiting Professor of Neurology, Univ. of Pennsylvania, 1966-67; Milton Shy Meml Prof., Univ. of Pennsylvania, 1970; Rockefeller Foundation Travelling Fellow, 1934; Hon. Member: Society for Psychiatry and Neurology, Vienna, 1948; American Neurological Assoc., 1952; Philadelphia Neurological Society, 1967; Hon. Foreign Member, French Neurological Society, 1949; Corresp. Member German Neurological Society, 1954; President, Neurological Section, Royal Society Medicine, London, 1953-54; President EEG Society, 1963-64. Hon. DSc, Edinburgh Univ., 1963; Gold Medal, Graz Univ., 1963; Honorary Alumnus, Neurological Inst., NY, 1966. *Publications:* The Cerebrospinal Fluid (with Dr J. G. Greenfield), 1925; articles in physiological, clinical and neurological journals. *Address:* 20 Lucastes Avenue, Haywards Heath, Sussex. *T:* Haywards Heath 4598. *Club:* Athenæum.

**CARMICHAEL, Harry John,** CMG 1943; Director: Abitibi Power and Paper Co. Ltd; Argus Corporation Ltd; Bank of Toronto, Toronto; Foster Wheeler Ltd; Massy-Harris Co. Ltd; Hiram Walkers Ltd; Continental Can Ltd; Brights Wines Ltd; Dover Coys Ltd; Hayes Wheel Ltd; *b* New Haven, Connecticut, 29 Sept. 1891; *s* of late William A. Carmichael and Mary Ann Moran; *m* 1942, Helen Marie Moran Woods. *Educ:* Lovell Sch., New Haven; New Haven High Sch. With McKinnon Industries Ltd, St Catharine's, Ontario, from 1912, and on acquisition by General Motors Corp., became President and General Manager, 1929; Vice-President and General Manager, General Motors of Canada, Ltd., 1936-41; Joint Dir-General of Munitions Production, Dept of Munitions and Supply, 1941-42; Co-ordinator of Production and Chm. War Production Board; Canadian Chm. of: Joint US-Canada War Production Board, 1942-45; Joint US-Canada Industrial Mobilization Planning Cttee, 1949. *Address:* 619 Avenue Road, Apartment 1601-2, Toronto 7, Ontario, Canada. *Clubs:* Canadian (New York); Rideau (Ottawa); Granite (Toronto); County of Buffalo (Williamsville, NY); Niagara (Niagara Falls, NY).

**CARMICHAEL, Ian (Gillett)**; *b* 18 June 1920; *s* of Arthur Denholm Carmichael, Cottingham, E Yorks, and Kate Gillett, Hessle, E Yorks; *m* 1943, Jean Pyman Maclean, Sleights, Yorks; two *d. Educ:* Scarborough Coll.; Bromsgrove Sch. Studied at RADA, 1938-39. Served War of 1939-45 (despatches). First professional appearance as a Robot in "RUR", by Karel and Josef Capek, The People's Palace, Stepney, 1939; stage appearances include: The Lyric Revue, Globe, 1951; The Globe Revue, Globe, 1952; High Spirits, Hippodrome, 1953; Going to Town, St Martin's, 1954; Simon and Laura, Apollo, 1954; The Tunnel of Love, Her Majesty's, 1958; The Gazebo, Savoy, 1960; Critic's Choice, Vaudeville, 1961; Devil May Care, Strand, 1963; Boeing-Boeing, Cort Theatre, New York, 1965; Say Who You Are, Her Majesty's, 1965; Getting Married, Strand, 1967; I Do! I Do!, Lyric, 1968. Films include: (from 1955) Simon and Laura; Private's Progress; Brothers in Law; Lucky Jim; Happy is the Bride; The Big Money; Left, Right and Centre; I'm All Right Jack; School for Scoundrels; Light Up The Sky; Double Bunk; The Amorous Prawn; Hide and Seek; Heavens Above!; Smashing Time. TV series include: The World of Wooster; Bachelor Father. *Recreations:* cricket, gardening, photography and reading. *Address:* c/o London Management, 235/241 Regent Street, W1A 2JT. *Clubs:* MCC; Lord's Taverners'.

**CARMICHAEL, James,** CMG 1950; DSc, MRCVS, Dip. Bact.; Chairman: Murphy Chemical Co. Ltd, 1955-68; Murphy & Son Ltd, Wheathampstead, since 1955; *s* of James Carmichael; *m* 1930, Kathleen Jackson, Scarborough, Yorks; one *s* one *d. Educ:* Denstone Coll.; Univ. of Edinburgh; Univ. of London. Veterinary Officer, Colonial Service, Uganda Protectorate, 1923; Veterinary Research Officer, 1930; Senior Veterinary Research Officer, 1937; retired from Colonial Service, 1945; Member various Scientific Advisory Cttees, Colonial Office, 1946-58. Member Council of Royal Society of Tropical Medicine and Hygiene, 1950-65. *Publications:* numerous publications in scientific journals on tropical veterinary medicine, tsetse fly problem, etc. *Recreations:* fishing, shooting, hunting, tennis, golf, etc. *Address:* Boarded Barns Farm, Ongar, Essex. *T:* Ongar 2573. *Club:* East India and Sports.

**CARMICHAEL, Sir John,** KBE 1955; Deputy Chairman, Fisons Ltd, since 1963 (Director, since 1961); Chairman, Jute Industries (Holdings) Ltd, since 1970 (Deputy Chairman, 1969, Director since 1966); Director: National Commercial Bank of Scotland Ltd, since 1965; Grampian Television, since 1967; Abbey National Building Society, since 1968; *b* 22 April 1910; *s* of late Thomas Carmichael and Margaret Doig Coupar; *m* 1940, Cecilia Macdonald Edwards; one *s* three *d. Educ:* Madras Coll., St Andrews; Univ. of St Andrews; Univ. of Michigan (Commonwealth Fund Fellow). Guardian Assurance Co., Actuarial Dept, 1935-36; Sudan Govt Civil Service, 1936-55; Member Sudan Resources Board and War Supply Dept, 1939-45; Secretary Sudan Development Board, 1944-48; Asst Financial Secretary, 1946-48; Dep. Financial Secretary, 1948-53; Director, Sudan Gezira Board, 1950-54; Chm. Sudan Light and Power Co., 1952-54; Acting Financial Secretary, then Permanent Under Secretary to Ministry of Finance, 1953-55; Financial and Economic Adviser to Sudan Government, 1955-59. Member of UK delegation to General Assembly of UN, 1959. Mem. Scottish Gas Board, 1960-70. Dep. Chm., ITA, 1960-64, Acting Chm. ITA, 1962-63; Chm. of the Herring Industry Board, 1962-65. *Recreations:* golf, gardening. *Address:* Magicwell, Balmullo, Leuchars, Fife. *T:* Balmullo 268. *Clubs:* New (Edinburgh); Royal and Ancient Golf (St Andrews).

**CARMICHAEL, Leonard;** Vice-President for Research and Exploration, National Geographic Society (Trustee, National Geographic Society, 1957-); *b* Philadelphia, Pennsylvania, 9 Nov. 1898; *s* of Thomas Harrison Carmichael and Emily Henrietta Leonard; *m* 1932, Pearl Kidston; one *d. Educ:* Germantown Friends Sch., Philadelphia; Tufts Coll. (BS 1921); Harvard Univ. (PhD 1924); Univ. Berlin. Instructor in Psychology, Princeton Univ. 1924-26; Asst Professor, 1926-27; Assoc. Professor of Psychology, Brown Univ., 1927-28; Professor, 1928-36; Director of Psychological Laboratory, 1927-36, and Director of Laboratory of Sensory Physiology, 1934-36; Chairman, Dept of Psychology, and Dean, Faculty of Arts and Science, Univ. of Rochester, 1936-38; President, Tufts Coll., and Director, Laboratory of Sensory Psychology and Physiology, 1938-52; Secretary (Director), Smithsonian Inst., 1953-63 (now Director Emeritus). Director, Nat. Roster of Scientific and Specialized Personnel, 1940-44; Chairman, American Council on Education, 1947-48; Member: Naval Res. Advisory Cttee, 1947-52; Advisory Cttee to Nat. Scientific Register; Nat. Advisory Cttee for Aeronautics, 1953-58; Nat. Acad. of Sciences; American Philosophical Soc., Philadelphia (Pres. 1970); American Acad. of Arts and Sciences; American Psychological Assoc.; Hon. LLD Harvard Univ., 1952; also Hon. Degrees from other Universities. Decorated by the Governments of Spain, Denmark, Italy and Germany. *Publications:* (with Dearborn and Lord) Special disabilities in learning to read and write, 1925; (with Warren) Elements of human psychology, 1930; The response mechanism (chapter in Boring, Langfeld and Weld, Introduction to Psychology), 1939; The Onset and early development of behaviour (Chapter in Carmichael L. (ed.), Manual of child psychology), 1946 (2nd edn, 1953); (with Dearborn) Reading and Visual Fatigue, 1947; Basic Psychology, 1957. Editorial Rep. of British Journal of Educational Psychology; many articles. *Address:* The National Geographic Society, 17th and M Streets, NW, Washington, DC 20036, USA. *Clubs:* St Botolph, Algonquin (Boston); Century Association (New York); Cosmos, Chevy Chase, Metropolitan (Washington).

**CARMICHAEL, Neil George;** MP (Lab) Woodside Division of Glasgow since 1962; *b* Oct. 1921; *m* 1948, Catherine McIntosh Rankin (*see* C. M. Carmichael); one *d. Educ:* Estbank Acad.; Royal Coll. of Science and Technology, Glasgow. Employed by Gas Board in Planning Dept. Past Member Glasgow Corporation. PPS to Minister of Technology, 1966-67; Jt Parly Sec., Min. of Transport, 1967-69; Parly Sec., Min. of Technology, 1969-70. *Address:* House of Commons, SW1; 53 Partick Hill Road, Glasgow, W1.

**CARMICHAEL-ANSTRUTHER, Sir W. E. F.;** *see* Anstruther.

**CARNAC;** *see* Rivett-Carnac.

**CARNARVON,** 6th Earl of, *cr* 1793; **Henry George Alfred Maurius Victor Francis Herbert;** Baron Porchester, 1780; Lieut-Colonel 7th Hussars; *b* 7 Nov. 1898; *o s* of 5th Earl and Almina (who *m* 2nd, 1923, Lieut-Colonel I. O. Dennistoun, MVO; she *d* 1969), *d* of late Frederick C. Wombwell; *S* father, 1923; *m* 1st,

1922, Catherine (who obtained a divorce, 1936, and *m* 2nd, 1938, Geoffrey Grenfell (decd), and *m* 3rd, 1950, D. Momand), *d* of late J. Wendell, New York, and Mrs Wendell, Sandridgebury, Sandridge, Herts; one *s* one *d*; 2nd, 1939, Ottilie (marr. diss.), *d* of Eugene Losch, Vienna. *Educ:* Eton. Owns about 4000 acres. *Heir: s* Lord Porchester, *qv*. *Recreations:* racing, and shooting. *Address:* Highclere Castle, near Newbury, Hants. *TA:* Carnarvon Highclere. *T:* Highclere 204. *Clubs:* White's, Portland.

*See also Sir B. C. Beauchamp.*

**CARNE, Colonel James Power,** VC 1953; DSO 1951; DL; *b* 11 April 1906; *s* of late G. N. Carne, Garras, Falmouth; *m* 1946, Mrs Jean Gibson, *widow* of Lt-Col J. T. Gibson, DSO, The Welch Regt; one *step s*. *Educ:* Imperial Service Coll.; Royal Military Coll., Sandhurst. Commissioned Gloucestershire Regt, 1925; seconded King's African Rifles, 1930-36; Adjutant 1st Bn Gloucestershire Regt, 1937-40. Served War of 1939-45: with KAR and on Staff, Madagascar, 1942, Burma, 1944; CO 6th and 26th Bns KAR, 1943-46. CO 5th Bn (TA) 1947-50, 1st Bn Gloucestershire Regt, 1950-51; retired 1957. Served Korean War of 1950-53 (DSO, VC). Freedom of Gloucester, 1953; Freedom of Falmouth, 1954. DSC (US), 1953. DL County of Gloucester, 1960. *Recreation:* fishing.

**CARNEGIE,** family name of **Duke of Fife** and of **Earls of Northesk** and **Southesk.**

**CARNEGY of Lour, Lt-Col (Ughtred) Elliott (Carnegy),** DSO 1919; MC; DL, JP Angus; Baron of Lour; late 3rd Dragoon Guards; *b* 13 June 1886; *o s* of late Major Francis Edward Joseph and late Isabella Carnegy, 10th of Lour, *o c* of Patrick Carnegy, CIE; by deed poll assumed the name of Carnegy, 1915, on his mother succeeding to the estate of Lour; *m* 1919, Violet (MBE, Order of Mercy) (*d* 1965), *y d* of late H. W. Henderson, West Woodhay, Berks; two *d* (and one *d* decd). *Educ:* Wellington Coll.; RMC, Sandhurst. Entered Army, 1907; Captain, 1914; Major, 1921; served European War as ADC to Maj.-General Hon. Sir Julian Byng, commanding 3rd Cavalry Division, and GSO 3rd Grade 3rd Cavalry Division in France; Staff Captain 22nd Mounted Brigade in Palestine (wounded 27 Nov. 1917); GSO 2nd Grade 21st Army Corps in Palestine and Syria, 1918; attached Staff of Gen. Sir R. Wingate, Residency, Cairo, 1919 (despatches twice, 1914 Star, MC and bar, DSO); Chevalier of Order of the Star of Roumania with Swords, 1920; served on General Staff, War Office, 1919-22; retired, 1922; commanded 20th (Fife and Forfar Yeomanry) Armoured Car Company, 1929-33; Member of HM's Bodyguard (Hon. Corps of Gentlemen-at-Arms), 1931-56; Bt Lt-Col, TA, 1932; County Director, Angus Branch British Red Cross, 1934-40; Member of Angus County Council, 1937-55; Member King's Body Guard for Scotland (the Royal Company of Archers), 1940-49; on outbreak of War joined volunteer Reserve of Royal Air Force and posted to Staff of late Air Vice-Marshal C. D. Breese, CB, AFC, commanding 18 Group, Coastal Command; Wing Comdr, 1941, commanded Central Area, Scotland, Air Training Corps, 1941-45. King's Jubilee Medal, 1935; Coronation Medal, 1937. *Recreation:* shooting. *Address:* Lour, Angus. *T:* Inverarity 237. *Clubs:* Cavalry, Pratt's, MCC; New (Edinburgh).

*See also Dame Beryl Oliver, J. L. E. Smith.*

**CARNER, Dr Mosco;** Music Critic of The Times, 1961-69; Member of the BBC Score Reading Panel since 1944; *b* 15 Nov. 1904; *m* 1962, Dr Elisabeth Bateman (*d* 1970). *Educ:* Vienna Univ. and Vienna Music Conservatory. Conductor at Danzig State Theatre, 1929-33. Resident in London since Autumn 1933, where active as conductor, musical author, critic and broadcaster. Music Critic of Time and Tide, 1949-62; Music Critic of The Evening News, 1957-61. Silver Medal of the Italian Government, 1964. *Publications:* A Study of 20th-Century Harmony, 1942; Of Men and Music, 1944; The History of the Waltz, 1948; Puccini, A Critical Biography, 1958 (Ital. edn, 1960, Japanese edn 1968). Contributions to New Oxford History of Music, and to Symposia on: Schubert, 1946; Schumann, 1952; The Concerto, 1952; Chamber Music, 1957; and Choral Music, 1963. *Recreations:* reading, motoring and swimming. *Address:* 14 Elsworthy Road, NW3. *T:* 01-586 1553.

**CARNEY, Most Rev. James F.;** *see* Vancouver, Archbishop of, (RC).

**CARNEY, Admiral Robert Bostwick,** Hon. CBE 1946; DSM (US), 1942 (and Gold Stars, 1944, 1946, 1955); and numerous other American and foreign decorations; United States Navy; retired; Chairman Board, Naval Historical Foundation; Director, several corporations; Corporation Consultant; *b* Vallejo, California, 26 March 1895; *s* of Robert E. and Bertha Carney; *m* 1918, Grace Stone Craycroft, Maryland; one *s* one *d*. *Educ:* United States Naval Acad., Annapolis, Md (BS). Served European War, 1914-18; Gunnery and Torpedo Officer aboard USS Fanning in capture of Submarine U-58 off coast of Ireland; War of 1939-45; North Atlantic, 1941-42; Commanding Officer, USS Denver, serving in Pacific, 1942-43; Chief of Staff to Admiral William Halsey (Commander, S. Pacific Force), 1943-45, participating in nine battle engagements. Deputy Chief of Naval Operations, 1946-50; President of US Naval Inst., 1950-51, 1954-56; Commander Second Fleet, 1950; Commander-in-Chief, United States Naval Forces, Eastern Atlantic and Mediterranean, 1950-52; Commander-in-Chief, Allied Forces, Southern Europe (North Atlantic Treaty Organisation), 1951-53; Chief of Naval Operations, 1953-55; retired 1955. Hon. LLD, Loras Coll., 1955. *Publications:* various professional. *Recreations:* field sports, music. *Address:* 2101 Connecticut Avenue (NW), Washington, DC 20008, USA. *Clubs:* Chevy Chase Country, Army and Navy Town (Washington, DC); The Brook (NY).

**CARNOCHAN, John Golder;** Under-Secretary, Ministry of Agriculture, Fisheries and Food, 1965-70; *b* Old Kilpatrick, 12 Sept. 1910; *s* of N. and M. G. Carnochan; *m* 1938, Helen Dewar, *y d* of A. A. and A. Ferguson, Doune; one *s*. ASAA 1936; ACA 1958; FCA 1959. Entered Ministry of Food, 1942; Dep. Accountant-General, 1948; Asst Secretary, 1949; Under-Secretary, 1965. *Address:* Pinecrest, Fir Tree Road, Leatherhead, Surrey. *T:* Leatherhead 3853. *Clubs:* Farmers', Civil Service, Authors'.

**CARNOCK,** 3rd Baron, *cr* 1916, of Carnock; **Erskine Arthur Nicolson,** 13th Bt of Nova Scotia, *cr* 1637; DSO 1919; JP; Captain, RN, retired; *b* British Legation, Athens, 26 March 1884; 2nd *s* of 1st Lord Carnock and Mary Catherine (*d* 1951), *d* of Captain Arch. Rowan Hamilton, Killyleagh, Co. Down; *S* brother, 1952; *m* 1919, Katharine (*d* 1968), *e d* of 1st Baron Roborough; one *s* (and one *s* killed in action 1942; one *d* decd). *Educ:* HMS Britannia; RN Staff Coll., 1913. War Staff Officer to the Light Cruiser Forces, 1914-19 (DSO, Légion d'honneur, St Anne with Swords, Crown of Italy); retired list, 1924.

*Recreation:* hunting. *Heir: s* Hon. David Henry Arthur Nicolson, *b* 10 July 1920. *Address:* Burrator, Sheepstor, Yelverton, S Devon.
*See also Baron St Levan.*

**CARNWATH, Andrew Hunter;** a Managing Director, Baring Brothers & Co. Ltd, since 1955; *b* 26 Oct. 1909; *s* of late Dr Thomas Carnwath, DSO, Dep. CMO, Min. of Health, and Margaret Ethel (*née* McKee); *m* 1939, Kathleen Mariaane Armstrong (*d* 1968); five *s* one *d*. *Educ:* Eton (King's Scholar). Served RAF (Coastal Comd Intelligence), 1939-45. Joined Baring Bros & Co. Ltd, 1928; rejoined as Head of New Issues Dept, 1945. Chm., Save and Prosper Group Ltd, 1961- (Dir, 1960-); Director: Equity & Law Life Assurance Soc. Ltd, 1955-; Law Reversionary Interest Soc. Ltd, 1955; Scottish Agricultural Industries Ltd, 1969-. Member: London Cttee, Hongkong and Shanghai Banking Corp., 1967-; Council, Inst. of Bankers, 1955- (Dep. Chm., 1969-70, Pres., 1970-); Cttee on Consumer Credit; Central Bd of Finance of Church of England (Chm., Investment Management Cttee, 1960-); Chm., Chelmsford Diocesan Bd of Finance, 1969- (Vice-Chm., 1967-68); Council, King Edward's Hosp. Fund for London, 1962- (Treasurer, 1965-); Royal Commn for Exhibn of 1851, 1964-; Council, Friends of Tate Gall., 1962- (Treasurer, 1966- ). Trustee, Imp. War Graves Endowment Fund, 1963-, Chm., 1964-. A Governor, Felsted Sch., 1965-. Chm., Saffron Walden Conservative Assoc. High Sheriff of Essex, 1965. FIB. *Publications:* lectures and reviews for Inst. of Bankers, etc. *Recreations:* music (playing piano, etc), pictures, travel, living in the country. *Address:* The Old Vicarage, Ugley, Bishop's Stortford, Herts. *T:* Rickling 283. *Club:* Athenæum.

**CARO, Anthony (Alfred),** CBE 1969; Sculptor; *b* 8 March 1924; *s* of Alfred and Mary Caro; *m* 1949, Sheila May Girling; two *s*. *Educ:* Charterhouse; Christ's Coll., Cambridge; Regent Street Polytechnic; Royal Acad. Schs, London. Asst to Henry Moore, 1951-53; taught part-time, St Martin's Sch. of Art, 1953-67; taught sculpture at Bennington Coll., Vermont, 1963, 1964, 1965. One-man Exhibitions: Galleria del Naviglio, Milan, 1956; Gimpel Fils, London, 1957; Whitechapel Art Gallery, London, 1963; Andre Emmerich Gallery, NY, 1964, 1966, 1968, 1970; Washington Gallery of Modern Art, Washington, DC, 1965; Kasmin Ltd, London, 1965, 1967; David Mirvish Gallery, Toronto, 1966; Galerie Bischofberger, Zurich, 1966; Kroller-Muller Museum, Holland, 1967; Hayward Gallery, London, 1969. Exhibited: First Paris Biennale, 1959 (sculpture Prize); Battersea Park Open Air Exhibitions, 1960, 1963, 1966; Gulbenkian Exhibition, London, 1964; Documenta III Kassel, 1965; Primary Structures, Jewish Museum, NY, 1966; Venice Biennale, 1966, David Bright Prize. *Recreation:* music. *Address:* 111 Frognal, Hampstead, NW3.

**CARÖE, Einar Athelstan Gordon,** CBE 1958; Grain Merchant and Broker, W. S. Williamson and Co., Liverpool since 1935; Consul for Denmark, in Liverpool, since 1931, also for Iceland since 1947; *b* 6 Oct. 1903; *s* of Johan Frederik Caröe and Eleanor Jane Alexandra Caröe (*née* Gordon); *m* 1st, 1934, Frances Mary Lyon (*d* 1947); two *s*; 2nd, 1952, Doreen Evelyn Jane Sandland; one *s* one *d*. *Educ:* Eton Coll. (King's Scholar); Trinity Coll., Cambridge (Scholar, BA). Chairman, Liverpool Savings Bank, 1947-48; Chairman Trustee Savings Banks Assoc., 1966- (Dep. 1951-66); President, Liverpool Consular Corps, 1952; Chairman, Liverpool Chamber of Commerce, 1950-51. Pres., Minton Ltd, Stoke-on-Trent, 1970- (Chm. 1956-70); Chairman: Maritime Insurance Co. Ltd, Liverpool, 1951-68; Liverpool Corn Trade Assoc., 1963-67; Richards-Campbell Tiles Ltd, 1967-68. Treasurer, Liverpool Univ., 1957-66; President 1966- (Dep. Treas., 1948-57); President, Lancashire County Lawn Tennis Assoc., 1953; Member Lawn Tennis Assoc. Council, 1954-66; President: Nat. Federation of Corn Trade Assocs, 1957-60; Internat. Savings Banks Inst., 1960-69 (Hon. Pres., 1969-). Officer, 1st Class, Order of Dannebrog, 1957 (Officer, 1945); Officer, Order of Icelandic Falcon, 1958; Comdr, Order of Crown of Belgium, 1966. King Christian X Liberty Medal, 1946. *Recreations:* lawn tennis (Lancashire doubles champion, 1933); philately (Fellow RSP(L) 1939). *Address:* Anthonys Close, Caldy Road, Caldy, West Kirby, Wirral, Cheshire. *T:* 051-625 7089. *Clubs:* Danish; British Pottery Manufacturers (Stoke-on-Trent); Liverpool Racquet, Palatine (Liverpool).

**CAROE, Sir Olaf (Kirkpatrick),** KCSI, 1945 (CSI 1941); KCIE, 1944 (CIE 1932); FRSL 1959; DLitt Oxon; late ICS and Officer Indian Political Service; Vice-President, Conservative Commonwealth Council, 1969 (Deputy Chairman, 1966-69); *e s* of late William Douglas Caroe and of Grace Desborough, *d* of John Rendall; *m* 1920, Frances Marion (Kaisar-i-Hind Gold Medal, 1947) (*d* 1969), *d* of late Rt Rev. A. G. Rawstorne, Bishop of Whalley; two *s*. *Educ:* Winchester; (Demy) Magdalen Coll., Oxford. Captain 4th Bn, The Queen's Regt (TF), 1914-19; entered ICS, 1919; served in Punjab till 1923, when posted to N. W. Frontier Province as Officer of Political Department; served as Deputy Commissioner, various Frontier Districts, including Peshawar, up to 1932; Chief Secretary to the Govt, of the NWFP, 1933-34; Deputy Secretary, Foreign and Political Dept, Government of India, 1934; officiated as Political Resident in the Persian Gulf, Resident in Waziristan, and as Agent to the Governor-General in Baluchistan, 1937-38 (despatches); Revenue Commissioner in Baluchistan, 1938-39; Secretary, External Affairs Dept, 1939-45; Governor North-West Frontier Province, India, 1946-47; left India Aug. 1947. Vice-Chairman Overseas League, 1951; visited US for British Information Services, 1952; Is President, Tibet Soc. of the UK, and Chairman, Tibet Cttee of British Orgs. for Aid to Refugees. *Publications:* Wells of Power, 1951; Soviet Empire, 1953 (republished 1966); The Pathans, 1958; From Nile to Indus (with Sir Thomas Rapp and Patrick Reid), 1960; Poems of Khushhal (with Sir Evelyn Howell), 1963; articles in The Round Table, Central Asian Society, and other Journals. *Address:* Newham House, Steyning, Sussex. *T:* Steyning, 2241. *Club:* Lansdowne.

**CARON, Leslie (Leslie Claire Margaret,** *née* Caron); film and stage actress; *b* 1 July 1931; *d* of Claude Caron and Margaret Caron (*née* Petit); *m* 1956, Peter Reginald Frederick Hall (marr. dissolved, 1965); one *s* one *d*; *m* 1969, Michael Laughlin. *Educ:* Convent of the Assumption, Paris. With Ballet des Champs Elysées, 1947-50, Ballet de Paris, 1954. *Films include:* American in Paris, 1950; subsequently, Lili; The Glass Slipper; Daddy Long Legs; Gaby; Gigi; The Doctor's Dilemma; The Man Who Understood Women; The Subterraneans; Fanny; Guns of Darkness; The L-Shaped Room; Father Goose; A Very Special Favour; Promise Her Anything; Is Paris Burning?; Head of the Family. *Plays:* Orvet, Paris, 1955; Gigi, London, 1956;

Ondine, London, 1961. *Recreation:* collecting antiques.

**CARPENTARIA, Bishop of,** since 1968; **Rt. Rev. Ernest Eric Hawkey;** *b* 1 June 1909; *s* of Richard and Beatrice Hawkey; *m* 1943, Patricia Spark. *Educ:* Trinity Grammar Sch., Sydney, NSW. *Recreations:* music, gardening. *Address:* The Bishop's House, Thursday Island, Queensland, Australia. *T:* 79.

**CARPENTER, Ven. Edward Frederick;** Archdeacon of Westminster since 1963, Treasurer since 1959, Canon since 1951; Lector Theologiae of Westminster Abbey, since 1958; *b* 27 Nov. 1910; *s* of Frederick James and Jessie Kate Carpenter; *m* Lilian Betsy Wright; three *s* one *d*. *Educ:* Strodes Sch., Egham; King's Coll., University of London. BA 1932, MA 1934, BD 1935, PhD 1943. Deacon, 1935; Priest, 1936; Curate, Holy Trinity, St Marylebone, 1935-41; St Mary, Harrow, 1941-45; Rector of Great Stanmore, 1945-51. Fellow of King's Coll., London University, 1954 (AKC 1935). Chairman Frances Mary Buss Foundation, 1956-; Chairman Governing Body of Camden Sch. for Girls, 1956-; Chairman of St Anne's Soc., 1958-; Joint Chm., London Soc. of Jews and Christians, 1960-; Member, Central Religious Advisory Cttee serving BBC and ITA, 1962-67; Chairman, Recruitment Cttee, ACCM, 1967; President: London Region of UNA, 1966-67; Modern Churchmen's Union, 1966; World Congress of Faiths, 1966. *Publications:* Thomas Sherlock, 1936; Thomas Tenison, His Life and Times, 1948; That Man Paul, 1953; The Protestant Bishop, 1956; (joint author) of Nineteenth Century Country Parson, 1954, and of History of St Paul's Cathedral, 1957; Common Sense about Christian Ethics, 1961; The Service of a Parson, 1965; Joint author: From Uniformity to Unity, 1962; The Church's Use of the Bible, 1963; The English Church, 1966; A House of Kings, 1966. *Recreations:* walking, talking, association football. *Address:* 5 Little Cloister, Westminster, SW1. *T:* 01-222 1445.

**CARPENTER, Sir Eric (Ashton),** Kt 1951; OBE 1948; Chairman and Managing Director, Greg Bros & Co. Ltd, 1929-69; Director: Industrial and General Trust Ltd, since 1953; Manchester Ship Canal Co., since 1956; *b* 12 Nov. 1896; *s* of Richard and Annie Carpenter; *m* 1951, Edith Elizabeth Mary, *d* of late William and Edith Sansom. *Educ:* Cheadle Hulme School. Director: Williams Deacon Bank Ltd, 1949-70 (Chm. 1952-64); Yorkshire Bank Ltd, 1952-64 (Chm. 1964-70); Lloyds Packing Warehouses (Holdings) Ltd (Chm. 1950-56); London & Lancashire Insurance Co. Ltd, 1951-70; Royal Insurance Co. Ltd, 1962-70; Liverpool & London & Globe Insurance Co. Ltd, 1962-70; Royal Bank of Scotland, 1952-68; British Wagon Co. 1958-64; Member: North Western Gas Board, 1949-67; General Council, Anglo-Dutch Trade, 1958-; Chm. Cotton and Rayon Merchants Assn, 1942-45; President Manchester Chamber of Commerce, 1948-50; President Association of British Chambers of Commerce, 1954-56 (Vice-Pres. 1951-54); Member Dollar Exports Council, 1949-60; British Member, Council of International Chamber of Commerce, 1949-61; President, The Inst. of Bankers, 1960-62. High Sheriff of Lancashire, 1959-60; JP City of Manchester, 1945-62. *Address:* Burrows Cross House, Gomshall, Guildford, Surrey. *T:* Shere 2441. *Club:* St James's (Manchester).

**CARPENTER, Rt. Rev. Harry James,** Hon. DD Oxford; *b* 20 Oct. 1901; *s* of William and Elizabeth Carpenter; *m* 1940, Urith Monica Trevelyan; one *s*. *Educ:* Churcher's Coll., Petersfield; Queen's Coll., Oxford. Tutor of Keble Coll., Oxford, 1927; Fellow, 1930; Warden of Keble Coll., 1939-55, Hon. Fellow, 1955; Hon. Fellow, Queen's Coll., Oxford, 1955; Canon Theologian of Leicester Cathedral, 1941-55; Bishop of Oxford, 1955-70. *Address:* 1 Meadow View, Baunton, Cirencester, Glos.

**CARPENTER, Rt. Hon. John Archibald B.;** *see* Boyd-Carpenter.

**CARPENTER, John McG. K. K.;** *see* Kendall-Carpenter.

**CARPENTER, Rhys,** MA Oxon, PhD, LittD; *b* Cotuit, Mass, USA, 5 Aug. 1889; *s* of William Henry Carpenter and Anna Morgan Douglass; *m* 1918, Eleanor Houston Hill, Evanston, Ill., USA; no *c*. *Educ:* Columbia Univ.; Balliol Coll., Oxford. Instructor in classical archæology in Bryn Mawr Coll., Penna, USA, 1913-15; Associate, 1915-16; Associate Professor, 1916-18; Professor, 1918-55; Professor Emeritus, 1955-. Attached to the American Commission to Negotiate Peace at Paris, 1918-19, as expert on Greco-Albanian territorial problems; Annual Prof. at American Acad., Rome, 1926-27; Director, American Sch. for Classical Studies at Athens, 1927-32 and 1946-48; Professor-in-charge, Classical School, American Academy in Rome, 1939-40; Sather Professor, Univ. of California, 1944-45; Corresponding Member, Hispanic Society of America, Pontifical Roman Academy of Archæology; Member Greek Archæological Society, German Archæological Institute, Austrian Archæological Institute, American Philosophical Society. Gold Medal, Amer. Inst. of Archaeology, 1969. *Publications:* Tragedy of Etarre, 1912; The Sunthief, and other Poems, 1914; The Plainsman, and other Poems, 1920; The Land Beyond Mexico, 1921; The Esthetic Basis of Greek Art, 1921 (2nd ed. 1959); The Greeks in Spain, 1925; The Sculpture of the Nike Temple Parapet, 1929; The Humanistic Value of Archæology, 1933; The Defenses of Acrocorinth, 1936; Folk Tale, Fiction and Saga in the Homeric Epics, 1946; Greek Sculpture: A Critical Review, 1960; Greek Art: A Study in the Evolution of Style, 1963; Discontinuity in Greek Civilization, 1966; Beyond the Pillars of Heracles, 1966; The Architects of the Parthenon, 1970; numerous articles on Greek Art in American Journal of Archæology and elsewhere. *Recreations:* mountain-climbing, archæological exploration. *Address:* Goose Walk, RD1, Chester Springs, Pa 19425, USA.

**CARPENTER, Trevor Charles;** Director of Posts, Scotland, since 1970; *b* 23 March 1917; *s* of late Walter Edward Carpenter and Florence Jane Carpenter, Newport, Mon.; *m* 1940, Margaret Lilian, *d* of Frederick James and May Ethel Day; one *s* five *d*. *Educ:* Alexandra Road Primary Sch., Newport; Newport High Sch. Exec. Officer, GPO, 1936; Higher Exec. Officer, 1947; Principal, 1951; Private Secretary to PMG, 1962; Dep. Director, Scotland, 1964; Director of Postal Personnel, GPO, 1967-70. *Recreations:* golf, Gaelic singing. *Address:* Postal Headquarters Scotland, 2-4 Waterloo Place, Edinburgh EH1 1PH.

**CARPENTIER, Général d'Armée Marcel Maurice;** Grand Croix de la Légion d'Honneur, 1956; Croix de Guerre (1914-18, 1939-45; Théâtres d'opérations exterieures) (thirteen times); Director and Editor-in-Chief of the General Military Review; *b* 2 March 1895; *m*; one *s*. *Educ:* Tours; Saint-Cyr. 2nd Lieut French Army, Aug. 1914; Lieut Nov. 1914; Captain 1915; Pilot's Certificate, 1916. Served

European War, 1914-18 (wounded, Legion of Honour, Croix de Guerre, five citations). Instructor, Saint-Cyr, 1919-23; Ecole de Guerre Supérieure, 1924; Military Attaché, Rio de Janeiro, and Inf. Prof., Brazilian War Academy, 1930-35; Chef de Bataillon, 1933; comd. Bn in Syria, 1936; Staff of HQ Levant Troops, Beyrouth, 1937; served War 1940-44 (Commander Legion of Honour, Croix de Guerre, seven citations); Chef de Cabinet Militaire, French High Comr, Levant States, 1939; Lt-Col, Staff of C-in-C French N. Africa, 1940; Colonel 1942; Comd. 7th Moroccan Tirailleurs Regt, N. Africa, 1942-43; Général de Brigade, 1943; Chief of Staff, French Exped. Corps, Italy, 1943-44; Chief of Staff, First French Army, 1944; Comdr. 2nd Moroccan Inf. Div. in liberation of Alsace and Rhine crossings, 1944-45; Général de Division, 1944. Comdr. XV Region, Marseille, 1945-46; C-in-C French Forces in Morocco, 1946-49; Général de Corps d'Armée, 1946; Member Conseil Supérieur de Guerre, since 1947; C-in-C French Forces, Indo-China, 1949-50 (Croix de Guerre); Dep. Chief of Staff, SHAPE, 1951-52; Inspector-General of French Inf. and Comdr of Strategic Reserves, Central Europe, 1952-53; Général d'Armée, 1953; Commander Allied Land Forces Central Europe, 1953-56. Vice-President Atlantic Treaty Association. American Legion of Merit, 1946; Commander Order of Leopold of the Belgians, 1948; Hon. CBE, 1949; Grand Officer, Portuguese Order of Military Merit, 1952; many other foreign decorations. *Publications:* Les Forces alliées en Italie, 1949; Un Cyrard au Feu, 1964; articles in military and academic journals. *Recreations:* fishing, swimming. *Address:* 1 Rue Blaise Desgoffe, Paris 6e. *T:* Babylone 16.99; Palais Beau Rivage, Juan-les-Pins, AM, France. *Club:* Cercle Internallié (Paris).

**CARPMAEL, Kenneth S.,** QC; *b* 12 July 1885; *s* of late Ernest Carpmael, KC, MA, Sutton, Surrey. *Educ:* Dulwich Coll. Entered Accountant Branch, Royal Navy, 1903; HMS Canterbury, Battle of Jutland; granted temporary commission as Sub-Lt, Dec. 1916, for period of hostilities; Lieut, 1917; retired as Paymaster Lt-Comdr, 1920; Paymaster Comdr (retired list), 1924; restored to active list RN, Sept. 1940 with rank of temp. Lt-Comdr, acting Comdr, Nov. 1940; on panel of Wreck Comrs (Eng.) under Merchant Shipping Acts, 1938-65. Reverted to retired list, March 1942, at own request; Mem. Admiralty Ferry Crew Organisation, 1943-60. Barrister, Middle Temple, 1919; Junior Counsel to Admiralty (Admiralty Court), 1931-35; KC 1935; Bencher of Middle Temple, 1942; Lent Reader, 1954; Treasurer, 1961; Governor of Dulwich Coll. (Lord Chancellor's representative), 1942; Estates Governor Dulwich, 1943; Governor James Allen's Girls' Sch., Dulwich, 1946-58. Barrister and KC (N Ire.), 1948. *Recreation:* yachting. *Address:* Queen Elizabeth Building, Temple, EC4. *T:* 01-353 5728; 20 Eyre Court, NW8. *T:* 01-722 1100. *Clubs:* Bath, Royal Cruising.

**CARR, Prof. (Albert) Raymond (Maillard);** Warden of St Antony's College, Oxford, since 1968 (Sub-Warden, 1966-68); Fellow since 1964; *b* 11 April 1919; *s* of Reginald and Marion Maillard Carr; *m* 1950, Sara Strickland; three *s* one *d*. *Educ:* Brockenhurst Sch.; Christ Church, Oxford. Gladstone Research Exhnr, Christ Church, 1941; Fellow of All Souls' Coll., 1946-53; Fellow of New Coll., 1953-64. Director, Latin American Centre, 1964-68. Chm. Soc. for Latin American Studies, 1966-. Prof. of History of Latin America, Oxford, 1967-68. Mem., Nat. Theatre Bd, 1968-. *Publications:* Spain 1808-1939, 1966; articles on Swedish, Spanish and Latin American history. *Recreation:* fox hunting. *Address:* St Antony's College, Oxford; 29 Charlbury Road, Oxford. *T:* 58136; Woolhanger Manor, Parracombe, Devon. *T:* 379. *Club:* United Hunts.

**CARR, Sir Bernard;** *see* Carr, Sir F. B.

**CARR, Catharine;** *see* Wade, Rosalind H.

**CARR, Air Marshal Sir (Charles) Roderick,** KBE, 1945 (CBE 1941); CB 1943; DFC; AFC; King of Arms, Order of British Empire, 1947-68; *b* 31 Aug. 1891; *s* of Charles Carr, Feilding, New Zealand; *m* Phyllis Isabel (*d* 1969), *d* of C. S. Elkington, Amersham; one *s*. *Educ:* Wellington Coll., NZ. Served European War, 1914-18, with NZ Forces, RNAS and RAF; North Russian Expedition, 1919; Chief of Air Staff, Lithuania, 1920; Shackleton's Antarctic Expedition, 1921-22; First RAF Long Distance Flight, England to Persian Gulf non-stop, 1927; RAF Egypt, 1929-33; HMS Eagle (Aircraft Carrier), China, 1936-39; Advanced Air Striking Force, RAF, France, 1939-40; AOC RAF in Northern Ireland, 1940-41; AOC No. 4 Group Bomber Command, 1941-45 (despatches); Deputy Chief of Staff (Air), Supreme HQ, Allied Exped. Force, 1945; AOC-in-C, India, 1946; retired list, 1947. Croix de Guerre (France); Commander: Legion of Honour (France); Order of St Anne, Order of St Stanislav (Russia). *Address:* Leighton Cottage, Bampton, Oxford. *Club:* International Sportsmen's.

**CARR, Prof. Charles Telford,** MA Manchester, DLitt St Andrews; Professor of German Language and Literature, University of St Andrews, since 1948; Master of St Salvator's College, since 1968; *b* 1905; *m* 1929, Marian Frances Hilton Roscoe (*d* 1948); one *s*; *m* 1952, Jean Margaret Berneaud; one *d*. *Educ:* Manchester Grammar Sch.; Univs of Manchester, Zürich and Vienna. Lectr in German: Birkbeck Coll., London, 1925-26; Univ. of Manchester, 1926-29; Univ. of of St Andrews, 1929-48; Dean of the Faculty of Arts, Univ. of St Andrews, 1955-59. *Publications:* Von Unsers Herren Liden, 1929; The German Influence on the English Vocabulary, 1934; Nominal Compounds in Germanic, 1939; countribs to modern languages jls. *Recreation:* golf. *Address:* 21 Hepburn Gardens, St Andrews, Fife. *T:* St Andrews 2764. *Club:* Royal and Ancient (St Andrews).

**CARR, Prof. Denis John;** Professor, Research School of Biological Sciences, Australian National University, Canberra, since 1968; *b* 15 Dec. 1915; *s* of James E. Carr and Elizabeth (*née* Brindley), Stoke-on-Trent, Staffs; *m* 1955, Stella G. M. Fawcett; no *c*. *Educ:* Hanley High Sch., Staffs; Manchester Univ. RAF, 1940-46. Manchester Univ.: undergraduate, 1946-49; Asst Lectr in Plant Ecology, 1949-53; Guest Research Worker at Max-Planck-Inst. (Melchers), Tübingen, 1952; Sen. Lectr in plant physiology, 1953, Reader, 1959, Melbourne; Prof. of Botany, Queen's Univ., Belfast, 1960-67. Hon. MSc Melbourne, 1958. *Publications:* numerous, in scientific journals. *Recreations:* research, music. *Address:* Research School of Biological Sciences, ANU Canberra, PO Box 475, ACT 2601, Australia.

**CARR, Edward Hallett,** CBE 1920; FBA 1956; *b* 28 June 1892. *Educ:* Merchant Taylors' Sch., London; Trinity Coll., Cambridge. Temporary Clerk Foreign Office, 1916; attached to the British Delegation to the Peace Conference, 1919; Temporary Sec. at British Embassy, Paris, for work with the Conference of Ambassadors, 1920-21; 3rd Sec. and transferred to Foreign Office, 1922; 2nd Sec.

and transferred to HM Legation at Riga, 1925; transferred to Foreign Office, 1929; Asst Adviser on League of Nations Affairs, 1930-33; First Sec., 1933; resigned, 1936; Wilson Prof. of International Politics, University Coll. of Wales, Aberystwyth, 1936-47. Director of Foreign Publicity, Min. of Information, Oct. 1939-April 1940. Asst Ed. of The Times, 1941-46. Tutor in Politics, Balliol Coll., Oxford, 1953-55; Fellow, Trinity Coll., Cambridge, 1955-; Hon. Fellow, Balliol Coll., Oxford, 1966. Hon. LittD: University of Manchester, 1964; University of Cambridge, 1967; Hon. Dr of Law, University of Groningen, 1964. *Publications:* Dostoevsky, 1931; The Romantic Exiles, 1933; Karl Marx: A Study in Fanaticism, 1934; International Relations since the Peace Treaties, 1937; Michael Bakunin, 1937; The Twenty Years' Crisis, 1919-39, 1939; Britain: A Study of Foreign Policy from Versailles to the Outbreak of War, 1939; Conditions of Peace, 1942; Nationalism and After, 1945; The Soviet Impact on the Western World, 1946; Studies in Revolution, 1950; A History of Soviet Russia: Vol. I, 1950, Vol. II, 1952, Vol. III, 1953 (all under title, The Bolshevik Revolution, 1917-1923), Vol. IV, 1954 (The Interregnum, 1923-24); Vol. V, 1958, Vol. VI, 1959; Vol. VII (in 2 parts), 1964 (Socialism in One Country, 1924-26); Vol. VIII (in 2 parts), 1969 (Foundations of a Planned Economy) in collaboration with R. W. Davies; German-Soviet Relations Between the Two World Wars, 1919-39, 1951; The New Society, 1951; What is History?, 1961; 1917: Before and After, 1968. *Address:* Trinity College, Cambridge; Dales Barn, Barton, Cambs.

**CARR, Frank George Griffith,** CB 1967; CBE 1954; MA, LLB; FSA; FRAS; Associate RINA; FIN; Director of the National Maritime Museum, Greenwich, SE10, 1947-66; *b* 23 April 1903; *e s* of Frank Carr, MA, LLD, and Agnes Maud Todd, Cambridge; *m* 1932, Ruth, *d* of Harold Hamilton, Burkitt, Ballycastle, Co. Antrim; no *c*. *Educ:* Perse and Trinity Hall, Cambridge. BA 1926; LLB 1928; MA 1939. Studied at LCC Sch. of Navigation and took Yacht Master's (Deep Sea) BoT Certificate, 1927; Cambridge Univ.: Squire Law Scholar, 1922; Capt. of Boats, Trinity Hall, 1926; Pres., Law Soc., 1924; Vice-Pres., Conservative Assoc., 1925; Pres., Nat. Union of Students, 1925; Ed., The Cambridge Gownsman, 1925. Asst Librarian, House of Lords, 1929-47. Served War of 1939-45, RNVR, Lt-Comdr. Chm., Cutty Sark Ship Management Cttee; Mem., HMS Victory Advisory Technical Cttee; Vice-President: Soc. for Nautical Research; Foudroyant Trust; Internat. Sailing Craft Assocn; HMS Unicorn Preservation Soc.; Governor, Dolphin Sailing Barge Museum Trust. *Publications:* Sailing Barges, 1931; Vanishing Craft, 1934; A Yachtsman's Log, 1935; The Yachtsman's England, 1936; The Yacht Master's Guide, 1940; numerous articles in yachting periodicals, etc. *Recreations:* yacht cruising; nautical research. *Address:* Lime Tree House, 10 Park Gate, Blackheath, SE3. *T:* 01-852 5181. *Clubs:* Athenæum, Royal Cruising, Cruising Association; Cambridge University Cruising (Cambridge).

**CARR, Sir (Frederick) Bernard,** Kt 1946; CMG 1944; *b* 5 April 1893; *s* of F. W. Carr; *m* 1933, Doreen Dadds; two *d*. *Educ:* Whitgift. TA Artists' Rifles and Middx Regt, 1911-18; seconded Royal West African Frontier Force, 1917-18; active service, Gibraltar, Egypt, France, East Africa. Colonial Administrative Service, 1919 (Nigeria); Chief Comr, Eastern Provinces, Nigeria, 1943; retired from Colonial Service, 1949. Chief Sec., Eritrea, 1949-50. *Address:* B36 San Remo Towers, Sea Road, Boscombe, Bournemouth, Hants.

**CARR, Henry Lambton,** CMG 1945; MVO 1957; retired 1961; *b* 28 Nov. 1899; *e s* of Archibald Lambton and Ella Carr, Archangel; *m* 1924, Luba, *d* of John George Edmund Eveleigh, London; two *s*. *Educ:* Haileybury Coll. Served N Russian Exped. Force (2nd Lieut), 1919. Foreign Office, 1920. HBM Passport Control Officer for Finland, 1927-41; Attaché at British Legation, Stockholm, 1941-45; attached to Foreign Office, 1945; First Sec., HM Embassy, Copenhagen, 1955; attached to Foreign Office, 1958. Chevalier (First Grade) of Order of Dannebrog, Denmark, 1957. *Recreation:* walking. *Address:* The Links, Forest Row, Sussex. *T:* Forest Row 2091; c/o Barclays Bank, Uppingham, Rutland. *Clubs:* Royal Automobile, Danish.

**CARR, Herbert Reginald Culling,** MA; Headmaster, The Grammar School, Harrogate, Yorks, 1934-60; retired; Director of Cullings' Antiques; *b* 16 July 1896; *s* of late Reginald Childers Culling Carr, OBE (ICS), and Enid Agnes Kenney Herbert; *m* 1927, Evelyn Dorothy Ritchie; one *d*. *Educ:* St Paul's Sch.; Pembroke Coll., Oxford (Open Scholar). Hons Modern History (2nd Class); Diplomas in Educn and Econs. Asst Master, Alleyn's Sch., Dulwich, 1927-31; Headmaster, Penrith Grammar Sch., Cumberland, 1931-34. sub-Lieut RNVR, 1915-19; Fl-Lieut RAFVR, 1940-44 (Africa Star). *Publication:* The Mountains of Snowdonia, 1925. *Recreation:* antiques. *Address:* Yew Tree Farm, Duntisbourne Abbots, near Cirencester, Glos. *T:* Miserden 378. *Club:* Alpine.

**CARR, Air Marshal Sir John Darcy B.;** *see* Baker-Carr.

**CARR, John Dickson;** author. *Publications:* The Wax Works Murder; The Eight of Swords; The Arabian Nights Murder; Black Spectacles; To Wake the Dead; The Burning Court; The Case of the Constant Suicides; The Four False Weapons; The Blind Barber; The Problem of the Wire Cage; Seat of the Scornful; Poison in Jest; The Man Who Could Not Shudder; The Emperor's Snuff Box; Till Death Do Us Part; He Who Whispers; The Hollow Man; The Sleeping Sphinx; The Crooked Hinge; Death Watch; The Life of Sir Arthur Conan Doyle; The Bride of Newgate; The Devil in Velvet, 1951; The Lost Gallows, 1952; The Nine Wrong Answers, 1952; Captain Cut-Throat, 1955; Patrick Butler for the Defence, 1956; Fire, Burn!, 1957; The Dead Man's Knock, 1958; Scandal at High Chimneys, 1959; A Dr Fell Omnibus, 1959; In Spite of Thunder, 1960; The Witch of the Low Tide, 1961; The Demoniacs, 1962; The Men Who Explained Miracles, 1964; Most Secret, 1964; The House at Satan's Elbow, 1965; The Third Bullet and other Stories, 1965; Panic in Box C, 1966; Dark of the Moon, 1968; The Mad Hatter Mystery, 1968; The Black Spectacles, 1969; Papa La-Bas, 1969; The Ghost's High Noon, 1970. *Address:* c/o Hamish Hamilton Ltd, 90 Great Russell Street, WC1.

**CARR, Rt. Hon. (L.) Robert,** PC 1963; MP (C) Mitcham since 1950; Secretary of State for Employment, since 1970; *b* 11 Nov. 1916; *s* of Ralph Edward and Katie Elizabeth Carr; *m* 1943, Joan Kathleen, *d* of Dr E. W. Twining; two *d* (and one *s* decd). *Educ:* Westminster Sch.; Gonville and Caius Coll., Cambridge. BA Nat. Sci. Hons, 1938; MA 1942. FIM 1957. Joined John Dale Ltd, 1938 (Dir, 1948-55; Chm., 1958-63); Director: Metal Closures Group Ltd, 1964-70 (Dep. Chm., 1960-63 and Jt Man. Dir, 1960-63); Carr, Day & Martin

Ltd, 1947-55; Isotope Developments Ltd, 1950-55; Metal Closures Ltd, 1959-63; Scottish Union & National Insurance Co. (London Bd), 1958-63; S. Hoffnung & Co., 1963, 1965-70; Securicor Ltd and Security Services Ltd, 1961-63, 1965-70; Mem., London Adv. Bd, Norwich Union Insurance Gp, 1965-70. PPS to Sec. of State for Foreign Affairs, Nov. 1951-April 1955, to Prime Minister, April-Dec. 1955; Parly Sec., Min. of Labour and Nat. Service, Dec. 1955-April 1958; Sec. for Technical Co-operation, 1963-64. Governor: St Mary's Hosp., Paddington, 1958-63; Imperial Coll. of Science and Technology, 1959-63; St Mary's Medical Sch. Council, 1958-63; Hon. Treas., Wright Fleming Inst. of Microbiology, 1960-63. *Publications:* (Jt) One Nation, 1950; (Jt) Change is our Ally, 1954; (Jt) The Responsible Society, 1958; (Jt) One Europe, 1965; articles in technical jls. *Recreations:* lawn tennis, music, gardening. *Address:* Monkenholt, Hadley Green, Herts. *T:* 01-449 5309. *Clubs:* Carlton, Brooks's.

**CARR, Raymond;** *see* Carr, A. R. M.

**CARR, Rt. Hon. Robert;** *see* Carr, Rt Hon. (L.) R.

**CARR, Air Marshal Sir Roderick;** *see* Carr, Air Marshal Sir C. R.

**CARR, Rupert Ellis;** Chairman: The Associated Biscuit Manufacturers Ltd, 1963-69; Peek, Frean & Co. Ltd, 1963-68; Meltis Ltd, 1963-68; *b* 16 Feb. 1910; *s* of Philip and Marjorie Carr; *m* 1949, Anna Louise Roncallo; one *s* one *d. Educ:* Rugby. Joined Peek, Frean & Co. Ltd, 1928; Dir, 1933; Man. Dir, 1940-63. Hon. Treas., Royal Warrant Holders' Assoc. (Pres., 1958); Pres., Cake and Biscuit Alliance Ltd, 1950-53; Chm. Standing Cttee and Mem. Council, Nat. Assoc. of Biscuit Manufacturers. *Recreations:* boats, gardening. *Address:* 37 Hyde Park Gate, SW7. *T:* 01-584 2595; Bembridge Lodge, Bembridge, IoW. *Club:* Royal Thames Yacht.

**CARR, William Compton;** solicitor; *b* 10 July 1918; *m*; two *s* one *d. Educ:* The Leys Sch., Cambridge. MP (C) Barons Court, 1959-64; PPS to Min. of State, Board of Trade, 1963; PPS to Financial Sec. to the Treasury, 1963-64. *Recreations:* reading, theatre-going, skin diving, eating, dieting.

**CARR, Sir William (Emsley),** Kt 1957; Chairman: News of the World Organisation, 1960-69; News of the World Ltd, 1952-69 (now Life President of the Companies and Consultant to the Board); Bees, Ltd, since 1970; *b* 30 May 1912; *y s* of late Sir Emsley and Lady Carr; *m* 1938, Jean Mary Forsyth; one *s* one *d. Educ:* Clifton Coll.; Trinity Coll., Cambridge (BA). News of the World, 1937-. Vice-Patron, Amateur Athletic Assoc.; President: Artisan Golfers' Assoc.; Press Golfing Soc.; London Newspapers Golf Soc.; Printing and Allied Trades Boxing Club; Counties Athletic Union; Vice-President: Professional Golfers' Assoc.; Sunday Newspapers Cricket League; Llangollen Eisteddfod; Cartoonists Club; Mem., National Greyhound Racing Club; Associate Mem., Amateur Rowing Assoc.; Hon. Member: British Canoe Union; Commonwealth Press Union. *Recreation:* sport. *Address:* Cliveden House, Cliveden Place, SW1; Bentley Wood, Halland, Sussex. *Clubs:* Buck's, Hamilton, Crockford's; Lucifer Golfing Society; Walton Heath Golf (Chm. 1948); Royal and Ancient Golf; Royal Liverpool Golf; Oxford and Cambridge Golfing Society.

**CARR, Brig. William Greenwood,** DSO 1941 and Bar, 1942; DL, JP; Lieutenant of the Queen's Bodyguard of the Yeomen of the Guard since 1970; *b* 10 March 1901; *s* of William Carr, DL, JP, Ditchingham Hall, Norfolk; *m* 1928, Donna Nennella, *d* of General Count Salazar, via Umbria, Rome; one *d. Educ:* Eton; University Coll., Oxford. Commnd in 12th Royal Lancers, 1922; Capt. and Adjt, 1925; comdg: 4th Co. of London Yeomanry, 1939; 22nd Armd Bde (8th Army), 1942; RACOCTU, Sandhurst, 1943; Brig. British Staff, GHQ, SW Pacific, 1944-45; retd 1946. Queen's Bodyguard Yeomen of the Guard: Exon, 1950; Ensign, 1954. Represented England at Olympic Games (riding), 1936. *Recreations:* hunting, shooting, sailing. *Address:* Ditchingham Hall, Norfolk. *T:* Woodton 226; 3 Chesterfield Street, Mayfair, W1. *T:* 01-629 5725. *Clubs:* Cavalry; Royal Yacht Squadron.

*See also Earl Ferrers.*

**CARR LINFORD, Alan,** RWS 1955 (ARWS 1949); ARE 1946; ARCA 1946; *b* 15 Jan. 1926; *m* 1948, Margaret Dorothea Parish; one *s* one *d. Educ:* Royal College of Art, and in Rome. Was awarded the Prix de Rome, 1947. *Recreation:* shooting. *Address:* Midfield, Lower Green, Wimbish, Saffron Walden, Essex. *T:* Radwinter 287.

**CARREL, Philip,** CMG 1960; OBE 1954; Under Secretary, Institute of Chartered Accountants in England and Wales; *b* 23 Sept. 1915; *s* of Louis Raymond Carrel and Lucy Mabel (*née* Cooper); *m* 1948, Eileen Mary Bullock (*née* Hainworth); one *s* one *d. Educ:* Blundell's; Balliol. Colonial Admin. Service, 1938, Zanzibar Protectorate. EA Forces, 1940. Civil Affairs, 1941-47 (OETA); Civilian Employee Civil Affairs, GHQ MELF, 1947-49 (on secondment from Som. Prot.); Colonial Admin. Service (Som. Prot.), 1947; Commissioner of Somali Affairs, 1953; Chief Sec. to the Government, Somaliland Protectorate, 1959-60. *Address:* Lych Gates, Chiltley Lane, Liphook, Hants. *T:* 2150.

**CARRERAS, Sir James,** Kt 1970; MBE 1945; Chairman and Chief Executive, Hammer Films, 1946-70; *b* 30 Jan. 1909; *s* of Henry and Dolores Carreras; *m* 1928, Vera St John; one *s. Educ:* privately. Deputy Chairman, Royal Naval Film Corporation, 1961; Chairman, Variety International, 1965. Knight Grand Band, Order of African Redemption (Liberia), 1968. *Recreation:* golf. *Address:* Court-in-Holmes, Forest Row, East Sussex. *Club:* Army and Navy.

**CARRICK,** 9th Earl of, *cr* 1748; **Brian Stuart Theobald Somerset Caher Butler;** Baron Butler (UK), 1912; Viscount Ikerrin, 1629; *b* 17 Aug. 1931; *o s* of 8th Earl of Carrick; *S* father, 1957; *m* 1951, (Mary) Belinda, *e d* of Major David Constable-Maxwell, TD, Bosworth Hall, near Rugby; one *s* one *d. Educ:* Downside. Chm. and Man. Dir, Ralli Bros & Coney Ltd, and Man. Dir, Ralli Brothers (Trading) Ltd. Member: Council of Cotton Research Corp.; British Cotton Growing Assoc. President: Liverpool Cotton Assoc. Ltd; Liverpool Cotton Futures Market; Director: Reynolds & Gibson ltd; Bacup Warehousing Co. Ltd; Khartoum Cotton Co. Ltd; Liverpool Uganda Co. Ltd; Ralucot (Tanzania) Ltd; Cowatex NV; Almelo; Cowatex GmbH. Nordhorn; Cotac, Le Havre. *Heir: s* Viscount Ikerrin, *qv. Address:* Roft Castle House, Marford, near Wrexham, N Wales. *T:* Rossett 567; Flat 3, No 2, Cadogan Gardens, SW3. *Club:* Pratt's.

**CARRICK, Edward;** *see* Craig, E. A.

**CARRIER, Philippe Leslie Caro,** CBE 1955; MD; Principal Medical Officer, Home Office, since 1958; *b* 14 Oct. 1893; *s* of Rev. E. T. Carrier; *m* 1925, Edith Gertrude Craig (*d* 1970); one *d*. *Educ:* Kingswood Sch., Bath; King's Coll., London. MRCS, LRCP 1916; MB, BS (London) 1922; MD (London) 1936; MRCP 1946. House Surgeon and Physician, Charing Cross Hosp., 1916. Capt. RAMC (SR), 1916-19. Private practice, 1919-27; Dist Med. Officer, Burma Rlys, 1927-36; Chief Med. Officer, 1936-48; Lieut-Col, RAMC, 1941-46, service in Burma and India. Home Office: Med. Officer, 1948-50; Principal Med. Officer, 1950-62. *Recreations:* fishing and sailing. *Address:* Ashdown House, St Ann's Hill, Lewes, Sussex. *T:* Lewes 531. *Club:* East India and Sports.

**CARRINGTON,** 6th Baron (Ireland) *cr* 1796, (Great Britain) *cr* 1797; **Peter Alexander Rupert Carington,** PC 1959; KCMG 1958; MC 1945; Secretary of State for Defence since 1970; *b* 6 June 1919; *s* of 5th Baron and Hon. Sibyl Marion (*d* 1946), *d* of 2nd Visc. Colville; *S* father, 1938; *m* 1942, Iona, *yr d* of late Sir Francis McClean; one *s* two *d*. *Educ:* Eton Coll.; RMC Sandhurst. Served NW Europe, Major Grenadier Guards. Parly Sec., Min. of Agriculture and Fisheries, 1951-54; Parly Sec., Min. of Defence, Oct. 1954-Nov. 1956; High Comr for the UK in Australia, Nov. 1956-Oct. 1959; First Lord of the Admiralty, 1959-63; Minister without Portfolio and Leader of the House of Lords, 1963-64; Leader of the Opposition, House of Lords, 1964-70. Chairman, Australia and New Zealand Bank Ltd, 1967-70, Australia and New Zealand Banking Group, 1970; former Director: Cadbury Schweppes Ltd; Amalgamated Metal Corpn Ltd; Hambros Bank; Barclays Bank. JP 1948, DL Bucks. Fellow of Eton Coll., 1966. *Heir: s* Hon. Rupert Francis John Carington, *b* 2 Dec. 1948. *Address:* 32a Ovington Square, SW3. *T:* 01-584 1476; The Manor House, Bledlow, near Aylesbury, Bucks. *T:* Princes Risborough 3499. *Clubs:* Turf, Beefsteak, Pratt's.

**CARRINGTON, Charles Edmund,** MC; writer and lecturer; *b* West Bromwich, 21 April 1897; *s* of late Very Rev. C. W. Carrington; *m* 1st, 1932, Cecil Grace MacGregor (marr. diss., 1954); one *d* decd; 2nd, 1955, Maysie Cuthbert Robertson. *Educ:* Christ's Coll., New Zealand; Christ Church, Oxford. Enlisted, 1914; first commission, 1915; Capt. 5th Royal Warwickshire Regt, 1917; served in France and Italy (MC); Major TA, 1927. BA Oxford, 1921; MA 1929; MA Cambridge, 1929. Asst Master, Haileybury Coll., 1921-24 and 1926-29; Lectr, Pembroke Coll., Oxford, 1924-25; Educational Sec. to the Cambridge Univ. Press, 1929-54. Military service, 1939, France, 1940; Lt-Col Gen. Staff, 1941-45. Prof. of British Commonwealth Relations at Royal Inst. of Internat. Affairs, 1954-62; organised unofficial Commonwealth conferences, New Zealand, 1959, Nigeria, 1962; Visiting Prof., USA, 1964-65. Mem. or past Mem. of: LCC Educn Cttee; Classical Assoc. Council; Publishers Assoc. Educational Group; Royal Commonwealth Soc. Council; Inter-Univ. Council; Overseas Migration Board, Islington Soc., etc; Chm. Shoreditch Housing Assoc., 1961-67. *Publications:* An Exposition of Empire, 1947; The British Overseas, 1950; Godley of Canterbury, 1951; Rudyard Kipling, 1955; The Liquidation of the British Empire, 1961; Soldier from the Wars Returning, 1965; A History of England (with J. Hampden Jackson), 1932; (under pen-name of Charles Edmonds) A Subaltern's War, 1929; T. E. Lawrence, 1935; contributor to: Camb. Hist. of the British Empire, 1959; An African Survey, 1957; Surveys of International Affairs, 1957-58 and 1959-60, etc. *Recreations:* historical studies, travel. *Address:* 56 Canonbury Park South, N1. *T:* 01-226 9486. *Club:* Travellers'.

**CARRINGTON, Most Rev. Philip,** MA, LittD, STD, DCL; Archbishop of Quebec and Metropolitan of the Province of Canada, 1944-60; *b* Lichfield, England, 6 July 1892; *s* of late Very Rev. Charles Walter Carrington; *m* 1919, Gwendolen Smith; no *c*. *Educ:* Christ's Coll., New Zealand; Canterbury Univ. Coll., NZ; Selwyn Coll., Cambridge. Chancellor's Gold Medal for English Verse, Carus, Member's, Hulsean Prizes; Deacon, 1918; Priest, 1919; specialised in boys' work; Boy Scout Commissioner for Canterbury; developed Soldiers of the Cross Scheme for children; Rector of Lincoln, NZ, 1922; Warden of St Barnabas Theological Coll., North Adelaide, South Australia, 1924-27; Speaker at Melbourne Church Congress, 1925; Dean of Divinity Bishop's Univ., Lennoxville, Quebec, 1927; Bishop of Quebec, 1935-44. Hon. STD Seabury-Western Seminary, Evanstown, Ill., 1933; Hon. DCL Lennoxville, 1933; LittD in course of New Zealand, 1934; Hon. DD: Durham; King's Coll., NS; Trinity Coll., Toronto; Wycliffe Coll., Toronto; Hon. D ès Lettres, Université de Laval, 1959. *Publications:* The Boy Scouts Camp Book, 1918; Christian Apologetics in the Second Century, 1921; Scoutcraft in the Church, 1921; The Soldier of the Cross, 1925; The Sign of Faith, 1930; The Meaning of the Revelation, 1931; The Road to Jerusalem, 1933; The Pilgrim's Way, 1937; The Primitive Christian Catechism, 1941; A Church History for Canadians, 1947; The Story of the Christ, 1957; The Early Christian Church, 1957; According to Mark, 1960; The Anglican Church in Canada, 1963. *Recreations:* cinephotography, literary. *Address:* Quebec Lodge, Little Somerford, Chippenham, Wilts.

**CARRINGTON, Richard;** author and biologist; *b* 10 June 1921; *s* of late Murray Carrington, actor, and Ethel McDowall, actress; *m* 1st, 1946, Audrey Barringer Sloan (marr. diss. 1952); 2nd, Mary Eden, *e d* of late C. O. Ellis. *Educ:* The Hall Sch., Hampstead; privately. Served War of 1939-45: Merchant Service, 1940; RAF, Britain and Far East, 1941-46. British Council, 1946-47; BBC, 1947-50; writing, scientific educn, and field work in biology, 1950-; res. on elephants in E Africa, 1955-56. Scientific FZS; FRAI; FRGS. Member: Internat. Oceanographic Foundn; Inst. of Archæology; Fauna Preservation Soc.; Egypt Exploration Soc. Founder and Editor of: The World Naturalist Series; The Advancement of Science Series; The Weidenfeld and Nicolson Natural History (Associate Editors: Dr L. Harrison Matthews and Prof. J. Z. Young); Manuals in Biology (Co-Editor, Dr L. Harrison Matthews). Founder and Director, Internat. Communications Centre, Nice, France, 1969. *Publications:* A Guide to Earth History, 1956; Mermaids and Mastodons, 1957; East from Tunis, 1957; Elephants, 1958; The Tears of Isis, 1959; A Biography of the Sea, 1960; The Mammals, 1963; A Million Years of Man, 1963; Great National Parks, 1967; (with Mary Eden) The Philosophy of the Bed, 1961; (with Dr A. d'A. Bellairs) The World of Reptiles, 1966; many foreign and braille edns. Educational books for children: The Dawn of History, 1955-61 (six titles): How Life Began, 1955; The Early Days of Man, 1955; Ancient Egypt, 1959; Ancient Sumer, 1959; Ancient Greece, 1961; Ancient Rome, 1961. Numerous articles and broadcasts. *Recreations:* music, friends, wine-tasting, reading. *Address:* c/o Royal

Geographical Society, 1 Kensington Gore, SW7.

**CARRINGTON, Roger Clifford,** MA, DPhil (Oxon); FRSA; Headmaster, St Olave's School, since 1937; *b* 16 Nov. 1905; *s* of Albert Carrington, Hastings; *m* Charlotte, *d* of Alexander Chalmers, Glasgow; one *s* one *d*. *Educ:* Wakefield Grammar Sch.; Queen's Coll., Oxford. Barclay Head Prize for Ancient Numismatics, 1930; Rome Student in Archæology at British Sch. at Rome, 1928-30; Asst Master, Haileybury Coll., 1930-34; Head of Classical Side, Dulwich Coll., 1934-37. *Publications:* Pompeii, 1936; Pompéi, 1937; Caesar's Invasions of Britain, 1938; Caesar's Gallic War, Book V, 1939; Two Schools, 1962; various articles. *Recreations:* walking, gardening, archæology. *Address:* Headmaster's House, St Olave's, Goddington Lane, Orpington, Kent.

**CARRINGTON, Sir William (Speight),** Kt 1958; Partner, Whinney Murray & Co., Chartered Accountants, 1932-70; Member of Council, Institute of Chartered Accountants in England and Wales, 1942-68 (President, 1955-56); *b* 1904; *s* of William Carrington, Blackpool; *m* 1932, Dorothy Mary, *d* of T. W. Fabian, Finchley; one *s*. *Educ:* Hebden Bridge, Yorks; Manchester Grammar Sch. Mem. Central Valuation Board and Panel of Referees Coal Nationalisation Act, 1946. Mem. Royal Commission on Taxation, 1951-55 and Millard Tucker Cttees, on Taxation of Trading Profits, 1949-51, and on Taxation treatment of provisions for Retirement, 1950-53; Chm. Dental Rates Study Group, 1961-. Younger Brother of Trinity House, 1952. *Publications:* various papers in professional journals at home and overseas. *Address:* 34 Cumberland Mansions, George Street, W1. *T:* 01-262 4808. *Clubs:* Junior Carlton, Gresham.

**CARROLL, Sir Alfred Thomas, (Sir Turi Carroll),** KBE 1962 (OBE 1950); farmer, New Zealand, since 1912; Chairman, New Zealand Maori Council, since 1961; *b* 24 Aug. 1890; *s* of Thomas Carroll and Mako Kaimoana; *m* 1922, Parehuia Shrimpton; one *d*. *Educ:* Te Aute Coll.; Wanganui Collegiate; Lincoln Agricultural Coll. Chm., Wairoa CC, 1938-59 (Mem., 1924-59); Past Chairman: Wairoa Co-op. Dairy Co. Ltd; Wairoa A. & P. Assoc.; East Coast Maori Trust Council; Maori Incorporated Blocks; Kahungunu Tribal Exec.; Wairoa Maori Trust; Wairoa Farmers' Union; and various sporting associations. Member: NZ Tuberculosis Assoc.; Wairoa Hosp. and Harbour Bd; Bd of Govs Wairoa Coll.; Wairoa Power Bd; Maori Educn Foundation. Bledisloe Medal, 1940. *Address:* Huramua Station, Wairoa, Hawkes Bay, New Zealand. *T:* A514. *Club:* Wairoa Gentlemen's.

**CARROLL, Rev. Canon Charles William Desmond;** Canon Residentiary of Blackburn Cathedral since 1964; *b* 27 Jan. 1919; *s* of Rev. William and Mrs L. Mary Carroll; *m* 1945, Doreen Daisy Ruskell; three *s*. one *d*. *Educ:* St Columba Coll.; Trinity Coll., Dublin. BA 1943; Dip. Ed. Hons 1945; MA 1946. Asst Master: Kingstown Grammar Sch., 1943-45; Rickerby House Sch., 1945-50; Vicar of Stanwix, Carlisle, 1950-59; Hon. Canon of Blackburn, 1959; Dir of Religious Education, 1959; Hon. Chaplain to Bishop of Blackburn, 1961. *Publication:* Management for Managers, 1968. *Address:* High Mount, 250 Preston New Road, Blackburn BB2 7AA. *T:* Blackburn 50156. *Clubs:* Royal Commonwealth Society; Rotary (Blackburn).

**CARROLL, Maj.-Gen. Derek Raymond,** OBE 1958; Chief Engineer, BAOR, since 1970; *b* 2 Jan. 1919; *er s* of late Raymond Carroll and Edith Lisle Carroll; *m* 1946, Bettina Mary, *d* of late Leslie Gould; one *s* two *d*. Student RIBA, 1936-39. Enlisted TA (Middx Yeo.), 1939; commnd into Royal Engineers, 1943; served Western Desert, 1941-43, Italy, 1943-44; psc 1945; various appts in Germany, 1946 and 1951-52; Sudan Defence Force, 1952-53; Libya, 1954; Chatham, 1955-56; WO, 1957-59; GSO1, 44 (Home Counties) Div./Dist, 1960-62; CRE 4 Div., 1962-64; Malaya, 1965-66; comd 12 Engr Bde, 1966-67; idc 1968; MoD, 1969-70. *Recreation:* sailing. *Address:* Headquarters BAOR, BFPO 40. *Club:* Royal Ocean Racing.

**CARROLL, Sir John (Anthony),** KBE 1953; MA, PhD; retired as Chief Scientist (Royal Navy); *b* 1899; *m* 1st, 1930; 2nd, 1951, Jean Leslie, *d* of W. Tudor Pole, OBE. *Educ:* King's Sch., Chester; Sidney Sussex Coll., Cambridge. Isaac Newton Student, 1922-25; Research Fellow, Sidney Sussex Coll., 1922-25; Asst Dir of Solar Physics Observatory, Cambridge, and Univ. Lectr in Astrophysics, 1924-30; Prof. of Natural Philosophy, Univ. of Aberdeen, 1930-45; Deputy for Research and Development to Controller of the Navy, and Scientific Adviser to Bd of Admiralty, 1946-64; Chief Scientist (RN), 1964, retd. Gresham Prof. in Astronomy, 1964-68. Eclipse-observing expeditions to California, Norway, Malay, Canada, and Siberia. Fellow: (sometime mem. Council) Royal Astronomical Soc.; Royal Society of Edinburgh; Cambridge Philosophical Soc.; American Physical Soc. Sometime Member: Board of Governors, Aberdeen Royal Infirmary; Aberdeen Univ. Court; Aberdeen Education Cttee. Mem. of various national and international scientific cttees; sometime Pres. of Commission on Instruments of International Astronomical Union. *Publications:* on mathematical, physical and astrophysical topics in journals of learned societies and technical publications. *Recreation:* golf. *Address:* 14 Belvedere Grove, Wimbledon, SW19. *T:* 01-947 1801. *Club:* Athenæum.

**CARROLL, Madeleine;** screen, stage, and radio actress; *d* of John Carroll, Co. Limerick, and Hélène de Rosière Tuaillon, Paris; *m* 1st, 1931, Capt. Philip Astley, MC (from whom she obtd a divorce, 1940); 2nd, 1942, Lieut Sterling Hayden, USMC (from whom she obtd a divorce, 1946); 3rd, 1946, Henri Lavorel (marr. diss.); 4th, 1950, Andrew Heiskell (marr. diss.); one *d*. *Educ:* private sch.; Birmingham Univ. (BA Hons French). Started theatrical career in touring company, playing French maid in The Lash; subsequently toured with Seymour Hicks in Mr What's his Name; became leading lady in British films as result of first screen test for The Guns of Loos; subsequently made Young Woodley, The School for Scandal, I was a Spy, and The Thirty Nine Steps; came to America in 1936 and made: The Case against Mrs Ames; The General Died at Dawn; Lloyds of London; On the Avenue; The Prisoner of Zenda; Blockade; Café Society; North-West Mounted Police; Virginia; One Night in Lisbon; Bahama Passage; My Favourite Blonde; White Cradle Inn; An Innocent Affair; The Fan. Radio appearances include the leading parts in: Cavalcade; Beloved Enemy; Romance; There's always Juliet. From 1941 until end of War, engaged exclusively in war activities. *Address:* 9484 Wilshire Boulevard, Beverly Hills, Calif. *TA:* Yeltsa, Los Angeles.

**CARROLL, Sir Turi;** *see* Carroll, Sir Alfred Thomas.

**CARROW, Comdr John Hinton,** CMG 1943; DSC; RN, retired; Senior Resident, Nigeria, retired; *b* 1890; *m* 1936, Gladys Lilian (Michael), MA Oxon, (marr. diss. 1963), *o d* of Anstruther Cardew-Rendle, MD (Cantab), DPH. *Educ:* Clifton Coll. Entered Royal Navy, 1905; served Battle of Jutland (DSC); invalided out, 1919; Colonial Administrative Service, Nigeria, 1919-47. *Address:* 40 Dorchester Road, Weymouth, Dorset. *Club:* East India and Sports.

**CARRUTHERS, Alwyn Guy;** Deputy Director of Statistics, Board of Trade, since 1968; *b* 6 May 1925; *yr s* of John Sendall and Lily Eden Carruthers, Grimsby; *m* 1950, Edith Eileen, *o d* of William and Edith Addison Lumb; no *c*. *Educ:* Wintringham Grammar Sch., Grimsby; King's Coll., London Univ. BA First Cl. Hons in Mathematics, Drew Gold Medal and Prize, 1945. RAE, Farnborough, 1945-46; Instructor Lieut, RN, 1946-49; Rothamsted Experimental Station, 1949. Postgraduate Diploma in Mathematical Statistics Christ's Coll., Cambridge, 1951. Bd of Trade, Statistics Division: Asst Statistician, 1951; Statistician, 1954; Chief Statistician, 1962; Asst Dir, 1968. *Recreations:* gardening, music. *Address:* 24 Red House Lane, Bexleyheath, Kent. *T:* 01-303 4898.

**CARSE, William Mitchell,** CBE 1953; *b* 23 Aug. 1899; *o s* of Robert Allison Carse, Hawkhead, Renfrewshire; *m* 1928, Helen Knox, *yr d* of J. B. Beaton, Milliken Park, Renfrewshire; one *s*. *Educ:* Glasgow High Sch.; Glasgow Univ.; Wellington Military Coll., Madras; St John's Coll., Cambridge. Passed Examination for RMC Sandhurst, 1917; proceeded to Wellington Military Coll., Madras, 1918; gazetted to Indian Army, 1918; served in South Persia until 1920; resigned Commission; entered HM Consular Service, 1923; served in USA, Guatemala, Germany, Portuguese East Africa, Portugal and Portuguese West Africa; Consul-Gen., Loanda, Angola, 1937-39; Consul at Teneriffe, 1939; Consul-Gen. at Reykjavik, Iceland, 1943; attached to British Political Mission in Hungary, 1945-46; Consul-Gen. at Tabriz, Persia, 1946-47, and at Ahwaz Persia, 1948, Deputy High Comr for the UK in Peshawar, Pakistan, 1948-51; Consul-Gen., São Paulo, Brazil, 1951-56, retd. Appointed to Distillers Company Ltd. (Industrial Group), London, 1957. *Recreations:* yachting, riding, chess. *Address:* Little Dene, St Alban's Road, Reigate, Surrey.

**CARSON, Hon. Edward;** Lieutenant Life Guards; *b* 17 Feb. 1920; *yr s* of Baron Carson, a Lord of Appeal in Ordinary; *m* 1943, Heather, *d* of Lt-Col Frank Sclater, OBE, MC; one *s* one *d*. *Educ:* Eton; Trinity Hall, Cambridge. MP (C) Isle of Thanet Div. of Kent, 1945-53. *Address:* Cleve Court, Minster-in-Thanet, near Ramsgate, Kent.

**CARSTAIRS, Charles Young,** CB 1968; CMG 1950; Under-Secretary, Construction Economics, Ministry of Public Building and Works, 1967-70; *b* 30 Oct. 1910; *s* of late Rev. Dr G. Carstairs, DD; *m* 1939, Frances Mary, *o d* of late Dr Claude Lionel Coode, Stroud, Glos; one *s* one *d*. *Educ:* George Watson's Boys' Coll., Edinburgh; Edinburgh Univ. Entered Home Civil Service, 1934, Dominions Office; transf. Colonial Office, 1935; Asst Private Sec. to Sec. of State for the Colonies, 1936; Private Sec. to Perm. Under-Sec. of State for the Colonies, 1937; Asst Sec., West India Royal Commn, 1938-39; Sec., Colonial Research Cttee, 1944-47; Administrative Sec., Development and Welfare Organisation, British West Indies, 1947-50; Sec., British Caribbean Standing Closer Assoc. Cttee, 1948-49; Dir of Information Services, Colonial Office, 1951-53, Asst Under-Sec., 1953-62; Deputy Sec., Medical Research Council, 1962-65; Under-Sec, Directorate-Gen., R and D, MPBW, 1965-67. *Address:* St Kea, Ridgegate Close, Reigate, Surrey. *T:* Reigate 44896. *Club:* Athenæum.

**CARSTAIRS, Prof. George Morrison,** MD; FRCPE; Professor of Psychological Medicine, University of Edinburgh, since 1961; Director, MRC Unit for Research on Epidemiological Aspects of Psychiatry, since 1960; *b* Mussoorie, India, 18 June 1916; *s* of late Rev. Dr George Carstairs, DD, K-i-H, and Elizabeth H. Carstairs; *m* 1950, Vera Hunt; two *s* one *d*. *Educ:* George Watson's Coll., Edinburgh; Edinburgh Univ. Asst Phys., Royal Edinburgh Hosp., 1942. MO, RAF, 1942-46. Commonwealth Fellow, USA, 1948-49; Rockefeller Research Fellow, 1950-51; Henderson Res. Schol., 1951-52; Sen. Registrar, Maudsley Hosp., 1953; Scientific Staff, MRC, 1954-60. Reith Lectr, 1962. Pres., World Federation for Mental Health, 1967-71. *Publications:* The Twice Born, 1957; This Island Now, 1963; chapters and articles in medical publications. *Recreations:* travel, theatre; formerly athletics (Scottish Champion 3 miler, 1937-39). *Address:* University Department of Psychiatry, Morningside Park, Edinburgh 10. *T:* 031-447 2011.

**CARSTEN, Prof. Francis Ludwig,** DPhil, DLitt Oxon; Masaryk Professor of Central European History in the University of London since 1961; *b* 25 June 1911; *s* of Prof. Paul Carsten and Frida Carsten (*née* Born); *m* 1945, Ruth Carsten (*née* Moses); two *s* one *d*. *Educ:* Heidelberg, Berlin and Oxford Univs. Barnett scholar, Wadham Coll., Oxford, 1939; Senior Demy, Magdalen Coll., Oxford, 1942; Lectr in History, Westfield Coll., Univ. of London, 1947; Reader in Modern History, Univ. of London, 1960. *Publications:* The Origins of Prussia, 1954; Princes and Parliaments in Germany from the 15th to the 18th Century, 1959; The Reichswehr and Politics, 1918-1933, 1966; The Rise of Fascism, 1967 (rev. edn, 1970); Ed. and Contributor, The New Cambridge Modern History, vol. V: The Ascendancy of France, 1961; articles in English Historical Review, History, Survey, Historische Zeitschrift, etc. *Recreations:* gardening, climbing, swimming. *Address:* 11 Redington Road, NW3. *T:* 01-435 5522.

**CARSWELL, John Patrick;** Assistant Under-Secretary of State, Department of Education and Science, since 1964; *b* 30 May 1918; *s* of Donald Carswell, barrister and author, and Catherine Carswell, author; *m* 1944, Ianthe Elstob; two *d*. *Educ:* Merchant Taylors' Sch.; St John's Coll., Oxford (MA). Served in Army, 1940-46. Entered Min. of National Insurance, 1946. Joint Sec., Cttee on Economic and Financial Problems of Provision for Old Age (Phillips Cttee), 1953-54; Asst Sec., 1955; Principal Private Sec. to Minister of Pensions and Nat. Insurance, 1955-56; Treasury, 1961-64; Under-Sec., Office of Lord Pres. of the Council and Minister for Science, 1964. Assessor to Robbins Cttee on Higher Education, 1963. *Publications:* The Prospector, 1950; The Old Cause, 1954; The South Sea Bubble, 1960; The Diary and Political Papers of George Bubb Dodington, 1965; The Civil Servant and his World, 1966; The Descent on England, 1969; contribs to Times Literary Supplement and other periodicals. *Address:* 32 Park Village East, NW1. *T:* 01-387 3920. *Clubs:* Oxford and Cambridge, Garrick.

**CARTER;** *see* Bonham-Carter and Bonham Carter.

**CARTER, Alexander Scott,** RCA 1927 (ARCA 1922); MRAIC; FRSA; architect and artist; *b* Harrow, Middx, 1879; *e s* of late Alexander Carter. *Educ:* Royal Academy Sch. of Architecture (two silver medals and other prizes). Practised architecture in London; went to Canada, 1912; exhibited at the Royal Academy, London, Royal Canadian Academy, The Art Gallery of Toronto, Canadian National Exhibition, Los Angeles Museum, etc; represented in the collections of The Queen, Duke of Devonshire, and others; represented in the National Gallery, Ottawa, the Art Gallery of Toronto, and in universities, churches, and large corporations in Canada and USA; Mem. of The Essex Archæological Soc. and the Soc. of Genealogists, London. Awarded The Royal Architectural Inst. of Canada and Allied Arts silver medal for 1959. FRSA. *Address:* 2 Washington Avenue, Toronto, Ont., Canada. *Clubs:* Arts and Letters, (Hon.) Faculty Union, University of Toronto (Toronto).

**CARTER, Arthur Herbert,** JP; Council of Royal Agricultural Society of England (Vice-President), Holland Agricultural Executive Committee (Chairman), Executive Committee and Council of Lincolnshire Agricultural Society, Council of Essex Pig Society (Chairman, 1946-47); Chairman Implements Committee, RASE; Governor, National College of Agricultural Engineering; Committee, National Power Farming Conference; *b* 1 June 1890; *er s* of Arthur Henry Carter, Wiggenhall, St Mary Magdalen, Norfolk; *m* 1916, Edith Mary Tindall; two *s.* Farmer and landowner in Lincolnshire and Cambridgeshire; High Sheriff Cambridgeshire and Huntingdon, 1940; Mem. Isle of Ely CC, 1922-47, Alderman 1933, resigned 1948; Council of Cambridgeshire and Isle of Ely Agricultural Society, 1923-48; Deeping Fen Drainage Board. Chairman County Civil Defence Cttee; Chairman Theatres and Cinemas Cttee; Vice-Chairman Finance Cttee; Member Holland (Lincs) War Agricultural Executive Cttee; Dep. Chairman HAEC and Chairman Labour Sub-Cttee and Housing; RASE representative on Rothamsted Trust Cttee. Freeman, City of London. *Recreations:* shooting, cricket. *Address:* The Manor House, Tydd St Giles, Wisbech, Cambs. *TA* and *T:* Long Sutton 3211.

**CARTER, Charles Frederick,** FBA 1970; Vice-Chancellor, University of Lancaster, since 1963; *b* Rugby, 15 Aug. 1919; *y s* of late Frederick William Carter, FRS; *m* 1944, Janet Shea; one *s* two *d. Educ:* Rugby Sch.; St John's Coll., Cambridge. Friends' Relief Service, 1941-45; Lectr in Statistics, Univ. of Cambridge, 1945-51; Fellow of Emmanuel Coll., 1947-51 (Hon. Fellow, 1965-); Prof. of Applied Economics, The Queen's Univ., Belfast, 1952-59; Stanley Jevons Prof. of Political Economy and Cobden Lectr, Univ. of Manchester, 1959-63. Chairman: Science and Industry Cttee, RSA, British Assoc. and Nuffield Foundn, 1954-59; Schools' Broadcasting Council, 1964; Joint Cttee of the Univs and the Accountancy Profession, 1964; Adv. Bd of Accountancy Educn, 1970; North-West Economic Planning Council, 1965-68; Sec.-Gen., Royal Econ. Soc., 1971-; Member: UN Expert Cttee on Commodity Trade, 1953; Capital Investment Advisory Cttee, Republic of Ireland, 1956; British Assoc. Cttee on Metric System, 1958; Council for Scientific and Industrial Research, 1959-63; Commn on Higher Education, Republic of Ireland, 1960-67; Heyworth Cttee on Social Studies, 1963; Advisory Council on Technology, 1964-66; North Western Postal Bd, 1970. Pres., Manchester Statistical Soc., 1967-69; Vice-Pres., Workers' Educational Assoc.; Dir, Friends' Provident and Century Life Office. Joint Editor: Journal of Industrial Economics, 1955-61; Economic Journal, 1961-70. Hon. Member, Royal Irish Academy; Trustee: Joseph Rowntree Mem. Trust, 1966; Sir Halley Stewart Trust, 1969. hon. DEconSc, NUI. *Publications:* The Science of Wealth, 1960; (with W. B. Reddaway and J. R. N. Stone) The Measurement of Production Movements, 1948; (with G. L. S. Shackle and others) Uncertainty and Business Decisions, 1954; (with A. D. Roy) British Economic Statistics, 1954; (with B. R. Williams) Industry and Technical Progress, 1957; Investment in Innovation, 1958; Science in Industry, 1959; (with D. P. Barritt) The Northern Ireland Problem, 1962; Wealth, 1968; articles in Economic Journal, etc. *Recreation:* gardening. *Address:* University House, Bailrigg, Lancaster. *T:* Lancaster 65201. *Club:* Athenæum.
*See also Professor G. W. Carter.*

**CARTER, Douglas,** CB 1969; Under-Secretary, Board of Trade, since 1963; *b* 4 Dec. 1911; 3rd *s* of Albert and Mabel Carter, Bradford, Yorks; *m* 1935, Alice, *d* of Captain C. E. Le Mesurier, CB, RN; three *s* one *d. Educ:* Bradford Grammar Sch.; St John's Coll., Cambridge (Scholar). First Cl. Hons, Historical Tripos Part I and Economics Tripos Part II. Wrenbury Research Scholarship in Economics, Cambridge, 1933. Asst Principal, Board of Trade, 1934; Sec., Imperial Shipping Cttee, 1935-38; Princ. BoT, 1939; Asst Sec., BoT, 1943; Chm., Cttee of Experts in Enemy Property Custodianship, Inter-Allied Reparations Agency, Brussels, 1946. Controller, Import Licensing Dept, 1949; Distribution of Industry Div., BoT, 1954; Industries and Manufacturers Div., 1957; Commercial Relations and Exports Div., 1960; Tariff Div., 1965. *Recreations:* reading, golf, bridge, travel. *Address:* Wychwood, The Drive, Belmont, Surrey. *T:* 01-642 0691. *Club:* Travellers'.

**CARTER, Edward Julian,** MA; ARIBA; FLA; *b* Grahamstown, South Africa, 10 June 1902; *s* of late Rev. Canon F. E. Carter; *m* 1930, Deborah Benson, *e d* of Bernard Howard, Loughton, Essex; one *s* four *d. Educ:* Lancing Coll.; Magdalene Coll., Cambridge; Architectural Assoc. Sch., London. Librarian-Editor, Royal Institute of British Architects, 1930-46. Head of Libraries Div., UN Educational, Scientific and Cultural Organisation (previously in UNESCO Preparatory Commn), 1946-57. Dir, Architectural Assoc., Bedford Square, 1961-67. Chairman, Assoc. Special Libraries and Information Bureaux, 1940-45. Vice-Chairman, Soc. for Cultural Relations with USSR, 1943-45. Hon. Fellow, Library Assoc., 1962. *Publication:* The Future of London, 1962. *Address:* Upper Kilcott, Hillsley, Glos. *Club:* Athenæum.

**CARTER, Edward Robert Erskine;** President and Chief Executive Officer, The Patino Mining Corporation, since 1958; Chairman and Director: Consolidated Tin Smelters Ltd; British Amalgamated Metal Investments Ltd; CDRH Ltd; The Southern Maryland Agricultural Association of Prince George's County, Maryland, Ltd; Dep. Chm., Chm. of Exec. Cttee and Dir, Amalgamated Metal Corporation Ltd; Vice-Chm., Mem. Exec. Cttee and Director, Rio Tinto Patino, SA; Pres. and Director, Advocate Mines Ltd; Director: Guildhall Insurance Co. of Canada;

Eastern Smelting Co. Ltd; Consolidated Tin Smelters (Australia) Pty Ltd; Williams, Harvey & Co. Ltd; Makeri Smelting Co. Ltd; The British Metal Corp. Ltd; Henry Gardner & Co. Ltd; Mountstar Metals Ltd; Wentworth Investment Corp. Ltd; Hardwicke Investment Corp. Ltd; First Investors Internat. Mining and Petroleum Fund; Member, Canadian Advisory Bd of Sun Alliance and London Insurance Gp; *b* 20 Feb. 1923; *s* of Arthur Norwood Carter, QC, and Edith Ireland; *m* 1947, Verna Leman Andrews; two *s* two *d*. *Educ:* Univ. of New Brunswick; (after War) Osgoode Hall, Toronto, Ont; Univ. of New Brunswick; Univ. of New Brunswick Law Sch. (BCL 1947); Rhodes Scholar for New Brunswick, 1947; Oxford Univ. (BCL 1949). Served War with Royal Canadian Artillery, 1942-44; on loan to 7th King's Own Scottish Borderers, First British Airborne Div., 1944; PoW, Sept. 1944-April 1945. Read Law with McMillan, Binch, Wilkinson, Berry & Wright, Toronto, Ont; called to Bar of New Brunswick, 1947; Ontario 1951; associated with A. N. Carter, QC in practise of law, St John, NB, 1949-53; Legal Officer, Abitibi Power & Paper Co. Ltd, Toronto, Ont, 1953-54; joined Fennell, McLean, Seed & Carter, 1954; Partner, 1955-58. Member: Law Soc. of Upper Canada; New Brunswick Barristers Soc. *Address:* (home) 331 Riverview Drive, Toronto 319, Ont, Canada; (office) Suite 1401, 7 King Street E, Toronto, Ont. *Clubs:* Buck's, (London, Eng.); Toronto, University (Toronto).

**CARTER, Elliott (Cook),** DrMus; composer; *b* New York City, 11 Dec. 1908; *m* 1939, Helen Frost-Jones; one *s*. *Educ:* Harvard Univ. (MA); Ecole Normale, Paris (DrMus). Professor of Greek and Maths, St John's Coll., Annapolis, 1940-42; Professor of Music: Columbia Univ., 1948-50; Yale Univ., 1960-61. Premiodelle Muse of City of Florence, 1969. *Compositions include:* First Symphony, 1942-43; Quartet for Four Saxophones, 1943; Holiday Overture, 1944; Ballet, The Minotaur, 1946-47; Woodwind Quintet, 1947; Sonata for Cello and Piano, 1948; First String Quartet, 1950-51; Sonata for Flute, Oboe, Cello and Harpsichord, 1952; Variations for Orchestra, 1953; Second String Quartet, 1960 (New York Critics' Circle Award; Pulitzer Prize; Unesco 1st Prize); Double Concerto for Harpsichord and Piano, 1961 (New York Critics' Circle Award); Piano Concerto, 1967; Concerto for Orchestra, 1970. Mem. Nat. Inst. of Arts and Letters, 1956; Mem. Amer. Acad. of Arts and Sciences (Boston), 1962. Sibelius Medal (Harriet Cohen Foundation), London, 1961. Holds hon. degrees. *Publications:* many articles in New Music Magazine, 1936-40. *Address:* Mead Street, Waccabuc, NY 10597, USA.

**CARTER, Eric Bairstow,** BSc(Eng); CEng, FIMechE, FRAeS, FIProdE; Director-General (Engine Research and Development), Ministry of Technology, since 1969; *b* 26 Aug. 1912; *s* of John Bolton Carter and Edith Carter; *m* 1934, Lily Roome; one *d*. *Educ:* Halifax Technical Coll. Workshop Supt and Lectr, Constantine Technical Coll., Middlesbrough, 1936; apptd to Air Min. (Engine Directorate), Sept. 1939; subseq. Air Min. appts to Industry (also to engine firms) and at HQ. Asst Dir (Research and Develt, Ramjets and Liquid Propellant Rockets), Dec. 1955; Dir (Engine Prod.), 1960; Dir (Engine Res. and Develt), 1963. MBIM, MAIAA. *Recreations:* work, sport (alas! now spectator). *Address:* 2 Graysfield, Welwyn Garden City, Herts. *T:* Welwyn Garden 25676. *Clubs:* Sportsman, Civil Service; Halifax Cricket.

**CARTER, Ernestine Marie, (Mrs John Waynflete Carter),** OBE 1964; Associate Editor, The Sunday Times, since 1968; *m* 1936, John Waynflete Carter, *qv*. *Educ:* Pape Sch., Savannah, Georgia; Wellesley Coll., Wellesley, Mass., USA (BA). Asst Curator of Architecture and Industrial Art, The Museum of Modern Art, New York, 1933-35, Curator, 1936-37; Specialist, Display and Exhibns Div., Min. of Information, 1939-41; US Office of War Information, London, 1941-44, in charge of exhibns and displays; Asst in Fashion Section, Britain Can Make It Exhibn, 1946; Fashion Editor, Harper's Bazaar, 1947-49; Contributor to The Observer, 1952-54; Women's Editor, The Sunday Times, 1955-68. Member: Council, Royal Coll. of Art, 1960-61; Nat. Council for Diploma in Art and Design, 1962-68; Selection Panel, Duke of Edinburgh's Prize for Elegant Design, 1965-67. FRSA 1964. *Publications:* Grim Glory, 1941; Flash in the Pan, 1953 (re-issued 1963); contributor to: The Intelligent Woman's Guide to Good Taste, 1958; Saturday Book, 1961. *Recreation:* sleep. *Address:* 26 Carlyle Square, SW3. *T:* 01-352 4344.

**CARTER, Francis Edward,** OBE 1937; Bailiff of the Royal Parks, 1928-47; *b* 18 Oct. 1886; *e s* of Francis Joseph Carter, Bristol; *m* 1917, Winifred, *d* of H. H. Stunt; two *s* one *d*. *Educ:* Colston Sch., Bristol. Entered Civil Service, 1907, retired 1947. Secretary, Government Hospitality Fund, 1914-16; Private Secretary to six successive First Commissioners of Works. *Recreation:* gardening. *Address:* 1 Grangelands, Knowle Drive, Sidmouth, Devon. *T:* Sidmouth 3452.

**CARTER, Francis Jackson,** CMG 1954; CVO 1963; CBE 1946; Under-Secretary of State of Tasmania and Clerk of Executive Council, 1953-64; also permanent head of Premier's and Chief Secretary's Department; *b* Fremantle, W Australia, 9 Sept. 1899; *s* of late Francis Henry Carter, formerly of Bendigo, Victoria; *m* 1926, Margaret Flora, *d* of late William Thomas Walker, Launceston; two *s* one *d*. *Educ:* Hobart High Sch.; Univ. of Tasmania. Entered Tasmanian Public Service, 1916; transferred to Hydro-Electric Dept, 1925; Asst Secretary, Hydro-Electric Commn, 1934; Secretary to Premier, 1935-39; Dep. Under-Secretary of State, 1939-53; served War of 1939-45 as State Liaison Officer to Commonwealth Dept of Home Security; Official Secretary for Tasmania in London, 1949-50; State Director for Royal Visit, 1954, 1958, 1963, and Thai Royal Visit, 1962. Executive Member, State Economic Planning Authority, 1944-55; Chairman, Fire Brigades Commn of Tasmania, 1945-70. Grand Master GL of Tasmania, 1956-59. FASA; FCIS. JP 1939. *Recreations:* music, golf and lawn bowls. *Address:* 568 Churchill Avenue, Sandy Bay, Hobart, Tasmania. *T:* Hobart 5.2382. *Clubs:* Royal Automobile of Tasmania, Masonic (Hobart).

**CARTER, Frank Ernest Lovell,** CBE 1956 (OBE 1949); Director General of the Overseas Audit Service since 1963; *b* 6 Oct. 1909; *s* of Ernest and Florence Carter; *m* 1966, Gerda (*née* Gruen). *Educ:* Chigwell Sch.; Hertford Coll., Oxford. Served in Overseas Audit Service in: Nigeria, 1933-42; Sierra Leone, 1943; Palestine, 1944-45; Aden and Somaliland, 1946-47; Tanganyika, 1950-54; Hong Kong, 1955-59; Deputy Director in London, 1960-62. *Address:* 8 The Leys, N2. *T:* 01-458 4684. *Club:* East India and Sports.

**CARTER, Prof. Geoffrey William,** MA; FIEE; Professor of Electrical Engineering, University of Leeds, since 1946; *b* 21 May

1909; *s* of late Frederick William Carter, FRS; *m* 1938, Freda Rose Lapwood; one *s* one *d*. *Educ:* Rugby Sch.; St John's Coll., Cambridge. MA 1937. Student Apprentice, British Thomson-Houston Co. Ltd, Rugby, 1932-35, Research Engineer, 1935-45; University Demonstrator in Engineering Science, Oxford, 1946. *Publications:* The Simple Calculation of Electrical Transients, 1944; The Electromagnetic Field in its Engineering Aspects, 1954 (rev. edn 1967); papers in Proc. IEE and elsewhere. *Recreations:* gardening, photography, playing the recorder. *Address:* 14 Oaklea Gardens, Leeds LS16 8BH. *T:* Leeds 673841.

*See also C. F. Carter.*

**CARTER, Maj.-Gen. James Norman,** CB 1958; CBE 1955; *b* 26 June 1906; *s* of late Captain N. H. Carter, RN, and Mrs N. H. Carter; *m* 1929, Barbara Violet Bovill; two *d*. *Educ:* Charterhouse; RMC Sandhurst. Commissioned The Dorset Regt, 1926; Captain, The Royal Warwickshire Regt, 1936; Lieut-Colonel, 1948; Colonel, 1950; Brigadier, 1954; Maj.-General, 1957. Asst Chief of Staff, Organisation and Training Div., SHAPE, 1955-58; Commander British Army Staff, British Joint Services Mission, Washington, 1958-60; Military Attaché, Washington, Jan.-July 1960; General Secretary, The Officers' Assoc., 1961-63. *Recreations:* golf, tennis, cricket. *Address:* c/o Lloyds Bank, Cox's and King's Branch, 6 Pall Mall, SW1.

**CARTER, Sir John,** Kt 1966; QC (Guyana) 1962; High Commissioner for Guyana in the United Kingdom, since 1970; *b* 27 Jan. 1919; *s* of Kemp R. Carter; *m* 1959, Sara Lou (formerly Harris); two *s*. *Educ:* University of London and Middle Temple, England. Called to English Bar, 1942; admitted to Guyana (late British Guiana) Bar, 1945; Member of Legislature of Guyana, 1948-53 and 1961-64; Pro-Chancellor, Univ. of Guyana, 1962-66; Ambassador of Guyana to US, 1966-70. *Recreations:* cricket, swimming. *Address:* 28 Cockspur Street, SW1; 2 Sandybabb Street, Kitty, Guyana, South America. *T:* 4802. *Club:* Georgetown (Guyana).

**CARTER, John Somers;** *b* 26 Feb. 1901; *s* of R. Carter. *Educ:* Edinburgh Academy; Bedford Sch.; Balliol Coll., Oxford, 1st Class Hon. Mods., 3rd Class Lit. Hum. Asst Master, Cheltenham Coll., 1924-32; Headmaster: St John's Sch., Leatherhead, 1933-47; Blundell's Sch., 1948-59. *Address:* Trelissick East, Feock, Truro, Cornwall, *T:* Feock 595.

**CARTER, John (Waynflete),** CBE 1956; Bibliographical consultant; Associate Director, Sotheby & Company, 34 New Bond Street, since 1955; Director, Parke-Bernet Galleries, Inc., 980 Madison Avenue, New York, since 1964; *b* 10 May 1905; *s* of Thomas Buchanan Carter and Margaret Teresa (*née* Stone), Eton; *m* 1936, Ernestine Marie Fantl (*see* Ernestine Carter); no *c*. *Educ:* Eton (King's Scholar; Keeper of the Wall); King's Coll., Cambridge (1st Cl. Classical Tripos). European representative of Scribners (New York) Rare Book Dept, 1927-39; Min. of Information, 1939-43; British Information Services, New York, 1944-45; Managing Director of Charles Scribners' Sons Ltd, London, 1946-53. Personal Asst to Hm Ambassador and Counsellor, British Embassy, Washington, 1953-55. Sandars Reader in Bibliography in the University of Cambridge, 1947. London Rose Bearer to Provost of King's Coll., Cambridge, 1947-. Member of Council, Arts Council of Great Britain, 1951-53. Member Court of Governors, University College of North Staffordshire, 1957-62. President, Bibliographical Society, 1968-69. Hon. Colonel, Commonwealth of Kentucky, 1963. Fellow of Eton Coll., 1967. *Publications:* Binding Variants in English Publishing 1820-1900, 1932; (anonymously) Victory in Burma, 1945; Taste and Technique in Book-collecting, 1948; ABC for Book-Collectors, 1952 (4th edn, 1966); Books and Book-Collectors, 1956; Edited: Sir T. Browne, Urne Buriall and the Garden of Cyrus, 1932, repr. 1958; Selected Prose of A. E. Housman; A Handlist of the Writings of Stanley Morison, 1950; (with Graham Pollard): An Enquiry into the Nature of Certain Nineteenth Century Pamphlets, 1934; The Firm of Charles Ottley, Landon & Co., 1948; (with John Sparrow) A. E. Housman, an annotated handlist, 1952; (with Percy H. Muir) Printing and the Mind of Man, 1967 (German trans. 1968). *Address:* 26 Carlyle Square, SW3. *T:* 01-352 4344. *Clubs:* Garrick, Beefsteak, Double Crown, Eton Ramblers; Grolier (New York); Rowfant (Cleveland); Barclay (Chicago).

**CARTER, Malcolm Ogilvy,** CIE 1943; MC 1918; Secretary, South-Western Regional Hospital Board, 1947-63, retired; *b* 2 July 1898; *s* of late Reginald Carter, MA, formerly Rector of Edinburgh Academy and Headmaster of Bedford Sch., and Mary Ogilvy Boyd; *m* 1921, Gwyneth Elaine, *d* of R. Platts, Bedford; one *d*; *m* 1944, Iris Cowgill, *d* of late Rev. T. A. Thomson, Shawell, Leicester. *Educ:* Edinburgh Academy; Bedford Sch.; Balliol Coll., Oxford. RFA 1917; served in France and Belgium, 1917-18 (MC); BA (Oxon), 1920; joined ICS in Bengal, 1921; Secretary to the Board of Revenue, 1934-35; District Magistrate, Midnapore and 24 Parganas, 1935-38; Director of Land Records, Aug.-Nov. 1938; Secretary to Floud Land Revenue Commission, Bengal, 1938-40; Director of Land Records, April-July 1940; Secretary to Governor of Bengal, 1940-42; Civil Representative of the Government of Bengal with Eastern Army, 1942-43; Commissioner Chittagong Division, Bengal and Liaison Officer to XIVth Army and Third Tactical Air Force, 1943-47. *Address:* Belvedere, Leigh Woods, Bristol 8. *Clubs:* Vincent's (Oxford); Saturday (Calcutta).

**CARTER, Air Cdre North,** CB 1948; DFC 1935; RAF retired; *b* 26 Nov. 1902; *s* of Lieut-Colonel G. L. Carter, CIE, Indian Army; *m* 1931, Kathleen Graham Machattie; one *s* one *d*. *Educ:* Wellington Coll.; RAF Coll., Cranwell. Commissioned from RAF Coll., 1922; No 5 Sqdn, India, 1923-27; RAF Depot, Iraq, 1929-32; No 56 Sqdn., North Weald, 1932-34; No 60 Sqdn., India, 1934 and 1935; RAF Staff Coll., 1936; Sqdn. Ldr, 1936; Staff Appointments, 1937-40; Wing Comdr, 1938; Commanded RAF Stations Dalcross, South Cerney, Pocklington and Castel Benito, 1941-45; Group Captain, 1946; Air Commodore, 1948; AOC Halton, 1949-50; SASO 205 Group Middle East Air Force 15, 1951-53; Provost Marshal and Chief of Air Force Police, 1953-54, retired 1954; Temp. Administrative Officer, Northern Region, Nigeria, 1955-63. *Address:* Gould's Bay, Hawkesbury River, PMB Brooklyn, NSW 2253, Australia.

**CARTER, Peers Lee,** CMG 1965; HM Ambassador to Afghanistan, since 1968; *b* 5 Dec. 1916; *s* of Peers Owen Carter; *m* 1940, Joan Eleanor Lovegrove; one *s*. *Educ:* Radley; Christ Church, Oxford. Entered HM Foreign Service, 1939. Joined the Army in 1940; served in Africa and Europe. HM Embassy, Baghdad, 1945; First Secretary, Commissioner-General's Office, Singapore, 1951; Counsellor HM Embassy, Washington, 1958; (Temp. duty) UK Delegation to UN, New York, 1961;

Head of UK Permanent Mission, Geneva, 1961; Inspector of Foreign Service Establishments, 1963-66; Chief Inspector of HM Diplomatic Service, 1966-68. *Address:* c/o Foreign and Commonwealth Office, King Charles Street, SW1. *Clubs:* Special Forces, Travellers'.

**CARTER, Peter Anthony,** CMG 1970; British High Commissioner in Mauritius, since 1970; *b* 16 Jan. 1914; *s* of Thomas Birchall Carter; *m* 1946, Mary Hutchison Heard; one *s* one *d*. *Educ:* Charterhouse; Sidney Sussex Coll., Cambridge. Metropolitan Police Office, 1936-39; Royal Tank Regt (Major), 1939-44; Colonial Office, 1947-60; Nyasaland, 1951-53; CRO, 1960-61; First Secretary, Dar-es-Salaam, 1961-64; Counsellor, Dublin, 1965-68; Head of British High Commission Residual Staff, Rhodesia, 1968-69. *Recreations:* golf, fishing, music. *Address:* Forth House, Beech Drive, Kingswood, Surrey; c/o Foreign and Commonwealth Office, SW1. *Club:* Royal Over-Seas League.

**CARTER, Raymond John;** MP (Lab) Birmingham (Northfield) since 1970; Electrical Engineer; *b* 17 Sept. 1935; *s* of John Carter; *m* 1959, Jeanette Hills; one *s* two *d*. *Educ:* Mortlake Co. Secondary Sch.; Reading Technical Coll.; Staffordshire Coll. of Technology. National Service, Army, 1953-55. Sperry Gyroscope Co.: Technical Asst, Research and Development Computer Studies, 1956-65. Electrical Engineer, Central Electricity Generating Bd, 1965-70. Mem. Easthampstead RDC, 1963-68 (Chm. Amenity Cttee); Governor, Garth Hill Comprehensive Sch. Contested: Wokingham, Gen. Elec., 1966; Warwick and Leamington, Bye-elec., March 1968. *Recreations:* football, athletics enthusiast, reading. *Address:* 146 Bullbrook Drive, Bracknell, Berkshire. *T:* Bracknell 20237.

**CARTER, Air Commodore Robert Alfred Copsey,** CB 1956; DSO 1942; DFC 1943; Royal Air Force, retired; *b* 15 Sept. 1910; *s* of S. H. Carter and S. Copsey; *m* 1947, Sally Ann Peters, Va, USA; two *s* one *d*. *Educ:* Portsmouth Grammar Sch.; RAF Coll., Cranwell. Cranwell Cadet, 1930-32; commissioned in RAF, 1932; served in India, 1933-36; grad. RAF School of Aeronautical Engineering, 1938; served in Bomber Command, 1940-45; commanded 103 and 150 Sqdns, RAF, GRimsby; grad. RAF Staff Coll., 1945; attended US Armed Forces Staff Coll., Norfolk, Va, USA, 1947; attached to RNZAF, 1950-53; comd. RAF Station, Upwood, 1953-55; SASO, RAF Transport Command, 1956-58; Director of Personal Services, Air Minsitry, 1958-61; AO i/c Admin., HQ, RAF Germany, 1961-64; retired 1964. AFRAeS, 1960; CEng, 1966. *Address:* The Old Cottage, Castle Lane, Whaddon, Salisbury, Wilts. *Club:* Royal Air Force.

**CARTER, Robert William Bernard,** CMG 1964; Deputy High Commissioner, Melbourne, since 1969; *b* 1913; 3rd *s* of late William Joseph Carter and late Lucy (*née* How); *m* 1945, Joan Violet, *o d* of Theodore and Violet Magnus; one *s* two *d* (and one *d* decd). *Educ:* St Bees Sch., Cumberland; Trinity Coll., Oxford (Scholar). Asst Master, Glenalmond, Perthshire, 1936. Served with the Royal Navy, 1940-46; Lieut, RNVR Administrative Assistant, Newcastle upon Tyne Education Cttee, 1946; Principal, Board of Trade, 1949; Trade Commissioner: Calcutta, 1952; Delhi, 1955; Accra, 1956; Principal Trade Commissioner, Colombo (Assistant Secretary), 1959; Senior British Trade Commissioner in Pakistan, 1961; Minister (Commercial), Pakistan, and Dep. High Comr, Karachi, 1967-68. *Recreations:* reading, travelling, collecting beer-mugs. *Address:* 53 Lansell Road, Toorak, Melbourne, Australia. *T:* 244540; c/o Foreign and Commonwealth Office, Downing Street, SW1. *Clubs:* Oriental, RNVR; Melbourne, Australian, Athenæum, Royal Automobile of Victoria (Melbourne).

**CARTER, Roland;** HM Ambassador in Ulan Bator, People's Republic of Mongolia, since 1969; *b* 29 Aug. 1924; *s* of Ralph Carter; *m* 1950, Elisabeth Mary Green; one *s* two *d*. *Educ:* Cockburn High Sch., Leeds; Leeds Univ. Served War of 1939-45: Queen's Royal Regt, 1944; 6th Gurkha Rifles, 1945; Frontier Corps (South Waziristan and Gilgit Scouts), 1946. Seconded to Indian Political Service, as Asst Political Agent, Chilas, Gilgit Agency, 1946-47; Lectr, Zurich Univ. and Finnish Sch. of Economics, 1950-53. Joined Foreign Service, 1953: FO, 1953-54; Third Sec., Moscow, 1955; Germany, 1956-58; Second Sec., Helsinki, 1959 (First Sec., 1962); FO, 1962-67; Kuala Lumpur, 1967-69. *Publication:* Näin Puhutaan Englantia (in Finnish; with Erik Erämetsä), 1952. *Recreations:* polo, music, linguistics, Indian studies. *Address:* c/o Lloyds Bank, Bromley, Kent.

**CARTER, His Honour Sir Walker (Kelly),** Kt 1965; QC 1951; an Official Referee of the Supreme Court of Judicature, since 1954; *b* 7 July 1899; *s* of Walter Carter, *qv*, and late Annie Elizabeth Carter; *m* 1925, Phyllis Iren, *d* of late Edward Ernest Clarke, Bank Bldgs, Simla, India; one *d*. *Educ:* Repton Sch.; Sidney Sussex Coll., Cambridge. RFA, 1918-19. Called to Bar, Inner Temple, 1924; Bencher, 1965. RA 1939-43. Chairman, Quarter Sessions for Parts of Lindsey, 1945-67, and for Parts of Kesteven, 1961-67; Chairman, Criminal Injuries Compensation Board, 1964-. *Address:* 65 Bedford Gardens, W8. *T:* 01-727 9862. *Club:* Reform.

*See also J. E. Vinelott.*

**CARTER, Walter,** CBE 1943; Chevalier of the Order of Vasa (Sweden); Chairman of London Committee of Management Board of Trade (War Damage Claims) and Hon. Adviser Board of Trade; *b* 9 April 1873; *s* of Charles Frederick Carter, Grimsby, Lincs; *m* 1st, Annie Elizabeth (*d* 1926), *d* of Henry Kelly, Cleethorpes, Lincs; one *s*; 2nd, 1931, Elsie Mary (*d* 1968), *d* of Alfred John Francis, Clifton, Bristol. Manager London Head Office, Royal Insurance Co. Ltd, to 1932. *Recreations:* golf, fishing. *Address:* The Grange, High Halden, Kent.

*See also Sir W. K. Carter.*

**CARTER, W. Horsfall,** MA Oxon; writer and lecturer on international political questions; retired European civil servant; *b* 25 March 1900; *s* of William Beazley Carter and Frances Esther Horsfall Rydal; *m* 1st, 1927, Doris Golby (*d* 1939); one *d*; 2nd, 1941, Esther Elizabeth Way Thacker (*d* 1942); one *s*; 3rd, 1944, Ethel Mary Mabbott (*d* 1970). *Educ:* Hurstpierpoint Coll., Sussex; St John's Coll., Oxford (Casberd Scholar). Heath Harrison Travelling Scholarship French, 1921, German, 1923; First Class Hons School of Modern Languages, 1922; Pres., Oxford Univ. French Club, 1922; Laming Travelling Fellow, Queen's Coll., Oxford, 1924-26; League of Nations Secretariat, Geneva, temporarily, 1924, 1928, 1930, 1937; on staff on The Spectator as assistant to the Editor and assistant leader-writer, 1928-30; on editorial staff of the Christian Science Monitor, 1931; Sec. of The New Commonwealth Soc., 1932-33; Editor: The New Commonwealth, 1932-36; The Fortnightly Review, 1937-39; leader-writing staff of The Manchester Guardian, 1940-42; European Publicity Officer, BBC, 1942-43; Foreign Office Research Dept, 1943-51; Head of Western Europe Section, 1947-51; Head of Publications Div., Secretariat, Council of Europe, Strasbourg, 1951-63. Contributor to all principal newspapers and periodicals; broadcasts on Spain. *Publications:* (with Mrs Krassin) The Life of Leonid Krassin, 1928; Speaking European, 1966; several translations from French, German and Spanish; numerous articles in monthly reviews. *Recreations:* talking foreign languages, lawn tennis, bridge. *Address:* 38 Kingsthorpe Grove, Northampton. *Club:* Savile.

**CARTER, Air Vice-Marshal Wilfred,** CB 1963; DFC 1943; AOA, HQ Bomber Command, 1965-67; *b* 5 Nov. 1912; *s* of late Samuel Carter; *m* 1950, Margaret Enid Bray; one *s* one *d*. *Educ:* Witney Grammar Sch. RAF, 1929. Served War of 1939-45 with Bomber Command in UK and Middle East. Graduate, Middle East Centre for Arab Studies, 1945-46. Air Adviser to Lebanon, 1950-53; with Cabinet Secretariat, 1954-55; OC, RAF, Ternhill, 1956-58; Sen. RAF Dir, and later Commandant, Jt Services Staff Coll.; Asst Chief of Staff, Cento, 1960-63; Asst Commandant, RAF Staff Coll., 1963-65. Gordon Shephard Memorial Prize (for Strategic Studies), 1955, 1956, 1957, 1961, 1965, 1967. Officer, Order of Cedar of Lebanon, 1953. *Recreation:* ski-ing. *Address:* c/o Bank of NSW, Kyneton, Victoria, Australia. *Clubs:* Royal Air Force; Weld (Perth).

**CARTER, William Stovold,** CMG 1970; CVO 1956; Secretary, Council on Tribunals, since 1970; *b* 10 Oct. 1915, *s* of late R. S. Carter, Bournemouth, Hants; *m* 1944, Barbara Alice Kathleen Dines; two *s* one *d*. *Educ:* Bec; Christ's Coll., Cambridge. Entered Colonial Administrative Service (Nigeria), 1939; retd as Administrative Officer, Class I (Resident), 1957. Entered Colonial Office, 1959; Asst Sec., 1965; joined Commonwealth Office, 1966; joined Foreign and Commonwealth Office, 1968; Head of Hong Kong Dept, 1965-70. *Recreation:* golf. *Address:* Broad Oak Farm, Chiddingly, near Lewes, Sussex. *T:* Chiddingly 267.

**CARTER-JONES, Lewis;** MP (Lab) Eccles since 1964; industrial training adviser; *b* Gilfach Goch, S Wales, 17 Nov. 1920; *s* of Tom Jones, Kenfig Hill, Bridgend, Glam.; *m* 1945, Patricia Hylda, *d* of late Alfred Bastiman, Scarborough, Yorks; two *d*. *Educ:* Bridgend County Sch.; University Coll. of Wales, Aberystwyth; BA (Chm. Student Finance Cttee). Served War of 1939-45 (Flight Sergeant Navigator, RAF). Head of Business Studies Dept, Yale Grammar-Technical Sch., Wrexham, Denbighshire. Contested (Lab) Chester, by-election, 1956, and general election, 1959. Mem., Estimates Cttee; Sec., Indo-British Parly Group. Special interest, application of technology for aged and disabled. *Address:* House of Commons, SW1.

**CARTIER, Rudolph;** Drama Producer, Television, since 1953; also Producer Television Operas, since 1956; *b* Vienna, Austria, 17 April 1908; *s* of Joseph Cartier; *m* 1949, Margaret Pepper; two *d*. *Educ:* Vienna Academy of Music and Dramatic Art (Max Reinhardt's Master-class). Film director and Scenario writer in pre-war Berlin; came to Britain, 1935; joined BBC Television. Productions include: Arrow to the Heart, Dybbuk, Portrait of Peter Perowne, 1952; It is Midnight, Doctor Schweitzer, L'Aiglon, The Quatermass Experiment, Wuthering Heights, 1953; Such Men are Dangerous, That Lady, Captain Banner, Nineteen-Eightyfour, 1954; Moment of Truth, The Creature, Vale of Shadows, Quatermass II, The Devil's General, 1955; The White Falcon, The Mayerling Affair, The Public Prosecutor, The Fugitive, The Cold Light, The Saint of Bleecker Street, Dark Victory, Clive of India, The Queen and the Rebels, 1956; Salome, Ordeal by Fire, Counsellor-at-Law, 1957; Captain of Koepenick, The Winslow Boy, A Tale of Two Cities, Midsummer Night's Dream, 1958; Quatermass and the Pit, Philadelphia Story, Mother Courage and her Children, (Verdi's) Othello, 1959; The White Guard, Glorious Morning, Tobias and the Angel (Opera), 1960; Rashomon, Adventure Story, Anna Karenina, Cross of Iron, 1961; Doctor Korczuk and the Children, Sword of Vengeance, Carmen, 1962; Anna Christie, Night Express, Stalingrad, 1963; Lady of the Camelias, The Midnight Men, The July Plot, 1964; Wings of the Dove, Ironhand, The Joel Brand Story, 1965; Gordon of Khartoum, Lee Oswald, Assassin, 1966; Firebrand, The Burning Bush, 1967; The Fanatics, Triumph of Death, The naked Sun, The Rebel, 1968; Conversation at Night, An Ideal Husband, 1969; Rembrandt, The Bear (Opera), The Year of the Crow, 1970. Prod. Film, Corridor of Mirrors. Directed Film, Passionate Summer. Guild of Television Producers and Directors "Oscar" as best drama producer of 1957. *Recreations:* motoring to far-away countries, mountaineering, colour photography, listening to serious music, going to films or watching television, stamp-collecting. *Address:* 26 Lowther Road, Barnes, SW13.

**CARTIER-BRESSON, Henri;** photographer; *b* 22 Aug. 1908. *Educ:* Ecole Fenélon; Lycée Condorcet, Paris; studied painting in the studio of André Lhote, 1929. Photographer, 1931; Asst Dir to Jean Renoir, 1937. Prisoner of War, 1940-43, escaped. Founded Magnum-Photos with Capa, Chim and Rodger, 1947; exhibitions: Museum of Modern Art, New York, 1947; Louvre, 1955 and 1969; Phillips Collection, Washington, 1964; Victoria and Albert Museum, 1969. Documentary film for CBS, Impressions of California, 1970. *Publications:* Images à la Sauvette (English title, The Decisive Moment); The Europeans; From one China to the other; Moscou; Flagrants Délits (English title, The World of Henri Cartier-Bresson). *Address:* c/o Magnum-Photos, 125 Faubourg St Honoré, Paris 8, France; 15 West 46th Street, New York, NY, USA.

**CARTLAND, Barbara (Hamilton), (Mrs Barbara McCorquodale);** authoress and playwright; *d* of late Major Bertram Cartland, Worcestershire Regiment; *m* 1st, 1927, Alexander George McCorquodale (whom she divorced, 1933; he *d* 1964), of Cound Hall, Cressage, Salop; one *d*; 2nd, 1936, Hugh (*d* 1963), 2nd *s* of late Harold McCorquodale, Forest Hall, Ongar, Essex; two *s*. Published first novel at the age of twenty-one, which ran into five editions; designed and organised many pageants in aid of charity, including Britain and her Industries at British Legion Ball, Albert Hall, 1930; carried the first aeroplane-towed glider-mail in her glider, the Barbara Cartland, from Manston Aerodrome to Reading, June 1931; 2 lecture tours in Canada, 1940; Hon. Junior Commander, ATS and Lady Welfare Officer and Librarian to all Services in Bedfordshire, 1941-49; Certificate of Merit, Eastern Command 1946; County Cadet Officer for St John Ambulance Brigade in Beds, 1943-47, County Vice-Pres. Cadets, Beds, 1948-50; organised and produced the St John Ambulance Bde Exhibn, 1945-50; Chm St John

Ambulance Bde Exhibn Cttee, 1944-51; County Vice-Pres.: Nursing Cadets, Herts, 1951; Nursing Div., Herts, 1966; CC Herts (Hatfield Div.), 1955-64; Pres. Herts Br. of Royal Coll. of Midwives, 1957. Founder, Barbara Cartland-Onslow Romany Gypsy Fund (with Earl of Onslow and Earl of Birkenhead) to Provide sites for Romany Gypsies, 1961 (first Romany Gypsy Camp at Hatfield); Dep. Pres., National Association of Health, 1965; Pres., 1966. CStJ 1953. *Publications: novels:* Jigsaw; Sawdust; If the Tree is Saved; For What?; Sweet Punishment; A Virgin in Mayfair; Just off Piccadilly; Not Love Alone; A Beggar Wished; Passionate Attainment; First Class Lady; Dangerous Experiment; Desperate Defiance; The Forgotten City; Saga at Forty; But Never Free; Bitter Winds; Broken Barriers; The Gods Forget; The Black Panther; Stolen Halo; Now Rough–Now Smooth; Open Wings; The Leaping Flame; Yet She Follows; Escape from Passion; The Dark Stream; After the Night; Armour against Love; Out of Reach; The Hidden Heart; Against the Stream; Again this Rapture; The Dream Within; If We Will; No Heart is Free; A Hazard of Hearts; A Duel of Hearts; A Knave of Hearts; The Enchanted Moment; The Little Pretender; A Ghost in Monte Carlo; Love is an Eagle; Love is the Enemy; Cupid Rides Pillion; Love Me For Ever; Elizabethan Lover; Desire of the Heart; The Enchanted Waltz; The Kiss of the Devil; The Captive Heart; The Coin of Love; Stars in My Heart; Sweet Adventure; The Golden Gondola; Love in Hiding; The Smuggled Heart; Love under Fire; The Messenger of Love; The Wings of Love; The Hidden Evil; The Fire of Love; The Unpredictable Bride; Love Holds the Cards; A Virgin in Paris; Love to the Rescue; Love is Contraband; The Enchanting Evil; The Unknown Heart; The Secret Fear; The Heartbreaker; *other books:* Sleeping Swords; Love is Mine; The Passionate Pilgrim; Blue Heather; Wings on My Heart; The Kiss of Paris; Love Forbidden; Lights of Love; The Thief of Love; The Sweet Enchantress; The Kiss of Silk; The Price is Love; The Runaway Heart; A Light to the Heart; Love is dangerous; Danger by the Nile; Love on the Run (all signed Barbara McCorquodale); *philosophy:* Touch the Stars; *sociology:* You in the Home; The Fascinating Forties; Marriage for Moderns; Be Vivid, Be Vital; Love, Life and Sex; Look Lovely, Be Lovely; Vitamins for Vitality; Husbands and Wives; Etiquette; The Many Facets of Love; Sex and the Teenager; Charm; Living Together; Woman the Enigma; The Youth Secret; The Magic of Honey; *biography:* Ronald Cartland, 1942; Bewitching Women; The Outrageous Queen; Polly, My Wonderful Mother, 1956; The Scandalous Life of King Carol; The Private Life of Charles II; The Private Life of Elizabeth, Empress of Austria; Josephine, Empress of France; Diane de Poitiers; Metternich; The Passionate Diplomat; *autobiography;* The Isthmus Years, 1943; The Years of Opportunity, 1947; I Search for Rainbows, 1967; We Danced All Night, 1919-1929, 1970. *plays:* Blood Money; French Dressing (with Bruce Woodhouse); *revue:* The Mayfair Revue; *radio play:* The Caged Bird; *television:* Portrait of Successful Woman, 1957; This is Your Life, 1958; Success Story, 1959; Midland Profile, 1961; No Looking Back–a Portrait of Barbara Cartland, 1967; The Frost Programme, 1968; *radio:* The World of Barbara Cartland, 1970. Editor of the Common Problem, by Ronald Cartland, 1943. *Address:* Camfield Place, Hatfield Herts. *T:* Essendon 226, 224.

*See also Countess of Dartmouth.*

**CARTLAND, Sir George (Barrington),** Kt 1963; CMG 1956; BA; Vice-Chancellor of the University of Tasmania since 1968; *b* 22 Sept. 1912; *s* of William Arthur and Margaret Cartland, West Didsbury, *m* 1937, Dorothy Rayton; two *s. Educ:* Manchester Central High Sch.; Manchester Univ.; Hertford Coll., Oxford. Entered Colonial Service, Gold Coast, 1935; served Colonial Office, 1944-49; Head of African Studies Br. and Ed. Jl of Afr. Adminis., 1945-49; Sec. London Afr. Conf., 1948; Admin. Sec., Uganda, 1949; Sec. for Social Services and Local Govt, Uganda, 1952; min. for Social Services, Uganda, 1955; Min. of Education and Labour, Uganda, 1958; Chief Sec., Uganda, 1960; Deputy Gov. of Uganda, 1961-62; Registrar of Univ. of Birmingham, 1963-67. Part-time Mem., West Midlands Gas Bd, 1964-67. OStJ 1956; awarded Belgian medal recognising services in connection with evacuation of the Congo, 1960. *Recreation:* mountaineering. *Address:* University of Tasmania, Hobart, Tasmania. *Clubs:* Athenæum; Tasmanian, Athenæum, Royal Tasmanian Yacht (all Hobart).

**CARTMEL, Lt-Col Alfred Edward,** CIE 1937; MM; late 20th Lancers; *b* 1893; *s* of Alfred Cartmel; *m* 1920, Flora May Macdonald; two *s* one *d. Educ:* St Albans Sch. Served European War, 1914-18, Egypt, Gallipoli, NWF, Egypt, Iraq with Herts Yeomanry (despatches, MM); transferred to Indian Army, 1918; served Afghanistan, 1919; Waziristan, 1919-20; NWF India, 1930-31; Burma, 1930-32; King's Police Medal, 1936; Major, 1936; Battalion Commandant: Burma Military Police, Lashio, 1931-36; Burma Frontier Force, Lashio, 1937; Remount Department, India, 1942-47; Lieut-Col 1944; Asst Director, Remounts, Eastern Command, 1944-46; retd, 1948. *Recreation:* golf. *Address:* 29 Fanshawe Street, Hertford. *T:* Hertford 2414. *Club:* Cavalry.

**CARTON DE WIART, Count Edmund,** KBE (hon.); Grand Maréchal (hon.) de la Cour de Belgique; President de la Commission Royale des Monuments de Belgique; *b* Brussels, 4 Jan. 1876; *s* of Constant Carton de Wiart, Brussels; *m* 1910, Louise, *d* of Baron de Moreau, former Minister of Foreign Affairs of Belgium; one *d. Educ:* Louvain; Paris; Oxford; Berlin. Doctor of Law and Social Sciences; Sec. of Mr Beernaert, former Prime Minister, 1897-1901; Prof. Louvain Univ., 1897-1901; Political Sec. of King Leopold, 1901-09; Belgian Plenipotentiary at several conferences. Financial Delegate of the Belgian Government in England during the War; Great Cross of Belgian Orders, Grand Officer of Légion d'Honneur, Great Cross, etc. *Publications:* The British Chartered Companies in the 19th Century; Leopold II, a Biography, etc. *Address:* Avenue de Tervueren 177, Brussels; Château de Brumagne, Namur, Belgium.

**CARTWRIGHT, Frederick;** *see* Cartwright, W. F.

**CARTWRIGHT, Rev. Canon James Lawrence,** FSA 1958; Canon Emeritus since 1966 (Residentiary Canon and Chancellor of Peterborough Cathedral, and Chapter Librarian, 1952-66); *b* Loughborough, 8 June 1889; *s* of James Cartwright and Harriet Macaulay Todd; *m* 1918, Ruth, *o d* of William Frederick Buck; two *d. Educ:* Loughborough Grammar Sch.; King's Coll., Cambridge. BA 1917 (2nd Class Hist. Tripos, Parts I and II); MA 1921. Admitted a Solicitor, 1911. Served European War, 1918-19, in France, Temp. 2nd Lieut Royal Sussex Regt. Deacon, 1919; Priest, 1920; Curate: St Peter's and Thorpe Acre, Loughborough, 1919-22; St John Baptist, Knighton, Leicester, 1922-25; Vicar:

Christ Church, Northampton, 1925-33; Oundle with Ashton, 1933-52; Rural Dean Oundle I, 1937-52; Non-Residentiary Canon of Peterborough, 1946-52; Select Preacher, University of Cambridge, 1964. *Recreations:* mountain walking, lettering, heraldry. *Address:* 129 Park Road, Peterborough. *T:* Peterborough 68396. *Club:* City and Counties (Peterborough).

**CARTWRIGHT, Rt. Hon. John Robert,** PC (Can.) 1967; MC 1917; Chief Justice of Canada, 1967-70; Judge, Supreme Court of Canada, 1949-70; *b* Toronto, Canada, 23 March 1895; *s* of James Strachan Cartwright, KC, MA, and Jane Elizabeth (*née* Young), Weymouth, England; *m* 1st, Jessie Carnegie, *d* of Thomas Alexander Gibson, KC, Toronto; one *d*; 2nd, Mabel Ethelwyn Tremaine, *widow* of late Brig. Arthur Victor Tremaine, CBE, CD, and *d* of George William Parmelee, LLD, DCL, of Quebec. *Educ:* Upper Canada Coll., Toronto; Osgoode Hall, Toronto. Served European War, 1914-18; enlisted Canadian Expeditionary Force, Aug. 1914; Lieut 1915; Capt. 1916; with 3rd Canadian Infantry Bn until Dec. 1915 (wounded twice); ADC to GOC 3rd Canadian Div., 1915, until demobilization in 1919; Called to bar, Ontario, 1920, with honours and Silver Medal. Appointed KC (Ont), 1933; Bencher of Law Society of Upper Canada, 1946; practised at Toronto with firm Smith, Rae, Greer & Cartwright. Hon. LLD: Toronto, 1959; Osgoode Hall, 1963; Queen's Univ., Kingston, Ont, 1967; York Univ., Toronto, 1969; Hon. DCL, Bishop's Univ., Lennoxville, 1970. *Recreations:* chess and reading. *Address:* 85 Range Road, Apt 707, Ottawa 2, Canada. *T:* 232-1990. *Clubs:* Rideau, Country (Ottawa); Toronto, Royal Canadian Military Institute (Toronto).

**CARTWRIGHT, Dame Mary Lucy,** DBE 1969; FRS 1947; ScD Cambridge 1949; MA Oxford and Cambridge; DPhil Oxford; Hon. LLD (Edin.) 1953; Hon. DSc: Leeds, 1958; Hull, 1959; Wales, 1962; Oxford, 1966; Visiting Professor: Claremont Graduate School, California, 1969-70; Case Western Reserve University, since 1970; *b* 1900; *d* of late W. D. Cartwright, Rector of Aynhoe. *Educ:* Godolphin Sch., Salisbury, and St Hugh's Coll., Oxford. Asst Mistress Alice Ottley Sch., Worcester, 1923-24, Wycombe Abbey Sch., Bucks, 1924-27; read for DPhil, 1928-30; Yarrow Research Fellow of Girton Coll., 1930-34; Fellow of Girton Coll., 1934-49; Univ. Lectr in Mathematics, Cambridge, 1935-59; Mistress of Girton Coll., Cambridge, 1949-68; Reader in the Theory of Functions, Univ. of Cambridge, 1959-68, Emeritus Reader 1968; Vis. Prof., Brown Univ., Providence, RI, 1968-69. Consultant on US Navy Mathematical Research Projects at Stanford and Princeton Universities, Jan.-May 1949. Fellow of Cambridge Philosophical Soc.; Pres. London Math. Soc., 1961-63; Pres. Mathematical Association, 1951-52. Sylvester Medal, Royal Soc., 1964; De Morgan Medal, London Mathematical Soc., 1968. Commandant British Red Cross Detachment, Cambridgeshire 112, 1940-44. Commander, Order of the Dannebrog. *Publications:* Integral Functions (Cambridge Tracts in Mathematics and Mathematical Physics), 1956; math. papers in various journals. *Address:* c/o Girton College, Cambridge CB3 0JG.
*See also W. F. Cartwright.*

**CARTWRIGHT, (William) Frederick,** DL, MIMechE; a Deputy Chairman, British Steel Corporation, since 1970; Group Managing Director, S Wales Group British Steel Corporation, since 1967; Chairman: The Steel Co. of Wales Ltd, 1967 (Managing Director, 1962-67); Richard Thomas and Baldwins, since 1967; *b* 13 Nov. 1906; *s* of William Digby Cartwright, Rector of Aynhoe; *m* 1937, Sally Chrystobel Ware; two *s* one *d*. *Educ:* Rugby Sch. Joined Guest, Keen and Nettlefold, Dowlais, 1929; gained experience at steelworks in Germany and Luxembourg, 1930; Asst Works Manager, 1931, Tech. Asst to Managing Director, 1935, Director and Chief Engineer, 1940, Director and General Manager, 1943, Guest, Keen and Baldwin, Port Talbot; Director and General Manager, Steel Co. of Wales, 1947; Asst Man. Dir and General Manager of the Steel Div., The Steel Co. of Wales Ltd, 1954. Dir, Lloyds Bank, and Chm., S Wales Cttee, 1968-. DL, County of Glamorgan; High Sheriff, Glamorgan, 1961. OStJ. Hon. LLD Wales, 1968. *Recreations:* riding and yachting. *Address:* Castle upon Alun, St Brides Major, near Bridgend, Glam. *T:* Southern-down 298. *Clubs:* Royal Ocean Racing; Royal Yacht Squadron.
*See also Dame Mary Cartwright.*

**CARUS-WILSON, Eleanora Mary,** FBA 1963; Emeritus Professor of Economic History in the University of London since 1965 (Professor, 1953-65); *b* Montreal, 27 Dec. 1897; *d* of late Prof. Charles Ashley Carus-Wilson and Mary L. G. Petrie, BA (London). *Educ:* St Paul's Girls' Sch.; Westfield Coll., London. BA 1921; MA with Distinction, 1926; Leverhulme Research Fellow, 1936-38; Head of Branch, Min. of Food, 1940-45; Lecturer at the London Sch. of Economics and Political Science, 1945; Reader in Economic History in the University of London, 1948. Trustee, Cassel Educational Trust, 1963; Ford's Lecturer in English History, University of Oxford, 1964-65; Pres., Economic History Soc., 1966-69; Pres., Medieval Archæology Soc., 1966-69; Assoc. Mem. Royal Flemish Academy, 1961. Hon. LLD, Smith Coll., 1968. *Publications:* The Overseas Trade of Bristol in the later Middle Ages, 1937; chapters on The Trade of Bristol and on The Iceland Trade in Studies in English Trade in the Fifteenth Century, 1933; Chapter on The Woollen Industry in the Cambridge Economic History of Europe, Vol. II, 1952; Medieval Merchant Venturers, 1954; (ed) Essays in Economic History, 1954, 1962; England's Export Trade, 1275-1547, 1963; The Expansion of Exeter at the Close of the Middle Ages, 1963; contributions to Medieval England, 1958, and to Victoria History of the County of Wiltshire, 1959; articles and reviews in the Economic History Review and other historical journals. *Recreations:* music, mountains. *Address:* 14 Lansdowne Road, W11.

**CARVELL, John Eric Maclean,** CBE 1950; *b* 12 Aug. 1894; *s* of John Maclean Carvell, MBE, MRCS, and Euphemia Sarah Avery; *m* 1918, Cicely Lilian, *y d* of F. S. Garratt, Reigate, Surrey; one *d*. *Educ:* Berkhamsted. Served European War, 2nd Lieut Queen's Westminster Rifles, 1914; France, 1915 (twice wounded); Instructor to Portuguese Army, 1917-18; Staff Capt., HQ London District, 1918-19; Vice-Consul, Lisbon, 1919, Cadiz, 1921; Chargé d'Affaires, Port-au-Prince, 1922; Consul (Local Rank), Brest, 1925; Vice-Consul, Munich, 1929; Consul, Porto Alegre, 1932, New York, 1934; Consul-General, Munich, 1938-39; Algiers, 1942-45; Los Angeles, 1945-47; Ambassador to Ecuador, 1950-51 (Minister, 1947-50); Minister to Bulgaria, 1951-54, retd from Foreign Service, 1954. *Address:* Pygle House, Askett, Aylesbury, Bucks.

**CARVER, David Dove,** OBE 1967; Secretary General, International PEN, since 1951; *b* 10

Aug. 1903; *s* of Henry George Dove and Alice Mary Carver; *m* 1945, Violet Blanche Hall (*née* Parlby), *widow* of Sir Gerald Boles, 2nd Bt; no *c*. *Educ:* Emanuel School, London. After short period as business executive studied singing (baritone) with Alfredo Morelli, Reinhold von Warlich and John Goss; recitals, Wigmore Hall, BBC, etc. War Service, Squadron-Leader RAFVR, 1940-45 (despatches); ADC to HRH the Duke of Windsor, Governor of the Bahamas, 1942-44. Resumed singing career, 1946. Director, Singers in Consort Male Voice Quintet, 1948-53. Secretary General, English Centre PEN and International PEN. Hon. DLitt Chang Ang Univ., Seoul, 1970. *Publications:* various songs and part songs, carols, etc. *Recreations:* music, travel, theatre. *Address:* 2 Elsworthy Terrace, Hampstead, NW3. *T:* 01-722 6772. *Clubs:* Savile, English-Speaking Union.

**CARVER, Gen. Sir (Richard) Michael (Power),** GCB 1970 (KCB 1966; CB 1957); CBE 1945; DSO 1943 and Bar 1943; MC 1941; Chief of the General Staff since 1971; *b* 24 April 1915; 2nd *s* of late Harold Power Carver and late Winifred Annie Gabrielle Carver (*née* Wellesley); *m* 1947, Edith, *d* of Lieutenant-Col Sir Henry Lowry-Corry, *qv*; two *s* two *d*. *Educ:* Winchester Coll.; Sandhurst. 2nd Lieut Royal Tank Corps, 1935; War of 1939-45 (despatches twice); GSO1, 7th Armoured Div., 1942; OC 1st Royal Tank Regt, 1943; Comdr 4th Armoured Brigade, 1944; Tech. Staff Officer (1), Min. of Supply, 1947; Joint Services Staff Coll., 1950; AQMG, Allied Land Forces, Central Europe, 1951; Col GS, SHAPE 1952; Dep. Chief of Staff, East Africa, 1954 (despatches); Chief of Staff, East Africa, 1955; idc 1957; Dir of Plans, War Office, 1958-59; Comdr 6th Infty Brigade, 1960-62; Maj.-Gen. 1962; GOC, 3 Div., 1962-64, also Comdr Joint Truce Force, Cyprus, and Dep. Comdr United Nations' Force in Cyprus, 1964; Dir, Army Staff Duties, Min. of Defence, 1964-66; Lt-Gen. 1966; comd FE Land Forces, 1966-67; Gen., 1967; C-in-C, Far East, 1967-69; GOC-in-C, Southern Command, 1969-71. Col Comdt: REME 1966-; Royal Tank Regt, 1968-; ADC (Gen.) 1969-. *Publications:* Second to None (History of Royal Scots Greys, 1919-45), 1954; El Alamein, 1962; Tobruk, 1964. *Address:* Shackleford Old Rectory, Eashing, Godalming, Surrey. *T:* Godalming 22483. *Club:* Anglo-Belgian.

**CARY,** family name of **Viscount Falkland.**

**CARY, Sir (Arthur Lucius) Michael,** KCB 1965 (CB 1964); Secretary, Housing and Construction, Department of the Environment, since Oct. 1970; *b* 3 April 1917; *e s* of late Joyce Cary; *m* 1946, Isabel Margaret Leslie; three *s* one *d*. *Educ:* Eton, Trinity Coll., Oxford, 1st Class Hon. Mods, 1st Class Litt. Hum. Asst Principal, Air Min., 1939. Joined RNVR, 1940; Radar Officer, HMS Illustrious, 1942-43. Principal, Air Min., 1945; Asst Sec., 1951. Counsellor UK Delegation to NATO, 1956-58; Asst Under Sec., Air Min., 1958-61; Dep. Sec. of the Cabinet, 1961-64; Second Permanent Under Sec. of State (RN), Min. of Defence, 1964-68; Permanent Sec., Min. of Public Building and Works, 1968-70. Comp. IEE 1967. Governor, Dragon Sch., 1965. Fellow of Eton Coll., 1967. *Recreation:* making clavichords and harpsichords. *Address:* 18 Morden Road, Blackheath, SE3. *T:* 01-852 3634. *Club:* Brooks's.

**CARY, Sir Michael;** *see* Cary, Sir A. L. M.

**CARY, Sir Robert (Archibald),** 1st Bt, *cr* 1955; Kt 1945; MP (C) Withington Division of Manchester since 1951; *b* 25 May 1898; *s* of Robert Cary; *m* 1924, Hon. Rosamond Mary Curzon, *d* of late Col Hon. Alfred Nathaniel Curzon and *sister* of 2nd Viscount Scarsdale, *qv*; one *s*. *Educ:* Ardingly; Royal Military Coll., Sandhurst. Served European War, 1916-18; 4th Dragoon Guards, 1916-23; Gen. Staff, Iraq, 1920; North Persia, 1921; rejoined 4th/7th Royal Dragoon Guards, Sept. 1939, and reappointed to Gen. Staff; MP (U) Eccles, 1935-45; PPS to Civil Lord of Admiralty, 1939; PPS to Sec. of State for India, 1942-44; a Lord Commissioner of the Treasury, 1945; PPS to Min. of Health, 1951-52; PPS to Lord Privy Seal and Leader of the House, 1951-64. Mem. of House of Commons Select Cttee on National Expenditure, 1941. *Heir: s* Roger Hugh Cary [*b* 8 Jan. 1926; Lieut, Gren. Guards (Res.); *m* 1st, 1948, Marilda, *d* of Major P. Pearson-Gregory, MC; one *d*; 2nd, 1953, Ann Helen Katharine, *e d* of Hugh Blair Brenan; two *s* one *d*]. *Address:* Wrotham Water, Wrotham, Kent. *T:* Fairseat 16. *Clubs:* Carlton, Turf, Pratt's.

**CARY, Maj.-Gen. Rupert Tristram Oliver,** CB 1948; CBE 1943 (MBE 1919); DSO 1943; late Royal Corps of Signals; *b* 1896. Served European War, 1916-19, France, Belgium, India (wounded, MBE, 3 medals); Persia and Iraq, 1941-43 (despatches, CBE); signal officer Eighth Army, 1943; Maj.-Gen. 1944; Commandant Sch. of Signals, 1945-46; ADC to the King, 1946-47; Comdr of Catterick sub-district, 1946-49; retired pay, 1949.

**CASADESUS, Robert;** concert pianist and composer; *b* Paris, 7 April 1899; *m* Gaby Lhote; two *s* one *d*. Studied harmony and piano, Paris Conservatory (first prize, piano, 1913, first prize, harmony, 1919; Diémer prize, 1921). Since 1921 has performed as soloist with orchestras in all principal cities in Europe and USA; has also given recitals throughout Europe, N Africa, Egypt, Brazil, Argentina, Mexico and the United States. Made American concert début with NY Philharmonic Symphony Orchestra (Arturo Toscanini, conductor), 1935. Director of American Conservatory of Fontainebleau, France, 1946-47 (Dir-Gen., 1948-). Composer of: numerous quartettes, trios, sonatas, concertos and pieces for piano; four orchestral suites; four symphonies. Awarded Gold Medal, World's Fair, Paris, 1937; Brahms Medal, Hamburg, 1958; Gold Medal, City of Paris, 1959. Comdr of Legion of Honour, France; Comdr of Order of Orange-Nassau, Netherlands. *Address:* Lawrenceville Road, Princeton, New Jersey, USA.

**CASALONE, Carlo D.;** *see* Dionisotti-Casalone.

**CASALS, His Excellency Pablo,** violoncellist; composer, conductor; *b* Vendrell, Tarragona, 1876; *m* 1914, Susan Metcalfe (decd); *m* 1957, Marta Montanez. *Educ:* Municipal School of Music, and Madrid Conservatoire; Barcelona Conservatoire (1st prize). Made début in England at Crystal Palace, 1898; Conductor of the Pau Casals Symphony Orchestra of Barcelona, Spain, founded, 1920; Founder Workers' Concert Soc. (Barcelona), 1923; Doctor Honoris Causa of The University of Edinburgh, 1934; Barcelona, 1939; Montpellier, 1946; Citizen of Honour of Barcelona; Citizen of Honour of Madrid, 1935; of Prades, 1941; of Perpignan, 1945; of Béziers, 1946; of Foix, 1947; of Narbonne, 1948; Mem. of Honour of the Spanish Academy, 1935; Mem. Academy Sciences et Lettres of Montpellier, 1947. Corresponding Mem. of The Hispanic Soc., New York. Beethoven gold medal: of Philharmonic Soc. of London; of Friends of Music, Vienna; Hon. Mem. of Friends of Music Soc. of Vienna (founded 1812), 1930; Hon. Mem. of Royal Philharmonic Soc. FRCM 1937; Gold Medal of the Worshipful Company of Musicians, London, 1937; Grand Cross of Isabella the Catholic; Grand Cross for services to the Republic of Austria; Grand Cross of the Republic of Spain; Grand Officer Legion of Honor, 1946; Medal of City of Toulouse, 1946; US Presidential Medal of Freedom, 1963. Holds Hon. Doctorates in Music and in Letters; Citizen of honour of several cities in Central America. *Publications:* symphonic and choral works, chamber music, etc. *Relevant Publications:* (by Lillian Littlehales) Pablo Casals (English-Spanish); (by Dr Rudolf von Jabel) Pablo Casals (German, French, etc.); (by Arthur Compte) Legende de Pablo Casals; (by Jose M. Corredor) Conversations with P. Casals, 1955 (German, English, French, Spanish, etc.); (by Bernard Gavoty) Pablo Casals, 1955 (French, German, Spanish); (by Joan Llangeres) Pau Casals (Catalan); (by Emil Ludwig) Galerie des Portraits; (by Navarro Costabella) Pablo Casals. *Address:* San Juan, Puerto Rico, USA.

**CASE, Air Vice-Marshal Albert Avion,** CB 1964; CBE 1957 (OBE 1943); General Secretary, Hospital Saving Association, since 1969; *b* Portsmouth, 5 April 1916; *s* of late Group Captain Albert Edward Case and Florence Stella Hosier Case, Amesbury, Wilts; *m* 1949, Brenda Margaret, *e d* of A. G. Andrews, Enfield, Middx; one *s* one *d*. *Educ:* Imperial Service Coll. Commd RAF, 1934; Sqdn Ldr, 1940; Wing Comdr, Commanding No. 202 Squadron, 1942; Group Capt., Maritime Ops HQ, ACSEA, 1945; OC, RAF, Koggala, Ceylon, 1945-46; JSSC, 1950-51; OC, RAF, Chivenor, 1953-55; OC, RAF, Nicosia, 1956-57; IDC, 1959; Air Cdre, 1959; Air Min., Dir, Operational Requirements, 1959-62; Air Vice-Marshal, 1962; AOC No. 22 Group RAF, Tech. Trg Comd, 1962-66; SASO HQ Coastal Comd, 1966-68; retd. MBIM. *Recreations:* swimming (RAF blue 1946), sailing. *Address:* 25 Kewferry Road, Northwood, Middx. *Clubs:* Royal Air Force, Royal Air Force Yacht.

**CASE, Captain Richard Vere Essex,** DSO 1942; DSC 1940; RD; RNR retired; Royal Naval Reserve ADC to the Queen, 1958; Chief Marine Superintendent, Coast Lines Ltd and Associated Companies, 1953-69; *b* 13 April 1904; *s* of late Prof. R. H. Case; *m* 1940, Olive May, *d* of H. W. Griggs, Preston, near Canterbury, Kent; one *s* one *d*. *Educ:* Thames Nautical Training Coll., HMS Worcester. Joined RNR 1920; commenced service in Merchant Service, 1920; Master's Certificate of Competency, 1928; Captain RNR, 1953; served War of 1939-45 (DSC and Bar, DSO). *Recreation:* bowls. *Address:* 5 The Serpentine, Grassendale, Liverpool L19 9DT. *T:* 051-427 1016. *Clubs:* Liverpool University, Liverpool Cricket.

**CASEY,** family name of **Baron Casey.**

**CASEY,** Baron *cr* 1960 (Life Peer); **Richard Gardiner Casey,** KG 1969; PC 1939; GCMG 1965; CH 1944; DSO 1918; MC; Governor-General of Australia, 1965-69; *b* 29 Aug. 1890; *s* of Richard Gardiner Casey, Shipley House, Melbourne, Australia; *m* 1926, Ethel Marian Sumner, *d* of Maj.-Gen. Sir Charles Ryan, KBE, CB; one *s* one *d*. *Educ:* Melbourne Church of England Grammar Sch.; Melbourne Univ.; Trinity Coll., Cambridge (BA 1913). Served European War, 1914-18, in Gallipoli and France (despatches, DSO, MC); Foreign Affairs Officer, Canberra, 1927; Liaison officer between the Australian Government and the Foreign Office, 1924-27 and 1927-31; Mem. of House of Representatives for Corio, 1931-40; and for Latrobe, 1949-60; Asst Federal Treasurer, 1933-35; Federal Treasurer, 1935-39; Minister in charge of Development, 1937-39; Minister for Supply and Development, 1939-40; Australian Minister to USA, 1940-42; Minister of State Resident in the Middle East and Mem. of War Cabinet of the UK, 1942-43; Governor of Bengal, 1944-46; Federal President, Liberal Party of Australia, 1947-49; Minister of Works and Housing, Australia, 1949-51 and of National Development, 1950-51 (Supply and Development 1949-50); Minister in Charge of the Commonwealth Scientific and Industrial Research Organisation, 1950-60; Minister for External Affairs, Australia, 1951-60. Represented Australia at Coronation and Imperial Conf. 1937 and at London Conf. on Conduct of the War, Nov. 1939. Hon. degrees from a number of Univs. KStJ. *Publications:* An Australian in India, 1947; Double or Quit, 1949; Friends and Neighbours, 1954; Personal Experience, 1939-46, 1962; The Future of the Commonwealth, 1963; Australian Father and Son, 1966. *Address:* Edrington, Berwick, Victoria 3806, Australia. *Clubs:* Athenæum, Oxford and Cambridge; Melbourne (Melbourne).

**CASEY, Most Rev. Eamonn;** *see* Kerry, Bishop of, (RC).

**CASEY, Rt. Rev. Patrick Joseph;** *see* Brentwood, Bishop of, (RC).

**CASEY, Dr Raymond,** FRS 1970; Senior Principal Scientific Officer (Special Merit), Institute of Geological Sciences, London, since 1964; *b* 10 Oct. 1917; *s* of Samuel Gardner Casey and Gladys Violet Helen Casey (*née* Garrett); *m* 1943, Norah Kathleen Pakeman; two *s*. *Educ:* St Mary's, Folkstone; Univ. of Reading. PhD 1958; DSc 1963. Geological Survey and Museum: Asst 1939; Asst Exper. Officer 1946; Exper. Officer 1949; Sen. Geologist 1957; Principal Geologist 1960. *Publications:* A Monograph of the Ammonoidea of the Lower Greensand, 1960-71; numerous articles on Mesozoic palaeontology and stratigraphy in scientific press. *Recreation:* research into early Russian postal and military history (Past Pres., British Soc. of Russian Philately). *Address:* 38 Reed Avenue, Orpington, Kent. *T:* Farnborough (Kent) 51728.

**CASH, Sir Thomas James,** KBE 1946; CB 1939; *b* 5 July 1888; *s* of late Thomas Cash; *m* 1929, Gladys Ann, *d* of late Charles Hopkins, Beckenham, Kent; one *s* one *d*. *Educ:* St Ignatius' Coll., Stamford Hill; Univ. Coll., London; Malden medal and Schol.; Hollier Scholarship in Greek; Bunnell Lewis Prizes for Latin verse. BA (Hons Classics), 1909; Fellow of University Coll., London. Barrister, Middle Temple, 1924. Entered War Office as Higher Div. Clerk, 1912; Principal, 1920; Asst Sec., 1925; Director of Finance and Assistant Under-Secretary of State, 1936; Deputy Under-Sec. of State for War, 1945-54; retired 1954. Chevalier, Legion of Honour, 1920; Comdr, Czechoslovakian Order of the White Lion, 1947. *Address:* Tressmere, Cobham, Surrey. *T:* 2875.

**CASHEL, Dean of;** *see* Wolfe, Very Rev. Charles William.

**CASHEL and EMLY, Archbishop of, (RC),** since 1960; **Most Rev. Thomas Morris,** DD; *b* Killenaule, Co. Tipperary, 16 Oct. 1914; *s* of James Morris and Johanna (*née* Carrigan). *Educ:* Christian Brothers Schs, Thurles; Maynooth Coll. Ordained priest, Maynooth, 1939; studied, Dunboyne Institute, 1939-41.

(DD). Professor of Theology, St Patrick's Coll., Thurles, 1942-Dec. 1959, Vice-Pres., 1957-60; appointed Archbishop, 1959; consecrated, 1960. Office-holder in Muintir na Tire (rural community movement). *Recreation:* reading. *Address:* Archbishop's House, Thurles, Co. Tipperary, Ireland. *T:* Thurles 242.

**CASHEL and EMLY, WATERFORD and LISMORE, Bishop of,** since 1968; **Rt. Rev. John Ward Armstrong;** *b* 30 Sept. 1915; *s* of John and Elizabeth Armstrong, Belfast; *m* 1941, Doris Winifred, *d* of William J. Harrison, PC and Florence Harrison, Dublin; two *s*. two *d* (and one *d* decd). *Educ:* Belfast Royal Academy; Trinity College, Dublin, BA, Respondent, 1938; Toplady Memorial Prize, Past. Theol Pr. and Abp. King's Prize (2) 1937; Biblical Greek Prize and Downes Prize (1) 1938; 1st Class Hons Hebrew, 1936 and 1937; 1st Class Divinity Testimonium, 1938; BD 1945; MA 1957 (SC). Deacon, then Priest, All Saints, Grangegorman, 1938; Hon. Clerical Vicar, Christ Church Cathedral, 1939; Dean's Vicar, St Patrick's Cathedral, 1944; Prebend. of Tassagard, St Patrick's Cathedral, 1950; Rector of Christ Church, Leeson Park, 1951; Dean of St Patrick's Cathedral, Dublin, 1958-68. Wallace Lecturer, TCD, 1954-65; Dean of Residences, University College, Dublin, 1954-63. Vice-Pres. Boys' Brigade, 1963-. Trustee, Nat. Library of Ireland, 1964-; Mem., British Council of Churches, 1966. *Publication:* contrib. to Church and Eucharist–an Ecumenical Study (Ed. Rev. M. Hurley, SJ), 1966. *Recreations:* carpentering and bird-watching. *Address:* Bishop's House, Newtown, Waterford, Ireland. *T:* Waterford 5005. *Club:* Friendly Brothers of St Patrick (Dublin).

**CASHMAN, Rt. Rev. David (John);** *see* Arundel and Brighton, Bishop of, (RC).

**CASHMORE, Herbert Maurice,** MBE 1948; FLA; Emeritus City Librarian, Birmingham; *b* London, 29 Jan. 1882; *s* of Herbert Henry Cashmore and Ellen Eliza Morris: unmarried. *Educ:* King Edward's Sch., Aston, Birmingham. Employed Birmingham Public Libraries since leaving sch.; Deputy Chief Librarian, 1912-28; City Librarian, 1928-47; war service 8th Royal Warwicks Regt, 1915-19; Vice-Pres. Internat. Federation of Library Assocs, 1947-; Past President: Birmingham and District Library Assoc.; Assoc. of Asst Librarians; Central Literary Assoc.; Midlands Arts Club (Hon. Treas., 1955-69); Délégué Touring Club de France; Fellow of Library Assoc. and mem. of its Council, 1928- (Hon. Treas. 1936-45; Pres. 1946; Hon. Fellow, 1947; Hon. Vice-Pres. 1964); Hon. Sec. and Treasurer, Regional Library Bureau (W Midland); Life Governor of Birmingham Univ.; Governor of Birmingham and Midland Institute (Vice-Pres. 1955-59); formerly Chm. Birmingham Sch. of Music; Mem. BBC Midland Area Council; Mem., Council of the Dugdale Soc.; Vice-President: Council of the British Records Assoc. and Business Archives Council; Unesco National Co-operating Body for Libraries; Coun. of Brit. Union Catalogue of Periodicals; Bryony House Management Cttee; Hon. Sec. and Treasurer of the Shakespeare Memorial Library Cttee, 1928-48, Chm., 1963-; Surveyed the Libraries of Eastern Europe for Library Association and Rockefeller Foundation, 1936; delegate to American Library Association Conference and toured USA and Canada at request of Foreign Office, 1941; Coronation Medal, 1937; Defence medal, 1946. *Publications:* Libraries of North-Eastern Europe, including Russia, 1938; compiled Birmingham Book of Remembrance, 1939-45; various contributions to the Central Literary Magazine and professional (library) periodicals, etc. *Recreations:* reading, philately. *Address:* 17 Greswolde Park Road, Acock's Green, Birmingham 27. *T:* 021-706 0042.

**CASHMORE, Rt. Rev. Thomas Herbert;** *b* 27 April 1892; *s* of Thomas James and Julia Cashmore; *m* 1919, Kate Marjorie Hutchinson; two *s* two *d* (and one *s* decd). *Educ:* Codrington Coll., Barbados, BWI (BA, Durham). Ordained, Barbados, for Chota Nagpur, India, 1917; SPG Missionary, Ranchi, Chota Nagpur, 1917-24; Principal St James's Coll., Calcutta, 1924-33; Vicar: St James's Parish, Calcutta, 1924-33; Holmfirth, Yorks, 1933-42; Brighouse, Yorks, 1942-46; Hon. Canon of Wakefield Cathedral, 1942-46; Canon Missioner, Diocese of Wakefield, 1946-54; Suffragan Bishop of Dunwich, 1955-67. Examining Chaplain to Bishop of St Edmundsbury and Ipswich, 1955-67. Awarded Kaisar-i-Hind (2nd Class), 1929. *Recreation:* motoring. *Address:* Lynton, Graham Avenue, Withdean, Brighton. *T:* Brighton 553005. *Club:* Royal Over-Seas League.

**CASLON, Vice-Adm. Clifford,** CB 1949; CBE 1942; RN (retired); *b* 11 May 1896; *s* of Sydney Herbert Caslon and Edith Elizabeth Thorpe; *m* 1930, Laurie Kathleen Walch; two *s*. *Educ:* Royal Naval Colls, Osborne and Dartmouth. Served in battleships Monarch and Malaya, European War, 1914-18. Qualified in Signals and W/T, 1920; Flag-Lieut and Signal Officer in cruisers Cardiff (med.) and Hawkins (China) and battle-cruiser Hood (Empire cruise), 1921-28; Fleet Signal Officer, Med. Fleet, 1929-30; Comdr 1930; Commanded destroyers Thruster, Viceroy and Blanche; Capt. 1937; qualified RN Staff Coll. and Imperial Defence Coll.; commanded 4th, 18th and 6th destroyer flotillas, 1938-42; Chief of Staff, Plymouth, 1943-44; commanded HMS Nelson, 1945-46; Naval ADC to the King, 1946-47; Rear-Adm. 1947; Flag Officer, Malaya, 1947-50; Vice-Adm. 1950; retd list, 1950. *Address:* 1 Maltravers Drive, Littlehampton, Sussex. *T:* 3119. *Club:* United Service.

**CASS, Edward Geoffrey,** OBE 1951; Assistant Under-Secretary of State (Programmes and Budget), Ministry of Defence, since 1965 (Air Ministry, 1963-64); *b* 10 Sept. 1916; *s* of Edward Charles and Florence Mary Cass; *m* 1941, Ruth Mary Powley; four *d*. *Educ:* St Olave's; Univ. Coll., London (Scholar); The Queen's Coll., Oxford (Scholar). BSc (Econ.) London (1st Cl.) 1937; George Webb Medley Scholarship, 1938; BA Oxon. (1st Cl. PPE) 1939. Lecturer in Economics, New Coll., Oxford, 1939. Ministry of Supply: Asst Director of Statistics, 1940; Temp. Principal, 1945; Asst Principal, 1947; Principal, 1948; Private Sec. to the Prime Minister, 1949; Asst Sec. (Chief Statistician), Ministry of Supply, 1952; Private Sec. to Minister of Supply, 1954; Imperial Defence Coll., 1958; Asst Sec., Ministry of Defence, 1959. *Address:* 60 Rotherwick Road, NW11. *T:* 01-455 1664.

**CASSEL, Sir Harold (Felix),** 3rd Bt *cr* 1920; QC 1970; Recorder of Great Yarmouth, since 1968; *b* 8 Nov. 1916; 3rd *s* of Rt Hon. Sir Felix Cassel, 1st Bt, PC, QC (*d* 1953), and Lady Helen Cassel (*d* 1947); *S* brother, 1969; *m* 1st, 1940, Ione Jean Barclay (marr. diss. 1963); three *s* one *d*; 2nd, 1963, Mrs Eileen Elfrida Smedley. Educ: Stowe; Corpus Christi Coll., Oxford. Served War of 1939-45, Captain, 1941, Royal Artillery. Called to Bar, Lincoln's Inn, 1946. JP, Herts, 1959-62; Dep. Chm., Herts QS, 1959-62. *Recreations:* shooting, swimming. *Heir:* *s* Timothy Felix Harold

Cassel, *b* 30 April 1942. *Address:* 49 Lennox Gardens, SW1. *T:* 01-584 2721. *Club:* Carlton.

**CASSELS, Field-Marshal Sir (Archibald) James (Halkett),** GCB 1961 (CB 1950); KBE 1952 (CBE 1944); DSO 1944; Chief of the General Staff, Ministry of Defence, 1965-68; *b* 28 Feb. 1907; *s* of late General Sir Robert A. Cassels, GCB, GCSI, DSO; *m* 1935, Joyce, *d* of late Brig.-Gen. Henry Kirk and Mrs G. A. McL. Sceales; one *s*. *Educ:* Rugby Sch.; RMC, Sandhurst. 2nd Lieut Seaforth Highlanders, 1926; Lieut 1929; Capt. 1938; Major, 1943; Col 1946; temp. Maj.-Gen. 1945; Maj.-Gen. 1948; Lieut-Gen. 1954; Gen. 1958. Served War of 1939-45 (despatches twice): BGS 1944; Bde Comd 1944; GOC 51st Highland Div., 1945; GOC 6th Airborne Div., Palestine, 1946 (despatches); idc, 1947; Dir Land/Air Warfare, War Office, 1948-49; Chief Liaison Officer, United Kingdom Services Liaison Staff, Australia, 1950-51; GOC 1st British Commonwealth Div. in Korea, 1951-52; Comdr, 1st Corps, 1953-54; Dir-Gen. of Military Training, War Office, 1954-57; Dir of Emergency Operations Federation of Malaya, 1957-59; PMN (Panglima Mangku Negara), 1958; GOC-in-C, Eastern Command, 1959; C-in-C, British Army of the Rhine and Comdr NATO Northern Army Group, 1960-63; Adjutant-Gen. to the Forces, 1963-64; Field-Marshal, 1968. ADC Gen. to the Queen, 1960-63. Col Seaforth Highlanders, 1957-61; Col Queen's Own Highlanders, 1961-66; Colonel Commandant: Corps of Royal Military Police, 1957-68; Army Physical Training Corps, 1961-65. *Recreations:* all forms of sport. *Address:* c/o Lloyds Bank Ltd, 6 Pall Mall, SW1; Pitearn, Alves, Forres, Moray. *Club:* United Service.

**CASSELS, Francis Henry,** TD 1945; **His Honour Judge Cassels;** Chairman, South West London Sessions, since 1965; *b* 3 Sept. 1910; 2nd *s* of Sir James Dale Cassels, *qv*; *m* 1939, Evelyn Dorothy Richardson; one *s* one *d*. *Educ:* Sedbergh; Corpus Christi Coll., Cambridge (MA). Called to the Bar, Middle Temple, 1932. Served Royal Artillery, 1939-45. Dep. Chm., County of London Sessions, 1954-65. *Recreations:* golf and snooker. *Address:* 14 Buckingham House, Courtlands, Richmond, Surrey. *T:* 01-940 4180. *Clubs:* Royal Wimbledon Golf; Constitutional (Putney).

**CASSELS, Field-Marshal Sir James;** *see* Cassels, Field-Marshal Sir A. J. H.

**CASSELS, Sir James Dale,** Kt 1939; Judge of Queen's Bench Division, High Court of Justice, 1939-61, retired; *b* 22 March 1877; *o s* of Robert Cassels; *m* 1900, Alice Jessie (*d* 1904), *d* of Josiah Stone; no *c*; *m* 1906, Bertha Frances (*d* 1957), *d* of Alfred Terry; one *s* (and two *s* decd) one *d*; *m* 1958, Mrs Deodora Croft, OBE, *widow* of Hon. Col C. M. Croft, DL, MICE, MIME. *Educ:* Westminster City Sch. MP (U) West Leyton, 1922-29; MP (U) NW Camberwell, 1931-35; Called to Bar, Middle Temple, 1908; KC 1923; Recorder of Guildford, 1927-29; of Brighton, 1929-39; Bencher of the Middle Temple since 1929; Treasurer, 1947. *Address:* 11 Marryat Road, Wimbledon, SW19. *T:* 01-946 8326.
*See also F. H. Cassels.*

**CASSELS, Prof. James Macdonald,** FRS 1959; Lyon Jones Professor of Physics, University of Liverpool, since Oct. 1960; *b* 9 Sept. 1924; *s* of Alastair Macdonald Cassels and Ada White Cassels (*née* Scott); *m* 1947, Jane Helen Thera Lawrence; one *s* one *d*. *Educ:* Rochester House Sch., Edinburgh; St Lawrence Coll., Ramsgate; Trinity College, Cambridge. BA, MA, PhD (Cantab.). Harwell Fellow and Principal Scientific Officer, Atomic Energy Research Establishment, Harwell, 1949-53. Lecturer, 1953, subseq. Senior Lecturer, University of Liverpool. Prof. of Experimental Physics, University of Liverpool, 1956-59; Visiting Prof., Cornell Univ., 1959-60. Mem. Council, Royal Soc., 1968-. *Publications:* contributions to scientific journals on atomic, nuclear and elementary particle physics. *Recreation:* travelling hopefully, by air and otherwise. *Address:* Overstrand, The Esplanade, Cressington Park, Liverpool L19 0PP. *T:* 051-427 1984.

**CASSELS, John Seton;** Under Secretary, National Board for Prices and Incomes, since 1968; *b* 10 Oct. 1928; *s* of Alastair Macdonald Cassels and Ada White Cassels (*née* Scott); *m* 1956, Mary Whittington; two *s* two *d*. *Educ:* Sedbergh Sch., Yorkshire; Trinity Coll., Cambridge. Rome Scholar, Classical Archaeology, 1952-54. Entered Ministry of Labour, Asst Principal, 1954; Principal, 1960; Assistant Secretary, 1965. Secretary of the Royal Commission on Trade Unions and Employers' Associations, 1965-68. *Address:* 10 Beverley Road, Barnes, SW13. *T:* 01-876 6270. *Club:* Oxford and Cambridge University.

**CASSELS, Prof. John William Scott,** FRS 1963; MA, PhD; Sadleirian Professor of Pure Mathematics, Cambridge University, since 1967; Head of Department of Pure Mathematics and Mathematical Statistics, since 1969; *b* 11 July 1922; *s* of late J. W. Cassels (latterly Dir of Agriculture in Co. Durham) and Mrs M. S. Cassels (*née* Lobjoit); *m* 1949, Constance Mabel Merritt (*née* Senior); one *s* one *d*. *Educ:* Neville's Cross Council Sch., Durham; George Heriot's Sch., Edinburgh; Edinburgh and Cambridge Univs. MA Edinburgh, 1943; PhD Cantab, 1949. Fellow, Trinity, 1949-; Lecturer, Manchester Univ., 1949; Lecturer, Cambridge Univ., 1950; Reader in Arithmetic, 1963-67. Dr (*hc*), Lille Univ., 1965. *Publications:* An Introduction to Diophantine Approximation, 1957; An Introduction to the Geometry of Numbers, 1959. Papers in diverse mathematical journals on arithmetical topics. *Recreations:* arithmetic (higher only), gardening (especially common vegetables). *Address:* 3 Luard Close, Cambridge CB2 2PL. *T:* 46108.

**CASSIDY, Sir Jack Evelyn,** Kt 1968, BA, LLB, QC, *b* 12 June 1894; *s* of J. W. Cassidy, Mudgee, NSW; *m* 1928, Gwyneth, *d* of Dr A. Waterhouse; one *s*. *Educ:* Mudgee Sch.; University of Sydney. Barrister-at-law, 1923; KC 1938. Vice-Pres., NSW Liberal Party, 1945-56. *Address:* 49 Cranbrook Road, Rose Bay, NSW, Australia.

**CASSIE, Arnold Blatchford David,** CBE 1955; Director of Research, Wool Industries Research Association, 1950-67, retired; *b* 17 May 1905; 3rd *s* of late D. A. Morris Cassie and late Mrs Cassie; *m* 1939, Catherine Dufour, *d* of late Surg. Capt. T. D. Halahan, OBE, RN; one *s* two *d*. *Educ:* Aberdeen Grammar Sch.; Edinburgh Univ.; Christ's Coll., Cambridge. Vans Dunlop Schol., Edin. Univ., 1926-29; Carnegie Research Schol., 1929-30; Post-grad. Research, University Coll., London, 1928-34; Scientific Officer: ICI Ltd, 1934-36, RAE, 1936-38; Chief Physicist, Wool Industries Research Assoc., 1938-40. Warner Memorial Medal 1949, Mather Lecturer 1962, Textile Institute; George Douglas Lectr, Soc. of Dyers and Colourists, 1961. Vice-Pres., Textile Institute, 1962-65; Governor, Bradford Institute of Technology, 1960-66. Hon. D.Tech. Bradford Univ., 1966. *Publications:* numerous in Proc. Royal Society, Trans. Faraday Soc., Jl of Textile Inst., etc. *Recreations:* gardening, golf, music. *Address:*

White Heather, Crescent Walk, Ferndown, Dorset. *T:* Ferndown 3705.

**CASSIE, Prof. W(illiam) Fisher,** CBE 1966; Partner, Waterhouse and Partners, Consulting Civil Engineers, since 1970; Professor of Civil Engineering, University of Newcastle upon Tyne (formerly King's College, University of Durham), 1943-70; *b* 29 June 1905; Scottish; *m* 1933, Mary Robertson Reid; no *c*. *Educ:* Grove Academy, Dundee; University of St Andrews. BSc (St Andrews), 1925. Asst Engineer, City Engineer and Harbour Engineer, Dundee; Research at University Coll., Dundee; PhD (St Andrews), 1930; first Senior Sir James Caird Scholarship in Engineering, 1930; Research and Study, University of Illinois (USA), 1930-31; MS (Ill.), 1931. Lectured at Queen's Univ., Belfast, University Coll., Cardiff, University Coll., London, 1931-40, King's Coll., Newcastle, University of Durham, 1940-70. Past Chm. Northern Counties Assoc. of Institution of Civil Engineers; Founder Chm. Northern Counties Branch Institution of Structural Engineers; Pres. Inst. Highways Engrs, 1967-68; FRSE; FICE; FIStructE; FInstHE; AMTPI; Mem. Sigma XI. Bronze Medallist, Instn of Struct. Engrs. *Publications:* Structural Analysis 1947; (with P. L. Capper), Mechanics of Engineering Soils, 1949; (with J. H. Napper) Structure in Building; Fundamental Foundations; Jls of Institution of Civil Engineers, Institution of Structural Engineers, and other tech. papers. *Recreations:* photography and traditional cultures of England. *Address:* 7 Main Street, Ponteland, Newcastle upon Tyne. *T:* Ponteland 2391.

**CASSILLIS, Earl of; Archibald Angus Charles Kennedy;** *b* 13 Sept. 1956; *s* and *heir* of 7th Marquess of Ailsa, *qv*.

**CASSIN, Prof. René,** Grand Croix Légion d'Honneur; Compagnon de la Libération; Médaille Militaire; Croix de Guerre; Membre du Conseil Constitutionnel since 1960; Hon. President, Conseil d'État; Member (ex-President) Human Rights Commission of United Nations since 1946 and first Reporter of the Universal Declaration; Judge (formerly President), European Court of Human Rights; President, International Institute of Human Rights, Strasbourg; Member of the French Institute since 1947; *b* Bayonne, 5 Oct. 1887; *s* of Henri Cassin; *m* 1917, Simone Yzombard; no *c*. *Educ:* Lycée de Nice; Facultés, Aix (Licencié ès lettres. Licencié en droit); Paris (Docteur ès Sciences juridiques, politiques et économiques); Agrégé des Facultés de Droit, 1919; Prof. of Civil Law, Lille, 1920-29; Agrégé then Prof., Faculty of Law, Paris, 1929-60! Prof. Hague Academy of Internat. Law, 1930, 1934, 1951; French Delegate to the League of Nations, 1924-38, and to Gen. Conference on disarmament, 1932-34; Legal Counsellor to Gen. de Gaulle, 1940; Permanent Sec. de Gaulle's Council of Defence of the Empire, 1940-41; Nat. Commr for Justice and Public Education, 1941-43; Prés. du Comité Juridique, 1943-45; Pres. legisl. sect. of Cons. Assembly, Algiers, 1944; Vice-Prés. du Conseil d'Etat, 1944-60; Pres. Prov Constitutional Cttee, 1958-59; French Delegate: to Conf. of Allied Ministers of Education, 1942-43; to UN Commission on War Crimes, 1943-45; to UN Assemblies, 1946-51, 1968, and to UNESCO, 1945-52-58-60-62; Founder, President and Hon. President Union Fédérale des Mutilés et Anciens Combattants; Founder, International Confederation of Wounded (CIAMAC). President: Supreme Court of Works Disputes, 1950-60; Soc. of Comparative Law, 1952-55; Internat. Institute of Administrative Sciences 1953-56; Institut d'études des relations internationales, 1955; Alliance israélite universelle 1944-; Friends of Paris Univ., 1952. Nobel Peace Prize, 1968; UN Human Rights prize, 1968. Hon. DCL, Oxford, Mainz, Jerusalem. *Publications:* L'Exception d'inexécution dans les rapports synallagmatiques, 1914; Les Droits de l'Etat dans les successions d'après le code civil, suisse, 1914; L'Interdiction du commerce avec l'ennemi (1917-19); La Nouvelle Conception du domicile dans le règlement des conflits de loi, 1931; La Déclaration universelle et la mise en œuvre des Droits de l'Homme, 1951; Le Conseil d'Etat, 1952; Founder of Etudes et Documents du Conseil d'Etat; numerous articles on civil, public and international law. *Address:* 36 Quai de Béthune, Paris Ive, France; Conseil Constitutionnel, 2 rue de Montpensier, Paris Ier, France.

**CASSIRER, Mrs Reinhold;** *see* Gordimer, Nadine.

**CASSON, Sir Hugh (Maxwell),** Kt 1952; RA 1970 (ARA 1962); RDI 1951; MA Cantab; FRIBA, FSIA; Professor of Interior Design, Royal College of Art, since 1953; Member Royal Danish Academy, 1954; Member, Royal Fine Art Commission, since 1960; *b* 23 May 1910; *s* of Randal Casson, ICS retd, Bassett, Southampton; *m* 1938, Margaret Macdonald, *d* of Dr James MacD. Troup, Pretoria, SA; three *d*. *Educ:* Eastbourne Coll.; St John's Coll., Cambridge. Craven Scholar, British Sch. at Athens, 1933; in private practice as architect since 1937 with late Christopher Nicholson; served War of 1939-45, Camouflage Officer in Air Ministry, 1940-44; Technical Officer Ministry of Town and Country Planning, 1944-46; private practice, 1946-48; Dir. of Architecture, Festival of Britain, 1948-51. Regular contributor as author and illustrator to technical and lay press. Mem. of Editorial Board, Architectural Review. *Publications:* New Sights of London (London Transport), 1937; Bombed Churches, 1946; Homes by the Million (Penguin), 1947; (with Anthony Chitty) Houses–Permanence and Prefabrication, 1947; Victorian Architecture, 1948; Inscape: the design of interiors, 1968. *Recreation:* sailing. *Address:* (home) 35 Victoria Road, W8; (office) 35 Thurloe Place, SW7. *T:* 01-584 4581.

**CASSON, Dame Sybil;** *see* Thorndike.

**CASTAING, J. C. de;** *see* Chastenet de Castaing.

**CASTELLANI, Professor Marchese Count Aldo,** DSC; Hereditary Count of Kisymaio; MD, FRCP; FACP; Hon. FRMS; FAmAcDerm; MD, Cairo (Hon.); Physician to Royal Houses of Savoy and of Aosta; Italian Medals (one silver, two bronze) for bravery on the Field; Italian Military Cross; Grand Cross, Crown of Italy; also Grand Cross: Order of Civil Merit (Spain); Order of George I (Greece); Order of the Nile (Egypt); Sovereign Order of Malta; Order of St Sava; Knight Officer Legion of Honour (France) and Serbian White Eagle; Comm. Polish Order Odrodzenia; Commander Order of Santiago de Espada (Portugal); Professor of Tropical Medicine, Lisbon Institute for Tropical Diseases; Emeritus Professor of Tropical Medicine, Ceylon Medical School; late Professor of Tropical Medicine Tulane University and Louisiana State University, New Orleans, USA, also Rome University and Naples University, Italy; late Director of Mycology, London School of Hygiene and Tropical Medicine; late Physician Italian Hospital, London; concerned with Sir William Simpson in foundation of Ross Institute; (Ross thanked them both in a letter to the Times, 18 Oct. 1928); *b* Florence, 8 Sept.

1877; *s* of Ettore Castellani; *m* Josephine, *d* of George Ambler Stead; one *d. Educ:* Univs of Florence and Bonn. Qualified 1899 (MD, highest honours); MRCP 1916. Mem. British Foreign Office and Royal Society's Commission on Sleeping Sickness in Uganda, 1902-03. Dir Govt Clinique for Tropical Diseases, and Physician Seamen's Ward, Gen. Hospital, Colombo, 1903-15. Milroy Lecturer, RCP, London, 1920; Gehrmann Lecturer, University of Illinois, 1926; Royal Italian Academy prize for Science, 1932; Bernhardt Nocht Medal for Tropical Med.; Pres. Internat. Soc. of Tropical Dermatology, 1960. Lieut-Col Royal Italian Med. Service (Balcanic zone, 1915-18) and Mem. Interallied Sanitary Commission; during Ethiopian War, 1935-36, Surgeon-Gen. to Italian Forces (Count of Kisymaio). Senator of the Kingdom of Italy, 1929-46. Fellow: Accademia Nazionale dei Lincei; Accad. dei Quaranta; Accad. Pontificia. Chiefly known for his discovery of the etiological agents of sleeping sickness and yaws, for the elucidation of the etiology of several other diseases, and for description of new tropical diseases and their causes; also for original work in dermatology (parasitic skin diseases) and bacteriology (absorption test, dilution method, combined vaccines, gas-fermentation, symbiotic phenomenon, new species of bacteria, fungi and protozoa). *Publications:* Manual of Tropical Medicine (with Dr A. J. Chalmers); Fungi and Fungal Diseases, 1928; Climate and Acclimatisation (2nd edn), 1938; Manuale di Clinica Tropicale (with Prof. Jacono), 1938; Malattie dell' Africa, 1947; Little Known Tropical Diseases, 1954 (Lisbon); Microbes, Men and Monarchs, 1960 (London) (3rd edn 1968), 1961 (New York, as: A Doctor in Many Lands); numerous scientific articles; formerly Ed. Jl Trop. Med. *Address:* Institute for Tropical Diseases, Junqueira, Lisbon, Portugal; Villa Azzurra, Cascais, Portugal. *Clubs:* Authors' (London); Caccia (Rome); Rotary (Lisbon).
*See also Baron Killearn.*

**CASTERET, Norbert;** Officier de la Légion d'Honneur, 1947; Croix de Guerre, 1917; archæologist, geologist, speleologist; *b* 19 Aug. 1897; *m* 1924, Elisabeth Martin (*d* 1940); one *s* four *d. Educ:* Lycée de Toulouse, Haute-Garonne. Bachelier; lauréat de l'Académie Française, 1934, 1936; lauréat de l'Académie des Sciences, 1935; mainteneur de l'Académie des Jeux Floraux, 1937; Grande Médaille d'Or de l'Académie des Sports, 1923; Médaille d'Or de l'Education Physique, 1947; Commandeur du Mérite de la Recherche et de l'Invention, 1956; Commandeur du Mérite sportif, 1958; Commandeur des Palmes académiques, 1964. *Publications:* 29 Works translated into 15 languages: Dix ans sous terre (English edn: Ten Years Under the Earth); Au fond des gouffres; Mes Cavernes (English edn: My Caves); En Rampant; Exploration (English edn: Cave Men New and Old); Darkness Under the Earth; Trente ans sous terre (English edn: The Descent of Pierre Saint-Martin), etc.; contributions to L'Illustration, Illustrated London News, Geographical Magazine, etc. *Recreation:* exploring caves. *Address:* Castel Mourlon, Saint-Gaudens, Haute-Garonne, France. *T:* St Gaudens 113.

**CASTLE, Rt. Hon. Barbara (Anne),** PC 1964; BA; MP (Lab) for Blackburn since 1955 (Blackburn East, 1950-55, Blackburn, 1945-50); *b* 6 Oct. 1911; *d* of Frank and Annie Rebecca Betts; *m* 1944, Edward Cyril Castle *qv*; no *c. Educ:* Bradford Girls' Grammar Sch.; St Hugh's Coll., Oxford. Elected to St Pancras Borough Council, 1937; Member Metropolitan Water Board, 1940-45; Asst Editor, Town and County Councillor, 1936-40; Administrative Officer, Ministry of Food, 1941-44; Housing Correspondent and Forces Adviser, Daily Mirror, 1944-45. Member of National Executive Cttee of Labour Party since 1950; Chairman Labour Party, 1958-59 (Vice-Chm. 1957-58). Minister of: Overseas Development, 1964-65; Transport, 1965-68; First Secretary of State and Secretary of State for Employment and Productivity, 1968-70. Hon. Fellow, St Hugh's Coll., Oxford, 1966. *Publication:* part author of Social Security, edited by Dr Robson, 1943. *Recreations:* poetry and walking.

**CASTLE, Edgar Bradshaw,** MA Oxon; Professor Emeritus, University of Hull; *b* 23 Dec. 1897; *s* of Frederick and Ellen Castle; *m* 1923, Mignon Marrable (*d* 1959); one *s* one *d*; *m* 1962, E. Ann Hodgkin. *Educ:* Bemrose Sch., Derby; Lincoln Coll., Oxford. Asst Master, Mill Hill Sch., 1923-28; Headmaster, Leighton Park Sch., Reading, 1928-47; Prof. of Education, University of Hull, 1948-61, Pro-Vice-Chancellor, 1956-59; Visiting Prof., University Coll. of Makerere, Uganda, 1961-65. Chm., Uganda Education Commission, 1963. *Publications:* Fathers and Sons, 1932; The Undivided Mind, 1941; Building the New Age, 1945; People in School, 1954; Moral Education in Christian Times, 1958; Ancient Education and To-Day, 1961; Approach to Quakerism, 1961; Principles of Education for Teachers in Africa, 1965; Growing Up in East Africa, 1966; Parents' Guide to Education, 1968; The Teacher, 1970. *Address:* Little Woolgarston Cottage, Corfe Castle, Wareham, Dorset.

**CASTLE, Edward Cyril;** journalist; *b* 5 May 1907; *m* 1944, Barbara Anne Betts (*see* Barbara Castle). *Educ:* Abingdon and Portsmouth Grammar Schools; served on newspapers in Portsmouth, Southampton, Newcastle, 1925-31; News Editor, Manchester Evening News, 1932; Asst Editor, Daily Mirror, 1943; Asst Editor, Picture Post, 1944-50; Editor of Picture Post, 1951-52. Alderman, GLC 1964-70. *Recreations:* walking, gardening. *Address:* Flat G, 19 John Spencer Square, N1.

**CASTLE, Mrs G. L.;** *see* Sharp, Margery.

**CASTLE STEWART,** 8th Earl, *cr* 1800 (Ireland); **Arthur Patrick Avondale Stuart;** Viscount Stuart, 1793; Baron, 1619; Bt 1628; *b* 18 Aug. 1928; 3rd but *e surv. s* of 7th Earl Castle Stewart, MC, and Eleanor May, *er d* of late S. R. Guggenheim, New York; *S* father, 1961; *m* 1952, Edna Fowler; one *s* one *d. Educ:* Brambletye; Eton; Trinity Coll., Cambridge. Lieut Scots Guards, 1949. *Heir: s* Viscount Stuart, *qv. Address:* Stone House Farm, East Pennard, Shepton Mallet, Somerset. *T:* Ditcheat 240; Stuart Hall, Stewartstown, Co. Tyrone. *T:* Stewartstown 208. *Club:* Carlton.

**CASTLEMAINE,** 7th Baron, *cr* 1812; **John Michael Schomberg Staveley Handcock;** Chairman, Mancunian Building Society, since 1967 (Director since 1957); Director, Irish International Bank Ltd, since 1967; *b* 10 March 1904; *s* of Robert John Handcock (*d* 1951), and Eleanoré Annie Esther Staveley; *S* kinsman 1954; *m* 1930, Rebecca Ellen, *o d* of William T. Soady, RN; one *s* two *d. Educ:* The Abbey, Tipperary. Joined Provincial Bank of Ireland Ltd, 1923, retired 1957. Served with Irish Defence Forces, Adjutant, 1939-45. *Recreations:* all sports, particularly sailing, shooting and fishing. Gardening and all forms of agriculture. *Heir: s* Hon. Roland Thomas John Handcock, The Parachute Regt [*b* 22 April 1943; *m* 1969, Pauline Anne, *e d* of John Taylor Bainbridge, Exeter]. *Address:*

Glanmore, Leixlip, Co. Kildare. *Clubs:* Dublin University, Bankers (Dublin).

**CASTLEREAGH, Viscount; Tristan Alexander Vane-Tempest-Stewart;** *b* 23 Oct. 1969; *s* and *heir* of Marquess of Londonderry, *qv.*

**CATARINICH, John,** CMG 1952; Consultant Psychiatrist; *b* Melbourne, 13 Nov. 1882; *s* of Capt. J. Catarinich, Dalmatia; *m* 1909, Nora J., *d* of J. Mouat; three *s* five *d. Educ:* St Patrick's Coll.; Melbourne Univ. (MB, BS). Joined Mental Hygiene Dept, State of Victoria, 1907; Medical Supt, Beechworth Mental Hospital, 1915-22, of Mont Park Mental Hospital, 1922-37; Director of Mental Hygiene, Victoria, 1937-51. *Address:* 18 Bradford Avenue, Kew, Melbourne, Victoria, Australia.

**CATCHESIDE, David Guthrie,** FRS 1951; DSc London; Director since 1967, Professor of Genetics, since 1964, Research School of Biological Sciences, Australian National University, Canberra; *b* 31 May 1907; *s* of David Guthrie Catcheside and Florence Susanna (*née* Boxwell); *m* 1931, Kathleen Mary Whiteman; one *s* one *d. Educ:* Strand Sch.; King's Coll., University of London. Asst to Professor of Botany, Glasgow Univ., 1928-30; Asst Lecturer, 1931-33, and Lecturer in Botany, University of London (King's Coll.), 1933-36; International Fellow of Rockefeller Foundation, 1936-37; Lecturer in Botany, University of Cambridge, 1937-50; Lecturer and Fellow, Trinity Coll., Cambridge, 1944; Reader in Plant Cytogenetics, Cambridge Univ., 1950-51; Prof. of Genetics, Adelaide Univ., S. Australia, 1952-55; Prof. of Microbiology, University of Birmingham, 1956-64. Research Associate, Carnegie Instn of Washington, 1958. Visiting Professor, California Inst. of Technology, 1961. Foundation FAA, 1954; FKC 1959. *Publications:* Botanical Technique in Bolles Lee's Microtomists' Vade-Mecum, 1937-50; Genetics of Micro-organisms, 1951. Papers on genetics and cytology. *Address:* Research School of Biological Sciences, ANU, Canberra, ACT 2601, Australia.

**CATCHPOOL, Egerton St John Pettifor,** CBE 1951; Member Workers Travel Association Management Committee, since its foundation, 1921; Chairman, Firbank Housing Society, since 1957; *b* 22 Aug. 1890; 4th *s* of Thomas K. Catchpool, Colchester; *m* 1920, Ruth Allason, 2nd *d* of Henry Lloyd Wilson, Birmingham; one *s* three *d* (and one *d* decd). *Educ:* Sidcot Sch.; Woodbrooke Quaker Coll.; Birmingham Univ. Secretary of Friends' Social Service Union, 1913-14; with Friends' War Victims Relief Cttee, 1915-19; Sub-Warden Toynbee Hall, first University Social and Educational Settlement, London, E1, 1920-29; First Secretary Youth Hostels Association England and Wales, 1930-50 (Vice-Pres. 1951-); retired 1950. Warden of Toynbee Hall, 1963-64. President Internat. Federation of Youth Hostels, 1938-50; Vice-President Internat. Friendship League; Member Society of Friends, Elder, 1946-. Co-opted Member LCC Education Cttee, 1925-31; Member Catering Wages Commn, 1947-50. Invited to Delhi by Govnt of India to advise on Social Service development, 1951. 15,000-mile tour of Africa, at invitation of British Council, advising on youth welfare, 1957. Fellow, Woodbrooke Coll., Birmingham, 1957. Royal Society of Arts Lecture, Leisure in an Affluent Society, 1964. Pres., Adventure Playpark Assoc., Welwyn Garden City, 1967-. Chevalier Order of Orange Nassau, 1948. *Publications:* Uniting Nations by means of Youth Hostels and International Work Camps; Candles in the Darkness, 1966. *Recreations:* walking, travelling and work camps. *Address:* Meadow Cottage, Welwyn Garden City, Herts. *T:* Welwyn Garden 22657.

**CATHCART,** family name of Earl Cathcart.

**CATHCART,** 6th Earl *cr* 1814; **Alan Cathcart,** DSO 1945; MC 1944; Viscount Cathcart, 1807; Baron Greenock (United Kingdom) and 15th Baron Cathcart (Scotland), 1447; Major-General, GOC Berlin (British Sector), since 1970; *b* 22 Aug. 1919; *o s* of 5th Earl and Vera, *d* of late John Fraser, of Cape Town; *S* father, 1927; *m* 1946, Rosemary, *yr d* of late Air Commodore Sir Percy Smyth-Osbourne, CMG, CBE; one *s* two *d. Educ:* Eton; Magdalene Coll., Cambridge. Served War of 1939-45 (despatches, MC, DSO). Adjt RMA Sandhurst, 1946-47; Regimental Adjt Scots Guards, 1951-53; Brigade Major, 4th Guards Brigade, 1954-56; Commanding Officer, 1st Battalion Scots Guards, 1957; Lt-Col comd Scots Guards, 1960; Colonel AQ Scottish Command, 1962-63; Imperial Defence Coll., 1964; Brigade Comdr, 152 Highland Brigade, 1965-66; Chief, SHAPEX and Exercise Branch SHAPE, 1967-68; GOC Yorkshire District, 1969-70; Brigadier, Queen's Body Guard for Scotland, Royal Company of Archers. *Heir: s* Lord Greenock, *qv. Address:* 14 Eaton Mews South, SW1. *T:* 01-235 4621. *Clubs:* Guards, Brooks's; Royal Yacht Squadron (Cowes).

**CATHERWOOD, Henry Frederick Ross;** Director-General, National Economic Development Council, 1966-May 1971; Director, John Laing & Son Ltd, from May 1971; *b* 30 Jan. 1925; *s* of Stuart and Jean Catherwood, Co. Londonderry; *m* 1954, Elizabeth, *er d* of Rev. Dr D. M. Lloyd Jones, late of Westminster Chapel, London; two *s* one *d. Educ:* Shrewsbury; Clare Coll., Cambridge. Articled Price, Waterhouse & Co.; qualified as Chartered Accountant, 1951; Secretary, Laws Stores Ltd, Gateshead, 1952-54; Secretary and Controller, Richard Costain Ltd, 1954-55; Chief Executive, 1955-60, Director, 1957; Asst Managing Director, British Aluminium Co. Ltd, 1960-62; Managing Director, 1962-64; Chief Industrial Adviser, Dept of Economic Affairs, 1964-66. Member of Council: British Institute of Management, 1961-66, 1969-; N. Ireland Development Council, 1963-64; Royal Institute of Internat. Affairs, 1964-; British Nat. Export Council, 1965-71; Nat. Economic Development Council, 1964-71. Vice-Pres., Inter-Varsity Fellowship (Pres. 1969-70). *Publications:* The Christian in Industrial Society, 1964; Britain With the Brakes Off, 1966; The Christian Citizen, 1969. *Recreations:* amusing the family, gardening, reading. *Address:* 25 Woodville Gardens, W5. *T:* 01-997 4117; Sutton Hall, Balsham, Cambridgeshire. *Club:* Oxford and Cambridge University.

**CATHIE, Ian Aysgarth Bewley,** MD, BS, MRCP, FRCPath; JP; *b* London, 3 Jan. 1908; 2nd *s* of George Cathie, Ewell, Surrey, and Lilly Pickford Evans; *m* 1938, Josephine, *o d* of Joseph Cunning, FRCS, Broome Park, Betchworth, Surrey; one *s* three *d. Educ:* Guy's Hospital; Zürich Univ. Asst path. to Ancoats Hospital, Manchester, 1932; demonstrator in path. in Manchester Univ. and registrar in path. to Manchester Royal Inf., 1934; path. and res. Fellow in path., Christie Hospital and Holt Radium Inst., also path. to Duchess of York Hospital for Babies, Manchester, 1936. Clinical Pathologist to The Hospital for Sick Children, Great Ormond Street, London, 1938-58, retired. Pathologist in EMS, 1939; war service in RAMC, 1940-46; captured in Tobruk, POW 1942-43. Hon. Member, British Pædiatric Association; Lord of the Manor of Barton-on-the-Heath, Warwickshire; CC Warwicks. *Publications:* Chapters in Moncrieff's Nursing and Diseases of Sick Children and (in collaboration) Garrod, Batten and Thursfield's Diseases of Children; also papers on pathology and pædiatrics in medical journals. Editor, Archives of Disease in Childhood, 1951-63. *Recreations:* gardening, hunting. *Address:* Barton House, Moreton-in-Marsh, Glos. *T:* Barton-on-the-Heath 303. *Clubs:* Chelsea Arts, Royal Automobile.

**CATLEDGE, Turner;** Director, The New York Times, since 1968; *b* 17 March 1901; *s* of Lee Johnson Catledge and Willie Anna (*née* Turner); *m* 1st; two *d*; 2nd, 1958, Abby Izard. *Educ:* Philadelphia (Miss.) High Sch.; Miss. State College. BSc 1922. Neshoba (Miss.) Democrat, 1921; Resident Editor, Tunica (Miss.) Times, 1922; Man. Editor, Tupelo (Miss.) Journal, 1923; Reporter, Memphis (Tenn.) Commercial Appeal, 1923-27; Baltimore (Md) Sun, 1927-29; New York Times: City Staff, 1929; Correspondent, Washington Bureau, 1930-36; Chief Washington news Correspondent, 1936-41; Chicago Sun: Chief Correspondent, 1941-42; Editor-in-Chief, 1942-43; Nat. Correspondent, New York Times, 1943-44; Managing Editor, 1951-64; Executive Editor, 1964-68 Vice-Pres., 1968-70. Member: Pulitzer Prizes Advisory Cttee, 1955-69; AP Managing Editors Assoc., 1954-64; Advisory Board, American Press Inst.; American Soc. of Newspaper Editors (Dir., Pres. 1961); Sigma Delta Chi. Hon. DLitt, Washington and Lee Univ.; Hon. Dr of Humane Letters, Southwestern at Memphis; Hon. LLD: Univ. of Kentucky; Tulane Univ. *Publication:* The 168 Days (with Joseph W. Alsop, Jr), 1937. *Address:* (office) 229 West 43rd Street, New York, NY 10036, US . *T:* 556-1234; (home) 2316 Prytania Street, New Orleans, La 70130, USA. *T:* 522-2429. *Clubs:* National Press, Gridiron, Metropolitan (Washington); Century, Players, Dutch Treat, Overseas Press, Silurians, Creek, The Links Golf (New York); Boston (New Orleans), New Orleans Country.

**CATLIN, Professor Sir George Edward Gordon,** Kt 1970; MA, PhD; FRSL; professor (retired) of political science and philosophy; *b* 29 July 1896; *s* of late Rev. George E. Catlin, sometime Vicar of St Luke's, Kew Gardens, Surrey, and of late Mrs Catlin, *née* Orton; *m* 1925, Vera Brittain (*d* 1970), one *s* one *d* (*see* Shirley Williams). *Educ:* Warwick; St Paul's Sch.; New Coll., Oxford (Exhibitioner in Modern History, 1914). Subsequently London Rifle Brigade. Oxford Modern History Sch. *cum laude*; Chancellor's English Essayist; *prox. accessit* Lothian Prize, 1920; Gladstone Prizeman, Matthew Arnold Memorial Prizeman, Oxford, 1921; Professor of Politics, Cornell Univ., 1924-35; acting Head of Dept, 1928; Foundation Lecturer: Yale Univ., 1938; Calcutta Univ., 1947; Lecturer: Peking Univ., Columbia Univ., University of California (Berkeley), Bologna, Cologne, etc.; Goethe Bicentenary Lecturer, Heidelberg Univ.; Kierkegaard Commemoration Address, University of Copenhagen, 1949; Weil Lecturer, University of N Carolina, 1957; Tagore Centenary Lecturer, Royal Society of Arts, 1961; Provost Mar Ivanios Coll., S India, India, 1951; Bronman Professor of Political Science, McGill Univ., 1956-60; Chairman of Dept; Walker-Ames Lecturer, University of Washington, 1964. Churchill Memorial Lectr, Fulton, Mo, 1969. Fellow and Vice-President of the World Academy of Arts and Sciences; Medallist, Soc. de l'Encouragement au Progrès (France); Vice-President, Anglo-German Assoc.; Director, Investigation into Eighteenth Amendment, US Constitution, under Rockefeller Foundation, 1926; editorial writer to Yorkshire Post, 1927-28, editor of People and Freedom, and special foreign correspondent, Germany, Russia, Spanish Civil War, Italy and India; co-founder, Realist Magazine, with H. G. Wells, Arnold Bennett and others. Contested (Lab.) Brentford Div., 1931, Sunderland Div., 1935; sometime Member Executive Cttee, Fabian Soc.; joint founder, America and British Commonwealth Assoc. (now E-SU); Technical adviser to Rt. Hon. Arthur Greenwood, 1939-40; Member Internat. Executive Cttee of Nouvelles Equipes Internationales (Internat. Cttee of Christian Socialist Parties) and rapporteur on European Union. Internat. Vice-President, Union Mondiale des Européens; Vice-President, War on Want. Sponsor, Martin Luther King Foundn. Mem., Inst. for Strategic Studies. Draftsman of Internat. Declaration in Support of Indian Independence, 1943. LDV, 1940. Comdr, Grand Cross, Order of Merit (Germany). *Publications:* Thomas Hobbes, 1922; The Science and Method of Politics, 1926, repr. 1964; Mary Wollstonecraft's Vindication: introd., 1928; Study of the Principles of Politics, 1929, repr. 1967; Liquor Control, 1931; Preface to Action, 1934; New Trends in Socialism, ed. 1935; War and Democracy, ed. 1938; (ed. and introd.) Durkheim's Rules of Sociological Method, 1938; Anglo-Saxony and its Tradition, 1939; The Story of the Political Philosophers, 1939; (8th edn, published in Britain as A History of the Political Philosophers, 1950); One Anglo-American Nation: The Foundation of Anglo-Saxony, 1941; Anglo-American Union as Nucleus of World Federation, 1942; The Unity of Europe, 1945; Above All Nations (Jointly), 1945; Mahatma Gandhi, 1948; What Does the West Want?, 1957; The Atlantic Community, 1959; Systematic Politics, 1962; Rabindranath Tagore centenary lectures, 1964; Political and Sociological Theory and its Applications, 1964; The Grandeur of England and the Atlantic Community, 1966; The Atlantic Commonwealth, 1969; Campaign (autobiography), 1969. Translations of above into various languages. *Address:* 4 Whitehall Court, SW1. *Clubs:* United Service, Pilgrims.
*See also B. O. Williams, Mrs Shirley V. T. B. Williams.*

**CATLING, Sir Richard (Charles),** Kt 1964; CMG 1956; OBE 1951; *b* 22 Aug. 1912; *y s* of late William Catling, Leiston, Suffolk; *m* 1951, Mary Joan Feyer (*née* Lewis). *Educ:* The Grammar School, Bungay, Suffolk. Palestine Police, 1935-48; Federation of Malaya Police, 1948-54; Commissioner of Police, Kenya, 1954-63; Inspector General of Police, Kenya, 1963-64. Colonial Police Medal, 1942; King's Police Medal, 1945. Officer Brother, OStJ, 1956. *Recreations:* fishing, sailing. *Address:* Hall Fen House, Irstead, Norfolk, Nor 38Z. *Club:* East India and Sports.

**CATNACH, Agnes,** CBE 1952; BA; *b* 8 Dec. 1891; *d* of Charles Burney Catnach, Newcastle upon Tyne. *Educ:* Polam Hall, Darlington; Royal Holloway Coll. Headmistress of Wallasey High Sch., 1926-34, of Putney County Sch., Mayfield, 1934-51. President of Assoc. of Headmistresses, 1942-44; Chairman of Joint Cttee of Four Secondary Associations, 1944-46; Member of Secondary Schools' Examinations Council, 1946-52; Member of General Nursing Council, 1943-58. *Address:* 3 Rusper House, Michel Grove, Eastbourne, Sussex. *T:* Eastbourne 31014. *Club:* University Women's.

**CATON-THOMPSON, Gertrude,** FBA 1944; Hon. LittD Cantab 1954; former Fellow of Newnham College, Cambridge; *o d* of late William Caton-Thompson and Mrs E. G. Moore. *Educ:* Miss Hawtrey's, Eastbourne; Paris. Employed Ministry of Shipping, 1915-19; Paris Peace Conference, 1919; student British School of Archæology in Egypt, 1921-26; excavated at Abydos and Oxyrhynchos, 1921-22; Malta, 1921 and 1924; Qau and Badari, 1923-25; on behalf of the British School in Egypt inaugurated the first archæological and geological survey of the Northern Fayum, 1924-26; continued work as Field Director for the Royal Anthropological Institute, 1927-28; appointed in 1928 by the British Assoc. to conduct excavations at Zimbabwe and other Rhodesian sites; Excavations in Kharga Oasis, 1930-33; South Arabia, 1937-38; Cuthbert Peek award of the Royal Geographical Society, 1932; Rivers Medallist of the Royal Anthropological Institute, 1934; Huxley medallist, 1946. Burton Medal of Royal Asiatic Society, 1954. Former Governor, Bedford Coll. for Women, and School of Oriental and African Studies, University of London; Member: Government Council British Inst. of History and Archæology in East Africa; Executive Cttee CPRE (Worcs). *Publications:* contributions to the Encyclopædia Britannica and various scientific journals; The Badarian Civilisation (part author), 1928; The Zimbabwe Culture, 1931 (repr. 1969); The Desert Fayum, 1935; The Tombs and Moon Temple of Hureidha, Hadramaut, 1944; Kharga Oasis in Prehistory, 1952. *Recreation:* idleness. *Address:* Court Farm, Broadway, Worcs. *Club:* English-Speaking Union.

**CATOR, Sir Geoffrey (Edmund),** Kt 1946; CMG 1936; *b* 14 Aug. 1884; *s* of Robert Cator and Evelyn Susan Sotheron Estcourt; *m* 1922, Elizabeth Margaret Wynne Mostyn (*d* 1967); one *s* one *d*. *Educ:* Bruton; Cambridge. BA 1906; Malayan CS 1907; various appointments in the Colonial Administrative Service, Agent for Malaya. Retired, 1948. *Address:* The Grange, Goring on Thames, Oxon.

**CATTELL, George Harold Bernard;** Director-General, National Farmers' Union, since 1970; *b* 23 March 1920; *s* of H. W. K. Cattell; *m* 1951, Agnes Jean Hardy; three *s* one *d*. *Educ:* Royal Grammar Sch., Colchester. Served Regular Army, 1939-58; psc 1954; despatches, Malaya, 1957; retired as Major, RA. Asst Director, London Engineering Employers' Assoc., 1958-60; Group Industrial Relations Officer, H. Stevenson & Sons, 1960-61; Director, Personnel and Manufacturing, Rootes Motors Ltd, 1961-68. Managing Director, Humber Ltd, Chm., Hills Precision Diecasting Ltd, Chm., Thrupp & Maberly Ltd, 1965-68. Dir, Manpower and Productivity Svcs, Dept of Employment and Productivity, 1968-70. AMN Federation of Malaya, 1958. *Recreations:* tennis, fishing. *Address:* Little Cheveney, Yalding, Kent. *T:* Hunton 365. *Club:* United Service.

**CATTERMOLE, Mrs James;** *see* Mitchell, Dr J. E.

**CATTERMOLE, Lancelot Harry Mosse,** ROI 1938; painter and illustrator; *b* 19 July 1898; *s* of Sidney and Josephine Cattermole; *g s* of George Cattermole, painter in water-colours and oils; *m* 1937, Lydia Alice Winifred Coles, BA; no *c*. *Educ:* Holmsdale House Sch., Worthing, Sussex; Odiham Grammar Sch., Hants. Senior Art Scholarship to Slade Faculty of Fine Art, University of London, and Central School of Arts and Crafts, London, 1923-26. Exhibitor RA, ROI, RBA, RP, etc., and Provincial Art Galleries. Signs work Lance Cattermole. *Recreations:* acting, reading and bridge. *Address:* Horizon, Palmers Way, 17 High Salvington, Worthing, Sussex. *T:* Worthing 60436.

**CATTO,** family name of **Baron Catto.**

**CATTO,** 2nd Baron, *cr* 1936, of Cairncatto; Bt *cr* 1921; **Stephen Gordon Catto;** a Managing Director, Morgan Grenfell & Co. Ltd; Director: Australian United Corporation Ltd (Melbourne); Australian Mutual Provident Society (London Board); The General Electric and English Electric Cos Ltd; Andrew Yule & Co. Ltd (Calcutta); Yule Catto & Co. Ltd; News of the World Organisation Ltd, and other companies; Member, London Advisory Committee, Hong Kong & Shanghai Banking Corporation; *b* 14 Jan. 1923; *o s* of 1st Baron Catto and Gladys Forbes, *d* of Stephen Gordon; *S* father 1959; *m* 1st, 1948, Josephine Innes (marr. diss. 1965), *er d* of G. H. Packer, Alexandria, Egypt; two *s* two *d*; 2nd, 1966, Margaret, *d* of J. S. Forrest, Dilston, Tasmania; one *s* one *d*. *Educ:* Eton; Cambridge Univ. Served with RAFVR, 1943-47. Member, Advisory Council, ECGD, 1959-65; part-time Mem., London Transport Bd, 1962-68. *Heir:* *s* Hon. Innes Gordon Catto, *b* 7 Aug. 1950. *Address:* Morgan Grenfell & Co. Ltd, 23 Great Winchester Street, EC2; 41 William Mews, Westminster, SW1. *Clubs:* Oriental; Melbourne (Australia).

**CATTON, Bruce;** Senior Editor, American Heritage Magazine, since 1959; *b* 9 Oct. 1899; *s* of George R. Catton; *m* 1925, Hazel Cherry; one *s*. *Educ:* Oberlin Coll. Newspaper Reporter in Cleveland, Boston and Washington, 1920-41. Asst Director of Information, US War Production Board, 1942-43, Director, 1944-45; Director of Information, US Dept of Commerce, 1945-47; Special Assistant, Secretary of Commerce, 1948; Asst Director of Information, US Dept of the Interior, 1950-52. Pulitzer Prize for history, 1954; National Book Award, 1954. Hon. LittD; Oberlin, 1956; Harvard, 1957; Northwestern Univ., 1957. Hon. LLD, Knox Coll., 1958. *Publications:* The War Lords of Washington, 1948; Mr Lincoln's Army, 1951; Glory Road, 1952; A Stillness at Appomattox, 1953; U. S. Grant and the American Military Tradition, 1954; Banners at Shenandoah, 1955; This Hallowed Ground, 1956; America Goes to War, 1958; Grant Moves South, 1960; The American Heritage Picture History of the Civil War, 1960; The Coming Fury, 1961; Terrible Swift Sword, 1963; Never Call Retreat, 1965; Grant Takes Command, 1969. *Recreations:* virtually none, except for unadorned loafing in the north woods of Michigan every summer. *Address:* 551 Fifth Avenue, New York, NY 10017, USA. *Clubs:* Players, Century, Lotos (New York).

**CAULFEILD,** family name of **Viscount Charlemont.**

**CAULFIELD, Hon. Sir Bernard,** Kt 1968; **Hon. Mr Justice Caulfield,** Judge of the High Court of Justice, Queen's Bench Division, since 1968; *b* 24 April 1914; 5th *s* of late John Caulfield and late Catherine Quinn, Haydock, Lancs; *m* 1953, Sheila Mary, *o d* of Dr J. F. J. Herbert; three *s* one *d*. *Educ:* St Francis Xavier's Coll.; University of Liverpool. LLB 1938, LLM 1940; Solicitor, 1940. Army Service, 1940-46; Home and MEF; Commnd, Dec. 1942, RAOC; released with Hon. rank of Major. Barrister-at-Law, Lincoln's Inn, 1947; joined Midland Circuit, 1949; QC 1961; Recorder of Coventry, 1963-68; Dep. Chairman QS, County of Lincoln (Parts of Lindsey), 1963-;

Leader, Midland Circuit, 1965-68; Member, General Council of Bar, 1965-68. Bencher, Lincoln's Inn, 1968. *Address:* Royal Courts of Justice, WC2.

**CAULTON, Rt. Rev. Sidney Gething,** MA; *b* 24 Aug. 1895; *s* of John Caulton, Ripley, Derby; *m* 1933, Beryl, *d* of Jospeh Guylee, Feilding, New Zealand; one *s*. *Educ:* St Chad's Coll., Durham (Exhibitioner). BA (2nd class Th.), 1922; MA 1927. Deacon, 1922; Priest, 1923; Curate of St Dunstan, Liverpool, 1922-29; Missionary in Diocese of Melanesia, 1927-37; Vicar of Whakatane, 1937-43; of Onehunga, 1943-46; of St Mary's Cathedral, Auckland, and Dean of Auckland, 1946-47; Bishop of Melanesia, 1947-54; Vicar of Northcote, 1954-57; Asst Bishop of Auckland, NZ, 1955-64; Vicar of St George, Epsom, NZ, 1957-62; Asst Bishop of Southwark, 1964-68. *Address:* 103 Churchill Road, Rothesay Bay, Auckland, NZ.

**CAUNTER, Brigadier John Alan Lyde,** CBE 1941; MC and Bar; *b* 17 Dec. 1889; *er s* of R. L. Caunter, MD, FRCS, and Mrs R. L. Caunter (*née* W. J. von Taysen); *m* 1920, Helen Margaret Napier (*d* 1942), *er d* of late Sir Walter Napier; one *s* one *d*; *m* 1945, Muriel Lilian Murphy (*née* Hicks). *Educ:* Uppingham Sch.; RMC, Sandhurst. 2nd Lieut Gloucestershire Regt, 1909; served European War, 1914-19 (MC and Bar, despatches, Brevet of Major); taken prisoner, 1914; escaped from Germany, July, 1917; operations France, Flanders, Macedonia, Turkey; Iraq Campaign, 1920-21; psc Camberley, 1923; transferred Royal Tank Corps, 1924; DAAG Rhine Army, 1925 and 1926; GSO2 Northern Command, 1927-28; DAA and QMG, N. Ireland, 1929-33; Bt. Lieut-Colonel, 1933; Lieut-Colonel, 1935; Comd 1st Bn (Light) Royal Tank Corps, 1935-39; Colonel and Temp. Brigadier 1939; Comdr 1st Army Tank Bde July-Oct. 1939; Cmdr Armoured Bde, Egypt, 1939-41; W. Desert Campaign, 1940-41, as Comdr 4th Armoured Bde (CBE, despatches); BGS, GHQ, India, 1941-43; retired 1944. Member Cornwall CC, 1952-67; Member for GB, Internat. Cttee of Internat. Game Fish Association (HQ at Fort Lauderdale, Fla, USA). *Publications:* 13 Days, 1918 (An Escape from a German Prison Camp); Shark Angling in Great Britain, 1961. *Recreations:* fishing, shooting, (present); past: Rugby football, cricket, hockey. *Address:* The Brentons, Hannafore, Looe, Cornwall. *T:* Looe 2427. *Club:* Shark Angling of Great Britain (President and Founder);(HQ at Looe).

**CAUSEY, Professor Gilbert,** FRCS; Sir William Collins Professor of Anatomy, Royal College of Surgeons, Professor of Anatomy, University of London, and Conservator of Hunterian Museum, 1952-70; *b* 8 Oct. 1907; 2nd *s* of George and Ada Causey; *m* 1935, Elizabeth, *d* of late F. J. L. Hickinbotham, JP, and of Mrs Hickinbotham; two *s* three *d*. *Educ:* Wigan Grammar Sch.; University of Liverpool. MB, ChB (1st Hons.), 1930; MRCS, LRCP, 1930; FRCS 1933; DSc 1964. Gold Medallist in Anatomy, Surgery, Medicine, and Obstetrics and Gynæcology; Lyon Jones Scholar and various prizes. Member of Anatomical and Physiological Societies. Asst Surgeon, Walton Hospital, Liverpool, 1935; Lecturer in Anatomy, University College, London, 1948; Rockefeller Foundation Travelling Fellow, 1950. FZS John Hunter Medal, 1964. *Publications:* The Cell of Schwann, 1960; Electron Microscopy, 1962; contributions to various scientific texts and journals. *Recreation:* music. *Address:* Orchard Cottage, Bodinnick-by-Fowey, Cornwall. *T:* Polruan 433. *Club:* Athenæum.

**CAUSLEY, Charles Stanley;** poet; teacher; broadcaster; *b* Launceston, Cornwall, 24 Aug. 1917; *o s* of Charles Causley and Laura Bartlett. *Educ:* Launceston National Sch.; Horwell Grammar Sch.; Launceston Coll.; Peterborough Training Coll. Served on lower-deck in Royal Navy (Communications Branch), 1940-46. Literary Editor, 1953-56, of BBC's West Region radio magazines Apollo in the West and Signature. Awarded Travelling Scholarships by Society of Authors, 1954 and 1966. FRSL 1958. Member Arts Council Poetry Panel, 1962-66. Awarded Queen's Gold Medal for Poetry, 1967. *Publications:* Hands to Dance, 1951; Farewell, Aggie Weston, 1951; Survivor's Leave, 1953; Union Street, 1957; Peninsula (ed), 1957; Johnny Alleluia, 1961; Dawn and Dusk (ed), 1962; Penguin Modern Poets 3 (with George Barker and Martin Bell), 1962; Rising Early (ed), 1964; Modern Folk Ballads (ed), 1966; Underneath the Water, 1968; Figure of 8, 1969; Figgie Hobbin, 1970. Contributor to many anthologies of verse in Great Britain and America. *Recreations:* the theatre; European travel; the re-discovery of his native town; playing the piano with expression. *Address:* 2 Cyprus Well, Launceston, Cornwall. *T:* Launceston 2731.

**CAUTE, (John) David,** MA, DPhil; writer; Reader in Social and Political Theory, Brunel University; *b* 16 Dec. 1936; *m* 1961, Catherine Shuckburgh; two *s*. *Educ:* Edinburgh Academy; Wellington; Wadham Coll., Oxford. Scholar of St Antony's Coll., 1959. Spent a year in the Army in the Gold Coast, 1955-56, and a year at Harvard Univ. on a Henry Fellowship, 1960-61. Fellow of All Souls Coll., Oxford, 1959-65. Visiting Professor, New York Univ. and Columbia Univ., 1966-67. *Plays:* Songs for an Autumn Rifle, staged by Oxford Theatre Group at Edinburgh, 1961; The Demonstration, Nottingham Playhouse, 1969. *Publications:* At Fever Pitch (novel), 1959 (Authors' Club Award and John Llewelyn Rhys Prize, 1960); Comrade Jacob (novel), 1961; Communism and the French Intellectuals, 1914-1960, 1964; The Left in Europe Since 1789, 1966; The Decline of the West (novel), 1966; Essential Writings of Karl Marx (ed), 1967; Fanon, 1970. *Address:* André Deutsch Ltd, 105 Great Russell Street, WC1.

**CAUTHERY, Harold William,** CB 1969; Director and Secretary and Member of the Land Commission since 1967; *b* 5 May 1914; *s* of Joseph Cauthery, Manchester; *m* 1938, Dorothy Constance, *d* of George E. Sawyer, Sutton Coldfield; one *s* one *d* (and one *d* decd). *Educ:* Bishop Vesey's Grammar Sch., Sutton Coldfield; Christ's College, Cambridge. Asst Inspector of Taxes, Inland Revenue, 1936; Asst Principal, Ministry of Health, 1937; Instructor-Lieut, RN, 1942-45; Principal, Ministry of Health, 1944; Asst Secretary: Ministry of Health, 1950; Ministry of Housing and Local Government, 1951; Under-Secretary, Min. of Transport, 1960-66; Dep. Secretary Min. of Land and Natural Resources, 1966. *Publications:* Parish Councillor's Guide, 10th Edition, 1958. *Recreations:* music (piano and double bass), gardening. *Address:* 1 Whetstone Green, Hexham, Northumberland. *T:* Hexham 3525.

**CAVALCANTI, Alberto de Almeida;** Film Director and Producer; Lecturer in the Film Department of Theatre Arts Faculty, University of California; *b* Rio de Janeiro, 6 Feb. 1897. *Educ:* Fine Arts Sch., Geneva (Architecture). Came into Films as an Art Director, then became Director in the French

Avant-Garde Group. Came to England in 1934 and worked in the Documentary School. Back to fictional films at Ealing in 1940. Films directed in France, 1924-34: Rien que les heures, En Rade, La P'tite Lilie, Yvette, Le Capitaine Fracasse, etc. Films directed or produced in Great Britain, 1934-46: North Sea, Men of the Lightship, The Foreman Went to France, Went the Day Well, Half-Way House, Champagne Charlie, Dead of Night, The Life and Adventures of Nicholas Nickleby, They Made Me a Fugitive, The First Gentleman, For Them That Trespass. Brazilian productions: Caicara, Painel, Terra é sempre Terra and Volta Redonda; directed: Simão o Caolho; O Canto do Mar, A Mulher de Verdade. Continental films: Brecht's Herr Puntila und sein Knecht Matti; Windrose (with Joris Ivens); Les Noces Venitiennes. Thus Spake Theodor Herzl (in Israel). For the Stage: Blood-wedding (in Spain); Fuente Ovejuna (in Israel); La Nuit. French TV, Les Empailles. *Publication:* Filme e realidade. *Address:* 26 rue des Abbesses, Paris XVIII, France. *Club:* Garrick.

**CAVALLERA, Rt. Rev. Charles;** *see* Marsabit, Bishop of, (RC).

**CAVAN,** 12th Earl of, *cr* 1647; **Michael Edward Oliver Lambart,** TD; DL; Baron Cavan, 1618; Baron Lambart, 1618; Viscount Kilcoursie, 1647; *b* 29 Oct. 1911; *o s* of 11th Earl of Cavan and Audrey Kathleen (*d* 1942), *o d* of late A. B. Loder; *S* father 1950; *m* 1947, Essex Lucy, *o d* of Henry Arthur Cholmondeley, Shotton Hall, Hadnall, Shropshire; two *d* (and one *d* decd). *Educ:* Radley College. Served War of 1939-45, Shropshire Yeomanry (despatches). Lieut-Colonel Commanding Shropshire Yeomanry, 1955-58. DL Salop, 1959. *Address:* Waters Upton Manor, Wellington, Shropshire. *T:* Great Bolas 384.

**CAVANAGH, John Bryan;** Dress Designer; Chairman and Managing Director, John Cavanagh Ltd; *b* 28 Sept. 1914; *s* of Cyril Cavanagh and Anne (*née* Murphy). *Educ:* St Paul's School. Trained with Captain Edward Molyneux in London and Paris, 1932-40. Joined Intelligence Corps, 1940, Captain (GS, Camouflage), 1944. On demobilisation, 1946, travelled throughout USA studying fashion promotion. Personal Assistant to Pierre Balmain, Paris, 1947-51; opened own business, 1952; opened John Cavanagh Boutique, 1959. Elected to Incorporated Society of London Fashion Designers, 1952 (Vice-Chm., 1956-59). Took own complete Collection to Paris, 1953; Gold Medal, Munich, 1954. *Recreations:* the theatre, swimming, travelling. *Address:* (home) 11 Pembridge Gardens, W2; (business) 26 Curzon Street, W1.

**CAVE;** *see* Verney-Cave.

**CAVE, Alexander James Edward,** OFM Tertiary; MD, DSc, FRCS, FLS, Emeritus Professor of Anatomy, University of London; *b* Manchester, 13 Sept. 1900; *e s* of late John Cave and of Teresa Anne d'Hooghe; *m* 1st, 1926, Dorothy M. Dimbleby (*d* 1961); one *d*; 2nd, 1970, Catherine Elizabeth FitzGerald. *Educ:* Manchester High Sch.; Victoria University of Manchester. MB, ChB (distinction Preventive Medicine) 1923; MD (commendation) 1937; DSc, 1944; FRCS, 1959; DSc London, 1967. Senior Demonstrator (later Lecturer) in Anatomy, University of Leeds, 1924-34; Senior Demonstrator of Anatomy and Curator of Anatomical Museum, University College, London, 1934-35; Asst Conservator of Museum (1935-46), Arnott Demonstrator (1936-46) and Professor of Human and Comparative Anatomy (1941-46), Royal College of Surgeons of England; Prof. of Anatomy, St Bartholomew's Hospital Medical Coll., University of London, 1946-67, now Member Board Governors. Arris and Gale Lecturer, 1932, 1941; Hunterian Trustee; Stopford Lecturer, 1967; Morrison Watson Research Fellow, 1961-70. Late Examiner in Anatomy, University of London, Royal University of Malta, Universities of Cambridge and Ireland. Primary FRCS and English Conjoint Board; Pres. Linnean Society; Fellow (late Vice-Pres. and Council Member) Zoological Society; Life-Member (late Council Mem., Hon. Secretary and Recorder, Vice-Pres.) Anatomical Society of Great Britain and Ireland; Member Ray Society; Member American Assoc. of Physical Anthropologists; *Publications:* various papers on human and comparative anatomy, physical anthropology and medical history. *Address:* 18 Orchard Avenue, Finchley, N3. *T:* 01-346 3340. *Club:* Athenæum.

**CAVE, Sir Charles (Edward Coleridge),** 4th Bt, *cr* 1896; *b* 28 Feb. 1927; *o s* of Sir Edward Charles Cave, 3rd Bt, and Betty, *o d* of late Rennell Coleridge, Salston, Ottery St Mary; *S* father 1946; *m* 1957, Mary Elizabeth, *yr d* of John Francis Gore, *qv*; four *s*. *Educ:* Eton. Lieut The Devonshire Regt, 1946-48. CC Devon, 1955-64; High Sheriff of Devonshire, 1969. FRICS. *Heir: s* John Carles Cave, *b* 8 Sept. 1958. *Address:* Sidbury Manor, Sidmouth, Devon. *T:* Sidbury 207.

**CAVE, Richard Guy,** MC 1944; Chief Executive and Managing Director, Smiths Industries Ltd, since 1968; Director, Thomas Tilling Ltd; *b* 16 March 1920; *s* of William Thomas Cave and Gwendolyn Mary Nichols; *m* 1957, Dorothy Gillian Fry; two *s* two *d*. *Educ:* Tonbridge; Gonville and Caius Coll., Cambridge. Joined Smiths Industries Ltd, 1946; Man. Dir, Motor Accessory Div., 1963. *Recreation:* sailing. *Address:* Thamescote, Chiswick Mall, W4. *T:* 01-994 8017.

**CAVE, Richard Philip,** MVO 1969; Fourth Clerk at the Table (Judicial), House of Lords, since 1965; Principal Clerk, Judicial Department, House of Lords, since 1959; Taxing Officer of Judicial Costs, House of Lords, since 1957; Crown Examiner in Peerage Cases since 1953; Secretary, Association of Lieutenants of Counties and Custodes Rotulorum, 1946-59, and since 1964; Founder and Chairman, Multiple Sclerosis Society of Great Britain and Northern Ireland, since 1953; Vice-President, International Federation of Multiple Sclerosis Societies, since 1967; *b* 26 April 1912; *s* of late Charles John Philip Cave and late Wilhelmina Mary Henrietta (*née* Kerr); *m* 1936, Margaret Mary, *e d* of Francis Westby Perceval; one *s*. *Educ:* Ampleforth Coll.; Trinity Coll., Cambridge (MA); Herts Institute of Agriculture; College of Estate Management. A Gold Staff Officer, Coronation of HM King George VI, 1937. Agent for Earl of Craven's Hamstead Marshall Estate, 1938-39. Royal Wilts Yeomanry (L. Corp.), 1939-40; The Rifle Bde (Captain; Officer i/c Cols. Comdt's Office, KRRC and Rifle Bde), 1940-45. Member Working Cttee, Society for Relief of Distress, 1955; a Governor, Nuffield Nursing Homes Trust, 1969. Gold Medal, Royal English Forestry Society, 1939; Silver Medal, RASE, 1939. Kt of St Gregory the Great, 1966. *Publications:* Elementary Map Reading, 1941; Article, Peerages and Dignities, in Atkin's Encyclopedia of Court Forms in Civil Proceedings, 1968. *Recreations:* hunting, shooting, cricket, hill-walking, collecting map postcards. *Address:* Watergate, Ham

Common, Richmond, Surrey. *T:* 01-940 8014. *Club:* Royal Commonwealth Society.

**CAVE-BROWNE-CAVE, Sir Robert,** 16th Bt, *cr* 1641; President of Cave & Co. Ltd, and of Seaboard Chemicals Ltd; *b* 8 June 1929; *s* of 15th Bt, and Dorothea Plewman, *d* of Robert Greene Dwen, Chicago, Ill; *S* father 1945; *m* 1954, Lois Shirley, *d* of John Chalmers Huggard, Winnipeg, Manitoba; one *s* one *d*. *Educ:* University of BC (BA 1951). *Heir: s* John Robert Charles Cave-Browne-Cave, *b* 22 June 1957. *Address:* 6087 Wiltshire Street, Vancouver, BC. *Clubs:* Royal Vancouver Yacht, Capilano Golf and Country (BC).

**CAVENAGH-MAINWARING, Captain Maurice Kildare,** DSO 1940; Royal Navy retired; joined Simpson (Piccadilly) Ltd, 1961, Advertising Manager since 1963; *b* 13 April 1908; *yr s* of Major James Gordon Cavenagh-Mainwaring, Whitmore Hall, Whitmore, Staffordshire; *m* Iris Mary, *d* of late Colonel Charles Denaro, OBE; one *s*. *Educ:* RN College, Dartmouth. Joint Services Staff College, 1951-52; HMS St Angelo and Flag Captain to Flag Officer, Malta, 1952-54; President, Second Admiralty Interview Board, 1955-56; Naval Attaché, Paris, 1957-60. ADC to the Queen, 1960. Retired from RN, 1960. Cross of Merit Sovereign Order, Knights of Malta, 1955; Comdr Légion d'Honneur, 1960. *Address:* 47 Cadogan Gardens, SW3. *T:* 01-584 7870. *Club:* United Service.

**CAVENDISH,** family name of **Baron Chesham,** of **Duke of Devonshire,** and of **Baron Waterpark.**

**CAVENDISH-BENTINCK,** family name of **Duke of Portland.**

**CAVENDISH-BENTINCK, Major Sir Ferdinand (William),** KBE, *cr* 1956; CMG 1941; Officier de la Couronne (Belgian); Member of: East African Production and Supply Council; East African Advisory Council on Agriculture, Animal Industry and Forestry; East African Agricultural, Forestry and Veterinary Research Organisations Committee; Chairman and Founder of Kenya Association, 1932; *b* 4 July 1889; *s* of late Frederick W. Cavendish-Bentinck; *heir-pres.* to 7th Duke of Portland, *qv*; *m* 1950, Gwyneth, *widow* of Colonel D. A. J. Bowie, RA. *Educ:* Eton; RMC, Sandhurst; Germany. Late 60th Rifles (KRRC); served Malta, India, and European War, 1914-18 (severely wounded, despatches); GSO War Office; Company Comdr, and later Asst Adjutant RMC, Sandhurst; worked for Vickers Ltd on Continent with HQ Brussels, 1923-24; Private Secretary to Governor of Uganda, 1925-27; Hon. Secretary Kenya Convention of Associations, 1930. Member for Agriculture and Natural Resources in Kenya Government, 1945-55; Speaker of Kenya Legislative Council, 1955-60 (MLC, and MEC, Kenya, 1934-60). Chairman of: Tanganyika League and African Defence Federation, 1938; Agricultural Production and Settlement Board, Kenya, 1939-45; Timber Controller for East Africa, 1940-45; Member of East African Civil Defence and Supply Council, 1940-45; a Delegate to Delhi Conference, 1940; contested South Kensington, 1922; Member of many Commissions and Select Cttees. *Publications:* articles on African subjects. *Address:* PO Box 7311, Nairobi, Kenya. *T:* Nairobi 5402. *Clubs:* Turf, Bath, Beefsteak; Muthaiga (Nairobi).

**CAVENDISH-BENTINCK, Victor Frederick William,** CMG 1942; Chairman: Bayer (UK) Ltd; FBA Pharmaceuticals Ltd; Baywood Chemicals Ltd; Bayer Dyestuffs Ltd, England; Bayer Chemicals Ltd; Director: Philip Hill Investment Trust, Ltd; Metrogate Property Holdings Ltd; Austro-Chematom Kernbrennstoff-GmbH (Austria); Farbenfabriken Bayer AG (Germany); NUKEM Nuklear-Chemie und-Metallurgie GmbH (Germany); SA Métallurgie et Mécanique Nucléaires (Belgium); *b* 18 June 1897; *s* of late Frederick Cavendish-Bentinck: *m* 1st, 1924 (marr. diss.); one *d* (one *s* decd); 2nd, 1948, Kathleen Elsie, *yr d* of Arthur Barry, Montreal. *Educ:* Wellington Coll., Berks. Attaché HM Legation, Oslo, 1915; 2nd Lieut, Grenadier Guards, 1918; 3rd Sec., HM Legation, Warsaw, 1919; transferred to Foreign Office, 1922; attended Lausanne Conference, 1922-23; 2nd Sec., HM Embassy, Paris, 1923; HM Legation, The Hague, 1924; transferred to Foreign Office, 1925; attended Locarno Conference, 1925; 1st Sec., HM Embassy, Paris, 1928; HM Legation, Athens, 1932; HM Embassy, Santiago, 1934; transferred to Foreign Office, 1937; Asst Under-Sec. of State, 1944; Ambassador to Poland, 1945-47; retired from Diplomatic Service, 1947. Chm. Council British Nuclear Forum. Grosses Verdienstkreuz (Germany). *Recreations:* travelling and antiques. *Address:* 21 Carlyle Square, SW3. *T:* 01-352 1258. *Clubs:* Turf, Beefsteak.

**CAWADIAS, Alexander Pocnagioti,** OBE; MD; FRCP; Knight Commander Royal Greek Order of Phoenix: Chairman Editorial Board, British Journal of Clinical Practice; Hon. Physician St John Clinic and Institute of Physical Medicine; Professor Emeritus of Medicine, Athens University (lecturing at the University, 1963); Fellow Academy of Athens; FRSM; *s* of Professor P. Cawadias, Gen. Dir of Antiquities and Fine Arts, Greece; *m* 1914, Sophie (*d* 1967), *d* of C. Constantinides, Alexandria; one *s* one *d*. *Educ:* Gymnasium, Athens; Universities of Paris, Bonn, and Heidelberg; Post-Graduate studies, London. Asst Physician, Paris teaching hospitals, 1910; Chief of Medical Clinic and Lecturer on Internal Diseases, Paris Univ., 1912; Senior Physician and Lecturer on Internal Diseases, Evangelismos Hospital, Athens, 1914; Mem. International Health Board, 1920; Pres. Royal Society of Medicine, Section of History, 1937-39; Pres. International Congress of Neo-Hippocratic Medicine, 1938; Thomas Vicary Lecturer, Royal College of Surgeons, 1941; during European War, 1914-18, Consulting Physician to the Greek Army, and major with Forces on Macedonian Front in charge of epidemics (Greek Military Cross, despatches); during War of 1939-45, Pres. Greek Red Cross. *Publications:* Diseases of the Intestines, 1927; Modern Therapeutics of Internal Diseases, 1931; Hermaphroditos, The Human Inter-sex, 1943; Clinical Endocrinology, 1947; and numerous papers on internal and constitutional diseases. *Recreations:* music and ballet. *Address:* 22 Academy Street, Athens, Greece.

**CAWDOR,** 6th Earl *cr* 1827; **Hugh John Vaughan Campbell,** FRICS; Baron Cawdor, 1796; Viscount Emlyn, 1827; *b* 6 Sept. 1932; *er s* of 5th Earl Cawdor, TD, FSA, and of Wilma Mairi, *e d* of late Vincent C. Vickers; *S* father, 1970; *m* 1957, Cathryn, 2nd *d* of Maj.-Gen. Sir Robert Hinde, *qv*; two *s* three *d*. *Educ:* Eton; Magdalen Coll., Oxford; Royal Agricultural Coll., Cirencester. High Sheriff of Carmarthenshire, 1964. *Heir: s* Viscount Emlyn, *qv*. *Address:* Golden Grove House, Broad Oak, Carmarthenshire. *Clubs:* St James', Pratt's.

**CAWLEY,** family name of **Baron Cawley.**

**CAWLEY,** 3rd Baron, *cr* 1918; **Frederick Lee Cawley,** 3rd Bt, *cr* 1906; Barrister-at-Law; *b* 27 July 1913; *s* of 2nd Baron and Vivienne, *d* of Harold Lee, Broughton Park, Manchester; *S* father 1954; *m* 1944, Rosemary Joan, *y d* of late R. E. Marsden; six *s* one *d*. *Educ:* Eton; New Coll., Oxford. BA Nat. Science 1935, MA 1942. Called to the Bar, Lincoln's Inn, 1938. Served War of 1939-45, Capt. RA Leicestershire Yeomanry (wounded). Mem. Woking UDC, 1949-57; Dep.-Chm. of Cttees, House of Lords, 1958-67. *Recreations:* gardening, shooting. *Heir: s* Hon. John Francis Cawley, *b* 28 Sept. 1946. *Address:* Openwood, Bagshot Road, Worplesdon, Guildford. *T:* 2191; New Court, Temple, EC4. *T:* 01-353 1769.

**CAWLEY, Sir Charles (Mills),** Kt 1965; CBE; Chief Scientist, Ministry of Power, 1959-67; a Civil Service Commissioner, 1967-69; *b* 17 May 1907; *s* of John and Emily Cawley, Gillingham, Kent; *m* 1934, Florence Mary Ellaline, *d* of James Shepherd, York; one *d*. *Educ:* Sir Joseph Williamson's Mathematical Sch., Rochester; Imperial Coll. of Science and Technology (Royal College of Sci.). ARCS, BSc (First Cl. Hons in Chem.), DIC; MSc; PhD; FRIC; FInstPet; DSc(London); FInstF; FRSA; Fellow, Imperial Coll. of Science and Technology. Fuel Research Station, DSIR, 1929-53. Imperial Defence Coll., 1949. A Dir, Headquarters, DSIR, 1953-59. Chm., Admiralty Fuels and Lubricants Advisory Cttee, 1957-64. Melchett Medal, Inst. of Fuel, 1968. *Publications:* Papers in various scientific and technical journals. *Address:* Springfield, Longlands, Worthing, Sussex.

**CAWLEY, Rev. Dr Frederick;** Principal Emeritus, Spurgeon's College, London, since Sept. 1955 (Principal, 1950-55); *b* Sept. 1884; *s* of S. R. and S. A. Cawley; *m* 1917, Mary Gold Coutts. *Educ:* Spurgeon's Coll., London; New Coll., Edinburgh. BA, BD (London); PhD (Edinburgh). Missionary: Baptist Missionary Soc., India, 1912-22 and Trinidad, West Indies, 1922-26. Baptist Minister: Falkirk, Scotland, 1926-35 and Camberwell, London, 1935-38; Penge, 1940-46. Senior Tutor, Spurgeon's Coll., London, 1938-47; Vice-Principal, 1947-50. Senator, University of London, 1951-56. *Publication:* The Transcendence of Jesus Christ, 1933. *Recreations:* motoring and fishing. *Address:* 23 Hillpark Road, Edinburgh EH4 7AN.

**CAWTHORN, Maj.-Gen. Sir Walter (Joseph),** Kt 1958; CB 1946; CIE 1943; CBE 1941; retired; *b* 18 June 1896; *s* of William Cawthorn, Rokeby, Victoria, Australia; *m* 1927, Mary Wyman Varley (*née* Gillison); (one *s* decd). *Educ:* Melbourne. Served European War, 1914-18, with 22 Battalion Australian Imperial Force, in Gallipoli, Egypt, France, and Belgium (wounded, despatches, 1914-15 Star, GS and Victory Medals); NW Frontier of India, 1930; Mohmand, 1935 (medal and clasp); War of 1939-45, Egypt, 1939-41 (CBE, despatches); Head of Middle East Intelligence Centre, 1939-41; Dir of Intelligence, India Command, 1941-45 and Dep Dir of Intelligence South-East Asia Command, 1943-45 (CIE, CB, despatches); Mem. India Delegation to UN conference, San Francisco, 1945; Representative of Comdr-in-Chief in India on Joint Chiefs of Staff in Australia, 1945-47; Dep. Chief of Staff, Pakistan Army, 1948-51; retd 1951. Dir, Jt Intelligence Bureau, Dept of Defence, Australia, 1952-54; High Comr for Austr. in Pakistan, 1954-58; High Commissioner for Australia in Ottawa, 1959-60; Dept of External Affairs, 1961-69. *Address:* Little Tocknells, Kallista, Victoria 3791, Australia. *Clubs:* United Service; Melbourne (Melbourne).

**CAWTHRA, Rear-Adm. Arthur James,** CB 1966; Admiral Superintendent, HM Dockyard, Devonport, 1964-66; *b* 30 Sept. 1911; *s* of James Herbert Cawthra, MIEE, and Margaret Anne Cawthra; *m* 1959, Adrien Eleanor Lakeman Tivy, *d* of Cecil B. Tivy, MCh, Plymouth; one *s* (and one *s* decd). *Educ:* abroad. Joined Royal Navy, 1930; Imperial Defence Course, 1956; HMS Fisgard, 1958-59; Dir Underwater Weapons, Admiralty, 1960-63. Capt. 1955; Rear-Adm. 1964. *Recreation:* sailing. *Address:* Lower Island, Blackawton, Totnes, Devon. *Club:* United Service.

**CAYFORD, Dame Florence Evelyn,** DBE 1965; JP; Mayor, London Borough of Camden, 1969; *b* 14 June 1897; *d* of George William and Mary S. A. Bunch; *m* 1923, John Cayford; two *s*. *Educ:* Carlton Road Sch.; St Pancras County Secondary Sch., Paddington Technical Institute. Alderman, LCC, 1946-52; Member: LCC for Shoreditch and Finsbury, 1952-64; GLC (for Islington) and ILEA, 1964-67. Chairman: Hospital and Medical Services Cttee LCC, 1948; (Health Cttee). Division 7, 1948-49, Division 2 in 1949; Health Cttee, 1953-60; Welfare Cttee, 1965, of LCC; Metropolitan Water Bd, 1966-67 (Vice-Chm., 1965-66). mem. Hampstead Borough Council, 1937-65 (Leader of Labour Group, 1945-58), Councillor for Kilburn until 1945, Alderman, 1945-65; Chairman: (Hampstead), Maternity and Child Welfare Cttee, 1941-45, Juvenile Court Panel, 1950-62; Dep. Mayoress, Camden Borough Council, 1967-68. Probation Cttee, 1959-; Leavesden Hosp. Management Cttee, 1948-63; Harben Secondary Sch., 1946-61. Member: Co-operative Political Party (ex-Chm. and Sec.); Co-operative Soc.; Labour Party; National Institute for Social Work Training, 1962-65; Min. of Health Council for Training of Health Visitors, 1962-65; Min. of Health Council for Training in Social Work, 1962-; Chm. of the London County Council, 1960-61. JP, Co. London, 1941-. Freeman of Borough of Hampstead, 1961. Noble Order, Crown of Thailand, 3rd Class, 1964. *Address:* 26 Hemstal Road, Hampstead, NW6. *T:* 01-624 6181.

**CAYLEY, Sir Digby (William David),** 11th Bt *cr* 1661; Assistant Classics Master, Portsmouth Grammar School, since 1968; *b* 3 June 1944; *s* of Lieut-Comdr W. A. S. Cayley, RN (*d* 1964) (*g g s* of 7th Bt), and of Natalie M. Cayley, BA; *S* kinsman, 1967; *m* 1969, Christine Mary Gaunt, BA, *o d* of late D. F. Gaunt and of Mrs A. T. Gaunt, Burley-in-Wharfedale, Yorks. *Educ:* Malvern Coll.; Downing Coll., Cambridge. *Recreations:* small bore shooting, archæology. *Heir: uncle* Cuthbert John Cayley [*b* 9 June 1907; *m* 1938, Cecil Lilla Iris, *d* of late Adm. George Cuthbert Cayley, CB]. *Address:* 61A Osborne Road, Southsea, Hants. *T:* Portsmouth 26746.

**CAYLEY, Henry Douglas,** OBE 1946; Chief General Manager, National & Grindlays Bank Ltd, 1964-69 (Director since 1966); Director, William Brandt Sons & Co. Ltd; *b* 20 Jan. 1904; *s* of late Cyril Henry Cayley, MD; *m* 1940, Nora Innes Paton, *d* of Nigel F. Paton; one *s* two *d*. *Educ:* Epsom Coll. Joined National Bank of India Ltd, London, 1922; Eastern Staff, 1926; Dep. Exchange Controller, Reserve Bank of India, 1939-48; rejoined National Bank of India, 1948; appointed to London Head Office, 1952; Asst Gen. Manager 1957, Dep. Gen. Manager 1960, Chief Gen. Manager 1964, National & Grindlays Bank Ltd. *Recreations:* gardening, walking. *Address:*

54 Southwood Park, Highgate Village, N6. *T:* 01-340 9580. *Clubs:* Oriental, Lansdowne.

**CAYZER,** family name of **Baron Rotherwick.**

**CAYZER, Hon. Anthony;** *see* Cayzer, Hon. M. A. R.

**CAYZER, Sir James Arthur,** 5th Bt, *cr* 1904; *b* 15 Nov. 1931; *s* of Sir Charles William Cayzer, 3rd Bt, MP, and Beatrice Eileen, *d* of late James Meakin and Emma Beatrice (later wife of 3rd Earl Sondes); *S* brother, 1943. *Educ:* Eton. *Heir: cousin,* Sir Nicholas Cayzer, *qv. Address:* Kinpurnie Castle, Newtyle, Angus. *T:* Newtyle 207. *Club:* Carlton.

**CAYZER, Hon. (Michael) Anthony (Rathborne);** shipowner; *b* 28 May 1920; 2nd *s* of 1st Baron Rotherwick; *m* 1952, Hon. Patricia Browne, *er d* of 4th Baron Oranmore and Browne, *qv,* and of Hon. Mrs Hew Dalrymple; three *d. Educ:* Eton; Royal Military Coll., Sandhurst. Commissioned Royal Scots Greys: served 1939-44 (despatches). Dep. Chairman: British & Commonwealth Shipping Co. Ltd; Union-Castle Mail Steamship Co. Ltd; Chairman, British Island Airways Ltd; Director: Cayzer, Irvine & Co. Ltd; Clan Line Steamers Ltd; Overseas Containers Ltd; Caledonia Investments Ltd; Sterling Industries Ltd, and other cos. Pres. Inst. of Shipping and Forwarding Agents, 1963-65. Pres., Chamber of Shipping of the United Kingdom, 1967. Past Mem. Mersey Docks and Harbour Bd. Chm. Liverpool Steamship Owners Assoc., 1956-57. Trustee, Nat. Maritime Museum, 1968-. *Address:* Great Westwood, Kings Langley, Herts. *T:* Kings Langley 62296. *Clubs:* Boodle's, Cavalry, Royal Aero, Royal Yacht Squadron.

**CAYZER, Sir (William) Nicholas,** 2nd Bt, *cr* 1921; Chairman of: British & Commonwealth Shipping Co. Ltd; Clan Line Steamers Ltd; Cayzer, Irvine & Co. Ltd; Caledonia Investments Ltd; Union-Castle Mail Steamship Co. Ltd and associated cos; Scottish Lion Insurance Co. Ltd; Deputy Chairman, Air Holdings Ltd; Director: Sun Alliance & London Insurance Ltd; Securities Agency; *b* 21 Jan. 1910; *s* of Sir August Cayzer, 1st Bt, and Ina Frances (*d* 1935), 2nd *d* of William Stancombe, Blounts Ct, Wilts; *S* father, 1943; *m* 1935, Elizabeth Catherine, *d* of late Owain Williams and *g d* of Morgan Stuart Williams, Aberpergwm and St Donat's Castle, Glamorgan; two *d. Educ:* Eton; Corpus Christi Coll., cambridge. Chm. Liverpool Steamship Owners Association, 1944-45; Pres. Chamber of Shipping of the UK, 1949; Pres. Inst. of Marine Engineers, 1963. Chm. Gen. Council of Brit. Shipping, 1959; Sometime Mem. Mersey Dock and Harbour Board; sometime Mem. National Dock Labour Board. Prime Warden, Shipwrights Company, 1969. *Heir: b* Major Bernard Gilbert Stancomb Cayzer, *b* 1914. *Address:* The Grove, Walsham-le-Willows. Suffolk. *T:* Walsham-le-Willows 263; 95j Eaton Square, SW1. *T:* Belgravia 5551. *Clubs:* City of London, Brooks's.

**CAZALET, Vice-Adm. Sir Peter Grenville Lyon,** KBE 1955; CB 1952; DSO 1945, and Bar 1949; DSC 1940; retired; Chairman, Navy League, 1960-67; President Association of Retired Naval Officers; *b* 29 July 1899; *e s* of late Grenville William Cazalet and Edith Lyon; *m* 1928, Elise, *d* of late J. P. Winterbotham, Cheltenham, Glos; four *s. Educ:* Dulwich. Midshipman in HMS Princess Royal, 1918; Lieut 1921; Comdr 1934; Capt. 1941; Rear-Adm. 1950; Vice-Adm. 1953. Served War of 1939-45 (despatches four times); Commanded: HMS Durban, 1941-42; 23rd Destroyer Flotilla, 1944-45; HMS London, 1949; Commodore Administration, Mediterranean Fleet, 1945-46; Dep. Dir of Plans, Naval Staff, 1946-47; Commodore RN Barracks, Chatham, 1949-50; Chief of Staff to Flag Officer Central Europe, 1950-52; Allied Chief of Staff to C-in-C Mediterranean, 1953-55; Flag Officer Comdg Reserve Fleet, 1955-56; retd 1957. ADC to the King, 1950. King Haakon VII Cross, 1946. *Address:* Forest Cottage, Duddleswell Manor, Sussex. *T:* Nutley 2879. *Club:* Army and Navy.

**CAZALET, Peter Victor Ferdinand,** DL; trainer of racehorses; *b* 15 Jan. 1907; *s* of late William Marshal Cazalet; *m* 1st, 1932, Leonora (*d* 1944), *o d* of Leonard Rowley; one *s* one *d*; 2nd, 1949, Zara (who *m* 1st, 1940, Major Hon. Alexander R. G. Strutt, now 4th Baron Belper; one *s*), *yr d* of late Sir Harry Mainwaring, Bt; two *s* (and one *s* decd). *Educ:* Eton; Christ Church, Oxford. Amateur rider, 1930-38; trainer, 1939; served War of 1939-45; RA 1939-40. Welsh Guards, 1940-45. JP 1954-69, High Sheriff, 1960, DL 1961, Kent. *Recreations:* ball games. *Address:* Fairlawne, Tonbridge, Kent. *T:* Plaxtol 326; 14 Eaton Row, SW1. *T:* 01-235 1826. *Clubs:* White's, Buck's.

**CAZALET-KEIR, Thelma,** CBE 1952; *d* of late W. M. Cazalet; *m* 1939, David (*d* 1969), *s* of Rev. Thomas Keir. Member of London County Council for East Islington, 1925-31; Alderman of County of London, 1931; contested by-election, East Islington, 1931; MP (Nat. C) East Islington, 1931-45; Parliamentary Private Secretary to Parliamentary Secretary to Board of Education, 1937-40; Parliamentary Secretary to Ministry of Education, May 1945. Member of Committee of Enquiry into conditions in Women's Services, 1942; of Committee on Equal Compensation (Civil Injuries), 1943; Chairman London Area Women's Advisory Committee, Conservative and Unionist Associations, 1943-46. Chairman Equal Pay Campaign Committee; Member Cost of Living Committee; Member Arts Council of Great Britain, 1940-49; Member Executive Committee of Contemporary Art Society; Member Transport Users Consultative Committee for London, 1950-52. A Governor of the BBC, 1956-61. Member Committee Royal UK Beneficent Association, 1962. President Fawcett Society, 1964. *Publication:* From the Wings, 1967. *Recreations:* music, lawn tennis. *Address:* Flat J, 90 Eaton Square, SW1. *T:* 01-235 7378.

**CAZENOVE, Philip Henry de Lerisson,** TD 1944; Major, Northamptonshire Yeomanry (retired); Stockbroker (retired); *b* 21 Dec. 1901; *yr s* of late Major Edward Cazenove; *m* 1942, Aurea Ethelwyn, *d* of C. I. L. Allix; three *s* one *d. Educ:* Eton. High Sheriff of Northants, 1949. *Recreations:* hunting, shooting, rackets, squash rackets, tennis, lawn tennis, golf. *Address:* Cottesbrooke, Northampton. *T:* Creaton 203. *Clubs:* White's, Bath, Pratt's, Royal Aero, MCC, All England Lawn Tennis.

**CEADEL, Eric Bertrand,** MA; University Librarian, University of Cambridge, since 1967; Fellow of Corpus Christi College, Cambridge, since 1962; *b* London, 7 Feb. 1921; *o s* of late Albert Edward Ceadel, FSS, and of Bertha Margaret (*née* Blackall); *m* 1946, Pamela Mary Perkins; three *s. Educ:* Bec Sch., London; Christ's Coll., Cambridge (Entrance Schol.). 1st cl. hons Class. Tripos, Pts I and II; BA 1941, MA 1945; Charles Oldham Class. Schol., 1941. Suffolk Regt, then Intelligence Corps, Capt., 1941-45. A. H. Lloyd Research Schol., Christ's Coll., 1945-47; Univ. Lectr in Japanese, University of Cambridge, 1947-67;

Vis Prof. of Japanese, University of Michigan, 1960, 1961; Sen. Tutor, Corpus Christi Coll., Cambridge, 1962-66; Sec., 1948-52, and Chm., 1963-65, Faculty Bd of Oriental Studies; Mem. Coun. of Senate, 1965-68; Curator in Oriental Literature, Univ. Library, Cambridge, 1954-67; Syndic of Univ. Library, 1961-67. *Publications:* (contrib. and ed.) Literatures of the East, 1953; Classified Catalogue of Modern Japanese Books in Cambridge University Library, 1962; articles in Class. Quarterly, Asia Major and other jls. *Address:* 20 Porson Road, Cambridge. *T:* 50053.

**CECIL,** family name of **Baron Amherst of Hackney, Marquess of Exeter, Baron Rockley,** and **Marquess of Salisbury.**

**CECIL, Lord David;** *see* Cecil, Lord E. C. D. G.

**CECIL, Lord (Edward Christian) David (Gascoyne);** CH 1949; Goldsmiths' Professor of English Literature, Oxford, 1948-70; Fellow of New College, Oxford, 1939-69, now Emeritus Fellow; *b* 9 April 1902; *yr s* of 4th Marquess of Salisbury, KG, GCVO; *m* 1932, Rachel, *o d* of late Sir Desmond MacCarthy; two *s* one *d*. *Educ:* Eton; Christ Church, Oxford. Fellow of Wadham Coll., Oxford, 1924-30. Trustee of National Portrait Gallery, 1937-51. Pres., The Poetry Soc., 1947-48; Rede Lecturer, Cambridge Univ., 1955. Hon. LittD Leeds, 1950; Hon. DLit London, 1957; Hon LLD Liverpool, 1951; St Andrews, 1951; Hon. DLitt Glasgow, 1962. *Publications:* The Stricken Deer, 1929; Sir Walter Scott, 1933; Early Victorian Novelists, 1934; Jane Austen, 1935; The Young Melbourne, 1939; Hardy, the Novelist, 1943; Two Quiet Lives, 1948; Poets and Story-Tellers, 1949; Lord M., 1954; The Fine Art of Reading, 1957; Max, 1964; Visionary and Dreamer: Two Poetic Painters–Samuel Palmer and Edward Burne-Jones, 1969; (ed) The Bodley Head Max Beerbohm, 1970. *Address:* 28 Charlbury Road, Oxford. *T:* 56933; Red Lion House, Cranborne, Wimborne, Dorset. *T:* Cranborne 244.

**CECIL, Henry;** *see* Leon, H. C.

**CECIL, Lord Martin;** *see* Cecil, Lord W. M. A.

**CECIL, Rev. Canon Philip Henry;** Vicar of Potton with Cockayne Hatley since 1967; Hon. Canon of St Albans 1965; *b* 27 July 1918; *s* of Rev. Henry Cecil and Elizabeth Cecil (*née* Spall); *m* 1945, Jessie Marie Barrick; one *s* four *d*. *Educ:* King Edward VII Sch., Sheffield; City of London Sch.; King's Coll., London (BD 2nd Class Hons, AKC 1940); Westcott House, Cambridge. University Prizes: Junior Wordsworth Prize for Latin, 1938; Bishop Collins Memorial Prize for Ecclesiastical History, 1939; Plumptre Prize for English Literature, 1940. Curate, Leeds Parish Church, 1941-45; Precentor and Sacrist, Durham Cath., 1945-48; Dean of Belize, Brit. Honduras, 1948-52; Rector, St Luke's, Old Street, 1952-54; Lectr, St Olave's, Hart Street, 1953-63, 1968-; Rector, Wormley, Herts, 1956-60; Proctor in Convocation, 1959-64; Exam. Chap. to Bp of St Albans 1960-; Dir Ordinands, dio. St Albans, 1960-63; Vicar, Bushey Heath, Herts, 1960-63; Principal, Bishops' Coll., Cheshunt, 1963-67, and Public Preacher Dio. St Albans. Limborough Lectr, St Botolph's, Aldgate, 1960-68; Queen's Chapel of the Savoy, 1969-. *Recreations:* listening to music, motoring, reading and writing comic verse, amateur theatricals, billiards, snooker. *Address:* Potton Vicarage, Sandy, Beds. *T:* Potton 261. *Club:* One Hundred and Eleven (Bray).

**CECIL, Robert,** CMG 1959; Reader in Contemporary German History, Reading University, since 1968; *b* 25 March 1913; *s* of late Charles Cecil; *m* 1938, Kathleen, *d* of late Col C. C. Marindin, CBE, DSO; one *s* two *d*. *Educ:* Wellington Coll.; Caius Coll., Cambridge. BA Cantab. 1935, MA 1961. Entered HM Foreign Service, 1936; served in Foreign Office, 1939-45; First Sec., HM Embassy, Washington, 1945-48; assigned to Foreign Office, 1948; Counsellor and Head of American Dept, 1951; Counsellor, HM Embassy, Copenhagen, 1953-55; HM Consul-Gen., Hanover, 1955-57; Counsellor, HM Embassy, Bonn, 1957-59; Dir-Gen., British Information Services, New York, 1959-61; Head of Cultural Relations Dept, FO, 1962-67. *Publications:* Levant and other Poems, 1940; Time and other Poems, 1955; Life in Edwardian England, 1969; contrib. to periodicals. *Recreations:* gardening, chess, etc. *Address:* Hambledon, Hants. *T:* Hambledon 669. *Clubs:* Athenæum, Royal Automobile.

**CECIL, V. A. G.;** *see* Gascoyne-Cecil.

**CECIL, Lord (William) Martin Alleyne;** *b* 27 April 1909; 2nd *s* of 5th Marquess of Exeter, KG, CMG (*d* 1956) and *b* and *heir-pres* to 6th Marquess of Exeter, *qv*; *m* 1st, 1934, Edith Lilian De Csanady (*d* 1954); one *s*; 2nd, 1954, Lillian Jane Johnson; one *d* (and one *d* decd). *Educ:* Royal Naval Coll., Dartmouth. *Address:* 100 Mile House, Cariboo Road, British Columbia. *T:* 604-395-2323.

**CECIL-WRIGHT, Air Commodore John Allan Cecil,** AFC, TD; DL; *b* 1886; *s* of Alfred Cecil Wright, Edgbaston; name changed by Deed Poll from Wright to Cecil-Wright, 1957; *m* 1946, Ethne Monica, *y d* of late Dr W. E. Falconar; two *s* (one of whom is by a former marriage). *Educ:* Winchester. 1st Vol. Bn Royal Warwicks Regt, 1905; served European War, 1914-19; joined RFC in 1916; Squadron Leader 605 (County of Warwick) Bomber Squadron, 1926-36; Comdt, Midland Command ATC, 1941-45; Hon. Air Cdre 605 (County of Warwick) Sq. Royal Aux. AF, 1946-55; Hon. Area Rep., RAF Benevolent Fund; Vice-Chm. (Air) Warwicks T & AFA, 1945-54. Dir, Warne Wright & Rowland, Ltd (Chm., 1920-63); Chm. H. J. Gray & Son Ltd; Dir The Decca Navigator Co. Ltd; Mem. Birmingham City Council, 1934-39; MP (Nat. U) Erdington div. of Birmingham, 1936-45; Pres. Erdington Conservative and Unionist Assoc., 1945-55; Pres. Sutton Coldfield Cons. and U. Assoc.; Patron, Aston Div. Cons. and U. Assoc. Mem., Warwicks CC 1958-61; DL, Warwicks, 1933-67; Mem. Exec. Cttee, Animal Health Trust; Pres., Cruft's Dog Show. *Address:* Long Range, Saltgrass Lane, Keyhaven, Lymington, Hants. *T:* Milford-on-Sea 2606; Flat 6, 7 Princes Gate, SW7. *T:* 01-584 4463. *Clubs:* Carlton, Royal Air Force, (Chm.) Kennel; Conservative (Birmingham).

**CELIBIDACHE, Sergiu;** Composer and Guest Conductor to leading Orchestras all over the World; *b* Rumania, 28 June 1912; *s* of Demosthene Celibidache; *m* Maria Celibidache. *Educ:* Jassy; Berlin. Doctorate in mathematics, musicology, philosophy and Buddhist religion. Conductor and Artistic Dir, Berlin Philharmonic Orchestra, 1946-51. Member: Royal Acad. of Music, Sweden; Acad. of Music, Bologna. German Critics' Prize, 1953; Berlin City Art Prize, 1955; Grand Cross of Merit, Federal Republic of Germany, 1954. *Recreations:* skiing, water-skiing. *Address:* c/o Camus, Via Boncompagni 12, Rome, Italy.

**CENTRAL TANGANYIKA, Bishop of,** since 1951; **Rt. Rev. Alfred Stanway;** *b* 9 Sept. 1908; *s* of Alfred Stanway, Millicent, S Australia, and Rosa Dawson; *m* 1939, Marjory Dixon Harrison. *Educ:* Melbourne High Sch.; Ridley Coll., Melbourne; Australian Coll. of Theology (ThL (Hons), 1934); Melbourne Teachers Coll. MA (Lamb), 1951. Diocese of Melbourne; Curate of St Albans, 1935-36; Mission of St James and St John, 1936-37; Diocese of Mombasa: Missionary, Giriama District, 1937-44; Principal Kaloleni Sch., 1938-44; Acting Gen. Sec., Victorian Branch, Church Missionary Soc., 1941; Hon. CF, 1942-46; Missionary, Maseno District, 1944-45; Rural Dean of Nyanza, 1945-47; Examining Chaplain to Bishop of Mombasa, 1945-51; Sec. African Council and African Education Board, Diocese of Mombasa, 1948-50; Commissary to Bishop of Mombasa, 1949-51; Archdeacon and Canon of Diocese of Mombasa, 1949-51. *Recreation:* chess. *Address:* PO Box 15, Dodoma, Tanzania, East Africa; c/o CMS, Cathedral Buildings, Flinders Lane, Melbourne, Vic. 3000, Australia.

**CERAM, C. W.;** *see* Marek, K. W.

**CERF, Bennett;** Chairman, Random House, Inc. since 1965 (President since firm was organized in 1927 until 1965); President, Modern Library Inc., since 1925; Director, RCA Inc., 1966-70; *b* 25 May 1898; *s* of Gustave Cerf and Fredericka Wise; *m* 1940, Phyllis Fraser; two *s*. *Educ:* Columbia Sch. of Journalism. BA Columbia Univ.; BLit Columbia Sch. of Journalism. Columnist for King Features, 1946-; Lecturer, 1946-. Panelist on American "What's My Line". Hon. Dr Lit: Coll. of Puget Sound, 1958; W Maryland Coll., 1966. *Publications:* Try and Stop Me, 1945; Encyclopædia of Modern American Humor, 1955; Reading for Pleasure, 1957; Treasury of Atrocious Puns, 1968; The Sound of Laughter, 1970, etc. *Recreations:* golf, tennis. *Address:* 201 E 50 Street, New York, USA. *T:* Plaza 1-2600. *Clubs:* Dutch Treat, Overseas Press, Raffles (New York).

**CHABAN-DELMAS, Jacques Pierre Michel;** Commander Légion d'Honneur; Prime Minister of France (apptd June) 1969; *b* Paris, 7 March 1915; *s* of Pierre Delmas and Georgette Delmas (*née* Barrouin); *m* 1947 (2nd marr.), Mme Geoffray (*née* Marie Antoinette Iōn) (*d* 1970); two *s* two *d*. *Educ:* Lycée Lakanal, Sceaux; Faculté de Droit, Paris; Ecole Libre des Sciences Politiques (Dip.). Licencié en droit. Journalist with l'Information, 1933. Served War of 1939-45: Army, 1939-40 (an Alpine Regt); joined the Resistance; *nom de guerre* of Chaban added (Compagnon de la Libération, Croix de Guerre); attached to Min. of Industrial Production, 1941; Inspector of Finance, 1943; Brig.-Gen., 1940; Nat. Mil. Deleg. (co-ord. mil. planning) Resistance, 1944; Inspector Gen. of Army, 1944; Sec-Gen., Min. of Inf., 1945. Deputy for Gironde (Radical), 1946. Mayor of Bordeaux, 1947-69. Leader of Gaullist group (Républicans Sociaux) in Nat. Assembly, 1953-56; also Mem. Consultative Assembly of Council of Europe; Minister of State, 1956-57; Minister of Nat. Defence, 1957-58; Pres., Nat. Assembly, 1958-69; etc. *Address:* Hotel Matignon, 57 rue de Varenne, Paris 7e, France.

**CHACKSFIELD, Air Vice-Marshal Sir Bernard,** KBE 1968 (OBE 1945); CB 1961; *b* 13 April 1913; *s* of Edgar Chacksfield Ilford, Essex; *m* 1937, Myrtle, *d* of Walter Matthews, Rickmansworth, Herts; two *s* two *d* (and one *s* decd). *Educ:* Co. High Sch., Ilford; RAF, Halton; RAF Coll., Cranwell. NW Frontier, 1934-37; UK, India, Burma, Singapore, 1939-45 (OBE); Air Min., 1945-48; Western Union (NATO), Fontainebleau, 1949-51; RAF Staff Coll., 1951-53; Fighter Command, 1954-55; Director, Guided Weapons (trials), Min. of Supply, 1956-58; IDC, 1959; SASO, Tech. Trg Comd, RAF, 1960; AOC No. 22 Group RAF Technical Training Command, 1960-62; Comdt-Gen., RAF Regiment and Inspector of Ground Defence, 1963-68; retired 1968. CEng, FRAeS, 1968. Order of Cloud and Banner with special rosette (Chinese), 1941. *Recreations:* scouting (HQ Comr, Air Activities, 1959-70; Chief Comr for England, 1970), sailing, fencing (Pres. RAF Fencing Union, 1963-68), gliding, walking, model aircraft (Pres. Soc. Model Aircraft Engs, GB, 1965-70), modern Pentathlon (Pres., RAF Pentathlon Assoc., 1963-68), shooting (Chm. RAF Small Arms Assoc., 1963-68); swimming; youth work, amateur dramatics. *Address:* Windwhistle, Bourne End, Bucks. *T:* Bourne End 20829. *Clubs:* Royal Air Force, Upper Thames Sailing.

**CHADDOCK, Prof. Dennis Hilliar,** CBE 1962; Professor of Engineering Design, University of Technology, Loughborough, since 1966; *b* 28 July 1908; *m* 1937, Stella Edith Dorrington; one *s* one *d* (and one *s* decd). *Educ:* University Coll. Sch. Engineering Apprentice, Sa Adolph Saurer, Switzerland, 1927-30; Research Engineer, Morris Commercial Cars Ltd, Birmingham, 1930-32; Asst Road Motor Engineer, LMS Railway Co., Euston, 1932-41. BSc (Eng) Hons, London, 1933; MSc (eng) London, 1938. HM Forces, 1941-46; Inspecting Officer, Chief Inspector of Armaments, 1941-43; Dep. Chief Inspecting Officer, 1943-45; Chief Design Officer, Armament Design Estabt, 1945-46; relinquished commission with rank of Lieut-Col, 1946. Superintendent, Carriage Design Branch of Armament Design Estabt, 1947-50; Imperial Defence Coll., 1951; Dep. Chief Engineer, 1952-55; Principal Superintendent, Weapons and Ammunition Div., Armament Research and Development Estabt, 1955-62; Dir of Artillery Research and Development, Ministry of Defence (Army) 1962-66. *Recreations:* model engineering; dinghy sailing. *Address:* 20 Paddock Close Quorndon, Leics. *T:* Quorn 2607.

**CHADWICK, Albert Edward,** CMG 1967; Director, formerly Chairman, Gas and Fuel Corporation of Victoria, since 1963; *b* 15 Nov. 1897; *s* of Andrew and Georgina Chadwick; *m* 1924, Thelma Marea Crawley; one *s* one *d*. *Educ:* Tungamah State Sch., Vic.; University High Sch., Vic. European War, 1914-18; served 1915-19 (MSM; despatches 1918); War of 1939-45: served RAAF, 1940-45 (Group Capt.). Engr, Robt Bryce & Co. Ltd, 1920-25; Lubricant Manager, Shell Co. of Aust. Ltd, 1925-35; Asst Gen. Man., Metropolitan Gas Co. Melbourne, 1935-51; Asst. Gen. Man., subseq. Gen. Man., Gas and Fuel Corp. of Vic., 1951-63. Chm., Overseas Telecommunications Commn (Australia), 1962-68. *Publications:* various technical and economic works. *Recreations:* golf, cricket, football, racing. *Address:* 413 Toorak Road, Toorak, Vic 3142, Australia. *T:* Melbourne 24-1163. *Clubs:* Athenæum, Naval and Military, Victorian Amateur Turf (Melbourne); Riversdale Golf; (Pres. 1964-) Melbourne Cricket.

**CHADWICK, Gerald William St John, (John Chadwick),** CMG 1961; First Director, Commonwealth Foundation, since 1966; Assistant Under-Secretary of State, CRO, 1960; *b* 28 May 1915; *s* of late John F. Chadwick, Solicitor; *m* 1938, Madeleine Renée Boucheron; two *s*. *Educ:* Lancing; St

Catharine's Coll., Cambridge (open Exhibitioner). Asst Principal, Colonial Office, 1938; transf. Dominions Office, following demobilisation, 1940; Sec., Parl. Mission to Newfoundland, 1943; further missions to Newfoundland and Bermuda, 1946 and 1947; attended United Nations, 1949; Office of UK High Commission, Ottawa, 1949-52; Counsellor, British Embassy, Dublin, 1952-53; UK Delegn to NATO, Paris, 1954-56; Asst Sec., CRO, 1956. *Publications:* The Shining Plain, 1937; Newfoundland: Island into Province, 1967; International Organisations, 1969; contrib. to: A Decade of the Commonwealth 1955-64, 1966; various articles. *Recreations:* travel; food. *Address:* 11 Cumberland House, Kensington Road, W8. *Club:* Athenæum.

**CHADWICK, Very Rev. Henry,** DD; FBA 1960; Dean of Christ Church, Oxford, since 1969; Regius Professor of Divinity and Canon of Christ Church, Oxford, 1959-69; *b* 23 June 1920; 3rd *s* of late John Chadwick, Barrister, Bromley, Kent, and Edith (*née* Horrocks); *m* 1945, Margaret Elizabeth, *d* of late W. Pemell Brownrigg; three *d. Educ:* Eton (King's Scholar); Magdalene Coll., Cambridge (Music Schol.). John Stewart of Rannoch Scholar, 1939. MusB. Asst Master, Wellington Coll., 1945; University of Camb.: Fellow of Queens' Coll., 1946-58; Hon. Fellow, 1958; Junior Proctor, 1948-49. Hon. Fellow, Magdalene Coll., 1962. Hulsean Lecturer, 1956; Visiting Prof., University of Chicago, 1957; Gifford Lectr, St Andrews Univ., 1962-64. Editor (with H. F. D. Sparks), Journal of Theological Studies, 1954-. Member, Jt Permanent Commn of the Roman Catholic Church and the Anglican Communion, 1969-. Forwood Lecturer, University of Liverpool, 1961; Hewett Lecturer, Union Theological Seminary, 1962; Birkbeck Lecturer, Cambridge, 1965. For. Hon. Mem., Amer. Acad. Arts and Sciences. Hon. DD, Glasgow and Yale; Hon. Teol Dr, Uppsala. *Publications:* Origen, Contra Celsum, 1953; Alexandrian Christianity (with J. E. L. Oulton), 1954; Lessing's Theological Writings, 1956; The Sentences of Sextus, 1959; The Circle and the Ellipse, 1959; St Ambrose on the Sacraments, 1960; The Vindication of Christianity in Westcott's Thought, 1961; Early Christian Thought and the Classical Tradition, 1966; The Early Church (Pelican), 1968; The Treatise on the Apostolic Tradition of St Hippolytus of Rome, ed G. Dix (rev. edn), 1968; The Enigma of St Paul, 1969; Reflections on Conscience, 1969. *Recreation:* music. *Address:* Christ Church, Oxford.
*See also Sir John Chadwick, W. O. Chadwick, Vice-Adm. Sir A. W. R. McNicoll.*

**CHADWICK, Sir James,** CH 1970; Kt 1945; FRS 1927; MSc (Vict); PhD (Cantab); Hon. DSc Reading, Dublin, Leeds, Oxford, Birmingham, Exeter, McGill; Hon. LLD Liverpool, Edinburgh; Fellow of Gonville and Caius Coll., Cambridge; *b* 20 Oct. 1891; *e s* of J. J. Chadwick; *m* 1925, Aileen, *e d* of H. Stewart-Brown, Liverpool; *twin d. Educ:* Manchester Secondary Sch.; Universities of Manchester, Berlin, and Cambridge. Formerly Lyon Jones Prof. of Physics in the University of Liverpool; Master of Gonville and Caius Coll., Camb., 1948-58. Mem., Pontifical Academy of Sciences; Assoc. Acad. Royal Belgium; Foreign Member; German Order Pour le Mérite; K. Ned Akad.Wet., Amsterdam; K. Danske Vid. Selskab.; Corr. Mem. Sächs. Akad. Wiss., Leipzig; Hon. Fellow: Inst. of Physics; Manchester Coll. of Science and technology; Amer. Physical Soc. Awarded Hughes Medal of Royal Society, 1932; Mackenzie Davidson Medal, 1932; Copley Medal, 1950; Nobel Laureate (Physics), 1935; US Medal for Merit, 1946; Trasenster Medal, 1946; Melchett Medal, 1946; Faraday Medal, 1950; Franklin Medal of Franklin Institute, Philadelphia, 1951; Guthrie Medal, IPPS, 1967. *Publications:* Radioactivity and Radioactive Substances, 1921; Radiations from Radioactive Substances (with Lord Rutherford and C. D. Ellis), 1930; various papers on radio-activity and connected problems. *Address:* 16 Grange Court, Pinehurst, Cambridge CB3 9BD. *T:* Cambridge 59326. *Clubs:* Athenæum; University (Liverpool).

**CHADWICK, John;** *see* Chadwick, G. W. St J.

**CHADWICK, John,** FBA 1967; MA; Perceval Maitland Laurence Reader in Classics, University of Cambridge, since 1969; Collins Fellow, Downing College, Cambridge, since 1960; *b* 21 May 1920; *yr s* of late Fred Chadwick; *m* 1947, Joan Isobel Hill; one *s. Educ:* St Paul's Sch.; Corpus Christi Coll., Cambridge. Editorial Asst, Oxford Latin Dictionary, Clarendon Press, 1946-52; Asst Lectr in Classics, 1952-54, Lectr in Classics, 1954-66, Reader in Greek Language, 1966-69, Univ. of Cambridge. Corresp. Mem., Deutsches Archäologisches Inst., 1957; Hon. Dr of Philosophical Sch., University of Athens, 1958; Hon. Dr, Université Libre de Bruxelles, 1969; Medal of J. E. Purkyně Univ., Brno, 1966. *Publications'* (jtly) The Medical Works of Hippocrates, 1950; (jtly) Documents in Mycenaean Greek, 1956; The Decipherment of Linear B, 1958, 2nd edn 1968 (trans. into 9 languages); The Pre-history of the Greek Language (in Camb. Ancient History), 1963; edns of Linear B Tablets, articles in learned jls on Mycenaean Greek. *Recreation:* travel. *Address:* Downing College, Cambridge; 52 Gough Way, Cambridge. *T:* Cambridge 56864.

**CHADWICK, Sir John (Edward),** KCMG 1967 (CMG 1957); Permanent UK Representative to OECD, Paris, since 1969; *b* 17 Dec. 1911; *e s* of late John Chadwick; *m* 1945, Audrey Lenfestey; one *s* two *d. Educ:* Rugby; Corpus Christi Coll., Cambridge (MA). Dept of Overseas Trade, 1934; Eastern Group Supply Council, Simla, 1941; Commercial Secretary, Washington, 1946-48; First Sec., Tel Aviv, 1950-53; Counsellor (Commercial) Tokyo, 1953-56; Minister (Economic), Buenos Aires, 1960-62, (Commercial), Washington, 1963-67; Ambassador to Rumania, 1967-68. *Address:* 69 Avenue Victor Hugo, Paris 16. *Clubs:* Travellers'; The Brook (New York).
*See also Very Rev. Henry Chadwick, W. O. Chadwick, Vice-Adm. Sir A. W. R. McNicoll.*

**CHADWICK, Lynn Russell,** CBE 1964; sculptor since 1948; *b* 24 Nov. 1914; *s* of late Verner Russell Chadwick and Marjorie Brown Lynn; *m* 1942, Charlotte Ann Secord; one *s*; *m* 1959, Frances Mary Jamieson (*d* 1964); two *d. Educ:* Merchant Taylors' Sch. Architectural Draughtsman, 1933-39; Pilot, FAA, 1941-44. Exhibitions have been held in London, in various galleries, and by the Arts Council; his works have also been shown in numerous international exhibitions abroad, including Venice Biennale, 1956. *Works in public collections:* Great Britain: Tate Gallery, London; British Council, London; Arts Council of Great Britain; Victoria and Albert Museum; Pembroke Coll., Oxford; City Art Gallery, Bristol; Art Gallery, Brighton; Whitworth Art Gallery, University of Manchester; France: Musée National D'Art Moderne, Paris; Holland: Boymans van Beuningen Museum, Rotterdam; Germany: Municipality of Recklinghausen; Staatliche Graphische Sammlung, Munich; Staatische

Kunstmuseum, Duisburg; Sweden: Art Gallery, Gothenburg; Belgium: Musées Royaux des Beaux-Arts de Belgique, Brussels; Italy: Galleria D'Arte Moderna, Rome; Museo Civico, Turin; Australia: National Gallery of SA, Adelaide; Canada: National Gallery of Canada, Ottawa; Museum of Fine Arts, Montreal; USA: Museum of Modern Art, New York; Carnegie Institute, Pittsburgh; University of Michigan; Albright Art Gallery, Buffalo; Art Institute, Chicago; Chile: Inst. de Artes Contemporáneas, Lima. *Address:* Lypiatt Park, Stroud, Glos.

**CHADWICK, Nora Kershaw,** CBE 1961; MA, FSA; FBA 1956; DLitt (Hon. Wales), 1958; DLitt (Hon., National University of Ireland), 1959; LLD (Hon., University of St Andrews), 1963; Hon. Life Fellow Newnham College, Cambridge, since 1958; *b* 28 Jan. 1891; *e d* of James Kershaw and Emma Clara Kershaw (*née* Booth); *m* 1922, Professor Hector Munro Chadwick (*d* 1947), Prof. of Anglo-Saxon, University of Cambridge; no *c*. *Educ:* Private School in Southport, Lancs; Newnham Coll., Cambridge. Medieval and Modern Langs. Tripos, Cl. II, 1913; Medieval and Modern Langs Tripos, (Part II, English Literature), Cl. I, 1914. Temp. post as Lecturer in English Language and Asst Lecturer in English Literature, University of St Andrews, 1914-19; returned to Cambridge, 1919, research work as a private student until marriage; continued writing and research work till the present day. Research Fellow, Newnham Coll., 1941-44; University Lecturer in the Early History and Culture of the British Isles, University of Cambridge, 1950-58. Director of Studies in Anglo-Saxon and Celtic subjects, in Newnham Coll., 1950-59, Girton Coll., 1951-62, Cambridge; O'Donnell Lecturer in Celtic Studies, Universities of Edinburgh, 1959, Wales, 1960, Oxford, 1961; Riddell Memorial Lecturer, University of Durham, 1960; Lecturer to British Academy, The Colonization of Brittany from Celtic Britain, 1965 (publ. 1966). *Publications:* Stories and Ballads of the Far Past, 1921; Anglo-Saxon and Norse Poems, 1922; an Early Irish Reader, 1927; Russian Heroic Poetry, 1932; Poetry and Prophecy, 1942; The Beginnings of Russian History, 1945; Poetry and Letters in Early Christian Gaul, 1955. (Ed. and contributor) Studies in Early English History, 1954; (Ed. and contributor) Studies in the Early British Church, 1958; (Ed. and contributor) Celt and Saxon: Studies in the Early British Border, 1963; Celtic Britain, 1963; The Age of the Saints in the Early Celtic Church, 1964; The Druids, 1966; The Celtic Realms (with Myles Dillon), 1967; (in collaboration with Professor H. M. Chadwick) The Growth of Literature, 3 vols, 1932-40; contributor to The Heritage of Early Britain, 1952; Irish Sagas (ed. Myles Dillon), 1959 (Dublin); Wales Through the Ages (ed. A. J. Roderick), 1959; Early Brittany, 1969; Celtic Britain, 1969; contrib. to learned journals. *Recreation:* exploring pre-Conquest Britain. *Address:* 7 Causewayside, Cambridge. *T:* Cambridge 55550.

**CHADWICK, Owen;** *see* Chadwick, W. O.

**CHADWICK, Sir R. Burton;** *see* Burton-Chadwick.

**CHADWICK, Rt. Rev. William Frank Percival;** *see* Barking, Bishop of.

**CHADWICK, (William) Owen;** Master of Selwyn College, Cambridge, since 1956, and Regius Professor of Modern History, since 1968; Vice-Chancellor, Cambridge University, 1969-71; Chairman: Trustees of University College, Cambridge, since 1965; Archbishops' Commission on Church and State, since 1966; *b* 20 May 1916; 2nd *s* of late John Chadwick, Barrister, Bromley, Kent, and Edith (*née* Horrocks); *m* 1949, Ruth Romaine, *e d* of B. L. Hallward, *qv*; two *s* two *d*. *Educ:* Tonbridge; St John's Coll., Cambridge. Asst Master at Wellington Coll., 1942-46; Fellow of Trinity Hall, Cambridge, 1947-56 (Dean, 1949-56); Hulsean Lecturer, 1949-50; Birkbeck Lecturer in Ecclesiastical History, 1956; Dixie Professor of Ecclesiastical History, 1958-68. DD 1955. FBA 1962. Hon. Fellow of Trinity Hall; Hon. Fellow of St John's Coll., Cambridge. Hon. DD St Andrews; Hon. DLitt, Kent. *Publications:* John Cassian, 1950; The Founding of Cuddesdon, 1954; From Bossuet to Newman, 1957; Western Asceticism, 1958; Creighton on Luther, 1959; Mackenzie's Grave, 1959; The Mind of the Oxford Movement, 1960; Victorian Miniature, 1960; The Reformation, 1964; The Victorian Church, 1966; ed. (with G. F. Nuttall) From Uniformity to Unity 1662-1962, 1962; contrib. to Studies in Early British History, 1954; articles and reviews in learned journals. *Recreations:* walking, music; Cambridge XV versus Oxford, 1936-38. *Address:* Master's Lodge, Selwyn College, Cambridge.
*See also Very Rev. Henry Chadwick, Sir John Chadwick, Vice-Adm. Sir A. R. W. McNicoll.*

**CHADWYCK-HEALEY, Sir Edward Randal,** 3rd Bt, *cr* 1919; MC 1917, bar to MC 1943; *b* 22 Jan. 1898; *e s* of Sir Gerald Chadwyck-Healey, 2nd Bt, CBE, and Mary Verena, *d* of G. A. Watson, East Court, Finchampstead, Berks; *S* father 1955; *m* 1924, Rachel Margaret, TD, formerly Chief Commander, ATS, *d* of L. C. W. Phillips, Unsted Park, Godalming. *Educ:* Eton; RMA, Woolwich. Commissioned RA, 1916; served European War, 1916-18; France, RFA and RHA. Served War of 1939-45: Field Artillery (France, North Africa, Italy); Major 1942; wounded twice. Chairman of Charrington & Co. (Brewers), 1949-59. A Trustee, City Parochial Foundation, since 1943; Prime Warden, Fishmongers' Company, 1953; President London Chamber of Commerce, 1955-57; President Freshwater Biological Assoc., 1960-; a Vice-Pres., Marine Biological Assoc., 1969-. Member, Council of Foreign Bondholders. Belgian Croix de Guerre, 1917. *Recreations:* fishing, shooting, swimming. *Heir:* *b* Charles Arthur Chadwyck-Healey, OBE [*b* 27 May 1910; *m* 1939, Viola, *d* of late Cecil Lubbock; three *s* two *d*]. *Address:* The Mill House, Hook, Basingstoke. *T:* Hook 2436. *Clubs:* Athenæum, Bath; Leander.

**CHAGALL, Marc,** Commander, Legion of Honour, 1965; Artist; *b* Vitebsk, Russia, 7 July 1889; *m* 1915, Bella Rosenfeld (decd); one *s* one *d*. *Educ:* Vitebsk, Russia. Left Russia, 1910, for Paris; returned to Russia, 1914; left again for Paris, 1922. Worked with Ambroise Vollard, famous art editor; left France for America, 1941; returned to France, 1948; has settled in the South of France. Has painted mural paintings besides easel pictures, ballet and theatre settings and costumes; at present working on ceramics; has done over 300 engravings. Retrospective exhibitions in the museums of London (Tate Gallery), Paris, Amsterdam, Chicago, New York, Venice, Jerusalem, and Tel Aviv, 1946-; International Prize for engraving, Biennale Venice, 1948; Erasmus Prize, 1960 (with A. Kokoschka). Salle Chagall founded in Paris Musée d'Art Moderne, 1950. *Publications:* Ma Vie, 1931; Illustrations for: Dead Souls, The Fables of La Fontaine, The Bible, The Arabian Nights, Stories from Boccaccio (verve), Burning Lights and the First Meeting, by Bella Chagall. *Address:* Les Collines, Vence, AM, France. *T:* 316 Vence.

**CHAGLA, Shri Mohomedali Currim,** BA (Oxon); Member of Parliament (Upper House), India; Indian lawyer and administrator; Barrister-at-law; *b* 30 Sept. 1900; *m* 1931, Meher-un-nissa (*d* 1961), *d* of Dharsi Jivraj; two *s* one *d*. *Educ:* St Xavier's High Sch. and Coll., Bombay; Lincoln Coll., Oxford. Hons. Sch. of Modern History, 1922; President: Oxford Asiatic Society, 1921; Oxford Indian Majlis, 1922; called to Bar, Indian Temple, 1922; practised on Original Side of High Court, Bombay, 1922-41; Professor of Constitutional Law, Government Law Coll., Bombay, 1927-30; Hon. Secretary, Bar Council of High Court of Judicature at Bombay, 1931-41; Puisne Judge, Bombay High Court, 1941-47; Chief Justice, 1947-58. Fellow Bombay Univ.; Hon. Fellow Lincoln Coll., Oxford, 1961. Went to New York as one of India's representatives to UNO Session and fought for Cause of Indians in S. Africa, 1946; Vice-Chancellor, Bombay Univ., 1947; President, Asiatic Society of Bombay, 1947-58; Chairman Legal Education Cttee, 1948; Member Law Commission, 1955-58; Shri Krishnarajendra Silver Jubilee Lecturer, 1954. Governor of Bombay, 14 Oct.-10 Dec. 1956. *Ad hoc* Judge International Court of Justice, The Hague, 1957-60; Chairman Life Insurance Corporation Enquiry Commission, 1958; Indian Ambassador to the United States, Mexico and Cuba, 1958-61; Indian High Commissioner in London and Ambassador to Ireland, 1962-63; Education Minister, 1963-66; Minsiter for External Affairs, Government of India, Nov. 1966-Sept. 1967. Member, Sikh Grievances Enquiry Commission, Sept. 1961. Leader, Indian Delegation to: Security Council for Kashmir Debate, 1964 and 1965; Commonwealth Conf., Ottawa, 1964; General Conf., UNESCO, 1964; UN General Assembly, 1967. Hon. LLD: University of Hartford, Hartford; Temple Univ., Philadelphia; Boston Univ., Boston; Dartmouth Coll., Hanover, NH; Leningrad Univ.; Panjab Univ.; Banaras Hindu Univ. *Publications:* The Indian Constitution, 1929; Law, Liberty and Life, 1950; The Individual and the State, 1958; An Ambassador Speaks, 1962; Education and the Nation, 1966; Unity and Language, 1967. *Recreations:* golf and bridge. *Address:* Pallonji Mansion, New Cuffe Parade, Bombay 5, India. *Clubs:* National Liberal; Willingdon (Bombay).

**CHAIN, Professor Sir Ernst (Boris),** Kt 1969; FRS 1949; FRSA 1963; MA Oxon; DrPhil Berlin; PhD Cambridge; DPhil Oxon; Professor of Biochemistry, University of London at Imperial College, since Oct. 1961; *b* Berlin, Germany, 19 June 1906; *s* of Dr Michael Chain, Chemist and industrialist (of Russian origin) and Margarete Eisner; *m* 1948, Dr Anne Beloff, *y d* of S. Beloff, NW3; two *s* one *d*. *Educ:* Luisengymnasium, Berlin; Friedrich-Wilhelm Univ., Berlin (Graduate in chemistry and physiology, 1930). Research in chemical dept of Institute of Pathology, Charité Hospital, Berlin, 1930-33; emigrated from Germany to England in 1933 because of racial persecution; research in the School of Biochemistry, Cambridge, under Sir Frederic Gowland Hopkins, OM, 1933-35; research in the Sir William Dunn School of Pathology, Oxford, since 1935. University Demonstrator and Lecturer in Chemical Pathology, University of Oxford, 1936-48; Scientific Director of International Research Centre for Chemical Microbiology, Istituto Superiore di Sanitã, Rome, 1948-64. Member Société Philomathique, Paris; Hon. Member New York Academy of Medicine; Foreign Member Accademia dei Lincei, Rome, Accademia dei XL; Associé Etranger, Académie Nationale de Médecine, Paris; Foreign Member, Real Acad. de Siencias, Madrid; For. Associate, Acad. des Sciences, Inst. de France; Hon. Life Member, New York Acad. of Science. Initiated, jointly with Professor H. W. Florey (later Lord Florey), work on penicillin that led to the remarkable curative properties of this substance; Nobel prize for Physiology and Medicine, 1945; Harmsworth Memorial Fund, 1946; Berzelius Medal in silver of Swedish Medical Society, 1946; Pasteur Medal of Institut Pasteur, Paris, 1946; Pasteur Medal of Société de Chimie biologique, 1946; Paul Ehrlich Centenary Prize, 1954; Dr hc Université de Liège, 1946, Université de Bordeaux, 1947, University of Turin, 1954, University of Paris, 1959; Albert Einstein College of Medicine, Yeshiva Univ., 1961; Universities of La Plata, Cordoba (Argentina), Montevideo (Uruguay), Brasil, 1962, Chicago, 1965; New York; Philadelphia College of Pharmacy. Hon. Fellow: Royal College of Physicians; Royal Society of Medicine; Institute of Biology; Weizmann Institute of Science, Rehovot, Israel; National Institute of Sciences, India; Societã Chimica Italiana; Microbiological Society of Israel; Finnish Biochemical Society; Fitzwilliam Coll., Cambridge; Societã delle Scienze Farmaceutiche, Milan; Deutsche Pharmazeutische Gesellschaft. Gold Medal for Therapeutics, Worshipful Society of Apothecaries of London, 1927; Marotta Medal (Societã Chimica Italiana); Carl Neuberg Medal. Commandeur de la Légion d'Honneur; Grande Ufficiale al merito della Repubblica Italiana. *Publications:* numerous on biochemical and chemical subjects in scientific journals. *Recreation:* music. *Address:* Department of Biochemistry, Imperial College of Science, Imperial Institute Road, SW7.

**CHAIR, S. de;** *see* de Chair.

**CHALDECOTT, John Anthony;** Keeper, Science Museum Library, South Kensington, since 1961; *b* 16 Feb. 1916; *o s* of Wilfrid James and Mary Eleanor Chaldecott; *m* 1940, Kathleen Elizabeth Jones; one *d*. *Educ:* Latymer Upper Sch., Hammersmith; Brentwood Sch.; Borough Road Coll., Isleworth; University College, London. BSc 1938, MSc 1949. Meteorological Branch, RAFVR, 1939-45 (despatches). Lecturer, Acton Technical Coll., 1945-48; entered Science Museum as Asst Keeper, Dept of Physics, 1949; Deputy Keeper and Secretary to Advisory Council, 1957. Vice-Pres., British Society for the History of Science. *Publications:* Science Museum handbooks; papers on the history of science. *Address:* 19 The Grove, Ratton Village, Eastbourne, Sussex. *Club:* Athenæum.

**CHALFONT,** Baron, *cr* 1964 (Life Peer); **(Alun) Arthur Gwynne Jones,** PC 1964; OBE 1961; MC 1957; *b* 5 Dec. 1919; *s* of Arthur Gwynne Jones and Eliza Alice Hardman; *m* 1948, Dr Mona Mitchell; no *c*. *Educ:* West Monmouth Sch. Commissioned into South Wales Borderers (24th Foot), 1940; served in: Burma 1941-44; Malayan campaign 1955-57; Cyprus campaign 1958-59; various staff and intelligence appointments; psc (Camberley), 1950; JSSC 1958; qual. as Russian interpreter, 1951; resigned commission, 1961, on appt as Defence Correspondent, The Times; frequent television and sound broadcasts on defence and foreign affairs, 1961-64; Minister of State, Foreign and Commonwealth Office, 1964-70; consultant on foreign affairs to BBC Television. UK Permanent Rep. to WEU, 1969. *Publications:* The Sword and The Spirit, 1963; various contribs to Journal Royal United Service Instn and other professional journals. *Recreations:* formerly Rugby football, cricket, lawn tennis; now music and theatre. *Address:* 27 Ormonde Gate, SW3. *Clubs:* Garrick; United Hunts.

**CHALLANS, Mary;** *see* Renault, Mary.

**CHALLE, Général d'Armée Aérienne Maurice;** *b* Le Pontet, Vaucluse, France, 5 Sept. 1905. *Educ:* Ecole Spéciale Militaire de Saint-Cyr, France. Pilot, 1925; Lieut, 1927; Captain, 1932. Ecole Supérieure de Guerre Aérienne, 1937-39. Served War of 1939-45; Sqdn Leader, with 8th Army, 1939-40; GHQ Air, 1940; Comdr, Reconnaissance Group 2/14, Avignon, Sept.-Dec. 1942; organised networks for the Resistance Movement. Lieut-Colonel 2nd Bde de Bombardement "Les Maraudeurs". 1945; Colonel, 1945; attached to Chief of Staff (Air), Cabinet, 1945; Deputy Chief of Staff (Air), 1946; Brig.-General (Air), Moroccan Air Command, 1949; Special Chief of Staff of Secretary of State for Air, 1951; Director, Centre d'Enseignement Supérieur Aérien and Comdr Ecole Supérieure de Guerre Aérienne, 1953; Lieut-General, Chief of Staff of Armed Forces, 1955; General, Flying Corps, 1957; Air Chief Marshal, Asst Chief of Staff of the Army, 1958; Asst C-in-C, Algeria, and Comdr 5th Aerial Region, Oct. 1958; C-in-C, Algeria, Dec. 1958. Member Conseil Supérieur de l'Air, 1958, 1960 (Secretary, 1951, 1952, 1953). Commander-in-Chief, Allied Forces Central Europe (NATO), May 1960-March 1961; led French Army revolt in Algeria, April 1961. Political prisoner, June 1961- (sentenced to 15 years' imprisonment). Grand Cross of Legion of Honour, 1960 (Grand Officer, 1952, Officer, 1945, Chevalier, 1940). War of 1939-45 (French Croix de Guerre). Holds several foreign decorations. *Address:* c/o Minister of Justice, Paris, France.

**CHALLENGER, Frederick,** BSc (London); PhD (Göttingen); DSc (Birmingham); FRIC; Professor of Organic Chemistry, the University, Leeds, 1930-53, Emeritus Professor, 1953; *b* Halifax, Yorks, 15 Dec. 1887; *s* of Rev. S. C. Challenger; *m* 1922, Esther Yates, MA (*d* 1969); two *d*. *Educ:* Ashville Coll., Harrogate; Derby Technical Coll.; University College, Nottingham; University of Göttingen. 1851 Exhibition Scholar, 1910-12; Asst Lecturer in Chemistry, University of Birmingham, 1912; Lecturer in Chemistry, 1915; Senior Lecturer in Organic Chemistry, University of Manchester 1920, Vice-President of Royal Institute of Chemistry, 1948-51. Governor: Giggleswick Sch.; Ashville Coll. *Publications:* Aspects of the Organic Chemistry of Sulphur, 1959; numerous publications, mostly in the Journal of the Chemical Society, Biochemical Journal and Journal of Institute of Petroleum, dealing with organo-metallic compounds (particularly of bismuth), organic thiocyanates and selenocyanates, aromatic substitution, sulphur compounds of shale oil, and other heterocyclic sulphur compounds, microbiological chemistry; mechanism of biological methylation (especially by moulds) as applied to arsenic, tellurium, selenium and sulphur compounds and checked by use of compounds containing isotopic carbon; sulphonium and other compounds of sulphur in plants and animals and in metabolic disturbances (homocystinuria); chemical biography. *Recreation:* walking. *Address:* 19 Elm Avenue, Beeston, Nottingham. *T:* Nottingham 257686.

**CHALLIS, Margaret Joan,** MA; Headmistress of Queen Anne's School, Caversham, since 1958; *b* 14 April 1917; *d* of R. S. Challis and L. Challis (*née* Fairbairn). *Educ:* Girton Coll., Cambridge. BA Hons., English Tripos, 1939, MA, 1943, Cambridge. English Mistress: Christ's Hospital, Hertford, 1940-44; Dartford Grammar School for Girls, 1944-45; Cheltenham Ladies' Coll., 1945-57. Housemistress at Cheltenham Ladies' Coll., 1949-57. *Recreations:* gardening, music, old churches. *Address:* Queen Anne's School, Caversham, Reading. *T:* Reading 71582. *Club:* English-Speaking Union.

**CHALMERS, Archibald MacDonald,** MC; Sheriff Substitute of Argyll at Oban, 1933-55, retired; Hon. Sheriff Substitute of Perthshire since 1956; *b* 26 Sept. 1883; *s* of James Chalmers and Caroline Berry Honey; *m* 1921, Mary, *o d* of late William T. Procter, DL Clackmannanshire; no *c*. *Educ:* Perth Academy; Glasgow Univ. Partner of firm of Robertson, Chalmers, Auld and Hunter, Solicitors, Glasgow; served European War, 1915-19, Major MGC (MC); Chairman, Court of Referees, Falkirk and Glasgow, 1927-30; Lecturer, Court Procedure and Negligence, Glasgow Atheneum, 1923-24. President Boy Scouts, Stirling, 1958-64. Hon. Vice-President, 1964-. *Recreations:* golf, fishing, etc. *Address:* Kilrock, Bridge of Allan. *T:* Bridge of Allan 2341. *Club:* Conservative (Glasgow).

**CHALMERS, Rev. Canon Reginald,** TD 1943; Vicar of Great Bowden and Welham 1948-65; Canon Residentiary of Leicester Cathedral, 1954-65; Member of Canterbury Convocation 1955-65; Rural Dean of Gartree Island, 1957-63; licensed to officiate on Carlisle Diocese; *b* 5 June 1893; *s* of Thomas William Chalmers, Ryde, IOW; *m* 1st, 1915, Gladys Lee Saunders, Hull (*d* 1944); one *s* one *d*; 2nd 1949, Mary Barron Robinson, Sunderland. *Educ:* Durham Univ. (MA). Officer, E. Yorks Regt, 1915-18. Ordained deacon, 1918, priest, 1919; Curate of Drypool, Hull, 1918-20; Vicar of St Luke's, Hull, 1920-24; CMS Staff, 1924-27; Vicar of St Paul, Newcastle upon Tyne, 1927-31; CMS, HQ London, 1931-35; Vicar of Holy Trinity, Leicester, 1935-48. CF (TA) 1927; on active service, 1939-45 (despatches, TD); DACG, 1943-45. Hon. Canon, Leicester Cathedral, 1945-54. *Recreations:* gardening, golf. *Address:* White Bridge, Grasmere, Westmorland. *T:* Grasmere 430.

**CHALMERS, Thomas Wightman,** CBE 1957; Special Assistant, Overseas and Foreign Relations, BBC, since 1964; *b* 29 April 1913; *s* of Thomas Wightman Chalmers and Susan Florence Colman; unmarried. *Educ:* Bradfield Coll.; King's Coll., London. Organ Scholar, King's Coll., London, 1934-36; BSc (Engineering), 1936. Joined BBC programme staff, 1936; successively announcer, Belfast and London; Overseas Presentation Director; Chief Assistant, Light Programme, 1945, Controller, 1948-50; Director, Nigerian Broadcasting Service, 1950-56, on secondment from BBC; Controller, North Region, BBC, 1956-58; Director of the Tanganyika Broadcasting Corporation, 1958-62; Deputy Regional Representative, UN Technical Assistance Board, East and Central Africa, 1962-64. *Recreations:* travelling, reading and music. *Address:* 5 All Souls Place, W1.

**CHALMERS, William John,** CBE 1954; Secretary and Director-General, Commonwealth War Graves Commission, since 1956; *b* 20 Oct. 1914; *s* of late William Chalmers, Inverness; *m* 1942, Jessie Alexandra Roy, *y d* of late George Johnston McGregor, Edinburgh; one *s* one *d*. *Educ:* Inverness Royal Academy; Edinburgh University. BL 1937; appointed staff Commonwealth War Graves Commission, 1938; served Queen's Own Cameron Highlanders, 1939-45; Bde Major 214th Infantry Bde, 1942-43 and 1944-45 (despatches); released to Commonwealth War Graves Commission, 1945; Assistant Secretary, 1948-56. Croix de Guerre, France, 1944; Coronation Medal, 1953. *Address:* 32 Grosvenor Gardens, SW1. *T:* 01-730 0751.

**CHALMERS, Rear-Admiral William Scott,** CBE 1939; DSC; retired; *b* 1 May 1888; *m* 1921, Muriel Violet Frances, *d* of Hon. Francis Agar; two *s*. *Educ:* Glasgow Academy; HMS Britannia; Dartmouth. Served European War, 1914-18, Royal Naval Siege Guns, Belgium (Croix de Guerre, France, DSC); HMS Lion and Queen Elizabeth, Battle of Jutland (despatches, British once, French twice); in command HMAS Australia, 1929-32, HMS Delhi, 1934-36; Director RN Staff Coll., 1937; Rear-Admiral and retired, 1939, and re-employed Admiralty Staff. *Publications:* The Life and Letters of David Beatty, 1951; Max Horton and the Western Approaches, 1954; Full Cycle (the biography of Admiral Sir B. H. Ramsay), 1959. *Address:* Guessens, Titchfield, Hants. *T:* Titchfield 3144. *Club:* United Service.

**CHALONER,** family name of Baron Gisborough.

**CHAMBERLAIN, Rev. Elsie Dorothea,** BD (London); *m* 1947, Rev. J. L. St C. Garrinton. *Educ:* Channing Sch.; King's Coll., London (BD). Asst Minister Berkeley Street, Liverpool, 1939-41; Minister: Christ Church, Friern Barnet, 1941-46; Vineyard Congregational Church, Richmond, 1947-54; BBC Religious Dept, 1950-67; Associate Minister, The City Temple, 1968-70. 1st woman chaplain, HM Forces, 1946-47. Chm., Congregational Union of England and Wales, 1956-57. *Publications:* (ed) Lift Up Your Hearts, 1959; (ed) Calm Delight: devotional anthology, 1959. *Recreations:* music, dress design. *Address:* Greensted Rectory, Ongar, Essex. *T:* Ongar 2630.

**CHAMBERLAIN, Rt. Rev. (Frank) Noel,** CB 1953; OBE 1949; MA (Lambeth), 1953; Hon. Assistant Bishop in the diocese of Portsmouth, since 1963 (Assistant Bishop, 1961-63); *b* 25 Dec. 1900; *y s* of late A. H. Chamberlain, Highgate; unmarried. *Educ:* Haberdashers' Sch.; King's Coll., London; AKC 1925; Fellow, King's Coll., London, 1953; Wells Theological Coll., Deacon, 1925; Priest, 1926; Curate Eton Mission, Hackney Wick, 1925-28; Chaplain, Royal Navy, 1928; Chaplain of the Fleet and Archdeacon of the Royal Navy, 1952-56; Hon. Chaplain to the Queen, 1952-56; Bishop of Trinidad and Tobago, 1957-61, resigned. Honorary Canon, Portsmouth Cathedral, 1962-64. *Recreation:* walking. *Address:* 1 Pembroke Chambers, Penny Street, Portsmouth. *Club:* Army and Navy.

**CHAMBERLAIN, George Digby,** CMG 1950; Chief Secretary, Western Pacific High Commission, 1947-52; *b* 13 Feb. 1898; *s* of Digby Chamberlain, late Knockfin, Knaresborough; *m* 1931, Kirsteen Miller Holmes; one *s* one *d*. *Educ:* St Catharine's Coll., Cambridge. War Service, 1917-19, with Rifle Brigade, Lieut RARO. Asst District Commissioner, Gold Coast, 1925; Asst Principal, Colonial Office, 1930-32; Asst Colonial Secretary, Gold Coast, 1932; Asst Chief Secretary, Northern Rhodesia, 1939; Colonial Secretary, Gambia, 1943-47; Acting Governor, Gambia, July-Nov. 1943, and June-Aug. 1944; Acting High Commissioner, Western Pacific, Jan.-April, and Sept. 1951-July 1952; retired 1952. *Recreations:* shooting, fishing. *Address:* 18 Douglas Crescent, Edinburgh 12. *Club:* New (Edinburgh).

**CHAMBERLAIN, Air Vice-Marshal George Philip,** CB 1946; OBE 1941; RAF, retired; Aviation and Electronics consultant; Director, Collins Radio Company of England; *b* 18 Aug. 1905; *s* of G. A. R. Chamberlain, MA, FLAS, FRICS, Enville, Staffordshire; *m* 1930, Alfreda Rosamond Kedward; one *s* one *d*. *Educ:* Denstone Coll.; Royal Air Force Coll., Cranwell. Commissioned RAF, 1925. On loan to Min. of Civil Aviation, 1947-48; Imperial Defence Coll., 1949; AOA 205 Group, MEAF, 1950; AOC Transport Wing, MEAF, 1951-52; Commandant, RAF Staff Coll., Andover, 1953-54; AO i/c A, HQ Fighter Command, 1954-57; Dep. Comtroller of Electronics, Min. of Supply, 1957-59, Min. of Aviation, 1959-60; Managing Director, Collins Radio Co. of England, 1961-66. *Recreations:* sailing, ski-ing, tennis. *Address:* Little Orchard, Adelaide Close, Stanmore, Middlesex. *Club:* Royal Air Force.

**CHAMBERLAIN, Sir Henry Wilmot,** 5th Bt, *cr* 1828; *b* 17 May 1899; *o s* of Sir Henry Chamberlain, 4th Bt, and Gwendolen (*d* 1928), *d* of J. Inglis Jones, Royal Horse Guards, Derry Ormond, Cardiganshire, and Lady Elizabeth Inglis Jones. *S* father 1936. *Address:* c/o Laurel Bank, 10 Clifton Hill, Dorking, Surrey.

**CHAMBERLAIN, Rt. Rev. Noel;** *see* Chamberlain, Rt Rev. F. N.

**CHAMBERLAIN, Professor Owen,** AB, PhD; Professor of Physics, University of California, since 1958; *b* San Francisco, 10 July 1920; *s* of W. Edward Chamberlain and Genevieve Lucinda Owen; *m* 1943, Babette Cooper; one *s* three *d*. *Educ:* Philadelphia; Dartmouth Coll., Hanover, NH (AB). Atomic research for Manhattan District, 1942, transferred to Los Alamos, 1943; worked in Argonne National Laboratory, Chicago, 1947-48, and studied at University of Chicago (PhD); Instructor in Physics, University of California, 1948; Asst Professor, 1950; Associate Professor, 1954. Guggenheim Fellowship, 1957; Loeb Lecturer in Physics, Harvard Univ., 1959. Nobel Prize (joint) for Physics, 1959. Fellow American Phys. Soc.; Mem., Nat. Acad. of Sciences, 1960. *Publications:* papers in Physical Review, Physical Review Letters, Nature, Nuovo Cimento. *Address:* Department of Physics, University of California, Berkeley, California, USA.

**CHAMBERLAIN, Hon. Sir Reginald Roderic St Clair,** Kt 1970; **Hon. Mr Justice Chamberlain;** Judge of the Supreme Court of South Australia, 1959-71; *b* 17 June 1901; *s* of late Henry Chamberlain; *m* 1929, Leila Macdonald Haining; one *d*. *Educ:* St Peter's Coll.; Adelaide Univ. Crown Prosecutor, 1928; KC 1945; Crown Solicitor, 1952-59; Chm., SA Parole Board. Chm., Anti-Cancer Foundn. *Recreations:* golf, bridge. *Address:* 72 Moseley Street, Glenelg South, South Australia. *T:* 95.2036. *Clubs:* Adelaide, Royal Adelaide Golf (Adelaide).

**CHAMBERLAIN, Ronald;** Lecturer and Housing Consultant; Governor, Middlesex Hospital; *b* 19 April 1901; *m* Joan Smith McNeill (*d* 1950), Edinburgh; one *s* one *d*; *m* 1951, Florence Lilian Illingworth, Cricklewood. *Educ:* Owens Sch., Islington; Gonville and Caius Coll., Cambridge (MA). Formerly Secretary to National Federation of Housing Societies and (later) Chief Exec. Officer to the Miners' Welfare Commission; later engaged on administrative work for the National Service Hostels Corporation. MP (Lab.) Norwood Division of Lambeth, 1945-50; Member of Middlesex County Council,

1947-52. *Recreation:* tennis. *Address:* 18 Basing Hill, Golders Green, NW11. *T:* 01-455 1491.

**CHAMBERLAYNE, Air Commodore Paul Richard Tankerville James Michael Isidore Camille,** CB 1945; AFC 1918; RAF, retired; *b* 15 May 1898; 2nd and *o surv. s* of late Major Tankerville James Chamberlayne, Chamberlainstown, Kells, Meath, Ireland, and late Donna Leopoldina, Princess Ruspoli; *m* 1935, Euphemia Caldwell Kerr; one *s* one *d.* 11th Hussars SR 1914; attached RFC 1915, RAF 1918; Wing Comdr 1937; Asst Air Attaché, Paris, 1937; Air Attaché, Lisbon, 1938; Group Captain, 1940; AOC 25 Group S Africa, 1943; AOC Training Delegation, Bordeaux, 1944-45; retired list, 1946. Order of Leopold (Belgium). *Recreation:* yachting. *Address:* Chamberlainstown House, Navan, Co. Meath, Eire.

**CHAMBERLIN, Sir Michael,** Kt 1964; OBE 1955; Director, National Trustees Executors and Agency Company Australasia Ltd, Melbourne, since 1933 (General Manager, 1933-67); *b* 30 Aug. 1891; *e s* of Richard Chamberlin, Essendon, Victoria, Australia; *m* 1924, Veronica Christina (*née* Erck). *Educ:* Christian Brothers and Central Coll., Geelong, Australia. Dep. Chancellor, Monash Univ., Vic., 1962-68. Hon. LLD Monash, 1969. *Recreation:* work. *Address:* 910 Glenferrie Road, Kew, Victoria, Australia; Monash University, Clayton, Victoria, Australia. *T:* 81-4817. *Club:* Athenæum (Melbourne).

**CHAMBERS, Professor George Haddon,** DSC 1946; MSc (Dunelm); Professor of Marine Engineering, University of Newcastle upon Tyne (formerly King's College, University of Durham), since 1956; *b* 7 Oct. 1912; *s* of Charles George Chambers and Ida May Ackling; *m* 1946, Joan Lilian Wilding; one *s* one *d. Educ:* Whitgift Sch.; HMS Erebus; RN Engineering Coll., Devonport; RN Coll., Greenwich. Engineer Officer in RN until retired as Commander, 1956. Career included, in addition to sea-going appts, service in Admiralty, with British Joint Services Mission, Washington, DC, and as Professor of Marine Engineering, RN Coll., Greenwich. *Address:* 4 Manor Road, Longbenton, Newcastle upon Tyne NE7 7XS. *T:* Newcastle upon Tyne 662656. *Club:* Naval.

**CHAMBERS, Sir Paul;** *see* Chambers, Sir S. P.

**CHAMBERS, Professor Robert Guy;** Professor of Physics, University of Bristol, since Oct. 1964; *b* 8 Sept. 1924; *s* of A. G. P. Chambers; *m* 1950, Joan Brislee; one *d. Educ:* King Edward VI Sch., Southampton; Peterhouse, Cambridge. Work on tank armament (Ministry of Supply), 1944-46; Electrical Research Association, 1946-47; research on metals at low temperatures, Royal Society Mond Laboratory, Cambridge, 1947-57; Stokes Student, Pembroke Coll., 1950-53; PhD 1952; ICI Fellow, 1953-54; NRC Post-doctoral Fellow, Ottawa, 1954-55; University Demonstrator, Cambridge, 1955-57; Senior Lecturer, Bristol, 1958-61; Reader in Physics, Bristol, 1961-64. *Publications:* various papers in learned journals on the behaviour of metals at low temperatures. *Recreation:* star-gazing. *Address:* 123 Redland Road, Redland, Bristol 6. *T:* 44982.

**CHAMBERS, Sir (Stanley) Paul,** KBE 1965; CB 1944; CIE 1941; Chairman: Liverpool & London & Globe Insurance Co. Ltd, since 1968; London & Lancashire Insurance Co. Ltd, since 1968; Royal Insurance Co. Ltd, since 1968; Imperial Chemical Industries Ltd, 1960-68; Director: National Westminster Bank Ltd, since Dec. 1968; Spey Investments, since 1970; *b* 2 April 1904; *s* of late Philip Joseph Chambers; *m* 1st, 1926, Dorothy Alice Marion (marr. diss. 1955), *d* of late T. G. B. Copp; 2nd, 1955, Mrs Edith Pollack, 2nd *d* of R. P. Lamb, Workington, Cumberland; two *d. Educ:* City of London Coll.; LSE (BCom 1928; MSc Econ 1934). Mem., Indian Income Tax Enquiry Cttee, 1935-36; Income Tax Adviser to Govt of India, 1937-40; Sec. and Comr, Bd of Inland Revenue, 1942-47; Chief of Finance Div., Control Commn for Germany, British Element, 1945-47; Dir, ICI Ltd, 1947; Dep. Chm., 1952-60. Dir, National Provincial Bank Ltd, 1951-69. President: Nat. Inst. of Economic and Social Res., 1955-62; British Shippers' Council, 1963-68; Inst. of Directors, 1964-68; Royal Statistical Soc., 1964-65; Advertising Assoc., 1968-. Chm., Cttee of Inquiry into London Transport, April 1953-Jan. 1955; Member: Cttee apptd to review organisation of Customs and Excise, Oct. 1951-Sept. 1953; Cttee on Departmental Records, June 1952-July 1954; NCB, 1956-60. A Vice-Pres., Liverpool Sch. of Tropical Medicine, 1969-. Treasurer, Open University, 1969-. (Jtly) Granada Guildhall Lectures, 1968; Beveridge Memorial Lecture, 1969. Hon. DSc Bristol, 1963; Hon. LLD Liverpool, 1967; Hon. DTech Bradford, 1967. *Address:* 1A Frognal Gardens, Hampstead, NW3. *Clubs:* Athenæum, Reform.

**CHAMBERS, Professor William Walker,** MBE 1945; William Jacks Professor of German, University of Glasgow, since 1954; Member, Commonwealth Scholarship Commission in Britain, 1962-66; Vice-Chairman, Governors of Jordanhill College of Education, 1962-67; *b* 7 Dec. 1913; *s* of William and Agnes Chambers; *m* 1947, Mary Margaret Best; one *s* one *d. Educ:* Wishaw Public Sch.; Wishaw High Sch.; Universities of Glasgow, Paris and Munich. MA (Glasgow) 1936; L. ès L. (Paris) 1940; PhD (Munich) 1939. Served War of 1939-45 (despatches, MBE); 2nd Lieut, RA, 1941; Intelligence Staff, HQ 8th Army, North Africa, Sicily, Italy and Austria, 1942-46; Asst Lecturer in German, University of Leeds, 1946-47, Lecturer 1947-50; Prof. of Modern Languages, University College, N. Staffs, 1950-54. President Assoc. of Univ. Teachers, 1962-63. FEIS, 1964. Verdienstkreuz Erste Klasse, 1967. *Publications:* (ed) Paul Ernst, Selected Short Stories, 1953; (ed) Fouqué, Undine, 1956; (ed) Paul Ernst, Erdachte Gespräche, 1958; (with J. R. Wilkie) A Short History of the German Language, 1970. *Recreations:* gardening, music. *Address:* 45 Newlands Road, Glasgow, S3. *T:* 041-632 1000.

**CHAMIER, Air Cdre Sir John Adrian,** Kt 1944; CB 1925; CMG 1919; OBE 1918; DSO 1917; Indian Army, retired; late RAF; Partner Radalarm Industries and Ship-Shape Industries, of Warsash, Hants; *b* 1883; *s* of late Maj.-General F. E. A. Chamier; *m* 1918, Edwina Ratcliff, *d* of E Lordly, Chester, Canada; one *s* (and one *s* decd). *Educ:* St Paul's Sch.; Royal Military Coll., Sandhurst. Served Somaliland, 1904; European War, 1914-18 (despatches, DSO); Dir of Technical Development, Air Ministry, 1927-28; Technical Dir Vickers and Supermarine Aviation Companies, 1929-32; recalled to RAF Sept. 1939; Commandant Air Training Corps, 1941. *Publication:* The Birth of the Royal Air Force, 1944. *Address:* c/o Midland Bank, High Street, Southampton. *Clubs:* Special Forces; Island Sailing (Cowes).

**CHAMIER, Lieut-Colonel (Hon. Colonel) Richard Outram,** CIE 1928; late Indian Army; *b* 24 Aug. 1888; *s* of late Maj.-General F. E. A.

Chamier, CB, CIE, formerly of the Bengal Staff Corps. *Educ:* Woodcote House, Windlesham, Surrey; St Paul's Sch.; RM Coll., Sandhurst. Joined Indian Army, 1909; served European War, 1914-18, Mesopotamia; Private Secretary to the Governor of Assam, 1922, to Governor of the United Provinces, India, 1924-27. *Club:* United Service.

**CHAMPERNOWNE, David Gawen,** MA; FBA 1970; Professor of Economics and Statistics, Cambridge University since 1970; Fellow of Trinity College, Cambridge, since Oct. 1959; *b* Oxford, 9 July 1912; *s* of late F. G. Champernowne, MA, Bursar of Keble Coll., Oxford; *m* 1948, Wilhelmina Dullaert; two *s*. *Educ:* The College, Winchester; King's Coll., Cambridge. 1st Class Maths, Pts 1 and 2; 1st Class Economics Pt 2. Asst Lecturer at London Sch. of Economics, 1936-38; Fellow of King's Coll., Cambridge, 1937-48; University Lecturer in Statistics at Cambridge, 1938-40; Asst in Prime Minister's statistical dept, 1940-41; Asst dir of Programmes, Ministry of Aircraft Production, 1941-45; Dir of Oxford Univ. Institute of Statistics, 1945-48; Fellow of Nuffield Coll., Oxford, 1945-59; Prof. of Statistics, Oxford Univ., 1948-59; Reader in Economics, Cambridge Univ., 1959-70. Editor, Economic Jl, 1971-. *Publication:* Uncertainty and Estimation in Economics (3 vols), 1969. *Address:* Trinity College, Cambridge; 230 Hills Road, Cambridge. *T:* Cambridge 47829.

**CHAMPION,** family name of **Baron Champion.**

**CHAMPION,** Baron, *cr* 1962, of Pontypridd (Life Peer); **Arthur Joseph Champion,** PC 1967; JP; Deputy Speaker and Deputy Chairman of Committees, House of Lords, since 1967; *b* 26 July 1897; *s* of William and Clara Champion, Glastonbury, Somerset; *m* 1930, Mary E. Williams, Pontypridd; one *d*. *Educ:* St John's Sch., Glastonbury. Signalman. MP (Lab.) Southern Division of Derbyshire, 1945-50, South-East Derbyshire, 1950-Sept. 1959; Parliamentary Private Secretary to Minister of Food, 1949-50, to Secretary of War, 1950-51; Joint Parliamentary Secretary, Ministry of Agriculture and Fisheries, April-Oct. 1951; Minister without Portfolio and Dep. Leader of the House of Lords, 1964-67. Formerly British Delegate to Consultative Assembly at Strasbourg; Govt appointed Director of the British Sugar Corporation, 1960-64, 1967-68. Hon. Assoc., RCVS, 1967. *Address:* 22 Lanelay Terrace, Pontypridd, Glam. *T:* Pontypridd 2349.

**CHAMPION, Professor Frank Clive;** Professor of Experimental Physics, University of London, King's College, since 1959; Fellow of King's Coll., 1970; *b* 2 Nov. 1907; *s* of Frank Charles Champion and Alice Champion (*née* Killick); *m* 1936, Joan Mingay (marr. diss., 1951). *Educ:* Royal Grammar Sch., Guildford; St John's Coll., Cambridge. (Scholar; Double 1st Class Natural Sciences Tripos (Physics); BA 1929, MA 1930, PhD 1932). Hockin Physics Prize and Hughes Prizeman, 1929. Asst Demonstrator, Cavendish Laboratory, 1929-32; Asst Lecturer in Physics, Nottingham Univ., 1932-34; Lecturer in Physics, King's Coll., London, 1934-48; Reader in Physics, 1941-59. Royal Society Visiting Professor, Malaysia, 1967. Scientific Adviser, Civil Defence, SE Div., 1946-51. Hon. Secretary, Atomic Scientists Assoc., 1945-48. FInstP 1932. FKC, 1970. *Publications:* (with N. Davy) Properties of Matter, 1936, 3rd edn 1959; University Physics, 1946, new edn 1960; Electronic Properties of Diamonds, 1963; research papers in nuclear physics and solid state physics in Proc. Royal Society, Proc. Physical Society, Physical Review, 1931-. *Recreations:* tennis, swimming, travel, music, literature (English and Spanish). *Address:* Physics Department, King's College, Strand, WC2. *T:* 01-836 5454.

**CHAMPION, Sir Harry George,** Kt, *cr* 1956; CIE 1941; MA, DSc; Professor Emeritus, Oxford University, since 1959; Emeritus Fellow, St John's College, Oxford; *b* 17 Aug. 1891. *Educ:* New Coll., Oxford. BA 1912; MA 1924; DSc 1950. Joined Indian Forest Service, 1915; Conservator of Forests, United Provinces, 1938; Professor of Forestry, Oxford Univ., 1940-59. *Address:* Windrush, Boars Hill, Oxford. *T:* 35240.

**CHAMPION, Rev. Sir Reginald Stuart,** KCMG 1946 (CMG 1944); OBE 1934; retired as Vicar of Chilham, Kent (1953-61); *b* 21 March 1895; *s* of late Philip Champion and Florence Mary Hulburd; *m* 1920, Margaret, *d* of late Very Rev. W. M. Macgregor, DD, LLD; two *s* one *d*. *Educ:* Sutton Valence Sch. Enlisted West Kent Yeomanry, 1912; Commissioned 3rd Bn E. Surrey Regt, 1913; European War, 1914-18; Occupied Enemy Territory Administration, Palestine, 1917-20; Colonial Administrative Service, 1920; District Officer, Palestine, 1920-28; Political Secretary, Aden, 1928-34; Secretary to Treaty Mission to the Yemen, 1933-34; Financial Adviser, Trans-Jordan, 1934-39; Dist Commissioner, Galilee, 1939-42; Political Mission to the Yemen, 1940; Chief Secretary, Aden, 1942-44, Gov. and C-in-C, 1944-51; retired from Colonial Service, 1951; ordained Deacon, Jan. 1952; Priest, Dec. 1952; Curate, All Saints', Maidstone, 1952. *Address:* 46 Chancellor House, Mount Ephraim, Tunbridge Wells, Kent. *T:* Tunbridge Wells 20719.

**CHAMPNEYS, Captain Sir Weldon D.;** *see* Dalrymple-Champneys.

**CHAMSON, André;** Member of the French Academy; Grand Croix de la Légion d'Honneur; Grand Officier de l'Ordre du Mérite; Curator of the Petit Palais since 1945; Directeur Général des Archives de France, since 1959; International President of the Pen, 1956; *b* 6 June 1900; *s* of Jean Chamson and Madeleine Aldebert; *m* 1924, Lucie Mazauric; one *d*. *Educ:* Ecole des Chartes. Joint Curator, Palais de Versailles, 1933-39. Served War of 1939-45 (Croix de Guerre, Médaille de la Résistance); Captain, Staff of 5th Army, 1939-40; Chef de bataillon, Bde Alsace Lorraine, 1944-45. Docteur *hc* Université Laval, Quebec. Commandeur de la Couronne, Belgium; Officer of Saint Sava, Norway; Officer of Merit, Italy; Grand Officier de l'Ordre du Soleil du Pérou; Grand Officier de l'Etoile Polaire de Suède; Grand Officier de l'Ordre National de la Côte d'Ivoire. *Publications:* Roux le bandit, 1925; Les Hommes de la route, 1927; Le Crime des justes, 1928; Les Quatre Eléments, 1932; La Galère, 1938; Le Puits des miracles, 1945; Le Dernier Village, 1946; La Neige et la fleur, 1950; Le Chiffre de nos jours, 1954; Adeline Vénician, 1956; Nos Ancêtres les Gaulois, 1958; Le Rendez-vous des Espérances, 1961; Comme une Pierre qui Tombe, 1964; La Petite Odyssée, 1965; La Superbe, 1967. *Address:* 35 rue Mirabeau, Paris XVIe. *Club:* Pen (Pres.)

**CHANCE, Major Geoffrey Henry Barrington,** CBE 1962; *b* 16 Dec. 1893; *s* of Ernest Chance, Burghfield, Berks; *m* 1st, 1914, Hazel Mary Louise Cadell (decd); two *d*; 2nd, 1933, Daphne Corona Wallace; one *s* one *d*. *Educ:* Eton. Engineering, 1913-14. Army, 1914-19. Qualified Chartered Accountant, 1928, practised, 1930-40; HM Treasury, 1941-45.

Company director. CC, Alderman (Wilts), 1955-67; Chairman Chippenham Conservative Assoc., 1955-62; High Sheriff of Wiltshire, 1965. *Recreations:* fishing, shooting. *Address:* Braydon Hall, Minety, Malmesbury, Wilts. *T:* Minety 214.

**CHANCE, Sir Hugh;** *see* Chance, Sir W. H. S.

**CHANCE, Ivan Oswald;** Chairman, Christie, Manson and Woods, since 1958; *b* 23 June 1910; *s* of Brig.-Gen. O. K. Chance, CMG, DSO, and Fanny Isabel, *d* of Sir George Agnew, 2nd Bt; *m* 1936, Pamela Violet, *d* of Everard Martin Smith. *Educ:* Eton. Joined Christie's, 1930; became a partner, 1935. Served War of 1939-45: 58 Middx AA Bn (TA), and Coldstream Guards (despatches, 1945). Chm., Georgian Group. *Recreation:* travel. *Address:* 50 Belgravia Court, Ebury Stree, SW1. *Clubs:* Brooks's, White's; Brook (New York).

**CHANCE, Kenneth Miles,** DSO 1916; DL; *b* 27 Jan. 1893; *y s* of late Sir F. W. Chance, KBE; *m* 1924, D. R. Shaw; two *d. Educ:* Repton; Hertford Coll., Oxford. High Sheriff, Cumberland, 1949; DL Cumberland, 1961. *Recreations:* shooting; golf. *Address:* The Glebe House, Wreay, Carlisle.

**CHANCE, Sir Roger (James Ferguson),** 3rd Bt, *cr* 1900; MC; *b* 26 Jan. 1893; *e s* of George Ferguson Chance (2nd *s* of 1st Bt) and Mary Kathleen, *d* of late Rev. Henry Stobart; *S* uncle 1935; *m* 1921, Mary Georgina, *d* of late Col William Rowney; one *s* two *d* (and one *s* decd). *Educ:* Eton; Trinity Coll., Cambridge (MA); London University (PhD). Served European War, Aug. 1914-April 1918; Capt. and Adjutant 4th (RI) Dragoon Guards, 1916-17; Capt. 1st Batt. The Rifle Brigade, 1918 (twice wounded, despatches twice, MC); Editor, Review of Reviews, 1932-33; Press Attaché, British Embassy, Berlin, 1938; Sqdn Leader RAFVR, 1940-41. *Publications:* Until Philosophers are Kings (political philosophy); Conservatism and Wealth (with Oliver Baldwin, politics); Winged Horses (fiction); Be Absolute for Death (fiction). *Heir; s* (George) Jeremy (ffolliott) Chance [*b* 24 Feb. 1926; *m* 1950, Cecilia Mary Elizabeth, *d* of Sir (William) Hugh (Stobart) Chance, *qv*; two *s* two *d*]. *Address:* 9 Eaton Square, SW1. *Club:* Athenæum.

*See also R. T. Armstrong.*

**CHANCE, Sir (William) Hugh (Stobart),** Kt 1945; CBE 1958; DL; *b* 31 Dec. 1896; 2nd *s* of George Ferguson Chance, Clent Grove, near Stourbridge, Worcs; *b* of Sir Roger Chance, 3rd Bt, *qv*; *m* 1st, 1926, Cynthia May (marr. diss.), *er d* of Major A. F. Baker-Cresswell, Cresswell and Harehope, Northumberland; two *s* three *d*; 2nd, 1961, Rachel Carr, *d* of late Cyril Cameron, RHA, and of Mrs Stormonth-Darling. *Educ:* Eton; Trinity Coll., Cambridge (MA). Dir, Chance Brothers Ltd, 1924-64. Served European War, 1914-18, Lieut Worcs Regt and Royal Flying Corps; Smethwick Borough Council, 1940-45; Chm. Smethwick Education Cttee, 1943-45; Worcs County Council, 1946, Vice-Chm., 1949-53; Chm. Education Cttee 1958-64; Pres. Assoc. of Technical Institutions, 1948-49; Chm. West Midlands Advisory Council for Further Education, 1949-61; Mem. of "Percy" Cttee on Higher Technological Education; Willis Jackson Cttee on Technical Teachers; Lord Chancellor's Cttee on Intestacy, 1951; Mem. Royal Commn. on Scottish Affairs, 1952; Pres. West Midlands Union of Conservative Associations, 1957-67. High Sheriff of Worcs, 1942; DL Worcs; Alderman Worcs CC 1953; Pres. Worcs Red Cross, 1958-67; Hon. Col (TA) Parsons Memorial Medal, 1946. *Recreations:* shooting; archery. *Address:* The Clock House, Birlingham, Pershore, Worcs. *T:* Eckington 223; 39 Seymour Walk, SW10. *Club:* Leander.

**CHANCELLOR, Sir Christopher (John),** Kt 1951; CMG 1948; MA; Director: Bristol Evening Post Ltd; Forte Holdings Ltd; Chairman, Madame Tussaud's Ltd; *b* 29 March 1904; *s* of late Sir John Robert Chancellor, GCMG, GCVO, GBE, DSO; *m* 1926, Sylvia Mary, *e d* of Sir Richard Paget, 2nd Bt, and Lady Muriel Finch-Hatton, *d* of 12th Earl of Winchilsea and Nottingham; two *s* two *d. Educ:* Eton Coll.; Trinity College., Cambridge (1st class in History). Joined Reuters in 1930; Reuters' Gen. Manager and Chief Corresp in Far East with headquarters in Shanghai, 1931-39; Gen. Manager of Reuters, Ltd, 1944-59, Trustee, 1960-65; Chm. Odhams Press Ltd, 1960-61 (Vice-Chm., 1959-60); Chm. and Chief Executive, The Bowater Paper Corporation Ltd and associated cos, 1962-69. Mem. Court, London Univ., 1956-62; Chm. Exec. Cttee of The Pilgrims Soc. of Great Britain, 1958-67; Mem. Board of Regents, Memorial Univ. of Newfoundland, 1963-68; Vice-Pres., National Council of Social Service, 1959-; Dep.-Chm., Council of St Paul's Cathedral Trust, 1954-62; Chm., Appeal and Publicity Cttee, King George VI National Memorial Fund, 1952-54; Dep.-Chm., Exec. Cttee, 1955-56. Mem. Council, Bath Univ.; Pres., Bath Preservation Trust. King Haakon VII Liberty Cross, 1947; Officer Order of Orange Nassau, 1950; Comdr Royal Order of Danebrog, 1951; Officer, Legion of Honour, 1951; Comdr Order of Civil Merit (Spain), 1952; Cross of Comdr Order of Phœnix, 1953; Comdr Order of Vasa, 1953; Comdr Order of Merit (Italy), 1959. *Address:* Hunstrete House, Pensford, Somerset; Hill Lodge, 14 Hillsleigh Road, W8. *Club:* Garrick.

**CHANDLER, Edwin George,** FRIBA, MPTI; City Architect, City of London, since 1961; *b* 28 Aug. 1914; *e s* of Edwin and Honor Chandler; *m* 1938, Iris Dorothy, *o d* of Herbert William Grubb; one *d. Educ:* Selhurst Grammar Sch., Croydon. Asst Architect, Hants County Council and City of Portsmouth, 1936-39. Served in HMS Vernon, Mine Design Dept, 1940-45. Gained distinction in thesis, ARIBA, 1942, FRIBA 1961. Dep. Architect and Planning Officer, West Ham, 1945-47; City Architect and Planning Officer, City of Oxford, 1947-61. Mem. RIBA Council, 1950-52; Mem. Univ. Social Survey Cttee, Oxford. *Publications:* Housing for Old Age, 1939; City of Oxford Development Plan, 1950. Articles contrib. to Press and professional jls. *Recreations:* landscaping, travel, swimming. *Address:* Guildhall, EC2. *T:* 01-606 3030; 36 Rouse Gardens, Alleyn Park, SE21. *T:* 01-670 4964. *Club:* Press.

**CHANDLER, George,** MA, PhD, FLA, FRHistS; City Librarian, Liverpool, since 1952; *b* 2 July 1915; *s* of W. and F. W. Chandler; *m* 1937, Dorothy Lowe; one *s. Educ:* Central Grammar Sch., Birmingham; Leeds Coll. of Commerce; University of London. Birmingham Public Libraries, 1931-37; Leeds Public Libraries, 1937-46; WEA Tutor Organiser, 1946-47; Borough Librarian, Dudley, 1947-50; Dep. City Librarian, Liverpool, 1950-52; Hon. Sec. Dudley Arts Club, 1948-50; Pres., Internat. Assoc. of Met. City Libraries, 1968-; Pres. 1962- (Hon. Sec. 1957-62), Soc. of Municipal and County Chief Librarians; Dir, 1962- (Hon. Sec. 1955-62), Liverpool and District Scientific, Industrial and Research Library, Advisory Council; Hon.

Librarian, 1957- (Hon. Sec. 1950-57), Historic Soc. of Lancs and Ches; Chm., Exec. Cttee, Library Assoc.; Hon. Editor, Internat. Library Review, 1969-. Unesco expert in Tunisia, 1964. Cavalier dell'Ordine Al Merito della Repubblica Italiana, 1962. *Publications:* Dudley, 1949; William Roscoe, 1953; Liverpool 1207-1957; Liverpool Shipping, 1960; Liverpool under James I, 1960; How to Find Out, 1963 (3rd edn 1967); Four Centuries of Banking: Martins Bank, Vol. I, 1964, Vol. II, 1968; Liverpool under Charles I, 1965; Libraries in the Modern World, 1965; How to Find Out About Literature, 1968; (Ed.) International Series of Monographs on Library and Information Science; contributions to educl and library press. *Recreations:* writing, research; walking; foreign travel. *Address:* 23 Dowsefield Lane, Liverpool L18 3JG. *T:* 051-428 2051. *Club:* (Hon. Librarian) Athenæum (Liverpool).

**CHANDOS,** 1st Viscount, *cr* 1954, of Aldershot; **Oliver Lyttelton, KG 1970;** PC 1940; DSO 1916; MC; late Grenadier Guards; President, Governing Body of Queen Elizabeth House, Oxford, since 1955; Chairman, Northern Ireland Development Council, 1955-65; a Trustee of the National Gallery, 1958-65; A Trustee of Churchill College, Cambridge, since 1958; Chairman, National Theatre Board since 1962, also Member, South Bank Theatre Board; *b* 15 March 1893; *o s* of late Right Hon. Alfred Lyttelton and late Hon. Mrs Alfred Lyttelton, GBE; *m* 1920, Lady Moira Godolphin Osborne, 4th *d* of 10th Duke of Leeds and Lady Katherine Frances Lambton (*d* 1952), *d* of 2nd Earl of Durham; two *s* (and one killed in action) one *d. Educ:* Eton; Trinity Coll., Cambridge. Joined army at outbreak of War, and Grenadier Guards, Dec. 1914; served continuously on active service, 1915-18; Adjutant 3rd Battalion, 15 Oct. 1915-18; Brigade Major 4th Guards Brigade, Feb. 1918; 2nd Guards Brigade, Sept. 1918 (despatches thrice, DSO, MC); Managing Dir, of the British Metal Corporation, Ltd; Controller of Non-Ferrous Metals, 1939-40. MP (U) Aldershot Div. of Hants 1940-54; Pres. of Board of Trade, 1940-41; Minister of State and Mem. of War Cabinet, 1941-42; Minister of Production and Member of War Cabinet, 1942-45; Pres. of Board of Trade and Minister of Production, May-July 1945; Chm. Associated Electrical Industries Ltd, 1945-51; Sec. of State for the Colonies, 1951-54; Chm., Associated Electrical Industries Ltd and subsidiaries, 1954-63; Director: Alliance Assurance Co. Ltd, 1954-69; I.C.I. Ltd, 1954-68. Pres. Institute of Directors, 1954-63; Pres., Manchester Coll. of Science and Technology, 1956-61. *Publications:* The Memoirs of Lord Chandos, 1962; From Peace to War: a study in contrast, 1857-1918, 1968. *Recreations:* golf, cricket, shooting; played golf for Cambridge Univ. 1913. *Heir: s* Hon. Antony Alfred Lyttelton [*b* 23 Oct. 1920; *m* 1949, Caroline Mary, *d* of Rt Hon. Sir Alan Lascelles, *qv*; two *s* two *d. Educ:* Eton; Trinity Coll., Cambridge. Served War of 1939-45 (despatches)]. *Address:* Trafalgar House, Downton, near Salisbury, Wilts; Chesham House, 30/31 Chesham Place, SW1. *Clubs:* Buck's; St James'; Grillions.

*See also Viscount Chaplin.*

**CHANDOS-POLE, Lt-Col John,** OBE 1951; JP; Lord Lieutenant of Northamptonshire since 1967; *b* 20 July 1909; *s* of late Brig.-Gen. Harry Anthony Chandos-Pole, CBE, DL, JP and late Ada Ismay, Heverswood, Brasted, Kent; *m* 1952, Josephine Sylvia, *d* of late Brig.-Gen. Cyril Randell Crofton, CBE, Limerick House, Milborne Port, near Sherborne; two step-*d. Educ:* Eton; Magdalene Coll., Cambridge (MA). 2nd Lieut Coldstream Guards, 1933; ADC: to Governor of Bombay, May-Nov., 1937; to Governor of Bengal, Nov. 1937-June 1938, Oct. 1938-Feb. 1939, also to Viceroy of India, June-Oct., 1938. Served War of 1939-45: France and Belgium (wounded); Palestine, 1948 (wounded, despatches); commanded 1st Bn, Coldstream Guards, 1947-48; Guards Depot, 1948-50; 2nd Bn, Coldstream Guards, 1950-52. Lieut-Col 1949; retired, 1953. A Member of the Hon. Corps of Gentlemen-at-Arms, 1956- (Harbinger, 1966-). DL 1965, JP 1957, Northants. *Recreations:* racing and travel. *Address:* Newnham Hall, Daventry, Northants. *T:* Daventry 2711. *Clubs:* Boodle's; Pratt's.

**CHANDOS-POLE, Major John Walkelyne,** DL, JP; *b* 4 Nov. 1913; *o s* of late Col Reginald Walkelyne Chandos-Pole, TD, JP, Radburne Hall; *m* 1947, Ilsa Jill, *er d* of Emil Ernst Barstz, Zürich; one *d* (one *s* decd). *Educ:* Eton; RMC, Sandhurst. Commissioned Grenadier Guards, 1933; ADC to Viceroy of India, 1938-39; retired, 1947. JP 1951, DL 1961, Derbys; High Sheriff of Derbys, 1959. *Recreation:* shooting. *Address:* Radburne Hall, Kirk Langley, Derby DE6 4LZ. *T:* Kirk Langley 246. *Clubs:* Boodle's; Pratt's; MCC; County (Derby).

**CHANDRA, Ram;** *see* Ram Chandra.

**CHANDRASEKHAR, Subrahmanyan,** FRS 1944; Morton D. Hull Distinguished Service Professor of Theoretical Astrophysics, University of Chicago, USA, since 1937; *b* 19 Oct. 1910; *m* 1936, Lalitha Doraiswamy. *Educ:* Presidency Coll., Madras; Trinity Coll., Cambridge (Government of Madras Research Scholar, PhD 1933, ScD 1942). Fellow of Trinity Coll., Cambridge, 1933-37. Managing Editor Astrophysical Journal, 1952-. Nehru Memorial Lecture, India, 1968. Mem. Nat. Acad. of Sciences, Amer. Philosophical Soc. and Amer. Acad. of Arts and Sciences (Rumford Medal, 1957); Bruce Gold Medal, Astr. Soc. Pacific, 1952; Gold Medal, Royal Astronomical Soc. London, 1953; Royal Medal, Royal Society, 1962; Nat. Medal of Science (USA), 1966. *Publications:* An Introduction to the Study of Stellar Structure, 1939; Principles of Stellar Dynamics, 1942; Radiative Transfer, 1950; Hydrodynamic and Hydromagnetic Stability, 1961; Ellipsoidal Figures of Equilibrium, 1969; various papers in current scientific periodicals. *Address:* Laboratory for Astrophysics and Space Research, 933 East 56th Street, Chicago, Illinois, USA. *T:* Chicago 752-3011. *Club:* Quadrangle (Chicago).

**CHANNON, Harold John,** CMG 1946; DSc London, BA London; FRIC; Fellow of University College, London; *b* 7 March 1897; *s* of W. J. Channon; *m* 1925, Hilda Alice Bond, MB, BS, DPH, Mem. Commn on Higher Educn in Malaya, 1938. *Educ:* Leathersellers Company Sch.; University Coll., London. Research Asst, Bio-chemical Dept, University Coll., London, 1922-24; Beit Memorial Fellow for Medical Research, 1923-26; Asst Biochemical Dept, University Coll., London, 1925-27; Biochemist, Dept of Experimental Pathology and Cancer Research, University of Leeds, 1927-31; Prof. of Biochemistry University of Liverpool, 1932-43; Research Manager, Unilever Ltd, 1943-55. Mem. Commission on Higher Education in the Colonies; Mem. Commission on Higher Education in West Africa, 1944; Mem. of Advisory Cttee on Education in the Colonies, 1939-44. Mem. Colonial Products Council, 1956-59. *Publications:* scientific papers mainly in The Biochemical Journal. *Recreations:* gardening; fishing. *Address:* Dunwood, Southway, Sidmouth, Devon. *T:* Sidmouth 2921. *Club:* Athenæum.

**CHANNON, (Henry) Paul (Guinness);** MP (C) for Southend West, since Jan. 1959; Parliamentary Under-Secretary of State, Department of the Environment, since Oct. 1970; *b* 9 Oct. 1935; *o s* of late Sir Henry Channon, MP, and of Lady Honor Svejdar (*née* Guinness), *e d* of 2nd Earl of Iveagh, KG; *m* 1963, Ingrid Olivia Georgia Guinness (*née* Wyndham); one *s* two *d. Educ:* Lockers Park, Hemel Hempstead; Eton Coll., Christ Church, Oxford. 2nd Lieut Royal Horse Guards (The Blues), 1955-56. Pres. of Oxford Univ. Conservative Association, 1958. Parly Private Sec. to: Minister of Power, 1959-60; Home Sec., 1960-62; First Sec. of State, 1962-63; PPS to the Foreign Sec., 1963-64; Parly Sec., Min. of Housing and Local Govt, June-Oct. 1970. Mem., Gen. Adv. Council to ITA, 1964-66; Conservative Spokesman on Arts and Amenities, 1967-. *Address:* 55 Chester Square, SW1. *T:* 01-730 4927; Kelvedon Hall, Brentwood, Essex. *T:* Ongar 2180. *Clubs:* Turf; Buck's; White's.

**CHANNON, Paul;** *see* Channon, H. P. G.

**CHANTLER, Philip,** CMG 1963; Chairman, North-West Economic Planning Board, 1965-69; *b* 16 May 1911; *s* of Tom and Minnie Chantler; *m* 1938, Elizabeth Margaret Pentney; one *d. Educ:* Manchester Central High Sch.; Manchester Univ.; Harvard Univ Commonwealth Fund Fellow, 1934-36; Asst Lectr in Public Admin., Manchester Univ., 1936-38; Tariffs Adviser, UK Gas Corp. Ltd, 1938-40. Served War of 1939-45: RA 1940-41; War Cabinet Secretariat, 1941-45; Economic Adviser, Cabinet Office, 1945-47; Economic Adviser, Ministry of Fuel and Power, 1947-60 (seconded as Economic Adviser, Government of Pakistan Planning Board, 1955-57); Under-Sec., Electricity Div., Min. of Power, 1961-65. *Publication:* The British Gas Industry: An Economic Study, 1938. *Recreations:* gardening; rambling; cycling; cine-photography; and domestic odd-jobbing. *Address:* The Gables, Woodbrook Road Alderley Edge, Cheshire; Tralong Cottage, West Cork, Eire.

**CHAPLIN,** family name of **Viscount Chaplin.**

**CHAPLIN,** 3rd Viscount, *cr* 1916, of St Oswalds, Blankney, in the county of Lincoln; **Anthony Freskyn Charles Hamby Chaplin;** Flight Lieutenant RAFVR; *b* 14 Dec. 1906; *er s* of 2nd Viscount and Hon. Gwladys Alice Gertrude Wilson, 4th *d* of 1st Baron Nunburnholme; *S* father, 1949; *m* 1st, 1933, Alvilde (marr. diss., 1951; she *m* 1951, James Lees Milne), *o d* of late Lieut-Gen. Sir Tom Bridges, KCB, KCMG; one *d*; 2nd, 1951, Rosemary, *d* of 1st Viscount Chandos, *qv*; two *d. Educ:* Radley. Occupied with Natural History and Music. Mem. Council, Zoological Soc. of London, 1934-38, 1950-; Sec., 1952-55. Voyage to New Guinea, to collect zoological material, 1935-36. Studied musical composition in Paris with Nadia Boulanger, 1937-39. Served RAF, 1940-46. *Publications:* 3 Preludes for piano; Toccata on a fragment of D. Scarlatti for piano; Cadenza for Mozart's piano concerto in C minor k. 491; various contributions to zoological journals. *Heir:* none. *Address:* Wadstray House, Blackawton, near Totnes, S Devon.

**CHAPLIN, Arthur Hugh,** CB 1970; Principal Keeper of Printed Books, British Museum, 1966-70; *b* 17 April 1905; *er s* of late Rev. Herbert F. Chaplin and Florence B. Lusher; *m* 1938, Irene Marcousé. *Educ:* King's Lynn Grammar Sch.; Bedford Modern Sch.; University Coll., London. Asst Librarian: Reading Univ. 1927-28; Queen's Univ., Belfast, 1928-29; Asst Keeper, Dept of Printed Books, British Museum, 1930-52; Dep. Keeper, 1952-59; Keeper, 1959-66. Exec. Sec., Organizing Cttee of Internat. Conference on Cataloguing Principles, Paris, 1961; Mem. Council, Library Association, 1964-; Pres., Microfilm Assoc. of GB, 1967-70. Fellow UCL, 1969. *Publications:* contributions to Jl Documentation, Library Assoc. Record, Library Quarterly, and to Cataloguing Principles and Practice (ed M. Piggott), 1954; Tradition and Principle in Library Cataloguing, 1966. *Recreations:* walking; motoring. *Address:* 44 Russell Square, WC1. *T:* 01-636 7217.

**CHAPLIN, Charles Spencer;** producer, and actor in films; *b* London, 16 April 1889; both parents (deceased) in theatrical profession; *s* of Charles Chaplin, variety comedian and Hannah (Lily Harley), singer; *m* 1st, 1918, Mildred Harris (marr. diss.); 2nd, 1924, Lolita McMurry (Lita Grey) (marr. diss.); one *s* (and one *s* decd); 3rd, 1936, Paulette Goddard (marr. diss.); 4th, 1943, Oona, *d* of late Eugene O'Neill; three *s* five *d.* Formed his own producing organisation and built Chaplin Studios, Hollywood, California, 1918. Was a founder of United Artists' Corporation (with Mary Pickford, Douglas Fairbanks, and D. W. Griffith) with British affiliation Allied Artists. Member, American Academy of Arts and Sciences, 1970. Films Include: Shoulder Arms, The Kid, The Gold Rush, The Circus, City Lights, Modern Times, The Great Dictator, Monsieur Verdoux, Limelight, A King in New York, A Countess from Hong Kong. Erasmus Prize, 1965. Hon. DLitt: Oxford, 1962; Durham, 1962. Officier de l'instruction Publique, République Française; Officer Legion of Honour. *Publication:* My Autobiography, 1964. *Address:* c/o United Artists Ltd, 142 Wardour Street, W1.

**CHAPLIN, Frederick Leslie;** Chairman, F. W. Woolworth & Co. Ltd, 1961-69; Director, F. W. Woolworth, USA, 1961-69; *b* 6 Dec. 1905; *s* of late Frederick and Marion Chaplin; *m* 1934, Vera Irene Townes; two *s. Educ:* St Osyth's Sch., Clacton. Joined Woolworth Company, 1928; Director, 1957; Managing Dir, 1960. *Recreations:* gardening; fishing; shooting. *Address:* Links View, 5 Broad Walk, Winchmore Hill, N21. *T:* 01-886 0244.

**CHAPLIN, Sir George (Frederick),** Kt 1962; CBE 1958; DL; JP; FRICS; FAI; Chairman of Essex County Council, 1961-65 (Member 1944-46; Vice-Chairman 1955-58); *b* 1900; *s* of late Jesse Chaplin, Leicester; *m* 1928, Doris Evelyn, *d* of William Henry Lee; one *s* two *d. Educ:* Leicester. Chm. Romford Divl Conservative Assoc., 1945-52 (Pres., 1952-66); Member: Romford Borough Council, 1937-52 (Mayor, 1946-47). Regional Dir, Lloyds Bank. Mem. Council of Govs for University of Essex; Gov., Brentwood Sch. Mem., Ct of Worshipful Co. of Innholders. JP 1952, DL 1963, Essex. *Recreation:* golf. *Address:* Great Ropers, Great Warley, Brentwood, Essex. *T:* Brentwood 2514. *Club:* Constitutional.

**CHAPLIN, William Robert,** CBE 1958; *b* 4 Feb. 1888; *s* of late William Robert Chaplin; *m* 1917, Tereora, *d* of Rev. J. J. Hutchin, Raratonga, Cook Islands; one *d.* Apprenticeship and Officer in sailing ships, Australian Naval Transport Service, 1914-18; commanded ships of the Australian Commonwealth Line, 1918-28. Elected an Elder Brother of Trinity House,

1928; retired, 1958. Member, Royal Commonwealth Society; FRGS. *Address:* Flat 2, 16 Stanhope Terrace, W2. *T:* 01-723 1575.

**CHAPLING, Norman Charles,** CBE 1954; Managing Director, Cable and Wireless Ltd, 1951-65, retd; *b* 11 Feb. 1903; *s* of late Charles Chapling; *m* 1933, Lenora, *d* of late Ernest Hedges; one *s.* Past Man. Dir: Cable & Wireless (Mid-East) Ltd; Cable & Wireless (West Indies) Ltd; Direct West India Cable Co. Ltd; Eastern Extension Australasia & China Telegraph Co. Ltd; Eastern Telegraph Co. Ltd; Eastern Telegraph Co. (France) Ltd; Halifax & Bermudas Cable Co. Ltd; Mercury House Ltd; West Coast of America Telegraph Co. Ltd; Western Telegraph Co. Ltd. Past Dir, SA Belge de Câbles Télégraphiques. *Address:* Treveal, Mawnan Smith, Falmouth, Cornwall. *Club:* Royal Automobile.

**CHAPMAN, (Anthony) Colin (Bruce),** CBE 1970; Chairman Group, Lotus Car Cos Ltd; Designer of sports and racing cars; *b* 19 May 1928; *s* of S. F. Kennedy Chapman; *m* 1954, Hazel Patricia Williams; one *s* two *d. Educ:* Stationers' Company's Sch., Hornsey; London Univ. (BSc Eng). Served as Pilot, RAF, 1950. Structural Engineer, 1951; Civil Engineer, Development engineer, British Aluminium Co., 1952. Formed own Company, Lotus Cars, manufacturing motor cars, 1955. FRSA 1968. *Recreation:* flying. *Address:* Lotus Cars Ltd, Norwich, Norfolk NOR 92W. *Clubs:* British Racing Drivers, British Automobile Racing; British Racing and Sports Car.

**CHAPMAN, Prof. Brian;** Professor of Government, University of Manchester, since 1961, and Dean, Faculty of Economic and Social Studies, since 1967; *b* 6 April 1923. *Educ:* Owen's Sch., London; Magdalen Coll. and Nuffield Coll., Oxford (DPhil, MA). Lieut, RNVR, 1942-45. Dept of Govt, University of Manchester, and Vis. Prof. at several European Univs, 1949-60; Foundn Prof. of Govt and Dir, Public Admin programme, University of W Indies, 1960-61. Mem. Council, Manchester Business School; Mem. Court, Cranfield Inst. of Technology; Jt Editor, Minerva Series. *Publications:* French Local Government, 1953; The Prefects and Provincial France, 1954; (with J. M. Chapman) The Life and Times of Baron Haussmann, 1956; The Profession of Government, 1959; (with P. Campbell) The Fifth Constitution, 1959; British Government Observed, 1963; The Police State, 1970; contributions to internat. learned jls, reviews and newspapers. *Address:* Department of Government, The University, Manchester 13. *T:* 061-273 3333. *Clubs:* Naval; Manchester Business School (Manchester).

**CHAPMAN, Colin;** *see* Chapman, A. C. B.

**CHAPMAN, Cyril Donald,** QC 1965; Recorder of Bradford, since 1969; *b* 17 Sept. 1920; *s* of Cyril Henry Chapman and Frances Elizabeth Chapman (*née* Braithwaite); *m* 1st, 1950, Audrey Margaret Fraser (*née* Gough) (marr. diss., 1959); one *s*; 2nd, 1960, Muriel Falconer Bristow; one *s. Educ:* Roundhay Sch., Leeds; Brasenose Coll., Oxford (MA). Served RNVR, 1939-45. Called to Bar, 1947; Harmsworth Scholar, 1947; North Eastern Circuit, 1947; Recorder of Huddersfield, 1965-69. Contested (C) East Leeds 1955, Goole 1964, Brighouse and Spenborough, 1966. *Recreation:* yachting. *Address:* Hill Top, Collingham, Wetherby, Yorks. *T:* Collingham Bridge 2813. *Clubs:* United University; Leeds (Leeds).

**CHAPMAN, Daniel Ahmling;** *see* Chapman Nyaho.

**CHAPMAN, Donald;** *see* Chapman, W. D.

**CHAPMAN, Fitzroy Tozer,** CBE 1942; DSc(Eng); BSc; MICE; FIEE; retired. *b* 6 Oct. 1880; *s* of Frederic Chapman; *m* 1906, Beatrice Maude Briggs (*d* 1968); *m* 1968, Amy Thomas. *Educ:* Leeds Modern Sch.; Leeds Univ. Electrical Designer, Greenwood & Batley Ltd, Leeds, 1901-11; Sen. Lectr and Supt, Testing Dept, Faraday House, London, 1911-20; District Technical Inspector, Board of Education, 1920-23; Divisional Inspector, 1933-36; Staff Inspector, 1936-39; seconded to War Office as temp. Brig., 1939-46; retired 1946. *Publications:* A Study of the Induction Motor, 1933; Electrical Engineering, 1956; miscellaneous papers on electrical subjects. *Recreation:* gardening. *Address:* 37 Military Road, Sandgate, Kent. *T:* Folkestone 38238. *Club:* Reform.

**CHAPMAN, Lieut-Col Frederick S.;** *see* Spencer Chapman.

**CHAPMAN, Prof. Garth;** Professor of Zoology, Queen Elizabeth College, University of London, since 1958; *b* 8 Oct. 1917; *o s* of E. J. Chapman and Edith Chapman (*née* Attwood); *m* 1941, Margaret Hilda Wigley; two *s* one *d. Educ:* Royal Grammar Sch., Worcester; Trinity Hall, Cambridge (Major Scholar). Telecommunications Research Establishment, Ministry of Aircraft Production, 1941-45. Asst Lecturer in Zoology, Queen Mary Coll., University of London, 1945-46; Lecturer in Zoology, Queen Mary Coll., University of London, 1946-58. *Publications:* various on structure and physiology of marine invertebrates. *Recreations:* gardening; wood-engraving. *Address:* Nunns, Coxtie Green, Brentwood, Essex.

**CHAPMAN, Prof. Guy Patterson,** OBE 1919; MC 1918; MA Oxon; BSc (Econ.) London; *b* 11 Sept. 1889; *o s* of George Walter Chapman, Beechwood, Cookham Dean, Berks, late Official Receiver in Bankruptcy; *m* 1926, Margaret Storm Jameson, *qv. Educ:* Westminster Sch.; Christ Church, Oxford; London Sch. of Economics, Barrister-at-Law, 1914. Served Royal Fusiliers, 1914-20, in France and Belgium, 1915-18 (despatches twice, OBE, MC), Major. Engaged in book-publishing, 1920-40. Served War of 1939-45, in Army Educational Corps, 1941-45; Lieut-Col Commandant Army Sch. of Education (Army Bureau of Current Affairs), 1943; Prof. of Modern History in the University of Leeds, 1945-53; Visiting Prof., University of Pittsburgh, Pa., 1948-49; Mem., Institute for Advanced Study, Princeton, NJ, 1957. FRSL. *Publications:* A Passionate Prodigality, 1933; Beckford, a biography, 1938; A Bibliography of the Works of William Beckford, 1931; Culture and Survival, 1940; The Dreyfus Case: A Reassessment, 1955; The Third Republic of France: the First Phase, 1963; Why France Collapsed, 1968. *Recreation:* travel. *Club:* Savile.

**CHAPMAN, Harold Thomas,** CBE 1951; FRAeS; MIMechE; formerly Director, Hawker Siddeley Group, retired 1969; *b* 4 Aug. 1896; 3rd *s* of Henry James and Elizabeth Chapman, Mornington, Wylam-on-Tyne; *m* 1923, Mabel Annie Graham. *Educ:* Rutherford Coll., Newcastle on Tyne. Served European War in RFC and RAF, 1917-19. Joined Armstrong Siddeley Motors Ltd as a Designer, 1926; Works Manager, 1936; Gen. Manager, 1945; Dir, 1946. *Recreations:* fishing, shooting, golfing. *Address:* Arlescote House, Arlescote, Banbury, Oxon. *T:* Edge Hill 248.

**CHAPMAN, Mrs Hester Wolferstan, (Mrs R. L. Griffin)**; *b* 26 Nov. 1899; *d* of T. Pellatt, Durnford Preparatory Sch., Dorset; *m* 1st, 1926, N. K. Chapman; 2nd, 1938, R. L. Griffin; no *c*. *Educ:* privately. Subsequently became mannequin in Paris; later in London, secretary, telephone operator, typist, companion, daily governess, schoolmistress. War of 1939-45: worked for Fighting French, American Red Cross and as waitress in a canteen at Combined Operations. *Publications: novels:* She Saw Them Go By, 1932; To Be a King, 1934; Long Division, 1943; I Will Be Good, 1945; Worlds Apart, 1947; Ever Thine, 1951; Falling Stream, 1954; The Stone Lily, 1957; Eugénie, 1961; Fear No More, 1968; *biographies:* Great Villiers, 1949; Mary II, Queen of England, 1953; Queen Anne's Son, 1954; The Last Tudor King, 1958; Two Tudor Portraits, 1960; Lady Jane Grey, 1962; The Tragedy of Charles II, 1964; Lucy, 1965; Privileged Persons, 1966; The Sisters of Henry VIII, 1969. *Recreations:* foreign travel, cinema and theatre, dress, interior decoration. *Address:* 13 Conway Street, W1. *T:* 01-636 3260.

**CHAPMAN, Air Vice-Marshal Hubert Huntlea,** CB 1958; CBE 1952; *b* 20 Feb. 1910; *s* of late Major George James Chapman, OBE, Bournemouth; *m* 1937, Phyllis Mary, *d* of late Cyril Smith Owbridge, Parkstone, Dorset; one *s*. *Educ:* Bedford Sch. Joined RAF, 1928; Fighter and Army Co-operation Squadrons and Signals Appointments, 1928-39; Signals Staff Appointments, 1940-43; Chief Telecommunications Officer, MAAF, 1944-45 (despatches twice); Dep. Dir of Signals Training, 1945-47; Chief Signals Officer, Air Command, Far East, 1947-48; Student, Jt Services Staff Coll., 1948; Sen. Air Staff Officer, HQ 43 Group, 1949-50; AOC, 43 Group, 1950-51; Dir of Signals Policy, 1952-53; Student, idc, 1954; Senior Air Staff Officer, Headquarters 90 (Signals) Group, RAF Medmenham, 1955-58; Dir-Gen. of Technical Services, Air Min., 1958-61; Air Officer-in-charge of Administration, Maintenance Command, 1961-63, retired, 1963. CEng, MIEE. Bronze Star (US), 1946. *Recreation:* photography. *Address:* Spencer Cottage, Spencer Road, Canford Cliffs, Dorset. *T:* Canford Cliffs 77830. *Clubs:* Royal Air Force; Parkstone Yacht (Dorset).

**CHAPMAN, John Henry Benjamin,** CB 1957; *b* 28 Dec. 1899; *s* of Robert Henry Chapman and Edith Yeo Chapman (*née* Lillicrap); *m* 1929, Dorothy Rowlerson; one *s* one *d*. *Educ:* HM Dockyard Sch., Devonport; RNC Greenwich. Dir of Naval Construction, Admiralty, 1958-61, retired. Dir, Fairfield S & E Co. Ltd, 1962-66; Consultant, Upper Clyde Shipbuilders, 1966-68. Mem. of Royal Corps of Naval Constructors; Vice-Pres., RINA. *Recreation:* sailing. *Address:* The Small House, Delling Lane, Old Bosham, Sussex. *T:* Bosham 3331. *Clubs:* Bath and County (Bath); Emsworth Sailing.

**CHAPMAN, Kathleen Violet,** CBE 1956; RRC 1953 (ARRC 1945); QHNS 1953-56; Matron-in-Chief, Queen Alexandra's Royal Naval Nursing Service, 1953-56, retired; *b* 30 May 1903; *d* of late Major H. E. Chapman, CBE, DL Kent, Chief Constable of Kent, and Mrs C. H. J. Chapman. *Educ:* Queen Anne's, Caversham. trained St Thomas's Hospital, 1928-32. *Address:* Holmfield, Compton Chamberlayne, Salisbury, Wilts.

**CHAPMAN, Mrs Murray, (Olive)**; FRGS; FRSA; *d* of late G. A. Garry Simpson, MRCS, and of Ethel Maud (*née* Gibbon); *m* late C. H. Murray Chapman, Flt-Lt RN. *Educ:* Queen's Coll.; Heatherley's Art Sch., London. Extensive travels both in the Artic and the East, including journey on horseback across Iceland; winter sledge journey through Lapland; and a journey among primitive tribes in Madagascar; has lectured on her expeditions before Royal Geog. Soc., Royal Scottish Geog. Soc., Royal Asiatic Soc., etc, and also in America; has held three one-man shows in Bond Street of her water-colour paintings and in 1933 produced a short sound travel film–Winter with the Laps–shown at the Academy Cinema, London, etc. *Publications:* Across Iceland, 1930; Across Lapland, 1932, in Penguin series 1939 (new edn 1947); Across Cyprus, 1937; Across Madagascar, 1943. *Address:* 24 Eaton Mansions, Cliveden Place, SW1.

**CHAPMAN, Prof. Norman Bellamy,** MA, PhD, FRIC; G. F. Grant Professor of Chemistry, Hull University, since Oct. 1956; *b* 19 April 1916; *s* of Frederick Taylor Chapman and Bertha Chapman; *m* 1949, Fonda Maureen Bungey; one *s* one *d*. *Educ:* Barnsley Holgate Grammar Sch.; Magdalene Coll., Cambridge (Entrance Scholar). 1st Cl. Parts I and II Nat. Sciences Tripos, 1937 and 1938. Bye-Fellow, Magdalene Coll., 1939-42; Univ. Demonstrator in Chemistry, Cambridge, 1945; Southampton Univ.: Lectr, 1947; Senior Lectr, 1949; Reader in Chemistry, 1955. R. T. French Visiting Prof., Univ. of Rochester, NY, 1962-63. BA 1938, MA 1942, PhD 1941, Cambridge. *Publications:* contribs to Jl Chem. Soc., Analyst, Jl Medicinal Chem., Tetrahedron, Jl Organic Chemistry, Chemistry and Industry. *Recreations:* music, gardening, cricket, rugby football. *Address:* 61 Newland Park, Hull. *T:* 42946.

**CHAPMAN, Mrs Olive M.**; *see* Chapman, Mrs Murray.

**CHAPMAN, Oscar Littleton;** attorney-at-law; *b* Omega, Virginia, 22 Oct. 1896; *s* of James Jackson Chapman and Rosa Archer Blount; *m* 1st, 1926, Olga Pauline Edholm (*d* 1932); 2nd, 1940, Ann Kendrick; one *s*. *Educ:* public schs, Va.; Randolph Macon Acad., Bedford, Va.; Univ. of Denver; Westminster Law Sch. (LLB). Enlisted in US Navy, 1918, served until 1920. Served for five years as asst and chief probation officer of Juvenile Court of Denver. Admitted to law practice, 1929; Mem. of Dist of Columbia Bar: admitted to practice before Supreme Court of US, 1934. Asst-Sec. of the Interior, 1933-46; Under-Sec. of the Interior, 1946-49; Sec. of the Interior, USA, 1949-53. Active in civic, political, and veterans' affairs, both in Denver and in Washington; has served at request of President, as head of Govt div. of Red Cross, Community Fund, and War Fund drives; appointed by late President Roosevelt to Interdepartmental Cttee to coordinate Health and Welfare Services of Govt, 1935; Cttee on Vocational Education, 1936; mem. of President's Advisory Cttee on Management Improvement in Govt; director: Franklin D. Roosevelt Foundation; Harry S. Truman Library. Has received several citations for service to US. Hon. Dr of Laws; Augustana Coll., 1934; Colorado State Coll. of Education, 1940; Howard Univ., 1949, Univ. of Denver, 1951; Western State Coll. of Colorado, 1961. Mem. American Judicature Soc. and of Phi Alpha Delta Law Fraternity. *Address:* Pennsylvania Building, Washington 4, DC, USA; 4975 Hillbrook Lane, Washington, DC. *Club:* City (Denver, USA).

**CHAPMAN, Sir Robin (Robert Macgowan),** 2nd Bt *cr* 1958; CBE 1961; TD and Bar, 1947; DL; JP; Partner in Chapman, Hilton, Hutchinson and Dunford, Chartered Accountants; Joint

Secretary, Shields Commercial Building Society, since 1939; Director: George Angus & Co. Ltd; Commercial Union Assurance Co. Ltd (Local Board); Manchester Dry Docks Co. Ltd; North Eastern Investment Trust Ltd (Manager); Shields Commercial Building Society; Chairman: James Hogg & Sons (North Shields) Ltd; John W. Pratt Ltd; *b* Harton, Co. Durham, 12 Feb. 1911; *er s* of 1st Bt and Lady Hélène Paris Chapman, JP (*née* Macgowan); *S* father, 1963; *m* 1941, Barbara May, *d* of Hubert Tonks, Ceylon; two *s* one *d*. *Educ:* Marlborough; Corpus Christi Coll., Cambridge (Exhibitioner). 1st Cl. Hons Maths, BA 1933; MA 1937. Chartered Accountant, ACA 1938; FCA 1945. Chm., Northern Counties Provincial Area Conservative Associations, 1954-57; Chm., Jarrow Conservative Association, 1957-60; Pres., Northern Soc. of Chartered Accountants, 1958-59, Mem. Cttee, 1949-60; Member: Police Authority, Co. Durham, 1955-59, 1961-65; Appeals Cttee, 1955-62; Durham Diocesan Conf., 1953-; Durham Diocesan Bd of Finance, 1953- (Chm. 1966); Durham County Territorial Assoc., 1948-68; N England Territorial Assoc., 1968 (Chm. 1966-70). Gov., United Newcastle Hospitals, 1957-64. TA Army officer, 1933-51; served War of 1939-45: RA Anti-Aircraft Command; GSO 2, 1940; CO 325 LAA regt, RA (TA), 1948-51; Hon. Col 1963; JP 1946, DL, 1952; High Sheriff of County Durham, 1960. *Recreation:* lawn tennis. *Heir: er s* David Robert Macgowan Chapman [*b* 16 Dec. 1941; *m* 1965, Maria Elizabeth de Gosztony-Zsolnay, *o d* of Dr N. de Mattyasovsky-Zsolnay, Montreal, Canada; one *s*]. *Address:* Cherry Tree House, Cleadon, near Sunderland. *T:* Boldon 7451. *Clubs:* Junior Carlton; County (Durham); Hawks (Cambridge).

**CHAPMAN, Air Chief Marshal Sir Ronald I.;** *see* Ivelaw-Chapman.

**CHAPMAN, Hon. Sir Stephen,** Kt 1966; QC 1955; **Hon. Mr Justice Chapman;** Judge of the High Court of Justice, Queen's Bench Division, since 1966; *b* 5 June 1907; 2nd *s* of late Sir Sydney J. Chapman, KCB, CBE, and of late Lady Chapman, JP; *m* 1963, Mrs Pauline Frances Niewiarowski, *widow* of Dmitri de Lobel Niewiarowski and *d* of late Lt-Col H. Allcard and late Mrs A. B. M. Allcard. *Educ:* Westminster; Trinity Coll., Cambridge. King's Scholar and Capt. Westminster; Entrance Scholar and Major Scholar, Trinity Coll., Cambridge; Browne Univ. Gold Medallist, 1927 and 1928; John Stuart of Rannoch Univ. Scholar, 1928; 1st Cl. Classical Tripos, Pt I, 1927, and in Pt II, 1929. Entrance Scholar, Inner Temple, 1929; Jardine student, 1931; 1st Cl. and Certificate of Honour, Bar Final, 1931; called to Bar, Inner Temple, 1931; SE Circuit, Herts-Essex Sessions; Asst Legal Adviser, Min. of Pensions, 1939-46; Prosecuting Counsel for Post Office on Se Circuit, 1947-50 (Leader, Circuit, 1962); Comr of Assize, Winchester, Autumn, 1961. Recorder of Rochester, 1959-61, of Cambridge, 1961-63; Judge of the Crown Court and Recorder of Liverpool, 1963-66. Dept. Chm. Herts QS, 1963. Mem. Bar Council, 1956; Hon. Treas. 1958; Vice-Chm. 1959-60. *Publications:* Auctioneers and Brokers, in Atkin's Encyclopædia of Court Forms, vol. 3, 1938; Insurance (non-marine), in Halsbury's Laws of England, 3rd edn, vol. 22, 1958; Statutes on the Law of Torts, 1962. *Recreation:* gardening. *Address:* Royal Courts of Justice, Strand, WC2; (private), 9 King's Bench Walk, Temple, EC4. *T:* 01-353 7966; The Manor House, Ware, Herts. *T:* Ware 2123. *Club:* Oxford and Cambridge University.

**CHAPMAN, Sydney Brookes,** ARIBA; AMTPI; MP (C) Handsworth Division of Birmingham since 1970; Senior Partner, Sydney Chapman Consultants, Chartered Architects and Town Planners; *b* 17 Oct. 1935. *Educ:* Rugby Sch.; Manchester University. DipArch 1958; ARIBA 1960; DipTP 1961; AMTPI 1962. Nat. Chm., Young Conservatives, 1964-66 (has been Chm. and Vice-Chm. at every level of Movt); Sen. Elected Vice-Chm., NW Area of Nat. Union of C and U Assocs, 1966-70; contested (C) Stalybridge and Hyde, 1964. Lectr in Arch. and Planning at techn. coll., 1964-70. *Publications:* political booklets. *Address:* House of Commons, SW1.

**CHAPMAN, (William) Donald;** *b* 25 Nov. 1923; *s* of Wm H. and Norah F. E. Chapman, Barnsley. *Educ:* Barnsley Grammar Sch.; Emmanuel Coll., Cambridge. MA (1st Cl. Hons) Economics, also degree in Agriculture; Senior Scholar of Emmanuel Coll. Research in Agric. Economics, Cambridge, 1943-46; Cambridge City Councillor, 1945-47; Sec., Trades Council and Labour Party, 1945-57; MP (Lab) Birmingham (Northfield), 1951-70. Research Sec. of the Fabian Soc., 1948-49; Gen. Sec., 1959-53. Formerly Labour Parliamentary Candidate for Hemel Hempstead. *Publications:* articles and Fabian pamphlets. *Recreation:* travel. *Address:* 2 Crescent Place, Brighton BN2 1AS. *T:* Brighton 684444.

**CHAPMAN-ANDREWS, Sir Edwin Arthur,** KCMG 1953 (CMG 1948); OBE 1936; retired as British Ambassador at Khartoum (1956-61); *b* 9 Sept. 1903; *er s* of Arthur John Chapman-Andrews and Ada Allen, Exeter; *m* 1931, Sadie Barbara Nixon, London; two *s* two *d*. *Educ:* Hele's Sch., Exeter; University College, London (Fellow, 1952); Sorbonne; St John's Coll., Cambridge (while a probationer Vice-Consul, to study oriental Languages). Probationer Vice-Consul, Levant Consular Service, 1926; Actg Vice-Consul, Port Said, Cairo and Suez, 1928-29; Actg Vice-Consul, Addis Ababa, 1930; FO, 1931-32; Vice-Consul at Kirkuk, Iraq and at Rowanduz, 1933-35; Actg Consul at Harar, 1935-36; Foreign Office, 1937; Asst Oriental Sec., Cairo, 1937-40. Hon. Commission in Royal Sussex Regt, 1940; Liaison Officer on staff of C-in-C, Middle East, with Emperor Haile Selassie; Foreign Office, 1942; Head of Personnel Dept, 1945; Inspector of Overseas Establishments, 1946; British Minister at Cairo, 1947-51; at Beirut, 1951; Ambassador, 1952. Adviser, Massey-Ferguson (Holdings) Ltd, 1962; Dir, Massey-Ferguson (Export), 1964-; Mitchell Cotts (Export), 1965. Member: Council of Lord Kitchener National Memorial Fund; British Nat. Export Council, 1965-68; Cttee for Middle East Trade (COMET), 1963-65 (Chm. 1965-68). KStJ; KCSG (Papal). *Recreation:* any change of occupation handy. *Address:* 2 The Leys, Brim Hill, N2. *Clubs:* Athenæum, Oriental.

**CHAPMAN-MORTIMER, William Charles;** author; *b* 15 May 1907; *s* of William George Chapman-Mortimer and Martha Jane McLelland; *m* 1934, Frances Statler; *m* 1956, Ursula Merits; one *d*. *Educ:* privately. *Publications:* A Stranger on the Stair, 1950; Father Goose, 1951 (awarded James Tait Black Memorial Prize, 1952); Young Men Waiting, 1952; Mediterraneo, 1954; Here in Spain, 1955; Madrigal, 1960. *Address:* Gisebo, 56100 Huskvarna, Sweden.

**CHAPMAN NYAHO, Daniel Ahmling,** CBE 1961; Executive Director, Pioneer Tobacco Co. Ltd, Ghana (Member of British-American Tobacco Group), since 1967; *b* 5 July 1909; *s* of William Henry Chapman and Jane Atsiamesi (*née* Atriki); *m* 1941, Jane Abam (*née* Quashie); two *s* four *d* (and one *d* decd). *Educ:* Bremen Mission Schs, Gold Coast and Togoland; Achimota Coll., Ghana; St Peter's Hall, Oxford. Postgraduate courses at Columbia Univ. and New York Univ.; Teacher, Government Senior Boys' School, Accra, 1930; Master, Achimota Coll., 1930-33, 1937-46. Area Specialist, UN Secretariat, Lake Success and New York, 1946-54; Sec. to Prime Minister and Sec. of Cabinet, Gold Coast/Ghana, 1954-57; Ghana's Ambassador to USA and Permanent Representative at UN, 1957-59; Headmaster, Achimota Sch., Ghana, 1959-63; Dir, UN Div. of Narcotic Drugs, 1963-66; Ambassador (Special Duties), Min. of External Affairs, Ghana, 1967. Gen. Sec., All-Ewe Conf., 1944-46; Commonwealth Prime Ministers' Conf., 1957. First Vice-Chm., Governing Council of UN Special Fund, 1959; Chairman: Mission of Indep. African States to Cuba, Dominican Republic, Haiti, Venezuela, Bolivia, Paraguay, Uruguay, Brazil, Argentina, Chile, 1958; Arts Council of Ghana, 1968-; Volta Union, 1968-. Vice-Chm., Commn on Univ. Educn in Ghana, 1960-61. Member: Board of Management, UN Internat. Sch., New York, 1950-54, 1958-59; UN Middle East and N. Africa Technical Assistance Mission on Narcotics Control, 1963; Political Cttee of Nat. Liberation Council, 1967; Board of Trustees of General Kotoka Trust Fund; Chm., Arts Council of Ghana, 1968-69. Darnforth Vis. Lectr, Assoc. Amer. Colls, 1969, 1970. Hon. LLD Greenboro Agric. and Techn. Coll., USA, 1958. Fellow, Ghana Acad. of Arts and Sciences. *Publications:* Human Geography of Eweland, 1946; Our HomelandBook I: South-East Gold Coast, 1945; (Ed.) The Ewe News-Letter, 1945-46. *Recreations:* music, gardening, walking. *Address:* (Office) Tobacco House, Liberty Avenue, PO Box 11, Accra, Ghana. *T:* 21111; (Home) No. 11 Ninth Avenue, Tesano, Accra, Ghana. *T:* 27180. *Clubs:* Royal Commonwealth Society (London); Accra (Ghana).

**CHAPPELL, William;** dancer, designer, producer; *b* Wolverhampton, 27 Sept. 1908; *s* of Archibald Chappell and Edith Eva Clara Blair-Staples. *Educ:* Chelsea School of Art. Studied dancing under Marie Rambert. First appearance on stage, 1929; toured Europe with Ida Rubinstein's company, working under Massine and Nijinska; danced in many ballets, London, 1929-34; joined Sadler's Wells Co., 1934, and has appeared there every season. Has designed scenery and costumes for ballets at Sadler's Wells, 1934-, including Les Rendezvous, Les Patineurs and Giselle; for many revues and London plays. Produced Lyric Revue, 1951, Globe Revue, 1952, High Spirits, Hippodrome, 1953, At the Lyric, 1953, Going to Town, St Martin's, 1954 (also arranging dances for many of these); An Evening with Beatrice Lillie, Lyric, Hammersmith, 1954 (asst prod.); Time Remembered, New, 1955; (with Orson Welles) Moby Dick, Duke of York's, 1955; The Buccaneer, Lyric, Hammersmith, 1955; Violins of St Jacques (also wrote libretto), Sadler's Wells; English Eccentrics; Love and a Bottle; Passion Flower Hotel; Travelling Light; Espresso Bongo; Living for Pleasure; Where's Charley?; appeared in and assisted Orson Wells with film The Trial. Illustrator of several books. *Publications:* Studies in Ballet; Fonteyn. *Recreations:* walking, reading, cinema, painting. *Address:* 40 Thurloe Square, SW7.

**CHAPPLE, Frank J.;** General Secretary, Electrical, Electronic and Telecommunication Union/Plumbing Trades Union, since Sept. 1966; *b* Shoreditch, 1921; *m*; two *s*. *Educ:* elementary school. Started as Apprentice Electrician; Member ETU, 1937-; Shop Steward and Branch Official; Member Exec. Council, 1958; Asst General Secretary, 1963-66. Member: National Exec. Cttee of Labour Party; Cttee of Inquiry into Shipping, 1967-. *Address:* Electrical Electronic and Telecommunication Union/Plumbing Trades Union, Hayes Court, West Common Road, Hayes, Bromley, Kent.

**CHAPPLE, Stanley;** Director of Symphony and Opera, University of Washington; *b* 29 Oct. 1900; *s* of Stanley Clements Chapple and Bessie Norman; *m* 1927, Barbara, *d* of late Edward Hilliard; no *c*. *Educ:* Central Foundation Sch., London. Began his musical education at the London Academy of Music at the age of 8, being successively student, professor, Vice-Principal, Principal until 1936; as a Conductor made début at the Queen's Hall, 1927, and has since conducted Symphony Orchestras in Berlin, Vienna, The Hague, Warsaw and Boston, St Louis, Washington, DC, and other American and Canadian cities. Assistant to Serge Koussevitzky at Berkshire Music Centre, 1940, 1941, 1942 and 1946; former conductor St Louis Philharmonic Orchestra and Chorus and Grand Opera Association. Hon MusDoc Colby Coll., 1947. *Publications:* Yorke Trotter Principles of Musicianship; Language of Harmony, Classway to the Keyboard. *Address:* 18311 47th Place NE, Seattle, Washington, USA.

**CHAPUT DE SAINTONGE, Rolland Alfred Aimé,** CMG 1953; Special Projects Officer, United Nations High Commission for Refugees, since March 1968; *b* Montreal, Canada, 7 Jan. 1912; *s* of Alfred Edward and Hélène Jeté Chaput de Saintonge; *m* 1940, Barbara Watts; one *s* two *d*. *Educ:* Canada; USA; Syracuse Univ., NY (BA, MA); Geneva Univ. (D ès Sc. Pol.). Extra-Mural Lecturer in International Affairs: University College of the South-West, Exeter, University of Bristol, University College of Southampton, 1935-40; Staff Speaker, Min. of Information, South-West Region, 1940; served Army, 1940-46; Lieut-Col (DCLI); Asst Secretary, Control Office for Germany and Austria, 1946-48; Head of Government Structure Branch, CCG and Liaison Officer to German Parliamentary Council, 1948-49; Head of German Information Dept, FO, 1949-58; Dep. Chief, Information and Public Relations Sect., UN High Commn for Refugees, 1960-64; Rep. in Senegal of UN High Comr for Refugees, Dec. 1964-Jan. 1966; Programme Support Officer, UNHCR, Feb. 1966-May 1967; Chief, N and W Europe Section, UNHCR, May 1967-March 1968. *Publications:* Disarmament in British Foreign Policy, 1935; British Foreign Policy Since the War, 1936; The Road to War and the Way Out, 1940; Public Administration in Germany, 1961. *Address:* 8 Minley Court, Somers Road, Reigate, Surrey.

**CHARLEMONT,** 11th Viscount *cr* 1665 (Ireland); **Charles St George Caulfeild;** Baron Caulfeild of Charlemont, 1620 (Ireland); retired as Manager of Bank of NSW, Cambooya, Queensland, 1945; *b* 23 Nov. 1884; *s* of Henry St George Caulfeild (*d* 1943) and Jane (*d* 1924), *d* of William Goldsmith; *S* brother, 1967; *m* 1915, Lydia Clara Kingston; two *d*. *Educ:* Private Grammar Sch., Bundaberg, Queensland. *Recreations:* gardening, stamp collecting. *Heir:* *b* Richard William St George Caulfeild [*b* 13 March 1887; *m* 1914, Dorothy Laura (*d* 1961), *d* of late Frank Giles; two *d*]. *Address:* 45 Amelia Street, Coorparoo, Brisbane, Queensland, Australia. *T:* Brisbane 97-1798.

**CHARLES, Anthony Harold,** ERD; TD; MA Cantab; MB; FRCS; FRCOG; Senior Obstetric and Gynæcological Surgeon, St George's Hospital; Senior Surgeon, Samaritan Hospital for Women (St Mary's); Consultant Gynæcologist, Royal National Orthopædic Hospital; Hon. Gynæcologist, Florence Nightingale Hospital and King Edward VII Hospital for Officers (Levy Wing); Consultant Gynæcologist, Caterham and District Hospital; Consulting Surgeon, General Lying-in-Hospital; *b* 14 May 1908; 2nd *s* of H. P. Charles; *m* 1962, Rosemary Christine Hubert; three *d. Educ:* Dulwich; Gonville and Caius Coll., Cambridge. Examiner in Midwifery and Gynæcology: Univ. of Cambridge; Soc. of Apothecaries; Royal College of Obstetricians and Gynæcologists, and London Univ. Member, Board of Governors, St Mary's Hospital. Past President: Chelsea Clinical Soc.; Sect. of Obstetrics and Gynæcology, RSM. Late Vice-Dean, St George's Hospital Medical Sch.; late Resident Asst Surgeon and Hon. Asst Anæsthetist, St George's Hospital. Colonel AMS; Hon. Colonel, late OC, 308 (Co. of London) General Hospital, T. & AVR. Hon. Surgeon to the Queen, 1957-59. Served 1939-45, Aldershot, Malta and Middle-East as Surgical Specialist; Officer-in-Charge, Surgical Division, 15 Scottish General Hospital and Gynæc. Adviser MEF. *Publications:* Women in Sport, in Armstrong and Tucker's Injuries in Sport, 1964; contributions since 1940 to Jl Obst. and Gyn., Postgrad. Med. Jl, Proc. Royal Soc. Med., Operative Surgery, BMJ. *Recreations:* golf, boxing (Middle-Weight, Cambridge *v* Oxford, 1930); Past President Rosslyn Park Football Club. *Address:* 90a Harley Street, W1. *T:* 01-935 4196; Gaywood Farm, Gay Street, Pulborough, Sussex. *Clubs:* Bath, Buck's; Hawks (Cambridge).

**CHARLES, Enid,** MA Cantab, PhD Cape Town; FRSE; Regional Adviser in Health Statistics, 1955-59, Consultant, 1961-64, WHO, South-East Asia; *b* Dec. 1894; *o d* of Rev. James Charles, Denbigh; *m* 1918, Lancelot Hogben (marr. diss. 1957); two *s* two *d. Educ:* Newnham Coll., Cambridge; Univ. of Liverpool. Leverhulme Research Fellow, 1937-39; Census Research Specialist, Dominion Bureau of Statistics, Ottawa, 1942-47; Chief Statistical Officer to the City Corporation, Birmingham, 1949-52. *Publications:* The Practice of Birth Control, 1932; The Twilight of Parenthood, 1935; The Changing Size of the Canadian Family, 1948; on comparative physiology, and mathematical genetics in Proc. Royal Soc. B, Quart. Jl Exper. Physiol., Jl Genetics, Jl Exper. Biol., etc; on vital statistics in London and Cambridge Economic Service Monographs, Economica, Sociological Review, Proc. Royal Soc. Edinburgh, and in Political Arithmetic. *Address:* 605 Greenwood Avenue, Iowa City, Iowa, USA.

**CHARLES, Very Rev. Harold John;** Dean of St Asaph, since 1957; *b* 26 June 1914; *s* of Rev. David Charles and Mary Charles, Carmarthenshire; *m* 1941, Margaret Noeline; one *d. Educ:* Welsh Univ. Aberystwyth; Keble Coll., Oxford. BA Wales 1935; BA Oxford 1938, MA 1943. Curate of Abergwili, Carms, 1938-40; Bishop's Messenger, Diocese of Swansea and Brecon, 1940-48; Warden of University Church Hostel, Bangor, and Lecturer at University College, Bangor, 1948-52; Vicar of St James, Bangor, 1952-54; Canon Residentiary of Bangor, 1953-54; Warden of St Michael's Coll., Llandaff, 1954-57; Canon of Llandaff, 1956-57. *Address:* The Deanery, St Asaph, Flintshire. *T:* St Asaph 2532.

**CHARLES, Sir John Alexander,** KCB 1955; Kt 1950; MD, FRCP, DPH; Chief Medical Officer to Ministry of Health, Ministry of Education and Home Office, 1950-60; *m* 1947, Madeleine Frances, *d* of late Sir W. E. Hume; one *s* one *d.* MB, BS (1st Class Hons.) 1916; DPH Cantab 1925; MD (Durham) 1930; FRCP 1935. Harveian Orator, Royal College of Physicians, 1955. (First) Rock Carling Fellow, 1962. President, 12th World Health Assembly, 1959. Jacques Parisot Lectr, WHO, 1970. Hon. DHY Durham. Leon Bernard Prize, WHO, 1962. *Address:* 25 Campden Hill Road, W8. *T:* 01-937 4527. *Club:* Athenæum.

**CHARLES, Sir Noel Hughes Havelock,** 3rd Bt *cr* 1928; KCMG 1941 (CMG 1937); MC; HM Ambassador to Turkey, 1949-51; *b* 20 Nov. 1891; 2nd *s* of Sir Richard Havelock Charles, 1st Bt, GCVO, KCSI; *S* brother, 1936; *m* 1st, Grace (*d* 1955), *d* of J. L. Bevir; 2nd, 1957, Gipsy Joan, 2nd *d* of late Sir Walter Lawrence, Hyde Hall, Sawbridgeworth, Herts. *Educ:* Rugby; Christ Church, Oxford, (MA). Served European War, 1914-18: France, 1915-18 (MC, despatches twice). Entered Diplomatic Service as 3rd Sec. at Brussels, 1919; 2nd Sec., 1920; 1st Sec., 1925; Bucharest; Tokyo, 1926; FO, 1929; Stockholm, 1931; Moscow, 1933; Counsellor, Brussels, 1936-37; Counsellor, Rome, 1937-39, Minister there, 1939-40; Minister at Lisbon, 1940-41; British Ambassador to Brazil, 1941-44; High Comr in Italy with rank of Ambassador, 1944-47; FO, 1947-49; retired, 1951. KStJ; 3rd Class Rising Sun. *Heir:* none. *Address:* c/o Coutts & Co., 440 Strand, WC2; St Christophe, Chateauneuf-de-Grasse, AM, France. *Clubs:* White's, Royal Automobile.

**CHARLES, Robert Lonsdale,** MC 1942; MA, FMA; Keeper, Department of Art, National Museum of Wales; *b* 19 Aug. 1916; *s* of late Robert Henry Charles, CBE; *m* 1946, Margaret Joy, *d* of late A. C. R. Stephenson; one *s* two *d. Educ:* Aysgarth Sch., Yorks; Shrewsbury; Corpus Christi Coll., Oxford. Royal Artillery, 1939-46; Control Commission for Germany, 1945-46. Assistant Keeper, National Museum of Wales, 1946; Keeper, 1952. *Publications:* Continental Porcelain of the 18th Century, 1964; articles and reviews. *Address:* National Museum of Wales, Cardiff. *T:* 26241.

**CHARLES, William Travers;** Special Lecturer in Law, Monash University, since 1966; Judge of the High Court, Zambia, 1963-66; *b* Victoria, Australia, 10 Dec. 1908; *s* of William James Charles and Elizabeth Esther Charles (*née* Payne); *m* 1940, Helen Gibson Vale; one *s* one *d. Educ:* St Thomas Grammar Sch., Essendon, Victoria; University of Melbourne. Called to bar, Victoria, 1932; practised at bar, 1932-39. Served Australian Army Legal Service including Middle East, 1940-42 (Lieut-Col), seconded AAG (Discipline), AHQ Melbourne, 1942-46. Chief Magistrate and Legal Adviser, British Solomon Islands Protectorate, 1946-51; Judicial Commn, British Solomon Islands, 1951-53; Magistrate, Hong Kong, 1954-56; District Judge, Hong Kong, 1956-58; Judge of the High Court, Western Nigeria, 1958-63. *Recreations:* cricket, football, music, history. *Address:* Department of Law, Monash University, Clayton, Victoria 3168, Australia.

**CHARLES-EDWARDS, Rt. Rev. Lewis Mervyn,** MA, DD; *b* 6 April 1902; *s* of Dr Lewis Charles-Edwards and Lillian Hill; *m* 1933, Florence Edith Louise Barsley; one *s* one *d. Educ:* Shrewsbury School; Keble College, Oxford; Lichfield Theological College. Curate, Christ Church, Tunstall, 1925-28; St Paul, Burton on Trent, 1928-31; Pontesbury, 1931-33; Vicar,

Marchington, 1933-37; Market Drayton, 1937-44; Newark on Trent, 1944-48; Rural Dean of Hodnet, 1938-44, of Newark, 1945-48; Vicar of St Martin in the Fields, London, WC2, 1948-56; Commissary to Bishop of Honduras, 1945-56; Chaplain to King George VI, 1950-52, to the Queen, 1952-56; Bishop of Worcester, 1956-70. Religious Adviser to Independent Television Authority, 1955-56. Chairman, Midland Region Religious Advisory Committee BBC, 1958-65. Member of Commission on Church and State, 1951. Chaplain and Sub-Prelate Order of St John of Jerusalem, 1965. Select Preacher, University of Cambridge, 1949; Oxford, 1964. *Publication:* Saints Alive!, 1953. *Address:* 9 Bell Lane, Ludlow, Shropshire.

**CHARLESTON, Robert Jesse;** Keeper of the Department of Ceramics, Victoria and Albert Museum since 1963; *b* 3 April 1916; *s* of Sidney James Charleston, Lektor, Stockholms Högskola; *m* 1941, Joan Randle; one *s* one *d*. *Educ:* Berkhamsted Sch., Herts; New College, Oxford. Army (Major, RAPC), 1940-46; Asst, Bristol Museum, 1947; Asst Keeper, Victoria and Albert Museum, 1948; Deputy Keeper, 1959. *Publications:* Roman Pottery, 1959; (ed) English Porcelain, 1745-1850, 1965; (ed) World Ceramics, 1968; numerous articles and reviews in The Connoisseur, Jl of Glass Studies, Burlington Magazine, etc. *Recreations:* foreign travel, music. *Address:* 1 Denbigh Gardens, Richmond, Surrey. *T:* 01-940 3592.

**CHARLESWORTH, John Kaye,** CBE 1957; DSc Leeds, PhD Breslau, MRIA, FRSE, FRGS, FGS; Professor of Geology, Queen's University, Belfast, 1921-54; Professor Emeritus, 1954; *b* 3 Jan. 1889; *e s* of late George Charlesworth, Burley, Leeds; *m* Janet Cumming, *e d* of late Rev. Alex. Gibson, MA, BD, Tarbolton; one *s* one *d*. *Educ:* Univs of Leeds, London, Breslau, Munich. Geologist on Scottish Spitsbergen Expedition of 1919; Senior Lectr in Geology in Univ. of Manchester, 1919-21; Member Senate, Queen's Univ., 1938-54; Member Charlemont Cttee on Industrial and Mineral Resources, NI, 1924-26; Mem. Scientific Research Grants Advisory Board, NI, 1929-32 (Chm. Board, 1935-41); Indep. Member several Trade Boards, NI, and Chairman several Wages Councils, NI, 1945-; Apptd Member Nat. Arbitration Tribunal, NI, 1941-59; Chairman, Sen. Certificate Examination enquiry, NI, 1948-50; Geological Adviser to Ministries of Agriculture, Commerce and Finance, NI, 1924-47; Mem. Unemployment Insurance Statutory Cttee, 1944-47; Mem. Nat. Insurance Advisory Cttee, 1947-60. Neill Prize Royal Society Edin., 1954; Prestwich Medal, Geological Soc., London, 1957. Hon. DSc Queen's Univ., Belfast, 1957. *Publications:* The Geology of Ireland: an introduction, 1953 (reprint 1966); The Quaternary Era, 1957 (reprint 1966); Historical Geology of Ireland, 1963; geological papers. *Address:* Corrig, Ballycastle, Co. Antrim, Northern Ireland.
*See also W. D. C. Lyddon.*

**CHARLESWORTH, Lilian E.,** CBE 1954; Director, Thomas Wall Trust. *Educ:* Clapham High Sch., GPDST; Royal Holloway Coll. Head Mistress of Kensington High Sch., 1931-39; Head Mistress, Sutton High Sch., GPDST, 1939-59. President of Assoc. of Headmistresses, 1948-50. Chairman: Joint Cttee of the Four Secondary Associations, 1952-54; Whitelands College Council; Member: Professional Classes Aid Council; Council, Queen Mary Coll. Hon. Director, Royal Academy of Dancing, Teachers' Training Course. *Address:* 46 Beaufort Mansions, SW3.

**CHARLEY, Sir Philip (Belmont),** Kt 1968; President, Royal Agricultural Society of NSW, 1965-69, Vice-Patron, 1969; *b* Richmond, NSW, 28 Dec. 1893; *s* of late P. Charley, Richmond, NSW; *m* 1st, 1923, N. M. Nivison; one *s* three *d*; 2nd, 1957, Myfanwy Rickard. *Educ:* Barker Coll., Hornsby, Sydney. Farming and dairying, Clarendon Park, from 1919. Served European War, 1914-18, as Gunner 5 Bde, AFA; served War of 1939-45: Lieut in AFC, Flt-Lieut ATC, RAAF, 1943-45. *Recreations:* racing, Rugby, cricket, swimming. *Address:* 59 Junction Road, Wahroonga, Sydney, Australia. *T:* Sydney 482000. *Clubs:* Union, Air Force Officers' (Sydney); Ex-Servicemen (Richmond).

**CHARLISH, Dennis Norman;** Under-Secretary, Ministry of Technology, since 1969; *b* 24 May 1918; *s* of Norman Charlish and Edith (*née* Cherriman); *m* 1941, Margaret Trevor, *o d* of William Trevor and Margaret Ann Williams, Manchester; one *d*. *Educ:* Brighton Grammar Sch.; London Sch. of Economics. Rosebery Schol., 1947; BSc (Econ) 1st class hons., 1951. Joined Civil Service as Tax Officer, Inland Revenue, 1936; Exec. Officer, Dept of Overseas Trade, 1937; Dep. Armament Supply Officer, Admty, 1941; Principal, BoT, 1949; Asst Secretary, 1959; Imperial Defence Coll., 1963; Under-Sec., BoT, 1967-69. *Address:* 28 Multon Road, SW18.

**CHARLTON, Bobby;** *see* Charlton, Robert.

**CHARLTON, Frederick Noel,** CB 1961; CBE 1946; Principal Assistant Solicitor (Litigation), Treasury Solicitor's Department, since Oct. 1956; *b* 4 Dec. 1906; *s* of Frederick William Charlton and Marian Charlton; *m* 1932, Maud Helen Rudgard; no *c*. *Educ:* Rugby School; Hertford Coll., Oxford Univ. (MA). Admitted a Solicitor, 1932; in private practice as Solicitor in London, 1932-39. War Service, 1939-46 (attained rank of Colonel, Gen. List). Joined Treasury Solicitor's Dept, 1946. Chairman, Coulsdon and Purley UDC, 1953-54 and 1964-65; Hon. Alderman, London Borough of Croydon. Bronze Star (USA), 1945. *Recreations:* golf, tennis, travel. *Address:* Windyridge, 11 Hillcroft Avenue, Purley, Surrey. *T:* 01-660 2802. *Club:* Junior Carlton.
*See also T. A. G. Charlton.*

**CHARLTON, George;** artist; Member of Staff of Slade School of Art, 1919-62; examiner for General School Examinations, University of London since 1931 and Associated Examining Board since 1959; *b* 1899; *s* of James William Charlton, London; *m* 1929, Daphne, *d* of Conrad Gribble, MICE, Weybridge. Student, Slade School, 1914, at age of fifteen (Slade and Robert Ross Scholarships). Served European War, 1917-19. Senior Lecturer in charge of Slade School, 1948-49; examiner for Board of Education Art Examinations, 1932-45, 1949-50-51; member of staff of Willesden School of Art, 1949-59; exhibitor at New English Art Club from 1915, member 1925-45, 1950-, Hon. Treasurer, 1958; works purchased by Tate Gallery, Contemporary Art Society and Bradford Art Gallery; exhibitor at London, provincial and overseas galleries. Formerly Governor: Camberwell School of Art; Trent Park Coll.; Farnham School of Art, 1950-60. *Publications:* Illustration for Wolff's Anatomy for Artists; for T. F. Powys' Mr Weston's Good Wine, 1st edn; for Richard Hughes' The Spider's Palace; articles on Prof. Henry Tonks and on Prof. Frederick Brown in Dictionary of

National Biography. *Address:* 40 New End Square, Hampstead, NW3.

**CHARLTON, Robert, (Bobby Charlton),** OBE 1969; Professional Footballer with Manchester United since 1954; *b* 11 Oct. 1937; *s* of Robert and Elizabeth Charlton; *m* 1961, Norma; two *d. Educ:* Bedlington Grammar Sch., Northumberland. FA Cup Winners Medal, 1963; FA Championship Medals, 1956-57, 1964-65 and 1966-67; World Cup Winners Medal (International), 1966; European Cup Winners medal, 1968. 100th England cap, 21 April 1970. *Publications:* My Soccer Life, 1965; Forward for England, 1967; This Game of Soccer, 1967; Book of European Football, 1969. *Recreation:* golf. *Address:* Oakdene, Brookfield Road, Lymm, Cheshire. *T:* Lymm 4225.

**CHARLTON, Thomas Alfred Graham,** CB 1970; Assistant Under-Secretary of State since 1960 (Ministry of Defence since 1964); *b* 29 Aug. 1913; 3rd *s* of Frederick William and Marian Charlton; *m* 1940, Margaret Ethel, *yr d* of A. E. Furst; three *d. Educ:* Rugby School; Corpus Christi Coll., Cambridge. Asst Principal, War Office, 1936; Asst Private Secretary to Secretary of State for War, 1937-39; Principal, 1939; Cabinet Office, 1947-49; Asst Secretary, 1949; International Staff, NATO, 1950-52. Coronation Medal, 1953. *Recreations:* golf, sailing, gardening. *Address:* Little Mynchen, Knotty Green, Bucks. *T:* Beaconsfield 3094. *Club:* Anglo-Belgian.

*See also Frederick Noel Charlton.*

**CHARLTON, Sir William Arthur,** Kt 1946; DSC; retired as General Marine Superintendent at New York, Furness Withy & Co. SS Lines, 1960; *b* 25 Feb. 1893; *s* of William and Augusta Pauline Charlton; *m* 1919, Eleanor Elcoat; two *s. Educ:* Blyth; Newcastle on Tyne. Master Mariner. DSC for service in N Africa landings, 1943. Younger Brother, Trinity House; Liveryman Hon. Company of Master Mariners; Fellow Royal Commonwealth Society. *Address:* 4 River Road, Scarsdale, New York, USA.

**CHARNLEY, John,** CBE 1970; DSc; FRCS; Consultant Orthopædic Surgeon and Director of Centre for Hip Surgery, Wrightington Hospital, near Wigan, Lancs; *b* 29 Aug. 1911; *m* 1957, Jill Margaret (*née* Heaver); one *s* one *d. Educ:* Bury Grammar Sch., Lancs. BSc 1932; MB ChB (Manch.) 1935; FRCS 1936; DSc 1964. Hon. Cons. Orthopædic Surgeon, Manchester Royal Infirmary, 1947. Hon. Lecturer in Clinical Orthopædics, Manchester Univ., 1959; Hon. Lecturer in Mechanical Engineering, 1966, Inst. of Science and Technology, Manchester Univ. Fellow of British Orthopædic Assoc.; Hon. Member: Amer. Acad. of Orthopædic Surgeons; American, French, Belgian, Swiss, Brazilian, and French-Canadian Orthopædic Assocs; S African Medical Assoc. *Publications:* Compression Arthrodesis, 1953; The Closed Treatment of Common Fractures, 1950 (German trans., 1968); Acrylic Cement in Orthopædic Surgery, 1970. *Recreations:* ski-ing two weeks per year–otherwise none. *Address:* Moss Lane, Tabley, Knutsford, Cheshire.

**CHARNLEY, William John,** MEng, CEng, FRAeS, FInstNav; idc; Deputy Controller of Guided Weapons, Ministry of Technology, since 1969; *b* 4 Sept. 1922; *s* of George and Catherine Charnley; *m* 1945, Mary Paden; one *s* one *d. Educ:* Oulton High Sch., Liverpool; Liverpool Univ. MEng 1945. Aerodynamics Dept, RAE Farnborough, 1943-55; Supt. Blind Landing Experimental Unit, 1955-61; Imperial Defence Coll., 1962; Head of Instruments and Electrical Engineering Dept, RAE Farnborough, 1965-68; Head of Research Planning, Min. of Technology, 1968-69. *Publications:* papers on subjects in aerodynamics, aircraft all weather operation, aircraft navigation. *Address:* Kirkstones, Brackendale Close, Camberley, Surrey. *T:* Camberley 22547.

**CHARQUES, Mrs Dorothy;** novelist since 1937; *b* 4 June 1899; *d* of Benjamin and Florence Margaret Taylor, Arrow, Alcester, Warwicks; *m* 1929, Richard Charques, author and critic; no *c*; *m* 1964, S. A. G. Emms, inventor and consultant engineer. *Educ:* Alcester Grammar Sch.; Sheffield Univ. BA Hons. Econ. (Sheffield); MA History. Asst Secretary and Research Secretary, Fabian Soc., 1924-29. *Publications:* with Richard Charques, 2 novels: Above and Below, 1929, After The Party, 1933; alone: The Tramp and His Woman, 1937; Between Sleeping and Waking, 1938; Time's Harvest (a trilogy comprising: Time's Harvest, 1940, The Returning Heart, 1943, Between the Twilights, 1946); Men Like Shadows, 1952; The Valley, 1954; The Dark Stranger, 1956; The Nunnery, 1959; A Wind from the Sea, 1970. *Recreations:* reading, walking; looking and seeing, generally out of doors. *Address:* 143 Loxley Road, Stratford upon Avon, Warwicks. *T:* Stratford upon Avon 5648.

**CHARRINGTON, Sir John,** Kt 1949; President, Charrington, Gardner, Locket & Co. Ltd, since 1964 (Chairman, 1940-64); *b* 1886; *s* of late John Charrington, Shenley, Herts, and Rose Georgiana Elizabeth Grainger; *m* 1912, Elizabeth Mary Dalbiac; two *s* three *d. Educ:* Haileybury. Served European War, 1914-18 (despatches). President: Coal Merchants Federation of Great Britain, 1930-31 and 1947-49; National Society for Clean Air; Coal Utilisation Council, 1967-68. *Recreation:* fishing. *Address:* High Quarry, Crockham Hill, Kent. *T:* Crockham Hill 313. *Club:* Carlton.

**CHARRINGTON, John Arthur Pepys;** President, Bass Charrington Ltd (formerly Chairman Charrington United Breweries Ltd from formation; previously Chairman Charrington & Co. Ltd); *b* 17 Feb. 1905; *s* of Arthur Finch Charrington and Dorothea Lethbridge; *m* 1932, Barbara Haliburton Cunard; three *s* two *d. Educ:* Eton; New College, Oxford. *Address:* Netherton House, Andover, Hampshire. *Clubs:* Boodle's, Bath; New (Edinburgh).

**CHARTERIS,** family name of **Earl of Wemyss.**

**CHARTERIS, Hugo Francis Guy,** MC; writer; *b* 11 Dec. 1922; *s* of late Hon. Guy Lawrence Charteris; *m* 1948, Virginia, *d* of Colin Gurdon Forbes Adam, *qv*; one *s* three *d* (and one *s* decd). *Educ:* Eton; Univ. of Oxford. Scots Guards, 1941-47; served in Italy (twice wounded); went as Public Relations Officer, Malaya, Java, etc, SEAC. Journalist, Daily Mail, London and Paris, 1948-51. Went to live in Sutherland, 1951-59. Formerly contributor, Sunday and Daily Telegraph. Scottish Arts Council Prize, 1969. *Publications:* A Share of the World, 1952; Marching with April, 1955; Picnic at Porokorro, 1958; The Lifeline, 1961; Pictures on the Wall, 1963; The River-Watcher, 1965; Clunie (for children), 1963; Staying with Aunt Rozzie, 1964; The Coat, 1966; The Indian Summer of Gabriel Murray, 1968. Television plays, including The Connoisseur, Toggle, Cradle Song, There is also Tomorrow. Short stories in Cornhill, London Magazine; translations, adaptations, etc. *Recreations:* photography, gardening, shooting. *Address:* The Grange, Elvington, York. *T:* Elvington 209.

**CHARTERIS, Leslie;** FRSA; author; *b* 1907; *m* 1st, Pauline Schishkin (divorced, 1937); one *d*; 2nd, Barbara Meyer (divorced, 1941); 3rd, Elizabeth Bryant Borst (divorced, 1951); 4th, Audrey Long. *Educ:* Rossall; Cambridge Univ. Many years of entertaining, but usually unprofitable, travel and adventure, and can still be had. After one or two false starts created character of "The Saint" (trans. into 15 languages besides those of films, radio, television, and the comic strip). *Publications:* Meet the Tiger, 1928; Enter the Saint; The Last Hero; Knight Templar; Featuring the Saint; Alias the Saint; She was a Lady (filmed 1938 as The Saint Strikes Back); The Holy Terror (filmed 1939 as The Saint in London); Getaway; Once More the Saint; The Brighter Buccaneer; The Misfortunes of Mr Teal; Boodle; The Saint Goes On; The Saint in New York (filmed 1938); Saint Overboard, 1936; The Ace of Knaves, 1937; Thieves Picnic, 1937; (trans., with introd.) Juan Belmonte, Killer of Bulls: The Autobiography of a Matador, 1937; Prelude for War, 1938; Follow the Saint, 1938; The Happy Highwayman, 1939; The First Saint Omnibus, 1939; The Saint in Miami, 1941; The Saint Goes West, 1942; The Saint Steps In, 1944; The Saint on Guard, 1945; The Saint Sees it Through, 1946; Call for the Saint, 1948; Saint Errant, 1948; The Second Saint Omnibus, 1952; The Saint on the Spanish Main, 1955; The Saint around the World, 1957; Thanks to the Saint, 1958; Señor Saint, 1959; The Saint to the Rescue, 1961; Trust the Saint, 1962; The Saint in the Sun, 1964; Vendetta for the Saint, 1965 (filmed 1968); The Saint on TV, 1968; The Saint Returns, 1969; The Saint and the Fiction Makers, 1969; The Saint Abroad, 1970; The Saint in Pursuit, 1970; Supervising Editor of the Saint Magazine, 1953-67; columnist, Gourmet Magazine, 1966-68; concurrently has worked as special correspondent and Hollywood scenarist; contributor to leading English and American magazines and newspapers. *Recreations:* eating, drinking, horseracing, sailing, fishing, and lying in the sun. *Address:* 8 Southampton Row, WC1. *Clubs:* Savage; Mensa, Yacht Club de Cannes.

**CHARTERIS, Hon. Sir Martin (Michael Charles),** KCVO 1962 (MVO 1953); CB 1958; OBE 1946; Assistant Private Secretary to the Queen since 1952; *b* 7 Sept. 1913; 2nd *s* of Hugo Francis, Lord Elcho (killed in action, 1916); *g s* of 11th Earl of Wemyss; *m* 1944, Hon. Mary Gay Hobart Margesson, *yr d* of 1st Viscount Margesson, PC, MC; two *s* one *d*. *Educ:* Eton; RMC Sandhurst. Lieut KRRC, 1936; served War of 1939-45; Lieut-Colonel, 1944. Private Secretary to Princess Elizabeth, 1950-52. *Recreation:* sculpting. *Address:* Appt 25, St James's Palace, SW1. *T:* 01-839 6920. *Clubs:* Travellers', White's.

**CHASE, Anya Seton;** *see* Seton, A.

**CHASE, Rt. Rev. George Armitage,** DD (*hc*), Cambridge, Leeds; STD (*hc*), Ripon College, USA; Bishop of Ripon, 1946-April 1959, retired; Fellow of Selwyn College, Cambridge; Hon. Fellow of Trinity Hall and Queen's College; *b* 3 Sept. 1886; 3rd *s* of late Rt Rev. Frederic Henry Chase. *Educ:* Rugby School; Queens' Coll., Cambridge (Carus Prize, 1909; Crosse Schol., 1910; Hulsean Prize, 1911). Ordained, 1911; Curate of Portsea, 1911-13; Fellow and Dean of Trinity Hall, 1913-34; Tutor, 1919-34; Master of Selwyn Coll., Cambridge, 1934-46; Univ. Lectr in Divinity, 1926-46; TCF, 1914-19; MC, 1917; Hon. Canon of Ely Cathedral, 1945-46. Examining Chaplain to Bishop of Ely, 1914-24 and 1935-46, to Bishop of Southwark, 1919-32, to Bishop of Winchester, 1932-42, to Archbishop of York, 1942-46. *Publication:* A Companion to the Revised Psalter, 1963. *Address:* 36 Millington Road, Cambridge.

**CHASE, Mary Ellen,** PhD; retired as Professor of English Literature, Smith College, Northampton, Mass.; Phi Beta Kappa, 1920; *b* 24 Feb. 1887; *d* of Edward Everett Chase and Edith Lord. *Educ:* Blue Hill Academy, Blue Hill, Maine; Univ. of Maine (BA 1909); Univ. of Minnesota (MA 1918, PhD 1922). Hon. LittD: Univ. of Maine, 1928; Bowdoin Coll., 1933; Hon. LHD: Colby Coll., 1937; Northeastern Univ., 1948; Smith Coll., 1949; Wilson Coll., 1957; Hon. LLD: Goucher Coll., 1960. *Publications:* Mary Christmas (novel), 1927; A Goodly Heritage, 1932; Mary Peters (novel), 1934; Silas Crockett (novel), 1935; Dawn in Lyonnesse (novel), 1937; A Goodly Fellowship, 1939; Windswept (novel), 1941; The Bible and the Common Reader, 1944; Jonathan Fisher: Maine Parson, 1948; The Plum Tree (novel), 1949; The White Gate, 1955; Life and Language in the Old Testament, 1956; The Edge of Darkness (novel), 1957; The Lovely Ambition (novel), 1960; The Psalms for the Common Reader, 1963; A Journey to Boston, 1965; A Walk on an Iceberg, 1966. *Address:* 16 Paradise Road, Northampton, Mass., USA.

**CHASE, Stuart;** author, social scientist; *b* Somersworth, New Hampshire, USA, 8 March 1888; *s* of Harvey Stuart and Aaronette Rowe Chase; *m* 1st, 1914, Margaret Hatfield (divorced, 1929); one *s* one *d*; 2nd, 1930, Marian Tyler. *Educ:* Massachusetts Inst. of Technology; Harvard Univ. SB cum laude, 1910; seven years in accounting work; CPA degree from Massachusetts, 1916; four years in Government Service, ending 1921; since 1921 has been chiefly engaged in economic research and writing books and articles; some public lecturing; consulting work for government agencies, business organizations, UNESCO, etc. Member National Inst. of Arts and Letters, Phi Beta Kappa; LittD American Univ., 1949; DHL Emerson Coll., Boston, 1970. *Publications:* The Tragedy of Waste, 1925; Your Money's Worth (with F. J. Schlink), 1927; Men and Machines, 1929; Prosperity: Fact or Myth?, 1929; The Nemesis of American Business, 1931; Mexico, 1931; A New Deal, 1932; The Economy of Abundance, 1934; Government in Business, 1935; Rich Land, Poor Land, 1936; The Tyranny of Words, 1938; The New Western Front, 1939; Idle Money, Idle Men, 1940; A Primer of Economics, 1941; The Road We Are Travelling, 1942; Goals for America, 1942; Where's the Money Coming From?, 1943; Democracy under Pressure, 1945; Men at Work, 1945; Tomorrow's Trade, 1945; For This We Fought, 1946; The Proper Study of Mankind, 1948 (revised, 1956); Roads to Agreement, 1951; Power of Words, 1954; Guides to Straight Thinking, 1956; Some Things Worth Knowing, 1958; Live and Let Live, 1960; American Credos, 1962; Money to Grow On, 1964; The Most Probable World, 1968; Danger–Men Talking, 1969; and many magazine articles for Harpers, Atlantic, The Saturday Review, etc. *Recreations:* tennis, ski-ing, sketching. *Address:* Georgetown, Conn 06829, USA. *Club:* Harvard (New York).

**CHASTENET de CASTAING, Jacques,** CBE 1938; Croix de Guerre, 1916; Grand Officier de la Légion d'Honneur, 1968; LLD Paris; historian and journalist; member of Académie française, 1956, and of Académie des Sciences morales et politiques, 1947; *b* 20 April 1893; *s* of G. Chastenet de Castaing, a French Senator; *m* 1919, Germaine Saladin; two *s*. *Educ:* Université de Paris. Served European

War, 1914-19; Liaison officer with the American EF, 1918; French Diplomatic Service, 1919; Attaché, 1919; General Secretary, Rhineland inter-allied High Commission, 1920; Secrétaire d'Ambassade, 1921; diplomatic correspondent, L'Opinion, 1926; Editor of Le Temps, 1931; Major, French Military Mission in Egypt, 1945. *Publications:* Du Sénat, 1919; William Pitt, 1941; Godoy, 1943; Wellington, 1945; Vingt Ans d'histoire diplomatique (1920-1940), 1945; Le Siècle de Victoria, 1947; Poincaré, 1948; La France de M. Fallieres, 1949; Histoire de la IIIe République, 7 Vols, 1952-62; Elizabeth the 1st, 1953; Winston Churchill et l'Angleterre du XX Siècle, 1956; Vie quotidienne au début du règne de Victoria, 1961; L'Angleterre d'aujourd'hui, 1965; En avant vers l'Ouest, 1967; Léon Gambettan, 1968, etc; contribs to l'Opinion, le Figaro, la Revue de Paris, le Temps, Paris-Presse, L'Aurore, etc. *Address:* 14 rue d'Aumale, Paris 9e. *Club:* L'Union (Paris).

**CHATAWAY, Rt. Hon. Christopher John,** PC 1970; MP (C), Chichester, since May 1969; Minister of Posts and Telecommunications, since 1970; broadcaster, journalist; *b* 31 Jan. 1931; *m* 1959, Anna Lett; two *s* one *d*. *Educ:* Sherborne Sch.; Magdalen Coll., Oxford. Hons. Degree, PPE. President OUAC, 1952; rep. Great Britain, Olympic Games, 1952 and 1956; briefly held world 5,000 metres record in 1954. Junior Exec. Arthur Guiness Son & Co., 1953-55; Staff Reporter, Independent Television News, 1955-56; Current Affairs Commentator for BBC Television, 1956-59. Elected for N Lewisham to LCC, 1958-61. MP (C) Lewisham North, 1959-66; PPS to Minister of Power, 1961-62; Joint Parly Under-Secretary of State, Dept of Education and Science, 1962-64; Alderman, GLC, 1967-70; Leader Educn Cttee, ILEA, 1967-69. Nansen Medal, 1960. *Publication:* (with Philip Goodhart) War Without Weapons, 1968. *Address:* Lordington Mill, Lordington, Chichester, Sussex.

**CHATER, Major-General Arthur Reginald,** CB 1941; CVO 1966; DSO 1918; OBE 1931; *b* 7 Feb. 1896, *s* of Thomas Addison Chater and Gertrude Lockyer Peel; *m* 1954, Diana, *o d* of late Edward Charles Daubeny, and *widow* of Maj.-Gen. Archibald Maxwell Craig. *Educ:* Aldenham. Entered Royal Marines as 2nd Lieut, 1913; served with RM Brigade in Flanders, 1914 (wounded at Antwerp); Gallipoli, 1915 (despatches, French Croix de Guerre); Grand Fleet, 1916-17; was Adjt of RM Bn which landed from HMS Vindictive at Zeebrugge on 23 April 1918 (DSO, Bt Major); served in Egyptian Army, 1921-25, and Sudan Defence Forces, 1925-31; commanded Sudan Camel Corps, 1927-30; commanded Military Operations in Kordofan, 1929-30 (despatches); Senior RM Officer, East Indies Station, 1931-33; Home Fleet, 1935-36; commanded Somaliland Camel Corps, 1937-40; commanded defence of British Somaliland, 1940 (despatches, CB); Military Governor and comd Troops, British Somaliland, 1941-43; comd Portsmouth Div. Royal Marines, 1943-44; Director of Combined Operations, India and SE Asia, 1944-45; MGGS, 1945-46, comd Chatham Group, Royal Marines, 1946-48; retired pay, 1948. One of HM's Body Guard of Hon. Corps of Gentlemen-at-Arms, 1949-66 and Harbinger, 1952-66; Col Comdt Somaliland Scouts, 1948-58. Member Berkshire CC, 1955-61. *Address:* 106 King's Road, Windsor, Berks. *T:* Windsor 66112. *Club:* United Service.

**CHATFIELD,** family name of **Baron Chatfield.**

**CHATFIELD,** 2nd Baron *cr* 1937, of Ditchling; **Ernle David Lewis Chatfield;** *b* 2 Jan. 1917; *s* of 1st Baron Chatfield, PC, GCB, OM, KCMG, CVO (Admiral of the Fleet Lord Chatfield), and Lillian Emma St John Matthews; *S* father, 1967; *m* 1969, (Felicia Mary) Elizabeth, *d* of late Dr John Roderick Bulman, Hereford. *Educ:* RNC Dartmouth; Trinity Coll., Cambridge. ADC to Governor-General of Canada, 1940-44. *Heir:* none. *Address:* Apartment 16, 46 Academy Road, Westmount, Quebec, Canada.
*See also Sir P. W. Donner.*

**CHATT, Joseph,** FRS 1961; ScD (Cantab); Director, Research Unit of Nitrogen Fixation, ARC, since 1963 (in Sussex since 1964); Professor of Chemistry, University of Sussex, since 1964; *b* 6 Nov. 1914; *e s* of late Joseph Chatt, Sebergham, Cumberland, and of Mrs M. E. Chatt, Carlisle, Cumberland; *m* 1947, Ethel, *y d* of Hugh Williams, St Helens, Lancs; one *s* one *d*. *Educ:* Nelson Sch., Wigton, Cumberland; Emmanuel Coll., Cambridge. Research Chemist, Woolwich Arsenal, 1941-42; Dep. Chief Chemist, later Chief Chemist, Peter Spence & Sons Ltd, Widnes, 1942-46; ICI Research Fellow, Imperial Coll., London, 1946-47; Head of Inorganic Chemistry Dept, Butterwick, later Ackers, Research Laboratories, ICI Ltd, 1947-60; Group Manager, Research Dept, Heavy Organic Chemicals Div., ICI Ltd, 1961-62; Distinguished Visiting Prof. of Chemistry, Pennsylvania State Univ., 1960; Visiting Prof. of Chemistry, Yale Univ., 1963; Prof. of Inorganic Chemistry, QMC, London Univ., 1964; Royal Society Leverhulme Visiting Prof., Univ. of Rajasthan, India, 1966-67; Vis. Prof., Univ. of S Carolina, 1968. Vice-Pres., Chemical Soc., 1962-65; Hon. Secretary: Chemical Soc., 1956-62; Chemical Council, 1958-60; Commn on Nomenclature of Inorganic Chemistry, Internat. Union of Pure and Applied Chemistry, 1959-63. Member of national and internat. cttees concerned with chemistry. *Publications:* scientific papers, mainly in Jl Chem. Soc. *Recreations:* antiques, numismatics, photography, travel. *Address:* 28 Tongdean Avenue, Hove, Sussex BN3 6TN. *T:* Brighton 554377.

**CHAU, Hon. Sir Sik Nin,** Kt 1960; CBE 1950; JP 1940; Chairman: Hong Kong Trade Development Council; Hong Kong Management Association; Hongkong Chinese Bank Ltd; The Dairy Farm, Ice & Cold Storage Co. Ltd; Wellcome Co. Ltd; Associated Dairies International Ltd; Hong Kong Marine Food Co. Ltd; Dairy Lane Ltd; Repulse Bay Enterprises Ltd; Far East Insurance Co. Ltd; Nin Fung Hong; Oriental Express Ltd; Sik Yuen Co. Ltd; Kowloon Motor Bus Company; Man Lee Cheung Co. Ltd; Pioneer Trade Development Co. Ltd; Director of numerous companies; *b* 1903; *s* of late Cheuk-Fan Chau, 1 Hing Hong Road, Hong Kong; *m* 1927, Ida Hingkwai, *d* of late Lau Siu-Cheuk; two *s*. *Educ:* St Stephen's Coll., Hong Kong; Hong Kong Univ.; London Univ.; Vienna State Univ. MB, BS, Hong Kong, 1923; DLO, Eng., 1925; DOMS 1926. LLD (Hon.), Hong Kong 1961. Member Medical Board, Hong Kong, 1935-41; Mem. Urban Council, 1936-41; Chm. Po Leung Kuk, 1940-41; MLC, Hong Kong, 1946-59; MEC, 1947-62. Dep. Chm., Subsid. British Commonwealth Parliamentary Assoc., Hong Kong, 1953-59. Chief Delegate of Hong Kong to ECAFE Conference in India, 1948, in Australia, 1949; Chairman ECAFE Conference in Hong Kong, 1955; President, Indo-Pacific Region, Internat. Scientific Management Assoc.; Fellow, Internat. Academy of Management; Member: Advisory

Board to Lingnan Inst. of Business Administration; Chinese Univ. of Hong Kong; Internat. Industrial Council, Stanford Univ.; Internat. Board of Electors of Insurance Hall of Fame; British Universities Selection Cttee; Council and Court of University of Hong Kong; Senior Member Board of Education Hong Kong, 1946-60; Chairman Hong Kong Model Housing Society; Vice-President, Hong Kong Anti-Tuberculosis Assoc.; Steward Hong Kong Jockey Club. Hon. President or Vice-President of numerous Assocs.; Hon. Adviser of Chinese General Chamber of Commerce; Permanent Dir Tung Wah Hospital Advisory Board. Coronation Medal, 1937; Defence Medal, 1945; Coronation Medal, 1953; granted permanent title of Honourable by the Queen, 1962. *Address:* IL 3547 Hatton Road, Hong Kong. *T:* 433695.

**CHAU TSUN-NIN, Sir,** Kt 1956; CBE 1938; *b* 22 Oct. 1893; *s* of late Hon. Chau Siu Ki and of Mrs Chau; *m* 1931, Elaine Leung; four *s* one *d.* *Educ:* St Stephen's Coll., Hong Kong; The Queen's Coll., Oxford (MA). Barrister-at-law, Middle Temple. Unofficial Member of Legislative Council, Hong Kong, 1931-53; Unofficial MEC, Hong Kong, 1946-59. Hon. LLD Univ. of Hong Kong. *Address:* No. 8, Queen's Road West, Hong Kong.

**CHAUNCY, Major Frederick Charles Leslie,** CBE 1958 (OBE 1953); Personal Adviser to Sultan of Muscat and Oman; *b* 22 Dec. 1904; *o s* of late Col C. H. K. Chauncy, CB, CBE, Indian Army; *m* 1932, Barbara Enid Miller; one *s.* *Educ:* Radley; Sandhurst. Commissioned British Army, 1924; transf. IA (45th Rattray's Sikhs), 1928; transf. IPS, 1930; served Persian Gulf, NWF India, Indian States; retired 1947; re-employed under HM's Foreign Office, 1949, as Consul-General at Muscat; retired 1958; appointed by Sultan of Muscat and Oman as his Personal Adviser, 1961. *Recreations:* Rugby football (Sandhurst); athletics (Sandhurst, Army, England, also UK in Olympic Games). *Address:* Adviser's House, Muscat, Gulf of Oman, Arabia. *Club:* United Service.

**CHAUVEL, Jean,** GCMG (Hon.) 1960; GCVO (Hon.) 1957; Grand Croix de la Légion d'Honneur; Grand Croix de l'Etoile Noire; Grand Croix de Malte; Hon. DCL Internat. Oxford; *b* Paris, 16 April 1897; *s* of Ferdinand Chauvel and Mme Chauvel (*née* Derrien); *m* 1926, Diane de Warzee d'Hermalle; two *s* two *d.* *Educ:* Université de Paris (Licencié en Droit). Foreign Affairs, 1921-40; subsequently, consecutively, Third, Second and First Secretary, Consul-General, and Minister. Founder of Study Group, Foreign Affairs (Resistance); Delegate in France of Commn of Foreign Affairs of Algiers, 1944; acting Sec.-Gen., Foreign Affairs Commn, Algiers, 1944; Ambassador of France and Sec.-Gen. of Foreign Affairs, 1945; Perm. Representative of France at Security Council, United Nations, 1949; Ambassador of France at Berne, 1951; Delegate at Conference of Geneva, 1954; Delegate at Manila Conference, 1954; Ambassador of France and High Commissioner in Austria, 1954; Ambassador of France in London, 1955-62; Delegate at the Geneva Conference (Laos), 1961-62; Diplomatic Counsellor of Govt, 1962-63. *Publications:* Préludes, 1945; D'une eau profonde, 1948; Labyrinthe, 1950; Infidèle, 1951; Imaginaires, 1952; Clepsydre, 1958; Sables, 1963. *Address:* 123 Rue de la Tour, Paris XVIe; Le Ruluat, Combrit, Finistère. *Clubs:* Union, Union Internalliée (Paris).

**CHAUVIRÉ, Yvette,** Chevalier de la Légion d'Honneur (palmes), académiques, 1964; Officier des Arts et des Lettres, 1967; ballerina; Artistic and Technical Adviser to Administrator of Paris Opera since 1963; *b* Paris, 22 April 1917. *Educ:* Ecole de la Danse de l'Opera, Paris. Paris Opera Ballet, 1930; first major rôles in David Triomphant and Les Créatures de Prométhée; Danseuse etoile, 1942; danced Istar, 1942; Monte Carlo Opera Ballet, 1946-47; returned to Paris Opera Ballet, 1947-49. Has appeared at Covent Garden, London; also danced in the USA, and in cities of Rome, Moscow, Leningrad, Berlin, Buenos Aires, Johannesburg, Milan, etc; official tours: USA 1948; USSR 1958, 1966, 1968; Canada 1967; Australia. Leading rôles in following ballets; Les Mirages, Lac des Cygnes, Sleeping Beauty, Giselle, Roméo et Juliette, Suite en Blanc, Le Cygne (St Saens), La Dame aux Camélias, etc. Choreographer: La Péri, Roméo et Juliette, Le Cygne. *Films:* La Mort du Cygne, 1937 (Paris); Carrousel Napolitain, 1953 (Rome). *Publication:* Je suis Ballerine. *Recreations:* Violon d'Ingre, painting and drawing, collections of swans. *Address:* 21 Place du Commerce, Paris 15e.

**CHAUX, Dr Victor M.;** *see* Mosquera-Chaux.

**CHAVAN, Yeshwantrao Balvantrao;** Minister of Finance, Government of India, since 1970; *b* 12 March 1913; *m* 1942, Venubai, *d* of late R. B. More, Phaltan, district Satara. *Educ:* Rajaram Coll., Kolhapur; Law Coll., Poona Univ. (BA, LLB). Took part in 1930, 1932 and 1942 Movements; elected MLA in 1946, 1952, 1957 and 1962; Parly Sec. to Home Minister of Bombay, 1946-52; Minister for Civil Supplies, Community Developments, Forests, Local Self Govt, 1952-Oct. 1956; Chief Minister: Bombay, Nov. 1956-April 1960; Maharashtra, May 1960-Nov. 1962; Defence Minister, Govt of India, 1962-66; Minister of Home Affairs, 1966-70. Member: Rajya Sabha, 1963-; Lok Sabha, 1963 and 1967. Mem. Working Cttee of All India Congress Cttee. Hon. Doctorate: Aligarh Univ.; Kanpur Univ., Marathwada Univ. *Address:* 1 Racecourse Road, New Delhi 11. *T:* 611614, (Office) 371800.

**CHAVASSE, Michael Louis Maude,** MA; QC 1968; Barrister-at-law; *b* 5 Jan. 1923; 2nd *s* of late Bishop C. M. Chavasse, OBE, MC, DD, MA and of Beatrice Cropper Chavasse (*née* Willink); *m* 1951, Rose Ethel, 2nd *d* of Vice-Adm. A. D. Read, *qv*; three *d.* *Educ:* Dragon Sch., Oxford; Shrewsbury Sch.; Trinity Coll., Oxford (Schol.). Enlisted in RAC, Oct. 1941; commnd in Buffs, 1942; served in Italy with Royal Norfolk Regt, 1943-45 (Lieut). 2nd cl. hons (Jurisprudence) Oxon, 1946. Called to Bar, Inner Temple, 1949. *Publications:* (jtly) A Critical Annotation of the RIBA Standard Forms of Building Contract, 1964; (with Bryan Anstey) Rights of Light, 1959. *Recreations:* shooting, photography. *Address:* 2 Paper Buildings, Temple, EC4; Park House, Chevening, Sevenoaks, Kent. *T:* Knockholt 2271.

**CHAYTOR, Sir William Henry Clervaux,** 7th Bt *cr* 1831; *b* 4 May 1914; *o s* of Sir Edmund Hugh Chaytor, 6th Bt and Isobel (who *m* 2nd, 1935, Edwin Burton Fiske, and died 1968), *d* of Thomas Scott, Darlington; *S* father, 1935; *m* 1947, Mrs Patricia Alderman; one *d.* *Educ:* Chillon Coll., Switzerland. *Heir:* *cousin* William Richard Carter Chaytor [*b* 10 Jan. 1881; *m* 1st, 1909, Anna Laura (*d* 1947), *d* of late George Fawcett; one *s* four *d*; 2nd, 1949, Clara Ethel (*d* 1966), *d* of John E. Parker]. *Address:* Flat 3, Bridlemere, Newmarket, Suffolk. *T:* 2491.

*See also Sir R. H. Lawson.*

**CHECKETTS, Sqdn-Ldr David John,** CVO 1969 (MVO 1966); Private Secretary to the Prince of Wales since 1970; Director, Neilson McCarthy Co.; *b* 23 Aug. 1930; 3rd *s* of late Reginald Ernest George Checketts and late Frances Mary Checketts; *m* 1958, Rachel Leila Warren Herrick; one *s* three *d*. Flying Training, Bulawayo, Rhodesia, 1948-50; 14 Sqdn, Germany, 1950-54; Instructor, Fighter Weapons Sch., 1954-57; Air ADC to C-in-C Malta, 1958-59; 3 Sqdn, Germany, 1960-61; Equerry to Duke of Edinburgh, 1961-66, to the Prince of Wales, 1967-70. *Recreations:* ornithology, shooting, squash. *Address:* Church Cottage, Winkfield, Windsor, Berks. *T:* Winkfield Row 2289. *Club:* Royal Aero.

**CHECKLAND, Prof. Sydney George,** MA, MCom, PhD; Professor of Economic History, University of Glasgow, since 1957; *b* 9 Oct. 1916; *s* of Sydney Tom and Fanny Selina Savory Checkland, Ottawa; *m* 1942, Edith Olive, *d* of Robert Fraser and Edith Philipson Anthony; two *s* three *d*. *Educ:* Lisgar Collegiate Inst., Ottawa; Birmingham Univ. Associate, Canadian Bankers' Assoc., 1937; BCom 1st Cl. 1941, MCom 1946, Birmingham; PhD Liverpool, 1953; MA Cambridge, 1953; Pres. Nat. Union of Students, 1941-42. Served in British and Canadian Armies; Lieut, Gov.-Gen.'s Foot Guards, Normandy (severely wounded). Asst Lecturer, Lecturer and Senior Lecturer in Economic Science, University of Liverpool, 1946-53; Univ. Lecturer in History, Cambridge, 1953-57; Lector in History, Trinity Coll., 1955-57. Member: East Kilbride Develt Corp.; Scottish Records Advisory Coun.; Nat. Register of Archives (Scotland). *Publications:* The Rise of Industrial Society in England, 1815-1885, 1964; The Mines of Tharsis, 1967; articles and reviews in economic and historical journals. *Address:* Number 5, The University, Glasgow, W2. *T:* 041-339 1801.

**CHEDLOW, Barry William,** QC 1969; Barrister-at-Law; *b* Macclesfield, 8 Oct. 1921; *m* Anne Sheldon, BA, DipEd; one *s* one *d*. *Educ:* Burnage High Sch.; Manchester Univ. Served RAF, 1941-46: USAAF, Flying Instructor, 1942; Flt-Lt 1943. Called to Bar, Middle Temple, 1947; Prizeman in Law of Evidence. Practises in London and on Midland Circuit; Asst to Recorders of Coventry and Lincoln. *Publications:* author and editor of various legal text-books. *Recreations:* languages, music, art. *Address:* 12 King's Bench Walk, Temple, EC4. *T:* 01-583 0811; Sheldon, Windsor Road, Gerrard's Cross, Bucks. *T:* Gerrard's Cross 83908.

**CHEESEMAN, Eric Arthur,** BSc (Econ), PhD (Med) (London); Professor of Medical Statistics, since 1961, The Queen's University of Belfast; *b* 22 Sept. 1912; 1st *s* of late Arthur Cheeseman and of Frances Cheeseman, London; *m* 1943, Henriette Edwina Woollaston; one *s*. *Educ:* William Ellis Sch.; London Univ. Mem. staff of Statistical Cttee of MRC, 1929-39. Served War of 1939-45, RA (TA); GSO3 21 Army Group, 1945. Research Statistician on staff of Statistical Research Unit of MRC and part-time lectr in Med. Statistics, London Sch. of Hygiene and Tropical Medicine, 1946-48; Lectr, later Reader, and Vice-Pres. (Finance), The Queen's Univ. of Belfast, 1948-. Statistical Adviser to Northern Ireland Hospitals Authority, 1948-; Mem. of Joint Authority for Higher Technicological Studies, 1965-. Consulting Statistician to Northern Ireland Tuberculosis Authority, 1950-59; Mem. of Statistical Cttee of Medical Research Council, 1950-61. Fellow Royal Statistical Soc.; Member: Statistical and Social Inquiry Soc. of Ireland; Soc. for Social Medicine; Biometrics Soc. *Publications:* Epidemics in Schools, 1950; (with G. F. Adams) Old People in Northern Ireland, 1951; various papers dealing with medical statistical subjects in scientific journals. *Recreation:* cricket. *Address:* 43 Beverley Gardens, Bangor, Co. Down, N Ireland. *T:* Bangor 2822.

**CHEETHAM, Canon Frederic Philip,** MA; Hon. CF; Vicar of Hartford, Cheshire, 1939-58, resigned; Canon Emeritus of Manchester Cathedral, 1939; Examining Chaplain to the Bishop of Manchester, 1924-47 and to the Bishop of Chester, 1945-58; *b* 1890; 2nd *s* of Walter and Ann Cheetham; *m* 1930, Helen Elizabeth, *y d* of J. D. MacIntosh, Woodford Green; one *s*. *Educ:* City of London Sch.; St John's Coll., Cambridge (Exhibitioner and Foundation Schol.); Ridley Hall, Cambridge. BA 1912; MA 1916; Browne Medallist, 1912; Carus Prizeman, 1913; Jeremie Prizeman, 1914. Deacon 1914; Priest, 1915. Curate, St Barnabas, Mitcham, 1914-16; Tutor, St Aidan's Coll., Birkenhead, 1916-20; Chaplain to Forces in France, 1918-19; Hon. CF 1920; Lecturer and Sub-Warden of Theological Hostel, King's Coll., London, 1920-24; Principal of Egerton Hall, Manchester, 1924-39; Hon. Canon of Manchester Cathedral, 1935-39; Rural Dean of Middlewich, 1951-57. Select preacher at Cambridge, 1941. *Address:* 515 The Ridge, St Leonards-on-Sea, Sussex.

**CHEETHAM, Sir Nicolas (John Alexander),** KCMG 1964 (CMG 1953); *b* 8 Oct. 1910; *s* of late Sir Milne Cheetham, KCMG, and of Mrs Nigel Law (*see* Anastasia Law); *m* 1st, 1937, Jean Evison Corfe (marr. diss. 1960); two *s*; 2nd, 1960, Lady Mabel Brooke (*née* Jocelyn). *Educ:* Eton College; Christ Church, Oxford. Entered HM Foreign Service, 1934; served in Foreign Office and at Athens, Buenos Aires, Mexico City and Vienna; UK Deputy Permanent Representative on North Atlantic Council, 1954-59; HM Minister to Hungary, 1959-61; Assistant Under-Secretary, Foreign Office, 1961-64; Ambassador to Mexico, 1964-68. *Recreations:* travelling, shooting, tennis, gardening. *Address:* Eyford Park, Bourton-on-the-Water, Glos. *Club:* Travellers'.

**CHEEVER, John;** writer, USA; *b* Quincy, Mass, 1912; *s* of Frederick Lincoln Cheever and Mary Liley Cheever; *m* 1941, Mary Winternitz; two *s* one *d*. *Educ:* Thayer Academy. *Publications:* The Way Some People Live; The Enormous Radio; The Housebreaker of Shady Hill; The Wapshot Chronicle; Some People, Places and Things that will Not Appear in my Next Novel; The Wapshot Scandal; The Brigadier and the Golf Widow; Bullet Park. *Recreations:* practically everything excepting big game. *Address:* Cedar Lane, Ossining, New York, USA. *T:* Wilson 1-0075. *Club:* Century (New York).

**CHEEVERS, William Harold;** Director of Engineering, Granada Television, since 1970; *b* 20 June 1918; *m* 1964, Shirley Cheevers; one *s*. *Educ:* Christ's Coll., London. Engineer, BBC Television, 1938-39. War Service, Army, PoW, 1941-45. Sen. Engr, BBC Television, 1946-54; Planning Engr, Radio-Corp. of America, in USA and Canada, 1954-55; Head of Engineering, Associated Rediffusion, 1955-60; Gen. Manager, Westward Television, Jt Man. Dir, 1963-67, Man. Dir, 1967-70; Dir, ITN News, 1967-70, and of IT Publications; also Director: Keith Prowse, 1963-70; Prowest, 1967-70; Direct Line Services, 1964-; Chm., British Regional Television Assoc., 1968-69. Fellow British Kinematograph Soc.; MInstD; MBIM; AssIEE. *Publications:* articles for most TV Jls, and Symposiums, at home and abroad. *Recreations:* boating, golf, reading. *Address:* The Old Coach House, Church Walk,

Modbury, S Devon. *T:* 450. *Club:* Royal Western Yacht Club of England (Plymouth).

**CHEGWIDDEN, Sir Thomas (Sidney),** Kt 1955; CB 1943; CVO 1939; Chevalier Légion d'Honneur, 1956; Chairman: Continental Ore Africa (Pvt) Ltd; Rhodesia United Air Carriers (Pvt) Ltd; Air Carriers Ltd; Victoria Falls Airways (Pvt) Ltd; Commercial Air Services (Rhodesia) (Pvt) Ltd; Rootes (CA) (Pvt) Ltd; Rawsons Motors (Pvt) Ltd; The Graham Publishing Co. (Pvt) Ltd; Rare Minerals (Pvt) Ltd; English Electric Co. (CA) (Pvt) Ltd; Director: English Electric Co. (CA) (Pvt) Ltd; Rare Minerals (Pvt) Ltd; *b* 7 Feb. 1895; *s* of late Thomas Chegwidden, 8 Wimborne Road, Bournemouth; *m* 1st, 1919, Kathleen Muriel, *d* of A. O. Breeds; 2nd, 1934, Beryl Sinclair, *d* of A. H. Nicholson; one *d*. *Educ:* Plymouth Coll.; Maidstone Grammar Sch.; Worcester Coll., Oxford. RMA Woolwich, 1916; Lieut RE, 1917-18. Resigned Commission and entered Upper Div. Civil Service, 1919; Asst Private Sec. to Dr T. J. Macnamara, Sir Montague Barlow, Mr Tom Shaw and Sir Arthur Steel-Maitland; Principal Private Sec. to Mr Oliver Stanley and Mr Ernest Brown; Under-Sec., Min. of Production, 1942-46; Civilian Dir of Studies, Imperial Defence Coll., 1946-47; Chm. of Public Services Bd and of Police Advisory Bd, S Rhodesia, 1947-53; Chm., Interim Federal Public Service Commission, Federation of Rhodesias and Nyasaland, 1953-55; Past Pres., Assoc. of Rhodesian Industries, 1958-61; Mem. Management Cttee, Assoc. of Rhodesian Industries; Chairman: Economic Affairs Cttee, Assoc. of Rhodesian Industries; Pres. and Fellow, Rhodesian Inst. of Management. *Publication:* The Employment Exchange Service of Great Britain (with G. Myrddin-Evans), 1934. *Address:* Claremont, Piers Road, Borrowdale, Rhodesia. *T:* Salisbury 882232. *Clubs:* Athenæum; Salisbury (Rhodesia).

**CHEKE, Dudley John,** CMG 1961; Ambassador to the Ivory Coast, Niger and Upper Volta, 1967-70; *b* 14 June 1912; *s* of late Thomas William Cheke, FRIC; *m* 1944, Yvonne de Méric, *d* of late Rear-Adm. M. J. C. de Méric, MVO; two *s*. *Educ:* St Christopher's, Letchworth; Emmanuel Coll., Cambridge. Entered HM Consular Service, 1934; served in Japan, Manchuria, Korea, 1935-41; served 1942-43, in East Africa and Ceylon; Foreign Office, 1944-49 and 1958-61; UK Delegate to OEEC, Paris, 1949-50; Commissioner-Gen.'s Office, Singapore, 1950-51; idc 1952; HM Consul-Gen., Frankfurt-am-Main, 1953-55, Osaka-Kobe, 1956-58; Mem. of Foreign Service Corps of Inspectors, 1961-63; Minister, Tokyo, 1963-67. *Recreations:* theatre, bird-watching. *Address:* c/o Foreign and Commonwealth Office, SW1. *Clubs:* Oxford and Cambridge University; Union Society (Cambridge).

**CHELMER,** Baron *cr* 1963 (Life Peer), of Margaretting; **Eric Cyril Boyd Edwards,** Kt 1954; MC 1944; TD; JP; *b* 9 Oct. 1914; *s* of Col C. E. Edwards, DSO, MC, TD, DL, JP, and Mrs J. Edwards; *m* 1939, Enid, *d* of F. W. Harvey; one *s*. *Educ:* Felsted Sch. Solicitor, 1937; LLB (London) 1937. Served Essex Yeomanry, 1940-54 (MC), Lieut-Col Commanding, 1945-46. JP Essex, 1950. Chm., Nat. Union of Conservative Associations, 1956, Pres., 1967; Chm., Nat. Exec. Cttee of Conservative and Unionist Assoc., 1957-65; Jt Treasurer of Conservative Party, 1965-; Political Cttee, Carlton Club, 1961; Cttee of Musicians' Benevolent Fund; Ralph Vaughan Williams Trust. *Recreations:* sailing, "improving". *Address:* Peacocks, Margaretting, Essex; 5 John Street, Bedford Row, WC1. *Clubs:* Carlton, United and Cecil, Royal Ocean Racing; Royal Burnham Yacht.

**CHELMSFORD,** 3rd Viscount *cr* 1921, of Chelmsford; **Frederic Jan Thesiger;** Baron Chelmsford, 1858; Lloyd's Insurance Broker; *b* 7 March 1931; *s* of 2nd Viscount Chelmsford and of Gilian, *d* of late Arthur Nevile Lubbock; *S* father, 1970; *m* 1958, Clare Rendle, *d* of Dr G. R. Rolston, Haslemere; one *s* one *d*. Formerly Lieut, Inns of Court Regt. *Heir: s* Hon. Frederic Corin Piers Thesiger, *b* 6 March 1962. *Address:* 26 Ormonde Gate, SW3; Hazelbridge Court, Chiddingfold, Surrey.

**CHELMSFORD, Bishop of,** since 1962; **Rt. Rev. John Gerhard Tiarks;** *b* 5 April 1903; *s* of late Rev. Hope Charles Tiarks, lately Rector of Donington, Salop, and late Evelyn Louisa, *d* of Capt. Charles Oakes Blackwood Hall, RN; *m* 1927, Gwyneth Mary, 2nd *d* of Rev. Griffith Matthews, BA; one *s* one *d*. *Educ:* Westminster (King's Scholar); Trinity Coll., Cambridge (Class. and Theological Triposes, BA 1925, MA 1929); Ridley Hall, Cambridge. Curate of Christ Church, Southport, 1926-29; 1st Vicar of Christ Church, Norris Green, Liverpool, 1930-34; Vicar of St Paul, Widnes, 1934-37; Vicar of St Helens, Lancs, 1937-44; Proctor in York Convocation, 1944; Vicar of Bradford and Provost of Bradford Cathedral, 1944-62. Chm., Missions to Seamen Council, 1965. *Recreations:* motoring, walking. *Address:* Bishopscourt, Chelmsford, Essex. *T:* Chelmsford 53053. *Club:* Athenæum.

**CHELMSFORD, Provost of;** *see* Price, Very Rev. H. M. C.

**CHELSEA, Viscount; Charles Gerald John Cadogan;** *b* 24 March 1937; *o s* of 7th Earl Cadogan, *qv*; *m* 1963, Lady Philippa Wallop, *d* of 9th Earl of Portsmouth, *qv*; one *s* one *d*. *Educ:* Eton. *Heir: s* Hon. Edward Charles Cadogan, *b* 10 May 1966. *Address:* 51 Chelsea Square, SW3. *T:* 01-352 8398; Marndhill, Ardington, near Wantage, Berks. *T:* East Hendred 273. *Clubs:* White's, Royal Automobile.

**CHELTENHAM, Archdeacon of;** *see* Hutchins, Ven. G. F.

**CHENEVIX-TRENCH, Anthony,** MA (Oxon); Head Master, Fettes College, Edinburgh, from Sept. 1971; *b* 10 May 1919; *s* of late C. G. Chenevix-Trench, CIE; *m* 1953, Elizabeth Chalmers, *e d* of late Capt. Sir Stewart Spicer, 3rd Bt, RN retd, and Lady Spicer, Chichester, Sussex; two *s* twin *d*. *Educ:* Shrewsbury Sch.; Christ Church, Oxford. Classical Schol. Christ Church, 1st Cl. Hon. Mods, De Paravicini Schol. Served War of 1939-45; joined RA 1939: seconded Indian Artillery (4th Hazara Mountain Battery, Frontier Force), 1940; served Malaya (Capt.; POW Singapore, 1942, released 1945). 1st Class Lit. Hum., and Prox. Acc., Craven and Ireland Scholarships, 1948. Asst Master, Shrewsbury Sch., 1948; Tutor in Classics, Christ Church, Oxford, 1951; House Master, Shrewsbury Sch. (Sch. House), 1952; Headmaster, Bradfield Coll., Berks, 1955-63. Mem., Robbins Cttee on Higher Education, 1961. FRSA. *Recreations:* shooting and general outdoor activities. *Address:* 86 West Lavant Cottages, West Lavant, near Chichester, Sussex. *Clubs:* Public Schools; Vincent's (Oxford).

**CHENEVIX-TRENCH, Brig. Ralph,** CB 1940; OBE 1919; MC; *b* 15 Dec. 1885; *s* of Col C. Chenevix-Trench; *m* 1916, Meriel Edith Jelf; one *s* one *d* (and one *s* killed in action, 1943). *Educ:* Wellington Coll.; RMA Woolwich.

Commissioned Royal Engineers, 1905; Asst Dir Posts and Telegraphs, Sudan, 1913-16; Darfur Campaign, 1916 (MC); European War in France and North Russia, 1917-19 (despatches thrice, OBE); transferred to Royal Signals, 1920; GSO1 and Dep. Dir Staff Duties, War Office, 1934-37; Comdt Signal Training Centre, 1938-39; Maj.-Gen. BEF, 1939-40 (CB); Signal Officer-in-Chief, Home Forces, 1940; retired pay, 1941. *Publications:* Gold Medal Essay of Royal United Service Institution, 1921; Bertrand-Steward Essay in Army Quarterly, 1931. *Recreation:* gardening. *Address:* Little Westport, Westport Road, Wareham, Dorset.

**CHENEY, Christopher Robert,** FBA; Professor of Medieval History, University of Cambridge, since Oct. 1955; Fellow, Corpus Christi College, Cambridge, 1955; *b* 1906; 4th *s* of George Gardner and Christiana Stapleton Cheney; *m* 1940, Mary Gwendolen Hall; two *s* one *d*. *Educ:* Banbury County Sch.; Wadham Coll., Oxford (Hon. Fellow, 1968). 1st class Modern History Sch., 1928; Asst Lectr in History, University Coll., London, 1931-33; Bishop Fraser Lectr in Ecclesiastical History, University of Manchester, 1933-37; Fellow of Magdalen Coll., Oxford, 1938-45; Univ. Reader in Diplomatic, 1937-45; Joint Literary Dir of Royal Historical Society, 1938-45; Prof. of Medieval History, Univ. of Manchester, 1945-55. Hon. Fellow, Wadham Coll., Oxford. Corresp. Fellow, Mediaeval Acad. of America; Corresp. Mem., Monumenta Germanae Historica. Hon. DLitt Glasgow, 1970. *Publications:* Episcopal Visitation of Monasteries in the 13th Century, 1931; English Synodalia of the 13th Century, 1941; Handbook of Dates, 1945; English Bishops' Chanceries, 1950; (with W. H. Semple) Selected Letters of Pope Innocent III, 1953; From Becket to Langton, 1956; (with F. M. Powicke) Councils and Synods of the English Church, Vol. II, 1964; Hubert Walter, 1967; (with M. G. Cheney) Letters of Pope Innocent III concerning England and Wales, 1967; articles and reviews in Eng. Hist. Rev., etc. *Address:* 236 Hills Road, Cambridge. *T:* Cambridge 47765.

**CHERENKOV, Prof. Pavel A.;** Soviet physicist; Member of the Institute of Physics, Academy of Sciences of the USSR; *b* 1904. *Educ:* Voronezh State Univ., Voronezh, USSR. Discovered the Cherenkov Effect, 1934. Awarded Stalin Prize, 1946; Nobel Prize for Physics (joint), 1958. *Address:* Institute of Physics, Academy of Sciences of the USSR, B Kaluzhskaya 14, Moscow, USSR.

**CHERKASSKY, Shura;** pianist; *b* 7 Oct. 1911; *s* of late Isaac and Lydia Cherkassky; *m* 1946, Genia Ganz (marr. diss. 1948). *Educ:* Curtis Institute of Music, Pa, USA (diploma). Plays with the principal orchestras and conductors of the world and is a constant soloist at Salzburg Festival. Has made numerous recordings. *Address:* c/o Ibbs & Tillett Ltd, 124 Wigmore Street, W1.

**CHERMAYEFF, Sergius,** FRIBA, FRSA; architect; abstract painter; Professor, Yale University, 1962-69, Emeritus, 1969; *b* 8 Oct. 1900; *s* of Ivan and Rosalie Chermayeff; *m* 1928, Barbara Maitland May; two *s*. *Educ:* Harrow Sch. Journalist, 1918-22; studied architecture, 1922-25; principal work in England; Studios BBC; Modern Exhibitions; Gilbey's Offices; ICI Laboratories; in Partnership: Bexhill Pavilion. Professor, Brooklyn Coll., 1942-46; Pres. and Dir, Inst. of Design, Chicago, 1946-51; Prof., Harvard Univ., 1953-62. In practice as Architect and Consultant, New Haven, Conn. Hon. Dr of Fine Art, Washington Univ. *Publications:* Architecture, Art and Architectural Criticism; ARP, 1939; Community and Privacy, 1963; Shape of Community, 1970. *Address:* 28 Lincoln Street, New Haven, Conn, USA.

**CHERMONT, Jayme Sloan,** KCVO (Hon.) 1968; Brazilian Ambassador to the Court of St James's, 1966-68, retired; *b* 5 April 1903; *s* of Ambassador E. L. Chermont and Mrs Helen Mary Chermont; *m* 1928, Zaïde Alvim de Mello Franco Chermont (decd); no *c*. *Educ:* Law Sch., Rio de Janeiro Univ. Entered Brazilian Foreign Office, 1928; served in Washington, 1930-32; Rio de Janeiro, 1932-37; London, 1937; transf. to Brazil, 1938; 1st Sec., 1941; Buenos Aires, 1943-45; transf. to Brazil, 1945; Counsellor, Brussels, 1948-50; Minister Counsellor, London (periodically Chargé d'Affaires), 1950-53; various appts, Brazilian FO, 1953-57; Consul-Gen., New York, 1957-60; Ambassador to Haiti, 1960-61; Head of Political and Cultural Depts, Brazil, 1961; Sec.-Gen., FO, 1962-63; Ambassador to Netherlands, 1963-66. Headed Brazilian Delegn to UN Gen. Assembly, 1962. Holds Orders from many foreign countries. *Recreations:* golf, chess, bridge, stamps, coins, books. *Address:* c/o Ministry of Foreign Affairs, Brasilia, Brazil. *Clubs:* White's, St James'; Jockey, Country, Itanhangá Golf (Rio).

**CHERNIAVSKY, Mischel;** cellist; *b* Uman, South Russia, 2 Nov. 1893; became British subject, 1922; *m* 1919, Mary Rogers, Vancouver, BC; four *s* (and one *s* decd). *Educ:* privately. Studied violoncello under David Popper and Herbert Walenn. Played before the Czar, Nicholas II, when seven years Old; at age of twelve performed Saint-Saëns concerto in presence of composer; toured the world with his brothers, Leo (violinist) and Jan (pianist), who with him formed the Cherniavsky Trio, 1901-23. Since 1925 has appeared in most countries of the world in recital and as soloist with orchestra. Entertained the Forces in Great Britain, 1939-42; organised concerts in Canada in aid of Mrs Churchill's Aid to Russia Fund, 1942-45; toured Union of South Africa, 1953. *Recreations:* golf, tennis, antique collecting. *Address:* Ferme des Moines, Le Bourg-Dun, Seine Maritime, France. *T:* Bourg-Dun 26. *Club:* Dieppe Golf.

**CHERRY, Prof. Colin;** *see* Cherry, Prof. E. C.

**CHERRY, Prof. (Edward) Colin;** Henry Mark Pease Professor of Telecommunication at Imperial College, University of London, since 1958; *b* 23 June 1914; *s* of Arthur and Margaret Cherry; *m* 1956, Heather Blanche White; two *d*. *Educ:* St Alban's; University of London. Student, with General Electric Company (Research Laboratories), 1932-36; studied for London BSc at the same time (as evening student at Northampton Polytechnic). BSc 1936, MSc 1940, DSc 1955. Research Staff of General Electric Company, 1936-45, being seconded during part of War years to Min. of Aircraft Production for radar research. Lectr, College of Technology, Manchester, 1945-47; Reader in Telecommunication, Imperial Coll. of Science and Technology, 1949-58. Hon. ACGI. *Publications:* On Human Communication, 1957; World Communication–Threat or Promise?, 1971; numerous scientific papers on theory of electric circuits, on telecommunication principles and on the psychology of speech and hearing. *Recreations:* gardening; foreign travel. *Address:* Tillingbrook, Rectory Lane, Shere, near Guildford, Surrey. *T:* Shere 2623.

**CHESHAM,** 5th Baron *cr* 1858; **John Charles Compton Cavendish,** PC 1964; *b* 18 June 1916; *s* of 4th Baron and Margot, *d* of late J. Layton Mills, Tansor Court, Oundle; *s* father, 1952; *m* 1937, Mary Edmunds, 4th *d* of late David G. Marshall, White Hill, Cambridge; two *s* two *d*. *Educ:* Eton; Zuoz Coll., Switzerland; Trinity Coll., Cambridge. Served War of 1939-45, Lieut Royal Bucks Yeomanry, 1939-42; Capt. RA (Air OP), 1942-45. JP Bucks 1946, retd. Delegate, Council of Europe, 1953-56. A Lord-in-Waiting to the Queen, 1955-59; Parly Sec., Min. of Transport, 1959-64. Chancellor, Primrose League, 1957-59. Executive Vice-Chm. Royal Automobile Club, 1966; Chm., British Road Federation, 1966; Hon. Sec., House of Lords Motor Club, 1966. *Heir: s* Hon. Nicholas Charles Cavendish [*b* 7 Nov. 1941; *m* 1965, Susan Donne (marr. diss. 1969), *e d* of Dr Guy Beauchamp]. *Address:* Bramdean Farmhouse, Alresford, Hants. *T:* Bramdean 212; Flat 6, 17 Cheyne Gardens, SW3. *T:* 01-352 0117. *Club:* Royal Automobile.

**CHESHIRE, Geoffrey Chevalier,** FBA 1945; DCL; Barrister-at-Law; Hon. Fellow of Merton College and of Exeter College, Oxford; Hon. Master of the Bench of Lincoln's Inn; Hon. LLD: Manchester University; London University; Jadavpur University, Calcutta; *b* Hartford, Ches, 27 June 1886; 2nd *s* of Walter Christopher Cheshire, Solicitor and Registrar of Northwich County Court, Ches; *m* 1st, 1915, Primrose Barstow (*d* 1962), 2nd *d* of Col T. A. A. Barstow, Seaforth Highlanders; two *s*; 2nd, 1963, Dame Mary (Kathleen) Lloyd (*see* Comdt Dame Mary Cheshire). *Educ:* Denstone Coll.; Merton Coll., Oxford. 1st Class Hon. Sch. of Jurisprudence, 1908; 2nd Cl. BCL 1910; Inns of Court Studentship, 1911. Lectr at University Coll. of Wales, Aberystwyth, 1909 and 1910; Fellow of Exeter Coll., Oxford, 1912-44; Bursar, 1919-33; All Souls Lecturer in Private International Law, 1922-33; All Souls Reader in English Law, 1933-44; Vinerian Prof. of English Law, Oxford, and Fellow of All Souls Coll., 1944-49; Mem. of Lord Chancellor's Cttee on Foreign Marriages, 1939; Deleg. to Hague Conf. on Codification of Private Internat. Law, 1951; Mem. Lord Chancellor's Cttee on Private Internat. Law, 1952-57; Mem. of the Inst. of Internat. Law, 1950-65. Served European War, Cheshire Regt, 1914-16; RFC (Kite-Balloon Section), 1916-18, Capt; Home Guard, 1940. *Publications:* Investigation of Charges in the RAF, 1919; Modern Real Property, 1925, 10th edn 1967; Private International Law, 1935, 7th edn 1965; (with C. H. S. Fifoot) The Law of Contract, 1945, 7th edn 1969; International Contracts, 1948; (Gen. Ed.) Stephen's Commentaries, 19th edn; The Private International Law of Husband and Wife, 1963. *Address:* Laundry Cottage, Empshott, Liss, Hants. *Club:* Athenæum.

*See also Group Capt. G. L. Cheshire.*

**CHESHIRE, Group Captain (Geoffrey) Leonard,** VC 1944; DSO 1940; DFC 1941; RAF retired; *b* 7 Sept. 1917; *s* of Geoffrey Chevalier Cheshire, *qv*; *m* 1959, Susan, *d* of Mrs Ryder, Clare, Suffolk; one *s* one *d*. *Educ:* Stowe Sch.; Merton Coll., Oxford. 2nd Class Hon. Sch. of Jurisprudence, 1939; OU Air Sqdn, 1936; RAFVR, 1937; Perm. Commn RAF, 1939; trained Hullavington; served War of 1939-45 (VC, DSO, DFC, two Bars to DSO); joined 102 Sqdn, 1940; Flying Officer, 1940; posted 35 Sqdn, 1941; Wing Comdr, Commanding 76 Sqdn, 1942; comd RAF Station, Marston Moor, 1943; 617 Sqdn, 1943; HQ Eastern Air Command, South-East Asia, 1944; British Joint Staff Mission, Washington, 1945; retired 1946; official British observer at dropping of Atomic Bomb on Nagasaki, 1945. Founder of Cheshire Foundation Homes for the Sick; Co-founder of Mission For the Relief of Suffering. *Publications:* Bomber Pilot, 1943; Pilgrimage to the Shroud, 1956; The Face of Victory, 1961. *Relevant publications:* Cheshire, VC, by Russell Braddon; No Passing Glory, by Andrew Boyle; New Lives for Old, by W. W. Russell. *Address:* Cavendish, Suffolk. *Clubs:* RAF Reserves, MCC.

**CHESHIRE, Leonard;** *see* Cheshire, G. L.

**CHESHIRE, Commandant Dame Mary (Kathleen),** DBE 1952 (OBE 1946); *b* 31 May 1902; *d* of late A. J. Lloyd and late Mrs Lloyd; *m* 1963, Geoffrey Chevalier Cheshire, *qv*. *Educ:* Ursuline Convent, Wimbledon. Joined WRNS, 1939; served as motor transport driver, and a writer, while a rating. Commissioned, 1940; Actg Supt, WRNS Portsmouth Command, 1946; Asst Dir Women's Royal Naval Service, 1948; Superintendent, Training and Drafting, HM Training Establishment Dauntless, Burghfield, near Reading, Berks; Superintendent, 1949; Dir Women's Royal Naval Service, 1950-54; Hon. Naval ADC to the Queen, 1952-54. *Address:* Laundry Cottage, Empshott, Liss, Hants.

**CHESHIRE, Air Chief Marshal Sir Walter (Graemes),** GBE 1965 (CBE 1949); KCB 1959 (CB 1955); idc; psa; Member, Commonwealth War Graves Commission, since 1968, Vice-Chairman since 1970; *b* 21 March 1907; *s* of late John F. Cheshire, Beckenham, Kent; *m* 1940, Mary, *d* of late Col E. W. Chance, OBE, TD; two *s*. *Educ:* Ipswich Sch.; Downing Coll., Cambridge. Commnd into RAF, 1926; Sqdn Ldr, 1937; RAF Staff Coll., 1938; various appts, Bomber Command; Air Attaché, Moscow; on staff HQ, ACSEA, 1939-45; AOC French Indo-China, 1945-46; idc 1949; AOC Gibraltar, 1950-52; Comdt RAF Staff Coll., Andover, 1952-53; Air Officer in charge of Administration, HQ 2nd TAF, 1953-55; AOC No 13 Group, Fighter Command, 1955-57; RAF Instructor at Imperial Defence Coll., 1957-59; AOC, RAF Malta, and Dep. C-in-C (Air), Allied Forces, Mediterranean, 1959-61; Mem. for Personnel, Air Council, 1961-64; Air ADC to the Queen, 1963-65; Air Mem. for Personnel, Min. of Defence, 1964-65; retired, 1965. *Recreations:* tennis, squash. *Address:* 30 Courtenay Place, Belmore Lane, Lymington, Hants. *Club:* Royal Air Force.

**CHESNEY, Kathleen,** MA, DPhil, DLitt; Principal, Westfield College (University of London), 1951-52; *b* 25 April 1899; *d* of Edward Shuldham Chesney. *Educ:* The Manor House, Brondesbury; Lady Margaret Hall, Oxford. MA 1926; DPhil Oxon, 1929; DLitt Oxon, 1953. Tutor in Modern Languages, St Hilda's Coll., Oxford, 1923, Fellow, 1924; University Lecturer in French, 1937; Vice-Principal of St Hilda's, 1941. Hon. Fellow of St Hilda's Coll., 1951, of Lady Margaret Hall, 1962, of Westfield Coll., 1963. *Publications:* Oeuvres Poëtiques de Guillaume Crétin (Paris), 1932; Fleurs de Rhétorique, from Villon to Marot (Oxford), 1950; Poëmes de Transition, Medium Ævum Monographs VIII, 1965; articles in Medium Ævum, French Studies, etc. *Address:* Barber's Cross, Watlington, Oxford. *Club:* University Women's.

**CHESSER, Eustace;** lecturer and consulting psychiatrist; *b* Edinburgh, 22 March 1902; 2nd *s* of Arthur Chesser; *m* 1st, 1926, Rose Morris, Durham (*d* 1960); one *s* one *d*; 2nd, 1961, Sheila Blayney-Jones. *Educ:* George Watson's, Edinburgh; Royal Colleges. LRCP, LRCS,

LRFPS, 1926. Hon. Sec. Soc. for Sex Education and Guidance (from inception until Dec. 1953). Member: The Royal Institution; Medico-Legal Council; Abortion Law Reform Assoc.; Married Women's Assoc.; Marriage Law Reform Soc. (Sponsor); Royal Medico-Psychological Soc.; Assoc. for Advancement of Psychotherapy; Brit. Exec. Cttee Internat. Union of Family Organizations; Brit. Social Biology Council; Soc. for Study of Addiction; International Cttee for Sexual Equality, Amsterdam (Mem. Council). Research Director, Research Council into Marriage and Human Relationships; Hon. Surgeon Dilke Mem. Hosp. FRSocMed. *Publications:* Love Without Fear, 1941; Marriage and Freedom, 1943; Unwanted Child, 1945; Grow Up-And Live, 1949; Successful Living, 1950; Cruelty to Children, 1951; Unquiet Minds, 1952; How to Make a Success of your Marriage, 1952; Humanly Speaking, 1954; The Sexual, Marital and Family Relationships of the English Woman, 1956; Live and Let Live, 1958; Psychology of Everyday Living, 1958; Woman, 1959; Outline of Human Relationships, 1959; Odd Man Out, 1959; Life is for Living, 1962; Woman and Love, 1962; Is Chastity Outmoded?, 1962; When and How to Stop Smoking, 1963; The Cost of Loving, 1964; Challenge of the Middle Years, 1964; Shelley and Zastrozzi: Self-revelation of a Neurotic, 1965; Unmarried Love, 1965; Living with Suicide, 1967; Sex and the Married Woman, 1969; Who Do You Think You Are?, 1970; contributor, Chambers's Encyclopædia. *Recreations:* ideas, places, people and things. *Address:* 17 Wimpole Street, W1. *T:* 01-580 4707; Apt 73, 40 Boulevard de Cessole, 06 Nice, France.

**CHESTER, Bishop of,** since 1955; **Rt. Rev. Gerald Alexander Ellison;** *b* 19 Aug. 1910; *s* of late Preb. John Henry Joshua Ellison, CVO, Chaplain in Ordinary to the King, Rector of St Michael's, Cornhill, and of Sara Dorothy Graham Ellison (*née* Crum); *m* 1947, Jane Elizabeth, *d* of late Brig. John Houghton Gibbon, DSO; one *s* two *d. Educ:* St George's, Windsor; Westminster Sch.; New Coll., Oxford; Westcott House, Cambridge. Curate, Sherborne Abbey, 1935-37; Domestic Chaplain to the Bishop of Winchester, 1937-39; Chaplain RNVR, 1940-43 (despatches); Domestic Chaplain to Archbishop of York, 1943-46; Vicar, St Mark's, Portsea, 1946-50; Hon. Chaplain to Archbishop of York, 1946-50; Canon of Portsmouth, 1950; Examining Chaplain to Bishop of Portsmouth, 1949-50; Bishop Suffragan of Willesden, 1950-55. Select Preacher: Oxford Univ., 1940 and 1961; Cambridge Univ., 1957. Chaplain, Master Mariners' Company, 1946; Chaplain, Glass Sellers' Company, 1951; Chaplain and Sub-Prelate, Order of St John. Mem. Wolfenden Cttee on Sport, 1960; Chairman: Westfield Coll., Univ. of London, 1953-67 (Fellow, 1968); Archbishops' Commn on Women and Holy Orders, 1963-66; Mem., Archbishops' Commn on Church and State, 1967; President: Actors Church Union; Pedestrians Assoc. for Road Safety. *Publications:* The Churchman's Duty, 1957; The Anglican Communion, 1960. *Recreations:* oarsmanship, walking. *Address:* Bishop's House, Chester. *Clubs:* Army and Navy; Leander.

**CHESTER, Dean of;** *see* Addleshaw, Very Rev. G. W. O.

**CHESTER, Archdeacon of;** *see* Fisher, Ven. L. G.

**CHESTER, Daniel Norman,** CBE 1951; MA; Warden of Nuffield College, Oxford, since Oct. 1954; Official Fellow of Nuffield College, 1945-54; *b* 27 Oct. 1907; *s* of Daniel Chester, Chorlton-cum-Hardy, Manchester; *m* 1936, Eva, *d* of James H. Jeavons. *Educ:* Manchester Univ. BA Manchester, 1930, MA 1933; MA Oxon, 1946. Rockefeller Fellow, 1935-36, Lecturer in Public Administration, 1936-45, Manchester Univ.; Mem. of Economic Section, War Cabinet Secretariat, 1940-45. Editor of jl of Public Administration, 1943-66. Mem. Oxford City Council, 1952-. Chairman: Oxford Centre for Management Studies; Police Promotion Examinations Bd, 1969; Cttee on Association Football, 1966-68; Oxfordshire Bridge Assoc. Vice-Pres. (ex-Chm.), Royal Inst. of Public Administration; Past Pres., Internat. Political Science Assoc. Hon. LittD Manchester, 1968. Corresp. Mem., Acad. des Sciences Morales et Politiques, Institut de France, 1967. *Publications:* Public Control of Road Passenger Transport, 1936; Central and Local Government: Financial and Administrative Relations, 1951; The Nationalised Industries, 1951; Lessons of the British War Economy (Ed.), 1951; The Organization of British Central Government (Ed.), 1914-56; (with Nona Bowring) Questions in Parliaments, 1962; articles in learned journals. *Address:* 136 Woodstock Road, Oxford. *Club:* Reform.

**CHESTER, Prof. Theodore Edward,** CBE 1967; Djur, MA (Econ) Manchester; Diploma in Commerce; Professor of Social Administration, University of Manchester, since 1955; Member, Council of Manchester Business School, since 1964; *b* 28 June 1908; *m* 1940, Mimi; one *s.* Teaching and research in law and administration, 1931-39. Service with HM Forces, 1940-45. Asst Man. in London city firm, 1946-48; Acton Soc. Trust: Senior Research Worker, 1948-52; Dir, 1952-55; Dean, Faculty of Economic and Social Studies, Univ. of Manchester, 1962-63. Research work into problems of large-scale Administration in private and public undertakings including the hosp. and educn service in Britain and comparative studies abroad as well as into the problems of training managers and administrators. Vis. Prof. at many foreign univs and institutions, notably in the United States and in Western Europe, 1959-; Kenneth Pray Vis. Prof., Univ. of Pa, 1968; first Kellogg Vis. Prof., Washington Univ., St Louis, 1969 and 1970. Ford Foundn Travelling Fellowships, 1960, 1967. WHO Staff Training Programme, 1963-; UN Res. Inst. for Economic and Social Studies, 1968. Member: National Selection Cttee for the recruitment of Sen. Hospital Administrative Staff, 1956-66; Advisory Cttee on Management Efficiency in the Health Service, 1959-65; Cttee of Inquiry into recruitment, training and promotion of clerical and administrative staffs in the Hospital Service, 1962-63; Programme Cttee of Internat. Hosp. Fedn and Chm. study group into problems of trng in hosp. admin, 1959-65; Pres. Corp of Secs, 1956-66; Trng Couns for Social Workers and Health Visitors, 1963-65; Cttee on Technical Coll. Resources, 1964-; Adviser: Social Affairs Div., OECD, 1965-66; Turkish State Planning Org. on Health and Welfare Problems, 1964. Broadcasts on social problems in Britain and abroad. *Publications:* (for Acton Soc. Trust) Training and Promotion in Nationalised Industry, 1951; Patterns of Organisation, 1952; Management under Nationalization, 1953; Background and Blueprint: A Study of Hospital Organisation under the National Health Service, 1955; The Impact of the Change (co-author), 1956; Groups, Regions and Committees, 1957; The Central Control of the Service, 1958; (with H. A. Clegg): The Future of Nationalization, 1953; Wage Policy and the Health Service, 1957; Post War

Growth of Management in Western Europe, 1961; Graduate Education for Hospital Administration in the United States: Trends, 1969; The British National Health Service, 1970; The Swedish National Health Service, 1970; Editor and contrib. Amer. Coll. Hosp. Administrators; regular contribs to scientific and other jls. *Recreations:* travel, music, swimming, detective stories. *Address:* Lisvane, 189 Grove Lane, Hale, Altrincham, Cheshire. *T:* 061-980 2828.

**CHESTER JONES, Prof. Ian,** DSc 1958; Professor of Zoology, University of Sheffield, since 1958; *b* 3 Jan. 1916; *s* of late H. C. Jones; *m* 1942, Nansi Ellis Williams; two *s* one *d*. *Educ:* Liverpool Institute High Sch. for Boys; Liverpool Univ. BSc 1938; PhD 1941. Served in Army, 1941-46. Commonwealth Fund Fellow, Harvard Univ., 1947-49. Senior Lecturer in Zoology, Univ. of Liverpool, 1955. Chm., Soc. for Endocrinology, 1966. Dr de l'Université de Clermont (*hc*), 1967. *Publication:* The Adrenal Cortex, 1957. *Address:* Department of Zoology, University of Sheffield.

**CHESTERFIELD, Archdeacon of;** *see* Cleasby, Ven. T. W. I.

**CHESTERFIELD, Arthur Desborough,** CBE 1962; Director: Woolwich Equitable Building Society since 1963; RoyWest Banking Corporation Ltd (Deputy Chairman), since 1965; Trust Corporation of Bahamas Ltd since 1967; Singer & Friedlander (Holdings) Ltd (Chairman) and Singer & Friedlander Ltd (Chairman), since 1967; Local Director (Inner London), National Westminster Bank, since 1969 (Director, Westminster Bank, 1963-69); Chairman of the City of London Savings Committee, since 1962; Fellow of the Institute of Bankers (Member of Council, 1950-65); *b* 21 Aug. 1905; *s* of Arthur William and Ellen Harvey Chesterfield; *m* 1932, Betty, *d* of John Henry Downey; two *s* three *d*. *Educ:* Hastings Grammar Sch. Entered Westminster Bank Ltd, Eastbourne, 1923; Joint Gen. Manager, 1947; Chief Gen. Manager, Westminster Bank, 1950-65, retired. Member: Export Guarantees Adv. Council, 1952-63; Nat. Savings Cttee, 1954-67. *Recreations:* music, gardening. *Address:* Woodlands Court, Withdean Road, Brighton 5, Sussex. *T:* Brighton 553043.

**CHESTERMAN, Dr Clement Clapton,** OBE 1919; Consulting Physician in Tropical Diseases since 1948; *b* 30 May 1894; 5th *s* of late W. T. Chesterman, Bath, and Elizabeth Clapton; *m* 1917, Winifred Lucy, *d* of late Alderman F. W. Spear; three *s* two *d*. *Educ:* Monkton Combe Sch.; Bristol Univ. MD London 1920; DTM and H, Cantab, 1920; FRCP 1952. Served European War, 1914-18 (despatches, OBE): Capt. RAMC (SR), 1917-19, Middle East. Medical Missionary, Belgian Congo, 1920-36; MO and Secretary, Baptist Missionary Soc., 1936-48. Lecturer in Tropical Medicine, Middlesex Hospital Medical Sch., 1944; Lecturer in Tropical Hygiene, University of London Institute of Education, 1956. Member Commn Royale Belge pour la Protection des Indigènes; Mem. Colonial Advisory Medical Cttee; Past Vice-Pres. Royal Society Tropical Medicine and Hygiene; Pres. Hunterian Society, 1967-68; Hon. Mem. Belgian Royal Society of Tropical Medicine. Occasional broadcasts on Medical Missions and Tropical Diseases. Serbian Red Cross Medal, 1915; Chevalier, Ordre Royal du Lion, 1938. *Publications:* In the Service of Suffering, 1940; A Tropical Dispensary Handbook (7th edn), 1960; articles in Transactions of Royal Society of Tropical Medicine and Hygiene, British Encyclopædia of Medical Practice, etc. *Recreation:* golf. *Address:* 7 Parsifal Road, NW6. *T:* 01-435 6475; 149 Harley Street, W1. *T:* 01-935 4444. *Clubs:* Royal Commonwealth Society; Highgate Golf.

**CHESTERMAN, Sir (Dudley) Ross,** Kt 1970; MSc, PhD; DIC; Warden of Goldsmiths' College (University of London) since 1953; Vice-Master of the College of Craft Education, since Dec. 1960 (Dean, 1958-60); *b* 27 April 1909; *s* of late Dudley and Ettie Chesterman; *m* 1938, Audrey Mary Horlick; one *s* one *d*. *Educ:* Hastings Grammar Sch.; Imperial College of Science, London (scholar). Acland English Essay Prizeman, 1930; 1st class hons BSc (Chem.), 1930; MSc 1932; Lecturer in Chemistry, Woolwich Polytechnic; PhD 1937; Science master in various grammar schools; Headmaster, Meols Cop Secondary Sch., Southport, 1946-48. Chief County Inspector of Schools, Worcestershire, 1948-53. Educational adviser to Haifa University Coll., Israel, 1966; Ford Foundation Travel Award to American Univs, 1966; Educational Consultant in Nigeria, 1969, 1970. Fellow *hc* of Coll. of Handicraft, 1958. Liveryman and Freeman of Goldsmiths' Co., 1968. *Publications:* The Birds of Southport, 1947; chapter in The Forge, 1955; chapter in Science in Schools, 1958; scientific papers in chemical journals; articles in educational periodicals. *Recreations:* music, painting, travel. *Address:* The Warden's Lodge, Goldsmiths' College, New Cross, SE14. *T:* 01-692 7171.

**CHESTERMAN, Sir Ross;** *see* Chesterman, Sir D. R.

**CHESTERS, Prof. Charles Geddes Coull,** BSc, MSc, PhD; FRSE; FLS; FInstBiol; Professor of Botany, University of Nottingham, since 1944; *b* 9 March 1904; *s* of Charles and Margaret Geddes Chesters; *m* 1928, Margarita Mercedes Cathie Maclean; one *s* one *d*. *Educ:* Hyndland Sch.; Univ. of Glasgow. Lecturer in Botany, 1930, Reader in Mycology, 1942, Univ. of Birmingham. *Publications:* scientific papers on mycology and microbiology, mainly in Trans. British Myc. Soc., Ann. Ap. Biol., Jl Gen. Microb. *Recreations:* photography and collecting fungi. *Address:* Grandage Cottages, Quenington, near Cirencester, Glos. *Club:* National Liberal.

**CHESTERS, Dr John Hugh,** OBE 1970; FRS 1969; Director, Corporate Laboratories of the British Steel Corporation (BISRA), since 1970; *b* 16 Oct. 1906; 2nd *s* of Rev. George M. Chesters; *m* 1936, Nell Knight, Minnesota, USA; three *s* one *d*. *Educ:* High Pavement Sch., Nottingham; King Edward VII Sch., Sheffield; Univ. of Sheffield. BSc Hons Physics, 1928; PhD 1931; DSc Tech 1945. Metropolitan-Vickers Research Schol., Univ. Sheff., 1928-31. Robert Blair Fellowship, Kaiser-Wilhelm Inst. für Silikatforschung, Berlin, 1931-32; Commonwealth Fund Fellowship, Univ. of Illinois, 1932-34; United Steel Cos Ltd: in charge of Refractories Section, 1934-45; Asst Dir of Research, 1945-62; Dep. Dir of Research, United Steel Cos Ltd, 1962-67, Midland Group, British Steel Corporation, 1967-70. President: Brit. Ceramic Soc., 1951-52; Inst. of Ceramics, 1961-63; Iron and Steel Inst., 1968-69. Iron and Steel Inst., Bessemer Gold Medal, 1966, etc. FInst Fuel, FIM, FICeram.; Fellow, Amer. Ceramic Soc. *Publications:* Steelplant Refractories, 1945 (1957); Iron and Steel, 1948. Numerous articles in Jl of Iron and Steel Inst., Trans Brit. Cer.Soc., Jl Amer. Cer.Soc., Jl Inst. of Fuel, etc. *Recreations:* foreign travel, fishing. *Address:* 21 Slayleigh Lane, Sheffield S10 3RF. *T:* Sheffield 301257.

**CHESTERTON, Sir Oliver (Sidney),** Kt 1969; MC 1943; Partner in Chesterton & Sons, Chartered Surveyors, London; Deputy Chairman, Trust Houses Group Ltd, since 1959; Vice-Chairman, Woolwich Equitable Building Society, since 1969; *b* 28 Jan. 1913; *s* of Frank and Nora Chesterton; *m* 1944, Violet Ethel Jameson; two *s* one *d*. *Educ:* Rugby Sch. Served War of 1939-45, Irish Guards. Vice-Chm., Council of Royal Free Med. Sch., 1964-; Crown Comr, 1969-. Past Pres., Royal Instn of Chartered Surveyors. *Recreations:* golf, fishing. *Address:* 7 York House, Kensington Church Street, W8. *Clubs:* White's; Rye Golf.

**CHETHAM-STRODE, Warren,** MC 1916; author and playwright since 1932; *b* 28 Jan. 1897; *yr s* of Dr Chetham-Strode; *m* 1927, Moira Hamilton Verschoyle; (one *s* decd). *Educ:* Sherborne Sch. Served War of 1914-18, Capt., 3rd Bn The Border Regt, 2nd Bn, and Tank Corps. British American Tobacco Co., 1919-22, USA and S India. In business, 1922-32. Attached Military Affairs Branch, MOI and WO, 1939; Commercial Relations Div. and Overseas General Div., MOI, 1940-45. *Publications: novels:* Mice and Management, 1932; Three Men and a Girl, 1958; Top off the Milk, 1959; The Years of Alison (USA), 1961; A Cat Called Tootoo (a book for children), 1966; Tootoo's Friends at the Farm, 1967; Tootoo the Travelling Cat, 1968; A Short Walk: an autobiography of youth; *plays:* Sometimes Even Now, Embassy, 1933; Man Proposes, Wyndhams, 1933; Heart's Content, Shaftesbury, 1936; The Day is Gone, Embassy, 1937; Strangers Road, on tour, 1942; Young Mrs Barrington, Winter Garden, 1945; The Guinea-Pig, Criterion, 1946; A Play for Ronnie, on tour, 1946; The Gleam, Globe, 1946; Background, Westminster, 1950; The Pet Shop, St Martin's, 1954; Silver and Gold, Connaught, Worthing, 1954; The Stepmother, St Martin's, 1958; *radio serial play:* The Barlowes of Beddington; *TV serial play:* The Happy Man; Sinister Street (adapted from the novel by Compton Mackenzie); *films:* Return to Night; The Gay Pursuit; The Guinea-Pig; Odette; The Lady with a Lamp; Background. *Address:* The Oast House, Playden, near Rye, Sussex. *T:* Iden 254. *Club:* Rye Dormy House.

**CHETWODE,** family name of **Baron Chetwode.**

**CHETWODE,** 2nd Baron *cr* 1945, of Chetwode; **Philip Chetwode;** Bt, 1700; *b* 26 March 1937; *s* of Capt. Roger Charles George Chetwode (*d* 1940; *o s* of Field Marshal Lord Chetwode, GCB, OM, GCSI, KCMG, DSO) and Hon. Molly Patricia Berry, *d* of 1st Viscount Camrose (she *m* 2nd, 1942, 1st Baron Sherwood, from whom she obtained a divorce, 1948, and *m* 3rd, 1958, Sir Richard Cotterell, 5th Bt, *qv*); *S* grandfather, 1950; *m* 1967, Mrs Susan Dudley Smith; two *s*. *Educ:* Eton. Commissioned Royal Horse Guards, 1956-66. *Heir: s* Hon. Roger Chetwode, *b* 29 May 1968. *Address:* Crowood House, Ramsbury, Wilts. *Clubs:* Turf, White's.

**CHETWYND,** family name of **Viscount Chetwynd.**

**CHETWYND,** 10th Viscount *cr* 1717 (Ireland); **Adam Richard John Casson Chetwynd;** Baron Rathdown, 1717 (Ireland); with Colonial Mutual Life Assurance Society Ltd, Salisbury, Rhodesia, since 1968; *b* 2 Feb. 1935; *o s* of 9th Viscount and of Joan Gilbert, *o c* of late Herbert Alexander Casson, CSI, Ty'n-y-coed, Arthog, Mer; *S* father, 1965; *m* 1966, Celia Grace, *er d* of Comdr Alexander Robert Ramsay, DSC, RNVR, Fasque, Borrowdale, Salisbury, Rhodesia; twin *s* one *d*. *Educ:* Eton. 2nd Lieut Cameron Highlanders, 1954-56. Freeman, Guild of Air Pilots and Air Navigators. *Recreations:* shooting, sailing. *Heir: s* Hon. Adam Douglas Chetwynd, *b* 26 Feb. 1969. *Address:* c/o Ouvry and Co., 53 Romney Street, SW1.

**CHETWYND, Sir (Arthur Henry) Talbot,** 7th Bt *cr* 1795; OBE 1919; MC; late Captain, 9th Lancers; *b* 13 April 1887; *s* of late Arthur Chetwynd; *S* cousin, 1938; *m* 1st, 1914, Evelyn Margaret (who obtained a divorce, 1940), *d* of late Leonard Andrews; 2nd, 1940, Violet Mary (*d* 1955), *d* of William Charles Cripps, Camden Park, Tunbridge Wells; 3rd, 1956, Frances Audrey Boumphrey, *o d* of late Dr Flawith-Smith. *Educ:* Wellington Coll., Berks. Served European War, 1914-19 (despatches twice, OBE, MC); Colonel Commanding Frontiers Camel Corps and Cars Patrols, 1924-30; War of 1939-45, Commandant War Reserve and Special Constabulary and Police Staff Officer for the County of Monmouthshire. 4th Class, Order of Nile, 1930. *Heir: n* Arthur Ralph Talbot Chetwynd [*b* 28 Oct. 1913; *m* 1940, Marjory May MacDonald, *e d* of late Robert Bruce Lang, Vancouver, BC; two *s*]. *Address:* Firs Cottage, Belmore Lane, Lymington, Hants. *T:* Lymington 4238. *Clubs:* Naval and Military; Royal Lymington Yacht.

**CHETWYND, George Roland,** CBE 1968; Chairman of Land Commission, 1970 (Deputy Chairman, 1967-70) Chairman of Governors, Queen Mary's (Roehampton) Hospital, 1952; Member, British Steel Corporation, since 1970; *b* 14 May 1916; *s* of George Chetwynd and Anne Albrighton. *Educ:* Queen Elizabeth Grammar Sch., Atherstone; King's Coll., London University. BA Hons History, 1939; Postgraduate Scholarship; enlisted Royal Artillery, 1940; commissioned Army Educational Corps, 1942. MP (Lab.) Stockton-on-Tees, 1945-62; Parliamentary Private Secretary to Minister of Local Government and Planning, 1950-51 (to Chancellor of Duchy of Lancaster, 1948-50); Director: North East Development Council, 1962-67; Northern and Tubes Group, BSC, 1968-. Delegate to Consultative Assembly, Council of Europe, 1952-54; Member: Nature Conservancy, 1950-62; General Advisory Council, ITA, 1964; North-East Advisory Cttee for Civil Aviation, 1964; Board of BOAC, 1966-. Freedom of Borough of Stockton-on-Tees, 1968. *Recreations:* walking, sea fishing. *Address:* The Briars, Thorpe Larches, Sedgefield, Stockton-on-Tees, Teesside. *T:* Stillington 336.

**CHETWYND, Sir Talbot;** *see* Chetwynd, Sir A. H. T.

**CHETWYND-TALBOT,** family name of **Earl of Shrewsbury and Waterford.**

**CHEVALIER, Maurice;** Officier, Légion d'Honneur, 1969; stage and film actor; *b* 12 Sept. 1888; *m* 1926, Yvonne Vallée (marr. diss. 1935); no *c*. *Educ:* Menilmontant Primary Sch., Paris. From small cafés in Paris at the age of twelve to a one-man show in the greatest theatres in the whole world. Croix de Guerre; Legion of Honour. *Films include:* The Innocents of Paris, The Love Parade, Merry Widow, I have Seven Daughters, Love in the Afternoon, Gigi, etc. *Publications:* Ma Route et Mes Chansons (ten books of autobiography). *Recreations:* walking, writing. *Address:* La Louque, Marnes-La-Coquette 92, France.

**CHEVASSUT, Rev. Canon Frederick George;** Canon Emeritus, Manchester, 1968; *b* 28 Jan. 1889; *e s* of late Rev. Canon Frederick George Chevassût; unmarried. *Educ:* Manchester

Univ. (BSc); Trinity Coll., Cambridge (Exhibitioner, æq. Abbott Scholarship, BA, Senior Optime, 1912; 2nd Class Theological Tripos Part 2, 1913; MA 1919; Ridley Hall, Cambridge. Asst Curate, Bolton Parish Church, 1913-15; served in Army (Lieut RFA), 1915-19; Warden of St Anselm Hall, Manchester Univ., 1919-22; Special Service Priest, Manchester Diocese, 1922-26; Rector of St George's, Hulme, Manchester, 1926-68; Hon. Canon of Manchester, 1955-68. Warden Toc H Hostel, Hulme, 1926; Sec. Manchester Corp. Advisory Cttee on Hulme Clearance, 1934-35. *Publications:* occasional articles and reviews. *Recreations:* general reading, mountain walking. *Address:* 155 Chester Road, Manchester M15 4JB.

**CHEVRIER, Hon. Lionel,** CC (Canada) 1967; PC (Can.); QC (Can.); Member, Legal Firm of Geoffrion & Prud'homme, 500 Place d'Armes, Montreal; Commissioner-General for State Visits to Canada, since 1967; Chairman, Canadian Economic Mission to Francophone Africa, since 1968; *b* 2 April 1903; *s* of late Joseph Elphège Chevrier and late Malvina DeRepentigny; *m* 1932, Lucienne, *d* of Thomas J. Brulé, Ottawa; three *s* three *d*. *Educ:* Cornwall College Institute; Ottawa Univ.; Osgoode Hall. Called to bar, Ontario, 1928; KC 1938; called to Bar, Quebec, 1957. MP for Stormont, Canada, 1935-54; MP for Montreal-Laurier, 1957-64. Dep. Chief Government Whip, 1940; Chm., Special Parly Sub-Cttee on War Expenditures, 1942; Parliamentary Asst to Minister of Munitions and Supply, 1943; Minister of Transport, 1945-54; Pres., St Lawrence Seaway Authority, 1954-57; Minister of Justice, 1963-64; High Commissioner in London, 1964-67. Delegate, Bretton Woods Conf., 1945; Chm., Canadian Delegn, UN General Assembly, Paris, 1948; Pres., Privy Council, Canada, 1957. Hon. degrees: LLD: Ottawa, 1946; Laval, 1952; Queen's, 1956; DCL, Bishops', 1964. *Publication:* The St Lawrence Seaway, 1959. *Recreations:* walking and reading. *Address:* 1321 Sherbrooke Street W, Montreal, Canada.

**CHEWTON, Viscount; James Sherbrooke Waldegrave;** *b* 8 Dec. 1940; *e s* of 12th Earl Waldegrave, *qv*. *Educ:* Eton Coll.; Trinity Coll., Cambridge. *Address:* Chewton House, Chewton Mendip, Bath.

**CHEYLESMORE,** 4th Baron (UK) *cr* 1887; **Francis Ormond Henry Eaton,** DSO 1917; Lieut-Colonel; late Captain 3rd Battalion Grenadier Guards; *b* 19 June 1893; *e s* of 3rd Baron and Elizabeth Richardson (*d* 1945), *d* of late F. O. French, New York; *S* father, 1925; *m* 1929, Pearl Margaret, *d* of late A. J. Sundberg, Alix, Alberta, Canada. *Educ:* Eton; Trinity Coll., Cambridge; RMC Sandhurst. Served European War, 1914-19 (DSO); served War of 1939-45, RCOC (CA), 1941-45. *Heir:* none. *Address:* Happy Valley Ranch, Alix, Alberta, Canada.

**CHEYNE, James,** CMG 1950; *b* 7 Oct. 1894; *s* of James Cheyne, Umtali, Rhodesia; *m* 1923, Minnie Mary Elizabeth Gordon, *d* of late George Barron Beattie, Aberdeen; one *d*. *Educ:* Robert Gordon's Coll., Aberdeen. Served European War, 1917-18; entered Colonial Service, Administrative Officer in Tanganyika Territory, 1918; Provincial Commissioner, 1941; Secretary for African Affairs, 1948; Mem. for Local Govt, Tanganyika Territory, 1950; retd 1951. *Address:* Glenwood, West Moors, Dorset. *T:* Ferndown 3102.

**CHEYNE, Major Sir Joseph (Lister Watson),** 3rd Bt *cr* 1908; *b* 10 Oct. 1914; *e s* of Sir Joseph Lister Cheyne, 2nd Bt, MC, and Nelita Manfield, *d* of Andrew Pringle, Borgue; *S* father, 1957; *m* 1st, 1938, Mary Mort (marr. diss. 1955; she *d* 1959), *d* of late Vice-Adm. J. D. Allen, CB; one *s* one *d*; 2nd, 1955, Cicely, *d* of T. Metcalfe, Padiham, Lancs; two *s* one *d*. *Educ:* Stowe Sch.; Corpus Christi Coll., Cambridge. Major, The Queen's Westminsters (KRRC), 1943; Italian Campaign. *Heir:* *s* Patrick John Lister Cheyne [*b* 2 July 1941; *m* 1968, Helen Louise Trevor, *yr d* of Louis Smith, Southsea; one *d*]. *Address:* Leagarth, Fetlar, Shetland; 28E Via Roma, Grottaferrata, Rome, Italy. *T:* Rome 9459519.

**CHIANG, Yee,** BSc; FRSA; FAAS; Professor of Chinese, Columbia University, USA, since 1970; *b* 19 May 1903; *s* of Chiang Ho-an and Tsai Hsiang-Lin. *Educ:* Nat. South-Eastern Univ., Nanking. Teacher of Chemistry in two different middle schools; Lecturer in Chemistry at National Chi-Nan Univ.; soldier in the Chinese Army for one year; Asst Editor of a daily newspaper at Hangchow in Chekiang province; District Governor of four districts, Kiukiang, Yushan, Tangtu, and Wuhu in Kiangsi and Anhui provinces; Lecturer in Chinese at Sch. of Oriental Studies, London Univ., 1935-38; in charge of Chinese Section at Wellcome Historical Medical Museum, 1938-40. Designed the décor and costumes for the Sadler's Wells Ballet, The Birds, 1942; Curator of Chinese Ethnology, Peabody Museum, Salem, Massachusetts, USA, 1956-; Ralph Waldo Emerson Fellow in Poetry, Harvard Univ., 1958-59. Mem. Sub-Cttee on New Art Center for Univ. of Virginia, 1962; Senior Specialist, East-West Center, 1967. *Publications:* a Book of poems in Chinese, 1935; The Chinese Eye, 1935; The Silent Traveller in Lakeland, 1937; Chinese Calligraphy, 1938; The Silent Traveller in London, 1938; Birds and Beasts, 1939; Chinpao and the Giant Panda, 1939; The Silent Traveller in Wartime, 1939; A Chinese Childhood, 1940; The Silent Traveller in the Yorkshire Dales, 1941; Lo Cheng, the Boy who wouldn't keep still, 1941; Chinpao at the Zoo, 1941; The Men of the Burma Road, 1942; The Story of Ming, 1943; The Silent Traveller in Oxford, 1944; Dabbitse, 1944; Yebbin, 1947; The Silent Traveller in Edinburgh, 1948; The Silent Traveller in New York, 1950; Chinese Painting, 1953; The Silent Traveller in Dublin, 1955; The Silent Traveller in Paris, 1956; The Silent Traveller in Boston, 1959; The Silent Traveller in San Francisco, 1964; Chinese Ch'an Poetry, 1966; The Silent Traveller in Japan, 1970; contributed many articles to various English and American papers and magazines. *Recreations:* calligraphy, painting, walking, travelling and climbing. *Address:* c/o Methuen & Co. Ltd, 11 New Fetter Lane, EC4.

**CHIANG KAI-SHEK, Generalissimo;** *b* 31 Oct. 1887; *s* of Chiang Sohan, Chekiang Province; *m* 1927, Mayling Soong (*see* madame Chiang Kai-Shek); (two *s* by a previous marriage). Visited Japan 1906, where he first met Dr Sun Yat-Sen and other revolutionary leaders; studied at National Military Acad., Paoting, North China, 1906, and at Tokyo Military Acad.; joined Dr Sun's revolutionary party, 1907; joined revolutionary army, Shanghai, on outbreak of Chinese Revolution, Oct. 1911; followed Dr Sun to Canton and attached to Gen. Headquarters, 1918-20; sent by Dr Sun to Soviet Russia to study military and social System, 1923; founder and principal, Whampoa Military Acad., Canton, 1924, which provided all officers to Northern Expeditionary Forces; elected member of Central Exec. Cttee of Kuomintang, 1926; C-in-C Northern Expeditionary Forces, 1926-28;

Chairman of State Council and Generalissimo of all fighting services, 1928, following establishment of National Govt at Nanking; resigned both posts, 1931; inaugurated New Life Movement, 1934; Tsungtsai (Director-General) of Kuomintang Party, Republic of China, 1938; Chairman of Supreme National Defence Council, 1939-47; Chairman of National Military Affairs Council, 1932-46; Chairman of People's Political Council (war-time parliament), 1939-40; Pres. of Executive Yuan, 1935-38 and 1939-45; Head of Supreme Policy Council, Canton, 1949. Chairman National Govt of Republic of China, 1943; elected President of Republic of China, 1948, under new constitution; retired, 1949; resumed Presidency (in Taiwan), 1950; elected for second term, 1954; re-elected President, 1960, 1966, Dir-Gen. 1969. chm. National Security Council, 1967. Hon. GCB, 1942. Holds many foreign orders and decorations, incl. Croix de Guerre. *Publications:* China's Destiny, 1943; Soviet Russia in China, 1957. *Address:* Office of the President, Taipei, Taiwan (Formosa). *T:* 23731.

**CHIANG KAI-SHEK, Madame (Mayling Soong Chiang);** Chinese sociologist; *y d* of C. J. Soong; *m* 1927, Chiang Kai-Shek, *qv. Educ:* Wellesley Coll., USA. LHD, John B. Stetson Univ., Deland, Fla, Bryant Coll., Providence, RI, Hobart and William Smith Colls, Geneva, NY; LLD, Rutgers Univ., New Brunswick, NJ, Goucher Coll., Baltimore, MD, Wellesley Coll., Wellesley, Mass, Loyola Univ., Los Angeles, Cal., Russell Sage Coll., Troy, NY, Hahnemann Medical Coll., Philadelphia, Pa, Wesleyan Coll., Macon, Ga, Univ. of Michigan, Univ. of Hawaii; Hon. FRCS. First Chinese woman appointed Mem. Child Labor Commn; Inaugurated Moral Endeavor Assoc.; established schools in Nanking for orphans of Revolutionary Soldiers; former Mem. Legislative Yuan; served as Sec.-General of Chinese Commission on Aeronautical Affairs; Member Chinese Commission on Aeronautical Affairs; Director-General of the New Life Movement and Chairman of its Women's Advisory Council; Founder and Director: National Chinese Women's Assoc. for War Relief; National Assoc. for Refugee Children; Chinese Women's Anti-Aggression League; Huashing Children's Home. Frequently makes inspection tours to all sections of Free China where personally trained girl workers carry on war area and rural service work; accompanies husband on military campaigns; first Chinese woman to be decorated by National Govt of China. Recipient of highest military and Civil decorations; Hon. Chm., British United Aid to China Fund, China; Hon. Chm., Soc. for the Friends of the Wounded; Hon. President, American Bureau for Medical Aid to China; Patroness, International Red Cross Commn; Hon. President, Chinese Women's Relief Assoc. of New York; Hon. Chairman, Canadian Red Cross China Cttee; Hon. Chairman, Board of Directors, India Famine Relief Cttee; Hon. Mem., New York Zoological Soc.; Hon. Pres., Cttee for the Promotion of the Welfare of the Blind; Life Mem., San Francisco Press Club and Associated Countrywomen of the World; Mem., Phi Beta Kappa, Eta Chapter; first Hon. Member, Bill of Rights Commemorative Society; Hon. Member, Filipino Guerrillas of Bataan Assoc. Medal of Honour, New York City Federation of Women's Clubs; YWCA Emblem; Gold Medal, New York Southern Soc.; Chi Omega Nat. Achievement Award for 1943; Gold Medal for distinguished services, National Institute for Social Sciences; Distinguished Service Award, Altrusa Internat. Assoc.; Churchman Fifth Annual Award, 1943; Distinguished Service Citation, All-American Conf. to Combat Communism, 1958; Hon. Lieut-Gen. US Marine Corps. *Publications:* China in Peace and War, 1939; China Shall Rise Again, 1939; This is Our China, 1940; We Chinese Women, 1941; Little Sister Su, 1943; Ten Eventful Years, for Encyclopædia Britannica, 1946; Album of Reproduction of Paintings, 1952; The Sure Victory, 1955; Madame Chiang Kai-Shek Selected Speeches, 1958-59. *Address:* Office of the President, Taipei, Taiwan (Formosa).

**CHIBNALL, Albert Charles,** FRS 1937; PhD (London); ScD (Cantab); Fellow of Clare College, Cambridge; Fellow of the Imperial College of Science and Technology, London; *b* 28 Jan. 1894; *s* of G. W. Chibnall; *m* 1st, 1931 (wife *d* 1936); two *d*; 2nd, 1947, Marjorie McCallum Morgan, DPhil, Fellow of Clare Hall; one *s* one *d. Educ:* St Paul's Sch.; Clare Coll., Cambridge; Imperial Coll. of Science and Technology; Yale Univ., New Haven, Conn. 2nd Lieut, ASC 1914; Capt., 1915; attached RAF, 1917-19, served Egypt and Salonika. Huxley Medal, 1922; Imperial Coll. Travelling Fellow, 1922-23; Seessel Fellow, Yale Univ., 1923-24; Hon. Asst in Biochemistry, University Coll., London, 1924-30; Asst Prof. 1930-36, Prof. 1936-43, Emeritus Prof. 1943, of Biochemistry, Imperial Coll.; Sir William Dunn Prof. of Biochemistry, Univ. of Cambridge, 1943-49. Silliman Lectr, Yale Univ., 1938; Bakerian Lectr, Royal Society, 1942. *Publications:* Protein Metabolism in the Plant, 1939; Richard de Baden and the University of Cambridge, 1315-1340, 1963; Sherington, fiefs and fields of a Buckinghamshire village, 1965; papers in scientific journals on plant biochemistry. *Address:* 6 Millington Road, Cambridge. *Clubs:* Athenæum, Savage.

**CHICHESTER,** family name of **Marquess of Donegall,** and of **Baron Templemore.**

**CHICHESTER,** 9th Earl of, *cr* 1801; **John Nicholas Pelham;** Bt 1611; Baron Pelham of Stanmer, 1762; *b* (posthumous) 14 April 1944; *s* of 8th Earl of Chichester (killed on active service, 1944) and Ursula (she *m* 2nd, 1957, Ralph Gunning Henderson), *o d* of late Walter de Pannwitz, de Hartekamp, Bennebroek, Holland; *S* father, 1944. *Recreations:* music, flying. *Heir: kinsman* Richard Anthony Henry Pelham, *b* Aug. 1952. *Address:* Little Durnford Manor, Salisbury, Wilts. *Club:* Turf.

**CHICHESTER, Bishop of,** since 1958; **Rt. Rev. Roger Plumpton Wilson,** DD (Lambeth), 1949; Clerk of the Closet to the Queen since 1963; *b* 3 Aug. 1905; *s* of Canon Clifford Plumpton Wilson, Bristol, and Hester Marion Wansey; *m* 1935, Mabel Joyce Avery, Leigh Woods, Bristol; two *s* one *d. Educ:* Winchester Coll. (Exhibitioner); Keble Coll., Oxford (Classical Scholar). Hon. Mods in Classics 1st Class, Lit. Hum. 2nd Class, BA 1928; MA 1932. Classical Master, Shrewsbury Sch., 1928-30, 1932-34; Classical Master, St Andrew's Coll., Grahamstown, S Africa, 1930-32. Deacon, 1935; Priest, 1936; Curacies: St Paul's, Prince's Park, Liverpool, 1935-38; St John's, Smith Square, SW1, 1938-39; Vicar of South Shore, Blackpool, 1939-45; Archdeacon of Nottingham and Vicar of Radcliffe on Trent, 1945-49; also Vicar of Shelford (in plurality), 1946-49; Bishop of Wakefield, 1949-58. Mem., Presidium, Conf. of European Churches, 1967-. *Recreations:* Oxford University Authentics Cricket Club, Oxford University Centaurs Football Club, golf. *Address:* The Palace, Chichester, Sussex. *T:* 82161. *Clubs:* Athenæum, Royal Commonwealth Society.

**CHICHESTER, Assistant Bishop of;** *see* Reeves, Rt Rev. R. A.

**CHICHESTER, Dean of;** *see* Hussey, Very Rev. J. W. A.

**CHICHESTER, Archdeacon of;** *see* Mason, Ven. L.

**CHICHESTER, Lieut-Col Arthur O'Neill Cubitt,** OBE 1941; MC 1918; *b* 14 July 1889; *s* of Canon E. A. Chichester and Hon. Mrs M. A. Chichester; *m* 1924, Hilda Grace, *d* of Rt Hon. W. R. Young, Galgorm Castle, Ballymena; three *d. Educ:* Wellington Coll.; Trinity Coll., Cambridge. Served European War, 1914-18, Surrey Yeomanry; Clerk, House of Lords, 1919-21; Clerk of Parliaments, N Ireland, 1928-45; served War, 1939-41, comdg 102 HAA Regts, RA; Director: Braidwater Spinning Co., Ballymena; Stevenson & Son, Dungannon; Chairman: Moygashel Ltd, 1952-63; County Cttee on Training and Employment, 1955-61; Pres., County Antrim Agricultural Assoc., 1957-64; Chairman and Vice-Chairman Co. Antrim Territorial Force Assoc., 1938-55; Mayor, Ballymena, 1948-52. Mem. ITA, 1955-59. *Recreation:* field sports. *Address:* Galgorm Castle, Ballymena, N Ireland. *T:* Ballymena 2365. *Clubs:* Royal Automobile; Ulster (Belfast).

**CHICHESTER, Sir (Edward) John,** 11th Bt *cr* 1641; *b* 14 April 1916; *s* of Comdr Sir Edward George Chichester, 10th Bt, RN, and Phyllis Dorothy, *d* of late Henry F. Compton, Minstead Manor, Hants; *S* father, 1940; *m* 1950, Hon. Mrs Anne Rachel Pearl Moore-Gwyn, *widow* of Capt. Howel Moore-Gwyn, Welsh Guards, and *d* of 2nd Baron Montagu of Beaulieu and of Hon. Mrs Edward Pleydell-Bouverie; two *s* three *d. Educ:* Radley; RMC Sandhurst. Commissioned RSF, 1936. Patron of one living. Served throughout War of 1939-45. Was employed by ICI Ltd, 1950-60. A King's Foreign Service Messenger, 1947-50. Formerly Capt., Royal Scots Fusiliers and Lieut RNVR. *Heir: s* James Henry Edward Chichester, *b* 15 Oct. 1951. *Address:* Battramsley Lodge, Boldre, Lymington, Hants. *Club:* Naval. *See also Sir C. S. B. Renshaw.*

**CHICHESTER, Sir Francis,** KBE 1967 (CBE 1964); FIN; Chairman, Francis Chichester Ltd, Map and Guide Publishers since 1945; air navigator and pilot; yachtsman; *b* 17 Sept. 1901; *m* 1st, 1923, Muriel Eileen Blakiston (*d* 1929); (one *s* decd); 2nd, 1937, Sheila Mary Craven; one *s. Educ:* Marlborough Coll. Emigrated to NZ, 1919; formed Godwin Chichester Aviation Co. Ltd, 1928; second person to fly solo to Australia, 1929; first E to W solo flight from New Zealand to Australia across Tasman Sea, 1931 (Johnston Memorial Trophy for 1931, for navigation); first long-distance solo seaplane flight (NZ-Japan), 1931; cruising flight in Puss Moth with one passenger Sydney to London *via* Peking, 1936. Served in RAF, 1941-45, as Sen. Navigation Officer, Empire Central Flying Sch., 1943-45. Director, Straight Aviation Training Ltd, 1946-49. Warden, Guild of Air Pilots and Air Navigators, 1960; winner of first Single-handed Trans-Atlantic Yacht Race, 1960; awarded Yachtsman of the Year Trophy, 1960; Blue Water Medal for 1960 (Cruising Club of America); Institute of Navigation Gold Medal, 1961; record solo East-West Crossing, Plymouth-New York, 1962; 2nd in Second Solo Trans-Atlantic Yacht Race, 1964; solo one-stop circumnavigation at record speed, 1966-67. Vice-Pres., Inst. of Navigation; Younger Brother of Trinity House, 1968. Membre d'Honneur, Yacht Club de France, 1967 (Special Centenary Award, 1967). Hon. Master of Bench, Middle Temple, 1967. Special Gold Medal, RGS; Special Award, Inst. of Navigation; Superior Achievement Award, American Inst. of Navigation; Aust. Inst. of Navigation Gold Medal, 1967. Marconi Memorial Medal of Honour, NY, 1967; Italian Polhena da Bravura, Sãn Rémo, 1967; Blue Water Medal (2nd Award), 1967; Special Bronze Medal, and Chichester Award, Royal Yacht Squadron, 1967. Gold Medal, Guild of Yachting Writers, 1967; Medal for Seamanship, Royal Cruising Club, 1967; Livingstone Gold Medal, Royal Scottish Geographical Soc., 1969. *Publications:* Navigation Notes for Instructors and Students (Air Ministry), 1941-43; Solo to Sydney, 1930; Seaplane Solo, 1932 (republished as Alone Over the Tasman Sea, 1946, and in Aviation Classics series, 1966); Ride on the Wind, 1937; Spotters' Hand Book, 1940; Astro-Navigation, 1940 (4 parts); Pinpoint the Bomber, 1941; Star Recognition, 1941; Alone Across the Atlantic, 1961 (published in France, Seul en Course, 1962); Atlantic Adventure, 1962; The Lonely Sea and the Sky, 1964; Along the Clipper Way, 1966; Gipsy Moth Circles the World, 1967; How to Keep Fit, 1969. *Address:* 9 St James's Place, SW1. *T:* 01-493 0931. *Clubs:* Royal Yacht Squadron, Royal Aero, Royal Ocean Racing, Ocean Cruising, Royal Cruising, RAF Yacht, Royal Thames Yacht, Royal London Yacht, Royal Western Yacht (Plymouth).

**CHICHESTER-CLARK, Rt. Hon. Major James Dawson,** PC (Northern Ireland ) 1966; Prime Minister of Northern Ireland since 1969; *b* 12 Feb. 1923; *s* of late Capt. J. L. C. Chichester-Clark, DSO and bar, DL, MP, and Mrs C. E. Brackenbury; *m* 1959, Moyra Maud Haughton (*née* Morris); two *d* one step *s. Educ:* Eton. Entered Army, 1942; 2nd Lieut Irish Guards, Dec. 1942; wounded, Italy, 1944; ADC to Governor-General of Canada (Field-Marshal Earl Alexander of Tunis), 1947-49; attended Staff Coll., Camberley, 1956; retired as Major, 1960. DL Co. Derry, 1954. MP for South Derry, Parliament of NI, July 1960-; Asst Whip, March 1963; Chief Whip, 1963-67; Leader of the House, 1966-67; Min. of Agriculture, 1967-69. *Recreations:* shooting, fishing, ski-ing. *Address:* Moyola Park, Castledawson, Co. Derry, N Ireland. *T:* Castledawson 239. *Club:* Guards.

**CHICHESTER-CLARK, Robert;** MP (UU), Londonderry City and County, since 1955; *b* 10 Jan. 1928; *s* of late Capt. J. L. C. Chichester-Clark, DSO and Bar, DL, MP, and Mrs C. E. Brackenbury; *m* 1953, Jane Helen Goddard; one *s* two *d. Educ:* Royal Naval Coll.; Magdalene Coll., Cambridge (BA Hons Hist. and Law). Journalist, 1950; Public Relations Officer, Glyndebourne Opera, 1952; Asst to Sales Manager, Oxford Univ. Press, 1953-55. PPS to Financial Secretary to the Treasury, 1958; Asst Government Whip (unpaid), 1958-60; a Lord Comr of the Treasury, 1960-61; Comptroller of HM Household, 1961-64; Chief Opposition Spokesman on N Ireland, 1964-70, on Public Building and Works, 1965-70. *Recreation:* fishing. *Address:* Ross House, Kells, Co. Antrim. *T:* Kells 239. *Club:* Carlton.

**CHICK, Sir (Alfred) Louis,** KBE, *cr* 1952; *b* 19 Jan. 1904; *s* of late Alfred Y. Chick; *m* 1948, Betty, *d* of Col C. J. D. Freeth, Lymington, Hants; one *s* three *d. Educ:* King's Sch., Canterbury; London School of Economics, London Univ. Entered Sudan Civil Service, 1930; Asst Financial Secretary, 1943-46; Dep. Financial Secretary, 1947-48; Financial Secretary, 1948-53; Fiscal Comr, Nigeria, 1953; Chief of Mission, International Bank

Mission to Malaya, 1954; Chairman, White Fish Authority, 1954-63. *Address:* Upper Bolney Cottage, Harpsden, Henley-on-Thames, Oxon. *T:* Henley 4784.

**CHICK, Prof. Arthur Oliver;** retired as Professor of Dental Prosthetics, University of London (1957-66); *b* 7 April 1914; *s* of Oliver and Alice Chick; *m* 1938, Dulcie Elizabeth Doudney; two *s* one *d*. *Educ:* Brentwood Grammar Sch.; Guy's Hospital Dental Sch., University of London. LDS RCS, 1936; MDS Bristol, 1950; PhD Bristol, 1953. House Surgeon and Jun. Staff appts, Guy's Hospital, 1936-38. Served as Army Dental Officer, 1941-46. Asst Lecturer in Dental Prosthetics, University of Bristol, 1946; Lecturer, 1948; Head of Dept, 1948; Sen. Lecturer, 1950-57; Hon. Dental Surgeon United Bristol Hospitals, 1948, and later Consultant. Formerly Examiner, Univs of Bristol, Birmingham and Manchester, also Royal College of Surgeons of England and City and Guilds of London Institute; Examiner, Univs of London and Belfast. *Publications:* scientific articles in British and foreign journals. *Recreation:* gardening. *Address:* c/o School of Dentistry, University of London, WC1.

**CHICK, Dame Harriette,** DBE 1949 (CBE 1932); DSc London; Hon. DSc Manchester; Fellow of University College, London; Member of the Scientific Staff of the Lister Institute, 1905-46, Hon. Member, 1946-70; *b* 1875; 3rd *d* of Samuel and Emma Chick, Ealing and Branscombe, Devon. *Educ:* Notting Hill High Sch.; University Coll., London (1851 Exhibitioner); University of Vienna. Engaged in researches on nutrition in Vienna, 1919-22. *Publications:* numerous papers on physiological and biochemical subjects in the Journal of Hygiene, Journal of Physiology, Biochemical Journal, British Journal of Nutrition. *Recreation:* walking. *Address:* 34 Storeys Way, Cambridge. *Club:* Cowdray.

**CHICK, Sir Louis;** *see* Chick, Sir A. L.

**CHIEF RABBI;** *see* Jacobovits, Rabbi Dr Immanuel.

**CHIEPE, Miss Gaositwe Keagakwa Tibe,** MBE 1962; High Commissioner of Botswana to the UK; also Ambassador to Denmark, Norway, Sweden, France and Germany; *b* 20 Oct. 1922; *d* of late T. Chiepe. *Educ:* Fort Hare, South Africa (BSc, EdDip); Bristol Univ., UK (MA (Ed)). Asst Educn Officer, 1948-53; Educn Officer and Schools Inspector, 1953-62; Sen. Educn Officer, 1962-65; Dep. Dir of Educn, 1965-67; Dir of Educn, 1968-70; Diplomat, 1970-. Member: Botswana Society, Botswana Girl Guide Assoc.; Internat. Fedn of University Women. *Recreations:* gardening, a bit of tennis, a bit of swimming (in Botswana), reading. *Address:* Botswana High Commission, 3 Buckingham Gate, SW1. *T:* 01-828 0445/6/7. *Club:* Notwane (Botswana).

**CHIESMAN, Sir Walter (Eric),** Kt 1960; CB 1955; MD, FRCP; Treasury Medical Adviser, 1945-65, retired; *b* July 1900; *m* 1930, Feodora Rennie; one *s* two *d*. *Educ:* Whitgift Sch.; Corpus Christi Coll., Cambridge; St Thomas's Hospital. MD Cambridge, 1934; FRCP 1947. Resident Asst Physician, 1928, 1st Asst, Medical Unit, 1929-33, St Thomas's Hospital; Medical Adviser to ICI, 1933-45; KHP 1950, QHP 1951. Past President Assoc. of Industrial Medical Officers. *Recreations:* gardening, fishing. *Address:* Little Prettymans, Edenbridge, Kent. *T:* Four Elms 237. *Club:* Oxford and Cambridge University.

**CHILCOTT, C. M.;** *see* Fordyce, C. M.

**CHILD, Clifton James,** OBE 1949; MA, PhM, FRHistS; Administrative Officer, Cabinet Office Historical Section, since 1969; *b* Birmingham, 20 June 1912; *s* of late Joseph and Georgina Child; *m* 1938, Hilde Hurwitz; two *s*. *Educ:* Moseley Grammar Sch.; Universities of Birmingham, Berlin and Wisconsin. Univ. of Birmingham: Entrance Schol., 1929; Kenrick Prizeman, 1930; BA 1st class hons, 1932; Francis Corder Clayton Research Schol., 1932-34; MA 1934. Univ. of Wisconsin: Commonwealth Fund Fellow, 1936-38; PhM 1938. Educn Officer, Lancs Community Council, 1939-40. Joined Foreign Office, 1941; Head of American Section, FO Research Dept, 1946-58; African Section, 1958-62; Dep. Librarian and Departmental Record Officer, 1962; Librarian and Keeper of the Papers, FO, 1965-69. FRHistS 1965. *Publications:* The German-Americans in Politics, 1939; (with Arnold Toynbee and others) Hitler's Europe, 1954; contribs to learned periodicals in Britain and US. *Recreations:* gardening, foreign travel. *Address:* Westcroft, Westhall Road, Warlingham, Surrey. *T:* Upper Warlingham 2540.

**CHILD, Major Sir (Coles) John,** 2nd Bt *cr* 1919, of Bromley Palace, Kent; DL; *b* 11 Feb. 1906; *o s* of 1st Bt and Eliza Caroline, *d* of late R. B. Barton, LLD; *S* father, 1929; *m* 1933, Sheila (*d* 1964), *e d* of Hugh Mathewson, 1570 Pine Avenue, Montreal; one *s* two *d*. ADC to Governor-Gen. of Dominion of Canada, 1931-33. Lieut Coldstream Guards R of O, re-employed 1939; Capt. 1940, Maj. 1941. DL Surrey, 1960. Lord of the Manor of Bromley. *Recreation:* won the Canadian Amateur Rackets, 1932, 1933, Singles and Doubles, and Doubles in 1934. *Heir:* *s* Coles John Jeremy Child, *b* 20 Sept. 1944. *Address:* Broomfield House, Westwood Road, Windlesham, Surrey. *T:* Bagshot 3743. *Clubs:* Guards, Pratt's.

**CHILD, Sir John;** *see* Child, Sir C. J.

**CHILD, Rev. Robert Leonard,** MA, BD, BLitt; Principal-Emeritus of Regent's Park College, Oxford; *b* 28 March 1891; *s* of Joseph Colin Child and Mary Ellen Sargent; unmarried. *Educ:* Chepstow Grammar Sch.; Newport Intermediate Boys' Sch. Civil Service as Second Division Clerk, and Officer of Customs and Excise, 1909-19. In training for Min. at Regent's Park Coll., London, Mansfield Coll., Oxford, and Marburg Univ. (Germany), 1919-26. Minister of St Andrew's Street Baptist Church, Cambridge, 1926-34; Minister of Broadmead Baptist Church, Bristol, 1934-42; Principal of Regent's Park Coll., Oxford, 1942-58; President, Baptist Union, 1954. *Publication:* A Conversation about Baptism, 1963. *Address:* 34 Lonsdale Road, Oxford. *T:* 59546.

**CHILD-VILLIERS;** *see* Villiers.

**CHILDS, Hubert,** CMG 1951; OBE 1943; *b* 6 July 1905; 3rd *s* of late Dr W. M. Childs, first Vice-Chancellor of the University of Reading. *Educ:* Oakham Sch.; University College, Oxford. Colonial Administrative Service, Nigeria, 1928-46, Sierra Leone, 1946-58. On Military service, 1941-46. Chief Comr, Protectorate, Sierra Leone, 1950-58. UK Plebiscite Administrator for Southern Cameroons, 1960-61; Official Observer, Malta Referendum, May 1964. *Address:* Brown's Gate, Bucklebury, Reading, Berks.

**CHILDS, Leonard,** CBE 1961 (OBE 1946); DL; JP; Chairman, Great Ouse River Authority, since 1949; *b* April 1897; *s* of Robert R. Childs, Grove House, Chatteris; *m* 1924, Mary M., *d* of John Esson, MIMinE, Aberdeen; three *s*.

*Educ:* Wellingborough. Served European War, 1914-18, in Royal Flying Corps and Artists' Rifles. County Councillor, Isle of Ely, 1922 (Chairman, 1946-49); Custos Rotulorum, 1952-65; High Sheriff, Cambs and Hunts, 1946; DL Cambs, 1950; JP Isle of Ely, 1932. *Recreation:* shooting. *Address:* South Park Street, Chatteris, Cambridgeshire. *T:* Chatteris 4.

**CHILE, BOLIVIA and PERU, Bishop in,** since 1963; **Rt. Rev. Kenneth Walter Howell,** MA; *b* 4 Feb. 1909; *s* of Frederick John and Florence Sarah Howell; *m* 1937, Beryl Mary Hope, *d* of late Capt. Alfred and Mrs Hope, Bedford; two *s* one *d. Educ:* St Olave's; St Peter's Hall, Oxford; Wycliffe Hall, Oxford. Curate of St Mary Magdalene, Peckham, 1933-37; Chaplain of Paraguayan Chaco Mission, 1937-38; Chaplain Quepe Mission, Chile, 1938-40; Superintendent of South American Missionary Society's Mission to Araucanian Indians in S Chile, 1940-47; Vicar of Wandsworth, 1948-63, Rural Dean, 1957-63; Hon. Canon of Southwark, 1962-63. Chaplain, Royal Hospital and Home for Incurables, Putney, 1957-63. *Address:* Diocesan Office, Casilla 675, Santiago, Chile.

**CHILSTON,** 3rd Viscount *cr* 1911, of Boughton Malherbe; **Eric Alexander Akers-Douglas;** Baron Douglas of Baads, 1911; *b* 17 Dec. 1910; *s* of 2nd Viscount and Amy (*d* 1962), *d* of late J. R. Jennings-Bramly, RHA; *S* father, 1947; *m* 1955, Marion (*d* 1970), *d* of late Capt. William Charles Howard, RE. *Educ:* Eton; Trinity Coll., Oxford. Formerly Flight Lieut RAFVR. *Publications:* part author, Survey of International Affairs, 1938 Vol. III, Hitler's Europe, Realignment of Europe (Royal Institute of International Affairs); Chief Whip: The Political Life and Times of A. Akers-Douglas, 1st Viscount Chilston, 1961; W. H. Smith, 1965. *Heir: cousin* Alastair George Akers-Douglas, *b* 6 Sept. 1946. *Address:* Chilston Park, Maidstone, Kent. *T:* Lenham 214. *Club:* Brooks's.

**CHILTON, Air Marshal Sir (Charles) Edward,** KBE 1959 (CBE 1945); CB 1951; RAF (retired); Chairman, Scott Anderson & Co.; Consultant and Director, IBM (Rentals) UK; *o s* of J. C. Chilton; *m* 1st, 1929, Betty Ursula (*d* 1963), 2nd *d* of late Bernard Temple Wrinch; one *s*; 2nd, 1964, Joyce Cornforth. Royal Air Force general duties branch; Air Commodore, 1950; Air Vice-Marshal, 1954; Air Marshal, 1959. Dep. Air Officer i/c Administration, Air Command, SE Asia, 1944; AOC Ceylon, 1946; Imperial Defence Coll., 1951; AOC Gibraltar, 1952; Asst Chief of the Air Staff (Policy), 1953-54; SASO, HQ Coastal Command, 1955; AOC Royal Air Force, Malta, and Dep. Comdr-in-Chief (Air), Allied Forces Mediterranean, 1957-59; AOC-in-C, Coastal Command and Maritime Air Commander Eastern Atlantic Area, and Commander Maritime Air, Channel and Southern North Sea, 1959-62. Specialist navigator (Air Master navigator certificate) and Fellow (Vice-Pres. 1949-51, 1959-61, 1963-65), Institute of Navigation. Pres. RAF Rowing Club, 1956; Vice-Adm. and Hon. Life Mem. RAF Sailing Assoc.; Hon. Vice-Pres. RAF Swimming Assoc. MInstD. Grand Cross of Prince Henry the Navigator (Portugal), 1960. *Address:* 11 Charles House, Phyllis Court Drive, Henley-on-Thames, Oxon. *Clubs:* Royal Air Force, United Service; (Vice-Patron) Royal Gibraltar Yacht; Phyllis Court.

**CHILTON, Donovan;** Keeper, Department of Electrical Engineering and Communications, Science Museum, London, since 1960; *b* 24 Feb. 1909; 5th *s* of Percy Chilton and Ada Grace Ryall; *m* 1937, Jane Margaret Saunders; two *s* (one *d* decd). *Educ:* Latymer Upper Sch.; Royal College of Science (Royal Scholar); University of Göttingen, Germany. BSc 1931; ARCS 1930; DIC 1931. Works physicist, Ilford Ltd, 1932-38; entered Science Museum, 1938; Dep. Keeper, 1949; Keeper, 1960. Air Ministry, Meteorological Office, 1939-45. FInstP; FMA. *Address:* Heathdale, 33 Park Avenue, Hutton, Essex. *T:* Brentwood 775.

**CHILTON, Brigadier Sir Frederick Oliver,** Kt 1969; CBE 1963 (OBE 1957); DSO 1941 and bar 1944; Chairman, Repatriation Commission, Australia, since 1958; *b* 23 July 1905. *Educ:* Univ. of Sydney (BA, LLB). Solicitor, NSW, 1929. Late AIF; served War of 1939-45, Libya, Greece, New Guinea and Borneo (despatches, DSO and bar); Controller of Joint Intelligence, 1946-48; Asst Sec., Dept of Defence, Australia, 1948-50; Dep. Sec., 1950-58. *Address:* c/o Repatriation Commission, Canberra, ACT, Australia. *Clubs:* Melbourne, Naval and Military (Melbourne), Imperial Service (Sydney).

**CHILVER, Amos Henry,** MA, DSc; Vice-Chancellor, Cranfield Institute of Technology, since 1970; *b* 30 Oct. 1926; *e s* of Amos H. Chilver and Annie E. Mack; *m* 1959, Claudia, *o d* of Sir Wilfrid Grigson; three *s* two *d. Educ:* Southend High Sch.; Bristol Univ. (Albert Fry Prize 1947). Structural Engineering Asst, British Railways, 1947; Asst Lecturer, 1950, Lecturer, 1952, in Civil Engineering, Bristol Univ.; Demonstrator, 1954, Lectr, 1956, in Engineering, Cambridge Univ.; Fellow of Corpus Christi Coll., Cambridge, 1958-61; Chadwick Prof. of Civil Engineering, UCL, 1961-69. Dir, Centre for Environmental Studies, 1967-69. Member: SRC, 1970- (Chm. Transport Cttee, 1970-, Aeronautical and Civil Engineering Cttee, 1968-70); ARC, 1967-70; Ferrybridge Enquiry Cttee, 1965; BSI Cttees on steel structures and cooling towers; Management Cttee, Inst. of Child Health, 1965-69. Telford Gold Medal, Institution of Civil Engineers, 1962. *Publications:* Problems in Engineering Structures (with R. J. Ashby), 1958; Strength of Materials (with J. Case), 1959; Thin-walled Structures (ed), 1967; papers on structural theory in engineering journals. *Address:* Cayley Lodge, Cranfield, Bedford. *T:* Cranfield 257; 2 Hampstead Square, NW3. *T:* 01-435 0675.

**CHILVER, Elizabeth Millicent, (Mrs R. C. Chilver);** Principal, Bedford College, University of London, 1964-71; Principal of Lady Margaret Hall, Oxford, from Sept. 1971; *b* 3 Aug. 1914; *o d* of late Philip Perceval Graves and late Millicent Graves (*née* Gilchrist); *m* 1937, Richard Clementson Chilver, *qv. Educ:* Benenden Sch., Cranbrook; Somerville Coll., Oxford. Journalist, 1937-39; temp. Civil Servant, 1939-45; Daily News Ltd, 1945-47; temp. Principal and Secretary, Colonial Social Science Research Council and Colonial Economic Research Cttee, Colonial Office, 1948-57; Director, Univ. of Oxford Inst. of Commonwealth Studies, 1957-61; Senior Research Fellow, Univ. of London Inst. of Commonwealth Studies, 1961-64. Mem. Royal Commn on Medical Education, 1965-68. Trustee, British Museum, 1970-. Médaille de la Reconaissance française, 1945. *Publications:* articles on African historical and political subjects. *Address:* 108 Clifton Hill, NW8. *T:* 01-624 2702.

**CHILVER, Prof. Guy Edward Farquhar,** MA, DPhil; Dean of Humanities and Professor of Classical Studies, University of Kent at Canterbury, since 1964, and Deputy Vice-Chancellor since 1966; *b* 11 Feb. 1910; *er s* of

late Arthur Farquhar Chilver and late Florence Ranking; *m* 1945, Sylvia Chloe, *d* of late D. P. Littell; no *c*. *Educ:* Winchester; Trinity Coll., Oxford. Harmsworth Sen. Scholar, Merton Coll., 1932-34. Queen's Coll., Oxford: Fellow and Prælector in Ancient History, 1934-63; Dean, 1935-39; Sen. Tutor, 1948-63; Emeritus Fellow, 1964-. Min. of Food, 1940-45; British Food Mission, Washington, 1943-45. Member Hebdomadal Council, Oxford Univ., 1949-63; Visiting Prof., University of Texas, 1963; Vice-Pres., Society for Promotion of Roman Studies, 1964-. *Publications:* Cisalpine Gaul, 1941; trans. (with S. C. Chilver), and annotated, Unesco History of Mankind, Vol. II, 1965; articles in learned journals. *Recreation:* bridge. *Address:* Oak Lodge, Boughton, near Faversham, Kent. *T:* Boughton 246. *Clubs:* Reform; Kent and Canterbury (Canterbury).
*See also R. C. Chilver, B. Davidson.*

**CHILVER, Richard Clementson,** CB 1952; Deputy Secretary, Ministry of Housing and Local Government since 1966; *b* 1912; *yr s* of Arthur Farquhar Chilver; *m* 1937, Elizabeth Chilver, *qv*. *Educ:* Winchester; New Coll., Oxford. Appointed to Air Ministry, 1934; Asst Under-Secretary of State, Air Ministry, 1946-55; Deputy Secretary: Cabinet Office, 1955-56; Ministry of Defence, 1956-61; Ministry of Transport, 1961-64; Ministry of Land and Natural Resources, 1964-66. *Address:* 108 Clifton Hill, NW8. *T:* 01-624 2702.
*See also Prof. G. E. F. Chilver, B. Davidson.*

**CHIMAY, Lt-Col Prince Alphonse de; Alphonse Marcel Jules Matteo Joseph de Riquet, Comte de Caraman;** TD; *b* 23 June 1899; *m* Brenda, *er d* of late Lord Ernest Hamilton; one *d*. *Educ:* Eton; RMC Sandhurst. Late Lieut Scots Guards; served European War, 1916-18; R of O 1920; Major TA 1939; Lt-Col 1942; commanded 2/7th Bn Middx Regt (DCO), 1942-45; AAG, AFHQ, CMF, 1945; served France, 1940, Africa, Sicily, Italy, 1943-45 (despatches). *Recreations:* sailing, golf, shooting. *Address:* The Garden House, Arrow, Alcester, Warwicks. *T:* Alcester 2513. *Club:* Guards.
*See also Marquess of Hertford.*

**CHINA, William Edward,** CBE 1959; MA, ScD, FIBiol; DipAgric Cantab; FRES; Keeper, Department of Entomology, British Museum (Natural History), 1955-61; Deputy Chief Scientific Officer, 1957-61; *b* 7 Dec. 1895; 2nd *s* of William Edwin China, London; *m* 1922, Lita Frances Gaunt, *d* of late A. R. Gaunt, Birmingham; one *s* twin *d*. *Educ:* Battersea Polytechnic; Trinity Hall, Cambridge (Open Scholar 1914). Entered British Museum as Asst, 1922; Asst Keeper, 1927; Dep. Keeper, 1944; Keeper, 1955. World authority on Hemiptera. Scientific Controller, International Trust, 1959-70, and Sec., International Commn, 1962-70, on Zoological Nomenclature. Foreign Mem. Soc. pro Faun. Flor. Fennica; Corresponding Mem. Entomological Soc. of Egypt. Served in France in Special Brigade (Poison Gas), RE, 1915-17; in 52 Squadron (Observer), RAF, 1918. Home Guard, 1940-45. *Publications:* over 200 scientific papers on the structure, taxonomy, evolution and zoogeography of the insect order Hemiptera. *Recreation:* gardening. *Address:* Mousehole, near Penzance, Cornwall. *T:* Mousehole 516.

**CHINN, Wilfred Henry,** CMG 1951; *b* 26 June 1901; *s* of Henry Chinn, Birmingham; *m* 1933, Rachel Mawd, *d* of Rev. Canon T. S. Dunn; two *d*. *Educ:* George Dixon Gram. Sch., Birmingham; University of Birmingham. Probation Officer, Birmingham, 1924-35; Principal Probation Officer, Palestine, 1935; Adviser on Social Welfare, Palestine, 1941; Dir of Social Welfare, Palestine, 1943; Adviser on Social Welfare to Sec. of State for the Colonies, 1947-61; Adviser on Social Development, Ministry of Overseas Development, 1964-66 (Dept of Technical Co-operation, 1961-64). *Address:* Yew Tree Cottage, Longnor, Shrewsbury, Salop. *T:* Dorrington 495.

**CHINNERY, E. W. Pearson;** teaching and research since 1949; *b* Waterloo, Vic., Australia, 5 Nov. 1887; *m* 1919, Sarah Johnston Neill, Belfast; four *d*. *Educ:* various schools; Christ's Coll., Cambridge; Diploma Anthropology Cantab. Magistrate British New Guinea, 1909-21; Government Anthropologist, New Guinea, 1924-32; Dir of District Services and Native Affairs, and Mem. of the Legislative and Executive Councils, New Guinea, 1932-38; Dir of Native Affairs, Northern Territory, 1938-46; Official Adviser in Native Matters to Commonwealth of Australia, 1938-47; explored new districts in Owen Stanley Range, British New Guinea, between Mt Obree and Mt Chapman, and took a leading part in the discovery and pacification of tribes and cannibals and head-hunters in various parts of the interior of New Guinea; Lieut AIF (Australian Flying Corps, observer); Medal Royal Humane Society; awarded Cuthbert Peek Grant, 1920, Royal Geographical Society; lectured in England, 1919-20, and in USA, England, Geneva, and Australia, 1930, 1934, 1947 and 1948. Delegate to Pan Pacific Science Congress, Australia, 1923, and International Pacific Health Conference, 1926; an Australian delegate to League of Nations (Permanent Mandates Commission) 18th Session Geneva, 1930 and 22nd Session, 1934; Delegate New Guinea and Australia International Anthropological Conf., London, July-Aug. 1934; Pres. Section Anthropology Australian and New Zealand Association for Advancement of Science, Sydney, 1932; an Australian Delegate to Trusteeship Council, United Nations, Lake Success, 1947; a mem. UN visiting mission to Ruanda Urundi and Tanganyika, 1948; Anthropologist, External Territories Dept, 1948-49. *Publications:* numerous papers and reports. *Address:* 15 Stevens Parade, Black Rock, Melbourne S9, Australia.

**CHINOY, Sir Sultan Meherally,** Kt 1939; Chairman: F. M. Chinoy & Co. Private Ltd; The Bombay Garage Private Ltd; Director, British India General Insurance Co. Ltd and other companies; *b* 16 Feb. 1885; *m* Sherbanoo; one *s* four *d*. *Educ:* Bharda New High Sch.; Elphinstone Coll. Mainly responsible for introduction of Wireless Telegraphy in India on a commercial scale and founded Indian Radio and Cable Communications Co. Ltd; Chm., Standing Cttee, Bombay Municipal Corporation, 1937-38; Mayor of Bombay, 1938-39; Mem., Bombay Board of Film Censors, 1938-39; Mem. Bombay Hospital Maintenance Fund Cttee; Cttee Mem. of Children's Aid Soc., Soc. for the Protection of Children in Western India; Mem., City Cttee, Bombay Branch Indian Red Cross Soc., etc; organised Pageants in 1937 and 1940 in aid of funds for Red Cross; Chm., Rupee Fund Cttee, King Emperor's Anti-Tuberculosis Fund, Bombay Presidency. Governor 89th District of Rotary International, 1944-45. *Publication:* Pioneering in Indian Business. *Recreation:* horse flesh. *Address:* Meher Buildings, Chowpatty, Bombay 7, India. *Clubs:* Willingdon Sports, Orient, Royal Western India Turf (Bombay).

**CHIPIMO, Elias Marko;** Executive Director, Standard Bank, since 1969; *b* 23 Feb. 1931; *s* of Marko Chipimo, Zambia (then Northern Rhodesia); *m* 1959, Anna Joyce Nkole Konie; four *s* two *d*. *Educ:* St Canisius, Chikuni, Zambia; Munali; Fort Hare Univ. Coll., SA; University Coll. of Rhodesia and Nyasaland. Schoolmaster, 1959-63; Sen. Govt Administrator, 1964-67; High Comr for Zambia in London, 1968-69; Perm. Sec., Min. of Foreign Affairs, 1969. Chm. Zambia Stock Exchange; Pres., Lusaka Branch, Zambia Red Cross; Mem., Zambia Univ. Council. *Publication:* Our Land and People, 1966. *Recreations:* reading, usually literature, philosophy and politics; chess; discussions. *Address:* PO Box 2238, Lusaka, Zambia.

**CHIPP, David Allan;** Editor in Chief of The Press Association since 1969; *b* 6 June 1927; *s* of late Thomas Ford Chipp and of Isabel Mary Ballinger; unmarried. *Educ:* Geelong Grammar Sch., Australia; King's Coll., Cambridge (MA). Served with Middlesex Regt, 1944-47; Cambridge, 1947-50. Joined Reuters as Sports Reporter, 1950; Correspondent for Reuters: in SE Asia, 1953-55; in Peking, 1956-58; various managerial positions in Reuters, 1960-68; Editor of Reuters, 1968. *Recreations:* coaching rowing; listening to Wagner. *Address:* Mile House, Ibstone, Bucks. *T:* Turville Heath 348. *Clubs:* Travellers', Press; Leander (Henley-on-Thames).

**CHIRICO, Giorgio de;** Italian artist; painter, theatrical designer and writer; *b* Greece, 10 July 1888; *s* of Evaristo and Gemma de Chirico; *m* Isabella Far. *Educ:* Polytechnic Institute, Athens; Academy of Fine Arts, Munich. During early career as a painter in Italy and Paris, began series of Italian townscapes; launched metaphysical School, Italy, 1917; Has designed scenery and costumes for ballet and operatic productions; other work includes murals, lithographs, book illustrations, designs etc. Known for his compositions of horses, gladiators, archaeological subjects, scenes of Greek mythology, portraits, still life. Since 1968, he has carried out his characteristic subjects in sculpture. Hon. RBA 1949. *Publications:* Hebdomeros, 1929; (with Isabella Far) Commedia dell'arte moderna, 1945, and other volumes of art criticism; Memorie della mia vita, 1945. *Address:* Piazza di Spagna 31, Rome, Italy.

**CHISHOLM, Ven. Alexander,** MA; Prebendary of Combe VI in Wells Cathedral since 1959; retired as Archdeacon of Carlisle (1947-Oct. 1958), also as Canon Residentiary of Carlisle Cathedral and Examining Chaplain to the Bishop of Carlisle; Archdeacon Emeritus, 1958; *b* 21 Jan. 1887; *s* of Alexander Chisholm, The Bank, Dolphinton. *Educ:* Hatfield Coll., Durham Univ. Curate of St Luke's, Bath, 1911-18; Vicar of Wedmore, 1918-36; Vicar of Yeovil with Preston Plucknett and Yeovil Marsh, 1936-40; Rector of Weston-super-Mare, 1940-47; Preb. of Whitchurch in Wells Cathedral, 1935-47; Sub-Dean of Wells Cathedral, 1946-47; Examining Chaplain to Bishop of Bath and Wells, 1938-47; OCF, 1939-47; Hon. Chaplain to Bishop of Bath and Wells, 1947-60. *Recreation:* music. *Address:* Abbey Close, Ditcheat, Shepton Mallet, Somerset. *T:* Ditcheat 314.

**CHISHOLM, Alexander Hugh,** OBE 1958; Chief Editor, Australian Encyclopædia; *b* Maryborough, Vic., 28 March 1890, of Scottish parents; *m* 1923, Olive Haseler, Brisbane; one *d*. *Educ:* State Sch., Maryborough Bushland. Sometime hon. lecturer in nature study in schools of Victoria and Queensland; Pres., Queensland Bird Lovers' League, 1919-22; Editor: Queensland Naturalist, 1920-22; The Emu, 1926-28; Victorian Naturalist, 1939-48; late Editor, The Australasian, Melbourne; Editor, The Argus, Melbourne, 1937-38; Adviser on Fauna Protection to Queensland Government; President: Field Naturalists' Club of Victoria; Royal Australasian Ornithologists' Union; Royal Australian Historical Soc.; holds honours from British, American, and Australian Ornithologists' Unions, Zoological Soc. of London, etc; Australian Nat. Hist. Medallion, 1940; Press Liaison Officer, March-July 1945, to the Duke of Gloucester. *Publications:* Bird Seeking in Queensland, 1922; Mateship with Birds, 1922; Feathered Minstrels of Australia, 1926; Birds and Green Places, 1929; Nature Fantasy in Australia, 1932; Bird Wonders of Australia, 1934; Strange New World, 1942; The Incredible Year, 1944; The Story of Elizabeth Gould, 1944; An Explorer and His Birds, 1945; The Making of a Sentimental Bloke, 1946; Fairy Wrens, 1948; News from Nature, 1948; Scots Wha Hae, 1950; The Romance of the Lyrebird, 1960; Ferdinand von Mueller, 1962; Australian Wild Life, 1966; The Joy of the Earth, 1969. *Recreation:* idling in green places. *Address:* History House, 8 Young Street, Sydney, Australia.

**CHISHOLM, Archibald Hugh Tennent,** CBE 1946; MA; The British Petroleum Co. Ltd; *b* 17 Aug. 1902; 2nd *s* of late Hugh Chisholm and Mrs Chisholm (*née* Harrison), Rush Park, Co. Antrim; *m* 1939, Josephine, *e d* of J. E. Goudge, OBE, ICS; one *s* two *d*. *Educ:* Westminster; Christ Church, Oxford. Wall Street Journal of NY, 1925-27; The British Petroleum Co. (then Anglo-Persian/Anglo-Iranian Oil Co.), Iran and Kuwait, 1928-36 and London, 1945-; Editor of The Financial Times, 1937-40; Army, 1940-45 (despatches twice, CBE). Vice-Pres. Iran Soc.; Mem. Council, Anglo-Arab Assoc.; FZS; FRSA; FInstPet. Chevalier, Légion d'Honneur. *Address:* Tragariff House, Bantry, Ireland. *T:* Bantry 74; 1 Stanhope Place, W2. *T:* 01-262 7521. *Clubs:* Athenæum, Bath, MCC; Cork and County.

**CHISHOLM, (George) Brock,** CC (Canada) 1967; CBE 1943; MC (and Bar); ED; MD; *b* 18 May 1896; *s* of Frank Herbert and Lisbeth McCraney Chisholm; *m* 1924, Grace McLean Ryrie; one *s* one *d*. *Educ:* Univ. of Toronto, Yale, etc. Psychiatrist, Toronto, Canada; OC Lorne Scots; OC 5th Infantry Bde; Comdt Northern Area, Military District 2; served 1940-45: GSO1; Dir of Personnel Selection; Deputy Adjt-Gen.; Dir-Gen. of Medical Services, Canadian Army, rank of Maj.-Gen.; Dep. Minister of Health, Department of National Health and Welfare, Canadian Government, 1945-46; Executive Sec., Interim Commission of the World Health Organisation, United Nations, 1946-48; Dir-Gen., WHO, 1948-53, United Nations, Palais des Nations, Geneva. Pres., World Federation for Mental Health, Aug. 1957-58; Vice-Pres., World Assoc. of World Federalists; Hon. Pres., World Federalists of Canada. Holds numerous hon. degrees, decorations and awards from organisations throughout the world. *Publications:* Prescription for Survival, 1957 (USA); Can People Learn to Learn?, 1958 (USA), 1959 (Eng.). *Address:* Apartment 202, 1400 Newport Avenue, Victoria, BC, Canada. *Club:* Union (British Columbia).

**CHISHOLM, Henry,** CBE 1965; MA, FCA; Chairman: Corby Development Corporation (New Town), since 1950; Ada (Halifax) Ltd, since 1961; *b* 17 Oct. 1900; *e s* of late Hugh

Chisholm and of Eliza Beatrix Chisholm (*née* Harrison); *m* 1st, 1925, Eve Hyde-Thomson; one *s*; 2nd, 1940, Audrey Viva Hughes (*née* Lamb); two *s*; 3rd, 1956, Margaret Grace Crofton-Atkins (*née* Brantom). *Educ:* Westminster (Schol.); Christ Church, Oxford (Scholar). 2nd Mods, 2nd Lit. Hum., BA 1923, MA 1960. Manager, Paris Office, Barton Mayhew & Co., Chartered Accountants, 1927-32; Partner, Chisholm Hanke & Co., Financial Consultants, 1932-38; Overseas Liaison Officer, Bowater-Lloyd Group, 1938-44; Dir, Bowater-Lloyd (Newfoundland) Ltd, 1940-44; Mem. and Chm. of Departmental Cttees on Organisation of Naval Supply Services, Admiralty, 1942-45; Dir and Financial Controller, The Metal Box Co. Ltd, 1945-46; Joint Managing Dir, A. C. Cossor Ltd, 1947-60. Mem., Monopolies Commn, 1966-69. Pres., London Flotilla, RNVSR, 1945-53; a Governor of Westminster Sch.; Founder Mem. British Institute of Management. *Recreations:* sailing, gardening, travel. *Address:* Scott's Grove House, Chobham, Woking, Surrey. *T:* Chobham 8660. *Clubs:* United Service, Royal Automobile, Naval, Royal Yacht Squadron, Royal Ocean Racing, (Hon. Life Member) Royal Thames Yacht.

**CHISHOLM, Rt. Rev. John Wallace;** *see* Melanesia, Bishop of.

**CHISHOLM, Roderick Æneas,** CBE 1946; DSO 1944; DFC and bar; AEA; ARCS; BSc; Chairman, Iranian Oil Services; *b* 23 Nov. 1911; *s* of Edward Consitt Chisholm and Edith Maud Mary Cary Elwes; *m* 1945, Phillis Mary Sanchia, *d* of late Geoffrey A. Whitworth, CBE; one *s* two *d*. *Educ:* Ampleforth Coll.; Imperial Coll. of Science and Technology, London. AAF, 1932-40; Royal Air Force, 1940-46 (Air Cdre). Hon. Treasurer, Georgian Group. *Publication:* Cover of Darkness, 1953. *Address:* 19 Tedworth Square, Chelsea, SW3. *Club:* Garrick.

**CHISHOLM, Ronald George;** TD 1944; late of HM Diplomatic Service; *b* 26 Jan. 1910; *s* of William Alexander Chisholm and Elizabeth George, both of Inverness; *m* 1st, 1937, Hilda (decd), *yr d* of James Gray, Aberdeen; 2nd, 1956, Elsie Mabel (Susan), *yr d* of James John Craik, Lewes; one *s* three *d*. *Educ:* Inverness High Sch.; Peterhead Acad. Sheriff Court Service, Scotland, 1929. Commnd in N Scottish Heavy Bde, RA, TA, 1929; TA Staff Coll. course, Camberley, 1939 (tsc); Staff appts, Scottish Comd, GHQ Home Forces and GHQ Middle East; demobilised, 1945, with rank of Major. Principal, Burma Office, 1945; transferred to India Office, 1946, and to Commonwealth Relations Office, 1947; First Sec., UK High Commission, Karachi, 1951; Actg Dep. High Commissioner for the UK in Peshawar, 1951-52, and in Dacca, 1952-53; UK Deleg. to Internat. Sugar Conf., 1953, Internat. Conf. on Polution of the Sea by Oil, 1954, and Volta River Conf., 1955; Dep. High Comr for the UK in Madras, 1957-60; CRO, 1960-63; British Dep. High Comr in Eastern Nigeria, 1963-65; London Secretariat, SEATO Ministerial Council Meeting, London, 1965. FSA Scot. 1954. Haakon VI Frihetsmedalji (Norway), 1945. *Recreation:* golf. *Address:* Little Buntings, Balcombe Road, Haywards Heath, Sussex. *T:* 50161. *Club:* Madras (Madras).

**CHITHAM, Sir Charles Carter,** Kt 1936; CIE 1934; JP; *b* 13 Sept. 1886. Joined Indian Police, 1906; Inspector-General of Police, Central Provinces, 1931; Federal Public Service Commissioner, Delhi, 1937, 1939; Acting Inspector of Constabulary, SW Region, 1940-45; King's Police Medal, 1931. *Address:* c/o Lloyds Bank, 6 Pall Mall, SW1; The Old Rectory, Great Cheverell, Devizes, Wilts. *T:* Lavington 2335.

**CHITTY, Anthony Merlott,** MA; FRIBA; AADipl.; AMTPI; architect and town-planning consultant since 1936; *b* 10 Dec. 1907; *s* of Rev. G. J. Chitty, Eton Coll., and Mary Dyson Hort, Cambridge; *m* 1938, Elizabeth Davis; two *s*. *Educ:* Eton; Trinity Coll., Cambridge. Chm. Board of Architectural Education, 1952-54; mem. of Sec. of State for the Colonies Advisory Cttee on Colonial Colleges of Art, Science and Technology, 1955-62; Mem. Governing Council, Kumasi Coll., Ghana, 1956-59; Architect Planner to new Universities at Nairobi, Kenya, and Lusaka, Zambia, 1965-. *Publications:* Curvature Refinements in Greek Architecture, 1932; Houses, Permanence and Prefabrication, 1945; Audio-visual aids in American Universities, 1966; Space Use Surveys in Universities, 1967. *Recreation:* sailing. *Address:* Collapit Creek House, Kingsbridge, Devon. *Clubs:* Reform; Leander.

**CHITTY, Letitia,** MA (Cantab), FRAeS, MICE; *b* 15 July 1897; *d* of Herbert Chitty, FSA and Mabel Agatha Bradby. *Educ:* mostly privately and Newnham Coll., Cambridge. Maths Tripos Part I, 1917; Mech. Science Tripos 1921. Associate of Newnham Coll. 1927-43 and 1958-70. Air Ministry, 1917-19; Airship Stressing Panel, 1922; Bristol Aeroplane Co., 1923-24; Asst to Prof. R. V. Southwell, 1926-32; Airship Analysis, 1933; Asst then Lectr, Civil Engrg, Imperial Coll., 1934-62; work on arch dams for Instn of Civil Engineers and Construction Industry Research and Information Assoc., 1962-69. Telford Gold Medal, ICE, 1969. FRAeS 1934; AMICE 1947. *Publications:* Abroad: an Alphabet of Flowers, 1948; technical contributions (mostly in collaboration) to Aero R. and M., Proc. Royal Society, Phil. Mag., RAeS Journal and Journal of ICE. *Address:* Flat 9, Imperial Court, 6 Lexham Gardens, W8. *T:* 01-370 1706.

**CHITTY, Sir Thomas Willes,** 3rd Bt *cr* 1924; author (as Thomas Hinde); *b* 2 March 1926; *e s* of Sir (Thomas) Henry Willes Chitty, 2nd Bt, and Ethel Constance, *d* of S. H. Gladstone, Darley Ash, Bovingdon, Herts; *S* father, 1955; *m* 1951, Susan Elspeth, *d* of R. Glossop; one *s* one *d*. *Educ:* Winchester; University Coll., Oxford. Royal Navy, 1944-47. Shell Petroleum Co., 1953-60. Granada Arts Fellow, Univ. of York, 1964-65; Visiting Lectr, Univ. of Illinois, 1965-67; Vis. Prof., Boston Univ., 1969-70. *Publications: novels:* Mr Nicholas, 1952; Happy as Larry, 1957; For the Good of the Company, 1961; A Place Like Home, 1962; The Cage, 1962; Ninety Double Martinis, 1963: The Day the Call Came, 1964; Games of Chance, 1965; The Village, 1966; High, 1968; Bird, 1970; *anthology:* Spain, 1963. *Heir: s* Andrew Edward Willes Chitty, *b* 20 Nov. 1953. *Address:* Bow Cottage, West Hoathly, Sussex.

**CHIVERS, Edgar Warren,** CB 1963; BSc; Director, Royal Armament Research and Development Establishment, 1962-67; *b* 7 Dec. 1906; *s* of E. Norton Chivers and Rose Chivers (*née* Warren); *m* 1934, Ruth, *d* of Rev. W. Simons; one *s* one *d*. *Educ:* Hampton Grammar Sch.; Queen Mary Coll., University of London. Joined Research Dept, Woolwich (War Office), 1928; Air Defence Experimental Establishment, 1931-40; Radar Research and Development Establishment, 1940-53; Supt of Ground Radar, 1947; Royal Radar Establishment, 1953-54; Head of Ground Radar Dept, 1953; Min. of Supply, Dir of Atomic Weapons (Development and Production), 1954-56; War Office, Royal

Armament Research and Development Estabt, 1956-; Head of Guided Weapons and Electronics, 1956; Dep. Dir, 1957. *Publications:* various in technical journals. *Recreations:* gardening, music, bee-keeping. *Address:* Neckfield, Crowborough, Sussex.

**CHIVERS, Stephen Oswald,** CBE 1945; MA, MInstT; formerly Chairman, Chivers & Sons Ltd; Member of Cambridgeshire and Isle of Ely CC; *b* 1899; *s* of John Chivers; *m* 1926, Marjorie Clarke; one *s*. *Educ:* Mill Hill Sch.; Christ's Coll., Cambridge. *Address:* Cawcutts, Impington, Cambridge. *T:* Histon 2553.

**CHOLMELEY, Francis William Alfred F.;** *see* Fairfax-Cholmeley.

**CHOLMELEY, John Adye,** FRCS; Surgeon, Royal National Orthopædic Hospital, 1948-70, Hon. Consultant Surgeon, since 1970; Chairman of Joint Examining Board for Orthopædic Nursing; *b* 31 Oct. 1902; *s* of Montague Adye Cholmeley and Mary Bertha Gordon-Cumming; unmarried. *Educ:* St Paul's Sch.; St Bartholomew's Hosp. MRCS, LRCP 1926; MB, BS London 1927; FRCS 1935; Resident appts St Bart's Hosp, 1928-30; Asst MO: Lord Mayor Treloar Cripples' Hosp., Alton, 1930-32; Alexandra Orth. Hosp., Swanley, 1933-34; Resident Surg. and Med. Supt, Country Br., Royal Nat. Orth. Hosp., Stanmore, 1940-48 (Asst Res. Surg., 1936-39); former Orthopædic Surg., Clare Hall Hosp., Neasden Hosp. Mem. Internat. Soc. of Orthopædic Surgery and Trauma (Société Internationale de Chirurgie Orthopédique et de Traumatologie, SICOT); FRSocMed (Pres. Orthopædic Sect., 1957-58); Fellow Brit. Orth. Assoc. *Publications:* articles on orthopædic subjects, particularly tuberculosis and poliomyelitis in med. jls. *Address:* Royal National Orthopædic Hospital, Brockley Hill, Stanmore, Mddx. *T:* 01-954 2300.

**CHOLMELEY, Sir Montague (John),** 6th Bt *cr* 1806; Captain, Grenadier Guards; *b* 27 March 1935; *s* of 5th Bt and Cecilia, *er d* of W. H. Ellice; *S* father, 1964; *m* 1960, Juliet Auriol Sally Nelson; one *s* two *d*. *Educ:* Eton. Grenadier Guards, 1954-64. *Heir:* *s* Hugh John Cholmeley, *b* 3 Jan. 1968. *Address:* Church Farm, Burton le Coggles, Grantham, Lincs. *T:* Corby Glen 329. *Clubs:* White's, Guards.

**CHOLMONDELEY,** family name of **Marquess of Cholmondeley,** and of **Baron Delamere.**

**CHOLMONDELEY,** 6th Marquess of, *cr* 1815; **George Hugh Cholmondeley,** MC 1943; DL; Bt 1611; Viscount Cholmondeley, 1661; Baron Cholmondeley of Namptwich (Eng.), 1689; Earl of Cholmondeley, Viscount Malpas, 1706; Baron Newborough (Ire.), 1715; Baron Newburgh (Gt Brit.), 1716; Earl of Rocksavage, 1815; late Grenadier Guards; Lord Great Chamberlain of England since 1966; *b* 24 April 1919; *e s* of 5th Marquess of Cholmondeley, GCVO, and Sybil (CBE 1946), *d* of Sir Edward Albert Sassoon, 2nd Bt; *S* father, 1968; *m* 1947, Lavinia Margaret, *d* of late Colonel John Leslie, DSO, MC; one *s* three *d*. *Educ:* Eton; Cambridge Univ. Served War of 1939-45: 1st Royal Dragoons, in MEF, Italy, France, Germany (MC). Retd hon. rank Major, 1949. DL Chester, 1955. *Heir:* *s* Earl of Rocksavage, *qv*. *Address:* Cholmondeley Castle, Malpas, Ches. *T:* Cholmondeley 202. *Clubs:* Turf, Cavalry, Guards, Royal Automobile.

**CHOPE, Robert Charles; His Honour Judge Chope;** Judge of County Courts, Cornwall and Plymouth (Circuit 59), since 1965; Deputy Chairman, Cornwall QS, since 1966; *b* 26 June 1913; *s* of Leonard Augustine Chope and Ida Florence (*née* Mair); *m* 1946, Pamela Durell; one *s* two *d*. *Educ:* St Paul's Sch.; University Coll., London. Called to Bar, Inner Temple, 1938. Served Royal Artillery, 1939-45. *Address:* 12 King's Bench Walk, Temple, EC4; Carclew House, Perranarworthal, Truro, Cornwall. *Club:* Royal Western Yacht.

**CHOPRA, Iqbal Chand,** CBE 1958 (OBE 1946); QC (Tanganyika) 1951; *b* 1 Dec. 1896; *s* of late Lala Ganga Ram; *m* 1919, Thelma Florence Campbell; two *s*. *Educ:* King's Inns, Dublin; Middle Temple, London. Practised at Lahore High Court, 1919-28, at Mwanza, Tanganyika, from 1928; MLC 1945-59, MEC 1953-59, Tanganyika. Mem., Tanganyika Railway Council, until 1941; Mem., East Africa Railway Cttee until 1959; Mem., Makerere Coll. Council until 1959. *Address:* 69 Chemin de Ruth, Cologny, Geneva, Switzerland. *T:* 521500.

**CHORLEY,** family name of **Baron Chorley.**

**CHORLEY,** 1st Baron *cr* 1945, of Kendal; **Robert Samuel Theodore Chorley,** QC 1961; JP; *b* Kendal, 1895; *e s* of late R. F. Chorley; *m* Katharine Campbell, *d* of late Edward Hopkinson, DSc; two *s* one *d*. *Educ:* Kendal Sch.; Queen's Coll., Oxford (Hastings Exhibitioner, Robert Herbert prize, MA). During European War served in Foreign Office; Cheshire Regt (HS), and Min. of Labour; called to Bar, 1920 (certificate of Honour); Pres. Hardwicke Soc., 1921-22; Tutor at the Law Society's School of Law, 1920-24; Lectr in Commercial Law, 1924-30; Sir Ernest Cassel Prof. of Commercial and Industrial Law in the Univ. of London, 1930-46; Dean of Faculty of Laws, London Univ., 1939-42; temporarily employed in Home Office, 1940-41; Acting Asst Sec., Min. of Home Security, 1941; Dep. Regional Comr for Civil Defence, NW Region, 1942-44; Chm. of Westmorland QS from 1944. Contested (Lab) Northwich Div., 1945; Member: Hobhouse Cttee (National Parks), 1945; Parly Delegn to India, 1945; Mocatta Cttee (Indorsements on Cheques), 1955. Lord in Waiting to the King, 1946-50. Former Mem. Council and Vice-Chm., National Trust; Hon. Sec. of Council for Preservation of Rural England, 1935-67; Pres., Fell Rock Climbing Club of English Lake District, 1935-37, Vice-Pres., 1969-; Assoc. of University Teachers: Mem. Coun. and Exec. Cttee, 1938-; Vice-Pres., 1945-47; Pres., 1947; Hon. Gen. Sec., 1953-65; President: Nat. Council for the Abolition of the Death Penalty, 1945-48; Sheffield and Peak District Branch, CPRE, 1946-; Friends of the Lake District, 1961-69 (Vice-Pres., 1946-56); Fire Service Research and Training Trust, 1946-; Pres., Holiday Fellowship, 1947-57; a Vice-Pres. of Howard League for Penal Reform, 1948-; Chm., Inst. for Study and Treatment of Delinquency, 1950-56 (Pres., 1956-); Pres., British Mountaineering Council, 1950-53; Pres., Ethical Union, 1950-54; Pres., Soc. of Public Teachers of Law, 1954-55; Vice-Pres., Alpine Club, 1956-58; Pres., Haldane Soc., 1957-; Pres., Commons and Footpaths Preservation Soc., 1961-. Hon. Fellow: Inst. of Bankers, 1960; LSE 1970. *Publications:* (jointly) Leading Cases in Mercantile Law; (jointly) Shipping Law; Law of Banking; (jointly) Leading Cases in the Law of Banking; (ed.) Arnould's Law of Marine Insurance (13th, 14th and 15th edns); General Editor Modern Law Review; various articles in the Law Quarterly Review, Modern Law Review, and elsewhere. *Recreations:* gardening, mountaineering and travel. *Heir:* *s* Hon. Roger Richard Edward Chorley [*b* 14 Aug. 1930; *m* 1964, Ann, *d* of late A. S. Debenham,

Ingatestone, Essex; two *s*]. *Address:* The Rookery, Stanmore, Mddx; London School of Economics, Clare Market, WC. *T:* 01-954 1845. *Club:* Alpine.

**CHORLEY, Charles Harold,** CB 1959; Second Parliamentary Counsel, 1968-69; *b* 10 June 1912; *o s* of late Arthur R. Chorley; *m* 1941, Audrey, *d* of R. V. C. Ash, MC; two *d. Educ:* Radley; Trinity Coll., Oxford. Called to Bar (Inner Temple), 1934. Joined Office of Parliamentary Counsel, 1938; one of the Parliamentary Counsel, 1950-68. *Address:* Paddock Wood, Tisbury, Salisbury, Wilts. *T:* Tisbury 325.

**CHOU EN-LAI;** Premier, State Council of the People's Republic of China since 1958; *b* Hwaiyin, Central Kiangsu, East China, 1898; *m* 1925, Teng Ying-ch'ao. *Educ:* Nankai High Sch. and Nankai Univ., China. Became active worker for Communist Party, 1921. Took part in Chinese National Revolution, 1924-27; mem. of Central Cttee of Chinese Communist Party, 1926-. Premier of Government Administration Council, Vice-Chm. People's Revolutionary Cttee, and Minister for Foreign Affairs, 1949-58. Has represented Chinese People's Republic at conferences abroad. *Address:* The Office of the Prime Minister, Peking, China.

**CHRIMES, Prof. Stanley Bertram,** MA, PhD, LittD; Professor of History and Head of Department of History, University College of South Wales and Monmouthshire, Cardiff, since 1953; Deputy Principal, 1964-66; Dean of Faculty of Arts, 1959-61; *b* 23 Feb. 1907; *yr s* of late Herbert Chrimes and Maude Mary (*née* Rose); *m* 1937, Mabel Clara, *o d* of late L. E. Keyser. *Educ:* Purley County Sch., Surrey; King's Coll., London (Lindley Student, BA, MA); Trinity Coll., Cambridge (Research Studentship, Senior Rouse Ball Student, PhD, LittD). Lectr, 1936, Reader, 1951, in Constitutional History, University of Glasgow. Temp. Principal, Ministry of Labour and National Service, 1940-45. Alexander Medal, Royal Hist. Society, 1934. *Publications:* English Constitutional Ideas in the XVth century, 1936 (American reprint, 1965); (translated) F. Kern's Kingship and Law in the Middle Ages, 1939 (repr. 1948, 1956); (ed and trans.) Sir John Fortescue's De Laudibus Legum Anglie, 1942 (repr. 1949); English Constitutional History, 1948 (4th rev. edn 1967; edn in Japan, 1963); (ed) The General Election in Glasgow, February 1950, 1950; An Introduction to the Administrative History of Mediæval England, 1952 (3rd rev. edn 1966); Some Reflections on the Study of History, 1954; (ed and cont. 7th edn) Sir W. Holdsworth's History of English Law, Vol. I, 1957; (ed, with A. L. Brown) Select Documents of English Constitutional History, 1307-1485, 1961; Lancastrians, Yorkists, and Henry VII, 1964 (2nd rev. edn 1966); articles and reviews in Trans Royal Hist. Soc., English Historical Review, Law Quarterly Review, etc. *Address:* University College, Cardiff. *T:* 20781.

**CHRIMES, Sir (William) Bertram,** Kt 1945; CBE 1939 (OBE 1930); JP; Chairman of Cooper's Stores, Grocers and Provision Merchants, Glasgow, Liverpool and London; *b* 6 Dec. 1883; *s* of Captain Henry Chrimes; *m* Mary (*d* 1952), *d* of John Holder, Liverpool; one *s* one *d*. Chm., Liverpool Cttee King's National Roll for Disabled Ex-Servicemen, 1922-45; Dir of War-time Meals Div., Min. of Food, 1940-47. Trustee, Bluecoat Hosp.; Mem., Liverpool Univ. Court; Vice-Pres., Liverpool Child Welfare Assoc.; Chm., Liverpool Advisory Cttee to Assistance Board, 1935-49; Liverpool Employment Cttee, 1937-56; Liverpool Disablement Advisory Cttee, 1945-55; Mem., Nat. Advisory Council on the employment of the disabled, 1951-55; Poppy Day Appeal, 1934-47. *Address:* 12 Church Street, Liverpool; Bryn y Glyn, Nantyglyn, Colwyn Bay, N Wales. *Clubs:* University, Athenæum, Lyceum (Liverpool).

**CHRIST, George Elgie,** CBE 1955; Parliamentary Liaison Officer, Conservative Party, and Editor Weekly News Letter, 1945-65; *b* 26 May 1904; *s* of late H. G. Christ, BSc, Dulwich Coll.; *m* 1938, Marianne Evans (*d* 1966). *Educ:* Christ's Hosp.; King's Coll., London Univ. Political Correspondent, Daily Telegraph, 1940-45; Governor of Christ's Hosp., 1937, and Almoner, 1945. Liveryman of Worshipful Company of Basketmakers, 1948. *Recreations:* gardening, cricket. *Address:* 5 Winterstoke Crescent, Ramsgate, Kent. *T:* Thanet 53736. *Clubs:* Savage, MCC.

**CHRISTCHURCH, Bishop of,** since 1966; **Rt. Rev. William Allan Pyatt,** MA; *b* Gisborne, NZ, 4 Nov. 1916; *e s* of A. E. Pyatt; *m* 1942, Mary Lilian Carey; two *s* one *d*. *Educ:* Gisborne High Sch.; Auckland Univ.; St John's Coll., Auckland; Westcott House, Cambridge. BA 1938 (Senior Sch. in History); MA 1939. Served War of 1939-45: combatant service with 2 NZEF; Major, 2 IC 20 NZ Armd Regt 1945. Ordained, 1946; Curate, Cannock, Staffs, 1946-48; Vicar: Brooklyn, Wellington, NZ, 1948-52; Hawera, 1952-58; St Peter's, Wellington, 1958-62; Dean of Christchurch, 1962-66. *Publications:* contribs to NZ Jl of Theology. *Recreations:* Rugby referee; political comment on radio; work among alcoholics. *Address:* Bishopscourt, 100 Park Terrace, Christchurch, NZ. *T:* 62.653. *Clubs:* Canterbury Officers (Christchurch).

**CHRISTELOW, Allan,** CMG 1950; Executive Vice-President and Director, Esso Standard Sekiyu KK; Director, TOA Nenryo KK; Director and Officer General, Sekiyu KK and General Gas KK; *b* 31 Jan. 1911; *s* of Joseph Christelow and Louisa Bateman, Bradford, Yorks; *m* 1942, Dorothy Beal; one *s* one *d*. *Educ:* Heckmondwike Sch.; Univ. of Leeds; Queen's Coll., Oxford; Princeton Univ. Asst Sec., War Cabinet Secretariat, 1944-45; Asst Sec. 1945-48, Under-Sec., 1948, HM Treasury Delegation to Washington, also Financial Counsellor, British Embassy, Washington, 1948. Acting Exec. Dir, Internat. Bank for Reconstruction and Development, 1948. Treasurer, Standard Vacuum Oil Co., 1959. Disabled and retired, 1963. *Address:* 341 Toquam Road, New Canaan, Conn 06840, USA. *Clubs:* American (Tokyo), Country (New Canaan), Tokyo Lawn Tennis.

**CHRISTENSEN, Arent Lauri, (A. Lauri Chris);** Norwegian painter and etcher; *b* 30 April 1893; *m* 1933, Hjordis Charlotte Lohren. *Educ:* The Royal Drawing Sch., Oslo. Began career as etcher and painter in Oslo; later travelled in the South, especially in Provence and Italy, and made a series of decorative landscape-etchings, which were exhibited in several countries; his interest in classic antiquity–especially the Grecian and Egyptian culture– inspired him to make various figure-compositions with incidents from the life in the antiquity and from Homer's Iliad; these compositions have been exhibited throughout Europe and America. Decorated Asker High Sch. with wall-paintings. Invented a new graphic method Chrisgrafia. The following museums have bought his works: British Museum, Victoria and Albert Museum, National Galleriet, Oslo, New York Free Arts

Library Museum, Bibliothèque Nationale, Paris, Brooklyn Museum, Brooklyn, etc; Mem. of the Soc. of Graphic Art, London, 1926. *Address:* Villa Chriss, Fjeldstadvn 16, Nesbru, Norway.

**CHRISTENSEN, Christian Neils,** CBE 1970; ERD; Chairman, Road Air Cargo Express (International) Ltd and Director, Tartan Arrow Services Ltd, since 1968; *b* 10 Dec. 1901; *s* of C. N. Christensen, Liverpool; *m* 1928, Elsie Florence Hodgson; one *s* one *d*. Shipping and forwarding, 1915-19; Man. Dir, Ex-Army Transport Ltd, 1919-39; army service, France, N Africa, Sicily, Italy, 1939-45 (Lt-Col, despatches twice); Man. Dir, North Western Transport Services Ltd and Dir, Transport Services (BTC) Ltd, 1945-49; Road Haulage Executive: Eastern Divisional Man., 1950-55; Midland Divisional Man., 1955-63; Man. Dir, British Road Services Ltd, and Chm., BRS (Contracts) Ltd, 1963-68. MInstT. Officer, Legion of Merit (US). *Recreation:* gardening. *Address:* Ellesmere, 22 Greensleeves Avenue, Broadstone, Dorset, BH18 8BL. *T:* Broadstone 4501.

**CHRISTENSEN, Eric Herbert,** CMG 1968; Secretary-General, President's Office, Permanent Secretary, Ministry of External Affairs, and Secretary to the Cabinet, The Gambia, since 1967; also Head of the Public Service since 1967; *b* 29 Oct. 1923; *s* of George Vilhelm Christensen and Rose Fleury; *m* 1951, Diana, *d* of Rev. J. Dixon-Baker; four *s* three *d*. Teacher, St Augustine's Sec. Sch., Bathurst, 1941-43; Military Service, W African Air Corps (RAF), Bathurst, 1944-45; Clerk, The Secretariat, Bathurst, 1946-47; Head of Chancery, then Vice-Consul, French Consulate, Bathurst, 1947-60; acted as Consul on several occasions; Attaché, Senegalese Consulate-Gen., Bathurst, 1961-65, acted as Consul-Gen. on several occasions; Asst Sec. (Ext. Affairs), Gambia Govt, 1965; Principal Asst Sec., Prime Minister's Office, Bathurst, 1966-67. Grand Officer, Order of the Brilliant Star of China (Taiwan), 1966; Officer, Order of Merit of Islamic Republic of Mauritania, 1967; Officer, Nat. Order of Republic of Senegal, 1967; Knight Commander's Cross, Badge and Star, Order of Merit of Federal Republic of Germany, 1968. *Recreations:* reading, photography, philately, chess. *Address:* 6 Kent Street, Bathurst, The Gambia. *T:* (office) Bathurst 243, (home) Bathurst 596.

**CHRISTIAN, Prof. John Wyrill;** Professor of Physical Metallurgy, Oxford University, since 1967; Fellow of St Edmund Hall, Oxford, since 1963; *b* 9 April 1926; *e s* of John Christian and Louisa Christian (*née* Crawford); *m* 1949, Maureen Lena Smith; two *s* one *d*. *Educ:* Scarborough Boys' High Sch.; The Queen's Coll., Oxford. BA 1946, DPhil 1949, MA 1950. Pressed Steel Co. Ltd Research Fellow, Oxford University, 1951-55; Lectr in Metallurgy, 1955-58; George Kelley Reader in Metallurgy, 1958-67. Visiting Prof.: Univ. of Illinois, 1959; Case Inst. of Technology, USA, 1962-63. Rosenhain medallist of Inst. of Metals, 1969. *Publications:* Metallurgical Equilibrium Diagrams (with others), 1952; The Theory of Transformations in Metals and Alloys, 1965; (Ed.) Structure Reports (Metals), 1962-64, (Brit. Ed.) Acta Metallurgica, 1967-. Papers in various scientific jls. *Address:* Strathdee House, 20 Linkside Avenue, Oxford. *T:* Oxford 58569.

**CHRISTIAN, Prof. Reginald Frank;** Professor of Russian, St Andrews University, since 1966; *b* 9 Aug. 1924; *s* of H. A. Christian, Liverpool; *m* 1952, Rosalind Iris Napier; one *s* one *d*. *Educ:* Liverpool Inst.; Queen's Coll., Oxford (MA). Hon. Mods Class. (Oxon), 1943; 1st cl. hons Russian (Oxon), 1949. Commnd RAF, 1944; flying with Atlantic Ferry Unit and 231 Sqdn, 1943-46. FO, British Embassy, Moscow, 1949-50; Lectr and Head of Russian Dept, Liverpool Univ., 1950-55; Sen. Lectr and Head of Russian Dept, Birmingham Univ., 1956-63; Vis. Prof. of Russian, McGill Univ., Canada, 1961-62; Prof. of Russian, Birmingham Univ., 1963-66; Exchange Lectr, Moscow, 1964-65. Pres., British Univs Assoc. of Slavists, 1967-70; Member, Internat. Cttee of Slavists, 1970-. *Publications:* Korolenko's Siberia, 1954; (with F. M. Borras) Russian Syntax, 1959; Tolstoy's War and Peace: a study, 1962; (with F. M. Borras) Russian Prose Composition, 1964; Tolstoy: a critical introduction, 1969; numerous articles and reviews in Slavonic and E European Review, Slavonic and E European Jl, Mod. Languages Review, Survey, Forum, Birmingham Post, Times Lit. Supp., etc. *Recreations:* tennis, squash, fell-walking, violin. *Address:* The Roundel, St Andrews, Fife. *T:* St Andrews 3322.

**CHRISTIANSEN, Michael Robin;** Editor, Sunday Mirror, since 1964; *b* 7 April 1927; *e s* of Arthur and Brenda Christiansen; *m* 1st, 1948, Kathleen Lyon (marr. diss.); one *s* one *d*; 2nd, 1961, Christina Robinson; one *s* one *d*. *Educ:* Hill Crest, Frinton; St Luke's, Conn., USA. Reporter, Daily Mail, 1943; Royal Navy, 1945-47; Chief Sub-Editor: Daily Mail, 1950; Daily Mirror, 1956; Dep. Ed., Sunday Pictorial, 1960; Asst Ed., Daily Mirror, 1961. *Recreations:* golf, coarse cricket. *Address:* Sunday Mirror, Holborn Circus, EC1. *T:* 01-353 0246.

**CHRISTIE, Agatha Mary Clarissa,** CBE 1956; Hon. DLitt; FRSL; *b* Torquay; *yr d* of Frederick Alvah Miller, New York; *m* 1st, 1914, Col Archibald Christie, CMG, DSO (from whom she obtained a divorce, 1928; he *d* 1962); one *d*; 2nd, 1930, Sir Max Mallowan, *qv*. *Educ:* home. *Publications: books:* The Mysterious Affair at Styles, 1920; The Secret Adversary; The Murder on the Links; Poirot Investigates; The Road of Dreams; The Man in the Brown Suit; The Secret of Chimneys; The Murder of Roger Ackroyd; The Big Four; The Mystery of the Blue Train; The Seven Dials Mystery; Partners in Crime; The Mysterious Mr Quin; The Murder at the Vicarage; The Sittaford Mystery; Peril at End House; The Thirteen Problems; Lord Edgeware Dies; The Hound of Death; Murder on the Orient Express; The Listerdale Mystery; Why Didn't They Ask Evans?; Parker Pyne Investigates; Three Act Tragedy; Death in the Clouds; The ABC Murders; Murder in Mesopotamia; Cards on the Table; Murder in the Mews; Dumb Witness; Death on the Nile; Appointment with Death; Hercule Poirot's Christmas; Murder is Easy; Ten Little Niggers; Sad Cypress; One, Two, Buckle My Shoe; Evil Under the Sun, 1941; N or M, 1941; The Body in the Library, 1942; Five Little Pigs; The Moving Finger, 1943; Towards Zero, 1944; Death comes as the End, 1945; Sparkling Cyanide, 1945; The Hollow, 1946; The Labours of Hercules, 1947; Taken at the Flood, 1948; Crooked House, 1949; A Murder is Announced, 1950; They Came to Baghdad, 1951; Mrs McGinty's Dead, 1952; They Do It With Mirrors, 1952; After the Funeral, 1953; A Pocket full of Rye, 1953; Destination Unknown, 1954; Hickory Dickory Dock, 1955; Dead Man's Folly, 1956; 4.50 from Paddington, 1957; Ordeal by Innocence, 1958; Cat among the Pigeons, 1959; The Adventure of the Christmas Pudding, 1960; The Pale Horse, 1961; The Mirror Crack'd from Side to Side, 1962; The Clocks, 1963; The Caribbean Mystery, 1964; At Bertram's Hotel, 1965; Star over Bethlehem (as Agatha Christie Mallowan), 1965; Third Girl, 1966; Endless Night, 1967; By the Pricking of my Thumbs, 1968; Hallowe'en Party, 1969; Passenger to Frankfurt, 1970; *plays:* Black Coffee; Alibi; Love from a Stranger; Peril at End House; Ten Little Niggers; Appointment with Death; Murder on the Nile; Murder at the Vicarage; The Hollow; The Mousetrap; Witness for the Prosecution; Spider's Web; Towards Zero; Verdict; The Unexpected Guest; Go Back for Murder; Rule of Three. *Recreations:* reading, travelling, bathing. *Address:* Winterbrook House, Wallingford, Berks.

**CHRISTIE, Charles Henry;** Headmaster, Brighton College, since 1963; *b* 1 Sept. 1924; *s* of late Lieut-Comdr C. P. Christie and Mrs C. S. Christie; *m* 1950, Naida Joan Bentley; one *s* three *d.* *Educ:* Westminster Sch. (King's Scholar); Trinity Coll., Cambridge (Exhibitioner). Served 1943-46, RNVR (despatches, 1945). Trinity Coll., Cambridge, 1946-49; Asst Master, Eton Coll., 1949-57; Under Master and Master of Queen's Scholars, Westminster Sch., 1957-63. *Address:* Brighton College, Eastern Road, Brighton BN2 2AL. *T:* Brighton 65788.

**CHRISTIE, George William Langham;** Chairman, Glyndebourne Productions Ltd; *b* 31 Dec. 1934; *o s* of John and Audrey Mildmay Christie; *m* 1958, Patricia Mary Nicholson; two *s* one *d.* *Educ:* Eton. Asst to Sec. of Calouste Gulbenkian Foundation, 1957-62. Chm. of Glyndebourne Productions from 1956 and of other family companies. *Address:* Glyndebourne, Lewes, Sussex. *T:* Ringmer 250. *Club:* Brooks's.

**CHRISTIE, Hon. Sir Harold George,** Kt 1964; CBE 1949; *b* 31 May 1896; *e s* of H. Christopher and Margaret Alice Christie; *m* 1959, Virginia (*née* Campbell), Palm Beach, Fla, USA. *Educ:* Nassau Gram. Sch. General Electric Company, Schenectady, NY, 1916; Canadian Air Force, 1917-18; Knickerbocker Press, Albany, NY, 1918-21; H. G. Christie, Real Estate, Nassau, NP, 1921-. Elected Bahamas House of Assembly, 1927; returned in all subsequent General Elections; mem. Governor's Exec. Council, 1939; retired, 1948, after being re-appointed three terms; permission to retain title as Honourable. Mem. Bahamas Air Board during War of 1939-45, a dep. Commissioner of Currency. *Recreations:* flying, sailing. *Address:* Cascadilla, Nassau, NP, Bahamas. *T:* 2-2020. *Clubs:* Royal Nassau Sailing, Bahamas Country, Lyford Cay (Nassau).

**CHRISTIE, John Belford Wilson;** Sheriff-Substitute of Perth and Angus at Dundee since Nov. 1955; Member, Parole Board for Scotland, since 1967; *b* 4 May 1914; *o s* of late J. A. Christie, Advocate, Edinburgh; *m* 1939, Christine Isobel Syme, *o d* of late Rev. J. T. Arnott; four *d.* *Educ:* Merchiston Castle Sch.; St John's Coll., Cambridge; Edinburgh Univ. Admitted to Faculty of Advocates, 1939. Served War of 1939-45, in RNVR, 1939-46. Sheriff-Substitute of Western Div. of Dumfries and Galloway, 1948-55. Member: Queen's Coll. Council, Univ. of St Andrews, 1960-67; Univ. Court, Univ. of Dundee, 1967-. *Recreations:* curling, golf. *Address:* Annsmuir Farm, Ladybank, Fife. *T:* Ladybank 480. *Clubs:* New (Edinburgh); Royal and Ancient (St Andrews).

**CHRISTIE, John Rankin;** Under-Secretary, Ministry of Technology, since 1967; *b* 5 Jan. 1918; *s* of Robert Christie and Georgina (*née* Rankin); *m* 1941, Constance May Gracie; one *s* two *d.* *Educ:* Ormskirk Gram. Sch.; London Sch. of Economics. War Office, 1936-39; Min. of Supply, 1939; Royal Artillery, 1943-47; Min. of Supply, 1947-54; Air Ministry, 1954; Private Sec. to Ministers of Supply, 1955-57; Asst Sec., 1957; British Defence Staffs, Washington, 1962-65; Under-Sec., Min. of Aviation, 1965-67. *Recreations:* travel, bird-watching. *Address:* Twitten Cottage, East Hill, Oxted, Surrey. *T:* Oxted 3047.

**CHRISTIE, John Traill;** Principal of Jesus College, Oxford, 1950-67, Hon. Fellow, 1967; Assistant Master, Westminster School, 1967-69; *b* 1899; 4th *s* of late C. H. F. Christie, DL, JP; *m* 1933, Lucie Catherine, *o d* of late T. P. Le Fanu, CB; two *d.* *Educ:* Winchester; Trinity Coll., Oxford (Scholar). 1st Class Class. Mods, 1920; 1st Class Lit. Hum., 1922. Sixth Form Master, Rugby Sch., 1922-28; Fellow and Tutor, Magdalen Coll., Oxford, 1928-32; Headmaster of Repton Sch., 1932-37; Headmaster of Westminster Sch., 1937-49. *Recreation:* walking. *Address:* 52 Elgin Crescent, W11. *Club:* Athenæum.

**CHRISTIE, Julie (Frances);** actress; *b* 14 April 1940; *d* of Frank St John Christie and Rosemary Christie (*née* Ramsden). *Educ:* Convent; Brighton Coll. of Technology; Central Sch. of Speech and Drama. *Films:* Crooks Anonymous, 1962; The Fast Lady, 1962; Billy Liar, 1963; Darling, 1964 (Oscar, NY Film Critics Award, Br. Film Academy Award, etc); Young Cassidy, 1964; Dr Zhivago, 1965 (Donatello Award); Fahrenheit 451, 1966; Far from the Madding Crowd, 1966; Petulia, 1967; In Search of Gregory, 1969. Motion Picture Laurel Award, Best Dramatic Actress, 1967; Motion Picture Herald Award, Best Dramatic Actress, 1967. *Address:* c/o Miss Olive Harding, International Famous Agency Ltd, 11 Hanover Street, W1. *T:* 01-629 8080.

**CHRISTIE, Group-Captain Malcolm Grahame,** CMG 1919; DSO 1917; MC 1916; Doktor-Ingenieur, Aachen; Consultant to Otto Simon-Carves Chemical Engineering Group, since 1950; *b* Edgbaston, Warwicks, 1881; 3rd *s* of J. A. Christie, banker, London; unmarried. *Educ:* Leamington; Malvern Coll.; Aachen Univ. (1st cl. hons). Became Gen. Manager and Dir, Otto Cokeoven Co. of Leeds and Pres., Otto Coking Corp., New York; Hon. Lecturer to Leeds Univ.; Royal Flying Corps, 1914-18; Royal Air Force, 1919-30; Air Attaché, Washington, USA, 1922-26, and Berlin, 1927-30; retired, 1930. *Publication:* The Nitrogen Compounds in Coal. *Recreations:* mountaineering, travel, aviation. *Address:* 58 Cranmer Court, Sloane Avenue, SW3. *Club:* Travellers'.

**CHRISTIE, Ronald Victor,** MD (Edin.); MSc (McGill); DSc (London); FACP; FRCP(C); FRCP; Professor of Medicine and Chairman of the Department, McGill University, since 1955; Dean of the Faculty of Medicine, since 1964; formerly Director Medical Professorial Unit and Physician, St Bartholomew's Hospital; Professor of Medicine, University of London, 1938-55; *b* 1902; *s* of late Dr Dugald Christie, CMG; *m* 1933, Joyce Mary Ervine (*d* 1967); one *s* one *d.* *Educ:* in China and later at George Watson's Coll.; Edinburgh Univ. House Physician and House Surg., Royal Infirmary, Edinburgh; Asst in Medicine, Rockefeller Institute for Medical Research, NY; Asst in Dept of Pathology, Freiburg Univ.; Research Associate, McGill Univ. Clinic, Royal Victoria Hosp., Montreal; Asst Dir of the Med. Unit and Asst Physician, London Hosp. Harveian Orator, RCP, 1969. Hon. FRCPEd; Hon. ScD, Dublin, 1962; Hon.

DSc, Edinburgh, 1970. *Publications:* papers in medical and scientific journals. *Address:* Office of the Dean, Faculty of Medicine, McGill University, Montreal, Canada.

**CHRISTIE, Walter Henry John,** CSI 1948; CIE 1946; OBE 1943; *b* 17 Dec. 1905; *s* of late Major H. G. F. Christie, IA; *m* 1934, Elizabeth Louise, *d* of late H. E. Stapleton; two *s* two *d*. *Educ:* Eton (KS, Newcastle Medallist); King's Coll., Cambridge (Winchester Reading Prize). Joined Indian Civil Service, 1928 and served in Bengal and New Delhi; Joint Private Sec. to the Viceroy, 1947; Adviser in India to Central Commercial Cttee, 1947-52; Vice-Chm., British India Corp. Ltd, 1952-58; Commonwealth Develt Finance Co. Ltd, 1959-68; Adviser, E African Develt Bank, 1969-70. Pres., Upper India Chamber of Commerce, 1955-56; Vice-Pres., Employers' Federation of India, 1956; Pres., UK Citizens Assoc., 1957; Steward, Indian Polo Assoc., 1951. *Address:* Quarry Ridge, Oxted, Surrey. *Clubs:* East India and Sports; Achilles.

**CHRISTIE, Sir William,** KCIE 1947 (CIE 1941); CSI 1945; MC; retired as Chairman, Bailey Meters & Controls Ltd Croydon; Director: Alaistair Watson & Co. Ltd; Summerson Holdings Ltd; *b* 29 Feb. 1896; *s* of late Rev. Alexander Mackenzie Christie; *m* Marjorie Haughton, 2nd *d* of late Henry Hall Stobbs; one *s* one *d*. *Educ:* Perth Acad., Perth; Bell Baxter Sch., Cupar, Fife; St Andrews Univ.; Clare Coll., Cambridge. Served Royal Scots, 1914-19 (MC). Joined Indian Civil Service, 1920; Finance Sec., UP, 1938-44; Chief Sec., UP, 1944-45; Chief Comr, Delhi, 1945-47. *Address:* Davan House, The Woodlands, Gerrards Cross, Bucks. *T:* Gerrards Cross 82246. *Club:* Caledonian.

**CHRISTISON, Gen. Sir (Alexander Frank) Philip,** 4th Bt *cr* 1871; GBE 1948 (KBE 1944); CB 1943; DSO 1945; MC (and Bar); DL; Chairman, Alban Timber Ltd; *b* 17 Nov. 1893; 2nd *s* of Sir Alexander Christison, 2nd Bt, and Florence (*d* 1949), *d* of F. T. Elworthy; *S* half-brother, 1945; *m* 1916, Betty, *d* of late Rt Rev. A. Mitchell, Bishop of Aberdeen and Orkney; (one *s* killed in action in Burma, 7 March 1942) three *d*. *Educ:* Edinburgh Academy; Oxford Univ. (BA). 2nd Lieut Cameron Highlanders, 1914; Capt. 1915; Bt Major, 1930; Bt Lt-Col 1933; Lt-Col Duke of Wellington's Regt, 1937; Col 1938; comd Quetta Bde, 1938-40; Comdt Staff Coll., Quetta, 1940-41; Brig. Gen. Staff, 1941; Maj.-Gen. 1941; Lt-Gen. 1942; Gen. 1947; comd XXIII and XV Indian Corps, 1942-45; Temp. Comdr 14th Army, 1945; C-in-C, ALFSEA, 1945; Allied Comdr Netherland East Indies, 1945-46; GOC-in-C Northern Command, 1946; GOC-in-C Scottish Command and Governor of Edinburgh Castle, 1947-49; ADC Gen. to the King, 1947-49; retired pay, 1949. Col, The Duke of Wellington's Regt, 1947-57; Col, 10th Princess Mary's Own Gurkha Rifles, 1947-57; Hon. Col, 414 Coast Regt Royal Artillery, 1950-57. DL Roxburghshire, 1956. President: Scottish Unionist Party, 1957-58; Earl Haig Fund; Army Cadet Force, Scotland; Vice-President: Burma Star Assoc.; Officers' Assoc.; Chm. Scottish Angling Fedn, 1969. FSA Scot, 1957. Chinese Order of Cloud and Banner with Grand Cordon, 1949. *Publications:* Birds of Northern Baluchistan, 1940; (with Aubrey Buxton) The Birds of Arakan, 1946. *Heir:* none. *Recreations:* ornithology (MBOU), Celtic languages, field sports. *Address:* The Croft, Melrose, Roxburghshire. *T:* Melrose 2456. *Clubs:* United Service; New (Edinburgh).

**CHRISTOFAS, Kenneth Cavendish,** CMG 1969; MBE 1944; HM Diplomatic Service; Minister in UK Delegation to European Economic Community, since 1969; *b* 18 Aug. 1917; *o s* of late Edward Julius Goodwin and of Lillian Christofas (*step-s* of Alexander Christofas); *m* 1948, Jessica Laura (*née* Sparshott); two *d*. *Educ:* Merchant Taylors' Sch.; University Coll., London. Served War of 1939-45 (MBE): commissioned in The Queen's Own Royal West Kent Regt, 1939; Adjt 1940; Staff Capt. 1941; DAAG 1942; Staff Coll., Quetta, 1944; AAG 1944; GSO1, War Office, 1946. Resigned from Army with Hon. rank of Lieut-Col and joined Sen. Br. of HM Foreign Service, 1948 (HM Diplomatic Service after 1965); served in Foreign Office, 1948-49 and 1951-55; Rio de Janeiro, 1949-51; Rome, 1955-59 and as Dep. Head of UK Delegn to European Communities, Brussels, 1959-61; seconded to CRO for service as Counsellor in the British High Commn, Lagos, 1961-64 and to Colonial Office as Head of Economic Dept, 1965-66; on sabbatical year at Univ. of London, 1964-65; Counsellor in Commonwealth Office, then in FCO, 1966-69. Order of Polonia Restituta (Poland), 1944. *Recreations:* railways and motoring. *Address:* c/o Foreign and Commonwealth Office, SW1. *Club:* Public Schools.

**CHRISTOFF, Boris;** opera singer (bass); *b* Plovdiv, near Sofia, Bulgaria, 18 May 1919; *s* of Kyryl and Rayna Teodorova; *m* Franca, *d* of Raffaello de Rensis. *Educ:* Univ. of Sofia (Doctor of Law). Joined Gussla Choir and Sofia Cathedral Choir as soloist. Obtained scholarship, through King Boris III of Bulgaria, to study singing in Rome under Riccardo Stracciari; made concert début at St Cecilia Academy in Rome, 1946 and operatic début, 1946; Covent Garden début, 1950, as Boris Godunov and Philip II; subsequently has appeared at all leading European and American opera houses; American début, Metropolitan Opera House, 1950; as Boris Godunov, San Francisco, 1956. Principal rôles include: Boris Godunov, King Philip, Galitzky, Konchak, Don Quixote, Dositheus, Ivan the Terrible, Ivan Susanin, Mephistopheles, Moses, Don Basilio, Pizarro. Has made numerous recordings, including opera and songs, winning many prix du disque. Hon. Mem. Théâtre de l'Opéra, Paris, Mem. La Scala, Milan. Holds foreign decorations. Commendatore della Repubblica Italiana. *Address:* Via Bertoloni 1, Rome, Italy.

**CHRISTOFFELSZ, Arthur Eric,** CMG 1949; BA, LLB Cantab; Barrister-at-Law, Gray's Inn; *b* 22 Aug. 1890; *s* of James Edwin Christoffelsz, ISO, and Eugenie Julia Weinman; *m* 1927, Edith Muriel Daniels. *Educ:* Royal College, Colombo; Queen's Coll., Cambridge. Called to the Bar, Gray's Inn, 1915; entered Ceylon Civil Service, 1915, and held various judicial and administrative appointments chief of which were: Govt Agent, North-Central Province, Ceylon, 1938-41; Comr of Labour, 1942-46; Principal Collector of Customs, 1947-49; Permanent Sec. to Minister of Labour and Social Services, 1949-51. *Address:* 8 Galle Face Court, Colombo 3, Ceylon. *T:* Colombo 25761. *Club:* Royal Commonwealth Society.

**CHRISTOPHER, Sir George Perrin,** Kt 1946; Member of Council, Chamber of Shipping, since 1927; *b* 1890; married. Formerly held the following positions: Dir, Peninsular & Oriental Steam Navigation Co.; Chm., Hain Steamship Co. Ltd; Chm. and Man. Dir, Union-Castle Mail Steamship Co. Ltd; Mem. General Cttee of Lloyd's Register of Shipping; Mem. Exec. Council of Shipping Federation

Ltd; Mem. Gen. Council, King George's Fund for Sailors; Mem. Cttee, HMS Worcester. Chm. Tramp Shipping Administrative Cttee, 1939, and London Gen. Shipowners' Soc., 1939; Dir of Commercial Services, Ministry of War Transport, 1941-45 (Dep.-Dir, 1939-41); Pres. of the Chamber of Shipping of the United Kingdom, 1948-49 (Vice-Pres., 1947-48); Jt Vice-Chm. of General Council of British Shipping, 1947-49; Liveryman Worshipful Co. of Shipwrights. *Address:* Trencrom, Raglan Road, Reigate, Surrey. *T:* Reigate 42530.

**CHRISTOPHERS, Brevet Col Sir Samuel Rickard,** Kt 1931; CIE 1915; OBE 1918; FRS 1926; MB; IMS retired; *b* 27 Nov. 1873; *s* of Samuel Hunt Christophers, Liverpool; *m* Elsie Emma, *d* of FitzRoy Sherman; one *s* one *d*. Member Malaria Commission, Royal Society and Colonial Office, 1898-1902; joined Indian Medical Service, 1902; Officer in Charge Central Malaria Bureau, India, 1910-22; Director Central Research Inst., Kasauli, India, 1922-32; KHP 1927-30; Professor of Malarial Studies, Univ. of London; Leverhulme Fellow, MRC, in charge Experimental Malaria Unit at the London School of Hygiene and Tropical Medicine, 1932-38. Buchanan Medal of Royal Society, 1952. *Publications:* Practical Study of Malaria; Reports to the Malaria Committee of the Royal Society; various publications on malaria, kalaazar and medical zoology, etc. *Address:* 20 Upper Golf Links Road, Broadstone, Dorset. *T:* Broadstone 2931.

**CHRISTOPHERSON, Sir Derman (Guy),** Kt 1969; OBE 1946; FRS 1960; DPhil (Oxon) 1941; AMICE, MIMechE; Vice-Chancellor and Warden of Durham University since 1960; *b* 6 Sept. 1915; *s* of late Derman Christopherson, Clerk in Holy Orders, formerly of Blackheath, and Edith Frances Christopherson; *m* 1940, Frances Edith, *d* of late James and Martha Tearle; three *s* one *d*. *Educ:* Sherborne Sch.; University Coll., Oxford. Henry Fellow at Harvard Univ., 1938; Scientific Officer, Research and Experiments Dept, Ministry of Home Security, 1941-45; University Demonstrator, Cambridge Univ. Engineering Dept, 1945, Lecturer, 1946; Professor of Mechanical Engineering, Leeds Univ., 1949-55; Prof. of Applied Science, Imperial Coll. of Science and Technology, 1955-60. Fellow of Magdalene Coll., Cambridge, 1945, Bursar, 1947. Mem. Council of Institution of Mechanical Engineers, 1950-53; Clayton Prize, Instn of Mechanical Engineers, 1963. Mem., Nat. Advisory Council for Training and Supply of Teachers, 1961; Chm., Cttee of Vice-Chancellors and Principals, 1967-70. Member: Board of Washington New Town Develt Corp., 1964; Science Research Coun., 1965-70. Fellow, Imperial Coll. of Science and Technology, 1966; Hon. Fellow, Magdalene Coll., Cambridge, 1969. Hon. DCL, Kent, 1966; Hon. DSc, Aston, 1967; Hon. LLD: Leeds, 1969; Royal Univ. of Malta, 1969. *Publications:* various papers in Proc. Royal Soc., Proc. IMechE, Jl of Applied Mechanics, etc. *Recreation:* chess. *Address:* Durham University, Old Shire Hall, Old Elvet, Durham. *Club:* Athenæum.

**CHRISTOPHERSON, Harald Fairbairn;** Commissioner of Customs and Excise since 1970; *b* 12 Jan. 1920; *s* of late Captain H. Christopherson, MN, and of Mrs L. G. L. Christopherson (*now* Christensen); *m* 1947, Joyce Winifred Emmett; one *s* two *d*. *Educ:* Heaton Grammar Sch., Newcastle upon Tyne; King's Coll., Univ. of Durham (BSc and DipEd). Served in RA, 1941-46, Captain 1945. Teacher and lecturer in mathematics, 1947-48. Entered administrative class, Home CS, Customs and Excise, 1948; seconded to Trade and Tariffs Commn, W Indies, 1956-58; Asst Sec., 1959; seconded to Treasury, 1965-66; Under Sec., 1969. *Recreations:* music, travel. *Address:* 57a York Road, Cheam, Surrey. *T:* 01-642 2444.

**CHRISTY, Ronald Kington,** CB 1965; HM Chief Inspector of Factories, 1963-67; *b* 18 Aug. 1905; *s* of William and Edna Christy; *m* 1931, Ivy, *y d* of W. Hinchcliffe, Whitchurch, Salop; one *s* one *d*. *Educ:* Strand Sch.; King's Coll., Univ. of London. Appointed HM Inspector of Factories, 1930; HM Superintending Inspector of Factories, 1953-59; HM Dep. Chief Inspector of Factories, 1959-63. Mem., Nuclear Safety Advisory Cttee, 1963-67. *Recreations:* gardening, travelling. *Address:* 6 Tyne Walk, Bembridge, IoW. *T:* Bembridge 2255. *Club:* Royal Automobile.

**CHUBB,** family name of **Baron Hayter.**

**CHUBB, Prof. Frederick Basil,** MA, DPhil; Professor of Political Science, Dublin University, Trinity College, since 1960; *b* 8 Dec. 1921; *s* of late Frederick John Bailey Chubb and Gertrude May Chubb, Ludgershall, Wilts; *m* 1946, Margaret Gertrude, *d* of late George Francis and Christina Rafther; no *c*. *Educ:* Bishop Wordsworth's Sch., Salisbury; Merton Coll., Oxford. BA 1946; MA (Oxon); MA (Dublin); DPhil (Oxon) 1950. Lecturer in Political Science, Trinity Coll., Dublin, 1948; Fellow in Polit. Sci., 1952; Reader in Polit. Sci., 1955; Bursar, 1957-62. Vice-Pres. Inst. of Public Administration, 1958; MRIA 1969. *Publications:* The Control of Public Expenditure, 1952; (with D. E. Butler (ed) and others) Elections Abroad, 1959; A Source Book of Irish Government, 1964; (ed with P. Lynch) Economic Development and Planning, 1969; The Government and Politics of Ireland, 1970; articles in learned jls. *Recreation:* fishing. *Address:* 19 Clyde Road, Ballsbridge, Dublin 4. *T:* 684625.

**CHURCH, Eric Edmund Raitt,** CMG 1967; CBE 1959; retired; *b* 18 Sept. 1907; *s* of James and Catherine Church, Chelsworth, Suffolk; *m* 1948, Diana Mary Lloyd Mawson; no *c*. *Educ:* Sudbury Gram. Sch.; Lincoln Coll., Oxford. Teaching appts in England, India and Brazil, 1928-36; Lectr, Univ. of Brazil, 1937; British Council: Rep., Brazil, 1939; Dir, Latin-American Dept, 1943; Asst Rep., Greece, 1947; Dir, Personnel Dept, 1948; Controller: Establishments Div., 1954; Overseas Div. B, 1962; Finance Div., 1964. *Address:* 31 Station Road, Sawbridgeworth, Herts. *T:* Sawbridgeworth 3023.

**CHURCH, Brig. Sir Geoffrey Selby,** 2nd Bt *cr* 1901; CBE 1940; MC; DL, JP; *b* 11 Jan. 1887; 2nd *s* of Sir William Selby Church, Bt, KCB, and Sybil Constance, *d* of Charles John Bigge, Linden, Northumberland; *S* father, 1928; *m* 1st, 1913, Doris Louise (*d* 1917), *d* of late Sir W. Somerville, KBE; 2nd, 1920, Helene Elizabeth (*d* 1962), *d* of John L. Trayner, Mich., USA; no *c*. *Educ:* Winchester; University Coll., Oxford. Sheriff of Herts, 1936; JP 1927, DL 1931, Herts. ADC (Additional) to King George VI, 1941-51. *Recreations:* outdoor sports. *Heir:* none. *Address:* St Michaels, Hatfield, Herts. *T:* Hatfield 62115. *Club:* United University.

**CHURCH, Richard (Thomas),** CBE 1957; FRSL; Vice-President, Royal Society of Literature; Past President: English Association; PEN; poet, novelist, and literary critic; *b* London, 26

March 1893; 2nd *s* of Thomas John Church and Lavinia Annie, *d* of Benjamin Orton; *m* 1st, Caroline Parfett; 2nd, Catherina Anna (*d* 1965), *d* of Carl Otto Schimmer; one *s* three *d*; 3rd, Dorothy Beale. *Educ:* Dulwich Hamlet Sch. *Publications: poetry:* Flood of Life, 1917; Hurricane, 1919; Philip, 1923; Portrait of the Abbot, 1926; The Dream, 1927; Theme and Variations, 1928; Mood without Measure, 1928; The Glance Backward, 1930; News from the Mountain, 1932; Twelve Noon, 1936; The Solitary Man, 1941; 20th Century Psalter, 1943; Poems of Our Time (Everyman's), 1945; The Lamp, 1946; Collected Poems, 1948; Poems for Speaking, 1949; Selected Lyrical Poems, 1951; The Prodigal, 1953; The Inheritors (winner of Foyle's Poetry Prize), 1957; North of Rome, 1960; The Burning Bush, 1967; *prose:* Mary Shelley, 1928; Oliver's Daughter, 1930; High Summer, 1931; The Prodigal Father, 1933; Apple of Concord, 1935; The Porch, 1937 (Femina-Vie Heureuse Prize); The Stronghold, 1939; Calling for a Spade, 1939; The Room Within, 1940; Eight for Immortality, 1941; Rufus, 1941; Plato's Mistake, 1941; The Sampler, 1942; Some Modern British Authors (for British Council), 1943; Green Tide, 1944; Kent, 1948; The Cave, 1950; The Growth of the English Novel, 1950; A Window on a Hill, 1951; The Nightingale, 1952; Portrait of Canterbury, 1953; Dog Toby, 1953; Over the Bridge, 1955 (awarded Sunday Times Prize for Literature, 1955); Small Moments, 1956; The Dangerous Years, 1956; The Golden Sovereign, 1957; Down River, 1958; A Country Window, 1958; The Crabapple Tree, 1959; The Bells of Rye, 1960; Calm October, 1961; Prince Albert, 1963; The Little Kingdom, 1964; The Voyage Home, 1964; A Stroll Before Dark, 1965; London: Flower of Cities All, 1966; Speaking Aloud, 1968; The White Doe, 1968; Little Miss Moffatt, 1969; The Wonder of Words, 1970; A Harvest of Mushrooms (essays), 1970. *Address:* The Priest's House, Sissinghurst Castle, Cranbrook, Kent. *Clubs:* Athenæum, Savile.

**CHURCH, Prof. Ronald James H.;** *see* Harrison-Church.

**CHURCHER, Maj.-Gen. John Bryan,** CB 1952; DSO 1944, Bar 1946; retired; Director and General Secretary, Independent Stores Association, since 1959; *b* 2 Sept. 1905; *s* of late Lieut-Col B. T. Churcher, Wargrave, Berks, and of Mrs Bryan Churcher; *m* 1937, Rosamond Hildegarde Mary, *y d* of late Frederick Parkin, Truro Vean, Truro, Cornwall; one *s* two *d*. *Educ:* Wellington Coll., Berks; RMC Sandhurst. Commissioned DCLI, 1925; Lieut, 1927; Capt. KSLI, 1936; Staff Coll., 1939; served War of 1939-45 (despatches, DSO and Bar); commanded: 1 Bn Hereford Regt, 1942-44; 159 Inf. Bde, 1944-46; 43 Div., 1946; Northumbrian Dist., 1946; 2 Div., 1946; 3 Div., 1946-47; 5 Div., 1947-48; Brig., Imperial Defence Coll., 1948; BGS, Western Command, 1949-51; Chief of Staff, Southern Comd, 1951-54; GOC, 3rd Inf. Div., 1954-57; Dir of Military Training at the War Office, 1957-59; retired, 1959. ADC to King George VI, 1949-52; ADC to the Queen to 1952. *Address:* Tudor Barn, Stanway, near Colchester, Essex. *T:* Marks Tey 294. *Club:* Army and Navy.

**CHURCHILL;** *see* Spencer-Churchill.

**CHURCHILL,** 2nd Viscount *cr* 1902; **Victor Alexander Spencer;** Baron 1815; Prince of the Holy Roman Empire; *b* 1 Aug. 1890; *s* of 1st Viscount and Lady Verena Maud Lowther, VA (*d* 1938), *d* of 3rd Earl of Lonsdale; godson of Queen Victoria; *S* father, 1934; *m* 1916, Kathleen (*d* 1943), *d* of Hon. Robert Beaven; *m* 1949, Joan (*d* 1957), *d* of Joseph Baron Black. *Educ:* Eton; Sorbonne, Paris. Page of Honour to King Edward VII, 1901-07; War of 1914-18, Major GSO (despatches); War of 1939-45, Staff Sergeant (1942-45), US Air Force. *Publication:* All My Sins Remembered. *Heir: half-b* Hon. Victor George Spencer, *b* 31 July 1934. *Address:* c/o National City Bank of New York, 17 Bruton Street, W1.

**CHURCHILL, Diana (Josephine);** actress, stage and screen; *b* Wembley, 21 Aug. 1913; *d* of Joseph H. Churchill, MRCS, LRCP and Ethel Mary Nunn; *m* Barry K. Barnes (*d* 1965). *Educ:* St Mary's Sch., Wantage; Guildhall Sch. of Music (scholarship). First professional appearance in Champion North, Royalty, 1931; subsequently in West End and in Repertory. Old Vic Season, 1949-50, New Theatre, as Rosaline in Love's Labour's Lost, Miss Kate Hardcastle in She Stoops to Conquer, Lizaveta Bogdanovna in A Month in the Country and Elise in The Miser; High Spirits, London Hippodrome, 1953; The Desperate Hours, London Hippodrome, 1955; Hamlet, Stratford-on-Avon Festival, 1956; Lady Fidget in The Country Wife, Royal Court Theatre, 1956; The Rehearsal, Globe Theatre, 1961; The Winter's Tale, Cambridge, 1966. Has also appeared in several films. *Address:* c/o Al. Parker Ltd, 50 Mount Street, W1.

**CHURCHILL, George Percy,** CBE 1924; *b* 14 Aug. 1877; *s* of Henry A. Churchill, CB; *m* 1906, Muriel (*d* 1967), *d* of Sir Alfred East, RA; two *s*. *Educ:* privately. Oriental Sec. to HM Legation at Teheran, with a Royal Commission, and given local rank of a 3rd Sec. in the Diplomatic Service, 1903: 2nd Sec., 1916; served in Persia until the end of European War; transferred to the Eastern Dept of the Foreign Office, 1919-24; British Consul-Gen. at Algiers, 1924-27; retired, 1937; employed by Home Office, 1939-41, as Sec. of Advisory Cttee, Defence Regulations 18B. Attached to the English Suite of the Shah of Persia during HM's State Visit to England in 1919, and was given the First Class of the Order of the Lion and the Sun of Persia. *Address:* 20 Abbey Road, NW8.

**CHURCHILL, Hon. Gordon,** PC (Canada); DSO 1945; ED; QC; Canadian barrister; Associate Counsel, firm of D'Arcy, Irving, Haig & Smethurst; *b* Coldwater, Ont, 8 Nov. 1898; *s* of Rev. J. W. and Mary E. Churchill; *m* 1922, Mona Mary, *d* of C. W. McLachlin, Dauphin, Man.; one *d*. *Educ:* Univ. of Manitoba. MA 1931, LLB 1950. Served European War, 1916-18, France; served War of 1939-45 (DSO), commanded First Canadian Armoured Carrier Regt, NW Europe. Principal of a Manitoba High Sch., 1928-38; Mem. Manitoba Legislature, 1946-49; called to Manitoba Bar, 1950; Member Federal Parlt for Winnipeg South Centre, 1951-68, retired; Federal Minister: for Trade and Commerce, 1957-60; of Veterans' Affairs, 1960-63; of National Defence, Feb.-April 1963. *Recreation:* golf. *Address:* 300-286 Smith Street, Winnipeg, Manitoba, Canada; 954 Palmerston Avenue, Winnipeg.

**CHURCHILL, Odette;** *see* Hallowes, O. M. C.

**CHURCHILL, Peter Morland,** DSO 1946; *b* 14 Jan. 1909; *s* of late W. A. Churchill, Consul General; *m* 1947, Mrs Odette Sansom (*see* Odette Hallowes) (marr. diss. 1955); *m* 1956, Jane Hoyle. *Educ:* Malvern; Caius Coll., Cambridge (BA mod. langs, French, Spanish, Italian). Served War of 1939-45, in French Resistance; Capt., DSO, Croix de Guerre,

1946. Author; estate agent on the Riviera. *Publications:* Of their own Choice, 1952; Duel of Wits, 1953; Spirit in the Cage, 1954; By Moonlight, 1959; All about the French Riviera, 1960. *Recreations:* swimming, golf; formerly ice-hockey (Capt. Cambridge Univ. Ice Hockey Team, 1932; International, 12 caps). *Address:* 06-Le Rouret, France. *T:* (93) 67.60.49.

**CHURCHILL, Maj.-Gen. Thomas Bell Lindsay,** CB 1957; CBE 1949; MC; *b* 1 Nov. 1907; 2nd *s* of late Alec Fleming Churchill, of PWD, Ceylon and Hong Kong, and late Elinor Elizabeth (*née* Bell); *m* 1st, 1934, Gwendolen Janie (*d* 1962), *e d* of late Lewis Williams, MD; one *s* one *d*; 2nd, 1963, Elizabeth Deirdre (marr. diss. 1967), *yr d* of late Bruce R. Campbell, Goorianawa, NSW; 3rd, 1968, Penelope Jane, *d* of Cecil G. Ormiston, Ringwood, Hants. *Educ:* Dragon Sch., Oxford; Magdalen Coll. Sch., Oxford; RMC Sandhurst. Gained Prize Cadetship to RMC Sandhurst, 1926; Prize for Mil. Hist., 1927. 2nd Lieut, Manchester Regt, 1927; Burma Rebellion, 1930-31 (despatches, MC); Adjt, 1931-34; instructor in interpretation of air photographs, RAF Sch. of Photography, 1934-39; Company Comdr, France, 1939-40; GSO1 Commandos, Sicily and Salerno Landings, 1943; comd 2nd Commando Bde, Italy, Jugoslavia, Albania, 1943-44; comd 11th and 138th Inf Bdes, Austria, 1945-46; Zone Comdr, Austria, 1947-49; DDPS, War Office, 1949-51; student, Imperial Def. Coll., 1952; Brig. i/c Admin, HQ Western Comd, 1953-55; Maj.-Gen. i/c Admin., GHQ, Far ELF, 1955-57; Vice-Quartermaster-Gen. to the Forces, 1957-60; Deputy Chief of Staff, Allied Land Forces, Central Europe, 1960-62, retd. Col The Manchester Regt, 1952-58; Col The King's Regt (Manchester and Liverpool). 1958-62. A Vice-Pres. of the Commando Assoc. and Trustee of the Commando Benevolent Fund; Dir, Great Britain-USSR Assoc., 1963-. *Publications:* Manual of Interpretation of Air Photographs, 1939; articles to Yorks Archæolog. Jl, 1935, to Army Quarterly and to Jl of RUSI. *Recreations:* genealogy, heraldry; fine arts. *Address:* 3 Ruvigny Mansions, The Embankment, SW15. *T:* 01-788 1605.

**CHURCHILL, Winston Spencer;** MP (C) Stretford (Lancs) since 1970; author; journalist; *b* 10 Oct. 1940; *s* of late Randolph Frederick Edward Spencer Churchill, MBE and of Hon. Pamela Beryl Digby, *e d* of 11th Baron Digby, KG, DSO, MC, TD; *m* 1964, Mary Caroline d'Erlanger, *d* of late Sir Gerard d'Erlanger, CBE, Chairman of BOAC; one *s* two *d*; *g s* of Baroness Spencer-Churchill, *qv*. *Educ:* Eton; Christ Church, Oxford (MA). Correspondent in: Yemen, Congo and Angola, 1964; Borneo and Vietnam, 1966; Middle East, 1967; Czechoslovakia, 1968; Biafra and Middle East, 1969. Lecture tours of the US and Canada, 1965, 1969. Contested Gorton Div. of Manchester in Bye-election, Nov. 1967. Correspondent of the Times, 1969-70. *Publications:* First Journey, 1964; (with late Randolph Churchill) Six Day War, 1967. *Recreations:* tennis, sailing, ski-ing. *Address:* Broadwater House, Chailey, Sussex. *Clubs:* White's, Buck's; St James's (Manchester).

**CHURSTON,** 4th Baron *cr* 1858; **Richard Francis Roger Yarde-Buller;** Bt 1790; VRD; Lieut-Comdr RNVR, retired; *b* 12 Feb. 1910; *er s* of 3rd Baron and Jessie (who *m* 2nd, 1928, Theodore William Wessel), *o d* of Alfred Smither; *S* father, 1930; *m* 1st, 1933, Elizabeth Mary (from whom he obtained a divorce, 1943, and who *m* 1943, Lieut-Col P. Laycock; she died 1951), 2nd *d* of late W. B. du Pre; one *s* one *d*; 2nd, 1949, Mrs Jack Dunfee. *Educ:* Eton Coll. *Heir:* *s* Hon. John Francis Yarde-Buller, *b* 29 Dec. 1934. *Address:* Woodcote, St Andrew, Guernsey, Channel Isles. *Clubs:* United Hunts; Royal Yacht Squadron.

*See also Earl Cadogan, Sir G. A. Lyle, Bt.*

**CHUTE, Marchette;** author; *b* 16 Aug. 1909; *d* of William Young Chute and Edith Mary Pickburn; unmarried. *Educ:* Univ. of Minnesota (BA). Doctor of Letters: Western Coll., 1952; Carleton Coll., 1957; Dickinson Coll., 1964. Mem., National Inst. of Arts and Letters, 1957. Outstanding Achievement Award, Univ. of Minnesota, 1958; co-winner of Constance Lindsay Skinner Award, 1959. *Publications:* Rhymes about Ourselves, 1932; The Search for God, 1941; Rhymes about the Country, 1941; The Innocent Wayfaring, 1943; Geoffrey Chaucer of England, 1946; Rhymes about the City, 1946; The End of the Search, 1947; Shakespeare of London, 1950; An Introduction to Shakespeare, 1951 (English title: Shakespeare and his Stage); Ben Jonson of Westminster, 1953; The Wonderful Winter, 1954; Stories from Shakespeare, 1956; Around and About, 1957; Two Gentle Men: the Lives of George Herbert and Robert Herrick, 1959; Jesus of Israel, 1961; The Worlds of Shakespeare (with Ernestine Perrie), 1963; The First Liberty: a history of the right to vote in America, 1619-1850, 1969; The Green Tree of Democracy, 1971; various articles in Saturday Review, Virginia Quarterly Review, etc. *Recreations:* walking, reading, talking. *Address:* 450 East 63rd Street, New York, New York 10021, USA. *T:* Templeton 8-8920. *Clubs:* Royal Society of Arts; PEN, Renaissance Society of America, Society of American Historians (New York).

**CILENTO, Sir Raphael West,** Kt 1935; MD, BS (Adelaide); DTM & H (England); (life) FRSanI (London); FRHistSoc, Queensland; Director-General of Health and Medical Services, Queensland, Australia, 1934-45; Hon. Professor of Tropical and Social Medicine, University of Queensland, 1937-45; Barrister Supreme Court, Queensland, since 1939; President, Royal Historical Society of Queensland, 1934-35, 1943-44, and since 1953; *b* 2 Dec. 1893; *s* of Raphael Ambrose Cilento and Frances Ellen Elizabeth West; *m* 1920, Phyllis Dorothy, *d* of late C. T. McGlew; three *s* three *d*. *Educ:* Adelaide High Sch.; Prince Alfred Coll., South Australia; Univ. of Adelaide. Colonial Medical Service (Federated Malay States), 1920-21; Duncan and Lalcaca medals, London Sch. of Tropical Medicine, 1922; Dir, Australian Inst. of Tropical Medicine, Townsville, North Queensland, 1922-28; Dir of Public Health, New Guinea, 1924-28; Rep. (Brit.) League of Nations Mission on Health Conditions in the Pacific with Dr P. Hermant (French rep.), 1928-29; Dir for Tropical Hygiene, Commonwealth of Australia, 1928-32 and Chief Quarantine Officer (General) NE Div., 1928-34, Brisbane, Qld; Pres., Royal Society Qld, 1933-34; Chm., State Nutritional Advisory Board, 1937; Pres., Med. Board of Qld, 1939; Assessor, Med. Assessment Tribunal, 1940; Senior Administrative Officer, Commonwealth Dept of Health, Canberra, ACT; Mem., Army Medical Directorates Consultative Cttee, 1941-45; Chm., National Survey, Health of Coal Miners, Australia, 1945; UNRRA Zone Dir, British occupied area Germany, Maj.-Gen., with assimilated status, BAOR, 1945-46; Dir, Div. of Refugees, 1946, of Div. of Social Activities, 1947-50, UN, NY. *Publications:* Malaria, 1924; White Man in the Tropics, 1925; Factors in Depopulation; NW Islands of the Mandated Territory of New Guinea, 1928; Health Problems in the Pacific, 1929; Anne

Mackenzie Oration, 1933; Second Sir Herbert Maitland Oration, 1937; Tropical Diseases in Australasia, 1940 (and 1942); Blueprint for the Health of a Nation, 1944. *Recreations:* international affairs, reading history. *Address:* Altavilla, 268 Vulture Street, South Brisbane, Queensland, Australia. *Clubs:* Johnsonian (Brisbane); Australasian Pioneers (Sydney).
*See also Sean Connery.*

**CIONA, Most Rev. James;** *see* Blantyre, Archbishop of, (RC).

**CITRINE,** family name of **Baron Citrine.**

**CITRINE,** 1st Baron *cr* 1946, of Wembley; **Walter McLennan Citrine,** PC 1940; GBE 1958 (KBE 1935); Comp. IEE; *b* Liverpool, 22 Aug. 1887; *m* 1913, Doris Slade; two *s.* Mersey District Sec. of Electrical Trades Union, 1914-20; Pres., Fed. Engineering and Shipbuilding Trades, Mersey District, 1917-18; Sec., 1918-20; Asst Gen. Sec., Electrical Trades Union, 1920-23; Asst Sec., TUC, 1924-25, Gen. Sec., 1926-46; Mem., Nat. Coal Board, 1946-47; Chm., Miners' Welfare Commn, 1946-47. Pres., Internat. Fed. of Trade Unions, 1928-45; Dir, Daily Herald (1929) Ltd, 1929-46; Mem., Nat. Production Advisory Council, 1942-46 and 1949-57; Past Mem., Reconstruction Jt Advisory Council; Treasury Consultative Council; Visiting Fellow, Nuffield Coll., 1939-47; Trustee of Imperial Relations Trust, 1937-49; Nuffield Trust for the Forces, 1939-46; Mem. of Cinematograph Films Council, 1938-48; Exec. Cttee of Red Cross, and St John War Organisation, 1939-46; Chm. of Production Cttee on Regional Boards (Munitions), 1942; Mem., Royal Commission on W Indies, 1938; Pres., British Electrical Development Assoc., 1948-52; Chm. Central Electricity Authority, 1947-57; Pres., Electrical Research Assoc., 1950-52 amd 1956-57; Pres. (1955) and Mem. of Directing Cttee, Union Internationale des Producteurs et Distributeurs d'Energie Electrique; Part-time Mem., Electricity Council, 1958-62. Part-time Mem. of UK Atomic Energy Authority, 1958-62. Hon. LLD, Manchester. *Publications:* ABC of Chairmanship; The Trade Union Movement of Great Britain; Labour and the Community; I Search for Truth in Russia, 1936 and 1938; My Finnish Diary; My American Diary, 1941; In Russia Now, 1942; British Trade Unions, 1942; Men and Work, 1964; Two Careers, 1967, etc. *Heir: s* Hon. N. A. Citrine, *qv.* *Address:* Dorislade, 59 Royston Park Road, Hatch End, Middx.

**CITRINE, Hon. Norman Arthur,** LLB; solicitor in general practice; author, editor, lecturer; *b* 27 Sept. 1914; *e s* and *heir* of 1st Baron Citrine, *qv*; *m* 1939, Kathleen Alice Chilvers; one *d.* *Educ:* University Coll. Sch., Hampstead; Law Society's Sch., London. Admitted solicitor of Supreme Court (Hons), 1937; LLB (London), 1938. Served War of 1939-45, Lieut RNVR, 1940-46. Legal Adviser to Trades Union Congress, 1946-51; entered general legal practice, 1951. *Publications:* War Pensions Appeal Cases, 1946; Guide to Industrial Injuries Acts, 1948; Trade Union Law, 1950, 3rd edn, 1968; Editor, ABC of Chairmanship, 1952. *Recreations:* boating, engineering, painting, carpentry. *Address:* Gorse Cottage, Berry Head, Brixham, Torbay, Devon. *T:* Brixham 3167. *Clubs:* Brixham Rotary; Brixham Yacht.

**CIVIL, Alan;** Principal Horn, BBC Symphony Orchestra, since 1966; *b* 13 June 1928; *m* Shirley Jean Hopkins; three *s* two *d.* *Educ:* Northampton, various schools. Principal Horn, Royal Philharmonic Orchestra, 1953-55; Philharmonia Orchestra, 1955-66. Guest Principal, Berlin Philharmonic Orchestra; international horn soloist; Prof. of Horn, Royal Coll. of Music, London; composer; founder of Alan Civil Horn Trio. Member: London Wind Soloists; London Wind Quintet; Music Group of London. *Recreations:* brewing, gardening, Baroque music. *Address:* Downe Hall, Downe, Kent. *T:* Farnborough (Kent) 52982. *Club:* Savage.

**CLAIR, René;** writer and film director; Member of The French Academy since 1960; Commandeur de la Légion d'Honneur; Hon. LLD, Cambridge, 1956; Hon. Dr RCA, 1967. *Films include:* The Italian Straw Hat; Sous les Toits de Paris; Le Million; A Nous la Liberté; Quatorze Juillet; The Ghost Goes West; I Married a Witch; It Happened Tomorrow; Le Silence est d'Or; La Beauté du Diable; Les Belles de Nuit; Les Grandes Manœuvers; Porte des Lilas; Tout l'Or du Monde; Les Fêtes Galantes. *Publications:* Star Turn; Reflections on the Cinema; La Princesse de Chine; Comédies et Commentaires. *Address:* SECA, 44 Champs-Elysées, Paris VIIIe.

**CLAMAGERAN, Alice Germaine Suzanne;** Director, School of Nurses and Social Workers, Centre Hospitalier Universitaire de Rouen, since 1942; President, International Council of Nurses, 1961-65; *b* 5 March 1906; *d* of William Clamageran, shipowner at Rouen and of Lucie Harlé. *Educ:* Rouen. Nursing studies: Red Cross School of Nurses, Rouen; Ecole Professionnelle d'Assistance aux Malades, Paris. Tutor, Red Cross Sch. for Nurses, Rouen, 1931-42 (leave, for course in Public Health at Florence Nightingale Internat. Foundn, London, 1934-35). War service (6 months), 1939-40. Pres. Bd of Dirs, Fondation Edith Seltzer (Sanatorium Chantoiseau, Briançon) for Nurses, Social Workers and Medical Auxiliaries; Hon. Pres. Nat. Assoc. of Trained Nurses in France. Médaille de Bronze de l'Enseignement Technique, 1960; Officier dans l'Ordre de la Santé Publique, 1961; Chevalier, Légion d'Honneur, 1962. *Address:* 1 rue de Germont, Rouen, France. *T:* Rouen 71-54-18.

**CLANCARTY,** 6th Earl of, *cr* 1803; **Richard Frederick John Donough Le-Poer-Trench;** Viscount Dunlo, 1801; Baron Kilconnel of Garbally, Co. Galway, 1797; Baron Trench (UK), 1815; Viscount Clancarty (UK), 1823; Marquess of Heusden in Kingdom of the Netherlands; *b* 27 Dec. 1891; *e s* of 5th Earl and Isabel Maude Penrice (*d* 1906), *d* of John G. Bilton, Charlton, Kent; *S* father, 1929; *m* 1st, 1915, Edith Constance (from whom he obtained a divorce, 1918), *d* of Major Alexander Albemarle Rawlinson; 2nd, 1918, Cora, *e d* of late H. H. Spooner and Mrs Philip Lindoe, Bourne Court, Bourne End; three *d.* Was in Royal Naval Air Force. *Heir: b* Hon. Greville Le-Poer-Trench, *b* 10 Dec. 1902. *Address:* Flint Place, Earnley, near Chichester, West Sussex. *T:* Birdham 337.

**CLANCY, Hon. Sir John (Sydney James),** KBE 1967; CMG 1964; Judge of Supreme Court of New South Wales, Australia, 1947-65; Chancellor of the University of New South Wales since 1960; *b* 30 May 1895; *s* of J. P. Clancy, Sydney; *m* 1923, Ethel Buckland; one *d.* *Educ:* Marist Brothers High Sch.; Sydney Univ. LLB, Hon. DLitt. Admitted Bar New South Wales, 1925; District Court Judge, 1931; Chm. Crown Employees Appeal Board, 1944. Served with 1st AIF, 1914-18, in New Guinea and France. *Address:* 53 Chelmsford Avenue, Lindfield, NSW, Australia. *T:* JM 3695. *Clubs:* Tattersall's, Rugby Union (Sydney).

**CLANMORRIS,** 7th Baron (Ireland), *cr* 1800; **John Michael Ward Bingham;** *b* 3 Nov. 1908; *o s* of 6th Baron Clanmorris; *S* father, 1960; *m* 1934, Madeleine Mary, *d* of late Clement Ebel, Copyhold Place, Cuckfield, Sussex; one *s* one *d*. *Educ:* Cheltenham Coll.; France and Germany. *Publications:* as John Bingham: My Name is Michael Sibley, 1952; Five Roundabouts to Heaven, 1953; The Third Skin, 1954; The Paton Street Case, 1955; Marion, 1958; Murder Plan Six, 1958; Night's Black Agent, 1960; A Case of Libel, 1963; A Fragment of Fear, 1965; The Double Agent, 1966; I Love, I Kill, 1968. *Heir: s* Hon. Simon John Ward Bingham, *b* 25 Oct. 1937. *Address:* 24 Abingdon Villas, W8. *Club:* Press.

**CLANWILLIAM,** 6th Earl of, *cr* 1776; **John Charles Edmund Carson Meade;** Bt 1703; Viscount Clanwilliam, Baron Gilford, 1766; Baron Clanwilliam (UK), 1828; Major Coldstream Guards (retired); *b* 6 June 1914; *o s* of 5th Earl of Clanwilliam; *S* father, 1953; *m* 1948, Catherine, *y d* of late A. T. Loyd, Lockinge, Wantage, Berks; six *d*. *Educ:* Eton; RMC Sandhurst. Adjt, 1939-42; Staff Coll., Haifa, 1942; Bde Major, 201 Guards Motor Brigade, 1942-43; Bde Major, 6 Guards Tank Brigade, 1944; Command and Gen. Staff Sch., Fort Leavenworth, USA, 1944; served in Middle East and France (despatches twice); retd, 1948. HM Lieut for Co. Down. *Heir: cousin* John Herbert Meade [*b* 27 Sept. 1919; *m* 1956, Maxine, *o d* of late J. A. Hayden-Scott; one *s* two *d*]. *Address:* Montalto, Ballynahinch, Co. Down. *T:* Ballynahinch 2296. *Clubs:* Carlton, Pratt's.

**CLAPHAM, Prof. Arthur Roy,** CBE 1969; FRS 1959; MA, PhD Cantab; FLS; Professor of Botany in Sheffield University, 1944-69, Professor Emeritus 1969; Pro-Vice-Chancellor, 1954-58, Acting Vice-Chancellor, 1965; Member of the Nature Conservancy since 1956, Chairman, Scientific Policy Committee since 1963; Member of Natural Environment Research Council, 1965-70; Chairman, British National Committee for the International Biological Programme; President: Derbyshire Naturalists' Trust; Linnean Society, 1967-70; *b* 24 May 1904; *o s* of George Clapham, Norwich; *m* 1933, Brenda North Stoessiger; one *s* two *d* (and one *s* decd). *Educ:* City of Norwich Sch.; Downing Coll., Cambridge (Foundation Scholar). Frank Smart Prize, 1925; Frank Smart Student, 1926-27; Crop Physiologist at Rothamsted Agricultural Experimental Station, 1928-30; University Demonstrator in Botany at Oxford Univ., 1931-44. *Publications:* (with W. O. James) The Biology of Flowers, 1935; (with T. G. Tutin and E. F. Warburg) Flora of the British Isles, 1952, 1962; Excursion Flora of the British Isles, 1959; various papers in botanical journals. *Address:* Cawood Cottage, Arkholme, Carnforth, Lancs. *T:* Hornby 640.

**CLAPHAM, Michael John Sinclair;** Deputy Chairman, Imperial Chemical Industries Ltd, since 1968; Member, Industrial Reorganization Corporation, since 1969; *b* 17 Jan. 1912; *s* of late Sir John Clapham, CBE and Lady Clapham, Cambridge; *m* 1935, Hon. Elisabeth Russell Rea, *d* of 1st Baron Rea of Eskdale; three *s* one *d*. *Educ:* Marlborough Coll.; King's Coll., Cambridge (MA). Apprenticed as printer with University Press, Cambridge, 1933-35; Overseer and later Works Man., Percy Lund Humphries & Co. Ltd, Bradford, 1935-38; joined ICI Ltd as Man., Kynoch Press, 1938; seconded, in conseq. of developing a diffusion barrier, to Tube Alloys Project (atomic energy), 1941-45; Personnel Dir, ICI Metals Div., 1946; Midland Regional Man., ICI, 1951; Jt Man. Dir, ICI Metals Div., 1952; Chm. 1959; Dir, ICI, 1961; served as Overseas Dir; Dir, ICI of Austr. & NZ Ltd, 1961-; Dir, Imp. Metal Industries Ltd, 1962-. Member: Standing Adv. Cttee on Pay of Higher Civil Service, 1968-; Review Body on Doctors' and Dentists' Remuneration, 1968-70. Mem., Birmingham Educn Cttee, 1949-56; W Mids Adv. Coun. for Techn., Commercial and Art Educn, and Regional Academic Bd, 1952; Life Gov., Birmingham Univ., 1955 (Mem. Coun., 1956-61); Mem. Court, Univ. of London, 1969-; Mem., Govt Youth Service Cttee (Albermarle Cttee), 1958; Mem. CNAA, 1964. *Publications:* Printing, 1500-1730, in The History of Technology, Vol. III, 1957; various articles on printing, personnel management and education. *Recreations:* sailing, canal boating, cooking. *Address:* 26 Hill Street, W1. *T:* 01-499 1240.

*See also B. D. Till.*

**CLAPPEN, Air Commodore Donald William,** CB 1946; RAF retired; *b* 30 June 1895; 2nd *s* of late E. S. Clappen and of Mrs F. Clappen, Westcliff-on-Sea; *m* 1917, Kathleen Mary Broughton Knight; one *s*. *Educ:* St John's Coll., Westcliff-on-Sea; Hurstpierpoint; University Coll., London. Joined Bleriot Aviation Co. as apprentice, 1910; flying pupil, 1912, gaining Pilot's Certificate No. 591 Aug. 1913, on Bleriot Monoplane; joined 1st Bn London Scottish (14th Bn Territorials), 1914; Commission Royal Flying Corps, 1916 (despatches); subsequently RAF, 1918; passed University and Engineer Course, 1922; various appointments including two overseas tours, Iraq prior to outbreak of war. Middle East, 1939-42; Officer Commanding RAF Cosford, near Wolverhampton, 1942-43; Senior Engineer Officer, Army Co-operation Command, 1943; Senior Air Staff Officer HQ 24 Gp, 1943-44; Air Officer Commanding RAF Station, St Athan, Wales, 1944-46; Senior Technical Staff Officer, HQ Bomber Command, 1946; retd 1949. *Recreations:* tennis, winter sports (ski-ing), forestry, cine-photography. *Address:* Three, The Garth, Great Missenden, Bucks. *T:* Great Missenden 4667. *Clubs:* Royal Air Force; Ski Club of Gt. Britain.

**CLARABUT, Maj.-Gen. Reginald Blaxland,** CB 1945; Indian Army, retired; *b* 7 Aug. 1893. Lieut Indian Army, 1917; Capt. 1919; Major, 1933; Bt Lieut-Col 1936; Lieut-Col 1939; Col 1940. AQMG Eastern Command, India, 1940-41; Deputy Dir, Supplies and Transport, India, 1941-44; Comd Nagpur District, 1944-45. *Address:* Oak Bank, Woodlands Close, Ottershaw, Surrey.

**CLARE, Ernest Elwyn S.;** *see* Sabben-Clare.

**CLARE, Neville Adolph St Louis;** *b* 19 Nov. 1900; *m* 1944, Dorothy Jean Depass; one *s* one *d*. *Educ:* Ruseas Secondary Sch.; Jamaica Coll., Kingston. Called to the Bar, Lincoln's Inn, 1941; Resident Magistrate, Jamaica, 1944; acted Judge, Supreme Court, Jamaica, 1954 and 1955; Puisne Judge of British Guiana, Oct. 1955-Nov. 1958, retd. Coronation Medal, 1953. Referee of Titles, Jamaica, 1963. Chm. Jamaica Civil Service Commn; Mem., Jamaica Defence Forces Commn. *Recreations:* reading, golf, music. *Address:* Montclare, Brownstown, Jamaica, WI.

**CLARENDON,** 7th Earl of, 2nd *cr* 1776; **George Frederick Laurence Hyde Villiers;** *b* 2 Feb. 1933; *o s* of Lord Hyde (*d* 1935) and Hon. Marion Féodorovna Louise Glyn (*see* Lady Hyde), *er d* of 4th Baron Wolverton; *S* grandfather, 1955. Page of Honour to King George VI, 1948-49; Lieut RHG, 1951-53. *Heir: uncle* Hon. (William) Nicholas Somers Laurence Hyde

Villiers [*b* 17 July 1916; *m* 1939, Mary Cecilia Georgina, *er d* of late Major Hon. E. A. C. Weld-Forester, CVO; three *d*]. *Address:* Freckenham House, Bury St Edmunds, Suffolk. *T:* Isleham 281; 8 Chelsea Square, SW3. *T:* 01-352 6338.

**CLARINGBULL, Gordon Frank,** BSc, PhD, AInstP, FGS, FMA; Director, British Museum (Natural History), since Dec. 1968; *b* 21 Aug. 1911; *s* of William Horace Claringbull and Hannah Agnes Cutting; *m* 1st, 1938, Grace Helen Mortimer (*d* 1953); one *s* one *d*; 2nd, 1953, Enid Dorothy Phyllis, *d* of late William Henry Lambert. *Educ:* Finchley County Grammar Sch.; Queen Mary Coll., Univ. of London (Fellow 1967). British Museum (Natural Hist.): Asst Keeper, 1935-48; Princ. Scientific Officer, 1948-53; Keeper of Mineralogy, 1953-68. Explosives res., Min. of Supply, 1940-43; special Scientific duties, War Office, 1943-45. Mineralogical Soc.: Gen. Sec., 1938-59; Vice-Pres, 1959-63; Pres., 1965-67; For. Sec., 1967-, Managing Trustee, 1969-. Visitor, Royal Institution, 1963-66. *Publications:* Crystal Structures of Minerals (with W. L. Bragg); papers in journals of learned societies on mineralogical and related topics. *Recreations:* craftwork, gardening, lettering. *Address:* 12 Broadlands Court, Kew Gardens Road, Richmond, Surrey. *T:* 01-948 0827; Padfield House, West Bradley, Glastonbury, Somerset. *T:* Baltonsborough 557. *Club:* Athenæum.

**CLARK,** family name of **Baron Clark.**

**CLARK;** *see* Chichester-Clark.

**CLARK,** Baron *cr* 1969 (Life Peer), of Saltwood; **Kenneth Mackenzie Clark,** CH 1959; KCB 1938; FBA 1949; Chancellor of University of York since 1969; *b* 13 July 1903; *o s* of late Kenneth McKenzie Clark and Margaret Alice McArthur; *m* 1927, Elizabeth Martin; two *s* one *d*. *Educ:* Winchester; Trinity College, Oxford (Hon. Fellow, 1968). Worked for two years with Mr Bernard Berenson, Florence; Keeper of Dept of Fine Art, Ashmolean Museum, Oxford, 1931-33; Director of National Gallery, 1934-45; Surveyor of the King's Pictures, 1934-44; Director of Film Div., later Controller, Home Publicity, Ministry of Information, 1939-41; Slade Professor of Fine Art, Oxford, 1946-50, and October 1961-62. Chairman Arts Council of Great Britain, 1953-60; Chairman of the ITA, 1954-57. Trustee, British Museum. Member: Advisory Council, Victoria and Albert Museum; Conseil Artistique des Musées Nationaux; Swedish Academy; Spanish Academy; Florentine Acad. Hon. LLD: Glasgow, Liverpool; Hon. DLit: Columbia, London, New York; Hon. DLitt: Oxford, Warwick; Hon. LittD: Cambridge, Sheffield; Hon. DUniv. York. Hon. FRIBA; Hon. FRCA. Serena Medal of British Academy (for Italian Studies), 1955; Gold Medal of New York University. HRSA. Comdr, Legion of Honour, France; Comdr, Lion of Finland; Order of Merit, Grand Cross, 2nd Cl., Austria. *Publications:* The Gothic Revival, 1929; Commemorative Catalogue of Exhibition of Italian Art, 1930 (part author and editor); Catalogue of Drawings of Leonardo da Vinci in the collection of His Majesty the King at Windsor Castle, 1935; One Hundred Details in the National Gallery, 1938; Leonardo da Vinci, 1939, new edn 1952; Last Lectures by Roger Fry, edited with an introduction, 1939; L. B. Alberti on Painting, 1944; Constable's Hay Wain, 1944; (Introduction to) Praeterita, 1949; Landscape into Art, 1949; Piero della Francesca, 1951; Moments of Vision, 1954; The Nude, 1955; Looking, 1960; Ruskin Today, 1964; Rembrandt and the Italian Renaissance, 1966; A Failure of Nerve, 1967; Civilisation, 1969. Numerous TV programmes, 1968-; TV series Civilisation, 1969. *Address:* B5 Albany, Piccadilly, W1. *Club:* St James'.

*See also Hon. A. K. M. Clark.*

**CLARK, Rt. Rev. Alan Charles;** Auxiliary Bishop of Northampton, (RC), since 1969; Titular Bishop of Elmham, since 1969; *b* 9 Aug. 1919; *s* of William Thomas Durham Clark and Ellen Mary Clark (*née* Compton). *Educ:* Westminster Cathedral Choir Sch.; Ven. English Coll., Rome, Italy. Priest, 1945; Curate, St Philip's, Arundel, 1945-46; postgrad. studies, Rome, 1946-48; Doctorate in Theol., Gregorian Univ., Rome, 1948; Tutor in Philosophy, English Coll., Rome, 1948-53, Vice-Rector, 1954-64; Parish Priest, St Mary's, Blackheath, SE3, 1965-69. *Peritus* at Vatican Council, 1962-65; Jt Chm., Jt Permanent Commn of the Roman Catholic Church and the Anglican Communion, 1969-. Freeman, City of London, 1969. *Recreation:* music. *Address:* The White House, Poringland, Norwich NOR 42W. *T:* Framingham Earl 202.

**CLARK, Hon. Alan Kenneth McKenzie;** historian; Governor, St Thomas' Hospital; *b* 13 April 1928; *s* of Baron Clark, *qv*; *m* 1958, Caroline Jane Beuttler; two *s*. *Educ:* Eton; Christ Church, Oxford (MA). Household Cavalry (Training Regt), 1946; RAAF, 1952-54. Barrister, Inner Temple, 1955. Mem., Inst. for Strategic Studies, 1963-; Mem., Exec., Conservative and Unionist Party (Poplar Divl Assoc.), 1968-. Mem., RUSI. *Publications:* The Donkeys, A History of the BEF in 1915, 1961; The Fall of Crete, 1963; Barbarossa, The Russo-German Conflict, 1941-45, 1965. *Address:* Seend Park, Wiltshire. *T:* Seend 215. *Club:* St James'.

**CLARK, Albert William;** Metropolitan Magistrate since 1970; *b* 23 Sept. 1922; *s* of William Charles Clark and Cissy Dorothy Elizabeth Clark; *m* 1951, Frances Philippa, *d* of Dr Samuel Lavington Hart, Tientsin; one *s* one *d*. *Educ:* Christ's Coll., Finchley. War service, 1941-46, Royal Navy. Called to Bar, Middle Temple, 1949; Clerk of Arraigns, Central Criminal Court, 1951-56; Clerk to the Justices, E Devon, 1956-70. *Recreations:* fly-fishing, walking, etc. *Address:* Coombe Cottage, Renfrew Road, Kingston Hill, Surrey. *T:* 01-942 8100.

**CLARK, Alec Fulton Charles,** CB 1960; Under-Secretary, Scottish Home and Health Department (retired); *b* 17 Dec. 1898; *yr s* of Charles and Mary Clark; *m* 1926, Mary, *er d* of David and Janet Watson; one *s* one *d*. *Educ:* Dunfermline High Sch.; Edinburgh Univ.; Lincoln Coll., Oxford. Asst Principal, Ministry of Agriculture and Fisheries, 1925; Principal, Ministry of Agriculture and Fisheries, 1934; Principal, Scottish Home Dept, 1939; Asst Sec. in Scottish Home Dept, 1942; promoted Under-Sec., 1953; retd 1963. *Recreation:* music. *Address:* 16 Lonsdale Terrace, Edinburgh 3. *T:* 031-229 7786. *Club:* Royal Over-Seas League (Edinburgh).

**CLARK, Sir Andrew Edmund James,** 3rd Bt *cr* 1883; MBE 1941; MC; QC 1943; *b* 18 July 1898; *o s* of Sir James Clark, 2nd Bt, CB, CMG, and Lilian Margaret, 2nd *d* of Robert Hopkins, Tidmarsh Manor, Berks; *S* father, 1948; *m* 1st, 1921, Angelica (*d* 1922), *d* of James Taylor, Strensham, Worcs; 2nd, 1924, Adeline Frances, *o d* of late Col A. D. Derviche-Jones, DSO; two *d*. *Educ:* Eton. 2nd Lieut Regular Army, RFA, 1916; served France and Belgium, 1916-18 (MC); Order of St John of Jerusalem;

retd, 1921. Called to Bar, Inner Temple, 1928, Lincoln's Inn, 1930; called up for service with Regular Army, 1939-45; Lieut-Col and Hon. Brigadier RARO. Bencher of Inner Temple, 1951; conducted Crichel Down Inquiry, 1954. *Publications:* The Way of Lucifer; God's Children; Selected Poems. *Recreations:* shooting, fishing, gardening. *Heir:* none. *Address:* Harcombe, near Chudleigh, S Devon. *T:* Chudleigh 2117. *Clubs:* Boodle's, MCC.

**CLARK, Arthur Campbell S.**; *see* Stuart-Clark.

**CLARK of Herriotshall, Arthur Melville,** MA (Hons); DPhil; DLitt; FRSE; FRSA; Reader in English Literature, Edinburgh University, 1946-60; *b* 20 Aug. 1895; 4th *s* of late James Clark and Margaret Moyes McLachlan, Edinburgh. *Educ:* Stewart's Coll., Edinburgh; Edinburgh Univ. (Sibbald Bursar and Vans Dunlop Scholar); Oriel Coll., Oxford (Scholar); MA First Class Hons and twice medallist, DLitt Edinburgh; DPhil Oxford. Lectr in English Language and Literature, Reading, 1920; Tutor to Oxford Home Students, 1921; Sec. of Oxford Union Soc., 1923; Pres. of Speculative Soc., 1926-29; Lectr in English Literature, Edinburgh Univ., 1928-46; Dir of Studies, Edinburgh Univ., 1931-47; Editor of Edinburgh University Calendar, 1933-45; External Examiner in English, St Andrews Univ., 1939-43, and Aberdeen Univ., 1944-46. Pres. of Scottish Arts Club, 1948-50. Pres. of Edinburgh Scott Club, 1957-58. Exhibitor RSA, SSA, etc. Chm., Scottish Students' Song Book Cttee Ltd. Knights's Cross, Order of Polonia Restituta, 1969. *Publications:* The Realistic Revolt in Modern Poetry, 1922; A Bibliography of Thomas Heywood (annotated), 1924; Thomas Heywood, Playwright and Miscellanist, 1931; Autobiography, its Genesis and Phases, 1935; Spoken English, 1946; Studies in Literary Modes, 1946; Two Pageants by Thomas Heywood, 1953; Sonnets from the French, and Other Verses, 1966; Sir Walter Scott: The Formative Years, 1969; contribs to Encyc. Brit., Collier's Encyc., Encyc. of Poetry and Poetics, Cambridge Bibl. of Eng. Lit., Library, Mod. Lang. Review, Classical Review, etc. *Recreations:* shooting, pastel-sketching. *Address:* 3 Woodburn Terrace, Edinburgh 10. *T:* 031-447 1240; Herriotshall, Oxton, Berwickshire. *Clubs:* New, Scottish Arts (Edinburgh); Union Society (Oxford).

**CLARK, Sir Beresford**; *see* Clark, Sir J. B.

**CLARK, Col Charles Willoughby,** DSO 1918; OBE 1945; MC 1916; DL; *b* 6 April 1888; *m* 1916; one *s* (one *d* decd). *Educ:* Atherstone Grammar Sch. Apprentice, Alfred Herbert Ltd, Coventry, 1904; Dir, 1934 (Chm. 1958-66). Served European War, 1914-18, France, Machine Gun Corps, Royal Tank Corps (MC, DSO, despatches twice). Chm. Coventry Conservative Assoc., 1945-48; Pres. Coventry Chamber of Commerce, 1951-53; Chm. Manufacturers' Section Cttee of Machine Tool Trades Assoc., 1946-55. Mem. Bd of Trade Machine Tool Advisory Council, 1957-66. Freeman of the City of London. Fellow Royal Commonwealth Society; FInstD; Mem. Inst of Export. DL Warwickshire, 1965. *Recreations:* shooting and fishing. *Address:* 49 Kenilworth Road, Leamington Spa, Warwickshire. *T:* Leamington Spa 2400; Brooklands Close, Ablington, near Bibury, Glos. *T:* Bidury 326. *Club:* Royal Automobile.

**CLARK, Colin Grant,** MA Oxon, MA Cantab; Research Fellow, Monash University, Melbourne, Australia; Director of Institute for Research in Agricultural Economics, Oxford, 1953-69; Fellow of the Econometric Society; *b* 2 Nov. 1905; *s* of James Clark, merchant and manufacturer, Townsville and Plymouth; *m* 1935, Marjorie Tattersall; eight *s* one *d*. *Educ:* Dragon Sch.; Winchester; Brasenose Coll., Oxford. Took degree in chemistry; Frances Wood Prizeman of the Royal Statistical Soc., 1928; Asst to late Prof. Allyn Young of Harvard; worked on the New Survey of London Life and Labour, 1928-29, and Social Survey of Merseyside, 1929-30; on Staff of Economic Advisory Council, Cabinet Offices, 1930-31; University Lectr in Statistics, Cambridge, 1931-37. Contested (Lab): North Dorset, 1929; Wavertree (Liverpool), 1931; South Norfolk, 1935. Visiting Lectr at Univs of Melbourne, Sydney, and Western Australia, 1937-38. Under-Sec. of State for Labour and Industry, Dir of Bureau of Industry, and Financial Adviser to the Treasury, Qld, 1938-52. Hon. ScD, Milan; Hon. DEcon, Tilburg, *Publications:* The National Income, 1924-31, 1932; (with Prof. A. C. Pigou) Economic Position of Great Britain, 1936; National Income and Outlay, 1937; (with J. G. Crawford) National Income of Australia, 1938; Critique of Russian Statistics, 1939; The Conditions of Economic Progress, 1940 (revised edns 1951 and 1957); The Economics of 1960, 1942; Welfare and Taxation, 1954; Australian Hopes and Fears, 1958; The Real Product of Soviet Russia, 1960; Taxmanship, 1964; (with Miss M. R. Haswell) The Economics of Subsistence Agriculture, 1964; Economics of Irrigation, 1967; Population Growth and Land Use, 1967; other pamphlets and numerous articles in Economic periodicals. *Recreations:* walking, gardening. *Address:* Mannix College, Monash University, Melbourne, Australia. *Club:* Johnsonian (Brisbane).

**CLARK, David Allen Richard**; *b* 18 July 1905; *s* of David Richard Clark and Sarah Ann Clark (*née* Clark); *m* 1932, Mary Kathleen, *y d* of Samuel Finney and Mary Ellen Finney (*née* Bagnall), Burslem, Stoke-on-Trent; three *s*. *Educ:* West Felton, Oswestry, C of E Sch.; Oswestry Boys' High Sch.; Oswestry Technical Coll.; Faculty of Technology, Manchester Univ. Stoney Prizeman, 1930; BScTech 1931; MScTech 1932. Apprentice fitter and turner, GWR Co., Oswestry Works, 1921-27; Asst, Surveyor's Office, Oswestry RDC, 1929; Draughtsman, Sentinel Steam Wagon Co. Ltd., Shrewsbury, 1930; Part-time Lectr, Manchester Coll. of Technology, 1931-32; Lectr, Heanor Mining and Technical Coll., 1932-36; Senior Lectr, Kingston-upon-Thames Technical Coll., 1936-39; Head of Engineering Dept, Luton Technical Coll., 1939-47; Principal, Constantine Technical Coll., Middlesbrough, 1947-55; Principal, Nottingham Regional Coll. of Technology, 1955-65. CEng, FIMechE. *Publications:* Materials and Structures, 1941; Advanced Strength of Materials, 1951; articles in technical and educational journals. *Recreation:* collection of old English pottery and porcelain. *Address:* Church Close, Great Wratting, Haverhill, Suffolk. *T:* Thurlow 229.

**CLARK, David (George)**; MP (Lab) Colne Valley since 1970; *b* 19 Oct. 1939; *s* of George and Janet Clark; *m* 1970, Christine Kirkby. *Educ:* Manchester Univ. (BA(Econ), MSc). Forester, 1956-57; Laboratory Asst in Textile Mill, 1957-59; Student Teacher, 1959-60; Student, 1960-63; Pres., Univ. of Manchester Union, 1963-64; Trainee Manager in USA, 1964; University Lecturer, 1965-70. Contested Manchester (Withington), Gen. Elec. 1966. *Publications:* The Industrial Manager, 1966; various articles on Management and Management Education. *Recreations:* fell-walking, ornithology. *Address:* House of Commons, SW1. *Clubs:* Golcar Socialist,

Honley Socialist, Slaithwaite Working Men's (all Yorks).

**CLARK, David S.**; *see* Stafford-Clark.

**CLARK, Desmond**; *see* Clark, John Desmond.

**CLARK, Mrs Edward**; *see* Lutyens, Elisabeth.

**CLARK, Sir Fife**; *see* Clark, Sir T. F.

**CLARK, Lt-Gen. Findlay**; *see* Clark, Lt-Gen. S. F.

**CLARK, Sir George Anthony**, 3rd Bt *cr* 1917; DL; Captain Reserve of Officers, Black Watch, 1939-64; Senator, N Ireland Parliament, 1951-69; *b* 24 Jan. 1914; *e s* of Sir George Ernest Clark, 2nd Bt and Norah Anne (*d* 1966), *d* of W. G. Wilson, Glasgow; *S* father 1950; *m* 1949, Nancy Catherine, 2nd *d* of George W. N. Clark, Carnabane, Upperlands, Co. Derry; one *d*. *Educ:* Canford. DL Belfast, 1961. *Recreations:* golf, tennis. *Heir: b* Colin Douglas Clark, MC, MA [*b* 20 July 1918; *m* 1946, Margaret Coleman, *d* of late Maj.-Gen. Sir Charlton Watson Spinks, KBE, DSO, and *widow* of Major G. W. Threlfall, MC; one *s* two *d*]. *Address:* Tullygirvan House, Ballygowan, Co. Down, Northern Ireland. *T:* Ballygowan 267. *Clubs:* Bath; Ulster (Belfast); Royal Ulster Yacht (Bangor, Co. Down); Kildare Street (Dublin).

**CLARK, Sir George (Norman)**, Kt 1953; DLitt, MA; Hon. LLD, Aberdeen; Hon. LitD, Utrecht; Hon. DLitt, Durham, Sheffield, Hull, Columbia; Hon. LittD, Dublin and Cambridge; Hon. Fellow: Trinity College, Dublin, 1953; Trinity College, Cambridge, 1955; Balliol and Oriel Colleges, Oxford, 1957; Trustee, British Museum, 1949-60; Member, University Grants Committee, 1951-58; President of the British Academy, 1954-58; President, Northamptonshire Record Society, 1958-65; *b* 27 Feb. 1890; *s* of late J. W. Clark, CBE, JP; *m* 1919, Barbara, *e d* of W. B. Keen; one *s* one *d*. *Educ:* Bootham Sch.; Manchester Grammar Sch.; Balliol Coll., Oxford; Brakenbury Scholar, 1908. 1st Cl. Lit. Hum., 1911; 1st Cl. Modern History, 1912; Fellow of All Souls Coll., 1912; 2nd Lieut Post Office Rifles, Aug. 1914; served in France; retd with rank of Capt., 1920; Fellow and Lectr of Oriel Coll., 1919-31; Tutor, 1922; Librarian, 1930; joined staff of English Historical Review, 1919; Editor, 1920-25; Joint Editor, 1925-26 and 1938-39; Univ. Lectr in Modern History, 1927-31; Proctor, 1929-30; Chichele Prof. of Economic History and Fellow of All Souls Coll., 1931-43; Regius Prof. of Modern History, and Fellow of Trinity Coll., Cambridge, 1943-47; Provost of Oriel Coll., Oxford, 1947-57, retd. Fellow of All Souls Coll., Oxford, 1961. Creighton Lectr, London Univ., 1948; Ford's Lectr, Oxford Univ., 1949-50; Murray Lectr, Glasgow Univ., 1952; Wiles Lectr, Queen's Univ., Belfast, 1956; Donnellan Lectr, Trinity Coll., Dublin, 1960; Whidden Lectr, McMaster Univ., 1960; Leslie Stephen Lectr, Cambridge Univ., 1965. FBA 1936; FRCP (Hon.) 1965. Mem., Royal Danish Acad. of Sciences; Foreign Mem., Royal Netherlands Academy of Sciences; Foreign Hon. Mem., American Acad. of Arts and Sciences and Amer. Historical Assoc. Comdr Order of Orange-Nassau. *Publications:* The Dutch Alliance and the War against French Trade, 1923; (with F. W. Weaver) Churchwarden's Accounts of Marston, etc, 1925; The Seventeenth Century, 1929; The Later Stuarts, 1934; Science and Social Welfare in the Age of Newton, 1937; Guide to English Commercial Statistics (1696-1782), 1938; (with W. J. M. van Eysinga) The Colonial Conferences between England and the Netherlands, 2 vols, 1940, 1951; The Wealth of England, 1946; Early Modern Europe, 1957; War and Society in the Seventeenth Century, 1958; The Campden Wonder, 1959; History of the Royal College of Physicians, 2 vols, 1964-66. *Address:* 7 Ethelred Court, Headington, Oxford OX3 9DA. *T:* Oxford 61028. *Club:* Athenæum.

**CLARK, Brig. George Philip**, CBE 1945; DSO 1940; *b* 25 March 1901; *e s* of late Rev. G. W. Clark; *m* 1st, 1936, Susan Caroline (*d* 1967), *o d* of late Major T. Close-Smith; one *s* one *d*; 2nd, 1969, Margaret Wheeler. *Educ:* Worcester; RMC Sandhurst. Joined Northamptonshire Regt, 1921; service in India and Sudan with Regiment; Capt. 1932; Major, 1938; Temp. Lieut-Col 1940; Temp. Col 1942; Temp. Brig. 1944; Col 1945. Served War of 1939-45 (despatches, DSO, CBE); retd pay, 1947. DL Suffolk, 1866-69. *Recreation:* hunting. *Address:* Stonehouse, Whitchurch, Aylesbury, Bucks. *T:* Whitchurch (Bucks) 555.

**CLARK, George Sidney R. K.**; *see* Kitson Clark.

**CLARK, Sir (Gordon Colvin) Lindesay**, KBE 1968; CMG 1961; MC; BSc; MME; Mining Engineer and Company Director, Australia; *b* 7 Jan. 1896; *s* of late Lindesay C. Clark, Launceston, Tas.; *m* 1922, Barbara J., *d* of A. C. Walch; one *s* two *d*. *Educ:* Church of England Grammar Sch., Launceston, Tasmania; Universities of Tasmania and Melbourne. Deputy-Controller of Mineral Production, Dept of Supply, Australia, 1942-44. Chairman: Western Mining Corp. Ltd, 1952; Central Norseman Gold Corp. NL, 1952; Gold Mines of Kalgoorlie (Aust.) Ltd, 1952; Broken Hill South Ltd, 1956; Dep. Chm., alcoa of Australia Ltd, 1970 (Chm., 1961-70); Director: North Broken Hill Ltd, 1953; Beach Petroleum NL, 1964; Central Norsman Minerals NL, 1969. Pres., Australasian Inst. of Mining and Metallurgy, 1959. Hon. DEng, Melbourne Univ., 1961. *Recreation:* golf. *Address:* (business) Collins House, 360 Collins Street, Melbourne, Victoria 3000, Australia. *T:* 67.7556; (private) 8 Moralla Road, Kooyong, Victoria 3144, Aust. *T:* 20.2675. *Clubs:* Melbourne, Australian (Melbourne); Tasmanian (Hobart); Weld (Perth).

**CLARK, Sir Henry Laurence**; *see* Urling Clark.

**CLARK, Henry Maitland**; Company director and public relations consultant; *b* 11 April 1929; *s* of Major H. F. Clark, Rockwood, Upperlands, Co. Londonderry; unmarried. *Educ:* Shrewsbury Sch.; Trinity Coll., Dublin; Trinity Hall, Cambridge. Entered Colonial Service and appointed District Officer, Tanganyika, 1951; served in various Districts of Tanganyika, 1951-59; resigned from Colonial Service, 1959. MP (UU) Antrim North (UK Parliament), Oct. 1959-1970; Vice-Chm. Conservative Trade and Overseas Develt Sub-Cttee; Member: British Delegation to Council of Europe and Western European Union, 1962-65; Advisory Council Food Law Res. Centre, Univ. of Brussels; Exec. Cttee, Lepra (British Leprosy Relief Assoc.); a Commonwealth Observer, Mauritius General Election, 1967. Vice-Pres., Dublin Univ. Boat Club. *Recreations:* rowing coach, sailing, shooting, golf, collecting old furniture. *Address:* Rockwood, Upperlands, Co. Derry, Northern Ireland. *T:* Maghera 237. *Clubs:* Royal Commonwealth Society; Leander; University (Dublin); Royal Portrush Golf.

**CLARK, Most Rev. Howard Hewlett**, DD; *b* 23 April 1903; *s* of Douglass Clark and Florence

Lilian Hewlett; *m* 1935, Anna Evelyn Wilson; one *s* three *d*. *Educ:* University of Toronto; Trinity College, Toronto. BA 1932. Christ Church Cathedral, Ottawa: Curate 1932. Priest-in-Charge, 1938, Rector 1939-54, Canon 1941; Dean of Ottawa, 1945; Bishop of Edmonton, 1954, Archibishop of Edmonton, 1959-61; Primate of Anglican Church of Canada, 1959-70; Metropolitan and Archbishop of Rupert's Land, 1961-69; Episcopal Canon of St George's Collegiate Church, Jerusalem, 1964-70. DD (*jure dignitatis*) Trinity College, Toronto, 1945; subsequently awarded numerous honorary doctorates in divinity and in civil law, both in Canada and abroad. *Publication:* The Christian Life According to the Prayer Book, 1957. *Address:* 252 Glenrose Avenue, Toronto 7, Ont, Canada.

**CLARK, James McAdam,** MC 1944; Consul-General, Paris, since 1970; *b* 13 Sept. 1916; *er s* of late James Heriot Clark, Wester Coltfield, and late Ella Catherine McAdam; *m* 1946, Denise Thérèse, *d* of late Dr Léon Dufournier, Paris; two *d*. *Educ:* Edinburgh Univ. BSc (Hons) Tech. Chemistry, 1938. Asst Lectr, Edinburgh Univ., 1938-39. Served Royal Artillery, 1939-46 (MC), rank of Capt.; Royal Mil. Coll. of Science, 1945-46 (pac). Min. of Fuel and Power, 1947-48. Entered Foreign (now Diplomatic) Service, 1948; FO, 1948-50; Head of Chancery, Quito, 1950-53; FO, 1953-56; Head of Chancery, Lisbon, 1956-60; Counsellor, UK Rep. to and Alternate Gov. of Internat. Atomic Energy Agency, Vienna, 1960-64; Head of Scientific Relations Dept, FO, 1964-66; Counsellor on secondment to Min. of Technology, 1966-70. Officer Order of Christ of Portugal, 1957. *Publications:* a number of poems and articles. *Recreations:* golf, sailing, music, disputation. *Address:* 23 Holland Park, W11. *T:* 01-727 8723; Tower House, Aldeburgh, Suffolk. *T:* Aldeburgh 2269; 2 rue de Miromesuil, Paris VIIIe, France. *T:* 265.06.99. *Clubs:* Travellers'; Aldeburgh Yacht, Aldeburgh Golf.

**CLARK, John,** OBE 1969; TD 1942; Chartered Surveyor; Partner (now Senior Partner) in J. M. Clark & Sons since 1925; *b* 11 June 1903; *s* of J. M. Clark, Haltwhistle, and Mrs Clark (*née* Jackson); *m* 1928, Audrey Irwin; one *s* three *d*. *Educ:* Oundle. Served 4th Bn, Royal Northumberland Fusiliers, 1922-43; retd as Lt-Col. President: Chartered Land Agents Soc., 1956; Royal Instn of Chartered Surveyors, 1969. *Recreation:* shooting. *Address:* Featherstone Castle, Haltwhistle, Northumberland. *Clubs:* National; Northern Counties (Newcastle upon Tyne).

**CLARK, John Allen;** Chairman, The Plessey Company Ltd, since 1970; *b* 14 Feb. 1926; *e s* of late Sir Allen Clark and Lady (Jocelyn) Clark, *d* of late Percy and Madeline Culverhouse; *m* 1952, Deirdre Kathleen (marr. diss. 1962), *d* of Samuel Herbert Waterhouse and Maeve Murphy Waterhouse; one *s* one *d*; *m* 1970, Olivia, *d* of H. Pratt and of Mrs J. A. Day. *Educ:* Harrow. Received early industrial training with Metropolitan Vickers and Ford Motor Co.; spent over a year in USA, studying the electronics industry. Served War of 1939-45; commissioned RNVR. Asst to Gen. Manager, Plessey International Ltd, 1949; Dir and Gen. Man., Plessey (Ireland) Ltd, and Wireless Telephone Co. Ltd, 1950; appointed to main board, The Plessey Co. Ltd, 1953; Gen. Man., Plessey Components Group, 1957; Man. Dir and Chief Executive, The Plessey Co. Ltd, 1962, Man. Dir, 1962-70, Dep. Chm., 1967-70; Dir, International Computers (Holdings) Ltd, 1968. Past Pres., Telecommunication Engineering and Manufacturing Assoc.; Vice-Pres., Inst. of Works Managers; Vice-Pres., Engineering Employers' Fedn. Companion, Instn of Elec. Engrs. *Recreations:* golf, shooting, swimming, flying helicopters. *Address:* The Plessey Co. Ltd, Ilford, Essex. *T:* 01-478 3040. *Club:* Bath.

*See also M. W. Clark.*

**CLARK, Brig.-Gen. John Arthur,** CMG 1919; DSO 1917; VD 1922; CD 1955; KC 1932; LLD 1952; Member, Advisory Board, Canada Trust Co. Ltd; Director, Stock Exchange Building Corp. Ltd; Hon. Member: American Bar Assoc.; Bar of Mons, Belgium; *b* Dundas, Ontario; *s* of William and Frances J. Clark; *m* Jean Abercrombie, *d* of late Donald McGillivray, Vancouver, BC; two *s* two *d*. *Educ:* Toronto Univ. (BA, LLB); Osgoode Hall. Practises Law, Clark, Wilson & Co., Vancouver, BC; Dominion Vice-Pres., Canadian Bar Assoc., 1950-51; Pres., Canadian Bar Assoc., 1951-52. Dir, Mutual Life Assurance Company, Canada, 1952-66. Commanded 72nd Seaforth Highlanders of Canada, 1915-18; commanded 7th Canadian Infantry Brigade, 1918, to demobilisation; Canadian Representative, British Mission to Italy, 1917 (CMG, DSO and two bars, despatches five times); Hon. Col Seaforth Highlanders of Canada; Citoyen d'Honneur: City of Mons; Province of Hainaut. Mem. Canadian House of Commons for Vancouver-Burrard, 1921-30; a Conservative. Chm., Canadian Nat. Inst. for the Blind, 1949-53, Hon. Counsel, 1953-; Hon. Solicitor, Vancover Red Cross, 1941-56. Gov., St George's Sch. *Recreation:* golf. *Address:* 475 Howe Street, Vancouver, BC. *Clubs:* Vancouver; Capilano Golf and Country.

**CLARK, Prof. J(ohn) Desmond,** CBE 1960; FBA 1961; FSA 1952; FRS (SA) 1959; PhD; Professor of Anthropology, University of California, Berkeley, USA, since 1961; *b* London, 10 April 1916; *s* of late Thomas John Chown Clark and Catharine (*née* Wynne); *m* 1938, Betty Cable, *d* of late Henry Lea Baume and late Frances M. S. (*née* Brown); one *s* one *d*. *Educ:* Monkton Combe Sch.; Christ's Coll., Cambridge. PhD in Archaeology (Cambridge), 1950. Dir, Rhodes-Livingstone Museum, Livingstone, N Rhodesia, 1938-61. Has conducted excavations in Southern, East and Equatorial Africa, the Sahara, and Syria, 1938-. Military Service in East Africa, Abyssinia, The Somalilands and Madagascar, 1941-46. Founder Mem. and Sec., N Rhodesia Nat. Monuments Commn, 1948-61. Corr. Mem. Scientific Coun. for Africa South of the Sahara, 1956-64, etc. Fellow, Amer. Acad. of Arts and Sciences, 1965. Comdr, Nat. Order of Senegal, 1968. *Publications:* The Prehistoric Cultures of the Horn of Africa, 1954; The Prehistory of Southern Africa, 1959; The Stone Age Cultures of Northern Rhodesia, 1960; Prehistoric Cultures of Northeast Angola and their Significance in Tropical Africa, 1963. (Ed.) Proc. 3rd Pan-African Congress on Pre-history, 1957; (comp.) Atlas of African Pre-history, 1967; (Ed., with W. W. Bishop) Background to Evolution in Africa, 1967; Kalambo Falls Prehistoric Site, vol. 1, 1969; The Prehistory of Africa, 1970; contribs to learned journals on prehistoric archaeology. *Recreations:* rowing, walking, photography. *Address:* 1941 Yosemite Road, Berkeley, Calif. 94707, USA. *T:* 525/4519 Area Code 415. *Club:* Royal Commonwealth Society.

**CLARK, Prof. John Grahame Douglas,** FBA 1951; MA, PhD, ScD (Cantab); Disney Professor of Archæology, Cambridge, since 1952; Head of Department of Archæology and Anthropology, Cambridge, 1956-61, and since 1968; Fellow of Peterhouse; *b* 28 July 1907; *s* of

Lt-Col Charles Douglas Clark and Maude Ethel Grahame Clark (*née* Shaw); *m* 1936, Gwladys Maude (*née* White); two *s* one *d*. *Educ:* Marlborough Coll.; Peterhouse, Cambridge. Research Student, 1930-32, and Bye-Fellow, 1933-35, of Peterhouse; Faculty Asst Lectr in Archæology, Cambridge, 1935-46, and Univ. Lectr, 1946-52. Served War of 1939-45, RAFVR, in Photographic Interpretation, 1941-43, and Air Historical Br., 1943-45. Munro Lectr in Archæology, Edinburgh Univ., 1949; Dalrymple Lectr in Archæology, Glasgow Univ., 1955; G. Grant MacCurdy Lectr, Harvard, 1957; William Evans Visiting Prof., Univ. of Otago, NZ, 1964; Commonwealth Visiting Fellow, Australia, 1964; Hitchcock Prof., Univ. of California, Berkeley, 1969. Reckitt Lecture, British Academy, 1954. mem. Ancient Monuments Board, 1954. Hon. Editor, Proceedings Prhistoric Soc., 1935-70. Hon. Corr. Mem., Royal Society Northern Antiquaries, Copenhagen, 1946, and of Swiss Prehistoric Soc., 1951; Fellow, German Archæological Inst., 1954; Hon. Mem., Royal Irish Academy, 1955; For. Mem., Finnish Archæological Soc., 1958; For. Hon. Mem., Amer. Acad. of Arts and Sciences, 1961; For. Mem., Royal Danish Acad. of Sciences and Letters, 1964; For. Mem., Royal Netherlands Acad. of Sciences, 1964; For. Fellow, Royal Society of Sciences, Uppsala, 1964; Mem., Royal Commission on Historical Monuments, 1957-69; Pres., Prehistoric Soc., 1958-62; Vice-Pres., Soc. of Antiquaries, 1959-62. Hodgkins Medal, Smithsonian Institution, 1967. Comdr, Order of the Danebrog, 1961. *Publications:* The Mesolithic Settlement of Northern Europe, 1936; Archæology and Society 1939, 1947 and 1957; Prehistoric England, 1940, 1941, 1945, 1948, 1962; From Savagery to Civilization, 1946; Prehistoric Europe, The Economic Basis, 1952; Excavations at Star Carr, 1954; The Study of Prehistory, 1954; World Prehistory, An Outline, 1961; (with Stuart Piggott) Prehistoric Societies, 1965; The Stone Age Hunters, 1967; World Prehistory, a new outline, 1969; Aspects of Prehistory, 1970; numerous papers in archæological journals. *Recreations:* gardening, travel, contemporary art. *Address:* 19 Wilberforce Road, Cambridge. *T:* Cambridge 59376. *Club:* Oxford and Cambridge University.

**CLARK, Leonard,** OBE 1966; poet and author; retired HM Inspector of Schools; *b* 1 Aug. 1905; *m* Jane, *d* of William Mark Callow, New Cross, and Annie Maria Callow (*née* Graham); one *s* one *d*. *Educ:* Monmouth Sch.; Normal Coll., Bangor. Teacher in Glos and London, 1922-28, 1930-36; Asst Inspector of Schools, Bd of Educn, 1936-45; HM Inspector of Schools, Min. of Educn (later DES), 1945-70; worked in SW, E and W Ridings, and Metropolitan Divisions; visits to Germany, Malta, Mauritius. Home Guard (Devon Regt), 1940-43. Consultant on Poetry for Seafarers' Educn Service, 1940-54; Mem., Literature Panel, Arts Council of GB, 1965-69. Member: Westminster Diocesan Schools Commn, 1970; Exec. Cttee, NBL, 1970. Liveryman of Haberdashers' Co., 1965; Freeman, City of London, 1965. Hon. Life Mem., NUT, 1970. FRSL, 1953. Kt, Order of St Sylvester, 1970. *Publications:* Poems, 1925; (ed) The Open Door: anthology of verse for juniors, 1937; Passage to the Pole, 1944; (ed) The Kingdom of the Mind: essays and addresses of Albert Mansbridge, 1945; (ed) Alfred Williams: his life and work, 1945; Rhandanim, 1945; XII Poems, 1948; The Mirror (poems), 1948; English Morning (poems), 1953; Walter de la Mare, a checklist, 1956; Sark Discovered, 1956; (ed) Andrew Young: prospect of a poet, 1957; (trans. jtly) Edmond de Goncourt, The Zemganno Brothers, 1957; Selected Poems, 1958; (ed) Quiet as Moss, 36 poems by Andrew Young, 1959; Walter de la Mare: a monograph, 1960; (ed) Collected Poems of Andrew Young, with bibliographical notes, 1960; (comp.) Drums and Trumpets: poetry for the youngest, 1962; Green Wood (autobiography), 1962; Daybreak (poems), 1963; When They Were Children, 1964; (comp.) Common Ground: an anthology for the young, 1964; Who Killed the Bears?, 1964; Andrew Young, 1964; (comp.) All Things New: anthology, 1965; (comp.) The Poetry of Nature, 1965; A Fool in the Forest (autobiography), 1965; The Year Round (poems), 1965; Robert Andrew Tells a Story, 1965; Robert Andrew and the Holy Family, 1965; Robert Andrew and Tiffy, 1965; Robert Andrew by the Sea, 1965; Robert Andrew and the Red Indian Chief, 1966; Robert Andrew and Skippy, 1966; Robert Andrew in the Country, 1966; Fields and Territories (poems), 1967; Prospect of Highgate and Hampstead, 1967; Grateful Caliban (autobiography), 1967; Flutes and Cymbals: an anthology for the young, 1968; (ed) Sound of Battle, 1969; (introd) Life in a Railway Factory by Alfred Williams, 1969; Near and Far (poems), 1969; Here and There (poems), 1969; (ed jtly) The Complete Poems of Walter de la Mare, 1970; (ed) Longmans Poetry Library (64 titles), 1970; Walking With Trees (poems), 1970; (comp.) Poems by Children, 1970; contrib. poems and articles to learned jls in GB and USA. *Recreations:* gardening, music, book collecting, writing. *Address:* 50 Cholmeley Crescent, Highgate, N6. *T:* 01-348 0092. *Clubs:* National Liberal, PEN.

**CLARK, Leslie Joseph,** BEM 1942; Chairman, Northern Gas Board, since 1967; *b* 21 May 1914; *s* of Joseph George Clark and Elizabeth (*née* Winslow); *m* 1940, Mary M. Peacock; one *s* one *d*. *Educ:* Stationers' Company's Sch.; King's Coll., London. BSc (Eng), 1st Cl. Hons, 1934; MSc 1948. Engineer, Gas Light & Coke Co., then North Thames Gas Board. Chief Engineer, North Thames Gas Board, 1962-65, Dep. Chm., 1965-67. Pres., Instn of Gas Engineers, 1965-66. *Publications:* technical papers to Instns of Gas Engineers and Mech. Engrs, Inst. of Fuel, World Power Conf., Internat. Gas Union, etc. *Recreations:* model engineering, walking, photography, music. *Address:* Hillway, New Ridley Road, Stocksfield, Northumberland. *T:* Stocksfield 2339. *Club:* Anglo-Belgian.

**CLARK, Sir Lindesay;** *see* Clark, Sir G. C. L.

**CLARK, Mrs Margaret;** *see* Storm, Lesley.

**CLARK, Marjorie,** (Pen-name, Georgia Rivers); journalist, writer of fiction; *b* Melbourne; *d* of George A. and Gertrude M. Clark. *Educ:* Milverton Girls' Grammar Sch. *Publications:* Jacqueline, 1927; Tantalego, 1928; The Difficult Art, 1929; She Dresses for Dinner, 1933; 12 full-length serials, numerous short stories and articles. *Recreation:* music. *Address:* 27 Moorhouse Street, East Camberwell, Vic., Australia. *Club:* PEN (Melbourne Centre).

**CLARK, Gen. Mark Wayne,** DSC (US); DSM (3 Oak Leaf Clusters) (US Army); DSM (US Navy); US Army, retired; President Emeritus, The Citadel, Military College of South Carolina (President, 1954-65); *b* Madison Barracks, New York, USA, 1 May 1896; *s* of Col Charles Carr and Rebecca Clark; *m* 1st, 1924, Maurine Doran (*d* 1966); one *s* (one *d* decd); 2nd, 1967, Mrs Mary Millard Applegate, Muncie, Ind. *Educ:* United States

Mil. Acad. (BS 1917); Infantry Sch. (grad. 1925); Comd and Gen. Staff Sch. (grad. 1935); Army War Coll. (grad. 1937). Served European War, 1917-18 (wounded); Dep. Chief of Staff, Civilian Conservation Corps, 1936-37; Mem. Gen. Staff Corps, March-June 1942; Chief of Staff for Ground Forces, May 1942; C-in-C Ground Forces in Europe, July 1942; led successful secret mission by submarine to get information in N Africa preparatory to Allied invasion, 1942; Comdr Fifth Army in Anglo-American invasion of Italy, 1943, capture of Rome, June 1944; Commanding Gen. 15th Army Group, Dec. 1944; Gen., 1945; US High Commissioner and Comdg Gen. US Forces in Austria, 1945-47; dep. US Sec. of State, 1947; sat in London and Moscow with Council of Foreign Ministers negotiating a treaty for Austria, 1947; Comdg Gen. 6th US Army, HQ San Francisco, 1947-49; Chief, US Army Field Forces, Fort Monroe, Virginia, 1949-52; 1952-53: Comdr-in-Chief, United Nations Command; C-in-C, Far East; Commanding Gen., US Army Forces in the Far East; Governor of the Ryukyu Islands. Thanks of US House of Representatives, 1945. Hon. KCB 1955; Hon. KBE 1944. Hon. DCL Oxford, 1945; many other awards and honours, both American and foreign. *Publications:* Calculated Risk, 1950; From the Danube to the Yalu, 1954. *Recreations:* fishing, hunting, golfing and hiking. *Address:* Francis Marion Hotel, Charleston, South Carolina 29402, USA. *T:* 722-5573.

**CLARK, Michael William;** Deputy Managing Director, Plessey Co. Ltd, since 1962; *b* 7 May 1927; *yr s* of late Sir Allen (George) Clark and late Lady (Jocelyn Anita Marie Louise) Clark (*née* Culverhouse); *m* 1955, Shirley (*née* MacPhadyen); two *s* two *d. Educ:* Harrow. 1st Foot Guards, Subaltern, 1945-48. Ford Motor Co., 1948-49; Bendix Aviation (USA), 1949-50; Plessey Co. Ltd, 1950- (Exec. Dir, 1951; formed Electronics Div., 1951; Main Bd Dir, 1953, and responsible for Electronic and Equipment Group); formed Plessey (UK) Ltd (Chm. and Man. Dir, 1962; Dir responsible for Corporate Planning, 1965; Dir responsible for Home Groups, 1969-). Comp. IEE, 1964; Comp. IERE, 1965. *Publications:* various articles. *Recreations:* shooting, fishing, forestry. *Address:* Braxted Park, Witham, Essex. *T:* Wickham Bishops 393. *Club:* Bath.
*See also J. A. Clark.*

**CLARK, Philip Lindsey,** DSO; FRBS; sculptor; *b* 1889; *m* 1917, Truda Mary Cainan (*d* 1952); six *s*; *m* 1962, Monica Mary Hansford. *Educ:* Douglas House Sch., Cheltenham. Studied sculpture at the Royal Academy Schs, London; served European War, 1914-18, Artists' Rifles, Royal Sussex Regt, rank of Capt. (despatches, DSO); War of 1939-45, Cameronians (Scottish Rifles), RAF Regt and RNVR, 1940-45. First exhibited sculpture at Royal Academy, 1920; Paris Salon, 1921. *Works:* The Cameronians (Scottish Rifles) War Memorial (1914-18), glasgow; St Saviour's (Southwark) War Memorial, Boro High Street; sculpture on Belgian Soldiers' Memorial (1914-18), Kensal Green, awarded Palm of Order of Crown of Belgium, 1932; sculpture in wood, stone and bronze works in Westminster Cathedral, Aylesford Priory, English Martyrs Church, Wallasey, and in and on many other churches and public buildings. *Address:* Flat 2, 6 Douglas Avenue, Exmouth, Devon. *T:* Exmouth 3570.

**CLARK, Ramsey;** Partner, law firm of Paul, Weiss, Goldberg, Rifkind, Wharton and Garrison, 345 Park Avenue, New York; *b* Dallas, Texas, 18 Dec. 1927; *s* of Thomas Campbell Clark, *qv*; *m* 1949, Georgia Welch, Corpus Christi, Texas; one *s* one *d. Educ:* Public Schs, Dallas, Los Angeles, Washington; Univ. of Texas (BA); Univ. of Chicago (MA, JD). US Marine Corps, 1945-46. Admitted to: State Bar of Texas, 1951; Bar of Supreme Court of US, 1956; Bar of the District of Columbia. Attorney General of the US, 1967-69. Member: Federal Bar Assoc.; Amer. Bar Assoc.; Amer. Judicature Soc. Engaged private practice of law, Dallas, 1951-61; Asst Attorney Gen., Lands Div., Dept of Justice, 1961-65; Dep. Attorney Gen., 1965-66; Actg Attorney Gen., 1966-67. *Address:* 6393 Lakeview Drive, Falls Church, Virginia, USA.

**CLARK, His Honour Reginald,** QC 1949; Judge of Clerkenwell, Middlesex, County Court Circuit 41, 1955-66, retired; *b* 18 March 1895; *y s* of J. T. Clark, Manchester; *m* 1923, Joan Marguerite, *y d* of R. Herbert Shiers, Bowdon, Ches.; three *d. Educ:* Trinity Hall, Cambridge. Called to Bar, Lincoln's Inn, 1920; Northern Circuit, 1920-23; practised Rangoon Bar, 1924-41; Judge, High Court, Madras, 1944; resigned from Madras High Court, 1948. Chm., N Midland District Valuation Board, Coal Nationalisation Act, 1948-49; Chm., Road and Rail Appeal Tribunal, 1949. Comr of Assize, North-Eastern, Western and South-Eastern Circuits, 1949; a County Court Judge, Circuit 58, Ilford, etc, 1950-55. Served in TF, European War, 1914-18, Gallipoli and France. Served in Army in Burma and India, 1942-44. *Recreations:* fishing and golf. *Address:* 25 Campden Hill Gate, Duchess of Bedford Walk, W8. *T:* 01-937 1460. *Club:* East India and Sports.

**CLARK, Very Rev. Robert James Vodden;** Dean of Edinburgh since 1967; Canon of Edinburgh Cathedral, 1962; Rector of St Leonard's, Lasswade, Midlothian, since 1969; *b* 12 April 1907; *s* of Albert Arther Clark and Bessie Vodden; *m* 1934, Ethel Dolina McGregor Alexander; one *d. Educ:* Dalry Normal Practising Episcopal Church Sch.; Edinburgh; Church Army Coll.; Coates Hall Theol. Coll. Ordained, 1941. Men's Social Dept, Church Army, 1926; varied work in homes for men; special work in probation trng home under Home Office, 1934-39; St Paul and St George, Edinburgh, 1941-44; Rector, St Andrew's, Fort William, 1944-47; seconded to Scottish Educn Dept as Warden-Leader of Scottish Centre of Outdoor Trng, Glenmore Lodge, 1947-49; Curate i/c St David's, Edinburgh, 1949-54; Rector of Christ Church, Falkirk, 1954-69. Mem., Royal Highland and Agric. Soc. *Recreations:* mountaineering (Mem., Scottish Mountaineering Club); photography (Mem., Falkirk Photographic Club). *Address:* St Leonard's Rectory, Dobbie's Road, Lasswade, Midlothian.

**CLARK, Lieut-Gen. (Samuel) Findlay,** CBE 1945; CD 1950; MEIC; PEng; President, World Wild Life Fund (Canada); Director, Royal Canadian Geographical Society; *b* 17 March 1909; *m* 1937, Leona Blanche Seagram. *Educ:* Univ. of Manitoba (BScEE); Univ. of Saskatchewan (BScME). Lieut, Royal Canadian Signals, 1933. Assoc. Prof. of Elec. and Mechan. Engrg (Capt.) at RMC Kingston, 1938. Overseas to UK, Aug. 1940 (Major); Comd 5th Canadian Armd Div. Sigs Regt (Lt-Col), 1941. GSO1 Can. Mil. HQ, London, 1942; Staff Course, Camberley, England (Col), 1942-43; CSO, HQ 2nd Canadian Corps until end of War (Brig. 1943). Dep. Chief of Gen. Staff, 1945; Imperial Defence Coll., 1948; Canadian Mil. Observer on Western Union Mil. Cttee; Maj.-Gen. 1949; Canadian Mil. Rep. NATO, London, 1949; Chm., Joint Staff. CALE, London, 1951; QMG of Canadian Army, 1951; GOC Central Comd, 1955; CGS, Sept. 1958-61. Chm., Nat.

Capital Commission, 1961-67. Col Comdt, Royal Canadian Corps of Signals. Legion of Merit (USA), 1945; Comdr Order of Orange Nassau (Netherlands), 1945. *Recreations:* fishing, shooting. *Address:* 3180 Midland Road, Victoria, BC, Canada. T: 382-6767. *Club:* Union (Victoria).

**CLARK, Ven. Sidney Harvie,** MA; Archdeacon of Stow since 1967 and Vicar of Hackthorn and Rector of Cold Hanworth since 1967; *b* 26 July 1905; *s* of John Harvie Clark and Minnie Young Hunter, Glasgow and Chiswick, London; *m* 1936, Sheilah Marjorie, *d* of late Dr G. C. L. Lunt, Bishop of Salisbury; one *s* one *d* (one *d* decd). *Educ:* St Paul's Sch., London; Jesus Coll. and Westcott House, Cambridge. Deacon, 1930; Priest, 1931; Curate, St Mary's, Gateshead, Co. Durham, 1930-34; St Mary's, Portsea, 1934-36; Rector, Jarrow-on-Tyne, 1936-40; St John's, Edinburgh, 1940-47; Rector of Wishaw, 1947-48; Archdeacon of Birmingham, 1947-67; Vicar of Harborne, 1948-67. *Recreations:* walking, camping. *Address:* Hackthorn Vicarage, Lincoln. *T:* Hackthorn 382. *Club:* Royal Commonwealth Society.

**CLARK, Sir Stewart S.;** *see* Stewart-Clark.

**CLARK, Stuart Ellis;** *b* 6 Feb. 1899; *s* of Robert and Susanah Clark, Dartford, Kent; *m* 1st, 1923, Mabel Olive Winspear (*d* 1932); one *s*; 2nd, 1935, Joan Bulley. *Educ:* Wilson's Sch. Acting Sec., Southern Rly Co., 1944; Asst Docks and Marine Manager, Southern Rly Co., Southampton Docks, 1947; Sec., Docks Executive, 1948; Sec., Docks and Inland Waterways Board of Management, British Transport Commission, 1950-55. *Recreations:* golf, swimming. *Address:* Knapp Cottage, Wambrook, near Chard, Somerset. *T:* Chard 2442.

**CLARK, Sir Thomas,** 3rd Bt *cr* 1886; DL; FRSE 1932; late senior partner, publishing firm of T. & T. Clark, Edinburgh; Major, Late 7th Battalion Royal Scots (the Royal Regiment); *b* 30 March 1886; *s* of 2nd Bt and Helen (*d* 1942), *d* of Rev. H. M. Douglas; *S* father, 1924; *m* 1914, Ellen Mercy, *o d* of late Francis Drake; two *s* two *d*. *Educ:* Edinburgh Academy; University Coll., Oxford. Chm., City of Edinburgh Territorial and Auxiliary Forces Assoc., 1947-50; late Hon. Col 414 (Forth) Coast Regt, RA TA; DL Edinburgh 1955. *Heir:* *s* John Douglas Clark, *b* 9 Jan. 1923. *Address:* 23 Wester Coates Avenue, Edinburgh 12. *T:* 031-337 1913. *Club:* Caledonian United Service and Northern (Edinburgh).

**CLARK, Thomas Archibald B.;** *see* Bennet-Clark.

**CLARK, Thomas Campbell, (Tom C. Clark);** a Justice of the Supreme Court, US, 1949; retired, 1967; former Director, Federal Judicial Center, Washington, DC; *b* 23 Sept. 1899; *s* of William H. Clark and Jennie Falls; *m* 1924, Mary Ramsey; one *s* one *d* (and one *s* decd). *Educ:* Grade Sch. and High Sch., Dallas, Texas; Virginia Military Inst.; Univ. of Texas (AB, LLB). Associated with Clark and Clark, Dallas, Texas, 1922-27; served European War, 1917-18, 153rd Inf. US Army. Civil District Attorney for Dallas County, Texas, 1927; Asst Attorney-Gen. in charge of Anti-trust Div., Dept of Justice, 1943; Asst Attorney-Gen. in charge of Criminal Div., Dept of Justice, 1943-45; Attorney-Gen., 1945-49. Fraternities: Delta Tau Delta, Phi Alpha Delta, Order of Coif. Holds numerous hon. doctorates in Law from Amer. Univs and Colls; Distinguished Alumnus Award, Univ. of Texas, 1962; Amer. Bar Assoc. Gold Medal, 1962, and other medals. *Address:* 2101 Connecticut Avenue, NW, Washington, DC. *T:* Decatur 2-2101; (business) Supreme Court Building, Washington, DC 20543. *T:* Executive 3-1640. *Clubs:* Chevy Chase (Md); Burning Tree; Alfalfa; University, National Lawyers' (Washington, DC).

*See also Ramsey Clark.*

**CLARK, Sir (Thomas) Fife,** Kt 1965; CBE 1949; Director-General, Central Office of Information, since 1954; *b* 1907; *m*; two *s* one *d*. *Educ:* Middlesbrough High Sch. (North Riding Scholar). Formerly Parly lobby corresp. and diplomatic correspondent, Westminster Press provincial newspapers. Public Relations and Principal Press Officer, Min. of Health, 1939-49; Controller, Home Publicity, COI, 1949-52; Adviser on Govt Public Relations and Adviser on Public Relations to the Prime Minister, 1952-55. Pres., Internat. Public Relations Assoc., 1955-57; Fellow and Past Pres., Inst. of Public Relations (President's Medal, 1967); Pres., Civil Service Horticultural Fedn, 1959-. Mem., Coun. of Management, Brighton Arts Festival, 1966-. *Address:* Wave Hill, Nevill Road, Rottingdean, Sussex. *T:* Brighton 33020.

**CLARK, Tom C.;** *see* Clark, Thomas Campbell.

**CLARK, Prof. Sir Wilfrid (Edward) Le Gros,** Kt 1955; FRS 1935; MA, DSc, Hon. DSc (Durham, Manchester, Edinburgh, Witwatersrand, S Africa); Hon. MD (Melbourne, Oslo); Hon. LLD (Malaya); FRCS; Professor of Anatomy, Oxford University, 1934-Oct. 1962; Director, MRC Unit for Research on Climatic and Working Efficiency, 1948-62; *b* Hemel Hempstead, 5 June 1895; *s* of Rev. Travers Clark; *m* 1st, 1923, Freda Constance Giddey (*d* 1963); two *d*; 2nd, 1964, Violet, *widow* of late Leonard Browne, MD. *Educ:* Blundell's Sch., Tiverton; St Thomas's Hospital. Capt. RAMC, 1918; Principal Medical Officer of Sarawak, Borneo, 1920-23; Reader in Anatomy, Univ. of London, 1924-27; Prof. of Anatomy, at St Bartholomew's Hosp., 1927-29, at St Thomas's Hosp., 1929-34; Mem., Anat., Physiol. and Zool. Soc. (Vice-Pres., Zool. Soc., 1942-44); Vice-Pres., Royal Anthropological Inst., 1939-42, 1947-52; Council, Royal Society, 1942-44; Mem., Medical Research Council, 1950-54; Pres. Anthropology Sect., British Assoc., 1939; Pres., Internat. Anat. Congress, 1950; Pres., British Assoc., 1961; Pres., Anatomical Soc., 1952-53; Mem., Norwegian Academy of Art and Science; For. Mem., Kungl. Vetenshaps. Soc. Uppsala; For. Assoc. Acad. Nacional Med. Buenos Aires; Hon. Mem., Royal Society New Zealand, 1954; Mem., Amer. Phil. Soc., Hon. Life Mem., New York Acad. Sc.; Mem, Nat. Acad. Sc., Washington. Doyne Memorial Medal, 1942; Viking Medal, 1956; Royal Medal, Royal Society, 1961. Arris and Gale Lect., RCS, 1932; Hunterian Prof., RCS, 1934, 1945; Henderson Lect., Edinburgh, 1936; Triennial Prize, RCS, 1947; Robert Boyle Lect., 1947; William Smith Lect., 1949; Earl Grey Mem. Lect., 1949; Hunter Mem. Lect., Sydney Univ., 1952; Munro Lectures, Edinburgh, 1953; Lady Jones Lectures, 1953; Ferris Lect., Yale Univ., 1956; Ferrier Lect., Royal Society, 1956; Maudsley Lect., 1957; Edridge-Green Lect., RCS, 1961; Harvey Lect., NY Acad. of Medicine. Past Examiner in Anatomy for RCS, and Univs of London, Durham, Wales and Bristol. Master Salters' Company, 1954. Hon. Fellow Hertford Coll., Oxford, 1962. *Publications:* Early Forerunners of Man, 1934; Morphological Aspects of the Hypothalamus, 1936; The Tissues of the Body, 6th edn 1970; Central Nervous System (Cunningham's

Anatomy), 1943, 1956; History of the Primates, 1949, 8th edn 1962; The Fossil Evidence for Human Evolution, 2nd edn 1964; The Antecedents of Man, 3rd edn 1970; Chant of Pleasant Exploration, 1968; numerous papers in Phil. Trans Royal Society and other scientific journals on neurology, anatomy, anthropology and palæontology; Editor, Jl Anat., 1940-45. *Address:* 16 Park Close, Templar Road, Oxford. *T:* Oxford 52716.

**CLARK, William Donaldson;** Director of Information and Public Affairs, International Bank for Reconstruction and Development, since 1968; *b* 28 July 1916; *y s* of John McClare Clark and Marion Jackson; unmarried. *Educ:* Oundle Sch.; Oriel Coll., Oxford (MA). 1st class Hons Mod. Hist., Gibbs Prize. Commonwealth Fellow and Lectr in Humanities, Univ. of Chicago, 1938-40; Min. of Information, and Brit. Inf. Services, Chicago, 1941-44; Press Attaché, Washington, 1945-46; London Editor, Encyclopædia Britannica, 1946-49; Diplomatic Corresp., Observer, 1950-55; Public Relations Adviser to Prime Minister, 1955-56; toured Africa and Asia for BBC and Observer, 1957; Editor of "The Week" in Observer, 1958-60; Dir, Overseas Development Inst., 1960-68. Frequent broadcasts and television appearances, including original Press Conference series (BBC), and Right to Reply (ATV). *Publications:* Less than Kin: a study of Anglo-American relations, 1957; What is the Commonwealth?, 1958; Number 10 (novel and (with Ronald Miller) play), 1966; Special Relationship (novel), 1968. *Recreations:* writing, talking, travel. *Address:* (office) World Bank, 1818 H Street NW, Washington, DC 20433, USA; (home) 3407 Rodman Street NW, Washington, DC 20008, USA. *T:* 363-0499; The Mill, Cuxham, Oxford. *T:* Watlington 381; Biniparell, Menorca, Baleares, Spain. *Clubs:* Athenæum, Savile; Tavern (Chicago).

**CLARK, William Gibson;** MP (C) East Surrey, since 1970; *b* 18 Oct. 1917; *m* 1944, Irene Dorothy Dawson Rands; three *s* one *d*. *Educ:* London. Mem. Association of Certified Accountants, 1941. Served in Army, 1941-46 (UK and India), Major. Mem. Wandsworth Borough Council, 1949-53 (Vice-Chm. Finance Cttee). Contested (C) Northampton, 1955; MP (C) Nottingham South, 1959-66. *Recreations:* tennis, gardening. *Address:* The Clock House, Box End, Bedford. *T:* Kempston 2361; 3 Barton Street, SW1. *T:* 01-930 5759. *Clubs:* Athenæum, Junior Carlton, Buck's.

**CLARK HUTCHISON, Alan Michael;** *see* Hutchison, A. M. C.

**CLARK-KENNEDY, Archibald Edmund,** MD (Cantab); FRCP; Fellow of Corpus Christi College, Cambridge, since 1919; Physician to the London Hospital, 1928-58; Dean of the London Hospital Medical College, 1937-53; *s* of late Rev. A. E. Clark-Kennedy (RN retired), Rector of Ewhurst, Surrey; *m* 1918, Phyllis, *d* of late Charles Howard Jeffree, Howard Lodge, Clapham Park; one *s* one *d*. *Educ:* Wellington Coll.; Corpus Christi Coll., Cambridge (exhibitioner, scholar). 1st class hons in Natural Science Tripos. Lieut, Queen's Royal West Surrey Regt (5th Territorial Bn), Aug. 1914; served as a combatant officer in India, then in Mesopotamia with IEF, D; returned to England, 1917; obtained diploma of MRCS and LRCP; commd in RAMC, 1918; served in France as MO to 158th Army RFA Bde. MRCP 1922; FRCP 1930. *Publications:* Stephen Hales, DD, FRS, an Eighteenth Century Biography, 1929; Medicine (two vols): Vol. I, The Patient and his Disease, 1947; Vol. II, Diagnosis, Prognosis and Treatment; Medicine in its Human Setting, 1954; Patients as People, 1957; Human Disease (a Pelican medical book), 1957; How to Learn Medicine, 1959; Clinical Medicine, The Modern Approach, 1960; The London: A Study in the Voluntary Hospital System (two vols): Vol. I, The First Hundred Years, 1740-1840, 1962; Vol. II, The Second Hundred Years, 1840-1948, 1963; Edith Cavell, Pioneer and Patriot, 1965; Man, Medicine and Morality, 1969; papers in medical and scientific journals. *Recreations:* mountaineering, sailing, hunting. *Address:* 8 Grange Road, Cambridge. *T:* Cambridge 52323.

**CLARKE, Arthur Charles;** *b* 16 Dec. 1917; *s* of Charles Wright Clarke and Norah Mary Willis; *m* 1953, Marilyn Mayfield (divorced, 1964). *Educ:* Huish's Grammar Sch., Taunton; King's Coll., London (BSc). HM Exchequer and Audit Dept, 1936-41. Served RAF, 1941-46. Instn of Electrical Engineers, 1949-50. Techn. Officer on first GCA radar, 1943; originated communications satellites, 1945. Chm., British Interplanetary Soc., 1946-47, 1950-53. Asst Ed., Science Abstracts, 1949-50. Since 1954 (with partner, Mike Wilson) engaged on underwater exploration on Gt Barrier Reef of Australia and coast of Ceylon. Extensive lecturing, radio and TV in UK and US. Unesco, Kalinga Prize, 1961; Acad. of Astronautics, 1961; World Acad. of Art and Science, 1962; Stuart Ballantine Medal, Franklin Inst., 1963; Westinghouse-AAAS Science Writing Award, 1969; *Publications: non-fiction:* Interplanetary Flight, 1950; The Exploration of Space, 1951; The Young Traveller in Space, 1954 (publ. in USA as Going into Space); The Coast of Coral, 1956; The Making of a Moon, 1957; The Reefs of Taprobane, 1957; Voice Across the Sea, 1958; The Challenge of the Spaceship, 1960; The Challenge of the Sea, 1960; Profiles of the Future, 1962; Voices from the Sky, 1965; (with Mike Wilson): Boy Beneath the Sea, 1958; The First Five Fathoms, 1960; Indian Ocean Adventure, 1961; The Treasure of the Great Reef, 1964; Indian Ocean Treasure, 1964; (with R. A. Smith) The Exploration of the Moon, 1954; (with Editors of Life) Man and Space, 1964; (Ed.) The Coming of the Space Age, 1967; The Promise of Space, 1968; (with the astronauts) First on the Moon, 1970; *fiction:* Prelude to Space, 1951; The Sands of Mars, 1951; Islands in the Sky, 1952; Against the Fall of Night, 1953; Childhood's End, 1953; Expedition to Earth, 1953; Earthlight, 1955; Reach for Tomorrow, 1956; The City and the Stars, 1956; Tales from the White Hart, 1957; The Deep Range, 1957; The Other Side of the Sky, 1958; Across the Sea of Stars, 1959; A Fall of Moondust, 1961; From the Ocean, From the Stars, 1962; Tales of Ten Worlds, 1962; Dolphin Island, 1963; Glide Path, 1963; Prelude to Mars, 1965; The Nine Billion Names of God, 1967; (with Stanley Kubrick) novel and screenplay, 2001: A Space Odyssey, 1968; papers in Electronic Engineering, Wireless World, Wireless Engineer, Aeroplane, Jl of British Interplanetary Soc., Astronautics, etc. *Recreations:* diving, photography, table-tennis. *Address:* 47/5 Gregory's Road, Colombo 7, Ceylon. *T:* Colombo 94255; c/o David Higham Associates, 76 Dean Street, London, W1. *Clubs:* Arts, British Sub-Aqua.

**CLARKE, Brig. Arthur Christopher L. S.;** *see* Stanley Clarke.

**CLARKE, Arthur Grenfell,** CMG 1953; *b* 17 Aug. 1906; *m* 1934, Rhoda McLean Arnott. *Educ:* Mountjoy Sch., Dublin; Dublin Univ. Appointed Cadet Officer, Hong Kong, 1929;

entered service of Hong Kong Government, 1929; interned in Stanley Camp during Japanese occupation; Financial Sec., 1952-62; retired, 1962. *Address:* Foxdene, Brighton Road, Foxrock, Co. Dublin. *T:* 894368.

**CLARKE, Captain Arthur Wellesley,** CBE 1946; DSO 1943; RN; *b* 16 April 1898; *s* of late Capt. Sir Arthur W. Clarke, KCVO, KBE, and Lady Clarke; *m* 1926, Kate Cicely Lance; one *s*. *Educ:* Merton Court Prep. Sch.; RN Colls Osborne and Dartmouth; Emmanuel Coll., Cambridge (6 months 1919). Midshipman, 1914; Lieut 1918; Comdr 1933; Capt. 1939; retired list, 1948 and re-employed at Admiralty. Served at sea throughout European War, 1914-18; Dardanelles, 1915 (despatches); Battle of Jutland, 1916; Atlantic and North Sea convoys. Between wars qualified as Navigating and Staff Officer; served at sea including in command at home and abroad; Asst Sec., Cttee of Imperial Defence, 1933-36. War of 1939-45: War Cabinet office, 1940, and later Addtl Naval Attaché, USA; commanded HMS Sheffield, Atlantic, North Russian and Malta convoys, N African landings and Barents Sea battle, 1941-43; Chief of Staff to Governor and C-in-C Malta, and later Naval Liaison Officer to Comdr, 8th Army, 1943; Chief of Staff to Head of Brit. Admty Delegn USA, 1944-46; comd HMS Ocean, 1946-48; Chief of Naval Information, Admty, 1948-57. Chairman: Marine Soc.; Shipwrecked Mariners' Soc.; Younger Brother, Trinity House. Officer, Legion of Merit (USA), 1946. *Recreation:* gardening. *Address:* 16 Yarborough Road, Southsea, Hants. *T:* Portsmouth 24539. *Clubs:* Brooks's; Royal Navy 1765-85; RNVR (Hon. Mem.).

**CLARKE, Sir Ashley;** *see* Clarke, Sir H. A.

**CLARKE, Austin,** MA; poet; *b* 1896; *s* of late Augustine Clarke and Ellen Patten Browne, Dublin. *Educ:* Belvedere Coll., Dublin; University Coll., Dublin. English Lectr at University Coll., Dublin, 1917-21; Asst Examiner in Matriculation, National Univ. of Ireland; Asst Editor of The Argosy Magazine during 1929; National Award for Poetry, Tailteann Games, 1932; Foundation Mem. of the Irish Academy of Letters, 1932, Pres., 1952-54; Pres., Irish PEN, 1939-42 and 1946-49; Chairman: Dublin Verse Speaking Soc.; Lyric Theatre Co. *Publications:* The Vengeance of Fionn (poems), 1917; The Fires of Baal (poems), 1920; The Sword of the West (poems), 1921; The Cattle-drive in Connaught (poems), 1925; The Son of Learning (a poetic comedy), 1927; Pilgrimage (poems), 1929; The Flame (a verse play), 1930; The Bright Temptation (novel), 1932; The Singing-Men at Cashel (novel), 1936; Collected Poems, 1936; Night and Morning (poems), 1938; Sister Eucharia (a verse play), 1939; Black Fast (a verse play), 1941; As the Crow Flies (a radio verse play), 1943; The Viscount of Blarney and other plays, 1944; First Visit to England (essays), 1945; The Second Kiss (a poetic comedy), 1946; The Plot Succeeds (a poetic comedy), 1950; Poetry in Ireland (a prose study), 1950; The Sun Dances at Easter (novel), 1952; The Moment Next to Nothing (a verse play), 1953; Ancient Lights (poems), 1955; Too Great a Vine (poems), 1957; The Horse-Eaters (poems), 1960; Collected Later Poems, 1961; Twice Round the Black Church (memoirs), 1962; Forget-me-not (verse), 1962; Collected Plays (verse), 1963; Flight to Africa (verse), 1963; Mnemosyne (verse), 1965; Beyond the Pale (memoirs), 1967; Old-Fashioned Pilgrimage, 1967; St Patrick's Purgatory, The Frenzy of Sweeney, The Silent Lover (all verse plays), 1967; The Third Kiss (a poetic comedy), 1967; A Penny in the Clouds, 1968; numerous reviews in daily, weekly, monthly press and quarterlies, and broadcasts. *Address:* Bridge House, Templeogue, Co. Dublin.

**CLARKE, Rev. Basil Fulford Lowther;** Vicar of Knowl Hill, Berks, since 1944; *b* 6 March 1908; *s* of late Rev. W. K. L. Clarke; *m* 1939, Eileen Noël Coates; one *s* two *d*. *Educ:* St John's Sch., Leatherhead; St John's Coll., Durham; Cuddesdon Theological Coll. BA 1930, MA 1933. Deacon 1932; Priest 1933. Curate of: St Andrew's, Coulsdon, Surrey, 1932-35; St Mary's, Monmouth, 1935-38; St James's, Watford, 1938-39; SS Philip and James's, Oxford, 1939-44. Member: Council for the Care of Churches, 1966; Adv. Bd for Redundant Churches, 1969. *Publications:* Church Builders of the 19th Century, 1938; Lesson Notes on the Prayer Book, 1943; My Parish Church, 1943; Clement Joins the Church, 1944; Anglican Cathedrals outside the British Isles, 1958; The Building of the 18th Century Church, 1963; (with John Betjeman) English Churches, 1964; Parish Churches of London, 1966. *Recreations:* visiting churches, and research in connexion with them. *Address:* Knowl Hill Vicarage, Reading, Berks. *T:* Littlewick Green 2643.

**CLARKE, Maj.-Gen. Sir Campbell;** *see* Clarke, Maj.-Gen. Sir E. M. C.

**CLARKE, Cyril Alfred Allen,** MA; Headmaster, Holland Park Secondary School, since 1957; *b* 21 Aug. 1910; *s* of late Frederick John Clarke; *m* 1934, Edna Gertrude Francis; three *s*. *Educ:* Langley Sch., Norwich; Culham Coll. of Educn; Birkbeck Coll., Univ. of London; King's Coll., Univ. of London. Entered London Teaching Service, 1933; Royal Artillery, 1940-46; Staff Officer (Major) in Educn Br. of Mil. Govt of Germany, 1945-46; Asst Master, Haberdashers' Aske's Hatcham Boys' Sch., 1946-51; Headmaster: Isledon Sec. Sch., 1951-55; Battersea Co. Sec. Sch., 1955-57. Governor, Langley Sch. FRSA. *Recreations:* photography, reading. *Address:* 22 Manor Drive North, New Malden, Surrey. *T:* 01-337 4223.

**CLARKE, Prof. Cyril Astley,** CBE 1969; FRS 1970; MD, ScD, FRCP, FRCOG; Professor of Medicine, since 1965, and Director, Nuffield Unit of Medical Genetics, since 1963, University of Liverpool; Consultant Physician, United Liverpool Hospitals (David Lewis Northern, 1946-58, Royal Infirmary since 1958) and to Broadgreen Hospital since 1946; *b* 22 Aug. 1907; *s* of Astley Vavasour Clarke, MD, JP, and Ethel Mary Clarke, *d* of H. Simpson Gee; *m* 1935, Frieda (Féo) Margaret Mary, *d* of Alexander John Campbell Hart and Isabella Margaret Hart; three *s*. *Educ:* Wyggeston Grammar Sch., Leicester; Oundle Sch.; Gonville and Caius Coll., Cambridge; Guy's Hosp. (Schol.). 2nd Class Hons, Natural Science Tripos Pt I; MD Cantab 1937; ScD Cantab 1963. FRCP 1949; FRCOG 1970. ho. Phys., Demonstr in Physiology and Clin. Asst in Dermatology, Guy's Hosp., 1932-36. Life Insurance practice, Grocers' Hall, EC2, 1936-39. Served, 1939-46, as Med Specialist, RNVR: HM Hosp. Ship Amarapoora (Scapa Flow and N Africa), RNH Seaforth and RNH Sydney. After War, Med. Registrar, Queen Elizabeth Hosp., Birmingham. Visiting Prof. of Genetics, Seton Hall Sch. of Med., Jersey City, USA, 1963; Lumleian Lectr, RCP, 1967; Ingleby Lectr, Univ. of Birmingham, 1968; Censor, RCP, 1967-69; Examr in Med., Dundee Univ., 1965-69. Pres., Liverpool Med. Instn, 1970-71; Member: MRC Working Party, 1966; Sub-Cttee of Dept of Health and

Social Security on prevention of Rhesus hæmolytic disease, 1967; Bd of Governors, United Liverpool Hosps, 1969. Gold Medal in Therapeutics, Worshipful Soc. of Apothecaries, 1970. *Publications:* Genetics for the Clinician, 1962; Selected Topics in Medical Genetics (ed), 1969; Human Genetics and Medicine, 1970; many contribs med. and scientific jls, particularly on prevention of Rhesus hæmolytic disease and on evolution of mimicry in swallowtail butterflies. *Recreations:* small boat sailing, breeding swallowtail butterflies. *Address:* Department of Medicine, The University, Ashton Street, PO Box 14J, Liverpool, L69 3BX. *T:* 051-709 4852; High Close, Thorsway, Caldy, Cheshire. *T:* 051-625 8811. *Clubs:* Athenæum; Oxford and Cambridge Sailing Society; West Kirby Sailing.

**CLARKE, Denzil Robert Noble;** Chairman, British-American Tobacco Co. Ltd, 1966-70 (Director, 1954-70; Vice-Chairman, 1962); Director, Sun Life Assurance Society, since 1966; *b* 9 July 1908; *er s* of late R. T. Clarke, ICS, LLD and late Mrs M. M. G. Clarke (*née* Whyte); *m* 1942, Ismay Elizabeth, *e d* of late Lt-Col Hon. R. M. P. Preston, DSO; one *s* two *d. Educ:* Stonyhurst Coll. Articled Clerk, Singleton Fabian & Co., Chartered Accountants, 1926; ACA 1932; FCA 1960. Joined British-American Tobacco Co. Ltd, 1932. War service, 1941-45; Far East; Lt-Col 1944. *Recreations:* gardening, tennis. *Address:* Puffins, South Drive, Wokingham, Berks. *T:* Wokingham 975. *Club:* Special Forces.
*See also Maj.-Gen. D. A. B. Clarke.*

**CLARKE, Maj.-Gen. Desmond Alexander Bruce,** CB 1965; CBE 1961 (OBE 1944); *b* 15 July 1912; *yr s* of late R. T. Clarke, ICS, LLD, Weybridge and late Mrs R. T. Clarke (*née* Whyte), Loughbrickland, Co. Down; *m* Madeleine, 2nd *d* of Rear-Adm. Walter Glyn Petre, DSO, Weybridge; three *s* two *d. Educ:* Stonyhurst Coll.; RMA Woolwich. Commissioned RA, 1932. Served War of 1939-45 (OBE): Middle East, India, France, Germany; AA and QMG, 59 (Staffs) Div., 1943; AA and QMG, 43 (Wessex) Div., Dec. 1944. Brig. i/c Administration, Southern Command, 1960-62; Dir of Personal Services, War Office, 1962-64; Dir of Personal Services (Army), Min. of Defence, 1964-66; retd Oct. 1966. Chevalier, Order of the Crown (Belgium), 1945; Croix de Guerre (Belgium), 1945. *Address:* Barford House, Wokingham, Berks.
*See also D. R. N. Clarke.*

**CLARKE, Brig. Dudley Wrangel,** CB 1945; CBE 1943 (OBE 1942); *b* 27 April 1899; *s* of late Sir Ernest Michael Clarke; unmarried. *Educ:* Charterhouse; RMA Woolwich. Royal Artillery, 1916-36; Gen. Staff, 1936-47; retired, 1947. With RFC and RAF, European War, 1914-18 (War and Victory Medals); Iraq Rebellion, 1920 (Medal and clasp); Palestine Rebellion, 1936 (Bt Major, Medal and clasp); Middle East Forces, 1939-40; Norway, 1940; Med. Theatre, 1940-45 (despatches, OBE, CBE, CB, Africa Star, Italy medal, US Legion of Merit). Head of Public Opinion Research Dept at Conservative Central Office, 1948-52. *Publications:* Seven Assignments, 1948; The Eleventh at War, 1952; Golden Arrow, 1955. *Recreations:* travel and the theatre. *Address:* 802 Raleigh House, Dolphin Square, SW1. *Club:* Cavalry.

**CLARKE, Edward,** QC 1960; **His Honour Judge Clarke;** Judge of the Central Criminal Court since 1964; *b* 21 May 1908; *s* of William Francis Clarke; *m* 1948, Dorothy May, *d* of Thomas Leask, Richmond, Surrey; three *s* one *d. Educ:* Sherborne Sch.; King's Coll., London. Called to Bar, Lincoln's Inn, 1935. Served War, 1943-46 in France, Belgium, Holland and Germany, Lieut-Col, Judge Advocate-General's Staff. Bencher, Lincoln's Inn, 1955; Dep. Chm., Herts Quarter Sessions, 1956-63; Dep. Chm., London Quarter Sessions, 1963-64. Fellow of King's Coll., London. 1965. President: Staines Amateur Regatta; King's Coll. London Assoc. (Laws Branch). *Publications:* (with Derek Walker Smith) The Life of Sir Edward Clarke; Halsbury's Laws of England (Criminal Law). *Recreations:* lawn tennis, criminology. *Address:* Central Criminal Court, EC4; 6 Norland Square, W11. *T:* 01-727 8343. *Clubs:* Garrick, MCC, Hurlingham.

**CLARKE, Maj.-Gen. Sir (Edward Montagu) Campbell,** KBE 1946 (CBE 1942); CB 1944; *b* 20 Nov. 1885; *m* 1914, Nancy (*d* 1948), *d* of S. M. Sheppard; one *s. Educ:* Rugby; RMA Woolwich. 2nd Lieut RA, 1905; Capt., 1914; Bt Major, 1917; Major, 1925; Bt Lt-Col, 1929; Col, 1933; Maj.-Gen., 1938; Dep. Supt Design Dept, Royal Arsenal, 1933-36; Mem. Ordnance Cttee, 1936-37; Vice-Pres., 1938; Dir of Artillery, 1938; Dir-Gen. of Artillery, 1942-45; retired pay, 1946. *Address:* c/o Lloyds Bank, 6 Pall Mall, SW1. *Club:* United Service.

**CLARKE, Elizabeth Bleckly,** CVO 1969; MA; Headmistress, Benenden School, Kent, since 1954; *b* 26 May 1915; *d* of Kenneth Bleckly Clarke, JP, MRCS, LRCP, Cranborne, Dorset, and Dorothy Milborough (*née* Hasluck). *Educ:* Grovely Manor Sch., Boscombe, Hants; St Hilda's Coll., Oxford, 1933-37. BA 1936, BLitt and MA 1940. Asst Mistress, The Grove Sch., Hindhead, 1937-39; Benenden Sch., 1940-47; called to the Bar, Middle Temple, 1949; Vice-Principal, Cheltenham Ladies' Coll., 1950-54. JP, County of Kent, 1956. *Recreation:* walking. *Address:* Benenden School, near Cranbrook, Kent. *T:* Benenden 592. *Club:* English-Speaking Union.

**CLARKE, Sir Ellis (Emmanuel Innocent),** Kt 1963; CMG 1960; HM Trinidad and Tobago Ambassador to the United States, since 1962, and to Mexico, since 1966; Permanent Representative to the United Nations, 1962-66; Representative on Council of Organisation of American States, since 1967; *b* 28 Dec. 1917; *o c* of late Cecil Clarke and of Mrs Elma Clarke; *m* 1952, Eyrmyntrude (*née* Hagley); one *s* one *d. Educ:* St Mary's Coll., Trinidad (Jerningham Gold Medal); London Univ. (LLB 1940); Gray's Inn. Private practice at Bar of Trinidad and Tobago, 1941-54; Solicitor-Gen., Oct 1954; Dep. Colonial Sec., Dec. 1956; Attorney-Gen., 1957-62. Chm. of Bd, British West Indian Airways, 1968-. *Address:* 7530 17th Street, NW, Washington, DC, USA. *Clubs:* Queen's Park Cricket (Port of Spain); Arima Race (Trinidad); Tobago Golf (President, 1970-).

**CLARKE, Ernest Meredyth H.;** *see* Hyde-Clarke.

**CLARKE, Brig. Frederick Arthur Stanley,** DSO 1918; psc† late The Essex Regiment; *b* 3 Oct. 1892; *s* of F. W. Clarke, Bushey, Herts, and A. E. Crees, Prittlewell, Essex; *m* 1917, Millicent, *d* of W. Charity, Wallington, Surrey; one *s* one *d* (and one *s* decd). *Educ:* Loughborough Sch.; abroad. Served 10th Bn London Regt, 1912; Lieut Essex Regt, 1916; Major TA, 1916-20; Capt. Essex Regt, 1925; Bt Major, 1933; Major, 1936; Bt Lt-Col, 1939; Lt-Col, 1942; Temp. Brig., 1940-41; Temp. Col., 1943; Temp. Brig., 1943-47; psc† 1929; GSO, Small Arms Sch., 1930-32; DAAG, HQ Western Commd, 1932-34; GSO2, Nigeria, 1935-38 (Local Lt-Col); Asst Comdt, Nigeria, 1938-39

(Local Col); DAAG, BEF, 1939-40; GSO2, and 1, BEF, 1940; DA & QMG, W Africa, 1940-41; Comdr, W Africa, 1941; AQMG, BNAF, 1942-43; ADQMG, BNAF, 1943; Comdr, BNAF, 1943-44; Comdr, CMF, 1944-45; Comdr, Home Forces, 1945-46; retired, 1947. Served European War, 1914-17, Gallipoli, Egypt, Palestine, India (1917-19 Star, British War Medal, Victory Medal, DSO, despatches); attached 57th Wildes Rifles, Frontier Force, 1918; served War of 1939-45, France, W Africa, N Africa, Italy (1939-45 Star, Africa Star (First Army Clasp), Italy Star, Defence Medal, War Medal). *Publications:* The History of the Royal West African Frontier Force, Part II, 1920-1961; articles in Service Journals; Bertrand Stewart Prize Essay, 1926; Gold Medal, Royal United Service Institution Essay, 1933. *Recreations:* various. *Address:* Ratcliffs, Black Notley, Essex.

**CLARKE, Sir Frederick (Joseph),** Kt 1967; Governor of St Lucia since 1967; *b* 21 May 1912; 2nd *s* of late R. G. H. Clarke; *m* 1944, Phyliss (*née* Lunn), *o c* of Henry and Elizabeth Lunn, Dosthill, Tamworth; one *s* two *d* (and one *s* decd). *Educ:* St Vincent Grammar Sch.; School of Medicine, Edinburgh. LRCPE, LRCSE, LRFPS (G) 1944. General Medical Practice, Peterborough, Northants, 1945; District Medical Officer, St Lucia, 1946, CMO, St Lucia, 1961. Retired from Civil Service Sept. 1963. Private Practice, 1963-67. Speaker of the Legislative Council, St Lucia, 1964-67. KStJ 1968. *Recreations:* cricket, bridge, gardening. *Address:* Government House, St Lucia. *Clubs:* Rotary, Press (St Lucia); St Lucia Cricket.

**CLARKE, Geoffrey,** ARA 1970; ARCA; artist and sculptor; *b* 28 Nov. 1924; *s* of John Moulding Clarke and Janet Petts; *m* 1947, Ethelwynne Tyrer; one *s*. *Educ:* Royal College of Art (Hons). Exhibitions: Gimpel Fils Gallery, 1952, 1955; Redfern Gallery, 1965; South Bank, 1951 (Icarus). Works in public collections: Victoria and Albert Museum; Tate Gallery; Arts Council; Museum of Modern Art, NY; etc. Prizes for engraving: Triennial, 1951; London, 1953, Tokyo, 1957. Commissioned work includes: grille, Martins Bank, Garrick Street; iron sculpture, Time Life Building, New Bond Street; cast aluminium relief sculpture (1000 sq. ft), Castrol House, Marylebone Road; mosaics, Liverpool Univ. Physics Block and Basildon New Town; stained glass windows for new Treasury, Lincoln Cathedral; bronze sculpture (80 ft high), Thorn Electric Building, Upper St Martin's Lane; relief sculpture on Canberra and Oriana; 3 (70 ft high) stained glass windows, high altar, cross and candlesticks (10 ft high cast silver), the flying cross and crown of thorns, all in Coventry Cathedral; sculpture, Nottingham Civic Theatre; UKAEA Culham; Westminster Bank, Bond Street; Univs of Liverpool, Exeter, Cambridge, Oxford, Manchester and Lancaster; screens in Royal Military Chapel, Birdcage Walk. Further work at Chichester, Newcastle, Manchester, Plymouth, Ipswich, Canterbury, Taunton, Winchester, St Paul, Minnesota, and Newcastle Civic Centre. *Address:* Stowe Hill, Hartest, Bury St Edmunds, Suffolk. *T:* Hartest 319.

**CLARKE, Gerald Bryan,** CMG 1964; ISO 1954; Secretary to the Cabinet and Secretary to the Prime Minister, Rhodesia, since 1955; *b* Gwelo, Rhodesia, 1 Nov. 1909; *s* of Francis Joseph Clarke and Margaret Shiel; *m* 1946, Eleanor, *widow* of B. C. Catella; one *s* one *d* (and one step *s*). *Educ:* St George's Coll., Salisbury, Rhodesia. Joined Southern Rhodesian Civil Service, 1927; Treasury, 1927-40. Served War, 1940-45: S Rhodesia Armoured Car Regt, E Africa and Abyssinia; Pretoria Regt, 6th SA Armoured Div., Italy. Chief Clerk, Treasury, 1945-48; Asst Sec., Public Services Board, 1948; Under-Sec., Cabinet Office, 1950. Attended Constitutional Confs on HMS Tiger, Dec. 1966, and HMS Fearless, 1968, as Mem. of Rhodesian Delegn. Comr of Oaths, Rhodesia. Coronation Medal, 1952. *Recreation:* rearing trees. *Address:* 58 Glamorgan Avenue, Salisbury, Rhodesia. *T:* Salisbury 82042; Juliasdale, Inyanga, Rhodesia. *T:* Juliasdale 0-0430.

**CLARKE, Guy Hamilton,** CMG 1959; HM Ambassador to Nepal, 1962-63, retired; *b* 23 July 1910; 3rd *s* of late Dr and Mrs Charles H. Clarke, Leicester. *Educ:* Wyggeston Grammar Sch., Leicester; Trinity Hall, Cambridge. Probationer Vice-Consul, Levant Consular Service, Beirut, 1933; transf. to Ankara, 1936; Corfu, 1940; Adana, 1941; Baltimore, 1944; has since served at: Washington, Los Angeles (Consul 1945), Bangkok, Jedda, Kirkuk (Consul 1949), Bagdad, Kirkuk (Consul-Gen. 1951); Ambassador to the Republic of Liberia, 1957-60, and to the Republic of Guinea, 1959-60; Mem. United Kingdom Delegation to United Nations Gen. Assembly, New York, 1960; HM Consul-General, Damascus, Feb. 1961, and Chargé d'Affaires there, Oct. 1961-Jan. 1962. *Address:* c/o Foreign and Commonwealth Office, SW1.

**CLARKE, Very Rev. (Harold George) Michael,** MA 1925; FRSA; *b* 1898; *s* of George Herbert Clarke, then second master of Hymer's Coll., Hull; *m* 1923, Katherine Beryl, *d* of late Barry Edward Girling, Algiers; two *s* one *d*. *Educ:* St Paul's Sch. (scholar); Trinity Coll., Cambridge (scholar). Served with 2nd Field Company RE in France, 1918. 1st Class Hons Mathematical Tripos, Pt 1, 1919, 2nd Class Hons History Tripos, Pt 2, 1921. Deacon, 1938; Priest, 1939. Asst Master at Winchester Coll., 1921-32; Headmaster of Rossall Sch., 1932-37; Headmaster of Repton Sch., 1937-44; Rector of Holy Trinity, St Marylebone, 1945-51. Chm., Standing Joint Cttee Public and Preparatory Schs, 1940-43; lectured in Canada, 1945, at invitation of Canadian Council of Churches; one of founders, and till 1961 Governor, of Administrative Staff Coll., Greenlands, Henley-on-Thames; Chm., Marriage Welfare Cttee of Family Welfare Assoc., 1948-51; Advisory Sec. to Bishop of London on Religious Drama, 1949-51; Rural Dean of St Marylebone, 1950-51; Provost of Birmingham, 1951-61. Master of the Glovers' Company, 1960. Chm. Home Cttee, SPG, 1961-64. Rector of Westonbirt with Lasborough, and Chaplain to Westonbirt Sch., 1961-68. Sub-Warden, Servants of Christ the King, 1963-70; Chaplain to Haberdashers' Co., 1970-. *Address:* Flint Cottage, Chipperfield, Herts.

*See also F. I. Kilvington.*

**CLARKE, Sir (Henry) Ashley,** GCMG 1962 (KCMG 1952; CMG 1946); GCVO 1961; Member: General Board, Assicurazioni Generali of Trieste, since 1964; Governing Body, Royal Academy of Music, since 1967; Advisory Council, Victoria and Albert Museum, since 1969; Council, British School at Rome, since 1962; Executive Committee, Keats-Shelley Association, since 1962; D'Oyly Carte Trust, since 1964; *b* 26 June 1903; *e s* of H. R. H. Clarke, MD; *m* 1st, 1937, Virginia (marr. diss. 1960), *d* of Edward Bell, New York; 2nd, 1962, Frances, *d* of John Molyneux, Worcs. *Educ:* Repton; Pembroke Coll., Cambridge. Entered Diplomatic Service, 1925; 3rd Sec., Budapest and Warsaw; 2nd Sec., Constantinople, FO and Gen.

Disarmament Conf, Geneva; 1st Sec., Tokyo; Counsellor, FO; Minister, Lisbon and Paris; Deputy Under-Sec., FO; Ambassador to Italy, 1953-62, retd. London Adviser, Banca Commerciale Italiana, 1962-70; Sec.-Gen., Europa Nostra, 1969-70. Governor: BBC, 1962-67; Brit. Inst. of Recorded Sound, 1964-67; Mem., Nat. Theatre Bd, 1962-66; Chairman: Italian Art and Archives Rescue Fund, 1966-70; Royal Acad. of Dancing, 1964-69. Hon. Dr of Political Science, Genoa, 1956; Hon. Academician, Accademia Filarmonica Romana, 1962; Hon. Fellow: Pembroke Coll., Cambridge, 1962; Ancient Monuments Soc., 1969. Knight Grand Cross of the Order of Merit of the Republic of Italy. *Recreation:* music. *Address:* Walton House, 1 Walton Street, SW3. *Clubs:* Athenæum, Garrick.

**CLARKE, Sir Henry O.;** *see* Osmond-Clarke.

**CLARKE, Sir Humphrey (Orme),** 5th Bt *cr* 1831; *b* 6 July 1906; *e s* of Sir Orme Bigland Clarke, 4th Bt, CBE, and Elfrida, *e d* of Alfred Roosevelt, New York; *S* father, 1949; *m* 1st, 1931, Frances Mary Powys, *d* of late Major Powys Sketchley, DSO; 2nd, 1938, Elisabeth, *d* of Dr W. A. Cook, Santa Barbara, Calif.; one *s*; 3rd, 1947, Constance Elizabeth, *d* of late Herbert Gibbs and of Mrs Gibbs, 32 Brechin Place, SW7; one *s*. *Educ:* Eton; Christ Church, Oxford. *Heir: er s* Charles Mansfield Tobias Clarke [*b* 8 Sept, 1939. *Educ:* Eton; Christ Church, Oxford]. *Address:* 18 Walton Street, SW3. *T:* 01-589 4738; The Church House, Bibury, Glos. *T:* Bibury 225. *Clubs:* Boodle's; Travellers', Jockey (Paris).

**CLARKE, Kenneth (Harry);** MP (C) Rushcliffe Division of Nottinghamshire since 1970; *b* 2 July 1940; *e c* of Kenneth Clarke, Nottingham; *m* 1964, Gillian Mary Edwards; one *s* one *d*. *Educ:* Nottingham High Sch.; Gonville and Caius Coll., Cambridge (BA, LLB). Chm., Cambridge Univ. Conservative Assoc., 1961; Pres., Cambridge Union, 1963; Chm., Fedn Conservative Students, 1963. Called to Bar, Gray's Inn 1963; practising Mem., Midland Circuit, 1963-. Research Sec., Birmingham Bow Group, 1965-66; Parly Candidate for Mansfield (Notts) in General Elections of 1964 and 1966. *Publications:* pamphlets published by Bow Group, 1964-. *Recreations:* modern Jazz music; watching Association Football. *Address:* 8 Amesbury Road, Moseley, Birmingham. *T:* 021-449 0594.

**CLARKE, Prof. Martin Lowther;** Professor of Latin, University College of North Wales, since 1948, Vice-Principal since 1967; *b* 2 Oct. 1909; *s* of late Rev. William Kemp Lowther Clarke; *m* 1942, Emilie de Rontenay Moon, *d* of late Dr R. O. Moon; two *s*. *Educ:* Haileybury Coll.; King's Coll., Cambridge. 1st class Classical Tripos, Parts I and II; Craven Scholar; Browne Medallist; Chancellor's Medallist; Craven Student. Asst, Dept of Humanity, Edinburgh Univ., 1933-34; Fellow of King's Coll., Cambridge, 1934-40; Asst Lecturer in Greek and Latin, University Coll., London, 1935-37. Foreign Office, 1940-45. Lecturer, 1946-47, and Reader, 1947-48, in Greek and Latin, University Coll., London; Vice-Principal, University Coll. of North Wales, 1963-65. *Publications:* Richard Porson, 1937; Greek Studies in England, 1700 to 1830, 1945; Rhetoric at Rome, 1953; The Roman Mind, 1956; Classical Education in Britain, 1500-1900, 1959; George Grote, 1962; Bangor Cathedral, 1969; papers in Transactions of Caernarvonshire Historical Soc. *Address:* 2 Coed Menai, Menai Avenue, Bangor, Caernarvonshire. *T:* Bangor 2460.

**CLARKE, Mary Gavin,** MA (Cantab and TCD), LLD (Aberdeen); *b* 29 Dec. 1881; *d* of late John Clarke, Lecturer in Education, Aberdeen Univ.; unmarried. *Educ:* Aberdeen High Sch. for Girls; Aberdeen Univ.; Girton Coll., Cambridge (Class I Med. and Mod. Langs Tripos); Cambridge Training Coll. After completion of training held research scholarship at Girton Coll. for two periods of a year each; Gamble Prize; taught Modern Languages for two years at Roedean Sch., Brighton; acted as Asst to Prof. of English Language and Literature in Aberdeen Univ., and as Asst Examiner to the Central Welsh Board in same subjects; Chief English Mistress, St Leonard's Sch., St Andrews; Headmistress of Edinburgh Ladies' Coll. (Mary Erskine Sch. for Girls), 1914-24; Headmistress of Manchester High Sch. for Girls, 1924-45. Special Lectr, Manchester Univ. Dept of Educn, 1948-53; Examiner, Manchester Univ. Sch. of Educn, 1949-59. Mem. Bd of Educn Investigation panel for Higher Sch. Certificate examination, 1937-38; Mem. of Board of Education Cttee (Norwood Cttee), 1941-43, on Secondary Sch. Examinations and Curriculum; special Lecturer for British Council in China, 1947; Mem. of Educational Board, Edinburgh Merchant Company, 1955-. *Publications:* Sidelights on Teutonic History during the Migration Period; The Headmistress Speaks (joint); Manchester and Salford Shaftesbury Society Lecture on Religious Education. *Address:* 3 Gordon Road, Edinburgh EH12 6NB. *T:* 031-334 2616.

**CLARKE, Very Rev. Michael;** *see* Clarke, Very Rev. H. G. M.

**CLARKE, Rear-Adm. Noel Edward Harwood,** CB 1959; *b* 21 Oct. 1904; *s* of Henry Trevisa Clarke and Margaret Evelyn Sale; *m* 1942, Katherine Miller, *d* of Harman Visger, France Lynch, near Stroud; two *s*. *Educ:* RN Colleges, Osborne and Dartmouth. RNEC Keyham, 1923-27; HMS Marlborough, 1927-29; HMS Kent, 1930-33; HMS Cairo, 1933-34; HM Dockyard, Portsmouth, 1934-36; HMS Sheffield, 1936-39; Admty, 1939-41; HMS Cumberland, 1942-43; HMS Excellent, 1943-47; HM Dockyard, Singapore, 1947-49; Admty, 1949-52; HM Dockyard, Gibraltar, 1952-56; Admty, 1957; Dir of Fleet Maintenance, Admty, 1958; Command Engineer Officer and Chief Staff Officer (Technical), on staff of C-in-C, Portsmouth, Nov. 1958-July 1960, retd; worked with Nat. Economic Development Office, 1963-68. County Councillor, IoW. *Recreation:* golf. *Address:* Seamark House, St Helens, Isle of Wight. *T:* Bembridge 2866. *Club:* Royal Naval (Portsmouth).

**CLARKE, Rt. Rev. Norman Harry,** MA; LLD (Hon.) Sheffield, 1956; Assistant Bishop, Canterbury Diocese, since 1962; Canon Emeritus of Southwark Cathedral since 1945; *b* Sheffield, 31 July 1892; *s* of Henry Stockdale Clarke; *m* 1919, Muriel, *d* of W. R. Locke; one *s* three *d*. *Educ:* Sheffield Univ. (BA 1st Class Hons Maths 1912); Ridley Hall, Cambridge. Diocesan Inspector of Schs, 1930-35; Canon Residentiary and Treasurer of Southwark Cathedral, 1940-45; Vicar of St Andrew's, Plymouth, 1945-51; Archdeacon of Plymouth, 1950-62; Suffragan Bishop of Plymouth, 1950-62. *Publication:* Thine is the Kingdom, 1941. *Recreations:* reading, gardening. *Address:* 4 Nailbourne Close, Kingston, Canterbury, Kent. *T:* Barham 202.

**CLARKE, Major Peter Cecil,** CVO 1969; Chief Clerk, Duchy of Lancaster, and Extra Equerry to HRH Princess Alexandra, the Hon. Mrs

Angus Ogilvy; *b* 9 Aug. 1927; *s* of late Captain E. D. Clarke, CBE, MC, Binstead, Isle of Wight; *m* 1950, Rosemary Virginia Margaret Harmsworth, *d* of late T. C. Durham, Appamattox, Virginia, USA; one *s* two *d*. *Educ:* Eton; RMA, Sandhurst. 3rd The King's Own Hussars and 14th/20th King's Hussars, 1945-64. Seconded as Asst Private Secretary to HRH Princess Marina, Duchess of Kent, 1961-64; Comptroller, 1964-68; Comptroller to HRH Princess Alexandra, 1964-69. *Recreations:* golf, fishing. *Address:* 6 Gordon Place, W8. *T:* 01-937 0356. *Clubs:* Cavalry, MCC.

**CLARKE, Reginald Arnold,** CMG 1962; OBE 1960; DFC 1945; *b* 6 May 1921; *s* of late John Leonard Clarke; *m* 1949, Dorithea Nanette Oswald; three *s* one *d*. *Educ:* Doncaster Grammar Sch. Royal Air Force, 1939-46; Provincial Administration, Nigeria, 1947-52; Financial Secretary's Office, Nigeria, 1952-57; Federal Ministry of Finance, Nigeria, 1957, Permanent Sec., 1958-63, retd; International Bank, Washington, DC, 1964. *Recreations:* travel, tennis, bridge. *Address:* c/o Midland Bank, Gosforth, Cumberland. *Club:* Royal Air Force Reserves.

**CLARKE, Sir Richard (William Barnes),** KCB 1964 (CB 1951); OBE 1944; Civil Service Department, since 1970; *b* 13 Aug. 1910; *s* of late William Thomas Clarke, schoolmaster, and late Helen Barnes; *m* 1950, Brenda Pile (*née* Skinner); three *s*. *Educ:* Christ's Hospital; Clare Coll., CAmbridge. BA; Wrangler, 1931; Frances Wood Prizeman, Royal Statistical Society, 1932. British Electrical and Allied Manufacturers' Association, 1932-33; Financial News, 1933-39; Visiting Lecturer, Cambridge Univ., 1935-36; Ministries of Information, Economic Warfare, Supply and Production, 1939-45: Combined Production and Resources Board (Washington), 1942-43; Asst Sec., HM Treasury, 1945; Under-Sec., 1947; Third Sec., 1955-62; Second Sec., 1962-66; Permanent Secretary: Min. of Aviation, 1966; Min. of Technology, 1966-70. Member Council, Manchester Business Sch., 1969-; Univ. of Cambridge Appointments Bd, 1969-. FBIM. *Publications:* The Economic Effort of War, 1939; The Management of the Public Sector of the National Economy (Stamp Memorial Lecture, 1964). *Address:* 3 Meadway Close, NW11. *T:* 01-455 7863. *Club:* Reform.

**CLARKE, Robin Mitchell,** MC 1944; Manager, Crawley, Commission for the New Towns, since 1962; *b* 8 Jan. 1917; *e s* of Joseph and Mary Clarke; *m* 1946, Betty Mumford; twin *s* and *d*. *Educ:* Ruckholt Central Sch., Leyton. Middleton and St Bride's Wharf, Wapping, 1932-34; Town Clerk's Office, City of Westminster, 1935-40. War of 1939-45: 12th Regt, RHA (HAC) and 142 (Royal Devon Yeomanry) Fd Regt, RA; Major, 1944; served Sicily and Italy (wounded, despatches, MC). Town Clerk's Office, Westminster, 1946-48; Crawley Development Corporation, 1948-62; Actg Chief Executive, 1961-62. ACIS 1949; FCIS 1959 (Mem. Nat. Council, 1968-). Past Chm., Sussex Council; Commandant, C Div., Sussex Special Constabulary. *Recreations:* gardening (of necessity), watching television. *Address:* Hillcrest, 40 Mount Close, Pound Hill, Crawley, Sussex. *T:* Pound Hill 2266.

**CLARKE, Roger Simon Woodchurch,** JP; Chairman, The Imperial Tobacco Co. Ltd, 1959-64; *b* 29 June 1903; *s* of late Charles S. Clarke, Tracy Park, Wick, Bristol; *m* 1936, Nancy Lingard, *d* of late William Martin, formerly of St Petersburg; no *c*. *Educ:* RN Colleges, Osborne and Dartmouth. Joined The Imperial Tobacco Co., 1922; Dir, 1944-68. JP Bristol, 1964. *Address:* Watts Barn, Codrington, Chipping Sodbury, Bristol. *T:* Badminton 228.

**CLARKE, Major Sir Rupert William John,** 3rd Bt *cr* 1882; MBE 1943; late Irish Guards; Director, National Bank of Australasia, since 1955; Chairman: United Distillers Co. since 1960 (Director 1958); Schweppes (Australia) since 1957 (late Vice-Chairman; Victory Reinsurance Co. of Australia; King Ranch Australia Pty Ltd; Vice-Chairman: Victoria Amateur Turf Club; Conzinc Riotinto of Australia Ltd; Director, Eastern Nitrogen Ltd; *b* 5 Nov. 1919; *s* of 2nd Bt and Elsie Florence (who *m* 2nd, 1928, 5th Marquess of Headfort), *d* of James Partridge Tucker, Devonshire; *S* father, 1926; *m* 1947, Kathleen, *d* of P. Grant Hay, Toorak, Victoria, Australia; two *s* one *d* (and one *s* decd). *Educ:* Eton; Magdalen Coll., Oxford (MA). Served War of 1939-45 (despatches, MBE). *Heir: s* Rupert Grant Alexander Clarke, *b* 12 Dec. 1947. *Address:* Bolinda Vale, Clarkefield, Vic 3430, Australia; Richmond House, 56 Avoca Street, South Yarra, Vic 3141. *Clubs:* Guards, Lansdowne; Melbourne, Athenæum, Australian (Melbourne); Union (Sydney); Queensland (Brisbane).

*See also Bt Col C. Gerard, Sir R. W. Knox.*

**CLARKE, Samuel Harrison,** CBE 1956; MSc; Hon. MIFireE; *b* 5 Sept. 1903; *s* of Samuel Clarke and Mary Clarke (*née* Clarke); *m* 1928, Frances Mary Blowers; one *s* two *d*. *Educ:* The Brunts Sch., Mansfield; University Coll., Nottingham (MSc London). Forest Products Res. Laboratory of DSIR, 1927; Fire Research Div., Research and Experiments Dept, Ministry of Home Security, 1940; Dir of Fire Research, DSIR, and Fire Offices Cttee, 1946-58; Dir of Fuel Research Station, DSIR, 1958; Dir, Warren Spring Laboratory, DSIR, 1958-63; Careers Officer, Min. of Technology, 1965-67 (DSIR, 1964-65); Mem. Stevenage Development Corporation, 1962-. *Publications:* papers in scientific and technical jls. *Recreations:* exchanging ideas, painting, gardening. *Address:* 57 Whitney Drive, Stevenage, Herts.

**CLARKE, Sir Selwyn S.;** *see* Selwyn-Clarke.

**CLARKE, Rev. Sydney Herbert;** *b* 7 May 1894; *s* of late Joseph Clarke; unmarried. *Educ:* Leeds Grammar Sch.; Trinity Coll., Cambridge (Senior Scholar); Cuddesdon Theological Coll. Preparatory Schoolmaster, 3 years; Deacon, 1919; Priest, 1920; Asst Master and Chaplain, Tonbridge Sch., Kent, 1919-34; Headmaster, St John's Coll., Johannesburg, 1935-54. Mem. Jt Matriculation Bd, Univ. of S Africa, 1936-54; Chm., 1943-44. Asst Master, Diocesan Coll., Rondebosch, Cape Town, 1955-62; Chaplain, Ardingly Coll., Sussex, 1963-64. Asst Priest (Hon.), St Saviour's Church, Eastbourne, 1964-. *Recreations:* walking, cricket, etc. *Address:* 10 Ripley Chase, The Goffs, Eastbourne, Sussex. *T:* Eastbourne 33966.

**CLARKE, Brig. Terence Hugh,** CBE 1943; *b* 17 Feb. 1904; *e s* of late Col Hugh Clarke, AM, Royal Artillery, and of Mrs Hugh Clarke, Bunces, Kennel Ride, Ascot; *m* 1928, Eileen Armistead, Hopelands, Woodville, NZ; two *d*. *Educ:* Temple Grove; Haileybury Coll.; RMA Sandhurst. 2nd Lieut Glos Regt, 1924; served India, 1924-27; China, 1928; India, 1928-31, in IA Ordnance Corps; England, 1931-33, Glos Regt; transferred to RAOC, 1933; Norway, 1940 (despatches); DDOS 1st Army, 1942, as Brig. (despatches, CBE); DDOS 2nd Army, 1944; Normandy to Luneberg, Germany (despatches); comd RAOC Training Centre,

1946; DDOS Southern Command, 1948-50; retired from Army, 1950, to enter industry as a Dir of public and private companies. MP (C) Portsmouth West, 1950-66; Prospective Parly Cand. (C) Portsmouth West. *Recreations:* capped six times for the Army at Rugby and boxed heavyweight for Army; sailing, ski-ing and horse racing. *Address:* Hollybank House, Emsworth, Hants. *T:* Emsworth 2256. *Club:* Army and Navy.

**CLARKE, Col Thomas Cecil Arthur,** DSO 1941; OBE 1945; MIMechE; late Royal Tank Regt; Secretary Royal Armoured Corps War Memorial Benevolent Fund, and Royal Tank Regt Assoc. and Benevolent Fund, 1951-62; *b* 24 Nov. 1898; *s* of Cecil Clarke, Hampstead; *m* 1932, Dorothy Leslie-Spinks, Bournemouth; one *s* one *d*. *Educ:* Dover Coll.; RMC Sandhurst. In Regular Army from 1917; served European War, 1917-19 (wounded); War of 1939-45 (DSO, OBE, despatches thrice, wounded); commanded 46th (Liverpool Welsh) RT Regt; retired 1951. *Recreations:* motoring, gardening. *Address:* Wendy's Wood, Lower Bourne, Farnham, Surrey.

**CLARKE, Thomas Ernest Bennett,** OBE 1952; screenwriter; *b* 7 June 1907; 2nd *s* of late Sir Ernest Michael Clarke; *m* 1932, Joyce Caroline Steele; one *d* (one *s* decd). *Educ:* Charterhouse; Clare Coll., Cambridge. Staff writer on Answers, 1927-35; editorial staff Daily Sketch, 1936; subsequently free-lance journalist. Wrote screen-plays of films: Johnny Frenchman, Hue and Cry, Against the Wind, Passport to Pimlico, The Blue Lamp, The Magnet, The Lavender Hill Mob (Academy and Venice Awards), The Titfield Thunderbolt, The Rainbow Jacket, Who Done It?, Barnacle Bill, A Tale of Two Cities, Gideon's Day, The Horse Without a Head. Other screen credits include For Those in Peril, Halfway House, Champagne Charlie (lyrics), Dead of Night, Train of Events, Encore, Law and Disorder, Sons and Lovers, A Man Could Get Killed. *Play:* This Undesirable Residence. *Publications:* Go South–Go West, 1932; Jeremy's England, 1934; Cartwright Was a Cad, 1936; Two and Two Make Five, 1938; Mr Spirket Reforms, 1939; What's Yours?, 1938; The World Was Mine, 1964; The Wide Open Door, 1966; The Trail of the Serpent, 1968. *Recreation:* racing. *Address:* Tanners Mead, Oxted, Surrey. *T:* Oxted 2183.

**CLARKE, William Malpas;** The Director, Committee on Invisible Exports, since 1966; Director: National & Grindlays Bank Ltd; UK Provident Institution; Cincinnati Milacron Ltd; Investeco Ltd; Consultant, The Banker (Editor March-Sept. 1966); Adviser, Bank of London & South America; *b* 5 June 1922; *o s* of late Ernest Clarke and of Florence Clarke; *m* 1946, Margaret, *y d* of late Reginald Braithwaite and of Lilian Braithwaite; two *d*. *Educ:* Audenshaw Grammar Sch.; Univ. of Manchester. Served Royal Air Force, 1941-46; Flying Instructor, 1942-44; Flight-Lieut, 1945. Editorial Staff, Manchester Guardian, 1948-55. Asst City Ed., The Times, 1955-57; City Ed., The Times, 1957-62; Financial and Industrial Ed., The Times, 1962-66. Mem. Council, RIIA. *Publications:* The City's Invisible Earnings, 1958; The City in the World Economy, 1965; Private Enterprise in Developing Countries, 1966; (ed, as Director of Studies) Britain's Invisible Earnings, 1967; The World's Money, 1970. *Recreations:* books, opera, lawn tennis. *Address:* 3 Streatley Place, Hampstead, NW3. *T:* 01-435 1852. *Clubs:* Reform, Hurlingham.

**CLARKE, Brig. William Stanhope,** CBE 1945; DSO 1944; psc; *b* 29 Dec. 1899; *s* of Capt. J. S. Clarke, RN, Dublin; *m* 1929, Roslyn Stewart, *d* of Dr E. S. Littlejohn, Sydney; two *s*. *Educ:* Wellington Coll. Joined RA, 1919; transferred to Royal Tank Corps, 1923; Major, Royal Tank Regt, 1938; served War of 1939-45, NW Europe (CBE, DSO); Lt-Col 1945; Col 1946; ADC to the Queen, 1952-54; retired, 1954. *Address:* Clint House, Ellisfield, Basingstoke, Hants. *Club:* Army and Navy.

**CLARKE HALL, Denis;** architect in private practice; President Architectural Association, 1958-59; Chairman, Architects Registration Council of the UK, 1963-64; *b* 4 July 1910; *m* 1936, Mary Garfitt; one *s* two *d*. *Educ:* Bedales. Has had his own practice, 1937-. Holds AA Dip. *Publications:* articles in Technical Journals. *Address:* 6 Masons Yard, Duke Street, St James's, SW1. *T:* 01-930 2951.

**CLARKE HALL, Lady, (Edna);** artist; *d* of late Rev. B. Waugh, founder of the NSPCC; *m* 1898, Sir W. Clarke Hall (*d* 1932); two *s*. *Educ:* The Slade Sch. (Slade Scholarship). Drawings, water-colours, etchings and lithographs. Represented at the Tate Gallery, British, Victoria and Albert and Fitzwilliam Museums and Manchester City Art Gallery. *Publications:* Poems, 1926; Facets, 1930. *Address:* Upminster Common, Essex.

**CLARKE TAYLOR, Air Vice-Marshal James;** *see* Taylor, Air Vice-Marshal J. C.

**CLARKSON, Derek Joshua,** QC 1969; Recorder of Rotherham since Oct. 1967; *b* 10 Dec. 1929; *o s* of Albert and Winifred Charlotte Clarkson; *m* 1960, Peternella Marie-Luise Ilse Canenbley; one *s* one *d*. *Educ:* Pudsey Grammar Sch.; King's Coll., Univ. of London. LLB (London) 1950. Called to Bar, Inner Temple, 1951; Nat. Service, RAF, 1952-54 (Flt-Lieut). In practice as Barrister, 1954-; Prosecuting Counsel to Post Office on North-Eastern Circuit, 1961-65; Prosecuting Counsel to Inland Revenue on North-Eastern Circuit, 1965-69. *Recreations:* book collecting; dialect study. *Address:* (chambers) 5 King's Bench Walk, Temple, EC4. *T:* 01-353 2882; 30 Park Square, Leeds 1. *T:* Leeds 33277/8; (home) 26 Cornwall Road, Harrogate, Yorks. *T:* Harrogate 4673.

**CLARKSON, (George Wensley) Anthony;** Chairman, Reveille Newspapers Ltd, since 1967; Director, Daily Mirror Newspapers Ltd, since 1967; *b* Christchurch, NZ, 21 April 1912; *s* of George Wensley and Nan O'Keeffe Clarkson, and *step s* of Percy Crisp; *m* 1st, 1935, Olive Oxley; 2nd, 1940, Pamela Minck; three *s*. *Educ:* St Bede's, Christchurch, NZ; King's Coll., Auckland, NZ. Reporter Auckland Sun, 1928-30; Founder-Editor, Challenge, 1933-35; Features Editor, Daily Mirror, 1937-40; served War of 1939-45, RN, 1940-46; Asst Eitor, John Bull, 1946-49, Associate Editor, 1949-52, Editor, 1952-53; Editor: Illustrated, 1953-55; Odhams Magazine Unit, 1955-57; Reveille, 1957-70; Dir, Reveille Newspapers Ltd, 1962-. *Recreation:* swimming. *Address:* 80 Warwick Gardens, W14. *T:* 01-603 3682; Windermere, New Road, Shoreham-by-Sea, Sussex. *T:* Shoreham-by-Sea 4316. *Clubs:* Press, Burma, Royal Automobile.

**CLARKSON, Rt. Rev. George William,** MA; *b* 13 Dec. 1897; *s* of William and Eliza Medley Clarkson. *Educ:* New Coll., Oxford. Deacon 1926, Priest 1927, diocese of Liverpool; Curate of Wigan, 1926-30; Vicar of St Elizabeth, Aspull, 1930-33; Fleetwood, 1933-36; Sub-Dean and Hon. Canon of John de Wheathampstead, Abbot, in St Albans Cathedral, 1936-39; Rector of Dunstable,

1939-44; Skegness, 1944-48; Vicar of Newark with Codington, Diocese of Southwell, 1948-54; Rural Dean of Dunstable, 1940-44; of Candleshoe, 1947-48; of Newark, 1948-54; Hon. Canon of Southwell Minster, 1952-54; Bishop Suffragan of Pontefract, 1954-61; Dean of Guildford, 1961-68, retd; an Asst Bishop, Diocese of Lincoln, 1968-. *Address:* 4 Syne Avenue, Skegness, Lincs.

**CLASEN, Andrew Joseph,** Hon. GCVO 1968; Commander with Crown, Adolphe Nassau; Commander Order of the Oaken Crown; Grand Cross: Order of Orange Nassau; Iceland Falcon; Luxembourg Ambassador in London since 1955 (Minister, 1944-55); *b* 5 Sept. 1906; *yr s* of late Bernard Clasen and Claire Duchscher; *m* 1944, Joan Mary Luke; one *s* one *d. Educ:* Beaumont Coll.; Univs of Oxford, London and Aix-la-Chapelle. DrIng, BSc; ARSM; Hon. FRIC. Acting Sec.-Gen. Luxembourg Foreign Affairs Ministry, Consul-Gen., Chargé d'Affaires, 1940-44. Luxembourg Delegate to Red Cross, UNRRA, European Council, UN, NATO and WEU. *Address:* Luxembourg Embassy, 27 Wilton Crescent, SW1. *T:* 01-235 6961. *Clubs:* Travellers', St James'.

**CLATWORTHY, Robert,** ARA 1968; sculptor; Visiting Tutor at Royal College of Art since 1960; Teacher at West of England College of Art Since 1967; *b* 1 Jan. 1928; *s* of E. W. and G. Clatworthy; *m* 1954, Pamela Gordon; two *s* one *d. Educ:* Dr Morgan's Grammar Sch., Bridgwater. Studied West of England Coll. of Art, Chelsea Sch. of Art, The Slade. Mem., Fine Art Panel of Nat. Council for Diplomas in Art and Design, 1961-. Exhibited: Hanover Gall., 1954, 1956; Waddington Galls, 1965; Holland Park Open Air Sculpture, 1957; Battersea Park Open Air Sculpture, 1960, 1963; Tate Gallery, British Sculpture in the Sixties, 1965. Work in Collections: Arts Council, Contemporary Art Soc., Tate Gallery, Victoria and Albert Museum, Greater London Council. *Address:* 1 Park Street, SE1.

**CLAUSON, Sir Gerard Leslie Makins,** KCMG 1945 (CMG 1933); OBE 1919; Grand Officer, Order of Orange Nassau, 1947; Vice-Chairman, Pirelli Ltd; Hon. Vice-President, Royal Archæological Institute; Past President, Royal Asiatic Society; *b* 28 April 1891; *e s* of late Major Sir John Eugene Clauson KCMG, CVO; *m* 1918, Honor Emily Mary, *d* of late Ernest Innis Husey, MVO; two *s* one *d. Educ:* Eton (Scholar); Corpus Christi Coll., Oxford (Scholar). Boden Sanskrit Scholar, 1911; Hall-Houghton Syriac Prizeman, 1913; James Mew Arabic Scholar, 1920; 2nd Lieut 7th Som. LI 1914; transferred to General List, 1915; served in Gallipoli, Egypt, Mesopotamia; Capt. Gen. Staff (despatches twice, French Croix de Guerre with Palms); 2nd Class Clerk, Board of Inland Revenue, Sept. 1914; transferred to Colonial Office on retirement from Army, 1919; Principal, 1920; Asst Sec., 1934; Asst Under-Sec. of State, 1940-51; retired, 1951. Mem. UK Delegn to: Imperial Economic Conference, Ottawa, 1932; Monetary and Economic Conference, London, 1933; Imperial Conf., 1937; Hot Springs Conf., 1943, and various other internat. meetings; Chm., Internat. Wheat Conf., 1947; and International Rubber Conf., 1951. FSA. Indiana Univ. Prize for Altaic Studies, 1969. *Publications:* Sanglax by Muhammad Mahdi Xan, 1960; Turkish and Mongolian Studies, 1962; papers on Turkish languages and history. *Recreations:* archæology and Oriental languages. *Address:* 28 Kensington Court Gardens, W8. *T:* 01-937 0378. *Club:* Athenæum.

**CLAVERING, Sir Albert,** Kt 1935; OBE 1941; an hon. adviser, National Savings Committee; *b* 17 April 1887; *s* of Isaac Clavering; *m* 1913, May Muriel Harris; one *s* two *d. Educ:* private. Dir of Companies, now retired. Mem. LCC, SE St Pancras, 1931-34. Hon. Organising Dir, Conservative and Unionist Films Assoc., 1930-45. *Address:* 2 Courtenay Gate, Kingsway, Hove, BN3 2WJ. *Clubs:* St Stephen's; Hove (Hove).

**CLAXTON, Rt. Rev. Charles R.;** *see* Blackburn, Bishop of.

**CLAXTON, John Francis,** CB 1969; Deputy Director of Public Prosecutions since Oct. 1966; *b* 11 Jan. 1911; *s* of Alfred John Claxton and Dorothy Frances O. Claxton (*née* Roberts); *m* 1937, Norma Margaret Rawlinson; no *c. Educ:* Tonbridge Sch.; Exeter Coll., Oxford (BA). Called to Bar, 1935. Joined Dept of Dir of Public Prosecutions, 1937; Asst Dir, 1956-66. *Recreations:* model making, gardening. *Address:* The White Cottage, Lock Road, Marlow, Bucks. *T:* Marlow 2744. *Club:* Oxford and Cambridge University.

**CLAXTON, Maj.-Gen. Patrick Fisher,** OBE 1946; Transport Officer-in-Chief (Army) since 1969; *b* 13 March 1915; *s* of Ernest William Claxton and Kathleen O'Callaghan Claxton, formerly Fisher; *m* 1941, Jōna Gudrūn Gunnarsdōttir; two *d. Educ:* Sutton Valence Sch.; St John's Coll., Cambridge (BA). Served GHQ, India, 1943-45; Singapore, 1945-46; WO, 1946-48; British Element Trieste Force, 1949-51; HQ, BAOR, 1952-54; RASC Officers' Sch., 1955-56; Amphibious Warfare HQ and Persian Gulf, 1957-58; Col, WO, 1959-60; Brig., WO, 1961-62; DST, BAOR, 1963-65; CTO, BAOR, 1965-66; Comdt, Sch. of Transport, and ADC to the Queen, 1966-68. MInstT 1967. *Address:* c/o Lloyds Bank Ltd, Cox's & King's Branch (Section F), 6 Pall Mall, SW1.

**CLAY, Sir Charles Travis,** Kt 1957; CB 1944, Hon. LittD; FSA; FBA 1950; Librarian, House of Lords, 1922-56; *b* 30 July 1885; *y s* of late John William Clay of Rastrick House, Yorks; *m* 1913, Hon. Violet, 2nd *d* of late Lord Robson; three *d. Educ:* Harrow; Balliol Coll., Oxford, 1st Class History. Asst private sec. to Marquess of Crewe at Colonial Office, 1909-10, and at India Office, 1910-14; Asst Librarian, House of Lords, 1914-22; Lieut Devon Yeo.; Major, Territorial Army Reserve; served European War (despatches twice, DAQMG). Pres., Yorks Archæological Soc., 1953-56. *Address:* 30 Queen's Gate Gardens, SW7. *T:* 01-584 0205. *Club:* Brooks's.

**CLAY, Sir Henry Felix,** 6th Bt *cr* 1841; Partner, McLellan and Partners, Consulting Engineers; *b* 8 Feb. 1909; *s* of Sir Felix Clay, 5th Bt, and Rachel, *er d* of Rt Hon. Henry Hobhouse; *S* father, 1941; *m* 1933, Phyllis Mary, *yr d* of late R. H. Paramore; one *s* two *d. Educ:* Gresham's Sch.; Trinity Coll., Cambridge. *Heir: s* Richard Henry Clay [*b* 2 June 1940; *m* 1963, Alison Mary, *o d* of Dr J. Gordon Fife; three *s* one *d*]. *Address:* Sheer House, West Byfleet, Surrey. *Club:* United University.

**CLAY, John Martin;** Director, Hambros Bank Ltd, since 1961; Chairman, Thos. Firth & John Brown Ltd, since 1966; Member, Commonwealth Development Corporation, since 1970; *b* 20 Aug. 1927; *s* of late Sir Henry Clay and Gladys Priestman Clay; *m* 1952, Susan Jennifer, *d* of Lt-Gen. Sir Euan Miller, *qv*; four *s. Educ:* Eton; Magdalen Coll., Oxford. *Recreation:* sailing. *Address:* Farningham House, Farningham, Dartford, Kent. *T:* Farningham 2266. *Club:* Royal Thames Yacht.

**CLAY, Gen. Lucius DuBignon;** US Army (retd); Senior Partner, Lehman Brothers, since 1963; Chairman, Federal National Mortgage Association; Director: Chase International Investment Corp.; Lehman Corp.; *b* 23 April 1897; *s* of Alexander Stephen and Francis White Clay; *m* 1918, Marjorie McKeown; two *s*. *Educ:* USMA, West Point, New York. Instructor, Officers' Training Camp, 1918-19; Engr Sch. of Application, 1919-20; Asst Prof. Mil. Science and Tactics, Alabama Poly. Inst., 1920-21; Constr Quartermaster and Post Engr Ft Belvoir, Va, 1921-24; Instr Dept Civil Engr, USMA, 1924-27; 11th Engrs Canal Zone, Field Mapping, 1927-30; Asst to Dist Engr Pittsburgh, in charge Construction Lock and Dam No. 2, Allegheny River, 1930-33; Asst to Chief of Engrs in River and Harbor Sec., 1933-37; Consultant on Devel. of Water Resources to Nat. Power Corp., Philippine Commonwealth, 1937-38; in charge constr. of Denison Dam, 1938-40; Asst to Administrator Civil Aeronautics Admin. on Airport Program, 1940-41; Dir of Matériel, ASF, 1942-44; commanded Normandy Base, 1944; Dep. Dir War Mobilization and Reconversion, 1945; Dep. Mil. Gov. of Germany, 1945-47; C-in-C, European Comd, and Military Governor of US Zone of Germany, 1947-49; retired, 1949. Personal Representative of the President, with rank of Ambassador, in Berlin, Aug. 1961-May 1962. Numerous hon. degrees, civic hons, medals, foreign decorations. Trustee: Presbyterian Hosp. of NY; Amer. Nat. Red Cross. *Publication:* Decision in Germany, 1950. *Recreations:* fishing, golf. *Address:* One William Street, New York, NY 10004, USA. *Clubs:* Army and Navy; University, Bohemian, Links, Pinnacle, Blind Brook.

**CLAYDEN, Rt. Hon. Sir (Henry) John,** PC 1963; Kt 1958; Chairman, Industrial Tribunals; *b* 26 April 1904; *s* of Harold William and Florence Hilda Clayden; *m* 1948, Gwendoline Edith Lawrance. *Educ:* Diocesan Coll., Capetown; Charterhouse; Brasenose Coll., Oxford. Called to Bar, Inner Temple, 1926; Advocate, South Africa, 1927; practised Johannesburg. Served War with S African Engineer Corps and SA Staff Corps, 1940-45. Apptd KC 1945; Judge, Supreme Court of South Africa, Transvaal Provincial Div., 1946-55, 1964-65. Judge of Federal Supreme Court, 1955; Chief Justice, Federation of Rhodesia and Nyasaland, Dec. 1960-April 1964. Chm. Southern Rhodesia Capital Commission, 1955; Federal Delimitation Commission, 1958; Hammarskjöld Accident Commission, 1962. Acting Gov.-Gen., Federation of Rhodesia and Nyasaland, May-June 1961. Hon. LLD Witwatersrand. *Address:* 8 Walton Street, SW3. *T:* 01-589 1300. *Clubs:* United Service; Rand, Salisbury (Rhodesia).

**CLAYE, Sir Andrew (Moynihan),** Kt 1960; Emeritus Professor of Obstetrics and Gynæcology, University of Leeds; *b* Brigg, Lincs, 18 July 1896; *o s* of Rev. Arthur Needham Claye and late Ada Augusta, *d* of Capt. Andrew Moynihan, VC; *m* 1928, Marjorie Elaine, MB, ChB, Leeds (1st Class Hons, Gold Medal), BA London, DCH, *yr d* of late Dr C. H. Knowles, Garforth, Leeds; two *d*. *Educ:* Lancing; Univ. of Leeds. Lieut 4th Dorset Regt, 1915-19; MRCS, LRCP, 1924; MB, ChB Leeds, 1924; MD Leeds, 1926; FRCS 1928; FRCOG 1934; BA London, 1964; MPhil Leeds, 1967. Formerly: Obstetric Surg., Leeds Maternity Hosp., and Surg., Hosp. for Women at Leeds; Hon. Consultant Surg., Royal Women's Hosp., Melbourne; MD Melbourne (*hc*), 1956; Sims-Black Travelling Prof. (Australia and New Zealand), RCOG, 1956; late Examiner, Univs of Oxford, Cambridge, Aberdeen, Belfast, Manchester and Conjoint Board in England; Pres., 1957-60, and late Examr, RCOG; Mem. of Council RCS (co-opted), 1950-55; late Mem., Central Midwives Board; Pres., 13th British Congress of Obstetrics and Gynæcology, 1952; Hon. Fellow and late Pres., North of England Obst. and Gynæcol. Soc.; Hon. Fellow, Edinburgh Obst. Soc.; Ed., British Obstetric Practice. *Publications:* The Evolution of Obstetric Analgesia, 1939; Management in Obstetrics, 2nd edn, 1956; (with Canon Adam Fox) English Well Used, 1968; articles on obstetric and gynæcological subjects. *Recreations:* reading the classics and music. *Address:* 247a Hills Road, Cambridge. *T:* 66161.

**CLAYSON, Christopher William,** OBE 1966; President, Royal College of Physicians of Edinburgh, 1966; Chairman, Scottish Council for Post-Graduate Medical Education, since 1970; *b* 11 Sept. 1903; *s* of Christopher Clayson and Agnes Lilias Montgomerie Hunter; *m* Elsie Webster Breingan. *Educ:* George Heriot's Sch.; Edinburgh University. MB, ChB 1926; DPH 1929; MD (Gold Medal) Edinburgh 1936; FRCPE 1951; FRCP 1967. Physician: Southfield Hosp., Edinburgh, 1931-44; Edinburgh City Hosp., 1939-44; Lectr in Tuberculosis Dept, Univ. of Edinburgh, 1939-44; Med. Supt, Lochmaben Hosp., 1944-48; Consultant Phys. in Chest Medicine, Dumfries and Galloway, 1948-68; retd from clinical practice, 1968. Served on numerous Govt and Nat. Health Service cttees, 1948-. Mem., Scottish Soc. of Physicians; Mem., Thoracic Soc.; Hon. FACP 1968; Hon. FRACP 1969. *Publications:* various papers on tuberculosis problem in leading medical jls. *Recreations:* gardening, fishing. *Address:* Cockiesknowe, Lochmaben, Lockierbie, Dumfriesshire. *T:* Lochmaben 231. *Clubs:* Caledonian; New (Edinburgh).

**CLAYSON, Sir Eric (Maurice),** Kt 1964; Chairman and Joint Managing Director, The Birmingham Post & Mail Ltd, and Chairman of subsidiaries, since 1957; Director: Associated Television Ltd, since 1964; ATV Network Ltd, since 1966; Alpha Television Services (Birmingham) Ltd, since 1964; Sun Alliance & London Insurance Group Ltd (Chairman, Birmingham Area Board) T. Dillon & Co. Ltd; Midland Air Tour Operators Ltd; Dir, Birmingham Regional Board, Lloyds Bank Ltd; Chairman, Midland Regional Local Board, Hill, Samuel & Co. Ltd; *b* 17 Feb. 1908; *yr s* of late Harry and Emily Clayson; *m* 1933, Pauline Audrey Wright; two *s*. *Educ:* Woodbridge Sch. Chartered Accountant, 1931; Dir, The Birmingham Post & Mail Ltd, 1944, Managing Dir, 1947, Jt Managing Dir, 1957. President: Birmingham Publicity Assoc., 1948-49 (Chm., 1947-48); W Midlands Newspaper Soc., 1949-50; The Newspaper Soc., 1951-52 (Hon. Treasurer, 1956-60); Birmingham Branch, Incorporated Sales Managers' Assoc., 1953-54; Birmingham and Midland Inst., 1967-68. Vice-Pres., Fédération Internationale des Editeurs de Journaux et Publications, 1954-67. Chairman: Exec. Cttee, British Industries Fair, 1956-57; Midlands Regular Forces Resettlement Cttee, 1961- (Mem., 1958-). Director: The Press Assoc. Ltd, 1959-66 (Chm., 1963-64); Reuters Ltd, 1961-66. Member: Council, Birmingham Chamber of Commerce, 1951- (Vice-Pres., 1953-54, Pres., 1955-56); Gen. Council of the Press, 1953-; BBC Midland Regional Adv. Council, 1954-57; W Midland Regional Economic Planning Council, 1965-68. Governor and Mem. Exec. Council, The Royal Shakespeare Theatre, Stratford-upon-Avon, 1963-; Life Governor, Birmingham Univ., 1956-, Mem. Council, 1959-; Mem. Convocation, Univ. of Aston in Birmingham,

1967-. President: Radio Industries Club of the Midlands, 1965-69; Midland Counties Golf Assoc., 1960-62; Vice-Pres., Professional Golfers' Assoc., 1959-. Guardian, Standard of Wrought Plate in Birmingham, 1969-. *Recreation:* reading newspapers. *Address:* The Poor's Piece, Linthurst Road, Barnt Green, Worcs. *T:* 021-445 1209.

**CLAYSON, Rev. Canon Jesse Alec Maynard,** AKC; Chaplain, HM's Household, since 1965; *b* 12 June 1905; *s* of Jesse and Lilian Clayson, St Margaret-at-Cliffe, Kent; *m* 1934, Gwendoline Mary, *d* of William and Olive Reed, Streatham; two *s* two *d. Educ:* Dover County Sch.; King's Coll., London. Deacon, 1934; Priest, 1935; Curate of St Stephen, Norbury, 1934-37; Chaplain RN (HMS Newcastle), 1937-38; Vicar of Holy Trinity, Dover, 1938-40; Vicar of St Stephen, Norbury, 1940-45; Sec., Canterbury Diocesan Bd of Finance, 1945-67; Archdeacon of Croydon, 1957-67; Hon. Canon of Canterbury Cathedral, 1951; Vicar of Bisley, 1967-69. *Address:* 27 Gorselands, Sedlescombe, Battle, Sussex. *T:* Sedlescombe 550.

**CLAYTON, Sir Arthur Harold,** 11th Bt of Marden, *cr* 1732; DSC 1945; Lt-Comdr RNR; *b* 14 Oct. 1903; *s* of Sir Harold Clayton, 10th Bt, and Leila Cecilia, *d* of Francis Edmund Clayton; *S* father, 1951; *m* 1st, 1927, Muriel Edith (*d* 1929), *d* of late Arthur John Clayton; 2nd, 1931, Alexandra Andreevsky (marr. diss. 1954); one *s* one *d*; 3rd, 1954, Dorothy (Jill) (*d* 1964), *d* of Arthur John Greenhalgh; 4th, 1965, Diana Bircham. *Educ:* Haileybury Coll. In business in London, 1923-41, 1946-50. Served War of 1939-45, RNVR, 1941-46 (despatches, DSC). *Recreations:* short and long distance sailing. *Heir: s* David Robert Clayton, *b* 12 Dec. 1936. *Address:* Colonsay, Kingswear, Dartmouth, Devon. *T:* Kingswear 243. *Clubs:* Albemarle; Royal Naval Sailing Association (Portsmouth); Brixham Yacht (Brixham); Royal Dart Yacht (Kingswear); Dartmouth Sailing.

**CLAYTON, Colin,** MA, LLB Cantab; Barrister-at-Law; a Master of the Supreme Court, Queen's Bench Division, 1951-67; *b* 13 Aug. 1895; 2nd *s* of Wheeler Welland Fielden Clayton, Morecambe and West Worthing; *m* 1937, Doris Marion, MBE, *widow* of Will. H. Moore and *d* of John Minshall. *Educ:* Brighton Grammar Sch.; Christ's Coll., Cambridge. Held commission in Royal Sussex Regt; served European War in France, 1915-18. Called to the Bar, Middle Temple, 1921. Law Ed. of The Times Law Reports, 1934-51. *Address:* Cloisters, Temple, EC4. *T:* 01-353 7818. *Club:* Oxford and Cambridge University.

**CLAYTON, Edwin,** ISO 1950; *b* 18 Sept. 1887; *s* of Henry Bell Clayton, Solicitor, Nottingham; *m* 1935, Gwendoline Douglas, *d* of Arthur Douglas Hay; one *s. Educ:* Nottingham; Huntingdon. Admitted a Solicitor, 1910; joined staff of Dir of Public Prosecutions, 1919; Asst Dir of Public Prosecutions, 1945-52; retired 1952. Served European War, 1914-18; joined RA, Aug. 1914; commissioned Dec. 1914, with the RFA; served overseas in France and Belgium; wounded at Passchendaele, 1917; Army of Occupation in Germany until 1919. *Recreations:* rowing, football, walking. *Address:* 128 Kenilworth Court, SW15. *T:* 01-788 2208.

**CLAYTON, Prof. Frederick William;** Professor of Classics since 1948, also Public Orator since 1965, University of Exeter; *b* 13 Dec. 1913; *s* of late William and Gertrude Clayton, Liverpool; *m* 1948, Friederike Luise Büttner-Wobst; two *s* two *d. Educ:* Liverpool Collegiate Sch.; King's Coll., Cambridge. Members' Essay Prizes (Latin and English), Porson Prize, Browne Medal, 1933; Craven Scholar in Classics, 1934; Chancellor's Medal for Classics, 1935; Fellow of King's Coll., 1937. Served War of 1939-45: Intelligence Corps, 1940-42; RAF, India, 1942-45. *Publications:* The Cloven Pine, 1942; various articles. *Address:* Halwill, Clydesdale Road, Exeter, Devon. *T:* Exeter 71810.

**CLAYTON, Air Marshall Sir Gareth (Thomas Butler),** KCB 1970 (CB 1962); DFC 1940, and Bar, 1944; Air Secretary, Ministry of Defence, since 1970; *b* 13 Nov. 1914; *s* of Thomas and Katherine Clayton; *m* 1938, Elisabeth Marian Keates; three *d. Educ:* Rossall Sch. Entered RAF, 1936; served in various Bomber and Fighter Squadrons, 1936-44; RAF Staff Coll., 1944; Air Attaché, Lisbon, 1946-48; various command and staff appts, 1948-58; idc 1959; Air Ministry, 1960-61; Air Officer Commanding No. 11 Group, RAF, 1962-63; Chief of Staff, Second Allied Tactical Air Force, Germany, 1963-66 Dir-Gen., RAF Personal Services, 1966-69; Chief of Staff, HQ RAF Strike Command, 1969-70. *Recreations:* shooting, fishing. *Address:* c/o Lloyds Bank Ltd, 263 Tottenham Court Road, W1. *Clubs:* Royal Air Force, Pathfinder.

**CLAYTON, Hon. Sir Hector (Joseph Richard),** Kt 1968; ED; BA, LLB; MLC, NSW, since 1937; former Upper House Opposition Leader (1960-62); Chairman, Australian Guarantee Corp. Ltd; *b* Sydney, 3 June 1885; *s* of late J. H. Clayton, Sydney, NSW; *m* 1917, Phyllis E., *d* of late A. Midwood; two *s* two *d. Educ:* Sydney Grammar Sch.; Univ. of Sydney. Admitted Solicitor, 1911; Mem. Clayton, Utz & Co., Sydney. AIF, overseas, 1914-19; AMF, 1939-45; Col comdg 1st Austr. Movement Control Gp; Hon. Col, retd. *Recreations:* bowls, gardening. *Address:* Parliament House, Sydney, NSW, Australia. *Clubs:* Australian, University, Royal Sydney Golf (all Sydney).

**CLAYTON, Jack;** film director; *b* 1921; *m* Christine Norden (marr. diss.); *m* Katherine Kath (marr. diss.). Entered film industry, 1935. Served War of 1939-45, RAF Film Unit. Production Manager: An Ideal Husband; Associate Producer: Queen of Spades; Flesh and Blood; Moulin Rouge; Beat the Devil; The Good Die Young; I am a Camera; Producer and Director: The Bespoke Overcoat, 1955; The Innocents, 1961; Our Mother's House, 1967; Director: Room at the Top, 1958; The Pumpkin Eater, 1964. *Address:* c/o Romulus Films Ltd, Brook House, Park Lane, W1.

**CLAYTON, John Pilkington,** MA, MB, BChir; Surgeon Apothecary to HM Household at Windsor since 1965; Surgeon Apothecary to HM Queen Elizabeth the Queen Mother's Household at the Royal Lodge, Windsor, since 1965; Senior Medical Officer: Eton College since 1965 (MO, 1962-); Royal Holloway College since 1966 (MO, 1962-); MO to Black and Decker Ltd, since 1956; *b* 13 Feb. 1921; *s* of late Brig.-Gen. Sir Gilbert Clayton, KCMG, KBE, CB, and Enid, *d* of late F. N. Thorowgood. *Educ:* Wellington Coll.; Gonville and Caius Coll., Cambridge; King's Coll. Hospital. RAFVR, 1947-49; Sqdn Ldr 1949. Senior Resident, Nottingham Children's Hosp., 1950. Div. Surg., St John's Amb. Bde, 1955-. *Address:* Town End House, Eton College, Windsor. *T:* Windsor 62257.

**CLAYTON, Lucie;** *see* Kark, Evelyn F.

**CLAYTON, Rev. Philip Thomas Byard,** CH 1933; MC; DD (Lambeth); MA; FSA; an Extra Chaplain to the Queen (formerly Chaplain to

King George V, to King George VI, and to the Queen); Chaplain to British Petroleum Oil Co.; Founder Padre of Toc H, when Toc H (Talbot House) began in Ypres Salient, 1915; Vicar, 1922-63, of All Hallows, Barking-by-the-Tower (bombed and burnt, 1940), the Guild Church of Toc H; *b* Queensland, 12 Dec. 1885; *y s* of late R. B. B. Clayton, JP; unmarried. *Educ:* St Paul's Sch. (Scholar); Exeter Coll., Oxford (Scholar). 1st Cl Theological Final, 1909. Curate of Portsea, 1910-14; Temp. CF 1915; Chaplain, 16th Gen. Hosp.; 16th Inf. Bde; Bde Chaplain, 6th Div.; opened Talbot House in Poperinghe, which was named after Gilbert Talbot, *y s* of the Bishop of Winchester, Dec. 1915; Chaplain and Tutor of Service Candidates' Sch. at Knutsford, 1919; refounded Talbot House, 1920, as Toc H (Royal Charter, 1922)–a movement to teach younger generation racial reconciliation and unselfish service; first planned and launched Tower Hill Improvement, 1926; secured opening of Tower Beach for children, 1934; brought Toc H to support Leprosy Relief; inaugurated Winant Volunteers (1948) and Osler Volunteers (1950) to help East End Clubs and Settlements. Toured the Empire, US, S America, on behalf of Toc H, 1922, 1925, 1927, 1952, 1956, 1963, 1966; Persia, 1932; Gold Coast and Nigeria, 1933; S Africa, 1934; India, 1925, 1934, 1939; US, 1947, 1949, 1959, 1961; Middle East, 1950-51. Mediterranean Fleet, 1935-37; Chaplain of Anglo-Saxon Tanker Fleet, 1941-43; Chaplain MN in Indian Ocean and Mediterranean, 1942-45. Order of the Crown of Belgium, 1965; Hon. Freeman of Poperinghe and Ypres. *Publications:* Encaustic Mediæval Tiles, 1910; The Work of a Great Parish, 1912; Tales of Talbot House, 1919; Plain Tales from Flanders, 1929; Earthquake Love, 1932; Letters from Flanders, 1932; Pageant of Tower Hill, 1963; much current, social, and religious writing, etc. *Recreation:* seafaring. *Address:* Wakefield House, 41 Trinity Square, Tower Hill, EC3. *T:* 01-488 3333. *Club:* Press.

**CLAYTON, Robert James,** CBE 1970 (OBE 1960); CEng, FIEE, FInstP, FRAeS; Technical Director, The General Electric & English Electric Companies Ltd, since 1968; Director of a number of GEC-EE operating companies; member of a number of government and industry committees on electronics, particularly research; *b* 30 Oct. 1915; *m* 1949, Joy Kathleen King; no *c. Educ:* Cambridge Univ. (MA). GEC Research Labs, 1937; Manager, GEC Applied Electronics Labs, 1955; Dep. Dir, Hirst Research Centre, 1960; Man. Dir, GEC (Electronics), 1963; Man. Dir, GEC (Research), 1966. Mem. Council, 1964-68, Chm. of Electronics Div., 1968-69, Vice-Pres., 1970-71, IEE. *Publications:* papers in Proc. IEE. *Recreations:* theatre, music. *Address:* Drumness, Church Road, Stanmore, Mddx. *T:* 01-954 0329. *Club:* Oxford and Cambridge University.

**CLAYTON, Prof. Stanley George,** MD, MS London; FRCS; FRCOG; Professor of Obstetrics and Gynæcology, King's College Hospital Medical School, since Oct. 1967; Hon. Consulting Surgeon: Queen Charlotte's Hospital; Chelsea Hospital for Women; *b* 13 Sept. 1911; *s* of Rev. George and Florence Clayton; *m* 1936, Kathleen Mary Willshire; one *s* one *d. Educ:* Kingswood Sch.; King's Coll. Hosp. Med. Sch. Qualified, 1934; FRCS 1936; Sambrooke Schol., Jelf Medal, Hallett Prize. Surg. EMS; Major RAMC. Obstetric Surg., Queen Charlotte's Hosp., 1946; Surg., Chelsea Hosp. for Women, 1953; Obstetric and Gynæcological Surg., King's Coll. Hosp., 1947-63; Prof. of Obst. and Gyn., Postgrad. Inst. of Univ. of London, 1963-67. Examiner, Univs of London, Oxford, Cambridge and Dublin, National Univ. of Wales and RCOG. Editor, Jl of Obstetrics and Gynaecology. *Publications:* Pocket Gynaecology, 1948, 6th edn 1967; Pocket Obstetrics, 6th edn 1967; jointly: Queen Charlotte's Text-Book, 11th edn 1965; Ten Teachers' Obstetrics, 12th edn 1970; Ten Teachers' Diseases of Women, 12th edn 1970; Rose and Carless' Surgery, 19th edn 1960; British Obstetric and Gynæcological Practice, 3rd edn 1964; articles in med. jls. *Address:* Fir Tree Lodge, Fir Tree Road, Leatherhead, Surrey.

**CLEALL, Ven. Aubrey Victor George;** Archdeacon of Colchester, 1959-69, now Archdeacon Emeritus; *b* 9 Dec. 1898; *s* of late George and Cecilia Cleall, Crewkerne, Somerset. *Educ:* Selwyn Coll., Cambridge; Wells Theological Coll. BA 1922, MA 1926, Cambridge; MA (*ad eund.*) 1947, TCD. Deacon; 1924; Priest, 1925; Curate of Crewkerne, 1924-28; Vicar of Waltham Abbey, 1929-59. Diocesan Inspector of Schools (Chelmsford Dio.), 1932-46. Saint Antholin's Lecturer (City of London), 1937-57. Officiating CF, 1940-46; Comd 6th Cadet Bn, The Essex Regt (Actg Major TARO), 1942-44. Rural Dean of Chigwell, 1946-59; Hon. Canon of Chelmsford Cathedral, 1949-59; Rector of Wickham St Paul with Twinstead, 1959-63. Member: Convocation of Canterbury and Church Assembly, 1965-69; Essex County Education Cttee, 1951-59 and 1961-67. Governor, Colchester Royal Grammar Sch., 1963-67. *Address:* 7 Orchard Close, Ansford, Castle Cary, Somerset. *T:* Castle Cary 404.

**CLEARY, Denis Mackrow,** CMG 1967; HM Diplomatic Service, retired; re-employed in Department of Health and Social Security since 1968; *b* 20 Dec. 1907; *s* of late Francis Esmonde Cleary and late Emmeline Marie Cleary (*née* Mackrow); *m* 1st, 1941, Barbara Wykeham-George (*d* 1960); 2nd, 1962, Mary Kent (*née* Dunlop), *widow* of Harold Kent; one step-*d. Educ:* St Ignatius Coll. and St Olave's Sch.; St John's Coll., Cambridge (Major Schol.). 1st Class Hons Pts I and II, Math. Tripos; BA 1930; MA 1934. Asst Principal, India Office, 1931; Principal, 1937; seconded to Min. of Home Security, 1940-44; Dep. Principal Officer to Regional Commissioner, Cambridge, March 1943-Sept. 1944; seconded to Foreign Office (German Section), 1946-49; Asst Sec., 1948; transferred to CRO and posted to Delhi as Counsellor, 1949-51; Dep. High Commissioner, Wellington, 1955-58; Mem. of British Delegn to Law of the Sea Conf., Geneva, 1960; Dep. High Comr, Nicosia, 1962-64; Head of Atlantic Dept, Commonwealth Office, 1964-68. Mem. Cttee for Exports to the Caribbean, 1965-67. *Recreations:* gardening, walking. *Address:* High Gate, Burwash Weald, Sussex. *T:* West Burwash 312.

**CLEARY, Rt. Rev. Joseph Francis;** Auxiliary Bishop of Birmingham, (RC), and Titular Bishop of Cresima, since 1965; *b* 4 Sept. 1912; *s* of William Cleary and Ellen (*née* Rogers). *Educ:* Dublin; Oscott Coll., Sutton Coldfield. Ordained Priest 1939. Asst, St Chad's Cathedral, 1939-41; Archbishop's Sec., 1941-51; Parish Priest, SS Mary and John's, Wolverhampton, 1951-; Diocesan Treasurer, 1963-65; Provost of Diocesan Chapter, 1966-. *Address:* Presbytery, Snow Hill, Wolverhampton, Staffs. *T:* Wolverhampton 21676.

**CLEARY, Sir Joseph Jackson,** Kt 1965; *b* 26 Oct. 1902; *s* of Joseph Cleary, JP; *m* 1945, Ethel McColl. *Educ:* Holy Trinity C of E Sch., Anfield, Liverpool; Skerry's Coll., Liverpool.

Alderman, 1941 JP, 1927 for Liverpool; Dep. Chm., Mersey Docks and Harbour Board; Lord Mayor of Liverpool, 1949-50. Contested East Toxteth Div., Liverpool, March 1929 and May 1929; West Derby, Oct. 1931; MP (Lab) Wavertree Div. of Liverpool, Feb.-Oct. 1935. Lecture tour to Forces in Middle East, 1945. Freeman, City of Liverpool, 1970. *Recreations:* football (Association), tennis. *Address:* 115 Riverview Heights, Liverpool 19. *T:* 051-422 2133.

**CLEARY, Sir William Castle,** KBE 1947; CB 1945; *b* 14 March 1886; *s* of Rev. Augustus Castle Cleary and Kate Wyon; *m* 1914, Rosalind Clara Gwendoline Crosbie (*d* 1965); one *s* one *d. Educ:* Bedford Sch.; Trinity Coll., Cambridge. Junior Inspector of Elementary Schs, Board of Education, 1910; Principal Private Sec. to H. B. Lees Smith, Sir Donald Maclean and Lord Halifax, Presidents of Board, 1931-35; Principal Asst Sec., Elementary Education, 1940; Dep. Sec., Min. of Education, 1945-50. *Address:* 29 Denbigh Gardens, Richmond, Surrey. *T:* 01-940 3397.

**CLEASBY, Ven. Thomas Wood Ingram;** Archdeacon of Chesterfield, since 1963; Rector of Morton, Derby, since 1970; *b* 27 March 1920; *s* of T. W. Cleasby, Oakdene, Sedbergh, Yorks, and Jessie Brown Cleasby; *m* 1st, 1956, Olga Elizabeth Vibert Douglas (*d* 1967); one *s* two *d*; 2nd, 1970, Monica, *e d* of the Bishop of Bristol, *qv. Educ:* Sedbergh Sch., Yorks; Magdalen Coll., Oxford; Cuddesdon Coll., Oxford. BA, MA (Hons Mod. History) 1947. Commissioned, 1st Bn Border Regt, 1940; served 1st Airborne Div., 1941-45, Actg Major. Ordained, Dio. Wakefield, 1949 (Huddersfield Parish Church). Domestic Chaplain to Archbishop of York, 1952-56; Anglican Chaplain to Univ. of Nottingham, 1956-63; Vicar of St Mary and All Saints, Chesterfield, 1963-70. *Recreations:* fell-walking, bird-watching, gardening, fishing. *Address:* Morton Rectory, Derby DE5 6GU. *T:* Tibshelf 402.

**CLEAVER, Leonard Harry,** JP; Director: A. W. Phillips Ltd; Yoxalls Ltd; *b* 27 Oct. 1909; *s* of late Harry Cleaver, OBE, JP; *m* 1938, Mary Richards Matthews; one *s. Educ:* Bilton Grange and Rugby. Chartered Accountant: articled Agar, Bates, Neal & Co., Birmingham; Sec. and Chief Accountant, Chance Bros Ltd, 1935-51; Partner, Heathcote & Coleman, 1951-59. MP (C) Yardley Div. of Birmingham, 1959-64; PPS to Parly Sec. to Min. of Housing and Local Govt, 1963-64; contested Yardley Div. of Birmingham, 1964, 1966. JP Birmingham, 1954. City Councillor, Yardley Ward, 1966-70. *Recreations:* Rugby football and fishing. *Address:* Camp House Farm, Beaudesert, Henley-in-Arden, Solihull, Warwicks. *T:* Henley-in-Arden 2113. *Clubs:* Carlton; Conservative (Birmingham).

**CLEAVER, Air Vice-Marshal Peter (Charles),** OBE 1945; Air Officer i/c Engineering, HQ Air Support Command, Royal Air Force, since 1969; *b* 6 July 1919; *s* of William Henry Cleaver, Warwick; *m* 1948, Jean, *d* of J. E. B. Fairclough, Ledbury; two *s. Educ:* Warwick Sch.; Coll. of Aeronautics (DCAe). Apprenticeship, Sir W. G. Armstrong Whitworth Aircraft Co. Ltd, 1935-39. War Service, RAF, mainly in Middle East, 1939-45. RAF Staff Coll., Haifa, 1945; HM Asst Air Attaché, Bucharest, 1947-49; Coll. of Aeronautics, Cranfield, 1950-52; Structural Research, RAE Farnborough, 1952-55; Min. of Supply, 1955-57; HQ FEAF, 1957-60; Maintenance Comd, 1960-63; OC, Central Servicing Develt Estabt, 1963-64; Air Officer Engineering, HQ Flying Trg Comd, 1964-65; idc 1966; Air Officer Engineering, HQ FEAF, 1967-69. FIMechE, FRAeS. *Recreation:* shooting. *Address:* Salmond House, Yorke Road, Upavon, Pewsey, Wilts. *T:* Upavon 351 (ext 290). *Club:* Royal Air Force.

**CLEE, Sir Charles (Beaupré Bell),** Kt 1947; CSI 1946; CIE 1938; *b* 5 Feb. 1893; *s* of J. B. B. Clee; *m* 1931, Rosemary Margaret Meredydd, *d* of late H. P. M. Rae; one *s. Educ:* Cambridge Univ. Nominated to Indian Civil Service, 1919, after serving with Suffolk Regt during European War; arrived India, 1919; Asst Collector and Magistrate, Bombay; Acting Dir of Information, 1924; Sec., Indian Tariff Board, 1925; Dep. Sec. to Govt Finance Dept, Bombay, 1928; Officiating Sec. to Govt, Home and Ecclesiastical Dept, Bombay, 1932; Officiating Sec. to Govt Finance Dept, 1933; Collector and Magistrate, 1935; Officiating Sec. to Govt Finance Dept, Bombay, 1936; Sec. to Govt Finance Dept, Sind, 1936; Officiating Chief Sec., 1938; Fin. Sec., 1939; Chief Sec. to Govt of Sind, 1940; Revenue Comr for Sind, 1943; retired, 1950. *Recreations:* shooting, cricket, golf. *Address:* c/o Lloyds Bank Ltd, Cox's & King's Branch, 6 Pall Mall, SW1.

**CLEEVE, Brig. Francis Charles Frederick,** CBE 1945; DSO 1940; MC; *b* 26 June 1896; *e s* of late Maj.-Gen. W. F. Cleeve, CB, and late Mrs Cleeve, Ty Gwyn, Abergavenny; *m* 1st, 1934, Vera (*d* 1949), 2nd *d* of James T. Daly, Raford, Leamington; 2nd, 1951, Helen, *d* of Mrs Arthur West. *Educ:* Cheltenham; Royal Military Academy, Woolwich. Entered Royal Artillery, 1914; served European War, 1915-18, Egypt, Balkans, France (MC, 1914-15 Star, Gen. Service and Allied War Medals); War of 1939-45, France (despatches twice, DSO, CBE). Retired, 1948, with hon. rank of Brig. *Address:* Throop Farm, Horsington, Templecombe, Som. *T:* Templecombe 349. *Club:* Naval and Military.

**CLEGG, Sir Alec, (Alexander Bradshaw Clegg),** Kt 1965; Chief Education Officer, West Riding County Council, since 1945; *b* 13 June 1909; *s* of Samuel and Mary Clegg, Sawley, Derbs; *m* 1940, Jessie Coverdale Phillips, West Hartlepool; three *s. Educ:* Long Eaton Gram. Sch.; Bootham Sch., York; Clare Coll., Cambridge (BA); London Day Training Coll.; King's Coll., London (MA). Asst Master, St Clement Danes Gram. Sch., London, 1932-36; Admin. Asst Birmingham Educn Cttee, 1936-39; Asst Educn Officer, Ches CC, 1939-42; Dep. Educn Officer, Worcs CC, 1942-45; West Riding, Jan.-Sept. 1945. Chevalier de l'ordre de l'Etoile Noire, 1961. *Address:* Saxton, Tadcaster, Yorks, WR. *T:* Barkston Ash 288.

**CLEGG, Sir Alexander Bradshaw;** *see* Clegg, Sir Alec.

**CLEGG, Sir Cuthbert (Barwick),** Kt 1950; TD; JP; *b* 9 Aug. 1904; *s* of Edmund Barwick Clegg, DL, JP, Shore, Littleborough, Lancs; *m* 1930, Helen Margaret, *y d* of Arthur John Jefferson, MD; one *s. Educ:* Charterhouse; Trinity Coll., Oxford (MA). Director: Barclays Bank Ltd, 1968-; Barclays Bank Trust Co. Ltd (Dep. Chm., 1969-); Stone-Platt Industries Ltd; Halifax Building Soc. Pres., British Employers Confederation, 1950-52; JP Lancs, 1946, Sheriff, 1955; Sheriff of Westmorland, 1969; Major (retired), Duke of Lancaster's Own Yeomanry. Member: Cotton Industry Working Party, 1946; Cotton Manufacturing Commission, 1947-49; Anglo-American Council on Productivity, 1948-52; Economic Planning Bd, 1949-53; British Productivity Council, 1952-54; Leader, UK Cotton Industry Mission to India, Hong Kong and

Pakistan, 1957. Hon. Life Governor, The Cotton, Silk and Man-Made Fibres Research Association (Pres., 1962-67); President: UK Textile Manufacturers' Assoc., 1960-69; Overseas Bankers' Club, 1966-67; Inst. of Bankers, 1968-69. Chm., Martins Bank Ltd, 1964-69. *Address:* Barn Close, Beetham, Milnthorpe, Westmorland. *T:* Milnthorpe 3191. *Clubs:* Bath; St James's (Manchester).

**CLEGG, Hugh Anthony,** CBE 1966; MA, MB Cantab; Hon. MD (TCD); Hon. DLit QUB; FRCP; Director, Office for International Relations in Medicine, RSM, since 1967; Editor, Tropical Doctor, a journal of medical practice in the tropics, since first publication, 1971; *b* 19 June 1900; *s* of Rev. John Clegg and Gertrude, *d* of John Wilson; *m* 1932, Baroness Kyra Engelhardt, *o d* of late Baron Arthur Engelhardt, Smolensk, Russia; one *s* one *d*. *Educ:* Westminster Sch. (King's Schol.); Trinity Coll., Cambridge (Westminster Exhibr, Senior Schol., in Nat. Science); St Bartholomew's Hospital. 1st Class Hons Part 1 Nat. Sci. Tripos; House Physician at St Bartholomew's Hosp.; House Physician at Brompton Hosp. for Diseases of the Chest; Medical Registrar, Charing Cross Hosp.; Sub-editor, British Medical Journal, 1931-34; Deputy Editor, 1934-46; Editor, 1947-65. Hon. Fellow, American Medical Assoc.; late Chm., UNESCO Cttee on Co-ordination of Abstracting in the Medical and Biological Sciences. Initiator and Sec., First World Conf. on Med. Educn, London, 1953, and Ed. of its Proceedings, 1954; Editor, Medicine a Lifelong Study (Proceedings of the Second World Conf. on Med. Educn, Chicago, 1959). Vice-Pres., L'Union Internationale de la Presse Médicale, and Pres. of its Third Congress, 1957; Mem. Med. Panel, British Council to 1965; Mem. Council, World Medical Assoc., 1957-61, and Chm. of its Cttee on Medical Ethics and author of first draft of code of ethics on human experimentation, subsequently modified as Declaration of Helsinki. Gold Medal of BMA, 1966. *Publications:* What is Osteopathy? (jointly), 1937; Brush up your Health, 1938; Wartime Health and Democracy, 1941; contributed medical terms Chambers's Technical Dictionary, 1940; How to Keep Well in Wartime (Min. of Information), 1943; Medicine in Britain (British Council), 1944; revised Black's Medical Dictionary, 1940-44; Advisory Editor medical section of Chambers's Encyclopædia. *Recreation:* reading reviews of the books I should like to read but haven't the time to. *Address:* Chandos House, 2 Queen Anne Street, W1. *T:* 01-580 2070, ext. 32; 19 Park Avenue, North End Road, NW11. *T:* 01-455 4785.

**CLEGG, Hugh Armstrong;** Professor of Industrial Relations, since 1967, and Director, Centre of Industrial and Business Studies, University of Warwick; Director, Industrial Relations Research Unit, Social Science Research Council, since 1970; Chairman of the Civil Service Arbitration Tribunal, since 1968; *b* 22 May 1920; *s* of late Rev. Herbert Hobson Clegg and of Mabel (*née* Duckering); *m* 1941, Mary Matilda (*née* Shaw); two *s* two *d*. *Educ:* Kingswood Sch., Bath; Magdalen Coll., Oxford. Served War, 1940-45; Official Fellow, Nuffield Coll., Oxford, 1949-66; Emeritus Fellow, 1966-. Member: Royal Commn on Trade Unions and Employers' Assocs, 1965-68; Ct of Inquiry into Seamen's Dispute, 1966-67; Nat. Board for Prices and Incomes, 1966-67; Ct of Inquiry into Council Workers' Pay Dispute, 1970. *Publications:* Labour Relations in London Transport, 1950; Industrial Democracy and Nationalisation, 1951; The Future of Nationalisation (with T. E. Chester), 1953; General Union, 1954; Wage Policy in the Health Service (with T. E. Chester), 1957; The Employers' Challenge (with R. Adams), 1957; A New Approach to Industrial Democracy, 1960; Trade Union Officers (with A. J. Killick and R. Adams), 1961; General Union in a Changing Society, 1964; A History of British Trade Unions (with A. Fox and A. F. Thompson), Vol. I, 1964; The System of Industrial Relations in Great Britain, 1970. *Recreations:* walking, beer. *Address:* 48 Amherst Road, Kenilworth, Warwicks. *T:* Kenilworth 54825.

**CLEGG, Walter;** MP (C) North Fylde since 1966; a Lord Commissioner, HM Treasury, since 1970; *b* 18 April 1920; *s* of Edwin Clegg; *m* 1951, Elise Margaret Hargreaves. *Educ:* Bury Grammar Sch.; Arnold Sch., Blackpool; Manchester Univ. Law Sch. Articled to Town Clerk, Barrow-in-Furness, 1937. Served in Royal Artillery, 1939-46 (commnd 1940). Qualified as Solicitor, 1947; subsequently in practice. Lancashire County Coun., 1955-61. Opposition Whip, 1967-69; Vice-Chm., Assoc. of Conservative Clubs; Hon. Sec., Cons. Housing and Local Govt Cttee. *Recreations:* fishing, shooting, reading. *Address:* Beech House, Raikes Road, Little Thornton, near Blackpool, Lancs. *T:* Thornton 2131. *Clubs:* Carlton, Constitutional.

**CLEGG-HILL,** family name of **Viscount Hill.**

**CLELAND, Brig. Sir Donald Mackinnon,** Kt 1961; CBE 1945; Administrator, Territory of Papua and New Guinea, 1953-66, and President Executive and Legislative Councils of Papua and New Guinea, 1951-64; *b* 28 June 1901; *m* 1928, Rachel Evans (CBE 1966); two *s*. *Educ:* Guildford Grammar Sch., Western Australia. Barrister and Solicitor, Western Australia, 1925-39. Served War of 1939-45: Middle East, Greece, Crete, Syria, New Guinea; Capt. 1939, Brig. 1942; Chief of Staff, Military Administration, Papua and New Guinea, and Chm. Australian-New Guinea Production Control Board, 1943-45. Dir, Federal Secretariat of Australian Liberal Party, 1945-51; Asst Administrator, Papua-New Guinea, 1951; Acting Administrator, 1952-53. Chancellor, Anglican Diocese of New Guinea, 1968; Pro-Chancellor, Univ. of Papua and New Guinea, 1969. Hon. Col of the Pacific Islands Regt, 1953-66. CStJ 1967. *Recreations:* gardening, golf. *Address:* Chester Street, Box 358, PO Port Moresby, Papua. *Clubs:* Australian, Royal Sydney Golf (Sydney); Weld (WA); Papua (Port Moresby).

**CLELAND, Sir John (Burton),** Kt 1964; CBE 1949; MD, ChM; Professor of Pathology, University of Adelaide, 1920; retd, 1948; *b* 22 June 1878; *e s* of late Dr Wm Lennox Cleland, of the Clelands of that ilk, and Matilda Lauder, *d* of late Dr John Hill Burton, Historiographer Royal for Scotland; *m*; one *s* four *d*. *Educ:* Univs of Adelaide and Sydney. House Surg., etc, PA Hospital, Sydney, 1900, and Resident Pathologist, 1901; visited China and Japan, 1903; Examin. with distinction London Sch. of Tropical Medicine, 1904; Cancer Research Scholar, London Hosp., 1904-05; Govt Pathologist and Bacteriologist, W Australia, 1906-09; Principal Asst Microbiologist, Govt Bureau of Microbiol. NSW, 1909-13; Principal Microbiol., Dept of Public Health, NSW, 1913-19; President: Royal Society of NSW, 1917; Royal Society of South Australia, 1928 and 1941. *Publications:* many papers in medical and scientific journals; Dengue and Papataci Fevers, in A System of Bacteriology in Relation to Medicine, Medical Research Council, 1930; Toadstools and Mushrooms and other Larger Fungi of South

Australia, Part I, 1934, Part II, 1935; (with R. V. Southcott) Injuries to Man from Marine Invertebrates in the Australian Region, 1965; Ecology, Environment and Diseases in Aboriginal Man in South and Central Australia, 1966. *Recreations:* ornithology and botany. *Address:* 1 Dashwood Road, Beaumont, Adelaide, S Australia.
*See also W. P. Cleland.*

**CLELAND, William Paton,** FRCP, FRCS, FACS; Surgeon, Brompton Chest Hospital, since 1948; Hon. Thoracic Surgeon, King's College Hospital; Senior Lecturer in Thoracic Surgery, Royal Postgraduate Medical School, since 1949; Civilian Consultant in Thoracic Surgery to the RN; Adviser in Thoracic Surgery to the Department of Health and Social Security; *b* 30 May 1912; *o s* of Sir John Cleland, *qv*; *m* 1940, Norah, *d* of George E. Goodhart; two *s* one *d. Educ:* Scotch Coll., Adelaide; Univ. of Adelaide, S Australia. MB, BS (Adelaide). Resident appts, Royal Adelaide and Adelaide Children's Hosps, 1935-36; MRCP 1939; House Physician and Resident Surgical Officer, Brompton Chest Hosp., 1939-41. Served in EMS as Registrar and Surgeon, 1939-45. FRCS 1946. Consulting Thoracic Surg., 1948-; Dir, Dept of Surgery, Inst. of Diseases of the Chest, Brompton Hosp. Member: Assoc. Thoracic Surgeons of Gt Brit. and Ire.; Thoracic Soc.; British Cardiac Soc.; FRSocMed. *Publications:* (jt author) Medical and Surgical Cardiology, 1969; chapters on thoracic surgery in British Surgical Practice, Diseases of the Chest (Marshall and Perry), Short Practice of Surgery (Bailey and Love), and Operative Surgery (Rob and Rodney Smith); articles on pulmonary and cardiac surgery in medical literature. *Recreations:* fishing, sailing, farming, photography. *Address:* Erskine Lodge, 50 Primrose Hill Road, Hampstead, NW3. *T:* 01-722 2977. *Club:* Royal Automobile.

**CLEMENS, Clive Carruthers,** MC 1946; Principal British Trade Commissioner, Vancouver, since 1970; *b* 22 Jan. 1924; British; *s* of M. B. Clemens, Imperial Bank of India, retired, and late Margaret Jane (*née* Carruthers); *m* 1947, Philippa Jane Bailey; three *s. Educ:* Blundell's Sch.; St Catharine's Coll., Cambridge. War Service 1943-46: commissioned in Duke of Cornwall's Light Infantry; served in India and Burma, 1944-45. Entered HM Foreign Service and apptd to FO, 1947; Third Sec., Rangoon, 1948; Third (later Second) Sec., Lisbon, 1950; FO, 1953; First Sec., Budapest, 1954; Brussels, 1956; Seoul, 1959; FO, 1961; Strasbourg (UK Delegn to Council of Europe), 1964; Counsellor, Paris, 1967. *Recreations:* birdwatching, photography, sailing. *Address:* c/o Foreign and Commonwealth Office, SW1.

**CLEMENT, David Morris,** FCA; Member, National Coal Board, since 1969; *b* 6 Feb. 1911; 2nd *s* of Charles William and Rosina Wannell Clement, Swansea; *m* 1938, Kathleen Mary, *o d* of Ernest George Davies, ACA, Swansea; one *d. Educ:* Bishop Gore's Grammar Sch., Swansea. Mem. Inst. Chartered Accountants, 1933. A. Owen John & Co., Swansea, and Sissons Bersey Gain Vincent & Co., London, Chartered Accts, 1933-35; ICI Ltd, Lime Gp, 1935-40; Chloride Electrical Storage Co. Ltd, 1941-46; National Coal Board: Sec., North Western Div., 1946-49; Chief Acct, Northern and Durham Divs, 1950-55; Dep. Dir-Gen. of Finance, 1955-61; Dir-Gen. of Finance, 1961-69. *Recreations:* golf, photography. *Address:* 19 The Highway, Sutton, Surrey. *T:* 01-642 3626. *Club:* Royal Automobile.

**CLÉMENT, René;** Chevalier de la Légion d'Honneur; Officier des Arts et des Lettres; film director since 1945; *b* Bordeaux, France, 1913; *m* 1940, Bella Guritch. *Educ:* in decorative and fine arts and architecture, Paris. Bataille du rail, 1946 (mise en scène and international jury prizes, Cannes); Les Maudits, 1947 (film d'aventures prize, Cannes); Walls of Malapaga, 1948 (mise en scène prize, Cannes; Oscar, 1950, Hollywood); Château de verre, 1950; Jeux interdits (Lion d'or, 1952, Venice; British award; Oscar, 1952, Hollywood, etc); Monsieur Ripois, 1954 (mise en scène prize, Cannes); Gervaise, 1956 (Critics prize, Venice; British award; Press prize, New York; 10 Best Direction in World, Tokyo, etc); Sea Wall, 1958; Quelle joie de vivre, 1960; Le jour et l'Heure, 1963; Les Félins, 1964; Is Paris Burning?, 1966; Le Passager de la Pluie, 1969. *Publication:* (with C. Audry) Bataille du rail, 1947. *Recreations:* antiques, painting, music. *Address:* 91 Avenue Henri Martin, Paris 16e. *T:* Trocadéro 30-93; 10 Avenue de St Roman, Monte Carlo. *T:* 30-59-35.

**CLEMENTI, Air Vice-Marshal Cresswell Montagu,** CBE 1968 (OBE 1946); Senior RAF Member, Royal College of Defence Studies (formerly Imperial Defence College), since Dec. 1969; *b* 30 Dec. 1918; *s* of late Sir Cecil Clementi, GCMG and Lady Clementi, MBE; *m* 1940, Susan, *d* of late Sir Henry Pelham, KCB and Hon. Lady Pelham; two *s* one *d. Educ:* Winchester; Magdalen Coll., Oxford (MA). Commnd in RAFVR, 1938; served War of 1939-45 as pilot in Bomber Comd and Air Armament specialist; CO, No. 214 (FMS) Sqdn, 1946-48; RAF Staff Coll., 1949; Air Min. (Bomber Ops Directorate), 1950-52; Wing Comdr i/c Flying, RAF Gunnery Centre for 2nd TAF, Sylt, Germany, 1953-54; jssc, Latimer, 1955; Directing Staff, 1955-57; attended nuclear weapons trials at Christmas Island, 1958; comd RAF Stn Bassingbourn, 1958-61; Gp Capt. Ops/Plans/Trng, Near East Air Force, Cyprus, 1961-63; idc 1964; Dir of Air Staff Plans, MoD (Air Force Dept), 1965-67; AOC No. 19 Gp, RAF Mount Batten, Plymouth, 1968-69. *Recreations:* riding, travel. *Address:* 8 Chiswick Staithe, W4. *T:* 01-995 9532. *Club:* Royal Air Force.

**CLEMENTS, Clyde Edwin,** CMG 1962; OBE 1958; Managing Director: C. E. Clements & Co. Pty Ltd, since 1962; C. E. Clements (Holdings) Ltd; President, Clements Peruana SA; Director, C. E. Clements (South East Asia) Sdn. Bhd.; *b* 2 Aug. 1897; *e s* of late Edwin Thomas Clements and late Mrs Clements; *m* 1919, Doris Gertrude Garrett; one *d. Educ:* Devonport Grammar Sch., Tasmania; Queen's Coll., Hobart, Tas. Served European War, 1914-18. Vice-Pres. Young Christian Workers, 1943-66; Dir Young Christian Workers Co-operative Soc. Ltd, 1948-62. Pres. Austr. AA, 1956-57; Mem. Bd, Austr. Nat. Travel Assoc., 1956-57; Mem. Bd, Tourist Develt Authority of Victoria, 1958-69; Vice-Pres. (OTA) World Touring Organization, 1958. Mem. Board of Management, Sir Colin MacKenzie Sanctuary, Healesville, Vic., 1962. Hon. Consul of Peru. *Recreations:* golf, angling. *Address:* 9 Cosham Street, Brighton, Vic 3186, Australia. *T:* 92.3974. *Clubs:* Royal Automobile of Victoria (Vice-Pres. 1942-44, 1952-53; Pres. 1955-61); RACV Country; Victoria Golf; Frankston Golf; West Brighton (Vic).

**CLEMENTS, Sir John (Selby),** Kt 1968; CBE 1956; FRSA; Actor, Manager, Producer; *b* 25 April 1910; *s* of late Herbert William Clements, Barrister-at-Law, and Mary Elizabeth (*née* Stephens); *m* 1st, 1936, Inga Maria Lillemor

Ahlgren (marr. diss. 1946); 2nd, 1946, Dorothy Katharine (*see* Kay Hammond), *d* of late Sir Guy Standing, KBE, and Dorothy Frances Plaskitt. *Educ:* St Paul's Sch.; St John's Coll., Cambridge. British Actors' Equity: Mem. Council, 1948, 1949; Vice-Pres., 1950-59; Trustee, 1958. Member: Arts Council Drama Panel, 1953-58; Council, RADA, 1957-. First stage appearance, Out of the Blue, Lyric, Hammersmith, 1930; subsequently appeared in: She Stoops to Conquer, Lyric; The Beaux' Stratagem, Royalty, 1930; The Venetian, Little, 1931; Salome, Gate Theatre, 1931; many Shakespearian parts under management of late Sir Philip Ben Greet; founded The Intimate Theatre, Palmers Green, London, 1935, and ran it as weekly repertory theatre until 1940, directing most of and appearing in nearly 200 plays; produced Yes and No, Ambassadors, 1937; appeared in: Skylark, Duchess, 1942; They Came to a City, Globe, 1943; (also produced) Private Lives, Apollo, 1944; (with Old Vic Co.) played Coriolanus, Petruchio and Dunois, New, 1947-48; appeared in Edward My Son, Lyric, 1948-49; as Actor-Manager-Producer, has presented and played in: The Kingmaker; Marriage à la Mode, St James's, 1946; The Beaux' Stratagem, Phoenix and Lyric, 1949-50; Man and Superman, New and Princes, 1951; (also author) The Happy Marriage, Duke of York's, 1952-53; Pygmalion, St Jame's, 1953-54; The Little Glass Clock, Aldwych, 1954-55; personal management of Saville Theatre, 1955-57, where presented and played in: The Shadow of Doubt; The Wild Duck, 1955-56; The Rivals, 1956; The Seagull; The Doctor's Dilemma; The Way of the World, 1956-57; Adviser on Drama to Associated Rediffusion Ltd, 1955-56, where produced films including: A Month in the Country; The Wild Duck; played in: (also co-presented and directed) The Rape of the Belt, Piccadilly, 1957-58; (also presented) Gilt and Gingerbread, Duke of York's, 1959; The Marriage-Go-Round, Piccadilly, 1959-60; produced Will You Walk a Little Faster?, Duke of York's, 1960; played in: J. B., Phœnix, 1961; The Affair, Strand, 1961; The Tulip Tree, Haymarket, 1962; Old Vic American tour, 1962; played in: (also co-presented and directed) The Masters, Savoy, 1963; Robert and Elizabeth, Lyric, 1964. Director, Chichester Festival Theatre: 1966 season, presented: The Clandestine Marriage; (also played in) The Fighting Cock (subseq. Duke of York's); The Cherry Orchard; (also played) Macbeth; 1967 season, directed: The Farmer's Wife; (also played Shotover) Heartbreak House (subseq. Lyric); presented: The Beaux' Stratagem; An Italian Straw Hat; 1968 season, presented: The Unknown Soldier and His Wife; The Cocktail Party (subseq. Wyndham's); (played Prospero) The Tempest; The Skin of our Teeth; 1969 season, presented: The Caucasian Chalk Circle; (also directed and played in) The Magistrate (subseq. Cambridge); The Country Wife; (also played Antony) Antony and Cleopatra; 1970 season, presented: Peer Gynt; Vivat! Vivat! Regina!; (also directed) The Proposal; Arms and the Man; The Alchemist. Entered films, 1934; films include: Things to Come; Knight Without Armour; South Riding; Rembrandt; The Four Feathers; Convoy; Ships With Wings; Undercover; They Came to a City; Train of Events; The Silent Enemy; The Mind Benders; Oh What a Lovely War!. *Address:* 7 Royal Crescent, Brighton, Sussex. *Club:* Garrick.

**CLEMENTS, Julia;** *see* Seton, Lady, (Julia).

**CLEMENTS, Rt. Rev. Kenneth John;** *see* Canberra and Goulburn, NSW, Bishop of.

**CLEMENTS, Richard Harry;** Editor of Tribune since 1961; *b* 11 Oct. 1928; *s* of Harry and Sonia Clements; *m* 1953, Bridget Mary MacDonald; two *s*. *Educ:* King Alfred Sch., Hampstead; Western High Sch., Washington, DC; Regent Street Polytechnic. Middlesex Independent, 1949; Leicester Mercury, 1951; Ed., Socialist Advance (Labour Party Youth paper), 1953; industrial staff, Daily Herald, 1954; joined Tribune, 1956. *Publication:* Glory without Power: a study of trade unions, 1959. *Recreation:* woodwork. *Address:* Tribune Publications Ltd, 24 St John Street, EC1. *T:* 01-253 2994.

**CLEMITSON, Rear-Adm. Francis Edward,** CB 1952; retired; *b* 9 Nov. 1899; *s* of William David and Helen Louisa Clemitson; *m* 1933, Kathleen Farquhar Shand; two *d*. *Educ:* Christ's Hospital. Entered Royal Navy as Cadet, 1917; Lieut (E), 1921; Commander (E), 1933; Capt. (E), 1943; Rear-Adm. (E), 1949; Deputy Engineer-in-Chief of the Fleet (Admin.), Admiralty, 1950-53; retired Oct. 1953. *Recreations:* tennis, golf, philately. *Address:* Tanhurst, Bramley, Surrey. *T:* Bramley 3148.

**CLEMO, G. R.,** DSc; FRS 1937; FIC; Professor of Organic Chemistry, King's College, University of Durham, 1925-54, Professor Emeritus, 1954; Director of Department of Chemistry, 1932-54. *Educ:* University Coll., Exeter; Queen's Coll., Oxford. Late asst to Prof. W. H. Perkin at Oxford; was in charge of the Research Department of the British Dyestuffs Corporation, Manchester. *Address:* Cherryburn, Mickley on Tyne, Northumberland.

**CLEMOES, Prof. Peter Alan Martin,** PhD (Cantab); Elrington and Bosworth Professor of Anglo-Saxon, Cambridge University, since Oct. 1969; Official Fellow of Emmanuel College, Cambridge, 1962-69, Professorial Fellow since 1969; *b* 20 Jan. 1920; *o s* of Victor Clemoes and Mary (*née* Paton); *m* 1956, Jean Elizabeth, *yr d* of Sidney Grew; two *s*. *Educ:* Brentwood Sch.; Queen Mary Coll., London; King's Coll., Cambridge. BA London (1st Cl. Hons English) 1950; Soley Student, King's Coll., Cambridge, 1951-53; Research Fellow, Reading Univ., 1954-55; PhD Cambridge 1956. Lectr in English, Reading Univ., 1955-61; Lectr in Anglo-Saxon, Cambridge Univ., 1961-69; Coll. Lectr in English, 1963-69 and Dir of Studies in English, 1963-65; Tutor, 1966-68; Asst Librarian, 1963-69. *Publications:* The Anglo-Saxons, Studies . . . presented to Bruce Dickins (ed and contrib.), 1959; General Editor of Early English Manuscripts in Facsimile (Copenhagen), 1963-, and co-editor of vol. XIII, 1966; textual and critical writings, especially on the works of Ælfric. *Address:* 14 Church Street, Chesterton, Cambridge. *T:* Cambridge 58655.

**CLERK, Sir John Dutton,** 10th Bt *cr* 1679; CBE 1966; VRD; JP; Vice-Lieutenant of Midlothian since 1965; Cdre RNR; retd; *b* 30 Jan. 1917; *s* of Sir George James Robert Clerk, 9th Bt, and Hon. Mabel Honor, *y d* of late Col Hon. Charles Dutton and *sister* of 6th Baron Sherborne, DSO; *S* father, 1943; *m* 1944, Evelyn Elizabeth Robertson; two *s* two *d*. *Educ:* Stowe. JP 1955, DL 1956, Midlothian. *Heir:* *s* Robert Maxwell Clerk [*b* 3 April 1945; *m* 1970, Felicity Faye, *yr d* of George Collins, Bampton, Oxford]. *Address:* Penicuik House, Penicuik, Midlothian, Scotland. *T:* Penicuik 4318. *Clubs:* Royal Over-Seas League; New (Edinburgh).

**CLERKE, Sir John Edward Longueville,** 12th Bt *cr* 1660; Captain Royal Wilts Yeomanry, RAC, TA; *b* 29 Oct. 1913; *s* of late Francis William

Talbot Clerke, *e s* of 11th Bt, and Albinia Mary, *er d* of Edward Henry Evans-Lombe (she *m* 3rd, 1923, Air Chief Marshal Sir Edgar Rainey Ludlow-Hewitt, *qv*); *S* grandfather, 1930; *m* 1948, Mary, *d* of Lt-Col I. R. Beviss Bond, Prosperity, Natal, S Africa and The Old Rectory, North Newnton, Marlborough, Wilts; one *s* two *d*. *Heir: s* Francis Ludlow Longueville Clerke, *b* 25 Jan. 1953. *Address:* Fairhill, Tokai, PO Retreat, Cape, South Africa.

**CLEVELAND, Archdeacon of;** *see* Linsley, Ven. Stanley Frederick.

**CLEVELAND, Harlan;** *see* Cleveland, J. H.

**CLEVELAND, (James) Harlan;** President, University of Hawaii, since 1969; *b* 19 Jan. 1918; *s* of Stanley Matthews Cleveland and Marian Phelps (*née* Van Buren); *m* 1941, Lois W. Burton; one *s* two *d*. *Educ:* Phillips Acad., Andover, Mass; Princeton Univ.; Oxford Univ. Farm Security Admin., Dept of Agric., 1940-42; Bd of Econ. Warfare (subseq. Foreign Econ. Admin.), 1942-44; Exec. Dir, 1944-45, Actg Vice-Pres., 1945-46, Econ. Sect., Allied Control Commn, Rome; Mem. US Delegn, UNRRA Council, London, 1945; Dept Chief of Mission, UNRRA Italian Mission, Rome, 1946-47; Dir, UNRRA China Office, Shanghai, 1947-48; Dir, China Program, Econ. Coop. Admin., Washington, 1948-49; Dept Asst Adminstr, 1949-51; Asst Dir for Europe, Mutual Security Agency, 1952-53; Exec. Ed., The Reporter, NYC, 1953-55, Publ., 1955-56; Dean, Maxwell Sch. of Citizenship and Pub. Affairs, Syracuse Univ., 1956-61; Asst Sec. for Internat. Orgn Affairs, State Dept, 1961-65. Holds hon. degrees and foreign orders; Freedom Medal (US), 1946. *Publications:* The Obligations of Power, 1966; (Jt Ed.) The Art of Overseasmanship, 1957; (jtly) The Overseas Americans, 1960; (Ed.) The Promise of World Tensions, 1961; (Jt Ed.) The Ethic of Power, 1962; Ethics and Bigness, 1962. *Address:* University of Hawaii, Honolulu, Hawaii 96822, USA. *Club:* Century (NY).

**CLEVELAND, Sydney Dyson,** OBE 1955; FMA; Director of Manchester City Art Galleries, 1952-62; *b* 11 April 1898; *m* 1923, Helen Plant; two *s*. *Educ:* Manchester Central Grammar Sch.; Regional College of Art. Hon. Sec., Arundel Soc. of Manchester, 1922-34; Keeper, Rutherston Loan Collection, 1927-37; Dep. Dir, Manchester City Art Galleries, 1937-52; Pres., North Western Fedn of Museums and Art Galleries, 1939; Hon. Treas., Museums Assoc., 1942-50; Pres., Museums Assoc., 1950-52; Mem., Arts Council art panel, 1953-55; Mem. British National Cttee of International Council of Museums. Hon. DA (Manchester) 1958; Hon. MA (Manchester) 1963, *Publications:* Guide to the Manchester Art Galleries: Arundel Soc. of Manchester Transactions; History of the Royal Manchester Institution; Heaton Hall, Heaton Park; Presidential Addresses to Museums Association; contribs to Studio, Connoisseur, Museums Journal, etc. *Recreation:* golf. *Address:* 6 Highfield Park, Heaton Mersey, Ches.

**CLEVERDON, (Thomas) Douglas (James);** Radio and Television Producer; *b* 17 January 1903; *er s* of Thomas Silcox Cleverdon, Bristol; *m* 1944, Elinor Nest, *d* of Canon J. A. Lewis, Cardiff; two *s* one *d* (and one *s* decd). *Educ:* Bristol Grammar Sch.; Jesus Coll., Oxford. Bookseller, and publisher of fine printing, Bristol, 1926-39. Free-lance acting and writing for BBC West Region, 1935-39; joined BBC (Children's Hour), 1939; W Regional Features Producer, 1939-43; Features Producer, London, 1943, until retirement in 1969; now free-lance Producer. Devised and co-produced BBC Brains Trust, 1941. BBC War Corresp. in Burma, 1945; from 1947, mainly concerned with productions for Third Programme. Co-directed stage prod. of Under Milk Wood, in Edinburgh and London, 1955; directed New York prod., 1957. Directed Poetry Festivals, Stratford-upon-Avon, 1966-67, and 1969-70. Associated with Chilmark Press, New York, in pubn of Clover Hill Edns (illustrated by contemporary engravers), 1964-. *Publications:* Engravings of Eric Gill, 1929; Growth of Milk Wood, 1969. *Recreations:* book-collecting; visual arts. *Address:* 27 Barnsbury Square, N1. *T:* 01-607 7392. *Club:* Savile.

**CLEWES, Howard Charles Vivian;** novelist; *b* York, 27 Oct. 1912; British parentage; *m* 1946, Renata Faccincani; one *d*. *Educ:* Merchant Taylors' Sch. Various advertising agents, 1931-37. Served War of 1939-45, infantry company Comdr Green Howards, then Major G2; Chief Press and Information Officer, Milan, Italy, 1945-47. Professional novelist, resident Florence, Rome, London, 1948-. *Publications:* (in UK, USA, etc) Dead Ground, 1946; The Unforgiven, 1947; The Mask of Wisdom, 1948; Stendhal, 1949; Green Grow the Rushes, 1950; The Long Memory, 1951; An Epitaph for Love, 1952; The Way the Wind Blows, 1954; Man on a Horse, 1964; *plays:* Quay South, 1947; Image in the Sun, 1955; *films:* The Long Memory, Steel Bayonet, The One that Got Away, The Day They Robbed the Bank of England, Mutiny on the Bounty, The Holiday, Up from the Beach, William the Conqueror, The Novice, The 40 Days of Musa Dagh, etc. *Recreations:* writing, fishing. *Address:* Wildwood, North End, NW3. *T:* 01-455 7110.

**CLEWORTH, Ralph,** QC 1947; MA, LLB (Cantab); *b* 31 Oct. 1896; *s* of late Rev. William Enoch Cleworth, MA (Cantab), AKC London, Vicar of Hanging Heaton, Dewsbury, Yorks, and late Jane Emily Burbey; *m* 1928, Eleanore, *d* of late George S. Greenwood, Batley, Yorks; one *s*. *Educ:* Wheelwright Grammar Sch., Dewsbury; Christ's Coll., Cambridge. Served European War, 1914-18, KOYLI. Middle Temple; practice on NE Circuit. Parliamentary Candidate West Leeds, 1929. Last Recorder of Berwick-upon-Tweed, 1947-51. Stipendiary Magistrate of Leeds, 1950-65. *Address:* 16 Driffield Terrace, The Mount, York.

**CLIBBORN, Donovan Harold,** CMG 1966; HM Ambassador to El Salvador, since 1971; *b* 2 July 1917; *s* of Henry Joseph Fairley Clibborn and Isabel Sarah Jago; *m* 1940, Margaret Mercedes Edwige Nelson (*d* 1966); one *s* two *d*. *Educ:* Ilford High Sch.; St Edmund Hall, Oxford (MA). Laming Travelling Fellow, Queen's Coll., Oxford, 1938-40. Entered Consular Service, 1939; Vice-Consul, Genoa, 1939-40. Army Service, 1940-45: Intelligence Corps and Royal Signals, Western Desert, Sicily, Italy, NW Europe (despatches); Major, 1944. Foreign Office, 1945-46; Consul, Los Angeles, 1946-48; Foreign Office, 1948-50; 1st Sec. (UK High Commn, India), Madras, 1950-52; 1st Sec. (Information), Rio de Janeiro, 1952-56; 1st Sec. (Commercial), Madrid, 1956-60; Consul (Commercial), Milan, 1960-62; Counsellor (Economic), Tehran, 1962-64; Counsellor, Rio de Janeiro, 1964-66; Consul-General, Barcelona, 1966-70. *Recreations:* reading, music. *Address:* c/o Foreign and Commonwealth Office, SW1.

**CLIBURN, Van, (Harvey Lavan Cliburn Jr);** Pianist; *b* Shreveport, La, 12 July 1934; *o c* of Harvey Lavan Cliburn and Rildia Bee (*née*

O'Bryan). *Educ:* Kilgore High Sch., Texas; Juilliard Sch. of Music, New York. Made début in Houston, Texas, 1947; subsequently has toured extensively in United States and Europe. Awards include first International Tchaikovsky Piano Competition, Moscow, 1958, and every US prize, for pianistic ability. *Recreation:* swimming. *Address:* c/o Hurok Attractions Inc., 730 Fifth Avenue, New York 19, USA.

**CLIFDEN,** 8th Viscount *cr* 1781 (Ireland); **(Arthur) Victor Agar-Robartes,** MC; Baron Clifden (Ireland), 1776; Baron Mendip (Great Britain), 1794; Baron Robartes, 1869; Major (retd) Grenadier Guards; *b* 9 June 1887; *o surv s* of Thomas Charles Agar-Robartes, 6th Viscount Clifden (*d* 1930) and of Mary (*d* 1921), *d* of late Francis Henry Dickinson, Kingweston, Som; *S* brother, 1966; *m* 1st, 1920, Patience Mary (*d* 1956), *d* of A. F. Basset; one *d*; 2nd, 1948, Margaret, *d* of L. Ray Carter. *Educ:* Eton; Brasenose Coll., Oxford. Served European War, 1914-18, Grenadier Guards, retiring with rank of Major (thrice wounded, MC). Partner, Roger Cunliffe Sons & Co., 1920, till amalgamation with Cater, Brightwen & Co. in 1941; Dir of Cater, Brightwen & Co., 1941-63, retired. *Recreations:* shooting and fishing. *Heir:* (to Viscountcy) none; (to Barony of Mendip in remainder) Earl of Normanton, *qv.* *Address:* 15 Grosvenor Square, W1. *T:* 01-629 0391; (seat) Lanhydrock, Bodmin, Cornwall. *T:* Bodmin 2818. *Club:* White's.

*See also Baron Derwent.*

**CLIFFORD,** family name of **Baron Clifford of Chudleigh.**

**CLIFFORD OF CHUDLEIGH,** 13th Baron *cr* 1672; **(Lewis) Hugh Clifford,** OBE 1962; DL; Hon. Colonel, The Devonshire Territorials, RAC, since 1968; *b* 13 April 1916; *o s* of 12th Baron and Amy (*d* 1926), *er d* of John A. Webster, MD; *S* father, 1964; *m* 1945, Hon. Katharine Vavasseur Fisher, 2nd *d* of 2nd Baron Fisher; two *s* two *d.* *Educ:* Beaumont Coll.; Hertford Coll., Oxford (BA). 2nd Lieut, Devonshire Regt, 1935. Served War of 1939-45: North Africa; Major, 1941 (prisoner of war, escaped). Retd, 1950. Lieut-Col, 1959; Col, 1961. ADC, 1964-69. DL Devon, 1964. *Recreation:* shooting. *Heir:* *s* Hon. Thomas Hugh Clifford, *b* 17 March 1948. *Address:* (seat) Ugbrooke Park, Chudleigh, South Devon; Morella, Montrose, Vic, Australia. *Clubs:* Army and Navy; Royal Yacht Squadron.

**CLIFFORD, Clark McAdams;** Secretary of Defense, USA, 1968-69; *b* 25 Dec. 1906; *s* of Frank Andrew Clifford and Georgia (*née* McAdams); *m* 1931, Margery Pepperell Kimball; three *d.* *Educ:* Washington Univ., St Louis (LLB). Served US Naval Reserve, 1944-46 (Naval Commendation Ribbon). Practised law in St Louis, 1928-43; specialised in trial cases, corporation and labour law; Special Counsel to President of US, 1946-50; Senior Partner: Clifford & Miller, 1950-68; Clifford, Warnke, Glass, McIlwain & Finney (law firm), 1969-. Director: National Bank of Washington; Phillips Petroleum Co. Trustee, Washington Univ., St Louis. Medal of Honor with Distinction, USA, 1969. *Recreation:* golf. *Address:* 815 Connecticut Avenue, Washington, DC 20006, USA.

**CLIFFORD, Sir (Geoffrey) Miles,** KBE 1949 (OBE 1939); CMG 1944; ED; *m* 1st, 1920, Ivy Dorothy ("Peta") (decd), *y d* of Arthur Robert Eland, Thrapston, Northants; no *c*; 2nd, Mary, *e d* of late Thomas Turner, Shelbyville, Ill., USA. *Educ:* privately. Served European War (France and Flanders), 1914-18; Army of the Rhine, 1919-20. Comd Nigerian European Defence Force, 1938-40 (Special Duty, 1941-42). Entered Colonial Administrative Service (Nigeria), 1921; Acting Resident, Adamawa, 1934-37; Principal Asst Sec., 1938-41; Colonial Sec., Gibraltar, 1942-44; Senior Resident, Nigeria, 1944; Chm. Salaries Commn, Cyprus, 1945; attached CO, 1946; Governor and C-in-C of Falkland Islands, 1946-54. Chief Warden, Westminster, 1954-57; Mem., LCC, 1955-58; Hon. Organiser, Mental Health Research Fund; Dir, Leverhulme Trust, 1956-65; Cttee of Management, Trans-Antarctic Expedition; Mem., Antarctic Sub-Cttee, International Geophysical Year; Chm., British National Cttee on Antarctic Research; Mem., Antarctic Cttee, NERC; a Vice-Pres., RGS, 1956-62; St Paul's Cathedral Trust Council; a Trustee of Toc H; Vice-Pres., African Medical and Research Foundn; Life Gov., Imperial Cancer Research Fund; Trustee, McIndoe Memorial Research Unit; Mem., Management Cttee (co-opted), Inst. of Basic Med. Sciences; Hon. Treasurer, Soc. for Health Educn; Mem., Porritt Working Party on Med. Aid to Developing Countries and Chm. Anglo-Amer. Conf. on same theme; Chm. Planning Cttee, Chelsea Group of Post-graduate Hospitals; Chm. Cttee of Management, Inst. Latin American Studies, London Univ.; Mem. Council and Exec. Cttee, Voluntary Service Overseas. Chairman: Nigerian Electricity Supply Corp.; United Nigeria Group. Mem. London Boards: East African Power & Light; Kenya Power. Fellow, UCL; Mem. Ct of Patrons, RCS; Chm., Conf. of Foundations, Ditchley, 1966; a Gov., United Westminster Schs. Hon. FRCS; Hon. FDS, RCS. *Publications:* A Nigerian Chiefdom; Notes on the Bassa-Komo Tribe; book reviews and occasional contribs to the Press. *Recreation:* photography. *Address:* Orchards, Brenchley, Kent. *Clubs:* Athenæum; (Hon. Mem.) Antarctic.

**CLIFFORD, Graham Douglas,** CMG 1964; FCIS; Director, The Institution of Electronic and Radio Engineers, since 1937; *b* 8 Feb. 1913; *s* of John William Clifford and Frances Elizabeth Reece; *m* 1937, Marjory Charlotte Willmot; two *d* (one *s* decd). *Educ:* London schs and by industrial training. Molins Machine Co. Ltd, 1929; Columbia Graphophone Co. Ltd, 1931; American Machinery Co. Ltd, 1934. Secretary: Radio Trades Exam. Bd, 1942-65 (Hon. Mem. 1965); Nat. Electronics Coun., 1961-65 (Mem. Coun., 1967). Editor of The Radio and Electronic Engineer. Hon. Mem., Assoc. of Engineers and Architects, Israel, 1966; Hon. Treasurer, UK Cttee for the Gandhi Centenary, 1969. Comdr, Order of Merit, Research and Invention, France, 1967. *Publications:* contribs to various technical journals. *Recreations:* photography, genealogy, music, but mainly work. *Address:* 45 West Park Lane, West Worthing, Sussex. *T:* Worthing 41423. *Clubs:* National Liberal, Royal Automobile.

**CLIFFORD, Prof. James Lowry;** William Peterfield Trent Professor of English, Columbia University, since 1964 (Professor of English, 1946-); President, Lichfield Johnson Society, 1958-59; *b* Evansville, Ind., USA, 24 Feb. 1901; *s* of George S. and Emily Orr Clifford; *m* 1940, Virginia Iglehart; two *s* one *d.* *Educ:* Wabash Coll. (AB); Massachusetts Inst. of Tech. (BS); Columbia Univ. (PhD). Manager, Young Car Co., Evansville, Indiana, 1926-28; English Master, Evans Sch., Tucson, Ariz., 1929-32; Graduate student, Columbia Univ., 1932-35; Travelling Fellow, Columbia Univ., 1935-36; Dept of English, Lehigh Univ.,

Bethlehem, Pa, 1938-44, Instructor to Associate Prof.; Associate Prof. of English, Barnard Coll., 1944-46; Guggenheim Fellowship, 1951-52 and 1965-66. Mem. Gen. Advisory Editorial Cttee, Yale Boswell Edition and Yale Edition of the Works of Samuel Johnson, also Mem. Adv. Cttee, Wesleyan Univ. Fielding Edn. Hon. Vice-Pres., Johnson Soc. of London; Hon. Mem., The Johnson Club, London and Johnson Soc., Oslo, Norway; Mem., The Johnsonians, NY. Hon. LittD, Evansville Coll., 1955; LHD, Wabash Coll., 1956; LHD, Indiana Univ., 1963. Phi Beta Kappa. FRSL 1956; FRSA 1970. *Publications:* Hester Lynch Piozzi (Mrs Thrale), 1941; Dr Campbell's Diary (edn), 1947; Pope and his Contemporaries (ed with Louis A. Landa), 1949; Johnsonian Studies, 1887-1950: a Survey and Bibliography, 1951 (rev. edn 1970); Young Samuel Johnson, 1955; Eighteenth Century English Literature: Modern Essays in Criticism (ed), 1959; Biography as an Art (ed), 1962; Smollett's Peregrine Pickle (ed), 1964; Man versus Society in 18th Century Britain (ed), 1968; Editor, Johnsonian News Letter, 1940-; various other editions for the Augustan Reprint Soc., and articles in scholarly jls. *Recreations:* baseball, music and theatre. *Address:* 25 Claremont Avenue, New York 27, NY, USA. *T:* New York-Monument 3-2233.

**CLIFFORD, Rev. Sir Lewis Arthur Joseph,** 5th Bt *cr* 1887; SJ; Headmaster of Beaumont College, Old Windsor, 1950-56 (formerly Bursar); *b* 9 April 1896; 3rd *surv. s* of Charles W. Clifford (3rd *s* of 1st Bt) and of Sicele Agnes De Trafford; *S* uncle, 1944. *Educ:* Beaumont Coll., Windsor, Berks. Served as Chaplain to the Forces during War of 1939-45, in France and Middle East. *Heir: b* Roger Charles Joseph Gerrard Clifford, *b* 1910. *Address:* Campion House, PO Box 54, Salisbury, Rhodesia.

**CLIFFORD, Sir Miles;** *see* Clifford, Sir G. M.

**CLIFFORD, Rev. Paul Rowntree,** MA; President, Selly Oak Colleges, Birmingham, since 1965; *b* 21 Feb. 1913; *s* of Robert and Harriet Rowntree Clifford; *m* 1947, Marjory Jean Tait; one *s* one *d. Educ:* Mill Hill Sch.; Balliol Coll., Oxford; Mansfield and Regents Park Colls, Oxford. MA (Oxon) 1939. West Ham Central Mission, London: Asst Minister, 1938-43; Supt Minister, 1943-53; McMaster Univ., Hamilton, Canada: Asst Prof. of Homiletics and Pastoral Theology, 1953-59; Dean of Men and Chm. of Dept of Religion, 1959-64; Prof. of Religion, 1964-65. *Publications:* The Mission of the Local Church, 1953; The Pastoral Calling, 1959; Now is the Time, 1970; articles in Jl of Religion, Metaphysical Review, Dialogue, Canadian Jl of Theology, Foundations, Religious Studies. *Recreations:* golf, gardening. *Address:* President's House, Selly Oak Colleges, Birmingham 29. *T:* 021-472 2462. *Club:* Reform.

**CLIFFORD, William Henry Morton,** CBE 1966; Solicitor to the Department of Health and Social Security (formerly Ministry of Social Security), since 1968; *b* 30 July 1909; *s* of Henry Edward Clifford, FRIBA, Glasgow, and Margaret Alice, *d* of Dr William Gibson, Campbeltown, Argyll; *m* 1936, Katharine Winifred, *d* of Rev. H. W. Waterfield, Temple Grove, Eastbourne; one *s* two *d. Educ:* Tonbridge Sch.; Corpus Christi Coll., Cambridge. Admitted a solicitor, 1936. Entered Solicitor's Department, GPO, 1937. Served in Army, 1939-45: Major GS, Army Council Secretariat, WO, 1944-45. Transferred to Solicitor's Office, Min. of National Insurance, 1945; Assistant Solicitor, Min. of Pensions and Nat. Insurance (later Min. of Social Security), 1953. *Recreations:* reading, listening to music (especially opera), genealogy, walking, sailing, Scottish country dancing. *Address:* Woodbrook, 7 Lake Road, Tunbridge Wells, Kent. *T:* Tunbridge Wells 21612. *Club:* Oxford and Cambridge.

**CLIFFORD-TURNER, Raymond;** Senior Partner, Clifford-Turner & Co.; Director: Transport Holding Co. since 1963; Banque de Paris et des Pays-Bas Ltd; *b* 7 Feb. 1906; *s* of Harry Clifford-Turner, solicitor; *m* 1933, Zoë Vachell; one *s* two *d. Educ:* Rugby Sch.; Trinity Coll., Cambridge. Solicitor, 1930; Partner, Clifford-Turner & Co., 1931. Wing Commander, RAFVR. *Recreations:* golf, racing. *Address:* 8a Hobart Place, SW1. *T:* 01-235 2443; Childown, Stonehill Road, Chertsey, Surrey. *Clubs:* Portland, St James'.
*See also Hon. A. G. Berry.*

**CLIFTON, Bishop of, (RC),** since 1949; **Rt. Rev. Joseph Edward Rudderham;** *b* 17 June 1899; *s* of William Rudderham and Agnes Mary Coan. *Educ:* St Bede's Coll., Manchester; St Edmund's Coll. Old Hall, Ware; Christ's Coll., Cambridge; Ven. English Coll., Rome. Priest, 1926 (by Cardinal Pompili in Rome); Curate at All Souls Church, Peterborough, 1927-32. Parish Priest, 1932-43; Administrator of Northampton Cathedral, 1943-49; Canon Penitentiary of Northampton Cathedral Chapter, 1946-49; Diocesan Inspector of Schs, 1941-49. *Address:* St Ambrose, Leigh Woods, Bristol BS8 3PW. *T:* Bristol 33072.

**CLIFTON, Henry Talbot de Vere;** *b* 16 Dec. 1907; *s* of late John Talbot Clifton and late Violet Mary (author, Mrs John Talbot Clifton). *Educ:* Christ Church, Oxford. Lord of the Manor of Anstey; Lord of the Manor of Lytham. Owner of Kildalton Castle, Islay, Scotland. *Publications:* Gleams Britain's Day, Dielma and other poems. *Recreations:* racing, fishing, music, horses, dogs. *Club:* Travellers'.

**CLIFTON, Leon James Thomas;** Under-Secretary, Ministry of Technology, since 1967; *b* 17 May 1912; *s* of William Clifton and Helen Florence Clifton (*née* Holloway); *m* 1937, Doris Camp; one *s* one *d. Educ:* Fulham Central. Air Min., 1929; Min. of Aircraft Production, 1940; Min. of Supply, 1946; Min. of Aviation, 1959 (Dir of Contracts, 1960-67). *Recreations:* gardening, fishing. *Address:* Rubicon, Kingsmead Road, Broadbridge Heath, Sussex. *T:* Horsham 61500.

**CLIFTON-BROWN, Anthony George,** TD; late Major RA; formerly Director: Royal Exchange Assurance; Westminster Bank Ltd; Westminster Foreign Bank Ltd; Bank of New South Wales (London Board); one of HM Lieutenants for City of London, 1950-60; *b* 11 Feb. 1903; *y s* of late Edward Clifton-Brown; *m* 1st, 1930, Delia Charlotte (*d* 1947), *y d* of late George Edward Wade; three *d*; 2nd, 1949, Phyllis Adrienne McCulloch, *d* of late Francis Harvey, Dublin. *Educ:* Eton; Trinity Coll., Cambridge. Mem. of Court of Assistants, Merchant Taylors' Company (Master, 1945-46; First Upper Warden, 1955-56); Sheriff of the City of London, 1957-58; Alderman of Broad Street Ward, 1950-60. Chm., Management Cttee, Royal London Homœopathic Hosp., 1948-61. Commendatore of Order of Merit of Italian Republic. *Address:* Via del Moro 7, 00153 Rome, Italy.

**CLIFTON-BROWN, Lt-Col Geoffrey Benedict;** *b* 25 July 1899; *m* 1927, Robina Margaret, *d* of late Rowland Sutton; two *s* (one *d* decd). *Educ:* Eton; RMC Sandhurst. 2nd Lieut 12th Lancers, 1918; Major, 1935; Lt-Col, 1940; served with 12th Lancers in France and

Belgium, 1939-40, evacuated Dunkirk (despatches). MP (C) Bury St Edmunds Div. of West Suffolk, 1945-50. *Address:* The Old Rectory, Cockfield, Bury St Edmunds, Suffolk. *T:* Cockfield Green 217. *Club:* Cavalry.

**CLINTON,** 22nd Baron *cr* 1299 (title abeyant 1957-65); **Gerard Nevile Mark Fane Trefusis;** landowner; *b* 7 Oct. 1934; *s* of Capt. Charles Fane (killed in action, 1940); assumed by deed poll, 1958, surname of Trefusis in addition to patronymic; *m* 1959, Nicola Harriette Purdon Coote; one *s* two *d. Educ:* Gordonstoun. Took seat in House of Lords, 1965. Mem., Prince of Wales's Councils, 1968-. *Recreations:* shooting, fishing, forestry. *Heir: s* Hon. Charles Patrick Rolle Fane Trefusis, *b* 21 March 1962. *Address:* Heanton Satchville, near Okehampton, North Devon. *T:* Dolton 224. *Club:* Boodle's.

**CLINTON, David Osbert F.;** *see* Fynes-Clinton.

**CLINTON, (Francis) Gordon,** FRCM; FBSM; baritone; Principal, Birmingham School of Music, since 1960; *b* 19 June 1912; *s* of Rev. F. G. Clinton, Broadway, Worcs; *m* 1939, Phyllis Jarvis, ARCM, GRSM; two *s* one *d. Educ:* Evesham Grammar Sch.; Bromley Sch. for Boys. Open Schol. RCM, 1935; Vicar Choral, St Paul's Cathedral, 1937-49; served War of 1939-45 in RAF; demobilised as Flt-Lieut. Appearances at major concerts and festivals, 1946-; joined staff, RCM, 1949. Examr on Associated Board, 1959-. Tours of America, Canada, Europe, Africa (singing, adjudicating, lecturing). *Recreations:* sport and motoring. *Address:* Birmingham School of Music, Dale End, Birmingham. *T:* 021-236 0338.

**CLINTON-BADDELEY, Madeleine Angela, (Angela Baddeley);** actress since 1915; *b* 4 July 1904; 3rd *d* of William Herman Clinton-Baddeley and Louise Bourdin; *m* 1st, 1921, Stephen Kerr Thomas (marr. diss.); one *d*; 2nd, 1929, Glencairn Alexander Byam Shaw, *qv*; one *s* one *d. Educ:* privately. First stage appearance, Old Vic, 1913, in Richard III and frequently on London stage until 1926; went to Australia with Dion Boucicault, 1926, during which tour parts included Mary Rose in the play of that name; reappeared in London, 1927, and continued on London stage in various parts including Katheryn Howard in The Rose Without a Thorn, Duchess, 1932, and Florrie in Sheppey, Wyndhams, 1933; played Olivia Grayne in Night Must Fall, Duchess, 1935, and the same part as her first appearance in New York, Barrymore Theatre, 1936. More recent London appearances include: Grace Fenning in Dear Octopus, Queen's, 1938; Cecily Cardew in The Importance of Being Earnest, 1939; Cattrin in The Light of Heart, Apollo, 1940, Globe, 1941; Miss Prue in Love for Love, Phoenix, 1943; Catherine Winslow in The Winslow Boy, Lyric, 1946; The Madwoman of Chaillot, St James's, 1951; Mrs Moxton (Moxie) in Relative Values, Savoy, 1951; Gina in The Wild Duck, Saville, 1955. Mem. Old Vic Company for 1949-50 Season, New Theatre; mem. Festival Company, Stratford, for 1955, 1958, 1959 seasons; Russian tour with Festival Company, 1958-59; Mae Peterson in Bye Bye Birdie, Her Majesty's, Haymarket, 1961-62; Mum in Day of the Prince, Royal Court, 1963; Lady Bracknell in The Importance of Being Earnest, 1964, and Madame Ranevsky in The Cherry Orchard, 1965, Playhouse, Nottingham; Zozyushka Savishna in Ivanov, Phœnix, 1965. Has appeared in films and on television (incl. Mrs Gamp in Martin Chuzzlewit, TV serial, 1965). *Recreation:* swimming. *Address:* 169 Ashley Gardens, SW1.

**CLINTON-THOMAS, Robert Antony,** CBE 1965; Consul-General, Antwerp, since 1970; *b* 5 April 1913; *s* of late Brig. R. H. Thomas, CSI, DSO, and Lady Couchman; *m* 1949, Betty Maria Clocca. *Educ:* Haileybury; Peterhouse, Cambridge (MA). Indian Civil Service, 1937-47; Foreign Office, 1947-49; 1st Sec. and Consul, Manila, 1949-53; Head of Chancery, HM Embassy, Tripoli, 1953-56; FO, 1956-57; Counsellor and Head of Chancery, HM Embassy, Addis Ababa, 1957-59; Counsellor and Head of Chancery, Political Office with the Near East Forces, Cyprus, 1959-61; Political Adviser to the C-in-C Middle East Comd, Aden, 1961-62; Counsellor, HM Embassy, Oslo, 1962-65; FCO (formerly CO), 1965-70. *Address:* c/o Foreign and Commonwealth Office, SW1.

**CLISSITT, William Cyrus,** OBE 1968; TD; JP; Editor, Evening Express, Liverpool, 1928-54; Secretary of the Press Council, 1960-68; *o s* of late Cyrus Thomas Clissitt, JP, Newport, Mon; *b* 1898; *m* 1923, Antoinette Mary, *e d* of late Joseph Herbert Canning, OBE, JP (Knight of Papal Order of St Gregory), Newport, Mon; one *s* two *d*. Editor Torbay Herald, Torquay, 1924; active service with Artists' Rifles OTC, European War, 1914-18; and Royal Artillery, 1939-45 (Lt-Col); inaugurated Weekly Wireless Talks on Sport for BBC at Cardiff, 1923; Founder Mem. Guild of British Newspaper Editors; selected Military Mem. West Lancs T & AFA; Hon. Col 626 (Liverpool Irish) HAA Regt RA, TA, 1950-55. JP Liverpool. *Publications:* Knowsley Hall; numerous newspaper articles on wide variety of subjects. *Recreation:* aerophilately. *Address:* 150 Stow Hill, Newport, Mon. *T:* Newport 65516.

**CLITHEROE,** 1st Baron *cr* (June) 1955, of Downham; Bt *cr* 1945 (succeeded to Btcy Sept. 1955); **Ralph Assheton,** PC 1944; JP; Vice-Lieutenant of Lancashire, since 1956; High Steward of Westminster since 1962; *b* 24 Feb. 1901; *o s* of Sir Ralph Assheton, 1st Bt; *m* 1924, Hon. Sylvia Benita Frances Hotham, FLAS, *d* of 6th Baron Hotham; two *s* one *d. Educ:* Eton; Christ Church, Oxford (MA). Called to Bar, Inner Temple, 1925; MP (Nat. U) Rushcliffe Div. of Notts, 1934-45; City of London, 1945-50; Blackburn West, 1950-55. Parly Sec., Min. of Labour and Min. of National Service, 1939-42; Parly Sec., Min. of Supply, 1942-43; Financial Sec. to the Treasury, 1943-44; Chm. Conservative Party Organisation, 1944-46; Chm. Public Accounts Cttee, 1948-50; Chm. Select Cttee on Nationalised Industries, 1951-53; Mem. Royal Commission on West Indies, 1938-39. Chm. Mercantile Investment Trust Ltd; Deputy Chairman: (Jt) National Westminster Bank (formerly a Dep. Chm., National Provincial Bank); John Brown & Co.; Tube Investments Ltd; Director: Coutts & Co.; Rio Tinto Zinc Corp. Ltd.; Borax Holdings Ltd; Tanganyika Concessions Ltd, and other companies. DL 1955, JP 1934, Lancashire; Mem. Council, Duchy of Lancaster. FSA. *Heir: s* Hon. Ralph John Assheton [*b* 3 Nov. 1929; *m* 1961, Juliet, *d* of Christopher Hanbury; two *s* one *d. Educ:* Eton; Christ Church (Scholar), Oxford (MA)]. *Address:* 17 Chelsea Park Gardens, SW3. *T:* 01-352 4020; Downham Hall, Clitheroe, Lancs. *T:* Chatburn 210. *Clubs:* Carlton, City of London, Royal Automobile, MCC.
*See also W. M. J. Worsley.*

**CLITHEROW, Rt. Rev. Richard George;** *see* Stafford, Bishop Suffragan of.

**CLIVE, Nigel David,** CMG 1967; OBE 1959; MC 1944; TD; Adviser to Secretary-General of OECD, since 1970; *b* 13 July 1917; *s* of late

Horace David and Hilda Mary Clive; *m* 1949, Maria Jeanne Tambakopoulou. *Educ:* Stowe; Christ Church, Oxford (Scholar). Commissioned 2nd Mddx Yeomanry, 1939; served in Middle East and Greece. Joined Foreign Office, 1946; served Athens, 1946-48; Jerusalem, 1948; FO, 1948-50; Baghdad, 1950-53; FO, 1953-58; Tunis, 1958-62; Algiers, 1962-63; FO, 1964-65; Head of Information Research Dept, FCO (formerly FO), 1966-69. *Recreations:* reading, travel. *Address:* 3 Cadogan Gardens, SW3. *T:* 01-730 1855; 1 rue Séguier, Paris 6e, France. *T:* Odéon 6914. *Clubs:* Brooks's, MCC.

**CLOAKE, John Cecil;** Counsellor (Commercial), British Embassy, Tehran, since 1968; *b* 2 Dec. 1924; *s* of late Dr Cecil Stedman Cloake, Wimbledon, and late Mrs Maude Osborne Cloake (*née* Newling); *m* 1956, Margaret Thomure Morris, Washington, DC, USA; one *s*. *Educ:* King's Coll. Sch., Wimbledon; Peterhouse, Cambridge. Served in Army, 1943-46 (Lieut RE). Foreign Office, 1948; 3rd Sec., Baghdad, 1949, and Saigon, 1951; 2nd Sec., 1952; FO, 1954; Private Sec. to Permanent Under-Sec., 1956, and to Parly Under-Sec., 1957; 1st Sec., 1957; Consul (Commercial), New York, 1958; 1st Sec., Moscow, 1962; FO, 1963; DSAO, 1965; Counsellor, 1966; Head of Accommodation Dept, 1967. *Recreations:* gardening, painting, architecture, local history, genealogy. *Address:* c/o Foreign and Commonwealth Office, SW1.

**CLOETE, (Edward Fairly) Stuart (Graham),** CIAL; *b* Paris, 23 July 1897; *s* of Laurence Cloete, Cape Town, and Edith Margaret Park, London; divorced; no *c*; *m* 1940, Mildred West, Elizabeth, New Jersey. *Educ:* Lancing Coll. 2nd Lieut Sept. 1914 (wounded twice); retired from Coldstream Guards, 1925; farmed in South Africa, 1925-35 and 1949-53. *Publications:* Turning Wheels, 1937; Watch for the Dawn, 1939; Yesterday is Dead, 1940; The Old Men and the Young (Poems), 1941; The Hill of Doves, 1941; Christmas in Matabeleland, 1942; Congo Song, 1943; Against These Three, 1945; The Third Way, 1946; The Curve and the Tusk, 1953; The African Giant, 1955; Mamba, 1956; Storm over Africa, 1956; The Mask, 1957; Gazella, 1958; The Soldiers' Peaches, 1959; The Fiercest Heart, 1960; The Silver Trumpet, 1961; West With the Sun, 1962; The Looking Glass, 1963; Rags of Glory, 1963; The Honey Bird, 1964; The 1001 Night of Jean Macaque, 1965; The Abductors, 1966; The Writing on the Wall, 1968; South Africa: the land and peoples, 1969; How Young They Died, 1969; stories, poems and articles to Saturday Evening Post, Collier's, Ladies' Home Journal, Argosy, Vogue, Saturday Review of Literature, Life and others. *Recreations:* farming, horses, cattle, painting, cooking, natural history. *Address:* c/o Curtis Brown Ltd, 13 King Street, Covent Garden, WC2. box 37, Hermanus, S Africa. *Clubs:* Guards, Savage; Coffee House, Explorers, National Arts, Overseas Press (New York).

**CLOGHER, Bishop of,** since 1970; **Rt. Rev. Richard Patrick Crosland Hanson, MA, DD;** *b* 1 Nov. 1916; *s* of late Sir Philip Hanson, CB, and Lady Hanson; *m* 1950, Mary Dorothy, *d* of late Canon John Powell; two *s* two *d*. *Educ:* Cheltenham Coll.; Trinity Coll., Dublin. 1st Hons BA in Classics also in Ancient Hist., 1938; BD with Theol. Exhibn, 1941; DD 1950; MA 1961. Asst Curate, St Mary's, Donnybrook, Dublin, and later in Banbridge, Co. Down, 1941-45; Vice-Principal, the Queen's Coll., Birmingham, 1946-50; Vicar of St John's, Shuttleworth, dio. Manchester 1950-52; on staff of Dept of Theol., University of Nottingham, as Lectr, Sen. Lectr and Reader, 1952-62; Lightfoot Prof. of Divinity, University of Durham, and Canon of Durham, 1962-64; Prof. of Christian Theology, Univ. of Nottingham, 1964-70; Hon. Canon of Southwell, 1964-70; Canon Theologian of Coventry Cathedral, 1967-70; Examining Chaplain to the Bishop of Southwell, 1968. *Publications:* Origen's Doctrine of Tradition, 1954; II Corinthians (commentary, Torch series), 1954; Allegory and Event, 1959; God: Creator, Saviour, Spirit, 1960; Tradition in the Early Church, 1962; (ed., abridged and trans.), Justin Martyr's Dialogue with Trypho, 1963; Contrib. to Institutionalism and Church Unity, 1963; The Anglican Synthesis, 1964; Vindications, 1966; (ed) Difficulties for Christian Belief, 1966; New Clarendon Commentary on Acts, 1967; Saint Patrick: his Origins and Career, 1968; (co-ed) Christianity in Britain 300-700, 1968; contribs to: A Dictionary of Christian Theology, 1969; Lambeth Essays on Ministry, 1969; Le Traité sur le Saint-Esprit de Saint Basile, 1969; Cambridge History of the Bible, vol. 1, 1970. Articles in: Jl of Theol. Studies, Vigiliae Christianae, Expository Times, Theology, Modern Churchman. *Recreations:* tennis, drama. *Address:* Thornfield, Fivemiletown, Co. Tyrone, N Ireland.

**CLOGHER, Bishop of, (RC),** since 1970; **Most Rev. Patrick Mulligan;** *b* 9 June 1912; *s* of James and Mary Martin. *Educ:* St Macartan's, Monaghan; Maynooth. Prof., St Macartan's, 1938; Bishop's Sec., 1943; Headmaster, Clones, 1948; Headmaster, St Michael's, Enniskillen, 1957; Parish Priest of Machaire Rois and Vicar General and Archdeacon, 1966. *Publications:* contribs to IER, JLAS, Seanchas Clochair. *Address:* Bishop's House, Monaghan, Ireland. *T:* Monaghan 19.

**CLORE, Charles;** Chairman: Sears Holdings Ltd; British Shoe Corporation Ltd; Sears Engineering Ltd; Lewis's Investment Trust Ltd; Selfridges Ltd; BSC Footwear Ltd; Sears Industries Inc.; Scottish Motor Traction Co. Ltd; Mappin & Webb Ltd; Princes Investments Ltd; The Bentley Engineering Group Ltd; *b* 26 Dec. 1904; *m* 1943, Francine Rachel Halphen (marr. diss.); one *s* one *d*. *Educ:* London. Is also Dir of Hill Samuel Group Ltd, Orange Free State Investment Co. Ltd and of a number of other public companies engaged in commercial and industrial enterprises. *Address:* 22 Park Street, Park Lane, W1. *T:* 01-499 3821.

**CLOSS, Prof. August,** MA, DPhil; Professor of German and Head of German Department, University of Bristol, 1931-64, now Emeritus; Dean of the Faculty of Arts, 1962 and 1963; *b* 9 Aug. 1898; 4th *s* of late A. Closs; *m* 1931, Hannah Margaret Mary (*d* 1953), novelist and art-critic, *d* of late Robert Priebsch, Prof. and Medievalist at UCL; one *d*. *Educ:* Berlin, Vienna, Graz, London. Lectured at Sheffield Univ., 1929-30; at University Coll., London, 1930-31. Guest-Prof. at univs of Amsterdam, Ghent, Berlin, Heidelberg, Frankfurt A/M, Bern, Vienna, Rome, Florence, etc, and in the USA at Univs of Columbia, Princeton, Yale, California and at Canadian and Indian Univs. Hon. Fellow Inst. of Technology, Hanover; Korresp. Mitglied der Deutschen Akademie; Membre Corresp. de l'Institut International des Arts et des Lettres (Zürich); Mem. of PEN. FRSL. Comdr, Cross of Order of Merit, West Germany, Austrian Cross of Merit *Litteris et Artibus*. *Publications:* Medieval Exempla: (Dame World) Weltlohn, 1934; The Genius of the German Lyric, 1938 (enlarged 2nd edn 1962, paperback edn 1965); German Lyrics of the Seventeenth Century, 1940,

1947; Hölderlin, 1942, 1944; Tristan und Isolt, 1944, 1947; Die Freien Rhythmen in der deutschen Dichtung, 1947; Novalis–Hymns to the Night, 1948; Die neuere deutsche Lyrik vom Barock bis zur Gegenwart, 1952, 1957; Deutsche Philologie in Aufriss; Woge im Westen, 1954; Medusa's Mirror; Reality and Symbol, 1957; The Harrap Anthology of German Poetry, 1957, new edn 1969; Reality and Creative Vision in German Lyrical Poetry (Symposium), 1963; Introductions to German Literature (4 vols), 1967; Twentieth Century German Literature, 1969; contribs to Times Literary and Educ. Supplements, German Life and Letters, Modern Lang. Rev., Euphorion, Rivista di Letterature Moderne, Reallexikon, Deutsches Literatur-Lexikon, Aryan Path, Germanistik, Universitas, and American journals. *Recreations:* music, collecting first editions. *Address:* 40 Stoke Hill, Stoke Bishop, Bristol 9. *T:* Bristol 682244. *Club:* University of Bristol.

**CLOTHIER, Cecil Montacute,** QC 1965; Recorder of Blackpool since 1965; *b* 28 Aug. 1919; *s* of Hugh Montacute Clothier, Liverpool; *m* 1943, Mary Elizabeth, *o d* of late Ernest Glover Bush; one *s* two *d. Educ:* Stonyhurst Coll.; Lincoln Coll., Oxford (BCL, MA). Enlisted, 1939; commissioned 1940, Royal Corps of Signals; 51 (H) Div., N Africa, Sicily; British Army Staff, Washington, DC; Hon. Lt-Col Royal Signals. Called to the Bar, Jan. 1950; Inner Temple; Mem., Gen. Council of the Bar. *Address:* Goldsmith Building, Temple, EC4. *T:* 01-353 7881. *Club:* East India and Sports.

**CLOTWORTHY, Stanley Edward,** CBE 1959; Chairman, Alcan Aluminium (UK) Ltd, since 1969; *b* 21 June 1902; *s* of Joseph and Fanny Kate Clotworthy; *m* 1927, Winifred Edith, *d* of J. Mercer Harris; one *s* one *d. Educ:* Peter Symonds Sch., Winchester; University Coll., Southampton. Student apprenticeship with B. T. H. Ltd, Rugby, 1923-26; Macintosh Cable Co., Liverpool, 1926-27; Alcan Industries Ltd (formerly Northern Aluminium Co.), 1927-67. Hon. DSc (Southampton Univ.). *Recreations:* shooting, gardening. *Address:* Kemano, Warreners Lane, St George's Hill, Weybridge, Surrey. *T:* Weybridge 42904.

**CLOUDSLEY-THOMPSON, John Leonard,** MA, PhD (Cantab), DSc (London); FRES, FLS, FZS, FIBiol, FWA; Professor of Zoology, University of Khartoum, and Keeper, Sudan Natural History Museum, since 1960; *b* Murree, India, 23 May 1921; *s* of Dr Ashley George Gyton Thompson, MA, MD (Cantab), DPH, and Muriel Elaine (*née* Griffiths); *m* 1944, Jessie Anne Cloudsley; three *s. Educ:* Marlborough Coll.; Pembroke Coll., Cambridge. War of 1939-45: commissioned into 4th Queen's Own Hussars, 1941; transf. 4th Co. of Lond. Yeo. (Sharpshooters); N Africa, 1941-42 (severely wounded); Instructor (Capt.), Sandhurst, 1943; rejoined regt for D Day, Caen Offensive, etc, 1944 (Hon. rank of Capt. on resignation). Lectr in Zoology, King's Coll., Univ. of London, 1950-60. Took part in: Cambridge Iceland Expedn, 1947; Expedn to Southern Tunisia, 1954; univ. expedns to parts central Africa, 1960-, incl. Trans-Sahara crossing, 1967. Liveryman, Worshipful Co. of Skinners, 1952-. Royal African Soc's Medal, 1969. *Publications:* Biology of Deserts (ed), 1954; Spiders, Scorpions, Centipedes and Mites, 1958 (2nd edn 1968); Animal Behaviour, 1960; Rhythmic Activity in Animal Physiology and Behaviour, 1961; Land Invertebrates (with John Sankey), 1961; Life in Deserts (with M. J. Chadwick), 1964; Desert Life, 1965; Animal Conflict and Adaptation, 1965; Animal Twilight, 1967; Microecology, 1967; Zoology of Tropical Africa, 1969. Many scientific articles in learned jls, etc. *Recreations:* music (especially opera), photography, travel. *Address:* Department of Zoology, University of Khartoum, Sudan; (permanent) c/o National Westminster Bank Ltd, 62 Victoria Street, SW1; (home) Flat 9, 4 Craven Hill, W2.

**CLOUGH, Prunella;** painter; *b* 1919; *d* of Eric Clough Taylor, poet and civil servant, and Thora Clough Taylor. *Educ:* privately; Chelsea Sch. of Art. Exhibited at Leger Gallery, 1947; Roland Browse & Delbanco, 1949; Leicester Galleries, 1953; Whitechapel Gallery, 1960; Grosvenor Gallery, 1964, 1968. *Address:* 65 Moore Park Road, SW6.

**CLOUSTON, Air Cdre (retd) Arthur Edmond,** CB 1957; DSO 1943; DFC 1942; AFC and Bar, 1939; RAF retd; *b* 7 April 1908; *s* of R. E. Clouston, mining engineer, Motueka, Nelson, NZ; *m* 1937, Elsie, *d* of late S. Markham Turner, Farnborough, Hants; two *d. Educ:* Rockville Sch.; Bainham Sch. Joined Royal Air Force, 1930. Record Flight, London-Capetown-London, 1937; Record Flight, London-NZ-London, 1938. Served War of 1939-45 (DFC, DSO), engaged in Research Test Flying, Fighter Comd, Coastal Comd; AOC, Singapore, 1954-57; Comdt, Aeroplane and Armament Experimental Establishment, Boscombe Down, Amesbury, 1957-60. Group Capt. 1947; Air Cdre 1954. *Publication:* The Dangerous Skies (autobiography). *Address:* Wings, Constantine Bay, Padstow, Cornwall.

**CLOUTMAN, His Honour Sir Brett (Mackay),** VC; Kt 1957; MC; QC; Senior Official Referee of the Supreme Court of Judicature, 1954-63; of Gray's Inn and Western Circuit; *b* 7 Nov. 1891; *s* of late Alfred B. Cloutman; *m* Margaret Hunter; two *d. Educ:* Berkhamsted Sch.; Bishops Stortford Coll.; London Univ. Served 1914-18 and 1939-45 Wars in France, Belgium, Syria, Egypt and Italy, in Royal Engineers; VC and MC while comdg 59th Field Co. RE in 5th Div., 1918; despatches, 1944. Called to Bar, 1926; KC 1946; Sen. Chm. War Pensions (Special Review) Tribunals, 1947; Official Referee, 1948. Master Worshipful Co. of Glass Sellers of London, 1939-40, 1965-66. Pres., Hornsey (N London) YMCA; Chm., Metropolitan Union of YMCA. Governor, Eltham Coll. *Publications:* (joint) The Law Relating to Authors and Publishers; The Law Relating to Printers. *Address:* 2 The Old Hall, Highgate, N6. *T:* 01-340 8205. *Club:* Athenæum.

**CLOVER, Robert Gordon,** TD 1951; QC 1958; JP; *His Honour Judge Clover;* Judge of County Courts since 1965; Deputy Chairman, Bucks Quarter Sessions, since 1969; *b* 14 Nov. 1911; *m* 1947, Elizabeth Suzanne (*née* McCorquodale); two *s. Educ:* Lancing Coll.; Exeter Coll., Oxford. MA, BCL Oxford. Called to Bar, 1935; practised on Northern Circuit, 1935-61; Recorder of Blackpool, 1960-61; Dep. Comr for purposes of Nat. Insurance Acts, 1961-65. Served in RA, 1939-45 (despatches, 1944). JP Bucks, 1969. *Address:* The Garth, Marlow, Bucks. *T:* Marlow 4170.

**CLOWES, Maj.-Gen. Norman,** CBE 1943; DSO 1918; MC; ADC to the King, 1946-49; retired Sept. 1949; *b* 7 Oct. 1893; *s* of late Albert Clowes, Warwick, Queensland; *m*; one *s. Croix de Guerre, France; Medal of Freedom, USA. Address:* Tanglin, Harefield Road, Middleton-on-Sea, Sussex.

**CLOYNE, Bishop of, (RC),** since 1957; **Most Rev. John J. Ahern;** *b* 31 Aug. 1911; *s* of James Ahern and Ellen Mulcahy. *Educ:* St Colman's

Coll., Fermoy; St Patrick's Coll., Maynooth; Irish Coll., Rome. Ordained, 1936. Prof. at St Colman's Coll., Fermoy, 1940-44; St Patrick's Coll., Maynooth, 1946-57. *Address:* Bishop's House, Cobh, Co. Cork, Ireland.

**CLUCAS, Kenneth Henry,** CB 1969; Secretary to the National Board for Prices and Incomes, since 1968; *b* 18 Nov. 1921; *o s* of late Rev. J. H. Clucas; *m* 1960, Barbara, *e d* of Rear-Adm. R. P. Hunter, USN (Retd), Washington, DC; one *d. Educ:* Kingswood Sch.; Emmanuel Coll., Cambridge. Royal Signals, 1941-46 (despatches). Joined Min. of Labour as Asst Principal, 1948; 2nd Sec. (Labour), British Embassy, Cairo, 1950; Principal, HM Treasury, 1952; Min. of Labour, 1954; Private Sec. to Minister, 1960-62; Asst Sec., 1962; Under-Sec., 1966-68. *Address:* Cariad, Knoll Road, Godalming, Surrey. *T:* Godalming 6430. *Club:* Oxford and Cambridge University.

**CLUER, Reginald Montagu;** former Puisne Judge; *b* 10 March 1891; *s* of A. R. Cluer, County Court Judge (Whitechapel and Shoreditch); *m* 1st, 1914, Hilda Egerton Hall; (one *s* killed in action, 1945); 2nd, 1936, Mary Bancroft (*d* 1960); two *s. Educ:* Clifton Coll.; Balliol Coll., Oxford. Barrister-at-law, 1915-32; Resident Magistrate, Jamaica, 1932-37; Dep. Public Prosecutor, FMS, 1938-39; Puisne Judge, Tanganyika, 1939-43; Puisne Judge, Jamaica, 1944-53. *Recreations:* numerous. *Address:* Le Verger, Trinity, Jersey, CI.

**CLUNIE, James;** *b* 20 March 1889; *m* 1912, Elizabeth Stewart. *Educ:* Lundin Links, Lower Largo. House painter and decorator. Mem. Exec. of Scottish Painters' Soc. for 18 years (Chm. three times). Mem. of Dunfermline Town Council, 1933-50; Magistrate 6 years. MP (Lab) Dunfermline, 1950-Sept. 1959. *Publications:* First Principles of Working Class Education, 1920; The Autobiography of a House Painter: Labour is my Faith, 1954, The Voice of Labour, 1958. *Recreations:* reading and book reviewing. *Address:* c/o Tate, 293 Henley Road, Ilford, Essex. *T:* 01-478 0380.

**CLUTTERBUCK, Vice-Adm. Sir David Granville,** KBE 1968; CB 1965; *b* Gloucester, 25 Jan. 1913; *m* 1937, Rose Mere Vaile, Auckland, NZ; two *d.* Joined RN, 1929. Served War of 1939-45 (despatches twice): navigating officer of cruisers HMS Ajax, 1940-42, HMS Newfoundland, 1942-46 (present Japanese surrender at Tokyo). Subsequently commanded destroyers Sluys and Cadiz; Naval Attaché at British Embassy, Bonn; Capt. (D) of Third Training Squadron in HMS Zest, Londonderry, 1956-58; commanded cruiser HMS Blake; Chief of Staff to C-in-C Home Fleet and C-in-C Allied Forces Eastern Atlantic, 1963-66; Rear-Adm., 1963; Vice-Adm. 1966; Dep. Supreme Allied Comdr, Atlantic, 1966-68. Administrative Dir, Business Graduates Assoc. Ltd, 1969-. *Address:* Long Acres, Prinsted, Emsworth, Hants. *Club:* United Service.

**CLUTTERBUCK, Sir (Peter) Alexander,** GCMG 1952 (KCMG 1946; CMG 1943); MC; *b* 27 March 1897; *e s* of late Sir Peter Clutterbuck, CIE, CBE, formerly Inspector Gen. of Forests, India and Burma; *m* 1921, Dorita, *y d* of Francis Seymour Weldon; one *d. Educ:* Malvern Coll. (Scholar); Pembroke Coll., Cambridge (Scholar). Served European War, Coldstream Guards, 1916-19 (despatches, MC); entered Civil Service as Asst Principal GPO, 1919; Colonial Office, 1922; additional Private Sec. to Parly Under-Sec. for the Colonies, 1924; Sec., Donoughmore Commn on Ceylon Constitution, 1927-28; Private Sec. to Permanent Under-Sec. of State, Dominions Office, 1928-29; Principal, Dominions Office, 1929; Mem. of UK Delegation to League of Nations Assembly, 1929, 1930, and 1931, negotiations with Egypt, 1930, and Reparations Conferences, London, 1931, Lausanne, 1932; Sec., Newfoundland Royal Commn, 1933; Dep. High Comr for UK, Union of South Africa, 1939-40; Asst Sec., Dominions Office, 1940; Asst Under-Sec. of State, 1942-46; High Comr for the UK in Canada, 1946-52, in India, 1952-55; HM Ambassador to the Republic of Ireland, 1955-59; Permanent Under-Sec. of State, CRO, 1959-61. Governor, Malvern Coll. Hon. DCL: Bishop's Univ., Quebec; Queen's Univ., Ont; Univ. of BC. *Address:* Upperton Farmhouse, Bury, Sussex. *T:* Bury 640. *Club:* Travellers'.

**CLUTTERBUCK, Maj.-Gen. Richard Lewis,** OBE 1958; Chief Army Instructor, Royal College of Defence Studies, since 1971; *b* London, 22 Nov. 1917; *s* of late Col L. St J. R. Clutterbuck, OBE, late RA, and late Mrs I. J. Clutterbuck; *m* 1948, Angela Muriel Barford; three *s. Educ:* Radley Coll.; Pembroke Coll., Cambridge. MA Cantab (Mech. Scis). Commd in RE, 1937; War Service: France, 1940; Sudan and Ethiopia, 1941; Western Desert, 1941-43; Italy, 1944; subseq. service in: Germany, 1946 and 1951-53; Italy, 1946; Palestine, 1947; Malaya, 1956-58; Christmas Island (Nuclear Trials), 1958; USA, 1961-63; Singapore, 1966-68. Instructor, British Army Staff Coll., 1953-56; Instructor, US Army Staff Coll., 1961-63; idc 1965; Chief Engr, Far East Land Forces, 1966-68; Engr-in-Chief (Army), 1968-70. FICE. *Publications:* Across the River (as Richard Jocelyn), 1957; The Long Long War, 1966; contribs to British and US jls. *Recreations:* sailing, canoeing, study of revolution. *Address:* Goodworth Cottage, Goodworth Clatford, Andover, Hants. *Clubs:* Royal Commonwealth Society, Army and Navy.

**CLUTTERBUCK, Maj.-Gen. Walter Edmond,** DSO 1943; MC; *b* 17 Nov. 1894; *s* of E. H. Clutterbuck, JP, Hardenhuish Park, Chippenham, Wilts; *m* 1919, Gwendolin Atterbury, *o d* of H. G. Younger, JP, Benmore, Argyllshire; one *s* three *d. Educ:* Horris Hill; Cheltenham Coll.; RMC Sandhurst. Commissioned Royal Scots Fusiliers, 1913; served European War, 1914-19, France, Gallipoli, Egypt, Palestine, and S Russia (wounded twice, MC and bar, Crown of Italy, 1914 Star and clasp, despatches twice); Bt Lt-Col 1939; War of 1939-45 commanded: 1st Royal Scots Fusiliers, 1939-40; 10th Inf. Bde, 1940-41; 1st Div., 1941-43, N Africa and Pantellaria (DSO, Legion of Honour); an Inf. Div. Home Forces, 1943. Chief of British Military Mission to Egypt, 1945-46; retired pay, 1946. *Recreations:* hunting, fishing, shooting. *Address:* Hornby Castle, Bedale, Yorks. *T:* Old Catterick 579. *Club:* Naval and Military.

**CLUTTON-BROCK, Prof. Alan Francis;** *m* 1936, Barbara Foy Mitchell; one *d. Educ:* Eton; King's College, Cambridge. Art Critic, The Times; Trustee of the National Gallery. Slade Professor of Fine Art, Univ. of Cambridge, 1955-58. *Address:* Chastleton House, Moreton-in-Marsh, Glos.

**CLUTTON-BROCK, Arthur Guy;** independent social worker since 1965; *b* 5 April 1906; *s* of late Henry Alan Clutton-Brock and late Rosa Clutton-Brock; *m* 1934, Francys Mary Allen; one *d. Educ:* Rugby Sch.; Magdalene Coll., Cambridge. Cambridge House, 1927; Rugby House, 1929; Borstal Service, 1933; Principal Probation Officer for the Metropolitan Police Court District, 1936; Head of Oxford House,

1940; Christian Reconstruction in Europe, 1946; Agricultural Labourer, 1947; Agriculturalist at St Faith's Mission, 1949; Field Worker of African Development Trust, 1959-65. *Publication:* Dawn in Nyasaland, 1959. *Address:* PO Box 2097, Salisbury, Rhodesia.

**CLUVER, Eustace Henry,** ED; MA; DM, ChB Oxon; DPH London; FRSH; Emeritus Professor of Medical Education, University of the Witwatersrand, Johannesburg, SA, since 1963; *b* 28 Aug. 1894; *s* of late Dr F. A. Cluver, Stellenbosch; *m* 1929, Eileen Ledger; three *d. Educ:* Victoria Coll., Stellenbosch; Hertford Coll., Oxford (Rhodes scholar). 1st class Final Hon. Sch. of Physiology, 1916. Elected to a Senior Demyship at Magdalen Coll., 1917; King's Coll. (Burney Yeo Scholarship, 1918). Served European War, 1914-18 (Capt. S Af. Med. Corps, BEF, France); War of 1939-45 (Col Dir of Pathology, S Af. Med. Corps). Prof. of Physiology, Univ. of the Witwatersrand, Johannesburg, 1919-26; Sec. for Public Health and Chief Health Officer for the Union of South Africa, 1938-40; Dir of S African Inst. for Med. Research and Prof. of Preventive Medicine, Univ. Witwatersrand, 1940-59. KStJ. *Publications:* Public Health in South Africa, 1934 (Textbook), 6th edn 1959; Social Medicine, 1951; Medical and Health Legislation in the Union of South Africa, 1949, 2nd edn 1960; papers in scientific and medical journals. *Address:* Mornhill Farm, Walkerville, Transvaal, South Africa.

**CLWYD,** 2nd Baron *cr* 1919; **John Trevor Roberts;** Bt, 1908; Assistant Secretary of Commissions, Lord Chancellor's Department of House of Lords, 1950-61; *b* 28 Nov. 1900; *s* of 1st Baron and Hannah (*d* 1951), *d* of W. S. Caine, MP; *S* father, 1955; *m* 1932, Joan de Bois, *d* of late Charles R. Murray, Woodbank, Partickhill, Glasgow; one *s* one *d. Educ:* Gresham's Sch.; Trinity Coll., Cambridge. BA 1922. Barrister, Gray's Inn, 1930. JP County of London, 1950. *Recreation:* fishing. *Heir: s* Hon. John Anthony Roberts [*b* 2 Jan. 1935; *m* 1969, Geraldine, *yr d* of C. E. Cannons, Sauderstead]. *Address:* 43 Campden Hill Square, W8. *T:* 01-727 7911; Tanyrallt, Abergele, Denbighshire. *T:* Abergele 2127.

**CLYDE, Rt. Hon. Lord; Rt. Hon. Lord Justice-General; James Latham McDiarmid Clyde,** PC 1951; DL; LLD, Edinburgh 1954, St Andrews 1955, Aberdeen 1960; Lord Justice-General of Scotland and Lord President of the Court of Session, since Dec. 1954; *b* 30 Oct. 1898; *e s* of late Lord Clyde, PC; *m* 1928, Margaret Letitia Du Buisson; one *s* one *d. Educ:* Edinburgh Academy; Trinity Coll., Oxford; Edinburgh Univ. Called to Scots Bar, 1925; KC (Scotland) 1936. Lord Advocate, 1951-54; Hon. Bencher, Middle Temple, 1958. MP (C) North Edinburgh, 1950-54. DL County of Kinross, 1965. *Address:* 14 Heriot Row, Edinburgh. *T:* 031-556 1264; Briglands, Rumbling Bridge, Kinross-shire. *Club:* New (Edinburgh).

*See also M. D. Butler.*

**CLYDE, Rt. Hon. James Latham McDiarmid;** *see* Clyde, Rt. Hon. Lord.

**CLYDE, Dr William McCallum,** CMG 1948; Senior Lecturer in English, Avery Hill College, 1958-70, retired; *b* 23 June 1901; *e s* of Rev. William A. Clyde; *m* 1931, Catherine Grace, *d* of Rev. D. D. Rees, Saltcoats, Scotland; four *s. Educ:* King Edward VII's Sch., Sheffield; St Andrews Univ. MA, 1st Class Hons, Eng. Lang. and Lit., St Andrews, 1925; Carnegie Research Fellowship, 1927-29; PhD St Andrews, 1929; Lectr in Eng. Lang. and Lit., St Andrews, 1929; Head of Dept of Eng. Lang. and Lit., University Coll., Dundee, 1935; Asst Div. Food Officer, East Scotland, 1939; Dep. Div. Food Officer, East Scotland, 1941; Adviser to Sec. of State for Colonies on wartime food supplies, 1942; Chm. of Nutrition, Food and Agricultural Unit to study food situation in Malaya in post-liberation period, 1945; Food Adviser to Special Commissioner in SE Asia, 1946; Leader, UK Delegn to UN FAO Meetings: Trivandrum, India, 1947; Baguio, Philippines, 1948; Singapore and Bangkok, 1949; Bandung, Indonesia, 1952; Tokyo and Rangoon, 1954; Dir of Economic Activities for Commissioner-Gen. for UK in SE Asia, Singapore, 1948-51; Vice-Chm., International Rice Commission, 1949, 1954; Rice Adviser to Foreign Office, 1951-56. Professor of English, Baghdad, 1956-58. *Publications:* The Freedom of the Press from Caxton to Cromwell, 1934; AE (George W. Russell): Poet, Essayist and Painter, 1935. *Recreation:* sketching. *Address:* 79 Queens Park Rise, Brighton, Sussex.

**CLYDESDALE, Marquess of Douglas and; Angus Alan Douglas Douglas-Hamilton;** *b* 13 Sept. 1938; *e s* of Duke of Hamilton and Brandon, *qv. Educ:* Eton; Balliol Coll., Oxford (BA). Flt Lieut RAF; retired, 1967. Chm., Intertech Developments Ltd. *Recreations:* motor racing, ski-ing, skin diving. *Address:* 8 Eccleston Mews, SW1. *T:* 01-235 7213; Lennoxlove, Haddington, E Lothian. *Club:* Royal Aero.

**CLYDESMUIR,** 2nd Baron *cr* 1948, of Braidwood; **Ronald John Bilsland Colville,** CB 1965; MBE 1944; TD; Lord Lieutenant, Lanarkshire, since 1963; Bt-Col Cameronians, TA; Brigadier Royal Company of Archers, Queen's Body Guard for Scotland; *b* 21 May 1917; *s* of 1st Baron Clydesmuir, PC, GCIE, TD, and Agnes Anne, CI 1947, Kaisar-i-Hind Gold Medal; *S* father, 1954; *m* 1946, Joan Marguerita, *d* of Lt-Col E. B. Booth, DSO, Darver Castle, Co. Louth; two *s* two *d. Educ:* Charterhouse; Trinity Coll., Cambridge. Served in The Cameronians (Scottish Rifles), 1939-45 (MBE, despatches). Commanded 6/7th Bn The Cameronians, TA, 1953-56. Director: Colvilles Ltd; British Linen Bank (Dep. Governor, 1966-); Bank of Scotland; Scottish Provident Instn; Scotbits Securities Ltd; The Scottish Western Investment Co.; Chm., Exec. Cttee, Scottish Council (Development and industry); President: Scottish Council of Physical Recreation; Scottish Br., National Playing Fields Assoc.; Vice-Chm. Council, Territorial, Auxiliary and Volunteer Reserve Assocs; Chm., Lanarkshire T&AFA, 1957-63, Pres. 1963-68; Pres. Lowland TA&VRA. Hon. Col, 52 Lowland Volunteers, T&AVR, 1970-. Scottish Outward Bound Assoc. DL Lanarkshire, 1955, Vice-Lieut, 1959-63. Hon. LLD Strathclyde, 1968. *Recreations:* shooting, fishing. *Heir: s* Hon. David Ronald Colville, *b* 8 April 1949. *Address:* Langlees House, Biggar, Lanarkshire. *T:* Biggar 57. *Clubs:* Caledonian; Western (Glasgow); New (Edinburgh).

*See also Capt. N. E. F. Dalrymple Hamilton.*

**COAD, Maj.-Gen. Basil Aubrey,** CB 1953; CBE 1950; DSO 1944 (Bar 1945); DL; *b* 27 Sept. 1906; *s* of late Engineer-Capt. H. J. Coad, RN, and late Mrs E. M. Coad; *m* 1st, 1935, Janet Octavia (*d* 1954); no *c*; 2nd, 1955, Mrs Clare Henley; one *d. Educ:* Felsted; RMC Sandhurst. Commissioned into Wilts Regt, 1926; served in India, 1926-28; Shanghai, 1929-30; Adjutant 2nd Bn Wilts Regt, 1934-37; Palestine, 1935-36; Adjt 4th Bn Wilts Regt, 1937-39; comd 5th Bn Dorsetshire Regt, 1942-44; Comdr 130 Infantry Bde, 1944-46; Staff Coll., 1946; comd 2nd Bn Wilts Regt, Dec. 1946-48; formed and comd 27 Infantry Bde, 1948-51; Hong Kong, 1949-50; Korea, 1950-51; Comdr 2nd Infantry Div., 1951-54; Pres., Regular Commissions Board, Westbury, Wilts, 1954-57, retired. Col The Wilts Regt (Duke of Edinburgh's), 1954-59; Col The Duke of Edinburgh's Royal Regt (Berks and Wilts), 1959-64. DL Wilts 1963. Officer, US Legion of Merit, 1954; American Silver Star, 1950. *Recreations:* golf, hockey and gardening. *Address:* Nursteed House, Devizes, Wilts. *Club:* Army and Navy.

**COADY, Aubrey William Burleton,** CMG 1959; Chairman, Electricity Commission of NSW, since 1959 (Member since 1950); *b* Singleton, NSW, 15 June 1915; *s* of W. A. Coady, Belmont; *m* 1964, Phyllis K., *d* of late G. W. Mathews. *Educ:* Newcastle High Sch.; Sydney Univ. (BA, BEc). Under-Sec. and Comptroller of Accounts, NSW Treasury, 1955-59. *Address:* 42 Rickard Avenue, Mosman, NSW 2088, Australia.

**COAKER, Maj.-Gen. Ronald Edward,** CBE 1963; MC 1942; Director of Military Operations, Ministry of Defence, since 1970; *b* 28 Nov. 1917; *s* of late Lieut-Col Vere Arthur Coaker, DSO, and Cicely Annie Coaker (*née* Egerton), Richard's Hill, Battle, Sussex; *m* 1946, Constance Aimée Johanna, *d* of Francis Newton-Curzon, Lockington Hall, Derby; one *s* two *d*. *Educ:* Wellington; RMC, Sandhurst. 2nd Lieut IA (Skinner's Horse), 1937; served War of 1939-45, Middle East, Italy and Burma; transf. 17th/21st Lancers, 1947; Lt-Col 1954; GSO1, 7th Armoured Div., 1954-56; comd 17th/21st Lancers, 1956-58; Col GS to Chief of Defence Staff, 1958-60; Brig. 1961; Commandant RAC Centre, 1961-62; Dir of Defence Plans (Army), 1964-66; Dep. Dir of Service Intelligence (Army), 1966-67; Assistant Chief of Staff (Intelligence), SHAPE, 1967-70. maj.-Gen. 1966. Col 17th/21st Lancers, 1965-. *Recreations:* field sports, riding, bridge, ski-ing, tennis. *Address:* Seaton Old Rectory, Uppingham, Rutland. *T:* Morcott 276. *Club:* Cavalry.

**COALES, Prof. John Flavell,** OBE 1945; FRS 1970; Professor of Engineering (Control), Cambridge University, since 1965; Fellow of Clare Hall since 1964; *b* 14 Sept. 1907; *s* of John Dennis Coales and Marion Beatrice Coales (*née* Flavell); *m* 1936, Mary Dorothea Violet, *d* of Rev. Guthrie Henry Lewis Alison; two *s* two *d*. *Educ:* Berkhamsted Sch.; Sidney Sussex Coll., Cambridge (MA). Admty Dept of Scientific Res., 1929-46; Res. Dir, Elliott Bros (London) Ltd, 1946; Engrg Dept, Cambridge Univ.: Asst Dir of Res., 1953; Lectr, 1956; Reader in Engrg, 1958; Prof., 1965. Part-time Mem., E Electricity Bd, 1967-. Mackay Vis. Prof. of Electrical Engrg, Univ. of Calif., Berkeley, 1963. Internat. Fedn of Automatic Control: MEC, 1957; Vice-Pres., 1961; Pres., 1963. Brit. Conf. on Automation and Computation: Gp B Vice-Chm., 1958; Chm., 1960. UK Automation Council: Chm. Res. and Develt Panel, 1960-63; Chm. For. Relations Panel, 1960-64; Vice-Chm., 1961-63; Chm., 1963-66. Instn of Electrical Engrs: Mem. Coun., 1953-55, 1964-; Chm., Measurement Section, 1953; Chm., Control and Automation Div., 1965, etc; Vice-Pres., 1966-. Pres., Soc. of Instrument Technology, 1958. Past Member: Gen. Bd and Exec. Cttee of Nat. Physical Laboratory; Adv. Coun., RMC of Science, 1963-; Educn Adv. Cttee for RAF, 1967-. Governor: Hatfield Coll. of Technology, 1951-68; Hatfield Polytechnic, 1969-; Mem. Governing Body, Nat. Inst. of Agricultural Engrg, 1970-. FIEE, FIEEE, FIAgrE, FInstP. *Publications:* (ed) Automatic and Remote Control (Proc. First Congr. of Internat. Fedn of Automatic Control), 1961; original papers on radio direction finding, radar, information theory, magnetic amplifiers, automatic control, automation and technical education. *Recreations:* mountaineering, farming, gardening. *Address:* 280 Hills Road, Cambridge; Mockerkin Hall, Cockermouth, Cumberland. *Club:* Athenæum.

**COATE, Maj.-Gen. Sir Raymond Douglas,** KBE 1967; CB 1966; Paymaster-in-Chief, 1963-67; *b* 8 May 1908; *s* of Frederick James and Elizabeth Anne Coate; *m* 1939, Frances Margaret Varley; two *s*. *Educ:* King Edward's Sch., Bath; RMC Sandhurst. Commissioned into Devonshire Regt, 1928; transferred to Royal Army Pay Corps, 1937; Col Comdt, RAPC, 1970-. *Address:* 18 Roehampton Close, Roehampton Lane, SW15. *Club:* Army and Navy.

**COATES, Sir Albert (Ernest),** Kt 1955; OBE 1946; MD, MS; LLD (*hc*); FRCS; FRACS; Consulting surgeon in private practice, Melbourne, Australia; Consulting Surgeon: Royal Melbourne, Royal Women's and Repatriation Hospitals, Melbourne; *b* 28 Jan. 1895; *s* of Arthur Coates, Ballarat, Vic.; *m* 1st, 1921, Harriet Josephine (*d* 1934), *d* of Elisha Hicks, Melbourne; 2nd, 1936, Catherine Martha, *d* of Alfred Anderson, Dunedin, NZ; two *s* three *d*. *Educ:* Ballarat; Univ. of Melbourne. MB, BS, Melbourne, 1924; MD 1926; MS 1927; FRACS 1932; FRCS (by election) 1953. Served European War, 1914-18: AIF, Gallipoli and France; Surg., Royal Melbourne Hosp., 1927-55. war Service, 1941-46 (despatches, OBE): Senior Surg. (Lt-Col) to AIF, Malaya; POW 1942; Chief MO in POW Hosp., Siam, 1944-45. Stewart Lectr in Surgery, Univ. of Melbourne, 1949-56. Mem. Dental Board, Vic., 1936-49; Pres. BMA, Vic., 1941 and 1947; Foundation Fellow, AMA; Mem. Council, Univ. of Melbourne, 1951-57; Pres., Nurses Memorial Centre, Melbourne, 1955-62; Chm. Board of Management, Fairfield Hosp., 1956-; Pres. Rotary Club, Melbourne, 1954-55; Mem. Olympics Civic Cttee, 1955-56. Hon. LLD, Melbourne, 1962. *Publications:* contribs on surgical subjects in Australian and other jls. *Recreation:* golf. *Address:* 2 Chastleton Avenue, Toorak, Vic 3142, Australia; 61 Collins Street, Melbourne, Vic 3000. *T:* MF4444. *Clubs:* Melbourne, Athenæum, Royal Melbourne Golf (Melbourne); Barwon Heads Golf.

**COATES, Captain Sir Clive Milnes-,** 2nd Bt *cr* 1911; OBE 1919; *b* 21 May 1879; *s* of 1st Bt and Edith, *e d* of Capt. Philip Woolley, Gravenhurst, Sussex; *S* father, 1921; changed names by deed poll to Sir Clive Milnes-Coates, 1946; *m* 1906, Lady Celia Hermione Crewe Milnes, 2nd *d* of 1st Marquis of Crewe, KG, PC; one *s* two *d* (and *yr s* killed in Normandy, 1944). *Educ:* Charterhouse; Exeter Coll., Oxford. Late 15th Hussars; Patron of one Living. *Heir: s* Robert Edward James Clive Milnes-Coates, Lt-Col Coldstream Guards, DSO [*b* 1907; *m* 1945, Lady Patricia Milnes-Gaskell, *er d* of 4th Earl of Listowel and *widow* of Lt-Col Charles Milnes-Gaskell, Coldstream Guards; one *s* (*b* 8 Dec. 1948), one *d*]. *Address:* 13 Hyde Park Gate, SW7. *T:* 01-584 8434; Helperby Hall, Helperby, York. *T:* Helperby 204.

*See also W. B. Harris.*

**COATES, Edith;** Principal Dramatic Mezzo-Soprano, Royal Opera, Covent Garden, 1947; *b* Lincoln, 31 May 1908; *d* of Percy and Eleanor Coates, Leeds; *m* 1933, Harry Powell Lloyd. *Educ:* Trinity Coll. of Music, London. Principal Mezzo, Sadler's Wells, 1935 (Carmen, Delilah, Azucena, Ortrud, Amneris, etc); Principal Mezzo, Covent Garden, 1937 (first appearance there under Sir Thomas Beecham, and in The Ring under Furtwängler, in Coronation season and 1938, 1939); Sadler's Wells, New Theatre and Provinces, singing many roles during War of 1939-45 and in Germany after war. Created role of Auntie in Britten's Peter Grimes, Sadler's Wells, 1945, and afterwards sang it at Paris Opera, Monnaie, Brussels and Covent Garden; has sung over 60 roles in opera; many oratorios, Royal Albert Hall, BBC and Provinces; many concerts and broadcasts; sang title role at Covent Garden in Tchaikowsky's Queen of Spades under Kleiber, 1950-51; sang in first English performances of Berg's Wozzeck, 1952; sang in first performance of Tippett's Midsummer Marriage, Covent Garden, 1955, Janacek's Jenufa, Covent Garden, 1956, and John Gardner's Moon and Sixpence, Sadler's Wells, 1957; played in Candide (Hillman-Bernstein after Voltaire), Saville, 1959; Countess in Queen of Spades, Covent Garden, 1961; sang in first performances of Grace Williams' Opera, The Parlour, Welsh National Opera, Cardiff, 1966; English Opera Group, 1963, 1965, 1967. *Recreations:* reading, walking. *Address:* Montrose, Cross Lane, Findon, Worthing, Sussex. *T:* Findon 2040. *Club:* Cowdray.

**COATES, Ernest William,** CMG 1970; State Director of Finance and Permanent Head of Victoria Treasury, Australia, since 1959; *b* 30 Nov. 1916; *s* of Thomas Atlee Coates; *m* 1943, Phyllis E. Morris; one *s* three *d*. *Educ:* Ballarat High Sch.; Univ. of Melbourne. Member: Bd of State Savings Bank of Victoria, 1960-; Nat. Debt Commn, Australia, 1963-; Australian Universities Commn, 1968-. *Recreations:* golf, music. *Address:* 64 Molesworth Street, Kew, Victoria 3101, Australia. *T:* 86 8226. *Club:* Athenæum (Melbourne).

**COATES, Brig. Sir Frederick (Gregory Lindsay),** 2nd Bt *cr* 1921; late Royal Tank Regiment; Defence Sales, since 1969; *b* 19 May 1916; *o s* of Sir William Frederick Coates, 1st Bt, Belfast, N Ireland; *S* father, 1932; *m* 1940, Joan Nugent, *d* of late Maj.-Gen. Sir Charlton Spinks, KBE, DSO; one *s* two *d*. *Educ:* Eton; Sandhurst. Served War of 1939-45, North Africa and NW Europe. Min. of Supply, 1947-53; Asst Military Attaché, Stockholm, 1953-56; British Joint Services Mission, Washington, 1956-58; Comdt, RAC School of Tank Technology, 1958-61; Asst Dir of Fighting Vehicles, War Office, 1961-64; Col GS, War Office and MoD (Army), 1964-66; Brig., British Defence Staff, Washington, DC, 1966-69. *Heir: s* David Charlton Frederick Coates, *b* 16 Feb. 1948. *Address:* Launchfield, Briantspuddle, Dorset; 66 Sussex Square, W2. *Clubs:* Naval and Military; RMYC; Island Sailing; RAC Yacht.

**COATES, Prof. Geoffrey Edward,** MA, DSc; Professor of Chemistry, University of Wyoming, since 1968; *b* 14 May 1917; *er s* of Prof. Joseph Edward Coates, *qv*; *m* 1951, Winifred Jean Hobbs; one *s* one *d*. *Educ:* Clifton Coll.; Queen's Coll., Oxford. Research Chemist, Magnesium Metal Corp., 1940-45; Univ. of Bristol: Lecturer in Chemistry, 1945-53; Sub-Warden of Wills Hall, 1946-51; Prof. of Chemistry, Univ. of Durham, 1953-68. *Publications:* Organo-metallic Compounds (monograph), 1956, new edns 1960, 1967; Principles of Organometallic Chemistry, 1968; papers in scientific journals. *Address:* Chemistry Department, University of Wyoming, Laramie, Wyoming 82070, USA. *Club:* Royal Commonwealth Society.

**COATES, Joseph Edward,** OBE 1919; DSc, FRIC; *b* 6 May 1883; *e s* of W. and M. J. Coates, Oakamoor, N Staffs; *m* 1915, Ada Maria Finney, MSc, FRIC (*d* 1968); two *s*. *Educ:* Alleyne's Grammar Sch., Uttoxeter; University Coll. of N Wales, Bangor. Fellow of Univ. of Wales, 1906-08; Research Asst to Prof. Haber, Karlsruhe, 1908-09; Lecturer in Chemistry, Univ. of Birmingham, 1910-20; Prof. of Chemistry, University Coll. of Swansea (University of Wales), 1920-48; retired 1948. Senior Technical Officer, RN Experimental Station, Stratford, London with rank of Lieut-Comdr, RNVR, 1915-19. *Publications:* papers in chemical journals. *Address:* Sabinal, Lucklands Road, Weston Park, Bath. *T:* Bath 23377.
*See also Prof. G. E. Coates.*

**COATES, Patrick Devereux;** Under-Secretary, Ministry of Housing and Local Government, since 1968; *b* 30 April 1916; *s* of H. H. H. Coates, OBE, and late Mrs F. J. Coates; *m* 1946, Mary Eleanor, *e d* of late Capt. Leveson Campbell, DSO, RN and of Mrs Cambell; one *s* one *d*. *Educ:* Trinity Coll., Cambridge. Entered Consular Service and served at Peking, Canton and Kunming, 1937-41; attached to Chinese 22nd Div. in Burma (despatches) and to Chinese forces in India, 1941-44; Actg Chinese Sec. to HM Embassy in China, 1944-46; 1st Sec., Foreign Office, 1946-50; transf. to Min. of Town and Country Planning, 1950; Asst Sec., Min. of Housing and Local Govt, 1955; Asst Under-Sec. of State, Dept of Economic Affairs, 1965-68. *Recreation:* getting into the fresh air. *Address:* c/o Ministry of Housing and Local Government, Whitehall, SW1.

**COATES, Reginald Charles;** Professor of Civil Engineering in the University of Nottingham since 1958; Deputy Vice-Chancellor, University of Nottingham, 1966-69; *b* 28 June 1920; *s* of Wilfrid and Margaret Anne Coates; *m* 1942, Doris Sheila; two *s* one *d*. *Educ:* New Mills Grammar Sch.; The Herbert Strutt Sch., Belper, Derbyshire; University Coll., Nottingham. Served War of 1939-45, corps of Royal Engineers. Lectr in Civil Engineering, University Coll., Nottingham, 1946, Senior Lectr in Civil Engineering, University of Nottingham, 1953. Mem. Council, Instn of Civil Engineers, 1969-. *Publications:* occasional articles in technical press. *Recreations:* cooking and idling. *Address:* University of Nottingham, Nottingham.

**COATS,** family name of **Baron Glentanar.**

**COATS, Sir Alastair Francis Stuart,** 4th Bt, *cr* 1905; *b* 18 Nov. 1921; *s* of Lieut-Col Sir James Stuart Coats, MC, 3rd Bt and of Lady Amy Coats, *er d* of 8th Duke of Richmond and Gordon; *S* father, 1966; *m* 1947, Lukyn, *d* of Capt. Charles Gordon; one *s* one *d*. *Educ:* Eton. Served War of 1939-45, Coldstream Guards (Capt.). *Heir: s* Alexander James Coats, *b* 6 July 1951. *Address:* Birchwood House, Durford Wood, Petersfield, Hants. *T:* Liss 2254.

**COATS, Air Cdre (retd) Rowland,** CB 1954; RAF retd; ICT 1958-65; *b* 26 May 1904; *m* 1959, Eva Gertrud Truemer; two *s* one *d* (triplets). *Educ:* Emmanuel Coll., Cambridge (MA); RAF Coll., Cranwell. 7 Squadron, 1925-28; spec. in Engrg; India, 1934-37; Staff Coll., 1938; War of 1939-45: Air Min.; Bomber Comd, Egypt; Stn Comdr, Bridgnorth, 1947-49; Air Cdre, 1949; AOC: Record Office, 1949-51; 62 Gp, 1951-53; AOA 205 Group, 1953-56; AOC 205 Group, 1956. *Address:* Lower Ebford, Barton, Topsham, Exeter. *T:* Topsham 3109.

**COBB, John Francis Scott,** QC 1962; Recorder of Sheffield, since 1970; *b* 15 Dec. 1922; *o s* of late J. H. Cobb, FRCS and Mrs E. M. Cobb (*née* Davidson); *m* 1951, Joan Mary, *o d* of W. H. Knapton, Whitgift, near Goole, Yorks, and of Mrs E. M. Knapton (*née* Silvester); two *s* two *d*. *Educ:* Winchester Coll.; Trinity Coll., Oxford. Commissioned Royal Artillery, 1942; Staff Capt. (Civil Affairs), Trieste, 1945-46; MA Oxon 1947; called to Bar, Inner Temple, 1948, Master 1969. Recorder of: Doncaster, 1961-64; Bradford, 1964-69; Hull, 1969-70. Asst Boundary Comr, 1965. *Recreations:* golf and gardening. *Address:* The Priory, Follifoot, near Harrogate, Yorks. *T:* Harrogate 81537; Flat 3, 14 Guilford Street, WC1. *T:* 01-242 4293. *Clubs:* Vincent's (Oxford); various provinical (Durham, York, Sheffield).

**COBB, John Leslie;** Director: Piccadilly Estate & Securities, since 1970; Warwick Securities, since 1970; *b* 25 Sept. 1923; *yr s* of Rev. John E. Cobb, Kirkburton, Yorks; *m* 1949, Pamela Teresa, *d* of late Arthur John Bareham, Chelmsford, Essex; one *d*. *Educ:* Burnage High Sch., Manchester; Thornes House, Wakefield. Served War of 1939-45: Ordinary Seaman, 1941; Midshipman, RNVR, 1943; Sub-Lieut, 1944; Lieut, 1945. Daily Express, 1949-52; Investors Chronicle, 1952-67, apptd Dep. Ed., 1957; Ed., Investors Chronicle and Stock Exchange Gazette following merger, 1967-70. *Address:* The Colnes, Coppins Close, Springfield, Chelmsford, Essex. *T:* Chelmsford 62454. *Club:* Reform.

**COBB, Richard Charles,** FBA 1967; Fellow and Tutor in Modern History, Balliol College, Oxford; Reader in French Revolutionary History, since 1969; *b* 20 May 1917; *s* of Francis Hills Cobb, Sudan Civil Service, and Dora Cobb (*née* Swindale); *m* 1963, Margaret Tennant; three *s* one *d*. *Educ:* Shrewsbury Sch.; Merton Coll., Oxford. Postmastership in History, Merton, 1934. HM Forces, 1942-46. Research in Paris, 1946-55; Lectr in History, UCW Aberystwyth, 1956-61; Sen. Simon Res. Fellow, Manchester, 1960; Lectr, University of Leeds, 1962. Chevalier des Palmes Académiques, 1956. *Publications:* L'armée révolutionnaire à Lyon, 1952; Les armées révolutionnaires du Midi, 1955; Les armées révolutionnaires, vol. 1, 1961, vol. 2, 1963; Terreur et Subsistances, 1965; A Second Identity: essays on France and French history, 1969; The Police and the People: French Popular Protest, 1789-1820, 1970. *Address:* Balliol College, Oxford. *Club:* Gridiron (Oxford).

**COBB, Rear-Adm. Robert,** CBE 1953 (OBE 1941); retired; *b* 18 Sept. 1900; *s* of late Lieut-Col Cobb; *m* 1930, Honor, *d* of late Sir C. Aubrey Smith; one *s* one *d*. *Educ:* All Saints, Bloxham; RN Colls, Osborne and Dartmouth. Joined Osborne, 1914; Midshipman, 1917; Comdr (E), 1934; Asst Naval Attaché, Europe, 1935-37; Capt. (E), 1944; Rear-Adm. (E), 1951; retired list 1954. War of 1939-45 (despatches twice, OBE). With British Council, 1954-59. *Address:* Hill Farm Cottage, 18 Highlands Road, Fareham, Hants. *T:* Fareham 3286.

**COBB, Timothy Humphry,** MA; Headmaster, Dover College, since 1958; *b* 4 July 1909; *s* of Humphry Henry Cobb and Edith Muriel (*née* Stogdon); *m* 1952, Cecilia Mary Josephine, *d* of W. G. Chapman; two *s* one *d*. *Educ:* Harrow; Magdalene Coll., Cambridge. Asst Master, Middlesex Sch., Concord, Mass, USA, 1931-32; Bryanston Sch., Blandford, Dorset, 1932-47, Housemaster, Head of Classics, Estate Bursar; Headmaster of King's Coll., Budo, Kampala, Uganda, 1947-58; formerly Sec., Uganda Headmasters' Association. *Publication:* Certificate English Language Practice, 1958. *Recreations:* music, golf, railway photography, producing plays. *Address:* The School House, Dover College, Dover, Kent. *T:* Dover 293. *Clubs:* MCC, Royal Commonwealth Society, Public Schools.

**COBBAN, James Macdonald,** TD; MA; DL; JP; Headmaster of Abingdon School, 1947-70; *b* 14 Sept. 1910; *s* of late A. M. Cobban, MIStructE, Scunthorpe, Lincs; *m* 1942, Lorna Mary (*d* 1961), *er d* of late G. S. W. Marlow, BSc, FRIC, barrister-at-law, Sydenham; four *d* (one *s* decd). *Educ:* Pocklington Sch.; Jesus Coll., Cambridge (Scholar); Univ. of Vienna. Classical Tripos, Part I, 1931, Part II, 1932; Sandys Student, 1932: Thirlwall Medallist and Gladstone Prizeman, 1935; MA, Cambridge; MA, Oxford (Pembroke Coll.). Asst Master, King Edward VI Sch., Southampton, 1933-36; Class. Sixth Form Master, Dulwich Coll., 1936-40, 1946-47. Intelligence Corps (TA), 1941; GSO3, Directorate of Mil. Intelligence, 1941; Intermediate War Course, Staff Coll., 1943; DAQMG, Combined Ops HQ, 1943; Staff Officer, CCG, 1944 (Lt-Col 1945). JP Berks, 1950; DL Berks, 1966. *Publications:* Senate and Provinces, 78-49 BC, 1935; (in collaboration) Civis Romanus, 1936; Pax et Imperium, 1938; Church and School, 1963. *Address:* The Old Vicarage, Steventon, Berks. *T:* Steventon 444.

**COBBOLD,** family name of **Baron Cobbold.**

**COBBOLD,** 1st Baron *cr* 1960, of Knebworth; **Cameron Fromanteel Cobbold, KG 1970;** PC 1959; GCVO 1963; Lord Chamberlain of HM Household since 1963; Chancellor of the Royal Victorian Order since 1963; Governor of Bank of England, 1949-61; one of HM Lieutenants for the City of London; Director: British Petroleum; Guardian Royal Exchange Assurance; Hudson's Bay Co.; *b* 14 Sept. 1904; *s* of late Lt-Col Clement Cobbold; *m* 1930, Lady (Margaret) Hermione (Millicent) Bulwer-Lytton, *er d* of 2nd Earl of Lytton, KG, PC, GCSI, GCIE; two *s* one *d*. *Educ:* Eton; King's Coll., Cambridge. Entered Bank of England as Adviser, 1933; Exec. Dir, 1938; Dep. Governor, 1945. Chairman: Stevenage Youth Trust; Hertfordshire Playing Fields Assoc.; Board of Governors, Middlesex Hospital and Medical Sch. Council. High Sheriff of County of London for 1946-47. Hon. Fellow Inst. of Bankers, 1961; Fellow of Eton, 1951-67. Chm. Malaysia Commission of Enquiry, 1962. Hon. LLD, McGill Univ., 1961. Hon. DSc (Econ.), London Univ., 1963. *Heir: s* Hon. David Antony Fromanteel Lytton-Cobbold [*b* 14 July 1937; assumed by deed poll, 1960, the additional surname of Lytton; *m* 1961, Christine Elizabeth, 3rd *d* of Major Sir Dennis Frederic Bankes Stucley, 5th Bt, *qv*; three *s*]. *Address:* Knebworth House, Knebworth, Herts. *T:* Knebworth 2310; St James's Palace, SW1. *T:* 01-930 4010. *Clubs:* Athenæum, White's.

**COBHAM,** 10th Viscount *cr* 1718; **Charles John Lyttelton,** KG 1964; PC 1967; GCMG 1957; TD; Baron Lyttelton, 1756 (renewed 1794); Baron Westcote, 1776; Bt 1618; Lord Lieutenant of Worcestershire since 1963; Lord Steward of HM Household since 1967; *b* 8 Aug. 1909; *s* of 9th Viscount, KCB and Violet Yolande (*d* 1966), *yr d* of Charles Leonard, Gloria, Cape Province; *S* father, 1949; *m* 1942, Elizabeth Alison, *yr d* of J. R. Makeig-Jones, Southerton House, near Ottery St Mary, Devon; four *s* four *d*. *Educ:* Eton; Trinity Coll., Cambridge. BA (Hons) Law Cambridge, 1932. Joined 100th (Worcs Yeo.) Fd Bde RA, TA, 1933; Capt. Worcs County Cricket Team, 1936-39; Vice-Capt., MCC New Zealand Tour, 1935-36. Served War of 1939-45, 53rd (Worcs

Yeo.) Anti-Tank Regt RA, France, 1940; seconded to 3rd Maritime Regt, RA, 1941; commanded 5th Regt Maritime RA, 1943-45. Parly Candidate (C) for Dudley and Stourbridge, 1948, but relinquished appointment upon death of his father, 1949. Governor-Gen. and C-in-C of New Zealand, 1957-62. President, MCC, 1954, Treasurer, 1963-64. Director: Lloyds Bank (and Chm., Birmingham Cttee); National Bank of New Zealand; Eagle Star Insurance Co. DL, Co. of Worcester, 1952-57 and 1963, when became Lord Lieut. Hon. Col The Queen's Own Warwicks and Worcs Yeomanry, TA, 1963-69. Pres., Nat. Inst. for the Blind, 1964-; Chm., Outward Bound Trust. *Recreations:* shooting, cricket, golf. *Heir:* *s* Hon. John William Leonard Lyttelton, *b* 5 June 1943. *Address:* Hagley Hall, Stourbridge, Worcs. *T:* Hagley 2408. *Club:* MCC.

*See also Sir J. C. Buchanan-Riddell, Baron Forester.*

**COBHAM, Barony of;** (abeyant).

**COBHAM, Sir Alan (John),** KBE 1926; AFC 1926; pioneer aviator; *b* 6 May 1894; *s* of Frederick Cobham and Elizabeth Burrows; *m* 1922, Gladys Lloyd (*d* 1961); two *s*. *Educ:* Wilson Grammar Sch. Pupilled, farming, 1912; commercial career, City, 1913; served European War, Aug. 1914 to Jan. 1919; served three years in France; commissioned 1917, RFC, later RAF; on demobilisation entered Civil Aviation; carried 5,000 passengers in 1919; joined the Aircraft Manufacturing Co. for aerial photography work, 1920; joined De Havilland Aircraft Co., 1921; did much aerial photography; Aug., flew 5,000 miles round Europe; Nov. 1921 started Spanish Air Line to Morocco; 1922, another 8,000 mile tour round Europe and North Africa; June 1922, flew Belgrade-London in day; 1923, flew 12,000 miles Europe, N Africa, Egypt, Palestine; awarded Britannia Trophy, first Britisher to cross Channel in light aeroplane; flew London-Brussels with 6-hp engine; 1924, won King's Cup Race; flew London-Rangoon and back; awarded Britannia Trophy for 1925; 1925, flew London-Cape Town and back (AFC); 1925, Royal Aero Club Gold Medal; Simms Gold Medal by Royal IAE; Aviation Gold Medal from Institute of Transport, 1926; flew from England to Australia and back, 1926; won Britannia Trophy, 1926; Comdr Pilot of flying boat expedition, flying round entire African continent for first time in history; promoter of Through African Air Route scheme, 1927-28; Air Ministry flight of survey with multi-engine seaplane, up Nile to Congo, 1931; organised National Aviation Day Ltd touring the British Isles, 1932 and 1933; organised National Aviation Displays Ltd, 1934, 1935; Pioneer of refuelling in the air; development and experimental work, 1936-46; introduced Cobham system of refuelling in flight into USAF, 1948; introduced Probe and Drogue System of Refuelling in flight to USAF, US Navy and Royal Air Force, 1951. Chm., Bournemouth Symphony Orchestra, 1956-57; Master, Guild of Air Pilots and Air Navigators, 1964-65. Hon. FRAeS, 1927. *Films:* With Cobham to the Cape and Back, With Cobham Round Africa, The Flight Commander, Cobham to Kivu and Back, The King's Cup. Has appeared on television, notably in series called The Flying Years. *Publications:* Skyways; My Flight to the Cape and Back; Australia and Back; Twenty Thousand Miles in a Flying Boat; numerous articles. *Recreations:* yachting, gardening. *Address:* c/o Tortola Shipyard Ltd, Fort Burt, Roadtown, Tortola, British Virgin Islands. *Clubs:* Royal Aero, Royal Air Force.

**COBHAM, Ven. John Oldcastle,** MA; Archdeacon of Durham and Canon Residentiary of Durham Cathedral, 1953-69, now Archdeacon Emeritus; Examining Chaplain to the Bishop of Wakefield, 1959-68; Member of Archbishop of Canterbury's Commission on Roman Catholic Relations, 1964-69; *b* 11 April 1899; *s* of late Ven. John Lawrence Cobham; *m* 1934, Joan (*d* 1967), *d* of late Rev. George Henry Cobham; no *c*. *Educ:* St Lawrence Coll., Ramsgate; Tonbridge Sch.; Corpus Christi Coll., Cambridge; Univ. of Marburg; Westcott House, Cambridge. Served in Royal Field Artillery, 1917-19; Curate at St Thomas', Winchester, 1926-30; Vice-Principal of Westcott House, Cambridge, 1930-34; Principal of The Queen's Coll., Birmingham, 1934-53; Vicar of St Benet's, Cambridge, 1940-45; Recognised Lectr, Dept of Theology, Birmingham Univ., 1946-53; Hon. Canon, Derby Cathedral, 1950-53. Chaplain to the Forces (EC), 1943-45. Select Preacher: Univ. of Cambridge, 1933 and 1940; Univ. of Birmingham, 1938; Univ. of Oxford, 1952-53; Examining Chaplain to the Bishop of Durham, 1953-66. Mem. of Liturgical Commission, 1955-62. George Craig Stewart Memorial Lecturer, Seabury-Western Theological Seminary, Evanston, Ill., 1963. *Publications:* Concerning Spiritual Gifts, 1933; co-translator of K. Barth in Revelation, a Symposium, 1937; contributor to: The Parish Communion, 1937; No Other Gospel, 1943; The Significance of the Barmen Declaration for the Oecumenical Church, 1943; DNB 1931-40 (E. C. Hoskyns), 1949; Theological Word Book of the Bible, 1950. *Recreations:* climbing, sketching. *Address:* Sands House, 5 Church Close, Aldeburgh, Suffolk IP15 5DY. *T:* Aldeburgh 2803. *Club:* Alpine.

**COBURN, Prof. Kathleen;** Professor of English, Victoria College, University of Toronto, since 1953; author; *b* 1905; *d* of Rev. John Coburn and Susannah Coburn. *Educ:* University of Toronto (MA); Oxford University (BLitt). Imperial Order of the Daughters of the Empire (IODE) Travelling Scholarship, 1930-31. Formerly Lecturer, Asst Prof., and Assoc. Prof. of English, Victoria College, University of Toronto. University Women's Internat. Senior Fellowship, 1948-49; John Simon Guggenheim Memorial Fellowship, 1953-54, renewed, 1957-58; Commonwealth Visiting Fellowship (Univ. of London), 1962-63. LLD, Queen's Univ., Kingston, Ont., 1964. FRSL 1954; FRSC 1958. Rose Mary Crawshay Prize for English Literature (Brit. Acad.), 1959. Hon. Fellow, St Hugh's Coll., Oxford, 1970. *Publications:* The Philosophical Lectures of S. T. Coleridge, 1949; Inquiring Spirit, 1951; The Letters of Sara Hutchinson, 1954; The Notebooks of S. T. Coleridge, vol. i, 1957, vol. ii, 1961, vol. iii, 1969; Coleridge: A Collection of Critical Essays, 1967; general editor, The Collected Coleridge, 1961-69. *Address:* Victoria College, Toronto, Canada.

**COCHRAN, William;** PhD, MA; FRS 1962; Professor of Physics, University of Edinburgh, since 1964; *b* 30 July 1922; *s* of James Cochran and Margaret Watson Cochran (*née* Baird); *m* 1953, Ingegerd Wall; one *s* two *d*. *Educ:* Boroughmuir Sch., Edinburgh; Edinburgh Univ. Asst Lectr, Edinburgh Univ., 1943-46; Demonstrator and Lectr, Univ. of Cambridge, 1948-62; Reader in Physics, Univ. of Cambridge, 1962-64. Fellow of Trinity Hall, Cambridge, 1951-64. Research fellowships abroad, 1950-51 and 1958-59. Guthrie medallist, Inst. Physics and Phys. Soc., 1966. *Publications:* Vol. III of The Crystalline State (with Prof. H. Lipson), 1954, new edn 1966; various publications on physics and chemistry of crystals. *Recreations:*

walking; family history. *Address:* Department of Natural Philosophy, The University, Drummond Street, Edinburgh; 71 Clermiston Road, Edinburgh.

**COCHRANE,** family name of **Earl of Dundonald** and **Baron Cochrane of Cults.**

**COCHRANE OF CULTS,** 3rd Baron *cr* 1919; **Thomas Charles Anthony Cochrane;** *b* 31 Oct. 1922; *s* of 2nd Baron Cochrane of Cults, DSO, and Hon. Elin Douglas-Pennant (*d* 1934), *y d* of 2nd Baron Penrhyn; *S* father, 1968. *Educ:* privately. *Heir: b* Hon. (Ralph Henry) Vere Cochrane [*b* 20 Sept. 1926; *m* 1956, Janet Mary Watson, *d* of late Dr W. H. W. Cheyne; two *s*]. *Address:* Balgownie, 18 Cliff Terrace, Buckie, Banffshire.

**COCHRANE, Lord; Iain Alexander Douglas Blair Cochrane;** *b* 17 Feb. 1961; *s* and *heir* of 14th Earl of Dundonald, *qv*.

**COCHRANE, Sir Desmond Oriel Alastair George Weston,** 3rd Bt *cr* 1903; Consul-General of Ireland to the Republics of Syria and The Lebanon since 1949; *b* 22 Oct. 1918; 2nd *s* of Sir Ernest Cochrane, 2nd Bt, and Elsa, *y d* of Erwin Schumacher; *S* father, 1952; *m* 1946, Yvonne, *o c* of late Alfred Bey Sursock and of Donna Maria Sursock; three *s* one *d*. *Educ:* Eton. Served War of 1939-45; Staff Captain: Northern Command, 1941; War Office, AG 12, 1942; GHQ Middle East Forces (Mil. Sec. Branch), 1943; Military Sec. to GOC 9th Army, 1944. *Heir: s* Henry Mark Sursock Cochrane, *b* 23 Oct. 1946. *Address:* Maison Sursock, Beyrouth, Lebanon. *Club:* Carlton.

**COCHRANE, Rear-Adm. Sir Edward Owen,** KBE 1943; *b* 17 Aug. 1881; *s* of Vice-Adm. Basil E. Cochrane and Cornelia Ramsay Robinson Owen; *m* 1908, Mary Lucy George (*d* 1955); (*s* Major RA, killed in Tunisia) one *d*. *Educ:* HMS Britannia. Midshipman, 1897; qualified as a Gunnery Lieut, 1905; Comdr, 1915; Capt., 1920; served at Admiralty as Asst Dir Gunnery Div. and Asst then Deputy Dir Naval Intelligence Div., 1921-24; Capt. of HMS Cairo, East Indies Station, 1924-26; of Devonport Gunnery Sch., 1927-29; Dir of Training and Staff Duties, 1929-31; Capt., HMS Repulse, 1931-32; Rear-Adm., 1933; retired list, 1933; employed as a Convoy Commodore with the rank of Commodore RNR, 1939-45. *Recreations:* interest: has been connected with work of Moral Re-Armament for many years. *Address:* 5 St George's Square, SW1. *T:* 01-828 5460. *Club:* United Service.

**COCHRANE, Maj.-Gen. James Rupert,** CB 1951; CBE 1947; retired; *b* 28 Nov. 1904; *s* of Brig.-Gen. J. K. Cochrane, CMG; *m* 1937, Hilary, *d* of H. W. Standen, Westways, Sevenoaks; one *s* one *d*. *Educ:* Charterhouse; RMA Woolwich. Commissioned Royal Artillery, 1925; Staff Coll., Camberley, 1939; Imperial Defence Coll., 1948. Served War of 1939-45 (despatches): in NW Europe, Italy and Middle East, on Staff and Commanding 191 (Herts and Essex) Yeomanry Fd Regt. Chief of Staff, HQ British troops in Palestine and Transjordan, 1945-47 (despatches). Commanded HAA Regt, 1947; Chief of Staff, HQ East Africa Command, 1949-52; Comd 51 (U) AA Brigade, 1952-53; Deputy Chief of Staff HQ Allied Land Forces, Central Europe, 1953-56; Principal Staff Officer to Deputy Supreme Allied Commander (Viscount Montgomery), Allied Powers in Europe, 1956-58; retired, 1959. *Recreations:* shooting and fishing. *Address:* Plestor House, Selborne, Alton, Hants. *Club:* United Service.

**COCHRANE, Hon. Lady, (Julia Dorothy),** CBE 1952; Chief Commissioner for England, Girl Guides Association, 1941-51, President, 1951-61; *e d* of 1st Baron Cornwallis, CBE, TD, DL, JP (*d* 1935); *m* 1926, Capt. the Hon. Sir Archibald Douglas Cochrane, GCMG, KCSI, DSO (*d* 1958); one *s* one *d*. Commander Sister of the Order of St John of Jerusalem. Red Cross Long Service Medal and clasp. *Address:* 17 Morpeth Mansions, Morpeth Terrace, SW1. *T:* 01-834 5700. *Club:* Guide.

**COCHRANE, Air Chief Marshal Hon. Sir Ralph (Alexander),** GBE 1950 (KBE 1945); KCB 1948; AFC 1919; *b* 24 Feb. 1895; *y s* of 1st Baron Cochrane of Cults; *m* 1930, Hilda Frances Holme Wiggin; two *s* one *d*. *Educ:* Osborne and Dartmouth. Entered Navy, 1912; transferred to newly created Airship branch 1915 and to RAF 1919; served in Egypt and Iraq, 1920-23, and at Aden, 1928-29; on the directing staff RAF Staff Coll., Andover, 1930-31, and at Air Ministry, 1932-33; Imperial Defence Coll., 1934. Seconded to New Zealand Govt to advise on air defence and became first Chief of the Air Staff of the Royal New Zealand Air Force, 1936-39. ADC to the King, 1939-40. Held various appointments covering intelligence and training, 1939-42; commanded Nos. 3 and 5 Bomber Groups, 1942-45; AOC-in-C Transport Command, 1945-47; AOC-in-C Flying Training Command, 1947-50; Vice-CAS, Air Ministry, 1950-52; retd Nov. 1952. Air ADC to the King, 1949; ADC to the Queen, 1952. RUSI Gold Medal Essay, 1935; Royal Aeronautical Soc. Edward Busk Memorial Prize, 1948. Joint Man. Dir Atlantic Shipbuilding Co., 1953-56; Rolls Royce Ltd, 1956-61; Chm. RJM Exports Ltd, 1962. *Address:* Grove Farmhouse, Shipton-under-Wychwood, Oxford OX7 6DG. *Clubs:* Brooks's, Royal Air Force.

**COCHRANE, Dr Robert Greenhill,** CMG 1969; Regional Leprosy Officer, Shinyanga Region, Tanzania, since 1969; Medical Superintendent, Kola Ndoto Leprosarium, Tanzania, since 1969; *b* 11 Aug. 1899; *s* of Dr Thomas Cochrane and Grace Hamilton Cochrane (*née* Greenhill); *m* 1st, 1927, Ivy Gladys Nunn (*d* 1966); two *s* one *d*; 2nd, 1968, Dr Martha Jeane Shaw. *Educ:* Sch. for Sons of Missionaries, Blackheath (now Eltham Coll.); Univ. of Glasgow; St Bartholomew's Hosp., London; London Sch. of Tropical Medicine. Dir, Leprosy Campaign and Dir of Leprosy Research, Madras State, India, 1941-51; Dir and Prin. Prof. of Medicine and Dermatology, and Dir, Rural Medicine, Christian Med. Coll., Vellore, S India, 1944-48; Adviser in Leprosy to Min. of Health, London, 1951-65; Vis. Med. Officer, Homes of St Giles, E Hanningfield, Essex, 1951-66; Tech. Med. Adviser, Amer. Leprosy Mission, Inc., 1953-64; Dir, Leprosy Study Centre, London, 1953-65; Med. Supt, Leprosy Hosp., Vadathorasalur, S Arcot, Madras, 1966-68. Pres., Internat. Leprosy Assoc., 1963-68, since when Pres. Emeritus. Kaisar-i-Hind gold medal (India), 1935. *Publications:* A Practical Textbook of Leprosy, 1947; Leprosy in Theory and Practice, 1959 (2nd edn 1964); Biblical Leprosy, A Suggested Interpretation, 1961; contribs to: Internat. Jl of Leprosy; Leprosy Review. *Address:* Kola Ndoto Hospital, PO Box 46, Shinyanga, Tanzania, East Africa; 606 Swede Street, Norristown, Pa 19401, USA. *Club:* Royal Commonwealth Society (London).

**COCK, Gerald,** MVO 1935; *b* 1887; *yr s* of late Alfred Cock, QC, Elm Court, Temple; unmarried. *Educ:* Tonbridge Sch.; Seafield Park. Travelled USA, British Columbia, Mexico, etc, 1909-15; returned to England, 1915; commissioned Royal Engineers, BEF,

France and Belgium, 1915-20 (Captain 1917); business in London, 1920-24; joined BBC, 1925 as first Dir of Outside Broadcasts; first Dir of Television, 1935; organised and directed the first television service to be established in Europe or America; North American representative of BBC, 1940-41; Pacific Coast representative of BBC, 1942-45; retired, 1946. *Publications:* articles on broadcasting and television. *Recreations:* travel, walking, riding. *Club:* Reform.

**COCKAYNE, Dame Elizabeth,** DBE 1955; Chief Nursing Officer, Ministry of Health, 1948-58, retired; *d* of William and Alice Cockayne, Burton-on-Trent. *Educ:* Secondary Sch., Burton-on-Trent, and privately. Gen. Hospital Training, Royal Infirmary, Sheffield; Fever Training, Mount Gold Hospital, Plymouth; Midwifery Training, Maternity Hospital, Birmingham. Former experience includes: Supervisor of Training Sch., LCC; Matron of West London Hosp., St Charles' Hosp., Royal Free Hosp. *Recreation:* gardening. *Address:* Rushett Cottage, Little Heath Lane, Cobham, Surrey.

**COCKBURN, Claud;** journalist; *b* 12 April 1904; *s* of Henry Cockburn, CB, and Elizabeth Stevenson; *m* 1940, Patricia Arbuthnot; three *s*. *Educ:* Berkhamsted Sch.; Keble Coll., Oxford; Universities of Budapest and Berlin. Travelling Fellow of The Queen's College, Oxford; Correspondent of The Times in New York and Washington, 1929-32; Editor, The Week, 1933-46; Diplomatic and Foreign Correspondent, the Daily Worker, 1935-46; since 1953 has written principally for Punch, New Statesman, Saturday Evening Post, and numerous other periodicals. *Publications:* High Low Washington, 1933; Reporter in Spain, 1936; Beat the Devil, 1952; Overdraft on Glory, 1955; (autobiog.) In Time of Trouble, 1956; Nine Bald Men, 1956; Aspects of History, 1957; (autobiog.) Crossing the Line, 1958; (autobiog.) View from the West, 1961; (autobiog.) I, Claud, 1967; Ballantyne's Folly, 1970. *Recreation:* travel. *Address:* Brook Lodge, Youghal, County Cork, Ireland.

**COCKBURN, Very Rev. James Hutchison,** DD; Minister of Dunblane Cathedral (Church of Scotland), 1918-45; Director, Department of Reconstruction and Inter-Church Aid, World Council of Churches, Geneva, 1945-48; Chaplain to King George VI, 1944-52, and to the Queen, 1952; now an Extra Chaplain to the Queen; *b* Paisley, 29 Oct. 1882; *s* of late George Hannah Cockburn, FEIS, schoolmaster, and late Isabella Brodie Marshall; *m* 1912, Amy Macloy; one *s* one *d*. *Educ:* Paisley Grammar Sch.; Glasgow Univ. (MA, BD, DD). Ministries: Mearns, 1908-14; Battlefield (Glasgow), 1914-18; War Service in France with YMCA and as Chaplain in Egypt and in East Africa; Offices held in Church of Scotland: Clerk, Union Cttee, 1927-29; Convener, Church and Nation Cttee, 1929-35; Clerk, Cttee on Restatement of Church's Faith, 1930-35; Convener of Business Cttee of the Gen. Assembly, 1936; Moderator of Gen. Assembly, 1941; Chm., Eastern Section of Presbyterian Alliance, 1939-44; Lecturer on Pastoral Theology, St Mary's Coll., St Andrews, 1931-34; Convener, Cttee on Inter-Church Relations, 1941-44; founded Society of Friends of Dunblane Cathedral, 1929; visited Canada and United States, 1942, during Moderatorship, speaking on spiritual issues of the war, and frequently since; Vice-Chm., British Council of Churches, 1942-44; William Belden Noble Lecturer, Harvard, 1942; Warrack Lecturer, Edinburgh, 1944-45; Hon. Prof., Buda-Pest Univ., 1946; DTh Prague, 1948; DD Yale, 1948, and Occidental, USA, 1950; LHD Wooster Coll., Ohio, 1953; Otts Lecturer, Davidson Coll., North Carolina, 1951; Mem. Royal Commission on Scottish Affairs, 1952-54. Order of White Lion (Czechoslovakia), 1948. *Publications:* Religious Freedom in Eastern Europe, 1951 (USA); The Celtic Church in Dunblane, 1954; The Medieval Bishops of Dunblane and their Church, 1959. *Recreation:* fishing. *Address:* The Cathedral, Dunblane, Perthshire.

**COCKBURN, Sir John (Elliot),** 12th Bt of that Ilk, *cr* 1671; Managing Director, Cellar Management Ltd; *b* 7 Dec. 1925; *s* of Lieut-Col Sir John Cockburn, 11th Bt of that Ilk, DSO and of Isabel Hunter, *y d* of late James McQueen, Crofts, Kirkcudbrightshire; *S* father, 1949; *m* 1949, Glory Patricia, *er d* of N. Mullings; three *s* two *d*. *Educ:* RNC Dartmouth; Royal Agricultural Coll., Cirencester. Served War of 1939-45, joined RAF, July 1944. *Recreation:* reading. *Heir: s* Charles Christopher Cockburn, *b* 19 Nov. 1950. *Address:* 48 Frewin Road, SW18. *Club:* Naval and Military.

**COCKBURN, Sir Robert,** KBE 1960 (OBE 1946); CB 1953; PhD, MSc; Fellow Commoner, Churchill College, Cambridge; Chairman, National Computing Centre, since 1970; *b* 31 March 1909; 2nd *s* of late Rev. R. T. Cockburn, Columba Manse, Belford, Northumberland; *m* 1935, Phyllis Hoyland; two *d*. *Educ:* Southern Secondary Sch. and Municipal Coll., Portsmouth; London Univ. BSc 1928, MSc 1935, PhD 1939, London. Taught Science at West Ham Municipal Coll., 1930-37; research in communications at RAE Farnborough, 1937-39; in radar at TRE Malvern, Worcs, 1939-45; in atomic energy at AERE Harwell, 1945-48; Scientific Adviser to Air Min., 1948-53; Princ. Dir of Scientific Research (Guided Weapons and Electronics), Ministry of Supply, 1954-55; Deputy Controller of Electronics, Ministry of Supply, 1955-56; Controller of Guided Weapons and Electronics, Ministry of Supply, 1956-59; Chief Scientist of Ministry of Aviation, 1959-64; Dir, RAE, Farnborough, 1964-69. Vice-Chm. of Space Cttee, Min. of Defence, 1964-65. Congressional Medal for Merit, 1947. *Publications:* scientific papers. *Recreation:* sailing. *Address:* 21 Fitzroy Road, Fleet, Hants. *T:* Fleet 5518. *Club:* Athenæum.

**COCKBURN-CAMPBELL, Sir Thomas;** *see* Campbell.

**COCKELL, Seton F.;** *see* Forbes-Cockell.

**COCKER, Prof. Ralph,** CBE 1968; MB, ChB, LDS (Victoria University Manchester), LRCP, MRCS, FDSRCS; Professor of Dental Surgery in the University of London, Director of Dental Studies, and Sub-Dean, King's College Hospital Medical School, University of London, since 1947; Consultant Dental Surgeon and Director of Dental Department, King's College Hospital, since 1947; *b* 18 April 1908; *er s* of Frank Barlow Cocker and Mary Wildman; *m* 1942, Margaret (*née* Jacques); one *s* two *d*. *Educ:* William Hulme's Grammar Sch., Manchester; Manchester Univ. Preston Prize and Medallist, Manchester Univ., 1930. private Practice, 1930-36; Asst Hon. Dental Surg., Manchester Dent. Hosp., 1933-36; Lectr in Clin. Dental Surg., Manchester Univ., 1936-45; Industrial Health Service (ICI Ltd), 1940-45; Lectr in Periodontia, Manchester Univ., 1945-47; Actg Cons. Dental Surg., Manchester Royal Infirmary, 1945-47; Past and present Examr in Dental Surgery, Univs of Manchester, London, Birmingham, Bristol, Sheffield, St Andrews; Chm. Bd of Examrs for Statutory Exam. (GDC), 1964-; Member: Bd of Faculty, RCS, 1955 (Vice-Dean, 1964-65) and Examr to Coll. for Dipl. and Final Fellowship in Dental Surgery; Standing Dental Adv. Cttee of Min. of Health, 1963- (Vice-Chm. 1965-); Dental Manpower Cttee (Min. of Health), 1960-; GDC, 1963-; Royal Soc. of Health, 1960-; Dental Educn Adv. Coun. of Gt Brit., 1947- (Chm., 1956-57; Treas., 1957-; Sec., 1967-); Dental Industry Standards Cttee (BSI); Founder Mem., King's Coll. Hosp. Med. Sch. Council and King's Coll. Hosp. Bd of Govs, 1948-; Mem. Bd of Dental Studies, London Univ., 1948- (Chm., 1967-); Adviser in Dental Surgery to Min. of Health, 1968; Temp. Adviser, WHO, 1970. *Recreations:* mountaineering, ski-ing, photography. *Address:* 10 Oaks Avenue, Gipsy Hill, SE19. *T:* 01-670 4068. *Club:* Alpine.

**COCKER, Sir William Wiggins,** Kt 1955; OBE 1946; JP; MA; LLD; Director of Cocker Chemical Co. Ltd; a Lloyd's Underwriter; *b* 17 Oct. 1896; *s* of Wiggins Cocker, Accrington; *m* 1922, Mary Emma Bowker, Accrington (*d* 1965); one *s* one *d*; *m* 1970, Mrs Rhoda Slinger, Accrington. Freedom of Borough of Accrington, 1958. *Address:* 384 Clifton Drive North, St Annes-on-Sea, Lancs.

**COCKERAM, Eric (Paul);** MP (C) Bebington since 1970; JP; Chairman, Watson Prickard Ltd; *b* 4 July 1924; *er s* of J. W. Cockeram; *m* 1949, Frances Irving, Birkenhead; two *s* two *d*. *Educ:* The Leys Sch., Cambridge. Served War, 1942-45: Captain The Gloucestershire Regt; "D Day" landings (wounded and discharged). Chm., Liverpool Stores Cttee, 1960-68; Pres., Menswear Assoc. of Britain, 1964-65. Mem., Bd of Governors, United Liverpool Hosps, 1965-; Chm., Liverpool NHS Exec. Council, 1970. Mem., Worshipful Co. of Glovers. Freeman: City of London; City of Springfield, Ill. JP, City of Liverpool, 1960. *Recreations:* golf, shooting, country walking. *Address:* House of Commons, Westminster, SW1; Woodstock, Burrell Road, Birkenhead, Cheshire L42 8NH. *T:* 051-608 3777. *Clubs:* Royal Automobile; Lyceum (Liverpool).

**COCKERELL, Sir Christopher (Sydney),** Kt 1969; CBE 1966; MA; FRS 1967; Consultant of Hovercraft Development Ltd, 1958-70 (Director, 1959-66); Chairman, Ripplecraft Co. Ltd, since 1950; *b* 4 June 1910; *s* of late Sir Sydney Cockerell; *m* 1937, Margaret Elinor Belsham; two *d*. *Educ:* Gresham's; Peterhouse, Cambridge. Pupil, W. H. Allen & Sons, Bedford, 1931-33; Radio Research, Cambridge, 1933-35; airborne and navigational equipment research and development, Marconi Wireless Telegraph Co. Ltd, 1935-50; inventor of and engaged on hovercraft since 1953; Consultant (hovercraft), Ministry of Supply, 1957-58. Pres., Internat. Air Cushion Engrg Soc.; Member, Min. of Technology's Adv. Cttee for Hovercraft, 1968-. A Trustee of National Portrait Gallery, 1967-. FRSA 1960; Fellow, Swedish Soc. of Aeronautics, 1963; Hon. Fellow: Soc. of Engineers, 1966; Manchester Inst. of Sci. and Tech., 1967; Downing Coll., Cambridge, 1969. Hon. Mem., Southampton Chamber of Commerce, 1967. Hon. DSc, Leicester, 1967; Hon. Dr RCA, 1968. Viva Shield, Worshipful Co. of Carmen, 1961; RAC Diamond Jubilee Trophy, 1962. Thulin Medal, Swedish Soc. of Aeronautics, 1963; Howard N. Potts Medal, Franklin Inst., 1965; Albert Medal, RSA, 1966; Churchill Medal, Soc. of Engineers, 1966; Royal Medal, Royal Soc., 1966; Mitchell Memorial Medal, Stoke-on-Trent Assoc. of Engineers, 1967; Columbus Prize, Genoa, 1968; John Scott Award, City of Philadelphia, 1968; Elmer A. Sperry Award, 1968; Gold Medal, Calais Chamber of Commerce, 1969; Bluebird Trophy, 1969. *Recreations:* antiquities, gardening, fishing. *Address:* 13 Ardnave Crescent, Southampton SO1 7FL. *T:* Southampton 69418. *Club:* Athenæum.

**COCKERELL, Sydney (Morris);** bookbinder; Senior Partner of D. Cockerell & Son since 1946; Visiting Lecturer, School of Librarianship, University College, London; *b* 6 June 1906; *er s* of late Douglas Cockerell and Florence Arundel; *m* 1931, Elizabeth Lucy Cowlishaw; one *s* two *d*. *Educ:* St Christopher Sch., Letchworth. Partnership with Douglas Cockerell, 1924. Assisted with repair and binding of Codex Sinaiticus Manuscript at British Museum, 1934; worked as electrical instrument maker, 1939-45. Has repaired and bound early manuscripts, including the Codex Bezae, 1965, and incunabula, designed and made numbers of tooled bindings, including Rolls of Honour for House of Lords, House of Commons, Household Brigade, London Transport, Metropolitan Police, American Air Force and ten vols. of Book of RAF at Church of St Clement Danes. Revived and developed craft of marbling paper. Visited Ceylon (under Commonwealth Plan), 1955, Canada, 1961, Florence and Lisbon, 1967, to advise on binding of flood-damaged books. Hon. Mem. Soc. of Scribes and Illuminators, 1956; Fellow International Institute for Conservation of Historic and Artistic Works, 1959; Master, Art Workers Guild, 1961. Mem., Double Crown Club. *Publications:* Marbling Paper, 1934; Appendix to Bookbinding and the Care of Books, 1943; The Repairing of Books, 1958; contributor to: Oxford Junior Encyclopædia, 1949; The Calligrapher's Handbook, 1956; Encyclopædia Britannica, 1963. *Address:* Riversdale, Grantchester, Cambridge. *T:* Trumpington 2124.

**COCKERTON, Rev. John Clifford Penn;** Principal, St John's College and Cranmer Hall, Durham, since 1970; *b* 27 June 1927; *s* of late William Penn Cockerton and Eleanor Cockerton. *Educ:* Wirral Grammar Sch.; Univ. of Liverpool; St Catherine's Society, Oxford; Wycliffe Hall, Oxford. Asst Master, Prenton Secondary Sch., 1949-51; Deacon 1954; Priest 1955; Asst Curate, St Helens Parish Church, 1954-58; Tutor 1958-60, Chaplain 1960-63, Cranmer Hall, Durham; Vice-Principal, St John's Coll., Durham, 1963-70. *Recreation:* music. *Address:* St John's College, Durham. *T:* Durham 2306. *Club:* Royal Commonwealth Society.

**COCKETT, Frank Bernard,** MS, FRCS; Consultant Surgeon to St Thomas' Hospital since 1954; Hon. Surgeon, Florence Nightingale Hospital, London, since 1960; *b* Rockhampton, Australia, 22 April 1916; *s* of late Rev. Charles Bernard Cockett, MA, DD; *m* 1945, Felicity Ann (*d* 1958), *d* of Col James Thackeray Fisher, DSO, Frieston, near Grantham, Lincs; one *s* two *d*; *m* 1960, Dorothea Anne Newman; twin *s*. *Educ:* Bedford Sch.; St Thomas's Hosp. Med. Sch. BSc (1st Cl. Hons), 1936; MRCS, LRCP 1939; MB, BS (London) 1940; FRCS (English) 1947; MS (London) 1953. Sqdn Ldr (Surgical Specialist) RAFVR, 1942-46; Surgical Registrar, St Thomas's Hosp., 1947-48; Resident Asst Surg., St Thomas's Hosp., 1948-50; Senior Lecturer in Surgery, St Thomas's Hosp. Med. Sch., 1950-54. Fellow Assoc. of Surgs of Gt Brit.; Mem. European Soc. of Cardiovascular Surgery. *Publications:* The Pathology and Surgery of the Veins of the Lower Limb, 1956; several contribs to Operative Surgery (ed. C. G. Rob and Rodney Smith), 1956; various papers in medical and surgical journals. *Recreations:* sailing, tennis, squash, gardening, collecting marine paintings. *Address:* 61 Harley Street, W1. *T:* 01-580 3612; 14 Essex Villas, Campden Hill, Kensington, W8. *T:* 01-937 9883. *Clubs:* Lansdowne, Little Ship; Island Sailing.

**COCKEY, Air Commodore Leonard Herbert,** CB 1945; Royal Air Force (retired); *b* 1893; *s* of late Rev. H. A. Cockey, Oldland Vicarage, Glos; *m* 1942, Eileen Anne, *d* of James A. Hogan, Tipperary; one *s* two *d*. *Educ:* Bristol Univ. Served European War, 1914-18 (French Croix de Guerre avec Palme, 1916). Qualified RAF Staff Coll. and idc. Served War of 1939-45 in Bomber Command and Southern Rhodesia; retired, 1945. *Address:* Sprayside, Banks Road, Sandbanks, Dorset. *Club:* Royal Air Force.

**COCKFIELD, Francis Arthur;** Managing Director and Chairman Executive Management Committee, Boots Pure Drug Co. Ltd, 1961-67, retired; *b* 28 Sept. 1916; 2nd *s* of late Lieut C. F. Cockfield and Louisa (*née* James). *Educ:* Dover County; London Sch. of Economics (LLB, BSc (Econ.)). Called to Bar, Inner Temple, 1942. Home Civil Service, Inland Revenue, 1938; Asst Sec. to Board of Inland Revenue, 1945; Commissioner of Inland Revenue, 1951-52; Dir of Statistics and Intelligence to Board of Inland Revenue, 1945-52; Finance Dir, Boots Pure Drug Co. Ltd, 1953-61; Mem., National Economic Development Council, 1962-64; Mem., Court of Governors, Univ. of Nottingham, 1963-67. Pres., Royal Statistical Soc., 1968-69. *Address:* Connaught House, Mount Row, Berkeley Square, W1. *Club:* Reform.

**COCKIN, Rt. Rev. George Eyles Irwin;** Rector of Bainton and Director of Post Ordination Training, Diocese of York, since 1969; Assistant Bishop of York, since 1969; *b* 15 Aug. 1908; *s* of late Charles Irwin Cockin, Solicitor, and of Judith Cockin. *Educ:* Repton; Leeds University (BA); Lincoln Theological College. Tutor, St Paul's College, Awka, Nigeria, 1933-40; Supervisor, Anglican Schools, E Nigeria, 1940-52. Deacon, 1953, Priest, 1954; Curate, Kimberworth, Rotherham, 1953-55; Sen. Supervisor, Anglican Schools, E Nigeria, 1955-58; Canon, All Saints Cathedral, Onitsha, 1957; first Bishop of Owerri, 1959-69. *Address:* The Rectory, Bainton, Driffield, Yorks. *T:* Middleton-on-the-Wolds 377.

**COCKING, Prof. John Martin,** MA; Professor of French Language and Literature, University of London, King's College, since 1952; Fellow of King's College since 1965; *b* 9 Nov. 1914; *s* of Matthew Maddern Bottrell Cocking and Annie Cocking; *m* 1941, May Parsons Wallis; one *s*. *Educ:* Penzance County Sch. for Boys; King's Coll., London; Sorbonne; British Institute in Paris. BA (Hons) French, 1935; Teacher's Diploma (London), 1936; Diplôme d'Etudes Universitaires (Sorbonne), 1937; MA (London), 1939. Lecturer in English Literature, British Institute in Paris, 1937-38, Lecturer in English and Asst to the Dir, 1938-39; Asst Lecturer in French, King's Coll., London, 1939-46 (including 5 years' absence on war service in the Army); Lecturer in French, King's Coll., London, 1946-52. *Publications:* Marcel Proust, 1956; articles in journals and reviews. *Address:* 12 Clorane Gardens, NW3. *T:* 01-435 9116.

**COCKRAM, Ben,** CMG 1948; OBE 1944; Jan Smuts Professor of International Relations, University of the Witwatersrand, 1961-70; *b* 1903; *s* of B. B. Cockram, St Helier's, Jersey, Channel Islands; *m* 1928, Doris Mary Holdrup; one *d*. *Educ:* Victoria Coll.; Taunton's Sch.; Queen's Coll., Oxford. BA (London); MA (Oxon); PhD (Michigan, USA). Asst Principal, Dominions Office, 1926; Private Sec. to Parly and Permanent Under-Secs of State, 1929-34; Principal, 1934-39; Political Sec. to UK High Comr in Union of S Africa, 1939-44; Counsellor, British Embassy, Washington, DC, 1944-49; Asst Sec., CRO, 1949-51; Dep. High Comr for the UK in Australia, 1952-54, and Acting High Comr, May-Oct. 1952; Dir of Information, CRO, 1954-57, Dir of Information Services, 1957-62. Adviser to UK delegs to Assembly and Council of League of Nations, 1935, 1936, 1937 and 1938, to Brussels Conference, on Far East, 1936, to San Francisco Conference, 1945, to Councils of UNRRA and FAO, to Peace Conference, Paris, 1946, the Assembly, Security, Economic and Social, and Trusteeship Councils of UN, 1946, 1947 and 1948; to Unesco Conferences, Paris, 1958 and 1960. Mem. of Far Eastern Commission on Japan, 1946-48; Mem. UK Delegation to Commonwealth Educational Conferences: at Oxford, 1959; at Delhi, 1962; Leader, UK Delegations to Unesco Confs on SE Asia, at Bangkok, 1960; on Latin America, at Santiago, Chile, 1961; on Africa, at Paris, 1962. South African Rep. at Nuclear Proliferation Conf., Toronto, 1966. *Publications:* Seen from South Africa, 1963; Problems of Southern Africa, 1964; The Conduct of British Foreign Policy, 1964; Rhodesia and UDI, 1966; The Population Problem and International Relations, 1970. *Recreation:* swimming. *Address:* Jan Smuts Memorial Building, University of the Witwatersrand, Johannesburg, South Africa.

**COCKRAM, Sir John,** Kt 1964; Director since 1952, General Manager since 1941, The Colne Valley Water Company; *b* 10 July 1908; *s* of Alfred John and Beatrice Elizabeth Cockram; *m* 1937, Phyllis Eleanor, *d* of Albert Henning; one *s* two *d*. *Educ:* St Aloysius Coll., Highgate. Chartered Accountant. Member: Herts CC, 1949- (Chm. 1961-65); Thames Conservancy, 1954-; Exec. Cttee, British Waterworks Assoc., 1948- (Pres., 1957-58); Chm., Water Companies Assoc., 1950-; Mem., Central Advisory Water Cttee, 1955-. Life Governor, Haileybury. *Recreations:* fishing, gardening. *Address:* Rebels' Corner, The Common, Chorleywood, Hertfordshire. *Club:* Bath.

**COCKS,** family name of **Baron Somers.**

**COCKS, Sir Barnett;** *see* Cocks, Sir T. G. B.

**COCKS, Rt. Rev. Francis William;** *see* Shrewsbury, Bishop Suffragan of.

**COCKS, Michael Francis Lovell;** MP (Lab) Bristol South since 1970; *b* 19 Aug. 1929; *s* of Dr H. F. Lovell Cocks; *m* 1954, Janet Macfarlane; two *s* two *d*. *Educ:* Bristol University. Various posts in education from 1954; Lectr, Bristol Polytechnic, 1968. Contested (Lab): Bristol West, 1959; South Gloucestershire, 1964, 1966. *Recreations:* swimming, listening to music, reading. *Address:* 6 Russell Grove, Bristol 6. *T:* 0272-44140.

**COCKS, Sir (Thomas George) Barnett,** KCB 1963 (CB 1961); OBE 1949; Clerk of the House of Commons since 1962. *Address:* House of Commons, SW1.

**CODE HOLLAND, R. H.;** *see* Holland, R. H. C.

**CODRINGTON, Sir Christopher William Gerald Henry,** 2nd Bt *cr* 1876; *b* 6 Oct. 1894; *s* of late Sir Gerald William Henry Codrington, 1st Bt, and Lady Edith Sybil Henrietta Denison (*d* 1945), *d* of 1st Earl of Londesborough; *S* father, 1929; *m* 1st, 1921, Joan (*d* 1961), 2nd *d* of T. Reginald Hague-Cook; one *s*; 2nd, 1963, Henrietta Desirée Moutray Read, *d* of late Major Beresford Moutray Read. *Educ:* Uppingham. Joined 19th Royal Hussars, 1914; served with 19th Hussars in France, 1914-18 (wounded); High Sheriff for Co. of Glos, 1938. *Recreations:* cricket, shooting, hunting. *Heir: s* Simon Francis Bethel Codrington [*b* 1923; *m* 1959, Pamela Joy Halliday, *d* of Major G. W. B. Wise, MBE; three *s*. Late Coldstream Guards]. *Address:* (seat) Dodington, Chipping Sodbury, Glos. *T:* Chipping Sodbury 2354; Castle Grove, Bampton, Tiverton, Devon. *Club:* Cavalry.

**CODRINGTON, Col Sir Geoffrey Ronald,** KCVO 1953 (CVO 1948); CB 1932; CMG 1951; DSO 1918; OBE 1919; TD; Extra Gentleman Usher to the Queen since 1967 (Gentleman Usher, 1952-66); *b* 13 May 1888; *s* of late Lt-Gen. Sir A. E. Codrington, GCVO, KCB; *m* 1923, Cecilia, *y d* of late Ernest James Wythes, CBE; two *s* two *d*. *Educ:* Harrow; Christ Church, Oxford (MA). Late The Leics Yeomanry. Served European War, 1914-18 (wounded, DSO, OBE, Order of SS Maurice and Lazarus, Italy), War of 1939-45 (American Bronze Star Medal). High Sheriff of Wilts, 1955-56. *Publication:* The Territorial Army, 1937. *Address:* Roche Court, Winterslow, Salisbury, Wilts. *T:* Winterslow 204. *Clubs:* Travellers'; Leander.

*See also Hon. R. T. Boscawen.*

**CODRINGTON, John Ernest Fleetwood,** CMG 1968; Commissioner for the Bahamas in London, since 1970; *b* 1919; *s* of late Stewart Codrington, Great Hormead Bury, Buntingford, Herts; *m* 1951, Margaret, *d* of late Sir Herbert Hall Hall, KCMG and of Lady Hall Hall; three *d*. *Educ:* Haileybury; Trinity Coll., Cambridge. Served RNVR, 1940-42: Sub-Lt, HMS Enchantress, HMS Vanity; Royal Marines, 1942-46: 42 (RM) Command (Capt.) Colonial Administrative Service, 1946; Asst District Comr, Gold Coast, 1947; Sen. Asst Sec., Governor's Office and Prime Minister's Office, 1952-55; Sec., Gold Coast Comr's Office, London, 1956; Actg Perm. Sec., Min. of Communications, Ghana, 1957; Administrative Officer, Nyasaland, 1958; Actg Sec. to Treasury, 1963-64; Financial Sec., Bahamas, 1964-70. *Recreation:* sailing. *Address:* Chequers Close, Lymington, Hants.

**CODRINGTON, Kenneth de Burgh;** Professor Emeritus of Indian Archæology in University of London (Institute of Archæology and School of Oriental and African Studies); *o s* of late Col H. de B. Codrington, IA; *m* 1927, Philippa Christine, *y d* of late E. V. Fleming, CB; one *s* one *d*. *Educ:* Sherborne Sch.; Cadet Coll., Wellington, India; Corpus Christi Coll., Cambridge; Wadham Coll., Oxford. Indian Army, 33rd QVO Light Horse, 1917; invalided, 1921; BA 1921; MA 1926. RAF Educational Staff, Cranwell, 1922; Prof. of Archæology and Fellow of the Graduate Sch., Univ. of Cincinnati, USA, 1925-26; Hon. Lecturer, University Coll., London and School of Oriental and African Studies, 1931; appointed Prof., 1948. Mem. Cttee of Management, Inst. of Archæology, 1944-67; Keeper, Indian Section, Victoria and Albert Museum, South Kensington, until 1948. London Division RNVR, 1924-39; Commander (S) retd, 1946. Joined J. Hackin, Dir of the French Archæological Delegation in Afghanistan, 1940. Catalogued and hung Burlington Fine Arts Club Exhibn of Indian Art (with Laurence Binyon), 1930; organised Tagore Society's Exhibn of Indian Art, London, 1944; Mem. Selection and Hanging Cttee, Royal Academy Exhibn of Art of India and Pakistan, Burlington House, 1947. Served on Councils of the Royal Asiatic Soc., Royal Anthropological Inst., and Museums Assoc.; Hon. Fellow, School of Oriental and African Studies. Chm., Civil Service Retirement Fellowship, Ashford and District. *Publications:* Ancient India, 1926; rev. edn of Vincent Smith's History of Indian Fine Art, 1930; An Introduction to the Study of Medieval Indian Sculpture, 1929; An Introduction to the Study of Islamic Art in India (India Soc.), 1934; The Wood of the Image; Cricket in the Grass; Birdwood and the Arts of India (Birdwood Lecture, RSA), 1969; papers on art, archæology and anthropology. *Address:* Rose Cottage, Appledore, Kent. *T:* Appledore 388. *Club:* Athenæum.

**CODRINGTON, Sir William (Alexander),** 8th Bt *cr* 1721; Cadet Training Officer, British and Commonwealth Group; *b* 5 July 1934; *e s* of Sir William Richard Codrington, 7th Bt, and Joan Kathleen Birellu, *e d* of Percy E. Nicholas, London, NW; *S* father, 1961. *Educ:* St Andrew Coll., S Africa; S African Naval Coll., General Botha. Joined Merchant Navy, 1952; joined Union Castle Mail Steamship Co., 1960; Master Mariner's Certificate of Competency, 1961. *Recreation:* sailing. *Heir: b* Giles Peter Codrington, *b* 28 Oct. 1943. *Address:* 99 St James Drive, Wandsworth Common, SW17. *Club:* Royal Southern Yacht.

**COE, Denis Walter;** *b* 5 June 1929; *s* of James and Lily Coe, Whitley Bay, Northumberland; *m* 1953, Margaret Rae, *d* of William F. Chambers, Middlesbrough; three *s* one *d*. *Educ:* Bede Trng Coll., Durham; London Sch. of Economics. Teacher's Certificate, 1952; BSc (Econ.) 1960; MSc (Econ.) 1966. National Service in RAF, 1947-50; Junior and Secondary Schoolmaster, 1952-59; Dep. Headmaster, Secondary Sch., 1959-61; Lectr in Govt, Manchester Coll. of Commerce, 1961-66. Contested (Lab) Macclesfield, 1964; MP (Lab) Middleton, Prestwich and Whitefield, 1966-70. *Recreations:* music, drama, walking. *Address:* 7 Aldersmead Road, Beckenham, Kent.

**COFFER, David Edwin,** OBE 1963; General Secretary, British Legion, since Oct. 1959; *b* 18 Sept. 1913; *s* of David Gilbertson Coffer and Florence Ellen Gard; *m* 1947, Edith Mary Moulton; three *d*. *Educ:* Colfe Grammar Sch. *Address:* 74 Ridgeway Drive, Bromley, Kent. *T:* 01-857 5483. *Clubs:* Royal Over-Seas League, Kennel.

**COFFEY, Christopher,** JP; *b* 8 Dec. 1902; *s* of Bernard and Thirza Coffey; *m* 1922, Doris May Coffey (*née* Scott); four *s* two *d*. *Educ:* St Catherine's, Sheffield. Employed in Railway Industry, Traffic Grade; NUR Trade Union Sec. (Branch); Nat. Conf. Sec.; Approved Soc. Branch Sec.; District Council Pres.; represented NUR at TUC and Labour Party Annual Conference, 1918-49; City Councillor, Nottingham, 1945-, Lord Mayor, 1953-54; JP 1947; Alderman, 1954; Labour Party Organising Sec., 1949-53. *Recreations:* fishing, football (soccer). *Address:* 55 Glapton Road, Nottingham. *T:* 85818.

**COFFIN, Cyril Edwin;** Under-Secretary, Ministry of Technology, since 1966; *b* 29 June 1919; *o s* of late Percy Edwin and Helena Constance Coffin; *m* 1947, Joyce Mary, *d* of C. R. Tobitt, Castle Hedingham; one *s* one *d* (and one *d* decd). *Educ:* King's Coll. Sch., Wimbledon; King's Coll., Cambridge (MA). Enlisted Royal Artillery, 1939; transf. Royal Scots, 1940; commnd RIASC, 1941. Temp. Asst Princ., Burma Office, 1946; Asst Princ., Min. of Food, 1947; Princ., 1948; jssc 1950; Asst, Sec., Min. of Agric., Fisheries and Food, 1957; seconded to Office of Minister for

Science, 1963; Alternate UK Governor, Internat. Atomic Energy Agency, 1964; transf. to Min. of Technology, 1966. *Recreation:* music. *Address:* 54 Cambridge Avenue, New Malden, Surrey. *T:* 01-942 0763. *Club:* Union (Cambridge).

**COGGAN, Rt. Hon. and Most Rev. F. Donald;** *see* York, Archbishop of.

**COGHILL, John Percival,** CBE 1951; Foreign Service, retired; Minister to Republic of Honduras, 1954-55; *b* 29 Nov. 1902; *s* of Percy de Geiger Coghill and Dr Agnes Irene Sinclair Coghill. *Educ:* Loretto Sch.; Cheltenham Coll.; Emmanuel Coll., Cambridge. Served at various Foreign Service posts in China. *Recreation:* walking. *Club:* Royal Commonwealth Society.

**COGHILL, Sir (Marmaduke Nevill) Patrick (Somerville),** 6th Bt *cr* 1778; TD 1947; DL Herts; Lieut-Col RA (TA), retd; *b* 18 March 1896; *s* of 5th Bt and Elizabeth Hildegarde Augusta, *d* of late Col Thomas Henry Somerville, Drishane, Skibbereen; *S* father, 1921. *Educ:* Haileybury. Joined RA 1915; served in France until Armistice and afterwards in Turkey and Iraq; Commanded 86th (Hertfordshire Yeomanry), Fd Regt RA TA, 1939-41, and served in Middle East, 1941-45 (despatches). Col, Arab Legion, Jordan, 1952-56. Order of Istiqlal, 2nd Class, Jordan, 1956. OStJ 1957. *Heir: b* Prof. Nevill Henry Kendal Aylmer Coghill, *qv*. *Address:* Savran House, Aylburton, Lydney, Glos. *Club:* Naval and Military.

**COGHILL, Prof. Nevill Henry Kendal Aylmer,** MA; Merton Professor of English Literature, Oxford, 1957-66; Fellow and Tutor in English Literature, Exeter College, Oxford, 1925-57; Emeritus Fellow: Exeter College, Oxford, 1957; Merton College, Oxford, 1966; *b* 19 April 1899; 2nd *s* of Sir Egerton Bushe Coghill, 5th Bt, and Elizabeth Hildegarde Augusta, *d* of late Col Thomas Henry Somerville, Drishane, Skibbereen; *heir-pres.* to Sir Patrick Coghill, 6th Bt, *qv*; *m* 1927, Elspeth Nora (marr. diss. 1933), *d* of Dr Harley, Inchture, Perthshire; one *d*. *Educ:* Haileybury; Exeter Coll., Oxford. Stapeldon Scholar (History), Exeter Coll., Oxford, 1916. Served European War, from 1917; 2nd Lieut RFA (BSF), 1918-19. Research Fellow, Exeter Coll., 1924, Official Fellow, 1925, and Tutor in English Literature; Sub-Rector, 1940-45; Dean of Degrees, 1940; Clark Lecturer, Trinity Coll., Cambridge, 1959. Mem. Oxford University Drama Commission, 1945; Dir, Friends of OUDS, 1940-47; produced: A Midsummer Night's Dream, Haymarket, 1945; Pilgrim's Progress, Covent Garden, 1951; Dr Faustus, University Theatre, Oxford, 1966; jt dir, Dr Faustus (film), 1967. FRSL 1950. Governor of Shakespeare Memorial Theatre, Stratford-upon-Avon, 1956. Pres., Poetry Soc., 1964-66. Hon. DLitt, Williams Coll., Mass, 1966. Has broadcast on Chaucer, Langland, etc. *Play:* (with Martin Starkie) Canterbury Tales, Phœnix Theatre, 1968. *Publications:* The Pardon of Piers Plowman (Gollancz Mem. Lecture, Br. Acad., 1945); Visions from Piers Plowman, 1949; The Poet Chaucer, 1949; The Canterbury Tales (in modern English), 1951; Geoffrey Chaucer, 1956; Shakespeare's Professional Skills, 1964, etc. *Recreations:* producing Shakespearian and other plays; music, etc. *Address:* Savran House, Aylburton, near Lydney, Glos. *T:* Lydney 2240; c/o Merton College, Oxford.

**COGHILL, Sir Patrick;** *see* Coghill, Sir M. N. P. S.

**COGMAN, Very Rev. Frederick Walter;** Dean of Guernsey since 1967; Rector of St Martin, Guernsey, since 1948; *b* 4 March 1913; *s* of William Frederick Cogman and Mabel Cozens; *m* 1940, Rose Hélène Mauger; one *s* one *d*. *Educ:* Rutlish Sch., Merton; King's Coll., London. Asst Priest, Upton-cum-Chalvey, Slough, 1938-42; Chaplain and Housemaster, St George's Sch., Harpenden, 1942-48. *Recreations:* music, painting. *Address:* The Deanery, Guernsey. *T:* Guernsey 38303.

**COHEN,** family name of **Barons Cohen** and **Cohen of Birkenhead.**

**COHEN,** Baron (Life Peer) *cr* 1951, of Walmer; **Lionel Leonard Cohen,** PC 1946; Kt 1943; a Lord of Appeal in Ordinary, 1951-60; *b* 1 March 1888; *s* of late Sir Leonard Lionel Cohen, KCVO; *m* 1918, Adelaide (*d* 1961), *y d* of late Sir Isidore Spielmann, CMG; two *s* one *d*. *Educ:* Eton; New Coll., Oxford. 1st class history, 1909, law 1910; called to Bar, Inner Temple, 1913; KC 1929; Bencher, Lincolns Inn, 1934 (Treasurer 1954); served in Min. of Economic Warfare, 1939-43; Judge of Chancery Div. of High Court of Justice, 1943-46; Lord Justice of Appeal, 1946-51. Chm., Company Law Amendment Cttee, 1943-45; Chm. of Royal Commission on awards to Inventors, 1946-56; Chm., Council on Prices, Productivity and Incomes, 1957-59. hon. Fellow of New Coll., Oxford, 1946; Hon. Fellow University Coll., London, 1955; Hon. LLD London Univ., 1962; Fellow of Eton Coll., 1950-60; Chm. College Cttee, UC London, 1953-63; Capt. Royal and Ancient, St Andrews, 1960-61. Mem. of Council, St Mary's Hospital Medical Sch. (Pres., 1961-66). Served European War, 1914-18, with 13th Princess Louise's Kensington Bn the London Regt and Staff. *Recreation:* golf. *Address:* 55 Porchester Terrace, W2. *T:* 01-723 5057. *Clubs:* White's, St James'.

*See also Hon. P. M. Samuel.*

**COHEN OF BIRKENHEAD,** 1st Baron *cr* 1956, of Birkenhead; **Henry Cohen,** Kt 1949; MD, ChB (Liverpool); FRCP; P and Hon. FRSH; Hon. FRCPE; Hon. FRCPI; Hon. FRCPGlas; Hon. FRCS; Hon. FRCOG; Hon. FRCGP; Hon. FDSRCS; Hon. FFARCS; Hon. FRIC; Hon. FACP; Hon. FRSM; Hon. DSc (NUI, Sussex, Nott.); Hon. ScD (Cambridge, Union Univ. of New York); Hon. LLD (Liverpool, London, Manchester, Hull, TCD, Wales); Hon. DCL Oxford; Hon. FFR; Hon. FBPsS; Hon. FAPHA; Hon FPS; Hon. FChS; FSA; FRSA; DL Lancs, JP; Chancellor of Hull University since 1970; Hon. Fellow, Jesus College, Cambridge; Professor of Medicine, University of Liverpool, 1934-65; Consulting Physician, Royal Infirmary, Liverpool, since 1934; President: General Medical Council, since 1961; Royal Society of Health, since 1958; Assoc. Study of Med. Educn, Internat. Acad. Hist. of Med.; (Life), Inst. of Health Education; Liverpool Playhouse, since 1961; Nat. Bureau for Co-operation in Child Care, since 1965; Children's Research Fund; Vis. Prof. of Med., NY State Univ., 1958; McGill Univ., Montreal, 1959; Chairman: Central Health Services Council, 1957-63; Standing Medical Advisory Cttee, Ministry of Health, 1948-63; several cttees and jt-cttees (Min. of Health), including Gen. Practice, Prescribing, Mental Nursing, Epilepsy, Welfare Foods, Poliomyelitis, Health Educn, Operational Research in Pharmaceutical Service, Safety of Drugs; Flour Panel, Ministry of Food, 1955; Jt-Cttee MRC and Nuffield Trust on Cortisone; RCP on Nomenclature; UK Foundation WHO; Advisory Res. Bd, Spastics Soc.; *b* 1900. *Educ:* Birkenhead; Univs of Liverpool and Paris. MB, ChB (1st Cl. Hons).

1922, MD (Special Merit), 1924, FRCP 1934. Several prizes, medals, fellowships, scholarships, etc. Beit Fellow, 1924. Editor-in-Chief, British Encyclopædia Med. Practice, 1955-70. Past Chairman: Min. of Health cttee on Rheumatism, Definition of Drugs and Food, etc; BMA cttees on Trng of a Doctor, and Gen. Practice; President: 5th British Congress on History of Medicine and Pharmacy, 1960; 10th European Institute on Alcoholism, 1964; King David Sch., Liverpool; Home for Aged; Nat. Soc. for Clean Air, 1961-63; BECC (SW Lancs); Brit. Diabetic Assoc.; Nat. Polio Foundn (Liverpool); Merseyside Multiple Sclerosis Soc.; Merseyside Council on Alcoholism; Wirral Assoc. for Mental Health; BMA Student's Trust, 1961-; Past President: BMA, 1950-52 (Gold Medal, 1967); 7th Internat. Congress of Biological Standards, 1961; RSM (Sect. of Medicine), 1953-55 (Sect. History Medicine, 1966); Liverpool Medical Inst., 1954-55; Heberden Soc., 1950-53; RSM, 1964-66; Assoc. of Physicinas of GB and Ireland, 1968-69; University Club, 1952-54; First World Conf. on Med. Educn, 1952, resigned; Jt Meeting BMA–CMA, Toronto (Section of Medicine), 1955. Pres., Brit. Soc. of History of Medicine; Vice-Pres., BMA, 1953-; National Assoc. for Mentally Handicapped Children; Crown Rep. GMC, 1945- (mem. deleg. to USA and Canada, 1946); Governing Trustee, Nuffield Provincial Hospitals Trust; Member: United Liverpool Teaching Hospitals and Liverpool Regional Hospitals Board; Assoc. Brit. Neurologists (Council, 1938-46); Physiological Soc.; Soc. Internat. de Médecine Interne; Soc. Internat. de Gastro-entérologie; Soc. Internat. d'Histoire de la Médicine; Expert Advisory Panel on Professional Educ., WHO, Br. Pharmacopœia Commn, 1948-53; Med. Adv. Cttee, Min. of Health, 1941-48; Councillor, RCP, 1943-46; rep. RCP on Negotiating Cttee for NHS; Examiner, RCP and Clinical Research Bd, MRC, 1954-57; Hon. Member: Assoc. of Phys., Gt Brit. and Ire.; York Med. Soc.; Harveian Soc.; Heberden Soc.; Montreal Clin. Soc.; Ophthalmological Soc.; Birkenhead Med. Soc.; Liverpool Arch. Soc.; New York Acad. Science; British Geriatric Soc.; Bedford Med. Inst. Lectures: Bradshaw, RCP, 1940; Skinner, Faculty of Radiologists, 1942; Lettsomian, Med. Soc., London, 1944; John Burns and Finlayson, RFPSG 1944; Samuel Hyde, RSM, 1947; Moynihan, RCS, 1949; Newsholme, Univ. of London, 1950; Harveian, 1950; Manson, Royal Inst. of Philosophy, 1951; Coronation, ERC, 1953; John Tate, Middx County Med. Soc., 1954; Sherrington, Univ. of Liverpool, 1955; Sydney Body, 1955; Hunterian Oration, 1955; Sir Charles Hastings, 1956; Henry Cavendish, 1956; Maurice Bloch, Glasgow Univ., 1957; Isaac Gilchrist, Aberdeen Univ., 1957, 1968; Paget, RDS, 1957; Crookshank (and Medallist), FAC. Radiol., 1958; Henry Wyld, 1958; Charles Tomes, RCS, 1959; Watson-Jones, RCS, 1959; Louis Gross, Montreal, 1959; Gilbert Scott, CRC, 1960; Founder's, RCN, 1960; Wilkinson, London Univ., 1960; Frederick William Price, RCPE, 1960; Founders and Benefactors, Univ. of Durham Dental Sch., 1960; Chadwick, RSH, 1961; Heberden (and medallist), 1961; Gideon de Laune, Soc. Apoth., 1962; John Snow, Assoc. of Anæsth., 1962; Osler Oration, CMA, 1963; Albee Memorial, USA, 1963; Croonian, RCP, 1964; Bowman Medal, Ophth. Soc., 1964; Lloyd-Roberts, RSM, 1964; Alpha Omega Alpha, Johns Hopkins, USA, 1964; Bengué, RIPHH, 1965; Winchester Address, BMA, 1965; Annual Oration, Med. Soc. London, 1966; Hastings Memorial, BMA, 1966; Astor, Middx Hosp., 1966; John Ash, Birmingham Univ., 1966; Abrahamson, RCSI, 1966; Nuffield Lectr and Medal, RSM, 1966; Trevor Lloyd Hughes, 1967; Ludwig Hektoen, Chicago, 1967; Wood Jones, Univ. of Manchester, 1967; Thomas Vicary, RCS, 1968; Roscoe, 1969; Upjohn, Univ. Sheffield, 1969; Kate Harrower Memorial, Med. Women's Fedn, 1969; Wiles, QUB, 1969. Harveian Oration, RCP, 1970. Bowman Medal, Ophth. Soc., 1964; Gold Medal, RSM, 1971. Hon. Freeman: Liverpool; Birkenhead; Soc. Apothecaries. Associate KStJ. *Publications:* New Pathways in Medicine, 1935; Nature, Method and Purpose of Diagnosis, 1943; Sherrington: Physiologist, Philosopher and Poet, 1958; The Evolution of Modern Medicine, 1958; contribs to many books, and medical and scientific journals. *Recreations:* Theatre (President of Board, Liverpool Repertory Theatre; Chm., 1948-61), Music, the arts. *Address:* 31 Rodney Street, Liverpool 1. *T:* Royal 2233; Cornercroft, Glendyke Road, Liverpool 18. *T:* Allerton 1981; 7 Princes Gate, SW7. *T:* 01-584 0203. *Clubs:* Athenæum, Savage (Hon. Life Mem.); University (Liverpool).

**COHEN, His Honour Judge Arthur;** *see* Cohen, N. A. J.

**COHEN, Arthur S.;** *see* Sefton-Cohen.

**COHEN, Sir B. N. W.;** *see* Waley-Cohen.

**COHEN, Clifford Theodore,** MC 1945; TD 1946; DL; **His Honour Judge Cohen;** County Court Judge since 1953; *b* 26 June 1906; *er s* of R. Cohen, Registrar, Stockton County Court; *m* 1961, Mrs Gladys Eileen Fielding, *yr d* of late Charles Allaun. *Educ:* Clifton Coll., Bristol; Magdalene Coll., Cambridge (MA). Called to Bar, Inner Temple, 1929. Practised on North-Eastern Circuit as barrister until Aug. 1939. Served War of 1939-45: 2nd Lieut with 1st Tyneside Scottish, The Black Watch, Royal Highland Regt; France; POW in Germany from May 1940 for nearly 5 years. Returned to work as barrister until July 1953. Hon. Col, 17 Bn The Parachute Regt, TA, 1963-67. DL Durham, 1958. *Recreation:* gardening. *Address:* Tanton Hall, Stokesley, North Yorks. *T:* Stokesley 300.

**COHEN, Sir Edgar (Abraham),** KCMG 1955 (CMG 1951); retired civil servant; *b* 5 Dec. 1908; *s* of late J. B. Cohen and Marthe Lewie; *m* 1967, Lillian Kathleen Langham. *Educ:* Manchester Grammar Sch.; Balliol Coll., Oxford (Scholar). 1st class Class. Hon. Mods., 1929, and Greats, 1931. Entered Board of Trade, 1932; Under-Sec., 1947; Second Sec. (Overseas), 1952; Permanent Deleg., with rank of Ambassador: to EFTA and GATT, Geneva, 1960-65; to OECD, Paris, 1965-68. *Address:* Heath Ridge, Graffham, Petworth. Sussex.

**COHEN, Sir Edward,** Kt 1970; Solicitor; Partner, Pavey, Wilson Cohen & Carter, Melbourne, Australia; Chairman: E Z Industries Ltd; Electrolytic Zinc Co. of Australasia Ltd; Commercial Union Assurance Co. of Australia Ltd; Derwent Metals Pty Ltd; Emu Bay Railway Co. Ltd; CUB Fibre Containers Pty Ltd; Carlton & United Breweries Ltd; The Foster Brewing Co. Ltd; Northern Australian Breweries Ltd; Director: Associated Pulp & Paper Mills Ltd; Burnie Timber Pty Ltd; Papermakers Ltd; The Shamrock Brewing Co. Ltd; Union Assurance Society of Australia Ltd; and other cos; *m* 1939, Meryl D. Fink; one *s*. *Educ:* Scotch Coll., Melbourne; (Exhibnr in Greek and Roman History) Ormond Coll., Univ. of Melbourne (LLB). Served, 1940-45: AIF, 2/12 Fd Regt, 9th Div. Artillery, Captain 1942. Past Member: Faculty of Law of Melbourne Univ.,

Council of Legal Education, and Bd of Examiners. Chm., Pensions Cttee of Melbourne Legacy, 1959-; Mem. Council (Past-Pres.) Law Inst. of Victoria, 1965-66. *Address:* 19 Russell Street, Toorak, Victoria 3142, Australia; (office) 390 Lonsdale Street, Melbourne, Victoria 3000, Australia. *Clubs:* Naval and Military, Victoria Racing, Royal Automobile (all in Melbourne).

**COHEN, George Cormack;** Sheriff-Substitute of the Lothians and Peebles at Edinburgh, 1955-66; *b* 16 Dec. 1909; *s* of J. Cohen and Mary J. Cormack, Melfort House, Bearsden, Dunbartonshire; *m* 1939, Elizabeth, *d* of James H. Wallace, Malvern; one *s* one *d.* *Educ:* Kelvinside Academy, Glasgow; Glasgow Univ. MA 1930, LLB 1934, Admitted to Scottish Bar, 1935; Sheriff-Substitute of Caithness at Wick, 1944-51; of Ayr and Bute at Kilmarnock, 1951-55. *Recreations:* golf, gastronomy, philately. *Address:* Sandlewood, Hadlow Park, Tonbridge, Kent. *T:* Hadlow 513. *Club:* Royal Automobile.

**COHEN, Sir Jack,** Kt 1965; OBE 1951; JP; Alderman, Borough of Sunderland, since 1935 and Councillor since 1929; Mayor, 1949-50; *b* 2 Nov. 1896; *s* of Samuel Cohen, Sunderland; *m* 1921, Kitty, *d* of Abraham Sinclair, Glasgow; one *s* one *d.* Served European War, 1914-18. JP Sunderland, 1939. *Address:* 16 Barnes Road, Sunderland, Durham. *T:* Sunderland 6628.

**COHEN, Prof. John,** PhD; Professor of Physiology, University of Manchester, since 1952; *b* 20 Jan. 1911; *s* of Joseph and Rebecca Cohen, Tredegar, Mon.; *m* 1st, 1939; one *s* one *d*; 2nd, 1955, Rosemarie Loss; three *s.* *Educ:* Tredegar Elementary and County Schs.; University Coll., London (MA, PhD). Research at: University Coll., London, 1933-40; Institute of Experimental Psychology, Oxford, 1940. RAC, 1940-41; attached to Offices of War Cabinet and Central Statistical Office, 1941-48; Joint Sec., Expert Cttee on Work of Psychologists and Psychiatrists in the Services, 1942-45; Mem., Working Party on Recruitment and Training of Nurses, 1946-47; Tech. Sec., Internat. Preparatory Commn for World Congress on Mental Health, 1948; Mem., Inter-professional Advisory Cttee to World Fedn for Mental Health, 1949-52; Consultant to UNESCO, 1948, 1950, 1967; Lectr in Psychology, Univ. of Leeds, 1948-49; Prof. of Psychology, Univ. of Jerusalem, 1949-51; Lectr in Psychology, Birkbeck Coll., Univ. of London, 1951-52. Mem. of Council, Brit. Psychological Soc., 1956-59. Hon. MA (Manchester), FBPsS 1943. Fellow, World Academy of Art and Science; Corr. Mem., Centre de Recherches de Psychologie Comparative. British Ed., Acta Psychologica; Member: Internat. Editorial Bd of Jl of Peace Research; Editorial Cttee of IKON Revue Internationale de Filmologie. *Publications:* Human Nature, War and Society, 1946; Report on Recruitment and Training of Nurses, 1948; co-editor: Human Affairs, 1937; Educating for Democracy, 1939; co-author: Risk and Gambling, 1956; Humanistic Psychology, 1958; Chance, Skill and Luck, 1960; Readings in Psychology (ed), 1964; Behaviour in Uncertainty, 1964; Human Robots in Myth and Science, 1966; A New Introduction to Psychology, 1966; Psychological Time in Health and Disease, 1967; Psychology: An Outline for the intending Student (ed), 1967; Causes and Prevention of Road Accidents (with B. Preston), 1968; (with I. Christensen) Information, Evidence and Choice, 1970; Elements of Child Psychology, 1970; numerous papers in psychological, medical, psychiatric and other learned jls. *Recreations:* travel, music. *Address:* Department of Psychology, The University, Manchester. *T:* 061-273 3333.

**COHEN, Sir John (Edward),** Kt 1969; Founder of Tesco Stores (Holdings) Limited and associated companies; First Life President since 1969 (formerly Chairman); *b* 6 Oct. 1898; *m* 1924, Sarah Fox; two *d.* *Educ:* Rutland Street LCC Sch. Served with RFC, 1917-19, France, Egypt, Palestine. Commenced in business on own account, 1919. Asst to Court, Worshipful Company of Carmen. FGI. *Recreations:* bridge, golf and world travel. *Address:* 22 Cumberland Terrace, Regent's Park, NW1. *T:* 01-935 1599; 01-935 9307. *Clubs:* Royal Automobile, City Livery.

**COHEN, John Michael,** FRSL 1957; critic and translator; *b* 5 Feb. 1903; *s* of late Arthur Cohen and Elizabeth (*née* Abrahams); *m* 1928, Audrey Frances Falk; four *s.* *Educ:* St Paul's Sch.; Queens' Coll., Cambridge. After short spell in publishing, joined family manufacturing business, 1925-40; war-time Schoolmaster, 1940-46; writing and translating from that date. *Publications:* (Penguin Classics): Don Quixote, 1950; Rousseau's Confessions, 1953; Rabelais, 1955; Life of Saint Teresa, 1957; Montaigne's Essays, 1958; Pascal's Pensées, 1961; Bernal Diaz, The Conquest of New Spain, 1963; The Spanish Bawd, 1964; Zarate, The Discovery and Conquest of Peru, 1968; The Four Voyages of Christopher Columbus, 1969; Penguin Book of Comic and Curious Verse, 1952; More Comic & Curious Verse, 1956; Penguin Book of Spanish Verse, 1956; History of Western Literature (Pelican Books), 1956; Robert Browning, 1952; Life of Ludwig Mond, 1956; Yet More Comic and Curious Verse, 1959; Poetry of This Age, 1959 (2nd, revised edn, 1966); Robert Graves, 1960; (with M. J. Cohen) Penguin Dictionary of Quotations, 1960; English Translators and Translations, 1962; The Baroque Lyric, 1963; (ed.) Latin American Writing Today (Penguin), 1967; Writers in the New Cuba (Penguin), 1967; other translations. *Recreations:* meditation; listening to music; gardening. *Address:* Knappswood, Upper Basildon, Reading, Berks. *T:* Upper Basildon 282.

**COHEN, Sir Karl Cyril,** Kt 1968; CBE 1963; *s* of Solomon Cohen, Leeds. *Educ:* Leeds University (LLB Hons 1935). Solicitor, 1940 (Partner, K. C. Cohen & Rhodes, Leeds). Councillor, Leeds City Council, 1952-. *Address:* Century House, South Parade, Leeds 1; 22 Gledhow Park Avenue, Leeds 7.

**COHEN, Comdr Kenneth H. S.,** CB 1954; CMG 1946; RN; European Adviser to United Steel Companies, 1953-66; Chairman, Franco-British Society, since 1967; Councillor of the RIIA; *b* 15 March 1900; *s* of late Herman Cohen, Barrister-at-Law, Inner Temple; *m* 1932, Mary Joseph, *d* of late Ernest Joseph, CBE, FRIBA; one *s* one *d.* *Educ:* Elstree Sch.; Eastbourne Coll. "Special Entry" RN Cadet, 1918, Midshipman, HMS Iron Duke; specialised in Torpedo Duties, 1926; RN Staff Coll., 1932; retired (Lt-Comdr), 1935; appointed HMS President, 1939; Comdr 1940. Attached Foreign Office, 1945. Officier de la Légion d'Honneur; Croix de Guerre avec palmes (France); Legion of Merit, Degree of Officer (USA); Officier de la Couronne (Belgium); Order of the White Lion (Czechoslovakia); Commandeur de l'Etoile Noire (France), 1960. *Publications:* articles in national press on problems of European integration. *Address:* 33 Bloomfield Terrace, SW1. *T:* 01-730 3228. *Clubs:* Garrick, MCC.

**COHEN, Marcel;** Directeur d'études à l'Ecole pratique des Hautes Etudes, 1919-55, retired 1955; Professeur à l'Ecole nationale des Langues Orientales Vivantes, 1911-50 (Hon. Prof. 1955); Directeur de recherches, 1937, 1938; Chargé de cours Institut d'ethnologie, Paris, 1926-59; *b* 6 Feb. 1884; *s* of Benjamin Cohen and Anna Bechmann; *m* 1913, Marguerite Bloch; three *c*. *Educ:* Paris. Agrégé de L'Université (Grammaire), 1908; Chargé de mission en Abyssinie, 1910-11; Docteur ès Lettres, 1924; Membre correspondant de l'Académie des Sciences de Berlin; Docteur *hc* Univs: Warsaw, Manchester, Prague. Membre d'honneur de l'Association phonétique internationale et de la Société de linguistique américaine; Lauréat du prix international Haile Selassie Ier, pour les études éthiopiennes, 1964. Chevalier de la Légion d'Honneur; Croix de Guerre, 1914-18, and 1939-45. *Publications:* Le Parler arabe des juifs d'Alger, 1912 (prix Volney); Le Système verbal sémitique et l'expression du temps, 1924 (prix Volney); Les Langues du Monde (direction avec A. Meillet), 1924 (1952); Instructions d'enquête linguistique et questionnaires linguistiques, 1928 (1951); Etudes d'éthiopien méridional, 1931; Traité de langue amharique, 1936; Nouvelles études d'éthiopien méridional, 1939; Le français en 1700 d'après le témoignage de Gile Vaudelin, 1946; Essai comparatif sur le vocabulaire et la phonétique du chamito-sémitique, 1947; Histoire d'une langue; le français, 1947 (1950, 1967); Linguistique et matérialisme dialectique, 1948; Grammaire française en quelques pages, 1948 (1966); Regards sur la langue française, 1950; Le Langage (Structure et évolution), 1950; L'écriture, 1953; Grammaire et Style, 1954; Cinquante années de recherches (bibliographie complète), 1955; (avec un groupe de linguistes) Français élémentaire? Non, 1955; Pour une Sociologie du langage, 1956; Notes de méthode pour l'histoire du français, 1958; La grande invention de l'écriture et son évolution, 1958; Le subjonctif en français contemporain, 1960 (1965); Etudes sur le langage de l'enfant (in collab.), 1962; Nouveaux regards sur la langue française, 1963; Encore des regards sur la langue française, 1966; Toujours des regards sur la langue française, 1970; Mélanges Marcel Cohen, 1970; numerous articles and mémoires. *Address:* 20 Rue Joseph Bertrand, 78 Viroflay, Yvelines, France. *T:* 926.5152. *Club:* Comité national des écrivains (Paris).

**COHEN, Myrella, (Mrs Mordaunt Cohen),** QC 1970; *b* 16 Dec. 1927; *d* of Samuel and Sarah Cohen, Manchester; *m* 1953, Lt-Col Mordaunt Cohen, TD; one *s* one *d*. *Educ:* Manchester High Sch. for Girls; Colwyn Bay Grammar Sch.; Manchester Univ. (LLB 1948). Called to the Bar, Gray's Inn, 1950. *Address:* 183 Queen Alexandra Road, Sunderland, Co. Durham. *T:* Sunderland 67082; 5 King's Bench Walk, EC4. *T:* 01-353 2882/4. *Club:* Royal Over-Seas League.

**COHEN, Lt-Col Nathan Leslie,** TD 1949; JP; Adjudicator (part-time) under Immigration Appeals Act; *b* 13 Jan. 1908; *s* of Reuben and Maud Cohen; unmarried. *Educ:* Stockton-on-Tees Grammar Sch.; Clifton Coll. In private practice as a Solicitor until 1939; called to the Bar, Lincoln's Inn, 1954. War Service, Aug. 1939-May 1945. Senior Legal Officer (Lt-Col), Military Govt, Carinthia, Austria, 1945-49; Pres. of Sessions Courts, Malaya, 1949-57; Justice of the Special Courts, Cyprus, 1958-59; Judge of HM Court of Soveriegn Base Areas of Akrotiri and Dhekalia, Cyprus, 1960-67. Vice-Pres., Northern Area, British Legion. JP Stockton-on-Tees, 1967. Diamond Jubilee Medal (Johore), 1955; Colonial Police Medal, 1956. *Recreations:* tennis, squash, shooting, reading. *Address:* 35 Richmond Road, Stockton-on-Tees, Teesside. *Club:* Royal Over-Seas League.

**COHEN, (Nathaniel) Arthur (Jim),** JP; **His Honour Judge Arthur Cohen;** County Court Judge, Circuit No 38, 1955-56, Circuit No 43, 1956-60, Circuit No 56, 1960-70, retired; *b* 19 Jan. 1898; 2nd *s* of late Sir Benjamin Arthur Cohen, KC, and Lady Cohen; *m* 1st, 1927, Judith Luard (marr. diss.); two *s*; 2nd, 1936, Joyce Collingridge. *Educ:* Rugby; CCC, Oxford (BA). Served European War, 1916-19, Royal Navy. Called to Bar, Inner Temple, 1923. War of 1939-45: recalled to RN and placed on Emergency List with rank of Commander. Legal Adviser to UNRRA, 1946-49; Dep. Chm., Foreign Compensation Commn, 1950-55. JP Surrey, 1958. *Recreations:* golf, music. *Address:* Gibb's Cottage, Limpsfield, Surrey. *T:* Limpsfield Chart 2223. *Club:* Oxford and Cambridge University.

**COHEN, Percy,** CBE 1936; Joint Director, Conservative Research Department, 1948-59; *b* London, 25 Dec. 1891; *e s* of M. Cohen; *m* 1917, Rosa Abrams; one *s* one *d*. *Educ:* Central Foundation Sch., London. Entered service of Conservative Central Office, 1911; Head of Library and Information Dept, 1928-48. Served first European War, France. Worked in 12 General Elections; Editor, Constitutional Year Book, 1929-39; Editor, Notes on Current Politics, 1942-59. *Publications:* British System of Social Insurance, 1932; Unemployment Insurance and Assistance in Britain, 1938; (ed) Conservative Election Handbook, 1945; (ed) Campaign Guide, 1950, 1951, 1955 and 1959. *Recreation:* walking. *Address:* 115 Grove Hall Court, St John's Wood, NW8. *T:* 01-286 2489. *Club:* Constitutional.

**COHEN, Reuben K.;** *see* Kelf-Cohen.

**COHEN, Sir Rex (Arthur Louis),** KBE 1964 (OBE 1944); Director: Barclays Bank London Local Board; Barclays Bank Trust Co.; Tribune Investment Trust; Chairman: Higgs & Hill Ltd; Meat and Livestock Commission; Member: Television Advisory Cttee; *b* 27 Nov. 1906; *s* of Rex David Cohen, Condover Hall, Shrewsbury; *m* 1932, Nina Alice Castello; one *d*. *Educ:* Rugby Sch.; Trinity Coll., Cambridge (BA). Commissioned KSLI (TA), 1938; Staff Capt. 159 Inf. Bde, 1940; DAQMG 53rd (W) Inf. Div., 1940; Staff Coll., 1941; Bde Major 160 Inf. Bde, 1942; AQMG 12th Corps, 1943; AQMG 2nd Army, 1945; Lt-Col, 1943. Past Mem., BoT Cttee for Consumer Protection. Past Chairman: Lewis's Investment Trust Group, 1958-65 (Joint Man. Dir, 1945); NAAFI, 1961-63. Officer, Order of Orange Nassau (Netherlands), 1944. *Recreations:* racing, horse breeding, shooting. *Address:* Ruckmans Farm, Oakwood Hill, near Dorking, Surrey. *T:* Oakwood Hill 255. *Clubs:* Garrick, White's; Jockey (Newmarket).

**COHEN, Dr Richard Henry Lionel,** CB 1969; Deputy Chief Medical Officer, Department of Health and Social Security, since 1967; *b* 1 Feb. 1907; *y s* of Frank Lionel and Bertha Hendelah Cohen; *m* 1934, Margaret Clarkson Deas; one *s*. *Educ:* Clifton Coll.; King's Coll., Cambridge; St Bartholomew's Hospital. Miscellaneous hosp. appts, 1940-46; MRC, 1948-62; Dep. Chief Med. Off., MRC, 1957-62; Dept of Health and Social Security (formerly Min. of Health), 1962-. *Address:* 8 Norfolk Road, NW8. *Club:* Reform.

**COHEN, Ruth Louisa,** CBE 1969; MA; Principal, Newnham College, Cambridge, since 1954; University Lecturer in Economics,

Cambridge, since 1945; Alternate Governor, Hebrew University of Jerusalem; *b* 10 Nov. 1906; *d* of late Walter Samuel Cohen and late Lucy Margaret Cohen. *Educ:* Hayes Court, Kent; Newnham Coll., Cambridge. Commonwealth Fund Fellow, Stanford and Cornell Univs., USA, 1930-32; Research Officer, Agricultural Economics Research Inst., Oxford, 1933-39; Fellow of Newnham Coll., Cambridge, 1939-54; Min. of Food, 1939-42; Board of Trade, 1942-45. Lay Mem., Gen. Medical Council, 1961. *Publications:* History of Milk Prices, 1936; Economics of Agriculture, 1939; articles in Economic Journal, etc. *Address:* Newnham College, Cambridge. *T:* Cambridge 62273. *Club:* University Women's.

**COHEN, Stanley;** MP (Lab) Leeds (South East) since 1970; *b* 31 July 1927; *s* of Thomas and Teresa Cohen; *m* 1954, Brenda P. Rafferty; three *s* one *d*. *Educ:* St Patrick's and St Charles' Schools, Leeds. Served in Royal Navy, 1947-49. Employed in Clothing Industry, 1943-47 and 1949-51; Clerical Officer with British Railways, 1951-70. Mem. Leeds City Council, 1952-; elected Alderman, 1968. Parly Candidate (Lab) Barkston Ash County Constituency, 1966. Mem., Duke of Edinburgh's Commonwealth Study Conf. to Australia, 1968. *Recreations:* walking, camping, driving. *Address:* 7 Marshall Terrace, Leeds 15. *T:* Leeds 649568. *Clubs:* Crossgates Recreational; Irish Centre (Leeds).

**COHN, Prof. Norman,** MA (Oxon); DLitt (Glasgow); FRHistS; author and historian; Director, The Columbus Centre (formerly Centre for Research in Collective Psychopathology), University of Sussex, and Professorial Fellow, University of Sussex, since 1966; late Professor of French, University of Durham; *b* London, 12 Jan. 1915; *yr s* of late August Cohn and Daisy Reimer; *m* 1941, Vera (*née* Broido); one *s*. *Educ:* Gresham's Sch., Holt (Scholar); Christ Church, Oxford (Scholar). 1st Class in Honour Sch. of Medieval and Mod. Languages, 1936. Hugh Le May Fellow, Rhodes Univ., 1950. Fellow, Center for Advanced Study in the Behavioral Sciences, Stanford, Calif, 1966. *Publications:* Gold Khan and other Siberian legends, 1946; The Pursuit of the Millennium, 1957 (revised edns 1961, 1970); Warrant for Genocide, 1967 (revised edn 1970; Anisfield-Wolf Award in Race Relations); contributor to Millennial Dreams in Action (ed. Thrupp), 1962; Caste and Race (ed. de Reuck and Knight), 1967; and to reviews and learned jls. *Recreations:* walking, travel. *Address:* 61 New End, NW3. *T:* 01-435 5755; (office) 3 Henrietta Street, WC2. *T:* 01-240 0278. *Club:* Athenæum.

**COIA, Jack Antonio,** CBE 1967; LLD 1970; BArch; FRIBA 1941; RSA 1962; AMPTI; architect; Commissioner, Royal Fine Art Commission for Scotland, since 1969; *b* 17 July 1898; *m* 1939, Eden Bernard; three *d*. *Educ:* St Aloysius Coll.; Glasgow Sch. of Art; Strathclyde Univ. Works include: immense contribution to RC Church Architecture in Scotland, 1936- (St Anne's Church, Glasgow); Catholic Pavilion, Post Office and Industry North Pavilion for the Empire Exhibition, Glasgow, 1938; Shipbuilding and Railways Section for the Festival of Britain Exhibition, Glasgow, 1951. Senior Partner of Gillespie Kidd and Coia whose works include: Flats at East Kilbride (Saltire Award 1953); and among several awards: from Civic Trust, Bellshill Maternity Hospital, 1962, Old Persons Housing and Home at Dumbarton, 1969; from RIBA: Bronze Medal and Regional Awards for Architecture in Scotland: St Bride's Church, East Kilbride, Church of Our Lady of Good Counsel, Dennistoun, 1966, St Peter's College at Cardross, 1967, Halls of Residence, The Lawns, Cottingham, for Hull University, 1968. Pres., Royal Incorpn of Architects in Scotland, 1967-68. Royal Gold Medal for Architecture, 1969. *Recreation:* golf. *Address:* 20 Park Circus, Glasgow C3. *Clubs:* Glasgow Art (Glasgow); Scottish Arts (Edinburgh).

**COKAYNE,** family name of **Baron Cullen.**

**COKE,** family name of **Earl of Leicester.**

**COKE, Dorothy Josephine,** RWS 1943 (ARWS 1935); artist; an official war artist, 1940, Women's Services subjects; *d* of Joseph Charles Coke and Edith Mary Price. *Educ:* The Slade School. Mem. of the New English Art Club. *Address:* 11 Eley Crescent, Rottingdean, Brighton, Sussex.

**COKE, Gerald Edward,** CBE 1967; JP; Treasurer, Bridewell Royal Hospital (King Edward's School, Witley), since 1946; Chairman, Glyndebourne Arts Trust, since 1955; Director, Royal Opera House, Covent Garden, 1958-64; Director, Royal Academy of Music, since 1957; a Governor of the BBC, 1961-66; Director: Rio Tinto-Zinc Corp. (Dep. Chm. 1962-66; Chm. Rio Tinto Co., 1956-62); S. G. Warburg & Co.; United Kingdom Provident Instn, and other companies; *b* 25 Oct. 1907; *o s* of late Major the Hon. Sir John Coke, KCVO, and late Hon. Mrs Coke; *m* 1939, Patricia, *e d* of late Rt Hon. Sir Alexander Cadogan, PC, OM, GCMG, KCB; three *s* one *d*. *Educ:* Eton; New Coll., Oxford (MA). JP Hants, 1952. Served War of 1939-45, Lieut-Col. Hon. FRAM 1968. *Address:* Jenkyn Place, Bentley, Hants. *T:* Bentley 3118. *Club:* Brooks's.

**COKE WALLIS, Leonard George,** CMG 1960; CIE 1945; late ICS; *b* 12 March 1900; *s* of late G. C. Wallis; *m* 1932, Frances Chieveley, *d* of late C. H. Coke; two *s* one *d*. *Educ:* University Coll., London; Christ's Coll., Cambridge. 1st class, BA Hons History, London; double first in Historical Tripos, Cambridge. Entered ICS 1924; Asst Magistrate and Sub-divisional Officer, Bengal, 1924-29; entered Political Service, 1929; served successively in NWF Province, on special duty in Political Dept Secretariat, in Eastern States Agency, Cooch Behar State, Central India, Hyderabad; Punjab Hill States; Resident for the Eastern States, 1944; Political Agent in Jaipur; Resident at Baroda and for Western India States, 1947; Dep. High Commissioner for UK in Pakistan, 1947-52; with National Savings Cttee, 1953-55; Chairman: Public Service Commission, Ibadan, W Region, Nigeria, 1956; Overseas Public Service Board, Nigeria House (West), London, 1961-66; London Selection Panel, Nigeria High Commission, 1966-67. *Publications:* articles on Nigerianisation of Public Services, and the Public Service Commission in Jl of African Administration, 1959, Incidi, 1960, Jl of Royal African Society, 1961. *Recreation:* golf. *Address:* 14 King's Close, Lyndhurtst, Hants. *T:* Lyndhurst 2543. *Club:* Oriental.

**COKER, Peter Godfrey,** ARA 1965; ARCA 1953; *b* 27 July 1926; *m* 1951, Vera Joyce Crook; one *s*. *Educ:* St Martin's Sch. of Art; Royal Coll. of Art (Royal Schol.). Brit. Inst. Schol., 1954. One-man Exhibitions: Zwemmer Gall., 1956, 1957, 1959, 1964, 1967; Magdalene Street Gall., Cambridge, 1968; Stone Gall., Newcastle, 1969; Thackeray Gall., London, 1970. Represented in Group Exhibitions: Tate Gall., 1958; Jordan Gall., Toronto, 1958; Northampton, 1960; Europaisches Forum,

Alpbach, Austria, 1960; Neue Galerie, Linz, 1960; RCA, 1952-62; Painters in E Anglia, Arts Council, 1966; Bicentenary Exhibn, Royal Acad., 1768-1968, 1968. Works in permanent collections: Art Coun.; Contemp. Art Soc., GB; Contemp. Art Soc., Wales; Birmingham Art Gall.; Herbert Gall., Coventry; Kettering Art Gall.; Batley Art Gall.; Rugby Library and Mus.; Rochdale Art Gall. and Museum; Leeds City Art Gall.; Ipswich Musuem and Art Gall.; Carlisle Musuem and Art Gall.; Southend Art Gall.; Educn Cttees of Nottingham, Essex, Derbyshire, Lancs, Inner London Authority; Texas Instruments (Bedford); British American Tobacco Co., and many private collections. Visiting Lecturer: St Martin's Sch. of Art; Colchester Sch. of Art. *Recreation:* music. *Address:* The Red House, Mistley, Manningtree, Essex. *T:* Manningtree 2179.

**COLBECK-WELCH, Air Vice-Marshal Edward Lawrence,** CB 1961; OBE 1948; DFC 1941; Royal Air Force, retired; *b* 29 Jan. 1914; *s* of Major G. S. M. Colbeck-Welch, MC, Collingham, Yorks; *m* 1938, Doreen, *d* of T. G. Jenkin, Sliema, Malta; one *s* two *d*. *Educ:* Leeds Grammar Sch. Commnd RAF, 1933; No. 22 Sqdn, RAF, 1934-37; CFS Instructor Course, 1937; Flying Instr RAuxAF Sqdns, 1937-39; Staff duties, 1940; OC No. 29 Night Fighter Sqdn, 1941-42; Staff Coll., 1942; Staff duties, 1943-44; Staff duties in 2nd TAF and OC No. 139 (Bomber) Wing, 1944-45; Air Min. Dep. Dir Air Defence, 1945-47; Staff duties in USA, 1947-50; OC Fighter Stations (2), 1950-53; Air Min. Personnel Staff duties, 1954-55; student, idc 1956; Comdt Central Fighter Estab., 1957-58; SASO, HQ No. 13 (F) Group, 1959; SASO, HQ Fighter Comd RAF, 1960-63. *Recreation:* sailing. *Address:* Chestnut Grove, St John, Jersey, CI. *Clubs:* United Service, Royal Air Force, Royal Automobile; Royal Air Force Yacht, Royal Channel Islands Yacht, St Helier Yacht.

**COLBERT, Claudette;** stage and film actress; *b* Paris, 13 Sept. 1905; *d* of Georges Chauchoin and Jeanne Loew; *m* 1st, Norman Foster (marr. diss.); 2nd, Dr Joel J. Pressman (*d* 1968). Went to America, 1908. First appearances; New York Stage, 1925; London stage, 1928. Returned to Broadway stage, 1958-60. After success on Broadway, entered films, 1929. *Plays include:* Wild Westcotts, The Marionette Man, We've Got to Have M0ney, The Cat Came Back, Leah Kleschna, High Stakes, A Kiss in the Taxi, The Ghost Train, The Pearl of Great Price, The Barker, The Mulberry Bush, La Gringa, Within the Law, Fast Life, Tin Pan Alley, Dynamo, See Naples and Die, The Marriage-Go-Round. *Films include:* For the Love of Mike, The Lady Lies, Manslaughter, The Smiling Lieutenant, Sign of the Cross, Cleopatra, Private Worlds, Maid of Salem, It Happened One Night, The Gilded Lily, I Met Him in Paris, Bluebeard's Eighth Wife, Zaza, Midnight, Drums Along the Mohawk, Skylark, Remember the Day, Palm Beach Story, No Time for Love, So Proudly We Hail, Without Reservations, The Secret Heart, The Egg and I, Sleep My Love, Three Came Home, The Secret Fury, The Planter's Wife, Destiny, Versailles, Parrish. *Address:* Bellerive, St Peter, Barbados, West Indies.

**COLBERT, John Patrick;** MSc (Econ.); economist; first Chairman and Managing Director, The Industrial Credit Company Ltd, 1933-52; *b* 12 Feb. 1898; *s* of late William Colbert, JP; *m* 1927, Helena, *d* of Hermann von Campe, Nachod, Czechoslovakia; one *s* two *d*. *Educ:* Rockwell Coll.; National Univ. of Ireland (University Coll., Cork). Joined staff of The Statist, 1920; Ed., 1923-28; first Chm. and Managing Dir, The Agricultural Credit Corporation Ltd, 1928-33; formerly Lecturer on Banking and Finance at University Coll., Dublin. *Publication:* Commentary on Misconceptions regarding Money and Bank Credit, 1942 (two edns). *Address:* Carysfort House, Grove Avenue, Blackrock, Co. Dublin. *T:* 881064.

**COLBORNE, Surgeon Rear-Adm. William John,** CB 1950; FRCS; Royal Navy, Retired, and an Hon. Surgeon to HM. MRCS, LRCP 1916; FRCS 1943; retired 1951. *Address:* Croft House, Yealmpton, Devon.

**COLCHESTER, Suffragan Bishop of,** since 1966; **Rt. Rev. Roderic Norman Coote,** DD; Archdeacon of Colchester, since 1969; *b* 13 April 1915; *s* of late Comdr B. T. Coote and late Grace Harriet (*née* Robinson); *m* 1964, Erica Lynette, *d* of late Rev. E. G. Shrubbs, MBE; two *d*. *Educ:* Woking County Sch.; Trinity Coll., Dublin. Curate Asst, St Bartholomew's, Dublin, 1938-41; Missionary Priest in the Diocese of Gambia and the Rio Pongas, 1942; Bishop of Gambia and the Rio Pongas, 1951-57; Suffragan Bishop of Fulham, 1957-66. *Recreations:* tennis, squash; piano (composer and broadcaster); Irish Champion 120 yds Hurdles. *Address:* The Bishop's House, 32 Inglis Road, Colchester, Essex.

**COLCHESTER, Archdeacon of;** *see* Colchester, Suffragan Bishop of.

**COLCHESTER, Halsey Sparrowe,** CMG 1968; OBE 1960; MA Oxon; Counsellor, British Embassy, Paris, since Nov. 1968; *b* 5 March 1918; *s* of late Ernest Charles Colchester; *m* 1946, Rozanne Felicity Hastings Medhurst, *d* of late Air Chief Marshal Sir Charles Medhurst, KCB, OBE, MC; four *s* one *d*. *Educ:* Uppingham Sch.; Magdalen Coll., Oxford. Served Oxf. and Bucks Lt Inf., 1940-43; 2nd SAS Regt, 1944-46 (despatches); Captain. Joined Diplomatic Service, 1947; FO 1948-50; 2nd Sec., Istanbul, 1950-54; FO 1954-56; Consul, Zurich, 1956-60; 1st Sec., Athens, 1960-64; FO 1964-68. *Recreations:* walking, theatre-going, wild flowers. *Address:* 15 Keats Grove, Hampstead, NW3. *T:* 01-435 2676. *Club:* Travellers'.

**COLCHESTER, Trevor Charles,** CMG 1958; Secretary, Commonwealth Association of Architects, London, since 1964; *b* London, 18 April 1909; *s* of Charles Colchester; *m* 1937, Nancy Joan Russell; one *d*. *Educ:* Corpus Christi Coll., Cambridge (MA). Colonial Service, 1931-64; in Kenya, Zanzibar, and Northern Rhodesia. Sec. to Cabinet, Kenya, 1954-57; Permanent Sec., Kenya, 1957-61. *Recreations:* fishing, gardening. *Address:* Plomesgate, Aldeburgh, Suffolk.

**COLDRICK, William;** Ex-Chairman of the Co-operative Party; Ex-Member of National Council of Labour; *b* 19 Feb. 1896; two *s* one *d*. *Educ:* Elementary and Continuation Classes and Labour Coll., London. MP (Lab. and Co-op.) Bristol North, 1945-50, North-East, 1950-Sept. 1959. Ex-Mem. Monmouthshire County Council. Trustee, Bristol Trustee Savings Bank; Mem. Central Exec., Co-op. Union; Mem. Advisory Cttee, Govt Dept of Technical Co-operation. Lecturer for National Council of Labour Colls. Sheriff of the City and County of Bristol, 1964. *Publications:* articles in various journals. *Recreations:* football, cricket. *Address:* 52 The Crescent, Sea Mills, Bristol 9. *T:* Bristol 682174.

**COLDSTREAM, Sir George (Phillips),** KCB 1955 (CB 1949); KCVO 1968; QC 1960; a special consultant to the Institute of Judicial Administration, New York University, since 1968; Hon. Reader in Judicial Administration, University of Birmingham, since 1969; *b* 20 Dec. 1907; *s* of late Francis Menzies Coldstream; *m* 1st, 1934, Mary Morna (marr. diss. 1948), *o d* of Major A. D. Carmichael, Meigle, Perthshire; one *d* (and one *d* decd); 2nd, Sheila Hope, *widow* of Lt-Col J. H. H. Whitty, DSO, MC. *Educ:* Rugby; Oriel Coll., Oxford. Called to the Bar, Lincoln's Inn, 1930. Bencher, 1954; Asst to Parly Counsel to Treasury, 1934-39; Legal Asst, Lord Chancellor's Office, 1939-44; Dep. Clerk of the Crown, 1944-54; Clerk of the Crown in Chancery and Permanent Sec. to the Lord Chancellor, 1954-68; Chm., Council of Legal Education, 1970-. Hon. LLD, Columbia Univ., 1966. *Address:* 11 Old Square, Lincoln's Inn, WC2. *T:* 01-242 5316; The Gate House, Seaford, Sussex. *T:* Seaford 2801. *Clubs:* Athenæum; Royal Cruising.

**COLDSTREAM, Sir William Menzies,** Kt 1956; CBE 1952; painter; Slade Professor of Fine Art, at University College, University of London, since 1949; Vice-Chairman, Arts Council of Great Britain, 1962-69 (Member, 1953); Chairman, National Advisory Council on Art Education, since 1958; Chairman, British Film Institute, since 1964; Fellow of University College, London; *b* 28 Feb. 1908; *yr s* of George Probyn Coldstream, MB, CM, and Lilian Mercer Tod; *m* 1st, 1931, Nancy Culliford Sharp (marr. diss. 1942); two *d*; 2nd, 1961, Monica Mary Hoyer, *d* of A. E. Monrad Hoyer; one *s* two *d*. *Educ:* privately; Slade Sch. of Fine Art, University Coll., London. Member: London Artists Assoc., 1931; London Group, 1933; work represented in exhibitions of: World's Fair, NY, 1938; British Art Since Whistler, Nat. Gallery, 1939; UN Internat. Exhibition, Paris, 1946; Retrospective Exhibition, South London Gallery, 1962; Painting and Sculpture of a Decade, Tate Gallery, 1964 (represented). Pictures in the collections of: Tate Gallery, National Gallery of Canada, National Museum of Wales, Ashmolean Museum, Imperial War Museum, Arts Council, British Council, Bristol Art Gallery, etc. Works purchased by Contemporary Art Soc. and Chantrey Bequest, 1940. In association with Claude Rogers and Victor Pasmore founded the Sch. of Drawing and Painting, Euston Road, 1937. Served War of 1939-45 with RE; official War Office Artist, Middle East and Italy, 1943-45. Trustee of National Gallery, 1948-55, 1956-63; Trustee of Tate Gallery, 1949-55, 1956-63; a Dir of Royal Opera House, Covent Garden, 1957-62; Chm., Art Panel of Arts Council, 1953-62; Hon. DLitt: Nottingham, 1961; Birmingham, 1962. *Address:* University College London, Gower Street, WC1. *T:* 01-387 7050. *Clubs:* Athenæum, MCC.

**COLDWELL-SMITH, Lieut-Col Frederick Lawrence,** MVO 1934; MC; psc; Australian Staff Corps (retired 1940); *b* 1895; *s* of late Frederick Coldwell-Smith, London; *m* 1920, Ina Beryl, *d* of late C. Fuller-Russell, London. *Educ:* Agricultural High Sch., Ballarat; RMC Duntroon. Commissioned in permt Forces, 1915; served European War, 1915-19; Capt. AIF on service, 1916-19; Capt. Australian Staff Corps, 1923; Major, 1935; Lt-Col, 1939. *Address:* 3 Young Street, Warrawee, NSW, Australia. *Club:* Imperial Service (Sydney).

**COLE,** family name of **Baron Cole** and of **Earl of Enniskillen.**

**COLE,** Baron *cr* 1965, of Blackfriars (Life Peer); **George James Cole;** Chairman, Unilever Ltd, 1960-70 (Director, 1948; Vice-Chairman, 1956); Vice-Chairman, Unilever NY since 1960 (Director, 1948); Director: The Niger Co. Ltd; Finance Corporation for Industry Ltd; Commonwealth Development Finance Co. Ltd; *b* 3 Feb. 1906; *s* of late James Francis Cole and late Alice Elizabeth Wheeler; *m* 1940, Ruth, *d* of late Edward Stanley Harpham and late Rosa Harriot Driscoll; one *s* one *d*. *Educ:* Raffles Sch., Singapore. Joined a Lever Brothers Ltd subsidiary, The Niger Co. Ltd (later merged into The United Africa Co. Ltd), 1923; various positions in London and Africa till 1939 when appointed Controller for British West Africa; Staff of Resident Minister, W Africa, as Commercial Mem. at Supply Centre, 1941; Dir, The United Africa Co. Ltd, 1945-63 (Joint Man. Dir, 1952-55). Taylor Woodrow (West Africa) Ltd, 1947-55; Chm., Palm Line Ltd, 1952-55 (Dir, 1949); on European Continent for Unilever Ltd, 1955. Trustee, Leverhulme Trust; Dep. Chm., London Sch. of Business Studies; Chm., Govt Advisory Cttee on Appointment of Advertising Agents; Mem. Council: RIIA; Royal African Society; Mem. Exec. Cttee, Council of UK South Africa Trade Assoc.; Vice-Pres., Hispanic Council; Vice-Pres., Luso-Brazilian Council; Mem. Internat. Adv. Cttee, Chase Manhattan Bank; Corresp. Mem., Nat. Industrial Conf. Bd (New York). Comdr, Order of Orange Nassau, 1963. *Address:* 50 Victoria Road, W8. *T:* 01-937 9085. *Clubs:* Athenæum, Travellers', Hurlingham.

**COLE, Viscount; Andrew John Galbraith Cole;** pilot, and company director; Captain Irish Guards, 1965; *b* 28 April 1942; *s* and *heir* of 6th Earl of Enniskillen, *qv*; *m* 1964, Sarah, *o d* of Maj.-Gen. J. Keith-Edwards, Nairobi; two *d*. *Educ:* Eton. *Address:* c/o William's Deacons Bank Ltd, 9 Pall Mall, SW1.

**COLE, (Alexander) Colin;** Windsor Herald of Arms since 1966 (Fitzalan Pursuivant of Arms Extraordinary, 1953; Portcullis Pursuivant of Arms, 1957); *b* 16 May 1922; *er s* of late Capt. Edward Harold Cole, and of Blanche Ruby Lavinia (*née* Wallis); *m* 1944, Valerie, *o d* of late Capt. Stanley Walter Card; four *s* three *d*. *Educ:* Dulwich; Pembroke Coll. Cambridge; Brasenose Coll., Oxford. BCL Oxon; MA Oxon. Served War of 1939-45, Capt. Coldstream Guards. Barrister-at-law (Inner Temple), 1949. One of the Court of Assistants of the Hon. Artillery Company; Major, RA(TAVR), OC Greater London Regt, Cadre RA (Volunteers). Mem. Court of Common Council of City of London (Castle Baynard Ward), 1964-. Freeman of City of London, Freeman and Liveryman, Scriveners' Company of London. Fellow Heraldry Soc. (Mem. Council); Hon. Heraldic Adviser, Monumental Brass Soc.; Sec., College of Arms Trust; Registrar and Librarian, College of Arms, 1967. Officer of Arms attendant, Imperial Soc. of Knights Bachelor. FSA (London). OStJ. *Publications:* articles on heraldry and kindred subjects in their appropriate journals; illus. Visitations of London (1568) and Wiltshire (1623) (Harleian Soc.). *Recreations:* art, archæology, architecture, parenthood and wine-bibbing. *Address:* College of Arms, Queen Victoria Street, EC4. *T:* 01-248 1188; Holly House, Burstow, Surrey. *Clubs:* Guards, City Livery.

**COLE, Prof. Boris Norman,** BSc(Eng) (London), PhD (Birmingham), WhSch, CEng, FIMechE; Professor of Mechanical Engineering and Head of Department of Mechanical Engineering, University of Leeds, since 1962; *b* 8 Jan. 1924; *s* of James Edward Cole and Gertrude Cole; *m* 1945, Sibylle Duijts; two *s* one *d*. *Educ:* King Edward's Sch., Birmingham. Apprenticed to Messrs Bellis and Morcom Ltd, Engineers,

Birmingham. Dept of Mech. Engrg, Univ. of Birmingham: Lectr, 1949-55; Sen. Lectr, 1955-58; Reader, 1958-62; Chm. of Faculty Bd of Applied Sciences, Birmingham Univ., 1955-57 and 1959-62. Mem., Smethwick Co. Borough Educn Cttee, 1957-60. Prizewinner, IMechE, 1953 and 1962. *Publications:* numerous in fields of solid and fluid mechanics and in engineering education. *Recreations:* walking, music, social history of engineering. *Address:* 399 Gledhow Lane, Leeds 7. *T:* Leeds 621306.

**COLE, Charles Woolsey,** MA, LHD, PhD, ScD, LittD, LLD; President Emeritus, Amherst College; *b* 8 Feb. 1906; *s* of Bertha Woolsey Dwight and Charles Buckingham Cole; *m* 1928, Katharine Bush Salmon; two *d. Educ:* Montclair (New Jersey) High Sch.; Amherst Coll., Amherst, Mass; Columbia Univ., NY, Univ. Fellow, Columbia, 1928-29; Instr History, Columbia Coll., 1929-35; Travelling Fellow of Social Science Research Council in Paris, 1932-33; Assoc. Prof. Economics, Amherst Coll., 1935-37; Prof. Economics, Amherst Coll., 1937-40; Prof. Hist. in graduate faculty, Columbia, 1940-46; Pres., Amherst Coll., 1946-60. Vice-Pres., Rockefeller Foundn, 1960-61; US Ambassador to Chile, 1961-64. Chief, Service Trades Branch, Office of Price Administration, Washington, DC, 1942; Regional Price Exec., New York Office of Price Administration, 1942-43; Columbia's Navy Sch. of Military Govt and Administration in addition to lecturing at Army Sch. of Mil. Govt in Charlottesville, Va, 1943-45; Vis. Lectr in Economics at Yale Univ., New Haven, Conn., 1938-39. Trustee: Merrill Trust; Clarke Sch. for the Deaf; Hampshire Coll. Dir, Federal Reserve Bank of Boston, 1966-68. Grand Cross, Order of Merit (Chile); Grand Officer, Order of Morazán (Honduras). *Publications:* French Mercantalist Doctrines Before Colbert, 1931; Colbert and a Century of French Mercantilism, 1939; Economic History of Europe (with S. B. Clough), 1941; French Mercantilism, 1683-1700, 1943; (with C. J. H. Hayes and M. Baldwin) History of Europe, 1949; History of Western Civilization, 1967; (with H. W. Bragdon and S. P. McCutchen): A Free People: the United States in the Formative Years, 1970; A free People: the United States in the Twentieth Century, 1970; edited Macmillan Career Books. *Recreation:* fly fishing for trout. *Address:* Box 66, Amherst, Mass, USA. *Clubs:* Century, Anglers' (New York).

**COLE, Claude Neville David,** JP; Managing Director, Newcastle Chronicle and Journal Ltd; Chairman, Celtic Press Ltd; Director: Thomson Regional Newspapers Ltd; Glamorgan County Times; H. W. Southey Ltd; Glamorgan Gazette Ltd; Guardian Press (Neath) Ltd; Pugh & Rowlands (Aberdare) Ltd; South Wales Gazette, Abertillery; *b* 4 June 1928; 2nd *s* of late W. J. Cole and of Mrs M. J. Cole; *m* 1951, Alma Gwlithyn Williams; one *s* one *d* (one *s* decd). *Educ:* Royal Masonic School; Harvard Business Sch. Journalist: Merthyr Express; South Wales Echo; Daily Graphic (Manchester); Daily Sketch (London); Daily Recorder; Empire News (Cardiff); Ed., Western Mail, Cardiff, 1956-59; Man. Dir, Western Mail and Echo Ltd, 1959-67. Chm., Cole Cttee on Recruitment of Nurses in Wales, 1961-63; Chm., Working Party on Welsh Tourism, 1963-64; Member: Court of Governors of Univ. of Wales, 1962-; Council of Univ. of Wales, 1962-; Council of Welsh National Sch. of Medicine, 1964-67; Governing Body of Cardiff Coll. of Music and Drama, 1963-67; Council of Welsh National Opera; Council of Cardiff New Theatre Trust, 1964-67; Welsh Nat. Theatre Cttee; Aberfan Disaster Fund, 1966-67; Welsh Hospitals Bd, 1962-67. Vice-Patron, Coun. for Wales, Brit. Empire and Commonwealth Games. Pres., Tenovus. OStJ. *Recreations:* Two of the three R's. *Address:* Newcastle Chronicle and Journal Ltd, Thomson House, Groat Market, Newcastle upon Tyne; Ellesmere North, 20 Granville Road, Jesmond, Newcastle upon Tyne. *Clubs:* East India and Sports; County (Cardiff); Northern Counties (Newcastle upon Tyne).

**COLE, Colin;** *see* Cole, A. C.

**COLE, David Lee,** CMG 1965; MC 1944; Assistant Under-Secretary of State (Deputy Chief Clerk), Foreign and Commonwealth Office, since 1970; *b* 31 Aug. 1920; *s* of late Brig. D. H. Cole, CBE, LittD, and Charlotte Cole (*née* Wedgwood); *m* 1945, Dorothy (*née* Patton); one *s. Educ:* Cheltenham Coll.; Sidney Sussex Coll., Cambridge. MA (1st Cl. Hons History). Served Royal Inniskilling Fusiliers, 1940-45. Dominions Office, 1947; seconded to Foreign Office for service with UK Delegn to UN, New York, 1948-51; First Sec., Brit. High Commn, New Delhi, 1953-56; Private Sec. to Rt Hon. the Earl of Home (Sec. of State for Commonwealth Relations and Lord President of the Council), 1957-60; Head of Personnel Dept, CRO, 1961-63; British Dep. High Comr in Ghana, 1963-64; British High Comr in Malawi, 1964-67; Minister (Political), New Delhi, 1967-70. *Recreation:* painting. *Address:* c/o Foreign and Commonwealth Office, SW1. *Club:* Travellers'.

**COLE, Edward Nicholas;** President and Chief Operating Officer, General Motors Corporation, since Nov. 1967; *b* Marne, Michigan, USA, 17 Sept. 1909; *s* of Franklin Benjamin Cole and Lucy Catherine Cole (*née* Blasen); *m* 1964, Dollie Ann McVey; one *s* (and one *s* one *d* by a previous marriage). *Educ:* Berlin (now Marne) High Sch., Marne, Mich; Pre-Law Course, Grand Rapids Junior Coll.; General Motors Inst., Flint, Mich (BSME). General Motors, Cadillac Motor Car Div.: Cooperative Student (Gen. Motors Inst.), 1930; various posts, 1933-42; then Chief Design Engr, 1943; Asst Chief Engr, 1944; Chief Engr, 1946; Works Manager, 1950; Plant Manager, Cadillac-Cleveland Tank Plant, 1950; Chief Engr, Chevrolet Motor Div., 1952, Gen. Manager, 1956. General Motors Corporation: Vice-Pres., 1956; Director, 1961; Gp Vice-Pres. in charge of Car and Truck Divs, 1961; Exec. Vice-Pres. in charge of Ops Staff Activities, 1965. Member: Soc. of Automotive Engrs; Nat. Acad. of Engineering; Pi Tau Sigma; Delta Sigma Pi; Sigma Xi; Tau Beta Pi; etc. Numerous other social and educational activities. Holds seven hon. degrees from US Univs and Colls. *Address:* General Motors Building, 3044 West Grand Boulevard, Detroit, Michigan 48202, USA. *Clubs:* Detroit Athletic, Detroit, Recess (all Detroit); Bloomfield Hills Country.

**COLE, Maj.-Gen. Eric Stuart,** CB 1960; CBE 1945; retired; Consultant Director, Granger Associates Ltd, Weybridge; *b* 1906; *s* of John William Cole; *m* 1942, Doris Cole. Served Palestine, 1936-39; War of 1939-45 in Italy, France, Greece (despatches, CBE); Maj.-Gen., 1958; Dir of Telecommunications, War Office, 1958-61. Col Comdt Royal Corps of Signals, 1962-67. *Address:* 28 Royal Avenue, Chelsea, SW3. *Club:* Army and Navy.

**COLE, Frank;** *see* Cole, (George) Francis.

**COLE, George;** actor on stage, screen, radio and television; *b* 22 April 1925; *m* 1st, 1954, Eileen Moore (marr. diss. 1966); one *s* one *d*; 2nd,

1967, Penelope Morrell; one *d. Educ:* Surrey County Council Secondary Sch., Morden. Made first stage appearance in White Horse Inn, tour and London Coliseum, 1939; Cottage to Let, Birmingham, 1940; West End and on tour, 1940-41; subseq. West End plays included Goodnight Children, New, 1942; Mr Bolfry, Playhouse, 1943. Served in RAF, 1943-47. Returned to stage in Dr Angelus, Phoenix, 1947; The Anatomist, Westminster, 1948; Mr Gillie, Garrick, 1950; A Phoenix too Frequent and Thor with Angels, Lyric, Hammersmith, 1951; Misery Me, Duchess, 1955; Mr Bolfry, Aldwych, 1956; Brass Butterfly, Strand, 1958; The Bargain, St Martin's, 1961; The Sponge Room and Squat Betty, Royal Court, 1962; Meet Me on the Fence (tour), 1963; Hedda Gabler, St Martin's, 1964; A Public Mischief, St Martin's, 1965; Too True To Be Good, Strand, 1965; The Waiting Game, Arts, 1966; The Three Sisters, Royal Court, 1967; Doubtful Haunts, Hampstead, 1968; The Passionate Husband, 1969. *Films include:* Cottage to Let, 1941; Morning Departure, Laughter in Paradise, Scrooge, Top Secret, 1949-51; Will Any Gentleman?, The Intruder, 1952; Happy Ever After, Our Girl Friday, 1953; Belles of St Trinian's, 1954; Quentin Durward, 1955; The Weapon, It's a Wonderful World, The Green Man, 1956; Blue Murder at St Trinian's, Too Many Crooks, Don't Panic Chaps, The Bridal Path, 1957-59; The Pure Hell of St Trinian's, Cleopatra, Dr Syn, 1961-62; One Way Pendulum, Legend of Dick Turpin, 1964; Great St Trinian's Train Robbery, 1965. TV Series include Life of Bliss (also radio), A Man of our Times. *Address:* Donnelly, Newnham Hill Bottom, Nettlebed, Oxon. *Club:* Royal Automobile.

**COLE, George Francis, (Frank);** Chairman: National Exhibition Centre Ltd; Alltransport Ltd; Cyprien-Fox Ltd; Davell & Rufford (Holdings) Ltd; Director, Shipping Industrial Holdings Ltd; *b* 3 Nov. 1918; *m* 1940, Gwendoline Mary Laver; two *s* one *d. Educ:* Manchester Grammar Sch. Dir and Gen. Manager, Clarkson Engineers Ltd, 1944-53; Gen. Man., Ariel Motors Ltd (BSA Group), 1953-55; Dir, then Man. Dir, Vono Ltd, 1955-67. Past Chairman: Grovewood Products Ltd; Portways Ltd; R. & W. H. Symington Holdings Ltd; Past Director, Duport Ltd. Pres., Birmingham Chamber of Commerce and Industry, 1968-69. Leader of Trade Missions to West Germany, Yugoslavia, Romania and Hungary. Member: Export Council for Europe; BNEC Denman Working Party; Brit. Inst. Management; Life Governor, Birmingham Univ.; Liveryman of City of London. Radio and Television appearances. *Publications:* press articles on economics, exports, etc. *Recreations:* tennis, oil painting. *Address:* Tudor Cottage, Barston, Solihull, Warwicks. *T:* Hampton-in-Arden 2724.

**COLE, Lieut-Gen. Sir George Sinclair,** KCB 1965 (CB 1962); CBE 1953; Vice-Chief of the Defence Staff, 1966-67, retired; *b* 12 March 1911; *s* of Capt. A. V. Cole, Fen Farm, Elmstead; *m* 1943, Sybil Irene Russell, *d* of W. R. Stoneham, JP; one *s* one *d. Educ:* Wellington Coll.; RMA Woolwich. Commissioned RA 1931; served War of 1939-45, BEF 1939-40; GSO1, Mil. Ops, WO, 1943-44; OC 58 LAA Regt RA, 21 Army Group, 1945; Military Assistant: to CIGS, 1946-48; to Chm. Western Europe Comdrs-in-Chief, 1949; jssc, Latimer, 1950; Dep. Chief of Staff, ALFCE, 1950-51; Head, Exercise Planning Staff, SHAPE, 1951-52; idc, 1953; OC 40 Fd Regt RA, Egypt and Cyprus, 1954-55; CRA 1 Inf. Div., 1956-59; Sec., Chiefs of Staff Cttee, 1959-61; Dir of Staff Duties, War Office, 1961-64; GOC-in-C, Eastern Command, 1965-66. Col Comdt, RA, 1965-70. *Recreations:* golf, fishing, bridge. *Address:* Moy Lodge, Old Avenue, West Byfleet, Surrey. *T:* Byfleet 46376. *Clubs:* Army and Navy; Jesters; Rye Golf; Woking Golf.

**COLE, Dr Herbert Aubrey,** CMG 1967; Director of Fishery Research, Ministry of Agriculture, Fisheries and Food, since 1958; *b* 24 Feb. 1911; *s* of Edwin Aubrey Cole, Farmer; *m* 1936, Elizabeth Lloyd; two *s* one *d. Educ:* Friars Sch., Bangor, N Wales; Univ. Coll. of N Wales. Entire career in Fishery Research, Min. of Agric., Fisheries and Food. *Publications:* numerous articles in learned jls. *Recreation:* gardening. *Address:* Garth, Normanston Drive, Lowestoft, Suffolk. *T:* Lowestoft 5839.

**COLE, Humphrey John Douglas;** Head, Regional Economics and Statistics Branch, Ministry of Technology, since 1969; *b* 30 Jan. 1928; *s* of late G. D. H. Cole and of Dame Margaret I. Cole, *qv*; *m* 1955, Hilda Annette Robinson; two *s* one *d. Educ:* Winchester Coll.; Trinity Coll., Cambridge. Research, Oxford Inst. of Statistics, 1950-61; Head, Economic Indicators and Foreign Trade, OECD Statistics Div., 1961-66; Dept of Economic Affairs: Senior Economic Adviser (Regional), 1966-67; Asst Dir of Economics, 1967-69. *Publications:* articles in Bulletin of Inst. of Statistics, 1950-61. *Recreations:* walking, family. *Address:* 3 The Mead, W13. *T:* 01-997 8285.

**COLE, John,** ROI; RBA; NEAC; landscape painter, especially of old shop fronts; *b* 2 Nov. 1903; *s* of late Rex Vicat Cole, ROI, RBC. Mem. Council, Artists' Gen. Benevolent Instn; Mem. Council of Management, Byam Shaw Sch. of Drawing and Painting Ltd; Chm., St James Art Soc. (for the Deafened); Chm., The Campden Hill Club. Paris Salon Silver Medal, 1952; Paris Salon Gold Medal, 1954. Works in public collections: Aberdeen; Manchester; Salford; Eastbourne; Greenock; Paisley; Newport (Mon.); Nat. Gall., Wellington, NZ; Hastings Corporation Art Gall.; Kensington (Leighton House). *Address:* The Duke of Sussex Studios, 44 Uxbridge Street, Kensington, W8.

**COLE, John Sydney Richard,** QC (Somaliland); BA; Barrister-at-Law; Lecturer, Law School, University of Dublin, since 1966; *b* 24 Jan. 1907; *o s* of late Rev. R. Lee Cole, MA, BD, Dublin; *m* 1st, 1931, Doreen Mathews (*d* 1966); one *s* one *d*; 2nd, 1968, Mrs Deirdre Gallet. *Educ:* Methodist Coll., Belfast; Cork Gram. Sch.; Trinity Coll., Dublin (Scholar and Moderator). Master, Royal Coll., Mauritius, 1930-36; Education Officer, Nigeria, 1936-40; Crown Counsel, Nigeria, 1940-46; Attorney-Gen., Bahamas, 1946-51, Somaliland Protectorate, 1951-56; Attorney-Gen. and Minister for Legal Affairs, Tanganyika, 1956-61; retired, 1961. English Legal Draftsman to Government of Republic of Sudan, 1962-65. Reid Prof. of Penal Legislation, Univ. of Dublin, 1965-66. *Publication:* (with W. N. Denison) Tanganyika - the Development of its Laws and Constitution, 1964. *Recreations:* walking, swimming. *Address:* 2 Rus in Urbe, Glenageary, Dublin. *Clubs:* Athenæum; University (Dublin).

**COLE, Leslie Barrett,** MA, MD Cantab, FRCP; Consultant Physician, Addenbrooke's Hospital, Cambridge; Fellow of King's College, Cambridge, 1949-66; Dean of Post Graduate Medical School, University of Cambridge, 1957-65; *b* 1898; *s* of Samuel Barrett Cole and Annie Gammon; *m* 1927, Mary, *d* of late Surg. Capt. H. W. Finlayson, DSO; three *s. Educ:* Leighton Park Sch.; King's

Coll., Cambridge (Exhibitioner). Served European War, 1916-18, RFA, India and Mesopotamia; RAMC 1939-41, BEF France. St Thomas's Hosp. (Medical Registrar and Resident Asst Physician; Mead Medal and Toller Prize); formerly Physician: W Suffolk Hosp.; Papworth Hosp. Assessor, MD Cttee, Univ. of Cambridge, 1958-65; Late Examiner: IN Medicine for MRCP and to Univs of Oxford, Cambridge and Bristol, also Conjoint Board; in Pharmacology, to Univ. of Cambridge; in Pathology to Conjoint Board. Royal College of Physicians: Councillor, 1950; Censor, 1960-62; Sen. Censor and Sen. Vice-Pres., 1964-65. Hon. Lt-Col RAMC. *Publications:* Dietetics in General Practice, 1939; numerous contribs to medical journals on cardiology, diabetes and general medical subjects and on tetanus to Quart. Jl of Medicine, Index of Treatment, British Encyclopædia of Medical Practice and Surgery of Modern Warfare. *Recreations:* riding, sailing. *Address:* 15 Fitzwilliam Street, Cambridge. *T:* Cambridge 50836. *Club:* Athenæum.

**COLE, Dame Margaret Isabel,** DBE 1970 (OBE 1965); author and lecturer; *b* Cambridge, 1893; *d* of Prof. J. P. Postgate, LittD, Prof. of Latin, Univ. of Liverpool, and Edith Allen; *m* 1918, G. D. H. Cole (*d* 1959); one *s* two *d. Educ:* Roedean Sch., Brighton; Girton Coll., Cambridge (1st class Hons Classical Tripos). Classical Mistress, St Paul's Girls' Sch., 1914-16; Asst Sec., Labour Research Dept, 1916-25; Lectr for Univ. Tutorial Classes, London, 1925-49, Cambridge, 1941-44; Contributor to Evening Standard, New Statesman, Guardian, Listener, etc; Hon. Sec., New Fabian Research Bureau, 1935-39; of Fabian Soc., 1939-53; Chm., 1955; Pres., 1963-; Mem., LCC Education Cttee, 1943-65; Alderman, 1952-65; Chm., Further Education Cttee, 1951-60 and 1961-65; Mem., ILEA Educn Cttee, 1965-67; Vice-Chm., Further and Higher Education Sub-Cttee, 1965-67. *Publications:* The Bolo Book (with G. D. H. Cole), 1923; Twelve Studies in Soviet Russia (ed), 1932; Roads to Success (ed), 1936; Women of To-Day, 1937; Marriage Past and Present, 1938; Books and the People, 1938; Democratic Sweden (ed.), 1938; Evacuation Survey (ed), 1940; Our Soviet Ally (ed), 1943; Beatrice Webb: a Memoir, 1945; (part Editor) Our Partnership, 1948; Makers of the Labour Movement, 1948; The Webbs and Their Work (ed), 1949; Growing up into Revolution, 1949; The Diaries of Beatrice Webb (ed), 1952; Robert Owen of New Lanark, 1953; The Diaries of Beatrice Webb II (ed), 1956; Servant of the County, 1956; The Story of Fabian Socialism, 1961; also detective novels and works on politics, etc, jointly with late G. D. H. Cole, for many years. *Recreations:* reading, looking at own and other countries. *Address:* 74 Addison Way, NW11. *T:* 01-455 0245. *Clubs:* Arts Theatre, English-Speaking Union.
*See also H. J. D. Cole.*

**COLE, Prof. Monica M.;** Professor of Geography, Bedford College, University of London, since 1964; *b* 5 May 1922; *d* of William Henry Parnall Cole and Dorothy Mary Cole (*née* Thomas). *Educ:* Wimbledon County Grammar Sch.; Bedford Coll., Univ. of London. Research Asst, Min. of Town and Country Planning, Cambridge, 1944-45; Postgrad. study, Univ. of London, 1945-46; Lectr in Geography: Univ. of Capetown, 1947; Univ. of Witwatersrand, 1948-51, Univ. of Keele, 1951-64. Assoc. Prof., Univ. of Idaho summer sch., 1952; Vis. Lectr, Univs of Queensland, Melbourne, and Adelaide, 1960. Mem. British delegn Internat. Geographical Congress in: Washington, 1952; Rio de Janeiro, 1956; London, 1964; New Delhi, 1968. Research vegetation/soils/geomorphology: S Africa, 1948-51; Brazil, 1956, 1965; Central and E Africa, 1959; Australia, 1960, 1962, 1963, 1965, 1966, 1967, 1968; Venezuela, 1964; Southern Africa, 1967, 1968. *Publications:* The Transvaal Lowveld, 1956; South Africa, 1961, 1966; contribs to Geograph. Jl, Geography, Trans. Inst. Brit. Geographers, S African Geograph. Jl, Trans. Instn Mining and Metallurgy, Proc. Royal Soc. *Recreations:* painting, photography, tennis, squash, walking, climbing. *Address:* Bedford College, Regents Park, NW1.

**COLE, Norman John,** VRD; RNVR since 1934; Lieutenant-Commander (S); *b* 1 June 1909; *s* of Walter John Cole and Maud Mary (*née* Thomas); *m* 1935, Margaret Grace, *d* of Arthur James Potter, Buxton, Derbyshire; one *s* two *d. Educ:* St John's Coll., Southsea. Served abroad War of 1939-45, with Royal Navy. Formerly held offices in Conservative Associations in Barnet Vale and Potters Bar. Mem. of Potters Bar Urban District Council, 1947-48. MP (L and C) South Division of Bedfordshire, 1951-66. Has served for many years on numerous youth, health, welfare and church cttees. *Recreations:* formerly Association football, cricket, tennis. *Address:* Derwent House, 50 Station Road, New Barnet, Herts. *T:* 01-449 5076.

**COLE, Ven. Ronald Berkeley;** Archdeacon of Leicester since 1963 (of Loughborough, 1953-63) and Vicar of St Philip, Leicester, since 1950; *b* 20 Oct. 1913; *s* of James William and Florence Caroline Cole; *m* 1943, Mabel Grace Chapman; one *s* one *d. Educ:* Bishop's Coll., Cheshunt. Registrar, London County Freehold and Leasehold Properties Ltd, 1934-40. Deacon, 1942; Priest, 1943; Curate, Braunstone, Leicester, 1942-48; Succentor, Leicester Cathedral, 1948-50. Hon. Chaplain, 1949-53, Examining Chaplain, 1956-, to Bishop of Leicester. *Recreations:* gardening, motoring. *Address:* St Philip's Vicarage, Leicester LE5 5TR. *T:* Leicester 736204.

**COLE, William Charles,** MVO 1966; DMus, FRAM, FRCM; FRCO; Secretary, Associated Board of the Royal Schools of Music, since 1962; The Master of the Music at the Queen's Chapel of the Savoy since 1954; Conductor, Leith Hill Musical Festival, since 1954; President, Surrey County Music Association, since 1958; Member Council, Royal College of Organists, since 1960 (Hon. Treasurer since 1964; President, 1970-71); Hon. Secretary, Royal Philharmonic Society, since 1969; *b* 9 Oct. 1909; *s* of Frederick George Cole and Maria (*née* Fry), Camberwell, London; *m* 1st, Elizabeth Brown Caw (*d* 1942); three *d*; 2nd, Winifred Grace Mitchell; one *s. Educ:* St Olave's Grammar Sch.; RAM. Organist and Choirmaster, Dorking Parish Church, 1930; Music Master, Dorking County Sch., 1931; served War of 1939-45, in Air Ministry; Hon. Musical Dir, Toynbee Hall, 1947-58; Prof. of Harmony and Composition, and Lectr in History of Music, Royal Academy of Music, 1945-62; Royal Academy of Dancing: Lectr, 1948-62; Chm. Music Cttee, 1961-68; Mem. Exec. Council, 1965-68; Conductor, People's Palace Choral Soc., 1947-63. Pres., The London Assoc. of Organists, 1963-66. Mem. Education Cttee, Surrey CC, 1951-62. *Publications:* Rudiments of Music, 1951; chapter on Development of British Ballet Music, in The Ballet in Britain, 1962; The Form of Music, 1959; articles in various musical jls. *Recreation:* stained glass. *Address:* 14 Bedford Square, WC1. *T:* 01-636 6379; Packways, Hindhead, Surrey. *T:* Hindhead 917. *Club:* Garrick.

**COLE, Maj.-Gen. William Scott,** CB 1949; CBE 1946; Army Officer, retired; *b* 29 March 1902; *s* of late W. Scott Cole; *m* 1948, Kathleen Winifred Coleing; one *d*. *Educ:* Victoria Coll., Jersey; RMA Woolwich. Commissioned into the Corps of Royal Engineers, 1921. Served War of 1939-45; Temp. Brig., 1943; Substantive Col, 1945; Subs. Brig., 1951; temp. Maj.-Gen., 1955; Subs. Maj.-Gen., 1956; retd 1958. *Club:* Army and Navy.

**COLE-HAMILTON, John,** CBE 1954; DL; *b* 15 Oct. 1899; *s* of late Col A. R. Cole-Hamilton; *m* 1930, Gladys Cowie; one *s* two *d*. *Educ:* Royal Academy, Irvine. Served European War, 1914-19, with RFC and RAF. Major, Home Guard, 1942. DL for County of Ayr, 1951. *Address:* Beltrim House, Kilwinning, Ayrshire.

**COLEBROOK, Edward Hilder,** CIE 1946; MC 1918; KPM 1924; Indian Police, retired; *b* 16 Oct. 1898; *s* of Edward Colebrook. Served European War, 1914-18, East Surrey Regt; Lieut, 1917-20; Indian Police, 1921-49, retired as Dep. Inspector-Gen. indian Police Medal, 1936. Mem. Guildford Borough Council, 1956-68. *Address:* Holly Mount, 21a Austen Road, Guildford, Surrey. *T:* Guildford 67727. *Club:* East India and Sports.

**COLEBROOK, Philip Victor Charles,** CEng, AMIChemE; Managing Director of Pfizer Ltd since 1958; Chairman and Managing Director of the Pfizer Group 1961-69; Vice-President, Pfizer International, since 1967; Managing Director of Calor Gas Holding Company, since 1969; *b* 8 March 1924; *s* of Frederick Charles Colebrook and Florence Margaret (*née* Cooper); *m* 1946, Dorothy Ursula Kemp; one *s* three *d*. *Educ:* Andover Grammar Sch.; Guildford Technical Coll.; Battersea Polytechnic, London. Served War of 1939-45, RNVR. Joined Pfizer as Works and Production Manager, 1952; appointed Dir, Pfizer Ltd, 1956. Mem., NHS Affairs Cttee, Assoc. of the British Pharmaceutical Industry, 1963-67. Trustee and Mem. of Steering Cttee, Univ. of Kent at Canterbury, 1964-65. *Recreations:* sailing, ski-ing, golf. *Address:* Greenway, Salisbury Road, St Margaret's Bay, Kent. *Clubs:* Reform; Royal Cinque Ports Yacht.

**COLEMAN, Arthur Percy;** Secretary, British Museum (Natural History), since 1965; *b* 8 Feb. 1922; *s* of Percy Coleman and Gladys May Coleman (*née* Fisher); *m* 1948, Peggy (*née* Coombs); two *d*. *Educ:* Wanstead Co. High Sch.; Bristol Univ. War Service in 1st King George V Own Gurkha Rifles, 1943-47; Min. of Public Building and Works, 1948-61; HM Treasury, 1961-64. *Recreations:* flowering shrubs, wild life, golf. *Address:* The Orchard, Vicarage Road, Coopersale, Epping, Essex. *T:* Epping 4180.

**COLEMAN, Lieut-Gen. Sir Charles;** *see* Coleman, Lieut-Gen. Sir Cyril F. C.

**COLEMAN, Lt-Gen. Sir (Cyril Frederick) Charles,** KCB 1957 (CB 1950); CMG 1954; DSO 1945; OBE 1944; Lieutenant-Governor and C-in-C of Guernsey, 1964-69; *b* Plymouth; *s* of late A. E. Coleman, Downderry, Cornwall; *m* 1935, Margaret Mary, *d* of late Bruce Petrie, Singapore; three *d*. *Educ:* Plymouth Coll.; RMC Sandhurst. 2nd Lieut The Welch Regt, 1923; Adjt 2nd Bn The Welch Regt, 1932-35; Service in China, Malaya, India; OC 4th Bn The Welch Regt, 1941-44; comd 160th Inf. Bde, 1944-46, in NW Europe (despatches); Staff Coll., 1946; comd 160th Inf. Bde, 1947-48; GOC South-Western District and 43rd (Wessex) Inf. Div., 1949-51; GOC Berlin (British Sector), 1951-54; Chief of Staff, Northern Army Group, BAOR, 1954-56; GOC-in-C Eastern Comd, 1956-59; retd 1959. Col The Welch Regt, 1958-65. Militaire Willemsorde (Netherlands), 1947. KStJ 1964. *Recreations:* shooting, hockey (Wales). *Address:* c/o Lloyds Bank Ltd, 6 Pall Mall, SW1. *Club:* Army and Navy.

**COLEMAN, Donald Richard;** MP (Lab) Neath since 1964; Parliamentary Private Secretary to the Secretary of State for Wales, since 1968; *b* 19 Sept. 1925; *s* of late Albert Archer Coleman and of Winifred Marguerite Coleman; *m* 1949, Phyllis Eileen (*née* Williams) (*d* 1963); one *s*; *m* 1966, Margaret Elizabeth Morgan; one *d*. *Educ:* Cadoxton Boys' Sch., Barry; Cardiff Technical Coll. Laboratory Technician, Welsh National Sch. of Medicine, Cardiff, 1940-42; Central Tuberculosis Laboratory, Cardiff, 1942-46; Sen. Technician, Swansea Technical Coll., 1946-50; University Coll., Swansea, 1950-54; Metallurgist, Research Dept, Steel Co. of Wales Ltd, Abbey Works, Port Talbot, 1954 until election to Parliament. PPS to Minister of State for Wales, 1967-68. *Address:* Penderyn, 18 Penywern Road, Bryncoch, Neath, Glamorgan. *T:* Neath 4599.

**COLEMAN, Laurence Vail;** Director Emeritus, American Association of Museums, since 1958; *b* 19 Sept. 1893; *s* of Thaddeus Vail Coleman and Kate Pratt; *m* 1917, Martine Weeks (decd); three *s*; *m* 1939, Susannah Armstrong. *Educ:* B. S. College of City of New York, 1915; MA Yale Univ., 1919; grad. work, Harvard Univ., 1919. Research Asst, NY State Commn on Ventilation, 1915; Asst in public health, American Museum Natural History, 1916; Asst in Zoology, Peabody Museum Natural History, 1917; US Army, 1918; Chief of Exhibits, American Museum Natural History, 1919-21; Dir, Safety Inst. America, 1921-23; Exec. Sec., American Assoc. of Museums, 1923-26; Dir, 1927-58. Trustee, Edward MacDowell Assoc., 1939-47; Hill-Stead Museum Trust, Connecticut, 1946-49; Mem. Executive Cttee, Internat. Museums Office, Paris, 1930-36; Educational Advisory Cttee, Pan-American Union, 1929-34; Jt Cttee on Materials for Research of American Council of Learned Societies and Social Science Research Council, 1931-40; Nat Cttee of USA on Intellectual Co-operation of the League of Nations, 1932-46; Cttee on Conservation of Cultural Resources, of National Resources Planning Board, 1941-43; US Nat. Cttee of Internat. Council of Museums, 1948-51. Hon. Fellow, The Museums Assoc. (British); Fellow, Rochester Museum Assoc.; Mid-west Museums Conf., USA; Charter Mem., Nat. Trust for Historical Preservation. Surveys of Museums in: USA, 1924 and 1932-34; Europe, 1927 and 1938; South America, 1928 and 1937; Canada, 1942. Received Alumni Service Medal, 1933, and Townsend Harris Medal, 1944, of College of City of New York; Distinguished Service Award of American Assoc. of Museums, 1940. *Publications:* Manual for Small Museums, 1927; Museums in South America, 1929; Historic House Museums, 1933; The Museum in America (3 vols), 1939, 1970; College and University Museums, 1942; Company Museums, 1942; Museum Buildings (vol. 1), 1950; (with Beardsley Ruml) Manual of Corporate Giving, 1952; contribs to educational magazines in US and Europe. *Address:* 3801 Connecticut Avenue NW, Washington, DC 20008, USA. *Clubs:* Cosmos (Emeritus Mem.) (Washington); Lake Placid (NY State).

**COLEMAN, Rt. Rev. William Robert,** DD; Professor of Humanities, York University, Toronto; *b* Ulverton, Quebec, 16 Aug. 1917; *s* of Rev. Stanley Harold Coleman and Mary Ann Coleman (*née* Armstrong); *m* 1947, Mary Elizabeth Charmes, *er d* of Thomas Summers and Marion Wilson; one *s* two *d*. *Educ:* St Mary's Collegiate Inst.; Brantford Collegiate Inst.; University Coll. and Wycliffe Coll. (BD); Univ. of Toronto (MA); Union Theological Seminary, New York (STM); Univs of Cambridge and Edinburgh. Deacon, 1942; Priest, 1943; Curate, Church of the Epiphany, Sudbury, Ont., 1942-43; Priest-in-charge, 1943-45; post-graduate study, 1945-47; Prof. of Religious Philosophy and Ethics, Wycliffe Coll., 1947-50; Dean of Divinity and Harold Prof., Bishop's Coll., Lennoxville, Quebec, 1950-52; Principal, Huron Coll., London, Ont., 1952-61; Bishop of Kootenay, 1961-65. FRSA, London. DD Wycliffe Coll., 1951. DD (Hon.) Huron Coll., 1961; DD (Hon.) Trinity Coll., Toronto, 1962. *Publications:* contributed to: In Such an Age (ed. W. C. Lockhart), 1951; The Church in the Sixties (ed. P. Jefferson), 1962. *Address:* 11 Catford Road, Apt 908, Downsview, Ontario, Canada.

**COLERAINE,** 1st Baron *cr* 1954, of Haltemprice; **Richard Kidston Law,** PC 1943; *b* Helensburgh, 27 Feb. 1901; *y s* of late Rt Hon. Andrew Bonar Law and Annie Pitcairn Robley; *m* 1929, Mary Virginia, *y d* of late A. F. Nellis, Rochester, NY; two *s*. *Educ:* Shrewsbury Sch.; St John's Coll., Oxford. Travelled in Asia Minor, India, Canada, United States, and South America; editorial staff, Morning Post, 1927; New York Herald-Tribune, 1928; Philadelphia Public Ledger, 1929; MP (U) SW Hull, 1931-45; (C) South Kensington Div., Nov. 1945-Feb. 1950; Haltemprice Div. of Kingston-on-Hull, 1950-54. Financial Sec., War Office, 1940-41; Parly Under-Sec. of State, Foreign Office, 1941-43; Minister of State, 1943-45; Minister of Education, 1945. Leader, UK Delegn Hotsprings Conf. on Food and Agriculture, 1943. Mem., Medical Research Council, 1936-40; Mem., Industrial Health Research Board, 1936-40; Chm. of Council of British Socs for Relief Abroad, 1945-49-54; Chm., Nat. Youth Employment Council, 1955-62; Chm., Central Transport Consultative Cttee, 1955-58; Chm., Mansfield House Univ. Settlement, 1953-66; Hon. Treas., British Sailors Soc., 1955-; Chm., Marshall Scholarship Commn, 1956-65; Chm., Standing Advisory Cttee on Pay of Higher Civil Service, 1957-61. Chm., Postgraduate Medical Sch. of London, 1958-. Chairman: Bromilow & Edwards Ltd; Victory Insurance Co.; Director, prudential Assurance Co. Ltd; and other public cos. Hon. LLD New Brunswick, 1951. *Publications:* The Individual and the Community in Ernest Barker's The Character of England, 1947; Return from Utopia, 1950; For Conservatives Only, 1970. *Recreations:* sailing, walking. *Heir:* *s* Hon. (James) Martin (Bonar) Law [*b* 8 Aug. 1931; *m* 1st, 1958, Emma Elizabeth (marr. diss, 1966), *o d* of late Nigel Richards and of Mrs H. C. C. Batten; two *d*; 2nd, 1966, Patricia, *yr d* of Maj.-Gen. Ralph Farrant; one *d*]. *Address:* 43b Sloane Street, SW1. *Clubs:* Carlton; Royal Yacht Squadron.

**COLERIDGE,** family name of **Baron Coleridge.**

**COLERIDGE,** 4th Baron *cr* 1873, of Ottery St Mary; **Richard Duke Coleridge,** CBE 1951 (OBE 1944); Captain Royal Navy, retired; Executive Secretary, NATO, Brussels, 1952-70; *b* 24 Sept. 1905; *e s* of 3rd Baron Coleridge and Jessie Alethea Mackarness (*d* 1957); *S* father, 1955; *m* 1936, Rosamund, *er d* of Admiral Sir W. W. Fisher, GCB, GCVO; two *s*. *Educ:* RNC Osborne and Dartmouth. Entered RN, 1919; RN Staff Course, 1938; invalided off Med. station and retd, 1939; rejoined, 1940, Asst Sec., Offices of War Cabinet and of Minister of Defence, with appt to GQG Vincennes, France; War Cabinet Office in London, July 1940-May 1941; Jt Staff Mission, Washington, May 1941; Dep. Sec. to Brit. Jt Staff and Combined Chiefs of Staff, 1942-45, and attended the Confs of Washington, Quebec (1942 and 1943), Cairo, Malta and Yalta; Council of Foreign Ministers, London Conf., Sept. 1945; UN Assembly in London, Jan. 1946; UK Sec. of Mil. Staff Cttee of UN, New York, 1946-48; Sec. to Brit. Jt Services Mission in Washington, 1948, and also Chief Staff Officer to Marshal of the RAF Lord Tedder (Chm. of Brit. Chiefs of Staff Cttee and Brit. Rep. on Standing Gp of NATO, 1950-51); rep. Brit. Chiefs of Staff on Temp. Cttee of Council of NATO, in Paris, 1951; attended Lisbon Conf., 1952. US Legion of Merit. *Heir:* *s* Hon. William Duke Coleridge, Major Coldstream Guards [*b* 18 June 1937; *m* 1962, Everild (Judy), *o d* of Lt-Col and Mrs Beauchamp Hambrough, Wisper's Farm, Nairobi; one *s* one *d*]. *Address:* The Chanter's House, Ottery St Mary, S Devon. *T:* Ottery St Mary 2417. *Club:* United Service.

**COLERIDGE, Lady (Marguerite) Georgina;** *b* 19 March 1916; *d* of 11th Marquess of Tweeddale; *m* 1941, Arthur Coleridge, *yr s* of John Duke Coleridge; one *d*. *Educ:* home, abroad as a child. Joined National Magazine Co.: Circulation Dept, 1937; Advertisement Dept., 1938; joined Country Life, 1945; Editor of Homes and Gardens, 1949-63; Chm., Inst. of Journalists (London District), 1954; Chm., Women's Press Club, 1959 (Pres., 1965-67). Dir, Country Life Ltd, 1962-; Dir, George Newnes Ltd, 1963; Publisher: Homes and Gardens, 1969-; Woman's Journal, 1969-; Ideal Home, 1970-. *Publications:* Grand Smashional Pointers (book of cartoons), 1934; I Know What I Like (clichés and platitudes), 1959. *Recreations:* flat-racing, detective stories, cooking; nothing highbrow. *Address:* 33 Peel Street, W8. *T:* 01-727 7732. *Clubs:* Writers' Press, PEN.

**COLES, Captain (RNR retired) Arthur Edward,** RD (with clasp); Commodore, Orient Line, retired; *b* 2 July 1902; *s* of late Arthur Coles, FCIS, and Ella May Coles; *m* 1940, Dorothy Blanche, *widow* of G. A. Griffin; no *c*. *Educ:* King Edward's Sch., Bath, Somerset. Cadet in Macandrew's Line, 1918. Joined RNR as probationary Sub-Lieut, 1927; joined Orient Line, 1928. Served Royal Navy, 1938-46; War of 1939-45 (despatches thrice, 1940; Dieppe, 1942; Normandy, 1944): HMS Malaya, 1939; Fleet Mine-sweepers; 9th Flotilla, 1941-42, 18th Flotilla, 1943-44; HMS Lochinvar (Trg Comdr), 1945-46. In command Orient Line ships, 1951-62. Younger Brother of Trinity House, 1951-. *Recreations:* motoring, photography. *Address:* Engleberg, 80 Dagger Lane, West Bromwich, Staffs. *T:* 021-553 0827. *Club:* Birmingham Conservative.

**COLES, Sir Arthur (William),** Kt 1960; *b* 6 Aug. 1892; *s* of George and Elizabeth Coles; *m* 1919, Lilian Florence Knight; two *s* three *d* (and one *s* decd). *Educ:* State Sch.; Geelong Coll. Served European War, 1914-18: 6th Bn, 1914, Gallipoli and France; commissioned, 1916; wounded thrice. Original partner in retail firm of G. J. Coles & Co., 1919; Dir and Gen. Man. on formation of Company, 1921; Managing Dir, 1931-44. JP 1934; Mem. Melbourne City Council, 1934-44; Lord Mayor of Melbourne, 1938-39-40; MP, Henty, Vic., 1940, resigned, 1946. Mem. Commonwealth War Workers Housing Trust, 1941-45; Chairman: Commonwealth War Damage Commn, 1942-48; Commonwealth Rationing Commn, 1942-

50; Austr. Nat. Airlines Commn, 1946-50; British Commonwealth Pacific Airlines, 1946-50; Geelong Coll. Council, 1939-68; Austr. Trustees, Northcote Immigration Trust, 1952. Vice-Chm., Trusts Corp. of Presbyterian Church of Vic., 1957-; Mem., Commonwealth Immigration Planning council, 1948-68; Part-time Mem. of Executive, CSIRO, 1956-65; Mem. Advisory Council, CSIRO, 1965; Australian Delegations to Commonwealth Agricultural Bureaux: Quinquennial Conf., London, 1960; Leader Delegn, 1965. *Recreation:* golf. *Address:* 48 Irving Road, Toorak, Victoria 3142, Australia. *T:* 20-6030. *Clubs:* Athenæum, Metropolitan Golf, Peninsula Country Golf (all in Victoria, Australia).

*See also Sir E. B. Coles, Sir G. J. Coles, Sir K. F. Coles.*

**COLES, Sir Edgar (Barton),** Kt 1959; Director, G. J. Coles & Co. Ltd, Melbourne; *b* St James, Vic, 3 June 1899; *s* of George Coles, Horsham, Vic.; *m* Mabel Irene, CBE 1965, *d* of Edward Johnson; one *s* two *d*. *Educ:* Scotch Coll., Launceston, Tasmania. Bank of NSW, 1916-19; G. J. Coles & Co.: joined, 1919; Sec., 1921-34; Dir, 1930-; Joint Managing Dir, 1940-44; Sole Managing Dir, 1944-61, Controlling Managing Dir, 1961-67, and Deputy Chm., 1958-61; Vice-Chm., 1961-63; Chm., 1963-68. Pres., Retail Traders Assoc. of Vic, 1946-48 and 1951-54. Pres., Australian Council of Retailers, 1952-54; Councillor of Royal Agricultural Soc., 1957-. *Recreations:* golf, photography. *Address:* Hendra, Mt Eliza, Vic 3930, Australia. *T:* Mt Eliza 71291; 236 Bourke Street, Melbourne, Vic 3000, Australia. *Clubs:* Athenæum (Melbourne); Victoria Racing; Victoria Amateur Turf; Melbourne Cricket; Lawn Tennis Assoc. of Victoria; Peninsula Golf.

*See also Sir A. W. Coles, Sir G. J. Coles, Sir K. F. Coles.*

**COLES, Sir George (James),** Kt 1957; CBE 1942; Founder and Director, G. J. Coles & Co.; *b* 28 March 1885; *s* of George Coles, Horsham, and Elizabeth Coles (*née* Scouler); *m* 1920, Margaret Gertrude, *d* of C. Herbert; one *s* three *d* (and one *d* decd). *Educ:* Beechworth Grammar Sch. Served War as L-Corp. 60th Bn AIF, 1916-18. Founded G. J. Coles and Co., 1914; Man. Dir, 1923-31; Chm., 1923-56. *Publication:* Chain Store Economics, 1927. *Recreations:* golf, bowls. *Address:* 55 Lansell Road, Toorak, Vic 3142, Australia. *T:* 24-4901. *Clubs:* Athenæum (Melbourne); Peninsula Country Golf.

*See also Sir A. W. Coles, Sir E. B. Coles, Sir K. F. Coles.*

**COLES, Gordon Robert;** General Manager, Antrim and Ballymena Development Commission, since 1968; *b* 24 Nov. 1913; *s* of Major Ernest A. Coles, MC, and late Florence L. B. Coles; *m* 1939, Georgina Elizabeth, *d* of late George Canning and Agnes Canning (*née* Watson), of Belfast; two *s* one *d*. *Educ:* St Albans Sch.; Imperial Coll., London Univ. DIC, BSc(Eng), ACGI. Civil Engineer, LMS Railway, 1935-37; HM Inspector of Factories, Home Office, 1937-39. Served War of 1939-45: Royal Engineers (Lt Col), England, Middle East (despatches), and India. HM Inspector of Factories, Min. of Labour, 1945-49; Principal, 1949, Asst Sec., 1956, Min. of Housing and Local Govt, 1949-68. *Recreations:* boats, golf, rifle shooting. *Address:* High Winds, Ballyclare, Co. Antrim, Northern Ireland. *T:* Doagh 328.

**COLES, Sir Kenneth (Frank),** Kt 1957; Director: G. J. Coles & Co. Ltd; Australian Oil and Gas Corp.; Permanent Trustee Company; Deputy Chairman, Rothmans of Pall Mall (Australia) Ltd; Chairman: Bankers & Traders Insurance Co. Ltd; Equitable Life & General Insurance; *b* 19 April 1896; *s* of George and Elizabeth Coles; *m* 1925, Marjorie Evelyn Tolley; one *s* two *d*. Entered G. J. Coles & Co. Ltd, 1920; appointed London Manager, 1926; State Manager for NS Wales, 1933; Dep. Chairman: G. J. Coles & Co. Ltd, 1945; Rothmans of Pall Mall (Australia) Ltd, 1957. pres., Internat. Soc. for Welfare of Crippled, 1957-60. *Recreation:* golf. *Address:* 83 Victoria Road, Bellevue Hill, Sydney, Australia. *T:* 36 4728. *Clubs:* Athenæum (Melbourne); Australian, Royal Sydney Golf, (Sydney); Elanora Country.

*See also Sir A. W. Coles, Sir E. B. Coles, Sir G. J. Coles.*

**COLES, Norman;** Deputy Chief Adviser (Research and Studies), Ministry of Defence, since 1969; *b* 29 Dec. 1914; *s* of Fred and Emily Coles; *m* 1947, Una Valerie Tarrant; five *s*. *Educ:* Hanson High Sch., Bradford; Royal College of Science; City and Guilds Coll. Head, Armament Dept, RAE, 1959; Dir Gen. Equipment Research and Development, Min. of Aviation, 1962; Dep. Controller: OF Aircraft (RAF), Min. of Technology, 1966-68; of Guided Weapons, Min. of Technology, 1968-69. *Recreations:* carpentry, crossword puzzles. *Address:* Shottery, Kingsley Avenue, Camberley, Surrey. *T:* Camberley 22953.

**COLES, Air Marshal Sir William (Edward),** KBE 1967 (CBE 1952); CB 1963; DSO 1944; DFC and Bar; AFC; Controller, Royal Air Force Benevolent Fund, since 1968; *b* 1913; *s* of late George Frederick Coles, Shenington, Banbury; *m* 1945, Eileen Marjorie, *d* of Ernest Wilberforce Hann; two *s*. *Educ:* Tysoe Secondary Sch. Entered Royal Air Force, 1938; served in 216, 233 and 117 Squadrons, Middle East, N Africa, Italy, Burma and European theatres, 1939-44; RAF Staff Coll., 1945; Air Min., 1946-48; Empire and Central Flg Sch., 1948-50; Comd RAF Middleton St George, 1950; Chief Instr CFS, 1951-53; Sen. RAF Liaison Officer and Air Advisor to UK High Comr in Austr., 1953-55; HQ, Flg Trg Comd, 1956; idc 1957; SASO, HQ No 3 Bomber Gp, RAF Mildenhall, Suffolk, 1957-60; AOC No 23 Gp, RAF Flg Trg Comd, 1960-63; Dir-Gen. of Personal Services (RAF), Min. of Defence, 1963-66; AOC-in-C, RAF Technical Training Comd, 1966-68. DFC (US) 1944. *Recreations:* golf, winter sports. *Address:* 3 Walpole Road, Surbiton, Surrey. *T:* 01-399 4625; Top Farm House, Shenington, Banbury, Oxon. *Clubs:* East India and Sports, Royal Air Force.

**COLEY, (Howard William) Maitland;** Stipendiary Magistrate for South Staffordshire since 1961; Deputy Chairman, Staffordshire Quarter Sessions, since 1959; *b* 14 July 1910; *s* of late W. Howard Coley; *m* 1940, Cecile Muriel (from whom he obtained a divorce, 1966), *d* of C. C. H. Moriarty, CBE; one *d*; *m* 1968, Jill Barbour-Simpson; one *s*. *Educ:* Rugby; Christ's Coll., Cambridge. Called to Bar, Middle Temple, 1934. Served RAF, 1940-45. Recorder of Wenlock, 1946; Recorder of Burton upon Trent, 1956-61. *Recreations:* golf, sailing. *Address:* New House Farm, Mamble, near Kidderminster, Worcs. *T:* Clows Top 236.

**COLFOX, Sir (William) John,** 2nd Bt *cr* 1939; JP; *b* 25 April 1924; *yr* and *o surv. s* of Sir (William) Philip Colfox, 1st Bt, MC, and of Mary (Frances) Lady Colfox; *S* father, 1966; *m* 1962, Frederica Loveday, *d* of Adm. Sir Victor Crutchley, *qv*; two *s* two *d*. *Educ:* Eton. Served in RNVR, 1942-46, leaving as Lieut. Qualified

Land Agent, 1950. JP Dorset, 1962, High Sheriff of Dorset, 1969. *Recreation:* outdoor sports. *Heir:* *s* Philip John Colfox, *b* 27 Dec. 1962. *Address:* Symondsbury Manor, Bridport, Dorset. *T:* Bridport 2685.

**COLGRAIN,** 2nd Baron *cr* 1946, of Everlands; **Donald Swinton Campbell,** MC 1917; JP; *b* 6 Nov. 1891; *e s* of 1st Baron Colgrain and Lady Angela Mary Alice, 2nd *d* of 4th Earl of Harrowby; *S* father, 1954; *m* 1917, Margaret Emily, *d* of P. W. Carver; three *s* one *d*. *Educ:* Eton Coll.; Trinity Coll., Cambridge. Served with West Kent Yeomanry, 1914-19, and with 8th Bn Royal West Kent Regt, 1940-41. JP Kent, 1942. *Recreation:* shooting. *Heir:* *s* Hon. David Colin Campbell [*b* 24 April 1920; *m* 1945, Veronica Margaret Webster (marr. diss. 1964); one *s* one *d*]. *Address:* Everlands, Sevenoaks, Kent. *T:* Sevenoaks 53303. *Clubs:* Bath, City University; Bombay Yacht.
*See also Hon. A. D. Campbell, Sir Ian Macdonald of Sleat.*

**COLHOUN, Prof. John;** Barker Professor of Cryptogamic Botany, University of Manchester, since 1960; *b* 15 May 1913; *yr s* of late James Colhoun and Rebecca Colhoun, Castlederg, Co. Tyrone; *m* 1949, Margaret, *e d* of Prof. G. Waterhouse, *qv*; three *d*. *Educ:* Edwards Sch., Castlederg, Co. Tyrone; The Queen's Univ. of Belfast; Imperial Coll. of Science, London Univ. BSc, MAgr (Belfast), PhD, DSc (London), MSc (Manchester), DIC. Min. of Agriculture for Northern Ireland: Research Asst, 1939-46; Senior Scientific Officer, 1946-50; Principal Scientific Officer, 1951-60. The Queen's Univ., Belfast: Asst Lecturer in Agricultural Botany, 1940-42; Asst Lectr 1942-45, Jun. Lectr 1945-46, Lectr 1946-54, Reader 1954-60, in Mycology and Plant Pathology. Warden of Queen's Chambers, 1942-49. FLS 1955. FIBiol 1963. Pres., British Mycological Soc., 1963; Chm., Fedn of British Plant Pathologists, 1968. *Publications:* Diseases of the Flax Plant, 1947; Club Root Disease of Crucifers caused by Plasmodiophora Bassicae Woron, 1958; numerous papers in Annals of Applied Biology, Annals of Botany, Trans Brit. Mycological Soc., Nature. *Address:* 12 Southdown Crescent, Cheadle Hulme, Cheshire. *T:* 061-485 2084. *Club:* Farmers'.

**COLIN, Rt. Rev. Gerald Fitzmaurice;** *see* Grimsby, Bishop Suffragan of.

**COLLAR, (Arthur) Roderick,** CBE 1964; FRS 1965; MA, DSc, CEng; FRAeS, FAIAA, FCASI; Sir George White Professor of Aeronautical Engineering, University of Bristol, since 1945; Pro-Vice-Chancellor, 1967-70 (Vice-Chancellor 1968-69); *b* 22 Feb. 1908; *s* of late Arthur Collar, JP, and Louie Collar; *m* 1934, Winifred Margaret Moorman; two *s*. *Educ:* Simon Langton Sch., Canterbury; Emmanuel Coll., Cambridge (Scholar). Aerodynamics Dept, Nat. Physical Laboratory, 1929-41; Structural and Mechanical Engineering Dept, Royal Aircraft Establishment, 1941-45. Pres., Royal Aeronautical Soc., 1963-64; Chairman: Aeronautical Research Council, 1964-68; Aeronautical Bd, CNAA. Chairman: Governors, Rolls-Royce Technical Coll.; Adv. Council, Royal Military Coll. of Science, Shrivenham. Member: Academic Adv. Council, Royal Defence Acad.; Academic Adv. Council, Cranfield Inst. of Technology; Clifton Coll. Council; Bd of Governors, United Bristol Hospitals (Chm., Nursing Services Cttee); SW Regional Hosp. Bd. Hon. LLD. R38 Memorial Prize (joint), 1932; George Taylor Gold Medal, 1947; Orville Wright Prize, 1958; J. E. Hodgson Prize, 1960; Gold Medal, RAeS, 1966. *Publications:* Elementary Matrices (joint), 1938; (joint ed.) Hypersonic Flow; numerous papers in technical press. *Recreations:* sport (onlooker), poetry, music. *Address:* Queen's Building, The University, Bristol BS8 1TR. *T:* Bristol 2-4161. *Club:* Athenæum.

**COLLARD, Prof. Patrick John;** Professor of Bacteriology and Director of Department of Bacteriology and Virology, University of Manchester, since 1962; *b* 22 April 1920; *s* of Rupert John Collard; *m* 1st, 1948, Jessie Robertson (marr. diss. 1955); one *s* one *d*; 2nd, 1956, Kathleen Sarginson; one *s* one *d*. *Educ:* St Bartholomew's Medical Coll., Univ. of London. Qualified MB, BS, 1942; House Appts, 1942-44. RAMC, 1944-48. Registrar, Westminster Hospital, 1941-50; Lectr, Guy's Hosp. Med. Sch., 1950-54; Prof. of Bacteriology, University Coll., Ibadan, Nigeria, 1954-62. *Publications:* papers in: BMJ, Lancet, Jl Soc. Gen. Microbiol., Jl of Hygiene, West African Med. Jl, etc. *Recreations:* talking, reading, playing chess, silver-smithing. *Address:* 9 Holmewood Court, Ballbrook Avenue, Didsbury, Manchester 20. *T:* 061-445 3479. *Club:* Athenæum.

**COLLES, Comdr Sir Dudley,** KCB 1953; KCVO 1949 (CVO 1943; MVO 1936); OBE 1919; RN (retd); Extra Equerry to The Queen since 1958; Deputy Treasurer to The Queen and Assistant Keeper of the Privy Purse, 1952-58 (Secretary, HM Privy Purse, 1932-52, and Deputy Treasurer to King George VI, 1941-52); *b* 1889; *s* of late Richard and late Selina Colles; *m* 1920, Jacqueline (*d* 1959), *d* of H. G. Norman, Gloucester; one *d*. *Educ:* Arnold House, Llandullas; Eastman's, Winchester. Royal Navy, 1906; Paymaster Comdr, 1928; Sec. to 3rd and 2nd Sea Lords and to Comdr-in-Chief America and West Indies Station; retired, 1932. *Address:* Wren House, Kensington Palace, W8. *Club:* Naval and Military.

**COLLETT, Rear-Adm. George Kempthorne,** CB 1957; DSC 1942; *b* 25 Jan. 1907; *s* of William George and Ruth Lilian Collett; *m* 1937, Rongnye, *e d* of Sir Charles A. Bell, KCIE, CMG; one *s* one *d*. *Educ:* RNC Osborne and Dartmouth. Comdr, 1939; Liaison Officer with Gen. de Gaulle, 1940; Executive Officer, HMS Trinidad, 1941-42; Staff Officer, Home Fleet, 1942-44; Naval Asst to First Sea Lord, 1944-45; CO, HMS Cardigan Bay, 1946-48; Min. of Supply, 1948-50; Joint Services Staff Coll., 1950-52; CO, HMS Bermuda, 1952-54; Vice Naval Deputy, SHAPE, Paris, 1955-57; retd 1958. Legion of Honour (officer), 1945. *Recreations:* gardening, golf. *Address:* Coombe Farm, Churt, Farnham, Surrey. *T:* Headley Down 2533. *Club:* United Service.

**COLLETT, Sir Henry Seymour,** 2nd Bt *cr* 1934, of Bridge Ward in the City of London; Member for Bridge Ward, Court of Common Council, 1958-70; *b* 14 Feb. 1893; *e s* of Sir Charles Collett, 1st Bt (Lord Mayor of London, 1933-34); *S* father, 1938; *m* 1920, Ruth Mildred, *e d* of late William Thomas Hatch, MICE; one *s* one *d* (and *er s* decd). *Educ:* Bishop's Stortford Coll. Textile Trade, London and Belgium; served European War: UPS Corps 1914; Lieut Suffolk Regt, 1915-16 (wounded); Lieut RFC France (wounded, prisoner 1918); Freedom of City of London, 1920; Liveryman, Worshipful Company of Glovers. Retail distributing trade, America, London and Provinces; retired as Dir of Colletts Ltd, 1964; Past Pres., City of London Retail Traders' Assoc.; FRSA. Comdr, Ordre National du Côte d'Ivoire, 1962; Comdr, Royal Order of the Phœnix (Greece), 1963.

*Recreations:* gardening, riding, swimming, etc. *Heir: g s* Ian Seymour Collett, *b* 5 Oct. 1953. *Address:* The Knoll, Stone Road, Bromley, Kent. *T:* 01-460 3068. *Clubs:* United Wards, Bridge Ward.
*See also Sir Charles G. Alexander, Bt, Sir Kingsley Collett.*

**COLLETT, Sir (Thomas) Kingsley,** Kt 1968; CBE 1956; Director, Adams Bros & Shardlow Ltd (Creative Printers), London and Leicester; *b* 7 March 1905; 6th *s* of late Sir Charles Collett, 1st Bt, Bromley, Kent (Lord Mayor of London, 1933-34); *m* 1930, Beatrice Olive, *d* of late Thomas H. Brown, Bickley, Kent. *Educ:* Bishop's Stortford Coll. Commn in RA (TA), 1923-28 (relinquished commn, disability); 54th Kent Bn, Home Guard, 1940-44; comd 51st Kent Home Guard Bn, 1952-57; Mem., City of London Territorial Auxiliary and Volunteer Reserve Assoc. Forces Association. HM Lieut for City of London, 1958. Freeman, City of London, 1930; Liveryman, Worshipful Co. of Distillers, 1934 (Master, 1960-61); Mem., Ct of Common Coun., City of London (Ward of Bridge), 1945-; Chairman: City of London Freemen's Sch. Cttee, 1949-52; Port of London Health Authority, 1953; City Lands Cttee and Chief Commoner, 1955; Special Cttee, 1956-66; Policy and Parly Cttee, 1967-. Corp. of London Rep. on Bd of Port of London Authority, 1959-67; Member: Pollution Control Cttee, PLA; Chairman's Steering Cttee of BNEC; Chm., Lord Mayor's Appeal Cttee; Kennedy Mem. Fund, 1964; Churchill fund, 1965; Vice-Chm., Lord Mayor's Appeal Cttee: cleaning St Paul's Cath, 1963-64; Attlee Mem. Fund, 1967. Governor, Royal Hospitals; Chm., Gov. Council, Bishop's Stortford Coll., 1964-. Chevalier, Mil. Order of Christ (Portugal), 1956. *Recreations:* gardening, golf, shooting. *Address:* Fairfax Cottage, Wilderness Road, Chislehurst, Kent. *Club:* East India and Sports (Chm., 1959-66).
*See also Sir H. S. Collett, Bt.*

**COLLEY, David Isherwood,** MA, FLA; MBIM; City Librarian, Manchester, since 1955; *b* 5 July 1916; *s* of Squire Colley and Ethel Isherwood; *m* 1947, Barbara Mary, *d* of Canon T. A. Child, Lincoln; four *d. Educ:* Holt Sch., Liverpool. Served Royal Corps of Signals, 1940-46. FLA 1947. Pres., NW Branch Library Assoc., 1963; Hon. Sec., NW Regl Library System, 1955-; Mem., Min. of Education Working Party on Public Libraries, 1961-62; Mem., Cons. Cttee for Nat. Library for Science and Technology, 1959-65; Hon. Librarian and Curator of Ancient Monuments Soc., 1955-; Hon. Librarian of Manchester Statistical Soc., 1955-; Mem., Manchester and Dist Advisory Council for Further Education, 1956-; Adviser to Libraries, Museums and Arts Cttee of Assoc. of Municipal Corporations, 1957-; Mem., Youth Development Coun., 1963-66; Hon. Sec., Manchester Soc. of Book Collectors, 1955-. MA (*hc*) Manchester, 1962. *Publications:* various articles in learned periodicals. *Recreations:* libraries, photography, young people; YMCA. *Address:* 5 Dalton Gardens, Davyhulme, Urmston, Manchester. *T:* 061-748 6626.

**COLLEY, Thomas,** MB, ChB (Victoria); MRCS, LRCP, FRCSE; DOMS; Emeritus Cons. Ophthalmologist, Wessex Regional Hospital Board; late Director of Ophthalmology to West Dorset Group of Hospitals; late Hon. Surgeon to Weymouth and Dorset County Royal Eye Infirmary; late Hon. Ophthalmic Surgeon to Dorset County Hospital, Dorchester and Weymouth and District Hospital; Ophthalmic Surgeon to EMS Hospital, Portwey, Weymouth (War Years); late Cons. Oculist to the Dorset CC and Weymouth Education Committee; *b* Dec. 1894; *s* of Thomas and Esther Colley, Preston; *m* Eleanor Mary, *e d* of late Rev. D. J. Thomas, OBE, MA, JP; two *d. Educ:* privately; Manchester Univ. (Dumville Surgical Prize, Medical Clinical Prize); Edinburgh University. House appointments Royal Infirmary, Manchester, Central Branch Royal Infirmary, Manchester, Hospital for Sick Children, Great Ormond Street, London, Royal London Ophthalmic Hospital (Moorfields). Chm., W Dorset Group Med. Adv. Cttee, 1948-54; Member: Med. Adv. Cttee to SW Metropolitan Regional Hosp. Bd, 1949-51, (Mem., Med. Adv. Cttee of Western Area, 1948-53); W Dorset Group Hospitals Management Cttee, 1948-61. FRSM (Mem. of Council, Section of Ophthalmology, 1938-42); Mem. of Ophthalmological Soc., BMA, etc. *Publications:* papers in medical journals. *Recreation:* philately. *Address:* 9 Westbury Court Road, Westbury-on-Trym, Bristol. *T:* 622683.

**COLLICK, Percy Henry;** Assistant General Secretary, Associated Society of Locomotive Engineers, 1940-57 (Organising Secretary, 1934-40). Contested (Lab) Reigate Division of Surrey, 1929 and 1931; MP (Lab) West Birkenhead, 1945-50, Birkenhead, 1950-64. General Purposes Cttee, TUC, 1930-34; National Executive, Labour Party, 1944; Joint Parly Sec., Min. of Agriculture, 1945-47. Mem. Council, Royal College of Veterinary Surgeons, 1949-53. Hon. Freeman of Birkenhead, 1965. *Address:* 142 Hendon Way, NW2.

**COLLIER,** family name, **Monkswell Barony.**

**COLLIER, Air Vice-Marshal Sir (Alfred) Conrad,** KCB 1947 (CB 1943); CBE 1941; retired as Chief Executive, Guided Weapons Division, English Electric Aviation Ltd, 1960; *b* 16 Nov. 1895; *m* 1st, 1920, G. M. C. Luis (*d* 1961); two *s* one *d*; 2nd, 1963, Kathleen, *d* of late Joseph Donaghy, JP, Londonderry. *Educ:* Sherborne Sch. 2nd Lieut 9th King's Own (RL) Regt, 1914; RFC, 1915 with subsequent continuous service in RFC and RAF; Air Attaché, Moscow, 1934-47; Dep. Dir of Plans, Air Min., 1938; Dir of Allied Air Co-operation, Air Min., 1940; Head of Air Section, British Military Mission to Moscow, 1941; Air Officer i/c Administration, AHQ, India, 1942-43; Deputy AOC-in-C Transport Comd, 1943-45; AOC No. 3 Group, Bomber Comd, 1946; Dir-Gen. of Technical Services, Min. of Civil Aviation, 1946-47; Air Vice-Marshal, 1946; Controller of Technical and Operational Services, Min. of Civil Aviation, 1947, resigned, 1948. A Governor, National Hospitals for Nervous Diseases, 1961-64. DL Kent, 1952-64. FRAeS. Order of White Lion, 2nd Class (Czechoslovakia); Grand Officer, Order of Orange Nassau (Netherlands); Officer, Legion of Honour, and Croix de Guerre (France). *Address:* Quinta Das Andorinhas, Mato Serrão, Lagoa, Algarve, Portugal. *Club:* Travellers'.

**COLLIER, Andrew James;** Under-Secretary (Establishment Officer), Civil Service Department, since 1968; *b* 12 July 1923; *s* of Joseph Veasy Collier and Dorothy Murray; *m* 1950, Bridget, *d* of George and Edith Eberstadt, London; two *d. Educ:* Harrow; Christ Church, Oxford. Served Army (RHA and Indian Artillery), 1943-46. Entered Treasury, 1948; Private Sec. to: Sir Henry Wilson Smith, 1950; Sir Leslie Rowan, 1951; Chancellors of the Exchequer, 1956-59; Asst Sec., 1961; Under-Sec., 1967. *Address:* 82 Old

Church Street, SW3. *T:* 01-352 5150. *Club:* Athenæum.

**COLLIER, Maj.-Gen. Angus Lyell,** CBE 1943; MC 1917; DL; JP; psc; *b* 10 Nov. 1893; *e s* of late Thomas Edward Collier; *m* 1922, Edith Dorothea Margaret, *yr d* of late George Edward Herne; one *s* one *d*. *Educ:* Sedbergh; Oriel Coll., Oxford (BA). 2nd Lieut Queen's Own Cameron Highlanders (Special Reserve), 1914; regular commission as Capt., 1917; served European War, 1914-19, in Belgium, France, Balkans and S Russia (MC, despatches twice, White Eagle of Serbia). Staff Coll., Camberley, 1927-28; Bt Major, 1930; Bt Lt-Col, 1936; Bt Col, 1938. War of 1939-45: GSO1 Scottish Comd; Infantry Bde Comdr; Mil. Sec., GHQ, Middle East Forces; Dist Comdr Cyrenaica, 1943; Dist Comdr, Italy, 1944; Dist Comdr, Home Forces, 1944-46 (CBE, despatches twice, French Légion d'Honneur, Officer, and Croix de Guerre avec palme). ADC to the King, 1945-46. DL Inverness-shire, 1950; JP 1953. *Address:* Glassburn, by Beauly, Inverness-shire. *Clubs:* United Service; Highland (Inverness).

**COLLIER, Air Vice-Marshal Sir Conrad;** *see* Collier, Sir A. C.

**COLLIER, Dorothy Josephine,** MA, BM, BCh Oxon; FRCS; retired, formerly Consultant Surgeon, Ear, Nose and Throat Department, Royal Free Hospital; Emeritus Consultant Surgeon, Ear, Nose and Throat Department, South London Hospital, formerly Associate Lecturer, Institute of Laryngology and Otology; Hunterian Professor, RCS, 1939; *b* 8 March 1894; *d* of late John Collier and late Agnes Mullins, Liverpool. *Educ:* Convent of Notre Dame, Southport; Oxford University; University Coll. Hosp. House Surgeon, King Edward VII Hosp., Windsor; House Surgeon, Registrar, and First Asst, Ear, Nose and Throat Dept, University Coll. Hosp.; Registrar, Central London Throat and Ear Hosp.; late Temp. Major, RAMC; (Specialist Otologist); served in N Africa and Italy. Fellow Royal Soc. of Medicine, late Pres., Section of Otology; late Sec., Section of Laryngology; Mem., late Mem. Council, Med. Women's Federation. *Publications:* (with J. D. MacLaggan) Diseases of the Ear, Nose and Throat, 1952 (trans. Spanish, Mexican Edn, 1955); articles on facial paralysis and other contribs to medical jls in England and USA. *Recreations:* travel in Spanish America and Middle East; orchid growing; gardening. *Address:* 25 Blenheim Road, St John's Wood, NW8. *T:* 01-624 6733.

**COLLIER, Air Commodore Kenneth Dowsett Gould,** CBE 1945; *b* 4 April 1892; *m* 1917; no *c*. *Educ:* privately. RFC 1915-18, RAF 1918 (despatches); India and Egypt, 1921-25; HMS Glorious, 1929-31; Admiralty, 1938-41; Air Ministry, 1941-47; Principal Scientific Officer, Ministry of Supply, 1947-53. Retired with the rank of Air Commodore, 1947. Bronze Star, USA, 1946. *Recreations:* sailing, garden. *Address:* Robin Hill, Fritham, New Forest, Hants. *T:* Cadnam 2312. *Club:* Naval and Military.

**COLLIER, Kenneth Gerald;** Principal, College of the Venerable Bede, Durham, since 1959; *b* 1910; *m* 1938, Gwendoline Halford; two *s*. *Educ:* Aldenham Sch.; St John's Coll., Cambridge. MA 1935; Diploma in Education (Oxon) 1945. Technical translation, Stockholm, 1931-32; Schoolmaster, 1933-41; Royal Ordnance Factories, 1941-44; Physics Master, Lancing Coll., 1944-49; Lectr, St Luke's Coll., Exeter, 1949-59. Editor, Education for Teaching, 1953-58. Chm., Assoc. Teachers in Colls and Depts of Education, 1964-65. Vis. Prof. of Education, Temple Univ., Philadelphia, 1965, 1968. *Publications:* The Science of Humanity, 1950; The Social Purposes of Education, 1959; New Dimensions in Higher Education, 1968; (contrib.) Sixth Form Citizens, 1950; Religious Faith and World Culture (New York), 1951; articles in educational and other jls. *Recreations:* local history; music; the film. *Address:* Principal's House, Bede College, Durham. *T:* 3502. *Club:* Reform.

**COLLIER, Sir Laurence,** KCMG 1944 (CMG 1934); *b* 13 June 1890; *s* of late Hon. John Collier and Ethel Gladys Huxley; *m* 1917, Eleanor Antoinette, *o d* of late William Luther Watson; one *s*. *Educ:* Bedales Sch.; Balliol Coll., Oxford (Brackenbury Scholar; 1st Class Modern History 1912). Clerk in Foreign Office, 1913; 2nd Sec. to HM Embassy, Tokyo, 1919; returned to Foreign Office, 1921; 1st Sec., 1923; Counsellor, 1932; Minister to Norway, 1941; British Ambassador to the Norwegian Govt, 1942-50; retired, 1951. *Publication:* Flight from Conflict, 1944. *Address:* Monkswell House, Blue House Lane, Limpsfield, Surrey. *T:* Oxted 3552. *Club:* Athenæum.

**COLLIER, Marie Elizabeth;** soprano; *b* Ballarat, Australia, 16 April 1927; *d* of Thomas Robinson Collier and Ann-Marie Bechaz; *m* 1952; three *s* one *d*. *Educ:* High Sch., Melbourne. Australian debut, 1954; Covent Garden, 1957; South America, 1961; USA, 1962. *Recreations:* conversation, food and wine. *Address:* 6 Cadogan Lane, SW1. *T:* 01-235 8306.

**COLLIER, Dr William Adrian Larry;** general practitioner in Halstead, Essex, since 1951; *b* 25 Nov. 1913; *s* of Hon. Gerald Collier, 2nd *s* of 2nd Baron Monkswell, and Lily Anderson; *S* uncle as 4th Baron Monkswell, 1964; disclaimed title, 7 April 1964; *m* 1945, Helen (*née* Dunbar, now Mrs Kemp); two *s*; *m* 1951, Nora Selby; one *s* one *d*. *Educ:* Fellowship Sch.; Odenwald Schule; Summerhill; Univs of Queensland, Edinburgh, London and Cambridge. IB 1937; MB, ChB Edinburgh 1943; DPH London 1947, PHLS (Trainee), 1947-50. Mem., Halstead UDC, 1954-67; Essex CC, 1958-61. FRSocMed. *Publications:* World Index of Imprints used on Tablets and other Solid Dose Forms, 1964 and 1967; contribs to Lancet and Pharmaceutical Journal. *Recreations:* swimming, camping, kids, local government, Essex River Authority. *Heir:* (*to disclaimed barony*); *s* Gerard Collier, *b* 28 Jan. 1947. *Address:* 30 Chapel Street, Halstead, Essex. *T:* Halstead 2029.

**COLLIGAN, John Clifford,** CBE 1963 (OBE 1957); Director-General, Royal National Institute for the Blind, since 1950; Secretary, British Wireless for the Blind Fund, since 1950; Hon. Treasurer and Deputy President, Executive World Council for the Blind, since 1969 (British Representative, 1954-69); *b* 27 Oct. 1906; *s* of John and Florence Colligan, Wallasey, Cheshire; *m* 1st, 1934, Ethel May Allton (*d* 1948); one *s* one *d*; 2nd, 1949, Frances Bird. *Educ:* Liscard High Sch., Wallasey. Dep. Sec., National Institute for the Blind, 1945-49. *Publications:* The Longest Journey, 1969; various articles on blind welfare. *Recreations:* fishing, gardening. *Address:* 3 Jonathans, Dene Road, Northwood, Mddx. *T:* Northwood 21988. *Club:* National Liberal.

**COLLINGS, Maj.-Gen. Wilfred d'Auvergne,** CB 1946; CBE 1941; *b* Guernsey, 8 Aug. 1893; 5th *s* of C. d'Auvergne Collings, MD, and Laura Josephine Williams; *m* 1928, Nancy Draper

Bishop; two *s* one *d*. *Educ:* Elizabeth Coll., Guernsey; RMC Sandhurst. Commissioned ASC 1914. Served in France, Gallipoli and Mesopotamia, 1914-18 (despatches twice); seconded for service with Egyptian Army, 1923-24 and Sudan Defence Force, 1925-30; on active service in Palestine, 1937-39; Dep. Dir of Supplies and Transport, Western Desert Force, 1940, British Forces in Greece, 1941, Eighth Army, 1941; Dir of Supplies and Transport, Persia and Iraq Force, 1942-43, 21st Army Group, 1944-45, and British Army of the Rhine, 1945-46; retired 1948. Chief of Supply and Transport Div., UN Relief and Works Agency in the Near East, 1949-53. Maj.-Gen. 1944. Commander, Order of Leopold II (Belgium); MC of Greece, Croix de Guerre of France and Belgium. *Address:* Beaumont, Albecq, Guernsey, Channel Islands. *Club:* Army and Navy.

**COLLINGWOOD, Rt. Rev. Mgr. Canon Cuthbert;** Parish Priest of Staines since 1954; Canon of the Metropolitan Chapter of Westminster since 1948; *b* 26 May 1908; *s* of late Austin Vincent Collingwood. *Educ:* St Edmund's College, Ware. Ordained by His Eminence Cardinal Bourne, 1934; Chaplain of Westminster Cathedral and Asst Master of Ceremonies, 1934-44, Master of Ceremonies, 1945-49; Editor of Westminster Cathedral Chronicle, 1940-45; Private Sec. to HE Cardinal Griffin, 1944-47; Administrator of Westminster Cathedral, 1947-54. Privy Chamberlain to HH the Pope, 1946, Domestic Prelate, 1968. Chm. of Catholic Truth Soc., 1948; Pres. of Metropolitan and City Catholic Police Guild, 1948. *Address:* 59 Gresham Road, Staines, Mddx. *T:* Staines 52381.

**COLLINGWOOD, Lt-Gen. Sir George;** *see* Collingwood, Lt-Gen. Sir R. G.

**COLLINGWOOD, Lawrance Arthur,** CBE 1948; Musical Adviser to the Gramophone Co.; *b* 14 March 1887; *s* of J. H. Collingwood; *m* 1914, Anna Koenig, St Petersburg, Russia; two *s* two *d*. *Educ:* Westminster Abbey Choir Sch.; Exeter Coll., Oxford; St Petersburg Conservatoire. For 25 years associated with work of The Old Vic and Sadler's Wells, first as repetiteur, then conductor; musical dir of Sadler's Wells Opera Co., 1940-47. *Address:* Ferniehurst, Waverley Drive, Camberley, Surrey. *T:* Camberley 5083.

**COLLINGWOOD, Lieut-Gen. (retired) Sir (Richard) George,** KBE 1959 (CBE 1951); CB 1954; DSO 1944; *b* 7 Oct. 1903; 4th *s* of Col C. G. Collingwood, Lilburn Tower and Glanton Pyke, Northumberland. *Educ:* RN Colls Osborne and Dartmouth; RMC Sandhurst. Entered Cameronians, 1923; Brigadier, 1944; served in Middle East and Burma. GOC 52 Lowland Division and Lowland District, Oct. 1952-55; Maj.-Gen. 1953; GOC, Singapore District, 1957-58; GOC-in-C, Scottish Command, 1958-61; Gov. of Edinburgh Castle, 1958-61. Col, The Cameronians (Scottish Rifles), 1964-68. A Mem. of the Jockey Club (Steward, 1960). Knight Grand Cross, Order of the Sword (Sweden), 1964. *Recreations:* hunting, shooting, racing. *Address:* Lilburn Tower, Alnwick, Northumberland. *T:* Wooperton 226. *Club:* Boodle's.

**COLLINGWOOD, Brig. Sydney,** CMG 1957; CBE 1945; MC 1917; retired; *b* 10 July 1892; *s* of late Sir William Collingwood, KBE, MICE, JP, Dedham Grove, near Colchester, Essex; *m* 1st, 1915, Charlotte Annie (decd), *d* of Colonel James Charles Oughterson, late 18th Royal Irish, Greenock; two *s* one *d*; 2nd, 1940, Eileen Mary, *widow* of late Major W. D. G. Batten, 3rd Gurkha Rifles, and *d* of A. Willson, Waldegrave Park, Twickenham. *Educ:* Liverpool Coll.; Royal Military Academy. 2nd Lieut, RA, 1912. Served European War, 1914-18. Major, 1930; Bt Lieut-Col 1934; Col, 1938; Brig., 1940; BGS, Southern Command, 1940-42; DDPS, War Office, 1942-46; retd, 1946. Regional Dir, Southern Region, Imperial War Graves Commission (Headquarters, Rome), 1946-57. Croix de Guerre, 1917. *Recreation:* rural preservation. *Address:* The Croft, Dedham, Colchester, Essex. *Club:* United Service.

**COLLINS,** family name of **Baron Stonham.**

**COLLINS, Brig. Arthur Francis St Clair,** CBE 1940 (OBE 1918); MC; *b* 10 March 1892; *s* of late Dr A. H. Collins, Edinburgh; one *d*. *Educ:* Bedford Sch. 3rd Bn Beds Regt, 1911-13; ASC 1913; Temp. Capt., 1914; Adjt, 1917-18; Acting Major, 1918-19; Adjt, 1927-28; Major, 1933; Lt-Col, 1939; Temp. Col, 1940; Col, 1943; Brig., 1941-46; served France and Belgium, 1914-21 (despatches twice, 1914 Star, MC, OBE); Germany and Upper Silesia, 1919-21; India, 1926; Shanghai, 1927; BEF France, 1939-40 and 1945 (CBE); retired pay, 1946; AMIME 1933. *Recreations:* Rugby, tennis, golf, rowing. *Address:* 17 Ingles Road, Folkestone, Kent. *Club:* Army and Navy.

**COLLINS, Arthur Jefferies;** President, Henry Bradshaw Society; *b* 30 Sept. 1893; *e s* of late Arthur and Beatrice Agnes Collins; *m* 1st, Winifred Alice (*d* 1924), *d* of D. Edward Higham; one *d*; 2nd, Mary Tindall, *d* of Robert Thornhill Harris; one *s*. *Educ:* Merchant Taylors' Sch.; Magdalene Coll., Cambridge (Exhibnr). BA (War Degree) 1915; MA 1961. European War, 1914-19; Capt. and Adjt, Royal North Devon Hussars; severely wounded with Devon Regt, 1917. Asst, British Museum, 1919; Dep. Keeper of Manuscripts, 1944-47; Lecturer in Palaeography to Sch. of Librarianship, London, 1947-55. Keeper of Manuscripts and Egerton Librarian, British Museum, 1947-55. *Publications:* Legal and Manorial Formularies (with B. Schofield), 1933; The Documents of the Great Charter of 1215 (Proc. Brit. Acad.); An Inventory of the Jewels and Plate of Queen Elizabeth I, 1574; Manuale ad usum Sarum (Henry Bradshaw Soc.); Bridgettine Breviary of Syon Abbey (Henry Bradshaw Soc.); articles in Antiquaries' JL, History, Times, etc. *Address:* Broughton Gorse, Hale Purlieu, near Fordingbridge, Hants. *T:* Downton 376.

**COLLINS, Bernard John,** CBE 1960; Joint Director of Planning and Transportation, Greater London Council, since 1969; *b* 3 July 1909; *s* of John Philip and Amelia Bounevialle Collins; *m* 1937, Grete Elisabeth, *e d* of H. A. Piehler; one *s* three *d*. *Educ:* Ampleforth. Served Royal Artillery, 1939-45, North Africa (despatches) and Italy. Ryde Memorial Prizeman, RICS, 1937. President, Town Planning Inst., 1957-58; Pres., International Fedn of Surveyors, 1967-69; Mem. Bureau, Internat. Fedn for Housing and Planning, 1962-66; Vice-Pres., RICS, 1968-; Mem. Board of Governors, Coll. of Estate Management, 1959-69; Vice-Chm. of Executive, Town and Country Planning Assoc., 1951-62; Chm., Assoc. of County Planning Officers, 1954-58; County Planning Officer, Middx, 1947-62; Sec. and Chief Exec. Commn for the New Towns, 1962-64; Dir of Planning, GLC, 1964-69; responsible for preparation of Greater London Develt Plan, 1969. chairman, Technical Panel: Conf. on London and SE Regional Planning, 1964-; Greater London and SE Regional Sports Council, 1966-. Hon. Mem., Deutscher Verein für

Vermessungswesen (German Soc. of Surveyors), 1965. *Publications:* Development Plans Explained (HMSO), 1951; Middlesex Survey and Development Plan, 1952; numerous articles and papers on town planning. *Address:* County Hall, SE1; Foxella, Matfield, Kent. *Club:* Athenæum.

**COLLINS, Sir Charles Henry,** Kt 1947; CMG 1941; *b* 10 Feb. 1887; *s* of late C. H. Collins, Torquay; *m* 1913, Florence E. Campkin (*d* 1968); two *d* (one *s* decd). *Educ:* King's Coll., Univ. of London. BA 1909. Entered Ceylon Civil Service, 1910; Dep. Chief Sec., 1940; Acting Financial Sec. in 1935, 1936, 1937, 1940, and 1943; Acting Chief Sec. in 1944, 1945 and 1947; retired, 1948. *Publications:* Public Administration in Ceylon, 1951; Public Administration in Hong Kong, 1952. *Recreations:* historical and archæological studies. *Address:* White House, Wix Hill, West Horsley, Surrey. *T:* Clandon 430.

**COLLINS, David Charles,** CBE 1969; Chairman and Chief Executive, Westland Aircraft Ltd; Chairman: British Hovercraft Corp. Ltd; FPT Industries Ltd; Draeger Normalair Ltd; Normalait-Garrett Ltd; Sandall Precision Co. Ltd; Westland Helicopters Ltd since 1968; *b* 23 Jan. 1908; *s* of Richard and Margaret Collins; *m* 1936, Dorothy Bootyman. *Educ:* private and gram. schs; Glamorgan Coll. of Technology. Student Apprentice, GWR and Aero Engines; Design Staff, Gloster Aircraft Ltd, 1928; Production Engr, Blackburn Aircraft Ltd, 1933; Fairey Aviation Ltd: Chief Planning Engr, 1941; Dep. Man., 1943; Man., 1946; joined Westland Aircraft Ltd as Works Dir, 1951; Dep. Man. Dir, 1959; Man. Dir, 1965; Director: British Hovercraft Assoc. Ltd; Coenraets SA; Normalair-Garrett (Holdings) Ltd; Normalair-Garrett Pty Ltd; Westland Engineers Ltd. Council Member: CBI; Soc. of British Aerospace Cos Ltd; SW Economic Planning Council. CEng, FIMechE, FIProdE, FRAeS, FInstD. *Recreations:* golf, fishing. *Address:* Orchard Way, Nether Compton, Sherborne, Dorset. *T:* Sherborne 2824. *Clubs:* Royal Aero; Sherborne Golf.

**COLLINS, Douglas;** perfumer; Founder and Chairman: Goya Ltd; National Seed Development Organisation; Director, Sutton & Sons Ltd; *b* 31 Aug. 1912; *s* of Richard Johnson Douglas Collins, Renfrew and Anascaul, Co. Kerry; *m* 1st, 1938, Patricia Backhouse (marr. diss. 1961); two *s* three *d*; 2nd, 1962, Elisabeth Worswick; one *s* two *d*. *Educ:* private schs, Sussex; state schs, Canada; Vevey; Zürich; Hanover; University, Perugia. Office boy in French hotels, 1928; clerk in paint works and stockbrokers, 1929-33; started unsuccessful businesses, 1933-36; started Goya Ltd, 1937. RNVR 1939; Navigator, HMS Gardenia; training Officers, HMS King Alfred; in command escort vessels; retd as Lt-Comdr, 1945. Chairman: British Lion Films Ltd and British Lion Studio Co. Ltd, 1958-61; Dir, National Film Finance Corporation, 1955-61. Owns and farms 500 acres at Great Missenden (cereals and pigs). *Publications:* Sailing in Helen, 1946; Mr Mole series of Children's Books, 1947-50; A Nose for Money, 1963. *Recreations:* ocean sailing, ski-ing, writing; repairing old furniture. *Address:* 14 Bourdon Street, W1. *T:* 01-629 4971. *Club:* Royal Cruising.

**COLLINS, Sir Geoffrey Abdy,** Kt 1952; *b* 5 June 1888; *y s* of Philip George and Susan Kate Collins; *m* 1936, Joan Mary, 2nd *d* of Albert Edward and Margaret Alice Ratcliffe; one *s* four *d*. *Educ:* Rugby; Christ's Coll., Cambridge (BA, LLB). Admitted solicitor, 1913. Served European War, 1914-18, in The Rifle Brigade (Capt.). Member: Royal UK Beneficent Assoc. Cttee, 1926-54 (Chm., 1950-54); Council of The Law Society, 1931-56, Pres., 1951-52. Past Master, Tylers and Bricklayers Co. *Address:* Mullion, 20 Ballard Estate, Swanage, Dorset. *T:* Swanage 2030.

**COLLINS, Henry Edward,** CBE 1948; Consulting Mining Engineer; *b* 4 Oct. 1903; *s* of James Collins; *m* 1934, Cecilia Harris; no *c*. *Educ:* Rotherham Grammar Sch.; Univ. of Sheffield (MEng). Sen. Lectr in Mining, Univ. of Sheffield, 1935-38; Manager, Rossington Main Colliery, Doncaster, 1939-42; Agent, Markham Colliery, Doncaster, 1942-44; Chief Mining Agent, Doncaster Amalgamated Collieries Ltd, 1944-45; Dir Coal Production, CCG, 1945-47; British Chm., UK/US Coal Control Gp, Germany (later Combined Coal Control Gp), 1947-50; Production Dir, Durham Div., NCB, 1950-56; Dir-Gen. of Reconstruction, NCB, 1956-57; Board Mem. for Production, NCB, 1957-67; Consultant to NCB, 1967-69. Mem., Govtl Cttee on Coal Derivatives, 1959-60; Chairman: NCB Opencast Executive, 1961-67; NCB Brickworks Executive, 1962-67; Whittlesea Central Brick Co. Ltd, 1966-67; Field Research Steering Cttee, Min. of Power, 1964-67; Past Director: Omnia Concrete Sales Ltd; Bradley's (Concrete) Ltd; Member: Minister of Power's Adv. Council on Research and Develt, 1963-67; Min. of Power Nat. Jt Pneumoconiosis Cttee, 1964-67; Safety in Mines (Adv.) Bd; Mining Qualifications Bd, 1962-69. Pres., Inst. of Mining Engineers, 1962. *Publications:* numerous papers on mining engineering subjects. *Address:* Rising Sun, 22a West Side, Wimbledon Common, SW19. *T:* 01-946 3949. *Club:* Athenæum.

**COLLINS, Vice-Adm. Sir John (Augustine),** KBE 1951; CB 1940; RAN retired; *b* Deloraine, Tasmania, 7 Jan. 1899; *s* of Michael John Collins, MD; *m* 1930, Phyllis Laishley, *d* of A. J. McLachlan; one *d*. *Educ:* Royal Australian Naval Coll. Served European War with Grand Fleet and Harwich Force, 1917-18; thereafter in various HM and HMA Ships abroad and in Australian waters; Squadron Gunnery Officer, HMA Squadrons; Liaison Officer for visit of Duke and Duchess of York to Australia; in command HMAS Anzac; staff course; Asst Chief of Naval Staff, Australia; Capt. HMAS Sydney (CB), 1939-41; Asst Chief of Staff to C-in-C, China, 1941 (despatches); Cdre comdg China Force, 1942 (Comdr of Order of Orange Nassau); Capt. HMAS Shropshire, 1943-44; Cdre comdg HM Australian Sqdn (wounded), 1944-46; idc 1947; Chief of Naval Staff and First Naval Mem., Australian Commonwealth Naval Bd, Melbourne, 1948-55; Australian High Comr to New Zealand, 1956-62. Officer of Legion of Merit (US); Royal Humane Society's Certificate for Saving Life at Sea. *Publication:* As Luck Would Have It, 1965. *Recreation:* golf. *Address:* 13 Dumaresq Road, Rose Bay, Sydney, NSW, Australia. *Club:* Royal Sydney Golf.

**COLLINS, Maj.-Gen. (Retd) Joseph Clinton,** CB 1953; CBE 1951 (OBE 1946); *b* 8 Jan. 1895; British; *m* 1925, Eileen Patricia Williams; two *d*. *Educ:* London Hosp. Served European War, 1914-18, France and Belgium, 1914; Surgeon Probationer, RNVR, 1915-16; Lieut, RAMC, 1917; Egyptian Army, 1923-33; DDMS, BAOR, 1946-49; DMS Far ELF, 1949-51; DMS Northern Command, 1951-53; KHS 1951-54; Dir Medical Services, BAOR, 1953-Dec. 1954, retired. CStJ 1948. 3rd Class Order of Nile. *Address:* c/o Glyn, Mills & Co., Whitehall, SW1.

**COLLINS, Gen. (retd) J(oseph) Lawton,** DSM 1942 (Oak Leaf Cluster, 1943, 1944, 1953); Silver Star, 1943 (Army Oak Leaf Cluster, and Navy Gold Star, 1944); Legion of Merit, 1943 (Oak Leaf Cluster, 1945); Bronze Star Medal, 1944; Director, Chas Pfizer & Co. Inc., 1957-69; Vice-Chairman, Pfizer International Subsidiaries since 1957; *b* New Orleans, La, 1 May 1896; *s* of Jeremiah Bernard Collins and Catherine Lawton; *m* 1921, Gladys Easterbrook; one *s* two *d.* *Educ:* Louisiana State Univ.; US Military Academy. 2nd Lieut, Infantry, 1917; 22nd Infantry, Fort Hamilton, NY, until Jan. 1918, graduated Inf. Sch. of Arms, Fort Sill, Oklahoma, 1918; went overseas and took command of bn of 18th Inf., Coblenz, 1919; Asst Chief of Staff, Plans and Training Div., American Forces in Germany, until 1921; Instr, US Mil. Acad., 1921-25; graduated: Inf. Sch., Fort Benning, Ga, 1926; Advanced Course, Field Artillery Sch., Fort Sill, Oklahoma, 1927; Instr, Inf. Sch., 1927-31; student, Comd and Gen. Staff Sch., Fort Leavenworth, Kansas, 1931-33; with 23rd Bde (Philippine Scouts), Fort William McKinley, and Asst Chief of Staff, Mil. Intell., Philippine Div., until 1936; Student: Army Industrial Coll., 1936-37; Army War Coll., 1937-38; Instr there, 1938-40. Served War of 1939-45; Office of Sec., War Dept Gen. Staff, 1940-41; Chief of Staff, VII Army Corps, 1941; Chief of Staff, Hawaiian Dept, 1941; Comdg Gen., 25th Inf. Div. in Guadalcanal ops, New Georgia Campaign, 1942-43; comd VII Army Corps, European Theater, for Invasion of France, 1944; and subseq. campaigns to end of hostilities, 1945; Dep. Comdg Gen. and Chief of Staff, HQ, Army Ground Forces, 1945; Dir of Information, War Dept, 1945; Dep. Chief of Staff, US Army, 1947, and Vice Chief of Staff (upon creation of that post), 1948; Chief of Staff, US Army, 1949-53; US Rep., Standing Group, NATO and US Mem. Mil. Cttee, 1953-56; US Special Rep. in Viet Nam with personal rank Ambassador, Nov. 1954-May 1955. Holds hon. degrees. Army of Occupation Medal, Germany, European War, 1914-18, and War of 1939-45; American Defense Service Medal; Asiatic-Pacific Medal; European-African-Middle Eastern Campaign Ribbon. (In addition to above US decorations) Hon. CB (British) 1945; Order of Suvorov, 2nd Class, twice (Russian); Croix de Guerre with Palm, Legion of Honor, Degree of Grand Officer (French); Order of Leopold II, Grand Officer Croix de Guerre with Palm (Belgian). *Address:* 1700 Pennsylvania Avenue, NW, Washington, DC 20006, USA. *T:* 659-1870. *Clubs:* Army and Navy (Washington, DC); Chevy Chase (Md).

**COLLINS, Rear-Adm. Kenneth St Barbe,** CB 1959; OBE 1945; DSC 1942; *b* 9 June 1904; *s* of late Charles Bury Collins, Col RE and late Ethel St Barbe; *m* 1932, Helen Mary Keen; one *s* one *d.* *Educ:* Lydgate House Sch., Hunstanton, Norfolk; RN Colls Osborne and Dartmouth. Midshipman, HMS Warspite, 1922, Vimiera, 1923; Sub-Lt, HMS Fitzroy, 1925; Lt and Lt-Comdr surveying ships Ormonde, 1927; Beaufort, 1929; Herald, 1930; Flinders, 1932; Endeavour, 1937; Seaplane Carrier, HMS Albatross, 1939; (as Comdr) Staff of Allied Naval Comdr Expeditionary Force, North Africa, 1942; staff of Allied Naval Comdr Expeditionary Force, Europe, 1943; surveying HMS Seagull, 1947; (as Capt.) surveying HMS Dampier, 1948; Cook, 1951; Vidal, 1954; Hydrographer of the Navy, 1955-60; Rear-Adm., 1957; retd 1960. Consultant to the Survey and Mapping Branch of Dept of Mines and Technical Surveys, Ottawa, 1960-63. *Address:* The Old Parsonage, Bentley, near Farnham, Surrey. *T:* Bentley 3227. *Club:* United Service.

**COLLINS, Canon Lewis John;** Canon since 1948, and Treasurer since 1970, of St Paul's Cathedral (Chancellor, 1948-53; Precentor, 1953-70); *b* 23 March 1905; *s* of Arthur Collins and Hannah Priscilla; *m* 1939, Diana Clavering Elliot; four *s.* *Educ:* Cranbrook Sch.; Sidney Sussex Coll. and Westcott House, Cambridge. Curate of Whitstable, 1928-29; Chaplain, Sidney Sussex Coll., Cambridge, 1929-31; Minor Canon of St Paul's Cathedral, 1931-34; a Dep. Priest-in-Ordinary to HM the King, 1931-34, Priest-in-Ordinary, 1934-35; Vice-Principal, Westcott House, Cambridge, 1934-37; Chaplain RAFVR, 1940-45; Dean of Oriel Coll., Oxford, 1938-48; Fellow Lecturer and Chaplain, 1937-48. Chairman: Christian Action, 1946-; Martin Luther King Foundn, 1969-; Pres., Internat. Defence and Aid Fund, 1964-. Order of Grand Companion of Freedom, Third Div., Zambia, 1970. *Publications:* The New Testament Problem, 1937; A Theology of Christian Action, 1949; Faith Under Fire, 1966; contributor, Three Views of Christianity, 1962. *Address:* 2 Amen Court, EC4. *T:* 01-248 3747. *Club:* Savile.

**COLLINS, Col Michael,** DFC (US); Colonel, USAF, retired; NASA Astronaut; Command Module Pilot, Apollo 11 rocket flight to the Moon, July 1969; Assistant Secretary of State for Public Affairs, US, since 1970; *b* Rome, Italy, 31 Oct. 1930; *s* of Maj.-Gen. and Mrs James L. Collins, Washington, DC, USA; *m* 1957, Patricia M. Finnegan, Boston, Mass; one *s* two *d.* *Educ:* St Albans Sch., Washington, DC (grad.). US Mil. Academy, West Point, NY (BSc). Served as an experimental flight test officer, Air Force Flight Test Center, Edwards Air Force Base, Calif; he was one of the third group of astronauts named by NASA in Oct. 1963; served as backup pilot for Gemini 7 mission; as pilot with John Young on the 3-day 44-revolution Gemini 10 mission, launched 18 July 1966, he shared record-setting flight (successful rendezvous and docking with a separately launched Agena target vehicle; he also competed two periods of extravehicular activity); subseq. assigned as Command Module Pilot for the third manned Apollo flight, and was in orbit 20 July 1969, when Neil Armstrong and Edwin Aldrin landed on the Moon. Member, Soc. of Experimental Test Pilots. Further awards include Presidential Medal of Freedom, NASA Exceptional Service Medal and Air Force Astronaut Wings. *Recreations:* fishing, handball. *Address:* c/o Department of State, Washington, DC 20520, USA.

**COLLINS, Miss Nina;** *see* Lowry, Mrs N. M.

**COLLINS, Norman Richard;** Deputy Chairman, Associated Television Corporation Ltd; Director: ATV Network Ltd; Independent Television News Co.; Watergate Productions Ltd; Independent Broadcasting Services Ltd; Governor, Sadler's Wells Foundation; Chairman: Central School of Speech and Drama; Loch Ness Investigation Burneau; *b* 3 Oct. 1907; *s* of late Oliver Norman Collins; *m* 1931, Sarah Helen, *d* of Arthur Francis Martin; one *s* two *d.* *Educ:* William Ellis Sch., Hampstead. At Oxford Univ. Press, 1926-29; Asst Literary Editor, News-Chronicle, 1929-33; Dep. Chm., Victor Gollancz Ltd, publishers, 1934-41. Controller Light Programme, BBC, 1946-47; late Gen. Overseas Service Dir, BBC; Controller Television, BBC, 1947-50, resigned. Governor, British Film Inst., 1949-51; Governor, Atlantic Inst.; Member: Council, English Stage Co.; Exec. Cttee, Nat. Book League, 1965-69. President: Appeals Cttee, Nat. Playing Fields Assoc.; Adoption Cttee for Aid to Displaced Persons; Radio Industries Club, 1950; Pitman

Fellowship, 1957; Regent Advertising Club, 1959-66. *Publications:* The Facts of Fiction, 1932; Penang Appointment, 1934; The Three Friends, 1935; Trinity Town, 1936; Flames Coming Out of the Top, 1937; Love in Our Time, 1938; "I Shall not want", 1940; Anna, 1942; London belongs to Me, 1945; Black Ivory, 1947; Children of the Archbishop, 1951; The Bat That Flits, 1952; The Bond Street Story, 1958; The Governor's Lady, 1968; The Captain's Lamp (play), 1938. *Address:* 1 Radlett Place, NW8. *Clubs:* Carlton, Turf, MCC.

**COLLINS, Stuart Verdun,** CB 1970; Chief Inspector of Audit, Ministry of Housing and Local Government, since 1968; *b* 24 Feb. 1916; *m* 1st, 1942, Helen Simpson (*d* 1968); two *d*; 2nd, 1970, Joan Mary Walmsley (widow); one *step s* two *step d*. *Educ:* Plymouth Coll. Entered Civil Service as Audit Assistant in the District Audit Service of the Ministry of Health, 1934; appointed District Auditor for the London Audit District, 1958. FIMTA, FBCS. *Recreations:* golf, do-it-yourself (provided not too arduous). *Address:* 37 The Spinneys, Bickley, Kent. *T:* 01-467 8269. *Club:* West Kent Golf (Captain 1970-71).

**COLLINS, Brig. Thomas Frederick James,** CBE 1945 (OBE 1944); JP; DL; Chairman, Essex County Council; *b* 9 April 1905; *s* of Capt. J. A. Collins and Emily (*née* Truscott); *m* 1942, Marjorie Morwenna, *d* of Lt-Col T. Donnelly, DSO; one *d*. *Educ:* Haileybury; RMC, Sandhurst. Gazetted to Green Howards, 1924; Staff College, 1938. Served War of 1939-45 (despatches twice, OBE, CBE): France, 1940, NW Europe, 1944-45. Retired, with rank of Brig., 1948. Essex County Council: CC, 1960; Vice-Chm., 1967; Chm., 1968. JP 1968, DL 1969, essex, 1968. Comdr, Order of Leopold II (Belgium), 1945. *Recreation:* shooting. *Address:* Ashdon Hall, Saffron Walden, Essex. *T:* Ashdon 232. *Club:* United Service.

**COLLINS, Sir William Alexander Roy,** Kt 1970; CBE 1966; Chairman and Managing Director, William Collins Sons & Co. Ltd, Publishers; *b* 23 May 1900; *s* of late William Alexander Collins, CBE, DSO and Grace Brander; *m* 1924, Priscilla Marian, *d* of late S. J. Lloyd, Pipewell Hall, Kettering; two *s* one *d* (and one *d* decd). *Educ:* Harrow; Magdalen Coll., Oxford. *Address:* 14 St James's Place, SW1. *T:* 01-493 5321; Hayle Farm House, Horsmonden, Tonbridge, Kent. *T:* Brenchley 2564. *Clubs:* MCC, All England Lawn Tennis; Rye Golf.

**COLLIS, John Stewart;** author; *b* 16 Feb. 1900; *s* of W. S. Collis and Edith (*née* Barton), Irish; *m* 1929, Eirene Joy; two *d*. *Educ:* Rugby Sch.; Balliol Coll., Oxford (BA). FRSL. *Publications:* include: Shaw, 1925; Forward to Nature, 1927; Farewell to Argument, 1935; The Sounding Cataract, 1936; An Irishman's England, 1937; While Following the Plough, 1946; Down to Earth, 1947 (Heinemann Foundation Award); The Triumph of the Tree, 1950; The Moving Waters, 1955; Paths of Light, 1959; An Artist of Life, 1959; Marriage and Genius, 1963; The Life of Tolstoy, 1969. *Recreation:* tennis. *Address:* 54 West Street, Ewell, Surrey. *T:* 01-393 6382.
*See also M. Collis, W. R. F. Collis.*

**COLLIS, Maurice;** ICS, retired; historian, biographer, novelist, dramatist, critic and art critic, formerly contributing to The Observer and Time and Tide and now occasionally to The Arts Review, The Sunday Telegraph, and to other publications; Founder Member, International Association of Art Critics; *b* 10 Jan. 1889; *s* of late W. S. Collis, JP, Kilmore, Killiney, Co. Dublin, Ireland, and Edith Barton; *m* 1912, Dorothy (marr. diss. 1917), *d* of Arthur Tilney-Bassett; two *s*; *m* 1922, Eleanor (*d* 1967), *d* of late Arthur Bourke; two *s* one *d*. *Educ:* Rugby Sch.; Corpus Christi Coll., Oxford. First class in Final Hons Sch. of Modern History; passed into Indian Civil Service in 1911 and was posted to Burma in 1912; served in Burma in various administrative and secretarial appointments for twenty-three years, being District Magistrate, Rangoon, in 1930, and Excise Commissioner in 1931; military service with the 35th Scinde Horse in India and active service with 1/70th Burma Rifles in Palestine, 1917-18; retired, 1936, when immediately began literary career. Took up painting, 1957; one man exhibition of gouaches, Kaplan Gallery, W1, Dec. 1959; exhibition of tempera paintings and stone figures at Gallery One, W1, April 1962. *Publications: on oriental subjects:* Siamese White, 1936; She was a Queen, 1937; Trials in Burma, 1938; Lords of the Sunset, 1938; Sanda Mala, 1939; The Dark Door, 1940; The Great Within, 1941; British Merchant Adventurers, 1942; The Land of the Great Image, 1943; The Motherly and Auspicious, 1943; The Burmese Scene, 1944; White of Mergen, 1945; Quest for Sita, 1946; Foreign Mud, 1946; Lord of the Three Worlds, 1947; The First Holy One, 1948; The Descent of the God, 1948; The Grand Peregrination, 1949; Marco Polo, 1950; The Mystery of Dead Lovers, 1951; The Journey Outward, 1952 and Into Hidden Burma, 1953 (first two vols of autobiography); Last and First in Burma, 1956; Wayfoong, 1965 (centenary vol. of Hongkong and Shanghai Banking Corp., commissioned, 1962); *on Mexico:* Cortés and Montezuma, 1954; *on English History and biography:* The Hurling Time, 1957; Nancy Astor, an informal biography, 1960; Stanley Spencer, a biography, 1962; Raffles (biography of Sir Stamford Raffles), 1966; Somerville and Ross, 1968; (many of above have been translated into one or more of following languages: Norwegian, Swedish, German, Danish, Dutch, French, Italian, Spanish, Portuguese, Rumanian, Bulgarian, Hindi, Tamil, Burmese, Siamese, Japanese, or publ. in America); *on art:* Alva, an introduction to his paintings, 1942; Introduction to the Drawings of Feliks Topolski, 1946; Alva, 1951; The Discovery of L. S. Lowry, 1951; Nicholas Egon; Some Beautiful Women of Today, 1952; *general:* The Three Gods, 1970; The Journey Up: Reminiscences 1934-68, 1970. *Address:* Bradford Lodge, Ray Park Road, Maidenhead, Berks. *T:* Maidenhead 21856.
*See also J. S. Collis, W. R. F. Collis.*

**COLLIS, William Robert FitzGerald,** MA, MD, FRCP, FRCPI, DPH; Professor of Pædiatrics, Medical College, Ahmadu Bello University, Zaria, N Nigeria, and Clinical Dean of Medical School, since 1967; *b* 16 Feb. 1900; *s* of William Stewart Collis and Edith Barton; *m*; three *s* one *d* (incl. one *s* one *d* adopted). *Educ:* Rugby Sch.; Trinity Coll., Cambridge; Yale Univ. (Davison scholar); King's Coll. Hosp., London (Burney Yeo scholar); Johns Hopkins Hosp., Baltimore (Rockefeller fellowship). Entered army, 1918; obtained commission in Irish Guards; graduated medical sch., 1924; held resident medical officer appts King's Coll. Hosp. and Hosp. for Sick Children, Great Ormond Street, 1924-27; Sec., Research Dept, Hosp. for Sick Children, Great Ormond Street, 1929-32; Dir, Dept of Pædiatrics, Rotunda Hosp., Physician to the National Children's Hosp., Dublin, 1932-57; Dir of Pædiatrics, University Coll. Hosp., Ibadan, Nigeria, 1959-61; Prof. of Pædiatrics, and Dir, Inst. of Child Health, Lagos, 1962-67. *Publications:* The Silver Fleece, an Autobiography, 1936; Clinical

Pædiatrics (The Baby), Text Book, 1938; Straight On, 1947; Modern Methods of Infant Management, 1948; Ultimate Value, 1951; The Lost and the Found; Fanconi and Wallgren's Textbook of Pædiatrics; African Encounter; A Doctor's Nigeria, 1960; papers in medical journals; *plays:* Marrowbone Lane; The Barrel Organ. *Recreations:* Rugby International, Ireland, 1924-26; riding. *Address:* Bo Island, Newtown Mount Kennedy, Co. Wicklow, Ireland; 54 West Street, Ewell, Surrey. *See also J. S. Collis, M. Collis.*

**COLLISHAW, Air Vice-Marshal Raymond,** CB 1941; DSO 1917; OBE (mil.), 1920; OBE (civil), 1946; DSC, DFC; *b* Canada, 22 Nov. 1893; *s* of John Edward Collishaw, Nanaimo, BC, Canada; *m* Juanita Eliza Trapp, New Westminster, BC. *Educ:* Naval Coll. and Staff Coll. Royal Canadian Navy (Fishery Protection Service), 1908-14; entered the RNAS 1915; commanded a number of squadrons in France, 1916-18; reached second place (with total of 60) in records for pilots of British Empire in number of hostile aircraft destroyed during Great War (despatches four times, DSO and bar); posted to Egypt, 1919; commanded RAF detachment with South Russian Expedition, 1919-20 (despatches); commanded RAF detachment with British Forces, North Persia, 1920; served in Iraq, 1921-23 (despatches); Senior Royal Air Force Officer, HMS Courageous, 1929-32; commanded RAF Stations, Bircham Newton, 1932-35, Upper Heyford, 1935, RAF in the Sudan, 1935-36, and Heliopolis, 1936-38; Air Officer commanding Egypt Group, RAF, 1939; retired, 1943; holds French Croix de Guerre with two palms, and Russian Orders St Stanislaus, St Anne, and St Vladimir. *Address:* 2627 Ottawa Avenue, West Vancouver, BC, Canada.

**COLLISON,** family name of **Baron Collison.**

**COLLISON,** Baron (Life Peer) *cr* 1964, of Cheshunt; **Harold Francis Collison,** CBE 1961; General Secretary, National Union of Agricultural Workers (now National Union of Agricultural and Allied Workers), since 1953; *b* 10 May 1909; *m* 1946, Ivy Kate Hanks. *Educ:* The Hay Currie LCC Sch.; Crypt Sch., Gloucester. Firstly, worked in a commercial office in London; farm worker in Glos, 1934-. National Union of Agricultural Workers: District Organiser in Gloucester and Worcs, 1944; Nat. Officer, 1946. Mem., TUC Gen. Coun., 1953-68, Chm., 1964-65. Chm., Social Insce and Industrial Welfare Cttee of TUC, 1957-69. member: Coun. on Tribunals, 1959-; Nat. Insce Adv. Cttee, 1959-; Governing Body of ILO, 1960-69; Pilkington Cttee on Broadcasting, 1960-62; Central Transport Consultative Cttee, 1962-70; Agric. Adv. Council, 1962-; Adv. Cttee on Agricultural Educn, 1963-; Royal Commn on Trades Unions and Employers' Assocs, 1965-68; Home-Grown Cereals Authority, 1965-; Industrial Health Adv. Cttee; Economic Develt for Agriculture; Industrial Consultative Cttee, Approach to Europe; Overseas Labour Consultative Cttee; Agric. Productivity Cttee, British Productivity Council; Vice-Chm., Land Settlement Assoc., 1964-; Chairman: Agric. Apprenticeship Council, 1968-; Supplementary Benefits Commn, 1969-; Mem., N Thames Gas Board (part-time), 1961-. *Recreations:* gardening, chess. *Address:* 96 Mill Lane, Cheshunt, Herts. *T:* Waltham Cross 24088; Headland House, 308 Gray's Inn Road, WC1. *T:* 01-278 7801.

**COLLISON, Levi,** JP; lately retired as Chairman of companies; *b* Preston, 1875; *s* of S. Collison, Preston; *m* (widower); two *s* two *d. Educ:* private school. Art publisher; founder of Collisons Ltd; contested Penrith Div. bye-election; MP (L) Penrith and Cockermouth Div., 1922-23; Trustee Preston Savings Bank. *Recreation:* golf. *Address:* Brooklands, Watling Street Road, Fulwood, Preston, Lancs. *Club:* Reform (Preston).

**COLLISON, Lewis Herbert,** TD; MA; JP; Headmaster of Liverpool College, 1952-70; *b* 30 July 1908; *s* of late Mr and Mrs W. H. Collison; *m* 1934, Edna Mollie Ivens; two *d. Educ:* Mill Hill Sch.; St John's Coll., Cambridge. Asst Master of Sedbergh Sch., 1931-40; Major in King's Own Royal Regt, 1940-45; Housemaster of Sedbergh Sch., 1946-52. Mem. Council, University of Liverpool, 1963-69. *Recreations:* pottery, sailing. *Address:* Ithaca, Boat Dyke Lane, Upton, Norfolk NOR 58Z. *Club:* Hawks (Cambridge).

**COLMAN, David Stacy,** MA; Librarian of Shrewsbury School, 1961-66; Master of Day Boys, 1949-61; Assistant Master, 1938-66; formerly Lieut, TA; *b* Broughty Ferry, Angus, 1 May 1906; *yr s* of Dr H. C. Colman; *m* 1934, Sallie Edwards (*d* 1970). *Educ:* Shrewsbury Sch.; Balliol Coll., Oxford (Scholar). 1st Class Hon. Mods, 1926; 1st Class Lit. Hum., 1928. Asst Master at Shrewsbury Sch., 1928-31 and 1935-36; Fellow of Queen's Coll., Oxford and Praelector in Classics and Ancient History, 1931-34; Headmaster, C of E Grammar Sch., Melbourne, 1937-38. Mem Council, Soc. for Promotion of Roman Studies, 1958-61, Classical Assoc., 1961-64. *Publication:* Sabrinae Corolla: The Classics at Shrewsbury School under Dr Butler and Dr Kennedy, 1950. *Address:* 19 Woodfield Road, Shrewsbury, Salop. *T:* 53749. *Clubs:* National Liberal; Leander; Shrewsbury (Shrewsbury).

**COLMAN, Elijah Alec,** JP; Chairman, E. Alec Colman Group of Companies; *b* Tipton, Staffs, 7 Jan. 1903; *s* of Abraham and Leah Colman; *m* 1956, Eileen Amelia Graham; no *c. Educ:* Tipton Green Coun. Sch., Staffs. Dir of numerous charitable organisations; concerned with rehabilitation of refugees throughout the world; Chm., British Friends of Bar-Ilan Univ.; Exec. Mem., Jt Palestine Appeal; Exec. Mem., Anglo-Israel Chamber of Commerce. JP Inner London, 1962. *Recreations:* reading, philosophy. *Address:* 67 Chesterfield House, Chesterfield Gardens, W1. *T:* 01-499 3284. *Clubs:* Devonshire, City Livery, Royal Automobile.

**COLMAN, Grace Mary,** MA; *b* 1892; *d* of Canon F. S. Colman. *Educ:* Newnham Coll., Cambridge. Formerly Tutor, Ruskin Coll., Oxford, and Staff Tutor, London Univ.; formerly Ed. of Educational Publications, Labour Party. MP (Lab.) Tynemouth, 1945-50. *Address:* 5 West Ford Road, Stakeford, Northumberland.

**COLMAN, Sir Michael (Jeremiah),** 3rd Bt *cr* 1907; *b* 7 July 1928; *s* of Sir Jeremiah Colman, 2nd Bt, and Edith Gwendolyn Tritton; *S* father, 1961; *m* 1955, Judith Jean Wallop, *d* of Vice-Adm. Sir Peveril William-Powlett, *qv*; two *s* three *d. Educ:* Eton. Director: Reckitt & Colman Ltd; Waterer's Sons & Crisp Ltd. Capt., Yorks Yeomanry, RARO, 1967. *Recreations:* farming, shooting. *Heir: s* Jeremiah Michael Powlett Colman, *b* 23 Jan. 1958. *Address:* Malshanger, Basingstoke, Hants. *T:* Oakley 241. *Club:* Cavalry.

**COLOMBO, Cardinal Archbishop of,** since 1965; **His Eminence Cardinal Thomas Benjamin Cooray,** OMI; BA, PhD, DD; Archbishop of Colombo, (RC), since 1946; *b* 28 Dec. 1901. *Educ:* St Joseph's Coll., Colombo; University

Coll., Colombo; The Angelicum, Rome. Created Cardinal, 1965; Pres., Ceylon Bishop's Conf.; Member: Sacred Congregation of Propaganda Fide and Oriental Churches; Pontifical Commn for Canon Law. *Address:* Archbishop's House, Borella, Colombo 8, Ceylon. *T:* 95471.

**COLOMBO, Bishop of,** since 1964; **Rt. Rev. Charles Harold Wilfred de Soysa;** *e s* of late Sir (Lambert) Wilfred (Alexander) de Soysa, and Evelyn Johanna Publina Fernando, OBE. *Educ:* Oriel Coll., Oxford; Cuddesdon Theol. College. BA 2nd class, Theology, 1932; MA 1945. Deacon, 1933; Priest, 1934. Church of St Jude, Hampstead Garden Suburb, 1933-36; Ceylon: St Paul, Kandy, 1936-40; Baddegama, 1940-41; Incumbent of Holy Emmanuel, Moratuwa, 1941-48; Sabbatical year, 1949-50; Principal of the Divinity Sch. of the Diocese of Colombo, 1950-64; Archdeacon of Colombo, 1955-64. Mem., Anglican-Roman Catholic Preparatory Commn, 1962-63. *Publication:* (Ed.) Church of Ceylon, her faith and mission, 1945. *Address:* Bishop's House, Steuart Place, Colombo, Ceylon. *Clubs:* United University; Havelock Golf (Colombo).

**COLQUHOUN, (Cecil) Brian (Hugh),** BSc (Eng) (London); FKC; FICE, FIStructE, MConsE, FASCE, MAICE, MEIC, MSocCE (France); Senior Partner, Brian Colquhoun & Partners, Consulting Engineers and Chartered Civil Engineers, 18 Upper Grosvenor Street, London W1, and at Manchester, Liverpool, Paris, Salisbury (Rhodesia), Blantyre, Lusaka, Ndola, Johannesburg, Teheran; seconded for 2 years as Engineering Adviser to the International Bank for Reconstruction and Development, Sept. 1954; Engineering Adviser to Parliamentary Channel Tunnel Committee, 1956-57; *b* 13 Nov. 1902; *yr s* of late Arthur Hugh Colquhoun, OBE; *m* 1936, Beryl Marquis, *y d* of late Lieut-Col H. G. Cowan, MBE, late of 22nd (Cheshire) Regt; two *s*. *Educ:* Felsted Sch.; London Univ., King's Coll. Joined Muirhead, Macdonald Wilson & Co. Ltd, Civil Engineering Contractors. Then joined C. H. Lobban, MInstCE. Spent four years in Mexico with Mexican Eagle Oil Co. Resident Engineer of Mersey Tunnel, 1930, and Resident Engineer-in-Charge, 1933-36. Engineer-in-Chief, Royal Ordnance Factories at Chorley, Risley and Kirkby, 1936-40, also Adviser on Maas (Rotterdam) tunnel, Tamar (Plymouth) tunnel and Rossall sea wall, 1935-39. Rehabilitation of war production factories in main industrial centres, 1940; Dir-Gen. of Aircraft Production Factories, 1941-44. Founded Brian Colquhoun and Partners, 1944. *Address:* 3 Fountain House, Park Lane, W1. *T:* 01-629 0041; Mill Farm, Milland, Sussex. *T:* Milland 314. *Clubs:* Royal Thames Yacht, Caledonian.

**COLQUHOUN, Maj.-Gen. Sir Cyril (Harry),** KCVO 1968 (CVO 1965); CB 1955; OBE 1945; late Royal Artillery; Secretary of the Central Chancery of the Orders of Knighthood, 1960-68; Extra Gentleman Usher to the Queen since 1968; *b* 1903; *s* of late Capt. Harry Colquhoun; *m* 1930, Stella Irene, *d* of late W. C. Rose, Kotagiri, India, and Cheam, Surrey; one *s*. Served War of 1939-45 (despatches, OBE); Palestine, 1946-48 (despatches); CRA 61st Div., 1945; CRA 6th Airborne Div., 1947-48; CRA 1st Infantry Div., 1949-50; Comdt, Sch. of Artillery, 1951-53; GOC 50th (Northumbrian) Infantry Div. (TA), and Northumbrian District, 1954-56; GOC Troops, Malta, 1956-59; retired 1960. Col Commandant: RA, 1962-69; Royal Malta Artillery, 1962-70. *Recreations:* gardening, shooting. *Address:* Longwalls, Shenington, Banbury, Oxon. *T:* Edgehill 246. *Club:* Army and Navy.

**COLQUHOUN, Rev. Canon Frank,** MA; Canon Residentiary and Chancellor of Southwark Cathedral since 1961; Principal, Southwark Ordination Course, since 1966; *b* 28 Oct. 1909; *s* of Rev. R. W. Colquhoun; *m* 1934, Dora Gertrude Hearne Slater; one *s* one *d*. *Educ:* Warwick Sch.; Durham Univ. LTh 1932, BA 1933, MA 1937, Durham. Deacon, 1933; Priest, 1934; Curate, St Faith, Maidstone, 1933-35; Curate, New Malden, Surrey, 1935-39; Vicar, St Michael and All Angels, Blackheath Park, SE3, 1939-46; Editorial Sec., Nat. Church League, 1946-52; Priest-in-Charge, Christ Church, Woburn Square, WC1, 1952-54; Vicar of Wallington, Surrey, 1954-61. Editor, The Churchman, 1946-53. *Publications:* Harringay Story, 1954; Your Child's Baptism, 1958; The Gospels, 1961; Total Christianity, 1962; The Catechism, 1963; Lent with Pilgrim's Progress, 1965; Christ's Ambassadors, 1965; The Living Church in the Parish (ed), 1952; Parish Prayers (ed), 1967; Hard Questions (ed), 1967. *Recreations:* writing, tennis, listening to music. *Address:* 77 Rectory Road, Beckenham, Kent. *T:* 01-650 0311.

**COLQUHOUN, Captain Sir Ivar (Iain),** 8th Bt of Luss, *cr* 1786; DL; JP; Chief of the Clan; Grenadier Guards; *b* 4 Jan. 1916; *s* of Sir Iain Colquhoun, 7th Bt, and Geraldine Bryde (Dinah), *d* of late F. J. Tennant; *S* father, 1948; *m* 1943, Kathleen, 2nd *d* of late W. A. Duncan and of Mrs Duncan, Gorhambury, St Albans; one *s*. one *d* (and one *s* decd). *Educ:* Eton. *Heir:* *s* Malcolm Rory Colquhoun, *b* 20 Dec. 1947. *Address:* Rossdhu, Luss, Dunbartonshire; Eilean de Mheinn, Crinan, Argyllshire; 37 Radnor Walk, SW3. *Clubs:* White's, Royal Ocean Racing.

*See also Marquess of Lorne.*

**COLSON, Phyllis Constance,** CBE 1964; retired; *b* 24 June 1904; *d* of late Charles Henry Colson, CBE, sometime Dep. Civil Engr-in-Chief, Admty and late Isabel Maude Colson. *Educ:* Huyton Coll. for Girls; Bedford Coll. of Physical Education. Teacher of Physical Educn, 1926-30; Organiser of Physical Educn, Nat. Assoc. of Girls' Clubs, 1930-33; Gen. Scheme; Le Titre Honorifique de la Féd. Internat. d'Educn Physique, 1945; King Gustavus Gold Medal, 1945; William Hyde Award for services to physical educn, 1953. *Recreations:* painting; interest in care of handicapped children and young adults. *Address:* 2 Forset Court, Edgware Road, W2. *Club:* English-Speaking Union.

**COLSTON-BAYNES, Dorothy Julia;** author; *d* of Sir Christopher Baynes, 4th Bt; assumed by deed poll, 1946, additional surname of Colston. *Publications:* Enter a Child; Andromeda in Wimpole Street; The Regent and his Daughter; Fountains of Youth (a Life of Marie Bashkirtseff); In Search of Two Characters (Book Society Recommendation; Royal Society of Literature Award); The Youthful Queen Victoria; (trans.) Poems from Paul Verlaine; work included in Lord David Cecil's Anthology of Modern Biography. *Address:* c/o Lt-Col J. C. M. Baynes, West Grindon, by Norham, Berwick-on-Tweed.

**COLT, Sir Edward (William Dutton),** 10th Bt *cr* 1694; MB, MRCP; *b* 22 Sept. 1936; *s* of Major John Rochfort Colt, North Staffs Regt (*d* 1944), and of Angela Miriam Phyllis (*née* Kyan; she *m* 1946, Capt. Robert Leslie Cock); *S* uncle, 1951; *m* 1966, Jane Caroline, *d* of James Histed Lewis, Geneva and Washington, DC. *Educ:* Stoke House, Seaford; Douai Sch.;

University Coll., London. Lately: Medical Registrar, UCH; House Physician, Brompton Hosp. Mem., BMA. *Recreation:* lawn tennis. *Heir:* none. *Address:* 11 Stafford Road, Seaford, Sussex.

**COLT, Samuel Sloan;** Director since 1930 (President, 1931-57), Bankers Trust Company, 16 Wall Street, New York City; *b* New York City, 13 July 1892; *s* of Richard Collins Colt and Mary Sloan; *m* 1st, 1918, Margaret Van Buren Mason; one *s* two *d*; 2nd, 1945, Anne Weld McLane. *Educ:* Groton Sch.; Yale Univ. (BA). Hon. LLD Colgate Univ. Entered employ Farmers' Loan & Trust Co., 1914; Vice-Pres. from 1925 until its affiliation with National City Bank; Vice-Pres., National City Bank, 1929-30; Vice-Pres., Bankers Trust Co., 1930; Director: General Foods Corp.; Provident Fire Insurance Co.; Mutual Life Insurance Co.; Royal Exchange Assurance; Gen. Electric Co.; American Can Co.; Chm., Eurofund Inc., 1959-. Treasurer, American Red Cross, Greater New York Chapter; Chm., Port of NY Authority; Hon. Trustee, Cttee for Economic Development. *Recreations:* golf, tennis, fishing, hunting. *Address:* 435 East 52nd Street, New York 22, NY. *TA:* Banktrust New York. *T:* Plaza 5-4919. *Clubs:* University, Yale, Links (New York), etc.

**COLTART, James Milne;** Chairman: Scottish Television Ltd, since 1969 (Managing Director, 1957-61, Deputy Chairman, 1961-69); Highland Printers Ltd, since 1959; Deputy Chairman: The Thomson Organisation Ltd, since 1964 (Managing Director, Thomson Newspapers Ltd, 1959-61); Thomson Television (International) Ltd, since 1962; The Scotsman Publications Ltd, since 1962 (Managing Director, 1955-62); Director: Thomson Printers Ltd; Thomson Publications Ltd; Times Newspapers Ltd; Welsh Dragon Securities Ltd; and of various other newspaper and television companies in Britain and overseas; Chairman of Trustees, The Thomson Foundation, since 1969 (Trustee since 1962); *b* 2 Nov. 1903; *s* of Alexander Coltart and Alice Moffat; *m* 1927, Margaret Shepherd (*d* 1956); one *s*; *m* 1961, Mary Fryer. *Educ:* Hamilton Cres., Glasgow. Accountant: Ioco Rubber Co. Ltd, 1926; Weir Housing Co. Ltd, 1927; Dir and Sec., Marr Downie & Co. Ltd, 1937; Man. Dir, Reid Bros Ltd, 1939; Asst Gen. Manager, Scottish Daily Express, 1950; Gen. Manager, Evening Citizen Ltd, 1955. Hon. LLD Strathclyde Univ., 1967. *Recreations:* golf, fishing. *Address:* (business) Thomson House, 200 Gray's Inn Road, WC1. *T:* 01-837 1234; 89 Piccadilly, W1. *T:* 01-499 5967; Wykhurst Farm, Ewhurst, Surrey. *T:* Ewhurst 412. *Club:* Western (Glasgow).

**COLTHURST, Sir Richard La Touche,** 9th Bt *cr* 1744; Underwriting Member of Lloyd's; *b* 14 Aug. 1928; *er s* of Sir Richard St John Jefferyes Colthurst, 8th Bt, and Denys Maida Hanmer West (*d* 1966), *e d* of Augustus William West; *S* father, 1955; *m* 1953, Janet Georgina, *d* of L. A. Wilson-Wright, Coolcarrigan, Co. Kildare; three *s* one *d*. *Educ:* Harrow; Peterhouse, Cambridge (MA). Dir, Atlantic Assurance Co. Ltd. Liveryman of Worshipful Company of Grocers. *Recreations:* forestry, cricket, tennis, swimming. *Heir:* *s* Charles St John Colthurst [*b* 21 May 1955. *Educ:* Eton]. *Address:* Turret Farm, Blarney, County Cork, Eire. *T:* Cork 85210; Wheatlands, Crockham Hill, Kent. *T:* Crockham Hill 260. *Clubs:* Buck's, City University, MCC; Kildare Street (Dublin); Cork and County (Cork).

**COLTON, Gladys M.;** Head Mistress, City of London School for Girls, since 1949; *b* 1909; *er d* of William Henry Colton. *Educ:* Wycombe High Sch.; University Coll., London. BA Hons, History; London Teacher's Diploma. Senior History Mistress, Ealing Girls' Grammar Sch., 1941-49. *Recreations:* music, walking. *Address:* 16 Coleherne Court, SW5. *T:* 01-370 3643. *Club:* English-Speaking Union.

**COLUM, Padraic;** author; *b* Longford, Ireland, 8 Dec. 1881; *m* 1912, Mary Maguire (*d* 1957). Associated with W. B. Yeats and Lady Gregory at beginning of Irish Theatre movement, 1902; wrote for Irish Theatre The Land, The Fiddler's House, Thomas Muskerry; went to America, 1914, lectured; invited by Hawaiian Legislature to make survey of native myth and folk-lore, and to make same over into stories for children of Hawaiian islands; went to Hawaii, 1923. First production of Balloon, 1946, Summer Theatre. Mem. of Irish Academy of Literature and American Academy of Arts and Letters. *Publications:* Three Plays; Wild Earth (poems); Dramatic Legends (poems); Castle Conquer (novel); many books for children, including The Adventures of Odysseus and The Tale of Troy; The King of Ireland's Son; The Golden Fleece; The Children of Odin; The Girl who Sat by the Ashes; The Boy Apprenticed to an Enchanter; The Children who Followed the Piper; The Voyagers; The Forge in the Forest; Hawaiian Tales and Legends; At the Gateways of the Day, The Bright Islands, The Road Round Ireland; The Fountain of Youth (Stories); Orpheus, or Stories from the Mythologies of the World; Balloon, a comedy in three acts; Cross Roads in Ireland; Collected Poems (1932); A Half-day's Ride, or Estates in Corsica (Essays), 1932; The Big Tree of Bunlahy: stories of my own countryside; The Legend of Saint Columba; The Story of Lowry Maen (narrative poem), 1937, Ten Poems, 1958; Our Friend James Joyce (with Mary Colum), 1959; Arthur Griffith, 1960; The Poet's Circuits, 1960; The Flying Swans (novel); Images of Departure (poems), 1968. *Recreation:* walking. *Address:* 11 Edenvale Road, Ranelagh, Dublin; 415 Central Park W, New York City 25.

**COLUMBIA, BRITISH, Metropolitan of;** *see* New Westminster, Archbishop of.

**COLUMBIA, BRITISH, Bishop of,** since 1969; **Rt. Rev. Frederick Roy Gartrell;** *b* 27 March 1914; *s* of William Frederick Gartrell and Lily Martha Keeble; *m* 1940, Grace Elizabeth Wood; three *s* one *d*. *Educ:* McMaster Univ. (BA); Wycliffe Coll. (LTh, BD). Deacon, 1938; Priest, 1939. Curate, St James the Apostle, Montreal, 1938; Rector, All Saints', Noranda, PQ, 1940; Senior Asst, St Paul's, Bloor Street, Toronto, 1944; Rector, St George's, Winnipeg, Manitoba, 1945; Archdeacon of Winnipeg, 1957; Rector, Christ Church Cathedral, Ottawa, and Dean of Ottawa, 1962-69. DD (*hc*): Wycliffe Coll., Toronto, 1962; St John's Coll., Winnipeg, 1965. *Recreation:* golf. *Address:* 3184 Woodburn Avenue, Victoria, BC, Canada.

**COLUMBIA, British, (Hon.) Assistant Bishop of;** *see* Martin, Rt Rev. Henry David.

**COLVILL, Lt-Col David Chaigneau,** DSO 1940; MC; Queen's Messenger, 1946-63, retd; late Oxfordshire and Bucks LI; *b* 4 July 1898; *y s* of late Robert Frederick Steuart Colvill, Coolock, Co. Dublin, and Sophia Maconchy; *m* 1954, Kathleen, *widow* of Paul Boissier. *Educ:* Winchester; RMC Sandhurst. 2nd Lieut, Oxon and Bucks Light Infantry, 1916; Capt., 1925; Major, 1938; Temp. Lt-Col, 1940; served European War, France, 1917-18 (wounded, MC); N Russia, 1919; India and Burma, 1926-35 (India General Service Medal with Clasp,

Burma, 1931); BEF, France and Belgium, 1939-40 (wounded, DSO); commanded 1st Bn (43rd Light Infantry), 1940-42; BLA, Normandy and Belgium, 1944-45; retired, 1946. *Address:* Gosling Green House, Groton, near Boxford, Suffolk. *Clubs:* Naval and Military; Kildare Street (Dublin).

**COLVILLE,** family name of **Viscount Colville of Culross** and of **Baron Clydesmuir.**

**COLVILLE OF CULROSS,** 4th Viscount *cr* 1902; **John Mark Alexander Colville,** 14th Baron (Scot.) *cr* 1604; 4th Baron (UK) *cr* 1885; *b* 19 July 1933; *e s* of 3rd Visc. and Kathleen Myrtle, OBE 1961, *e d* of late Brig.-Gen. H. R. Gale, CMG, RE, Bardsey, Saanichton, Vancouver Island; *S* father, 1945; *m* 1958, Mary Elizabeth, *o d* of Col M. H. W. Webb-Bowen, Camrose, Stockton, Norwich; four *s*. *Educ:* Rugby; New Coll., Oxford (MA). Lieut Grenadier Guards Reserve. Barrister-at-law, Lincoln's Inn, 1960. Mem., Royal Company of Archers (Queen's Body Guard for Scotland). Hon. Mem., Rating and Valuation Assoc. *Heir: s* Master of Colville, *qv*. *Address:* Worlingham Hall, Beccles, Suffolk. *T:* Beccles 3191; Fawsyde, Kinneff, Inverbervie, Kincardineshire, Scotland. *T:* Catterline 208; 54 Cathcart Road, SW10. *T:* 01-352 2400. *See also Baron Carrington.*

**COLVILLE, Master of; Hon. Charles Mark Townshend Colville;** *b* 5 Sept. 1959; *s* and *heir* of 4th Viscount Colville of Culross, *qv*.

**COLVILLE, Sir Cecil;** *see* Colville, Sir H. C.

**COLVILLE, Maj.-Gen. Edward Charles,** CB 1955; DSO 1944, Bar, 1945; DL; JP; retired; *b* 1 Sept. 1905; *s* of late Admiral Hon. Sir Stanley Colville, GCB, GCMG, GCVO, and of The Lady Adelaide Colville (*d* 1960), *d* of 4th Earl Clanwilliam, GCB, KCMG, RM; *m* 1934, Barbara Joan Denny; two *d*. *Educ:* Marlborough; Sandhurst. ADC to Governor-Gen., Canada, 1932-34; Brigade Comd, 1944-46 (despatches); Military Adviser to UK High Comr, Canada, 1946-47; Comd Inf. Bde, TA, 1949-52; BGS, HQ Northern Army Group, 1952-54; Chief of Staff, Far East Land Forces, 1954-55; Comdr 51st Highland Div., 1956-59; retired, 1959. JP West Sussex, 1960; DL Co. Sussex, 1962. *Address:* Old Bartons, Stoughton, near Chichester, Sussex. *T:* Compton 278. *Club:* Army and Navy. *See also Sir A. B. C. Edmonstone, Bt.*

**COLVILLE, Sir (Henry) Cecil,** Kt 1962; MS (Melbourne), FRACS; private surgical practice, Melbourne; *b* 27 Aug. 1891; *s* of John William Colville and Mary Newman; *m* 1916, Harriet Elizabeth Tatchell; two *d*. *Educ:* Melbourne Church of England Grammar Sch. MB, BS (Melbourne) 1914; MS (Melbourne) 1920; FRACS 1931. War service, RAMC and AAMC, 1915-17. Pediatric Surg., Alfred Hospital, Melbourne, 1924-51. Pres., Federal Council of BMA, 1955-62; Pres. AMA, 1962-64. *Address:* 1045 Burke Road, Hawthorn, Vic 3123, Australia. *T:* Melbourne 82-5252. *Clubs:* Naval and Military, Metropolitan Golf (Melbourne).

**COLVILLE, John Rupert,** CB 1955; CVO 1949; Director: Hill, Samuel and Co.; Coutts and Co.; Ottoman Bank; National & Grindlays Bank; *b* 28 Jan. 1915; *s* of late Hon. George Colville and Lady Cynthia Colville; *m* 1948, Lady Margaret Egerton (*see* Lady Margaret Colville); two *s* one *d*. *Educ:* Harrow; Trinity Coll., Cambridge. Page of Honour to King George V, 1927-31. 3rd Sec., Diplomatic Service, 1937; Asst Private Sec. to Mr Neville Chamberlain, 1939-40; to Mr Winston Churchill, 1940-41 and 1943-45, and to Mr Clement Attlee, 1945. Served War of 1939-45, Pilot, RAFVR, 1941-44. private Sec. to Princess Elizabeth, 1947-49; 1st Sec., British Embassy, Lisbon, 1949-51; Counsellor, Foreign Service, 1951; Joint Principal Private Sec. to the Prime Minister, 1951-55. Officier, Légion d'Honneur. *Publications:* Fools' Pleasure, 1935; contrib. to Action This Day–Working with Churchill, 1968. *Address:* The Old Rectory, Stratfield Saye, Reading, Berks. *T:* Turgis Green 203; 32 Hyde Park Square, W2. *T:* 01-262 3891. *Clubs:* White's, Pratt's.

**COLVILLE, Lady Margaret;** *b* 20 July 1918; *d* of 4th Earl of Ellesmere and Violet, Countess of Ellesmere; *m* 1948, John Rupert Colville, *qv*; two *s* one *d*. Served War of 1939-45 in ATS (Junior Subaltern). Lady in Waiting to the Princess Elizabeth, Duchess of Edinburgh, 1946-49. *Address:* The Old Rectory, Stratfield Saye, Reading, Berks. *T:* Turgis Green 203; 32 Hyde Park Square, W2. *T:* 01-262 3891. *See also Duke of Sutherland.*

**COLVILLE, Norman Robert;** *b* 11 Sept. 1893; *o surv. s* of late David Colville, JP, Jerviston House, Lanarkshire; *m* 1st, 1915, Marjorie Southworthe (*d* 1937), 2nd *d* of late P. H. Edelston, Penwortham House, Lancs; (one *s* killed in action, 1941) one *d*; 2nd, 1938, Audrey Manuella Alexandre Joaquina (*d* 1940), formerly wife of Raymond Cecil Parr, and *d* of late Germain Bapst, Paris; 3rd, 1951, Diana Evelyn (she *m* 1st, 1945, 4th Earl of Kimberley, from whom she obt. a divorce, 1948), *o d* of late Lt-Col Hon. Sir Piers Walter Legh, GCVO, KCB, CMG, CIE, OBE; one *s*. *Educ:* Fettes; Clare Coll., Cambridge. Served European War, 1914-18, with Argyll and Sutherland Highlanders (MC, despatches twice); Capt. 1917; retd 1919; Group Comdr Home Guard, 1940-41. High Sheriff of Cornwall, 1940-41. FSA 1968. *Recreations:* hunting, shooting, golf, travel. *Address:* Penheale Manor, Launceston, Cornwall. *T:* North Petherwin 241; 11 Kensington Square, W8. *T:* 01-937 8942. *Club:* Travellers'.

**COLVILLE, Comdr Sir Richard,** KCVO 1965 (CVO 1953; MVO 1950); CB 1960; DSC 1943; Royal Navy retd; Extra Equerry to the Queen since 1968; *b* 26 Sept. 1907; 3rd *s* of late Adm. Hon. Sir Stanley Colville, GCB, GCMG, GCVO; *m* 1933, Dorothy, *d* of late Brig.-Gen. Halhed B. Birdwood; one *s* two *d*. *Educ:* Harrow. Joined Royal Navy, 1925. Served War of 1939-45, Mediterranean. Comdr (S), 1944. Press Secretary to King George VI, 1947-52, to the Queen, 1952-68. *Address:* Inchreed, Jarvis Brook, Sussex.

**COLVIN, Hon. Arthur Edmund,** CBE 1935; MC; MB; ChM; FRACS; Hon. Colonel RAAMC; MLC New South Wales, 1932-55, retired; OStJ; *b* 24 April 1884; *s* of Rev. Edmund Alexander Colvin and Gertrude Elizabeth Reynolds Huntley; *m* 1910, Edith Jaques Stack. *Educ:* Newington Coll.; The King's Sch.; Univ. of Sydney; Post Graduate work, Europe, America and Canada. Resident Medical Officer, Sydney Hosp., 1907-09; practised medical profession, Orange, New South Wales; served European War, 1915-18; Gas Officer 1st Div. AIF; later ADMS to DMS Maj.-Gen. Sir Neville Howse, VC (MC, despatches); served War of 1939-45; ADGMS, Army HQ, 1939; seconded, 1943, as Medical Services Adviser to Dir Gen. of Man Power; retired list, 1945, with rank of Hon. Col. Nine years Mayor of Orange, NSW; 21 years an Alderman, Municipal Council of Orange; Vice-Chm. Hospitals Commn ten years; Mem. NSW Med. Bd prior to War of 1939-45; Mem. of

Upper House Parliament 23 yrs. Hon. Surg. to Duke of Gloucester during visit of HRH to NSW, 1934. Hon. Col 6th NSW Mounted Rifles, 1949, retd 1955, retaining rank of Hon. Col. Mem. Council, Fairbridge Farm Schs of NSW; Life Governor, Sydney Hospital; Life Mem. of Returned Sailors', Soldiers' and Airmen's Imperial League of Australia. *Recreation:* golf. *Address:* The Astor, 123 Macquarie Street, Sydney, New South Wales, Australia. *Clubs:* Union, Australian, Royal Sydney Golf (Sydney).

**COLVIN, Howard Montagu,** CBE 1964; FBA 1963; MA; Senior Research fellow of St John's College, Oxford, since 1948, Librarian since 1950, Tutor in History since 1957; Reader in Architectural History, Oxford University, since 1965; Member, Royal Fine Art Commission, since 1962; Member, Royal Commission on Historical Monuments, since 1963; *b* 15 Oct. 1919; *s* of late Montagu Colvin; *m* 1943, Christina Edgeworth, *d* of late H. E. Butler, Prof. of Latin at University Coll., London; two *s. Educ:* Trent Coll.; University Coll., London. Served in RAF, 1940-46 (despatches); Asst Lecturer, Dept of History, University Coll., London, 1946-48. Hon. ARIBA. *Publications:* The White Canons in England, 1951; A Biographical Dictionary of English Architects 1660-1840, 1954 (Sir Banister Fletcher prize, 1957); The History of the King's Works, Vols. 1 and 2 (with R. Allen Brown and A. J. Taylor), 1963; A History of Deddington, 1963; Catalogue of Architectural Drawings in Worcester College Library, 1964; Architectural Drawings in the Library of Elton hall (with Maurice Craig), 1964; (ed with John Harris) The Country Seat, 1970; articles on mediæval and architectural history in Archaeological Journal, Architectural Review, etc. *Address:* 50 Plantation Road, Oxford. *T:* Oxford 57460. *Club:* Oxford and Cambridge University.

**COLVIN, John Horace Ragnar,** CMG 1968; Foreign and Commonwealth Office (formerly Foreign Office), London, since 1968; *b* Tokyo, 18 June 1922; *s* of late Adm. Sir Ragnar Colvin, KBE, CB and of Lady Colvin; *m* 1st, 1948, Elizabeth Anne Manifold (marr. diss., 1963); one *s* one *d*; 2nd, 1967, Moranna Sibyl de Lerisson Cazenove; one *s* one *d. Educ:* RNC Dartmouth; University of London. Royal Navy, 1935-51; HM Diplomatic Service, 1951-; HM Embassies, Oslo, 1951-53 and Vienna, 1953-55; British High Commn, Kuala Lumpur, 1958-61; HM Consul-General, Hanoi, 1965-67. *Recreation:* oriental ceramics. *Address:* The Old Parsonage, Pamber Heath, near Basingstoke, Hants. *T:* Silchester 253. *Club:* St James'.

**COLVIN, Brigadier Dame Mary Katherine Rosamond,** DBE 1959 (OBE 1947); TD; Extra Lady in Waiting to the Princess Royal, 1964-65 (Lady in Waiting, 1962-64); *b* 25 Oct. 1907; *d* of Lt-Col F. F. Colvin, CBE. Commissioned 1939; Commanded Central Ordnance Depot, ATS Gp, Weedon, Northants, 1943-44; subsequently held staff appointments in Military Government, Germany; Comdt WRAC Sch. of Instruction, 1948-51; Asst Dir, WRAC, HQ. Scottish Comd, 1951-54; Inspector of Recruiting (Women's Services), War Office, 1954-56; Dep. Dir, WRAC, HQ Eastern Command, 1956-57; Dir of the Woman's Royal Army Corps, 1957-61. Hon. ADC to the Queen, 1957-61, retd. *Address:* Pasture House, North Luffenham, Oakham, Rutland.

**COLWYN,** 3rd Baron, *cr* 1917; **Ian Anthony Hamilton-Smith;** Bt 1912; Dental Surgeon since 1966; *b* 1 Jan. 1942; *s* of 2nd Baron Colwyn and Miriam Gwendoline, *d* of Victor Ferguson; *S* father 1966; *m* 1964, Sonia Jane, *d* of P. H. G. Morgan, The Eades, Upton-on-Severn; one *s* one *d. Educ:* Cheltenham Coll.; Univ. of London. BDS London 1966; LDS, RCS 1966. *Recreations:* Rugby Union, motoring, music. *Heir: s* Hon. Craig Peter Hamilton-Smith, *b* 13 Oct. 1968. *Address:* Yew Tree Cottage, Dumbleton, near Evesham, Worcs. *T:* Ashton-under-Hill 383; (practice) Painswick House, Cheltenham, Glos.

**COLYER, Air Marshal Douglas,** CB 1942; CMG 1958; DFC 1918; MA; *b* 1 March 1893; *y s* of Henry Charles Colyer, HM Customs, and Charlotte, *d* of Owen Hill, Greenhithe, Kent; *m* Violet, *d* of Charles Zerenner. *Educ:* St Dunstan's Coll. and St Catharine's Coll., Cambridge. 2nd Lieut Lincolnshire Regt, 1915; transf. to RFC, 1916; permanent commission in Royal Air Force, 1919; Air Adviser, Latvian Govt, 1930-31; Air Attaché Paris, Madrid, Lisbon, 1936-40; RAF Mem., Combined Chiefs of Staff, Washington, 1945-46; Civil Air Attaché, Paris, 1947-52; Civil Aviation Representative, Western Europe, 1952-60; retd, 1960. Officer of Legion of Honour, 1938; Order of Polonia Restituta, 2nd Class, 1941; Commander of Legion of Merit (USA), 1946; Grand Officer, Order of Orange-Nassau (Holland), 1946. *Address:* c/o National Westminster Bank, Cambridge.

**COLYER-FERGUSSON, Sir James Herbert Hamilton,** 4th Bt, *cr* 1866; *b* 10 Jan. 1917; *s* of Max Christian Hamilton Colyer-Fergusson (*d* on active service, 1940) and Edith Jane (*d* 1936), singer, *d* of late William White Miller, Portage la Prairie, Manitoba; *S* grandfather, 1951. *Educ:* Harrow; Balliol Coll., Oxford. BA 1939; MA 1945. Formerly Capt., The Buffs; served War of 1939-45 (prisoner-of-war, 1940). Entered service of former Great Western Railway Traffic Dept, 1947, later Operating Dept of the Western Region of British Rlys, 1957; Personal Asst to Chm. of British Transport Commission, 1961; Passenger Officer in SE Division of Southern Region, British Railways, 1967; Parly and Public Correspondent, British Railways Bd, 1968; Deputy to Curator of Historical Relics, BRB. *Heir: uncle* William Porteous Colyer-Fergusson, *b* 18 Oct. 1893. *Address:* 61 Onslow Square, SW7. *Club:* Bath.

*See also Sir Basil Goulding, Bt, Viscount Monckton of Brenchley.*

**COLYTON,** 1st Baron, *cr* 1956, of Farway and of Taunton; **Henry Lennox d'Aubigne Hopkinson,** PC 1952; CMG 1944; Chairman, Tanganyika Concessions Ltd; Director: London Tin Corporation; Union Minière and other companies; *b* 3 Jan. 1902; *e s* of late Sir Henry Lennox Hopkinson, KCVO; *m* 1st, 1927, Alice Labouisse (*d* 1953), *d* of Henry Lane Eno, Bar Harbor, Maine, USA; one *s*; 2nd, 1956, Mrs Barbara Addams, *d* of late Stephen Barb, New York. *Educ:* Eton Coll.; Trinity Coll., Cambridge (BA History and Modern Languages Tripos). Entered Diplomatic Service, 1924; 3rd Sec., Washington, 1924; 2nd Sec., Foreign Office, 1929; Stockholm, 1931; Asst Private Sec. to Sec. of State for Foreign Affairs, 1932; Cairo, 1934; 1st Sec., 1936; Athens, 1938; War Cabinet Secretariat, 1939; Private Sec. to Permanent Under-Sec. for Foreign Affairs, 1940; Counsellor, Office of Minister of State in the Middle East, 1941; Minister Plenipotentiary, Lisbon, 1943; Dep. Brit. High Comr in Italy, 1944-46. Resigned from Foreign Service to enter politics, 1946; Head of Conservative Parly Secretariat and Jt Dir, Conservative Research Dept, 1946-50; MP (C) Taunton Div. of Somerset, 1950-56; Sec. for

Overseas Trade, 1951-52; Minister of State for Colonial Affairs, 1952-Dec. 1955; Mem., Consultative Assembly, Council of Europe, 1950-52; Delegate, General Assembly, United Nations, 1952-55; Chm., Anglo-Egyptian Resettlement Board, 1957-60; Chm., Joint East and Central African Board, 1960-65. Royal Humane Society's Award for saving life from drowning, 1919. OStJ 1959. *Heir:* *s* Hon. Nicholas Henry Eno Hopkinson [*b* 18 Jan. 1932; *m* 1957, Fiona Margaret, *o d* of Sir Torquil Munro, *qv*; two *s*]. *Address:* Netherton Hall, near Colyton, Devon. *TA:* Farway. *T:* 261; 27½ Smith Terrace, SW3. *T:* 01-352 0655. *Clubs:* Buck's White's, Beefsteak; Royal Cornwall Yacht (Falmouth).

**COMAY, Michael;** Ambassador of Israel to the Court of St James's since 1970; *b* Cape Town, 7 Oct. 1908; *s* of Alexander and Clara Comay; *m* 1935, Joan Solomon; one *s* one *d*. *Educ:* Univ. of Cape Town (BA, LLB). Barrister, 1931-40. Served with S African Army, Middle East and UK, 1940-45 (Major). Settled Palestine as representative S African Zionist Fedn, 1945; Adviser, Political Dept Jewish Agency, 1946-48; Dir, British Commonwealth Div., Israel Foreign Min., 1948-51; Asst Dir-Gen., Israel For. Min., 1951-53 and 1957-59; Minister, then Ambassador to Canada, 1953-57; Perm. Rep. and Ambassador of Israel to UN, 1960-67; Political Adviser to For. Minister and Ambassador-at-Large, 1967-70. *Recreations:* walking, painting. *Address:* Israel Embassy, 2 Palace Green, W8.

**COMBE, Air Vice-Marshal Gerard,** CB 1946; retired; *b* 15 Feb. 1902; 3rd *s* of late Percy Combe, Cobham, Surrey; *m* 1930, Brenda Mary, *er d* of Capt. Hugh Bainbridge, Killeen, Bournemouth; two *s*. *Educ:* King's College Sch.; RAF Coll., Cranwell. Flying duties in No 31 Sqdn India (NWFP), 1922-26; on return to UK in 1926 specialised in Armament; Armament Staff duties until 1932; Flying duties in No 30 Sqdn, Iraq, 1932-33 (Barzan Operations, Northern Kurdistan); Staff Coll. (psc), 1934; Armament and Chemical Warfare duties, 1935-38; commanded No 52 (Bomber) Sqdn, 1939; Armament Staff duties, Advanced Air Striking Force, 1939-40 (despatches). During 1941-45; Vice-Pres. (Air) Ordnance Board; Chief Superintendent Chemical Defence Experimental Station, Porton; Dir of Armament Development (MAP); Dir-Gen. of Armament, Air Ministry, 1945-47; Senior Air Staff Officer, RAF, HQ MEAF, 1947-49; Pres. of The Ordnance Board, 1950-51; AOA, HQ Maintenance Command, 1951-52; Air Officer Commanding, No 41 Group, 1953-55, retd 1955. United States Legion of Merit, Degree of Commander, 1946. *Recreation:* sailing. *Address:* Woodpeckers Cottage, Brockenhurst, Hants. *T:* Brockenhurst 3360. *Clubs:* Royal Lymington Yacht, Lymington Town Sailing.

**COMBERMERE,** 5th Viscount, *cr* 1826; **Michael Wellington Stapleton-Cotton;** Bt 1677; Baron Combermere, 1814; postgraduate student; *b* 8 Aug. 1929; *s* of 4th Viscount Combermere and Constance Marie Katherine (*d* 1968), *d* of Lt-Col Sir Francis Dudley W. Drummond, KBE; *S* father, 1969; *m* 1961, Pamela Elizabeth, *d* of Rev. R. G. Coulson; one *s* two *d*. *Educ:* Eton; King's Coll., Univ. of London. Palestine Police, 1947-48; Royal Canadian Mounted Police, 1948-50; Short-service commn as gen. duties Pilot, RAF, 1950-58, retd as Flt-Lt; Sales Rep., Teleflex Products Ltd, 1959-62; read Theology, KCL, 1962-67 (BD, MTh). *Heir:* *s* Hon. Thomas Robert Wellington Stapleton-Cotton, *b* 30 Aug. 1969. *Address:* 46 Smith Street, SW3. *T:* 01-352 1319. *Club:* Royal Automobile.

**COMBS, Willis Ide,** CMG 1962; HM Diplomatic Service; Ambassador to Indonesia, since 1970; *b* Melbourne, 6 May 1916; *s* of Willis Ide Combs, Napier, New Zealand; *m* 1942, Grace Willis; two *d*. *Educ:* Dannevirke High Sch.; Victoria Coll., NZ; St John's Coll., Cambridge. Served in HM Forces, 1940-46. Apptd Mem. Foreign Service, 1947; transf. to Paris as 2nd Sec. (Commercial), Dec. 1947; 1st Sec., Nov. 1948; transf. to Rio de Janeiro, as 1st Sec., 1951; to Peking as 1st Sec. and Consul, 1953 (Chargé d'Affaires, 1954); Foreign Office, 1956; to Baghdad as Counsellor (Commercial), 1959; Diplomatic Service Inspector, 1963; Counsellor, British Embassy, Rangoon, 1965; Asst Under-Sec. of State, FCO, 1968. *Address:* Sunset, Wadhurst Park, Wadhurst, Sussex. *Club:* United University.

**COMFORT, Alexander;** poet and novelist; Hon. Research Associate, Department of Zoology, University College, London, since 1951; Director, Medical Research Council Group on Ageing, University College, since 1966; *b* 10 Feb. 1920; *s* of Alexander Charles and Daisy Elizabeth Comfort; *m* 1943, Ruth Muriel Harris; one *s*. *Educ:* Highgate Sch.; Trinity Coll., Cambridge (Robert Styring Scholar Classics, and Senior Scholar, Nat. Sciences); London Hospital (Scholar). 1st Cl. Nat. Sc. Tripos, Part I, 1940; 2nd Cl. Nat. Sc. Tripos, 1st Div. (Pathology), 1941; MRCS, LRCP 1944; MB, BCh Cantab 1944; MA Cantab 1945; DCH London 1945; PhD London 1949 (Biochemistry); DSc London 1963 (Gerontology). Refused military service in war of 1939-45. Lectr in Physiology, London Hospital Medical Coll., 1948-51. Pres., Brit. Soc. for Research on Ageing, 1967. *Publications:* The Silver River, 1937; No Such Liberty (novel), 1941; Into Egypt (play), 1942; France and Other Poems, 1942; A Wreath for the Living (poems), 1943; Cities of the Plain (melodrama), 1943; The Almond Tree (novel), 1943; The Powerhouse (novel), 1944; Elegies, 1944; The Song of Lazarus (poems, USA), 1945; Letters from an Outpost (stories), 1947; Art and Social Responsibility (essays), 1947; The Signal to Engage (poems), 1947; Gengulphus (play), 1948; On this side Nothing (novel), 1948; First Year Physiological Technique (textbook), 1948; The Novel and Our Time (criticism), 1948; Barbarism and Sexual Freedom (essays), 1948; Sexual Behaviour in Society (social psychology), 1950; The Pattern of the Future (broadcast lectures), 1950; Authority and Delinquency in the Modern State (social psychology), 1950; And all but He Departed (poems), 1951; A Giant's Strength (novel), 1952; The Biology of Senescence (textbook), 1956; Darwin and the Naked Lady (essays), 1961; Come Out to Play (novel), 1961; Haste to the Wedding (poems), 1961; Are you Sitting Comfortably? (songs), 1962; Sex and Society (social psychology), 1963; Ageing, the Biology of Senescence (textbook), 1964; The Koka Shastra (translation), 1964; The Process of Ageing (science), 1965; Nature and Human Nature (science), 1966; The Anxiety Makers (med. history), 1967. *Address:* 44 The Avenue, Loughton, Essex.

**COMFORT, Anthony Francis;** Inspector of Diplomatic Service Establishments, 1965-68; *b* Plymouth, 12 Oct. 1920; *s* of Francis Harold Comfort and Elsie Grace (*née* Martin); *m* 1948, Joy Margaret Midson; two *s* one *d*. *Educ:* Bristol Grammar Sch.; Oriel Coll., Oxford. Entered Foreign Service, 1947; 2nd Sec. (Commercial), Athens, 1948-51; Consul, Alexandria, 1951-53; 1st Sec. (Commercial), Amman, 1953-54; Foreign Office, 1954-57; seconded to Colonial Office, 1957-59; 1st Sec.

(Commercial), Belgrade, 1959-60; 1st Sec. and Consul, Reykjavik, 1961-65. *Recreations:* walking, gardening. *Address:* Little Wheelers, Sarratt, Rickmansworth, Herts. *T:* Kings Langley 3074.

**COMFORT, Charles Fraser,** RCA, LLD, FRSA; artist and Author; Emeritus director, National Gallery of Canada, 1965. *b* Edinburgh, 22 July 1900; *m* 1924, Louise Chase, Winnipeg; two *d. Educ:* Winnipeg Sch. of Art and Art Students' League, New York. Cadet Officer, Univ. of Toronto Contingent of Canadian OTC, 1939; Commnd Instr in Infantry Weapons, 1940; Sen. Canadian War Artist (Army) Major, 1942-46 (UK, Italy and NW Europe). Head of Dept of Mural Painting, Ontario Coll. of Art, 1935-38; Associate Prof., Dept of Art and Archaeology, Univ. of Toronto, 1946-60 (Mem. staff, 1938); Dir, Nat. Gall. of Canada, 1959. Gold Medal and cash award, Great Lakes Exhibn, Albright Gall., Buffalo, NY, 1938; has travelled widely in Europe; Royal Society Fellowship to continue research into problems of Netherlandish painting, 1955-56; studied under Dr William Heckscher of Kunsthistorisch Inst., Utrecht. *Works include:* landscape painting and portraiture (oils and water colour); mural paintings and stone carvings in many public buildings. Pres., Royal Canadian Academy of Arts, 1957-60; Past Pres. and Charter Mem., Canadian Soc. of Painters in Water Colour; Past Pres. and Charter Mem., Canadian Group of Painters; Mem., Ontario Soc. of Artists. Dr of Laws *hc,* Mount Allison Univ., 1958. Medaglia di benemerenza culturale (Italy), 1963; Univ. of Alberta National Award in painting and related arts, 1963. *Publications:* Artist at War, 1956 (Toronto); contrib. to Royal Commsission Studies Report on National Development in the Arts, Letters and Sciences, Vol. II, 1951; contrib. various art and literary publications. *Address:* 28 Boulevard Alexandre Taché, Hull, PQ, Canada.

**COMMAGER, Henry Steele,** MA Oxon; MA Cantab; Professor of American History, Amherst College, since 1956; Professor of History, Columbia University, 1938-56; Hon. Professor, University of Santiago de Chile; *b* 25 Oct. 1902; *s* of James W. Commager and Anna Elizabeth Dan; *m* 1928, Evan Carroll; one *s* two *d. Educ:* Univ. of Chicago; Univ. of Copenhagen. AB, Univ. of Chicago, 1923; MA, 1924; PhD, 1928; Scholar Amer-Scand. Foundation, 1924-25; taught History New York Univ., 1926-29; Prof. of History, 1929-38. Lectr on American History, Cambridge Univ., 1942-43; Hon. Fellow, Peterhouse; Pitt Prof. of Amer. Hist., Cambridge Univ., 1947-48; Lectr, Salzburg Seminar in Amer. Studies, 1951; Harold Vyvyan Harmsworth Prof. of American History, Oxford Univ., 1952; Gotesman Lectr, Upsala Univ., 1953; Special State Dept lectr to German Univs, 1954; Zuskind Prof., Brandeis Univ., 1954-55; Prof., Univ. of Copenhagen, 1956; Visiting Prof., Univ. of Aix-Provence, summer 1957; Lectr, Univ. of Jerusalem, summer 1958; Commonwealth Lectr, Univ. of London, 1964; Harris Lectr, Northwestern Univ., 1964; Visiting Prof., Harvard, Chicago, Calif, etc. Editor-in-Chief, The Rise of the American Nation; Consultant, Office War Information in Britain and USA; Mem. US Army War Hist. Commn; Mem. Historians Commn on Air Power; special citation US Army; Consultant US Army attached to SHAEF, 1945. Trustee; American Scandinavian Foundation; American Friends of Cambridge Univ. Mem. of the Amer. Acad. of Arts and Letters, USA. Hon degrees: EdD, Rhode I; LittD, Washington, Ohio Wesleyan, Pittsburgh, Marietta, Hampshire Coll., 1970; DLitt, Cambridge, Franklin-Marshall, W Virginia, Michigan State; LHD, Brandeis, Puget Sound, Hartford, Alfred; LLD, Merrimack, Carleton; Dickinson Coll., 1967; Franklin Pierce Coll., 1968; Columbia Univ., 1969; Ohio State, 1970; DHL Maryville Coll., 1970. Knight of Order of Dannebrog (Denmark), 1957 (1st cl.). *Publications:* Theodore Parker, 1936; Growth of the American Republic, 1930, 2 vols 1939; sub-ed (with S. E. Morison) Documents of American History, 1934, 7th edn 1963; Heritage of America (with A. Nevins), 1939; America: Story of a Free People (with A. Nevins), 1943, new edn 1966; Majority Rule and Minority Rights, 1944; Story of the Second World War, 1945; ed Tocqueville, Democracy in America, 1947; ed America in Perspective, 1947; ed The St Nicholas Anthology, 1947; The American Mind, 1950; The Blue and the Gray, 2 vols 1950; Living Ideas in America, 1951; Robert E. Lee, 1951; Freedom, Loyalty, Dissent, 1954 (special award, Hillman Foundation); Europe and America since 1942 (with G. Bruun), 1954; Joseph Story, 1956; The Spirit of Seventy-Six, 2 vols (with R. B. Morris); Crusaders for Freedom; History: Nature and Purpose, 1965; Freedom and Order, 1966; Search for a Usable Past, 1967; Was America a Mistake?, 1968; The Commonwealth of Learning, 1968; The American Character, 1970; America and the Enlightenment, 1971. Edited: Atlas of American Civil War; Winston Churchill, History of the English Speaking Peoples; Why the Confederacy Lost the Civil War; Major Documents of the Civil War; Theodore Parker, an Anthology; Immigration in American History; Lester Ward and the Welfare State; The Struggle for Racial Equality; Joseph Story, Selected Writings and Judicial Opinions; Winston Churchill, Marlborough, 1968; Selections from Thomas Paine, 1971. *Recreation:* music. *Address:* Amherst, Mass, USA; (summer) Linton, Cambs, England. *Clubs:* Athenæum, Lansdowne (London); Century (New York); St Botolph (Boston); (former Pres.) PEN (American Centre).

**COMPSTON, Nigel Dean,** MA, MD, FRCP; Consulting Physician: Royal Free Hospital, since 1954; Royal Masonic Hospital, since 1960; St Mary Abbot's Hospital, since 1957; King Edward VII Hospital for Officers, since 1965; *b* 18 April 1918; *s* of George Dean Compston and Elsie Muriel Robinson; *m* 1942, Diana Mary (*née* Standish); two *s* one *d. Educ:* Royal Masonic Sch.; Trinity Hall, Cambridge; Middlesex Hospital. BA Cantab 1939; MRCS, LRCP 1942; MB, BCh Cantab 1942; MRCP 1942; MA, MD Cantab 1947; FRCP 1957. RAMC, 1942-47 (Temp. Lt-Col). Research Fellow, Middlesex Hosp. Medical Sch., 1948-51; E. G. Fearnsides Scholar, Cambridge, 1951; Mackenzie Mackinnon Research Fellow, RCP, 1951; Asst Prof. Medicine, Middlesex Hosp., 1952-54; formerly Asst Registrar, RCP. examiner: Pharmacology and Therapeutics, Univ. of London, 1958-63, Medicine, 1968; Medicine, RCP, 1965-. Vice-Dean, Royal Free Hosp. Sch. of Medicine, 1968-70; Mem. Bd of Governors, The Royal Free Hosp. Hon. Editor Proc. RSM, 1966. *Publications:* Multiple Sclerosis (jtly), 1955; Recent Advances in Medicine (jtly), 1964, 1968. Contributions to learned jls. *Recreations:* sailing, ski-ing, squash. *Address:* Monkswood Cottage, Camlet Way, Hadley Wood, Herts. *T:* 01-449 3814; 149 Harley Street, W1. *T:* 01-935 4444. *Clubs:* Oriental, MCC.

**COMPSTON, Vice-Adm. Sir Peter (Maxwell),** KCB 1970 (CB 1967); Deputy Supreme Allied

Commander, Atlantic, 1968-70, retired; *b* 12 Sept. 1915; *s* of Dr G. D. Compston; *m* 1st, 1939, Valerie Bocquet (marr. diss); one *s* one *d*; 2nd, 1953, Angela Brickwood. *Educ:* Epsom Coll. Royal Navy, 1937; specialised in flying duties. Served 1939-45, HMS Ark Royal, Anson, Vengeance; HMCS Warrior, 1946; HMS Theseus, 1948-50 (despatches); Directorate of RN Staff Coll., 1951-53; Capt. 1955; in comd HMS Orwell and Capt. 'D' Plymouth, 1955-57; Imperial Defence Coll., 1958; Naval Attaché, Paris, 1960-62; in comd HMS Victorious, 1962-64; Rear-Adm., Jan. 1965; Chief of British Naval Staff and Naval Attaché, Washington, 1965-67; Flag Officer Flotillas, Western Fleet, 1967-68. *Recreations:* theatre, country life. *Address:* Holmwood, Stroud, near Petersfield, Hants. *Clubs:* Army and Navy; Royal Navy (Portsmouth); Seaview Yacht (Seaview, Isle of Wight).

**COMPTON,** family name of **Marquess of Northampton.**

**COMPTON, Earl; Spencer Douglas David Compton;** *b* 2 April 1946; *s* and *heir* of 6th Marquess of Northampton, *qv*; *m* 1967, Henriette Luisa Maria, *o d* of late Baron Bentinck; one *d*. *Educ:* Eton. *Address:* 8 Kensington Palace Gardens, W8; Castle Ashby, Northampton. *T:* Yardley Hastings 232. *Club:* Turf.

**COMPTON, Denis Charles Scott,** CBE 1958; professional cricketer, retired 1957; *b* 23 May 1918; *m* 1st; one *s*; 2nd; two *s*. *Educ:* Bell Lane Sch., Hendon. First played for Middlesex, 1936. First played for England *v* New Zealand, 1937; *v* Australia, 1938; *v* West Indies, 1939; *v* India, 1946; *v* S Africa, 1947. Played in 78 Test matches; made 122 centuries in first-class cricket. Association football: mem. of Arsenal XI; England XI, 1943. *Publications:* Playing for England, 1948; End of an Innings, 1958. *Recreation:* golf. *Address:* 15 Charterhouse Street, EC1. *T:* 01-242 4388. *Clubs:* Royal Automobile; Wanderers (Johannesburg).

**COMPTON, Sir Edmund (Gerald),** KCB 1965 (CB 1948); KBE 1955; MA; Parliamentary Commissioner for Administration since 1967, and in Northern Ireland since 1969; *b* 30 July 1906; *er s* of late Edmund Spencer Compton, MC, Pailton House, Rugby, and Mrs Compton, Valparaiso, Chile; *m* 1934, Betty Tresyllian, 2nd *d* of late Hakewill Tresyllian Williams, DL, JP, and of Mrs Williams, Churchill Court, Kidderminster; one *s* four *d*. *Educ:* Rugby (Scholar); New Coll., Oxford (Scholar). 1st Class Lit. Hum., 1929; entered Home Civil Service, Administrative Grade, 1929; Colonial Office, 1930; transf. to HM Treasury, 1931; Private Sec. to Financial Sec. to Treasury, 1934-36; seconded to Min. of Aircraft Production as Private Sec. to Minister, 1940; Min. of Supply, 1941; Asst Sec., HM Treasury, 1942, Under-Sec., 1947, Third Sec., 1949-58; Comptroller and Auditor General, Exchequer and Audit Dept, 1958-66. Chairman: Irish Sailors and Soldiers Land Trust, 1946; Central Bd of Finance of C of E, 1965; Governing Body, Rugby Sch., 1969; Governors, St Mary's Sch., Calne; Mem. Governing Body, Royal Acad. of Music. Hon. FRAM 1968. *Recreations:* music, fly-fishing. *Address:* 53 Evelyn Gardens, SW7. *T:* 01-370 3220. *Clubs:* Athenæum, Boodle's.

**COMPTON, Edward (Robert Francis);** DL West Riding, Yorks, late Major Royal Scots Greys; *b* 14 Dec. 1891; *e s* of late Lord Alwyne Compton; *m* 1st, 1918, Sylvia (*d* 1950), *y d* of late A. H. Farquharson; two *s* one *d*; 2nd, 1952, Mrs Allan Wilson (*d* 1957), Little Court, Bracknell, Berks; 3rd, 1958, Lady Sysonby, Kitale, Kenya. *Address:* Newby Hall, Ripon, Yorks; Torloisk, Aros, Isle of Mull, Scotland. *Clubs:* Bath; New (Edinburgh); Muthaiga (Nairobi).

**COMPTON, Eric Henry,** CVO 1954; Retired Commissioner, New Zealand Police; *b* 14 March 1902; *s* of William Henry Compton and Harriet Compton (*née* Morgon); *m* 1925, Nona Audrey Muriel Cole; five *s* one *d*. *Educ:* Hastings High Sch., NZ. Joined NZ Police Force, 1923; Detective Sergt, 1939, Chief Detective, 1946, Sub-Insp., 1952, Asst Comr, 1952, Comr, 1953; retired on superannuation, 1956. Chm., British Sailors' Soc., Wellington, 1952-; Dep. Chm., NZ British Sailors' Soc., 1952-; Management Cttee, Christian Business Men's Assoc., 1951; Hon. Sec., NZ Fellowship of Peruvian Bible Schs. Lady Godley Medal 1919; Coronation Medal 1953. *Recreation:* bowls (indoor). *Address:* Old West Road, No 4 RD Palmerston North, New Zealand. *T:* 81-645.

**COMPTON, Fay;** *b* London, 18 Sept. 1894; *d* of Edward Compton and Virginia Bateman; *m* 1st, Harry Gabriel Pélissier (*d* 1913); one *s*; 2nd, Lauri de Freece (*d* 1921); 3rd, 1922, Leon Quartermaine (marr. diss., 1942; he died 1967); 4th, 1942, Ralph Champion Shotter (marr. diss., 1946). *Educ:* Leatherhead Court, Surrey. First appearance on stage, 1911; America, 1914; London music-hall stage (Coliseum), 1939. Has played Titania, Ophelia, Calpurnia, Paulina, and other Shakespearean parts, and had many successes in leading rôles of great variety, including: name part in Mary Rose, 1920 and 1926; Fanny Grey in Autumn Crocus, Lyric, 1931 (subsequently on tour); Dorothy Hilton in Call it a Day, Globe, 1935-37 (subsequently touring in the same part); Mary in Family Portrait, on tour 1940, and Strand, 1948 (Ellen Terry Award); Ruth in Blithe Spirit, Piccadilly, 1941-42; Martha Dacre in No Medals, Vaudeville, 1944-46; name part in Candida, Piccadilly, 1947; Gina Ekdal in The Wild Duck, St Martin's, 1948, etc. Old Vic Company, 1953-54 (having first appeared at Edinburgh Festival of 1953 with the Company): Gertrude in Hamlet; Countess of Rossillion in All's Well That Ends Well; Constance of Bretagne in King John; Volumnia in Coriolanus; Juno in The Tempest. Lady Bracknell in The Importance of Being Earnest, Old Vic, 1959; visited USA, 1959, playing lead in God and Kate Murphy; Comtesse de la Brière in What Every Woman Knows, Old Vic, 1960; Acted, Chichester Festival Theatre, 1962, 1963; A Month in the Country, Guildford (Yvonne Arnaud), 1965. Film career began 1917; has appeared in several notable films including, more recently, The Story of Esther Costello; Town on Trial; The Virgin and the Gipsy; has broadcast, and first appeared on television, 1952, since when has played numerous important rôles in plays and serials (including The Forsyte Saga, 1967). *Publication:* Rosemary: Some Remembrances, 1926. *Address:* The Crossways, 4 Clamp Hill, Stanmore, Mddx.

*See also Sir Compton Mackenzie.*

**COMPTON, Maurice;** engaged in research in Department of Development Studies, University of Sussex; *b* 26 March 1908; *s* of late S. Compton; *m* 1936, Maureen Ebie Reed; one *s*. *Educ:* Liverpool Univ.; King's Coll., Cambridge. Family Business, 1924-29; Universities, 1929-34; Min. of Agriculture, 1934-39; Min. of Food, 1939-51; Asst Sec., Min. of Agric., Fisheries and Food, 1951-65; Under-Sec. and Comr for Administration and Finance, Forestry Commn, 1965-69; retd. *Publications:* (with Hugh Bott) British Industry, 1940; contrib. to Economic

Reconstruction, by J. R. Bellerby, 1943; articles in economic periodicals. *Recreations:* reading, gardening, the theatre. *Address:* 42 Whittingehame Gardens, Surrenden Road, Brighton, Sussex. *Club:* Royal Automobile.

**COMPTON, Robert Herbert K.;** *See* Keppel-Compton.

**COMPTON, Air Vice-Marshal William Vernon C.;** *see* Crawford-Compton.

**COMPTON MILLER, Sir John (Francis),** Kt 1969; MBE 1945; TD; MA Oxon; Barrister-at-Law; Senior Registrar, Principal Probate Registry, since 1964 (Registrar, 1946-64); *b* 11 May 1900; 3rd *s* of Frederick Richard Miller, MD and Effie Anne, *d* of Samson Rickard Stuttaford; *m* 1st, 1925, Alice Irene Mary (*d* 1931), *er d* of John Scales Bakewell; one *s*; 2nd, 1936, Mary, *e d* of Rev. Alexander MacEwen Baird-Smith; one *s* one *d*. *Educ:* St Paul's Sch.; New Coll., Oxford. Called to Bar, Inner Temple, 1923; went the Western Circuit, practised Criminal, Common Law, Probate and Divorce Courts. Major, Inns of Court Regt, TA, 1936. A Deputy Judge Advocate, United Kingdom and North West Europe. Examiner, Council of Legal Education, 1951-64. UK Rep., Council of Europe Sub-Cttee on Registration of Wills. *Publications:* I tried my hand at Verse, 1968; Further Verse, 1970. *Recreations:* painting and versing. *Address:* 2 Crown Office Row, Temple, EC4. *T:* 01-583 1352. *Club:* Garrick.

**COMYN, James,** QC 1961; Recorder of Andover since 1964; *b* Co. Dublin, 8 March 1921; *o s* of late James Comyn, QC, Dublin and late Mary Comyn; *m* 1967, Anne, *d* of late Philip Chaundler, MC, Biggleswade, and of Mrs Chaundler, Cambridge. *Educ:* Oratory Sch.; New Coll., Oxford (MA). Ex-Pres. of Oxford Union. Inner Temple, 1942; called to Irish Bar, 1947. Master of the Bench, Inner Temple, 1968-. A Governor of the Oratory Sch., 1964. Owner of the "Clareville" herd of pedigree Aberdeen-Angus and the "Beaufield" herd of pedigree Herefords. *Recreations:* farming, golf. *Address:* Queen Elizabeth Building, Temple, EC4. *T:* 01-353 5432; Belvin, Tara, Co. Meath, Ireland. *T:* Navan 25111. *Clubs:* Athenæum, Oxford and Cambridge University.

**CONACHER, Mungo;** retired as Director and Chief General Manager, Martins Bank Ltd (1955-66); Director: Barclays Bank Ltd; Anglo Portuguese Bank Ltd; Butlers Bank Ltd, Nassau; Wyresdale Anglers Ltd; Chairman; North Western Region, National Savings Committee; Member, National Savings Committee; *b* 24 March 1901; *o s* of late Thomas and Margaret Conacher, Luss, Dunbartonshire; *m* 1930, Florence Victoria Fuller; two *d*. *Educ:* mainly in Scotland. Entered Bank of Liverpool at Newcastle upon Tyne, 1917; Joint Gen. Manager, Martins Bank Ltd, 1945; Dep, Chief Gen. Manager, 1950; Chief Gen. Manager, 1955; Dir, 1965. Member of Council: Univ. of Liverpool; Liverpool Sch. of Tropical Medicine; Liverpool Council of Social Service Inc.; and several other charities. *Recreations:* foreign travel, golf, gardening, fishing. *Address:* Pine Grove, Mountwood Road, Prenton, Birkenhead, Cheshire. *T:* 051-608 1194. *Clubs:* Caledonian; Royal Liverpool Golf.

**CONAN DOYLE, Air Commandant Dame Jean L. A.;** *see* Bromet, Air Comdt Dame Jean.

**CONANT, James Bryant,** Hon. CBE 1948; PhD; Author and Educational Consultant, in US, since 1965; President Emeritus, Harvard University; *b* 26 March, 1893; *s* of James Scott Conant and Jennett Orr Bryant; *m* 1921, Grace Thayer Richards; two *s*. *Educ:* Roxbury Latin Sch.; Harvard, AB, 1913, PhD, 1916; Instructor in Chemistry, Harvard, 1916-17; Lieut Sanitary Corps, USA, 1917; Major, Chemical Warfare Service, 1918; Asst Prof., Harvard, 1919-25; Assoc. Prof., 1925-27; Sheldon Emery Prof., Organic Chemistry, 1928-33; Chm., Dept of Chemistry, 1931-33; Pres., 1933-53, retired. US High Commissioner, 1953-55, Ambassador, 1955-57, Federal Republic of Germany. *Hon. degrees:* LLD: Univ. of Chicago, 1933, New York Univ., 1934, Princeton Univ., 1934, Yale, 1934, Amherst, 1935, Coll. of Charleston, 1935, Coll. of William and Mary, 1936, Williams, 1938, Dartmouth, 1938, Tulane, 1939, Univ. of Calif, 1940, Univ. of Pa, 1940, Bristol Univ. (England), 1941, Queen's Univ., 1941, Jewish Theolog. Seminary, 1951, Univ. of NC, 1945, Univ. of Toronto, 1945, Baylor Univ., Univ. of Ill., Univ. of State of New York, 1947, Northeastern Univ., Univ. of Mass, 1948, Univ. of Michigan, Yeshiva Univ., Wesleyan Univ., 1949, Swarthmore Coll., 1950, Jewish Theolog. Seminary, 1951, Univ. of Birmingham, England, 1954; Harvard, Edinburgh, and Michigan State Univs, 1955, Leeds Univ., 1956; Univ. of New Hampshire, 1966; LHD, Boston Univ., 1934; ScD: Columbia Univ., Stevens Inst., Tufts Coll., 1934, Univ. of Wisconsin, 1935, Cambridge Univ. (England), 1941, McGill Univ., 1945, Free Univ. of Berlin, 1954; DCL: Oxford Univ. (England), 1936, Colgate Univ., 1952; LittD: Univ. of Algiers, 1944, Hamilton Coll., 1947; DSc: Univ. of London, 1946, Univ. of Lyons (France), 1947, Canterbury University Coll., NZ, 1951; FEIS 1947; admitted to Univ. of Adelaide *ad eundem gradum*, 1951. Lectures: Univ. of Calif, 1924; Sachs, Teachers' Coll., 1945; Terry, Yale, 1946; Stafford-Little, Princeton, 1957; Godkin, Harvard, 1958; Stimpson, Goucher Coll., 1951; Page Barbour, Univ. Va, 1952, Stevenson, LSE, 1952; Morrow, Smith Univ., 1959; Inglis, Harvard, 1959; Pollack, Harvard, 1959; Jefferson, Univ. of Calif, 1960. Research Associate California Technical, 1927. Mem. Educational Policies Commn of NEA, 1941-46, 1947-50, 1957-63; Chairman: National Defence Research Cttee and Dep. Dir, Office of Scientific Research and Development, 1941-46; Steering Cttee for Manhattan Dist charged with production of atomic bombs, 1942-45; Gen. Advisory Cttee of AEC, 1947-52. Member: Nat. Acad. of Sciences; Amer. Chem. Soc.; Mass. Historical Soc.; Amer. Acad. of Art and Sciences, Amer. Philosophical Soc.; Nat. Science Foundation, 1950-53; Science Advisory Cttee, 1951-53. For. Member: Royal Society; Royal Institute of Chemistry; RSE; Hon. FCS; awarded Chandler Medal, Columbia Univ., 1932; Nichols Medal, 1932; Priestley Medal, Amer. Chem. Soc., 1944; Medal of Merit with Oak Leaf Cluster, 1948; Woodrow Wilson Award for Distinguished Service, 1959; Presidential Medal of Freedom, 1963; Great Living American Award, 1965; Sylvanus Thayer Award, 1965; Arches of Science Award, 1967; Atomic Pioneer Award, 1970. Hon. Fellow, Emmanuel Coll., Cambridge. Comdr, Legion of Honor. *Publications:* Practical Chemistry (with N. H. Black); Organic Chemistry; Chemistry of Organic Compounds; Our Fighting Faith, 1942; On Understanding Science, 1947; Education in a Divided World, 1948 (Gleichkeit der Chancen, 1955); Fundamentals of Organic Chemistry (with A. H. Blatt), 1950; Science and Common Sense, 1951; Modern Science and Modern Man, 1952; Education and Liberty, 1953; The Citadel of Learning, 1956; Germany and Freedom, 1958; The American

High School Today, 1959; The Child, The Parent, and the State, 1959; Education in the Junior High School Years, 1960; Slums and Suburbs, 1961; Thomas Jefferson and the Development of American Public Education, 1962; The Education of American Teachers, 1963; Two Modes of Thought, 1964; Shaping Educational Policy, 1964; The Comprehensive High School, 1967; Scientific Principles and Moral Conduct, 1967; My Several Lives, 1970; Editor: Vols II and IX Organic Syntheses; Harvard Case Histories in Experimental Science; papers in scientific journals on researches in organic chemistry. *Address:* (office) c/o TIAA, 730 Third Avenue, New York, NY, USA; (home) 200 East 66th Street, New York. *Clubs:* Athenæum; Tavern, Harvard; Century, Chemists, Harvard (New York); Cosmos (Washington).

**CONANT, Sir Roger John Edward,** 1st Bt *cr* 1954; CVO 1953; *b* 28 May 1899; *e s* of late E. W. P. Conant, Lyndon Hall, Oakham; *m* 1920, Daphne, *d* of A. E. Learoyd; three *s*. *Educ:* Eton; RMC Sandhurst. Grenadier Guards, 1917-21 and 1939-45; served European War (wounded); MP (C) Chesterfield, 1931-35, Bewdley Div. of Worcs, 1937-50, Rutland and Stamford, 1950-Sept. 1959. Comptroller of HM Household, 1951-54. *Heir:* *s* John Ernest Michael Conant [*b* 24 April 1923; *m* 1950, Periwinkle Elizabeth, *d* of late Dudley Thorp, Kimbolton, Hunts; two *s* two *d* (and one *s* decd)]. *Address:* Manor House, Harringworth, Corby, Northants. *Club:* Carlton.

**CONCANNON, John Dennis;** MP (Lab) Mansfield since 1966; *b* 16 May 1930; *m* 1953, Iris May Wilson; two *s* two *d*. *Educ:* Rossington Sec. Sch. Coldstream Guards, 1947-53; Mem. Nat. Union of Mineworkers, 1953-66; Branch Official, 1960-65. Mem., Mansfield Town Council, 1962-66. Asst Govt Whip, 1968-70; Opposition Whip, 1970-. *Recreations:* cricket, basket-ball. *Address:* 84 Langford Road, Mansfield, Notts. *T:* Mansfield 27235.

**CONDLIFFE, John Bell,** MA, DSc, LLD, LittD; Consultant, Stanford Research Institute, Menlo Park; Professor of Economics, 1940-60, now Emeritus, University of California, Berkeley; *b* Melbourne, Australia, 23 Dec. 1891; *s* of Alfred B. and Margaret Condliffe; *m* 1916, Olive Grace, *d* of Charles Mills; two *s* one *d*. *Educ:* Canterbury Coll., University of NZ; Gonville and Caius Coll., Cambridge (Sir Thomas Gresham Research Student). Prof. of Economics, Canterbury Coll., 1920-26; Research Sec., Institute of Pacific Relations, 1927-31; Visiting Prof. of Economics, Univ. of Mich, 1930-31; Economic Intelligence Service, League of Nations, 1931-36; Univ. Prof. of Commerce, LSE, 1936-39; Associate-Dir, Div. of Economics and History, Carnegie Endowment for International Peace, 1943-48; Research Associate, Institute of International Studies, Yale Univ., 1943-44; Fulbright Research Scholar, Cambridge Univ., 1951; Consultant, Reserve Bank of New Zealand, 1957; Adviser, National Council of Applied Economic Research, New Delhi, 1959-60; Henry E. Howland Memorial Prize, 1939; Wendell L. Willkie Memorial Prize, 1950. FRSA, 1949; Fellow Amer. Assoc. for the Advancement of Science, 1953. Gold Cross, Royal Order of Phœnix (Greece), 1954. *Publications:* The Life of Society, 1922; A Short History of New Zealand, 1925; Problems of the Pacific, 1928; New Zealand in the Making, 1930 (rev. edn, 1959); Problems of the Pacific, 1929, 1930; China To-day–Economic, 1933; World Economic Survey, 1931-32, 1932-33, 1933-34, 1934-35, 1935-36, 1936-37; The Reconstruction of World Trade, 1940; Agenda for a Post-War World, 1942; The Common Interest in International Economic Organization (with A. Stevenson), 1944; The Commerce of Nations, 1950; Point Four and the World Economy, 1950; The Welfare State in New Zealand, 1958; Foreign Aid Re-examined, 1963; The Development of Australia, 1964; Foresight and Enterprise, 1965; Economic Outlook for New Zealand, 1969; articles in journals, etc. *Address:* 1801 Broadway, San Francisco, Calif, USA. *Clubs:* Bohemian (San Francisco); Cosmos (Washington).

**CONDON, Denis David,** OBE 1964; Senior Representative at Lloyd's of London for Neilson McCarthy, Consultants; *b* 23 Oct. 1910; *s* of Capt. D. Condon and Mrs A. E. Condon; *m* 1933, Mary Marson; one *d*. *Educ:* Paston Grammar Sch., North Walsham, Norfolk. Journalist until 1939. War Service with Royal Artillery, UK and Burma (Major). Joined India Office, 1946; CRO, 1947; served India, Ceylon, Australia, Nigeria; Head of News Dept, CO, 1967-68. *Recreations:* fishing, bird-watching, gardening. *Address:* 2 A'Becket's Avenue, Aldwick Bay, Sussex. *T:* Pagham 2406. *Clubs:* Oriental, Civil Service; Gymkhana (Delhi); Australasian Pioneers (Sydney).

**CONDON, Prof. Edward Uhler,** PhD; Professor of Physics, University of Colorado, Boulder, Colorado, since 1963; Editor, Reviews of Modern Physics, 1957-68; *b* 2 March 1902; *s* of late William Edward Condon, civil engineer; *m* 1922, Emilie Honzik; two *s* one *d*. *Educ:* Univ. of Calif, Berkeley, Calif. National Research Fellow, Göttingen and Munich, 1926-27; Lectr in Physics, Columbia Univ., 1927-28; Asst Prof. of Physics, Princeton Univ., 1928-29; Prof. of Theoretical Physics, Univ. of Minn., 1929-30; Assoc. Prof. of Physics, Princeton Univ., 1930-37; Assoc. Dir of Research, Westinghouse Electric Corp., 1937-45; Dir, National Bureau of Standards, US Dept of Commerce, Washington, DC, 1945-51. Dir of Research and Development, Corning Glass Works, 1951-54; Prof. of Physics, Washington Univ., St Louis, Mo, 1956-63. Scientific Adviser to US Senate Special Cttee on Atomic Energy 79th Congress. President: American Physical Soc., 1946; Amer. Assoc. for Advancement of Science, 1953; Amer. Assoc. of Physics Teachers, 1964; Soc. for Social Responsibility in Science, 1968-69. Visiting Prof. of Physics: Univ. of Pa, 1955-56; Oberlin Coll., 1962-63. DSc (hon.): Delhi (India); New Mexico Sch. of Mines; American Univ.; Alfred Univ. *Publications:* Quantum Mechanics (with P. M. Morse), 1929; The Theory of Atomic Spectra (with G. H. Shortley), 1935; Handbook of Physics (with H. Odishaw), 1958; Scientific Study of Unidentified Flying Objects, 1969; numerous research papers, mostly published in Physical Review. *Address:* 761 Cascade Avenue, Boulder, Colo, USA. *Clubs:* Cosmos (Washington, DC); University (Boulder).

**CONESFORD,** 1st Baron, *cr* 1955, of Chelsea; **Henry George Strauss,** QC 1946; *b* London, 1892; *o s* of late A. H. Strauss; *m* 1927, Anne, *yr d* of late J. Bowyer Nichols, Lawford Hall, Manningtree. *Educ:* Rugby (Scholar); Christ Church, Oxford (Scholar). MA (1st class Classical Hon. Mods; 1st class Lit. Hum.). Junior Treasurer, Oxford Union Soc., 1914; enlisted, 1914; invalided; served in Government Depts; called to Bar, Inner Temple, 1919; Hon. Bencher, 1969. MP (C) Norwich, 1935-45, Combined English Universities, 1946-50, Norwich South, 1950-April 1955. Parliamentary Private Sec. to the Attorney-Gen., 1936-42; Joint Parliamentary

Sec., Ministry of Works and Planning, 1942-43; Parliamentary Sec., Ministry of Town and Country Planning, 1943-45, when he resigned office in disagreement with the decisions of the Crimea Conference; Parliamentary Sec., Board of Trade, 1951-55; Pres., London Soc.; Past Pres.: Architecture Club; Design and Industries Assoc. Hon. FRIBA, 1965. *Publication:* Trade Unions and the Law, 1946. *Heir:* none. *Address:* 25 Cheyne Walk, SW3. *T:* 01-352 1984. *Clubs:* Carlton, Beefsteak, Pratt's; Norfolk (Norwich).

**CONEY, Rev. Canon Harold Robert Harvey,** MA Oxon; *b* 28 Oct. 1889; *s* of John Harvey and Hope Josephine Coney; *m* 1925, Edith Mary Carpenter; three *s* one *d. Educ:* Keble Coll., Oxford; Cuddesdon Coll. Formerly an Architect; served in France, 1915-17, Civil Service Rifles (despatches); Meritorious Service Medal, 1916; deacon, 1920; priest, 1921; Curate of Bermondsey, 1920-23; Warden of Caius Coll. Mission, Battersea, 1923-28; Vicar of Felkirk, 1928-37; Canon Missioner of Wakefield Cathedral, 1937-40; Champney Lecturer in Christian Evidence, 1937-40; Campden Lecturer, Wakefield Cathedral, 1937-40; Rector of Thornhill, Dewsbury, 1940-61 and Rural Dean of Dewsbury, 1947-61; Hon. Canon of Wakefield Cathedral, 1937-61, Canon Emeritus, 1961; Curate of Coonamble, NSW, Australia, 1961-63; Permission to officiate, Bath and Wells, 1963-69, Brisbane, 1969. *Recreation:* laughing. *Address:* 49 Salisbury Road, Ipswich, Queensland 4305, Australia.

**CONGLETON,** 8th Baron *cr* 1841; **Christopher Patrick Parnell;** Bt 1766; *b* 11 March 1930; *s* of 6th Baron Congleton (*d* 1932) and Hon. Edith Mary Palmer Howard (MBE 1941) (she *m* 2nd, 1946, Flight Lieut A. E. R. Aldridge, who died 1950), *d* of late R. J. B. Howard and late Lady Strathcona and Mount Royal; *S* brother, 1967; *m* 1955; Anna Hedvig, *d* of G. A. Sommerfelt, Oslo, Norway; two *s* three *d. Educ:* Eton; New Coll., Oxford. *Heir: s* Hon. John Patrick Christian Parnell, *b* 17 March 1959. *Address:* Ebbesbourne Wake, Salisbury, Wilts.

**CONLAN, Bernard;** MP (Lab) Gateshead (East) since 1964; Engineer; *b* 24 Oct. 1923; *m*; one *d. Educ:* Manchester Primary and Secondary Schs. Mem., AEU, 1940-, Officer, 1943-. Mem., Manchester City Coun., 1954-. Joined Labour Party, 1942; contested (Lab) High Peak, 1959. *Address:* House of Commons, SW1.

**CONN, Prof. John Farquhar Christie,** DSc; CEng; MRINA; John Elder Professor of Naval Architecture, University of Glasgow, since 1957; *b* 5 July 1903; *s* of Alexander Aberdein Conn and Margaret Rhind Wilson; *m* 1935, Doris Maude Yeatman; one *s* one *d. Educ:* Robert Gordon's Coll., Aberdeen; Glasgow Univ. Apprenticeship at Alexander Hall and Co. Ltd, Aberdeen, 1920-25; employed in several shipyards; Scientific staff, Ship Div., National Physical Laboratory, 1929-44; Chief Naval Architect, British Shipbuilding Research Association, 1945-57. *Publications:* various papers in Trans. of Instn of Naval Architects and other learned societies. *Recreations:* music, reading. *Address:* The University, Glasgow, W2; 30 Colquhoun Drive, Bearsden, Glasgow. *T:* 041-942 4640.

**CONNELL, Mrs A. B.;** *see* de Valois, Dame Ninette.

**CONNELL, Sir Charles,** Kt 1956; DL; Chairman, Charles Connell & Co. Ltd, since 1949; Director Upper Clyde Shipbuilders, since 1967; *b* 15 May 1900; *s* of late Charles Broadfoot Connell; *m* 1924, Audrey Menzies Raymond; one *s* two *d. Educ:* Fettes; Clare Coll., Cambridge. Joined Charles Connell & Co. 1921, Dir, 1930. Chairman: Alscot Shipping Co.; Iron Trades Employers' Insurance Assoc. Ltd; Director: St Andrews Shipping Co.; Scottish Ore Carriers Ltd; G. & J. Weir; etc. President: Clyde Shipbuilders Assoc., 1949; Shipbuilding Employers' Federation, 1950-51; Shipbuilding Conference, 1952-53; British Employers' Confederation, 1954-56. Mem., Anglo-American Council of Productivity, 1951-53; Vice-Pres., British Productivity Council, 1955; Joint Chm., Technical Cttee, Lloyd's Register of Shipping, 1955-65. Mem., Admiralty Shipbuilding Advisory Cttee, 1953-54; Chm. of Council, British Shipbuilding Research Assoc., 1954-56, and again 1957, 1959; Mem., Iron and Steel Board, 1953-62; Chm., Scottish Cttee, Council of Industrial Design, 1958-61; Mem., Royal Fine Art Commission for Scotland, 1964-; Vice-Pres., Royal Highland and Agricultural Soc. of Scotland, 1969-70. Prime Warden, Shipwrights' Co., 1965-66. MA, MRINA, MIES; Hon. Comdr, RNR; DL Dunbartonshire, 1957. Comdr Royal Norwegian Order of St Olav, 1958. *Address:* Craigallian, Milngavie, Dunbartonshire. *T:* Milngavie 1676; Colquhalzie, Auchterarder, Perthshire. *T:* Auchterarder 59; 42 Upper Brook Street, W1. *T:* 01-629 8628. *Clubs:* Travellers'; Western (Glasgow).

**CONNELL, Sir Charles (Gibson),** Kt 1952; with Connell & Connell, WS, 10 Dublin Street, Edinburgh; *b* 11 March 1899; *s* of late Sir Isaac Connell, SSC, and Mary Jane (*née* Gibson); *m* 1927, Constance Margaret Weir; one *s* one *d. Educ:* Melville Coll., Edinburgh; Edinburgh Univ. 2nd Lieut RFA, 1917-19. WS 1923; BL Edinburgh, 1923. JP City of Edinburgh, 1933. Secretary: Royal Scottish Agricultural Benevolent Instn, 1935-66; Scottish Agricultural Arbiters Assoc., 1935-66; Director: Commercial Union Assurance Co. Ltd (Chm., Edinburgh Board); Dominion & General Trust Ltd (Chm.); The Edinburgh Building Soc.; Melville Coll. Mem., Nature Conservancey (Chm. Scottish Cttee); Chm., scottish Wildlife Trust. Pres., Scottish Unionist Assoc., 1944-45; Joint Hon. Sec., 1938-54. *Publications:* Ed 3rd, 4th and 5th Edns (1961) of Connell on the Agricultural Holdings (Scotland) Acts. *Recreations:* wildlife conservation, gardening. *Address:* 12 Abbotsford Park, Edinburgh. *T:* 031-447 2026. *Clubs:* Caledonian, New (Edinburgh).

**CONNELL, Charles Percy;** Puisne Judge, Kenya Colony, 1951-64, retired; *b* 1 Oct. 1902; *s* of late C. R. Connell, Barrister-at-Law and late K. Adlard; *m* 1946, Mary O'Rourke. *Educ:* Charterhouse; New Coll., Oxford (Hons, Jurisprudence). Called to Bar, Lincoln's Inn, 1927. Joined Kenya Judicial Service, 1938 (Resident Magistrate). Served War of 1939-45 (8th Army Clasp and war medals); commissioned King's African Rifles, 1941; British Military Administration (Legal and Judicial), Eritrea and Tripolitania, 1942-46. Acting Puisne Judge, Kenya, 1950. *Recreations:* tennis, cricket and trout fishing. *Address:* c/o National Westminster Bank, 14 Sloane Square, SW1.

**CONNELLAN, Joseph;** MP (N) County Down South, Northern Ireland Parliament, since 1949; Journalist; Editor "Frontier Sentinel," Newry; working-class parentage; *m* 1937, Nellie, *d* of late Daniel and Brigid O'Hare, Cloughrea, Bessbrook, Co. Armagh. MP (N) S Armagh, 1929-33. Several times elected to many local public boards. One of earliest followers of Arthur Griffith, founder of Sinn Fein; a pioneer of that movement in North of Ireland and for a lengthy period active in Gaelic League and Gaelic Athletic Assoc. Senior Vice-Pres., Ulster Council of National Athletic and Cycling Assoc. (Ireland). Member: County Armagh Diocesan Hist. Soc.; Louth Archæolog. Soc.; Brönte Soc. (England), and other national literary and cultural bodies. *Address:* Dūin Mhuire, Dublin Road, Newry, N Ireland. *T:* Newry 2505.

**CONNELLY, Marc;** playwright; *b* 13 Dec. 1890; *s* of Patrick Joseph Connelly and Mabel Louise Fowler Cook. *Educ:* Trinity Hall, Washington, PA. Member of Authors' League of America (Past Pres.) and of National Inst. of Arts and Letters (Past Pres.). Prof. of Playwriting, Yale (retired). LittD (Hon.) Bowdoin. *Publications:* Plays: The Wisdom Tooth, The Green Pastures (awarded Pulitzer Prize, 1930), and others; co-author: Dulcy, Merton of the Movies, Beggar on Horseback, To the Ladies, Farmer Takes a Wife, and others; several musical comedies; A Souvenir from Qam (novel), 1965; Voices Offstage (memoirs), 1968; contributor of verse, articles and fiction to magazines, including Coroner's Inquest (awarded O. Henry short-story prize). *Address:* 25 Central Park West, New York City, NY, USA. *TA:* Marconel NY. *T:* Circle 7-2147. *Clubs:* Savage; Players' (New York).

**CONNER, Cyril;** *b* 26 Feb. 1900; *m* 1st, 1930, Mary Stephanie Douglass; two *d*; 2nd, 1946, Margaret Isobel Hunt (*née* Murison); one *d* (one step *s* adopted). *Educ:* Haileybury; Merton Coll., Oxford. MA Greats and Law. Commn in RGA 1918. Called to Bar, Inner Temple, and practised at Common Law Bar, London, 1924-38; Arbitrator for Milk Marketing Board, 1934-38; BBC Dir for NE England, 1938; Head of BBC's Commonwealth and Foreign Relations, 1941-60, except Jan.-July 1953, when BBC Controller for Northern Ireland. Mem., Administrative Council of European Broadcasting Union, 1951-60. Delegate to Commonwealth Broadcasting Confs, 1946, 1952, 1956, 1960. Chm. of Frances Martin Coll., London, 1950 and 1951. Dep. Chm., West Sussex QS, 1963-; JP West Sussex, 1963-. Chm., Rent Assessment Cttee for Surrey and Sussex, 1966-. *Publications:* contributions to Juridical Review and other legal journals. *Address:* Lovehill House, Trotton, near Rogate, West Sussex. *T:* Midhurst 3665. *Clubs:* Athenæum, Special Forces.

**CONNER, Rearden;** (pen-name of **Patrick Reardon Connor**), MBE 1967; novelist and short-story writer; *b* 19 Feb. 1907; *s* of John and Bridie Connor; *m* 1942, Malinka Marie Smith; no *c*. *Educ:* Christian Brothers Schs; Presentation Coll., Cork. Worked in Min. of Aircraft Production, during War, in Research and Development of Equipment. Carried on in this field, after war, in Min. of Supply, and later in Min. of Aviation and Min. of Technology. Critic of fiction, The Fortnightly, 1935-37, also on Books of the Month; Reader of fiction for Cassell, 1948-56. Work has been included in: Best Short Stories Anthology (twice); Pick of To-Day's Short Stories; Whit Burnett anthology (USA), Stories of the Forties. *Publications:* Shake Hands with The Devil, 1933 (Literary Guild Selection in USA; filmed, 1958); Rude Earth, 1934; Salute to Aphrodite, 1935 (USA); I am Death, 1936; Time to Kill, 1936 (USA); Men Must Live, 1937; The Sword of Love, 1938; Wife of Colum, 1939; The Devil Among the Tailors, 1947; My Love to the Gallows, 1949; Hunger of the Heart, 1950; The Singing Stone, 1951; The House of Cain, 1952; (under *pseudonym* Peter Malin): To Kill is My Vocation, 1939; River, Sing Me a Song, 1939; Kobo the Brave, 1950. *Recreations:* listening to music; going to the theatre. *Address:* 25 Victoria Street, Brighton 1, Sussex. *T:* Brighton 27900.

**CONNERY, Sean, (Thomas Connery);** actor; *b* 25 Aug. 1930; *s* of Joseph and Euphamia Connery; *m* 1962, Diane, *d* of Sir Raphael West Cilento, *qv*, and Lady Cilento; one *s* (and one step *d*). Served Royal Navy. Has appeared in films: No Road Back, 1956; Action of the Tiger, 1957; Another Time, Another Place, 1957; Hell Drivers, 1958; Tarzan's Greatest Adventure, 1959; Darby O'Gill and the Little People, 1959; On the Fiddle, 1961; The Longest Day, 1962; The Frightened City, 1962; Woman of Straw, 1964; The Hill, 1965; A Fine Madness, 1966; Shalako, 1968; The Molly Maguires, 1968; The Red Tent (1st Russian co-production), 1969; *as James Bond:* Dr No, 1963; From Russia With Love, 1964; Goldfinger, 1965; Thunderball, 1965; You Only Live Twice, 1967. *Recreations:* oil painting, golf, reading, cooking. *Address:* c/o Richard Hatton Ltd, 17a Curzon Street, W1.

**CONNOLLY, Cyril (Vernon),** Author and Journalist; Chevalier de la Légion d'Honneur; *b* 10 Sept. 1903; *o s* of Major Matthew Connolly, Bath, and Muriel Vernon; *m* 1959, Deirdre, *o c* of Hon. P. W. D. Craig, MBE, and Mrs Aline Hanbury; one *s* one *d*. *Educ:* Eton (scholar); Balliol Coll., Oxford (Brackenbury Scholar). Has written for New Statesman and other periodicals, 1927-; founded Horizon, 1939, and ed, 1939-50; Literary Editor, Observer, 1942-43; contributes weekly to Sunday Times. *Publications:* The Rock Pool (fiction), 1935; Enemies of Promise, 1938; The Unquiet Grave, 1944-45; The Condemned Playground, 1944; Put Out the Light (translation), 1944; Ideas and Places, 1953; The Missing Diplomats, 1953; (ed) The Golden Horizon, 1953; (ed) Great English Short Novels, 1953; (with Jerome Zerbe) Les Pavillons, 1962; Previous Convictions, 1963; The Modern Movement, 1965. *Recreation:* travel. *Address:* 48 St John's Road, Eastbourne, Sussex. *Clubs:* White's, Pratt's.

**CONNOLLY, Joseph;** *b* Belfast, 19 Jan. 1885; *s* of John and Margaret Connolly; *m* 1916, Roisin MacGavock; four *s* four *d*. *Educ:* St Malachy's Coll., Belfast. Manufacturer of furniture; active in Sinn Fein and Irish Independence Movement from youth; arrested and imprisoned after 1916 Rising; sent as Consul-Gen. to USA by Republican Govt, 1921; resigned following the Treaty, 1922; Chm. Reorganized Sinn Fein, 1923; elected to Senate in 1928 and leader of the Senate Group of Fianna Fail, 1928-36; Minister for Posts and Telegraphs, 1932-33; Minister for Lands and Forestry, 1933-36; Delegate to League of Nations, 1932-33; Minister and Head of Delegation to World Economic Conference, London, 1933; Chm., Commissioners of Public Works, 1936-50, retd 1950. *Address:* Melford, Westfield Road, Dublin.

**CONNOR, Bishop of,** since 1969; **Rt. Rev. Arthur Hamilton Butler,** MBE 1944; DD; MA; *b* 8 March 1912; *s* of George Booker and Anne Maude Butler; *m* 1938, Betty, *d* of Seton Pringle, FRCSI; one *s*. *Educ:* Friars School, Bangor; Trinity Coll., Dublin. Curate: Monkstown, Dublin, 1935-37; Christ Church, Crouch End, N8, 1937; Holy Trinity, Brompton, SW3, 1938-39. Army, 1939-45: Chaplain, 2nd DCLI, 1939-43; Senior Chaplain, 1st Div., 1943-45. Incumbent of Monkstown, 1945-58; Bishop of Tuam, Killala and Achonry, 1958-69. *Recreations:* golf, fishing. *Address:* Bishop's House, 22 Deramore Park, Belfast 9. *Clubs:* Ulster (Belfast); University, Royal Irish Yacht (Dublin).

**CONNOR, Patrick Reardon;** *see* Connor, Rearden.

**CONOLLY-CAREW,** family name of **Baron Carew.**

**CONRAN, (George) Loraine;** Director, Manchester City Art Galleries, since 1962; Member: British National Committee, International Council of Museums; Court, Royal College of Art; *b* 29 March 1912; *o s* of Col George Hay Montgomery Conran; *m* 1938, Jacqueline Elspeth Norah Thullier O'Neill Roe; one *s* one *d* (and one *d* decd). *Educ:* RNC Dartmouth. Museum and Art Gallery, Birmingham, 1935; Walker Art Gallery, Liverpool, 1936; Southampton Art Gallery, 1938; Curator, The Iveagh Bequest, Kenwood, 1950. Chm., Jt Cttee of Museums Assoc. and Carnegie UK Trust. Served War of 1939-45 (despatches). *Address:* City Art Gallery, Mosley Street, Manchester 2. *Club:* Athenæum.

**CONRAN, Terence Orby;** Joint Chairman, Ryman Conran Ltd, since 1968; Chairman, Conran Holdings Ltd, 1965-68; *b* 4 Oct. 1931; *m*; two *s*; *m* 1963, Caroline Herbert; one *s* one *d*. *Educ:* Bryanston, Dorset. Mem., Council of Industrial Design. RSA Presidential Medal for Design Management to Conran Group. *Recreation:* gardening. *Address:* 9 St Andrew's Place, NW1. *T:* 01-935 7443.

**CONROY, Sir Diarmaid (William),** Kt 1962; CMG 1960; OBE 1955; TD 1946; QC (Gibraltar) 1953; (Kenya) 1956; President, Industrial Tribunals for England and Wales, since 1965; Chief Justice, N Rhodesia, 1961-65; *b* 22 Dec. 1913; *m* 1939, Alice Lilian Elizabeth Craig; one *s* two *d*. *Educ:* Mount St Mary's; Gray's Inn. Practised at Bar, 1935-39; served War, 1939-46, with London Irish Rifles (Major, wounded); Crown Counsel, N Rhodesia, 1946; Legal Draftsman, N Rhodesia, 1949; Attorney-Gen., Gibraltar, 1952; Permanent Sec. of Ministry of Legal Affairs, Solicitor-Gen. and Dep.-Speaker, Kenya, 1955-61. *Recreations:* sailing, fishing. *Address:* 8 Fairburn Court, St Johns Avenue, SW15. *T:* 01-789 4121. *Club:* Royal Thames.

**CONRY, Brigadier John de Lisle,** CIE 1937; Indian Army, retired; *b* 14 April 1882; *y s* of late Thomas Conry, Staff Surgeon, RN, Clonryn, Longford, Ireland, and late Isabella Mary Conry, later of Spestos Grange, Bow, Devon; *m* 1921, Dorothy, *o d* of late Rev. G. H. Marwood, Royal Navy, Plymouth, Devon; (one *s* killed in action, 1945). *Educ:* Mannamead Sch., Plymouth; Royal Naval Sch., Eltham; Sandhurst. 1st Bn The Dorset Regt, 1901; transferred 96th Berar Inf., Indian Army, 1903; Adjt and CO; served 3½ years in Burma Military Police, NE frontier of India; Instructor, later Senior Instructor, Senior Officers Sch., Belgaum; Comdr, Mhow Brigade Area; late Col 2/19th Hyderabad Regt; served European War, Mesopotamia (despatches twice). *Address:* South Efford House, Aveton Gifford, Kingsbridge, South Devon. *T:* Loddiswell 384.

**CONSTABLE, Sir Henry M. S.;** *see* Strickland-Constable.

**CONSTABLE, William George;** MA, Hon. DCL Durham; Hon. LittD Nottingham, New Brunswick; FSA; Curator of Paintings, Boston Museum of Fine Arts, 1938-57; late Director, Courtauld Institute of Art, London University; Barrister-at-law; Chevalier, Legion of Honour; Commendatore of Crown of Italy; Corresponding Member, Academy of Fine Arts, Brussels; Officier de l'Ordre des Arts et des Lettres; Hon. Phi Beta Kappa; Fellow: American Academy of Arts and Sciences; International Institute for Conservation of Museum Objects (President 1958); Hon. Fellow, St John's College, Cambridge; *b* Derby, 1887; *m* Olivia, *d* of A. Carson Roberts; two *s*. *Educ:* Derby Sch.; St John's Coll., Cambridge (Fellow; Whewell Scholar in the University); Slade Sch. In the Army, 1914-18, Major, 16th Sherwood Foresters; 2 i/c, 11th Lancs Fusiliers (despatches). Lecturer, Wallace Collection; Asst, National Gallery, 1923-28; Lecturer in Art, Bristol University, 1928; Ferens Lecturer in Fine Art, University Coll., Hull, 1929-30; Asst Dir, National Gallery, 1929-31; Slade Prof. of Fine Art, Cambridge Universty, 1935-37; Sydney Jones Lecturer in Art, Liverpool Univ.; Ryerson Lecturer, Yale Univ. *Publications:* Contributions to Essays in Adult Education, 1919; Catalogue of British Primitives Exhibition, 1924; Catalogue of the Marlay Bequest, Fitzwilliam Museum, 1927; Catalogue of Italian Pictures in the W. H. Woodward Collection, 1928; John Flaxman, 1928; Commemorative Catalogue of the Dutch Exhibition, 1929 (pictures: with Dr H. Schneider); Commemorative Catalogue of the Italian Exhibition, 1930 (with Lord Balniel and K. Clark); English Painting 1500-1700, 1930 (with C. H. Collins Baker); general editor Commemorative Catalogue; French Exhibition, 1932; British Exhibition (with Charles Johnson and others); contrib. to Cambridge Medieval History; Mantegna (W. H. Charlton lecture), 1936; Art History and Connoisseurship; Catalogue of English XII Cent. Mural Paintings ( with E. W. Tristram), 1944; Venetian Painting, 1949; Richard Wilson, 1953; The Painter's Workshop, 1954; Canaletto, 1962; Art Collecting in the United States, 1964; contributions to the principal art periodicals. Was art critic of New Statesman and Saturday Review, and is on the consultative cttee of Burlington Magazine. *Address:* 23 Craigie Street, Cambridge, Mass, USA. *Club:* Athenæum.

**CONSTANT, Antony;** Head of the Group Training Department, the Delta Group of Companies; *b* 1918; *s* of Frederick Charles and Mary Theresa Constant; *m* 1947, Pamela Mary Pemberton; one *s*. *Educ:* Dover Coll.; King's Coll., Cambridge. Asst master, Oundle Sch., 1939-45; Staff of Dir of Naval Intelligence, Admiralty, 1940-44; Educational Adviser to the Control Commission, Germany, 1945. Asst Master, and Asst House Master of School House, Rugby Sch., 1945-49; Rector of Royal Coll., Mauritius, 1949-53; Dir of Studies, RAF Coll., Cranwell, 1953-59; Educational Adviser to the Ministry of Defence and Chm. of Joint-Services Working Party, 1959-62. *Publications:* various papers on historical geography. *Recreations:* ornithology, sailing. *Address:* Delta Metal Co. Ltd, Dartmouth Street, Birmingham 7.

**CONSTANTINE,** family name of **Baron Constantine.**

**CONSTANTINE,** Baron *cr* 1969 (Life Peer), of Maraval and Nelson; **Learie Nicholas Constantine,** Kt 1962; MBE 1945; Member, Race Relations Board, since 1966; *b* 21 September 1901; *s* of Lebrun Constantine and Anna Pascal; *m* 1927, Norma Agatha Cox, Port of Spain, Trinidad; one *d*. *Educ:* St Ann's RC, Trinidad. Solicitor's Clerk, 1917-22; Civil Servant, 1922-25; Clerk, Oil Company, 1925-

29; Professional Cricketer, 1929-40; ARP Equipment Clerk, Nelson, Lancs, also Billeting Officer, 1940-42; Welfare Officer, Min. of Labour and Nat. Service, 1942-47 (MBE); broadcast during War, including several times, BBC Brains-Trust. Lecturer, HM Forces, NW Region. Student, Middle Temple, 1949 (Hon. Master of the Bench, 1963); qualified in Law, Sept. 1954; called to Trinidad Bar, 1955. Asst to Legal Adviser, Oil Co., Trinidad, 1955-56. Entered local politics; fought election Tunapuna constituency; became Minister of Works and Transport in first Party Government, 1956; High Commissioner for the Government of Trinidad and Tobago, in London, 1962-64. Member: Sports Council, 1965-; General Adv. Council of BBC; a Governor of BBC, 1968-71. Honorary Freedom of Nelson, Lancashire, 1963. Rector of Univ. of St Andrews, 1968- (Hon. LLD 1968). *Publications:* Cricket and I; Cricket in the Sun; How to play Cricket; Cricketers' Carnival; Cricket Crackers; Colour Bar: The Young Cricketer's Companion; (with Denzil Batchelor) The Changing Face of Cricket. Contributions to The Listener, John Bull, and leading papers and magazines in London. *Recreations:* cricket, football. *Address:* 11 Kendal Court, Shoot-up Hill, Hampstead, NW2. *T:* 01-452 8462. *Clubs:* MCC, Lord's Taverners'; The XL; Esher (Surrey) Cricket; Bootle (Liverpool); Fulwood and Broughton (Preston); Windhill (Shipley, Yorks); Chinghoppers (Chingford).

**CONSTANTINE, Air Chief Marshal Sir Hugh (Alex),** KBE 1958 (CBE 1944); CB 1946; DSO 1942; Co-ordinator, Anglo-American Community Relations, Ministry of Defence (Air), since 1964; *b* 23 May 1908; *s* of Fleet Paymaster Henry Constantine, RN, and Alice Louise Squire; *m* 1937, Helen, *d* of J. W. Bourke, Sydney, Australia; one *d. Educ:* Christ's Hosp.; Royal Air Force Coll., Cranwell. Pilot Officer in RAF, 1927; 56 (F) Sqdn, 1928-29; Flying Instructor, RAF Coll., 1930-31; CFS Instructor, 1932-33 and 1936-37; No 1 Armoured Car Co. (Iraq), 1934-36 (Palestine, despatches); Sqdn Ldr, 1936; 214 Bomber Sqdn, 1936-38; graduated Staff Coll., Andover, 1940; served in Bomber Comd, 1940-45 (despatches, four times); Air Vice-Marshal, Jan. 1945, and commanded No 5 (B) Group Bomber Command; Chief Intelligence Officer, BAFO and Control Commission, Germany, 1946; idc, 1947; SASO, 205 Gp (Egypt), 1948-49; Dir of Intelligence, Air Min., 1950-51; AO i/c A, Fighter Comd, 1952-54; AOC No 25 Group, Flying Training Command, 1954-56; Deputy Chief of Staff (Plans and Operations), SHAPE, NATO, 1956-59; AOC-in-C, Flg Trg Comd, 1959-61; Commandant, Imperial Defence Coll., 1961-64. Air Marshal, 1958; Air Chief Marshal, 1961. Gov., Christ's Hospital, 1963. Order of Polonia Restituta (2nd Class), 1945. *Recreations:* Rugby (English Trial, 1934), Eastern Counties, RAF and Leicester; golf. *Address:* 4 Chester Row, SW1. *T:* 01-730 0700. *Clubs:* Royal Air Force; Swinley Forest.

**CONSTANTINE, Sir Theodore,** Kt 1964; CBE 1956; *b* 15 March 1910; *er s* of Leonard and Fanny Louise Constantine; *m* 1935, Sylvia Mary, *y d* of Wallace Henry Legge-Pointing; one *s* one *d. Educ:* Acton Coll. Personal Asst to Chm. of public company, 1926-28; Executive in industry, 1928-38; Managing Dir of public company subsidiary, 1938-39. Served War of 1939-45, Auxiliary Air Force. Resumed pre-war Directorships, Oct. 1945. Dir of Industrial Holding Company, 1956-59; Chm. of Public Companies, 1959-68. Organisational work for Conservative Party as Constituency Chm., Area Chm., Mem. Nat. Exec. Cttee, Nat. Advisory Cttee on Publicity. Chm., Nat. Union Cons. and Unionist Assocs, 1967-68. Trustee, Sir John Wolstenholme Charity; Mem., Court of Assts, Worshipful Co. of Coachmakers; Freeman of City of London. High Sheriff of Greater London, 1967; DL Greater London, 1967. *Recreations:* (now spectator) motor racing, power boats. *Address:* Hunters Beck, Uxbridge Road, Stanmore, Middx. *T:* 01-954 0624. *Clubs:* Carlton, Gresham, Royal Automobile; British Automobile Racing.

**CONSTANTINOPLE, Archbishop of and Oecumenical Patriarch;** *see* Athenagoras.

**CONWAY, Brig. Albert Edward,** CB 1945; OBE 1940; New Zealand Forces (retired list); *b* 7 April 1891; *s* of Edward J. J. P. and Ann J. Conway; *m* 1916. Alice Rose Hinemoa Francis; two *s* one *d. Educ:* Reefton District High School. NZ Volunteers, 1907 and NZ Territorial Force, 1911; commissioned 12th (Nelson) Regt 1911, 13th (NC & W) Regt 1912; Canterbury Regt 1st NZEF, European War, incl. landing at Gallipoli, 1914-19 (twice wounded, despatches); NZ Staff Corps, 1919. Comdt, Central Military Dist Sch. of Instruction, Trentham, 1937; Dir of Mobilization, 1939; Dir of Military Training, May 1940. Capt. 1914; Major, 1927; Lt-Col, 1939; Temp. Col, 1940; Temp. Brig., 1941; Col, 1946; Brig., 1947; Adjt-Gen., NZ Military Forces and 2nd Military Mem., NZ Army Board, 1940-46; Hon. ADC to Governor-Gen., 1940-46; retired list, 1947. Councillor, NZ Golf Assoc., 1925-26-27, Vice-Pres., 1961. Sec.-Treas., Bay of Plenty District Golf Assoc., 1951-61. Patron, Bay of Plenty Eagles Golfing Soc., 1962-69; Mem. Cttee, Manawatu Golf Club, 1964. American Legion of Merit (Officer), 1946. *Recreations:* golf, sea fishing. *Address:* 51 Te Awe Awe Street, Palmerston North, New Zealand. *T:* 76-832.

**CONWAY, Hugh Graham,** CBE 1964; Group Managing Director, Gas Turbines, Rolls Royce Ltd, since 1970; Director, Rolls Royce Ltd; *b* 25 Jan. 1914; *s* of G. R. G. Conway; *m* 1937, Eva Gordon Simpson; two *s. Educ:* Merchiston Castle Sch., Edinburgh; Cambridge Univ. Joined aircraft industry, 1938; Man. Dir, Bristol Engine Division, Rolls Royce Ltd, 1964-70. Mem., Decimal Currency Board, 1967-. *Publications:* several technical books. *Recreation:* vintage motoring. *Address:* 10 Clarendon Mews, W2.

**CONWAY, James;** General Secretary, Amalgamated Union of Engineering and Foundry Workers (formerly Amalgamated Engineering Union), since 1964; *b* 7 Oct. 1915; British; *m* 1951, Sylvia; one *s.* Member: Sec. of State for Educn and Science's Cttee for Adult Educn; Machine Tools Cttee; Machine Tools EDC, 1966-. *Publications:* articles in newspapers and AEU Jl; Editor: AEU Journal; The Way (AEU). *Recreation:* moorland walking. *Address:* Camden Cottage, Wilderness Road, Chislehurst, Kent BR7 5EY.

**CONWAY, His Eminence Cardinal William;** *see* Armagh, Cardinal Archbishop of.

**CONYNGHAM,** family name of **Marquess Conyngham.**

**CONYNGHAM,** 6th Marquess, *cr* 1816; **Frederick William Burton Conyngham;** Baron Conyngahm, 1780; Viscount Conyngham, 1789; Earl Conyngham, Viscount Mount-Charles, 1797; Earl of Mount-Charles, Viscount Slane, 1816; Baron Minster (UK), 1821; *b* 24 June 1890; *s* of 4th Marquess and Hon. Frances Eveleigh de Moleyns (who *m*

2nd, 1899, J. R. B. Cameron; she *d* 1939), *e d* of 4th Baron Ventry; *S* brother, 1918; *m* 1922, Antoinette Winifred (*d* 1966), *er d* of late J. W. H. Thompson; one *s* (one *s* one *d* decd); *m* 1966, Stella, *d* of Francis Barrallier Thompson, and *widow* of Robert Newton Tory. Late Inniskilling Fusiliers and Westmorland and Cumberland Yeomanry and served in the North Irish Horse; Capt. commanding No. 1 Independent Platoon. 1st Ross-shire Home Guard in war of 1939-45. *Heir: s* Earl of Mount Charles, *qv. Address:* Les Prés, St Lawrence, Jersey, CI. *Club:* Boodle's.

*See also Sir T. Ainsworth, Bt, Baron Croft, Baron Holm Patrick.*

**COOK, Prof. Alan Hugh,** FRS 1969; Professor of Geophysics, University of Edinburgh, since Sept. 1969; *b* 2 Dec. 1922; *s* of late Reginald Thomas Cook, OBE, and of Ethel Cook; *m* 1948, Isabell Weir Adamson; one *s* one *d. Educ:* Westcliff High Sch. for Boys; Corpus Christi Coll. Cambridge. MA, PhD, ScD. Admty Signal Estabt, 1943-46; Research Student, then Res. Asst, Dept of Geodesy and Geophysics, Cambridge, 1946-51; Metrology Div., Nat. Physical Laboratory, Teddington, 1952. Vis. Fellow, Jt Inst. for Laboratory Astrophysics, Boulder, Colorado, 1965-66; Supt, Standards (subseq. Quantum Metrology) Div., Nat. Physical Laboratory, 1966-69. FInstP; FRSE 1970. C. V. Boys Prize, Inst. of Physics, 1967. *Publications:* Gravity and the Earth; many contribs learned jls on gravity, artificial satellites, precise measurement, fundamental constants of physics and astronomy. *Recreations:* amateur theatre, travel, painting. *Address:* Department of Geophysics, 6 South Oswald Road, Edinburgh EH9 2HX. *T:* 031-667 3434; 1 Frogston Terrace, Edinburgh EH10 7AD. *T:* 031-445 2976.

**COOK, Air Vice-Marshal Albert Frederick,** CBE 1955 (OBE 1946); *b* 26 Aug. 1901; *s* of Charles Neville Cook, Dun Laoghaire, Co. Dublin; *m* 1929, Cecil Phyllis (*d* 1967), *d* of Lionel McEnnery, Dublin; two *d*; *m* 1969, Penelope, *d* of late K. B. Anderson, Weybridge. *Educ:* Kingstown Sch.; Royal College of Surgeons, Dublin. LRCP, LRCS, Ireland, 1924; DPH 1935. Joined RAF, 1925; served War of 1939-45: Middle East, France and Germany; Principal Medical Officer, BAFO, Germany, 1949-51; PMO, Flying Trg Comd, 1951-55; PMO, Bomber Comd, 1955-56. QHP 1956; PMO, MEAF, 1957-59; retired, 1959. *Publication:* 2nd Tactical Air Force Narrative, in Medical History of Second World War (RAF Medical Services, vol. ii). *Address:* Crown Cottage, Worplesdon, Surrey. *Club:* Royal Air Force.

**COOK, Alexander Edward,** CMG 1955; *b* 3 April 1906; *s* of Edward Arthur Cook and M. J. Cook (*née* Wreford); *m* 1936, Ethel Catherine Margaret (*née* Mayo); one *s* two *d. Educ:* Imperial Service Coll., Windsor; Pembroke Coll., Cambridge. Entered Colonial Service as a Cadet, Nigeria, 1928; Asst District Officer, District Officer, Asst Sec.; Financial Sec., Gibraltar, 1945; Financial Sec., Eastern Region, Nigeria, 1953; Permanent Sec., Ministry of Finance, Eastern Region, Nigeria, 1954; retired 1956; Mem., British Caribbean Federal Capital Commn, 1956. Attached Fed. Govt of UK of Libya as Economic Adviser, under auspices of UN Tech. Assistance Admin., 1959-60. *Recreations:* fishing and golf. *Address:* Knollside, Uplyme, Lyme Regis, Dorset. *T:* Lyme Regis 3185. *Clubs:* United University, Royal Over-Seas League.

**COOK, (Alfred) Melville,** MusDoc, FRCO; Organist and Choirmaster of the Metropolitan United, Toronto, since 1967; *b* 18 June 1912; *s* of Harry Melville and Vera Louis Cook; *m* 1944, Marion Weir Moncrieff; no *c. Educ:* King's Sch., Gloucester. Chorister, 1923-28, Asst Organist, 1932-37, Gloucester Cathedral. Organist and Choirmaster: All Saints, Cheltenham, 1935-37; Leeds Parish Church, 1937-56. MusDoc Durham, 1940. Served War in RA, 1941-46. Organist and Master of the Choristers, Hereford Cathedral, 1956-66. Conductor, Three Choirs Festival, Hereford, 1958, 1961, 1964; Conductor, Hereford Choral Soc., 1957-66. Organist and Choirmaster, All Saints', Winnipeg; Conductor of the Winnipeg Philharmonic Choir, Canada, 1966. *Recreations:* walking, swimming. *Address:* Metropolitan United Church, 51 Bond Street, Toronto, Canada.

**COOK, Arthur Herbert,** FRS 1951; DSc, PhD, FRIC; Director, Brewing Industry Research Foundation, Nutfield, Surrey, since 1958, Assistant Director, 1949-58; *b* London, 10 July 1911; *s* of Arthur Cook, London. *Educ:* Owen's Sch., Islington, London; Universities of London (Imperial Coll. of Science and Technology) and Heidelberg. Joined staff of Imperial Coll., 1937; Asst Prof. and Reader in the University, 1947-49. Hon. DSc Heriot-Watt. *Publications:* (with late Prof. F. Mayer) Chemistry of the Natural Colouring Matters. Numerous articles, mainly in Journal of Chemical Soc. Editor, The Chemistry and Biology of Yeasts, 1958; Barley and Malt: Biology, Biochemistry, Technology, 1962. *Recreations:* gardening, photography. *Address:* The Lodge, Lyttel Hall, Nutfield, Redhill, Surrey. *T:* Nutfield Ridge 2297. *Club:* Athenæum.

**COOK, Bernard Christopher Allen,** CMG 1958; OBE 1945; *b* 20 July 1906; *s* of late Sir Edward Cook, CSI, CIE; *m* 1933, Margaret Helen Mary, *d* of Rt Rev. C. E. Plumb, DD; two *d* (and one *s* decd). *Educ:* Radley Coll. (Open Scholarship); Brasenose Coll., Oxford (Open Scholarship). ICS 1929; held various posts in UP; Govt of India: Finance and Commerce Cadre, 1938; Custodian of Enemy Property, 1939-41; Actg Joint Sec., Finance Dept, and Mem. Central Legislative Assembly, 1946; Indian Trade Comr, London, 1946-47; Foreign Service, 1947; Control Commn, Germany (currency reform), 1948-49; Political Adviser, Asmara, 1949-51; First Sec. (Commercial), Paris, 1951-53; Counsellor (Commercial), Rangoon, 1953-57; Counsellor (Commercial), HBM Embassy, Mexico City, 1957-59; HM Consul-General, Barcelona, 1959-66; retired, 1966; re-employed, 1967-69. *Address:* c/o National and Grindlay's Bank, 13 St James's Square, SW1. *Club:* Oriental.

**COOK, Brian Hartley K.;** *see* Kemball-Cook.

**COOK, Charles Alfred George,** MC 1945; GM 1945; FRCS; Consultant Ophthalmic Surgeon: Guy's Hospital, since 1954; Moorfields Eye Hospital, since 1956; Teacher of Ophthalmology, University of London (Guy's Hospital and Institute of Ophthalmology), since 1955; *b* 20 Aug. 1913; *s* of late Charles F. Cook and Beatrice Grist; *m* 1939, Edna Constance Dobson; one *s* one *d. Educ:* St Edward's Sch., Oxford; Guy's Hospital. MRCS LRCP, 1939; DOMS (Eng.), 1946; FRCS, 1950. Capt. and Major RAMC, 1939-45. Moorfields Eye Hospital: Clinical Asst, 1946-47; Ho. Surg., 1948-49; Sen. Resident Officer, 1950; Chief Clin. Asst, 1951-55. Sen. Registrar, Eye Dept, Guy's Hospital, 1951-55; Moorfields Research Fellow, Inst. of Ophthalmology, 1951-58; Ophthalmic Surg., West Middlesex Hospital, 1954-56. Mem., Court of Examrs, RCS; Examr for DOMS,

RCP and RCS; Examr Brit. Orthoptic Board; Sec., Ophthalmological Soc. of UK, 1956-57; Vice-Dean, Inst. of Ophthalmology, 1959-62. Freeman, City of London. *Publications:* Articles in Brit. Jl of Ophthalmology, Trans. Ophthalmological Soc., Jl of Pathology and other Med. Jls. *Recreations:* swimming, reading; an interest in all outdoor recreations. *Address:* Rooks Hill House, Rooks Hill, near Seal, Sevenoaks, Kent. *T:* Sevenoaks 61320; 96 Harley Street, W1. *T:* 01-935 9555. *Clubs:* Athenæum, Garrick.

**COOK, Ven. Edwin Arthur,** MA; Archdeacon of Bath, 1947-62, now Emeritus; Prebendary of Whitelackington, 1947-62; Rector of Bath Abbey, 1947-60, retired; *b* 9 July 1888; *s* of George Thomas and Mary Ann Cook; *m* 1920, Marion Elliott; one *s* one *d*. *Educ:* Maidstone Grammar Sch.; Queens' Coll. and Ridley Hall, Cambridge. Curate, Holy Trinity, Margate, 1911; CMS Missionary Western China, 1913; Rector, St James's, Dover, 1926; Vicar, Holy Trinity, Margate, 1929; Vicar, Christ Church, Folkestone, 1939; Vicar (in Plurality), Holy Trinity, Folkestone, 1942; Rural Dean of Elham, 1943; Proctor in Convocation, 1945; Hon. Canon of Canterbury, 1946. *Address:* 1 Cranhill Road, Bath, Somerset. *T:* 22368.

**COOK, Vice-Admiral Eric W.;** *see* Longley-Cook.

**COOK, Sir Francis Ferdinand Maurice,** 4th Bt, *cr* 1886; *b* 21 Dec. 1907; *s* of Sir H. F. Cook, 3rd Bt, and Hon. Mary Hood, *e d* of 2nd Viscount Bridport; *S* father, 1939, also as Visconde de Monserrate in Portugal; *m* 1937, Joan Loraine Ashton-Case (marr. diss., 1942), *d* of Hon. Mrs Herbert Eaton; one *s*; *m* 1951, Jane Audrey Nott (marr. diss., 1956), *er d* of Mrs Turnbull and step *d* of Lieut-Comdr S. G. L. Turnbull, RN (retd); one *d*; *m* 1956, Mrs Bridget Polland (*née* Lynch). *Educ:* Bradfield Coll., Berks, and privately. FRSA; Member: Chelsea Art Soc.; Jersey Soc. of Artists; Jersey Artists' Group; St Ives Soc. of Artists, Cornwall. Gold Medallist, 1934. Exhibited works at RA, RBA, London Portrait Soc., London Group, etc., and provinces. Represented in the permanent collections Walker Art Gall., Liverpool, Manchester, Northampton, and Bournemouth. *Recreation:* architecture. *Heir:* *s* Christopher Wymondham Rayner Herbert Cook, *b* 1938. *Address:* Le Coin, La Haule, St Aubin, Jersey, CI; (Studio) The Cloister Studio and Galleries, Route de Lisle, La Haule, St Aubin, Jersey, CI. *T:* Jersey Central 41234. *Clubs:* Arts, Royal Automobile; Victoria (St Helier).

**COOK, Francis John Granville,** MA Cantab; Headmaster of Campbell College, Belfast, since 1954; *b* 28 Jan. 1913; *o s* of late W. G. Cook and Nora Braley; *m* 1942, Jocelyn McKay, *d* of late John Stewart, Westholm, Dunblane, Perthshire; one *s* two *d*. *Educ:* Wyggeston Sch.; Downing Coll., Cambridge. Historical and Law Triposes; Squire Scholar; Tancred Studentship, Lincoln's Inn. Asst Master, Rossall Sch., 1937; served War, 1940-46, with Royal Navy; Headmaster of Junior Sch., Rossall Sch., 1949-54. *Recreations:* gardening, fishing, painting. *Address:* Headmaster's House, Campbell College, Belfast. *T:* Belfast 63076; Avonmore House, Carlingford, Co. Louth. *Clubs:* RNVR; Ulster (Belfast).

**COOK, Frank,** BSc, MB, BS London, FRCS, FRCOG; Consulting Obstetric Surgeon Emeritus, Guy's Hospital; Consulting Surgeon, Chelsea Hospital for Women; Hon. Consulting Gynæcologist and Obstetrician to Orpington and Sevenoaks Hospitals; Fellow of Royal Society of Medicine; Freeman of the Society of Apothecaries; *b* 6 Nov. 1888; *o s* of late Frank Plant Cook of Mansfield Woodhouse, Notts; *m* 1917, Edith Harriette Wallace, *yr d* of late Rev. James Reid, Co. Clare; one *s*. *Educ:* Bedford Modern Sch.; Guy's Hospital; University of London; Scholarship and Research Studentship in Physiology, University of London; First Class Hons in BSc (Physiology); Beit Memorial Research Fellow; Dean of the Institute of Obstetrics and Gynæcology; Examiner in Obstetrics and Gynæcology to the Universities of Cambridge, London, Glasgow and Bombay, and to the Royal College of Obstetricians and Gynæcologists; Mem., SW Metropolitan Regional Hosp. Board; Member: Boards of Governors, St Thomas' Hosp., and Queen Charlotte's and Chelsea Hosps. Col RAMC. Served in both Great Wars; France, Belgium and Mesopotamia (1914 Star with Bar); Palestine, Greece, Sudan, Egypt and India. Hunterian Prof., Royal College of Surgeons, 1917 and 1924: Consulting Gynæcologist to Queen Alexandra Military Hosp., Millbank and to King Edward VII Sanatorium, Midhurst; Medical Inspector of the High Court, Divorce Division; Demonstrator of Pathology, Surgical Registrar and tutor, etc., Guy's Hosp. *Publications:* Midwifery, 1948; (joint) Diseases of Women, 1949; various papers on physiological, surgical, and obstetric subjects. *Address:* 25c Lansdowne Road, Tunbridge Wells, Kent. *T:* Tunbridge Wells 22038.

**COOK, Frank Allan Grafton,** CBE 1959 (OBE 1942); retired; *b* 13 June 1902; *s* of George and Lucy Cook; *m* 1934, Phyllis Mary, *y d* of H. W. Blunt, MA, of Oxford; three *d*. *Educ:* Nottingham High Sch.; Gonville and Caius Coll., Cambridge. Entered the Levant Consular Service, 1924; served in Egypt, Hejaz, Morocco, Greece; Consul at Mosul, 1939; served in Persia and Abyssinia; Chargé d'Affaires at Addis Ababa, 1945-46; Consul-Gen., Berlin, 1947; Counsellor and Consul-Gen., Rangoon, 1948-49; Consul-Gen., Basra, 1949-53; Antwerp, 1953-57; Izmir, 1957-59; retired, 1959. *Address:* 409 The Ridge, Hastings, Sussex.

**COOK, George Steveni L.;** *see* Littlejohn Cook.

**COOK, Rt. Rev. Henry George;** *see* Athabasca, Bishop Suffragan of.

**COOK, Cdre Henry Home;** Defence Adviser to British High Commissioner, Ottawa, since 1970; *b* 24 Jan. 1918; *o s* of George Home Cook, Edinburgh; *m* 1943, Theffania, *yr d* of A. P. Saunders, Gerrards Cross; two *s* two *d*. *Educ:* St Laurence Coll., Ramsgate; Pangbourne College. Entered RN as Paymaster Cadet, 1936; Comdr 1955; Captain 1963; Cdre 1970. Naval Sec. to Vice-Adm. Sir Guy Sayer, 1953-59; Sqdn Supply Officer, 1st S/m Sqdn, 1959; Comdr, RNC Greenwich, 1961; Naval Attaché, Ankara, 1964; Dir of Public Relations (RN), 1966. *Recreations:* fencing, swimming, sailing. *Address:* Ramblers Cottage, Layters Green, Chalfont St Peter, Bucks. *T:* Gerrards Cross 83724. *Club:* Army and Navy.

**COOK, Sir James (Wilfred),** Kt 1963; FRS 1938; DSc, PhD (London); FRIC; Vice-Chancellor, University of East Africa, 1966-70; *b* 10 Dec. 1900; *s* of late Charles William and late Frances Cook; *m* 1st, 1930, Elsie Winifred (*d* 1966), *d* of late Major Griffiths; three *s*; 2nd, 1967, Vera Elizabeth Ford. *Educ:* Sloane Sch., Chelsea; University Coll., London (Tuffnell Scholar). Lectr in Organic Chemistry, The Sir John Cass Tech. Inst., 1920-28; Research Chemist, DSIR, 1928-29; Research Chemist,

The Royal Cancer Hosp. (Free), 1929-39; Reader in Pathological Chemistry, University of London, 1932-35; Prof. of Chemistry, Univ. of London, 1935-39; Professorial Lectr in Chemisty, Chicago Univ., 1938; Regius Prof. of Chemistry, Glasgow Univ., 1939-54; Principal, University Coll. of the South West, Exeter, 1954-55; Vice-Chancellor, Exeter Univ., 1955-66. Member: University Grants Cttee, 1950-54; Cttee on cost of Nat. Health Service, 1953-56; Cttee of Enquiry into Pharmaceutical Ind., 1965-66; Member Council: DSIR, and Chm. Post-graduate Training Awards Cttee, 1960-65; University Coll. of Rhodesia, 1955-68. Hon. Dir, MRC Carcinogenic Substances Res. Unit, 1956-66; Chairman: Chemical Council, 1959-63; Cttee on Composition of Milk, 1958-60; Advisory Cttee on Pesticides and other Toxic Chemicals, 1962-66; Advisory Cttee on Scientific and Technical Information, 1965-66. President: Royal Inst. of Chemistry, 1949-51; Section B, British Assoc., 1957, Section X, 1966; Hon. Member: Polish Chem. Soc.; Chilean Chem. Soc.; Corr. Mem. Nat. Acad. of Exact Sciences of Buenos Aires. Awarded, jointly with Prof. Sir Ernest Kennaway, prize of Union Internationale contre le Cancer, 1936; part recipient of first award of Anna Fuller Memorial Prize, 1939; recipient of Katherine Berkan Judd Prize (Mem. Hosp., New York) for 1940; Davy Medallist, Royal Society, 1954; Pedler Lectr., Chem. Soc., 1950. Fellow, University Coll., London. Hon. ScD, Dublin; Hon. DSc, Nigeria; Hon. D de l'U, Rennes; Hon. LLD, Exeter. Officier de l'Ordre de Léopold. *Publications:* numerous papers on organic chemistry, especially in relation to cancer, hormones, polycyclic compounds, bile acids, etc., published mainly in the Journal of the Chemical Society and the Proceedings of the Royal Society. Ed Progress in Organic Chemistry, Vols I-VII. *Address:* The Burn, 15a Knowle Road, Budleigh Salterton, Devon EX9 6AR. *Club:* Athenæum.

**COOK, John Edward E.**; *see* Evan-Cook.

**COOK, John Gilbert,** CVO 1970; CBE 1963; HM Treasury Valuer, 1950-69, retd; *b* 16 May 1911; *s* of late John Andrew Cook; *m* 1937, Doreen Violet Mary Harrington; two *s* two *d*. *Educ:* Bedford Sch. Articled to Sir H. Trustram Eve, 1929-32. Member: Royal Institution of Chartered Surveyors; Chartered Auctioneers' and Estate Agents' Institute. *Recreations:* Rugby football (English International and Barbarian; Captain of Bedford, 1936-39), golf, cricket (mem. MCC). *Address:* Summerville, 15 Harold Grove, Frinton-on-Sea, Essex. *T:* Frinton-on-Sea 4254. *Clubs:* MCC, Pathfinder; Frinton Golf.

**COOK, Prof. John Manuel;** FSA; Professor of Ancient History and Classical Archæology, Bristol University, since 1958 (formerly Reader); *b* 11 Dec. 1910; *s* of late Rev. C. R. Cook; *m* 1939, Enid May, *d* of Dr W. A. Robertson; two *s*. *Educ:* Marlborough; King's Coll., Cambridge. Sir William Browne's Medal for Greek Ode, 1933; Members' Latin Essay Prize, 1933; Augustus Austen Leigh Student in King's Coll., 1934; Asst in Humanity and Lectr in Classical Archæology, Edinburgh Univ., 1936-45; Dir of British Sch. of Archæology at Athens, 1946-54; Dean, Faculty of Arts, Bristol Univ., 1966-68. C. E. Norton Lectr of the Archaeological Inst. of America, 1961-62; Visiting Prof., Yale Univ., 1965; Gray Memorial Lectr, Cambridge, 1969. Served in Royal Scots Force 133, and HQ Land Forces, Greece. *Address:* 4 Edgecumbe Road, Redland, Bristol 6.

**COOK, Joseph,** FRIC; Deputy Controller, Royal Ordnance Factories, Ministry of Defence, since 1966; *b* 7 April 1917; *y s* of Joseph Cook, MBE, JP, and Jane Cook (*née* Adams), Cumberland; *m* 1950, Betty, *d* of James and Elizabeth Barlow, Standish, Lancs; two *d*. *Educ:* Whitehaven Grammar Sch.; Univ. of Liverpool (BSc, DipEd). RAF, 1939-40. Posts in Ministries of Supply, Aviation, Technology and Defence (incl. Factory Develt Officer, ROF, Chorley, Lancs), 1943-49; ROF, Burghfield: Manager, 1950-58; Dir, 1959-65; Group Dir, Ammunition Production, 1966. *Recreations:* swimming, golf. *Address:* Abbots-wood, Bramley Road, Pamber End, near Basingstoke, Hants. *T:* Monk Sherborne 304.

**COOK, Melville;** *see* Cook, Alfred Melville.

**COOK, Norman Charles,** BA; V-PSA, FMA; Director: Guildhall Museum since 1950; Museum of London, since 1970; *b* 24 Jan. 1906; *s* of George and Emily Cook; *m* 1934, Dorothy Ida Waters; one *s* one *d*. *Educ:* Maidstone Grammar Sch. Maidstone Museum, 1924-37; Morven Institute of Archaeological Research, Avebury, 1937-39; Curator, Southampton Museum, 1947-50. Hon. Sec., 1954-59, Pres., 1964-65, Museums Assoc. Vice-Pres., Soc. of Antiquaries, 1967-. *Recreation:* archæology. *Address:* 113a Mayow Road, SE26. *T:* 01-778 3906. *Club:* Arts.

**COOK, Brig. Richard Arthur,** CBE 1961; *b* 26 May 1908; *m* 1940, Sheila Mary Ostell Prosser; two *s*. *Educ:* St Paul's; RMA, Woolwich. Commissioned, Royal Artillery, 1928. Posted to India, 1933. Served War of 1939-45 in India and Burma: Staff Coll., 1941; Regimental Comd, 1943; Joint Services Staff Coll., 1947; Col, 1948; Col Administrative Plans, GHQ, MELF, 1948-51; CRA (Brig.) 16th Airborne Div., 1954-56; NATO Defence Coll., 1957; BGS, Southern Command, 1958-61; retired from Army, 1961. *Address:* Drove End House, West Grimstead, near Salisbury, Wilts. *T:* Farley 205; 20 Rosary Gardens, SW7. *T:* 01-373 4866. *Club:* Army and Navy.

**COOK, Prof. Robert Manuel;** Laurence Professor of Classical Archaeology, University of Cambridge, since 1962; *b* 4 July 1909; *s* of Rev. Charles Robert and Mary Manuel Cook; *m* 1938, Kathleen, *d* of James Frank and Ellen Hardman Porter. *Educ:* Marlborough Coll.; Cambridge Univ. Walston Student, Cambridge Univ., 1932; Asst Lectr in Classics, Manchester Univ., 1934; Lectr, 1938; Sub-warden, St Anselm's Hall, Manchester, 1936-38; Laurence Reader in Classical Archaeology, Cambridge Univ., 1945, Ord. Mem., German Archaeological Inst., 1953. *Publications:* Corpus Vasorum Antiquorum, British Museum 8, 1954; Greek Painted Pottery, 1960; The Greeks till Alexander, 1962; (with Kathleen Cook) Southern Greece: an archaeological guide, 1968. *Address:* 15 Wilberforce Road, Cambridge. *T:* Cambridge 52863.

*See also Prof. J. M. Cook.*

**COOK, William Birkett,** MA; Headmaster of Durham School since 1967; *b* 30 Aug. 1931; *e s* of William James and Mildred Elizabeth Cook, Headington, Oxford; *m* 1958, Marianne Ruth, *yr d* of late A. E. Taylor, The Schools, Shrewsbury; one *s* one *d* (and one *d* decd). *Educ:* Dragon Sch.; Eton (King's Schol.); Trinity Coll., Cambridge (Schol.). National Service, 1950-51 (commnd in RA). Porson Prizeman, 1953; 1st cl. Classical Tripos Pt I, 1953, Pt II, 1954; Henry Arthur Thomas Student, 1954. Asst Master, Shrewsbury Sch., 1955-67, and Head of Classical Faculty, 1960-

67. *Recreation:* music, especially singing. *Address:* School House, Durham School, Durham. *T:* Durham 4783.

**COOK, Sir William (Richard Joseph),** KCB 1970 (CB 1951); Kt 1958; FRS 1962; Chief Adviser (Projects and Research) to the Minister of Defence (Equipment), since 1968; *b* 10 April 1905; *s* of John Cook; *m* 1929, Grace (*née* Purnell); one *d*; *m* 1939, Gladys (*née* Allen); one *s* one *d*. *Educ:* Trowbridge High Sch.; Bristol Univ. Entered CS, 1928; various scientific posts in Research Estabs of WO and Min. of Supply, 1928-47; Dir of Physical Research, Admiralty, 1947-50; Chief of Royal Naval Scientific Service, 1950-54; Deputy Dir, Atomic Weapons Research Establishment, Aldermaston, 1954-58; Mem. for Reactors, Atomic Energy Authority, 1961-64 (Mem. for Development and Engineering, 1959-61, for Engineering and Production, 1958-59); Dep. Chief Scientific Adviser, Ministry of Defence, 1964-67. *Address:* Ministry of Defence, Main Building, Whitehall, SW1; Adbury Springs, Newbury, Berks. *T:* Newbury 409. *Club:* Athenæum.

**COOKE, (Alfred) Alistair;** Chief Correspondent in the United States of The Guardian since 1948; *b* 20 Nov. 1908; *s* of Samuel Cooke and Mary Elizabeth Byrne; *m* 1st, 1934, Ruth Emerson; one *s*; 2nd, 1946, Jane White Hawkes; one *d*. *Educ:* Blackpool Grammar Sch.; Jesus Coll., Cambridge (Scholar); Yale Univ.; Harvard. Founded Cambridge University Mummers, 1928; First Class, English Tripos, 1929; Second Class, 1930. Editor, The Granta, 1931; Commonwealth Fund Fellow, 1932-34. BBC Film Critic, 1934-37; London Correspondent for NBC, 1936-37; Commentator on American Affairs for BBC, 1938-; Special Correspondent on American Affairs, The London Times, 1938-40; American Feature Writer, The Daily Herald, 1941-43; UN Correspondent of the Manchester Guardian (which changed name to Guardian, 1959), 1945-48. Master of ceremonies: Ford Foundation's television programme, Omnibus, 1952-61; of UN television programme, International Zone, 1961-67. Peabody Award for internat. reporting, 1952. *Publications:* (ed) Garbo and the Night Watchmen, 1937; Douglas Fairbanks: The Making of a Screen 1954; (ed) The generation on Trial: USA v Alger Hiss, 1950; Letters from America, 1951; Christmas Eve, 1952; A Commencement Address, 1954; (ed) The Vintage Mencken, 1955; Around the World in Fifty Years, 1966; Talk about America, 1968. *Recreations:* golf, photography, music, fishing, travel, chess. *Address:* 1150 Fifth Avenue, New York City; Nassau Point, Cutchogue, Long Island, NY, USA. *Clubs:* Savile; Royal and Ancient (St Andrews); National Press (Washington).

**COOKE, Alistair;** *see* Cooke, Alfred A.

**COOKE, Cecil;** *see* Cooke, R. C.

**COOKE, Sir Charles (Arthur John),** 11th Bt, *cr* 1661; *b* 12 Nov. 1905; *yr s* of 10th Bt and Lady Mildred Adelaide Cecilia Denison; *S* father, 1964; *m* 1932, Diana, *o d* of late Maj.-Gen. Sir Edward Maxwell Perceval, KCB, DSO, JP; one *s* one *d*. *Educ:* Wellington Coll.; RMC Sandhurst. Served War of 1939-45, 4/7th Dragoon Guards, France (prisoner, 1940). Capt., 1945, Major, 1952, 4/7th Dragoon Guards; retired from Army, 1953. *Recreations:* shooting and fishing. *Heir:* *s* David William Perceval Cooke [*b* 28 April 1935; *m* 1959, Margaret Frances, *d* of Herbert Skinner, Knutsford, Cheshire; three *d*]. *Address:* 15 Esplanade, Fowey, Cornwall.

**COOKE, Charles Fletcher F.;** *see* Fletcher-Cooke.

**COOKE, Christopher Herbert,** CIE 1946; *b* 29 May 1899; *s* of late F. J. Cooke, ICS (retired); *m* 1929, Beryl Gourley Ainsley; one *s* one *d*. *Educ:* Clifton; Christ Church, Oxford (MA). Indian Civil Service (United Provinces), 1922; Joint Magistrate, Collector, Settlement Officer, 1922-39; Revenue Sec., Finance Sec., Settlement Commissioner, 1939-44; Commissioner, Lucknow Division, 1945-47; retired from ICS, 1947; Settlement Commissioner for Forest Reserves, Ghana, 1951-57. *Recreation:* golf. *Address:* Redholme, Great Missenden, Bucks. *T:* Great Missenden 2580. *Club:* East India and Sports.

**COOKE, Air Marshal Sir Cyril Bertram,** KCB, *cr* 1947 (CB 1945); CBE 1941; retired; *b* 28 June 1895; *s* of late John Cooke, Chalkcliffe, Dorking; *m* 1918, Elizabeth Amelia Phyllis, *d* of John Benjamin Davies, Bank House, Pembroke; one *s* one *d*. *Educ:* Dorking High Sch.; Northampton Engineering Coll., London. Temp. 2nd Lieut RGA, 1914; transferred to RFC, 1915; Flight-Comdr and Temp. Capt., 1916: Sqdn Comdr and Acting Major, 1918; Permanent Commission RAF as Flight-Lieut, 1919; Squadron Leader, 1924; Wing-Comdr, 1935; Group Capt., 1939; Acting Air Cdre, 1940; Temp. Air Cdre, 1941; Subst. Air Cdre, 1944; Acting Air Vice-Marshal, 1944; Air Vice-Marshal, 1946; Actg Air Marshal, 1947; Air Marshal, 1947. Served European War, 1914-18, in Egypt, Sudan, Salonika and Home Defence; India, 1922-25; NW Frontier, 1925; Iraq, 1931-33; War of 1939-45, served in Middle East, 1941-42, North Africa and Italy, 1944-45 (despatches, CBE, CB); commanded No. 206 Group in Middle East, 1941-42; Chief Maintenance Staff Officer, MAAF, 1944-45; AOC No. 43 Group, Maintenance Command, RAF, 1945-46; Dir-Gen., Servicing and Maintenance, Air Min., 1946-47; AOC-in-C Maintenance Command, 1947-49, retd. *Recreation:* represented RAF at cricket, 1927-37. *Address:* North Barn, Old Manor Road, Rustington, Sussex. *T:* 4831.

**COOKE, Deryck Victor;** Senior Assistant, Music Information, BBC, since 1965; *b* 14 Sept. 1919; *s* of Henry Victor Cooke and Mabel Cooke (*née* Judd); *m* 1966, Jacqueline Etienne. *Educ:* Selwyn Coll., Cambridge. ARCM 1937; BA 1940, MA 1943, Cantab; ARCO 1946. Gunner, RA, 1940-45. Asst, Music Div., BBC, 1947-59; Free-lance Writer, 1959-65. Responsible for Realisation of Mahler's Tenth Symphony, first performed London, 1964. Kilenyi Mahler Medal, 1964. *Publications:* The Language of Music, 1959; Mahler 1860-1911, 1960. *Address:* 76 Eton Place, Eton College Road, NW3. *T:* 01-722 7992.

**COOKE, George William,** FRS 1969; Deputy Director since 1962, and Head of Chemistry Department since 1956, Rothamsted Experimental Station, Harpenden; *b* 6 Jan. 1916; *s* of late William Harry Cooke and late Sarah Jane Cooke (*née* Whittaker); *m* 1944, Elizabeth Hannah Hill; one *s* one *d*. *Educ:* Loughborough Grammar Sch.; University Coll., Nottingham. BSc (Chem.) London Univ., 1937, PhD London, 1940. Awarded Min. of Agric. Research Schol., tenable at Rothamsted Experimental Station, 1938; apptd Scientific Officer there, 1941, and Prin. Sc. Officer, 1951. Chairman, Agriculture Group of Soc. of Chem. Industry, 1956-58; Pres., Fertiliser Soc., London, 1961-62. Research Medal of Royal Agricultural Soc., 1967. *Publications:* Fertilizers and Profitable Farming, 1960; The Control of Soil Fertility,

1967; many papers in scientific jls on soil science, crop nutrition and fertilizers. *Recreations:* boats, canoes. *Address:* 33 Topstreet Way, Harpenden, Herts. *T:* Harpenden 2899. *Club:* Farmers'.

**COOKE, Rev. Canon Greville (Vaughan Turner),** MA, MusB Cantab; FRAM; FSA; Rector of Buxted since 1956; Canon Emeritus, Peterborough Cathedral, since 1956; Composer, Author, Poet, Broadcaster; Adjudicator at Musical Festivals; *b* 14 July 1894; *s* of William Turner Cooke, Chief Clerk of Central Office of Royal Courts of Justice, London, and Adeline Hannah, *d* of David Johnson, MD. *Educ:* Hamilton House, Ealing; Royal Academy of Music (Schol. Exhibitioner); Christ's Coll., Cambridge (Organ Schol.); Ridley Hall, Cambridge (Theol. Studentship); ARAM 1913; BA 1916; MusBac 1916; MA 1920. Ordained, 1918; Curate, Tavistock, 1918, Ealing, 1920; Dep. Minor Canon of St Paul's Cathedral, 1920-21; Vicar of Cransley, Northants, 1921-56. Canon Non-residentiary of Peterborough Cathedral, 1955. Prof., Royal Academy of Music, 1925-59, FRAM 1927; FSA 1962. Dir of Music, London Day Training Coll. Examiner for LRAM Diploma, Associated Board Exams, 1927; Lectr for London Univ., Royal Institution of Great Britain, League of Arts, Music Teachers' Association, Sussex Archæological Soc. (Mem. Council), London Appreciation Soc., RSCM, RSA, Shell-Mex, IBM. *Publications:* The Theory of Music, 1928; Art and Reality, 1929; Tonality and Expression, 1929; Poems, 1933; Cransley Broadcast Sermons, 1933; The Light of the World, 1949 (USA 1950, paperback 1965); A Chronicle of Buxted, 1960 (paperback 1965); The Grand Design, 1964; Thus Saith the Lord: a Biblical anthology, 1967; musical publications include: *orchestral:* Prelude for Strings; *songs:* Three Songs; Day-dreams; The Shepherdess; Bereft; Eileen Aroon; But Yesterday; Your Gentle Care; My Heaven; Weep you no more; The Bells of Heaven; Shepherd Boy's Song; *choral:* Nobody Knows; Deep River; Jillian of Berry; Oh, to be in England; How can I help England; Claribel; Oh, Hush Thee My Baby; Cobwebs; *anthems:* Drop, Slow Tears; Let us with a gladsome mind; This Joyful Eastertide; Bread of the World; Lo! God is Here; *pianoforte:* High Marley Rest; Time Keepers; Meadowsweet; La Petite; Pets' Corner; Up the Ladder; A Day at the Sea; Bargain Basement; Reef's End; Cormorant Crag: Song Prelude; Whispering Willows; Haldon Hills; In the Cathedral; Gothic Prelude; *violin and piano:* High Marley Rest; *'cello and piano:* Sea Croon. Composer of several Hymns and contributor to Hymns Ancient and Modern, BBC Hymn Book, Baptist Hymn Book, etc. *Address:* Buxted Rectory, Uckfield, Sussex. *T:* Buxted 2287.

**COOKE, Sir Henry Frank,** Kt 1969; Chairman, Western Australian Division, Australian Red Cross, since 1961; *b* 10 Oct. 1900; *s* of F. V. Cooke; *m* 1926, Jean, *d* of B. L. Clarkson; two *s* three *d*. *Educ:* Hale School. Chairman: W Aust. Bd, Commercial Union Assurance Co.; Terrace Arcade Ltd. Vice-Chairman, Chamberlain Industries. Member of Senate, Univ. of W Aust. Hon. Treasurer, Pastoralists' and Graziers' Assoc. *Address:* 5 Brae Road, Claremont, W Australia 6010, Australia.

**COOKE, Jean Esme Oregon, (Mrs John Bratby),** ARA 1965; (professional name Jean E. Cooke); Lecturer in Painting, Royal College of Art, since 1964; *b* 18 Feb. 1927; *d* of Arthur Oregon Cooke, Grocer, and of Dorothy Emily Cooke (*née* Cranefield); *m* 1953, John Randall Bratby, *qv*; three *s* one *d*. *Educ:* Blackheath High Sch.; Central Sch. of Arts and Crafts; Goldsmiths' Coll. Sch. of Art; Royal Coll. of Art. NDD in Sculpture, 1949. Pottery Workshop, 1950-53. Purchase of self-portrait, Chantry Bequest, 1959; Portrait of Dr Egon Wellesz for Lincoln Coll., Oxford. One-man shows: Establishment Club, 1963; Leicester Gall., 1964; Bear Lane Gall., Oxford, 1965; Arun Art Centre, Arundel; Ashgate Gall., Farnham; Moyan Gall., Manchester; Bladon Gall., Hampshire, 1966; Lane Gall., Bradford, 1967; Gallery 66, Blackheath, 1967; Motley Gall., Lewisham, 1968. Works exhibited: Furneaux Gall., 1968; Upper Grosvenor Gall., 1968. *Recreations:* gardening, biology, swimming, walking. *Address:* 7 Hardy Road, Blackheath, SE3. *T:* 01-858 6288.

**COOKE, Rear-Adm. John Ernest,** CB 1955; CEng, FIMechE; Royal Navy, retired; *b* 1899; *s* of Arthur Cockerton Cooke; *m* 1923, Kathleen Mary, *d* of Walter James Haward; one *s* one *d*. *Educ:* Owen's Sch. Entered Royal Navy, 1915; served War of 1939-45, HMS Furious and HMS Anson; Capt., 1946; Manager of the Engineering Dept, HM Dockyard, Malta, 1950-53; Rear-Adm., 1953; Manager of the Engineering Dept, HM Dockyard, Portsmouth, 1954-57; retired. General Manager, Production, Messrs Bailey (Malta) Ltd, 1959-61. *Address:* c/o Lloyds Bank Ltd, Commercial Road, Portsmouth, Hants. *Club:* Royal Commonwealth Society, United Service; Union (Malta), Royal Malta Yacht.

**COOKE, Sir John F.;** *see* Fletcher-Cooke.

**COOKE, Rear-Adm. John Gervaise Beresford,** CB 1965; DSC 1940; Naval Secretary, 1966-67, retired; *b* 19 Oct. 1911; *s* of late (Judge) John Fitzpatrick Cooke, Londonderry, Northern Ireland, and Eleanora Lucia Caroline Macky; *m* 1941, Helen Beatrice Cameron; three *s* one *d*. *Educ:* Royal Naval Coll., Dartmouth. Entered Navy, 1925; served in Destroyers; qualified in gunnery, 1938; Commanded HM Ships Modeste and Finisterre, 1947; Comdr 1947; Admiralty, 1948-49; commanded HM Ships Broadsword and Battleaxe, 1950-51; Staff of C-in-C Med., 1952-54. Capt., 1954; Admiralty, 1955-57; idc 1958; commanded Admiralty Surface Weapons Establishment, 1959-60; Chief of Staff to Commander, British Navy Staff and Asst Naval Attaché, Washington, 1961-63; Rear-Adm., 1963; Asst Chief of Naval Staff (Warfare), 1963-66. *Recreations:* tennis, golf, shooting, fishing. *Address:* Downstead House, Twyford, Hants. *T:* Owslebury 209. *Club:* Naval and Military.

**COOKE, Kenneth;** *see* Cooke, R. K.

**COOKE, Sir Leonard,** Kt 1965; OBE 1951; President and Chairman, Co-operative Wholesale Society Ltd, 1960-66; *b* 6 May 1901; *s* of late Ernest Llewellyn Cooke and of Elizabeth Anne Cooke; *m* 1927, Florence Ellen Nunn; one *d*. *Educ:* Bishop Wordsworth Sch., Salisbury. Managing Sec., Macclesfield Co-operative Soc., 1933-38; Director: Co-operative Wholesale Soc., 1938-66; Co-operative Insurance Soc., 1945-66. Chm., NW Passenger Transport Co-ordinating Cttee, 1966-69; Vice-Chairman: Sugar Bd, 1969- (Mem., 1967-).; SE Lancs and NE Cheshire Passenger Transport Authority, 1969-; Member: BR (London Midland) Board, 1955-; North Western Regional Economic Planning Council, 1965-; Board of BTA, 1965-; NW Gas Board, 1967-; Merseyside Passenger Transport Authority, 1969-. Comdr, Order of the Dannebrog, 1962. *Recreations:* golf, bridge. *Address:* Sunning Hey, Tytherington,

Macclesfield, Cheshire. *T:* Macclesfield 2524. *Club:* Royal Commonwealth Society.

**COOKE, Col Philip Ralph D.**; *see* Davies-Cooke.

**COOKE, Major Randle Henry;** Equerry to the Duke of Edinburgh since Oct. 1968; *b* 26 April 1930; *o s* of Col H. R. V. Cooke, Dalicote Hall, Bridgnorth, Salop and Mrs E. F. K. Cooke, Brodawel, Tremerchion, N Wales; *m* 1961, Clare Bennett; one *s* one *d. Educ:* Heatherdown, Ascot; Eton College. 2nd Lieut, 8th King's Royal Irish Hussars, 1949; served Korea, 1950-53 with Regt and USAF (POW); ADC to GOC 7th Armoured Div., 1955; Regimental Adjt, 1957; Instructor, RMA Sandhurst, 1960; Sqdn Comdr, Queen's Royal Irish Hussars, Malaya, Borneo and Germany, 1963; GSO3 (SD), HQ 1st Div., 1965. *Recreations:* equitation and practically everything to do with water. *Address:* c/o Coutts & Co., 440 Strand, WC2. *Club:* Cavalry.

**COOKE (Richard) Kenneth,** OBE 1945; Metropolitan Stipendiary Magistrate since 1970; *b* 17 March 1917; *s* of Richard and Beatrice Mary Cooke; *m* 1945, Gwendoline Mary Black; no *c. Educ:* Sebright Sch., Wolverley; Birmingham Univ. Admitted Solicitor (Hons), 1939; Birmingham Law Soc. Prizeman. Sqdn Leader, RAFVR, 1939-45. Solicitor in private practice specialising in Magistrates' Courts, 1945-52; Clerk: to Prescot and St Helens Justices, 1952-57; to Rotherham County Borough and WR Justices, 1957-64; to Bradford City Justices, 1964-70. *Publications:* contribs to Criminal Law Review, Justice of the Peace and Local Govt Review, etc. *Recreations:* trout fishing, choral singing, sampling bin ends. *Address:* c/o Wells Street Magistrates' Court, 59-65 Wells Street, W1. *T:* 01-580 2454/7.

**COOKE, Robert (Gordon),** MA (Oxon); MP(C) Bristol West, since March 1957; *b* 29 May 1930; *er s* of Robert V. Cooke, *qv*; *m* 1966, Jenifer Patricia Evelyn, *yr d* of Evelyn Mansfield King, *qv*; one *s* one *d. Educ:* Harrow; Christ Church, Oxford. President: Oxford Univ. Conservative Assoc., 1952; Curzon Club, 1952-53; Editor, Oxford Tory, 1952-53. Councillor, City and Co. of Bristol, 1954-57; contested Bristol SE at Gen. Election, 1955. Parliamentary Private Secretary to: Minister of State, Home Office, 1958-59; Minister of Health, 1959-60; Minister of Works, 1960-62; introduced: Fatal Accidents Act, 1959; Historic Buildings Bill, 1963; Motorways Commn Bill, 1968. State Dept Foreign Leader Visitor in USA, 1961. Chm., Bristol Political Educn Cttee, 1955-57; Vice-Chm., Arts and Amenities Cttee of Conservative Party, 1959-62 and 1964-; Member: Estimates Cttee, 1964; Services Cttee, House of Commons, 1967-; Adv. Cttee on Works of Art in Palace of Westminster, 1964; Exec. Cttee, UN Parly Group, 1965-; Chm., Cons. Broadcasting and Communications Cttee, 1962-64. Member: Historic Houses Cttee, BTA; Georgian Group; Victorian Soc. Treasurer and Chm., Gen. Purposes Cttee of Primrose League. Director, Westward Television, 1970-. Lord of Manor and Patron of Living of Athelhampton and Burleston. *Publication:* West Country Houses, 1957. *Recreations:* architecture, building, gardening. *Address:* Athelhampton, Dorchester, Dorset. *T:* Puddletown 363. *Clubs:* Carlton, Pratt's, Farmer's, St Stephen's, Royal Automobile Clifton, Constitutional (Bristol).

**COOKE, Brig. Robert Thomas,** CBE 1943; psc†; *b* 23 Jan. 1897; *o s* of Capt. Robert George Cooke and Sarah Louisa, *d* of Thomas Connolly, Dundalk, Co. Louth; *m* 1922, Löie Howard, *d* of Frank Shawcross-Smith, Buxton, Derbyshire; two *d. Educ:* Warwick Sch.; RMC Sandhurst; Staff Coll., Camberley. 2nd Lieut ASC, 1915; Capt., 1926; Bt Major, 1937; Major, 1938; Lieut-Col, 1940; Col, 1942; Brig., 1943. Served France, Belgium, Egypt and Syria, 1914-19 (severely wounded twice). Staff Coll., 1930-31; Staff Appointments: Aldershot Command, 1932-34; Southern Command, 1934-36; Active Service, Palestine Rebellion, 1937-38; GSO2, War Office, 1938-40. AA & QMG, Narvik, March 1940; AA & QMG 54 Div., July 1940; AQMG (ops) Eastern Command, 1941; DQMG 1st Army, Aug. 1942; DQMG, AFHQ, N Africa, Dec. 1942; DA & QMG 9 Corps BNAF, March 1943; Brig. "Q" 15 Army Group, July 1943; DA & QMG 5 Army, Italy, Sept. 1943; Brig. i/c Administration, HQ L of C 21st Army Group, Nov. 1943-Feb. 1945; Col i/c Admin. S Wales District, 1945-46; Brig. "Q" GHQ, Middle East, 1946-47; Brig. i/c Administration, British Troops in Egypt, 1947; retired pay, 1949. Croix de Guerre, 1944. *Recreations:* hunting, golf, tennis. *Address:* 35 Egerton Road, Queen's Park, Bournemouth, Hants; c/o Lloyds Bank Ltd, Bournemouth, Hants.

**COOKE, Robert Victor,** FRCS 1929; Senior Surgeon: Bristol Royal Hospital; Bristol Homoeopathic Hospital; Tetbury and Almondsbury District Hospitals; *b* Berkeley, Glos, 17 May 1902; *e s* of John Cooke and Rose Eva (*née* O'Neill); *m* 1st, 1929, Elizabeth Mary (*d* 1964), MD, MRCP, *d* of Hugh Gordon Cowie, MD, Banff, Scotland; two *s*; 2nd, 1970, Dr Mavis Coutts. *Educ:* Lydney Grammar Sch., Glos; Bristol Univ.; Bristol Gen. Hosp. (ChM 1930); Middlesex Hosp.; Guy's Hosp. House appointments in Bristol and London; Asst to Prof. of Surgery, Univ. of Wales, 1929-33; Hon. Asst Surgeon, Bristol Gen. Hosp. and Bristol Children's Hosp., 1933-. Royal College of Surgeons: Mem. Council; Mem. Court of Examiners; Hunterian Prof.; Representative, Central Consultants and Specialists Cttee; Vice-Pres., 1969. British Medical Association: Mem.; Pres., Section of Surgery, Oxford, 1963; Pres., 1967-68. Pres., Proctological and Surgical Sections, RSM. Formerly Examiner in Surgery, Univs of Glasgow, Birmingham, Wales, Bristol, Oxford and Liverpool. A. B. Mitchell Memorial Lectr, Belfast, 1966; Bradshaw Lectr, RCS, 1970; (first) De Silva Memorial Lecture, Colombo, 1970. Mem., Bd of Governors, Bristol Royal Hosp. Hon. Secretary: Bristol Medico-Chirurgical Soc., 1935-46; Moynihan Chirurgical Club, 1950-59. FRSM; Fellow, Assoc. of Surgeons of Great Britain and Ireland. Liveryman, Soc. of Apothecaries of London. Hon. MD 1967. Cecil Joll Award, 1963; Lawrence Abel Cup, BMA, 1965. *Publications:* papers on intravenous pyelography, blood vessel injuries, goitre surgery, surgery of colon and biliary tract; chapter on intestinal resection and anastomosis in Textbook of British Surgery, 1956. *Recreations:* gardening (FRHS, and Mem. Iris, Rose and Delphinium Socs); Antiquary (Collector of English furniture; Mem., Bristol and Glos Archaeological Soc.); golf. *Address:* Litfield House, Clifton Down, Bristol 8. *T:* Bristol 36363; Athelhampton, Dorchester, Dorset.

*See also Robert Gordon Cooke.*

**COOKE, (Roland) Cecil,** CMG 1959; CBE 1952; Director of Exhibitions, Central Office of Information, 1946-61, retired; *b* 28 June 1899; *m* 1924, Doris Marjorie, *d* of Reginald Fewings. Architectural Asst, LCC, 1921; Dir of Publicity, Catesbys, Ltd, 1935; Dir of Exhibitions Div., Ministry of Information,

1945. Dir of Exhibitions, Festival of Britain, 1949-51; Dir, Festival Gardens Co., 1951; Dir of Exhibitions, British Government Pavilion, Brussels, 1958; UK representative, International Jury, Brussels Exhibition, 1958. Comr Gen., British Pavilion, Seattle World's Fair. *Publications:* contrib. to periodicals and press, illustrated stories for children, political and strip cartoons. *Recreation:* painting. *Address:* Greenbanks, Fairmile Lane, Cobham, Surrey. *T:* Cobham (Surrey) 2557.

**COOKE, Maj.-Gen. Ronald Basil Bowen Bancroft,** CB 1950; CBE 1943; DSO 1944; *b* 1 Sept. 1899; *s* of late Lieut-Col Sydney Cooke, Orwell Lodge, Horsham, and Alice Elizabeth Bancroft; *m* 1933, Joan, *d* of late Major Claude Chichester, Tunworth Down House, Basingstoke; two *s* one *d* (one *s* decd). *Educ:* Charterhouse; RMC. 2nd Lieut 17th Lancers, 1918; Major, 1937; Chief Instr, RAC Tactical Sch., 1939; CO, E Riding Yeomanry, 1940; AQMG, GHQ Home Forces, 1941; GSO1, 6 Armd Div. and 1st Armd Gp, 1941-42; Brig. RAC 1st Army, 1942; Brig.–Gen. Staff, 10 Corps, 1943-44; Comdr 9 Armd Bde, 1944-45; Lieut-Col and Col, 1945; Chief of Staff, Allied Commn, Austria, 1946-47; Comdr, 8 Armd Bde, 1948; Maj.-Gen., 1949; Comdr 49 Armd Div. and North Midland District, 1949-52; Dir of the Royal Armoured Corps, War Office, 1952-55; Dir of Civil Defence for Wales, 1956-60; Comdt Civil Defence Staff Coll., Sunningdale, 1960. High Sheriff of Hampshire, 1966. Mem., Hampshire CC, 1967. Comdr US Legion of Merit, 1944 and 1946. *Recreations:* polo, hunting and shooting. *Address:* Poland Court, Odiham, Hants; 13 Bolton Gardens, SW5. *Club:* Cavalry.

**COOKE, Rupert C.;** *see* Croft-Cooke.

**COOKE, Sir Samuel Burgess Ridgway,** Kt 1967; QC 1960; **Hon. Mr Justice Cooke;** Judge of the High Court of Justice, Queen's Bench Division, since 1967; *b* 16 March 1912; *o s* of Samuel and Jessie Lennox Cooke; *m* 1st, Isabel Nancy, *d* of late E. F. Bulmer, Adams Hill, Hereford; 2nd, Diana, *d* of late George Witherby, Burley, Hants. *Educ:* Gonville and Caius Coll., Cambridge (schol.). 1st Class Hons Classical Tripos Pt I and Law Tripos Pt II; Pres., Cambridge Union Soc., 1934. Cholmeley Schol., Lincoln's Inn; called to Bar (cert. of honour), 1936; Asst to Parly Counsel to Treasury, 1938-45; Parly Counsel, 1945-46; private practice, 1946; Jun. Counsel to Min. of Lab. and Nat. Service, 1950-60. Bencher of Lincoln's Inn; Mem., Senate of the Four Inns of Court, 1966-68. *Address:* 3 Well Road, Hampstead, NW3. *T:* 01-435 1282; Rectory Farm, Plumpton, Northants. *T:* Blakesley 271. *Club:* Athenæum.

**COOKE, Maj.-Gen. Sidney Arthur,** CB 1953; OBE 1943; retired; *b* 21 July 1903; *s* of late Major Arthur Cooke, 13th Hussars, and late Mrs Kezia Cooke; unmarried. *Educ:* Warwick; RMC, Sandhurst. British Army: Gazetted to Lincolnshire Regt, 1924; Lieut, 1926; Capt. 1935; Major 1941; Lieut-Col 1947; Col 1948; Maj.-Gen. 1951; retired, 1957. Order of Al Istiqlal (First Class) Jordan, 1953; Order of Al Kawkab (First Class) Jordan, 1957. *Address:* The Wilderness, 62 Grove Lane, Holt, Norfolk. *T:* Holt (Norfolk) 3258.

**COOKE, William Charles Cyril,** MA Cantab; Headmaster, Northampton School, 1921-44; *b* 26 March 1881; *s* of late Rev. W. C. Cooke, Histon, Cambs. *Educ:* King Edward's Sch., Birmingham; Queens' Coll., Cambridge. 2nd Class Classical Tripos, 1903 (Cambridge Univ. Athletics, 1903); Classical master, King's Sch., Peterborough, 1903; Caldy Grange Grammar Sch., 1908; Northampton Sch., 1910-21; 4th Bn Northants Regt 1915-19; Member, HMC, IAHM. *Publications:* occasional articles and verses. *Recreations:* walking and the Education Act, 1944. *Address:* 19 Abington Grove, Northampton. *T:* 54071-1.

**COOKSLEY, Clarence Harrington,** QPM 1969; Chief Constable of Northumberland since 1969; *b* 16 Dec. 1915; *e s* of Clarence Harrington Cooksley and Elsie Cooksley, Nottingham; *m* 1940, Eunice May White, Nottingham; two *s*. *Educ:* Nottingham. Joined Nottinghamshire Constabulary, 1938. Served Duke of Wellington's Regt and Dep. Asst Provost Marshal, Special Investigation Branch, Royal Corps of Military Police, 1942-46. Dir. of Dept of Law, Police Coll., Bramshill, 1961; Dep. Chief Constable of Hertfordshire, 1961-63; Chief Constable of Northumberland County Constabulary, 1963-69. OStJ 1966. *Address:* North Moor, Stannington, Morpeth, Northumberland. *T:* Stannington 259. *Clubs:* Royal Commonwealth; Northern Counties (Newcastle upon Tyne).

**COOKSON, Clive;** *b* 16 Sept. 1879; 3rd *s* of Norman Charles Cookson; *m* 1913, Marion Amy James (*d* 1961); two *s* one *d*. *Educ:* Harrow. A Vice-Pres., FBI (now CBI). Hon. DCL Durham. *Recreations:* gardening, shooting, fishing. *Address:* Nether Warden, Hexham, Northumberland. *T:* 3277. *Clubs:* Brooks's; Northern Counties, Union (Newcastle upon Tyne).
*See also Prof. R. C. Cookson.*

**COOKSON, Prof. Richard Clive,** FRS 1968; MA, PhD, FRIC; Professor of Chemistry in the University of Southampton since 1957; *b* 27 Aug. 1922; *s* of Clive Cookson, *qv*; *m* 1948, Ellen Fawaz; two *s*. *Educ:* Harrow Sch.; Trinity Coll., Cambridge. BA 1944; MA, PhD Cantab 1947. Research Fellow, Harvard Univ., 1948; Research Div. of Glaxo Laboratories Ltd, 1949-51; Lectr, Birkbeck Coll., London Univ., 1951-57. *Publications:* papers, mainly in Jl Chem. Soc. *Address:* Chemistry Department, The University, Southampton. *T:* 56331.

**COOKSON, Roland Antony,** OBE 1946; Chairman: Lead Industries Group Ltd, since 1967 (Goodlass Wall and Lead Industries Ltd, 1962-67); Consett Iron Co. Ltd, 1966-67 (Director 1955; Acting Chairman 1964); Director of Lloyds Bank Ltd since 1964 (Chairman, Northern Regional Board); *b* 12 Dec. 1908; *s* of late Bryan Cookson; *m* 1931, Rosamond Gwladys, *er d* of late Sir John S. Barwick, 2nd Bt; one *d*. *Educ:* Harrow; Magdalen Coll., Oxford. Vice-Chm., Northern Regional Board for Industry, 1949-65; Mem., Northern Economic Planning Council, 1965-68; Pres., Tyneside Chamber of Commerce, 1955-57; Chm., Northern Regional Council, CBI, 1970- (Vice-Chm., 1968-70); Mem., Port of Tyne Authority, 1968-. Mem., Court and Council, Univ. of Newcastle upon Tyne; Chm., Appointments Board, Univs of Newcastle upon Tyne and Durham. *Recreations:* music, fishing, shooting. *Address:* Howden Dene, Corbridge, Northumberland. *T:* Corbridge 2422. *Clubs:* Brooks's; Northern Counties (Newcastle upon Tyne).
*See also Sir Richard Barwick, Bt.*

**COOLIDGE, William David,** BS, PhD, DSc, MD, LLD, DEng; Director Emeritus of the Research Laboratory, General Electric Co., Schenectady, New York; *b* 23 Oct. 1873; *s* of Albert E. Coolidge and Martha Alice; *m* 1st, 1908, Ethel Westcott Woodard (*d* 1915); one *s* one *d*; 2nd, 1916, Dorothy Elizabeth MacHaffie (*d* 1969). *Educ:* Massachusetts

Institute of Technology; University of Leipsic. Instructor Phys. Chem., Mass. Inst. of Tech., 1901-03; Asst Prof. Phys. Chem. Research, Mass. Inst. of Tech., 1904-05; Phys. Chem., Research Lab., GEC, 1905-07; Asst Dir, 1908-28; Assoc. Dir, 1928-32; Dir, 1932-40; Vice-Pres. and Dir of Research, 1940-44. Member: Nat. Acad. of Sciences; Amer. Acad. of Arts and Sciences, etc, etc; Honorary or Corresponding Mem. numerous Socs both in USA and abroad. *Medals and Awards:* Rumford Medal, 1914; Howard N. Potts Medal, 1926; Louis Edward Levy Gold Medal, 1926; Gold Medal (Amer. Coll. of Radiology), 1927; Hughes Medal, 1927; Edison Medal, 1927; John Scott Award, 1937; Faraday Medal, 1939; Duddell Medal, 1942; Franklin Medal, 1944; K. C. Li Medal and Award (Columbia Univ.), 1952 (first recipient). Orden al Merito, Chilean Government, 1942. Roentgen Medal, 1963. *Publications:* articles in specialist journals. *Recreations:* photography and travel. *Address:* 1480 Lenox Road, Schenectady 8, NY, USA. *T:* 4-7491. *Clubs:* Mohawk (Schenectady); Engineers (Dayton).

**COOLS-LARTIGUE, Alexander Raphael,** QC (Windward Islands), 1945; *b* 25 Oct. 1899; *e s* of Theodore Cools-Lartigue and Emily Cools-Lartigue (*née* Giraud); *m* 1927, Alexandra Sybil Potter; two *s* four *d. Educ:* St Mary's Coll., St Lucia; Dominica Grammar Sch., WI. Called to the Bar, Gray's Inn, 1924; practised at the Bar of the Leeward Islands, 1924-35. Crown Attorney, Dominica, 1935; Attorney-General: St Lucia, 1938; Windward Islands, 1942; Puisne Judge, Supreme Court of the Windward Islands and Leeward Islands, 1949-53; Senior Puisne Judge, Jamaica, 1958-64 (Puisne Judge, 1953-64). *Recreations:* tennis and golf. *Address:* Supreme Court, Kingston, Jamaica. *Clubs:* various in St Vincent, Grenada and St Lucia, WI.

*See also Sir Louis Cools-Lartigue.*

**COOLS-LARTIGUE, Sir Louis,** Kt 1968; OBE 1955; Governor of Dominica since Nov. 1967; *b* 18 Jan. 1905; *s* of Theodore Cools-Lartigue and Emily (*née* Giraud); *m* 1932, Eugene (*née* Royer); two *s* four *d. Educ:* Convents, St Lucia and Dominica; Dominica Gram. Sch. Clerk, Dominica Civil Service, 1924; Chief Clerk to Administrator and Clerk of Councils, 1932; Colonial Treas., Dominica, 1940, St Vincent, 1945; Asst Administrator, St Lucia, 1949; Chief Sec., Windward Is, 1951, retd, 1960 on abolition of office; performed duties of Governor's Dep., Windward Is, over fifty times; Speaker of Legislative Coun., Dominica, 1961-67; Speaker of House of Assembly, Dominica, March-Oct. 1967. *Recreations:* tennis, swimming. *Address:* Government House, Roseau, Dominica, West Indies.

*See also A. R. Cools-Lartigue.*

**COOMARASWAMY, Sir Velupillai,** Kt, *cr* 1952; CMG 1947; High Commissioner for Ceylon in Canada since 1958; *b* 25 Sept. 1892; *s* of late S. Velupillai, Vaddukoddai, Jaffna, Ceylon; *m* 1926, Nesamany, *d* of W. H. T. Bartlett, formerly Asst Supt of Surveys, Ceylon; one *s* one *d. Educ:* Victoria Coll., Jaffna; Trinity Coll., Kandy. Entered CCS, 1913; formerly Registrar-Gen., Dir of Commercial Intelligence, Food Controller, Controller of Imports, Exports and Exchange, Dir of Food Supplies and Control, Govt Agent, Western and Eastern Provinces, Permanent Sec. to Ministry of Home Affairs and Rural Development, Ceylon; Dep. High Comr for Ceylon in UK, 1948-53; Minister Plenipotentiary and Envoy Extraordinary for Ceylon in Burma, 1953-54; Chm., Ceylon prohibition commn, 1955-57; Delegate of Ceylon to 14th Gen. Assembly of the United Nations. *Address:* 28 Range Road, Ottawa. *T:* CE 5-5256. *Clubs:* Orient (Colombo), Colombo (Colombo).

**COOMBS, Derek Michael;** MP (C) Yardley Division of Birmingham since 1970; *b* 12 Aug. 1931; *s* of Clifford and Mary Coombs; *m* 1959, Patricia O'Toole; one *s* one *d. Educ:* Rydal Prep. Sch.; Bromsgrove School. S&U Stores Ltd: Dir 1960; Jt Man. Dir 1970 (also of subsids). *Publications:* various papers on economics and foreign affairs. *Recreations:* ski-ing, theatre, collecting Greco-Roman antiquities. *Address:* 14 Chester Street, SW1. *T:* 01-235 8765; Shottery Grange, Shottery, Stratford-on-Avon, Warwicks. *T:* Stratford-on-Avon 5249.

**COOMBS, Herbert Cole,** MA, PhD; FAA; Chairman: Australian Council for Aboriginal Affairs, since 1968; Australian Council for Arts, since 1968; Chancellor, Australian National University, since 1968; *b* 24 Feb. 1906; *s* of Francis Robert Henry and Rebecca Mary Coombs; *m* 1931, Mary Alice Ross; three *s* one *d. Educ:* Univ. of Western Australia, Perth, WA (MA); LSE (PhD). Asst Economist, Commonwealth Bank of Australia, 1935; Economist to Commonwealth Treasury, 1939; Mem., Commonwealth Bank Board, 1942; Dir of Rationing, 1942; Dir-Gen. of Post-War Reconstruction, 1943; Governor, Commonwealth Bank of Australia, 1949-60; Chm., Commonwealth Bank Board, 1951-60; Governor and Chm. of Board, Reserve Bank of Australia, 1960-68; Chm., Australian Elizabethan Theatre Trust, 1954-68. Hon. LLD: Melbourne; ANU; Sydney; Hon. DLitt WA; Hon. Fellow LSE, 1961. *Recreation:* golf. *Address:* 119 Milson Road, Cremorne, NSW 2090, Australia.

**COOMBS, Robert Royston Amos,** ScD; FRS 1965; Quick Professor of Biology, and Head, Immunology Division, Department of Pathology, University of Cambridge, since 1966; Fellow of Corpus Christi College; *b* 9 Jan. 1921; *s* of Charles Royston Amos and Edris Owen Amos (formerly Coombs); *m* 1952, Anne Marion Blomfield; one *s* one *d. Educ:* Diocesan Coll., Cape Town; Edinburgh and Cambridge Univs. BSc, MRCVS Edinburgh 1943; PhD Cambridge 1947; Stringer Fellow, King's Coll., Cambridge, 1947. Asst Director of Research, Dept of Pathology, University of Cambridge, 1948; Reader in Immunology, University of Cambridge, 1963-66. Fellow of CCC, 1962. *Publications:* (with Anne M. Coombs and D. G. Ingram) Serology of Conglutination and its relation to disease, 1960; (ed with P. G. H. Gell) Clinical Aspects of Immunology, 1963; numerous scientific papers on immunology. *Recreation:* retreat to the country. *Address:* 6 Selwyn Gardens, Cambridge. *T:* Cambridge 52681.

**COOPER,** family name of **Viscount Norwich** and **Baron Cooper of Stockton Heath.**

**COOPER;** *see* Ashley-Cooper.

**COOPER OF STOCKTON HEATH,** Baron *cr* 1966, of Stockton Heath (Life Peer); **John Cooper,** MA; General Secretary and Treasurer, National Union of General and Municipal Workers, since Jan. 1962; Member, Thames Conservancy, since 1955; Chairman, British Productivity Council, 1965-66; *b* 7 June 1908; *s* of John Ainsworth Cooper and Annie Lily Cooper (*née* Dukes); *m* 1934, Nellie Spencer (marr. diss. 1969); three *d*; *m* 1969, Mrs Joan Rogers. Educ: Stockton Heath Council Sch.; Lymm Grammar Sch., Cheshire. Employed Crosfields Soap Works, Warrington, 1924-28;

NUGMW, 1928-, District Sec., Southern Dist, 1944-61; Chm., 1952-61. Member: Manchester CC, 1936-42; LCC, 1949; Alderman, 1952-53; London Labour Party Executive; MP (Lab) Deptford, 1950-51; PPS to Sec. of State for Commonwealth Relations, 1950-51. Member: Fabian Soc.; NEC Labour Party, 1953-57; TUC Gen. Council, 1959-; NEDC; Governor various instns, etc. Visiting Fellow, Nuffield Coll., Oxford; MA Oxon. Prix de la Couronne Française, 1970. *Address:* Room 43, Ruxley Towers, Claygate, Esher, Surrey. *T:* Esher 62081.

**COOPER, Sqdn Ldr Albert Edward,** MBE 1946; MP (C) Ilford South, 1950-66 and since 1970; Managing Director, Dispersions Ltd; Director, Ault & Wiborg (Export) Ltd; *b* 23 Sept. 1910; *s* of Albert Frederick Smith and Edith Alice Cooper, Withernsea, Yorks; *m* 1933, Emily Muriel, *d* of William John Nelder, Launceston; one *d. Educ:* London Coll. for Choristers; Australia. Entered politics, 1935, when elected to Ilford Borough Council; Chairman: Electricity and Lighting Cttee; Education (Finance) and Legal and Parliamentary Cttees; Alderman, 1947. Served War of 1939-45; enlisted in RAF, 1940, and served as navigator in Coastal Command. Contested (C) Dagenham, Gen. Election, 1945; PPS to President of the Board of Trade, 1952-54. *Recreations:* cricket, swimming, bridge, and motoring. *Address:* 14 Chartwell, 80 Wimbledon Parkside, SW19. *Club:* 1900.

**COOPER, Andrew Ramsden,** CBE 1965; Industrial Consultant and Company Director, since 1966; Member for Operations and Personnel, Central Electricity Generating Board, 1959-66; *b* 1 Oct. 1902; *s* of Mary and William Cooper, Rotherham, Yorks. *Educ:* Rotherham Grammar Sch.; Sheffield Univ. Colliery Engineer, Yorks and Kent, 1916-28; Chief Electrical Engineer, Pearson & Dorman Long, 1928; Personal Asst to G. A. Mower, London, 1935; joined Central Electricity Board Operation Dept, NW England and N Wales, 1936; transf. to HQ, 1937; Operation Engineer, SE and E England, 1942; Chief Operation Engineer to Central Electricity Board, 1944; Controller, Merseyside and N Wales Div. (Central Electricity Authority), 1948-52; NW Div., 1952-54; N West, Mersyside and N Wales Div., 1954-57; Mem. and Regional Dir, CEGB, 1957-59. Faraday Lectr, 1952-53. MEng; CEng; FIEE; MBIM; MRI; FInstF. Pres., Conférence Internationale des Grands Réseaux Electriques, 1966-. Mem. Assoc. of Mining, Electrical and Mechanical Engineers. Hon. Master of Engineering, Liverpool Univ., 1954. *Publication:* Load Dispatching, with Special Reference to the British Grid System (a paper receiving John Hopkinson Award, 1948, and Willans Medal, 1952, IEE). *Recreations:* golf, writing, broadcasting. *Address:* 15 Strathmore Court, 143 Park Road, NW8. *T:* 01-586 0869. *Clubs:* Savile; Royal Wimbledon Golf.

**COOPER, Capt. Archibald Frederick,** CBE 1944 (OBE 1919); Royal Navy; *b* 7 March 1885; 3rd *s* of Major T. F. Cooper, Royal Artillery. *Educ:* abroad; Brighton Grammar Sch. Sec. to Naval Sec. to First Lord of the Admiralty, 1927-29; Sec. to C-in-C, East Indies, 1929-32; to C-in-C, Plymouth, 1932-35. Deputy Judge-Advocate of the Fleet, 1935-46; retired, 1946. Special Service in Germany, Oct.-May 1947. Naval Gen. Service Medal Bar, 1909-14 (Persian Gulf), 1914-15 Star, British and Allied war medals; Officer of the Crown of Belgium, 1918; Star of Ethiopia 3rd Class, 1930; Jubilee Medal, 1935; Coronation Medal, 1937; France and Germany War Medal; Defence Medal; British War Medal. *Recreations:* ski-ing and gardening. *Address:* Horns Hill Lodge, Squerryes Park, near Westerham, Kent. *T:* Westerham 3114.

**COOPER, Sir Charles (Eric Daniel),** of Woollahra, 5th Bt, *cr* 1863; *b* 5 Oct. 1906; *s* of Sir Daniel Cooper, 4th Bt, and Lettice Margaret, *y d* of 1st Viscount Long; *S* father 1954; *m* 1st, 1931, Alice Estelle (*d* 1952), *y d* of late William Manifold, Victoria, Australia; 2nd, 1953, Mary Elisabeth, *e d* of Capt. J. Graham Clarke, Frocester Manor, Glos; two *s. Educ:* Harrow; RMC Sandhurst. Lieut 1st The Royal Dragoons, 1926; Capt., 1935; Major, 1945. Served War of 1939-45. *Recreations:* hunting and shooting. *Heir: s* William Daniel Charles Cooper, *b* 5 March 1955. *Address:* East Challoch, Dunragit, Stranraer, Wigtownshire. *Club:* Cavalry.

**COOPER, Lady Diana, (Diana, Viscountess Norwich);** 3rd *d* of 8th Duke of Rutland, KG (*d* 1925), and Violet Lindsay (*d* 1937); *m* 1919 (as Lady Diana Manners) A. Duff Cooper, 1st Viscount Norwich (*cr* 1952), PC, KCMG, DSO (*d* 1954); one *s* (*see* 2nd Viscount Norwich). Nurse at Guy's Hospital during European War, 1914-18. Took leading part in Max Reinhardt's play, The Miracle, that showed, on and off, for 12 years in London and provincial towns, in USA (New York and all the great cities), and on the Continent (Prague, Buda-Pest, Vienna, Dortmund, Salzburg). Pres., Order of Charity. *Publications:* The Rainbow Comes and Goes, 1958; The Light of Common Day, 1959; Trumpets from the Steep, 1960. *Address:* 10 Warwick Avenue, W2; Le Marget-Gaterie des Pâtres, Uzès, Gard, France.

**COOPER, Douglas;** Art Historian and Critic: Slade Professor of Fine Art, Oxford University, 1957-58; Flexner Lecturer, Bryn Mawr, 1961; *b* London, 20 Feb. 1911. *Educ:* various European Univs. Dep.-Dir, Monuments and Fine Arts Branch, Control Commn for Germany, 1944-46; Lectr, Courtauld Institute of Art. Chevalier de la Légion d'Honneur. *Publications:* Letters of Van Gogh to Emile Bernard, 1937; The Road to Bordeaux, 1940; Paul Klee, 1949; Turner, 1949; Juan Gris, 1949; Leger, 1949; Degas Pastels, 1954; Catalogue of the Courtauld Collection, 1954; Van Gogh Water Colours, 1955; Toulouse-Lautrec, 1956; Graham Sutherland, 1961; De Staël, 1962; Picasso: Les Déjeuners, 1962; Picasso: Theatre, 1968; The Cubist Epoch, 1970. *Address:* Château de Castille, Argilliers, Gard, France.

**COOPER, Sir Francis Ashmole, (Sir Frank),** 4th Bt *cr* 1905; Chairman, Ashmole Investment Trust Ltd, since 1969; *b* 9 Aug. 1905; s of Sir Richard Ashmole Cooper, 2nd Bt, and Alice Elizabeth (*d* 1963), *d* of Rev. E. Priestland, Spondon; *S* brother, 1970; *m* 1933, Dorothy F. H., *d* of Emile Deen, Berkhamsted, and Maggie Louise Deen; one *s* three *d. Educ:* Lancing Coll.; King's Coll., Cambridge (MA); University Coll., London (PhD). Joined Cooper, McDougall and Robertson Ltd, 1926; on leave to University College, 1931-36; Technical Director, 1940-62; retired, 1962. *Recreation:* yachting. *Heir: s* Richard Powell Cooper, *b* 13 April 1934. *Address:* Littleheath Great Farm, Berkhamsted, Herts. *T:* Berkhamsted 3234. *Clubs:* Carlton, Royal Thames Yacht; Royal Motor Yacht (Sandbanks, Poole).

**COOPER, Frank,** CB 1970; CMG 1961; a Deputy Secretary, Civil Service Department, since 1970; *b* 2 Dec. 1922; *s* of late V. H. Cooper, Fairfield, Manchester; *m* 1948, Peggie, *d* of F. J. Claxton; two *s* one *d. Educ:*

Manchester Grammar Sch.; Pembroke Coll., Oxford. War of 1939-45: Pilot, Royal Air Force, 1941-46. Asst Principal, Air Ministry, 1948; Private Secretary: to Parly Under-Sec. of State for Air, 1949-51; to Permanent Under-Sec. of State for Air, 1951-53; to Chief of Air Staff, 1953-55; Asst Sec., Head of the Air Staff, Secretariat, 1955-60; Dir of Accounts, Air Ministry, 1961-62; Asst Under-Sec. of State, Air Min., 1962-64, Min. of Defence, 1964-68; Dep. Under-Sec. of State, Min. of Defence, 1968-70. *Recreations:* tennis, sailing. *Address:* Delafield, Camden Park Road, Chislehurst, Kent.

**COOPER, Wing-Comdr Geoffrey;** President: Raydel Ltd (a property company in Nassau, Bahamas); Estate Developers Ltd; Land Title Clearance Ltd; *b* 18 Feb. 1907; *s* of Albert Cooper, Leicester, and Evelyn J. Bradnam, Hastings; *m* 1951, Mrs Tottie Resch, Blanc Pignon, Jersey, CI. *Educ:* Wyggeston Gram. Sch., Leicester; Royal Grammar School, Worcester. Accountancy, business management. Auxiliary Air Force, 1933; Imperial Airways, 1939. Served Royal Air Force 1939-45, Pilot. MP (Lab) for Middlesborough West Div., 1945-51. *Publications:* Cæsar's Mistress (exposé of BBC and nationalisation); articles in England, Bahamas and USA on civil aviation, business management and government methods. *Recreations:* portrait and landscape painting, swimming, tennis, ski-ing and horse riding. *Address:* PO Box 4305, Nassau, Bahamas. *Club:* Royal Air Force.

**COOPER, George Edward;** Chairman, North Thames Gas Board, since 1970; *b* 25 Jan. 1915; *s* of H. E. Cooper and R. A. Jones, Wolverhampton; *m* 1941, Dorothy Anne Robinson; one *s*. *Educ:* Wolverhampton Municipal Grammar Sch. Wolverhampton and Walsall Corp., 1933-40. Served War, 1940-45, with RA in Middle East (Bimbashi Sudan Defence Force), Captain. Qualified as Accountant, Inst. of Municipal Treasurers and Accountants, 1947; Hemel Hempstead Development Corp., 1948-50; W Midlands Gas Bd (finally Dep. Chm.), 1950-70. FIMTA, 1965; CIGasE, 1968. *Recreations:* photography, geology, golf. *Address:* 78 Lillington Road, Leamington Spa, Warwickshire. *T:* Leamington Spa 21888. *Club:* Belfry.

**COOPER, Dame Gladys,** DBE 1967; (Dame Gladys Merivale); actress; *b* 18 Dec. 1888; *m* 1st, H. J. Buckmaster (marr. diss.); one *s* one *d*; 2nd, 1928, Sir Neville Pearson, *qv* (marr. diss.); one *d*; 3rd, 1937, Philip Merivale (*d* 1946). First appearance on stage, Theatre Royal, Colchester, Dec. 1905; first London appearance, Vaudeville Theatre, 1906; subsequent successes at London theatres, notably as: Paula in revival of The Second Mrs Tanqueray, 1922; Magda in revival of Magda, 1923; Peter Pan, 1923 and 1924; Dora, in revival of Diplomacy, 1924; Mrs Cheyney in The Last of Mrs Cheyney, 1925; Leslie Crosbie in The Letter, 1927; Felicity, Countess of Marshwood, in Relative Values, Savoy, 1951; Grace Smith in A Question of Fact, Piccadilly, 1953; Lady Yarmouth in The Night of the Ball, New, 1955; Mrs Gantry in The Bird of Time, Savoy, 1961. Conducted management of Playhouse, 1927-33. First New York appearance, as Marcelle Linden in The Shining Hour, 1934; also, in New York: Lady Macbeth in Macbeth, 1935; Tiny Fox Collier in Spring Meeting, 1938; Mrs Parrilow in The Morning Star, 1942; Mrs St Maugham in The Chalk Garden, 1955; A Passage to India, 1962; The Sacred Flame, 1967; Out of the Question, 1968; His, Hers and Theirs, 1969. *Films include:* Rebecca; That Hamilton Woman; Now, Voyager; The Song of Bernadette; Mrs Parkington; The White Cliffs of Dover; Love Letters; The Green Years; Green Dolphin Street; The Bishop's Wife; Madame Bovary. *Relevant Publications:* Gladys Cooper, 1931; Without Veils, 1953. *Address:* Barn Elms, Henley-on-Thames, Oxon.

*See also Robert Morley.*

**COOPER, Sir Guy;** *see* Cooper, Sir H. G.

**COOPER, Harold H.;** *see* Hinton-Cooper.

**COOPER, Sir (Harold) Stanford,** Kt, *cr* 1945; FCA; retired; *b* 26 Aug. 1889; *s* of late Rev. James Rides Cooper, Wimbledon, and Bessie Pomeroy; *m* 1st, 1916; two *d*; 2nd, 1939; 3rd, 1952, Joan Bretten. *Educ:* private tuition. Served in RNVR, 1916-19. Member: Scott Cttee on Land Utilisation in Rural Areas, 1941-42; Exec. and Council, Royal Society of St George. Governor, brit. Soc. for Internat. Understanding. Vice-Pres., Brit. Atlantic Cttee; Member: Council in England of Council of Christians and Jews; World Brotherhood, Europe. Formerly: Permanent Lay Mem. of Restrictive Practices Court; Vice-Chm., Ford Motor Co. Ltd; Chm. of various European Ford Cos. FRGS. Liveryman, Glaziers' and Coachmakers' Cos; Knight of the Round Table; Premier Comdr of Finnish Lion Order; Knight of Swedish North Star; Comdr of Order of Dannebrog; Knight of Order of Leopold. *Recreation:* country life. *Address:* 35 Campden Hill Gate, Duchess of Bedford Walk, W8. *Clubs:* Carlton, Pilgrims, MCC, Anglo-Belgian, Hurlingham.

**COOPER, Henry Ford;** *b* 22 June 1904; *s* of John W. and S. A. Cooper; *m* 1948, Elsie Zahn; two *s* one *d*. *Educ:* Liberia Coll., Monrovia. Entered Liberian Foreign Service State Dept, 1922; Liberian Consul-Gen. for Gt Britain, 1931-36, for German Reich, 1936-42. Manager Liberia Govt Import Export Corp., 1943-46; Liberian Minister in Paris, 1947-52, to Madrid, 1950-52; Liberian Ambassador in London, 1952-56. Chm., Liberian Delegn to 3rd, 6th, 7th and 8th Sessions UN Gen. Assembly. *Recreation:* fishing. *Address:* Camp Johnson Road, Monrovia, Liberia, West Africa.

**COOPER, Sir (Henry) Guy,** Kt 1941; MC; DCM; *b* 1890; *s* of late Rev. H. S. Cooper, MA Oxon; *m* 1922, Charlotte (Kaisar-i-Hind Gold Medal, 1941), *e d* of late William Meek, OBE, St Andrews, Fifeshire; two *d*. *Educ:* St Edmunds, Canterbury; Keble Coll., Oxford. Served European War, 1914-18, with Royal Corps of Signals and 130th KGO Baluchis, IA (despatches thrice, DCM, MC); Pres., Karachi Chamber of Commerce, 1930; Bengal Legislative Assembly, 1934-35; Bengal Chamber of Commerce Cttee, 1936-42; Gen. Manager of Burmah-Shell, India, 1936-44. Chm., Indian Petroleum Industry Cttee, 1939-44; British Petroleum Co., 1945-56. *Address:* Priory Acres, Boscombe Village, near Salisbury, Wilts. *Club:* Oriental.

**COOPER, James Lees;** Publisher and Editor in Chief, The Globe and Mail, Toronto, since 1963; Director, The Globe and Mail Ltd; *b* Darwen, Lancs, 6 March 1907; *s* of James William and Alice (Lees) Cooper; *m* 1930, Ruby Smith; one *d*. *Educ:* Darwen Grammar Sch. Articled to Darwen News as journalist; worked as reporter, Ashton-under-Lyne; Allied Newspapers, Manchester, and Daily Express, London. War Correspondent, 1941-45: Malta Convoys, Western Desert, Madagascar, Sicily, Italy campaigns. First staff correspondent in Canada for Daily Express, 1947-55; Chief of New York Bureau,

1955-57; organized Overseas Edn of Globe and Mail and its printing and distribution by The Times of London (first overseas edn of a Canadian newspaper), 1958; returned to Canada as Asst to Editor and Publisher, 1959. Trustee, Toronto Gen. Hosp.; Dir, Imperial Trust, Montreal; Chm., Canadian Section, Commonwealth Press Union. *Address:* 140 King Street West, Toronto 1, Ont, Canada. *T:* 368-7851.

**COOPER, Joan Davies;** Chief Inspector in the Children's Department of the Home Office since 1965; *b* 12 Aug. 1914; *d* of late Valentine Holland Cooper and of Wynnefred Louisa Cooper; unmarried. *Educ:* Fairfield High Sch., Manchester; University of Manchester (BA). Asst Dir of Educn, Derbyshire CC, 1941; Children's Officer, E Sussex CC, 1948. *Publications:* contribs to social work jls. *Recreations:* golf, gardening. *Address:* The Garden House, Paine's Twitten, Lewes, Sussex. *T:* Lewes 2604. *Club:* English-Speaking Union.

**COOPER, Joshua Edward Synge,** CB 1958; CMG 1943; retired from the Foreign Office; *b* 3 April 1901; *e s* of late Richard E. Synge Cooper and Mary Eleanor, *y d* of William Burke; *m* 1934, Winifred, *d* of Thos F. Parkinson; two *s*. *Educ:* Shrewsbury; Brasenose Coll., Oxford; King's Coll., London. Civil Service, 1925; Trans. Air Min. (attached FO), 1936; returned to FO, 1943; retired, 1961. *Publication:* Russian Companion, 1967. *Address:* Kingsfield, Cobbler's Hill, Great Missenden, Bucks. *T:* Great Missenden 2400.

**COOPER, Maj.-Gen. Kenneth Christie,** CB 1955; DSO 1945; OBE 1943; psc; idc; retired; *b* 18 Oct. 1905; 4th *s* of E. C. Cooper; *m* 1933, Barbara Harding-Newman; one *s* one *d*. *Educ:* Berkhamsted Sch. 2nd Lieut, Royal Tank Corps, 1927; India, 1930-34; Adjt, 6 RTR, Egypt, 1935-38; Staff Coll., 1939; Bde Major, 23 Armd Bde, 1939-40; CO Fife and Forfar Yeomanry, 1941-42; GSO1, 9 Corps, N Africa, 1942-43; BGS, AFHQ, N Africa-Italy, 1943-44; Comdr, 7 Armoured Bde, 1945-46; Brig., Royal Armoured Corps, N Comd, 1947-48; Chief of Staff, West Africa Comd, 1948-50; idc 1951; Asst Comdt, Staff Coll., 1952-53. GOC 7th Armoured Div., Dec. 1953-March 1956; Chief of Staff to the Comdr-in-Chief Allied Forces, Northern Europe, 1956-59; retired, 1959. *Recreations:* Rugby, hockey, lawn tennis, shooting. *Address:* West End House, Donhead St Andrew, Shaftesbury, Dorset. *Club:* Army and Navy.

**COOPER, Prof. Kenneth Ernest;** Emeritus Professor of Bacteriology, Bristol University, 1968; *b* 8 July 1903; *s* of E. Cooper; *m* 1930, Jessie Griffiths; no *c*. *Educ:* Tadcaster Grammar Sch.; Leeds Univ. BSc 1925, PhD 1927 Leeds; LRCP MRCS 1936; FIBiol. Leeds University: Research Asst in Chemotherapy, 1928-31; Research Asst in Bacteriology, 1931-36; Lectr in Bacteriology, 1936-38; Bristol University: Lectr in Bacteriology, 1938-46; Reader in Bacteriology, 1946-50; Prof. of Bacteriology, 1951-68; Dep. Dean of the Faculty of Science, 1955-58. Hon. Gen. Sec. of Soc. for Gen. Microbiology, 1954-60, Hon. Treas., 1961-68, Hon. Mem., 1969. *Publications:* numerous papers in medical, chemical and bacteriological journals. *Recreation:* golf. *Address:* Fairfield, Clevedon Road, Tickenham, Clevedon, Somerset BS21 6RB. *T:* Nailsea 2375. *Club:* English-Speaking Union.

**COOPER, Lance Harries,** MBE 1944; FCA; Chairman, Mond Nickel Company, Ltd, 1951-59; *b* 7 May 1890; *o s* of late William White and late Edith Lydia Cooper; *m* 1st, 1920, Mary (*d* 1933), *e d* of late Nathaniel Kinch; one *s* one *d*; 2nd, 1937, Greta Mary, *o d* of late Walter Roff. *Educ:* University Coll. Sch., London; University Coll., Reading. Served European War, 1914-18, RFA. Accountant at Guest, Keen & Nettlefolds, Ltd, Dowlais Works & Collieries, Merthyr Tydfil, Glam., 1920-26; The Mond Nickel Company, Ltd: Chief Accountant, 1926; Sec., 1928; Dir, 1945; Vice-Pres., International Nickel Co. of Canada Ltd, 1954, Dir, 1958-61; retd, 1961. Formerly Mem., Internat. Nickel Adv. Cttees, New York and London. OStJ. *Recreations:* cricket and other games; the theatre and music. *Address:* Newlands, 10 Grove End Road, NW8. *T:* 01-286 0344. *Club:* MCC.

**COOPER, Dr Leslie Hugh Norman,** FRS 1964; FRIC, FIBiol, FGS, FRMetS; Deputy Director, Marine Biological Laboratory, Plymouth; *b* 17 June 1905; *s* of Charles Herbert Cooper and Annie Cooper (*née* Silk), Austral, Woodland Park, Prestatyn, Flints; *m* 1935, Gwynedd Daloni Seth Hughes, Bryngwynt, Bangor, Caerns; four *s* one *d*. *Educ:* John Bright Grammar Sch., Llandudno; University Coll. of North Wales, Bangor. PhD 1927, DSc 1938, Univ. of Wales. Chemist, Rubber Research Assoc., 1927-29; Chemist, Imperial Chemical Industries, 1929-30; Chemist at the Marine Biological Laboratory, Plymouth, engaged on the study of the physics and chemistry of the ocean as a biological environment, 1930-. *Publications:* numerous papers on oceanography. *Address:* 2 Queens Gate Villas, Lipson, Plymouth. *T:* Plymouth 61174.

**COOPER, Louis Jacques B.;** *see* Blom-Cooper.

**COOPER, Malcolm Edward;** Chairman: Allied Suppliers Ltd (formerly The Home and Colonial Stores Ltd), since 1959; Allied Services Ltd; Solicitor; *b* 21 Nov. 1907; *m* 1935, Christine Joan Metcalfe (*d* 1967); two *d*. Joined Allied Suppliers Group, Jan. 1931, on the legal side; transferred to Secretarial side, 1934, and to Management, 1946. *Address:* 179/189 City Road, EC1. *T:* 01-253 2000.

**COOPER, Prof. Malcolm McGregor,** CBE 1965; Professor of Agriculture and Rural Economy, and Dean of the Faculty of Agriculture, University of Newcastle upon Tyne, since 1954; *b* Havelock North, New Zealand, 17 Aug. 1910; *s* of Laurence T. Cooper, farmer, and Sarah Ann Cooper; *m* 1937, Hilary Mathews, Boars Hill, Oxford; three *d*. *Educ:* Napier Boys High Sch., NZ; Massey Agricultural Coll., Palmerston North, NZ; University Coll., Oxford. BAgrSc (NZ), 1933; Rhodes Scholarship, 1933; Oxford, 1934-37; Diploma Rural Econ., 1935; BLitt in Agric. Economics, 1937. Returned to NZ 1937; Mem. of Staff, Dept of Scientific and Industrial Research, till 1940, when appointed Lecturer in Dairy Husbandry at Massey Agric. Coll. Served War of 1939-45, with NZ Mil. Forces, 1941-46; in Italy with 2 NZ Div. in an Infantry battalion, 1943-45; rank of Major on demobilisation; returned to Massey as Head of Dept of Dairy Husbandry, 1946; Prof. of Agriculture, Univ. of London, 1947-54. Pres., British Grassland Soc., 1958-59; Member, Nature Conservancy Council; formerly member: Agricultural Advisory Council; Advisory Board, Pig Industry Development Authority; Agricultural Research and Advisory Cttee for Government of Sudan; Scientific Advisory Panel of the Minister of Agriculture; Agricultural Cttee of UGC; Chm., Beef Recording Assoc. (UK) Ltd. FRSE 1956, Hon. FRASE 1969. *Publications:*

(in collaboration) Principles of Animal Production (New Zealand), 1945; Beef Production, 1953; Competitive Farming, 1956; Farm Management, 1960; Grass Farming, 1961; Sheep Farming, 1965; technical articles on agricultural topics. *Recreations:* Rugby football (Rugby Blue, 1934, 1935 and 1936; Capt. OURFC 1936, and Sec. 1935; capped for Scotland, 1936); summer sports, reading, farming. *Address:* School of Agriculture, The University, Newcastle upon Tyne 1. *Club:* Farmers'.

**COOPER, Martin Du Pré;** Music Editor of the Daily Telegraph since 1954; *b* 17 Jan. 1910; *s* of late Cecil Henry Hamilton Cooper, sometime Dean of Carlisle, and late Cecil Stephens; *m* 1940, Mary, *d* of late Lieut-Col Douglas Stewart, DSO, and late Mabel Elizabeth Ponsonby; one *s* three *d*. *Educ:* Winchester; Oxford. Studied music in Vienna, 1932-34, with Egon Wellesz; Asst Editor, Royal Geographical Soc. Journal, 1935-36; Music Critic: London Mercury, 1934-39; Daily Herald, 1945-50; The Spectator, 1946-54; joined music staff of Daily Telegraph, 1950; Editor of Musical Times, 1953-56. Pres., Critics' Circle, 1959-60. Mem., Editorial Bd of New Oxford History of Music, 1960. Hon. FTCL. *Publications:* Gluck, 1935; Bizet, 1938; Opéra Comique, 1949; French Music from the death of Berlioz to the death of Fauré, 1950; Russian Opera, 1951; Les Musiciens anglais d'aujourd'hui, 1952; Ideas and Music, 1966; Beethoven–the Last Decade, 1970. *Address:* 12 Campden Hill Court, W8.

**COOPER, Sir Patrick Graham Astley,** 6th Bt *cr* 1821; Director, Crendon Concrete Co. Ltd, Long Crendon, since 1959; *b* 4 Aug. 1918; *s* of late Col C. G. A. Cooper, DSO, RA and I. M. M. A. Cooper, Abergeldie, Camberley, Surrey; *S* cousin, Sir Henry Lovick Cooper, 5th Bt, 1959; *m* Audrey Ann Jervoise, *d* of late Major D. P. J. Collas, Military Knight of Windsor; one *s* two *d*. *Educ:* Marlborough Coll. Qualified ALAS, 1949; Sen. Asst Land Comr, Min. of Agric., Fisheries and Food, 1950-59. Served 1939-40, Gunner, RA, 52 AA Bde TA (invalided out). *Recreation:* tennis. *Heir: s* Alexander Paston Astley Cooper, *b* 1 Feb. 1943. *Address:* Monkton Cottage, Monks Risborough, Aylesbury, Bucks. *T:* Princes Risborough 2810. *Clubs:* Farmers', Directors.

**COOPER, Robert William,** OBE 1919; MC, JP; past Director, Ferranti Ltd; past Chairman, British Aluminium Co. Ltd; *b* 6 March 1877; *s* of late Robert Cooper, JP, Bexley; *m* 1904, Violet (*d* 1950), *e d* of late Maj.-Gen. H. B. Hayward; one *s*. *Educ:* Cheltenham. DAQMG, 1914-18. Croix de Guerre, with Silver Star, 1916; Order of Comdr of St Olav (Norway), 1933. *Recreation:* shooting. *Address:* Wood Hill House, Warninglid, near Haywards Heath, Sussex. *T:* Warninglid 284.

**COOPER, Sir Stanford;** *see* Cooper, Sir H. S.

**COOPER, Hon. Sir Walter (Jackson),** Kt 1959; MBE 1918; Member Australian Country Party; *b* 23 April 1892; *s* of Joseph Pollitt Cooper; *m* 1918, Louie Dorothy Marion Crick; no *c*. *Educ:* John Wyggeston Sch., Leicester; University of Leeds. Arrived Australia from England, 1910; acquired grazing property NW Qld, 1914. Served War, Australian Forces, 1914-18 (wounded, losing leg, France); subseq joined Australian sect., RFC, 1917; served England, France, Germany (despatches); discharged rank Capt. Senator for Queensland, 1928-32 and 1934-68; Mem., Public Works Cttee, 1937-47; Jt Cttee on Social Security; Temp. Chm. of Cttees, 1938-47; Mem., Standing Cttee on Broadcasting, 1942-47; Jt Cttee on War Gratuity, 1944-45-48; Historic Memorials Cttee, 1947, 1948. Leader of Opposition in the Senate, 1947-49; Minister for Repatriation, Dec. 1949-Dec. 1960. Member: Empire Parly Assoc. Delegn to UK, 1948; Jt Parly Cttee on Foreign Affairs, 1962-68; Printing Cttee, 1962-68; Cttee of Disputed Returns and Qualifications, 1962-68. *Recreations:* gardening, fishing, swimming, riding. *Address:* Molena, Gordon Parade, Manly, Qld. *T:* 96.1417. *Clubs:* United Service, Queensland Masonic, Commercial Travellers' Assoc., Air Force, Royal Automobile of Queensland, Royal Queensland Aero, Brisbane Legacy (all in Brisbane).

**COOPER, Wilfred Edward S.;** *see* Shewell-Cooper.

**COOPER, William;** novelist; Personnel Consultant to: UK Atomic Energy Authority since 1958; Central Electricity Generating Board, since 1962; *b* 1910 (real name H. S. Hoff); married; two *d*. Assistant Commissioner, Civil Service Commission, 1945-58. *Publications:* (as H. S. Hoff) Trina, 1934; Rhéa, 1935; Lisa, 1937; Three Marriages, 1946; (as William Cooper) Scenes from Provincial Life, 1950; The Struggles of Albert Woods, 1952; The Ever-Interesting Topic, 1953; Disquiet and Peace, 1956; Young People, 1958; C. P. Snow (British Council Bibliographical Series, Writers and Their Work, No 115) 1959; Prince Genji (a play), 1960; Scenes from Married Life, 1961; Memoirs of a New Man, 1966; You Want The Right Frame of Reference, 1971. *Address:* 14 Keswick Road, SW15. *Club:* Savile.

**COOPER, Very Rev. William Hugh Alan;** Provost of Bradford since 1962; *b* 2 June 1909; *s* of William and Ethel Cooper; *m* 1940, Barbara (*née* Bentall); one *s* two *d*. *Educ:* King's Coll. Sch., Wimbledon; Christ's Coll., Cambridge; St John's Hall, London. Curate of Lee, 1932-36; Holy Trinity, Cambridge, 1936-38; CMS Missionary and Diocesan Missioner of Dio. Lagos, 1938-41; Curate of Farnham, 1941-42; Rector of Ashtead, 1942-51; Vicar of St Andrew, Plymouth, 1951-62; Preb. of Exeter Cath., 1958-62. *Address:* Provost's House, Parsons Road, Bradford 9. *T:* Bradford 44020.

**COOPER, Prof. Sir William M.;** *see* Mansfield Cooper.

**COOPER-KEY, Sir Neill,** Kt 1960; *b* 26 April 1907; *er s* of late Captain E. Cooper-Key, CB, MVO, Royal Navy; *m* 1941, Hon. Lorna Harmsworth, *er d* of 2nd Viscount Rothermere, *qv*; one *s* one *d*. *Educ:* RNC, Osborne, Dartmouth. Served War of 1939-45, Irish Guards. Director: Associated Newspapers Ltd; London & Aberdeen Investment Trust Ltd; Price Brothers Ltd, Canada; Chm., Transport Group (Holdings) Ltd and subsidiaries; Mem., Cttee of Management, RNLI. MP (C) Hastings, 1945-70. Chm., Parly Tourist and Resorts Cttee, 1955-65; sponsored Univs and Colls Estates Bill, 1964. *Recreations:* hunting, farming. *Address:* Burnt Wood, Battle, Sussex. *Clubs:* White's, Guards; East Sussex (St Leonards-on-Sea).

*See also Sir James G. Le N. King.*

**COOPLAND, George William,** MA; BSc(Econ.); LittD; Hon. LittD Fouad I University; Emeritus Professor, 1940; *b* 8 July 1875; *m* 1902; one *d*. *Educ:* University Coll., Liverpool. Various Secondary Schs., 1896-1913; Lecturer in Mediæval History, University of Liverpool, 1913; Lecturer in charge of Dept of Mediæval History, 1914-37; Prof. of Mediæval History,

Egyptian University, Cairo, 1929-30; Prof. of Mediæval History, University of Liverpool, 1937-40; in charge of Dept of Mediæval History, University of Liverpool, 1940-45; Lecturer in Dept Mediæval History, University of Liverpool, 1945-46; retired, 1946; Visiting Prof., Farouk I University, Alexandria, 1946-47, 1948, 1954-55, Fouad I Univ., Cairo, 1949, 1950-51. Sometime Sec. to University Extension Board, Liverpool, Chm. of Faculty of Arts, Examiner for Matriculation, Higher Sch. Certificate etc. *Publications:* The Abbey of St Bertin and its Neighbourhood, 900-1350, 1914 (Oxford Studies in Social and Legal History, ed Vinogradoff); Notes on Domainal Administration (Mackay Miscellany), 1914; The Franco-Belgian Frontier, (Geographical Teacher, 1916); The Tree of Battles and some of its Sources (Revue d'Histoire du Droit, 1923); An Unpublished Work of John of Legnano, The Somnium of 1372 (Nuovi Studi Medievali, 1925); Eustache Deschamps and Nicholas Oresme (Romania, 1926); Nicholas Oresme's Livre Contre Divinacion (The Monist, 1927); Serfdom and Feudalism, Harmsworth Universal History, 1928; The Tree of Battles, 1949; Nicole Oresme and the Astrologers, 1952; Le Jouvencel Revisited (Symposium, 1951); Le Songe du Vieil Pèlerin of Philippe de Mézières, 1969; Articles and Reviews on Mediæval Life and Thought in Manchester Guardian, Liverpool Post, etc. *Recreations:* travel, country life. *Address:* Fairholme, Broad Oak, Rye, Sussex. *Club:* University (Liverpool).

**COORAY, Edmund Joseph,** CMG 1955; OBE 1952; Chairman, Browns Group, Colombo; *b* 16 Nov. 1907; 2nd *s* of M. E. Cooray, Wadduwa, Ceylon; *m* 1933, Eileen de S. Wijeyeratne; two *s* two *d. Educ:* St Joseph's Coll., Colombo, Ceylon; University of London (BA Hons 1927; LLB Hons 1930; LLM 1931). Barrister-at-Law, Lincoln's Inn, 1931; passed Ceylon Civil Service Examination, 1931 (1st in order of merit); served in Ceylon Civil Service, 1931-53; Senator, Ceylon, 1955-61; Minister of Justice, 1960. *Recreations:* tennis, gardening. *Address:* 14 Dawson Road, Colombo 5, Ceylon. *T:* Colombo 88203. *Club:* 80 (Colombo).

**COORAY, His Eminence Cardinal Thomas Benjamin;** *see* Colombo, Cardinal Archbishop of.

**COOTE, Captain Sir Colin (Reith),** Kt 1962; DSO 1918; journalist; Managing Editor of the Daily Telegraph and Morning Post 1950-64 (deputy editor, 1945-50); *er s* of late Howard Coote. *Educ:* Chilverton Elms, Dover; Rugby; Balliol Coll., Oxford. BA 1914. Served European War, 1914-18 (wounded and gassed). MP (CL) Isle of Ely Division, 1917-22. Legion of Honour, 1958. *Publications:* Italian Town and Country Life, 1925; In and About Rome, 1926; Maxims and Reflections of The Rt Hon. Winston Churchill, 1948; (with R. H. Mottram) Through Five Generations: The History of the Butterley Company, 1950; (with P. D. Bunyan) Sir Winston Churchill: A Self-Portrait, 1954; A Companion of Honour: The Story of Walter Elliot, 1965; Editorial, 1965; The Government We Deserve, 1969. *Address:* 16 Bigwood Road, NW11.

**COOTE, John Oldham;** Captain, RN; Managing Director, Beaverbrook Newspapers Ltd, since 1968; *b* 13 Aug. 1921; *o s* of Frederick S. and Edith F. Coote; *m* 1944, Sylvia Mary (*née* Syson); three *d. Educ:* Felsted. Royal Navy 1940-60 (despatches 1944). Joined Beaverbrook Newspapers, 1960; Gen. Manager, Sunday Express, 1963; Managing Dir and Gen. Manager, Evening Standard, 1965. *Recreations:* sailing, golf. *Address:* 47 Caversham Street, SW3. *Clubs:* Royal Ocean Racing, Royal Yacht Squadron.

**COOTE, Rear-Adm. Sir John Ralph,** 14th Bt, *cr* 1621; CB 1957; CBE 1946; DSC; RN retired; *b* 10 Jan. 1905; *s* of Sir Ralph Coote, 13th Bt, and Alice, *y d* of late Thomas Webber of Kellyville, Queen's Co.; *S* father 1941; *m* 1927, Noreen Una, JP Wilts 1950, *o d* of late Wilfred Tighe of Rossanagh, Ashford, Co. Wicklow; two *s. Educ:* Royal Naval Colls, Osborne and Dartmouth. Retired 1958. *Heir: s* Christopher John Coote [*b* 22 Sept. 1928; *m* 1952, Anne Georgiana, *d* of Lt-Col Donald Handford, Guyers House, Corsham, Wilts; one *s* one *d*]. *Address:* Monkton House, near Melksham, Wilts. *T:* Melksham 2286. *Club:* United Service.

**COOTE, Rt. Rev. Roderic Norman;** *see* Colchester, Suffragan Bishop of.

**COPAS, Most Rev. Virgil;** *see* Port Moresby, Archbishop of, (RC).

**COPE, Prof. F(rederick) Wolverson,** DSc; FGS; CEng, FIMinE; Professor of Geology and Head of Geology Department, University of Keele, since 1950; *b* 30 July 1909; *e s* of Fred Cope and late Ida Mary Cope (*née* Chappells), Macclesfield; *m* 1st, 1935, Ethel May Hitchens, BSc (*d* 1961); one *s* two *d*; 2nd, 1962, Evelyn Mary Swales, BA, AKC, *d* of late John Frederick Swales and of Ada Mary Swales, Kingston-upon-Hull; one *d. Educ:* The King's Sch., Macclesfield; Univs of Manchester (DSc 1946) and London. Brocklehurst Scholar, 1928; John Dalton Prize, 1930; BSc with First Class Honours in Geology, 1931; MSc, Mark Stirrup Scholar, Manchester, 1932. Demonstrator in Geology, Bedford Coll., Univ. of London, 1933-34; Daniel Pidgeon Fund, Geol. Soc. of London, 1937; Prin. Geologist in Geological Survey of GB, 1934-50; Murchison Award of Geol. Soc. of London, 1948; Vis. Prof. of Geology, Univ. of Pisa, 1964. FGS 1934; CEng 1968; FIMinE 1969. *Publications:* The North Staffordshire Coalfields, in Coalfields of Great Britain (ed. by late Sir Arthur Trueman), 1954. Various research publications mainly in the fields of stratigraphy and palaeontology. *Recreations:* cars, ornithology, Italy. *Address:* 5 Church Plantation, Keele, Staffordshire ST5 5AY. *T:* Keele Park 393.

**COPE, John Wigley,** MA, MB, BChir Cantab, FRCS; Surgeon in charge Ear, Nose and Throat Department, St Bartholomew's Hospital; *b* 1 Nov. 1907; *o s* of J. J. Cope, Widney Manor, Warwicks; *m* 1937, Muriel Pearce Brown, Reading; two *s* one *d. Educ:* King Edward's Sch., Birmingham; Trinity Coll., Cambridge; St Bartholomew's Hosp., London. Demonstrator in Anatomy, St Bartholomew's Med. Coll., 1935. Served with RAFVR (Med. Branch) as Aural Specialist, 1940-45 (Sqdn-Ldr). Aural Surgeon, Royal Waterloo Hosp., 1946; Surgeon, Royal National Throat, Nose and Ear Hosp., 1946. Dean, St Bartholomew's Hosp. Med. Coll., 1962-68. Pres., Section of Otology, RSM (formerly Sec.). *Recreations:* shooting, rock-climbing, gardening, golf. *Address:* Owls Hatch Cottage, Seale, near Farnham, Surrey. *T:* Runfold 2456. *Club:* Bath.

**COPE, Maclachlan Alan Carl S.;** *see* Silverwood-Cope.

**COPE, Sir Mordaunt (Leckonby),** 16th Bt *cr* 1611; MC 1915; retired; *b* 12 Feb. 1878; 4th *s* of Sir Anthony Cope, 13th Bt; *S* nephew, 1966; *m*

1st, 1917, Frances Muriel (*d* 1935), *o surv c* of A. E. W. Darby, DL, JP, of Shropshire; 2nd, 1936, Eveline, *d* of late Alfred Bishop, Gloucester; no *c*. *Educ:* Prior Park Coll., Bath. Captain, late Rifle Brigade; formerly Egyptian Camel Corps. Served European War, 1914-18 (wounded, despatches, MC). *Recreations:* one-time polo, tennis and usual general sports. *Heir:* none. *Address:* 41 Grove End Gardens, St John's Wood, NW8.

**COPE, Sir (Vincent) Zachary,** Kt 1953; BA, MD, MS London, FRCS; Hon. FRSM; Consulting Surgeon to St Mary's Hospital, Paddington, and to Bolingbroke Hospital, Wandsworth Common; Vice-President, BMA; *b* Hull, 14 Feb. 1881; *m* 1st, 1909, Agnes Dora (*d* 1922), *d* of late James Newth; 2nd, 1923, Alice May (*d* 1944), *d* of late J. Watts and Ellen Watts, King's Lynn; one *d*. *Educ:* Westminster City Sch.; St Mary's Hospital Medical Sch. MB, BS with distinction in Surgery and Forensic Medicine, 1905; Hunterian Prof., Royal Coll. of Surgeons, 1916, 1920, 1925, and 1927; Arris and Gale Lecturer, RCS, 1922; Bradshaw Lecturer, 1949; Tomes' Lecturer and Vicary Lecturer, 1952; served as Capt. and temp. Major RAMCT, attached to 3rd London General Hospital, and saw active service in Mesopotamia, 1916-18 (despatches); formerly: Sector Hospital Officer, EMS; Hon. Librarian, Royal Society of Medicine; President, Lettsomian Lecturer and Orator, Medical Soc. of London; Chm., National Medical Manpower Cttee; Vice-Pres. and Mem. of Council (ex-Court of Examiners), RCS; Examiner at London, Manchester, and Birmingham Universities. *Publications:* The Surgical Aspect of Dysentery, 1921; The Early Diagnosis of the Acute Abdomen, 1st edn 1922, 13th edn 1968; Clinical Researches in Acute Abdominal Disease, 2nd edn, 1927; The Treatment of the Acute Abdomen, 2nd edn, 1928; Human Actinomycosis, 1938; The Versatile Victorian (the life of Sir Henry Thompson, Bt), 1951; William Cheselden, 1953; Florence Nightingale and the Doctors, 1958; Editor, the two clinical volumes, Official History of War of 1939-45; A History of the Royal College of Surgeons of England, 1959; A History of the Acute Abdomen, 1965; Almroth Wright, 1966; various articles in medical journals. *Address:* 170 Chiltern Court, Baker Street, NW1. *T:* 01-486 1946. *Club:* Athenæum.

**COPEMAN, William Sydney Charles,** CBE 1965 (OBE 1945); TD; JP (Co. London); MA, MD. FRCP; Emeritus Physician, Middlesex and West London Hospitals, and Hospital of St John and St Elizabeth; President, Arthritis and Rheumatism Council; Chairman: Kennedy Research Institute; Faculty of History of Medicine, Society of Apothecaries; *b* 29 July 1900; *o s* of late Dr S. Monckton Copeman, FRS, MD, FRCP, and Ethel, *d* of Sir (Thomas) William Boord, Bt, MP; *m* Helen, *d* of late W. W. Bourne of Garston Manor, Herts; one *s* two *d*. *Educ:* Lancing College; Caius College, Cambridge; Paris; St Thomas' Hospital. FRCP, 1937; Asst Etranger to Prof. of Pædiatrics, University of Paris; House Physician, Hospital for Sick Children, Great Ormond Street; Medical Registrar and Medical Registrar to Out-Patients, St Mary's Hospital; Mem. Council (and FitzPatrick Lectr), Royal Coll. of Physicians, and Vice-Pres., 1969; Mem., Assoc. of Physicians; late Pres., Epidemiological and Historical, and Vice-Pres., Medicine Sections, Royal Society of Medicine; late Hunterian Prof. and Vicary Lectr, Royal Coll. of Surgeons; Woodward Lectr, Yale Univ.; late Chm., Med. Res. Council Rheum. Cttee; Past Pres. (Late Orator and Hon. Fellow) Hunterian Soc. and Heberden Socs, Osler Club, and West London Medical Soc.; past Master of Apothecaries' Company; Chm., Faculty of History of Medicine; ex-Chm., Chartered Soc. of Physiotherapy; late Research Grantee, British Medical Assoc.; President and Vice-Pres., Ligue Européenne et Internationale contre le Rhumatisme. Ensign, Coldstream Guards, European War, 1914-18; Lieut-Col RAMC, War of 1939-45 (despatches twice, OBE); Adviser in Medicine, Malta Command, 1943; Heberden Research Medallist, 1940; awarded Gold Key of Amer. Congress of Physical Med., 1941; Triennial Gold Medallist, W London Med. Soc., 1970. CStJ. Comdr Order of Merit, Knights of Malta. Patron living of Hadleigh, Essex. *Publications:* A Text-book of the Rheumatic Diseases (4th Edn), 1968; (Editor) The Treatment of Rheumatism in General Practice (4th Edn), 1939; Cortisone and ACTH in Clinical Practice, 1954; Doctors and Disease in Tudor Times, 1960; A History of the Gout, 1964; Apothecaries: a History of the Worshipful Society of Apothecaries of London, 1617-1967, 1968; contribs to Chief Medical Journals; article, Diseases of Locomotor System, Price's Text-book of Medicine, and British Encyclopædias of Medicine, and Surgery. Editor, Annals of Rheumatic Diseases. *Recreations:* shooting and travelling. *Address:* 129 Harley Street, W1 *T:* 01-935 3470; Rapleys, Ockley, Surrey. *Club:* Athenæum.

**COPISAROW, Alcon Charles,** DSc; FInstP; CEng; FIEE; Director and Vice-President, McKinsey & Company, Inc., since 1966; *b* 25 June 1920; *o s* of late Dr Maurice Copisarow, Manchester; *m* 1953, Diana, *y d* of Ellis James Castello, MC, Bucklebury, Berks; two *s* two *d*. *Educ:* Manchester Central Grammar Sch.; University of Manchester; Imperial Coll. of Science and Technology; Sorbonne, Paris. Council of Europe Research Fellow. Served War, 1942-47; Lieut RN, 1943-47; British Admiralty Delegn, Washington, 1945. Home Civil Service, 1946-66; Office of Minister of Defence, 1947-54. Scientific Counsellor, British Embassy, Paris, 1954-60. Dir, Forest Products Research Laboratory, Dept of Scientific and Industrial Research, 1960-62; Chief Technical Officer, Nat. Economic Development Council, 1962-64. Chief Scientific Officer, Min. of Technology, 1964-66; Head of Internat. Div., 1964-65. Head of Electrical, Chemical Plant and Materials Industries Div., 1965-66. Chairman: Commonwealth Forest Products Conf., Nairobi, 1962; CENTO Conf. on Investment in Science, Teheran, 1963; Cttee for Research on Dental Materials and Equipment, 1966; Member: Scientific Manpower Cttee, Advisory Council on Scientific Policy, 1963-64; Econ. Develt Cttees for Electronics Industry, 1963-64, and for Heavy Electrical Industry, 1966-67; Trop. Prod. Adv. Cttee, 1965-66; Cabinet (Official) Cttees. *Address:* The White House, Denham, Bucks. *Clubs:* Athenæum, United Service.

**COPLAND, Aaron;** American composer; *b* Brooklyn, NY, 14 Nov. 1900; *s* of Harris M. Copland and Sarah Mittenthal; unmarried. *Educ:* Boys' High Sch., Brooklyn, NY; studied music privately; Fontainebleau Sch. of Music, France; Paris (with Nadia Boulanger). Guggenheim Fellow, 1925, 1926. Lecturer on music, New School for Social Research, NY, 1927-37; organised Copland-Sessions Concerts, which presented American music, 1928-31; tour of Latin-American countries, as pianist, conductor and lecturer in concerts of American music, 1941 and 1947; Charles Eliot Norton Prof. of Poetry, Harvard Univ., 1951-52. *Principal works:* Symphony for Organ and

Orchestra, 1924; First Symphony (orch.), 1928; Short Symphony (No. II), 1933; El Salon Mexico (orch.), 1936; Billy the Kid (ballet), 1938; Piano Sonata, 1941; Lincoln Portrait (speaker and orch.), 1942; Rodeo (ballet), 1942; Sonata for Violin and piano, 1943; Appalachian Spring (ballet, Pulitzer Prize), 1944; Third Symphony, 1946; Clarinet Concerto, 1948; Piano Quartet, 1950; Twelve Poems of Emily Dickinson, 1950; The Tender Land (Opera), 1954; Symphonic Ode (1929, rev. 1955); Piano Fantasy, 1957; Orchestral Variations 1958; Nonet, 1960; Connotations for Orchestra, 1962; Music for a Great City, 1964; Emblems for Symphonic Band, 1964; Inscape for Orchestra, 1967; various film scores. Member: National Institute of Arts and Letters; American Academy of Arts and Sciences; President of the Edward MacDowell Assoc., 1962; American Soc. of Composers, Authors and Publishers; Hon. Mem., Accademia Santa Cecilia, Rome; Hon. Mem., RAM, 1959; Hon. Dr of Music, Princeton Univ., 1956, Harvard Univ., 1961; Hon. Dr of Humane Letters, Brandeis Univ., 1957. FRSA 1960. Presidential Medal of Freedom, Washington, 1964; Howland Prize, Yale Univ., 1970. *Publications:* What to listen for in music, 1939 (revised 1957); Our New Music, 1941; Music and Imagination, 1952; Copland on Music, 1960; The New Music 1900-1960, 1968. *Address:* c/o Boosey and Hawkes, 30 West 57 Street, New York, USA. *Clubs:* Harvard, Century Association (New York).

**COPLAND, Very Rev. Charles McAlester;** Provost of St John's Cathedral, Oban, since 1959; *b* 5 April 1910; *s* of Canon Alexander Copland and of Violet Williamina Somerville McAlester; *m* 1946, Gwendoline Lorimer Williamson; two *d*. *Educ:* Forfar Academy; Denstone Coll.; Corpus Christi Coll., Cambridge (MA); Cuddesdon College. Curate, Peterborough Parish Church, 1934-38; Mission Priest, Chanda, CP, India, 1938-53 (Head of Mission, 1942-53); Canon of Nagpur, 1952; Rector, St Mary's, Arbroath, 1953-59; Canon of Dundee, 1953. *Recreations:* formerly Rugby football, athletics; rifle shooting (shot for Cambridge, for Scotland 1932-69). *Address:* The Rectory, Oban, Argyll. *T:* Oban 2323.

**COPLAND, Sir Douglas Berry,** KBE, *cr* 1950; CMG 1933; MA, DSc (NZ); LittD, Melbourne, Queensland, Harvard; LLD McGill, Carleton, Clark, BC, Adelaide, Tasmania, Melbourne, Australian National University; DCL Bishop's University; Economic Consultant and Company Director; Founder, Committee for Economic Development of Australia, 1960-67; *b* Timaru, New Zealand, 24 Feb. 1894; *s* of Alexander Copland; *m* 1919, Ruth Victoria, *y d* of F. W. S. Jones, Waimate, NZ; two *d*. *Educ.* Waimate District High Sch.; Canterbury Coll. MA with first-class honours in Economics, 1915; DSc for research in Currency and Finance, 1925; Lecturer in History and Economics and Dir of Tutorial Classes, University of Tasmania, 1917; Prof. of Economics, University of Tasmania, 1920-24; Sidney Myer Prof. of Commerce and Dean of the Faculty of Commerce, University of Melbourne, 1924-44; Truby Williams Prof. of Economics, University of Melbourne, 1944-45, Prof. Emeritus, 1946; Commonwealth Prices Commr, 1939-45; Econ. Consultant to Prime Minister, 1941-45; Australian Minister in China, 1946-48; First Vice-Chancellor, Australian Nat. Univ., Canberra, 1948-53. Editor, Economic Record, 1925-45; Commr, Victorian State Savings Bank, 1940-45; Chm., State Econ. Cttee of Victoria, 1938-45; served on many govtl cttees, Australia and NZ, and was Chm., Cttee of Economists and Under Treasurers which reported to Australian Loan Council 1931 and initiated Premiers' Plan; Marshall Memorial Lecturer, Cambridge Univ., 1933; Godkin Lecturer. Harvard, 1945; Sidney Ball Lecturer, Oxford, 1953; Finlay Lecturer, University Coll., Dublin, 1953; Beatty Lecturer, McGill Univ., 1961; Shann Memorial Lecturer, Univ. of Western Australia, 1962. High Comr for Australia in Canada, 1953-56; First Principal, Australian Administrative Staff Coll. (Founded 1956), 1956-60; Leader, Australian Trade Mission to Canada, 1960. Mem., Amer. Philosophical Soc., 1948. Mem., ANZAAS (President, 1952). *Publications:* Monetary Policy and its Application to Australia, 1926; Australia in the World Crisis– 1929-33, 1934; The Australian Economy, Sixth Edition, 1947; Towards Total War, 1942; The Road to High Employment, 1945; Report to Prime Minister on Economic Conditions in United Kingdom, United States and Canada, 1945; Back to Earth in Economics; Australia, 1948; Inflation and Expansion, 1951. With E. O. G. Shann: The Crisis in Australian Finance, 1931; The Battle of the Plans, 1931; The Australian Price Structure, 1933. With C. V. Janes: Cross Currents in Australian Finance, 1937; Australian Marketing Problems, 1938; Australian Trade Problems, 1938. With R. H. Barback, The Conflict of Expansion and Stability, 1957. The Adventure of Growth, 1960; The Changing Structure of the Western Economy (Beatty Lectures, McGill Univ.), 1963; numerous articles in Economic Journals. *Recreations:* golf and tennis. *Address:* Mount Macedon, Victoria 3441, Australia. *Club:* Melbourne (Melbourne).

**COPLAND, Harold W.;** *see* Wallace-Copland.

**COPLAND SIMMONS, Rev. F. P.;** *see* Simmons.

**COPLESTON, Ernest Reginald,** CB 1954; Secretary, University Grants Committee, 1963-69 (Deputy Secretary, 1957-63); retired; *b* 16 Nov. 1909; *s* of F. S. Copleston, former Chief Judge of Lower Burma; *m* Olivia Green. *Educ:* Marlborough Coll.; Balliol Coll., Oxford. Inland Revenue Dept, 1932; Treasury, 1942. Under-Sec., 1950. *Address:* 6 The Park, NW11. *T:* 01-455 3875.

**COPLESTON, Rev. Frederick Charles,** SJ; MA Oxon, DPhil Rome, Gregorian Univ.; FBA 1970; Principal of Heythrop College, London, since 1970; *b* 10 April 1907; *s* of F. S. Copleston, former Chief Judge of Lower Burma, and N. M. Little. *Educ:* Marlborough Coll.; St John's Coll., Oxford. Entered Catholic Church, 1925; Soc. of Jesus, 1930; ordained 1937. Prof. of History of Philosophy: Heythrop Coll., 1939-70; Gregorian Univ., Rome, 1952-68. *Publications:* Friedrich Nietzsche, Philosopher of Culture, 1942; St Thomas and Nietzsche, 1944; Arthur Schopenhauer, Philosopher of Pessimism, 1946; A History of Philosophy (vol. 1, Greece and Rome, 1946; revised 1947; vol. 2, Augustine to Scotus, 1950; vol. 3, Ockham to Suarez, 1953; vol. 4, Descartes to Leibniz, 1958; vol. 5, Hobbes to Hume, 1959; vol. 6, Wolff to Kant, 1960; vol. 7, Fichte to Nietzsche, 1963; vol. 8, Bentham to Russell, 1966); Medieval Philosophy, 1952; Existentialism and Modern Man, 1948; Aquinas (Pelican), 1955; Contemporary Philosophy, 1956; The Meaning of Metaphysics, 1970; articles in learned journals. *Address:* Heythrop College, 11 Cavendish Square, W1M 0AN. *T:* 01-580 6941.

**COPLESTONE-BOUGHEY, John Fenton; His Honour Judge Coplestone-Boughey;** Judge of the County Courts since 1969; *b* 5 Feb. 1912; *o s* of late Comdr A. F. Coplestone-Boughey, RN; *m* 1944, Gilian Beatrice, *e d* of late H. A. Counsell, Appleby; one *s* one *d*. *Educ:* Shrewsbury School; Brasenose Coll., Oxford (Open Exhibitioner, Matthew Arnold Prizeman). Inner Temple, Entrance Scholar 1934, Barrister 1935. Legal Assistant, Min. of Health, 1937-40. Royal Artillery, 1940-46; Advanced Class, Military Coll. of Science, 1945. Chester Chronicle & Associated Newspapers, Ltd: Dir, 1947-56; Dep. Chm., 1956-65. Chairman, Nat. Insurance Tribunals (SW London), 1951-69; Referee, Nat. Service and Family Allowances Acts, 1957-69. Battersea etc Hospital Management Cttee, Member 1960-69, Chairman 1969. *Publications:* contrib. to Halsbury's Laws of England. *Recreations:* walking, travel. *Address:* 82 Oakley Street, SW3. *T:* 01-352 6287. *Club:* Athenæum.

**COPNALL, (Edward) Bainbridge,** MBE 1944; FRBS 1948; President, Royal Society of British Sculptors, 1961-66; *b* 29 Aug. 1903; *s* of E. W. Copnall, photographer, and Emily Bainbridge, Wellington, NZ; *m* 1927, Edith Muriel Dancy, LRAM; one *s* one *d* (and one *s* decd). *Educ:* Goldsmiths' Coll.; Royal Academy Schs. Served War of 1939-45: (rank Major, GS; Western Desert and Italy with 8th Army). First exhibited Royal Academy, 1924, as painter; exhibited Royal Scottish Acad., Paris Salon, and at most London Galls and Provincial Galls; many portraits painted until 1928; became sculptor, 1929; master: Liverpool Coll. of Art, 1928-30; Rochester Coll. of Art, 1935-38; Headmaster, Sir John Cass Coll. of Art, 1945-53. One-man Exhibitions: Horsham, Worthing, Folkestone, Liverpool, Wertheim, Goupil, Alwin and Maidstone Galls, Rangoon, and Toronto. Sculptures: RIBA, 1930-34; Queen ships, 1938 and 1946; many sculptures for London buildings; Liverpool (3 churches); Luton; Southampton; Plymouth; Portsmouth; Cardiff; Sunderland; Hull; Billingham, etc; statue of Gen. Aung San (Burma, 1954; Bronze); figure of Ven. Nynaung Sayadaw (Burma, 1955; bronze); again architectural sculpture, London; fountains at Victoria Park and Crawley New Town; Stag in Stag Pl., London; group in fibre glass for Dudley, Worcs; Glass Screen for Dudley (Churchill Memorial); Growing Family, Billingham. Founder Mem., Soc. of Portrait Sculptors, 1947; Mem., Art Workers Guild, 1968; Hon. Member: Nat. Soc., 1968; Liverpool Artists Club, 1969; Hon. Corresp. Mem., Nat. Soc. of Sculptors of America, 1967. Master Glass Painter, 1968. FRSA 1968. Broadcasts on BBC (TV) experiences and work. Winner, Constance Fund, 1949. Silver Medal, RBS, 1962. *Publications:* A Sculptor's Manual, 1970; articles and reproductions in most architectural journals and Listener (mainly sculpture); paper, RSA, 1966, etc. *Recreations:* painting and Rugby football. *Address:* Lee Priory, Littlebourne, Canterbury, Kent. *Clubs:* Chelsea Arts, Architectural Association; Artists' (Liverpool); Richmond RFC; Liverpool RFC.

**COPPEL, Dr Elias Godfrey,** CMG 1965; QC (at the Bar of Victoria and Tasmania); *b* 7 Oct. 1896; *s* of Albert Coppel; *m* 1925, Marjorie Jean Service; two *s* (and one *s* decd). *Educ:* Melbourne Grammar Sch.; Melbourne Univ. Served European War, 1st Australian Imperial Force, France, 1915-19. Admitted to the Bar, 1922; LLD 1936; KC 1945. Acting Justice, Supreme Court, Victoria, 1950-52; Acting Justice, Supreme Court, Tasmania, 1956 and 1958; Warden of Convocation, University of Melbourne, 1950-59; Mem. of University Council, 1959-. *Publication:* The Law Relating to Bills of Sale, 1935. *Address:* 152 Finch Street, Glen Iris, Victoria 3146, Australia.

**COPPLESON, Sir Lionel (Wolfe),** Kt 1969; Chairman, Managing Director and Director of Companies; retd as Chairman of Custom Credit Corporation Group, but remained on Boards, 1969; *b* Wee Waa, NSW, 29 May 1901; *s* of Albert and Siba Coppleson; *m* 1929, Edith Maude, *d* of Alfred Bamford; one *s* one *d*. *Educ:* Sydney Grammar Sch. Joined Coppleson Ltd (merchants), Wee Waa, 1918; Manager, 1924; estab. Finance Construction Ltd, builders, Sydney, 1927; acquired George Ward Pty Ltd, roofing engrs, 1930; estab. George Ward Pty Ltd, Melbourne, 1933; apptd Special Distributor for John Lysaght Ltd in NSW and Vic, 1938; estab. 3 factories for war supplies, 1940; apptd to advise John Lysaght Ltd, England, 1946; estab. George Ward Distributors Pty Ltd, also George Ward Pty Ltd Registered Master Builders, 1947; estab. Wilkins Servis Pty Ltd, washing machine manufrs (Chm.), 1948; Foundation Dep. Chm.: Custom Credit Corp. Ltd, 1953; Nat. & Gen. Ins. Co. Ltd, 1954; Custom Life Assce Co. Ltd, 1957; First Nat. Reinsurance of Aust. Ltd and Custom Factors Ltd, 1958; Chm., 1962: Custom Credit Group of Cos; Addenbrooke Pty Ltd; Copanco Pty Ltd; Bamford Services Pty Ltd; Cokeson Pty Ltd; Foundation Pres.: Inst. of Urology, Sydney, 1964; Aust. Kidney Foundation, 1968. Mem. cttee for appeals, various organisations, etc. *Recreations:* played: football, cricket, tennis, golf, bowls, snooker; swimming and life-saving (surf) champion; racing, trotting, boxing, horticulture, orchid growing, agricultural shows. *Address:* Addenbrooke, 21 Cranbrook Road, Bellevue Hill, NSW 2023, Australia. *T:* 36 6475. *Clubs:* Newcastle, Royal Prince Alfred Yacht, Australian Golf, Royal Motor Yacht, Pioneers, Australian Jockey, American National, Tattersalls (all in NSW); Stock Exchange (Melbourne).

**COPPOCK, Sir Richard,** Kt 1951; CBE 1942; Hon. ARIBA; retired as General Secretary, National Federation of Building Trades Operatives, 1961; *b* 21 Feb. 1885; *s* of Joseph Coppock and Hannah Woodward; *m* 1st, 1908; 2nd, 1926, Ursula M'Loughlin; one *s* one *d*. *Educ:* Didsbury National Sch.; Manchester Technical Sch. Bricklayer and Trade Union Official; International work for the trade unions in the Building trade; Pres. of same for many years; has travelled extensively throughout Europe and America; Mem. of Manchester City Council, 1919-21; Alderman, London County Council, and also Councillor and Chm. of Parks, Highways, and Parliamentary Cttees, 1925-52; Chm. of LCC, 1943-44 (Vice-Chm. 1939-40); Chm., Fire Bde Cttee, 1951-58. *Publications:* many pamphlets dealing with organisation of Building Trade, Workmen and Rationalisation, etc. *Recreations:* reading, music, and propaganda. *Address:* Little Wanborough, Wanborough Lane, Cranleigh, Surrey. *T:* 4391.

**COPSON, Prof. Edward Thomas,** MA Oxford, DSc Edinburgh, FRSE; Emeritus Professor of Mathematics, St Andrews University; *b* 21 Aug. 1901; *s* of late T. C. Copson; *m* 1931, Beatrice Mary, *er d* of late Prof. Sir Edmund Whittaker, FRS; two *d*. *Educ:* King Henry VIII Sch., Coventry; St John's Coll., Oxford. Lecturer, University of Edinburgh, 1922-29; St Andrews, 1930-34; Asst Prof., RNC, Greenwich, 1934-35; Prof. of Mathematics, University Coll., Dundee, 1935-50; Regius Prof. of Mathematics, St Andrews Univ.,

1950-69. Keith Prize, Royal Society of Edinburgh, 1939-41. Master of St Salvator's Coll., St Andrews, 1954-57. *Publications:* The Theory of Functions of a Complex Variable, 1935; The Mathematical Theory of Huygens' Principle (with Prof. Bevan Baker), 1939; Asymptotic Expansions, 1965; Metric Spaces, 1968; papers in various mathematical periodicals. *Address:* 42 Buchanan Gardens, St Andrews, Fife. *T:* St Andrews 2708.

**CORAH, Sir John (Harold),** Kt 1952; late Chairman, N. Corah & Sons Ltd, Leicester (from 1926); *b* 25 Dec. 1884; *s* of Alfred Corah of Scraptoft Hall, Leicestershire; *m* 1st, 1913, Vivienne Woodhouse (*d* 1942); one *d*; 2nd, 1951, Edmée Pattera. *Educ:* Marlborough. JP 1924; High Sheriff of Leicestershire, 1933; Dep. Chm., County Bench, 1942-51. *Recreations:* sailing and cruising. *Address:* Number One Glebe Mount, 1 Glebe Road, Stoneygate, Leicester. *T:* Leicester 705799. *Club:* Royal Motor Yacht (Sand Banks, Dorset).

**CORBET, Mrs Freda (Kunzlen), (Mrs Ian McIvor Campbell),** BA; JP; MP (Lab) Peckham Division of Camberwell since 1950 (NW Camberwell, 1945-50); *b* 1900; *d* of James Mansell; *m* 1925, William Corbet (*d* 1957); *m* 1962, Ian McIvor Campbell. *Educ:* Wimbledon County Sch.; University Coll., London. Called to Bar, Inner Temple, 1932. JP, Co. London, 1940. *Address:* House of Commons, SW1; 39 Gravel Road, Bromley, Kent.

**CORBET, Lieut-Col Sir John (Vincent),** 7th Bt, *cr* 1808; MBE 1946; DL; JP; RE (retired); *b* 27 Feb. 1911; *s* of Archer Henry Corbet (*d* 1950) and Anne Maria (*d* 1951), *d* of late German Buxton; *S* kinsman, Sir Gerald Vincent Corbet, 6th Bt, 1955; *m* 1st, 1937, Elfrida Isobel Francis; 2nd, 1948, Doreen Elizabeth Stewart (*d* 1964), *d* of Arthur William Gibbon Ritchie; 3rd, 1965, Annie Elizabeth Lorimer, MBE, Dunedin, NZ. *Educ:* Shrewsbury Sch.; RMA; Magdalene Coll., Cambridge. BA Cambridge 1933. 2nd Lieut, RE, 1931; served North-West Frontier, India, 1935, and War of 1939-45 in India, Burma and Malaya (despatches, MBE); Lieut-Col, 1953; retd 1955. DL County of Salop, 1961; JP 1957; High Sheriff of Salop, 1966; CC Salop. OStJ; Mem., Church Assembly, 1960; Mem. Board of Visitors, Stoke Heath Borstal. *Address:* Acton Reynald, near Shrewsbury, Salop. *T:* Clive 259. *Clubs:* United Service, Royal Thames Yacht.

**CORBET, Air Vice-Marshal Lancelot Miller,** CB 1958; CBE 1944; RAF retired; *b* Brunswick, Vic., Australia, 19 April 1898; *s* of late John Miller and late Ella Beatrice Corbet, Caulfield, Vic., Australia; *m* 1924, Gwenllian Elizabeth, *d* of late Thomas Powell and late May Maria Bennett, Claremont, Western Australia; one *s*. *Educ:* Melbourne High Sch.; Scotch Coll., Melbourne; Melbourne Univ. (MB, BS 1922). RMO, Perth (WA) Hospital, 1922-23, Perth Children's Hospital 1923; Hon. Asst Anæsthetist, Perth Hospital, 1931; Clinical Asst to Out-Patient Surgeon, Perth Hospital, 1931-32. Was Major AAMC; commanded 6th Field Hygiene Sect., 1930-32; entered RAF 1933; served in UK and India, 1933-37; Principal MO, W Africa, 1941-43; Principal MO, Transport Command, RAF, 1943-45; Principal MO, Malaya, 1945-46; Principal MO, British Commonwealth Air Forces, Japan, 1946-48; OC, RAF Hospital, Nocton Hall, 1949-52; Principal MO, HQBF, Aden, 1952-54; Principal MO, 2nd Tactical Air Force, 1954-56; Dep. Dir-Gen. of Medical Services, Air Ministry, 1956-58, retired. KStJ. *Recreations:* lacrosse, tennis, squash, golf, etc. *Address:* 24 Hensman Street, South Perth, West Australia. *T:* Perth 67-3025. *Club:* Naval and Military (Perth, West Australia).

**CORBETT,** family name of **Baron Rowallan.**

**CORBETT, Captain Hugh Askew,** CBE 1968; DSO 1945; DSC 1943; RN; Warden of University Centre, Cambridge University, since 1969; *b* 25 June 1916; *s* of late Rev. F. St John Corbett, MA, FRSL, FRHistS, St Georges-in-the-East, London and late Elsie L. V. Askew; *m* 1945, Patricia Nancy, *d* of Thomas Patrick Spens, OBE, MC, LLD; three *s*. *Educ:* St Edmund's Sch., Canterbury. Joined Royal Navy, 1933; served War of 1939-45 in Destroyers as Lieut (despatches, 1940); commanded HMS: Wheatland, 1943-45 (Lieut); Charity, 1951 (Comdr); Cockade, 1951-53 (Comdr); Cæsar as Capt. (D), 8th Destroyer Sqdn, 1961-63; Staff of Chief of Defence Staff, 1963-65; comd HMS Fearless, 1965-67 (Capt.); Head of Naval Manpower Future Policy Div., 1967-69. Naval Staff Coll., 1945; Army Staff Coll., 1946; Imp. Def. Coll., 1960. MBIM 1967. *Address:* Holly Cottage, Clare Road, Cambridge. *T:* Cambridge 57735.

**CORBETT, Prof. John Patrick,** MA; Professor of Philosphy, University of Sussex, since Oct. 1961; *b* 5 March 1916; *s* of E. S. H. and K. F. Corbett; *m* 1st, 1940, Nina Angeloni; two *s*; 2nd, 1968, Jan Adams; one *d*. *Educ:* RNC, Dartmouth; Magdalen Coll., Oxford. Lieut, RA, 1940; POW in Germany, 1940-45. Fellow of Balliol, 1945-61; Jowett Lectr in Philosophy. Council of Europe Fellow, 1957; Visiting Lectr, Yale Univ., 1958; NATO Fellow, 1960; Vis. Prof., Univ. of Toronto, 1968. *Publications:* Europe and the Social Order, 1959; Ideologies, 1965. *Address:* 84 Fort Road, Newhaven, Sussex.

**CORBETT, Prof. Peter Edgar;** Yates Professor of Classical Art and Archaeology in the University of London (University College), since 1961; *b* 19 June 1920; 2nd *s* of Ernest Oliver Corbett and Margaret Edgar. *Educ:* Bedford Sch.; St John's Coll., Oxford. Royal Artillery, 1940-41, RAFVR, 1942-45. Thomas Whitcombe Greene Scholar, and Macmillan Student of British School at Athens, 1947-49; Asst Keeper in Dept of Greek and Roman Antiquities, British Museum, 1949-61. Lectr in Classics, Univ. of Calif, Los Angeles, 1956. *Publications:* The Sculpture of the Parthenon, 1959; articles in Jl of Hellenic Studies, Hesperia, Annual of Brit. School at Athens, Brit. Mus. Quarterly. *Address:* University College, Gower Street, WC1.

**CORBETT, Rupert Shelton,** MA, MChir Cantab; FRCS; retired 1961; *b* 11 Feb. 1893; 2nd *s* of late Henry Shelton Corbett. *Educ:* Diocesan Coll., South Africa; Stubbington House, Hampshire; Cambridge Univ.; St Bartholomew's Hosp., London. MRCS, lrcp 1917; FRCS; MA Cantab 1922; BCh 1922; MB 1923; MChir 1927; formerly: Surgeon, St Bartholomew's Hosp.; Surgeon, St Andrew's Hosp., Dollis Hill; Consulting Surgeon, Chalfonts and Gerrards Cross Hosp.; Examiner in Surgery, Universities of Cambridge and London; Mem. of Examining Board, Royal Coll. of Surgeons; First Gordon-Watson Memorial Lectr., 1958; Mem. Council, Assoc. of Surgeons of Great Britain and Ireland, 1957-59; Pres., Chiltern Medical Soc., 1960-61. Vice-President: Jersey Branch, Royal Commonwealth Soc.; St John Ambulance Assoc., Jersey. *Publications:* contributions in British Surgical Practice; various articles in med. jls. *Address:* Katrina, Beaumont Hill, St Peter, Jersey. *T:* Central 20065.

**CORBETT, Lieut-Gen. Thomas William,** CB 1941; MC and Bar; psc; *b* 2 June 1888; *m* 1st, 1915, Flora Margaret McDonell (*d* 1951); 2nd, 1952, S. N. E., *widow* of Lieut-Col H. H. C. Withers, DSO, RE; one *d*. 2nd Lieut Indian Army, 1908; Capt., 1915; Bt. Major, 1919; Major, 1922; Bt Lieut-Col 1930; Lieut-Col, 1933; Col, 1935; Maj.-Gen., 1940; served European War, 1914-19 (MC); a Corps Comdr, Middle East, 1942; CGS, Middle East, 1942; retired, 1943. *Address:* Panthill, Barcombe, Sussex.

**CORBETT, Lt-Col Uvedale,** DSO 1944; *B* 12 Sept. 1909; *s* of Major C. U. Corbett, Stableford, Bridgnorth, Shropshire; *m* 1st, 1935, Veronica Marian Whitehead (marr. diss., 1952); two *s* one *d*; 2nd, 1953, Mrs Patricia Jane Walker. *Educ:* Wellington (Berks); RMA, Woolwich. Commissioned Royal Artillery, 1929; relinquished command 3rd Regt RHA 1945; retired. MP (C) Ludlow Div. of Shropshire, 1945-51. *Address:* Shobdon Court, Leominster, Herefordshire. *T:* Kingsland 260. *Club:* Army and Navy.

**CORBETT ASHBY, Dame Margery (Irene),** DBE 1967; LLD; Hon. President, International Alliance of Women; Hon. President, British Commonwealth League; *b* 1882; *d* of C. H. Corbett of Woodgate, Danehill, Sussex, and Marie, *d* of George Gray, Tunbridge Wells; *m* 1910, Arthur Brian Ashby, barrister, Inner Temple; one *s*. *Educ:* Home; Newnham Coll., Cambridge. Sec. to the National Union of Suffrage Societies on leaving college; lectured on education and land questions from Liberal platforms; Liberal candidate, 1918, 1922, 1923, 1924, 1929 General Elections; 1937 and 1944 by-elections; substitute delegate for UK to Disarmament Conference, 1931-35; travelled and lectured all over Europe, in India, Pakistan, Near East, United States and Canada, speaking in English, French, and German. *Recreations:* gardening and travelling. *Address:* Wickens, Horsted Keynes, Sussex. *T:* Chelwood Gate 264. *Club:* University Women's.

**CORBETT-WINDER, Col John Lyon,** OBE 1949; MC 1942; JP; RARO 1958; Lord Lieutenant of Montgomeryshire since 1960; *b* 15 July 1911; *o s* of Major W. J. Corbett-Winder, Vaynor Park, Berriew, Montgomery; *m* 1944, Margaret Ailsa, *d* of Lt-Col J. Ramsay Tainsh, CBE, VD; one *s* two *d*. *Educ:* Eton; RMC Sandhurst. 2nd Lieut, 60th Rifles, 1931; Lt-Col, 1942. Served War of 1939-45, Western Desert and N Africa, 1939-43 (despatches twice); Commanded: 44 Reconnaissance Regt; 1st Bn 60th Rifles; GSO1 Infantry Directorate, WO, 1944-47; commanded 2nd Bn 60th Rifles, Palestine, 1947-48 (despatches); AAG, HQ Southern Command, 1948-51; GSO1, HQ 53 Welsh Inf. Div., 1952-55; Col Gen. Staff, SHAPE Mission to Royal Netherlands Army, 1955-57; Dep. Mil. Sec., HQ, BAOR, 1957-58; retd 1958. JP Montgomeryshire, 1959. Mem., Parly Boundary Commn for Wales, 1963-. Commander, Order of Orange Nassau, 1958. KStJ 1970 (CStJ 1966). *Recreations:* gardening, forestry, shooting. *Address:* Vaynor Park, Berriew, Welshpool, Montgomeryshire. *T:* Berriew 204.

**CORBIN, Maurice Haig Alleyne; Hon. Mr Justice Corbin;** Puisne Judge, Supreme Court, Trinidad and Tobago, since 1957; *b* 26 May 1916; *s* of L. A. Corbin; *m* 1943, Helen Jocelyn Child; one *s* two *d*. *Educ:* Harrison Coll., Barbados; Queen's Royal Coll., Trinidad. Solicitor, 1941; appointed Magistrate, Trinidad, 1945; called to the Bar, Middle Temple, 1949; Crown Counsel, 1953; Registrar, Supreme Court, 1954. *Recreations:* tennis, sports broadcasting. *Address:* 45 Ascot Road, Goodwood Park, Trinidad, West Indies. *Club:* Union (Port of Spain, Trinidad).

**CORBISHLEY, Rev. Thomas,** SJ; *b* 30 May 1903; *s* of William and Catherine Corbishley. *Educ:* Catholic Coll., Preston; Campion Hall, Oxford. 1st in Mods; 1st in Greats. Entered Soc. of Jesus, 1919; Priest, 1936; Master of Campion Hall, 1945-58; Superior of Farm Street Church, W1, 1958-66. *Publications:* Agnosticism, 1936; The Divine Majesty (trans. from German), 1948; Roman Catholicism, 1950; Religion is Reasonable, 1960; Spiritual Exercises of St Ignatius (trans.), 1963; Ronald Knox the Priest, 1964; The Contemporary Christian, 1966; contributed to: Catholic Commentary on Holy Scripture, 1953; Religion in the Modern World, 1952; We believe in God, 1968; contributions to Journal of Roman Studies, Journal of Theological Studies, Klio, Month, Dublin Review, etc. *Address:* 114 Mount Street, W1. *T:* 01-493 7811.

**CORDEAUX, Lt-Col John Kyme,** CBE 1946; *b* 23 July 1902; *yr s* of late Col E. K. Cordeaux, CBE; *m* 1928, Norah Cleland (who obtained a divorce, 1953); one *s* (and one *s* decd); *m* 1953, Mildred Jessie Upcher. *Educ:* Royal Naval Colleges Osborne and Dartmouth. Served Royal Navy 1916-23; transf. Royal Marines (Lieut), 1923; RN Staff Coll., 1937. Served War, 1939-46; Naval Intelligence Div., 1939-42; Major, 1940; Actg Lieut-Col 1941; temp. Col, 1942; seconded to Foreign Office, 1942-46; Lieut-Col 1946. Contested (C), Bolsover Div. of Derbyshire, 1950 and 1951; prospective Conservative Candidate, North Norfolk Div., 1952-53; MP (C), Nottingham Central, 1955-64; promoted, as Private Member's Bill, Landlord and Tenant Act, 1962. Commander, Order of Orange-Nassau (Netherlands), 1944; Commander, Order of Dannebrog (Denmark), 1945; Haakon VII Liberty Cross (Norway), 1946. *Publication:* Safe Seat (novel), 1967. *Recreations:* Association football; cricket. *Address:* 11 Hyde Park Gardens, W2. *Club:* MCC.

**CORDEIRO, Most Rev. Mgr Joseph;** *see* Karachi, Archbishop of, (RC).

**CORDIER, Dr Andrew Wellington;** President, Columbia University, since 1969 (Acting President, 1968-69) and Dean, School of International Affairs, since 1962; *b* 3 March 1901; *s* of Wellington J. Cordier and Ida May Anstine; *m* 1924, Dorothy Elizabeth Butterbaugh; one *s* one *d*. *Educ:* Hartville High Sch.; Manchester Coll., Indiana; Univ. of Chicago; Graduate Inst. of Internat. Studies, Geneva. BA Manchester, 1922; MA 1923, PhD 1926, Chicago. Teacher, Greentown High Sch., 1919-21; Chm., Dept of History and Polit. Sci., Manchester Coll., 1927-44, and Lectr in Social Scis for Indiana Univ. Extension Div., 1929-44; travelled extensively, 1928-41; US Dept of State, 1944-46 (drafting new Charter for UN); Techn. Expert, US Delegn at founding conf., San Francisco; Exec. Asst to Sec.-Gen. of UN, 1946-61 (Under-Sec.); Under-Sec. i/c General Assembly and Related Affairs, 1961-62; Principal Adviser to all Presidents of Gen. Assembly of UN since inception; Special Rep. of Sec.-Gen.: Korea, 1952; in connection with Mount Scopus problem, 1958; Congo, 1960. Consultant to Dept of State; Mem., Council on Foreign Relations; Trustee: Carnegie Endowment for Internat. Peace; Internat. House; Manchester College. Holds numerous hon. degrees, medals and awards incl.: Alumni Medal, Chicago Univ.; Ohioan Career Medal for 1959; Walter

W. Van Kirk Award; Ohio Governor's Award, 1962; Mayor's Award of City of New York. *Address:* Colombia University, New York, NY 10027, USA. *T:* 280-4604. *Clubs:* Century Association, University (New York).

**CORDINGLEY, Maj-Gen. John Edward,** OBE 1959; Major-General, Royal Artillery, British Army of the Rhine, since 1968; *b* 1 Sept. 1916; *s* of Air Vice-Marshal Sir John Cordingley, *qv*; *m* 1st, 1940, Ruth Pamela (marr. diss. 1961), *d* of late Major S. A. Boddam-Whetham; two *s*; 2nd, 1961, Audrey Helen Anne, *d* of Maj-Gen. F. G. Beaumont-Nesbitt, *qv*; two step *d*. *Educ:* Sherborne; RMA, Woolwich. 2nd Lieut RA, 1936; served War of 1939-45, Europe and India. Brigade Comdr, 1961-62; Imperial Defence Coll., 1963; Dir of Work Study, Min. of Defence (Army), 1964-66; Dep. Dir, Royal Artillery, 1967-68; Maj-Gen., 1968. Fellow, Inst. of Work Study Practitioners, 1965; MBIM, 1966. *Recreations:* golf and gardening. *Address:* Groom's Cottage, Palace Yard, Much Hadham, Herts. *T:* Much Hadham 2853. *Clubs:* United Hunts, Ski of Great Britain.

**CORDINGLEY, Air Vice-Marshal Sir John (Walter),** KCB 1946 (CB 1943); KCVO 1962; CBE 1937 (OBE 1919); RAF, retd; *b* 10 Dec. 1890; *m* 1st, 1913, Elizabeth Ruth Carpenter (*d* 1938); one *s*; 2nd, 1944, Mrs Joan Isabel Morton. RNVR 1905-13; RND 1914-17; Air Bd 1918; Air Ministry, 1918-22; Admiralty and Air Ministry mentions for service, European War, 1914-18. Officer-in-Charge Records, RAF, 1922-39; Dir-Gen. of Manning, Air Ministry, 1939-47; Controller, RAF Benevolent Fund, 1947-62; Wing Comdr, 1924; Group Capt., 1931; Air Commodore, 1941 (Acting, 1939); Air Vice-Marshal, 1947 (Acting 1943); retired list, 1947. vice-Patron of National Association for Employment of Regular Sailors, Soldiers and Airmen; a Dir of United Services Trustee, 1947-; a Vice-President: Officers' Assoc.; Royal Wolverhampton Sch.; Jamaica Legion; Member Councils of: RAF Benevolent Fund; League of Rememberance; Governor Star and Garter Home; Mem., BBC Appeals Advisory Cttee, 1957-60. *Address:* 147b Ashley Gardens, SW1. *T:* 01-828 8916. *Club:* Royal Thames Yacht.
*See also Maj.-Gen. J. E. Cordingley.*

**CORDINGLY, Rt. Rev. Eric William Bradley;** *see* Thetford, Suffragan Bishop of.

**CORDLE, John Howard;** MP (C) Bournemouth East and Christchurch since Oct. 1959; Chairman: E. W. Cordle & Son Ltd since 1968 (Managing Director, 1946-68); Euro Exports Ltd; *b* 11 Oct. 1912; *s* of late Ernest William Cordle; *m* 1st, 1938 (marr. diss., 1956); three *s* (one *d* decd); 2nd, 1957, *e d* of Col A. Maynard, OBE; one *s* four *d*. *Educ:* City of London Sch. Served RAF (commissioned), 1940-45. Dir, Church of England Newspaper, 1959-; Dir, Church Soc., 1951-. Member: Archbishops of Canterbury and York Commission on Evangelism, 1945-46; Church Assembly, 1946-53; Oxford Trust of Churches Patronage Board, 1947-. Prospective Candidate (C) for NE Wolverhampton, 1949; contested (C) Wrekin Div., 1951. Mem. of Lloyd's, 1952; Mem. Founders Livery Company and Freeman of City of London, 1956. Director: Amalgamated Developers Ltd; Surgical Medical Supplies Ltd. Chairman: West Africa Cttee, Conservative Commonwealth Council; Anglo-Libyan Parly Group; Vice-Chm., Crafts Council of Great Britain. Life Governor: St Mary's and St Paul's Coll., Cheltenham; Epsom Coll.; Mem. Court of University of Southampton. Gold Staff Officer, Coronation, 1953. Grand Band, Order of the Star of Africa (Liberia), 1964. *Recreations:* shooting, tennis, golf, gardening. *Address:* Malmesbury House, The Close, Salisbury, Wilts. *T:* Salisbury 27027. *Clubs:* Carlton, National, English-Speaking Union, Royal Commonwealth Society.

**CORFIELD, Sir Conrad Laurence,** KCIE 1945 (CIE 1937); CSI 1942; MC; ICS (retired); *s* of late Rev. Egerton Corfield, MA, Rector of Finchampstead, Berks; *m* 1922, Phyllis Betha (*d* 1932), *d* of late L. P. E. Pugh, KC; one *s* one *d*; *m* 1961, Mrs Sylvia Daunt, *widow* of Lt-Col C. O'B. Daunt, OBE, MC, Central India Horse. *Educ:* St Lawrence; St Catharine's Coll., Cambridge. Capt. 1st Cambridgeshire Regt; served European War, France; joined ICS 1920; Asst Comr Punjab; Asst Private Sec. to the Viceroy, 1921-22; joined Political Dept 1925; served in Kathiawar, Baluchistan, Rajputana, Central India, and Hyderabad; Vice-Pres., Rewa State Council, 1933-34; Joint Sec., Political Dept, Simla, 1934-38; Officiating Political Sec., June-Sept. 1937; Resident at Jaipur, 1938-40; officiating Resident for Rajputana, May-Oct. 1939; Resident for the Punjab States, 1941-45; Political Adviser to the Viceroy as Crown Representative, 1945-47. Governor and Vice-Pres., St Lawrence Coll. Chm., Wokingham Div. Conservative Assoc., 1950-54 (Pres. 1954-62). Chm. Wessex Area, 1960-63; former Chairman: Yateley Industries for Disabled Girls, 1954-64; St John Council for Berks, 1944-62; St Crispin's Sch., Wokingham, 1954-67; Finchampstead Parish Council, 1955-61. CStJ. *Recreations:* (past) Captain, Cambridge Univ. Hockey, 1919-20; English Hockey International, 1920; gardening. *Address:* 15 Heather Road, Heatherlands, George, Cape Province, South Africa. *T:* George 5128. *Clubs:* Travellers', Army and Navy.

**CORFIELD, Rt. Hon. Captain Frederick Vernon,** PC 1970; MP (C) South Gloucester, since 1955; Minister of Aviation Supply, since Oct. 1970; *b* 1 June 1915; *s* of late Brig. F. A. Corfield, DSO, OBE, IA, and M. G. Corfield (*née* Vernon); *m* 1945, Elizabeth Mary Ruth Taylor; no *c*. *Educ:* Cheltenham Coll. (Scholar); RMA, Woolwich. Royal Artillery, 1935; 8th Field Regt, RA, India, 1935-39; served War of 1939-45; Actg Capt., 23rd Field Regt, BEF, 3rd Div., 1939; Adjutant, 23rd Field, 51st (Highland) Div., 1940 (despatches); prisoner of war, Germany, 1940-45. Called to Bar, Middle Temple, 1945 (Middle Temple Scholarship); JAG's Branch, WO, 1945-46; retired, 1946; farming, 1946-56. Jt Parly Sec., Min. of Housing and Local Govt, 1962-64; Minister of State, Board of Trade, June-Oct. 1970. Barrister. *Publication:* Corfield on Compensation, 1959. *Recreations:* gardening, fishing. *Address:* 2 Paper Buildings, Temple, EC4; Wordings Orchard, Sheepscombe, near Stroud, Glos. *T:* Painswick 3367. *Club:* Carlton.

**CORI, Prof. Carl Ferdinand;** Biochemist at Massachusetts General Hospital, Harvard Medical School, Boston, Mass. since 1967; Professor of Biochemistry, Washington University School of Medicine, St Louis, Mo, 1931-67; *b* Prague, Czechoslovakia, 5 Dec. 1896; *s* of Carl Cori and Maria Lippich; went to US, 1922; naturalised, 1928; *m* 1920, Gerty T. (*d* 1957), *d* of Otto Radnitz; one *s*; *m* 1960, Anne Fitz-Gerald Jones. *Educ:* Gymnasium, Trieste, Austria; (German) University of Prague (MD). Asst in Pharmacology, University of Graz, Austria, 1920-21; Biochemist State Inst. for Study of Malignant Disease, Buffalo, NY, 1922-31. Mem. Nat. Acad. of Sciences, Royal Society etc. Shared Nobel Prize in Medicine and Physiology, 1947.

DSci Western Reserve, 1946, Yale, 1946, Boston Univ., 1948, Cambridge, 1949. Mid-West Award, 1946, Squibb Award, 1947; Sugar Research Foundation award, 1947 and 1950; Willard Gibbs Medal, 1948. Hon. DSc: Monash, 1966; Granada, 1967; Brandeis, 1965; Gustavus Adolphus Coll., 1965; Washington, 1966; St Louis, 1966. *Publications:* articles in scientific journals. *Address:* Massachusetts General Hospital, Fruit Street, Boston, Mass, USA.

**CORK, Bishop of, (RC),** since 1952; **Most Rev. Cornelius Lucey;** and **Ross, Bishop of,** since 1954; *b* Windsor, Co. Cork. *Educ:* Maynooth; Innsbruck. Priest, 1927. Co-Founder and Pres., Christus Rex Soc. for priests; Founder and Superior, La Sociedad de Santo Toribio (missionary and welfare organisation for the barriadas of Peru). *Address:* Bishop's House, Cork, Eire.

**CORK, Dean of;** *see* Johnston, Very Rev. F. M. K.

**CORK and ORRERY,** 13th Earl of, *cr* 1620. **Patrick Reginald Boyle;** Baron Boyle of Youghall, 1616; Viscount Dungarvan, 1620; Viscount Kinalmeaky, Baron Boyle of Bandon Bridge and Baron Boyle of Broghill (Ireland), 1628; Earl of Orrery, 1660; Baron Boyle of Marston, 1711; writer, artist and broadcaster; *b* 7 Feb. 1910; *s* of Major Hon. Reginald Courtenay Boyle, MBE, MC (*d* 1946), and of Violet, *d* of late Arthur Flower; *S* uncle, 12th Earl of Cork and Orrery, 1967; *m* 1952, Dorothy Kate, *o d* of late Robert Ramsden, Meltham, Yorks. *Educ:* Harrow Sch.; Royal Military College, Sandhurst. Royal Ulster Rifles, 1930-33; Capt. London Irish Rifles, Royal Ulster Rifles (TA), 1935-38. Served War of 1939-45 with Royal Ulster Rifles, Burma Rifles, Cameronians (Scottish Rifles) in Special Force (Chindits) (severely wounded) and Parachute Regt. Now Hon. Major, late Army Air Corps. Life Governor, Christian Faith Soc. FRSA 1947. *Publications:* (author and illustrator) Sailing in a Nutshell, 1935; (jointly) Jungle, Jungle, Little Chindit, 1946. Contribs to the Hibbert Jl. *Recreations:* sailing, oil-painting, gardening. *Heir:* *b* Hon. John William Boyle, DSC [*b* 12 May 1916; *m* 1943, Mary Leslie, *d* of late Gen. Sir Robert Gordon Finlayson, KCB, CMG, DSO; three *s*]. *Address:* Orchard Cottage, Upperton, Petworth, Sussex.

**CORK, CLOYNE, and ROSS, Bishop of,** since 1957; **Rt. Rev. Richard Gordon Perdue;** *b* 13 Feb. 1910; *s* of Richard Perdue; *m* 1943, Evelyn Ruth Curry, BA; two *d*. *Educ:* Trinity Coll., Dublin. BA 1931; MA and BD 1938. Deacon 1933, priest 1934, Dublin. Curate of Drumcondra with N Strand, 1933-36; Rathmines, 1936-40; Incumbent of Castledermot with Kinneagh, 1940-43; Roscrea, Diocese of Killaloe, 1943-54; Archdeacon of Killaloe and Kilfenora, 1951-54; Examining Chaplain to Bishop of Killaloe, 1951-54; Bishop of Killaloe, Kilfenora, Clonfert and Kilmacduagh, 1953-57. *Address:* The Palace, Bishop Street, Cork.

**CORLETTE, Brig. James Montagu Christian,** CMG 1919; DSO; VD; Chevalier Légion d'Honneur; BE, DEng, MICE, Hon MIEAust; Consulting Engineer; Brigadier (retired) Australian Military Forces; *b* 25 Aug. 1880; *s* of Rev. Canon J. C. Corlette, DD Oxon, and Mrs F. E. Corlette, *d* of late Sir William Montagu Manning, KCMG, etc; *m* 1914, Ruby, *d* of Paterson J. Saunders, Newcastle, NSW; one *s*. *Educ:* Sydney Grammar Sch.; University of Sydney; graduate BE in Civil and Mining Engineering. Over 40 years service with Australian Military Forces; i/c first 750 sq. miles of Australian Military Topographical Survey, 1910-11; attached Army in India, 1911-12; served European War, 1914-18, with Aust. Engineers; left with first contingent from Australia; Gallipoli, France, and Belgium; CRE 2nd Australian Div., 1917-18 (CMG, DSO, Chevalier Légion d'Honneur, despatches five times, 1914-15 Star); commanded 1 Infantry Bde, 1926-34, 1 Div., 1932-34; Group Comdr (Col) on staff of Volunteer Defence Corps, War of 1939-45. Chief Engineer of Water Supply and Sewerage Board, Newcastle, NSW, 1925-45. Pres. Instn of Engineers, Australia, 1930 (Warren Memorial prizeman, 1945; P. N. russell Memorial medallist, 1947; Hon. Mem., 1960). Hon. DEng Newcastle Univ., NSW, 1966. *Publication:* articles on engineering subjects. *Recreation:* football blue at University. *Address:* The Terrace, Newcastle, NSW, Australia. *T:* 2.2035. *Clubs:* University (Sydney); Newcastle, United Service (Newcastle, NSW).

**CORLEY, Michael Early Ferrand; His Honour Judge Corley;** County Court Judge, since 1967; *b* 11 Oct. 1909; *s* of Ferrand Edward Corley, late of Christian College, Madras, and Elsie Maria Corley. *Educ:* Marlborough; Oriel Coll., Oxford. Called to Bar, 1934. War Service, RNVR, 1940-46. *Recreation:* cruising under sail. *Address:* 3 Brockley Grove, Hutton, Brentwood, Essex.

**CORMACK, James Maxwell Ross,** MA; Regius Professor of Greek, University of Aberdeen, since 1965; *b* 20 July 1909; *s* of Benjamin Cormack and Frances Helen Ross; *m* 1st, 1938, Isabel Ogg Catto, MA (*d* 1968); 2nd, 1968, Sybil Phyllis Dadley, BA; one *s*. *Educ:* Robert Gordon's Coll., Aberdeen; Aberdeen Univ. (1st Cl. Hons in Classics, 1932); Trinity Coll., Cambridge (Senior Scholar and Research Scholar); Vienna Univ.; British Sch. at Athens. Cambridge Classical Tripos: 1st Cl. Pt I, 1933, 1st Cl. Part II, with distinction in Literature, 1935; Fullerton Scholar and Wilson Fellow of Aberdeen Univ., 1935-37; Lecturer in Classics, University of Reading, 1937-46; Prof. of Classics, University of Reading, 1946-65; Dean of Faculty of Letters, 1948-54; Dep. Vice-Chancellor, 1954-64; Acting Vice-Chancellor, Oct. 1963-March 1964. Review Editor of Jl of Hellenic Studies, 1948-51. FRNS. *Publications:* The Inscribed Monuments of Aphrodisias, 1955; Monumenta Asiae Minoris Antiqua, vol. viii (jt editor), 1962; articles on Greek Epigraphy, with particular reference to Asia Minor and Macedonia, in Journal of Roman Studies, Annual of the British Sch. at Athens, American Journal of Archæology, Harvard Theological Review, Proceedings of British Academy, and Hesperia, 1940 onwards. *Address:* The Department of Greek, King's College, Aberdeen.

**CORMACK, Sir Magnus (Cameron),** KBE 1970; Senator for Victoria; *b* Caithness, Scotland, 12 Feb. 1906; *s* of William Petrie Cormack and Violet McDonald Cameron; *m* 1935, Mary Gordon Macmeiken; one *s* three *d*. *Educ:* St Peter's Sch., Adelaide, S Aust. Farmer and Grazier. Served War, 1940-44; Aust. Imperial Forces, SW Pacific Area, Major. Pres., Liberal Party Organisation, 1947-49; Senator for Victoria, 1951-53 and 1962-. *Recreation:* deep sea sailing. *Address:* Lower Crawford, via Heywood, Victoria 3304, Australia. *Clubs:* Australian, Naval and Military (Melbourne, Victoria); Hamilton (Victoria).

**CORMACK, Patrick Thomas;** MP (C) Cannock since 1970; *b* 18 May 1939; *s* of Thomas Charles and Kathleen Mary Cormack, Grimsby; *m*

1967, Kathleen Mary MacDonald; one *s*. *Educ:* St James' Choir School and Havelock School, Grimsby; Univ. of Hull (BA Hons English and History). Second Master, St James' Choir School, Grimsby, 1961-66; Company Education and Training Officer, Ross Group Ltd, Grimsby, 1966-67; Assistant Housemaster, Wrekin College, Shropshire, 1967-69; Head of History, Brewood Grammar School, Stafford, 1969-70. *Recreations:* old English silver, walking, visiting old churches. *Address:* Somerford Grange, Brewood, Stafford. *T:* Brewood 203. *Club:* Constitutional.

**CORNBERG, Mrs Sol;** *see* Gaskin, Catherine.

**CORNELL, Katharine;** Actress-Manager, Producer, Actress; retired; *b* 16 Feb. 1898; *d* of Peter C. Cornell, MD, and Alice Gardner Plimpton; *m* 1921, Guthrie McClintic (*d* 1961); no *c*. *Educ:* Private schs in Buffalo, NY; Oaksmere, Mamaroneck, NY. Made her debut, 1916, with Washington Square Players in Bushido, and remained with this company two years, following which she spent two seasons with Jessie Bonstelle stock company at Buffalo and Detroit. Her first and only appearance on the London stage was as Jo in Little Women, New Theatre, 1919. Subsequently, in America, appeared in Nice People, A Bill of Divorcement, Will Shakespeare, The Enchanted Cottage, Casanova, The Way Things Happen, The Outsider, Tiger Cats, Candida, The Green Hat (in which she became a star), The Letter, The Age of Innocence, Dishonored Lady; became America's only actress-manager, with her presentation of The Barretts of Wimpole Street, 1931; since then she has produced and appeared in Lucrece, Alien Corn, Romeo and Juliet, Flowers of the Forest, Saint Joan, The Wingless Victory, Candida, Herod and Mariamne, No Time for Comedy, The Doctor's Dilemma, Rose Burke, The Three Sisters, Lovers and Friends, Antigone, Antony and Cleopatra, That Lady, Captain Carvallo, The Constant Wife, The Prescott Proposals, The Dark is Light Enough, The Firstborn (Habimah Theatre, Tel Aviv, Israel, July 1958), Dear Liar. Her late husband, a producer in his own right, directed all her plays since The Green Hat (exc. Prescott Proposals; directed by a co-author, Howard Lindsay). Television debut in The Barretts of Wimpole Street, 1956, There Shall be No Night, 1957. Holds numerous hon. degrees and awards. Medals include: Medal of Merit (US Govt); Medal, Amer. Academy of Arts and Letters. *Publications:* I wanted to be an Actress, the autobiography of Katharine Cornell, 1938; Curtain Going Up, 1941. *Recreations:* music, reading. *Address:* Palisades, New York, USA. *Clubs:* Colony, Cosmopolitan (New York); Garrett (Buffalo, NY).

**CORNER, Edred John Henry,** FRS 1955; FLS; Fellow, Sidney Sussex College, Cambridge; Professor of Tropical Botany, University of Cambridge, since 1966; *b* 12 Jan. 1906; *s* of late Edred Moss Corner and Henrietta Corner (*née* Henderson); *m* 1953, Helga Dinesen Sondergoord; one *s* two *d* (by 1st *m*). *Educ:* Rugby Sch. Asst Dir, Gardens Dept, Straits Settlements, 1929-45; Principal Field Scientific Officer, Latin America, Unesco, 1947-48; Lecturer in Botany, Cambridge, 1949-59; Reader in Plant Taxonomy, 1959-65. Member: American Mycological Soc.; Brit. Mycological Soc.; French Mycological Soc.; Fellow, American Assoc. for the Advancement of Science; Corr. Member: Botanical Soc. of America; Royal Netherlands Botanical Soc.; Hon. Mem., Japanese Mycological Soc. Mem., Governing Body of Rugby Sch., 1959-. Darwin Medal, Royal Soc., 1960; Patron's Medal, Royal Geographical Society, 1966; Gold Medal, Linnean Soc. of London, 1970. *Publications:* Wayside Trees of Malaya (2 vols), 1940 and 1952; A Monograph of Clavaria and allied genera, 1950; Life of Plants, 1964; Natural History of Palms, 1966; Monograph of Cantharelloid Fungi, 1966. *Address:* 91 Hinton Way, Great Shelford, Cambs CB2 5AH. *T:* Shelford 2167.

**CORNER, Frank Henry;** Ambassador of New Zealand to United States of America since 1967; *b* 17 May 1920; *y s* of Charles William Corner, Napier, NZ, and Sybil Corner (*née* Smith); *m* 1943, Lynette Robinson; two *d*. *Educ:* Napier Boys' High Sch.; Victoria Univ. of Wellington. MA, 1st cl. History; James Macintosh and Post-graduate Scholar. External Affairs Dept, NZ, and War Cabinet Secretariat, 1943; 1st Sec., NZ Embassy, Washington, 1948-51; Sen. Counsellor, NZ High Commn, London, 1952-58; Dep. Sec. NZ Dept of External Affairs, 1958-62; Perm. Rep. (Ambassador) to UN, 1962-67. Mem., NZ Delegn to Commonwealth Prime Ministers' Meetings, 1944, 1946, 1951-57; Deleg. to UN Gen. Assembly, 1949-52, 1955, and 1960-68; NZ Rep. to UN Trusteeship Council, 1962-66 (Pres., 1965-66; Chm., UN Vis. Mission to Micronesia, 1964); NZ Rep. on UN Security Coun., 1966; Adviser, NZ Delegn: Paris Peace Conf., 1946; Geneva Conf. on Korea, 1954; numerous other internat. confs as adviser or delegate. *Recreations:* music, walking, tennis. *Address:* 27 Observatory Circle, NW, Washington, DC 20008, USA. *T:* CO5-1721. *Club:* Chevy Chase (Washington).

**CORNER, George Washington;** Executive Officer, American Philosophical Society, Philadelphia, Pennsylvania, since 1960; *b* 12 Dec. 1889; *s* of George Washington Corner, Jr, and Florence Elmer (*née* Evans); *m* 1915, Betsy Lyon Copping, *d* of Rev. Bernard Copping and Cora (*née* Lyon); one *s* (one *d* decd). *Educ:* Boys' Latin Sch., Baltimore; Johns Hopkins Univ., Baltimore (AB 1909, MD 1913). Asst in Anatomy, Johns Hopkins Univ., 1913-14; Resident House Officer, Johns Hopkins Hosp., 1914-15; Asst Prof. of Anatomy, University of Calif., 1915-19; Associate Prof. of Anatomy, Johns Hopkins, 1919-23; Prof. of Anatomy, Univ. of Rochester, 1923-40; Dir, Dept of Embryology, Carnegie Instn of Washington, Baltimore. 1940-55; Historian, Rockefeller Inst., New York, 1956-60. George Eastman Visiting Prof., Oxford, and Fellow, Balliol Coll., 1952-53; Vicary Lectr, RCS, 1936; Vanuxem Lecturer, Princeton, 1942; Terry Lecturer, Yale, 1944. Passano Award, 1958. Member: United States National Academy of Sciences (Vice-Pres., 1953-57); American Philosophical Soc. (Vice-Pres. 1953-56). Hon. Fellow Royal Society, Edinburgh; Foreign Mem., Royal Society, London. Dr (*hc*) Catholic Univ., Chile, 1942; Hon. DSc: Rochester, 1944; Boston Univ., 1948; Oxford, 1950; Chicago, 1958; MA (by decree) Oxford, 1952; Hon. LLD: Tulane 1955; Temple, 1956; Hon. DMedScience, Woman's Med. Coll., 1958; Hon. LittD Pa, 1965. *Publications:* Anatomical Texts of Earlier Middle Ages, 1927; Anatomy (a history), 1930; Hormones in Human Reproduction, 1942; Ourselves Unborn, 1944; ed The Autobiography of Benjamin Rush, 1948; Anatomist at Large, 1958; George Hoyt Whipple and His Friends, 1963; Two Centuries of Medicine, 1965; History of the Rockefeller Inst., 1965; numerous articles on histology, embryology, physiology of reproduction, history of medicine. *Recreations:* travel, photography. *Address:* American Philosophical Society, 104 South Fifth Street, Philadelphia, PA 19106,

USA. *Clubs:* Tudor-Stuart (Baltimore); Franklin Inn (Philadelphia); Century (NY).

**CORNFORD, Edward Clifford,** CB 1966; Controller of Guided Weapons and Electronics, Ministry of Aviation Supply (formerly Ministry of Technology), since 1969; *b* 6 Feb. 1918; *s* of John Herbert Cornford; *m* 1945, Catherine Muir; three *s* three *d*. *Educ:* Kimbolton Sch.; Jesus Coll., Cambridge (BA). Joined RAE, 1938. Operational Research with RAF, 1939-45. Guided Weapons Res. at RAE, 1945-60; jssc 1951; Head of Guided Weapons Dept, RAE, 1956-61; Min. of Defence: Chm., Def. Res. Policy Staff, 1961-63; Asst Chief Scientific Adviser, 1963-64; Chief Scientist (Army), Mem. Army Board, Ministry of Defence, 1965-67; Chm. Programme Evaluation Group, MoD, 1967-Jan. 1968 Dep. Chief Adviser (Research and Studies), MoD, 1968-69. FRAeS. *Publications:* on aeronautical subjects in jls of learned socs and technical publications. *Recreation:* travelling. *Address:* Woodside, Waverley Drive, Camberley, Surrey. *T:* 22289.

**CORNFORTH, John Warcup,** FRS 1953; DPhil; Associate Professor in Molecular Sciences, University of Warwick, since 1965; Director, Shell Research Milstead Laboratory of Chemical Enzymology, since 1962; *b* 7 Sept. 1917; *er s* of J. W. Cornforth, Sydney, Aust.; *m* 1941, Rita, *d* of W. C. Harradence; one *s* two *d*. *Educ:* Sydney High Sch.; Universities of Sydney and Oxford. BSc Sydney (Univ. Medal in Organic Chemistry), 1937; MSc Sydney, 1938; 1851 Exhibition Overseas Scholarship, 1939-42; DPhil Oxford, 1941; scientific staff of Med. Research Coun., 1946-62. Lectures: Pedler, Chem. Soc., 1968-69; Andrews, Univ. of NSW, 1970; Max Tishler, Harvard Univ., 1970. Chemical Society's Corday-Morgan Medal and Prize, 1953; (with G. J. Popjak) CIBA Medal of the Biochem. Soc., 1965; Chem. Soc. Flintoff Medal, 1966; Stouffer Prize, 1967; Ernest Guenther Award, 1969; (with G. J. Popjak) Davy Medal, Royal Soc., 1968. Has been deaf since boyhood. *Publications:* (part author) The Chemistry of Penicillin, 1949; numerous papers on organic chemical and biochemical subjects. *Recreations:* lawn tennis, chess, gardening. *Address:* Ingleside, 187 Ufton Lane, Sittingbourne, Kent.

**CORNISH, Prof. Ronald James;** Consultant, C. S. Allott & Son, Sale, Cheshire, since 1970; *b* Exeter, Devon, 30 Dec. 1898; *s* of William Henry Cornish and Eva Maud Eliza (*née* Horrell); *m* 1927, Edith Oliver Oliver; twin *d*. *Educ:* Hele's Sch., Exeter; Exeter Sch., Exeter; Manchester Univ. RGA, 1917-19; engineer, Messrs Mather & Platt, Ltd, Manchester, 1922-25; Manchester University: Asst Lecturer, 1925-29; Lecturer, 1929-34; Head of Dept of Municipal Engineering, 1934-53; Prof. of Municipal Engineering, 1953-61; Prof. Emeritus, 1966; seconded, Jan.-June 1960, as Prof. of Engineering in University Coll. of Ibadan, Nigeria; Prof. of Civil Engineering, Indian Institute of Technology, Hauz Khas, New Delhi, 1961-66; Head of Civil Engrg Dept, Malta Coll. of Arts, Science and Technology, 1966-70. FICE (Ex-Mem. Council); FIStructE (Ex-Mem. Council); MIMechE; FIMunE; MIE (Ind.). Hon. FIPHE; FRSH (Ex-Mem. Council). *Publications:* papers in Proc. Royal Soc., Philosophical Magazine, Jls of Engineering Instns, etc. *Address:* 20 Oakdene Road, Marple, Stockport SK6 6PJ.

**CORNISH, William Herbert,** CB 1955; Receiver for the Metropolitan Police District, 1961-67; *b* 2 Jan. 1906; *s* of late Rev. Herbert H. Cornish and Susan Emerson; *m* 1938, Eileen May Elizabeth Cooney; two *d*. *Educ:* Wesley Coll., Dublin; Trinity Coll., Dublin. Scholar, 1st Cl. Moderator with Large Gold Medal in Modern History and Political Science. Entered Home Office, 1930; Asst Sec., 1942; Asst Under-Sec. of State, 1952-60. *Recreations:* gardening and music. *Address:* 2 Tormead, Dene Road, Northwood, Mddx. *T:* Northwood 21933.

**CORNWALL, Archdeacon of;** *see* Young, Ven. Peter Claude.

**CORNWALL, Ian Wolfran,** PhD London; Reader in Human Environment, University of London, since 1965; *b* 28 Nov. 1909; *s* of Lt-Col J. W. Cornwall, CIE, IMS, and Effie E. C. (*née* Sinclair), *d* of Surg.-Gen. D. Sinclair, IMS; *m* 1937, Anna Margareta (*née* Callear) (*d* 1967); two *s*. *Educ:* private sch.; Wellington Coll., Berks; St John's Coll., Cambridge (BA). Teaching, clerking, pharmaceutical manufacturing, selling, 1931-39; Postal and Telegraph Censorship, Press Censorship, MOI, 1939-45. London Univ. Inst. of Archaeology: Student, 1945-47 (Diploma, 1947); Secretary, 1948-51. University teacher and researcher, 1951- (PhD London, 1952). Member: Zoological Soc.; Geologists' Assoc.; Prehistoric Soc.; Royal Anthropological Inst. Henry Stopes Memorial Medal, Geologists' Assoc., 1970. *Publications:* Bones for the Archaeologist, 1956; Soils for the Archaeologist, 1958; The Making of Man, 1960 (Carnegie Medal of Library Assoc.); The World of Ancient Man, 1964; Hunter's Half Moon (fiction), 1967; Prehistoric Animals and their Hunters, 1968; Ice Ages, 1970. Contribs to specialist jls. *Recreations:* geology, gardening, photography. *Address:* Flat 8, 11 Netherhall Gardens, NW3.

**CORNWALL, Gen. Sir J. H. M.;** *see* Marshall-Cornwall.

**CORNWALL, Rt. Rev. Nigel Edmund,** CBE 1955; Assistant Bishop of Winchester and Canon Residentiary of Winchester Cathedral, since 1963; *b* 13 Aug. 1903; *s* of late Alan Whitmore Cornwall, priest, sometime Archdeacon of Cheltenham; *m* 1959, Mary, *d* of Rev. C. R. Dalton. *Educ:* Marlborough Coll; Oriel Coll., Oxford. BA, 3rd class History, 1926; MA 1930. Cuddesdon Theological Coll., 1926-27; Deacon, Diocese of Durham, 1927; Curate, St Columba's, Southwick, Sunderland, 1927-30; Priest, Durham, 1928; Chaplain to Bishop of Colombo, 1931-38; Curate, St Wilfred's, Brighton, 1938-39; Missionary Priest of Diocese of Masasi, 1939-49; Headmaster, St Joseph's Coll., Chidya, 1944-49; Bishop of Borneo, 1949-62. Commissary to Bishop of Kuching, in England, 1963-. *Address:* 11 The Close, Winchester. *T:* 4504.

**CORNWALL-JONES, Brig. Arthur Thomas,** CMG 1949; CBE 1945 (OBE 1943); *b* 21 July 1900; *s* of Rev. E. Cornwall-Jones (sometime Canon of Aberdeen); *m* 1929, Marie Evelyn Joan, *d* of late Lieut-Col R. H. Hammersley-Smith, CBE; four *s*. *Educ:* Trinity Coll., Glenalmond. IA, 1920-47; 2nd Bn 5th Royal Gurkha Rifles (FF); Asst Sec. Offices of War Cabinet and Minister of Defence, 1939-41 and 1943-44; Sec. Middle East Defence Cttee, 1941-43; British Sec. Combined Chiefs of Staff, 1944-46; Senior Asst Sec. (Military) of the Cabinet, 1946-50. British Army since Aug. 1947 (Gen. List, Supernumerary); retired pay, 1950. Served with British, Australian and Pakistan Administrative Staff Colls and Philippine Executive Academy, 1950-68. US Legion of Merit (Comdr) 1946. *Address:* The Paddock, Waltham St Lawrence, Berks. *T:* Shurlock Row 453. *Club:* Army and Navy.

**CORNWALL-LEGH, C. L. S.**; *see* Legh.

**CORNWALLIS,** family name of **Baron Cornwallis.**

**CORNWALLIS,** 2nd Baron, *cr* 1927, of Linton, Kent, in County of Kent; **Wykeham Stanley Cornwallis,** KCVO 1968; KBE 1945; MC; Lord Lieutenant of Kent since 1944 and Custos Rotulorum; HM's Lieutenant for City and County of Canterbury; Pro-Chancellor, University of Kent at Canterbury; one of HM's Lieutenants for City of London; Chairman: Fremlin's Ltd; Isherwood, Foster & Stacey; Warden Insurance Co.; Director: Royal Insurance Co. (Chairman Kent Board, formerly Chairman London Board); London & Liverpool & Globe Insurance Co. (Chairman London Board); London and Lancashire Insurance Co.; Barclays Bank (Local Director Kent district); Whitbread Investment Co.; *b* 14 March 1892; *s* of 1st Baron and Mabel (*d* 1957), *d* of O. P. Leigh, Belmont Hall, Cheshire; *S* father, 1935; *m* 1st, 1917, Cecily Etha Mary (*d* 1943), *d* of Sir James Walker, 3rd Bt of Sand Hutton; one *s* (one *d* decd); 2nd, 1948, Esmé Ethel Alice (*d* 1969), *widow* of Sir Robert Walker, 4th Bt, Sand Hutton. *Educ:* Eton; RMC Sandhurst. Served European War, 1914-18, Royal Scots Greys and General Staff, France and Belgium (wounded, despatches, MC). Hon. Colonel: 5th Bn The Buffs, E Kent Regt, 1956-67; 415 Coast Regt RA (TA), 1935-56; 8th Bn (Territorial), The Queen's Regt, 1967-68. President: Inst. of Packaging, 1961-64; Kent County Boy Scouts Assoc; Kent County Playing Fields Assoc.; Kent County Agricultural Soc.; Kent Assoc. of Workmen's Clubs; Patron, Kent Assoc. of Boys' Clubs; Vice-Patron: Kent County Society; Assoc. of Men of Kent and Kentish Men; Trustee of MCC (Pres. 1948); Trustee RASE; Kent County Council: Vice-Chm., 1931-35; Chm., 1935-36, late Alderman; Chm. Kent War Agricultural Executive Cttee, 1939-46; DL, JP Kent; Vice-Pres., SE District T&AVR. Hon. DCL Univ. of Kent at Canterbury, 1968. Hon. Freeman, Borough of Maidstone. Provincial Grand Master, Masonic Province of Kent. Edward Hardy Gold Medal, for service to County of Kent. KStJ. Knight Comdr, Order of Dannebrog (Denmark). *Recreations:* Capt., Kent Cricket XI, 1924-25-26. *Heir:* *s* Hon. Fiennes Neil Wykeham Cornwallis, OBE 1963 [*b* 1921; *m* 1st, 1942, Judith (marr. diss., 1948), *o d* of late Lt-Col Lacy Scott Ashcroft, Wadhurst, Sussex; one *s* (one *d* decd); 2nd, 1951, Jean, *y d* of Capt. H. R. Landale, Ewell Manor, West Farleigh, Kent; one *s* three *d*. Served War of 1939-45, in Coldstream Guards]. *Address:* Ashurst Park, Tunbridge Wells, Kent. *T:* Fordcombe 212; Dundurn House, St Fillans, Perthshire. *Clubs:* Cavalry, Devonshire, MCC (Pres. 1948); (Patron) Kent County (Maidstone), etc.

*See also Hon. Lady Cochrane, Major Sir F. William S. Steel, Bt.*

**CORNWELL, David John Moore, (John Le Carré);** writer; *b* 19 Oct. 1931; *s* of Ronald Thomas Archibald Cornwell and Olive (*née* Glassy); *m* 1954, Alison Ann Veronica Sharp; three *s*. *Educ:* Sherborne; Berne Univ.; Lincoln Coll., Oxford. Taught at Eton, 1956-58. Mem. of HM Foreign Service, 1960-64. *Publications:* Call for the Dead, 1961 (filmed as The Deadly Affair, 1967); A Murder of Quality, 1962; The Spy Who Came in from the Cold, 1963; The Looking-Glass War, 1965; A Small Town in Germany, 1968. *Address:* c/o A. P. Watt and Son, 26-28 Bedford Row, WC1. *Club:* Savile.

**CORNWELL, Ven. Leonard Cyril,** MA, BD, Hon. CF; Archdeacon of Swindon, 1947-63, now Emeritus; *b* 28 March 1893; 2nd *s* of T. E. D. Cornwell and Alice Warner; *m* 1927, Grace Annie, *d* of R. E. D. Rudman and Alice Pike; four *s*. *Educ:* Fitzwilliam House and Ridley Hall, Cambridge. BA Cambridge, 1914; MA 1918; BD London, 1921. Curate St Augustine, Plymouth, 1916-18; Temp. Army Chaplain, 1918-21; Curate of St Paul, Chippenham, 1921-26; Curate-in-Charge, St Christopher, Brislington, Bristol, 1926-31, and first Vicar, 1931-36; Rector of St Paul, Chippenham, Wilts, 1936-50; Rector of Brinkworth, Wilts, 1950-60. Hon. Clerical Sec., Bristol Diocesan Conf., 1928-47; Editor, Bristol Diocesan Directory, 1929-32; Hon. Chaplain to Bishop of Bristol, 1942-47; Hon. Canon of Bristol Cathedral, 1945-47, and 1962-63. Sub-Chaplain of Order of St John of Jerusalem, 1954-63. *Address:* Causeway House, Brinkworth, Chippenham, Wilts. *T:* Brinkworth 202.

**CORRIE, W(allace) Rodney;** Chairman, North West Economic Planning Board, since 1969; *b* 25 Nov. 1919; *o c* of late Edward and Mary Ellen Corrie; *m* 1952, Helen Margaret (*née* Morice), *widow* of Flt-Lt A. H. E. Kahn; one *s* one *d*. *Educ:* Leigh Grammar School; Christ's Coll., Cambridge (BA 1941, MA 1944). Served Royal Signals, 1940-46 (despatches). Entered Civil Service, Min. of Town and Country Planning, 1947; Min. of Housing and Local Govt, 1951; Asst Secretary, 1961; Assistant Under-Secretary of State, DEA, 1969; Under-Sec., Min. of Housing and Local Govt, 1969-. *Recreations:* fell-walking exploring byways. *Address:* Windgather, Wainwright Road, Altrincham, Cheshire.

**CORRIGAN, Very Rev. Terence Edward;** Provincial of the Society of Jesus in England, 1964-70; *b* Brislington, Bristol, 30 Sept. 1915; *s* of Joseph Corrigan and Ann (*née* Tunks). *Educ:* Christian Brothers. Ordained priest, 1948. Master at Stonyhurst Coll., 1944-46, 1951-52; Procurator and Bursar at Stonyhurst Coll., 1952-59; Regular Superior of Salisbury Mission of Soc. of Jesus in S Rhodesia, 1959-64. *Address:* 114 Mount Street, W1.

**CORRY**; *see* Lowry-Corry.

**CORRY, Sir James Perowne Ivo Myles,** 3rd Bt, *cr* 1885; a Vice-President of King George's Fund for Sailors; The Royal Alfred Merchant Seamen's Society, and of Royal Merchant Navy School; *b* 10 June 1892; *s* of 2nd Bt and Charlotte, *d* of late J. Collins; *S* father, 1926; *m* 1st, 1921, Molly Irene (marr. diss., 1936), *y d* of late Major O. J. Bell; one *s* two *d*; 2nd, 1946, Cynthia, *widow* of Capt. David Polson, and *o d* of late Capt. F. H. Mahony and Mrs Francis Bliss; one *d*. *Educ:* Eton; Trinity Coll., Cambridge. *Heir:* *s* Lt-Comdr William James Corry, RN [*b* 1924; *m* 1945, Diana (*née* Lapsley); four *s* two *d*]. *Address:* Dunraven, Fauvic, Jersey, CI. *Clubs:* Lansdowne, Leander.

**CORSON, Rear-Adm. Eric Reid,** MVO 1922; DSC 1914; Commander Greek Order of the Redeemer, 1933; Royal Navy (retired); *b* 1887; *s* of late George Corson, Dumfries and Leeds; *m* 1924, Marjorie (*d* 1969), *d* of late James Winants, New Jersey, USA; three *s*. *Address:* 17 Lowndes Close, Belgravia, SW1. *T:* 01-235 7221.

**CORTAZZI, Henry Arthur Hugh,** CMG 1969; Royal College of Defence Studies, 1971; *b* 2 May 1924; *m* 1956, Elizabeth Esther Montagu; one *s* two *d*. *Educ:* Sedbergh Sch.; St Andrews and London Univs. Served in RAF, 1943-47; joined Foreign Office, 1949; Third Sec., Singapore, 1950-51; Third/Second Sec., Tokyo, 1951-54; FO, 1954-58; First Sec.,

Bonn, 1958-60; First Sec., later Head of Chancery, Tokyo, 1961-65; FO, 1965-66; Counsellor (Commercial), Tokyo, 1966-70. *Recreations:* collecting, reading. *Address:* c/o FCO, King Charles Street, SW1; (home) 8 Browning Close, Randolph Avenue, W9. *Club:* Travellers'.

**CORTLANDT, Lyn,** BA; FIAL, FRSA; artist, United States; *d* of late Graf Karl Gustav von Lubieński and late Mrs Elinor Ernestine (Thiel) Cortlandt. *Educ:* Los Angeles: Chouinard and Jepson Art Insts; New York: Art Students' League of NY; Art Sch. of Pratt Inst.; Columbia Univ. Sch. of Painting and Sculpture; Hans Hofmann Sch. of Fine Arts; China Inst. in America followed by private instruction. Phi Beta Kappa, Phi Kappa Phi. National exhibitions in USA include: Pennsylvania Academy of Fine Arts, National Academy of Design, Brooklyn Museum and many others; also numerous exhibitions in Europe, Japan, S America. Represented in Collections: Metropolitan Museum of Art, New York; Museum of Fine Arts, Boston; Fogg Museum of Art; Art Inst. of Chicago; Brooklyn Museum; Baltimore Museum of Art; Cincinnati Art Museum; Springfield Museum of Fine Arts, Mass; Musée National d'Art Moderne, Paris, France; Stedelijk Museum, Amsterdam, Holland; New York Public Library, Boston Public Library; and other important public and private collections. Toured extensively in Brazil and Argentina by invitation, 1963. Solo exhibitions, Museums in São Paulo, Buenos Aires, etc, 1964-65. Radio: Moderator, Panel Forums on Art Subjects. Lectured on Contemporary Art and on various National Ideologies, in foreign countries. Member: Allied Artists of America; The Painters' and Sculptors' Soc. of NJ; Creative Club; Philadelphia Water Color Club; Internat. Platform Assoc.; Amer. Acad. of Political and Social Science; Acad. of Political Science; Amer. Judicature Soc.; UN/USA; Nat. Trust for Historic Preservation; Comitato Internazionale: Centro Studi e Scambi Internazionali; Accademia Internazionale Leonardo da Vinci; New York Zoological Soc. Adv. Mem., Marquis Library Soc., etc. Recipient of numerous awards. CSSI Medal of Honor. *Recreations:* reading, music, travel, tennis. *Address:* 1070 Park Avenue, New York, NY 10028, USA. *T:* Atwater 9-6370. *Clubs:* Pen and Brush; Le Cercle d'Or.

**CORVEDALE, Viscount; Edward Alfred Alexander Baldwin;** *b* 3 Jan. 1938; *o s* and *heir* of 3rd Earl Baldwin of Bewdley, *qv. Educ:* Eton; Trinity Coll., Cambridge (MA). *Address:* Bushey House, Apperley, Glos.

**CORY, Ven. Alexander;** Archdeacon Emeritus (retired, 1961); *b* 19 March 1890; *s* of Rev. Alexander Arthur Cory, Vicar of Tipton, Staffs; *m* 1st, 1917, Dorothy Frances Barnard (*d* 1958); one *s* one *d*; 2nd, 1958, Kathleen, *d* of J. A. Emily, Vancouver, BC. *Educ:* S John's Sch., Leatherhead; Keble Coll., Oxford (MA); Cuddesdon Theological Coll., Oxford. Curate of Portsea, 1914-17; TCF, 1917-19; Rector of Burton Overy, Leics, 1919-23; Vicar of S Mary's, Far Cotton, Northampton, 1923-28; Vicar of Fareham, Hants, 1928-38; Vicar of Hayling Island, 1938-46; Rural Dean of Havant, 1943-46; Vicar of All Saints, Ryde, IW, 1946-52; Rural Dean of East Wight, 1948-51; Hon. Canon of Droxford in Portsmouth Cathedral, 1948-52; Archdeacon of the Isle of Wight, 1952-61; Hon. Canon of Portsmouth Cathedral 1961. *Recreations:* gardening and handicrafts. *Address:* Garthland, Dudsbury Crescent, Ferndown, Dorset. *T:* Ferndown 4717. *Club:* (Hon. Mem.) Royal Victoria Yacht (Ryde, IW).

**CORY, Sir Clinton James Donald,** 4th Bt, *cr* 1919; *b* 1 March 1909; 2nd *s* of Sir Donald Cory, 2nd Bt, shipowner of Llandaff, Glam, and Gertrude, *d* of Henry Thomas Box; *S* brother, 1941; *m* 1935, Mary, *o d* of Dr A. Douglas Hunt, Park Grange, Derby; one *s*. *Educ:* Brighton Coll.; abroad. *Recreations:* shooting, fishing, golf. *Heir: s* Clinton Charles Donald Cory, *b* 13 Sept. 1937. *Address:* Baytree Cottage, Hinxworth, near Baldock, Herts. *T:* Ashwell 209.

**CORY-WRIGHT, Sir Richard (Michael),** 4th Bt *cr* 1903; *b* 17 Jan. 1944; *s* of Capt. A. J. J. Cory-Wright (killed in action, 1944), and of Susan Esterel (who *m* 2nd, 1949, Lt-Col J. E. Gurney, DSO, MC), *d* of Robert Elwes; *S* grandfather, 1969. *Educ:* Eton; Birmingham Univ. *Heir:* Michael Cory-Wright [*b* 5 March 1920; *m* 1954, Elizabeth, *d* of late Major J. A. Morrison, DSO]. *Address:* Tacolneston Hall, Norwich, Norfolk NOR 87W. *Club:* Cavalry.

**CORYTON, Air Chief Marshal Sir (William) Alec,** KCB 1950 (CB 1942); KBE 1945; MVO 1919; DFC 1922; RAF retired; *b* 16 Feb. 1895; 3rd *s* of late William Coryton, Pentillie Castle, Cornwall; *m* 1925, Philippa Dorothea, *e d* of late Daniel Hanbury, Castle Malwood, Lyndhurst, *g d* of Sir Thomas Hanbury of La Mortola, Italy; three *d. Educ:* Eton; Cambridge. Rifle Brigade; wounded, 1915; RAF 1917; Flying Instructor to the Duke of York, 1919 (MVO); India N-WF 1920 (DFC); Dir of Operations (Oversea), Air Ministry, 1938-41 (CB); AOC Bomber Group, 1942-43; Air Ministry, 1943-44, Asst Chief of the Air Staff (Operations); Air Comdr, Third Tactical Air Force, and Bengal, Burma, SEAC, 1944-45 (KBE); Controller of Supplies (Air) Min. of Supply, 1946-50; Chief Exec. Guided Weapons, Min. of Supply, 1950-51; retired list, 1951. Managing Dir Engine Div., Bristol Aeroplane Co. Ltd 1951; Chm. and Man. Dir Bristol Aero-Engines, Ltd, 1955; Dep. Chm. (Resident in Bristol), Bristol Siddeley Engines Ltd, 1950-64, retired. *Address:* Two Leas, Langton-Matravers, Dorset.

*See also Sir Michael Nall, Bt.*

**COSBY, Brig. Noel Robert Charles,** CIE 1945; MC; Indian Army, retired; *b* 26 Dec. 1890; *s* of Robert Parkyn Cosby; *m* 1st, 1938, May Margrit Kellersberger (*d* 1942), Berne, Switzerland; no *c*; 2nd, 1960, Margaret Esther Remon Bunting. *Educ:* HMS Worcester, Greenhithe, Kent, for competitive entry to RN. Commissioned Indian Army, Jan. 1915 and posted 5th Royal Gurkhas FF in Egypt; served Turkish attack on Suez Canal, 1915; Gallipoli, May-Dec. 1915 (evacuated wounded, despatches twice, MC); Mesopotamia, 1917-19 (despatches); almost continuous service on NW Frontier, India, regimentally and with Frontier Corps, 1921-45; Mohmand Ops, 1935 (despatches); Waziristan Ops, 1939-40 (wounded, despatches); retired 1945 after four years as Inspector-Gen. Frontier Corps with rank of Brig. *Recreations:* sailing, shooting, gardening. *Address:* The Val House, Alderney, CI. *Club:* Naval and Military.

**COSGRAVE, Rev. Francis Herbert,** MA; DCL (Hon.) Bishop's University, Lennoxville, PQ, 1927; LLD (Hon.) Queen's University, Kingston, 1929, McMaster University, Hamilton, 1933, University of Toronto, 1945; DD (Hon.) Victoria University, Toronto, 1936; formerly Provost and Vice-Chancellor of the University of Trinity College, Toronto; *b* 11 July 1880; 5th *s* of late Frederick Cosgrave, JP, Glebelands, Kilsallaghan, Co. Dublin; *m* Annie Leila, *d* of late Dr J. Metcalf, Kingston, Ont. *Educ:* Corrig Sch., Kingstown, Co. Dublin; Trinity Coll., Dublin. *Address:* 561

Avenue Road, Toronto 7, Canada. *T:* WA 1.6821. *Clubs:* Royal Canadian Yacht: Faculty of University (Toronto).

**COSGRAVE, Liam;** Member of Dail Eireann since 1943; Leader of Fine Gael Party since 1965; *b* April 1920; *s* of late William T. Cosgrave; *m* 1952, Vera Osborne; two *s* one *d.* *Educ:* Synge Street Christian Brothers; Castlenock College, Dublin; King's Inns. Served in Army during Emergency. Barrister-at-Law, 1943; Senior Counsel, 1958. chairman Public Accounts Committee, 1945; Parliamentary Secretary to Taoiseach and Minister for Industry and Commerce, 1948; Minister for External Affairs, 1954-57. Leader first delegation from Ireland to the UN Assembly. Hon. LLD Duquesne Univ., Pittsburg, Pa, and St John's Univ., Brooklyn, 1956. Knight Grand Cross of Pius IX. Hon. LLD de Paul Univ., Chicago, 1958. *Address:* Beechpark, Templeogue, Co. Dublin.

**COSGRAVE, Col L. Moore,** DSO 1916; ED; retired as Economic Adviser, Mercantile Bank of Canada, Montreal; *b* Toronto, 28 Aug. 1890; *s* of Lawrence Joseph Cosgrave, Toronto, and Kate Ellen Forbes, Port Hope, Ont; *m* 1916, Beryl Hunter Jones, Windsor, Canada, and Honolulu; one *s* one *d.* *Educ:* Royal Military Coll., Kingston; McGill Univ., Montreal. Commissioned rank, Canadian Field Artillery, 1914; Capt. 1915; Major, 1916 (DSO and bar, despatches thrice, ED (Canada), French Croix de Guerre); Lieut-Col and OC 1st Can. Arty Bde, 1918; Canadian Govt Trade Comr, Wembly Exhibition, England, 1922-24; Canadian Govt Trade Commissioner to China, 1925-35; Group Comr Shanghai Volunteer Corps, 1932-35; Senior Canadian Government Trade Commissioner to Australia, 1935-42; Canadian Military Attaché South-West Pacific area attached High Commissioner for Canada in Australia, 1942; Official Signatory for Canada at surrender of Japan on Board USS Missouri, 2 Sept. 1945; Mem. Canadian Delegation, Far East Advisory Council to Japan, Jan. 1946; Commercial Counsellor Canadian Embassy, China, 1947; Western Representative, Foreign Trade Service, 1949-52; Chargé d'Affaires *ad interim,* Canadian Legation, Lisbon, Aug. 1952-June 1956, retired. *Publication:* Afterthoughts of Armaggeddon, 1919. *Recreations:* golf and hunting. *Address:* Mercantile Bank of Canada, Montreal, Quebec, Canada. *Clubs:* Royal Commonwealth Society; United Services, English-Speaking Union (Montreal); University (Toronto, Ont); Royal British (Lisbon).

**COSLETT, Air Marshal Sir Norman;** *see* Coslett, Air Marshal Sir T. N.

**COSLETT, Air Marshal Sir (Thomas) Norman,** KCB 1963 (CB 1960); OBE OBE 1942; MIMechE; idc; psc; *b* 8 Nov. 1909; *s* of Evan Coslett; *m* 1938, Audrey Garrett. *Educ:* Barry Grammar Sch.; Halton; Cranwell. Dep. Dir of Engineering Plans, Air Ministry, 1954; Senior Technical Staff Officer, HQ Coastal Command, 1957; Commandant, No 1 School of Technical Training, 1958-61; AOC No 24 Group, 1961-63; AOC-in-C, RAF Maintenance Command, 1963-66. Air Cdre, 1957; Air Vice-Marshal, 1962; Air Marshal, 1963; retired, 1966. Dir, Flight Refuelling (Holdings) Ltd, 1966-. *Recreation:* farming. *Address:* c/o A R 8b, Adastral House, Theobald's Road, WC1; 28 Lower Park, Putney Hill, SW15.

**COSSLETT, Dr Vernon Ellis;** Reader in Electron Physics, University of Cambridge, since 1965; Fellow of Corpus Christi College, Cambridge, since 1963; *b* 16 June 1908; *s* of Edgar William Cosslett and Anne Cosslett (*née* Williams); *m* 1940, Anna Joanna Wischin (*d* 1969); one *s* one *d.* *Educ:* Cirencester Grammar Sch.; Bristol Univ. BSc Bristol 1929; PhD Bristol 1932; MSc London 1939; ScD Cambridge 1963. Research at: Bristol Univ., 1929-30; Kaiser-Wilhelm Institut, Berlin, 1930-31; University Coll., London, 1931-32; Research Fellow, Bristol Univ., 1932-35; Lectr in Science, Faraday House, London, 1935-39; Research (part-time), Birkbeck Coll., London, 1936-39; Keddey-Fletcher-Warr Research Fellow of London Univ. (at Oxford), 1939-41; Lectr in Physics, Electrical Laboratory, Oxford Univ., 1941-46; ICI Fellow, Cavendish Laboratory, Cambridge, 1946-49; Lectr in Physics, Univ. of Cambridge, 1949-65. Past Pres., Royal Microscopical Soc.; Past Vice-Pres., Inst. of Physics; Past Pres., Assoc. of Univ. Teachers. Hon. DSc (Tübingen), 1963. *Publications:* Introduction to Electron Optics, 1946 (1951); Practical Electron Microscopy, 1951; X-ray Microscopy (with W. C. Nixon), 1960; Modern Microscopy, 1966; many scientific papers. *Recreations:* gardening, mountain walking, listening to music. *Address:* 31 Comberton Road, Barton, Cambridge. *T:* Comberton 2428.

**COSTAIN, Albert Percy;** MP (C) Folkestone and Hythe since 1959; Director, Richard Costain Ltd; *b* 5 July 1910; *s* of William Percy Costain and Maud May Smith; *m* 1933, Joan Mary, *d* of John William Whiter; one *s* one *d.* *Educ:* King James, Knaresborough; Coll. of Estate Management. Production Dir on formation of Richard Costain Ltd, 1933. Chm., Richard Costain Ltd, 1956-69; Chm., Pre-stressed Concrete Development Group, 1952. London Treasurer, National Children's Home, 1950-60. FIOB Author of Home Safety Act, 1961; Parly Priv. Sec. to Minister of Public Bldg and Works, 1962-64. Mem. Cttee of Public Accts, 1961-64. Mem. Estimates Cttee, 1960-61, 1965-; Mem. Estimates Sub-Cttee on Building and Natural Resources, 1965-. Joint Vice-Chm., Conservative Party Transport Cttee, 1964. Jt Sec., Conservative Housing and Local Govt Cttee, 1964-65, Jt Vice-Chm., 1965-66; All Party Tourists and Resorts Cttee: Sec., 1964-66; Vice-Chm., 1966-69; Chm., 1970-; Vice-Chm., Conservative Party Arts, Public Building and Works Cttee, 1965-. *Recreations:* sailing, golf. *Address:* Inwarren, Kingswood, Surrey. *T:* Mogador 2443. *Clubs:* Carlton, Royal Thames Yacht; Walton Heath Golf.

**COSTANZI, Edwin J. B.;** *see* Borg-Costanzi.

**COSTAR, Sir Norman (Edgar),** KCMG 1963 (CMG 1953); *b* 18 May 1909. *Educ:* Battersea Grammar School; Jesus Coll., Cambridge. Asst Principal, Colonial Office, 1932; Private Sec. to Permanent Under Sec., Dominions Office, 1935; served in UK High Commissioner's Offices, Australia, 1937-39, New Zealand, 1945-47. Principal, 1938; Asst Sec., 1946. Dep. High Commissioner, Ceylon, 1953-57; Asst Under-Sec., Commonwealth Relations Office, 1958-60; Dep. High Commissioner in Australia, 1960-62; High Commissioner: Trinidad and Tobago, 1962-66; Cyprus, 1967-69. *Club:* United University.

**COSTELLO, John Aloysius,** SC; *b* Dublin, 20 June 1891; *s* of John Costello and Rose Callaghan; *m* 1919, Ida Mary O'Malley (*d* 1956); three *s* two *d.* *Educ:* Christian Brothers' Schs and University Coll., Dublin. BA 1911, LLB 1914; called to Bar, 1914; called to Inner Bar, 1925; Senior Bencher of Honourable Soc. of King's Inns; Mem. of Royal Irish Academy, 1948. Hon. LLD: University of Montreal,

Ottawa Univ. and Fordham Univ., 1948; Catholic Univ. of America, St John's Univ., NY, and Iona Coll., New Rochelle, NY, 1956. Hon. Life Member Canadian Bar Association. Asst to Law Officer, Provisional Govt, 1922; Asst to Attorney-Gen., Irish Free State, 1922-26; Attorney-Gen. IFS, 1926-32; Taoiseach, 1948-51 and Minister for Health, April-June, 1951; Leader of the Opposition in Dáil Eireann, 1951-54, Taoiseach, 1954-57; again Leader of the Opposition in Dáil Eireann, 1957-59. TD, Co. Dublin, 1933-37, Dublin Townships, 1937-43 and 1944-48, Dublin South (East), 1948-69. *Address:* 20 Herbert Park, Ballsbridge, Dublin 4.

**COSTELLO, Sir Leonard (Wilfred James),** Kt 1935; CBE 1946; JP; Member Devon Agricultural Wages Committee, 1956-62; President: Devon Old Peoples Welfare Committee; Devon and Cornwall Liberal Federation; Tiverton Division Liberal Association; Chairman General Commissioners of Income Tax for E Budleigh and Clinton Division of Devon, 1954-64; Commissioner for E Exminster Division; Chairman Devon Branch, Magistrates Association, 1954-63; Past Member Council (also of Executive Legal and Mental Health Committees), Magistrates Association, also of joint Committee of that Association and BMA; Vice-President and Member of Committees, Devon Community Council; Member Central Executive Committee and Chairman Exeter, Mid and E Devon Branch of NSPCC; Vice-President Devon Branch of Forces Help Society and Lord Roberts Workshops; Member Council, Alexandra Rose Day (Hon. Treasurer 1941-48); Member Exeter Cathedral Restoration Fund Committee; Past Chairman Directors, Exeter Theatre Co. Ltd; *b* London, 25 Aug. 1881; *e s* of late James Edward and late Alice Eliza Costello; *m* 1st, 1907, Winifred Avery (*d* 1950), *e d* of Thomas and Sarah Belgrave; two *d*; 2nd, 1952, Joan Barbara Alice Piper, *d* of George Earle Hewitt. *Educ:* Dulwich Coll.; Peterhouse, Cambridge. ba, LLB, 1902; MA 1906. Called to Bar, Inner Temple, 1903; practised in London and on Midland Circuit, 1903-26; Lectr in Common Law, University Coll., Nottingham, 1906-08; served European War, 1916-18, Capt. RASC; Judge, High Court, Calcutta, 1926-40; Acting Chief Justice of Bengal, May-Aug. 1937, and July-Aug. 1939; Chm. of a Home Office Advisory Cttee on Aliens in the Isle of Man, 1941; Mem. Managing Cttee of Elizabeth Garrett Anderson Hospital, 1941-50; Pres. of All India and of Calcutta Societies for the Prevention of Cruelty to Animals, 1933-41; Pres. of Soc. for the Protection of Children in India, 1927-37; twice Pres. of Bengal Flying Club, Calcutta. Mem., first Exec. Cttee of League of Young Liberals, 1907, and later Chm. of London Council and Mem. of London Liberal Council; Prospective Lib Candidate, N Islington, 1912-14; contested (L) Strand Div. of Westminster, Jan. 1910; Exeter, 1918 and 1922; MP (L) Huntingdonshire, 1923-24; contested Huntingdon, 1924. High Sheriff of Devon, 1945-46; Hon. Legal Adviser Devon County Army Welfare Services, 1941-46 (Defence Medal); Dep. Chm. Devon Quarter Sessions, 1940-47; Mem. Rating Appeal Cttee, 1940-50; Dep. Chm. County Justices Cttee, 1941-46; Chm. 1946-56; Mem. Devon Standing Joint Cttee, 1946; Vice-Chm., 1952-56; Chm. of Devon Quarter Sessions, 1947-56; Mem. Bd of Visitors, HM Prison, Dartmoor, 1950-61; Chm. County Confirming and Compensation Cttees, 1951-56; Mem. Exeter Prison Visiting Justices Cttee, 1946-56 and for five years Pres. Conf. of Prison and Borstal Visiting Justices; Mem. Devon Magistrates Courts Cttee from its inception till 1956; JP Devon, 1940-. Chm. Agric. Land Tribunal for SW Region of England, 1948-58. Has given evidence before various Royal Commissions. *Publications:* articles on policies and economics; Law relating to Enquiries Profiteering Act, 1919. *Recreations:* formerly golf and tennis, now croquet and studying foreign languages. *Address:* Grantlands, Uffculme, Devon. *T:* Cradock 418. *Clubs:* National Liberal; Exeter and County (Exeter); Royal Calcutta Turf (Calcutta).

**COSTIGAN, Rev. John,** SJ; MA; *b* Feb. 1916. *Educ:* Stonyhurst; Oxford. Joined the Soc. of Jesus, 1934; ordained, 1949. Rector of: Beaumont Coll., 1958-64; St Aloysius' Coll., Glasgow, 1964-70. *Address:* c/o 45 Hill Street, Glasgow C3.

**COSTIN, Maj.-Gen. Eric Boyd,** DSO 1917; late Royal Canadian Regiment, West yorkshire Regiment and Manchester Regiment; *b* 1889; *yr s* of late Capt. Charles Costin, 14th Foot (W Yorks Regt); *m* 1922, Violet Constance, *e d* of late Sir George Saltmarsh; one *s* one *d*. *Educ:* Christ's Hospital, Hertford, London and Horsham. Served European War, 1914-18 (despatches, DSO, Chevalier Légion d'Honneur, Brevet of Major); psc; Brevet Lieut-Col, 1934; commanded 2nd Bn The Manchester Regt, 1935-38; served War of 1939-45; retired, 1946. Col The Manchester Regt, 1948-54. *Address:* Bessborough House, St Mawes, Cornwall. *T:* St Mawes 220. *Club:* Royal Cornwall Yacht (Falmouth).

**COSTLEY-WHITE, Cyril Grove,** CMG 1953; Historical Section, India Office Library and Records, since 1968; *b* 30 Oct. 1913; *s* of late Very Rev. H. Costley-White, DD; *m* 1st, 1938, Elizabeth Delmore (marr. diss. 1955); two *s* one *d*; 2nd, 1955, Elisabeth Marianne, *d* of late Rev. Noel Braithwaite Chard and of Lady Janet Chard; two *s*. *Educ:* Eton; Balliol Coll., Oxford. Joined Colonial Office (after competitive examination), 1937; transferred, 1940, to Dominions Office. Served on Staff of UK High Commissioner in Canada, 1941-44, and New Zealand, 1944-46; Deputy United Kingdom High Commissioner in Ceylon, 1949-50; Asst Sec., CO (formerly CRO), 1951-68; retd 1969. *Address:* 129a Ashley Gardens, SW1. *T:* 01-828 8159.

**COTES, Peter, (Sydney Arthur Boulting);** play producer, film and television director; *e s* of Arthur Boulting and Rose Bennett; *m* 1st, 1938, Myfanwy Jones (marr. diss.); 2nd, 1948, Joan Miller. *Educ:* Taplow; Brighton and privately. Was for some years an actor; made theatrical debut, Portsmouth Hippodrome, in the arms of Vesta Tilley. Formed own independent play-producing co. with Hon. James Smith, 1949, presented Rocket to the Moon, St Martin's Theatre, and subsequently produced, in association with Arts Council of Great Britain, seasons in Manchester and at Embassy and Lyric Theatres, Hammersmith. Founded: New Lindsey, 1946; New Boltons, 1951. Productions include: Pick Up Girl, 1946; The Animal Kingdom, 1947; The Master Builder, 1948; Miss Julie, 1949; The Biggest Thief in Town, 1951; The Mousetrap, 1952; The Man, 1952; The Father, 1953; Happy Holiday, 1954; A Pin to see the Peepshow (produced New York); Hot Summer Night, 1958; Epitaph for George Dillon (Holland), 1959; The Rope Dancers, 1959; Girl on the Highway, 1960; A Loss of Roses, 1962; The Odd Ones, 1963; Hidden Stranger (New York), 1963; What Goes Up. . .!, 1963; So Wise, So Young, 1964; Paint Myself Black, 1965; The Impossible Years, 1966; Staring at the Sun, 1968; Janie Jackson, 1968; The Old Ladies,

1969. Films: The Right Person; The Young and the Guilty; has prod. and adapted numerous plays for BBC Television and ITV; was Sen. Drama Dir, Associated Rediffusion Ltd, 1955-58; producing stage plays and films, 1959-60; Supervising Producer of Drama Channel 7, Melbourne, 1961; produced and adapted plays for Anglia TV, 1964; produced first TV series of P. G. Wodehouse short stories, on BBC; wrote George Robey centenary Tribute, BBC Omnibus series, 1969; wrote and dir. in One Pair of Eyes series, BBC, 1970. FRSA. *Publications:* No Star Nonsense, 1949; The Little Fellow, 1951; A Handbook of Amateur Theatre, 1957; I Meantersay!, 1970. *Recreations:* cricket, cycling. *Address:* 27 Cathcart Road, SW10. *T:* 01-352 4252. *Club:* Savage.

**COTT, Hugh Bamford,** ScD Cantab, DSc Glasgow; FRPS, FZS; Fellow of Selwyn College, since 1945; *b* 6 July 1900; *s* of late Rev. A. M. Cott, Ashby Magna; *m* 1928, Joyce Radford; one *s* one *d. Educ:* Rugby Sch.; RMC, Sandhurst; Selwyn Coll., Cambridge. Joined 1st Bn the Leics Regt; served in Ireland, 1919-21. 2nd class, Nat. Sciences Tripos, Pt I, 1925. Carried out zoological expeditions to SE Brazil, 1923; Lower Amazon, 1925-26; Zoological Society's Expedition to the Zambesi, 1927, Canary Islands, 1931, Uganda, 1952, Zululand, 1956, Central Africa, 1957; Lecturer in Hygiene, Bristol Univ., 1928-32; Asst and Lecturer in Zoology, Glasgow Univ., 1932-38; Strickland Curator and Lectr in the University of Cambridge, 1938-67; Lectr, 1945-67, and Dean, 1966-67, of Selwyn Coll., Cambridge. War of 1939-45: Mem. Advisory Cttee on Camouflage, 1939-40; Capt. and Major (RE) MEF; served Western Desert, 1941 (despatches); Chief Instructor, Middle East Camouflage Sch., 1941-43; GSO 2 (Cam) Mountain Warfare Trg Centre, 1943-44. *Publications:* Adaptive Coloration in Animals, 1940; Zoological Photography in Practice, 1956; Uganda in Black and White, 1959; various scientific papers on adaptive coloration, feeding habits of tree frogs, camouflage, edibility of birds, ecology of crocodiles, etc published in Trans and Proc. of Zool Soc. London, Proc. R. Ent. Soc. London, Photographic Jl, Engineers' Jl etc. *Recreations:* travel, pen drawing, photography. *Address:* Selwyn College, Cambridge; Denebanks, Netherbury, Bridport, Dorset. *T:* Netherbury 348.

**COTTENHAM,** 8th Earl of, *cr* 1850; **Kenelm Charles Everard Digby Pepys;** Bt 1784 and 1801; Baron Cottenham, 1836; Viscount Crowhurst, 1850; *b* 27 Nov. 1948; *s* of 7th Earl of Cottenham and Lady Angela Isabel Nellie Nevill, *d* of 4th Marquess of Abergavenny; *S* father, 1968. *Educ:* Eton. *Address:* 28 Chalfont House, Cadogan Lane, SW1; The Hollies, Eridge Green, Tunbridge Wells, Kent.
*See also Baron McGowan.*

**COTTER, Lieut-Col Sir Delaval James Alfred,** 6th Bt, *cr* 1763; DSO 1944; late 13th/18th Royal Hussars; *b* 29 April 1911; *s* of 5th Bt and Ethel Lucy (*d* 1956), *d* of Alfred Wheeler; *S* father, 1924; *m* 1st, 1943, Roma (marr. diss., 1949), *widow* of Sqdn Ldr K. A. K. MacEwen and *o d* of late Adrian Rome, Dalswinton Lodge, Salisbury, SR; two *d*; 2nd, 1952, Mrs Eveline Mary Paterson, *widow* of Lieut-Col J. F. Paterson, OBE, and *d* of late E. J. Mardon, ICS (retired). *Educ:* Malvern Coll; RMC, Sandhurst. Served War of 1939-45 (DSO); retired, 1959. JP Wilts, 1962-63. Now lives in Southern Ireland. *Heir: n* Patrick Laurence Delaval Cotter, *b* 21 Nov. 1941. *Address:* Castle Widenham, Castletownroche, Co. Cork, Eire. *Clubs:* Cavalry; Kildare Street (Dublin).

**COTTERELL, Geoffrey;** author; *b* 24 Nov. 1919; *yr s* of late Graham Cotterell and of Millicent (*née* Crews). *Educ:* Bishops Stortford College. Served War of 1939-45, Royal Artillery, 1940-46. *Publications:* Then a Soldier, 1944; This is the Way, 1947; Randle in Springtime, 1949; Strait and Narrow, 1950; Westward the Sun, 1952; The Strange Enchantment, 1956; Tea at Shadow Creek, 1958; Tiara Tahiti, 1960; Go, said the bird, 1966; Bowers of Innocence, 1970. *Recreation:* golf. *Address:* 2 Fulbourne House, Blackwater Road, Eastbourne, Sussex. *Clubs:* Savage, Cooden Beach Golf.

**COTTERELL, Lt-Col Sir Richard (Charles Geers),** 5th Bt, *cr* 1805; CBE 1965; Lord Lieutenant and Custos Rotulorum for County of Hereford, 1945-57; a Forestry Commissioner (unpaid), 1945-64; *b* 1 June 1907; *s* of Sir J. R. G. Cotterell, 4th Bt, and Lady Evelyn Amy Gordon Lennox, *e d* of 7th Duke of Richmond and Gordon; *S* father, 1937; *m* 1st, 1930, Lady Lettice Lygon (marr. diss. 1958), *e d* of 7th Earl Beauchamp; two *s* two *d*; 2nd, 1958, Patricia Lady Sherwood, *d* of 1st Viscount Camrose. *Educ:* Eton; Sandhurst. Entered Royal Horse Guards, 1927; retd on to Reserve of Officers, 1932; entered Shropshire Yeo., 1935; Major, 1937; commanded 76th Shropshire Yeomanry Medium Regt RA in Middle East and Italy, 1943-45 (despatches). JP 1938. *Heir: s* John Henry Geers Cotterell [*b* 8 May 1935; *m* 1959, Vanda Alexandra Clare Bridgewater; three *s* one *d*]. *Address:* Garnons, Hereford. *T:* Bridge Sollers 232. *Club:* White's.
*See also Viscount Camrose, Baron Chetwode, Sir Terence Falkiner, Baron Sinclair.*

**COTTESLOE,** 4th Baron (UK) *cr* 1874; **John Walgrave Halford Fremantle,** GBE 1960; TD; Bt 1821; Baron of Austrian Empire, *cr* 1816; *b* 2 March 1900; *s* of 3rd Baron Cottesloe, CB and Florence (*d* 1956), *d* of Thomas Tapling; *S* father 1956; *m* 1st, 1926, Lady Elizabeth Harris (marr. diss., 1945), *o d* of 5th Earl of Malmesbury; one *s* one *d*; 2nd, 1959, Gloria Jean Irene Dunn; one *s* two *d. Educ:* Eton; Trinity Coll., Cambridge. BA (Hons) Mechanical Sciences 1921; MA 1924. DL of County of London; Chairman: Thomas Tapling & Co. Ltd; Yiewsley Engineering Co. Ltd; formerly Vice-Chm. of Port of London Authority; Chairman: South Bank Theatre Board; Advisory Council and Reviewing Cttee on Export of Works of Art; Hammersmith and St Mark's Hospital; British Postgraduate Medical Fedn; Nat. Rifle Assoc. Served as OC 251 (Bucks) AA Battery RA (TA), 1938-39; GSO 1 att. 2nd Armoured Division, 1940; Senior Military Liaison Officer to Regional Commissioner, NE Region, 1940-41; GSO 1 (Technical) AA Command, 1941-42; Commanding Officer, 20 LAA Regt RA, 1942-44; GSO 1 (Radar) War Office, 1944-45. Mem. LCC, 1945-55. Chairman: Royal Postgraduate Medical Sch., 1949-58; NW Met. Regional Hospital Bd, 1953-60; Tate Gallery, 1959-60; Arts Council of Gt Britain, 1960-65; Hon. Sec. Amateur Rowing Assoc., 1932-46; a Steward of Henley Royal Regatta; Pres., Leander, 1957-62. *Recreations:* rowed in winning crews in Oxford and Cambridge Boat Race, 1921 and 1922 and in Grand Challenge Cup, Henley, 1922; has shot in English VIII for Elcho Shield at Bisley on 37 occasions and won Match Rifle Championship six times, with many other first prizes for long-range shooting. *Heir: s* Comdr Hon. John Tapling Fremantle, (RN retd) [*b* 22 Jan. 1927; *m* 1958, Elizabeth Ann, *d* of Lieut-Col Henry Shelley Barker, Walcote House, Walcote, Rugby; one *s* two *d*]. *Address:* 21

Lyndhurst Road, NW3. *T:* 01-435 6626. *Clubs:* Travellers', Leander.

**COTTINGHAM, Dame Margaret;** *see* Teyte, Dame Maggie.

**COTTON, Sir Charles Andrew,** KBE 1959; DSc, LLD; FRSNZ; Emeritus Professor of Geology, Victoria University of Wellington, New Zealand, 1955 (Professor, 1921-54); *b* 24 Feb. 1885; *s* of Charles Henry Cotton; *m* 1926, Hilda Mary Josephine Gibbons; one *s* one *d.* *Educ:* Otago Univ. DSc 1915 (1st cl. hons). Dir Coromandel Sch. of Mines, 1908; Lecturer in charge of Dept of Geology, Victoria Coll., Wellington, 1909. Dumont Medal and Hon. Mem. Geol Soc. of Belgium; Victoria Medal of RGS; Hon. Fellow Geol Soc. America; For. and C'wealth Mem. Geol Soc. London; Hon. Fellow Edinburgh Geol Soc. Hon. LLD, University of New Zealand, 1955. *Publications:* Geomorphology of New Zealand. 1922; Landscape, 1941; Geomorphology, 1942; Climatic Accidents, 1942; Volcanoes as Landscape Forms, 1944; Earth Beneath, 1945; New Zealand Geomorphology, 1955. Papers in Trans Royal Society of NZ; NZ Geographer; NZ Jl of Science and Technology; NZ Science Review; NZ Jl of Geology and Geophysics; Geographical Jl; Scottish Geographical Jl; Jl of Geology; Geolog. Magazine; Amer. Jl of Science; Science; Scientific Monthly; Bulletin of Geolog. Soc. of America, and in learned jls of other foreign countries; reports of Internat. Geographical Congresses, etc. *Address:* 2 Manuka Avenue, Lower Hutt, New Zealand. *T:* 60-815.

**COTTON, Christopher P.;** *see* Powell-Cotton.

**COTTON, Prof. H.,** MBE 1918; DSc; *b* 17 June 1889; *s* of John Thomas and Sophia Cotton; *m* 1915, Lilian Hall; one *s.* *Educ:* Manchester Univ., resident at Hulme Hall. Asst Lecturer in Electrical Engineering and in Physics at Technical Coll., Huddersfield; Lecturer in Electrical Engineering at Technical Sch., St Helens; Lecturer at University Coll., Nottingham; Emeritus Prof. of Electrical Engineering at Nottingham Univ.; retired 1954; three years in France with the Meteorological Section RE during the war; practical training in Electrical Engineering at the Hanley Power Station and with the Westinghouse Electrical Co. Ltd. *Publications:* Electricity Applied to Mining; Mining Electrical Engineering; Design of Electrical Machinery; Advanced Electrical Technology; Electrical Transmission and Distribution; Electric Discharge Lamps; Principles of Illumination; Applied Electricity; Vector and Phasor Analysis of Electric Fields and Circuits; contributor to Journal of Institution of Electrical Engineers, World Power, Electrician, Electrical Review and Electrical Times. *Recreation:* music. *Addresss:* St George's Lodge, Cherry Tree Road, Woodbridge, Suffolk. *T:* 3111.

**COTTON, Henry;** *see* Cotton, T. H.

**COTTON, Sir John Richard,** KCMG 1969 (CMG 1959); OBE 1947; retired from HM Diplomatic Service, 1969; Adjudicator, Immigration Appeals; *b* 22 Jan. 1909; *s* of late J. J. Cotton, ICS, and late Gigia Ricciardi Arlotta; *m* 1937, Mary Bridget Connors, Stradbally, County Waterford, Ireland; three *s.* *Educ:* Wellington Coll.; RMC, Sandhurst (prize Cadet and King's India Cadet). Commissioned 1929; 8th King George's Own Light Cavalry (IA), 1930-34; transferred to Indian Political Service, 1934; served in: Aden, Abyssinia (Attaché HM Legation, 1935), Persian Gulf, Rajputana, Hyderabad, Kathiawar, Baroda, New Delhi (Dep. Sec. Political Dept). Transferred to HM Foreign Service, 1947; served in Karachi (First Sec.), 1947-48, Foreign Office, 1949-51, Madrid (Counsellor [Commercial] HM Embassy), 1951-54; Consul-Gen., Brazzaville, 1954-55, Leopoldville, 1955-57; Counsellor (Commercial), HM Embassy, Brussels, 1957-62. Consul-Gen., São Paulo, Brazil, 1962-65; Ambassador to Congo Republic (Kinshasa), and to Burundi, 1965-69. *Recreations:* golf, tennis, photography. *Address:* Lansing House, Hartley Wintney, Hants. *T:* Hartley Wintney 2681. *Club:* United Service.

**COTTON, Leonard Thomas,** MCh; FRCS; Surgeon, King's College Hospital, since 1957; Surgeon, Queen Victoria Hospital, East Grinstead, and St Luke's Nursing Home for the Clergy; *b* 5 Dec. 1922; *s* of Edward Cotton and Elizabeth (*née* Webb); *m* 1946, Frances Joanna Bryan; one *s* two *d.* *Educ:* King's College Sch., Wimbledon; Oriel Coll., Oxford; King's Coll. Hospital. MRCS, LRCP 1946; BM, BCh Oxon 1946; FRCS 1950; MCh Oxon 1957. House Surgeon, King's College Hospital, 1946; Resident Surgical Officer, Royal Waterloo Hospital, 1947; Resident Surgical Officer, Weymouth and District Hospital, 1948; National Service, Surgical Specialist RAMC, 1949-51; Senior Registrar and Registrar, King's College Hospital, 1951-57; Surgical Tutor, King's Coll. Hospital Medical Sch., 1957-65. FRSM; Mem., Surgical Research Soc., Association of Surgeons. *Publications:* (ed) Hey Groves' Synopsis of Surgery; co-author, short text-book of Surgery; contributions to medical journals. *Recreations:* gardening, reading, squash. *Address:* 126 College Road, SE19. *T:* 01-670 7156; Private Wing, King's College Hospital, Denmark Hill, SE5. T: 01-274 8670.

**COTTON, Michael James,** ARIBA, AMTPI; Director of Defence Services II, Ministry of Public Building and Works, since 1969; *b* 22 Dec. 1920; *s* of Clifford Cotton and Mildred L. (*née* Palmer); *m* 1945, Dorsey Jane (*née* Thomas); one *d.* *Educ:* School of Architecture and Dept of Civic Design, Liverpool University. War Service, 1940-46, Royal Marines 42 Commando (Captain). Asst Town Planner, Staffs CC, 1949-50; Architect Planner, Stevenage Development Corp., 1950-52; Asst Town Planner, Fedn of Malaya, 1952-54; Architect and Sen. Architect, Public Works Dept, Singapore, 1954-59; Sen. Architect, Directorate of Works, WO, 1959-64; Chm. Joint Post Office/MPBW R&D Group, 1964-66; Chief Architect, Scottish Office, 1966-67; Asst Dir Overseas Services, MPBW, 1967-69. *Recreation:* golf. *Address:* 14 Rectory Close, Merrow, Guildford, Surrey. *T:* Guildford 68808.

**COTTON, (Thomas) Henry,** MBE 1946; late Flight Lieutenant RAFVR (invalided, 1943); golfer; Golf Manager, Penina Golf Hotel; Professional Golf Correspondent of Golf Illustrated; Director and Founder Golf Foundation for development of youthful golfers; attached Temple Golf Club, Maidenhead (as Professional); Golf Course Architect: Abridge, Felixstowe, Canons Brook, Ampfield, Megève and Deauville (France), Penina and Val de Lobo (Portugal), Castle Eden Golf Club, Eaglescliffe, Mountain Springs (Ireland), Stirling, Gourock, Windmill Hill, Bletchley, Sene Valley, Folkstone, etc; *b* Holmes Chapel, Cheshire, 26 Jan. 1907; *m* 1939, Mrs Maria Isabel Estanguet Moss. *Educ:* Alleyn's Sch. Played in first Boys' Golf Championship, 1921; asst at Fulwell, 1924; Rye, 1925; Cannes, 1926; professional Langley Park, 1927; Waterloo, Brussels, 1933;

Ashridge, 1936; won Kent Professional Championship, 1926-27-28-29-30; Belgian Open, 1930, 1934, 1938; Dunlop Tournament, 1931, 1932, 1953, runner-up, 1959; News of the World Tournament, 1932 and 1939; British Open, 1934, 1937 and 1948 (1934 was First British win for 11 years); Italian Open, 1936; German Open, 1937-38-39; Silver King Tournament, 1937; Czechoslovak Open, 1937-38; Harry Vardon Trophy, 1938; Daily Mail £2000 Tournament, 1939; Penfold Tournament, 1939 and 1954; News Chronicle Tournament, 1945; Star Tournament, 1946; Prof. Golfers' Assoc. Match Play Champion, 1946; French Open Champion, 1946 and 1947; Vichy Open Champion, 1946; represented Great Britain v America, 1929, 1937, 1947, 1953; Ryder Cup Team Capt., 1939, 1947 and 1953; Spalding Tournament, 1947; visited USA in 1929, 1931, 1947, 1948, 1956 and 1957; visited Argentine 1929, 1948, 1949 and 1950; lowest record round in Open Championships (65), held until 1964. Collected over £70,000 for Red Cross and other war charities in 130 matches organised by himself. Hon. Life Mem., Professional Golf Assoc. Vice-Pres., National Golf Clubs Advisory Bureau. *Publications:* Golf, 1932; This Game of Golf, 1948; My Swing, 1952; (Henry Cotton's) My Golfing Album, 1960; Henry Cotton Says, 1962; Studying the Golf Game, 1964; The Picture World of Golf, 1965; Golf in the British Isles, 1969. *Recreations:* painting, motoring, photography. *Address:* Penina Golf Hotel, Portimas, Portugal.

**COTTON, Lt-Col (Bt Col) Vere Egerton,** CBE 1937; TD; Hon. LLD; retired; Member, Liverpool Cathedral Committee; *b* 5 May 1888; *s* of late Charles Calveley Cotton; *m* 1922, Elfreda Helen, *d* of W. F. Moore; three *s.* *Educ:* Repton; Magdalene Coll., Cambridge (Exhibitioner; MA). Served in Artillery, TA, 1911-36; European War, France, Belgium and Italy, 1915-19 (despatches thrice, OBE, Croix de Guerre, Croce di Guerra); commanded 59th (4th W Lancs) Medium Bde RA TA, 1932-36. Hon. Col 470 LAA Regt (TA), 1952-56. Pro-Chancellor, Liverpool Univ., 1942-54; Chm., Liverpool Libraries, Museums and Arts Cttee, 1939-55; Mem. of Arts Council, 1954-59; Co-opted Mem., Art and Culture Cttee, Liverpool City Council; Lord Mayor of Liverpool, 1951-52; High Sheriff of County Palatine of Lancashire, 1956-57; Hon. Alderman, Liverpool, 1964. Hon. LLD Liverpool, 1953. *Publication:* Book of Liverpool Cathedral. *Recreation:* travel. *Address:* Langdale, Grassendale Park, Liverpool L19 0LP. *T:* 051-427 1196. *Clubs:* Old Hall, Exhange, Palatine (Liverpool).

**COTTON, STAPLETON-,** family name of **Viscount Combermere.**

**COTTRELL, Dr Alan Howard,** FRS 1955; Deputy Chief Scientific Adviser to HM Government, since 1968; *b* 17 July 1919; *s* of Albert and Elizabeth Cottrell; *m* 1944, Jean Elizabeth Harber; one *s.* *Educ:* Moseley Grammar Sch.; University of Birmingham. BSc 1939; PhD 1942. Lectr in Metallurgy, University of Birmingham, 1943; Prof. of Physical Metallurgy, University of Birmingham, 1949-55; retired March 1955. Deputy Head of Metallurgy Division, Atomic Energy Research Establishment, Harwell, Berks, 1955-58; Goldsmiths' Prof. of Metallurgy, Cambridge Univ., 1958-65; Dep. Chief Scientific Adviser (Studies), Min. of Defence, 1965-67, Chief Adviser, 1967. Part-time Mem., UKAEA, 1962-65; Member: Adv. Council on Scientific Policy, 1963-64; Central Adv. Council for Science and Technology, 1967-. A Vice-Pres., Royal Society, 1964. Fellow Royal Swedish Academy of Sciences; Hon. Fellow, Christ's Coll., Cambridge, 1970 (Fellow, 1958-70). foreign Hon. Mem., American Academy of Arts and Sciences, 1960; Hon. DSc: Columbia Univ., 1965; Newcastle Univ., 1967; Liverpool Univ., 1969; Manchester, 1970. Rosenhain Medallist of the Inst. of Metals; Hughes Medallist, Royal Society, 1961; Inst. of Metals (Platinum) Medal, 1965; Réamur Medal, Société Française de Métallurgie, 1964; James Alfred Ewing Medal, ICE, 1967; Holweck Medal, Société Française de Physique, 1969; Albert Sauveur Achievement Award, Amer. Soc. for Metals, 1969. *Publications:* Theoretical Structural Metallurgy, 1948, 2nd edn 1955; Dislocations and Plastic Flow in Crystals, 1953; The Mechanical Properties of Matter, 1964; Theory of Crystal Dislocations, 1964; An Introduction to Metallurgy, 1967; scientific papers to various learned journals. *Recreation:* music. *Address:* 19 Madingley Road, Cambridge. *Club:* Athenæum.

**COTTRELL, Sir Edward (Baglietto),** Kt 1957; CBE 1946 (OBE 1943); JP; Chairman of Saccone & Speed Ltd since 1938; retired as British Consul, Algeciras, Spain; *b* 5 May 1896; *s* of late Capt. William Henry Cottrell, CMG, OBE, RNVR; *m* 1926, Josephine, *o d* of late Dr J. Baggetto; two *s* two *d.* *Educ:* King's Sch., Canterbury. Dir Gibraltar Chamber of Commerce, 1923, Vice-President, 1943; Authorised Officer Exports and Imports, 1939; Chm. and Officer Administration City Council, 1940-45; Chm. Evacuation Cttee, 1940; Unofficial Mem. Executive Council, 1941-51. JP Gibraltar, 1939. Former President, Sandpits Lawn Tennis Club. *Recreations:* shooting, tennis. *Address:* 4 Library Street, Gibraltar. *T:* A4571. *Clubs:* Royal Gibraltar Yacht, Mediterranean Racing (Gibraltar).

**COTTRELL, Kathleen Lila,** MA Cantab; JP; Headmistress, Manchester High School for Girls, since 1959; *b* 4 Dec. 1914; *d* of W. George Cottrell, JP, Company Dir, and Dorothy K. Cottrell. *Educ:* Colston's Girls' Sch., Bristol; Girton Coll., Cambridge. Asst Mistress (Classics), 1937-49: Elmhurst Sch., Street, Som; Swansea High Sch.; St George's Sch., Edinburgh. Head Mistress: Ackworth Sch., Yorks, 1949-52; Carlisle and County High Sch., 1952-59. JP Manchester City, 1968. *Recreations:* music, gardening, daydreaming. *Address:* 7 Rodmill Court, 24a Wilbraham Road, Manchester 14. *T:* 061-224 7044.

**COTTRELL, Leonard;** author; writer and producer for radio and television; *b* Tettenhall Staffs, 21 May 1913; *s* of William and Beatrice Cottrell; *m* 1940, Doris Swain (marr. diss., 1960); no *c*; *m* 1965, Diana, *d* of Roy and Deidre Randolph. *Educ:* King Edward's Grammar Sch., Birmingham. Worked first in manufacturer's advertising dept and as free-lance writer for BBC. Joined BBC as writer/producer (Features), 1942. War Correspondent, 1944-45; Sen. Producer, 1946; seconded UNESCO, 1951-53; joined BBC Television (Drama) as writer/producer, 1956; resigned to concentrate on authorship and free-lance radio and television writing, 1960. *Publications:* All Men are Neighbours, 1947; The Lost Pharaohs, 1950; The Bull of Minos, 1953; Madame Tussaud, 1954; Life under the Pharaohs, 1955; Seeing Roman Britain, 1956; The Mountains of Pharaoh, 1956; Lost Cities, 1957; The Great Invasion, 1958; Anvil of Civilisation, 1958; Concise Encyclopaedia of Archæology (ed), 1960; Land of the Pharaohs, 1960; Enemy of Rome, 1961; Wonders of Antiquity, 1961; The Tiger of Ch'in, 1962; Lost Worlds, Land of the Two Rivers, 1962;

The Lion Gate, 1963; Guide to Egypt, Digs and Diggers, Tutankhamun, 1964; Land of Shinar, 1965; Queens of the Pharaohs, 1966; The Warrior Pharaohs, 1968; Reading the Past, 1969. *Recreations:* archæology, music, history, fast cars. *Address:* 217 Station Road, Knowle, Solihull, Warwicks. *T:* Knowle 5789. *Club:* Savile.

**COTTRELL, Tom Leadbetter;** first Principal and Vice-Chancellor of Stirling University since 1965; *b* 8 June 1923; *s* of late Allin Cottrell and of Mrs Lily Cottrell; *m* 1950, Marie, *e d* of E. A. Findlay, Fairlie; two *s*. *Educ:* George Watson's Boys' Coll.; Edinburgh Univ. BSc 1943, DSc 1958. Joined Research Dept ICI (Explosives) Ltd, 1943; seconded to do research at the Physical Chemistry Laboratory, Oxford, 1946-48; research on Physical Chemistry and Blasting Explosives with Nobel Division of ICI, 1948-58; on Directorate Staff of ICI, 1958-59; Prof. of Chem., University of Edinburgh, 1959-66. Mem., Council for Scientific Policy, 1969-. Meldola Medalist, 1952. *Publications:* The Strengths of Chemical Bonds, 1954, 2nd edn 1958; (with J. C. McCoubrey) Molecular Energy Transfer in Gases, 1961; Chemistry, 1963; Dynamic Aspects of Molecular Energy States, 1965; papers in various scientific jls. *Recreations:* yacht racing, looking at pictures. *Address:* The University of Stirling, Stirling. *Clubs:* Scottish Arts (Edinburgh); Royal Forth Yacht.

**COTTS, Sir Crichton Mitchell;** *see* Cotts, Sir R. C. M.

**COTTS, Sir (Robert) Crichton Mitchell,** 3rd Bt, *cr* 1921; *b* 22 Oct. 1903; *yr s* of Sir William Dingwall Mitchell Cotts, 1st Bt, KBE, MP (*d* 1932), and Agnes Nivison (*d* 1966), 2nd *d* of late Robert Sloane; *S* brother, 1964; *m* 1942, Barbara, *o d* of late Capt. Herbert J. A. Throckmorton, Royal Navy; two *s* three *d*. *Heir: s* Richard Crichton Mitchell Cotts, *b* 26 July 1946. *Address:* 37 Queen's Grove, NW8.

**COUCH, William Charles Milford,** CB 1956; CBE 1946; FIEE; Deputy Director of Electrical Engineering, Admiralty, 1941-59; *b* 24 Aug. 1894; *s* of Samson H. E. Couch, RN; *m* 1919, Dorothy, *d* of Henry Charles Mosson, Gillingham, Kent; one *s* one *d*. *Educ:* Mathematical Sch., Rochester; HM Dockyard Sch., Chatham; RN Coll., Greenwich. Dockyard apprentice, 1909-14; Admiralty Scholarship, RN Coll., Greenwich, 1914-16; sea service, 1920-22; successive ranks in electrical engineering dept, serving at Admiralty Engineering Laboratory, West Drayton, Chatham and Malta; at Admiralty as Asst Dir of Electrical Engineering, 1937-41. *Address:* Kenilworth, Hayesfield Park, Bath. *T:* Bath 22888.

**COUCHMAN, Dame Elizabeth (May Ramsay),** DBE 1961 (OBE 1941); JP; BA; *b* 1878; *d* of late Archibald Tannock and Elizabeth Ramsay Tannock; *m* 1917, Claude Ernest Couchman (decd). *Educ:* University of Western Australia (BA). President, Australian Women's National League, 1927-45; Mem., Australian Broadcasting Commission, 1932-42; Senior Vice-Pres., Royal Commonwealth Soc., 1950-61; office-bearer in many educational, patriotic and social-service organisations. Life Member: National Council of Women (Vic.); Liberal Party (Vic.). *Publications:* articles in the press on Liberal politics and current topics. *Address:* 51 Mathoura Road, Toorak, Melbourne, Australia. *T:* 24 3841. *Clubs:* Lyceum, Australian Women's Liberal (Melbourne).

**COUCHMAN, Adm. (retired) Sir Walter (Thomas),** KCB 1958 (CB 1954); CVO 1953; OBE 1939; DSO 1942; *b* 1905. *s* of Malcolm Edward Couchman, CSI, and Emily Elizabeth Ranking; *m* 1937, Phyllida Georgina Connellan (marriage dissolved, 1965); one *s* two *d*; *m* 1965, Mrs Hughe Hunter Blair, *widow* of Lieut-Col D. W. Hunter Blair. *Educ:* RN Colleges Osborne and Dartmouth. Specialised in Naval Aviation, 1928; Staff Coll., 1935; Comdr 1938; Capt. 1942; qualified Naval Pilot; comd HMS Glory, 1946; Dir of Naval Air Org. and Trg, Admty, 1947; Flag Officer Flying Trg, 1951; Rear-Adm., 1952; Flag Officer, Aircraft Carriers, 1954; Deputy Controller of Supplies (Air), Ministry of Supply, 1955-56; Vice-Adm. 1956; Flag Officer Air (Home), 1957-60; Adm. 1959; Vice-Chief, Naval Staff, Admiralty, 1960. *Address:* Moultons, Clopton Corner, Woodbridge, Suffolk. *Club:* United Hunts.

**COUDENHOVE-KALERGI, Richard N.,** DrPhil, Count; President Paneuropean Union; formerly Professor at New York University, and at Tokyo; *b* 16 Nov. 1894; *s* of Count Henri Coudenhove-Kalergi and Mitsou Aoyama; *m* Ida Roland (*d* 1951); one *d*; *m* 1952, Countess Alix Tiele-Bally (*d* 1968). *Educ:* Theresianic Acad., Vienna, DrPhil; founded Paneuropean Union and started PE Movement, 1923; first PE Congress, Vienna, 1926; second Congress, Berlin, 1929; third Congress, Basel, 1932; fourth Congress, Vienna, 1935; fifth Pan-European Congress, New York, 1943; sixth Pan-European Congress, Baden Baden, 1954; seventh Pan-European Congress, Baden Baden, 1955; eighth Congress Bad Ragaz, 1957; ninth Congress, Nice, 1960; founded European Parliamentary Union, 1947; European Parliamentary Congresses: first, Gstaad, 1947; second, Interlaken, 1948; third, Venice, 1949; fourth, Constance, 1950. Awarded first Charlemagne Prize (with gold medal), by City of Aachen, 1950; Sonning Prize, Copenhagen University, 1965; Japanese Peace Prize, 1967. Hon. Citizen of Frankfurt Univ., 1953; Hon. Chairman: European Movement, 1952; Yuai Movement, Tokyo, 1954. french Legion of Honour, 1954 (officer, 1963); Grand Cross of Merit, 1955; Grand Silver Decoration with star (Austria), 1962. *Publications:* Ethik U Hyperethik; Krise der Weltanschauung; Praktischer Idealismus; Paneuropa; Held oder Heiliger; Los vom Materialismus; Kampf um Paneuropa; Gebote des Lebens; Stalin and Co.; Revolution durch Technik; Europa Erwacht!, 1934; Europa ohne Elend, 1936; The Totalitarian State Against Man, 1938; Europe Must Unite, 1939; Crusade for Pan Europe, 1943; Europe seeks Unity, 1949; Kampf um Europa, 1949; An Idea conquers the World, 1953; In Memoriam Ida Roland, 1951; Die Europaeische Nation, 1953; Vom ewigen Krieg zum grossen Frieden, 1956; Eine Idee erobert Europa, 1958; From War to Peace, 1959; Die Wiedervereinigung Europas, 1964. Revue: (1924-38) Paneuropean (in French and German). *Address:* Leonhardsgraben 16, Bâle, Switzerland.

**COUGHTRIE, Thomas,** CBE 1958; Chairman, Bruce Peebles Industries Ltd, and Bruce Peebles Ltd, Edinburgh, 1961-67; *b* 28 Oct. 1895; *m* 1918, Mary Morrison; one *s* two *d*. *Educ:* Royal Coll. of Science, Glasgow. Founded Belmos Co. Ltd, Elect. Engrs, 1919 (merged with Bruce Peebles & Co. Ltd, Edinburgh, 1961); Mem. Royal Fine Art Commn for Scotland, 1962-67; Chm. Valuation Appeals Cttee, Co. Lanark, 1956-; Director: Scottish Mutual Assurance Soc.; Ailsa Investment Trust Ltd; Alva Investment Trust Ltd. JP Lanark, 1959. Hon. LLD Glasgow, 1959; Hon. DSc Heriot-Watt, 1968.

*Recreations:* golf, gardening, reading. *Address:* Orchard House, Crossford, Carluke, Lanarkshire. *T:* Crossford 203. *Clubs:* Athenæum, Devonshire; Western (Glasgow).

**COULDREY, Robert Charles,** CBE 1942; *b* 5 June 1890; *e s* of late Henry Robert and Josephine Couldrey; *m* 1931, Honorine Oonagh, *o d* of late Travers Blackley; one *s* one *d*. *Educ:* United Services Coll., Windsor. Served European War, France, 1915-18; Capt. RFA 1917 (despatches); seconded Egyptian Army, 1918; Sudan Government, 1918; Dir Commercial Intelligence Branch, 1931; Dir of Customs, 1935; Pres. Sudan Resources Board, 1940; Mem. of Governor-General's Council, 1940-44; Controller-Gen. of War Supply, Sudan Government, 1941-44 (despatches); Ministry of Supply, 1944; Board of Trade, 1947; retired 1953. Order of the Nile, 1936. *Address:* Sparks Cottage, Northiam, Sussex. *T:* Staplecross 352. *Clubs:* Royal Commonwealth Society; Sudan (Khartoum).

**COULSHAW, Rev. Leonard,** CB 1949; MC 1917; FKC; *b* 24 Feb. 1896; *s* of late Percy Dean Coulshaw and late Alice Maud Hatt; *m* 1932, Yvonne Cecilia Joan, *d* of Rev. C. Hanmer-Strudwick, Rector of Slawston, Leics; no *c*. *Educ:* Southend-on-Sea High Sch. for Boys; King's Coll., London; Ely Theological Coll. Served European War, 1914-18, Essex Regiment, 1914-20 (MC, despatches); left Army with rank of Captain. Ordained, 1923; Curate, St Andrew's, Romford, Essex; commissioned as Chaplain, RN, 1927; served in HMS Cyclops, 1927-29; RN Barracks, Portsmouth, 1929; HMS Iron Duke, 1929-30; HMS Effingham (Flagship East Indies Station), 1930-32; Royal Hospital Sch., Holbrook, 1932-34; Senior Chaplain HMS Ganges, 1934-37; HMS Royal Sovereign, 1937 (present at Coronation Review, Spithead); HMS Revenge, 1937. Chaplain Royal Naval Hospital, Malta, 1937-40; RM Depot, Lympstone, 1940-42; Senior Chaplain, RN Base, Lyness, 1942-44; Chaplain HM Dockyard, Sheerness, 1944-46; RM Barracks, Portsmouth, 1946-47; Chaplain of the Fleet and Archdeacon of the Royal Navy, 1948-52; KHC, 1948-52; QHC, 1952; Vicar of: West End, Southampton, 1952-54; Frensham, 1954-65. *Recreation:* gardening. *Address:* 4 Pound Close, Hilland, Headley, Bordon, Hants. *T:* Headley Down 2519.

**COULSHED, Dame (Mary) Frances,** DBE 1953 (CBE 1949); TD 1951; Brigadier, Women's Royal Army Corps, retired; *b* 10 Nov. 1904; *d* of Wilfred and Maud Coulshed. *Educ:* Parkfields Cedars, Derby; Convent of the Sacred Heart, Kensington. Served War of 1939-45 (despatches); North-West Europe, 1944-45, with General Headquarters Anti-Aircraft Troops and at Headquarters Lines of Communications; Deputy Dir, Anti-Aircraft Command, 1946-50; Dep. Dir, War Office, July-Dec. 1950; ADC to the King, 1951, to the Queen, 1951-54; Dir, WRAC, 1951-Sept. 1954. Order of Leopold I of Belgium with palm, Croix de Guerre with palm, 1946. *Address:* 815 Endsleigh Court, Upper Woburn Place, WC1.

**COULSON, Charles Alfred,** FRS 1950; MA, PhD Cantab; DSc St Andrews; FRSE; FInstP; FIMA; Rouse Ball Professor of Mathematics at Oxford University, and Fellow of Wadham College, Oxford, since 1952; *b* 1910; *m* 1938, Eileen Florence Burrett; two *s* two *d* (and one *s* decd). Formerly: Fellow of Trinity Coll., Cambridge; Lecturer, Department of Mathematics, University of St Andrews, at University Coll., Dundee; College Lecturer in Mathematics, University Coll., Oxford; ICI Fellow in Chemistry, Physical Chemistry Laboratory, Oxford; Prof. of Theoretical Physics, King's Coll., University of London, 1947-52. Firth Vis. Prof., Sheffield, 1969. Lectures: Riddell, Newcastle, 1953; Rede, Cambridge, 1954; McNair, Chapel Hill, NC, USA, 1954; Bruce Preller, Royal Society of Edinburgh, 1956; Firth, Nottingham, 1957; Eddington Memorial, 1958; Fisher Baker, Cornell Univ., 1959; George B. Pegram, Brookhaven, 1961; Silvanus Thompson, 1963; Sir D. Owen Evans, Aberystwyth, 1966; Faraday, London, 1967; Freemantle, Oxford, 1968. Member: Council, Royal Society, 1964-65; Central Cttee, World Council of Churches, 1962-68; Pres., Mathematical Assoc., 1968-69; Vice-Pres. Methodist Conference, 1959. Pierre Lecomte de Nouy Prize, 1955. Hon. Member: American Academy of Arts and Sciences, 1963; New York Academy of Sciences, 1956; Royal Socs of Liège and Brussels. Chm. of Oxfam, 1965-. Hon. DSc: E Anglia; Leicester; Dunedin; Hon. DTech Bradford, 1970. *Publications:* four scientific textbooks and about 350 research papers, chiefly in the fields of quantum theory and theoretical chemistry; 3 general books and many articles on relation between science and religion. *Address:* Mathematical Institute, 24-29 St Giles, Oxford OX1 3LB; Wadham College, Oxford; 64 Old Road, Headington, Oxford OX3 7LN. *T:* Oxford 62825.

**COULSON, (James) Michael;** Barrister-at-Law; Deputy Chairman: Northern Agricultural Land Tribunal, since 1967; Quarter Sessions, North riding of Yorks, since 1968; a Chairman of Industrial Tribunals, since 1968; *b* 23 Nov. 1927; *s* of William Coulson, Fulwith Grange, Harrogate; *m* 1955, Dilys Adair, *d* of David Webster Jones, Knapton Hall, Malton, Yorkshire; one *s*. *Educ:* Fulneck Sch., Yorks; Merton Coll., Oxford; Royal Agricultural Coll., Cirencester. Served E Riding Yeomanry (Wenlocks Horse); Queen's Own Yorks Yeomanry (Major). Called to Bar, Middle Temple, 1951; Mem. North Eastern Circuit. Former Mem., Tadcaster RDC. Sometime Sec. Bramham Moor and York and Ainsty Point to Point Race Meetings. MP (C) Kingston-upon-Hull North, 1959-64; Mem., Executive Cttee, Conservative Commonwealth Council; Parliamentary Private Sec. to the Solicitor-Gen., 1962-64. Asst Recorder of Sheffield, 1965-. *Recreations:* hunting, reading, travel. *Address:* Elm House, Coxwold, York; 5 King's Bench Walk, Temple, EC4. *Clubs:* Cavalry; Yorkshire.

**COULSON, Sir John Eltringham,** KCMG 1957 (CMG 1946); Secretary-General of EFTA since Nov. 1965; *b* 13 Sept. 1909; *er s* of H. J. Coulson, Bickley, Kent; *m* 1944, Mavis Ninette Beazley; two *s*. *Educ:* Rugby; Corpus Christi Coll., Cambridge. Entered Diplomatic Service in 1932. Served in Bucharest, Min. of Econ. Warfare, War Cabinet Office, Foreign Office and Paris. Sometime Dep. UK representative to UN, New York; Asst Under-Sec., Foreign Office, 1952-55; Minister British Embassy, Washington, 1955-57; Asst to Paymaster-Gen., 1957-60; Ambassador to Sweden, 1960-63; Dep. Under-Sec. of State, Foreign Office, 1963-65; Chief of Administration of HM Diplomatic Service, Jan.-Sept. 1965. *Recreations:* fishing, golf. *Address:* EFTA, Geneva, Switzerland; The Old Mill, Selborne, Hants. *Club:* St James'.

**COULSON, Prof. John Metcalfe;** Professor of Chemical Engineering, University of Newcastle upon Tyne (formerly University of Durham), since 1954 (on leave of absence to Heriot-Watt University, 1968-69); *b* 13 Dec. 1910; *m* 1943, Clarice Dora Scott (*d* 1961); two *s*; *m* 1965, Christine Gould; one *d*. *Educ:*

Clifton Coll.; Christ's Coll., Cambridge; Imperial Coll. Royal Arsenal, Woolwich, 1935-39; Asst Lectr, Imperial Coll., 1939; Ministry of Supply, 1939-45; Lectr in Chem. Engineering, Imperial Coll., 1945-52; Reader, 1952-54. *Publications:* Chemical Engineering Vol. I and Vol. II (with Prof. J. F. Richardson), 1954 and 1955, 2nd edn 1964. Contrib. Instn of Chem. Eng, Chem. Eng Science, etc. *Recreations:* chess, photography. *Address:* 12 Northumberland Avenue, Newcastle upon Tyne NE3 4XE. *T:* Newcastle 856855.

**COULSON, Michael;** *see* Coulson, J. M.

**COULSON, Maj.-Gen. Samuel M.;** *see* Moore-Coulson.

**COULTAS, William Whitham,** CBE 1943; *b* 17 Feb. 1890; *s* of Rev. G. W. Coultas; *m* 1919, Joyce Visger Lloyd; one *s* (one *d* decd). *Educ:* St Lawrence Coll.; Sidney Sussex Coll., Cambridge. Student interpreter in Thailand, 1913; Consul at Medan, 1930; Chiengmai, 1933; Consul-Gen., Saigon, 1937-38; Counsellor of Legation and HBM Consul-Gen. at Bangkok, 1938-41. *Recreations:* golf, gardening. *Address:* The Field House, Fleet, Hants. *T:* Fleet 6310.

**COULTHARD, William Henderson,** CBE 1968; MSc, CEng, FIMechE, FRPS; Deputy Director, Royal Armament Research and Development Establishment, since 1962; *b* 24 Nov. 1913; *s* of William and Louise Coulthard, Flimby, Cumberland; *m* 1942, Peggie Frances Platts Taylor, Chiselhurst; one *d* (one *s* decd). *Educ:* Flimby, Workington Schs; Armstrong Coll., University of Durham. Mather Schol., University of Durham, 1932. Linen Industry Research Assoc., 1934; Instrument Dept, Royal Aircraft Estabt, 1935; Air Ministry HQ, 1939; Sqdn Ldr RAFVR, 1944; Official German Translator, 1945; Air Photography Div., RAE, 1946; Supt, later Dep. Dir, Fighting Vehicles Research and Development Estabt, 1951. *Publications:* Aircraft Instrument Design, 1951; Aircraft Engineer's Handbook, 1953; (trans.) Mathematical Instruments (Capellen), 1948; (trans.) Gyroscopes (Grammel), 1950; articles in technical journals. *Recreations:* art history (Diploma in History of Art, London Univ., 1964); languages. *Address:* Argyll, Francis Close, Ewell, Surrey. *T:* 01-337 4909.

**COUNSELL, John William;** Director of the Theatre Royal, Windsor, since 1938; *b* 24 April 1905; *s* of Claude Christopher Counsell and Evelyn Counsell (*née* Fleming); *m* 1939, Mary Antoinette Kerridge; twin *d. Educ:* Sedbergh Sch.; Exeter Coll., Oxford. Mem. of the OUDS, 1923-26; formerly engaged as a tutor. First appearance on professional stage, Playhouse, Oxford, 1928; two tours of Canada with Maurice Colbourne in Shavian Repertory, 1928-29; leading juvenile, Northampton and Folkstone Repertory Cos, 1929-30; Stage Manager for Baliol Holloway's production of Richard III, New, 1930; Stage Dir, Scenic Artist and eventually Producer, Oxford Repertory Company, 1930-33; Producer and Joint Man.-Dir, Windsor Repertory Company, 1933-34; Lover's Leap, Vaudeville, 1934; toured as Tubbs in Sweet Aloes, 1936; toured S Africa in The Frog, 1936-37; refounded Windsor Repertory Co., 1938. Called to the Colours as Territorial reservist, 1940; served in N Africa, France and Germany, 1942-45; Mem. planning staff of SHAEF; demobilised, 1945, rank of Lieut-Col. Resumed direction of Theatre Royal, Windsor. Has, in addition, produced: Birthmark, Playhouse, 1947; Little Holiday, 1948; Captain Brassbound's Conversion, Lyric, Hammersmith, 1948; The Man with the Umbrella, Duchess, 1950; Who Goes There!, Vaudeville, 1951; His House in Order, 1951; Waggon Load of Monkeys, Savoy, 1951; For Better for Worse, Comedy, 1952; Anastasia, St James's, 1953; Grab Me a Gondola, Lyric, 1956; Three Way Switch, Aldwych, 1958; How Say You?, Aldwych, 1959. Governor, E Berks Coll. of Further Educn. *Publication:* Counsell's Opinion (autobiography), 1963. *Recreations:* gardening, photography. *Address:* 3 Queen's Terrace, Windsor, Berks. *T:* Windsor 65344. *Club:* Green Room.

**COUPER, Sir Guy,** 4th Bt, *cr* 1841; *b* 12 March 1889; *s* of Sir Ramsay Couper, 3rd Bt and Norah (*d* 1925), *d* of Horatio Wilson Scott; *S* father 1949. Served European War, 1916-18. *Heir: kinsman* George Robert Cecil Couper [*b* 15 Oct. 1898; *m* 1941, Margaret Grace, *d* of late R. G. D. Thomas; one *s* one *d*(*twins*)]. *Address:* 350 Station Street, Box Hill, Melbourne, Vic., Australia.

**COUPLAND, Prof. Rex Ernest;** Professor of Human Morphology, University of Nottingham, since 1967; *b* 30 Jan. 1924; *s* of Ernest Coupland, company dir; *m* 1947, Lucy Eileen Sargent; one *s* one *d*. *Educ:* Mirfield Grammar Sch.; University of Leeds. MB, ChB with honours, 1947; MD with distinction, 1952; PhD 1954; DSc 1970. House appointments, Leeds General Infirmary, 1947; Demonstrator and Lecturer in Anatomy, University of Leeds, 1948, 1950-58; Asst Prof. of Anatomy, University of Minnesota, USA, 1955-56; Prof. of Anatomy, Queen's Coll., Dundee, University of St Andrews, 1958-67. Medical Officer, RAF, 1948-50. FRSE 1960. Mem., Biological Research Board of MRC, 1964-. *Publications:* The Natural History of the Chromaffin Cell, 1965; papers in jls of anatomy, physiology, endocrinology, pathology and pharmacology on endocrine and nervous systems; chapter on Anatomy of the Human Kidney, on Renal Disease (ed Black), 1962; Asst Editor, Gray's Anatomy (ed Davies), 1967. *Recreations:* tennis, photography, gardening. *Address:* Olive Quill, Nottingham Road, Ravenshead, near Nottingham. *T:* Blidworth 3518.

**COURAGE, Edward Raymond,** CBE 1964; Director: National Westminster Bank Ltd; Courage, Barclay & Simonds Ltd; Midland Marts Ltd; *b* 29 Sept. 1906; *er s* of Raymond Courage; *m* 1948, Hermione Mary Elizabeth, *er d* of Lt-Col Sir John Reynolds, 2nd Bt, MBE; one *s. Educ:* Eton; Trinity Coll., Cambridge. High Sheriff of Northants, 1953-54. *Recreations:* racing, shooting, fishing. *Address:* Edgcote, Banbury, Oxfordshire; 31 Abbotsbury House, Abbotsbury Road, W14. *Clubs:* Garrick, Jockey.

**COURAGE, Richard Hubert,** JP; Chairman of Courage, Barclay & Simonds Ltd (formerly Courage & Barclay Ltd), since 1959; *b* 23 Jan. 1915; *s* of Raymond Courage and Mildred Frances Courage (formerly Fisher); *m* 1941, Jean Elizabeth Agnes Watson, *d* of late Sir Charles Cuningham Watson, KCIE, CSI, ICS; two *s* (and one *s* decd). *Educ:* Eton. Served War of 1939-45: Northants Yeomanry, 1939-46, Major (despatches). Dir, Courage & Co, 1948; Chm. Courage, Barclay & Simonds Ltd, 1959; Dir, Fowler Ltd, 1959; Mem. London Advisory Board, Norwich Union Insurance Group. JP Essex, 1955. *Recreations:* yachting and shooting. *Address:* Fitzwalters, Shenfield, Essex. *T:* Brentwood 191.

**COURATIN, Rev. Canon Arthur Hubert;** Sixth Canon and Chapter Librarian, Durham

Cathedral, since 1962; Examining Chaplain to Bishop of Southwark since 1959; *b* 1902; *s* of Arthur Louis and Marian Couratin. *Educ:* Dulwich Coll.; Corpus Christi Coll., Oxford (Scholar); S Stephen's House, Oxford. 1st Cl. Classical Moderations; 2nd Cl. Literae Humaniores; 2nd Cl. Hons Sch. of Theology; BA 1925; MA 1927. Deacon, 1926; priest, 1927; Asst Curate, S Saviour's, Roath, 1926-30 (in charge of S Francis', roath, 1927-30); Vice-Principal, Queen's Coll., Birmingham, 1930; Asst Curate, S Stephen's, Lewisham (in charge of Church of the Transfiguration, Lewisham), 1930-35; Chaplain, S Stephen's House, Oxford, 1935-36, Vice-Principal, 1936, Principal, 1936-62; Junior Chaplain, Merton Coll., Oxford, 1936-39. Hon. Canon of Christ Church, 1961-62. *Address:* No 7, The College, Durham. *T:* Durham 4767.

**COURCEL, Baron de; (Geoffroy Chodron de Courcel);** Grand Officier, Légion d'Honneur, 1969; Compagnon de la Libération, 1943; Croix de Guerre, 1939-45; French diplomatist; Ambassador of France to the Court of St James's since 1962; *b* Tours, Indre-et-Loire, 11 Sept. 1912; *s* of Louis Chodron de Courcel, Officer, and Alice Lambert-Champy; *m* 1954, Martine Hallade; two *s*. *Educ:* Stanislas Coll.; University of Paris. DenDr, LèsL, Dip. Ecole des Sciences Politiques. Attaché, Warsaw, 1937; Sec., Athens, 1938-39; Armée du Levant, 1939; joined Free French Forces, June 1940; Chef de Cabinet, Gén. de Gaulle, London, 1940-41; Captain 1st Spahis marocains Regt, Egypt, Libya and Tunisia, 1941-43; Dep.-Dir of Cabinet, Gén de Gaulle, Algiers, 1943-44; Mem. Conseil de l'Ordre de la Libération, 1944; Regional Comr for Liberated Territories, 1944; in charge of Alsace-Lorraine Dept, Min. of Interior, 1944-45; Counsellor, 1945; in Min. of Foreign Affairs: Dep. Dir Central and N European Sections, 1945-47; First Counsellor, Rome, 1947-50; Minister Plen., 1951; Dir Bilateral Trade Agreements Section, 1951; Dir African and ME Section, 1953; Dir Gen., Polit. and Econ. Affairs, Min. of Moroccan and Tunisian Affairs, 1954; Perm. Sec., Nat. Defence, 1955-58; Ambassador, Perm. Rep. to NATO, 1958; Sec.-Gen. Présidence de la République, 1959. Ambassadeur de France, 1965 Hon. DCL Oxon, 1970. MC (Great Britain) 1943; Grand Cross of Royal Victorian Order (Hon. GCVO), 1950, etc. *Publication:* L'influence de la Conférence de Berlin de 1885 sur le droit Colonial International, 1936. *Recreations:* shooting, swimming. *Address:* 11 Kensington Palace Gardens, W8; 7 rue de Médicis, Paris 6e; La Ravinière, Fontaines en Sologne, Loir et Cher, France.

**COURCY;** *see* de Courcy.

**COURNAND, André Fréderic,** MD; Professor Emeritus of Medicine, Columbia University College of Physicians and Surgeons, New York, since 1964 (Professor of Medicine, 1951-60); *b* Paris, 24 Sept. 1895; *s* of Jules Cournand and Marguérite Weber; *m* Sibylle Blumer (*d* 1959); three *d* (one *s* killed in action, 1944); *m* 1963, Ruth Fabian. *Educ:* Sorbonne, Paris. BA Faculté des Lettres, 1913; PCB Faculté des Sciences, 1914; MD Faculté de Médecine, 1930. Interne des Hôpitaux de Paris, 1925-30. Came to US in 1930; naturalized American Citizen since 1941. Director, Cardio-Pulmonary Laboratory, Columbia University Division, Bellevue Hospital; Visiting Physician, Chest Service, Bellevue Hospital, 1952. Member: American Physiological Soc.; Assoc. of Amer. Physicians; National Acad. of Sciences (USA), 1958; Hon. Member: British Cardiac Soc.; Swedish Soc. Internal Medicine; Swedish Cardiac Soc.; Soc. Médicale des Hôpitaux, Paris; Foreign Corresp., Académie Royale de Médecine de Belgique, 1956; For. Member: Académie des Sciences, Institut de France, 1957; Académie Nationale de Médecine, Paris, 1958. Laureate: Andreas Retzius Silver Medal of Swedish Soc. Internal Medicine, 1946; Lasker Award, US Public Health Assoc., 1949. croix de Guerre (1914-18) France, three stars; Commandeur de la Légion d'Honneur, 1957. Nobel Prize for Medicine and Physiology (jointly), 1956; Jimenez Diaz Fondacion Prize, 1970. Doctor (*hc*): University of Strasburg, 1957; University of Lyons, 1958; Université libre de Bruxelles 1959; University of Pisa, 1961; University of Birmingham, 1961; Gustaphus Adolphus, Coll., Minnesota, 1963; University of Brazil, 1965; Columbia Univ., 1965. *Publications:* Cardiac Catheterization in Congenital Heart Disease, 1949; L'Insuffisance cardiaque chronique; very numerous articles on human physiopathology of lungs and heart. *Recreations:* Groupe de la Haute Montagne du Club Alpin Français, 1929, and American Alpine Club. *Address:* 1361 Madison Avenue, New York, NY 10028, USA. *T:* Atwater 9-4456. *Club:* Century Association (New York).

**COURT, Prof. Seymour Donald Mayneord,** CBE 1969; James Spence Professor of Child Health, University of Newcastle upon Tyne, since 1955; Physician to Royal Victoria Infirmary, and Babies' Hospital, and Paediatric Physician to Princess Mary Maternity Hospital, Newcastle upon Tyne; *b* 4 Jan. 1912; *s* of David Henry and Ethel Court; *m* 1939, Dr Frances Edith Radcliffe; two *s* one *d*. *Educ:* Adams Grammar Sch., Wem; Birmingham Univ. Resident Hosp. appts Birmingham Gen. Hosps, and Hosp. for Sick Children, London, 1936-38; Paediatric Registrar, Wander Scholar, Westminster Hosp., 1938-39; Physician, EMS, 1939-46; Nuffield Fellow in Child Health, 1946-47; Reader in Child Health, University of Durham, 1947-55. *Publications:* (jointly) Growing Up in Newcastle upon Tyne, 1960; (ed) The Medical Care of Children, 1963. Contributions to special jls and text books on respiratory infection in childhood. *Recreations:* walking, natural history, poetry. *Address:* 26 Northumberland Avenue, Gosforth, Newcastle upon Tyne 3. *T:* Newcastle upon Tyne 851637.

**COURT, William Henry Bassano;** FBA 1968; Professor of Economic History, University of Birmingham, 1947-70; *b* Cirencester, Glos, 12 Oct. 1904; *m* 1940, Audrey Kathleen, *d* of Rev. A. E. Brown, CIE; three *d*. *Educ:* Cirencester and Newbury Grammar Schs; Downing Coll., Cambridge. Choate Fellow and Rockefeller Fellow, Harvard Univ., 1927-29; AM (Harvard), 1928. Successively Lecturer, Reader, and Prof. of Economic History at University of Birmingham; Dean of the Faculty of Commerce and Social Science, 1956-59; Acting Dean, Feb.-July, 1960; Dep. Dean, May-Sept. 1970. Temporary Civil Servant, 1941-45, attached to Ministry of War Transport, later to Historical Section, War Cabinet Office. Pres., Economic History Soc., 1969. Visiting Fellow: Institute of Advanced Studies, Princeton, NJ, USA, 1954; Australian National Univ., 1959. Hon. Fellow Downing Coll., Cambridge, 1965. *Publications:* The Rise of the Midland Industries, 1938; Coal (History of the Second World War, United Kingdom Civil Series), 1951; Concise Economic History of England from 1750 to recent times, 1954; contrib. Economic History, to Approaches to History, by H. P. R. Finberg, 1962; British Economic History, 1870-1914: Commentary and Documents, 1965; Scarcity and Choice in History, 1970; articles in learned jls. *Address:*

113 Selly Park Road, Birmingham 29. *T:* 021-472 1758.

**COURTENAY,** family name of **Earl of Devon.**

**COURTENAY, Lord; Hugh Rupert Courtenay;** Assistant with Messrs Stratton & Holborow, Chartered Surveyors and Chartered Land Agents, Exeter; *b* 5 May 1942; *o s* of 17th Earl of Devon, *qv*; *m* 1967, Dianna Frances, *er d* of J. G. Watherston, Jedburgh, Roxburghshire; one *d*. *Educ:* Winchester; Magdalene Coll., Cambridge (BA). ARICS. *Recreation:* riding. *Address:* The Stables House, Powderham, near Exeter, Devon. *T:* Starcross 370. *Club:* University Pitt (Cambridge).

**COURTENAY, Thomas Daniel, (Tom Courtenay);** actor; *b* 25 Feb. 1937; *s* of Thomas Henry Courtenay and late Anne Eliza Quest; single. *Educ:* Kingston High Sch., Hull; University Coll., London. RADA, 1958-60; started acting professionally, 1960; Old Vic, 1960-61: Konstantin Treplieff, Poins, Feste and Puck; Billy Liar, Cambridge Theatre, June 1961-Feb. 1962 and on tour; Andorra, National Theatre (guest), 1964; The Cherry Orchard, and Macbeth, Chichester, 1966; Century Theatre, Manchester, 1967; Hamlet, Edinburgh, 1968; She Stoops to Conquer, Garrick, 1969. Began acting in films, 1962. *Films:* The Loneliness of the Long Distance Runner; Private Potter; Billy Liar; King and Country (Volpi Cup, 1964); Operation Crossbow; King Rat; Dr Zhivago; The Night of the Generals; The Day the Fish Came Out; A Dandy in Aspic; Otley. Has appeared on Television. Best Actor Award, Prague Festival, 1968; TV Drama Award (for Oswald in Ghosts), 1968. *Recreations:* listening to music (mainly classical and romantic); watching sport (and occasionally taking part in it, in a light-hearted manner). *Address:* Fulham, SW6. *Clubs:* Savile, Garrick.

**COURTNEIDGE, Cicely,** CBE 1951; *b* Sydney, NSW, 1 April, 1893; *d* of late Robert Courtneidge and Rosaline May Adams; *m* Jack Hulbert, *qv*. First appearance on stage, Prince's Theatre, Manchester, 1901; on London stage, Apollo, 1907; appeared in variety theatres with great success, from 1916; has made popular broadcasts; Gaiety Theatre, New York, 1925; commenced film career, 1929; has appeared successfully in several notable films. *Plays include:* The House that Jack Built, Adelphi, 1929; Folly to be Wise, Piccadilly, 1931; Hide and Seek, Hippodrome, 1937; Under Your Hat, Palace, 1938; Full Swing, Palace, 1942; Under the Counter, Phoenix, 1945, New York, 1947, Australia, 1947-48; Her Excellency, Hippodrome, 1949; Gay's the Word, Saville, 1951; Over the Moon, Piccadilly, 1953; The Bride and the Bachelor, Duchess, 1956; Fool's Paradise, Apollo, 1959; The Bride Comes Back, Vaudeville, 1960; High Spirits, Savoy, 1964; Dear Octopus, Haymarket, 1967. *Publication: autobiography:* Cicely, 1953. *Address:* 18a Charles Street, W1.

**COURTNEY, Comdr Anthony Tosswill,** OBE 1949; RN; author and lecturer; General Manager, New English Typewriting School, since 1969; *b* 16 May 1908; *s* of Basil Tosswill Courtney and Frances Elizabeth Courtney (*née* Rankin); *m* 1st, 1938, Elisabeth Mary Cortlandt Stokes (*d* 1961); no *c*; 2nd, 1962, Lady (Elizabeth) Trefgarne (marr. diss. 1966), *widow* of 1st Baron Trefgarne. *Educ:* Royal Naval Coll., Dartmouth. Midshipman, HMS Ramillies, 1925; world cruise in HMS Renown with the Duke and Duchess of York, 1927; Sub-Lieut HMS Cornwall, 1930; Lieut HMS Malaya, 1931-33; qualified as Interpreter in Russian after language study in Bessarabia, 1934; qualified in Signals and W/T at Signal Sch., Portsmouth, 1935; served at Admiralty and on staff of C-in-C, Plymouth, 1936; Flag Lieut to Rear-Adm. comdg Third Cruiser Sqdn, Mediterranean Fleet, 1937-39; Staff of Adm. comdg 3rd Battle Squadron and N Atlantic Escort Force, 1939-41; Naval Mission in Russia, 1941-42; Flag Lieut and Signals Officer to Adm. comdg Aircraft Carriers, 1943; Staff of Adm. comdg S Atlantic Station, 1944; Staff of Rear-Adm., Gibraltar, 1945; Intelligence Div., Naval Staff, Admiralty, 1946-48; Chief Staff Officer (Intelligence) Germany, 1949-51; qualified as Interpreter in German; Intelligence Div., Naval Staff, Admiralty, 1952-53; retd with rank of Comdr, 1953. Entered business as Export Consultant (ETG Consultancy Services), until 1965. Contested (C) Hayes and Harlington, 1955. MP (C) Harrow East, 1959-66. Vice-Chm. Conservative Navy Cttee, 1964. Chm. Parliamentary Flying Club, 1965. *Publication:* Sailor in a Russian Frame, 1968. *Recreations:* shooting, sailing and flying. *Address:* 9 Alford House, Stanhope Road, Highgate, N6. *T:* 01-348 3216. *Clubs:* White's, Carlton.

**COURTNEY, Air Chief Marshal Sir Christopher (Lloyd),** GBE, *cr* 1945 (CBE 1919); KCB, *cr* 1939 (CB 1932); DSO 1917; *b* 27 June 1890; *y s* of late W. L. Courtney, MA, LLD; *m* 1926, Constance Rayson, *d* of G. E. Greensill. *Educ:* Bradfield Coll. Entered HMS Britannia as Naval Cadet, 1905; joined RN Air Service, 1912; served European War, 1914-18 (despatches, DSO, Legion of Honour); transferred to RAF, 1918; Directing Staff, RAF Staff Coll., Andover, 1925-28; served Southern Kurdistan, 1931 (CB); Chief Staff Officer, Iraq Command, 1931-33; Dir of Training, Air Ministry, 1933-34; Dir of Staff Duties, 1934-35; Dir of Operations and Intelligence and Dep. Chief of Air Staff, 1935-36; Air Officer Commanding British Forces in Iraq, 1937-38; commanding Reserve Command RAF, 1939-40; Air Mem. for Supply and Organisation on the Air Council, 1940-45 (Legion of Merit, US); retired, 1945. A Governor of Star and Garter Home, 1952-. Master of Vintners' Company, 1964-65 (Court, 1958). *Address:* 104 Bryanston Court, W1. *T:* 01-262 9030. *Clubs:* United Service, Royal Air Force.

**COURTNEY, Group Captain Ivon Terence,** CBE 1919; RAF (retired); *b* Oct. 1885; *y s* of late William McDougall Courtney, Stormonstown, Co. Dublin; *m* 1915, Emily Lilian (*d* 1964), *y d* of Alfred Campbell Courtney, Danesfield, Clontarf, Co. Dublin; one *s*. *Educ:* Tonbridge; Rossall. Commissioned Royal Marine Light Infantry, 1904; seconded to Naval Wing, RFC, 1912 for flying duty and to RNAS, 1914; permanently transferred to RAF, 1919; retired list, 1932.

**COURTNEY, Dame Kathleen (D'Olier),** DBE 1952 (CBE 1946); Joint President United Nations Association, 1951; *b* 11 March 1878; *d* of Major D. C. Courtney, RE, Nullamore, Milltown, Co. Dublin, and Alice Margaret Mann. *Educ:* private schs; Lady Margaret Hall, Oxford. Hon. Sec. Nat. Union Women's Suffrage Socs, 1911-14; relief work in Europe during and after European War, 1914-18. Joined Exec. Cttee, League of Nations Union, 1928, Vice-Chm., 1939; Dep.-Chm. of UNA, 1945, Chm. 1949. During War of 1939-45 visited USA twice to lecture on behalf of MOI. *Recreations:* travelling, walking. *Address:* 3 Elm Tree Court, Elm Tree Road, NW8. *T:* 01-286 3691. *Club:* University Women's.

**COURTNEY, Victor Desmond,** JP; Member Federal Immigration Planning Council, 1951-

56; Trustee Soldiers' Dependants Appeal Fund (WA); *b* Raymond Terr., NSW, 1894; *m* 1937, Thela, *d* of late John Richards, Perth; one *d*. Has been all his life in journalism, and has contributed to a number of Australian papers. Man. Dir Western Press Ltd and associated companies until he disposed of his interests in Dec. 1954; now author and publisher, and Dir, Craft Print Ltd. *Publications;* Random Rhymes, 1941; Cold is the Marble, 1948; All I May Tell, 1956; Life of J. J. Simons, 1961; Perth and All This!, 1962; As We Pass By, 1963. *Recreations:* motoring, swimming. *Address:* 45 North Beach Road, North Beach, Western Australia. *Clubs:* Reelers, Perth Football, Royal Automobile. National Football League (WA).

**COURTOWN,** 8th Earl of, *cr* 1762; **James Montagu Burgoyne Stopford,** OBE 1950 (MBE 1945); TD and clasp; Viscount Stopford, 1762; Baron Courtown (Ireland), 1758; Baron Saltersford (Great Britain), 1796; DL County of London, 1951; *b* 24 Nov. 1908; *e s* of 7th Earl of Courtown and Cicely Mary Birch; *S* father, 1957; *m* 1st, 1934, Christina Margaret (marriage dissolved, 1946), 3rd *d* of late Adm. J. Ewen Cameron, CB, MVO; two *d*; 2nd, 1951, Patricia, 3rd *d* of Harry S. Winthrop, Auckland, NZ; two *s* one *d*. *Educ:* Eton. Served War of 1939-45 (MBE). Lieut-Col commanding 1st Bn London Irish Rifles (Royal Ulster Rifles) (TA), 1947-51; Bt Col 1951. *Heir: s* Viscount Stopford, *qv*. *Address:* Beech Shade, Cambridge Road, Beaconsfield, Bucks. *T:* Beaconsfield 3417; Marlfield, Gorey, Co. Wexford, Ireland. *T:* Gorey 124. *Club:* Travellers'.

*See also Brig. W. H. Brooks.*

**COUSIN, Prof. David Ross;** Emeritus Professor of Philosophy, University of Sheffield; *b* 28 Jan. 1904; *s* of John William Cousin and Marion Miller Young; *m* 1930, Beatrice Elizabeth Connell; three *s*. *Educ:* Merchiston Castle Sch., Edinburgh; The Queen's Coll., Oxford (BA). Class. Mods 1925; Lit Hum 1927; Philosophy, Politics and Economics, 1928. Asst, Dept of Logic, University of Glasgow, 1928; Lecturer, 1930; Senior Lecturer, 1948. Board of Trade (temp. Principal), 1941-45. Prof. of Philosophy, Univ. of Sheffield, 1949-69; Dean of Faculty of Arts, 1958-61. *Publications:* contributions to learned jls. *Address:* 16 Cobden Crescent, Edinburgh EH9 2BG.

**COUSINS, Rt. Hon. Frank,** PC 1964; Chairman, Community Relations Commission, since 1968; *b* Bulwell, Notts, 8 Sept. 1904; *m* 1930, Annie Elizabeth Judd; two *s* two *d*. *Educ:* King Edward Sch., Doncaster. Mem. Institute of Transport; Organiser, Rd Transport Section, TGWU, 1938; Nat. Officer (Rd Tr. Section), 1944; Nat. Sec. (Rd Tr. Section), 1948; Asst Gen. Sec. TGWU, 1955; General Secretary, TGWU, 1956-69 (seconded, as Minister of Technology, Oct. 1964-July 1966). MP (Lab) Nuneaton, Jan. 1965-Dec. 1966. Elected Mem., Gen. Council of TUC, 1956-69. Member: British Transport Jt Consultative Council, 1955-63; Min. of Labour Nat. Jt Advisory Council, 1956; Exec. Council Internat. Transport Workers Federation, 1956 (Pres., 1958-60, 1962-64); Colonial Labour Advisory Cttee, 1957-62; London Travel Cttee, 1958-60; Political Economy Club, 1957; Council for Scientific and Industrial Research, 1960-64; National Economic Development Council; Central Advisory Council for Science and Technology, 1967-; Nat. Freight Corp., 1969-; Governor, Nat. Inst. of Economic and Social Research, 1958; Chm., Central Training Council, 1968-. *Recreations:* gardening, reading. *Address:* Ropers Lane, Wrington, Somerset.

**COUSINS, Norman;** Editor, The Saturday Review, since 1940; *b* 24 June 1915; *s* of Samuel and Sara Cousins; *m* 1939, Ellen Kopf; four *d*. *Educ:* Teachers Coll., Columbia Univ. Educational Editor, New York Evening Post, 1935-36; Managing Editor, current History Magazine, 1936-39 (World War II edn, USA); Chm., Conn Fact-Finding Commission on Education, 1948-51. Vice-Pres. PEN Club, American Center, 1952-55; National Press and Overseas Press Clubs; Lectr for US Dept of State; co-Chm., National Cttee for a Sane Nuclear Policy, 1957-63. Pres. United World Federalists, 1952-54 (Hon. Pres., 1955-). Pres., World Assoc. of World Federalists, 1965-. Chm., Bd of Directors, Nat. Educational Television, 1969-70; Mem. Bd of Directors: National Educational Television and Radio Center; Educational Broadcasting Corp.; Vice-Pres., Dir, Chm., Edit. Cttee of McCall Corp.; US Govt Rep. at dedication Nat. Univ., Addis Ababa, 1962; co-Chm., Citizens' Cttee for a Nuclear Test-Ban Treaty, 1963; Chm., Cttee for Culture and Intellectual Exchange, for International Co-operation Year, 1965; US Presidential Rep. at Inauguration of Pres. of Philippines, 1966; US Govt Rep. at Internat. Writers Conf., Finland, 1966. Chm. Mayor's Task Force on Air Pollution, NYC, 1966-. Holds various hon. degrees. Awards include: Benjamin Franklin Award for Public Service in Journalism, 1956; Eleanor Roosevelt Peace Award, 1963; Overseas Press Club Award for best interpretation of foreign affairs in magazine writing, 1965, etc. *Publications:* The Good Inheritance, 1941; (ed) A Treasury of Democracy, 1941; Modern Man is Obsolete, 1945; (ed jtly) Poetry of Freedom, 1946; Talks with Nehru, 1951; Who Speaks for Man?, 1953; Saturday Review Treasury (ed. sup.), 1957; In God We Trust (ed), 1958; March's Thesaurus (ed. sup.), 1958; Dr Schweitzer of Lambaréné, 1960; In Place of Folly, 1961; Present Tense, 1967. *Recreations:* music (especially organ), sports, reading, chess. *Address:* (office) 380 Madison Avenue, NYC 10017, USA; (home) 160 Silvermine Road, New Canaan, Conn 06840, USA. *Clubs:* Coffee House, Century (New York).

**COUSTEAU, Jacques-Yves;** Officier, Légion d'Honneur; Croix de Guerre with Palm; Officier du Mérite Maritime; Chevalier du Mérite Agricole; Officier des Arts et des Lettres; Capitaine de Corvette in French Navy; undersea explorer; author; archæologist; *b* 11 June 1910; *m* 1937, Simone Melchior; two *s*. *Educ:* Stanislas, Paris; Navy Academy, Brest. Served as gunnery officer; commanded French Navy Base at Shanghai, 1935-36. Was partly responsible for invention of the Aqualung, a portable breathing device for divers. Has made film records of his undersea expeditions since 1942; various awards for submarine colour photography. Established the Undersea Research Group in 1945. In 1950 formed and became Pres. of Campagnes Océanographiques Françaises; created and became Pres. of Office Français de Recherches Sous Marines Marseille, 1952 (Centre d'Etudes Marines Avancées, 1968); since 1951, on his famous ship Calypso, every year makes long oceanographic expeditions, using underwater television. In July 1956 made world's record anchorage of his ship Calypso in the Atlantic (7,500 metres for 2 days). Took part in making of the Bathyscaphe (first with Picard, then with French Navy, but declined to be in charge of it). Promoted Conshelf saturation dive programme, 1965: Conshelf 3, 6 men lived and worked 3 weeks 370 feet below water surface, 1965. Dir Musée

Océanographique, Monaco, Nov. 1956- Foreign Associate, Nat. Acad. of Sciences, USA. Gold Medal, RGS, 1963. *Publications:* Par 18 mètres de fond, 1946; La Plongée en Scaphandre, 1949; (with Frédéric Dumas) The Silent World, 1953 (New York and London), first published in English, then in other languages (film awarded Oscar for best documentary feature film of 1956; Grand Prix, Gold Palm, Festival Cannes, 1956); (ed with James Dugan) Captain Cousteau's Underwater Treasury, 1960 (London); The Living Sea, 1963 (London); World Without Sun, 1965 (film awarded Oscar, 1966). Articles in National Geographic Magazine. *Film:* The Golden Fish, awarded Oscar for best short film, 1960. *Address:* Villa Richard, Monaco; Villa Baobab, Sanary-sur-Mer (Var), France. *Clubs:* Club des Explorateurs (Paris); Club Alpin Sous Marin; Yacht Club de France.

**COUTANCHE;** family name of **Baron Coutanche.**

**COUTANCHE,** Baron, *cr* 1961, of St Brelade and of the City of Westminster (Life Peer); **Alexander Moncrieff Coutanche,** Kt 1945; Bailiff of Jersey, 1935-61; *b* Jersey, 9 May 1892; *yr s* of Adolphus Arnold Coutanche, notary, Jersey, and of Ina Finlayson, Glasgow; *m* 1924, Ruth Sophia Joan, CStJ, *o c* of Leicester Gore; one *s*. *Educ:* Victoria Coll., Jersey; privately. Entered Middle Temple, 1912; called to Jersey Bar, 1913; English Bar, 1915; gazetted, general list, 1917; Claims Commission, France and Belgium, 1917-20; Staff Capt., 1919 (despatches, Chevalier de l'Ordre de la Couronne and Croix de Guerre, Belgium); Dep. of St Helier in States of Jersey, 1922-25; Solicitor-Gen. for Jersey, 1925-31; Attorney-Gen., 1931-35; Hon. Doctor, University of Caen (France), 1938; Hon. Bencher of the Middle Temple, 1961. Knight of Grace, Order of St John of Jerusalem, 1946; Silver Medal, RSPCA, 1939. *Publication:* (joint) Dictionary of Anglo-Belgian Law, 1920. *Address:* Clos des Tours, St Aubin, Jersey. *T:* Jersey, Central 41178. *Clubs:* Athenæum, Royal Commonwealth Society (Vice-Pres.), Royal Automobile (Hon.), Royal Aero (Hon.); Victoria (Jersey).

**COUTTS;** *see* Money-Coutts.

**COUTTS, Frederick,** CBE 1967; General of The Salvation Army, 1963-69; *b* 21 Sept. 1899; British; *m* 1925, Bessie Lee (*d* 1967); one *s* three *d*. *Educ:* Leith Academy and Whitehill. RFC, 1917-18. Officer, The Salvation Army, 1920. Literary Sec. to the General, 1952. Training Principal, International Training Coll., 1953-57; Territorial Comdr, Eastern Australia, 1957-63. *Publications:* The Timeless Prophets, 1944; He had no Revolver, 1944; The Battle and the Breeze, 1945; Portrait of a Salvationist, 1955; Jesus and Our Need, 1956; The Call to Holiness, 1957; Essentials of Christian Experience, 1969. *Recreation:* reading. *Address:* 3 Dubrae Close, St Albans, Herts. *T:* St Albans 59655.

**COUTTS, John Archibald;** Professor of Jurisprudence in the University of Bristol; *b* 29 Dec. 1909; *e s* of Archibald and Katherine Jane Coutts; *m* 1940, Katherine Margaret Alldis; two *s*. *Educ:* Merchant Taylors', Crosby; Downing Coll., Cambridge (MA, LLB). Barrister Gray's Inn, 1933; lectured in Law: University Coll., Hull, 1934-35; King's Coll., London, 1935-36; Queen's Univ., Belfast, 1936-37; Trinity Coll., Dublin, 1937-50; Prof. of Laws, University of Dublin, 1944-50. Fellow, Trinity College, Dublin, 1944-50. Visiting Prof., Osgoode Hall Law Sch., Toronto, 1962-63. *Publications:* The Accused (ed); contributions to legal journals. *Address:* 22 Hurie Crescent, Clifton, Bristol 8. *T:* Bristol 36984.

**COUTTS, Sir Walter (Fleming),** GCMG 1962 (KCMG 1961; CMG 1953); Kt 1961; MBE 1949; Assistant Vice-Chancellor (Administration), University of Warwick, since 1969; Director: Assam & African Investments; Mackenzie Dalgety & Co.; Amgoorie Tea Co.; Pergamon Press; *b* Aberdeen, 30 Nov. 1912; *s* of late Rev. John William Coutts, MA, DD, and Mrs R. Coutts, Crieff; *m* 1942, Janet Elizabeth Jamieson, CStJ, 2nd *d* of late A. C. Jamieson and of Mrs M. E. Jamieson, Welwyn, Herts; one *s* one *d*. *Educ:* Glasgow Academy; St Andrews Univ.; St John's Coll., Cambridge. MA St Andrews, 1934. District Officer Kenya, 1936; Secretariat Kenya, 1946; District Commissioner, 1947; Administrator, St Vincent, 1949; Minister for Education, Labour and Lands, Kenya, 1956-58, Chief Sec., 1958-61; Special Commissioner for African Elections, Feb. 1955; Governor of Uganda, Nov. 1961-Oct. 1962; Governor-Gen. and C-in-C, Uganda, 1962-63. Sec. to Dulverton Trust, 1966-69. KStJ. *Recreations:* golf, fishing. *Address:* 38 Binswood Avenue, Leamington Spa, Warwicks. *T:* Leamington Spa 24416.

**COUTTS DONALD, William,** CA; Chairman, Urwick, Orr & Partners Ltd; Director, Urwick, Currie Ltd; *b* Forfar, Scotland, 11 March 1906; *s* of James Donald and Betsy Milne Coutts; *m* 1936, Dora Eleanor Tiso; one *s*. *Educ:* Forfar Acad.; St Andrews Univ. Henderson & Loggie, CA, 1923-28; Chief Accountant, Forsters Glass Co. Ltd, 1928-30; Sec. and Chief Accountant, Scribbans & Co. Ltd, 1930-36; Urwick, Orr & Partners Ltd, 1936-: Dir 1940; Man. Dir, 1952-63; Chm., 1963. CA 1928, FCWA 1936, FBIM 1945. Pres., Inst. of Management Consultants, 1969-70; Chm., Management Consultants Assoc., 1960 and 1964; Member: NEDC, 1964-66; Council of British Inst. of Management, 1967-; formerly Mem., Council of Cost and Works Accountants. *Publications:* several pamphlets and articles on financial and cost accounting. *Recreations:* golf, cricket. *Address:* 16 The Downsway, Sutton, Surrey. *T:* 01-642 5683. *Clubs:* Devonshire; Effingham Golf, Harborne Golf (Birmingham).

**COUVE DE MURVILLE, Maurice;** Commandeur de la Légion d'Honneur; Prime Minister of France, 1968-69; *b* 24 Jan. 1907; *m* 1932, Jacqueline Schweisguth; three *d*. *Educ:* Paris Univ. Inspecteur des finances, 1930; directeur des finances extérieures, 1940; membre du Comité français de la libération nationale (Alger), 1943; représentant de la France, Conseil consultatif pour l'Italie, 1944; Ambassador in Rome, 1945; directeur général des affaires politiques, Ministère des Affaires Etrangères, 1945-50; Ambassador in Egypt, 1950-54; French Permanent Rep., NATO, Sept. 1954-Jan. 1955; Ambassador in the US, 1955-56; Ambassador of France to the Federal Republic of Germany, 1956-58; Ministre des Affaires Etrangères, 1958-68, de l'Economie et des Finances, June-July 1968. *Address:* 44 rue du Bac, Paris 7e.

**COVELL, Maj.-Gen. Sir Gordon,** Kt 1946; CIE 1939; MD; IMS, retired; *b* 20 Oct. 1887; *s* of late Edwin Louis Covell; *m* Oona, *d* of late Col Kenneth Macleod, IMS; two *s* one *d*. *Educ:* King's Sch., Canterbury; Guy's Hosp. MB, BS 1913; DTM & H Eng 1922; DPH 1929; MD 1923. Maj.-Gen. 1944; late Dir Malaria Institute of India; retired, 1947; KHP, 1944-47. Walter Reed Medal for achievement in Tropical Medicine, 1960; Darling Medal for

Malaria Research, 1961. *Address:* The End House, Sandy Way, Cobham, Surrey.

**COVENEY, Prof. James;** Professor of Modern Languages and Head of School of Modern Languages, University of Bath, since 1969; Joint Director, Centre for European Industrial Studies, University of Bath, since 1969; *b* 4 April 1920; *s* of James and Mary Coveney; *m* 1955, Patricia Yvonne Townsend; two *s*. *Educ:* St Ignatius Coll., London; Univs of Reading and Strasbourg. Served War of 1939-45, Flt-Lt (Pilot), RAF. BA, 1st cl. hons French, Reading, 1950; DrUniv Strasbourg, 1953. Univ. of Strasbourg: French Govt Research Scholar, 1950-51; Lecteur d'Anglais, 1951-53; Lectr in French, Univ. of Hull, 1953-58; Asst Dir of Exams (Mod. Langs), Civil Service Commn, 1958-59; UNO Secretariat, New York, 1959-61; NATO Secretariat, 1961-64; Sen. Lectr i/c of Mod. Langs, Univ. of Bath, 1964-68; Language Cons. to McKinsey & Co. Inc., Management Consultants, 1967-. *Publications:* La Légende de l'Empereur Constant, 1955; articles in British and French periodicals. *Address:* 40 Westfield Close, Bath, Somerset. *T:* Bath 63670. *Club:* Reform.

**COVENTRY,** family name of **Earl of Coventry.**

**COVENTRY,** 11th Earl of *cr* 1697; **George William Coventry;** Viscount Deerhurst, 1697; *b* 25 Jan. 1934; *o s* of 10th Earl and Hon. Nesta Donne Philipps, *e d* of 1st Baron Kylsant; *S* father, 1940; *m* 1955, Marie Farquhar-Medart (marriage dissolved, 1963); one *s*. *Educ:* Eton; RMA, Sandhurst. *Heir:* *s* Viscount Deerhurst, *qv*.
*See also Earl of Harrowby.*

**COVENTRY, Bishop of,** since 1956; **Rt. Rev. Cuthbert Killick Norman Bardsley,** CBE 1952; DD 1957; *b* 28 March 1907; *yr s* of late Canon J. U. N. Bardsley and Mabel Killick. *Educ:* Eton; New Coll., Oxford. Curate of All Hallows, Barking by the Tower, 1932-34; Rector of Woolwich, 1940-44; Provost of Southwark Cathedral, 1944-47; Suffragan Bishop of Croydon, 1947-56; Hon. Canon in Canterbury Cathedral, 1948-56; Archbishop of Canterbury's Episcopal Representative with the three Armed Forces, 1948-56; Hon. Chaplain Siemens Bros, 1943-46; Proctor in Convocation, 1945-46. Select Preacher, University of Cambridge, 1958. *Publications:* Bishop's Move, 1952; Sundry Times, Sundry Places, 1962; Him We Declare, 1967; I Believe in Mission, 1970. *Recreations:* golf, sketching. *Address:* The Bishop's House, Coventry. *Club:* United Service.

**COVENTRY, Assistant Bishop of;** *see* McKie, Rt Rev. J. D.

**COVENTRY, Archdeacon of;** *see* Buchan, Ven. Eric Ancrum.

**COVENTRY, Rev. John Seton,** SJ; Lecturer in Theology, Heythrop College; *b* 21 Jan. 1915; *yr s* of late Seton and Annie Coventry, Barton-on-Sea, Hants. *Educ:* Stonyhurst; Campion Hall, Oxford. MA Oxon 1945. Entered Society of Jesus, 1932; ordained, 1947; Prefect of Studies, Beaumont, 1950; Rector, Beaumont, 1956-58; Provincial, English Province of Soc. of Jesus, 1958-64. *Publications:* Morals and Independence, 1946; The Breaking of Bread, 1950; Faith Seeks Understanding, 1951; The Life Story of the Mass, 1959; The Theology of Faith, 1968. *Address:* Heythrop College, Cavendish Square, W1. *T:* 01-636 2387.

**COWAN, Prof. Charles Donald,** MA Cantab, PhD London; Professor of the History of South-East Asia in the University of London since 1961; Chairman, Centre of South East Asian Studies; *b* London, 18 Nov. 1923; *s* of W. C. Cowan and Minnie Ethel (*née* Farrow); *m* 1st, 1945, Mary Evelyn, *d* of Otto Vetter, Perth, WA (marriage dissolved, 1960); two *d*; 2nd, 1962, Daphne Eleanor, *d* of Walter Rishworth Whittam, Rangoon. *Educ:* Kilburn Grammar Sch.; Peterhouse, Cambridge. Served Royal Navy, 1941-45. Lecturer in History, Raffles Coll., Singapore, 1947-48, and University of Malaya, 1948-50; Lectr in the History of South-East Asia, Sch. of Oriental and African Studies, University of London, 1950-60. Visiting Prof. of South-East Asian History, Cornell Univ., 1960-61. *Publications:* Nineteenth Century Malaya, 1961; The Economic Development of South-East Asia (ed), 1964; The Economic Development of China and Japan (ed), 1964; numerous articles on Asian history and politics. *Address:* School of Oriental and African Studies, University of London, WC1.

**COWAN, Sir Christopher (George) Armstrong,** Kt 1958; JP; *b* 6 April 1889; *s* of late William James Cowan and Frances Isabella Cowan, Wood Green, London; *m* 1912, Bertha Lydia Caroline, *d* of late James and Emma Ross; one *s* (and one *s* decd). *Educ:* Merchant Taylors' Sch. Barrister-at-Law, Middle Temple, 1927; SE Circuit, Surrey and S London Sessions. Mem. Ruislip-Northwood Urban Dist Council, 1936-49. Mddx CC: Councillor, 1937, Alderman, 1951-58, Vice-Chm., 1955-56, Chm., 1956-57; Alderman, 1961-65; High Sheriff, Mddx, 1960; JP, 1942; Chm. Uxbridge Bench, 1947-64 (Dep.-Chm. 1944-47). Ex-Member: Standing Jt Cttee; Magistrates' Courts Cttee; Advisory Cttee; Agricultural Wages Cttee; NW Home Counties Regional Advisory Water Cttee, 1945-58, 1961-65; Northwood and Pinner Hosp. Bd, 1936-48 (Chm.). Member: Harefield and Northwood Group Hosp. Management Cttee, 1948-63; NW Metrop. Reg. Hosp. Bd, 1957-63; Chm. Nat. Assistance Tribunals, 1934-49; Chm. Cowan Brothers (Stratford) Ltd until 1968. *Address:* Kiln Farm, Northwood, Mddx. *T:* Northwood 21122.

**COWAN, Maj.-Gen. David Tennant,** CB 1945; CBE 1945; DSO 1942, Bar 1944; MC; Indian Army (retired); late RARO; *b* 8 Oct. 1896; *s* of Charles Thomas and Kate Cowan; *m* 1920, Anne Elliot Dunlop; one *d* (one *s* killed in action). *Educ:* Reading; Glasgow Univ. 2nd Lieut Argyll and Sutherland Highlanders, 1915; Capt. 1920; Bt Major, 1933; Major, 1934; Bt Lt-Col 1938; Lt-Col 1940; Brig. 1941; Maj.-Gen. 1942. Served European War, 1914-18 (despatches, MC); 3rd Afghan War; Waziristan Ops, 1919-20 (despatches) and 1937 (despatches). 6th Gurkha Rifles, 1917-40; Chief Instructor, Indian Military Academy, 1932-34; Comdt 1/6 Gurkha Rifles, 1939-40; DDMT GHQ, India, 1941; Offg DMT, GHQ, India, 1941-42. War of 1939-45 in Burma (despatches, DSO and bar, CBE, CB). Served with Argyll and Sutherland Highlanders and 6th Gurkha Rifles; GOC 17th Indian Div., 1942-45, and British and Indian Div., British Commonwealth Occupation Force, Japan, 1945-46. Retd 1947, RARO 1948. Commandant, Devon Army Cadet Force, 1948-58. Chm. Approved Sch., Devon, 1951-60; Sec. (part-time) Assoc. of Managers of Approved Schs. DL Devon, 1960. Hon. Commandant Empire Village, VIth British Empire and Commonwealth Games, Wales, 1958. *Recreations:* games, fishing. *Address:* Oakley, Burley, Hants. *T:* Burley 3278. *Clubs:* Army and Navy; Royal Lymington Yacht.

**COWAN, Sir (Henry) Kenneth,** Kt 1958; FRSE 1956; Chairman, Cruden Investments Ltd;

Vice-Chairman, Crudens Ltd, Musselburgh, since 1969 (Chairman, 1967-69); Director: Cruden Foundation, since 1964; Eskside Securities Ltd; Tannochside Bonding Co. Ltd; Thistle Industrial Holdings Ltd; Trustee, Scottish Hospital Endowments Research Trust; Member, Industrial Injuries Advisory Council; *b* 17 June 1900; *e s* of Henry Cowan, Belfast; *m* 1933, Elinor Margaret Graham (*d* 1966), *er d* of George Craig, JP, Drumcovitt House, Feeny, Londonderry; no *c*. *Educ:* Royal Belfast Academical Instn; Queen's Univ., Belfast, MB, BCh, BAO, 1921; DPH 1924; MD 1925. Asst Medical Officer of Health, Belfast, 1923, Leicester, 1928; Dep. County MO, Leics, 1933; County MOH, Glos, 1937, Essex, 1949-54; late Chief MO, Dept of Health for Scotland; Hon. Physician to the Queen, 1956-59. Mem., General Medical Council, 1955-63. Chm. Public Health Cttee, BMA, 1951-54; Mem. Standing Med. Advisory Cttee, Central Health Services Council, 1951-54. Smith Award, 1955. MRCPE 1956; FRCPE 1957; FRCPS(G) (Hon.), 1961. Hon. LLD Glasgow Univ., 1964. *Publications:* articles in various medical journals. *Recreation:* golf. *Address:* Claremont, Longniddry, East Lothian. *T:* Longniddry 3176.

**COWARD, David John,** CMG 1965; OBE 1962; Registrar General, Kenya, since 1955; *b* 21 March 1917; *s* of late Robert J. Coward, Exmouth, Devon; *m* 1954, Joan, *d* of late Reginald Frank, Doncaster; three *d*. *Educ:* Exmouth Grammar Sch. and Law Society's Sch. of Law. Admitted a solicitor, 1938. Joined RN as a rating at outbreak of war, 1939; commissioned, 1941; demobilized as Lieut-Comdr (S) RNVR, 1947. ADC to Governor of Trinidad, 1947. Joined Colonial Legal Service, 1948, Asst Registrar Gen., Kenya; Dep. Registrar Gen., 1952; Registrar Gen., Official Receiver and Public Trustee, 1955. Acted as Permanent Sec. for Justice and Constitutional Affairs, 1963-64. Served in Kenya Police Reserve, 1949-63, latterly as Senior Superintendent i/c Nairobi Area. Colonial Special Constabulary Medal, 1954. *Recreation:* golf. *Address:* PO Box 231, Nairobi, Kenya. *T:* Nairobi 20660. *Clubs:* Naval; Nairobi and Limuru Country (Kenya).

**COWARD, Sir Noel,** Kt 1970; *b* Teddington, 16 Dec. 1899; *s* of late Arthur Coward and Violet Veitch. *Educ:* Chapel Road Sch.; privately. Made first appearance on stage, 1910. and has made many other successful stage appearances in London and New York, also in cabaret in London and Las Vegas. Played King Magnus in The Apple Cart, Haymarket, 1953. FRSL. Plays: I'll Leave it to you, 1920; The Young Idea, 1921; The Vortex, 1924; Easy Virtue, 1925; Fallen Angels, 1925; Hay Fever, 1925; The Queen was in the Parlour, 1926; This was a Man, 1926; The Marquise, 1927; On with the Dance (revue), 1925; Home Chat, 1927; Sirocco, 1927; This Year of Grace (revue), 1928; Bitter Sweet (operette), 1929; Private Lives, 1930; Cavalcade, 1931; Words and Music (revue), 1932; Design for Living, 1932; Conversation Piece, 1934; Point Valaine, 1935; To-Night at Eight-Thirty, 1936; Operette, 1938; Blithe Spirit, 1941; Present Laughter, 1942; This Happy Breed, 1943 (written 1939); Sigh No More (revue), 1945; Pacific 1860 (musical play), 1946; Peace In Our Time, 1947; Ace of Clubs (musical play), 1950; Relative Values (play), 1951; Quadrille, 1952; After the Ball (musical play), 1954; South Sea Bubble, 1956; Nude with Violin, 1956; Look After Lulu, 1959; London Morning (ballet), 1959; Waiting in the Wings (play), 1960; Sail Away (musical play), 1961 (prod. USA), 1962 (prod. Savoy Theatre); The Girl Who Came to Supper (prod. USA), 1963; High Spirits (prod. USA, London), 1964; A Song at Twilight; Shadows of the Evening; Come into the Garden Maud, 1966; *Films:* In Which We Serve, 1942; This Happy Breed, 1944; Brief Encounter, 1945; Blithe Spirit, 1945; The Astonished Heart, 1950; Around The World in 80 Days, 1957; Our Man in Havana, 1959; Surprise Package, 1960; Bunny Lake is Missing, 1965; Boom, 1968. *Publications:* Collected Sketches and Lyrics, 1931; Present Indicative (autobiography), 1937; To Step Aside, 1939; Middle East Diary, 1945; Star Quality, 1951; Noël Coward's Song Book, 1953; Future Indefinite (autobiography), 1954; Pomp and Circumstance (novel), 1960; The Collected Short Stories of Noël Coward, 1962; Pretty Polly Barlow (novel), 1964; Lyrics of Noël Coward, 1965; Bon Voyage (short stories), 1967; Not Yet the Dodo (verse), 1967. *Address:* Les Avants, sur Montreux, Switzerland. *Clubs:* Athenæum, Garrick.

**COWDEROY, Most Rev. Mgr Cyril Conrad;** *see* Southwark, Archbishop and Metropolitan of, (RC).

**COWDRAY,** 3rd Viscount, *cr* 1917; **Weetman John Churchill Pearson,** TD; Bt, *cr* 1894; Baron, *cr* 1910; Captain, Sussex Yeomanry; *b* 27 Feb. 1910 (twin); *s* of 2nd Viscount and Agnes Beryl (*d* 1948), *d* of Lord Edward Spencer Churchill; *S* father, 1933; *m* 1st, 1939, Lady Anne Bridgeman (from whom he obtained a divorce, 1950), *d* of 5th Earl of Bradford; one *s* two *d*; 2nd, 1953, Elizabeth Georgiana Mather, 2nd *d* of A. H. M. Jackson; one *s* two *d*. *Educ:* Eton; Christ Church, Oxford. Parliamentary Private Sec. to Under-Sec. of State for Air, 1941-42. *Recreations:* hunting, polo, shooting, fishing. *Heir:* *s*. Hon. Michael Orlando Weetman Pearson, *b* 17 June 1944. *Address:* Cowdray Park, Midhurst. *T:* Midhurst 2461; Dunecht, Aberdeenshire. *T:* Lyne of Skene 244. *Clubs:* Cavalry, White's.
*See also Duke of Atholl, Viscount Blakenham, Hon. Mrs Angela Campbell-Preston, Baron Cranworth.*

**COWDREY (Michael) Colin;** *b* 24 Dec. 1932; *s* of Ernest Arthur Cowdrey and Kathleen Mary Cowdrey (*née* Taylor); *m* 1956, Penelope Susan Cowdrey (*née* Chiesman); three *s* one *d*. *Educ:* Homefield, Sutton, Surrey; Tonbridge; Brasenose Coll., Oxford. Cricket: 5 years Tonbridge Sch. XI (Capt., 1949-50); Public Schs (Lord's) (Capt. 1950); (3 years) Oxford XI (Capt. 1954); Kent Cap, 1951 (Captain, 1957-70); 104 appearances for England (first 1954; Capt. 23 times); 9 Overseas Tours; 23 Test-Centuries. Runner-up Amateur Rackets Title, Queen's Club, 1953 and Doubles, 1965. Mem., MCC Cttee and Cricket Council. dir, Charlton Athletic Football Club. Freeman, City of London, 1962. *Publications:* Cricket Today, 1961; Time for Reflection; Tackle Cricket This Way, 1969; The Incomparable Game, 1970. *Recreations:* rackets, golf. *Address:* Kentish Border, Limpsfield, Surrey. *T:* Limpsfield Chart 2377. *Clubs:* MCC, Royal Automobile.

**COWDRY, Rt. Rev. Roy Walter Frederick;** Assistant Bishop of Grahamstown, since 1965; Rector of St Cuthbert's, Port Elizabeth, since 1964; *b* 28 April 1915; *s* of Frederick William Thomas Cowdry and Florence Emma (*née* Roberts); *m* 1964, Elizabeth Melene, *d* of Rt Rev. B. W. Peacey, *qv*; two *s*. *Educ:* King's Coll., London. Deacon, 1941; Priest, 1942. Asst Curate: St Nicholas, Perivale, 1941-44; Christ Church, Ealing, 1944-50; Domestic Chaplain to Archbishop of Cape Town, 1950-58; Asst Bishop of Cape Town, 1958-61; Bishop Suffragan of Cape Town, 1961-64. Chaplain, Cape Town Gaol, 1951-57.

Chaplain, OStJ, 1961. *Address:* St Cuthbert's Rectory, 24 Westbourne Road, Port Elizabeth, CP, S Africa. *T:* 32526. *Club:* Royal Over-Seas League.

**COWE, (Robert George) Collin;** Fellow and Senior Bursar, Magdalen College, Oxford, since 1970; *b* 24 Sept. 1917; *s* of Peter and Annie Cowe, Berwick-upon-Tweed; *m* 1943, Gladys May, *d* of William Greenwood Wright and Jessie Wright, Bingley, Yorks; one *d*. *Educ:* The Duke's Sch., Ainwick; The Grammar Sch., Berwick-upon-Tweed; Edinburgh Univ. MA (Hons Classics) 1939; MA Oxon, 1970. Served Royal Regiment of Artillery, Field Branch, 1939-46; Major, RA, 1944-46. National Coal Board, 1947-; Private Sec. to Chm., 1947-49; Principal Private Sec. to Chm., 1949-52; Sec., East Midlands Div., 1952-55; Staff Dir, North-Eastern Div., 1955-58; Dep.-Sec. to NCB, 1958-59; Sec., 1960-67; Man. Dir, Associated Heat Services Ltd (associate co. of NCB), 1967-69. *Recreations:* riding, swimming. *Address:* Brookside Cottage, Brook End, Chadlington, Oxford OX7 3NF. *T:* Chadlington 373. *Club:* Caledonian.

**COWELL, Maj.-Gen. Sir Ernest Marshall,** KBE 1944 (CBE 1939); CB 1940; DSO 1918; TD; MD, BS London; FRCS; AMS(T); Legion of Merit, rank of Commander, 1944; Commander of the Grand Priory of the Hospital of St John of Jerusalem, 1945; Officier de la Légion d'Honneur, 1943; Croix de Guerre with palm; Hon. Member of Military Surgeons, USA; *b* 24 Feb. 1886; *s* of Jasper Cowell, Steyning, Sussex; *m* 1st, 1912, Dorothie (*d* 1962), *d* of Arthur Miller, ISO, late of India Office; one *s* two *d*; 2nd, 1963, Mary K. Ebeling, *d* of Thomas Ebeling of Guernsey. *Educ:* Steyning Gram. Sch.; University Coll., London. MRCS, LRCP, MB, BS London, 1907; MD 1909; FRCS 1910. Surgical Specialist, BEF 1915-18 (DSO, despatches twice); Lieut-Col OC No. 1, CCS, BEF 1918-19; Commandant 1st Army Sch. of Instruction, RAMC; County Dir and County Controller, BRCS Surrey, 1927-38; ADMS 44th (Home Counties) Div. 1934-40; DDMS 3 Corps BEF, 1940; DDMS 2 Corps, 1940-42; DMS Allied Forces, North Africa, 1942, Maj.-Gen. (despatches); DDMS Northern Command, 1944. PMO Control Commn for Germany; Dir of Health Div., UNRRA Mission to Greece; late KHS Fellow of University Coll., London, 1918; Arris and Gale Lecturer, RCS, 1919; late Surg. Croydon Gen. Hosp., 1922; Hunterian Prof. Royal College of Surg., 1927; Freeman Borough of Croydon, 1945; Freeman of City of London, 1953; Mem: of Worshipful Company of Coopers. DL Surrey, 1927-68. *Publications:* Hernia, 1927; Pocket Book of First Aid in Accidents and Chemical Warfare, 1937; Field Service Notes for Regimental Officers, 1939; (with P. S. Mitchiner) Medical Organisation in Air Raids, 2nd edn 1941. *Recreations:* walking, gardening, fishing. *Address:* Stuart Lodge, Sausmarez Road, St Martin, Guernsey, CI.

**COWELL, Frank Richard,** CMG 1952; BA, BSc (Econ), PhD (London); retired Civil Servant; Secretary United Kingdom National Commission for UNESCO, 1946-58; *b* 16 Nov. 1897; *s London; William Frank Cowell and E. A. Pearce; m* 1927, Lilian Margaret (*d* 1970), *d* of Rev. A. E. Palin; two *s*. *Educ:* Roan Sch., Greenwich: King's Coll., London; London Sch. of Economics. BA 1919, BSc (Econ) 1927. Rockefeller Foundation Fellow in the Social Sciences, 1929-31; PhD 1938. Served in HM Stationery Office, 1921-39; Foreign Office, 1939-46. Dep. Sec. Gen. British Council, May-Nov. 1940; served on British Mission to French National Cttee, 1940-43. *Publications:* Brief Guide to Government Publications, 1938; Cicero and the Roman Republic, 1948, 5th edn (Penguin), 1968; History, Civilization and Culture, 1952; Culture, 1959; Everyday Life in Ancient Rome, 6th edn 1970; Revolutions of Ancient Rome, 1962; Leibniz, 1970; Values in Human Society, 1970; The Dominance of Rome, 1970. *Address:* Crowdleham House, Kemsing, Kent. *T:* Sevenoaks 61192. *Club:* Athenæum.

**COWELL, Stuart Jasper,** MA, MB, BCh Cantab; FRCP; Professor Emeritus in the University of London; *b* 9 Feb. 1891; *s* of Jasper Cowell, Steyning, Sussex; *m* 1925, May Penelope (*d* 1961), *d* of late Cecil Archibald Smith, CIE, MICE; one *s* two *d*. *Educ:* Steyning and Brighton Grammar Schs; Queens' Coll., Cambridge; University Coll. Hosp. Medical Sch., London. 1st Cl. Natural Science Tripos, 1912; Asst in Med. Unit, University College Hosp. Med. Sch., 1921; clinical asst to Sir Edward Mellanby (Medical Research Council) at Sheffield, 1923. Associate Ed. of Biochemical Journal, 1939-43; Editorial Board, Nutrition Abstracts and Reviews, 1954-56, and British Journal of Nutrition; Mem. of North-West Metropolitan Regional Hosp. Board, 1947-56; late Chm. Catering and Nutrition Cttee of King Edward Hosp. Fund for London. *Publications:* papers in scientific journals. *Recreations:* gardening, prawning, sailing. *Address:* The Flagstaff, Northam, N Devon. *T:* Bideford 2076.

**COWEN, Alan Biddulph,** CMG 1961; OBE 1945; retired as Deputy Chairman of Standards Association of Rhodesia and Nyasaland; *b* 26 Sept. 1896; *m*; two *s*. *Educ:* St John's Coll., Johannesburg, S Africa; Sch. of Mines and Technology. Formerly Chm., Southern Rhodesian Electricity Supply Commission; Mem. of Federal Power Board. CEng; FIEE; M(SA)IEE. *Address:* 307 Main Road, Eastcliff, Hermanus, Cape Province, S Africa.

**COWEN, John David,** MC 1943; TD 1944; MA; FSA; Director, Barclays Bank Ltd, since 1965; *b* 1904; *e s* of John Edward Cowen, Minsteracres, Northumberland; *m* 1944, Rhoda Susan Harris; one *s* two *d*. *Educ:* Rugby (scholar); Hertford Coll., Oxford (scholar). Final Law Soc. Exams (Hons), 1931. Entered Barclays Bank Ltd, 1931; Gen. Manager (Staff), 1948-49; Gen. Manager, 1950-65. Fellow, Inst. of Bankers (Mem. Council, 1950-59); Chairman: Inter-Bank Cttee on Electronics, 1955-61; Inter-Bank Working Party on Negotiating Machinery in Banking, 1965-67. Joined Northumberland Hussars Yeomanry, 1929; Major, 1942; served in North Africa, Sicily (despatches), France and Germany. Dir, Newcastle upon Tyne and Gateshead Gas Co., 1934-47 (Chm. 1947). Mem., Standing Commn on Museums and Galls, 1966-; Governor, Museum of London, 1965-67; Treas., Soc. of Antiquaries of London, 1964-; Pres., The Prehistoric Soc., 1966-70; Pres. Soc. of Antiquaries of Newcastle upon Tyne, 1966-68 (Hon. Curator, 1933-39, 1947-48); Corr. Mem. German Archaeolog. Inst.; Hon. DCL (Durham), 1961. *Publications:* articles in banking and archaeological jls (Brit. and foreign). *Recreations:* prehistory, travel. *Address:* 35 Argyll Road, W8. *T:* 01-937 2127; Over Court, Bisley, near Stroud, Glos. *T:* Bisley 209. *Clubs:* Athenæum, Cavalry.

**COWEN, Prof. Zelman,** CMG 1968; Vice-Chancellor of Queensland University, since 1970; *b* 7 Oct. 1919; *s* of Bernard and Sara Cowen; *m* 1945, Anna Wittner; three *s* one *d*. *Educ:* Scotch Coll., Melbourne; University of Melbourne; Oxford Univ. BA 1939, LLB 1941,

LLM 1942, Melbourne; BCL, MA 1947, DCL 1968, Oxford. Lieut, RANVR, 1941-45. Called to Bar, Gray's Inn, 1947; called to Vic (Aust.) Bar, 1951. Victorian Rhodes Schol., 1941; Vinerian Schol., Oxford Univ., 1947. Fellow and Tutor, Oriel Coll., Oxford, 1947-50; Prof. of Public Law and Dean of Faculty of Law, University of Melbourne, 1951-66; Dominion Liaison Officer to Colonial Office (UK), 1951-66; Prof. Emer., University of Melbourne, 1967; Vice-Chancellor and Professor, Univ. of New England, Armidale, NSW, 1967-70. Vis. Professor: University of Chicago, 1949; Harvard Univ., 1953-54 and 1963-64; Fletcher Sch. of Law and Diplomacy, 1954 and 1964; University of Utah, 1954; University of Ill, 1957-58; Washington Univ., St Louis, 1959. Mem., Social Science Res. Coun. of Aust., 1952-; For. Hon. Mem., Amer. Acad. of Arts and Sciences, 1965. Broadcaster on radio and TV on nat. and internat. affairs; Mem. and Chm., Victorian State Adv. Cttee of Australian Broadcasting Commn (at various times during 1950's and 1960's); Mem., Chief Justice's Law Reform Cttee, 1951-66; President: Asthma Foundn of Victoria, 1963-66; Adult Educn Assoc. of Australia, 1968-. Mem. Bd of Governors, Hebrew Univ. of Jerusalem, 1969-. Hon. LLD, Hong Kong, 1967. *Publications:* (ed jtly) Dicey's Conflict of Laws, 1949; Australia and the United States: Some Legal Comparisons, 1954; (with P. B. Carter) Essays on the Law of Evidence, 1956; American-Australian Private International Law, 1957; Federal Jurisdiction in Australia, 1959; (with D. M. da Costa) Matrimonial Causes Jurisdiction, 1961; Sir John Latham and other papers, 1965; British Commonwealth of Nations in a Changing World, 1965; Isaac Isaacs, 1967; The Private Man, 1969; articles and chapters in legal works in UK, US, Canada, Germany, Australia. *Recreations:* tennis, squash, music, theatre. *Address:* University of Queensland, St Lucia, Brisbane, Queensland 4067, Australia. *Clubs:* University (Sydney); Armidale (Armidale); Royal Automobile of Victoria (Melbourne).

**COWERN, Raymond Teague,** RA 1968 (ARA 1957); RWS; RE; ARCA; RWA; artist (painter and etcher); Principal, Brighton College of Art and Crafts; *b* 12 July 1913; *s* of George Dent Cowern and Elsie Ellen Teague; *m* Margaret Jean Trotman; one *s* two *d. Educ:* King Edward's Grammar Sch., Aston, Birmingham. Studied Central Sch. of Art, Birmingham, Royal Coll. of Art, London. Worked with Sakkarah Expedition of the Oriental Institute of Chicago; Rome Scholar in Engraving, 1937-39; commissioned by Pilgrim Trust Scheme for Recording Britain. Served in the Army, 1940-46. Represented by work at British Museum and in public collections Glasgow, Liverpool, Birmingham, Oxford, Cambridge, Bristol and museums abroad. *Address:* Church Lodge, Patcham, Brighton. *T:* Brighton 56704. *Club:* Chelsea Arts.

**COWIE, Mervyn Hugh,** CBE 1960; ED 1954; *b* 13 April 1909; *s* of Capt. Herbert Hugh Cowie, JP; *m* 1st, 1934, Erica Mary Beaty (*d* 1956); two *s* one *d*; 2nd, 1957, Valori Hare Duke; one *s* one *d. Educ:* Brighton Coll.; Brasenose Coll., Oxford. Hon. Game Warden, 1932-; Mem. Nairobi District Council, 1932-36; KAR, Reserve of Officers, 1932-38 (3rd and 5th Battalions); Kenya Regt, 1939; served War of 1939-45; Abyssinia, Middle East, Madagascar (retd Lieut-Col). MLC Kenya, 1951-60; Dir of Manpower, Mau-Mau Emergency, 1953-56. Founder and Dir, Royal National Parks of Kenya, 1946-66. Vice-Pres. E African Tourist Travel Assoc., 1950-65; Mem. Nat. Parks Commn, Internat. Union for Conservation of Nature, 1959-66; Hon. Trustee, Uganda Nat. Parks, 1950-; Vice-Pres., Fauna Preservation Soc., London; Trustee, East African Wild Life Soc. TV and Radio (BBC Natural History Section). FCA; FZS (London). Editor, Royal Nat. Parks of Kenya Annual Reports, 1946-65. Lectures (Tours USA and Britain). *Publications:* Fly Vulture, 1961; I Walk with Lions (USA), 1964; African Lion, 1965. Contributor to International Journals and Conferences. *Recreations:* big game photography, mountaineering, flying and wild life conservation. *Address:* PO Box 505, Nairobi, Kenya. *T:* Langata 210. *Clubs:* East India and Sports, Shikar; Explorer's (New York); Muthaiga Country (Nairobi); Nairobi Rotary (Past Pres.); Mountain Club of Kenya; Aero Club of East Africa.

**COWIE, William Lorn Kerr,** QC (Scotland) 1967; *b* 1 June 1926; *s* of Charles Rennie Cowie, MBE and late Norah Slimmon Kerr; *m* 1958, Camilla Henrietta Grizel Hoyle; two *s* two *d. Educ:* Fettes Coll.; Clare Coll., Cambridge; Glasgow Univ. Sub-Lieut RNVR, 1944-47; Cambridge, 1947-49; Glasgow Univ., 1949-51; Mem., Faculty of Advocates, 1952. *Address:* 20 Blacket Place, Edinburgh 9. *T:* 031-667 8238.

**COWLES, Virginia,** OBE 1947; writer; *b* USA, 24 Aug. 1912; *d* of Florence Wolcott Jaquith and Edward Spencer Cowles; *m* 1945, Aidan M. Crawley, *qv*; two *s* one *d. Educ:* privately. Newspaper correspondent, 1937-41 and 1943-45; Special Asst to the American Ambassador, American Embassy, London, 1942-43. *Publications:* Looking for Trouble, 1941; How America is Governed, 1944; No Cause for Alarm, 1949; Winston Churchill: The Era and the Man, 1953; Edward VII and His Circle, 1956; The Phantom Major, 1958; The Great Swindle, 1960; The Kaiser, 1963; 1913: The Defiant Swan Song, 1967; The Russian Dagger, 1969. *Recreation:* politics. *Address:* 19 Chester Square, SW1. *T:* 01-730 3030.

**COWLES-VOYSEY, Charles,** FRIBA, retired; *b* 24 June 1889; *e s* of Charles Francis Annesley Voysey, FRIBA, architect; *m* 1912, Dorothea Denise Cowles; no *c. Educ:* private sch.; University Coll., London. Architect for: Worthing Civic Centre; White Rock Pavilion, Hastings; the Guildhall, Cambridge; Watford Town Hall; Bromley (Kent), Town Hall Extensions; Bridgeton Halls, Glasgow; Municipal Offices, High Wycombe; Kingsley Hall, Bow; Bognor Regis Municipal Offices; Hampshire County Council Offices, Winchester, and other public buildings and private houses; Consulting Architect to various local authorities. *Recreation:* landscape painting. *Address:* 2 Bunkers Hill, NW11. *T:* 01-455 7274. *Club:* Athenæum.

**COWLEY,** 6th Earl *cr* 1857; **Richard Francis Wellesley;** Baron Cowley, 1828; Viscount Dangan, 1857; *b* 12 June 1946; *s* of 5th Earl Cowley and Elizabeth Anne, *yr d* of Lieut-Col Pelham Rawstorn Papillon, DSO; *S* father, 1968. *Educ:* Wellesley House, Broadstairs; Eton. *Heir: uncle* Hon. Garret Graham Wellesley [*b* 30 July 1934; *m* 1960, Elizabeth Suzanne Lennon; one *s* one *d*]. *Address:* 3 Market Mews, W1.

**COWLEY, Rev. Canon Colin Patrick;** Rector of Wonston, Winchester, since 1955; Canon of Winchester, 1950-55, Hon. Canon, 1955; *b* 3 Aug. 1902; *er s* of Rev. H. G. B. Cowley; *m* 1930, Dorothea Minna Pott, 69 Victoria Road, Kensington, W8; three *d. Educ:* Winchester; Hertford Coll., Oxford. Curate at St Mary's, Bridport, 1926-28; Curate at St Mary Abbots, Kensington, 1928-35; Rector of Shenfield, Essex, 1935-50. Chaplain to the Forces, 1940-45. *Recreations:* golf and walking. *Address:*

Wonston Rectory, Sutton Scotney, Hants. *T:* Sutton Scotney 240.

**COWLEY, Denis Martin,** QC 1965; Barrister-at-Law; *b* 30 Jan. 1919; *s* of late Sir William Percy Cowley, CBE; *m* 1940, Margaret Hazel, *d* of Hugo Teare, Ramsey, Isle of Man; one *s* two *d*. *Educ:* Radley Coll.; Exeter Coll., Oxford (BA (Hons Jurisprudence)). Served RAFVR, 1939-45. Called to Bar, Inner Temple, 1946. Midland Circuit. *Recreations:* shooting, sailing. *Address:* 2a Huntingdon Drive, The Park, Nottingham. *T:* 42948; 52 Elm Park Road, Chelsea, SW3. *T:* 01-352 5395; Seal Rock Cottage, Castletown, Isle of Man. *T:* Castletown 3532; Francis Taylor Buildings, Temple, EC4. *T:* 01-353 9942. *Clubs:* United University; Nottinghamshire County.

**COWLEY, Horace W.;** *see* Wyndham, Horace Cowley.

**COWLEY, Maj.-Gen. John Cain;** Paymaster-in-Chief and Inspector of Army Pay Services since 1967; *b* 17 July 1918. Served War of 1939-45; Royal Army Pay Corps: Lieut, 1945; Capt., 1946; Major, 1953; Lieut-Col and Staff Paymaster, (1st class), 1955; Colonel and Chief Paymaster, 1960; Dep. Paymaster-in-Chief, War Office, 1960; Brig., 1966; jssc; psc. *Address:* Ministry of Defence, Whitehall, SW1.

**COWLEY, Lt-Gen. Sir John Guise,** KBE 1958 (CBE 1946; OBE 1943); CB 1954; Albert Medal, 1935; late RE; Chairman, Bowmaker Ltd, since 1962; Director: C. T. Bowring and Co. Ltd, since 1969; British Oxygen Co. Ltd; Alastair Watson & Co.; *b* 20 Aug. 1905; *s* of Rev. Henry Guise Beatson Cowley, Fourgates, Dorchester, Dorset; *m* 1941, Irene Sybil, *d* of Percy Dreuille Millen, Berkhamsted, Herts; one *s* three *d*. *Educ:* Wellington Coll.; RMA Woolwich. 2nd Lieut RE 1925; Capt. 1936; Major 1940; Lieut-Col 1941; Brig. 1943; Maj.-Gen. 1953; Lieut-Gen. 1957. Served War of 1939-45, Middle East, Italy, and North-West Europe (despatches four times, OBE). Chief of Staff, Headquarters, Eastern Command, 1953-56; Vice-Quartermaster-Gen., 1956-57; Controller of Munitions, Ministry of Supply, 1957-60; Master-Gen. of the Ordnance, War Office, 1960-62; retd, 1962. Col Commandant: Royal Pioneer Corps, 1961-67; Royal Engineers, 1961-70. Vice-Pres., wellington Coll., 1969; Governor, brockenhurst Grammar Sch., 1969-; Chm. of Governors, Eagle House Sch., 1968-. Knight Comdr Order of Orange Nassau (Netherlands). *Recreations:* golf, bridge. *Address:* Whitemoor, Burley, Ringwood, Hants. *T:* Burley 2357. *Club:* Army and Navy.

**COWLEY, Kenneth Martin,** CMG 1963; OBE 1956; *b* 15 May 1912; *s* of late Robert Martin Cowley, OBE, and late Mabel Priscilla Cowley (*née* Lee); *m* 1948, Barbara (*née* Tannahill); one *s* (and one step *s*). *Educ:* Merchant Taylors' Sch., Crosby; Exeter Coll., Oxford. District Officer, Kenya, 1935-44; Asst Sec., 1944-46; District Comr, 1946-49; Actg Native Courts Officer, 1949-53; Sec. for African Affairs, 1953-56; Provincial Commissioner, Southern Province, Kenya, 1956-63; Sec., Kenya Regional Boundaries and Constituencies Commns, 1962; Sen. Administrative Manager, Express Transport Co. Ltd, Kenya, 1963-70, retd. *Recreations:* riding, natural history. *Address:* c/o Lloyds Bank Ltd, 40 Victoria Street, Douglas, Isle of Man. *Club:* Nairobi (Kenya).

**COWLING, Donald George,** MBE 1945; JP; Chairman, City of Leeds Conservative Association, 1957-67 (Deputy Chairman 1956); *b* 27 Oct. 1904; *m* 1928, Muriel, *o c* of late Charles Richard Chambers; one *s* one *d*. Mem. Leeds City Council, 1930; Chm. Transport Cttee, 1938-41 and 1949-53; Mem. Local Price Regulation Cttee for NE Region, 1940-41; resigned from Council to join RAF 1941; released as Sqdn Ldr, 1945, and re-elected to City Council, 1946; Chm. Central Div. (Conservative Party), 1948-53, Chm. of SE Leeds Div., 1953-57; Dep. Lord Mayor, 1951-52; Lord Mayor of Leeds, 1953-54; Alderman of City of Leeds, 1949-55; resigned 1955; Hon. Alderman, 1967. Mem. Court and Council University of Leeds; Mem. House Cttee Gen. Infirmary at Leeds, 1955-59; Mem. Cttee Leeds Triennial Music Festival, 1955-59; Mem. Company of Poulters; Pres. Nat. Fedn of Wholesale Poultry Merchants, 1955-61 (Chm., 1939-41 and 1949-55). Pres. Leeds Branch of Royal Society of St George, 1958-66. *Recreation:* golf. *Address:* Gatescroft, Headingley, Leeds 6. *T:* 51175; Sandsend Court, Sandsend, N Yorks. *T:* Sandsend 328. *Clubs:* Leeds; Alwoodley Golf.

**COWLING, Thomas George,** FRS 1947; Professor of Applied Mathematics, Leeds University, 1948-70; *b* 17 June 1906; *s* of George and Edith Eliza Cowling; *m* 1935, Doris Moffatt; one *s* two *d*. *Educ:* Sir George Monoux Sch., Walthamstow; Oxford Univ. Teacher of mathematics, Imperial Coll. of Science, University Coll., Swansea, University Coll., Dundee, Manchester Univ., and at University Coll., Bangor (Prof. of Mathematics, 1945-48). Gold Medallist, Royal Astronomical Soc., 1956, Pres., 1965-67. Hon. Fellow, Brasenose Coll., Oxford, 1966. Halley Lectr, Oxford Univ., 1969. *Publications:* (with S. Chapman) The Mathematical Theory of Non-Uniform Gases, 1939; Molecules in Motion, 1950; Magneto-hydrodynamics, 1957; also a number of papers, chiefly astronomical and atmospheric. *Recreation:* gardening. *Address:* 19 Hollin Gardens, Leeds LS16 5NL. *T:* 53342.

**COWPER. Brig. Anthony William,** CBE 1964 (OBE 1945); retired; *b* 10 May 1913; *s* of Walter Taylor Cowper, solicitor, Southgate, London, and West Burton, Yorks; *m* 1949, Margaret Mary, *d* of Clarence W. Fry, Upminster, Essex; no *c*. *Educ:* Merchant Taylors' Sch. Joined Christie's, Fine Art Auctioneers, 1932. Commissioned from TA (HAC) into West Yorks Regt, Nov. 1939; War Service in India, Burma, Ceylon and Singapore, 1940-45 (OBE). Granted regular commn, 1947; served overseas almost continuously (mainly Far East) in Regtl and Staff appts (despatches, Malayan Emergency, 1954); Col 1961; Brig. 1965; Defence Adviser to British High Comr in Malaysia, 1967; retd 1969. Freeman of City of London. *Recreations:* fly fishing, small boat sailing, antiques, Far East affairs. *Address:* West Burton, Leyburn, Yorkshire. *T:* Aysgarth 306. *Club:* United Service.

**COWPER, Sir Norman (Lethbridge),** Kt 1967; CBE 1958; Senior Partner, Allen, Allen & Hemsley, solicitors, Sydney, Australia; *b* 15 Sept. 1896; *yr s* of Cecil Spencer de Grey Cowper; *m* 1925, Dorothea Huntly, *d* of Hugh McCrae; three *d*. *Educ:* Sydney Grammar Sch.; University of Sydney (BA, LLB). Served War of 1939-45, 2nd AIF, Lt-Col. Solicitor, Supreme Court of NSW, 1923. Partner, Allen, Allen & Hemsley, 1924. Dir, Australian Inst. of Polit. Science, 1932-; Mem. Council, Australian National Univ., 1955-; Mem. Board of Trustees, Sydney Grammar Sch., 1935 (Chm. 1957); Chm., Council on New Guinea Affairs, 1965. *Publications:* occasional articles: Australian Quarterly, Australian Outlook,

Australian Dictionary of Biography. *Recreations:* tennis, reading, gardening. *Address:* Wivenhoe, Millewa Avenue, Wahroonga, Sydney, Australia. *T:* 48 2336. *Clubs:* Australian, University (Sydney).

**COWPERTHWAITE, Sir John James,** KBE 1968 (OBE 1960); CMG 1964; Financial Secretary, Hong Kong, since 1961; *b* 25 April 1915; *s* of late John James Cowperthwaite and of Jessie Wemyss Barron Jarvis Cowperthwaite, Algarve, Portugal; *m* 1941, Sheila Mary, *d* of Alexander Thomson, 19 Seafield Drive East, Aberdeen; one *s*. *Educ:* Merchiston Castle Sch.; St Andrews Univ; Christ's Coll., Cambridge. Entered Colonial Administrative Service, Hong Kong, 1941; seconded to Sierra Leone, 1942-45. *Address:* 45 Shouson Hill Road, Hong Kong. *T:* 92455. *Clubs:* Royal Hong Kong Jockey, Royal Hong Kong Golf; Royal and Ancient.

**COWTAN, Maj.-Gen. Frank Willoughby John,** CBE 1970 (MBE 1947); MC 1942 and Bar, 1945; Deputy Quartermaster-General, Ministry of Defence (AD), since 1970; *b* 10 Feb. 1920; *s* of late Air Vice-Marshal F. C. Cowtan, CB, CBE, KHS and late Mrs N. A. Cowtan (*née* Kennedy); *m* 1949, Rose Isabel Cope; one *s* one *d*. *Educ:* Wellington Coll.; RMA Woolwich. 2nd Lieut Royal Engineers, 1939; served War of 1939-45, BEF, N Africa, Italy, NW Europe (Captain); Palestine, Kenya, Middle East, 1945-50 (Major); psc 1951; Middle East, UK, BAOR, 1952-58; Liaison Officer to US Corps of Engrs, USA, 1958-60 (Bt Lt-Col); CO 131 Parachute Engr Regt, 1960-62; CO Victory Coll., RMA Sandhurst, 1962-65 (Lt-Col); Comd 11 Engr Bde, BAOR, 1965-67 (Brig.); ndc (Canada) 1967-68; Dir of Quartering (Army), 1968-70. *Recreations:* golf, shooting, wildfowling, sailing, travel, languages. *Address:* Sandford, Shortheath, Farnham, Surrey. *T:* Farnham 4134.

**COX;** *see* Roxbee Cox.

**COX, Arthur Henry,** CMG 1938; *b* 8 Nov. 1888; *s* of Henry Thompson Cox, RN, Inspector-Gen. of Hospitals and Fleets; *m* 1929, Marjorie Thorpe Lewis; one *s*. *Educ:* Felsted (scholar); Corpus Christi Coll., Cambridge, MA (BA Mod. Langs). Asst District Commissioner, Uganda, 1911; Aide-de-Camp to Sir Robert Coryndon, Governor, Uganda, 1918-19; 1st Grade Administrative Officer, 1922; Dep. Provincial Commissioner, 1928; Acting Provincial Commissioner, July 1929 and June 1932; Asst Chief Sec., Uganda, 1930; Acting Dep. Chief Sec., March 1930-Oct. 1931; Provincial Commissioner, 1932; Resident of Buganda and Mem. of Executive Council, Uganda, 1932-44; retired, 1944; Civil Dispersals Officer, Uganda; discharged troops in Kenya, 1944-45; employed Colonial Office, 1947-49. *Address:* Rowlands, Old Hunstanton, Norfolk. *T:* Hunstanton 2375.

**COX, Sir Christopher (William Machell),** GCMG 1970 (KCMG 1950; CMG 1944); Educational Adviser, Ministry of Overseas Development, 1964-70; *b* 17 Nov. 1899; *e s* of late A. H. Machell Cox, Chevin Close, St Audries, Somerset. *Educ:* Clifton Coll.; Balliol Coll., Oxford. 2nd Lieut RE (Signals), 1918; 1st class Classical Moderations; 1st class Lit Hum, 1923; War Memorial Student, Balliol Coll., 1923-24; Craven Fellow, Oxford Univ., and Senior Demy, Magdalen Coll., 1924-26; archæological exploration in Turkey, 1924, 1925, 1926, 1931; Fellow of New Coll., Oxford, 1926-70, Hon. Fellow, 1970. sub-Warden, 1931; Dean, 1934-36; visited Africa, 1929; Persia, 1936; Dir of Education, Anglo-Egyptian Sudan, and Principal of Gordon Coll., Khartoum, 1937-39; Mem. of Governor-General's Council, 1938-39; Educational Adviser to the Sec. of State for the Colonies, 1940-61; Educational Adviser, Dept of Technical Co-operation, 1961-64. Pres., Education Sect., British Assoc., 1956. Hon. DLit Belfast, 1961; Hon. LLD Hong Kong, 1961; Hon. LLD Leeds, 1962; Hon. DCL Oxford, 1965. *Publications:* Monumenta Asiae Minoris Antiqua, Vol V (with A. Cameron), 1937; occasional papers. *Club:* Athenæum.

**COX, Prof. David Roxbee,** PhD; Professor of Statistics, Imperial College of Science and Technology, since 1966; Head of Department of Mathematics, since 1970; *b* 15 July 1924; *s* of S. R. Cox, Handsworth, Birmingham; *m* 1948, Joyce (*née* Drummond), Keighley, Yorks; three *s* one *d*. *Educ:* Handsworth Grammar Sch., Birmingham; St John's Coll., Cambridge (MA). PhD Leeds, 1949. Posts at Royal Aircraft Establishment, 1944-46; Wool Industries Research Assoc., 1946-50; Statistical Laboratory, Cambridge, 1950-55; Visiting Prof., University of N Carolina, 1955-56; Reader in Statistics, Birkbeck College, 1956-60, Professor of Statistics, 1961-66. Editor of Biometrika, 1966-. *Publications:* Statistical Methods in the Textile Industry, 1949 (jt author); Planning of Experiments, 1958; Queues, 1961 (jt author); Renewal Theory, 1962; Theory of Stochastic Processes, 1965 (jt author); Statistical Analysis of Series of Events, 1966 (jt author); Analysis of Binary Data, 1970; papers in Jl of Royal Statistical Society, Biometrika, etc. *Address:* Imperial College, SW7. *T:* 01-589 5111.

**COX, Sir (Ernest) Gordon,** KBE 1964; TD; FRS 1954; FRIC; FInstP; DSc; Secretary of the Agricultural Research Council since 1960; *b* 24 April 1906; *s* of Ernest Henry Cox and Rosina Ring; *m* 1st, 1929, Lucie Grace Baker (*d* 1962); one *s* one *d*; 2nd, 1968, Mary Rosaleen Truter, DSc, *d* of Dr D. N. Jackman. *Educ:* City of Bath Boys' Sch.; University of Bristol. Research Asst, Davy-Faraday Laboratory, Royal Institution, 1927; Chemistry Dept, Univ. of Birmingham, 1929-41 (Reader in Chemical Crystallography, 1940); Prof. of Inorganic and Structural Chemistry, University of Leeds, 1945-60; commissioned in Territorial Army, 1936; special scientific duties, War Office, 1942-44; attached to HQ staff of 21 Army Group, France and Germany, as Technical Staff Officer, Grade I, 1944-45. Vice-Pres., Institute of Physics, 1950-53; Mem. Agric. Research Council, 1957-60. DSc (*hc*), Newcastle and Birmingham, 1964; Hon. LLD Bristol, 1969. *Publications:* numerous scientific papers in jls of various learned societies, chiefly on the crystal structures of chemical compounds. *Recreations:* music, gardening, natural history. *Address:* 117 Hampstead Way, NW11. *T:* 01-455 2618. *Clubs:* Athenæum, English-Speaking Union, Lansdowne.

**COX, Euan Hillhouse Methven;** *b* 19 June 1893; *o c* of Alfred W. Cox, Glendoick, Glencarse, Perthshire, and late Helen Salmon; *m* 1925, Norah Helen Cox; one *s* one *d*. *Educ:* Cargilfield; Rugby; Trinity Hall, Cambridge. Temp. Lieut Royal Marines, 1914-16; explored in Upper Burma, 1919, with Reginald Farrer; Gardening Editor, Country Life, 1922-27; Editor, The Garden, 1924-26; Founder and Editor, The New Flora and Silva, 1928-38. *Publications:* Rhododendrons for Amateurs, 1924; Farrer's Last Journey, 1926; The Evolution of a Garden, 1927; Primulas for Garden and Greenhouse (with G. C. Taylor), 1928; Wild Gardening, 1929; The Plant Introductions of Reginald Farrer, 1930; The

Gardener's Chapbook, 1931; A History of Gardening in Scotland, 1935; A History of Plant Collecting in China, 1945; Modern Rhododendrons (with P. A. Cox), 1956; Modern Shrubs (with P. A. Cox), 1958; Modern Trees (with P. A. Cox), 1961. *Recreations:* gardening, botanical exploration, fishing, photography. *Address:* Glendoick, Perth. *T:* Glencarse 205.

**COX, Sir Geoffrey (Sandford),** Kt 1966; CBE 1959 (MBE 1945); Deputy Chairman, Yorkshire Television, since 1968; *b* 7 April 1910; *s* of Sandford Cox, Wellington, NZ, and Mary Cox (*née* MacGregor); *m* 1935, Cecily Barbara Talbot Turner; two *s* two *d. Educ:* Southland High Sch., New Zealand; Otago Univ., New Zealand (MA); Rhodes Scholar, 1932-35; Oriel Coll., Oxford (BA). Reporter, Foreign and War Corresp. News Chronicle, 1935-37, Daily Express, 1937-40. Enlisted New Zealand Army, 1940; commissioned, Dec. 1940; served in 2 New Zealand Div., Greece, Crete, Libya, Italy; Major, Chief Intelligence Officer, Gen. Freyberg's staff (despatches twice). First Sec. and Chargé d'Affaires, NZ Legation, Washington, 1943; NZ Rep., first UNRRA Conf., 1943; Political Corresp., News Chronicle, 1945; Asst Editor, News Chronicle 1954. Regular Contributor, BBC radio and TV, 1945-56; Editor and Chief Exec., Independent Television News, 1956-68; founded News at Ten, 1967. Vice-Chm., Internat. Broadcast Inst. TV Producers' Guild Award Winner, 1962; TV Soc. Silver Medal, 1963. *Publications:* Defence of Madrid, 1937; The Red Army Moves, 1941; The Road to Trieste, 1946. *Recreations:* fishing, golf. *Address:* 20 Chesterford Gardens, NW3. *T:* 01-435 1592. *Club:* Garrick.

**COX, Sir (George) Trenchard;** *see* Cox, Sir Trenchard.

**COX, Sir Gordon;** *see* Cox, Sir E. G.

**COX, Harry Bernard,** CBE 1956; Deputy Chairman, Thos Wyatt & Son (West Africa) Ltd, since 1967; Consultant, Knight, Frank & Rutley, since 1967; *b* 29 Nov. 1906; *e surv s* of Rev. Charles Henry Cox, BSc; *m* 1955, Joan, *e d* of P. Munn, Brighton; one *s* one *d. Educ:* Upholland Grammar Sch.; Keble Coll., Oxford. Colonial Administrative Service, Nigeria, 1930; Dir of Commerce and Industries, Nigeria, 1949; Acting Development Sec., Nigeria, 1953-54; Acting Commissioner for Nigeria, 1955; Principal Sec. to the Commissioner for Nigeria in the United Kingdom, 1955. John Holt & Co. (Liverpool) Ltd, 1958; Chm., John Holt (Nigeria) Ltd, 1962. *Recreation:* golf. *Address:* Great Pollards, Ashurst, Tunbridge Wells, Kent. *T:* Fordcombe 216. *Club:* Oriental.

**COX, Sir Herbert Charles Fahie,** Kt 1946; JP; Chief Justice of Basutoland, the Bechuanaland Protectorate, and Swaziland, 1956-61; *b* 1893; 2nd *s* of late Sir Charles T. Cox, KCMG, of British Guiana; *m* 1st, 1919, Dorothy, *o d* of late Sir Maurice Berkeley; one *s* one *d*; 2nd, 1933, Mabel, *o d* of late T. Wright, MD, Lee-on-the-Solent; one *s* one *d.* Barrister-at-Law, 1915; KC Nigeria, 1936; British Guiana Police, 1913-19; served European War, 1917-19; Asst Attorney-Gen., British Guiana, 1920-25; Attorney-Gen., Bahamas, 1925-29; MLC, 1926; Attorney-Gen., Gibraltar, 1929-33; Solicitor-Gen., Nigeria, 1933-35; Attorney-Gen., Nigeria, 1935-46; Chief Justice of N Rhodesia, 1946-52 (Chm. Northern Rhodesia Police Commission of Enquiry, 1946-47), Tanganyika, 1952-56. Chm., Commission of Enquiry into Provincial Disturbances, Sierra Leone, 1956. JP Wilts, 1963. CC, Dorset, 1963-69; Dep. Chm., Wilts QS, 1964-68. *Recreations:* tennis, golf, cricket. *Address:* Pentridge House, Pentridge, near Salisbury, Wilts. *Clubs:* Royal Commonwealth Society, East India and Sports.

*See also N. J. G. Ramsay.*

**COX, Major Horace B. T.;** *see* Trevor Cox.

**COX, Ian Herbert,** CBE 1952; MA; FGS; FRGS; FZS; General Treasurer, British Association for the Advancement of Science, 1965-70; *b* 20 Feb. 1910; *e s* of late Herbert Stanley Cox and Elizabeth Dalgarno; *m* 1945, Susan Mary, *d* of late Lieut Comdr N. G. Fowler Snelling and *widow* of Flt Lieut D. S. S. Low; two *s* two *d. Educ:* Oundle; Magdalene Coll., Cambridge (Exhibnr). Geologist, Oxford Univ. Hudson Straits Expedition, 1931; research, Dept of Geology, Cambridge, 1932-36; with BBC 1936-39; served War of 1939-45 (Comdr, RNVR); BBC 1946; Science Corresp., London Press Service, 1947-48; Dir of Sc., Festival of Britain Office, 1948-51; Shell Internat. Pet. Co., 1952-70 (Hd Sc. and Develt TR Div., Convener Shell Grants Cttee); Mem. Council, RGS, 1953-57, 1959-62; Mem. Management Cttee, Scott Polar Research Inst., 1955-57; Vice-Pres., Geol. Soc., 1966-68. A Governor, Chelsea Coll., Univ. of London; Mem. Court, RCA. *Publications:* papers on geology and palæontology of the Arctic; (ed) The Queen's Beasts, 1953; The Scallop, 1957; monographs in World Land Use Survey. *Recreations:* working with wood and stone; gardening. *Address:* Shepherd's House, The Sands, Farnham, Surrey. *T:* Runfold 2080. *Clubs:* Athenæum, Hanstown; Arctic.

**COX, Sir John (William),** Kt 1951; CBE 1946; Member, 1930-68, and Speaker of the House of Assembly, Bermuda, 1948-68; *b* 29 April 1900; *s* of Henry James and Ellen Augusta Cox; *m* 1926, Dorothy Carlyle, *d* of J. D. C. Darrell; three *s. Educ:* Saltus Grammar Sch., Bermuda. Merchant; Partner of the firm of Pearman, Watlington & Co., Hamilton, Bermuda, General and Commission Merchants. Hon. Consul of the Netherlands at Hamilton, Bermuda. Comdr, Royal Netherlands Order of Orange Nassau, 1956. *Address:* The Grove, Devonshire Parish, Bermuda. *T:* 2-0303. *Clubs:* Royal Bermuda Yacht, Royal Hamilton Amateur Dinghy, Mid Ocean (Bermuda).

**COX, Air Vice-Marshal Joseph,** CB 1957; OBE 1950; DFC 1940; retired; *b* 25 Oct. 1904; *m* 1933, Dorothy Thomas; one *d. Educ:* Peter Symond's Sch., Winchester, Hants. Commissioned, RAF, 1928; various appts at home and abroad, 1929-39. War of 1939-45: Examining Officer (flying), Central Flying Sch., 1939-40; comd No 15 (Bomber) Sqdn, June-Dec. 1940; Chief Instructor No 33 Service Flying Training Sch., Canada, 1941-42; commanded No 31 Bombing and Gunnery Sch., Canada, 1942-43; commanded No 12 Advanced (Pilot) Flying Unit, and Stn Comdr RAF Spitalgate (Grantham), 1943-45. Comd No 8302 Air Disarmament Wing in Germany, 1945-46; comd RAF Fuhlsbuttel (Hamburg), 1946-48; Senior Personnel Staff Officer, HQ Maintenance Comd, 1948-51; Stn Comdr RAF Finningley, 1951-52; AOC, RAF, Ceylon, 1952-55; Senior Air Staff Officer, Flying Training Command, 1955-58; retired, 1958. *Recreations:* tennis, swimming, cricket, (in younger days) soccer, hockey, squash, badminton, water polo, riding. *Address:* Pippins, 19 Highmoor Road, Caversham, Reading, Berks. *T:* 72761. *Clubs:* MCC, Royal Air Force, Royal Air Force Reserves; Adastrian Cricket.

**COX, Dr Leonard Bell,** CMG 1968; Consulting Neurologist since 1927; *b* 29 Aug. 1894; *s* of Rev. Edward Thomas Cox and Isabella Bell; *m* 1925, Nancy Compson Trumble; one *d* (and one *d* decd). *Educ:* Wesley Coll., Melbourne; Melbourne Univ. MB, BS Melbourne 1916; MRCPE 1919; MD Melbourne 1920; FRACP 1938. Hon. and Consulting Neurologist, Alfred Hosp., Melbourne, 1934-; Cons. Neurologist, Queen Victoria Hosp., 1948. Served European War, 1914-18, Capt. AAMC, 1917; War of 1939-45, Wing Comdr, Consultant in Neurology to RAAF. Foundation Pres., Aust. Assoc. of Neurologists, 1950. Chairman: Trustees of Nat. Gallery of Victoria, 1957-65; Nat. Gallery and Cultural Centre Building Cttee, 1957-64; Member: Felton Bequests Cttee, 1958-; Commonwealth Research Adv. Cttee, 1948. *Publications:* Ars Vivendi, 1942; (jt) Human Torulosis, 1946; articles on neurology and neuropathology in med jls. *Recreations:* Chinese art, country gardening. *Address:* Folly Farm, Falls Road, Olinda, Vic 3788, Australia. *T:* 751110. *Clubs:* Melbourne, Melbourne Cricket (Melbourne).

**COX, Dame Marjorie (Sophie),** DBE 1950 (CBE 1943; OBE 1937); *b* 13 Dec. 1893; Fellow of University College, London; retired; *d* of late Albert and Amelia Cox, Trowbridge, Wilts. *Educ:* University Coll., London. BA London. Entered Civil Service as temp. clerk in 1915 and became established through Lytton examination in 1921; Mem. Beveridge Cttee on Social Security; Dep. Sec. Min. of Pensions (later of Pensions and National Insurance), 1946-54. *Recreation:* gardening. *Address:* 10 The Paragon, Wannock Lane, Willingdon, Eastbourne, Sussex. *T:* Polegate 4159. *Club:* Oxford and Cambridge University.

**COX, Maj.-Gen. Maurice L.;** *see* Lea-Cox.

**COX, Norman Ernest;** Counsellor (Commercial), British Embassy, Moscow, since 1969; *b* 28 Aug. 1921; *s* of late Ernest William Cox and late Daisy Beatrice (*née* Edmonds); *m* 1945, Maruja Margarita (*née* Cruz); one *s* one *d*. *Educ:* Lycée Français de Madrid; King's Coll., London. Tax Officer, Inland Revenue, 1938-41; Army, Intell. Corps, 1941-45: Gibraltar, 1942-45; Attaché, Madrid, 1945-47; FO, 1947-50; 2nd Sec., Sofia, 1950-52; 2nd Sec., Montevideo, 1952-54; FO, 1954-57; Dep. Regional Information Officer for SE Asia, Singapore, 1957-60; FO, 1960-62: Laos Conf., Geneva, 1961; Sec. to UK Conf. Delegn to ECSC, Luxemburg, 1962-63; 1st Sec. (Commercial), Madrid, 1963-66; Counsellor (Information), Mexico, Regional Information Officer for Central American Republics, PRO to Duke of Edinburgh for 1968 Olympics, 1966-68. *Recreations:* swimming, walking, climbing, travelling; archaeology, history, linguistics, comparative religion. *Address:* 36 Meadow Road, Malvern Link, Worcs; Commercial Department, British Embassy, Kutuzovsky Prospect, Moscow, USSR. *T:* Moscow 241-10-33. *Club:* Royal Automobile.

**COX, Peter Richmond;** Deputy Government Actuary since 1963; *b* 3 Sept. 1914; *s* of Richard R. Cox, Civil Servant, and Nellie D. (*née* Richmond). *Educ:* King's Coll. Sch., Wimbledon. Entered Government Actuary's Dept, 1933. Qualified as Fellow, Institute of Actuaries, 1939. Joint Hon. Sec., Institute of Actuaries, 1962-64 (Vice-Pres., 1966-68). Pres., Eugenics Soc., 1970 (Hon. Librarian, 1965-70). *Publications:* Demography, 1950 (4 edns); (with R. H. Storr-Best) Surplus in British Life Assurance, 1962; various papers on actuarial and demographic subjects. *Recreations:* music, painting, gardening. *Address:* Braeside, Headley Drive, Epsom, Surrey. *T:* Burgh Heath 53555. *Club:* Reform.

**COX, Philip (Joseph),** DSC 1943; QC 1967; *b* 28 Sept. 1922; *s* of Joseph Parriss Cox, Rugby; *m* 1951, Margaret Jocelyn Cox, *d* of R. C. H. Cox, Purley, Surrey; one *s* one *d*. *Educ:* Rugby Sch; Queens' Coll., Cambridge. RNVR, 1942-46 (Lieut). Called to Bar, Gray's Inn, 1949; practised at Bar, Birmingham, 1949-67. Mem. County Court Rules Cttee, 1962-68; Dep. Chm., Northants QS, 1963-; Dep. Chm., Warwicks QS, 1966-. Legal Assessor to Disciplinary Cttee, RCVS, 1969-. *Recreation:* sailing. *Address:* (home) 40 George Road, Edgbaston, Birmingham 15. *T:* 021-454 2656; (chambers) 1 King's Bench Walk, Temple, EC4. *Clubs:* RNVR; Union (Birmingham); Royal Cruising, Bar Yacht.

**COX, Thomas Michael;** MP (Lab) Wandsworth Central since 1970; *b* London, 1930. *Educ:* state schools; London Sch. of Economics. Electrical worker. Former Mem., Fulham Borough Council; contested (Lab) GLC elections, 1967; contested (Lab) Stroud, 1966. Member: ETU; Co-operative Party. *Address:* House of Commons, SW1.

**COX, Thomas Richard Fisher,** CMG 1955; Bursar, St Andrew's College, Dublin, since 1962; *b* 21 Feb. 1907; *s* of late Rev. James Fisher Cox; *m* 1st, 1933, Doreen Alice Rae; one *s* two *d*; 2nd, 1968, Rowena Mary Figgis; one *s*. *Educ:* Portora Royal Sch.; TCD; University Coll., Oxford. Provincial Admin., Uganda, 1930; acted as Sec. for African Affairs, 1949-50; Chm. Languages Board, Uganda, 1950-60; Provincial Comr, Uganda, 1950-61. *Publications:* articles in Uganda Jl and Jl of African Admin. *Recreations:* golf, gardening; formerly boxing (boxed for Oxford Univ. *v* Cambridge Univ., 1930). *Address:* 21 Hyde Park, Dalkey, Co. Dublin. *T:* 804596. *Clubs:* Friendly Brothers (Dublin); East Africa House.

**COX, Sir Trenchard,** Kt 1961; CBE 1954; MA; FRSA (Vice-President 1964-68); FMA; FSA; Director and Secretary, Victoria and Albert Museum, 1956-66; *b* 31 July 1905; *s* of late William Pallett Cox and Marion Beverley; *m* 1935, Mary Désirée, *d* of late Sir Hugh Anderson, Master of Gonville and Caius Coll., Cambridge. *Educ:* Eton; King's Coll., Cambridge. Worked as volunteer at the National Gallery and Brit. Museum (Dept of Prints and Drawings), 1929-32; spent a semester at the University of Berlin in the Dept of Arts, 1930; Asst to the Keeper, Wallace Collection, 1932-39; seconded for war-time duties, to Home Office, 1940-44; Dir of Birmingham Museum and Art Gallery, 1944-55. Mem., Ancient Monuments Board for England, 1959-. Hon. DLitt (Birmingham) 1956. Chevalier, Légion d'Honneur, 1967. *Publications:* The National Gallery, a Room-to-Room Guide, 1930; Jehan Foucquet, Native of Tours, 1931; part editor of the Catalogue to the Exhibition of French Art at Burlington House, Jan.-March 1932; The Renaissance in Europe, 1933; A General Guide to the Wallace Collection, 1933; A Short Illustrated History of the Wallace Collection and its Founders, 1936; David Cox, 1947; Peter Bruegel, 1951; Pictures: a Handbook for Curators, 1956. *Recreations:* reading, play-going, travelling. *Address:* 33 Queen's Gate Gardens, SW7. *T:* 01-584 0231. *Clubs:* Athenæum, Beefsteak.

**COX, Maj.-Gen. William Reginald,** CB 1956; DSO 1945; Director Territorial Army, Cadets and Home Guard, 1958-60, retired; *b* 13 June 1905; *e s* of late Major W. S. R. Cox; *m* 1947,

Dorothy Irene Cox; no *c*. *Educ:* Wellington Coll. Commissioned KSLI, 1925; Adjutant, 2nd Bn, 1931-34; Staff Coll., Camberley, 1938; served War of 1939-45: Bde Major 114 Inf. Bde, 1940; Instr, Staff Coll., Camberley, 1941; GSO 1 Northern Comd, York, 1942; comd 1 Worcs. Regt, 1942-43; GSO 1, 21 Army Gp, 1943-44; comd 7 Green Howards, 1944; 131 Lorried Inf Bde, 1944; 129, 146 and 31 Inf. Bdes, 1945-47; BGS Western Comd, 1948; idc 1949; DAG, GHQ, MEF, 1950-52; Dep. Dir Infty, War Office, 1952-54; Chief of Staff, Southern Command, 1954-55; GOC 53rd (Welsh) Div., TA, and Mid-West District, 1955-58. Col, KSLI, 1957-63. Order of White Lion of Czechoslovakia (3rd Cl.); Military Cross of Czechoslovakia, 1945. *Recreations:* tennis, golf. *Address:* c/o National Provincial Bank, Ross, Herefordshire. *Club:* Naval and Military.

**COX, William Robert;** Deputy Under-Secretary of State, Home Office, and Director-General of the Prison Service, since 1970; *b* 2 Jan. 1922; *s* of late William Robert and Berthe Marie Cox, Winchester; *m* 1948, Elizabeth Anne Priestley Marten; one *s* one *d*. *Educ:* Peter Symonds' Sch., Winchester; Christ's Coll., Cambridge. Foreign Office (German Sect.), 1946; Min. of Town and Country Planning, 1950; Min. of Housing and Local Govt, 1952-69 (Under-Sec., 1965); Asst Under-Sec. of State, Office of Sec. of State for Local Govt and Regional Planning, 1969-70. *Recreations:* chess, music. *Address:* Home Office, Whitehall, SW1. *Club:* Athenæum.

**COX, William Trevor;** *see* Trevor, W.

**COXETER, Harold Scott Macdonald,** FRS 1950; PhD Cambridge, 1931; Professor of Mathematics, University of Toronto, since 1948; *b* 9 Feb. 1907; *s* of Harold Samuel Coxeter and Lucy (*née* Gee); *m* 1936, Hendrina Johanna Brouwer, The Hague; one *s* one *d*. *Educ:* King Alfred Sch., London; St George's Sch., Harpenden; Trinity Coll., Cambridge. Entrance Scholar, Trinity Coll., 1926; Smith's Prize, 1931. Fellow Trinity Coll., Cambridge, 1931-36; Rockefeller Foundation Fellow, Princeton, 1932-33; Procter Fellow, Princeton, 1934-35; Asst Prof., 1936-43, Associate Prof., 1943-48, University of Toronto. Visiting Professor: Notre Dame, 1947; Columbia Univ., 1949; Dartmouth Coll., 1964; University of Amsterdam, 1966; University of Edinburgh, 1967; University of East Anglia, 1968; ANU, 1970. Editor Canadian Jl of Mathematics, 1948-57. Pres., Canadian Mathematical Congress, 1965-67. Hon. LLD Alberta, 1957; Hon. DMath Waterloo, 1969. *Publications:* Non-Euclidean Geometry, 1942 and 1965; Regular Polytopes, 1948 and 1963; The Real Projective Plane, 1949, 1955 and 1959; (with W. C. J. Moser) Generators and Relations, 1957 and 1964; Introduction to Geometry, 1961, new edn 1969; Projective Geometry, 1964; (with S. L. Greitzer) Geometry Revisited, 1967; Twelve Geometric Essays, 1968; various mathematical papers. *Recreations:* music, travel. *Address:* 67 Roxborough Drive, Toronto 287, Canada.

**COXWELL-ROGERS, Maj.-Gen. Norman Annesley,** CB 1944; CBE 1943 (OBE 1933); DSO 1940; *b* 29 May 1896; *s* of late Henry Annesley Coxwell-Rogers, Asst Inspector-General Royal Irish Constabulary, Dowdeswell, Glos, and late Mary Georgina, *d* of Edmund Waller, Dundrum and Bray, Co. Dublin; *m* 1928, Diana Coston; one *s* one *d*. *Educ:* Cheltenham Coll.; Royal Military Academy, Woolwich. 2nd Lieut Royal Engineers, 1915; service at home, Gibraltar and India; served France and Belgium, 1915-18 (wounded, despatches twice); NW Frontier, Mohmand Operations, 1933, served as Field Engineer in charge of construction of Gandab Road (OBE, despatches); Mohmand Operations, 1935, as CRE (Bt Lieut-Col); War of 1939-45, BEF, France, Sept. 1939-June 1940, N Africa, Sicily, and Italy, 1943, Chief Engineer Allied Armies in Italy (despatches twice, DSO, CBE, CB, Legion of Merit (USA)); Colonel, 1941; Maj.-Gen. 1943; retired pay, 1946. Col Comdt RE, 1956-61. *Address:* Rossley Manor, near Cheltenham, Glos.. *T:* Andoversford 233. *Club:* United Service.

**COYNE, James E.;** Canadian banker; *b* Winnipeg, 17 July 1910; *s* of James Bowes Coyne and Edna Margaret Coyne (*née* Elliott). *Educ:* University of Manitoba (BA); University of Oxford (BCL). Admitted to the Bar, Manitoba, 1934; solicitor and barrister in Manitoba, 1934-38; Financial Attaché, Canadian Embassy, Washington, DC, 1941; Mem. War-time Prices and Trade Board, Ottawa, 1942 (Dep.-Chm.). Bank of Canada, Ottawa: Asst to the Governors, 1944-49; Deputy-Governor, 1950-54; Governor, 1955-61. *Address:* 29 Ruskin Row, Winnipeg, Manitoba, Canada.

**COZENS, Brig. Dame (Florence) Barbara,** DBE 1963; RRC 1958; *b* 24 Dec. 1906; *d* of late Capt. A. Cozens, S Staffs. *Educ:* Seabury Sch., Worthing. Nurse Training: The Nightingale Sch., St Thomas' Hosp., London, 1928-32. Joined QAIMNS, 1933. Served War of 1939-45, England and Continent. Lieut-Col 1954; Col 1958; Brig. 1960; Matron-in-Chief and Dir of Army Nursing Services, 1960-64, retd; Chief Nursing Officer to St John Ambulance Brigade, 1965-. Col Commandant, QARANC, 1966-69. CStJ. *Recreations:* gardening, golf. *Address:* 174 Old Dover Road, Canterbury, Kent. *Club:* United Nursing Services.

**COZENS, Air Cdre Henry Iliffe,** CB 1946; AFC 1939; RAF retired; *b* 13 March 1904; *m* 1956, Gillian Mary, *o d* of Wing Comdr O. R. Pigott, Wokingham, Berks; one *s* two *d*. *Educ:* St Dunstan's Coll.; Downing Coll., Cambridge. MA 1934. commissioned in RAF, 1923; Mem. of British Arctic Air Route Expedition, 1930-31. Served War of 1939-45 (AFC, CB). idc 1947. Bursar, Ashorne Hill Coll. *Address:* Horley Manor, Banbury, Oxon. *Club:* Royal Air Force.

**COZENS-HARDY,** family name of **Baron Cozens-Hardy.**

**COZENS-HARDY,** 4th Baron, *cr* 1914, of Letheringsett; **Herbert Arthur Cozens-Hardy,** OBE 1966; JP, DL; a Director of Pilkington Brothers Ltd, glass manufacturers, St Helens, since 1938; *b* 8 June 1907; *o s* of 3rd Baron Cozens-Hardy and Gladys Lily, *d* of Arthur Wrigley Cozens-Hardy; *S* father, 1956; unmarried. *Educ:* Winchester; Worcester Coll., Oxford. Pilkington Brothers Ltd, 1932-. Chairman: St Helens Savings Cttee, 1950-60; Lancashire Magistrates Court Cttee, 1952-; Prescot Magistrates, 1953-; Huyton Coll., Liverpool, 1956-. JP 1939, DL 1953, Lancs. KJStJ 1952: Chm., St John Council for Lancashire, 1947-. Pres., Royal Lancs Agricultural Soc., 1959-63, Chm., 1965-. *Recreations:* usual. *Heir:* none. *Address:* Parkside, Knowsley Park, Prescot, Lancs. *T:* 051-426 5522; Letheringsett Hall, Norfolk. *T:* Holt 3222. *Club:* Royal Automobile.

**COZZENS, James Gould;** US author; *b* Chicago, USA, 19 Aug. 1903; *s* of Henry William Cozzens and Bertha Wood; *m* 1927. Bernice Baumgarten. *Educ:* Kent Sch., Connecticut;

Harvard University. *Publications:* Confusion, 1924; Michael Scarlett, 1925; Cockpit, 1928; The Son of Perdition, 1929; SS San Pedro, 1931; The Last Adam, 1933; Castaway, 1934; Men and Brethren, 1936; Ask Me Tomorrow, 1940; The Just and the Unjust, 1942; Guard of Honour, 1949; By Love Possessed, 1958; Children and Others, 1965; Morning, Noon and Night, 1968. *Recreation:* writing. *Address:* Shadowbrook, Williamstown, Mass, USA.

**CRABBE, Sir Cecil (Brooksby),** Kt 1956; JP; *b* 24 June 1898; *s* of late Rev. Henry Brooksby Crabbe, Bradford, Yorks; *m* 1925, Margaret, *d* of late Rev. Herbert Henry Willmott, Rector of Rivenhall, Essex; one *s* one *d* (and one *s* decd). *Educ:* Trent Coll., Derbyshire; Royal Military Coll., Sandhurst. Served with Indian Army, NW Frontier and Iraq, 1918-22; admitted Solicitor, 1924; Legal Asst, Registry of Friendly Societies, 1925; Asst Registrar of Friendly Societies, 1940; Deputy Industrial Assurance Commissioner, 1947; Chief Registrar of Friendly Societies and Industrial Assurance Commissioner, 1954-63, retd. Hon. Fellow Building Societies Inst., 1955; Vice-Pres. Building Societies Assoc., 1963; Mem., Trustee Savings Banks Inspection Cttee, 1964-; Dir, Chelsea and South London Building Society, 1964-. Mem., Croydon and Warlingham Park Hosp. Management Cttee, 1963- (Chm., 1965-). JP Croydon, 1961-. *Address:* 54 Croham Park Avenue, South Croydon, Surrey CR2 7HL. *T:* 01-688 1705. *Club:* Athenæum.

**CRABBE, Reginald James Williams,** FIA, FSS; Chairman and Managing Director, Provident Life Association of London Ltd, since 1967; Chairman: United Standard Insurance Co. Ltd, since 1967; Vigilant Assurance Co. Ltd, since 1970; *b* 22 June 1909; *e s* of late Harry James and Annie Martha Crabbe; *m* 1948, Phyllis Maud Smith; two *d. Educ:* Chigwell Sch., Essex. Entered National Mutual Life Assurance Soc., 1926; FIA 1933; joined Provident Life as Asst Actuary, 1935. Chm., Life Offices' Assoc., 1965, 1966. *Publication:* (with C. A. Poyser, MA, FIA) Pension and Widows' and Orphans' Funds, 1953. *Recreations:* reading, gardening, music, art. *Address:* Fairways, 166 Lower Green Road, Esher, Surrey. *T:* Esher 62219.

**CRACROFT, Air Vice-Marshal Peter Dicken,** CB 1954; AFC 1932; *b* 29 Nov. 1907; *s* of Lt-Col H. Cracroft, Bath; *m* 1932, Margaret Eliza Sugden Patchett; two *s. Educ:* Monkton Combe Sch., Bath. Commissioned RAF 1927; Fleet Air Arm, 1928-31; Central Flying Sch. Instructors' Course, 1931; Flying Instructor, Leuchars, 1931-35; Adjt HMS Courageous, 1936-37; Chief Flying Instructor, Oxford Univ. Air Sqdn, 1937-39; RAF Stn Mount Batten, 1939-40; Air Staff, Coastal Command, 1940-41; OC RAF Station, Chivenor, 1941-43; SASO 19 Gp (later 17 Gp), 1933-44; OC 111 Op. Trg Unit, Bahamas, 1944-45; SASO HQ Air Comd, SE Asia, Mil. Gov. Penang, 1945; AOC Bombay, 1945-46; SASO, HQ 19 Gp, 1946-48; RAF Dir and CO, Jt Anti-Submarine Sch., Londonderry, 1948-50; Sen. Air Liaison Officer, S Africa, 1950-52; AOC 66 Gp, Edinburgh, 1952-53; Senior Air Staff Officer, Headquarters Coastal Command, 1953-55; AOC Scotland and 18 Group, 1955-58; retired from RAF, Dec. 1958. *Recreations:* tennis, fishing, shooting. *Address:* Watercombe, West Milton, near Bridport, Dorset. *T:* Powerstock 241.

**CRACROFT-AMCOTTS, Lt-Col Sir Weston,** Kt 1954; MC 1917; DL, JP; Chairman Lindsey County Council, 1951-64; *b* 7 Nov. 1888; *er s* of Major F. A. Cracroft-Amcotts, late V Dragoon Guards, and of Mrs F. A. Cracroft-Amcotts, *d* of Anthony Willson, Rauceby, Lincs; *m* 1927, Rhona, *d* of late E. C. Clifton-Brown, Burnham Grove, Burnham, Bucks; four *d. Educ:* Eton; RMA Woolwich. Commissioned RE, 1908; served European War, 1914-18; retired with rank of Major, 1920; commissioned as Major, 46th Bn Lincs Regt, (RE), TA, 1938; retired with rank of Lieut-Col, 1942; Lieut-Col, Home Guard, 1942-45. JP Lindsey, Lincs, 1924; DL Lincs, 1936; High Sheriff of Lincolnshire, 1954. *Address:* Hackthorn Hall, Lincoln. *T:* Hackthorn 212.

**CRADDOCK, George;** *b* 26 Feb. 1897; *s* of late Amos George Craddock and of Athey Alpheaus Craddock, Northampton; *m* 1962, Margaret, *d* of late Mr and Mrs G. Morris, Bangor. *Educ:* Fircroft Coll.; Birmingham Univ. Joined Labour Party, 1918; Vice-Pres. Sparkbrook Divisional Labour Party; Pres. King's Norton Div. Labour Party. Contested Balsall Heath Ward, Birmingham City Council Elections, 1926, 1927, 1928. Labour Agent Thornbury Parly Div., 1929-36; Area Organiser Nat. Union Distributive and Allied Workers, 1936-49; MP (Lab) South Bradford, Dec. 1949-1970. treas. Sheffield Trades and Labour Council, 1942-43; rep. Darnall Ward on Sheffield City Council, 1945-. *Recreations:* motoring, walking, reading; philatelist. *Address:* 25 High Trees, Dore, Sheffield. *T:* Sheffield 362842.

**CRADDOCK, Sir (George) Beresford,** Kt 1960; practising barrister; *b* 7 Oct. 1898; *m* 1936, Ethel Martin Bradford. *Educ:* St Andrews Univ. MA Economics and Philosophy; BSc Chemistry and Physics, with First Class Hons and special distinction in Chemistry; ARIC. Barrister-at-Law, Gray's Inn, 1947; chambers in Middle Temple. Held important executive posts in business at home, in India and in Africa, 1921-39. European War, 1914-18, Staff Lieut, RE Chemical Warfare Staff, having first served in RGA; War of 1939-45, Asst Dir, Ministry of Supply. Contested (Nat. Govt) Lichfield, Staffs, 1938 (by-election), and 1945; MP (C) Spelthorne Div. of Mddx, 1950-70; PPS to Rt Hon. Harold Watkinson, as Minister of Transport and Civil Aviation, 1956-59, and as Minister of Defence, 1959-62. Mem., Speaker's Panel of Chairmen, 1966-70. *Recreations:* golf and music. *Address:* 9 The Grove, Highgate Village, N6. *T:* 01-348 1494. *Club:* Carlton.

**CRADDOCK, Lieut-Gen. Sir Richard Walter,** KBE 1963 (CBE 1954; MBE 1940); CB 1959; DSO 1944; Lieutenant of HM Tower of London, 1966-69; *b* 3 Aug. 1910; *s* of Sir Walter Craddock, *qv*; *m* 1943, Josephine Pamela Ann (*née* Love); one *s* one *d. Educ:* Charterhouse; Royal Military Coll., Sandhurst. 2nd Lieut The Buffs, 1930; Col, 1951; Temp. Brig., 1951; Dir of Plans, War Office, 1951-53; Brigadier and Maj.-Gen., 1957; Maj.-Gen. i/c Administration, British Army of the Rhine, 1957-59; Director of Military Operations, War Office, 1959-62; Lieut-Gen. 1963; Comdr, British Forces, Hong-Kong, 1963-64; GOC-in-C, Western Comd, 1964-66. Mem. Cttee, Corps of Commissionaires, 1969-. Deputy Col The Queen's Own Buffs, 1965-66; Col The Queen's Regt, 1966-. *Address:* Upcote, Chilbolton, Hants. *Club:* United Service.

**CRADDOCK, Sir Walter Merry,** Kt 1935; DSO 1919; MC; OStJ; *b* 1883; 2nd *s* of late Frederick Charles Craddock; *m* 1909, Margaret Amy (*d* 1948), *d* of late Anthony Henry Ten-Broeke; one *s.* Served European War, 1914-19, Lieut-Col 2/20th Bn London Regt (despatches thrice, MC, DSO). Commanded Calcutta

Scottish IAF 1924-28; lately Sheriff of Calcutta. ADC to the King, 1925; Col, 1925; re-employed, 1940. High Sheriff of Glos, 1949. *Address:* Barns Close, Amberley, near Stroud, Glos. *T:* 2267. *Club:* Bengal (Calcutta).
*See also Lieut-Gen. Sir R. W. Craddock.*

**CRADOCK, Percy,** CMG 1968; Foreign and Commonwealth Office, since 1969; *b* 26 Oct. 1923; *m* 1953, Birthe Marie Dyrlund. Served Foreign Office, 1954-57; First Sec., Kuala Lumpur, 1957-61, Hong Kong, 1961, Peking, 1962; Foreign Office, 1963-66; Counsellor and Head of Chancery, Peking, 1966-68; Chargé d'Affaires, Peking, 1968-69. *Address:* Foreign and Commonwealth Office, SW1. *Club:* Reform.

**CRADOCK-HARTOPP, Sir J. E.;** *see* Hartopp.

**CRAGG, Rt. Rev. (Albert) Kenneth,** DPhil; Hon. Canon of Canterbury; Assistant Bishop to the Archbishop in Jerusalem, since 1970; *b* 8 March 1913; *yr s* of Albert and Emily Cragg; *m* 1940, Theodora Melita, *yr d* of John Wesley Arnold; three *s* (one *d* decd). *educ:* Blackpool Grammar Sch.; Jesus Coll., Oxford; Tyndale Hall, Bristol. BA Oxon 2nd Cl. Hons Mod. Hist., 1934; MA Oxon 1938; DPhil 1950. Ellerton Theol. Essay Prize, Oxford, 1937; Green Moral Philos. Prize, Oxford, 1947. Deacon, 1936; Priest, 1937; Curate, Higher Tranmere Parish Church, Birkenhead, 1936-39; Chaplain, All Saints', Beirut, Lebanon, 1939-47; Warden, St Justin's House, Beirut, 1942-47; Asst Prof. of Philos., Amer. University of Beirut, 1942-47; Rector of Longworth, Berks, 1947-51; Sheriff's Chap., Berks, 1948; Prof. of Arabic and Islamics, Hartford Seminary, Conn, USA, 1951-56; Rockefeller Travelling Schol., 1954; Res. Canon, St George's Collegiate Church, Jerusalem, 1956-61; Fellow, St Augustine's Coll., Canterbury, 1959-60, Sub-Warden, 1960-61, warden, 1961-67; Examng Chaplain to Archbishop of Canterbury, 1961-67. Select Preacher: Cambridge, 1961; Dublin, 1962. Proctor in Convocation, Canterbury, 1965-68; Visiting Prof., Union Theological Seminary, New York, 1965-66; Lectr, Faculty of Divinity, Cambridge, 1966; Jordan Lectr, Sch. of Oriental and African Studies, University of London, 1967; Vis. Prof., University of Ibadan, Nigeria, 1968; Bye-Fellow, Gonville and Caius Coll., Cambridge, 1968-. Editor, The Muslim World Quarterly, 1952-60. *Publications:* The Call of the Minaret, 1956; Sandals at the Mosque, 1959; The Dome and the Rock, 1964; Counsels in Contemporary Islam, 1965; Christianity in World Perspective, 1968; The Privilege of Man, 1968; The House of Islam, 1969; Alive to God, 1970; translated: City of Wrong, 1959; The Theology of Unity, 1965; Contributor: Journal of World History, 1957; Religion in the Middle East, 1969. *Address:* 59 Prospect Road, Southborough, Tunbridge Wells, Kent. *T:* Tunbridge Wells 28236; c/o Jerusalem and the East Mission, 12 Warwick Square, SW1; Gonville and Caius College, Cambridge.
*See also Ven. H. W. Cragg.*

**CRAGG, Ven. Herbert Wallace,** MA; Archdeacon of Bromley since 1969; Vicar of Christ Church, Beckenham, since 1957; Hon. Canon of Rochester since 1963; *b* 18 Nov. 1910; *s* of Albert and Emily Cragg; *m* 1938, Elsie Emery; three *d. Educ:* Tyndale Hall, Bristol; St John's Coll., Durham. LTh 1932, BA 1933, MA 1938. Curate: St Mary, Kirkdale, Liverpool, 1933-37; Cheadle Parish Church, Cheshire, 1937-38; Vicar: The Saviour, Blackburn, 1938-44; St James, Carlisle, 1944-57. Hon. Canon of Carlisle, 1956-57; Proctor in Convocation: for Carlisle, 1951-57; for Rochester, 1959-69. *Publications:* The Sole Sufficiency of Jesus Christ, 1961; The Holy Spirit and the Christian Life, 1962; The Encouragement of the Believer, 1964; Victory in the Christian Life, 1964. *Address:* Christ Church Vicarage, 61 Hayes Lane, Beckenham, Kent BR3 2RE.
*See also Rt Rev. A. K. Cragg.*

**CRAGG, James Birkett;** Vice-President (Academic) since 1970, and director, Environmental Sciences Centre; Kilham Memorial Professor and Professor of Biology, University of Calgary, Alberta, since 1966; *b* 8 Nov. 1910; *s* of late A. W. Cragg, N Shields; *m* 1937, Mary Catherine Macnaughtan (marr. diss. 1968); five *s* (one *d* decd); *m* Jean Moore. *Educ:* private sch.; Tynemouth High Sch.; Durham Univ. BSc King's Coll., University of Durham, 1933; DThPT, 1934; MSc, 1937; DSc Newcastle, 1965. Demonstrator, Physiology Dept, Manchester Univ., 1935; Asst Lecturer, and later Lecturer, in Zoology, University Coll. of North Wales, 1937; seconded to Agricultural Research Council, 1942; Scientific Officer, ARC Unit of Insect Physiology, 1944; Reader in Zoology, Durham Colls, in University of Durham, 1946; Prof. of Zoology, University of Durham, 1950-61; Dir, Merlewood Research Station (Nature Conservancy), Grange-over-Sands, Lancs, 1961-66; Chairman: Commn for Ecology; Internat. Union for Conservation of Nature; Convenor, Internat. Biological Programme PT Cttee; Mem., Internat. Biological Programme Cttees; Consultant, Ford Foundation, 1965. Commonwealth Prestige Fellow (New Zealand), 1964. *Publications:* papers in scientific periodicals; (ed) Advances in Ecological Research. *Recreation:* books. *Address:* 3312 Underhill Drive, Calgary 44, Alberta, Canada. *Club:* Athenæum.

**CRAGG, Rev. Canon Kenneth;** *see* Cragg, Rev. Canon A. K.

**CRAGGS, Prof. James Wilkinson,** BSc, PhD; Professor of Engineering Mathematics, University of Southampton, since 1967; *b* 3 Feb. 1920; *s* of Thomas Gibson Craggs and Margaret (*née* Wilkinson); *m* 1946, Mary Baker; two *s* one *d. Educ:* Bede Collegiate Sch., Sunderland; University of Manchester. BSc 1941, PhD 1948, Manchester; PhD Cambridge, 1953. Junior Lectr, Royal Military Coll. of Science, 1941-45; Asst Lectr, University of Manchester, 1947-49; Lecturer, queen's Coll., Dundee, 1951-52; King's Coll., Newcastle upon Tyne: Lectr, 1952-56; Senior Lecturer, 1956-60; Reader in Mathematics, 1960-61; Prof. of Mathematics, University of Leeds, 1961-63; Prof. of Applied Mathematics, Melbourne Univ., 1963-67. *Publications:* contrib. learned journals regarding the mechanics of solids and fluids. *Recreation:* Methodist lay preacher. *Address:* University of Southampton, Highfield, Southampton.

**CRAGGS, Prof. John Drummond,** MSc, PhD, FInstP; Professor of Electronic Engineering, University of Liverpool, since 1955; *b* 17 May 1915; *s* of Thomas Lawson Craggs and Elsie Aidrienne Roberts; *m* 1941, Dorothy Ellen Margaret Garfitt; two *d. Educ:* Huddersfield Coll.; University of London. Research Student, King's Coll., London Univ., 1937-38; Metropolitan-Vickers High Voltage Research Laboratory, Manchester, 1938-48; University of California, Radiation Laboratory, 1944-45; apptd Sen. Lectr, 1948, and, later, Reader, Dept of Electrical Engineering, University of Liverpool. *Publications:* Counting Tubes, 1950 (with S. C. Curran); Electrical Breakdown of Gases, 1953 (with J. M. Meek); High Voltage Laboratory Technique, 1954 (with J. M. Meek); papers in various professional jls.

*Address:* Stone Cottage, Newton-cum-Larton, West Kirby, Wirral, Cheshire. *T:* 051-625 5055.

**CRAIG,** family name of **Viscount Craigavon.**

**CRAIG, Albert James Macqueen;** Visiting Fellow, St Antony's College, Oxford, since 1970; *b* 13 July 1924; *s* of James Craig and Florence Morris; *m* 1952, Margaret Hutchinson; three *s* one *d*. *Educ:* Liverpool Institute High Sch.; Univ. of Oxford. Queen's Coll., Oxford (Exhibr), 1942; 1st cl. Hon. Mods Classics, 1943 (Hon. Schol.); Army, 1943-44; 1st cl. Oriental Studies (Arabic and Persian), 1947; Sen. Demy, Magdalen Coll., 1947-48; Lectr in Arabic, Durham Univ., 1948-55; seconded to FO, 1955 as Principal Instructor at Middle East Centre for Arab Studies, Lebanon; joined Foreign Service substantively, 1956; served: FO, 1958-61; HM Political Agent, Trucial States, 1961-64; 1st Sec., Beirut, 1964-67; Counsellor and Head of Chancery, Jedda, 1967-70. *Address:* c/o Foreign and Commonwealth Office, SW1. *Club:* Travellers'.

**CRAIG, Very Rev. Archibald Campbell,** MC 1918; DD (Hon.); *b* 3 Dec. 1888; *yr s* of Rev. Alexander McRae Craig; *m* 1950, Mary Isobel Laidlaw, *d* of Rev. John Laidlaw; no *c*. *Educ:* Kelso High Sch.; Edinburgh Univ.; New Coll., Edinburgh. Served European War, 1914-18, 13th Royal Scots and Intelligence Corps, 1914-19. Pastorates in Galston and Glasgow, 1921-30; Chaplain to University of Glasgow, 1930-39; Sec. to the Churches' Commission on International Friendship and Social Responsibility, 1939-42; Gen. Sec., British Council of Churches, 1942-46; Asst Leader, Iona Community, 1946-47; Lecturer in Biblical Studies, Glasgow Univ., 1947-57. Moderator of the Gen. Assembly of the Church of Scotland, May 1961-62. Hon. DD: Edinburgh, 1938; Glasgow, 1961; Dublin, 1961. *Publications:* University Sermons, 1937; Preaching in a Scientific Age (Warrack Lectures), 1954; God Comes Four Times, 1957. *Recreation:* gardening. *Address:* St John's, Doune, Perthshire. *T:* Doune 386.

**CRAIG, Sir Arthur John Edward,** Kt 1938; DL, JP; Custos Rotulorum of the Soke of Peterborough; *b* 9 June 1886; *s* of John Robert Craig; *m* 1908, Gertrude Ethel Rowe (*d* 1959); one *s* one *d*. *Educ:* St Peter's Coll. Mayor of City of Peterborough, 1928-29; five times Deputy Mayor; ex-Chm. Soke of Peterborough County Council; ex-Chm. County Finance and Gen. Purposes Cttee; ex-Chm. Governors Deacon's Sch., Peterborough; ex-Chm. ATC; Hon. Surveyor British Red Cross and Order of St John; Pres. Peterborough and North Northants Conservative Assoc.; Dir Woolwich Equitable Building Soc. Fellow Chartered Auctioneers and Estate Agents Inst. Chm. Arthur E. Craig & Co. Ltd, etc. Hon. Freeman of City of Peterborough. *Recreations:* billiards, golf. *Address:* Thorpefields, Peterborough. *Clubs:* Royal Automobile; City and Counties (Peterborough).

**CRAIG, Mrs Barbara Denise,** MA Oxon; Principal of Somerville College, Oxford, since 1967; *b* 22 Oct. 1915; *o d* of John Alexander Chapman and Janie Denize (*née* Callaway); *m* 1942, Wilson James Craig; no *c*. *Educ:* Haberdashers' Aske's Girls' Sch., Acton; Somerville Coll., Oxford. Craven Fellow, 1938; Goldsmiths' Sen. Student, 1938; Woolley Fellow in Archæology of Somerville Coll., 1954-56. Temp. Asst Principal, Mins of Supply and Labour, 1939-40; Asst to Prof. of Greek, Aberdeen Univ., 1940-42; Temp. Asst Principal, Min. of Home Security, 1942; Temp. Principal, Min. of Production, 1943-45. Unofficial work as wife of British Council officer in Brazil, Iraq, Spain, Pakistan, 1946-65; from 1956, archæological work on finds from British excavations at Mycenae and participation in joint Hellenic-British excavations at Mycenae. *Recreations:* bird-watching (Mem. Brit. Ornithologists' Union); walking. *Address:* Somerville College, Oxford. *T:* Oxford 55880. *Club:* University Women's.

**CRAIG, Charles (James);** opera singer (tenor); *b* 3 Dec. 1920; *s* of James and Rosina Craig; *m* 1946, Dorothy Wilson; one *s* one *d*. *Educ:* in London. Protégé of Sir Thomas Beecham; Principal Tenor with Carl Rosa Opera Co., 1953-56; joined Sadler's Wells Opera Co., 1956. Appears regularly at Internat. Opera Houses, incl. Covent Garden, Milan, Rome, Vienna, Paris, Berlin, Buenos Aires, etc; repertoire of 48 operas, incl. Otello, Aida, Turandot, Norma, Andrea Chenier, Die Walküre, Götterdämmerung, Lohengrin, etc. Concerts, TV and radio, and records. International Opera Medal Award, 1962. *Recreations:* motoring, cooking. *Address:* Whitfield Cottage, Whitfield, Northants.

**CRAIG, Clifford,** CMG 1951; radiologist; President, National Trust of Australia (Tasmania), since 1963; *b* 3 Aug. 1896; *s* of Dr W. J. Craig, Box Hill, Victoria, Australia; *m* 1927, Edith Nance Bulley; two *s* one *d*. *Educ:* Scotch Coll., Melbourne; University of Melbourne. MB, BS, 1924; MD Melbourne, 1926; MS Melbourne, 1930; FRACS 1930; DDR 1954. Surgeon Superintendent, Launceston General Hospital, 1926-31; Hon. Surgeon, Launceston General Hospital, 1932-41; Surgeon Superintendent, 1941-51. Pres., Tasmanian Branch, BMA, 1941; Mem. Federal Council, BMA, 1941-47. Pres. Rotary International, Launceston, 1950; Pres., Medical Council, Tasmania, 1954-66; Chairman, Tasmanian Cancer Cttee. Served European War, 1914-18, 1st AIF (Palestine), 1916-18; War of 1939-45, RAAF, 1940-45. *Publications:* The Engravers of Van Diemen's Land, 1961; Old Tasmanian Prints, 1964; History of the Launceston General Hospital, 1963; articles in medical jls. *Recreations:* Cricket Blue, Melbourne Univ.; tennis, golf. *Address:* 21 High Street, Launceston, Tasmania 7250, Australia. *T:* 24182. *Clubs:* Launceston (Launceston); Tasmanian (Hobart).

**CRAIG, Prof. David Parker,** FRS 1968; FAA 1969; FRIC; Professor of Chemistry, Australian National University, since 1967; *b* 23 Dec. 1919; *s* of Andrew Hunter Craig, Manchester and Sydney, and Mary Jane (*née* Parker); *m* 1948, Veronica, *d* of Cyril Bryden-Brown, Market Harborough and Sydney; three *s* one *d*. *Educ:* Sydney Church of England Grammar Sch.; University of Sydney; University Coll., London. MSc (Sydney) 1941, PhD (London) 1950, DSc (London) 1956. Commonwealth Science Scholar, 1940. War Service: Capt., Australian Imperial Force, 1941-44. Lectr in Chemistry, University of Sydney, 1944-46; Turner and Newall Research Fellow, 1946-49, and Lectr in Chemistry, University Coll., London, 1949-52; Prof. of Physical Chemistry, Univ. of Sydney, 1952-56; Prof. of Chemistry, University Coll., London, 1956-67. Pres. Sydney University Union, 1955; Fellow of University Coll., London, 1964-. *Publications:* original papers on chemistry in scientific periodicals. *Address:* Research School of Chemistry, Australian National University, Box 4 PO Canberra, ACT 2600, Australia.

**CRAIG, Edward Anthony** (works also under name of Edward Carrick), FRSA; writer and lecturer, designer for film and theatre; independent film art director; *b* 3 Jan. 1905; *s* of late Edward Gordon Craig, CH; *m* 1960, Mary, *d* of late Lieut-Col H. A. Timewell, OBE. Studied art, the theatre and photography in Italy, 1917-26; has discovered numerous documents of great value to the history of the theatre; Art Dir to the Welsh Pearson Film Co., 1928-29; Art Dir for Associated Talking Pictures, 1932-36; Supervising Art Dir, Criterion Film, 1937-39; established AAT Film Sch., 1937; Art Dir to the Crown Film Unit (Ministry of Information), 1939-46; Executive Art Dir, Independent Producers (Rank), 1947-49; wood-engravings, oil paintings, and scene designs exhibited at: the St George's Gallery, 1927 and 1928; at the Redfern Gallery, 1929, 1931, 1938; The Grubb Group, 1928-38; also in the principal Galleries of Canada and North America; designer of scenes and costumes for numerous London productions and at Stratford-upon-Avon, 1949. *Official Purchasers:* the British Museum; Victoria and Albert Museum; Metropolitan Museum, New York; Yale Univ., USA; The University, Austin, Texas. *Publications:* Designing for Moving Pictures, 1941; Meet the Common People, 1942; Art and Design in British Films, 1948; Designing for Films, 1949; Gordon Craig, The Story of his Life, 1968. *Illustrations:* The Georgics of Virgil, 1931, etc; books of verse by John Keats, Edith Sitwell, Edmund Blunden, W. H. Davies, etc. *Recreations:* books and music. *Address:* Cutlers Orchard, Bledlow, Aylesbury, Bucks.

**CRAIG, Elizabeth Josephine;** Cookery Expert: Scottish Field; People's Friend, etc; lecturer; *d* of late Rev. John Mitchell Craig, The Manse, Memus, Forfar, Angus, and Katherine Nichol; *m* 1919, A. E. Mann, American War Correspondent and broadcaster; no *c*. *Educ:* George Watson's Ladies' Coll., Edinburgh. Editor of Woman's Life, 1915-18; Freelance from then onward, contrib. to daily, weekly, and monthly periodicals. Mem. Inst. Hygiene (MIH); Fellow of the Cookery and Food Association (ACFA); FRHS; FRSA; Chevalière de Coteaux; Dame de la Chaine des Rôtisseurs. *Publications:* Cooking with Elizabeth Craig; Entertaining with Elizabeth Craig; Wine in the Kitchen; Simple Cooking; Simple Gardening; Woman, Wine and a Saucepan; Economical Cookery; Keeping House with Elizabeth Craig; Gardening with Elizabeth Craig; Needlecraft; Madeira (with André Simon); Beer and Vittels; Court Favourites; Scottish Cookery; Family Cookery; The Scandinavian Cookery Book; The Cook's Guide to Wine; Cook Continentale; What's Cooking in Scotland; The Art of Irish Cooking. *Recreations:* gardening, travelling. *Address:* St Catherine's, Botesdale, Diss, Norfolk. *T:* Botesdale 434. *Clubs:* Pen, Women's Press, Arts Theatre.

**CRAIG, Hamish M.;** *see* Millar-Craig.

**CRAIG, Prof. John,** MB, FRCPE; FRAScot; Professor of Child Health, University of Aberdeen, 1948-63, now Emeritus; *b* 4 Sept. 1898; *s* of John and Jane Craig; *m* 1929, Margaret, *y d* of late H. F. Morland Simpson, LLD; two *s*. *Educ:* Robert Gordon's Coll., Aberdeen; University of Aberdeen; Paris. Thompson Travelling Fellow of University of Aberdeen. Asst Physician, 1924, then Senior Physician, Royal Aberdeen Hosp. for Sick Children; Asst Physician, then Physician, Aberdeen Royal Infirmary, 1932-47. Paediatrician to Maternity Hosp. and City Hosp., Aberdeen; Pres., British Paediatric Assoc., 1956-57. Hon. Fellow, Amer. Acad. of Pediatrics. Hon. LLD. *Publications:* Pædiatrics in the North-Eastern Region of Scotland; A Short History of the Royal Aberdeen Hospital for Sick Children; articles in medical journals. *Recreations:* golf, archaeology. *Address:* 5 Albyn Terrace, Aberdeen. *T:* Aberdeen. 26024.

**CRAIG, Sir John Herbert McCutcheon,** KCVO 1949; Kt 1946; CB 1935; LLD; Deputy Master and Comptroller, Royal Mint, and ex-officio Engraver of the King's Seals, 1938-49, retired 1949; *b* 9 Feb. 1885; *s* of Robert James Craig, JP, and Anna Maria Millar; *m* 1920, Vera M. Worsfold. *Educ:* Foyle Coll., Derry; Trinity Coll., Dublin (Classical Scholar). BA (Senior Moderator, University Student and Double Large Gold Medallist), 1907; LLD (jure dig.), 1946. Entered Treasury, 1908; Principal Asst Sec., Treasury, 1931. Freeman of City of London and Liveryman of Goldsmiths' Company, 1943. Chm. and Treasurer Sir John Cass's Foundation, 1950-57. *Publications:* Newton at the Mint, 1946; History of London Mint, 1953; A History of Red Tape, 1955; articles in Nature, Notes and Records of Royal Society, Proc. Royal Instn, etc. *Address:* 8 Clareville Court, Clareville Grove, SW7.

**CRAIG, Thomas Rae,** CBE 1969 (OBE 1945); TD; Board Member, British Steel Corporation, since 1967; *b* 11 July 1906; *s* of Sir John Craig, CBE, and Jessie Craig (*née* Sommerville); *m* 1931, Christina Gay (*née* Moodie); three *s* one *d*. *Educ:* Glasgow Academy; Lycée Malherbe, Caen, Normandy. Served War of 1939-45: Lt-Col 6th Cameronians; AA and QMG 52nd (Lowland) Div. Dir of Colvilles Ltd, 1935; Man. Dir, 1958; Dep. Chm., 1961; Chm. and Man. Dir, 1965-68. Dir, Bank of Scotland, and other cos. Trustee of Scottish Hospital Endowments Research Trust; Mem. of Convocation of Strathclyde Univ.; Mem., BR (Scottish) Bd (formerly Scottish Railways Bd), 1966-. Hon. LLD: Strathclyde, 1968; Glasgow, 1970. *Recreation:* farming. *Address:* (business) 48 St Vincent Street, Glasgow C2. *T:* 041-248 2560; (home) Invergare, Rhu, Dunbartonshire. *T:* Rhu 427. *Clubs:* Naval and Military; Western, Royal Scottish Automobile (Glasgow).

**CRAIG, Rt. Hon. William,** PC (N Ire.) 1963; MP (U) Larne Division of Antrim, Parliament of Northern Ireland, since 1960; Minister of Home Affairs, Northern Ireland, 1966-68; *b* 2 Dec. 1924; *s* of late John Craig and Mary Kathleen Craig (*née* Lamont); *m* 1960, Doris Hilgendorff; two *s*. *Educ:* Dungannon Royal Sch.; Larne Grammar Sch.; Queen's Univ., Belfast. Served War of 1939-45, Royal Air Force, 1943-46. Qualified as solicitor, 1952. Chief Whip, Parliament of Northern Ireland, 1962-63; Minister of Home Affairs, 1963-64; Minister of Health and Local Government, 1964; Minister of Development, 1965-66. *Recreations:* travel, motoring, shooting, golf, photography, reading. *Address:* Parliament Buildings, Stormont, Belfast 4, Northern Ireland; (home) 23 Annadale Avenue, Belfast 7. *T:* (home) Belfast 644096. *Club:* Royal North of Ireland Yacht (Cultra, Belfast).

**CRAIG, Prof. William Stuart McRae;** Professor of Paediatrics and Child Health, University of Leeds, 1946-68, now Emeritus; *b* 19 July 1903; *s* of William Craig, MB, and Katherine Jane Stuart; *m* 1934, Beatrice Anne Hodgson. *Educ:* Bingley Grammar Sch.; Watson's Coll., Edinburgh; Universities of Edinburgh and Glasgow. BSc (Naval Architecture) Glasgow, 1924; Buchanan Scholarship, 1930; MB, ChB Edinburgh, 1930; MD Edinburgh, 1933; FRCPEd 1936; FRSE 1937; FRCP 1956. Formerly: Asst Paediatrician, Simpson

Memorial Hosp., and Western Gen. Hosp., Edinburgh; Asst Pathologist, Royal Hosp. for Sick Children, Edinburgh; Children's Physician, Livingstone Dispensary, Edinburgh; Lectr and First Asst to Professor of Child Life and Health, University of Edinburgh; Hospital Officer and Medical Officer, Ministry of Health; EMS; Senior Paediatrician various Leeds hospitals; Consultant Adviser to City of Leeds Child Welfare and Sch. Health Cttees; Member: BMA; Yorks Council for Community Relations; Bd of Govs, Holly Bank Special Sch., Huddersfield; Chm., Leeds and District Spastic Soc. Honeyman Gillespie Lectr, 1952; first Charles McNeil Lectr, RCPE, 1969. Hon. Member: British Paediatric Assoc., 1969; Scottish Paediatric Soc., 1969. Corresponding Mem., Sociedade Portuguesa de Pediatria, 1952. Formerly Examiner in Child Health, Universities of Bristol, Aberdeen, Glasgow and Edinburgh, and RCPE. John Thomson Memorial Medal, 1931. *Publications:* Child and Adolescent Life in Health and Disease, 1946; Care of the Newborn, 4th Edn 1969; John Thomson, Pioneer and Father of Scottish Paediatrics, 1968; various reference books, medical and nursing periodicals. *Address:* Braidview, Gifford, East Lothian. *Club:* Caledonian (Edinburgh).

**CRAIGAVON,** 2nd Viscount (UK), *cr* 1927, of Stormont, County Down (NI); **James Craig,** Bt, *cr* 1918; *b* 2 March 1906; *s* of 1st Viscount and Dame Cecil Mary Nowell Dering, later Dowager Viscountess Craigavon, DBE (*d* 1960); *S* father, 1940; *m* 1939, Angela Fiona, *yr d* of Percy Tatchell, MRCS, LRCP; one *s* two *d*. *Educ:* Eton. Lieut-Comdr RNVR (retd). *Heir: s* Hon. Janric Fraser Craig, *b* 9 June 1944. *Address:* 27 Launceston Place, W8. *T:* 01-937 7615.

**CRAIGIE, Dr Hugh Brechin,** CBE 1965; Principal Medical Officer, Mental Health Division, Scottish Home and Health Department; *b* 19 May 1908; *s* of late Hugh Craigie; *m* 1st, 1933, Lillia Campbell (*d* 1958), *d* of Dr George Campbell Murray; three *s*; 2nd, 1962, Eileen (MBE 1950), *d* of F. S. Lyons. *Educ:* Manchester Grammar Sch.; Manchester Univ. House Physician, Manchester Royal Infirmary, 1931-32; Asst Medical Officer, Monsall Fever Hosp., Manchester, 1932-33; Senior Medical Officer, County Mental Hosp., Lancaster, 1933-46; Dep. Med. Supt, County Mental Hosp., Whittingham, 1946; HM Senior Medical Commissioner, General Board of Control for Scotland, 1947. Served War of 1939-45 (despatches), RAMC (Hon. Lieut-Col). *Publications:* various papers on psychiatry. *Address:* Belmont Cottage, Gullane, East Lothian.

**CRAIGIE, James,** OBE 1946; FRS 1947; MB, ChB, PhD, DPH; LLD St Andrews 1950; *b* 25 June 1899; *s* of James Craigie and Frances Stewart McHardy; *m* 1929, Margaret Kerr Scott Fotheringham; two *d*. *Educ:* Perth Acad.; University of St Andrews. Asst Medical Officer, Murray Royal, Perth, 1923; Asst in Bacteriology, University of St Andrews, 1927; Research Associate, Connaught Laboratories, Toronto, 1931, Research Mem., 1943; successively Lecturer in Epidemiology, 1932, Associate Prof. of Virus Infections, 1940, prof. of Virus Infections, 1946, and Sec., 1935-45, at the Sch. of Hygiene, University of Toronto. Mem. of Scientific Staff, Imperial Cancer Research Fund, 1947-64; Mem., Joint United States-Canadian Commission (Rinderpest), 1942-46; Pres., Soc. of American Bacteriologists, 1946; FRS Canada, 1946; United States of America Typhus Commission Medal, 1946; Medal of Freedom, 1947; Stewart Prize (BMA), 1950. *Publications:* on bacteriology, virus diseases, typhoid phage-typing and experimental oncology. *Address:* Ridgehurst, Christmas Common, Watlington, Oxon.

**CRAIGIE, John Hubert,** SM 1967; FRS 1952; *b* 8 Dec. 1887; *s* of John Yorston Craigie and Elizabeth Mary Pollock; *m* 1926, Miriam Louise, *d* of Allen R. Morash and Clara Louise (*née* Smith). *Educ:* Harvard Univ. (AB); University of Minnesota (MSc); University of Manitoba (PhD). Dalhousie Univ., 1914. served European War, 1914-18, Canadian Expeditionary Force, 1915-18; Indian Army, 1918-20. canada Dept of Agriculture: Plant Pathologist, 1925-27; Senior Plant Pathologist, 1927-28; Officer-in-Charge (of Laboratory), Dominion Laboratory of Plant Pathology, Winnipeg, 1928-45; Associate Dir, Science Service, Canada Dept of Agriculture, Ottawa, 1945-52; retired 1952. Hon. DSc: University of British Columbia, 1946; University of Manitoba, 1959; Hon. LLD: University of Saskatchewan, 1948; Dalhousie Univ., 1951. *Publications:* papers in scientific journals. *Address:* 479 Kensington Avenue, Ottawa 3, Canada. *T:* 722-1511.

**CRAIGMYLE,** 3rd Baron, *cr* 1929, of Craigmyle; **Thomas Donald Mackay Shaw;** Director of Inchcape & Co. Ltd; Chairman of Hooker, Craigmyle & Co. Ltd; Secretary, Catholic Union of Great Britain; *b* 17 Nov. 1923; *s* of 2nd Baron and Lady Margaret Cargill Mackay (*d* 1958), *e d* of 1st Earl of Inchcape; *S* father, 1944; *m* 1955, Anthea Esther Christine, *y d* of late E. C. Rich; two *s* three *d*. *Educ:* Eton; Trinity Coll., Oxford (MA). Served RNVR, 1943-46. FRSA. *Recreations:* Scottish country dancing and piping. *Heir: s* Hon. Thomas Columba Shaw, *b* 19 Oct. 1960. *Address:* 18 The Boltons, SW10; Scottas, Knoydart, Inverness-shire. *Clubs:* Caledonian; Royal Thames Yacht; Bengal (Calcutta).

*See also W. B. Dean.*

**CRAIGTON,** Baron, *cr* 1959 (Life Peer); **Jack Nixon Browne,** PC 1961; CBE 1944; *b* 3 Sept. 1904. *Educ:* Cheltenham Coll. Served War of 1939-45, RAF (Balloon Command), Actg Group Capt. Contested (C) Govan Div., Glasgow, in 1945; MP (C) Govan Div., 1950-55; MP (C) Craigton Div. of Glasgow, 1955-Sept. 1959; Parly Private Sec. to Sec. of State for Scotland, 1952-April 1955; Parly Under-Sec., Scottish Office, April 1955-Oct. 1959; Minister of State, Scottish Office, Nov. 1959-Oct. 1964. City of Westminster Chamber of Commerce (formerly Westminster Chamber of Commerce): Mem., General Purposes Cttee, 1948; Mem., Exec. Cttee, 1950; Chm., 1954; Pres., 1966-. Chm., United Biscuits (Holdings) Ltd, 1967-. *Recreation:* gardening. *Address:* Bank House, 67 High Street, Staines, Middx. *T:* Staines 54284. *Clubs:* Carlton, Buck's, Boodle's.

**CRAM, Alastair Lorimer,** MC 1945; **Hon. Mr Justice Cram;** Appellate Judge, Supreme Court of Appeal, Malawi, 1964-68, retired; in private practice at Scots Bar, Edinburgh; *b* 25 Aug. 1909; *m* 1951, Isobel Nicholson; no *c*. *Educ:* Perth Academy; Edinburgh University (LLB). Solicitor, 1933; private practice, 1935-39; admitted Scots Bar, 1946. Served in HM Army, 1939-48: POW, successful escapes; RA, SAS, Intelligence Corps, Counsel War Crimes Group NW Europe, Major; GSO 2. Resident Magistrate, Kenya, 1948; Actg Puisne Judge, 1953-56; Sen. Resident Magistrate, Kenya, 1956; Temp. Puisne Judge, 1958-60; Puisne Judge, High Court of Nyasaland, 1960; acting Chief Justice and (briefly) Governor-General,

Malawi, 1965. Athlete, climber, and traveller: in Alps, 1930-60, and Himalayas, 1960 and 1963; in African, Asian and South American deserts, 1940-66; in Amazon basin and Peruvian Andes, 1966. *Publications:* Editor, Kenya Law Reports, 1952-56; contribs law reports, legal and mountaineering jls. *Recreations:* shooting, sound-recordings, photography (still and cine), orchid-collecting, languages. *Address:* 5 Upper Dean Terrace, Edinburgh. *T:* 031-332 5441. *Clubs:* Alpine; Scottish Mountaineering (Edinburgh); Kenya Mountain (Nairobi).

**CRAMER, Hon. Sir John (Oscar),** Kt 1964; FREI; QRV; MHR (L) for Bennelong, New South Wales, since 1949; Senior Partner, Cramer Brothers, real estate auctioneers; Managing Director, Higgins (Buildings) Ltd; *b* Quirindi, NSW, 18 Feb. 1897; *s* of J. N. Cramer, Quirindi; *m* 1921, Mary, *d* of William M. Earls; two *s* two *d. Educ:* State public schs; business coll. Mayor of North Sydney, 1940-41; Member: Sydney County Council, 1935- (Chm., 1946-49); Statutory Cttee on Public Works, 1949-56 (Chm., 1955-56); Executive Building Industry Congress of New South Wales; Executive of Liberal Party of Australia, NSW Division (a founder of Provisional Exec.). Minister for the Army, 1956-63. *Recreation:* bowls. *Address:* Parliament House, Canberra, ACT, Australia. *Club:* Rotary.

**CRAMPTON SMITH, Alec;** *see* Smith, Alexander C.

**CRANBORNE, Viscount; Robert Edward Peter Cecil;** Captain Grenadier Guards; *b* 24 Oct. 1916; *s* and *heir* of 5th Marquess of Salisbury, *qv*; *m* 1945, Marjorie Olein (Mollie), *d* of late Capt. Hon. Valentine Wyndham-Quin; five *s* one *d.* MP (C) Bournemouth West, 1950-54. *Address:* Manor House, Cranborne, Dorset.

**CRANBROOK,** 4th Earl of, *cr* 1892; **John David Gathorne-Hardy,** CBE 1955; Viscount Cranbrook, 1878; Baron Medway, 1892; DL, JP Suffolk; Hon. MA Cantab; Treasurer: Linnean Society; University of East Anglia; Trustee, British Museum (Natural History), since 1963; Member: Nature Conservancy, since 1967; East Suffolk County Council (Chairman, 1950-57); *b* 15 April 1900; *e s* of 3rd Earl and Lady Dorothy Boyle, *y d* of 7th Earl of Glasgow; *S* father, 1915; *m* 1st, 1926, Bridget (who obtained a divorce 1930), *o d* of late Rupert D'Oyly Carte; 2nd, 1932, Fidelity (JP Suffolk), *o d* of late Hugh E. Seebohm; two *s* three *d. Educ:* Eton; RMA, Woolwich. Gunner RFA, 1918-19; Lieut, RFA, 1921-32; Alderman LCC, 1928-30; Parliamentary Private Sec. to HM First Commissioner of Works (Earl Peel), 1927-28; Deputy Regional Commissioner for Eastern Civil Defence Region, 1940-45. Hon. Air Cdre 3619 (Suffolk) Fighter Control Unit, Royal Aux. AF, 1950-61; Chm. East Anglian Regional Hospital Board, 1947-59. KStJ. *Heir: s* Lord Medway, *qv. Address:* Red House Farm, Great Glemham, Saxmundham, Suffolk. *T:* Rendham 424.

*See also Hon. R. Gathorne-Hardy.*

**CRANE, Prof. Francis Roger;** Professor of Law and Dean of the Faculty of Law, Queen Mary College, London, since 1965; *b* 19 Dec. 1910; *s* of late Francis Downing Crane and Elizabeth Mackintosh; *m* 1938, Jean Berenice, *d* of Kenneth Hadfield; two *s* one *d. Educ:* Highgate Sch.; University Coll., London. LLB 1933; Solicitor, 1934, Clifford's Inn Prize. Lecturer in Law; King's Coll. and private practice, 1935-38; Lecturer in Law, University of Manchester, 1938-46; Prof. of Law, University of Nottingham, 1946-52; Prof. of English Law, King's Coll., London, 1952-65. visiting Professor: Tulane Univ., 1960; University of Khartoum, 1963; Dean of the Faculty of Law and Visiting Prof., University of Canterbury (New Zealand), 1964. Served War of 1939-45: Royal Corps of Signals, Major, 1944. *Publications:* (jointly) A Century of Family Law, 1957; articles and notes in legal periodicals. *Address:* 10 Myddelton Park, Whetstone, N20. *T:* 01-445 4642.

**CRANE, Sir Harry (Walter Victor),** Kt 1966; OBE 1949; JP; Industrial Relations Consultant since 1965; *b* 12 Feb. 1903; *s* of William and Ann Crane; *m* 1930, Winefride Mary, *d* of Thomas and Lucy Wing; one *s. Educ:* Nottingham. Engineer Fitter. NUGMW: District Officer, 1934; Nat. Officer, 1943; District Sec., 1957; retd from Union service, 1965. Member: Catering Commn, 1950-52; Catering Hygiene Cttee, 1949-52; Food Hygiene Adv. Coun.; Workers' Travel Assoc. Management Cttee, 1960-; (pt-time) E Midlands Electricity Bd, 1965-; Milk Marketing Bd, 1966-. Director (part-time), Transport Holding Co., Ministry of Transport, 1966-. Chairman: Labour Party Conference Arrangements Cttee, 1954-65; Industrial Injuries Advisory Council, 1967; Sec. or Chm. of Joint Industrial Councils during Trade Union career. FREconS 1944. JP 1961. *Recreations:* swimming, gardening, reading. *Address:* Riverain, 22 Cliff Drive, Radcliffe-on-Trent, Nottingham. *T:* Radcliffe-on-Trent 2683. *Club:* Royal Commonwealth Society.

**CRANE, Morley Benjamin,** FRS 1947; ALS, VMH; formerly Deputy Director and Head of Pomology Department of the John Innes Horticultural Institution; *b* 17 March 1890. *Publications:* (with Sir Daniel Hall) The Apple, 1933; (with W. J. C. Lawrence) The Genetics of Garden Plants, 4th edn 1952; many research papers on origin, genetics and breeding of cultivated fruits and plants. *Address:* Plovers Dip, Fishponds Way, Haughley, Suffolk.

**CRANKO, John;** Ballet Director, Wuerttembergische Staatsoper, Stuttgart, since 1961; Ballet Director, Munich, since 1968; *b* 15 Aug. 1927. *Educ:* Highlands North Sch., Johannesburgh. Started as dancer and choreographer, University of Cape Town Ballet and Cape Town Ballet Club; joined Sadler's Wells Ballet as a dancer, 1946; Resident Choreographer, 1951-57. Many ballets in repertoire of both Companies of the Royal Ballet; also for New York City Ballet, Ballet de l'Opéra de Paris, Ballet Rambert, and many opera ballets; produced Peter Grimes, Covent Garden, 1953. First revue, Cranks, written and produced Nov. 1952, at St Martin's Theatre, 1956. First British commissioned three-act ballet, The Prince of the Pagodas (score by Benjamin Britten), Royal Opera House, 1956, also La Scala, Milan and Metropolitan, New York, 1957; Ballets for Royal Opera House: Antigone, 1959; Brandenburg Concertos 2 and 4; Ballets for Stuttgart: Daphnis et Chloë, 1962; The Seasons, 1962; Romeo and Juliet, 1962; Leatro Armonico, 1963; Firebird, 1964; Jeu des Cartes, 1965; Onegin, 1965; Opus 1, 1965; Concerto for Flute and Harp, 1966; Nutcracker, 1966; Sonata for Cello Solo, 1967; Presence, 1968; Song of the Nightingale, 1968; Concerto, 1968; The Taming of the Shrew, 1969 Brouillard, 1970; Poème de l'extase, 1970; Orfeus, 1970; Rossiniana, 1970. *Address:* 19 Alderney Street, SW1. *T:* 01-828 9516.

**CRANKSHAW, Edward,** TD; FRSL; writer; Correspondent on Soviet Affairs for The Observer, 1947-68; *b* 3 Jan. 1909; *s* of Arthur and Amy Crankshaw; *m* 1931, Clare, *d* of late E. A. Carr. *Educ:* Bishop's Stortford Coll. Commissioned 4th Bn Queen's Own Royal West Kent Regt (TA), 1936; GSO1 attached Brit. Mil. Mission, Moscow, 1941-43. Ehrenkreuz für Wissenschaft und Kunst, 1st Class (Austria). *Publications:* Joseph Conrad: Aspects of the Art of the Novel, 1936; Vienna: the Image of a Culture in Decline, 1938; Britain and Russia, 1945; Russia and the Russians, 1947; Russia by Daylight, 1951; The Forsaken Idea: a study of Viscount Milner, 1952; Gestapo: Instrument of Tyranny, 1956; Russia without Stalin, 1956; Krushchev's Russia, 1959; The Fall of the House of Habsburg, 1963; The New Cold War: Moscow v. Pekin, 1963; Krushchev: a Biography, 1966; Maria Theresa, 1969; *novels:* Nina Lessing, 1938; What Glory?, 1939; The Creedy Case, 1954; contribs to many periodicals and symposia in UK and USA. *Recreations:* fishing, music. *Address:* Church House, Sandhurst, Kent. *T:* 293. *Clubs:* Brooks's, Beefsteak, Savile.

**CRANLEY, Viscount; Michael William Coplestone Dillon Onslow;** *b* 28 Feb. 1938; *s* and *heir* of 6th Earl of Onslow, *qv*; *m* 1964, Robin Lindsay, *o d* of Major Robert Lee Bullard III, US Army, and of Lady Aberconway; one *s* one *d*. *Educ:* Eton; Sorbonne. Life Guards, 1956-60, served Arabian Peninsula. Insurance Broker. *Heir: s* Hon. Rupert Charles William Bullard Onslow, *b* 16 June 1967. *Address:* 28 Moore Street, SW3. *T:* 01-584 4615. *Club:* Beefsteak.

**CRANMER, Prof. Philip,** FRCO; Professor of Music, University of Manchester, since 1970; *b* 1 April 1918; *s* of Arthur Cranmer and Lilian Phillips; *m* 1939, Ruth Loasby; one *s* three *d*. *Educ:* Wellington; Christ Church, Oxford (BMus, MA). Asst Music Master, Wellington Coll. 1938-40; served RA, 1940-46; Major, Education Officer, Guards Div., 1946; Dir of Music, King Edward's Sch., Birmingham, 1946; Staff Accompanist, Midland Region, BBC, 1948; Lectr in Music, Birmingham Univ., 1950; Hamilton Harty Prof. of Music, Queen's Univ., Belfast, 1954-70. Pres., INcorporated Soc. of Musicians, 1971. FRCO 1947. Hon. RAM 1967. Chevalier de l'Ordre de Léopold II, 1947; Croix de Guerre Belge, 1947. *Publication:* The Technique of Accompaniment, 1970. *Recreation:* squash. *Address:* Faculty of Music, The University, Manchester 13.

**CRANSTON, Prof. Maurice (William);** Professor of Political Science at the London School of Economics, since 1969; *b* 8 May 1920; *o c* of William Cranston and Catherine Harris; *m* 1958, Baroness Maximiliana von und zu Fraunberg; two *s*. *Educ:* London Univ.; St Catherine's, Oxford. Lecturer (part-time) in Social Philosophy, London Univ., 1950-59; Reader (previously Lecturer) in Political Science at London Sch. of Economics, 1959-69. Visiting Prof. of Government: Harvard Univ., 1965-66; Dartmouth Coll., USA, 1970-71. Vice-Pres. de l'Alliance Française en Angleterre, 1964-. Literary Adviser to Methuen Ltd, 1959-69. MA, BLitt, FRSL. Foreign Hon. Mem., Amer. Acad. of Arts and Sciences, 1970-. *Publications:* Freedom, 1953; Human Rights Today, 1954 (revised edn 1962); John Locke: a biography, 1957 (James Tait Black Memorial Prize); Jean-Paul Sartre, 1962; What Are Human Rights? (New York), 1963; Western Political Philosophers (ed), 1964; A Glossary of Political Terms, 1966; Rousseau's Social Contract, 1967; Political Dialogues, 1968; La Quintessence de Sartre (Montreal), 1969; Language and Philosophy (Toronto), 1969; The New Left, 1970. *Recreation:* walking. *Address:* 1 Kent Terrace, Regent's Park, NW1. *T:* 01-262 2698. *Clubs:* Travellers', Garrick.

**CRANSTON, Prof. William Ian;** Professor of Medicine, St Thomas's Hospital Medical School, since 1964; *b* 11 Sept. 1928; *s* of Thomas and Margaret Cranston; *m* Pamela Isabel Pearson; four *s*. *Educ:* High Sch. for Boys, Glasgow; Aberdeen Grammar Sch.; Boys' High Sch., Oswestry; University of Aberdeen, FRCP London 1965 (MRCP 1952); MB, ChB (Hons), 1949; MD Aberdeen 1957; MA Oxon. 1962. Royal Infirmary, Aberdeen: House Physician, 1949-50; Medical Registrar, 1952-53; Asst in Medical Unit, St Mary's Hospital, Paddington, 1953-56; 1st Asst in Dept of Regius Prof. of Med., Radcliffe Inf., Oxford, 1961-64. Mem., Med. Res. Soc. *Recreations:* reading, gardening, painting. *Address:* St Thomas's Hospital Medical School, Albert Embankment, Westminster Bridge, SE1.

**CRANSWICK, Rt. Rev. Geoffrey Franceys,** BA, ThD; *b* 10 April 1894; *s* of late Canon E. G. Cranswick, Sydney; *m* 1927, Rosamund Mary, 3rd *d* of late Blews Robotham, The Knoll, Littleover, Derby; one *s*. *Educ:* The King's Sch., Parramatta; Church of England Grammar Sch., N Sydney; University of Sydney (BA 1916); Ridley Hall, Cambridge. Tutor, Moore Theological Coll., Sydney, 1916; Travelling Sec., Australian Student Christian Movement, 1918; Curate, Parish Church, West Ham, 1920; Missionary CMS, Bengal, India, 1923, as Principal of King Edward's Sch., Chapra, Bengal; Organising Sec. CMS in Canterbury, Rochester and Chichester Dioceses, 1938; India Sec. at HQ CMS, 1938-43; Chm., India Cttee, Conference of British Missionary Socs, 1941; Bishop of Tasmania, 1944-63, retd. Mem., UNA Exec. (Tasmania). *Recreations:* bowls, gardening. *Address:* 361 Davey Street, Hobart, Tasmania 7000, Australia. *Club:* Rotary (Hobart).

**CRANWORTH,** 3rd Baron, *cr* 1899; **Philip Bertram Gurdon;** Lieutenant, Royal Wiltshire Yeomanry; *b* 24 May 1940; *s* of Hon. Robin Gurdon (killed in action, 1942) and Hon. Yoskyl Pearson (she *m* 2nd, 1944, as his 2nd wife, Lieut-Col. Alistair Gibb, and 3rd, 1962, as his 2nd wife, 1st Baron McCorquodale of Newton, *qv*), *d* of 2nd Viscount Cowdray; *S* grandfather, 1964; *m* 1968, Frances Henrietta Montagu Douglas Scott, *d* of late Lord William Scott and of Lady William Scott, Beechwood, Melrose; one *s* one *d*. *Educ:* Eton; Magdalene Coll., Cambridge. *Heir: s b* 12 Aug. 1970. *Address:* Grundisburgh Hall, Woodbridge, Suffolk.

*See also C. M. T. Smith-Ryland.*

**CRASKE, Rt. Rev. Frederick William Thomas;** Assistant Bishop in diocese of London since 1961; Chairman of the Prison Chaplaincies Council of the Church Assembly, since 1961; *b* 11 May 1901; *s* of William James Craske; *m* Nellie, *d* of late Harold Wilson; two *s*. *Educ:* King's Coll. (City Exhibitioner), University of London (BA). Jelf Prize and AKC 1927; FKC 1954. Deacon, 1927; Priest, 1928; Curate of St Chrysostum, Victoria Park, Manchester, 1927-29; International Sec., 1929-30, London Sec., 1930-32, Student Christian Movement; Curate of All Hallows, Lombard Street, London, 1929-32; Lecturer, King's Coll., London, 1932; Vicar of: Read-in-Whalley, 1932-35; St John the Evangelist, Blackburn, 1935-39; Education Sec., Missionary Council of Church Assembly, 1939-50; Gen. Sec., Church of England Youth Council, 1942-44; Select Preacher, Cambridge Univ., 1943; Representative of British Council of Churches in Germany, 1950-53; Examining Chaplain to Bishop of Leicester, 1950-53; Bishop of Gibraltar, 1953-59; Moderator of the Central Advisory Council for the Ministry, 1960-65. Chaplain and Sub-Prelate, Order of St John of Jerusalem, 1956-. *Address:* 106 Grand Drive, Raynes Park, SW20.

**CRASTER, Sir John Montagu,** Kt 1955; JP, CA Northumberland; *b* 5 June 1901; *s* of late Thos William Craster; *m* 1936, Vera Gwendolin, 5th *d* of late Robert Durward; no *c*. *Educ:* Clifton Coll.; Gonville and Caius Coll., Cambridge. High Sheriff of Northumberland, 1944. Chairman: Assoc. of Sea Fisheries Cttees for England and Wales, 1939-70; Northumberland Sea Fisheries Cttee, 1929-70; Alnwick Petty Sessions; Berwick-on-Tweed Conservative Assoc., 1946-49, 1953-56 (Pres., 1965-67); Alnwick RDC, 1945-48; CC Northumberland, 1947-57; CA, 1957-67. Alnwick NFU, 1932 and 1948; Northumberland Playing Fields Assoc., 1946-48; Member: Nat. Health Act Exec. Cttee, 1948-49; Northumberland Agric. Exec. Cttee, 1945-65; Exec. Cttee Northumberland Central Landowners' Assoc., 1934-64; North Sunderland Harbour Commn, 1942-67; Vice-Chm., Farne Island Cttee of Nat. Trust, 1947-67; Mem. Home Office Advisory Cttee for Wild Birds' Protection Act, 1954-69; Pres. of Fisheries Organisation Soc., 1956-69; Member: Bledisloe Cttee Salmon and Freshwater Fisheries Acts, 1957-61; Humane Traps Panel, Dept of Agriculture for Scotland. Coronation Medal, 1953. *Publications:* Chapter XII, The Birds of Northumberland, in The Three Northern Counties of England, 1938; Naturalist in Northumberland, 1969; nature articles and notes to Cornhill Magazine, etc. *Recreations:* shooting, fishing, and ornithology. *Address:* Craster West House, Northumberland. *TA:* Craster, Craster. *T:* Embleton 225. *Club:* Farmers'.

**CRATHORNE,** 1st Baron *cr* 1959, of Crathorne; **Thomas Lionel Dugdale,** 1st Bt, *cr* 1945; PC 1951; TD; Vice-Lieutenant, North Riding of Yorkshire, since 1957; R of O, Royal Scots Greys, 1928; Major Yorkshire Hussars Yeomanry, 1931; JP North Riding of Yorkshire; *b* 20 July 1897; *o s* of late J. Lionel Dugdale and late Maud Violet, *d* of G. W. P. Woodroffe, late Royal Horse Guards; *m* 1936, Nancy (*d* 1969), OBE 1961, *d* of Sir Charles Tennant, 1st Bt; two *s*. *Educ:* Eton; RMC Sandhurst. Joined Royal Scots Greys, 1916, and served European War, 1917-18; Capt. 1923; Adjt, Yorks Hussars (Yeomanry), 1927; War of 1939-45, on active service, 1939-41. MP (U) Richmond, Yorks, 1929-59; Parliamentary Private Sec. to Sir Philip Cunliffe Lister (when Pres. of Board of Trade, Aug.-Oct. 1931; Sec. of State for the Colonies, 1931-35 and Sec. of State for Air, 1935); Parliamentary Private Sec. to Mr Stanley Baldwin when Prime Minister, 1935-37; a Lord of the Treasury, 1937-40, and Dep. Chief Government Whip, 1941-42; Vice-Chm., Conservative Party Organisation, 1941-42, Chm., 1942-44. Pres. Nat. Union of Conservative and Unionist Assocs, 1951; Minister of Agriculture and Fisheries, 1951-54, resigned. UK Deleg., Council of Europe and W European Union, 1958-59, 1961-65; Delegate to NATO Parliamentarians Conf., 1958 (Pres., 1962-63) (Mem. Standing Cttee, 1958-65); Chairman UK National Cttee for Atlantic Congress, 1959; Mem. Adv. Commn on Central Africa, 1960; Chm. Deptl Cttee on the Law on Sunday Observance, 1961-64; Steward of Jockey Club, 1960-62 (Senior Steward, 1962); Mem., The Horserace Betting Levy Board, 1964-; Chm. Political Honours Scrutiny Cttee, 1961-; Chm. North of England Adv. Cttee for Civil Aviation, 1964-. *Recreations:* shooting, fishing. *Heir:* *s* Hon. Charles James Dugdale, [*b* 12 Sept. 1939; *m* 1970, Sylvia Mary, *yr d* of Arthur Montgomery, Wimbledon]. *Address:* Crathorne Hall, Yarm, Yorks. *T:* Eaglescliffe 3235; 14 Bedford Gardens, W8. *T:* 01-727 6942. *Clubs:* Carlton, White's; Jockey (Newmarket).

**CRAUFURD, Sir Robert (James),** 9th Bt *cr* 1781; Member of the London Stock Exchange, associated with Messrs Phillips and Drew; *b* 18 March 1937; *s* of Sir James Gregan Craufurd, 8th Bt and of Ruth Marjorie, *d* of Frederic Corder; *S* father, 1970; *m* 1964, Catherine Penelope, *yr d* of late Captain Horatio Westmacott, Torquay; three *d*. *Educ:* Harrow; University College, Oxford. Joined Phillips and Drew on leaving Oxford University, 1960; elected Member of the London Stock Exchange, 1969. *Recreations:* gardening, local history, music and Commonwealth coins. *Address:* Brightwood, Aldbury, Tring, Herts. *Club:* English-Speaking Union.

**CRAVEN,** family name of **Earl of Craven.**

**CRAVEN,** 7th Earl of, *cr* 1801; **Thomas Robert Douglas Craven;** Viscount Uffington, 1801; Baron Craven, 1665; *b* 24 Aug. 1957; *e s* of 6th Earl of Craven and of Elizabeth (*née* Johnstone-Douglas); *S* father, 1965. *Heir:* *b* Hon. Simon George Craven, *b* 16 Sept. 1961. *Address:* The Dower House, Hamstead Marshall, Newbury, Berks.

**CRAVEN, Archdeacon of;** *see* Sephton, Ven. A.

**CRAVEN, Prof. Avery O.,** LLD (Hon.), LittD (Hon.); Professor of History, The University of Chicago, since 1928; Professor of American History and Institutions, Cambridge, England, 1952-53; *b* 1886; *s* of Oliver and Mary Pennington Craven; *m* 1936, Georgia Watson; one *d*. *Educ:* Simpson Coll (AB); University of Chicago (PhD); Harvard Univ. (MA). MA Cambridge, 1952. Instructor, Simpson Coll., 1908-11; Asst Prof., College of Emporia, 1920-23; Associate Professor: Michigan State Coll., 1924-25; University of Ill, 1925-27; University of Chicago, 1927-28; Prof. of History, University of Sydney (Australia), 1948-49. Hon. DHL Wayne State Univ., USA. *Publications:* Soil Exhaustion as a factor in History of Virginia and Maryland, 1925; Edmond Ruffin, Southerner, 1931; The Repressible Conflict, 1936; Democracy in American Life, 1938; The Coming of the Civil War, 1942; The United States, Experiment in Democracy, 1947; An Historian and the Civil War, 1964; Reconstruction, 1969. *Address:* Dune Acres, RFD3, Chesterton, Indiana, USA. *T:* Chesterton 4722. *Club:* Quadrangle (Chicago, Ill).

**CRAVEN, Marjorie Eadon,** RRC 1941 (1st Class); *b* 21 March 1895; *yr d* of late John Alfred Craven and Susannah Eadon Craven, Sheffield, Yorks. *Educ:* Roedean Sch. SRN; SCM; RNT; Health Visitor, District Nurse (Leeds). Mem. St John VAD, 1915-17; Leeds Gen. Infirmary, 1917-26; studied nursing administration: Bedford Coll., London, Royal College of Nursing, 1926; Teachers' Coll., Columbia Univ., NY City, 1927-28. Matron, West London Hospital, 1929-38 and 1947-53; Matron and Principal Matron, TANS, 1939-44; Matron-in-Chief, British Red Cross Soc. and Joint Cttee, Order of St John and BRCS, 1953-62, retd. Vice-Pres., W. L. H. Nurses' League; Vice-Pres., National Florence Nightingale Memorial Cttee. Officer (Sister) Order of St John, 1957. Florence Nightingale Medal, 1961. *Recreation:* music. *Address:* 5 Pembroke Close, Grosvenor Crescent, SW1. *Clubs:* Cowdray, VAD Ladies'.

**CRAVEN, Air Marshal Sir Robert Edward,** KBE 1970 (OBE 1954); CB 1966; DFC 1940; Commander, Maritime Air Force, since 1969; *b* 16 Jan. 1916; *s* of Gerald Craven, Port Elizabeth, S Africa, and Edith Craven, York; *m* 1940, Joan Peters; one *s* one *d*. *Educ:* Scarborough Coll. MN, 1932-37; Pilot Officer, RAF, 1937; 201, 210, 228 Sqdns, 1937-41; RAF Staff Coll., 1942; Staff Appts: Coastal Command, 1942 (despatches thrice); Directing Staff, RAF Staff Coll., 1944; HQ, Mediterranean and Middle East, Cairo, 1945; CO Eastleigh, Kenya, 1946; RN Staff Coll., 1948; Directing Staff, Joint Services Staff Coll., 1949; Standing Group, NATO Washington, 1951; RAF St Eval, 1954; Directing Staff, RAF Staff Coll., 1957; Group Capt. 1957; CO RAF Lyneham, 1959; Director, Personal Services, RAF, 1961; Air Cdre 1961; Air Officer Admin., Transport Comd, 1964; Air Vice-Marshal, 1965; SASO, Flying Training Comd, 1967-68, Training Comd, 1968-69. Order of Menelik (Ethiopia), 1955. *Recreations:* fishing, antique furniture restoration and reproduction. *Address:* Milverton Lodge, Sandy Lane, Northwood, Mddx. *Club:* Royal Air Force.

**CRAWFORD,** 28th Earl of, *cr* 1398, and **BALCARRES,** 11th Earl of, *cr* 1651; **David Robert Alexander Lindsay,** KT 1955; GBE, *cr* 1951; DL; Baron Lindsay of Crawford before 1143; Baron Lindsay of Balcarres, 1633; Earl of Balcarres, Lord Lindsay and Balniel, 1651; Baron Wigan (UK), 1826; Premier Earl of Scotland; Head of House of Lindsay; Deputy Governor, Royal Bank of Scotland, since 1962; Trustee of: British Museum since 1940; National Gallery, Oct. 1935-Dec. 1941, June 1945-June 1952, June 1953-July 1960 (Chairman, Jan. 1938-Dec. 1939 and May 1946-Dec. 1948); National Galleries of Scotland since 1947 (Chairman, 1952-); The Pilgrim Trust since 1949; Chairman: Royal Fine Art Commission, 1943-57; National Trust, 1945-65; National Art-Collections Fund; National Library of Scotland; *b* 20 Nov. 1900; *e s* of 27th Earl of Crawford and 10th of Balcarres and Constance (*d* 1947), *y d* of Sir Henry Pelly, 3rd Bt, MP, and the Lady Lilian Yorke; *S* father, 1940; *m* 1925, Mary, 3rd *d* of late Rt Hon. Lord Richard Cavendish, PC, CB, CMG; three *s*. *Educ:* Eton; Magdalen College, Oxford. MP (C) Lonsdale Div. of Lancs, 1924-40. Tate Gallery, 1932-41; Mem. of Standing Commission on Museums and Galleries, 1937; Rector of St Andrews Univ., 1952-55. DL Fifeshire, 1953. Hon. LLD: St Andrews; Cambridge; Hon. LittD Manchester; Hon. DLit London; Hon. DLitt Exeter; Hon. DCL: Oxford; Warwick; Amherst Coll., Mass; Hon. DUniv York. RSA, FRIBA, FSA, FSAScot. *Heir: s* Lord Balniel, *qv*. *Address:* Balcarres, Colinsburgh, Fife. *Clubs:* Athenæum, Travellers'.

*See also Hon. James Lindsay, Viscount Dilhorne, M. H. Mason, Sir Godfrey Nicholson, Bt.*

**CRAWFORD, Brig. Alastair Wardrop Euing;** *b* 1896; *s* of Col E. R. Crawford, DL, of Auchentroig, Buchlyvie; *m* 1924, Helena Beatrice, *d* of Adm. Sir Charles Dundas of Dundas, KCMG; one *s* two *d*. *Educ:* Glenalmond; RMC Sandhurst. Served European War, 1916-18; 2nd Lieut Royal Scots Greys, 1916; retired as Major, 1937. Recalled, 1939; Lt-Col Comdg 43rd Reconnaissance Regt, RAC, 1942-43; served in NW Europe, 1944-46, with HQ VIII Corps (despatches), Brig., 1945; retired, 1946. Mem. of Queen's Body Guard for Scotland (Royal Company of Archers), 1949. DL 1947-65, JP 1951-65. Vice-Lieut, 1964-65, Stirlingshire. *Recreations:* shooting, hunting. *Address:* La Fougeraie, Archirondel, Gorey, Jersey, CI. *T:* East 504. *Clubs:* Cavalry; New (Edinburgh); Stirling and County.

**CRAWFORD, Sir (Archibald James) Dirom,** Kt 1957; Hon. Treasurer Western Area Conservative and Unionist Association since 1959 (President, 1956-59; Chairman, 1951-56); *b* 1899; *s* of Malcolm M. Crawford and Ethel Elizabeth Crawford, *d* of Andrew Wernicke; unmarried. *Educ:* Winchester; RMC Sandhurst. Served as Subaltern, 6th Inniskilling Dragoons, then RARO; invalided out of Service, 1939. Chairman: Bridgwater Div. Conservative and Unionist Assoc., 1948-51; Somerset County Federation of Conservative and Unionist Assocs, 1950-51. Pres., Somerset County Cttee, British Legion, Dec. 1957- (Hon. Treasurer, 1953-57). *Address:* Park House, Over Stowey, Bridgwater, Somerset. *T:* Nether Stowey 269. *Club:* Cavalry.

**CRAWFORD, Sir Dirom;** *see* Crawford, Sir A. J. D.

**CRAWFORD, Sir Douglas Inglis,** Kt 1964; CB 1952; DSO 1945; TD 1942; DL; Vice-Chairman, United Biscuits Ltd; Chairman, D. S. Crawford Ltd; Deputy Chairman, Martins Bank Ltd; *b* 22 March 1904; *e s* of Archibald Inglis and Mary Forsyth Crawford; unmarried. *Educ:* Uppingham; Magdalene Coll., Cambridge. Served War of 1939-45 in Field Artillery; Comd 87 (Field) Army Group RA (TA), 1947-51; Director: Royal Insurance Co. Ltd; Liverpool & London & Globe Insce Co.; London and Lancs Insurance Co. Ltd; Liverpool Exchange Co. Ltd. Mem. of Royal Artillery Institution. DL Lancs, 1951; Sheriff of the County Palatine of Lancaster, 1969-. *Recreations:* golf, shooting. *Address:* Fernlea, Mossley Hill, Liverpool 18. *T:* Allerton 2013. *Clubs:* White's, Boodle's, Army and Navy; New (Edinburgh); Royal and Ancient, Hon. Company of Edinburgh Golfers.

**CRAWFORD, Sir Ferguson;** *see* Crawford, Sir W. F.

**CRAWFORD, Sir Frederick,** GCMG 1961 (KCMG 1953; CMG 1951); OBE 1945; Director Resident, Anglo American Corporation of South Africa Ltd, Salisbury, Rhodesia; *b* 9 March 1906; *s* of James Mansfield Crawford, MD, Hull; *m* 1st, 1936, Maimie Alice (*d* 1960), *d* of John Harold Green, London and Cape Town; two *s*; 2nd, 1962, Clio, *widow* of Vasso Georgiadis, Uganda, and *d* of Jean Colocotronis, Athens. *Educ:* Hymers Coll., Hull; Balliol Coll., Oxford (BA). Colonial Civil Service; Cadet, Tanganyika, 1929; Asst District Officer, 1931; District Officer, 1941; seconded E African Governors' Conference, 1942-43 and 1945-46; Exec. Officer, Economic Control Board, Tanganyika, 1944-45. Economic Sec., N Rhodesia, 1947; Dir of Development, N Rhodesia, 1948-50. Governor and Comdr-in-Chief, Seychelles, 1951-53; Dep. Governor of Kenya, 1953-56; Governor of Uganda, 1956-Oct. 1961. Retired. KStJ 1958. *Publication:* Review of the Northern Rhodesia Development Plan, 1948. *Recreations:* fishing, golf. *Address:* Charter House, Box 1108, Salisbury, Rhodesia. *Clubs:* Brooks's; Royal and Ancient Golf (St Andrews).

**CRAWFORD, Maj.-Gen. George Oswald,** CB 1956; CBE 1944; Director of Ordnance Services, War Office, 1958-61; *b* 1902; *s* of late Col Arthur Gosset Crawford, Nailsworth, Glos; *m* Sophie Cecilia, *d* of J. C. Yorke, JP, Langton, Dwrbach, Pembs; two *s* one *d*. *Educ:* Bradfield; RMC. 2nd Lieut Glos Regt, 1922;

transf. RAOC 1928. Served CMF, 1942-45; Lieut-Col 1942; Brig. 1943; Dep. Dir of Ordnance Services, Western Command, 1947-51; DDOS, Southern Command, 1951-55; ADC to the Queen, 1954-55; Maj.-Gen. 1955; Inspector, Royal Army Ordnance Corps, 1955-57; Commandant Mechanical Transport Organisation, Chilwell, 1957-58; Col Comdt RAOC, 1960-66. *Club:* United Service. *See also Wilson Stephens.*

**CRAWFORD, Hugh Adam,** RSA 1958 (ARSA 1938); Painter; *b* 28 Oct. 1898; *s* of John Cummings and Agnes Crawford; *m* 1934, Kathleen Mann, ARCA, *d* of late Archibald and Rosamond Mann, Old Coulsdon, Surrey; two *s* (one *d* decd). *Educ:* Garelochhead Public Sch.; Glasgow Sch. of Art. Served in European War, 1915-19. Dipl. Glasgow Sch. of Art, 1923; studied in London, 1923-25. Runner-up, Prix de Rome, 1926. Lectr, 1926, Head of Drawing and Painting Dept, 1936, Glasgow Sch. of Art; Head of Gray's Sch. of Art, Aberdeen, 1948; Princ., Duncan of Jordanstone Coll. of Art, Dundee, 1953. Commissions include portraits of: Lord Strathclyde; Lord Hughes; Sir Hector Maclennan; Sir Patrick Dolan; Sir Alexander King, etc.; also portraits for War Records. *Publications:* contribs to Scottish Library Review of criticisms of books on art. *Recreation:* study of magnetism. *Address:* Carronmor, Blanefield, Stirlingshire. *T:* Blanefield 512. *Clubs:* Savile, Chelsea; Scottish Arts (Edinburgh); Art (Glasgow).

**CRAWFORD, James,** CBE 1956; Full-time Member National Coal Board, 1957-62 (Part-time Member, 1956-57), retired; Member, General Council of Trades Union Congress, 1949-57; Chairman, British Productivity Council, 1955-56; *b* Maybole, 1 Aug. 1896; *s* of late James Crawford; *m* 1st, 1929, Mary McInnes (*d* 1944), *d* of James McGregor; two *s*; 2nd, 1945, Agnes Crossthwaite, *d* of William Sheal; one *s*. *Educ:* Cairn Sch.; Carrick Academy, Maybole. Served European War, 1914-18, 6th Highland Light Infantry, and 2nd and 10th Cameronians. Mem. of Glasgow City Council, 1930-38; Magistrate, 1935-38. Contested (Lab.) Kilmarnock Div. of Ayr and Bute, 1935; Mem. Advisory Council, Dept of Scientific and Industrial Research, 1950-55; Gen. Pres., National Union of Boot and Shoe Operatives, 1944-57. *Recreation:* bowls. *Address:* 118 Northampton Road, Earls Barton, Northampton. *T:* Earls Barton 282.

**CRAWFORD, Joan;** Actress; *b* 23 March; *d* of Thomas Le Sueur; *m* 1st, Douglas Fairbanks, jun. (divorced); 2nd, Franchot Tone (divorced); 3rd, 1942, Phillip Terry, actor (divorced, 1946); 4th 1955, Alfred N. Steele (*d* 1959); (one *s* three *d*, adopted). *Educ:* Kansas City. Won dancing contests; in chorus of Chicago revue; signed by J. J. Shubert for New York musical production; signed by Metro-Goldwyn-Mayer Studios; later at Warner Brothers Studios; now free-lancing; appeared in Our Modern Daughters, Our Blushing Brides, Our Dancing Daughters, Possessed, Sadie McKee, Forsaking All Others, Gorgeous Hussy, Love on the Run, Last of Mrs Cheyney, The Bride Wore Red, Mannequin, The Women, No More Ladies, A Woman's Face, Reunion in France, Above Suspicion, Mildred Pierce, Humoresque, The Damned Don't Cry, Harriet Craig, This Woman is Dangerous, Torch Song, Johnny Guitar, Female on the Beach, Queen Bee, Autumn Leaves, The Story of Esther Costello; The Best of Everything; The Caretakers; Whatever Happened to Baby Jane?; Strait-Jacket; I Saw What You Did; Berserk! *Publication:* (with Jane Kesner Ardmore) A Portrait of Joan, 1963. *Recreations:* theatre, dancing. *Address:* 8008 W Norton Avenue, Los Angeles, Calif. 90046, USA.

**CRAWFORD, Sir John (Grenfell),** Kt 1959; CBE 1954; MEc (Sydney); FAIAS; Vice-Chancellor, Australian National University, since 1968; *b* 4 April 1910; *s* of Henry and Harriet Crawford, Sydney; *m* 1935, Jessie Anderson Morgan; one *d*. *Educ:* Sydney Univ.; Harvard Univ.; Research Fellow, University of Sydney, 1933-35; Lectr, Agricultural Economics, University of Sydney (Part-time), 1934-41; Commonwealth Fund Fellow, USA, 1938-40; Economic Adviser, Rural Bank of NSW, 1935-43; Director, Commonwealth Bureau of Agricultural Economics, 1945-50; Sec., Dept of Commerce and Agriculture, 1950-56; Sec., Dept of Trade, Commonwealth of Australia, 1956-60; resigned from Civil Service, 1960. Dir and Prof. of Economics, Research Sch. of Pacific Studies, Australian National Univ., 1960-67, and Fiscal Adviser to the Univ. Vice-Chm., Commonwealth Cttee of Economic Enquiry, 1962-64, 1966-67. Mem. World Bank Economic Mission to India, 1964-65. Hon. DSc Newcastle, NSW, 1966; Hon. DEc New England, NSW, 1969. *Publications:* Australian National Income (with Colin Clark), 1938; Australian Trade Policy 1942-66; A Documentary History, 1968; articles in Economic Record, Journal of Public Administration, Australian Outlook; several edited books on Australian Economic Affairs and several published lectures on trade and educn policy. *Recreations:* tennis, reading. *Address:* Australian National University, Box 4, GPO, Canberra, ACT. *Clubs:* Commonwealth (Canberra); Union (Sydney); Melbourne (Melbourne).

**CRAWFORD, Maj.-Gen. John Scott,** CB 1945; CBE 1940; CEng, FIMechE; *b* 6 Feb. 1889; *s* of John Paton Crawford; *m* 1916, Amy Middleton-Andrews; two *s*. *Educ:* Liverpool Coll.; Campbell Coll., Belfast. RASC 1915-28; RAOC, 1928-39. Dir of Mechanization on formation of Ministry of Supply; Dep. Dir-Gen. of Tanks and Transport, and in 1943, Dep. Dir-Gen. of Armaments Production. Mem. of Council SMM & T (Vice-Pres., 1948-50; Hon. Treas. 1953-57). Mem. Inst. Engineering Inspection (Pres. 1953-54). Pres. Rubber Research Assoc., 1952-54. Vice-Pres. Liverpool Coll., Mem. Court of Worshipful Co. of Carmen, Master, 1957-58. Comdr, Order of Leopold II (Belgium), 1963. *Recreations:* golf, fishing. *Address:* 11 Glenmore House, Richmond Hill, Surrey. *T:* 01-940 1225. *Club:* Royal Automobile.

**CRAWFORD, Captain John Stuart,** DSO 1940; Royal Navy, retired; HM Consul, Tromsö, Norway, 1956-70, retired; *b* 24 March 1900; *s* of late John Crawford, MD, BS, and late Christian Patricia Blackstock; *m* 1927, Katherine Macdonald; one *d* (and one *s* decd). *Educ:* Dollar Academy; RNC, Osborne and Dartmouth. Midshipman, 1916-18; HMS Valiant; Lieut, 1920; Lieut-Comdr, 1928; Comdr, 1934; Capt., 1940. Naval Attaché Angora, 1946-48; retired list, 1950. County Civil Defence Officer, Northants, 1951; Asst Commissioner of Police (in charge of Marine Police Branch), Malaya, 1951-55. Younger Brother of Trinity House, 1961-. *Recreation:* sailing. *Address:* The Gardens, West Stafford, Dorchester, Dorset. *Club:* Naval and Military.

**CRAWFORD, Sir (Robert) Stewart,** KCMG 1966; (CMG 1951); CVO 1955; Deputy Under-Secretary of State, Foreign and Commonwealth Office, since 1970; *b* 27 Aug. 1913; *s* of late Sir William Crawford, KBE, head of W. S. Crawford Ltd, advertising agents; *m* 1938, Mary Katharine, *d* of late Eric

Corbett, Gorse Hill, Witley, Surrey; three *s* one *d* (and one *s* decd). *Educ:* Gresham's Sch., Holt; Oriel Coll., Oxford. Home Civil Service (Air Ministry), 1936; Private Sec. to Chief of Air Staff, 1940-46; Asst Sec., Control Office for Germany and Austria, 1946; Foreign Office, 1947; Counsellor, British Embassy, Oslo, 1954-56; Counsellor, later Minister, British Embassy, Baghdad, 1957-59; Dep. UK Delegate to OEEC Paris, 1959-60; Asst Under Sec., Foreign Office, 1961-65; Political Resident, Persian Gulf, 1966-70. *Recreations:* tennis, golf. *Address:* 5a Manchester Street, W1. *Club:* Oxford and Cambridge.

**CRAWFORD, Sir Stewart;** *see* Crawford, Sir R. S.

**CRAWFORD, Prof. Theodore;** Professor of Pathology in the University of London, since 1948; Director of Pathological Services, St George's Hospital and Medical School, since 1946; *b* 23 Dec. 1911; *s* of late Theodore Crawford and late Sarah Mansfield; *m* 1938, Margaret Donald Green, MD; two *s* three *d*. *Educ:* St Peter's Sch., York; Glasgow Academy; Glasgow Univ. BSc, 1932; MB, ChB, 1935; FRFPS, 1938; MD 1941; Bellahouston Gold Medal (Glasgow Univ.), 1941; MRCP 1960; FRCP Glas 1962; FRCPath 1963, FRCP 1964; Hall Tutorial and Research Fellow, 1936-38. Asst Physician, Glasgow, Royal Hosp. for Sick Children, 1936-38; Lecturer in Pathology (Glasgow Univ.), 1939-46. Served War of 1939-45, Major RAMC, 1941-45. Mem. of the Medical Research Council, 1960-64; Registrar, Coll. of Pathologists, 1963-68; Consultant Adviser in Pathology to Dept of Health and Social Security and Chm. of its Central Pathology Cttee, 1969-. Royal Society of Medicine (Pres. Section of Pathology, 1961-62). Pres., Royal Coll. of Pathologists, 1969- (Vice-Pres., 1968-69); Mem., Pathological Soc. of Great Britain, etc.; Chm., Scientific Cttee, British Empire Cancer Campaign, 1969- (Hon. Sec., 1955-67; Hon. Sec. of the Campaign, 1967-70). Member: Council Epsom Coll.; Standing Medical Advisory Cttee, Health Services Council, 1964-69; Army Pathology Adv. Cttee, 1970-. *Publications:* (ed) Modern Trends in Pathology, 1967; scientific papers in Lancet, British Medical Journal, British Journal of Surgery, Archives of Disease in Childhood, British Journal of Opthalmology, Journal of Pathology and Bacteriology, etc. *Recreations:* horticulture, hill walking, music. *Address:* 26 Corkran Road, Surbiton. *T:* 01-399 7540; St George's Hospital, SW1. *T:* 01-235 7727; Garrien, Strathlachlan, Strachur, Argyll. *T:* Strachur 205. *Clubs:* Royal Automobile, Hanstown.

**CRAWFORD, Sir (Walter) Ferguson,** KBE 1958 (OBE 1921); CMG 1950; *b* 11 April 1894; *s* of H. F. Crawford, Melbourne, Vic., Australia; *m* 1927, Marjorie Vivienne Shirley; one *s* one *d*. *Educ:* Sydney Grammar Sch., Sydney, NSW; Sydney Univ.; New Coll., Oxford, NSW Rhodes Scholar, 1915. Served European War, 1914-18, in Argyll and Sutherland Highlanders, 1915-18 (despatches). Irak Political Service, 1919-21; Sudan Political Service, 1921-44; Governor Northern Province, Sudan, 1942-44; Palestine Govt Liaison Officer, 1944-46; Head of British Middle East Development Div. (Foreign Office), 1946-60. Dir-Gen., Middle East Assoc., 1960-64. *Recreation:* golf. *Address:* Baidland, Shant Lane, Churt, Surrey.

**CRAWFORD, Vice-Adm. Sir William (Godfrey),** KBE 1961; CB 1958; DSC 1941; *b* 14 Sept. 1907; *s* of late H. E. V. Crawford, Wyld Court, Axminster, and late Mrs M. E. Crawford; *m* 1939, Mary Felicity Rosa, *d* of Sir Philip Williams, 2nd Bt; three *s* one *d*. *Educ:* RN Coll., Dartmouth. Lieut RN, 1929; specialised in gunnery, 1932; Lieut-Comdr, 1937; Gunnery Officer, HMS Rodney, 1940-42; Comdr Dec. 1941; Exec. Officer, HMS Venerable, 1944-46; Capt. 1947; in comd HMS Pelican and 2nd Frigate Flotilla, Med., 1948-49; Dep.-Dir RN Staff Coll., 1950-52; in comd HMS Devonshire, 1952-53; in comd RN Coll., Dartmouth, 1953-56; Rear-Adm. 1956; Imperial Defence Coll., 1956-58; Flag Officer, Sea Training, 1958-60; Vice-Adm. 1959; Comdr British Navy Staff and Naval Attaché Washington, 1960-62; retired list, 1963. Overseas Office Inspector of BTA, 1964-. *Recreations:* sailing, fishing. *Address:* 20 Hornton Court, W8. *T:* 01-937 7711. *Clubs:* United Service; Cruising (Naval Member).

**CRAWFORD-COMPTON, Air Vice-Marshal William Vernon,** CB 1965; CBE 1957; DSO 1943, Bar 1945; DFC 1941, Bar, 1942; RAF retired, 1969; General Manager, Sampsons Mushrooms, since 1969; *b* 2 March 1915; *s* of William Gilbert Crawford-Compton; *m* 1949, Chloe Clifford-Brown; two *d*. *Educ:* New Plymouth High Sch., New Zealand. Joined RAF, 1939; served War of 1939-45 (DFC and Bar, DSO and Bar); 11 Group and 2nd TAF Group Capt., 1955; SASO, 11 (Fighter) Group; Student, Imperial Defence Coll., 1961; Air Officer in Charge of Administration, Near East Air Force, 1962-63; SASO 1963-66. Air Vice-Marshal, 1963. Legion of Honour (France); Croix de Guerre (France); Silver Star (USA). *Recreations:* golf, tennis, fishing. *Address:* Church Farm House, Yapton, Sussex.

**CRAWLEY, Aidan Merivale,** MBE; Chairman, London Weekend Television, since 1967; Director, Television Advisers, since 1968; *b* 10 April 1908; *s* of late Canon A. S. Crawley; *m* 1945, Virginia Cowles, *qv*; two *s* one *d*. *Educ:* Harrow; Oxford. Journalist, 1930-36; Educational Film Producer, 1936-39. AAF, 601 Sqdn, 1936-40; Asst Air Attaché, Ankara, Belgrade (resident Sofia), May 1940-May 1941; joined 73 (F) Sqdn, Egypt; shot down July 1941; prisoner until May 1945. MP (Lab.) Buckingham Div. of Bucks, 1945-51; Parliamentary Private Sec. to successive Secs of State for the Colonies, 1945 and 1946-47; Parliamentary Under-Sec. of State for Air, 1950-51; Resigned from the Labour Party, 1957; MP (C) West Derbyshire, 1962-67. Ed.-in-Chief, Independent Television News Ltd, 1955-56; making television documentaries for BBC, 1956-60; Mem. Monckton Commission on Federation of Rhodesia and Nyasaland, 1960. *Publication:* Escape from Germany, 1956; De Gaulle: A Biography, 1969. *Recreation:* cricket. *Address:* 19 Chester Square, SW1. *T:* 01-730 3030. *Club:* White's.

**CRAWLEY, Mrs Aidan Merivale;** *see* Cowles, Virginia.

**CRAWLEY, Charles William;** Emeritus Fellow of Trinity Hall, 1966; University Lecturer in History, 1931-66; Vice-Master of Trinity Hall, Cambridge, 1950-66; *b* 1 April 1899; *s* of Charles Crawley, barrister of Lincoln's Inn, and Augusta, *d* of Rt Rev. Samuel Butcher, Bishop of Meath; *m* 1930, Kathleen Elizabeth, *d* of Lieut-Col H. G. Leahy, OBE, RA; four *s* one *d*. *Educ:* Winchester (Scholar); Trinity Coll., Cambridge (Scholar). Fellow of Trinity Hall, 1924-66. Asst Tutor, 1927, Acting Senior Tutor, 1940, Senior Tutor, 1946-58. Vice-Master, 1950. *Publications:* The Question of Greek Independence, 1821-1833, 1930, repr. 1970; (ed) New Cambridge Modern History, Vol IX, 1965; articles in historical journals. *Recreation:* walking. *Address:* 1 Madingley Road, Cambridge. *T:* 52849. *Club:* Athenæum.

**CRAWLEY, Desmond John Chetwode,** CMG 1964; CVO 1961; HM Minister to the Holy See, since 1970; *b* 2 June 1917; *s* of late Lieutenant-Colonel C. G. C. Crawley, OBE; *m* 1945, Daphne Lesly, *y d* of Sir Vere Mockett, *qv*; two *s* one *d*. *Educ:* King's Sch., Ely; Queen's Coll., Oxford. Entered Indian Civil Service, serving in Madras Presidency, 1939; entered Indian Political Service, serving in Baluchistan, 1946; entered Commonwealth Relations Office, 1947, and served in London, Calcutta, and on loan to the Foreign Office in Washington; British Dep. High Commissioner in Lahore, Pakistan, 1958-61; Imperial Defence Coll., 1962; British High Commissioner in Sierra Leone, 1963-66; Ambassador to Bulgaria, 1966-70. *Address:* c/o Foreign and Commonwealth Office, SW1; 35 Chartfield Avenue, SW15. *T:* 01-788 9529. *Club:* Oxford and Cambridge University.

**CRAWLEY, John Cecil,** MBE 1944; Editor of News and Current Affairs, BBC, since 1967; *b* 1909; *s* of John and Kathleen Crawley; *m* 1933, Constance Mary Griffiths; two *d*. *Educ:* William Ellis Sch. War Service, Army, 1939-45. Journalism: Reynolds, 1927; Central News Agency, 1928; National Press Agency, 1929; Press Secretaries, 1933; BBC: Sub-Ed., 1945; Foreign Correspondent, New York, 1959-63; Foreign News Ed., 1963-67. *Recreations:* walking, bird-watching. *Address:* 157 Clarence Gate Gardens, NW1. *T:* 01-723 6876.

**CRAWLEY-BOEVEY, Sir Thomas (Michael Blake),** 8th Bt *cr* 1784; Editor, Money Which?, since 1968; *b* 29 Sept. 1928; *er s* of Sir Launcelot Valentine Hyde Crawley-Boevey, 7th Bt, and of Elizabeth Goodeth, *d* of Herbert d'Auvergne Innes, late Indian Police; *S* father, 1968; *m* 1957, Laura Coelingh; two *s*. *Educ:* Wellington Coll.; St John's Coll., Cambridge (BA 1952, MA 1956). 2nd Lieut, Durham Light Infantry, 1948. With Shipping Agents, 1952-61; with Consumers' Association, 1961-. *Recreations:* gardening, bicycling, looking at buildings. *Heir: er s* Thomas Hyde Crawley-Boevey, *b* 26 June 1958. *Address:* 29 Lonsdale Square, N1. *T:* 01-607 5575.

**CRAWSHAW,** 4th Baron, *cr* 1892; **William Michael Clifton Brooks,** Bt, *cr* 1891; *b* 25 March 1933; *s* of 3rd Baron and Sheila (*d* 1964), *o d* of late Lieut-Col P. R. Clifton, CMG, DSO; *S* father, 1946. *Educ:* Eton; Christ Church, Oxford. Jt Master, Oxford Univ. Drag Hounds, 1952-53. Treasurer, Loughborough Div. Conservative Assoc., 1954-58; County Commissioner, Leics Boy Scouts, 1958-. Lord of the Manor of Long Whatton. *Heir: b* Hon. David Gerald Brooks [*b* 14 Sept. 1934; *m* 1970, Belinda Mary, *d* of George Burgess, Melbourne, and of Mrs J. P. Allen, Coleman's Hatch, Sussex. *Educ:* Eton; Royal Agricultural College, Cirencester]. *Address:* Whatton, Loughborough, Leics. *TA:* Kegworth. *T:* Hathern 225. *Club:* MCC.

**CRAWSHAW, Sir (Edward) Daniel (Weston),** Kt 1964; QC (Aden) 1949; *b* 10 Sept. 1903; British; *m* 1942, Rosemary Treffry; one *s* two *d* (and one *s* decd). *Educ:* St Bees Sch.; Selwyn Coll., Cambridge. Solicitor, Supreme Court of Judicature, England, 1929; Barrister-at-Law, Gray's Inn, 1946; Solicitor, Northern Rhodesia, 1930-32; Colonial Legal Service, Tanganyika, 1933-39; Zanzibar, 1939-47; Attorney-Gen., Aden, 1947-52; Puisne Judge, Tanganyika, 1952-60; Justice of Appeal, Court of Appeal for Eastern Africa, 1960-65. Commissioner, Foreign Compensation Commission, 1965-. Brilliant Star of Zanzibar, 1947; Coronation Medal, 1953. *Recreations:* sailing, golf. *Address:* 1 Fort Road, Guildford, Surrey. *T:* Guildford 2496. *Clubs:* Oxford and Cambridge, Royal Over-Seas League; County (Guildford).

**CRAWSHAW, Philip,** CBE 1959 (MBE 1948); Director-General, Royal Over-Seas League, since 1959; *b* 25 Nov. 1912; twin *s* of R. Crawshaw; *m* 1947, June Patricia, *d* of E. D. K. Mathews; two *d*. *Educ:* Repton. Travelling Sec., Over-Seas League, 1936; Asst Sec., 1940; Sec., 1946; Sec.-Gen., 1956. *Recreation:* golf. *Address:* Over-Seas House, St James's, SW1. *T:* 01-493 5051; 73 Albert Drive, Wimbledon, SW19. *T:* 01-788 1494.

**CRAWSHAW, Lt-Col Richard,** OBE 1958; TD 1958; MA, LLB; DL; Barrister-at-Law; MP (Lab) Toxteth Division of Liverpool since 1964; *b* 25 Sept. 1917; *s* of Percy Eli Lee Crawshaw and Beatrice Lavinia (*née* Barritt); *m* 1960, Audrey Frances Lima; no *c*. *Educ:* Pendleton Gram. Sch.; Tatterford Sch.; Pembroke Coll., Cambridge (MA); London Univ. (LLB). Clerk, 1931-33; Engineer, 1933-36; Theological Student, 1936-39; Royal Artillery and Parachute Regt, 1939-45; Pembroke Coll., Cambridge, 1945-47; called to Bar, Inner Temple, 1948; Northern Circuit. Liverpool City Council, 1948-65. DL Lancaster, 1970. *Recreations:* climbing, walking and youth activities. *Address:* The Orchard, Aintree Lane, Liverpool 10. *T:* 051-526 7886.

**CRAXTON, Harold,** OBE 1960; Hon. RAM, Hon. RCM; Professor of Pianoforte, Royal Academy of Music, 1919-60; *b* 30 April 1885; *e s* of Thomas Robert Craxton, Devizes, Wilts; *m* 1914, Essie May Faulkner; five *s* one *d*. *Educ:* Latymer Upper Sch., Hammersmith. Accompanist to Madam Albani, Dame Clara Butt, Kennerley Rumford, Dame Nellie Melba and Elena Gerhardt, etc; has given many pianoforte recitals of early English music. *Publications:* pianoforte pieces and transcriptions of early writers. *Recreation:* golf. *Address:* 14 Kidderpore Avenue, NW3. *T:* 01-435 2965.

**CREAGH, Maj.-Gen. Edward Philip Nagle,** CB 1954; retired; *b* 29 Feb. 1896; *s* of late P. W. Creagh, Fermoy, Co. Cork and Mrs S. H. Creagh; *m* 1927, Ethel Frances Montgomery; one *s* one *d*. *Educ:* St Augustine's Coll., Ramsgate; University Coll. of Cork, NUI. MB, BCh 1917; MRCP 1931. Commissioned RAMC, 1917; Captain 1918; Major 1929; Lt-Col 1943; Col 1948; Brig., 1951; Maj.-Gen., 1953; QHP 1953. War of 1939-45 (despatches). Retired, Feb. 1956. Col Comdt, RAMC, 1956-63. *Recreations:* amateur rider (up to 1927); trout fishing, golf. *Address:* Te Whare, Birch, near Colchester, Essex. *T:* Birch 210.

**CREAGH, Maj.-Gen. Sir Kilner Rupert B.;** *see* Brazier-Creagh.

**CREAGH, Maj.-Gen. Sir Michael O'Moore,** KBE 1941; MC; *b* 16 May 1892. 2nd Lieut 7th Hussars, 1911; Captain, 1918; Major, 15th/19th Hussars, 1924; Bt Lt-Col 1931; Lt-Col 1934; Col 1938; Maj.-Gen. 1941; served European War, 1914-18 (despatches, MC); War of 1939-45, Operations in Middle East (despatches, KBE); retired pay, 1944; UNRRA, 1944-46; Dep. Chief of Greece Mission; Chief of Emergency Supply Unit, European Regional Office; Chief of European Regional Office Voluntary Soc. Liaison Unit. *Address:* Pigeon Hill, Homington, Salisbury, Wilts.

**CREAMER, Amos Albert,** DFC 1943; Under-Secretary, Civil Service Department, since 1968; *b* 6 May 1917; *s* of late Amos and Anne

Creamer; *m* 1946, Margaret Lloyd; one *s* one *d*. *Educ:* Owens Sch.; King's Coll., London. 1st class Hons LLB 1939. Entered Treasury, 1935, Inland Revenue, 1936. Served in RAF, Bomber and Training Comds (Sqdn Ldr), 1941-46. Entered Min. of Works, 1946; Asst Sec., 1956; Under-Sec., 1965; Under-Sec., Treasury, 1967. *Address:* 5 Wildcroft Gardens, Edgware, Mddx.

**CREAMER, Brian;** Physician, St Thomas' Hospital, London, and Senior Lecturer in Medicine, St Thomas's Hospital Medical School, since 1959; *b* 12 April 1926; *s* of L. G. Creamer and late Mrs Creamer, Epsom; *m* 1953, Margaret Holden Rees; two *s* one *d*. *Educ:* Christ's Hosp.; St Thomas' Hosp. MB, BS Hons London, 1948; MD London, 1952; FRCP 1966 (MRCP 1950); Research Asst, Mayo Clinic, Rochester, USA, 1955-56. Sir Arthur Hurst Memorial Lectr, 1968. Mem., British Soc. of Gastroenterology. *Publications:* (ed) Modern Trends in Gastroenterology, vol. 4, 1970; contributions to med. jls. *Recreations:* gardening, domestic bliss and gastroenterological musing. *Address:* Tetherdown, Oxshott Rise, Cobham, Surrey. *T:* Cobham 3994.

**CREASEY, John,** MBE 1946; author; *b* 17 Sept. 1908; *s* of Joseph Creasey and Ruth Creasey (*née* Creasey); *m* 1st, 1935, Margaret Elizabeth Cooke; 2nd, 1941, Evelyn Jean Fudge. *Educ:* Fulham Elementary Sch.; Sloane Sch., Chelsea. Various clerical posts, 1923-35. Began writing, 1925; full time writing, 1935-; mostly crime novels; some travel. Liberal candidate, Bournemouth, 1950. Founder, All Party Alliance Movement, 1967; contested (APA) Nuneaton, 1967; Brierley Hill, April 1967; Gorton, Manchester, 1967. Founder Chm., Crime Writers' Assoc., 1953; Mem. Board of Mystery Writers of America, 1957-60 (Pres., 1966-67); Mem. Western Writers of America. Dir, Robert Sommerville Ltd (Literary Agents). *Publications:* 464 between 1932 and 1968; Toff series (50 titles); Dept Z series (30 titles); West of the Yard series (36 titles); Dr Palfrey series (24 titles); *pseudonyms:* as J. J. Marric, Gideon series (13 titles) (Gideon's Fire won 1961 "Edgar" for year's best crime novel, award of Mystery Writers of America); also books as Michael Halliday, Gordon Ashe, Anthony Morton (Baron series); as Norman Deane, and Jeremy York; *travel books:* Round the World in 465 Days, 1952; Let's Look at America, 1956; *philosophical:* Good, God and Man, 1968. *Recreation:* motoring. *Address:* New Hall, Bodenham, near Salisbury, Wilts. *T:* Bodenham 249. *Clubs:* National Liberal, Royal Automobile, Paternosters.

**CREASY, Admiral of the Fleet Sir George Elvey,** GCB 1953 (KCB 1949; CB 1944); CBE 1943; DSO 1940; MVO 1934; DL; *b* 13 Oct. 1895; *s* of late Leonard and late Ellen Maud Creasy; *m* 1924, Monica Frances Ullathorne; one *s*. *Educ:* RNC Osborne and Dartmouth. Joined HM Navy, 1908; Sub-Lt 1915; Lieut 1916; Comdr 1930; Capt. 1935; Rear-Adm. 1943; Vice-Adm. 1948; Adm. 1951; Adm. of the Fleet, 1955; Asst Dir of Plans, Naval Staff, 1936-38; comd 1st Destroyer Flotilla, 1938-40; Dir of Anti-Submarine Warfare, Naval Staff, 1940-42; commanded HMS Duke of York, 1942-43; Chief of Staff to the Allied Naval Commander-in-Chief, 1943-44; Admiral (Submarines), 1944-46; Flag Officer, Air, Far East, 1947; Fifth Sea Lord and Deputy Chief of Naval Staff (Air), 1948-49; Lord Commissioner of the Admiralty and Vice-Chief of Naval Staff, 1949-51; Commander-in-Chief, Home Fleet, 1952-54, and also Commander-in-Chief, Eastern Atlantic, under NATO, 1952-54; Commander-in-Chief, Portsmouth, 1954-57; also Commander-in-Chief, Home Station, Designate, 1954-57, and Allied C-in-C Channel Comd, under NATO, 1954-57. DL Essex, 1959. Comdr of the Order of Orange Nassau, 1942; Order of Polonia Restituta, 3rd class, 1942; Legion of Merit Degree of Comdr, 1946. *Address:* Old House, Great Horkesley, near Colchester, Essex. *T:* Great Horkesley 291. *Club:* United Service.

**CREASY, Sir Gerald Hallen,** KCMG 1946 (CMG 1943); KCVO 1954; OBE 1937; *b* 1 Nov. 1897; *y s* of Leonard and Ellen Maud Creasy; *m* 1925, Helen Duff, *y d* of Reginald B. Jacomb; one *s* one *d*. *Educ:* Rugby. On Military Service (RA), 1916-19; entered Colonial Office, 1920; Chief Sec. to the West African Council, 1945-47; Governor and C-in-C, Gold Coast, 1947-49; Governor and C-in-C, Malta, 1949-54, retired 1954. GCStJ 1970 (KStJ 1949). LLD (*hc*) Royal University of Malta, 1954. *Address:* 30 Ashburnham Road, Eastbourne, Sussex. *T:* Eastbourne 27147.

**CREDITON, Bishop of,** since 1954; **Rt. Rev. Wilfrid Arthur Edmund Westall;** *b* 20 Nov. 1900; *s* of Rev. A. St Leger and Jessie Margaret Westall; *m* 1927, Ruth, *d* of Frank and Beatrice Evans; one *s* three *d*. *Educ:* Merchant Taylors' Sch.; St Chad's Coll., Durham Univ. (BA). Priest, 1925; Asst Curate, St Aidan's, Birmingham, 1925-27, of the Church of the Good Shepherd, Brighton, 1927-30; Vicar of St Wilfrid's, Brighton, 1930-41; Rector of Hawnby-with-Old Byland, Yorks, 1941-45; Vicar of Shaldon, Devon, 1945-51; Archdeacon of Exeter and Canon Residentiary of Exeter Cathedral, 1951-58. Prebendary of Exeter Cathedral, 1951-60; Warden of the Exeter Diocesan Mission; Proctor in Convocation, 1949-64; Select Preacher to Oxford Univ., 1967; Examining Chaplain to Bishop of Exeter; Chaplain and Sub-Prelate of the Order of St John of Jerusalem; Vice-Chm. of the Additional Curates' Soc.; Pres. of the Church Union; Fellow, Corp. of St Mary & St Nicholas (Woodard Schs); Pres., Exeter Civic Soc. *Recreations:* sketching, railways and travel. *Address:* 10 The Close, Exeter, Devon. *T:* Exeter 73509.

*See also C. T. Evans, C. F. Evans.*

**CREE, Brig. Gerald Hilary,** CBE 1946; DSO 1945; Colonel, The Prince of Wales's Own Regiment of Yorkshire, 1960-70; *b* 23 June 1905; *s* of late Maj.-Gen. Gerald Cree; *m* 1945, Joan Agnes, *d* of late Lt-Col W. R. Eden, RA; one *d*. *Educ:* Kelly Coll.; RMC Sandhurst. Commissioned, The West Yorks Regt, 1924; King's African Rifles, 1931-36; comd 2nd Bn West Yorks Regt, 1942-44; 1st Bn 1946-48; Comdr 25 (East African) Infantry Bde, 1944-45 and Brig. 1953. Served Palestine, East Africa, Abyssinia, Western Desert, Iraq, Burma, 1938-45. Commander 127 (East Lancs) Infantry Brigade (TA), 1953-56; Col, The West Yorks Regt, 1956-57, retd. *Address:* Yetson House, Ashprington, Totnes, Devon. *Club:* United Service.

**CREED, Albert Lowry,** MA; Headmaster of Kingswood School, 1959-70; *b* 16 July 1909; *s* of Rev. Albert H. Creed; *m* 1943, Joyce Marian (*née* Hunter), Leeds; two *s* one *d*. *Educ:* Kingswood Sch.; Downing Coll., Cambridge. MA Cantab 1931. Asst Master: Stretford Grammar Sch., 1932-35; Bishop's Stortford Coll., 1935-39; Housemaster, Christ's Hospital, 1939-42; Headmaster: Staveley-Netherthorpe Grammar Sch., 1942-46; Truro Sch., Cornwall, 1946-59. Chm., West Cornwall Hospital Management Cttee, 1957-59; Vice-Pres., Methodist Conf., 1962-63; a Dir, The Methodist Recorder. FRSA. *Recreations:* Rugby football, tennis, walking, travel.

*Address:* Trevor House, Langford, near Lechlade, Glos. *Club:* Royal Commonwealth Society.

**CREEDY, Sir Herbert (James),** GCB 1933 (KCB 1919; CB 1915); KCVO 1923 (CVO 1917; MVO 1911); MA; Secretary and Registrar of the Distinguished Service Order since 1933; Member of Council, Union Jack Services Clubs; Member, Executive Committee, Lord Kitchener National Memorial Fund; *b* 3 May 1878; *m* 1904, Mabel Constance (*d* 1958), *d* of S. J. Lowry; one *d. Educ:* Merchant Taylors' Sch.; St John's Coll., Oxford (Scholar). 1st Class Classical Mods; 1st Class Lit. Hum.; Senior Scholar of St John's Coll., 1901-05; Hon. Fellow of St John's Coll., 1931; appointed to the War Office as Clerk of the Higher Division, 1901; seconded for special duty in S Africa, 1903; Resident Clerk, 1903-04; Private Sec. to Sir Edward Ward, Permanent Under-Sec. of State for War, 1903-08; Clerk to Comrs of Income Duty for Army Services, 1907-08; Asst Principal, War Office, 1908-20; Private Sec. to successive Secretaries of State for War (Col Seely, Mr Asquith, Earl Kitchener, Mr Lloyd George, Earl of Derby, Viscount Milner, and Mr Churchill), 1913-20; Asst to the Sec. of the War Office, 1916-20; Sec. of the War Office, 1920-24; Permanent Under-Sec. of State for War, 1924-39; Mem. and Sec. of the Army Council, 1920-39; retired from the Civil Service, 1939; re-employed with the Security Executive, 1940-45 (Chm., 1943-45). JP Co. of London, 1928-39; Governor of Wellington Coll., 1939-53, and Hon. Treas., 1941-50; a Comr Royal Hospital, Chelsea, 1945-57; a Trustee of Imperial War Museum, 1942-59; Member of various Cttees of the National Council, YMCA, 1939-64. OStJ 1931; Comdr Legion of Honour; Officer of the Belgian Order of the Crown; 2nd Class of the Russian Order of St Anne. *Address:* 93 Woodstock Road, Oxford. *T:* Oxford 55897. *Club:* United Service.

**CREESE, Nigel Arthur Holloway;** Headmaster, Melbourne Grammar School, since 1970; *b* 4 June 1927; *s* of late H. R. Creese; *m* 1951, Valdai (*née* Walters); two *s* two *d. Educ:* Blundell's Sch.; Brasenose Coll., Oxford. Assistant Master: Bromsgrove Sch., 1952-55; Rugby Sch., 1955-63; Headmaster, Christ's Coll., Christchurch, NZ, 1963-70. *Address:* Melbourne Church of England Grammar School, Domain Road, South Yarra, Victoria 3141, Australia.

**CREIGHTON, Prof. Donald Grant,** CC (Canada) 1967; University Professor, University of Toronto, since 1967; Professor of History since 1945, and Chairman, Department of History, 1955-59, University of Toronto; *b* 1902; 2nd *s* of late Rev. William B. Creighton and of Laura Harvie; *m* 1926, Luella Sanders Browning Bruce; one *s* one *d. Educ:* Victoria Coll., University of Toronto; Balliol Coll., Oxford. Univ. Lectr, Dept of History, Univ. of Toronto, 1927; John Simon Guggenheim Memorial Fellowship, 1940-41; Rockefeller Fellowship, 1944-45; Nuffield Travelling Fellowship, 1951-52. Chm., Canadian Cttee, Encyclopedia Americana, 1956-63; Commonwealth Mem., Monckton Advisory Commn on Central Africa, 1959; Member: Ontario Adv. Cttee on Confedn, 1965-; Historic Sites and Monuments Bd of Canada, 1958-. Sir John A. Macdonald Prof., 1965. Fellow, Royal Soc. of Canada, 1946; Pres., Canadian Historical Assoc., 1956-57; Corres. Mem., Royal Historical Soc., 1966. Tyrrell Medal, Royal Soc. Canada, 1951; Governor-General's Medal for Academic Non-Fiction, 1952 and 1955; Univ. of British Columbia's Medal for Biography, 1955; National Award in Letters, Univ. of Alberta, 1957. Molson Prize, awarded by Canada Council, 1964. Hon. LLD: Universities of New Brunswick, 1949; Queen's, Kingston, Ontario, 1956; Saskatchewan, 1957; British Columbia, 1959; St Francis Xavier, 1967; Victoria, BC, 1967; Dalhousie, 1970; Hon. DLitt: Manitoba, 1957; McGill, 1959. *Publications:* The Commercial Empire of the St Lawrence, 1937; Dominion of the North: A History of Canada, 1944; John A. Macdonald: The Young Politician, 1952; John A. Macdonald: The Old Chieftain, 1955; The Story of Canada, 1959; The Road to Confederation, 1964; Canada's First Century, 1970. *Address:* 15 Princess Street, PO Box 225, Brooklin, Ont, Canada. *Club:* Athenæum.

**CREMIN, Cornelius Christopher;** Irish Permanent Representative at UN since 1964; *b* 6 Dec. 1908; 2nd *s* of D. J. Cremin and Ann (*née* Singleton), Kenmare, Co. Kerry; *m* 1935, Patricia Josephine, 2nd *d* of late P. C. O'Mahony, Killarney; one *s* three *d. Educ:* National Univ. of Ireland. BComm 1930; MA (Classics) 1931. Travelling studentship (Classics), NUI, 1931-34; Brit. Sch. at Athens and Rome, 1932; Dipl. in Class. Archaeol., Oxford, 1934; 3rd Sec., Dept of External Affairs, 1935; 1st Sec., Irish Legation, Paris, 1937-43; Chargé d'Affaires, Berlin, 1943-45; Chargé d'Affaires, Lisbon, 1945-46; Couns., Dept of External Affairs, Dublin, 1946-48; Asst Sec., 1948-50; Minister to France, March-Sept. 1950; Ambassador to France, 1950-54; Head of Irish Delegn, OEEC, 1950-54, and Vice-Chm. of OEEC Council (official), 1952-54; Ambassador to the Holy See, 1954-56; Sec. of the Dept of External Affairs, Dublin, 1958-62; Irish Ambassador to Britain, 1963-64 (and 1956-58). LLD *hc* National Univ. of Ireland, 1965. Grand Officer of the Legion of Honour, 1954; Knight Grand Cross of the Order of Pius, 1956; Grand Cross of Merit (Fed. Germany), 1960. *Recreations:* golf, boating. *Address:* 1 East End Avenue, New York, USA.

**CRERAR, Hon. Thomas Alexander,** PC (Canada); LLD; Member of Canadian Senate since 1945; *b* Molesworth, Ont., 17 June 1876; *s* of William S. Crerar, Scotch-Canadian, and Margaret McTavish, Scotch-Irish-Canadian; *m* 1906, Jessie, *d* of Alexander Hamilton, Solsgirth, Manitoba; one *d. Educ:* public schs and collegiate, Portage la Prairie, Manitoba. Teacher, farmer, grain elevator operator; invited to enter Union Government, 1917; PC Canada, 1917; Minister of Agriculture, 1917-19; MP Marquette, Manitoba, 1917-25; Leader of Progressive Party, 1921-22; MP Brandon, 1930; Minister of Railways and Canals, 1929-30; Minister of Mines and Resources, Canada, 1935-45; Mem. of delegation representing Canadian Government at coronation of Their Majesties, 1937 and to Imperial Conference following; Representative of Canadian Government at Conference of Dominions' Ministers to consider co-ordination of War effort, London, Nov. 1939; resigned from Govt in April 1945 when called to Senate of Canada; ex-President: United Grain Growers Ltd; Grain Growers Export Co. Ltd; Public Press Ltd; and Country Guide Publishing Co. Ltd; Director: Modern Dairies, Winnipeg; Algoma Steel Corp.; Canada Steamships Ltd; The Eastern Trust Co. Ltd; a Liberal; a Presbyterian. Hon. LLD, Manitoba, 1954. *Recreation:* golf. *Address:* Winnipeg, Manitoba, Canada. *Clubs:* Manitoba, St Charles Country (Winnipeg); Rideau (Ottawa).

**CRESPIN, Régine;** soprano singer; *b* 23 Feb.; *d* of Henri Crespin and Marguerite (*née* Meirone); *m* 1962, Lou Bruder, French novelist, critic, poet, translator. *Educ:* Nîmes;

Conservatoire National, Paris (Baccalauréat). Has been working at the Opera, Paris, from 1951, in all the famous opera houses of Europe and all over the World, giving concerts, recitals, etc. Officer des Arts et des Lettres. *Recreations:* sea, sun, sleep, books, theatre; and my dog! *Address:* 3 Avenue Frochot, Paris 9e.

**CRESSWELL, Rev. Cyril Leonard,** KCVO 1959 (CVO 1946); MA, FSA, FRSA; Chaplain of The Queen's Chapel of the Savoy, 1933-61; Chaplain Emeritus of the Royal Victorian Order since 1961 (Chaplain, 1938-61); *b* 1890; *s* of late Rev. John Cresswell; *m* 1924, Madeleine Aglaé Blanche, *d* of late Walter Southwell Jones. *Educ:* private; Emmanuel Coll., Cambridge; Ridley Hall, Cambridge. Curate of Holy Trinity, St Marylebone, 1919-23; Rector of St George's, Birmingham, 1923-26; Chaplain, St Mary's Hosp., Paddington, 1926-31; Mem. Governing Bd and Finance Cttee, 1931-48; Hon. Chaplain, 1931; Hon. Organising Sec., Anglican Evangelical Group Movement, 1941, Chm. 1942-43; Hon. Sec., Cromer Convention, 1927-34; Hon. Auditor, Clergy Orphan Corporation; Asst Grand Chaplain, Grand Lodge of England, 1946; Chaplain, Sancta Maria Lodge and Prince of Wales Lodge; Provincial Grand Chaplain, Middlesex, 1952; Mem. Executive, The Grenfell Assoc. of Great Britain and Ireland, 1930; Pres., Paddington and St Marylebone Rotary Club, 1934-35; Mem. Community Service Cttee of Rotary International Assoc. for Great Britain and Ireland, 1935; Burgess of the Manor and Liberty of the Savoy, 1934; Mem. Propaganda Cttee, King Edward's Hospital Fund for London, 1934; National Council of Social Service, 1935; Council of Bishop Wilson Theological Coll.; Court of the Corporation of the Sons of the Clergy; Trustee, Hyndman Bounty Trust, 1941-51; Council of Jerusalem and the East Mission, 1938-62; Gov., Cheltenham C of E Training Colls; Fellow, Royal Empire Soc.; Chaplain, The Saddlers' Co., 1942; Chaplain, Ven. Order of St John of Jerusalem, and Ecclesiastical Representative on Chapter Gen., 1962; Golden Lectr, 1944-45 and 1945-46; Worshipful Co. of Weavers, 1947; Chaplain to the Company and Limborough Lectr, 1948-51; Freeman of City of London, 1948; Chaplain, Worshipful Co. of Farmers, 1949-67, and Mem. Court, 1949; Chaplain, Instn Electrical Engineers, 1951-61; Hon. Chaplain, Assoc. of Lancastrians in London, 1953-62 (Vice-Pres., 1962); Chaplain: Farmers' Club, 1951-67; Nat. Farmers' Union, 1955; Royal Agricultural Benevolent Instn, 1955; Royal Coll. of Veterinary Surgeons, 1956-62; Coun., The Fleming Memorial Fund for Medical Research, 1959; Vice-Pres., Univ. of London Assoc. of Lancastrians, 1960. *Recreations:* agriculture and farming, motoring, shooting, riding. *Address:* Three Barrows Place, Elstead, Surrey. *T:* Elstead 3286. *Clubs:* Athenæum, The Pilgrims, Royal Automobile.

**CRESSWELL, William Foy,** CBE 1956; Senior Official Receiver in Bankruptcy, 1948-56; *b* 2 Nov. 1895; *s* of Edward Cresswell and Annie Maria (*née* Foy); *m* 1922, Olive May Barham; two *d*. *Educ:* Portsmouth Secondary Sch. Entered Civil Service as Boy Clerk, 1911. Served with Hon. Artillery Company 2nd Inf. Bn in France, Italy and Austria, 1916-19. Appointed to Bankruptcy Department, Board of Trade, 1921; Asst Official Receiver, High Court, 1931; Official Receiver, Swansea and district, 1934; Official Receiver, Bradford, Yorks, 1936; recalled to London to assist with BoT War Damage Insurance Schemes, 1941. Retired, Dec. 1956. *Recreations:* walking, gardening, the open air. *Address:* 27 Sullington Gardens, Worthing, Sussex. *T:* Findon 2065.

**CRESTON, Dormer** (pen-name); *see* Colston-Baynes, D. J.

**CRESWELL, Sir Archibald;** *see* Creswell, Sir K. A. C.

**CRESWELL, Prof. Sir (Keppel) Archibald (Cameron),** Kt 1970; CBE 1955 (MBE 1919); FBA 1947; FSA; Hon. DLitt Oxford; Hon. LitD Princeton; Hon. ARIBA; Professor of Muslim Architecture at the American University, Cairo, since 1956; Professor of Muslim Art and Archæology, at the Egyptian University, 1931-51; Rockefeller Foundation Fellowship, 1952-54; Order of Ismail (Comdr); Syrian Order of Merit, First Class; *b* 13 Sept. 1879; *o s* of Keppel Creswell, of Lloyd's, and Margaret, *d* of Thomas Henderson, Solicitor, Rugby. *Educ:* Westminster Sch. Studying Muslim art since 1910; served European war, 2/Lieut RFC, 1916; Staff Capt. RAF Middle East, 1918 (despatches thrice); Inspector of Monuments, Occupied Enemy Territory (Syria and Palestine), 1919-20; since then domiciled in Cairo; Cambridge Univ. Extension Lectr, 1924; on Cttee of Persian Exhibition, London, 1931; delivered Forlong Lectures (6), 1931; invited to Bicentennial of Princeton Univ. as Leader in Section of Near Eastern Art, 1947; awarded Sir Percy Sykes Memorial Medal by Royal Central Asian Society, 1948; Triennial Gold Medal of Royal Asiatic Society, 1959; Mem. Higher Council of Arabic Monuments and of Museum of Muslim Art; Mem. Council of Coptic Museum and of Coptic Archæological Soc.; Hon. Mem. Royal Central Asian Soc., American Oriental Soc. and Archäologisches Institut des Deutschen Reiches; Hon. Corresponding Mem. of Archæological Survey of India. Trustee Palestine Museum of Antiquities, 1949-54. Has travelled extensively in Syria, Palestine, Transjordan, Iraq, Eastern Turkey and Tunisia. *Publications:* Brief Chronology of the Muslim Monuments of Egypt, 1919; Origin of the Cruciform Plan of Cairene Madrasas, 1922; Archæological Researches at the Citadel of Cairo, 1924; The Works of Sultan Bibars, 1926; Early Muslim Architecture, vol. 1, 1932 (enl. edn in 2 vols, 1970), vol. 2, 1940; The Muslim Architecture of Egypt, Vol. 1, Fātimids, 1952, Vol. 2, Ayyūbids and Early Bahrite Mamlūks, 1959; A Short Account of Early Muslim Architecture (Pelican Book), 1958; A Bibliography of the Architecture, Arts and Crafts of Islam, 1961; also contributions to Burlington Magazine, The Indian Antiquary, Journal of RAS, Syria, Iraq, Ars Islamica, Byzantion, The Year-Book of Oriental Art, Archæologia, Ars Orientalis, the Encyclopaedia of Islam, new edn, The Ency. Brit., new edn, The Urdu Encyclopaedia of Islam, The Enciclopedia Universale dell' Arte, etc. *Address:* 2 rue Baehler, Qasr en-Nil, Cairo; School of Oriental Studies, The American University, Cairo. *T:* 40936. *Clubs:* Athenæum, Royal Automobile.

**CRESWELL, Sir Michael Justin,** KCMG 1960 (CMG 1952); Ambassador to Argentine Republic, 1964-69; retired; *b* 21 Sept. 1909; *s* of late Col Edmund William Creswell, RE; *m* 1st, 1939, Elizabeth Colshorn; one *s*; 2nd, 1950, Baroness C. M. thoe Schwartzenberg; one *s*. *Educ:* Rugby; New Coll., Oxford. Laming Travelling Fellow, Queen's Coll., Oxford, 1932. Entered Foreign Service, 1933; 3rd Sec., Berlin, 1935-38; 2nd Sec., Madrid, 1939-44, Athens, 1944; Foreign Office, 1944-47; Counsellor, Tehran, 1947-49, Singapore, 1949-51; Minister, British Embassy, Cairo, 1951-54; Ambassador to Finland, 1954-58; Senior

Civilian Instructor, Imperial Defence Coll., 1958-60; Ambassador to Yugoslavia, 1960-64. *Recreations:* stalking, travelling. *Address:* Copse Hill, Ewhurst, near Cranleigh, Surrey. *Clubs:* Brooks's, Pratt's; Shikar.

**CRESWICK, Harry Richardson,** MA; Librarian Emeritus of Cambridge University; *b* 1902; *m* Agnes Isabel, *d* of late J. W. Stubbings, Bradwell-on-Sea, Essex. *Educ:* Barnet Grammar Sch.; Trinity Coll., Cambridge. On staff of University Library, Cambridge, 1926-38; Deputy Librarian, Bodleian Library, Oxford, 1939-45; Bodley's Librarian and Student of Christ Church, 1945-47; Librarian of Cambridge Univ. and Professorial Fellow of Jesus Coll., 1949-67. Hon. LittD, Trinity Coll., Dublin. *Address:* Conington Hall, near Cambridge.

**CRETNEY, Sir (William) Godfrey,** Kt 1966; (first) Headmaster, The Regis School, Tettenhall, Wolverhampton, since 1955; *b* 24 Aug. 1912; *s* of Robert William and Amy E. Cretney; *m* 1940, Nancy Margaret, *d* of Lewis H. and Nancy Chesterton, Wallasey, Ches; two *s* one *d*. *Educ:* Douglas High Sch., IOM; Liverpool Univ. (BA Hons English, Dipl. Educn). War Service, Royal Corps of Signals, India Comd, 1940-46 (Major). Resident Master, Arnold Sch., Blackpool, 1934-38; Sen. English Master, Liverpool Inst. High Sch., 1939-48; (first) Headmaster, Castle Rushen High Sch., IOM, 1948-54. Member: Sec. of State's Consultative Cttee on Research into Comprehensive Educn, 1965; Govt Cttee on Speech Therapy, 1969. Life Mem., Court of Governors of Birmingham, 1970. *Recreations:* walking, reading, sport. *Address:* Arbory, 29 Lowlands Avenue, Tettenhall, Wolverhampton, Staffs. *T:* Wolverhampton 51012.

**CREW, Air Vice-Marshal Edward Dixon,** DSO 1944 and Bar 1950; DFC 1941 and Bar 1942; Deputy Controller, National Air Traffic Control Services, since 1969; *b* 24 Dec. 1917; *er s* of F. D. Crew, MB, MRCS, LRCP; *m* 1945, Virginia Martin; one *s*. *Educ:* Felsted Sch.; Downing Coll., Cambridge (MA). Commissioned RAFVR, 1939; served War of 1939-45: night fighter sqdns; 604 sqdn, 85 Sqdn; Comd 96 Sqdn; permanent commission, 1945. Malayan Emergency, Comd No. 45 Sqdn, 1948-50; on exchange, RCAF, 1952-54; CFE, 1954-56; Comd RAF Brüggen, Germany, 1959-62; Comdr, Air Forces Borneo, 1965-66; AOC Central Reconnaissance Estabt, 1968; various Air Staff jobs at Air Min. and MoD. *Recreations:* shooting, tennis. *Address:* c/o National Westminster Bank Ltd, 10 Benet Street, Cambridge. *Club:* Royal Air Force.

**CREW, Francis Albert Eley,** FRS; TD; MD, DSc, PhD, DIH, FRCPE, FRSE; OStJ; Hon. DSc Benaras Hindu University; Hon. LLD Edinburgh University; Order of Polonia Restituta; Foreign Member Czecho-Slovakian Academy of Agriculture; Hon. Member National Veterinary Medical Association and Physiological Society of India; Member American Genetic Association; Hon. Member Polish Society of Arts and Sciences Abroad; Brigadier RAMC TA; late Commander, Edinburgh Special Constabulary; late Chairman Board of Governors, Royal (Dick) Veterinary College; *b* 1886; *m* 1913, Helen Campbell Dykes, MB, ChB; one *s* one *d*. *Educ:* King Edward VI's High Sch., Birmingham; Univs of Birmingham and Edinburgh, MB, ChB 1912. Served European War, India and France, 1914-18; 6th Bn The Devonshire Regt and No. 3 FA, RAMC Guards Div.; ADMS Edinburgh Area, 1940-42; Dir Medical Research, WO, 1942-46; Service Sub-Editor Official Medical History of the War. Asst in Natural History Dept, Univ. of Edinburgh, 1919-21; Buchanan Prof. of Animal Genetics, 1928-44 and Dir of Inst. of Animal Genetics, 1921-44, Univ. of Edinburgh; Prof. of Public Health and Social Medicine, Edinburgh Univ., 1944-55; Prof. of Preventive and Social Medicine, Ein Shams Univ., Cairo, Feb.-Nov. 1956; WHO Vis. Prof. of Prev. and Social Med., Univ. of Rangoon, 1957-58, Topiwala Nat. Med. Coll., Univ. of Bombay, 1959-60. Adviser in Genetics to Dir, Central Family Planning Inst., New Delhi, (for ODM), 1966-67. OC, Edinburgh Univ. OTC med. unit, 1920-29; Keith prizeman, RSE, 1937-39; Lt-Col Comdg 1st Edinburgh Bn Home Guard, 1954-56. Mem. Army Health Adv. Cttee, 1946-56; Chm. Board of Management, Edinburgh Central Group of Hospitals, 1946-56. 1st William Withering Lectr, Univ. of Birmingham, 1927; Milroy Lectr, RCP, 1928; Galton Memorial Lectr, Eugenics Soc., 1953; Charles Hastings Memorial Lectr, BMA, 1954; George Frederic Still Memorial Lectr, British Pædiatric Assoc., 1955; Nursing Mirror Lectr, Univ. of Edinburgh, 1962. Pres., 2nd Internat. Congress of Sex Research, 1930; Section D British Assoc., 1937; Assoc. of British Zoologists, 1937; Genetical Soc., 1938-39; VIIth Internat. Genetical Congress, 1939. Freeman, City of London, in Co. of Apothecaries. *Publications:* Official (Army) Medical History of the War; Health, its Nature and Conservation, 1965; The Foundations of Genetics, 1965; text-books on animal genetics, genetics of sexuality, organic inheritance in man, sex-determination, genetics of the budgerigar, genetics in relation to clinical medicine, essays in social medicine, hygiene; numerous papers dealing with these and related matters. *Recreations:* books, gardening, Mendelian experimentation with bantams and Australian finches. *Address:* Upton's Mill, Framfield, Sussex. *T:* Framfield 336. *Club:* Athenæum.

**CREWDSON, Bt-Col William Dillworth,** CB 1947; TD; DL, JP; Member Westmorland County Council, 1924, Alderman, 1943, retired 1970; *b* 6 Nov. 1897; *e s* of late Canon Crewdson; *m* 1907, Cicely Maud (*d* 1966), *d* of John Bruce Nichols, Holmwood; three *d*. *Educ:* Marlborough Coll.; Trinity Coll., Cambridge. MA, LLB; Barrister-at-law; served European War, 1914-18, 4th Bn Border Regt; commanded 4th Bn The Border Regt 1919-25; commanded 11th Bn Westmorland Home Guard, 1940-45. *Address:* Helme Lodge, Kendal, Westmorland. *T:* Kendal 172.

**CREWE, Albert V.,** PhD; Professor, Department of Physics and the Enrico Fermi Institute of The University of Chicago, since 1963 (Assistant Professor, 1956-59; Associate Professor, 1959-63); *b* 18 Feb. 1927; *m* 1949, Doreen Patricia Blunsdon; one *s* three *d*. *Educ:* Univ. of Liverpool (BS, PhD). Asst Lectr, 1950-52, Lectr, 1952-55, Univ. of Liverpool; Div. Dir, Particle Accelerator Division, Argonne National Laboratory, 1958-61; Dir, Argonne National Laboratory, 1961-67. Named Outstanding New Citizen by Citizenship Council of Chicago, 1962; received Immigrant's Service League's Annual Award for Outstanding Achievement in the Field of Science, 1962; Illinois Sesquicentennial Award, 1968. *Publications:* Research USA (with J. J. Katz), 1964; contribs to: Proc. Royal Soc.; Proc. Phys. Soc.; Physical Review; Science; Physics Today; Jl of Applied Physics; Reviews of Scientific Instruments, etc. *Address:* 63 Old Creek Road, Palos Park, Illinois, USA. *T:* Gibson 8-8738. *Clubs:*

Cosmos (Washington DC); Quadrangle, Wayfarers' (Chicago).

**CREWE, Bertie Gibson,** CBE 1948 (OBE 1930; MBE 1926); *b* 15 Oct. 1884; *e s* of Frederick Crewe; *m* 1920, Ethel Emily Ireland (*d* 1960); two *d. Educ:* Bancroft's Sch., Woodford Wells. Secretary to British Empire Patents Conf., 1922, Patents Cttee of Imperial Economic Conf., 1923, Dating of Patents Cttee, 1926 and Copyright Royalty (Mechanical Musical Instruments) Enquiry, 1928; member of UK Delegation: to Conf. of Internat. Industrial Property Union at The Hague, 1925, Berne, 1926, London, 1934 and Neuchatel, 1947; to Confs of Internat. Copyright Union at Rome, 1928, Brussels, 1948; to Internat. Conf. on German-owned Patents at London, 1946; Asst Comptroller, HM Patent Office, 1938-50, UK Mem. Cttee of Copyright Experts of UNESCO, 1949. *Address:* Little Pentrelew Annexe, Restronguet Point, Feock, Truro, Cornwall. *T:* Feock 693.

**CRIBB, Air Cdre Peter Henry,** CBE 1957; DSO 1942, and Bar, 1944; DFC 1941; JP; Chairman, Capricorn Investments Pty Ltd; *b* 28 Sept. 1918; *s* of late Charles B. Cribb and Mrs Ethel Cribb; *m* 1949, Vivienne Janet, *yr d* of Col S. T. J. Perry, MC, TD, DL, Oxton, Birkenhead, Ches; three *s. Educ:* Bradford Grammar Sch.; Prince Henry's Sch., Otley. Flt Cadet, RAF Coll., 1936-38; Flying duties in Bomber Comd, 1938-45 (Comd No. 582 Sqdn, RAF Little Staughton); Comdg RAF Salbani, RAF Peshawar, India and Staff No. 1 Indian Gp, 1945-47; OC 203 Sqdn, 1947, and HQ Staff, 1950, Coastal Comd; RAF Staff Coll., Bracknell, 1951; Asst Dir Tech. Intell., Air Min., 1951-53; Gp Capt. Plans and Policy, HQ Bomber Comd, 1953-57; 2nd TAF, Germany (OC Oldenburg, Ahlhorn and Gutersloh), 1957-60; Air Min., Dep. Dir Air Staff Briefing, 1959-61, Dir, 1961-62; SASO, Air Forces, Middle East, 1962-63; IDC, 1964; Deputy to Asst Chief of Defence Staff (Joint Warfare), MoD 1965-66; retired, 1966. Administrative Manager, Goldsworthy Mining Ltd, 1966-68. Associate Fellow, Australian Inst. of Management. JP Western Australia. *Recreations:* sailing, fishing. *Address:* 193 Lockhard Street, Como, Western Australia 6152, Australia. *Clubs:* Royal Air Force; Royal Freshwater Bay Yacht (Perth).

**CRICHTON,** family name of **Earl of Erne.**

**CRICHTON, Sir Andrew Maitland-Makgill-,** Kt 1963; Chairman, Overseas Containers Ltd; Director, P&OSN Co., since 1957; Vice-Chairman, Port of London Authority, since 1967 (Member, 1964-67); Chairman, EDC for General Post Office, since Dec. 1965; Member Council, Chamber of Shipping in the UK; *b* 28 Dec. 1910; *S* Lt-Col D. M.-M.-Crichton, Queen's Own Cameron Highldrs, and Phyllis (*née* Cuthbert); *m* 1948, Isabel, *d* of Andrew McGill, Sydney, NSW. *Educ:* Wellington Coll. Joined Gray, Dawes & Co., 1929; transf. India to Mackinnon Mackenzie & Co. (Agents of BI Co. and for P & O on Indian Continent and in parts of Far East), 1931. Joined IA, 1940; DDM (Shipping), Col, at GHQ India, 1944. Mackinnon Mackenzie, Calcutta, 1945-48; P&O Co., UK (Gen. Manager, 1951). Chairman: Nat. Assoc. Port Employers, 1958-65; Vice-Chm., British Transport Docks Bd, 1963-68; a Vice-Pres., Inst. of Transport; Member: Nat. Freight Corp., 1969-; Council, Chamber of Shipping of UK; Police Council for GB; Industrial Court. dir several shipping cos, etc. *Recreations:* golf, collecting paintings, music. *Address:* 55 Hans Place, Knightsbridge, SW1. *T:* 01-584 1209; The Mill House, Earl Soham, Suffolk. *T:* Earl Soham 330. *Clubs:* City of London, Caledonian, Oriental, Anglo-Belgian.

*See also Maj.-Gen. Edward Maitland-Makgill-Crichton.*

**CRICHTON, Hon. Arthur Owen;** 3rd *s* of 4th Earl of Erne; *b* 15 Aug. 1876; *m* 1906, Katharine Helen Elizabeth (*d* 1964), 3rd *d* of late Col Hon. Walter Rodolph Trefusis, CB; one *s* one *d. Educ:* Eton; Christ Church, Oxford. Late Lieut 3rd Battalion Gordon Highlanders; served South African War; European War (despatches, Order of the Crown of Belgium). Chairman of Association of Investment Trusts, 1941-52. *Club:* Carlton.

**CRICHTON, David George,** MVO 1968; British Consul-General, Nice, since 1970; *b* 31 July 1914; *e s* of late Col Hon. Sir George Crichton, GCVO and *cousin* and *heir* of 6th Earl of Erne, *qv*; *m* 1941, Joan Fenella, *d* of late Col D. W. Cleaver; one *s* one *d. Educ:* Eton. Worked as journalist, Reading and Manchester, and on Daily Telegraph, Paris and London, 1933-39; served War of 1939-45 in Derbyshire Yeomanry (despatches); Major 1944; entered Foreign Service, 1946; served in Belgrade, Singapore, Alexandria, Miami, La Paz and Santiago. *Address:* Villa Carina, Boulevard Général de Gaulle, 06-St Jean Cap Ferrat, France. *T:* 06-56-95. 77 Cadogan Gardens, SW3. *T:* 01-589 5054. *Club:* Boodle's.

**CRICHTON, Maj.-Gen. Edward Maitland-Makgill-,** OBE 1948 (MBE 1945); GOC 51st Highland Division, 1966-68, retired; *b* 23 Nov. 1916; *s* of Lt-Col D. E. Maitland-Makgill-Crichton, Queen's Own Cameron Highlanders and Phyllis (*née* Cuthbert); *m* 1951, Sheila Margaret Hibbins, Bexhill-on-Sea; three *s. Educ:* Bedford Sch.; RMC SAndhurst. 2nd Lieut Queen's Own Cameron Highlanders, 1937; Adjt 5th Bn Cameron Highlanders, 1939; served with 5th Cameron Highlanders and 51 (Highland) Div., N Africa, Sicily, Normandy, NW Europe, 1940-45; GSO 1, HQ British Commonwealth Occupation Force, Japan, 1946-47; Mobilisation Br., WO 1948-50; 1st Bn Cameron Highlanders, Tripoli and Canal Zone, 1950-52; Jt Services Staff Coll., 1953; GSO 1, 3rd Inf. Div. (UK Strategic Reserve), Canal Zone, Egypt, UK and Suez, 1953-57; with 1st Bn Cameron Highlanders, Aden, 1957; comd 1st Liverpool Scottish, 1958-61; Comdr 152 (Highland) Inf. Bde, 1962-64; Dep. Dir Army Staff Duties, MoD, 1965-66. *Recreations:* shooting, golf, gardening, fishing. *Address:* Hill House, Brenchley, Kent. *T:* Brenchley 2339. *Club:* Army and Navy.

*See also Sir Andrew Maitland-Makgill-Crichton.*

**CRICHTON, Hon. Sir (John) Robertson (Dunn),** Kt 1967; **Hon. Mr Justice Crichton;** Judge of the High Court of Justice, Queen's Bench Division, since 1967; *b* 2 Nov. 1912; *s* of Alexander Cansh and Beatrice Crichton, Wallasey, Ches; *m* 1944, Margaret Vanderlip, *d* of Col Livingston Watrous, Washington, DC, and Nantucket, Mass, USA; two *s* one *d. Educ:* Sedbergh Sch.; Balliol Coll., Oxford. Called to the Bar, Middle Temple, 1936; Bencher, 1959. Served War of 1939-45, RA (TA). KC 1951; QC 1952. Recorder of Blackpool, 1952-60; Judge of Appeal of the Isle of Man, 1956-60; Recorder of Manchester and Judge of Crown Court at Manchester, 1960-67. *Recreations:* gardening, painting, fishing. *Address:* Royal Courts of Justice, Strand, WC2; Hempfield, Dunham Massey, Altrincham, Cheshire. *T:* 061-928 6101. *Club:* Oxford and Cambridge University.

**CRICHTON, Hon. Sir Robertson;** *see* Crichton, Hon. Sir J. R. D.

**CRICHTON, Col Walter Hugh,** CIE 1941; MB, ChB Edinburgh 1919; DPH London 1934; IMS (retired); School Medical Officer, Essex; *b* 24 July 1896; *m* 1920, Dorothy Martindale, Trinity, Edinburgh; one *s* one *d.* Apptd Indian Medical Service, 1920; Foreign Political Dept, 1930; Vice-Consul, Seistan, Persia; Agency Surgeon Kurram Valley, NWFP, 1932; MOH, Simla, 1934; Chief Health Officer, Delhi Prov., 1936; on active service Paiforce, 1941; ADMS, Basra, 1942; Mil. Gov., CMF, 1943; Dir PH Mil. Gov., 21 Army Group, BLA, 1944-45; Dir Public Health, Cp and Berar, 1945-47; MOH Kent Co. Dists, 1948-50; Chief WHO Mission, Korea, 1950; PH Administrator WHO East Med. Region, until 1956; ACMO Norfolk; Freeman Naples City, 1944; Cross of Merit (1st Class) Order of Malta, 1944; Kt Comdr Order of Orange-Nassau, 1946. *Address:* Carousel, Polstead Heath, near Colchester, Essex. *T:* Hadleigh (Suffolk) 2374. *Club:* Naval and Military.

**CRICHTON MAITLAND;** *see* Maitland.

**CRICHTON-MILLER, Donald,** TD; MA; *b* 1906; *s* of late Hugh Crichton-Miller, MA, MD, FRCP; *m* 1931, Monica, *d* of late B. A. Glanvill, JP, Bromley, Kent; two *s* one *d. Educ:* Fettes Coll., Edinburgh; Pembroke Coll., Cambridge (Exhibitioner). Played Rugby Football for Cambridge and Scotland; Asst Master: Monmouth Sch., 1929-31; Bryanston Sch., 1931-34; Stowe Sch., 1934-36; Head Master: Taunton Sch., Somerset, 1936-45; Fettes Coll., 1945-58; Stowe Sch., 1958-63. Carried out education surveys in Pakistan, 1951, and Malta, 1956. HM Comr, Queen Victoria Sch., Dunblane. *Recreations:* games and sports of various kinds. *Address:* Westridge House, Compton, Berks. *Club:* Athenæum.

**CRICHTON-STUART,** family name of **Marquess of Bute.**

**CRICK, Prof. Bernard,** BSc (Econ.), PhD (London); Professor of Political Theory and Institutions, Sheffield University, since 1965; Director of the Morrell Studies in Toleration (Acton Society), since 1969; *b* 16 Dec. 1929; *s* of Harry Edgar and Florence Clara Crick; *m* 1953, Joyce Pumfrey Morgan; two *s. Educ:* Whitgift Sch.; University Coll., London. Research student, LSE, 1950-52; Teaching Fellow, Harvard, 1952-54; Asst Prof., McGill, 1954-55; Vis. Fellow, Berkeley, 1955-56; Asst Lectr, later Lectr, later Sen. Lectr, LSE, 1957-65. Jt Editor, Political Quarterly, 1966-. Joint Sec., Study of Parlt Gp, 1964-68. *Publications:* The American Science of Politics, 1958; In Defence of Politics, 1962, 2nd edn 1964 (trans. German, Japanese, Spanish, Italian); The Reform of Parliament, 1964, 2nd edn 1968; (ed) Essays on Reform 1967, 1967. *Recreations:* polemicising, lecturing, city-walking and theatre-going. *Address:* 24 Denning Road, NW3. *T:* 01-435 9404; The Basement, 19 Collegiate Crescent, Sheffield 10. *Clubs:* Reform; Attercliffe (Non-Political) Workingmen's (Sheffield).

**CRICK, Rt. Rev. Douglas Henry,** DD; Hon. Assistant Bishop, Diocese of Gloucester, 1957-67; Bishop of Chester, 1939-55; 2nd *s* of Rev. Philip Crick, MA, Waresley Vicarage, near Sandy; *m* 1st, 1914, Evelyn (*d* 1960), 2nd *d* of Rev. J. C. Vernon, Sherburn Vicarage, Malton, E Yorks; one *s* three *d*; 2nd 1961, Mary, 2nd *d* of Rev. B. Wright, Catbrook, Chipping Campden, Glos. *Educ:* Winchester Coll. (scholar); New Coll., Oxford (scholar). Ordained 1908; Chaplain, Mersey Mission to Seamen, 1908-12; Maltby Main Colliery Village, 1912-16; Asst Master Winchester Coll., 1916-17; Housemaster Bradfield Coll., 1917-18; Vicar of Wednesbury, Staffs, 1918-24; Rector of Stoke on Trent, 1924-35; Archdeacon of Stoke on Trent, 1932-35; Bishop Suffragan of Stafford, 1934-39; Rector of Edgmond, 1935-39; Prebendary of Lichfield Cathedral, 1929-39; Chaplain and Sub-Prelate Order of St John of Jerusalem; Chairman of Industrial Christian Fellowship, 1947-55. *Recreation:* reading. *Address:* The Haven, Chipping Campden, Glos. *T:* Campden 679.
*See also Very Rev. I. D. Edwards.*

**CRICK, Francis Harry Compton,** FRS 1959; BSc London, PhD Cantab; Laboratory Scientist at Medical Research Council Unit for Molecular Biology, Cambridge, since 1949; *b* 8 June 1916; *e s* of late Harry Crick and late Annie Elizabeth (*née* Wilkins); *m* 1st, 1940, Ruth Doreen Dodd (divorced, 1947); one *s*; 2nd, 1949, Odile Speed; two *d. Educ:* Mill Hill Sch.; University Coll., London; Caius Coll., Cambridge. Scientist in Admiralty, 1940-47; Strangeways Laboratory, Cambridge, 1947-49; Brooklyn Polytechnic, NY, USA, 1953-54. Vis. Lectr Rockefeller Inst., NY, USA, 1959; Vis. Prof., Chemistry Dept, Harvard, 1959; Fellow, Churchill Coll., Cambridge, 1960-61; Vis. Biophysics Prof., Harvard, 1962; Non-resident Fellow, Salk Inst. for Biological Studies, San Diego, 1962-. Fellow, University Coll., London, 1962; For. Hon. Mem., Amer. Acad. of Arts and Sciences, 1962; Hon. Mem., Amer. Soc. Biological Chem., 1963; Hon. MRIA, 1964; Hon. Fellow, Churchill Coll., Cambridge, 1965; FAAAS 1966; Hon. FRSE; For. Associate, US Nat. Acad. of Sciences, 1969. Bloor Lectr, Rochester, USA, 1959; (with J. D. Watson) Warren Triennial Prize Lectr, Boston, USA, 1959; Herter Lectr, Johns Hopkins Sch. of Medicine, USA, 1960; Franklin Harris Lectr, Mount Zion Hosp., 1962; Holme Lectr, London, 1962; Henry Sidgewick Memorial Lectr, Cambridge, 1963; Harveian Lectr, London, 1963; Graham Young Lectr, Glasgow, 1963; Robert Boyle Lectr, Oxford, 1963; James W. Sherrill Lectr, Scripps Clinic, 1964; Elisha Mitchel Memorial Lectr, North Carolina, 1964; Vanuxem Lectr, Princeton, 1964; William T. Sedgwick Memorial Lectr, MIT, 1965; A. J. Carlson Memorial Lectr, Chicago, 1965; Failing Lectr., Univ. of Oregon, 1965; Robbins Lectr, Pomona Coll., 1965; John Danz Lectr, Univ. of Washington, 1966; Sumner Lectr, Cornell, 1966; Royal Society Croonian Lectr, 1966; Cherwell-Simon Memorial Lectr, Oxford, 1966; Genetical Soc. Mendel Lectr, 1966; Rickman Godlee Lectr, University College, London, 1968; Shell Lectr, Stanford Univ., 1969. lasker Award (jointly), 1960; Prix Charles Léopold Mayer, French Académies des Sciences, 1961; Research Corp. Award (with J. D. Watson), 1962; Gairdner Foundation Award, Toronto, 1962; Nobel Prize for Medicine (jointly), 1962. *Publications:* Of Molecules and Men, 1966; papers and articles on molecular biology in scientific journals. *Recreation:* conversation, especially with pretty women. *Address:* The Golden Helix, 19 Portugal Place, Cambridge.

**CRICK, R(onald) Pitts,** FRCS, DOMS; Senior Ophthalmic Surgeon, King's College Hospital, since 1950; Recognised Teacher in the Faculty of Medicine, University of London, since 1960; *b* 5 Feb. 1917; *yr s* of Owen J. Pitts Crick and Margaret Daw, Minehead, Som; *m* 1941, Jocelyn Mary Grenfell Robins, *yr d* of Leonard A. C. Robins and Geraldine Grenfell, Hendon; four *s* one *d. Educ:* Latymer Upper Sch., London; King's Coll. and (Science Schol.) King's Coll. Hosp. Med. Sch., Univ. of London. MRCS, LRCP 1939. Surgeon, MN, 1939-40; Surg. Lieut, RNVR, 1940-46. Ophthalmic Registrar, King's Coll. Hosp.,

1946-48; DOMS 1946. Surgical First Asst, Royal Eye Hosp., 1947-50; Ophth. Surg., Epsom County Hosp., 1948-49; Ophth. Registrar, Belgrave Hosp. for Children, 1948-50; Ophth. Surg., Sevenoaks Hosp., 1948-50; Sen. Ophthalmic Surg., Royal Eye Hosp., 1950-69; Ophthalmic Surg., Belgrave Hosp. for Children, 1950-66. Examr to RCS for Diploma in Ophthalmology, 1961-68. FRCS, 1950. Hon. Ophth. Surg., Royal London Soc. for the Blind, 1954-57. FRSocMed, Vice-Pres. Ophthalmological Section, 1964, and Mem. Council Ophthalmolog. Section, 1953-54 and 1956-58. Member: Ophthalmolog. Soc. of the UK; Faculty of Ophthalmologists; Oxford Ophthalmolog. Congress; Southern Ophthalmolog. Soc. (Vice-Pres., 1969; Pres., 1970). *Publications:* Cardiovascular Affections, Ateriosclerosis and Hypertension (Section in Systematic Ophthalmology, ed A. Sorsby), 1950 and 1958; medical and opthalmic contribs to Brit. Jl Ophthalmology, BMJ, Jl RN Med. Service, Trans Ophthalmolog. Soc. of the UK, etc. *Recreations:* cinematography, motoring, sailing. *Address:* Private Consulting Rooms, King's College Hospital, SE5. *T:* 01-274 8570; Pembroke House, Sevenoaks, Kent. *T:* Sevenoaks 53633. *Clubs:* Royal Automobile; Royal Motor Yacht.

**CRICK, Very Rev. Thomas,** CB 1943; CBE 1937; MVO 1922; MA; Dean Emeritus, 1958 (Dean of Rochester, 1943-58); permission to officiate in the Diocese of London, 1958; Chaplain to the High Sheriff of Kent, 1959; *b* 1885; *s* of late Rev. Thomas Crick, and *g s* of late Rev. Thomas Crick, Public Orator of Cambridge Univ. and Pres. of St John's Coll.; *m* 1921, Elena Marjorie, *d* of Charles Morgan, Barcelona; one *s. Educ:* St Edmund's Sch., Canterbury; Brasenose Coll., Oxford. Curate of Wigan, 1909; Chaplain, Royal Navy, 1911; served in HMS King Edward VII, Flagship of International Force at occupation of Scutari, 1913; HMS Malaya (Battle of Jutland, wounded); HMS New Zealand (Naval Mission, under Earl Jellicoe, to India and the Dominions), 1919-20; HMS Malaya (Duke of Connaught's visit to India), 1920-21; HMS Renown (Prince of Wales' visit to India and Japan), 1921-22; Senior Chaplain of RNC, Dartmouth, 1923-26, and 1929-32; Chaplain of HM Dockyard and Royal Marine Barracks, Chatham, 1926-28; of HMS Excellent, HM Gunnery Sch., Portsmouth, 1932-35; HM Dockyard, Portsmouth, 1935-38; Hon. Chaplain to the King, 1935-40; Chaplain of the Fleet and Archdeacon for Royal Navy, 1938-43; Chaplain to the King, 1940-43. Hon. Chaplain, Royal Naval Association, 1952; Hon. Chaplain, Royal Marine Assoc., 1954. President St Bartholomew's Hospital, Rochester, 1943-58. Gold Badge of the British Legion, 1958. *Address:* c/o Westminster Bank, Kingston-on-Thames, Surrey. *Club:* United Service.

**CRIDLAND, Charles Elliot Tapscott;** Vice-Chairman, The Aero Group, 1969-70; *b* Glos, 21 July 1900; *s* of S. L. Cridland; *m* 1st, 1923, Kathleen (*d* 1957), *d* of Capt. Bell, Cheltenham; two *d*; 2nd, 1968, Joan Gardiner, *d* of late G. A. McLennan and Mrs E. Coy. *Educ:* Trent Coll., Long Eaton; Faraday House Engineering Coll., London. Chm. and Managing Director: Rye & Co., Lincoln, 1927-30; Eclair Doors Ltd, 1937-47; Aldis Bros Ltd, 1946-57; Automatic Changers Ltd, 1956-57; Chairman: Hawkes & Snow (Curtaincraft) Ltd, 1949-63; Portable Balers Ltd, 1953-61; Aero Heat Treatment Ltd, 1947-69; Hard Coating Ltd, 1951-69; Chisholm, Gray and Co. Ltd, 1956-69; Aerotaps Ltd, 1958-69; Aerocoldform Ltd, 1956-69; Broadstone Ballvalve Co. Ltd, 1959-69; Bendz Ltd, 1962-69; Quality Machined Parts, Ltd, 1964-69; Kinsman Ltd, 1965-69. Vice-Chm., Mercian Builders Merchants Ltd, 1965-67. Dir, A. D. Foulkes Ltd, 1958-65. Mem. Org. Cttee, Birmingham Productivity Assoc., 1955-63. Chm. Organisation Cttee, National Farmers' Union, Glos Branch, 1946; Chm., Skel Rolling Shutter Assoc., 1945-46. Scientific Instrument Manufacturers' Assoc. of Gt Brit. Ltd: Mem. Council, 1949-57, Vice-Pres., 1953 and 1957, Pres., 1954-56; Chm., Transport Users' Consultative Cttee, W Midlands Area, 1960-69; Mem., Central Transport Consultative Cttee, 1963-69. Mem. Court of Assistants, The Worshipful Co. of Scientific Instrument Makers, 1955; elected Master, 1956 and 1957; Freeman, City of London, 1955. *Ex-officio* Mem. Bd of Govs, Faraday House Engrg Coll., 1961-63; Vice-Pres. and Hon. Treas. Faraday House Old Students Assoc., 1960, Pres. 1962-63. Served War, RAF, 1918-19. *Recreations:* golf (played for Warwicks and Glos), and farming. *Address:* Manor Cottage, Abbotts Morton, Worcester WR7 4NA. *T:* Inkberrow 357.

**CRIPPS,** family name of **Baron Parmoor.**

**CRIPPS, Anthony L.;** *see* Cripps, M. A. L.

**CRIPPS, Hon. Frederick Heyworth,** DSO 1918; TD; DL; 2nd *s* of 1st Baron and *heir-pres* to 2nd Baron Parmoor, *qv*; *b* 4 July 1885; *m* 1927, Violet, Duchess of Westminster (marriage dissolved, 1951), *d* of Sir William Nelson, 1st Bt; one *s. Educ:* Winchester; New Coll., Oxford. Dir of Russian and English bank in Petrograd until 1914; Royal Bucks Hussars Yeomanry, 1904; served European War, Gallipoli (wounded); Senussi campaign, Palestine (DSO and bar) and France (Belgian croix de guerre); commanded regt from Aug. 1917. War of 1939-45, Lieut-Comdr RNVR, 1939. DL Bucks. *Publication:* Life's a Gamble, 1958. *Recreations:* shooting and fishing. *Address:* Southridge, Wash Common, Newbury, Berks. *T:* 388. *Club:* White's.

**CRIPPS, Dame Isobel,** GBE 1946; *b* 25 Jan. 1891; 2nd *d* of late Harold William Swithinbank, FRGS, DL, JP, RN, Denham Court, Bucks; *m* 1911, Rt Hon. Sir Stafford Cripps, PC, CH, FRS, QC (*d* 1952); one *s three d.* FRSA. Special Grand Cordon of Order of Brilliant Star, 1st class, China, 1946. *Address:* Greyholme, Minchinhampton, Stroud, Glos GL6 9HA. *T:* Brimscombe 3089. *Club:* Cowdray. *See also J. S. Cripps.*

**CRIPPS, John Stafford,** CBE 1968; Editor, The Countryman, since 1947; Chairman, Countryside Commission, since 1970; *b* 10 May 1912; *s* of late Rt Hon. Sir Stafford Cripps, PC, CH, FRS, QC, and Isobel (*see* Dame Isobel Cripps); *m* 1936, Ursula, *d* of late Arthur C. Davy; four *s* two *d. Educ:* Winchester; Balliol Coll., Oxford. 1st Class Hons Politics, Philosophy and Economics (Modern Greats). Filkins Parish Councillor; Witney Rural District Councillor; Chairman: Rural District Councils' Association, 1967-70; Rural Cttee of Nat. Council of Social Service; Member: Oxfordshire Planning Cttee, 1948-69; W Oxfordshire Technical Coll. Governors, 1951-70; South East Economic Planning Council; Exec. Cttee, Nature Conservancy; Exec. Cttee, Council for the Preservation of Rural England, 1963-69; Inland Waterways Amenity Advisory Council. *Publication:* Milk Distribution, 1937. *Address:* Filkins, Lechlade, Glos. *TA:* Filkins. *T:* Filkins 209. *Club:* Farmers'.

**CRIPPS, (Matthew) Anthony Leonard,** DSO 1943; TD 1947; QC 1958; Recorder of

Nottingham since 1961; Master of the Bench, Middle Temple, since 1965; Judge of (ecclesiastical) Court of Arches, since 1969; *b* 30 Dec. 1913; *s* of late Major Hon. L. H. Cripps; *m* 1941, Dorothea Margaret (Surrey CC 1965-67), *d* of G. Johnson Scott, Ashby-de-la-Zouch; three *s*. *Educ:* Eton; Christ Church, Oxford; Army and RAF Staff Coll., Haifa. Roy. Leicestershire Regt, TA, 1933. Served War of 1939-45: Norway, Sweden, Finland, Iceland, N Africa, Italy, Egypt, 1939-44 (Capt. to Lt-Col); Staff Officer, Palestine and Syria, 1944-46. Barrister-at-law, Middle Temple, 1938, and Inner Temple, 1961. Contested (C) Bosworth (Leics) Div., 1950. Chairman: Disciplinary Cttees, Milk Marketing Bd, 1956-, Potato and Egg Marketing Bds, 1956-67; Isle of Man Govt Commn on Agricultural Marketing, 1961-62; Home Sec.'s Adv. Cttee on Service Candidates, 1966- (Dep. Chm., 1965). Member: Agricultural Wages Bd, 1964-67; Northumberland Cttee of Inquiry into Foot and Mouth Disease, 1968-69. Chairman: Reigate Conservative Assoc., 1961-64; Res. Cttee, Soc. of Conservative Lawyers, 1966-68; Conservative Cttee of Inquiry into Discrimination against Women in Law and Administration, 1968-69. Vice-Chm., SE Area Conservative Assoc., 1964-66. Mem., National Exec. Cttee of Conservative Party, 1964-. Vice-Pres., Bonaventure Investments Ltd (Canada). Chm., Billbrook Finance Ltd; Dir, Caledonian African Investment Trust (Pty) Ltd (S Africa). A Governor, Thomas Coram Foundn; Chm., Alpine Sun for British Children. Hon. Mem., Birmingham Fraud Squad. *Publications:* Agriculture Act 1947, 1947; Agriculture Holdings Act, 1948, 1948. (Ed.) 9th edn, Cripps on Compulsory Purchase: Powers, Procedure and Compensation, 1950. Legal articles, especially on agricultural matters, for Law Jl and Encyclopaedia Britannica. *Recreations:* family life and gardening. *Address:* Alton House, Felbridge, East Grinstead, Sussex. *T:* 23238; 1 Harcourt Buildings, Temple EC4. *T:* 01-353 9421. *Clubs:* Brooks's, Lansdowne; County, United Services (Nottingham).

**CRIPPS, William Parry,** CBE 1964; *b* 23 June 1903; *o s* of late Captain Egerton Tymewell Cripps, MC, South Cerney Manor, Cirencester; *m* 1941, Catherine Isabel, 2nd *d* of late Rev. C. A. Sturges-Jones and *widow* of Major C. J. Oldridge de la Hey; (one *s* decd). *Educ:* Wellington. Dir H. & G. Simonds Ltd, Reading, retired 1962; Chm. Cirencester Benefit Soc. CC Glos, 1961-; High Sheriff, Glos, 1963. *Address:* Stratton Cleeve, Cirencester, Glos. *T:* 3464.

**CRISHAM, Air Vice-Marshal William Joseph,** CB 1953; CBE 1944; RAF retired; General Secretary, British Leprosy Relief Association; *b* 19 Nov. 1906; *m* 1946, Maureen Teresa Bergin, Dublin; three *s* three *d*. *Educ:* in Ireland. Served War of 1939-45; commanded Nos 13 and 23 Sqdns; Comdt Central Fighter Establishment, 1950-53; AOC No. 12 Group Fighter Command, Nov. 1953-56; AOC RAF Levant MEAF, 1956-58; AOC RAF Germany (2nd TAF), 1958-61; retired 1961. *Club:* Royal Air Force.

**CRISP, Col Rev. Alan Percy,** DSO 1918; OBE 1944; VD; LLB; JP; Assistant Parish Priest, St George, Hobart, Tasmania, since 1970; *b* 23 Dec. 1889; *s* of late Samuel Percy and Myra Gertrude Crisp, Hobart; *m* Doris Lillian, 2nd *d* of late William Henry Ellis and Emily Selina Ellis, Dysart House, Kempton, Tasmania; one *s*. *Educ:* University of Tasmania. Enrolled a practitioner of the Supreme Court of Tasmania, 1912; Lieut in 3rd Field Artillery Brigade, Australian Imperial Forces, 1914; served on Gallipoli, 1915 (promoted Capt.); served in France and Belgium, 1916-18 (promoted Major, despatches thrice, DSO, Croix de Guerre); promoted Lieut-Col AMF; commanded 6th Field Artillery Bde, 1924-28 and 1939-40; ADC to Gov.-Gen. of Australia (Lord Gowrie), 1939-40; comd a Field Regt Royal Australian Artillery, 1940-42; Staff Officer with 2nd AIF, 1942-46 (Temp. Col, 1945); served Palestine, Egypt, New Guinea, Solomon Islands and Dutch East Indies; transferred to R of O, AMF, 1946, with rank of Hon. Col; Retired List, with rank of Hon. Col, 1948. Retired from active practice as Barrister and Solicitor, 1948. Police Magistrate, 1953-65; Chm. Licensing Court (Tasmania), 1954-65. Ordained Deacon of Church of England in Tasmania, 1969; Priest, 1970. *Recreation:* walking. *Address:* 4 Albuera Street, Hobart, Tasmania. *Clubs:* Royal Automobile of Tasmania, Naval and Military (Hobart).

**CRISP, Prof. Dennis John,** ScD; FRS 1968; Professor in Department of Marine Biology, University College of North Wales; Director, Natural Environment Research Council Unit of Marine Invertebrate Biology, since 1970 (Hon. Director, 1965-70); *b* 29 April 1916; *m* 1944, Ella Stewart Allpress; one *s* one *d*. *Educ:* St Catharine's Coll., Cambridge. Research Asst, Dept of Colloid Science, Univ. of Cambridge, 1943-46; ICI (Paints Div.), i/c of Marine Paints Res. Stn, Brixham, Devon, 1946-51; Dir, Marine Science Laboratories, University Coll. of N Wales, 1951-70. *Publications:* (ed) Grazing in Terrestrial and Marine Environments, 1964; papers in Proc. Royal Soc., Jl Marine Biol. Assoc., Jl Experimental Biology, Jl Animal Ecology, etc. *Recreations:* travel, photography. *Address:* Craig y Pîn, Llandegfan, Menai Bridge, Anglesey. *T:* Menai Bridge 775.

**CRISP, Sir (John) Peter,** 4th Bt *cr* 1913; *b* 19 May 1925; *o s* of Sir John Wilson Crisp, 3rd Bt, and Marjorie, *d* of F. R. Shriver; *S* father, 1950; *m* 1954, Judith Mary, *d* of late H. E. Gillett; three *s* one *d*. *Educ:* Westminster. *Heir: s* John Charles Crisp, *b* 10 Dec. 1955. *Address:* Hollyhocks, Cranleigh, Surrey.

**CRISP, Hon. Sir (Malcolm) Peter,** Kt 1969; a Justice of the Supreme Court of Tasmania since 1952; Senior Puisne Judge since 1968; *b* Devonport, Tasmania, 21 March 1912; *s* of late T. M. Crisp, Burnie, (legal practitioner), and Myrtle May (*née* Donnelly); *m* 1935, Edna Eunice (*née* Taylor); two *d*. *Educ:* St Ignatius Coll., Riverview, Sydney; Univ. of Tasmania (LLB). Admitted legal practitioner, Tas, 1933; Crown Prosecutor, 1940. Served AIF, 1940-46 (in Australia, UK and Borneo, 2/1 Tank Attack Regt and Staff appts; rank of Colonel on discharge). Crown Solicitor, 1947-51; Solicitor-Gen. and KC, 1951. Lecturer in Law of Real Property, Univ. of Tasmania, 1947-52; Mem. Univ. Council, 1948-55; Chm., State Library Bd, 1956-; Mem. Council, Nat. Library of Aust., 1960-; Pres., Library Assoc. of Aust., 1963-66; Royal Commissioner, Fluoridation of Public Water Supplies, 1966-68. *Recreations:* cruising, angling. *Address:* 10 Anglesea Street, Hobart, Tasmania. *T:* Hobart 235639. *Clubs:* Commonwealth (Canberra); Tasmanian, Royal Yacht Club of Tasmania (Hobart).

**CRISP, Sir Peter;** *see* Crisp, Sir (John) P.

**CRISP, Hon. Sir Peter;** *see* Crisp, Hon. Sir M. P.

**CRISPIN, Geoffrey Hollis,** QC 1961; Recorder of Rochester since 1968; Deputy Chairman,

Hertfordshire Quarter Sessions, since 1965; *b* 15 May 1905; *s* of Harry Crispin, Rochester; *m* 1931, Winifred, 4th *d* of A. J. Baldwin, Berkhamsted; two *s* one *d*. *Educ:* Rochester Mathematical Sch.; London Univ. Barrister-at-Law, 1937. Comr of Assize, 1963, 1965. *Address:* The Tile House, Chipperfield, Herts. *T:* Kings Langley 2264. *Club:* MCC.

**CRITCHETT, Sir Ian (George Lorraine)**, 3rd Bt *cr* 1908; BA Cantab; *b* 9 Dec. 1920; *s* of Sir Montague Critchett, 2nd Bt, and Innes, 3rd *d* of late Col F. G. A. Wiehe, The Durham Light Infantry; *S* father, 1941; *m* 1st, 1948, Paulette Mary Lorraine, *e d* of Col H. B. Humfrey (*d* 1962); 2nd, 1964, Jocelyn Daphne Margret, *e d* of Comdr C. M. Hall, Wellow House, Wellow, Bath; one *s* one *d*. *Educ:* Harrow; Clare Coll., Cambridge. RAFVR, 1942-46. Joined Foreign Office, 1948; 3rd Sec. (Commercial), at Vienna, 1950-51; 2nd Sec. (Commercial) at Bucharest, 1951-53; 2nd Sec. at Cairo, 1956. *Heir: s* Charles George Montague Critchett, *b* 2 April 1965. *Address:* Uplands Lodge, Pains Hill, Limpsfield, Surrey. *Clubs:* Carlton, Travellers', Pratt's, MCC.

**CRITCHLEY, Alexander;** accountant; *b* 17 Dec. 1893; *s* of William Edwin and Elizabeth Alice Critchley; *m* 1925, Lucy Lindasy; one *s* two *d*. *Educ:* Liverpool. FSAA 1924. Formerly Mem., Liverpool City Council; MP (U) Edgehill Div. of Liverpool, 1935-45; Dep. Chm. Electricity Cttee, Liverpool City Council, 1922. *Recreations:* golf, tennis. *Address:* The Laurels, 454 Aigburth Road, Liverpool 19. *T:* 051-427 1364. *Clubs:* St Stephen's; Constitutional, Lyceum (Liverpool).

**CRITCHLEY, Julian Michael Gordon;** MP (C) Aldershot and North Hants since 1970; writer and journalist; *b* 8 Dec. 1930; *s* of Dr Macdonald Critchley, *qv*; *m* 1955, Paula Joan Baron (divorced 1965); two *d*; *m* 1965, Mrs Heather Goodrick; one *s* one *d*. *Educ:* Shrewsbury; Sorbonne; Pembroke Coll., Oxford (MA). MP (C) Rochester and Chatham, 1959-64; contested Rochester and Chatham, 1966. Chm. of the Bow Group, 1966-67. Pres., Atlantic Assoc. of Young Political Leaders, 1968-. *Recreations:* watching boxing, the countryside, reading military history. *Address:* 41 Castle Street, Farnham, Surrey. *Clubs:* Garrick, Coningsby; Oxford Union Society.

**CRITCHLEY, Macdonald,** CBE 1962; MD, ChB 1st Class Hons (Bristol), FRCP; MD (Zürich) *hc*; D en M (Aix-Marseille) *hc*; FACP (hon.); Consulting Neurologist; *s* of Arthur Frank and Rosina Matilda Critchley; *m* 1927, Edna Auldeth Morris; two *s*. *Educ:* Christian Brothers Coll.; Univ. of Bristol (Lady Haberfield Scholarship in Medicine, Markham Skerritt Prize for Original Research). Goulstonian Lectr, RCP, 1930; Hunterian Prof., RCS, 1935; Royal Coll. of Physicians: Bradshaw Lectr, 1942; Croonian Lectr, 1945; Harveian Orator, 1966; Pres., World Fedn of Neurology; Hon. Consulting Neurologist, King's Coll. Hosp.; Hon. Consulting Physician, National Hosp., Queen Square; formerly Dean, Inst. of Neurology; Neurological Physician, Royal Masonic Hosp.; formerly Neurologist to Royal Hosp. and Home for Incurables, Putney. Temp. Surgeon-Capt. RNVR and Consulting Neurologist to Royal Navy; Long Fox Lectr, Univ. of Bristol, 1935; William Withering Lectr, Univ. of Birmingham, 1946; Tisdall Lectr, Univ. of Manitoba, 1951; Semon Lectr, Univ. of London, 1951; Sherrington Lectr, Univ. of Wisconsin; Orator, Medical Soc. of London, 1955. Pres. Harveian Soc., 1947. Hunterian Orator, 1957; Doyne Memorial Lectr, 1961; Victor Horsley Memorial Lectr, 1963; Honyman Gillespie Lectr, 1963; Schorstein Lectr, 1964; Hughlings Jackson Lectr and Medallist, RSM, 1964; Gowers Lectr and Medallist, 1965; Veraguth Gold Medallist, Bern, 1968; Arthur Hall Memorial Lectr, 1969; Rickman Godlee Lectr, 1970. Pres. Assoc. of British Neurologists, 1962-64; Second Vice-Pres., RCP, 1964. Hon. Corresp. Mem. Académie de Médecine de France, Norwegian Academy of Science and Letters, Royal Academy of Medicine, Barcelona, and Neurological Socs. of France, Switzerland, Holland, Turkey, Uruguay, US, Canada, Australia, Brazil, Argentine, Germany, Chile, Spain, Roumania, Norway, Czechoslovakia, Greece, Italy, Bulgaria and Hungary. Visiting Prof., Univs of: Istanbul, 1949; California, 1950 and 1964; Hawaii, 1966. Master, Worshipful Soc. of Apothecaries, 1956-57. Served European War, 1917-18. *Publications:* Mirror Writing; Neurology of Old Age; Observations on Pain; Language of Gesture; Shipwreck-survivors; Sir William Gowers; The Parietal Lobes; Developmental Dyslexia; The Black Hole; Aphasiology; The Dyslexic Child; various articles on nervous diseases. *Address:* Private Consulting Room, National Hospital, Queen Square, WC1. *T:* 01-837 3611. *Clubs:* Athenæum, Garrick.

*See also J. M. G. Critchley.*

**CROAN, Thomas Malcolm;** Sheriff Substitute of Aberdeen, Kincardine and Banff at Banff and Peterhead, since 1969; *b* 7 Aug. 1932; *s* of John Croan and Amelia Sydney; *m* 1959, Joan Kilpatrick Law; one *s* two *d*. *Educ:* St Joseph's Coll., Dumfries; Edinburgh University. MA 1953; LLB 1955. Admitted to Faculty of Advocates, 1956; Standing Junior Counsel: to Queen and Lord Treasurer's Remembrancer, 1963-64; to Scottish Develt Dept, 1964-65 and (for highways work) 1967-69; Advocate Depute, 1965-66. Mem. of Legal Aid Supreme Court Cttee, 1968-69. *Recreations:* golf, woodworking, reading. *Address:* Belvedere, Sandyhill Road, Banff. *T:* Banff 2578.

**CROCKER, Antony James Gulliford;** Assistant Under-Secretary of State, Supplementary Benefits Commission, Department of Health and Social Security, since 1968; *b* 28 Oct. 1918; *s* of late Cyril James Crocker and Mabel Kate Crocker; *m* 1st, 1943, E. S. B. Dent; 2nd, 1949, Nancy Wynell, *d* of late Judge Gamon and Eleanor Margaret Gamon; two *s* one *d*. *Educ:* Sherborne Sch. (Scholar); Trinity Hall, Cambridge (Major Scholar, MA). Served War, 1939-46, Dorsetshire Regt (Major). Asst Princ. 1947, Princ. 1948, Min. of Nat. Insurance. Sec., Nat. Insce Advisory Cttee, 1955-56; Asst Sec., Min. of Pensions and Nat. Insce, 1956, Under-Sec., War Pensions Dept, 1964 (Min. of Social Security, 1966-). *Recreations:* horticulture, philately. *Address:* Wealdover, Guildown Avenue, Guildford, Surrey. *T:* 66555. *Club:* Oxford and Cambridge University.

**CROCKER, Walter Russell,** CBE 1955; Australian diplomat, retired 1970; *b* 25 March 1902; *e s* of late Robert Crocker and Alma Bray, Parnaroo, SA; *m* 1950, Claire (marr. diss. 1968), *y d* of F. J. Ward, Headmaster of Prince Alfred Coll., Adelaide, and *widow* of Dr John Gooden, Physicist; two *s*. *Educ:* University of Adelaide; Balliol Coll., Oxford; Stanford University, USA. Entered Colonial Administrative Service (Nigeria), 1930; transf. to League of Nations, 1934, and to ILO (Asst to Dirs-Gen). Served War, 1940-45 (Lt-Col, Croix de Guerre avec palme, Ordre royal du Lion, Belgium). Farming at Parnaroo, 1946; UN Secretariat (Chief of Africa Sect.), 1946-49; Prof. of Internat. Relations, Aust. Nat.

Univ., 1949-52; Actg Vice-Chancellor, 1951; High Commissioner for Australia to India, 1952-55; Ambassador of Australia to Indonesia, 1955-57; High Comr to Canada, 1957-58; High Comr for Australia to India and Ambassador to Nepal, 1958-62; Amb. of Australia to the Netherlands and Belgium, 1962-65; Ambassador to Ethiopia and High Commissioner to Kenya and Uganda, 1965-67; Ambassador to Italy, 1967-70. L'Ordre royal du Lion (Belgium), 1945. *Publications:* The Japanese Population Problem, 1931; Nigeria, 1936; On Governing Colonies, 1946; Self-Government for the Colonies, 1949; Can the United Nations Succeed?, 1951; The Race Question as a factor in International Relations, 1955; Nehru, 1965. *Recreations:* gardening, walking, music; previously ski-ing, tennis. *Address:* The Peak Farm, Giles Corner, South Australia, Australia. *Clubs:* Oxford and Cambridge University, Reform; Gymkhana (Delhi); Circolo della Caccia (Rome).

**CROCKER, Sir William Charles,** Kt, *cr* 1955; MC; solicitor (retired); *b* 19 May 1886; *s* of T. E. Crocker; *m* 1st, Mary Madeline (*d* 1953), *d* of A. H. Tailby; one *s* five *d*; *m* 2nd, 1956, Ruth, *d* of Harry Chandler, Los Angeles, Calif., and *widow* of Col James G. Boswell. Served articles with father; admitted solicitor, 1912; Mem. of Disciplinary Cttee under Solicitors Act, 1949-60; Pres., Law Soc., 1953-54. Served European War, Artists Rifles; 2nd Lieut 4th Dorset Regt (MC). Hon. Mem. American Bar Assoc., 1958. *Publication:* Far from Humdrum, 1967. *Recreations:* travel, reading. *Address:* Crockers', Seal Chart, Kent. *T:* Sevenoaks 61458; 1155 Oak Grove Avenue, San Marino, Calif., USA. *T:* Sycamore 32079. *Clubs:* Arts, Royal Automobile.

**CROCKFORD, Brig. Allen Lepard,** CBE 1955 (OBE 1945); DSO 1943; MC 1916; TD 1942; late Hon. Colonel RAMC 54 and 56 Division (TA); *b* 11 Sept. 1897; *s* of late J. A. V. Crockford, West Worthing, Sussex; *m* 1924, Doris Ellen Brookes-Smith; one *s* two *d. Educ:* Gresham's Sch.; King's Coll., Cambridge; St Thomas's Hosp. Glos Regt, BEF (Capt.; wounded), 1915-19. BA Cantab, 1920; MA 1926; MB, BCh Cantab, 1922; Gen. Practice, 1924-39; RAMC (TA): served with 43rd, Guards Armoured, 46th and 56th Divs, BNAF and CMF (Col), 1939-45; Gen. Practice, 1945-46; Medical Sec., St Thomas's Hosp. Medical Sch., London, SE1, 1946-64. Col (TA), ADMS, 56 Armoured Div., 1947; Brig. (TA); DDMS AA Comd, 1949; KHS 1952; QHS 1952-57; OStJ 1954. *Recreations:* sailing, gardening. *Address:* The Oast House, Trottiscliffe, West Malling, Kent. *T:* Fairseat 478. *Club:* Royal Ocean Racing.

**CROFT,** family name of **Baron Croft.**

**CROFT,** 2nd Baron *cr* 1940, of Bournemouth; **Michael Henry Glendower Page Croft;** Bt 1924; Barrister, called to the Bar, Inner Temple, 1952; *b* 20 Aug. 1916; *s* of 1st Baron Croft, PC, CMG, and Hon. Nancy Beatrice Borwick (*d* 1949), *y d* of 1st Baron Borwick; *S* father, 1947; *m* 1948, Lady Antoinette Fredericka Conyngham (*d* 1959), *o d* of 6th Marquess Conyngham, *qv*; one *s* one *d. Educ:* Eton; Trinity Hall, Cambridge (BA). Served War of 1939-45, Capt. RASC. Director: Henry Page & Co. Ltd, 1946-57; Ware Properties Ltd, 1958-65. Mem. Exec. Cttee, Contemporary Arts Soc., 1960-68 and 1970-. *Heir: s* Hon. Bernard William Henry Page Croft [*b* 28 Aug. 1949. *Educ:* Stowe]. *Address:* 8 Hereford Square, SW7; Croft Castle, near Leominster, Herefordshire. *Clubs:* Bath, Hurlingham.

**CROFT, Sir Bernard Hugh (Denman),** 13th Bt *cr* 1671; *b* 24 Aug. 1903; *s* of Sir Hugh Matthew Fiennes Croft, 12th Bt, and Lucy Isabel, *e d* of Frederick Taylor, Terrible Vale, near Uralla, NSW; *S* father, 1954; *m* 1931, Helen Margaret, *d* of H. Weaver; three *s* two *d. Educ:* Armidale Sch., NSW. Rep. NSW Rugby Union in NZ, 1928. *Recreations:* football, tennis, golf. *Heir: s* Owen Glendower Croft [*b* 26 April 1932; *m* 1959, Sally, *d* of Dr T. M. Mansfield, Brisbane, Queensland; one *s* one *d*]. *Address:* Salisbury Court, Uralla, NSW, Australia. *T:* Uralla 24.

**CROFT, (John) Michael;** Director, National Youth Theatre, since 1956; *b* 8 March 1922. *Educ:* Plymouth Grove Elem. Sch. and Burnage Gram. Sch., Manchester; Keble Coll., Oxford (BA Hons). War Service in RAF and RN, 1940-45. After short career as actor, took up teaching, 1949; Asst English Master, Alleyn's Sch., 1950-55 (prod. series of Shakespeare plays with large schoolboy cos); founded Youth Theatre with group from Alleyn's Sch., 1956; this grew rapidly into nat. organisation with provincial branches; rep. Gt Brit. at Paris Festival, 1960 and W Berlin Festival, 1961; appeared at Old Vic, 1965. Also Dir Shakespeare for leading cos in Belgium and Holland, 1960-65. Productions: Zigger Zagger, Strand, 1968, Berlin Festival, 1968, Holland Festival, 1970; Little Malcolm and his Struggle, Holland Festival, 1968; Fuzz, Berlin Festival, 1970. *Publications:* (novel) Spare the Rod, 1954; (travel book) Red Carpet to China, 1958; contribs to various periodicals on theatre, education. *Recreations:* sport, travel, motoring. *Address:* 81 Eccleston Square, SW1. *T:* 01-834 4714. *Club:* Savile.

**CROFT, Sir John William Graham,** 4th Bt, *cr* 1818; Lieutenant late RHA; *b* 30 May 1910; *s* of late William Graham Croft, 4th *s* of 2nd Bt, and Marjorie, *d* of late Rev. T. G. S. Hall; *S* uncle 1930. *Educ:* Stowe. *Heir: cousin* Major John Archibald Radcliffe Croft [*b* 27 March 1910; *m* 1953, Lucy Elizabeth Jupp; one *s*]. *Address:* 57 Chester Row, Eaton Square, SW1.

**CROFT, Michael;** *see* Croft, J. M.

**CROFT, Col Noel Andrew Cotton,** DSO 1945; OBE 1970; MA Oxon; Essex Regiment; Commandant, Metropolitan Police Cadet Corps, since 1960; *b* 30 Nov. 1906; *s* of late Rev. Canon R. W. Croft, MA; *m* 1952, Rosalind, 2nd *d* of late Comdr A. H. de Kantzow, DSO, RN; three *d. Educ:* Lancing Coll.; Stowe Sch.; Christ Church, Oxford; Sch. of Technology, Manchester. Cotton Trade, 1929-32; Mem. British Trans-Greenland Expedition, 1933-34; ADC to Maharajah of Cooch Behar, India, 1934-35; Second-in-Command, Oxford Univ. Arctic Expedition to North-East Land, 1935-36; Ethnological Exped. to Swedish Lapland, 1937-38; Sec. to Dir of Fitzwilliam Museum, Cambridge, 1937-39. Served War of 1939-45, Capt. 1939; WO Mission to Finno-Russian War, 1939-40; Bde Intelligence Officer Independent Companies, Norwegian Campaign, 1940; Combined Ops, 1940-41; Major, 1941; Asst Mil. Attaché, Stockholm, 1941-42; sea or parachute ops in Tunisia, Corsica, Italy, France, and Denmark, 1943-45; Lieut-Col 1945; Asst Dir Scientific Research, War Office, 1945-49; WO Observer on Canadian Arctic Exercise "Musk-Ox", 1945-46, and on NW Frontier Trials, India, 1946-47; attached Canadian Army, 1947-48. GSO1, War Office, 1949-51; Liaison Officer HQ Continental Army, USA, 1952-54; comd The Infantry Junior Leaders Bn, 1954-57; Comdt Army Apprentices Sch., Harrogate, 1957-60. Corresp. Fellow, Arctic Inst. of North America; Chm., Friends of Scott Polar Research Inst. Polar Medal (clasp Arctic,

1935-36), 1942; Back Award, RGS, 1946. *Publications:* (with A. R. Glen) Under the Pole Star, 1937; Polar Exploration, 1939. *Recreations:* mountaineering, ski-ing, sailing, photography. *Address:* River House, Strand-on-the-Green, W4. *T:* 01-994 6359. *Clubs:* Alpine, hurlingham.

**CROFT-COOKE, Rupert,** BEM; novelist, playwright, biographer, writer of books on travel, food and wine, circus, gypsies; *b* Edenbridge, Kent, 20 June 1903; *s* of late Hubert Bruce Cooke, London Stock Exchange, and late Lucy, *d* of Dr Alfred Taylor. *Educ:* Tonbridge Sch.; Wellington Coll., Salop (now Wrekin Coll.). Founded and edited weekly, La Estrella, Argentina, 1923-24; antiquarian bookseller, 1929-31; Lecturer in English Institute Montana, Zugerberg, Switzerland, 1931, etc. Joined Intelligence Corps, 1940; served Madagascar campaign (BEM), 1942; commnd 3rd (Queen Alexandra's Own) Gurkha Rifles, 1943; Capt. (Field Security Officer) Poona Dist, 1944; Instr, Intell. Sch., Karachi, 1945; FSO, Delhi Dist, 1945-46. Book Critic, The Sketch, 1947-53. *Publications:* four early books of poems; Twenty Poems from the Spanish of Becquer, 1926; Some Poems, 1929; Troubadour, 1930; Banquo's Chair (play), 1930; Give him the Earth, 1930; Tap Three Times (play), 1931; Night Out, 1932; Cosmopolis, 1932; Release the Lions, 1933; Picaro, 1934; Shoulder the Sky, 1934; Deliberate Accident (play), 1934; Blind Gunner, 1935; Crusade, 1936; God in Ruins, 1936; Kingdom Come, 1937; The World is Young (autobiog.), Rule, Britannia, 1938; Darts, 1938; Pharaoh with his Wagons, 1938; How to get more out of Life, 1938; The Man in Europe Street (autobiog.), 1939; Same Way Home, 1939; Major Road Ahead (ed.), 1939; The Circus has no Home (autobiog.), 1940; Glorious, 1940; Octopus, 1946; Ladies Gay, 1946; The Circus Book (ed.), 1947; The Moon in My Pocket (autobiog.), 1948; Rudyard Kipling (English Novelists Series), 1948; Wilkie, 1948; Brass Farthing, 1950; Three Names for Nicholas, 1951; Cities, 1951; The Sawdust Ring, 1951; Nine Days with Edward, 1952; The Life for Me (autobiog.), 1953; The Blood-Red Island (autobiog.), 1953; Harvest Moon, 1953; The Verdict of You All (autobiog.), 1955; A Few Gypsies, 1955; Fall of Man, 1955; Sherry, 1955; Seven Thunders, 1956 (film, 1957); The Tangerine House (autobiog.), 1956; Port, 1957; Barbary Night, 1958; The Gardens of Camelot (autobiog.), 1958; Smiling Damned Villain; The Quest for Quixote (autobiog.), 1959; The Altar in the Loft (autobiog.); Thief, 1960; The Drums of Morning (autobiog.); English Cooking; Madeira, 1961; The Glittering Pastures (autobiog.); Wine and Other Drinks, 1962; The Numbers Came (autobiog.), 1963; Bosie, 1963; Clash by Night (film), 1963; The Last of Spring (autobiog.); The Wintry Sea (autobiog.), 1964; Paper Albatross, 1965; The Gorgeous East, 1965; The Purple Streak (autobiog.), 1966; The Wild Hills (autobiog.), 1966; The Happy Highways (autobiog.), 1967; Feasting with Panthers, 1967; The Ghost of June, 1968; The Sound of Revelry, 1969; Wolf from the Door, 1969; Exotic Food, 1969; Exiles, 1970. *Recreations:* all. *Address:* c/o A. M. Heath and Co. Ltd, 35 Dover Street, W1X 4EB.

**CROFT-MURRAY, Edward,** CBE 1966; Keeper, Department of Prints and Drawings, British Museum, since 1954; *b* Chichester, 1 Sept. 1907; *s* of Bernard Croft-Murray; *m* 1960, Rosemary Jill Whitford-Hawkey; one *d*. *Educ:* Lancing Coll.; Magdalen Coll., Oxford. Asst Keeper, Dept of Prints and Drawings, Brit. Museum, 1933; Dep. Keeper, 1953. Served War, 1939-46: Admiralty, 1939-40; Civilian Officer, Military Intelligence, War Office, 1940-43; Major, Allied Control Commission (Monuments and Fine Arts Section), Italy and Austria, 1943-46. Trustee, Cecil Higgins Museum, Bedford; Member: (Rep. Oxford Univ.), Brit. Instn Fund; Central Council for the Care of Churches; Musicians' Union. FSA 1940. *Publications:* Catalogue of British Drawings in the British Museum, Vol. I (with Paul Hulton), 1960; Decorative Painting in England, 1537-1837, Vol. I, 1962; papers in Walpole Society, Burlington Magazine, and Country Life. *Recreations:* music (especially that of the XVIIIth and early XIXth century); study of wall-painting in England. *Address:* 4 Maids of Honour Row, Richmond Green, Surrey. *T:* 01-940 2548; Croft Castle, near Leominster, Herefordshire. *Clubs:* Athenæum, Beefsteak.

**CROFTON,** family name of **Baron Crofton.**

**CROFTON,** 5th Baron *cr* 1797; **Edward Blaise Crofton;** Bt 1758; *b* 31 May 1926; *o s* of late Hon. Edward Charles Crofton and Cecilia Mabel, *d* of John T. Day and *widow* of Alexander Francis Macdonald; *S* grandfather, 1942; *m* 1st, 1948, Ann (marr. diss. 1963), *e d* of Group Capt. Charles Tighe, Ballina Park, Co. Wicklow; three *s* one *d* (and one *s* decd); 2nd, 1964, Mrs Mary Irvine Flach. Sub-Lt RN, retired, 1947. *Heir: s* Hon. Charles Edward Piers Crofton, *b* 27 April 1949. *Address:* 31 Cadogan Place, SW1.

*See also Sir Geoffrey Hughes-Onslow.*

**CROFTON, Denis Hayes,** OBE 1948 (MBE 1943); retired Home and Indian Civil Servant; *b* 14 Dec. 1908; *s* of late Richard Hayes Crofton, Colonial Civil Service and Mabel Annie Crofton (*née* Smith); *m* 1933, Alison Carr, *d* of late Andrew McClure and Ethel McClure; three *s* one *d*. *Educ:* Tonbridge Sch.; Corpus Christi Coll., Oxford (Class. Mods, Lit. Hum., MA). Indian Civil Service, 1932; served in Bihar; subdivisional Magistrate, Giridih, 1934, Jamshedpur, 1935; Under-Sec. to Govt of Bihar, Polit. and Appt Depts, 1936; Under-Sec. to Govt of India, Dept of Labour, 1939; Private Sec. to Indian Mem., Eastern Gp Supply Council, 1941; Dist Mag. and Collector, Shahabad, Bihar, 1942; Sec. to Gov. of Bihar, 1944; apptd to Home Civil Service, 1947; Principal, Min. of Fuel and Power, Petroleum Div. 1948; Asst Sec., Petroleum Div. and Chm., OEEC Oil Cttee, Paris, 1950-53; Asst Sec., Monopolies and Restrictive Practices Commn, 1953; Asst Sec., Min. of Fuel and Power, Electricity Div., 1956; Petroleum Div., 1961; Accountant General and Under-Secretary for Finance, 1962-68. *Recreations:* reading, gardening. *Address:* Tile Barn House, 147 Hadlow Road, Tonbridge, Kent. *T:* Tonbridge 3465. *Club:* Royal Commonwealth Society.

**CROFTON, Prof. John Wenman;** Professor of Respiratory Diseases and Tuberculosis, University of Edinburgh, since 1952; Dean of Faculty of Medicine, 1964-66; Vice-Principal since 1969; *b* 1912; *s* of Dr W. M. Crofton; *m* 1945, Eileen Chris Mercer; two *s* three *d*. *Educ:* Tonbridge; Sidney Sussex Coll., Cambridge; St Thomas's Hosp. Medical qualification, 1936; War of 1939-45, RAMC; France, Middle East, Germany. Lecturer in Medicine, Postgraduate Medical Sch. of London, 1947-51, Senior Lecturer, 1951; Part-time Tuberculosis Unit, Medical Research Council, Brompton Hosp., 1947-50. Weber-Parkes Prize, RCP, 1966. *Publications:* (jt author) Respiratory Diseases, 1969; contributor to BMJ, Lancet, Thorax, etc. *Recreations:* conversation, family life, mountains. *Address:* 7 Pentland Avenue,

Colinton, Edinburgh 13. *T:* 031-441 3730. *Club:* University Staff (Edinburgh).

**CROFTON, Sir Malby (Sturges),** 5th Bt, *cr* 1838 (orig. *cr* 1661); Partner, Messrs Fenn & Crosthwaite; Member of the London Stock Exchange since 1957; *b* 11 Jan. 1923; *s* of Sir Malby Richard Henry Crofton, 4th Bt, DSO and Bar, and Katharine Beatrix Pollard; *S* father, 1962. *Educ:* Eton (King's Scholar); Trinity Coll., Cambridge (scholar). Served with Life Guards, 1942-46, in Middle East and Italy. Mem. Kensington Borough Council, 1962, Chm. Finance Cttee, 1965. *Recreations:* tennis, swimming, motoring, planting trees, farming. *Heir: kinsman* Brig. Roger Crofton, *qv. Address:* 75 Victoria Road, W8; Longford House, Co. Sligo, Eire.

**CROFTON, Sir Patrick Simon,** 7th Bt *cr* 1801; *b* 2 Dec. 1936; *o s* of Major Morgan G. Crofton (*d* 1947); *S* grandfather, 1958; *m* 1967, Mrs Lene Eddowes, *d* of Kai Augustinus, Copenhagen, and Mrs R. Tonnesen, Port Elizabeth, SA; one *d. Educ:* Eton Coll. 2nd Lieut Welsh Guards, 1955-57. Entered Steel Industry, 1957; became Public Relations Consultant, 1961. Joint Managing Dir, Crofton Mohill Holdings Ltd; Dir, Blair Eames Suslak, Sir Patrick Crofton Ltd, Advertising Agents; Managing Dir, Sir Patrick Crofton Developments Ltd. *Recreations:* ski-ing, motoring, music, political argument. *Heir: uncle* Hugh Denis Crofton, *b* 10 April 1937. *Address:* Carbrook, Curridge, near Newbury, Berks. *Clubs:* Guards, East India and Sports.

**CROFTON, Brig. Roger,** CIE 1942; MC; Indian Army (retired); *b* 13 March 1888; *s* of late Col Malby Edward Crofton; *m* 1914, Stella Clifton (*d* 1916), *d* of Judge T. G. Carver, KC; *m* 1921, Dorothy Frances (*d* 1953), *d* of Col H. M. Hatchell, DSO; one *s*; *m* 1954, Marjorie, *widow* of J. Johnston May. *Educ:* Rossall Sch.; RMA Woolwich. RA, 1907-32; served European War (MC, Bt Major, despatches twice); IA, 1932-42; Dir of Artillery (afterwards Armaments), 1938-42. *Address:* c/o Lloyds Bank Ltd, 6 Pall Mall, SW1. *Club:* Army and Navy.
*See also Sir Malby Crofton.*

**CROFTS, John Ernest Victor;** *b* 6 May 1887; *e s* of Rev. John Crofts, vicar of Dalton, near Southport; *m* 1915, Sibyl Ann, *d* of Rev. C. Hony, Woodborough, Wilts; two *s. Educ:* Magdalen Coll. Sch.; Queen's Coll., Oxford (Bible Clerk). First class hons in English Language and Literature, 1909; BLitt 1914; Senior Demy, Magdalen Coll., 1913-15; Asst Lecturer in English at University Coll., Reading, 1912-19; served with 101st Field Ambulance, 1915-18 (corporal); Winterstoke Prof. of English in the University of Bristol, 1919-41; Public Orator, University of Bristol, 1929-36; co-opted mem. of Bristol Education Cttee, 1938-41; mem. of John Lewis Partnership Ltd (Partners' Counsellor), 1941-52. *Publications:* Field Ambulance Sketches, by a Corporal, 1920; Gray, Poetry and Prose, 1926; Shakespeare and the Posthorses, 1927; Romeo and Juliet (The Warwick Shakespeare, 1938); Packhorse, Waggon and Post, 1967. *Address:* Stonethwaite, Borrowdale, Keswick, Cumberland.

**CROKE, Air Commodore Lewis George Le Blount,** CBE 1941; late Royal Air Force; *b* 28 July 1894; *s* of C. W. Le B. Croke, Solicitor; *m* 1925, Phyllis Mary, *d* of late George Churcher; two *d. Educ:* Merchant Taylors' Sch., London. Merchant Service, 1910-14; European War, Royal Naval Reserve, till 1917; RNAS and RAF Observer, 1917; took Wings, 1923; served in various Home Stations and abroad as Flight Comdr and Sqdn Comdr till 1939; Sqdn Leader, 1929; Wing Comdr, 1936; Group Capt., 1939; Air Commodore, 1941; retired list, 1945. *Recreations:* fencing and shooting. *Address:* White Cottage, Frampton, Dorchester, Dorset.

**CROLL, Hon. David Arnold,** QC; BA, LLB; Senator; *b* Moscow, 12 March 1900; *s* of Hillel and Minnie Croll; *m* 1925, Sarah Levin; three *d. Educ:* public schs and Patterson Collegiate Institute, Windsor; Osgoode Hall, Toronto; University of Toronto. Emigrated to Canada with family, 1906, settling at Windsor, Ont; first and only commercial venture operation of news-stand, which greatly facilitated secondary education; after high school and course articled to solicitor; graduation from Osgoode Hall law sch. followed by practice at Windsor, 1925-30; presently senior partner in Croll and Croll, Windsor, Ont., and Croll, Borins and Shiff, Toronto, Ont. Mayor of Windsor, Ont., 1930-34, 1939-40; Mem. for Windsor-Walkerville, Ont. Legislature, 1934-44; late Minister of Labour, Public Welfare and Municipal Affairs for the Province of Ont.; was youngest and first Jewish Cabinet Minister and first Jewish Senator, in Canada. Mem. of House of Commons for Toronto Spadina, 1945-55 when appointed to Senate. Served War of 1939-45, with Canadian Army overseas, enlisting as Private in Sept. 1939 and discharged in rank of Col in Sept. 1945. *Recreations:* golf and the more strenuous sports. *Address:* Toronto-Dominion Centre, Box 192, Suite 3503, Toronto, Ont, Canada. *Club:* Primrose (Toronto).

**CROLY, Brig. Henry Gray,** CBE 1958; JP; Assistant Secretary of Commissions, Lord Chancellor's Office, since Dec. 1966; *b* 7 June 1910; *s* of late Lt-Col W. Croly, DSO, late RAMC, Ardvarna, Tralee; *m* 1939, Marjorie Rosanne, *er d* of Major J. S. Knyvett, late R Warwickshire Regt, Clifford Manor Road, Guildford; two *s* two *d. Educ:* Sherborne Sch.; RMA Woolwich. 2nd Lieut RA, 1930; served in India: Mohmand Ops, 1935; Waziristan, 1936-37 (despatches); served War of 1939-45, mostly India and Burma; GSO1, British Mil. Mission to France, 1946-47; 2nd-in-Comd 26 Medium Regt RA, 1947-48; jssc 1949; GSO1, WO, 1950-51; Col GS, SHAPE, 1952; OC 26 Field Regt Suez Canal Zone, 1953-55; Dep. Sec., Chiefs of Staff Cttee, 1955-58; UK Nat. Mil. Rep. to SHAPE, 1959-61; retd 1962. Sec., Health Visitor Trng Council and Council for Trng in Social Work, 1963-66. JP Surrey, 1968. *Recreations:* golf, gardening, reading. *Address:* Heatherwood, Lower Bourne, Farnham, Surrey. *T:* Farnham 4851. *Clubs:* Army and Navy, MCC; Hankley Common Golf.

**CROMARTIE,** 4th Earl of *cr* 1861; **Roderick Grant Francis Mackenzie,** MC 1945; TD 1964; JP; CC; Major Seaforth Highlanders, retired; Viscount Tarbat of Tarbat, Baron Castlehaven and Baron MacLeod of Leod, *cr* 1861; *b* 24 Oct. 1904; *er surv. s* of Lt-Col Edward Walter Blunt-Mackenzie, DL (*d* 1949) and Countess of Cromartie, (3rd in line); *S* mother, 1962, having discontinued use of surname of Blunt, for himself and son, and reverted to Mackenzie; *m* 1st, 1933, Mrs Dorothy Downing Porter (marr. diss. 1945), *d* of Mr Downing, Kentucky, USA; two *d*; 2nd, 1947, Olga (Mendoza) (marr. diss. 1962), *d* of late Stuart Laurance, Paris; one *s*; 3rd, 1962, Lilias Richard, MB, ChB, *d* of Prof. (James) Walter MacLeod, *qv. Educ:* Charterhouse; RMC Sandhurst. Commissioned to 1st Bn Seaforth Highlanders in Ireland, 1924; transferred to 2nd Bn Seaforth Highlanders, in India, 1925; seconded to Nigeria Regt of RWAFF, 1928-29; rejoined 2nd Seaforth Highlanders, 1930;

Operations North-West Frontier, India, 1930-31; in France in 1940 with 4th Seaforth Highlanders (MC). JP Ross and Cromarty, 1937; CC Ross and Cromarty, 1963; Hon. Sheriff Substitute. FSA Scot. *Heir:* *s* Viscount Tarbat, *qv*. *Address:* Castle Leod, Strathpeffer, Ross and Cromarty, Scotland. *Clubs:* Army and Navy, Pratt's.

**CROMBIE, George Edmond,** CMG 1950; HM Diplomatic Service, retired; *b* 14 June 1908; *s* of Dr James M. P. Crombie, Aberdeen. *Educ:* Fettes Coll., Edinburgh; Aberdeen Univ. Asst Principal, India Office, 1931; Principal, 1937. war of 1939-45, Lieut 1st Frontier Force Regt, Indian Army, 1942-45; served in Italy (despatches). Returned to India Office, 1945; Asst Sec., Burma Office, 1947; UK Dep. High Comr, Rangoon, 1947; Counsellor, HM Embassy, Rangoon, 1948-49; Dep. High Commissioner for UK, Madras, 1951-53; Counsellor, UK High Commission, Ottawa, 1955-58; Dep. High Commissioner for UK in Federation of Malaya, 1959-60; Counsellor, British Embassy, Dublin, 1961-65; British High Commissioner in The Gambia, 1965-67. *Recreations:* golf, swimming. *Address:* 212 Queen's Road, Aberdeen AB1 8DJ. *Clubs:* University (Aberdeen); Stephen's Green (Dublin).

**CROMBIE, Rear-Adm. (Retd) John Harvey Forbes,** CB 1952; DSO 1943; *b* 16 Feb. 1900; *o s* of late James Forbes Crombie, Woodside, Aberdeenshire; *m* 1934, Rosamond, *e d* of late Brig.-Gen. Rodney Style, Wierton Grange, Boughton Monchelsea, Kent; one *s* three *d*. *Educ:* St Aubyn's, Rottingdean; RN Colls Osborne and Dartmouth. Served European War, HMS Queen Elizabeth and HMS Oak, 1916-18. Qualified in Signals, 1924; later served on staffs of Adm. Sir Maurice Fitzmaurice, Adm. Sir Frederic Dreyer, Adm. Sir Howard Kelly, Adm. Sir William Fisher. Served War of 1939-45, HMS Repulse (despatches), 1939-41; Capt., 1941; Senior Officer Minesweepers, N Russia, 1941-43 (HMS Bramble); Dir of Minesweeping, 1943-46; HMS Vengeance, in command, 1946-48; HMS Mercury, in command, 1948-50; Rear-Adm. 1950; Flag Officer, Scotland, and Adm. Supt, Rosyth, 1951-53. ADC to King George VI, 1950; Mem. Queen's Body Guard for Scotland (The Royal Company of Archers). Order of Alexander Nevsky, 1943; Legion of Merit (USA), 1944; Order of Orange Nassau, 1945. *Address:* Gateside House, Gullane, East Lothian. *T:* Gullane 3139. *Clubs:* United Service; New (Edinburgh).

**CROMER,** 3rd Earl of, *cr* 1901; **George Rowland Stanley Baring;** Viscount, *cr* 1898; Baron, *cr* 1892; PC 1966; MBE 1945; DL; Chairman and Managing Director, Baring Brothers & Co. Ltd, since 1967; Chairman: IBM UK Holdings Ltd, since 1967; London Multinational Bank Ltd, since 1970; one of HM Lieutenants for the City of London, since 1967; *b* 28 July 1918; *o s* (to whom King George V stood sponsor) of 2nd Earl of Cromer, PC, GCB, GCIE, GCVO, and Lady Ruby Elliot, 2nd *d* of 4th Earl of Minto; *S* father, 1953; *m* 1942, Hon. Esmé Harmsworth, 2nd *d* of Viscount Rothermere, *qv*; two *s* one *d*. *Educ:* Eton; Cambridge Univ. Served War of 1939-45 (despatches, MBE); Lt-Col, Grenadier Guards, 1945. Page of Honour to King George V, 1931-35; Private Sec. to Marquess of Willingdon on official visits to S America, 1938, and to Australia and NZ, 1940; Managing Dir, Baring Brothers & Co. Ltd, 1947-61 (on leave, 1959-61); Mem., Inter-Parly Mission to Brazil, 1954; British Economic Minister and Head of Treasury Delegn in Washington, and UK Exec. Dir of Internat. Monetary Fund, Internat. Bank for Reconstruction and Develt, and Internat. Finance Corp., 1959-61; Bank of England: part-time Dir, Jan.-July 1961; Governor, 1961-66; Dir, Bank of Internat. Settlements, Basle, 1961-66; UK Governor, Internat. Bank for Reconstruction and Develt, Internat. Finance Corp., and Internat. Develt Assoc., 1963-66. Dir, Union Carbide Corp., NY; formerly Director: Daily Mail & General Trust Ltd; Anglo-Newfoundland Develt Co. Ltd; Royal Insurance Co. Ltd. DL Kent, 1968. Hon. LLD New York Univ., 1966. *Heir:* *s* Viscount Errington, *qv*. *Address:* Frenchstreet Farm, Westerham, Kent; 8 Bishopsgate, EC2. *T:* 01-588 2830. *Clubs:* Brooks's, Beefsteak, MCC; Brook (NY); Metropolitan (Washington).

*See also J. D. Hills.*

**CROMPTON-INGLEFIELD, Col Sir John (Frederick),** Kt 1963; TD; DL; Chairman, Inglefield Group of Companies; *b* 1904; *e s* of Adm. Sir F. S. Inglefield, KCB, DL; *m* 1926, Rosemary, *d* of Adm. Sir Percy Scott, 1st Bt, KCB, KCVO, LLD; three *d*. *Educ:* RN Colls Osborne and Dartmouth. Retired from Royal Navy, 1926. Derbyshire Yeomanry (Armoured Car Co.), Lieut 1936, Major 1939. Served War of 1939-45, with 1st Derbyshire Yeo. and 79th Armoured Div. (despatches) Africa and Europe. Lt-Col Comdg Derbyshire Yeo, 1950-53; Bt Col 1954; Hon. Col, Leics and Derbyshire Yeo., 1962-70. Chm. W Derbyshire Conservative and Unionist Assoc., 1951-66; Vice-Chm., 1957-64, Chm., TA, Derbyshire, 1964-69. CC 1932-55, JP 1933, DL 1953, and High Sheriff, 1938, Derbyshire. OStJ. *Recreation:* shooting. *Address:* Parwich Hall, near Ashbourne, Derbyshire. *T:* Parwich 229; 15 Beaufort Gardens, SW3. *T:* 01-589 0650. *Clubs:* United Service, Cavalry, Royal Automobile; Malta Union.

**CROMWELL,** 6th Baron, *cr* 1375 (called out of abeyance 1923); **David Godfrey Bewicke-Copley;** Partner in Mullens & Co. since 1960; *b* 29 May 1929; *s* of 5th Baron Cromwell, DSO, MC, and of Lady Cromwell (Freda Constance, *d* of Sir F. W. B. Cripps, DSO); *S* father, 1966; *m* 1954, Vivian Penfold, *y d* of H. de L. Penfold, South Africa; two *s* two *d*. *Educ:* Eton; Magdalene Coll., Cambridge. Called to the Bar, Inner Temple, 1954. Mem. London Stock Exchange, 1956-. *Heir:* *s* Hon. Godfrey John Bewicke-Copley, *b* 4 March 1960. *Address:* The Manor House, Great Milton, Oxfordshire. *T:* Great Milton 230.

**CRONE, Anne;** author: Modern Languages Mistress, Princess Gardens School, Belfast, since 1948; *b* 16 Sept. 1915; *d* of William Crone, MBE, former Asst Sec., Ministry of Commerce for NI, and Mary Jane Plunkett. *Educ:* Methodist Coll., Belfast; Somerville Coll., Oxford (MA, BLitt). Three Prizes (Somerville); 1st Cl. Final Hon. Sch. Mod. Langs; Grad. Schol. Modern Languages Mistress, Victoria Coll., Belfast, 1938-45. *Publications:* *novels:* Bridie Steen, 1948 (New York), 1949 (London); This Pleasant Lea, 1951 (New York), 1952 (London); My Heart and I, 1955 (London). *Address:* 10 King's Road, Knock, Belfast 5. *T:* 653112.

**CRONE, Col Desmond Roe,** CIE 1946; OBE 1941; MSc; *b* 24 Sept. 1900; 4th *s* of late John Smythe Crone, LRCPI, Willesden; *m* 1932, Margaret, 2nd *d* of late Rev. W. E. Wilkie Brown, MA, KIH, Edinburgh; three *s*. *Educ:* Kilburn Grammar Sch.; RMA Woolwich. Commissioned Royal Engineers, 1920; joined Survey of India, 1924; served with Indo-Afghan Boundary Commission, 1932; Operations NW Frontier, 1930 and 1933; Captain, 1931; Major 1938; Lt-Col 1945; retired 1948, Hon. Col. Senior Lectr in

Surveying, University of the Witwatersrand, Johannesburg, 1947-49, and Queen's Univ., Belfast, 1954-62. FRSA 1934. *Publication:* Elementary Photogrammetry, 1963. *Recreations:* yachting, gardening. *Address:* 22 Pioneer Street, Mittagong, MSW 2575, Australia. *Club:* Royal Commonwealth Society.

**CRONIN, Archibald Joseph,** MD (Glasgow), MRCP, DPH London; novelist; *b* 19 July 1896; *s* of Patrick Cronin and Jessie Montgomerie; *m* Agnes Mary Gibson, MB, ChB; three *s. Educ:* Glasgow Univ. Served European War, Surgeon Sub-Lieut, RNVR; graduated MB, ChB, with hons, 1919; Physician to Out-Patients Bellahouston War Pensions Hospital; Medical Superintendent Lightburn Hospital, Glasgow; general practice South Wales, 1921-24; Medical Inspector of Mines for Great Britain, 1924; MD (hons) 1925; Report on First-Aid Conditions in British Coal Mines, 1926, published by HM Stationary Dept, also Report on Dust Inhalation in Haematite Mines; practised medicine in London, 1926-30; in 1930 decided to give up medicine, follow natural bent and devote himself to literature; first novel, Hatter's Castle, published in 1931, was instantaneous success; first play, Jupiter Laughs, produced 1940. Hon. DLitt, Bowdoin Univ., Hon. DLitt, Lafayette Univ. *Publications:* Hatter's Castle, 1931; Three Loves, 1932; Grand Canary, 1933; The Stars Look Down, 1935; The Citadel, 1937; The Keys of the Kingdom, 1942; The Green Years, 1944; Shannon's Way, 1948; The Spanish Gardener, 1950; Adventures in Two Worlds, 1952; Beyond this Place, 1953; Crusader's Tomb, 1956; The Northern Light, 1958; The Judas Tree, 1961; A Song of Sixpence, 1964; A Pocketful of Rye, 1969; Creator of Dr Finlay's Casebook. *Recreations:* golf, tennis, gardening, fishing. *Address:* Champ-Riond, Baugy sur Clarens, Vaud, Switzerland. *Clubs:* Pilgrims, University, Links (New York).
*See also V. A. P. Cronin.*

**CRONIN, Henry Francis,** CBE 1944; MC; BSc (Eng.); FCGI; MInstCE, MInstWE; President Institution of Civil Engineers, 1952-53; Chief Engineer, Metropolitan Water Board, London, 1939-59, retired; *b* 12 May 1894; *s* of Dominic and Annie Cronin; *m* 1926, Beatrice Warburton Stent; one *s. Educ:* Beaumont Coll.; Brighton Municipal Technical Coll.; City and Guilds Engineering Coll., South Kensington. Served European War, 1914-18, in Infantry and Royal Engineers (despatches, twice wounded, MC); entered service of Metropolitan Water Board in 1920; held various positions on Engineering Staff; Deputy Chief Engineer in 1933; Pres. Institution of Water Engineers, 1945-46. *Address:* Little Barnfield, Hawkhurst, Kent. *Club:* Athenæum.

**CRONIN, John Desmond,** FRCS; MP (Lab) Loughborough since 1955; Consultant Surgeon; *b* 1 March 1916; *s* of John Patrick Cronin and Beatrice Cronin (*née* Brooks); *m* 1941, Cora, *d* of Rowland Mumby-Croft; one *s* two *d. Educ:* London Univ. MRCS, LRCP 1939; MB, BS (London) 1940; FRCS 1947. House Surgeon, St Bartholomew's Hosp., 1939-40; Surgeon EMS, Royal Free Hosp., 1941-42. Served RAMC, 1942-46, France, Germany and Burma campaigns; Surgical Specialist, Major (Actg Lt-Col 1945). Asst Orthopædic Surgeon, Prince of Wales's Hosp., 1947-51; Orthopædic Surgeon, French Hosp., 1948-. Vice-Chm., North St Pancras Labour Party, 1950. Member LCC, 1952-55. Opposition Whip, House of Commons, 1959-62. Director: Racal Electronics Ltd, 1965-; Knight Wegenstein Ltd, 1969-70. Officier, Légion d'Honneur, 1967 (Chevalier, 1960). *Publications:* contributions to British Med. Journal and Proceedings Royal Soc. Medicine, and to the national press; Report on the Medical Services of Malta (pub. Central Office of Information, Govt of Malta). *Recreations:* sailing, shooting, riding, tennis. *Address:* 14 Wimpole Street, W1. *T:* 01-580 2460. *Club:* Hurlingham.

**CRONIN, Vincent Archibald Patrick;** author; *b* 24 May 1924; *s* of Archibald Joseph Cronin, *qv*; *m* 1949, Chantal, *d* of Comte Jean de Rolland; two *s* three *d. Educ:* Ampleforth; Harvard; Trinity Coll., Oxford. Rifle Bde, 1943-45. *Publications:* The Golden Honeycomb, 1954; The Wise Man from the West, 1955; The Last Migration, 1957; A Pearl to India, 1959; The Letter after Z, 1960; Louis XIV, 1964; Four Women in Pursuit of an Ideal, 1965; The Florentine Renaissance, 1967; The Flowering of the Renaissance, 1970. *Address:* 44 Hyde Park Square, W2.

**CRONNE, Prof. Henry Alfred;** Professor of Medieval History in the University of Birmingham, 1946-70; Dean of the Faculty of Arts, 1952-55; *b* 17 Oct. 1904; *o c* of late Rev. James Kennedy Cronne, Portaferry, Co. Down, N Ireland; *m* 1936, Lilian Mey, *er d* of E. F. Seckler, Bishops Tawton, Barnstaple; one *d. Educ:* Campbell Coll., Belfast; Queen's Univ. of Belfast; Balliol Coll., Oxford; Inst. of Historical Research. MA Belfast; MA Oxon; MA Birmingham, *jure officii*; FRHistSoc. Asst Lecturer in History, QUB, 1928-31; Lecturer in Medieval History, King's Coll., London, 1931, and subsequently Lecturer in Palaeography and Reader in Medieval History. War of 1939-45, served in Home Guard and Somerset Special Constabulary. *Publications:* Bristol Charters, 1378-1499, 1946; The Reign of Stephen, 1970; (ed with Charles Johnson) Regesta Regum Anglo-Normannorum, Vol. II, 1100-1135, 1956, (ed with R. H. C. Davis), Vol. III, 1135-1154, 1968, and Vol. IV, 1969; contribs to historical jls. *Recreations:* fly-fishing, walking, boats. *Address:* Winswood Cottage, Cheldon, Chulmleigh, N Devon. *Club:* University Staff (Chm. 1952-59).

**CRONYN, Capt. St John,** CBE 1951; DSO 1941; Royal Navy; *b* 20 May 1901; *yr s* of Dr J. G. Cronyn, Dublin; *m* 1937, Lilias Marion, *er d* of late P. W. Wake; no *c. Educ:* Royal Naval Colls, Osborne and Dartmouth; Gonville and Caius Coll., Cambridge. Midshipman, HMS Orion, 1917; served Yangtsze gunboat flotilla, Mediterranean station and Training Establishments; RN Staff Coll., 1934; Comdr, 1937; minesweeping, 1939-41 (DSO, despatches); Eastern Fleet, 1942-43; Capt., 1943; Tactical Division, Admiralty, 1944-45; Dir RN Tactical Sch., 1945-48; HMS Devonshire, 1948-50; Chief Staff Officer, Gibraltar, 1951-52 (CBE) (Ammunition Explosion); ADC to the Queen, 1952; retired list, 1953. *Recreations:* hockey, cricket, tennis. *Address:* 24 Swan Court, Chelsea, SW3. *Club:* Naval and Military.

**CROOK,** family name of **Baron Crook.**

**CROOK,** 1st Baron *cr* 1947, of Carshalton, Surrey; **Reginald Douglas Crook;** *b* 2 March 1901; *s* of Percy Edwin Crook; *m* 1922, Ida G. Haddon; one *s. Educ:* Strand Sch. Local Govt Service; Organising Sec. of Poor Law Officers' Union and Ed., Poor Law Gazette, 1920-24; Gen. Sec., Min. of Labour Staff Assoc., 1925-51, and Ed., Civil Service Argus, 1929-51; Sec., Fedn of Min. of Labour Staff, 1944-51; Mem., National Whitley Council for Civil Service, 1925-51; Mem., Min. of Labour Departmental Whitley Council, 1925-51; Hon. Sec., Labour

Parliamentary Assoc., 1945-47; a Dep. Chm. of Cttees, House of Lords, 1949-; Mem., Ecclesiastical Cttee of Parliament, 1949-; Chm. of Interdeptl Cttee of Enquiry as to Optical Services, appointed by Min. of Health, 1949-52; Mem., Parl. Delegn to Denmark, 1949; Deleg. to Finland, 1950; Mem., Police Wages Council, 1951; Chm., National Dock Labour Board, 1951-65, also Chm., National Dock Labour Board (Nominees) Ltd and Chm., National Dock Labour Board Pensions Trustees Ltd; Delegate, United Nations General Assembly, 1950; Mem., United Nations Administrative Tribunal, 1951-71, Vice-Pres., 1952-71; Mem., UK Goodwill Mission to 350th Anniversary of Virginia, 1957; President: (also Fellow) Brit. Assoc. of Industrial Editors, 1953-61; Assoc. of Optical Practitioners (also Pres., 1959-65); Cystic Fibrosis Research Foundation Trust; The Pre-Retirement Assoc.; Vice-Pres., Royal Soc. for the Prevention of Accidents; Vice-Pres. and Fellow, Inst. of Municipal Safety Officers. Member: Inst. of Neurology; Gen. Practice Finance Corp., 1966-; London Electricity Board, 1967-. Chm., London Electricity Consultative Council, 1967-. Master, Worshipful Co. of Spectacle Makers, 1963-65; an Apothecary and Freeman of City of London. Warden, Guild of Freemen of City of London. JP Surrey. KStJ 1955. Mem. Chapter-Gen. of St John, 1957-. *Heir: s* Hon. Douglas Edwin Crook [*b* 19 Nov. 1926; *m* 1954, Ellenor Rouse; one *s* one *d*]. *Address:* Breedene, Princes Avenue, Carshalton, Surrey. *T:* 01-643 2620.

**CROOK, Arthur Charles William;** Editor, The Times Literary Supplement, since 1959; *b* 16 Feb. 1912; *m* 1948, Sarita Mary Vivien Bushell; one *s* two *d*. Editorial staff of The Times; Asst Editor, The Times Literary Supplement, 1951-59. *Recreation:* theatre. *Address:* 70 Regent's Park Road, NW1. *T:* 01-722 8446. *Club:* Garrick.

**CROOK, Eric Ashley,** FRCS; Consulting Surgeon; *b* 25 April 1894; *s* of Thomas Ashley and Emma Daisy Crook; *m* 1924, Elizabeth Grace Garratt; one *s* one *d*. *Educ:* Winchester; New Coll., Oxford (MA, MCh). FRCS 1922. Cons. Surgeon: Charing Cross Hosp., Gordon Hosp., Putney Hosp., Royal Masonic Hosp. Served European War, 1914-18, Surg. Lieut, RN. *Address:* Silver Mist, Harmans Cross, Swanage, Dorset.

*See also W. H. C. Frend.*

**CROOK, Kenneth Roy;** Counsellor, Foreign and Commonwealth Office, since 1967; *b* 30 July 1920; *s* of Alexander Crook, Prescot, Lancs, and Margaret Kay Crook; *m* 1943, Freda Joan Vidler; two *d*. *Educ:* Prescot Grammar Sch., Lancs; Skerry's Coll., Liverpool. Appointed to: Board of Trade, 1937; Min. of War Transport, 1939. Royal Navy, 1941-46. Board of Trade, 1946-49; Commonwealth Relations Office, 1949; Second Sec., Canberra, 1951-54; First Sec., Madras, 1956-59; Deputy High Commissioner: Peshawar, W Pakistan, 1962-64; Dacca, E Pakistan, 1964-67. *Recreations:* walking, gardening, golf. *Address:* Foreign and Commonwealth Office, King Charles Street, SW1; 16 Burntwood Road, Sevenoaks, Kent. *T:* Sevenoaks 52774.

**CROOK, Brig. Paul Edwin,** CBE 1965 (OBE 1946); DSO 1957; Commander, Rhine Area, since 1969; *b* 19 April 1915; *s* of late Herbert Crook and Christine Crook, Lyme Regis; *m* 1st, 1944, Joan (marr. diss. 1967), *d* of late William Lewis; one *d*; 2nd, 1967, Betty, *d* of late John William Wyles. *Educ:* Uppingham Sch.; Emmanuel Coll., Cambridge. BA 1936, MA 1946. Commnd into QORWK Regt, 1935; served: India and Palestine, 1937-39; War of 1939-45, Africa, NW Europe, Burma; Chief Civil Affairs Officer (Col), Netherlands East Indies, 1946; comd 3rd Bn The Parachute Regt, 1954-57; Suez Ops, 1956; comd Army Airborne Trng and Develt Centre, 1959-62; Comdr and Chief of Staff, Jamaica Defence Force, 1962-65; Security Ops Advisor to High Comr for Aden and S Arabia, 1965-67; Royal Naval War Coll., Greenwich, 1968. ADC to The Queen, 1965. Bronze Star (US), 1945. *Recreations:* cricket, sailing, jazz. *Address:* HQ Rhine Area, BFPO 34. *Clubs:* United Service, MCC; Jamaica (W Indies).

**CROOKENDEN, Lt-Gen. Sir Napier,** KCB 1970 (CB 1966); DSO 1945; OBE 1954; AFRAeS 1967; GOC-in-C, Western Command, since 1969; *b* 31 Aug. 1915; 2nd *s* of late Col Arthur Crookenden, CBE, DSO; *m* 1948, Patricia Nassau, *d* of 2nd Baron Kindersley, *qv*; two *s* two *d*. *Educ:* Wellington Coll.; RMC, Sandhurst. Commissioned, Cheshire Regt, 1935; Bde Major, 6th Airlanding Bde, 1943-44; CO, 9th Bn, The Parachute Regt, 1944-46; GSO1 (Plans) to Dir of Ops, Malaya, 1952-54; Comdr, 16th Parachute Bde, 1960-61; idc 1962; Dir, Land/Air Warfare MoD (Army Dept), 1964-66; Commandant, RMCS, Shrivenham, 1967-69. Col, The Cheshire Regt, 1968-. *Address:* Eccleston Hill, Chester. *Clubs:* United Service, Ski Club of Great Britain.

**CROOKS, James,** CVO 1958; FRCS; Hon. Consulting Ear, Nose and Throat Surgeon, The Hospital for Sick Children, Great Ormond Street; *b* 2 Oct. 1901; *s* of James amd Margaret Crooks, Loanhead, Midlothian; *m* 1931, Irene G. Heath (whom he divorced 1950); two *d*; *m* 1970, Caroline A. Woollcombe. Educ: University, Edinburgh; Royal Infirmary, Edinburgh; St Bartholomew's Hospital, London. MB, ChB, Edinburgh 1923; FRCS 1928. House Surgeon, Royal Infirmary, Edinburgh, 1924; House Physician, Casualty Officer, Resident Medical Supt, Surgical Registrar, The Hospital for Sick Children, 1924-31, Chm. Med. Cttee, 1950-53; Chm., Building Cttee, 1948-67. Kirk-Duncanson Research Scholar in USA, Vienna, Paris, Copenhagen, 1929-31; Fellow Royal Society of Medicine; Mem. Royal Medical Society Edinburgh; Hon. Mem. Brit. Paed. Assoc. *Publications:* The Ear, Nose and Throat in Garrod, Batten and Thursfield's Diseases of Children; Accessory Nasal Sinusitis in Childhood, 1936; Chronic Running Ear in Childhood, 1938; Tonsils and Adenoids: evaluation of removal in 50 Doctors' children; (with S. E. T. Cusdin) Suggestions and Demonstration Plans for Hospitals for Sick Children, 1947. *Recreations:* painting, sailing. *Address:* Private Consulting Rooms, The Hospital for Sick Children, 34 Great Ormond Street, WC1. *T:* 01-405 2943; Meadow Farm, Ringshall, near Berkhamsted, Herts. *T:* Little Gaddesden 2295.

**CROOKS, Air Vice-Marshal Lewis M.;** *see* Mackenzie Crooks.

**CROOKSHANK, Henry,** CIE 1946; DSc (Dublin); BAI; BA, FNISc India, FGS, etc; *b* 13 Feb. 1893; *s* of Charles Henry Crookshank, Judge Commissioner, Land Commission, N Ireland; *m* 1921, Eileen Mary Somerville Lodge; three *d*. *Educ:* St Columba's, Rathfarnham; Trinity Coll., Dublin. Royal Dublin Fusiliers and Royal Engineers, 1914-18 (despatches); Geological Survey of India, 1920; recalled Royal Engineers, 1940-44; wounded Razmak, 1941; Offg Dir, Geological Survey of India, 1944-45; States Liaison Officer, Geological Survey of India, Calcutta, 1946, retd. Dir, Geological Survey of Pakistan,

1948-56. *Publications:* The True Story of the Giant's Causeway, 1946; many papers to Geological Survey of India publications, etc. *Recreations:* golf, tennis, shooting. *Address:* c/o National and Grindlays Bank Ltd, 13 St James's Square, SW1; Kilbogget Corner, Ballybrack, Co. Dublin.

**CROOM-JOHNSON, David Powell,** DSC 1944; VRD 1953; QC 1958; Judge of Courts of Appeal of Jersey and Guernsey, since 1966; Recorder of Winchester, since 1962; *b* 28 Nov. 1914; 3rd *s* of late Hon. Sir Reginald Powell Croom-Johnson, sometime a Judge of the High Court, and late Lady (Ruby) Croom-Johnson; *m* 1940, Barbara Douglas, *y d* of late Erskine Douglas Warren, Toronto; one *d*. *Educ:* The Hall, Hampstead; Stowe Sch.; Trinity Hall, Cambridge. Called to Bar, Gray's Inn, 1938; Master of the Bench, 1964; Western Circuit. Mem. Gen. Council of the Bar, 1958-62; Mem. Senate of Inns of Court, 1966-. RNVR (London Div.), 1936-53. Served with Royal Navy, 1939-46. Lieut-Comdr RNR (Retired). Council, Oakdene Sch. 1956-. *Recreations:* books, music. *Address:* 28 Rutland Street, SW7. *T:* 01-589 8681; 12 King's Bench Walk, EC4. *T:* 01-583 0811. *Club:* Garrick.

*See also H. P. Croom-Johnson.*

**CROOM-JOHNSON, Henry Powell,** CMG 1964; CBE 1954 (OBE 1944); TD 1948; Assistant Director-General, The British Council, since 1966; *b* 15 Dec. 1910; *e s* of late Hon. Sir Reginald Croom-Johnson, sometime Judge of High Court, and of late Lady (Ruby) Croom-Johnson; *m* 1947, Jane, *er d* of late Archibald George Mandry; two *s*. *Educ:* Stowe Sch.; Trinity Hall, Cambridge. Asst Master, Bedford Sch., 1932-34. Joined staff of British Council, 1935. Served with Queen's Westminsters and King's Royal Rifle Corps, 1939-46 (staff Sicily, Italy, Greece; Lt-Col). Rejoined British Council, 1946; Controller Finance Div., 1951; Controller European Div., 1956; Representative in India, 1957-64; Controller, Overseas Div. B, 1964. *Recreations:* climbing, books, music. *Address:* 3a Ravenscourt Square, W6. *T:* 01-748 3677; The Cottage, Hillesden, Buckingham. *T:* Steeple Claydon 391. *Club:* Savile.

*See also D. P. Croom-Johnson.*

**CROOME, (John) Lewis,** CMG 1957; Chief Overseas Relations Officer, UK Atomic Energy Authority, since 1958; *b* 10 June 1907; *s* of John and Caroline Croome; *m* 1st, 1931, Honoria Renée Minturn (*née* Scott; as Honor Croome, Editorial Staff of The Economist) (*d* 1960); four *s* one *d* (and one *s* decd); 2nd, 1961, Pamela Siola, *o d* of Lt-Col Tyrrel Hawker, Hurstbourne Priors, Hants; one *s*. *Educ:* Henry Thornton Sch., Clapham; London Sch. of Economics. Imperial Economic Cttee, 1931-39; Ministry of Food, 1939-48; Deputy (later Head), British Food Mission, Ottawa, 1942-46; HM Treasury (Central Economic Planning Staff), 1948-51; Min. of Food, 1951-54; UK Delegation to OEEC, Paris, 1954-57; Ministry of Agriculture, Fisheries and Food, 1957-58. *Recreations:* painting, gardening. *Address:* Pearmain, Ruxley, Claygate, Surrey. *T:* Esher 62597. *Club:* Reform.

**CROOME, Lewis;** *see* Croome, J. L.

**CROOT, Sir (Horace) John,** Kt 1965; CBE 1962; Consultant Surgeon; *b* 14 Oct. 1907; *s* of Horace Croot, LDS, RCS and Winifred Croot; *m* 1st, 1944, Ruth Martyn; 2nd, 1955, Irene Linda Louvain Burley; no *c*. *Educ:* Haileybury; Guy's Hosp. Med. Sch. MRCS, LRCP and MB, BS (London), 1930. Resident Posts, Guy's Hospital etc, 1930-32; medical practice, Hong Kong and Canton, 1932-36; Surgeon, Chinese Maritime Customs, 1935-36; post-grad. study, London, FRCS, 1938. Lt-Col RAMC, 1940-46, mainly India and Burma (despatches), 1944. Sen. Lectr in Surgery, Univ. of Bristol, and Hon. Consultant Surgeon, United Bristol Hosps, 1946-50; Prof. of Surgery, Univ. of E Africa, 1951-58; Minister of Health and Labour, Uganda, 1958-61; Sen. Consultant Surgeon, Mulago Hosp., Kampala, 1961-69. Pres., Assoc. of Surgeons of E Africa, 1956 and 1962. Mem., Pensions Appeal Tribunals, 1970-. *Publications:* contribs to Lancet and Brit. Jl of Surgery. *Address:* 29 Knole Wood, Devenish Road, Sunningdale, Berks. *T:* Ascot 23651.

**CROSBY, Harry L., (Bing);** singer; motion picture actor; *b* Tacoma, Washington; *s* of Harry L. and Catherine Crosby; *m* 1st, Wilma Wyatt (Dixie Lee) (*d* 1952); four *s*; 2nd, 1957, Kathryn Grant; two *s* one *d*. *Educ:* Gonzaga Univ., Spokane, Washington. 2 years vaudeville, 4 years vocal trio with Paul Whiteman band; over 20 years radio and records and motion pictures; over 200,000,000 record sales by 1960; with Paramount Production Incorporated, 1931-. Best Actor Award (Oscar), 1944. Hon. DMus, Gonzaga Univ. *Publications:* Call Me Lucky, 1953; popular songs. *Relevant Publication:* Bing (by Ted and Larry Crosby). *Address:* 170 N Robertson Boulevard, Beverly Hills, Calif 90211, USA. *Clubs:* Lakeside Golf (Hollywood); Burlingame County; San Francisco Golf; Cypress Point; Royal and Ancient (St Andrews).

**CROSFIELD, Very Rev. George Philip Chorley;** Provost of St Mary's Cathedral, Edinburgh, since 1970; *b* 9 Sept. 1924; *s* of James Chorley Crosfield and Marjorie Louise Crosfield; *m* 1956, Susan Mary Jullion (*née* Martin); one *s* two *d*. *Educ:* George Watson's Coll., Edinburgh; Selwyn Coll., Cambridge. Royal Artillery, 1942-46 (Captain). Priest, 1952; Asst Curate: St David's, Pilton, Edinburgh, 1951-53; St Andrew's, St Andrews, 1953-55; Rector, St Cuthbert's, Hawick, 1955-60; Chaplain, Gordonstoun School, 1960-68; subseq. Canon and Vice Provost, St Mary's Cathedral, Edinburgh. *Recreations:* walking, reading, oboe, carpentry. *Address:* 8 Lansdowne Crescent, Edinburgh, EH12 5EQ. *T:* 031-225 2978.

**CROSLAND, Rt. Hon. Anthony;** *see* Crosland, Rt Hon. C. A. R.

**CROSLAND, Rt. Hon. (Charles) Anthony (Raven),** PC 1965; MP (Lab) Grimsby since Oct. 1959; *b* 29 Aug. 1918; *s* of late Joseph Beardsel Crosland, CB, and of Jessie Crosland; *m* 1st, 1952, Hilary Anne (marr. diss. 1957), *d* of Henry Sarson, Newbury, Berks; 2nd, 1964, Mrs Susan Catling, *d* of Mark Watson, Baltimore, Maryland. *Educ:* Highgate Sch.; Trinity Coll., Oxford (Scholar). First Class, Philosophy, Politics and Economics; Chm., Oxford Univ. Democratic Socialist Club; Pres., Oxford Union, 1946. Served War of 1939-45, fusilier, Royal Fusiliers, 1940; commissioned Royal Welch Fusiliers, 1941; joined Parachute Regt, 1942, and served N Africa, Italy, France, Austria; Capt., 1943-45. Fellow and lectr in Economics, Trinity Coll, Oxford, 1947-50; MP (Lab) South Glos, 1950-55; Minister of State for Economic Affairs, 1964-65; Sec. of State for Educn and Science, 1965-67; President of the Bd of Trade, 1967-69; Secretary of State for Local Government and Regional Planning, 1969-70. Hon. Fellow, Trinity Coll., Oxford, 1966. Sec. of the Indept Commn of Inquiry into the Co-operative Movement, 1956-58, Chm. of Fabian Soc.,

1961-62; Coun. Mem. of Consumers' Assoc., 1958-63. *Publications:* (contributor) New Fabian Essays, 1952; Britain's Economic Problem, 1953; The Future of Socialism, 1956; The Conservative Enemy, 1962. *Address:* 37 Lansdowne Road, W11.

**CROSLAND, Brig. Harold Powell,** CB 1955; CBE 1943; MC 1918; TD; DL; late RA; Chairman: Lead Development Assoc.; Zinc Development Assoc.; London Metal Exchange; President of the Board (late Chairman and Managing Director) of Metal Traders Ltd; Director of Metal Market & Exchange Co. Ltd; *b* 1893; *s* of Walter Crosland, JP, The Grange, Eaton Hastings, Faringdon, Berks; *m* 1916, Lilian Edith (*d* 1960), *d* of late Lieut-Col William Henry Hippisley, Scots Greys, Sparsholt Manor, Wantage, Berks; one *s* one *d. Educ:* Malvern. Joined Berkshire Yeomanry, 1912; served European War, 1914-18 in Gallipoli, Egypt, Palestine and Syria (wounded, despatches twice, MC); Capt., 1916; Major, 1920; Lieut-Col 99 Bucks and Berks Yeo. Field Brigade, RA, 1933-38; Bt Col, 1937; retired, 1938; re-employed, 1939. Chm. Berks T&AFA; DL Berks 1936. *Address:* Satwell Spinneys, Rotherfield Greys, near Henley-on-Thames, Oxon.

**CROSS,** family name of **Viscount Cross.**

**CROSS,** 3rd Viscount, *cr* 1886; **Assheton Henry Cross;** late Lieut Scots Guards; *b* 7 May 1920; *e s* of 2nd Viscount and Maud Evelyn (who *m* 2nd, 1944, Guy Hope Coldwell (*d* 1948), Stoke Lodge, Ludlow, Salop), *d* of late Maj.-Gen. Inigo Jones, CVO, CB, Kelston Park, Bath; *S* father, 1932; *m* 1952, Patricia Mary (marr. diss., 1957; she *m* 1960, Comdr G. H. H. Culme-Seymour), *e d* of E. P. Hewetson, JP, The Craig, Windermere, Westmorland; two *d. Educ:* Shrewsbury; Magdalene Coll., Cambridge. *Heir:* none. *Address:* Eccle Riggs, Broughton-in-Furness, Lancs. *T:* 243. *Club:* Guards.

**CROSS, Alexander Galbraith,** MA, MD, FRCS; Ophthalmic Surgeon; lately Dean of the Medical School, St Mary's Hospital; Civilian Consultant in Ophthalmology, RN, since 1946; Consultant Surgeon, Moorfields Eye Hospital, since 1947; Consultant Ophthalmic Surgeon, St Mary's Hospital, since 1946; Consultant Ophthalmic Surgeon, Royal National Throat, Nose, and Ear Hospital, since 1954; Ophthalmic Surgeon, Royal Masonic Hospital, since 1961; Ophthalmic Surgeon, St Dunstan's, since 1946; Hon. Consultant Ophthalmologist, Royal National Institute for the Blind, since 1968; *b* 29 March 1908; *er s* of late Walter Galbraith Cross and late Mary Stewart Cross, Wimbledon; *m* 1939, Eileen Longman, twin *d* of late Dr H. B. Corry, Liss, Hants; one *d. Educ:* King's Coll. Sch.; Gonville and Caius Coll., Cambridge; St Mary's Hosp., London (university Scholar). Meadows Prize, 1932, Broadbent and Agnes Cope Prizes, 1933, Cheadle Gold Medallist, 1933, St Mary's Hospital. House Phys. and House Surg., St Mary's, 1933-35; House Surg. and Sen. Res. Officer, Moorfields Eye Hosp., 1937-39; Ophth. Surg., West Middlesex Hosp., 1938-48; Ophth. Surg., Tite Street Children's Hosp., 1939-48; Ophth. Surg., Princess Beatrice Hosp., 1939-47. Wing Comdr, RAFVR, 1941-46 and Adviser in Ophthalmology, South-East Asia Air Forces. Examiner in Fellowship and in Diploma of Ophthalmology for RCS and in Ophthalmology for Univ. of Bristol; Recognised Teacher of Ophthalmology, University of London. Co-opted Mem. Council Royal College of Surgeons, 1963-68. Mem. Bd of Govs: St Mary's Hosp., 1951-60; Moorfields Eye Hosp., 1962-65 and 1968. Mem. Paddington Group Hosp. Management Cttee, 1952-60. Vice-Pres. Ophthalmological Soc. of UK, 1963- (Sec. 1949-51); Member: Royal Soc. of Medicine (Sec. 1951, Ophthalmic Section, Vice-Pres., 1960); BMA (sec. 1948, Ophthalmic Section, Vice-Pres., 1957). Mem. Council, Faculty of Ophthalmologists, 1963-65, Vice-Pres. 1964, Pres. 1968; Dean, Inst. of Ophthalmology, 1967 (Deputy Dean, 1966-67). *Publications:* 12th Edn, May and Worth's Diseases of the Eye; articles in British Jl of Ophthalmology, the Lancet, and other med. jls, dealing with ophthalmology. *Recreations:* gardening, lawn tennis, golf, squash racquets. *Address:* 27 Harley Street, W1. *T:* 01-580 3614; 4 Cottenham Park Road, Wimbledon, SW20. *T:* 01-946 3491.

**CROSS, Prof. (Alfred) Rupert (Neale),** FBA 1967; Vinerian Professor in the University of Oxford since Oct. 1964; *b* 15 June 1912; *s* of Arthur George Cross and Mary Elizabeth (*née* Dalton); *m* 1937, Aline Heather Chadwick; no *c. Educ:* Worcester Coll. for the Blind; Worcester Coll., Oxford. DCL 1958. Solicitor, 1939. Tutor, Law Soc., 1945-48; Fellow of Magdalen Coll., Oxford, 1948-64; Visiting Prof., Univ. of Adelaide, 1962, and Sydney, 1968. *Publications:* Evidence (3rd edn), 1967; Precedent in English Law (2nd edn), 1968; (with P. Asterley Jones) Introduction to Criminal Law (6th edn), 1968; Cases in Criminal Law (4th edn); 1968; (with Nancy Wilkins) An Outline of the Law of Evidence (2nd edn), 1968; articles in Law Quarterly Review, Modern Law Review and Criminal Law Review. *Recreation:* chess. *Address:* All Souls College, Oxford. *T:* Oxford 49641.

**CROSS, Beverley;** playwright; *b* 13 April 1931; *s* of George Cross, theatrical manager, and Eileen Williams, actress; *m* 1st, 1955, Elizabeth Clunies-Ross (marr. diss.); two *d*; 2nd, 1965, Gayden Collins. *Educ:* Nautical Coll., Pangbourne; Balliol Coll., Oxford. Mem. Shakespeare Memorial Theatre Company, 1954-56; then began writing plays. One More River, Duke of York's, 1959; Strip the Willow, Arts, Cambridge, 1960; The Singing Dolphin, Oxford, 1960; The Three Cavaliers, Birmingham Rep., 1960; Belle, or The Ballad of Dr Crippen, Strand, 1961; Boeing-Boeing, Apollo, 1962; Wanted On Voyage, Marlowe, Canterbury, 1962; Half A Sixpence, Cambridge, London, 1963; Jorrocks, New, London, 1966. *Libretti:* The Mines of Sulphur, Sadler's Wells, 1965; All the King's Men, 1969; Victory, Covent Garden, 1970; The Rising of the Moon, Glyndebourne, 1970. *Screen plays of:* Jason and the Argonauts, 1962; The Long Ships, 1963; Genghis Khan, 1965; Half A Sixpence, 1966. *Television plays:* The Nightwalkers, 1960; The Dark Pits of War, 1960; Catherine Howard, 1969. Arts Council Drama Award, 1960. *Directed:* Boeing-Boeing, Sydney, 1964; The Platinum Cat, Wyndham's, 1965. *Publications:* Mars in Capricorn, 1955; The Nightwalkers, 1956; Plays For Children, 1960. *Recreations:* rough shooting, ocean racing. *Address:* c/o Curtis Brown Ltd, 13 King Street, WC2. *T:* 01-240 2488; Skiathos, Greece. *Clubs:* MCC, Greenroom; Royal Ocean Racing.

**CROSS, Clifford Thomas;** Commissioner (and Joint Secretary), Customs and Excise, since 1970; *b* 1 April 1920; *o s* of late Arthur and Helena Cross; *m* 1942, Ida Adelaide Barker; one *s* two *d. Educ:* Latymer Upper Sch., Hammersmith; Univ. of London (LLB). Joined Inland Revenue, 1939; Customs and Excise, 1946; Asst Sec. 1959; Comr 1970. *Recreations:* squash rackets, bonsai culture, watching television, etc. *Address:* Monkton Combe, 10 Drake Road, Westcliff-on-Sea, Essex. *T:* 01-626 1515.

**CROSS, Frederick Victor,** CMG 1949; Assistant Secretary, Ministry of Transport, since 1949; Director, Sitmar Line (London) Ltd; Navigation & Coal Trade Co. Ltd; Alva Steamship Co. Ltd; *b* 19 April 1907; *m* 1932, Gwendoline Horton; one *s* one *d*. *Educ:* RNC Greenwich. INA scholarship, 1927. Shipping Attaché, British Embassy, Washington, DC, 1946-49. *Address:* 21 Durham Avenue, Bromley, Kent.

**CROSS, Rt. Hon. Sir Geoffrey,** PC 1969; Kt 1960; **Rt. Hon. Lord Justice Cross;** a Lord Justice of Appeal since 1969; *b* 1 Dec. 1904; *e s* of late Arthur George Cross and Mary Elizabeth Dalton; *m* 1952, Joan, *d* of late Major Theodore Eardley Wilmot, DSO, and *widow* of Thomas Walton Davies; one *d*. *Educ:* Westminster; Trinity College, Cambridge. Craven Scholar, 1925. Fellow of Trinity College, 1927-31; called to the Bar, Middle Temple, 1930; QC 1949. Master of the Bench, Middle Temple, 1958. Chancellor of the County Palatine of Durham, 1959. A Judge of the Chancery Div. of the High Court of Justice, 1960-69. *Publications:* Epirus, 1932; (with G. R. Y. Radcliffe) The English Legal System (4th edn 1964). *Address:* 66 Oakwood Court, W14. *T:* 01-602 2131.

**CROSS, Hannah Margaret;** barrister-at-law; *b* 25 April 1908; *o d* of late F. J. K. Cross and Eleanor Mary Cross (*née* Phillimore); *m* 1936, Edmund Gordon Wright, barrister-at-law; one *s* one *d*. *Educ:* Downe House Sch.; St Hilda's Coll., Oxford. BA 1929. Called to Bar, Lincoln's Inn, 1931; first woman Mem. of Gen. Council of Bar, 1938-45; Civil Defence, 1939-45. *Address:* 9 Old Square, Lincoln's Inn, WC2. *T:* 01-405 4038; The Quay House, Sidlesham, near Chichester, Sussex. *T:* Sidlesham 258.

**CROSS, James Richard;** Senior British Trade Commissioner, Montreal, since 1968; *b* 29 Sept. 1921; *s* of J. P. Cross and Dinah Cross (*née* Hodgins); *m* 1945, Barbara Dagg; one *d*. *Educ:* King's Hosp., Dublin; Trin. Coll., Dublin. Scholar, First Cl. Moderatorship Economics and Polit. Science. RE (Lieut). Asst Principal, Bd of Trade, 1947; Private Sec. to Parly Sec., 1947-49; Principal, 1950; Trade Commissioner: New Delhi, 1953-56; Halifax, 1957-60; Winnipeg, 1960-62; Asst Sec., 1962; Sen. Trade Comr, Kuala Lumpur, 1962-66; Bd of Trade, 1966-67; Under Sec., 1968. *Recreations:* theatre, bridge, camping. *Address:* c/o FCO, King Charles Street, SW1; British Government Office, 635 Dorchester Boulevard West, Montreal 101, PQ, Canada. *Clubs:* Travellers'; St James's (Montreal).

**CROSS, Joan,** CBE 1951; opera singer; *b* Sept. 1900. *Educ:* St Paul's Girls' Sch. Principal soprano, Old Vic and Sadler's Wells, 1924-44; Dir of Opera, Sadler's Wells, 1941-44; subsequently Principal, National Sch. of Opera (Ltd), Morley Coll., London, resigned. *Address:* 2 Cavendish Avenue, NW8.

**CROSS, Air Chief Marshal Sir Kenneth (Brian Boyd),** KCB 1959 (CB 1954); CBE 1945; DSO 1943; DFC 1940; *b* 4 Oct. 1911; *s* of Pembroke H. C. Cross and Mrs Jean Cross; *m* 1945, Brenda Megan, *d* of Wing-Comdr F. J. B. Powell; two *s* one *d*. *Educ:* Kingswood Sch., Bath. Pilot Officer, RAF, 1930; Flying Badge, 1931; 25 Fighter Sqdn, 1931; Flying Officer, 1932; Flying Instructor, No 5 FTS Sealand and Cambridge Univ. Air Sqdn, 1934; Flt Lt 1935; Sqdn Ldr 1938; commanded No 46 Fighter Sqdn UK, Norway, 1939-40; Wing Comdr 1940; posted Middle East, 1941; Actg Group Capt. 1941; Actg Air Commodore, 1943; Director Overseas Operations, Air Ministry, 1944; Imperial Defence Coll., 1946; reverted Group Capt., 1946; Group Capt. Operations HQ BAFO Germany, 1947; OC Eastern Sector Fighter Command, 1949; Dir of Weapons, Air Ministry, 1952; subs. Air Cdre, 1953; Dir of Ops, Air Defence, 1954-Dec. 1955; Air Vice-Marshal, 1956; AOC No 3 (Bomber) Group, 1956-59; Air Marshal, 1961; AOC-in-C, Bomber Comd, 1959-63; Air Chief Marshal, 1965; AOC-in-C, Transport Comd, 1963-66, retd. Dir Suffolk Branch, British Red Cross Soc., 1968. Norwegian War Cross, 1941; USA Legion of Merit, 1944; French Legion of Honour, 1944; French Croix de Guerre, 1944; Dutch Order of Orange Nassau, 1945. *Recreations:* Rugby football and golf (colours RAF). *Clubs:* Royal Air Force, Army and Navy.

**CROSS, Prof. Kenneth William,** MB, DSc, FRCP; Professor of Physiology, London Hospital Medical College since 1960; Hon. Physiologist to The London Hospital; *b* 26 March 1916; *s* of late George Cross, Ealing; *m* 1942, Joyce M. Wilson (*née* Lack, *d* 1970); one step *d*; *m* 1970, Dr Sheila R. Lewis. *Educ:* St Paul's Sch.; St Mary's Hospital Medical Sch. Qualified, 1940; House appointments in St Mary's Hospital Sector; graded Physician EMS Amersham Emergency Hosp. 1945; Friends' Ambulance Unit, China, 1946-47. Lecturer in Physiology, 1947, Reader, 1952, St Mary's Hosp. *Publications:* contrib. to Journal of Physiology. *Recreation:* sailing. *Address:* London Hospital Medical College, Turner Street, E1.

**CROSS, Rev. Leslie Basil,** MA Oxon; Fellow, 1927-47, formerly Chaplain, Tutor and Junior Bursar of Jesus College, Oxford, Fellow Emeritus, 1960; *b* 18 April 1895; *s* of John James Cross, formerly Rector of Revesby, Lincs, and Mary Emma Aspden; *m* 1927, Gertrude, 4th *d* of Walter Savill, Finches, Lindfield, Sussex. *Educ:* Trent Coll.; Keble Coll., Oxford; Wycliffe Hall, Oxford. Asst Master, Lake House Preparatory Sch., Bexhill-on-Sea, 1916-17; Housemaster, Stamford Grammar Sch., 1918-19; Headmaster, Trent Coll. Preparatory Sch., 1922-23; Chaplain and Lecturer in Theology, Jesus Coll., Oxford, 1923-26; Lecturer in Theology, to St Peters Hall, Oxford, 1928-33; Examining Chaplain to Archbishop of York, 1925-28; Examining Chaplain to Bishop of Manchester, 1929-39; and Truro, 1935-54; Vice-Principal, Ripon Hall, Oxford, 1933-54; Select Preacher, Oxford, 1935 and 1937; Proctor for University of Oxford in Convocation of Canterbury, 1936; Public Examiner in Final Honour Sch. of Theology, 1937-39; Estates Bursar, Jesus Coll., 1941-43, Senior Tutor, 1945-47; Junior Proctor, Oxford Univ., 1943-44. *Publications:* Essay in The Atonement in History and in Life; articles in The Modern Churchman, etc, and pamphlets. *Recreations:* fishing, shooting, gardening. *Address:* 27 Linton Road, Oxford.

**CROSS, Brigadier Lionel Lesley,** CBE 1950; Secretary of the Commonwealth Press Union, 1959-70; *b* 7 June 1899; *yr s* of Charles Frederick Cross, FRS, and Edith, *d* of Maj.-Gen. Charles Stainforth, CB; *m* 1940, Rose Blanche Margaret, *d* of Sir Robert Taylor, Kytes, Herts; no *c*. *Educ:* Wellington Coll.; RMA Woolwich. Commissioned RFA, 1918; France and Belgium, 1918. Adjutant Bucks and Berks Yeo. Artillery, 1925-29; retd 1929. Rejoined Army, 1939; Staff Capt. RA 1939; France and Belgium, 1940; Major 1941; Lieut-

Col 1942; Asst Dir of Public Relations, War Office, 1942-46; Brig. 1946; Dep. Dir of Public Relations, War Office, 1946-50; Chief of Public Information, SHAPE, 1954-58 (Dep., 1951-54); retired, 1958. *Recreations:* racing, bridge. *Addresss:* 15 Cedar House, Marloes Road, W8. *T:* 01-937 0112. *Club:* Army and Navy.

**CROSS, Prof. Robert Craigie,** MA Glasgow, MA Oxford; Regius Professor of Logic, University of Aberdeen, since 1953; *b* 24 April 1911; *s* of Matthew Cross and Margaret Dickson; *m* 1943, Peggy Catherine Elizabeth Vernon; two *d.* *Educ:* Glasgow Univ.; Queen's Coll., Oxford. MA 1st Cl. Hons Classics, Glasgow, 1932; 1st Cl. Hons Classical Mods, Oxford, 1934; 1st Cl. Lit. Hum., Oxford, 1936. Fellow and Tutor in Philsophy, Jesus Coll., Oxford, 1938; served War, 1941-45, Navy and Admiralty; Senior Tutor, Jesus Coll., Oxford, 1948-53. Trustee, Scottish Hospital Endowments Research Trust, 1968-; Mem., University Grants Cttee, 1965-; Mem., North Eastern Regional Hospital Bd, 1958-65. *Publications:* (with A. D. Woozley) Plato's Republic: A Philosophical Commentary, 1964; contributions to learned jls. *Address:* 14 Westfield Terrace, Aberdeen. *T:* 22470. *Club:* United University.

**CROSS, Rupert;** *see* Cross, A. R. N.

**CROSSE, Rev. Frank Parker;** Rector of Upton Magna, Shrewsbury, 1960-67; *b* 24 Oct. 1897; *s* of Edmund Francis Crosse and Margaret Laldlaw Selby; *m* 1925, Isabel McIver McIntyre; two *d.* *Educ:* St Bees; RMC Sandhurst. Commissioned Regular Army, South Staffs Regt, 1916 (MC). Priest 1924; Vicar, Christ Church, Derry Hill, Wilts, 1926; Private Chaplain to Marquess of Lansdowne, 1927; Vicar, St Aldhelm's, Branksome, Bournemouth, 1931; Dean and Archdeacon of Grahamstown, 1934-44; Rector of Barlborough, 1944-51; Rector of Morton, Derby, 1951-60; Custos, Denstone Coll., 1955; Canon of Derby Cathedral, 1956-60. Vice-Provost and Senior Chaplain (Midland Div.) Woodard Schs, 1962. *Publication:* Intercessions in Time of War, 1939. *Address:* 24 Preston Trust Homes, Preston, Telford, Salop. *T:* Kinneasley 669.

**CROSSE, Gordon;** composer; Music Fellow, University of Essex, since 1969; *b* 1 Dec. 1937; *s* of Percy and Marie Crosse; *m* 1965, Elizabeth Bunch. *Educ:* Cheadle Hulme Sch.; St Edmund Hall, Oxford; Accad. di S Cecilia, Rome. Three Operas: Purgatory, 1966; The Grace of Todd, 1967; The Story of Vasco, 1970. Concerto da Camera, 1962; Meet My Folks, 1963; "Symphonies" I, 1964; Second Violin Concerto, 1970; much other orchestral, vocal and chamber music. *Address:* Brant's Cottage, Wenhaston, Halesworth, Suffolk. *T:* Blythburgh 354.

**CROSSLAND, Prof. Bernard,** MSc (London); PhD (Bristol); DSc; FIMechE; FIProdE; Professor and Head of Department of Mechanical Engineering, The Queen's University, Belfast, since 1959; *b* 20 Oct. 1923; *s* of R. F. Crossland and K. M. Rudduck; *m* 1946, Audrey Elliott Birks; two *d.* *Educ:* Simon Langton's, Canterbury. Apprentice, Rolls Royce Ltd, 1940-41; Nottingham Univ., 1941-43; Technical Asst, Rolls Royce, 1943-45; Asst Lectr, Lectr and then Senior Lectr in Mechanical Engineering, Univ. of Bristol, 1946-59. George Stephenson and Thomas Hawksley Medals, IMechE. *Publications:* An Introduction to the Mechanics of Machines, 1964; various papers on fatigue of metals and effect of very high fluid pressures on properties of materials; strength of thick-walled vessels, explosive welding, friction welding, and design. *Recreations:* sailing, walking. *Address:* The Queen's University, Belfast BT7 1NN. *T:* Belfast 45133.

**CROSSLAND, Sir Leonard,** Kt 1969; Chairman, Ford Motor Co. Ltd, since 1968; *b* 2 March 1914; *s* of Joseph and Frances Crossland; *m* 1st, 1941, Rhona Marjorie Griffin; two *d*; 2nd, 1963, Joan Brewer. *Educ:* Penistone Grammar Sch. Purchase Dept, Ford Motor Co. Ltd, 1937-39. Royal Army Service Corps, 1939-45. Ford Motor Co. Ltd: Purchase Dept, 1945-50; Chief Buyer, Tractor and Implement Dept, 1950-57; Chief Buyer, Car and Truck Dept, 1957-59; Asst Purchase Manager, 1959-60; Purchase Manager, 1960-62; Exec. Dir, Supply and Services, 1962-66; Dir, Manufacturing Staff and Services, 1966; Asst Man. Dir, 1966-67; Man. Dir, 1967; Dep. Chm., 1967. *Recreations:* shooting, fishing, golf. *Address:* Rivenhall Old Rectory, Witham, Essex. *T:* Witham 2116. *Clubs:* City Livery, Royal Automobile.

**CROSSLAND, Prof. Ronald Arthur;** Professor of Greek, University of Sheffield, since 1958; *b* 31 Aug. 1920; *s* of Ralph Crossland, BSc, and Ethel Crossland (*née* Scattergood). *Educ:* Stanley Road Elementary Sch., Nottingham; Nottingham High Sch.; King's Coll., Cambridge. Major Scholar in Classics, King's Coll., Cambridge, 1939-41 and 1945-46. National Service in Royal Artillery, 1941-45. Henry Fellow, Berkeley Coll., Yale Univ., 1946-47; Instructor in Classics, Yale Univ., 1947-48; Senior Student of Treasury Cttee for Studentships in Foreign Languages and Cultures (for research in Hittite Philology and Linguistics), 1948-51; Hon. Lectr in Ancient History, University of Birmingham, 1950-51; Lecturer in Ancient History, King's Coll., University of Durham, Newcastle upon Tyne, 1951-58. Harris Fellow of King's Coll., Cambridge, 1952-56. Vis. Prof., Univ. Texas, 1962; Collitz Vis. Prof., Univ. Michigan, 1967. *Publications:* chapter, Immigrants from the North, in Cambridge Ancient History, rev. edn, 1967; articles in Trans Philological Soc., Archivum Linguisticum, Past and Present. *Recreations:* music, travel. *Address:* 6 Causeway Head Road, Dore, Sheffield S17 3DT. *T:* Sheffield 368182, 78555.

**CROSSLEY,** family name of **Baron Somerleyton.**

**CROSSLEY, Sir Christopher John,** 3rd Bt *cr* 1909; Lieutenant-Commander Royal Navy, retired; *b* 25 Sept. 1931; *s* of late Lt-Comdr Nigel Crossley, RN (*s* of late Eric Crossley, OBE, 2nd *s* of 1st Bt); *S* great uncle (Sir Kenneth Crossley, 2nd Bt), 1957; *m* 1959, Carolyne Louise (marr. diss. 1969), *d* of late L. Grey Sykes; two *s.* *Educ:* Canford Sch. Entered Royal Navy, 1950. *Recreations:* royal tennis, squash. *Heir:* *s* Nicholas John Crossley, *b* 10 Dec. 1962.

**CROSSLEY, Prof. Eric Lomax;** Professor of Dairying, University of Reading, 1947-68, now Professor Emeritus; *b* 15 Sept. 1903; British; *m* 1933, Janet Hircombe Sutton; one *s.* *Educ:* Nottingham High Sch.; High Pavement Sch., Nottingham; University Coll., Nottingham. Research work bacteriology and biochemistry at University Coll., Nottingham and Nat. Inst. for Research in Dairying, Shinfield, Reading, 1923-25; Advisory Dairy Bacteriologist, Min. of Agriculture, at Harper Adams Agricultural Coll., Newport, Salop, 1925-29; Chief scientific and technical adviser, dir of laboratories, Aplin & Barrett Ltd, Yeovil, Som and associated Cos, 1929-47. Has been engaged in scientific investigation (particularly bacteriology) of milk processing and manufacture of dairy and other food products. Part-time Consultant, FAO. President: Soc. Dairy Technology, 1953-54; Internat. Commn for Dried and Condensed Milks, 1960-65; Inst. of Food Science and Technology, 1967-69. *Publications:* The United Kingdom Dairy Industry; original papers in scientific journals. *Recreations:* entomology and music. *Address:* Cliffdene, Shooters Hill, Pangbourne, Berks. *T:* Pangbourne 2967.

**CROSSLEY, Geoffrey Allan;** Counsellor, HM Embassy, Oslo, since 1969; *b* 11 Nov. 1920; *s* of Thomas Crossley and Winifred Mary Crossley (*née* Ellis); *m* 1925, Aline Louise Farcy; two *s* one *d. Educ:* Penistone; abroad; Gonville and Caius Coll., Cambridge. Served War of 1939-45: Min. of Supply, 1941-; Foreign Office, 1942-; in Algeria and France. Foreign Service, 1945-: Second Sec., Paris, 1945-48; FO, 1948-49; Alternate UK Deleg. on UN Balkans Commn, Greece, 1949-52; Dep. Regional Inf. Officer with Commissioner-Gen. for SE Asia, Singapore, 1952-55; FO, 1955-57; Consulate-Gen., Frankfurt, for Saar Transition from France to Germany, 1957-59; Political Office, NE Command, Cyprus (later in charge), 1959-61; Head of Chancery, Berne, 1961-65; on secondment to Min. of Overseas Development, as Head of W and N African Dept, 1965-67; Dep. High Comr, Lusaka, 1967-69. *Recreations:* tennis, squash, ski-ing, swimming, water-skiing, hacking, painting, music. *Address:* c/o Foreign and Commonwealth Office, SW1.

**CROSSLEY, Sir Julian (Stanley),** Kt 1964; Director, Barclays Bank Ltd, Barclays Bank DCO (Chairman, 1947-64); Chairman, Dominion Students' Hall Trust; Governor (Vice-President, 1960-66), Wellington College; Governor, Queen Elizabeth House; Vice-President, Commonwealth Institute; Hon. Treasurer, The Pilgrims Society of Great Britain; *b* 3 Jan. 1899; *s* of Charles Wheatley Crossley, Longfield, Triangle, Halifax, and Caroline Smedley Marsden-Smedley; *m* 1928, Barbara Mary, *d* of Frederick Craufurd Goodenough; three *s* one *d. Educ:* Wellington Coll.; New Coll., Oxford. Midshipman RN, 1917-19. Entered service of Barclays Bank Ltd, 1921. *Address:* Severals, Alresford, Hants. *Clubs:* Brooks's; Royal Yacht Squadron.

**CROSSLEY, Wing-Comdr Michael Nicholson,** DSO 1940; OBE 1946; DFC; Fighter Command; farming in South Africa since 1955; *b* 29 May 1912; *s* of late Major E. Crossley, OBE; *m* 1957, Sylvia Heyder; one *s* two *d. Educ:* Eton Coll.; Munich. Commissioned in RAF, 1935. *Recreations:* golf, tennis, squash, ski-ing. *Address:* Loughrigg, White River, E Transvaal, S Africa. *Clubs:* United Hunts; Rand (Johannesburg).

**CROSSMAN, Douglas Peter,** TD 1944; DL; Director, Huntingdon Steeplechases Ltd; *b* 25 Sept. 1908; *s* of late Percy Crossman, Gt Bromley Hall, Colchester; *m* 1st, 1932, Monica, *d* of late C. F. R. Barnett; two *s* one *d*; 2nd, 1939, Jean Margaret, *d* of late Douglas Crossman, Cokenach, Royston. *Educ:* Uppingham; Pembroke Coll., Cambridge. Commission Warwicks Yeomanry, 1934-45. Chairman: Mann Crossman Paulin Ltd, 1961-65; Watney Mann Ltd, 1965-70. President: Licensed Victuallers' Sch., 1958; Shire Horse Soc., 1958; Beer and Wine Trade Benev., 1960; Licensed Victuallers' Nat. Homes, 1963; Hunts Agricultural Soc., 1965; Chairman: Govs, Dame Alice Owen's Sch., 1951-65; Hunts Conservative Assoc., 1954-61; Eastern Area, Nat. Union of Conservative Party, 1965; Nat. Union of Conservative Party, 1969. Master, Brewers' Co., 1950. Chairman, Brewers' Soc., 1968, 1969. DL Huntingdonshire, 1958. Master: Essex and Suffolk Foxhounds, 1938-40; Cambridgeshire Foxhounds, 1947-49. *Recreations:* hunting, shooting, fishing, gardening. *Address:* Tetworth Hall, Sandy, Beds. *T:* Gamlingay 212. *Clubs:* Carlton, Cavalry.

**CROSSMAN, Rt. Hon. Richard (Howard Stafford),** PC 1964; OBE 1945; MA; MP (Lab) Coventry East since 1945; Editor of the New Statesman since 1970; *b* 15 Dec. 1907; *s* of late Mr Justice Crossman and late Helen Howard; *m* 1954, Anne Patricia, *d* of late A. P. McDougall; one *s* one *d. Educ:* Winchester (Schol.); New Coll., Oxford (Scholar, first in Mods and first in Greats). Fellow and Tutor of New Coll., Oxford, 1930-37; Asst Editor, New Statesman and Nation, 1938-55; Lecturer for Oxford Univ. Delegacy for Extra Mural Studies, and Workers' Educational Assoc., 1938-40; Leader of Labour group on Oxford City Council, 1934-40. Dep. Dir Psychological Warfare, AFHQ Algiers, 1943; Asst Chief Psychological Warfare Div. SHAEF, 1944-45; Mem. Anglo-American Palestine Commn, 1946; Mem. Malta Round Table Conf., 1955; Mem. Labour Party Exec., 1952-67; Chm. working party on Nat. Superannuation, 1956; on Science, 1963. Minister of Housing and Local Government, 1964-66; Leader of the House, and Lord President of the Council, 1966-68; Secretary of State for Social Services, i/c Dept of Health and Social Security, 1968-70. *Publications:* Plato Today, 1937; Socrates, 1938; Government and the Governed, 1939; How we are Governed, 1939; Palestine Mission, 1947; (editor) The God that Failed, 1950; (editor and contributor) New Fabian Essays, 1952; The Charm of Politics, 1958; A Nation Reborn, 1960; Planning for Freedom, 1965. *Address:* 9 Vincent Square, SW1. *T:* 01-834 6414; Prescote Manor, Banbury, Oxon. *Clubs:* Athenæum, Farmers'.

**CROSTHWAIT, Timothy Leland,** CMG 1964; MBE 1944; British Ambassador to the Malagasy Republic, since 1970; *b* 5 Aug. 1915; *s* of Lt-Col L. G. Crosthwait, Survey of India; *m* 1959, Anne Marjorie, *d* of Col T. M. M. Penney. *Educ:* Wellington Coll.; Peterhouse, Cambridge (MA). Appointed to Indian Civil Service, 1937; Asst Private Sec. to Viceroy, 1942-44; Air Min., 1948-55; Commonwealth Relations Office, 1955; British Deputy High Commissioner in Ceylon, 1957-61; Asst Sec., CRO, 1961-63; British High Commissioner, Zanzibar, 1963-64; British Deputy High Commissioner, Malta, 1965-66; British High Commissioner, Guyana, 1966-67; FCO, 1967-70. *Address:* c/o Foreign and Commonwealth Office, SW1.

**CROSTHWAITE, Sir Bertram Maitland,** Kt 1935; VD; *b* 9 Oct. 1880; *s* of late Rev. Samuel Maitland Crosthwaite and late Kate Bennett Colnett; *m* 1921, Nora Marsden, *d* of late Charles Earnest Higgin; one *s* one *d.* Joined Burma Railways Co. Ltd as Asst Traffic Supt, 1898; District Traffic Supt, 1905; Traffic Manager, 1924; commanded Burma Railways Bn (Indian Defence Force) with rank of Lt-Col; Hon. ADC to Viceroy; Mem. Railway Board (India), 1927; transferred to Indian State Railway Service, 1929; General Manager, Burma Railways, 1932; retired, 1935. *Address:* Kirkham Court, Denton Road, Eastbourne. *T:* Eastbourne 23363.

**CROSTHWAITE, Sir Moore;** *see* Crosthwaite, Sir P. M.

**CROSTHWAITE, Sir (Ponsonby) Moore,** KCMG 1960 (CMG 1951); *b* 13 Aug. 1907; *o s* of late P. M. Crosthwaite, MICE, and late Agnes Alice, *y d* of J. H. Aitken, Falkirk, Stirlingshire. *Educ:* Rugby; CCC, Oxford. Laming Fellowship, Queen's Coll., 1931. Entered Diplomatic Service, 1932; has served in Bagdad, Moscow, Madrid, Athens and Foreign Office; Deputy UK Representative to United Nations, New York, 1952-58; Ambassador to the Lebanon, 1958-63; Ambassador to Sweden, 1963-66. *Recreations:* travel, the arts. *Address:* 17 Crescent Grove, SW4. *Club:* Athenæum.

**CROSTHWAITE-EYRE, Sir Oliver (Eyre),** Kt 1961; DL; Verderer of New Forest since 1945; Chairman: Eyre & Spottiswoode Ltd; Associated Book Publishers Ltd; *b* 14 Oct. 1913; *e s* of Major J. S. Crosthwaite-Eyre and Dorothy Muriel Eyre; *m* 1939, Maria Alexandra Puthon; two *s* three *d. Educ:* Downside; Trinity Coll., Cambridge. Served War of 1939; enlisted private, 1940; commissioned, April 1940; served Norway, Middle East, and NW Europe (despatches). MP (C) New Forest Div. of Hants, 1950-68 (New Forest and Christchurch Div., 1945-50). DL Southampton, 1954. *Address:* 114 Roebuck House, Palace Street, SW1. *T:* 01-828 4080; Warrens, Bramshaw, Lyndhurst, Hants. *T:* Cadman 2247. *Clubs:* Carlton, Boodle's.

**CROUCH, David (Lance);** MP (C) Canterbury since 1966; Director: David Crouch & Co. Ltd; Noble and Samson Ltd; Pfizer Ltd; *b* 23 June 1919; *s* of Stanley Crouch and Rosalie Kate Crouch (*née* Croom); *m* 1947, Margaret Maplesden, *d* of Major Sydney Maplesden Noakes, DSO and Norah Parkyns Maplesden Noakes (*née* Buckland), Shorne, Kent; one *s* one *d. Educ:* University Coll. Sch. Served in City of London Yeomanry (TA), 1938-39; served War of 1939-45, Royal Artillery: Major 1943; attached RAF Staff (GSO2), 1944-45. Joined British Nylon Spinners Ltd, 1946; ICI Ltd, 1950; Dir of Publicity, Internat. Wool Secretariat, 1962-64. Formed own co., David Crouch & Co. Ltd, as international marketing and public relations consultants (Chairman); Mem., Inst. of Marketing and Sales Management. Contested (C) West Leeds, 1959. *Recreations:* cricket, tennis, golf. *Address:* Barton Manor, Westmarsh, near Canterbury, Kent. *Clubs:* Carlton, Arts, MCC.

**CROUSAZ, Engineer Rear-Adm. Augustus George,** CB 1937; *b* 13 April 1884; *s* of William de Prelaz Crousaz, Guernsey; *m* 1911, Dorothy Constance Skerry; one *d. Educ:* Elizabeth Coll., Guernsey. Royal Navy; Asst Engineer-in-Chief of the Fleet, 1932-36; retired list, 1939; Deputy Engineer-in-Chief of the Fleet, 1936-39. *Recreation:* tennis. *Address:* 33 Burgh Heath Road, Epsom, Surrey.

**CROUT, Dame Mabel,** DBE 1965; JP; Alderman, London Borough of Greenwich; *b* 6 Jan. 1890. Member of Woolwich Borough Council, 1919-64; Mem. of London Borough of Greenwich, 1964-. JP, London, 1920-. Mem. of London County Council, 1949-55. Freeman of Woolwich, 1959. *Address:* 112 Strongbow Crescent, Eltham, SE9. *T:* 01-850 3444.

**CROWDER, F(rederick) Petre,** QC 1964; MP (C) Ruislip-Northwood since 1950; Recorder of Colchester since 1967; Chairman, Hertfordshire Court of Quarter Sessions, since 1963 (Deputy Chairman, 1959-63); barrister-at-law; *b* 18 July 1919; *s* of late Sir John Ellenborough Crowder; *m* 1948, Hon. Patricia Stourton, *d* of 25th Baron Mowbray, MC (also 26th Baron Segrave and 22nd Baron Stourton); two *s. Educ:* Eton; Christ Church, Oxford. Served War of 1939-45; joined Coldstream Guards, 1939, and served in North Africa, Italy, Burma; attained rank of major. Contested North Tottenham, 1945. Called to the Bar, Inner Temple, 1948. South Eastern Circuit; North London Sessions. Recorder of Gravesend, 1960-67. PPS to Solicitor-Gen., 1952-54; PPS to Attorney General, 1954-62. *Address:* 2 Harcourt Buildings, Temple, EC4. *T:* 01-236 2112; (residence) 8 King's Bench Walk, Temple, EC4. *T:* 01-353 8101; Lodge Farm, Knebworth, Herts. *T:* Knebworth 3169. *Clubs:* Carlton, Pratt's, Turf.

**CROWE, Sir Colin Tradescant,** KCMG 1963 (CMG 1956); United Kingdom Permanent Representative to the United Nations, since 1970; *b* 7 Sept. 1913; *s* of late Sir Edward Crowe, KCMG; *m* 1938, Bettina Lum. *Educ:* Stowe Sch.; Oriel Coll., Oxford. Served at HM Embassy, Peking, 1936-38 and 1950-53; Shanghai, 1938-40; HM Embassy, Washington, 1940-45; Foreign Office, 1945-48, 1953-56; UK Delegn to OEEC, Paris, 1948-49; HM Legation, Tel Aviv, 1949-50; Imperial Defence Coll., 1957; Head, British Property Commn, Cairo, 1959; British Chargé d'Affaires, Cairo, 1959-61; Deputy UK Representative to the UN, New York, 1961-63; Ambassador to Saudi Arabia, 1963-64; Chief of Administration, HM Diplomatic Service, 1965-68; High Comr in Canada, 1968-70. Supernumerary Fellow, St Antony's Coll., Oxford, 1964-65. *Address:* c/o Foreign and Commonwealth Office, King Charles Street, SW1; Pigeon House, Bibury, Glos. *Club:* Travellers'.

**CROWE, Prof. Percy Robert,** BSc Econ. (London); PhD (Glasgow); MA (Manchester); Professor in Geography, University of Manchester, since 1953; a Pro-Vice-Chancellor since 1968; *b* 2 March 1904; *m* 1931, Margaret D. J. Robertson; two *s* one *d. Educ:* Henry Thornton Sch., Clapham, London; London Sch. of Economics and Political Science. Asst to Lecturer in Geography, Glasgow Univ., 1925-28; Commonwealth Fund Fellow, 1928-30; Lectr in Geography, Glasgow Univ., 1928-47; Technical Officer, Meteorological Office, 1939-41; Commission in RAF 1944-45; Reader in Geography, University of London, and Head of Geography Dept, Queen Mary Coll., 1947-53. *Publications:* Concepts in Climatology, 1970; articles in geographical and meteorological jls. *Recreations:* hill walking, chess. *Address:* 239 Bramhall Lane South, Bramhall, Cheshire. *T:* 061-439 1134.

**CROWE, Hon. Philip Kingsland,** Bronze Star (US Army) 1945; Ambassador of USA to Norway since 1969; *b* 7 Jan. 1908; *s* of Earle Rosman Crowe and Kathleen McMullin Higgins Crowe; *m* 1937, Irene Pettus; three *d. Educ:* St Paul's Sch., Concord; Univ. of Virginia. Reporter and Editor, New York Evening Post, 1929-32; Broker, Milmine Bodman & Co., NY, 1932-35; Explorer, French Indo-China, 1935-36; Life and Fortune, 1936-40; with USAF HQ, England, 1940-42; Chief, Secret Intell. Office of Strategic Services in India, Burma and China; Exec. Off., S China Comd of OSS; Special Rep. of Econ. Co-operation Mission to China, 1948-49; Rep. of USA to 10th Session of Econ. Commn (E Asia) of UN; US Deleg. to ECAFE Conf., 1954; Ambassador to Ceylon, 1953-57; Special Asst to Sec. of State, 1957-59; Ambassador to Union of S Africa, 1959-61; led expedns for wildlife conservation to 57 nations in Asia, Africa, S America, Australia, 1962-68. Director: World Wildlife Fund (Internat.); World Wildlife Fund (USA); African Wildlife Leadership Foundn; Amer. Cttee for Internat. Wildlife Protection; Trustee, Sch. of Advanced Internat. Studies of Johns Hopkins

Univ. FRGS; Life Member: Royal Asiatic Soc.; Ceylon Wildlife Protection Soc.; Member: Council on Foreign Relations (NY); Soc. of Cincinatti; Soc. of Colonial Wars; Huguenot Soc.; St Nicholas Soc. Officer, Legion of Honour (France), 1959; Yun Hui of Cloud and Banner, 1st cl. (Rep. of China), 1961; Mil. Order of Christ, 1st cl. (Portugal), 1960. *Publications:* Sport is Where You Find It, 1954; Diversions of a Diplomat in Ceylon, 1957; Sporting Journeys in Asia and Africa, 1966; The Empty Ark, 1968; World Wildlife: the last stand, 1970; Out of the Mainstream, 1970. *Recreations:* fishing, shooting, hunting. *Address:* American Embassy, Oslo, Norway. *T:* 56-68-80. *Clubs:* Boodle's, Flyfishers'; Brook, Century, Racquet and Tennis, Explorers, Anglers, Boone and Crocket (New York); Metropolitan, Dacor (Washington); Harvard Travellers (Boston); Chesapeake Bay Yacht (Easton, Md); Lakota, Round Table (Woodstock, Vt); Rand (Johannesburg); Hill (Ceylon); Norske Selskab (Oslo).

**CROWE, Sylvia,** CBE 1967; landscape architect in private practice since 1945; *b* 1901; *d* of Eyre Crowe; unmarried. *Educ:* Berkhamsted; Swanley Hort. Coll. Designed gardens, 1927-39. Served FANY and ATS, 1939-45. Since 1945, private practice as landscape architect has included: work as consultant to: Harlow and Basildon New Town Corporations; Imperial Coll., South Kensington; Central Electricity Generating Board, for Trawsfynydd and Wylfa Nuclear Power Stations; Forestry Commission; reclamation of land after 1952 floods and design of public gardens at Mablethorpe and Sutton on Sea; churchyard at St Mary's, Banbury; gardens for Oxford Univ., various Colls and Commonwealth Inst., London; Sec., Internat. Federation Landscape Architecture, 1948-59; Vice-Pres., 1964; Pres., Inst. Landscape Architects, 1957-59. Hon. FRIBA, 1969. *Publications:* Tomorrow's Landscape, 1956; Garden Design, 1958; The Landscape of Power, 1958; Landscape of Roads, 1960; Forestry in the Landscape, 1966. *Recreations:* walking and gardening. *Address:* 182 Gloucester Place, NW1. *T:* 01-723 9968.

**CROWLEY, Sir Brian Hurtle,** Kt 1969; MM; Chairman, Australian Jockey Club Committee, since 1962; *m* 1922, Dorothy, *d* of L. Sweet; one *s* two *d*. *Educ:* Scots College, Sydney. Served with Aust. Imperial Forces, 1916-19. *Address:* 3 Bedford Crescent, Collaroy, NSW 2097, Australia.

**CROWLEY, Rear-Adm. George Clement,** CB 1968; DSC 1942, and Bar 1944; Official Fellow and Bursar of Corpus Christi College, Oxford University, since 1969; *b* 9 June 1916; *s* of Charles Edmund Lucas Crowley and Beatrice Cicely Crowley; *m* 1948, Una Margaret Jelf; two *s*. *Educ:* Nautical Coll., Pangbourne. Cadet, HMS Frobisher, 1933; served in China and New Zealand, 1934-39; served War of 1939-45, destroyers; comdg HMS Walpole, 1943-45; comdg HMS Tenacious, 1945-46 (despatches); RN Staff Course, 1947; Staff appts, 1948-53; Exec. Off., HMS Newfoundland, 1953-55; Drafting Comdr, Chatham, 1955-57; Asst Dir Plans, 1957-59; Capt. (D) 7th Destroyer Sqdn, 1959-61; CO New Entry, Trng Estab. HMS Raleigh, 1961-63; Capt. of Fleet to Flag Off. C-in-C Far East Fleet, 1963-64; Staff of Jt Exercise Unison, 1964-65; Staff of Defence Operational Analysis Estab., W Byfleet, 1965-66; Director-General, Naval Personal Services, 1966-68. Capt. 1957; Rear-Adm. 1966. *Recreations:* fishing, tennis, gardening. *Address:* c/o Corpus Christi College, Oxford OX1 4JF. *T:* Oxford 49431. *Club:* Army and Navy.

**CROWLEY-MILLING, Air Vice-Marshal Denis,** CBE 1963; DSO 1943; DFC 1941, Bar 1942; Air Officer Commanding No 38 Group, RAF Odiham, since 1970; *b* 22 March 1919; *s* of T. W. and G. M. Crowley-Milling (*née* Chinnery); *m* 1943, Lorna Jean Jeboult (*née* Stuttard); two *d* (one *s* decd). *Educ:* Malvern Coll., Worcs. RAF Volunteer Reserve, 1937-39; served with Fighters and Fighter Bombers, Nos 615, 242, 610 and 181 Sqdns, 1939-44; Air Ministry Operational Requirements, 1945-47; OC No 6 Sqdn, Middle East, 1947-50; Personal Staff Officer C-in-C Fighter Comd, 1950-52; Wing Comdr Flying, RAF Odiham, 1952-54; Directing Staff, RAF Staff Coll., Bracknell, 1954-57; Flying Coll., RAF Manby, 1957-58; Plans Staff Fighter Comd, 1958-59; Group Capt. Operations Central Fighter Establishment, 1959-62; OC RAF Hong Kong, 1964-66; Dir Operational Requirements, MoD (Air), 1966-67; Comdr, RAF Staff and Principal Air Attaché, Washington, 1967-70. *Recreations:* golf and shooting. *Address:* c/o Barclays Bank Ltd, Colwyn Bay, Denbighshire. *Club:* Royal Air Force.

**CROWN, Mrs Leon;** *see* Vyvyan, Jennifer B.

**CROWTHER,** family name of **Baron Crowther.**

**CROWTHER,** Baron *cr* 1968 (Life Peer), of Headingley; **Geoffrey Crowther;** Kt 1957; Chairman: Commission on the Constitution, since 1969; Committee on Consumer Credit, since 1968; Chancellor, The Open University, since 1969; Chairman: The Economist Newspaper Ltd; Trust Houses Forte Ltd (lately Trust Houses Group Ltd); Director: Commercial Union Assurance Co. Ltd; Royal Bank of Canada; Member Governing Bodies: Charterhouse; London School of Economics; *b* 13 May 1907; *s* of late Charles Crowther; *m* 1932, Margaret, *d* of E. H. Worth, Claymont, Delaware, USA; two *s* three *d* (and one *d* decd). *Educ:* Leeds Grammar Sch.; Oundle Sch.; Clare Coll., Cambridge (MA; Hon. Fellow, 1958); Yale Univ.; Columbia Univ. Pres. of Cambridge Union, 1928; Commonwealth Fund Fellow, 1929-31. Joined staff of The Economist, 1932; Asst Ed., 1935; Ed., 1938-March 1956. Wartime service in Min. of Supply, 1940-41, Min. of Information, 1941-42, and as Dep. Head of Joint War Production Staff, Min. of Production, 1942-43. Chm., Central Advisory Council for Education (England), 1956-60. Hon. LLD Nottingham, 1951; Hon. DSc (Econ.), London, 1954; Hon. LLD: Swarthmore, 1957; Dartmouth, 1957; Michigan, 1960; Liverpool, 1961; Hon. LittD Leeds, 1970. *Publications:* An Introduction to the Study of Prices (with Sir W. T. Layton), 1935; Ways and Means, 1936; Economics for Democrats, 1939; Ways and Means of War, 1940; An Outline of Money, 1941. *Recreations:* places, music, and history. *Address:* 25 St James's Street, SW1. *T:* 01-839 5520; 51 Hyde Park Gate, SW7. *T:* 01-584 9497. *Clubs:* Brooks's; Links, Yale (New York).

**CROWTHER, Edward,** CBE 1951; Chairman, Northern Gas Board, 1949-62, retired; *b* 7 Oct. 1897; *er s* of John Henry Crowther, Wallasey, Ches; *m* 1927, Gwyneth Ethel, *er d* of R. T. Lewis, Stoke-on-Trent; one *d*. *Educ:* Wallasey Gram. Sch.; Liverpool Univ. (Master of Engineering). Various appts in gas industry; Gen. Manager, Chief Engineer and Dir of Newcastle upon Tyne and Gateshead Gas Co. immediately prior to nationalisation of gas industry; Pres., Institution of Gas Engineers, 1948-49. *Publications:* contributions to technical literature of gas industry. *Recreation:* golf. *Address:* 52 Beulah Road, Rhiwbina, Cardiff CF4 6LX. *T:* Cardiff 68234.

**CROWTHER, Eric (John Ronald);** Metropolitan Magistrate, since 1968; *b* 4 Aug. 1924; *s* of Stephen Charles Crowther, company secretary, and Olive Beatrix Crowther (*née* Selby); *m* 1959, Elkē Auguste Ottilie Winkelmann; one *s* one *d*. *Educ:* University College Sch., Hampstead. Royal Navy, 1943-47 (Medit. Area of Ops). Awarded Tancred Studentship in Common Law, 1948; Called to Bar, Lincoln's Inn, 1951; winner of Inns of Court Contest in Advocacy, 1951; Lecturer on English Life and Institutions for Brit. Council, 1952-69; Lecturer on Elocution and Advocacy for Council of Legal Educn, 1955-. Joined Inner Temple *ad eundem*, 1960. Practised at Criminal Bar, 1951-68. Member: SE Circuit; Surrey and S London Sessions; Mddx Sessions, Central Criminal Court. *Recreations:* travel, transport, the theatre, debating, student welfare. *Address:* 21 Old Buildings, Lincoln's Inn, WC2.

**CROWTHER, Francis Harold;** retired from Diplomatic Service, 1966; *b* Umtali, Southern Rhodesia, 25 May 1914; *s* of A. D. Crowther; *m* 1952, Mary Eleanor, *d* of F. G. Forman; two *d*. *Educ:* Plumtree Sch., Southern Rhodesia; Univ. of Cape Town; Christ Church, Oxford. Entered Consular Service, Japan, 1938; served in Japan, India, Ceylon, Singapore, Indochina, Korea, Foreign Office, Yugoslavia, Morocco, Mozambique and the Netherlands. *Address:* 59 Sloane Gardens, SW1.

**CROWTHER, Sir William (Edward Lodewyk Hamilton),** Kt 1964; CBE 1955; DSO 1919; VD; FRACP; medical practitioner; Past President of Medical Council of Tasmania; *b* 9 May 1887; *s* of Edward L. Crowther, MD; *m* Joyce Nevett Mitchell, Tunallock, NSW; one *s*. *Educ:* Ormond Coll.; University of Melbourne. Late CO 5th Field Ambulance AIF (despatches, wounded, DSO, 1914-15 star, two medals); Hon. Consulting Physician, Hobart General Hosp.; Consulting Physician, Queen Alexandra Hosp. Halford Oration, 1933; Archibald Watson Memorial Lecture, 1951; Roentgen Oration, 1953. *Publications:* series on the extinct Tasmanian race and on history of medicine in Tasmania, to scientific journals. *Recreations:* yachting, historical research. *Address:* 190 Macquarie Street, Hobart, Tas. *Club:* Tasmanian (Hobart).

**CROXTON-SMITH, Claude;** President, Institute of Chartered Accountants in England and Wales, June 1970-71; *b* 24 Aug. 1901; *m* 1928, Joan Norah Bloss Watling; two *d*. *Educ:* Dulwich Coll.; Gonville and Caius Coll., Cambridge. The Sales Staff, Anglo American Oil Co. Ltd, 1924-31; Articled Clerk, Inst. of Chartered Accountants in England and Wales, 1932-36; Chartered Accountant, 1936-39. Served War of 1939-45, RAOC (Major). Chartered Accountant in Public Practice (Bristol), 1946-. *Recreations:* walking, reading. *Address:* 18 Hughenden Road, Clifton, Bristol BS8 2TT. *T:* Bristol 34708. *Club:* Bristol (Bristol).

**CROYDON, Suffragan Bishop of,** since 1956; **Rt. Rev. John Taylor Hughes;** also Bishop to the Forces, since 1966; Archdeacon of Croydon since 1967; *b* 12 April 1908; *s* of Robert Edward and Annie Hughes. *Educ:* Castle Hill Sch., Ealing; Uxbridge County Sch.; Bede Coll., University of Durham. Ordained 1931; Asst Chaplain and Tutor, Bede Coll., Durham, 1931-34; Lecturer, Bede Coll., 1934-35; Curate, St John's, Shildon, Co. Durham, 1934-37; Vicar, St James, West Hartlepool, 1937-48; Canon Residentiary and Missioner of Southwark Cathedral, Warden of Diocesan Retreat House, Southwark, 1948-56. Pres., Norman Houses. *Recreations:* drama, golf, rowing. *Address:* 26 Birdhurst Rise, South Croydon, Surrey CR2 7ED. *T:* 01-688 6686.

**CROYDON, Archdeacon of;** *see* Croydon, Suffragan Bishop of.

**CROYSDALE, Sir James,** Kt 1953; *b* 15 June 1886; *s* of Charles Croysdale, worsted manufacturer, Leeds; *m* 1915, Jessie Gladys, *d* of Alfred Verity, Leeds; one *d*. *Educ:* Ilkley Grammar Sch. Admitted Solicitor, 1909; Pres. Leeds Law Soc., 1943. Leeds City Council, 1930-64; Leader, 1941-45 and 1951-53; Chm. Finance Cttee, 1941-45 and 1951-53; formerly Chm. of other cttees; Lord Mayor of Leeds, 1955-56; President: Leeds Conservative Assoc.; Northern Counties Chess Assoc., 1939-48; Mem. Bd of Management: Leeds Skyrac; Morley Trustees Savings Bank; Chm. Trustees, Leeds Children's Holiday Camp. *Address:* 39 Foxhill Court, Leeds LS16 5PN. *T:* Leeds 675101. *Club:* Leeds and County Conservative (President).

**CROZIER, Douglas James Smyth,** CMG 1957; Assistant Educational Adviser, Ministry of Overseas Development, 1963-68; Director of Education, Hong Kong, 1951-61; *b* 20 March 1908; *yr s* of late Thomas James Crozier, JP and Myra Elizabeth Crozier; *m* 1934, Ann Hobbs; one *s* one *d*. *Educ:* Portora Royal School; The Queen's Univ. of Belfast. Master, Education Dept, Hong Kong, 1931; POW in Japanese hands, 1941-45; Temp. Senior Inspector of Schools, 1949. MLC, Hong Kong, 1951; MEC, 1956-61. Governor, Hong Kong House, London; Vice-Pres., Asia Christian Colls Assoc. (Pres., N Ireland Branch). Mem., World Bank Economic Mission to Yemen Arab Republic, 1970. Hon. LLD: Hong Kong, 1961; Chinese Univ. of Hong Kong, 1969. *Recreations:* fishing and walking. *Address:* Rose Cottage, Tandragee, Co. Armagh. *T:* Tandragee 543. *Club:* Hong Kong (Hong Kong).

**CROZIER, Eric John;** writer and theatrical producer; *b* 14 Nov. 1914; *s* of John and Ethel Mary Crozier, London; *m* 1st, 1936, Margaret Johns (marriage dissolved, 1949); two *d*; 2nd, 1950, Nancy Evans. *Educ:* University Coll. Sch., London; Royal Academy of Dramatic Art; British Institute, Paris. Play producer for BBC Television Service, 1936-39. Produced plays and operas for Sadler's Wells Opera, Stratford-on-Avon Memorial Theatre, Glyndebourne Opera and other theatres, 1944-46. Closely associated with Benjamin Britten as producer or author of his operas, 1945-51, and was co-founder with him of The English Opera Group, 1947, and The Aldeburgh Festival of Music and the Arts, 1948. *Publications:* Christmas in the Market Place (adapted from French of Henri Ghéon), 1944; (with Benjamin Britten) Albert Herring, a comic opera in three acts, 1947, Saint Nicolas, a cantata, 1948, Let's Make an Opera, an entertainment for children, 1949; The Life and Legends of Saint Nicolas, 1949; Noah Gives Thanks, a play, 1950; (with E. M. Forster and Benjamin Britten) Billy Budd, an opera in four acts, 1951; Rab the Rhymer, a play with songs, 1953; (with Lennox Berkeley) Ruth, a lyrical opera, 1956; The Story of Let's Make an Opera, 1962; The Mastersingers of Nuremberg, 1963; The Magic Flute, 1963. *Recreation:* listening to music. *Address:* Church Field Cottage, Great Glemham, Saxmundham, Suffolk. *T:* Rendham 471.

**CRUDDAS, Maj.-Gen. Ralph Cyril,** CB 1953; DSO and Bar, 1943; retired; *b* 26 Aug. 1900; 2nd and *o surv. s* of late Rev. W. S. Cruddas and late Catharine, *d* of J. H. Peter-Hoblyn; *m* 1940, Edwina Marjorie Clare, 2nd *d* of Sir

Charles Hanson, 2nd Bt; three *d. Educ:* Cheltenham Coll.; Royal Military College, Sandhurst. 2nd Lieut DCLI, 1919; Private Sec. to the Governor of Assam, 1933-35; served War of 1939-45, in Middle East, Italy and NW Europe; commanded 7th Battalion Oxford and Bucks Light Infantry, 1941-43; commanded: Cyrenaica District, 1947-48; Tactical Wing Sch. of Infantry, 1948-49; 133 Infantry Brigade, 1949-51; GOC Land Forces, Hong Kong, 1951-54; retired 1955. *Address:* Springfield House, Nunney, near Frome, Somerset. *T:* Nunney 309. *Club:* United Service.

**CRUFT, John Herbert;** Music Director, Arts Council of Great Britain, since 1965; *b* 4 Jan. 1914; *er s* of Eugene and Winifred Cruft; *m* 1938, Mary Margaret Miriam, *e d* of late Rev. and of Mrs Pat McCormick; two *s. Educ:* Westminster Abbey Choir Sch.; Westminster Sch.; Royal College of Music (K. F. Boult Conducting Scholar). Oboist in BBC Television, London Philharmonic and Suisse Romande Orchestras, 1936-40. Served with Royal Corps of Signals, 1940-46. London Symphony Orchestra: Oboist, 1946-49; Sec., 1949-59; British Council: Dir of Music Dept, 1959-61; Dir of Drama and Music Dept, 1961-65. FRCM. *Address:* 7 Phene Street, Chelsea, SW3.

**CRUICKSHANK, Andrew John Maxton,** MBE 1945; actor; *b* 25 Dec. 1907; *m* 1939, Curigwen Lewis; one *s* two *d. Educ:* Aberdeen Grammar Sch. With Baynton Shakespearean Company, 1929; appeared in Richard of Bordeaux, New York, 1934; Mary Tudor, London Playhouse, 1935; Lysistrata, Gate, 1936; Macbeth, Old Vic, 1937 (Mem. of Old Vic Company, 1937-40). Served Royal Welch Fus., and GS, 1940-45. Spring 1600, Lyric, Hammersmith, 1945-46; The White Devil, Duchess, 1947; The Indifferent Shepherd, Criterion, 1949; Memorial Theatre, Stratford (Parts included Wolsey, Kent and Julius Caesar), 1950; St Joan, Cort Theatre, New York, 1951; Dial M for Murder, Westminster Theatre, 1952; Dead on Nine, Westminster, 1955; The House by the Lake, Duke of York's, 1956; Inherit The Wind, 1960; Look Homeward Angel, 1960; The Lady From the Sea, Queen's, 1961; The Master Builder, Ashcroft Theatre, Croydon, 1963; Alibi for a Judge, Savoy, 1965. Has appeared in many films, also in radio and on television. *Address:* 33 Carlisle Mansions, Carlisle Place, SW1. *Club:* Garrick.

**CRUICKSHANK, Herbert James,** CBE 1969; CEng, MIMechE; FIOB; FBIM; Joint Deputy Chairman, Bovis Holdings Ltd, since 1970 (Group Managing Director, 1966); Member, Metrication Board, since 1969; *b* 12 July 1912; *s* of late James William Cruickshank and of Dorothy Alicia Cruickshank; *m* 1939, Jean Alexandra Payne; no *c. Educ:* Charlton Central Sch.; Regent Street Polytechnic (Schol.). Bovis Ltd: Staff Trainee, 1931; Plant and Labour Controller, 1937; Dir, 1964; Gilbert-Ash Ltd: (formed within Bovis Gp), 1945; Director, 1949; Civil Engineering Works in Nyasaland, 1949-55; Managing Dir, UK, 1960-63; Chm. and Man. Dir, 1964. Director: National Building Agency; The Building Centre; Mem., NEDC on the Building Industry. Chm., National Consultative Council's Working Party on Metrication. *Recreations:* singing, photography, sketching. *Address:* 45 Bidborough Ridge, Tunbridge Wells, Kent. *T:* Tunbridge Wells 27270. *Clubs:* Oriental, MCC.

**CRUICKSHANK, Prof. John;** Professor of French, University of Sussex, since 1962; *b* Belfast, N Ireland, 18 July 1924; *s* of Arthur Cruickshank, parliamentary reporter, and Eva Cruickshank (*née* Shummacher); *m* 1949, Kathleen Mary Gutteridge; one *s. Educ:* Royal Belfast Academical Institution; Trinity Coll., Dublin. Awarded Mod. Lang. Sizarship, TCD, 1943; Cryptographer in Mil. Intell., 1943-45; 1st class Moderatorship in Mod. Langs (French and German) and 2nd class Moderatorship (Mental and Moral Science), TCD, 1948; Lecteur d'Anglais, Ecole Normale Supérieure, Paris, 1948-49; Asst Lectr in French and German, Univ. of Southampton, 1951; Sen. Lectr in French, Univ. of Southampton, 1961. Mem., UGC, 1970-. *Publications:* Albert Camus and the Literature of Revolt, 1959; Critical Readings in the Modern French Novel, 1961; The Novelist as Philosopher, 1962; Montherlant, 1964; (ed) French Literature and Its Background: vols 1-6, 1968-70; articles in: French Studies; Modern Language Review; Essays in Criticism; Chicago Review; Symposium; Letterature Moderne; London Magazine; Twentieth Century, etc. *Recreations:* painting in oils, watching football and cricket. *Address:* 29 Windermere Court, East Drive, Brighton 7. *T:* Brighton 682156.

**CRUICKSHANK, Flight-Lieut John Alexander,** VC 1944; late RAF; with National and Grindlay's Bank Ltd, London (Overseas Staff); *b* 20 May 1920; *s* of James C. Cruickshank, Aberdeen, and Alice Bow, Macduff, Banffshire; *m* 1955, Marian R. Beverley, Toronto, Canada. *Educ:* Aberdeen Grammar Sch.; Daniel Stewart's Coll., Edinburgh. Entered Commercial Bank of Scotland, 1938; returned to banking, 1946. Mem. of Territorial Army and called for service, Aug. 1939, in RA; transferred to RAF 1941 and commissioned in 1942; all RAF service was with Coastal Command. ADC to Lord High Commissioner to the Gen. Assembly of the Church of Scotland, 1946-48. *Address:* 40 St Clair Terrace, Edinburgh 10. *T:* 031-447 5323.

**CRUICKSHANK, Prof. Robert,** CBE 1966; MD (Aberdeen); FRCP; FRCPEd; DPH; FRSE; Professor of Preventive Medicine, University of the West Indies, Kingston, Jamaica, 1966-68; *b* Sept. 1899; *m* 1929, Margaret Petrie; one *s* one *d. Educ:* Univ. of Aberdeen. Anderson Travelling Fellowship, Univ. of Glasgow, 1922-24; Resident Med. Officer, Royal Hosp. for Sick Children, Glasgow, 1925, Belvidere Hosp. for Infectious Diseases, Glasgow, 1925-27; McRobert Lectr in Malignant Diseases, Univ. of Aberdeen, 1927-28; Lectr in Bacteriology, Univ. of Glasgow, and Bacteriologist to Glasgow Royal Infirmary, 1928-36; Pathologist in charge of LCC Group Laboratory, 1936-45; Dir, Central Public Health Laboratory of Public Health Laboratory Service, 1945-48; Prof. of Bacteriology in Univ. of London at St Mary's Hosp. Med. Sch., 1949-57, and Principal of Wright Fleming Inst. of Microbiology, 1955-57; Prof. of Bacteriology, Univ. of Edinburgh, 1958-66, now Emeritus; Prof. of Preventive Medicine, Univ. of West Indies, Kinston, Jamaica, 1966-68. Hon. LLD, Aberdeen, 1968. *Publications:* (ed.) Modern Trends in Immunology, 1963; (ed.) Medical Microbiology (11th edn), 1965; articles in med. jls embodying researches on the diagnosis and control of infectious diseases. *Recreation:* golf. *Address:* 17 Greenhill Gardens, Edinburgh 10. *Club:* Athenæum.

**CRUIKSHANK, John Merrill,** CMG 1951; OBE 1937; *b* 4 Sept. 1901; *s* of J. P. and J. E. Cruikshank (*née* Crombie); *m* 1930, Elaine Strong; one *s. Educ:* McGill Univ. (MD, CM, DPH). Colonial Medical Service; Surgeon,

Bahamas, 1928-30; Chief Medical Officer, Bahamas, 1930-40; DMS Bahamas Military Forces, 1939-41; RCAF, 1941-46; Asst Medical Adviser, Colonial Office, 1946-48; Insp.-Gen., S Pacific Health Service, and DMS, Fiji, 1948-56; WHO Area Representative for S Pacific, 1956-59. Subseq Dir, Medical Services, Belmont, Calif; retd. Certificate Tropical Medicine, London; Fellow: Amer. Coll. Surgeons; Amer. Coll. Physicians; Royal Sanitary Inst. OStJ 1950. *Publications:* articles in medical journals. *Recreation:* radio engineering. *Address:* 707 Royal Avenue, Calgary, Alberta, Canada. *T:* 262-6789. *Club:* Corona.

**CRUM, Maj.-Gen. Vernon Forbes E.**; *see* Erskine Crum.

**CRUMP, Maurice,** CBE 1959; Deputy Director of Public Prosecutions, 1958-66; *b* 13 Jan. 1908; *s* of William Hamilton Crump and Jean Morris Alan Crump (*née* Esplen); *m* 1946, Mary Arden, *d* of Austin Stead, Montreal, PQ, Canada. *Educ:* Harrow; Oxford. Called to Bar, 1931, practised Western Circuit. RAF Reserve, 1929-35; recommissioned RAF Volunteer Reserve, 1940; served War of 1939-45, as pilot, 1940-45; Capt. in Command on North Atlantic Return Ferry, 1944-45. In Dept of Dir of Public Prosecutions, 1945; Asst Dir, 1951-58. *Recreations:* flying, travelling. *Address:* Dorval, Punta de la Mona, Almuñecar, P. de Granada, Spain. *Clubs:* Oxford and Cambridge University, Royal Aero.

**CRUMP, Norris Roy,** ME, DEng, DCL, LLD, DSc; Chairman, Member Executive Committee and Director, Canadian Pacific Railway Company; Chairman and Chief Executive Officer, Canadian Pacific Investments Ltd; Chairman and Director, Canadian Pacific Securities Ltd; President and Director, Commandant Properties Ltd; Director: Bank of Montreal; Canadian Pacific Steamships Ltd; Mutual Life Assurance Co., Canada; Canadian Pacific Air Lines Ltd; Canadian Pacific (Bermuda) Ltd; International Nickel Co. of Canada; Midland Simcoe Elevator Co. Ltd (Vice-President); Canadian Fund Incorporated; Canadian Investment Fund, Ltd; Cominco Ltd; Soo Line Railroad Co.; Grand River Railway Co.; Lake Erie and Northern Railway Co.; Canadian Pacific de Mexico; MacMillan Bloedel, Ltd; Marathon Realty Co. Ltd; *b* Revelstoke, BC, 30 July 1904; *s* of Thomas Huntley Crump; *m* 1930, Stella Elvin; two *d*. *Educ:* public schs, Vancouver, BC; high schs, Revelstoke, BC; Purdue Univ., Lafayette (BSc, ME). Joined CPR Co., 1920; Vice-Pres. and Gen. Manager, Eastern Lines, 1947; Vice-Pres. E Region, 1947; Vice-Pres., Jurisdiction all lines, Montreal, 1948; Director, CPR, 1949; Vice-Pres. and Mem. Exec. Cttee, MTL, 1949; Pres. CPR Co., 1955, Chm. and Pres., 1961-64; Chm. and Chief Exec. Officer, 1964; Chm., 1969. Member: Canadian Chamber of Commerce; Internat. Chamber of Commerce (Dir Cdn Council); Canadian Exporters Assoc., Montreal (Mem. Bd of Govs); BoT, Montreal; BoT, Toronto; Amer. Assoc. of Railroad Superintendents; Engrg Inst. of Canada; Newcomen Soc. of England (in Canada); Professional Engineers of Quebec; Nat Industrial Conf. Bd, New York. Holds many hon. degrees. KStJ. *Recreations:* boating, handicrafts, gun-collecting. *Address:* 12 Kilburn Crescent, Montreal 254, Quebec, Canada. *T:* Hunter 6-2257; Windsor Station, Montreal 101, Quebec. *Clubs:* Canadian Railway, St James's, St-Denis, Canadian, Mount Royal, Mount Stephen (Montreal); Toronto Railway, York (Toronto); Rideau (Ottawa); Seigniory (Montebello); Royal St Lawrence yacht; Laval-sur-le-lac.

**CRUMP, Rt. Rev. William Henry Howes;** *see* Saskatchewan, Bishop of.

**CRUMP, William Maurice Esplen;** *see* Crump, Maurice.

**CRUSE, Rt. Rev. John Howard;** *see* Knaresborough, Bishop Suffragan of.

**CRUTCHLEY, Brooke,** CBE 1954; Printer of the University of Cambridge since 1946; Fellow of Trinity Hall; *b* 31 July 1907; *yr s* of late Ernest Tristram Crutchley, CB, CMG, CBE, and Anna, *d* of James Dunne; *m* 1936, Diana, *d* of late Lt-Col Arthur Egerton Cotton, DSO, and Beryl Marie (who *m* 2nd, John Lee Booker); two *s* one *d*. *Educ:* Shrewsbury; Trinity Hall, Cambridge. Editorial Staff of Yorkshire Post, 1929-30; Asst Univ. Printer at Cambridge, 1930-45; Secretary's Dept of the Admiralty, 1941-45. *Address:* 2 Courtyards, Little Shelford, Cambs. *T:* Shelford 2389. *Clubs:* Athenæum, Double Crown.

**CRUTCHLEY, Adm. Sir Victor Alexander Charles,** VC 1918; KCB 1946 (CB 1945); DSC 1918; RN retired; DL; *b* 2 Nov. 1893; *s* of late Percy Edward Crutchley and late Hon. Frederica Louisa, 2nd *d* of 3rd Baron Southampton; *m* 1930, Joan Elizabeth Loveday, *y d* of late William Coryton, Pentillie Castle, Cornwall, and late Mrs William Coryton; one *s* one *d*. *Educ:* Osborne and Dartmouth. Served European War in HMS Centurion, Battle of Jutland; in HMS Brilliant in attempt to block Ostend Harbour, 22-23 April 1918 (DSC); in HMS Vindictive in similar attempt, 9-10 May 1918 (VC, Croix de Guerre); commanded HMS Diomede, New Zealand; Senior Officer, First Minesweeping Flotilla, 1935-36; Capt. Fishery Protection and Minesweeping Flotilla, 1936-37; commanded HMS Warspite, 1937-40; Commodore RN Barracks, Devonport, 1940-42; commanded Australian Naval Squadron, 1942-44; Flag Officer Gibraltar, 1945-47; retired, 1947, as Adm. DL Dorset, 1957. Chief Comdr Legion of Merit (USA), 1944; Polonia Restituta, 1942. *Address:* Mappercombe Manor, Powerstock, Bridport, Dorset. *Club:* United Service.

*See also Sir William John Colfox, Bt.*

**CRUTE, Robert;** Town Clerk, Leeds, 1952-64; *b* 28 May 1907; 6th *s* of late Richard Rutter Crute, Solicitor, Sunderland, Co. Durham, and late Mary A. G. Crute; *m* 1936, Eleanor Haswell, *er d* of late William Moore and late Mary Moore, Newcastle upon Tyne; two *s*. *Educ:* Bede Collegiate Sch., Sunderland; Durham Univ. Asst Solicitor, County Borough of Sunderland, 1930-34; Chief Asst Solicitor, Sunderland, 1934-38; Dep. Town Clerk and Dep. Clerk of the Peace, Bolton, Lancs, 1938-47; Dep. Town Clerk, Leeds, 1947-52. Chm., Associate Sect., Soc. of Town Clerks, 1950-51. *Clubs:* Royal Over-Seas League; Leeds (Leeds).

**CRUTTWELL, Mrs Geraldine;** *see* McEwan, Geraldine.

**CRUTTWELL, Hugh (Percival);** Principal of Royal Academy of Dramatic Art since 1966; *b* 31 Oct. 1918; *s* of Clement Chadwick Cruttwell and Grace Fanny (*née* Robin); *m* 1953, Geraldine McEwan, *qv*; one *s* one *d*. *Educ:* King's Sch., Bruton; Hertford Coll., Oxford. *Address:* 93 Abingdon Road, W8. *T:* 01-937 9726.

**CRYMBLE, Percival Templeton**, MB, FRCS; Hon. FICS; Emeritus Professor of Surgery, Queen's University, Belfast, since 1948 (Professor of Surgery, 1933-48); late Examiner in Surgery, London University; *b* Belfast, 1880; *s* of George Crymble; *m* Norah Ireland; one *s* two *d*. *Educ:* Academical Institution, Belfast; Queen's Univ., Belfast. Post-Graduate study in London and Vienna; BEF France, 1915-16. *Publications:* Quain's Anatomy, Section on Peritoneum; Current Surgery; articles in medical journals. *Recreations:* golf, music. *Address:* 28 Golf Links Road, Newcastle, Co. Down. *T:* Newcastle 2443.

**CUBBON, Brian Crossland;** Controller (Administration), Prison Department, Home Office, since 1969; *b* 9 April 1928; *m* 1956, Elizabeth Lorin Richardson; three *s* one *d*. *Educ:* Bury Grammar Sch.; Trinity Coll., Cambridge. Entered Home Office, 1951; Private Sec. to Permanent Under Sec. of State, 1953-55; Cabinet Office, 1961-63; Private Sec. to Home Sec., 1968-69; Asst Under Sec. of State, 1969. *Address:* Brook Farm House, Capel, near Tonbridge, Kent. *T:* Paddock Wood 2534. *Club:* United University.

**CUBBON, Maj.-Gen. John Hamilton,** CB 1962; CBE 1958 (OBE 1940); DL; *b* 15 March 1911; *s* of Joseph Cubbon; *m* 1951, Amelia Margaret Yates; two *s* one *d*. *Educ:* St Bees Sch.; RMC Sandhurst. 2nd Lieut Ches Regt, 1931; Commanded: 1st Bn The Parachute Regt, 1946-49; 1st Bn The Ches Regt, 1951-54; 18th Infantry Bde, Malaya, 1956-57. Maj.-Gen. 1960; GOC SW Dist, 1960-63; GOC Land Forces, Middle East Command, 1963-65. DL Devon, 1969. *Recreation:* sailing. *Address:* Treetops, West Hill, Ottery St Mary, Devon.

**CUBITT,** family name of **Baron Ashcombe.**

**CUBITT, Hon. (Charles) Guy,** DSO 1943; TD; DL; *b* 13 Feb. 1903; 3rd *surv. s* of 2nd Baron Ashcombe, CB; *m* 1927, Rosamond Mary Edith, *d* of Sir Montagu Cholmeley, 4th Bt; one *s* two *d*. *Educ:* Eton; RMC Sandhurst. Partner, Cubitt and West; Chm., Cummins & Co. Lt-Col Surrey Yeomanry (despatches, DSO); Hon. Col Surrey Yeomanry, 1951. Formerly Chm., The Pony Club. High Sheriff of Surrey, 1955; Surrey County Council, 1955 (Alderman, 1965); DL Surrey, 1956. *Address:* High Barn, Effingham, Leatherhead, Surrey. *T:* Bookham 2632. *Club:* Cavalry.
*See also Baron Carew.*

**CUBITT, James William Archibald,** MBE 1945; FRIBA; architect; Senior Partner of James Cubitt and Partners, London, Nigeria, Burma, Malaya, since 1948; *b* 1 May 1914; *s* of James Edward and Isabel Margaret Cubitt; *m* 1st, 1939, Ann Margaret Tooth (marr. diss. 1947); one *s* one *d*; 2nd, 1950, Constance Anne (*née* Sitwell); one *s*. *Educ:* Harrow; Brasenose Coll., Oxford; Architectural Association Sch. of Architecture. BA Oxon 1935; ARIBA 1940; FRIBA 1955. Army, 1940-45. In private practice as architect from 1948. Main works in England: exhibition and shop design; schools for Herts CC, W Riding CC, LCC, Leeds Corporation. Has also designed many public buildings, schools, offices and private houses in Ghana; now works in Nigeria, Burma, Singapore, Brunei and Libya. Architect for the University of Libya and for Medical Centre, Malaya. Writes articles and reviews. Council of Architectural Assoc., 1960- (Pres., 1965-66). Sculpture: one-man show, John Whibley Gallery, March 1962; Burgos Gallery, New York, March 1966. *Address:* 25 Gloucester Place, W1. *T:* 01-935 0288.

**CUDLIPP, Hugh,** OBE 1945; Chairman: International Publishing Corporation Ltd, since 1968 (Deputy Chairman, 1964-68); International Publishing Corporation Newspaper Division, since 1970; Deputy Chairman (editorial), Reed International Board, since 1970; Director, Associated Television Ltd; *b* 28 Aug. 1913; *s* of William Cudlipp, Cardiff; *m* 2nd, 1945, Eileen Ascroft (*d* 1962); 3rd, 1963, Jodi, *d* of late John L. Hyland, Palm Beach, Fla, and Mrs D. W. Jones, Southport. *Educ:* Howard Gardens Sch., Cardiff. Provincial newspapers in Cardiff and Manchester, 1927-32; Features Ed., Sunday Chronicle, London, 1932-35; Features Ed., Daily Mirror, 1935-37; Ed., Sunday Pictorial, 1937-40. Military Service, 1940-46. Ed., Sunday Pictorial, 1946-49; Managing Ed., Sunday Express, 1950-52; Editorial Dir, Daily Mirror and Sunday Pictorial, 1952-63; Joint Managing Dir, Daily Mirror and Sunday Pictorial, 1959-63; Chm., Odhams Press Ltd, 1961-63; Chm., Daily Mirror Newspapers Ltd, 1963-68. *Publications:* Publish and be Damned!, 1955; At Your Peril, 1962. *Address:* Daily Mirror Newspapers Ltd, Holborn Circus, EC1.

**CUDLIPP, Reginald;** Director, Anglo-Japanese Economic Institute, London, since 1961; *b* Cardiff, 11 Dec. 1910; *s* of William Cudlipp, Cardiff; *m* 1945, Rachel Joyce Braham. *Educ:* Cardiff Technical Coll. Began journalistic career on Penarth News, Glamorgan; Sub-Ed., Western Mail, Cardiff; joined News of the World Sub-Editorial Staff, 1938; served War, 1940-46; rejoined News of the World and became Special Correspondent in USA, 1946-47; Features Ed., 1948-50, Dep. Ed., 1950-53, Ed., 1953-59; Dir, News of the World Ltd, 1955-60. Extensive industrial tours of Japan at invitation of Japanese Govt. Member: Japan Soc.; RCAS; RSA; RIIA. Ed. Japan (quarterly review and monthly survey), and special publications on Japanese industry. Lecturer and writer on Japan's economic and industrial progress; also first-hand study of developing nations and economic co-operation, especially in Africa and SE Asia. *Publications:* numerous contribs to newspapers and periodicals, on Japan and Anglo-Japanese affairs. *Recreations:* music, travel, and reading, writing and talking about Japan. *Address:* 342 Grand Buildings, Trafalgar Square, WC2. *T:* 01-930 5567.

**CUDMORE, Hon. Sir Collier Robert,** Kt 1958; Leader of Liberal and Country Party, Legislative Council, South Australia, 1944-59; barrister; *b* 13 June 1885; *s* of Daniel H. Cudmore, Wentworth, NSW, and Victor Harbour, S Australia; *m* 1922, Phyllis, *d* of Dr A. E. Wigg; one *s* one *d*. *Educ:* St Peter's Coll., Adelaide; Adelaide Univ.; Magdalen Coll., Oxford (BA). Called to bar, Inner Temple, 1910; practised as barrister and solicitor, Adelaide, 1912-55. Served European War, 1915-18, RFA, France (wounded twice); Bn Comdr Volunteer Defence Corps, 1940. Dir, Elder Smith & Co. Ltd; Local Dir, North British and Mercantile Insurance Co.; Mem. Council, University of Adelaide; a Governor of St Peter's Coll., Adelaide. *Recreations:* rowing (rowed Oxford VIII, 1908-09; won Olympic Fours, 1908); bowls. *Address:* 5 Acacia Street, Medindie, South Australia. *Clubs:* Adelaide (Adelaide); Vincent's (Oxford); Leander.

**CULHANE, Rosalind, (Lady Padmore),** MVO 1938; OBE 1949; Treasury Welfare Adviser, 1943-64; *y d* of late F. W. S. Culhane, MRCS, Hastings, Sussex; *m* 1964, Sir Thomas Padmore, *qv*. Joined Treasury in 1923 and attached to office of Chancellor of Exchequer; Asst Private Sec. to Mr Chamberlain, 1934, Sir

John Simon, 1937, Sir Kingsley Wood, 1940. *Address:* 39 Cholmeley Crescent, N6. *T:* 01-340 6587.

**CULLEN OF ASHBOURNE,** 2nd Baron *cr* 1920; **Charles Borlase Marsham Cokayne,** MBE 1945; Major, Royal Signals; *b* 6 Oct. 1912; *e s* of 1st Baron and Grace Margaret, *d* of Rev. Hon. John Marsham; *S* father, 1932; *m* 1942, Valerie Catherine Mary (marr. diss. 1947), *o d* of late W. H. Collbran; one *d*; *m* 1948, Patricia Mary, *er d* of late Col S. Clulow-Gray and late Mrs Clulow-Gray, Marsham Court, SW1. *Educ:* Eton. Served War of 1939-45 (MBE). Amateur Tennis Champion, 1947, 1952. *Heir: b* Hon. Edmund Willoughby Marsham Cokayne [*b* 18 May 1916; *m* 1943, Janet Manson, *d* of late William Douglas Watson and of Mrs Lauritson, Calgary]. *Address:* 75 Cadogan Gardens, SW3. *T:* 01-589 1981. *Clubs:* MCC, Queen's.

**CULLEN, Prof. Alexander,** OBE 1960; DSc(Eng), FIEE, FIEEE, FInstP, FCGI; Pender Professor of Electrical Engineering, University College, London, since 1967; *b* 20 April 1920; *s* of Richard and Jessie Cullen, Lincoln; *m* 1940, Margaret, *er d* of late Alexander Lamb, OBE; two *s* one *d*. *Educ:* Lincoln Sch.; City and Guilds Coll., London. Staff of Radio Dept, RAE Farnborough, working on development of radar, 1940-46; Lectr in Electrical Engineering, University Coll., London, 1946-55 (title of Reader conferred 1955); Prof. of Electrical Engineering, University of Sheffield, 1955-67. Kelvin premium of IEE, 1952; Extra premium of IEE, 1953 (with Prof. H. M. Barlow and Dr A. E. Karbowiak); Radio Sect. premium of IEE, 1954; Ambrose Fleming premium of IEE, 1956 (with J. C. Parr); Duddell premium of IEE, 1957 (with Dr H. A. French); Electronics and Communications Sect. premium of IEE, 1959. Member: Electronics Research Council, Min. of Technology; Station Cttee, Radio and Space Research Station (SRC); Engineering Advisory Cttee, BBC. *Publications:* Microwave Measurements (jointly with Prof. H. M. Barlow), 1950; a number of papers on electromagnetic waves and microwave measurement techniques in IEE proceedings and elsewhere. *Recreations:* music and reading. *Address:* Dept of Electronic and Electrical Engineering, University College, London, Torrington Place, WC1.

**CULLEN, Brian;** *see* Cullen, J. B.

**CULLEN, (James) Brian,** CBE 1964; *b* 2 Nov. 1905; *s* of late J. Bertram Cullen and Emily (*née* Shaw); *m* 1936, Kathleen, *d* of late Thomas Jones; two *s* one *d*. *Educ:* King William Coll., Isle of Man. Entered Civil Service, 1940; Principal, Ministry of Supply, 1941; Asst Sec., Ministry of Supply, 1951; transferred to Board of Trade, 1954; seconded to Foreign Office, 1957 (HM Diplomatic Service, 1965); British Commercial Counsellor, Stockholm, 1957, Washington, DC, 1960; retired, 1966. *Publications:* numerous contribs to fishing jls, etc. *Recreations:* fishing, bird-watching, cooking. *Address:* Thie Vane, Malew, Isle of Man.

**CULLEN, James Reynolds;** *b* 13 June 1900; *s* of Rev. James Harris Cullen, London Missionary Society; *m* 1931, Inez, *e d* of M. G. Zarifi, MBE; one *s* two *d*. *Educ:* Weimar Gymnasium; Tonbridge Sch.; Balliol Coll., Oxford (Scholar). Hertford Schol., 1919; Craven Schol., 1920; 1st class Hon. Mods, 1920; 2nd class Lit. Hum. 1922; MA 1925. Asst Master, Winchester Coll., 1922-30; archæological expeditions to Asia Minor, 1925, and Mytilene, 1930; Dir of Education, Cyprus, 1930-45; Dir of Education, Uganda, 1945-52; Asst Master, Oundle Sch., 1953-60, Cranbrook and Benenden Schs, 1960-68. *Address:* Weathercock House, Hawkhurst, Kent. *Club:* Royal Commonwealth Society.

**CULLEN, Raymond;** Chairman, The Calico Printers' Association Ltd and subsidiaries, 1964-68; *b* 27 May 1913; *s* of late John Norman Cullen and Bertha (*née* Dearden); *m* 1940, Doris, *d* of A. W. Paskin; two *d*. *Educ:* King's Sch., Macclesfield; St Catharine's Coll., Cambridge (Scholar, MA). Joined The Calico Printers' Assoc. Ltd Commn Printing, 1934; transf. overseas, 1938; service in India and China. Dir, W. A. Beardsell & Co. (Private) Ltd, Madras, 1946 (Chm. and Man. Dir, 1949-55); Chm. and Man. Dir, Mettur Industries Ltd, 1949-55; Chm. and Man. Dir, Marshall Fabrics Ltd, 1955-62; Director: Calico Printers' Assoc. Ltd, 1962-68; Barclays Bank Ltd Manchester Local Bd, 1965-69. Member: Textile Coun., 1967-69; Coun., Inst. of Directors, 1967; NW Economic Planning Coun., 1968-69; Governor, Manchester Grammar Sch. *Recreations:* fishing, golf. *Address:* Cranford, Ladybrook Road, Bramhall, Cheshire. *T:* 061-485 3204. *Clubs:* Public Schools; St James's (Manchester).

**CULLEY, Group Captain Stuart Douglas,** DSO 1918; retired; Representative British and American Industries, Italy, since 1946; owner and sole director Messrs Stuart Culley, Milan; *b* 22 Aug. 1895; *s* of Walter J. Culley and Mabel A. Stather; *m* 1936, Marguerite Henriette Vulliamy, *d* of late Lieut-Col W. H. Battle, FRCS, RAMC (T). *Educ:* America, Canada, England. Joined RNAS, 1917; Grand Fleet and Sea Patrol, 1917-18 (DSO, despatches); Baltic Force, 1919; (despatches) Iraq, 1920-22 (GS medal with clasp, Iraq); Palestine, 1922-24; Staff Coll., 1930; India, 1931-35; Khajuri Plain, 1930-31 (Indian GS medal with clasp); Mohmand Operations, 1935 (despatches); Syrian Campaign, 1941 (despatches); Inspector, Royal Iraqi Air Force, British Military Mission to Iraq, 1937-40; OC Royal Air Force, Palestine and Transjordan, 1940-41; Air Min., 1941-42; N Africa, Italy, 1943-44; India, 1945; retired Dec. 1945. *Address:* Villa Stuart, Salò, Lago di Garda, Italy. *Club:* Royal Air Force, Naval and Military.

**CULLINGFORD, Rev. Cecil Howard Dunstan,** MA; FRSA; Vicar of Stiffkey with Morston, since 1967; *b* 13 Sept. 1904; *s* of Francis James and Lilian Mabel Cullingford; *m* 1933, Olive Eveline, *d* of Lieut-Col P. H. Collingwood, Clifton, Bristol; one *s* one *d*. *Educ:* City of London Sch.; Corpus Christi Coll., Cambridge (Foundation Scholar). 1st Class Hons in Classical Tripos, Parts 1 and 2, and Historical Tripos, Part 2. VIth Form Master, Brighton Coll., 1928-32; Vice-Principal, Clifton Theological Coll., 1932-34; Chaplain of Oundle Sch., 1935-46. Army Chaplain, 1939-45; Guards Armoured Div., 1939-43; Staff Chaplain, 21st Army Group, 1943-44; Senior Chaplain, 79th Armoured Div., 1944-45. Headmaster of Monmouth Sch., 1946-56; Lectr in Naval History at Britannia, RNC Dartmouth, 1957-60; Chaplain: St John's Sch., Leatherhead, 1960-64; St Michael's Sch., Limpsfield, 1964-67. Pres., Silleren Ski Club, 1966. *Publications:* Exploring Caves, 1951; (ed) British Caving: an Introduction to Speleology, 1953 (2nd edn 1961); (ed) A Manual of Caving Techniques, 1969. *Recreations:* hockey, pot-holing, music, archæology. *Address:* The Rectory Flat, Stiffkey, Wells-next-the-sea, Norfolk. *T:* Binham 351.

*See also E. C. M. Cullingford.*

**CULLINGFORD, Eric Coome Maynard,** CMG 1963; Labour Attaché, British Embassy, Bonn; *b* 15 March 1910; *s* of Francis James and Lilian Mabel Cullingford; *m* 1938, Friedel Fuchs; two *s* one *d*. *Educ:* City of London Sch.; St Catharine's Coll., Cambridge (Exhibitioner). Entered Ministry of Labour as Third Class Officer, 1932; Principal, 1942. Served with Manpower Div. of CCG, 1946-50. Asst Sec., Min. of Labour, 1954. Labour Attaché, Bonn, 1961-65. Regional Controller, Eastern and Southern Region, Dept of Employment and Productivity, 1966-68. *Address:* Oaklands, Furze Field, Oxshott, Surrey.

*See also Rev. C. H. D. Cullingford.*

**CULLINGWORTH, Prof. John Barry;** Director of Centre for Urban and Regional Studies, University of Birmingham, since 1966; *b* 11 Sept. 1929; *s* of Sidney C. and Winifred E. Cullingworth; *m* 1951, Betty Violet (*née* Turner); one *s* two *d*. *Educ:* High Pavement Sch., Nottingham; Trinity Coll. of Music, London; London Sch. of Economics. Research Asst, Asst Lectr and Lectr, Univ. of Manchester, 1960-63; Sen. Lectr and Reader, Univ. of Glasgow, 1963-66. Member: Central Housing Adv. Cttee for England and Wales; Scottish Housing Adv. Cttee; Chairman: Cttee on Community Facilities in Expanding Towns (Report, The Needs of New Communities, 1967); Cttee on Unfit Housing in Scotland (Report, Scotland's Older Houses, 1967); Cttee on Allocation of Council Houses, 1968; Birmingham COPEC House Improvement Soc. *Publications:* Housing Needs and Planning Policy, 1960; Housing in Transition, 1963; Town and Country Planning in England and Wales, 1964; English Housing Trends, 1965; Housing and Local Government, 1966; Scottish Housing in 1965, 1967; A Profile of Glasgow Housing, 1968; (with V. Karn) Ownership and Management of Housing in New Towns, 1968; Housing and Labour Mobility, (Paris) 1969. *Address:* University of Birmingham, PO Box 363, Birmingham 15. *Club:* National Liberal.

**CULLIS, Michael Fowler,** CVO 1955; Director, Arms Control and Disarmament Research, Foreign Office, since 1967; *b* 22 Oct. 1914; *s* of late Prof. Charles Gilbert Cullis, Imperial Coll. of Science and Technology, London Univ., and of Winifred Jefford Cullis (*née* Fowler), 63 Kingston House, Princes Gate, SW7; *m* Catherine Robertson, Arbroath, Scotland. *Educ:* Wellington Coll. (scholar); Brasenose Coll., Oxford (Hulme Scholar). MA, classics. Law (Lincoln's Inn), and journalism, 1938-39. Military Intelligence, Gibraltar, 1939-40; served Min. of Economic Warfare (London, Spain and Portugal), 1940-44; joined Foreign Office as head of Austrian Section, 1945; Political Adviser on Austrian Treaty negotiations (London, Moscow, Vienna, Paris, New York), 1947-50; Special Asst, Schuman Plan, 1950; First Sec., British Embassy, Oslo, 1951-55; Regional (Information) Counsellor for the five Nordic countries, British Embassy, Copenhagen, 1955-58; Adviser to Gov. of Malta, 1959-61; Sen. Research Associate, Atlantic Institute, Paris, 1962-65; writing, lecturing, etc, at various European centres, 1965-66. Comdr of Order of Dannebrog, 1957. *Recreations:* squash rackets, music, travel, Siciliana, chess. *Address:* County End, Bushey Heath, Herts. *T:* 01-950 1057. *Club:* Athenæum.

**CULLWICK, Prof. Ernest Geoffrey,** OBE 1946; Capt. (L) RCN(R), retired; MA, DSc, FIEE, FRSE; Watson-Watt Professor of Electrical Engineering in the University of Dundee since 1967 (University of St Andrews, Queen's College, Dundee, 1949-67); Dean of the Faculty of Engineering and Applied Science; *b* Wolverhampton, 24 May 1903; *s* of late Herbert Ernest Cullwick and Edith Ada Ascough; *m* 1929, Mamie Ruttan, *o d* of G. B. Boucher, Peterborough, Ontario; one *s* one *d*. *Educ:* Wolverhampton Grammar Sch.; Downing Coll., Cambridge (Mathematical Scholar, Foundation Scholar in Engineering). Mathematical and Mechanical Sciences Tripos, Industrial Bursar of the Royal Exhibition of 1851; with British Thomson Houston Co. and Canadian General Electric Co.; Asst Prof. of Electrical Engineering, Univ. of British Columbia, Vancouver, 1928-34; Lectr in Electrical Engineering, Military Coll. of Science, Woolwich, 1934-35; Associate Prof. of Electrical Engineering, Univ. of British Columbia, 1935-37; Prof. and Head of Dept of Electrical Engineering, Univ. of Alberta, Edmonton, 1937-46; Dir of Electrical Engineering, RCN, 1942-47; Dir, Electrical Research Div. Defence Research Board, Ottawa, 1947-49. Dean, Faculty of Applied Science, Univ. of St Andrews, 1955-60, 1965-67. Coun., Royal Soc. of Edinburgh, 1958-61; Chm. Scottish Centre IEE, 1961-63; Mem., Athlone Fellowships Managing Cttee. *Publications:* technical, scientific and educational papers; The Fundamentals of Electromagnetism, 1939; Electromagnetism and Relativity, 1957. *Recreations:* golf, bookbinding, philately. *Address:* 516 Perth Road, Dundee, Scotland.

**CULME-SEYMOUR, Comdr Sir Michael;** *see* Seymour.

**CULSHAW, John (Royds),** OBE 1966; Head of Music Programmes, BBC Television, since 1967; *b* 28 May 1924; *s* of Percy Ellis Culshaw and late Dorothy Royds Culshaw. *Educ:* King George V Sch., Southport, Lancs. RNAS (Fleet Air Arm), Lieut, 1942-46. The Decca Record Co. Ltd (Classical Recordings), 1946-54; Capitol Records Inc., Hollywood, USA, 1954-56; The Decca Record Co. Ltd (Manager, Classical Recordings), 1956-67. Vienna Philharmonic Orchestra: Nicolai Medal, 1959; Schalk Medal, 1967. *Publications:* Sergei Rachmaninov, 1949; The Sons of Brutus, 1950; A Century of Music, 1951; A Place of Stone, 1952; Ring Resounding, 1967. Contributor: The Gramophone, Saturday Review (USA), High Fidelity (USA), etc. *Recreation:* flying. *Address:* 16 Arlington Avenue, N1. *T:* 01-359 2837.

**CULVER, Roland Joseph;** actor; *b* 31 Aug. 1900; *s* of Edward Culver and Florence Tullege; *m* 1st, 1934, Daphne Rye (marr. diss.); two *s*; 2nd, 1947, Nan Hopkins. *Educ:* Highgate Coll.; Royal Academy of Dramatic Art. First appearance on stage, Hull Rep. Theatre, as Paul, in Peter and Paul, 1924; first London appearance, Century Theatre, with Greater London Players, 1925; there followed continuous parts in plays in West End theatres. Played Lieut-Comdr Rogers, in French Without Tears, Criterion, Nov. 1936 until 1939; Ford, in Believe It or Not, New, 1940; Viscount Goring, in An Ideal Husband, Westminster, 1943; George Wayne, in Another Love Story, Phoenix, 1944. First English actor to go to Hollywood after end of 1939-45 War; on returning to England appeared as Ronald Knight, MA, in Master of Arts, Strand, 1949; Oscar, in Who is Sylvia?, Criterion, 1950; William Collyer, in The Deep Blue Sea, Duchess, 1952; prod revival of Aren't We All?, Haymarket, 1953. First appearance on New York stage at Coronet, 1953, as Philip, in The Little Hut; Simon Foster in Simon and Laura, Strand, London, 1954; Stanley Harrington in Five Finger

Exercise, Comedy Theatre, London, 1958, New York and US tour, 1959-61; Sir Richard Conyngham, PC, MP, in Shout for Life, Vaudeville, 1963; Dr Parker in Carving a Statue, Haymarket, 1964; Lebedyev in Ivanov, Phœnix, 1965, New York and United States tour 1966; Getting Married, Strand, 1967; Hay Fever, Duke of York's, 1968; His, Hers and Theirs, Apollo, 1969; My Darling Daisy, Lyric, 1970. Wrote and appeared in his own play, A River Breeze, 1956. Has appeared on BBC TV and ITV. Entered films, 1931, and has appeared in numerous successful pictures. *Films include:* French without Tears, On Approval, The First of the Few, Secret Mission, To Each His Own, Down to Earth, Emperor Waltz, Trio, Quartette. *Publication:* A River Breeze (play), 1957. *Recreations:* painting, golf, hacking and writing. *Address:* The Old School, Fawley, Henley-on-Thames, Oxon. *T:* Henley 3778. *Clubs:* Garrick, Green Room.

**CUMBER, John Alfred,** CMG 1966; MBE 1954; TD; HM Overseas Civil Service, retired; Commissioner in Anguilla, 1969; Administrator of the Cayman Islands, 1964-68; *b* 30 Sept. 1920; *s* of A. J. Cumber, FRIBA, AMICE; *m* 1945, Margaret Anne Tripp. *Educ:* Richmond County Sch.; LSE. Served War of 1939-45 (Major). Joined Colonial Service, 1947; served Kenya: District Officer, 1947; District Comr, 1950; Senior District Comr, 1960; Senior Asst Sec., 1961-63. *Recreations:* art, photography, music, swimming. *Address:* c/o Barclays Bank Ltd, Canterbury, Kent.

**CUMBER, William John,** CBE 1943; farmer; *b* 21 Dec. 1878; *s* of William and Ellen Cumber; *m* 1904, Elizabeth (*d* 1965), *d* of Sir Edward Brown; one *s* five *d. Educ:* Kendrick Sch., Reading. Farms 2000 acres in Berks and Wilts; Mem. of Berks War Agric. Cttee, 1916-19, and 1939-64; Chm. of Farmers' Club, 1939-46; Pres., Shire Horse Soc., 1939-46; Chm., Council of Agriculture for England, 1940; Mem. Luxmore Cttee on Agricultural Education, 1941-42; for many years Alderman Berks CC (Chm., 1954-57) and Chm. Agricultural Cttee of County Councils' Assoc. Pres., British Horse Soc., 1948, 1949; Pres., Smithfield Club, 1949-50; Pres., Shorthorn Soc., 1953-54. Hon. Fellow RASE; Master Worshipful Company of Farmers, 1956. *Address:* Conkers, Theale, Berks. *T:* Theale 410. *Club:* Farmers'.

**CUMBERBATCH, Arthur Noel,** CMG 1953; CBE 1942 (MBE 1933); Minister (Commercial), Cairo, 1948-54, retired from Foreign Service, 1954; *b* 25 Dec. 1895. *Educ:* King's Coll. Sch.; Paris. Served European War, 1914-18 (despatches). Employed in Commercial Secretariat, Athens, 1920; Asst to the Commercial Sec., Athens, 1931; Commercial Secretary, Athens, 1934. Served, later, in Cairo, Tehran and again in Athens. *Address:* 16 Buckingham Palace Mansions, SW1. *T:* 01-730 4238.

**CUMBERBATCH, Isaac William,** CBE 1955 (OBE 1950); *b* Silverdale, Staffs, 11 Jan. 1888; *m*; one *s. Educ:* Church of England Sch., Silverdale; High Sch. and Sutherland Inst., Longton; North Staffs Technical Coll., Stoke-on-Trent. 1st class Hons in Principles of Mining (Bd of Educn). Formerly; Pres. N Staffs Br. Nat. Assoc. of Colliery Managers; Pres. N Staffs Inst. of Mining Engineers; Vice-Pres. Inst. of Mining Engineers; Pres. and Chm. N Staffs. Colliery Owners' Assoc. An Hon. Technical Mining Adviser on Manpower and Production, attached to Mines Dept, 1941; Production Dir, Cannock Chase Coalfield. Pioneer in research work carried out at Sneyd Colliery in N Staffs Coalfield on dust suppression. Chm. West Midlands Division National Coal Board, 1950-55. Member: Cttee to enquire into, and find a remedy for, dangers arising from Coal Dust in Mines; Cttee on Recruitment, Education and Training (responsible for Report published by Mining Assoc., 1945). JP Borough of Newcastle-under-Lyme; MInstME. *Publications:* a number of papers before Nat. Assoc. of Colliery Managers and Inst. of Mining Engineers. *Address:* Highfields, Clayton Road, Newcastle, Staffs. *T:* Newcastle, Staffs, 67091.

**CUMBERLEGE, Geoffrey Fenwick Jocelyn,** DSO 1917; MC 1918; *b* 18 April 1891; 3rd *s* of late Henry Mordaunt and Blanche Cumberlege, Walsted Place, Lindfield, Sussex; *m* 1927, Vera Gladys, 3rd *d* of Major Sir A. D. Gibbons, 7th Bt; three *s* one *d. Educ:* Charterhouse; Worcester Coll., Oxford; MA. Hon. Fellow Worcester Coll., Oxford; Hon. DCL, Durham, 1953. Served France, 1915-18, Italy, 1918-19 (Croce di Guerra); substantive Capt. in Oxford and Bucks LI, Oct. 1917 (DSO, MC, despatches thrice); Manager of Oxford University Press in India, 1919-27, in USA, 1927-34. Publisher to the Univ. of Oxford, 1945-56. *Address:* Idlehurst, Birch Grove, Horsted Keynes, Sussex. *T:* Chelwood Gate 224. *Clubs:* Athenæum, United Service; Royal Bombay Yacht (Bombay).

**CUMING, Frederick George Rees,** ARA 1969; ARCA 1954; NDD 1948; NEAC 1960; painter; *b* 16 Feb. 1930. *Educ:* University School, Bexley Heath; Sidcup Art School; Royal College of Art. Has exhibited in many galleries, London, New York, etc. Work purchased by official bodies, including: Ministry of Works, RA, Kent Education Cttee, Scunthorpe Art Gallery, Scunthorpe Education Cttee. *Address:* Egerton House, Egerton, Ashford, Kent.

**CUMING, Mariannus Adrian,** CMG 1962; Chairman, Cuming Smith & Co. Ltd, Melbourne, since 1945, and associated fertiliser companies; Director: Broken Hill Pty Co. Ltd and subsidiaries; Imperial Chemical Industries of Australia and New Zealand Ltd; Victorian Board AMP Society; *b* 26 Nov. 1901; *s* of J. Cuming, Melbourne; *m* 1926, Wilma Margaret, *d* of W. C. Guthrie; three *s* one *d. Educ:* Melbourne Grammar Sch.; Melbourne Univ. (BSc); Imperial Coll., London (Dip.). Dir, Alfred Hospital, Melbourne, 1945-. *Recreations:* golf, fishing. *Address:* 29 Stonnington Place, Toorak, Vic 3142, Australia. *T:* Melbourne 20 5319. *Clubs:* Australian, Melbourne, Royal Melbourne Golf (Melbourne); Weld (Perth).

**CUMINGS, Sir Charles (Cecil George),** KBE 1951; *b* 30 March 1904; *s* of late Capt. C. E. G. Cumings and E. M. Cumings, OBE; *m* 1942, Enid Gethen; one *s* one *d. Educ:* St Andrew's Coll. and Rhodes University Coll., Grahamstown, S Africa; New Coll., Oxford. Called to the Bar, Inner Temple, 1927; Sudan Political Service, 1927-30; Legal Dept, Sudan Govt, 1930; Advocate-Gen., 1943; Chief Justice, 1945; Legal Sec., 1947-54. Lectr in Law, Rhodes Univ., 1953-55. Resident Dir in Africa, British South Africa Company, 1957-59. *Recreation:* tennis. *Address:* 56 Aberdeen Road, Avondale, Rhodesia.

**CUMINGS, Prof. John Nathaniel,** MD, FRCP; Professor of Chemical Pathology, University of London, at the Institute of Neurology, National Hospital for Nervous Diseases, since 1958; *b* 4 Oct. 1905; *s* of Arthur N. Cumings; *m* 1940, Mary P. Parish; one *s* one *d. Educ:* King's

Coll. and King's Coll. Hosp. Qualified King's Coll. Hosp., 1927; House Appts, and Asst Pathologist, King's Coll. Hosp.; MD 1931; Asst Pathologist, National Hosp., 1933; Clinical Pathologist, National Hospital, 1945; FRCP 1953. Hughlings Jackson Lecture, RSM, 1970. *Publications:* Cerebral Lipidosis, 1957; Heavy Metals and the Brain, 1959. *Address:* 17 Elm Grove Road, Ealing, W5. *T:* 01-567 4466.

**CUMMING, Brig. A. E.,** VC 1942; OBE 1942; MC 1918; *b* 18 June 1896; *m* 1922, Elizabeth Doris Brown; (one *s* died of wounds in Italy, 1944). *Educ:* privately; Cadet Coll., Quetta. 2nd Lieut Indian Army, 1915; served in Mesopotamia and Palestine with 53rd Sikhs, Frontier Force, 1917-20 (MC); NW Frontier, India, with 3rd Royal Bn 12th Frontier Force Regt, 1921-22 and 1936-37; Comdt, 2nd Bn 12th Frontier Force Regt, 1940; served in Malaya, 1941-42 (wounded, VC); Bde Comdr, 1942 (OBE); Eastern Frontier, India, 1943; Comdr Dehra Dun Sub-Area, 1944-47; retired, 1947. Supt of Police, Kyrenia, Cyprus, Sept. 1956-59. *Recreation:* touring. *Address:* 2 Scotland Street, Edinburgh 3.

**CUMMING, Sir Duncan (Cameron),** KBE 1953 (CBE 1946); CB 1948; *b* 10 Aug. 1903; *s* of late Dr R. Cumming; *m* 1930, Nancy Acheson Houghton; one *d. Educ:* Giggleswick; Caius Coll., Cambridge. Sudan Political Service, 1925; Chief Administrator, Cyrenaica (Brig.), 1942; Chief Civil Affairs Officer, Middle East (Maj.-Gen.), 1945-48. Governor, Kordofan Province, Sudan, 1949. Deputy Civil Sec., Sudan Government, 1950-51; Chief Administrator of Eritrea, 1951-52. Man. Dir, BOAC Associated Companies Ltd, 1955-59; BOAC Adviser on African Affairs, 1959-64. KStJ. *Address:* 41 Gilston Road, SW10. *Club:* Athenæum.

**CUMMING, Lieut-Col Malcolm Edward Durant,** CB 1961; OBE 1945; attached War Office, 1934-65; *b* 27 Sept. 1907. *Educ:* Eton; Royal Military Coll., Sandhurst. Served with 60th Rifles, 1927-34. *Recreations:* fishing and rural interests generally. *Address:* Lydwicke, Slinfold, Sussex. *T:* Slinfold 443. *Club:* Greenjackets.

**CUMMING, Lieut-Col Sir Ronald Stuart,** Kt 1965; TD; Chairman, Distillers Company Ltd, 1963-67 (Dir 1946-67); *b* April 1900; *s* of John F. Cumming, OBE, DL, JP, Aberlour, Banffshire; *m* 1924, Mary, OBE 1953, *d* of late Col Wm Hendrie, Hamilton, Ont.; two *d. Educ:* Uppingham; Aberdeen Univ. Grenadier Guards, 1918-19; Dir, John Walker & Sons Ltd, 1931-39; Joint Man. Dir, James Buchanan & Co. Ltd, 1939-46; served Seaforth Highlanders (TA), 1939-45; Man. Dir, James Buchanan & Co. Ltd, 1946-51; Chm., Booth's Distilleries Ltd, 1953-63; Chm., John Walker & Sons Ltd, 1957-63; Chm. Coun, Scotch Whisky Assoc., 1961-67. *Recreations:* fishing, shooting, golf. *Address:* Sourden Brae, Rothes, Morayshire. *Clubs:* Boodle's; New (Edinburgh).

**CUMMING, Roualeyn Charles Rossiter,** CIE 1942; *b* 2 Nov. 1891; *e s* of Roualeyn Charles Cumming, Calne, Wilts; *m* 1st, 1916, Pauline Grace (*d* 1952), *y d* of Edward Hagarty Parry, Stoke Poges; 2nd, 1958, Eileen Mary (*née* Steel), *widow* of Comdr E. D. Michell, DSC, RN. *Educ:* St Paul's Sch. Entered Indian Police, 1911; Personal Assistant to Chief Comr of Assam, 1914-16; Political Officer, NE Frontier, India, 1927-30; Deputy Inspector-Gen. of Police, Assam, 1935-37; Inspector Gen. of Police and Joint Sec. in Home Dept, Govt of Assam, 1937-46. King's Police Medal, 1940. *Recreation:* golf. *Address:* Post Mead, Bishop's Waltham, Hampshire. *Club:* East India and Sports.

**CUMMING, Sir William Gordon G.;** *see* Gordon Cumming.

**CUMMING, William Richard,** CVO 1954; Assistant Secretary, Prime Minister's Office, Canberra, Australia, since 1966; *b* 15 Oct. 1911; *e s* of George Cumming, Coorparoo, Qld; *m* 1939, Evelyn Joyce, *o d* of late George Paul, Epping, NSW; one *s* one *d. Educ:* Gregory Terr., Brisbane; Univs of Queensland and Sydney. BA Queensland, LLB, DipPubAd Sydney. Admitted to NSW Bar, 1941. Enlisted in AIF and served War of 1939-45 with AAPC, Major. Adviser, Federal Taxation Dept, 1947-51; Senior Executive Officer, Prime Minister's Dept, Australia, 1951-55; Asst Secretary, Prime Minister's Dept, 1955-60; Official Sec., Australian High Commissioner's Office, London, 1960-66; Acting Deputy High Commissioner, 1965-66; Extra Gentleman Usher to the Queen, 1962-66; Dir, Royal Visits, ACT, 1953-54, 1956, 1957-58; Dir-Gen., Australia, Royal Visit, 1959. Secretary: Commonwealth Literary Fund, 1955-60, 1967-; Commonwealth Historic Memorials Cttee, 1955-60, 1967-; Commonwealth Art Advisory Bd, 1955-60, 1967-; Commonwealth Assistance to Australian Composers, 1967-; Council, Australian Nat. Gallery, 1968-. Member: Council, Nat. Library of Australia, 1967; Council, Australian Inst. of Aboriginal Studies, 1969-. *Recreations:* collecting antiques and Australian art, motoring. *Address:* Prime Minister's Department, Canberra, ACT, Australia. *Club:* University (Sydney).

**CUMMING-BRUCE, Hon. Sir Francis Edward Hovell-Thurlow-,** KCMG 1961 (CMG 1957); Governor and C-in-C of the Bahamas since 1968; *b* 9 March 1912; *s* of 6th Baron Thurlow and Grace Catherine, *d* of Rev. Henry Trotter; *b* and *heir-pres* to 7th Baron Thurlow, *qv*; *m* 1949, Yvonne Diana Aubyn Wilson, CstJ 1969; two *s* two *d. Educ:* Shrewsbury Sch.; Trinity Coll., Cambridge. Asst Principal, Dept of Agriculture for Scotland, 1935; transferred to Dominions Office, 1937; Asst Private Sec. to Sec. of State, 1939; Asst Sec., Office of UK High Comr in NZ, 1939; Asst Sec., Office of UK High Comr in Canada, 1944; Secretariat, Meeting of Commonwealth Prime Ministers in London, 1946; served with UK Delegn at Paris Peace Conf., 1946, and at UN Gen. Assemblies, 1946 and 1948; Principal Private Sec. to Sec. of State, 1946; Asst Sec., CRO, 1948; Head of Political Div., Office of UK High Comr in New Delhi, 1949; Establishment Officer, CRO, 1952; Head of Commodities Dept, CRO, 1954; Adviser on External Affairs to Governor of Gold Coast, 1955; Deputy High Comr for the UK in Ghana, 1957; Asst Under-Sec. of State, CRO, April 1958; Deputy High Comr for the UK in Canada, 1958; High Comr for UK: in New Zealand, 1959-63; in Nigeria, 1964-67. KStJ 1969. *Recreations:* fishing, golf. *Address:* Government House, Nassau, Bahamas. *Club:* Travellers'. *See also Hon. Sir J. R. H.-T.-Cumming-Bruce.*

**CUMMING-BRUCE, Hon. Sir (James) Roualeyn Hovell-Thurlow-,** Kt 1964; MA; **Hon. Mr Justice Cumming-Bruce;** Judge of the High Court of Justice, Probate, Divorce and Admiralty Division, since 1964; Judge of the Restrictive Practices Court, since 1968; *b* 9 March 1912; *s* of 6th Baron Thurlow and Grace Catherine, *d* of Rev. Henry Trotter; *m* 1955, Lady (Anne) Sarah Alethea Marjorie Savile, *d* of 6th Earl of Mexborough; two *s* one *d. Educ:* Shrewsbury; Magdalene Coll., Cambridge. Barrister, Middle Temple, 1937 (Harmsworth Scholar);

Master of the Bench, 1959. Served War of 1939-45 (Lt-Col RA). Chancellor of Diocese of Ripon, 1954-57; Recorder of Doncaster, 1957-58; Recorder of York, 1958-61; Junior Counsel to the Treasury (Common Law), 1959-64. *Address:* 1 Mulberry Walk, Chelsea, SW3. *T:* 01-352 5754; Leigh House, Winsham, Somerset. *T:* Winsham 279. *Clubs:* Pratt's, United University.
*See also Hon. Sir F. E. H.-T.-Cumming Bruce.*

**CUMMINGS, Constance;** actress; *d* of Kate Cummings and Dallas Vernon Halverstadt; *m* 1933, Benn Wolfe Levy, *qv*; one *s* one *d*. *Educ:* St Nicholas Girls Sch., Seattle, Washington, USA. Began stage work, 1932; since then has appeared in radio, television, films and theatre. Plays include: The Petrified Forest; Return to Tyassi; Goodbye, Mr Chips; The Good-Natured Man; St Joan; Romeo and Juliet; The Taming of the Shrew; Lysistrata; The Rape of the Belt; JB; Who's Afraid of Virginia Woolf?; Justice is a Woman; Fallen Angels; A Delicate Balance; Hamlet. Has appeared Albert Hall, performing with orchestra Peter and the Wolf and Honegger's Jeanne d'Arc au Bûcher. Mem., Arts Coun., 1965-; Chm., Young People's Theatre Panel, 1966-. *Recreations:* anthropology and music. *Address:* 66 Old Church Street, SW3. *T:* 01-352 0437.

**CUMMINS, Geraldine Dorothy;** author; *d* of late Prof. Ashley Cummins, MD, and Jane Constable; *b* 1890. *Educ:* home. *Publications:* The Land They Loved, Fires of Beltane, Irish novels; Variety Show (short stories); The Scripts of Cleophas; Paul in Athens; The Great Days of Ephesus; The Childhood of Jesus; Beyond Human Personality; The Road to Immortality, They Survive (with E. B. Gibbes); When Nero was Dictator; After Pentecost; Healing the Mind (with Dr Connell); Travellers in Eternity; I Appeal Unto Caesar; The Manhood of Jesus; Dr E. Œ. Somerville (biography); Unseen Adventures (autobiographical); The Fate of Colonel Fawcett; Mind in Life and Death; Swan on a Black Sea; plays produced: Till Yesterday Comes Again, three Irish plays (with S. R. Day); Broken Faith, Fox and Geese, The Way of the World; two books trans. into four languages; has contributed short stories or articles to periodicals and magazines. *Recreations:* gardening, tennis, music, played in the Irish International Hockey team. *Address:* Woodville, Glanmire, Co. Cork.

**CUNARD, Sir Harry (Palmes),** 6th Bt *cr* 1859; *b* 12 Sept. 1909; *s* of late Capt. Alick May Cunard (*s* of William Samuel Cunard, a *g s* of 1st Bt) and Muriel Palmes; *S* kinsman, Sir Edward Cunard, 5th Bt, 1962. *Educ:* Eton; Trinity Coll., Cambridge. BA Hons 1931. *Heir: b* Major Guy Alick Cunard, *b* 2 Sept. 1911. *Address:* 23 Place Newton, Wintringham, Malton, Yorks. *T:* Rillington 286. *Club:* Cambridge Union.

**CUNDALL, Charles,** RA 1944 (ARA 1937); RWS 1941 (ARWS 1935); *b* 6 Sept. 1890; *s* of Charles Hellyar Cundall and Elizabeth Mary Fletcher; *m* 1923, Jacqueline Pietersen; one *d*. *Educ:* Ackworth Sch.; Royal Coll. of Art and Slade Sch.; Paris. Served in Royal Fusiliers, European War, 1914-17; Official War Artist to RN and RAF, 1940-45. Mem. of the New English Art Club, Royal Soc. of Portrait Painters, and Manchester and Bristol Academies of Fine Arts; pictures purchased by Tate Gallery, Contemporary Art Soc., Liverpool, Manchester, Bristol, and other galleries. *Recreations:* travelling, reading. *Address:* Great Cheyne Studio, Cheyne Row, Chelsea, SW3. *T:* 01-352 9704; Barnyard Cottage, South Lane, Houghton, near Arundel, Sussex. *T:* Bury 529. *Clubs:* Arts, Garrick.

**CUNDIFF, Major Frederick William;** Director of Chesters Brewery Co. Ltd; *s* of late Sir William Cundiff. MP (C) Rusholme Div. of Manchester, 1944-45; Withington Div. of Manchester, 1950-51. *Address:* Easedale, Prestbury, Cheshire.

**CUNEO, Terence Tenison;** portrait and figure painter, ceremonial, military and engineering subjects; *b* 1 Nov. 1907; *s* of Cyrus Cuneo and Nell Marion Tenison; *m* 1934, Catherine Mayfield Monro, *yr d* of Major E. G. Monro, CBE; two *d*. *Educ:* Sutton Valence Sch.; Chelsea and Slade. Served War of 1939-45: RE, and as War Artist; special propaganda paintings for Min. of Information, Political Intelligence Dept of FO, and War Artists Advisory Cttee; representative of Illustrated London News, France, 1940. Royal Glasgow Inst. of Fine Arts; Pres. of Industrial Painters Group; Exhibitor, RA, RP, ROI Paris Salon (Hon. Mention, 1957). Has painted extensively in North Africa, South Africa, Rhodesia, Canada and USA; one-man exhibition, Underground Activities in Occupied Europe, 1941; one-man exhibition, RWS Galleries, london, 1954 and 1958. Best known works include: Garter Ceremony, 1964; Equestrian portrait of HM the Queen as Colonel-in-Chief, Grenadier Guards, 1963; Queen Elizabeth II at Guildhall Banquet after Indian Tour, 1961; Queen Elizabeth II at RCOG, 1960; Coronation of Queen Elizabeth II in Westminster Abbey (presented to the Queen by HM's Lieuts of Counties), 1955; Queen Elizabeth II at the Mansion House after Commonwealth Tour, 1955; The Queen's Coronation Luncheon, Guildhall, 1953; The Duke of Edinburgh at Cambridge, 1953; Visit to Lloyd's of Queen Elizabeth II with the Duke of Edinburgh, to lay Foundation Stone of Lloyd's New Building, 1952; The Queen's State Visit to Denmark, 1957; Memorial Paintings, El Alamein, The Royal Engineers, 1950, The Rifle Brigade, 1951; King George VI at The Royal Artillery Mess, Woolwich, 1950; King George VI and Queen Elizabeth at The Middle Temple Banquet, 1950; Portraits of Viscount Allendale KG, as Canopy Bearer to Her Majesty, 1954. Engineering Mural, Science Museum, 1957. *Publications:* articles in The Studio, The Artist, Art and Industry. *Recreations:* writing, sketching, travel, riding. *Address:* 201 Ember Lane, East Molesey, Surrey. *T:* 01-398 1986. *Club: Junior Carlton.*

**CUNINGHAME, Sir John Christopher Foggo Montgomery-,** 12th Bt *cr* 1672, of Corsehill, Ayrshire and Kirktonholm, Lanarkshire; is working in Charterhouse, Japhet & Thomasson Ltd; *b* 24 July 1935; 2nd *s* of Col Sir Thomas Montgomery-Cuninghame, 10th Bt, DSO (*d* 1945), and of Nancy Macaulay (his 2nd wife), *d* of late W. Stewart Foggo, Aberdeen (she *m* 2nd, 1946, Johan Frederik Christian Killander); *b* of Sir Andrew Montgomery-Cuninghame, 11th Bt; *S* brother, 1959; *m* 1964, Laura Violet, *d* of Sir Godfrey Nicholson, Bt, *qv*; two *d*. *Educ:* Fettes; Worcester Coll., Oxford (BA). 2nd Lieut, Rifle Brigade (NS), 1955-56; Lieut, London Rifle Brigade, TA, 1956-. *Recreation:* fishing. *Heir:* none. *Address:* 28 Kelso Place, W8. *T:* 01-937 1835.

**CUNINGHAME, Sir William Alan Fairlie-,** 15th Bt *cr* 1630; MC; BE (Sydney); retired as Research Officer, National Standards Laboratory, Sydney; *b* 31 Jan. 1893; *s* of 13th Bt and Georgiana Maud, *d* of late Edward Hardman Macartney; *S* brother, 1939; *m* 1929,

Irene Alice, *d* of late Henry Margrave Terry; one *s*. *Educ:* Sydney Univ. Served European War, 1915-19 (MC). *Heir:* *s* William Henry Fairlie-Cuninghame, *b* 1930. *Address:* 45 Wyvern Avenue, Chatswood, Sydney, NSW, Australia.

**CUNLIFFE,** family name of **Baron Cunliffe.**

**CUNLIFFE,** 3rd Baron *cr* 1914, of Headley; **Roger Cunliffe;** Director, Architectural Association, since 1969; *b* 12 Jan. 1932; *s* of 2nd Baron and Joan Catherine Lubbock; *S* father, 1963; *m* 1957, Clemency Ann Hoare; two *s* one *d*. *Educ:* Eton; Trinity Coll., Cambridge (MA); Architectural Association (AA Dipl.). With Robert Matthew & Johnson-Marshall, London, 1957-59; own practice, London, 1960; with Harry Weese & Associates, Chicago, 1961-63; with Leonard Manasseh & Partners, London, 1964-65; with Robert Matthew, Johnson-Marshall & Partners, 1966-69. ARIBA 1959. *Publication:* (with Leonard Manasseh) Office Buildings, 1962. *Heir:* *s* Hon. Henry Cunliffe, *b* 9 March 1962. *Address:* 1 Hurst Avenue, N6.

**CUNLIFFE, Christopher Joseph; His Honour Judge Christopher Cunliffe;** a County Court Judge since 1966; *b* 28 Feb. 1916; *s* of Lt-Col E. N. Cunliffe, OBE, RAMC, Buckingham Crescent, Manchester, and Harriet Cunliffe (*née* Clegg); *m* 1942, Margaret Hamer Barber; two *d*. *Educ:* Rugby Sch.; Trinity Hall, Cambridge. BA 1937. Called to the Bar, Lincoln's Inn, 1938. Legal Cadet, Br. North Borneo Civil Service. 1939-40. Served RAFVR, 1941-46; Intelligence, Judge Advocate General's Branch. Practised on Northern Circuit, 1946; Dep. Coroner, City of Liverpool, 1953; Chairman: National Insurance Tribunal, Bootle, 1956-; Mental Health Review Tribunal for SW Lancs and W Ches, 1961-. *Recreations:* golf, gardening. *Address:* Durford Hatch, Durford Wood, Petersfield, Hants. *Clubs:* Carlton Masonic (Liverpool); Nuffield United Services Officers' (Portsmouth).

**CUNLIFFE, Sir David Ellis,** 9th Bt *cr* 1759; *b* 29 Oct. 1957; *s* of Sir Cyril Henley Cunliffe, 8th Bt and of Lady Cunliffe (Eileen, *d* of Frederick William and Nora Anne Parkins); *S* father, 1969. *Heir:* *b* Andrew Mark Cunliffe, *b* 17 April 1959. *Address:* 17 Gurney Court Road, St Albans, Herts.

**CUNLIFFE, Hon. Geoffrey;** *b* 26 Aug. 1903; 2nd *s* of 1st Baron Cunliffe and Edith Boothby (later Dowager Baroness Cunliffe, *d* 1965); *m* 1st, 1922, Patrick Sidney (*d* 1940), *o d* of late Robert B. Frend, Ardsallagh, Co. Tipperary; one *s* (and *er s* killed in action, 1945); 2nd, 1941, Gavrelle (marr. diss. 1947), *d* of William Arthur Thomas, and *widow* of Christopher Hobhouse; one *s* one *d*; 3rd, 1947, Barbara Waring, *d* of late Dr J. A. Gibb, Maidstone, Kent. *Educ:* Eton; Trinity Coll., Cambridge. Controller of Aluminium, Min. of Supply and Min. of Aircraft Production, 1939-41; Mem., Industrial and Export Council, Board of Trade, 1941; Dir of Office Machinery, BoT, 1941-42; Dep. Chm. and Man. Dir, British Aluminium Co. Ltd, 1947-59; Man. Dir of Norcros Ltd, 1959-63. A Dep. Pres., British Standards Instn, 1965- (Chm. Finance Cttee, 1959-61; Pres. of the Instn, 1961-63; Chm. Gen. Council, 1961-64). *Address:* Poyntzfield House, by Conon Bridge, Ross-shire.

**CUNLIFFE, Prof. Marcus Falkner;** Professor of American Studies, University of Sussex since 1965; *b* 5 July 1922; *s* of Keith Harold and Kathleen Eleanor Cunliffe; *m* 1949, Mitzi Solomon, NY; one *s* two *d*. *Educ:* Oriel Coll., Oxford. Commonwealth Fund Fellow, Yale Univ., 1947-49; Lecturer in American Studies, University of Manchester, 1949-56; Senior Lecturer, 1956-60. Fellow, Center for Advanced Study in the Behavioral Sciences, Stanford, Calif., 1957-58; Visiting Prof. in American History, Harvard Univ., 1959-60. Prof. of American History and Institutions, University of Manchester, 1960-64. *Publications:* The Royal Irish Fusiliers, 1793-1950, 1953; The Literature of the United States, 1954; History of the Royal Warwickshire Regiment, 1919-53, 1957; George Washington: Man and Monument, 1958; The Nation Takes Shape, 1789-1837, 1959; Soldiers and Civilians: The Martial Spirit in America, 1775-1865, 1968; American Presidents and the Presidency, 1969. *Recreation:* filling in questionnaires. *Address:* 8 Lewes Crescent, Brighton BN2 1FH. *T:* Brighton 61617.

**CUNLIFFE, Capt. Robert Lionel Brooke,** CBE 1944; Royal Navy, retired; *b* 15 March 1895; *s* of Col Foster Cunliffe and Mrs Cunliffe (*née* Lyon); *m* 1926, Barbara Eleanor Cooper (*d* 1970); three *d*. *Educ:* RN Colls Osborne and Dartmouth. Comdr 1930; Capt. 1936; commanded HMS Milford, 1938-39; RNC Dartmouth, 1939-42; Commodore, Dover, 1942; commanded HMS Illustrious, 1942-44 (despatches); Cdre, RN Barracks, Devonport, 1944-46; Retd, 1946. Naval Asst to UK High Comr, Canada, 1946-48. Grand Officer Order of Leopold II, Belgium, 1948. *Recreations:* cricket, shooting. *Address:* The Garden House, Pakenham, Bury St Edmunds, Suffolk. *T:* Pakenham 236. *Club:* United Service. *See also Baron Sackville.*

**CUNLIFFE, Thomas Alfred; His Honour Judge Cunliffe;** County Court Judge since 1963 (Birkenhead and Chester Circuit since 1966; Bolton, Burnley, etc., 1963-66); *b* 9 March 1905; *s* of Thomas and Elizabeth Cunliffe, Preston; *m* 1938, Constance Isabella Carden; one *s* one *d*. *Educ:* Lancaster Royal Grammar Sch.; Sidney Sussex Coll., Cambridge (Classical Scholar). Inner Temple: Profumo Prize, 1926; Paul Methven Prize, 1926. Called to the Bar, 1927; Yarborough Anderson Scholar, 1927. Practised Northern Circuit, 1927-63; Dep. Chm., Lancs County Quarter Sessions, 1961; Recorder, Barrow-in-Furness, 1962. RAFVR (Squadron Leader), 1940-45. *Recreations:* music, gardening. *Address:* 39 Dee Park Road, Gayton, Wirral, Cheshire L60 3RG. *Club:* Union (Cambridge).

**CUNLIFFE-JONES, Rev. Prof. Hubert,** DD (Hon.); Professor of Theology, University of Manchester, since 1968; *b* Strathfield, Sydney, NSW, Australia, 30 March 1905; *s* of Rev. Walter and Maud Cunliffe-Jones; *m* 1933, Maude Edith Clifton, BSc, DipEd Sydney; two *s* two *d*. *Educ:* Newington Coll., Sydney; Sydney and Oxford Univs; Camden Coll., Sydney; Mansfield Coll., Oxford. Congregational Minister, Warrnambool, Vic., Australia, 1928-29; Travelling Sec., Australian SCM 1929-30; Congregational Minister, Witney, Oxon, 1933-37; Tutor in Systematic Theology, Yorks United Independent Coll., Bradford, 1937-47; Principal Yorks United Independent Coll., Bradford, 1947-58; Associate Principal, Northern Congregational Coll., Manchester, 1958-66; Prof., History of Doctrine, Univ. of Manchester, 1966-68 (Lectr, 1958-66). Chm. of the Congregational Union of England and Wales, 1957-58. Hon. DD Edinburgh, 1956. *Publications:* The Holy Spirit, 1943; The Authority of the Biblical Revelation, 1945; Deuteronomy, 1951; Jeremiah, 1960; Technology, Community and Church, 1961; Christian Theology since 1600,

1970; articles in Theology, Expository Times, etc. *Recreation:* drama. *Address:* 5 Wood Road, Manchester M16 9RB.

**CUNLIFFE-LISTER,** family name of **Baroness Masham of Ilton** and **Earl of Swinton.**

**CUNLIFFE-OWEN, Sir Dudley (Herbert),** 2nd Bt, *cr* 1920; Managing Director: Palace & Derby Castle Ltd: Palace Hotel & Casino Ltd; Palace Entertainments Ltd; *b* 27 March 1923; 2nd (but *o surv*) *s* of Sir Hugo Cunliffe-Owen, 1st Bt and Helen Elizabeth Cunliffe-Owen (*d* 1934), *d* of James Oliver, New York; *S* father 1947; *m* 1st, 1947, Mary Maud (*d* 1956), *e d* of R. R. Redgrave; 2nd, 1956, Hon. Juliana Eveline Nettlefold (*née* Curzon) (marr. diss., 1962), 3rd *d* of 2nd Viscount Scarsdale, *qv*; one *d*; 3rd, 1964, Jean, *o d* of late Surg. Comdr A. N. Forsyth, RN; one *s* one *d*. *Educ:* RN Coll., Dartmouth. Served War, 1939-46 (despatches); Lieut Royal Navy; retired 1947. *Recreation:* yachting. *Heir: s* Hugo Dudley Cunliffe-Owen, *b* 16 May 1966. *Address:* Eyreton House, Quarterbridge, Douglas, Isle of Man. *T:* Douglas 4545. *Club:* Royal Thames Yacht.

**CUNNANE, Most Rev. Joseph;** *see* Tuam, Archbishop of, (RC).

**CUNNINGHAM, Gen. Sir Alan Gordon,** GCMG 1948; KCB 1941 (CB 1941); DSO 1918; MC 1915; LLD; *b* 1 May 1887; *s* of Prof. D. J. Cunningham, FRS, and Elizabeth Cumming Browne; *m* 1951, Margery, *widow* of Sir Harold Edward Snagge, KBE. *Educ:* Cheltenham; Royal Military Academy, Woolwich. First commission, 1906; served European War, France, 1914-18; Brigade Major and Gen. Staff Officer 2nd Grade (despatches 5 times, DSO and MC); Gen. Staff Officer, Straits Settlements, 1919-21; passed Naval Staff Coll., 1925; Brevet Lt-Col 1928; Instructor, Machine Gun Sch., 1928-31; Lt-Col 1935; Imperial Defence Coll., 1937; Comdr Royal Artillery, 1st Div., 1937-38; Maj.-Gen., 1938; Comdr 5th Anti-Aircraft Div. TA, 1938; commanded 66th, 9th and 51st Divs, 1940; GOC East Africa Forces, 1940-41; GOC-in-C 8th Imperial Army in Middle East, 1941; Commandant Staff College, Camberley, 1942; Lt-Gen. 1943; GOC Northern Ireland, 1943-44; GOC-in-C Eastern Command, 1944-45; Gen., 1945; High Commissioner and C-in-C for Palestine, 1945-48; Col Commandant Royal Artillery, 1944-54. Pres., Council of Cheltenham Coll., 1951-63. Comdr American Legion of Merit, 1945; Brilliant Star of Zanzibar (1st class), 1941; Ordre de la Couronne (1st Class), Belgium, 1950; Order of Menelik (1st Class), 1954, etc. *Recreations:* gardening, fishing. *Club:* Army and Navy.

**CUNNINGHAM, Air Cdre Alexander Duncan,** CB 1941; CBE 1919 (OBE 1919); late RAF; *m* 1918, Hilda Carter (*d* 1954); *m* 1965, Mrs Gladys Way, September Cottage, Bourne End Bucks. Served European War, 1914-19 (despatches, OBE, CBE); Air Commodore, 1933; retired list, 1938. Re-employed, 1939-45 (despatches), Air Vice-Marshal, 1940. *Address:* c/o Ministry of Defence (Air), Whitehall, SW1.

**CUNNINGHAM, Sir Charles (Craik),** KCB 1961 (CB 1946); KBE 1952; CVO 1941; Deputy Chairman, United Kingdom Atomic Energy Authority, since 1966; *b*Dundee, 7 May 1906; *s* of late Richard Yule Cunninghum, Abergeldie, Kirriemuir, and Isabella Craik; *m* 1934, Edith Louisa Webster; two *d*. *Educ:* Harris Acad., Dundee; University of St Andrews. Entered Scottish Office, 1929; Private Sec. to Parliamentary Under Sec. of State for Scotland, 1933-34; Private Sec. to Sec. of State for Scotland, 1935-39; Asst Sec., Scottish Home Dept, 1939-41; Principal Asst Sec., 1941-42; Dep. Sec., 1942-47; Sec., 1948-57; Permanent Under-Sec. of State, Home Office, 1957-66. Hon. LLD St Andrews, 1960. *Address:* 5 Stanford Court, Cornwall Gardens, SW7. *Clubs:* Athenæum, Reform; New (Edinburgh).

**CUNNINGHAM, Ebenezer,** MA; Fellow, St John's College, Cambridge; *b* 7 May 1881; *m* 1908, Ada Collins (*d* 1969); one *s* one *d*. *Educ:* Owen's Sch., Islington; St John's Coll., Cambridge. Senior Wrangler, 1902; Smith's Prizeman, 1904; Fellow of St John's Coll., 1904; Lecturer in Mathematics, Liverpool University, 1904-07; University Coll., London, 1907-11; St John's Coll., Cambridge, 1911-46. Chm., Congregational Union of England and Wales, 1953-54. *Publications:* Principle of Relativity, 1914; Relativity and Electron Theory, 1915. *Address:* Wayside, 141 Huntingdon Road, Cambridge. *T:* 53545.
*See also Prof. R. C. Browne.*

**CUNNINGHAM, George,** BA, BSc; MP (Lab) South West Islington since 1970; *b* 10 June 1931; *s* of Harry Jackson Cunningham and Christina Cunningham, Dunfermline; *m* 1957, Mavis, *d* of Harold Walton; one *s* one *d*. *Educ:* Dunfermline High Sch.; Blackpool Grammar Sch.; Univs of Manchester and London. Nat. Service in Royal Artillery (2nd Lieut), 1954-56; on staff of Commonwealth Relations Office, 1956-63; 2nd Sec., British High Commn, Ottawa, 1958-60; Commonwealth Officer of Labour Party, 1963-66; on staff of Min. of Overseas Development, 1966-69; Overseas Development Inst., 1969-70. Contested (Lab) Henley Div. of Oxfordshire, 1966. *Publications:* (Fabian pamphlet) Rhodesia, the Last Chance, 1966; (ed) Britain and the World in the Seventies, 1970. *Address:* 17 Copthall Gardens, Twickenham, Mddx. *T:* 01-892 5972.

**CUNNINGHAM, Prof. George John,** MBE 1945; Professor of Pathology, Medical College of Virginia, and Chief of Laboratory Service, McGuire VA Hospital, Richmond, Virginia, since 1968; Conservator of Pathological Collection, Royal College of Surgeons; Consultant Pathologist to South East and South West Metropolitan Hospital Boards; *b* 7 Sept. 1906; *s* of George S. Cunningham and Blanche A. Harvey; *m* 1957, Patricia Champion, Brisbane, Australia. *Educ:* Royal Belfast Academical Institution; Dean Close Sch., Cheltenham; St Bartholomew's Hospital Medical Coll. MRCS, LRCP, 1931; MB, BS London, 1933; MD London, 1937; FCPath 1964. Asst Pathologist, Royal Sussex County Hosp., Brighton, 1934-42. War Service, RAMC, Middle East and Italy (temp. Lt-Col). Senior Lectr in Pathology, St Bartholomew's Hosp., London, 1946-55; Sir William Collins Prof. of Pathology, Univ. of London, at RCS, 1955-68. Dorothy Temple Cross Travelling Fellow in America, 1951-52; Vis. Prof., New York State Univ., 1961; Vis. Prof., Cairo Univ., 1963. Past Pres., Assoc. Clin. Path., Internat. Acad. of Pathology, Quekett Microscopical Club. Freeman, City of London. *Publications:* chap. on Gen. Pathology of Malignant Tumours in Cancer, Vol. 2, 1957; chap. on Microradiography, in Tools of Biological Research, Vol. 2, 1960; and several articles on Pathology, in medical press. *Recreations:* squash rackets, growing carnations. *Address:* 300 West Franklin Street, Apartment 1203-E, Richmond, Va 23220, USA. *T:* 703 643-1012. *Clubs:* National Liberal; Surrey County Cricket; Downtown, Hermitage Country (Richmond, Va).

**CUNNINGHAM, Sir Graham,** KBE 1946; Kt 1943; LLB London; FSGT; *b* 19 May 1892; *s* of Daniel Cunningham and Charlotte Eliza Galetti; *m* 1st, 1924, Marjorie Minshaw Harris (decd); two *s* one *d*; 2nd, 1934, Olive St John Williams (*d* 1958); 3rd, 1958, Edith Ellen Smith. *Educ:* Bancrofts Sch., Woodford Wells, Essex. Chm., 1935-61 (Managing Dir, 1929-60) Triplex Safety Glass Company, Ltd; Chm. Shipbuilding Advisory Cttee, 1946-60; Mem. Economic Planning Bd, 1947-61; Dep. Chm. Royal Commission on the Press, 1961-62. Crown Governor, Dep. Chm. and Hon. Fellow, Imperial Coll. of Science and Technology; Past Pres. Soc. of British Gas Industries (1956); Past Pres., Soc. Glass Technology; Dep. Dir-Gen. Children's Overseas Reception Board, 1940; Dir of Claims, War Damage Commission, 1941; Chief Executive and Controller-Gen. Munitions Production, Ministry of Supply, 1941-46; Chm., Scrap Steel Investigation Cttee, 1946; US Medal of Freedom with Silver Bar, 1945; Chm. Dollar Exports Board, 1949. Liveryman of the Coach Makers and Harness Makers Company; Past Master, Curriers Company; Past Master, Glaziers Company. *Recreation:* gardening. *Address:* Woolmers, Mannings Heath, near Horsham, Sussex. *T:* Horsham 3809. *Club:* Junior Carlton.

**CUNNINGHAM, Rt. Rev. James;** *see* Hexham and Newcastle, Bishop of, (RC).

**CUNNINGHAM, Group Captain John,** CBE 1963 (OBE 1951); DSO 1941; DFC; Chief Test Pilot for de Havilland Aircraft Co., since 1946; Executive Director, Hawker Siddeley Aviation, since 1963; *b* 27 July 1917; *s* of late A. G. Cunningham and of E. M. Cunningham. *Educ:* Whitgift. Apprenticed to De Havilland Aircraft Co., Hatfield, 1935-38; employed, 1938-Aug. 1939, with De Havillands, Light Aircraft Development and Test Flying. Called up Aug. 1939; joined AAF, 1935; commanded 604 Sqdn, 1941-42; Staff job, 1942-43; commanded 85 Sqdn, 1943-44 (DSO and two bars, DFC and bar); Group Capt. Night Operations HQ 11 Group, 1944. International Record Flight, 16 Oct. 1957: London to Khartoum direct; distance 3,064 statute miles in 5 hrs 51 mins, by Comet 3; average speed 523 statute mph. Derry and Richards Memorial Medal of Guild of Air Pilots and Air Navigators for 1965. *Address:* Hawker Siddeley Aviation, Hatfield Aerodrome.

**CUNNINGHAM, Dr John A.;** MP (Lab) Whitehaven, Cumberland, since 1970; *b* 4 Aug. 1939; *s* of Alderman Andrew Cunningham, JP; *m* 1964, Maureen; one *d*. *Educ:* Jarrow Grammar Sch.; Bede Coll., Durham Univ. Hons Chemistry, 1962; PhD Chemistry, 1966. Formerly: Research Fellow in Chemistry, Durham Univ.; School Teacher; Trades Union Officer. Chm., Chester-le-Street Youth Centre; Member: Duke of Edinburgh's Study Gps for Industry; Exec., Tyneside Productivity Assoc. Mem. Chester-le-Street UDC. *Recreations:* golf, squash, gardening, classical and folk music, reading. *Address:* House of Commons, SW1.

**CUNNINGHAM, Sir Knox;** *see* Cunningham, Sir S. K.

**CUNNINGHAM, Sir (Samuel) Knox,** 1st Bt, *cr* 1963; QC; *b* 3 April 1909; 4th *s* of late Rt Hon. Samuel Cunningham and late Janet McCosh; *m* 1935, Dorothy Enid, JP, *d* of late Edwin Riley. *Educ:* Royal Belfast Academical Institution; Fettes; Clare Coll., Cambridge. Business in Ulster, 1931-37; called to Bar, Middle Temple, 1939; Inn of Court of N Ireland, 1942. Served War of 1939-45, Scots Guards. Contested (U) West Belfast, 1943 and 1945; MP (UU) South Antrim, 1955-70; Parliamentary Private Secretary: to the Financial Sec. to the Treasury, 1958-59; to the Prime Minister, Rt Hon. Harold Macmillan, 1959-63. UK Deleg. to Council of Europe and WEU, 1956-59. Member: Ulster Unionist Council, 1943-; National Executive of Conservative Party, 1959-66. Pres., Old Fettesian Assoc., 1967-70; Chm., Nat. Council of YMCAs, 1949-67; Member: World Alliance of YMCAs, 1947-69; Court of the Drapers' Company; Oprington UDC, 1954-55; Governor, Queen Mary Coll., University of London. *Recreations:* formerly boxing (Heavyweight Boxing Champion, Cambridge Univ., 1931), rifle shooting and travel. *Address:* Derhams House, Minchinhampton, Stroud, Glos. *T:* Brimscombe 3278; 2 Essex Court, Temple, EC4. *T:* 01-353 6956. *Clubs:* Carlton, St Stephen's; MCC; Ulster (Belfast); Gainsford Boxing (President).

**CUNNINGHAM-REID, Captain Alec Stratford,** DFC; *m* 1927, Ruth Mary Clarisse (from whom he obtained a divorce, 1940), *yr d* of 1st Baron Mount Temple, PC; two *s*; *m* 1944, Angela Williams (from whom he obtained a divorce, 1949); one *s* one *d*. *Educ:* University Coll., London; Clare Coll., Cambridge. Served European War, 1914-18; Royal Engineers and RFC (despatches, DFC); MP (U) Warrington, Lancs, 1922-23 and 1924-29; MP St Marylebone, 1932-45; (Independent, 1942-45); Parliamentary Private Sec. to Sir John Baird, Bt, First Commissioner of Works, 1922; promoted League of Youth and Liberty (LOYAL), 1923; Parliamentary Private Sec. to Rt Hon. Col Wilfrid Ashley, PC, MP, Minister of Transport, 1924. *Publications:* Planes and Personalities; Besides Churchill–Who?; Blame the Old Gang!; Will it be Peace?. *Address:* La Petite Ferme, 06 Valbonne, France. *T:* Valbonne 67-00-41. *Club:* Bath.

**CUNNINGHAME GRAHAM of Gartmore, Adm. Sir Angus (Edward Malise Bontine),** KBE, *cr* 1951 (CBE 1944); CB 1947; JP: Lord Lieutenant of Dunbartonshire, 1954-68; Keeper of Dumbarton Castle, since 1955; *b* 1893; *s* of Comdr C. E. F. Cunninghame Graham, MVO, Royal Navy; *m* 1924, Mary Patricia, *d* of late Col Lionel Hanbury, CMG; one *s* one *d*. *Educ:* Osborne and Dartmouth. HM Yacht Victoria and Albert, 1914; served in Grand Fleet, 1914-18; SNO West River, China, 1936-38; Capt. of HM Signal Sch., 1939-41; Capt. of HMS Kent, 1941-43; Commodore Royal Naval Barracks, Chatham, 1943-45; ADC to King George VI; Rear-Adm, 1945; Rear-Adm. Comdg 10th Cruiser Squadron, and 2nd in Comd Home Fleet, 1945-46; Flag Officer, Scotland, 1950-51, and Admiral Superintendent, Rosyth, 1947-51; Vice-Adm. 1948; retd list, 1951; Adm., 1952. An Ensign in Royal Company of Archers (Queen's Body Guard for Scotland). Hon. Sheriff Substitute, 1959. Vice-Pres., RNLI; Trustee for National Library of Scotland; Commissioner of Queen Victoria Sch. A Vice-Pres. National Trust for Scotland. DL Dunbartonshire, 1952-55. JP 1955. *Address:* Ardoch, Cardross, Dunbartonshire, Scotland. *T:* Dumbarton 2905. *Clubs:* United Service; Royal Yacht Squadron (Naval Member); New (Edinburgh). *See also Baron Polwarth.*

**CUNNISON, David Keith,** CIE 1933; formerly Secretary, Bengal Chamber of Commerce, Calcutta; *b* 1881; *m* 1914, Helena, *d* of late George North, South Thoresby, Lincs; one *d*. *Educ:* George Watson's Coll. and Univ., Edinburgh, (MA, LLB). *Address:* Ravenscroft, Bulstrode Way, Gerrards Cross, Bucks.

**CUNYNGHAME, Sir (Henry) David St Leger Brooke Selwyn,** 11th Bt (of Milncraig), *cr* 1702; *b* 7 Feb. 1905; *s* of Lieut-Col Sir Percy Francis Cunynghame, 10th Bt, OBE, DL, JP, and Maud Albinia Margaret (*d* 1948), *o d* of Major Selwyn-Payne, Badgeworth Court, Gloucester; *S* father, 1941; *m* 1941, Hon. Pamela Margaret Stanley, *qv*; three *s*. *Educ:* Eton. Mem. of Board of Dirs of various British Motion Picture Producing and Distributing Companies. Served as Sqdn Ldr; RAFVR during War of 1939-45. *Recreation:* shooting. *Heir:* *s* Andrew David Francis Cunynghame, *b* 25 Dec. 1942. *Address:* 15 Madeline Road, SE20. *T:* 01-778 7740. *Club:* Carlton.

**CUNYNGHAME, James Ogilvy B.;** *see* Blair-Cunynghame.

**CURE, (George) Nigel C.;** *see* Capel Cure.

**CURIE, Eve, (Mrs Henry R. Labouisse),** writer and journalist; *b* Paris, 6 Dec. 1904; *d* of late Marie and Pierre Curie; *m* 1954, Henry Richardson Labouisse, *qv*. *Educ:* by governesses, generally Polish; Sévigné College, Bachelor of Science and Bachelor of Philosophy. Accompanied her mother in her tour of the US 1921; devoted several years to the study of the piano and gave her first concert in 1925 in Paris; later she took up musical criticism and under a pseudonym acted for several years as musical critic of the weekly journal Candide; after the death of her mother in 1934 she collected and classified all the papers, manuscripts, and personal documents left by Mme Curie and went to Poland in 1935 to obtain material as to Mme Curie's youth; wrote Mme Curie's biography; went to America again in 1939 and has gone several times since on lecture tours; was a co-ordinator of the women's war activities at the Ministry of Information in Paris at the beginning of the war, until she went on a lecture tour in the USA; came back to Paris 2 May 1940; after the French capitulation went to live in London for six months, then to America for her third lecture tour; Vichy Govt deprived her of French citizenship in April 1941; in 1942, travelled, as a war correspondent to the battlefronts of Libya, Russia, Burma, China; enlisted in the Fighting French corps, Volontaires Françaises, 1943, as a private; received basic training in England; 2nd Lieut 1943; 1st Lieut 1944. Co-publisher of Paris-Presse, an evening paper in Paris, 1944-49. Special Adviser to the Sec. Gen. of NATO, Paris, Aug. 1952-Nov. 1954. *Publications:* Madame Curie (in US), 1937 (trans. into 32 langs); Journey Among Warriors, 1943. *Recreation:* swimming. *Address:* 1 Sutton Place South, New York, NY 10022, USA.

**CURLE, John Noel Ormiston,** CMG 1966; CVO 1956; Ambassador to the Philippines, since 1970; *b* 12 Dec. 1915; *s* of Major W. S. N. Curle, MC, Melrose, Scotland; *m* 1st, 1940, Diana Deane; one *s* one *d*; 2nd, 1948, Pauline, *widow* of Capt. David Roberts; one step *s* two step *d*. *Educ:* Marlborough; New Coll., Oxford. 1st Class Hons, MA, Laming Travelling Fellow of Queen's Coll. Diplomatic Service, 1939; Irish Guards, 1939; War Cabinet Secretariat, 1941-44. Has served in Lisbon, Ottawa, Brussels, Stockholm (Counsellor), Athens (Counsellor); Boston (Consul-Gen., 1962-66); Ambassador to: Liberia, 1967-70 and Guinea, 1968-70. Comdr, Order of the North Star (Sweden), 1956. *Recreation:* skiing (represented Oxford *v* Cambridge, and British Univs *v* Swiss Univs). *Address:* British Embassy, Manila, Philippines; Appletree House, near Byfield, Rugby. *T:* Chipping Warden 211. *Club:* Guards.

**CURLEWIS, His Honour Judge Sir Adrian (Herbert),** Kt 1967; CBE 1962; Judge of the District Court, New South Wales, Australia, since 1948; *b* 13 Jan. 1901; *s* of late Judge Herbert R. Curlewis and late Ethel Turner, Authoress; *m* 1928, Beatrice Maude Carr; one *s* one *d*. *Educ:* Sydney Church of England Grammar Sch.; Univ. of Sydney. Called to Bar of NSW, 1927. Served War of 1939-45, Capt. 8 Div. AIF, Malaya. President: Surf Life Saving Assoc. of Australia, 1933-; International Surf Life Saving Council, 1956-; Chairman: Australian Outward Bound Trust (Founder and Past Pres.), 1956-; National Fitness Council, New South Wales, 1948-; National Co-ordinator, Duke of Edinburgh's Award in Australia, 1958-; Pres., Royal Humane Soc. (NSW), 1968. Youth Policy Adv. Cttee to NSW Government, 1961-63. Chm. and Royal Commissioner on various Government Enquiries. *Recreations:* surfing, gardening. *Address:* 5 Hopetoun Avenue, Mosman, NSW, Australia. *T:* 96-5365. *Clubs:* University (Sydney); Elanora Country (NSW).

**CURRALL, Alexander,** CB 1970; CMG 1965; Director, Department for National Savings, since 1968; *b* 30 Jan. 1917; *s* of late R. T. Currall, Edinburgh; *m* 1940, Madeleine Crombie Saunders; one *s*. *Educ:* George Watson's Coll., Edinburgh; Edinburgh Univ. Min. of Supply, 1939-40; Royal Artillery and Indian Artillery, 1940-46. Successively in Min. of Supply, Min. of Materials and Board of Trade, concerned mainly with internat. economic negotiations, excepting the period 1950-54, when responsible for public trading in non-ferrous metals, and 1954-55, when holding a Commonwealth Fellowship for travel and study in USA. Seconded to Foreign Office as Dep. Consul-Gen., New York, and Dir of British Industrial Development Office, 1960-62; Minister (Commercial), British High Commn, Ottawa, 1962-66; Under-Secretary: Board of Trade, 1966-67; DEA 1967-68. *Address:* 5 Spencer Hill, SW19. *Club:* Caledonian.

**CURRAN, Charles;** MP (C) Uxbridge, 1959-66 and since 1970; *b* 1903; *m* Mona Regan; one *s*. *Educ:* Cardiff High Sch.; Stonyhurst. Called to Bar, Gray's Inn. Journalist. Fleet Street, 1928-55: London Evening News (Chief Sub-Editor, Asst Editor); Evening Standard (Features Editor, Asst Editor); Daily Mirror (Asst Editor); Contested (C): West Walthamstow, 1945; Uxbridge, 1951 and 1955. *Publication:* You Know You Can Trust Me (novel). *Address:* 9 Stone Buildings, Lincoln's Inn, WC2. *T:* 01-405 0975; 70 Park Mansions, Knightsbridge, SW1. *T:* 01-584 7845. *Clubs:* Press, Savage, Carlton.

**CURRAN, Charles John;** Director-General of the BBC since April 1969; *b* 13 Oct. 1921; *s* of Felix Curran and Alicia Isabella (*née* Bruce); *m* 1949, Silvia Meyer; one *d*. *Educ:* Wath-on-Dearne Gram. Sch., S Yorks; Magdalene Coll., Cambridge. Indian Army, 1941-45. Producer, Home Talks, BBC, 1947-50; Asst Editor, Fishing News, 1950-51; BBC, 1951-, including appts as Canadian Rep., 1956-59 and Sec., 1963-66; Dir of External Broadcasting, 1967-69. *Recreation:* refereeing coarse Rugby. *Address:* British Broadcasting Corporation, Broadcasting House, W1A 1AA. *T:* 01-580 4468. *Club:* Oxford and Cambridge University.

**CURRAN, Desmond,** CBE 1961; FRCP; Lord Chancellor's Medical Visitor, 1967; Hon. Consulting Psychiatrist, St George's Hospital, since 1967; formerly Professor of Psychiatry, St George's Hospital Medical School, University of London; Civil Consultant in Psychological Medicine to the

Royal Navy; *b* 14 Feb. 1903; *s* of late J. P. Curran; *m* 1938, Marguerite (*née* Gothard); two *s*. *Educ:* Wellington Coll.; Trinity Coll., Cambridge; St George's Hosp.; Johns Hopkins Hosp., Baltimore. MB, BChir Cambridge, 1928; MRCP 1928, FRCP 1937; MRCS, LRCP 1927; DPM London 1930; Rockefeller Travelling Fellowship, 1930-31; Gaskell Gold Medal Psychological Medicine, 1933. War of 1939-45: Consultant in Psychological Medicine to Royal Navy (Temp. Surg. Capt. RNVR), 1939-46. Croonian Lecturer, RCP 1948. President: Psychiatric Section, RSM; 1951-52; Royal Med. Psychological Assoc., 1963-64. Member: (Franklin) Deptl Cttee on Punishments, Prisons and Borstals, etc, 1948-51; (Wolfenden) Deptl Cttee on Homosexuality and Prostitution, 1954-57; (Representative RCP), Gen. Med. Council, 1961-67. Distinguished Fellow, Amer. Psychiatric Assoc., 1966. *Publications:* (jointly) Psychological Medicine, 6th edn 1969; articles and papers in medical text books and journals. *Recreation:* golf. *Address:* 77 Clarence Gate Gardens, NW1. *Clubs:* Athenæum, United University.

**CURRAN, Harry Gibson,** CMG 1953; *b* 1901; *s* of late James P. and Jessie M. Curran; *m* 1962, Betty, *d* of Harold Beazley. *Educ:* Royal Naval College, Dartmouth; University College, Oxford (MA). Served War of 1939-45, Middle East (despatches). Treasury Representative, South Asia, 1950-53; Canada, 1953-56; Head of Economic Mission, Ecuador, 1956-58; Representative World Bank, India, 1959-61; Dep. Dir, European Office, World Bank, 1961-66. *Address:* Waterstock Mill, near Wheatley, Oxford. *Club:* Travellers'.

**CURRAN, Rt. Hon. Sir Lancelot E.,** PC (N Ireland) 1957; Kt 1964; BA, LLB (QUB); QC (N Ireland) 1943; Lord Justice of Appeal, Supreme Court of Judicature, Northern Ireland, since 1956; *b* 8 March 1899; 4th *s* of late Miles Curran, Myrtlefield Park, Belfast; *m* 1924, Doris Lee; two *s* (one *d* decd). *Educ:* Royal Belfast Academical Institution. Barrister, King's Inns, 1923; Bencher, Inn of Court of N Ireland, 1946. MP Carrick Div., Co. Antrim, NI Parlt, April 1945 (re-elected June 1945)-1949; Parly Sec., Min. of Finance and Chief Whip, 1945. Served European war, 1917-18, RFC and RAF; War of 1939-45, Major, Army. Lecturer in Contract and Tort, Queen's Univ., Belfast; Chm. Court of Referees and Dep. Umpire under Unemployment Pensions Acts, 1926-45; Senior Crown Prosecutor for Co. Down; Attorney-Gen., NI, 1947-49; Judge of High Courts of Justice, NI, 1949-56. *Recreation:* golf. *Address:* Wentworth, Deramore Park, Belfast 9. *T:* 668922. *Club:* Royal Co. Down Golf.

**CURRAN, Prof. Robert Crowe,** MD; FRSE 1962; Leith Professor of Pathology, Birmingham University, since 1966; Chairman, Division of Pathological Studies, since 1968; Hon. Consultant Pathologist to the United Birmingham Hospitals; *b* 28 July 1921; *s* of John Curran and Sarah Crowe, Netherton, Wishaw, Lanarkshire; *m* 1947, Margaret Marion Park; one *s* one *d*. *Educ:* Glasgow Univ. MB, ChB 1943, MD 1956; FRCPath 1967; FRCP 1969. RAMC, 1945-47. Lectr in Pathology, Glasgow Univ., 1950-55. Sen. Lectr and Cons. Pathologist, Sheffield Univ., 1955-58; Prof. of Pathology, St Thomas's Hospital Medical Sch., 1959-66. Registrar, Royal Coll. of Pathologists. *Publications:* Atlas of Histopathology; scientific papers on structure and disorders of connective tissue, etc. *Recreations:* golf, music. *Address:* 12 Hintlesham Avenue, Edgbaston, Birmingham 15.

*See also Sir S. C. Curran.*

**CURRAN, Sir Samuel (Crowe),** Kt 1970; FRS 1953; FRSE 1947; DSc; DL; Principal and Vice-Chancellor, University of Strathclyde, since 1964; *b* 23 May 1912; *s* of John Curran, Kinghorn, Fife, and Sarah Owen Crowe, Ballymena, Ulster; *m* 1940, Joan Elizabeth, *yr d* of Charles William Strothers and Margaret Beatrice (*née* Millington); three *s* one *d*. *Educ:* Glasgow Univ.; St John's Coll., Cambridge. DSc Glasgow 1950; MA; BSc, PhD Glasgow, 1937; Cavendish Laboratory, 1937-39; PhD Cantab, 1941; RAE, 1939-40; Min. of Aircraft Production and Min. of Supply, 1940-44; Manhattan Project (Min. of Supply), Univ. of California, 1944-45 (Invention of Scintillation Counter, 1944). Researches in nuclear physics. Natural Philosophy, Glasgow Univ. 1945-55; UK Atomic Energy Authority, 1955-58; Chief Scientist, AWRE, Aldermaston, Berks, 1958-59. Principal, Royal Coll. of Science and Technology, Glasgow, 1959-64. Pres., Scottish Soc. for Mentally Handicapped Children, 1954-. Member: Council for Scientific and Industrial Research, 1962-65; Science Research Council, 1965-68; Adv. Council on Technology, 1965-; Chairman: Adv. Cttee on Med. Research, 1962-; Adv. Bd on Relations with Univs, 1966-; Mem. Council, Royal Society of Edinburgh, 1961-64; Mem., Scottish Econ. Planning Council, 1965-68; Chief Scientific Officer to the Sec. of State for Scotland, 1967-. Director: Scottish Television, 1964-; D-Mac Ltd; Hall-Thermotank, 1969-; Gen. Steels Div., BSC, 1970-. FRCPS (Hon.) 1964; Hon. LLD, Glasgow, 1968. Freeman, Motherwell and Wishaw, 1966. DL Glasgow, 1969. Comdr, St Olav (Norway), 1966; Officer of Polonia Restituta, 1970. *Publications:* (with J. D. Craggs) Counting Tubes, 1949; Luminescence and the Scintillation Counter, 1953; Alpha, Beta and Gamma Ray Spectroscopy, 1964; papers on nuclear researches and education in Proc. Royal Soc., London, Proc. Royal Soc. Edinburgh, Philosophical Magazine, Physical Review, Nature, etc. *Recreation:* sailing. *Address:* Livingstone Tower, University of Strathclyde, Glasgow, C1. *Clubs:* Athenæum, Caledonian; Royal Scottish Automobile (Glasgow).

*See also R. C. Curran.*

**CURRER BRIGGS, D. H.;** *see* Briggs, D. H. C.

**CURREY, Rear-Adm. Edmund Neville Vincent,** CB 1960; DSO 1944; DSC 1941; *b* 1 Oct. 1906; *s* of Dr and Mrs E. F. N. Currey, Lismore, Co. Waterford, Ireland; *m* 1941, Rosemary Knight; one *d*. *Educ:* Royal Naval Colls, Osborne and Dartmouth. Joined RNC Osborne 1920; served in submarines and destroyers as junior officer; served War of 1939-45; commanded HM ships Wrestler, Escapade and Musketeer; Comdr, 1942; Capt., 1949; subsequently served with British Naval Mission to Greece; Naval Asst to Adm. Commanding Reserves; in command of HMS Bermuda; Naval Asst to Second Sea Lord; Rear-Adm., 1958. Chief of Staff to C-in-C, Portsmouth, 1958-61, retired. Polish Gold Cross of Merit, with swords, 1943. *Recreation:* golf. *Address:* Glendower House, Clifton Park, Bristol 8. *T:* Bristol 35492.

**CURREY, Rear-Adm. Harry Philip,** CB 1956; OBE 1941; *b* 18 Sept. 1902; *s* of Hon. H. L. Currey; *m* 1928, Rona Gwenllian Harkness; one *s* one *d*. *Educ:* RN Colls Osborne and Dartmouth. Served War of 1939-45: Western Approaches, GHQ, Cairo, E Indies Stn, Eastern Fleet, Mediterranean, British Pacific Fleet. Admty, 1945-47; Capt. of Dockyard, HM Dockyard, Devonport, 1948-50; HMS

Bermuda, 1951-53; Flag Officer, Gibraltar and Adm. Supt, HM Dockyard, Gibraltar, 1953-56; retired, 1956. *Recreations:* fishing, gardening. *Address:* Pond Cottage, Newton Valence, near Alton, Hants. *T:* Tisted 281.

**CURREY, Ronald Fairbridge,** MC, MA, Hon. LLD; *b* 23 Oct. 1894; *s* of late Hon. H. L. Currey and Ethelreda (*d* 1942), *d* of late C. A. Fairbridge; *m* 1924, Dorothy White; three *s*. *Educ:* Diocesan Coll., Rondebosch; S Andrews Coll., Grahamstown; Rhodes Univ. Coll., Grahamstown; Trinity Coll., Oxford; Rhodes Scholar, 1912. Served 1914-18, Argyll and Sutherland Highlanders (attached Black Watch), France and Belgium (MC and Bar); Asst Master, Rugby Sch., 1920-21; S Andrews Coll., Grahamstown, 1922-26; Joint Headmaster, Ridge Preparatory Sch., Johannesburg, 1927-30; Rector of Michaelhouse, Balgowan, Natal, 1930-38; Headmaster of S Andrews Coll., Grahamstown, S Africa, 1939-55; Headmaster, Ruzawi Sch., Marandellas, S Rhodesia, 1956-61; Lectr in Classics, Rhodes Univ., Grahamstown, until 1965. *Publications:* (with others) Coming of Age–Studies in South African Politics, Economics, and Citizenship, 1930; Some Notes on The Future of the South African Church Schools, 1942; Rhodes: a Biographical Footnote, 1946; (with others) The South African Way of Life, 1953; S Andrews College, 1855-1955, 1955; Rhodes University, 1904-1970, 1970. *Address:* 34 Hill Street, Grahamstown, South Africa.

**CURRIE, Prof. Alastair Robert,** FRCPE, FRCP Glasgow, FRSE; Regius Professor of Pathology, University of Aberdeen, since 1962; *b* 8 Oct. 1921; *s* of late John Currie and of Margaret MacTaggart; *m* 1949, Jeanne Marion Clarke, MB, ChB; three *s* two *d*. *Educ:* High Sch. and Univ. of Glasgow. BSc 1941; MB, ChB Glasgow, 1944; MRCPE 1947, FRCPE 1957; MCPath 1963; FCPath 1965; FRCP Glasgow, 1964; FRSE 1964; MRCP 1966. RAMC 1949-51; Lectr in Pathology, Univ. of Glasgow 1947-54; Sen. Lectr in Pathology, Univ. of Glasgow, and Cons. Pathologist, Royal Infirmary, Glasgow, 1954-59; Head, Div. of Pathology, Imperial Cancer Research Fund, London, 1959-62. Chm., Standing Adv. Cttee on Laboratory Services; Member: MRC, 1964-68; Scottish NE Regional Hosp. Bd; Scottish Health Services Council. *Publications:* papers in scientific and med. jls. *Recreations:* golf, fishing. *Address:* 45 Don Street, Old Aberdeen. *T:* Aberdeen 43516. *Club:* Athenæum.

**CURRIE, Sir George (Alexander),** Kt 1960; retired as Vice-Chancellor, University of New Zealand (May 1952-Dec. 1961); *b* Banffshire, Scotland, 13 Aug. 1896; *s* of George Currie, farmer, and Mary Currie; *m* 1923, Margaret, *d* of Alexander Smith; two *s*. *Educ:* University of Aberdeen (BscAg, DSc). War Service, Gordon Highlanders, 1915-18. Manager, Salter Estate Co. Ltd, N Queensland, 1923-26; Scientific Officer, Dept Agric., Queensland, 1926-29; Principal Research Officer, Council for Scientific and Industrial Research, Australia, 1929-39; Prof. of Agriculture, University of Western Australia, 1939-40; Vice Chancellor, Univ. of Western Australia, 1940-52. Chm. Commn on Higher Educn for Papua and New Guinea, 1963-64. Hon. LLD: Aberdeen, 1948; Melbourne, 1954; Dalhousie, Canada, 1958; Papua, New Guinea, 1967. Hon. DLitt, University of Western Australia, 1952. *Publications:* The Origins of CSIRO, 1901-26, 1966; some 20 bulletins, pamphlets and articles on scientific research; articles on univ. educn and admin. *Address:* 20 Chermside Street, Canberra, Australia.

**CURRIE, George Boyle Hanna,** MBE 1946; *b* 19 Dec. 1905; *s* of late Very Rev. William John Currie, BA, DD; *m* 1933, Stephanie Maud Evelyn Costello; two *s* two *d*. *Educ:* Campbell Coll., Belfast; Trinity Coll., Dublin (BA, MA, LLB). Called to Bar, Middle Temple, 1932; Northern Circuit, 1932; Councillor, Wirral UDC, 1934-50 (Chm. Council, 1938); contested (C) East Flintshire, 1950 and 1951; MP (UU) North Down, 1955-70. Served War, 1939-46; RAFVR (Sqdn Ldr). *Recreations:* salmon fishing, golf. *Address:* (Chambers) 2 Pump Court, Temple, EC4. *T:* 01-353 3106, 7540; (Residence) 1 Pump Court, Temple, EC4. *T:* 01-583 1594; Rathdune House, Downpatrick, Co. Down. *T:* Downpatrick 2544. *Club:* County (Downpatrick).

**CURRIE, Lieut-Col George Selkirk,** CMG 1944; DSO 1918; MC 1916; member, firm of McDonald, Currie & Company, chartered accountants, 630 Dorchester Boulevard West, Montreal; *b* 17 Oct. 1889; *m* 1927, Louisa Hope, *d* of George H. Napier, Montreal; two *s* two *d*. *Educ:* Perth, Ontario; McGill Univ. (BA). Served European War, 1914-18 (despatches twice, MC, DSO). Deputy Minister of National Defence (Army), Canada, 1942-44. *Address:* 695 Aberdeen Avenue, Westmount 217, Quebec, Canada. *Clubs:* University, Montreal Racquet, Royal Montreal Golf (Montreal).

**CURRIE, Sir James,** KBE 1967 (OBE 1950); CMG 1958; retired from HM Diplomatic Service, 1967; Commonwealth Foundation, since 1967; *b* 6 May 1907; *o s* of Charles Howat Currie and Rebecca Ralston, Glasgow; *m* 1945, Daisy Mowat; one *s*. *Educ:* Glasgow Academy; Glasgow Univ.; Balliol Coll., Oxford; London School of Economics. William Hollins & Co. Ltd, 1931-34; National Milk Publicity Council, 1934-39; Ministry of Economic Warfare, 1939. Commercial Secretary: Rio de Janeiro, 1941; Ankara, 1944; First Secretary (Commercial), Istanbul, 1945; Santiago, Chile, 1947; Commercial Counsellor, Washington, 1949; Commercial Counsellor and Consul-General, Copenhagen, 1952; Consul-General: São Paulo, 1956; Johannesburg, 1962. Member: Community Relations Commn, 1970-; London Council of Univ. of Witwatersrand. *Publication:* Professional Organisations in the Commonwealth, 1970. *Recreations:* fishing and golf. *Address:* 2 Westbury Road, W5. *T:* 01-998 2683. *Club:* Reform.

**CURRIE, Rear-Adm. Robert Alexander,** CB 1957; DSC 1944, bar 1945; DL; *b* 29 April 1905; 5th *s* of John Currie, Glasgow, and Rachel Thomson, Dundee; *m* 1944, Lady (Edith Margaret) Beevor, *widow* of Sir Thomas Beevor, 6th Bt, and *d* of Frank Agnew, Eccles, Norfolk; one step *s* (*see* Sir Thomas Beevor, 7th Bt) three step *d*. *Educ:* RN Colleges, Osborne and Dartmouth. Captain RN, 1945; Captain (D) Fifth Flotilla, 1948-49; idc 1950; Director, Royal Naval Staff Coll., 1951-52; Comdg Officer, HMS Cumberland, 1953; Rear-Adm., 1954; Chief of Staff to Chairman, British Joint Service Mission, Washington, DC, 1954-57; retired, 1957. Member, Cttee of Enquiry into the Fishing Industry, 1958-60. DL, Suffolk, 1968. King Haakon VII Liberty Cross, Norway, 1945. *Recreations:* shooting, fishing. *Address:* Thorpe Morieux Hall, near Bury St Edmunds. *T:* Cockfield Green 276. *Clubs:* United Service; West Suffolk.

**CURRIE, Sir Walter Mordaunt Cyril,** 5th Bt, *cr* 1846; Member of the Performing Rights Society; *b* 3 June 1894; *s* of 4th Bt and Bertha (*d* 1951), *d* of T. A. Mitford Freeman; *S* father, 1941. *Educ:* Sherborne. Served European War,

1915-16, with RAOC. *Publications:* Some 25 lyrics and part songs, 2 cantatas; choral symphony, Odysseus; Nativity Play, The Three Kings, music by C. Armstrong Gibbs. *Address:* Chasefield Cottage, Wickham Bishops, Witham, Essex.

**CURRY, Thomas Peter Ellison;** *b* 22 July, 1921; *s* of Maj. F. R. P. Curry; *m* 1950, Pamela Joyce, *d* of late Group Capt. A. J. Holmes, AFC, JP; two *s* two *d*. *Educ:* Tonbridge; Oriel Coll., Oxford. BA 1948; MA 1951. Served War of 1939-45; enlisted 1939; commnd, 1941; 17th Indian Div., India and Burma, 1941-45. War Office, 1946. Called to Bar, Middle Temple, 1953. QC 1966. Solicitor, 1968; partner in Freshfields, Solicitors, 1968-70; returned to Bar, 1970. Rep. Army and Sussex at Squash Racquets, also Oxford, 1946-48 (triple blue); British Steeplechase champion, Olympic Games, 1948. Served on AAA Cttee of Inquiry, 1967. *Publications:* (Joint Editor) Palmer's Company Law, 1959; (Joint Editor) Crew on Meetings, 1966. *Recreations:* rackets; research into causes and course of civil wars and mutinies; engaged on history of American Civil War; gardening. *Address:* Cedar House, Vicarage Lane, Send, Surrey. *T:* Ripley 3019. *Club:* MCC.

**CURSITER, Stanley,** CBE 1948 (OBE 1919); RSW; RSA 1937 (now Hon. retired Academician); FRSE; FEIS; FRIAS; HM's painter and limner in Scotland since 1948; *b* Kirkwall, Orkney Isles, 1887; *s* of J. Scott Cursiter; *m* Phyllis Eda, *d* of David Hourston of Greenfield; one *d*. Represented in permanent collections of the Corporations of Liverpool, Oldham, Paisley, Cork; Scot. Mod. Arts; Director of National Galleries of Scotland, 1930-48. Served European War with Scottish Rifles and 4th Batt. Field Survey Royal Engineers (OBE, despatches twice). Freeman of City and Royal Burgh of Kirkwall, 1948. Hon. LLD Aberdeen, 1959. *Address:* 70 Victoria Street, Stromness, Orkney.
*See also J. M. Hunter.*

**CURSLEY, Norman Sharpe;** *b* 13 April 1898; *s* of David and Mary Cursley; *m* 1922, Alice Nelly Hill; one *s* one *d*. *Educ:* Newark Sch., Leicester. Formerly: Reporter, Leicester Daily Mercury, 1921; Special Writer, The Globe, 1922; Reporter, Daily Sketch, 1923; Reporter and News Editor, Westminster Gazette, 1924-28; News Editor, Daily News (Manchester), 1929-48; News Editor, News Chronicle (London), 1948; Asst Editor, News Chronicle, 1951, Editor and Director of the News Chronicle, 1958-60. *Recreations:* golf, motoring. *Address:* The Old Orchard, Puttenham, near Guildford, Surrey. *T:* Puttenham 298. *Club:* Press.

**CURSON, Bernard Robert,** CMG 1967; HM Diplomatic Service; Consul-General, Atlanta, USA, since 1970; *b* 14 Nov. 1913; *e s* of late Robert and Mabel Curson; *m* 1949, Miriam Olive Johnson, Lynchburg, Virginia; one *s*. *Educ:* University College School. asst Private Secretary to Secretary of State for India, 1943-44 and 1945-46; Member UK delegation to UN Assembly, 1946, 1947, 1948; Private Secretary to Secretary of State for Commonwealth Relations, 1948-50; Office of UK High Commissioner, Ceylon, 1950-52; Member UK delegation to UN Wheat Conference, Geneva, 1956; Member UK delegation to Colombo Plan Consultative Cttee, Wellington, 1956 and Saigon, 1957; Regional Information Officer, British Information Services, Canada, 1958-64; Head of: Information Policy Dept, CRO, 1964-65; Jt Information Administration Dept, 1965-68; Information Policy Dept, FCO, 1968-70. *Address:* c/o National & Grindlay's Bank Ltd, 13 St James's Square, SW1. *Club:* Travellers'.

**CURTEIS, Capt. Sir Gerald,** KCVO, *cr* 1954 (MVO 1927); RN, retired, Elder Brother of Trinity House from 1936, Deputy Master of the Corporation, 1948-61; Court of The London Assurance, 1953-63; *b* 16 Oct. 1892; *s* of late Robert Mascall Curteis, Piltdown, Uckfield; *m* 1st, Lettice (*d* 1918), *d* of late Canon Foster, Groombridge; no *c*; 2nd, 1936, Dolla, *o d* of late Walter G. Darby, Markly, Sussex; one *s* two *d*. *Educ:* Parkside, Ewell; RN Colleges, Osborne and Dartmouth. Entered Navy, 1906; served European War in HM Ships Blonde, Warspite, Boadicea, Godetia; served in HMS Renown during tour of Duke and Duchess of York to New Zealand and Australia, 1927; Comdr, 1927; Captain, 1934; retired list, 1936; served War of 1939-45, in RN. Hon. Member Worshipful Company of Feltmakers. *Address:* Broomwood, Sevenoaks, Kent. *Clubs:* United Service, MCC; (Hon. Member) Royal Corinthian Yacht.

**CURTHOYS, Roy Lancaster,** CMG 1958; Chief Australian Correspondent, Times and New York Times, 1927-57, retired; *b* Ballarat, 4 Oct. 1892; *er s* of late Alfred George Curthoys, Perth, W. Australia; unmarried. *Educ:* privately; Hale Sch., Perth. Member, literary staff, Perth Daily News, 1910-16; West Australian, Perth, 1916-18; Melbourne Herald, 1919-20; joined Melbourne Argus Staff, 1920; on staff Australian Press Association, London, 1922-23; Asst Editor of Argus, 1925-28; Editor, 1929-35; Member of Federal Council of Australian Journalists Association, 1918-20. *Recreations:* music, walking. *Address:* 56 Walsh Street, South Yarra, Victoria 3141, Australia.

**CURTIN, Rt. Rev. Mgr. Canon Jeremiah John,** DD; Rector, Pontificio Collegio Beda, Rome, since 1961; Priest-Director and Ecclesiastical Adviser, Universe Enquiry Bureau, since 1953; Canon of Southwark Diocesan Chapter since 1958; Domestic Prelate to HH Pope John XXIII since 1961; *b* Sileby, Leics, 19 June 1907; *e s* of late Jeremiah John Curtin and Mary Bridget Curtin (*née* Leahy). *Educ:* Battersea Polytechnic; Wimbledon Coll.; St Joseph's Coll., Mark Cross; St John's Seminary, Wonersh; Gregorian Univ., Rome. BA London 1927; DD Rome 1933 (Gregorian Univ.). Priest, 1931; Prof. of Philosophy and Theology, St John's Seminary, Wonersh, 1933-48; Vice-Rector, 1947-48; Parish Priest, St Paul's, Hayward's Heath, 1948-56; Parish Priest, Our Lady of Ransom, Eastbourne, 1956-61. *Recreations:* archæology, music. *Address:* Pontificio Collegio Beda, Viale di San Paolo 18, Roma 00146, Italy. *T:* 551.700. *Club:* Athenæum.

**CURTIS, Maj.-Gen. Alfred Cyril,** CB 1944; DSO 1942; MC; ADC to the King, 1944; *b* 2 Nov. 1894. Lieut, Indian Army, 1915; Capt., 1918; Maj., 1932; Bt Lieut-Col, 1936; Lieut-Col, 1938; Colonel, 1940; temp. Maj.-Gen., 1944. Comdr Lucknow District, 1946; retired, 1948 as hon. Maj.-Gen.

**CURTIS, Colin Hinton Thomson,** CVO 1970; ISO 1970; Agent-General for Queensland in London, since 1970; *b* 25 June 1920; *s* of A. Curtis, Brisbane; *m* 1943, Anne Catherline Drevesen; one *s*. *Educ:* Brisbane Grammar School. RANR Overseas Service, 1940-45. Sec. and Investigation Officer to Chm., Sugar Cane Prices Board, 1948-49; Asst Sec. to Central Sugar Cane Prices Board, 1949; Sec. to Premier of Queensland, 1950-64; Mem., Qld Trade Missions to SE Asia, 1963 and 1964; Asst Under-Sec., Premier's Dept, 1961-64;

Assoc. Dir and Dir of Industrial Development, 1964-66; Under-Sec., Premier's Dept and Clerk of Exec. Council, 1966-70; State Dir, Royal Visit, 1970. *Recreations:* squash, sailing, swimming, tennis. *Address:* Queensland Government Offices, 392/3 Strand, WC2. *T:* 01-836 3224. *Club:* Royal Automobile.

**CURTIS, Sir (Edward) Leo,** Kt 1965; Lord Mayor of Melbourne, Australia, 1963-64 and 1964-65; *b* London, 13 Jan. 1907; *m* 1938, Elvira Lillian Prahl. Joined Melbourne City Council, Dec. 1955; Member of various cttees. Past President of Retail Traders Association of Victoria. *Address:* 5 Kenley Court, Toorak, Victoria 3142, Australia. *Clubs:* Athenæum (Melbourne); various sporting.

**CURTIS, Rt. Rev. Ernest Edwin;** *see* Mauritius and Seychelles, Bishop of.

**CURTIS, Brig. Francis Cockburn,** CBE 1945; MA; MIEE; Fellow Emeritus, Trinity Hall, Cambridge, since 1961; *b* 2 May 1898; *s* of late Lieut-Col J. G. C. Curtis, Oxford and Bucks Light Infantry, Walmer, Kent; *m* 1933, Dorothy Joan Grant; two *s* one *d*. *Educ:* Bedales Sch.; RMA, Woolwich; King's Coll., Cambridge. Commissioned RE 1917; served in Flanders (despatches), Iraq and Palestine; transferred to Royal Signals, 1923; served on General Staff in War Office and Aldershot Command, and in Home Office (ARP Dept); OC 38th (Welsh) Divisional Signals, 1940-41; Army Council Secretariat (Secretary Standing Cttee on Army Administration), 1941; Joint Planning Staff, 1942; Colonel 1943; Dep. Director of Military Operations, 1943-44; Director of Post-Hostilities Plans, War Office, 1944; Brigadier, General Staff (Plans and Ops), GHQ, MELF, 1945-48; Director for European Inter-Allied Planning, War Office, 1948-51; retired 1951; Fellow and Bursar, Trinity Hall, Cambridge, 1952-59; Treasurer, 1959-61. *Recreation:* fishing. *Address:* 16 Marlborough Court, Cambridge. *Club:* United Service.

**CURTIS, Sir George (Harold),** Kt 1955; CB 1950; Chief Land Registrar, HM Land Registry, 1947-63; *b* 12 June 1902; *s* of Dr John Cyril Curtis and Mabel Curtis; *m* 1928, Susan Phyllis Elmer; no *c*. *Educ:* Swansea Grammar Sch.; Keble Coll., Oxford. BA (hons) 1923; Boxing Blue, 1924; BCL 1924. Bacon Scholar, Gray's Inn, 1924; called to the Bar, 1925; HM Land Registry, 1926; transferred to HM Treasury, 1940; Asst Secretary, 1945. President Caterham and Dist. Residents Assoc., 1957-61. Chairman, Cttee for secession of Nyasaland from Federation of Rhodesia and Nyasaland, March 1963, and of Cttee for dissolution of the Federation, Aug.-Dec. 1963; Member panel of Chairmen of Industrial Tribunals, 1965-67; President, Mumbles Chamber of Trade, 1966-. *Recreations:* golf in intervals from gardening. *Publication:* (with T. B. F. Ruoff) The Law and Practice of Registered Conveyancing, 1958. *Address:* Tyrnant, 14 West Cross Lane, West Cross, Swansea.

**CURTIS, John S.;** *see* Sutton Curtis.

**CURTIS, Sir Leo;** *see* Curtis, Sir E. L.

**CURTIS, Michael Howard;** Executive Aide to HH The Aga Khan; Chairman, East African Printers and Publishers, Nairobi, Kenya, since 1959; *b* 28 Feb. 1920; *e s* of Howard and Doris May Curtis; *m* 1st, 1947, Barbara Winifred Gough; two *s* two *d*; 2nd, 1961, Marian Joan Williams. *Educ:* St Lawrence Coll.; Sidney Sussex Coll., Cambridge (MA). Eastern Daily Press, Norwich, 1945; News Chronicle: Leader Writer, 1946; Dep. Editor, 1952; Editor, 1954-57; Dir, News Chronicle Ltd, 1954-57; Personal Aide to HH The Aga Khan, 1957-59. *Address:* 77 Boulevard de Montmorency, Paris 16e, France. *Clubs:* Garrick, Travellers'; Muthaiga (Nairobi).

**CURTIS, Dame Myra,** DBE, *cr* 1949 (CBE 1942); MA; Principal, Newnham College, Cambridge, 1942-Sept. 1954, retired; *b* 2 Oct. 1886. *Educ:* Winchester School for Girls (now St Swithun's); Newnham Coll., Cambridge. Civil Servant, 1915-41. Commissioner, War Damage Commission, 1943-59; Chairman of Interdepartmental Cttee on Children deprived of a normal home life, 1945-46; Member Central Land Board, 1947-59; Member General Medical Council, 1955-60. *Publication:* Modern Money (with Hugh Townshend), 1937. *Address:* 5a Northgate, Chichester, Sussex.

**CURTIS, Percy John,** CB 1960; CBE 1955; Secretary, Exchequer and Audit Department, 1955-63; *b* 3 Oct. 1900; *s* of J. H. Curtis, Trimdon, Co. Durham; *m* 1st, 1924, Dorothy Hilda Ford Hayes (*d* 1954); one *s*; 2nd, 1958, Joyce Irene Potter. *Educ:* Rye Grammar Sch. Entered Exchequer and Audit Dept, 1920. *Address:* 2 Rigault Road, SW6. *T:* 01-736 4072. *Club:* Reform.

**CURTIS, Sir Peter,** 6th Bt, *cr* 1802; *b* 9 April 1907; *s* of late Edward Beaumont Cotton Curtis; *S* cousin, 1943; *m* 1934, Joan Margaret Nicholson; one *s* two *d*. *Educ:* Winchester Coll. Lieut 16/5 Lancers, 1926-28 (SR); Lieut 16/5 Lancers, 1928-34. Served 1939-45 Shropshire Yeomanry, Div. HQ Armoured Div. and 38 (W) Infantry Div., and Pioneer Corps. *Recreations:* hunting, shooting, fishing, racing (horse). *Heir:* *s* William Peter Curtis, *b* 9 April 1935. *Address:* Little Manor, Bishop's Waltham, Hants. *Club:* Cavalry.

**CURTIS, Peter;** *see* Lofts, Norah.

**CURTIS, Richard James Seymour,** OBE 1962; *b* 22 Oct. 1900; *s* of late Sir George Curtis, KCSI, ICS, and of late Lady Curtis, OBE, La Frégate, Dinard, France; *m* 1929, Mary Margaret, *o d* of late Rev. and Mrs H. J. Boyd, St Paul's Vicarage, St Leonards-on-Sea; one *s* one *d*. *Educ:* Haileybury; King's Coll., Cambridge; University of Caen. Hons degree in History, Cambridge, 1922. Appointed Assistant Anglais at Lycée Corneille, Rouen, by Board of Education, Oct. 1922; Asst Master, Hurst Court, Sept. 1923, partner, 1926, Headmaster, 1933-61. Incorporated Assoc. of Preparatory Schools (Vice-Chm. IAPS, 1946; Chm. 1957). Asst Secretary and Secretary, Common Entrance Examination Board, 1961-67. Member Hastings Borough Council, 1952-61; President Soc. of Schoolmasters, 1962. *Publications:* (with A. R. Slater) Latin and French Revision Papers, 1948. Translator of The Revolutionaries, by Louis Madelin; Russia Unveiled, by Panait Istrati; Murder Party, by Henry Bordeaux; The Corsairs of St Malo, by Dupont. *Address:* The Wychert, Haddenham, Bucks. *T:* Haddenham 7136. *Club:* Royal Automobile.

**CURTIS, Air Vice-Marshal Walter John Brice,** CB 1946; CBE 1941 (OBE 1919); *b* 9 Nov. 1888; *m* 1917, Kathleen Osman Mullery; one *s* one *d* (and one *s* Flight-Lieut killed in action, Middle East, 1943). *Educ:* Lewisham House, Weston-super-Mare; Brighton Grammar Sch. RFC 1914; RAF 1918; Air Ministry, 1920-24; Iraq, 1924-27; Middle East, 1927-28; Coastal Command, 1930-32; India, 1933-38; Air Ministry, 1938-44; Dep. Director of Equipment, 1938-39; Director of Equipment, Air Commodore, 1940-44; AOC 55 (M) Wing,

1944-45; AOC 42 Group, July-Nov. 1945; AOC 40 Group, 1945-47; retired, 1947. Despatches 1941. *Recreations:* hockey, tennis, golf. *Address:* The Meads, Grange Road, Uckfield, Sussex. *T:* Uckfield 2882.

**CURTIS, Air Marshal Wilfred Austin,** SM 1967; CB 1946; CBE 1943; DSC 1917; ED 1945; Commander, US Legion of Merit; Chevalier, French Legion of Honour; Croix de Guerre with palm; LLD 1948; retired; *b* 21 Aug. 1893; *s* of Colin Mackenzie and Margaret Alice Sherwin; *m* 1924, Pearl Burford (decd); two *s* one *d*; *m* 1962, Mrs Maiola Englebright. *Educ:* Toronto Public and Technical Schools. Joined Canadian Army, 1915; transferred to Royal Naval Air Service, 1916; served as fighter pilot, France, 1917 and 1918; operated General Insurance business in own name at Toronto until outbreak of war, 1939; Director of Postings and Careers, 1940-41; Comd Uplands Air Training Station, 1941; Dep. C-in-C, RCAF overseas, Nov. 1941-44; Air Member Air Staff, Jan. 1944; Senior RCAF Member, Permanent Joint Board on Defence, Jan. 1944-Sept. 1947; Chief of Air Staff, Canada, 1947-53. Chancellor, York Univ., Toronto, 1960-68. Mem., Royal Canadian Military Inst. *Recreation:* golf. *Address:* Towers of Cable Beach, PO Box 4939, Nassau, Bahamas. *T:* 78-343. *Clubs:* York, Rosedale Golf (Toronto).

**CURTIS, Wilfred Harry,** CB 1953; CBE 1950; *b* 23 May 1897; retired as Assistant Under-Secretary of State, War Office, 1958. *Educ:* Summerleaze, Harptree, Somerset. JP County of London, 1950-58. *Address:* Woodlands, Curdridge, near Southampton. *T:* Botley 2125.

**CURTIS BROWN, Spencer;** President, Curtis Brown Ltd, London, literary agents; *b* 1906; *s* of A. Curtis Brown and Caroline Lord; *m* 1928, Jean, *d* of Rev. W. Watson, DD; one *d*. *Educ:* Harrow; Magdalene Coll., Cambridge (History Exhibitioner). Personal Adviser to General Sikorski, Polish Prime Minister, 1941-43; Intelligence Corps (Special Services); assisted in reorganizing book trade in liberated countries, 1945; served on various Government Cttees concerned with book distribution. *Publications:* (jt author) The Dark Side of the Moon, 1946. Contributed to various jls in England and America. *Recreation:* listening to other people. *Address:* 13 King Street, WC2. *T:* 01-240 2488. *Club:* Travellers'.

**CURTIS-RALEIGH, Nigel Hugh; His Honour Judge Curtis-Raleigh;** Judge of County Courts, since 1966; *b* 8 Nov. 1914; *s* of late Capt. H. T. R. Curtis-Raleigh; *m* 1964, Jean Steadman, MB, DPM; three *s*. *Educ:* Wellington; Queen's Coll., Oxford (History Exhibitioner, Kitchener Scholar). Called to the Bar, Middle Temple (Harmsworth Law Scholar), 1939. Served HAC, 1939-40. *Recreations:* music, chess, poker.

**CURWEN, Dame (Anne) May,** DBE, *cr* 1949 (CBE 1943); MA Cantab; President, British Council for Aid to Refugees; Vice-President, UNA, UK Committee; Vice-Chairman, National Council of Social Service; *b* 7 May 1889; *d* of William Curwen and Emma Cook. *Educ:* Birkenhead High Sch.; Harrogate Coll.; Newnham Coll., Cambridge. Hons Historical Tripos, Parts I and II, MA 1920; History Mistress, Orme Girls' Sch., Newcastle, Staffs, 1914-16; Organising Secretary, Scottish Women's Hospitals, 1916-19; in Serbia in connection with inquiry into condition of women and children there, 1918-19; joined staff National YWCA in finance dept, 1919; Education Secretary, YWCA, 1920-30; National General Secretary, YWCA of Great Britain, 1930-49; Chairman, Women's Group on Public Welfare, 1948-60; HM Govt Delegate to the UN Refugee Fund, 1954-58 (Chairman, 1958); Vice-Chairman World Refugee Year, UK Cttee, June 1959-June 1960; UN Nansen Medal award, 1964. Jugo-Slav Order of St Sava (3rd Class), 1922; Order of Polonia Restituta, 1970. *Recreations:* reading, cooking. *Address:* Cedarwood Cottage, Barton House, Barton-on-Sea, Hants. *T:* New Milton 3718.

**CURZON;** *see* Roper-Curzon.

**CURZON,** family name of **Earl Howe** and **Viscount Scarsdale.**

**CURZON, Clifford (Michael),** CBE 1958; FRAM; Pianist; *b* 18 May 1907, of British parents; *m* 1931, Lucille Wallace, American harpsichordist; two adopted *s*. *Educ:* Royal Academy of Music (Thalberg Scholar and Potter Exhibitioner); studied under Prof. Chas Reddie at Royal Academy of Music, Schnabel (Berlin), Katherine Goodson, and Landowska and Boulanger (Paris); concert tours in England, Europe and USA; in 1936 and 1938 toured Europe under the auspices of the British Council; Soloist at the Royal Philharmonic, BBC and Promenade Concerts, etc.; also Colonne and Société Philharmonique Concerts, Paris. 1st performance of Alan Rawsthorne's Piano Concerto No. 2, commnd by Arts Council for Festival of Britain, 1951. Formed (with Szigeti, Primrose and Fournier) the Edinburgh Festival Piano Quartet, 1952. American Tours, 1948-70, including solo appearances with New York Philharmonic Orchestra under Bruno Walter, the Philadelphia Orchestra, Pittsburgh and Toronto Orchestras, etc.; Soloist Holland Festival, 1953; Zürich Festival, 1953; tour of Continent as soloist with BBC Symphony Orchestra under Sir Malcolm Sargent, 1954; Soloist Bergen and Munich Festivals, 1954. Soloist Beethoven Festival, Bonn, Salzburg, Edinburgh and Prades Festivals. *Recreations:* gardening and swimming. *Address:* The White House, Millfield Place, Highgate, N6. *T:* 01-340 5348; The Close, Glenridding, Cumberland.

**CURZON, Francis John Nathaniel;** late Captain, Scots Guards; *b* 28 July 1924; *o s* of late Hon. Francis Nathaniel Curzon, 3rd *s* of 4th Baron Scarsdale, and late Winifred Phyllis (*née* Combe); *heir pres* to 2nd Viscount Scarsdale, *qv*; *m* 1st, 1948, Solange (marr. diss., 1967), *yr d* of late Oscar Hanse, Belgium; two *s* one *d*; 2nd, 1968, Helene Gladys Frances, *o d* of late Maj. William Ferguson Thomson, Kinellar, Aberdeenshire; two *s*. *Educ:* Eton. *Recreations:* piping, photography. *Address:* Weston Lodge, Kedleston, Derby. *T:* Duffield 2665. *Club:* Guards.

**CURZON, Leonard Henry,** CB 1956; Assistant Under Secretary of State, Ministry of Defence, since 1964; *b* 4 Jan. 1912; *s* of late Frederick Henry Curzon; *m* 1935, Greta, *e d* of late Willem and Anny van Praag; one *s*. *Educ:* Sir Walter St John's Sch.; Jesus Coll., Cambridge (Scholar, BA, LLB). Asst Principal, Import Duties Advisory Cttee, 1934; Air Ministry, 1938; Ministry of Aircraft Production, 1940; Ministry of Supply, 1946; Ministry of Aviation, 1959; idc 1947. *Address:* 69 Christchurch Mount, Epsom, Surrey. *T:* Epsom 22732. *Club:* United University.

**CUSACK, Henry Vernon,** CMG 1955; CBE 1947; HM Overseas Civil Service (retired); Deputy Director General of the Overseas Audit Service, 1946-55; *b* 26 June 1895; 2nd *s* of late Edward Cusack, Bray, Co. Wicklow, and of Constance Louisa Vernon, *e d* of late Col

Vernon, DL, JP, Clontarf Castle, Dublin; unmarried. *Educ:* Aravon Sch., Ireland. Served European War, 1914-19 (General Service and Victory medals), France, Belgium and North Russia, as Captain, RASC, attached RGA; entered Colonial Audit Service, 1920; Asst Auditor: Sierra Leone, 1920-22, Nigeria, 1922-28; Sen. Asst Auditor, Nyasaland, 1928-33; Asst Director, Central Office, Colonial Audit Dept London, 1933-37; Auditor, Gold Coast, 1937-46; a Governor of the King's Hospital Sch., Dublin (Chm., 1964-69). FRGS. Coronation Medal, 1953. *Address:* Clonalon, Meath Road, Bray, Co. Wicklow. *T:* Dublin 862412. *Clubs:* Naval and Military; University (Dublin); Royal St George Yacht (Dun Laoghaire, Co. Dublin).

**CUSACK, Hon. Sir Ralph Vincent,** Kt 1966; **Hon. Mr Justice Cusack;** Judge of the High Court of Justice (Queen's Bench Division) since 1966; *b* 13 April 1916; *s* of late His Honour John Cusack, KC, and late Dora, *d* of R. Winder, Solicitor; unmarried. *Educ:* King's Coll. Sch.; University of London; and in Italy. LLB 1939; Barrister, Gray's Inn, 1940; Bencher, 1966. Served in Army, 1940-46; Staff Capt., HQ Eastern Command, 1943-44; Dep. Asst Military Secretary (Major), War Office, 1944-46. Freeman, City of London, 1949; Member General Council of the Bar, 1953-57, 1960-64; QC 1960; Recorder of Gloucester, 1961-64; of Wolverhampton, 1964-66; Comr of Assize, South Eastern Circuit, July 1965; Leader of the Oxford Circuit, 1964-66. Deputy Chairman, Berkshire Quarter Sessions, 1962-68. *Address:* 221 Ashley Gardens, Westminster, SW1. *T:* 01-834 5610; Royal Courts of Justice, Strand, WC2. *Clubs:* Athenæum, Garrick.

**CUSDEN, Victor Vincent,** OBE 1943; *b* 26 Jan. 1893; *s* of James Cusden and Elizabeth Susan Wakelyn; *m* 1927, Aimée Louise Charlotte Pauwels; one *s* (one *d* decd). *Educ:* Christ's Hospital. Interned during war at Ruhleben Camp, Germany, where studied for Consular Service; granted Civil Service Certificate as a Probationer Vice-Consul in the Consular Service, 1919; appointed to Salonica, 1919; transferred to Antwerp, 1920; acting Vice-Consul at Charleroi, 1920-21; given substantive rank of Vice-Consul, 1921; acting Consul-General at Antwerp, 1921-22-23; acting Vice-Consul at Ghent, 1921; transferred to Valparaiso, 1924; acting Consul-General at Valparaiso, 1924-25 and 1927; transferred to Barcelona, 1928; acting Consul-General at Barcelona in 1928, 1929 and 1930; acting Consul at Malaga, 1929; in charge of Consulate General at Dakar, 1930; Consul at Nantes, 1930 (did not proceed); Consul-General at Dakar, 1931; at Loanda, 1941; Izmir (Smyrna), Turkey, 1946-51; Retired, 1951. Coronation Medal, 1937. *Address:* Mayfield, Avisford Park Road, Walberton, Arundel, Sussex.

**CUSDIN, Sidney Edward Thomas,** OBE 1946; DSc (Hong Kong); FRIBA, AADip; Senior Partner in Firm of Cusdin, Burden and Howitt, Architects; *b* 28 July 1908; *s* of Sidney Herbert Cusdin, London; *m* 1936, Eva Eileen (Peggy), *d* of F. P. Dorizzi, London; no *c*. *Educ:* Municipal School of Arts and Crafts, Southend-on-Sea, Essex; Architectural Assoc., London. AA Holloway Scholarship, 1927; Fifth Year Travelling Studentship, 1929; joined staff of Stanley Hall & Easton and Robertson: British Pavilions at Brussels Internat. Exhibition and Johannesburg Exhibition; elected Member of AA Council, 1937, and worked on RIBA Cttees. Served War of 1939-45, RAF, on staff of HQ, No. 26 Group (despatches twice, OBE). Re-joined firm of Easton & Robertson, 1946 (firm later known as Easton & Robertson, Cusdin, Preston and Smith, until 1965 when this partnership was dissolved). Pres. AA, 1950-51; Mem. Council RIBA, 1950-51. Awarded Henry Saxon Snell Prize and Theakston Bequest, 1950; Principal works: London: Development of the Hosp. for Sick Children, Great Ormond Street, British Postgraduate Medical Fedn, and London Univ., Inst. of Child Health; Medical Coll. of St Bartholomew's Hosp., New Hostel and Labs; Middlesex Hosp. Medical Sch.; New Sch. Buildings and Astor Coll.; National Inst. for Medical Research Develt, Mill Hill; Cambridge: Dept of Engineering, New Workshops and Laboratories; Univ. Chemistry Laboratories; United Cambridge Hosps, Addenbrooke's Hosp., Hills Rd, New Develt; MRC, extension of Lab. of Molecular Biology; Harlow: Princess Alexandra Hosp.; Belfast: Queen's Univ. of Belfast, Inst. of Clin. Science; Royal Victoria Hosp. Develt; Royal Belfast Hosp. for Sick Children, alterations and additions; Malaya: plans for Develt of Univ. of Malaya; Hong Kong; plans for develt of Univ. of Hong Kong; Cons. Architect for Queen Elizabeth Hosp., Hong Kong (awarded RIBA Bronze Medal); Cons. Architect to The Imperial Cancer Research Fund, London. *Publications:* (with James Crooks) Suggestions and Demonstration Plans for Hospitals for Sick Children, 1947. *Recreations:* theatre, travel, fishing; spending time in believing that "WS" was Shakespeare. *Address:* 1-4 Yarmouth Place, Piccadilly, W1Y 8JQ. *T:* 01-493 8913; 34 Ringshall, Little Gaddesden, near Berkhamsted, Herts. *Clubs:* Savile, The Sette of Odd Volumes.

**CUSHION, Air Vice-Marshal Sir William Boston,** KBE 1947 (CBE 1942; OBE 1927); CB 1944; RAF, retired; *b* 30 Jan. 1891; *s* of late William Cushion, Surlingham, Norwich; *m* 1917, Esther Jane Kenyon-Spooner; two *d*. *Educ:* Gresham's Sch., Holt; Faraday House, London, WC1. 2nd Lieut Manchester Regt, 1914; attached Royal Flying Corps, 1915; served France, 1915-18; permanent commission, Royal Air Force, 1919, as Flight Lieut; Sqdn Leader, 1921; served India, 1922-27; Wing Comdr, 1930; Iraq, 1933-35; Group Capt., 1937; Air Commodore, 1940; Temp. Air Vice-Marshal, 1942; late Director-General of Equipment, Air Ministry; British Overseas Airways Corp., retired, 1956. *Address:* 146 Rivermead Court, SW6. *T:* 01-736 4687. *Club:* Hurlingham.

**CUSSEN, Edward James Patrick;** Senior Prosecuting Counsel to the Crown at the Central Criminal Court, since 1964; *b* 21 Oct. 1904; *e s* of Patrick David Cussen and Mary (*née* Enright); *m* 1948, Veronica FitzSimon Hewett; one *d*. *Educ:* Beaumont Coll., Old Windsor; St John's Coll., Oxford. Called to the Bar, Inner Temple, 1931; Bencher of the Inner Temple, 1959. Civil Assistant, attached to the General Staff, War Office, 1940; Intelligence Corps, 1941-46 (Lieut-Colonel). Prosecuting Counsel to the Crown at North London Sessions, 1950; a Junior Prosecuting Counsel to the Crown at Central Criminal Court, 1953; Second Senior Prosecuting Counsel to the Crown, Central Criminal Court, 1959. *Recreation:* tennis. *Address:* 1 Dr Johnson's Buildings, Temple, EC4. *T:* 01-353 1662.

**CUST,** family name of **Baron Brownlow.**

**CUSTANCE, Michael Magnus Vere,** CB 1959; Deputy Under-Secretary of State, Department of Health and Social Security (formerly Ministry of Social Security), since

1966; *b* 3 Jan. 1916; *e s* of late Mrs Arthur Long (Marjorie Bowen, novelist); *m*; one *s* one *d*. *Educ:* St Paul's; The Queen's Coll., Oxford. Asst Principal, Board of Trade, 1938; Ministry of Shipping, 1939; Royal Air Force, 1941-45; Principal, Ministry of War Transport, 1943; Asst Sec., Min. of Transport, 1948; Under-Sec., Min. of Transport and Civil Aviation, 1956; Dep. Sec., Min. of Transport and Civil Aviation, 1958; in Ministry of Aviation, 1959-63; in Ministry of Transport, 1963-66. IDC (1952 Course). *Address:* c/o Department of Health and Social Security, 10 John Adam Street, WC2.

**CUTFORTH, Maj.-Gen. Sir Lancelot Eric,** KBE 1958 (CBE 1949; OBE 1945); CB 1953; Chairman: London Area Transport Users' Consultative Committee, since 1964; London Transport Passengers Committee, since 1970; *b* 14 Aug. 1899; *s* of G. H. Cutforth; *m* 1925, Vera Reffell; two *d*. *Educ:* St Peter's Sch., York; Royal Military Academy, Woolwich. 2nd Lieut RA, 1918; AAG, War Office, 1941; DDOS 1942; DOS, HQ BAOR, 1946; DDOS, War Office, 1948; DOS, MELF, 1951; Maj.-Gen., 1951; Inspector, RAOC, War Office, 1953-55; Director of Ordnance Services, War Office, 1955-58, retired; Colonel Comdt RAOC, 1957-65; Director-General of Inspection, Ministry of Supply, 1958-60; Asst Master-Gen. of Ordnance (Inspection), WO, 1960-62. *Address:* Earleydene, Sunninghill, Ascot, Berks. *T:* Ascot 20923. *Club:* Army and Navy.

**CUTHBERT, Lady, (Betty Wake),** CBE 1946 (OBE 1943); OStJ 1944; *d* of Guy Shorrock and Emma Wake; *m* 1928, Vice-Adm. Sir John Cuthbert, *qv*; no *c*. Joined Auxiliary Fire Service, London, as driver, 1938; Fire Staff, Home Office, 1941; Chief Woman Fire Officer, National Fire Service, 1941-46. Nat. Chairman, Girls' Venture Corps, 1946-67 (President 1967); Member Hampshire CC 1967. Member Council Chest and Heart Assoc. *Address:* Ibthorpe Manor Farm, Hurstbourne Tarrant, Andover, Hants.

**CUTHBERT, Vice-Adm. Sir John (Wilson),** KBE 1957 (CBE 1945); CB 1953; *b* 1902; *s* of William Cuthbert, Glasgow; *m* 1928, Betty Wake, *d* of Guy Shorrock (*see* Lady Cuthbert); no *c*. *Educ:* Kelvinside Acad.; RN Colleges. Midshipman, 1919; Commander, 1936; Captain, 1941; Rear-Adm., 1951; Vice-Adm., 1954. Commanded: HMS Glasgow, 1942; Ajax, 1944-46; Vengeance, 1949-50; Joint Planning Staff, London, 1942-44; Deputy Controller Admiralty, 1951-53; Flag Officer Flotillas, Home Fleet, 1953-54. Admiral Commanding Reserves, 1955-56; Flag Officer, Scotland, 1956-58. Retired List, 1958. Member Royal Company of Archers (Queen's Body Guard for Scotland). JP. *Address:* Ibthorpe Manor Farm, Hurstbourne Tarrant, near Andover, Hants. *T:* Hurstbourne Tarrant 237. *Club:* United Service.

**CUTHBERTSON, Sir David (Paton),** Kt 1965; CBE 1957; MD, DSc Glasgow; FRSE, FRCPE; Hon. Research Fellow in Pathological Biochemistry, Glasgow University, in the Biochemical Department of the Royal Infirmary, Glasgow; late Director Rowett Research Institute, 1945-65; *b* 9 May 1900; *s* of John Cuthbertson, MBE, Kilmarnock; *m* 1928, Jean Prentice, *d* of late Rev. Alexander P. Telfer, MA, Tarbet, Dunbartonshire; two *s* one *d*. *Educ:* University of Glasgow. BSc 1921; MB, ChB, 1926; DSc, 1931; MD, 1937. Bellahouston Gold Medallist. 2nd Lieut (temp.) Royal Scots Fusiliers, 1919. Lecturer in Pathological Biochemistry and Clinical Biochemist, Royal Infirmary and University of Glasgow, 1926-34; Grieve Lecturer in Physiological Chemistry, University of Glasgow, 1934-45; Arris and Gale Lecturer Royal College of Surgeons, 1942. Lieut-Col and Zone Medical Advisor (No. 1) Glasgow Home Guard, 1941-43; seconded to Administrative Headquarters, Medical Research Council, 1943-45. Consultant Director Commonwealth Bureau of Animal Nutrition, 1945-65; Hon. Consultant in Physiology and Nutrition to the Army, 1946-65. Member: UK Agricultural Mission to Canada, 1950; Tech. Cttee, Scottish Agricultural Improvement Council, 1951-64; Advisory Cttee on Pesticides and other Toxic Chemicals, 1966-. Chairman: General and Organising Cttees, 9th International Congress of Animal Production, 1966; ARC Tech, Cttee on Nutrient Requirements of Livestock, 1959-. President: International Union of Nutritional Sciences, 1960-66; Sect. I (1953) and Sect. M (1958) of British Assoc.; Nutrition Soc., 1962-65; British Soc. of Animal Production, 1966-67. Scientific Governor, British Nutrition Foundn, 1968-. Baxter Lectr, American Coll. of Surgeons, 1959. Hon. Member: American Institute of Nutrition; Society Biochemistry, Biophysics et Microbiol. Fenniae. Hon. DSc Rutgers, 1958; Hon. LLD Glasgow, 1960; Dr *hc* Zagreb, 1969. Hon. FRCSE 1967. *Publications:* papers on Physiology of Protein Nutrition and Metabolism and on Metabolic Response to Injury, Ruminant Digestion, etc. *Recreations:* water-colour painting and golf. *Address:* Glenavon, 11 Willockston Road, Troon, Ayrshire. *T:* Troon 704. *Clubs:* Athenæum; Strathcona (Bucksburn).

**CUTHBERTSON, Prof. Joseph William,** DSc, FIM, MIEE; retired as Cripps Professor of Metallurgy, University of Nottingham (1954-66), now Emeritus Professor; *b* 27 Feb. 1901; *s* of late William Edward Cuthbertson, MRCS, LRCP, and late Kathleen Cuthbertson; *m* 1933, Milly Beatrix Nelson; no *c*. *Educ:* Manchester Grammar Sch., University of Manchester. Asst, ultimately Senior Lecturer, Dept of Metallurgy, Manchester Univ., 1929-44; seconded to Ministry of Supply, 1942-46; Asst Director of Research, Tin Research Institute, 1944-54. *Publications:* numerous scientific papers, progress reviews, and articles on metallurgy and electro-metallurgy. *Recreations:* motoring, gardening. *Address:* Sandbanks, Methven Close, Grange-over-Sands, Lancs. *T:* Grange-over-Sands 2852.

**CUTLER, Sir (Arthur) Roden,** VC; KCMG 1965; KCVO 1970; CBE, 1957; Governor of New South Wales, since 1966; *b* 24 May 1916; *s* of Arthur William Cutler and Ruby Daphne (*née* Pope); *m* 1946, Helen Gray Annetta (*née* Morris); four *s*. *Educ:* Sydney High Sch.; University of Sydney (BEc). Public Trust Office (NSW), 1935-42; War of 1939-45 (VC). State Secretary, RSS & AILA (NSW), 1942-43; Mem., Aliens Classification and Adv. Cttee to advise Commonwealth Govt, 1942-43; Asst Dep. Dir, Security Service, NSW, 1943; Asst Comr Repatriation, 1943-46; High Comr for Australia to New Zealand, 1946-52; High Comr for Australia to Ceylon, 1952-55; HM's Australian Minister to Egypt, 1955-56; Secretary General, SEATO Conference, 1957; Chief of Protocol, Dept of External Affairs, Canberra, 1957-58; State President of RSS AILA (Aust. Cap. Territory), 1958; Australian High Comr to Pakistan, 1959-61; Australian Representative to Independence of Somali Republic, 1960; Australian Consul-General, New York, 1961-65; Ambassador to the Netherlands, 1965. Hon. Col, Royal New South Wales Regt, 1966; Hon. Col, Sydney Univ. Regt, 1966; Hon. Air Cdre 22 Squadron

RAAF. Hon. LLD, Univ. of Sydney; Hon. DSc: Univ. of New South Wales; Univ. of Newcastle. KStJ 1965. *Recreations:* swimming, shooting, yachting. *Address:* Government House, Sydney, NSW, Australia.

**CUTLER, Horace Walter,** OBE 1963; Member of Greater London Council since 1964, Deputy Leader since 1967; *b* London, N16, 28 July 1912; *s* of Albert Benjamin and Mary Ann Cutler; *m* 1957, Christiane, *d* of Dr Klaus Muthesius; two *s* three *d*. *Educ:* Harrow Grammar Sch.; Hereford. Served War of 1939-45: RNVR, 1941-46, Lieut. Harrow Borough Council: elected 1952; Chm. Planning Cttee, 1954; Chm. Housing Cttee, 1955-58; Dep. Mayor, 1958; Alderman, 1959; Mayor, 1959-60; Leader of Council, 1961-65; Chm., Gen. Purposes Cttee, 1962-65; Middlesex CC: elected, 1955; Vice-Chm., Estates and Housing Cttee, 1957; Chm. Planning Cttee, 1961-65; Dep. Leader of CC, 1962; Leader, 1963-65; Greater London Council: elected (Harrow), 1964; Dep. Leader of Opposition, 1964-67; Dep. Leader of GLC (C), and Chm. Housing Cttee, 1967-70; Policy and Resources Cttee, 1970-. Member: Milton Keynes New City Develt Corp. (Chm., Housing Cttee, 1969-); Land Commn, London and SE Regional Adv. Cttee; Central Housing Adv. Cttee, Min. of Housing and Local Govt; Nat. Housing and Town Planning Exec. Cttee (Vice-Chm., London Region, 1968). Adopted prospective Parly Candidate (C) Willesden East, 1967; Pres., Harrow West Conservative Assoc., 1964- (Chm., 1961-64). *Recreations:* golf, ski-ing, classical music, travel. *Address:* Hawkswood, Hawkswood Lane, Gerrards Cross, Bucks. *T:* Fulmer 3182; Flat 43, 2 Hyde Park Square, W1. *T:* 01-723 6954. *Club:* Constitutional.

**CUTLER, Sir Roden;** *see* Cutler, Sir A. R.

**CUTTELL, Rev. Canon Colin;** Vicar of All Hallows, Barking-by-the-Tower, Guild Church of Toc H, since 1963; *b* 24 Sept. 1908; *s* of late Maurice John Cuttell, Cheltenham, Glos., and Blanche Vickers; unmarried. *Educ:* Bishop's Univ., Lennoxville (BA; STM 1968). Deacon, 1937; Priest, 1938. Missioner of Wabamun, Canada, 1937-42; Domestic Chaplain to the Archbishop of Quebec, 1942-43; Chaplain to the Forces, 1943-44; Priest Vicar, Southwark Cathedral, 1945-49; Bishop of Southwark's Chaplain for Industrial Relations, 1948-; Commissary for Bishop of Qu'Appelle, 1951-; Founder and Senior Chaplain, S London Industrial Mission, 1950-. Canon Residentiary and Librarian of Southwark Cathedral, 1954-63. Acting Chaplain, Lincoln Coll., Oxford. Sabbatical year, 1960; Acting Provost, Southwark, 1961. Field Commissioner, Toc H 1962; Deputy Admin. Padre, Toc H, 1963-. Editor of Over the Bridge, 1948-. *Publication:* Ministry Without Portfolio, 1962. *Recreations:* swimming, sketching, walking. *Address:* Home Farm Lodge, Everlands, Sevenoaks, Kent. *T:* Sevenoaks 55424; The Porch Room, Byward Street, EC3. *T:* 01-709 2929. *Club:* Royal Commonwealth Society.

**CZIFFRA, Gyorgy;** Pianist; *b* Budapest, Hungary; *m* 1942, Madame Sulejka Cziffra; one *s*. *Educ:* Conservatoire of Music, Budapest. Has given recitals and taken part in concerts at the Festival Hall, London, and throughout the world: USA, Canada, France, Israel, Benelux, Italy, Switzerland, also BBC and BBC Television, London. Records for HMV: Liszt, Greig, Tchaikowski, Beethoven, Schumann, paraphrases by G. Cziffra, etc. Founded, 1968, biennial Concours International de Piano, Versailles, for young pianists. *Address:* 4 rue de Montigny, Cormeilles en Parisis, S et O, France.

# D

**d'ABREU, Prof. Alphonso Liguori,** CBE 1968 (OBE 1944); DL; Surgeon, United Birmingham Hospitals since 1946; Dean of Medical School 1959-63, Professor of Surgery, since Oct. 1963 (of Cardiac Surgery, 1960-63), University of Birmingham; Hon. Consultant in Thoracic Surgery to the Army since 1964; Member Central Health Services Council, since 1964; Member Council, Royal College of Surgeons, since 1963; Member Medical Sub-Committee of University Grants Committee, since 1964; *b* 5 Aug. 1906; *s* of Dr John Francis d'Abreu and Teresa d'Abreu; *m* 1935, Elizabeth Throckmorton (*d* 1970); three *d*. *Educ:* Stonyhurst Coll.; Univ. of Birmingham. MB ChB Birmingham 1930; MRCS, LRCP 1930; FRCS 1932; ChM Birmingham 1936; FRCP 1968. House Surgeon and Surgical Registrar, Gen. Hospital, Birmingham; Jun. Asst, Surgical Unit, Cardiff Royal Infirmary, University of Wales, 1930-33, Asst Dir, 1933-39; Acting Prof. of Surgery, 1945-46. Lieut RAMC (Supp. Reserve), 1939; served War of 1939-45 (despatches), Major, RAMC 1939, Lt-Col, 1942-45; retd. Hunterian Prof., RCS, 1939 and 1946, Mem. Court of Examiners, 1957-63. vis. Lectr in Surgery, Med. Sch., Harvard Univ., USA, 1951; John Alexander Lectr, Univ. of Michigan, 1965; McLauchlin Gallie Vis. Prof., Canada, 1966; Vis. Prof., Boston City Hosp. (Harvard Unit), 1967. FRSocMed 1946- (Pres., Sect. of Surgery, 1966-67). Hon. Col, RAMC (48 Div. TA, W Midland District, 1963-67). DL Warwicks, 1967. *Publications:* (with Prof. Lambert Rogers) Everyday Surgery, 1938; A Practice of Thoracic Surgery, 1st edn 1953, 2nd edn 1958; Intrathoracic Crises (with A. Brian Taylor and David B. Clarke), 1968; ed and contrib. Thoracic Surgery, (Butterworth's) Clinical Surgery, Contributions to med. journals. *Recreations:* fishing; Vice-Pres. Warwicks County Cricket Club. *Address:* Ford House, Coughton, near Alcester, Warwicks. *Clubs:* Athenæum, Forty Club.
*See also* F. A. d'Abreu.

**d'ABREU, Francis Arthur,** ERD 1954; Surgeon, Westminster Hospital, since 1946, and Hospital of St John and St Elizabeth, since 1950; Surgeon to Jockey Club and National Hunt Committee, since 1964, and to Horserace Betting Levy Board; *b* 1 Oct. 1904; *s* of Dr John Francis d'Abreu and Teresa d'Abreu; *m* 1945, Margaret Ann Bowes-Lyon; one *s* two *d*. *Educ:* Stonyhurst Coll.; Birmingham Univ. MB, ChB Birmingham 1929; MRCS, LRCP 1929; FRCS, 1932; ChM Birmingham 1935. House Surgeon, Gen. Hosp., Birmingham, 1929; Res. Surgical Officer, Gen. and Queen's Hosps, Birmingham, 1930-34; Surg. Registrar, St Bartholomew's Hosp., London, and Westminster Hosp., 1934-39. Mem., Ct of Examiners RCS; Examiner to Soc. of Apothecaries; formerly Examiner to Univs of Cambridge and London. Lieut RAMC (Supp. Reserve), 1939. Served War of 1939-45: Major, RAMC, 1939, Lt-Col 1942-45. Kt of Magistral Grace, Sov. and Mil. Order of Malta. *Publications:* contrib. to various medical jls. *Recreations:* ski-ing, squash, tennis. *Address:* 37 Chester Terrace, Regent's Park, NW1; 82 Harley Street, W1. *T:* 01-580 3161. *Club:*

Hurlingham.
*See also Prof. A. L. d'Abreu.*

**DACCA, Archbishop of, (RC),** since 1967; **Most Rev. Theotonius A. Ganguly,** CSC, DD, PhD; *b* Hashnabad, Dacca, Pakistan, 18 Feb. 1920; *s* of Nicholas K. Ganguly. *Educ:* Little Flower Seminary, Dacca, Bengal; St Albert Seminary, Ranchi, India. PhD Notre Dame Univ., USA, 1951. Priest, 1946; Mem. of Congregation of Holy Cross, 1951; Prof., Notre Dame Coll., Dacca, 1952-60; Principal, Notre Dame Coll., 1960; Auxiliary Bishop of Dacca, 1960; Coadjutor Archbishop of Dacca, 1965. *Address:* Archbishop's House, PO Box 3, Dacca 2, Pakistan. *T:* Dacca 242379.

**DACCA, Bishop of,** since 1956; **Rt. Rev. James Douglas Blair;** *b* 22 Jan. 1906; *s* of Rev. A. A. Blair; unmarried. *Educ:* Marlborough; Keble Coll., Oxford; Cuddesdon Coll. 2nd class Lit. Hum., 1928. Deacon, Penistone, Yorks, 1929; Priest, 1930; Oxford Mission Brotherhood of the Epiphany, Calcutta, 1932-; Asst Bishop of Calcutta, with charge of East Bengal, 1951; Bishop of East Bengal, 1956; title of diocese changed to Dacca, 1960. *Recreation:* walking. *Address:* St Thomas' Church, Victoria Park, Dacca, East Pakistan.

**DACIE, Prof. John Vivian,** FRS 1967; MD, FRCP; Professor of Haematology, Royal Post-graduate Medical School of London, University of London, since 1957; *b* 20 July 1912; British; *s* of John Charles and Lilian Maud Dacie, Putney; *m* 1938, Margaret Kathleen Victoria Thynne; three *s* two *d. Educ:* King's Coll. Sch., Wimbledon; King's Coll., London: King's Coll. Hospital, London. MB, BS London 1935; MD 1952; MRCP 1936; FRCP 1956; MD (Hon.) Uppsala, 1961; FRCPath. Various medical appointments, King's Coll. Hospital, Postgraduate Medical Sch. and Manchester Royal Infirmary, 1936-39. Pathologist, EMS, 1939-42; Major, then Lieut-Col, RAMC, 1943-46. Senior Lecturer in Clinical Pathology, then Reader in Haematology, Postgraduate Medical Sch., 1946-56. *Publications:* Practical Haematology, 1950, 2nd edn, 1956, 4th edn (jointly), 1968; Haemolytic Anaemias, 1954, 2nd edn, Part I, 1960, Part II, 1962, Parts III and IV, 1967; various papers on anaemia in medical journals. *Recreations:* music, entomology, gardening. *Address:* 10 Alan Road, Wimbledon, SW19. *T.* 01-946 6086.

**da COSTA, Harvey Lloyd,** CMG 1962; QC Jamaica 1959; Attorney-General of the West Indies, 1959-62; *b* 8 Dec. 1914; *s* of John Charles and Martha da Costa. *Educ:* Calabar High Sch., Jamaica; St Edmund Hall (Sen. Exhibnr; Rhodes Schol.), Oxford. BA (Hons) London; MA, BLitt Oxon, Practised at Chancery Bar, 1950-52; Crown Counsel, Jamaica, 1952-54; Sen. Crown Counsel, Jamaica, 1954-56; Asst Attorney-Gen., Jamaica, 1956-59. *Recreations:* swimming, tennis, cricket. *Address:* 18 Mona Road, Liguanea, PO Jamaica, West Indies. *Clubs:* West India; Trinidad Country (Port-of-Spain).

**da COSTA, Sergio Corrêa;** Grand Officer, Military Order of Aeronautical Merit, Brazil, 1967; Grand Officer, Order of Naval Merit, Brazil, 1967; GCVO; Brazilian Ambassador to the Court of St James's since 1968; *b* 19 Feb. 1919; *s* of Dr I. A. da Costa and Lavinia Corrêa da Costa; *m* 1943, Zazi Aranha; one *s* two *d. Educ:* Law Sch., Univ. of Brazil; post grad. UCLA; Brazilian War Coll. Career diplomat; Sec. of Embassy, Buenos Ayres, then Washington, 1944-48; Acting Deleg., Council of OAS, Wash., 1946-48; Inter-American Econ. and Social Coun., Washington, 1946-48; Dep. Head, Economic Dept, Min. of Ext. Relations, 1952; Actg Pres., Braz. Nat. Techn. Assistance Commn, 1955-58; Minister-Counsellor, Rome, 1959-62; Permanent Rep. to FAO, Rome, 1960; Mem., Financial Cttee of FAO, 1962-63; Amb. to Canada, 1962-65; Asst Sec.-Gen. for Internat. Organizations at Min. Ext. Relations, 1966; Sec.-Gen. Min. of Ext. Relations, 1967-68. Grand Cross of Victorian Order (Hon. GCVO), Gt Britain, 1968; also numerous Grand Crosses, etc, of Orders, from other countries, 1957-. *Publications:* (mostly in Brazil): As 4 Coroas de Pedro I, 1941; Pedro I e Metternich, 1942; Diplomacia Brasileira na Questao de Leticia, 1943; A Diplomacia do Marechal, 1945; Every Inch a King–A biography of Pedro I, Emperor of Brazil, 1950 (1964), (New York). *Recreations:* reading, writing, boating. *Address:* 54 Mount Street, London, W1. *T:* 01-629 0507. *Clubs:* White's, Travellers' (London); Rideau, Country (Ottawa); Circolo della Caccia (Rome).

**DACRE,** Baroness (27th in line), *cr* 1321; **Rachel Leila Douglas-Home;** *b* 24 Oct. 1929; *er* surv. *d* of 4th Viscount Hampden, CMG (*d* 1965) (whose Barony of Dacre was called out of abeyance in her favour, 1970) and of Leila Emily, *o d* of late Lt-Col Frank Evelyn Seely; *m* 1951, Hon. William Douglas-Home, *qv*; one *s* three *d. Heir: s* Hon. James Thomas Archibald Douglas-Home, *b* 16 May 1952. *Address:* Drayton House, East Meon, Hants.

**da CUNHA, John Wilfrid; His Honour Judge da Cunha;** Judge of County Courts since 1970; JP; *b* 6 Sept. 1922; 2nd *s* of Frank C. da Cunha, MD, DPH, and Lucy (*née* Finnerty); *m* 1953, Janet, MB, ChB, JP, *d* of Louis Savatard, (Hon.) MSc, LSA, and Judith Savatard, MB, BS; one *s* four *d. Educ:* Stonyhurst Coll., Lancs; St John's Coll., Cambridge. MA Cantab 1954. Served 1942-47, 23rd Hussars (RAC) and Judge Advocate Gen. (War Crimes), Hon. Major. Called to Bar, Middle Temple, 1948; Northern Circuit. Chm., Local Appeal Tribunal, Min. of Social Security (Wigan), 1964-69. Asst Recorder, Oldham County Borough QS, 1966-70; Chm., Industrial Tribunals, 1966-70; Dep. Chm., Lancs County QS, 1968-; JP Lancs 1968. *Recreations:* gardening, walking, pottering. *Address:* Beech Cottage, Mobberley, Knutsford, Cheshire. *T:* Mobberley 3320. *Club:* National Liberal.

**DAENIKER, Dr Armin;** Swiss Ambassador to the Court of St James's, 1957-63, retired; *b* 24 Feb. 1898; *m* 1938; no *c. Educ:* Universities of Zürich, Berne, Geneva, London Sch. of Economics (doctor juris utriusque, Zürich). Vice-Consul, Riga, 1927; Shanghai, 1930; Swiss Chargé d'Affaires, Tokio, 1933, Teheran, 1936; Head of Administrative Div., Federal Political Dept, Berne, 1946; Swiss Minister, New Delhi, 1948, and concurrently in Bangkok, 1950; Swiss Minister, Stockholm 1952; Swiss Mem., Neutral Nations Commn for Repatriation of Prisoners of War in Korea, 1953-54; Swiss Minister to the Court of St James's, 1955; Vice-Pres., Swiss Winston Churchill Foundation. *Address:* Villa Sonnenhof, 2 Jolimontstrasse, Berne, Switzerland.

**D'AETH, Rev. Narbrough Hughes,** CB 1951; CBE 1943; Priest-in-Charge, Midland and Swan Parishes, Perth, since 1967; *b* 7 Jan. 1901; *s* of late Capt. Reginald Hughes D'Aeth and late Lady Nina Hughes D'Aeth; *m* 1934, Mary Colbeck, *d* of late E. W. Davis; three *d. Educ:* Royal Naval Colls, Osborne and Dartmouth. Served European War, 1914-18, with Grand Fleet, 1917-19; transferred to RAF, 1920;

Malta, 1924; China, 1926-28; British Arctic Air Route Expedn in E Greenland, 1930-31; Polar Medal, 1932; Aden, 1934-36; War of 1939-45 in UK and N Africa (despatches thrice, CBE); Air Officer Commanging, RAF, Malta, 1949-52; AO i/c Administration at Headquarters, Technical Training Command, 1952-54; Senior Air Staff Officer, Headquarters, Home Command, 1954-56. Group Capt., 1941; Air Commodore, 1943; Air Vice Marshal, 1950; retired, 1956. Lincoln Theological Coll., 1956-57. Ordained Deacon, Dec. 1957; Curate, St John the Baptist, Crowthorne, Dec. 1957-59; Rector: East Langdon with Guston, Kent, 1959-60; Flinders Islands, 1960-67. American Legion of Merit, 1945; Czechoslovak Medal of Merit, 1945. *Address:* The Rectory, 6 Burgess Street, Midland, Western Australia.

**DAGGETT, William Ingledew;** late Senior Ear, Nose and Throat Surgeon to King's College Hospital; Consulting Ear, Nose and Throat Surgeon to Leatherhead Hospital and St Luke's Hostel for Clergy; late Chairman King's College Hospital Group Medical Committee; late Brigadier RAMC; Consultant in Otolaryngology to Army; *b* 2 Oct. 1900; *s* of Dr H. Ingledew Daggett, Boroughbridge; *m* 1928, Eileen Hilda (marr. diss., 1947), *d* of Col T. W. Simpson; no *c. Educ:* Sedbergh (Exhibitioner); Caius Coll., Cambridge (Scholar, 1st Class Hons Nat. Sci. Tripos); King's Coll. Hosp. (Scholar), MA, MB, BChir Cantab; FRCS; recognised teacher University of London. *Publications:* in medical and surgical journals. *Address:* 15 Devonshire Close, W1. *T:* 01-580 5366. *Club:* Bath.

**DAHL, Rev. Canon Murdoch Edgcumbe;** Canon Theologian (formerly Canon Residentiary) of St Albans Cathedral, since 1965; *b* 11 March 1914; *s* of Oscar Horace and Edith Gladys Dahl; *m* 1940, Joan, *d* of Daniel Charles and Edith Marion Woollaston; three *s*. *Educ:* Royal Grammar Sch., Newcastle upon Tyne; Armstrong Coll. (subsq. King's Coll.), Newcastle upon Tyne; St John's Coll., Durham. BA 1936, MA 1956, Durham. Deacon 1937; Priest 1938. Curate of: St Paul, Astley Bridge, 1937-39; Fallowfield, 1939-43; Harpenden, 1943-49; Vicar of Arlesey and Rector of Astwick, 1949-51; Minister, St Oswald's, Croxley Green, 1951-56; Vicar of Great with Little Hormead and Rector of Wyddial, 1956-65; Examining Chaplain to Bishop of St Albans, 1959-; Hon. Canon of St Albans, 1963-65. *Publications:* Resurrection of the Body, 1962; Sin Streamlined, 1966; The Christian Materialist, 1968. *Address:* 2 Sumpter Yard, St Albans, Herts. *T:* St Albans 61744.

**DAHL, Robert Henry,** TD 1950; MA Oxford; Head Master of Wrekin College, since 1952; *b* 21 April 1910; *y s* of Murdoch Cameron Dahl, London, and Lilian May Edgcumbe; *m* 1936, Lois Helen Allanby; three *s. Educ:* Sedbergh Sch.; Exeter Coll., Oxford. Asst Master (Modern Langs) at Merchant Taylors' Sch., 1934-38. Asst Master and Housemaster at Harrow Sch., 1938-52. Served War of 1939-45: intelligence Corps, Middle East, 1941-43; Major, 1943; Political Intelligence Dept of Foreign Office, 1943-46. *Publication:* Joint Editor, Selections from Albert Schweitzer, 1953. *Recreations:* golf, music. *Address:* Wrekin College, Wellington, Salop. *T:* Wellington 4963.

**DAHRENDORF, Prof. Ralf,** PhD, DrPhil; Member, European Economic Commission, Brussels, since 1970; *b* Hamburg, 1 May 1929; *s* of Gustav Dahrendorf and Lina Dahrendorf (*née* Witt); *m* 1954, Vera Banister; two *d. Educ:* several schools, including Heinrich-Hertz Oberschule, Hamburg; studies in philosophy and classical philology, Hamburg, 1947-52; DrPhil 1952; postgrad. studies at London Sch. of Economics, 1952-54; Leverhulme Research Schol., 1953-54; PhD 1956. Habilitation, and University Lecturer, Saarbrücken, 1957; Fellow at Center for Advanced Study in the Behavioural Sciences, Palo Alto, USA, 1957-58; Prof. of Sociology, Hamburg, 1958-60; Vis. Prof. Columbia Univ., 1960; Prof. of Sociology, Tübingen, 1960-64; Vice-Chm., Founding Cttee of Univ. of Konstanz, 1964-66; Prof of Sociology, Konstanz, 1966-69; Parly Sec. of State, Foreign Office, W Germany, 1969-70. Sidney Ball Lecturer, Oxford, 1965; Journal Fund Award for Learned Publication, 1966; Henry Failing Distinguished Lecturer, Oregon, 1966. *Publications:* Marx in Perspektive, 1953; Industrie und Betriebssoziologie, 1956; Soziale Klassen und Klassenkonflikt, 1957; Homo sociologicus, 1959; Sozialstruktur des Betriebes, 1959; Gesellschaft und Freiheit, 1961; Über den Ursprung der Ungleichheit, 1961; Die angewandte Aufklärung, 1963; Das Mitbestimmungsproblem in der deutschen Sozialforschung, 1963; Arbeiterkinder an deutschen Universitäten, 1965; Bildung ist Bürgerrecht, 1965; Gesellschaft und Demokratie in Deutschland, 1965; Markt und Plan, 1966; Conflict After Class, 1967; Essays in the Theory of Society, 1967; Pfade aus Utopia, 1967; Die Soziologie und der Soziologe, 1967; Für eine Erneuerung der Demokratie in der Bundesrepublik, 1968. *Address:* European Economic Commission, 200 rue de la Loi, Brussels, Belgium. *T:* Brussels 35 00 40; Konstanz, Zur Torkel 10. *T:* 6 38 14. *Club:* PEN.

**DAICHES, David,** MA Edinburgh; MA, DPhil Oxon; PhD Cantab; FRSL; Professor of English, University of Sussex, since 1961, and Dean of the School of English Studies, 1961-68; *b* 2 Sept. 1912; *s* of Rabbi Dr Salis Daiches and Flora Daiches (*née* Levin); *m* 1937, Isobel J. Mackay; one *s* two *d. Educ:* George Watson's Coll., Edinburgh; Edinburgh Univ. (Vans Dunlop Schol., Elliot Prize); Balliol Coll., Oxford (Elton Exhibnr). Asst in English, Edinburgh Univ., 1935-36; Andrew Bradley Fellow, Balliol Coll., Oxford, 1936-37; Asst Prof. of English, Univ. of Chicago, 1939-43; Second Sec., British Embassy, Washington, 1944-46; Prof. of English, Cornell Univ., USA, 1946-51; University Lecturer in English at Cambridge, 1951-61; Fellow of Jesus Coll., Cambridge, 1957-62. Visiting Prof. of Criticism, Indiana Univ., USA, 1956-57; Elliston Lectr, University of Cincinnati, Spring 1960; Whidden Lectr, Mcmaster Univ., Canada, 1964; Hill Foundation Visiting Prof., Univ. of Minnesota, Spring 1966; Ewing Lectr, Univ. of California, 1967; Carpenter Memorial Lectr, Ohio Wesleyan Univ., 1969. Fellow, Centre for the Humanities, Wesleyan Univ., Middletown, Conn, 1970. Hon. LittD, Brown Univ. *Publications:* The Place of Meaning in Poetry, 1935; New Literary Values, 1936; Literature and Society, 1938; The Novel and the Modern World, 1939 (new edn, 1960); Poetry and the Modern World, 1940; The King James Bible: A Study of its Sources and Development, 1941; Virginia Woolf, 1942; Robert Louis Stevenson, 1947; A Study of Literature, 1948; Robert Burns, 1950 (new edn 1966); Willa Cather: A Critical Introduction, 1951; Critical Approaches to Literature, 1956; Two Worlds: An Edinburgh Jewish Childhood, 1956; Literary Essays, 1956; John Milton, 1957; The Present Age, 1958; A Critical History of English Literature, 1960; George Eliot's Middlemarch, 1963; The Paradox of Scottish Culture, 1964; The Idea of a New University (ed), 1964; English

Literature (Princeton Studies in Humanistic Scholarship), 1965; More Literary Essays, 1968; Some Late Victorian Attitudes, 1969; Scotch Whisky, 1969. *Recreations:* talking, music. *Address:* Downsview, Wellhouse Lane, Burgess Hill, Sussex. *Club:* Oxford and Cambridge University.
*See also L. H. Daiches.*

**DAICHES, Lionel Henry,** QC (Scot) 1956; *b* 8 March 1911; *s* of late Rev. Dr. Salis Daiches, Edinburgh, and Mrs Flora Daiches; *m* 1947, Dorothy Estelle Bernstein; two *s. Educ:* George Watson's Coll., Edinburgh; Edinburgh Univ. (MA, LLB). Pres., Edinburgh Univ. Diagnostic Soc., 1931; Convener of Debates, Edinburgh Univ. Union, 1933; Editor, The Student, 1933. Served 1940-46 in N Stafford Regt and Major, JAG Branch in N Africa and Italy, including Anzio Beach-head. Admitted Scots Bar, 1946. Contested (L) Edinburgh South, 1950; Standing Junior Counsel to Board of Control, Scotland, 1955-66; Sheriff-Substitute of Lanarkshire at Glasgow, 1962-67. *Publication:* Russians at Law, 1960. *Recreations:* walking and talking. *Address:* 10 Heriot Row, Edinburgh. *T:* 031-556 4144. *Clubs:* Puffin's (Edinburgh); Art (Glasgow).
*See also D. Daiches.*

**DAIN, Rt. Rev. Arthur John;** Coadjutor Bishop, Diocese of Sydney, since 1965; *b* 13 Oct. 1912; *s* of Herbert John Dain and Elizabeth Dain; *m* 1939, Edith Jane Stewart, MA, *d* of Dr Alexander Stewart, DD; four *d. Educ:* Wolverhampton Gram. Sch.; Ridley Coll., Cambridge. Missionary in India, 1935-40; 10th Gurkha Rifles, 1940-41; Royal Indian Navy, 1941-47; Gen. Sec., Zenana Bible and Medical Mission, 1947-59; Overseas Sec., British Evangelical Alliance, 1950-59; Federal Sec., CMS of Australia, 1959-65; Hon. Canon of St Andrew's Cathedral, 1963. *Publications:* Mission Fields To-day, 1956; Missionary Candidates, 1959. *Recreation:* sport. *Address:* Barker House, 33 Fairfax Road, Bellevue Hill, NSW 2023, Australia. *T:* 36-3320.

**DAINTON, Prof. Frederick Sydney,** FRS 1957; MA, BSc Oxon, PhD, ScD Cantab; Dr Lee's Professor of Chemistry, Oxford University, since 1970; *b* 11 Nov. 1914; *y s* of late George Whalley and Mary Jane Dainton; *m* 1942, Barbara Hazlitt, PhD, *o d* of late Dr W. B. Wright, Manchester; one *s* two *d. Educ:* Central Secondary Sch., Sheffield; St John's Coll., Oxford; Sidney Sussex Coll., Cambridge. Open Exhibitioner, 1933; Casberd Prizeman, 1934, Casberd Scholar, 1935, Hon. Fellow 1968, St John's Coll., Oxford; Goldsmiths' Co. Exhibitioner, 1935, 1st class Hons Chemistry, 1937, University of Oxford; Research Student, 1937, Goldsmiths' Co. Senior Student, 1939, University Demonstrator in Chemistry, 1944, H. O. Jones Lecturer in Physical Chemistry, 1946, University of Cambridge. Fellow, 1945, Praelector, 1946, Hon. Fellow 1961, St Catharine's Coll., Cambridge. Prof. of Physical Chemistry, University of Leeds, 1950-65; Vice-Chancellor, Nottingham Univ., 1965-70. Visiting Prof., University of Toronto, 1949; Tilden Lecturer of Chemical Soc., 1950; Peter C. Reilly Lecturer, University of Notre Dame, Ind., USA, 1952; Arthur D. Little Visiting Prof., MIT, 1959; George Fisher Baker Lectr, Cornell Univ., 1961; Boomer Lectr, Univ. of Alberta, 1962. Chairman: Assoc. for Radiation Research, 1964-66; Adv. Cttee on Sci. and Tech. Information, 1966-70. President: Faraday Soc., 1965-67; Assoc. for Science Education, 1967. Member: Council for Scientific Policy, 1965- (Chm. 1969-); Central Advisory Council for Science and Technology, 1967-. Sylvanus Thompson Medal, British Institute of Radiology, 1958; Davy Medal, Royal Soc., 1969. Hon. ScD: Lódz, 1966; Dublin, 1968; Hon. DSc: Bath Univ. of Technology, 1970; Loughborough Univ. of Technology, 1970; Heriot-Watt, 1970; Warwick, 1970. *Publications:* Chain Reactions, 1956; papers on physico-chemical subjects in scientific jls. *Recreations:* walking, colour photography. *Address:* Physical Chemistry Laboratory, South Parks Road, Oxford OX1 3QZ. *T:* Oxford 53324. *Club:* Athenæum.

**DAINTREE JOHNSON, Harold;** *see* Johnson, H. D.

**DAKERS, Mrs Andrew;** *see* Lane, Jane.

**DAKERS, Lionel Frederick,** FRCO; Organist and Master of the Choristers, Exeter Cathedral, since Sept. 1957; Examiner to the Associated Board of the Royal Schools of Music, since 1958; Special Commissioner, Royal School of Church Music, since 1958; Condustor; Exeter Musical Society, since 1957; Exeter Chamber Orchestra, since 1959; *b* Rochester, Kent, 24 Feb. 1924; *o s* of Lewis and Ethel Dakers; *m* 1951, Mary Elisabeth, *d* of Rev. Claude Williams; four *d. Educ:* Rochester Cathedral Choir Sch. Studied with H. A. Bennett, Organist of Rochester Cathedral, 1933-40, with Sir Edward Bairstow, Organist of York Minster, 1943-45, and at Royal Academy of Music, 1947-51. Organist of All Saints', Frindsbury, Rochester, 1939-42. Served in Royal Army Educational Corps, 1943-47. Cairo Cathedral, 1945-47; Finchley Parish Church, 1948-50; Asst Organist, St George's Chapel, Windsor Castle, 1950-54; Asst Music Master, Eton Coll., 1952-54; Organist of Ripon Cathedral, 1954-57; Conductor Ripon Choral Soc. and Harrogate String Orchestra, 1954-57; Hon. Conductor, Exeter Diocesan Choral Association, 1957; Lectr in Music, St Luke's Coll., Exeter, 1958-70. Mem., Organs Adv. Cttee of Council for Care of Churches of C of E, 1970. ARCO, 1944; FRCO, 1945; ADCM, 1952; BMus Dunelm, 1951; ARAM 1955; FRAM, 1962; FRSCM 1969. Compositions: church music, etc. *Publication:* Church Music at the Crossroads, 1970. *Recreations:* book collecting, gardening, continental food, travel. *Address:* 11 The Close, Exeter, Devon EX1 1EZ. *T:* Exeter 77521. *Club:* Savage.

**DALDRY, Sir Leonard (Charles),** KBE 1963 (CBE 1960); Chairman of the Nigeria Board of Barclays Bank DCO, 1961-63, retired; *b* 6 Oct. 1908; *s* of Charles Henry Daldry; *m* 1938, Joan Mary, *d* of John E. Crisp; no *c.* Joined Barclays Bank DCO 1929. Local Dir in W Africa at Lagos, 1952. Assoc. Inst. of Bankers, 1936. Mem. Nigerian Railway Corp., 1955-60; Special Mem., Nigerian House of Reps, 1956-59; Senator, Federal Legislature, Nigeria, 1960-61. Chm., St Loye's Coll. for the Disabled, Exeter, 1969-. *Address:* Prospect House, Budleigh Salterton, Devon. *Club:* Athenæum.

**DALE, Rt. Rev. Basil Montague,** MA; *b* 12 April 1903; *er s* of late Rev. Canon Harold Montague Dale; *m* 1927, Kathleen, *d* of Lieut-Col C. A. E. O'Meara, CIE; one *s. Educ:* Dean Close Sch.; Queens' Coll., Cambridge; Westcott House Theological Coll. Historical and Theological Tripos, MA Cambridge. Ordained Diocese of Southwark, 1927; Curate, St Andrew's, Catford, 1927-29; in charge of All Saints, Putney, 1929-32; Vicar, St Andrew's, Handsworth, Birmingham, 1932-35; Vicar, Paignton, Devon, 1936-44; Chaplain to the King, 1948; Rector of Hatfield, Herts, 1945-49; Rural Dean of Hertford, 1948-49;

Domestic Chaplain to the Marquess of Salisbury, 1946-49; Bishop of Jamaica, 1950-55; Rector of Haslemere, 1955-62; Asst Bishop of Guildford, 1955-67; Hon. Canon of Guildford Cathedral, 1961. Mission of Help to Diocese of British Honduras with Central America, 1947. *Recreations:* gardening, walking. *Address:* Brownscombe Cottage, Hindhead Road, Haslemere, Surrey.

**DALE, Francis Richard,** CBE 1950; DSO 1919; MC; MA; Hon. MA London, 1948; *b* 7 March 1883; *s* of J. F. Dale, Coleshill, Warwicks; *m* 1909, Mary, *d* of E. J. M. Phillips, Liverpool; two *s* (and one *s* killed in action, 1943) two *d*. *Educ:* Oundle; Trinity Coll., Cambridge. Classical VI Form Master, Leeds Grammar Sch., 1906-19; The Royal Welch Fusiliers, 1916-19; demobilised, Feb. 1919; Headmaster, Plymouth Coll., 1920-29; Headmaster, City of London Sch., 1929-Aug. 1950; Pres., the Virgil Soc., 1952-54; Pres., Headmasters' Assoc., 1939-40. Temp. Lectr in Classics, King's Coll., London, 1953-55, 1959, Westfield Coll., 1960-62, 1964. Vice-Pres., Classical Association. *Publications:* On the Teaching of Latin; Paginæ Primæ. *Recreations:* trans. of ancient verse into quantity in English; tape recordings of Latin and Greek. *Address:* Dingle Ridge, Arkley, Barnet, Herts. *T:* 01-449 6468.

**DALE, Sir William (Leonard),** KCMG 1965 (CMG 1951); General Counsel to UNRWA, Near East, since 1968; Legal Adviser, Commonwealth Office, 1966 (CRO, 1961-66), retired; *b* 17 June 1906; *e s* of late Rev. William Dale, Rector of Preston, Yorks; *m* 1966, Mrs Gloria Spellman Finn, Washington, DC; one *d*. *Educ:* Hymers Coll., Hull; London (LLB); Barrister, Gray's Inn, 1931. Asst Legal Adviser, Colonial and Dominions Offices, 1935; Ministry of Supply, 1940-45; Dep. Legal Adviser, Colonial and Commonwealth Relations Offices, 1945; Legal Adviser, United Kingdom of Libya, 1951-53; Legal Adviser, Min. of Educn, 1954-61. *Publications:* Law of the Parish Church, 1932 (4th edn, 1967); contributions to journals. *Recreations:* music (except Wagner); Italian and the Italians. *Address:* UNRWA Headquarters, Museitbeh Quarter, Beirut, Lebanon. *Club:* Travellers'.

**DALGARNO, Prof. Alexander,** PhD; Professor of Astronomy, Harvard University, and Member of Smithsonian Astrophysical Observatory, since 1967; *b* 5 Jan. 1928; *s* of William Dalgarno; *m* 1957, Barbara Kane; two *s* two *d*. *Educ:* Southgate Grammar Sch.; University Coll., London. BSc Maths, 1st Cl. Hons London, 1947; PhD Theoretical Physics London, 1951; AM Harvard, 1967. The Queen's University of Belfast: Lectr in Applied Maths, 1952; Reader in Maths, 1956; Dir of Computing Lab, 1960; Prof. of Quantum Mechanics, 1961; Prof. of Mathematical Physics, 1966-67. Chief Scientist, Geophysics Corp. of America, 1962-63. Fellow, Amer. Acad. of Arts and Sciences, 1968. *Publications:* numerous papers in scientific journals. *Recreations:* squash, books. *Address:* c/o Harvard College Observatory, Cambridge, Mass. 02138, USA.

**DALGETTY, James Simpson,** MA, LLB; Solicitor to Secretary of State for Scotland and Solicitor in Scotland to HM Treasury since 1964; *b* 13 Aug. 1907; *s* of late Rev. William Dalgetty and Elizabeth Reid Dalgetty (*née* Simpson); *m* 1936, Mary Macdonald; one adopted *d*. *Educ:* George Watson's Coll., Edinburgh; Edinburgh Univ. Legal Asst, Dept of Health for Scotland, 1937; Asst Solicitor, 1944; Asst solicitor, Office of Solicitor to Sec. of State for Scotland, 1946; Senior Legal Draftsman to Govt of Nyasaland, and acting Solicitor-Gen., 1962-64. *Recreations:* photography, travel, reading. *Address:* Glenora, Marine Parade, North Berwick. *T:* North Berwick 3112.

**DALGETY, Arthur William Hugh;** *b* Nov. 1899; 2nd *s* of late Major F. J. Dalgety and Hon. Mrs Dalgety of Lockerley Hall, Romsey; *m*; one *s*. *Educ:* Harrow; Sandhurst. Lieut 9th Queen's Royal Lancers, retired. Master: Dunston Harriers, 1923; Vine Hunt, 1924-29; own Staghounds, 1926; New Forest Buckhounds, 1936-38 and 1944-47; Southdown Foxhounds, 1929-52; Meynell Foxhounds, 1952-55; Isle of Wight Foxhounds, 1955-59; Hursley Foxhounds, 1959-64; Tedworth Foxhounds, 1964-65; Ormond Foxhounds, 1965-; North Tipperary Foxhounds, 1965-68; own Beagles, 1950-63. *Address:* Balsdean, Brighton, Sussex. *T:* Brighton 33640; Lockerley Hall, Romsey, Hants; Emmel Castle, Cloughjordan, Co. Tipperary, Ireland. *Clubs:* Cavalry, United Hunts.

**DALGLISH, Captain James Stephen,** CVO 1955; CBE 1963; Welfare Officer, Metropolitan Police, since 1963; *b* 1 Oct. 1913; *e s* of late Rear-Adm. Robin Dalglish, CB; *m* 1939, Evelyn Mary, *e d* of late Rev. A. Ll. Meyricke, formerly Vicar of Aislaby, near Whitby; one *s* one *d*. *Educ:* RN Coll., Dartmouth. Commanded HMS Aisne, 1952-53; HM Yacht Britannia, 1954, HMS Woodbridge Haven and Inshore Flotilla, 1958-59; HMS Excellent, 1959-61; HMS Bulwark, 1961-63; jssc 1950; idc 1957. Retired from RN, 1963. *Recreations:* Rugby football, gardening, painting. *Address:* Park Hall, Aislaby, Whitby, Yorks. *T:* Sleights 213; 2 End House, Coleherne Mews, SW10. *T:* 01-373 5551. *Club:* United Service.

**DALHOUSIE,** 16th Earl of, *cr* 1633; **Simon Ramsay,** GBE 1957; MC 1944; LLD; Baron Ramsay, 1619; Lord Ramsay, 1633; Baron Ramsay (UK), 1875; Lord Chamberlain to the Queen Mother, 1965; Governor-General, Federation of Rhodesia and Nyasaland, 1957-63; Lord Lieutenant, County of Angus, since 1967; *b* 17 Oct. 1914; 2nd *s* of 14th Earl (*d* 1928) and Lady Mary Adelaide Heathcote Drummond Willoughby (*d* 1960), *d* of 1st Earl of Ancaster; *S* brother, 1950; *m* 1940, Margaret Elizabeth, *d* of Brig.-Gen. Archibald and Hon. Mrs Stirling of Keir; three *s* two *d*. *Educ:* Eton; Christ Church, Oxford. Served TA, Black Watch, 1936-39; embodied, 1939. MP (C) for County of Angus, 1945-50; Conservative Whip, 1946-48 (resigned). Hon. Col St Andrews Univ. OTC, 1963. Knight Pres., Hon. Soc. of Knights of The Round Table, 1964. *Heir: s* Lord Ramsay, *qv*. *Address:* Brechin Castle, Brechin. *T:* Brechin 2176. Dalhousie Castle, Bonnyrigg, Midlothian; 5 Margaretta Terrace, SW3. *T:* 01-352 6477. *Club:* White's.

*See also Maj.-Gen. Sir G. F. Johnson, Adm. Hon. Sir A. R. M. Ramsay, Earl of Scarbrough.*

**DALI, Salvador (Felipe Jacinto);** Spanish painter; stage-designer; book-illustrator; writer; interested in commercial art and films; *b* Figueras, Upper Catalonia, 11 May 1904; *s* of Salvador Dali, notary and Felipa Dome (Doménech); *m* 1935, Gala (*née* Elena Diaranoff); she *m* 1st, Paul Eluard. *Educ:* Academy of Fine Arts, Madrid; Paris. First one-man show, Barcelona, 1925; became prominent Catalan painter by 1927; Began surrealist painting in Paris, 1928; first one-man show, Paris, Nov. 1929; first one-man show, New York, Nov. 1933. Visited United States, 1934, 1939, 1940; lectured in Museum of Modern Art, New York, 1935; later, came to London; first visited Italy, 1937. Designer of scenery and costumes for ballet, etc., also of film scenarios. Has held exhibitions of paintings in many American and European Cities; Exhibition of jewels, London, 1960. *Publications:* Babaouo (ballet and film scenarios), 1932; Secret Life of Salvador Dali, 1942; Hidden Faces (novel), 1944; Fifty Secrets of Magic Craftsmanship, 1948; Diary of a Genius, 1966. *Address:* c/o Carstairs Gallery, 11 E 57th Street, New York 22; Hotel St Regis, 5th Avenue, and 55th Street, New York 22; Port-Lligat, Cadaqués, Spain.

**DALITZ, Prof. Richard Henry,** FRS 1960; Royal Society Research Professor at Oxford University, since 1963; *b* 28 Feb. 1925; *s* of Frederick W. and Hazel B. Dalitz, Melbourne, Australia; *m* 1946, Valda (*née* Suiter) of Melbourne, Australia; one *s* three *d. Educ:* Scotch Coll., Melbourne; Univ. of Melbourne; Trinity Coll., Univ. of Cambridge, PhD Cantab, 1950. Lecturer in Mathematical Physics, Univ. of Birmingham, 1949-55; Research appointments in various Univs, 1953-55; Reader in Mathematical Physics, Univ. of Birmingham, 1955-56; Prof. of Physics, Univ. of Chicago, 1956-66. Maxwell Medal and Prize, Institute of Physics and the Physical Soc., 1966. *Publications:* Strange Particles and Strong Interactions, 1962 (India); Nuclear Interactions of the Hyperons, 1962 (India); numerous papers on theoretical physics in various British and American scientific jls. *Recreations:* mountain walking, travelling. *Address:* 12 Parks Road, Oxford; All Souls College, Oxford. *Club:* Quadrangle (Chicago).

**DALKEITH, Earl of; Walter Francis John Montagu Douglas Scott;** DL; VRD; Lieutenant-Commander, RNR; MP (C) Edinburgh North, since 1960; Brigadier the Queen's Body Guard for Scotland, Royal Company of Archers; *o s* and *heir* of 8th Duke of Buccleuch, *qv*; *b* 28 Sept. 1923; *m* 1953, Jane, *d* of John McNeill, QC, Appin, Argyllshire, and Hongkong; three *s* one *d. Educ:* Eton; Christ Church, Oxford. Served War of 1939-45, RNVR. PPS to the Lord Advocate, 1961-62 and to the Sec. of State for Scotland, 1962-64. DL, Selkirk 1955, Midlothian 1960, Roxburgh 1962. *Heir: s* Lord Eskdaill, *qv. Address:* Eildon Hall, Melrose, Roxburghshire. *T:* St Boswells 2705; 46 Bedford Gardens, W8. *T:* 01-727 4358. *Clubs:* White's; Conservative, New (Edinburgh).

**DALLAPICCOLA, Prof. Luigi;** composer; piano teacher at Conservatorio Musicale, Florence, 1934-67; *b* 3 Feb. 1904; *s* of Pio Dallapiccola and Domitilla Alberti; *m* 1938, Laura Luzzatto; one *d. Educ:* Ginnasio-Liceo, Pisino d'Istria; Conservatorio Musicale, Florence. Became Italian Citizen, 1918. First visited London, 1938; again in 1946, and various European capitals during these years; USA: 1951, 1952, 1956, 1959, 1962, 1964, 1967, 1969. Member: Accad. S Cecilia, Rome, 1939; Accad. Filarmonica Romana, 1947; also of various foreign academies, 1953-, incl. RAM. Dr hc Univ. of Michigan, Ann Arbor, 1967. Grosser Kunstpreis des Landes Nordrhein-Westfalen für Musik, Düsseldorf, 1962; Musikpreis Ludwig Spohr, Braunshweig, 1964. Verdienstkreuz 1 Klasse des Verdienstordeus des Bundesrepublik Deutschland, 1968. Has written since 1925; *works include:* Sei Cori di Michelangelo Buonarroti il Giovane, 1933-36; Divertimento in Quattro Esercizi, 1934; Musica per tre Pianoforti, 1935; Volo di Notte, 1937-39; Canti di Prigionia, 1938-41; Piccolo Concerto per Muriel Couvreux, 1939-41; Marsia, 1942-43; Liriche Greche, 1942-45; Il Prigioniero, 1944-48; Ciaccona Intermezzo e Adagio, 1945; Job, 1950; Tartiniana, 1951; Canti di Liberazione, 1951-55; Quaderno Musicale di Annalibera, 1952; Goethe-Lieder, 1953; Variazioni per Orchestra, 1954; An Mathilde, 1955; Cinque Canti, 1955; Tartiniana Seconda, 1956; Concerto per la Notte di Natale dell' Anno 1956, 1957; Requiescant, 1957-58; Dialoghi, 1960; Preghiere, 1962; Parole di San Paolo 1964; Ulysses, opera, 1968. Many of his works have been recorded. *Address:* Via Romana 34, 50125 Firenze, Italy. *T:* 227698.

**DALLARD, Berkeley Lionel Scudamore,** CMG 1948; JP; FIANZ; *b* Waikari, Christchurch, New Zealand, 27 Aug. 1889; *s* of Geo. Joseph Dallard, Settler, born Tewkesbury, England, and Saria Maria, born Cheltenham, England; *m* 1915, Agnes Rowan Inglis; three *d. Educ:* Waikari Public Sch.; Rangiora High Sch.; Victoria University Coll. Entered Civil Service, NZ, 1907; served in Stamp Office, Audit Office, Board of Trade, Public Service Commissioner's Office (Asst Public Service Commr, 1929), Justice Dept; Controller Gen. of Prisons, and Chief Probation Officer, NZ, 1925-48; Under Sec. for Justice and Registrar Gen., NZ, 1934-48; retd, 1948. Govt Mem. of Govt Service Tribunal, 1949-60, retd. City Councillor, Wellington, 1949-62. Chairman: Wellington Hospital Board, 1962; Combined Purchasing Cttee for NZ Hosps. *Publications:* miscellaneous brochures on Criminology and Law. *Recreations:* bowls and gardening. *Address:* 94 Upland Road, Kelburn, Wellington, NZ. *TA* and *T:* Wellington 26209. *Clubs:* (Past Pres.) Savage, (Past Pres.) Rotary (Wellington, NZ).

**DALLEY, Christopher Mervyn,** MA Cantab; FInstPet; Chairman of Iraq Petroleum Co., Qatar Petroleum Co., Abu Dhabi Petroleum Co. and other associated companies, since 1970; *b* 26 Dec. 1913; *er s* of late Christopher Dalley; *m* 1947, Elizabeth Alice, *yr d* of Lt-Gen. Sir James Gammell, *qv*; one *s* three *d. Educ:* Epson Coll., Surrey; Queens' Coll., Cambridge. Served in RN, 1939-45 (Lt-Comdr). Joined British Petroleum Co., 1946; Chief Engineer, BP Refinery (Llandarcy), 1952; joined Iranian Oil Operating Companies in Iran 1954: Asst Gen. Managing Dir, 1958; joined Iraq Petroleum Co. and associated companies, 1962; Man. Dir. 1963. Pres., Inst. of Petroleum, 1970; Mem. Council, World Petroleum Congress, 1970. Order of Homoyoun (Iran), 1963. *Address:* Mead House, Woodham Walter, near Maldon, Essex. *T:* Danbury 2404; 6 Godfrey Street, SW3. *T:* 01-352 8260.

**DALLING, Sir Thomas,** Kt 1951; FRCVS, FRSE; Veterinary Consultant with the United Nations Food and Agriculture Organisation; *b* 23 April 1892. *Educ:* George Heriot's Sch., Edinburgh; Royal (Dick) Veterinary College. MRCVS 1914; Fitzwygram and Williams Memorial Prizes. Served with RAVC in France, 1916-18 (despatches), Major. Joined Staff of Glasgow Veterinary Coll., 1919, and later became Chief Investigator of Animal Diseases Research Assoc.; Veterinary Superintendent, Wellcome Physiological Research Laboratories, 1923; Prof. of Animal Pathology, University of Cambridge, 1937 (MA); Dir, Ministry of Agriculture and Fisheries Laboratories, Weybridge, 1942; Chief Veterinary Officer, Ministry of Agriculture and Fisheries, 1948-52; Hon. FRCVS, 1951; Hon. degrees: DSc Belfast, 1951; LLD Glasgow, 1952; DSc Bristol, 1952; LLD Edinburgh, 1959. Dalrymple-Champneys Cup and Medal, 1935; John Henry Steele Memorial Medal in gold, 1950; Thomas Baxter Prize, 1951. Mem. Council Royal Coll. of Veterinary Surgeons, since 1938 (Pres. 1949-

50, 1950-51. Vice-Pres., 1951-52, 1952-53); late Mem. Agricultural Research Council. *Publications:* many veterinary and scientific articles. *Address:* United Nations Food and Agriculture Organisation, Viale delle Terme di Caracalla, Rome. *Club:* Farmers'.

**DALRYMPLE,** family name of **Earl of Stair.**

**DALRYMPLE, Viscount; John David James Dalrymple;** *b* 4 Sept. 1961; *s* and *heir* of 13th Earl of Stair, *qv.*

**DALRYMPLE, Sir (Charles) Mark,** 3rd Bt, *cr* 1887; RAuxAF; Market Gardener; *b* 13 May 1915; *s* of Sir David Charles Herbert Dalrymple, 2nd Bt, of Newhailes, and Margaret Anna (*d* 1962) (who obtained a divorce, 1919, and *m* 2nd, 1925, Sir Patrick Graham Blake, 5th Bt, who *d* 1930), *y d* of late Sir Mark Mactaggart Stewart, 1st Bt; *S* father, 1932; *m* 1946, Lady Antonia Marian Amy Isabel Stewart, *o d* of 12th Earl of Galloway, *qv. Educ:* Canford Sch., Wimborne, Dorset. Lieut 4th/5th (Queen's Edinburgh) Royal Scots (TA), (52nd Searchlight Regt) The Royal Regt, 1937-40 (discharged due to insufficiently good eyesight). Aircraftman RAFVR, 1941-46 (1939-45 Star, France and Germany Star, Defence Medal, War Medal, 1939-45). *Heir:* none. *Address:* Newhailes, Musselburgh, Midlothian, Scotland. *T:* Musselburgh 2812; 26 Chelsea Square, SW3. *T:* 01-352 6919. *Clubs:* Lansdowne, Royal Over-Seas League; New (Edinburgh).

**DALRYMPLE, Sir Hew (Fleetwood) Hamilton-,** 10th Bt, *cr* 1697; DL; late Major, Grenadier Guards; Chairman, Mackinlay-McPherson Ltd; Assistant Managing Director, Scottish & Newcastle Breweries; Director, scottish American Investment Company; *b* 9 April 1926; *er s* of Sir Hew (Clifford) Hamilton-Dalrymple, 9th Bt, JP; *S* father, 1959; *m* 1954, Lady Anne-Louise Mary Keppel, 3rd *d* of 9th Earl of Albemarle, *qv*; four *s. Educ:* Ampleforth. Brig. and Adjutant, Queen's Body Guard for Scotland (Royal Company of Archers). DL East Lothian, 1964. *Heir: e s* Hew Richard Hamilton-Dalrymple, *b* 3 Sept. 1955. *Address:* Leuchie, North Berwick, East Lothian. *T:* North Berwick 2903. *Club:* New (Edinburgh).

**DALRYMPLE, Ian Murray,** FRSA; Film Producer, Writer and Director; *b* 26 Aug. 1903; *s* of late Sir William Dalrymple, KBE, LLD; *m* 2nd, Joan Margaret, *d* of late James Douglas Craig, CMG, CBE; one *s* and one *d* of previous marriage and two *s. Educ:* Rugby Sch.; Trinity Coll., Cambridge (Editor of The Granta, 1924-25). Executive Producer, Crown Film Unit, Min. of Information, 1940-43; subseq. op. through Wessex Film Productions Ltd and Ian Dalrymple (Advisory) Ltd. Chm. Brit. Film Acad., 1957-58. Film Editor, 1927-35. Screen writer, 1935-39, films including The Citadel, South Riding, Storm in a Teacup, The Lion Has Wings. Produced for Crown Film Unit; Fires Were Started, Western Approaches, Coastal Command, Ferry Pilot, Close Quarters, Wavell's 30,000, Target for To-Night, London Can Take It, etc. Independent productions: The Woman in the Hall, Esther Waters, Once a Jolly Swagman, All Over The Town, Dear Mr Prohack, The Wooden Horse, Family Portrait, The Changing Face of Europe (series), Royal Heritage, Raising a Riot, A Hill in Korea. Commissioned productions include: The Heart of the Matter, The Admirable Crighton, A Cry from the Streets, Bank of England (Educational Films), The Boy and the Pelican. Film Adviser, Decca Ltd, 1967-68. Supervising Film Projects, Argo Record Co. Ltd (Div. of Decca Ltd), 1969. Prod Chaucer's Tale, 1970.

**DALRYMPLE, Sir Mark;** *see* Dalrymple, Sir C. M.

**DALRYMPLE-CHAMPNEYS, Captain Sir Weldon,** 2nd Bt, *cr* 1910; CB 1957; MA, DM, BCh, DPH Oxon; Fellow and former Member of Council (Milroy Lecturer, 1950), Royal College of Physicians, London; Captain, Grenadier Guards (retired); Deputy Chief Medical Officer, Ministry of Health, 1940-56; President: Section of Epidemiology and Public Health, Royal Society of Medicine, 1943-45; Section of Comparative Medicine, 1954-55; Section of History of Medicine, 1957-59; Vice-President Emeritus, Royal Society of Health; Ex-Chairman, Royal Veterinary College; Member of Council, Animal Health Trust; President, Federation of Civil Service Photographic Societies; President Hæmophilia Society; *b* 7 May 1892; *o surv s* of Sir Francis Henry Champneys, 1st Bt, and Virginia Julian (*d* 1922), *o d* of late Sir John Warrender Dalrymple, 7th Bt, of North Berwick; *S* father, 1930; *m* 1924, Anne, OBE 1948 (*d* 1968), *d* of late Col A. Spencer Pratt, CB, CMG, Broom Hall, Kent. *Educ:* Oriel Coll., Oxford (Hon. Fellow, 1967). Served European War, 1914-19 (wounded); Senior Asst MOH, Willesden UDC; Hon. Physician to the King, 1941-44; Lord of the Manor of Stanwick (Northants); assumed additional surname of Dalrymple by deed poll, 1924. Ex-Chm., Vegetable Drugs Cttee, Ministry of Supply. Past Pres., Joint Food and Agriculture Organisation/World Health Organisation Expert Cttee on Brucellosis. *Publications:* Reports to Ministry of Health on the Accommodation for the Sick provided at certain Public Schools for Boys in England, 1928; Undulant Fever, 1929; Bovine Tuberculosis in Man, with special reference to infection by milk, 1931; The Supervision of Milk Pasteurising Plants, 1935; Undulant Fever, a Neglected Problem (Milroy Lectures, Royal College of Physicians), 1950; Brucella Infection and Undulant Fever in Man, 1960; also numerous articles in scientific journals. *Recreations:* yachting, swimming, travelling, photography, etc. *Heir:* none. 6a Moreton Road, Oxford. *T:* Oxford 58171. *Clubs:* Athenæum, Guards.

**DALRYMPLE-HAMILTON, Adm. Sir Frederick Hew George,** KCB, *cr* 1945 (CB 1941); DL; JP; *b* 27 March 1890; *s* of late Col Hon. North de Coigny Dalrymple-Hamilton, MVO, of Bargany, Girvan, Ayrshire; *m* 1918, Gwendolen, *d* of Sir Cuthbert Peek, 2nd Bt; one *s* two *d. Educ:* HMS Britannia. Entered Royal Navy, 1905; served European War, 1914-18; Capt. 1931; Capt. Royal Naval Coll., Dartmouth, 1936-39; Capt. HMS Rodney, 1939-41, present at destruction of German battleship Bismarck (CB); Rear-Adm, 1941; Adm. Commanding Iceland, 1941-42; Naval Secretary to First Lord of Admiralty, 1942; Vice-Adm. 1944; Vice-Adm. Commanding 10th Cruiser Squadron and 2nd in Command, Home Fleet, 1944-45 (KCB); Vice-Adm. Malta and Flag Officer Central Mediterranean, 1945-46; Flag Officer Comdg Scotland and North Ireland, 1946-48; Adm., 1948; Adm., British Joint Services Mission, Washington, USA, 1948-50; retd list 1950. Mem., Queen's Body Guard for Scotland, Royal Company of Archers, 1969-. JP and DL for Wigtownshire, 1952. *Address:* Bargany, Girvan, Ayrshire. *T:* Old Dailly 242. *Clubs:* United Service; New (Edinburgh).

*See also Capt. N. E. F. Dalrymple Hamilton.*

**DALRYMPLE HAMILTON, Captain North Edward Frederick,** CVO 1961; MBE 1953; DSC 1943; Royal Navy, retired; *b* 17 Feb. 1922; *s* of Admiral Sir Frederick Dalrymple-Hamilton, *qv*; *m* 1949, Hon. Mary Colville, *d* of 1st Baron Clydesmuir, PC, GCIE, TD; two *s*. *Educ:* Eton. Entered Royal Navy, 1940; Comdr 1954; Capt. 1960. Comdg Officer HMS Scarborough, 1958; Executive Officer, HM Yacht Britannia, 1959; Capt. (F) 17th Frigate Squadron, 1963; Dir of Naval Signals, 1963; Dir, Weapons Equipment Surface, 1966; retd, 1970. Brig., Royal Company of Archers, Queen's Body Guard for Scotland. *Address:* Lovestone, Girvan, Ayreshire. *T:* Old Dailly 227. *Clubs:* United Service, Pratt's.

**DALRYMPLE-HAY, Sir James Brian,** 6th Bt, *cr* 1798; Estate Agent; *b* 19 Jan. 1928; *e s* of Lt-Col Brian George Rowland Dalrymple-Hay (*d* on active service, 1943) and Beatrice (*d* 1935), *d* of A. W. Inglis; *S* cousin, 1952; *m* 1958, Helen Sylvia, *d* of late Stephen Herbert Card and of Molly M. Card; three *d*. *Educ:* Hillsbrow Preparatory Sch., Redhill; Blundell's Sch., Tiverton, Devon. Royal Marine, 1946-47; Lieut Royal Marine Commando, 1947-49; Palestine Star, 1948. Estate Agent and Surveyor's Pupil, 1949; Principal, 1955-. *Recreations:* cricket, Rugby football, swimming. *Heir: b* John Hugh Dalrymple-Hay [*b* 16 Dec. 1929; *m* 1962, Jennifer, *d* of late Brig. Robert Johnson, CBE; one *s*]. *Address:* The Red House, Church Road, Warnham, near Horsham, Sussex.

**DALRYMPLE-SMITH, Captain Hugh,** RN (retired); *b* 27 Sept. 1901; *s* of late Arthur Alexander Dalrymple-Smith and late Mary Glover; *m* 1939, Eleanor Mary Hoare; two *s* one *d*. *Educ:* Ovingdean; Osborne; Dartmouth. Midshipman, 1917; Ronald Megaw Prize for 1921-22; qualified gunnery 1925, advanced course, 1928. Capt. 1941 (despatches); Admiralty Operations Div., 1942-43; commanding HMS Arethusa, including Normandy landings, 1943-45 (despatches). Naval Attaché, Nanking, 1946-48; commanding HMS King George V, 1948-49. Retired, Dec. 1950, and recalled as Actg Rear-Adm.; Chief of Staff to C-in-C Allied Forces, Northern Europe, 1951-53; retired as Captain. Dir, Television Audience Measurement Ltd, 1958-66. *Recreation:* painting. *Address:* Crossfield, Bovingdon, Herts. *T:* Bovingdon 3179.

**DALRYMPLE-WHITE, Sir Henry Arthur Dalrymple,** 2nd Bt, *cr* 1926; DFC 1941 and Bar 1942; *b* 5 Nov. 1917; *o s* of Lieut-Col Sir Godfrey Dalrymple-White, 1st Bt, and Hon. Catherine Mary Cary, *d* of 12th Viscount Falkland; *S* father 1954; *m* 1948, Mary (marr. diss. 1956), *o d* of Capt. Robert H. C. Thomas; one *s*. *Educ:* Eton; Magdalene Coll., Cambridge; London Univ. Formerly Wing Commander RAFVR. Served War of 1939-45. *Heir: s* Jan Hew Dalrymple-White, *b* 26 Nov. 1950. *Address:* c/o Brown, Shipley Ltd, Founders Court, Lothbury, EC2. *Club:* Junior Carlton.

**DALTON, Alfred Hyam;** Commissioner of Inland Revenue since 1970; *b* 29 March 1922; *m* 1946, Elizabeth Stalker; three *d*. *Educ:* Merchant Taylors' Sch., Northwood; Aberdeen Univ. Served War, REME, 1942-45 (despatches). Entered Inland Revenue, 1947; Asst Sec., 1958; Sec. to Board, 1969. *Recreations:* bridge, carpentry. *Address:* 18a Cotsford Avenue, New Malden, Surrey. *T:* 01-942 1045.

**DALTON, Maj.-Gen. Sir Charles (James George),** Kt 1967; CB 1954; CBE 1949 (OBE 1941); *b* 28 Feb. 1902; *s* of late Maj.-Gen. James Cecil Dalton, Col Comdt, RA, and late Mary Caroline, *d* of late Gen. Sir George Barker, GCB; *m* 1936, Daphne, *d* of Col Llewellyn Evans, and late Mrs F. A. Macartney; one *s* two *d* (and one *s* decd). *Educ:* Aysgarth Sch., Yorks; Cheltenham Coll.; RMA Woolwich. Commissioned, RA, 1921; Staff Coll., Camberley, 1935-36; served in Egypt and India, 1922-39; staff appts in India and Burma, 1939-45 (CRA 26 Ind. Div., BGS 33 Ind. Corps, CRA 14 Ind. Div.); served with CCG, 1946; War Office (Brig. AG Coordination), 1946-49; Comdr 8 AA Bde, 1949-51; Services Relations Adviser to UK High Comr Control Commn for Germany, 1951-54; Dir of Manpower Planning, War Office, 1954-57, retired. Capt. 1934, Major 1939, Lt-Col 1946, Col 1947, Brig. 1951, Maj.-Gen. 1954. Col Comdt RA, 1960-65. Dir-Gen. of Zoological Soc. of London, 1957-67. OStJ. *Recreations:* shooting and fishing. *Address:* The Hutts, Grewelthorpe, Ripon. *T:* Kirkby Malzeard 355. *Club:* Army and Navy.

**DALTON, Maj.-Gen. John Cecil D'Arcy,** CB 1954; CBE 1948; DL; High Sheriff of Yorkshire, 1970-71; *b* 2 Mar. 1907; *yr s* of late Maj.-Gen. J. C. Dalton, Col Comdt RA, and of late Mrs Dalton; *m* 18 July 1942, Pamela Frances, *d* of late Brig.-Gen. W. H. E. Segrave, DSO; two *s*. *Educ:* Cheltenham Coll.; RMA Woolwich, 2nd Lieut RA, 1926; psc 1939; served War of 1939-45; France and Flanders, 1940; N Africa, 1942-43; NW Europe, 1944. Maj.-Gen., 1958; Maj.-Gen. i/c Administration, Gen. HQ, Far East Land Forces, 1957-59; Dir of Quartering War Office, 1959-60; Vice-Quartermaster-Gen., War Office, 1960-62, retired 1962. CC N Riding Yorks, 1964-70, DL North Riding Yorks, 1967. *Address:* Hauxwell Hall, Leyburn, Yorks.

**DALTON, Vice-Adm. Sir Norman (Eric),** KCB 1959 (CB 1956); OBE 1944; *b* 1 Feb. 1904; *s* of late William John Henry Dalton, Portsmouth; *m* 1927, Teresa Elizabeth, *d* of late Richard Jenkins, Portsmouth; one *s* one *d*. *Educ:* RN Colls Osborne and Dartmouth. Joined RN, 1917; Capt. 1946; Rear-Adm. 1954; Vice-Adm. 1957. Deputy Engineer-in-Chief of the Fleet, 1955-57; Engineer-in-Chief of the Fleet, 1957-59; Dir-Gen. of Training, 1959-60; retired 1960. Vice-Pres., Vocational Guidance Association, 1967. *Address:* New Lodge, Peppard Lane, Henley-on-Thames, Oxon. *T:* Henley 5552. *Club:* Army and Navy.

**DALTON, Peter Gerald Fox,** CMG 1958; Deputy Head of International Secretariat (Shipping); *b* 12 Dec. 1914; *s* of late Sir Robert (William) Dalton, CMG; *m* 1944, Josephine Anne Helyar; one *s* one *d*. *Educ:* Uppingham Sch.; Oriel Coll., Oxford. HM Embassy, Peking 1937-39; HM Consulate-Gen., Hankow, 1939-41; HM Embassy, Chungking, 1941-42; Foreign Office, 1942-46; HM Legation, Bangkok, 1946; HM Embassy, Montevideo, 1947-50; Foreign Office, 1950-53; Political Adviser, Hong Kong, 1953-56; Foreign Office, 1957-60; HM Embassy, Warsaw, 1960-63; HM Consul-General: Los Angeles, 1964-65; San Francisco, 1965-67; Minister, HM Embassy, Moscow, 1967-69; retd from HM Diplomatic Service, 1969. *Address:* Cat Street House, Upper Hartfield, Sussex. *T:* Forest Row 2491. *Club:* Travellers'.

**DALTON, Philip Neale;** Deputy President, Immigration Appeal Tribunal; *b* 30 June 1909; *o s* of late Sir Llewelyn Dalton, MA; *m* 1947, Pearl, *d* of Mark Foster, Kenya; one *s* two *d*. *Educ:* Downside Sch.; Trinity Coll., Cambridge. Barrister-at-law. Inner Temple, 1933; Resident Magistrate, Ghana, 1937;

military service, 1939-45; Crown Counsel, Ghana, 1945-51; Solicitor-Gen., Fiji, 1951-53; Attorney-Gen., British Solomon Islands, and Legal Adviser, Western Pacific High Commission, 1953-56; Attorney-Gen., Zanzibar, 1957-63. Puisne Judge, Kenya, 1963-69. Order of the Brilliant Star (second class) Zanzibar, 1963. *Recreations:* cricket, golf. *Address:* 7 The Glebe, Standlake, Oxon. *Clubs:* Royal Commonwealth Society; Nairobi (Nairobi).

**DALTON, Thomas Wilson Fox,** CB, 1946; Chairman, James Miller & Co. Ltd, West India Merchants; *b* 28 Dec. 1886; *s* of late Rev. Edwin Dalton, DD, and Mary Eliza Dalton; *m* 1913, Mabel Louise, *d* of late Rev. James Pickett; three *d*. *Educ:* Central High Sch., Leeds. Entered Board of Trade (Second Division Clerk), 1907; Ministry of Labour, 1916; Finance Officer to Commissioner for the Special Areas (England and Wales), Dec. 1934-Sept. 1939; Accountant-Gen., 1943-Dec. 1951, Min. of Labour and Nat. Service. *Address:* 2 Warren Close, Worthing, Sussex. *T:* Worthing 65288. *Club:* National Liberal.

**DALTON-MORRIS, Air Marshal Sir Leslie,** KBE 1959 (CBE 1944); CB 1952; psa; retired as AOC-in-C, Royal Air Force Maintenance Command (1961-63); *b* 7 April 1906; *m* Marion, 2nd *d* of late A. G. Ellis, Bromley, Kent; one *d*. Entered Royal Air Force, 1924; experimental and test pilot, Martlesham Heath, 1926-28; Signals Course, Cranwell, 1929-30; RAF, Staff Coll., 1937; HQ No. 2 Group, 1938-39; served War of 1939-45 (despatches, CBE); Deputy Chief Signals Officer, HQ Fighter Command, 1939-41. Bomber Command, 1941-43; SASO No. 26 Group, 1943-44; Comd Signals Officer, HQ, Bomber Command, 1944-45; Dir of Radio and later Signals, Air Ministry, 1945-47; Commandant Central Signals Establishment, 1948-49; Comd Signals Officer, Middle East Air Force, 1949; Asst Chief of the Air Staff (Signals), 1952-56; AOC, No. 90 Group, 1956-58; AOC-in-C, Signals Command, 1958-61. *Recreation:* golf. *Address:* 12 Charles House, Phyllis Court Drive, Henley-on-Thames, Oxon. *Clubs:* Royal Air Force; Phyllis Court.

**DALWOOD, Hubert;** Sculptor; *b* 2 June 1924; *s* of Cyril Herbert Dalwood and Edith Mary (*née* Mitchell); *m* 1963, Caroline Gaunt; two *s* (two *d* by a previous *m*). *Educ:* Bath Acad. of Art. Gregory Fellow of Sculpture, Univ. of Leeds, 1955-58. First one-man exhibn, London, 1954; 1st Prize for Sculpture, John Moore's Exhibition, Liverpool, 1960; British Pavilion, Venice, 1962 (John Bright Prize-winner); Internat. Sculpture Symposium, Toronto, 1967. Vis. Prof., Univ. of Wisconsin, 1967-68. Commissions for: Liverpool Univ.; Leeds Univ.; Nuffield Coll., Oxford; Wolverhampton Polytechnic; Birmingham Plytechnic. Work in collections; Tate Gallery; Museum of Modern Art and Guggenheim Museum, New York; Carnegie Inst., Pittsburgh; etc. Address: c/o Gimpel Fils, 50 South Molton Street, W1.

**DALY, Ashley Skeffington,** FRCS; FFARCS; DA England; Consulting Anæsthetist London Hospital; late Anæsthetist to Royal Masonic Hospital; Brigadier, Consulting Anæsthetist to the Army; *b* 12 July 1882; *s* of late Frederick H. Daly, MD, JP, of Hackney; *m* Maude, *d* of Arthur C. James of Paignton; one *s* one *d*. *Educ:* Merchant Taylors' Sch.; London Hospital. MRCS, LRCP, 1905; DA England 1935; FRCS 1944; FFARCS 1948. Held various Resident Hospital appointments, 1903-09. *Publications:* articles on Anæsthetics, House-Surgeon's Vade Mecum and Manual of War Surgery. *Address:* 6 Cotlands, Sidmouth, Devon. *T:* Sidmouth 2998. *Club:* MCC.

**DALY, Most Rev. Cahal Brendan;** *see* Ardagh and Clonmacnois, Bishop of, (RC).

**DALY, Harry John,** CMG 1966; FRACP; FFARCS 1949; FFARACS; Retired Anæsthetist; *b* 3 Aug. 1893; *s* of Henry and Victoria Daly, both Irish; *m* 1921, Jean Edmunds, Sydney. *Educ:* St Ignatius Coll., Sydney, Australia, MB, ChM Sydney, 1918; FRACP 1946; FFARACS Melbourne 1952. Gen. Practice, Haberfield NSW; Specialist Anæsthetist, Sydney, 1929; Hon. Consulting Anæsthetist to Lewisham, Sydney and St Vincent's Hospitals. Dean, Faculty of Anæsthetists, RACS, 1954. Hon. Member: Royal Society of Medicine; Liverpool Soc. Anæsthetists, 1935. Orton Medallion, RACS, 1969. *Publications:* numerous scientific articles in med. jls, 1932-56. *Recreations:* fishing, gardening. *Address:* 8 The Parapet, Castlecrag, NSW, Australia. *T:* 955957. *Club:* Royal Sydney Golf.

**DALY, Ivan de Burgh,** CBE 1959; FRS 1943; MA, MD Cambridge, MD Birmingham, FRCP; *b* 14 April 1893; *s* of late James Thomas Daly and Amy Pritchard; *m* Beatrice Mary, *e d* of Alfred Leetham, Ganton, Yorks; one *s* (and one *s* decd). *Educ:* Rossall; Gonville and Caius Coll., Cambridge; St Bartholomew's Hospital, 1st Class Natural Science Tripos Part I, 1914. Private RAMC, 1914; Flight Sub-Lieut RNAS, 1915-17; Capt. RAFMS; Mem. of Invaliding Medical Board, Hampstead and York, 1918; Asst in Department of Physiology, University Coll., London, 1919-23; Beit Memorial Research Fellow, junior 1920, 4th year 1923; Lecturer in Experimental Physiology in Univ. of Wales, Cardiff, 1923; Prof. of Physiology in the University of Birmingham, 1927-32; Prof. of Physiology, University of Edinburgh, 1933-47; Dir of Institute of Animal Physiology, Agricultural Research Council, 1948-58; Dir Medical Research Council's Physiological Laboratory, Armoured Fighting Vehicle Training Sch., Lulworth, Dorset, 1942-45; Mem. Agricultural Research Council, 1945-47; Wellcome Trust Research Fellow, 1958-62. Hon. Fellow Soc. Reg. Med., Budapest; Hon. Member: Thoracic Soc. (Pres., 1954-55); Physiological Soc., 1969. Harvey Lecturer, New York, 1936; Lyon Lecturer, Univ. of Minnesota, USA, 1951; Louis Abrahams Lecturer, RCP, 1956. Thruston Medal, Caius Coll., Cambridge, 1928; Baly Medal, RCP, 1959. Co-Editor of Quarterly Journal Experimental Physiology. *Publications:* (with Catherine Hebb) Bronchial and Pulmonary Vascular Systems, 1966; Physiological papers on the Cardiovascular System and Pulmonary Circulation in scientific jls. *Address:* 25 High Street, Long Crendon, Aylesbury, Bucks. *T:* Long Crendon 298. *Club:* Athenæum.

*See also Michael de Burgh Daly.*

**DALY, Rt. Rev. John Charles Sydney;** Assistant to the Bishop of Coventry, and Priest-in-charge of Honington with Idlicote and Whatcote, since 1968; *b* 13 Jan. 1903; *s* of S. Owen Daly. *Educ:* Gresham's Sch., Holt; King's Coll., Cambridge; Cuddesdon Coll., Oxford. Curate, St Mary's Church, Tyne Dock, South Shields, 1926-29; Vicar, Airedale with Fryston, Yorks, 1929-35; Bishop of Gambia, 1935-51; Bishop of Accra, 1951-55; Bishop in Korea, 1955-65, of Taejon (Korea), 1965-68. *Address:* Idlicote Rectory, Shipston-on-Stour, Warwicks.

**DALY, Lawrence;** General Secretary, National Union of Mineworkers, since 1968; *b* 20 Oct. 1924; *s* of James Daly and Janet Taylor; *m* 1948, Renée M. Baxter; four *s* one *d*. *Educ:* primary and secondary schools. Glencraig

Colliery (underground), 1939; Workmen's Safety Inspector, there, 1954-64. Part-time NUM lodge official, Glencraig, 1946; Chm., Scottish NUM Youth Committee, 1949; elected to Scottish Area NUM Exec. Cttee, 1962; Gen. Sec., Scottish NUM, 1964; National Exec., NUM, 1965. *Publications:* (pamphlets): A Young Miner Sees Russia, 1946; The Miners and the Nation, 1968. *Recreations:* literature, politics, folk-song. *Address:* 222 Euston Road, NW1. *T:* 01-387 7631. *Club:* Jewel Miners' (Edinburgh).

**DALY, Dame Mary Dora,** DBE 1951 (CBE 1949; OBE 1937); Victorian President of Catholic Welfare Organisation since 1941; *b* Cootamundra, NSW; *d* of late T. P. MacMahon, Darling Point, Sydney; *m* 1923, Dr John J. Daly, Melbourne; one *s* one *d. Educ:* Loreto Abbey, Ballarat, Vic. Mem. of Council, Vic. Div. of Australian Red Cross Soc. since 1936. War of 1939-45; Mem. of finance and advisory cttees, Australian Comforts Fund; Mem. executive cttees, Lord Mayor of Melbourne's appeals for food for Britain, toys for Britain, Victorian Government fat for Britain drive. Mem. Victorian Council Girl Guides Assoc., 1954. Pres., Australian Catholic Relief, Archdiocese of Melbourne. Cross, Pro Ecclesia et Pontifice, 1952. *Address:* 6 Henry Street, Kew, Victoria 3101, Australia.

**DALY, Michael de Burgh,** MA, MD, ScD Cambridge; Professor of Physiology in the University of London, at St Bartholomew's Hospital Medical College, since 1958; *b* 7 May 1922; *s* of Ivan de Burgh Daly, *qv*; *m* 1948, Beryl Esmé, *y d* of late Wing Commander A. J. Nightingale; two *s. Educ:* Loretto Sch., Edinburgh; Gonville and Caius Coll., Cambridge; St Bartholomew's Hospital. Nat. Science Tripos. Part I, 1943, Part II, 1944, Physiology. House-physician, St Bartholomew's Hospital, 1947; Asst Lecturer, 1948-50, and Lecturer, 1950-54, in Physiology, University Coll., London; Rockefeller Foundation Travelling Fellowship in Medicine, 1952-53; Locke Research Fellow of Royal Soc., 1954-58; former Co-Editor of Journal of Physiology. FRSM. Mem. Physiological Soc. Schafer Prize in Physiology, University Coll., London, 1953; Thruston Medal, Gonville and Caius Coll., 1957; Sir Lionel Whitby Medal, Cambridge Univ., 1963. *Publications:* contributor to Winton and Bayliss' Human Physiology and to Starling's Principles of Human Physiology; papers on the reflex control of respiration and the cardiovascular system in Journal of Physiology. *Recreation:* model engineering. *Address:* 7 Hall Drive, Sydenham, SE26. *T:* 01-778 8773.

**DALY, Lt-Gen. Sir Thomas (Joseph),** KBE 1967 (CBE 1953; OBE 1944); CB 1965; DSO 1945, Chief of the General Staff, Australia, since 1966; *b* 19 March 1913; *s* of Lt-Col T. J. Daly, DSO, VD, Melbourne; *m* 1946, Heather, *d* of late James Fitzgerald, Melbourne; three *d. Educ:* St Patrick's Coll., Sale; Xavier Coll., Kew, Vic; RMC, Duntroon. Attached 3rd LH, 1934; attached for training 16/5 Lancers, India, 1938; Adj, 2/10 Aust. Inf. Bn, 1939; Bde Major, 18 Inf. Bde, 1940; GSO1 5 Aust. Div., 1942; CO 2/10 Inf. Bn, AIF, 1944; Instr, Staff Coll., Camberley, UK, 1946; Joint Services Staff Coll., Latimer, 1948; Dir of Mil. Art, RMC Duntroon, 1949; Dir of Infantry, AHQ, 1951; Comd 28 Brit. Commonwealth Inf. Bde, Korea, 1952; Dir, Ops and Plans, AHQ, 1953; IDC, London, 1956; GOC Northern Command, Australia, 1957-60; Adjt Gen., 1961-63; GOC, Eastern Command, Australia, 1963-66. Legion of Merit (US), 1953. *Recreations:* golf, tennis, cricket. *Address:* 116 Empire Circuit, Yarralumia, ACT, Australia. *T:* 731224. *Clubs:* Australian (Sydney); Naval and Military (Melbourne).

**DALY LEWIS, Edward;** *see* Lewis.

**DALYELL, Tam;** MP (Lab) West Lothian, since 1962; *b* 9 Aug. 1932; *s* of Gordon and Eleanor Dalyell; *m* 1963, Kathleen, *o d* of Baron Wheatley, *qv*; one *s* one *d. Educ:* Eton; King's Coll., Cambridge; Moray House Teachers' Training Coll., Edinburgh. Trooper, Royal Scots Greys, 1950-52; Teacher, Bo'ness High Sch., 1956-60. Contested (Lab) Roxburgh, Selkirk, and Peebles, 1959. Dep.-Director of Studies on British India ship-school, Dunera, 1961-62. Member Public Accounts Cttee, House of Commons, 1962-66; Secretary, Labour Party Standing Conference on the Sciences, 1962-64; PPS to Minister of Housing, 1964-65; Chm. Parly Labour Party Education Cttee, 1964-65; Chm. Parly Labour Party Sports Group, 1964-; Mem. House of Commons Select Cttee on Science and Technology, 1967-69. PPS to Rt Hon. R. H. S. Crossman, MP, 1967-. *Publications:* The Case of Ship-Schools, 1960; Ship-School Dunera, 1963. *Recreations:* tennis, swimming. *Address:* The Binns, Linlithgow, Scotland. *T:* Philipstoun 255. *Club:* Arts (Edinburgh).

**DAM, (Carl Peter) Henrik,** DrSc; Professor of Biochemistry and Nutrition, Polytechnic Institute, Copenhagen (appointed while in the USA), 1941-65, and leader of biochemical division, Danish Fat Research Institute, 1956-63; *b* Copenhagen, Denmark, 21 Feb. 1895; *s* of Emil Dam and Emilie Peterson; *m* 1924, Inger Olsen; no *c. Educ:* Polytechnic Institute (MS Chemistry 1920) and University, Copenhagen (DrSc Biochemistry 1934). Instructor of Chemistry, Royal Agricultural Sch., Copenhagen, 1920; Instructor of Biochemistry, Univ. of Copenhagen, 1923; Asst Prof., Biochemistry, 1928, Associate Prof., Biochemistry, 1931-41, Univ. of Copenhagen; Senior Research Associate, Univ. of Rochester, 1942-45; Associate Member, Rockefeller Institute, 1945-48. went to the US on a lecture tour, 1940, lectured in the US and in Canada, 1940-41; returned to Denmark, 1946; 2nd lecture tour in US and Canada, 1949. Worked with F. Pregl, Graz, Austria, 1925; with Rudolf Schoenheimer, Freiburg, Germany, 1932-33 (Rockefeller Fellow); with P. Karrer, Zürich, 1935 and later. Awarded share of 1943 Nobel Prize for Physiology and Medicine, 1944. Member: Danish Academy of Technical Sciences, 1947; Kgl. Danske Videnskabernes Selskab, 1948; Foreign Corresp. Member Royal Academy Medicine, Belgium, 1951; Gesellschaft für Ernährung, Germany, 1961. Fellow, American Institute of Nutrition, 1964. Hon. FRSE, 1953. Norman Medal, German Fat Research Society, 1960; Dr Sc (*hc*) University of St Louis, 1965. *Publications:* over 270 papers on biochemical subjects in British, other European, and American journals. Main subjects: Cholesterol Metabolism, The Discovery and further Investigation of Vitamin K, Studies on Vitamin E and Lipids, growth, gall stone formation, etc. *Recreations:* travels in Europe, the US and Canada. *Address:* Polytechnic Institute, østervoldgade 10III, Copenhagen 1350, Denmark.

**d'AMBRUMENIL, Sir Philip,** Kt 1945; *b* 28 Dec. 1886; 2nd *s* of Benerice Henry and Isabella d'Ambrumenil; *m* 1921, Gertrude Merriel, *e d* of C. H. Bailey, Newport, Mon.; one *s* one *d. Educ:* Rugby School. Entered Lloyd's, 1904; Gold Medal for services to Corporation of Lloyd's, 1943; Dep. Chairman War Risks

Insurance Office (Ministry of War Transport, 1939-44; Dep. Chairman of Lloyd's, 1945, 1946; Chairman, 1947; Dep. Chairman Lloyd's Register of Shipping, 1948, 1949. Officier de l'Ordre de la Couronne, 1947; Officer of the Order of Orange Nassau, 1948; Knight of the 1st degree, Order of St Olav, 1948; Commander, Order of George 1st (Greece). *Address:* 1312 Minster House, St James's Court, SW1. *T:* 01-834 2360.

**DAMER;** *see* Dawson-Damer.

**DANCE, James,** ERD 1954; MP (C) Bromsgrove, since 1955; *b* 5 May 1907; *s* of late Sir George Dance; *m* 1st, Charlotte (decd), *d* of George Herbert Strutt, Bridgehill, Belper; 2nd, 1934, Anne (CBE 1962), *d* of Colonel Arthur Travis Walker; one *s* three *d*. *Educ:* Eton Coll. Major, The Queen's Bays (2nd Dragoon Guards); served in France, Middle East and Italy, 1940-45. Chairman Rugby Division Conservative Assoc., 1946-48. Contested (C) Rugby, 1950 and 1951. PPS to Secretary of State for Air, 1957-60. *Recreations:* cricket, real tennis, golf. *Address:* Moreton House, Moreton Morrell, Warwickshire. *T:* Moreton Morrell 235; 8 York House, Turk's Row, SW3. *T:* 01-730 1343. *Clubs:* White's, MCC.

**DANCKWERTS, Rt. Hon. Sir Harold Otto,** PC 1961; Kt 1949; a Lord Justice of Appeal, 1961-69; *b* 23 Feb. 1888; *s* of William Otto Danckwerts, KC, and Mary Caroline Lowther; *m* 1st, 1918, Florence Mary Pride (*d* 1969); one *s* one *d*; 2nd, 1969, Ella Hamilton Marshall, Glasgow. *Educ:* Winchester Coll.; Balliol Coll., Oxford (MA); Harvard Univ., USA. Called to Bar, Lincoln's Inn, 1913 (Certificate of Honour), Bencher, 1941, Treasurer, 1962. During European War, 1914-19, served with E Riding of Yorkshire Yeomanry and Machine Gun Corps (Captain); Tutor to Law Society, 1914-23; Reader to Law Society, 1923-41; Junior Counsel to Treasury and Board of Trade in Chancery matters and Junior Counsel to Attorney-General in Charity matters, 1941-49; Judge of the High Court of Justice (Chancery Division), 1949-61. *Address:* 4 Stone Buildings, Lincoln's Inn, WC2. *Clubs:* Oxford and Cambridge University, Kennel.

**DANCKWERTS, Prof. Peter Victor,** GC 1940; MBE 1943; FRS 1969; MIChemE; Shell Professor of Chemical Engineering, Cambridge University, since 1959; Fellow of Pembroke College, Cambridge, since 1959; *b* 14 Oct. 1916; *s* of late Vice-Adm. V. H. Danckwerts and Joyce Danckwerts; *m* 1960, Lavinia, *d* of Brig.-Gen. D. A. Macfarlane. *Educ:* Winchester Coll.; Balliol Coll., Oxford; Massachusetts Inst. of Technology. BA (chemistry) Oxon, 1938; SM (Chemical Engineering Practice), MIT, 1948; MA Cantab 1948. RNVR, 1940-46. Commonwealth Fund Fellow, MIT, 1946-48; Demonstrator and Lecturer, Dept of Chemical Engineering, Cambridge Univ., 1948-54; Deputy Director of Research and Development, Industrial Group, UK Atomic Energy Authority, 1954-56; Prof. of Chemical Engineering Science, Imperial College of Science and Technology, 1956-59. MIChemE 1955 (President, 1965-66). *Address:* Department of Chemical Engineering, Pembroke Street, Cambridge. *T:* Cambridge 58231. *Club:* Oxford and Cambridge.

**DANCY, John Christopher,** MA; Master of Marlborough College, since Sept. 1961; *b* 13 Nov. 1920; *e s* of Dr J. H. Dancy and late Dr N. Dancy; *m* 1944, Angela Bryant; two *s* one *d*. *Educ:* Winchester (Scholar); New Coll., Oxford (Scholar, MA). 1st Class, Classical Hon. Mods., 1940; Craven Scholar, 1946; Gaisford Greek Prose Prize, 1947; Hertford Scholar, 1947; Arnold Historical Essay Prize, 1949. Served in Rifle Brigade, 1941-46; Capt. GSO(3)I, 30 Corps, 1945; Major, GSO(2)I, 1 Airborne Corps, 1945-46. Lecturer in Classics, Wadham Coll., 1946-48; Asst Master, Winchester Coll., 1948-53; Headmaster of Lancing Coll., 1953-61. Member, Public Schools' Commission, 1966-68. *Publications:* Commentary on 1 Maccabees, 1954; The Public Schools and the Future, 1963. *Address:* Marlborough College, Wilts. *T:* Marlborough 2140.

**DANDIE, James Naughton,** CBE 1961; MC 1918; MA, LLB, SSC; Partner of Hill & Robb, Solicitors, Stirling; *b* 2 June 1894; *s* of Alexander Dandie, Art Master, Edinburgh; *m* 1929, Anne Bonelly, *o d* of John Alexander Aitchison Calder; two *s*. *Educ:* George Watson's Coll., Edinburgh; Edinburgh University (1912-14 and 1919-22). On service with 1/1 Highland (Fife) RGA(T), 1914-19, retiring as Captain (France); despatches, 1917; MC 1918. President, Scottish Lawn Tennis Assoc., 1935. Hon. Sheriff Substitute, 1951; Council of Law Society of Scotland, 1950-66 (President, 1958-61); Legal Aid Central Cttee (Chairman, 1955-58); Law Reform (Scotland) Cttee, 1954-64; Council, Scottish Universities Law Institute; Hon. Member American Bar Assoc.; Hon. FRIAS, 1963. *Publications:* articles to legal journals. *Recreations:* photography; curling. *Address:* 16 Abercromby Place, Stirling. *T:* Stirling 2777. *Club:* Caledonian (Edinburgh).

**DANDY, James Edgar,** MA Cantab; Keeper of Botany, British Museum (Natural History), 1956-66; *b* 24 Sept. 1903; *e s* of late John James Dandy, Preston, Lancs.; *m* 1929, Joyce Isabelle Glaysher; one *s*. *Educ:* Preston Grammar Sch.; Downing Coll., Cambridge. Entered Herbarium, Royal Botanic Gardens, Kew, 1925; joined Dept of Botany, British Museum (Natural History), 1927. *Publications:* books and papers in scientific publications, chiefly on systematic botany. *Recreations:* angling, gardening. *Address:* Rowans, Grove Road, Tring, Herts. *T:* Tring 3122.

**DANE, William Surrey,** CBE 1953; MC; Patron, The Association of Independent Hospitals (Chairman, 1960-63; President, 1963-69); Member Board of Governors, Hospital for Sick Children, Great Ormond Street, for 24 years (Vice-Chairman 1957-67); Member Committee of Management, Institute of Child Health, University of London, 1955-67; Member Council, Charing Cross Hospital Medical School, 1956-67; Life Vice-President Printers' Pension Corporation; Hon. Vice-President Lloyd Memorial (Printers) Convalescent Home (President, 1950-61); a Vice-Chairman and Managerial Consultant of Odhams Press Ltd, printers and publishers of Long Acre, WC2, 1959-March 1961 (Joint Managing Director, 1947-57, Managing Director, 1958); Chairman, Daily Herald, 1949-60; Member, General Advisory Council of the BBC, 1956-62; *b* 1892; *e s* of James Surrey Dane, Adelaide, SA; *m* 1919, Dorothy Mary, *d* of late Rev. W. A. Armstrong, MA, Funtington Vicarage, near Chichester; one *s* two *d*. Served European War, 1914-19, Captain and Adjt, Seaforth Highlanders (despatches, MC); during War of 1939-45 was a Director at Min. of Information, 1939, and Min. of Supply, 1941-45. *Address:* Apple Porch, Peaslake, near Guildford. Surrey. *T:* Dorking 730235.

**DANIEL, Adm. Sir Charles (Saumarez),** KCB 1948 (CB 1945); CBE 1941; DSO 1939; *b* 23 June 1894; *s* of late Lieut-Colonel C. J. Daniel,

CBE, DSO; *m* 1919, Marjory Katharine (*d* 1958), *d* of Arthur C. Wilson, MB, ChB, Formby; one *d*; *m* 1963, Mrs Pares Wilson, The Manor House, Little Shelford, Cambridge. *Educ:* Southcliffe Sch., Filey; RN Colleges, Osborne and Dartmouth. HMS Orion, Home Fleet and Grand Fleet, 1912-18 (despatches, Jutland, 1914-15 Star, 2 medals); specialised in Signals and Wireless, 1918; Commander, 1928; Experimental Commander HM Signal Sch., 1928-30; passed RN and RAF Staff Colleges, 1931-32; Commander HMS Glorious, 1933-34; Captain, 1934; passed Imperial Defence Coll., 1935; Plans Div., Admiralty, for Joint Planning Cttee, 1936-38; Captain D 8th Destroyer Flotilla, 1938-40, European War (DSO); Director of Plans, Naval Staff, Admiralty, 1940-41 (CBE); In Command HMS Renown, 1941-43; Rear-Adm. 1943. Flag Officer, Combined Operations, 1943; Vice-Adm. (Admin.) British Pacific Fleet, Rear-Adm. Commanding 1st Battle Squadron, British Pacific Fleet, 1944-45 (CB); Third Sea Lord and Controller of the Navy, 1945-49 (KCB); Vice-Adm. 1946; Commandant Imperial Defence Coll., 1949-51; Admiral 1950; retired list, 1952. Chairman, Television Advisory Cttee, 1952-62. A Director of Blaw Knox Ltd, 1953-66. *Address:* The Manor House, Little Shelford, Cambridge. *T:* Shelford 3253. *Club:* United Service.

**DANIEL, Glyn Edmund,** MA, LittD; Fellow of St John's College, Cambridge, since 1938; University Lecturer in Archaeology, since 1948; *b* 23 April 1914; *o s* of John Daniel and Mary Jane (*née* Edmunds); *m* 1946, Ruth, *d* of late Rev. R. W. B. Langhorne, Exeter. *Educ:* Barry County Sch.; University College, Cardiff; St John's Coll., Cambridge (Scholar; BA 1st Class Hons with Distinction, Archaeological and Anthropological Tripos). Strathcona Student, 1936; Allen Scholar, 1937; Wallenberg Prizeman, 1937; Research Fellowship, St John's Coll., 1938; PhD 1938; MA 1939. Intelligence Officer, RAF, 1940-45; in charge Photo Interpretation, India and SE Asia, 1942-45 (despatches); Wing Comdr, 1943. Faculty Asst Lectr in Archaeology, 1945-48; Steward of St John's Coll., 1946-55; Leverhulme Research Fellow, 1948-50. Lecturer: Munro, Archaeology, Edinburgh Univ., 1954; Rhys, British Acad., 1954; O'Donnell, Edinburgh Univ., 1956; Josiah Mason, Birmingham Univ., 1956; Gregynog University College, Wales, 1968; Ballard-Matthews, University Coll. of North Wales, 1968. Visiting Prof., Univ. Aarhus, 1968; Ferrens Prof., Univ. Hull, 1969. Pres., South Eastern Union of Scientific Socs, 1955. LittD 1962. Pres., Bristol and Gloucestershire Archaeological Soc., 1962-63. Hon. Mem. Istituto Italiano di Preistoria e Protostoria, Corresponding Fellow, German Archaeological Institute, Corresponding Mem., Jutland Archaeological Soc. Editor, Ancient Peoples and Places, and of Antiquity, since 1958. Director: Anglia Television, Ltd; Antiquity Publications Ltd; Cambridge Arts Theatre. FSA 1942. Knight (First Class) of the Dannebrog, 1961. *Publications:* The Three Ages, 1942; A Hundred Years of Archaeology, 1950; The Prehistoric Chamber Tombs of England and Wales, 1950; A Picture Book of Ancient British Art (with S. Piggott), 1951; Lascaux and Carnac, 1955; ed Myth or Legend, 1955; Barclodiad y Gawres (with T. G. E. Powell), 1956; The Megalith Builders of Western Europe, 1958; The Prehistoric Chamber Tombs of France, 1960; The Idea of Prehistory, 1961; The Hungry Archaeologist in France, 1963; New Grange and the Bend of the Boyne (with late S. P. O'Riordain), 1964; (ed with I. Ll. Foster), Prehistoric and Early Wales, 1964; Man Discovers his Past, 1966; The Origins and Growth of Archaeology, 1967; The First Civilisations, 1968; Archaeology and the History of Art, 1970; and articles in archaeological journals. *Recreations:* travel, walking, swimming, food, wine, writing detective stories (The Cambridge Murders, 1945; Welcome Death, 1954). *Address:* The Flying Stag, 70 Bridge Street, Cambridge. *T:* 56082; La Marnière, Zouafques-par-Tournehem, 62 France. *T:* Calais 35.61.40. *Club:* United University.

**DANIEL, Sir Goronwy Hopkin,** KCVO 1969; CB 1962; DPhil Oxon; Principal, Aberystwyth University College, since 1969; *b* 21 March 1914; *s* of David Daniel, ME; *m* 1940, Lady Valerie, *d* of 2nd Earl Lloyd George; one *s* two *d*. *Educ:* Pontardawe Secondary Sch.; Amman Valley County Sch.; University College of Wales, Aberystwyth; Jesus Coll., Oxford. Fellow of University of Wales; Meyricke Scholar, Jesus Coll.; Oxford Institute of Statistics, 1937-40; Lecturer, Dept of Economics, Bristol Univ., 1940-41; Clerk, House of Commons, 1941-43; Ministry of Town and Country Planning, 1943-47; Ministry of Fuel and Power, Chief Statistician, 1947-55; Under-Sec., Coal Div., 1955-62, Gen. Div., 1962-64; Permanent Under-Sec. of State, Welsh Office, 1964-69. *Publications:* papers in statistical, fuel and power, and other journals. *Recreations:* country pursuits. *Address:* Plas Penglais, Aberystwyth, Cardiganshire. *T:* Aberystwyth 3583. *Club:* Travellers'.

**DANIEL, Henry Cave;** *b* 16 Aug. 1896; *s* of late H. T. Daniel, Manor House, Stockland, Bridgwater; *m* 1931, Barbara, *d* of late Mrs Blain, King's Barrow, Wareham, Dorset; one *s* one *d*. *Educ:* Eton; RMC, Sandhurst. Joined 17th Lancers, 1914, and served European War, 1914-18, with that regiment, retiring in 1920. Rejoined Army, 1939, and served War of 1939-45, in France and England until invalided out in 1941. High Sheriff of Somerset, 1949. *Recreations:* hunting and shooting. *Address:* Woodlands, Holford, Bridgwater. *T:* Holford 203. *Clubs:* Cavalry; Somerset County (Taunton).

**DANIEL, (John) Stuart,** QC 1961; *b* 17 Feb. 1912; *s* of Walter John Daniel and Nena Nithsdale Newall. *Educ:* Haileybury; Merton Coll., Oxford. Called to Bar, Middle Temple, 1937. Member, Lands Tribunal, 1967-. *Address:* 39c Randolph Avenue, W9. *T:* 01-286 8322.

**DANIEL, Prof. Peter Maxwell,** MA, MB, BCh Cambridge; MA, DM Oxon; DSc London; FRCP; FCPath; FInstBiol; Professor of Neuropathology, University of London, at the Institute of Psychiatry, Maudsley Hospital, since 1957; Hon. Consultant Neuropathologist, the Bethlem Royal and Maudsley Hospitals; *b* 14 Nov. 1910; *s* of Peter Daniel, FRCS, surgeon to Charing Cross Hospital, and Beatrice Laetitia Daniel. *Educ:* Westminster Sch.; St John's Coll., Cambridge; New Coll., Oxford. Hon. Consultant Pathologist, Radcliffe Infirmary, 1948-56; Senior Research Officer, University of Oxford, 1949-56; Hon. Consultant in Neuropathology to the Army at Home, 1952-. John Hunter Medal and Triennial Prize, 1946-48, and Erasmus Wilson Lectr, 1964, RCS. Editorial Board of Jl of Physiology, 1958-65; Jl of Neurology, Neurosurgery and Psychiatry, 1953-64; Journal of Neuroendocrinology, 1966-. President, British Neuropathological Society, 1963-64; Member, Council: Assoc. of British Neurologists, 1966-69; Neurological Section, RSM, 1965- (Vice-Pres. of Section, 1968); Pres., Harveian Soc. London, 1966;

Mem. Council, Royal Microscopical Soc., 1968-. Member: Bd of Govs, Bethlem Royal and Maudsley Hosps, 1966-; Council, Charing Cross Hosp. Medical Sch. Chm., Academic Bd, Inst. of Psychiatry, 1966-. *Publications:* (jointly) Studies of the Renal Circulation, 1947; papers in various medical and scientific journals. *Address:* Department of Neuropathology, Institute of Psychiatry, Maudsley Hospital, Denmark Hill, SE5. *Clubs:* Athenæum, Garrick, Savage.

**DANIEL, Stuart;** *see* Daniel, J. S.

**DANIELL, Brig. Averell John,** CBE 1955; DSO 1945; *b* 19 June 1903; *s* of late Lt-Col Oswald James Daniell, QO Royal West Kent Regt, and late May Frances Drummond Daniell (*née* Adams); *m* 1934, Phyllis Kathleen Rhona Grove-Annesley; two *s* one *d*. *Educ:* Wellington Coll.; RM Acad., Woolwich. Commissioned, Royal Field Artillery, 1923; Captain, RA, 1936; Major, 1940; Lt-Col, 1943. Served War of 1939-45; Middle East, Iraq, Burma. Col, 1948; Brig., 1952; retired, 1955. Administrative Officer, Staff Coll., Camberley, 1955-61. Colonel Commandant, Royal Artillery, 1956-66. *Address:* Oak Lodge, Hythe, Kent. *T:* Hythe 66494.

**DANIELL, Peter Averell,** TD 1950; Senior Government Broker, since 1963; *b* 8 Dec. 1909; *s* of R. H. A. Daniell and Kathleen Daniell (*née* Monsell); *m* 1935, Leonie M. Harrison; two *s* one *d*. *Educ:* Eton Coll.; Trinity Coll., Oxford (MA). Joined Mullens & Co., 1932. Partner, 1945. Served KRRC, 1939-45, Middle East and Italy. *Recreations:* shooting, fishing, golf. *Address:* Glebe House, Buckland, Surrey. *T:* Betchworth 2320. *Clubs:* United University, Alpine.

**DANIELL, Ralph Allen,** CBE 1965 (OBE 1958); Deputy High Commissioner Wellington, since 1967; *b* 26 Jan. 1915; 2nd *s* of late Reginald Allen Daniell; *m* 1943, Diana Lesley (*née* Tyndale); one *s* three *d*. *Educ:* Lancing Coll.; University College, Oxford. Appointed to Board of Trade, 1937. Joined HM Forces, 1942; served with Royal Tank Regt in North Africa and Italian campaigns, 1943-45. Appointed to HM Foreign Service as First Secretary, 1946; Mexico City, 1946; Rome, 1949; Foreign Office, 1951; Helsinki, 1953; Promoted to Counsellor, 1958; Washington, 1958; New York, 1959; Cairo, 1962. *Address:* 2 Molesford Road, SW6. *Club:* Oxford and Cambridge University.

**DANIELL, Roy Lorentz,** CBE 1957; Barrister-at-Law; Charity Commissioner, 1953-62; *s* of late Edward Cecil Daniell, Abbotswood, Speen, Bucks; *m* 1936, Sheila Moore-Gwyn, *d* of late Maj. Moore-Gwyn, Clayton Court, Liss, Hants. *Educ:* Gresham's Sch., Holt; New Coll., Oxford. *Address:* Abbotswood, Speen, near Aylesbury, Bucks. *T:* Hampden Row 333. *Club:* Oxford and Cambridge University.

**DANIELLI, Prof. James Frederic,** FRS 1957; PhD, DSc, MIBiol; Director, Center for Theoretical Biology, since 1965 and Assistant to the President, since 1969, State University of New York at Buffalo (formerly University of Buffalo, New York; *b* 13 Nov. 1911; *s* of James Frederic Danielli; *m* 1937, Mary Guy; one *s* one *d*. *Educ:* Wembley County Sch.; London, Princeton and Cambridge Univs. Commonwealth Fund Fellow, 1933-35; Beit Medical Research Fellow, 1938-42; Fellow of St John's Coll., Cambridge, 1942-45; Physiologist to Marine Biological Assoc., 1946; Reader in Cell Physiology, Royal Cancer Hospital, 1946-49; Prof. of Zoology, King's Coll., London, 1949-62; Chm., Dept of Biochemical Pharmacology, Univ. of Buffalo, 1962-65; Provost for Faculty of Natural Sciences and Mathematics, 1967-69. *Publications:* Permeability of Natural Membranes (with H. Davson), 1943; Cell Physiology and Pharmacology, 1950; Cytochemistry: a critical approach, 1953; Editor, Journal of Theoretical Biology. *Address:* State University of New York at Buffalo, Center for Theoretical Biology, 4248 Ridge Lea Road, Amherst, New York 14226, USA; Tangnefedd, Dinas Cross, Pembs.

**DANIELS, David Kingsley,** CBE 1963 (OBE 1945); retired as Secretary-General, Royal Commonwealth Society (1958-67); *b* 17 Feb. 1905; *y s* of late E. Daniels and Anne M. Daniels; unmarried. *Educ:* Kent Coll., Canterbury; St Edmund Hall, Oxford. Colonial Administrative Service, Tanganyika, 1928; King's African Rifles, 1940; Chief Staff Officer, Military Admin., Somalia, 1941 (despatches); Senior Civil Affairs Officer, Reserved Areas, Ethiopia, 1943-45 (OBE); Chief Secretary (Colonel), Military Administration, Malaya, 1945-46; Principal Asst Secretary, Singapore, 1947-49; Under Secretary, Singapore, 1950-52; Dep. Chief Secretary, Federation of Malaya, 1952-55; Director, Malayan Students Dept in UK, 1956-58. *Address:* Little Oaten, 28 Oaten Hill, Canterbury, Kent. *T:* Canterbury 63029. *Clubs:* Royal Commonwealth Society, MCC.

**DANIELS, Harold Albert;** Under-Secretary, Ministry of Posts and Telecommunications, since 1969; *b* 8 June 1915; *s* of Albert Pollikett Daniels and Eleanor Sarah Maud Daniels (*née* Flahey); *m* 1946, Frances Victoria Jerdan; one *s*. *Educ:* Mercers' Sch.; Christ's Coll., Cambridge. BA 1937; Wren Prize 1938; MA 1940. Asst Principal, Post Office, 1938; Admiralty, 1942; Post Office, 1945; Principal, 1946; Asst Sec., 1950; Under-Sec., 1961. *Address:* Lyle Court Cottage, Bradbourne Road, Sevenoaks, Kent. *T:* Sevenoaks 54039.

**DANIELS, Prof. Henry Ellis;** Professor of Mathematical Statistics, University of Birmingham, since 1957; *b* 2 Oct. 1912; *s* of Morris and Hannah Daniels; *m* 1950, Barbara Edith Pickering; one *s* one *d*. *Educ:* Sciennes Sch., Edinburgh; George Heriot's Sch., Edinburgh; Edinburgh Univ.; Clare Coll., Cambridge. MA Edinburgh 1933, BA Cantab 1935, PhD Edinburgh 1943. Statistician, Wool Industries Research Assoc., 1935-47; Ministry of Aircraft Production, 1942-45; Lecturer in Mathematics, University of Cambridge, 1947-57. Fellow Inst. of Mathematical Statistics; elected Mem. Internat. Statistical Inst., 1956. Guy Medal (Silver) Royal Statistical Society. *Publications:* papers in Journal of the Royal Statistical Society, Annals of Mathematical Statistics, Biometrika, etc. *Recreations:* playing the piano, repairing watches. *Address:* 253 Northfield Road, Kings Norton, Birmingham 30. *T:* 021-458 1467.

**DANILOVA, Alexandra,** lecturer, teacher and choreographer; *b* Pskoff, Russia, 20 Nov. 1906; *d* of Dionis Daniloff and Claudia Gotovzeffa; *m* 1st, 1931, Giuseppe Massera (*d* 1936); 2nd, 1941, Kazimir Kokic (marr. annulled, 1949). *Educ:* Theatrical Sch., Petrograd. Maryinski Theatre, Leningrad, 1923-24; Diaghileff Company, 1925-29; Waltzes from Vienna, 1931; Colonel de Basil Company, 1933-37; Prima Ballerina, Ballet Russe de Monte Carlo, 1938-58. Teacher (on Faculty) of School of American Ballet. Guest artist Royal Festival Hall, London, 1955; Ballerina in Oh Captain (Musical), New York, 1958. With own Company has toured West Indies, Japan, Philippines, USA, Canada and S

Africa. Capezio Award (for outstanding services to Art of the Dance), 1958; Guest Choreographer Metropolitan Opera House, Guest Teacher and Choreographer, Germany (Krefeld Festival of Dance) and Amsterdam, 1959-60; Choreographed Coppelia for La Scala di Milano, 1961; Lecture performances throughout US; Guest Choreographer, Washington Ballet, 1962-64. *Recreations:* needlework, ping-pong, gardening. *Address:* Apartment 2 P, Carnegie House, 100 West 57 Street, New York City 19, USA; RFD 2, Church Road, Lakewood, New Jersey, USA.

**DANINOS, Pierre;** French Author; *b* Paris, 26 May 1913; *m* 1st, 1942, Jane Marrain; one *s* two *d*; 2nd, 1968, Marie-Pierre Dourneau. *Educ:* Lycée Janson de Sailly, Paris. Began to write for newspapers, 1931; reporter for French press in England, USA, etc. Liaison agent with British Army, Dunkirk, 1940. Published first book in Rio de Janeiro, 1940; returned to France, 1942, from South and Central America, Chronicler for Le Figaro. *Publications:* Méridiens (novel), 1945; Passeport pour la nuit, 1946; Les Carnets du Bon Dieu (Prix Interallié 1947); L'Eternel Second, 1949; Sonia les autres et moi (Prix Courteline, 1952) (English trans., Life with Sonia, 1958); Les Carnets du Major Thompson, 1954 (English trans., Major Thompson Lives in France, 1955); Le Secret du Major Thompson (English trans., Major Thompson and I, 1957), 1956; Vacances à Tous Prix, 1958; Un certain Monsieur Blot, 1960 (English trans., 1961); Le Jacassin, 1962; Snobissimo, 1964; Le 36ème dessous, 1966; Le Major Tricolore, 1968; Ludovic Morateur, 1970. *Recreations:* tennis, ski-ing, collecting British hobbies. *Address:* 81 rue de Grenelle, Paris 7e, France.

**DANKS, Sir Alan (John),** KBE 1970; Chairman, (NZ) University Grants Committee, since 1966; *b* 9 June 1914; *s* of T. E. Danks; *m* 1943, Loma Beryl Hall (*née* Drabble). *Educ:* West Christchurch High Sch.; Univ. of Canterbury, NZ. Teaching profession, 1931-43; Economics Dept of Univ. of Canterbury, 1943-66; Prof., 1962; Pro-Vice Chancellor of Univ. of Canterbury, 1964. *Address:* 38 Wadestown Road, Wellington, New Zealand. *T:* 47094. *Club:* Wellington, NZ.

**DANKWORTH, Mrs C. D.;** *see* Laine, Cleo.

**DANKWORTH, John Philip William,** ARAM 1969; musician; *b* 20 Sept. 1927; British; *m* 1960, Cleo Laine, *qv*; one *s* one *d*. *Educ:* Monoux Grammar Sch. Studied Royal Academy of Music, 1944-46. Closely involved with post-war development of British jazz, 1947-60; formed large jazz orchestra, 1953. Composed works for combined jazz and symphonic musicians including: Improvisations (with Matyas Seiber, 1959), and Escapade (commissioned by Northern Sinfonia Orch., 1967). Many important film scores (1964-) including: Saturday Night and Sunday Morning, Darling, The Servant, Morgan, Accident. *Recreations:* driving, household maintenance. *Address:* The Old Rectory, Wavendon, near Bletchley, Buckinghamshire. *T:* Woburn Sands 3151. *Clubs:* Savage, Ronnie Scott's.

**DANN, Howard Ernest,** CBE 1965; Commissioner, Snowy Mountains Hydro-Electric Authority, since 1967; *b* 27 April 1914; *m* 1946, Marjorie Bush; two *s*. *Educ:* Brighton Grammar Sch. (Dux); University of Melbourne (BMechE). AIF, 1940-44; Major RAEME. Supt. Engineer, Electric Authority of NSW, 1946-50; Member Commonwealth and States Snowy River Cttee, 1946-49 (NSW Representative, Techn. Cttee); Chief Engineer Investigations, Snowy Mountains Hydro-Electric Authority, prior to Associate Comr, Snowy Mountains Hydro-Electric Authority, 1959-67. FIEAust, MASCE. *Publications:* papers in journals of Instn of Engrs (Australia) and American Society of Civil Engineers. *Recreation:* golf. *Address:* 9 Moloola Avenue, Cooma North, New South Wales, Australia. *T:* 21-777.

**DANN, Rt. Rev. Robert William;** Co-Adjutor Bishop, Diocese of Melbourne, since 1969; *b* 28 Sept. 1914; *s* of James and Ruth Dann; *m* 1949, Yvonne (*née* Newnham); one *s* two *d*. *Educ:* Trinity Coll., Univ. of Melbourne. BA Hons Melbourne 1946. Deacon, 1945; Priest, 1946. Dir of Youth and Religious Education, Dio. Melbourne, 1946; Incumbent: St Matthew's, Cheltenham, 1951; St George's, Malvern, 1956; St John's, Footscray, 1961; Archdeacon of Essendon, 1961; Dir of Evangelism and Extension, Dio. Melbourne, 1963. *Recreation:* squash racquets. *Address:* 8 Canterbury Road, Camberwell, Victoria 3124, Australia. *T:* 826714. *Club:* Royal Automobile of Victoria (Melbourne).

**DANNATT, Sir Cecil,** Kt 1961; OBE 1943; MC 1917; FIEE; MIMechE; Director, Associated Electrical Industries, 1954-63, retired (Vice-Chairman, 1960-62); *b* 21 Sept. 1896; *s* of late Mark and Hannah Dannatt; *m* 1925, Winifred Ethel Flear; two *s*. *Educ:* Burton-on-Trent Grammar Sch.; Durham Univ. DSc University of Durham, 1936. Research Engineer, 1921-40; Prof. of Electrical Engineering, Birmingham Univ., 1940-44. Managing Director Metropolitan-Vickers Electrical Co., 1954-60. *Publications:* Electrical Transmission and Interconnection, 1926; prize papers, IEE. *Recreation:* golf. *Address:* The Willows, Oxshott, Surrey. *T:* Oxshott 2424. *Club:* Royal Automobile.

**DANNAY, Frederic;** co-author with Manfred B. Lee, *qv*, under pseudonym of Ellery Queen. Visiting Professor at University of Texas, 1958-59. *Publications:* Roman Hat Mystery, 1929; French Powder Mystery, 1930; Dutch Shoe Mystery, 1931; Greek Coffin Mystery, Egyptian Cross Mystery, 1932; American Gun Mystery, Siamese Twin Mystery, 1933; Chinese Orange Mystery, Adventures of Ellery Queen, 1934; Spanish Cape Mystery, 1935; Halfway House, 1936; Door Between, 1937; Devil to Pay, Four of Hearts, Challenge to the Reader, 1938; Dragon's Teeth, 1939; New Adventures of Ellery Queen, 1940; 101 Years' Entertainment, 1941; Calamity Town, The Detective Short Story (a bibliography), Sporting Blood, 1942; There was an Old Woman, Female of the Species, 1943; Misadventures of Sherlock Holmes, Best Stories from Ellery Queen's Mystery Magazine, 1944; Case Book of Ellery Queen, Murderer is a Fox, Rogues' Gallery, 1945; The Queen's Awards (1946), To the Queen's Taste, 1946; The Queen's Awards (1947), Murder By Experts, 1947; 20th Century Detective Stories, The Queen's Awards (1948), Ten Days' Wonder, 1948; The Queen's Awards (1949), Cat of Many Tails, 1949; The Queen's Awards (Fifth Series), Literature of Crime, Double, Double, 1950; Origin of Evil, Queen's Quorum, The Queen's Awards (Sixth Series), 1951; Calendar of Crime, King is Dead, The Queen's Awards (Seventh Series), 1952; Scarlet Letters, The Queen's Awards (Eighth Series), 1953; Glass Village, Ellery Queen's Awards (Ninth Series), 1954; QBI: Queen's Bureau of Investigation, Ellery Queen's Awards (Tenth Series), 1955; Inspector Queen's Own Case, Ellery Queen's Awards (Eleventh Series), 1956; In the Queens' Parlor,

Ellery Queen's Awards (Twelfth Series), 1957; The Finishing Stroke, Ellery Queen's 13th Annual, 1958; Ellery Queen's 14th Mystery Annual, 1959; Ellery Queen's 15th Mystery Annual, 1960; Ellery Queen's 16th Mystery Annual, 1962; Quintessence of Queen, To Be Read Before Midnight, 1963; Player on the Other Side, Ellery Queen's Mystery Mix, 1963; And on the Eighth Day, Double Dozen, 1964; Queens Full, The Fourth Side of the Triangle, Ellery Queen's 20th Anniversary Annual, 1965; Face to Face, 1967; Ellery Queen's Murder Menu, 24th Mystery Annual, 1970. Co-author with Manfred B. Lee, *qv*, under pseudonym of Barnaby Ross; *publications:* Tragedy of X, Tragedy of Y, 1932; Tragedy of Z, Drury Lane's Last Case, 1933. All four Barnaby Ross publications reissued as by Ellery Queen, 1940-42. Co-author with Manfred B. Lee, *qv*, of Ellery Queen, Jr juvenile mysteries and of Radio and Television Programs (Adventures of Ellery Queen). Co-editor with Manfred B. Lee, *qv*, of 14 collections of short stories by Dashiell Hammett, Stuart Palmer, John Dickson Carr, Margery Allingham, Roy Vickers, and O. Henry. Co-editor with Manfred B. Lee, *qv*, of Ellery Queen's Mystery Magazine (24th year of publication). Under author's name of Daniel Nathan; *publication:* The Golden Summer, 1953. The following address is for all names (Frederic Dannay, Ellery Queen, Barnaby Ross, Daniel Nathan). *Address:* Larchmont, New York, USA.

**DANNREUTHER, Rear-Adm. Hubert Edward,** DSO 1916; *b* 12 Dec. 1880; *y s* of late Prof. Edward Dannreuther; *m* 1916, Janie, *y d* of late J. Hay Thorburn; three *s*. *Educ:* privately; HMS Britannia. Joined HMS Britannia, 1895; chief cadet Captain, 1896; Lieut, 1902; Gunnery Lieut of Exmouth, Flagship of Mediterranean Fleet, 1911-12; commanded Guard of Honour on official landing of the King at Malta, Jan. 1912; 1st and Gunnery Lieut of Invincible, in action of Heligoland Bight, 28 Aug. 1914; also of Invincible when Flagship of Vice-Adm. Sturdee at Battle of Falkland Islands, 8 Dec. 1914 (despatches, promoted to Commander); Senior of six survivors from HMS Invincible, 1916 (despatches, DSO); Order of St Anne, 3rd Class, with Swords; French Croix de Guerre with palms, 1917; Commander HMS Renown, 1916-19; HMS Excellent, 1919-20; Captain, 1920; Vice-President, Chemical Warfare Cttee, 1920-23; HMS Dauntless, 1924-26; Captain Superintendent of Training and in command of the Flinders Naval Depôt, Australia, 1927-29; HMS Eagle, 1929-31; Commodore of RN Barracks, Portsmouth, 1931-32; Rear-Adm. 1932; retired list, 1932. *Address:* Windycroft, Hastings, Sussex. *T:* Hastings 744.

**DANTER, Harold Walter Phillips;** *b* 31 March 1886; *s* of late Lieut-Col F. W. Danter, VD, RE, JP, Gerrards Cross, Bucks; unmarried. *Educ:* Christ's Hospital, Hertford, London, and West Horsham. Clerk in the Bank of England, 1904-14. Held commission in 5th East Surrey Regt, 1908-10. Student at Lichfield Theological Coll., 1914-16; Deacon, 1916; Priest, 1917. Work with Church Army, BEF, France, 1918-19. Curate: St Paul's, Stafford, 1917-19; Holy Trinity, Woolwich, 1919-21; SS Mary and John, Oxford, 1921-28; Vicar of Pattishall, Northants, 1928-33; Rural Dean, Brackley III deanery, 1933-53; Vicar of Brackley, 1933-56; Non-residentiary Canon of Peterborough Cathedral, 1955-56; Canon Emeritus of Peterborough Cathedral, 1956-58. Received into the Roman Catholic Church, March 1958. *Publication:* The Hill of Daydreams (Poems), 1917. *Recreation:* general interest in art and literature. *Address:* 32 Thorncliffe Road, Oxford. *T:* Oxford 55598.

**DARBY, Henry Clifford,** OBE 1946; LittD 1960; FBA 1967; Professor of Geography in the University of Cambridge, since 1966; Fellow of King's College, Cambridge; *b* 7 Feb. 1909; *s* of Evan Darby, Resolven, Glamorgan; *m* 1941, Eva Constance Thomson; two *d*. *Educ:* Neath County Sch.; St Catharine's Coll., Cambridge. 1st Class Geographical Tripos, Parts I, 1926, II, 1928; PhD 1931; MA 1932. Lecturer in Geography, University of Cambridge, 1931-45; Ehrman Fellow, King's Coll., Cambridge, 1932-45; Intelligence Corps, 1940-41 (Capt.); Admiralty, 1941-45; John Rankin Prof. of Geography, University of Liverpool, 1945-49; Prof. of Geography, University Coll. London, 1949-66; Leverhulme Research Fellow, 1946-48; Visiting Prof. Univ. of Chicago, 1952, Harvard Univ., 1959, 1964-65, and Univ. of Washington, 1963; Mem. Council, English Place-Name Soc., 1953-; Mem., Royal Commission on Historical Monuments (England), 1953-; Mem., National Parks Commn, 1958-63; Mem., Water Resources Board, 1964-68. Pres. Institute of British Geographers, 1961; Pres., Section E British Assoc., 1963. Hon. Member: Croatian Geog Soc., 1957; Royal Netherlands Geog. Soc., 1958; Hon. Fellow, St Catharine's Coll., Cambridge, 1960. Victoria Medal, RGS, 1963. Daly Medal, American Geog. Soc., 1963. Hon. LHD Chicago, 1967; Hon. LittD Liverpool, 1968; Hon. DLitt Durham, 1970. *Publications:* An Historical Geography of England before AD 1800 (Editor, and Contributor), 1936; The Cambridge Region (Editor and Contributor), 1938; The Medieval Fenland, 1940; The Draining of the Fens, 2nd edn, 1956; The University Atlas (with H. Fullard), 12th edn, 1967; The Library Atlas (with H. Fullard), 7th edn, 1960; The New Cambridge Modern History Atlas (with H. Fullard), 1970; General Editor and Contributor, The Domesday Geography of England, 5 vols, 1952-67; articles in geographical and historical journals. *Address:* 60 Storey's Way, Cambridge. *T:* Cambridge 54745.

**D'ARCY, Very Rev. Martin Cyril,** SJ; MA; Hon. LLD Georgetown University, USA; Hon. DLitt, Fordham University, USA; Hon. LittD, Marquette University, USA; Hon. DLitt, National University of Ireland; FRSL; *b* Bath, 15 June 1888; *s* of Martin Valentine D'Arcy and Madoline Keegan and *gs* of Nicholas D'Arcy of Ballyforan, Co. Roscommon. *Educ:* Stonyhurst; Oxford (1st Class. Lit. Hum., Charles Oldham Prize, John Locke Scholarship, Greek Moral Philosophy Prize); Gregorian Univ., Rome. Priest, 1921; taught at Stonyhurst and worked at Farm Street Church, W1; The Master of Campion Hall, Oxford, 1932-45; Provincial of English Province of Soc. of Jesus, 1945-50. Conventual Chaplain to the Knights of Malta, 1956. Foreign Hon. Mem., Amer. Acad. of Arts and Sciences, 1960. *Publications:* The Mass and the Redemption; Catholicism; Christ as Priest and Redeemer; The Spirit of Charity; Thomas Aquinas; The Nature of Belief; Death and Life; part author of God and the Supernatural, God and the Universe, A Monument to St Augustine, The Life of the Church; Mirage and Truth; The Problem of Evil; The Mind and Heart of Love; Communism and Christianity; The Meeting of Love and Knowledge; The Sense of History; No Absent God; Facing God; Of God and Man; Facing the Truth; Humanism and Christianity. *Address:* 114 Mount Street, W1. *Club:* Athenæum.

**D'ARCY, Surgeon Rear-Adm. Thomas Norman,** CB 1953; CBE 1950; retired; *b* 12 Feb. 1896; *s* of Dr S. A. D'Arcy, Rosslea, County Fermanagh, Ireland; *m* 1922, Eleanor Lennox Broadbent, Port Said; two *s* two *d*. *Educ:* Royal School, Cavan; RCS Dublin. Qualified, 1919; Surgeon Probationer RNVR, 1915-18; Surgeon Lieut RN, 1919; Surgeon Lieut-Comdr 1925; Surgeon Comdr 1930; Surgeon Capt. 1943; Surgeon Rear-Adm., 1951; Medical Officer in Charge, RN Hospital, Plymouth, and Command Medical Officer, 1951-54. KHS 1951; QHS 1952-54. CStJ 1953. Gilbert Blane medal, 1929. *Publications:* surgical articles to Jl of RN Medical Service (Co-Editor, 1946-47). *Recreations:* hockey (old Irish International), caravanning, fishing. *Address:* South Wind, Witley, Surrey. *T:* Godalming 5751.

**DARCY DE KNAYTH,** Baroness (18th in line), *cr* 1332; **Davina Marcia Ingrams** (*née* **Herbert**); *b* 10 July 1938; *d* of late Squadron Leader Viscount Clive (*d* on active service, 1943), and of Vida, *o d* of late Capt. James Harold Cuthbert, DSO, Scots Guards (she *m* 2nd, 1945, Brig. Derek Schreiber, *qv*); *S* to father's Barony, 1943; *m* 1960, Rupert George Ingrams (*d* 1964), *s* of late Leonard Ingrams and of Mrs Ingrams; one *s* two *d*. *Heir: s* Hon. Caspar David Ingrams, *b* 5 Jan. 1962. *Address:* Camley Corner, Stubbings, Maidenhead, Berks.

**D'ARCY HART, P. M.;** *see* Hart, P. M. D.

**DARELL, Brig. Sir Jeffrey (Lionel),** 8th Bt, *cr* 1795; MC 1945; Commandant, Mons Officer Training School, since 1970; Commander, 56 Infantry Brigade (TA), since 1965; *b* 2 Oct. 1919; *s* of late Lt-Col Guy Marsland Darell, MC (3rd *s* of 5th Bt); *S* cousin, 1959; *m* 1953, Bridget Mary, *e d* of Maj.-Gen. Sir Allan Adair, 6th Bt, *qv*; one *s* two *d*. *Educ:* Eton; RMC, Sandhurst. Lt-Col, Coldstream Guards. Served War of 1939-45: ADC to GOC-in-C, Southern Comd, 1942; Bde Major, Guards Bde, 1953-55; Officer Comdg 1st Bn Coldstream Guards, 1957-59; GSO1, PS12, War Office, 1959; College Comdr RMA Sandhurst, 1961-64; Comdg Coldstream Guards, 1964-65; Vice-Pres., Regular Commns Bd, 1968-70. *Recreations:* normal. *Heir: s* Guy Jeffrey Adair Darell, *b* 8 June 1961. *Address:* 17 Welbeck House, Welbeck Street, W1. *T:* 01-935 4941. *Club:* Guards.

**DARESBURY,** 2nd Baron, *cr* 1927, of Walton, Co. Chester; **Edward Greenall,** Bt, *cr* 1876; late Life Guards; *b* 12 Oct. 1902; *o surv. s* of 1st Baron Daresbury, CVO, and late Frances Eliza, OBE 1945, *d* of Capt. Wynne-Griffith, 1st Royal Dragoons; *S* father 1938; *m* 1st 1925, Joan Madeline (*d* 1926), *d* of Capt. Robert Thomas Oliver Sheriffe, of Goadby Hall, Melton Mowbray; 2nd, 1927, Josephine (*d* 1958), *y d* of Brig.-Gen. Sir Joseph Laycock, KCMG, DSO; one *s*; 3rd, 1966, Lady Helena Hilton Green (*née* Wentworth-Fitzwilliam) (*d* 1970), 4th *d* of 7th Earl Fitzwilliam. *Educ:* Wixenford; Eton. *Heir: s* Hon. Edward Gilbert Greenall [*b* 27 Nov. 1928; *m* 1952, Margaret Ada, *y d* of late C. J. Crawford and of Mrs Crawford, Wayside, St Andrews; three *s* one *d*]. *Address:* Clonshire House, Adare, Co. Limerick, Eire.

**DARGIE, Sir William Alexander,** Kt 1970; CBE 1969 (OBE 1960); FRSA 1951; artist; portrait, figure and landscape painter; Chairman, Commonwealth Art Advisory Board, Prime Minister's Department, since 1969 (Member since 1953); *b* 4 June 1912; *s* of Andrew and Adelaide Dargie; *m* 1937, Kathleen, *d* of late G. H. Howitt; one *s* one *d*. *Educ:* Melbourne, and in studio of A. D. Colquhoun. Offical War Artist (Capt.) with AIF in Middle East, Burma, New Guinea, India, 1941-46. Dir, National Gallery of Victoria Art Schs, 1946-53. Member: Internat. Council of Nat. Gallery Canberra, 1968-; Nat. Capital Planning Cttee, Canberra, 1970-; Aboriginal Arts Adv. Cttee, 1970-; Trustee, Native Cultural Reserve, Port Moresby, Papua-New Guinea, 1970-. Archibald Prize for portraiture, 1941, 1942, 1945, 1946, 1947, 1950, 1952, 1956; Woodward Award, 1940; McPhillimy Award, 1940; McKay Prize, 1941. Painted portrait of The Queen for Commonwealth of Aust., 1954; the Duke of Gloucester, 1947; the Duke of Edinburgh for City of Melbourne, 1956. Portraits of Sir Macfarlane Burnet, Sir William Ashton, Sir Lionel Lindsay, acquired for Commonwealth Nat. Collection. Rep. in public and private collections in Aust., NZ, England and USA. One-man exhibition, Leger Galls, London, 1958. Exhibits with RA and Royal Soc. of Portrait Painters. *Publication:* On Painting a Portrait, 1956. *Recreations:* books, chess, tennis. *Address:* 19 Irilbarra Road, Canterbury, Victoria 3126, Australia. *T:* 83 3396 Melbourne. *Clubs:* Melbourne, Savage (Melbourne).

**DARKE, Harold Edwin,** CBE 1966; Hon. MA Cantab; DMus Oxon; FRCM, FRCO; Hon. RAM; Professor, Royal College of Music, London, 1919-69; *b* 29 Oct. 1888; *s* of Samuel and Arundel Darke; *m* 1918, Dora Garland, the violinist who was first woman to lead Queen's Hall Orchestra; two *s*. *Educ:* Owen's Sch., Islington; Royal College of Music (Organ and Composition Scholar, Tagore Gold Medal). Pupil of Parratt and Stanford; Asst Organist, Temple Church, 1919; Organist, Stoke Newington Presbyterian Church, 1904; Organist, Emmanuel Church, West Hampstead, 1906; St James, Paddington, 1911; St Michael's Cornhill, 1916-66; Conductor, City of London Choral Union, 1925-31; Founder and Conductor of St Michael's Singers, 1919-66; Founder and Conductor of Wartime Choir, Drop in and sing, 1940; Pres., Royal Coll. of Organists, 1940-41; Pres., Cambridge Organist Assoc., 1941-45; Acting-Organist, King's Coll., Cambridge, 1941-45; Conductor, Cambridge Univ. Madrigal Soc., 1941-45. Fellow, King's Coll., Cambridge, 1945-49. Adjudicator of chief Musical Competitive Festivals; Toured US and Canada, 1938, 1949, Africa, 1955, W Indies, 1960, 1963, as Examiner for Royal Schools of Music and gave Organ Recitals. Fellow, Royal School of Church Music. Hon. Freeman Worshipful Company of Musicians, 1957; Freeman of the City of London. *Publications:* choral works: As the leaves fall, 1917; The Kingdom of God, 1921; Ring out ye crystal Spheres (St Michael's Festival), 1928; The Sower, 1929; O Lord, Thou art my God (Festival of Sons of Clergy), 1931; An Hymn of Heavenly beauty (Worcester Festival), 1935; The Love which passeth Knowledge, 1939; Adventante Deo (St George's, Windsor), 1949; A Song of David (St Michael's and Worcester Festivals), 1956; Propers of the Communion (Coventry Consecration), 1961; Be strong and of a good Courage (Chelmsford Jubilee), 1964; I Will greatly rejoice (Winchester Choral Association), 1966. Communion Service (Buffalo, USA, 1965); Festal Te Deum (Blackburn Cathedral), 1965; Six Miniatures for Oboe and Piano, 1969. *Recreations:* photography, motoring. *Address:* 24 Widecombe Way, N2. *T:* 01-455 5087.

**DARLING,** family name of **Baron Darling.**

**DARLING,** 2nd Baron, *cr* 1924, of Langham; **Robert Charles Henry Darling;** Major retired, Somerset Light Infantry; *b* 15 May 1919; *s* of late Major Hon. John Clive Darling, DSO; *S* grandfather, 1936; *m* 1942, Bridget Rosemary

Whishaw, *d* of Rev. F. C. Dickson; one *s* two *d*. *Educ:* Wellington Coll.; RMC Sandhurst. Retired, 1955. Sec., Bath and West and Southern Counties Soc. *Recreations:* fishing, gardening. *Heir: s* Hon. Robert Julian Henry Darling [*b* 29 April 1944; *m* 1970, Janet, *yr d* of Mrs D. M. E. Mallinson, Richmond, Yorks]. *Address:* Puckpits, Limpley Stoke, Bath, Somerset. *T:* Limpley Stoke 2146.

**DARLING, Prof. Arthur Ivan;** Professor of Dental Medicine, University of Bristol, since 1959 (of Dental Surgery, 1947-59); Director of Dental Studies in the University of Bristol since 1947; Hon. Director, Dental Unit (formerly Dental Research Unit), of MRC since 1961; Pro-Vic-Chancellor, since 1968; *b* 21 Nov. 1916; *s* of John Straughan Darling and Henrietta Jeffcoat; *m* 1948, Kathleen Brenda Pollard; one *s* three *d*. *Educ:* Whitley Bay and Monkseaton Grammar Sch.; King's Coll., Univ. of Durham, LDS Dunelm, 1937, BDS Dunelm, 1938; Parker Brewis Research Fellow, 1938-41; MDS Dunelm, 1942. Lecturer: in Operative Dental Surgery, 1941, in Oral Anatomy, 1943, in Dental Materia Medica, 1945, University of Durham; Dean of Med. Faculty, Univ. of Bristol, 1963-66. LRCP, MRCS 1947; FDS, RCS 1948; DDSc Dunelm 1957; FFD, RCSI 1964; FRCPath 1967. *Publications:* scientific papers on professional subjects in journals. *Recreations:* music and gardening. *Address:* 7 Rylestone Grove, Bristol 9.

**DARLING, Rev. Charles Brian Auchinleck,** CMG 1949; MA Cantab; *b* 5 March 1905; *s* of late Ven. James George Reginald Darling, sometime Archdeacon of Suffolk and Norah Lilian Loxdale Auchinleck; *m* 1939, Rachel Middleton Lankester, *d* of Capt. Cyril Lankester Paul, RA; one *s* one *d*. *Educ:* Framlingham Coll.; Jesus Coll., Cambridge. Colonial Admin. Service, 1928, Gold Coast Colony; seconded Colonial Office, 1939; Principal, Dominions Office, 1940-45; Asst Chief Secretary: East African Governors' Conference, 1945; East Africa High Commission, 1948; retd 1951; ordained, 1952; retd 1966. *Recreation:* fly-fishing. *Address:* Fallow Hill, Bromeswell, Woodbridge, Suffolk. *T:* Eyke 222.

**DARLING, Maj.-Gen. Douglas Lyall,** CB 1968; DSO 1943 and Bar, 1945; MC 1941 and Bar, 1942; GOC 53 (Welsh) Division (TA)/Wales District, Dec. 1963-May 1968, retired; *b* 3 Oct. 1914; *s* of late George Kenneth Darling, CIE; *m* 1953, Elizabeth Anne Forsyth; two *d*. *Educ:* Eton; Sandhurst. Commissioned into Rifle Bde, 1934. Served War of 1939-45 with Rifle Bde, and commanded 7th Bn The Rifle Bde, 1942-45. Comd Eaton Hall OCTU, 1945-48; GSO1, Plans, Min. of Defence, 1952-53; School of Infantry, 1954-55. GSO1, Staff Coll., 1956-58; Comd 133 Infantry Brigade, 1959-61; Imperial Defence Coll., 1962-63; Chief, British Commanders-in-Chief Mission to the Soviet Forces in Germany, 1963. *Recreations:* hunting, combined training and horse trials, sailing. *Address:* Darley House, Hullavington, Chippenham, Wilts. *T:* Hullavington 241. *Clubs:* Army and Navy; Royal Channel Islands Yacht.
*See also General K. T. Darling.*

**DARLING, Sir Frank F.;** *see* Fraser Darling.

**DARLING, Rt. Hon. George;** PC 1966; MP (Co-op and Lab), Hillsborough Division of Sheffield, since 1950; Journalist; Minister of State, Board of Trade, 1964-68; *b* 1905; *s* of F. W. Darling, Co-operative shop asst; *m* 1932, Dorothy, *d* of T. W. Hodge, farmer; one *s* one *d*. *Educ:* Elementary Sch., Crewe; Liverpool and Cambridge Univs. Engineer; market research executive; newspaper reporter; BBC Industrial Correspondent; author. *Recreation:* gardening. *Address:* 17 Amersham Road, Beaconsfield, Bucks. *T:* Beaconsfield 3352.

**DARLING, Gerald Ralph Auchinleck,** RD 1967; QC 1967; MA; *b* 8 Dec. 1921; *er s* of late Lieut-Col R. R. A. Darling and Moira Moriarty; *m* 1954, Susan Ann, *d* of Brig. J. M. Hobbs, OBE, MC; one *s* one *d*. *Educ:* Harrow Sch. (Reginald Pole Schol.); Hertford Coll., Oxford (Baring Schol., Kitchener Schol.; MA 1948). Served with RNVR, 1940-46: Fleet Fighter Pilot, N Africa, Sicily, Salerno landings, Malta convoys; Test Pilot, Eastern Fleet; Chief Test Pilot, British Pacific Fleet; RNR until 1967; Lt-Comdr (retd). Called to Bar, Middle Temple, 1950 (Harmsworth Law Schol.); Barrister, Northern Ireland, 1957; QC Hong Kong 1968. Panel of Lloyd's Arbitrators in Salvage Cases, 1967, Panel of Wreck Commissioners, 1967. *Publication:* (contrib.) Halsbury's Laws of England (Admiralty and Ship Collisions). *Recreations:* fly fishing, shooting. *Address:* Crevenagh, Omagh, Northern Ireland; Queen Elizabeth Building, Temple, EC4. *T:* 01-353 5728. *Clubs:* Naval and Military; Tyrone County (Omagh).

**DARLING, Henry Shillington,** CBE 1967; Principal of Wye College, London University, since 1968; *b* 22 June 1914; *s* of late J. S. Darling, MD, FRCS, and Marjorie Shillington Darling, BA, Lurgan, N Ireland; *m* 1940, Vera Thompson Chapman, LDS, Belfast; one *s* two *d*. *Educ:* Watts' Endowed Sch.; Greenmount Agric. Coll., N Ireland; Queen's Univ., Belfast; Imp. Coll. Tropical Agriculture, Trinidad. BSc (1st Hons), 1938, BAgr (1st Hons) 1939, MAgr 1950, Belfast; AICTA 1942; PhD London, 1959. Middle East Anti-Locust Unit, Iran and Arabia, 1942-44; Research Div., Dept of Agriculture: Uganda, 1944-47; Sudan, 1947-49; Faculty of Agriculture, University Coll., Khartoum, 1949-54; Head of Hop Research Dept, Wye Coll., London Univ., 1954-62; Prof. of Agriculture and Dir of Inst. for Agric. Research, Ahmadu Bello Univ., Zaria, Nigeria, 1962-68; Dep. Vice-Chancellor, Ahmadu Bello Univ., 1967-68. FInstBiol 1968. Hon. DSc Ahmadu Bello Univ. Order of the Hop, 1959. *Publications:* many papers in jls and reports dealing with applied biology, entomology and agricultural science. *Recreations:* reading, walking, golf, Christian dialogue. *Address:* The Principal's House, Coldharbour, Wye, Ashford, Kent. *T:* Wye (Kent) 350. *Clubs:* Athenæum, farmers'; Samaru (Nigeria).

**DARLING, Sir James Ralph,** Kt 1968; CMG 1958; OBE 1953; MA Oxon; MA (Hon.) Melbourne; DCL (Hon.) Oxon; FACE; Headmaster, Geelong Church of England Grammar School, Corio, Victoria, Australia, 1930-61; *b* 18 June 1899; *s* of late Augustine Major Darling and Jane Baird Nimmo; *m* 1935, Margaret Dunlop, *er d* of late John Dewar Campbell; one *s* three *d*. *Educ:* Repton Sch.; Oriel Coll., Oxford. 2nd Lieut Royal Field Artillery, 1918-19, France and Germany; Asst Master Merchant Taylors' Sch., Crosby, Liverpool, 1921-24; Asst Master Charterhouse Sch., Godalming, 1924-29; in charge of Public Schs Empire Tour to NZ, 1929; Hon. Sec. Headmasters' Conference of Australia, 1931-45, Chm., 1946-48; Member: Melbourne Univ. Council; Commonwealth Univs Commission, 1942-51; Commonwealth Immigration Advisory Council; Australian Broadcasting Control Board, 1955-61. Pres. Australian Coll. of Educn, 1959-63 (Fellow 1959); Chairman: Australian Road Safety Council; Australian Frontier Commission; Australian

Broadcasting Commission, 1961-67; Commonwealth Immigration Publicity Council; Vice-Pres., Elizabethan Trust. *Publications:* The Education of a Civilized Man, 1962; Timbertop (with E. H. Montgomery) 1967. *Address:* 11 Maple Grove, Toorak, Victoria 3142, Australia. *T:* 20.6262. *Clubs:* Australian (Sydney); Melbourne (Melbourne).

**DARLING, J. C. S.;** *see* Stormonth Darling.

**DARLING, Gen. Sir Kenneth (Thomas),** GBE 1969 (CBE 1957); KCB 1963 (CB 1957); DSO 1945; Commander-in-Chief, Allied Forces, Northern Europe, 1967-69, retired; *b* 17 Sept. 1909; *s* of late G. K. Darling, CIE; *m* 1941, Pamela Beatrice Rose Denison-Pender. *Educ:* Eton; Royal Military College, Sandhurst. Commissioned 7th Royal Fusiliers, 1929; jssc 1946; idc 1953. Served NW Europe, 1944-45: Comd 5th Parachute Bde, 1946; Comd Airborne Forces Depot, 1948; Comd 16th Parachute Bde, 1950; Brig. A/q 1st (Br) Corps, 1954; Chief of Staff 1st (Br) Corps, 1955; Chief of Staff 2nd Corps, 1956. Dep. Dir of Staff Duties (D), WO, 1957-58; GOC Cyprus District and Dir of Ops, 1958-60; Dir of Infantry, 1960-62; GOC 1st (Br) Corps, 1962-63; GOC-in-C, Southern Command, 1964-66. Colonel: The Royal Fusiliers (City of London Regt), 1963-68; The Royal Regt of Fusiliers, 1968-; Col Comdt, The Parachute Regt, 1965-67. ADC Gen., 1968-69. *Recreation:* riding. *Address:* Vicarage Farmhouse, Chesterton, Bicester, Oxon. *T:* Bicester 2092. *Club:* Army and Navy. *See also Maj.-Gen. D. L. Darling.*

**DARLINGTON, Instructor Rear-Adm. Sir Charles (Roy),** KBE 1965; BSc; Director of the Naval Education Service and Head of Instructor Branch, Royal Navy, Oct. 1960-Oct. 1965, retired; on staff of Haileybury, since Oct. 1965; *b* 2 March 1910; *o s* of C. A. Darlington, Newcastle under Lyme, Staffs; *m* 1935, Nora Dennison Wright, Maulds Meaburn, Westmorland; one *s* one *d*. *Educ:* Orme Sch., Newcastle under Lyme; Manchester Univ. (BSc). Double First in Maths 1931; Sen. Maths Master, William Hulme's Gram. Sch., 1937-40. Entered Royal Navy, 1941 (Instructor Lieut); served in: HM Ships Valiant and Malaya during War, and later in HM Ships Duke of York, Implacable, Vanguard and Tyne. On Staff of C-in-C Home Fleet, 1954-55, as Fleet Meteorological Officer; for various periods in Admty, HMS Excellent and HMS Collingwood. Rear-Adm. 1960. *Recreations:* cricket, hill-walking, mathematics and trying to avoid ignorance of the arts, and particularly of history. *Address:* Southfield, Hailey Lane, Hertford. *T:* Hoddesdon 65185. *Club:* Army and Navy.

**DARLINGTON, Cyril Dean,** DSc; FRS 1941; Sherardian Professor of Botany, University of Oxford, since 1953; also Keeper, Oxford Botanic Garden; Fellow of Magdalen College; *b* 19 Dec. 1903; *m* Margaret Upcott; one *s* three *d* (and one *s* decd); 2nd, Gwendolen Harvey (*née* Adshead). *Educ:* St Paul's Sch.; Wye Coll. Rockefeller Fellow in Pasadena, 1932, in Kyoto, 1933. Royal Medal of Royal Society, 1946; Pres. Genetical Soc., 1943-46. Pres. Rationalist Press Assoc., 1948; Dir, John Innes Horticultural Institution, 1939-53; Fellow of Wye Coll. For. Mem. Acc. Lincei and Royal Danish Academy of Sciences. Joint Founder of Heredity, 1947. *Publications:* Chromosomes and Plant Breeding, 1932; Recent Advances in Cytology, 3rd edn 1965; Evolution of Genetic Systems, 1939, 1958; The Conflict of Science and Society, 1948; The Facts of Life, 1953; Chromosome Botany and the Origins of Cultivated Plants, 1956, 1963; Darwin's Place in History, 1959; Genetics and Man, 1964; The Evolution of Man and Society, 1969; (jointly): The Handling of Chromosomes, 5th edn, 1969; Chromosome Atlas of Flowering Plants, 1945, 1956; The Elements of Genetics, 1949; Genes, Plants and People, 1950; edited: Teaching Genetics, 1963; Chromosomes Today, 1966. *Recreation:* gardening. *Address:* Woodside, Frilford Heath, Berks.

**DARLINGTON, Reginald Ralph,** PhD; FBA 1954: Professor of History in University of London (Birkbeck College), 1945-69, retired, Emeritus Professor 1969; Fellow of Birkbeck College, since 1970; *b* 6 Nov. 1903. *Educ:* University Coll., Reading. Lecturer in History, Bedford Coll. (University of London), 1927-36; Reader in Medieval History in University of London, 1936-39; Prof. of History, University Coll., Exeter, 1939-45. Creighton Lecturer, University of London, 1962. FRHistS; FSA. *Publications:* Vita Wulfstani, 1928; Darley Cartulary, 1945; VCH Wilts vol. ii, 1955; The Norman Conquest, 1963; Worcester Cartulary, 1968; papers in English Historical Review, History, etc. *Address:* Warrenhurst, 25 Wargrave Road, Twyford, Reading. *T:* Twyford 109.

**DARLINGTON, William Aubrey,** CBE 1967; MA; author, journalist, and dramatist; dramatic critic of the Daily Telegraph, 1920-68; Member, Editorial Staff of the Daily Telegraph; *b* Taunton, 20 Feb. 1890; *o s* of late Thomas Darlington, HMIS Board of Education; *m* Marjorie, *y d* of late Sydney Sheppard; one *d*. *Educ:* Shrewsbury; St John's Coll., Cambridge (Classical Scholar); Honours in Classics and in English Literature. Was a schoolmaster 1913-14; during war, held commission in 7th Northumberland Fusiliers (TF); began contributing to Punch and other periodicals in 1916; took up journalism as profession in 1919, being asst editor and afterwards editor of The World; joined staff of the Daily Telegraph as dramatic critic, 1920; for many years Mem. of Advisory Cttee for Diploma in Dramatic Art, London Univ.; Lecturer on Playwriting at East London Coll., London Univ., 1926-27; Pres., Critics' Circle, 1930; London Theatre Correspondent of New York Times, 1939-60. *Publications: novels:* Alf's Button; Wishes Limited; Egbert; Alf's Carpet; Mr Cronk's Cases; Alf's New Button; *theatre books:* Through the Fourth Wall; Literature in the Theatre; Sheridan; J. M. Barrie; The Actor and his Audience; The World of Gilbert and Sullivan; Six Thousand and One Nights; Laurence Olivier; *autobiography:* I Do What I Like; *plays:* Alf's Button; Carpet Slippers; Marcia Gets Her Own Back; The Key of the House; English version of A Knight Passed By, by Jan Fabricius; burlesque version of The Streets of London. *Recreation:* golf. *Address:* Monksdown, Bishopstone, Sussex. *T:* Seaford 2657. *Club:* Garrick.

**DARNLEY,** 10th Earl of, *cr* 1725; **Peter Stuart Bligh;** Baron Clifton of Leighton Bromswold, 1608; Baron Clifton of Rathmore, 1721; Viscount Darnley, 1723; late Major, Dragoon Guards; *b* 1 Oct. 1915; *s* of 9th Earl and Daphne Rachel, *d* of late Hon. Alfred Mulholland; *S* father 1955. *Educ:* Eton; Royal Military College, Sandhurst. Served War of 1939-45 (prisoner). *Heir: half-brother* Hon. Adam Ivo Stuart Bligh [*b* 8 Nov. 1941; *m* 1965, Susan Elaine, *y d* of Sir Donald Anderson, *qv*; one *s*]. *Address:* Cobham Hall, Cobham, Kent.

**DART, Raymond Arthur;** United Steelworkers of America Professor of Anthropology, The

Institutes for the Achievement of Human Potential, Philadelphia, since 1966; Emeritus Professor since 1959, Professor of Anatomy, 1923-58, and Dean of the Faculty of Medicine, 1925-43, University of the Witwatersrand, Johannesburg; *b* Toowong, Brisbane, Australia, 4 Feb. 1893; *s* of Samuel Dart and Eliza Anne Brimblecombe; *m* 1936, Marjorie Gordon Frew, Boksburg, Transvaal; one *s* one *d*. *Educ:* Ipswich Grammar Sch., Queensland (Scholarship holder); University of Queensland (Scholarship holder and Foundation scholar); graduated BSc (Hons) 1913; MSc 1915; Sydney Univ., 1914-17; graduated MB, ChM (Hons) 1917; MD 1927; Demonstrator of Anatomy and Acting Principal of St Andrew's Coll., Sydney, 1917; House Surgeon at Royal Prince Alfred Hospital, Sydney, 1917-18; Capt., AAMC, Australia, England, France, 1918-19; Senior Demonstrator of Anatomy, University Coll., London, 1919-20; Fellow of Rockefeller Foundation, 1920-21; Senior Demonstrator of Anatomy and Lecturer in Histology, University Coll., London, 1921-22; Capt., SAMC, 1925; Major, 1928; Lieut-Col Reserve Officers, 1940; Pres. of Anthropological Section SAAAS, 1926 (Gold Medal, 1939); Vice-Pres., SAAAS, 1952; Vice-Pres. of Anthropological Section, BAAS, Johannesburg, 1929; Mem. of International Commission on Fossil Man since 1929; Fellow of Royal Society of South Africa, 1930, and Mem. of Council, 1938, Vice-Pres. 1938-39, 1939-40, 1950-51; Mem. Board, SA Institute for Medical Research, 1934-48; Mem. SA Med. Council, 1935-48, Executive Cttee, 1940-48; Mem. SA Nursing Council from its inception in 1944 until 1951; Mem. Medical Advisory Cttee, SA Council for Scientific and Industrial Research, 1946-48; Pres. Anthropological Section, First Pan-African Congress of Prehistory, 1947-51; guest-lecturer at The Viking Fund Seminar, New York, and public lecturer of The Lowell Inst., Boston, 1949; Inaugural Lecturer, John Irvine Hunter Memorial, Univ. of Sydney, NSW, 1950; Woodward Lecturer, Yale Univ., USA, 1958; Inaugural Van Riebeeck Lecturer. SA Broadcasting Corp., 1959. Pres. SA Archaeological Soc., 1951; Pres. SA Assoc. for Advancement of Science, Bulawayo, S Rhodesia, 1953; Vice-Pres., Fourth Pan-African Congress of Prehistory, 1959-62; Pres. SA Museums Assoc., 1961-62; Vice-Pres., Assoc. Scientific and Technical Socs of S Africa, 1961-62, 1962-63, Pres., 1963-64; Pres. SA Soc. of Physiotherapy, 1961-68, Hon. Life Vice-Pres., 1968-; Mem., Internat. Primatological Cttee, 1963-; Mem., Municipal Library Advisory Cttee, Johannesburg, 1964-. Coronation Medal, 1953; Sen. Capt. Scott Memorial Medal, SA Biological Soc., 1955; Viking Medal and Award for Physical Anthropology, Wenner-Gren Foundation of New York, 1957; Simon Biesheuvel Medal (Behavioural Sciences), 1963. Hon. DSc: Natal, 1956; Witwatersrand, 1964; La Salle, 1968. Fellow Odontological Soc. of SA, 1937; Fellow Institute of Biology, 1964. Raymond Dart Lectureship in Institute for Study of Man in Africa, estab. 1964; Museums of Men and Science, Johannesburg, initiated 1966, Board of Governors, 1968. Hon. Life Member: Dental Assoc. of South Africa, 1958, Medical Assoc. of South Africa, 1959, Anatomical Society of Great Britain and Ireland, 1961, Anatomical Soc. of Southern Africa, 1970, S African Nursing Assoc., 1970. *Publications:* Racial Origins, chapter in The Bantu-speaking Tribes of South Africa, 1937; chapters on genealogy and physical characters, in Bushmen of the Southern Kalahari, 1937. Ed Africa's Place in the Human Story, 1954; The Oriental Horizons of Africa, 1955; Adventures with the Missing Link, 1959; Africa's Place in the Emergence of Civilisation, 1960; Beyond Antiquity, 1965; over 200 articles on anthropological, archaeological, neurological and comparative anatomical subjects in scientific and lay periodicals. *Recreations:* swimming, music. *Address:* 20 Eton Park, Eton Road, Sandhurst, Johannesburg, South Africa. *T:* 45.4241. *Clubs:* Associated Scientific and Technical, Country (Johannesburg).

**DART, Thurston;** King Edward Professor of Music, King's College, University of London, since 1964; Artistic Director of Philomusica of London (formerly Boyd Neel Orchestra), 1955-59; *b* 3 Sept. 1921; *s* of H. T. Dart. *Educ:* Hampton Grammar School; Chapel Royal, Hampton Court (chorister); Royal College of Music. ARCM 1942; BA London, 1942; Operational Research for RAF, 1942-45 (despatches). Cambridge University: Asst Lectr in Music, 1947-52; Lectr, 1952-62; Prof. of Music, 1962-64. Editor, Galpin Soc. Jl, 1947-55; Sec., Musica Britannica, 1950-64; Fellow, Jesus Coll., Cambridge, 1953-64. Visiting Lectr, Harvard Univ., 1954. Cobbett Medal, 1957. *Publications:* The Interpretation of Music, 1954; contributions to Grove's Dictionary (5th edn); Co-editor: Dowland's Ayres for Four Voices, 1953; Jacobean Consort Music, 1955; (ed) Bull's Keyboard Music, II, 1963; articles and reviews in Music and Letters, etc. *Recreation:* organology. *Address:* King's College, Strand, WC2. *Club:* Savile.

**DARTMOUTH,** 9th Earl of, *cr* 1711; **Gerald Humphry Legge;** Baron Dartmouth, 1682; Viscount Lewisham, 1711; *b* 26 April 1924; *s* of 8th Earl of Dartmouth, CVO, DSO; *S* father, 1962; *m* 1948, Raine (*see* Countess of Dartmouth), *d* of late Alexander McCorquodale; three *s* one *d*. *Educ:* Eton. Served War, 1943-45, Coldstream Guards, Italy (despatches). FCA 1951. Dir, Rea Bros Ltd, Bankers, 1958 (Vice-Chm. 1963). Hon. LLD Dartmouth Coll., USA, 1969. *Heir: s* Viscount Lewisham, *qv*. *Address:* 40a Hill Street, W1. *Clubs:* Buck's, Bath.
*See also Baron Herschell.*

**DARTMOUTH, Countess of; Raine Legge;** Member for Richmond upon Thames, GLC, since 1967; Chairman of GLC Historic Buildings Board since 1968; *b* 9 Sept. 1929; *d* of late Alexander George McCorquodale and of Barbara Cartland, *qv*; *m* 1948, Earl of Dartmouth, *qv*; three *s* one *d*. Westminster City Councillor, 1954-65 (served on various cttees); Mem. for Lewisham West, LCC, 1958-65 (served on Town Planning, Parks, Staff Appeals Cttees); Mem. Environmental Planning Cttee, Covent Garden Develt Cttee, Strategic Planning Cttee and Arts Sub-Cttee, GLC. Vice-Pres., Nat. Assoc. for Health; Patron, West Lewisham Con. Assoc.; Pres., Barnes Day Club for Old People; Patron, 59th Westminster Scouts The Countess of Dartmouth's Own. Formerly: LCC Voluntary Care Cttee Worker, Wandsworth and Vauxhall; Mem. Citizen's Advice Bureaux Cttee for Central London. Hon. Dr Law, Dartmouth Coll., USA. *Address:* 40a Hill Street, W1. *T:* ex-Directory.

**DARVALL, Frank Ongley,** CBE 1954; retired from HM Diplomatic Service, 1970; Dean of Academics, Alvescot College, since 1970; a Governor, Sulgrave Manor; Member Council of Haileybury and Imperial Service College; *b* 16 April 1906; 5th *s* of late R. T. Darvall and Annie E. Johnson, Reading; *m* 1931, Dorothy, *er d* of Harry Edmonds and late Jane Quay, NY City; one *s* decd. *Educ:* Dover Coll.; Reading (BA); London (BA, PhD); Columbia (MA).

President Nat. Union of Students, 1927-29; Commonwealth Fund Fellow, 1929-31; Assoc. Sec. for Internat. Studies, Internat. Students Service, 1931-32; Dir, Geneva Students Internat. Union, 1933. Lecturer in Economics and History, Queen's Coll., Harley Street, 1933-36; Director Research and Discussion, English-Speaking Union, 1936-39; Dep. Director American Div., Ministry of Information, 1939-45; British Consul, Denver, 1945-46; 1st Secretary HM Embassy, Washington, 1946-49; Vice-Chairman Kinsman Trust, 1949-56; Editor, The English-Speaking World, 1950-53; Director-General, English-speaking Union of the Commonwealth, 1949-57; Chairman, Congress of European-American Assoc., 1954-57. European Editor, World Review, 1958-59. Hon. Dir, UK Cttee, Atlantic Congress, 1959; Attached British High Commn, Cyprus, 1960-62; Dir, British Information Services, Eastern Caribbean, 1962-66; attached, British Consulate-Gen., Barcelona, 1966; Consul, Boston, 1966-68; FCO (formerly CO), 1968-70. Contested (L) Ipswich, 1929, King's Lynn, 1935, Hythe bye-election, 1939. Extension Lecturer and Tutorial Classes Tutor, Cambridge and London Universities, 1933-39. *Publications:* Popular Disturbances and Public Order in Regency England, 1934; The Price of European Peace, 1937; The American Political Scene, 1939. *Address:* The Old Rectory, Alvescot, Oxon. *Club:* Travellers'.

**DARVILL, Harold Edgar;** a Deputy Chairman of Barclays Bank Ltd, 1968-70 (Director and Vice-Chairman 1966-68, General Manager, 1959-66); Governor, Royal National Throat, Nose and Ear Hospital, 1967-70; *b* 1908; 2nd *s* of Edgar Darvill, Thames Ditton; *m* 1933, Constance Nellie, *d* of Joseph Clack, Bulawayo; one *s*. *Educ:* Dunstable Grammar Sch. Entered Barclays Bank 1932, after service with Barclays Bank DCO in Rhodesia. Served with RAF in N Africa, Sicily, France, and with RAAF until 1951. Fellow, Institute of Bankers; Dep. Chairman of Council, 1963-65. Chairman, Management Cttee, Institute of Laryngology and Otology, 1960-70. *Recreations:* travel, gardening. *Address:* Clac's Ley, Halstead, Kent. *T:* Knockholt 3247.

**DARWEN,** 2nd Baron, *cr* 1946, of Heys-in-Bowland; **Cedric Percival Davies;** Publisher; Chairman and Managing Director of Darwen Finlayson Ltd, Publishers, since 1954; Chairman of Hollybank Engineering Co. Ltd; *b* 18 Feb. 1915; *e s* of 1st Baron and M. Kathleen Brown; *S* father 1950; *m* 1934, Kathleen Dora, *d* of George Sharples Walker; three *s* one *d*. *Educ:* Sidcot; Manchester Univ. BA Hons English Lit. and Language, Manchester, 1947. Engaged in Cotton Industry, 1932-40. On staff of school for Maladjusted Children, 1942-44. Manchester Univ., 1944-48, Teaching Diploma, 1948. Warden of Letchworth Adult Education Centre, 1948-51; Secretary to Training and Education Dept of National Assoc. for Mental Health, 1951-53. Dep. Editor of John O'London's, 1959-62. *Recreations:* boats, painting, cinephotography. *Heir:* *s* Hon. Roger Michael Davies, *b* 28 June 1938. *Address:* White Lodge, Sandelswood End, Beaconsfield, Bucks. *T:* Beaconsfield 3355.

**DARWIN, Henry Galton,** MA; Legal Counsellor, Foreign and Commonwealth Office, since 1970; *b* 6 Nov. 1929; *s* of late Sir Charles Darwin, KBE, FRS; *m* 1958, Jane Sophia Christie; three *d*. *Educ:* Marlborough Coll.; Trinity Coll., Cambridge. Called to Bar, Lincoln's Inn, 1953. Asst Legal Adviser, FO, 1954-60 and 1963-67; Legal Adviser, British Embassy, Bonn, 1960-63; Legal Counsellor, UK Mission to UN, 1967-70. *Publications:* contribs in Report of a Study Group on the Peaceful Settlement of International Disputes, 1966 and International Regulation of Frontier Disputes, 1970; notes in British Yearbook of International Law and American Jl of International Law. *Address:* 30 Hereford Square, SW7. *T:* 01-373 1140. *Club:* Athenæum.

**DARWIN, Sir Robin, (Robert Vere Darwin),** Kt 1964; CBE 1954; ARA 1966; Painter; Rector and Vice-Provost, Royal College of Art, 1967-71 (Principal, 1948-67); Fellow of University College, London; Hon. Fellow, Society of Industrial Artists; Member: Royal Mint Advisory Committee; Arts Advisory Council, Institute of Directors; *b* 7 May 1910; *s* of late Bernard Darwin, CBE; *m* 1st, Yvonne, *d* of late H. J. Darby (marr. diss.); 2nd, Ginette, *d* of late F. W. Hewitt and Adriana Hugh-Smith. *Educ:* Eton Coll.; Slade Sch. Asst Master, Eton Coll., 1933-38; camouflage directorate, Ministry of Home Security, 1939-44; staff of Council of Industrial Design, 1945-46 (Member Council, 1947-55, and 1962-67); Professor of Fine Art, Univ. of Durham, 1946-47. Has held one-man shows at Redfern Galleries, 1933 and 1944; Messrs Agnews, 1935, 1938, 1940, 1951, 1952, 1955, 1961, 1964; Leicester Galleries, 1946. Pictures purchased by Contemporary Art Society and by Manchester, Leeds and other provincial Galleries. Member: Science Museum Adv. Council, 1951-59; Council, RSA, 1954-59; Nat. Adv. Council on Art Educn, 1959-69; Nat. Council for Diplomas in Art and Design, 1961-69; Governing Body Imp. Coll. of Science and Technology. Hon. DLitt: Newcastle 1964; Birmingham, 1966. Bicentenary Medal, RSA, 1962. *Address:* Royal College of Art, SW7. *T:* 01-584 5020; 8 Redcliffe Road, SW10. *T:* 01-352 2697; The Old Rectory, Ham, near Marlborough, Wilts. *T:* Inkpen 239.

**DARWIN, Ruth,** CBE 1938; *d* of late Sir Horace Darwin; *m* 1948, William Rees-Thomas, *qv*. Hon. Commissioner, 1921-31, Commissioner, 1931-32, a Senior Commissioner of Board of Control, 1932-49. *Address:* High Hackhurst, Abinger Hammer, Dorking, Surrey.

**DARYNGTON,** 2nd Baron, *cr* 1923, of Witley; **Jocelyn Arthur Pike Pease;** *b* 30 May 1908; *s* of 1st Baron Daryngton, PC and Alice (*d* 1948), 2nd *d* of Very Rev. H. Mortimer Luckock, sometime Dean of Lichfield; *S* father 1949. *Educ:* Eton; privately; Trinity Coll., Cambridge (MA). Member Inner Temple, 1932. *Heir:* none. *Address:* The Street, Monks Eleigh, near Ipswich, Suffolk.

*See also N. E. Archer.*

**DAS, Sudhi Ranjan;** Chairman, Board of Directors of the Statesman Ltd, since 1968; *b* 1 Oct. 1894; *e s* of late Rakhal Chandra Das; *m* 1919, Swapana, 2nd *d* of late Rai Bahadur S. B. Majumdar; two *s* one *d*. *Educ:* Tagores Sch., Santiniketan; Bangabasi Coll., Calcutta; University Coll., London. Graduated Calcutta Univ., 1915; LLB London 1st class 1st, 1918; called to Bar, Gray's Inn, 1918; joined Calcutta Bar, 1919; Lecturer University Law College; Additional Judge, Calcutta High Court, 1942; Puisne Judge, Calcutta High Court, 1944; Chief Justice of East Punjab High Court, 1949; Judge, Federal Court of India, 1950; Judge, Supreme Court of India, 1950-56; Chief Justice of India, 1956-59. Vice-Pres., Indian Council for Cultural Relations, 1964-65. Mem., Univ. Grants Commn, 1962-. Vice-Chancellor, Visva-Bharati (University founded by Dr Rabindra Nath Tagore), 1959-65. LLD hc: Calcutta Univ., 1957; Allahabad Univ., 1958; Dr *hc* Visva-Bharati, 1966. Fellow of University Coll., London, 1961. *Address:* Swapanpuri, Kalimpong, West Bengal, India.

**DASH, Sir Arthur (Jules),** Kt 1952; CIE 1938; *b* York, 24 April 1887; *s* of Jules Janin Dash; *m* 1922, Greta Brancepeth Wardale; one *d*. *Educ:* Worcester Cathedral King's Sch.; Christ Church, Oxford. Entered Indian Civil Service 1910 and posted to Bengal; joined Indian Army Reserve of Officers in 1915 and served on Frontier and in the Punjab; on return to Bengal served as District Magistrate, 1919-27 and sometime as Political Agent to the Tripura State; Secretary to Govt of Bengal in the Education Dept, 1928-31; in various Divisions as Commissioner from 1932; retired from ICS, 1942; Chairman, Bengal Public Service Commission, 1942-47 and of Eastern Pakistan Commission, Dacca, 1947-51. *Address:* Barton Lodge, Rolvenden, Cranbrook, Kent. *Clubs:* East India and Sports; Himalayan (New Delhi).

**DASH, Sir Roydon Englefield Ashford,** Kt, *cr* 1945; DFC; Hon. LLD (London); FAI; Chairman of the Stevenage Development Corporation, 1953-62; *b* 3 March 1888; *s* of late Roland Ashford Dash, FSI; *m* 1933, Joan Pritchett Harrison. *Educ:* Haileybury Coll., Herts. Chief Valuer, Board of Inland Revenue, retired 1951. *Recreations:* golf and motoring. *Address:* 52 The Shimmings, Boxgrove Road, Guildford, Surrey.

**DASHWOOD, Sir Francis (John Vernon Hereward),** 11th Bt, *cr* 1707; (Premier Baronet of Great Britain); *b* 7 Aug. 1925; *s* of Sir John Lindsay Dashwood, 10th Bt, CVO, and Helen Moira Eaton; *S* father, 1966; *m* 1957, Victoria Ann Elizabeth Gwynne de Rutzen; one *s* three *d*. *Educ:* Eton; Christ Church, Oxford; Harvard Business Sch., USA. BA 1948, MA 1953. Foreign Office, 1944-45. Aluminium Company of Canada Ltd, 1950-51; EMI Ltd, 1951-53. Member of Buckinghamshire County Council, 1950-51; Member Lloyd's, 1956. Contested (C) West Bromwich, 1955, Gloucester, 1957. *Heir: s* Edward John Francis Dashwood, *b* 25 Sept. 1964. *Address:* West Wycombe Park, Buckinghamshire. *T:* High Wycombe 23720. *Club:* Brooks's.

**DASHWOOD, Sir Henry George Massy,** 8th Bt, *cr* 1684; *b* 11 May 1908; *s* of Sir Robert Henry Seymour Dashwood, 7th Bt, and late Margaret Helen, *e d* of late Lieut-Gen. G. Henry, CB; *S* father, 1947; *m* 1948, Susan Mary, *e d* of late Maj. Victor Montgomerie-Charrington, Grey Court, King's Sutton, Northamptonshire; one *s* one *d*. *Educ:* privately. *Heir: s* Richard James Dashwood, *b* 14 Feb. 1950. *Address:* Ledwell House, Sandford St Martin, Oxford. *TA* and *T:* Great Tew 267.

**da SILVA, John Burke,** CMG 1969; Foreign and Commonwealth Office since 1969; *b* 30 Aug. 1918; *o s* of John Christian da Silva and Gabrielle Guittard; *m* 1st, 1940, Janice Margaret Mayor (decd); one *d*; 2nd, 1963, Jennifer Jane Parker; one *s* two *d*. *Educ:* Stowe Sch.; Trinity Coll., Cambridge (MA). Served Army, 1940-46: Major, Intell. Corps (despatches). Control Commission, Germany, 1946-50; Foreign Office, 1951; 2nd Sec., Rome, 1954; Consul, Hamburg, 1956; FO, 1958; 1st Sec., Bahrein, 1960; on Staff of C-in-C, Middle East, Aden, 1963; Counsellor, Washington, 1966. *Recreation:* Oriental Art. *Address:* Copse Close, Virginia Water, Surrey. *T:* Wentworth 2342. *Club:* Bath.

**DATAR SINGH, Sardar Bahadur Sir,** Kt 1939; Adviser to CCG, Ministry of Food and Agriculture, India. *Educ:* India; went to England and took training in agriculture and dairy farming, 1919-21. Returned to India, 1921, and started career as agriculturist and dairy farmer in Montgomery District, Punjab, where he built up a big estate and pedigreed Sahiwal dairy herd; Vice-Chairman, Indian Council of Agric. Research, 1933-50; ex-Member Export Advisory Council; Food Advisory Council, and Selection Cttee for Armed Forces, War of 1939-45. Represented India at International Dairy Congress, Copenhagen, 1931, Berlin, 1937; Non-official Adviser to Govt of India for Trade Negotiations between British Govt and Govt of India and was sent to England in 1937 on this duty; led Indian Industrial Delegation to Australia and New Zealand, 1945; Indian delegate to International Wheat Agreement 1948; Indian delegate at third FAO Conference, USA, 1948; Member FAO Council and Cttee, 1948-52. Pioneer in scientific breeding and dairy farming in India; Chairman Cattle Preservation and Development Cttee appointed by Govt of India, 1947; led Indian Delegation to FAO Livestock Conf., 1950 (Chm.); Chm. ISO Conf. on Shellac, New Delhi, 1950; Indian Deleg. to FAO Co-ordinating Cttee, and Council Meetings, 1952; Leader Indian Delegation to International Dairy Congress, Hague, 1953; to FAO Council, Rome, 1953. Formerly: Production Commissioner and Additional Secretary, in charge Production Division, Ministry of Food and Agriculture, Govt of India; Vice-President All India Cattle Show Society; Cattle Utilization Adviser to Govt of India and Vice-Chairman Indian Council of Agricultural Research; President: Indian Central Cotton, Jute, Sugarcane, Lac Cess Arecanut, Tobacco and Oilseeds Cttees; Development Adviser and Additional Sec. for Kashmir, Min. of Home Affairs, 1955. Sardar Bahadur, 1937. Awarded Medal by International Dairy Congress, 1949; FRSA; NDD. *Publications:* Reorganization of Goshalas and Pinjrapoles in India; several contributions on agricultural questions. *Address:* Bairagarh, Bhopal, MP, India. *Club:* Gymkhana (New Delhi).

**DATE, William Adrian;** Puisne Judge, British Guiana, 1956-64, retired; *b* 1 July 1908; *er s* of James C. Date; *m* 1933, Dorothy MacGregor Grant; two *d*. *Educ:* Queen's Royal Coll., Trinidad; Grenada Boys' Secondary Sch.; Lodge Sch., Barbados; Middle Temple, London. Magistrate and District Govt Officer, St Lucia, 1933-39; Crown Attorney, St Vincent, 1939-44; Legal Draughtsman, Jamaica, 1944-47; Chief Secretary, Windward Islands, 1947-50; Puisne Judge of the Supreme Court of the Windward and Leeward Islands, 1950-56. *Recreations:* golf, tennis, bridge. *Address:* St George's, Grenada, West Indies.

**DAUBE, Prof. David,** FBA 1957; MA, DCL, PhD, Dr jur; Director of the Robbins Hebraic and Roman Law Collections and Professor-in-Residence at the School of Law, University of California, Berkeley, since 1970; Member, academic Board, Institute of Jewish Studies, London, since 1953; *b* Freiburg, 8 Feb. 1909; 2nd *s* of Jakob Daube; *m* 1936 (marr. diss., 1964); three *s*. *Educ:* Berthold-gymnasium, Freiburg; Universities of Freiburg, Göttingen and Cambridge. Fellow of Caius Coll., 1938-46; Lecturer in Law, Cambridge, 1946-51; Professor of Jurisprudence at Aberdeen, 1951-55; Regius Prof. of Civil Law, Oxford Univ., 1955-70; former Fellow of All Souls Coll., Oxford. Senior Fellow, Yale Univ., 1962; Delitzsch Lecturer, Münster, 1962; Gifford Lecturer, Edinburgh, for 1962 and 1963 (lectures delivered, 1963-64); Olaus Petri Lecturer, Uppsala, 1963; Ford Prof., Univ. of California, Berkeley, 1964; Riddell Lectr, Newcastle, 1965; Gray Lectr, Cambridge,

1966; Vis. Prof., Univ. of Constance, 1966; Lionel Cohen Lectr, Jerusalem, 1970. Corresp. Mem., Akad. Wiss., Göttingen, 1964, Bayer. Akad. Wiss., Munich, 1966; Hon. Mem. Royal Irish Acad., 1970. Hon. LLD: Edinburgh, Leicester; Dr *hc* Paris. *Publications:* Studies in Biblical Law, 1947; The New Testament and Rabbinic Judaism, 1956; Forms of Roman Legislation, 1956; The Exodus Pattern in the Bible, 1963; The Sudden in the Scriptures, 1964; Collaboration with Tyranny in Rabbinic Law, 1965; Roman Law, 1969; ed Studies in memory of F. de Zulueta, 1959; (with W. D. Davies) Studies in honour of C. H. Dodd, 1956, and articles. *Address:* School of Law, University of California, Berkeley, Calif 94720, USA.

**DAUBENY, Peter Lauderdale,** CBE 1967 (OBE 1961); Artistic Director of the World Theatre Season; *b* Wiesbaden, 16 April 1921; *s* of Col Cyril Daubeny and Margaret Duncan; *m* 1948, Mary Vyvyan Kempster; one *s* one *d. Educ:* Marlborough. Joined repertory company, at Playhouse, Liverpool, under William Armstrong. Served War of 1939-45: Coldstream Guards (Lieut); invalided out, 1943. Formed play-producing company Peter Daubeny Ltd; productions included: But for the Grace of God, The Late Edwina Black, Fallen Angels, We proudly Present. In 1951 he began to present Opera, Theatre and Ballet Companies including: Rosario and Antonio; Katherine Dunham; Martha Graham; Moscow State Dance Company's Beryoska and Moiseyev; Moscow Puppet Theatre; Classical Theatre of China; Mozart Opera Company, Salzburg; Hungarian State Dance Company; Théâtre National Populaire; Berthold Brecht Company; Edwige Feuillère Company; Maurice Chevalier; Jean Louis Barrault-Renaud Company; recent productions and presentations: Moscow Art Theatre at Sadler's Wells; The Comédie Française at Princes Theatre; Ibsen's Ghosts (Old Vic Prod.); Faust, at Princes Theatre (Ingmar Bergman's prod.); Jerome Robbins Ballets, USA; Compagnie Marie Bell; The House by the Lake (Duke of York's); The Aspern Papers (Queen's); Chin Chin (Wyndham's), 1961; Connection (Duke of York's), 1961; Photo Finish (Saville), 1962; Micheál Mac Liammóir, Vittorio Gassman, and Teatro Popolare Italiano (Aldwych), 1963; produced for Royal Shakespeare Company. World Theatre Seasons, 1964-, including: Peppino de Filippo, Comédie Française; Schiller, Greek Art, Abbey, Moscow Art and Polish Contemporary Theatres; Théâtre de France, Compagnia dei Giovani, Habimah, Actors' Studio and Czech National Theatres; National Theatre of Greece, Polish Popular Theatre, Gorki Theatre, Leningrad, National Theatre of Poland, Noh Theatre of Japan, Bremen Theatre, Cameri Theatre of Israel, Piccolo Theatre of Milan, Czech Theatre on the Balustrade, Rome Stabile Theatre, Royal Dramatic Theatre of Sweden, Bunraku National Theatre of Japan, Théâtre de la Cité, Theatre Behind the Gate from Prague, New York Negro Ensemble Co., Anna Magnani, Cinohemi Klub of Praque, Catania Stabile Theatre of Sicily. Consultant Director, Royal Shakespeare Company, 1966-. Chevalier of the Legion of Honour, 1957; Gold Cross of the Royal Order of King George I of Greece; Order of Merit, Republic of Italy, 1966; Gold Medal of Czechoslovakia, 1968. *Publication:* Stage by Stage, 1952. *Recreation:* travelling. *Address:* 26 Chester Square, SW1. *Club:* Garrick.

**DAUBNEY, Robert,** CMG 1939; OBE 1937; MSc; MRCVS; Veterinary Consultant to the FAO of the United Nations from 1951; *b* 1891; *s* of Robert Daubney, Southampton; *m* 1919, Jean Ethel Winifred, *d* of Thomas J. D. Ker, Hampstead. *Educ:* Manchester Grammar Sch.; Liverpool Univ.; George Washington Univ.; Cambridge Univ.; Royal Veterinary Coll., London. Served European War, 1914-19; Helminthologist Ministry of Agriculture, 1920; entered Colonial Service, 1925; Director of Veterinary Services, Kenya, 1937-47, of E African Central Veterinary Research Institute, 1939-47, retired; Veterinary Adviser to Egyptian Govt until 1951. *Publications:* Numerous on original research in Helminthology and Bacteriology (virus diseases). *Address:* c/o Glyn Mills & Co. (Holt's Branch), Whitehall, SW1.

**DAUNT, Maj.-Gen. Brian,** CB 1956; CBE 1953; DSO 1943; late RA; *b* 16 March 1900; *s* of Dr William Daunt, Parade House, Hastings; *m* 1938, Millicent Margaret, *d* of Capt. A. S. Balfour, Allermuir House, Colinton, Edinburgh; two *d* (one *s* decd). *Educ:* Tonbridge; RMA, Woolwich. Commissioned RA, 1920; served NW FRontier, India, 1929-30; War of 1939-45; France, 1940, as 2 i/c Regt; CO Anti-Tank Regt, 1941; Italy, as CO 142 Field Regt, RA, Royal Devon Yeo., 1943 (DSO); CRA: 1st Armoured Div., 1944; 46 Div., 1944; 10 Indian Div., 1946; Italy, 1945 (despatches). Has had various Brigadier's appts. Commandant Coast Artillery Sch. and Inspector Coast Artillery, 1950-53; General Officer Commanding Troops, Malta, 1953-Nov. 1956; retired, 1957; Controller, Home Dept, British Red Cross Society, 1957-66. Col Comdt RA, 1960-65. CStJ 1966. *Recreations:* shooting, fishing, sailing, gardening. *Address:* Blackstone House, Sotwell, near Wallingford, Berks. *T:* Wallingford 3060. *Club:* Army and Navy.

**DAVEN-THOMAS, Rev. Canon Dennis;** *see* Thomas, Rev. Canon Dennis D.

**DAVENPORT;** *see* Bromley-Davenport.

**DAVENPORT, Rear-Adm. Dudley Leslie,** CB 1969; OBE 1954; *b* 17 Aug. 1919; *s* of late Vice-Adm. R. C. Davenport, CB, Catherington, Hants; *m* 1950, Joan, *d* of late Surg. Comdr H. Burns, OBE; two *s. Educ:* RNC, Dartmouth. Naval Cadet, 1933; Midshipman, 1937; served in Destroyers, Mediterranean and Atlantic, 1939-45; commanded HMS Holmes, 1945 and HMS Porlock Bay, 1946; served in HMS Sheffield, 1947-48; at HMS Ganges, 1949-51; Naval Staff Course, 1951; Naval Instructor, Indian Defence Services Staff Coll., 1951-53; comd HMS Virago, 1954-55; NATO Defence Course, 1955-56; Comdr RN Barracks, Chatham, 1956-57; Captain, 1957; Staff of Admiral Comdg Reserves, 1958-60; Captain Inshore Flotilla Far East, 1960-62; Director Naval Officers Appointments (Seaman Officers), 1962-64; comd HMS Victorious, 1964-66; Rear-Admiral, 1967; Flag Officer, Malta, 1967-69; retd, 1969. *Recreations:* golf, gardening. *Address:* Rose Cottage, Halnaker, Chichester, Sussex. *T:* Halnaker 210. *Club:* United Service.

**DAVENTRY,** 2nd Viscount, *cr* 1943; **Robert Oliver Fitz Roy,** Captain RN; retired; *b* 10 Jan. 1893; *er s* of late Captain Rt Hon. Edward Algernon Fitz Roy, MP and of 1st Viscountess Daventry, CBE; *S* mother, 1962; *m* 1916, Grace Zoë, *d* of late Claude Hume Campbell Guinness; five *d. Educ:* Royal Naval Colleges, Osborne, Dartmouth. Joined Royal Navy, 1906; Captain, 1936. Served European War, 1914-18; served War of 1939-45: comd HMS Rodney (despatches). High Sheriff, Rutland, 1956-57. *Heir: b* Hon. John Maurice Fitz Roy Newdegate, Commander RN retired [*b* 1897;

*m* 1919, Lucia Charlotte Susan, OBE, *d* of Sir Francis Newdigate Newdegate, GCMG; one *s* two *d*]. *Address:* Stoke Dry House, Uppingham, Rutland. *T:* Uppingham 3380. *Club:* Carlton.

*See also Sir Geoffrey Bates, Bt.*

**DAVEY, Jocelyn;** *see* Raphael, Chaim.

**DAVEY, Roy Charles;** Headmaster, King's School, Bruton, since 1957; *b* 25 June 1915; *s* of William Arthur Davey and Georgina (*née* Allison); *m* 1940, Kathleen Joyce Sumner; two *d. Educ:* Christ's Hospital; Brasenose Coll., Oxford (Open Scholar). Asst Master, Weymouth Coll., 1937-40. War Service, Royal Artillery, 1940-46. Senior Master, 1946-49, Warden, 1949-57, The Village Coll., Impington. *Recreations:* poetry, botany, gardening, games. *Address:* Park Wall, Bruton, Somerset. *T:* Bruton 2330. *Club:* Public Schools.

**DAVEY, Prof. Thomas Herbert,** OBE 1941; *b* 30 June 1899; *s* of Rev. Charles Davey, DD, Belfast, N Ireland; *m* 1935, Irene Margaret Cottom; one *s. Educ:* Royal Belfast Academical Institution; Queen's Univ., Belfast. War service, 1917-18; MB, BCh, BAO Belfast, 1925; MD 1934; Liverpool School of Tropical Medicine, 1929; Professor of Tropical Diseases of Africa, Liverpool School of Tropical Medicine, and Director of Sir Alfred Lewis Jones Research Laboratory, Freetown, Sierra Leone, 1938; Prof. of Tropical Hygiene, Liverpool School of Tropical Medicine, Liverpool Univ., 1945-61, now emeritus. *Publications:* (with Dr W. P. H. Lightbody) Control of Disease in the Tropics, 1956; Blacklock and Southwell's Guide to Human Parasitology, 1957. *Recreation:* gardening. *Address:* 78 Ashley Drive, Bangor, Co. Down, N. Ireland. *T:* Bangor 3912.

**DAVID, Mrs Elizabeth;** 2nd *d* of Rupert Sackville Gwynne, MP, and Hon. Stella Ridley; *m* 1944, Lt-Col Ivor Anthony David (marr. diss., 1957). *Publications:* A Book of Mediterranean Food, 1950; French Country Cooking, 1951; Italian Food, 1954; Summer Cooking, 1955; French Provincial Cooking, 1960. *Address:* c/o Elizabeth David Ltd, 46 Bourne Street, Pimlico, SW1. *T:* 01-730 3123.

**DAVID, Herman Francis,** CBE 1968; Chairman and Managing Director, Diamond Development Co. Ltd, since 1952; Chairman and/or Director of other Companies; Chairman, All England Lawn Tennis and Croquet Club and Chairman, Committee of Management of The Championships, Wimbledon, since 1959; *b* 26 June 1905; *er s* of late Herman David and Gertrude Florence David (*née* Feeny); *m* 1934, Mavis Jeanne, *er d* of late Lt-Col W. J. Evans, DSO, JP; one *s* two *d. Educ:* Stonyhurst Coll.; New Coll., Oxford (BA 1927). Oxford Half-Blue, Lawn Tennis, 1927. Rep. GB in Davis Cup, 1932, and in various international matches, 1930-39; Non-playing Captain, British Davis Cup, 1953-58. Served War, 1939-45, RAFVR; Fighter Comd Operations Controller; demobilised with rank of Wing Comdr. *Recreations:* lawn tennis, croquet, bridge. *Address:* 7 Parkside Gardens, Wimbledon Common, SW19. *T:* 01-946 4651. *Clubs:* Royal Air Force, All England Lawn Tennis and Croquet, Queen's; Royal Wimbledon Golf; Edgbaston Priory Lawn Tennis, Tally-Ho Lawn Tennis (Birmingham); International Lawn Tennis Clubs of Great Britain, France, America, Australia, Belgium, Denmark.

**DAVID, Richard (William),** CBE 1967; Publisher to the University, Cambridge University Press, since 1970; Fellow of Clare Hall, Cambridge; *b* 28 Jan. 1912; *e s* of Rev. F. P. and Mary W. David, Winchester; *m* 1935, Nora, *o surv d* of G. B. Blakesley, Ashby-de-la-Zouch; two *s* two *d. Educ:* Winchester Coll. (Scholar); Corpus Christi Coll., Cambridge (Scholar). Joined editorial staff, CUP, 1936. Served RNVR, 1940-46, in Mediterranean and Western Approaches; qualified navigator, 1944; Lt-Comdr, 1945. Transferred to London Office of CUP, 1946; London Manager, 1948-63; Sec. to the Syndics of the Press, 1963-70. Member of Council of Publishers Assoc., 1953-63; Chairman of Export Research Cttee, 1956-59; President, 1959-61. *Publications:* The Janus of Poets, 1935; Love's Labour's Lost (The Arden Edition of Shakespeare), 1951. Articles on the production of Shakespeare's plays, Shakespeare Survey and other periodicals. *Recreations:* music, botanising, sailing. *Address:* 41 Barton Road, Cambridge. *T:* Cambridge 50376. *Club:* Garrick.

**DAVID, Robin (Robert) Daniel George,** QC 1968; **His Honour Judge David; Chairman, Cheshire Quarter Sessions, since 1968;** *b* 30 April 1922; *s* of late Alexander Charles Robert David and Edrica Doris Pole David (*née* Evans); *m* 1944, Edith Mary David (*née* Marsh); two *d. Educ:* Christ Coll., Brecon; Ellesmere Coll., Salop. War Service, 1943-47, Captain, Royal Artillery. Called to Bar, Gray's Inn, 1949; joined Wales and Chester Circuit, 1949. Dep. Chairman, Cheshire QS, 1961; Dep. Chairman, Agricultural Land Tribunal (Wales), 1965-68. *Recreations:* caravanning, boating. *Address:* (home) Hallowsgate House, Kelsall, Cheshire. *T:* Kelsall 456; (chambers) 4 Paper Buildings, Temple, EC4. *T:* 01-353 8408, 01-353 0196; (chambers) 40 King Street, Chester. *T:* Chester 23886. *Club:* National Liberal.

**DAVIDSON,** family name of **Viscount Davidson.**

**DAVIDSON,** 1st Viscount, *cr* 1937, of Little Gaddesden; **John Colin Campbell Davidson,** PC 1928; GCVO, *cr* 1935; CH 1923; CB 1919; President Anglo-Argentine Society; Patron Maida Vale Hospital for Nervous Diseases; *o s* of late Sir James Mackenzie Davidson, MB, CM; *b* Aberdeen, 23 Feb. 1889; *m* 1919, Joan (*see* Viscountess Davidson), *y d* of 1st Baron Dickinson, PC, KBE; two *s* two *d. Educ:* Westminster; Pembroke Coll., Cambridge. Called to Bar, Middle Temple, 1913; Private Secretary to Lord Crewe, Secretary of State for Colonies, 1910; to Rt Hon. L. Harcourt, 1910-15; to Rt Hon. A. Bonar Law, 1915-16; to Chancellor of Exchequer and Leader of House of Commons, 1916-20; MP (U) Hemel Hempstead Division of Herts, Nov. 1920-Dec. 1923, and 1924-37; PPS to Leader of House of Commons, Nov. 1920-March 1921; to Rt. Hon. S. Baldwin, President Board of Trade, 1921-22; to Mr Bonar Law, 1922-23; Chancellor, Duchy of Lancaster, 1923-24; Parliamentary Secretary to Admiralty, Nov. 1924-27; Chairman Unionist Party, 1927-30; Chancellor, Duchy of Lancaster, 1931-37; Hon. Adviser, Commercial Relations, 1940, and Controller of Production, MOI, 1941; official tour of S. America, 1942. Chairman Indian States Inquiry Cttee, 1932; Investigator Distressed Areas (W. Cumberland), 1934; Chairman Ordnance Survey Inter-deptl Cttee, 1935; Chairman, Goodwill Trade Mission to Iraq, Syria, Lebanon and Cyprus, 1946. Pres. Hispanic and Luso-Brazilian Councils, 1944-69, now Founder Pres. Dominican Grand Cross Order of Merit of Duarte, Sanchez and Mella, 1957; Grand Cross, La Orden El Sol, Peru, 1960; Grand Cross, Order of Merit, El Orden de Mayo al merito, Argentina, 1960; Grand Cross, Order Al Merito, Chile. *Relevant* *publication:* Memoirs of a Conservative, 1969. *Recreations:* gardening, motoring, and travel. *Heir:* *s* Hon. John Andrew Davidson [*b* 22 Dec. 1928; *m* 1956, Margaret Birgitta, *o d* of Maj.-Gen. C. H. Norton, *qv*; four *d* (including twin *d*)]. *Address:* Said House, Chiswick Mall, Chiswick, W4. *T:* 01-994 8111 and 01-994 4342. *Club:* United University.

*See also Ven. B. G. B. Fox, Hon. C. R. Strutt.*

**DAVIDSON, Viscountess (Frances Joan),** Baroness (Life Peeress), *cr* 1963, under title of Baroness Northchurch; DBE 1952 (OBE 1920); *y d* of 1st Baron Dickinson, PC, KBE; *m* 1919, Viscount Davidson, *qv*; two *s* two *d*. MP (U) Hemel Hempstead Division of Herts, 1937-Sept. 1959. *Recreations:* gardening, walking. *Address:* Said House, Chiswick Mall, Chiswick, W4. *T:* 01-994 4342, 8111.

**DAVIDSON, Alan Eaton;** Head of Chancery, UK Delegation to NATO, Brussels, since 1968; *b* 30 March 1924; *s* of William John Davidson and Constance (*née* Eaton); *m* 1951, Jane Macatee; three *d*. *Educ:* Leeds Grammar Sch.; Queen's Coll., Oxford. 1st class hons Class. Mods. and Greats. Served in RNVR (Ordinary Seaman, later Lieut) in Mediterranean, N Atlantic and Pacific, 1943-46. Member of HM Foreign Service, 1948; served at: Washington, 1950-53; The Hague, 1953-55; FO, 1955-59; First Secretary, British Property Commission, and later Head of Chancery, British Embassy, Cairo, 1959-61; Head of Chancery and Consul, Tunis, 1962-64; FO, 1964; Counsellor, 1965; Head, Central Dept, FO, 1966-68. *Publications:* Seafish of Tunisia and the Central Mediterranean, 1963; Snakes and Scorpions Found in the Land of Tunisia, 1964. *Recreations:* walking, painting, cookery. *Address:* 56a Avenue Hamoir, 1180 Brussels, Belgium. *T:* 74.71.11.

**DAVIDSON, Air Vice-Marshal (retired) Sir Alexander Paul,** KBE, *cr* 1950 (CBE 1941); CB 1946; Director-General Organisation, Air Ministry, 1947-51, retired; *b* 26 July 1894; *s* of late Alexander Davidson, Walton-on-Thames; *m* 1933, Jane Elizabeth Dahlstrand, Malmö, Sweden; one *s*. *Educ:* City of London Sch.; RMC, Sandhurst. Commissioned Highland Light Infantry; Seconded RFC 1916; served throughout 1914-18 with RFC and RAF; transferred RAF 1923; HQ Iraq; ADC Governor-General Australia, Lord Stonehaven, 1925-28; psa 1930; Coastal Area RAF 1931-33; HQ Palestine and Transjordan, 1933-37; Staff Officer to Inspector-General, RAF, 1938; served War of 1939-45 (despatches four times, CBE, Polish Cross of Valour); Air Attaché Poland, Lithuania, Latvia and Estonia, 1939-40; Bomber Command, 1940-41; HQ Levant, 1942; HQ Middle East, 1942-43; AOA Malta, 1943; AOA Coastal Air Force, 1943-44; AOC Iraq and Persia, 1944; Air Ministry, Post-Hostilities Planning; Deputy Chief of Air Division, Control Commission, Germany, 1946; Chief of Combined Service Div., CCG, 1947. *Recreations:* squash and tennis. *Address:* Rock Cottage, Slapton, Kingsbridge, Devon. *T:* Torcross 386. *Club:* Royal Air Force.

**DAVIDSON, Very Rev. (Andrew) Nevile,** DL; MA Edinburgh, Hon. DD Glasgow; Minister of Glasgow Cathedral, 1935-67; Moderator, General Assembly of the Church of Scotland, May 1962-May 1963; an Extra Chaplain to the Queen in Scotland since 1969 (Chaplain, 1952-69); Chaplain, Convention of Royal Burghs of Scotland; Scottish Prelate, Order of St John of Jerusalem; Governor Royal Society for the Relief of Indigent Gentlewomen; Convener Church and Nation Committee of Church of Scotland General Assembly, 1954-60; *b* 13 Feb. 1899; *s* of Rev. James Davidson, BD, and Constance, *d* of Sir Andrew Agnew of Lochnaw, 8th Bt, and Lady Louisa Noel; *m* 1944, Margaret Helen de Carteret, *er d* of late Colonel C. de C. Martin, MD, IMS. *Educ:* North Berwick; Edinburgh Univ. Vans Dunlop Scholarship in Philosophy; Asst Lecturer in Logic and Metaphysics, University of Edinburgh, for three years; studied divinity at New Coll., Edinburgh; Asst St George's, Edinburgh, 1924-25; Minister of St Mary's, Old Aberdeen, 1925-32; St Enoch's, Dundee, 1932-34; Joint-Founder in 1928 of the Dunkeld Fellowship and Founder in 1938, of the Friends of Glasgow Cathedral; served as Chaplain to the Forces with 52nd (Lowland) Div., 1940-42; Joint-Convenor of the Special Cttee which produced the Church of Scotland's Report on Evangelism, Into All the World, 1944-46; President: Scottish Church Society, 1945-47, and 1967-70; Church Service Society, 1948-50; a Chaplain to King George VI in Scotland, 1946-52; President New Coll. Union, 1953-55; Chairman BBC Scottish Religious Advisory Cttee, 1950-56; President Scottish Ecclesiological Society, 1956-57; Chairman Scottish Churches Ecumenical Cttee, 1950-63. Attended inauguration of United Church of S. India on 27 Sept. 1947, as official representative of Church of Scotland; at request of Foreign Mission Cttee, spent winter, 1947-48, visiting Mission Stations of Church of Scotland throughout India and Pakistan; Chairman Commn on Spiritual Healing appointed by General Assembly, 1954-58. Winner of St Mungo Prize, 1958-61 (triennially awarded). Vice-President British Council of Churches, 1963-65; President, Society of Friends of Glasgow Cathedral, 1967; Convener, Inter-Church Relations Cttee of the Church of Scotland, 1964-69. Macneil-Fraser Lectr, Trinity Coll., Glasgow. DL Glasgow, 1962. *Publications:* Reflections of a Scottish Churchman, 1965; book reviews and occasional contributions periodicals. *Recreations:* reading, motoring, travel. *Address:* Seafield House, West Barns, East Lothian. *T:* Dunbar 3236; Forest House, Nethy Bridge, Inverness-shire. *T:* Nethy Bridge 218.

**DAVIDSON, Arthur;** MP (Lab) Accrington since 1966; *b* 7 Nov. 1928. *Educ:* Liverpool Coll.; King George V Sch., Southport; Trinity Coll., Cambridge. Served in Merchant Navy. Barrister, Middle Temple, 1953. Trinity Coll., Cambridge, 1959-62; Editor of the Granta. Contested (Lab) Blackpool S, 1955, and Preston N, 1959. PPS to Solicitor-General, 1968-70. Hon. Legal Advisor, Southport Trades Council. *Recreations:* lawn tennis, ski-ing, theatre, modern jazz; formerly Member Cambridge Univ. athletics team. *Address:* House of Commons, SW1; 56 Courtenay Street, SE11.

**DAVIDSON, Basil Risbridger,** MC 1945; author and journalist; *b* 9 Nov. 1914; *s* of Thomas and Jessie Davidson; *m* 1943, Marion Ruth Young; three *s*. Served War of 1939-45 (despatches twice, MC, US Bronze Star, Jugoslav Zasluge za Narod); British Army, 1940-45 (Balkans, N Africa, Italy); Temp. Lt-Col demobilised as Hon. Major. Editorial staff of The Economist, 1938-39; The Star (diplomatic correspondent, 1939); The Times (Paris correspondent, 1945-47; chief foreign leader-writer, 1947-49); New Statesman (special correspondent, 1950-54); Daily Herald (special correspondent, 1954-57); Daily Mirror (leader-writer, 1959-62). Student of African affairs (contrib. to many periodicals); a Vice-Pres., Anti-Apartheid Movement, 1969-. Freeman of City of Genoa, 1945. *Publications: novels:* Highway Forty, 1949; Golden Horn, 1952; The Rapids, 1955;

Lindy, 1958; The Andrassy Affair, 1966; *non-fiction:* Partisan Picture, 1946; Germany: From Potsdam to Partition, 1950; Report on Southern Africa, 1952; Daybreak in China, 1953; The New West Africa (ed.), 1953; The African Awakening, 1955; Turkestan Alive, 1957; Old Africa Rediscovered, 1959; Black Mother, 1961; The African Past, 1964; Which Way Africa?, 1964; The Growth of African Civilisation: West Africa AD 1000-1800, 1965; Africa: History of a Continent, 1966; A History of East and Central Africa to the late 19th Century, 1967; Africa in History: Themes and Outlines, 1968; The Liberation of Guiné, 1969; The Africans, An Entry to Cultural History, 1969. *Address:* c/o Barclays Bank Ltd, 19 Fleet Street, EC4. *Club:* Savile.

**DAVIDSON, Brian,** CBE 1965; Solicitor with Gas Council, since 1969; *b* 14 Sept. 1909; *o s* of late Edward Fitzwilliam Davidson and late Esther Davidson (*née* Schofield); *m* 1935, Priscilla Margaret, *d* of late Arthur Farquhar and Florence Chilver; one *s* one *d* (and one *s* decd). *Educ:* Winchester Coll. (Scholar); New Coll., Oxford (Scholar). Gaisford Prize for Greek Verse; 1st class Honour Mods.; 2nd class LitHum; President, Oxford Union Society; President OU Conservative Assoc.; BA 1932. Cholmeley Student Lincoln's Inn; Barrister-at-Law, 1933; Law Society Sheffield Prize; Solicitor, 1939; Air Ministry and Ministry of Aircraft Production, 1940. With Bristol Aeroplane Co., 1943-: Business Manager, 1946; Director, 1950-68; Director: Bristol Siddeley Engines Ltd, 1959-68; Bristol Siddeley Whittle Tools Ltd. Member: Monopolies Commission, 1954-68; Gloucestershire CC (and Chairman Rating Valuation Appeals Cttee), 1953-60; Cttee Wine Society, 1966-. *Recreations:* fox-hunting, sailing (represented Oxford Univ.), Scottish country dancing, bridge. *Address:* 13a South Eaton Place, SW1. *T:* 01-730 3160; Hill Court, Berkeley, Gloucestershire. *T:* Falfield 488. *Clubs:* Travellers', Hurlingham.

*See also Prof. G. E. F. Chilver, R. C. Chilver.*

**DAVIDSON, Charles Kemp,** QC (Scot.) 1969; *b* Edinburgh, 13 April 1929; *s* of Rev. Donald Davidson, DD, Edinburgh; *m* 1960, Mary, *d* of Charles Mactaggart, Campbeltown, Argyll; one *s* two *d*. *Educ:* Fettes Coll., Edinburgh; Brasenose Coll., Oxford; Edinburgh Univ. Admitted to Faculty of Advocates, 1956. *Address:* 22 Dublin Street, Edinburgh 1. *T:* 031-556 2168.

**DAVIDSON, Hon. Sir Charles (William),** KBE 1964 (OBE 1945); retired; *b* 14 Sept. 1897; *s* of Alexander Black Davidson and Marion Perry; *m* 1929, Mary Gertrude Godschall Johnson; one *s* two *d*. *Educ:* Townsville Grammar Sch., Townsville. Served European War, 1914-18: 42 Bn AIF, 1916-19; Lieut; France (wounded); served War of 1939-45: 42 Bn AIF, 1939-44; Lt-Col; Hon. Colonel 42 Inf. Bn, 1955. Dairy farmer, 1921-25; sugar farming from 1925. MHR for Capricornia (Queensland), 1946-49, and for Dawson (Queensland), 1949-63, retired; Postmaster-General, 1956-63; Minister for Navy, 1956-58; Dep. Leader, Parliamentary Country Party, 1958-63. *Recreations:* bowls, golf, fishing, gardening. *Address:* 439 Brisbane Corso, Yeronga, Brisbane, Queensland, Australia. *T:* Brisbane 48.4264. *Clubs:* United Service, Masonic (Brisbane); Mackay Civic.

**DAVIDSON, Francis,** CBE 1961; Finance Officer, Singapore High Commission, London; *b* 23 Nov. 1905; *s* of James Davidson and Margaret Mackenzie; *m* 1937, Marial Mackenzie, MA; one *s* one *d*. *Educ:* Millbank Public Sch., Nairn; Nairn Academy. Commercial Bank of Scotland Ltd, 1923-29; Bank of British West Africa Ltd, 1929-41; Colonial Service (Treasury), 1941-61; retired from Colonial Service, Nov. 1961, as Accountant-General of Federation of Nigeria. *Recreations:* tennis, philately. *Address:* 39 Charterhouse Road, Orpington, Kent. *T:* Orpington 30071. *Club:* Royal Over-Seas League.

**DAVIDSON, Maj.-Gen. Francis Henry Norman,** CB 1942; DSO 1919; MC (and Bar); *b* 1 April 1892; *s* of late Sir Leybourne Davidson; *m* Edna Mildred, *d* of J. G. Counsel, Bombay; two *s*. *Educ:* Marlborough; RMA. Entered Army 1911; served European War, 1914-19 (wounded, despatches four times, MC and bar, DSO); Bt Major, 1929; Major 1929; Bt Lt-Col, 1933; Colonel, 1938; Maj.-General 1941; GSO2, AHQ India, 1925-27; Brig. Major 12th Indian Inf. Bde, 1927-29; GSO2, War Office, 1930-34; Imperial Defence Coll. Course, 1935-36; GSO 2nd Grade Staff Coll., Camberley, 1937-38; GSO 1st Grade 2nd Division, Aldershot, 1938-39; CCRA 1st Corps BEF 1939-40; BGS X Corps, 1940; Director of Military Intelligence, War Office, 1940-44; MGGS British Army Staff, Washington, USA, 1944-46; retired pay, 1946. Colonel Comdt Intelligence Corps, 1952-60. *Address:* 82 Chelsea Park Gardens, SW3. *Clubs:* English-Speaking Union; Hurlingham.

**DAVIDSON, Howard William,** CMG 1961; MBE 1942; *b* 30 July 1911; *s* of late Joseph Christopher Davidson, Johannesburg, and Helen, *d* of James Forbes; *m* 1st, 1941, Anne Elizabeth, *d* of late Captain R. C. Power; one *d*; 2nd, 1956, Dorothy, *d* of late Sir Wm Polson, KCMG; one *step s*. *Educ:* King Edward VII Sch., Johannesburg; Witwatersrand Univ.; Oriel Coll., Oxford. Cadet, Colonial Admin. Service, Sierra Leone, 1935; District Commissioner, 1942; Dep. Fin. Secretary, 1949; Fin. Secretary, Fiji, 1952; Fin. Secretary, N Borneo, 1958; State Financial Secretary and Member Cabinet, Sabah, Malaysia, 1963-64; Financial Adviser, 1964-65; Member of Inter-Governmental Cttee which led to establishment of new Federation of Malaysia; retired, 1965. Inspector (part-time) Min. of Housing and Local Government, 1967-70. Appointed Panglima Darjah Kinabalu (with title of Dato') in first Sabah State Honours List, 1963. *Recreations:* cricket, gardening, fishing. *Address:* Glebe Cottage, Tillington, Petworth, Sussex. *Clubs:* East India and Sports; Sussex County Cricket.

**DAVIDSON, Ian Douglas,** CBE 1957; Director: Canadian Imperial Bank of Commerce; Western Assurance Co.; British American Assurance Co.; Interlink Investments Ltd; Debhold (Canada) Ltd; Cerro Corp.; Schering Corp. Ltd; Chairman, Clarke Institute of Psychiatry; Member, Board of Governors, University of Toronto; *b* 27 Oct. 1901; *s* of Rev. John Davidson, JP, and Elizabeth Helen (*née* Whyte); *m* 1st, 1936, Claire Louise (*d* 1937), *d* of E. S. Gempp, St Louis, Missouri; one *d*; 2nd, 1938, Eugenia, *d* of late Marques de Mohernando and Lorenza, Marquesa de Mohernando; one *d*. *Educ:* King Williams's Coll. Royal Dutch Shell Group of Companies, 1921-61; President: Mexican Eagle Oil Co., 1936-47; Cia. Shell de Venezuela, 1953-57; Canadian Shell Ltd, 1957-61. Order of St Mark (Lebanon), 1957; Orden del Libertador (Venezuela), 1957. *Address:* 115 Riverview Drive, Toronto 12, Ontario, Canada. *Clubs:* Caledonian (London); Toronto, York (Toronto); Links (NY).

**DAVIDSON, Ivor Macauley;** Director, National Gas Turbine Establishment, since 1970; *b* 27

Jan. 1924; *s* of late James Macauley and Violet Alice Davidson; *m* 1948, Winifred Lowes; four *s* one *d*. *Educ:* Bellahouston Sch.; Univ. of Glasgow. Royal Aircraft Establishment, 1943; Power Jets (R&D) Ltd, 1944; attached RAF, 1945; National Gas Turbine Establishment, 1946: Dep. Dir, 1964. *Publications:* numerous, scientific and technical. *Recreations:* music, gardening, business. *Address:* Monksway, Pirbright Road, Farnborough, Hants. *T:* Farnborough 44686.

**DAVIDSON, James,** MB, ChB, FRCP Edinburgh; FSAScot.; late Senior Lecturer on Pathology, University of Edinburgh and Consultant Pathologist to the Edinburgh Southern Hospitals and The Royal Victoria and Associated Hospitals; *b* 3 Feb. 1896; *s* of James Davidson and Isabella Slater Shaw; *m* 1927, Constance Ellen Cameron; two *d*. *Educ:* University of Edinburgh. House Physician, Royal Infirmary, Edinburgh; Tutor in Clinical Medicine, University of Edinburgh; Lecturer on Morbid Anatomy and Senior Asst to Prof. of Pathology, University of Edinburgh; Senior Pathologist to Royal Infirmary, Edinburgh; Asst to Prof. of Medical Jurisprudence, University of Edinburgh; Lecturer on Forensic Medicine, London Hospital Medical Coll.; Director of Metropolitan Police Laboratory, Hendon, NW9. *Publications:* various papers on subjects dealing with Pathology and Forensic Science; (joint) text-book, Practical Pathology, 1938. *Recreations:* gardening, golf and fishing. *Address:* Linton Muir, West Linton, Peebles-shire. *Clubs:* New, Caledonian (Edinburgh).

**DAVIDSON, James Duncan Gordon,** MVO 1947; Chief Executive, Royal Highland and Agricultural Society of Scotland, since 1970; *b* 10 Jan. 1927; *s* of Alastair Gordon Davidson and M. Valentine B. Davidson (*née* Osborne); *m* 1955, Catherine Ann Jamieson; one *s* two *d*. *Educ:* RN Coll., Dartmouth; Downing Coll., Cambridge. Active List, RN, 1944-55; Senior Sub-Lieut, HMS Vanguard, Royal Cruise to S Africa, 1947; various appointments as a Watchkeeping, Navigating and Intelligence Officer; Asst Naval Attaché, Moscow and Helsinki, 1952-54; Navigator, HMS St Kitts, 1954-55; placed on Retired List at own request, 1955. Subseq. farming, and political work; contested (L) West Aberdeenshire, 1964; MP (L) West Aberdeenshire, 1966-70. Editor and Chairman of Cttee which produced A Plan for the North East, 1964. *Recreations:* family, farming, ski-ing, climbing. *Address:* Tillychetly, Alford, Aberdeenshire. *T:* Alford 2246. *Clubs:* National Liberal; Scottish Liberal (Edinburgh).

**DAVIDSON, Prof. (James) Norman,** CBE 1967; MD, DSc; FRS 1960; FRSE; FRCPE FRCPGlas; FRIC; Gardiner Professor of Biochemistry, Glasgow University, since 1947, and Director of the Biochemical Laboratories; *b* 5 March 1911; *s* of late James Davidson, FRSE, Edinburgh; *m* 1938, Morag McLeod, BSc, PhD, *d* of late Alexander Mathers McLeod, SSC, Edinburgh; two *d*. *Educ:* George Watson's Coll., Edinburgh; Edinburgh Univ. BSc (1st Class Hons Chemistry) 1934; MB, ChB (Hons) 1937; Vans Dunlop Entrance Scholar in Medicine, Robert Wilson Memorial Prizeman, Wellcome Gold Medallist; MD 1939; DSc (Edinburgh), 1945; Carnegie Research Fellow in Biochemistry at Kaiser Wilhelm Institut für Zellphysiologie, Berlin-Dahlem, 1937-38; Lecturer in Biochemistry, University of St Andrews, at University College, Dundee, 1938-40; Lecturer in Biochemistry, University of Aberdeen, 1940-45; Member Scientific Staff of Medical Research Council at National Institute for Medical Reasearch, Hampstead, NW3, 1945-46; Prof. of Biochemistry in University of London at St Thomas's Hospital Medical Sch., 1946-47; guest lecturer: Ghent, Brussels, Liège, 1954, Oslo and Uppsala, 1953, Paris, 1952, USA 1947, 1956, 1960, 1961, 1964, 1966, 1968, Warsaw, 1959, Moscow, 1961, Brazil, 1963, Malaysia, 1963. Formerly Examiner for Universities of St Andrews, Oxford, Cambridge, London, Leeds, Liverpool, Aberdeen, Birmingham, Singapore, Bristol; Member: Editorial Board of British Journal of Nutrition; Biological Research Board, MRC, 1964-68; European Molecular Biology Organisation; Board of Management, Glasgow Royal Infirmary, 1948-70. President: Royal Society, Edinburgh, 1958-59, 1964-67 (Vice-Pres., 1955-58); Assoc. Clinical Biochemists, 1963-66; Mem. Council, Royal Soc., 1968-70. Vice-President, Saltire Society, 1959-62. Chairman: Scottish Council Inst. Biology, 1959-60; Biochemical Society (Sec., 1946-52, Chm., 1961-63). Vice-Chairman, Advisory Cttee for Medical Research, Scotland, 1961-67. FRSM; FIBiol (Vice-Pres., 1961-63); FCS. Hon. Fellow, Soc. Ital. Biol. Sperimentale. Makdougall-Brisbane Prize, RSE, 1969. *Publications:* The Biochemistry of the Nucleic Acids, 6th edition, 1969; (with G. H. Bell and H. Scarborough) Text-book of Physiology and Biochemistry, 7th edition, 1968; (with E, Chargaff) The Nucleic Acids: Chemistry and Biology, 1955; numerous biochemical papers in medical and scientific journals. *Recreations:* fishing, foreign travel, Scottish cultural activities. *Address:* Biochemistry Department, The University of Glasgow, Glasgow W2; Penlee, Ledcameroch Road, Bearsden, Dunbartonshire. *T:* 041-942 4371. *Clubs:* Athenæum; New (Edinburgh).

**DAVIDSON, James Wightman,** MA; PhD; Professor of Pacific History, Australian National University, since 1949; *b* 1 Oct. 1915; *s* of late George Wightman Davidson and late Edith Mabel Davidson (*née* Brown), both of Wellington, NZ; unmarried. *Educ:* Waitaki Sch., NZ; Victoria, University Coll., Wellington, NZ; St John's Coll., Cambridge; MA (NZ), 1st class hons in history, 1938; PhD Cantab, 1942. Research Assistant, Nuffield Coll., Oxford, 1941-42. Served in NZ Public Service, Internal Affairs Dept, 1938; External Affairs Dept, 1947; in UK Civil Service, Admiralty (Naval Intelligence Division), 1942-45; Colonial Office, 1945; Fellow of St John's Coll., Cambridge, 1944-51; University Lecturer in History, 1946-50; MLA, Western Samoa, 1949-50; Trusteeship Officer to Govt of Western Samoa, 1949-50. Assisted New Zealand Govt in working out proposals for constitutional reform in Western Samoa, 1947; Constitutional Adviser to Governments of: Western Samoa, 1959-61; the Cook Islands, 1963; Nauru, 1967-68; Consultant to Future Political Status Commn, Congress of Micronesia, 1969. *Publications:* The Northern Rhodesian Legislative Council, 1948; The Study of Pacific History, 1955; Samoa mo Samoa, 1967; articles in various historical and political journals. *Recreations:* tennis, swimming, sailing. *Address:* Australian National University, Canberra, ACT. *T:* Canberra 959.323.

**DAVIDSON, John Wallace Ord,** CMG 1936; OBE 1926; member of London Stock Exchange, 1949-59; *b* 9 Nov. 1888; *s* of late George Greenshields Davidson; *m* 1935, Edith, *d* of late James Cory, Cory Manor, N. Devon. *Educ:* Christ's Hospital. HM Consular Service, China, 1909; served European War, Chinese Labour Corps, France, 1917-18; Acting Chinese Secretary, HM Legation, Peking, 1928-29; Acting Consul-General,

Shanghai, 1933 and 1937; Consul-General, 1938; Counsellor, FO, 1945, Head of Prisoners of War Dept, 1945-46, and of Consular Dept, FO, 1946-48; retired on pension, 1948; a Governor of Christ's Hospital. *Address:* Cory Manor, near Holsworthy, N Devon. *T:* Bradworthy 318.

**DAVIDSON, Maj.-Gen. Kenneth Chisholm,** CB 1948; MC; psc; late Infantry; *b* 1897; *m* 1934, Diana Blanche Wilson; one *s* one *d*. *Educ:* Newbury Grammar Sch. 2nd Lieut Gordon Highlanders, 1915; served European War, 1914-19 (wounded twice); War of 1939-45, Persia and Iraq Force (despatches), Sicily (despatches), Italy (despatches). Lieut-Col, 1942; Col, 1942; Brig., 1947; actg Maj.-Gen., 1943; retired pay, 1949 (with hon. rank of Maj.-Gen.). *Address:* Rooklands, Tangley, near Andover, Hants. *T:* Chute Standen 612.

**DAVIDSON, Sir (Leybourne) Stanley (Patrick),** Kt 1955; FRSE; Professor of Medicine, University of Edinburgh, 1938-59, retired; Physician to the Queen in Scotland, 1952-61, an Extra Physician to HM in Scotland, since 1961; *b* 3 March 1894; 2nd *s* of late Sir L. F. W. Davidson; *m* Isabel Margaret, *e d* of late Hon. Lord Anderson; no *c*. *Educ:* Cheltenham Coll.; Trinity Coll., Cambridge; Edinburgh Univ.; BA (Cambridge), MB, ChB 1919, Edinburgh Univ., 1st class hons, MD, awarded gold medal for thesis; MD Oslo; FRCP (London), 1940; FRCP (Edinburgh), 1925. Pres., 1953-56; LLD (Edinburgh Univ.) 1962. Regius Prof. of Medicine, University of Aberdeen, 1930-38; Sen. Phys. Royal Infirmary, Aberdeen, 1932-38, etc. Hon. Physician to King George VI in Scotland, 1947-52. Hon. LLD Aberdeen. *Publications:* Pernicious Anæmia, monograph (with Prof. G. L. Gulland), 1930; A Textbook of Medical Treatment (with D. M. Dunlop and Stanley Alstead), 1963; The Principles and Practice of Medicine (with Staff of Edinburgh Univ. Dept of Medicine), 1963; Human Nutrition and dietetics (with R. Passmore), 1963; articles in medical journals. *Recreations:* tennis, golf, fishing, shooting. *Address:* 28 Barnton Gardens, Davidson's Mains, Edinburgh 4. *Club:* New (Edinburgh).

**DAVIDSON, Very Rev. Nevile;** *see* Davidson, Very Rev. Andrew N.

**DAVIDSON, Norman;** *see* Davidson, J. N.

**DAVIDSON, Mrs Paul;** *see* Cairns, Julia.

**DAVIDSON, Lady Rachel;** *see under* Pepys, Lady (Mary) Rachel.

**DAVIDSON, Roger Alastair McLaren,** CMG 1947; Secretary of the Scottish Universities Entrance Board, 1953-66; *b* 6 Feb. 1900; *s* of late Rev. R. S. Davidson, The Manse, Kinfauns, Perthshire; *m* 1928, Elsie Stuart, *d* of late J. A. Y. Stronach, Edinburgh; one *s* one *d*. *Educ:* Fettes Coll., Edinburgh; University of Edinburgh. Served European War, 1914-18, 2nd Lieut Royal Highlanders, 1918-19; entered Colonial Education Service, 1924; Nigeria, 1924-37; Asst Dir of Education, Tanganyika, 1937-40; seconded to Colonial Office, 1941-43; Asst Dir of Education, Southern Provinces, Nigeria, 1943-44; Dir of Education, Nigeria, 1944-51; Inspector-Gen. of Education, Nigeria, 1951-53. *Address:* Longrigg, St Andrews. *T:* 2345. *Club:* Royal and Ancient (St Andrews).

**DAVIDSON, Sir Stanley;** *see* Davidson, Sir L. S. P.

**DAVIDSON, William Bird;** Director and Chief Executive, National Westminster Bank Limited, since 1968; *b* 18 May 1912; 2nd *s* of J. N. Davidson; *m* 1941, Christina M. Ireton; two *s*. *Educ:* Queen Elizabeth Grammar Sch., Penrith. War Service, Royal Artillery, 1939-45. Entered Nat. Provincial Bank, 1929; Jt Gen Manager, 1961; Chief Gen. Manager, 1967-68; Dir, 1968. Director: Westminster Foreign Bank Ltd; Ulster Bank Ltd. FIB. *Recreation:* golf. *Address:* Rose Cottage, 9 Starrock Road, Coulsdon, Surrey. *T:* Downland 53687.

**DAVIDSON-HOUSTON, Major Aubrey Claud;** portrait painter since 1952; *b* 2 Feb. 1906; *s* of late Lt-Col Wilfred Bennett Davidson-Houston, CMG, and Annie Henrietta Hunt; *m* 1938, Georgina Louie Ethel (*d* 1961), *d* of late Capt. H. S. Dobson; one *d*. *Educ:* St Edward's Sch., Oxford; RMC, Sandhurst; Slade Sch. of Fine Art. 2nd Lieut, Royal Sussex Regt, 1925; ADC to Governor of Western Australia, 1927-30; Nigeria Regt, RWAFF, 1933-37; PoW (Germany), 1940-45; Sch. of Infty, 1946-47; MS Branch, WO, 1948-49; retd, 1949. Slade Sch. of Fine Art, 1949-52 (diploma). *Portraits include:* The Queen, for RWF; The Duke of Edinburgh, for 8th King's Royal Irish Hussars and for Duke of Edinburgh's Royal Regt; Queen Elizabeth, The Queen Mother, for Black Watch of Canada; The Princess Royal, for WRAC; The Duke of Gloucester, for Royal Inniskilling Fusiliers, for Scots Guards and for Trinity House; also portraits for Lincoln Coll. and Keble Coll., Oxford, and for Selwyn Coll., Cambridge; also for a number of other regts and for City Livery cos, schools, etc. A Governor, St Edward's School, Oxford. *Address:* Hillview, West End Lane, Esher, Surrey. *T:* Esher 64769; 4 Chelsea Studios, 412 Fulham Road, SW6. *T:* 01-385 2569. *Clubs:* Buck's, Chelsea Arts, Naval and Military, MCC.

**DAVIE, Alan;** painter, poet, jazz musician and designer of jewellery; *b* 1920. *Educ:* Edinburgh Coll. of Art. Gregory Fellowship, Leeds Univ., 1956-59. One-man exhibitions, since 1946, at: Edinburgh; Whitechapel Art Gallery; Pittsburgh; Gimpel Fils; New York; Los Angeles; Zürich; Salon de Mai, Paris; Documenta, Germany; Rome; Palazzo Grassi, Venice; Graves Art Gallery, Sheffield, and at leading art galleries in Germany and other European countries. Prize for Best Foreign Painter, VII Bienal de São Paulo, 1963. Work represented in exhibitions: in Australia, 1958-59; in Moscow, 1960; in Mexico City, 1960; Dunn International Exhibition, London, 1963; Gulbenkian Painting and Sculpture of an Age Exhibition, Tate Gallery, 1964, Zürich, 1964; Salon de Mai, Paris, yearly since 1964. Official purchases include Tate Gallery; Gulbenkian Foundn, London; Stuyvesant Foundn, London; Stedelijk Mus., Amsterdam; Carnegie Inst., USA; Mus. of Modern Art, New York. *Relevant publication:* Alan Davie (Ed Alan Bowness), 1967. *Address:* Gamels Studio, Rush Green, Hertford.

**DAVIE, Rev. Sir (Arthur) Patrick;** *see* Ferguson Davie.

**DAVIE, Cedric Thorpe,** OBE 1955; FRAM; Master of Music and Reader in Music, University of St Andrews, since 1945; composer (especially for film, theatre, radio); *b* 30 May 1913; *s* of Thorpe and Gladys Louise Davie; *m* 1937, Margaret Russell Brown; two *s*. *Educ:* High Sch. of Glasgow; Royal Scottish Academy of Music; Royal Academy of Music; Royal College of Music. Member: Scottish Arts Council, 1965; Arts Council of Great Britain, 1968. FRAM, 1949. Hon. LLD (Dundee), 1969. *Publications:* Musical Structure and Design, 1949; Oxford Scottish

Song Book, 1969. Articles and reviews in learned jls. *Recreations:* eating and drinking; travel Northwards in search of sunshine. *Address:* 5 North Street, St Andrews, Fife. *T:* St Andrews 3950.

**DAVIE, Prof. Donald Alfred;** Professor of English, Stanford University, California, since 1968; *b* 17 June 1922; *s* of George Clarke Davie and Alice (*née* Sugden); *m* 1945, Doreen John; two *s* one *d*. *Educ:* Barnsley Holgate Gram. Sch.; St Catharine's Coll., Cambridge. BA 1947; PhD 1951. Served with Royal Navy, 1941-46 (Sub-Lieut RNVR). Lecturer in Dublin Univ., 1950-57; Fellow of Trinity Coll., Dublin, 1954-57; Visiting Prof., University of Calif., 1957-58; Lecturer, Cambridge Univ., 1958-64; Fellow of Gonville and Caius Coll., Cambridge, 1959-64; George Elliston Lecturer, University of Cincinnati, 1963; Prof. of Literature, University of Essex, 1964-68, and Pro-Vice-Chancellor, 1965-68. *Publications;* poetry: Brides of Reason, 1955; A Winter Talent, 1957; The Forests of Lithuania, 1959; A Sequence for Francis Parkman, 1961; Events and Wisdoms, 1964; Essex Poems, 1969; criticism and literary history: Purity of Diction in English Verse, 1952; Articulate Energy, 1957; The Heyday of Sir Walter Scott, 1961; Ezra Pound: Poet as Sculptor, 1965; Introduction to The Necklace by Charles Tomlinson, 1955; anthologies: The Late Augustans, 1958; (with Angela Livingstone) Modern Judgements: Pasternak, 1969. *Recreations:* verse-translation; Literary politics; travel. *Address:* 989 Cottrell Way, Stanford, Calif, USA. *Clubs:* Savile; Union (Cambridge).

**DAVIE, Sir Paul (Christopher),** Kt 1967; Remembrancer, City of London, 1953-67; *b* 30 Sept. 1901; *s* of Charles Christopher Davie and Beatrice Paulina Mabel (*née* Walrond); *m* 1938, Betty Muriel, *d* of late Captain Ronald Henderson, MP for Henley div. of Oxfordshire, 1924-32, of Studley Priory, Oxon.; one *s* one *d*. *Educ:* Winchester; New Coll., Oxford. Called to Bar, Lincoln's Inn, 1925; 2nd Asst Legal Advisor, Home Office, 1936; Asst Legal Advisor, 1947. *Publications:* Silicosis and Asbestosis Compensation Schemes, 1932; Joint Managing Ed., Encyclopædia of Local Government Law and Administration, 1934. *Recreations:* history, gardening. *Address:* The Old Rectory, Bentley, Hants. *T:* Bentley 3128. *Club:* Travellers'.

**DAVIES,** family name of **Barons Darwen, Davies,** and **Davies of Leek.**

**DAVIES;** *see* Llewelyn-Davies.

**DAVIES,** 3rd Baron, *cr* 1932, of Llandinam; **David Davies;** *b* 2 Oct. 1940; *s* of 2nd Baron and Ruth Eldrydd (*d* 1966), 3rd *d* of Major W. M. Dugdale, CB, DSO; *S* father (killed in action), 1944. *Educ:* Eton; King's Coll., Cambridge. *Heir: b* Hon. Jonathan Hugh Davies [*b* 25 Jan. 1944; *m* 1966, Veronica, *er d* of Sir Godfrey Agnew, *qv*; one *s* one *d*]. *Address:* Plas Dinam, Llandinam, Montgomeryshire.

**DAVIES OF LEEK,** Baron *cr* 1970 (Life Peer), of Leek, Staffordshire; **Harold Davies,** PC 1969; *b* July 1904; *m* Jessie Elizabeth Bateman, BSc, London; one *d*. *Educ:* Lewis Grammar Sch., Pengam, Glam. Trained for teaching; Schoolmaster and Tutor in Adult Education; several lecture tours in USA and Canada; Lecturer to various organisations and Labour Movement. MP (Lab) Leek Div. of Staffs, 1945-70; formerly Member several Parliamentary Cttees; Joint Parliamentary Secretary, Ministry of Social Security, 1966-67 (Ministry of Pensions and National Insurance, 1965-66). Special Envoy (of Prime Minister) on Peace Mission to Hanoi, 1965. FRGS. *Publications:* various Press articles on Social and Educational Problems, etc.; numerous writings and pamphlets on Far East, SE Asia, etc. *Recreations:* was keen on all sports and played most of them, now interested in foreign affairs (Far East), agriculture, education, economic affairs. *Address:* 81 Trentham Road, Longton, Stoke-on-Trent, Staffs. *T:* Stoke-on-Trent 39976.

**DAVIES, Air Commodore Adolphus Dan,** CB 1953; CBE 1947; psa; *b* 14 Oct. 1902; *m* 1925, Kathleen Hobbs (*d* 1969); one *d*. Cranwell, 1921-23; Air Ministry, Dep. Directorate War Organisation, 1938; Commanded Scampton, Bomber Command, 1943; Fiskerton, Bomber Command, 1944; Air Ministry, Directorate Gen. of Manning, 1944; Air Officer Commanding Royal Air Force, Hong Kong, 1948; Air Cdre 1949; Air Officer in charge of Administration, Coastal Command, 1951-54; retired Aug. 1954. *Address:* 54 Azalea Walk, Eastcote, Pinner, Middx. *T:* 01-868 0257.

**DAVIES, Alan B.;** *see* Bowen-Davies.

**DAVIES, Air Cdre Alan Cyril,** CBE 1967; Director of Air Plans, Ministry of Defence, since 1969; *b* 31 March 1924; *s* of Richard Davies, Maidstone; *m* Julia Elizabeth Ghislaine Russell; two *s* (and one *s* decd). Enlisted RAF, 1941; commnd 1943; comd Joint Anti-Submarine School Flight, 1952-54; comd Air Sea Warfare Development Unit, 1958-59; comd No 201 Sqdn, 1959-61; Air Warfare Coll., 1962; Dep. Dir, Operational Requirements, MoD, 1964-66; comd RAF Stradishall, Suffolk, 1967-68; idc 1969. *Address:* R3 Section, Lloyds Bank Ltd, 6 Pall Mall, SW1. *Club:* Royal Air Force.

**DAVIES, (Albert) Meredith;** Musical Director, Vancouver Symphony Orchestra, since 1964; Musical Director, English Opera Group, 1963-65; Guest Conductor, Royal Opera House, Covent Garden, and Sadler's Wells; also BBC; *b* 30 July 1922; 2nd *s* of Reverend E. A. Davies; *m* 1949, Betty Hazel, *d* of late Dr Kenneth Bates; three *s* one *d*. *Educ:* Royal College of Music; Stationers' Company's Sch.; Keble Coll., Oxford; Accademia di S. Cecilia, Rome. Junior Exhibitioner, RCM, 1930; Organist to Hurstpierpoint Coll., Sussex, 1939; elected Organ Scholar, Keble Coll., 1940. Served War of 1939-45, RA, 1942-45. Conductor St Albans Bach Choir, 1947; Organist and Master of the Choristers, Cathedral Church of St Alban, 1947-49; Musical Dir, St Albans Sch., 1948-49; Organist and Choirmaster, Hereford Cathedral, and Conductor, Three Choirs' Festival (Hereford), 1949-56; Organist and Supernumerary Fellow of New Coll., Oxford, 1956; Associate Conductor, City of Birmingham Symphony Orchestra, 1957-59; Dep. Musical Dir, 1959-60; Conductor, City of Birmingham Choir, 1957-64. *Address:* 50 Fishpool Street, St Albans, Herts.

**DAVIES, (Alfred William) Michael,** QC 1964; Recorder of Derby since 1965; Leader of Midland Circuit since 1968; *b* 29 July 1921; *er s* of Alfred Edward Davies, Stourbridge; *m* 1947, Margaret, *y d* of Robert Ernest Jackson, Sheffield; one *s* three *d*. *Educ:* King Edward's Sch., Birmingham; University of Birmingham (LLB). Called to Bar, Lincoln's Inn, 1948; Dep. Chm. Northants QS, 1962-. Chm. Mental Health Review Tribunal, for Birmingham Area, 1965-; Mem., Gen. Council of the Bar, 1968-. Recorder of Grantham, 1963-65. *Recreations:* golf and the theatre. *Address:* 2 Harcourt Buildings, Temple, EC4. *T:* 01-353 4746; 20 Old Buildings, Lincoln's Inn, WC2. *T:*

01-405 1125; 1a Arthur Road, Edgbaston, Birmingham 15. *T:* 021-454 7965. *Clubs:* Garrick; Nottinghamshire (Nottingham); County (Northampton).

**DAVIES, Alun B. O.**; *see* Oldfield-Davies.

**DAVIES, Alun Talfan,** QC 1961; MA; LLB; barrister-at-law; Recorder of Cardiff since 1969; Deputy Chairman, Cardiganshire Court of Quarter Sessions, since 1963; Judge of the Courts of Appeal, Jersey and Guernsey, since 1969; *b* Gorseinon, 22 July 1913; *s* of late Rev. W. Talfan Davies, Presbyterian Minister, Gorseinon; *m* 1942, Eiluned Christopher, *d* of late Humphrey R. Williams, Stanmore, Middx; one *s* three *d*. *Educ:* Gowerton Gram. Sch.; Aberystwyth Univ. Coll. of Wales (LLB); Gonville and Caius Coll., Cambridge (MA, LLB). Called to the Bar, Gray's Inn, 1939; Bencher, 1969-. Practised on Wales and Chester circuit. Participates in Legal Aid Scheme. Contested (Ind.) University of Wales (by-elec.), 1943; contested (L): Carmarthen Div., 1959 and 1964; Denbigh, 1966. Mem. Court of University of Wales and of Courts and Councils of Aberystwyth and Swansea University Colls. Recorder: of Merthyr Tydfil, 1963-68; of Swansea, 1968-69. Mem., Commn on the Constitution, 1969-. Chm., Aberfan Disaster Fund, 1969-. *Address:* 62 Eaton Crescent, Swansea. *T:* Swansea 57021; 5 King's Bench Walk, Temple, EC4. *T:* 01-353 4713. *Clubs:* National Liberal; Ffynnone, Bristol Channel Yacht (Swansea).

**DAVIES, Rear-Adm. Anthony,** CB 1964; Royal Navy, retired; Warden, St George's House, Windsor Castle, since 1966; *b* 13 June 1912; *s* of James Arthur and Margaret Davies; *m* 1940, Lilian Hilda Margaret, *d* of Admiral Sir H. M. Burrough, *qv*; two *s* two *d*. *Educ:* Royal Naval College, Dartmouth. Midshipman, HMS Danae, 1930-32; Sub-Lieut, HMS Despatch, 1934; Lieut, HMS Duncan, 1935-37; Gunnery course, 1938; HMS Repulse, 1939; HMS Cossack 1940-41; Lieut-Comdr, HMS Indefatigable, 1943-45; Comdr, HMS Triumph, 1950; HMS Excellent, 1951-54; Capt., HMS Pelican, 1954-55; Dep. Dir, RN Staff Coll., 1956-57; Far East Fleet Staff, 1957-59; Dep. Dir, Naval Intelligence, 1959-62; Head of British Defence Liaison Staff, Canberra, Australia, 1963-65. *Address:* 25 The Cloisters, Windsor Castle, Berks. *T:* Windsor 64842.

**DAVIES, Rt. Hon. Sir Arthian**; *see* Davies, Rt Hon. Sir (William) Arthian.

**DAVIES, Prof. Arthur;** Reardon-Smith Professor of Geography, University of Exeter, since 1948; Deputy Vice-Chancellor, University of Exeter, 1969-71; *b* 13 March 1906; *s* of Richard Davies, Headmaster, and Jessie Starr Davies, Headmistress; *m* 1933, Lilian Margaret Morris; one *d*. *Educ:* Cyfarthfa Castle Sch.; University Coll. of Wales, Aberystwyth, 1st cl. Hons in Geography and Anthropology, 1927; MSc Wales 1930; Fellow, University of Wales, 1929-30, Asst Lecturer in Geography, Manchester Univ., 1930-33; Lecturer in Geography, Leeds Univ., 1933-40. Served War of 1939-45, RA 1940-45, Normandy (despatches twice, Major); Mem., High Mil. Tribunal of Hamburg, 1945. *Publications:* Yugoslav Studies, Leplay Soc., London, 1932; Polish Studies, Leplay Soc., London, 1933; contrib. to Encyclopaedia Britannica and geographical and historical learned journals. *Recreations:* gardening and architecture. *Address:* Morlais, Winslade Park, Clyst St Mary, Devon. *T:* Topsham 3296.

**DAVIES, (Arthur Edward) Miles,** CB 1956; *b* 26 Nov. 1903; *s* of Edward M. and Margaret Davies; *m* 1934, Elspeth Lang. *Educ:* University of Liverpool. Under Sec. Ministry of Education, 1950-58. *Address:* 6 Strathearn Place, W2. *Club:* Reform.

**DAVIES, Brian H.**; *see* Humphreys-Davies.

**DAVIES, Caleb William,** CMG 1962; MRCS; LRCP; DPH; Principal Assistant Senior Medical Officer, South-Western Regional Hospital Board, since 1966 (Assistant SMO, 1963-66); *b* 27 Aug. 1916; *s* of Caleb Davies, KIH, MB, ChB, and Emily (*née* Platt); *m* 1939, Joan Heath; three *s* one *d*. *Educ:* Kingswood Sch., Bath; University Coll. and University Coll. Hosp. Med. Sch., London; Edinburgh Univ.; London Sch. of Hygiene and Tropical Med. Kenya: MO, 1941; MOH, Mombasa, 1946; Tanganyika: Sen. MO, 1950; Asst Dir of Med. Services, 1952; Uganda: Dep. Dir of Medical Services, 1958; Permanent Sec. and Chief Medical Officer, Ministry of Health, 1960; retired 1963. *Recreations:* squash, tennis, swimming, photography. *Address:* Abbey View House, Abbey View, Bath, Somerset. *T:* Bath 4566.

**DAVIES, Carlton Griffith,** CMG 1953; MC 1915; *b* 2 Aug. 1895; *o surv s* of late Walter Davies, MBE, Calcutta and Ealing; *m* 1926, Florence Evelyn, *y d* of late Robert MacSymon, Greenock and Liverpool; two *s* (and one *s* and one *d* decd). *Educ:* Rugby Sch.; Exeter Coll., Oxford. Served European War, 1914-19, London Regt (The Queen's), and Machine-Gun Corps (MC, despatches). Asst District Comr, Sudan Political Service, 1920; Comr, Gezira Area, 1930; Asst Civil Sec., 1935-36; Asst Financial Sec., 1936-40; seconded to Sudan Defence Force, 1939-40 (despatches). Governor, Upper Nile Province, 1940-45; Sudan Agent in London, 1951-55. 4th Class Order of the Nile (Egypt), 1930; Officer of the Order of Leopold (Belgium), 1949. *Recreations:* golf, sailing and gardening. *Address:* Three Lanes End Farm, Wisborough Green, Billingshurst, Sussex. *T:* Wisborough Green 375. *Clubs:* Royal Over-Seas League, Royal Commonwealth Society.

**DAVIES, Ven. Carlyle W.**; *see* Witton-Davies.

**DAVIES, (Claude) Nigel (Byam)**; *b* 2 Sept. 1920; unmarried. *Educ:* Eton. Studied at Aix en Provence University, 1937, and at Potsdam, 1938. Entered Sandhurst, 1939, and later commissioned Grenadier Guards. Served Middle East, Italy and Balkans, 1942-46. Formerly Managing Dir of Windolite Ltd from 1947. MP (C) Epping Div. of Essex, 1950-51. *Recreation:* travel. *Club:* Carlton.

**DAVIES, Cuthbert Collin,** PhD; Reader Emeritus in Indian History in the University of Oxford, since 1965; *b* 16 April 1896; *o s* of D. C. Davies, Narberth, Pembs; *m* 1918, Rachel Eleanor, *er d* of Rees Davies, JP, Carmarthen; one *s* one *d* (and one *d* decd). *Educ:* Narberth Grammar Sch.; University of Wales (Aberystwyth); Peterhouse, Cambridge. BA 1st Class Hons. Hist. Wales, 1923; PhD Cambridge, 1926. Temp. commn 15th W Yorks Regt, 1915; France, 1916-17 (twice wounded); Regular Commn 2/1st Gurkha Rifles, IA, 1918; Third Afghan War, 1919; ops in Waziristan, 1921-22; Comdg Dharamsala, 1922. Flt Lieut RAF, 1940. Lectr in Indian Hist., Sch. Oriental and African Studies, London Univ., and Supervisor of Indian Civil Service Probationers, 1929; Visiting Prof. Boulder, Colorado, 1939; Visiting Prof. in South Asian History, University Wis., 1965. FRHistS, 1932; MA Balliol Coll., Oxford,

1936; Reader in Indian History, Oxford Univ., 1936-63; Corresponding Mem. Historical MSS. Commn, Government of India, 1953. Sir Jadunath Sarkar Gold Medal, Asiatic Soc. Bengal, 1959. *Publications:* The Problem of the North-West Frontier, 1932; Warren Hastings and Oudh, 1939; Benares Diary of Warren Hastings, 1948; Historical Atlas of the Indian Peninsula, 1949 (2nd edn 1959); Private Correspondence of Lord Macartney, 1950; Bharateeya Aitihasik Atlas, 1954. Contrib. to Cambridge History of India; New Cambridge Modern History; Army Quarterly; Eng. Historical Review; Journal E India Assoc.; Ency. Britannica; Ency. of Islam; Ency. Hebraica, History; Indian Archives; Annales Historiques de la Révolution Française; Handbuch der Weltgeschichte, etc. *Recreations:* fishing and walking. *Address:* 100 Divinity Road, Oxford. *T:* Oxford 43750.

**DAVIES, David Arthur;** Secretary-General, World Meteorological Organization, Geneva, Switzerland, since 1955; *b* 11 Nov. 1913; *s* of Garfield Brynmor Davies and Mary Jane Davies (*née* Michael); *m* 1938, Mary Shapland; one *s* two *d*. *Educ:* University of Wales (MSc) (1st cl. Hons Maths; 1st cl. Hons Physics). Technical Officer, Meteorological Office, 1936-39. War Service, RAF, 1939-47 (despatches). Principal Scientific Officer, Met. Office, 1947-49; Dir, E African Met. Dept, Nairobi, 1949-55; Pres. World Meteorological Organization Regional Assoc. for Africa, 1951-55. Hon. Mem., Amer. Meteorological Soc. FInstP. *Publications:* various meteorological papers and articles dealing mainly with artificial stimulation of rain. *Recreations:* music, painting. *Address:* 34 Avenue Krieg, Geneva, Switzerland. *T:* Geneva 35 07 79. *Club:* Anglo-Belgian.

**DAVIES, David Cyril,** BA, LLB; Headmaster, Woodberry Down School, since 1967; *b* 7 Oct. 1925; *s* of D. T. E. Davies and Mrs G. V. Davies, JP; *m* 1952, Joan Rogers, BSc; one *s* one *d*. *Educ:* Lewis Sch., Pengam; UCW Aberystwyth. Asst Master, Ebbw Vale Gram. Sch., 1951-55; Head, Lower Sch., Netteswell Bilateral Sch., 1955-58; Sen. Master and Dep. Headmaster, Peckham Manor Sch., 1958-64; Headmaster, Greenway Comprehensive Sch., 1964-67. *Recreations:* reading, Rugby and roughing it. *Address:* 9 Plaxtol Close, Bromley, Kent. *T:* 01-464 4187.

**DAVIES, David Henry;** General Secretary, Iron and Steel Trades Confederation, since 1967; *b* 2 Dec. 1909; British; *m* 1934, Elsie May Battrick; one *s* one *d* (and one *d* decd). *Educ:* Ebbw Vale, Mon. Organiser, 1950, Asst. Gen. Sec., 1953-66, Iron and Steel Trades Confederation. Chm., Jt Adv. Cttee on Safety and Health in the Iron and Steel Industry, 1965-67; Vice-Chm., Nat. Dock Labour Bd, 1966-68; Hon. Treas. WEA, 1962-69 (Mem. Central Coun. and Central Exec. Cttee, 1954-69); Hon. Treas., British Labour Party, 1965-67 (Chm., 1963; Mem. Nat. Exec., 1954-67); Hon. Sec., Brit. Sect., Internat. Metalworkers Federation, 1960-; Member: Ebbw Vale UDC, 1945-50; Royal Institute of International Affairs, 1954-; Iron and Steel Operatives Course Adv. Cttee, City and Guilds of London Institute Dept of Technology, 1954-; Iron and Steel Industry Trng Bd, 1964-; Constructional Materials Gp, Economic Development Cttee for the Building and Civil Engrg Industries, 1965-68; Iron and Steel Adv. Cttee, 1967-. Governor: Ruskin Coll., Oxford, 1954-; Iron and Steel Industry Management Trng Coll., Ashorne Hill, Leamington Spa, 1966-. Mem. TUC Gen. Coun., 1967-. *Address:* Swinton House, 324 Gray's Inn Road, WC1. *T:* 01-837 6691.

**DAVIES, Rt. Rev. David Henry S.;** *see* Saunders-Davies.

**DAVIES, D(avid) H(erbert) Mervyn,** MC 1944; TD 1946; QC 1967; Barrister-at-law; *b* 17 Jan. 1918; *s* of Herbert Bowen Davies and Esther Davies, Llangunnor, Carms; *m* 1951, Zita Yollanne Angelique Blanche Antoinette, 2nd *d* of Rev. E. A. Phillips, Bale, Norfolk. *Educ:* Swansea Gram. Sch. Solicitor, 1939 (Daniel Reardon Prize, Travers Smith Schol.). Commissioned Welch Regt (TA), 1936; served War of 1939-45, 18th Bn Welch Regt and 2nd London Irish Rifles, Africa, Italy and Austria. Called to Bar, Lincoln's Inn, 1947. *Publication:* The Copyright Act 1956, 1957. *Address:* 5 New Square, Lincoln's Inn, WC2. *T:* 01-405 6430; 7 Stone Buildings, Lincoln's Inn, WC2. *T:* 01-242 8061.

**DAVIES, David John Denzil;** MP (Lab) Llanelli since 1970; *b* 9 Oct. 1938; *s* of G. Davies, Conwil Elfed, Carmarthen; *m* 1963, Mary Ann Finlay, Illinois; one *s* one *d*. *Educ:* Queen Elizabeth Grammar Sch., Carmarthen; Pembroke Coll., Oxford. Bacon Scholar, Gray's Inn, 1961; BA (1st cl. Law) 1962; Martin Wronker Prize (Law), 1962. Teaching Fellow, Univ. of Chicago, 1963; Lectr in Law, Leeds Univ., 1964; called to Bar, Gray's Inn, 1964. *Address:* House of Commons, SW1.

**DAVIES, Sir David (Joseph),** Kt 1969; Chairman, Wales Tourist Board, 1965-70; Director and Chairman of Nolton Estates Ltd since 1939, and associated companies; *b* 30 Aug. 1896; *s* of David and Catherine Davies; *m* 1924, Eleanor Irene Davies (*née* Bowen); one *s*. *Educ:* Maesteg Higher Grade and Bridgend County Schools. Served in Welch Regt, 1915-19, Acting Captain. Director: E. I. Davies Ltd, 1926-36; W. S. Lowe Ltd, 1936-48; Chm. and Man. Dir, Mackross Ltd, 1948-59. Mem. Court, University Coll., Cardiff, 1959-; Mem. Court and Council, National Museum of Wales, 1961-. *Recreations:* painting in oils, world travel. *Address:* 28 Queen Anne Square, Cardiff CF1 3ED. *T:* Cardiff 22695. *Club:* Cardiff and County (Cardiff).

**DAVIES, David Lewis,** DM; Physician, Bethlem Royal and Maudsley Hospital, since 1948; *b* 16 April 1911; *s* of late Harry Davies and the late Anne Davies; *m* 1945, Celia Marjorie Rapport, MB, FFA RCS; three *s*. *Educ:* Manchester Grammar Sch.; St John's Coll., Oxford (Scholar). BA Oxford (1st Cl. Hons Physiology), 1933; BM, BCh 1936; DPMEng 1943; MA 1944; DM 1948; MRCP 1964; FRCP 1970. RAMC (Temp. Major), 1942-46; Dean, Institute of Psychiatry, University of London, 1950-66. Member: Standing Mental Health Sub-cttee, Central Health Services Council; Area Nurse Training Cttee, SE Metropolitan Regional Hosp. Bd. Hon. Mem., Venezuelan Psychiatric Association, 1964. *Publications:* (ed jtly) Psychiatric Education, 1964; (ed jtly) Studies in Psychiatry, 1968; papers on psychiatric subjects in med. jls. Chapters in Louis Wain: the man who drew cats, 1968. Wrote script and commentary for film, Victorian Flower Paintings, 1967. *Recreations:* gardening, carpentry. *Address:* 31a Alleyn Park, Dulwich, SE21. *T:* 01-670 3670.

**DAVIES, Prof. David Richard Seaborne,** MA Cantab; LLB Wales; JP Liverpool; Dean of the Faculty of Law, University of Liverpool, since 1946; Professor of the Common Law since 1946 (Pro-Vice Chancellor, 1956-60); Warden of Derby Hall since 1947; Member Citizenship Deprivation Tribunal; Member Standing Committee on Criminal Law Revision; Governor: Liverpool College; Rydal School, Colwyn Bay; *b* 26 June 1904; *er s* of late David

S. and Claudia Davies, Pwllheli. *Educ:* Pwllheli Gram. Sch.; University Coll., Aberystwyth; St John's Coll., Cambridge. (McMahon and Strathcona Studentships). First Class Hons LLB (Wales); Law Tripos, 1927 (Class I, Div. I); Yorke Prize, Cambridge Univ., 1928; Lecturer in University of London from 1929; late Reader in English Law in University of London at London Sch. of Economics; Nationality Div., Home Office, 1941-45; Sec. of the Naturalization (Revocation) Cttee, 1944-48; Mem. Oaksey Departmental Cttee on Police Conditions, 1948-49; Chm., Departmental Cttee on Agricultural Diploma Education in Wales, 1956. MP (L) Caernarvon Boroughs, April-July 1945. Pres., Soc. of Public Teachers of Law, 1960-61. Lucien Wolf Memorial Lecturer, 1952. British delegate, SEATO Universities Conference, Karachi, 1961. Cooley Lecturer, University of Mich., 1962. BBC (Wales) Annual Lecture, 1967. Examiner for Oxford, Cambridge, London, Birmingham, Manchester, Leeds, Exeter, Dublin, Nottingham, The Law Society, the Civil Service, etc. Public Orator, Liverpool Univ., 1950-55. Chm., Liverpool Licensing Planning Cttee, 1960-63; High Sheriff of Caernarvonshire, 1967-68. *Publications:* articles in Law Quarterly Review, Modern Law Review, Nineteenth Century, The Annual Survey of English Law, 1930-41. Journal of the Soc. of Public Teachers of Law, etc. *Recreation:* gardening. *Address:* Derby Hall, North Mossley Hill Road, Liverpool 18. *T:* 051-724 2418; y Garn Pwllheli, N Wales. *T:* Pwllheli 2109.

**DAVIES, David Ronald,** MB, BS, FRCS; Surgeon, University College Hospital, London, since 1946; *b* Clydach, Swansea, 11 May 1910; 3rd *s* of late Evan Llewelyn and Agnes Jane Davies; *m* 1940, Alice Christine, 2nd *d* of Rev. John Thomson; three *s*. *Educ:* University Coll. and University Coll. Hosp., London. MRCS, LRCP 1934; MB BS London, 1934; FRCS, 1937; House appts at University Coll. Hosp., 1937-39; Asst Surg. EMS at University Coll. Hosp. and Hampstead Gen. Hosp., 1939-41; served RAMC; Surgical Specialist and Officer-in-Charge Surgical Div., 1941-46; Surgeon: Queen Mary's Hospital, Roehampton, 1947-61; Harrow Hosp., 1946-69. Fellow University Coll.; Fellow Assoc. of Surgeons. *Publications:* The Operations of Surgery (with A. J. Gardham); Progress in Clinical Surgery, Section on Hyperparathyroidism. *Address:* 5 Upper Wimpole Street, W1. *T:* 01-935 1525; 36 Steele's Road, NW3. *T:* 01-722 3808; Newland Farm, Withypool, Somerset. *T:* Exford 352. *Club:* Athenæum.

**DAVIES, Derek G. G.;** *see* Gill-Davies.

**DAVIES, Sir Edmund;** *see* Davies, Sir H. E.

**DAVIES, Ednyfed Hudson;** *b* 4 Dec. 1929; *s* of Rev. E. Curig Davies. *Educ:* University College of Swansea; Balliol Coll., Oxford. Lecturer in Dept of Extra-Mural Studies, University of Wales, Aberystwyth, 1957-61; Lecturer in Political Thought, Welsh Coll. of Advanced Technology, Cardiff, 1961-66. MP (Lab) Conway, 1966-70. BBC Welsh Motoring Correspondent, and on contract to BBC, Cardiff, as TV and Radio Commentator and Interviewer on Current Affairs, 1962-66.

**DAVIES, Elidir (Leslie Wish),** FRIBA, FRSA; Chartered Architect in private practice; Vice-Chm., Internat. Assoc. of Theatre Technicians, 1963; Vice-Chm., Assoc. of British Theatre Technicians, 1964; *b* 3 Jan. 1907; *yr s* of Rev. Thomas John Landy Davies and Hetty Boucher (*née* Wish); *m* Vera (*née* Goodwin). *Educ:* privately; Colchester Sch.; Bartlett Sch. of Architecture, University of London (under Prof. Albert Richardson). Min. of Supply Air Defence, 1939-44; Min. of Town and Country Planning, London and Wales, 1944-47; University Lectr and Cons. to Argentinian and Uruguay Govts on planning and low cost housing, 1947-49; private practice (Devereux and Davies); rebuilding of Serjeants' Inn, Fleet Street; Royal Vet. Coll., London Univ. (Research and Field Labs); King's Coll. Sch., Wimbledon (Jun. Sch. and Sci. Labs); St James's Hosp., Balham (Out-patients' and other Depts); St Benedict's Hosp. (Hydrotherapy Dept), 1950-61. West Indies: 5-year Hospital progr. for Trinidad (incl. new gen. and maternity hosps, trg schs, specialist depts, and hosp. services). Cons. Arch. Hosps to Govts of Guiana, Barbados and Grenada, 1957-63. Private practice (Elidir L. W. Davies & Partners). Architect to: St David's Coll., Lampeter, restoration and new bldgs; London Borough of Camden; new Central Library, theatre and arts centre; St David's Theatre for Wales; Mermaid Theatre; Royal Court Theatre, London; Dynevor Castle, Carmarthen, Wales–New arts centre for drama and films; rebuilding of Wren's church, St Michael Paternoster Royal; Cons. Architect to City of Cambridge (new Music and drama centre); Govt Offices, Century House, Waterloo; private houses and housing developments in London and the country. Bronze Medal, RIBA, 1953. *Publications:* lectures and articles; contrib. to pubn relating to hospital architecture. *Recreations:* theatre, travel, sailing, visual arts. *Address:* (private) 19 Marlborough Place, St John's Wood, NW8; (office) 100 Wigmore Street, W1. *T:* 01-486 3841. *Clubs:* Garrick, Art Workers' Guild.

**DAVIES, Elwyn,** MA; Hon. LLD Wales; MSc, PhD Manchester; Secretary for Welsh Education, Department of Education and Science, 1964-69; Vice-President, National Library of Wales (Member Council, 1957-; Treasurer, 1959-64); a Governor: National Museum of Wales, since 1957 (Member Council, 1959-); University of Wales, since 1966; University College of South Wales and Monmouthshire, Cardiff since 1963; a Governor and Member Council, University College of Wales, Aberystwyth, since 1965; Member Council Hon. Society Cymmrodorion since 1964; Member Schools Broadcasting Council for Wales since 1964; *b* 20 Sept. 1908; *e s* of late Rev. Ben Davies, Llandeilo, Carms; *m* 1940, Margaret, *o d* of late Matthew Henry Dunlop, Bury, Lancs; no *c*. *Educ:* Llandysul and Llandeilo Grammar Schs; Universities of Wales (Aberystwyth Coll.) and Manchester. Asst Lectr and Lectr in Geography, University of Manchester, 1934-45, seconded Intelligence Div. Naval Staff, 1941-45; Sec. to the Council, University of Wales, Sec. of the University Press Board and the Board of Celtic Studies, 1945-63; Sec. University Bd for Training Colls, 1945-48, and Univ. Educn Bd, 1948-49; Sec., Univ. Extension Bd, 1945-61; Permanent Sec., Welsh Dept, Min. of Educn, 1963-64. Mem. Pilkington Cttee on Broadcasting, 1960-62. Mem. Standing Commission on Museums and Galleries, 1960-64. *Publications:* Cyfarwyddiadau i Awduron (A Guide for Authors), 1954; (ed) A Gazetteer of Welsh Place-Names, 1957; (ed) Celtic Studies in Wales, 1963; (ed with Alwyn D. Rees) Welsh Rural Communities, 1960; papers in anthropological and geographical periodicals. *Recreations:* watching Rugby football and cricket, walking. *Address:* Butts Field, Tenby, Pembrokeshire.

**DAVIES, Emlyn Glyndwr,** MSc; Forensic Science Adviser, Home Office, since 1963; *b* 20

March 1916; *yr s* of late William and Elizabeth Davies; *m* 1940, Edwina, *d* of late Lemuel and Alice Morgan, Blaengarw; two *s*. *Educ:* Bargoed Grammar Sch.; Maesycwmmer Grammar Sch.; University Coll of Wales, Aberystwyth (MSc). Asst Master, Ardwyn Sch., 1939-42; Ministry of Supply, 1942-44; Forensic Science Laboratory, Cardiff, 1944-58; Director, Forensic Science Laboratories: Nottingham, 1958-59; Preston, 1959-63. *Publications;* contribs to scientific jls. *Recreation:* Rugby football. *Address:* Home Office, SW1.

**DAVIES, Ernest Albert John;** Journalist, author; *b* London, 18 May 1902; *s* of late Alderman Albert Emil Davies; *m* 1st, 1926, Natalie Rossin, New York (marriage dissolved, 1944; she *d* 1955); two *s* one *d*; 2nd, 1944, Peggy Yeo (*d* 1963); one *d*. *Educ:* Wycliffe Coll.; London Univ. (Diploma in Journalism). Editor, Traffic Engineering and Control, 1960-; Managing Editor, Antique Finder, 1962-; Editor Clarion, 1929-32; Associate Editor, New Clarion, 1932. Served on Fabian Soc. Exec., 1940; Gov. National Froebel Foundation, 1938-40. With British Broadcasting Corporation, 1940-45, and its North American Service Organiser, 1944-45. Contested (Lab) Peterborough, 1935; MP (Lab) Enfield Division of Middx, 1945-50, East Enfield, 1950-59. Parl. Private Sec. to Min of State, 1946-50; Parliamentary Under-Sec. of State, Foreign Office, 1950-51. Chm. Transport Group Parliamentary Labour Party, 1945-50 and 1951-59; Jt Chm. Parliamentary Roads Study Group, 1957-59. Mem. Select Cttee on Nationalised Industries, 1952-59, Chm. British Yugoslav Soc., 1957-; Mem., Exec. Cttee, European-Atlantic Gp, 1958-65 (Vice-Pres., 1966-). Mem. British Delegation to Gen. Assembly, UN, 1947, 1948-49 and 1950; Dep. Leader British Deleg. to UN Conf. on Freedom of Information, 1948; Mem. British Deleg. to London Conf. 1950; Leader UK Deleg., Economic Commn for Europe, Geneva, 1950; UK Representative at Foreign Ministers' Deputies' Four Power Talks, Paris, 1951. Vice-Chm., British Parking Assoc., 1969- (Mem. Council, 1968-); Hon. Mem., Instn of Highway Engineers; Associate: Institute of Transport; Institute of Traffic Admin; Director: Printerhall Ltd; Antique Finder Ltd. *Publications:* How Much Compensation, 1935; National Capitalism, 1939; The State and the Railways, 1940; American Labour, 1943; British Transport, 1945; National Enterprise, 1946; Problems of Public Ownership, 1952; (ed) Roads and Their Traffic, 1960; Transport in Greater London, 1962; (ed) Traffic Engineering Practice, 1963, new edn 1968. *Address:* 6f Observatory Gardens, Kensington, W8. *T:* 01-937 4769. *Club:* Wig and Pen.

**DAVIES, Dr Ernest Arthur,** JP; *b* 25 Oct. 1926; *s* of Daniel Davies and Ada (*née* Smith), Nuneaton; *m* 1956, Margaret Stephen Tait Gatt (marr. diss. 1967), *d* of H. Gatt, Gamesley, near Glossop; no *c*. *Educ:* Coventry Jun. Techn. Coll.; Westminster Trng Coll., London; St Salvator's Coll., University of St Andrews; St John's Coll., Cambridge. PhD Cantab 1959; AInstP 1959. RAF Aircraft Apprentice, 1942-43 (discharged on med. grounds). Westminster Trng Coll., 1946-48; Teacher, Foxford Sch., Coventry, 1948-50; University of St Andrews, 1950-54 (1st cl. hons Physics, Neil Arnott Prize, Carnegie Schol.); subseq. research in superconductivity, Royal Society Mond Lab., Cambridge; AEI Research Scientist, 1957-63; Lectr in Physics, Faculty of Technology, University of Manchester, 1963-66. MP (Lab) Stretford, 1966-70; Parliamentary Private Secretary to: PMG (Mr Edward Short), Nov.-Dec. 1967; Foreign Secretary (Mr George Brown), Jan.-Mar. 1968; Foreign and Commonwealth Sec. (Mr Michael Stewart), 1968-69; Jt Parly Sec., Min. of Technology, 1969-70. Co-Vice-Chm., Parly Labour Party's Defence and Services Group; Mem., Select Cttee on Science and Technology, 1966-67, 1967-68, 1968-69; Parly Deleg. to 24th Gen. Assembly of UN (UK Rep. on 4th Cttee). Councillor, Borough of Stretford, 1961-67; JP Lancs, 1962. *Publications:* contribs to Proc. Royal Society, Jl of Physics and Chem. of Solids. *Recreations:* reading, walking. *Address:* 29 Dudley Road, Whalley Range, Manchester 16. *T:* 061-865 2831. *Club:* Stretford Trades and Labour (Stretford).

**DAVIES, Rev. Ernest William;** Rector of Piddlehinton, 1957-64; Rural Dean of Bere Regis, 1961-64; retired; *b* 23 May 1901; *s* of late Ernest James Davies; *m* 1928, Winifred Lancashire, Hythe, Kent; two *s* two *d*. *Educ:* Dulwich Coll.; St John's Coll., Oxford (Open Classical Scholar); 1st Class Hon. Mods 1922, 2nd Class Lit. Hum., 1924, BA 1924, MA 1927, Oxford Univ. Diploma in Education, 1934. Ordained priest, 1955. Headmaster, King's Sch., Rochester, 1935-57. *Address:* Weyside Cottage, Upwey, Weymouth, Dorset. *T:* Upwey 2011.

**DAVIES, Evan Tom,** DSc, PhD London; Dottore in Matematica Rome; MSc Wales; Professor of Mathematics, University of Calgary, since 1969; *b* 24 Sept. 1904; *yr s* of Thomas and Elizabeth Davies, Pencader, Carmarthenshire; *m* 1st, 1941, Margaret Helen Picton (*d* 1944); no *c*; 2nd, 1955, Hilda Gladys Boyens; one *s*. *Educ:* Llandyssul County Sch.; University Coll., Aberystwyth; University Coll., Swansea; University of Rome; Sorbonne and Collège de France. Lecturer, King's Coll., London, 1930-46; Prof. of Mathematics, Univ. of Southampton (formerly University Coll., Southampton), 1946-69 (Emeritus, 1969); Dep. Vice-Chancellor, Southampton Univ., 1954-57. *Publications:* papers in mathematical journals. *Recreations:* caravanning, foreign travel. *Address:* Mathematics Department, University of Calgary, Calgary 44, Alberta, Canada; 2 Uplands Way, Southampton. *T:* Southampton 56836.

**DAVIES, Rev. Canon George Colliss Boardman,** DD; Proctor in Convocation, Diocese of Worcester, since 1964; Canon Residentiary of Worcester since 1963; *b* 7 Dec. 1912; *y s* of late Ven. George Middlecott Davies and Berta Mary, *d* of late Admiral F. R. Boardman, CB; *m* 1951, Edith Mavis, *d* of late J. D. Maitland-Kirwan; one *d*. *Educ:* Monkton Combe Sch.; St Catharine's Coll., Cambridge, 2nd cl. Historical Tripos pt 1, 1934; MA 1938; BD 1947; DD 1951; Curate of Woking, 1937-39; permission to officiate Diocese of Ely, 1939-40; Rector of St Clement with St Edmund and St George, Colegate, Norwich, 1940-42; Rector of North Tamerton, 1942-51; Rector of Kingham, 1951-56; Beresford Prof. of Ecclesiastical History, Trinity Coll. Dublin, 1956-63, and Professor of Pastoral Theology, 1960-63; Canon and Treasurer of St Patrick's Cathedral, Dublin, 1962-63. Mem. Gen. Synod of ch. of Ireland, 1961-63. Commissary to Bp of Kimberley and Kuruman, 1968-. Trinity Coll., Dublin, MA and DD (*ad eund*), 1959. *Publications:* The Early Cornish Evangelicals, 1951; Henry Phillpotts, Bishop of Exeter, 1954; Men for the Ministry: The History of the London College of Divinity, 1963. Contribs to The Church Quarterly Review, The Churchman. *Address:* The Old Precentory, College Yard, Worcester. *T:* Worcester 24874. *Club:* Royal Commonwealth Society.

**DAVIES, George Francis,** CMG 1962; Chairman and Managing Director Davies Brothers Ltd since 1954; *b* 26 Jan. 1911; *yr s* of late C. B. Davies, CBE, MIEA, and late Ruby A. Davies: *m* 1935, Margaret Ingles; one *s* three *d*. *Educ:* Clemes Coll., Hobart, Tasmania. Gen. Man., Davies Brothers Ltd, 1940; Chm. Dirs, Commercial Broadcasters Pty Ltd, 1950; Chm. and Man. Dir, Davies Brothers Ltd, 1954; Dir, Australian Newsprint Mills Ltd, 1954; Dir, Australian Elizabethan Theatre Trust, 1955; Chm. Dirs, Tasmanian Television Ltd, 1959; Dir, Tasmanian Containers Pty Ltd, 1959; Dir, National Heart Foundation of Australia, 1961. Trustee Tasmanian Museum and Art Gallery, 1955. *Recreations:* golf, fishing, racing. *Address:* 301 Sandy Bay Road, Hobart, Tasmania. *T:* 5.1141. *Clubs:* Tasmanian, Athenæum (Hobart); Launceston (Launceston).

**DAVIES, George Peter H.;** *see* Humphreys-Davies.

**DAVIES, Gwen F.;** *see* Ffrangcon-Davies.

**DAVIES, (Gwilym) E(dnyfed) Hudson;** *see* Davies, Ednyfed H.

**DAVIES, Gwilym Elfed;** MP (Lab) Rhondda East since Oct. 1959; *b* 9 Oct. 1913; *s* of David Davies and Miriam Elizabeth (*née* Williams); *m* 1940, Gwyneth Rees, *d* of Daniel and Agnes Janet Rees; two *s* one *d*. *Educ:* Tylorstown Boys' Sch. Branch Official Tylorstown Lodge, NUM, 1935-59. Member Glamorgan CC, 1954-61. Chairman Local Government Cttee, 1959-61. PPS to Minister of Labour, 1964-68, to Minister of Power, 1968. *Recreations:* Rugby football and cricket. *Address:* Maes-y-Ffrwd, Ferndale Road, Tylorstown, Rhondda, Glam. *T:* Ferndale 254.

**DAVIES, Gwilym Prys;** Chairman of Welsh Hospitals Board, since 1968; Member of Welsh Council, since 1968; Member of Welsh Advisory Committee, ITA, since 1966; *b* 8 Dec. 1923; *s* of William and Mary Matilda Davies; *m* 1951, Llinos Evans; three *d*. *Educ:* Towyn Sch., Towyn, Merioneth; University College of Wales, Aberystwyth. Served RN, 1942-46. Faculty of Law, UCW, Aberystwyth, 1946-52; President of Debates, Union UCW, 1949; President Students' Rep. Council, 1950; LLB 1949; LLM 1952. Admitted Solicitor, 1956; Partner, firm of Morgan Bruce & Nicholas, Solicitors of Cardiff, Pontypridd and Porth, 1957-. Contested (Lab) Carmarthen, 1966. Hon. Solicitor to various Welsh charitable and educational foundations. Member: Regional Studies Assoc.; Ct of Governors, UCW, Aberystwyth. OStJ. *Publications:* A Central Welsh Council, 1963; Y Ffermwr a'r Gyfraith, 1967. *Address:* Lluest, 78 Church Road, Tonteg, Pontypridd, Glam. *T:* Newtown Llantwit 462.

**DAVIES, Rev. Gwynne Henton;** Principal, Regent's Park College, Oxford, since 1958; *b* 19 Feb. 1906; *m* 1935, Annie Bronwen (*née* Williams); two *d*. *Educ:* Perse Sch., Cambridge; University College of South Wales, Cardiff; Oxford; Marburg/Lahn, Germany. Minister West End Baptist Church, London, W6, 1935-38; Tutor Bristol Baptist Coll., 1938-51; special Lecturer in Hebrew, University of Bristol, 1948-51; (First) Prof. of Old Testament Studies, Faculty of Theology, Durham Univ., 1951-58; Select Preacher to the Universities of Cambridge and Oxford. OT Editor, The Teachers' Commentary (revised 7th edn), 1955. Secretary, Society for Old Testament Study, 1946-62 (President, 1966); Vice-Pres., Baptist Union of GB and Ireland, 1970-71. Hon. DD: Glasgow, 1958; Stetson. *Publications:* (with A. B. Davies) The Story in Scripture, 1960; Exodus, 1967; Genesis, in The Broadman Bible Commentary, 1969; Who's Who in the Bible, 1970. *Address:* 55 St Giles, Oxford.

**DAVIES, Handel,** CB 1962; MSc; CEng; FRAeS; FAIAA; Technical Director, British Aircraft Corporation, since 1969; *b* 2 June 1912; *m* 1942, Mary Graham Harris. *Educ:* Aberdare Grammar Sch.; University of Wales. Royal Aircraft Establishment and Ministry of Aircraft Production, 1936-47; Head of Aerodynamics Flight Division, RAE, 1948-52. Chief Superintendent, Aeroplane and Armament Experimental Establishment, Boscombe Down, 1952-55; Scientific Adviser to Air Ministry, 1955-56; Dep. Director-General, then Director-General, Scientific Research (Air), Ministry of Supply, 1957-59; Dep. Director, RAE, Farnborough, 1959-63. Dep. Controller of Aircraft, (R&D), Ministry of Aviation, 1963-67, Ministry of Technology, 1967-69. Member of Council, RAeS, 1955-59, 1967. *Publications:* papers in Reports and Memoranda of Aeronautical Research Council and in Journal of Royal Aeronautical Society. *Recreation:* sailing. *Address:* British Aircraft Corporation Ltd, Weybridge, Surrey; Keel Cottage, Woodham Road, Horsell, Woking, Surrey. *T:* Woking 4192. *Clubs:* Royal Aero; Royal Air Force yacht (Hamble).

**DAVIES, Harold Haydn,** CB 1956; MC 1917; Chairman Welsh Board of Health, 1952-57; retired; *b* 27 Dec. 1897; *s* of late John Davies, Ammanford, and London; *m* 1926, Cecilia, *er d* of late Morgan Michael, Pontardulais, Glam.; one *s* one *d*. *Educ:* London; Pembroke Coll., Cambridge. Asst Secretary (Dep. Establishment Officer) Ministry of Housing and Local Govt, 1951; Ministry of Health, 1921-51. Gazetted to Royal Northumberland Fusiliers, 1917; served European War, 1914-18; BEF, France, 1917-18 (MC; prisoner of war, March 1918). Mem., NW Surrey Hospital Management Cttee; National Assessor for senior administrative appointments in the Hospitals Service. OStJ 1957. *Address:* Woodlands, Coombe Park, Kingston Hill, Surrey. *T:* 01-546 2030.

**DAVIES, Haydn;** *b* 8 May 1905; *o s* of late A. Davies, Abertysswg, Mon.; *m* 1936, Mary, *e d* of late J. Dodd, Ealing; one *d*. *Educ:* Lewis Sch., Pengam, Glam.; University College of Wales, Aberystwyth; London School of Economics. BA (Hons) Wales. LCC Schoolmaster, 1926; President, London Schoolmasters Assoc.; Education Correspondent News Chronicle; Industrial Correspondent, The Star, 1935, and again 1952; MP (Lab.) SW St Pancras, 1945-50; contested York, 1950. Member National Union of Journalists. Worked during War of 1939-45 in Ministry of Economic Warfare and Board of Trade. *Address:* 20 Wendover Way, Countess Wear, Exeter, Devon.

**DAVIES, Hector Leighton,** CBE 1941; JP, DL; *b* Sebastapol, near Griffithstown, Mon, 18 April 1894; *e s* of late Sir John Cecil Davies, CBE, of the Mount, Gowerton, and later Stelvio, Newport, Mon; *m* 1924, Miss Ballantyne Poulton le Fylde; one *s* one *d*. *Educ:* Malvern Coll.; Technical Education, Swansea and Germany. Chm., Swansea Pilotage Authority; Past President of Council of Iron and Steel Institute; Past Chairman: Swansea Employment Cttee; Welsh Bd of Industry; Industrial Estates Management Corporation of Wales; S Wales Regional Industrial Advisory Cttee of National Savings Movement; Industrial Welfare Society. JP 1927; DL Mon, 1956. *Address:* Cobwebs,

Penmaen, Gower, Glam. *Clubs:* Royal Automobile; Bristol Channel Yacht (Swansea).

**DAVIES, Maj.-Gen. Henry Lowrie,** CB 1945; CBE 1942 (OBE 1941); DSO 1934; MC; psc; *b* 25 Jan. 1898; *s* of Lieut-Colonel H. Davies, CMG; *m*; one *s* two *d*; *m* 1948, Margaret Jane Blomfield Plowden. *Educ:* Dover Coll.; RMC, Sandhurst. Joined 18th Royal Garhwal Rifles in India, 1916; served European War (Mesopotamia, Army of Black Sea); on NWF of India in Waziristan operations, 1922-23; in Mohmand operations NWF of India, 1933; passed Staff Coll., Quetta, 1928 and 1929; GSO3 Northern Command, 1931-32; Brigade Major Peshawar Brigade, 1933-35; GSO2 Military Dept, India Office, 1937; a Divisional Commander, Indian Army, 1942; served in Iceland (GSO1 Iceland Force), Burma (BGS Burma Army and Burcorps, 1942), Arakhan (Div. Comd), during War of 1939-45; Deputy CGS, GHQ, India; Comdt Staff Coll., Quetta; Deputy CGS, Pakistan Army, HQ; retired, 1948. Asst Director, Investigation Div., Ministry of Agriculture, Fisheries and Food, 1948-62; Historian, Cabinet Office (Historical Section), Nov. 1962-. *Recreations:* racing, golf. *Address:* 102 Latymer Court, W6. *T:* 01-748 5171. *Clubs:* Naval and Military; Royal Mid-Surrey Golf.

**DAVIES, Rt. Hon. Sir (Herbert) Edmund,** PC 1966; Kt 1958; **Rt. Hon. Lord Justice Edmund Davies;** a Lord Justice of Appeal, since 1966; Life Governor and Fellow, King's College, London University; Hon. Fellow, Exeter College, Oxford; Hon. LLD University of Wales; Chairman of the Court of Quarter Sessions for Denbighshire, 1953-64; Lieutenant-Colonel Royal Welch Fusiliers; *b* 15 July 1906; 3rd *s* of Morgan John Davies and Elizabeth Maud Edmunds; *m* 1935, Eurwen Williams-James; three *d*. *Educ:* Mountain Ash Grammar Sch.; King's Coll., London; Exeter Coll., Oxford. LLB (London) and Postgraduate Research Scholar, 1926; LLD London, 1928; BCL (Oxon) and Vinerian Scholar, 1929; called to Bar, Gray's Inn, 1929; Bencher, 1948; Treasurer, 1965, 1966; Lecturer and Examiner, Faculty of Laws, London Univ., 1930-31; Army Officers' Emergency Reserve, 1938; Infantry OCTU and thereafter commissioned in Royal Welch Fusiliers, 1940; later seconded to JAG's Dept; QC 1943; Recorder of Merthyr Tydfil, 1942-44; of Swansea, 1944-53; of Cardiff, 1953-58; Judge of High Court of Justice, Queen's Bench Division, 1958-66; Asst Judge Advocate-General, 1944-45; Chairman: Lord Chancellor's Cttee on Limitation of Actions, 1961; Tribunal of Inquiry into Aberfan Disaster, 1966; Council of Law Reporting; Member, Home Secretary's Criminal Law Revision Cttee (Chairman 1968-). President University College of Swansea, 1965-(Member Court of Governors, 1948-). Hon. Life Member, Canadian Bar Assoc. *Publications:* Law of Distress for Rent and Rates, 1931; miscellaneous legal writings. *Address:* Royal Courts of Justice, WC2. *Clubs:* Reform; Cardiff and County (Cardiff); City (Chester); Bristol Channel Yacht.

**DAVIES, Humphrey;** *see* Davies, Morgan Wynn Humphrey.

**DAVIES, Rev. Canon Hywel Islwyn,** BA; PhD; Rector of Collyweston, since 1969; *b* 14 Feb. 1909; *s* of Rev. H. J. Davies and Mary Davies, Loughor, Swansea; *m* 1st, 1940, Beti Lewis Beynon (decd); one *d*; 2nd, 1956, Glenys Williams. *Educ:* Gowerton Grammar Sch.; University of Wales; Gonville and Caius Coll., Cambridge; St Michael's Coll., Llandaff. BA 1st Class Philosophy, 1932 Pierce Scholar; PhD University of Cambridge; Lord Rhondda Scholar, 1936. Ordained, 1936; Curacy, Merthyr Tydfil; Lecturer, 1940, Tutor 1942, St David's Coll., Lampeter; Vicar, Llanstephan, Carms, and Tutor, Trinity Coll., Carmarthen, 1945; Director Adult Education, Diocese of St David's, 1946; Examining Chaplain Bishop of Monmouth; Vicar Llanbadarn Fawr and Lecturer, University College of Wales, Aberystwyth, 1947; Vicar of Llanelly and Canon of St David's Cathedral, 1950; Dean of Bangor, 1957-61; Head of Dept of Religion and Philosophy, Univ. of Ife, 1961-69, Prof. 1966-69, Mem. Univ. Council and Dean of Faculty of Arts, 1963-69. Examining Chaplain to Archbishop of Wales and to Bishop of Bangor, 1957. Public Preacher: Dio. Lagos, Ibadan, and N Nigeria; Examining Chaplain to Bishops of Ibadan and Northern Nigeria; Canon, St James's Cathedral, Ibadan, 1966, Canon Emeritus 1969. Governor, Immanuel Theolgical Coll., Ibadan. Examiner: Univ. of Ibadan; Univ. of Lagos. Mem. Adv. Panel, W African Sch. Certificate. *Publications:* various, in philosophical, theological, Welsh, English, and African journals. *Recreation:* Celtic Bygones. *Address:* The Rectory, Collyweston, Stamford, Lincs. *T:* Duddington 238.

**DAVIES, Ifor;** MP (Lab) Gower since Oct. 1959; *b* 9 June 1910; *s* of Jeffrey and Elizabeth Jane Davies; *m* 1950, Doreen Griffiths; one *s* one *d*. *Educ:* Gowerton; Swansea Technical; Ruskin Coll., Oxford. Oxford Diploma, Economics and Politics. Accountant, 1931-39; Personnel Officer, ICI, 1942-47; Ministry of Labour, Statistics Dept, 1947-48; Personnel Officer, Aluminium Wire and Cable Co. Ltd, 1948-59; Opposition Whip (Welsh), 1961-64; a Lord Commissioner of the Treasury and Govt Whip, 1964-66; Parly Under-Sec. of State, Welsh Office, 1966-69. Executive Member South Wales District, WEA, 1950-60; Secretary Gowerton Welsh Congregational Chapel, 1948; Hon. Secretary Gower Constituency Labour Party, 1948-59; Member Glamorgan County Council, 1958-61. *Recreations:* walking and listening to music. *Address:* Ty Pentwyn, Three Crosses, Swansea, Glam. *T:* Gowerton 2222.

**DAVIES, Iforwyn Glyndwr;** Formerly Senior Principal Medical Officer, Ministry of Health; QHP 1957-59; *b* 11 June 1901; *s* of Richard and Margaret Davies, Porth, South Wales; *m* 1930, Lillian May, *d* of Evan James, Cardiff, South Wales; one *s*. *Educ:* The County Sch., Porth; University College, Cardiff; St Bartholomew's Hospital, London. MRCS, LRCP, 1923; MB, BS London, 1924; MD London, 1944; MRCP, 1926; FRCP, 1954. Formerly: Tuberculosis Physician, City of Nottingham, 1933; Deputy MOH, City and County of Bristol, 1937; Lecturer in Public Health, University of Bristol, 1937; Dep. Director, Preventive Medicine Laboratories; Prof., of Public Health, University of Leeds, 1947, also Medical Officer of Health and School Medical Officer, City of Leeds. *Publications:* Text-Book: Modern Public Health for Medical Students, 1955 (2nd edition, 1963); contrib. to Lancet, Medical Officer, Public Health. *Recreation:* music. *Address:* Amberley, Well Meadows, Shaw, Newbury, Berks. *T:* Newbury 2055.

**DAVIES, Very Rev. Ivor Gordon;** Dean of Lewisham, since 1970; Residentiary Canon of Southwark Cathedral and Diocesan Missioner since 1957; Proctor in Convocation, since 1965; *b* 21 July 1917; *m* 1946, Kristine Wiley, SRN; one *s* two *d*. *Educ:* University of Wales (BA); Oxford; London (BD). Deacon 1941,

Priest 1942, Llandaff; Curate of St Paul's, Cardiff, 1941-44; CF 1944-47; Curate of St John the Baptist, Felixtowe, 1947-49; Vicar of St Thomas', Ipswich, 1950-57. *Address:* 97 Kingsmead Road, Tulse Hill, SW2. *T:* 01-674 6091.

**DAVIES, Jack Gale Wilmot,** OBE 1946; Executive Director of the Bank of England, since 1969; *b* 10 Sept. 1911; *s* of Langford George Davies, MD, BCh, MRCS, LRCP, and Lily Barnes Davies; *m* 1949, Georgette O'Dell (*née* Vanson); one *s*. *Educ:* Tonbridge Sch.; St John's Coll., Cambridge. Nat. Institute of Industrial Psychol., 1935-39. Regimental service, The Middlesex Regt, 1940-42; Chief Psychologist, Directorate for Selection of Personnel, War Office, 1942-46. Bureau of Personnel, UN Secretariat, 1946-48; Secretariat, Human Factors Panel, Cttee on Industrial Productivity, 1948-49; Staff Training Section, UN Secretariat, 1950-52; Secretary, Cambridge Univ. Appointments Board, 1952-68; Asst to the Governor, Bank of England, 1968. FBPsS 1946. Fellow St John's Coll., Cambridge, 1959-68. *Publications:* articles in Occupational Psychology and similar journals. *Recreations:* cricket, golf, music. *Address:* 31 Wingate Way, Cambridge. *Clubs:* Royal Automobile, MCC.

**DAVIES, Dame Jean;** *see* Lancaster, Dame J.

**DAVIES, John;** *see* Davies, L. J.

**DAVIES, Rt. Hon. John (Emerson Harding),** PC 1970; MBE 1946; MP (C) Knutsford since 1970; Secretary of State for Trade and Industry and President of the Board of Trade, since Oct. 1970; *b* 8 Jan. 1916; *s* of Arnold Thomas Davies, FCA, and Edith Minnie (*née* Harding); *m* 1943, Vera Georgina Bates; one *s* one *d*. *Educ:* St Edward's Sch., Oxford. Enlisted RASC, 1939; Commissioned 2nd Lieut, RASC, 1940; G2 (Tech.) Combined Ops Experimental Establishment (COXE), 1945-46. Joined Anglo-Iranian Oil Co., 1946; served in Stockholm, London and Paris, 1946-55; General Manager, Markets, 1956-60; Director BP Trading, 1960; Vice-Chairman and Managing Director, Shell Mex and BP, 1961-65; Director-General, CBI, 1965-69. Director: Hill Samuel Group, 1969-70; Black and Decker, 1970. Minister of Technology, July-Oct. 1970. Member: NEDC, 1964-69; Nat. Joint Advisory Council, Dept of Employment and Productivity (formerly Min. of Labour), 1965-69; British Productivity Council, 1965-69; British National Export Council, 1966-69; Council of Industrial Design, 1966-; Public Schools Commission, 1966-68. Member Council, University of Sussex; Governor: St Edward's Sch., Oxford; Windlesham House School Trust. DUniv Essex, 1967. FCA 1961 (ACA 1939); FRSA 1964; JDipMA 1965. *Recreations:* travel and music. *Address:* 114 Rivermead Court, SW6. *T:* 01-736 4817. *Clubs:* Oriental, Hurlingham.

**DAVIES, Rev. John Gordon,** MA, DD; Edward Cadbury Professor of Theology and Head of Department of Theology, University of Birmingham, since Oct. 1960; Director of Institute for Study of Worship and Religious Architecture, University of Birmingham, since 1962; *b* 20 April 1919; *s* of late A. G. Davies and of Mrs Davies, Chester; *m* 1945, Emily Mary Tordoff; one *s* two *d*. *Educ:* King's Sch., Chester; Christ Church, Oxford; Westcott House, Cambridge. Curate of Rotherhithe, Dec. 1942-Sept. 1948; Univ. of Birmingham: Asst Lecturer in Theology, 1948-50; Lecturer, 1950-57; Senior Lecturer, 1957-59; Reader, 1959-60; Dean of Faculty of Arts, 1967-70. ba oxon., 1942; MA 1945; BD 1946; DD 1956; MA (Official) Birmingham, 1952; Hon. DD St Andrews, 1968. Hereditary Freeman, City of Chester; Brother of Ancient and Worshipful Company of Skinners and Felt Makers. Bampton Lecturer, 1958. Hon. Canon, Birmingham, 1965. Hon. Mem., Guild for Religious Architecture, USA. Conover Memorial Award, New York, 1967. *Publications:* The Theology of William Blake, 1948 (USA 1966); The Origin and Development of Early Christian Church Architecture, 1952 (USA 1953); Daily Life in the Early Church: Studies in the Church Social History of the First Five Centuries, 1952 (reprinted 1955); Daily Life of Early Christians, 1953; Social Life of Early Christians, 1954; The Spirit, the Church, and the Sacraments, 1954; La Vie quotidienne des premiers chrétiens, 1956; Members One of Another; Aspects of Koinonia, 1958; He Ascended into Heaven: A Study in the History of Doctrine (Bampton Lectures, 1958), 1958; Der Heilige Geist, die Kirche und die Sakramente, 1958; The Making of the Church, 1960; Intercommunion, 1961; The Architectural Setting of Baptism, 1962; Holy Week, A Short History, 1963; The Early Christian Church, 1965; A Select Liturgical Lexicon, 1965; La Chiesa delle Origini, 1966; Worship and Mission, 1966; As Origens do Cristianismo, 1967; Dialgo con el Mundo, 1967; The Secular Use of Church Buildings, 1968; Liturgiskt Handlexikon, 1968; co-author: An Experimental Liturgy, 1958; translator: Essays on the Lord's Supper, 1958; The Eucharistic Memorial Vol. I, 1960, Vol. II, 1961; Mission in a Dynamic Society, 1968. Contributor to: Becoming a Christian, 1954; The Teachers' Commentary, 1955; The Concise Encyclopædia of Living Faiths, 1959; Making the Building Serve the Liturgy, 1962; The Modern Architectural Setting of the Liturgy, 1964; A Manual for Holy Week, 1967; Journal of Theological Studies; Journal of Hellenic Studies; Vigilae Christianae; Harvard Theological Review; Encyclopædia Britannica, etc. *Recreation:* sailing. *Address:* 28 George Road, Edgbaston, Birmingham 15. *T:* 021-454 6254.

**DAVIES, John Howard Gay;** Deputy Editorial Director, Thomson Regional Newspapers Ltd; *b* 17 Jan. 1923; *er s* of late E. E. Davies, Nicholaston Hall, Gower, Glamorgan; *m* 1st, 1948, Eira Morgan (marr. dissolved, 1953); 2nd, 1955, Betty Walmsley; one *s*. *Educ:* Bromsgrove Sch.; Wadham Coll., Oxford. Welsh Guards, 1942-46 (despatches). Daily Telegraph, 1952-55; Deputy Editor, Western Mail, 1955-58; an Assistant Editor, Sunday Times, 1958-62; Exec. Assistant to Editorial Director, Thomson Newspapers Ltd, 1962-64; Editor, Western Mail, 1964, 1965. *Address:* 14 Woodborough Road, SW15. *T:* 01-788 4563.

**DAVIES, John L.;** *see* Langdon-Davies.

**DAVIES, J(ohn) R(obert) Lloyd,** CMG 1953; Assistant Secretary, Department of Employment and Productivity; *b* 24 March 1913; *o s* of J. R. Davies and late Mrs Davies, Muswell Hill; *m* 1943, Margery, *o d* of Mrs McClelland and late Major McClelland, Nottingham; one *s* one *d*. *Educ:* Highgate Sch.; Oriel Coll., Oxford. Joined staff of Ministry of Labour, 1936; Private Secretary to Sir Thomas Phillips, 1940. Served War of 1939-45: Royal Navy; Lieut RNVR; service in Far East; Dep. Labour Attaché, HM Embassy, Washington, 1945-47; Asst Secretary, Ministry of Labour, London, Oct. 1947; Labour Attaché, HM Embassy, Paris, 1956-60. *Recreations:* music, geology and reading. *Address:* 35 Grange Gardens, Pinner, Middlesex. *T:* 01-866 9526. *Club:* Oxford and Cambridge.

**DAVIES, Prof. John Tasman,** PhD, DSc London; MA, ScD Cantab; Professor of Chemical Engineering and Head of Department, University of Birmingham, since 1960; *b* 1 May 1924; *m* 1948, Ruth Batt; two *s*. *Educ:* Boys' High Sch., Christchurch, NZ; Canterbury University Coll.; London Univ. MA Cantab. 1955; PhD London 1949; DSc London 1955. Worked with Sir Eric Rideal, FRS, Royal Institution London, 1946-48; Research Associate and Bristol-Myers Fellow, Stanford Univ., Calif. (USA) (worked with late Prof. J. W. McBain, FRS), 1948-49; Beit Mem. Fellow for Medical Research, Royal Instn and KCL, 1949-52; Lectr in: Chemistry, KCL, 1952-55; Chemical Engineering, Cambridge Univ., 1955-60. Overseas guest lecturer at Gordon Conference on Surface Activity, USA, 1956. Visiting Prof., University of Minnesota, 1963. Member: UN Consultative Commn to Indian Inst. of Petroleum, 1967-70; UNESCO Advisory Group on Petroleum Technology, Arab States, 1967; (part-time) West Midlands Gas Board, 1968-. Member Sigma-Xi, 1949 (USA), MIChemE. *Publications:* (with Sir Eric Rideal, FRS) Interfacial Phenomena, 1961; The Scientific Approach, 1965; many on Surface Phenomena and Chemical Engineering. *Address:* Department of Chemical Engineering, The University, Birmingham 15. *T:* 021-472 1301.

**DAVIES, Rev. (John) Trevor,** MA, BD Edinburgh, PhD London; Minister, Richmond Hill Congregational Church, Bournemouth, since 1951; Chairman, Congregational Union of England and Wales, 1960-61; *b* Mountain Ash, 2 May 1907; *s* of Thomas Davies, Neath, Glam.; *m* 1933, Alice Hitchen, Lancs; one *s*. *Educ:* County Sch., Neath; Yorkshire United Coll., Bradford; Edinburgh and London Universities. Formerly Minister of Congregational Churches: Heaton, Newcastle on Tyne; Clarendon Road, Watford; Cliff Town, Southend-on-Sea. Lecturer in: Philosophy of Religion, New Coll., London, 1948-51; Psychology, King's Coll., London, 1950-51. Preaching tours in USA, 1954, 1958, 1964, and Canada, 1962. *Publications:* Sublimation, 1945; Lord of All, 1951; Corner Pieces, 1953; Richmond Hill Story, 1956; Is Anyone There?, 1960. Has written weekly column, in Christian World, since 1949. *Recreations:* golf, motoring. *Address:* The Manse, Richmond Hill Congregational Church, Bournemouth, Hants. *T:* Bournemouth 20161. *Club:* Royal Over-Seas League.

**DAVIES, Col Joseph Marie,** QC 1962; Recorder of Birmingham, since 1970; Chairman, Cumberland County Quarter Sessions, since 1963 (Deputy Chairman, 1956-63); *b* 13 Jan. 1916; *s* of Joseph and Mary Davies, St Helen's; *m* 1948, Eileen Mary (*née* Dromgoole); two *s* two *d*. *Educ:* Stonyhurst Coll.; Liverpool Univ. Called to Bar, Gray's Inn, Nov. 1938; practice in Liverpool. Served War of 1939-45; The King's Regt, Nov. 1939-Dec. 1941; RIASC and Staff Allied Land Forces, SE Asia, Dec. 1941-April 1946. Returned to practice in Liverpool until May 1962; now practice in London. *Address:* 4 Elm Grove, Eccleston Park, Prescot, Lancs. *T:* 051-426 5415. *Club:* Athenæum (Liverpool).

**DAVIES, Kenneth;** *see* Davies, S. K.

**DAVIES, Kenneth Arthur,** CMG 1952; OBE 1946; Commonwealth Geological Liaison Officer, 1954; *b* 28 Jan. 1897; *s* of William and Alice Davies; *m* 1932, Edna Myfanwy, *d* of Rev. T. Rowlands; one *s*. *Educ:* Pontypridd Grammar Sch.; University Coll., Wales, Aberystwyth; Trinity Coll., Cambridge. Served European War, 1914-18, with RFA in France and Belgium, 1916-19; 1st Class Hons Geology BSc, University Coll., Aberystwyth. Research Scholar, 1923-26; Fellow of University of Wales, 1926; MSc 1925; PhD (Cantab.), 1928. Field Geologist, Govt of Uganda, 1929; Senior Geologist, 1936; Director, Geological Survey, 1939, retired 1951. Adviser on Mineral Development to Uganda Govt, 1952-54. Dep.-Dir Overseas Geological Surveys, 1957-65. Adviser to United Nations, 1966. Fellow, Geological Society, 1928; Member of Institution of Mining and Metallurgy, 1950. Murchison Medallist, Geological Society, 1954. *Publications:* various on Stratigraphy of Central Wales and graptolites in British Geological journals, and on African Geology in British and American journals. *Recreations:* tennis, gardening. *Address:* Park Cottage, Somerset Road, SW19.

**DAVIES, Lewis,** OBE 1948; Chairman of Staffordshire County Council, 1949-58, retired; *b* 1 July 1886; *m* 1904, Bertha Griffiths; one *s* one *d* (also one adopted *s*). *Educ:* Brownhills Council Sch. Methodist: Sunday Teacher, 1904, Lay Preacher, 1908; all offices in Methodist Church, open to Laymen, to present time. CC 1925, CA, 1938; County Magistrate, 1934-. Chairman, County Magistrates, Lichfield and Brownhills Division, 1951-. Member CC Assoc., 1946-58; Chairman of a number of School Governing Bodies, member Labour Party, 1919-. Vice-President, North Staffs Univ. *Recreations:* bowls; formerly tennis, cricket, football. *Address:* Griffith House, Chasetown, near Walsall, Staffs. *T:* Brownhills 3121.

**DAVIES, (Lewis) John,** QC 1967; *b* 15 April 1921; *s* of William Davies, JP, and Esther Davies; *m* 1956, Janet Mary Morris; one *s* two *d*. *Educ:* Pontardawe Grammar Sch.; University College of Wales, Aberystwyth; Trinity Hall (Common Law Prizeman, 1943; Scholar, 1943-44), Cambridge. 1st class hons: LLB Wales, 1942; BA, Cantab, Cantab llb cantab, 1944. Asst Principal, HM Treasury, 1945-46; Senior Law Lecturer, Leeds Univ., 1946-48; Administrative Asst, British Petroleum, 1949-52. Called to the Bar, 1948; Mem., Bar Council, 1969-. *Recreations:* gardening, golf. *Address:* Old Manor Cottage, 24 Park Road, Teddington, Middx. *T:* 01-977 3975.

**DAVIES, Lewis Mervyn,** CMG 1966; OBE 1962; Chief Secretary, Western Pacific High Commission, since 1965; *b* 5 Dec. 1922; *s* of late Rev. Canon L. C. Davies; *m* 1950, Ione Podger; one *s*. *Educ:* St Edward's Sch., Oxford. Served with Fleet Air Arm, 1941-46: Lieut A, RNVR. District Commissioner, Gold Coast, 1948; Western Pacific: Senior Asst Secretary, 1956-62; Financial Secretary, 1962-65. Lay Canon, Cathedral Church of St Barnabas, Honiara, 1965. Commandeur de l'Ordre National du Mérite, 1966. *Recreations:* sailing, tennis. *Address:* c/o National Westminster Bank Ltd, 28 High Street, Nantwich, Cheshire.

**DAVIES, Lloyd;** *see* Davies, J. R. L.

**DAVIES, Col Lucy Myfanwy,** CBE 1968 (OBE 1962); Deputy Controller Commandant, WRAC, since 1967; *b* 8 April 1913; *d* of late Col A. M. O. Anwyl-Passingham, CBE, DL, JP, and late Margaret Anwyl-Passingham; *m* 1955, Major D. W. Davies, TD, RAMC (*d* 1959); no *c*. *Educ:* Francis Holland Graham Street Sch. Driver FANY, 1939; commnd ATS, 1941; served in Egypt, 1945-48; Asst Director, WRAC Middle East (Cyprus), 1957-59; Comdt WRAC Depot, 1961-64; Dep. Director

WRAC, 1964-68; retired, 1968. OStJ 1938. *Recreations:* travel, racing, reading. *Address:* 6 Elm Place, SW7. *T:* 01-373 5731. *Clubs:* Curzon House, Hamilton, United Hunts; Sandown Park, Lingfield Park.

**DAVIES, Marcus John A.**; *see* Anwyl-Davies.

**DAVIES, Martin,** CBE 1965; FBA 1966; FSA; FMA; Director of the National Gallery, since 1968; *b* 22 March 1908; *s* of Ernest Davies and Elizabeth Eleanor Taylor. *Educ:* Rugby; King's Coll., Cambridge. Became Assistant Keeper of the National Gallery, 1932; Deputy Keeper, 1947; Keeper, 1960. Hon. DLitt Exon, 1968. *Address:* 16 Rupert House, Nevern Square, SW5. *Club:* Reform.

**DAVIES, Meredith;** *see* Davies, Albert Meredith.

**DAVIES, Michael;** *see* Davies A. W. M.

**DAVIES, Michael John,** CMG 1961; OBE 1957; Secretary, Imperial College of Science and Technology, and Clerk to the Governing Body, since 1962; *b* 7 Oct. 1918; *y s* of late David Alexander Davies; *m* 1949, Elizabeth Eve Burridge; two *s* one *d*. *Educ:* Diocesan Coll., Cape Town; University of Cape Town; Trinity Coll., Oxford. (MA) as a Rhodes Scholar. Joined Colonial Service (now HM Overseas Civil Service) in Tanganyika, as an Administrative Officer, 1940. Private Secretary to the Governor, 1943-47; seconded to the Colonial Office, 1947-49. Assistant Special Representative for Tanganyika at Trusteeship Council of United Nations, 1958 and 1959; Minister: for Constitutional Affairs in Tanganyika, 1959; for Security and Immigration, 1959-60; for Information Services, 1960-61 (until date of Self Government in Tanganyika, May 1st). Acting Chief Secretary May-Aug., 1960; retired from HM Overseas Civil Service, 1962. Médaille de la Belgique Reconnaissante (for services to Belgian Refugees), 1961. *Recreations:* watching Rugby football (Welsh International, 1938 and 1939); playing golf; gardening. *Address:* Lanrick, Cross-in-Hand, Sussex. *T:* Heathfield 3499.

**DAVIES, Miles;** *see* Davies, A. E. M.

**DAVIES, Prof. (Morgan Wynn) Humphrey,** MScEng, FIEE; Professor of Electrical Engineering, Queen Mary College, University of London, since 1956; *b* 26 Dec. 1911; *s* of late Richard Humphrey Davies, CB; *m* 1944, Gwendolen Enid, *d* of late Canon Douglas Edward Morton, Camborne, Cornwall; one *s*. *Educ:* Hill Crest, Swanage; Westminster Sch.; University College of N. Wales, Bangor; Charlottenburg Technische Hochschule, Berlin. Grad. Apprentice with Metropolitan-Vickers, 1933; Lecturer in Electrical Engineering, University of Wales, 1935-42; Commonwealth Fellow, Mass. Institute of Technology, 1938-39; University Lecturer in Electrical Engineering, College of Technology, Manchester, 1943; Education Officer to Instn of Electrical Engineers, 1944-47; Lecturer, 1947, and University Reader, 1952, in Electrical Engineering, Imperial Coll., University of London, 1947-56. Member: Council, IEE, 1948-51, 1958-61 (Chm., Science and Gen. Div. 1964-65). Council, City & Guilds of London Inst., 1952-; Engineering Adv. Cttee, BBC, 1965-; Computer Bd for Univs and Res. Councils, 1968-. *Publications:* Power System Analysis (with J. R. Mortlock), 1952. Papers in Proc. of Instn of Electrical Engineers. *Recreation:* travel. *Address:* Wych Cross, Keston, Kent. *T:* Farnborough (Kent) 53212. *Club:* Athenæum.

**DAVIES, Nigel;** *see* Davies, Claude N. B.

**DAVIES, Oswald Vaughan L.;** *see* Lloyd-Davies.

**DAVIES, P(eter) Maxwell;** freelance composer; conductor; *b* 8 Sept. 1934. *Educ:* Leigh Grammar Sch.; Manchester Univ.; Royal Manchester Coll. of Music. MusB (Hons), 1956. Studied with Goffredo Petrassi in Rome (schol. 1957); Harkness Fellow, Grad. Music Sch., Princetown Univ., NJ, 1962. Dir of Music, Cirencester Grammar Sch., 1959-62; Lecture tours in Europe, Australia and New Zealand, 1965; Visiting Composer, Adelaide Univ., 1966; Co-Dir, with Harrison Birtwistle, of Pierrot Players, 1967-; has conducted many concerts with this ensemble in Britain and abroad. Series for Schools Broadcasts, BBC Television. *Publications:* Trumpet Sonata, 1955; Five Pieces for Piano, 1956; St Michael Sonata, for 17 Wind Instruments, 1957; Alma Redemptoris Mater for 6 Wind Instruments, 1957; Five Motets for Sorprano, Contralto, Tenor and Bass soli, double Choir and Instruments, 1959; Prolation for Orchestra, 1959; Ricercar and Doubles on 'To Many a Well', 1959; O Magnum Mysterium, 1960 (Instrumental parts); Four Carols from O Magnum Mysterium for unaccopanied chorus, 1960; Fantasia on O Magnum Mysterium for organ, 1960; Te Lucis Ante Terminum, 1961; String Quartet, 1961; First Fantasia on an In Nomine of John Taverner, 1962 (commissioned by BBC); Leopardi Fragments, 1962; Sinfonia, 1962; The Lord's Prayer for SATB choir, 1962; Four Carols, 1962; Five Little Pieces for Piano Solo, 1962-64; Veni Sancte Spiritus for Soprano, Contralto and Bass soli, mixed Chorus and small Orchestra, 1963; Second Fantasia on John Taverner's In Nomine for Orchestra, 1964; Shakespeare Music for Chamber Ensemble, 1964; Ecce Manus Tradentis for mixed Chorus and Instruments, 1965; Seven in Nomine for Instruments, 1963-65; The Shepherd's Calender for Young Singers and Instrumentalists, 1965; Revelation and Fall for Soprano solo and Instruments, 1965; Antechrist for Chamber Ensemble, 1967; L'Homme Armé for Chamber Ensemble, 1968; Shall I Die For Mannis Sake?, Carol for Soprano and Alto Voices and Piano, 1966; Five Carols for Soprano and Alto Voices, unacompanied, 1966; Hymnos for Clarinet and Piano, 1967; Fantasia and Two Pavans (Purcell, real. Davies), 1968-69; Eight Songs for a Mad King, 1969; St Thomas Wake–Foxtrot for Orchestra (commnd by City of Dortmund), 1969; Worldes Bliss, 1969; Eram Quasi Agnus, 1969; Cauda Pavonis, 1969; Solita for flute solo, 1969. *Address:* c/o Boosey & Hawkes, PO Box 1BR, W1.

**DAVIES, Reginald,** CMG 1950; *b* 17 Nov. 1887; *y s* of late Rev. Owen Davies; *m* 1928, Gwenllyan Kathleen Butler Dew; one *s* one *d*. *Educ:* Hymers Coll., Hull; St Catharine's Coll., Cambridge (Scholar). BA (Hons Maths), 1909; rowed for Cambridge, 1910. Entered Sudan Political Service, 1911; Resident, Dar Masalit, 1920; Director of Intelligence, 1927; Asst Civil Secretary, 1929; Dep. Financial Secretary, 1930; Secretary for Economic Development, 1931; Chairman of the Board of Economics and Trade and Member of Governor-General's Council, 1934; retired 1935. Order of the Nile, 3rd Class, 1932. Dep. Director-General, Alexandria Municipality, 1935-39; Director Publicity Section of HM Embassy, Cairo, 1939-42. Finance Officer, The British Council, 1942-47. Asst Director-General, The British Council, 1947; retired 1953. *Publications:* The Camel's Back: Service in the Rural Sudan, 1957; various contributions to Sudan Notes and Records. *Recreation:* foreign travel.

*Address:* 2 Stratton Audley Manor, near Bicester, Oxfordshire. *Club:* Leander.

**DAVIES, Rhys,** OBE 1968; novelist and short story writer; *b* 9 Nov. 1903; *s* of Thomas R. and Sarah A. Davies. *Educ:* Porth Co. Sch. *Publications:* The Withered Root, 1927; A Pig in a Poke, 1931; Count Your Blessings, 1932; The Red Hills, 1932; Love Provoked, 1933; Honey and Bread, 1935; The Things Men Do, 1936; A Time to Laugh, 1937; My Wales, 1937; Jubilee Blues, 1938; Under the Rose, 1940; Tomorrow to Fresh Woods, 1941; A Finger in Every Pie, 1942; The Story of Wales, 1943; The Black Venus, 1944; The Trip to London, 1946; The Dark Daughters, 1947; Boy With a Trumpet, 1949; Marianne, 1951; The Painted King, 1954; No Escape (play), 1954; Collected Stories, 1955; The Perishable Quality, 1957; The Darling of Her Heart, 1958; Girl Waiting in the Shade, 1960; The Chosen One, 1967; Print of a Hare's Foot, 1969. Contributions to numerous British and American periodicals. *Recreations:* theatre; living in London; cultivating ruined characters. *Address:* c/o Curtis Brown Ltd, 13 King Street, Covent Garden, WC2.

**DAVIES, Rt. Rev. Robert Edward;** *see* Tasmania, Bishop of.

**DAVIES, Prof. Robert Ernest,** FRS 1966; University of Pennsylvania: Benjamin Franklin Professor of Molecular Biology, since 1970 (Professor of Biochemistry, School of Medicine, 1955); Chairman, Department of Animal Biology, School of Veterinary Medicine, since 1962; Chairman, Graduate Group Committee on Molecular Biology, since 1962; Professor of Biochemistry, Graduate School of Medicine, since 1962; *b* 17 Aug. 1919; *s* of William Owen Davies and Stella Davies; *m* 1961, Helen C. (*née* Rogoff); two *step s. Educ:* Manchester Grammar Sch.; University of Manchester and University of Sheffield. BSc(Chem.) Manchester, 1941; MSc Manchester 1942; PhD Sheffield 1949; DSc Manchester 1952; MA Oxon 1956. Temp. Asst Lecturer in Chemistry, University of Sheffield. Half-time research (Ministry of Supply, Chemical Defence Research Dept), 1942; Full-time research on temp. staff, Medical Research Unit for Research in Cell Metabolism, 1945. Apptd to Estab. Staff of Medical Research Council, 1947; Hon. Lecturer in Biochemistry, University of Sheffield, 1948-54. Visiting Prof., Pharmakologisches Inst., University Heidelberg, March-May 1954. *Publications:* very many: in chemistry, biochemistry, physiolog. and biology journals concerning secretion, muscle contraction, kidneys, etc. *Recreations:* mountaineering, caving, underwater swimming. *Address:* Department of Animal Biology, School of Veterinary Medicine, University of Pennsylvania, Pa 19104, USA. *T:* (office) 594-7861; 7053 McCallum Street, Philadelphia, Pa 19119, USA. *Clubs:* Fell and Rock-climbing Club of the English Lake District; Cave Diving Group; Manchester Univ. Mountaineering.

**DAVIES, Roy Dicker Salter,** CBE 1967; a Chief Inspector of Schools, Department of Education and Science, 1958-68, retired; *b* 24 March 1906; *yr s* of Ernest Salter Davies, CBE, and Evelyn May Lile. *Educ:* Tonbridge Sch.; Magdalen Coll., Oxford (MA). Served RE, 1939-40, RA, 1940-45. Appointed HM Inspector of Schools, 1934; Staff Inspector, 1951. Mem., Departmental Cttee on Adult Educn, 1969-. *Recreations:* watching Rugby football; cricket. *Address:* Wick House, Stogumber, Taunton, Somerset. *T:* Stogumber 422.

**DAVIES, Rev. Rupert Eric;** Principal, Wesley College, Bristol, since 1967; designated President of the Methodist Conference, 1970-71; *b* 29 Nov. 1909; *s* of Walter Pierce and Elizabeth Miriam Davies; *m* 1937, Margaret Price Holt; two *s* two *d. Educ:* St Paul's Sch.; Balliol Coll. (Class. Scholar), Oxford; Wesley House, Cambridge; Univ. of Tübingen, Germany. First cl. in Honour Mods, Classics, 1930; second cl. in Lit. Hum., 1932; first cl. in Theology, Pt II, 1934 (Wesley House); trav. schol. in Germany, 1934-35; BD (Cantab) 1946. Chaplain, Kingswood Sch., Bath, 1935-47; Methodist Minister, Bristol, 1947-52; Tutor, Didsbury Coll., Bristol, 1952-67. Select Preacher to Univs of: Cambridge, 1962; Oxford, 1969; Mem. Exec. Cttee, World Methodist Council, 1956-; Mem., Anglican-Methodist Unity Commn, 1965-68; World Council of Churches: Faith and Order Commn, 1965-; Deleg. to Fourth Assembly, 1968. *Publications:* The Problem of Authority in the Continental Reformers, 1946; Catholicity of Protestantism (ed), 1950; Approach to Christian Education (ed), 1956; John Scott Lidgett (ed), 1957; The Church in Bristol, 1960; Methodists and Unity, 1962; Methodism, 1963; History of the Methodist Church in Great Britain (ed), vol. I, 1965; We Believe in God (ed), 1968; Religious Authority in an Age of Doubt, 1968. *Recreations:* golf, theatre. *Address:* Ridgewood, 11 Northover Road, Westbury-on-Trym, Bristol BS9 3LN. *T:* Bristol 626580.

**DAVIES, (Stanley) Kenneth,** CBE 1951; Chairman, Excelsior Ropes Ltd, Cardiff; *b* 25 April 1899; 2nd *s* of late Sir John Davies, CBE, JP; *m* 1938, Stephanie Morton; one *s* one *d. Educ:* Christ Coll., Brecon; Blundell's; Royal Military Academy, Woolwich. Founder Member, Cardiff Aeroplane Club, 1929. Private pilot's licence, 1931-61. Formed Cambrian Air Services Ltd, 1936, Managing Director, 1936-51. Member Cttee Royal Aero Club of United Kingdom, 1935 (Vice-Chm., 1948-51, Chm. 1952-58, Vice-Pres., 1958-); Member Board British European Airways Corporation, 1951-67; Dep. Chairman BEA Helicopters Ltd, 1965-67; Chairman Welsh Advisory Council for Civil Aviation, 1948-60; Chairman Cardiff Airport Consultative Cttee, 1956-63; Member Welsh Cttee of Arts Council of Great Britain, 1954-67; Member Consultative Cttee, Sadler's Wells Trust, 1962-; Chairman of Contemporary Art Society of Wales, 1966-; Liveryman of the Guild of Air Pilots and Air Navigators; Vice-President, FAI (Federation Aeronautique Internationale), rep. UK; Member Cttee, Dublin Theatre Festival, 1967; Life Member: Iron & Steel Institute; S Wales Inst. of Engineers; Royal Agricultural Society; Royal Dublin Society. FRSA; MInstT. *Recreations:* aviation and gastronomy (Member Cttee of Management of Internat. Wine and Food Society). *Address:* Killoughter, Ashford, Co. Wicklow. *T:* Wicklow 4126; Collingdon Road, Cardiff. *T:* 21693. *Clubs:* Buck's, Turf, Royal Aero; County (Cardiff); Kildare Street (Dublin).

**DAVIES, Stephen Owen;** MP (Ind Lab) Merthyr Tydfil since 1970 (MP (Lab), 1934-70, for same constituency); lately chief Organiser to South Wales Miners' Federation; *b* Nov. 1886; *s* of late Thomas and late Esther Owen Davies; *m* 1934, Seph Davies, Gwauncaegurwen; two *s* three *d. Educ:* University College, Cardiff; Royal College of Science. Coalminer at 12 years of age; matriculated from coalface; graduated in Arts and returned to colliery as collier; check-weigher, 1913. Was trained as a Mining Engineer. Miners' Agent under S Wales Miners' Federation at Dowlais, 1918-34;

Vice-President SWMF, 1924-33; represented Welsh Miners on MFGB 1924-34; Member Court of Governors of National Library of Wales, National Museum of Wales, University of Wales; presented evidence before several Government inquiries, etc. *Recreations:* walking, swimming. *Address:* Gwynfryn, Merthyr Tydfil, Glam. *T:* Merthyr 3410.

**DAVIES, Stuart Duncan,** CBE 1968; FRAeS, BSc; Technical Director, Dowty Rotol Ltd; *b* 5 Dec. 1906; *s* of William Lewis Davies and Alice Dryden Duncan; *m* 1935, Ethel Rosalie Ann Radcliffe; one *d. Educ:* Westminster City Sch.; London Univ. (BSc Eng.). Vickers (Aviation) Ltd, 1925-31; Hawker Aircraft Ltd, 1931-36; A. V. Roe and Co. Ltd, 1938-55, Chief Designer, 1945-55; with Dowty Group Ltd, 1955-58, as Managing Director of Dowty Fuel System Ltd; Technical Director, Hawker Siddeley Aviation Ltd, 1958-64. British Gold Medal for Aeronautics, 1958. *Address:* 16 Wilthyholt Court, Moorend Road, Cheltenham, Glos. *T:* Cheltenham 29216. *Club:* Royal Aero.

**DAVIES, Thomas A.;** *see* Anwyl-Davies.

**DAVIES, Rev. Trevor;** *see* Davies, Rev. John Trevor.

**DAVIES, Trevor Arthur L.;** *see* Lloyd Davies.

**DAVIES, Wilfred Horace;** Director: Cable & Wireless Ltd, 1968; East African External Telecommunications Ltd, 1968; Nigeria External Telecommunications Ltd, 1968; Sierra Leone External Telecommunications Ltd, 1969; *b* 7 March 1917; *s* of late Gerald Edward Davies and Editha Lucy (*née* Sweet-Escott); *m* 1st, Helen Rose Gillam; one *s* one *d*; 2nd, Eva Nancy Berry; two *s. Educ:* Aldenham Sch. Cable & Wireless Ltd, 1935: Asst Staff Manager, 1957; Dep. Staff Manager, 1961; Staff Manager, 1962; Dir, 1968. MBIM. *Recreations:* golf, gardening. *Address:* (office) Mercury House, Theobolds Road, WC1. *T:* 01-242 4433; (home) Hartrow, Kingsdale Road, Berkhamsted, Herts. *T:* Berkhamsted 4346. *Clubs:* Royal Commonwealth Society, Exiles.

**DAVIES, Rt. Hon. Sir (William) Arthian,** PC 1961; Kt 1952; DL; **Rt. Hon. Lord Justice Davies;** a Lord Justice of Appeal since 1961; Chairman of Buckinghamshire Quarter Sessions, since 1961; *b* 10 May 1901; *s* of late Arthian Davies; *m* 1933, Mary Bailey, *d* of late Henry Liptrot; one *d. Educ:* Dulwich; Trinity Coll., Oxford (MA). Barrister, 1925; QC 1947; sometime Exr and Asst Reader to Council of Legal Education and Gresham Lecturer in Law; Junior Counsel to Ministry of Labour and National Service, 1934-47; Recorder of Merthyr Tydfil, 1946-49, Chester, 1949-52. JP (Bucks), 1948; DL 1967; Dep. Chairman Quarter Sessions: Co. Cardigan, 1949-52, Bucks, 1951-61. Bencher, Inner Temple, 1952; Judge of High Court of Justice, Probate, Divorce, and Admiralty Division, 1952-59; Judge of High Court of Justice, Queen's Bench Div., 1959-61. Dep. Chairman Parliamentary Boundary Commn for Wales, 1958-61; Chairman Home Office Cttee on Matrimonial Proceedings in Magistrates' Courts, 1958. Hon. Fellow, Trinity Coll., Oxford, 1969. *Address:* Royal Courts of Justice, WC2; Ballinger Lodge, Great Missenden, Bucks. *Club:* Oriental.

**DAVIES, William John,** CMG 1943; OBE 1929; *b* Carmarthen, 21 Feb. 1891; *s* of William and Sarah Davies; *m* 1921, Miriam Ellen Brown, Usk, Mon.; no *c. Educ:* Queen Elizabeth Grammar Sch., Carmarthen; University, Aberystwyth (BA 1912). Entered Japan Consular Service, 1913; Asst Japanese Secretary and Second Secretary to HM Embassy, Tokyo, 1918-34; Consul, Tokyo, 1934-37; Acting Counsellor of Embassy, 1936; Consul in Foreign Office, 1938; Consul-General at Harbin, 1939-41; Consul-General at Kobe, 1941; Foreign Office, 1943-45; Japanese Language Supervisor, BBC, 1946-50; external examiner in Japanese, University of London, 1948-51. *Recreations:* motoring, gardening. *Address:* Tudor Cottage, 9 Westmeston Avenue, Rottingdean, Sussex. *T:* Brighton 32013.

**DAVIES, William Rupert R.;** *see* Rees-Davies.

**DAVIES, William Tudor,** CBE 1963 (OBE 1960); FREconS; FBIM; JP; Barrister at Law and Economist; Independent Chairman and Adviser of Trade Associations; Adviser on indutrial legislation and conciliation and international cartels; *b* Nantyglo, Mon.; *o s* of John Pritchard Davies; *m* 1937, Iva Mary, *yr d* of Philip Kyle, OBE. *Educ:* University of Wales, Aberystwyth; University of Bristol; University of Manchester. BA 1st Class Honours; 1st Class Diplomas in Theory and Practice of Education; Founder Member and Fellow, British Institute of Management; Research Medallist, University of Bristol; Post-Graduate Research, University of Manchester; Post-Graduate Reserach, University of Cambridge; Lecturer in Economics; Editorial staff Manchester Guardian; Parliamentary candidate, 1922 and 1923; Editorial staff Financial News; Chairman of Joint Cttee of Building and Civil Engineering Industries set up under Control of Employment Act, 1939; Independent Chairman of Joint Industrial Council of Distributive Trades; Chairman of Wages Councils; Chairman, Reinstatement in Civil Employment Tribunals; Member: Further Education and Training Tribunal; London Conscientious Objectors' Tribunal, 1940-60; Chairman of National Insurance Tribunals; Independent Chairman of the National Conciliation Board for the Co-operative Service; Chairman of Boards of Inquiry under Ministry of Labour; Independent Chairman Local Appeal Boards; Independent Chairman Joint Cttee of North Wales Coal Industry; Chairman, Road Transport Inquiries under Road Traffic Acts, 1961, and Compulsory Purchase orders; Hearing Appeals from Licensing Authorities and Public Inquiries, Ministry of Transport; Member Isle of Man Traffic Tribunal; Commissioner of Inquiry in Nigeria for Secretary of State for the Colonies; Barrister and Solicitor of Supreme Court, Federation of Nigeria, etc. *Publications:* National Essay Prize on The Creation of an International Police Force (Welsh National Eisteddfod, Caernarvon, 1921); The Rationalisation of Industry, 1928; The Economic Task, 1931; The Economics of Plenty, 1934; Trade Associations and Industrial Co-ordination, 1938-39; Personnel Management and Essential Work Orders, 1944; National Insurance, Law of Tribunals, 1950. *Recreations:* golf, walking. *Address:* 2 Harcourt Buildings, Temple, EC4. *T:* 01-353 7202; Sunhaven, Links Avenue, Gidea Park, Essex. *T:* Romford 41026. *Club:* National Liberal.

**DAVIES, William Watkin,** MA, Barrister-at-law; retired as Lecturer in International Politics, Birmingham University; *b* 1895; *o s* of Rev. J. Gwynoro Davies, and Jane Mary, *d* of William Watkin, JP, Criccieth; *m* 1925, Cecily Dorothea, MB, BS, *e d* of Lieut-Col Cecil Crosskey, DL. *Educ:* Barmouth; Aberystwyth Coll.; St John's Coll., Oxford (Casberd Exhibitioner). Honour School of Modern

History; Barrister-at-law, Gray's Inn, North Wales Circuit. History Master, Friends Sch., Saffron Walden, 1915-17; Barmouth County Sch., 1917-19; Lecturer in History and Economics for WEA, 1919-21; Lecturer in History, Bristol Univ., 1919-21; Lecturer for League of Nations Union; lectured at the International Summer School, Salzburg, 1921; Examiner in History for the Central Welsh Board, 1917-22; for the Northern Universities, 1922; Internal Examiner at Bristol Univ., 1921-22; Extension Lecturer for London Univ., 1925-27; member of various learned societies. *Publications:* Gladstone and the Unification of Italy; How to Read History (Japanese translation); Chapters in Outline of Literature and Art; Wales; A World Outlook; A Wayfarer in Wales; Lloyd George, 1863-1914; Articles in numerous journals; Editor of Welsh Outlook, 1925-27. *Recreations:* walking, foreign travel, music. *Address:* 77 Wentworth Road, Harborne, Birmingham 17.

**DAVIES, Wyndham Matabele,** QC 1946; BA, LLB; Stipendiary Magistrate of Pontypridd, 1949-66; Chairman Glamorgan QS, 1961-66 (Dep. Chairman, 1950-61); *s* of David John and Jane Davies; *m* 1936, Enid Maud, *d* of James Jenkins, JP, and Catherine Jenkins; one *s.* Called to Bar, Lincoln's Inn, 1922. European War, 1914-18, served in France, Belgium, mainly with 1st S. Wales Borderers, 1915-19; War of 1939-45, Royal Corps of Signals, 1939-40. Special Divorce Commissioner, 1946-49. *Recreations:* fishing, golf. *Address:* The Long House, Lisvane, Glamorgan. *T:* Cardiff 756654. *Club:* Cardiff and County (Cardiff).

**DAVIES, Dr Wyndham Roy;** Director, Medical Economic Research Institute, since 1968; *b* 3 June 1926; *s* of late George Edward Davies, LLB, Llangadock, Carms, and of Ellen Theresa (*née* Merris), Treaford Hall, Birmingham. *Educ:* King Edward's, Birmingham; Birmingham and London Universities. LRCP 1948; MB, ChB, 1949; DPH 1958; DIH 1959. House Surgeon, General Hospital, Birmingham, 1949; Receiving Room Officer, Children's Hospital, Birmingham, 1949; Resident Medical Officer, Little Bromwich Hospital, Birmingham, 1950. Entered RN, 1950; HMS Surprise, 1950-51; HMS St Angelo, 1951-53; Squadron Medical Officer, 4th Destoyer Sqdn, Home Fleet, 1953-54; Research Assistant, St George's Hospital Medical Sch. (MRC), 1955; Admiralty Medical Board and HMS Dauntless (WRNS), 1956-57; stood by building of HMS Albion, HMS Malcolm, 1957; HMS Glory, 1957; London School of Hygiene and Tropical Medicine, 1958; RN Medical Sch., 1958-59; habitability trials, HMS Centaur and HMS Bulwark, 1959-60; Joint Services Amphib. Warfare Centre, 1960-63; qual. shallow water diver, 1960; Chemical Defence Exper. Establishment, 1963; retired as Surgeon Lieut-Comdr, 1963. Adopted Prospective Parliamentary Candidate for Birmingham Perry Barr Div., 1963; MP (C) Perry Barr Div. of Birmingham, 1964-66. Joint Secretary, Party Education and Sc. Cttee, 1965-66; Vice-President, Birmingham Cons. and Unionist Assoc., 1965-. Hon. Medical Adviser, British Sub-Aqua Club, 1959-66; Hon. Medical Adviser, British Safety Council, 1962-64; Governor, Royal Humane Society, 1962-; Chairman Organizing Cttee, World Congress of Underwater Activities, 1962; Cttee, Poole and Dorset Adventure Centre, 1961-64; Island Comdr for Sea Scouts, Malta, 1951-53; ADC, Boy Scouts, City of Westminster, 1957-62; Founder Member Old Edwardians BP Guild, 1948-; Hon. Secretary, Houses of Parliament BP Guild, 1964-66. Medical Officer British Schools Exploring Society Exped. to Labrador, 1958; Medical Commn on Accident Prevention, 1963-; Founder, Society for Underwater Technology; BMA Rep. for Birmingham, 1968-; Exec. Council, Monday Club, 1965-69; Chairman: Health Cttee, 1965-69; University Liaison Cttee, 1967-68. *Publications:* Expired Air Resuscitation, 1959; Skin Diving, 1959; Collectivism or Individualism in Medicine, 1965; Reforming the National Health Service, 1967; The Pharmaceutical Industry, A Personal Study, 1967; articles in The Practitioner and Physiological Journal. *Recreations:* all sports on, in or under water, travel, exploring, painting. *Address:* 20 Spur Hill Avenue, Poole, Dorset. *T:* Parkstone 4642. *Clubs:* Carlton; British Schools Exploring.

**DAVIES-COOKE, Col Philip Ralph,** CB 1958; TD 1937; DL; JP; *b* 27 Nov. 1896; *s* of Major P. T. Davies-Cooke, OBE, DL, JP; *m* 1924, Kathleen Mabel Cooke (OBE 1964); two *s* one *d.* *Educ:* Eton; Royal Military Coll., Sandhurst. Served European War, 1915-18, with 1st The Royal Dragoons, also Ireland, 1920-23; with 5 RWF, 1924-29; QO Yorks Dragoons, 1930-45; and served War of 1939-45. Hon. Col 4 RWF, 1950-61; Chairman Denbigh/Flint T&AFA), 1950-61; Rep. Chairman for Wales on Council T&AFA, 1955-61. Chairman N. Wales Regional Advisory Cttee (Forestry), 1952-61. JP 1925, Vice-Lieutenant of County of Flintshire, 1957; DL 1947, High Sheriff, Flintshire, 1949; Chairman Petty Sessions Div. Magistrates, 1952-. Landowner: N Wales and Yorks. *Publication:* Flintshire Shrievalty, 1949. *Recreations:* hunting, shooting. *Address:* Gwysaney, Mold, N Wales. *T:* Mold 34; Owston Hall, Doncaster, Yorks. *Clubs:* Cavalry, International Sportsmen's.

**d'AVIGDOR-GOLDSMID, Major Sir Henry Joseph,** 2nd Bt, *cr* 1934; DSO 1945; MC 1945; TD; DL, JP; MP (C) Walsall South since 1955; Bullion Broker; Major RAC TA, late Royal West Kent Regiment; *b* 10 June 1909; *s* of Sir Osmond Elim d'Avigdor-Goldsmid, 1st Baronet; *S* father, 1940; *m* 1940, Rosemary Margaret Horlick, *d* of C. R. I. Nicholl; one *d* (and one *d* decd). *Educ:* Harrow; Balliol Coll., Oxford, MA, 1938. Served War of 1939-45 (despatches twice, MC, DSO). Alderman of Kent CC, 1951 (CC 1946); DL, JP Kent, 1949; High Sheriff of Kent, 1953. Parliamentary Private Secretary to Minister of Housing and Local Government, 1955-56. Chairman, Anglo-Israel Bank Ltd, 1961-. *Heir:* *b* Maj.-Gen. James Arthur d'Avigdor-Goldsmid, *qv.* *Address:* Somerhill, Tonbridge, Kent. *Clubs:* White's, Carlton.

**d'AVIGDOR-GOLDSMID, Maj.-Gen. James Arthur,** CB 1965; OBE 1955; MC 1944; MP (C) Lichfield and Tamworth since 1970; *b* 19 Dec. 1912; *s* of Sir Osmond d'Avigdor-Goldsmid, 1st Bt, and Alice Lady d'Avigdor-Goldsmid; *heir-pres* to brother (Maj. Sir Henry Joseph d'Avigdor-Goldsmid, 2nd Bt, *qv*); unmarried. *Educ:* Harrow; RMC, Sandhurst. 2nd Lieut 4th/7th Royal Dragoon Guards, 1932. Served War of 1939-45, France and Germany (wounded). Commanded: 4th/7th Royal Dragoon Guards, 1950-53; 20th Armoured Brigade Group, 1958-61; Director, Royal Armoured Corps, War Office, subseq. Ministry of Defence, 1962-65; President, Regular Commissions Board, Feb.-Sept. 1965 Director TA and Cadets, 1966-68. Col of 4th/7th Royal Dragoon Guards, 1963. Chm., Kent TA&VRA; Vice-Chm., SE TA&VRA. *Address:* 101 Mount Street, W1. *T:* 01-499 1989. *Clubs:* Cavalry, Turf, Jockey.

**DAVIS, Alfred George Fletcher H.;** *see* Hall-Davis.

**DAVIS, Anthony Ronald William James;** Editor of Building (formerly The Builder), since 1970; *b* 26 July 1931; *e s* of Donald William Davis, Barnes and Mary Josephine Davis (*née* Nolan-Byrne), Templeogue Mill, Co. Dublin; *m* 1960, Volande Mary June, *o d* of Patrick Leonard, retd civil engr; two *d*. *Educ:* Hamlet of Ratcliffe and Oratory; Regent Street Polytechnic. Joint Services School for Linguists on Russian course as National Serviceman (Army), 1953-55; Architectural Asst, Housing Dept, Mddx County Architect's Dept, 1956-58; Sub-Editor, The Builder, 1959; Editor, Official Architecture and Planning, 1964; Mem. Board of Architecture and Planning Publications Ltd, 1966. *Publications:* contribs to various, architectural and technical. *Recreations:* collecting porcelain, music and dreaming. *Address:* 8 Blake Close, Dowles Green, Wokingham, Berks. *T:* West Forest 5046. *Clubs:* Savage, Architectural Association.

**DAVIS, Anthony Tilton,** MA; Head Master, Reading School, since 1966; *b* 14 Aug. 1931; *o s* of J. W. Davis; unmarried. *Educ:* St Bartholomew's Grammar Sch., Newbury; Reading Univ.; St John's Coll., Cambridge (Scholar). 1st class hons Class. Tripos Part I, 1954; 1st class hons (with distinction in Ancient History) Class. Tripos Part II, 1955. Sub-Lieut, RNVR, 1955-57. Asst Master and Classical Sixth Form Master, Harrow Sch., 1957-66 (Head of Latin, 1964-66). *Publications:* Sallust, Catiline, 1967; articles and reviews in Greece and Rome and Didaskalos. *Recreations:* cricket (Captain, Berks CCC, 1960-70); music, antiques, water colours, ski-ing. *Address:* The Head Master's Lodge, Reading School, Reading, Berks. *T:* Reading 81886.

**DAVIS, Archibald William;** *b* 20 May 1900; *s* of late G. W. Davis, Crayford, Kent; *m* 1930, Eunice, *d* of late W. Pidd, Westwood, Coventry; one *s*. *Educ:* Bablake Sch., Coventry; University College, London; Balliol Coll., Oxford; Emmanuel Coll., Cambridge. Entered HM Levant Consular Service, 1922; served at Consular posts in Persia, Turkey, Syria and Iraq; Political Officer, Aleppo (N Syria), 1941-42, with rank of Lt-Col; HM Consul-General, Basra, Iraq, 1946-49; Seville, Spain, 1950-53; retired 1953. *Address:* Rowanduz, Mendip Edge, Bleadon Hill, Weston-super-Mare, Somerset. *T:* Bleadon 830.

**DAVIS, Bette;** Actress; *b* Lowell, Mass. *Educ:* Cushing Academy, Ashburnham. Mass. Stage experience in Wild Duck, Broken Dishes, Solid South; entered films, 1930. Pictures she has appeared in: Dangerous (Academy Award of 1935 won 1936); The Petrified Forest, The Golden Arrow, 1936; Marked Woman, Kid Galahad, It's Love I'm After, That Certain Woman, 1937; Jezebel (Academy Award of 1938 won 1939); The Sisters, 1938; Dark Victory, Juarez, The Old Maid, Private Lives of Elizabeth and Essex, 1939; All This and Heaven Too, 1940; The Letter, The Great Lie, The Bride came COD, The Man who came to Dinner, The Little Foxes, 1941; In This our Life, Watch on the Rhine, Old Acquaintance, 1942; Mr Skeffington; The Corn is Green; A Stolen Life; Deception; Winter Meeting; June Bride; The Story of a Divorce; All about Eve; Another Man's Poison; The Star; The Virgin Queen; Wedding Breakfast; The Scapegoat, Pocketful of Miracles; Whatever Happened to Baby Jane?; Dead Image; Where Love Has Gone; Hush . . . Hush, Sweet Charlotte; The Nanny; The Anniversary. *Publication:* The Lonely Life, 1963. *Recreations:* swimming and horseback riding. *Address:* Westport, Conn, USA.

**DAVIS, Sir Charles (Sigmund),** Kt 1965; CB 1960; Legal Adviser and Solicitor to Ministry of Agriculture, Fisheries and Food, and Forestry Commission, since 1957; *b* London, 22 Jan. 1909; *y s* of late Maurice Davis (*b* Melbourne, Australia) and Alfreda Regina Davis; *m* 1940, Pamela Mary, *er d* of late J. K. B. Dawson, OBE, and Phyllis Dawson; two *d*. *Educ:* Trinity Coll., Cambridge. Double 1st Cl. Hons, Law Tripos; Sen. Schol., Exhibitioner and Prizeman of Trinity, 1927-30; MA 1934. Called to the Bar, Inner Temple (Studentship and Certif. of Honour), 1930, and in Sydney Australia, 1931; practised as barrister in London, 1931-34; entered Legal Branch, Ministry of Health, 1934; held legal posts in various public offices, 1938-46 (Corporal, Home Guard, 1940-45); Asst Solicitor, Min. of Agric. and Fisheries, 1946-55; Prin. Asst Solicitor, Min. of Agriculture, Fisheries and Food, 1955-57. *Recreations:* music (LRAM, ARCM) and much else. *Address:* c/o Ministry of Agriculture, Fisheries and Food, Whitehall Place, SW1. *T:* 01-839 7711. *Club:* Farmers'.

**DAVIS, Clinton;** *see* Davis, S. C.

**DAVIS, Colin (Rex),** CBE 1965; Chief Conductor, BBC Symphony Orchestra, since Sept. 1967; Musical Director designate, Royal Opera House, Covent Garden (from Sept. 1971); *b* 25 Sept. 1927; *s* of Reginald George and Lillian Davis; *m* 1949, April Cantelo (marr. diss., 1964); one *s* one *d*; *m* 1964, Ashraf Naini; two *s*. *Educ:* Christ's Hospital; Royal College of Music. Orchestral Conductor, Freelance wilderness, 1949-57; Asst Conductor, BBC Scottish Orchestra, 1957-59. Conductor, Sadler's Wells, 1959; Principal Conductor, 1960-65; Musical Director, 1961-65. Artistic Director, Bath Festival, 1969. Conducted at Metropolitan Opera House, New York, 1969. *Recreations:* anything at all. *Address:* c/o Pears-Phipps Management, 8 Halliford Street, N1.

**DAVIS, Brig. Cyril Elliott,** CBE 1941; *b* 15 March 1892; *y s* of late O. J. H. Davis, Ford Park, Plymouth, Devon; *m* 1st, 1918, Fay (*d* 1957), *y d* of Leathes Prior, Eaton, Norwich; two *s*; 2nd, 1958, Helen, *widow* of Rev. T. V. Garnier, OBE. *Educ:* Alton Sch.; Plymouth Coll. Regular Commission in ASC, 1912, from 3rd DCLI (SR); served European War, 1914-18, France, Belgium, Greek Macedonia, Serbia, Bulgaria, European Turkey, Egypt, Palestine (1914 Star and Clasp, BWM and Victory Medal); Palestine Campaign, 1937 (Palestine Gen. Service Medal); Lieut-Col 1939 and posted to Singapore. Temp. Col 1940; Col 1941; Dep. Dir of Supplies and Transport, Malaya Command (acting Brig.), 1941; transferred to S Western Pacific Command, Java, Jan. 1942; Ceylon, March 1942; retired April 1946. A General Comr of Income Tax, 1958-. King George V Jubilee Medal, 1935; Comdr Order of Leopold II (Belgium), 1951. *Address:* Outer Finches, Buckfast, Devon. *T:* 3231.

**DAVIS, David;** *see* Davis, William Eric.

**DAVIS, Edward David Darelan,** FRCS, LDS, RCS; retired as Consultant Surgeon and Lecturer, Nose, Throat, and Ear Department, Charing Cross Hospital; Surgeon EMS; Consultant Surgeon: Military Hospital, Millbank; Royal Dental Hospital; Metropolitan Ear, Nose, & Throat Hospital; Curator Ferens Institute, Middlesex Hospital; *b* 11 Aug. 1880; *s* of late Wm Davis; *m* 1911,

Alice Mildred, *d* of H. C. Russell, JP; two *s* one *d*. *Educ:* Queen's Coll., Taunton; University Coll., Cardiff; Charing Cross Hospital. Graduated at Charing Cross Hospital, 1903, and held posts of House Physician, House Surgeon, Demonstrator of Anatomy and Clinical Asst to Nose, Throat, and Ear Dept; Senior Clinical Asst Throat Hospital, Golden Sq.; Clinical Asst to Surgical Out-patients and Ear Dept, Children's Hospital, Gt Ormond Street; Clinical Asst and Surgeon Laryngologist, Mt Vernon Hospital for Consumption; Mem. of the Council of the Otological Section (Pres.) and Laryngological Section (Pres.) of the Royal Society of Medicine; Semon Lecturer, 1947. Consulting Surgeon (nose, throat, and ear), Military Hospitals of London District; Surgeon Maxillo-Facial Red Cross Hospital and Officers' Hospitals; Surgeon 22 CCS, BEF. Late Treas. Medical Defence Union; FRSocMed, etc. *Publications:* various papers to Medical Journals and Transactions of Medical Societies. *Recreations:* golf, ski-ing, billiards. *Address:* 17 Priory Court, Granville Road, Eastbourne, Sussex. *T:* Eastbourne 29435. *Clubs:* Athenæum; Devonshire (Eastbourne).

**DAVIS, (Ernest) Howard,** CMG 1969; OBE 1960; Financial and Development Secretary, Gibraltar, since 1965; *b* 22 April 1918; *m* 1948, Marie Davis (*née* Bellotti); two *s*. *Educ:* Christian Brothers Schs, Gibraltar and Blackpool; London Univ. (BA 1st cl. hons). Gen. Clerical Staff, Gibraltar, 1936-46; Asst Sec. and Clerk of Councils, 1946-54; seconded Colonial Office, 1954-55; Chief Asst Sec., Estabt Officer and Public Relations Officer, Gibraltar, 1955-62; Director of Labour and Social Security, 1962-65. *Recreations:* cricket, gardening. *Address:* 6 Mount Road, Gibraltar. *T:* A.4503.

**DAVIS, Francis John,** CMG 1970; OBE 1966; Chairman of Commission, Commonwealth Service Laboratories, since 1967; *b* 13 April 1900; *s* of Albert Henry Davis and Caroline Billing; *m* 1933, Thelma Doris Cox. *Educ:* State Schools, Victoria. Member of Parliament of Australia for Deakin, Vic, Dec. 1949-Nov. 1966 (Liberal). *Recreations:* travelling, walking, reading. *Address:* 5a/12 Marine Parade, St Kilda, Victoria 3182, Australia. *T:* 94-6164.

**DAVIS, Sir Gilbert,** 2nd Bt, *cr* 1946; Director: Atlas Stone Co. Ltd, SW1, since 1922; Eastwoods Ltd, 1953-62; one of HM's Lieutenants, City of London, 1946-69; *b* 2 Aug. 1901; *er s* of Sir Charles Davis, 1st Bt, and Lady (Elsie) Davis (*née* Keeble) (*d* 1967), Barrington Hall, Cambridge; *S* father, 1950; *m* 1927, Kathleen Ford (marriage dissolved, 1944); one *s* one *d*. *Educ:* Clifton Coll.; Cambridge Univ. Freeman, Grocers' Company, 1922, Liveryman, 1926; Mem. of Common Council, City of London (Broad Street Ward), 1946-69; Chm. City of London Police Cttee, 1952 and Labour Cttee, 1953-56. Dep. Governor of the Hon. The Irish Soc., 1960. Was until 1958 Mem. Council London Chamber of Commerce; Mem. of Lloyds, 1934-. Vice-Pres., Inst. of Quarrying (Chm., London Branch, 1960-63); Chm. Admiralty Ferry Crew Assoc., 1960-63. Served War of 1939-45; Royal Navy. MIChemE, 1924-67. *Recreation:* sailing. *Heir:* *s* John Gilbert Davis [*b* 17 Aug. 1936; *m* 1960, Elizabeth, *d* of Robert Smith Turnbull, Falkirk; two *d*. *Educ:* Oundle; Royal Naval Coll., Dartmouth]. *Address:* 7 Marina Court, Deal, Kent. *Clubs:* East India and Sports, Royal Automobile.

**DAVIS, Harold Sydney,** FRCP; Consultant Physician: Royal Free Hospital, London, since 1954; King Edward VII Hospital, Windsor, since 1945; Hampstead General Hospital since 1946; Florence Nightingale Hospital, London, since 1947; Hon. Physician to the Queen, T & AVR, 1967-68; *b* 6 Aug. 1908; *s* of Harold Adamson Davis and Edith May Davis, Jamaica, WI; *m* 1940, Molly, *d* of Herbert Percy Stimson, London; one *d*. *Educ:* Jamaica Coll., WI; Dulwich Coll., London; Gonville and Caius Coll., Cambridge; Charing Cross Hosp., London (Exhibr). BA 1930, MB, BChir 1935, MA 1936, Cantab.; LRCP, MRCS 1933; MRCP 1936; FRCP 1954. Held usual resident appts in various London hosps, 1933-39. Commissioned into RAMC, March 1939 (Lieut); seconded as Physician, Ashridge Hosp. (EMS), 1940. OC 308 (Co. London) Gen. Hosp. RAMC/AER, 1964 (Col). Examr in Medicine, London Univ.; Lectr in Medicine, Royal Free Hosp. Sch. of Medicine, London Univ., 1962; Mem. Bd of Govs, Royal Free Hosp., 1963. Pres., Eagle Ski Club, 1960-63. *Publications:* contrib. learned jls. *Recreation:* ski-mountaineering. *Address:* Fingest Hill Cottage, near Henley-on-Thames, Oxon. *T:* Turville Heath 275; 90a Harley Street, W1. *T:* 01-935 8033. *Clubs:* Bath, Ski Club of Gt Britain (Vice-Pres. 1964), Kandahar Ski.

**DAVIS, Sir Herbert,** Kt 1943; CBE 1941; Vice-Chairman Unilever Ltd until 1956; *b* 12 March 1891; *m* 1912, Eva FitzGerald Radford; one *d* (and one *d* decd). *Educ:* St John's Coll., Cambridge. *Recreation:* golf. *Address:* East Court, Effingham, Surrey. *T:* Bookham 111.

**DAVIS, Howard;** *see* Davis, E. H.

**DAVIS, J. C. A.;** *see* Ainsworth-Davis.

**DAVIS, Air Chief Marshal Sir John (Gilbert),** GCB 1968 (KCB 1964; CB 1953); OBE 1945; psc 1946; idc 1955; RAF, retired; Lieutenant-Governor and Commander-in-Chief of Jersey since 1969; *b* 24 March 1911; *e s* of late John Davis, Whitby, Yorks; *m* 1937, Doreen, *d* of Arthur Heaton, Hinckley, Leics; one *s* one *d*. *Educ:* Whitby Grammar Sch.; Queens' Coll., Cambridge, MA 1937. First Commnd RAF, 1934; SASO, Bomber Command HQ, 1958-59; Air Officer Commanding No. 1 Group, Bomber Command, 1959-61; Air Officer Commanding Malta, and Dep. Comdr-in-Chief (Air), Allied Forces Mediterranean, 1961-63; Air Mem. for Supply and Organisation, 1963-66; Air Officer Commanding-in-Chief: Flying Trng Comd, 1966-68; Trng Comd, 1968-69. Air ADC to the Queen, 1967-69. MBOU. KStJ 1969. *Recreations:* ornithology, fishing, tennis and golf. *Address:* Government House, Jersey, Channel Islands. *Clubs:* United Service; Royal Air Force; Union Society (Cambridge).

**DAVIS, John Henry Harris;** Chairman and Chief Executive since Oct. 1962, The Rank Organisation Ltd, Subsidiary and Associated Cos; Chairman: Southern Television Ltd, since 1968; The Children's Film Foundation Ltd; Director: Eagle Star Insurance Co. Ltd; Xerox Corporation (USA); *b* 10 Nov. 1906; *s* of Sydney Myering Davis and Emily Harris; *m* 1st, 1926, Joan Buckingham; one *s*; 2nd, 1947, Marion Gaved; two *d*; 3rd, 1954, Dinah Sheridan (marr. diss. 1965). *Educ:* City of London Sch. British Thomson-Houston Group, 1931-38. Joined Odeon Theatres (predecessor of The Rank Organisation); Chief Accountant, Jan. 1938; Sec., June 1938; Jt Managing Dir, 1942; Man. Dir, 1948-62 and Dep. Chm., 1951-62, The Rank Organisation Ltd. Governor: Central Sch. of Speech and Drama; British Film Inst. FCIS 1939; KStJ. *Recreations:* farming, gardening, reading, travel, music. *Address:* Crowhurst Place, Lingfield, Surrey. *Club:* Royal Automobile.

**DAVIS, Leslie Harold Newsom,** CMG 1957; Director, Guthrie Estates Ltd; *b* 6 April 1909; *s* of Harold Newsom Davis and Aileen Newsom Davis (*née* Gush); *m* 1950, Judith Anne, *d* of L. G. Corney, CMG; one *s* two *d. Educ:* Marlborough; Trinity Coll., Cambridge. Apptd to Malayan Civil Service, 1932; Private Sec. to Governor and High Comr, 1938-40; attached to 22nd Ind. Inf. Bde as Liaison Officer, Dec. 1941; interned by Japanese in Singapore, 1942-45; District Officer, Seremban, 1946-47; British Resident, Brunei, 1948; Asst Adviser, Muar, 1948-50; Sec. to Mem. for Education, Fed. of Malaya, 1951-52. Mem. for Industrial and Social Relations, 1952-53; Sec. for Defence and Internal Security, Singapore, 1953-55; Permanent Sec., Min. of Communications and Works, Singapore, 1955-57; Special Rep., Rubber Growers' Assoc. in Malaya, 1958-63. *Recreation:* golf. *Address:* Berrywood, Heyshott, near Midhurst, Sussex. *Club:* Oxford and Cambridge.

**DAVIS, Leslie John,** MD Ed.; FRCP London, Edinburgh and Glasgow; Professor Emeritus, University of Glasgow, 1961; Hon. Consulting Physician, Glasgow Royal Infirmary; *b* 1899; *s* of late John Davis; *m* 1938, Marjorie Adelaide, *yr d* of late Arthur Cleveland. *Educ:* University Coll. Sch.; Edinburgh Univ. Served at sea, 1918; MB, ChB, Edinburgh 1924; House Surgeon, Royal Infirmary, Edinburgh, 1925; Research Student, London Sch. of Tropical Medicine, 1926; Asst Bacteriologist, Wellcome Tropical Research Laboratories, 1927-30; Prof. of Pathology, Hong-Kong Univ., 1931-39; Dir, Medical Laboratory, Bulawayo, 1939-40; Asst and later Lecturer, Dept of Medicine, Edinburgh Univ.; Temp. Asst Physician, Royal Infirmary, Edinburgh, and later Physician, Municipal Hospitals, Edinburgh, 1940-45; Muirhead Prof. of Medicine, University of Glasgow, 1945-61; Consulting Physician to the Royal Navy, 1954-61. *Publications:* The Megaloblastic Anaemias (with A. Brown), 1953; numerous contribs to medical and scientific journals mainly on pathological and haematological subjects. *Recreations:* yachting, fishing, model engineering. *Address:* Norton Brook, Yarmouth, Isle of Wight. *T:* Yarmouth 474. *Club:* Royal Solent Yacht.

**DAVIS, Dame Margaret;** *see* Rutherford, Dame Margaret.

**DAVIS, Morris Cael,** CMG 1970; MD, FRACP; Consultant Physician, 110 Collins Street, Melbourne, since 1938; *b* 7 June 1907; *s* of David and Sarah Davis; *m* 1933, Sophia Ashkenasy (*d* 1966); two *s. Educ:* Melbourne High Sch.; Univ. of Melbourne. MB, BS (1st cl. hons) Melbourne, 1930; MD 1932; MRCP 1938; FRACP 1946. Univ. of Melbourne: Prosector in Anatomy, 1927; Beaney Schol. in Pathology, 1932-33; Lectr in Pathology, 1933; Lectr in Medicine, Dental Faculty, 1940-63; Bertram Armytage Prize for Med. Res., 1934 and 1942; Fulbright Smith Mundt Schol., 1953-54. Alfred Hosp., Melbourne: Acting Pathologist, 1933-35; Physican to Out-Patients, 1938-46; Phys. to In-Patients, 1946-67; Cons. Phys., 1967-; Foundn Chm., Cardiovascular Diagnostic Service, 1959-67; Dir and Founder, Dept of Visual Aids, 1954-67; Chm. Drug Cttee, 1960-67. Travelled Nuffield Sponsorship, 1954; Litchfield Lectr, Oxford Univ., 1954; Hon. Consultant, Dental Hosp., Melbourne, 1946-. Pres., Victorian Friends of Hebrew Univ., Jerusalem, 1953-64; Federal Pres., Australian Friends Hebrew Univ., 1964; Alternate Governor, Hebrew Univ., 1961-63. Founder, Australian Medical Assoc. Arts Group, Pres. 1959-. *Publications:* papers on medicine, medical philosophy and medical educn in Australian Med. Jl, Australian Dental Jl, student jls. *Recreations:* painting, music, book collecting, garden. *Address:* 177 Finch Street, Glen Iris, Victoria 3146, Australia. *T:* Melbourne 502423. *Clubs:* University House, Australia America Association, Australia America Club, National Gallery Society (Melbourne).

**DAVIS, Nathanael Vining;** President and Director of Alcan Aluminium Limited since 1947; *b* 26 June 1915; *s* of Rhea Reineman Davis and late Edward Kirk Davis; *m* 1941, Lois Howard Thompson; one *s* one *d. Educ:* Harvard Coll.; London Sch. of Economics. With Alcan group since 1939 with exception of 3 years on active duty with US Navy. *Address:* Box 6090, Montreal 101, Quebec, Canada. *T:* 877-2340. *Clubs:* Mount Royal, St James's (Montreal); University, The Links (New York); Somerset (Boston); Rolling Rock (Ligonier, Pa); Country (Brookline, Mass).

**DAVIS, Prof. Norman,** MBE 1945; FBA 1969; Merton Professor of English Language and Literature, University of Oxford, since 1959; *b* Dunedin, NZ, 16 May 1913; *s* of James John and Jean Davis; *m* 1944, Magdalene Jamieson Bone; no *c. Educ:* Otago Boys' High Sch., Dunedin; Otago Univ.; Merton Coll., Oxford. MA NZ 1934; BA Oxon 1936, MA 1944; NZ Rhodes Scholar, 1934. Lecturer in English, Kaunas, Lithuania, 1937; Sofia, Bulgaria, 1938. Government service mainly abroad, 1939-46. Lecturer in English Language, Queen Mary Coll., University of London, 1946; Oriel and Brasenose Colls., Oxford, 1947; Oxford Univ. Lectr in Medieval English, 1948; Prof. of English Language, University of Glasgow, 1949. Hon. Dir of Early English Text Soc., 1957-. Jt Editor, Review of English Studies, 1954-63. *Publications:* Sweet's Anglo-Saxon Primer, 9th edn 1953; The Language of the Pastons (Sir Israel Gollancz Memorial Lectures, British Academy, 1954), 1955; Paston Letters (a selection), 1958; Beowulf facsimile ed. Zupitza, 2nd edn 1959; English and Medieval Studies (ed with C. L. Wrenn), 1962; The Paston Letters (a selection in modern spelling), 1963; Glossary to Early Middle English Verse and Prose (ed J. A. W. Bennett and G. V. Smithers), 1966; rev. edn, Tolkien-Gordon: Sir Gawain, 1967; Non-Cycle Plays and Fragments (EETS), 1970; Paston Letters and Papers of the Fifteenth Century, Part 1, 1971; reviews and articles in jls. *Address:* Merton College, Oxford.

**DAVIS, Ralph Henry Carless;** Professor of Medieval History, University of Birmingham, since 1970; Editor of History since 1968; *b* 7 Oct. 1918; *s* of late Prof. Henry William Carless Davis and Rosa Jennie Davis; *m* 1949, Eleanor Maud Megaw; two *s. Educ:* Leighton Park Sch.; Balliol Coll., Oxford. Friends' Ambulance Unit, 1939-45. Asst Master, Christ's Hosp., Horsham, 1947-48; Lectr, University Coll., London, 1948-56; Fellow and Tutor, Merton Coll., Oxford, 1956-70; Mem. Hebdomodal Council, Oxford Univ., 1967-69. *Publications:* The Mosques of Cairo, 1944; (ed) The Kalendar of Abbot Samson of Bury St Edmunds, 1954; A History of Medieval Europe, 1957; King Stephen, 1967; (ed with H. A. Cronne) Regesta Regum Anglo-Normannorum, vol. iii, 1968, vol. iv, 1969; articles in historical and archæological jls. *Recreations:* travel, archæology, architecture. *Address:* c/o School of History, University of Birmingham, PO Box 363, Birmingham 15.

**DAVIS, Maj.-Gen. Ronald A. B.**; *see* Bramwell Davis.

**DAVIS, Sir Rupert C. H.**; *see* Hart-Davis.

**DAVIS, S(tanley) Clinton;** MP (Lab) Hackney Central since 1970; *b* 6 Dec. 1928; *s* of Sidney Davis; *m* 1954, Frances Jane Clinton Davis (*née* Lucas); one *s* three *d*. *Educ:* Hackney Downs Sch.; Mercers' Sch.; King's Coll., London University. LLB 1950; admitted Solicitor 1953. Mem. Exec. Council, Nat. Assoc. of Labour Student Organisations, 1949-50. Councillor, London Borough of Hackney, 1959; Mayor of Hackney, 1968. Contested (Lab): Langstone Div. of Portsmouth, 1955; Yarmouth, 1959 and 1964. *Recreations:* golf, association football, reading biographical histories. *Address:* 354 Finchley Road, NW3. *T:* 01-435 4976.

**DAVIS, Thomas Frederick;** Metropolitan Magistrate, 1947-63, retired; *b* 9 Feb. 1891; *m* 1915, Rose Kipping (*d* 1966); one *s*; *m* 1967, Nora Gwendoline Roche. *Educ:* various; King's Coll., London. Served European War, 1914-18, France; Lieut East Surrey Regt, 1915-16 (wounded); Lieut Observer, RFC, 1916-17 (wounded); Capt. (Admin.) RAF, 1917-19. Barrister-at-Law, 1921-47. *Recreations:* golf, gardening and music. *Address:* 21 Stanford Court, Cornwall Gardens, SW7. *T:* 01-937 7356; Ardenwood, Copthorne, Crawley, Sussex. *T:* Copthorne 2320.

**DAVIS, William;** Editor of Punch since 1968; *b* 6 March 1933; *m* 1967, Sylvette Jouclas. *Educ:* City of London Coll. On staff of Financial Times, 1954-59; Ed. of Investor's Guide, 1959-60; City Ed. of Evening Standard, 1960-65 (with one Year's break as City Ed. of Sunday Express); Financial Editor, The Guardian, 1965-68. *Publication:* Three Years Hard Labour: the road to devaluation, 1968; Merger Mania, 1970; (ed) Pick of Punch, 1969, 1970. *Recreations:* books, travelling, tennis. *Address:* Flat 97, 25 Porchester Place, W2. *T:* 01-402 5711.

**DAVIS, William Eric,** (professionally known as **David Davis**), MBE 1969; MA Oxon; LRAM, ARCM; *b* 27 June 1908; *s* of William John and Florence Kate Rachel Davis; *m* 1935, Barbara de Riemer; one *s* two *d*. *Educ:* Bishop's Stortford Coll.; The Queen's Coll., Oxford (MA). Schoolmaster, 1931-35; joined BBC as mem. of Children's Hour, 1935. Served with RNVR Acting Temp. Lieut, 1942-46. BBC, 1946-70; Head of Children's Hour, BBC, 1953-61; Head of Children's Programmes (Sound), BBC, 1961-64; Producer, Drama Dept, 1964-70. *Publications:* various songs, etc. including: Lullaby, 1943; Fabulous Beasts, 1948; Little Grey Rabbit Song Book, 1952; various speech recordings, including The Tales of Beatrix Potter. *Recreations:* children, cats, growing roses. *Address:* 18 Mount Avenue, W5. *T:* 01-997 8156. *Club:* Garrick.

**DAVIS, Rt. Rev. William Wallace;** *see* Nova Scotia, Bishop of.

**DAVIS, Adm. Sir William (Wellclose),** GCB 1959 (KCB 1956; CB 1952); DSO 1944, and Bar, 1944; DL; Chairman: Gloucestershire Community Council; King George's Fund for Sailors; Board of Governors, Ladies' College, Cheltenham; President, Gloucestershire Branch of British Institute of Management; Vice-President and Treasurer, Royal Institution of Great Britain; *b* 11 Oct. 1901; *s* of late W. S. Davis, Indian Political Service; *m* 1934, Lady Gertrude Elizabeth Phipps, 2nd *d* of 3rd Marquis of Normanby; two *s* two *d*. *Educ:* Summerfields, Oxford; Osborne and Dartmouth Naval Colls. Midshipman, 1917; Lieut, 1921; Comdr, 1935; Capt., 1940; Rear-Adm., 1950; Acting Vice-Adm. and Vice-Adm., 1953; Adm. 1956, Dep. Dir of Plans and Cabinet Offices, 1940-42; commanded HMS Mauritius, 1943-44; Dir of Under Water Weapons, Admiralty, 1945-46; Imperial Defence Coll., 1947; Chief of Staff to C-in-C Home Fleet, 1948-49. The Naval Sec., Admiralty, 1950-52; Flag Officer 2nd in Command Mediterranean, 1952-54; Vice-Chief of the Naval Staff, Admiralty, 1954-57; Comdr-in-Chief, Home Fleet, and NATO Comdr-in-Chief, Eastern Atlantic Area, 1958-60; First and Principal Naval ADC to the Queen, 1959-60, retired. Member: Royal United Service Institution; European-Atlantic Group; British Atlantic Cttee; Gloucestershire County Education Cttee; Diocesan Council of Education. Chm., Gloucestershire Scouts Assoc.; Pres., Gloucestershire Outward Bound. DL Glos 1963. *Recreations:* golf, fishing, shooting. *Address:* Coglan House, Longhope, Glos. *T:* Longhope 282. *Clubs:* United Service; Ends of the Earth; Royal Wimbledon Golf.

**DAVIS-GOFF**; *see* Goff, Sir E. W. D.

**DAVISON,** family name of **Baron Broughshane.**

**DAVISON, John A. B.**; *see* Biggs-Davison.

**DAVISON, Rev. Leslie,** BD (London); General Secretary, Home Mission Department of the Methodist Church, since 1965 (Secretary, 1957-65); *b* 8 June 1906; *s* of George Robert Davison and Naomi (*née* Beardsmore); *m* 1937, Irene Florence Lilley (*d* 1963). *Educ:* The Bede, Sunderland; Victoria Park United Methodist Coll., Manchester. Probationer at: Camelford and Wadebridge, 1927-28; Cheltenham, 1928-30; Waverley Park, London, 1930-37. Ordained, 1931; S London Mission, 1937-44. Alderman of Bermondsey, 1940-44; London County Councillor, 1942-44. Superintendent of Walsall Mission, 1944-50; Chm., Wolverhampton and Shrewsbury District, 1950-57; Sec. Home Mission Dept, Methodist Church, 1957-65. Pres., Methodist Conference, 1962-63. Hon. degrees: LHD, Kansas Wesleyan Univ.; DD, Dickinson Coll., Pa. *Publications:* Ballads of Bermondsey, 1942; The Cross in the Club, 1943; The Principles of Penal Reform, 1960. Ed, The Christian Replies, 1960; (jointly) The Pattern of Prayer, 1961; Preacher's Gold, 1962; Sender and Sent, 1969. *Recreation:* walking. *Address:* (home) 11 Hitherwood Court, SE19. *T:* 01-670 7940; (office) Methodist Church Home Mission Department, 1 Central Buildings, Westminster, SW1. *T:* 01-930 5911.

**DAVISON, Ralph,** OBE 1970; QPM 1962; Chief Constable of Teesside Constabulary since 1968; *b* 25 March 1914; *s* of Ralph Dixon Davison and Elizabeth (*née* Bulmer), Saltburn, Yorks; *m* 1939, Joyce, *d* of George Smith and Winifred (*née* Elstob), Spennymoor, Co. Durham; one *s* one *d*. *Educ:* Sir William Turner's Sch., Redcar. School Teacher, 1932; Liverpool City Police, 1934-56; Chief Constable, Middlesbrough, 1956-68. Coronation Medal, 1953; Police Long Service and Good Conduct Medal, 1956. SBStJ 1965. *Recreations:* photography, boating, music. *Address:* 571 Marton Road, Middlesbrough, Teesside. *T:* Middlesbrough 36056.

**DAVITT, Cahir;** President of the High Court, Eire, 1951-66, retired (Hon. Mr Justice Davitt); *b* 15 Aug. 1894; *s* of Michael Davitt and Mary Yore; *m* 1925, Sarah Gertrude Lynch; four *s* one *d*. *Educ:* O'Connell Sch. and

University Coll., Dublin, BA, NUI, 1914; LLB, 1916; Barrister, King's Inns, Dublin, 1916, Bencher, 1927. Judge of the Dail Courts, 1920-22; Judge-Advocate Gen., Irish Free State Defence Forces, 1922-26; Temp. Judge, Circuit Court, 1926-27; Circuit Judge, City and County of Dublin, 1927-45; (Puisne) Judge of the High Court, 1945-51. Mem. of Judiciary Cttee, 1923-24, to advise Irish Free State Executive in relation to the establishment of Courts of Justice under the IFS Constitution; Chairman: Civil Service Compensation Board, 1929-66; Commission of Inquiry into Derating, 1930; Med. Bureau of Road Safety, 1969-. President: Irish Rugby Football Union, 1936-37; Irish Squash Rackets Assoc., 1936. *Recreation:* golf. *Address:* 88 Lower Churchtown Road, Dublin 14. *T:* 981831. *Clubs:* Milltown Golf, Fitzwilliam Lawn Tennis (Dublin).

**DAVSON, Sir Geoffrey Leo Simon,** 2nd Bt; *see* Glyn, Sir Anthony, 2nd Bt.

**DAVY, Brig. George Mark Oswald,** CB 1945; CBE 1943; DSO 1941; US Legion of Merit; *b* 22 Sept. 1898; *s* of late Capt. G. C. H. Davy; *m* 1932, Isabel Gwendolen (*d* 1970), *d* of late E. Alan Hay, Bengeo House, Hertford; one *s.* European War, 1914-18, France and Belgium: RFA and RHA; transferred to 3rd Hussars, 1931; Staff Coll., Camberley, 1932-33; Bde Major, 150 Inf. Bde, 1935-36; Company Comdr RMC, Sandhurst, 1937-38; Naval Staff Coll., Greenwich, 1939; France and Belgium, 1939-40; Western Desert, 1940-41; Greece, April 1941; commanded 3rd and 7th Armoured Bdes in Desert, 1941; Director of Military Operations GHQ, Middle East, 1942-44; Dep. Asst Chief of Staff (Operations), AFHQ Algiers, 1944; commanded Land Forces Adriatic, 1944-45; War Office representative with the Polish Forces, 1945-47; retd 1948; recommissioned for military service, 1956; retd again 1959. Sculptor. Painter of horses in oils and of landscapes and seascapes in water colours; Mem., Coun., Chelsea Art Soc. Gold Cross of Merit with Swords, Poland. *Publication:* The Seventh and Three Enemies, 1958. *Recreations:* fishing, sailing. *Address:* 4 Queens Elm Square, SW3. *T:* 01-352 8845. *Club:* Cavalry.

**DAVY, Georges Ambroise,** Hon. KBE 1955; Grand Officier, Légion d'Honneur; Commandeur des Palmes académiques; Commandeur d'Orange-Nassau, Commandeur de l'étoile de Sud; Grand Officier du Nichan-Iftikhar; D. ès L.; Member, Institut de France (Académie des Sciences Morales et Politiques); Hon. Dean of Faculty of Letters, University of Paris; Member, Board, Centre National de la Recherche Scientifique: Director of Foundation Thiers; Président de l'Institut Internationale de Philosophie politique; *b* 31 Dec. 1883; *s* of Jean-Marie Davy and Isabelle Piquois; *m* 1918, Marie-Rose Vial; four *c. Educ:* École Normale Supérieure, University of Paris. Agrégé de Philosophie, Docteur ès Lettres. Prof. of Literature, Dijon, 1919-30. Dean of the Faculty, 1922-30; Rector of Rennes Univ., 1931-38; Inspector-Gen. of Education, 1938-44. Prof. Fac. of Letters, University of Paris, 1944-55; Dean of Faculty of Letters, Paris, 1950-55. Prof. *hc* University of Brazil. Assoc. Mem. Belgian Royal Academy. Dr *hc* University of Brussels. *Publications:* La Foi jurée, 1922; Le Droit, l'idéalisme et l'expérience, 1923; Sociologie politique, 1925; Sociologues d'hier et d'aujourd'hui, 1935, Des clansoux Empires, etc. *Address:* Fondation Thiers, 5 Rond Point Bugeaud, Paris, 16e, France.

**DAWBARN, Graham Richards,** CBE 1948; MA; FRIBA (retired); FRAeS; RIBA Distinction in Town Planning; *b* London, 8 Aug. 1893; *s* of late R. A. Dawbarn, MICE, MIEE; *m* 1923, Olive, *d* of late John Topham, Barrister-at-Law; two *d. Educ:* The King's Sch., Canterbury; Corpus Christi Coll., Cambridge. Served European War, 1914-17; Public Works Dept, Hong Kong, 1921-23; won in open competition Raffles Coll., Singapore (with Cyril Farey), 1924, and Constantine Technical Coll., Middlesbrough, 1925; awarded Henry Saxon Snell prize for hospital design, 1927, and Godwin and Wimperis Bursary for executed works, 1931; flew in light aeroplane with late Sir Nigel Norman 8000 miles through USA studying airports; founded with him firm of Norman & Dawbarn, 1933, and remained a senior partner in it until 1958; MOH Housing Medal, 1949; two architectural awards by Council of Festival of Britain, 1951; Bronze Medal, Paris Salon, 1957; President AA and member of RIBA Council, 1945-47; Hon. Corresponding member Danish Assoc. of Architects; member of professional and technical cttees including Business Buildings Cttee, London Airport Layout Panel and Terminal Buildings Cttee; Work (mainly in partnership) includes numerous Airport Buildings layouts and reports; Housing for three New Towns and various Boroughs; University and Medical Sch. for West Indies, the expansion scheme for the Imperial Coll., London, Adult Training Colleges and Schools; and with their Cons. Civil Engineer, the BBC Television Centre at Wood Lane. *Address:* Marymead, Chieveley, Newbury, Berks. *Club:* Athenæum.

*See also A. M. Prestt.*

**DAWBARN, Simon Yelverton;** HM Diplomatic Service; British Embassy, Athens, since 1968; *b* 16 Sept. 1923; *s* of Frederic Dawbarn and Maud Louise Mansell; *m* 1948, Shelby Montgomery Parker; one *s* two *d. Educ:* Oundle Sch.; Corpus Christi Coll., Cambridge. Served in HM Forces (Reconnaissance Corps), 1942-45. Reckitt & Colman (Overseas), 1948-49. Joined Foreign Service, 1949. Foreign Office, 1949-53; Brussels, 1953; Prague, 1955; Tehran, 1957; seconded to HM Treasury, 1959; Foreign Office, 1961; Algiers, 1965. *Address:* c/o Foreign and Commonwealth Office (Athens), King Charles Street, SW1. *Club:* Travellers'.

**DAWES, Charles Ambrose William,** MC 1942; Chairman, New Zealand Shipping Co. Ltd, and Federal Steam Navigation Co. Ltd, since 1966; Member of Lloyd's since 1950; Fruit Farmer since 1961; *b* 30 March 1919; *s* of Edwyn Sandys Dawes and Joan Prideaux (*née* Selby); *m* 1940, Mary Neame Finn; one *s* three *d. Educ:* Stowe. Joined W. A. Browne & Co., Chartered Accountants, 1938. 2nd Lieut (TA), 97th (Kent Yeomanry) Field Regt, RA, 1939; served in France and Middle East, 1939-42; RA Training Regt, Cromer, 1943-46; Captain, 1942. Joined J. B. Westray & Co. Ltd, 1946: Director, 1949; joined New Zealand Shipping Co. Ltd, 1953: Director, 1955; Dep. Chairman, 1961; Chairman, 1966. Director: Australian and New Zealand Banking Group Ltd; Mercantile & General Reinsurance Co. Ltd, 1963; Peninsula & Oriental Steam Navigation Co., 1966. *Recreations:* shooting, tennis, gardening. *Address:* Mount Ephraim, near Faversham, Kent. *T:* Boughton 310. *Clubs:* Bath, City of London.

**DAWES, Edgar Rowland,** CMG 1958; Vice-Chairman Australian Broadcasting Commission, 1945-67; Governor, Adelaide Festival of Arts, since 1965; Member of Board: Royal Adelaide Hospital; Queen Elizabeth

Hospital; *b* 28 Nov. 1902; *s* of George and Gertrude Dawes, Norwood, SA; *m* 1926, Adeline Melba Hurcombe (decd); one *s* one *d*; *m* 1966, Patricia M., *d* of W. Henderson. *Educ:* Public and High Sch., Norwood; Adelaide Univ. Secretary, Australian Society of Engineers, 1926-39; MHA, SA, 1929-32; Director Industries Corp., 1935-39; Member Board, Inst. Medical and Veterinary Sciences, 1935-. Area Management Board (Govt Appt), Min. of Munitions, 1939-45; also Asst Controller, Gun Ammunition; Controller, Ordnance Production and Chief Technical Officer. Member first Council of National Univ., Canberra, 1953-57; Commonwealth Govt Delegate to UNSCAT Conference, Geneva, 1963. Director of private companies (Engineering), 1945-. Chm. and Comr, Charitable Funds, SA, 1967-; Dep. Chm., Inst. of Med. and Veterinary Science (IMVS), SA, 1967. *Recreations:* fishing and boating. *Address:* 18 St Georges Avenue, Glandore, South Australia. *T:* LF 2673. *Club:* Naval and Military.

**DAWES, Dr Geoffrey Sharman;** Director of Nuffield Institute for Medical Research, Oxford, since 1948; *b* 21 Jan. 1918; *s* of Rev. W. Dawes, Thurlaston Grange, Derbyshire; *m* 1941, Margaret Monk; two *s* two *d*. *Educ:* Repton Sch.; New Coll., Oxford. BA 1939; BSc 1940; BM, BCh 1943; DM 1947. Rockefeller Travelling Fellowship, 1946; Fellow, Worcester Coll., Oxford, 1946; University Demonstrator in Pharmacology, 1947; Foulerton Research Fellow, Royal Society, 1948. FRCOG 1969. Max Weinstein Award, 1963; Gairdner Foundation Award, 1966. *Publications:* Foetal and Neonatal Physiology, 1968; various publications in physiological and pharmacological journals. *Recreation:* fishing. *Address:* 8 Belbroughton Road, Oxford. *T:* Oxford 58131.

**DAWICK, Viscount; Alexander Douglas Derrick Haig;** *b* 30 June 1961; *s* and *heir* of 2nd Earl Haig, *qv*.

**DAWKINS, Dr Charles John Massey;** Senior Anæsthetist, University College Hospital, since 1946; *b* 13 July 1905; *s* of C. W. Dawkins, CBE; *m* 1930, Dr Sylvia Mabel Ransford; one *s* two *d*. *Educ:* Mill Hill Sch.; Emmanuel Coll., Cambridge. MA, MD Cantab.; DA Eng. 1936; FFARCS Eng. 1948. Dental Anæsthetist, Middlesex Hospital, 1931-48; Anæsthetist: Hampstead General Hospital, 1932-; Paddington Green Children's Hospital, 1933-; University College Hospital, 1939-; Maidenhead Hospital, 1945-; St Columba's Hospital, 1946-. FRSocMed; Mem. Council, Section of Anæsthetics, Royal Society Med.; Hon. Member Finnish Society of Anæsthetists. *Publications:* Incidence of Anæsthetic Complications, 1937; contributor to Proc. Royal Society Med., etc. *Recreations:* sailing and gardening. *Address:* 27 Well Walk, NW3. *T:* 01-435 6633; River View, Bradwell-juxta-mare, Essex. *T:* Bradwell-on-Sea 243. *Club:* United Hospitals Sailing.

**DAWNAY,** family name of **Viscount Downe.**

**DAWNAY, Lt-Col Christopher Payan,** CBE 1946; MVO 1944; Chairman: Dalgety and New Zealand Loan Ltd; Guardian Royal Exchange Assurance Company; Managing Director Lazard Bros & Co. Ltd; Director of other public companies; *s* of late Maj.-Gen. Guy P. Dawnay, CB, CMG, DSO, MVO, and Mrs Cecil Dawnay; *m* 1939, Patricia, *d* of Sir Hereward Wake, 13th Bt, CB, CMG, DSO; two *s* two *d*. *Educ:* Winchester; Magdalen Coll., Oxford. With Dawnay Day & Co. Ltd, Merchant Bankers, 1933-39 and 1946-50. War service with Coldstream Guards and in various staff appointments, 1939-45. Partner Edward de Stein & Co., Merchant Bankers, 1951-60; Director Lazard Bros & Co. Ltd, 1960; Chm., Guardian Assurance Co., 1967-68. US Legion of Merit. *Recreations:* fishing, shooting and sailing. *Address:* Longparish House, Andover, Hants. *T:* Longparish 204. *Club:* Brooks's.
*See also Capt. O. P. Dawnay.*

**DAWNAY, Maj.-Gen. (retired) Sir David,** KCVO 1968; CB 1952; DSO 1943 (Bar 1945); Secretary to the Ascot Authority and Clerk of the Course, Ascot, 1957-69; Commander 56th Armoured Division, 1954-57; *b* 10 July 1903; *s* of Maj. Hon. Hugh Dawnay, DSO, and Lady Susan Beresford; *m* 1926, Lady Katharine Nora Beresford; twin *s* one *d* (and one *d* decd). *Educ:* Eton Coll.; RMC, Sandhurst. Rifle Bgde, 1924; transferred 10th R. Hussars, 1924; Capt. 1930; War of 1939-45; Major, 1940; 2nd in Comd, North Irish Horse, 1940; CO 2nd Reconnaissance Regt, 1941; CO North Irish Horse, 1941; 2nd in Comd, 23rd and 26th Armoured Bdes, 1943; Comdr: 21 Tank Bde, 1943; 26 Armoured Bde, 1945; 86 Area, Venice, 1946; student, Staff Coll., Camberley, 1946; Comdr, 2nd Armoured Bde, 1947; Dep. Comdr, North Midland District, 1948; Comdr 8 Armoured Bde, 1948; Commandant, RMA, Sandhurst, 1951-54. Hon. Colonel, North Irish Horse, 1947-69, T&AVR, 1969-; Colonel: 10th Royal Hussars (Prince of Wales's Own), 1962-69; Royal Hussars, 1969-. Joint Master, Waterford Hounds, 1957-69. *Recreations:* hunting, cricket, lawn tennis, polo. *Address:* Whitfield Court, Waterford, Ireland. *T:* Waterford 84102. *Club:* Cavalry.

**DAWNAY, Hon. George William ffolkes,** MC 1944; DL; Coldstream Guards; Director, Barclays Bank Ltd since 1956; *b* 20 April 1909; *s* of 9th Viscount Downe, CMG, DSO and Dorothy, *o c* of Sir William ffolkes, 3rd Bt; *m* 1945, Rosemary Helen (*d* 1969), *d* of late Lord Edward Grosvenor and of late Lady Dorothy Charteris; two *s* two *d*. *Educ:* Eton. DL Norfolk, 1961. *Address:* Hillington Hall, King's Lynn, Norfolk. *T:* Hillington 304.

**DAWNAY, Captain Oliver Payan,** CVO 1953; Partner in Grieveson, Grant & Co., Stockbrokers; *b* 4 April 1920; *s* of late Maj.-General Guy Payan Dawnay, CB, CMG, DSO, MVO; *m* 1st, 1944, Lady Margaret Dorothea Boyle (marr. diss. 1962), *y d* of 8th Earl of Glasgow, DSO; two *s* one *d*; 2nd, 1963, Hon. Iris Irene Adele Peake, *e d* of 1st Viscount Ingleby, PC; one *d*. *Educ:* Eton; Balliol Coll., Oxford. Parliamentary and Press section, Ministry of Economic Warfare, 1939-40. Served War of 1939-45: Coldstream Guards, 1940-46; Adjt 1st Batt., 1943-44; seconded to Foreign Office, Conference Dept, 1945-46; demobilised, as Captain, 1946. Messrs Dawnay Day and Co., Merchant Bankers, 1946-50. Private Secretary and Equerry to Queen Elizabeth the Queen Mother, 1951-56; Extra Equerry, 1956-62. *Address:* Flat 5, 32 Onslow Square, SW7. *Clubs:* Brooks's, MCC.
*See also Lt-Col C. P. Dawnay.*

**DAWNAY, Vice-Adm. Sir Peter,** KCVO 1961 (MVO 1939); CB 1958; DSC 1944; Royal Navy, retired; an Extra Equerry to the Queen since 1958; Director, Morland & Co. Ltd, 1965; *b* 14 Aug. 1904; *s* of Maj. Hon. Hugh and Lady Susan Dawnay; *m* 1936, Lady Angela Montagu-Douglas-Scott, *d* of 7th Duke of Buccleuch; one *s* one *d*. *Educ:* Osborne and Dartmouth. Legion of Merit (USA). In command HMS Saintes and 3rd Destroyer Flotilla, 1950-51; in command HMS Mercury (HM Signal Sch.), 1952-53; in command HMS Glasgow, 1954-56. Deputy Controller of the Navy, Admiralty,

1956-58; Flag Officer, Royal Yachts, 1958-62; retired, 1962. *Address:* Hattingley House, Medstead, Alton, Hampshire. *T:* Medstead 2294. *Clubs:* White's, United Service.

**DAWSON, Christopher William,** CMG 1947; *b* 31 May 1896; *s* of Rev. H. Dawson, MA, and Tertia Dean; *m* 1924, Jill, *d* of Prof. R. G. McKerron, Aberdeen Univ.; no *c. Educ:* Dulwich Coll.; Brasenose Coll., Oxford. Joined East Surrey Regt, 1915; served in India (NW Frontier) and Mesopotamia; demobilised with rank of Captain, 1919. Joined Malayan Civil Service 1920 and served in various parts of Malaya until 1942. Called to Bar, Gray's Inn, 1929. Secretary for Defence Malaya, 1941-42; interned by Japanese in Singapore, 1942-45; Chief Secretary and Officer Administering the Govt, Sarawak, 1946-50; retired, 1950; Deputy Chief Secretary, British Administration, Eritrea, 1951-52. President: British Assoc. of Malaya, 1957-58; Sarawak Assoc., 1962. *Address:* Corner Cottage, Vanzell Road, Midhurst, Sussex. *T:* Midhurst 3333.

**DAWSON, Frank Harold,** CBE 1948; MC 1917; Director, The Cunard Steam-Ship Company Ltd, 1950-62, retired (General Manager, 1950-59); *b* 14 Feb. 1896; *m* 1924, Florence Kathleen, *d* of Captain James C. Barr, CB; two *d. Educ:* Liverpool Institute High Sch. Joined the Cunard Steam-Ship Co. Ltd, 1912. Served European War, 1914-20 (MC, despatches), Capt., The King's Regt (Liverpool). Chairman, Employers' Assoc. of the Port of Liverpool, 1954-57; Chairman, The Liverpool Steam-Ship Owners' Assoc., 1955-56. Hon. Captain RNR. *Address:* Berwyn, North Close, Bromborough, Cheshire. *T:* 051-334 2193.

**DAWSON, Comdr Sir Hugh Trevor,** 2nd Bt, *cr* 1920; CBE 1950; Royal Navy, retired; *b* 17 Jan. 1893; *o surv. s* of Sir Trevor Dawson, 1st Bt, and Louise (*d* 1935), *d* of John Miller Grant; *S* father 1931; *m* 1918, Vera Anne Loch, *d* of late Sir F. L. Halliday; one *s* three *d. Educ:* Royal Naval Coll., Osborne and Dartmouth. *Heir: s* Hugh Halliday Trevor Dawson [*b* 6 June 1931; *m* 1955, Caroline Jane, *d* of Antony Acton; two *s*]. *Address:* Casina Lodge, 8 Park Village West, NW1. *T:* 01-387 2020. *Club:* United Service.

*See also Brig. Ralph Micklem.*

**DAWSON, John Alexander,** CBE 1942; FICE; *b* 24 March 1886; *s* of Alexander Dawson, Aberdeen; *m* 1910, Margaret, *er d* of late Alexander M. Cruickshank, Bloemfontein, SA; two *s* one *d. Educ:* Robert Gordon's Coll., Aberdeen; Aberdeen and Glasgow Universities, BSc (Engineering) Glasgow. Entered Admiralty as Asst Civil Engineer, 1912; served at Portsmouth, Admiralty, Ostend (1919) and Rosyth; transferred to Air Ministry, 1921; served at Air Ministry, Inland Area, Singapore, Coastal Command; Chief Engineer Air Defence of Great Britain; Chief Engineer Bomber Command; Dep. Director of Works, 1938; Director of Works, Air Ministry, 1940-48; Chief Resident Engineer, London Airport, 1948-54, retired 1954. *Address:* Girdleness, Bedford Road, Moor Park, Northwood, Middx. *T:* Northwood 21163. *Club:* Moor Park Golf (Rickmansworth).

**DAWSON, (Sir) Lawrence Saville,** 2nd Bt, *cr* 1929; does not use the title, and his name is not on the Official Roll of Baronets.

**DAWSON, Richard Leonard Goodhugh,** MB, FRCS; Plastic Surgeon, Mount Vernon Centre for Plastic Surgery, Northwood, and Royal National Orthopædic Hospital, London, since 1953; Plastic Surgeon, Royal Free Hospital, London, since 1958; *b* 24 Aug. 1916; *s* of L. G. Dawson and Freda Hollis; *m* 1945, Betty Marie Freeman-Mathews; two *s. Educ:* Bishop's Stortford Coll., Herts; University Coll., London; University College Hospital. MRCS, LRCP 1939; MB London 1940; FRCS 1947; BS London 1948. Royal Army Medical Corps, 1941-46; service in England and Far East (4 years); POW in Japanese hands, 1942-45. Member British Assoc. Plastic Surgeons. *Publications:* Chapters in Operative Surgery, 1957; numerous contributions to Lancet, BMJ, British Journal Plastic Surgery and other journals. *Recreations:* squash, golf, gardening. *Address:* (Office) 99 Harley Street, W1. *T:* 01-935 0066; (Home) Wellingrove House, Woodcock Hill, Rickmansworth, Herts. *T:* Rickmansworth 72117. *Clubs:* Junior Carlton; River.

**DAWSON, Maj.-Gen. Robert Boyd,** CB 1969; CBE 1965; DSO 1941; Chief of the General Staff, New Zealand Army, 1967-70, retired; *b* 21 July 1916; British, NZ Citizen (as also parents); *m* 1st, 1942, Valeska Christina Bess McIntosh (*d* 1961); one *s* (one *d* decd); 2nd, 1964, Doreen Margaret Gawden Bickford. *Educ:* Rotorua High Sch.; RMC, Duntroon, Aust. Commissioned into NZ Army, Dec. 1938. Served overseas with NZ Expedny Force, in Middle East, 1940-43 (despatches twice, DSO); commanded Infantry Bn in Occupation Forces, Japan, 1947-48; various staff appts, NZ Army HQ; JSSC, UK, 1953; NZ Chief Planner, SEATO Mil. Planning Office, Bangkok, 1957-59; QMG, NZ Army HQ, 1960-62; Comdr 28 Commonwealth Infty Bde Gp, Malaysia, 1963-64; IDC, London, 1965. *Recreations:* golf, gardening. *Address:* Allawah, 1 Waitui Crescent, Lower Hutt, New Zealand. *T:* Wellington 696-308. *Clubs:* Wellesley, United Services' Officers (Wellington, NZ).

**DAWSON, Col Rupert George,** CB 1945; TD; JP, Perthshire; *b* 13 July 1887; *s* of late Peter Dawson, Drum Coille, Braco; *m* 1912, Juliette (*d* 1962), *er d* of late Senator J. M. Wilson, Montreal; two *s* two *d* (and one *s* and one *d* decd). *Educ:* Stonyhurst. Served European War, 1914-19 (despatches twice); Lt-Col, 1920; Bt Colonel, 1924; Member Queen's Body Guard for Scotland (Royal Company of Archers) since 1938; Chairman TA Assoc., Perthshire, 1936-46. Served War of 1939-45, 1939-41. DL Perthshire, 1937-47. Privy Chamberlain of the Sword and Cape to the Pope, 1939, re-appointed (to HH Pope John XXIII) Dec. 1958 and (to HH Pope Paul VI) Sept. 1963. Seigneur de La Hague; Knight of Magistral Grace, Military Order of Malta; Knight Commander, Order of the Holy Sepulchre. *Address:* La Hague Manor, St Peter, Jersey, Channel Islands. *Club:* Caledonian.

**DAWSON, Air Chief Marshal Sir Walter Lloyd,** KCB 1954 (CB 1945); CBE 1943; DSO 1948; Director, Southern Electricity Board, since 1961; *b* 6 May 1902; *s* of late W. J. Dawson, Sunderland; *m* 1927, Elizabeth Leslie, *d* of late D. V. McIntyre, MA, MB, ChB; one *s* one *d.* AOC Levant, 1946-48; Commandant, School of Land/Air Warfare, Old Sarum, 1948-50; idc, 1950-51 (RAF Instructor); Asst Chief of the Air Staff (Policy), 1952-53; Deputy Chief of Staff (Plans and Operations), SHAPE, 1953-56; Inpector-General of RAF, 1956-57; Air Member for Supply and Organisation, 1958-60, retired. Chm., Handley Page, 1966-69 (Vice-Chm., 1964-66). *Address:* Woodlands, Heathfield Avenue, Sunninghill, Berks. *Club:* Royal Air Force.

**DAWSON, William Siegfried;** Professor of Psychiatry, University of Sydney, 1927-51; Hon. Consultant Psychiatrist, Royal Prince Alfred Hospital, Sydney, since 1951; *b* Skipton-in-Craven, 27 April 1891; *s* of late William Harbutt Dawson, and of late Anna (*née* Gruetz); *m* 1927, Gladys Lyle, *er d* of late W. G. Lauder Paton. *Educ:* Skipton Grammar Sch.; Sedbergh; Dulwich; Trinity Coll., Oxford; St Thomas's Hospital. MA and DM; FRCP; Foundation Fellow RACP; Gold Medallist, Royal Medico-Psychological Assoc. of Great Britain; Rockefeller Medical Fellow, 1925. late Senior Assistant Maudsley Hospital, London, and Teacher in Psychological Medicine, University of London; President Australasian Assoc. of Psychiatrists, 1946-47; Corresp. Member American Psychiat. Assoc.; Hon. Fellow Australian and New Zealand College of Psychiatrists. Lt-Col AAMC, retired. *Publications:* papers dealing with mental disorders. *Recreation:* travel. *Address:* 36 Salisbury Crescent, Oxford OX2 7TL.

**DAWSON-DAMER,** family name of **Earl of Portarlington.**

**DAWSON-MORAY, Edward Bruce,** CMG 1969; Principal, Civil Service Department, since 1969; *b* 30 June 1909; *s* of late Alwyn Bruce Dawson-Moray and late Ada (*née* Burlton); *m* 1st, 1933, Ursula Frances (*née* Woodbridge) (marr. diss.); one *s* two *d*; 2nd, Beryl Barber. *Educ:* Cranbrook Sch.; University of London (BA Hons). Housemaster, Chillon Coll., Switzerland, 1938-42. British Legation, Berne, 1942; 3rd Secretary, 1944; 3rd Secretary and Vice-Consul, Rome, 1947-48; Consul: Leopoldville, 1948-50; Detroit, 1950-51; 1st Secretary and Consul, Rangoon, 1952-54; Information Officer and Consul, Naples, 1954-56; Foreign Office, 1956-60; Consul, Casablanca, 1960-63; Chief Establishment Officer, Diplomatic Wireless Service, 1963-69. Senior Editor, Foreign Office List, 1957-60. *Recreations:* literature, photography, opera, travel. *Address:* 2 Pennypiece, Cleeve Road, Goring-on-Thames, Reading, Berks RG8 9BY. *T:* Goring-on-Thames 3314; Civil Service College, Sunningdale Park, Ascot, Berks. *T:* Ascot 23711. *Club:* Royal Overseas League.

**DAWTRY, Alan Graham,** CBE 1968 (MBE 1945); TD 1948; Town Clerk of Westminster, since 1956; Hon. Secretary of the London Boroughs Association; Member: Clean Air Council; Metrication Board since 1969; *b* 8 April 1915; *s* of Melancthon and Kate Nicholas Dawtry, Sheffield; unmarried. *Educ:* King Edward VII Sch., Sheffield; Sheffield Univ. (LLB). Admitted Solicitor, 1938; Asst Solicitor, Sheffield, 1938-48; Deputy Town Clerk, Bolton, 1948-52; Deputy Town Clerk, Leicester, 1952-54; Town Clerk, Wolverhampton, 1954-56. Served War of 1939-45: Commissioned RA; Campaigns France, North Africa, Italy (MBE, despatches twice); released with rank of Lieut-Colonel. Foreign orders: Honour (Austria); Leopold II (Belgium); Merit (Chile); Legion of Honour (France); Merit (W. Germany); the Phœnix (Greece); Merit (Italy); Homayoun (Iran); the Star (Jordan); African Redemption (Liberia); the Right Hand (Nepal); the Two Niles (Sudan); the Crown (Thailand). *Address:* 806 Collingwood House, Dolphin Square, SW1.

**DAY, Prof. Alan Charles Lynn;** Professor of Economics, London School of Economics, University of London, since 1964; *b* 25 Oct. 1924; *s* of Henry Charles Day, MBE, and Ruth Day; *m* 1962, Diana Hope Bocking; no *c*. *Educ:* Chesterfield Grammar Sch.; Queens' Coll., Cambridge. Asst Lecturer, then Lecturer, LSE, 1949-54; Economic Adviser, HM Treas., 1954-56; Reader in Economics, London Univ., 1956-64. Ed., National Inst. Econ. Review, 1960-62; Econ. Correspondent, The Observer, intermittently, 1957-. Part-time Economic Advisor on Civil Aviation, BoT, 1968-. Member: Council, Consumers' Assoc., 1963; Board, British Airports Authority, 1965-68; SE Region Econ. Planning Council, 1966-69; Road Research Laboratory Traffic Research Cttee, 1966; Ministry of Housing Preservation Policy Group, 1966; Home Office Cttee on the London Taxicab Trade, 1967. *Publications:* The Future of Sterling, 1954; Outline of Monetary Economics, 1956; The Economics of Money, 1959; (with S. T. Beza) Wealth and Income, 1960. *Recreations:* travel, eating. *Address:* 2 Regent Square, WC1. *T:* 01-837 0665; 11 Christchurch Hill, NW3. *T:* 01-435 4584; Old Post Office Cottage, Lake, near Salisbury, Wilts. *T:* Amesbury 3100. *Club:* Reform.

**DAY, Sir Albert James Taylor,** Kt *cr* 1954; CBE 1947 (OBE 1941); *b* 9 Feb. 1892; *s* of Albert Henry and Elizabeth Day; *m* 1919, Dorcas Gosling; one *s* (and one *s* decd). *Educ:* Church and Secondary Schools. Civil Servant (PO), 1908-23; Asst Secretary Association of Executive Officers and other Civil Servants, 1923-29; General Secretary, 1929-30; General Secretary Society of Civil Servants, 1930-46; CS National Whitley Council: part-time Chairman Staff Side, 1939-46; Chairman Staff Side, 1947-56. *Address:* Stone End, Fox Hill Close, Haywards Heath, Sussex. *T:* 4222.

**DAY, Derek Malcolm;** Head of Personnel Operations Department, Foreign and Commonwealth Office, since 1969; *b* 29 Nov. 1927; *s* of late Alan W. Day and of Mrs A. W. Day; *m* 1955, Sheila Nott; three *s* one *d*. *Educ:* Hurstpierpoint Coll.; St Catharine's Coll., Cambridge. Royal Artillery, 1946-48; St Catharine's Coll., 1948-51. Entered HM Foreign Service, Sept. 1951; Third Sec., British Embassy, Tel Aviv, 1953-56; Private Sec. to HM Ambassador, Rome, 1956-59; Second, then First Sec., FO, 1959-62; First Sec., British Embassy, Washington, 1962-66; First Sec., FO, 1966-67; Asst Private Sec. to Sec. of State for Foreign Affairs, 1967-68. *Recreations:* hockey (rep. Great Britain, Olympic Games, Helsinki, 1952); gardening, and the family. *Address:* Falconhurst, Lingfield, Surrey. *T:* Lingfield 2538. *Club:* United Universities.

**DAY, Edith;** actress; *b* Minneapolis, USA, 10 April 1896; *d* of Oscar Day and Ella Mahla; *m* 1st, Carle E. Carlton (marr. dissolved); 2nd, Pat Somerset (marr. dissolved). First appearance on stage, Shubert Theatre, St Paul, Minn., Sept. 1915; Empire Theatre, London, 1920, as Irene O'Dare in Irene (which she had played at the Vanderbilt Theatre, New York); Jenny, in Jenny, Empire, 1922. Subsequently she played in New York and in London, etc. Later successes include: Nina Benedetto, in Wildflower, Casino, 1923; Rose Marie La Flamme, in Rose Marie, Drury Lane, 1925 (for 2 years); Margot Bonvalet, in The Desert Song, Drury Lane, 1927-28 and Magnolia, in Show Boat, 1928-29; Rose Marie (revival), 1929-30. She appeared in Variety Theatres with Robert Naylor, in a repertory of songs, 1931-32. The Desert Song (revival), London Coliseum, 1936; Lolita, in Sunny River, Piccadilly, 1943. In Noel Coward's Waiting in the Wings, Duke of York's, 1960. First appeared in films, 1917. Has made numerous broadcasts.

**DAY, James Wentworth;** author, journalist and publicist; Chairman and Managing Director of News Publicity Ltd; Lord of the Manors of

Exning Hall and Coggishall in Exning; *b* Marsh House, Exning, Suffolk, 21 April 1899; *s* of late J. T. Wentworth Day, Lacies Court, Abingdon, Berks, and Martha Ethel Staples of Wicken; *m* 1943, Marion Edith, *d* of late Hamish McLean, Mount Hutt Estates, S. Island, NZ, and of Mrs Hamish McLean, Christchurch, NZ; one *d*. *Educ:* Newton Coll.; Cambridge. Served European War, 1917-18; Daily Express, Publicity Manager, 1923; Asst Editor Country Life, 1925; acting Editor of the Field, 1930-31; Dramatic Critic, Sunday Express, 1932, and Editor of English Life; as Personal Representative of Lady Houston, 1933-34, was on exec. of Houston-Mount Everest flight, negotiated purchase of Saturday Review (editor, 1934), conducted High Tory campaign in nine bye-elections. Editor, Illustrated Sporting and Dramatic News, 1935-36-37; Propaganda Adviser to Egyptian Government, 1938-39; Publicity Adviser to Anglo-Turk Relief Cttee, 1940; War Correspondent in France, 1940, and with minesweepers; Near East Correspondent to BBC, 1941. Contested (C) Hornchurch Div. of Essex, 1950 and 1951. Editor, East Anglia Life, 1962-66. Member Society of Authors; Member Inst. of Journalists; FRSA. Owns a large part of Adventurers' Fen and a few good old Masters, mainly of the Wentworth family. *Publications:* The Lure of Speed, 1929; The Life of Sir Henry Segrave, 1930; Speed, the Life of Sir Malcolm Campbell, 1931; My Greatest Adventure (for Sir Malcolm Campbell), 1932; Kaye Don the Man, 1934; The Modern Fowler, 1934; A Falcon on St Paul's, 1935; King George V as a Sportsman, 1935; Sporting Adventure, 1937; The Dog in Sport, 1938; Sport in Egypt, 1939; Farming Adventure, 1943; Harvest Adventure, 1945; Gamblers' Gallery, 1948; Wild Wings, 1949; Coastal Adventure, 1949; Marshland Adventure, 1950; Broadland Adventure, 1951; The New Yeomen of England, 1952; Rural Revolution, 1952; The Modern Shooter, 1953; Norwich and the Broads, 1953; The Wisest Dogs in the World, 1954; A History of the Fens, 1954; Ghosts and Witches, 1954; They Walk the Wild Places, 1956; Poison on the Land, 1957; The Angler's Pocket Book, 1957; The Dog Lover's Pocket Book, 1957; Lady Houston, DBE–The Woman Who Won the War, 1958; A Ghost Hunter's Game Book, 1958; HRH Princess Marina, Duchess of Kent (The First Authentic Life Story), 1962; The Queen Mother's Family Story, 1967; Portrait of the Broads, 1967; In Search of Ghosts, 1969. Edited Best Sporting Stories (anthology). Contributions to Great Georgians; The English Counties; 50 Great Ghost Stories, 1966; 50 Great Horror Stories, 1969; Treasures of Britain (Readers Digest), 1968, etc; has broadcast and written many articles on politics, the Near East, field sports, natural history, agriculture, dogs, flying, motoring, racing, shipping, etc, in the leading newspapers and journals. *Recreations:* taking the Left Wing intelligentsia at its own valuation; shooting (especially wildfowling), riding, fishing, sailing, natural history, and old furniture. *Address:* Ingatestone, Essex. *T:* Ingatestone 3035. *Club:* Public Schools.

**DAY, John King,** TD; MA, BSc; Principal, Elizabeth College, Guernsey, CI, since 1958; *b* Ipoh, Perak, FMS, 27 Oct. 1909; *s* of Harold Duncan Day, Mining Engineer, and Muriel Edith Day; *m* 1935, Mary Elizabeth Stinton, *er d* of late Tom Stinton, Headmaster of the High Sch., Newcastle-under-Lyme; three *s*. *Educ:* Stamford Sch.; Magdalen Coll., Oxford. Demy 1928-32. Honour School of Natural Science (Chemistry) Class 2. Assistant Master, Kendal Sch., Westmorland, 1932; Asst Master and Housemaster, Gresham's Sch., 1933-57; served Royal Norfolk Regt (7th Bn) and Military College of Science, 1939-45. *Recreations:* walking, fishing and sketching. *Address:* Elizabeth College, Guernsey, Channel Islands. *T:* Guernsey 24483. *Clubs:* English-Speaking Union, Royal Commonwealth Society.

**DAY, Robin;** Television Journalist; *b* 24 Oct. 1923; *s* of late William and Florence Day; *m* 1965, Katherine Mary, *d* of R. I. Ainslie, DSO, QC, Perth, WA. *Educ:* Bembridge Sch.; St Edmund Hall, Oxford. Military service, 1943-47; commd RA, 1944. Oxford, 1947-51: Union debating tour of American universities, 1949; President Union, 1950; BA Hons (Jurisprudence), 1951. Middle Temple: Blackstone Entrance Scholar, 1951; Harmsworth Law Scholar, 1952-53; called to Bar, 1952. Information Asst, British Embassy Press Office, Washington, 1953-54; free-lance broadcasting and journalism, 1954-55; BBC Talks Producer (radio), 1955; Newscaster and Parliamentary Correspondent, Independent TV News, 1955-59; Guild of TV Producers' Merit Award, Personality of the Year, 1957; columnist in News Chronicle, 1959; joined BBC TV programme Panorama, 1959, specializing in political interviews and foreign film assignments as reporter/director; Introducer of Panorama, 1967-. FRSA 1970. *Publications:* Television: A Personal Report, 1961; The Case for Televising Parliament, 1963. *Recreations:* reading, talking, ski-ing. *Address:* c/o BBC TV Studios, Lime Grove, W12. *Club:* Garrick.

**DAY, Theodora,** MA; *d* of late Stanley Day, FIA, Blackheath. *Educ:* Girton Coll., Cambridge. Principal Brighton Diocesan Training Coll., 1927-38; Principal Maria Grey Training Coll., NW6, 1938-49. *Address:* Nynehead Court, Wellington, Somerset.

**DAY-LEWIS, Cecil,** CBE 1950; MA Oxon; CLit; FRSL; FRSA; Author (C. Day Lewis); Poet Laureate, since 1968; Director, Chatto & Windus Ltd; *b* 27 April 1904; *s* of Rev. F. C. Day-Lewis and Kathleen Blake Squires; *m* 1st, 1928, Constance Mary King (marr. dissolved, 1951); two *s*; 2nd, 1951, Jill Angela Henriette Balcon; one *s* one *d*. *Educ:* Sherborne Sch. (scholar); Wadham Coll., Oxford (exhibitioner). Asst Master at Sumerfields, Oxford, 1927-28; Larchfield, Helensburgh, 1928-30; Cheltenham Coll., 1930-35. Editor of books and pamphlets, Ministry of Information, 1941-46; Clark Lecturer, Trinity Coll., Cambridge, 1946; Professor of Poetry, Oxford Univ., 1951-56. Charles Eliot Norton Prof. of Poetry, Harvard Univ., 1964-65. Compton Lectr, Hull Univ., 1968. Vice-President: Royal Society of Literature, 1958-; London Library, 1968. Member: Arts Council, 1962-68; Irish Academy of Letters, 1968. Hon. Member, American Academy of Arts and Letters, 1966; Hon. Fellow, Wadham Coll., Oxford, 1968. Hon. DLitt: Exeter; Hull, 1970; Hon. LittD TCD, 1968. *Publications:* The Buried Day; Collected Poems, 1954; A Hope for Poetry; Poetry for You; The Poetic Image; Pegasus and other Poems, The Gate and other Poems; The Room and other Poems, 1965; The Whispering Roots, 1970, etc; translations: The Georgics of Virgil; The Aeneid of Virgil; The Eclogues of Virgil. Also detective novels under pseudonym of Nicholas Blake. *Relevant publication:* Cecil Day-Lewis, the Poet Laureate: a bibliography, 1968. *Address:* c/o Chatto & Windus, Ltd, 40 William IV Street, WC2. *Club:* Athenæum.

**DAYSH, Prof. George Henry John,** BLitt Oxon; DCL; Deputy Vice-Chancellor of University of Newcastle upon Tyne and Professor of

Geography in the University, 1963-66; Emeritus Professor, since Oct. 1966 (Professor of Geography, King's College, University of Durham, Newcastle upon Tyne, 1943-63; Sub Rector, King's College, 1955-63); Chairman, Tyne Tees Television, since 1968; *b* 21 May 1901; *s* of Alfred John Daysh and Margaret (*née* Campbell); *m* 1927, Sheila Guthrie, *er d* of Dr A. F. A. Fairweather; one *s* one *d*. *Educ:* Eggars Grammar Sch.; University College, Reading; Wadham Coll., Oxford. Housemaster, Pocklington Sch., E. Yorks, 1924-27; Lecturer in Geography, Bedford Coll., University of London, 1927-29; Lecturer-in-charge, Dept of Geography, 1930-38, Reader of Geography, 1938-43, King's Coll., Newcastle upon Tyne. Seconded for special duties with Dist Comr for special area of Cumberland, 1938; Senior Research Officer, Ministry of Town and Country Planning, 1943-45. Member of Exec. of NE Development Board, 1934-39, Vice-President NE Industrial and Development Assoc.; Chairman Research Cttee of NEIDA; Secretary Commn on Ports of International Geographic Union, 1947-51; Chairman University of Durham Matriculation and Sch. Examination Board, 1953-63. Part-time Member Northern Gas Board, 1956-70. Chairman, newcastle upon Tyne Hospital Management Cttee, 1968-. Visiting Prof. Fouad I Univ., 1951. Chairman, Triennial Grants Cttee, University College of Sierra Leone, 1960. Consultant to Cumberland Development Council, 1966-69. Fellow of Royal Geographical and American Geographical Societies. Hon. DCL (Newcastle), 1964. FRSA. *Publications:* Southampton–Points in its Development, 1928; A Survey of Industrial Facilities of the North-East Coast, 1936 (rev., 1940 and 1949); West Cumberland with Alston–a Survey of Industrial Facilities, 1938 (revised 1951); (ed) Studies in Regional Planning, 1949; (ed) Physical Land Classification of North-East England, 1950; (with J. S Symonds) West Durham, 1953; (ed) A Survey of Whitby, 1958; contribs to Geographical Journal, Geography, Economic Geography, Geographical Review, etc. *Recreations:* gardening, field sports, travel and exploration. *Address:* 2 Dunkirk Terrace, Corbridge, Northumberland. *T:* Corbridge-on-Tyne 2154.

**DEACON, Lt-Col Edmund Henry;** DL 1953; JP 1954; *b* 1902; *s* of late Col E. Deacon, DL, Sloe House, Halstead, Essex; *m* 1927, Betty, *d* of late Brig.-Gen. J. E. C. Livingstone-Learmonth, CMG, DSO; one *d*. *Educ:* Wellington; Trinity Coll., Cambridge; Master Newmarket and Thurlow Hounds, 1934-42. Joint Master East Essex Hounds, 1947-50. Commanding 15 Bn Essex Home Guard, 1952; Chairman of Governors of Felsted Sch., 1952-65. *Address:* Brick House, Steeple Bumpstead, Haverhill, Suffolk. *Clubs:* Cavalry, Pratt's, United Hunts.

**DEACON, George Edward Raven,** CBE 1954; FRS 1944; FRSE 1957; FRAS; FRGS; DSc; Director, National Institute of Oceanography since 1949; Foreign Member, Swedish Royal Academy of Sciences, 1958; *b* 21 March 1906; *m* 1940, Margaret Elsa Jeffries (*d* 1966); one *d*. *Educ:* City Boys' Sch., Leicester; King's Coll., London. FKC. Served on Scientific Staff of the Discovery Cttee, in England and in the Royal Research Ships William Scoresby and Discovery II, 1927-39. Hon. DSc: Liverpool, 1961; Leicester, 1970. Polar Medal, 1942; Alexander Agassiz Medal, US National Academy of Sciences, 1962. Royal Medal, Royal Soc., 1969. Hon. Member, Royal Society of New Zealand, 1964; President, Institute of Navigation, 1961-64; Vice-President, RGS, 1965-70. *Publications:* Oceanographical papers in the Discovery Reports, etc. *Address:* Flitwick House, Milford, Surrey. *T:* Godalming 5929.

**DEACON ELLIOTT, Air Vice-Marshal Robert,** CB 1967; OBE 1954; DFC 1941 (2 mentions); Bursar, Civil Service College, Sunningdale Park, since 1969; *b* 20 Nov. 1914; British; *m* 1948, Grace Joan Willes, Leamington Spa; two *s* one *d*. *Educ:* Northampton. 72 Fighter Sqdn (Dunkirk and Battle of Britain), 1939-41; HQ Fighter Comd, 1942-43; 84 Group 2 ATAF, 1944-46; Air Ministry (OR 5), 1946-48; OC Flying Wing and OC 26 APC in Cyprus, 1948-51; HQ Fighter Comd, Head of Admin. Plans, 1951-54; Army Staff Coll., on Directing Staff, 1954-56; CO, RAF Leconfield, 1956-57; CO, RAF Driffield, 1957-58; Air University USAF, Maxwell AFB, USA, 1958-61; Commandant, Officer and Aircrew Selection Centre, 1962-65; AOC, RAF Gibraltar, 1965-66; AOC, RAF Malta, and Dep. C-in-C (Air), Allied Forces Mediterranean, 1966-68, retd. *Recreations:* squash rackets, shooting, photography. *Address:* Beech Hanger, Windmill Lane, Alton, Hants. *Clubs:* Royal Air Force; Royal Gibraltar Yacht.

**DEADMAN, Ronald;** Editor, Teachers' World, since 1968; Member of the Press Council since 1969; *b* 28 May 1919; *s* of Thomas Deadman and Margaret Healey; *m* 1952, Joan Evans; no *c*. *Educ:* Hinguar Street Sch., Shoeburyness; Oakley Coll., Cheltenham. Served RAF, 1937-45. Teaching, 1950-66; Features Editor, The Teacher, 1966-67; Editor, Everyweek, 1967-68. *Publications:* Enjoying English, Bk 1, 1966, Bk 2, 1968; (novel, for children) The Happening, 1968; (ed, short stories) The Friday Story, 1966; Contrasts, 1971; contribs to New Statesman, Guardian, BBC, Where magazine, Education and Training. *Recreation:* brooding. *Address:* 54 Arundel Terrace, Barnes, SW13. *T:* 01-748 9734.

**DEAKIN, Maj.-Gen. Cecil Martin Fothergill,** CB 1961; CBE 1956; *b* 20 Dec. 1910; *m* 1934, Evelyn, *e d* of late Sir Arthur Grant, Bt of Monymusk, Aberdeenshire; one *s* one *d*. *Educ:* Winchester Coll. Commissioned into Grenadier Guards, 1931. Served with Regt NW Europe, 1944-45 (despatches). Commanded: 2nd Bn Grenadier Guards, 1945-46; 1st Bn, 1947-50; 32nd Guards Bde, 1953-55; 29th Infantry Bde, 1955-57 (Suez Expedition, despatches); Brigadier, General Staff, War Office, 1957-59; Director of Military Training, 1959; GOC 56th London Div., TA, 1960; Director Territorial Army, Cadets and Home Guard, 1960-62; Commandant of the JSSC, Latimer, 1962-65. Director, Mental Health Research Fund, 1967. President, Grenadier Guards Assoc. *Recreations:* numerous. *Address:* Stocks Farm House, Beenham, Berks. *Clubs:* Guards; Royal Yacht Squadron.

*See also Sir A. B. C. Edmonstone, Bt.*

**DEAKIN, Frederick William Dampier,** DSO 1943; MA; Warden of St Antony's College, Oxford, 1950-68, retired; Hon. Fellow, 1969; *b* 3 July 1913; *e s* of Albert Witney Deakin, Aldbury, Tring, Herts; *m* 1st, 1935, Margaret Ogilvy (marr. dissolved, 1940), *d* of late Sir Nicholas Beatson Bell, KCSI; two *s*; 2nd, 1943, Livia Stela, *d* of Livin Nasta, Bucharest. *Educ:* Westminster Sch.; Christ Church, Oxford. 1st Class, Modern History, 1934; Amy Mary Preston Read Scholar, 1935. Fellow and Tutor, Wadham Coll., Oxford, 1936-49; Research Fellow, 1949; Hon. Fellow, 1961. Served War of 1939-45; with Queen's Own Oxfordshire Hussars, 1939-41; seconded to Special Operations, War Office, 1941; led first British Military Mission to Tito, May 1943.

First Secretary, HM Embassy, Belgrade, 1945-46. Russian Order of Valour, 1944; Chevalier de la Légion d'Honneur, 1953; Grosse Verdienstkreuz, 1958; Yugoslav Partisan Star (1st Class), 1969. *Address:* Le Castellet, Var, France. *Clubs:* St James', White's.

**DEAKINS, Eric Petro;** MP (Lab) Walthamstow (West) since 1970; *b* 7 Oct. 1932; *er s* of Edward Deakins and late Gladys Deakins. *Educ:* Tottenham Grammar Sch.; London Sch. of Economics. BA (Hons) in History, 1953. Executive with FMC (Meat) Ltd, 1956; General Manager, Pigs Div., FMC (Meat) Ltd, 1969. *Publication:* A Faith to Fight For, 1964. *Recreations:* writing, cinema, squash, football. *Address:* Flat 1, 35 Haymarket, SW1. *T:* 01-930 2669.

**DEAN, (Arthur) Paul;** MP (C) Somerset North since 1964; Parliamentary Under-Secretary of State, Department of Health and Social Security, since 1970; Director, Howard Panton Ltd, since 1967; *b* 14 Sept. 1924; *s* of Arthur Percival Dean and Jessie Margaret Dean (*née* Gaunt); *m* 1957, Doris Ellen Webb. *Educ:* Ellesmere Coll., Shropshire; Exeter Coll., Oxford (MA, BLitt). Former President Oxford Univ. Conservative Assoc. and Oxford Carlton Club. Served War of 1939-45, Capt. Welsh Guards; ADC to Comdr 1 Corps BAOR. Farmer, 1950-56. Resident Tutor, Swinton Conservative Coll., 1957; Conservative Research Dept, 1957-64, Assistant Director from 1962; a Front Bench Spokesman on Health and Social Security, 1969-. Formerly Member Governing Body of Church in Wales. *Publications:* contributions to political pamphlets. *Recreation:* fishing. *Address:* Richmonte Lodge, East Harptree, near Bristol; House of Commons, SW1. *Clubs:* St Stephen's; Bath and County; Keynsham Conservative.

**DEAN, Sir Arthur (William Henry),** Kt 1946; CIE 1941; MC; ED; retired; *b* 7 Feb. 1892; *e s* of William James and Mary Elizabeth Dean, Brackley, Northants; *m* 1st, 1916, Ivie Stella (*d* 1950), 2nd *d* of late George Martin, Merton, Surrey; three *s* (one *d* decd); 2nd, 1951, Marjorie Ella, *o d* of late E. C. D. Robins, Southend. *Educ:* Rutlish Sch., Merton; Imperial Coll., London Univ. Bessemer Medallist, 1913; BSc (Eng.); Asst Engineer Troityzk Goldfields, Kotchkar, Russia, 1913-15; Military Service, 1915-19, temp. Commission RE, Tunnelling Companies (MC and Bar, despatches); Asst, Exec., Superintending, Additional Chief and Chief Engineer Govt of India, Public Works Dept, 1919-46; Chairman Delhi Improvement Trust, 1946-48; Chief Civil Engineer, Foreign Office Administration of African Territories, London, 1949-52; Gen Manager, Libyan Development Agency, Tripoli, 1952-62. CStJ 1946. Order of Istiklal (2nd Class), Libya, 1959. *Publications:* Proceedings Institution of Civil Engineers; 1934, Construction of a submersible road bridge over the Narbudda River (Cooper's Hill Medal and Telford Premium); 1939, Anti-Malarial Operations in the Delhi Urban Area; various papers to Indian Roads Congress. *Address:* 66 The Avenue, Worcester Park, Surrey. *T:* 01-337 4701.

**DEAN, Basil,** CBE 1947 (MBE 1918); Governing Director of B. D. Enterprises Ltd, since 1939, and of Basil Dean Productions, Ltd, 1926-64; Member of Council of RADA. Organised and was First Controller of Liverpool Repertory Theatre (The Playhouse) until 1913; Cheshire Regt, 1914; Captain, 1916; Director Entertainment branch, Navy and Army Canteen Board, 1917; Joint Managing Director of Drury Lane Theatre, 1924-25; Managing Director of Reandean co., St Martin's Theatre, London, 1919-25; founded and was first Chairman and Joint Managing Director Associated Talking Pictures, Ltd, ATP Studios, Ltd (re-named Ealing Studios), and their subsidiary companies, 1929-36; General European Representative of the Radio Keith Orpheum Corporation (USA); Chairman and Managing Director of Radio Keith Orpheum, Ltd, 1930-32; Shute Lecturer, Liverpool Univ., 1932-33; Director of National Service Entertainment, 1941; founder and director-general of Entertainments National Service Assoc. (ENSA), 1939; Director of Entertainments Navy, Army, and Air Force Institutes, 1939; produced Flecker's Hassan (musical score by Delius), His Majesty's, 1923; A Midsummer Night's Dream, Drury Lane, 1924; other productions include The Skin Game, 1920; A Bill of Divorcement, 1921; Loyalties, 1922; The Constant Nymph, 1926; Young Woodley, 1928; The Circle of Chalk, 1929; Autumn Crocus, 1931; Call it a Day, 1935; When we are Married, 1938; Johnson over Jordan, 1939; The Diary of a Nobody, 1954; Who Cares?, 1956; Touch It Light, 1958; devised and presented Cathedral Steps before St Paul's Cathedral, and Coventry Cathedral, 1942, Salute to the Red Army, for Ministry of Information, Albert Hall, 1943; re-produced Hassan for South African National Theatre, 1950 and for Dublin Drama Festival, 1960. *Publications:* Various Plays and Pamphlets, including Marriages are made in Heaven (Manchester, 1908); Mother to be, Effie (Manchester, 1909); The Love Cheats (London, 1910); (with Barry Jackson) Fifinella (London, 1919); part author (with Margaret Kennedy) of Come with Me, 1928; (with George Munro), Murder Gang, 1933; The Actor and his Workshop, 1922; The Theatre in Emergency, 1939; The Theatre in Reconstruction, 1945; wrote official history of ENSA (The Theatre at War), 1956; Seven Ages: an autobiography, 1888-1927, 1970; *dramatisations:* The Constant Nymph (with Margaret Kennedy), 1926; Beau Geste (with P. C. Wren, 1928); Sleeveless Errand (with Norah James), 1933; The Heart of the Matter (with Graham Greene), 1949; The Diary of a Nobody (original book of George and Weedon Grossmith), 1954; *Address:* 18 Norfolk Road, NW8. *T:* 01-722 7979. *Clubs:* Garrick, Royal Automobile.

*See also W. B. Dean.*

**DEAN, Commander Brian,** DSO 1940; RN (retired); *b* 12 Feb. 1895; *e s* of late Captain F. W. Dean, RN (retired); *m* Hilda (*d* 1968), *yr d* of late John Saliba. *Educ:* Stratheden House, Blackheath; RN Colleges, Osborne and Dartmouth. Midshipman, 1912; Lieut, 1916; Comdr. (retired), 1940; wounded in Sept. 1915; spent most of European War in destoyers; Officer of Watch in HMS Lion at surrender of German Fleet, 1918; made a chart of River Orinoco, 1922; at defence of Hankow in Jan. 1927; qualified as Instructor in Chemical Warfare and as Interpreter in Spanish; Commanded HMS Sabre (destroyer), 1937-Dec. 1940; in her took part in evacuation of BEF from Dunkirk, making 10 trips and transporting 5,000 troops (DSO). Invalided on account of war injuries, 1947; served on Staff of Flag Officer, Scotland, as Deputy Command Mine-watching Service Officer, 1953-61. *Recreation:* small boat sailing. *Address:* PO Box 22, Otane, Hawke's Bay, New Zealand.

**DEAN, (Charles) Raymond,** QC 1963; Recorder of Kingston-upon-Hull, since 1970; *b* 28 March 1923; *s* of late Joseph Irvin Gledhill Dean and late Lilian Dean (*née* Waddington); *m* 1948,

Pearl Doreen (*née* Buncall); one *s* one *d*. *Educ:* Hipperholme Grammar Sch.; The Queen's Coll., Oxford (1941-42 and 1945-47). RAF Flying Duties, 1942-45 (Flt Lieut). BA (Jurisprudence) 1947, MA 1948; called to Bar, Lincoln's Inn, 1948; Deputy Chairman, West Riding QS, 1961-65; Recorder: of Rotherham, 1962-65; of Newcastle upon Tyne, 1965-70. *Recreations:* fishing, motoring, reading, Rugby Union (now non-playing), golf. *Address:* 30 Davies Avenue, Leeds, Yorks. *T:* Leeds 663205. *Clubs:* United Universities; Sheffield (Sheffield); Durham County (Durham).

**DEAN, Col Donald John,** VC 1918; OBE 1961; TD; DL; JP; *b* 1897; *m* 1923, Marjorie, *d* of late W. R. Wood; one *s* one *d*. Served European War, 1914-18 (despatches, VC); War of 1939-45 (despatches). JP 1951, DL 1957, Kent. Comdr Royal Danish Order of the Dannebrog. *Address:* 1 Park Avenue, Sittingbourne, Kent.

**DEAN, Eric Walter,** CB 1968; CBE 1958; retired; *b* 5 March 1906; *s* of late Thomas W. Dean, London; *m* 1935, Joan Mary, *d* of late L. A. Stanley, Folkestone; one *d*. *Educ:* Forest Sch.; Exeter Coll., Oxford. Called to Bar, Inner Temple, 1931. Solicitors Dept, Board of Trade, 1935-68; Asst Solicitor, 1947-61; Principal Asst Solicitor, 1961-68, retired. *Recreations:* music, horse-racing. *Address:* 30 Bowen Court, The Drive, Hove, Sussex. *T:* Brighton 731823. *Club:* Bath.

**DEAN, Frederick Harold;** Vice Judge Advocate General since 1968; *b* 5 Nov. 1908; *o c* of late Frederick Richard Dean and Alice Dean (*née* Baron), Manchester; *m* 1st, 1939, Gwendoline Mary Eayrs Williams (marr. diss., 1966), 3rd *d* of late Rev. W. Williams, Kingsley, Staffs; one *s* one *d*; 2nd, 1966, Sybil Marshall Dennis, *o d* of late Col F. B. M. Chatterton, CMG, CBE. *Educ:* Manchester Grammar Sch.; Manchester Univ. LLB 1930; LLM 1932. Called to Bar, Middle Temple, 1933. Practised on Northern Circuit, 1934-40 and 1945-50. Served in RAFVR, 1940-45 in UK, Iraq, Egypt and E Africa (Sqdn Ldr). AJAG, 1950; DJAG: Far East, 1954-57 and 1962-65; Middle East, 1958-61; Germany, 1967-68. *Publication:* Bibliography of the History of Military and Martial Law (in composite vol., A Nation at War), 1968. *Recreations:* travel, walking, music, reading. *Address:* The Old Farmhouse, Lower Street, Quainton, Aylesbury, Bucks. *T:* Quainton 263. *Club:* Oxford and Cambridge University.

**DEAN, Henry Edwin,** MBE 1943; JP; retired; *b* 29 Aug. 1881; *s* of George Dean and Eliza Blundell; *m* 1912, Olive Marie Bussey; one *s* one *d*. *Educ:* Village Sch., West Derby. Clerk, Judge Sir Alfred A. Tobin, 1896-1902; South African Constabulary, 1902-07; Fencing Dept, EAP, 1908; Transport Officer EAP, 1908-11; Office Superintendent Public Works Dept EAP, 1911-16; Accountant Public Works Dept EAP, 1916-21; Chief Accountant, Public Works Dept Tanganyika Territory, 1921-25; Gold Coast, 1925-32; Treasurer, Dominica, 1932-36; Mem. Council, Roseau, Dominica, 1932-36; Treasurer, St Lucia, 1940-44; late Member of Executive and Legislative Councils, Dominica and St Lucia; also formerly JP, Special JP, and Vis. JP, Dominica and St Lucia. *Recreations:* gardening, bowls and crosswords. *Address:* 206 The Gateway, Dover, Kent.

**DEAN, Sir John (Norman),** Kt 1957; *b* 13 Dec. 1899; *s* of late George Dean; *m* 1935, Charlotte Helen Audrey, *d* of late Thomas Atkinson Walker; one *s*. *Educ:* Felsted; King's Coll., London University. BSc London (Hons Chemistry). Flying Officer, RNAS and RAF, 1916-19. Chairman: The Telegraph Construction and Maintenance Co. Ltd, 1954-61; Submarine Cables Ltd, 1960-63; Asst to President, General Cable Corporation of New York, USA, 1964-69, retd. ARIC; FIRI; Comp. IEE. *Publications:* important papers on thermoplastics and submarine cables, to technical and scientific bodies. *Recreation:* horse racing. *Address:* Winkhurst Green, Ide Hill, Sevenoaks, Kent. *T:* Ide Hill 245. *Club:* Army and Navy.

**DEAN, Sir Maurice (Joseph),** KCB 1957 (CB 1946); KCMG 1949; Assistant Managing Director, British Printing Corporation, since 1969 (Director since 1966); *b* 16 Sept. 1906; *y s* of late W. J. Dean, Purley, Surrey; *m* 1943, Anne, *d* of W. F. Gibson, Cardiff; one *s* one *d*. *Educ:* St Olave's; Trinity Coll., Cambridge. Mathematical Tripos Part I, 1926; Part II, 1928; Mayhew Prize. asst Principal, Air Ministry, 1929; Asst Under-Secretary of State, 1943; Deputy Secretary, Control Office for Germany and Austria, 1946; Deputy Under-Secretary of State, Foreign Office (German Section), 1947-48; Deputy Secretary, Ministry of Defence, 1948-52; Third Secretary, HM Treasury, 1952; Second Secretary, Board of Trade, 1952-55; Permanent Under-Secretary of State, Air Ministry, 1955-63; a Second Secretary, HM Treasury, Nov. 1963-64; Joint Permanent Under-Secretary of State, Dept of Education and Science, April-Oct. 1964; Permanent Secretary, Ministry of Technology, 1964-66. Co-opted, Member Cambridge Univ. Appointments Board, 1957-60; Member Cambridge Univ. Women's Appointments Board, 1963. Chairman, London Advisory Board, Salvation Army, 1968. Visiting Prof., Dept of Industrial Administration, Strathclyde Univ., 1966. Hon. LLD Strathclyde, 1970. *Address:* 27 Bathgate Road, SW19. *T:* 01-946 0290. *Clubs:* Oxford and Cambridge; Royal Wimbledon (Golf).

**DEAN, Sir Patrick (Henry),** GCMG 1963 (KCMG 1957; CMG 1947); Director, Taylor Woodrow, since 1969; Chairman, Crowell Collier & Macmillan Ltd; *b* 16 March 1909; *o s* of late Professor H. R. Dean and Irene, *d* of Charles Arthur Wilson; *m* 1947, Patricia Wallace, *y d* of late T. Frame Jackson; two *s*. *Educ:* Rugby Sch.; Gonville and Caius Coll., Cambridge. Classical Scholar, Gonville and Caius Coll., 1928; First Class Hons, Classical Tripos Part I; Law Tripos Parts 1 and 2, 1929-32; Fellow of Clare Coll., Cambridge, 1932-35; called to the Bar, 1934; Barstow Law Scholar, Inns of Court, 1934; practised at Bar, 1934-39; Asst Legal Adviser, Foreign Office, 1939-45; Head of German Political Dept, FO, 1946-50; Minister at HM Embassy, Rome, 1950-51; Senior Civilian Instructor at Imperial Defence Coll., 1952-53; Asst Under-Secretary of State, Foreign Office, 1953-56; Dep. Under-Secretary of State, Foreign Office, 1956-60; Permanent Representative of the United Kingdom to the United Nations, 1960-64; Ambassador in Washington, 1965-69. Hon. Fellow, Clare Coll. and Gonville and Caius Coll., Cambridge, 1965. Hon. Bencher, Lincoln's Inn, 1965. Hon. LLD Lincoln Wesleyan Univ., 1961, Chattanooga Univ., 1962, Hofstra Univ., 1964, Columbia Univ., 1965, University of South Carolina, 1967, College of William and Mary, 1968. *Publications:* various articles and notes in the Law Quarterly Review. *Recreations:* mountains, swimming. *Address:* 5 Bentinck Mansions, Bentinck Street, W1. *T:* 01-935 0881. *Clubs:* Brooks's, Beefsteak.

**DEAN, Paul;** *see* Dean, A. P.

**DEAN, Rt. Rev. Ralph Stanley;** *see* Cariboo, Bishop of.

**DEAN, Raymond;** *see* Dean, C. R.

**DEAN, Prof. William Reginald,** MA Cambridge; *b* 5 Nov. 1896; *er s* of late W. J. Dean, Purley, Surrey; *m* 1926, Dorothy, *er d* of late C. R. Terrett, Swansea; one *s* one *d. Educ:* Christ's Hospital; Trinity Coll., Cambridge. Mathematical Tripos, Part I, 1919; Part II, 1921; Rayleigh Prize, 1923; Adams Prize, 1951. Fellow of Trinity Coll., 1923-. Asst Prof., Imperial Coll. of Science, 1924-29; Lecturer, Trinity Coll., Cambridge, and University Lecturer in Mathematics, 1929-52; Goldsmid Prof. of Mathematics, University College, London, 1952-64. Visiting Prof., University of Arizona, USA, 1964-67. *Publications:* various papers on hydrodynamics and elasticity. *Address:* 43 Woodstock Road North, St Albans, Herts. *T:* St Albans 53834. *Club:* Oxford and Cambridge.

**DEAN, Winton (Basil);** author and musical scholar; *b* Birkenhead, 18 March 1916; *e s* of Basil Dean, *qv*, and Esther, *d* of A. H. Van Gruisen; *m* 1939, Hon. Thalia Mary Shaw, 2nd *d* of 2nd Baron Craigmyle; one *s* one adopted *d* (and two *d* decd). *Educ:* Harrow; King's Coll., Cambridge. Translated libretto of Weber's opera *Abu Hassan* (Arts Theatre, Cambridge) 1938. Served War of 1939-45: in Admiralty (Naval Intelligence Div.), 1944-45. Member: Music Panel, Arts Council, 1957-60, Cttee of Handel Opera Society (London), 1955-60; Council, Royal Musical Assoc., 1965-. Ernest Bloch Prof. of Music, University of California (Berkeley), 1965-66. *Publications:* The Frogs of Aristophanes (trans. of choruses to music by Walter Leigh), 1937; Bizet (Master Musicians), 1948; Carmen, 1949; Introduction to the Music of Bizet, 1950; Franck, 1950; Hambledon *v* Feathercombe, the Story of a Village Cricket Match, 1951; Handel's Dramatic Oratorios and Masques, 1959; Shakespeare and Opera (Shakespeare in Music), 1964; Georges Bizet, His Life and Work, 1965; Handel and the Opera Seria, 1969. Contributed to Grove's Dictionary of Music and Musicians (5th edn) and to musical periodicals and learned journals. *Recreations:* cricket, shooting; naval history. *Address:* Hambledon Hurst, Godalming, Surrey. *T:* Wormley 2644.

**DEANE,** family name of **Baron Muskerry.**

**DEANE, Major Donald Victor,** CIE 1947; CBE 1959 (OBE 1941); RE (retired); Consultant to International Nickel Ltd, since 1961; *b* 19 Oct. 1902; *s* of late V. M. Deane, Braiswick, Colchester, Essex; *m* 1929, Dorothy Doreen Cuerden; two *d. Educ:* Gresham's Sch., Holt; RMA, Woolwich. Commissioned into RE, 1922; proceeded to India, 1925; selected for special employment in Indian Mints, 1932; Mint Master, Calcutta, 1938. Retired from Army, 1947. Senior Master of the Indian Govt Mints, 1947-57, retired. 1939-45 Star; India General Service, Silver Jubilee, War, and India Service medals. *Recreation:* golf. *Address:* Tara, Fauvic, Jersey, CI. *Club:* Royal Jersey Golf.

**DEANE, Nora Bryan,** CBE 1957 (MBE 1947); Matron, Bristol Maternity Hospital, 1934-63, retired; *b* 1902; *d* of Stuart and Kathleen Deane, Rosscarbery, Co. Cork. *Educ:* privately. General Training, Prince of Wales's General Hospital, N15, 1924-28; Midwifery Training, Rotunda Hospital, Dublin, 1928-29. President: Royal College of Midwives, 1952-58; International Confederation of Midwives, 1954-57; National Council of Women of Great Britain, 1962-64; Vice-President, International Council of Women, 1966-. Coronation Medal, 1953. Hon. MA Bristol Univ., 1963. *Recreations:* travel, reading. *Address:* 1 Cotham Lawn Road, Bristol 6. *Club:* Cowdray.

**DEANE, William,** CBE 1952; *b* 4 Nov. 1894; 2nd *s* of W. H. Deane and Martha Deane (*née* Copeland), Hart, Co. Durham; unmarried. *Educ:* Grammar Sch., West Hartlepool. Post Office Savings Bank, GPO, 1910. Served European War, 1914-18, Royal Air Force; Air Ministry, 1919; Head, Parliamentary and Air Council Branch, 1940-45; Director of Administration and Finance, RAF Delegation, Washington, DC, 1945-46; Director of Accounts, Air Ministry, 1947-54, retired 1954. *Recreation:* œnology. *Address:* 54 Bishopric Court, Horsham, Sussex. *T:* Horsham 62921. *Club:* Reform.

**DEANE-DRUMMOND, Maj.-Gen. Anthony John,** CB 1970; DSO 1960; MC 1942 and Bar, 1945; Assistant Chief of the Defence Staff (Operations), 1968-70; *b* 23 June 1917; *s* of late Col J. D. Deane-Drummond, DSO, OBE, MC; *m* 1944, Mary Evangeline Boyd; four *d. Educ:* Marlborough Coll.; RMA, Woolwich. Commissioned Royal Signals, 1937. War Service in Europe and N Africa; POW, Italy, 1941 (escaped, 1942); Staff Coll., 1945; Bde Major, 3rd Parachute Bde, 1946-47; Instructor, Sandhurst, 1949-51 and Staff Coll., 1952-55; CO, 22 Special Air Service Regt, 1957-60; Bde Comdr, 44 Parachute Bde, 1961-63; Asst Comdt, RMA, Sandhurst, 1963-66; GOC 3rd Division, 1966-68. *Publication:* Return Ticket, 1951. *Recreations:* gliding (Pilot, British Team, 1958, 1960, 1963, 1965; British Gliding Champion, 1957; Chairman Army Gliding Assoc.); Helicopter pilot. *Address:* c/o Glyn Mills & Co., 67 Lombard Street, EC3. *Clubs:* Special Forces, Airborne, Army and Navy.

**DEANESLY, Margaret,** MA; DLitt Lambeth; FSA; Professor of History, University of London, 1942-50, now Emeritus; *b* 5 March 1885; *d* of Samuel and Clara Maria Deanesly; unmarried. *Educ:* Godolphin Sch., Salisbury; Newnham Coll. Cambridge History Tripos, Part I, 1st Class, 1911; part II, 1st Class, 1912; Arthur Hugh Clough Scholarship, 1912; MA (Manchester), 1915; Marion Kennedy research studentship, 1916-17; Mary Bateson research fellowship, Newnham, 1917-20; lecturer in history, Armstrong Coll., Newcastle, 1920, Manchester, 1922-26; lecturer at R. Holloway Coll., University of London, 1936-39, at Bedford Coll., 1939-42. Birkbeck Lecturer, Cambridge, 1951. DLitt, Lambeth, 1962. *Publications:* The Incendium Amoris of Richard Rolle of Hampole, 1915; The Lollard Bible, 1920; History of the Medieval Church, 1925, 2nd edn 1929, 3rd edn 1934, 4th edn 1947; preface to Burton Abbey, Staffs Record Society, 1936; A History of Europe from 476-911, 1956; The pre-Conquest Church in England, 1961; Sidelights on the Anglo-Saxon Church, 1962; Augustine of Canterbury, 1964; contributions to learned journals. *Recreations:* history of art, and archæology. *Address:* 196 Clarence Gate Gardens, NW1. *T:* 01-723 0912.

**de ARAMBURU, don Gonzalo N.;** Peruvian Ambassador to the Court of St James's, 1962-69; *b* 10 March 1899; *s* of Narciso de Aramburu and Victoria Rosas y de la Puente; *m* 1928, Mercedes Gonzalez; no *c. Educ:* Lima Inst.; Universidad Nacional Mayor de San Marcos, Lima; Central Univ., Madrid. Min. of Foreign Affairs, Lima, 1920; 2nd Secretary, Washington, Berlin, Rome, 1922-29; 1st Secretary, Madrid, Rio de Janeiro, 1929-36;

Counsellor, London, 1936-40; Director of Protocol, Lima, 1940-43; Delegate to French Cttee of National Liberation, Algiers, 1943-44; Minister in Paris, 1944-46; Ambassador to Colombia, Ecuador, Federal Republic of Germany, Uruguay and Netherlands, 1946-62. Grand Officer, Légion d'Honneur, France, 1946; Grand Cross, Order Al Mérito por Servicios Distinguidos, Peru, 1952; various other foreign orders. *Clubs:* White's; Nacional (Peru), etc.

**DEARNLEY, Christopher Hugh,** MA (Oxon), BMus, FRCO; Organist of St Paul's Cathedral since 1968; *b* 11 Feb. 1930; 3rd *s* of Rev. Charles Dearnley; *m* 1957, Bridget (*née* Wateridge); three *s* one *d*. *Educ:* Cranleigh Sch., Surrey; Worcester Coll., Oxford. Organ Scholar, Worcester Coll., Oxford, 1948-52. Asst Organist, Salisbury Cathedral, and Music master, the Cathedral Sch., Salisbury, 1954-57; Organist and Master of the Choristers, Salisbury Cathedral, 1957-67. Pres., Incorporated Assoc. of Organists, 1968-70. *Publications:* The Treasury of English Church Music, Vol. III, 1965; English Church Music 1650-1750, 1970. *Recreations:* sketching, travel, walking or bicycling in London. *Address:* 5 Amen Court, EC4.

**DEARNLEY, Gertrude,** MD, BS London; FRCOG; Gynæcological Surgeon, retired; *d* of late Rev. T. W. Dearnley, MA Oxon, *Educ:* Liverpool High Sch.; London (Royal Free Hospital) School of Medicine for Women. *Recreation:* gardening. *Address:* Mill Cottage, Ewood, Newdigate, Surrey.

**DEAS, (James) Stewart,** MA, BMus, Hon. FTCL; Music Correspondent, Country Life, since 1966; James Rossiter Hoyle Professor of Music in the University of Sheffield, 1948-68 (Dean of the Faculty of Arts, 1955-58); Emeritus Professor 1969; *b* 19 June 1903; *e s* of John Mackenzie Deas, Asst Keeper HM General Register House, Edinburgh and Elizabeth Bryce Cooper; *m* 1936, Hilda Jamieson; one *s* two *d*. *Educ:* George Watson's Coll.; Edinburgh Univ. MA 1924, BMus 1929, Bucher Scholar, 1926-30, in Berlin and Basle. Studied with Sir Donald Tovey and Felix Weingartner. Conductor Edinburgh Opera Co., 1931-33; music critic, Glasgow Evening Times, 1934-35; Director of South African Coll. of Music and Prof. of Music, University of Cape Town, 1935-38; war service Foreign Office and BBC; music critic, The Scotsman, London, 1939-44, Edinburgh (Editorial Staff), 1944-48; Conductor Edinburgh Chamber Orchestra, 1946-48; Member BBC Scottish Music Advisory Cttee, 1947-48; Member Council, Programme Cttee, Edinburgh International Festival, 1946-48; has been Guest Conductor of various orchestras including Hallé, London Symphony, Royal Philharmonic, BBC Scottish, Cape Town Municipal and Hovingham Festival. Conductor, Sheffield Chamber Orchestra, 1951-68; Chairman, Sheffield Bach Society, 1959-63. *Publications:* In Defence of Hanslick, 1940; Or Something, 1941; articles in Music and Letters and other periodicals. *Address:* 1 The Slade, Froxfield, near Petersfield, Hants. *T:* Hawkley 346. *Club:* Savile.

**DEAVIN, Stanley Gwynne,** OBE 1958; FCA; Chartered Accountant; Chairman, North Eastern Gas Board, since 1966 (Dep. Chairman, 1961-66); *b* 8 Aug. 1905; *s* of Percy John Deavin and Annie (*née* Crayton); *m* 1934, Louise Faviell; one *s* one *d*. *Educ:* Hymer's Coll., Hull. Firm of Chartered Accountants, 1921-33; Secretary and Accountant, Preston Gas Co., 1933-49; North Western Gas Board: Secretary, 1949-61; Member Board, 1960-61. *Recreations:* cricket, Rugby football, theatre. *Address:* 50 Hookstone Drive, Harrogate, Yorks. *T:* Harrogate 84301. *Clubs:* Royal Automobile; Lancs County Cricket; Yorks County Cricket.

**DE AZCARATE, Pablo;** *see* Azcarate.

**DE BAKEY, Prof. Michael Ellis,** MD, MS; President and Chief Executive Officer, Baylor College of Medicine, since 1969 (Professor of Surgery and Chairman of Department of Surgery since 1948, Chief Executive Officer, 1968-69; Baylor University College of Medicine; Vice-President for Medical Affairs, Baylor University, 1968-69); Surgeon-in-Chief, Ben Taub General Hospital, Houston, Texas; Director, Cardiovascular Research Center, Methodist Hospital (Houston), since 1968; Consultant in Surgery to various Hospitals etc., in Texas, and to Walter Reed Army Hospital, Washington, DC; *b* 7 Sept. 1908; *s* of Shaker Morris and Raheiga Zerba De Bakey; *m* 1936, Diana Cooper; four *s*. *Educ:* Tulane Univ., New Orleans, La., USA. Residency in New Orleans, Strasbourg, and Heidelberg, 1933-36; Instructor, Dept of Surgery, Tulane Univ., 1937-40; Asst Prof. of Surgery, 1940-46; Associate Prof. of Surgery, 1946-48. Colonel Army of US (Reserve). In Office of Surgeon-General, 1942-46, latterly Director Surgical Consultant Div. Chairman, President's Commission on Heart Disease, Cancer and Stroke, 1964; has served on governmental and university cttees, etc., concerned with public health, research and medical education. Member and Hon. Member of medical societies, including: American Assoc. for Thoracic Surgery (Pres. 1959); International Cardiovascular Society (Pres. 1959); BMA (Hon. Foreign Corresp. Member 1966); Royal Society Med., London. Has received numerous awards from American and foreign medical institutions, and also honorary doctorates. *Publications:* The Blood Bank and the Technique and Therapeutics of Transfusions, 1942; (with B. M. Cohen) Buerger's Disease, 1962; contributions to standard textbooks of medicine and surgery, Current Therapy, and many symposia; Editor, Year Book of General Surgery; etc.; numerous articles in medical journals. *Recreations:* hunting, music. *Address:* Baylor College of Medicine, 1200 Moursund Avenue, Houston, Texas, USA. *T:* JA-94951; 5323 Cherokee, Houston, Texas, USA. *T:* JA-82508. *Clubs:* Cosmos, University Federal (Washington, DC); River Oaks Country (Houston, Texas).

**de BEER, Esmond Samuel,** CBE 1969; FBA 1965; FSA, FRSL, FRHistSoc; historical scholar, specialising in seventeenth-century English history; *b* 1895; *s* of I. S. de Beer and Emily, *d* of Bendix Hallenstein, Dunedin, NZ. *Educ:* Mill Hill Sch.; New Coll., Oxford (MA); University College, London (MA). Studied under late Sir Charles Firth. A Trustee, National Portrait Gallery, 1959-67. Independent Member, Reviewing Cttee on Export of Works of Art, 1965-70. Fellow University College, London, 1967. Hon. Fellow, New Coll., Oxford; Hon. DLitt (Durham, Oxford); Hon. LittD (Otago). Hon. Vice-President: The Historical Association; Hakluyt Society, 1966-. *Publications:* first complete edition of Diary of John Evelyn, 1955; articles and reviews in learned periodicals, etc.; now editing John Locke's correspondence. *Address:* 31 Brompton Square, SW3. *T:* 01-584 5687. *Club:* Athenæum.

**de BEER, Sir Gavin (Rylands),** Kt 1954; FRS; FSA; MA, DSc Oxon; Hon. ScD Cantab; Hon. D.-ès-L. Lausanne; Hon. D. de l'Univ.

Bordeaux; Chev. Lég. d'Hon.; Editorial Consultant, Thomas Nelson Ltd; *b* 1 Nov. 1899; *o s* of Herbert Chaplin de Beer and Mabel, *d* of John Rylands; *m* 1925, Cicely Glyn, *yr d* of Rev. Sir Hubert Medlycott, Bt. *Educ:* Ecole Pascal, Paris; Harrow Sch.; Magdalen Coll., Oxford. Lieut Grenadier Guards, 1918-19; Fellow of Merton Coll., 1923-38; Jenkinson Lecturer in Embryology, Oxford, 1926-38; served 1939-45, Lieut-Colonel Grenadier Guards, GSO1, Psychological Warfare at HQ 21 Army Group; Prof. of Embryology, University College, London, 1945-50; Director, British Museum (Natural History), 1950-60. President: Linnean Society, 1946-49; XV International Congress of Zoology, 1958. Trustee, National Portrait Gallery, 1961-67. Corres. Member: Académie des Sciences, Institut de France; Société d'histoire et d'archéologie de Genève; Société neuchâteloise d'histoire et d'archéologie; Societé vaudoise d'histoire et d'archéologie; Member: Institut International d'Embryol.; British Council; Hon. Member Society Zool. France, Société Royale Zool. Belgique, and Zool. Society, India. Geoffroy-St-Hilaire Gold Medal, 1954; Darwin medal, 1958; Linnean Gold Medal, 1958; Mendel Medal, 1965; Kalinga Prize, UNESCO, 1968. *Publications:* Growth, 1924; Introduction to the Study of Genetics, 1924; Comparative Anatomy, Histology and Development of the Pituitary Body, 1926; Introduction to Experimental Embryology, 1926 (Greek edn 1942); Vertebrate Zoology, 1928; Embryology and Evolution, 1930 (French edn 1933); Early Travellers in the Alps, 1930, new edn 1966; Alps and Men, 1932; The Elements of Experimental Embryology (with J. S. Huxley), 1933; A German Reader for Biology Students (with H. G. Fiedler), 1934; Le Voyage en Suisse de Mme Roland, 1937; Development of the Vertebrate Skull, 1937; On Shelley (with E. Blunden and S. Norman), 1938; Embryos and Ancestors, 1940 (3rd rev. edn 1962); Escape to Switzerland, 1945; Thomas Pennant's Tour on the Continent, 1948; Travellers in Switzerland, 1949; Beaujolois Campbell's Journey to Florence, 1951; Journal du voyage de Gibbon en Suisse, 1952; Speaking of Switzerland, 1952; Sir Hans Sloane and the British Museum, 1953; Archæopteryx, 1954; Alps and Elephants, 1955; The First ascent of Mont Blanc (with T. G. Brown), 1957 (Italian ed., 1961); The Sciences were never at War, 1960; Reflections of a Darwinian, 1962; Charles Darwin, 1963; Atlas of Evolution, 1964; Rede Lecture, Genetics and Prehistory, 1965; Hannibal's March, 1967; Voltaire's British Visitors, 1967; Gibbon and his World, 1968; Hannibal, 1969; Streams of Culture, 1969. Editor and part author of Evolution: Essays presented to E. S. Goodrich, 1938; General Editor, British Men of Science; articles in Encyclopædia Britannica, Chambers's Encyclopædia, and papers in various scientific, military, literary, and alpine journals. *Recreation:* wandering about. *Address:* La Colline, 1880 Bex, Switzerland. *T:* (025)5.20.52.

**DEBENHAM, Sir Gilbert Ridley,** 3rd Bt, *cr* 1931; *b* 28 June 1906; 2nd *s* of Sir Ernest Ridley Debenham, 1st Bt, JP; *S* brother, Sir Piers Debenham, 2nd Bt, 1964; *m* 1935, Violet Mary, *e d* of late His Honour Judge (George Herbert) Higgins; three *s* one *d*. *Educ:* Eton; Trinity Coll., Cambridge. *Heir: s* George Andrew Debenham, *b* 10 April 1938. *Address:* Tonerspuddle Farm, Dorchester, Dorset.

**DEBRE, Michel Jean-Pierre;** Minister of Defence, France, since 1969; *b* 15 Jan. 1912; *s* of Prof. Robert Debré and Dr Jeanne Debré (*née* Debat-Ponsan); *m* 1936, Anne-Marie Lemaresquier; four *s*. *Educ:* Lycée Louis-le-Grand; Faculté de Droit de Paris (LLD); Ecole Libre des Sciences Politiques; Cavalry Sch., Saumur. Auditeur, Conseil d'Etat, 1934; French Army, 1939-44; Commissioner, Angers region, 1944-45; Saar Economic Mission, 1947; Secretary-General for German and Austrian Affairs, 1948. Senator from Indre et Loire, 1948, re-elected 1955; Minister of Justice, 1958-59; Prime Minister, 1959-62; Deputy from St Denis, La Réunion, 1963, re-elected 1967, 1968; Minister of Economic Affairs and Finances, 1966-68; Minister for Foreign Affairs, 1968-69. Member Union des Démocrats pour la Vème République. Officer Légion d'Honneur, Croix de Guerre, Rosette of Résistance, Medal of Escaped Prisoners. *Publications:* Refaire la France 1944; Demain la Paix, 1945; La Mort de l'Etat Républicain, 1948; La République et son Pouvoir, 1950; La République et ses Problèmes, 1951; Ces Princes qui nous Gouvernent, 1957; Au Service de la Nation, 1963; Jeunesse, quelle France te faut-il?, 1965. *Recreation:* equitation. *Address:* 18 rue Spontini, Paris 16e.

**DE BRIGARD, Camilo;** Grand Officer, Order of Boyacá, Colombia; Ambassador of Colombia to the Court of St James's since 1970; *b* 24 Dec. 1906; *m* 1970, Imelda Restrepo de Brigard. *Educ:* Colegio Nacional de San Bartolome and Univ. Nacional, Bogotá, Colombia. MHR, 1930-36; Senator of the Republic, 1936-40; Mem. Adv. Commn of Min. for Foreign Affairs, 1936-40; Prof. of Internat. Public Law and Diplomatic History, Univ. Pontificia Javeriana, Bogotá, 1928-48; Sec.-Gen., IX Inter-American Conf., 1948; Colombian Lawyer to Internat. Court of Justice, The Hague, 1950; Colombian Ambassador to West Germany, 1952-57. Past Deleg. to Gen. Assemblies of the UN. Dir, (newspaper) El Siglo, Bogotá, up to 1969. Mem. Academia de la Lengua, Colombia. Holds foreign Orders of high degree. *Publications:* Los Límites entre Colombia y el Brasil, 1936; Estudios de Derecho Internacional Colombiano, 1940; El Contrato Colectivo de Trabajo, 1968; several articles in internat. and Colombian newspapers and magazines. *Address:* 73 Eaton Square, SW1; Calle 70 No 4-60, Bogotá, Colombia. *Clubs:* White's; Jockey, Country (Bogotá).

**de BROGLIE,** 7th Duc; **Louis Victor de Broglie;** Member of the Institut de France, Académie Française since 1944, Académie des Sciences since 1933; Professor, Faculté des Sciences, Paris, since 1932; Permanent Secretary, Académie des Sciences, since 1942; Foreign Member Royal Society (London) since 1953; *b* Dieppe, 15 Aug. 1892; *s* of Victor, Duc de Broglie; *S* brother, Duc Maurice, 1960; unmarried. *Educ:* Lycée Janson de Sailly, Paris. Licencié ès Lettres, 1910; Licencié ès Sciences, 1913; served Radio-télégraphie Militaire, 1914-19; Docteur ès Sciences, 1924; Maître de Conférences, Faculté des Sciences, Paris, 1928. Nobel Prize for Physics, 1929. *Publications:* Thèse de doctorat sur la théorie des Quanta, 1924; nombreux mémoires, articles, livres sur la physique, en particulier sur la théorie de Quanta et la mécanique ondulatoire et sur la philosophie des sciences. *Address:* 94 Rue Perronet, Neuilly-sur-Seine, France. *T:* Maillot 76.09.

**de BROKE;** *see* Willoughby de Broke.

**de BRUYNE, Dr Norman Adrian,** FRS; President of Techne Inc., since 1967; *b* 8 Nov. 1904; *s* of Pieter Adriaan de Bruyne and Maud de Bruyne (*née* Mattock); *m* 1940, Elma Lilian Marsh; one *s* one *d*. *Educ:* Lancing Coll.; Trinity Coll., Cambridge. MA 1930, PhD 1930. Fellow of

Trinity Coll., Cambridge, 1928-44. Managing Director: Aero Research Ltd, 1934-48; Ciba (ARL) Ltd, 1948-60; Techne (Cambridge) Ltd, 1964-67. Awarded Simms Gold Medal, RAeS, 1937. FInstP 1944; FRAeS 1955; FRS 1967. *Recreation:* inventing. *Address:* RD3 No. 661 Brunswick Pike, Princeton, New Jersey 08540, USA. *T:* 609-452 9275.

**de BUNSEN, Sir Bernard,** Kt 1962; CMG 1957; MA Oxon; Principal of Chester College, Chester, since 1966; *b* 24 July 1907; *s* of late L. H. G. de Bunsen, and late Victoria de Bunsen (*née* Buxton). *Educ:* Leighton Park Sch.; Balliol Coll., Oxford. Schoolmaster, Liverpool Public Elementary Schools, 1930-34; Asst Director of Education, Wiltshire CC, 1934-38; HM Inspector of Schools, Ministry of Education, 1938-46; Director of Education, Palestine, 1946, until withdrawal of British administration, 1948; Professor of Education, Makerere University College, East Africa, 1948, acting Principal, Aug. 1949, Principal, 1950-64, Hon. Fellow, 1968. Vice-Chancellor of University of East Africa, 1963-65; Chairman: Africa Educational Trust, 1967-; Archbishops' Working Party on Future of Theological Colleges, 1967-68. Hon. LLD St Andrews, 1963. *Address:* Chester College, Chester. *Club:* Athenæum.

**de BURGH, Capt. Charles,** DSO 1917; RN (retired); retired as Agent to Dean and Chapter of Durham Diocese, Lord Crewe Trustees, and Croxdale Estates (1933-52); *b* 17 July 1886; *s* of late Lieut-Colonel T. J. de Burgh of Oldtown, Naas, Co. Kildare; *m* 1910, Isabel Caroline Berkeley (*d* 1968), *d* of late Rev. Edward Fitzhardinge Campbell; two *d. Educ:* Tonbridge Castle; Stubbington. Entered Navy, 1902; joined the submarine service 1908; served submarines till 1914; HMS Antrim till 1915; rejoined submarine service, taking command of submarines, 1915; served subsequently in command of HM submarines during war (DSO) until 1923; Mobilisation Dept, Admiralty, 1923-25; commander HMS Valiant and Queen Elizabeth, 1925-26; in command, HMS Cyclops, 1926-27, 6th S/M Flotilla, 1928-29; CO Anti-submarine school (HMS Lucia), 1929-30; Officer Instructor to RNVR Tyne Div., 1930-32; retired, 1932; Naval Officer in Control of Shipping and Convoys, 1939-46. *Address:* Coolattin Lodge, Seaforde, Co. Down. *T:* Seaforde 24.

*See also Sir Robert Kinahan.*

**de BURGH, General Sir Eric,** KCB 1941 (CB 1932); DSO 1916; OBE; idc; psc; Indian Army, retired; *b* Oldtown, Naas, Ireland, 10 May 1881; *s* of late Lieut-Colonel Thomas John de Burgh, of Oldtown, Naas, Co. Kildare; *m* 1923, Mary (*d* 1934), *d* of late Lieut-Gen. Sir E. A. Fanshawe, KCB; two *d. Educ:* St Mark's Sch., Windsor; Marlborough Coll. 2nd Lieut, and Lieut, 3rd Royal Dublin Fusiliers (Militia); 2nd Lieut Manchester Regt 1903; Lieut, Captain, Major, 9th Hodson's Horse; Colonel Indian Army. 1923; Maj.-General, 1934; Lieut-General, 1938; General, 1940; served South Africa, 1902 (Queen's medal, 4 clasps); World War (1914 Star, GS and Victory Medals, despatches, DSO, Brevets of Major and Lieut-Colonel); Afghanistan and NWF, 1919 (despatches, medal and clasp); Waziristan, 1922 (despatches, OBE, clasp); Commanded, 1st Indian Div., Waziristan, 1937 (despatches, medal and clasp); GSO1, Staff Coll., Quetta, 1928-30; Brig., Gen. Staff, Eastern Command, India, 1930-31; Comm. 1st Risalpur Cavalry Brigade, India, 1931-34; Comdr, Lahore District, 1934-35; Deputy Chief of the Gen. Staff, Army Headquarters, India, 1935-36; Commander Rawalpindi District, 1936-38; Chief of Gen. Staff, India, 1939-41; retired, 1941. *Address:* Bargy Castle, Tomhaggard, Wexford, Ireland. *T:* Tomhaggard 3. *Clubs:* Special Forces; Kildare Street (Dublin).

**DE BUTTS, Brig. Frederick Cromie,** CB 1943; DSO 1917; MC; Indian Army, retired; *b* 6 Nov. 1888; *s* of Capt. F. R. McC. De Butts, RA, and CM, *d* of Capt. Dalgairns Travers, 17th Foot; *m* 1st, K. P. M. (*d* 1916), *d* of O. O'Donnell, of Hintlesham, Suffolk; one *s*; 2nd, 1920, Sybil Katherine, *d* of late Canon H. W. Beauchamp of Copdock, Suffolk. *Educ:* Wellington Coll.; RMC, Sandhurst. Lieut-Colonel, 1933; Colonel, 1938; Brigadier, 1940; retired, 1943. *Address:* Swallowfield Park, Reading, Berks. *T:* Reading 882383.

*See also Colonel F. M. De Butts.*

**DE BUTTS, Col Frederick Manus,** CMG 1967; OBE 1961 (MBE 1943); Defence Attaché, British Embassy, Cairo, since 1968; *b* 17 April, 1916; *s* of Brig. F. C. De Butts, *qv; m* 1944, Evelyn Cecilia, *d* of Sir Walter Halsey, 2nd Bt; one *s* one *d. Educ:* Wellington Coll.; Oriel Coll., Oxford. Commissioned into Somerset LI, 1937. Served War of 1939-45, in Middle East, Italy, France and Germany. Staff Coll., 1944; Joint Services Staff Coll., 1954; Bt Lieut-Colonel, 1957; Commanded 3rd Bn Aden Protectorate Levies, 1958-60; Bde Colonel, Light Infantry, 1961-64; Comdr, Trucial Oman Scouts, 1964-67; HQ Home Counties District, Shorncliffe, Kent, 1967-68. *Recreations:* tennis, sailing, riding, shooting. *Address:* British Embassy, Cairo; c/o Foreign and Commonwealth Office, King Charles Street, SW1. *Club:* Army and Navy.

**de CANDOLE, Eric Armar Vully,** CMG 1952; CBE 1950; MA; Sudan Political Service (retired); *b* 14 Sept. 1901; *e s* of late Rev. Armar Corry Vully de Candole, Rector of Ayot Saint Lawrence, Hertfordshire and late Edith Hodgson; *m* 1932, Marian Elizabeth Pender, *d* of Maj. H. Constable Roberts, DSO, MVO; three *s. Educ:* Colet Court; Aldenham Sch.; Worcester Coll., Oxford (Exhibitioner). Hons, Modern History, 1923, BA 1924, MA 1946. Joined Sudan Political Service, 1923; served in Education Dept as Tutor, Gordon Coll., 1923-27; Acting Warden, 1927-28; Berber, Khartoum and Darfur Provinces as Dist Comr and Magistrate, 1928-36; Resident, Dar Masalit, 1936-44; Dep.-Governor, Northern Province, 1944-46; seconded to British Military Administration as Chief Secretary, Cyrenaica, 1946-48; Chief Administrator, Somalia, 1948; Chief Administrator, Cyrenaica, 1948-49; HBM's Resident in Cyrenaica, 1949-51. With Kuwait Oil Co. Ltd, 1952-66. Order of the Nile, Egypt (4th class), 1934; Order of Istiqlal, Libya (1st class), 1954. *Publications:* articles on Middle East. *Recreations:* gardening, riding and travel. *Address:* Shootwood, Burley, Hants. *T:* Burley 2330. *Club:* Travellers'.

**de CANDOLE, Rt. Rev. Henry Handley Vully;** *b* 25 May 1895; *s* of late Very Rev. H. L. C. V. de Candole, Dean of Bristol, and late Helen Edith, *d* of Sir Henry Thompson, 1st Bt; *m* 1937, Frances Sophia Cornwall, *d* of late Ven. A. W. Cornwall, Archdeacon of Cheltenham; no *c. Educ:* Marlborough Coll.; King's Coll. and Westcott House, Cambridge. Deacon, 1920; Priest, 1921; Asst Chaplain, Marlborough Coll., 1920-22; Resident Chaplain to Archbishop (Davidson) of Canterbury, 1923-26; Asst Curate of St John's, Newcastle on Tyne, 1926-31, Vicar, 1931-32; Chaplain of Peterhouse, Cambridge, 1932-34; Dean, 1933-34; Chaplain of Theological Coll., Chichester, 1934-37; Liturgical Missioner, diocese of Chichester, 1937-49; Priest-in-charge, Wiston with

Buncton, Sussex, 1939-40; Vicar of Henfield, Sussex, 1940-49; Prebendary of Bracklesham in Chichester Cathedral, 1945-49; Bishop Suffragan of Knaresborough, 1949-65. *Publications:* The Church's Offering, 1935; The Sacraments and the Church, 1935; The Church's Prayers, 1939; The Story of Henfield, 1947; Lent with the Church, 1952; The Christian Use of the Psalms, 1955. *Address:* 21 Brunswick Drive, Harrogate, Yorks. *T:* Harrogate 3632.

**de CHAIR, Somerset;** *b* 22 Aug. 1911; *s* of late Admiral Sir Dudley de Chair, Governor of NSW; *m* 1st, 1932, Thelma Arbuthnot (marr. diss. 1950); one *s* (and one *s* decd); 2nd, 1950, Carmen Appleton (*née* Bowen) (marr. diss. 1958); two *s*; 3rd, 1958, Mrs Margaret Patricia Manlove (*née* Field-Hart); one *d. Educ:* King's Sch., Paramatta, New South Wales; Balliol Coll., Oxford. MP (Nat C) for S. West Norfolk, 1935-45; Parliamentary Private Secretary to Rt Hon. Oliver Lyttleton, MP, Minister of Production, 1942-44; MP (C) South Paddington, 1950-51. 2nd Lieut Supp. Res. RHG, 1938; served with Household Cavalry in the Middle East, during Iraqi and Syrian campaigns (wounded), IO to 4th Cavalry Bde, 1940-41; Captain GS (I), 1942; Chairman National Appeal Cttee of UN Assoc., and member of National Exec., 1947-50. *Publications:* The Impending Storm, 1930, and Divided Europe, 1931 (on International situation); Peter Public, 1932 (a political extravaganza); Enter Napoleon, 1935 (a novel); Red Tie in the Morning (a novel), 1937; The Golden Carpet (Iraq Campaign), 1943; The Silver Crescent (Syrian Campaign), 1943; A Mind on the March, 1945; Editor of Napoleon's Memoirs (2 vols), 1945; edited and translated Supper at Beaucaire by Napoleon, 1945; The First Crusade (edited and translated from Gesta Francorum), 1946; The Teetotalitarian State (a novel), 1947; The Dome of the Rock (a novel), 1948; The Millennium (poems), 1949; Julius Caesar's Commentaries (new edn), 1952; The Story of a Lifetime (novel), 1954; The Waterloo Campaign, 1957; Editor of Admiral de Chair's memoirs, The Sea is Strong, 1961; Bring Back the Gods (novel), 1962; Collected Verse, 1970. *Address:* St Osyth Priory, St Osyth, Essex; Farm of the Running Waters, Kortright, Delaware County, New York, USA. *Club:* Carlton.

**DECIES,** 6th Baron *cr* 1812; **Arthur George Marcus Douglas de la Poer Beresford;** Ex-Flying Officer, RAFVR (DFC, USA); *b* 24 April 1915; *s* of 5th Baron Decies and Helen Vivien (*d* 1931), *d* of late George Jay Gould; *S* father, 1944; *m* 1937, Ann Trevor (*d* 1945); *m* 1945, Mrs Diana Galsworthy; one *s* two *d. Heir: s* Hon. Marcus Hugh Tristram de la Poer Beresford [*b* 5 Aug. 1948; *m* 1970, Sarah Jane, *o d* of Col Basil Gunnell, New Romney, Kent]. *Address:* Château de Betouzet, Andrein, Sauveterre de Bearn, Basses Pyrenées, France.

**DE CLIFFORD,** 26th Baron *cr* 1299; **Edward Southwell Russell,** OBE 1955; Colonel (retired) REME, TA; *b* 30 Jan. 1907; *o s* of 25th Baron and Evelyn Victoria Anne, *d* of Walter Robert Chandler [she *m* 2nd, 1913, Capt. Arthur Roy Stock (*d* 1915); 3rd, G. V. Tate, MC]; *S* father, 1909; *m* 1926, Dorothy Evelyn Meyrick; two *s. Educ:* Eton; Engineering Coll. of London Univ. *Heir: s* Hon. John Edward Southwell Russell [*b* 8 June 1928; *m* 1959, Bridget Jennifer, *yr d* of Duncan Robertson, Llangollen, Denbs]. *Address:* The Birches, Silvington, Cleobury Mortimer, Kidderminster, Worcs.

*See also His Honour Judge T. Elder-Jones.*

**de COURCY,** family name of **Baron Kingsale.**

**de COURCY, Kenneth Hugh;** *b* 6 Nov. 1909; 2nd *s* of late Stephen de Courcy of Co. Galway and Hollinwood Mission, and late Minnie de Courcy; *m* 1950, Rosemary Catherine, *o d* of late Comdr H. L. S. Baker, OBE, RN (retired), Co. Roscommon, Eire; two *s* two *d. Educ:* King's College Sch. and by travelling abroad. 2nd Lieut, 3rd City of London Regt (Royal Fusiliers) TA (Regular Army Candidate), 1927. 2nd Lieut Coldstream Guards (Supplementary Reserve), 1930; Lieut and resigned, 1931; Hon. Secretary to late Sir Reginald Mitchell-Banks' unofficial cttee on Conservative policy, 1933; 1934, formed with Earl of Mansfield, late Viscount Clive, late Lord Phillimore, and with Sir Victor Raikes, KBE, Imperial Policy Group and was Hon. Secretary 1934-39; travelled as Group's chief observer of Foreign Affairs in Europe and America, 1935-39; special visit of enquiry to Mussolini, Doctor Beneš, Dr Schuschnigg, 1936; to King Boris of Bulgaria, etc., 1938; to Italy and King Boris, 1939-40; adviser on War Intelligence to United Steel Companies Ltd, 1944-45. Formerly published monthly serial memoranda on Foreign Affairs and Strategy, (1938-); was Proprietor of: Intelligence Digest; The Weekly Review, 1958-66; Director of Ringrone Newspapers Ltd, 1966. Editor, Bankers Digest, 1969-. Lord of the Manors of Stow-on-the-Wold and Maugersbury, Glos. Hon. Citizen of New Orleans, La, USA, 1950. *Publications:* Review of World Affairs (23 vols since 1938); various articles on Strategy and Foreign Affairs. *Recreation:* climbing. *Address:* c/o Ward Bowie & Co., 2 Clements Inn, WC2.

**DE COURCY-IRELAND, Lt-Col Gerald Blakeney,** MVO 1917; MC 1916; The Worcestershire Regt; *b* 1895; *m* 1924, Helen Beresford, *e d* of late John Stapleton-Martin, MA, barrister-at-law, and late Mrs Stapleton-Martin, Wood Hall, Norton, Worcester; one *d. Educ:* Sherborne; Clare Coll., Cambridge. Temp. 2nd Lieut King's Royal Rifle Corps, 1914; temp. Lieut 1915; temp. Captain, 1916; Acting Major, 1917; Adjutant, 9th Service Batt., 1918; relinquished Commission, 1920; Lieut The Worcestershire Regt, 1916; Captain, 1925; Major, 1938; retired pay, 1946. *Recreation:* shooting. *Address:* Greenways, 1 Bank Farm Road, Shrewsbury SY3 9DH. *T:* Shrewsbury 2993. *See also J. R. T. Hooper.*

**DEDIJER, Vladimir,** DJur, MA Oxon; Order of Liberation, of Yugoslavia, etc.; Yugoslav Author; *b* 4 Feb. 1914; *m* 1944, Vera Krizman; one *s* two *d* (and two *s* decd). *Educ:* Belgrade Univ. Served War from 1941, Tito's Army, Lieut-Colonel; Yugoslav Delegate to Peace Conference, Paris, 1946, and to UN General Assemblies, 1945, 1946, 1948, 1949, 1951, 1952. Member Central Cttee, League of Communists of Yugoslavia, 1952-54, when expelled (defended right of M Djilas to free speech, 1954; sentenced to 6 months on probation, 1955). Prof. of Modern History, Belgrade Univ., 1954-55. Simon Senior Fellow, Manchester Univ., 1960; Research Fellow, St Antony's Coll., Oxford, 1962-63; Research Associate, Harvard Univ., 1963-64; Visiting Prof., Cornell Univ., 1964-65. Hon. Fellow, Manchester Univ.; Member Historical Institute of Serbian Academy of Science, 1964. President International War Crimes Tribunal, 1966. Member, Serbian Acad. of Science. *Publications:* Partisan Diary, 1945; Notes from the United States, 1945; Paris Peace Conference, 1948; Yugoslav-Albanian Relations, 1949; Tito, 1952; Military Conventions, 1960; The Beloved Land, 1960; Road to Sarajevo, 1966; The Battle Stalin Lost, 1969. Contrib. to Acta Scandinavica. *Address:* Gorkičeva 16, Ljubljana, Yugoslavia. *T:* 61-729.

**DEE, Philip Ivor,** CBE 1946 (OBE 1943); FRS 1941; MA Cantab; Professor of Natural Philosophy at University of Glasgow since 1943; *b* Stroud, Glos., 8 April 1904; *s* of Albert John Dee, Stroud; *m* 1929, Phyllis Elsie Tyte; two *d*. *Educ:* Marling Sch., Stroud; Sidney Sussex Coll., Cambridge (Scholar). Stokes Student at Pembroke Coll., Cambridge, 1930-33; Lecturer in Physics at Cavendish Laboratory and Fellow of Sidney Sussex Coll., Cambridge, 1934-43; Superintendent, Telecommunications Research Establishment, Ministry of Aircraft Production, 1939-45. Advisory Council DSIR, 1947-52. Hughes Medal of Royal Society, 1952. *Publications:* scientific papers in Proceedings of Royal Society, etc. *Address:* Department of Natural Philosophy, University of Glasgow, Glasgow W2.

**DEED, Basil Lingard,** OBE 1946; TD; MA. Headmaster of Stamford School, 1947-68; *b* 1909; *s* of late S. G. Deed, Maldon; *m* 1937, Elizabeth Mary, *d* of S. P. Cherrington, Berkhamsted; four *d*. *Educ:* Haileybury Coll.; Peterhouse, Cambridge. 2nd Class Classical Tripos Part I; 1st class Classical Tripos Part II. Asst Master, Berkhamsted School, 1931-37; Asst Master, Shrewsbury Sch., 1937-47; served War of 1939-45, mostly on General Staff; Lieut-Colonel MEF, 1943; Italy, 1944-45. *Address:* Bendor, Warborough, Oxon. *T:* Warborough 514. *Clubs:* National Liberal; Blackwater Sailing.

**DEEDES, Maj.-Gen. Charles Julius,** CB 1968; OBE 1953; MC 1944; Chief of Staff, Eastern Command, 1965-68, retired; *b* 18 Oct. 1913; *s* of General Sir Charles Deedes, KCB, CMG, DSO; *m* 1939, Beatrice Murgatroyd, Brockfield Hall, York; three *s*. *Educ:* Oratory Sch.; Royal Military Coll., Sandhurst. Served War of 1939-45 (despatches); Asst Military Secretary, GHQ Middle East, 1945; Officer Comdg Glider Pilot Regt, 1948; GSO1 War Office, 1950; Officer Comdg 1st Bn KOYLI, 1954 (despatches); Colonel General Staff, War Office, 1956; Comd 146 Infantry Brigade (TA), 1958; Deputy Director, Ministry of Defence, 1962. Colonel of the KOYLI, 1966-68. Dep. Colonel, The Light Infantry (Yorks), 1968-. Military Cross (Norway), 1940. *Recreations:* hunting, tennis. *Address:* Lea Close, Brandsby, York. *T:* Brandsby 239. *Club:* United Service.

**DEEDES, Percy Gordon,** CMG 1962; OBE 1958; *b* 2 July 1899; twin *s* of late Gordon Frederic Deedes, Hythe, Kent, England; *m* 1927, Audrey Winifred (*d* 1968), *d* of late Alfred Riva Harvey, Salisbury, Rhodesia; one *d*. *Educ:* Repton. Served European War, 1917-19, RNAS and RAF as Flt Lieut. In business Kenya, 1920-23; Union of South Africa, 1923-28; farming in S Rhodesia, 1928-51. Served War, 1940-42, RAF as Flt Lieut, in Greece and Middle East. Chm., Natural Resources Board of Rhodesia, 1951-65. *Address:* Saltwood, P.O. Box 50, Penhalonga, Rhodesia.

**DEEDES, Rt. Hon. William Francis,** PC 1962; MC 1944; MP (C) Ashford Division of Kent since 1950; DL; *b* 1 June 1913; *s* of William Herbert Deedes; *m* 1942, Evelyn Hilary Branfoot; two *s* three *d*. *Educ:* Harrow. Parliamentary Sec., Ministry of Housing and Local Government, Oct. 1954-Dec. 1955; Parliamentary Under-Sec., Home Dept., 1955-57; Minister without Portfolio, 1962-64. DL, Kent, 1962. *Address:* New Hayters, Aldington, Kent. *T:* Aldington 269. *Club:* Junior Carlton.

**DEEGAN, Joseph William,** CMG 1956; CVO 1954; Inspector-General of Colonial Police, 1966-67; *b* 8 Feb. 1899; *s* of John and Sarah Deegan; *m* 1926, Elinor Elsie Goodson; one *s* two *d*. *Educ:* St Paul's and St Gabriel's Schs, Dublin. Army, 1919-25 (seconded to King's African Rifles, 1922-25); Tanganyika Police, 1925-38; Uganda Police, 1938-56 (Commissioner of Police, 1950-56); Dep. Inspector-Gen. of Colonial Police, 1956-61, 1963-65. Colonial Police Medal, 1942; King's Police Medal, 1950. *Address:* Tuffshard, Cuckmere Road, Seaford, Sussex. *T:* Seaford 4180.

**DEER, George,** OBE 1944; *b* 29 March 1890; *m* 1916, Olive Stoakes (*see* Olive G. Deer); one *s* one *d*. *Educ:* Elementary. Trade Union Official for 30 years with Workers' Union, later Transport and General Workers' Union. Alderman and Councillor Lincoln City Council, 1922-38, 1945-50; Mayor of Lincoln, 1933-34; Sheriff of Lincoln, 1943-44. MP (Lab) Lincoln, 1945-50, Newark Div. of Notts, 1950-64. *Address:* 13 Hunsley Crescent, Grimsby. *T:* Cleethorpes 63624.

**DEER, Mrs Olive G.;** Member of Grimsby Borough Council, 1964-67; *b* Grimsby, 31 July 1897; *m* 1916, George Deer, *qv*; one *s* one *d*. *Educ:* Barcroft Street Sch., Cleethorpes, Lincs. Member: Min. of Labour Exchange Cttees, 1921-45; Bd of Guardians, 1922-25; Bracebridge Mental Hosp. Cttee, 1933-47; Lincoln City Council, 1945-49; Sheffield Regional Hosp. Bd, 1948-50; Bd of Nat. Hosp., Queen Square, 1950; S Eastern Metrop. Regional Hosp. Bd, 1957. Dir, 1940-50, Chm., 1946-48, Lincoln Co-operative Soc. Alderman, LCC, 1952-58; Councillor, LCC (Shoreditch and Finsbury), 1958-64. Chm. LCC Welfare Cttee, 1955-62; Chm. of the London County Council, 1962-63. *Address:* 13 Hunsley Crescent, Grimsby. *T:* Cleethorpes 63624.

**DEER, Prof. William Alexander,** MSc Manchester, PhD Cantab; FRS 1962; FGS; Professor of Mineralogy and Petrology, Cambridge University, since Oct. 1961; Master of Trinity Hall, Cambridge, since 1966; *b* 26 Oct. 1910; *s* of William Deer; *m* 1939, Margaret Marjorie, *d* of William Kidd; two *s* one *d*. *Educ:* Manchester Central High Sch.; Manchester Univ.; St John's Coll., Cambridge. Graduate Research Scholar, 1932, Beyer Fellow, 1933, Manchester Univ.; Strathcona Studentship, St John's Coll., Cambridge, 1934; Petrologist on British East Greenland Expedition, 1935-36; 1851 Exhibition Senior Studentship, 1938; Fellow, St John's Coll., Cambridge, 1939; served War of 1939-45, RE, 1940-45. Murchison Fund Geological Soc. of London, 1945; Junior Bursar, St John's Coll., 1946; Leader NE Baffin Land Expedition, 1948; Bruce Medal, Royal Society of Edinburgh, 1948; Tutor, St John's Coll., 1949; Prof. of Geology, Manchester Univ., 1950-61; Fellow of St John's Coll., Cambridge, 1961-66, Hon. Fellow, 1969. Percival Lecturer, Univ. of Manchester, 1953; Joint Leader East Greenland Geological Expedition, 1953; Leader British East Greenland Expedition, 1966. Trustee, British Museum (Natural History), 1967. President: Mineralogical Soc., 1968-69; Geological Soc., 1970-; Mem., NERC, 1968-. *Publications:* papers in Petrology and Mineralogy. *Recreation:* gardening. *Address:* The Master's Lodge, Trinity Hall, Cambridge. *T:* Cambridge 52396.

**DEERHURST, Viscount; Edward George William Coventry;** *b* 24 Sept. 1957; *s* and *heir* of 11th Earl of Coventry, *qv*.

**DEEVES, Thomas William,** CMG 1953; CBE 1949; MC 1917, and Bar 1918; Civil Service, 1911-54; *b* 19 March 1893; *s* of S. Deeves,

Kilcooly, Thurles, Co. Tipperary; *m* 1921 Lilian Mary Thornton (*d* 1969); one *s* one *d*. *Educ:* Lurgan Coll., N Ireland. Served European War, 1914-18. Formerly Asst Sec., Ministry of Food and Foreign Office. *Recreation:* fishing. *Address:* Crossways, Gerrards Cross, Bucks. *T:* Gerrards Cross 83279. *Club:* English-Speaking Union.

**de FARIA, Antonio Leite;** Grand Cross of Christ (Portugal), 1949; Portuguese Ambassador to the Court of St James's, since 1968; *b* 23 March 1904; *s* of Dr Antonio B. Leite de Faria and Dona Lucia P. de Sequeira Braga Leite de Faria; *m* 1926, Dona Herminia Cantilo de Faria; two *s*. *Educ:* Lisbon University (Faculty of Law). Attaché to Min. of Foreign Affairs, 1926; Sec. to Portuguese Delegn, League of Nations, 1929-30; 2nd Sec., Rio de Janeiro, 1931, Paris, 1933, Brussels, 1934; 1st Sec., London, 1936; Counsellor, London, 1939; Minister to Exiled Allied Govts, London, 1944; Minister to The Hague, 1945; Dir Gen., Political Affairs, and Acting Sec. Gen., Min. of Foreign Affairs, 1947; Ambassador: Rio de Janeiro, 1950; NATO, 1958; Paris, 1959; Rome (Holy See), 1961; London, 1968. Holds many foreign decorations. *Address:* 12 Belgrave Square, SW1. *T:* 01-235 3688; Rua da Horta Seca 11, Lisboa. *T:* 32 25 38; Casa do Bom Retiro, S Pedro de Azurem, Guimarães. *T:* 40408.

**de FERRANTI, Basil Reginald Vincent Ziani;** Executive Director, International Computers Ltd; Director, Ferranti Ltd; *b* 2 July 1930; *yr s* of Sir Vincent de Ferranti, *qv*; *m* 1st, 1956, Susan Sara (from whom he obtained a divorce, 1963; she *m* 1963, Peter Henriques), *d* of late Christopher and of Lady Barbara Gore; three *s*; 2nd, 1964, Simone, *d* of late Col and of Mrs H. J. Nangle; one *d*. *Educ:* Eton; Trinity Coll., Cambridge. Served 4th/7th Royal Dragoon Guards, 1949-50. Man., Domestic Appliance Dept, Ferranti Ltd, 1954-57. Contested Exchange Div. of Manchester, Gen. Election, 1955; MP (C) Morecambe and Lonsdale Div. of Lancaster, Nov. 1958-Sept. 1964. Dir of overseas operations, Ferranti Ltd, 1957-62; Parliamentary Sec., Ministry of Aviation, July-Oct. 1962; resigned, to return to firm of Ferranti Ltd. Dep. Man. Dir, Internat. Computers and Tabulators, Sept. 1963 until Managing Dir, 1964. Pres., British Computer Soc., 1968-69; Chm., UK Automation Council, 1968-. Member of Council: Instn of Electrical Engineers, 1962-65; Cheltenham Coll., 1959-66. *Publications:* contrib. Brit. Computer Soc. Jl and Procs. Internat. Fedn for Information Processing. *Recreation:* skiing. *Address:* ICL House, Putney, SW15. *T:* 01-788 7272; 16 Chelsea Park Gardens, SW3. *T:* 01-352 1011; Adders Moss, Over Alderley, Macclesfield, Cheshire. *T:* Alderley Edge 3237.

*See also S. B. J. Z. de Ferranti.*

**de FERRANTI, Sebastian Basil Joseph Ziani;** Chairman and Managing Director, Ferranti Ltd, since 1963 (Managing Director, 1958; Director 1954); *b* 5 Oct. 1927; *er s* of Sir Vincent de Ferranti, *qv*; *m* 1953, Mona Helen, *d* of T. E. Cunningham; one *s* two *d*. *Educ:* Ampleforth. Served 4th/7th Royal Dragoon Guards, 1947-49. Trained with Brown Boveri, Switzerland, and Alsthom, France; joined Transformer Dept, Ferranti Ltd, 1950. President: Electrical Research Assoc., 1968-69; BEAMA, 1969-. Mem., Nat. Defence Industries Council, 1969-. Hon. DSc, Salford Univ., 1967. *Address:* Kerfield House, Knutsford, Cheshire. *Clubs:* Athenæum, Cavalry.

*See also B. R. V. Z. de Ferranti.*

**de FERRANTI, Sir Vincent Ziani,** Kt 1948; LLD (*hc*); DEng (*hc*); FIEE; Chairman, Ferranti Ltd, 1930-63; *b* 16 Feb. 1893; *s* of Dr Sebastian Ziani de Ferranti, FRS and Gertrude Ruth Ince; *m* 1919, Dorothy H. C. Wilson; two *s* three *d*. *Educ:* Repton. Served European War, 1914-19, Royal Engineers, Capt. (MC); War of 1939-45, Major Comdg Field Coy. RE, France, 1939-40. Lieut-Col Comdg 63rd County of Lancs Bn Home Guard, 1940-44. Hon. Col 123 Field Engr Regt RE, TA, 1948-57. Chairman: International Executive Council, and British National Cttee, World Power Conference, 1950-62; Brit. Electrical and Allied Mfctrs Assoc., 1938-39. Vice-Pres. 1946-57, Pres. 1957-59; Pres. Instn of Electrical Engineers, 1946-47; Pres. British Electrical Power Convention, 1949-50; Pres. Television Soc., 1954-57. *Address:* Henbury Hall, Macclesfield, Cheshire. *T:* Macclesfield 2400. *Clubs:* Athenæum, Devonshire, Royal Aero.

*See also B. R. V. Z. and S. B. J. Z. de Ferranti.*

**de FISCHER-REICHENBACH, Henry-Béat,** Dr jur.; Swiss Ambassador to the Court of St James's, 1964-66; *b* 22 July 1901; *s* of Henry B. de Fischer-Reichenbach, bailiff-delegate of the Sov. Order of Malta in Switzerland, and Caroline Falck-Crivelli; *m* 1949, Madeleine de Graffenried; three *d*. *Educ:* Stella Matutina Jesuit Coll., Feldkirch; Universities of Fribourg, Munich, Paris and Berne. Entered Federal Political Dept, Berne, 1929; Attaché, Swiss Legation, The Hague, 1931; Second Secretary, Buenos-Aires and Montevideo, 1933; First Secretary: Warsaw, 1939; Bucharest, 1940; Chargé d'affaires successively Riga, Kowno, Reval, Helsinki, 1940; Counsellor: Bucharest, 1941; Cairo and Beirut, 1947; Minister: Cairo, 1949; Ethiopia, 1952; Lisbon, 1954; Ambassador, Vienna, 1959. Mem. Board of Patrons, C. G. Jung Inst., Zurich. President: Fondation pour l'histoire des Suisses à l'étranger; Swiss Assoc., Knights of Malta; Comité exécutif international pour l'assistance aux Lépreux de l'Ordre de Malte. *Publications:* Contributions à la Connaissance des relations suisses-égyptiennes, 1956; Dialogue luso-suisse, 1960; Camões-Price, 1961. The Swiss presence in the United Kingdom during the 18th Century, 1967. *Recreations:* history, architecture, psychology. *Address:* Le Pavillon, Thunplatz 52, Berne. *T:* 44.15.09; Clos Soleil, Vufflens-le-Château, Vaud, Switzerland. *Clubs:* Travellers'; Grande Société (Berne).

**de FONBLANQUE, Maj.-Gen. Edward Barrington,** CB 1948; CBE 1945; DSO 1944; Assistant Commissioner, Civil Defence, Federation of Malaya, 1951; *b* 29 May 1895; *s* of Lester Ramsay de Fonblanque and Constance Lucy Kerr; *m* 1934, Elizabeth Sclater; two *s* one *d*. *Educ:* Rugby. Joined Royal Artillery 1914; served European War, 1914-18 (despatches); Instructor Equitation Sch., Weedon, 1921-25; Capt., Royal Horse Artillery, 1923-31; Instructor, Staff Coll., Quetta, 1934-38; Commanded B/O Battery RHA, 1938-39; Commanded 2 RHA, 1939-40; GSO 1, 2 Div., 1940; CRA 45 Div., 1940-41; Chief of Staff 10 Corps and 10 Army, 1941-43 (despatches); CCRA 5 Corps, 1944-45; Chief of Staff I Corps, 1946; Chief Administrative Officer, Control Commission Germany, 1947; ADC to the King, 1947; Comdr, Salisbury Plain District, 1948-51; retired, 1951. Inspector-Gen., Federal Home Guard, Malaya, 1952-58. Col Comdt, RA 1952; Representative Col Comdt 1959; retd 1960. Comdr, Legion of Merit. *Recreation:* sailing. *Address:* The Cottage, Bank, near Lyndhurst, Hants; c/o Lloyds Bank, 6 Pall Mall, SW1. *Club:* Army and Navy.

**de FREITAS, Rt. Hon. Sir Geoffrey Stanley,** PC 1967; KCMG 1961; MP (Lab) Kettering since 1964; President of Assembly of Council of Europe 1966-69; Barrister-at-law, Lincoln's Inn (Cholmeley Schol.); Director, Laporte Industries, since 1968; *b* 7 April 1913; *s* of Sir Anthony Patrick de Freitas, OBE, and Maud, *d* of Augustus Panton Short; *m* 1938, Helen Graham, *d* of Laird Bell, KBE (Hon.), LLD (Hon.) Harvard of Illinois, USA; three *s* one *d*. *Educ:* Haileybury; Clare Coll., Cambridge (Hon. Fellow); Yale Univ. (Mellon fellow). Pres. of Cambridge Union, 1934. Shoreditch Borough Council (Lab), 1936-39; Bar Council, 1939. RA 1939, RAF, 1940-45. MP (Lab) Central Nottingham, 1945-50, Lincoln, 1950-61; Parliamentary Private Sec. to Prime Minister, 1945-46; Under-Sec. of State for Air, 1946-50; Under-Sec. of State, Home Office, 1950-51. Shadow Minister of Agriculture, 1960-61. British High Comr in Ghana, 1961-63; designated (1963) British High Comr in East African Federation when formed; British High Comr in Kenya, 1963-64. Delegate: to UN, 1949 and 1964; to Council of Europe, 1951-54 and 1965 (Leader of UK Delegn); to NATO Parly Conf., 1955-60, 1965, 1969 (Leader of UK Delegn). Chairman: Gauche Européenne, 1966-; Labour Cttee for Europe; European-Atlantic Group; Party's Defence Cttee, 1964-; Soc. of Labour Lawyers, 1955-58; Vice-Chairman: Nature Conservancy, 1954-58; British Council; Churches Social Responsibility Cttee, 1956-61; Council: Royal Society of Arts, 1958-61, Agricultural Cooperative Association, 1964-69. Farmed at Bourn, Cambs, 1953-69. *Recreations:* the countryside; formerly games and athletics (full blue CUAC). *Address:* 11 Trumpington Road, Cambridge. *Clubs:* Reform, Garrick, Guild of Air Pilots (Liveryman); Hawks (Cambridge).

**DE FREYNE,** 7th Baron *cr* 1851; **Francis Arthur John French;** Knight of Malta; *b* 3 Sept. 1927; *s* of 6th Baron and Victoria, *d* of Sir J. Arnott, 2nd Bt; *S* father 1935; *m* 1954, Shirley Ann, *o c* of late D. R. Pobjoy; two *s* one *d*. *Educ:* Ladycross, Glenstal. *Heir:* *s* Hon. Fulke Charles Arthur John French, *b* 21 April 1957. *Address:* Corke Little, Bray, Co. Wicklow, Eire. *T:* Bray 2671. *Clubs:* St James'; Kildare Street (Dublin).

**de GAULLE, General Charles André Joseph Marie;** President of the French Republic, 1959-69; *b* 22 Nov. 1890; *s* of Henri de Gaulle and Jeanne Maillot-Delannoy; *m* 1921, Yvonne Vendroux; one *s* one *d* (and one *d* decd). *Educ:* Saint-Cyr Academy. Served as Captain, European War, 1914-18; served War of 1939-45 as Gen. of Brigade, and Comdr 4th Armoured Div., 1940; Under-Sec. National Defence, June 1940; Chief of Free French, the Pres. of French National Cttee, London and Brazzaville, 1940-42; Pres. of French Cttee of National Liberation, Algiers, 1943; Pres. of Provisional Government of the French Republic and Head Chief of Armies, 1944-46; Founder of "Rassemblement du peuple français", 1947. Pres. of French Government 2 June 1958-8 Jan. 1959. Royal Victorian Chain, 1960. *Publications:* La Discorde Chez l'ennemi, 1924; Le fil de l'Epée, 1932; Vers l'Armée de métier, 1934; La France et son Armée, 1938 (Eng. edn, 1945); Discours et Messages, 1947; Mémoires de guerre: l'Appel, Vol. 1, 1954 (Eng. trans., The Call to Honour, 1955); Vol. II, l'Unité, 1956; Vol. III, Le Salut, 1959 (Eng. trans., Salvation, 1960). *Address:* La Boisserie, Colombey-les-Deux-Eglises, Haute-Marne, France.

**de GEX, Maj.-Gen. George Francis,** CB 1964; OBE 1949; Director, Royal Artillery, 1964-66, retired; *b* 23 April 1911; *s* of late Brig.-Gen. F. J. de Gex, CB, CMG; *m* 1946, Ronda Marianne, *d* of late C. F. Recaño; one *d*. *Educ:* Wellington Coll., Berks; Trinity Hall, Cambridge (MA). 2nd Lieut RA 1931; served War of 1939-45: BEF, 1940 (despatches); NW Europe, 1944. Lt-Col 1953; Col 1954; Brig. 1959; Comd 1 AGRA, 1958-59; DMS(B), War Office, 1959-60. Comdr Artillery, Northern Army Group, 1961-64. Col Comdt, RA 1967-. DSC (USA), 1945. *Recreations:* shooting, ski-ing, reading. *Address:* Flat 13, 3 Hans Crescent, SW1. *Club:* Army and Navy.

**de GREY,** family name of **Baron Walsingham.**

**de GREY, Roger,** RA 1969 (ARA 1962); Senior Tutor, Royal College of Art, since 1953; *b* 18 April 1918; *s* of Nigel de Grey, CMG, OBE, and Florence Emily Frances (*née* Gore); *m* 1942, Flavia Hatt (*née* Irwin); two *s* one *d*. *Educ:* Eton Coll.; Chelsea Sch. of Art. Served War of 1939-45: Royal West Kent Yeomanry, 1939-42; RAC, 1942-45 (US Bronze Star, 1945). Lecturer, Dept of Fine Art, King's Coll., Newcastle upon Tyne, 1947-51; Master of Painting, King's Coll., 1951-53. Pictures in the following public collections: Arts Council; Contemporary Arts Society; Chantrey Bequest; Queensland Gallery, Brisbane; Manchester, Carlisle, Bradford and other provincial galleries. Hon. ARCA, 1959. *Address:* 5 and 6 Camer Street, Meopham, Kent. *T:* 2327.

**de GUINGAND, Maj.-Gen. Sir Francis W.,** KBE 1944 (CBE 1943; OBE 1942); CB 1943; DSO 1942; Chairman: Rothmans of Pall Mall (UK); Carreras Ltd, 1967-68, and other Cos; Director and International Director of the Rothmans Group; *b* 28 Feb. 1900; *s* of late Francis J. de Guingand; *m* 1942, Arlie R., *widow* of Major H. D. Stewart, West Yorks Regt (marr. diss., 1957); one *d*. *Educ:* Ampleforth Coll.; RMC, Sandhurst. Joined W Yorks Regt, 1919; seconded to KAR, 1926-31; OC Troops Nyasaland, 1930-31; Adjt 1st Bn W Yorks Regt, 1932-34; Staff Coll., Camberley, 1935-36; Mil. Asst to Sec. of State for War (Mr Hore-Belisha), 1939-40; Dir Mil. Intell., Middle east, 1942; Chief of Staff: 8th Army, 1942-44; 21st Army Group, 1944-45; retd pay, 1947. DSM (USA); CL of M (USA); Legion of Honour (France); Croix de Guerre (France); Order of Kutuzov 1st Grade (Russia); Order of Orange Nassau (Dutch). *Publications:* Operation Victory, 1947; African Assignment, 1953; Generals at War, 1964. *Recreations:* shooting, fishing, golf, sailing. *Address:* c/o Carreras Ltd, 27 Baker Street, W1; PO Box 52056, Saxonwold, Johannesburg, SA. *T:* Johannesburg 42-8203. *Clubs:* Army and Navy, Royal Automobile, White's; Rand; Country (Johannesburg).

**de HAVILLAND, Olivia Mary, (Mme. P. P. Galante);** actress; *b* Tokyo, Japan, 1 July 1916; *d* of Walter Augustus de Havilland and Lilian Augusta (*née* Ruse); *m* 1st, 1946, Marcus Aurelius Goodrich (marr. diss., 1953); one *s*; 2nd, 1955, Pierre Paul Galante; one *d*. *Educ:* in California. Played Hermia in Max Reinhardt's stage production of Midsummer Night's Dream, 1934. *Legitimate theatre* (USA): Juliet in Romeo and Juliet, 1951; Candida, 1951 and 1952; A Gift of Time, 1962. Began film career 1935, Midsummer Night's Dream. Nominated for Academy Award, 1939, 1941, 1946, 1948, 1949; Acad. Award, 1946, 1949; New York Critics' Award, 1948, 1949; San Francisco Critics' Award, 1948, 1949; Women's National Press Club Award for 1949, Belgian Prix Femina, 1957, etc. *Important Films:* Gone With the Wind, 1939; Hold Back the Dawn, 1941; Princess O'Rourke, 1943; To Each His Own, 1946; The Dark Mirror, 1946; The Snake Pit,

1948; The Heiress, 1949; My Cousin Rachel, 1952; Not as a Stranger, 1955; The Ambassador's Daughter, 1956; Proud Rebel, 1957; The Light in the Piazza, 1961; Lady in a Cage, 1963; Hush . . . Hush, Sweet Charlotte, 1965. Also TV. Pres. of Jury, Cannes Film Festival, 1965. Amer. Legion Humanitarian Medal, 1967. *Publication:* Every Frenchman Has One, 1962. *Address:* BP 156-16, Paris, France.

**de HAVILLAND, Maj.-Gen. Peter Hugh,** CBE 1945; DL; *b* 29 July 1904; *s* of late Hugh de Havilland, JP, CA, Gt Horkesley, Essex; *m* 1930, Helen Elizabeth Wrey, *d* of W. W. Otter-Barry, *qv*; two *s*. *Educ:* Eton; RMA, Woolwich. 2nd Lieut, RA, 1925; Lieut RHA, 1933-36; Adjt 84th (East Anglian) Field Bde, RA (TA), 1936-38; served War of 1939-45 (despatches thrice, CBE); France, Middle East, N Africa, NW Europe; Brig. i/c Administration, 1 Corps, 1945-47; Dep. Regional Comr, Land, Schleswig Holstein, 1948; Dep. Head, UK Deleg. Five Power Military Cttee, 1949; UK Mil. Rep., SHAPE, 1951; Chief of Staff, Northern Comd, 1953-55, retd 1955. DL Essex, 1962. Comdr Order of Leopold II, 1945. *Recreations:* shooting, hunting. *Address:* King's Farm, Little Horkesley, Colchester. *T:* Great Horkesley 209. *Club:* Army and Navy.

**DEHLAVI, Samiulla Khan;** Ambassador of Pakistan to France, since 1968; *b* 14 Sept. 1913; *s* of late Sir Ali Mohomed Khan Dehlavi, JP, Barrister-at-Law; *m* 1938, Genevieve (*née* Chantrenne); two *s*. *Educ:* Rugby; University of Oxford (PPE). BA 1935; MA. Entered ICS, 1938; served as Dist and Secretariat officer in Undivided Bengal before Independence; entered Pakistan Foreign Service, 1949; Dep. Sec., Min. of Foreign Affairs, 1950; Chargé-Counsellor, Paris, until 1953; Jt Sec., Foreign Affairs, 1953-57; Ambassador to Rome (concurrently to Tunisia), 1957-61. Foreign Sec., Pakistan, 1961-63; Ambassador to Cairo (concurrently to Libya and Yemen), 1963-65; Ambassador to Switzerland, 1965-66; concurrently to Albania, 1966; High Comr in London, concurrently Ambassador to Ireland, 1966-68. Grand Cross of Merit of Italian Republic, 1961. Order of Sitara-e-Pakistan, 1967. *Recreations:* riding, tennis, big game hunting (India, Pakistan, Kenya, Sudan). *Address:* Pakistan Embassy, 18 rue Lord Byron, Paris 8e.

**DEHN, Conrad Francis,** QC 1968; Barrister; *b* London, 24 Nov. 1926; *o s* of late C. G. Dehn, Solicitor and Cynthia (*née* Fuller: Francyn the painter); *m* 1954, Sheila, *y d* of late W. K. Magan; two *s* one *d*. *Educ:* Charterhouse (Sen. Exhibr); Christ Church, Oxford (Holford Exhibr). Served RA, 1945-48; 2nd Lieut 1947. Lord Justice Holker Jun. Schol., Gray's Inn, 1949; Slade Exhibn, Christ church, 1950; 1st cl. hons PPE Oxon. 1950, MA 1952; Holt Schol., Gray's Inn, 1951; Lord Justice Holker Sen. Exhibn, Gray's Inn, 1952; Pres., Inns of Court of Students Union, 1951-52. WEA Tutor, 1951-55. Called to Bar, Gray's Inn, 1952. Mem. Governing Body, United Westminster Schs, 1953-57. *Publication:* contrib. to Ideas, 1954. *Recreations:* talking, reading, walking, tennis, squash. *Address:* 15 Sydenham Hill, SE26; 2 Crown Office Row, Temple, EC4. *T:* 01-353 1878. *Club:* Reform.

**DEHN, Paul (Edward);** poet; author; *b* 5 Nov. 1912; *e s* of Frederick and Helen Dehn. *Educ:* Shrewsbury Sch.; Brasenose Coll., Oxford. Film-Critic and columnist Sunday Referee, 1936-39; HM Forces (Major), 1939-45; Film-critic: Sunday Chronicle, 1945-53; News Chronicle, 1954-60; Daily Herald, 1960-63. Won Hollywood Academy award as co-author story for film Seven Days to Noon, 1952; commentary Festival documentary Waters of Time (Venice Award 1952); Libretto for Lennox Berkeley's One-Act Opera, A Dinner Engagement (prod. Aldeburgh and Sadler's Wells, 1954); screen-play for Anthony Asquith's Glyndebourne film, On Such a Night, 1955; won British Film Academy Award (Best British Screen-play) for screenplay of Anthony Asquith's Orders to Kill, 1958; commentary Basil Wright's documentary, A Place For Gold, 1960; Lyrics for Terence Rattigan's musical comedy, Joie de Vivre, 1960 (prod. Queen's Theatre, 1960); wrote book and lyrics of Virtue in Danger, a musical version of Vanbrugh's The Relapse (prod. Mermaid and Strand Theatres, 1963). With Richard Maibaum, co-author of screenplay, Goldfinger, 1964. Wrote screenplays: The Spy Who Came In From The Cold; The Deadly Affair, 1965. Wrote screenplay for Zeffirelli's film-version of Shakespeare's The Taming Of The Shrew, 1966. Co-author screenplay, The Night Of The Generals, 1967. Wrote *Libretti* for two one-act operas, William Walton's The Bear and Lennox Berkeley's Castaway, Aldeburgh and Sadler's Wells, 1967. Wrote screenplays: Beneath The Planet Of The Apes, and A Fragment of Fear (also Associate Producer), 1968-69. Pres., Critics' Circle, 1956. Former Councillor, Royal Society for The Protection of Birds. Cheltenham Festival Poetry Prize, 1957. *Publications:* The Day's Alarm (poems), 1949; Romantic Landscape (poems), 1952. Adaptation of Oscar Wilde's A Woman of No Importance (produced Savoy, 1953), 1954; For Love and Money (a miscellany), 1956; Quake, Quake, Quake (verses), 1960; The Fern on the Rock (collected poems), 1965. Many songs and sketches for West End revues. *Recreation:* ornithology. *Address:* 19 Bramerton Street, Chelsea, SW3.

**de HOGHTON, Sir (Henry Philip) Anthony (Mary),** 13th Bt *cr* 1611; *b* 19 April 1919; *e s* of Sir Cuthbert de Hoghton, 12th Bt, JP, and Helen (*d* 1943), *o d* of late Major Duncan Macdonald of Glencoe; *S* father 1958. *Educ:* Beaumont; Magdalen Coll., Oxford. *Heir: b* Charles James Gilbert de Hoghton [*b* 5 July 1930; *m* 1957, Winifred Valerie Maud, *yr d* of W. R. Glynn Thomas; one *d*. *Educ:* Ampleforth; Trinity Coll., Cambridge). *Address:* Hoghton Tower, Hoghton, Lancs. *T:* Hoghton 452.

**de JERSEY, Rear-Adm (retired) Gilbert Carey,** CB 1959; *b* 5 Oct. 1905; British (Guernsey); *m* 1932, Patricia Wyndham Lee; two *s* three *d*. *Educ:* Elizabeth Coll., Guernsey; RNC's Osborne, Dartmouth and Keyham. Served as Cadet until 1923; successively Midshipman, Sub-Lieut and Lieut, 1923-34; Lieut-Comdr: Portsmouth Dockyard, 1936; HMS Malaya, 1938; Comdr: Admiralty, 1941; Singapore Dockyard, 1945; HMS Illustrious, 1948; Captain: Admiralty Overseeing, 1950; Admiralty, 1952; Singapore Dockyard, 1956; Admiralty, 1957; Rear-Adm. 1958; Director of Naval Ordnance, Admiralty, 1958-60, retired. Jurat of Royal Court, Guernsey, 1960. *Recreations:* walking, boat sailing. *Address:* (Home) Côte des Vardes, Montville Road, Guernsey, Channel Islands. *T:* Guernsey 20895.

**de JONG, Major Nicholas Charles Callard;** Director of Planning and Mechanisation, Postal Headquarters, since 1967; *b* 15 Oct. 1911; *s* of David de Jong, Wallasey, Cheshire and Jessie Florence de Jong (*née* Callard), Totnes, Devon; *m* 1937, Olwen May East, Milford Haven; one *d*. *Educ:* Queen Elizabeth's, Crediton; Techn. Coll., Cardiff;

University of South Wales. BSc(Eng) 1st cl. hons (London); CEng, MICE, FIMechE, FIEE. L. G. Mouchell & Co. Ltd, Bridge design and building, 1932-34; entered GPO service by open competition, 1934; served in various grades and places, incl.: Telephone Man., Preston, 1953-57; Controller, N Ire., 1957-61; overseas consultancy work in W Indies and Cyprus; various posts in Engrg Dept of P.O.: Dep. Engr-in-Chief, 1966. Officer, Order of Orange Nassau, 1946; Bronze Star (USA), 1946. *Recreations:* boats, golf, travel. *Address:* 33 Mount Avenue, Westcliff-on-Sea, Essex. *T:* Southend 75824.

**DEKOBRA, Maurice;** Officer of the Legion of Honour; Grand Cross of St John the Baptist; Grand Officer of the Nicham Iftikar; Doctor of Letters, *hc*; novelist and playwright; *b* Paris, 1885; unmarried. *Educ:* College Rollin; Paris Univ. Corresp. for leading Paris newspapers in Europe, America, Africa; Lectr at Berlin Univ.; motored through Europe for the Figaro; mobilised during the war as liaison officer with the British, Indian and American Armies at the front; writes cosmopolitan novels which are translated in thirty languages, since 1924. Member: Internat. Acad., Washington, DC; Bolivian Acad. *Publications:* Messieurs les Tommies; Au Pays du Fox-Trot; Prince ou Pitre; Tu seras courtisane; Minuit . . . Place Pigalle: Mon Cœur au Ralenti; La Madone des Sleepings; La Gondole aux chimères; Flammes de Velours; Serenade au Bourreau; Le Sphinx a parlé; L'Archange aux pieds fourchus; Phryné, 1931; Perfumed Tigers, 1931; La Volupté éclairant le Monde, 1932; Rue des Bouches Peintes, 1933; Confucius en pull over, 1934; Princess Brinda, 1934; His Chinese Concubine, 1935; A Frenchman in Japan, 1936; Blood and Caviare, 1937; The Widow with the Pink Gloves, 1938; Written with Lipstick, 1938; Death requests the pleasure . . ., 1939; Emigrants de Luxe, 1942; The Romance of a Coward, 1943; The Madonna in Hollywood, 1945; Shanghai Honeymoon, 1946; Hell is Sold Out, 1948; Operation Magali, 1952; Poison at Plessis, 1953; The Man Who Died Twice, 1954; Chinese Puzzle, 1955; The Lady is a Vamp, 1958; The 7th Wife of Prince Hassan, 1961. *Recreations:* riding, fencing, thought reading. *Address:* 12 rue Beaujon, Paris, France. *T:* Macmahon 07.33.

**de la BEDOYERE, Count Michael;** Editor: Search Newsletter, 1962-68; Catholic Herald, 1934-62; *b* 16 May 1900; *s* of Comte Yvon de la Bedoyere, and Sybil Emily, *d* of Dr A. W. Thorold, sometime Bishop of Winchester; *m* 1st, 1930, Catherine (*d* 1959), *d* of Algar Labouchere Thorold; four *s* one *d*; 2nd, 1961, Charlotte Halbik; two *s*. *Educ:* Stonyhurst; Oxford Univ. (MA 1st Class Honours Modern Greats). Asst master at Beaumont Coll., 1928-29; Lecturer in Philosophy in University of Minnesota, USA, 1930-31; Asst Ed. of the Dublin Review, 1932-34. *Publications:* The Drift of Democracy, 1931; Lafayette, a Revolutionary Gentleman, 1933; George Washington, an English Judgment, 1935; Sociology: Vol. 5 of European Civilization: Its Origin and Development, 1936; Christian Crisis, 1940; Christianity in the Market Place, 1943; No Dreamers Weak, 1944; Catherine, Saint of Siena, 1946; The Life of Baron von Hügel, 1951; Living Christianity, 1954; The Layman in the Church, 1955; Cardinal Griffin, 1955; The Archbishop and the Lady, 1956; The Meddlesome Friar, 1958; The Cardijn Story, 1958; François de Sales, 1959; Francis, Saint of Assisi, 1962. Ed., Objections to Roman Catholicism, 1964; ed., The Future of Catholic Christianity, 1966. *Address:* Elylands, Edenbridge, Kent.

**DE LA BERE, Brig. Sir Ivan,** KCVO 1959 (CVO 1950); CB 1957; CBE 1944 (OBE 1934); BA Cantab; CStJ 1950; Secretary, Central Chancery of the Orders of Knighthood, St James's Palace, 1946-60; Extra Gentleman-Usher to the Queen, since 1961; *b* 25 April 1893; *s* of John De La Bere, Battledown Manor, Cheltenham, Glos; *m* 1923, Marjorie Minton Haines; (one *d* decd). 2nd Lieut Dorset Regt, 1913; Lieut-Col Dorset Regt, 1939; Brig. 1941; Acting Maj.-Gen., 1944; retired. Foreign decorations (1946-60): Comdr Order of Merit (W Germany); Comdr, Order of Merit (Italy); Officer, Legion of Honour (France); Comdr, Order of White Elephant (Siam); Officer, Order of: Orange (Netherlands); Rafidan (Iraq); Danebrog (Denmark); Christ (Portugal); North Star (Sweden); personal order of Shah of Persia. *Publication:* The Queen's Orders of Chivalry, 1961. *Address:* Kingston House, Corfe Castle, Dorset.

**DE la BERE, Sir Rupert,** 1st Bt, *cr* 1953; KCVO 1953; Kt 1952; President, Proprietors of Hay's Wharf Ltd and other Companies; Alderman of City of London for Ward of Tower; *b* 16 June 1893; *s* of Lillian Margaret and Reginald De la Bere; *m* 1919, Marguerite (*d* 1969), *e d* of late Sir John Humphery; two *s* three *d*. *Educ:* Tonbridge Sch. Captain East Surrey Regt; served European War 1914-18, India, Mesopotamia, Egypt; seconded to RFC and RAF; graduated at Aboukir, Egypt. MP (C) Evesham Div. of Worcs, 1935-50, South Worcs, 1950-55; Sheriff of City of London, 1941-42; Lord Mayor of London, 1952-53. KStJ 1953. Knight Comdr, Order of the Dannebrog (Denmark), 1954; Knight Comdr Order of the North Star (Sweden), 1954. *Heir:* *s* Cameron De la Bere [*b* 12 Feb. 1933; *m* 1964, Clairemonde, *o d* of Casimir Kaufmann, Geneva; one *d*]. *Recreations:* aviation and squash racquets. *Address:* Crowborough Place, Crowborough, Sussex. *T:* Crowborough 103. *Club:* Carlton.

**DELACOMBE, Maj.-Gen. Sir Rohan,** KCMG 1964; KCVO 1970; KBE 1961 (CBE 1951; MBE 1939); CB 1957; DSO 1944; Governor of Victoria, Australia, since 1963; *b* 25 Oct. 1906; *s* of late Lieut-Col Addis Delacombe, DSO, Shrewton Manor, near Salisbury; *m* 1941, Eleanor Joyce, *d* of late R. Lionel Forster, JP, Egton Manor, York; one *s* one *d*. *Educ:* Harrow; RMC Sandhurst. 2nd Lieut The Royal Scots, 1926; served Egypt, N China, India and UK, 1926-37; active service Palestine, 1937-39 (despatches, MBE); France, Norway, Normandy, Italy, 1939-45; Lieut-Col comd 8th Bn and 2nd Bn The Royal Scots, 1943-45; GSO1, 2nd Infantry Div., Far East, 1945-47; Colonel GS, HQ, BAOR, 1949-50; Brig. Comd 5 Inf. Bde, 1950-53, Germany; Dep. Mil. Sec., War Office, 1953-55; Maj.-Gen. 1956. Col The Royal Scots, 1956-64; GOC 52 Lowland Div. and Lowland District, 1955-58; GOC Berlin (Brit. Sector) 1959-62. Mem. Queen's Body Guard for Scotland, Royal Company of Archers, 1957. KStJ, 1963. Hon. Col 1st Armoured Regt (Australian Army); Hon. Air Cdre RAAF, LLD *hc* Melbourne. *Recreations:* normal. *Address:* Government House, Melbourne, Australia; Shrewton Manor, near Salisbury, Wilts. *T:* Shrewton 253. *Club:* United Service.

**DELACOURT-SMITH,** Baron *cr* 1967 (Life Peer) of New Windsor; **Charles George Percy Smith,** PC 1969; General Secretary, Post Office Engineering Union, since 1953; Adviser, Prison Officers' Association, since 1956; *b* 25 April 1917; *o s* of Charles and Ethel Smith, Windsor, Berks; *m* 1939, Margaret Hando, Newport, Mon.; one *s* two *d*. *Educ:* County

Boys' Sch., Windsor; Wadham Coll., Oxford (Scholar). Librarian, Oxford Union; Research Asst, New Fabian Research Bureau, 1938-39. Entered army (RE) in the ranks, July 1940; Commissioned Jan. 1943, RASC (despatches). MP (Lab) Colchester Div. of Essex, 1945-50; Mem., Executive, Labour Research Dept, 1947-51; Parliamentary Private Sec. to Sec. of State for Commonwealth Relations, 1947-49; Asst Sec. Civil Service Clerical Assoc., 1939-53. Chm., Civil Service Nat. Whitley Council (Staff Side), 1962-64. Mem. (part-time) British Airports Authority, 1965-69; Minister of State, Min. of Technology, 1969-70. member: Shipbuilding Inquiry Cttee, 1965-66; Cttee on engagement and use of labour in construction, 1967-68. World Pres., Postal, Telegraph, and Telephone International, 1969-. JP London, 1960-69. *Publications:* Britain's Food Supplies in Peace and War, 1940; (with John Parker, MP) Modern Turkey, 1940; edited (with M. I. Cole) Democratic Sweden, 1938. *Recreations:* reading, music, theatre. *Address:* 62 Marlborough Mansions, Cannon Hill, NW6.

**de LACRETELLE, Jacques;** French Writer; Member of Académie Française; *m* 1933, Yolande de Naurois; three *c.* First book published in 1920; Prix Femina, 1922; Grand Prix du roman de l'Académie Française, 1927. *Publications:* Silvermann; La Bonifas; Amour Nuptial; Les Hauts Ponts; Le Pour et le Contre, etc.; Translation of Precious Bane by Mary Webb and Wuthering Heights by Emily Brontë. *Address:* 49 Rue Vineuse, Paris, XVIe. *T:* Kléber 78-67.

**DELAFIELD, Max Everard,** MC, MB, BCh, DPH; Professor Emeritus University of London; *b* 23 March 1886; *m* 1910; one *s*; *m* 1940, May, *d* of A. A. Purry, Hampstead. *Educ:* Merchant Taylors' Sch., London; Jesus Coll., Cambridge; St Thomas's Hosp. Late Prof. of Chemistry as applied to Hygiene at London Sch. of Hygiene and Tropical Medicine; formerly Head of Dept of Hygiene and Bacteriology, Queen Elizabeth Coll., Lecturer at University Coll. Hospital Medical Sch. and University Coll. *Recreations:* home and gardening. *Address:* 14 Lyttelton Court, N2. *T:* 01-455 2873.

**de la Lanne-Mirrlees, Robin Ian Evelyn Stuart;** *see* Mirrlees.

**de la MARE, Sir Arthur (James),** KCMG 1968 (CMG 1957); HM Diplomatic Service; British High Commissioner in Singapore, 1968-70; *b* 15 Feb. 1914; *s* of late Walter H. de la Mare, Trinity, Jersey, Channel Islands, and late Laura Vibert Syvret; *m* 1940, Katherine Elisabeth Sherwood; three *d. Educ:* Victoria Coll., Jersey; Pembroke Coll., Cambridge. Joined HM Foreign Service, 1936. HM Vice-Consul: Tokyo, 1936-38; Seoul, Korea, 1938-39; USA 1942-43; First Sec., Foreign Service, 1945; HM Consul, San Francisco, 1947-50; HM Embassy, Tokyo, 1951-53; Counsellor, HM Foreign Service, 1953-63; Head of Security Dept, Foreign Office, 1953-56; Counsellor, HM Embassy, Washington, 1956-60; Head of Far Eastern Dept, Foreign Office, 1960-63; Ambassador to Afghanistan, 1963-65; Asst Under-Sec. of State, Foreign Office, 1965-67. *Recreations:* gardening, golf. *Address:* c/o Foreign and Commonwealth Office, SW1. *Clubs:* Royal Commonwealth Society; Tokyo (Tokyo, Japan).

**de la MARE, Prof. Peter Bernard David,** MSc NZ; PhD London; DSc London; Professor of Chemistry, University of Auckland, New Zealand, since 1967; *b* 3 Sept. 1920; *s* of late Frederick Archibald and of Sophia Ruth de la Mare, Hamilton, NZ; *m* 1945, Gwynneth Campbell, *yr d* of Alexander and late Daisy Gertrude Jolly, Fairview, Maraekakaho, Hastings, NZ; two *d. Educ:* Hamilton High Sch., Hamilton, NZ; Victoria University Coll. (University of NZ); University Coll., London. BSc NZ, 1941; MSc NZ, 1942; PhD London, 1948; DSc London, 1955. Agricultural Chemist, NZ Govt Dept of Agriculture, 1942-45; Shirtcliffe Fellow (University of NZ) at University Coll. London, 1946-48; University Coll. London: Temp. Asst Lecturer, 1948; Lecturer, 1949; Reader, 1956; Prof. of Chemistry, Bedford Coll., University of London, 1960-67. *Publications:* (with J. H. Ridd) Aromatic Substitution–Nitration and Halogenation, 1959; (with W. Klyne) Progress in Stereochemistry 2, 1958, 3, 1962; (with R. Bolton) Electrophilic Addition to Unsaturated Systems, 1966; scientific papers and reviews. *Recreations:* cricket, chess, table tennis, etc. *Address:* Chemistry Department, University of Auckland, Auckland, New Zealand.

**de la MARE, Richard Herbert Ingpen;** Chairman: Faber & Faber Ltd since 1960; Faber & Faber (Publishers) Ltd; Faber Music Ltd; Fine Art Engravers Ltd; Latimer Trend & Co. Ltd (Printers); *b* 4 June 1901; *e s* of late Walter John de la Mare, OM, CH, and Constance Elfrida Ingpen; *m* 1930, Amy Catherine (*d* 1968), *er d* of late Rev. S. A. Donaldson, DD, Master of Magdalene College, Cambridge; three *s* one *d. Educ:* Whitgift Sch., Croydon; Keble Coll., Oxford. Joined Faber & Gwyer Ltd, 1925, Dir 1928; succeeded by Faber & Faber Ltd, 1929, Dir 1929-45, Vice-Chm. 1945. *Publications:* essays and addresses on typography. *Recreations:* listening to music, oriental art, gardening. *Address:* Much Hadham Hall, Herts. *T:* Much Hadham 2663. *Club:* Athenæum.

*See also Baron Donaldson of Kingsbridge.*

**DELAMERE,** 4th Baron *cr* 1821; **Thomas Pitt Hamilton Cholmondeley;** Captain Welsh Guards; Director, Proved Securities Ltd; *b* 19 Aug. 1900; *e s* of 3rd Baron and Lady Florence Cole (*d* 1914), 4th *d* of 4th Earl of Enniskillen; *S* father, 1931; *m* 1st, 1924, Phyllis Anne (marriage dissolved, 1944), *e d* of late Lord George Scott, OBE; one *s* two *d*; 2nd, 1944, Ruth Mary Clarisse, (marriage dissolved, 1955), *yr d* of 1st Baron Mount Temple; 3rd, 1955, Diana Colvile, *yr d* of late Seymour Caldwell and of Mrs Caldwell, The Red House, Hove, Sussex. *Educ:* Eton. *Heir: s* Hon. Hugh George Cholmondeley [*b* 18 Jan. 1934; *m* 1964, Mrs Ann Willoughby Tinne, *o d* of late Sir Patrick Renison, GCMG; one *s*]. *Address:* Soysambu, Elementeita, Kenya. *Clubs:* White's, Turf.

*See also Major Sir Evelyn Delves Broughton.*

**DELANEY, Colin John,** CVO 1954; CBE 1962; Commissioner of Police, NSW, 1952-62; *b* 28 Feb. 1897; *m* 1919, Gladys Viola Meyers (*d* 1966); one *s* (and one *s* decd). *Recreations:* golf, bowls. *Address:* 9 Bareena Avenue, Wahroonga, New South Wales, Austalia.

**DELANEY, Shelagh;** playwright; *b* Salford, Lancs, 1939; one *d. Educ:* Broughton Secondary Sch. *Plays:* A Taste of Honey, Theatre Royal, Stratford, 1958 and 1959, Wyndhams, 1959, New York, 1960 and 1961 (Charles Henry Foyle New Play Award, Arts Council Bursary, New York Drama Critics' Award); The Lion in Love, Royal Court 1960, New York 1962. *Films:* A Taste of Honey, 1961 (British Film Academy Award, Robert Flaherty Award); Charlie Bubbles, 1968 (Writers Guild Award for best original film writing). *Publications:* A Taste of Honey, 1959 (London and New York); The Lion in Love,

1961 (London and New York); Sweetly Sings the Donkey, 1963 (new York), 1964 (London). *Address:* c/o Hope Leresche and Steele, 11 Jubilee Place, SW3; c/o CMA, 555 Madison Avenue, New York, NY 10022, USA; c/o CMA, 99 Park Lane, W1.

**DELARGY, Captain Hugh James;** MP (Lab) Platting Division of Manchester, 1945-50, Thurrock Division of Essex since 1950; *b* 1908; *s* of Bernard Delargy, Co. Antrim. *Educ:* France and Italy. Enlisted, 1941; five years' service in Royal Artillery; Capt. 1944 (despatches). An Asst Govt Whip (unpaid), 1950-51; an Opposition Whip, 1951-52. *Address:* House of Commons, SW1.

**de la RUE, Sir Eric (Vincent),** 3rd Bt, *cr* 1898; *b* 5 Aug. 1906; *s* of Sir Evelyn Andros de la Rue, 2nd Bt, and Mary Violet (*d* 1959), *e d* of John Liell Francklin of Gonalston, Notts; *S* father 1950; *m* 1st, 1945, Cecilia (*d* 1963), *d* of late Lady Clementine Waring; two *s*; 2nd, 1964, Christine Schellin, Greenwich, Conn., USA; one *s*. *Educ:* Oundle. Served War of 1939-45. Capt. Notts Yeomanry, 1942-45. *Heir: s* Andrew George Ilay de la Rue, *b* 3 Feb. 1946. *Address:* Caldra, Duns, Scotland. *T:* Duns 94.

**DE LA WARR,** 9th Earl *cr* 1761; **Herbrand Edward Dundonald Brassey Sackville,** PC 1936; GBE 1956; Baron De La Warr, 1209 and 1572; Baron West, 1342; Viscount Cantelupe, 1761; Baron Buckhurst (UK), 1864; JP, East Sussex; DL Sussex; *b* 20 June 1900; *e s* of 8th Earl and Hon. Muriel Agnes Brassey (*d* 1930), 2nd *d* of 1st Earl Brassey; *S* father, 1915; *m* 1st, 1920, Diana (*d* 1966), *d* of late Gerard Leigh and of late Mrs Reginald Halsey; one *s* one *d* (and one *s* missing, presumed killed, War of 1939-45); 2nd, 1968, Sylvia, Countess of Kilmuir (*see* Countess De La Warr). *Educ:* Eton; Magdalen Coll., Oxford. Served as a sailor during the War; Parly Under-Sec., War Office, 1929-30; Parliamentary Sec., Ministry of Agriculture, and Dep. Minister of Fisheries, 1930-31 and 1931-35; Parliamentary Sec., Board of Education, 1935-36; Parliamentary Under-Sec. of State for the Colonies, 1936-37; Lord Privy Seal, 1937-38; Pres. of the Board of Education, 1938-40; First Commissioner Office of Works and Public Buildings, April-May, 1940; Chm. Estate Cttee, National Trust, 1950-51, and 1955-70; Postmaster-Gen., 1951-April 1955; Chm. Agricultural Research Council, 1944-49; Lord-in-Waiting to HM 1924 and 1929-31; Mayor of Bexhill, 1932-33, 1933-34, and 1934-35. Chm. Joint East and Central Africa Board, 1955-58; Chm. Royal Commonwealth Society, 1960. FRSA 1962. *Heir: s* Lord Buckhurst, *qv*. *Address:* Fishers Gate, Withyham, Sussex. *T:* Hartfield 246; 1 Buckingham Mews, Stafford Place, SW1. *T:* 01-834 0477. *Clubs:* Turf, Allies; Sussex (Eastbourne).

*See also Countess of Erroll, Maj.-Gen. Sir S. G. Menzies.*

**DE LA WARR, Countess; Sylvia Margaret Sackville,** DBE 1957; *d* of William Reginald Harrison, Liverpool; *m* 1st, 1925, David Patrick Maxwell Fyfe (later Earl of Kilmuir, *cr* 1962, PC, GCVO) (*d* 1967); two *d* (and one *d* decd); 2nd, 1968, Earl De La Warr, *qv*. *Address:* Fishers Gate, Withyham, Sussex.

**DELAY, Professeur Jean,** Commandeur de la Légion d'Honneur; Grand Officier de l'Ordre national du Mérite; Professor of Mental Diseases, Faculté de Médecine de Paris, since 1946; Member of the Académie de Médecine since 1955; Member of the Académie Française since 1959; *b* Bayonne, Basses-Pyrénées, 14 Nov. 1907; *m* 1933, Marie-Madeleine Carrez; two *d*. *Educ:* Faculté de Médecine and Faculté des Lettres Sorbonne. DèsL Sorbonne. Former Director L'Institut de Psychologie, Sorbonne; Mem. French Section Unesco. Hon. Member, Royal Society Med.; Dr hc Univs of Zürich, Montreal and Barcelona. Hon. Mem. numerous Foreign Socs. *Publications:* scientific: Les Dissolutions de la mémoire, 1942; Les Dérèglements de l'humeur, 1946; Les Maladies de la mémoire, 1947; La Psycho-Physiologie humaine, 1945; Aspects de la psychiatrie moderne, 1956; Etudes de psychologie médicale, 1953; Méthodes biologiques, 1950, psychométriques, 1956, chimiothérapiques, 1961, en psychiatrie; Introduction à la médecine psychosomatique, 1961; Abrégé de psychologie, 1962; Les démences tardives, 1962; L'électoencéphalographie clinique, 1966; Le syndrome de Korsakoff, 1969; literary: La Cité grise, 1946; Hommes sans nom, 1948; Les Reposantes, 1947; La Jeunesse d'André Gide (grand prix de la Critique), Vol. I, 1956, Vol. 2, 1957; Une Amitié (André Gide et Roger Martin du Gard), 1968. *Address:* 53 avenue Montaigne, Paris VIIIe. *T:* Elysees 77-07.

**DELBRIDGE, Rt. Rev. Graham Richard;** a Bishop Coadjutor of Sydney since 1969; Bishop in Wollongong since 1969; *b* 22 May 1917; *s* of Richard and Evelyn Delbridge; *m* 1943, Audrey Doris Traversi; one *s* three *d*. *Educ:* Moore Theological College, NSW. Scholar in Theology, Australian College of Theology, 1955. Director of Youth Work, Sydney, 1943-52; Rector, Holy Trinity, Adelaide, 1952-57; Rector, St Matthew's, Manly, 1957-60; Archdeacon and Senior Chaplain to the Primate of Australia, 1963-68. *Recreation:* bush walking. *Address:* Bishop's Lodge, 20 Reserve Street, Wollongong, NSW, Australia. *T:* Wollongong 26927. *Club:* Royal Automobile (Australia).

**DELBRÜCK, Prof. Max;** Professor of Biology, California Institute of Technology, since 1947; *b* 4 Sept. 1906; *s* of Hans Delbrück and Lina Thiersch; *m* 1941, Mary Bruce; two *s* two *d*. *Educ:* Univs of Tübingen, Berlin, Bonn and Göttingen. PhD 1930. Visiting Prof., 1946, and Acting Prof., 1961-63, Cologne Univ. Mem., Nat. Acad. of Sciences; Fellow: Leopoldina Acad., Halle; Royal Danish Acad.; Foreign Mem., Royal Soc. Kimber Gold Medal (Genetics), US Nat. Acad. of Sciences; Nobel Prize for Physiology or Medicine (jtly), 1969. Hon. PhD: Copenhagen; Chicago. *Address:* 1510 Oakdale Street, Pasadena, California, USA.

**DELDERFIELD, Ronald Frederick,** Dramatist and Author; *b* 12 Feb. 1912, *s* of William James Delderfield and Alice (*née* Jones), London; *m* 1936, May Evans; one *s* one *d*. *Educ:* West Buckland Sch. Newspaper reporter, sub-ed., and ed., Exmouth Chronicle, 1929-39; served in RAF, 1940-45; Air Min. Staff as Public Relations Officer, 1944; Europe, 1944-45; resigned editorship Exmouth Chronicle, 1947. First play, Spark in Judaea, produced Ambassadors by New Plays and privately performed, 1937; Twilight Call (comedy), Birmingham Rep., 1939; Printer's Devil, Q and Embassy, London, 1939; This is my Life (with Basil Thomas), 1943; Spinster of South Street (York Drama Festival Play and tour), 1945; Worm's Eye View, Embassy and Whitehall, 1945 (filmed, 1950); Peace Comes to Peckham, Embassy and Prince's, 1947; All Over The Town, Playhouse, 1947; (filmed, 1948); The Queen Came By, Duke of York's, 1949; Wagonload o' Monkeys, Savoy, 1951; Where there's a Will, Garrick, 1951 (filmed 1953); Glad Tidings, 1952 (filmed); Golden Rain, 1952; All on a Summer's Day, 1953; The Orchard Walls, St Martin's, 1953; The Mayerling Affair (Pitlochry Festival), 1957;

(with Michael Pertwee) Now and Forever (film), 1956; various broadcast sketches and short plays. *Publications:* All Over the Town (novel), 1947; Seven Men of Gascony (novel) (USA and Britain), 1949; Farewell the Tranquil Mind (novel) (USA and Britain), 1950; Nobody Shouted Author (reminiscences), 1951; Bird's Eye View (autobiography); The Adventures of Benn Gunn (novel and TV serial), 1956; The Dreaming Suburb (novel and Radio serial), 1958; The Avenue Goes to War, 1958; There Was a Fair Maid Dwelling (published under title Diana, USA), 1960, The Unjust Skies (sequel); Napoleon in Love (novel and TV play), 1959, staged Pitlochry Festival, 1960; Stop at a Winner (filmed as On the Fiddle, 1961); The March of the Twenty-Six, 1962; My Dearest Angel (Pitlochry Festival); The Spring Madness of Mr Sermon (novel), 1963; The Golden Millstones (biography), 1964; Too Few For Drums (novel), 1964; Under an English Sky (travel), 1965 (USA 1967); A Horseman Riding By (novel), 1966; Cheap Day Return (novel), 1967; The Retreat from Moscow, 1967; The Green Gauntlet (novel), 1968; For My Own Amusement (essays), 1968; Imperial Sunset: the Fall of Napoleon, 1813-1814, (history), 1969 (USA 1968); Come Home Charlie and Face Them (novel), 1969; God is an Englishman (novel), 1970; Overture for Beginners (autobiography), 1970. *Recreation:* swimming. *Address:* Sidmouth, E Devon.

**DELFONT, Bernard;** Chairman and Chief Executive, Associated British Picture Corporation; Chairman: Associated British Cinemas; ABC Television Films Ltd; EMI-MGM, Elstree Studios, since 1970; The Grade Organisation Ltd; Managing Director, Bernard Delfont Ltd; Director: EMI Ltd; Grade Organisation; Forte's Holdings Ltd; Blackpool Tower Co. Ltd; *b* Tokmak, Russia, 5 Sept. 1909; *s* of Isaac and Olga Winogradsky; *m* 1946, Carole Lynne; one *s* two *d.* Entered theatrical management, 1941; assumed management of: Wimbledon Theatre, 1942; Whitehall Theatre and St Martin's Theatre, 1943; (with Mala de la Marr) Winter Garden, 1944; Saville Theatre, 1946; New Royalty Theatre, 1960; took over lease of Prince of Wales Theatre, 1958; assumed management of Comedy Theatre and Shaftesbury Theatre, 1964; converted London Hippodrome into Talk of the Town, Theatre Restaurant, 1958, and presents entertainment there; controls more than 30 cos (theatre, film, television, music, property interests). Presents pantomimes and summer shows in many cities and towns in England, Past Barker (Pres.), Variety Club of GB, 1969; Pres., Variety Artistes' Fedn, for which (with Leslie A. Macdonnell), presents annual Royal Variety Performance. Companion, Grand Order of Water Rats. *Address:* 30-31 Golden Square, W1R 4AA. *T:* 01-437 9234.

**DELHI, Archbishop of, (RC),** since 1967; **Most Rev. Angelo Fernandes;** Secretary General of Catholic Bishops' Conference of India, since 1960; Chairman, National Justice and Peace Committee; Consultor, Vatican Justice and Peace Commission; Member, Vatican Secretariat for Non-Believers; *b* 28 July 1913; *s* of late John Ligorio and Evelyn Sabina Fernandes. *Educ:* St Patrick's, Karachi; St Joseph's Seminary, Mangalore; Papal University, Kandy, Ceylon (STL). Secretary to Archbishop Roberts of Bombay, 1943-47; Administrator of Holy Name Cathedral, Bombay, 1947-59; Coadjutor Archbishop of Delhi, 1959-67. Hon. DD Vatican, 1959. *Publications:* Apostolic Endeavour, 1962; articles in Clergy Monthly, World Justice, Religion and Society, Social Action, Reality, etc. *Recreations:* music, especially classical, and wide travel on the occasion of numerous meetings in many countries of the world. *Address:* Archbishop's House, Alexandra Place, New Delhi 1, India. *T:* 48029.

**DE L'ISLE,** 1st Viscount, *cr* 1956; **William Philip Sidney,** VC 1944; KG 1968; PC 1951; GCMG 1961; GCVO 1963; Baron De L'Isle and Dudley, 1835; Bt 1806; Bt 1818; Chancellor, Order of St Michael and St George, since 1968; Governor-General of Australia, 1961-65; *b* 23 May 1909; *o s* of 5th Baron De L'Isle and Dudley and Winifred (*d* 1959), *e d* of Roland Yorke Bevan and Hon. Agneta Kinnaird, 4th *d* of 10th Baron Kinnaird; *S* father, 1945; *m* 1st 1940, Hon. Jacqueline Corinne Yvonne Vereker (*d* 1962), *o d* of late Field Marshal Viscount Gort of Hamsterley, VC, GCB, CBE, DSO, MVO, MC; one *s* four *d*; 2nd 1966, Margaret Lady Glanusk, JP, *widow* of 3rd Baron Glanusk, DSO (whom she *m* 1942). *Educ:* Eton; Magdalene Coll., Cambridge. Commissioned Supplementary Reserve, Grenadier Guards, 1929, and served War of 1939-45 with Regt. MP (C) Chelsea, 1944-45; Parliamentary Sec., Ministry of Pensions, 1945; Sec. of State for Air, Oct. 1951-Dec. 1955. Chairman: Phoenix Assurance Co. Ltd (previously Dep. Chm.); First National Finance Corpn Ltd; Council, Churchill Memorial Trust. Hon. Fellow Magdalene Coll., Cambridge, 1955. FCA; Hon. FRIBA. Hon. LLD Sydney, 1963. KStJ 1961. *Heir: s* Hon. Philip John Algernon Sidney [*b* 21 April 1945. Commissioned 2nd Lieut Grenadier Guards, 1966]. *Address:* Penshurst Place, near Tonbridge, Kent; Glanusk Park, Crickhowell, Brecon.

**DELL, Rt. Hon. Edmund,** PC 1970; MP (Lab) Birkenhead since 1964; *b* 15 Aug. 1921; *s* of late Reuben and Frances Dell; *m* 1963, Susanne Gottschalk. *Educ:* Elementary schls; Owen's Sch., London; Queen's Coll., Oxford (Open Schol.). 1st Cl. Hons Mod. Hist., BA and MA 1947. War Service, 1941-45, Lieut RA (Anti-tank). Lecturer in Modern History, Queen's Coll., Oxford, 1947-49; Executive in Imperial Chemical Industries Ltd, 1949-63. Mem., Manchester City Council, 1953-60. Contested (Lab) Middleton and Prestwich, 1955. Pres., Manchester and Salford Trades Council, 1958-61. Simon Research Fellow, Manchester Univ., 1963-64. Parly Sec., Min. of Technology, 1966-67; Jt Parly Under-Sec. of State, Dept of Economic Affairs, 1967-68; Minister of State: Board of Trade, 1968-69; Dept of Employment and Productivity, 1969-70. Boys' Chess Champion of London, 1936. *Publications:* ed (with J. E. C. Hill) The Good Old Cause, 1949; Brazil: The Dilemma of Reform (Fabian Pamphlet), 1964; articles in learned journals. *Recreation:* listening to music. *Address:* 4 Reynolds Close, NW11.

**DELLER, Alfred,** OBE 1970; singer; *b* Margate, Kent, 31 May 1912; *s* of Thomas William Deller and Mary Cave; *m* 1937, Kathleen Margaret Lowe; two *s* one *d. Educ:* secondary sch. Lay-Clerk, Canterbury Cathedral, 1941-47; Vicar-Choral, St Paul's Cathedral, 1947-61. Soloist in BBC Third Programme inaugural concert, 1946; sang role of Oberon in first perf. of A Midsummer Night's Dream (opera by Britten), 1960. Formed Deller vocal ensemble Consort, 1950; Deller Consort tours of Australia, NZ, and USA, 1964, 1967, 1969. Concert tours of America with Desmond Dupré, 1955, 1957, 1959, 1962. Founder and Artistic Dir, Stour Music Festival, 1963. Festivals: Edinburgh, Aldeburgh, Three Choirs, Royal Danish, Vienna, Stuttgart, Graz, Lucerne, Hitzacker, etc. Hon. Music Adviser, Univ. of Kent. Pres., Catch Club of

America. *Relevant publication:* Hardwick: Alfred Deller, a Singularity of Voice, 1968. *Recreations:* conversation and country life. *Address:* Barton Cottage, The Street, Kennington, Ashford, Kent. *T:* Ashford 23838.

**DELLER, Capt. Harold Arthur;** Commodore of Union Castle Mail SS Co. Ltd, 1960-62, retired; *b* 28 Aug. 1897; *s* of William John Deller, RN, and Edith Deller; *m* 1922, Mary Phyllis Elizabeth Deller (cousin); one adopted *d. Educ:* King Edward VII Sch., North Shields (Tynemouth), Northumberland. At sea as Cadet, SS Austrian Prince, from 1911. Served European War (Gen. Service and Merchant Service Medals) until captured at sea, July 1915. Joined Union Castle Mail SS Co., 1919, as Junior Officer. War of 1939-45 (Medal for Gen. Service, 1939-45 Star, Atlantic Star); first command, 1938. Capt. of various Mail Vessels from 1947, finally to Flagship, Pendennis Castle (RMS), 1960. Consultant, James A. Silver Ltd. Royal Order of Phoenix (Greece), 1941. *Publications:* contributor to South African Personality, and to English Digest. *Recreation:* painting. *Address:* 8 Reynolds Court, Romsey, Hants. *T:* Romsey 2449. *Clubs:* Southampton Master Mariners' (Southampton); Royal Motor Yacht (Poole).

**DEL MAR, Norman Rene,** ARCM; FGSM; Hon. RAM; *b* 31 July 1919; *m* 1947, Pauline Mann; two *s. Educ:* Marlborough; Royal College of Music. Asst Sir Thomas Beecham, Royal Philharmonic Orchestra, 1947; Principal Conductor, English Opera Group, 1949; Conductor and Prof. of conducting, Guildhall Sch. of Music, 1953; Conductor, Yorshire Symphony Orchestra, 1954; Conductor, BBC Scottish Orchestra, 1960-65. *Publication:* Richard Strauss, Vol. 1, 1962, Vol. 2, 1969. *Recreation:* philately. *Address:* Witchings, Hadley Common, Herts. *T:* 01-449 4836.

**DELMAS, J. P. M. C.;** *see* Chaban-Delmas.

**DELMER, (Denis) Sefton,** OBE 1946; writer on foreign affairs; *b* 24 May 1904; *s* of late Prof. F. S. Delmer, Hobart, Tasmania, English lecturer at Berlin Univ.; *m* 1935, Isabel (marriage dissolved, 1946), *d* of late Capt. P. O. Nicholas; *m* 1948, Zoë Ursula Black; one *s* one *d. Educ:* St Paul's Sch.; Lincoln Coll., Oxford. Joined Daily Express, 1927; Berlin Correspondent of Daily Express, 1928-33; Paris Correspondent, 1933-36; War Correspondent during Spanish Civil War, July 1936-Sept. 1938; Chief European Reporter of the Daily Express from 1937; War Correspondent, Poland 1939, France, 1939-40, with French Army; Foreign Office, 1941-45; rejoined Daily Express, as Chief Foreign Affairs Reporter, 1945-59. Editorial adviser to Der Spiegel, Hamburg, 1963-64. *Publications:* Trail Sinister, 1961; Black Boomerang, 1962; Die Deutschen und ich, 1962. *Address:* The Valley Farm, Lamarsh, near Bures, Suffolk. *T:* Twinstead 222. *Clubs:* Garrick, Press, Lansdowne.

**DELMER, Sefton;** *see* Delmer, D. S.

**de los ANGELES, Victoria;** Cross of Lazo de Dama of Order of Isabel the Catholic, Spain; Condecoración Banda de la Orden Civil de Alfonso X (El Sabio), Spain; Opera and Concert-Artiste (singing in original languages), Lyric-Soprano, since 1944; *b* Barcelona, Spain, 1 Nov. 1923; *m* 1948, Enrique Magrina; two *s. Educ:* Conservatorium of Barcelona; University of Barcelona. Studied until 1944 at Conservatorium, Barcelona; first public concert, in Barcelona, 1944; dĕbut at Gran Teatro del Liceo de Barcelona, in Marriage of Figaro, 1945; concert tours in Spain and Portugal, 1945 and 1946; winner of first prize at Concours International of Geneva, 1947; Paris Opera first appearance, and dĕbut at the Scala, Milan, also South-American concert-tour, 1949; first tour in Scandinavia, first appearance at Covent Garden, and Carnegie Hall Dĕbut, 1950; first United States concert tour, and Metropolitan Opera of New York season, 1951. Since 1951 has appeared at the most important opera theatres and concert halls of Europe, South and Central America and Canada; first tour in S Africa, 1953; first tour in Australia, 1956; first appearance, Vienna State Opera, 1957. Opening Festival, Bayreuth, with Tannhäuser, 1961. Gold Medal, Barcelona, 1958; Silver Medal, province of Barcelona, 1959; Medal Premio Roma, 1969, etc. *Address:* Victoria de los Angeles de Magriñá, c/o E. Magriñá, Paseo de Gracia, 87-7-D, Barcelona, Spain.

**de LOTBINIERE, Lt-Col Sir Edmond;** *see* Joly de Lotbinière.

**de LOTBINIERE, Seymour Joly,** CVO 1956; OBE 1953; *b* 21 Oct. 1905; *s* of late Brig.-Gen. H. G. Joly de Lotbinière, DSO; *m* 1944, Mona Lewis; one *s. Educ:* Eton; Trinity Coll., Cambridge. Called to Bar, Lincoln's Inn. On BBC staff, 1932-67. Governor, Bristol Old Vic Trust, 1963-67. *Address:* Brandon Hall, Brandon, Suffolk.

*See also Lt-Col Sir Edmond Joly de Lotbinière.*

**DEL RE, Arundel;** OBE 1920; MA London, MA Oxon, Balliol College; LittD, Tokyo University of Education, Japan; Professor Emeritus Nanzan Catholic University, Nagoya; Tutor and Lecturer, Victoria University, Wellington, New Zealand, 1958-67; *b* 29 Jan. 1892; *o s* of Capt. Pietro del Re (Royal Italian Army) and Bertha Fremoult Hill; *m* 1923; two *d. Educ:* Florence; University Coll., London. University Lecturer in Italian, Oxford, 1920-27; King's College, London University, 1922-27; Prof. of English Literature, Tokyo Imperial Univ. and Imperial Univ., Taihoku (Formosa), 1927-41; Adviser to the Civil Information and Educn Section, GHQ, SCAP, in Japan, 1945-51. Order of the Sacred Treasure, third class (Japan), 1963. *Publications:* John Florio's Firste Fruites, 1936; Commentary to Bridges' Testament of Beauty (Introduction), 1938; Creation Myths of the Formosan Savages, 1951, etc. *Address:* 17 Barnet Street, Highett, Melbourne, 3190, Australia.

**DELVE, Sir Frederick (William),** Kt 1962; CBE 1942; Chief Officer, London Fire Brigade, 1948-62, retired; Director: Securicor Ltd; NU-Swift International Ltd; Sound Diffusion Ltd; *b* 28 Oct. 1902; *s* of Frederick John Delve, Master Tailor, Brighton; *m* 1924, Ethel Lillian Morden; no *c. Educ:* Brighton. Royal Navy, 1918-23; Fire Service since 1923; Chief Officer, Croydon Fire Brigade, 1934-41; Dep. Inspector-in-Chief of NFS, 1941-43; Chief Regional Fire Officer, No. 5 London Region, National Fire Service, 1943-48. Pres., Institution of Fire Engineers, 1941-42; King's Police and Fire Services Medal, 1940. *Recreations:* all outdoor games, gardening. *Address:* 53 Ashley Court, Grand Avenue, Hove, Sussex.

**DELVIN, Lord; William Anthony Nugent;** Captain, RA, retired; *b* 21 Nov. 1928; *s* and *heir* of 12th Earl of Westmeath, *qv*; *m* 1963, Susanna Margaret, *o d* of J. C. B. W. Leonard, *qv*; two *s. Educ:* Marlborough Coll. *Heir: s* Hon. Sean Charles Weston Nugent, *b* 16 Feb. 1965. *Address:* Farthings, Rotten Row Hill, Bradfield, Berks. *T:* Bradfield 426.

**DELYSIA, Alice;** *d* of M. Lapize and Mme. Mathilde Douce; *m* 1944, Captain Kolb-Bernard, DSC, Agent Consulaire (for France). *Educ:* Convent des Sœurs de Nevers. Began under C. B. Cochran in Odds and Ends, 1914; More Pell Mell, Carminetta, As You Were, Afgar; went to America with Afgar, came back to London in Mayfair and Montmartre; went again to America in the Schubert revue Topics of 1924; came back to London in first straight play; successes: Her Past, Princess Charming, A Pair of Trousers, The Cat and The Fiddle, and Mother of Pearl, etc; first appearance in Australia, 1934; returned to London and made several subsequent tours; entered films, 1934, and appeared in Evensong. Enlisted with ENSA, May 1941, acting for troops in whole Middle East, then Normandy, Belgium, Holland, until end of war. King's Medal for Freedom; Africa Star, 8th Army; French Recognition Medal for War Services; Free French Medal; Order of Merit (Lebanon and Syria). *Recreations:* horse riding, walking, swimming.

**de MANIO, Jack,** MC 1940; Broadcaster; Presenter of BBC programme *Today* since 1958; *b* 26 Jan. 1914; *s* of Jean and Florence de Manio; *m* 1st, 1935, Juliet Gravaeret Kaufmann, New York (marriage dissolved, 1946); one *s*; 2nd, 1946, Loveday Elizabeth Matthews (*widow, née* Abbott). *Educ:* Aldenham. Served War of 1939-45, Royal Sussex Regt; 7th Bn, BEF, 1939-40; 1st Bn, Middle East Forces, 1940-44; Forces Broadcasting, Middle East, 1944-46. Joined Overseas Service, BBC, 1946; BBC Home Service, 1950; resigned to become freelance, 1964. *Publication:* To Auntie with Love, 1967; Life Begins Too Early, 1970. *Recreation:* fishing. *Address:* 105 Cheyne Walk, SW10. *T:* 01-352 0889. *Clubs:* St James', Hurlingham, MCC.

**DEMANT, Rev. Vigo Auguste,** DLitt; BSc; Canon of Christ Church and Regius Professor of Moral and Pastoral Theology in Oxford University since 1949; Canon Residentiary, 1942-49, Treasurer, 1948-49, of St Paul's Cathedral; *b* 8 Nov. 1893; *s* of late T. Demant, linguist, of Newcastle on Tyne, and Emily Demant; *m* 1925, Marjorie, *d* of late George Tickner, FZS, Oxford; one *s* two *d*. *Educ:* Newcastle on Tyne; Tournan, France; Armstrong Coll., Durham Univ.; Manchester Coll. and Exeter Coll., Oxford; Ely Theological Coll. Curacies: S Thomas, Oxford, S Nicholas, Plumstead, S Silas, Kentish Town; Vicar of S John-the-Divine, Richmond, Surrey, 1933-42; Dir of Research to Christian Social Council, 1929-33. Ex-Mem. Departmental Cttee on Homosexual Offences and Prostitution. Gifford Lecturer, St Andrews, 1957-58. *Publications:* This Unemployment, 1931; God, Man and Society, 1933; Christian Polity, 1936; The Religious Prospect, 1939; Theology of Society, 1947; Religion and the Decline of Capitalism, 1952; A Two-way Religion, 1957; Christian Sex Ethics, 1963. *Recreation:* carpentry. *Address:* Christ Church, Oxford.

**de MARGERIE, Roland,** CVO 1938; Ambassador of France; Hon. conseiller d'Etat; *b* 6 May 1899; *s* of late P. de Margerie, KBE, French Ambassador in Berlin, 1922-31, and Jeanne Rostand, sister of the Playwright Edmond Rostand, Mem. of the French Academy; *m* 1921, Jenny, *d* of Edmond Fabre-Luce, Vice-Chm. of the Crédit Lyonnais; two *s* one *d*. *Educ:* Sorbonne; Ecole des Sciences Politiques, Paris. Joined Foreign Office, 1917; Lieut 17th Bn of Chasseurs Alpins, 1918-21; Attaché to French Embassy, Brussels, 1921; Sec., Berlin, 1923; 1st Sec. to the French Embassy, London, 1933-39; mem. of the mission attached to their Majesties during their State visit to France, 1938; Counsellor, 1939; Capt. 152nd Regt of the Line, Sept. 1939-Feb. 1940; ADC to Gen. Gamelin, Feb.-March 1940; Private Sec. to the Minister for Foreign Affairs, March 1940; French Consul-Gen., Shanghai, 1940-44; Chargé with the office of the French Embassy in Peking, 1944-46. Asst deleg. negotiations for Brussels Pact, 1948; Minister plenipotentiary, 1949; Director-Gen. of Political Affairs, France, 1955; French Ambassador to the Holy See, 1956-59; to Spain, 1959-62; to the Federal Republic of Germany, 1962-65; Conseiller d'Etat, 1965-70. Comdr Legion of Honour; holds various foreign orders. *Address:* 14 rue St Guillaume, Paris 7. *Club:* Jockey (Paris).

**de MAULEY,** 6th Baron, *cr* 1838; **Gerald John Ponsonby;** *b* 19 Dec. 1921; *er s* of 5th Baron de Mauley and Elgiva Margaret, *d* of late Hon. Cospatrick Dundas and Lady Cordeaux; *S* father, 1962; *m* 1954, Helen Alice, *d* of late Hon. Charles W. S. Douglas and *widow* of Lieut-Col B. L. L. Abdy Collins, OBE, MC, RE. *Educ:* Eton; Christ Church, Oxford (MA). Served War of 1939-45, France; Lieut Leics Yeo., Captain RA. Called to Bar, Middle Temple, 1949. *Heir:* *b* Major Hon. Thomas Maurice Ponsonby, Royal Glos Hussars [*b* 2 Aug. 1930; *m* 1956, Maxine Henrietta, *d* of W. D. K. Thellusson; two *s*]. *Address:* Langford House, Little Faringdon, Lechlade, Glos.

**DE MEL, Most Rev. Hiyanirindu Lakdasa Jacob;** *see* Calcutta, Bishop of.

**de MENDIETA, Rev. Dr Emmanuel Alexandre A.;** *see* Amand de Mendieta.

**de MILLE, Agnes George (Mrs W. F. Prude);** Choreographer and Author; *b* New York City; *d* of William C. and Anna George de Mille; *m* 1943, Walter F. Prude; one *s*. *Educ:* University of Calif. (AB *cum laude*). Dance concerts USA, England, Denmark, France, 1929-40; Choreographed: Black Crook, 1929; Nymph Errant, 1933; Romeo and Juliet 1936; Oklahoma, 1943; One Touch of Venus, 1943; Bloomer Girl, 1944; Carousel, 1945; Brigadoon, 1947; Gentlemen Prefer Blondes, 1949; Paint Your Wagon, 1951; The Girl in Pink Tights, 1954; Oklahoma (film), 1955; Goldilocks, 1958; Juno, 1959; Kwamina, 1961; One Hundred and Ten in the Shade, 1963; Come Summer, 1968. Founded and directed Agnes de Mille Dance Theatre, 1953-54. Directed: Allegro, 1947; The Rape of Lucretia, 1948; Out of This World, 1950; Ballets composed: Black Ritual, 1940; Three Virgins and a Devil, 1941; Drums Sound in Hackensack, 1941; Rodeo, 1942; Tally-Ho, 1944; Fall River Legend, 1948; The Harvest According, 1952; The Rib of Eve, 1956; The Bitter Wierd, 1963; The Wind in the Mountains, 1965; The Four Marys, 1965; The Golden Age, 1966, etc. Television shows, for Omnibus, etc. Mem., Nat. Adv. Council of the Arts, 1965-66; Pres., Soc. for Stage Directors and Choreographers, 1966-67. Hon. Degrees: Mills Coll., 1952; Russell Sage College, 1953; Smith Coll., 1954; Northwestern Univ., 1960; Goucher Coll., 1961; University of Calif., 1962; Clark Univ., 1962; Franklin and Marshall Coll., 1966; Western Michigan Univ., 1967. New York Critics Award, 1943, 1944, 1945; Antoinette Perry Award, 1962; and numerous other awards, 1943-58. *Publications:* Dance to the Piper, 1952; And Promenade Home, 1958; To a Young Dancer, 1962; The Book of the Dance, 1963; Lizzie Borden, Dance of Death, 1968; articles in Vogue, Atlantic Monthly, Good Housekeeping, New York Times,

McCall's, Horizon, Esquire. *Club:* Merriewold Country (NY).

**DE MOLEYNS;** *see* Eveleigh-de-Moleyns.

**de MONTHERLANT, Henri;** *see* Montherlant.

**de MONTMORENCY, Sir Reginald (D'Alton Lodge),** 18th Bt, *cr* 1631; *b* 13 March 1899; *y s* of John Kiddell de Montmorency and Ada Margaret Ligonier Balfour; *S* cousin, 1963; *m* 1928, Dorothy Victoria, 2nd *d* of Gilbert Walter Robinson. *Educ:* privately in England and Bruges for art. Served European War 1914-18: Hon. Artillery Co. and Royal Horse Artillery, 1917-19. P. & O., 1915-17, shore service at home and abroad, 1919-25; Manager: (in Bombay) for Bell, Russ & Co. (East India merchants), 1925-33; A. Besse of Arabia and Manager of the Halal Shipping Co., 1933-35. Joined the staff of The Times, 1936 and retired 1967. Travelled widely in Commonwealth and other countries in connection with his work. *Recreations:* swimming, riding, walking and drawing. *Heir: cousin* Arnold Geoffroy de Montmorency, *b* 27 July 1908. *Address:* Bristol Cottage, Putney Heath, SW15. *T:* 01-788 2102. *Club:* Royal Commonwealth Society.

**DEMPSEY, James;** MP (Lab) Coatbridge and Airdrie since Oct. 1959; *b* 6 Feb. 1917; *s* of late James Dempsey; *m* 1945, Jane, *d* of late John McCann; four *s*. *Educ:* Holy Family Sch., Mossend; Co-operative Coll., Loughborough; National Council of Labour Colls. Served War of 1939-45: Auxiliary Military Pioneer Corps. Member Hospital Board of Management and Board for Industry and Executive Council, National Health Service, National Assistance Board. JP Lanarkshire, 1954; CC Lanarkshire, 1945-. *Address:* The House of Commons, SW1; 113 Thorndean Avenue, Bellshill, Lanarkshire. *T:* 2712.

**DENBIGH,** 11th Earl of, *cr* 1622 and **DESMOND,** 10th Earl of, *cr* 1622; **William Rudolph Michael Feilding;** *b* 2 Aug. 1943; *s* of 10th Earl of Denbigh and Verena Barbara, *d* of W. E. Price; *S* father, 1966; *m* 1965, Caroline Judith Vivienne, *o d* of Lt-Col Geoffrey Cooke; two *d*. *Educ:* Eton. *Heir: cousin* William David Feilding, *b* 12 Aug. 1939. *Address:* Pailton House, Rugby; 19 Essex Villas, W8. *T:* 01-937 9911.

**DENBIGH, Prof. Kenneth George,** FRS 1965; MA Cantab, DSc Leeds; Principal of Queen Elizabeth College, University of London, since 1966; *b* 30 May 1911; *s* of late G. J. Denbigh, MSc, Harrogate; *m* 1935, Kathleen Enoch; two *s*. *Educ:* Queen Elizabeth Grammar Sch., Wakefield; Leeds University. Imperial Chemical Industries, 1934-38, 1945-48; Lecturer, Southampton Univ., 1938-41; Ministry of Supply (Explosives), 1941-45; Lecturer, Cambridge Univ., Chemical Engineering Dept, 1948-55; Professor: of Chemical Technology, Edinburgh, 1955-60, of Chemical Engineering Science, London Univ., 1960-61; Courtauld's Prof., Imperial Coll., 1961-66. Hon. DèsSc Toulouse, 1960; Hon. DUniv. Essex, 1967. *Publications:* The Thermodynamics of the Steady State, 1951; The Principles of Chemical Equilibrium, 1955; Science, Industry and Social Policy, 1963; Chemical Reactor Theory, 1965; various scientific papers. *Address:* Queen Elizabeth College, Campden Hill Road, W8. *T:* 01-937 5411.

**DENCH, Judith Olivia, (Judi Dench),** OBE 1970; actress (theatre, films and television); *b* 9 Dec. 1934; *d* of Reginald Arthur Dench and Eleanora Olave Dench (*née* Jones). *Educ:* The Mount Sch., York; Central Sch. of Speech and Drama. *Theatre:* Old Vic seasons, 1957-61: parts incl.: Ophelia in Hamlet; Katherine in Henry V; Cecily in The Importance of Being Earnest; Juliet in Romeo and Juliet; also 1957-61: two Edinburgh Festivals; Paris-Belgium-Yugoslavia tour; America-Canada tour; Venice (all with Old Vic Co.). Subseq. appearances incl.: Royal Shakespeare Co., 1961-62: Anya in The Cherry Orchard, Aldwych; Isabella in Measure for Measure, Stratford-on-Avon; Nottingham Playhouse tour of W Africa, 1963; Oxford Playhouse, 1964-65: Irina in The Three Sisters; Doll Common in The Alchemist; Nottingham Playhouse, 1965: Saint Joan; The Astrakhan Coat (world première); Variety London Critics' Best Actress of the Year Award for perf. as Lika in The Promise, Fortune, 1967; Sally Bowles in Cabaret, Palace, 1968; 1969; London Assurance, Aldwych, 1970; Major Barbara, Aldwych, 1970; Associate Mem., Royal Shakespeare Co., Stratford-on-Avon, incl. Bianca in Women Beware Women, Viola in Twelfth Night, doubling Hermione and Perdita in The Winter's Tale; tour of Nigeria and Ghana. *Films:* He Who Rides a Tiger; A Study in Terror; Four in the Morning (Brit. Film Acad. Award for Most Promising Newcomer, 1965); A Midsummer Night's Dream. TV appearances, 1957- (Best Actress of the Year Award from Guild of Television Dirs for Talking to a Stranger, 1967). Awards incl. British and foreign, for theatre, films and TV. *Recreations:* painting, swimming, picking up odds and ends. *Address:* 4 Prospect Place, Holly Walk, Hampstead, NW3.

**DENHAM,** 2nd Baron, *cr* 1937, of Weston Underwood; **Bertram Stanley Mitford Bowyer,** 10th Bt, *cr* 1660, of Denham; 2nd Bt, *cr* 1933 of Weston Underwood; a Lord-in-Waiting to The Queen, 1961-64 and since 1970; *b* 3 Oct. 1927; *s* of 1st Baron and Hon. Daphne Freeman-Mitford, 4th *d* of 1st Baron Redesdale; *S* father 1948; *m* 1956, Jean, *o d* of Kenneth McCorquodale, Fambridge Hall, White Notley, Essex; three *s* one *d*. *Educ:* Eton; King's Coll., Cambridge. Joined Grenadier Guards, 1945; commissioned Oxford & Bucks LI, 1946; demobilised, 1948. Mem. Westminster CC, 1959-61. *Recreations:* field sports. *Heir: s* Hon. Richard Grenville George Bowyer, *b* 8 Feb. 1959. *Address:* Laundry Cottage, Weston Underwood, Olney, Bucks. *T:* Olney 535. *Clubs:* Buck's, Pratt's.

**DENHAM, Capt. Henry Mangles,** CMG 1945; RN, retired; *b* 9 Sept. 1897; *s* of Henry Mangles Denham and Helen Clara Lowndes; *m* 1924, Estelle Margaret Sibbald Currie; one *s* two *d*. *Educ:* RN Coll., Dartmouth. Went to sea at beginning of European War, serving at Dardanelles in HMS Agamemnon and destroyer Racoon; occupation of the Rhine in HM Rhine Flotilla; round the world cruise with the Prince of Wales in HMS Renown, 1921; served in Mediterranean for long period largely in HMS Queen Elizabeth and Warspite; at Staff Coll., 1935; Comdr of HMS Penelope, 1936-39. Naval Attaché, Denmark, 1940; Naval Attaché, Stockholm, 1940-47; retd list, 1947. *Publications:* The Aegean, 1963; Eastern Mediterranean, 1964; The Adriatic, 1967; The Tyrrhenian Sea, 1969. *Recreation:* yachting. *Clubs:* United Service, Royal Automobile, Royal Ocean, Royal Cruising, Royal Yacht Squadron (Cowes).

**DENHAM, Maurice;** Actor since 1934; *b* 23 Dec. 1909; *s* of Norman Denham and Winifred Lillico; *m* 1936, Margaret Dunn; two *s* one *d*. *Educ:* Tonbridge Sch. Hull Repertory Theatre, 1934-36; theatre, radio and television, 1936-39. Served War of 1939-45: Buffs, 1939-43; Royal Artillery, 1943-45; despatches, 1946. Theatre, films, radio and television, 1946-. *Recreations:* painting, conducting gramophone records. *Address:* 29 Bedford Gardens, W8. *T:* 01-727 6112. *Clubs:* Garrick, Green Room.

**DENHOLM, Sir John (Carmichael),** Kt 1955; CBE 1947; President of J. & J. Denholm Ltd; *b* 24 Dec. 1893; *s* of John Denholm and Jane Miller, Greenock, Scotland; *m* 1926, Mary Laura, *d* of Peter Kerr, Greenock; no *c*. *Educ:* Greenock Acad. Joined family firm, J. & J. Denholm Ltd, 1910; Dir 1922; RNVR: Midshipman, 1910; Sub-Lieut, 1912; Lieut temp. 1915, perm. list 1917; Lieut-Comdr 1925; resigned 1926; served European War, 1914-18; RN Div. Antwerp and Gallipoli, 1914-15; RN HMS Ladybird, 1916-19 (despatches); Regional Shipping Rep. for West Coast Scotland, Ministry of Shipping and Min. of War Transport, 1940-45. Council of Chamber of Shipping: Mem. 1936; Vice-Pres, 1953; Pres. 1954-55. Chm., David Macbrayne Ltd, 1963-64. *Recreation:* golf. *Address:* Glendower, Skelmorlie, Ayrshire. *T:* Wemyss Bay 2120 *Clubs:* Western, Royal Scottish Automobile (Glasgow).

*See also Col Sir William Denholm.*

**DENHOLM, Col Sir William (Lang),** Kt 1965; TD; Chairman, J. & J. Denholm Ltd; Chairman, Shipping Federation, 1962-65; Joint Chairman, National Maritime Board, 1962-65; President, International Shipping Federation, 1962-67; *b* 23 Feb. 1901; *s* of John Denholm and Jane Miller, Greenock; *m* 1925, Dorothy Jane, *d* of Robert Ferguson, Greenock; two *s* one *d*. *Educ:* Greenock Academy; Greenock Collegiate. Joined family firm J. & J. Denholm Ltd, 1918. 2nd Lieut 77th (H) Field Regt, RA (TA), 1921; in command, 1939-40; Hon. Col 1945-60. Mem. Gen. and Scottish Cttees, Lloyd's Register of Shipping, 1935. Mem. Council, Shipping Federation, 1936; Vice-Chm., 1950-62. Vice-Chm, Glasgow Royal Infirmary and Assoc. Hospitals, 1949-60; Chm., 1960-64. DL County of Renfrew, 1950. Chevalier of the Order of St Olav (Norway). *Recreation:* golf. *Address:* Glenmill, Kilmacolm, Renfrewshire. *T:* Kilmacolm 2535. *Clubs:* Western, Royal Scottish Automobile (Glasgow); Royal Clyde Yacht.

*See also Sir John Denholm.*

**DENING, Sir (Maberly) Esler,** GCMG, *cr* 1955 (KCMG, *cr* 1950; CMG 1945); OBE 1939 (MBE 1919); HM Foreign Service, retired; *b* 21 April 1897; *o surv s* of late Walter Dening, Ottery St Mary, Devon, and Lydia James. Enlisted in Australian Imperial Forces, 1915, and served in Egypt and France; demobilised 1919 with rank of Lieut; joined HM Consular Service, 1920, and served in Tokyo, Osaka and Kobe in Japan, Seoul (Korea), Manila (Philippines), Dairen and Harbin (Manchuria), 1920-38; appointed to Foreign Office, 1938; a First Sec. in HM Embassy, Washington, 1941. Served in the Home Guard (35th London), 1940-43; Chief Political Adviser to Supreme Allied Commander, South-East Asia, 1943-46; an Asst Under-Sec. of State, FO, 1946-50; special mission to Asia with rank of Ambassador, 1950-51; UK Political Representative in Japan, 1951-52; HM Ambassador to Japan, 1952-57. Head of UK Delegn to Antarctic Treaty Conference, Washington, 1959. Chairman, Royal Central Asian Soc., 1967-70. Order of the Rising Sun First Class (Japan), 1964. *Publication:* Japan, 1960. *Address:* 99b Elm Park Gardens, SW10. *T:* 01-352 8585. *Clubs:* Boodle's, Beefsteak, Royal Automobile.

**DENING, Maj.-Gen. Roland,** CB 1942; MVO 1935; MC 1918; DL; IA; psc; retired; *b* 13 Sept. 1888; *s* of late Lt-Gen. Sir Lewis Dening, KCB, DSO, and late Beatrice Catherine Scott; *m* 1917, Clare de Burgh (Kaisar-i-hind Gold Medal, 1942; DGStJ, 1963), *d* of J. H. Garratt, Greystones, Co. Wicklow; one *s* two *d*. *Educ:* Wellington Coll., Berks; RMA Woolwich. Entered Royal Field Artillery, 1907; Transferred to 18th Bengal Lancers, Indian Army, 1911; served European War 18th (KGO) Lancers, France 1914-18, Palestine and Syria 1918; DAAG 4th Cavalry Div. EEF 1918; DAAG Northforce EEF 1919; Instructor Cavalry Sch., Saugor, 1920-21; Attended Staff Coll., Quetta, 1922; Brigade Major, 1st Risalpur Cavalry Brigade, 1924-28; Commandant, Equitation Sch., Saugor, 1931-34; Commandant, 19th KGO Lancers, 1934-36; Gen. Staff Officer 1st Grade, Peshawar District, 1936-38; Comm. Jullunder Brig. Area, India, 1938; Comdr 1st Abbotabad Inf. Bde, 1940; Maj.-Gen. 1940; Comdr Peshawar District, 1940-43; retired, 1944, Col 19th King George V's Own Lancers, 1945-49. Chm. Housing Cttee, Ottery St Mary UDC, 1948-51; Chm. British Legion Devon County, 1950-54; County Cadet Officer (Ambulance), St John Ambulance Brigade, Devon, 1951-61; Officer Brother, Order of St John of Jerusalem, 1958. Pres. Honiton and District Agricultural Assoc., 1957. DL Devonshire, 1954. *Recreations:* polo, tennis, rackets. *Address:* Tipton Lodge, Tipton St John, near Sidmouth, East Devon. *T:* Ottery St Mary 2027.

**DENINGTON, Mrs Evelyn Joyce,** CBE 1966; Chairman, Stevenage Development Corporation, since 1966; Deputy Leader of the Opposition, Greater London Council, since 1967; *b* 9 Aug. 1907; *d* of Phillip Charles Bursill and Edith Rowena Bursill; *m* 1935, Cecil Dallas Denington. *Educ:* Blackheath High Sch.; Bedford Coll., London. Journalism, 1927-31; Teacher, 1933-45; Gen. Sec., Nat. Assoc. of Labour Teachers, 1938-47; Member: St Pancras Borough Coun., 1945-59; LCC, 1946-65 (Chm. New and Expanding Towns Cttee, 1960-65); GLC, 1964- (Chm. Housing Cttee, 1964-67); Stevenage Development Corp., 1950-66; Central Housing Adv. Cttee, 1955- (Chm. Sub-Cttee prod. report Our Older Homes); SE Economic Planning Coun., 1966-. Hon. FRIBA. *Address:* Weale House, 29 Crescent Grove, Clapham, SW4. *T:* 01-622 1275.

**DENISON,** family name of **Baron Londesborough.**

**DENISON, Dulcie Winifred Catherine; (Dulcie Gray);** actress, playwright, authoress; *b* 20 Nov. 1920; *d* of late Arnold Savage Bailey, CBE, and of Kate Edith (*née* Clulow Gray); *m* 1939, Michael Denison, *qv*. *Educ:* England and Malaya. In Repertory in Aberdeen, 1st part Sorrel in Hay Fever, 1939; Repertory in Edinburgh, Glasgow and Harrogate, 1940; BBC Serial, Front Line Family, 1941; Shakespeare, Regents Park; Alexandra in The Little Foxes, Piccadilly; Midsummer Night's Dream, Westminster, 1942; Brighton Rock, Garrick; Landslide, Westminster, 1943; Lady from Edinburgh, Playhouse, 1945; Dear Ruth, St James's; Wind is 90, Apollo, 1946; on tour in Fools Rush In, 1946; Rain on the Just, Aldwych, 1948; Queen Elizabeth Slept Here, Strand, 1949; The Four-poster, Ambassadors, 1950 (tour of S Africa, 1954-55); See You Later (Revue), Watergate, 1951; Dragon's Mouth, Winter Garden, 1952; Sweet Peril, St James's, 1952; We Must Kill Toni, Westminster; The Diary of a Nobody, Arts, 1954; Alice Through the Looking Glass, Chelsea Palace, 1955. Appeared in own play, Love Affair, Lyric Hammersmith, 1956; South Sea Bubble, Cape

Town, 1956; Tea and Sympathy, Melbourne and Sydney, 1956; South Sea Bubble, Johannesburg, 1957; Double Cross, Duchess, 1958; Let Them Eat Cake, Cambridge, 1959; Candida, Piccadilly and Wyndham's, 1960; Heartbreak House, Wyndham's, 1961; A Marriage Has Been Arranged, and A Village Wooing (Hong Kong); Shakespeare Recital (Berlin Festival); Royal Gambit for opening of Ashcroft Theatre, Croydon, 1962; Where Angels Fear to Tread, Arts and St Martin's, 1963; An Ideal Husband, Strand, 1965; On Approval, St Martin's, 1966; Happy Family, St Martin's, 1967; Number 10, Strand, 1967; Out of the Question, St Martin's, 1968; Three, Fortune, 1970. *Films include:* They were Sisters, 1944; Wanted for Murder, 1945; A Man about the House, 1946; Mine Own Executioner, 1947; My Brother Jonothan, 1947; The Glass Mountain, 1948; The Franchise Affair, 1951; Angels One Five, 1952; There was a Young Lady, 1953. Has appeared in television plays and radio serials. *Publications: play:* Love Affair; *books:* Murder on the Stairs; Murder in Melbourne; Baby Face; Epitaph for a Dead Actor; Murder on a Saturday; Murder in Mind; The Devil Wore Scarlet; No Quarter for a Star; The Murder of Love; Died in the Red; The Actor and His World (with Michael Denison); Murder on Honeymoon; For Richer, For Richer. *Recreations:* golf, embroidery, swimming, butterflies. *Address:* Shardeloes, Amersham, Bucks.

**DENISON, John Law,** CBE 1960 (MBE 1945); FRCM; General Manager, Royal Festival Hall, since 1965; Council Member, Arts Educational Trust Ltd; *b* 21 Jan. 1911; *s* of late Rev. H. B. W. and Alice Dorothy Denison; *m* 1st, 1936, Annie Claudia Russell Brown (marriage dissolved, 1946); 2nd, 1947, Evelyn Mary Donald (*née* Moir) (*d* 1958), *d* of John and Mary Scott Moir, Edinburgh; one *d*; *m* 1960, Audrey Grace Burnaby (*née* Bowles) (*d* 1970). *Educ:* Brighton Coll.; Royal Coll. of Music. Played horn in BBC Symphony, London Philharmonic, City of Birmingham, and other orchestras, 1934-39. Served War of 1939-45; gazetted Somerset Light Inf., 1940; DAA and QMG 214 Inf. Bde and various staff appts, 1941-45 (despatches). Asst Dir, Music Dept, British Council, 1946-48; Music Dir, Arts Council of Great Britain, 1948-65. *Publications:* articles for various musical publications. *Address:* Royal Festival Hall, SE1.

**DENISON, (John) Michael (Terence Wellesley);** Actor; *b* 1 Nov. 1915; *s* of Gilbert Dixon Denison and Marie Louise (*née* Bain); *m* 1939, Dulcie Gray (*see* D. W. C. Denison). *Educ:* Harrow; Magdalen Coll., Oxford. Dramatic Sch., 1937-38; Westminster Theatre, 1938; Aberdeen Repertory, 1939. First film, 1940. Served War of 1939-45, Royal Signals and Intelligence Corps, 1940-46. Has appeared in following plays: Ever Since Paradise, 1946; Rain on the Just, 1948; Queen Elizabeth Slept Here, 1949; The Four-poster, 1950; Dragon's Mouth, 1952; Sweet Peril, 1952; The Bad Samaritan, 1953; Alice Through the Looking Glass, 1953, and 1955; We Must Kill Toni, 1954; tour of S Africa, 1954-55; Memorial Theatre, Stratford-on-Avon, 1955; prod. and acted in Love Affair, 1956; A Village Wooing and Fanny's First Play (Edinburgh and Berlin festivals), 1956; Meet Me By Moonlight, 1957; Let Them Eat Cake, 1959; Candida, 1960; Heartbreak House, 1961; My Fair Lady, Melbourne; A Village Wooing (Hong Kong); Shakespeare Recital (Berlin Festival), 1962; Where Angels Fear to Tread, 1963; Hostile Witness, 1964; An Ideal Husband, 1965; On Approval, 1966; Happy Family; Number 10, 1967; Out of the Question, 1968; Three, Fortune, 1970. *Films include:* My Brother Jonathan, 1947; The Glass Mountain, 1948; Landfall, 1949; The Franchise Affair, 1950; Angels One Five, The Importance of Being Earnest, 1951; The Truth About Woman, 1957. Many television appearances including title role Boyd, QC, 1957-61 and 1963. On Council British Actors Equity Assoc., 1959-70 (Vice-Pres. 1952, 1961-63). *Publication:* (with Dulcie Gray) The Actor and His World, 1964. *Recreations:* golf, painting, watching cricket, gardening, motoring. *Address:* Shardeloes, Amersham, Bucks. *Clubs:* Richmond Golf (Richmond); Middlesex County Cricket.

**DENISON, Michael;** *see* Denison, J. M. T. W.

**DENISON-PENDER,** family name of **Baron Pender.**

**de NIVERVILLE, Air Vice-Marshal Joseph Lionel Elphege Albert,** CB 1945; RCAF retired; Assistant Deputy Minister (Air), Department of Transport, Ottawa, Canada, retired, 1964; *b* Montreal, Quebec, 31 Aug. 1897; *s* of Napoleon de Niverville; *m* 1920, Eméla Noël. *Educ:* La Salle Academy, Ottawa. RFC and RAF, 1917-19; Canadian Air Board and RCAF 1920-45; Air Officer Commanding No. 3 Training Command, Montreal, 1941-43; Member of Air Council for Training, RCAF, 1943; retired list, Aug. 1945. *Recreations:* golf, fishing, hunting. *Address:* 111 Wurtemburg Street, Ottawa, Ont, Canada. Canada.

**DENMAN,** family name of **Baron Denman.**

**DENMAN,** 4th Baron *cr* 1834, **Thomas Denman;** *b* 2 Aug. 1905; *o s* of 3rd Baron Denman, PC, GCMG, KCVO, and Hon. Gertrude Mary Pearson, GBE (*d* 1954), *o d* of 1st Viscount Cowdray; *S* father 1954. *Educ:* Eton; Trinity Coll., Cambridge. *Heir: cousin,* Capt. Sir Charles Spencer Denman, 2nd Bt, *qv.*

**DENMAN, Sir Charles Spencer,** 2nd Bt *cr* 1945; MC 1942; *b* 7 July 1916; *e s* of Hon. Sir Richard Douglas Denman, 1st Bt; *S* father 1957; also *heir-pres* to cousin, 4th Baron Denman, *qv*; *m* 1943, Sheila Anne, *d* of late Lt-Col Algernon Bingham Anstruther Stewart, DSO, Seaforth Highlanders, of Ornockenoch, Gatehouse of Fleet; three *s* one *d*. *Educ:* Shrewsbury. Served War of 1939-45 with Duke of Cornwall's Light Infantry (TA), India, Middle East, Western Desert and Dodecanese Islands; Major, 1943. Contested (C) Leeds Central, 1945. Chairman: Overseas Marketing Corporation Ltd; Tennant Budd & Roderick Pratt Ltd. Dep. Chm., marine and General Mutual Life Soc. Ltd; Director: C. Tennant Sons & Co. Ltd; NMA Co. of New Zealand Ltd; Consolidated Gold Fields; British Bank of the Middle East; Member: Council of Middle East Trade, 1963; Advisory Council of Export Credit Guarantee Department, 1963-68; British National Export Council, 1965; Cttee on Invisible Exports, 1965-67; Lord Kitchener Nat. Meml Fund. *Heir: s* Richard Thomas Denman, *b* 4 Oct. 1946. *Address:* Highden House, Washington, Pulborough, Sussex. *T:* Findon 2102. *Club:* Brooks's.

**DENMAN, Prof. Donald Robert;** Professor of Land Economy, Cambridge University, since 1968; Head of Department of Land Economy, Cambridge, since 1962; Fellow of Pembroke College, Cambridge, since 1962; *b* 7 April 1911; 2nd *s* of Robert Martyn Denman and Letitia Kate Denman, Finchley; *m* 1941, Jessica Hope, 2nd *d* of Richard H. Prior, Chichester; two *s*. *Educ:* Christ's Coll., Finchley; London University. BSc (London) 1938; MSc 1940; PhD 1945; MA Cantab 1948; FRICS 1949.

Dep. Exec. Off., Cumberland War Agricultural Exec. Cttee, 1939-46; University Lectr, Cambridge Univ., 1948-68. Land Management Cttee of Agricultural Improvement Coun., 1953-60; Member: Church Assembly, 1957-; Standing Cttee of Istituto de Diritto Agrario Internazionale e Comparato, Florence, 1960-; Dilapidations Legislation Commn, Church Assembly, 1958-64; Cttee of CNAA, 1966-; Advisor on Academic devt of land economy to University of Science and Technology, Kumasi, Ghana and University of Nigeria, 1963-; Advisor to Min. of Land Reform and Rural Co-operation, Iran. Vice-Pres., Conservation Soc. Governor, Canford Sch. *Publications:* Tenant Right Valuation: In History and Modern Practice, 1942; Tenant Right Valuation and Current Legislation, 1948; Estate Capital: The Contribution of Landownership to Agricultural Finance, 1957; Origins of Ownership: A Brief History of Landownership and Tenure, 1958 (2nd edn 1959); Bibliography of Rural Land Economy and Landownership 1900-1957 (*et al*), 1958; (jtly) Farm Rents: A Comparison of Current and Past Farm Rents in England and Wales, 1959; (Ed and contrib.) Landownership and Resources, 1960; (Ed and contrib.) Contemporary Problems of Landownership, 1963; Land in the Market, 1964; (jtly) Commons and Village Greens: A Study in Land Use, Conservation and Management Based on a National Survey of Commons in England and Wales 1961-66, Financed by the Nuffield Foundation, 1967; (Ed and contrib.) Land and People, 1967; The Case for Capitalism (Capitalism and Property), 1967; Rural Land Systems: A General Classification of Rural Land Systems in Relation to the Surveyors' Profession and Rural Land Reform, 1968; Land Use and the Constitution of Property, 1969; numerous monograpns, articles and papers in academic and professional jls and nat. press in Britain and abroad. *Recreation:* travel. *Address:* Pembroke College, Cambridge; 12 Chaucer Road, Cambridge. *T:* Cambridge 57725. *Club:* Carlton.

**DENMAN, George Roy,** CMG 1968; Deputy Secretary, Board of Trade, since 1970 (Under-Secretary, 1967-70); *b* 12 June 1924; *s* of Albert Edward and Gertrude Ann Denman; *m* 1966, Moya Lade; one *s*. *Educ:* Harrow Gram. Sch.; St John's Coll., Cambridge. War Service 1943-46; Major, Royal Signals. Joined BoT, 1948; Asst Private Sec. to successive Presidents, 1950-52; 1st Sec., British Embassy, Bonn, 1957-60; UK Delegn, Geneva, 1960-61; Counsellor, Geneva, 1965-67. Mem. negotiating delegn with European Communities, 1970-. *Address:* 26 St Luke's Street, SW3. *T:* 01-352 3199. *Club:* United University.

**DENMAN, John Leopold,** JP, FSA; FRIBA; Architect practising in Brighton, Sussex; *b* 15 Nov. 1882; *s* of Samuel Denman and Elizabeth Harriet Morley; *m* 1912, Constance Winifred Bluett; one *s* two *d*. *Educ:* Brighton Grammar Sch.; Architectural Association Sch. Awarded 1st Premium in open competition for–Women's Hospital, Brighton, and New Senior Sch. at Rickmansworth for Royal Masonic Institution for Girls; other Architectural works include: Eridge Castle, Sussex; renovation of Holy Trinity Church, Eridge Green; St Martin's Priory, Canterbury; Christ Church Cathedral Library and other destroyed property in precincts of Canterbury Cathedral; new Diocesan Offices, Canterbury; Harewood Court, flats for the aged at Hove for Royal Masonic Benevolent Institution; the new Sussex Eye Hospital, Brighton; Holiday Home and housing development, South Heighton, for Guinness Trust; rebuilding of tower at St Michael's Church, Southwick; Housing Scheme at Lindfield for Cuckfield UDC; Barclays Bank Ltd, Local Head Offices at Brighton; numerous church renovations incl. Brighton and Arundel parish churches. Pres., Regency Soc. of Brighton and Hove; Past-Pres. South-Eastern Society of Architects; Past Vice-Pres., RIBA. RIBA Distinction in Town Planning. Served with RE during European War, 1914-18. *Address:* Oldways, Hurstpierpoint, Sussex. *T:* Hurstpierpoint 2138.

**DENNELL, Prof. Ralph;** Beyer Professor of Zoology, University, Manchester, since 1963; *b* 29 Sept. 1907; *m* 1932, Dorothy Ethel Howard; no *c*. *Educ:* Leeds Grammar Sch.; University of Leeds. Demonstrator in Zoology, University of Leeds, 1929; Grisedale Research Student, University of Manchester, 1932; Asst Lecturer in Zoology, University of Manchester, 1935; Asst Lecturer in Zoology, and Lecturer in Zoology, Imperial Coll., 1937-46; Reader in Experimental Zoology, 1946-48, Prof. of Experimental Zoology, 1948-63, University of Manchester. *Publications:* papers on crustacea and insect physiology, in various zoological periodicals. *Address:* Department of Zoology, The University, Manchester 13.

**DENNING,** Baron (Life Peer) *cr* 1957, of Whitchurch; **Alfred Thompson Denning,** PC 1948; Kt 1944; Master of the Rolls since 1962; Hon. Fellow of Magdalen College, Oxford, 1948; Hon. LLD Ottawa, 1955; Glasgow, 1959; Southampton, 1959; London, 1960; Cambridge, 1963; Leeds, 1964; McGill, 1967; Dallas, 1969; Dalhousie, 1970; Hon. DCL, Oxford, 1965; *b* 23 Jan. 1899; *s* of Charles and Clara Denning; *m* 1st, 1932, Mary Harvey (*d* 1941); one *s*; 2nd, 1945, Joan, *d* of J. V. Elliott Taylor, and *widow* of J. M. B. Stuart, CIE. *Educ:* Andover Grammar Sch.; Magdalen Coll., Oxford (Demy). 1st Class Mathematical Moderations; 1st Class Mathematical Final School; 1st Class Final Sch. of Jurisprudence; Eldon Scholar, 1921; Prize Student Inns of Court; called to the Bar, 1923; KC 1938; Judge of the High Court of Justice, 1944; a Lord Justice of Appeal, 1948-57; a Lord of Appeal in Ordinary, 1957-62. Chancellor of Diocese of London, 1942-44; and of Southwark, 1937-44; Recorder of Plymouth, 1944; Bencher of Lincoln's Inn, 1944; Nominated Judge for War Pensions Appeals, 1945-48; Chm. Cttee on Procedure in Matrimonial Causes, 1946-47; Chm., Royal Commission on Historical MSS, 1962-. Held enquiry into circumstances of resignation of Mr J. D. Profumo, Sec. of State for War, 1963. Chairman: Cttee on Legal Education for Students from Africa; British Institute of International and Comparative Law; Adv. Cttee on Appointment of JP's for Inner London. Pres., Birkbeck Coll.; Treas., Lincoln's Inn, 1964. Served in RE 1917-19 (BEF France). *Publications:* Joint Editor of Smith's Leading Cases, 1929; of Bullen and Leake's Precedents, 1935; Freedom under the Law, (Hamlyn Lectures), 1949; The Changing Law, 1953; The Road to Justice, 1955. *Address:* 11 Old Square, Lincoln's Inn, WC2. *T:* Holborn 5896; The Lawn, Whitchurch, Hants. *T:* 2144. *Club:* Athenæum.

*See also Vice-Adm. Sir N. E. and Lieut-Gen. Sir R. F. S. Denning.*

**DENNING, Vice-Adm. Sir Norman (Egbert),** KBE 1963 (OBE 1945); CB 1961; Secretary, Services, Press and Broadcasting Committee, since 1967; *b* 19 Nov. 1904; *y s* of late Charles and Clara Denning, Whitchurch, Hants; *m* 1933, Iris, *d* of late Capt. R. Curtis, Singapore, and of Mrs Curtis, now of Gisborne, New Zealand; two *s* one *d*. *Educ:* Andover Grammar

Sch., Hampshire. Capt. 1951. Dir of Administrative Planning Admty, 1952; Dir, RN Coll., Greenwich, 1956. Rear-Admiral, 1958; Dep. Chief of Naval Personnel, 1958; Dir-Gen. of Manpower, 1959; DNI, 1960-64. Vice-Adm., 1961; Chief Naval Supply and Secretariat Officer, 1962-64; Deputy Chief of the Defence Staff (Intelligence), 1964-65. *Address:* Rose Cottage, Micheldever, Hants. *T:* 268. *Club:* Royal Automobile.

*See also Baron Denning, Lieut-Gen. Sir R. F. S. Denning.*

**DENNING, Lt-Gen. Sir Reginald (Francis Stewart),** KBE 1946; CB 1944; *b* 12 June 1894; 2nd *s* of Charles and Clara Denning, Whitchurch, Hants; *m* 1927, Eileen Violet (OBE 1969), *d* of late H. W. Currie, 12 Hyde Park Place, W2; two *s* one *d. Educ:* privately. 2nd Lieut Bedfordshire Regt, 1915; European War, 1914-18 (severely wounded, despatches). Adjutant, Bedfs and Herts Regt, 1922-25; Adjutant, 2 Bedfs and Herts Regt, 1926-29; Student Staff Coll., Camberley, 1929-30; Bt Major, 1934; Bt Lt-Col, 1939; Brig., 1941; Subst. Col, 1942; Acting Maj.-Gen., 1943; Maj.-Gen., 1944; Lieut-Gen., 1949; Maj.-Gen. i/c Administration South-Eastern Command, 1943-44; Principal Administrative Officer to the Supreme Allied Commander, South-East Asia, 1944-46; Chief of Staff, Eastern Command, 1947-49; GOC Northern Ireland, 1949-52; retired pay, 1952. Col, Bedfs and Herts Regt, 1948 3rd East Anglian Regt (16th/44th Foot), 1958, Royal Anglian Regt, 1964-66. Chm. SSAFA, 1953. DL, County of Essex, 1959-68. CStJ 1946; Commander Legion of Merit (USA), 1946. *Recreations:* hunting, polo, riding. *Address:* Delmonden Grange, Hawkhurst, Kent. *T:* 2286. *Clubs:* Army and Navy, MCC.

*See also Baron Denning, Vice-Adm. Sir N. E. Denning.*

**DENNINGTON, Dudley,** FICE; Traffic Commissioner and Director of Development, Dept of Planning and Transportation, GLC, since 1970; *b* 21 April 1927; *s* of John Dennington and Beryl Dennington (*née* Hagon); *m* 1951, Margaret Patricia Stewart; two *d. Educ:* Clifton Coll., Bristol; Imperial Coll., London Univ. (BSc). ACGI 1947. National Service, 2nd Lieut, RE, 1947-49; Sandford Fawcett and Partners, Consulting Engineers, 1949-51; D. & C. Wm Press, Contractors, 1951-52; AMICE 1953; Manager, Design Office, George Wimpey & Co., 1952-65; GLC 1965-; Asst Chief Engineer, Construction, 1965-67; Chief Engineer, Construction, 1967-70; FICE 1966. *Recreations:* gardening, mathematics, history. *Address:* 25 Corkran Road, Surbiton, Surrey. *T:* 01-399 2977.

**DENNIS, Nigel Forbes;** writer; Joint Editor, Encounter, 1967-70; *b* 1912; *s* of Lieut-Col M. F. B. Dennis, DSO, and Louise (*née* Bosanquet); *m* 1st, Mary-Madeleine Massias; 2nd, Beatrice Ann Hewart Matthew; two *d. Educ:* Plumtree Sch., S Rhodesia; Odenwaldschule, Germany. Secretary, Nat. Bd of Review of Motion Pictures, NY, 1935-36; Asst Editor and Book Reviewer, The New Republic, NY, 1937-38; Staff Book Reviewer, Time, NY, 1940-58; Dramatic Critic, Encounter, 1960-; Staff Book Reviewer, Sunday Telegraph, 1961-. *Publications:* Boys and Girls Come out to Play, 1949; Cards of Identity, 1955; Two Plays and a Preface, 1958; Dramatic Essays, 1962; Jonathan Swift, 1964 (RSL Award, 1966); A House in Order, 1966; Exotics (poems), 1970. *Plays:* Cards of Identity, Royal Court, 1956; The Making of Moo, Royal Court, 1957; August for the People, Royal Court and Edinburgh Festival, 1962. *Recreation:* gardening. *Address:* c/o A. M. Heath & Co., 35 Dover Street, W1. *Club:* Casino Maltese (Malta).

**DENNISON, Mervyn William,** CBE 1967; MC 1944; JP; Secretary, Fermanagh County Council, N Ireland; *b* 13 July 1914; *er s* of Reverend W. Telford Dennison and Hester Mary (*née* Coulter); *m* 1944, Helen Maud, *d* of Claud George Spiller, Earley, Berks; one *s* one *d. Educ:* Methodist Coll., Belfast; Queen's Univ., Belfast (BA); Middle Temple. Called to Bar of Northern Ireland, 1945; Middle Temple, 1964. Served War of 1939-45, with Royal Ulster Rifles and Parachute Regt (POW Arnhem, 1944). Crown Counsel, N Rhodesia, 1947; Legal Draftsman, 1952; Senior Crown Counsel and Parliamentary Draftsman, Federal Govt of Rhodesia and Nyasaland, 1953; Federal Solicitor-Gen., 1959; QC (N Rhodesia) 1960. High Court Judge, Zambia, 1961-67. Formerly: Chm., Road Service Bd (N Rhodesia); Mem. Central African Air Authority. Hon. Col, The Zambia Regt. CStJ 1964. *Recreations:* fishing, sailing. *Address:* County Buildings, Enniskillen, Northern Ireland. *Clubs:* Army and Navy; Salisbury (Rhodesia).

**DENNISON, Adm. Robert Lee;** DSM (US); Legion of Merit (Gold Star); US Navy; Commander in Chief, Atlantic and US Atlantic Fleet and Supreme Allied Commander Atlantic, 1960-63, retired; Vice-President, The Copley Press Inc., since 1963, Member Board of Directors, since 1964; *b* 13 April 1901; *s* of Ludovici Waters and Laura Florence Lee Dennison; *m* 1937, Mildred Mooney; one *s* one *d. Educ:* US Naval Acad.; Pa State Coll. (MS); Johns Hopkins Univ. (EngD). Ensign, 1923; advanced through grades to Admiral, 1959. Served with Atlantic, Pacific and Asiatic Fleets; comd Ortolan, 1935-37, Cuttlefish, 1937-38; John D. Ford, 1940-41, Missouri, 1947-48; mem. jt war plans cttee of Jt Chiefs of Staff, 1944-45; Asst Chief of Naval Ops (polit-mil. affairs), 1945-47; naval aide to Pres. of USA, 1948-53; Cdr Cruiser Div. 4 Atlantic Fleet, 1953-54; Dir Strategic Plans Div., Asst Chief of Naval Ops (Plans and Policy), mem. jt strategic plans cttee of Jt Chiefs of Staff, 1954-56; Cdr First Fleet, Pacific Fleet, 1956-58; Dep. Chief Naval Ops (Plans and Policy), 1958-59; C-in-C, US Naval Forces, E Atlantic and Mediterranean, 1959-60. Hon. OBE 1946; Commander: Order of Naval Merit (Brazil); Order of the Crown (Belgium); Legion of Honour (France); Grand Cross, Order of Orange-Nassau (Netherlands), Grand Cross, Military Order of Aviz (Portugal). *Address:* c/o Trust Department Office, The Riggs National Bank, Washington, DC, USA. *Clubs:* Ends of the Earth, American (London); Metropolitan, Army-Navy, Chevy Chase (Washington, DC); New York Yacht.

**DENNISON, Prof. Stanley Raymond,** CBE 1946; David Dale Professor of Economics, University of Newcastle upon Tyne, since 1962; Pro-Vice-Chancellor since 1966; *b* 15 June 1912; *o s* of late Stanley Dennison and Florence Ann Dennison, North Shields; unmarried. *Educ:* University of Durham; Trinity College, Cambridge. Lecturer in Economics, Manchester University, 1935-39; Professor of Economics, University Coll. of Swansea, 1939-45; Lecturer in Economics, Cambridge Univ., 1945-58; Fellow of Gonville and Caius Coll., 1945-58; Prof. of Economics, Queen's Univ. of Belfast, 1958-61. Chief Economic Asst, War Cabinet Secretariat, 1940-46. Member: University Grants Cttee, 1964-68; North Eastern Electricity Board; Review Body on Remuneration of Doctors and Dentists (to 1970); Verdon Smith Cttee on Marketing and Distribution of Fatstock and Carcase Meat, 1964; Scott Cttee on Land Utilisation in Rural Areas, 1942 (Minority Report); Beaver Cttee on Air Pollution, 1954; Waverley Cttee on Med. Services for the Armed Forces, 1955. Chm. of Wages Councils. Chm. Governors, Royal Grammar Sch., Newcastle upon Tyne, 1969-. *Publications:* The Location of Industry and the Depressed areas, 1939; (with Sir Dennis Robertson) The Control of Industry, 1960; various articles, etc, on economic questions. *Recreation:* music. *Address:* The University, Newcastle upon Tyne NE1 7RU. *Club:* Reform.

**DENNISON, Thomas Andrews;** Retired, 1957, as Puisne Judge of HM Supreme Court of Ghana; *b* 18 Sept. 1906; *s* of late Robert John Andrews Dennison; *m* 1937, Diana Mary Talbot; one *s*. *Educ:* Coleraine Academical Institution; Newcastle High Sch., Staffs; Trinity Coll., Dublin (BA). Called to Irish Bar, 1931; joined Colonial Legal Service as Crown Counsel, Kenya Colony, 1935. Acted as Solicitor-Gen., Kenya, and nominated mem. of Legislative Council on various occasions. District Magistrate, Gold Coast, 1948. War of 1939-45, 1940-42, Lieut 4th Bn The King's African Rifles. *Recreations:* golf, swimming and photography. *Address:* PO Box 24867, Karen, Nairobi, Kenya. *Clubs:* University (Dublin); Muthaiga Country (Nairobi).

**DENNY, Sir Alistair (Maurice Archibald),** 3rd Bt, *cr* 1913; *b* 11 Sept. 1922; *er s* of Sir Maurice Edward Denny, 2nd Bt, KBE and of Lady Denny, Gateside House, Drymen, Stirlingshire; *S* father 1955; *m* 1949, Elizabeth *y d* of Sir Guy Lloyd, Bt, *qv*; three *s*. *Educ:* Marlborough. Started engineering training with William Denny & Bros. Served War in Fleet Air Arm, 1944-46. Continued engineering training with Alexander Stephen & Sons, Glasgow, and Sulzer Bros., Winterthur, Switzerland; returned to William Denny & Bros, 1948; left, Sept. 1963, when firm went into liquidation. *Recreations:* golf, ski-ing, gardening, photography. *Heir:* *s* Charles Alistair Maurice Denny, *b* 7 Oct. 1950. *Address:* Damside of Strathairly, Upper Largo, Fife. *T:* Upper Largo 214. *Club:* RNVR.

**DENNY, Sir Anthony Coningham de Waltham,** 8th Bt, *cr* 1782, of Tralee Castle, Co. Kerry, Ireland; Partner in Verity and Beverley, Architects and Design Consultants, since 1959; *b* 22 April 1925; *s* of Rev. Sir Henry Lyttleton Lyster Denny, 7th Bt, and Joan Lucy Dorothy, *er d* of Major William A. C. Denny, OBE; *S* father 1953; *m* 1949, Anne Catherine, *e d* of S. Beverley, FRIBA; two *s*. *Educ:* Clayesmore Sch. Served War of 1939-45: Middle East, RAF (Aircrew), 1943-47. Anglo-French Art Centre, 1947-50; Mural Painter and Theatrical Designer, 1950-54. Hereditary Freeman of City of Cork. *Recreations:* architecture and painting. *Heir:* *s* Piers Anthony de Waltham Denny, *b* 14 March 1954. *Address:* 4 Heath Villas, Vale of Health, Hampstead, NW3. *T:* 01-435 4191.

**DENNY, James Runciman,** MBE 1944; MA, MusB Cantab; West Riding Professor of Music, Leeds University, since 1950; *b* 9 May 1908; *m* 1934, Agatha Nash; one *s* two *d*. *Educ:* Gresham's Sch., Holt; Royal College of Music; Christ's Coll., Cambridge. Music Dir, Bedford Sch., 1933-37; Music Asst, BBC, Belfast, 1937-39; Head of Midland Regional Music, BBC, and Conductor BBC Midland Chorus and Singers, 1946-50; Leeds Guild of Singers, 1952-55. Pres., Incorporated Soc. of Musicians, 1964. Hon. RAM. Served War of 1939-45, Royal Warwicks Regt; GSO1, India Command. *Publications:* The Oxford School Harmony Course, 1960; Hymn to Christ the King, 1963. *Address:* The University, Leeds 2. *Club:* Athenæum.

**DENNY, Alderman Sir J(onathan) Lionel P(ercy),** GBE 1966; Kt 1963; MC 1918; Hon. DSc; Lord Mayor of London for 1965-66; Alderman, Ward of Billingsgate; *b* 5 Aug. 1897; *s* of late J. Percy Denny, Putney; *m* 1920, Doris, *d* of R. George Bare, FSI, Putney; one *s*. *Educ:* St Paul's Sch. Served European War, 1915-19, Lieut E Surrey Regt; active service in France (wounded thrice, MC); Sqdn Leader RAFVR and RAF Regt, 1940-45. Mem. Court of Common Council, since 1941, for Ward of Billingsgate (Dep., 1951; Alderman, 1957); Chief Commoner, 1954. One of HM Lieuts for the City of London, 1951-; JP Co. of London, 1951-; JP City of London, 1957-. An almoner of Christ's Hosp. Livery Companies: Barber-Surgeons (Master, 1938-39); Vintners' (Master, 1960-61); Company of Watermen and Lightermen (Master, 1967). "Elected" Mem. Council, London Chamber of Commerce, 1948-. Chm. London Court of Arbitration, 1958-59. Sheriff, City of London, 1961-62. First Chancellor, The City Univ., London, 1966. Jt Hon. Col 254 (City of London) Regt RA (TA), 1965-66. KStJ 1966 (OStJ 1961). Chevalier, Légion d'Honneur, 1967 and other orders from Liberia, Ivory Coast, Senegal, Austria and Jordan. Hon. DSc The City Univ., 1966. *Recreation:* motor-cruising. *Address:* 901 Grenville House, Dolphin Square, SW1. *T:* 01-834 4048. *Clubs:* City Livery (Pres. 1959-60), Eccentric, Royal Thames Yacht.

**DENNY, Sir Lionel;** *see* Denny, Sir J. L. P.

**DENNY, Margaret Bertha Alice, (Mrs E. L. Denny),** OBE 1946; Under Secretary, Ministry of Transport and Civil Aviation, 1957-58; *b* 30 Sept. 1907; *o d* of late Edward Albert Churchard and late Margaret Catherine (*née* Arnold) and step-*d* of late William Ray Lenanton, JP; *m* 1957, Edward Leslie Denny, JP, formerly Chm., William Denny Bros, Shipbuilders, Dumbarton. *Educ:* Dover County Sch.; Bedford Coll. for Women, London Univ. (BA Hons PhD). Entered Civil Service as Principal Ministry of Shipping, 1940; Asst Sec., 1946. Gov., Bedford Coll., University of London. Member: Scottish Adv. Coun. for Civil Aviation, 1958-67; Western Regional Hospital Board, Scotland; Scottish Cttee, Coun. of Industrial Design; Gen. Advisory Council, BBC, 1962-66; Gen. Nursing Council, Scotland, 1962; Board of Management, State Hosp., Carstairs. County Comr, Girl Guides, Dunbartonshire, 1958-68. Officer, Order of Orange Nassau, 1947. *Address:* Ash House, Gartocharn, by Alexandria, Dunbartonshire. *T:* Gartocharn 272. *Clubs:* English-Speaking Union; Kelvin (Glasgow).

**DENNY, Adm. Sir Michael (Maynard),** GCB 1954 (KCB 1950; CB 1940); CBE 1944; DSO 1945; Consultant, Cammell Laird (Chairman 1959-66); *b* Kempley, Glos, 3 Oct. 1896; *y s* of late Canon Edward Denny, MA; *m* 1923, Sara Annie Esmé, *d* of late Col Loftus Welman, Royal Irish Rifles; no *c*. *Educ:* RN Colls, Osborne and Dartmouth. Naval Cadet, 1909; midshipman, 1914; Sub-Lieut 1916; Lieut 1917; Comdr 1930; Capt. 1936; Rear-Adm. 1945; Vice-Adm. 1948; Adm. 1952; served European War, 1914-19, in North Sea, HMS Neptune and Royal Sovereign; specialised in Gunnery, 1920, and awarded the Egerton Memorial prize; when not in sea appointment spent all service in gunnery experimental work, HMS Excellent; Fleet Gunnery Officer on staff of Adm. Sir W. W. Fisher,

Mediterranean Fleet, 1932-34; Asst. and Dep. Dir of Naval Ordnance, Admiralty, 1937-40; commanded cruiser Kenya, 1940-42; Chief of Staff to C-in-C Home Fleet, 1942-43; commanded aircraft-carrier Victorious, 1944-45; Asst Chief of Naval Personnel and Dir of Personal Services, 1946-47; Flag Officer (Destroyers), Mediterranean Fleet, 1947-49; a Lord Commissioner of Admiralty, Third Sea Lord and Controller of the Navy, 1949-53; Commander-in-Chief Home Fleet, and Commander-in-Chief, Eastern Atlantic (NATO), 1954-55; Chm., British Joint Services Mission, Washington, DC, and UK Representative on Standing Group of NATO Military Cttee, 1956-59; retired, 1959. *Recreations:* yachting, tennis. *Address:* 79 Cadogan Square, SW1. *Club:* United Service.

**DENNY-BROWN, Derek Ernest,** OBE 1942; MD NZ, DPhil Oxon, FRCP; AM Hon Harvard; LLD Hon. Wayne; Dr *hc* Brazil; Hon. DSc Otago; Professor of Neurology, Harvard University; Hon. Col RAMC; *b* 1901; *s* of Charles Denny-Brown; *m* 1937, Sylvia Marie, *d* of late Dr J. O. Summerhayes, DSO; four *s*. *Educ:* New Plymouth High Sch., NZ; Otago Univ., NZ; Magdalen Coll., Oxford. Beit Memorial Research Fellow, 1925-28; Rockefeller Travelling Fellow, 1936, formerly Neurologist to St Bartholomew's Hosp., London, Asst Physician National Hosp., Queen Square, and sometime Registrar to Dept for Nervous Diseases, Guy's Hosp.; former Dir, Neurol. Unit, Boston City Hosp. Hon. Fellow, RSM, 1958. Gran Oficier, Order of Hippolite Unanue (Peru), 1963. Sherrington Medal, Royal Society Medicine London, 1962; Jacoby Award, Amer. Neurol. Assoc., 1968. *Publications:* Selected Writings of Sir Charles Sherrington, 1939; Diseases of Muscle (part author), 1953; The Basal Ganglia, 1962; Cerebral Control of Movement, 1966. Papers on neurological subjects in scientific journals. *Address:* New England Primate Center, Southborough, Mass 01772, USA; 3 Mercer Circle, Cambridge, Mass 02138, USA.

**DENNYS, Cyril George,** CB 1949; MC 1918; retired as Under-Secretary; *b* 25 March 1897; *s* of Lieut-Col A. H. Dennys, IA, and Lena Mary Isabel (*née* Harrison); *m* 1920, Sylvia Maitland (*née* Waterlow); two *d* (and one *d* decd). *Educ:* Malvern Coll.; Trinity Coll., Oxford. Served European War, 1914-18, as Lieut, RGA, 1917-18. Entered Ministry of Labour as Asst Principal, 1919; Principal Private Sec. to Minister of Labour, 1938; Asst Sec., 1938; Principal Asst Sec., Ministry of Supply, 1942-45; Under-Secretary: Ministry of Labour, 1946; Ministry of National Insurance, 1946; Ministry of Pensions and National Insurance, 1953; retired 1962. *Recreation:* golf. *Address:* 38 Belsize Grove, Hampstead, NW3. *T:* 01-722 3964. *Clubs:* Oxford and Cambridge; Hadley Wood Golf (Barnet).

**DENNYS, Rodney Onslow,** MVO 1969; OBE 1943; FSA; Somerset Herald of Arms, since 1967; *b* 16 July 1911; *s* of late Frederick Onslow Brooke Dennys, late Malayan Civil Service; *m* 1944, Elisabeth Katharine, *d* of late Charles Henry Greene; one *s* two *d*. *Educ:* Canford Sch.; LSE. Apptd to FO, 1937; HM Legation, The Hague, 1937-40; FO, 1940-41. Commissioned in Intell. Corps, 1941; Lt-Col 1944; RARO, 1946. Reapptd, FO, 1947; 1st Sec. British Middle East Office, Egypt, 1948-50; 1st Sec. HM Embassy: Turkey, 1950-53; Paris, 1955-57; resigned, 1957. Rouge Croix Pursuivant of Arms, 1961-67. Served on Earl Marshal's Staff for State Funeral of Sir Winston Churchill, 1965, and for the Prince of Wales' Investiture, 1969. Freeman of City of London and Liveryman of Scriveners Co. *Publications:* Flags and Emblems of the World; (jt) Royal and Princely Heraldry of Wales; articles in jls on heraldry and kindred subjects. *Recreation:* sailing. *Address:* College of Arms, EC4. *T:* 01-248 1912; Heaslands, Steep, near Crowborough, Sussex. *T:* Crowborough 61328.

*See also Graham, Sir Hugh, and Raymond, Greene.*

**de NORMANN, Sir Eric,** KBE 1946; CB 1941; Chairman, Ancient Monuments Board for England, 1955-64; *b* 26 Dec. 1893; *s* of Albert de Normann and Irene Wood; *m* 1921, Winifred Leigh (*d* 1968); one *s*. *Educ:* Château du Rosey, Switzerland; University Coll. of South Wales. Served European War, 1915-19 (despatches twice); Office of Works, 1920; Imperial Defence Coll., 1935. Dep. Sec., Ministry of Works, 1943-54. FSA. *Address:* Aylesham, Old Avenue, Weybridge, Surrey. *T:* Weybridge, 42682. *Club:* Athenæum.

**DENSON, John;** Editor, Los Angeles Herald-Examiner, 1963-65; Executive Editor, New York Journal-American, 1965-66; *b* Arcadia, La, 25 July 1903; *s* of John Lee Denson and Annie Laurie (*née* Tarver); *m* 1935, Katherine Alvord. *Educ:* Briarley Hall Military Acad., Poolesville, Md. Journalist, Washington and Mid-West, 1921-27; Washington Corresp., New York Herald Tribune, 1927-29; Reporter, New York World, New York World Telegram, 1930-33; Asst Managing Editor: Washington Post, 1934-35; Chicago Times, 1936-37; Washington Ed., Internat. News Service, 1937-39; Publicity News Ed., Columbia Broadcasting System, 1939-41; Asst Chief in Washington, Time Magazine, 1941-44; Asst Exec. Ed., Chicago American, 1945; Associate Ed., Fortune, 1946; Man. Ed., Kiplinger Magazine, 1947-48; Managing and Foreign Ed. and War Corresp., Collier's Magazine, 1949-52; Ed., Newsweek, 1953-61; Ed., New York Herald Tribune, 1961-62. Ed. (geo-history), The Five Worlds of our Lives. *Address:* 570 North Rossmore Street, Apt 311, Los Angeles, Calif, USA. *Clubs:* Overseas Press, Deadline, Dutch Treat, Coffee House (NY); National Press (Washington).

**DENSON, John Boyd,** OBE 1965; Chargé d'Affaires, Peking, since 1969; *b* 13 Aug. 1926; *o s* of late George Denson and of Mrs Alice Denson (*née* Boyd); *m* 1957, Joyce Myra Symondson; no *c*. *Educ:* Perse Sch.; St John's Coll., Cambridge. Royal Regt of Artillery, 1944; Intelligence Corps, 1946; Cambridge, 1947-51 (English and Oriental Langs Triposes). Joined HM Foreign (now Diplomatic) Service, 1951. Served in Hong Kong, Tokyo, Peking, London, Helsinki, Washington; Asst Head of Far Eastern Dept, Foreign Office, 1965-68. *Recreations:* looking at pictures, the theatre, wine. *Address:* 19 Gainsborough Court, College Road, Dulwich, SE21. *T:* 01-693 8361.

**DENT,** family name of **Furnivall Barony.**

**DENT, Alan Holmes,** FRSA 1970; author, critic and journalist; *b* Ayrshire, Scotland, 7 Jan. 1905; *s* of John Dent, Westmorland, and Margaret Holmes, Yorks. *Educ:* Carrick Academy; Glasgow Univ. London dramatic critic of The Manchester Guardian, 1935-43; dramatic critic of Punch, 1942-43 and again in 1963. Served War of 1939-45, in RN Hosp., 1943-45. Dramatic Critic of News Chronicle, 1945-60; Film Critic of: the Sunday Telegraph, 1961-63; Illustrated London News, 1947-68. Frequent broadcaster since 1942. Shute Lecturer in the Art of the Theatre, Liverpool Univ., 1956. Pres. The Critics' Circle, 1962. Lectured on The Fine Art of Criticism at

Toronto Univ., at Boston, at Vassar, at Princeton, and at Long Island and New York Universities, Nov. and Dec., 1966. Text-ed. of Sir Laurence Olivier's films of Henry V, Hamlet, and Richard III (text-adviser). Ed., Bernard Shaw and Mrs Patrick Campbell: their Correspondence, 1952. *Publications:* Preludes and Studies, 1942; Nocturnes and Rhapsodies, 1950; My Dear America . . ., 1954; Mrs Patrick Campbell: a biography, 1961; Robert Burns in his Time, 1966; My Covent Garden, 1970; Vivien Leigh: a biography, 1970. *Address:* 85 Aylesbury End, Beaconsfield, Bucks. *T:* Beaconsfield 2102.

**DENT, Prof. Charles Enrique,** FRS 1962; Professor of Human Metabolism, University College Hospital Medical School, since 1956; Hon. Consultant Physician, University College Hospital; *b* 25 Aug. 1911; *m* 1944, Margaret Ruth Coad; one *s* five *d. Educ:* Bedford Sch.; Wimbledon Coll.; Imperial Coll. of Science; University Coll., London. Research chemist, Imperial Chemical Industries (Dyestuffs Group), 1934-37. A/Capt. Intelligence Corps, BEF, 1939-40. Asst, Medical Unit, University Coll. Hosp. Medical Sch., 1944-51. Reader in Medicine, 1951-56. Humphry Davy Rolleston Lectr, RCP, 1962. MD Louvain 1966. Gairdner Foundn Award, 1965. *Address:* 77 Eaton Rise, Ealing, W5. *T:* 01-997 3703.

**DENT, Dr Frederick (James),** OBE 1958; FRS 1967; Director, Gas Council Midlands Research Station, 1952-67, retired; *b* 12 Oct. 1905; *s* of Frederick Dent and Sarah Liddell Dent; *m* 1942, Jean Marie Macvean; one *s* one *d. Educ:* Leeds Modern Sch.; Leeds Univ. BSc 1927; PhD 1929; DSc 1944. In charge of Gas Production Research, Jt Res. Cttee of Instn of Gas Engrs and Leeds Univ., 1929-41; Joint Asst Dir, Gas Research Bd, 1941-52. *Publications:* contribs to Trans Instn Gas Engineers. *Recreations:* sailing, photography. *Address:* 13 Valley View Court, Zaccheus Street, Msida, Malta.

**DENT, Harold Collett;** *b* 14 Nov. 1894; *s* of Rev. F. G. T. and Susan Dent; *m* 1922, Loveday Winifred Martin; one *s* one *d. Educ:* Public elementary schs; Kingswood Sch., Bath; London Univ. (external student). Asst Master in secondary schs, 1911-25 (War Service, 1914-19); Head of Junior Dept, Brighton, Hove and Sussex Grammar Sch., 1925-28; first headmaster, Gateway School, Leicester, 1928-31; freelance journalist, 1931-35; asst ed., Book Dept Odhams Press, 1935-40; Ed., The Times Educational Supplement, 1940-51; Educational Correspondent, The Times, 1952-55; Professor of Education and Dir of the Inst. of Education, University of Sheffield, 1956-60; Senior Research Fellow, Inst. of Education, University of Leeds, 1960-62; Lecturer and Asst Dean, Inst. of Education, University of London, 1962-65; Visiting Prof., University of Dublin, 1966; BA; FRSA; Hon. FCP; Hon. FEIS. *Publications:* A New Order in English Education, 1942; The Education Act, 1944; Education in Transition, 1944; To be a Teacher, 1947; Secondary Education for All, 1949; Secondary Modern Schools, 1958; The Educational System of England and Wales, 1961; Universities in Transition, 1961; British Education, 1962; 1870-1970, Century of Growth in English Education, 1970. *Recreation:* gardening. *Address:* Riccards Spring, Whatlington, Battle, Sussex. *Club:* Athenæum.

**DENT, Rear-Adm. John,** CB 1956; OBE 1941; *b* 5 Aug. 1899; *s* of late Thomas Dent, Yorks; *m* Nancy Alys Mary, *d* of late Mortimer Brutton Ford, Exmouth; one *s. Educ:* Sedbergh Sch. Joined RN, 1917; HMS Princess Royal, 1917-19; Naval Base, Constantinople, 1919-22; RN Coll., Dartmouth, 1924-29; Sec. to: Flag Officer (Submarines), 1929-31; C-in-C, East Indies, 1932-34; Second Sea Lord and Chief of Naval Personnel, 1935-38; C-in-C, Plymouth, 1938-39; C-in-C, Western Approaches, 1939-40; Vice-Controller of Navy, 1940-43 (OBE); HMS Devonshire, 1943-45; BSO, Singapore, 1945-46; HMS Ceres, 1946-47; idc 1948; Asst Dir of Plans, Admiralty, 1949-51; RN Barracks, Portsmouth, 1951-53; Staff of C-in-C Mediterranean, 1953-54; Chief Staff Officer (Administration), The Nore, 1954-58, retired. *Recreations:* golf and gardening. *Address:* Many Trees, Sway, Hants. *T:* Sway 379.

**DENT, Leonard Maurice Edward,** DSO 1914; Chairman and Managing Director Abco Products, Ltd; Member: City & Guilds Art School Committee (Chairman 1958-70); Council, Queen's College, London; governing body of Oundle Sch.; Council and Executive Committee, City and Guilds of London Institute; Council of University of Reading (Treasurer, 1959-63); Berks Branch, Coun. for Preservation of Rural England (Chairman 1950-64); *b* 18 June 1888; *s* of Edward and Mabel P. Dent; *m* 1920, Hester Anita, *d* of Col Gerard Clark, 4 Sussex Gardens, W2; one *s* four *d. Educ:* Eton; Trinity Coll., Cambridge, BA. Served European War, 1914-18 (wounded, despatches thrice, DSO, Chevalier Légion d'Honneur); Master of the Grocers' Company 1935-36; Berks CC, 1946-58; High Sheriff of Berks, 1948-49. Mem. KCH Bd of Governors, 1950-63; Chm. Belgrave Hosp. for Children, 1947-63. *Recreations:* photography, music, art collecting. *Address:* Hillfields, Burghfield Common, near Reading. *T:* Burghfield Common 2495. *Clubs:* United University, MCC.

**DENT, Sir Robert (Annesley Wilkinson),** Kt 1960; CB 1951; *b* 27 Jan. 1895; *e s* of late R. W. Dent, JP, Flass, Maulds Meaburn, Penrith, and late Edith Vere, OBE, *d* of Rev. F. H. Annesley Clifford Chambers, Glos; *m* 1927, Elspeth Muriel, *d* of Sir Alfred Tritton, Bt, Upper Gatton Park, Reigate; one *s.* three *d. Educ:* Eton; Trinity Coll., Cambridge. Served European War, 1914-18, with King's Royal Rifle Corps (Lieutenant) in France and Flanders, (wounded, despatches). Rejoined 1940 and served War of 1939-45, with GHQ Home Forces and at the War Office AQMG (Temporary Lieut-Col), 1943-45. Clerk of Public Bills, House of Commons, retired 1959. High Sheriff, Westmorland, 1960. *Recreations:* shooting, gardening. *Address:* Flass, Maulds Meaburn, Penrith, Cumberland. *T:* Ravensworth (Penrith) 225. *Clubs:* Army and Navy; Cumberland County.

**DENT, (Robert) Stanley (Gorrell),** RE 1946 (ARE 1935); ARCA (London) 1933; RWA 1954 (ARWA 1951); ASIA(Ed.), 1967; Principal of the Gloucestershire College of Art and Design at Cheltenham and Gloucester; *b* 1 July 1909; *o c* of Robert and Hannah Dent; *m* Doris, *o c* of Clement and Mabel Wenban; two *s. Educ:* The Newport Technical Coll.; The Newport, Mon., Sch. of Art and Crafts; Royal College of Art. Volunteered for service in Royal Engineers, 1942, invalided out, 1944. Runner up in Prix-de-Rome Scholarship, 1935; awarded the British Institution Scholarship in Engraving for the year 1933; Works exhibited at the Royal Academy, The Royal Scottish Academy, The New English Art Club, The Royal Society of British Artists, The Art Institute of Chicago, The International Print Makers Exhibition, Calif., and other leading Art Exhibitions. Ministry of Education Intermediate Assessor, 1957-60. Panel Mem.

(Fine Art), National Council for Diplomas in Art and Design, 1962-65. Vice-Pres., Cheltenham Group of Artists. *Recreations:* gardening and all forms of sport; gramophile. *Address:* Wenbans, Ashley Road, Battledown, Cheltenham. *T:* Cheltenham 24742.

**DENT-BROCKLEHURST, Mrs Mary,** JP; *b* 6 Feb. 1902; *d* of late Major J. A. Morrison, DSO, and late Hon. Mary Hill-Trevor; *m* 1924, Major John Henry Dent-Brocklehurst, OBE (*d* 1949), Sudeley Castle, Glos; one *s* three *d*. *Educ:* at home. JP and CC, 1949, CA 1958, Glos; High Sheriff, County of Gloucester, 1967. *Recreations:* gardening, beekeeping, travelling, archæology. *Address:* Hawling Manor, Andoversford, Cheltenham, Glos. *T:* Guiting Power 362.

**DENTON, Eric James,** FRS 1964; ScD; Royal Society Research Professor, University of Bristol, since Oct. 1964; Physiologist, Laboratory of Marine Biological Association, Plymouth, since 1956; *b* 30 Sept. 1923; *s* of George Denton and Mary Anne (*née* Ogden); *m* 1946, Nancy Emily, *d* of Charles and Emily Jane Wright; two *s* one *d*. *Educ:* Doncaster Grammar Sch.; St John's Coll., Cambridge; University Coll., London. Research in Radar, TRE Malvern, 1943-46; Biophysics Research Unit, University Coll., London, 1946-48; Lectr in Physiology, University of Aberdeen, 1948-56; Carnegie Fellow at Muséum National d'Histoire Naturelle, Paris, 1954-55. Fellow, University Coll., London, 1965. Hon. Sec., Physiological Soc., 1963-69. *Publications:* scientific papers in Jl of Marine Biological Assoc., etc. *Recreation:* gardening. *Address:* Fairfield House, St Germans, Cornwall. *T:* St Germans (Cornwall) 204.

**DENTON-THOMPSON, Aubrey Gordon,** OBE 1958; MC 1942; Senior Agricultural Adviser, United Nations Development Programme, Korea, since 1968; Food and Agriculture Organisation Country Representative, since 1970; *b* 6 June 1920; *s* of late M. A. B. Denton-Thompson; *m* 1944, Ruth Cecily Isaac (*d* 1959); two *s* (one *d* decd); *m* 1961, Barbara Mary Wells. *Educ:* Malvern Coll. Served in RA 1940-44; seconded to Basutoland Administration, 1944; apptd to HM Colonial Service, 1945; transferred to Tanganyika as Asst District Officer, 1947; seconded to Colonial Office, 1948-50, District Officer; seconded to Secretariat, Dar es Salaam, as Asst Sec., 1950; Colonial Sec., Falkland Islands, 1955-60; Dep. Permanent Sec., Ministry of Agriculture, Tanganyika, 1960-62; retired from Tanganyika Civil Service, 1963. Man. Dir, Tanganyika Sisal Marketing Assoc. Ltd, 1966-68 (Sec. 1963). *Recreations:* ornithology and golf. *Address:* UN Development Programme, Central Post Office Box 143, Seoul, Korea.

**d'ENTRÈVES, Alexander Passerin,** FRHistS; Professor of Political Theory, University of Turin, since 1958; *b* 26 April 1902; 4th *s* of Count Hector Passerin d'Entrèves et Courmayeur; *m* 1931, Nina Ferrari d'Orsara; one *s* one *d*. *Educ:* University of Turin, Italy; Balliol Coll., Oxford. Doctor of Law, Turin, 1922; DPhil Oxon, 1932; Lecturer, University of Turin, 1929; Prof. University of Messina, 1934, Pavia, 1935, Turin, 1938; Prefect of Aosta, April-May 1945; Mem. of Council of Val d'Aosta, Dec. 1945. Serena Prof. of Italian Studies, University of Oxford, 1946-57; Fellow Magdalen Coll., Oxford, 1946-57. Vis. Prof., Harvard Univ., 1957; Yale Univ., 1960-64. Fellow, Amer. Acad. Arts and Sciences; Member: Société Académique St Anselme, Aosta; Accademia delle Scienze, Turin; Accademia dei Lincei, Rome; Académie de Savoie, Chambéry. *Publications:* The Medieval Contribution to Political Thought, 1939; Reflections on the History of Italy, 1947; Aquinas, Selected Political Writings, 1948; Alessandro Manzoni, 1949; Natural Law, An Introduction to Legal Philosophy, 1951; Dante as a Political Thinker, 1952; The Notion of the State, An Introduction to Political Theory, 1967; other publications in Italian and French. *Recreation:* rambling in the Alps. *Address:* Strada al Ronchi 48, Cavoretto, Torino, Italy; Castello di Entrèves, Courmayeur, Val d'Aosta, Italy.

**de PASS, Col Guy Eliot,** DSO 1918; OBE 1945; late 4th Dragoon Guards; Director Vereeniging Estates, Springfield Collieries, Coronation Collieries, Amalgamated Collieries of South Africa (all in Sth Africa); Chairman, Cedar Investment Trust; Director: Indian & General Investment Trust, Atlas Electric & General Investment Trust, International Investment Trust, Trust & Agency of Australasia (all in GB); *b* 30 Oct. 1898; *yr s* of late John de Pass; *m* 1925, Winifred Dorothy, *d* of late Westcott Featherstonehaugh and late Mrs Featherstonehaugh, Durban, Natal; three *d*. *Educ:* St Andrews, Eastbourne; Eton; Sandhurst. Served European War, 1914-18 (despatches, DSO), 4th Royal Dragoon Guards; Major 4th Batt. Oxford Bucks Light Infantry (TA), 1938; Military Asst to the Quartermaster-Gen. of the Forces, 1940; 2nd in Command 4th Bn Oxford and Bucks Light Infantry, 1939-40; Asst Commandant, Donnington, Salop, 1941; Sub-Area Comdr, Preston, 1943; Dep. Dir Labour 2nd Army (HQ), May 1943-45, NW Europe Campaign (OBE). *Recreation:* shooting. *Address:* Upper House Farm, near Henley-on-Thames, Oxfordshire. *T:* Rotherfield Greys 378. *Club:* Cavalry.

**de PEYER, Charles Hubert,** CMG 1956; retired Under-Secretary, Ministry of Fuel and Power (Served with Foreign Office, with rank of Minister in United Kingdom Delegation to European Coal and Steel Community, 1952-56); Borough Councillor, Hemel Hempstead, since 1964; *b* 24 Oct. 1905; 2nd *s* of Everard Charles de Peyer and Edith Mabel Starkey; *m* 1st, 1930, Flora Collins, singer, New York; one *s* one *d*; 2nd, 1953, Mary Burgess; two *s* one *d*. *Educ:* Cheltenham Coll.; Magdalen Coll., Oxford (Hons PPE). Entered Civil Service, Mines Dept, 1930. *Recreations:* gardening, music. *Address:* Holly House, Leverstock Green, Hemel Hempstead, Herts. *Club:* Reform.

**de PEYER, Gervase;** Solo Clarinettist; Conductor; 1st Clarinet, London Symphony Orchestra, since 1955. Founder Member, The Melos Ensemble of London; *b* London, 11 April 1926; *m* 1950, Sylvia Southcombe; one *s* two *d*. *Educ:* King Alfred's London; Bedales; Royal College of Music. Served HM Forces, 1945 and 1946. Prof., Royal Acad. of Music, 1959-61. ARCM; Hon. ARAM. Medallist, Worshipful Co. of Musicians, 1948. Has made recordings; Dir, Melos Ensemble's recording programme. *Recreations:* motoring, sport, theatre. *Address:* 70 Wood Vale, Highgate, N10. *T:* 01-883 4688.

**de PIRO, Alan C. H.,** QC 1965; *b* 31 Aug. 1919; *e s* of late J. W. de Piro; *m* 1947, Mary Elliot (marr. diss.); two *s*; 1964, Mona Addington; one step *s* one step *d*. *Educ:* Repton; Trinity Hall, Cambridge (Sen. Scholar). MA 1947 (Nat. Sci. and Law). Royal Artillery, 1940-45 (Capt.); West Africa. Called to Bar, Middle Temple, 1947; Inner Temple, 1962. Mem., Gen. Council of the Bar, 1961-65, 1966-; Dep.

Chairman: Beds QS, 1966-; Warwicks QS, 1967-. Vice-Pres., L'Union Internationale des Avocats, 1968-. Member: Coun. Internat. Bar Assoc., 1967-. Editorial Advisory Cttee, Law Guardian, 1965-; Law Panel British Council, 1967-. *Recreations:* conversation, opera, inland waterways. *Address:* 1 Harcourt Buildings, Temple, EC4; Bascote Top Lock Cottage, near Southam, Warwicks. *Clubs:* Garrick; Hawks (Cambridge).

**de POLNAY, Peter;** author; *b* 8 March 1906; *m* 1942, Margaret Mitchell-Banks (*d* 1950); one *s*; *m* 1955, Maria del Carmen Rubio y Caparo. *Educ:* privately in England, Switzerland and Italy. Farmed in Kenya. First began to write in Kenya in 1932; was in Paris when Germans entered, worked with early French Resistance, escaped back to England after imprisonment under Vichy Government. *Publications:* Angry Man's Tale, 1938; Children My Children!, 1939; Boo, 1941; Death and Tomorrow, 1942; Water on the Steps, 1943; Two Mirrors, 1944; The Umbrella Thorn, 1946; A Pin's Fee, 1947; The Moot Point, 1948; Into an Old Room, a Study of Edward Fitzgerald, 1949; Somebody Must, 1949; An Unfinished Journey, 1952; Death of a Legend: The True Story of Bonny Prince Charlie, 1953; Fools of Choice, 1955; Before I Sleep, 1955; The Shorn Shadow, 1956; The Clap of Silent Thunder, 1957; Peninsular Paradox, 1958; The Crack of Dawn, 1960; The Gamesters, 1960; Garibaldi, 1961; No Empty Hands, 1961; The Flames of Art, 1962; A Man of Fortune, 1963; Three Phases of High Summer, 1963; A Home of One's Own, 1964; The Plaster Bed, 1965; The World of Maurice Utrillo, 1967; Aspects of Paris, 1968; A Tower of Strength, 1969; The Patriots, 1969; A Tale of Two Husbands, 1970; Napoleon's Police, 1970. *Recreation:* shooting. *Address:* c/o A. M. Heath & Co. Ltd, 35 Dover Street, W1.

**de PUTRON, Air Commodore Owen,** CB 1951; CBE 1946; RAF retired; *b* 4 July 1893; *s* of late Captain Beaumont de Putron, Guernsey, CI; *m* 1918, Phyllis Patricia, *d* of late Frederick Bestow, Kent; one *d*. *Educ:* private school. Dominion Service, 1910; seconded to Army, 1914; commissioned Durham Light Infantry, 1914; permanent commn, RAF, 1919; served European War, 1914-18, in France, 1914-15 (very severely wounded); attached to RFC, 1917; SO III, Ireland, 1918-20 (despatches); Sqdn Leader, 1930; Staff Official, Iraq, 1930-33; Staff Officer, ADGB, 1933-35; OC Army Co-op. Sqdn, 1935-36; Wing Comdr, 1937; Group Capt., 1940; Air Cdre, 1943; Air ADC, 1945-47, ADC, 1948-51, to King George VI. Provost Marshal and Chief of the Air Force Police, 1942-51; retired, 1951. As Provost Marshal visited many times all Theatres of War, 1943-45, and introduced RAF Police Dogs for guard duties in 1943. *Recreation:* gardening. *Address:* Bluehayes, Beer, Devon. *Club:* Royal Air Force.

**DERAMORE,** 6th Baron *cr* 1885; **Richard Arthur de Yarburgh-Bateson,** Bt 1818; Partner, Cherry and Deramore, Chartered Architects; Director of, and Design Consultant to, Rodway Smith Advertising Ltd; *b* 9 April 1911; *s* of 4th Baron Deramore and of Muriel Katherine (*née* Duncombe); *S* brother, 1964; *m* 1948, Janet Mary, *d* of John Ware, MD, Askham-in-Furness, Lancs; one *d*. *Educ:* Harrow; St John's Coll., Cambridge. AA Diploma, 1935; MA Cantab 1936; ARIBA 1936. Served as Navigator, RAFVR, 1940-45: 14 Sqdn, RAF, 1942-44 and 1945. County Architect's Dept, Herts, 1949-52. Governor, Tudor Hall Sch., Banbury. *Publications:* occasional contribs to Architectural Journals. *Recreation:* water-colour painting. *Heir:* none. *Address:* Heath Close, Hyde Heath, Amersham, Bucks. *T:* Chesham 3001. *Clubs:* Royal Air Force, Royal Automobile.

**DE RAMSEY,** 3rd Baron *cr* 1887; **Ailwyn Edward Fellowes;** TD; Captain RA; Lord Lieutenant of Huntingdon and Peterborough, 1965-68 (of Hunts, 1947-65); *b* 16 March 1910; *s* of late Hon. Coulson Churchill Fellowes and Gwendolen Dorothy, *d* of H. W. Jefferson; *S* grandfather, 1925; *m* 1937, Lilah, *d* of Frank Labouchere, 15 Draycott Avenue, SW; two *s* two *d*. Served War of 1939-45 (prisoner). Pres. Country Landowners' Assoc., Sept. 1963-65. *Heir: s* Hon. John Ailwyn Fellowes, *b* 27 Feb. 1942. *Address:* Abbots Ripton Hall, Huntingdon. *T:* Abbots Ripton 234. *Clubs:* Buck's, Brooks's.

*See also Lord Ailwyn, Lord Fairhaven.*

**DERBY,** 18th Earl of *cr* 1485; **Edward John Stanley,** MC 1944; Bt 1627; Baron Stanley 1832; Baron Stanley of Preston, 1886; Major late Grenadier Guards; *b* 21 April 1918; *s* of Lord Stanley, PC, MC (*d* 1938), and Sibyl Louise Beatrix Cadogan (*d* 1969), *e d* of Henry Arthur, late Viscount Chelsea, and Lady Meux; *g s* of 17th Earl of Derby, KG, PC, GCB, GCVO; *S* grandfather, 1948; *m* 1948, Lady Isabel Milles-Lade, *yr d* of late Hon. Henry Milles-Lade, and sister of 4th Earl Sondes. *Educ:* Eton; Oxford Univ. Left Army with rank of Major, 1946. Former Pres., British Cotton Growing Assoc. and Cotton Research Corpn; President: Liverpool Chamber of Commerce, 1948-; NW Area Conservative Assoc., 1969-. Hon. LLD Liverpool Univ., 1949. Pro-Chancellor, Lancaster Univ., 1964-. Lord Lieut and Custos Rotulorum of Lancaster, 1951-68. Alderman, Lancashire CC, 1968-. Commanded 5th Bn The King's Regt, TA, 1947-51, Hon. Col, 1951-67; Hon. Captain, Mersey Div. RNVR, 1955; Hon. Col 1st Bn The Liverpool Scottish Regt, TA, 1964-67; Hon. Col, Lancastrian Volunteers, 1967-. *Heir: b* Captain Hon. Richard Oliver Stanley, *qv*. *Address:* Knowsley, Prescot, Lancs. *T:* 051-489 6147; Stanley House, Newmarket, Suffolk. *T:* Newmarket 3011. *Clubs:* White's; Jockey (Newmarket).

**DERBY, Bishop of,** since 1969; **Rt. Rev. Cyril William Johnston Bowles;** *b* Scotstoun, Glasgow, 9 May 1916; *s* of William Cullen Allen Bowles, West Ham, and Jeanie Edwards Kilgour, Glasgow; *m* 1965, Florence Joan, *d* of late John Eastaugh, Windlesham. *Educ:* Brentwood Sch.; Emmanuel Coll., Jesus Coll. (Lady Kay Scholar) and Ridley Hall, Cambridge. 2nd cl., Moral Sciences Tripos, Pt. I, 1936; 1st cl., Theological Tripos, Pt. I, and BA, 1938; 2nd cl., Theological Tripos, Pt. II, 1939; MA 1941. Deacon 1939, Priest 1940, Chelmsford; Curate of Barking Parish Church, 1939-41; Chaplain of Ridley Hall, Cambridge, 1942-44; Vice-Principal, 1944-51; Principal, 1951-63; Hon. Canon of Ely Cathedral, 1959-63; Archdeacon of Swindon, 1963-69. Select Preacher: Cambridge, 1945, 1953, 1958, 1963; Oxford, 1961; Dublin, 1961. Exam. Chaplain to Bishop of Carlisle, 1950-63; to Bishops of Rochester, Ely and Chelmsford, 1951-63; to Bishop of Bradford, 1956-61; to Bishop of Bristol, 1963-69. Hon. Canon, Bristol Cathedral, 1963-69; Surrogate, 1963-69; Commissary to Bishop of the Argentine, 1963-69. Vice-Pres., Church Missionary Soc., 1952-; Member: Archbishops' Liturgical Commn, 1955-; Council for Women's Ministry in the Church, 1970 (Chm.); C of E Council on Foreign Relations, 1965; Governor of Brentwood School; Life Governor of Dean Close School and of Cheltenham Training Colleges. *Publications:* contributor: The Roads Converge, 1963; A Manual for Holy Week, 1967. *Address:* Bishop's House, Turnditch,

Derby DE5 2LH. *T:* (office) Derby 46744; (home) Cowers Lane 464.

**DERBY, Assistant Bishop of;** *see* Parfitt, Rt. Rev. T. R.

**DERBY, Archdeacon of;** *see* Richardson, Ven. J. F.

**DERBYSHIRE, Sir Harold,** Kt 1934; MC; QC 1928; *b* 1886; *s* of James Derbyshire, Cherry Tree, Lancs; *m* 1915, Dorothea Alice, *d* of John Taylor, Crosshill, Blackburn; one *s* one *d*. *Educ:* Queen Elizabeth's Grammar Sch., Blackburn; Sidney Sussex Coll., Cambridge (Scholar); 1st Class Natural Science Tripos, MA, LLB. Barrister, Gray's Inn, 1911 (1st Cl. Bar Final and Certificate of Honour); practised Northern Circuit; Judge of Appeal, Isle of Man, 1933-34; Chief Justice, High Court, Calcutta, 1934-46; Jurisdiction: Bengal (now W Bengal and East Pakistan) and Assam, Population, 1946, seventy million, now divided among 3 High Courts at Calcutta, Dacca, and Gauhati. 1934-46: Fellow, Calcutta Univ.; Trustee, Victoria Memorial; Chm., Mayo Hosp. Bencher Gray's Inn 1931, Treasurer, 1948. Contested (L) Clitheroe, 1923, Royton, 1929. Served European War, 1914-19 (MC); served in France and Belgium, comdg first a Battery and later a Bde of Artillery; Liaison Officer between RA and RAF. Now fruit farmer. *Address:* Lindsey Lodge Farm, Hadleigh, Suffolk. *T:* Boxford 207.

**DE RENZY-MARTIN, Lieut-Col Edward Cuthbert,** CMG 1919; DSO 1917; MC; Commander of Order of Skanderbeg; retired; *b* 1883; *s* of late Lieut-Gen. Sir A. R. Martin, KCB; *m* 1st, 1912, Winifred Grace Alicia (*d* 1937), *d* of late E. C. P. Hull, of Park Gate House, Ham Common; one *s* three *d*; 2nd, 1942, Margaret Grant, MBE, *e d* of late Dr A. C. Reid, 16 Pelham Road, Nottingham; one *s* one *d*. *Educ:* Wellington; RMC Sandhurst. Served European War, 1914-18 (despatches, CMG, DSO, MC, Bt Major; wounded, POW, 1918); Inspector of Albanian Gendarmerie, 1927-34; Hon. Attaché and Sec., British Embassy, Madrid, 1938-40. *Address:* Yew Tree Cottage, High Lorton, Cockermouth, Cumberland. *T:* Lorton 253. *See also C. E. Tilney.*

**DERHAM, Prof. David Plumley,** CMG 1968; MBE 1945; BA, LLM Melbourne; Vice-Chancellor of the University of Melbourne since 1968; *b* 13 May 1920; *s* of Dr A. P. Derham, CBE, MC, ED, MD, FRACP; *m* 1944, Rosemary, *d* of late Gen. Sir Brudenell White, KCB, KCMG, KCVO, DSO; one *s* two *d*. *Educ:* Scotch Coll., Melbourne; Ormond Coll., Melbourne Univ. AIF, 1941-45 (Major). Solicitor, 1948; Barrister, 1948-51; Melbourne University: Tutor in Law, Queen's Coll., and Independent Lectr, Constitutional Law, 1949-51; Prof. of Jurisprudence, 1951-64; Vis. Fellow, Wadham Coll., Oxford, 1953; Carnegie Trav. Fellow, 1953-54; Constitutional Consultant, Indian Law Inst, 1958-59; Sen. Res. Fellow and Vis. Lectr, Chicago Univ. Law Sch., 1961; Vis. Prof. Northwestern Univ. Law Sch., 1961; Dean of Faculty of Law, Monash Univ., 1964-68. Mem. Commonwealth Cttee on Future of Tertiary Educn in Australia, 1962-64; Mem. Australian Univs Commn, 1965-68. Hon. LLD Monash. *Publications:* (Ch. 1) Legal Personality and Political Pluralism, 1958; (Ch. 6) Essays on the Australian Constitution, (2nd edn) 1961; Paton, Textbook of Jurisprudence (Ed. 3rd edn) 1964; (with F. K. H. Maher and Prof. P. L. Waller) Cases and Materials on the Legal Process, 1966; (with F. K. H. Maher and Prof. P. L. Waller) An Introduction to Law, 1966; articles in legal jls. *Recreations:* tennis, lawn tennis. *Address:* University of Melbourne, Parkville, Melbourne, Vic., 3052, Australia. *T:* 34-4222. *Clubs:* Melbourne, Naval and Military, Melbourne Beefsteak, Royal Melbourne Tennis.

**de RHÉ-PHILIPE, Maj.-Gen. Arthur Terence,** CB 1944; OBE 1943; Corps of Royal Engineers; Col Commandant, Royal Corps of Transport; Chairman, GEC-Elliott Mechanical Handling Ltd; Managing Director, Spencer (Melksham) Ltd; *b* 2 Sept. 1905; *s* of late George William Vitalli de Rhé-Philipe, OBE; *m* Moira Evelyn, *d* of late Captain A. L. Cameron; two *d*. *Educ:* Cheltenham; RMA, Woolwich; Clare Coll., Cambridge. 2nd Lieut RE 1926; Capt. 1936; Temp. Major, 1939; Temp. Lieut-Col 1941; Temp. Col 1942; Temp. Brig. 1943; Col 1948; Brig., 1953; temp. Maj.-Gen. 1953; Maj.-Gen. 1954. Dir of Movements, War Office, Sept. 1953-Dec. 1955, retired., Served War of 1939-45 in Great Britain, North Africa and Italy (OBE, CB). Legion of Merit (US) 1943. *Recreations:* golf, cricket. *Address:* Keyford, Upton Scudamore, Warminster, Wilts.

**DERING, Lieut-Col Sir Rupert (Anthony Yea),** 12th Bt, *cr* 1626; *b* 17 Oct. 1915; *s* of late Capt. Rupert Chomeley Yea Dering, KOSB (killed in action, 1915); *S* cousin (Sir Anthony Myles Cholmeley Dering) 1958; *m* 1940, Betty Bridgett, *o d* of Lieut-Col V. P. Druce, Charminster, Dorset; one *d*. *Educ:* Downside; RMC, Sandhurst. 2nd Lieut, King's Own Scottish Borderers, 1935; retd through ill-health, 1947. *Heir:* none. *Address:* Bellings, Midhurst, Sussex. *T:* Midhurst 3404.

**d'ERLANGER, Leo Frederic Alfred;** Banker: Director of public companies; *b* 2 July 1898; *s* of Baron François Rodolphe d'Erlanger and Elizabetta Barbiellini-Amidei; *m* 1930, Edwina Louise Pru; one *s* one *d*. *Educ:* Eton; Royal Military Coll., Sandhurst. War of 1914-18, Active Service First Bn Grenadier Guards. Officier de la Légion d'Honneur. *Address:* 44 Upper Grosvenor Street, W1. *Clubs:* Bath, Bucks.

**de ROS,** 27th Baroness (in her own right; Premier Barony of England) *cr* 1264; **Georgiana Angela Maxwell;** *b* 2 May 1933; *er d* of Lieut-Comdr Peter Ross, RN (killed on active service, 1940) and *g d* of 26th Baroness de Ros (*d* 1956); *S* grandmother, 1958 (on termination of abeyance); *m* 1954, Comdr John David Maxwell, RN; one *s* one *d*. *Educ:* Wycombe Abbey Sch., Bucks; Studley Agricultural Coll., Warwicks. NDD 1955. *Heir:* *s* Hon. Peter Trevor Maxwell, *b* 23 Dec. 1958. *Address:* Old Court, Strangford, N Ireland.

**de ROTHSCHILD;** *see* Rothschild.

**DERRY, Bishop of, (RC),** since 1939; **Most Rev. Neil Farren,** DD, DCL; *b* 25 March, 1893; *s* of John Farren and Margaret McLaughlin. *Educ:* St Columb's Coll., Derry; University Coll. (NUI) Dublin; Maynooth Coll., Rome. Prof. St Columb's Coll., Derry, 1920-27 (Maths and Science), Pres., 1927-39. An Asst to Papal Throne. *Publications:* Domicile and Quasi-domicile, 1920. *Address:* Bishop's House, St Eugene's, Derry. *TA:* Bishop of Derry. *T:* Derry 2302.

**DERRY, Thomas Kingston,** MA DPhil Oxon; *b* 5 March 1905; *y s* of late Rev. W. T. Derry, Wesleyan Minister; *m* 1930, Gudny, *e d* of late Hjalmar Wesenberg, Commander of Order of Vasa, Oslo, Norway. *Educ:* Kingswood Sch., Bath; Queen's Coll., Oxford (Bible Clerk and

Taberdar). 1st Class, Classical Moderations, 1925; 1st Class, Final Sch. of Modern History, 1927; Senior George Webb Medley Scholar, 1927; Gladstone Prizeman, 1928; Sixth Form Master and Chief History Master, Repton Sch., 1929-37; Headmaster, Mill Hill School, 1938-40; Political Intelligence Dept of Foreign Office, 1941-45 (Chief Intelligence Officer, Scandinavia); Asst Master, St Marylebone Grammar Sch., 1945-65; Visiting Prof., Wheaton Coll., Mass, 1961-62. *Publications:* The Campaign in Norway (official military history); A Short History of Norway; (with T. I. Williams) A Short History of Technology; The United Kingdom Today; A Short Economic History of Britain; (with E. J. Knapton) Europe 1815-1914; Europe 1815 to the Present; (with T. L. Jarman and M. G. Blakeway), The Making of Britain, 3 vols. *Address:* Nils Lauritssons vei 27, Oslo 8, Norway.

**DERRY, Warren,** MA; *b* 19 Oct. 1899; *e s* of late Rev. W. T. Derry, Wesleyan minister; *m* 1930, Lorna Adeline, *yr d* of Reginald H. Ferard; one *s* two *d*. *Educ:* Kingswood Sch., Bath; Magdalen Coll., Oxford (Demy). 2nd Class Hons Classical Moderations, 1920; 1st Class Hons. Final Sch. of English Language and Literature, 1922; Passmore Edwards Scholar, 1922; Asst Master, the Edinburgh Academy, 1922-28; Headmaster Wolverhampton Grammar Sch., 1929-56. *Publication:* Dr Parr, a Portrait of the Whig Dr Johnson, 1966. *Address:* 11 Abbey Court, Edward Street, Bath.

**DERRY AND RAPHOE, Bishop of,** since 1970; **Rt. Rev. Cuthbert Irvine Peacocke,** TD; MA; *b* 26 April 1903; *er s* of late Rt Rev. Joseph Irvine Peacocke, DD; *m* 1931, Helen Louise Gaussen; one *s* one *d*. *Educ:* St Columba's Coll., Dublin; Trinity Coll., Dublin, Curate, Seapatrick Parish, 1926-30; Head of Southern Mission, 1930-33; Rector, Derriaghy, 1933-35; Rector, St Mark's, Dundela, 1935-56; CF, 1939-45; Archdeacon of Down, 1950-56, Dean of St Anne's Cathedral, Belfast, 1956-69. *Publication:* The Young Parson, 1936. *Recreations:* games, garden and reading. *Address:* See House, Culmore Road, Londonderry, N Ireland.

**DERWENT,** 4th Baron *cr* 1881; **Patrick Robin Gilbert Vanden-Bempde-Johnstone,** Bt 1795; *b* 26 Oct 1901; *y s* of late Hon. Edward Henry Vanden-Bempde-Johnstone, 2nd *s* of 1st Baron and Hon. Evelyn Agar-Ellis (*d* 1952), *d* of 5th Viscount Clifden; *S* brother 1949; *m* 1929, Marie-Louise, *d* of late Albert Picard, Paris; one *s*. *Educ:* Charterhouse; RMC, Sandhurst. Commissioned KRRC, 1921; Major, KRRC. Director: Yorkshire Insurance Co.; National Safe Deposit and Trustee Co. Ltd; past Chm., Reinsurance Corp.; ex-Mem., Horserace Totalisator Bd, Tote Investors Ltd; Past Chm., British Road Fedn. Junior Opposition Whip in House of Lords, 1950-51; Minister of State, Bd of Trade, 1962-63; Minister of State, Home Office, 1963-64. *Recreations:* shooting and fishing. *Heir:* *s* Hon. Robin Evelyn Leo Vanden-Bempde-Johnstone, MVO 1957 [*b* 30 Oct. 1930; *m* 1957, Sybille de Simard de Pitray, *d* of Vicomte de Simard de Pitray and Madame Jeannine Hennessy; one *s* three *d*]. *Address:* Hackness Hall, Scarborough, Yorks; 10 Wilton Place, SW1. *Club:* Beefsteak.

*See also Earl of Listowel.*

**DESAI, Shri Morarji Ranchhodji,** BA; Deputy Prime Minister and Minister of Finance, Government of India, 1967-69; *b* 1896. *Educ:* Wilson Coll., Bombay. Entered Provincial Civil Service of Govt of Bombay, 1918; resigned to join the Civil Disobedience Campaign of Mahatma Gandhi, 1930; convicted for taking part in the Movement during 1930-34; Sec., Gujarat Pradesh Congress Cttee, 1931-37 and 1939-46; Minister for Revenue, Co-operation, Agriculture and Forests, Bombay, 1937-39; convicted, 1940-41, and detained in prison, 1942-45; Minister for Home and Revenue, Bombay, 1946-52; Chief Minister of Bombay, 1952-56; Minister for Commerce and Industry, Government of India, 1956-58. Treasurer, All India Congress Cttee, 1950-58; Minister of Finance, Government of India, 1958-63, resigned from Govt (under plan to strengthen Congress) Aug. 1963. Hon. Fellow, College of Physicians and Surgeons, Bombay, 1956; Hon. LLD, Karnatak Univ., 1957. *Address:* 5 Dr Rajendra Prasad Road, New Delhi, India. *T:* 381600.

**DE SAUMAREZ,** 6th Baron *cr* 1831; **James Victor Broke Saumarez;** Bt 1801; *b* 28 April 1924; *s* of 5th Baron de Saumarez and Gunhild, *d* of late Maj.-Gen. V. G. Balck, Stockholm; *S* father, 1969; *m* 1953, Julia, *d* of D. R. Charlton, Gt Holland-on-Sea, Essex; twin *s* one *d*. *Educ:* Eton Coll.; Millfield; Magdalene Coll., Cambridge (MA). Farmer; Director, Shrubland Health Clinic Ltd. *Recreations:* swimming, gardening, photography. *Heir:* *s* Hon. Eric Douglas Saumarez, *b* 13 Aug. 1956. *Address:* Shrubland Vista, Coddenham, Ipswich, Suffolk. *T:* Claydon 220.

**DESBOROUGH, Vincent Robin d'Arba,** FBA 1966; FSA 1956; Senior Research Fellow, New College, Oxford, since 1968; *b* 19 July 1914; *s* of Maximilian Julius Praetorius, PhD (killed on active service, European War, 1914-18), and of Violet Mary Francesca (*née* Parker; who changed the surname for herself and dependants from Praetorius to a family name of Desborough, by deed-poll, after the death of her husband and the Russian Revolution); *m* 1950, Mary Hobson Appach; one *d* (one *s* decd). *Educ:* Downside Sch.; New Coll., Oxford. BA 1936; BLitt 1939; Charles Oldham Prize, 1939; MA 1949. Macmillan Student, British Sch. of Archæology at Athens, 1937-39. Served War of 1939-45, Royal Artillery (Temp. Captain, 1944). British Coun. (Sec. Registrar, Brit. Inst., Athens), 1946-47; Asst Dir, Brit. Sch. of Archæology at Athens, 1947-48; University of Manchester, 1948-68. Corresp. Mem., German Archæological Institute. Chm., Man. Cttee, British Sch. at Athens, 1968-. *Publications:* Protogeometric Pottery, 1952; The Last Mycenaeans and their Successors, 1964; contrib. to revised edn of Cambridge Ancient History; articles and reviews in archæological and classical jls. *Address:* 13 Field House Drive, Woodstock Road, Oxford. *T:* Oxford 52285.

**de SEGONZAC, A. D.;** *see* Dunoyer de Segonzac.

**des FORGES, Sir Charles Lee,** Kt, *cr* 1944; CBE 1941; *b* 20 July 1879; *s* of Walter Harry des Forges, Hull and Nottingham; *m* 1905, Alice Mary Stretton (*d* 1947); two *s*; *m* 1948, Doreen Clarke. *Educ:* privately at Hull and Nottingham. Asst Solicitor and Dep. Clerk of the Peace, Nottingham, 1902-12; Town Clerk and Clerk of the Peace, Rotherham County Borough, 1912-46; Secretary, Rotherham Region Joint Town Planning Cttee, 1922; Clerk to Rotherham Assessment Cttee, 1926; Clerk to South-West Yorks. Joint Board for the Mentally Defective, 1928-46. *Recreations:* fly-fishing, golf. *Address:* Bentwater, Churt, Surrey. *T:* Frensham 2604.

**DESHMUKH, Sir Chintaman Dwarkanath,** Kt 1944; CIE 1937; President, India International Centre, New Delhi, since 1959; Chairman, Administrative Staff College of India, Hyderabad, since 1959; Member, Board of Trustees, UN Institute for Training and Research since 1965; *b* Bombay Presidency, 14 January 1896; *s* of D. G. Deshmukh, lawyer; *m* 1st, 1920, Rosina, *d* of Arthur Silcox, London; one *d*; 2nd, 1953, Srimathi Durgabai. *Educ:* Elphinstone High Sch.; Elphinstone Coll., Bombay; Jesus Coll., Cambridge. National Science Tripos, pt 1, Frank Smart Prize in Botany, 1917; BA 1918; first in Indian Civil Service Examination, London (open competitive), 1918; passed UK Bar Examination in 1919 and was called to Bar, Inner Temple, 1963. Asst Commissioner, 1920-24; Under Sec. to CP Government, 1924-25; Deputy Commissioner and Settlement Officer, 1926-30; Joint Sec. to 2nd Round Table Conference, 1931; Revenue Sec. to CP Govt, 1932-33; Financial Sec. to Govt of CP and Berar, India, 1933-39; Joint Sec. to the Government of India; Dept of Education, Health and Lands; Officer on Special Duty, Finance Dept, Govt of India; Custodian of Enemy Property, 1939; Sec. to Central Board of Reserve Bank of India, Bombay, 1939-41; Deputy-Governor, 1941-43; Gov., 1943-49, retired, 1949. Pres., Indian Statistical Inst., Calcutta, 1945-64. India's delegate to the World Monetary Conference at Bretton Woods, 1944. Governor, World Bank and Fund, for India, Washington, 1946; Financial Rep. in Europe and America of Govt of India, 1949-50; Chm. Joint Board of Governors of World Bank and International Monetary Fund, 1950; Mem. Planning Commn, 1950; Minister of Finance, Govt of India, 1950-56, resigned 1956. Chairman: University Grants Commission, India, 1956-60; Indian Institute of Public Administration, 1964; Central Sanskrit Bd, 1967-68. Vice-Chancellor, Univ. of Delhi, 1962-67. Ramon Magsaysay Award (Philippines), 1959. *Recreation:* gardening. *Address:* India International Centre, 40 Lodi Estate, New Delhi, India.

**DE SICA, Vittorio;** Italian film director and actor; *b* 7 July 1901; *s* of Umberto and Teresa De Sica; *m*; one *d*. Productions (in some of which he had acted) include: The Little Martyr; Tomorrow Is Too Late; Shoe Shine; Bicycle Thieves; Miracle in Milan; Umberto D; Bread, Love and Dreams; Bread, Love and Jealousy; The Sign of Venus; Scandal in Sorrento; Like Father, Like Son; Il Tetto; L'Oro di Napoli; Anna of Brooklyn; La Ciociara; The Last Judgement; Marriage, Italian Style; Woman Times Seven; Sunflower.

**de SILVA, Hon. Hethumuni Ayadoris,** CMG 1951; Puisne Justice, Supreme Court, Ceylon, since 1950; *b* 29 June 1891; *s* of late de Silva Hethumuni Harmanis, proprietary planter, and late Oino de Silva; *m* 1919, Rosamond, de Silva Gunasekera; two *s* one *d*. *Educ:* Royal Coll., Colombo; Middle Temple, London. Called to the English Bar, 1916; enrolled as an advocate, Supreme Court, Ceylon, 1917, practised until 1934; District Judge in many towns, 1934-50. President of Ceylon Judicial Service Association, 1946-50. *Recreations:* tennis, planting, reading. *Address:* 103 Rosmead Place, Cinnamon Gardens, Colombo, Ceylon. *T:* 9929.

**DESIO, Prof. Ardito;** Professor of Geology and Director of Geological Institute of the University of Milan and of Applied Geology at the Engineering School of Milan since 1931; *b* 18 April 1897; *m* 1932; one *s* one *d*. *Educ:* Udine and Florence. Grad. Univ. of Florence in Nat. Sciences. Asst, University of Pavia, 1923, also Engineering Sch., Milan, 1924-25 to 1930-31; Lectr in Phys Geography, University of Milan, 1929-30 and in Palaeontology there until 1935. Pres., Italian Geological Cttee, 1966-. Director: Rivista Italiana di Paleontologia e Stratigrafia, 1942; Geologia Tecnica, 1967. Hon. Member: Gesellschaft für Erdkunde zu Berlin, 1941; Italian Geog. Soc., 1955. Faculty of Sciences University of Chile, 1964; Member: Institut d'Egypte, 1936; Accademia Naz. Lincei, 1948; Ist. Lombardo Accad. Scienze Lettere, 1949; New York Academy of Sciences, 1961; For. Mem., Geological Soc. of London, 1964. Led expedition to K2 (8611 m, 2nd highest peak in the World; reached on 31 July 1954), and 16 expeditions in Africa and Asia. Gold Medal of the Republic of Pakistan, 1954; Gold Medal of the Sciences, Letters and Arts, of Italy, 1956; Patrons: Medal of Royal Geog. Soc. of London, 1957. Cav. Grand Cross, 1955. *Publications:* about 320, among them: La spedizione geografica Italiana al Karakoram 1929, 1936; Le vie delle sete, 1950; Geologia applicata all' ingegneria, 1958; Ascent of K2, 1956 (11 languages, 15 editions); I ghiacciai del gruppo Ortles-Cevedale (Alpi centrali), 1967. *Recreation:* alpinist. *Address:* (Office) Piazzale Gorini 15, Milano. *T:* 292726; (Residence) Viale Maino 14, Milano. *T:* 709845. *Clubs:* Internat. Rotary; Panatlon.

**de SMITH, Prof. Stanley Alexander,** MA, PhD; Downing Professor of the Laws of England, and Fellow, Fitzwilliam College, University of Cambridge, since 1970; *b* 27 March 1922; *s* of Joseph de Smith and Jane Alexander; *m* 1946, Catherine Joan Natley (marr. diss. 1965); two *s* two *d*; 1967, Barbara Lillywhite. *Educ:* Southend High School; St Catharine's Coll., Cambridge. BA 1942, MA 1946; PhD London, 1959. Asst Lectr in Law London Sch. of Economics and Political Science, 1946; Lectr, 1948; Reader in Public Law, 1954. Military service, 1942-46; with 77th (DLOY) Medium Regt, RA, in NW European Campaign; subseq. on intelligence duties in Germany; despatches, 1945. Order of Leopold II, Croix de Guerre (1940) with palms, 1945; Captain 1946. Sec., Buganda Constitutional Cttee and Namirembe conf., 1954 Prof. of Public Law, Univ. of London, 1959-70; Constitutional Commissioner, Mauritius, 1961-68; Visiting Fellow, Research Sch. of Social Sciences, Australian National Univ., 1962; Visiting Prof., NY Univ. Sch. of Law, and Senior Fellow, NY Univ. Center for International Studies, 1967-68. *Publications:* Joint editor, Commonwealth and Dependencies, Halsbury's Laws of England (3rd edition), 1953; The Vocabulary of Commonwealth Relations, 1954; Judicial Review of Administrative Action, 1959 (2nd edn 1968); The Lawyers and the Constitution, 1960; The New Commonwealth and its Constitutions, 1964; Microstates and Micronesia, 1970. *Address:* Fitzwilliam College, Cambridge; 2 Gog Magog Way, Stapleford, Cambs.

**DESMOND, Astra, (Lady Neame),** CBE 1949; BA London; Hon. RAM; Mezzo-soprano singer; Professor of Singing at Royal Academy of Music, 1947-63; President Incorporated Society of Musicians, 1950; President Society of Women Musicians, 1952-56; Member Arts Council Music Panel, 1953-59; Member of Carl Rosa Trust Council, 1956-58; *b* Torquay, 10 April 1893; *m* 1920, Sir Thomas Neame, *qv*; two *s* (and one *s* deceased). *Educ:* Notting Hill High Sch. (Sch. Scholar); Westfield Coll., (Classical Scholarship); singing with Blanche Marchesi (Mary South Scholarship) and Louise Trenton; and Grenzebach and von Bos in Berlin. Has appeared at leading Festivals and Concerts since 1920; especially associated with Elgar's works, frequently under the composer's direction; sang in first broadcast of Stravinsky's Oedipus Rex in 1928; has appeared in Opera with Carl Rosa Company; as guest artist at Sadler's Wells (Delilah and Carmen), Covent Garden (Ortrud and Fricka), and Glastonbury festivals; has toured in Scandinavia, Holland, France, the Balkans, Iberia, and New York both independently and for the British Council; sang in recitals and with the National Orchestra of Athens in April 1940 and again in 1946; in November 1941 was sent by the British Council on a tour of Portugal and Spain. Medal of S Olav (Norway), 1943. *Publications:* Grieg's Songs (Music and Letters, Oct. 1941); Dvořák's Songs, 1942; Sibelius' Songs, 1945; New English Version of Dvořák's Biblical Songs, 1949. *Recreation:* study of foreign languages. *Address:* Preston Lea, Faversham, Kent. *T:* Faversham 2012. *Club:* Cowdray.

**de SOUZA, Carlos Alves;** Brazilian Ambassador to the Court of St James's 1964-66; *b* Rio de Janeiro, 19 May 1901; *m* Clelia, *d* of President Arthur Bernades; one *s* one *d*. Served in Brazilian Forces (War Service and Military Service Cross). A Cabinet Minister during 1926. 2nd Sec., Rio de Janeiro, 1924; 1st Sec., Paris, 1926; Vienna, 1934; Mexico, 1935; Counsellor, Foreign Office, Rio de Janeiro, 1936; Minister in Belgrade, 1939-41; Head of Administrative Department of Foreign Office, Rio de Janeiro, 1943; Ambassador in: Havana, 1945-49; Rome, 1949-56; Paris, 1956-63. Has served on many Commissions; holds foreign decorations. *Address:* c/o Ministry of Foreign Affairs, Rio de Janeiro, Brazil.

**de SOYSA, Rt. Rev. Charles Harold Wilfred;** *see* Colombo, Bishop of.

**de THIER, Jacques;** Grand Officer, Order of Léopold II; Commander, Order of Léopold and Order of the Crown, Belgium; Civic Cross (1914-18); Grand Cross of Royal Victorian Order (Hon. GCVO); Director, Compagnie Financière et de Gestion pour l'Etranger (Cometra), Brussels, since 1966; *b* Heusy, Belgium, 15 Sept. 1900; *m* 1946, Mariette Negroponte; three *step s*. *Educ:* University of Liège. Doctor of Laws (University of Liège), 1922; Mem. Bar (Liège and Verviers), 1923-29. Attached to Prime Minister's Cabinet, Brussels, 1929-32; entered Diplomatic Service, 1930; Attaché, Belgian Legation, Berlin, 1932; Chargé d'Affaires in Athens, 1935, Teheran, 1936; First Sec., Berlin, 1937-38; First Sec., then Counsellor, Washington, 1938-44; Chargé d'Affaires, Madrid, 1944-46; Asst to Dir-Gen., Polit. Dept, Min. of Foreign Affairs, Brussels, 1947, then Asst Head of Belgian Mission in Berlin; Consul-Gen. for Belgium, NY, 1948-55; Pres., Soc. of Foreign Consuls in New York, 1954; Belgian Ambassador: to Mexico, 1955-58; in Ottawa, 1958-61; Mem. Belgian Delegns to Gen. Assemblies of UN, 1956, 1957, 1959 and 1960; Belg. Rep. to Security Council, Sept. 1960; Belgian Ambassador to Court of St James's, 1961-65, and concurrently Belgian Perm. Rep. to Council of WEU, 1961-65. Holds foreign decorations. *Recreation:* golf. *Address:* 38 avenue des Klauwaerts, Brussels 5. *Clubs:* Anglo-Belgian; Cercle Royal Gaulois, Royal Golf de Belgique (Brussels).

**de THIEUSIES, Vicomte A.;** *see* Obert de Thieusies.

**de TRAFFORD, Dermot Humphrey,** VRD 1963; Chairman GHP Group Ltd, since 1966; *b* 19 Jan. 1925; *s* of Rudolph de Trafford, *qv*, and June Lady Audley (*née* Chaplin); *m* 1946, Patricia Mary Beeley; three *s* six *d*. *Educ:* Harrow Sch.; Christ Church, Oxford (MA). Trained as Management Consultant, Clubley Armstrong & Co. Ltd and Orr & Boss and Partners Ltd, 1949-52; Dir, Clubley Armstrong & Co. Ltd, Brentford Transformers Ltd (now Brentford Electric Ltd), Hugh Smith & Co. (Possil) Ltd (now Hugh Smith (Glasgow) Ltd), Counting Instruments Ltd, 1953. Man. Dir, GHP Group Ltd, 1961. *Recreations:* yachting, ski-ing. *Address:* 51 Hyde Park Gate, SW7. *T:* 01-589 6122. *Clubs:* White's, Pratt's, Royal Ocean Racing; Royal Yacht Squadron, Island Sailing.

**de TRAFFORD, Captain Sir Humphrey Edmund,** 4th Bt, *cr* 1841; MC 1916; JP, DL late Coldstream Guards; *b* 30 Nov. 1891; *e s* of 3rd Bt and Violet (*d* 1925), *d* of late Capt. Franklin, 77th Regt; *S* father, 1929; *m* 1917, Hon. Cynthia Cadogan (*d* 1966), 3rd *d* of late Viscount Chelsea and Hon. Lady Meux; four *d*. *Educ:* Oratory Sch.; RMC Sandhurst. Served European War, 1914-18 (MC); a Steward of the Jockey Club, 1934, 1944 and 1951. JP 1944; DL 1946; High Sheriff 1945-46, Herts. *Heir: b* Rudolph de Trafford, *qv*. *Address:* Newsells Park, Barkway, Royston, Herts.

*See also Sir Max Aitken, Bt, Maj.-Gen. F. J. C. Bowes-Lyon, Mrs A. Parker Bowles.*

**de TRAFFORD, Rudolph Edgar Francis,** OBE 1919; *b* 31 Aug. 1894; *b* of Sir Humphrey de Trafford, 4th Bart; *m* 1st, 1924, June (who obtained a divorce, 1938), *o d* of Lieut-Col Reginald Chaplin; one *s* (*see* D. H. de Trafford); 2nd, 1939, Katherine, *e d* of W. W. Balke, Cincinnati, USA. *Educ:* Downside Sch.; Trinity Coll., Cambridge, BA. Served European War, 1914-18; Intelligence Corps and Gen. Staff GHQ. *Address:* 70 Eaton Square, SW1. *T:* 01-235 1823. *Club:* White's.

**DEUTSCH, André;** Managing Director, André Deutsch Ltd, since 1951; *b* 15 Nov. 1917; *s* of late Bruno Deutsch, and of Maria Deutsch (*née* Havas); unmarried. *Educ:* Budapest; Vienna; Zurich. First job in publishing, with Nicholson & Watson, 1942; started publishing independently under imprint of Allan Wingate (Publishers) Ltd, 1945; started for second time André Deutsch Limited, in 1951. Founded: African Universities Press, Lagos, Nigeria, 1962; East Africa Publishing House, Nairobi, Kenya, 1964. Dir, Book Develt Council, 1966-70. *Recreations:* travel, ski-ing, publishing, talking. *Address:* 5 Selwood Terrace, London, SW7.

**DEUTSCH, Dr John James,** CC (Canada) 1969; Vanier Medal 1968; FRSC; Principal and Vice-Chancellor, Queen's University, Kingston, Ontario, since 1968; *b* 26 Feb. 1911; *s* of Carl and Elizabeth Deutsch; *m* 1940, Stephanie Frances Heaggerty; one *d*. *Educ:* Primary Sch., Quinton, Sask.; Campion Coll., Regina; Queen's Univ., Kingston (BCom). Research Asst, Bank of Canada, Ottawa, 1936; Asst Dir of Research, Rowell-Sirois Commn, Ottawa, 1937; special wartime Asst to Under-Sec. of State for External Affairs, Dept of External Affairs, Ottawa, 1942; Mem. of Editorial Dept, Winnipeg Free Press, 1945; Dir, Internat. Economic Relations Div., Dept of Finance, Ottawa, 1946; Asst Dep. Minister of Finance, Ottawa, 1953; Sec. of Treasury Board, Govt of Canada, 1954; Head of Dept of Economics and Political Science, Univ. of British Columbia, 1956; Queen's Univ., Kingston: Vice-Princ. (Administration) and Prof. of Economics, 1959; Vice-Princ., 1962; Principal-Elect and Prof. of Econs, 1967. Chm., Economic Council of Canada, 1963. Mem. Royal Commn on Newfoundland Finances 1957; Chm., Royal Commn on Natural Gas Distribution of Greater Winnipeg, 1958; Industrial Inquiry Comr,

Labour Dispute in the Forest Industry of BC, 1959; Econ. Adviser, Special Senate Cttee on Manpower and Employment, 1960; Chm., Royal Commn on Higher Educn in New Brunswick, 1961; Member: Special Commn of Inquiry into Unemployment Insce Act, 1961; Adv. Group on Executive Compensation in the Public Service, Ottawa, 1968; Royal Commn on Post-Secondary Educn, Ontario; J. W. Dafoe Foundn; Trustee Canada Studies Foundn; Special Adviser, Maritime Union Study, 1968. Director: Canadian Imperial Bank of Commerce, 1967; International Nickel Co. of Canada Ltd, 1967; Canadian Nuclear Assoc., 1968; Assocn of Univs and Colls of Canada. Hon. LLD. many Canadian univs. *Publications:* (jtly) The Canadian Economy: Selected Readings; (jtly) The American Economic Impact on Canada. *Address:* Summerhill, Queen's University Campus, Kingston, Ontario, Canada. *Clubs:* Rideau (Ottawa); Cataraqui Golf and Country (Kingston).

**DE VALERA, Eamon,** FRS 1968; President of Ireland since 1959, re-elected 1966; Chancellor of National University of Ireland since 1921; *b* New York, USA, 14 Oct. 1882; *o c* of Vivion de Veléra (*b* Spain) and Catherine Coll (*b* Ireland); following his father's death was brought to Co. Limerick, as a child; *m* 1910, Sinéad Ni Fhlannagáin; four *s* two *d* (and one *s* decd). *Educ:* Nat. Sch., Bruree; Christian Brothers' Sch., Rathluirc, Co. Cork; Blackrock Intermediate and University Colls, Dublin; grad. former RUI, postgrad. studies in that University in the NUI and in TCD. BA, BSc, HDip. in Ed. Secondary sch. teacher and Teachers' Training Coll. and Univ. lectr; for many years an active mem. of Gaelic League. Joined Irish Volunteers at foundn, 1913; OC 3rd Bn and Adj. Dublin Bde, Irish Volunteers, 1915-16, and Comdt in Irish National Uprising, Easter 1916; sentenced to death, commuted to penal servitude for life; released, Gen. Amnesty, June 1917; elected Sinn Féin MP, East Clare, 1917; President, Sinn Féin, 1917-26; Pres., Irish Volunteers, 1917-22; re-imprisoned, May 1918; escaped from Lincoln Gaol, Feb. 1919; Pres. of Irish Republic, 1919-22; visited the USA, seeking official recognition for Republic, 1919-20, and raised external loan of six million dollars for Irish Republican Government; rejected Anglo-Irish Treaty, Dec. 1921-Jan. 1922; founded Fianna Fáil, 1926; Pres. Fianna Fáil, 1926-59. Parly. rep for East Mayo 1918-21; MP for Down (N Ireland) 1921-29 and S Down (N Ireland), 1933-37; Leader of Opposition, IFS Parliament, 1927-32; Pres. Exec. Council IFS and Minister for External Affairs, 1932-37; introduced Constitution of Ireland Dáil Eireann, 1937; following enactment by the people, and coming into operation, of the new Constitution, became Taoiseach (Head of Government) and Minister for External Affairs in Government of Ireland, 1937-48, and Minister for Education, 1939-40; Leader of Opposition, Dáil Eireann, 1948-51 and 1954-57; Taoiseach again 1951-54 and 1957-59. Pres. of Council of League of Nations at its 68th and Special Sessions, Sept. and Oct. 1932; Pres. of Assembly of League of Nations, 1938. Holds hon. degrees (LLD, PhD, ScD); MRIA; Hon. Bencher, Hon. Soc. of King's Inns; Hon. FRCSI. Decorations include: Grand Cross of: Order of Pius IX, 1933; Order of Charles, 1961; Supreme Order of Christ, 1962; Grand Cordon, Order of Leopold, 1968. *Address:* Aras an Uachtaráin, Dublin 8.

**de VALOIS, Dame Ninette,** DBE, *cr* 1951 (CBE 1947); Director of the Royal Ballet, 1931-63; Governor of the Royal Ballet (formerly the Sadler's Wells Ballet, Royal Opera House, Covent Garden, and the Sadler's Wells Theatre Ballet, Sadler's Wells Theatre); Founder of The Royal Ballet School (formerly The Sadler's Wells School of Ballet); *b* Baltiboys, Blessington, Co. Wicklow, 6 June 1898; 2nd *d* of Lieut-Col T. R. A. Stannus, DSO, Carlingford; *m* 1935, Dr A. B. Connell. Prima ballerina the Royal Opera Season Covent Garden (International), May to July 1919 and again in 1928. Première danseuse British National Opera Company, 1918; mem. The Diaghileff Russian Ballet, 1923-26; choreographic dir to the Old Vic, the Festival Theatre, Cambridge, and The Abbey Theatre, Dublin, 1926-30; Founder of The National Sch. of Ballet, Turkey, 1947. Principal choreographic works: Job, The Rake's Progress, Checkmate, and Don Quixote. Hon. MusDoc London, 1947; Hon. DLitt Reading, 1951; Oxford, 1955; Hon. DMus, Sheffield, 1955; Hon. MusD Trinity Coll., Dublin, 1957; Hon. Doc Fine Arts, Smith Coll., Mass, USA, 1957; Hon. LLD Aberdeen, 1958; FRAD 1963. Chevalier of the Legion of Honour, 1950. Gold Albert Medal, RSA, 1964. *Publications:* Invitation to the Ballet, 1937; Come Dance with Me, 1957. *Address:* c/o Royal Ballet School, 153 Talgarth Road, W14.

**de VAUX, Father Roland;** Dominican; Dr Theol; Director of French Biblical and Archæological School, Jerusalem, 1945-65; *b* 17 Dec. 1903. *Educ:* Paris. Prof., French Biblical and Archæological Sch., Jerusalem, 1933. Leader of Archæological Missions at Tell el Far'ah and Khirbet Qumrân; Co-dir of the Excavations in Jerusalem. Head of internat. team publishing Dead Sea Scrolls held in Jordan. Mem., Académie des Inscriptions et Belles Lettres, Paris; Hon. FSA; Corresp. FBA. Hon. DD: Dublin 1954; Louvain, 1964; Vienna, 1965; Hon. LLD, Aberdeen, 1964; Hon. DHL, Yale, 1965. *Publications:* La Genèse, 1951 (2nd edn 1962); Samuel, 1953 (2nd edn 1961); Rois, 2nd edn, 1959; Bible de Jérusalem; Les Institutions de l'Ancien Testament, I 1958, II 1960; Les Sacrifices de l'Ancien Testament, 1964; Studies in Old Testament Sacrifice, 1964; Bible et Orient, 1967; Histoire ancienne d'Israël, vol. I, 1971. *Address:* Ecole Biblique et Archéologique Française, POB 178, Jerusalem.

**DEVENISH, Rev. Robert Cecil Silvester,** MA; *b* 22 Nov. 1888; 3rd *s* of late Very Reverend R. J. S. Devenish, Dean of Cashel, Ireland; *m* 1923, Lily Darley, 2nd *d* of late Right Rev. W. R. Moore, Bishop of Kilmore, Elphin and Ardagh; two *d. Educ:* Midleton Coll.; Dublin University. Deacon, 1912; Priest, 1913; TCF, 1915-19; HCF, 1919; Chaplain Indian Ecclesiastical Establishment, 1919-43; Archdeacon of Lahore, 1934-40; Rector of St Paul's Naval and Garrison Church, Esquimalt, 1941-46; Chaplain of the Upper Chine Sch., Shanklin, I of W, 1946; Asst-Priest, St Mary Abbots Church, Kensington, W8, 1951-59; part-time help, Worplesdon, 1959-63. *Address:* The Anchorage, Fordens Lane, Holcombe, Dawlish, Devon.

**DEVENPORT, Martyn Herbert,** MA; Headmaster, Victoria College, Jersey, CI, since Sept. 1967; *b* 11 Jan. 1931; *s* of Horace Devenport and Marjorie Violet (*née* Fergusson); *m* 1957, Mary Margaret Lord; three *s* one *d. Educ:* Maidstone Gram. Sch.; Gonville and Caius Coll., Cambridge. Asst Master at Eton Coll., 1957-67. *Recreations:* photography, squash, sailing. *Address:* Victoria College, Jersey, CI. *T:* Central 22350.

**DEVERELL, Sir Colville (Montgomery),** GBE 1963 (OBE 1946); KCMG 1957 (CMG 1955); CVO 1953; retired from Government Service,

Nov. 1962; Secretary-General, International Planned Parenthood Federation, 1964-69; *b* 21 Feb. 1907; *s* of George Robert Deverell and Maude (*née* Cooke); *m* 1935, Margaret Wynne, *d* of D. A. Wynne Wilson; three *s*. *Educ:* Portora Sch., Enniskillen, Ulster; Trinity Coll., Dublin (LLB); Trinity Coll., Cambridge. District Officer, Kenya, 1931; Clerk to Exec. and Legislative Councils, 1938-39; civil affairs Branch, E Africa Comd, 1941-46, serving Italian Somaliland, British Somaliland, Ethiopia; Mem. Lord de la Warr's Delegation, Ethiopia, 1944; seconded War Office in connection Italian Peace Treaty, 1946. Sec., Development and Reconstruction Authority, Kenya, 1946; acted as Financial Sec. and Chief Native Comr, 1949; Administrative Secretary, Kenya, 1949; Colonial Sec., Jamaica, 1952-55; Governor and Comdr-in-Chief, Windward Islands, 1955-59; Governor and Comdr-in-Chief, Mauritius, 1959-62. Chm. UN(FP) Mission to India, 1965. Constitutional Adviser, Seychelles, 1966. LLD *jure dignitatis*, Dublin, 1964. *Recreations:* cricket, tennis, squash, golf and fishing. *Address:* 46 Northfield End, Henley-on-Thames, Oxon. *Clubs:* East India and Sports; MCC; Nairobi (Kenya).

**DEVEREUX,** family name of **Viscount Hereford.**

**DEVERS, Gen. Jacob L.;** United States Army (retired); Chairman, American Battle Monuments Commission, 1959-69; *b* 8 Sept. 1887; *s* of Philip Kissinger Devers and Ella Kate Loucks; *m* 1911, George Hays Lyon; one *d*. *Educ:* York High Sch., York, Pa; US Military Academy, West Point, NY. Chief of Staff, Panama Canal Dept, 1939-40; Cdg Gen., 9th Infantry Division, 1940-41; Cdg Gen. of the Armored Force, 1941-43; Cdg Gen. European Theatre of Operations, US Army, 1943; Deputy Supreme Allied Comdr, Mediterranean Theatre, and Cdg Gen. North African Theatre of Operations, United States Army, 1944; commanded Sixth Army Group in France, 1944-45; Commanding General, Army Ground Forces, USA, 1945-48; Chief Army Field Forces, USA, 1948-49; retired from US Army, 1949. Managing Dir, AAA Foundation for Traffic Safety, Washington, DC 1950. *Recreations:* polo, baseball, golf. *Address:* 1430 33rd Street, Northwest, Washington, DC 20007, USA. *Clubs:* Cosmos, Army-Navy (Washington, DC).

**de VESCI,** 6th Viscount, *cr* 1776; **John Eustace Vesey;** *b* 25 Feb. 1919; *s* of Lt-Col Hon. Thomas (Eustace) Vesey (*d* 1946) (*b* of 5th Viscount), and of Lady Cecily (Kathleen) Vesey (a Lady-in-Waiting to the Duchess of Gloucester, 1947-51, a Woman of the Bedchamber to Queen Mary, 1951-53, and an Extra Lady-in-Waiting to the Duchess of Gloucester 1953-), *d* of 5th Earl of Kenmare; *S* uncle 1958; *m* 1950, Susan Anne, *d* of late Ronald (Owen Lloyd) Armstrong Jones, MBE, QC, DL, and of the Countess of Rosse; one *s* two *d* (and one *d* decd). *Educ:* Eton; Trinity Coll., Cambridge. Served War of 1939-45 with Irish Guards, Narvik (wounded), North Africa and Italy. Followed career of Land Agent; now managing own property and forestry consultancy. FLAS(O), FRICS. *Heir:* *s* Hon. Thomas Eustace Vesey, *b* 8 Oct. 1955. *Address:* Abbeyleix, Ireland. *T:* Abbeyleix 31162. *Clubs:* White's, Buck's; Kildare Street (Dublin).

*See also Earl of Rosse.*

**de VIGIER, William Alphonse;** Chairman and Managing Director (also founder), Acrow (Engineers) Ltd; Chairman: Thos. Storey (Engineers) Ltd, Stockport; Adamson & Hatchett Ltd, Dukinfield; E. H. Bentall & Co. Ltd, Maldon; S. H. Heywood & Co. Ltd, Reddish; Crawley Bros Ltd, Saffron Walden; Acrow Automation Ltd, Harefield; Acrow Australia Ltd; Acrow Engineers (Pty) Ltd, South Africa; *b* 22 Jan. 1912; *m* 1939, Betty Kendall; two *d*. *Educ:* La Chataigneraie, Coppet, Switzerland. Director: Vigier Cement SA, Switzerland; Acrow Argentina SA; Acrow Peru SA; Acrow India Ltd; Richmond Screw & Anchor Co., Canada; Inland Steel Pty, South Africa; Pres., Acrow Corp. of America; Partner, Acrow-Wolff GmbH, Germany; Knight of Star of the North (Sweden); Grand Commander, Order of Star of Africa. *Recreations:* tennis, skiing, swimming. *Address:* Tinkers Lodge, Marsh Lane, Mill Hill, NW7; Acrow (Engineers) Ltd, 8 South Wharf, W2. *T:* (business) 01-262 3456. *Clubs:* Devonshire, St James'.

**de VILLIERS,** 3rd Baron, *cr* 1910; **Arthur Percy de Villiers;** *b* 17 Dec. 1911; *s* of 2nd Baron and Adelheid, *d* of H. C. Koch, Pietermaritzburg, Natal; *S* father 1934; *m* 1939, Lovett (marr. diss. 1958), *d* of Dr A. D. MacKinnon, Williams Lake, BC; one *s* two *d*. *Educ:* Magdalen Coll., Oxford. Barrister, Inner Temple, 1938. Farming in New Zealand. Admitted as a barrister to the Auckland Surpreme Court, 1949. *Heir:* *s* Hon. Alexander Charles de Villiers, *b* 29 Dec. 1940. *Address:* Huapai, Kumeu, Auckland, NZ.

**DE VITO, Gioconda;** Violinist; Professor of Violin at Accademia Di Santa Cecilia, Rome, 1935; *b* 26 July 1907; *d* of Giacomo and Emilia De Vito (*née* De Giudice), Martina Franca Puglia, Italy; *m* 1949, James David Bicknell; no *c*. *Educ:* Conservatorio Di Musica Rossini, Pesaro. Began to play violin at age of 8½; final examinations (distinction), Conservatorio Pesaro, 1921; first concert, 1921; first prize, Internat. Competition, Vienna, 1932. World wide musical activitites since debut with London Philharmonic Orchestra, 1948; Royal Philharmonic Soc., 1950; Edinburgh Festival, 1949, 1951, 1953 (took part, 1953, in Festival of the Violin with Yehudi Menuhin and Isaac Stern), and 1960; played at Bath Fest. and Festival Hall with Yehudi Menuhin, 1955; Jury Tchaikowsky Internat. Violin Competition, Moscow, and recitals Moscow and Leningrad. 1958; Soloist, Adelaide Centenary Fest., and toured Australia, 1960; concerts, Buenos Aires, 1961; retired, 1961. Last concerts, Gt Brit., Swansea Festival, Oct. 1961; Continent, Basle Philharmonic, Nov. 1961. Diploma di Medaglia d'Oro del Ministero della Pubblica Istruzione for services to Art, 1957. *Recreation:* bird watching. *Address:* Via Cassia 595, Rome. *T:* 3070937; Flint Cottage, Loudwater, Rickmansworth, Herts. *T:* 2865.

**DEVITT, Lt-Col Sir Thomas Gordon,** 2nd Bt, *cr* 1916; Partner of Devitt & Moore, Shipbrokers; Chairman of the National Service for Seafarers; *b* 27 Dec. 1902; *e s* of Arthur Devitt (*d* 1921) *e s* of 1st Bt and Florence Emmeline (*d* 1951), *e d* of late William Forbes Gordon, Manar, NSW; *S* grandfather, 1923; *m* 1st, 1930, Joan Mary (who obtained a divorce, 1936), 2nd *d* of late Charles Reginald Freemantle, Hayes Barton, Pyrford, Surrey; 2nd, 1937, Lydia Mary (marriage dissolved, 1953), *o d* of late Edward Milligen Beloe, King's Lynn, Norfolk; two *d*; 3rd, 1953, Janet Lilian, *o d* of late Col H. S. Ellis, CBE, MC; one *s* one *d*. *Educ:* Sherborne; Corpus Christi Coll., Cambridge. 1939-45 War as Lt-Col, Seaforth Highlanders and OC Raiding Support Regt. Royal Order of Phœnix of Greece with swords. Chm. Macers Ltd, 1961-70. Chm., Board of Governors, The Devitt and Moore Nautical Coll., Pangbourne, 1948-61; Governor, Sherborne Sch. *Heir:* *s* James Hugh

Thomas Devitt, *b* 18 Sept, 1956. *Recreation:* shooting. *Address:* Cooks Mill, Fordham Heath, Essex. *T:* Fordham 242; 5 Rembrandt Close, Holbein Place, SW1. *T:* 01-730 2653. *Club:* MCC.

**DEVLIN,** family name of **Baron Devlin.**

**DEVLIN,** Baron (Life Peer) *cr* 1961, of West Wick; **Patrick Arthur Devlin,** PC 1960; Kt 1948; FBA 1963; Chairman of the Press Council, 1964-69; *b* 25 Nov. 1905; *e s* of W. J. Devlin; *m* 1932, Madeleine, *yr d* of Sir Bernard Oppenheimer, 1st Bt; four *s* two *d. Educ:* Stonyhurst Coll.; Christ's Coll., Cambridge. President of Cambridge Union, 1926. Called to Bar, Gray's Inn, 1929; KC 1945; Master of the Bench, Gray's Inn, 1947; Treasurer of Gray's Inn, 1963. Prosecuting Counsel to the Mint, 1931-39. Legal Dept, Min. of Supply, 1940-42; Junior Counsel to the Ministries of War Transport, Food and Supply, 1942-45; Attorney-Gen., Duchy of Cornwall, 1947-48; Justice of the High Court, Queen's Bench Div., 1948-60; Pres. of the Restrictive Practices Court, 1956-60; a Lord Justice of Appeal, 1960-61; a Lord of Appeal in Ordinary, 1961-64, retd; High Steward of Cambridge Univ., 1966-. Chm. of Council, Bedford Coll., University of London, 1953-59; Chairman: Wilts Quarter Sessions, 1955-; Cttee of Inquiry into the Dock Labour Scheme, 1955-56; Cttee of inquiry into the port transport industry, 1964-65; Jt Bd for the National Newspaper Industry, 1965-69; Nyasaland Inquiry Commission, 1959. Pres., Brit. Maritime Law Assoc., 1962-. A Judge of the Administrative Tribunal of the ILO, 1964-; Chm., Commn apptd under constn of ILO to examine complaints concerning observance by Greece of Freedom of Assoc. and similar Conventions of 1948, 1949. Chm. Assoc. Average Adjusters, 1966-67. Hon. LLD: Glasgow 1962; Toronto 1962; Cambridge 1966; Leicester, 1966; Sussex 1966; Durham, 1968; Liverpool, 1970; Hon. DCL Oxon, 1965. *Publications:* Trial by Jury, 1956 (Hamlyn Lectures); The Criminal Prosecution in England (Sherrill Lectures), 1957; Samples of Lawmaking (Lloyd Roberts and other lectures), 1962; The Enforcement of Morals, (Maccabean and other lectures), 1965; The House of Lords and the Naval Prize Bill, 1911 (Rede Lecture), 1968. *Address:* West Wick House, Pewsey, Wilts.
*See also William Devlin.*

**DEVLIN, Bernadette;** MP (Ind Unity), Mid Ulster, since April 1969; *b* 23 April 1947; *d* of late John James Devlin and Elizabeth Devlin. *Educ:* St Patrick's Girls' Acad., Dungannon; psychology student at Queen's Univ., Belfast, 1966-. Youngest MP in House of Commons when elected at age of 21. *Publication:* The Price of my Soul (autobiog.), 1969. *Recreations:* walking, folk music, doing nothing, swimming. *Address:* House of Commons, SW1.

**DEVLIN, William;** Actor; *b* Aberdeen, 5 Dec. 1911; *y s* of William John Devlin, ARIBA, and Frances Evelyn Crombie; *m* 1936, Mary Casson (marr. diss.); one *d. m* 1948, Meriel Moore. *Educ:* Stonyhurst Coll.; Merton Coll., Oxford (BA). Sec. OUDS, 1932-33; studied at Embassy Theatre Sch., 1933-34. New Theatre with John Gielgud, 1934-35 (Hamlet and Noah); Old Vic Company, 1935-36 (Peer Gynt, Cassius, Richard III, Leontes, Lear, etc.); except for war period has appeared for Old Vic in every year, 1935-53 (Shylock, Macbeth, Claudius, Brutus, Dogberry, Fluellen, etc.). Parnell in The Lost Leader, Abbey Theatre, Dublin, 1937; Zola, Clemenceau, Gladstone in biogr. plays about them, 1937-38; Ransom in Ascent of F6 and Seth in Mourning becomes Electra!, New Theatre, 1938. Joined HM Forces, Sept. 1939, as a Trooper in Horsed Cavalry; commnd in Royal Wilts Yeom. and served with 8th Army in Africa and Italy for 4½ years; released as Major, Nov. 1945. Leading man with Old Vic at Theatre Royal, Bristol, 1945-48. Memorial Theatre, Stratford-on-Avon, seasons 1954 and 1955. First appeared in New York as Bohun, QC in You Never Can Tell, Martin Beck Theatre, 1948; subseq. at Boston as Lear and Macbeth. Played Clemenceau in The Tiger, the first play to be televised in 1936, and has appeared regularly in this medium and also in Sound Broadcasting. Mem., Equity Council, 1957-65. Mem., Monksilver Parish Council, 1967, Clerk 1970. *Recreations:* golf and fishing. *Address:* Bird's Hill Cottage, Monksilver, Taunton, Som. *T:* Stogumber 389.
*See also Baron Devlin.*

**DEVON,** 17th Earl of, *cr* 1553; **Charles Christopher Courtenay,** Bt 1644; RARO Lieutenant (W/Captain) Coldstream Guards; *b* 13 July 1916; *o surv. s* of 16th Earl and Marguerite (*d* 1950), *d* of late John Silva; *S* father, 1935; *m* 1939, Venetia, Countess of Cottenham, *d* of Captain J. V. Taylor; one *s* one *d. Educ:* Winchester; RMC, Sandhurst. Served war of 1939-45 (despatches). *Recreations:* shooting and fishing. *Heir: s* Lord Courtenay, *qv. Address:* Powderham Castle, Exeter. *T:* Starcross 253.
*See also Col E. St J. Birnie, Earl of Halifax.*

**DEVONPORT,** 2nd Viscount, *cr* 1917, of Wittington, Bucks; **Gerald Chester Kearley;** Baron, *cr* 1910; 2nd Bt, *cr* 1908; *b* 16 Sept. 1890; *er s* of 1st Viscount and Selina (*d* 1931), *y d* of Edward Chester, Bilsworth; *S* father, 1934; *m* 1938, Sheila Isabel, *e d* of Lieut-Col C. Hope Murray, Morishill, Beith, Ayrshire; one *s* one *d. Educ:* Eton; Exeter Coll., Oxford. War of 1914-18: RN Division; transf. to Scots Guards, 1916 (Lieut); seconded to Army Remount Services, France 1918; War of 1939-45: Head Observer Royal Observer Corps; Bomb Reconnaissance Officer ARP Service; Mem. of Lloyd's. *Recreations:* travelling, shooting. *Heir: s* Hon. Terence Kearley [*b* 29 Aug. 1944; *m* 1968, Elizabeth Rosemary, *d* of J. G. Hopton]. *Address:* Peasmarsh Place, Sussex. *Clubs:* Carlton, Beefsteak.

**DEVONS, Prof. Samuel;** FRS 1955; Professor of Physics, Columbia University, New York, since 1960 (Chairman, Dept of Physics, 1963-67); *b* 1914; *s* of Rev. David I. Devons and E. Edleston; *m* 1938, Celia Ruth Toubkin; four *d. Educ:* Trinity Coll., Cambridge. BA 1935; MA, PhD 1939. Exhibition of 1851 Senior Student, 1939. Scientific Officer, Senior Scientific Officer, Air Ministry, MAP, and Ministry of Supply, 1939-45. Lecturer in Physics, Cambridge Univ., Fellow and Dir of Studies, Trinity Coll., Cambridge, 1946-49; Prof. of Physics, Imperial Coll. of Science, 1950-55; Langworthy Prof. of Physics and Dir of Physical Laboratories, Univ. of Manchester, 1955-60. Royal Soc. Leverhulme Vis. Prof., Andhra Univ., India, 1967-68. Rutherford Medal and Prize, Inst. of Physics, 1970. *Publications:* Excited States of Nuclei, 1949; (ed) Biology and Physical Sciences, 1969; (ed) High Energy Physics and Nuclear Structure, 1970; contributions to Proc. Royal Society, Proc. Phys. Soc., etc. *Recreations:* plastic arts, travel. *Address:* Department of Physics, Columbia University, New York, NY 10027, USA.

**DEVONSHIRE,** 11th Duke of *cr* 1694; **Andrew Robert Buxton Cavendish,** PC 1964; MC; Baron Cavendish, 1605; Earl of Devonshire, 1618;

Marquess of Hartington, 1694; Earl of Burlington, 1831; Baron Cavendish (UK) 1831; Vice-Lieut of the County of Derby since 1957; Chancellor of Manchester University since 1965; President: The Royal Hospital and Home for Incurables; Derbyshire Boy Scouts' Assoc.; Vice-President Building Societies Association (President 1954-61); Chairman Grand Council, British Empire Cancer Campaign, 1956; a Trustee of the National Gallery, 1960; *b* 2 Jan. 1920; *o surv s* of 10th Duke of Devonshire, KG, and Lady Mary Cecil (*see* Dowager Duchess of Devonshire), *d* of 4th Marquess of Salisbury, KG, GCVO; *S* father, 1950; *m* 1941, Hon. Deborah Vivian Freeman-Mitford, *d* of 2nd Baron Redesdale; one *s* two *d*. *Educ:* Eton; Trinity Coll., Cambridge. Served War of 1939-45, Coldstream Guards (MC). Contested (C) Chesterfield Div. of Derbyshire, 1945 and 1950. Parliamentary Under-Sec. of State for Commonwealth Relations, Oct. 1960-Sept. 1962; Minister of State, Commonwealth Relations Office, Sept. 1962-Oct. 1964 and for Colonial Affairs, 1963-Oct. 1964. Executive Steward of the Jockey Club, 1966-69. Mayor of Buxton, 1952-54; Pres. of the Lawn Tennis Assoc., 1955-61. Hon. LLD: Manchester; Sheffield; Hon. Dr Law, Memorial Univ. of Newfoundland. *Heir:* *s* Marquess of Hartington, *qv*. *Address:* 4 Chesterfield Street, W1. *T:* 01-499 5803; Chatsworth, Bakewell, Derbyshire. *T:* Baslow 2204; Lismore Castle, Co. Waterford, Eire. *T:* Lismore 20. *Clubs:* Brooks's, Jockey, White's, Devonshire.
*See also Lady Maud Baillie, Rt Hon. Harold Macmillan, Viscount Stuart of Findhorn.*

**DEVONSHIRE, Dowager Duchess of, (Mary Alice),** GCVO, *cr* 1955; CBE 1946; Mistress of the Robes to The Queen, 1953-66; Chancellor of the University of Exeter since 1956; *b* 29 July 1895; *d* of 4th Marquis of Salisbury, KG, PC, GCVO, and Lady Cicely Alice Gore (*d* 1955), 2nd *d* of 5th Earl of Arran; *m* 1917, as Lady Mary Cecil, 10th Duke of Devonshire, KG; one *s* (*see* 11th Duke of Devonshire) two *d* (*er s* killed in action, 1944). *Address:* 5 Cheyne Walk, SW3. *T:* 01-352 2097; Moorview, Edensor, Bakewell, Derbyshire. *T:* Baslow 2204.

**DE VRIES, Peter;** writer; *b* Chicago, 27 Feb. 1910; *s* of Joost and Henrietta (*née* Eldersveld) de Vries; *m* 1943, Katinka Loeser; two *s* one *d*. *Educ:* Calvin College, Michigan (AB); Northwestern University. Editor, community newspaper, Chicago, 1931; free lance writer, 1931-; associate editor Poetry Magazine, 1938; co-editor, 1942; joined editorial staff New Yorker Magazine, 1944. Mem., Nat. Inst. of Arts and Letters. *Publications:* No But I saw the Movie, 1952; The Tunnel of Love, 1954; Comfort Me with Apples, 1956; The Mackerel Plaza, 1958; The Tents of Wickedness, 1959; Through the Fields of Clover, 1961; The Blood of the Lamb, 1962; Reuben, Reuben, 1964; Let Me Count the Ways, 1965; The Vale of Laughter, 1967; The Cat's Pajamas and Witch's Milk, 1968. *Address:* c/o New Yorker Magazine, 25 W 43rd Street, NYC; (home) 170 Cross Highway, Westport, Conn, USA.

**De WAAL, Brig. Pieter,** CB 1946; CBE 1944; *b* 31 Dec. 1899; *s* of Paul J. De Waal; *m* 1930, Isobel Peebles McLaggan; two *s*. *Educ:* Zeerust, Transvaal; Pretoria; Camberley Staff Coll. (psc); Imperial Defence Coll. (idc). BSc Transvaal University Coll. (University of South Africa), 1920. Commissioned in South African Permanent Force, 1922; OC SA Permanent Garrison Artillery, 1930-31; OC Cape Command, 1932; OC Roberts Heights Command, OC Special Service Battalion and Commandant Military Coll., 1933; Dir of Military Operations and Training, Defence Headquarters, 1934-39; UDF Liaison Officer on staff of GOC East Africa Command, 1940; Dep. Chief of Staff, Defence HQ, Pretoria, 1941-43; attached to SHAEF, 1944-45; Quartermaster-Gen. UDF, 1945-50; Naval and Marine Chief of Staff, UDF, 1951-52; Military and Naval Attaché to Union of South Africa Embassy, Washington, DC, USA, and Military, Air and Naval Adviser to High Commissioner for the Union of South Africa at Ottawa, Canada, 1953-54. Retd from R of O, S African Defence Forces, 1960. *Recreation:* woodwork. *Address:* Hope Cottage, Church Street, George, Cape Province, South Africa. *Club:* Civil Service (Cape Town).

**DEWAR,** family name of **Baron Forteviot.**

**DEWAR, Donald Campbell;** *b* 21 Aug. 1937; *m* 1964, Alison McNair; one *s* one *d*. *Educ:* Glasgow Univ. MP (Lab) South Aberdeen, 1966-70. *Address:* 11 Royal Terrace, Glasgow.

**DEWAR, George Duncan Hamilton;** chartered accountant; Partner, Peat, Marwick, Mitchell & Co., Glasgow, since 1949; *b* 11 Sept. 1916; *s* of George Readman Dewar and Elizabeth Garrioch Sinclair Hamilton; *m* 1940, Elizabeth Lawson Potts Lawrie; one *s* one *d*. *Educ:* High Sch. of Glasgow. Mem. Inst. Chartered Accountants of Scotland (admitted, 1940; Mem. Coun., 1960-65; Vice-Pres., 1969-70; Pres., 1970-71). *Recreations:* golf, sailing, gardening. *Address:* (office) 135 Buchanan Street, Glasgow, C1. *T:* 041-248 7191; (home) 82 Langside Drive, Glasgow S3. *T:* 041-637 1734. *Clubs:* Caledonian; Conservative, Royal Scottish Automobile (Glasgow); Scottish Conservative (Edinburgh).

**DEWAR, Rev. Canon Lindsay,** MA, BD; *b* 1891; *y s* of John Dewar, LRCP and S, Edinburgh; *m* 1926, Edith Marjorie (*d* 1968), *e d* of John William Hudson; one *s* one *d*. *Educ:* Westminster; King's Coll., London; Keble Coll., Oxford. Deacon, 1914; Priest, 1915; Asst Curate of Wimbledon, 1914-16; Temp. CF, 1916-18; lectr Bishop's Coll., Cheshunt, 1918-19; licensed preacher diocese of Oxford, 1919-21; Warden of St Anselm's Hall, Manchester, 1921-27, Vicar of St Marks, Witton, Blackburn, 1927-30; Canon of York Minster, 1930-35, Chancellor, 1933-35; Canon Missioner of Gloucester, 1935-37; Examining Chaplain to Archbishop of York, 1930-42; to Bishop of St Albans, 1954-55; Principal of Bishop's Coll., Cheshunt, 1937-55; Hon. Canon of St Albans, 1937-67; Canon Emeritus, 1967-; Rector of Much Hadham, 1955-67. *Publications:* Magic and Grace, 1929; (with C. E. Hudson) A Manual of Pastoral Psychology, 1932; Imagination and Religion, 1933; Man and God, 1935; Does God Care?, 1936; (with others) An Introduction to Pastoral Theology, 1937; (ed.) Training in Prayer, 1937; What is the Purpose of Life?, 1938; Learning to Think, 1939; (with Phyllis Dent) Training in Worship, 1942; (with C. E. Hudson) Christian Morals, 1946; Psychology and the Parish Priest, 1949; Outline of New Testament Ethics, 1949; The Moral Conduct of a Christian, 1951; The Holy Spirit and Modern Thought, 1959; Moral Theology in the Modern World, 1964; An Outline of Anglican Moral Theology, 1968. *Address:* St Andrews, 3 Green Lane Close, Linton, Cambs. *T:* Linton 896.

**DEWAR, Prof. Michael James Steuart,** FRS 1960; MA, DPhil Oxon; Robert A. Welch Prof. of Chemistry, University of Texas, since 1963; *b* 24 Sept. 1918; *s* of Francis D. Dewar, ICS, and Nan B. Keith; *m* 1944, Mary Williamson; two *s*. *Educ:* Winchester Coll. (First Scholar); Balliol Coll., Oxford (Brackenbury, Frazer and

Gibbs Scholar). ICI Fellow in Chemistry, Oxford, 1945; Courtaulds Ltd, Fundamental Research Laboratory, 1945-51; Reilly Lecturer at Notre Dame Univ., USA, 1951; Prof. of Chemistry and Head of Dept of Chemistry at Queen Mary Coll., University of London, 1951-59; Prof. of Chemistry, University of Chicago, 1959-63. Tilden Lecturer, Chemical Soc., 1954. Visiting Prof. at Yale Univ., USA, 1957. Hon. Sec. Chemical Soc., 1957-59. Harrison Howe Award of Amer. Chem. Soc., 1961. Falk-Plaut Lecturer, Columbia Univ., 1963; Daines Memorial Lecturer, University of Kansas, 1963; Glidden Company Lecturer, Western Reserve Univ., 1964; Arthur D. Little, Visiting Prof., MIT, 1966; Marchon Visiting Lectr, University of Newcastle upon Tyne, 1966; Glidden Company Lectr, Kent State Univ., 1967; Gnehm Lectr, Eidg. Tech. Hochschule, Zurich, 1968; Barton Lectr, Univ. of Oklahoma, 1969; Kahlbaum Lectr, Univ. of Basel, 1970. Fellow, Amer. Acad. of Arts and Sciences, 1966. *Publications:* The Electronic Theory of Organic Chemistry, 1949; Hyperconjugation, 1962; Introduction to Modern Chemistry, 1965; The Molecular Orbital Theory of Organic Chemistry, 1969; Computer Compilation of Molecular Weights and Percentage Compositions, 1970; papers in scientific journals. *Address:* Department of Chemistry, University of Texas, Austin, Texas 78712, USA. *T:* (512) 471-5053.

**DEWAR, Brig. Michael Preston Douglas,** CB 1958; CBE 1956; retired; *b* 1 Oct. 1906; *s* of late Vice-Admiral R. G. D. Dewar, CBE, and Mrs S. E. Dewar (*née* Churchill); *m* 1935, Winifred Elizabeth (*née* Murphy); one *s* one *d*. *Educ:* Winchester Coll. Commissioned 2nd Lieut, The Buffs, 1926; Captain, 1938; Staff Coll., 1939; Major, 1943; OC Home Counties Bde Trg Centre, 1946-47; GSO 1, 6th Airborne Div., 1947-48; Lt-Col, 1948; Jt Services Staff Coll., 1948-49; Col GS, E Africa, 1949-51; Col, 1951; Col Administrative Plans, GHQ, MELF, 1951-52; Dep. Dir Manpower Planning, War Office, 1952-55; Brig., 1955; UK Nat. Military Rep., SHAPE, 1955-58, retired 1959. *Recreations:* golf; gardening; bridge. *Address:* Further Down, Westfield, Hastings, Sussex. *T:* Hastings 51075. *Club:* Army and Navy.

**DEWAR, Robert James,** CMG 1969; CBE 1964; Agriculturalist, Agricultural Projects Department, International Bank for Reconstruction and Development, since 1969; *b* 1923; *s* of late Dr Robert Scott Dewar, MA, MB, ChB, Dumbreck, Glasgow, and of Mrs Roubaix Dewar, Aberdovey, N Wales; *m* 1947, Christina Marianne, *d* of late Olof August Ljungberger, Stockholm, Sweden; two *s* one *d*. *Educ:* High Sch. of Glasgow; Edinburgh Univ. (BSc, Forestry); Wadham Coll., Oxford. Asst Conservator of Forests, Colonial Forest Service, Nigeria and Nyasaland, 1944-55; Dep. Chief Conservator of Forests, Nyasaland, 1955-60; Chief Conservator of Forests, Dir of Forestry and Game, Nyasaland (now Malawi), 1960-64; Mem. Nyasaland Legislative Council, 1960. Permanent Secretary, Malawi: Min. of Natural Resources, 1964-67 and 1968-69; Min. of Economic Affairs, 1967-68; Min. of Agriculture, 1969. Mem. Nat. Development Council, Malawi, 1966-69; retired from Malawi Civil Service, 1969. *Recreations:* golf, angling, shooting. *Address:* 7612 Edenwood Court, Carderock Springs, Bethesda, Md 20034, USA. *T:* 301 469-6569. *Clubs:* Travellers', Royal Commonwealth Society.

**DEWAR, Thomas; His Honour Judge Dewar;** Judge of the County Court (Circuit 41, Clerkenwell) since 1966; *b* 5 Jan. 1909; *s* of James Stewart Dewar and Katherine Rose Dewar; *m* 1950, Katherine Muriel Johnson; one *s*. *Educ:* Penarth Intermediate School; Cardiff Technical Coll.; Sch. of Pharmacy, University of London; Birkbeck Coll., University of London. Pharmaceutical Chemist, 1931; BPharm 1931, PhD 1934, BSc (Botany, 1st cl. hons). 1936, London. Called to Bar, Middle Temple, 1939; Blackstone Pupillage Prize, 1939. Admin. staff of Pharmaceutical Soc., 1936-40; Sec., Middx Pharmaceutical Cttee, 1940-41; Asst Dir, Min. of Supply, 1943; Sec., Wellcome Foundation, 1943-45. Mem. of Western Circuit, 1945-62; Judge of the County Court (Circuit 59, Cornwall and Plymouth), 1962-65, (circuit 38, Edmonton, etc), 1965-66. Presided over inquiry into X-ray accident at Plymouth Hosp., 1962. *Publications:* Textbook of Forensic Pharmacy, 1946 and four subsequent editions; scientific papers in Quarterly Jl of Pharmacy and Pharmacology. *Recreations:* horticulture, travel. *Address:* 1 Garden Court, Temple, EC4. *T:* 01-353 3326; Goldenhurst Cottage, Aldington, Kent. *T:* Aldington 420. *Club:* Reform.

**DEWAR, William McLachlan,** CBE 1970 (OBE 1955); FRSE 1958; MA; Headmaster, George Heriot's School, Edinburgh, 1947-70; *b* 19 April 1905; *s* of James McLachlan Dewar and Annie Kempie Cuthbert, Crieff; *m* 1935, Mary Sinclair, *d* of late John Anderson, Lerwick; two *s* one *d*. *Educ:* Morrison's Academy, Crieff; Edinburgh Univ.; Rome. MA 1928 (1st Cl. Classics), Vans Dunlop Scholar (Classics), 1927; John Edward Baxter Scholar, 1928. Asst Master, Aberdeen Grammar Sch., 1929-32; Senior Classics Master, Dumfries Academy, 1933-41; Rector, Greenock Academy, 1941-47. Commissioned RAF (VR), 1941; Mem. Scottish Air Cadet Council, 1948; Air Cadet Council, 1965-68. President: Scottish Schoolmasters' Assoc., 1944; Scottish Secondary Teachers' Assoc., 1947-49; Headmasters' Assoc. of Scotland, 1958-60; Member: Cttee on Grants to Students, 1958-60; Scottish Certificate of Education Examination Board, 1964. Scottish Council for Training of Teachers, 1959-67; Departmental Cttees on Secondary Sch. Curriculum, etc. Dir, Edinburgh Chamber of Commerce, 1964-67; Chm. Governors, Moray House Coll. of Education. FRSA 1968. Hon. DLitt, Heriot-Watt, 1970. Chevalier des Palmes Académiques, 1961. *Publications:* The Law and The Teacher, 1955; numerous papers on classical and educational subjects. *Recreations:* study of puns; teacher politics; formerly hockey. *Address:* 35 Craiglockhart Grove, Edinburgh 11. *T:* 031-443 3287.

**de WARDENER, Prof. Hugh Edward,** MBE 1946; MD, FRCP; Professor of Medicine, University of London, Charing Cross Hospital, since 1960; *b* 8 Oct. 1915; *s* of Edouard de Wardener and Becky (*née* Pearce); *m* 1st, 1939, Janet Lavinia Bellis Simon (marr. diss, 1947); one *s*; 2nd, 1947, Diana Rosamund Crawshay (marr. diss., 1954); 3rd, 1954, Jill Mary Foxworthy (marr. diss., 1969); one *d*; 4th, 1969, Josephine Margaret Storey, MBE. *Educ:* Malvern Coll. St Thomas's Hosp., 1933-39; RAMC, 1939-45; St Thomas's Hosp., 1945-60, Registrar, Senior Lecturer, Reader. MRCP 1946, MD 1949, FRCP 1958. Pres. Internat. Soc. of Nephrology, 1969-. *Publications:* The Kidney: An Outline of Normal and Abnormal Structure and Function, 1967. Papers in various scientific journals. *Recreations:* normal and scything. *Address:* 9 Dungarvan Avenue, Barnes, SW15. *T:* 01-878 3130.

**de WATTEVILLE, John Edward,** CBE 1946; JP; *b* 26 Jan. 1892; *s* of Walter de Watteville, MD, Kingussie; *m* 1922, Alexis Charlotte Margaret, *d* of Charles Bishopp, London; two *d* (and one *s* killed in action 1945). *Educ:* Merchiston Castle; Edinburgh Univ. First Class Hons Classics, 1915. Served European War, 1914-18, Cameron Highlanders (Lieut), RFC and RAF (Flying Officer), 1915-19, wounded in France, 1917. Asst Principal, Scottish Office, 1919; Principal, 1921; Asst Sec., 1931; Under-Sec. (Scottish Home Dept), 1946; Dep. Sec., 1948; Sec. of Commissions for Scotland, 1953-66. JP City of Edinburgh. Croix de Guerre with Palm, 1917. *Address:* 12 Murrayfield Drive, Edinburgh EH12 6EB. *T:* 031-337 6674.

**DEWDNEY, Duncan Alexander Cox,** CBE 1968; Executive Director, Rio Tinto Zinc Corporation, since 1968; Chairman: RTZ Britain, since 1969; Anglesey Aluminium, since 1968; *b* 22 Oct. 1911; *o s* of late Claude Felix Dewdney and of Annie Ross Cox; *m* 1935, Ann, *d* of Walter Riley and Emily Sterratt; two *d*. *Educ:* Bromgrove Sch., Worcs; University of Birmingham (BSc Hons, Cadman Medallist). Served War of 1939-45; RAF, 1940-45 (Wing Comdr). British Petroleum Co., 1932-36; International Assoc. (Pet. Ind.) Ltd, 1936-40; Research Man., Esso Development Co., 1945-51; joined Esso Petroleum Co., 1951; Dir, 1957; Man. Dir, 1963-67; Vice-Chm., 1968. Seconded to NBPI as Jt Dep. Chm., 1965-66, part-time Mem. Bd, 1967-69. Chm., Irish Refining Co. Ltd, 1958-65; Dir, Esso Chemicals SA, 1964. Chm., National Economic Devt Cttee for the Mechanical Engrg Industry, 1964-68. Legion of Merit, 1945. *Recreations:* reading, riding, repose. *Address:* Salters, Harestock, Winchester, Hants. *T:* Winchester 2034. *Club:* Travellers'.

**de WET, Dr Carel;** Minister of Mines and Health, Government of South Africa, since 1967; *b* Memel, OFS, S Africa, 25 May 1924; *g s* of Gen. Christian de Wet; *m* 1949, Rina Maas, BA; one *s* three *d*. *Educ:* Vrede High Sch., OFS; Pretoria Univ. (BSc); University of Witwatersrand (MB, BCh). Served at Nat. Hosp., Bloemfontein; subseq. practised medicine at Boksburg, Transvaal, at Winburg, OFS, and, from 1948, at Vanderbijlpark, Transvaal. Mayor of Vanderbijlpark, 1950-52; MP for Vanderbijlpark, 1953-64, when he was Mem. various Parly and Nat. Party Cttees; South African Ambassador to the Court of St James's, 1964-67. *Recreations:* golf, rugby, cricket. *Address:* 12 Bryntirion, Pretoria, S Africa. *Clubs:* Travellers', Royal Automobile, Devonshire, Hurlingham, Wentworth; Here XVII (Cape Town), Constantia (Pretoria), Club RSA (Johannesburg).

**DEWEY, Sir Anthony Hugh,** 3rd Bt, *cr* 1917; JP; *b* 31 July 1921; *s* of late Major Hugh Grahame Dewey, MC (*e s* of 2nd Bt), and of Marjorie Florence Isobell (who *m* 2nd, 1940, Sir Robert Bell, KCSI; he died 1953), *d* of Lieut-Col Alexander Hugh Dobbs; *S* grandfather, 1948; *m* 1949, Sylvia, *d* of late Dr J. R. MacMahon, Branksome Manor, Bournemouth; two *s* three *d*. *Heir:* *s* Rupert Grahame Dewey, *b* 29 March 1953. *Address:* Silton Lodge, Gillingham, Dorset. *T:* Bourton 324. *Club:* Army and Navy.

**DEWEY, Cyril Marston;** retired, 1969; Director and Deputy General Manager, Anchor Line Ltd, 1956-69; a Director, Walter Runciman & Co. Ltd, 1958-69; Shipping Adviser to Australian Commonwealth Government, 1949-51; *b* 28 Oct. 1907; *s* of late Marston Dewey and Lucie Cazaly; *m* 1935, Alicia P. Maldonado; two *d*. *Educ:* Streatham Grammar Sch. Asst Manager: Blue Star Line, Buenos Aires, 1935-45; Blue Star Line Ltd, London, 1946-49; Gen. Manager, Australian Shipping Board, 1951-55. *Recreation:* golf. *Address:* c/o Barclays Bank Ltd, 122 Leadenhall Street, EC3.

**DEWEY, Thomas Edmund;** Partner, Dewey, Ballantine, Bushby, Palmer and Wood, since 1955; *b* 24 March 1902; *s* of George Martin Dewey and Annie Thomas; *m* 1928, Frances E. Hutt (*d* 1970); two *s*. *Educ:* Univ of Michigan (AB 1923); Columbia Univ., New York (LLB 1925). Admitted to New York Bar, 1926; Chief Asst US Attorney, Southern District of NY, 1931-33; US Attorney, 1933; private practice, 1934-35; Counsel Assoc. of Bar for removal of Municipal Court Judge, 1934; Special Asst Attorney-Gen. of US in special matters, 1934-45; Special Prosecutor Investigation of Organised Crime, New York, 1935-37; District Attorney, New York County, 1938-41; Governor of New York, 1942-54. Republican candidate for Presidency of US, 1944, 1948. Trustee of various charities. Holds numerous honorary degrees. *Publications:* Case Against the New Deal, 1940; Journey to the Far Pacific, 1952; Thomas E. Dewey on the Two Party System; contributor to magazines. *Address:* 141 East 72nd Street, New York, USA; Pawling, NY, USA. *Clubs:* Recess, Downtown, Links, Blindbrook, Indian Creek, City Mid Day, Augusta National, Quaker Hill (USA).

**DEWHURST, Comdr Ronald Hugh,** DSO 1940; RN retired; *b* 10 Oct. 1905; *s* of late Robert Paget Dewhurst, ICS, and late Florence Frances Maud Dewhurst; *m* 1928, Torquilla Macleod Lawrence (*d* 1953); one *s* one *d*; *m* 1954, Marion Isabel Dahm; one *d*. *Educ:* Abberley Hall; Osborne; Dartmouth. Joined Royal Navy, 1919; served in submarines, 1927-53; commanded HM submarines H. 33, Seahorse, and Rorqual (DSO and two Bars); Amphion, Taciturn, and RN Detention Quarters, 1953-55; retired to New Zealand, 1955. *Recreation:* country life. *Address:* Kerikeri, Bay of Islands, NZ.

**DEWING, Maj.-Gen. Maurice Nelson,** CB 1950; CBE 1944; DSO 1943; MC 1918; late Royal Artillery; *b* 11 Nov. 1896; *s* of late Rev. R. S. Dewing, Stowlangtoft, Bury St Edmunds, Suffolk; *m* 1921, Sheila, *d* of late E. R. Hawkins, JP, Squires Hill, Tilford, Surrey; two *s*(and one *s* decd). *Educ:* Malvern Coll.; RMA, Woolwich. Served European War, 1914-18, with RA, 2nd Lieut, 1915; France and Belgium (MC, 1914-15 Star, two medals); War of 1939-45, in Middle East and Italy (despatches, DSO, CBE); Temp. Brigadier, 1942; Lt-Col, 1943; Col, 1946; Maj.-Gen., 1948; GOC 2nd AA Group, 1948-51; retired pay, 1951. *Address:* Tulse Hill, Zeals, Wiltshire.

**DEWING, Maj.-Gen. Richard Henry,** CB 1941; DSO 1917; MC 1915; psc; retired; *b* 15 Jan. 1891; *e surv s* of Rev. R. S. Dewing and Dora, *d* of R. J. Pettiward, of Finborough Hall, Suffolk; *m* 1920, Helen, *e d* of Lieut-Col A. J. Wogan-Browne, 33rd Cavalry; one *s* (and *e s* killed in action in Libya, 2nd *s* decd, *o d* decd). *Educ:* Haileybury. Commd in RE, 1911; joined 2nd QVO Sappers and Miners, 1914; Capt., 1917; Bt Major, 1919; Major, 1926; Bt Lieut-Col, 1930; Lieut-Col, 1934; Col 1936; Maj.-Gen., 1939; served in Mesopotamia and Persia, 1915-19 (DSO, MC); Peace Service India, 1913-14, 1920-21; GSO 2 Royal Military Coll., Kingston, Canada, 1927-29; OC 54th Field Co., Bulford; GSO2 Southern Command, 1931-33; Imperial Defence Coll., 1934; Gen. Staff Officer, 1st Grade, War Office, 1936-37; Army Instructor Imperial Defence Coll., 1937-39; Dir of Military Operations, 1939-40; Chief of Staff, Far East, 1940-41; Military Mission, Washington, 1942; Chief of Army–RAF Liaison Staff, Australia, 1943-44; SHAEF Mission to Denmark, 1945. Grand Cross Order of Dannebrog (Denmark); Officer Legion of Merit (USA). *Address:* Nigg, Tain, Ross-shire.

**DE WOLF, Vice-Adm. Harry George,** CBE 1946; DSO 1944; DSC 1944; *b* 1903; *s* of late Harry George De Wolf, Bedford, NS; *m* 1931, Gwendolen Fowle, *d* of Thomas St George Gilbert, Somerset, Bermuda; one *s* one *d.* Served War of 1939-45. Asst Chief of Naval Staff, Canada, 1944-47; Sen. Canadian Naval Officer Afloat, 1947-48; Flag Officer, Pacific Coast, 1948-50; Vice-Chief of Naval Staff, 1950-52; Chm. of Canadian Joint Staff Washington, 1953-55; Chief of Naval Staff, Canada, 1956-60, retired. Hon. DSc (M), Royal Military College of Canada, 1966. *Address:* 119 Minto Place, Rockcliffe Park, Ottawa, Ont., Canada; Old Post Office, Somerset, Bermuda.

**de WOLFF, Brig. Charles Esmond,** CB 1945; CBE 1919 (OBE 1919); LLB; *b* 25 Nov. 1893; *s* of C. L. de Wolff; *m* 1920, Ada Marjorie, *d* of Henry Arnold, Hatch End. Served European War, 1914-19 (despatches four times, OBE, CBE, Russian Order of Vladimir); 2nd Lieut Royal Sussex Regiment, 1914; transferred RAOC War of 1939-45 (CB); retd pay, 1946. OStJ 1952. *Clubs:* Army and Navy, Union (Malta).

**DEXTER, Harold,** FRCO; Organist; Professor and Head of General Musicianship Department, Guildhall School of Music and Drama; Organist, St Botolph's, Aldgate; Music Editor, International Music Co. Ltd; *b* 7 Oct. 1920; *s* of F. H. and E. Dexter; *m* 1942, Faith Grainger; one *d. Educ:* Wyggeston Grammar Sch., Leicester; Corpus Christi Coll., Cambridge, 1939-41 and 1946. ARCO 1938; College Organ Scholar; John Stewart of Rannoch Scholar, 1940; FRCO 1940; ARCM 1941. BA, MusB 1942; MA 1946; RCO Choirmaster's Diploma; John Brook Prize, 1946; ADCM, 1948. Royal Navy and RNVR 1941-46. Organist, Louth Parish Church and Music-Master, King Edward VI Grammar Sch., Louth, 1947-49; Organist, Holy Trinity, Leamington Spa, 1949-56; Music Master, Bablake Sch., Coventry, 1952-56; Master of the Music, Southwark Cathedral, 1956-68. FGSM 1962, FRSCM 1964 (Hon. diplomas). *Address:* 20 St Mary's Gardens, SE11. *T:* 01-735 6936.

**de YARBURGH-BATESON,** family name of **Baron Deramore.**

**D'EYNCOURT, Sir (Eustace) Gervais T.;** *see* Tennyson D'Eyncourt.

**DE ZOYSA, Sir Cyril,** Kt 1955; Proctor of the Supreme Court, Justice of the Peace and Unofficial Magistrate; *b* 26 Oct. 1897. *Educ:* Royal College, Ceylon. Gov. Dir, Associated Motorways Group of Cos; Chairman: Sri Lanka Asbestos Products Ltd; Ceylon Synthetic Textiles Ltd; Pearl Textiles Ltd; President: Young Men's Buddhist Assoc.; Ceylon Nat. Assoc. for the Prevention of Tuberculosis; Boy Scouts Assoc.; Insts of the Rubber Industry, Ceylon. Dep. Pres. of the Ceylon Senate, 1952-55, Pres., 1955-62. Pres., Incorporated Law Soc. of Ceylon, 1956-62; Mem., Council of Legal Educn, 1956-. *Recreation:* cricket (Royal College, Colombo, etc). *Address:* Park Flats, Park Street, Colombo 2, Ceylon. *T:* Colombo 22478. *Clubs:* Sinhalese Sports, Kalutara Town (Ceylon).

**de ZULUETA, Sir Philip Francis;** *see* Zulueta.

**D'HARCOURT, Robert;** Légion d'Honneur; Médaille Militaire; University Professor; Member of the French Academy since 1946; *b* 23 Nov. 1881; *m* Ghislaine de Caraman-Chimay; three *s* one *d.* Voluntary service, European War, 1914-18 (twice wounded, Médaille Militaire, Légion d'Honneur). Professor Université Catholique Libre, 1920. *Publications:* works on Schiller and Goethe; contributions to the Revue de Paris, Revue des Deux Mondes. *Address:* 52 Avenue de Saxe, Paris. *T:* Suffren 00.94.

**DHAVAN, Shanti Swarup;** Governor of West Bengal, India, since 1969; *b* 2 July 1905; *m* Shakuntala Kapur, *d* of Malik Basant Lal Kapur; two *s* one *d. Educ:* Punjab Univ.; Emmanuel Coll., Cambridge. BA, 1st Cl. Hons History, Punjab Univ., 1925. Hist. Tripos 1931, Law Tripos 1932, Cambridge Univ.; Pres. Cambridge Union, 1932. Called to the Bar, Middle Temple, 1934; Advocate of High Court, Allahabad, 1937, and Senior Advocate of Supreme Court of India, 1958; Lecturer in Commercial Law, Allahabad Univ., 1940-54; Senior Standing Counsel of Govt of Uttar Pradesh, 1956-58; Judge of Allahabad High Court, 1958-67; High Commissioner in UK, 1968-69. Founder-mem. and Sec., Bernard Shaw Soc., formed 1949. Pres. Indo-Soviet Cultural Soc., Uttar Pradesh Sect., 1965-67. Leader of cultural delegation to Soviet Union, 1966. *Publications:* The Legal system and theory of the State in Ancient India, 1962; Doctrine of sovereignty and colonialism, 1962; Secularism in Indian Jurisprudence, 1964; also papers on Indian Judicial system, UNO and Kashmir, and the Nehru Tradition. *Recreations:* study of Indian jurisprudence, journalism. *Address:* Raj Bhavan, Calcutta, India.

**DHENIN, Air Vice-Marshal Geoffrey Howard,** AFC 1953 and Bar, 1957; GM 1943; QHP 1970; MA, MD, DPH; Deputy Director General Medical Services, RAF, since 1970; *b* 2 April 1918; *s* of Louis Richard Dhenin and Lucy Ellen Dagg; *m* 1946, Claude Andree Evelyn Rabut; two *s* two *d. Educ:* Hereford Cathedral Sch.; St John's Coll., Cambridge; Guy's Hosp., London. Joined RAF; various sqdn and other med. appts, Bomber Comd, 2nd TAF, 1943-45 (despatches 1945); pilot trng, 1945-46; various med. officer pilot appts, 1946-58; Staff Coll., Bracknell, 1958-59; comd Princess Mary's RAF Hosp. Akrotiri, Cyprus, 1960-63; comd RAF Hosp. Ely, 1963-66; PMO Air Support Comd, 1966-68; Dir of Health and Research, RAF, 1968-70. *Recreations:* golf, ski-ing, sub-aqua. *Address:* Ruxbury Lodge, St Ann's Hill, Chertsey, Surrey. *T:* Chertsey 3624. *Club:* Royal Air Force.

**DHRANGADHRA, Maharaja Sriraj of Halvad-, His Highness Shri Shaktimant Jhaladhip Mahamandlesvar Maharana Sriraj Meghrajji III,** KCIE 1947; 45th Ruler (dynastic salute of 13 guns), Head of Jhala-Makhvana Clan and of Shaktimant Order; MP for Jhalwar (Gujarat State), since 1967; *b* 3 March 1923; *s* of HH Maharaja Sriraj Ghanshyamsinhji Saheb, GCIE, KCSI, late Ruler, and HH Maharani Srirajni Anandkunvarba Saheba, Rajmata Saheba; *S* to the Gaddi, 1942, assumed government 1943 on termination of political minority; *m* 1943, Princess Brijrakunvarba Sahiba, *d* of Air Cdre HH Raj-rajeshvar Sarmd-i-Hind Maharajadhiraj Shri Umaidsinhji, GCSI, GCIE, KCVO, Maharaja Sahib of Marwar (Jodhpur); three *s. Educ:* Heath Mount Sch.; Haileybury Coll.; St Joseph's Academy, Dehra Dun. Joined the Shivaji Military Sch., Poona, to train for joining the Indian Military Academy, Dehra Dun; spent nearly a year acquiring administrative experience at Baroda, then at Dhrangadhra; philosophy course, Christ Church, Oxford, 1952-54; took Diploma in Social Anthropology, 1954-55; research in Indian Sociology, 1955-58 (BLitt Oxon.). FRAS, FRAI; Associate, Royal Historical Soc. Mem. Standing Cttee of Chamber of Princes, 1945; pursued active policy of social and economic reform; was prime mover in Confederation of States scheme, 1945; first state in Saurashtra to accept participation in Constituent Assembly of India; signed Instrument of Accession to India 1947; First Mem. of Presidium of United State of Saurashtra, later Vice-Pres. Perm. Pres., Girassia Educ. Trust; Pres., Marwar Regency Council, 1965-68; and of Governing Council, Rajkumar Coll., Rajkot, 1966-; Chm. Board of Rulers, Saurashtra States Conf., 1966-. Mem. Gujarat Legislative Assembly (from Dhrangadhra), Feb.-March 1967, resigned. *Heir: s* Tikaraj Saheb of Halvad-Dhrangadhra, Namdar Jhalavrit Maharajkumar Shri Sodhsalji, *cr* Tikaraj (Yuvaraj), 1961, *b* 22 March 1944. *Address:* Ajitniwas Palace, Dhrangadhra, Jhalawar, Gujarat State, India; Dhrangadhra House, Poona 16, India; A/6 Rashmi, Carmichael Road, Bombay 26, India; 3 Tyagaraja Marg, New Delhi 11, India.

**DIAMAND, Peter;** Director, Edinburgh International Festival, since 1965; Artistic Adviser, Holland Festival; *b* 1913; *m* 1947, Maria Curcio, Italian pianist. *Educ:* Schiller-Realgymnasium, Berlin; Berlin Univ. Studied Law and Journalism in Berlin. Left Germany, 1933; became Private Sec. to Artur Schnabel, pianist. Personal Asst to Dir of Netherlands Opera, Amsterdam, 1946, subsequently Artistic Adviser until 1965; Gen. Manager of Holland Festival, 1948-65. Mem. Board of Netherlands Chamber Orchestra, 1955-. Knight, Order of Oranje Nassau, Holland, 1959; Grosses Ehrenzeichen fuer Verdienste, Austria, 1964; Medal of Merit, Czechoslovakia, 1966. *Address:* 29 St James's Street, SW1. *T:* 01-839 2611. *Club:* Arts (Edinburgh).

**DIAMOND,** family name of **Baron Diamond.**

**DIAMOND,** Baron *cr* 1970 (Life Peer), of the City of Gloucester; **John Diamond,** PC 1965; *b* 30 April 1907; *s* of Henrietta and Rev. S. Diamond, Leeds; *m*; two *s* two *d*. *Educ:* Leeds Grammar Sch. Qualified as Chartered Accountant, 1931, and commenced practice as John Diamond & Co. MP (Lab) Blackley Div. of Manchester, 1945-51, Gloucester, 1957-70; Chief Secretary to the Treasury, 1964-70 (in the Cabinet, 1968-70); formerly PPS to Minister of Works. Chm. of Finance Cttee, Gen. Nursing Council, 1947-53; Dir of Sadler's Wells Trust Ltd, 1957-64; Hon. Treas., Fabian Soc., 1950-64. *Recreation:* music. *Address:* Flat 4, 15 Greycoat Place, SW1. *T:* 01-799 2573.

**DIAMOND, Arthur Sigismund,** MM 1918; Master of the Supreme Court, Queen's Bench Division, 1952-59; *b* 23 Dec. 1897; *s* of Rev. S. and Mrs Diamond, Leeds; *m* 1st, 1928, Gladys Elkah (*d* 1946), *d* of Edward Lumbrozo Mocatta: one *s* two *d*; 2nd, 1952, Sybil Grace, *d* of Edward Lumbrozo Mocatta. *Educ:* Leeds Grammar Sch.; Trinity Coll., Cambridge (MA, LLD). Called to the Bar, 1921. *Publications:* The Law of Master and Servant, 1st edn 1932; Primitive Law, 1st edn 1935; The Evolution of Law and Order, 1951; The History and Origin of Language, 1959. FRAI. *Recreation:* gardening. *Address:* 9 Bracknell Gardens, NW3. *T:* 01-435 4201.

**DIAMOND, George Clifford,** OBE 1955; MA; Head Master, Cardiff High School for Boys, retired 1966; *b* 27 Nov. 1902; *m*; two *s*. *Educ:* Cardiff High Sch.; The Leys Sch., Cambridge; Queen's Coll., Cambridge (Scholar). English Tripos, Class I, History Tripos, Part II Class II. Asst Master, Mill Hill Junior Sch., 1926-27; Senior English Master, Leys Sch., 1927-34. Pres., Welsh Secondary Schools' Assoc., 1957. *Address:* Flat 9A, The Cathedral Green, Llandaff, Glamorgan.

**DIAMOND, Prof. Jack,** CBE 1969; Whitworth Scholar, MSc (Cambridge and Manchester); FCGI; FIMechE; MIMarE; Beyer Professor of Mechanical Engineering, Manchester University, since 1953; Pro-Vice-Chancellor, since 1970; Member: University Grants Committee, since 1965; National Research Development Corporation, since 1966; *b* 22 June 1912; *s* of late Alfred John Diamond and Jessie M. Kitchingham; *m* 1943, Iris Evelyn Purvis; three *d*. *Educ:* Chatham Technical Sch.; Royal Dockyard School, Chatham; City and Guilds Coll., London; St John's Coll., Cambridge. Engineering apprenticeship, HM Dockyard, Chatham, 1928-32; Whitworth Scholar, 1932; BSc, ACGI, Wh. Sch. (sen.), 1935. Research in Heat Transfer, University Eng. labs and St John's, Cambridge, 1935-37; MSc 1937; Univ. Demonstrator in Engineering, Cambridge, 1937-39. RN (temp. Engr Officer), 1939-44. RN Scientific Service on loan to Ministry of Supply in Canada and at AERE, Harwell, 1944-53. Member: Governing Board of Nat. Inst. for Research in Nuclear Science, 1957-60; Council, IMechE, 1958- (Vice-Pres. 1967); Pres., Section B, British Acad., 1970. FCGI 1968. *Publications:* various, in engineering publications. *Address:* The University, Manchester 13. *T:* 061-273 3333. *Clubs:* Athenæum; RNVR.

**DIBDEN, Commissioner Edgar;** Chief of the Staff (Second-in-Command) of The Salvation Army, 1953-57; *b* 4 Dec. 1888; *s* of Henry and Frances Dibden; *m* 1914, Helena Bennett; one *s*. *Educ:* Grammar Sch.; The Salvation Army Training Coll., London. Salvation Army Officer, 1910. Formerly Vice-Chm. Salvation Army Trustee Co. Vice-President: Salvation Army Assurance Soc. Ltd; Reliance Bank Ltd; Salvation Army Fire Insurance Corp. Ltd; Salvationist Publishing & Supplies Ltd. Has held important administrative and financial positions in The Salvation Army; formerly: ADC to Gen. George Carpenter; Chancellor of the Exchequer of The Salvation Army. *Address:* 52 Village Way, Beckenham, Kent. *T:* Beckenham 3215.

**DIBLE, James Henry,** LLD; MB, ChB (Glasgow); FRCP; FCPath; late Director, Department of Pathology, British Post-Graduate Medical School, 1937-57; Professor Emeritus, London University, 1955; *s* of Samuel Dible, Southampton, and Ellen Bell, Itchen; *m* Marjorie Yeo, *d* of S. J. Allen, Strines, Derbyshire; two *s* one *d*. *Educ:* King Edward VI School, Southampton; Glasgow Univ.; Hons graduate in medicine, 1912. Lieut RAMC, 1914 (1914-15 star); Capt. RAMC, 1915; Commanded No. 7 Mobile Laboratory, 1915-18, in French and Italian theatres of War (Czecho-Slovak Military Medal, 1st Class). George Holt Prof. of Pathology, Liverpool Univ., 1929-37; late Pres. Institute of Medical Laboratory Technology and Sims Woodhead Medallist; Humphrey Davy Rolleston Lecturer, RCP; Pres., Internat. Soc. of Geographical Pathology, 1961-63. Hon. Fellow: Royal Soc. of Medicine, 1962; Coll. of Pathology, 1967. Hon. LLD Glasgow, 1954. *Publications:* Recent Advances in Bacteriology, 3rd edn 1951 (with J. D. Maclennan); Pathology, 3rd edn 1950; Peripheral Vascular Disorders (with others),

1956; The Pathology of Limb Ischaemia, 1967; various papers in scientific and medical journals. *Address:* Nettleton House, Gerrard's Cross, Bucks. *T:* Gerrard's Cross 82692.

**DIBLE, James Kenneth Victor;** *b* 24 May 1890; *y s* of late William and Margaret Anne Dible, Bitterne Park, Southampton; *m* 1st, 1914, Muriel McQuade (decd); 2nd, Mabel Louise, *widow* of Rev. A. H. Hildesley, KIH (1st Class), MA. *Educ:* Haileybury Coll.; RMC Camberley. Entered Army 1909; retd, 1919, on appointment to HM Consular Service; Probationer Vice-Consul at Algiers, 1919; Vice-Consul, 1921; Acting Consul-Gen. there, 1921-22; transferred to Strasbourg, 1922; Acting Consul-Gen. there in 1922, and also in each year from 1924 to 1927; in charge of Vice-Consulate at Lima, 1927; definitely transferred there, 1928; Acting Consul at Callao, 1928; Consul at Lima, 1928; acted as Chargé d'Affaires in 1929; transferred to Lille, 1930, and to Oporto, 1936; Consul-Gen. at Amsterdam, 1938; transferred to Bordeaux, 1939; seconded to Home Office, 1940-41; to Board of Trade, 1942-44; promoted Consul-Gen., attached Supreme Headquarters, Allied Expeditionary Force (with rank of Maj.-Gen.), 1944-45; Consul-Gen. at Valparaiso, 1945-50, retired 1950. *Address:* The Cottage, Buckden, Huntingdon PE18 9TF. *T:* Buckden 347.

**DIBLE, William Cuthbert,** CIE 1938; late ICS; *b* 18 June 1886; *s* of William Dible, Southampton; *m* 1926, Florence H. B. Johnson (*d* 1948), Culpepper, Va, USA; *m* 1949, Dorothy Lings, Didsbury, Lancs. *Educ:* Charterhouse; Corpus Christi Coll., Oxford. Entered ICS 1910, as Asst Magistrate and Collector, United Provinces; served as Magistrate and Collector; Divisional Commissioner, 1934-42; Mem. Board of Revenue, United Provinces, India, 1942-45; Chm., Road-Lands Enquiry Cttee, War Transport Dept, Government of India; retired, 1946. *Address:* Cotton Wood, East Cliff, Bournemouth, Hants. *T:* Bournemouth 23352.

**DICK, Alick Sydney;** industrial consultant; *b* 20 June 1916; *s* of Dr W. Dick, Chichester, Sussex; *m* 1940, Betty Eileen Melinda Hill; three *s*. *Educ:* Chichester High Sch.; Dean Close, Cheltenham. Managing Dir, Standard Triumph International Ltd, Coventry, 1954-61. Pres. of Soc. of Motor Manufacturers and Traders, 1957. Governor: University of Birmingham, 1959; Coll. of Aeronautics, Cranfield, 1960-63. Benjamin Franklin Medal (RSA), 1961. Governor, Dean Close Sch., Cheltenham, 1964. *Recreations:* tennis, boats. *Address:* The Old Farm House, Hill Wootton, Warwicks. *T:* Kenilworth 54416.

**DICK, Prof. George (Williamson Auchinvole),** MD (Edinburgh), DSc (Edinburgh), FRCPE, FRCP, FRCPath, MPH (Johns Hopkins); Bland-Sutton Professor of Pathology, Middlesex Hospital Medical School, since 1966; *b* 14 Aug. 1914; *s* of Rev. David Auchinvole Dick and Blanche Hay Spence; *m* 1941, Brenda Marian Cook; two *s* two *d*. *Educ:* Royal High School, Edinburgh; Univ. of Edinburgh; Johns Hopkins Univ., Baltimore, Md. BSc (1st Class Hons Path.) 1939; MD (Gold Medal) 1949. Asst Pathologist, Royal Infirmary, Edinburgh, 1939-40; Pathologist, RAMC, 1940-46 (Lt-Col); Pathologist, Colonial Med. Research Service, 1946-51; Rockefeller Foundation Fellow (International Health Div.), 1947-48; Research Fellow, Johns Hopkins Univ., 1948-49; Scientific Staff, MRC, 1951-54; Prof. of Microbiology, Queen's Univ., Belfast, 1955-65. Pres., Inst. of Medical Technology; Member: Jt Cttee on vaccination and immunisation; Central and Scottish Health Svcs Councils. FIBiol; Fellow, Inst. of Med. Laboratory Technology. Singapore Gold Medal, 1952 and 1958. *Publications:* papers on yellow fever and other arbor viruses, encephalitis, poliomyelitis, hepatitis, multiple sclerosis, smallpox vaccine and poliomyelitis and combined vaccines, etc in Jl Immunol.; Tr. Royal Society Trop. Med. Hyg.; Br. Jl Exp. Path.; Jl Path. and Bact.; BMJ; Lancet, etc. *Recreations:* gardening, painting. *Address:* The Middlesex Hospital Medical School, Mortimer Street, W1. *Clubs:* Athenæum, Royal Commonwealth Society.
*See also J. A. Dick.*

**DICK, James Brownlee,** MA, BSc, FInstP; Director, Building Research Station, since 1969; *b* 19 July 1919; *s* of James Brownlee Dick and Matilda Forrest; *m* 1944, Audrey Moira Shinn; two *s*. *Educ:* Wishaw High Sch.; Glasgow Univ. Royal Naval Scientific Service, 1940. Building Research Station: Physics Div., 1947; Head of User Requirements Div., 1960; Head of Production Div., 1963; Asst Dir, 1964; Dep. Dir., 1969. *Publications:* various papers in professional and scientific jls. *Recreations:* reading, gardening, golf. *Address:* 4 Murray Road, Berkhamsted, Herts. *T:* Berkhamsted 2580.

**DICK, John Alexander,** MC 1944; QC (Scotland) 1963; Sheriff Substitute of the Lothians at Edinburgh, since 1969; *b* 1 Jan. 1920; *y s* of Rev. David Auchinvole Dick and Blanche Hay Spence; *m* 1951, Rosemary Benzie Sutherland; no *c*. *Educ:* Waid Academy, Anstruther; University of Edinburgh. Under-graduate, 1937; enlisted in London Scottish, 1940; commissioned Royal Scots, 1942; Italy, 1944; Palestine, 1945-46; released 1946, hon. rank of Major. MA (1st Cl. Hons Economics) 1947, LLB (with distinction) 1949, Univ. of Edinburgh. Called to Scots Bar, 1949; Lecturer in Public Law, Univ. of Edinburgh, 1953-60; Junior Counsel in Scotland to HM Commissioners of Customs and Excise, 1956-63. *Recreations:* golf, hill-walking, photography. *Address:* 66 Northumberland Street, Edinburgh 3. *T:* 031-556 6081. *Club:* Royal Scots (Edinburgh).
*See also Prof. George Dick.*

**DICK, John Kenneth,** FCA, FRSA; Chairman and Managing Director, Mitchell Cotts Group Ltd; *b* 5 April 1913; *s* of John Dick and Beatrice May Dick (*née* Chitty); *m* 1942, Pamela Madge, 3rd *d* of late Maurice Salmon and Katie Salmon (*née* Joseph); two *s* (and one *s* decd). *Educ:* Sedbergh. Qual. with Mann Judd & Co., Chartered Accountants, 1936; Partner, Mann Judd & Co., 1947; Mitchell Cotts Group Ltd: Jt Man. Dir, 1957; Sole Man. Dir, 1959; Dep. Chm., 1964; Chm., 1966. Mem., Commonwealth Devt Corp., 1967; Gov., City of London Soc.; Mem., British Nat. Export Cttee, 1968; Chm., Cttee for Middle East Trade, 1968; a Vice-Pres., Middle East Assoc., 1970. *Recreation:* golf. *Address:* Langleys, Queens Drive, Oxshott, Surrey. *T:* Oxshott 2409, (office) 01-283 1234. *Clubs:* Caledonian, City of London; Rand (Johannesburg).

**DICK, Commodore John Mathew,** CB 1955; CBE 1945; VRD; RNVR, retired; Solicitor to Secretary of State for Scotland, 1946-64 (and in Scotland to Treasury); *b* 2 Aug. 1899; *s* of late Mathew Dick, Campbeltown, Argyll, and Margaret Barr; *m* 1930, Anne Moir (*d* 1959), *d* of late Ralph Hill Stewart, Edinburgh; one *s*. *Educ:* Campbeltown Gram. Sch.; Edinburgh Academy. Entered Royal Naval Volunteer Reserve, 1917; served in Mediterranean and Grand Fleet, 1917-19 (despatches, Order of Crown of Roumania); Lieut RNVR 1924;

Comdr 1935 (commanded Edinburgh RNVR 1927-39); Capt. 1940 (Coastal Forces and Admiralty); RNVR ADC to the King, 1943-45; retired list, 1946. *Address:* 35 Dick Place, Edinburgh. *Club:* New (Edinburgh).

**DICK, Rear-Adm. Royer Mylius,** CB 1951; CBE 1943; DSC 1918; Commissioner-in-Chief, St John Ambulance Brigade, 1962-67; *b* 14 Oct. 1897; *s* of Louis Henry Mylius Dick and Edith Alice Guy; *m* 1928, Agnes Mary Harben; one *d* (one *s* decd); *m* 1955, Vera, *widow* of Col Bertram Pott. *Educ:* RN Colls, Osborne and Dartmouth. Midshipman, 1914; at sea, 1914-18 (DSC); Lieut, 1918; Comdr, 1933; Capt, 1940; Commodore 1st cl. 1942; Rear-Adm. 1949. Dep. Chief of Staff, Mediterranean Station, 1940-42; British Admty Delegn to Washington, 1942; Chief of Staff, Mediterranean Stn, 1942-44 (despatches twice, CBE); HMS Belfast, 1944-46; Dir Tactical and Staff Duties, Admiralty, 1947-48; Chief of Staff to Flag Officer, Western Europe, 1948-50; Flag Officer, Training Sqdn, 1951-52; Standing Group Liaison Officer to North Atlantic Council, 1952-55; Vice-Adm. Acting, 1953; retired list, 1955. Dep. Comr-in-Chief, SJAB, 1957-62. Dep. Chm., Horticultural Marketing Council, 1960-63; Chm., Royal United Service Institution, 1965-67. KStJ 1961; Bailiff Grand Cross, Order of Hosp. of St John of Jerusalem, 1967. Officer Legion of Merit (US), 1943; Officer Legion of Honour, 1943; Croix de Guerre avec palme, 1946; Naval ADC to the King, 1949. *Clubs:* United Service, Royal Automobile.

**DICK-LAUDER, Sir George;** *see* Lauder.

**DICKENS, Prof. Arthur Geoffrey,** FBA 1966; Director, Institute of Historical Research and Professor of History in the University of London, since 1967; *b* 6 July 1910; *er s* of Arthur James Dickens and Gertrude Helen Dickens (*née* Grasby), both of Hull, Yorks; *m* 1936, Molly, *er d* of Walter Bygott; two *s*. *Educ:* Hymers Coll., Hull; Magdalen Coll., Oxford. Demy, 1929-32, Senior Demy, 1932-33, of Magdalen Coll.; BA with 1st Class Hons in Mod. Hist., 1932; MA 1936. Fellow and Tutor of Keble Coll., Oxford, 1933-49; Oxford Univ. Lecturer in Sixteenth Century English History, 1939-49. Served in RA, 1940-45; demobilised as Staff Capt. G. F. Grant Prof. of History, Univ. of Hull, 1949-62; Dep. Principal and Dean of Faculty of Arts, 1950-53; Pro-Vice-Chancellor, 1959-62; Prof. of History, King's Coll., Univ. of London, 1962-67. Pres., Ecclesiastical History Soc., 1966-68. Member: Advisory Council on Public Records, 1968-; Adv. Council on Export of Works of Art; Records Cttee, Essex CC, 1965-. Chm., Victoria History of the Counties of England, 1967-68. Sec., British Nat. Cttee of Historical Sciences, 1967-; Foreign Sec., British Acad., 1969-; Vice-Pres., Royal Historical Soc., 1969-. Editor, Bulletin of the Inst. of Historical Research, 1967-. Visiting Prof., Univ. of Rochester, NY, 1953-54; Birkbeck Lectr, Trinity Coll., Cambridge, 1969-70. Fellow, Folger Library, Washington, DC, 1954. FRHistS 1947; FSA 1962. DLit London, 1965. *Publications:* Lübeck Diary, 1947; The Register of Butley Priory, 1951; The East Riding of Yorkshire, 1954; Lollards and Protestants, 1959; Thomas Cromwell, 1959; Tudor Treatises, 1960; Clifford Letters, 1962; The English Reformation, 1964; Reformation and Society in 16th Century Europe, 1966; Martin Luther and the Reformation, 1967; The Counter-Reformation, 1968; research articles in: English Historical Review, Church Quarterly Review, Yorkshire Archæological Jl, Cambridge Antiquarian Jl, Bodleian Library Record, Archiv. für Reformationsgeschichte; Britain and the Netherlands, Victoria County History, York, etc. *Recreations:* travel, collecting pictures. *Address:* 26 Grange Road, Highgate, N6. *Club:* Athenæum.

**DICKENS, Frank,** FRS 1946; MA Cambridge, DSc, PhD London; DIC; FIBiol.; Consultant to the Tobacco Research Council, since 1969; *b* 1899; *s* of late John Dickens and Elizabeth Dickens, Northampton; *m* 1925, Molly, *o d* of late A. W. and Norah Jelleyman, Northampton; two *d*. *Educ:* Northampton Grammar Sch.; Magdalene Coll., Cambridge (Scholar). Res. in Organic Chemistry at Imperial Coll. of Sciences, 1921-23; Lectr in Biochemistry, Middlesex Hospital Medical Sch., whole-time worker for MRC, 1929; Mem. Scientific Staff, MRC, 1931; Research Dir North of England Council of British Empire Cancer Campaign, 1933-46; Philip Hill Professor of Experimental Biochemistry, Middlesex Hosp. Med. Sch., 1946-67, now Emeritus; Dir, Tobacco Research Council Labs, Harrogate, 1967-69. Research for Royal Naval Personnel Cttee of MRC, Nat. Inst. for Medical Research, 1943-44. An Editor of Biochemical Journal, 1937-47; Chm., Biochemical Soc., 1950. Mem. Scientific Advisory Cttee of the British Empire Cancer Campaign. Chm., British Nat. Cttee for Biochemistry; Mem. Internat. Relations Cttee of Royal Society, 1964-66. Hon. Fellow: King's Coll. (University of Newcastle); Leeds Univ. *Publications:* Chemical and Physiological Properties of the Internal Secretions (with E. C. Dodds); translation of the Metabolism of Tumours (by O. Warburg); ed, Oxygen in the Animal Organism (with E. Neil); Carbohydrate Metabolism and its Disorders (with P. J. Randle and W. J. Whelan); numerous scientific papers mainly in Biochemical Jl. *Recreations:* fishing, photography. *Address:* 15 Hazelhurst Crescent, Findon Valley, Worthing, Sussex. *T:* Findon 2022.

**DICKENS, James McCulloch York;** Assistant Director of Manpower Planning, National Freight Corporation, since 1970; *b* 4 April 1931; *e s* of A. Y. Dickens and I. Dickens (*née* McCulloch); *m* 1st, 1955, M. J. Grieve (marr. diss. 1965); 2nd, 1969, Mrs Carolyn Casey. *Educ:* Shawlands Academy, Glasgow; Newbattle Abbey Coll., Dalkeith, Midlothian; Ruskin Coll. and St Catherine's Coll., Oxford. Administrative Asst, National Coal Board, 1956-58; Industrial Relations Officer, National Coal Board, 1958-65; Management Consultant, 1965-66; MP (Lab) West Lewisham, 1966-70. *Recreations:* music, theatre, the countryside. *Address:* 32 Hall Drive, Sydenham, SE26. *T:* 01-778 8677.

**DICKENS, Sir Louis (Walter),** Kt 1968; DFC 1940; AFC 1938; DL; *b* 28 Sept. 1903; *s* of C. H. Dickens; *m* 1939, Ena Alice Bastable; one *s* one *d*. *Educ:* Clongowes Wood Coll.; Cranwell Cadet Coll. Bomber Sqdn, 1923-27; Flying Trng, 1927; Egypt, 1932; Personnel, Air Min., 1932-35; subseq. Flying Instructor, Cranwell; Bomber Comd, France, 1940; Flying Instructor, Canada, 1941-42; Bomber Comd, 1943-44; SHAEF France, 1944-45; retired, 1947. Chm. Berks CC, 1965-68; DL Berks, 1966. *Recreation:* golf. *Address:* Fairway, Devils Highway, Crowthorne, Berks. *T:* Crowthorne 2668. *Club:* Royal Air Force.

**DICKENS, Monica Enid, (Mrs R. O. Stratton);** *b* 10 May 1915; *d* of late Henry Charles Dickens, Barrister-at-law, and Fanny Runge; *m* 1951, Comdr Roy Olin Stratton, US Navy; two *d*. *Educ:* St Paul's Girls' Sch., Hammersmith.

*Publications:* One Pair of Hands, 1939; Mariana, 1940; One Pair of Feet, 1942; The Fancy, 1943; Thursday Afternoons, 1945; The Happy Prisoner, 1946; Joy and Josephine, 1948; Flowers on the Grass, 1949; My Turn to Make the Tea, 1951; No More Meadows, 1953; The Winds of Heaven, 1955; The Angel in the Corner, 1956; Man Overboard, 1958; The Heart of London, 1961; Cobbler's Dream, 1963; Kate and Emma, 1964; The Room Upstairs, 1966; The Landlord's Daughter, 1968; The Listeners, 1970. *Recreations:* riding, gardening. *Address:* North Falmouth, Mass, USA.

**DICKENS, Air Commodore Thomas Charles,** CB 1955; CBE 1946; AFRAeS; RAF retired; Aero-Engine Division, Rolls Royce, Derby, since 1962; *b* 11 March 1906; *s* of T. J. Dickens; *m* 1936, Joyce Muriel Adamson; two *s*. *Educ:* Hymers Coll. Cadet Coll., Cranwell, 1925-26; Engineering Course, Henlow, 1931-33; Staff Coll., Andover, 1938. Served War of 1939-45 (despatches twice): Advanced Air Striking Force, 1939-40; Chief Engineer, RCAF Eastern Air Command, 1942-43; Bomber Command Stations, 1944-45; Staff of Officers' Advanced Training Sch., 1946-47. SASO N1 (B) Group, 1948-49; Air War Coll., USA, 1950; A/AOA, Fighter Command, 1951; idc 1952; Asst Chief of Staff, Logistics (Aircent), Fontainebleau, 1953-56; General Manager, Hong Kong Aircraft Engineering Co. Ltd, 1956-61. Congressional Silver Life Saving Medal (USA), 1950. *Address:* c/o Lloyds Bank Ltd, 260 Union Street, Torquay, Devon. *Clubs:* Royal Air Force; Hong Kong.

**DICKENSON, Aubrey Fiennes T.;** *see* Trotman-Dickenson.

**DICKENSON, Lt-Col Charles Royal,** CMG 1965; Postmaster-General of Rhodesia, 1964-68, retired; local company director; *b* 17 June 1907; *e s* of Charles Roland and Gertrude Dickenson; *m* 1950, Hendrika Jacoba Margaretha Schippers; two *d*. *Educ:* Shaftesbury Grammar Sch., Dorset. Entered British Post Office as Engineering Apprentice, 1923; British Post Office HQ, 1932-39. Served War in Royal Signals, 1939-45, attaining rank of Lieut-Col. BPO NW Regional HQ as Asst Controller of Telecommunications, 1945-47; BPO HQ, London, 1947-50; loaned to S Rhodesia Govt, 1950-54; Controller of Telecommunications. Ministry of Posts, Federation of Rhodesia and Nyasaland, 1954-57; Regional Controller for N Rhodesia, Fedn of Rhodesia and Nyasaland, 1957-61; Dep. Postmaster-Gen., Rhodesia and Nyasaland, 1961-62; Postmaster-Gen., Rhodesia and Nyasaland, 1962-63. Hon. Mem., S Africa Inst. of Electronic and Radio Engineers (Hon. M(SA) IERE), 1966. *Recreations:* growing orchids, photography. *Address:* 8 Shiri Road, Greendale, Salisbury, Rhodesia. *T:* Salisbury (Rhodesia) 46264.

**DICKEY, Edward Montgomery O'Rorke,** CBE 1952; MA; Hon. FRCA; *b* Belfast, 1894; *s* of Edward O'Rorke Dickey and Emily Monteith; *m* 1922, Eunice Howard; one *s*. *Educ:* Wellington; Trinity Coll., Cambridge. Served War of 1914-18 in RGA. Art Master, Oundle, 1924-26; Prof. of Fine Art and Dir of the King Edward VII Sch. of Art, King's Coll., University of Durham, 1926-31; Staff Inspector for Art, Ministry of Education, 1931-57; first Curator of the Minories, Colchester (Victor Batte-Lay Trust), 1957-62. *Publications:* The Isle of Pheasants, 1926; A Picture Book of British Art, 1931; Industry and Art Education on the Continent (with W. M. Keesey), 1934. *Address:* Little Birchwood, Beverley Avenue, West Mersea, Colchester.

**DICKIE, Rev. Edgar Primrose,** MC; MA, BD (Edinburgh); BA Oxon; DD (Edinburgh); Emeritus Professor of Divinity, St Mary's College, University of St Andrews, since 1967 (Professor, 1935-67, retired); Extra Chaplain to the Queen in Scotland since 1967 (Chaplain, 1956-67, retired); *b* 12 Aug. 1897; *y* and *o surv. s* of William Dickie, editor of Dumfries and Galloway Standard, and Jane Paterson; *m* 1927, Ishbel Graham Holmes, *d* of Andrew Frier Johnston and Magdalene Ross Holmes, Edinburgh. *Educ:* Dumfries Academy; Edinburgh University; Christ Church, Oxford; New Coll., Edinburgh; Marburg; Tübingen. Served with rank of Capt., 3rd and 1/5th KOSB, Palestine, Flanders, France (wounded, MC). MA Edinburgh, First Class Hons in Classics; Vans Dunlop Scholar; BA Oxford, First Class in Literae Humaniores; at New Coll., Edinburgh, Hamilton Scholar; Fullarton Scholar in Hebrew; Tutor in Greek, 1925-26; Hons Diploma; Senior Cunningham Fellow, 1926; Asst Minister, New North Church, Edinburgh; Ordained, 1927; Minister of St Cuthbert's Church, Lockerbie, 1927-33; Minister of St Anne's Church, Corstorphine, Edinburgh, 1933-35; External Examiner in Biblical Criticism, Edinburgh Univ., 1931-34 and 1934-35; in New Testament Greek, New Coll., Edinburgh, 1931-34; in History of Doctrine, Univ. of Manchester, 1939-41; in Ethics, Queen's Univ., Belfast, 1941; in Systematic Theology, Univ. of Aberdeen, 1942; in Theology, Univ. of Glasgow, 1948, Belfast, 1953. Kerr Lectr in 1936-39; Murtle Lectr, Univ. of Aberdeen, 1941; Gen. Supt of work of Church of Scotland in BEF, 1940, and with BLA, 1944-45 (despatches). Capt. St Andrews Univ. Senior Training Corps, 1941; Convener, Church of Scotland Youth Cttee, 1945-50. Founder-mem., Studiorum Novi Testamenti Societas, 1937. Pres. Scottish Sunday School Union, 1955-57; Vice-Pres. Scottish Universities Athletic Club. Governor, St Leonards Sch. Hon. LLD St Andrews, 1969. Hon. Life Mem., Students' Union, St Andrews; Hon. Blue, Athletic Union, St Andrews. Companion of Merit, Order St Lazarus of Jerusalem. *Publications:* Psammyforshort: Rex. Imp.: A Nonsense Story, 1928; The New Divine Order, 1930; translation of Karl Heim's Die Neue Welt Gottes; The Seven Words from the Cross, 1931; Spirit and Truth, 1935; translation of Heim's Das Wesen des Evangelischen Christentums; God Transcendent; translation of Heim's Glaube und Denken (3rd edn); Revelation and Response, 1938; One Year's Talks to Children, 1940; Scottish Life and Character, 1942; A Second Year's Talks to Children, 1943; The Paper Boat, 1943; The Obedience of a Christian Man, 1944; Normandy to Nijmegen, 1946; The Fellowship of Youth, 1947; Mister Bannock: A Nonsense Story, 1947; I Promise (Girl Guides), 1949; It was New to me (Church of Scotland), 1949; God is Light: Studies in Revelation and Personal Conviction, 1953; Thou art the Christ, 1954; A Safe Stronghold, 1955; introductory essay to McLeod Campbell The Nature of the Atonement, 1959; The Unchanging Gospel, 1960; The Father Everlasting, 1965; Remembrance, 1966; occasional articles in Punch, The Scots Magazine, and other periodicals. *Recreations:* hill-walking, winter sports. *Address:* Surma, Hepburn Gardens, St Andrews, Fife. *T:* St Andrews 3617.

**DICKINS, Basil Gordon,** CBE 1952 (OBE 1945); BSc, ARCS, DIC, PhD; Deputy Controller of Guided Weapons, Ministry of Technology, 1966-68; *b* 1 July 1908; *s* of late Basil Dickins; *m* 1935, Molly Aileen (*d* 1969), *d* of late H. Walters Reburn. *Educ:* Royal Coll. of Science,

London. Royal Aircraft Establishment, 1932; Air Min., 1936, later Min. of Aircraft Production; Head of Operational Research Section, HQ Bomber Command, 1941; Asst Scientific Adviser, Air Ministry, 1945; Dir of Tech. Personnel Administration, Min. of Supply, 1948; Dep. Scientific Adviser to Air Ministry, 1952; Dir of Guided Weapons Research and Development, Min. of Supply, 1956; Dir-Gen. of Atomic Weapons, Min. of Supply, 1959; Dir-Gen. of Guided Weapons, Ministry of Aviation, 1962. *Publications:* papers in Proc. Royal Society and Reports and Memoranda of Aeronautical Research Council. *Address:* Hillside, Daddyhole Road, Torquay, Devon.

**DICKINS, Bruce,** MA Cantab; Hon. LittD Manchester; Hon. DLitt Edinburgh; FBA; Elrington and Bosworth Professor of Anglo-Saxon, Cambridge University, Jan. 1946-Sept. 1957, since when Emeritus Professor; Fellow of Corpus Christi College, since 1946; *b* 26 Oct. 1889; *e s* of Henry Everard and Constance Dickins, Nottingham; *m* Mary Geraldine, *e d* of late Sir Herbert J. C. Grierson; one *s* one *d.* *Educ:* Nottingham High Sch.; Magdalene College, Cambridge (Scholar). 2nd Class (Div. 1) History Tripos, Pt 1; 1st Class, Mediæval and Modern Languages Tripos; Allen Scholar. Acted for two years as Censor in War Office; served as 2nd Lieut, Hampshire Regt; Capt. on staff of Leeds Group and Sector, Home Guard, 1940-43; Lecturer, 1919-25, and Reader, 1925-31, in English Language, Edinburgh Univ.; Professor of English Language, Leeds Univ., 1931-45; sometime Donaldson Bye-Fellow for Research of Magdalene Coll., Cambridge; Pres. Yorks Soc. for Celtic Studies, 1936-38; Pres. Viking Soc., 1938-39; Pres. John Mason Neale Soc., 1952-57; Pres. Cambridge Antiquarian Soc., 1953-55. Sandars Reader in Bibliography, 1968-69; Sandars Lectr in Bibliography, 1969. Sir Israel Gollancz Memorial Prize (British Academy), 1955. *Publications:* Runic and Heroic Poems of the Old Teutonic Peoples, 1916, 1968; Robert Henryson, The Testament of Cresseid, 1925; Scots Poems by Robert Fergusson, 1925; The Runic Inscriptions of Maeshowe, 1930; The Dream of the Rood (with Alan S. C. Ross), 1934; The Conflict of Wit and Will, 1937; John Mitchell Kemble and Old English Scholarship, 1940; (jointly) The Place-names of Cumberland, 1950-52; (with R. M. Wilson) Early Middle English Texts, 1951; Henry, First Duke of Lancaster, 1966; (with Alfred Fairbank) The Italic Hand in Tudor Cambridge, 1962; contribs to various linguistic, literary, bibliographical, and archæological jls; Jt Editor, Leeds Studies in English and Kindred Languages, 1932-40; Editor, Yorkshire Celtic Studies, 1938-40; Dir and Gen. Editor, English Place-Name Soc., 1946-51; Pres. Cambridge Bibliographical Soc., 1951-57, and Jt Editor of its Transactions, 1949-68. *Address:* Flat 3, 1 Newnham Walk, Cambridge. *T:* Cambridge 52209.

**DICKINS, Brig. Frederick,** CIE 1936; *b* 25 Nov. 1879; *s* of F. V. Dickins, CB; *m* 1st, 1906, Florence Mackay (*d* 1949); two *s*; 2nd, 1949, Audrey May Adam (*d* 1950). *Educ:* St Paul's Sch.; Scoones's. 2nd Lieut RA 1900; Indian Ordnance Dept, 1906; DADOS 2nd Indian Cavalry Div., France, 1914-16; Chief Ordnance Officer, Aden Field Force, 1918-19 (despatches); ADOS, AHQ, India, 1929; Dir of Ordnance Services, AHQ, India, 1935-36; retired 1936; Non-Intervention Board, Spain (Gibraltar), 1938; HM Consul at Cadiz, 1939; Censorship Dept, Sept. 1939; Min. of Economic Warfare, 1940-41; Schoolmaster, 1943-46. *Address:* c/o National & Grindlays Bank, 13 St James's Square, SW1.

**DICKINSON,** family name of **Baron Dickinson.**

**DICKINSON,** 2nd Baron *cr* 1930, of Painswick; **Richard Clavering Hyett Dickinson;** *b* 2 March 1926; *s* of late Hon. Richard Sebastian Willoughby Dickinson, DSO (*o s* of 1st Baron) and May Southey, *d* of late Charles Lovemore, Melsetter, Cape Province, S Africa; *S* grandfather, 1943; *m* 1957, Margaret Ann, *e d* of Brig. G. R. McMeekan, *qv*; two *s.* *Heir:* *s* Hon. Martin Hyett Dickinson, *b* 30 Jan. 1961. *Address:* Painswick House, Painswick, Glos. *T:* Painswick 3207.

*See also Viscount Davidson.*

**DICKINSON, Arthur Harold,** CMG 1946; OBE 1938; *b* 5 Oct. 1892; *s* of late Walter Dickinson, formerly of Leighton Hall, Caversham, and of Mary Mechan; *m* 1920, Ethel Constance Kitchen (*d* 1961); one *s* one *d.* *Educ:* Bromsgrove Sch. Cadet Colonial Police Service, 1912; served in Straits Settlements; Inspector-Gen. of Police, Straits Settlements, 1939, and in addition Civil Security Officer, Malaya; Prisoner of War in Singapore, Feb. 1942-Aug. 1945; retired Nov. 1946. King's Police Medal, 1928. *Address:* Martins, Maidenhead Court, Berks. *Club:* Royal Automobile.

**DICKINSON, Basil Philip Harriman;** Under Secretary, Ministry of Transport, since 1959; *b* 10 Sept. 1916; *yr s* of F. H. and I. F. Dickinson; *m* 1941, Beryl Farrow; three *s* one *d.* *Educ:* Cheltenham Coll.; Oriel Coll., Oxford. *Address:* 27 York Avenue, Hove 2, Sussex. *T:* Brighton 738966.

**DICKINSON, Rt. Rev. John Hubert,** MA; Vicar of Chollerton since 1959; Hon. Canon in Newcastle Cathedral since 1947; *m* 1937, Frances Victoria, *d* of late Rev. C. F. Thorp; two *d.* *Educ:* Jesus Coll., Oxford; Cuddesdon Coll. Deacon, 1925; Priest, 1926; Curate of St John, Middlesbrough, 1925-29; SPG Missionary, South Tokyo, 1929-31; Asst Bishop of Melanesia, 1931-37; Vicar of Felkirk-with-Brierley, 1937-42; Vicar of Warkworth, 1942-59. *Address:* Chollerton Vicarage, Hexham, Northumberland.

**DICKINSON, Rear-Adm. (retired) Norman Vincent,** CB 1953; DSO 1942, and Bar, 1944; DSC 1920; *b* 29 May 1901; *s* of late Dr Thomas Vincent Dickinson, MD, and Beatrice Frances Evans; *m* 1930, Rosamond Sylvia, *d* of late Vice-Admiral L. W. Braithwaite, CMG; two *s.* *Educ:* RN Colls, Osborne and Dartmouth. Midshipman, HMS Royal Sovereign, 1917-20; Lieut S Africa Station, 1923-25; specialised in Physical Training, 1926; Training Special Entry Cadets, HMS Erebus, 1927; Term Lieut RNC Dartmouth, 1931; 1st Lieut Boys' Training Establishment HMS Ganges, 1934; Comdr, 1936; Asst Dir Physical Training Admiralty, 1937; served War of 1939-45 (despatches thrice); Atlantic Convoys, 1940; Capt., 1942; North Africa landing, 1942; Sicily landing, 1943; Salerno landing, 1943; Sen. Officer Inshore Sqdn, Corsica, 1943; Senior Naval Officer, Northern Adriatic, 1944; Senior Officer 18 Minesweeping Flotilla operating from Southern Ireland, 1945; Head of Naval Branch, Berlin, 1947; HMS Victorious (Training Squadron), 1948; Capt. of Royal Naval Coll., Dartmouth, 1949-51; Rear-Adm., 1951; Flag Officer (Flotillas) Indian Fleet, 1951-53; retired, 1954. Chevalier Légion d'Honneur, 1944; Croix de Guerre with Palm, 1944; Officer, Legion of Merit, 1944. *Recreation:* gardening. *Address:* Dials Close,

Lower Wield, near Alresford, Hants. *T:* Preston Candover 269. *Club:* Special Forces.

**DICKINSON, Patric (Thomas);** poet, playwright and freelance broadcaster; *b* 26 Dec. 1914; *s* of Major A. T. S. Dickinson, 51 Sikhs, FF, IA, and Eileen Constance Kirwan; *m* 1946, Sheila Dunbar Shannon; one *s* one *d. Educ:* St Catharine's Coll., Cambridge (Crabtree Exhibitioner). Asst Schoolmaster, 1936-39. Artists' Rifles, 1939-40. BBC, 1942-48 (Feature and Drama Dept); Acting Poetry Editor, 1945-48. Sometime Gresham Prof. in Rhetoric at the City University. Atlantic Award in Literature, 1948. *Publications:* The Seven Days of Jericho, 1944; Theseus and the Minotaur and Poems, 1946; Stone in the Midst and Poems, 1948; The Sailing Race (poems), 1952; The Scale of Things (poems), 1955; The World I See (poems), 1960; This Cold Universe (poems), 1964; A Round of Golf Courses, 1951; Aristophanes Against War, 1957; The Aeneid of Vergil, 1960; A Durable Fire (play), 1962. Anthologies: Soldiers' Verse, 1945; Byron (selected), 1949; Poems to Remember, 1958; The Good Minute (autobiog.), 1965; Poet's Choice (jt editor), 1967; Selected Poems, 1968; More Than Time (poems), 1970; Aristophanes (translation), vols I and II, 1970. *Recreation:* golf (Cambridge Blue, 1935). *Address:* 38 Church Square, Rye, Sussex. *T:* Rye 2194. *Clubs:* Savile, Rye Golf.

**DICKINSON, Prof. Robert Eric;** Professor of Geography, University of Arizona; formerly Professor of Geography, University of Leeds, 1958, and Research Professor, 1963; *b* 9 Feb. 1905; *m* 1941, Mary Winwood; no *c. Educ:* Upholland Grammar Sch., near Wigan; Leeds University. BA Hons (1st Cl. Geog.), Leeds, 1925; DipEd, Leeds, 1926; MA (Geog.), Leeds, 1928; PhD London, 1932. Asst Lectr in Geography, University Coll., Exeter, 1926-28; University Coll., London: Asst Lectr, 1928-32, Lectr, 1932-41, Reader in Geog., 1941-47; Prof. of Geog., Syracuse Univ., NY, 1947-58. Visiting Prof. at Univs of: California, 1960-61; Washington, 1963; Nebraska, 1963; Kansas State Univ., 1964; Arizona, 1967; Laval, 1968. Rockefeller Fellow, 1931-32 (USA), 1936-37 (Europe); Guggenheim Fellow, 1957-58. *Publications:* Making of Geography, 1932; The German Lebensraum, 1943; The Regions of Germany, 1944; City, Region and Regionalism, 1945; The West European City, 1951; Germany: A General and Regional Geography, 1952; The Population Problem of Southern Italy, 1955; City and Region, 1964; City and Region in Western Europe, 1967; Makers of Modern Geography, 1969. *Address:* Department of Geography, University of Arizona, Tucson, Arizona 85721, USA.

**DICKINSON, Ronald Arthur,** CMG 1964; Under-Secretary, Export Credits Guarantee Department, since Dec. 1965; *b* 7 Nov. 1910; *s* of J. H. Dickinson, JP, Cartmel and Oldham, Lancs; *m* 1939, Helen, *d* of Joseph Severs, Oldham, Lancs. *Educ:* schools and univs. *Recreation:* any sport. *Address:* 86 Regency Lodge, NW3. *T:* 01-722 2655; Export Credits Guarantee Department, 59-67 Gresham Street, EC2. *Club:* Overseas Bankers.

**DICKINSON, Ronald Sigismund Shepherd,** CMG 1967; Civil Aviation Division, Board of Trade, since 1969; *b* 30 March 1906; *o s* of Walter Sigismund Dickinson and Janet (*née* Shepherd); *m* 1932, Vida Evelyn, 4th *d* of Roger Hall and Maud (*née* Seaton); one *d. Educ:* Dulwich Coll.; London Sch. of Economics. AIB 1936. Min. of Aircraft Production, 1941; Principal, 1943; Civil Aviation Dept, Air Min., 1944; Min. of Civil Aviation, 1946; Asst Sec., 1947; Rees-Jeffreys Post-Graduate Research Student, LSE, 1950-51; Civil Air Attaché, British Embassy, Washington, 1952-54; Civil Aviation Adviser to Fedn of W Indies, Trinidad, 1961-62; UK Representative on Council of ICAO, Montreal, 1962-69. 1st Vice-Pres. of Council of ICAO, 1966-67. *Address:* c/o Board of Trade, The Adelphi, John Adam Street, WC2. *Club:* Royal Commonwealth Society.

**DICKINSON, Prof. Thorold (Barron);** Professor of Film in the University of London (Slade School of Fine Arts), since 1967; *b* Bristol, 16 Nov. 1903; *s* of Ven. Charles Henry Dickinson, sometime Archdeacon of Bristol, and Beatrice Vindhya (*née* Thorold); *m* 1929, Irene Joanna Macfadyen, ARIBA, AA Dipl. *Educ:* Clifton Coll.; Keble Coll., Oxford. Entered film industry, 1926; film editor, subseq. film director and script writer. Directed (among others): Gaslight, 1940; The Next of Kin, 1941. Organised Army Kinematograph Service Production Group and produced 17 military training films, 1942-43. Directed Men of Two Worlds, 1944-45; collab. scripts of: Mayor of Casterbridge; Then and Now; directed: The Queen of Spades, 1949; Secret People, 1951; Hill 24 Doesn't Answer, 1953-55. Produced Power Among Men, 1958-59, and many short films for UN. Mem. of Cttee, Nat. Film Archive, 1950-56; Chm., Brit. Film Acad., 1952-53; Mem., Cttee administering Brit. Film Inst. Experimental Fund, 1952-56; Chief, Film Services Office of Public Information, UN, NY, 1956-60; Senior Lecturer in Film, Slade School of Fine Arts, UCL, 1960-67. Consultant to Amer. Film Inst., 1968. Mem. Board, New York Film Council, 1958-60. Pres., International Federation of Film Societies, 1958-66, Hon. Pres., 1966-. *Publications:* (with Catherine de la Roche) Soviet Cinema, 1947; contribs to periodicals: Sight and Sound, Bianco e Nero, Geog. Mag., Soviet Studies. *Recreations:* theatre, film, walking, reading. *Address:* 17 Queensborough Mews, Porchester Terrace, W2. *T:* 01-229 6100; Sheepdrove Cottage, Lambourn, Berks. *T:* Lambourn 393.

**DICKINSON, William Michael,** MBE 1960; publisher; *b* 13 Jan. 1930; *s* of Comdr W. H. Dickinson, RN, retd, and late Ruth Sandeman Betts. *Educ:* St Edward's Sch., Oxford. Army Service, 1948-51; 2/Lieut, Ox. and Bucks LI, Sept. 1948; seconded Somaliland Scouts; Lieut 1950; Colonial Service Devonshire Course, 1951-52; Somaliland Protectorate: Admin. Officer, 1952; Dist. Officer, 1953-54; Asst Sec. (Political), 1955-56; seconded to British Liaison Org., Ethiopia, as Sen. Asst Liaison Officer, 1957-59; Brit. Liaison Officer in charge, 1959; transf. N Rhodesia as Dist Officer, 1960; Dist Comr, 1961; seconded to Foreign Office as HM Consul-Gen., Hargeisa, 1961-63; Principal, External Affairs Section, Office of Prime Minister, N Rhodesia, during 1964; Senior Principal, Ministry of Foreign Affairs, Government of Zambia. *Recreations:* tennis, reading. *Address:* c/o Africa Research Ltd, 1 Parliament Street, Exeter. *T:* Exeter 76190. *Club:* Public Schools.

**DICKSON, Alexander Graeme,** CBE 1967 (MBE 1945); MA Oxon; Hon. Director (Founder), Community Service Volunteers, since 1962; *b* 23 May 1914; *y s* of late Norman Bonnington Dickson and Anne Agnes Higgins, Wimbledon Park; *m* 1951, Mora Agnes Hope Robertson, Moffat, artist and writer. *Educ:* Rugby; New Coll., Oxford. Private Sec. to late Sir Alec Paterson, 1935; editorial staff: Yorkshire Post, 1936-37; Daily Telegraph, 1937-38, Germany; refugee relief, Czechoslovakia, winter 1938-39. Served War of 1939-45: Cameron Highlanders; 1st KAR (Abyssinian

Campaign); E Africa Comd. Displaced Persons Directorate, Berlin, 1946-48; introd Mass Educn, Gold Coast, 1948-49; founded Man O' War Bay Training Centre, Cameroons and Nigeria, 1950-54; Chief Unesco Techn. Assistance Mission, Iraq, 1955-56; refugee relief, Austro-Hungarian frontier, winter 1956-57; founded Voluntary Service Overseas, 1958, and Community Service Volunteers, 1962; Consulted by: US Peace Corps, 1961, 1969; Indian Govt and Hong Kong Govt, 1968; Nigerian Govt, 1969. Hon. LLD Leeds, 1970. *Publications:* (with Mora Dickson) A Community Service Handbook, 1967; School in the Round, 1969; articles on community development and youth service. *Recreations:* identical with workinvolving young people in community service, at home or overseas. *Address:* 19 Blenheim Road, W4. *T:* 01-994 7437.

*See also M. G. Dickson.*

**DICKSON, Arthur Richard Franklin; Hon. Mr Justice Dickson;** Judge of the High Court, Uganda; Judge, High Court of Lagos, Nigeria, 1958-62, retd; *b* 13 Jan. 1913; British subject; *m* 1949, Joanna Maria Margaretha van Baardwyk; four *s. Educ:* Rusea's Secondary Sch. and Cornwall Coll., Jamaica. Called to the Bar, Lincoln's Inn, 1938. Judicial Service. HM Overseas Civil Service: Jamaica, 1941; Magistrate, Turks and Caicos Islands, 1944-47; Asst to Attorney-Gen., and Legal Draftsman, Barbados, 1947-49; Magistrate: British Guiana, 1949-52; Nigeria, 1952-54; Chief Magistrate, Nigeria, 1954; Chief Registrar, High Court, Lagos, 1956. Temp. appointment, Solicitors Dept, GPO London, 1962-63; served Northern Rhodesia (latterly Zambia), 1964-67. *Publication:* Revised Ordinances (1909-1941) Turks and Caicos Islands, 1944. *Recreations:* gardening, walking, swimming, riding. *Address:* The High Court, PO Box 7085, Kampala, Uganda; 31 Prince Charles Drive, Kampala, Uganda; 51 Central Drive, St Albans, Herts. *Clubs:* Royal Commonwealth Society; Kampala.

**DICKSON, Bertram Thomas,** CMG 1960; BA, PhD; *b* Leicester, 20 May 1886; *s* of J. T. Dickson of Leicester; *m* 1910, Florence (decd), *d* of W. Roberts; one *s* one *d. Educ:* Queen's Univ., Kingston, Ontario (BA); Cornell Univ.; McGill Univ., Montreal (PhD). Served European War, 1914-18: Agricultural Officer, 1st British Army, 1917-18; Commandant, 1st British Army Sch. of Agriculture, 1918-19. Professor of Economic Botany, McGill Univ., 1919-26; Prof. of Plant Pathology, McGill Univ., 1926-27; Chief, Division of Plant Industry, CSIRO, Canberra, 1927-51; Delegate, 2nd Session, FAO Conference, Copenhagen, 1946; Mem., UNESCO Arid Zone Advisory Cttee, 1952-57; UN Adviser, Desert Research Institute of Egypt, 1958-59. Pres., Canberra Repertory Soc., 1932-41; Exec. Mem., Australian National Research Council, 1932-47; Pres., Legacy Club, Canberra, 1933; Pres., Australian Institute of Agricultural Science, 1945-46 (Vice-Pres., 1935-39); Chm., Canberra Univ. Coll., 1954-60. Pres., Australian Royal Society, 1957, 1958. *Address:* Ewos Parade, Cronulla, NSW, Australia.

**DICKSON, Bonner William Arthur,** CBE 1953; A Governor of the College of Aeronautics since 1953; *b* 1887; *s* of Francis George Dickson; *m* 1915, Harriet Olive (*d* 1968), *d* of Samuel Turney Johnson; (one *s* decd). Sometime Dir and Gen. Manager, Vickers-Armstrongs Ltd. (Aircraft Section); Acting Prin., Coll. of Aeronautics, Cranfield, July 1954-Sept. 1955. *Address:* 70 Rivermead Court, Hurlingham, SW6. *Clubs:* Royal Aero, Hurlingham.

**DICKSON, Dr David,** CB 1969; Director, W. & R. Chambers Ltd, since 1969; *b* 1 Nov. 1908; *s* of Robert and Elizabeth Dickson, Crieff, Perthshire; *m* 1935, Isabella Sword Grant, *d* of A. P. Grant, Easterhouse, Lanarkshire; one *s*. *Educ:* Morrison's Acad., Crieff; University of Edinburgh. Asst Classics Teacher, Royal High Sch., Edinburgh, 1931-38; Principal Classics Teacher, Alloa Acad., 1938-40; HM Inspector of Schools, 1940; HM Chief Inspector of Schools, 1955; HM Senior Chief Inspector of Schools, Scottish Educn Dept, 1966-69. Governor, Donaldson's School for the Deaf, 1969-. *Recreations:* golf, gardening. *Address:* 7 Albert Place, Stirling. *T:* Stirling 4760.

**DICKSON, Air Vice-Marshal Edward Dalziel,** CB 1953; CBE 1946; RAF (Medical Branch), Retired; MD, FRCSE; Hon. Civilian Consultant in Oto-Laryngology to the Royal Air Force since 1955; *b* 10 Feb. 1895; *s* of late Dr E. D. Dickson, Physician, HBM Embassy, Constantinople; *m* Ethel Sinclair, *d* of J. E. Grey, Pres. Royal College of Veterinary Surgeons, Edinburgh; one *s*. *Educ:* privately; Edinburgh Univ.; London; Paris. MD (Edinburgh) 1951; MB, ChB (Edinburgh) 1918; FRCSE 1922; DLO RCPS Eng. 1925. Served European War, 1914-18, Capt. RAMC; ENT Specialist, 1918-22, Salonika, Serbia, Turkey. Hon. Aural Surg. British Hosp. (82nd Gen.), Constantinople, 1922; late Asst OP Dept, Central London Throat, Nose and Ear Hosp. Joined RAF 1923; Sqdn Ldr 1929; Wing Comdr 1935; Group Capt. 1940; Air Commodore, 1947; Air Vice-Marshal, 1951. KHS, 1948-52; QHS 1952-55. Senior Consultant, RAF, 1951-55. Consultant in Oto-Laryngology, RAF, 1938-55. FRSM (Pres. Section of Otology, 1952-53); Mem. Scottish Oto-Laryngological Soc.; Mem. Otological Sub-Cttee, Flying Personnel Research Cttee, and Mem. Council, British Assoc. of Oto-Laryngologists; Mem. Editorial Board of Excerpta Medica; Chm. Royal National Institute for the Deaf. Pres., IX Internat. Congress in Audiology, London, 1968. Sir William Dalby Prize in Otology, Royal Society of Medicine (jointly); Silver Medal for Distinguished Service (Serbia), 1920; Medal of Merit 1st Class (Czecho-Slovakia), 1946. *Publications:* contrib. to Aviation Oto-Laryngology (jointly), 1947; chapter on intense sound and ultrasound, in Industrial Medicine and Hygiene, Vol. II, 1954; numerous papers and reports on aviation otology and rhinology in learned journals. *Recreations:* gardening, music, conjuring. *Address:* 126 West Heath Road, Hampstead, NW3. *T:* 01-455 4211. *Clubs:* Royal Air Force, Savage; Magic Circle; University Union (Edinburgh).

**DICKSON, Eileen Wadham, (Mrs C. F. Dickson);** *d* of John Edward Latton, Librarian to Inner Temple, and Ethel Letitia Baker; *m* 1931, Charles Frederick Dickson, OBE. *Educ:* Convent of the Sacred Heart, Roehampton; Bruges, Belgium. Served War of 1939-45 with WVS and on Executive Council of Stage Door Canteen. Joined Harper's Bazaar, 1949; Fashion Editor, 1951; Editor, 1953-65. *Recreations:* theatre, reading, racing, gardens. *Address:* 54 Eaton Square, SW1. *T:* 01-235 7676; Grimsdyke, Aldworth, Berks. *T:* Compton 247.

**DICKSON, Dr Gordon Ross;** Farms Director for the Duke of Norfolk, 1958-71; Principal of Royal Agricultural College, Cirencester, from Sept. 1971; *b* 12 Feb. 1932; *s* of T. W. Dickson, Tynemouth; *m* 1956, Dorothy Stobbs; two *s* one *d. Educ:* Tynemouth High Sch.; Durham Univ. BSc (Agric) 1st cl. hons 1953, PhD (Agric) 1958, Dunelm. Tutorial Research

Student, Univ. Sch. of Agric., King's Coll., Newcastle upon Tyne, 1953-56; Asst Farm Dir, Council of King's Coll., Nafferton, Stocksfield-on-Tyne, 1956-58. *Address:* Wepham House, Burpham, Arundel, Sussex. *T:* Arundel 2153; (from Sept. 1971) Bailey Lodge, Royal Agricultural College, Cirencester, Glos. *Club:* Farmers'.

**DICKSON, (Horatio Henry) Lovat;** writer and literary consultant; *b* 30 June 1902; *s* of Gordon Fraser Dickson and Josephine Mary Cunningham; *m* 1934, Marguerite Isabella, *d* of A. B. Brodie, Montreal; one *s. Educ:* Berkhamsted Sch.; University of Alberta (MA). Lecturer in English, Univ. of Alberta, 1927-29; Associate Editor, Fortnightly Review, 1929-32; Editor of Review of Reviews, 1930-34; Managing Dir of Lovat Dickson Ltd (Publishers), 1932-38; Director: Macmillan & Co. (publishers), 1941-64; Pan Books Ltd, 1946-64; Reprint Soc., 1939-64. *Publications:* The Green Leaf, 1938; Half-Breed, The Story of Grey Owl, 1939; Out of the West Land, 1944; Richard Hillary, 1950; two vols of autobiog.: Vol. I, The Ante-Room, 1959; Vol. II, The House of Words, 1963; H. G. Wells, 1969. *Address:* c/o Macmillan & Co. Ltd, 4 Little Essex Street, WC2. *Club:* Garrick.

**DICKSON, Ian Anderson,** WS; Sheriff-Substitute of Lanarkshire, at Hamilton, since Dec. 1961; *b* Edinburgh, 1905; *s* of Robert Anderson Dickson, DDS, and Marie Anne Morris; *m* 1943, Margaret Forbes, *o d* of James John and Annabella Florence Ross, Glenfuir, Falkirk; four *s. Educ:* Edinburgh Academy; Harrow; Edinburgh Univ. (BL). A practising Solicitor, first in Edinburgh and, 1934-61, in Coatbridge; Mem. Coatbridge Town Council, 1937-44; Burgh Prosecutor, Coatbridge, 1944-60; Hon. Sheriff-Substitute of Lanarkshire at Airdrie, 1955-61. *Recreations:* golf, Scouting, motoring. *Address:* 9 Cleveden Gardens, Glasgow W2. *T:* 041-339 7731; Rockview, Elie, Fife. *T:* 234. *Clubs:* Western (Glasgow); Royal Burgess Golfing Society (Edinburgh); Golf House (Elie).

**DICKSON, Jennifer (Joan), (Mrs R. A. Sweetman),** ARA 1970; RE 1965; Director, Graphics Atelier, Saidye Bronfman Centre, Montreal, since 1969; *b* 17 Sept. 1936; 2nd *d* of John Liston Dickson and Margaret Joan Turner, S Africa; *m* 1962, Ronald Andrew Sweetman; one *s. Educ:* Goldsmith's College Sch. of Art, Univ. of London; Atelier 17, Paris. Taught at Eastbourne Sch. of Art, 1959-62 (French Govt Schol., to work in Paris under S. W. Hayter). Directed and developed Printmaking Dept, Brighton Coll. of Art, 1962-68. Vis. Artist, Ball State Univ., Muncie, Indiana, 1967; Artist in Residence at Univ. of the West Indies, Kingston, Jamaica, 1968. Has lived in Montreal since 1969. Founder Mem., Brit. Printmakers' Council; Mem., Engraving Faculty of Brit. Sch. at Rome. Prix des Jeunes Artistes (Gravure), Biennale de Paris, 1963. *Publications:* suites of original etchings: Genesis, 1965; Alchemic Images, 1966; Eclipse, 1968; Song of Songs, 1969; Out of Time, 1970. *Address:* 1270 Herron Road, Villa 225, Dorval, Quebec Province, Canada. *T:* 514-631-3859.

**DICKSON, John Abernethy,** CB 1970; Director-General and Deputy Chairman, Forestry Commission, since 1968; *b* 19 Sept. 1915; *yr s* of late John and Williamina Dickson; *m* 1942, Helen Drummond, *o d* of Peter Drummond Jardine; two *d. Educ:* Robert Gordon's Coll., Aberdeen; Aberdeen Univ. MA 1936; BSc (For.) 1938. Joined Forestry Commn, 1938; District Officer, 1940; seconded to Min. of Supply, Home Grown Timber Production Dept, 1940-46; Divisional Officer, 1951; Conservator, 1956; Dir (Scotland), 1963; Comr Harvesting and Marketing, 1965. Hon. LLD Aberdeen, 1969. *Recreation:* golf. *Address:* (home) 56 Oxgangs Road, Edinburgh 10. *T:* 031-445 1067. *Club:* Caledonian.

**DICKSON, Lovat;** *see* Dickson, H. H. L.

**DICKSON, Murray Graeme,** CMG 1961; *b* 19 July 1911; *s* of Norman and Anne Dickson. *Educ:* Rugby; New Coll., Oxford. Prison Service (Borstals), 1935-40. Served War of 1939-45, in Force 136. Entered Colonial Service, 1947; Education Officer, Sarawak, 1947, Deputy Dir of Education, 1952, Dir of Education, 1955-66; retd. Unesco adviser on educl planning to Govt of Lesotho, 1967-68. *Address:* c/o National Westminster Bank, 250 Wimbledon Park Road, SW19.
*See also A. G. Dickson.*

**DICKSON, Marshal of the Royal Air Force Sir William (Forster),** GCB 1953 (KCB 1952; CB 1942); KBE 1946 (CBE 1945; OBE 1934); DSO 1918; AFC 1922; idc; psa; *b* 24 Sept. 1898; *s* of late C. C. Forster Dickson, Chancery Registrar's Office, Royal Courts of Justice, and of late Agnes Nelson Dickson, Northwood, Mddx; *m* 1932, Patricia Marguerite, *d* of late Sir Walter Allen, KBE; one *d* (and one *d* decd). *Educ:* Bowden House, Seaford; Haileybury Coll. Royal Naval Air Service, 1916-18 (DSO, despatches thrice); transferred to RAF, 1918; Permanent Commn in RAF, 1919; employed on Naval Flying work, 1919-21; Test Pilot, RAF, 1921-22; Air Ministry, 1923-26; No. 56 (Fighter) Sqdn, 1926-27; RAF Staff Coll., Andover, 1927-28; posted to India, 1929; served on NW Frontier, 1929-30 and at HQ RAF Delhi (despatches); commanded RAF Station, Hawkinge, and No. 25 (Fighter) Squadron, 1935-36; Directing Staff, Staff Coll., 1936-38; Imperial Defence Coll., 1939; Dir of Plans, Air Ministry, 1941-42; commanded Nos 9 and 10 Groups in Fighter Comd, 1942-43; commanded No. 83 Group in TAF, 1943-44; commanded Desert Air Force, 1944; Asst Chief of Air Staff (Policy), Air Ministry, 1945-46; Vice-Chief of Air Staff, Air Ministry, 1946-48; C-in-C, MEAF, 1948-50; Mem. for Supply and Organisation, Air Council, 1950-52; Chief of the Air Staff, 1953-56; Chm. of the Chiefs of Staff Cttee, 1956-59; Chief of Defence Staff, 1958-59. Pres. Royal Central Asian Soc., 1961-65; Pres. Ex-Services Mental Welfare Soc., 1960-; Haileybury Soc., 1962. Master, The Glass Sellers' Co., 1964. Russian Order of Suvarov, 1944; USA Legion of Merit. *Address:* Foxbriar House, Cold Ash, Newbury, Berks. *Club:* Royal Air Force.

**DICKSON MABON, Jesse;** *see* Mabon, J. D.

**DICKSON WRIGHT, Arthur;** *see* Wright, A. D.

**DIDSBURY, Brian,** MB, ChB, DPH, DPA; Senior Principal Medical Officer, Department of Education and Science, since 1969; *b* 27 March 1926; *s* of Abraham Didsbury and Minnie Elizabeth Walker; *m* 1952, Dorothy Lewis; three *s* two *d. Educ:* Salford Grammar Sch. Miscellaneous hosp. appts, 1950-52; Malayan Med. Service, 1952-55; Asst MOH, Smethwick Co. Borough, 1956-58; Dep. MOH, Co. Boroughs of Gt Yarmouth, 1958-60, and West Ham, 1960-64; SMO, Min. of Health, 1964-65; PMO, Dept of Health and Social Security, 1965-69. *Publications:* contrib. Lancet. *Address:* 56 The Charter Road, Woodford Green, Essex. *T:* 01-504 2718.

**DIEFENBAKER, Rt. Hon. John (George),** PC 1957; PC (Can.) 1957; MA; QC; LLD, DCL and LittD (Hon.); Doctor of Humanities (Hon.); FRSC; MP for Prince Albert, Sask., since Aug. 1953 (Lake Centre, 1940-53); lawyer; Leader of Canadian Progressive Conservative Party, Dec. 1956-Sept. 1967; Leader of HM Loyal Opposition, Parliament of Canada, during Spring 1957, and again April 1963-Sept. 1967; Prime Minister of Canada, June 1957-April 1963; *b* Grey County, Ont., 18 Sept. 1895; *s* of William Thomas Diefenbaker and Mary Florence (*née* Bannerman); *m* 1st, 1929, Edna Brower (*d* 1950); 2nd, 1953, Olive Evangeline, LLD, DCL, *d* of Rev. Dr C. B. Freeman; one step *d. Educ:* Univ. of Saskatchewan, Saskatoon. BA 1915, MA 1916, in Political Science; served overseas with 196th Bn, as a Lieut, invalided 1917; LLB 1919, University of Saskatchewan. Called to the Bar of Saskatchewan, 1919; KC 1929; QC (Ont.) 1960. Admitted to Bars of Ontario, Alberta and BC; Hon. Bencher: Gray's Inn; Law Society of Upper Canada; Law Soc. of Saskatchewan; Hon. Mem., Illustre Nacional Colegio de Abogados (Mexico). Private practice or in partnerships (senior partner), Prince Albert, from 1919. Mem. of Council of Canadian Bar Association (Vice-Pres., 1939-42; became Hon. Life Mem., 1957). Contested (Conservative) Prince Albert, 1925, 1926; elected MP Lake Centre, 1940. Chm. of first British Commonwealth Conf., at which Delegates from Congress of US attended, Ottawa, 1943; attended UN Assembly, as Adviser to Progressive Conservative Representative on Canadian Delegn, San Francisco, 1945; Mem. Canadian Delegn of Empire Parliamentary Assoc. in Bermuda and in Washington, DC, 1946; Mem. Canadian Delegn to Commonwealth Parl. Assoc. in New Zealand and Australia, 1950; Mem. Canadian Delegn to UN, 1952; Mem. Canadian Delegn to NATO Parliamentary Assoc., 1955. Minister in Attendance on the Queen, during her visit to N America, 1957; accompanied her on visit to Chicago, Royal Tour of 1959. Leader of Canadian Delegn to Conf. of Commonwealth Prime Ministers, London, 1957, 1960, 1961, 1962. Made World Tour of Commonwealth and NATO countries, 1958. Hon. Col. North Saskatchewan Regt, Royal Canadian Inf. Corps; Hon. Freeman, City of London, 1963. Hon. Chief: Cree Indians (Frog Lake) (Chief Great Eagle); Sioux (Chief Walking Buffalo); Kainai Chieftains (Chief Many Spotted Horses). Holds 35 hon. degrees from universities and colleges both in Canada and abroad. Hon. FRSC; FRAIC. *Address:* House of Commons, Ottawa, Canada; 246 19th Street West, Prince Albert, Saskatchewan, Canada.

**DIESKAU, Dietrich F.;** *see* Fischer-Dieskau.

**DIETRICH, Marlene;** actress; *b* Berlin, 27 Dec. 1904; *d* of Eduard von Losch and Josephine Felsing; *m* Rudolph Sieber; one *d. Educ:* Berlin; Weimar. Max Reinhardt Sch. of theatre; Stage, Berlin and Vienna; First notable film, The Blue Angel; films in America since 1930; naturalised as an American, 1937; numerous stage and cabaret appearances in Europe, Great Britain and America. *Recreation:* tennis. *Address:* Paramount Studio, Hollywood, California.

**DIGBY,** family name of **Baron Digby.**

**DIGBY,** 12th Baron (Ire.) *cr* 1620, and 5th Baron (GB) *cr* 1765; **Edward Henry Kenelm Digby,** JP; Vice-Lieutenant, Dorset, since 1965; Captain, late Coldstream Guards; *b* 24 July 1924; *o s* of 11th and 4th Baron Digby, KG, DSO, MC, and Hon. Pamela Bruce, OBE, *y d* of 2nd Baron Aberdare; *S* father, 1964; *m* 1952, Dione Marian, *yr d* of Rear-Adm. Robert St Vincent Sherbrooke, *qv*; two *s* one *d. Educ:* Eton; Trinity Coll., Oxford; RMC. Served War of 1939-45. Capt., 1947; Malaya, 1948-50; ADC to C-in-C: FARELF, 1950-51; BAOR, 1951-52. Mem. Council, Royal Agricultural Soc. England, 1954; Dorchester Rural District Councillor, 1962; Dorset County Councillor, 1966; Mem. Dorset Agric. Exec. Cttee. DL 1957, JP 1959, Dorset. *Recreations:* ski-ing, shooting, racing, tennis. *Heir: s* Hon. Henry Noel Kenelm Digby, *b* 6 Jan. 1954. *Address:* Minterne, Dorchester, Dorset. *T:* Cerne Abbas 370. *Clubs:* Turf, Pratt's; Kildare Street (Dublin).

**DIGBY, Adrian,** CBE 1964; MA Oxon; FSA; Keeper, Department of Ethnography, British Museum, 1953-69; excavated Maya site of Las Cuevas, British Honduras, 1957; *b* 13 June 1909; *s* of late William Pollard Digby, FInstP, MIME, MIEE; *m* 1939, Sylvia Mary, *d* of late Arnold Inman, OBE, KC; two *d. Educ:* Lancing; Brasenose Coll., Oxford. Entered British Museum as Asst Keeper, 1932. Hon. Asst Sec. of International Congress of Anthropological and Ethnological Sciences, London, 1934; Hon. Sec. of International Congress of Americanists, Cambridge, 1952. Served in Intelligence Division Naval Staff, Admiralty, 1942-44; Hydrographic Dept, Admiralty, 1944-45. Vis. Prof. in Archaeology, Univ. de Los Andes, Bogota, 1970. Pres. Sect. H of The British Association for the Advancement of Science, 1962; Vice-Pres. Royal Anthropological Inst., 1962, 1966. *Publications:* Ancient American Pottery (with G. H. S. Bushnell), 1955; Maya Jades, 1964; articles on anthropological subjects in Man and in Chambers's Encyclopædia. *Address:* The Paddocks, Eastcombe, Stroud, Glos. *T:* Bisley (Glos) 409. *Club:* Athenæum.

**DIGBY, George F. Wingfield;** Keeper of Department of Textiles, Victoria and Albert Museum, since 1947; *b* 2 March 1911; 2nd *s* of late Col F. J. B. Wingfield Digby, DSO; *m* 1935, Cornelia, *d* of Prof. H. Keitler, University of Vienna; one *s* (decd). *Educ:* Harrow; Trinity Coll., Cambridge; Grenoble Univ.; Sorbonne; Vienna. Asst Keeper, Dept of Textiles, Victoria and Albert Museum, 1934; seconded to Education Office, Jamaica (Jamaica Coll.), 1941-45; Asst Keeper (1st class), Victoria and Albert Museum, 1946. *Publications:* The Work of the Modern Potter in England, 1952; Meaning and Symbol in Three Modern Artists, 1955; Symbol and Image in William Blake, 1957; Elizabethan Embroidery, 1963; (jointly) History of the West Indian Peoples (4 vols for schools); (part author) The Bayeux Tapestry, 1957; (contributor) Brussels Colloque International: La Tapisserie flamande au XVII-XVIII siècle, 1959; (contributor) Colston Research Soc. Papers: Metaphor and Symbol, 1960; The Devonshire Hunting Tapestries, 1971; contributor to Apollo, Burlington, Connoisseur, etc. *Recreations:* oriental ceramics and contemporary hand-made pottery. *Address:* 72 Palace Gardens Terrace, W8.

*See also S. W. Digby.*

**DIGBY, Very Rev. Richard Shuttleworth Wingfield,** MA; Dean of Peterborough since 1966; *b* 19 Aug. 1911; *s* of late Everard George Wingfield Digby and Dorothy (*née* Loughnan); *m* 1936, Rosamond Frances, *d* of late Col W. T. Digby, RE; two *s* one *d. Educ:* Nautical Coll., Pangbourne; Royal Navy; Christ's Coll., Cambridge; Westcott House, Cambridge. BA 1935; MA 1939. Asst Curate of St Andrew's, Rugby, 1936-46. Chaplain to the Forces (4th

Cl. Emergency Commn), 1940-45; POW, 1940-45. Vicar of All Saints, Newmarket, 1946-53; Rector of Bury, Lancs, 1953-66; Rural Dean of Bury, 1962-66. Pres. and Chm., Bury Trustee Savings Bank, 1953-66; Dep. Chm., Trustee Savings Bank Assoc., North-West Area, 1965-66. Hon. Canon of Manchester Cath., 1965; Hon. Chaplain to Regt XX, The Lancs Fusiliers, 1965. *Recreations:* walking, golf. *Address:* The Deanery, Peterborough. *T:* Peterborough 62780. *Club:* Army and Navy.

**DIGBY, Simon Wingfield,** TD; DL; MA; MP (U) West Dorset since 1941; *b* 1910; *s* of late Col F. J. B. Wingfield Digby, DSO; *m* 1936, Kathleen Elizabeth, *d* of late Hon. Mr Justice Courtney Kingstone, Toronto, Canada; one *s* one *d*. *Educ:* Harrow Sch.; Trinity Coll., Cambridge. Delegate to International Studies Conference, 1934. Prospective Conservative Candidate for West Dorset, Jan. 1937-June 1941; returned, 1941; a Conservative Whip, 1948-51. Barrister-at-law, Inner Temple; served in Army (TA), Aug. 1939-June 1945 in UK and NW Europe; Major, 1943. Civil Lord of the Admiralty, 1951-57. Mem. of Empire Parl. Delegn to East Africa, 1948 and Inter-Parliamentary Union Delegation to Chile, 1962. Pres., Wessex Young Conservatives, 1947-50; Chairman: Conservative Forestry Sub-Cttee, 1959-67; Shipping and Shipbuilding Cttee, 1964-. Mem., Coastal Pollution Select Cttee, 1966-68. Delegate, Council of Europe Assembly and Assembly of WEU, 1968. Order of Leopold and Order of White Lion. *Recreations:* fishing, bloodstock breeding. *Address:* Sherborne Castle, Sherborne, Dorset. *T:* Milborne Port 265; Coleshill House, Coleshill, near Birmingham. *Club:* Carlton.
*See also G. F. W. Digby.*

**DIGBY, Ven. Stephen Basil W.;** *see* Wingfield-Digby.

**DIGGINES, Christopher Ewart;** Counsellor (Commercial), Lusaka, since 1969; *b* 2 July 1920; *s* of late Sir William Diggines; *m* 1946, Mary Walls; one *s* one *d*. *Educ:* Haileybury Coll.; Trinity Coll., Oxford. Army, 1940-46. Senior History Master, Birkenhead Sch., 1948-49; apptd to CRO, 1949; Office of the UK High Comr in India (Madras), 1952-56; Canadian National Defence Coll., 1958-59; UK Mission to UN (1st Sec.), 1959-62; British Deputy High Commissioner, Kingston, Jamaica, 1962-64; Foreign and Commonwealth Office (formerly Commonwealth Office), 1964-69. *Address:* c/o Foreign and Commonwealth Office, SW1.

**DIGGLE, Rev. Reginald Fraser,** CBE 1946; MC; MA; Hon. CF; *b* 18 June 1889; *s* of John William and Edith Diggle. *Educ:* Marlborough; Merton Coll., Oxford. Ordained, 1913; Domestic Chaplain to Bishop of Carlisle, 1913-14; Curate of St Martin's, Birmingham, 1914-15; Temp. Chaplain to Forces, 1918-19; Sec. and Domestic Chaplain to Bishop of Carlisle, 1915-20; Curate of St John's, Great Yarmouth, 1921-25; Rector of St Clement's, Worcester, 1925-37; Rural Dean of Worcester, 1932-37; Private Chaplain to Bishop of Worcester, 1934; Examining Chaplain to Bishop of Worcester, 1937; Hon. Canon of Worcester, 1936; Vicar of St Giles's, Oxford, 1937-60. Chaplain RAFVR, 1940-46; Asst Chaplain in Chief, RAF India, 1942-46. *Recreation:* gardening. *Address:* 55 Osler Road, Headington, Oxford. *T:* Oxford 61694.

**DIKE, Kenneth Onwuka,** MA, PhD; Chairman, Planning Committee, University of Port Harcourt, since 1967; *b* 17 Dec. 1917; *s* of late Nzekwe Dike, merchant; *m* 1953, Ona Patricia, *d* of R. R. Olisa, MBE; two *s* three *d* (and one *d* decd). *Educ:* Dennis Memorial Grammar Sch., Onitsha; Achimota Coll., Ghana; Fourah Bay Coll., Sierra Leone; Univ. of Durham (BA); Univ. of Aberdeen (MA); London Univ. (PhD). Appointed Lecturer in History, University Coll., Ibadan, 1950-52; Senior Research Fellow, W African Inst. of Social and Economic Research, 1952-54; University Coll., Ibadan: Sen. Lectr, Dept of History, 1954-56; Prof. of History, 1956-60; Vice-Principal, 1958-60. Founder and Dir, National Archives of Nigeria, 1951-64; Chm. Nigerian Antiquities Commn, 1954-; Pres., Historical Soc. of Nigeria, 1955-; Vice-Chancellor, University of Ibadan, Oct. 1960-67; Dir, Inst. of African Studies, University of Ibadan, 1962-67; Chm., Assoc. of Commonwealth Univs, 1965-66. Chm., Commn for Review of Educational System in Eastern Region; Mem. Ashby Commn on Higher Educn in Nigeria; Chm. Organising Cttee, Internat. Congress of Africanists. FRHistS 1956. Hon. LLD: Aberdeen, 1961; Northwestern, 1962; Leeds, 1963; London, 1963; Columbia, 1965; Princeton, 1965; Hon. DLitt: Boston, Mass, 1962; Birmingham, 1964; Ahmadu Bello, 1965; Hon. DSc, Moscow, 1963. FKC 1962. *Publications:* Trade and Politics in the Niger Delta, 1830-1885, 1956; Report on the Preservation and Administration of Historical Records in Nigeria, 1953; A Hundred Years of British Rule in Nigeria, 1957; The Origins of the Niger Mission, 1958; also articles in learned journals on Nigerian and West African history. *Address:* PO Box 59, Awka, via Enugu, Eastern Region, Nigeria. *T:* Awka 59. *Clubs:* Royal Commonwealth Society; Metropolitan (Lagos, Nigeria).

**DILHORNE,** 1st Viscount *cr* 1964, of Green's Norton; **Reginald Edward Manningham-Buller;** Baron, 1962; Bt, 1866; PC 1954; Kt 1951; DL; a Lord of Appeal in Ordinary since 1969; *b* 1 Aug. 1905; *o s* of Lt-Col Sir Mervyn Manningham-Buller, 3rd Bt; *S* to father's Baronetcy, 1956; *m* 1930, Lady Mary Lilian Lindsay, 4th *d* of 27th Earl of Crawford, KT, PC; one *s* three *d*. *Educ:* Eton; Magdalen Coll., Oxford. BA 1926. Called to Bar, Inner Temple, 1927. KC 1946. MP (C) Daventry Div. of Northamptonshire, 1943-50, and for South Northants, 1950-62. Parliamentary Sec. to Min. of Works, May-Aug. 1945; Mem., Rushcliffe Cttee on Legal Aid, 1944-45; Mem., Parliamentary Delegn to USSR, 1945, and Anglo-American Cttee on Palestine, 1946. Solicitor Gen., 1951-54; Attorney-Gen., Oct. 1954-July 1962; Lord High Chancellor of Great Britain, 1962-64. Recorder of Kingston-upon-Thames, Jan.-July 1962. Hon. DCL, South Methodist Univ., Dallas, Texas; Hon. LLD, McGill Univ., Canada. DL, Northants, 1967. *Heir: s* Hon. John Mervyn Manningham-Buller, late Coldstream Guards [*b* 28 Feb. 1932; *m* 1955, Gillian Evelyn, *d* of Col George Stockwell; two *s* one *d*]. *Address:* 6 Kings Bench Walk, Temple, EC4. *T:* 01-583 0022; Horninghold Manor, near Market Harborough, Leicestershire. *T:* Hallaton 641. *Clubs:* Carlton, Pratt's, Buck's.

**DILKE;** *see* Fetherston-Dilke.

**DILKE, Sir John Fisher Wentworth,** 5th Bt *cr* 1862; formerly on staff of The Times, Government Information Services, and BBC Foreign Service; *b* 1906; *e s* of Sir Fisher Wentworth Dilke, 4th Bt, and Ethel Clifford (*d* 1959); *S* father, 1944; *m* 1st, 1934, Sheila (marr. diss. 1949), *d* of Sir William Seeds, *qv*; two *s*; 2nd, 1951, Iris Evelyn, *d* of late Ernest Clark. *Heir: s* Charles John Wentworth Dilke, *b* 21 Feb. 1937. *Address:* Metcombe House, Ottery St Mary, Devon.

**DILL, Sir (Nicholas) Bayard,** Kt 1955; CBE 1951; *b* 28 Dec. 1905; *s* of Thomas Melville and Ruth Rapalje Dill; *m* 1930, Lucy Clare Dill; two *s*. *Educ:* Saltus Grammar Sch., Bermuda; Trinity Hall, Cambridge. Law Tripos Cantab, 1926. Mem. Colonial Parliament (for Devonshire Parish), 1938-68; MLC, 1968; Mem. HM Exec. Council, 1944-54; Chairman: Board of Trade, 1935-42, also Bd of Educn, 1940, and Board of Works, 1942-48, Bermuda; St David's Island Cttee, 1940-43; Public Works Planning Commn, 1942-49; Board of Civil Aviation, 1948-, 1956-, 1960-; Bermuda Trade Development Bd, 1957-59. Served as Capt., Bermuda Volunteer Engs, 1936-44. Chancellor of Diocese of Bermuda. *Recreations:* sailing, golf. *Address:* Edey's Hill, Devonshire, Bermuda. *T:* 2-0560. *Clubs:* Royal Thames Yacht; Royal Bermuda Yacht, Mid-Ocean, Royal Hamilton Amateur Dinghy (Bermuda); India House, Canadian, Cruising of America (NYC).

**DILLISTONE, Rev. Canon Frederick William,** DD; Fellow and Chaplain, Oriel College, Oxford, 1964-70; Canon Emeritus of Liverpool Cathedral since 1964; Examining Chaplain, Diocese of Liverpool, since 1964, to Bishop of Salisbury since 1964, to Bishop of London since 1967, and to Bishop of Wakefield, since 1968; *b* 9 May 1903; *s* of late Frederick Dillistone; *m* 1931, Enid Mary, *d* of late Rev. Cecil Francis Ayerst; two *s* one *d*. *Educ:* Brighton Coll.; BNC, Oxford (Scholar). BA 1924; BD 1933; DD 1951. Deacon, 1927; Priest, 1928; Vicar of St Andrew, Oxford, 1934-38; Prof. of Theology, Wycliffe Coll., Toronto, 1938-45; Prof. of Theology, Episcopal Theological Sch., Cambridge, Mass, 1947-52; Canon Residentiary and Chancellor of Liverpool Cathedral, 1952-56; Dean of Liverpool, 1956-63. Hulsean Preacher, Cambridge, 1953; Select Preacher, Oxford, 1953-55; Select Preacher, Cambridge, 1960; Stephenson Lectr, Univ. of Sheffield, 1966; Bampton Lectr, Univ. of Oxford, 1968. Asst Editor, Theology Today, 1951-61. Hon. DD: Knox Coll., Toronto, 1946; Episcopal Theological Sch., Cambridge, Mass, 1967. Chaplain OStJ, 1958. *Publications:* The Significance of the Cross, 1945; The Holy Spirit in the Life of To-day, 1946; Revelation and Evangelism, 1948; The Structure of the Divine Society, 1951; Jesus Christ and His Cross, 1953; Christianity and Symbolism, 1955; Christianity and Communication, 1956; The Novelist and the Passion Story, 1960; The Christian Faith, 1964; Dramas of Salvation, 1967; The Christian Understanding of Atonement, 1968; Editor, Scripture and Tradition, 1955; Editor, Myth and Symbol, 1966; contributor to: The Doctrine of Justification by Faith, 1954; A Companion to the Study of St Augustine, 1955; Steps to Christian Understanding, 1958; The Ecumenical Era in Church and Society, 1959; Metaphor and Symbol, 1961; The Theology of the Christian Mission, 1961; Christianity and the Visual Arts, 1964; Mansions of the Spirit, 1966; Christianity in its Social Context, 1967; Studies in Christian History and Interpretation, 1967; Christ for us Today, 1968; Grounds of Hope, 1968; Man, Fallen and Free, 1969; Sociology, Theology and Conflict, 1969. *Recreation:* gardening. *Address:* Oriel College, Oxford; 15 Cumnor Rise Road, Oxford. *T:* Cumnor 2071.

**DILLON,** family name of **Viscount Dillon.**

**DILLON,** 20th Viscount *cr* 1622; **Michael Eric Dillon;** Count in France, *cr* 1711; local Lt-Col retired, RHG; *b* 13 Aug. 1911; *o s* of 19th Viscount, and Juanita (*d* 1962), *d* of Brig.-Gen. Charles Edward Beckett, CB; *S* father, 1946; *m* 1939, Irène Marie France, *y d* of René Merandon du Plessis, Whitehall, Mauritius; four *s* three *d* (and one *d* decd). *Educ:* Eton; RMC Sandhurst. 2nd Lieut 15/19th Hussars, 1931; seconded to Transjordan Frontier Force, 1935; Lieut RHG, 1937; Capt., 1939; Major, 1946; retired, 1952. Knight of the Sovereign Order of Malta; Officer of Order of Orange-Nassau (Netherlands). *Heir:* *s* Hon. Charles Henry Robert Dillon [*b* 18 Jan. 1945. *Educ:* Downside; RMA Sandhurst; Royal College of Art, Kensington]. *Address:* Rath House, Termonfeckin, Drogheda, Co. Louth, Ireland. *Clubs:* Challoner; Kildare Street (Dublin).

**DILLON, C(larence) Douglas;** *b* Geneva, Switzerland, 21 Aug. 1909; *s* of Clarence Dillon; *m* 1931, Phyllis Elsworth; two *d*. *Educ:* Groton Sch.; Harvard Univ. (AB). Mem., NY Stock Exchange, 1931-36; US and Foreign Securities Corporation and US and International Securities Corporation, 1937-53 (Dir, 1938-53; Pres., 1946-53); Dir, Dillon, Read & Co. Inc., 1938-53 (Chm. of Bd, 1946-53); American Ambassador to France, 1953-57; Under-Sec. of State for Economic Affairs, USA, 1957-59, Under-Sec. of State, USA, 1959-61; Sec. of the Treasury, USA, 1961-65. Served US Naval Reserve, 1941-45 (Lieut-Comdr; Air Medal, Legion of Merit). Mem. Bd of Governors: NY Hosp.; Metropolitan Museum of Art (President, 1969-). Hon. Dr of Laws: New York Univ., 1956; Lafayette Coll., 1957; Univ. of Hartford, Conn., 1958; Columbia Univ., 1959; Harvard Univ., 1959; Williams Coll., 1960; Rutgers Univ., 1961; Princeton Univ., 1961; University of Pennsylvania, 1962; Bradley Univ., 1964; Middleburg Coll., 1965. *Address:* Far Hills, New Jersey, USA.

**DILLON, George Brian Hugh,** QC 1965; Barrister-at-Law; *b* 2 Oct. 1925; *s* of late Capt. George Crozier Dillon, RN; *m* 1954, Alisoun, *d* of late Hurbert Samuel Lane, MC; two *s* two *d*. Called to the Bar, Lincoln's Inn, 1948. *Address:* 13 Old Square, Lincoln's Inn, WC2.

**DILLON, Sir Robert William Charlier,** 8th Bt *cr* 1801; Baron of the Holy Roman Empire, 1782; *b* 17 Jan. 1914; *s* of Robert Arthur Dillon (*d* 1925) and Laura Maud (*d* 1915), *widow* of J. Lachlin McCliver, New Zealand; *S* kinsman, 1925; *m* 1947, Synolda, *d* of late Cholmondeley Butler Clarke and of Mrs Cholmondeley-Clarke, late of Holywell, Co. Tipperary. *Heir:* none. *Address:* Lismore, Knocknacree Road, Dalkey, Co. Dublin.

**DILLON, Thomas;** Professor of Chemistry, University College, Galway, 1919-54; *b* Inniscrone, Co. Sligo, 1884; *s* of late J. B. Dillon, Ballina, Co. Mayo, and Elizabeth Sullivan; *m* 1916, Geraldine, *d* of Count Plunkett; two *s* three *d*. *Educ:* Clongowes Wood Coll.; Queen's (now Univ.) Coll., Cork; RCS, Dublin. MA NUI, 1908; DSc 1910; ScD Dublin (*hc*) 1954; MRIA; Pres., Inst. of Chemistry of Ireland for 1954-56. Asst to Prof. of Chemistry, University Coll., Dublin, 1909-19. Mem. Executive Council, Sinn Fein, 1917-22 (Hon. Sec. 1917). *Publications:* papers on chemical subjects in Proc. Royal Dublin Soc. and RIA, and other scientific jls. *Address:* 13 Marlborough Road, Donnybrook, Dublin. *T:* Dublin 680365.

**DILLWYN-VENABLES-LLEWELYN, Brig. Sir C. M.;** *see* Venables-Llewelyn.

**DILWORTH-HARRISON, Ven. Talbot;** Archdeacon of Chesterfield Emeritus and Vicar of Edingley with Halam, Newark, since 1963; *b* 5 July 1886; *s* of James and Louisa

Dilworth-Harrison; unmarried. *Educ:* Dean Close, Cheltenham; Keble Coll., Oxford; Cuddesdon. Lecturer S Boniface Coll., Warminster, 1907-08; Asst Curate S Mary's, Prestwich, 1909-17; Vicar of Ringley, Lancs, 1917-27; Vicar of S Bartholomew's, Brighton, 1927-34; Commissary to: Bishop of Trinidad, 1922-58; Archbishop of Brisbane, 1935-43; Bishop of Accra, 1936; Examining Chaplain to Bishop of Derby, 1934-63; Archdeacon, Vicar and Lecturer of Chesterfield, 1934-63. *Publications:* Three Centuries of a Village Sanctuary; A Scrapbook of Prayer; Everyman's Story of the Oxford Movement; The Catholic Faith and this Generation; Every Boy's/Girl's Confirmation Book; John Bull Considers his Church; Everyman's Confirmation Book. *Address:* Halam Vicarage, Newark, Notts.

**DIMECHKIE, Nadim;** Ambassador of Lebanon to the Court of St James's, since 1966; *b* Lebanon, 5 Dec. 1919; *s* of Badr and Julia Dimechkie; *m* 1946, Margaret Alma Sherlock; two *s*. *Educ:* American Univ. of Beirut (BA, MA Economics). Deleg., Jt Supply Bd for Syria and Lebanon, 1942-44; Dir Gen., Min. of Nat. Economy, 1943-44; Counsellor, Lebanese Embassy, London, 1944-49; Consul-Gen., Ottawa, 1950; Dir, Economic and Social Dept, Min. of Foreign Affairs, 1951-52; Chargé d'Affaires, Cairo, 1952; Minister, 1953-55; Minister, Switzerland, 1955-57; Ambassador to USA, 1958-62; Dir, Economic Affairs, Min. of Foreign Affairs, 1962-66. Lebanese Order of Cedars, UAR Order of Ismail and Order of Merit; Syrian Order of Merit; Tunisian Order of Merit; Greek Order of Phoenix. *Address:* 21 Kensington Palace Gardens, W8. *T:* 01-229 7265. *Clubs:* Travellers', Hurlingham, Royal Automobile; Metropolitan, Chevy Chase (Washington); Cercle de Beirut, Aero (Beirut).

**DIMMOCK, Peter,** CVO 1968; OBE 1961; General Manager and Head of Outside Broadcasts, BBC Television, since 1954; Sports Adviser, European Broadcasting Union, since 1959; responsible for Liaison between BBC and Royal Family since 1963; *b* 6 Dec. 1920; *e s* of late Frederick Dimmock, OBE, and of Paula Dimmock (*née* Hudd); *m* 1960, Mary Freya (Polly), *e d* of late Sir Richard Elwes, OBE, TD; three *d*. *Educ:* Dulwich Coll.; France. TA; RAF pilot, instr, and Air Ministry Staff Officer, 1939-45. After demobilisation became Press Association correspondent; joined BBC as Television Outside Broadcasts Producer and commentator, 1946; produced both studio and outside broadcasts, ranging from documentaries to sporting, theatrical and public events; has produced or commentated on more than 500 television relays, including Olympic Games 1948, Boat Race 1949, first international television relay, from Calais, 1950, King George VI's Funeral, Windsor, 1952. Produced and directed television outside broadcast of the Coronation Service from Westminster Abbey, 1953; first TV State Opening of Parliament, 1958; first TV Grand National, 1960; TV for Princess Margaret's Wedding, 1960. Created BBC Sportsview Unit and introduced new television programme Sportsview, 1954, regular compère of this weekly programme, 1954-64. *Publications:* Sportsview Annuals, 1954-65; Sports in View, 1964. *Recreations:* flying, gliding, winter sports, golf. *Address:* 41 Addison Avenue, Holland Park, W11. *Clubs:* St James', Turf, Garrick.

**DIMOLINE, Hon. Brig. Harry Kenneth,** CBE 1943 (MBE 1938); DSO 1942; TD; *b* 6 Sept. 1903; British; *s* of late C. A. F. Dimoline; *m* 1928, Amy Sybil Heap; one *s* one *d*. *Educ:* Sedbergh. Formed 68 Med. Regt, RA, 1939; campaigns: Eritrea, Western Desert, Alamein, Tripoli, Tunis, Italy, Burma (despatches four times, DSO, CBE); CRA 4 Indian Div., 1942-44 (Divisional Comdr, 1944); CRA 47 (London) Inf. Div., 1944; CRA 17 Indian Div. SEAC, Nov. 1944. Chief Commandant Malayan Police Volunteer Reserve, 1949-57. Colonial Police Medal, 1955. *Recreations:* hunting, riding. *Address:* High Compton, Donhead St Andrew, Shaftesbury, Dorset.

**DIMSDALE, Mrs Helen Easdale,** FRCP; Neurologist, Royal Free Hospital, since 1950; Hon. Consultant Physician, Maida Vale Hospital (National Hospitals); *b* 2 July 1907; *d* of late John Harold Brown and late Ellen Carse Easdale; *m* 1930, Wilfrid Hampden Dimsdale; one *s*. *Educ:* Hayes Court, Kent; Girton Coll., Cambridge; UCH, London. MA Cl. I Nat. Sci. Tripos I, 1929; MD Cantab 1946; FRCP 1949. Resident appointments, University Coll. Hosp.; Medical Registrar, Elizabeth Garrett Anderson Hosp., 1938; Med. Registrar, 1940, and Neuropathologist, 1942, Maida Vale Hosp. for Nervous Diseases; First Asst, Dept of Neurology, London Hosp., 1942. Late Neurologist and Physician, Elizabeth Garrett Anderson Hosp., 1946; late Tutor in Medicine, Royal Free Hosp. Sch. of Med., 1952. Member: Assoc. of British Neurologists; Assoc. of Physicians. *Publications:* section on Diseases of the Nervous System, The Practice of Medicine (ed. J. S. Richardson Churchill), 1956; chapter (Acute Encephalomyelitis of Virus Origin) in Modern Trends in Neurology 2nd series (ed. D. Williams), 1957; contribs to medical periodicals. *Recreation:* sailing. *Address:* Private Consulting Rooms, National Hospital, Queen Square, WC1. *T:* 01-837 1900; Flat 2, 123 Harley Street, W1. *T:* 01-935 6446.

**DIMSDALE, Sir John Holdsworth,** 3rd Bt *cr* 1902; *b* 31 Dec. 1901; *s* of 2nd Bt and Edith Kate (*d* 1911), *d* of late John Connacher; *S* father, 1923; *m* 1949, Gisela Panova (*d* 1969). *Address:* 4 Moorhill Gardens, Thornhill, Southampton. *T:* West End 3212.

**DINESEN, Thomas,** VC 1918; French Croix de Guerre; Civil Engineer; *b* 1892; *e s* of late Capt. W. Dinesen; *m* 1926, Jonna Lindhardt; two *s* two *d*. *Educ:* Rungsted Sch.; Polytechnical Sch., Copenhagen. Served European War, 1917-19, with Royal Highlanders of Canada; farmer in Kenya Colony, 1920-23. *Publications:* No Man's Land, 1929 (translated from Danish into English under the title Merry Hell); Twilight on the Betzy (Denmark, Norway, Sweden and Finland), 1951, (England and Holland), 1952; The Axe (Denmark), 1959. *Recreations:* yachting, travelling. *Address:* Leerbaek, Vejle, Denmark.

**DINEVOR;** *see* Dynevor.

**DINGLE, Herbert,** DSc, ARCS; Professor Emeritus of History and Philosophy of Science, University College, London, 1955 (Professor, 1946-55); formerly Professor of Natural Philosophy, Imperial College of Science and Technology, South Kensington; *b* 2 Aug. 1890; *s* of James Henry Dingle and Emily Jane Gorddard; *m* 1918, Alice (*d* 1947), *d* of late Frederick Westacott; one *s*. *Educ:* Plymouth Science, Art, and Technical Schs; Imperial Coll. of Science and Technology. Mem. of British Government Eclipse Expeditions, 1927, 1932 and 1940 (cancelled owing to war); Mem. Internat. Astronomical Union, 1928-; Vice-Pres. Internat. Union for the History of Science, 1953-56; Pres. Brit. Soc. for History of Science, 1955-57; Pres., Royal Astronomical Society, 1951-53, Hon.

Sec., 1929-32, Vice-Pres., 1938-39, 1942-44, 1948-50, 1953-54; Lowell Lecturer, Boston, USA, 1936; Corresp. Member: Inst. of Coimbra; Inst. of Advanced Studies, Cordoba, Argentina. *Publications:* Relativity for All, 1922; Modern Astrophysics, 1924; Science and Human Experience, 1931; Through Science to Philosophy, 1937; The Special Theory of Relativity, 1940; Mechanical Physics, 1941; Subatomic Physics, 1942; Science and Literary Criticism, 1949; Practical Applications of Spectrum Analysis, 1950; The Scientific Adventure, 1952; The Sources of Eddington's Philosophy, 1954; (with 1st Visc. Samuel) A Threefold Cord, 1961; scientific papers in Proc. Royal Soc., Monthly Notices of Royal Astronomical Soc., Nature, Brit. Jl for the Philosophy of Science, Encyclopædia Britannica, etc; part author: Splendour of the Heavens, 1923; Life and Work of Sir Norman Lockyer, 1929; The New World Order, 1932; The New Learning, 1933; Science To-Day, 1934; (ed) A Century of Science, 1951; (ed jtly) Chemistry and Beyond: essays by F. A. Paneth, 1965. *Address:* 104 Downs Court Road, Purley, Surrey CR2 1BD. *T:* 01-660 3581. *Club:* Athenæum.

**DINGLE, Sir Philip (Burrington),** Kt 1964; CBE 1954; Town Clerk of Manchester, 1944-66; *b* 19 Sept. 1906; *s* of Frederick Burrington Dingle and Jessie Roberta Elizabeth (*née* Needham); *m* 1938, Kathleen Mary, *d* of late Cecil Hurst, Sheffield; one *s* one *d*. *Educ:* Cheltenham Coll.; Sheffield Univ. LLM Sheffield, 1928. Articled to late Sir William Hart, Town Clerk of Sheffield, 1924-28; admitted Solicitor, 1928; Asst Solicitor to Sheffield Corporation, 1928-37; Dep. Town Clerk, Manchester, 1938-44; Member: Advisory Council on Child Care, 1948-52; Advisory Council on Clean Air, 1957-67; Council of Cheltenham Coll., 1956-70 (Life Mem., 1965). Pres., Soc. of Town Clerks, 1961-62. Chm., City of Manchester Boy Scouts, 1946-66, Pres., 1968-70. Hon. LLD Manchester, 1960. *Address:* Darley, The Bent Curbar, Derbyshire. *T:* Grindleford 407. *Club:* National Liberal.

**DINGLE, Prof. Robert Balson,** PhD; FRSE; Professor of Theoretical Physics, University of St Andrews, since 1960; *b* 26 March 1926; *s* of late Edward Douglas Dingle and Nora Gertrude Balson; *m* 1958, Helen Glenronnie Munro; two *d*. *Educ:* Bournemouth Secondary Sch.; Cambridge University. PhD 1951. Fellow of St John's Coll., Cambridge, 1948-52; Theoretician to Royal Society Mond. Lab., 1951-52; Chief Asst in Theoretical Physics, Technical Univ. of Delft, Holland, 1952-53; Fellow, Nat. Research Council, Ottawa, 1953-54; Reader in Theoretical Physics, Univ. of WA, 1954-60. *Publications:* contribs to learned journals. *Recreations:* local history, music and gastronomy. *Address:* 6 Lawhead Road East, St Andrews, Fife, Scotland. *T:* St Andrews 4287.

**DINGLEY, Allen Roy,** FRCS; Consulting Surgeon, Royal National Throat, Nose and Ear Hospital, London; Consulting Aural Surgeon, Sutton Hospital; *b* 28 Oct. 1892; *s* of Allen Dingley, FRCS. *Educ:* Leys Sch., Cambridge. Brackenbury Surgical Scholar, St Bart's Hospital, 1916. Surgical Specialist, Mesopotamia Exped. Force, 1917-20. Late Chief Asst, Throat Department, St Bart's Hospital. *Publications:* articles in medical journals on otolaryngology. *Recreation:* golf. *Address:* 49 The Avenue, Cheam, Surrey. *T:* 01-580 1163. *Club:* Walton Heath Golf.

**DINGWALL, Baroness;** *see* Lucas of Crudwell and Dingwall.

**DINGWALL, Eric John,** MA, DSc (London), PhD (London, Faculty of Science); anthropologist; Hon. Assistant Keeper of Printed Books, British Museum; Hon. Vice-President, Magic Circle; *s* of Alexander Harvey Dingwall, Ceylon. *Educ:* privately; Pembroke Coll., Cambridge. Formerly on staff, Cambridge Univ. Library; Dir, Dept of Physical Phenomena, American Soc. for Psychical Research, New York, 1921; Research Officer, Soc. for Psychical Research, 1922-27, investigating many American and European mediums in New York, Boston, Paris, Copenhagen, Warsaw, Munich, Gratz, etc, publishing results in Proc. and Jl of the SPR; toured Spain, 1935; went to the West Indies, 1936, to study special social and religious conditions in Trinidad and Haiti with reference to abnormal mental phenomena; went to Poland, S America, W Indies, and USA, 1937. Attached to Ministry of Information and to a Dept, Foreign Office, 1941-45. *Publications:* Joint Editor, Revelations of a Spirit Medium, 1922; Studies in the Sexual Life of Ancient and Mediæval Peoples, I, Male Infibulation, 1925; How to Go to a Medium, 1927; Ghosts and Spirits in the Ancient World, 1930; The Girdle of Chastity, 1931; Artificial Cranial Deformation, 1931; How to Use a Large Library, 1933; Editor of English edn of Woman (Ploss-Bartels), 1935; Racial Pride and Prejudice, 1946; Some Human Oddities, 1947; Very Peculiar People, 1950; (with K. M. Goldney and T. H. Hall) The Haunting of Borley Rectory, 1956; (with J. Langdon-Davies) The Unknown–is it nearer?, 1956; The American Woman, 1956; (with T. H. Hall) Four Modern Ghosts, 1958; The Critics' Dilemma, 1966; Editor of and contributor to: Abnormal Hypnotic Phenomena, 1967-68; contributions to English and foreign publications. *Recreations:* bibliography, studying rare and queer customs, collecting queer and unusual clocks, watches and automata. *Address:* Pine Hill, Crowhurst, Sussex. *T:* Crowhurst 217. *Club:* National Liberal.

**DINGWALL, John James,** OBE 1964; HM Inspector of Constabulary for Scotland, 1966-70; *b* 2 Sept. 1907; *s* of James Dingwall, Bannockburn, Stirling; *m* 1932, Jane Anne, *d* of James K. Halliday, Falkirk; two *d*. *Educ:* Bridge of Allan and Stirling. Stirlingshire Constabulary, 1927-49; Stirling and Clackmannan Police Force, 1949-55; seconded as Dir of Studies, Scottish Police Coll., 1953-55; Chief Constable of Angus, 1955-66. *Recreations:* angling, shooting, golf. *Address:* 2 Hillpark Crescent, Edinburgh 4.

**DINGWALL, Walter Spender,** MA; Secretary Chichester Diocesan Fund, 1946-61, retired; *b* 14 Dec. 1900; *s* of late Rev. Walter Molyneux Dingwall and Sophia Spender; *m* 1932, Olive Mary Loasby; no *c*. *Educ:* Marlborough Coll.; Christ Church, Oxford. Sixth Form Master at St Edward's Sch., Oxford, 1923-37; nine years Bursar of the Sch., ten years Housemaster; Headmaster, Hurstpierpoint Coll., Sussex, 1937-45; Hon. Sec. and Treasurer, Public Schools Bursars' Assoc., 1932-38. *Address:* The White House, Woodmancote, near Henfield, Sussex.

**DINGWALL-SMITH, Ronald Alfred;** Secretary (Finance), Scottish Office, since 1970; *b* 24 Feb. 1917; *m* 1946; one *s* one *d*. *Educ;* Alleyn's Sch., Dulwich; London School of Economics (evening classes). Entered Civil Service as Clerical Officer, Ministry of Transport, 1934; Asst Auditor, Exchequer and Audit Dept, 1935, Auditor, 1940; Asst Principal 1947, Principal 1949, Asst Sec. 1955, Under-Sec.

1965-70, Scottish Development Department. *Recreations:* golf, bowls, gardening. *Address:* 2 Mortonhall Road, Edinburgh EH9 2HW. *T:* 031-667 5817. *Clubs:* Royal Commonwealth Society, Civil Service.

**DINKEL, Ernest Michael,** RWS 1957; ARCA; Head of The School of Design, Edinburgh College of Art, 1947-60, retired; *b* 24 Oct. 1894; *s* of Charles and Lucy Dinkel; *m* 1st, 1929, Kathleen Hanks; 2nd, 1941, Emmy Keet; two *s* two *d* (and one *s* decd). Huddersfield Sch. of Art; War Service abroad, 1916-19 (general and war service medals). Royal Coll. of Art, 1921-25, Student. RIBA Owen Jones Scholarship, 1926. Asst to Prof. Robert Anning Bell and Prof. Tristram, at Royal Coll. of Art, 1925-40; Head of Stourbridge Sch. of Art, 1940-47; Exhibitor: Royal Academy, Royal Scottish Academy, Royal Society of Painters in Water Colours. *Recreations:* glass engraving; pottery, sculpture; wide interest in art subjects. *Address:* The Grange, Bussage, near Stroud, Glos. *T:* Brimscombe 2368.

**DINSDALE, Richard Lewis;** Chairman, West of England Newspapers Ltd, since 1969; *b* 23 June 1907; *m* 1930, Irene Laverack; one *d.* *Educ:* Hull Technical Coll. Joined Hull Daily Mail as reporter, 1926; Editorial posts: Newcastle Evening World; Chief Sub-editor, Manchester Evening News; Dep. Chief Sub-editor, Daily Express, Manchester; Evening News, London; Daily Mirror, 1940-42; War Service, 1942-46; Copy-taster, Daily Mirror, 1946, successively Chief Sub-editor, Dep. Night Editor, Night Editor; Dep. Editor, 1955; seconded Daily Herald as Editorial Adviser, 1961; Dep. Editor, Daily Herald, 1962; Dep. Editor, The Sun, 1964, Editor, 1965-69. *Recreations:* sea fishing, golf. *Address:* West of England Newspapers Ltd, 55-57 Exeter Street, Plymouth PL4 0AJ. *T:* Plymouth 62831.

**DINWIDDIE, Melville,** CBE 1943 (OBE 1919); DSO 1917; MC 1915; DD; Controller, Scotland, British Broadcasting Corp., 1933-57, retired; *b* 18 July 1892; 2nd *s* of late Rev. J. L. Dinwiddie, Ruthwell; *m* 1920, Arna, *e d* of late Alexander Guild, WS, Edinburgh. Served European War, 1914-18 (despatches, DSO, OBE, MC); retd, 1924; was Asst at South Leith Parish Church; Minister of St Machar's Cathedral, Aberdeen, 1925-33. *Address:* 22 Polwarth Terrace, Edinburgh EH11 1NB. *Club:* New (Edinburgh).

**DINWIDDY, Thomas Lutwyche;** Master of the Supreme Court (Chancery Division) since 1958; *b* 27 Aug. 1905; *o c* of late Harry Lutwyche Dinwiddy, Solicitor, and late Ethel Maude (*née* McArthur); *m* 1935, Ruth, *d* of late Charles Ernest Rowland Abbott, Barrister-at-Law and Bencher of Lincoln's Inn; three *s.* *Educ:* Winchester; New Coll., Oxford (BA). Solicitor, Dec. 1930; Partner in Frere Cholmeley & Co., 28 Lincoln's Inn Fields, WC2, 1933-57. Council of Law Soc., 1953-57. Served RA (TA), 1939-45; Staff Coll., Camberley, 1943; demobilised as Major. *Recreations:* golf, watching cricket, motoring (preferably in Scotland). *Address:* Little Hafton, Pine Road, Hook Heath, Woking, Surrey. *Club:* United University.

**DIONISOTTI-CASALONE, Carlo;** Professor of Italian, Bedford College (formerly Bedford College for Women), University of London, 1949-70; *b* 9 June 1908; *s* of Eugenio Dionisotti-Casalone and Carla Cattaneo; *m* 1942, Maria Luisa Pinna-Pintor; three *d* (and one *d* decd). *Educ:* Turin, Italy. Dottore in lettere, Univ. of Turin, 1929; Libero Docente di Letteratura Italiana, Univ. of Turin, 1937; Asst di Letteratura Italiana, Univ. of Rome, 1943; Italian Lectr, Univ. of Oxford, 1947; MA Oxon, 1947. *Publications:* Indici del giornale storico della letteratura italiana (Turin), 1945; Guidiccioni-orazione ai nobili di Lucca (Rome), 1946; Bembo-Savorgnan, Carteggio d'amore (Florence), 1950; Oxford Book of Italian Verse (revised edn), 1952; Bembo, Prose e Rime (Turin), 1960; Geografia e storia della letter. ital. (Turin), 1967. *Address:* 44 West Heath Drive, NW11.

**DIPLOCK,** Baron (Life Peer) *cr* 1968, of Wansford; **(William John) Kenneth Diplock,** PC 1961; Kt 1956; a Lord of Appeal in Ordinary since 1968; Member of Lord Chancellor's Law Reform Committee, since 1952; *b* 8 Dec. 1907; *s* of W. J. Hubert Diplock, Croydon; *m* 1938, Margaret Sarah, *d* of George Atcheson, Londonderry. *Educ:* Whitgift; University Coll., Oxford. Barrister, Middle Temple, 1932; Sec. to Master of the Rolls, 1939-48. Served War of 1939-45, RAF, 1941-45. KC 1948; Recorder of Oxford, Dec. 1951-Jan. 1956. Master of the Bench, Middle Temple, 1956; Judge of High Court of Justice, Queen's Bench Div., 1956-61; a Lord Justice of Appeal, 1961-68. Judge of Restrictive Practices Court, 1960-61 (Pres., 1961). Hon. Fellow of University Coll., Oxford, 1958. Pres., Nat. Assoc. of Parish Councils, 1962-66; Vice-Pres., Brit. Maritime Law Assoc., 1964; Chairman: Advisory Bd (Comparative Law), Brit. Inst. of Internat. and Comparative Law, 1959-67; Council of Legal Education, 1969-70 (Chm., Bd of Studies, 1963-69); Law Advisory Cttee, Brit. Council, 1966; Dep. Chm., Boundary Commn for England, 1958-61. Hon. Fellow, American Bar Foundation, 1969. *Recreation:* hunting. *Address:* 1 Crown Office Row, Temple, EC4; Wansford in England, Peterborough. *Club:* Athenæum.

**DIRAC, Paul Adrien Maurice,** FRS 1930; BSc Bristol, PhD Cantab; Lucasian Professor of Mathematics, Cambridge, 1932-69, now Professor Emeritus; Fellow of St John's College, Cambridge; *b* 8 Aug. 1902; *m* 1937, Margit Wigner, Budapest. Mem. Pontifical Academy of Sciences, 1961. Nobel Prize in Physics for 1933; Royal Medal of Royal Society, 1939; Copley Medal of Royal Society, 1952. *Publications:* Principles of Quantum Mechanics: papers on quantum theory. *Address:* St John's College, Cambridge.

**DISBREY, Air Vice-Marshal William Daniel,** CB 1967; CBE 1945 (OBE 1943); AFC 1939; Manager, Technical Training Institute, Airwork Services, Saudi Arabia, since 1970; *b* London, 23 Aug. 1912; *s* of Horace William Disbrey; *m* 1939, Doreen Alice, *d* of William Henry Ivory, Stevenage; two *d.* *Educ:* Minchenden Secondary Sch. Joined RAF as an Apprentice, 1928; gained Cadetship to RAF Coll., Cranwell, 1931; Commnd, 1935. No. 3 Fighter Sqdn, 1933-34; Fleet Air Arm, 1934-37; Engrg Specialist Course, Henlow, 1937-39; Engr Officer, No. 13 Group HQ, 1940-41; Engr Officer, HQ Fighter Comd, 1941-43; Chief Engr Officer, 2nd TAF, 1943-46; Staff Coll. Course, 1946; CO, No. 12 Sch. of Technical Training, 1946-48; Sen. Technical Officer, Royal Indian Air Force, 1948-51; Min. of Supply, 1951-54; Chief Engr Officer, Bomber Comd, 1954-57; Imperial Defence Coll., 1957; Dir of Research and Development, Bombers, Min. of Aviation, 1958-61; Comdt, No. 1 Radio Sch., Locking, 1961-64; Dir-Gen. of Engineering (RAF), 1964-67 AO Engineering, Bomber Comd, 1967, Strike Comd, 1968-70. CEng; FIMechE; FRAeS. *Recreations:* golf, sailing. *Address:* Old Heatherwode, Buxted, Sussex. *T:* Buxted 2104. *Club:* Royal Air Force.

**DISNEY, Harold Vernon,** CBE 1956; Manager, Engineering Division, Reactor Group, UK Atomic Energy Authority, since 1969; *b* 2 July 1907; *s* of Henry Disney and Julia Vernon; *m* 1936, Lucy Quinton; two *d. Educ:* Hallcroft Higher Standard Sch., Ilkeston; Nottingham Univ. Coll. Internat. Combustion, 1931-35; ICI (Alkali), 1935-46. On loan to Min. of Supply (RFF's), 1941-46. Dept of Atomic Energy, 1946-54; UKAEA: Asst Dir, Defence Projects, Industrial Gp, 1954; Dir of Engineering, Industrial Gp, 1958; Man. Dir, Engineering Gp, Risley, 1962. FIMechE 1947. *Recreation:* gardening. *Address:* Delph House, Delphfields Road, Appleton, Warrington, Lancs. *T:* Warrington 62984. *Club:* National Liberal.

**DISNEY, Lieut-Col Henry Anthony Patrick;** *b* 1893; *s* of Henry William Disney, Barrister-at-law, Metropolitan Police Magistrate, and Isabel Power; *m* 1915, Kathleen Maud Suffern; two *s* (and two *s* decd including one killed in War of 1939-45). *Educ:* Marlborough; Caius Coll., Cambridge (BA). Served European War, Cambridgeshire Regt; Pilot RFC, War Office Staff; DAQMG Italy; Wing Comdr RAF 1918. Dir Standard Telephones and Cables Ltd, Kolster Brandes Ltd, Creed and Co. Ltd, Standard Radio Relay Services Ltd, International Telephone and Telegraph Co. Ltd, 1919-32; joined Staff of E. K. Cole Ltd, 1932; Dir of Aeronautical Production, Air Min., 1936-38; Dir of Armament and Equipment Production, Air Min., 1938; left Min. of Aircraft Production, 1940, and rejoined RAF. Pilot Officer 1940; Wing Comdr 1941; Group Capt. 1944; released 1945; served in India, 1943-45. Dir of Brit. Export Trade Research Organisation, resigned, 1949; Staff Personnel Adviser, Rootes Group of Companies, 1950; Consultant Management Selection Ltd, 1957; John Tyzack & Partners Ltd, 1960; retired, 1962. Fellow Royal Commonwealth Society. Officer, Order of Crown of Italy. *Recreation:* philately. *Address:* Headbourne Worthy House, Headbourne Worthy, Winchester, Hants.

**DITCHBURN, Robert William,** FRS 1962; Professor of Physics, University of Reading, 1946-68, now Emeritus; *b* 14 Jan. 1903; *e s* of William and Martha Kathleen Ditchburn; *m* 1929, Doreen May, *e d* of Arthur Samuel Barrett; one *s* three *d. Educ:* Bootle Secondary Sch.; Liverpool Univ.; Trinity Coll., Cambridge (Entrance and Senior Scholar, Hooper Prizeman, Isaac Newton Student). Fellow of Trinity Coll., Dublin, 1928-46; Prof. of Natural and Experimental Philosophy in Dublin Univ., 1929-46; Temp. Principal Experimental Officer, Admiralty, 1942-45. Mem. of Royal Irish Academy, 1931; Registrar for Social Studies, Trinity Coll., Dublin, 1940-44; Vice-Pres. Physical Soc., 1958; Vice-Pres. Inst. of Physics and Physical Soc., 1960-62. Fellow Inst. of Physics. *Publications:* Light, 1952; and scientific papers. *Recreations:* walking, music. *Address:* 14 Betchworth Avenue, Earley, Reading RG6 2RJ.

**DIVERRES, Prof. Armel Hugh;** Carnegie Professor of French, University of Aberdeen, since 1958; *b* Liverpool, 4 Sept. 1914; *o s* of late Paul Diverres and Elizabeth (*née* Jones); *m* 1945, Ann Dilys, *d* of late James and Enid Williams; one *s* two *d. Educ:* Swansea Grammar Sch.; University Coll., Swansea; Univ. of Rennes; Sorbonne, Paris. MA (Wales), LèsL (Rennes), Docteur de l'Université de Paris. Fellow of University of Wales, 1938-40; served in RA and Int. Corps, 1940-46, Capt. Asst Lectr in French, University of Manchester, 1946-49; Lectr, 1949-54; Sen. Lectr in French, University of Aberdeen, 1954-57. *Publications:* Voyage en Béarn by Froissart (ed), 1953; La Chronique métrique attribuée à Geffroy de Paris (ed), 1956; Chatterton by A. de Vigny (ed), 1967; articles and reviews in learned journals. *Recreation:* hill walking. *Address:* 202 Queen's Road, Aberdeen AB1 8DD. *T:* 36121.

**DIVERS, Brig. Sydney Thomas,** CB 1955; CBE 1944 (OBE 1940); DSO 1942; TD; company director; *b* 30 Jan. 1896; *s* of William and Alice Divers, Greenwich, Kent; *m*; two *s* two *d. Educ:* Greenwich Central Sch. Served Army, 1914-18, 1939-45 (USA Bronze Star, 1944; despatches 5 times); TA, 1914-19, 1924-51. Royal Observatory, Greenwich, 1910-14; HM Customs and Excise, 1919-34; Assistance Board, 1935-46; Ministry of Pensions and National Insurance, 1946-54 (Controller, Newcastle upon Tyne, 1951-54); Under-Sec.: Min. of Supply, 1956; Admiralty, 1957-59; UN Adviser, Administration: Burma, 1954-55; Nepal, 1959-62; Asia and Far East, 1962-64; UN Adviser, Social Security: Iraq, 1965-66; Trinidad 1967. Inst. of Public Administration; British Inst. of Management. *Recreations:* fishing, gardening. *Address:* RD 2, Winton, Southland, New Zealand. *Club:* National Liberal.

**DIVINE, Arthur Durham,** OBE 1946; DSM 1940; (**David Divine**); author and journalist; formerly War Correspondent, now Defence Correspondent, Sunday Times; *b* 27 July 1904; 2nd *s* of Arthur Henry and Mabel Divine, Cape Town; *m* 1931, Elizabeth Ann, 2nd *d* of Sir Ian MacAlister; two *d. Educ:* Rondebosch High Sch., Cape Town; Kingswood Coll., Grahamstown, S Africa. Cape Times, 1922-26 and 1931-35, where founded daily column of World Comment; has travelled extensively in Europe, Africa, Asia, N and S America, and the Pacific. *Publications:* Sea Loot, 1930; They Blocked the Suez Canal, 1936; The Pub on the Pool, 1938; Tunnel from Calais, 1943, and many other thrillers; The Merchant Navy Fights, The Wake of the Raiders, Behind the Fleets, 1940, in conjunction with Ministry of Information; Destroyer's War, 1942; Road to Tunis, 1944; Navies in Exile, 1944; Dunkirk, 1945, and many boys' books; under pseudonym of David Rame: Wine of Good Hope, 1939; The Sun Shall Greet Them, 1941; under name of David Divine: The King of Fassarai, 1950; Atom at Spithead, 1953; The Golden Fool, 1954; Boy on a Dolphin, 1955; The Nine Days of Dunkirk, 1959; These Splendid Ships, 1960; The Iron Ladies, 1961; The Daughters of the Pangaran, 1963; The Blunted Sword, 1964; The Broken Wing, 1966; The Stolen Seasons, 1967; The Key of England, 1968; The North-West Frontier of Rome, 1969; The Three Red Flares, 1970; Mutiny at Invergordon, 1970; *Films:* Atom at Spithead; Boy on a Dolphin; Dunkirk. *Address:* 24 Keats Grove, Hampstead, NW3. *T:* 01-435 6928.

**DIX, Victor Wilkinson,** MA, MB, BChir Cantab, FRCS, MRCP; retired; Professor Emeritus, University of London. Assistant Surgeon, The London Hospital, 1930-37; Surgeon, The London Hospital, 1937-64. *Address:* 8 Shandon Close, Tunbridge Wells, Kent. *T:* Tunbridge Wells 30839.

**DIXEY, Dr Frank,** CMG 1949; OBE 1929; FRS 1958; DSc; FGS; Geological Adviser and Director of Colonial Geological Surveys, Colonial Office, 1947-59; *b* 7 April 1892; *m* 1919, Helen Golding (*d* 1961); one *d* (decd); *m* 1962, Cicely Hepworth. *Educ:* Barry Grammar Sch.; University of Wales. Served European War, 1914-18, RGA, 1915-18; Govt Geologist, Sierra Leone, 1918-21; Dir of Geological Survey, Nyasaland, 1921-39; Dir of Water

Development, N Rhodesia, 1939-44; Dir of Geological Survey, Nigeria, 1944-47. Geological Soc. Murchison medallist, 1953; Geol. Soc. S Africa Draper medallist, 1945 and Hon. Mem., 1959; Corresponding Mem. Geological Soc., Belgium, 1947, Hon. Mem., 1958. Alexander du Toit Memorial Lecturer, Johannesburg, 1955. Hon. Mem. Inst. Min. and Met., 1958. *Publications:* Practical Handbook of Water Supply, 1931, 2nd Edn 1950; official reports and scientific papers on geology, geomorphology, and mineral resources of African States. *Address:* Woodpecker Cottage, Bramber, Steyning, Sussex. *T:* Steyning 2313. *Club:* Athenæum.

**DIXEY, Marmaduke;** *see* Howard, Geoffrey.

**DIXEY, Paul (Arthur Groser);** Deputy Chairman of Lloyd's, 1967, 1969; *b* 13 April 1915; *e s* of late Neville Dixey, JP (Chairman of Lloyd's, 1931, 1934 and 1936), and Marguerite (*née* Groser); *m* 1939, Mary Margaret Baring, 2nd *d* of Geoffrey Garrod, *qv*; four *s* one *d. Educ:* Stowe; Trinity Coll., Cambridge. Elected an Underwriting Mem. of Lloyd's, 1938. Served War of 1939-45, Royal Artillery. Member: London Insce market delegn to Indonesia, 1958; Dunmow RDC, 1958-64; Cttee, Lloyd's Underwriters' Assoc., 1962-; Cttee, Salvage Assoc., 1962-; Cttee, Lloyd's, 1964-70; Gen. Cttee, Lloyd's Register of Shipping, 1964-; Chm., Salvage Assoc., 1964-65. Mem. Council, Morley Coll., 1952-62; Chm. Governors, Vinehall Sch., 1966-. *Recreations:* riding, fly-fishing. *Address:* Easton Glebe, Little Easton, Dunmow, Essex. *T:* Great Dunmow 2840.

**DIXIE, Sir (Alexander Archibald Douglas) Wolstan,** 13th Bt *cr* 1660; *b* 8 Jan. 1910; *s* of Sir Douglas Dixie, 12th Bt, and Margaret Lindsay, *d* of Sir A. Jardine, 8th Bt of Applegirth; *s* father, 1948; *m* 1st, 1940, Phyllis Pinnel (marr. diss. 1950), *d* of late Lt-Col Percy John Probyn, DSO; 2nd, 1950, Dorothy Penelope King-Kirkman; two *d. Educ:* St Joseph's Coll., Dumfries; Prior Park Coll., Bath. Hereditary Governor, Dixie Grammar Sch., 1948; Windsor Rural District Council, 1956-58. *Recreations:* cricket, tennis, squash. *Address:* Bosworth Park, Leics; Manor Park, Old Windsor, Berks.

**DIXON,** family name of **Baron Glentoran.**

**DIXON, Bernard;** former Chairman and Managing Director of Flowers Breweries Ltd (1947-58); chairman and director of a number of brewing and malting companies; *b* Redcar, Yorks, 23 Dec. 1906; 3rd *s* of late Capt. Thomas Robert Dixon and Lily Jane (*née* Barry), Thriplow Place, near Royston, Herts; *m* 1930, Olive Marie, *d* of G. H. Watts, Cambridge; four *d. Educ:* Campbell Coll., Belmont, Belfast, NI; British Sch. of Malting and Brewing; University of Birmingham. Sometime examiner, Institute of Brewing, Mem. Publications Cttee, Journal of Inst. of Brewing, Chm. London Section, Inst. of Brewing, 1939-40. Winner numerous awards at home and abroad for brewery products, including championship, London, 1929 and 1930 and Grand Prix, Brussels, Prague, Pilsen. Patentee of inventions used throughout brewing industry. Formerly Hon. Sec. Bedfordshire Brewers' Assoc. and Mem. Brewers' Soc. Cttee on Replanning. Commissioned, Cambs Regt, 1929; Sports Officer, 1930; commissioned, Home Guard, 1940. Breeder of pure-bred Arabian Horses which have been exported to Government studs in all parts of the world; Governor of the Arab Horse Soc. Past Pres. Old Campbellian Soc. *Publications:* technical papers to various sections of Institute of Brewing and Incorporated Brewers' Guild. *Recreations:* hunting, farming, golf. *Address:* Grey Gates, Harpenden, Herts. *T:* Harpenden 3122. *Clubs:* Bath, royal Automobile; Kildare Street (Dublin).

**DIXON, Dr Bernard;** Editor of New Scientist since 1969 (Deputy Editor, 1968-69); *b* Darlington, 17 July 1938; *s* of late Ronald Dixon and Grace Peirson; *m* 1963, Margaret Helena Charlton; two *s* one *d. Educ:* Queen Elizabeth Grammar Sch., Darlington; King's Coll., Univ. of Durham; Univ. of Newcastle upon Tyne. BSc, PhD. Luccock Res. Fellow, 1961-64, Frank Schon Fellow, 1964-65, Univ. of Newcastle; Asst Editor, 1965-66, Dep. Editor, 1966-68, World Medicine. Mem. Cttee, Assoc. of British Science Writers, 1969- . Mem., Soc. for General Microbiology, 1962; MIBiol 1965. *Publications:* (ed) Journeys in Belief, 1968; The Health Watch, 1971; numerous articles in scientific and general press on microbiology, and other scientific topics; research papers in Jl of General Microbiology, etc, mostly on microbial biochemistry. *Recreation:* running a Scottish country dance band. *Address:* 21 Dane Road, Chelmsford, Essex. *T:* Chelmsford 59631.

**DIXON, Maj.-Gen. Bernard Edward Cooke,** CB 1947; CBE 1944; MC 1917; *b* 7 Sept. 1896; *s* of late George Frederick Dixon, MRCS, MRCP; *m* 1923, Elizabeth Norah Fitzpatrick (*née* Gibson); two *d. Educ:* Bedford Sch.; RMA Woolwich. Commissioned in RE, 1915; served in France, 1916-19 (despatches, MC); Lieut-Col 1939; Col 1942; Temp. Brig. 1940; Temp. Maj.-Gen. 1944; Brig. 1947; Middle East, 1940-43 (despatches twice); Italy, 1943-44 (CBE); E-in-C, GHQ Middle East, 1944-47 (CB); CE, HQ Western Command, 1947-48; retired, 1948, with hon. rank of Maj.-Gen. *Recreation:* yachting. *Address:* Kilima, East Stour, Gillingham, Dorset. *T:* East Stour 250.

**DIXON, Cecil Edith Mary,** MBE 1939; formerly Professor of Piano and Accompaniment, RCM, retired; *b* 27 Nov.; *d* of James Dickson and Margaret Emily Dixon. *Educ:* New Zealand and Australia. Was on the original staff of the BBC, remained there until Sept. 1943; toured for CEMA as a free-lance pianist till 1946; studied piano under Herbert Sharpe and the Royal College of Music and later with Tobias Matthay. *Recreations:* dogs and country walks. *Address:* 17 Milner Street, SW3. *T:* 01-589 0030.

**DIXON, Sir Charles William,** KCMG 1945 (CMG 1932); KCVO 1961; OBE 1924; *b* 29 April 1888; *s* of John W. Dixon, Leeds, and Alice, *d* of Charles Hainsworth, Bramley, Yorks. *Educ:* Clifton; Balliol Coll., Oxford (Exhibitioner). 1st Class Classical Mods, 1909; 1st Class Lit. Hum., 1911. Entered Colonial Office, 1911; Private Sec. to the Permanent Under-Sec. of State (Sir George Fiddes), 1917-19; Asst Under-Sec. of State, Dominions Office (afterwards Commonwealth Relations Office), 1940-48; Adviser, Commonwealth Relations Office (now Commonwealth Office), 1948-67. *Address:* Balholm Grange, Branksome Park, Bournemouth, Hants. *T:* Westbourne 61449.

**DIXON, Sir (Francis Wilfred) Peter,** KBE 1959 (CBE 1952); MB, BS; FRCS; Air Vice-Marshal retired; Consultant in Surgery to the RAF, retired 1966; *b* 4 Oct. 1907; *s* of Frederick Henry Dixon, New Norfolk, Tas.; *m* 1940, Pamela Ruby, *d* of Brig. Charles C. Russell, MC, RA (Retd), London; two *s* one *d. Educ:* Newman Coll.; Melbourne Univ. MB, BS, Melbourne, 1930; FRCS Ed. 1937; FRCS 1949; DO Oxford, 1936. House Surgeon, St

Vincent's Hosp., Melbourne. Joined RAF 1930; Wing-Comdr 1943; served War of 1939-45; Aden, Normandy, SW Pacific; Air Cdre 1949; Air Vice-Marshal, 1957. Civilian Consultant in Surgery, RAF, 1966-. Lady Cade Medal, RCS, 1963. *Publications:* contribs to medical journals. *Recreation:* sailing. *Address:* Hill House, Snape Bridge, near Woodbridge, Suffolk. *T:* Snape 404.

**DIXON, Guy Holford,** JP; Barrister-at-Law; Recorder of Newark-on-Trent since 1965; *b* 20 March 1902; *s* of late Dr Montague Dixon, Melton Mowbray; unmarried. *Educ:* Abbotsholme Sch., Derbs; Repton Sch.; University Coll., Oxford. BA (History) Oxon, 1925. Called to the Bar, Inner Temple, 1929. Deputy Chairman: Leics QS, 1960; Northampton County QS, 1966. Lay Canon, Leicester Cathedral, 1962. JP Leics, 1960. *Recreation:* looking at and collecting pictures. *Address:* The Old Rectory, Brampton Ash, Market Harborough, Leics. *T:* Dingley 200; Burton Overy, Leics. *T:* Great Glen 2274. *Clubs:* Reform; Leicestershire (Leicester).

**DIXON, Hubert John,** MC, MA; retired as Headmaster of King's College School, Wimbledon (1934-60); *b* 5 June 1895; *s* of William Arthur and Caroline Dixon; *m* 1st, 1922, Mary Frances Arnold (*d* 1960); one *s* one *d*; 2nd, 1962, Yvonne Muriel Price. *Educ:* King Edward's Sch., Birmingham; Queen's Coll., Cambridge (Classical Exhibitioner). Sixth Form Master: Fettes Coll., Edinburgh, 1920-21; Dulwich Coll., 1921-34. Served with 1st Bn Royal Warwicks Regt in France, 1916-19 (MC, despatches). *Recreation:* reading. *Address:* 1 Lancaster Gardens, Wimbledon, SW19.

**DIXON, Sir John,** 2nd Bt *cr* 1919; *b* 13 June 1886; *s* of 1st Bt and Emily Katherine, 2nd *d* of G. Beacham Cole of Twickenham; *S* father, 1924; *m* 1910, Gwendolen Anna, *d* of Sir J. L. E. Spearman, 2nd Bt; two *s* one *d*. *Heir: s* John George Dixon [*b* 17 Sept. 1911; *m* 1947, Caroline, *er d* of C. T. Hiltermann, 31 Melbury Court, London; one *d*]. *Recreations:* hunting, fishing and shooting. *Address:* Astle Cottage, Chelford, Cheshire. *TA:* Chelford.

**DIXON, Most Rev. John Harkness.** *Educ:* Univ. of Toronto (BA); Trinity Coll., Toronto (Scholar, BD). Deacon, 1912; Priest, 1913. Curate, Fenaghvale, Ont., 1912-13; Christ Church Cathedral, Ottawa, 1914-22; Minor Canon, Ottawa, 1913-22; Rector: S Bartholomew, Ottawa, 1922-32; Grace Church, Toronto, 1932-40; Dean and Rector, Christ Church Cathedral, Montreal, 1940-43; Bishop of Montreal, 1943-60; Archbishop of Montreal and Metropolitan of the Province of Canada, 1960-62; retired Sept. 1962. *Address:* Apt 304, 6201 Sherbrooke Street West, Montreal 28, Que., Canada.

**DIXON, John Reginald;** Managing Director, 1923-66, Chairman, 1927-66, Cleveland Bridge & Engineering Co. Ltd; retired; *b* 19 Jan. 1886; *s* of Charles F. Dixon and Amy Beckett; *m* 1913, Elsie Margaret Gunion; two *s* (and *e s* killed AAF Dunkirk, 1940). *Educ:* Marlborough Coll. Joined Cleveland Bridge & Engineering Co., 1903; Works Manager, 1912. *Recreations:* gardening, shooting, travel; skiing in younger days. *Address:* Pitminster Lodge, Pitminster, Taunton, Som. *Clubs:* Junior Carlton, Ski Club of Great Britain, Alpine Ski.

**DIXON, Leslie C. G.;** *see* Graham-Dixon.

**DIXON, Malcolm,** FRS 1942; MA, PhD, ScD Cantab; Emeritus Professor of Enzyme Biochemistry, Cambridge University, since 1966; *b* 18 April 1899; *s* of Allick Page and Caroline Dewe Dixon. *Educ:* Emmanuel Coll., Cambridge. BA 1920; commenced research in biochemistry under Sir F. G. Hopkins, 1921; 1851 Exhibition Senior Student, 1924-27; Senior Demonstrator in Biochemistry, University of Cambridge, 1923-27; University Lecturer in Biochemistry, 1928-44; Reader in Enzyme Biochemistry, Cambridge University, 1945-65; Prof. of Enzyme Biochemistry, 1966; Dir of Sub-Dept of Enzyme Biochemistry, Cambridge Univ., 1945-66; Fellow of King's Coll., Cambridge, 1950-66, Hon. Fellow, 1968. Pres. of the Commission on Enzymes of the Internat. Union of Biochemistry, 1956-61. *Publications:* Manometric Methods, 1934, 3rd edn 1951; Multi-enzyme Systems, 1949; Enzymes (with Prof. E. C. Webb), 1958, 2nd edn 1964; numerous papers dealing with the subject of enzymes, with special reference to biological oxidation processes and cell-respiration. *Recreation:* music. *Address:* Biochemical Laboratory, Cambridge. *T:* Cambridge 51781. *Club:* Athenæum.

**DIXON, Margaret Rumer H.;** *see* Haynes Dixon.

**DIXON, Michael George,** OBE 1964; Chief Passport Officer, Foreign Office, since 1967; *b* 10 March 1920; *s* of Sidney Wilfrid and Elsie Dixon. *Educ:* Enfield Grammar Sch. Foreign Office, 1937. HM Forces, 1940-46 (POW, Far East). *Recreation:* gardening. *Address:* 9 Ridge Crest, Enfield, Mddx. *T:* 01-363 3408.

**DIXON, Rt. Hon. Sir Owen,** PC 1951; OM 1963; GCMG 1954 (KCMG 1941); Chief Justice of Australia, 1952-64; *b* 28 April 1886; *s* of late Joseph William Dixon, Melbourne, Solicitor, and Edith Annie, *d* of late Edward Owen, Sydney; *m* 1920, Alice Crossland, *d* of Rev. H. A. Brooksbank; two *s* two *d*. *Educ:* Hawthorn Coll., Melbourne; University of Melbourne. Called to Bar, Victoria 1910; KC 1922; Acting Judge of the Supreme Court of the State of Victoria, 1926; Justice, High Court of Australia, 1929-52; Chm. of Central Wool Cttee, 1940-42; Chm. of Shipping Control Board, 1941-42; Chm. of Commonwealth Marine War Risks Insurance Board, 1941-42; Chairman of: Marine Salvage Board, 1942; Allied Consultative Shipping Council in Australia, 1942; served as Envoy Extraordinary and Minister Plenipotentiary of the Commonwealth of Australia at Washington, 1942-44; served as UN Mediator between India and Pakistan, Kashmir dispute, 1950. Howland Prize, Yale, 1955. Corres. Fellow, British Academy, 1970. Hon. DCL Oxford, 1958; Hon. LLD: Harvard, 1958; Melbourne, 1959; ANU 1964. *Address:* 4 Higham Road, Hawthorn, Melbourne, E3, Australia. *Clubs:* Melbourne, Australian (Melbourne); Australian (Sydney).

**DIXON, Sir Peter;** *see* Dixon, Sir (F. W.) P.

**DIXON, Piers;** MP (C) Truro since 1970; Stockbroker; *b* 29 Dec. 1928; *s* of late Sir Pierson (John) Dixon, GCMG, CB (British Ambassador in New York and Paris) and of Lady (Ismene) Dixon; *m* 1960, Edwina, *d* of Rt Hon. Duncan Sandys, *qv*; two *s*. *Educ:* Eton (schol.); Magdalene Coll., Cambridge (exhibnr); Harvard Business Sch. Grenadier Guards, 1948. Calvin Bullock, investment bankers, New York and London, 1954; Philip Hill, Higginson, merchant bankers, 1958; S. G. Warburg and Co., merchant bankers, 1961; Sheppards and Chase, stockbrokers, 1964-. Contested (C) Brixton, 1966. *Publication:* Double Diploma, 1968. *Recreation:* history. *Address:* Tregullow, Scorrier, Redruth, Cornwall. *T:* St Day 534; 14 South Eaton Place, SW1. *T:* 01-730 6646. *Clubs:* Brooks's,

City University; Racquet and Tennis (New York).

**DIXON, Stanley;** Chairman, Midland-Yorkshire Tar Distillers Ltd, since 1968; *b* 12 Aug. 1900; *m* 1936, Ella Margaret Hogg; two *s. Educ:* Leeds Grammar Sch.; Queen's Coll., Oxford. Articled to Leather & Veale, Chartered Accountants in Leeds, 1924-27; Manager, Leather & Veale (later Peat, Marwick, Mitchell & Co.), Leeds, 1927-35; Sec., Midland Tar Distillers Ltd, 1935-66; Dir, Midland Tar Distillers Ltd (now Midland-Yorkshire Tar Distillers Ltd), 1943-. Pres., Inst. of Chartered Accountants in England and Wales, 1968-69. *Publication:* The Case for Marginal Costing, 1967. *Recreations:* Church affairs, gardening and music. *Address:* 83 Norton Road, Stourbridge, Worcs. *T:* Stourbridge 5672.

**DIXON-NUTTALL, Major William Francis,** DSO 1916; TD; late RE (TF); JP; retired as Director United Glass Ltd, 8 Leicester Street, WC2 (1926-54), Dec. 1954; Commissioner for Income Tax; *e s* of late F. R. Dixon-Nuttall, JP; *m* 1917, Gladys Lena, *o d* of W. Henry Gregory, Caldecott, Aughton, and Glenorchy Lodge, Dalmally; one *s. Address:* Esher Place Avenue, Esher, Surrey. *Club:* Junior Carlton.

**DOAK, Sir James,** Kt 1945; CA (Glasgow); Director: Legal & General Assurance Society Ltd; J. H. Fenner & Co. (Holdings); *b* 1904; *m* 1931, Helen Gaylord; one *s* (and one *s* decd). *Address:* Jacobs Farm, Sedlescombe, Battle, East Sussex.

**DOBB, Major Erlam Stanley,** CB 1963; TD; a Deputy Director-General, Agricultural Development and Advisory Service, since 1971; *b* 16 Aug. 1910; *m* 1937, Margaret Williams; no *c. Educ:* Ruthin; University Coll. of N Wales. Chartered Surveyor and Land Agent, Anglesey, Denbigh and Merioneth, 1930-35; Asst Land Comr, 1935-40 (*in absentia* War Service); Land Comr, 1940-47; Regional Land Comr, 1947-52; Dep. Dir, Agricultural Land Service, 1952-59, Dir, 1959-70, MAFF. Governor, Royal Agricultural College. Royal Welch Fusiliers (TA), 1938-46, Major. FRICS. *Publications:* professional contributions to journals of learned societies. *Recreations:* golf, gardening. *Address:* Churchgate, Westerham, Kent. *T:* Westerham 2294. *Clubs:* Crowborough Beacon Golf, Limpsfield Chart Golf, Golfers'.

**DOBB, Maurice Herbert,** MA Cantab; PhD (London); DrEconSc (Prague); Emeritus Reader in Economics, University of Cambridge; Fellow of Trinity College, Cambridge; *b* 1900; *s* of Walter Herbert Dobb and Elsie Annie Moir, London; *m* Barbara Marian Nixon. *Educ:* Charterhouse; Pembroke Coll., Cambridge (Exhibitioner and Scholar). 1st Class Parts I and II, Econs Tripos. Research Student, LSE, 1922-24; Visiting Lectr in Russian Economic Studies, Univ. of London Sch. of Slavonic Studies, 1943-46; Visiting Prof. at Sch. of Economics, Univ. of Delhi, 1951. *Publications:* Capitalist Enterprise and Social Progress, 1925; Russian Economic Development since the Revolution, 1928; Wages, 1928 (revised edn 1956); Political Economy and Capitalism, 1937 (revised edn 1940); Soviet Economy and the War, 1941; Soviet Planning and Labour in Peace and War, 1942; Studies in the Development of Capitalism, 1946; Development of Soviet Economy since 1917, 1948 (rev. edn 1966); collaborated in ed. Works and Correspondence of David Ricardo, 1951-55; On Economic Theory and Socialism, Collected Papers, 1955; An Essay on Economic Growth and Planning, 1960; Papers on Capitalism, Development and Planning, 1967; Welfare Economics and the Economics of Socialism, 1969; contributor to Chambers's Encyclopædia, Encyclopædia of the Social Sciences; articles and reviews in the Economic Journal, Economica, Soviet Studies, etc. *Address:* Trinity College, Cambridge; College Farmhouse, Fulbourn, Cambs. *T:* Fulbourn 298.

**DOBBIE, Mitchell Macdonald,** CB 1951; Secretary of Commissions for Scotland since 1966; *b* 2 Oct. 1901; *s* of James Dobbie, Ayr, and Jean Macdonald; *m* 1931, Evelyn Willison (*d* 1967), *e d* of R. W. Grieve, Edinburgh. *Educ:* Ayr Academy; University of Edinburgh (MA, LLB). Called to Bar, Gray's Inn, 1927. Entered Inland Revenue Dept, 1925; Ministry of Labour, 1928; Private Sec. to Parl. Sec., 1934; transferred to Dept of Health for Scotland, 1938; Asst Sec., 1939; Principal Asst Sec., 1945; seconded to Ministry of Home Security as Principal Officer, Scotland Civil Defence Region, 1943-45; Under-Sec., Min. of Housing and Local Govt, 1948; Principal Establishment Officer, 1956-63; retd 1963, and re-employed in Scottish Development Dept., 1963-66; JP City of Edinburgh. *Address:* 13 Eton Terrace, Edinburgh 4. *T:* 031-332 3150. *Clubs:* New, Scottish Arts (Edinburgh).

**DOBBIE-BATEMAN, Rev. Arthur Fitzroy,** CB 1948; Auxiliary Priest, St John's, Frome, since 1969; *b* 1897; *s* of Richmond Bateman; *m* 1923, Margaret Laing Dobbie, MB, ChB, Edinburgh, DIH (*hc*), LSA. *Educ:* Bristol Grammar Sch.; Wadham Coll., Oxford; St George's, Windsor. Civil Service, 1923-52; Asst Curate, St John's, Frome, 1952-55; Rector of Whatley with Chantry, Frome, 1955-69. *Publication:* St Seraphim of Sarov, 1936. *Address:* The Hermitage, Gentle Street, Frome, Somerset. *T:* Frome 2502.

**DOBBS, Joseph Alfred,** OBE 1957 (MBE 1945); TD 1945; HM Consul-General, Zagreb, since 1969; *b* Abbeyleix, Ireland, 22 Dec. 1914; *s* of John L. Dobbs and Ruby (*née* Gillespie); *m* 1949, Marie, *d* of Reginald Francis Catton; four *s. Educ:* Worksop Coll.; Trinity Hall, Cambridge (Schol.). Pres., Cambridge Union Soc., 1936. Served War of 1939-45, Major, Royal Artillery (despatches). Joined Foreign Office, 1946; served Moscow, 1947-51, 1954-57 and 1965-68; FO, 1951-54; Delhi, 1957-61; Warsaw, 1961-64; Rome, 1964-65. *Recreations:* riding, golf, ski-ing. *Address:* c/o Foreign and Commonwealth Office, SW1. *Club:* Oxford and Cambridge.

**DOBBS, Mattiwilda;** Order of North Star (Sweden), 1954; opera singer (coloratura soprano); *b* Atlanta, Ga, USA; *d* of John Wesley and Irene Dobbs; *m* 1957, Bengt Janzon, Swedish journalist and public relations man; no *c. Educ:* Spelman Coll., USA (BA); Columbia Univ., USA (MA). Studied voice in NY with Lotte Leonard, 1946-50; special coaching Paris with Pierre Bernac, 1950-52. Marian Anderson Schol., 1948; John Hay Whitney Schol., 1950; 1st prize in singing, Internat. Comp., Geneva Conservatory of Music, 1951. Appeared Royal Dutch Opera, Holland Festival, 1952. Recitals, Sweden, Paris, Holland, 1952; appeared in opera at La Scala, Milan, 1953; Concerts, England and Continent, 1953; Glyndebourne Opera, 1953-54, 1956, 1961; Covent Garden Opera, 1953, 1954, 1956, 1958; command performance, Covent Garden, 1954. Annual concert tours: US, 1954-; Australia, New Zealand, 1955, 1959, and 1968; Israel, 1957 and 1959; USSR concerts and opera (Bolshoi Theater), 1959; San Francisco Opera, 1955; début Metropolitan Opera, 1956; there annually,

1956-. Appearances Hamburg State Opera, 1961-63; Royal Swedish Opera, 1957 and subseq. annually; Norwegian and Finnish Operas, 1957-64. *Address:* Vastmannagatan 50, Stockholm, Sweden. *T:* 34-83-00.

**DOBBS, Richard Heyworth,** MD, FRCP; Consulting Pædiatrician: London Hospital since 1946; Queen Elizabeth Hospital for Children since 1939; Southend Hospital Group since 1946; *b* 10 May 1905; of British parentage; *m* 1930, Phyllis Leon; one *s* one *d*. *Educ:* Bedales Sch.; Downing Coll., Cambridge; London Hosp. MRCS, LRCP 1930; MB Cantab 1931; MD 1941; MRCP 1936; FRCP 1947. Pres., British Paediatric Assoc., 1970. Editor, Archives of Disease in Childhood, 1954-69. *Publications:* (in collab.) Midwifery, 1940, 5th edn 1962; Leigh's Subacute Encephalopathy; Hyperammonaema, 1969. *Recreations:* gardening and travel. *Address:* 3 Oakhill Way, Hampstead, NW3. *T:* 01-435 4010.

**DOBIE, Marryat Ross,** CBE 1953; BA; *b* Bellary, India, 1888; *s* of Surg. Lieut-Col Stanley Locker Dobie, IMS; *m* Grace Vera Patmore; two *d*. *Educ:* Fettes Coll., Edinburgh; Wadham Coll., Oxford. Asst in British Museum, 1912-14; Private in London Scottish, 1914-15; Officer in Intelligence Corps, 1915-19; Official of the Inter-Allied Rhineland High Commission, 1919-24; Official of the Inter-Allied Commission of Government and Plebiscite in Upper Silesia, 1921-22; Asst in National Library of Scotland, 1929-31; Keeper of Manuscripts, 1931-46; Librarian, 1946-53. Officer, Intelligence Corps, 1940-44. *Address:* 15 Church Road, Duffus, Elgin, Morayshire. *T:* Hopeman 674.

**DOBINSON, Prof. Charles Henry,** CMG 1969; Professor of Education, University of Reading, 1951-68, now Emeritus; *b* 7 Oct. 1903; *s* of late Henry Mark Dobinson, and late Florence Gertrude (*née* Agate); *m* 1929, Dorothy Maude Shooter; one *s* one *d*. *Educ:* Brockley County Grammar Sch., London; Wadham Coll., Oxford (MA). 2nd Cl. Hons Hon. Mods Maths; 1st Cl. Hons Oxford Hon. Sch. of Nat. Science (Geology); Diploma in Educn, Oxford; BSc London. Biology Master, Mill Hill Sch., 1927-33; Headmaster, King Edward VI Grammar Sch., Five Ways, Birmingham, 1933-45; Reader in Education, Oxford Univ., 1945-51. An adviser to UK first delegation to Unesco, 1946; Chm. Educn Cttee, Nat. Fedn of Community Assocs, 1949-62; a Governor of Unesco Internat. Inst. of Educn, Hamburg, 1950-65; Member: Banjo Commn on Education in Western Region of Nigeria, 1960-61; Advisory Commn on Higher Teacher Training in the Sudan, 1964. Visiting Prof., Summer Schs of Syracuse, New York, 1950, Arkansas, 1950, 1952, 1967, Syracuse, 1955, 1957, Cornell, 1959, Alberta, 1960, Missouri, 1961, 1963, 1964, 1966, 1968, 1970, Calgary, 1969. FGS. *Publications:* (ed) Education in a Changing World, 1950; Technical Education for Adolescents, 1951; Schooling 1963-1970, 1963; Jean-Jacques Rousseau, 1969; various school text-books between 1929 and 1966; articles in educational press of UK, USA, France and Sweden. *Recreations:* gardening and reading. *Address:* The Old Barn, Sonning Common, near Reading, Berks. *T:* Kidmore End 2191.

**DOBRÉE, Lt-Col Bonamy,** OBE 1929; late RA; Professor of English Literature, University of Leeds, 1936-55; *b* 1891; *s* of Bonamy Dobrée and Violet Chase; *m* 1913, Valentine (Gladys), *d* of Sir Alexander Brooke-Pechell, 7th Bt; one *d*. *Educ:* Haileybury; RMA Woolwich; Cambridge. Commissioned in RFA 1910; resigned 1913; rejoined Aug. 1914; served European War in France and Palestine (despatches); served also 1939-45. Cambridge 1920, Capt. of fencing team; BA 1921; MA 1926; resided abroad, 1921-25; Lecturer, London Univ., 1925-26; Prof. of English, Egyptian Univ., Cairo, 1926-29; Mem. Central Advisory Council for Education (England), 1944-53; Clark Lecturer, 1953; Gresham Prof. in Rhetoric, 1955-61; Lord Northcliffe Memorial Lecturer, 1963. Hon. Docteur de Dijon. Hon. DLitt, Kent at Canterbury, 1968. *Publications:* Restoration Comedy, 1924; Essays in Biography; Histriophone; Timotheus, 1925; Nonesuch Vanbrugh; Sarah Churchill, 1927; World's Classics Congreve, 1928; Restoration Tragedy, The Lamp and the Lute, 1929; (with Herbert Read) The London Book of English Prose, 1931; Variety of Ways; William Penn; St Martin's Summer: Letters of Lord Chesterfield, with Life, 1932; John Wesley, 1933; Giacomo Casanova, 1933; As Their Friends Saw Them, 1933; Modern Prose Style, 1934; (with G. E. Manwaring) The Floating Republic, 1935; (ed) The Letters of King George III, 1935; (ed) From Anne to Victoria, 1937; English Revolts, 1937; (with Edith Batho) The Victorians and After (Introduction to English Literature Series), 1938; The Unacknowledged Legislator, 1942; English Essayists (Britain in Pictures), 1947; (with Herbert Read) The London Book of English Verse, 1949; Alexander Pope, 1951; The Broken Cistern, 1954; The Early Eighteenth Century: Oxford History of English Literature, 1959; Three Eighteenth Century Figures, 1962; Rudyard Kipling, 1967; Milton to Ouida: a Collection of Essays, 1970. *Recreation:* gardening. *Address:* 15 Pond Road, Blackheath, SE3. *T:* 01-852 0679. *Club:* Athenæum.

**DOBREE, John Hatherley,** MS, FRCS; Consultant in Ophthalmology, St Bartholomew's Hospital, London, EC1, since 1956; Senior Ophthalmic Surgeon, North Middlesex Hospital, N18, since 1947; *b* 25 April 1914; *s* of Hatherley Moor Dobree, OBE, and Muriel Dobree (*née* Hope); *m* 1941, Evelyn Maud Smyth; two *s*. *Educ:* Victoria Coll., Jersey; St Bartholomew's Hosp. MS London 1947; FRCS 1950. House Physician, Metropolitan Hosp., E8, 1938-39; House Surgeon, Western Ophthalm. Hosp., 1940. Served in RAMC, 1940-46, in MEF, as RMO and Ophthalmic Specialist. Chief Asst, Eye Dept, St Bartholomew's Hosp., 1946-51. FRSocMed (Past Sec., Sect. of Ophthalmology); Past Hon. Sec. Ophthalmological Soc. of UK. *Publication:* The Retina (with Sir Stewart Duke-Elder). *Address:* 113 Harley Street, W1. *T:* 01-935 9189.

**DOBROSIELSKI, Marian,** PhD Zurich; Knight Cross of the Order of Polonia Restituta, 1964; Ambassador of Poland to the Court of St James's since 1969; *b* 25 March 1923; *s* of Stanislaw and Stefania Dobrosielski; *m* 1950; one *d*. *Educ:* Univ. of Zurich; Univ. of Warsaw. Served in Polish Army in France, War of 1939-45. With Min. of Foreign Affairs, 1948-; Polish Legation, Bern, 1948-50; Head of Section, Min. of Foreign Affairs, 1950-54; Asst Prof., Warsaw Univ. and Polish Acad. of Sciences, 1954-57; Mem., Polish delegn to UN Gen. Assembly, 1952, 1953, 1958, 1966. first Sec., Counsellor, Polish Embassy in Washington, 1958-64; Min. of Foreign Affairs: Counsellor to Minister, 1964-69; Acting Dir, Research Office, 1968-69; Associate Prof., Univ. of Warsaw, 1966; Vice-Dean of Faculty of Philosophy, Univ. of Warsaw, 1966-68; Chm., Scientific Council, Inst. of Philosophy, Univ. of Warsaw, 1969; Chm., Editorial Bd of Studia

Filozoficzne, 1968-69; Sec., Polish Philos. Soc., 1955-57 and 1965-69. Mem. Polish United Workers Party (Sec. Party Org., Univ. of Warsaw, 1956-57, 1968-69). Hon. Vice-Pres., Scottish-Polish Cultural Assoc., Glasgow, 1969-. *Publications:* A Basic Epistemological Principle of Logical Positivism, 1947; The Philosophical Pragmatism of C. S. Peirce, 1967; On some contemporary problems: Philosophy, Ideology, Politics, 1970; numerous articles on philosophy and internat. problems in professional jls. *Recreation:* tennis. *Address:* Polish Embassy, 47 Portland Place, London, W1. *T:* 01-580 4324.

**DOBRY, George Leon Severyn,** QC 1969; *b* 1 Nov. 1918; *m* 1948, Margaret Headley Smith, *e d* of Joseph Quartus Smith, JP, Woolpits, Saling, Essex; two *d*. *Educ:* Edinburgh Univ. (MA). Served War of 1939-45: Air Force (F/O), 1942-46. Called to Bar, Inner Temple, 1946. Mem. Council, Justice, 1956-68. *Publications:* Woodfall's Law of Landlord and Tenant, 25th edition (one of the Editors), 1952; Blundell and Dobry, Town and Country Planning, 1962; Blundell and Dobry Planning Appeals and Inquiries, 1962. *Recreations:* reading, walking. *Address:* 2 Paper Buildings, Temple, EC4. *T:* 01-353 5835; (Residential Chambers) 1 Harcourt Buildings. *T:* 01-583 6208; The New House, Saling, Essex. *T:* Shalford Green 614. *Club:* Reform.

**DOBSON, Maj.-Gen. Anthony Henry George,** CB 1968; OBE 1953; MC 1944; BA Cantab; Inspector, Ministry of Housing and Local Government; *b* 15 Dec. 1911; *s* of late Col Arthur Curtis Dobson, DSO, Royal Engineers, and late Susanna (*née* Oppenheim); *m* 1945, Nellie Homberger; two *s* two *d*. *Educ:* Cheltenham Coll.; Royal Military Academy, Woolwich; Clare Coll., Cambridge. Commissioned Royal Engineers, 1931; hons degree (mech. science), Cambridge, 1934; service in UK, 1934-37; seconded to RAF for survey duties, Iraq, 1938-39. Served War of 1939-45: Middle East (Egypt, Turkey, Iraq), 1939-42; Prisoner of War, Italy, 1942-43; interned in Switzerland after escape, 1944; North-West Europe (Holland and Germany), 1945. Germany, 1945-50; Manpower planning Dept, War Office, 1950-53; in comd, Engineer Regt, Hong Kong, 1953-56; Engr branch, War Office, 1956-59; Chief Engr, HQ Eastern Comd, UK, 1959-62; DQMG, HQ BAOR, 1962-64; Chief Engr, HQ North AG/BAOR, 1964-67, retd. Lt-Col 1945; Col 1956; Brig. 1959; Maj.-Gen. 1964. *Recreations:* ski-ing, gliding. *Address:* Ramillies, Compton Way, Moor Park, Farnham, Surrey. *T:* Runfold 2350. *Clubs:* United Service, Ski Club of Great Britain; Kandahar Ski.

**DOBSON, Christopher Selby Austin,** FSA; Librarian, House of Lords, since 1956; *b* 25 Aug. 1916; *s* of late Alban Tabor Austin Dobson, CB, CVO, CBE; *m* 1941, Helen Broughton, *d* of late Capt. E. B. Turner, Holyhead; one *s* one *d*. *Educ:* Clifton Coll.; Emmanuel Coll., Cambridge (BA). With National Council of Social Service, 1938-39. Served War of 1939-45, Lieut Middx Regt (despatches). Asst Principal (Temp.), Ministry of Education, 1946-47; Asst Librarian, House of Lords, 1947-56. *Publication:* (ed) Oxfordshire Protestation Returns 1641-42, 1955. *Recreations:* collecting books, mezzotints, stamps, etc. *Address:* 60 Homefield Road, Bromley, Kent BR1 3AL. *T:* 01-460 2303. *Clubs:* Athenæum; (Hon.) Rowfant (Cleveland).

**DOBSON, Cowan;** portrait painter; *s* of late H. J. Dobson, RCA; *m* 1931, Phyllis, *e d* of Lancelot Bowyer. Studied Edinburgh, Paris, London. Works hung in world's leading galleries. *Recreation:* legerdemain. *Address:* Studio, 62 South Edwardes Square, W8. *T:* 01-937 7544. *Club:* Hurlingham.

**DOBSON, Sir Denis (William),** KCB 1969 (CB 1959); OBE 1945; Clerk of the Crown in Chancery and Permanent Secretary to the Lord Chancellor, since 1968; *b* 17 Oct. 1908; *s* of late William Gordon Dobson, Newcastle upon Tyne; *m* 1st, 1934, Thelma (marr. diss. 1947), *d* of Charles Swinburne, Newcastle upon Tyne; one *s* one *d*; 2nd, 1948, Mary Elizabeth, *d* of J. A. Allen, Haywards Heath; two *s* one *d*. *Educ:* Charterhouse; Trinity Coll., Cambridge (MA, LLB). Solicitor, 1933. Served in RAF, 1940-45 (Desert Air Force, 1942-45). Called to the Bar, Middle Temple, 1951; Bencher, 1968. Dep. Clerk of the Crown in Chancery and Asst Permanent Sec. to Lord Chancellor, 1954-68. *Address:* 50 Egerton Crescent, SW3. *T:* 01-589 7990. *Club:* Athenæum.

**DOBSON, Prof. Eric John,** MA, DPhil Oxon; Professor of English Language, Oxford University, since 1964; *b* 16 Aug. 1913; *o s* of John and Lottie Frances Dobson; *m* 1940, Francis Margaret Stinton; two *s* one *d*. *Educ:* North Sydney High Sch.; Wesley Coll., Sydney Univ.; Merton Coll., Oxford. BA (1st cl. Hons English) Sydney, 1934; 1st in Final Hon. Sch. of English 1937, DPhil 1951, Oxford. Tutor in English, Sydney Univ., 1934-35; Wentworth Travelling Fellow of Sydney Univ., 1935-38; Harmsworth Sen. Schol. of Merton Coll., 1938-40; Lecturer in English, University of Reading, 1940-48. Served in Intelligence Div., Naval Staff, Admiralty, 1943-45. Lecturer in English, Jesus Coll. and St Edmund Hall, Oxford, 1948-54; Reader in English Lang., Oxford Univ., 1954-64 (title of Prof. from 1960); Professorial Fellow of Jesus Coll., Oxford, 1954-. *Publications:* English Pronunciation 1500-1700, 1957; The Phonetic Writings of Robert Robinson, 1957; Edition of Hymn to the Virgin in Trans. of Cymmrodorion Soc., 1954; The Affiliations of the MSS of Ancrene Wisse, in English and Medieval Studies, 1962; The Date and Composition of Ancrene Wisse (Gollancz Memorial Lecture, Brit. Acad., 1966); articles and reviews in journals. *Address:* 9 Davenant Road, Oxford. *T:* Oxford 56222.

**DOBSON, Gordon Miller Bourne,** CBE 1951; FRS 1927; DSc; formerly Reader in Meteorology, University of Oxford; *b* 25 Feb. 1889; *s* of late Thos Dobson, MD, Windermere; *m* 1st, 1914, Winifred Duncombe Rimer (*d* 1952); two *s* one *d*; 2nd, 1954, Olive M. Bacon. *Educ:* Sedbergh; Caius Coll., Cambridge. *Publications:* Photographic Photometry; Exploring the Atmosphere; papers on geophysical subjects. *Address:* Watch Hill, The Ridings, Shotover, Oxford OX3 8TB. *T:* Oxford 62511.

**DOBSON, Commodore John Petter,** CBE 1961; DSC 1940; RD 1940; RNR (retired); *b* 2 Sept. 1901; *s* of Lieut-Comdr John Dobson, RNR and Alice Martha (*née* Petter); *m* 1942, Edith Agnes Ferguson; one *d*. *Educ:* Middlesbrough High Sch.; Liverpool Coll.; HMS Conway. Midshipman, RNR, 1917; Cadet, Canadian Pacific, 1919; Submarines, 1924; Navigator, RMS Empress of Australia; with Royal trip to Canada and US; subsequently called up, 1939. Minesweeping, 1939-42; Cdre of Convoys, 1942-44, including Normandy Landings; Admiralty Berthing Officer, Sydney, NSW, 1944-45. In command CPS, 1946-61; Master, Empress of Canada (Flagship of Canadian Pacific Steamships Ltd), 1961-62; retired.

1962. Mem., Whitby RDC; Member: Hon. Company of Master Mariners; NE Advisory Council for Sport and Recreation; NE Fisheries Board. Freeman and Liveryman of City of London. *Recreation:* collecting antiques. *Address:* Cleveland House, Goldsborough, near Whitby, Yorks. *T:* Sandsend 222. *Club:* Whitby Conservative.

**DOBSON, Patrick John H.;** *see* Howard-Dobson.

**DOBSON, Raymond Francis Harvey;** Industrial Relations Consultant, Caledonian Airways, since 1970; *b* 26 April 1925; *s* of Tom Noel Dobson; *m* 1947, Vivienne Joyce Martin; three *s* one *d*. *Educ:* Purbrook Park Sch., Portsmouth. Radio Officer, Merchant Navy, 1940-47; Post Office, 1947-66. Trade Union Official, Postal Workers' Union, 1950-66 (Mem. Nat. Exec., 1960-66). MP (Lab) Bristol North-East, 1966-70; PPS, Min. of Technology, 1967-69; Asst Govt Whip, 1969-70; Member: Select Cttee of Estimates, 1966-67; Select Cttee for Science and Technology, 1969. *Address:* Hunters Moon, Highlands Road, Long Ashton, Bristol. *T:* Long Ashton 3092. *Club:* Ashton Court Country (Bristol).

**DOBSON, Richard Portway;** Chairman, British American Tobacco Co. Ltd; *b* 11 Feb. 1914; *s* of Prof. J. F. Dobson; *m* 1946, Emily Margaret Carver; one step *d*. *Educ:* Clifton Coll.; King's Coll., Cambridge. Flt-Lt, RAF, 1941-45 (Pilot). Joined British American Tobacco Co. Ltd, 1935: served in China, 1936-40; China, Rhodesia and London, 1946-; Dir, 1955; Dep. Chm., 1962; Vice-Chm., 1968; Chm., 1970. *Publication:* China Cycle, 1946. *Recreations:* fly fishing, golf. *Address:* 16 Marchmont Road, Richmond upon Thames, Surrey. *T:* 01-940 1504. *Club:* United University.

**DOBSON, Sydney George;** formerly Chairman of the Board, The Royal Bank of Canada; *b* 20 Sept. 1883; *s* of J. W. Dobson and Harriett Martell; *m* 1913, Beatrice, *d* of S. G. Chambers; one *s* one *d*. *Educ:* Sydney Public Schs. Joined The Merchants Bank of Halifax at Sydney, NS, 1900; transferred to The Royal Bank of Canada, Truro, NS, 1904; Accountant, Winnipeg, 1906; Asst Manager, Truro, 1909; Accountant, Toronto, 1910; Manager, Sydney, 1911; Asst Manager, Montreal, 1915; Manager, Vancouver, 1916; Actg Supervisor, Winnipeg, 1918; Gen. Inspector at Head Office, 1919; Asst Gen. Manager, 1922; Gen. Manager, 1934; Dir, 1939; Vice-Pres. and Gen. Manager, 1942; Exec. Vice-Pres., 1945; Pres., 1946. Dir of BC Power Corp. Ltd, Shawinigan Water & Power Co., and BC Electric Co. Ltd. Formerly Governor of McGill Univ. *Recreations:* golf, yachting, motoring. *Address:* 1321 Sherbrooke Street West, Montreal, Canada. *Clubs:* Mount Royal, St James's, Montreal, Royal St Lawrence Yacht, Mount Bruno Golf and Country, Royal Montreal Golf (Montreal); Rideau (Ottawa).

**DOCKER, Sir Bernard (Dudley Frank),** KBE 1939; *o s* of late Frank Dudley Docker, CB; *m* 1949, Norah, *widow* of Sir William Collins. *Educ:* Harrow. *Recreations:* golf, shooting, yachting. *Address:* Rozel Bay, St Helier, Jersey, Channel Islands. *Clubs:* Royal London Yacht; St Helier Yacht.

**DODD, Charles Edward Shuter;** *b* 2 May 1891; *s* of H. W. Dodd, FRCS, Harley Street, London; *m* 1921, Elizabeth Mabel, *d* of Sir Henry Birchenough, 1st Bt, GCMG; one *s* one *d*. *Educ:* Harrow; Balliol Coll., Oxford. Exhibitioner and Hon. Scholar of Balliol; Hertford, Craven and Ireland Univ. Scholarships. Served European War, 1914-19, in Royal Welch Fusiliers (TF), Welsh Guards and Intelligence Corps; Third Sec., Diplomatic Service, 1919; 2nd Sec., 1920; 1st Sec., 1924; Counsellor, 1937; Envoy Extraordinary and Minister Plenipotentiary at Panama, 1939-43. Municipal Councillor (Progressive) for Lansdown Ward, Bath, 1952-61. *Address:* 7 The Circus, Bath.

**DODD, Rev. Charles Harold,** CH 1961; MA (Oxford, Cambridge, Manchester); Hon. DD (Oxford, Cambridge, London, Manchester, Glasgow, Aberdeen and Wales); Hon. DLitt, Oxford; Hon. STD (Harvard); Hon. DTheol (Oslo); Docteur hc (Strasbourg); FBA 1946; Hon. Fellow, Jesus College, Cambridge, since 1949; Hon. Fellow, University College, Oxford, since 1951; *b* Wrexham, Denbighshire, 7 April 1884; *e s* of late Charles Dodd, FGS, and Sarah, *d* of Edward Parsonage, Wrexham; *m* 1925, Phyllis Mary, *widow* of John Elliott Terry, and *y d* of late George Stockings, Bournemouth; one *s* one *d*. *Educ:* Wrexham; University Coll., Oxford (Classical Scholar); Berlin; Senior Demy, Magdalen Coll., 1907-11; studied Theology meanwhile at Mansfield Coll., Oxford. Ordained, 1912; Minister of the Independent or Congregational Church at Warwick, 1912-15, 1918-19; Yates Lectr in New Testament Greek and Exegesis, Mansfield Coll., 1915-30; Univ. Lectr in New Testament Studies, Oxford, 1927-30; Grinfield Lectr on the Septuagint, Oxford, 1927-31; Rylands Prof. of Biblical Criticism and Exegesis, Manchester, 1930-35; Speaker's Lectr in Biblical Studies, Univ. of Oxford, 1933-37; Shaffer Lecturer, Yale Univ., 1935; Ingersoll Lecturer, Harvard Univ., 1935, 1950; Norris-Hulse Prof. of Divinity, Cambridge, 1935-49; Fellow of Jesus Coll., Cambridge, 1936-49; Hewett Lecturer, Episcopal Theological Seminary, Cambridge, USA, 1938; Olaus Petri Lecturer, University of Uppsala, 1949; Bampton Lecturer in America, Columbia Univ., 1950; Stone Lecturer, Princeton Theological Seminary, 1950; Visiting Prof. of Biblical Theology, Union Theological Seminary, New York, 1950; Gen. Dir, New Translation of the Bible, 1950-65; Joint Dir, 1966-70; Editor, Texts and Studies, 1953-62. Sarum Lectr, Oxford, 1954-55. Hon. Freeman, Wrexham, 1964. *Publications:* The Meaning of Paul for To-day, 1920; The Gospel in the New Testament, 1926; The Authority of the Bible, 1928; Ephesians, Colossians, and Philemon (Abingdon Commentary), 1929; The Bible and Its Background, 1931; The Epistle to The Romans (Moffatt Commentary), 1932; There and Back Again, 1932; The Bible and the Greeks, 1935; Parables of the Kingdom, 1935; The Apostolic Preaching and its Developments, 1936; The Present Task in New Testament Studies (Inaugural Lecture), 1936; History and the Gospel, 1937; The Johannine Epistles (Moffatt Commentary), 1946; The Bible To-day, 1946; Benefits of His Passion, 1947; About the Gospels, 1950; The Coming of Christ, 1951; Gospel and Law, 1951; Christianity and the Reconciliation of the Nations, 1952; According to the Scriptures, 1952; The Interpretation of the Fourth Gospel, 1953; New Testament Studies, 1953; Historical Tradition in the Fourth Gospel, 1963; More New Testament Studies, 1968; The Founder of Christianity, 1970; Israel and the Arab World, 1970. *Address:* 1 Wellington Place, St Giles', Oxford.

**DODD, Harold,** MB, ChM (Liverpool), FRCS, LRCP; Consulting Surgeon (retired) to: St Mary's Hospital Group, Paddington; King George Hospital, Ilford; Royal Hospital, Richmond; Royal London Homoeopathic Hospital; Hon. Curate (Deacon), All Soul's

Church, W1; Past President, Association of Consultants and Specialists of Regional Board Hospitals; *b* 13 March 1899; *e s* of Alfred Ledward Dodd and Annie Elizabeth Marshall; *m* 1945, Mary, *yr d* of late R. H. Bond; one *s*. *Educ:* University of Liverpool; Guy's Hosp. Lieut, RAF (pilot), 1918-19; MB, ChB (Distinction in Surgery) Liverpool, 1922, O. T. Williams Prizeman for 1923; House Surgeon, House Physician, Surgical Tutor and Registrar, Liverpool Royal Infirmary, 1923-26; Asst Medical Superintendent, St Luke's Hosp., Chelsea, 1926-28; Surgical Clinics, Univ. of Berlin, 1926 and 1937; Resident Medical Officer, Royal Northern Hosp., N7, 1928-30. Fellow, Assoc. of Surgeons of Great Britain; FRSM (Ex-Pres. Section of Proctology). Chm., Management Cttee, Royal Med. Benevolent Fund. *Publications:* (with F. B. Cockett) Pathology and Surgery of the Veins of the Lower Limb, 1956; surgical papers in medical journals. *Address:* 27 Wimpole Street, W1. *T:* 01-580 4121; (home) 22 Campden Hill Gate, Duchess of Bedford's Walk, W8. *T:* 01-937 9297.

**DODD, Prof. James Munro,** DSc, PhD; FRSE; Professor of Zoology, University College of North Wales, since 1968; *b* 26 May 1915; *m* 1951, Margaret Helen Ingram Macaulay (*née* Greig), BSc (Aberdeen), PhD (Harvard); three *s*. *Educ:* The White House Sch., Brampton, Cumberland; Univ. of Liverpool. BSc hons (Cl. 1) 1937; DipEd 1938. PhD St Andrews, 1953; DSc St Andrews, 1968. Biology Master, Cardigan Grammar Sch., 1938-40. Royal Air Force (Navigator and Staff Navigator), 1940-46. Asst in Zoology, Univ. of Aberdeen, 1946-47; Lectr in Zoology, Univ. of St Andrews, in charge of Gatty Marine Laboratory, 1947-57; Reader in Zoology, Univ. of St Andrews, and Dir of Gatty Marine Laboratory, 1957-60; Prof. of Zoology, Leeds Univ., 1960-68. FRSE 1957. *Publications:* contributor to Marshall's Physiology of Reproduction, The Thyroid Gland, The Pituitary Gland, and to zoological and endocrinological jls. *Recreations:* fishing, photography, music. *Address:* c/o Department of Zoology, University College of North Wales, Bangor.

**DODD, Sir John (Samuel),** Kt 1947; TD; engineer; *b* 13 Oct. 1904; *s* of late William Dodd, JP, Keldwith, Windermere; *m* 1937, Margaret McDougall, *d* of late William Hamilton, Glasgow; four *s*. *Educ:* Uppingham; Rouen; Christ's Coll., Cambridge (MA). Contested Oldham (L) 1929 and (LNat) 1945; MP (LNat) Oldham, 1935-45. MIME; FRGS; Fellow, Royal Philatelic Society, London; Past Pres., Assoc. of British Chambers of Commerce; Mem., Central National Service Cttee for Great Britain, 1939-40; Hon. Adviser on Tank Production and Chm. of Tank Production Groups, Ministry of Supply, 1940-41; Hon. Mem. Administrative Council, Cotton Research Corporation; Underwriting Mem. of Lloyd's; Late Major Royal Tank Regt TA. Chm. of Exec. Cttee of Nat. Liberal Council, 1947-49; Mem. of Lord Chancellor's Cttee on County Court Procedure, 1947-49. *Publications:* contribs to various periodicals and trade journals. *Recreations:* travel, yachting, mountaineering, philately. *Address:* La Maison Maret, Trinity, Jersey, Channel Islands. *T:* Jersey North 24. *Clubs:* Naval and Military; Royal Windermere Yacht; Royal Lytham and St Anne's Golf; Royal Channel Islands Yacht.

**DODD, Kenneth Arthur, (Ken Dodd);** professional entertainer, comedian, singer and actor, since 1957; *b* 1931; *s* of Arthur and Sarah Dodd; unmarried. *Educ:* Holt High Sch., Liverpool. Frequently appears at the Palladium, London, etc. Pantomime, Robinson Crusoe, Coventry Theatre 1969-70. *Recreations:* racing, soccer, reading. *Address:* 76 Thomas Lane, Knotty Ash, Liverpool 14.

**DODDS, Sir Charles;** *see* Dodds, Sir E. C.

**DODDS, Denis George,** LLB (London); CompIEE; Solicitor; Chairman, Merseyside and North Wales Electricity Board, since 1962 (Deputy Chairman, 1960-62); *b* 25 May 1913; *s* of Herbert Yeaman Dodds and Violet Katharine Dodds; *m* 1937, Muriel Reynolds Smith; two *s* three *d*. *Educ:* Rutherford Coll., Newcastle upon Tyne; King's Coll., Durham Univ. Asst Solicitor and Asst Town Clerk, Gateshead, 1936-41. Served Royal Navy (Lieut RNVR), 1941-46. Dep. Town Clerk and Dep. Clerk of the Peace, City of Cardiff, 1946-48; Sec., S Wales Electricity Board, 1948-56; Chief Industrial Relations Officer, CEA and Industrial Relations Adviser, Electricity Council, 1957-59. *Recreations:* music and gardening. *Address:* Arley, 27 Dowhills Road, Blundellsands, Liverpool L23 8SJ. *T:* 051-924 6001.

**DODDS, Sir (Edward) Charles,** 1st Bt, *cr* 1964; Kt 1954; MVO 1929; DSc (London); FRS 1942; FRSE; FRCP, FRCPSG; FRIC; Emeritus Professor of Biochemistry, University of London (Courtauld Professor of Biochemistry and Director, Courtauld Institute of Biochemistry at Middlesex Hospital Medical School, 1927-65); *b* 1899; *o s* of late Ralph Edward and Jane Dodds, Darlington and London; *m* 1923, Constance Elizabeth (*d* 1969), *o d* of late J. T. and Katharine Jordan, Darlington; one *s*. *Educ:* Harrow Co. Sch.; Middx Hosp. Med. Sch. (MD, PhD). Pathologist, Royal Nat. Orthopædic Hosp. Lectures: Goulstonian, RCP, 1934; Harvey, New York Univ., 1935; Harben, Royal Inst. of Public Health, London, 1937; Cantor, RSA, 1939; Bertram Louis Abrahams, RCP, 1950; Purser, TCD, 1950; Sanderson-Wells, Middx Hosp., 1953; Dorothy Platt, King's Coll., 1953; Cavendish, W London Med. Chirurgical Soc., 1955; Guiteras, Amer. Urological Soc., Boston, 1956; Lane, Stanford Univ., 1956; Crookshank, RCS, 1959; Addison, Guy's Hosp., 1946, 1960; Linacre, St John's Coll., Cambridge, 1960; Comfort Crookshank, Middx Hosp., 1960. William Julius Mickle Fellowship, Univ. of London, 1943; Sims Travelling Prof., RCS, 1952. President: RCP, 1962-66; 4th Internat. Congress in Endocrinology, 1968; a Vice-Pres. and Mem. Council, Royal Soc., 1957-59; Vice-President: Eugenics Soc.; Arthritis and Rheumatism Council (Chm., Planning Sub-Cttee). Formerly Chairman: Scientific Adv. Cttee, British Empire Cancer Campaign; Governing Body, Lister Inst.; Science Cttee, British Heart Foundn. Formerly Chairman: Cttee of Management of Cancer Res. Inst., Royal Cancer Hosp.; Tropical Products Inst. Cttee, DSIR; Food Additives and Contaminants Sub-Cttee of Food Standards Cttee, and Adv. Cttee on Poisonous Substances used in Agriculture and Food Storage, Min. of Agriculture, Fisheries and Food; Scientific Adv. Cttee, Fleming Memorial Fund for Med. Res.; Adv. Council on Scientific Res. and Technical Develt, Mem., Heberden Soc.; formerly Mem., Nat. Res. Develt Corp. Hon. Member: Assoc. of Physicians; Pathological Soc. of Manchester; Amer. Soc. of Clinical Pathologists; Amer. Assoc. for Cancer Res.; New York Acad. of Sciences; Chilean Chem. Soc.; Chilean Med. Soc.; Biological Soc. of Chile; Radiological Soc. of Chile; Chilean League against Cancer; Soc. of Chemical Industry of France; Finnish Med. Soc.

Duodecim; Royal Med. Acad. of Barcelona; Italian Chemical Soc.; Danish Soc. of Internal Medicine; Med. Soc. of Gothenburg. Foreign Corresp. Mem., Nat. Acad. of Medicine of France; Hon. Councillor, Consejo Superior de Investigaciones Cientificas of Spain. FInstBiol; Hon. FRCS, hon. FRCOG, Hon. FRCPSG, Hon. FRACP, Hon. FRCPath; Hon. Fellow: Royal Coll. of Physicians and Surgeons (Canada); Australian Postgraduate Fedn in Medicine. Hon. MD: Melbourne; Birmingham; Hon. ScD Cambridge; Hon. DSc Chicago; Hon. LLD Glasgow; Hon. Dr Bologna. Past Master, Worshipful Soc. of Apothecaries. KStJ. Gold Medal for Therapeutics, W London Med. Soc., 1938; Cameron Prizeman, Univ. of Edinburgh, 1940; Charles L. Meyer Prize and Walker Prize, RCS, 1946; Garton Prize and Medal, British Empire Cancer Campaign, 1948; Berzelius Medal, Swedish Med. Soc.; Medals of Univs of Ghent and Brussels; Pasteur Medal, Congress of Biological Chemistry of Société de Chimie Biologique Française; Gold Medal in Therapeutics, Soc. of Apothecaries, 1951; Gold Medal, Soc. of Chemical Industry, 1951; Harben Medal, Royal Inst. of Public Health, 1952. *Publications:* (with G. E. Beaumont) Recent Advances in Medicine; (with F. Dickens) Chemical and Physiological Properties of Internal Secretions; (with L. E. H. Whitby) The Laboratory in Surgical Practice; articles on biochemical subjects in various scientific jls. *Heir: s* Ralph Jordan Dodds [*b* 25 March 1928; *m* 1954, Marion, *er d* of late Sir Daniel Davies, KCVO; two *d*]. *Address:* 49 Sussex Square, W2. *T:* 01-723 0498. *Clubs:* Athenæum, Savage, Bath.

**DODDS, Eric Robertson,** MA Oxon; Hon. DLitt (Manchester, Dublin, Edinburgh and Belfast); FBA; Corresponding Member of Academia Sinica, Bavarian Academy, American Academy of Arts and Sciences; Hon. Fellow, University College, Oxford; Hon. Student of Christ Church, Oxford; Regius Professor of Greek, University of Oxford, 1936-60; *b* 26 July 1893; *o s* of Robert Dodds, Headmaster of Banbridge Academy; *m* 1923, Annie, *yr d* of late Rev. Canon A. D. Powell. *Educ:* Campbell Coll., Belfast; University Coll., Oxford. Lectr in Classics at University Coll., Reading, 1919-24; Prof. of Greek in the University of Birmingham, 1924-36. *Publications:* Select Passages Illustrative of Neoplatonism, 2 vols, 1923 and 1924; Thirty-two Poems, 1929; Proclus' Elements of Theology, 1933; Journal and Letters of Stephen MacKenna, 1936; Euripides' Bacchae, 1944; The Greeks and the Irrational, 1951; Plato's Gorgias, 1959; Pagan and Christian in an Age of Anxiety, 1965. *Recreation:* psychical research. *Address:* Cromwell's House, Old Marston, Oxford.

**DODDS, George Christopher Buchanan;** Assistant Under-Secretary of State, Ministry of Defence, since 1964; *b* 8 Oct. 1916; *o s* of George Hepple Dodds and Gladys Marion (*née* Ferguson), Newcastle upon Tyne; *m* 1944, Olive Florence Wilmot Ling; no *c*. *Educ:* Rugby; Gonville and Caius Coll., Cambridge (BA). Entered Secretary's Dept, Admiralty, 1939; Royal Marines, 1940-41; Private Sec. to Sec. of the Admiralty, 1941-43; Asst Private Sec. to Prime Minister, June-Aug. 1944; Asst Sec., 1951; idc, 1959. *Recreations:* bird-watching, walking, golf, bridge. *Address:* 5 Bryanston Square, W1. *T:* 01-262 2852. *Clubs:* United University; Royal Mid-Surrey Golf.

**DODDS, George Elliott;** Consultant Editor and Director, Huddersfield Examiner; *b* 4 March 1889; *yr s* of George William and Elizabeth Anne Dodds, Sydenham, Kent; *m* 1918, Frances Zita MacDonald, *yr d* of Rev. Joseph Johnson, Sale, Ches; two *d*. *Educ:* Mill Hill Sch.; New Coll., Oxford. Pres. Liberal Party Organisation, 1948-49; contested York City, 1922 and 1923, Halifax, 1929, Rochdale, 1931 and 1935. Pres., Unservile State Group. *Publications:* Is Liberalism Dead?, 1919; Liberalism in Action, 1922; The Social Gospel of Liberalism, 1926; Let's Try Liberalism, 1944; The Defence of Man, 1947; The Logic of Liberty (with Erna Reiss), 1966. *Recreation:* golf. *Address:* Belhaven, 230 Somerset Road, Huddersfield. *T:* Huddersfield 30597. *Clubs:* Reform, National Liberal; Old Millhillians.

**DODDS, Gladys Helen,** MD, FRCS, FRCSE, FRCOG; Medical Director, Family Planning Association, Hong Kong; Hon. Consultant Obstetrician and Gynæcologist, Queen Charlotte's and North East Metropolitan Hospitals, London; *b* Kirkcaldy, Fife, 1898; *d* of James Dodds and Elizabeth Paterson. *Educ:* High Sch., Dunfermline; Univ. of Edinburgh. House Surg., Royal Maternity Hosp. and Royal Hosp. for Sick Children, Edinburgh; 1st Asst, Obstetric Unit, University Coll. Hosp., London. *Publications:* Gynecology for Nurses, 1946; Midwives' Dictionary; contributions to the Encyclopædia of Medical Practice and to medical journals. *Address:* B 26 Po Shan Mansions, 10 Po Shan Road, Hong Kong.

**DODDS, Harold Willis;** President, Princeton University, 1933-June 1957; *b* Utica, Penna, 28 June 1889; *s* of Samuel Dodds and Alice Dunn; *m* 1917, Margaret Murray. *Educ:* AB Grove City (Pa) Coll., 1909; AM Princeton, 1914; PhD Pennsylvania, 1917. Instructor in Economics, Purdue Univ., 1914-16; Asst Prof. of Political Science, Western Reserve Univ., 1919-20; Sec., National Municipal League, 1920-28; Editor, National Municipal Review, 1920-33; Prof. of Politics, Princeton Univ., 1927-33; Executive Sec., US Food Administration, Pa, 1917-19; Electoral Adviser to Govt of Nicaragua, 1922-24; Technical Adviser to President, Tacna-Arica Plebiscitary Commn, 1925-26; Chief Adviser to President, National Board of Elections of Nicaragua, 1928; Consultant to Cuban Govt in Election Law Procedure, 1935; Chm., American Delegation, Anglo-American Conf. on the Refugee Problem, 1943, Bermuda; Chm., The President's Cttee on Integration of Medical Services in the Armed Forces, 1946; Mem., The President's Advisory Commn on Universal Training, 1947. Pres., Assoc. of American Univs, 1952-54; Chm., Personnel Task Force of Commn on Organization of Exec. Branch of the Govt, 1954-55; Chm., Joint Congressional Commn on James Madison Memorial. *Publications:* Out of This Nettle . . . Danger, 1943; The Academic President: Educator or Caretaker, 1962; various reports, pamphlets and articles on political and public administration. *Recreations:* golf and gardening. *Address:* 87 College Road W, Princeton, NJ, USA. *Clubs:* Athenæum (London); Century, Princeton (New York); University (Washington); Nassau (Princeton).

**DODDS, Sir James Leishman,** KCMG 1950 (CMG 1938); *b* 1891; *s* of late Sir James Miller Dodds, KCB; *m* 1927, Etelka, *y d* of late Brig.-Gen. Sir Conyers Surtees, CB, CMG, and *widow* of Edward Bell, New York; one *d*. *Educ:* Marlborough; Wadham Coll., Oxford (Classical Exhib.). Served European War, 1915-19; entered Diplomatic Service, 1919; served Tokyo, 1919, Madrid 1923, Stockholm 1925, The Hague 1929, Berne 1933; Counsellor of Embassy, Japan, 1938-40; Envoy Ext. and Min. Plen. Bolivia, 1940-43; Cuba, 1944-49; Ambassador to Peru, 1949-51; retd, 1951.

*Address:* Church House, Beckley, Sussex. *T:* Beckley 276. *Club:* Athenæum.

**DODDS, James Pickering,** CB 1954; Assistant Under-Secretary of State, Department of Health and Social Security, since 1968 (Under-Secretary, Director of Establishments and Organisation, Ministry of Health, 1965-68); *b* 7 Feb. 1913; *s* of James Thompson and Elizabeth Fingland Dodds; *m* 1942, Ethel Mary Gill; two *d. Educ:* Queen Elizabeth's Grammar Sch., Darlington; Jesus Coll., Cambridge. Entered Ministry of Health, 1935; Nuffield Home Civil Service Travelling Fellowship, 1950; Under-Sec., 1951. *Address:* 21 Luttrell Avenue, Putney, SW15.

**DODDS-PARKER, Arthur Douglas;** MA (Oxford); MP (C) Cheltenham since 1964; company director since 1946; *b* 5 July 1909; *o s* of A. P. Dodds-Parker, FRCS, Oxford; *m* 1946, Aileen, *d* of late Norman B. Coster and late Mrs Alvin Dodd, Grand Detour, Ill., USA; one *s. Educ:* Winchester; Magdalen Coll., Oxford. BA in Modern History, 1930; MA 1934. Entered Sudan Political Service, 1930; Kordofan Province, 1931-34; Asst Private Sec. to Governor-General, Khartoum, 1934-35; Blue Nile Province, 1935-38; Public Security Dept, Khartoum, 1938-39; resigned 1938; joined Grenadier Guards, 1939; employed on special duties, March 1940; served in London, Cairo, East African campaign, North Africa, Italy and France, 1940-45. MP (C) Banbury Div. of Oxon, 1945-Sept. 1959. Jt Parly Under-Sec. of State for Foreign Affairs, Nov. 1953-Oct. 1954, Dec. 1955-Jan. 1957; Parly Under-Sec. for Commonwealth Relations, Oct. 1954-Dec. 1955. Chairman: British Empire Producers Organisation; Joint East and Central Africa Board, 1947-50; Conservative Commonwealth Council, 1962-64. Col, 1944 (despatches, French Legion of Honour, Croix de Guerre). *Address:* 9 North Court, Great Peter Street, SW1; Yew Tree Cottage, Prestbury, Glos. *Clubs:* Carlton; Leander.

**DODGE, Bayard,** DD, LLD, MA, BD; Retired; *b* New York City, 5 Feb. 1888; *s* of late Cleveland Hoadley Dodge and Grace Parish; *m* 1914, Mary Williams Bliss; two *s* two *d. Educ:* Browning Sch., New York City; Princeton Univ.; Union Theological Seminary and Columbia Univ., New York City. Mem. of the Faculty of the American Univ. of Beirut, 1913-19; Acting Executive Secretary, 1919-20; Managing Dir of the Syria-Palestine Area of the Near East Relief, 1920-21; returned to American Univ., Beirut, 1921-22; Pres., American Univ. of Beirut, 1923-48. Mem. of the Trustee Board of the League of Nations for Settlement of the Assyrians, 1936-42; Adviser, UN Relief for Palestine Refugees, Nov. 1948. Visiting Prof., Columbia Univ., 1949-54; Lecturer Princeton Univ., 1951-55; Cultural Affairs Officer, Cairo, 1955-56; Visiting Prof., American Univ. at Cairo, 1956-59. Corresp. Mem. Arab Acad., Syrian Republic, 1956. Hon. LLD: Occidental Coll., 1926; Yale Univ., 1949; Hon. DD, Princeton Univ., 1928; Hon. LittD, American Univ. of Beirut, 1966. Chevalier, Légion d'Honneur, 1927; Mérite Libanais, 1937; Mérite Syrien, 1937; Grand Officier de l'Ordre Royal du Phénix, 1937; Ordre de l'Instruction Publique, Lebanese Republic, 1942; Décoration de l'Instruction Publique de l'Iran, 1942; Hon. OBE, 1946; Commander, Pologna Restituta, 1947; Grand Officer, Order of Cedar (Lebanon), 1948; Commander, Order of Ismail (Egypt), 1948; Syrian Order of Umayya, 1948. *Publications:* The American University of Beirut, 1958; Al-Azhar, a Millennium of Muslim Learning, 1961; Muslim Education in Medieval Times, 1962. *Address:* 19 Alexander Street, Princeton, New Jersey 08540, USA.

**DODGE, John V.;** Vice-President, Editorial, Encyclopædia Britannica Inc., since 1970; *b* 25 Sept. 1909; *s* of George Dannel Dodge and Mary Helen Porter; *m* 1935, Jean Elizabeth Plate; two *s* two *d. Educ:* Northwestern Univ., Evanston, Ill., USA; Univ. of Bordeaux, Bordeaux, France. Free-lance writer, 1931-32; Editor, Northwestern Alumni News and Official publications of Northwestern Univ., 1932-35; Exec. Sec., Northwestern Univ. Alumni Assoc., 1937-38; Asst Editor, Encyclopædia Britannica, and Associate Editor, Britannica Book of the Year, 1938-43. US Army, 1943-46 (Intelligence). Associate Editor, Ten Eventful Years and Asst Editor, Encyclopædia Britannica, 1946-50; Editor, Britannica World Language Dictionary, 1954; Managing Editor, Encyclopædia, 1950-60; Executive Editor, 1960-64; Senior Vice-Pres., Editorial, 1964-65; Senior Editorial Consultant, 1965-70. Conseiller Editorial, Encyclopædia Universalis (Paris), 1968-. *Recreations:* gardening and bowling. *Address:* 1499 Shermer Road, Northbrook, Ill 60062, USA. *T:* Crestwood 2-0254.

**DODS, Sir Lorimer (Fenton),** Kt 1962; MVO 1947; Emeritus Professor of Child Health, University of Sydney, since 1960; Chairman, Children's Medical Research Foundation, Sydney, since 1966 (Hon. Director, 1960-66); *b* 7 March 1900; British; *m* 1927, Margaret Walsh; one *s* one *d. Educ:* Sydney Church of England Gram. Sch., N Sydney; St Paul's Coll., University of Sydney (1918-23). Served 1st AIF, 1918. Gen. Med. Practice, 1926-37; Pædiatric Practice, 1937-39 and 1945-49. Served 2nd AIF, RAAMC, Lt-Col, Middle East and New Guinea. Prof. of Child Health, University of Sydney, and Dir of Commonwealth Inst. of Child Health, 1949-60. *Publications:* various pædiatric contribs. *Address:* 8 Albert Street, Edgecliff, NSW 2027, Australia. *T:* FB 2152. *Clubs:* Union, Royal Sydney Golf (Sydney).

**DODSON,** family name of **Baron Monk Bretton.**

**DODSON, Derek Sherborne Lindsell,** CMG 1963; MC 1945; HM Diplomatic Service; Ambassador to Hungary since 1970; *b* 20 Jan. 1920; *e* and *o surv. s* of Charles Sherborne Dodson, MD, and Irene Frances Lindsell; *m* 1952, Julie Maynard Barnes; one *s* one *d. Educ:* Stowe; RMC Sandhurst. Commissioned as 2nd Lieut in Royal Scots Fusiliers, 1939, and served in Army until Feb. 1948. Served War of 1939-45 (MC): India, UK, Middle East, and with Partisans in Greece and N Italy. Mil. Asst to Brit. Comr, Allied Control Commn for Bulgaria, July 1945-Sept. 1946; GSO 3, War Office, Oct. 1946-Nov. 1947; apptd a Mem. HM Foreign Service, 1948; 2nd Sec., 1948; Acting Vice-Consul at Salonika, Sept. 1948; Acting Consul Gen. there in 1949 and 1950; Second Sec., Madrid, 1951; promoted First Sec., Oct. 1951; transferred to Foreign Office, Sept. 1953; apptd Private Sec. to Minister of State for Foreign Affairs, 1955; First Sec. and Head of Chancery, Prague, Nov. 1958; Chargé d'Affaires there in 1959, 1960, 1961, 1962; promoted and apptd Consul at Elisabethville, 1962; Transf. FO and apptd Head of the Central Dept, 1963; Counsellor, British Embassy, Athens, 1966-69. *Recreations:* shooting, fishing, walking. *Address:* 47 Ovington Street, SW3. *T:* 01-589 5055; The Three Gables, Leadenham, near Lincoln. *T:* Fulbeck 212. *Clubs:* Boodle's, Travellers'.

**DODSWORTH, Sir John Christopher S.;** *see* Smith-Dodsworth.

**DODWELL, David William,** CIE 1946; BA (Hons) Oxon, MA, PhD, Columbia; Economic Adviser to Joseph Lucas Ltd, Birmingham, 1948-63, retd; *b* 13 Dec. 1898; *s* of Frederick William Dodwell and Martha Ann Williams Dodwell (*née* Carpenter), Banbury, Oxon; *m* 1924, Marcia Ada Bausor Bradley (later Rev. M. A. B. Dodwell, MA Oxon, of the Christian Community, Birmingham; she *d* 1964), *d* of late W. Harris Bradley, Wolverhampton; two *s* one *d* (and one adopted *d*). *Educ:* Grimsbury Council Sch., Banbury; Banbury Grammar Sch.; Balliol Coll., Oxford. Brackenbury Scholar of Balliol in Modern History, 1915. 2nd Lieut, Worcs Regt, served in Egypt, 1917-19. BA Oxon, 2nd class Hons Mod. Hist., 1921. Entered ICS and arrived Madras, 1922; served as Asst Collector, Sub-Collector and Collector in various districts of Madras Province, 1922-25, 1928-32, and 1934-35. Tutor to HH the Maharajah of Travancore, 1925-28. Beit Prize of Oxford Univ. for essay on British Nationality, 1929; granted special leave to hold a Commonwealth Fund Service Fellowship at Graduate Sch. of Economics, Columbia Univ., New York, 1932-34; MA 1933, PhD 1934, Columbia, in economics; attached to Finance Dept of Madras Govt, 1935; Finance Sec. to the Govt of Madras, 1942-48; retd, 1948. Mem. OEEC Mission to USA to study motor industry, 1952. *Publications:* Treasuries and Central Banks, 1934; Ways and Means Procedure, 1936. *Recreations:* gardening, music. *Address:* 2 Blackwell Close, Towcester, Northants.

**DOGGART, James Hamilton,** MA, MD, FRCS; Consulting Surgeon, Moorfields, Westminster and Central Eye Hospital and Hospital for Sick Children, Great Ormond Street; Immediate Past Chairman, British Orthoptic Board; FRSM; Livery of the Society of Apothecaries of London; Ophthalmological Society, Société belge d'Ophtalmologie, Société franc. d'Ophtalmologie; Hon. Member: Australian, NZ and Peruvian Ophthalmological Societies; Oto-Neuro-Ophth. Soc. of the Argentine; Canadian Ophthalmological Society; Lecturer, Institute of Ophthalmology; Examiner: for British Orthoptic Board; (in Fellowship of Ophthalmology) RCSI; formerly: Faculty of Ophth. representative on Council of RCS; Examiner in Ophthalmology, Royal Coll. of Surgeons and Physicians, University of Belfast, and for FRCS, 1954-60; formerly Pres. and Mem. Council, Faculty of Ophthalmologists and Fellow and Councillor, Hunterian Society; Hon. Secretary, Editorial Committee, British Journal Ophthalmology; surgeon-oculist in London since 1929; *b* 22 Jan. 1900; *s* of late Arthur Robert Doggart, Bishop Auckland; *m* 1st, 1928, Doris Hilda Mennell; one *d*; 2nd, 1938, Leonora Sharpley Gatti; one *s*. *Educ:* Bishop's Stortford Coll.; King's Coll., Cambridge (Scholar); St Thomas's Hospital. Surg. Sub-Lt, RNVR, 1918; Schol., King's Coll., Cambridge, 1919-22; Mem. Anglo-American Physiological Exped. to Andes, 1921; Ophth. Ho. Surg., St Thomas's Hosp., 1923-24; Ho. Surg., Casualty Officer, Royal Northern Hosp., 1925-26; appts at Royal Westminster Ophthalmic Hosp.; Clinical Asst, Refraction Asst, Chief Clin. Asst and Pathologist, 1926-30; appts at Moorfields Eye Hosp.; Clin. Asst, Refraction Asst, Chief Clin. Asst, 1927-34, Asst Med. Officer to Physico-Therapy Dept, 1930-31, Lang Research Schol., 1930-33; Clin. Asst, London Hosp., 1929-34; Ophth. Surg., East Ham Memorial Hosp., 1930-31; appts at St George's Hosp.: Asst Ophth. Surg., 1931-46, Ophth. Surg., 1946-49; Lectr in Ophthalmology, St George's Hosp. Med. Sch., University of London, 1931-49; Ophth. Surg., Lord Mayor Treloar Hosp., 1932-37; Asst Surgeon, Central London Ophthalmic Hosp., 1934-38; Ophth. Surg., Hosp. Hosp.: Sick Children, Great Ormond Street, 1936-63; Lectr in Ophth., Inst. of Child Health, 1936-63; Hon. Secretary: Section of Ophthalmology, RSM, 1935-37; Ophthalmological Soc., 1939-40, 1946-47. Chm., Cttee of Horatian Soc., 1965-69. Sq/Ldr, W/Cdr, RAF, Med. Br., 1940-45. CStJ 1962. *Publications:* Diseases of Children's Eyes, 1947, 2nd edn, 1950; Children's Eye Nursing, 1948; Ocular Signs in Slit-Lamp Microscopy, 1949; Ophthalmic Medicine, 1949; Chapters in: Moncrieff's Nursing of Sick Children, 1948; Garrod Batten and Thursfield's Diseases of Children, 1949; Stallard's Modern Practice in Ophthalmology, 1949; Berens' Diseases of the Eye, 1949; Parsons and Barling's Diseases of Children, 1954; Treves and Rogers' Surgical Applied Anatomy, 1952; Gaisford and Lightwood's Pædiatrics for the Practitioner, 1955; Thérapeutique Médicale Oculaire; articles in British Encyclopædias of Medical and Surgical Practice; papers in Brit. Jl Ophth., etc. *Recreations:* travelling, walking, reading. *Address:* Flat 90, 22 Park Crescent, W1. *T:* 01-636 4948; 42 Sheffield Terrace, W8. *Clubs:* Brooks's, Garrick, MCC; Hawks (Cambridge).

**DOGGETT, Frank John,** CB 1965; Deputy Secretary (A), Ministry of Aviation Supply (formerly Ministry of Technology) since 1967; *b* 7 Jan. 1910; *s* of Frank Hewitt and Charlotte Doggett; *m* 1st, 1940, Clare Judge (*d* 1956); one *d*; 2nd, 1957, Mary Battison. *Educ:* Mathematical Sch., Rochester; University of London (LLB). Inland Revenue, 1929; Air Ministry, 1938; MAP, 1940; MOS, 1946, Under-Sec., 1957-59; Under-Sec., Min. of Aviation, 1959-66, Dep. Sec., 1966-67. *Address:* The Jays, Ridgeway Road, Dorking, Surrey. *T:* Dorking 5819.

**DOIG, Sir James (Nimmo Crawford),** Kt 1970; Chairman and Managing Director, U. E. B. Industries Ltd; *b* 21 Aug. 1913; *s* of David Dickson Doig; *m* 1943, Rita Elizabeth Lowe; two *s* one *d*. *Educ:* Alan Glen's School and Royal Technical College, Glasgow. Managing Director, U.E.B. Industries Ltd, 1948-; Chairman, 1965-. *Recreations:* yachting, painting. *Address:* 48 Paritai Drive, Auckland, New Zealand. *Clubs:* Northern, Wellesley, Royal NZ Yacht Squadron (all NZ).

**DOIG, Peter Muir;** MP (Lab) West Dundee since Nov. 1963; *b* 27 Sept. 1911; *m* 1938, Emily Scott; two *s*. *Educ:* Blackness Sch., Dundee. Sales Supervisor with T. D. Duncan Ltd, Bakers, Dundee. Mem. of Dundee Town Council, 1953-63, Hon. Treasurer, 1959-63. *Recreations:* tennis, chess. *Address:* 29 Riverside Road, Wormit, Fife.

**DOIG, Ralph Herbert,** CVO 1954; Public Service Commissioner, Western Australia, since 1965; *b* 24 Feb. 1909; *s* of late William and Rose Doig; *m* 1937, Barbara Crock; two *s* four *d*. *Educ:* Guildford Grammar Sch.; University of Western Australia (BA, DipCom). Entered Public Service of WA, 1926; Private Sec. to various Premiers, 1929-41; Asst Under-Sec., Premier's Dept, 1941; Under-Sec., Premier's Dept, and Clerk of Executive Council, Perth, Western Australia, 1945-65. State Director: visit to Western Australia of the Queen and the Duke of Edinburgh, 1954; visit of the Duke of Edinburgh for British Empire and Commonwealth Games, 1962; visit of the Queen and the Duke of Edinburgh, 1963. *Recreation:* bowls. *Address:* Public Service Commissioner's Office, Perth, Western Australia 6000. *T:* 21.8251.

**DOISY, Prof. Edward A.;** Professor Emeritus of Biochemistry and Director Emeritus of Edward A. Doisy Department of Biochemistry, St Louis University School of Medicine, since 1965; *b* Hume, Ill., 13 Nov. 1893; *s* of Edward Perez and Ada Alley Doisy; *m* 1st, 1918, Alice Ackert (*d* 1964); four *s*; 2nd, 1965, Margaret McCormick. *Educ:* Univ. of Illinois (AB 1914, MS 1916); Harvard (PhD 1920). Hon. ScD: Yale, 1940; Washington, 1940; Chicago, 1941; Central Coll., 1942; Illinois, 1960; Gustavus Adolphus Coll., 1963; Hon. Dr, Paris, 1945; Hon. LLD, St Louis, 1955. Asst in Biochemistry, Harvard Medical Sch., 1915-17; Army Service, 1917-19; Instructor, Associate and Associate Prof. in Biochemistry, Washington Univ. Sch. of Medicine, 1919-23; Prof. of Biochemistry and Chm. of Dept, St Louis Univ. Sch. of Medicine, 1923-65, Distinguished Service Prof., 1951-65. Member: American Soc. of Biological Chemists (Pres. 1943-45); American Chem. Soc.; Endocrine Soc. (Pres. 1949-50); American Assoc. for the Advancement of Science; Soc. for Experimental Biology and Medicine (Pres. 1949-51); National Academy of Sciences; American Philosophical Soc.; Amer. Acad. Arts and Sci.; Pontifical Acad. of Sci.; Foundation or Memorial Lectr at New York, Kansas, Pittsburgh, Chicago, Cleveland, Minnesota, Rochester; several medals and awards; shared the Nobel Prize in Physiology and Medicine for 1943 with Dr Henrik Dam. *Publications:* more than 100 papers in medical and scientific journals. *Recreations:* golf, hunting and fishing. *Address:* Apt. 4b, Colonial Village Apts, Webster Groves, Mo. 63119, USA; St Louis University School of Medicine, 1402 South Grand Boulevard, St Louis, Missouri 63104. *T:* 865-2288, ext. 448.

**DOKE, Dr Clement Martyn,** MA, DLitt; Professor Emeritus of Bantu Philology, University of the Witwatersrand; retired; *b* Bristol, 1893; *s* of late Rev. J. J. Doke, Baptist Minister; *m* 1919, Hilda F. Lehman (*d* 1948); one *s* four *d*. *Educ:* Transvaal Univ. Coll., Pretoria; London Univ. Came to S Africa, 1903; Staff of SA Baptist Mission Soc. in Lambaland, North Rhodesia, 1914-21; completed translation of New Testament into Lamba, 1918; appointed to staff of Univ. of the Witwatersrand, 1923; undertook research trip to NW Kalahari to study Phonetics of Qhung Bushman, 1925; research in NW Rhodesia in Phonetics among the Lamba, 1926; research in NW Rhodesia among the Ila, 1927; seconded by S Rhodesian Govt for linguistic survey of native languages of S Rhodesia, and awarded Carnegie travelling fellowship for the year 1929; Editor of the South African Baptist, 1922-47; Joint-editor of Bantu Studies, 1931-41; Joint-editor of African Studies, 1942-53. Chm. of the Central Orthography Cttee of the Union Government Advisory Cttee on African Studies, 1929; Chm. of the Inter-University Cttee on African Studies, 1935; Pres., Baptist Union of S Africa, 1949-50. *Publications:* The Grammar of the Lamba Language; Hygiene Reader in Lamba, 1922; Dissertation on the Phonetics of the Zulu Language, 1923; Outline of Phonetics of the Language of the Qhung Bushmen, 1925; The Phonetics of the Zulu Language, Outline of Lamba Phonetics, 1926; Lamba Folklore and Proverbs (American Folklore Soc.) Text-Book of Zulu Grammar, 1927, 6th edn 1961; (ed) Grammar of the Sesuto Language (Jacottet); An Outline of Ila Phonetics, 1928; (with Rev. B. H. Barnes) The Pronunciation of the Bemba Language; The Problem of Word-division in Bantu, 1929; The Unification of the Shona Dialects (Govt Blue-Book); The Lambas of Northern Rhodesia; A Comparative Study in Shona Phonetics, 1931; (ed) Xhosa Baptist Hymnal, 1932; English-Lamba Vocabulary, 1933, 2nd rev. edn; Bantu Linguistic Terminology, 1935; Text-Book of Lamba Grammar, 1938; Bantu: Modern Grammatical, Phonetical, and Lexicographical Studies since 1860, 1945; (ed) Longman's Zulu Readers: Imvulamlomo, Ingqaqamazinyo, Ufundukhuphuke, 1946; Unokuhlekisa, Unozizwe, Usokuzula, 1947; Izinkamb'eAfrika, 1949; Ukuhlakaniph'eAfrika, 1950; (with late B. W. Vilakazi) Zulu-English Dictionary, 1948; The Southern Bantu Languages, 1954; Zulu Syntax and Idiom, 1955; (with late S. M. Mofokeng) Text-Book of Southern Sotho Grammar, 1957; (with D. McK. Malcolm and J. M. A. Sikakana) English and Zulu Dictionary, 1958; Lamba Bible Dictionary, 1959; trans. Bible into Lamba, 1959. *Address:* 5 Recreation Road, Alice, CP, South Africa.

**DOLCI, Danilo;** Coordinator Centro Studi e Iniziative, since 1958 (Founder); *b* Sesana, Trieste, 1924; *s* of Enrico Dolci and Mely Kontely; *m* 1952, Vincenzina Mangano; two *s* three *d*. *Educ:* University of Rome; University of Milan. Came to Sicily to Work for improvement of social conditions, 1952; arrested and tried for non-violent "reverse strike" to find work for unemployed, 1958. Mem. Internat. Council of War Resisters' International, 1963. Hon. DPhil, Univ. of Berne, 1968; Lenin Peace Prize, 1958; Benemerenza Antonio Feltrinelli Gold Medal, Accademia Nazionale dei Lincei, 1969. *Publications:* Banditi a Partinico, 1955; Inchiesta a Palermo, 1956; Spreco, 1960; Conversazioni, 1962; Verso un mondo nuovo, 1964 (trans. A New World in the Making, 1965); Chi Gioca Solo, 1966; Inventare il futuro, 1968; Il limone lunare (poema per la radio dei poveri cristi). *Address:* Centro Studi, Largo Scalia 5, Partinico (PA), Italy. *T:* 781905. *Club:* Instituto Nazionale Urbanistica (Rome).

**DOLIN, Anton, (Patrick Healey-Kay);** dancer and choreographer; *b* Slinfold, Sussex, 27 July 1904; *s* of H. G. Kay and Helen Maude Kay (*née* Healey). Joined Diaghilev's Russian Ballet Company in 1923, creating a number of roles; in 1927 danced with Karsavina at the London Coliseum in Le Spectre de la Rose; and later in the year founded the Nemchinova-Dolin Ballet with Nemchinova; rejoined the Diaghilev Company in 1929 (prominently associated with the Camargo Soc.); principal dancer with the Vic-Wells Ballet Company, 1931-35; with Markova-Dolin Ballet Co., 1935-37; organised (with Julien Braunsweg) London's Festival Ballet, 1950; led Festival Ballet in 19-week tour of United States and Canada, 1954-55, and in tour of Europe, 1958; has danced principal rôle in all classical and many modern works; has worked also for films, and in revue, etc. His choreographic works for the ballet include: Hymn to the Sun, The Nightingale and the Rose, Rhapsody in Blue, Espagnol, The Pas de Quatre, Variations for Four, Ravel's Bolero, The Swan of Tuonela (Sibelius). Guest Dir of Ballet, Rome Opera. Awarded The Order of The Sun by the Pres. of Peru, 1959. *Publications:* Divertissement, 1930; Ballet Go Round, 1939; Pas de Deux, 1950; Markova, 1953; Autobiography, 1960; The Sleeping Ballerina, 1966. *Recreation:* travel. *Address:* c/o Martins Bank, 5 Hanover Square, W1.

**DOLL, Richard;** *see* Doll, W. R. S.

**DOLL, William Alfred Millner,** CMG 1943; *b* 19 Dec. 1885; *s* of Charles FitzRoy Doll, JP, and Emily Frances Doll, Hadham Towers, Much

Hadham, Herts; *m* 1st, Walburga, *d* of Philip Eber, Arben, Switzerland; 2nd, Sybil, *d* of Richard Cunningham, Wadhurst, Sussex. *Educ:* Charterhouse (Scholar); Trinity Hall, Cambridge (Scholar); Bonn, Freiburg, Geneva, and Florence. BA 1907; MA 1912. N. M. Rothschild & Sons, 1912-24; served European War, 1914-19 (despatches, MSM; Orders of St Anne and St Stanislas, 3rd Cl); Inter-allied Commission in Bulgaria, 1925-30; British Delegate, 1926-30; Pres., 1926 and 1929; Financial Observer, State of Parana, Brazil, 1930-33; negotiated for Metropolitan Vickers financial agreement with Govt of Brazil for electrification of Central Railway, 1933-34; Financial Adviser, Ministry of Finance, Siam, 1936-42 (Order of Crown of Siam, 1st Cl.). Advisory Attaché, Bank of England, 1942-45; Financial Mem. of the De La Warr Mission to Ethiopia, 1944; Currency Adviser to Lord Louis Mountbatten's Command, South East Asia, 1945-46; Financial Adviser to Siamese Government, 1946-51. Légion d'Honneur, 1950. *Recreations:* music, natural history, philately, outdoor sports. *Address:* c/o Westminster Bank Ltd, Aldersgate Branch, EC1. *Club:* MCC.

**DOLL, Prof. (William) Richard (Shaboe),** OBE 1956; FRS 1966; DM, MD, FRCP, DSc; Regius Professor of Medicine, University of Oxford, since 1969; *b* Hampton, 28 Oct. 1912; *s* of Henry William Doll and Amy Kathleen Shaboe; *m* 1949, Joan Mary Faulkner, MB, BS, MRCP, DPH; one *s* one *d*. *Educ:* Westminster Sch.; St Thomas's Hosp. Med. Sch., London. MB, BS 1937; MD 1945; FRCP 1957; DSc London 1958. RAMC, 1939-45. Appts with Med. Research Council, 1946-69; Mem. Statistical Research Unit, 1948; Dep. Dir, 1959; Dir, 1961-69. Hon. Associate Physician, Central Middlesex Hosp., 1949-69; Teacher in Medical Statistics and Epidemiology, University Coll. Hosp. Med. Sch., 1963-69; Member: MRC, 1970-; Scientific Council of Internat. Cancer Research Agency, 1966-70. Hon. Lectr London Sch. of Hygiene and Tropical Med., 1956-62; Milroy Lectr, RCP, 1953; Marc Daniels Lectr, RCP, 1969; William Julius Mickle Fellow, Univ. of London, 1955. David Anderson Berry Prize (jt), RSE 1958; Bisset Hawkins Medal, RCP, 1962; UN award for cancer research, 1962. Hon. DSc Newcastle. *Publications:* Prevention of Cancer: Pointers from Epidemiology, 1967; articles in scientific journals on aetiology of lung cancer, leukaemia and other cancers, also aetiology and treatment of peptic ulcer; author (jt) Med. Research Council's Special Report Series, 1951, 1957, 1964. *Recreations:* food and conversation. *Address:* 13 Norham Gardens, Oxford. *T:* Oxford 55207. *Club:* New Arts.

**DOLLAR, Dr Jean Marguerite,** FRCS; Surgeon Royal Eye Hospital; Ophthalmic Surgeon Elizabeth Garrett Anderson Hospital, Royal Free Hospital, and St Olave's Hospital, Bermondsey. *Educ:* London Sch. of Medicine for Women. MRCS, LRCP 1926; MB, BS 1927; DOMS 1929; MS London 1935; FRCS 1936. Formerly: Surgical Registrar, Royal Eye Hosp.; House Surgeon, Elizabeth Garrett Anderson Hospital, and King Edward VII Hospital, Windsor; Hunterian Professor Royal College of Surgeons of England. *Publications:* contribs to medical press. *Address:* 6 Devonshire Place, W1. *T:* 01-935 6168.

**DOLLEY, Christopher;** Director: Pearson Longman Ltd, since 1971; Penguin Publishing Co. Ltd; Managing Director, Penguin Books Ltd; *b* 11 Oct. 1931; *yr s* of Dr Leslie George Francis Dolley and Jessie, Otford, Kent; *m* 1966, Christine Elizabeth Cooper; two *s*. *Educ:* Bancrofts Sch.; Corpus Christi Coll., Cambridge. Joined Unilever, 1954; with Unilever subsidiaries, 1954-62: G. B. Ollivant Ltd, 1954-59; United Africa Co., 1959-62. Joined Penguin Books Ltd as Export Manager, 1962; Dir, Penguin Books Ltd, 1964; Exec. Vice-Pres., Penguin Books Inc., Baltimore, 1966; Jt Man. Dir, Penguin Publishing Co., 1969. *Publication:* (ed) The Penguin Book of English Short Stories, 1967. *Recreations:* golf, gardening, collecting. *Address:* Fulwood House, Bolton Avenue, Windsor, Berks. *T:* Windsor 66961. *Club:* 14 West Hamilton Street (Baltimore, Md).

**DOLMETSCH, Carl Frederick,** CBE 1954; Director of Haslemere Festival since 1940; specialist and authority on early music and instruments; *b* 23 Aug. 1911; *s* of Arnold Dolmetsch and Mabel Johnston; *m* 1937, Mary Douglas (marr. diss. 1961), one *s* two *d* (and one *s* decd). *Educ:* privately. Began studying music with Arnold Dolmetsch at age of 4; first performed in public at 7, first concert tour at 8, first broadcast on violin and viol, 1925, at 14 years of age; virtuoso recorder-player at 15. Toured and broadcast in America, 1935 and 1936; recorder recitals, Wigmore Hall, Feb. and Nov. 1939, and annually, 1946-; toured and broadcast in Holland, 1946; Italy and Switzerland, 1947; Sweden, 1949; New Zealand, 1953; France, 1956; America, 1957; Switzerland, Austria, Germany, Holland, 1958; Belgium, America, 1959; Sweden, Austria, Germany, 1960; Australia, 1965; Colombia, 1966; France, Sweden, 1967; Alaska and Canada, 1969; America (yearly), 1961-70. Frequent broadcasts in this country and abroad. Musical Dir of Soc. of Recorder Players, 1937; Mem. Incorporated Soc. of Musicians; Mem. Art Workers' Guild, 1953; Patron Early Music Soc., University of Sydney. Hon. Fellow of Trinity Coll. of Music, 1950. Hon. DLitt University of Exeter, 1960. Hon. Fellow London Coll. of Music, 1963. *Publications:* Recorder Tutors, 1957, 1962 and 1970; edited and arranged numerous publications of 16th-, 17th- and 18th-century music; articles on many aspects of early music and instruments. *Recreations:* ornithology, natural history. *Address:* Jesses, Haslemere, Surrey. *T:* Haslemere 3818.

**DOLPHIN, Albert Edward;** *b* 8 Feb. 1895; *m* 1915, Emily Hazeltine, Todmorden, Yorks; two *s*. *Educ:* University of Saskatchewan. Went to Canada in 1913; after specialising in Finance and Economics, University of Saskatchewan, was associated in business with International Correspondence Schools; returned to England Dec. 1921 and joined Encyclopædia Britannica Co. Ltd; Dir, 1934. Administrateur of Encyclopædia Britannica SARL, France; Dir, Encyclopædia Britannica (South Africa) Pty. Ltd; Vice-Chm. and Managing Dir, Encyclopædia Britannica Ltd, 1947-53. Member: Chartered Institute of Secretaries; Association of Certified and Corporate Accountants. *Recreation:* philately. *Address:* Le Chalet, Mount Road, Thundersley, Essex.

**DOLPHIN, Rear-Adm. George Verner Motley,** CB 1957; DSO 1944; retd; *b* 1902; *s* of late Capt. George Manaton Dolphin, Royal Navy, and late Anne Clare Savory; *m* 1926, Phyllis Margaret Dickinson; one *s*. *Educ:* RN Colls Osborne and Dartmouth. Entered RN, 1916; served in destroyers, 1924-32; Term Lieut, RNC Dartmouth, 1930; Comdr RNC Dartmouth, 1944. Served War of 1939-45: HMS Sheffield, on Northern Patrol, 1939; HMS Hermione, in Malta Convoys, 1940-41 (despatches); HMS Ramillies, E Africa, 1943; Capt. GG3 and Naval Officer in charge Gold

Area for Normandy landings (DSO); Capt. of RNAS Rattray, 1945. admiralty, Bath (DNE), 1946; Capt. of Dockyard, Portsmouth, 1948; Sen. Officer (Afloat), New Zealand Navy and Capt. of HMNZS Bellona and Black Prince, 1950; Cdre, Harwich, 1953; Admiral Superintendent, HM Dockyard, Chatham, 1954-58. *Recreations:* sailing, tennis, golf. *Address:* Hurst Cottage, Hurst, near Petersfield, Hants. *T:* Harting 336.

**DOLPHIN, John Robert Vernon,** CBE 1956; part-time Consultant; TD; *b* 1 Oct. 1905; *s* of H. E. Dolphin and Dorothy Dolphin, Christleton, Chester; *m* 1966, Mary Evelyn Fisher. *Educ:* Marlborough Coll.; Loughborough Engineering Coll. (DLC). Student Apprentice, Hydraulic Engineering Co., Chester, 1926-28; Inspector, Selection Trust Ltd, 1929-30; Man., Austin Hoy and Co. Ltd, 1930-34; Sales Manager and Engineer, Sheepbridge Coal and Iron Co. Ltd; John Dolphin Ltd, Consultants, 1938. Army, 1939, Lieut TA; Lieut-Col 1940; Commanding Officer Inter-Services Research Station, Welwyn. Managing Dir, Corgi Motor Cycle Co. Ltd, Dolphin Industrial Developments Ltd, and Hydraulic Developments Ltd, 1946-50; Chief Engineer, Atomic Weapons Research Establishment, 1951-57; Engineer-in-Chief, Research Gp, UKAEA, 1957-59; Joint Managing Dir, Lansing Bagnall Ltd and J. E. Shay Ltd, 1959-64. Director, TI (Group Services) Ltd, 1964-68. FInstF 1939. *Inventions include:* Welman One-man Submarine; Welbike Parachutists' Motorcycle; Corgi Motorcycle; Harrier Folding Jeep; Hoy Double Box Coal Cutter Chain; Lina-Loda Freight Handling Machine; Turret (3-way reach) Truck. *Recreations:* swimming and yachting. *Address:* The Mill, Whitchurch-on-Thames, Oxon. *T:* Pangbourne 2480. *Clubs:* Royal Automobile; Upper Thames Motor Yacht.

**DOMB, Prof. Cyril,** PhD; Professor of Theoretical Physics, King's College, University of London, since Oct. 1954; *m* Shirley Gallinsky; three *s* three *d*. *Educ:* Hackney Downs Sch.; Pembroke Coll., Cambridge. Major Open Schol., Pembroke Coll., 1938-41; Radar Research, Admiralty, 1941-46; MA Cambridge, 1945; Nahum Schol., Pembroke Coll., 1946; PhD Cambridge, 1949; ICI Fellowship, Clarendon Laboratory, Oxford, 1949-52; MA Oxon, 1952; University Lecturer in Mathematics, Cambridge, 1952-54. *Publications:* articles in scientific journals. *Recreation:* walking. *Address:* c/o King's College, Strand, WC2.

**DOMVILE, Adm. Sir Barry Edward,** KBE 1934; CB 1922; CMG 1917; RN (retired); *b* 1878; *e s* of Adm. Sir Compton Domvile, GCB; *m* 1916, Alexandrina (*d* 1950), *d* of Mr von der Heydt; one *s* one *d* (and one *s* killed in action, 1941). *Educ:* HMS Britannia. Entered RN 1892; specially promoted Lieut, 1898; Beaufort Testimonial; Ryder Prize; Goodenough Gold Medal; Comdr. 1909; Capt. 1916; Rear-Adm. 1927; Gold Medallist, Royal United Service Institution, 1906; Asst Sec., Cttee of Imperial Defence, 1912-14; served European War in comd of HM Ships, 1914-19 (CMG); Dir of Plans Div., Admiralty, 1920-22; Chief of Staff, Mediterranean (Commodore, 2nd Class), 1922-25; Commanded HMS Royal Sovereign, 1925-26; Dir of Naval Intelligence Div., 1927-30; Rear-Adm. and Vice-Adm. commanding 3rd Cruiser Sqdn, Mediterranean, 1931-32; Pres., RNC Greenwich, and Vice-Adm. Commanding War Coll., 1932-34; Adm. and retired list, 1936. *Publications:* By and Large, 1936; Look to Your Moat, 1937; From Admiral to Cabin Boy, 1947. *Recreation:* outdoor sports. *Address:* Robin's Tree, Roehampton Vale, SW15. *T:* 01-788 3830. *Club:* Royal Yacht Squadron (Cowes).

**DOMVILLE, Sir Gerald Guy,** 7th Bt *cr* 1814; Lieut-Comdr RNVR; *b* 3 March 1896; 3rd *s* of late Rear-Adm. Sir William Cecil Henry Domville, CB, 4th Bt, and Moselle (*d* 1957), *d* of Henry Metcalf Ames, Linden, Northumberland; *S* brother, 1930; *m* 1920, Beatrice Mary (who obtained a divorce, 1930), *o c* of late Brig.-Gen. R. S. Vandeleur, CB, CMG; no *c*. *Educ:* Wellington Coll. Served European War, 1915-19 and War of 1939-45. *Heir:* none. *Address:* 60 Knightsbridge, SW1. *T:* 01-730 2121. *Clubs:* Royal Thames Yacht, Portland.

**DON, Kaye Ernest;** managing director of engineering co.; *b* 10 April 1891; *s* of Charles Frederick Don; *m* 1932, Eileen, *d* of Leonard F. Martin, New York; two *s* one *d*. *Educ:* Wolverhampton Grammar Sch. Commenced career in the rubber industry, with which was associated until 1915, when joined HM Forces; demobilised, 1919; first served in the Army Service Corps and was discharged on medical grounds; rejoined Royal Flying Corps as pilot in 1916; after serving on the Western Front was posted to British Mission; before the War, raced motor cycles, and took up motor car racing in 1920 and high speed motor boat racing in 1931; travelled extensively in America, South America, Australia, South Africa and Europe. *Recreation:* golf. *Address:* Marton, Chobham, Surrey.

**DON-WAUCHOPE, Sir P. G.;** *see* Wauchope.

**DONALD, Craig Reid Cantlie,** CMG 1963; OBE 1959; Bursar of Malvern College, since 1964; *b* 8 Sept. 1914; *s* of Rev. Francis Cantlie and Mary Donald, Lumphanan, Aberdeenshire; *m* 1945, Mary Isabel Speid; one *d*. *Educ:* Fettes; Emmanuel Coll., Cambridge (Scholar). BA 1937, MA 1947. Administrative Officer, Cyprus, 1937. Military Service, 1940-46, Lieut-Col. Commissioner, Famagusta, 1948. Registrar, Cooperative Societies, 1951; Deputy Financial Sec., Uganda, 1951; Sec. to the Treasury, 1956-63. *Recreation:* country pursuits. *Address:* Thirlstane House, Thirlstane Road, Malvern, Worcs. *T:* Malvern 61446. *Club:* Travellers'.

**DONALD, Air Marshal Sir (David) G.;** *see* Donald, Sir Grahame.

**DONALD, Douglas Alexander;** Sheriff-Substitute of Inverness, Moray, Nairn, and Ross and Cromarty, at Inverness, since 1956. Sheriff Substitute of Inverness, Elgin and Nairn at Portree, 1940-45; of Argyll at Dunoon and of Bute at Rothesay. *Address:* Sheriff Court House, Inverness.

**DONALD, Air Marshal Sir Grahame,** KCB 1944 (CB 1941); DFC; AFC; MA; *b* 1891; *s* of David Donald, MD; *m* 1916, Gwynneth Adrienne (*d* 1946), *d* of J. W. Martin, Filey; (one *s* killed in action, 1940; one *d* decd); *m* 1947, Ailsa Stevenson; one *d*. *Educ:* Dulwich Coll.; University Coll., Oxford. Served European War, 1914-18, with RNAS; joined RAF 1918. AOC-in-C Maintenance Command, 1942-47; retired, 1947. *Address:* The Manor Cottage, Tilford, Farnham, Surrey. *T:* Frensham 2135. *Club:* Royal Air Force.

**DONALD, Prof. Ian,** MBE 1946; MD; FRCS (Glasgow); FRCOG; FCO&G (SA); Regius Professor of Midwifery, University of Glasgow, since 1954; *b* 27 Dec. 1910; British; *m* 1937, Alix Mathilde de Chazal Richards; four *d*. *Educ:* Warriston Sch., Moffat; Fettes Coll.,

Edinburgh; Diocesan Coll., Rondebosch, Cape. BA Cape Town, 1930; MB, BS London, 1937; MD London, 1947; MRCOG 1947; FRCOG 1955; FRCS (Glasgow) 1958; FCO&G (South Africa) 1967. Served War of 1939-45 with Royal Air Force (Medical), 1942-46 (despatches). Reader in Obstetrics and Gynæcology, St Thomas's Hosp. Medical Sch., 1951; Reader, University of London, Inst. of Obstetrics and Gynæcology, 1952; Leverhulme Research Scholar, 1953; Blair Bell Memorial Lecturer, RCOG, 1954. Eardley Holland Gold Medal, 1970; Blair Bell Gold Medal, RSM, 1970. *Publications:* Practical Obstetric Problems, 1955, 4th edn 1969; articles on respiratory disorders in the newborn, in Lancet and Jl of Obst. and Gynæc. Brit. Empire, and on ultrasonics in diagnosis, in Lancet. *Recreations:* sailing, music, painting. *Address:* 9 Hamilton Drive, Glasgow, W2. *T:* 041-339 5050.

**DONALD, Sir James Bell,** Kt 1969; JP (Auckland, NZ); Managing Director, A. B. Donald Ltd, Auckland, NZ, and subsidiary Cos since 1900; *b* 13 Oct. 1879; 2nd *s* of late Alexander Bell Donald and Charlotte Donald; *m* 1968, Doris Sadie Olive Fair; no *c. Educ:* Queen's College, Auckland, NZ. Elected MP, 1929, and apptd Minister of the Crown, holding portfolios of Minister of Customs, Postmaster-Gen., Minister of Marine; Mem., Auckland Harbour Bd, 1935 (Chm., 1946-47); retd Oct. 1947. *Publication:* The Inheritance of the Lord, or the Israel of God, 1964. *Recreations:* bowls, Rugby football. *Address:* 34 Arney Road, Remuera, Auckland, NZ. *T:* Auckland 547726. *Clubs:* Auckland, Northern (Auckland).

**DONALD, Prof. Kenneth William,** DSC 1940; MA, MD, DSc, FRCP, FRCPE, FRSE; Professor of Medicine, University of Edinburgh, since 1959; Senior Physician, Royal Infirmary, Edinburgh; Physician to the Queen in Scotland since 1967; *b* 25 Nov. 1911; *s* of Col William Donald, MC, RA and Julia Jane Donald, Sandgate; *m* 1942, Rēthe Pearl, *d* of D. H. Evans, Regents Park. *Educ:* Cambridge Univ.; St Bartholomew's Hosp. Kitchener Scholar and State Scholar, 1930; Senior Scholar, Emmanuel Coll., Cambridge, 1933. Served with Royal Navy, 1939-45: Senior MO, 1st and 5th Flotilla of Destroyers; Senior MO, Admiralty Experimental Diving Unit. Chief Asst, Med. Prof. Unit and Cattlin Research Fellow, St Bartholomew's Hosp., 1946-48; Rockefeller Travelling Research Fellow, Columbia Univ., 1948-49; Senior Lecturer in Medicine, Inst. Diseases of the Chest, Brompton Hosp., 1949-50; Reader in Medicine, Univ of Birmingham and Physician, Queen Elizabeth Hosp., Birmingham, 1950-59. Scientific Consultant to the Royal Navy. Physician to the Royal Navy in Scotland. Medical Consultant to Scottish Dept of Home and Health; Member: Commonwealth Scholarship Commn; Medical Sub-Cttee, UGC; RN Personnel Research Cttee (Chm.) and Hyperbaric Oxygen Therapy Cttee of MRC; Scottish Adv. Cttee on Med. Research; Council and Scientific Adv. Cttee, British Heart Foundn; Chairman: Under-Water Physiology Sub-Cttee of MRC; Physiology Adv. Cttee, NCB. Mem. Council, RCPEd; Gov., Inst. of Occupational Medicine, Edinburgh. *Publications:* contribs to scientific and medical jls concerning normal and abnormal function of the lungs, the heart and the circulation and high pressure physiology in relation to diving and submarines, drowning, resuscitation. *Recreations:* reading, theatre, fishing. *Address:* Department of Medicine, The Royal Infirmary, Edinburgh EH3 9YW. *T:* 031-229 2477. *Club:* Naval and Military.

**DONALD, Prof. Maxwell Bruce,** SM (MIT); ARCSc; Hon. MIChemE; FRIC; Emeritus Professor of Chemical Engineering in the University of London; *b* 20 July 1897. *Educ:* Felsted Sch.; Royal Coll. of Science; Massachusetts Inst. of Technology. Served European War, Lieut and ADC, RA, 1915-19. Sir Alfred Yarrow Scholar, 1921; Demonstrator in Physical Chemistry, Royal College of Science, 1923; Chemical Engineer, Chilean Nitrate Producers Assoc., 1925; Adviser on bitumen emulsions, Royal Dutch-Shell Group, 1929; Lecturer in Chemical Engineering, University Coll., London, 1931; Reader, 1947; Ramsay Memorial Prof., 1951-65. Hon. Sec., Institution of Chemical Engineers, 1937-49, Moulton medallist, 1937, Osborne Reynolds medallist, 1940; Vice-Pres. 1950. DSIR Visitor to British Baking Research Assoc., 1949. *Publications:* (with H. P. Stevens) Rubber in Chemical Engineering, 1933 and 1949; Elizabethan Copper, 1955; Elizabethan Monopolies, 1961. *Address:* Rabbit Shaw, 6 Stagbury Avenue, Chipstead, Surrey CR3 3PA. *T:* Downland 53365.

**DONALD, William C.**; *see* Coutts Donald.

**DONALDSON,** family name of **Baron Donaldson of Kingsbridge.**

**DONALDSON OF KINGSBRIDGE,** Baron *cr* 1967 (Life Peer), of Kingsbridge; **John George Stuart Donaldson,** OBE 1943; retired farmer; *b* 9 Oct. 1907; *s* of Rev. S. A. Donaldson, Master of Magdalene, Cambridge, and Lady Albinia Donaldson (*née* Hobart-Hampden); *m* 1935, Frances Annesley Lonsdale; one *s* two *d. Educ:* Eton; Trinity Coll., Cambridge. Pioneer Health Centre, Peckham, 1935-38; Road Transport, 1938-39. Royal Engineers, 1939-45. Since then farming in Glos, and later Bucks. Mem., Glos Agric. Exec. Cttee, 1953-60. Hon. Sec. Nat. Assoc. Discharged Prisoners Aid Socs, 1961; Chairman: Nat. Assoc. for the Care and Resettlement of Offenders, 1966; Bd of Visitors, HM Prison, Grendon, 1963; Consumer Council, 1968-; Nat. Cttee Family Service Units, 1968-; Cttee of Enquiry into conditions of service for young servicemen, 1969. Member, SE Regional Planning Council, 1966. Director: Royal Opera House, Covent Garden, 1958; Sadler's Wells, 1963; British Sugar Corp., 1966. *Recreations:* music in general, opera in particular, tennis. *Address:* 1 Chalcot Crescent, NW1. *Clubs:* Brooks's, Farmers:.

*See also R. H. I. de la Mare.*

**DONALDSON, David Abercrombie,** RSA 1962 (ARSA 1951); RP 1964; Painter; Head of Painting School, Glasgow School of Art, since 1967; *b* 29 June 1916; *s* of Robert Abercrombie Donaldson and Margaret Cranston; *m* 1949, Maria Krystyna Mora-Szorc; one *s* two *d. Educ:* Coatbridge Sec. Sch.; Glasgow Sch. of Art. Travelling Scholarship, 1938. Joined Staff of Glasgow Sch. of Art, 1940. Paintings in private collections in America and Europe and public collections in Scotland. Sitters include: The Queen, 1968; Sir Hector Hetherington; Dame Jean Roberts; Sir John Dunbar; Lord Binning; Rev. Lord McLeod; Mrs Winifred Ewing; Miss Joan Dickson; Earl of Haddo. *Recreation:* painting. *Address:* 15 Cleveden Gardens, Glasgow W2. *T:* 041-339 5082. *Club:* Art (Glasgow).

**DONALDSON, Sir Dawson,** KCMG 1967; CEng, FIEE; Chairman, Commonwealth Telecommunications Board, 1962-69, retired; *b* 29 Dec. 1903; *s* of Dawson Donaldson and Ada M. Gribble; *m* 1928, Nell Penman; two *s* two *d. Educ:* Auckland Grammar Sch.; New Zealand Univ. New Zealand Post and Tels

Dept, 1922-62; Executive Engineer, 1928-48; Superintending Engineer, 1948-54; Dep. Dir Gen., 1954-60; Dir Gen., 1960-62. *Recreations:* bowls and garden. *Address:* 2 Ridd Crescent, Karori, Wellington, New Zealand.

**DONALDSON, Air Cdre Edward Mortlock,** CB 1960; CBE 1954; DSO 1940; AFC 1941 (and bar 1947); Air Correspondent, The Daily Telegraph, since 1961; *b* 22 Feb. 1912; *s* of C. E. Donaldson, Malay Civil Service; *m* 1st, 1936, Winifred Constant (marr. diss., 1944); two *d*; 2nd, 1944, Estellee Holland (marr. diss., 1956); one *s*; 3rd, 1957, Anne, Sofie Stapleton. *Educ:* King's Sch., Rochester; Christ's Hosp., Horsham; McGill Univ., Canada. Joined RAF, 1931; 3 Sqdn, Upavon, Kenley and Sudan until 1936; Flight Comdr, 1 Sqdn, 1936-38; Flight-Lieut 1936; Sqdn Leader 1938; Comdr, 151 Sqdn, 1938-40; Chief Instructor, 5 Flying Training Sch., 1941; Wing Comdr, 1940; went to US to build four air Gunnery Schs, 1941, and teach USAF combat techniques; Group Capt., 1942; Mem. USAF Board and Directing Staff at US Sch. of Applied Tactics, 1944; Comdr RAF Station, Colerne, RAF first jet station, 1944; in comd RAF Station, Milfield, 1946; in comd RAF High Speed Flight, 1946; holder of World's Speed Record, 1946; SASO, No. 12 Group, 1946-49; in comd Air Cadet Corps and CCF, 1949-51; in comd RAF Station, Fassberg, Germany, 1951-54; Joint Services Staff Coll., 1954; Dir of Operational Training, Air Ministry, 1954-56; Air Cdre, 1954; Dep. Comdr Air Forces, Arabian Peninsular Command, 1956-58; Commandant, Royal Air Force Flying Coll., Manby, 1958-61; retd. Legion of Merit (US), 1948. *Recreations:* shooting, sailing, golf. *Address:* 41 Princes Gate Mews, SW7. *Clubs:* Royal Air Force, RAF Yacht.

**DONALDSON, Prof. Gordon;** Professor of Scottish History and Palæography, University of Edinburgh, since 1963; *b* 13 April 1913; *s* of Magnus Donaldson and Rachel Hetherington Swan. *Educ:* Royal High Sch., Edinburgh; Universities of Edinburgh and London. Asst in HM Gen. Register House, Edinburgh, 1938; Lecturer in Scottish History, University of Edinburgh, 1947, Reader, 1955. Mem. Royal Commission on the Ancient and Historical Monuments of Scotland, 1964-. *Publications:* The Making of the Scottish Prayer Book of 1637, 1954; A Source Book of Scottish History, 1952-61; Register of the Privy Seal of Scotland, vols v-viii, 1957-66; Shetland Life under Earl Patrick, 1958; Scotland: Church and Nation through sixteen centuries, 1960; The Scottish Reformation, 1960; Scotland–James V to James VII, 1965; The Scots Overseas, 1966; Northwards by Sea, 1966; Scottish Kings, 1967; The First Trial of Mary Queen of Scots, 1969; Memoirs of Sir James Melville of Halhill, 1969; Contribs to Scottish Historical Review, English Historical Review, Transactions of Royal Historical Society, etc. *Address:* 24 East Hermitage Place, Edinburgh EH6 8AD. *T:* 031-554 1076.

**DONALDSON, John Coote,** CIE 1939; MC; Indian Civil Service, retired; *b* 24 May 1895; *s* of late John Donaldson, KC, Dublin; *m* 1933, Barbara Maud, *d* of late Hon. Sir Charles Henry Bayley Kendall; one *s* one *d*. *Educ:* Felsted; Trinity Coll., Dublin (MA). Entered Indian Civil Service, 1920. *Address:* Medlars, Fairy Road, Seaview, IoW. *T:* Seaview 2379.

**DONALDSON, Hon. Sir John (Francis),** Kt 1966; **Hon. Mr Justice Donaldson;** Judge of the High Court of Justice, Queen's Bench Division, since 1966; *b* 6 Oct. 1920; *er s* of Malcolm Donaldson, *qv* and Evelyn Helen Marguerite Maunsell; *m* 1945, Dorothy Mary, *d* of late Reginald George Gale Warwick; one *s* two *d*. *Educ:* Charterhouse; Trinity Coll., Cambridge. Sec. of Debates, Cambridge Union Soc., 1940; Chm. Federation of University Conservative and Unionist Assocs, 1940; BA (Hons) 1941; MA 1959. Commissioned Royal Signals, 1941; served with Guards Armoured Divisional Signals, in UK and NW Europe, 1942-45; and with Military Government, Schleswig-Holstein, 1945-46; Hon. Lieut-Col, 1946. Called to Bar, Middle Temple, 1946; Harmsworth Law Scholar, 1946; QC 1961; Bencher 1966; Mem. Gen. Council of the Bar, 1956-61, 1962-66, Junior Counsel to Registrar of Restrictive Trading Agreements, 1959-61; Dep. Chm., Hants QS, 1961-66; Mem. Council on Tribunals, 1965-66. Mem. Croydon County Borough Council, 1949-53. Vice-Pres., British Maritime Law Assoc., 1969-. *Publications:* Jt Ed., Lowndes and Rudolf on General Average and the York-Antwerp Rules (8th edn), 1955 and (9th edn), 1964; contributor to title Insurance, in Halsbury's Laws of England (3rd edn), 1958. *Recreations:* sailing, do-it-yourself. *Address:* 1 Essex Court, Temple, EC4. *T:* 01-583 5131; Over the Water, Walhampton, Lymington, Hants. *T:* 2655; Royal Courts of Justice, Strand, WC2. *Clubs:* Royal Cruising, Bar Yacht, Royal Lymington Yacht.

**DONALDSON, Malcolm,** MA Cantab; FRCS MB, BCh Cantab, FRCOG; FIHE; Consulting Physician Accoucheur, St Bartholomew's Hospital; Hon. Director Cancer Information Association, Oxford; Vice-President, British Cancer Campaign; late Vice-Chairman National Radium Commission; late Director of Cancer Department, St Bartholomew's Hospital; Consulting Gynæcologist, Mount Vernon Hospital, Northwood; Consulting Gynæcologist, Royal Northern Hospital; Cottage Hospital, Brentford; Potters Bar; etc; *b* 27 April 1884; *s* of John Donaldson, Chiswick; *m* 1st, 1919, Evelyn Helen Marguerite Gilroy; two *s*; 2nd, 1940, Mia (*d* 1970), *widow* of Gregory J. M. Whyley, MA, LLB. *Educ:* Charterhouse; Trinity Coll., Cambridge; Natural Science Tripos. Served War of 1914-18, Major RAMC (despatches). Entered St Bartholomew's Hospital, 1906, and was appointed to the staff 1921; late examiner in Midwifery and Gynæcology, Cambridge Univ., London MB, and Central Midwives Board. *Publications:* Early Diagnosis and Treatment of Cancer, Institute of Public Health, 1929; Radiotherapy in Diseases of Women, 1933; Early Diagnosis of Malignant Disease (jointly), 1936; The Cancer Riddle, 1962; many articles dealing with Education of the Lay Public concerning Cancer and other medical papers. *Recreation:* rowing, won the University Sculls and rowed for the University against Oxford and later in the same year against Harvard University. *Address:* 337 Woodstock Road, Oxford. *Clubs:* Athenæum, Leander.

*See also Sir John Francis Donaldson.*

**DONALDSON, Rear-Adm. Vernon D'Arcy;** *b* 1 Feb. 1906; *s* of Adm. Leonard Andrew Boyd Donaldson, CB, CMG, and of Mary Mitchell, *d* of Prof. D'Arcy Thompson, Queen's Coll., Galway; *m* 1946, Mrs Monypenny of Pitmilly (Joan Cranfield Monypenny), *d* of James Egerton Howard Monypenny. *Educ:* RN Colls, Osborne and Dartmouth. Entered Royal Navy, Sept. 1919; Midshipman, 1923; Sub-Lieut 1927, Lieut 1928; specialised in Torpedoes and served as Torpedo Officer in HMS Vernon, 8th Dest. Flot., China Stn, and HMS Glorious; Comdr Dec. 1939, and served in Plans Div. Admlty, as exec. officer HM Ships Birmingham and Frobisher in Eastern Fleet, and on staff of C-in-C Eastern Fleet; Capt. Dec. 1944. Asst-Dir, TASW Div., Naval

Staff, 1945-47; Naval Attaché, China, 1948-49; commanded HMS Gambia, 1950-51; Dir TASW div., Naval Staff, 1952-54; ADC to the Queen, 1953-54; Dep. Chief of Supplies and Transport, Admiralty (acting Rear-Adm.), 1955-57; retired, 1957. *Address:* 36 Tregunter Road, SW10; Moor Wood Cottage, Benenden, Kent. *Clubs:* United Service, United Hunts.

**DONCASTER, Archdeacon of;** *see* Rogers, Ven. E. J. G.

**DONCASTER, John Priestman,** CBE 1967; MA; formerly Keeper, Department of Entomology, British Museum (Natural History), 1961-68, retired; *b* 20 Nov. 1907; *s* of Charles Doncaster and Hilda Priestman; *m* 1938, Frances Julia Gaynesford Walter; one *d*. *Educ:* St Catharine's Coll., Joined British Museum as Asst Keeper in charge of Exhibition Section, 1937; Entered Dept of Entomology, 1951; Dep. Keeper, 1955. *Publications:* papers, etc. on Aphididæ, in scientific journals. *Address:* 3 Devonshire Road, Harpenden, Herts.

**DONE, His Honour William Edward Pears,** MC; FSA; retired County Court Judge; JP Middlesex, Hertford and West Sussex; *b* 10 March 1883; *s* of late William and M. E. Done, Groombridge, Sussex; *m* 1st, 1917, Beatrice Helen Sharpley (*d* 1952); one *d*; 2nd, 1954, Gladys Bagley. *Educ:* Elizabeth Coll., Guernsey; Pembroke Coll., Oxford. Called to Bar, 1910; practised Common Law Bar and Western Circuit. Commission 5th Royal Sussex Regt, Sept. 1914; served in France, Belgium and Italy; Staff Capt. 145 Infantry Brigade, 1917 (despatches, MC, Croce di Guerra); returned to practice, 1919. Appointed County Court Judge, April 1945; circuits: Lambeth 1945, Edmonton 1945, Clerkenwell 1950; retired 1955. *Publications:* Looking back in Sussex, 1953; Chichester as the Romans called it, 1957; The Parish Church of St Peter and St Paul, West Wittering. *Recreations:* gardening, botany and local history. *Address:* Westringes, West Wittering, Chichester.

**DONEGALL,** 6th Marquis of (*cr* 1791), **Edward Arthur Donald St George Hamilton Chichester;** Hereditary Lord High Admiral of Lough Neagh; Viscount Chichester and Baron of Belfast, 1625; Earl of Donegall, 1647; Earl of Belfast, 1791; Baron Fisherwick (Gt Britain), 1790; *b* 7 Oct. 1903; *o c* of 5th Marquess and 2nd wife, Violet Gertrude, (*d* 1952), *o d* of Henry St George Twining, Halifax, NS; *S* father, 1904; *m* 1968, Mrs Maureen McKenzie. *Educ:* Eton; Christ Church, Oxford. A Journalist; Lt-Col in the Army Cadet Force; British War Correspondent, 1939-45. *Heir:* Baron Templemore, *qv*. *Address:* Lord Donegall's Office, The Studio, 39 Clabon Mews, SW1. *T:* 01-589 6688. *Clubs:* Carlton, Press, MCC.

**DONEGAN, Rt. Rev. H. W. B.;** *see* New York, Bishop of.

**DONERAILE,** 9th Viscount, *cr* 1785; **Richard St John St Leger;** Baron Doneraile, 1776; *b* 29 Oct. 1923; *o s* of 8th Viscount and of Sylvia St Leger; *S* father 1957; *m* 1945, Melva Jean Clifton; three *s* two *d*. *Educ:* George Washington Sch., USA. In lumber business and real estate. *Heir: s* Hon. Richard Allen St Leger, *b* 17 Aug. 1946. *Address:* 501 E Katella Apartment 21C, Orange, Calif 92667, USA. *T:* (714) 633-1146.

**DONIACH, Prof. Israel,** MD (London); FCPath 1963; FRCP 1968; Professor of Morbid Anatomy in University of London, London Hospital, since 1960; *b* 9 March 1911; *yr s* of Aaron Selig and Rahel Doniach; *m* 1933, Deborah Abileah; one *s* (one *d* decd). *Educ:* University Coll. and Hosp., London. Asst Pathologist, St Mary's Hosp., London, 1935-37; Clinical Pathologist and Cancer Research Asst, Mount Vernon Hosp., Northwood, 1937-43; Senior Lecturer in Morbid Anatomy, Postgraduate Medical Sch. of London, 1943-59, Reader, 1959-60. *Publications:* papers in morbid anatomy and experimental pathology in various journals. *Address:* 25 Alma Square, NW8. *T:* 01-286 1617.

**DONKIN, Air Cdre Peter Langloh,** CBE 1946; DSO 1944; retired; *b* 19 June 1913; *s* of Frederick Langloh and Phyllis Donkin; *m* 1941, Elizabeth Marjorie Cox; two *d*. *Educ:* Sherborne; RAF Coll., Cranwell. Commissioned RAF, 1933; No. 16 Sqdn, 1933-38; British Mission in Poland, 1939; CO 225 Sqdn, 1940; CO 239 Sqdn, 1941-42; CO 35 Wing, 1943-44; Sch. Land Air Warfare, 1945; HQ, RAF Levant, 1946; RCAF Staff Coll., 1948-49; Exchange USAF, 1950; CO, RAF Chivenor, 1951-53; Air Attaché, Moscow, 1954-57; Asst Chief of Staff, HQ Allied Air Forces, Central Europe, 1957-58; idc, 1959; AOC, RAF, Hong Kong, 1960-62. *Recreations:* shooting, yachting. *Address:* Coombe Cross, Templecombe, Som. *Club:* Carlton.

**DONLEAVY, James Patrick;** Author; *b* 23 April 1926; *m* Mary Wilson Price; one *s* one *d*. *Educ:* schs in USA; Trinity Coll., Dublin. *Publications:* The Ginger Man (novel), 1955; Fairy Tales of New York (play), 1960; What They Did In Dublin With The Ginger Man (introd. and play), 1961; A Singular Man (novel), 1963 (play, 1964); Meet My Maker The Mad Molecule (short stories), 1964; The Saddest Summer of Samuel S (novella), 1966 (play, 1967); The Beastly Beatitudes of Balthazar B (novel), 1968. *Address:* Balsoon House, Bective, Co. Meath, Ireland.

**DONNELLY, Desmond Louis;** Journalist; Adviser to the David Brown Corporation since 1954, to Philips Industries since 1965, to Metropolitan Pensions Association since 1969 and to other corporations; Director of cos; *b* 16 Oct. 1920; *o s* of late L. J. Donnelly, Assam, India, and Aimée Tucker; *m* 1947, Rosemary, *d* of late Dr John Taggart, Belfast; one *s* two *d* (of whom one *s* one *d* are twins). *Educ:* Bembridge Sch., Isle of Wight. Served War of 1939-45. RAF, 1940-46, Flight Lieut. Contested (Common Wealth), Evesham, 1945, (Lab), County Down, 1946; MP (Lab) Pembroke, 1950-68; resigned Labour Whip, 1968; MP (Ind) 1968-70. Editor, Town and Country Planning, 1946-49; Dir of the Town and Country Planning Assoc., 1948-50. *Publications:* The March Wind, 1959; Trade With Communist Countries (with Alec Nove), 1960; David Brown's: The Story of a Family Business, 1960; No Gains without Pains, 1960; Years Ahead, 1964; Struggle for the World, 1965; The Nearing Storm, 1968; Gadarene '68, 1968; There is Another Britain, 1970. *Recreations:* swimming, walking and cricket. *Address:* Pant-y-Beudy, Trefasser, near Goodwick, Pembs. *T:* St Nicholas 223; Flat 16, 88 Portland Place, W1. *T:* 01-581 7890. *Clubs:* Royal Air Force, Chelsea Arts; Pembrokeshire County (Haverfordwest).

**DONNER, Frederic Garrett;** Chairman of the Board of Trustees, Alfred P. Sloan Foundation; Director, General Motors Corporation (formerly Chairman of General Motors Corporation, 1958-67); *b* 1902; *s* of Frank Donner and Cornelia (*née* Zimmerman); *m* 1929, Eileen Isaacson; one *s* one *d*. *Educ:* University of Michigan, Ann Arbor, Michigan, USA. General Motors Corporation; joined

1926; retired 1967. Dir, Communications Satellite Corporation; Trustee: Presbyterian Hosp., New York City; Sloan-Kettering Inst. for Cancer Research, New York City. Holds hon. doctorates and foreign decorations. *Address:* Room 25, 50, 630 Fifth Avenue, New York, NY 10020, USA. *Clubs:* Links, University (NY City); Creek Country, North Hempstead Country (Long Island, NY).

**DONNER, Sir Patrick William,** Kt, *cr* 1953; MA; *b* 1904; *s* of late Ossian Donner and Violet Marion McHutchen, Edinburgh; *m* 1938, Hon. Angela Chatfield (*d* 1943), *er d* of 1st Baron Chatfield, GCB, OM, KCMG, CVO, Admiral of the Fleet; *m* 1947, Pamela *y d* of Rear Adm. Herbert A. Forster, *qv*; one *s* two *d*. *Educ:* Exeter Coll., Oxford. Studied Imperial development and administration, 1928-30; MP (C) West Islington, 1931-35; Basingstoke Div. of Hants, 1935-55; Hon. Sec., India Defence League, 1933-35; Parliamentary Private Sec. to Sir Samuel Hoare, Home Sec., 1939; Mem. Advisory Cttee on Education in the Colonies, 1939-41; Parliamentary Private Sec. to Col Oliver Stanley, Sec. of State for the Colonies, 1944; Dir, National Review Ltd, 1933-47; Mem. Executive Council Joint East and Central African Board, 1937-54. Volunteered RAFVR 1939; Acting Sqdn Leader, 1941. Chm. Executive Cttee of the Men of the Trees, 1959-62. Mem., Art Panel of the Arts Council, 1963-66. High Sheriff of Hants, 1967-68. *Recreations:* music, Dutch painting, arboriculture. *Address:* Hurstbourne Park, Whitchurch, Hants. *T:* Whitchurch 2230.

**DONNISON, Prof. David Vernon;** Director, Centre for Environmental Studies, since 1969; *b* 19 Jan. 1926; *s* of F. S. V. Donnison, *qv*; *m* 1950, Jean Elizabeth (*née* Kidger); two *s* two *d*. *Educ:* Marlborough Coll., Wiltshire; Magdalen Coll., Oxford. Asst Lecturer and Lecturer, Manchester Univ., 1950-53; Lecturer, Toronto Univ., 1953-55; Reader, London Sch. of Economics, 1956-61; Prof. of Social Administration, 1961-69. Chm., Public Schs Commission, 1968-70. *Publications:* The Neglected Child and the Social Services, 1954; Welfare Services in a Canadian Community, 1958; Housing since the Rent Act, 1961; Social Policy and Administration, 1965; The Government of Housing, 1967. *Address:* 38 Douglas Road, N1. *T:* 01-226 7956.

**DONNISON, Frank Siegfried Vernon,** CBE 1943; Indian Civil Service (retired); *b* 3 July 1898; *s* of Frank Samuel and of Edith Donnison; *m* 1923, Ruth Seruya Singer, MBE, JP (*d* 1968); one *s* one *d*. *Educ:* Marlborough Coll.; Corpus Christi Coll., Oxford. Served with Grenadier Guards, 1917-19; ICS (Burma), 1922; Chief Sec. to Govt of Burma, 1946; military service, Burma, 1944-45 (despatches). Historian, Cabinet Office, Historical Section, 1949-66. *Publications:* Public Administration in Burma, 1953; British Military Administration in the Far East, 1943-46, 1956; Civil Affairs and Military Government, North-West Europe, 1944-46, 1961; Civil Affairs and Military Government, Central Organization and Planning, 1966; Burma, 1970. *Recreation:* music. *Address:* Lower Cross Farmhouse, East Hagbourne, Didcot, Berks. *T:* Didcot 3314. *Club:* Royal Automobile.

*See also Professor D. V. Donnison.*

**DONOUGHMORE,** 7th Earl of (*cr* 1800), **John Michael Henry Hely-Hutchinson;** Baron Donoughmore, 1783; Viscount Suirdale, 1800; Viscount Hutchinson (UK), 1821; *b* 12 Nov. 1902; *er s* of 6th Earl of Donoughmore, KP, PC, and Elena (*d* 1944), *d* of late M. P. Grace, New York; *S* father, 1948; *m* 1925, Dorothy Jean (MBE 1947), *d* of late J. B. Hotham; two *s* one *d*. *Educ:* Winchester; Magdalen Coll., Oxford. MP (C) Peterborough Div. of Northants, 1943-45. Grand Master, Freemasons' Grand Lodge of Ireland, 1964. *Heir:* *s* Viscount Suirdale, *qv*. *Address:* Knocklofty, Clonmel, Ireland.

**DONOVAN,** family name of **Baron Donovan.**

**DONOVAN, Baron,** *cr* 1964 (Life Peer); **Terence Norbert Donovan,** PC 1960; Kt 1950; a Lord of Appeal in Ordinary since 1963; *b* 13 June 1898; *m* 1925, Marjorie, *d* of Charles and Leah Murray, Winchester; two *s* one *d*. Called to Bar, Middle Temple, 1924; commenced to practise, 1932; QC 1945. Served in France, 1917-18, with Beds Regt, and later, with RAF. Called to Bar of Southern Rhodesia, 1937; entered Civil Service, 1920, leaving in 1932. Chm., Brit. Govt Legal Mission to Greece, 1945; Member: Denning Cttee on Divorce procedure, 1946; Lewis Cttee on Court Martial procedure, 1946-48; Chm.: Criminal Appeals Cttee, 1964; Royal Commission on Trade Unions and Employers' Assocs, 1965-68. MP (Lab) East Leicester, 1945-50; North East Leicester, Feb.-July 1950; Judge of King's Bench Div., High Court of Justice, 1950-60; a Lord Justice of Appeal, 1960-63. JP Hants. *Address:* House of Lords, SW1. *Club:* Athenæum.

**DONOVAN, Prof. Desmond Thomas;** Yates-Goldsmid Professor of Geology and Head of Department of Geology, University College, London, since 1966; *b* 16 June 1921; *s* of T. B. Donovan; *m* 1959, Shirley Louise Saward; two *s*. one *d*. *Educ:* Epsom Coll.; University of Bristol. BSc 1942; PhD 1951; DSc 1960. Asst Lectr in Geology, University of Bristol, 1947; Lectr in Geology, Bristol, 1950; Prof. of Geology University of Hull, 1962. *Publications:* Stratigraphy: An Introduction to Principles, 1966; (ed) Geology of Shelf Seas, 1968; papers on fossil cephalopods, Jurassic stratigraphy, Pleistocene deposits. *Address:* University College, Gower Street, WC1E 6BT. *T:* 01-387 7050. *Clubs:* Athenæum, national Liberal.

**DONOVAN, Dame Florence (May);** *see* Hancock, Dame Florence.

**DONOVAN, Hedley (Williams);** Editor-in-Chief, Time Inc., since 1964; *b* 24 May 1914; *s* of Percy Williams Donovan and Alice Dougan Donovan; *m* 1941, Dorothy Hannon; two *s* one *d*. *Educ:* University of Minnesota; Hertford Coll., Oxford. BA (*magna cum laude*) Minn., 1934; BA Oxon. 1936. Hon. LittD: Pomona Coll., 1966, Boston, 1968. Hon. DHL: Southwestern at Memphis, 1967; Rochester, 1968; Hon. LLD, Carnegie-Mellon, 1969. US Naval Reserve, active duty, 1942-45 (Lieut-Comdr). Reporter, Washington Post, 1937-42; Writer and Editor, 1945-53, Managing Editor, 1953-59, Fortune; Editorial Dir, Time Inc., 1959-64. Phi Beta Kappa; Rhodes Scholar. *Address:* Time Inc., Time & Life Building, Rockefeller Center, New York, NY 10020, USA. *T:* Judson 6-1212. *Clubs:* University (New York); Manhasset Bay Yacht (Long Island); Sands Point Golf.

**DONOVAN, John,** CBE 1953; MInstT; retired; *b* 25 Dec. 1891; *s* of John Donovan, stevedore; *m* 1911, Annie Louise Burke; two *s* four *d*; *m* 1964, Dame Florence May Hancock, *qv*. *Educ:* St Joseph's, Swansea, Dockworker, 1906-15. Served European War, 1914-18, Welsh Regt, 1915-19. Dockworker, 1919-25; Trade Union Sec., Cornwall, 1925-32; Trade Union Area Sec., 1932-40; National Docks Sec., Transport and Gen. Workers Union, 1940-47; Mem., Management Board, British Transport Docks,

1947-58. Mem. Falmouth Town Council, 1928-32; mem. Bristol City Council, 1937-40. *Recreations:* music, swimming, Rugby football. *Address:* 4 Melita Road, St Andrew's, Bristol 6. *T:* Bristol 43880.

**DONOVAN, John Thomas,** CIE 1931; BA RUI; Barrister-at-law; *y s* of late William Donovan, Galway; *b* 12 Dec. 1885; *m* Sara, *d* of C. Devane, Limerick; two *s* two *d*. *Educ:* Clongowes Wood Coll.; Queen's Coll., Galway; Trinity Coll., Dublin. Entered Indian Civil Service, 1910; Registrar of Co-operative Socs, Bengal, 1916-21; Dep. Commissioner of Darjeeling, 1921-22; Sec. to Govt of Bengal Agriculture and Industries Dept, and Mem. of the Bengal Legislative Council, 1922-24; Mem. of the Legislative Assembly of India, and District Magistrate, Hooghly, 1925-27; District Magistrate Bakarganj District, 1927-31; retired from Indian Civil Service, 1932; Organising Sec., Irish Bank Officials' Association, 1932-48; Hon. Fellow of Institute of Bankers of Ireland, 1935. *Address:* Fernhurst, Shrewsbury Road, Dublin. *T:* Dublin 692774.

**DOOLITTLE, Lt-Gen. James H.;** Hon. KCB 1945; Trustee since 1965 (Chairman of Executive Committee and Vice-Chairman, Board of Trustees, 1965-69), Aerospace Corporation; Chairman of Board, Space Technology Laboratories, Inc., 1959-62; Director: Mutual of Omaha Insurance Co.; United Benefit Life Insurance Co.; Companion Life Insurance Co.; Tele-Trip Co., Inc.; *b* 14 Dec. 1896; *s* of Frank H. Doolittle and Rosa C. Shephard; *m* 1917, Josephine E. Daniels; two *s*. *Educ:* University of California (AB); MIT (MS, ScD). US Army Air Force, 1917-30; Manager, Aviation Dept, Shell Oil Co., 1930-40; USAAF, 1940-45. Dir, Shell Oil Company, 1946-67 (Vice-Pres., 1946-59). *Publications:* various scientific. *Recreations:* shooting, fishing. *Address:* 5225 Wilshire Boulevard, Room 702, Los Angeles, Calif 90036, USA.

**DORATI, Antal;** composer and conductor; Chief Conductor: Stockholm Philharmonic Orchestra since 1966; National Symphony Orchestra, Washington, DC, since 1970; *b* Budapest, 9 April 1906; *s* of Alexander Dorati and Margit (*née* Kunwald). *Educ:* Royal Academy of Music, Budapest; University of Vienna. Conductor: Royal Opera House, Budapest, 1924-28; Münster State Opera, 1929-32; Musical Director: Ballet Russe de Monte Carlo, 1932-40; Ballet Theatre, NY, 1940-42; New Opera Co., NY, 1942-43; Musical Dir and Conductor: Dallas Symph. Orch., 1944-49; Minneapolis Symph. Orch., 1944-60; Chief Conductor, BBC Symphony Orchestra, 1963-66. Guest conductor of major orchestras of the world, Salzburg, Holland, Venice, Lucerne, Berlin Festivals, etc; London Symphony, New Philharmonia, London Philharmonic, Royal Philharmonic, Israel Philharmonic orchestras, etc. Holder of 9 recording awards in America and Europe. DrMus, Macalister Coll., St Paul, 1958. Mem., Royal Swedish Academy of the Arts. Compositions include: Le Chemin de la Croix (dramatic cantata); Symphony I; Missa Brevis; The two enchantments of Li-Tai-Pe; String Quartet; Cello Concerto; Nocturne and Capriccio for oboe and strings; Magdalena (ballet); Madrigal Suite; String Octet; Largo Concertato for String Orch.; Chamber-Music Song Cycle for Sopr. and small orch., etc. *Recreations:* painting, sketching, reading, art collecting. *Address:* c/o Ibbs & Tillet, 124 Wigmore Street, W1; c/o Hurok Attractions, 730 Fifth Avenue, New York 19, NY, USA.

**DORCHESTER, Suffragan Bishop of,** since 1956; **Rt. Rev. David Goodwin Loveday,** MA; *b* 13 April 1896; 6th *s* of late J. E. T. Loveday, JP, of Williamscote, near Banbury, Oxon; unmarried. *Educ:* Shrewsbury Sch. (Careswell Exhibitioner); Magdalene Coll., Cambridge (Sizar), 2nd cl. Class. Tripos, Part I, 2nd Class, Theol. Tripos, Part I. Deacon, 1923; Priest, 1924; Asst Master, Malvern Coll., 1917-19; Asst Master and Chaplain, Aldenham Sch., 1922-25; Clifton Coll., 1925-31; Headmaster of Cranleigh Sch., 1931-54; Archdeacon of Dorking and Examining Chaplain, Guildford, 1954-56. Select Preacher: Cambridge 1933 and 1954, Dublin, 1951, Oxford, 1955 and 1957. *Address:* Wardington, Banbury, Oxon. *T:* Cropredy 219. *Clubs:* Oxford and Cambridge; County (Guildford).

**DOREY, Edgar Aleck,** CBE 1945; Jurat of Royal Court of Jersey since 1935; Juge d'Instruction (Magistrate) for Jersey since 1947; *b* 21 Oct. 1886; *s* of Thomas Dorey; *m* 1919, Olive Kathleen Giffard; one *s* one *d*. *Educ:* High Sch., Jersey. Capital and Counties Bank, 1902-18; retired to Jersey, 1931. *Address:* Stella Maris, Samares, Jersey. *T:* Central 22687. *Club:* United (Jersey).

**DOREY, Stanley Fabes,** CBE 1946; FRS 1948; DSc, CEng, FInstCE, Hon. FIMechE, FRINA, FIMarE, etc.; Chief Engineer Surveyor of Lloyd's Register of Shipping, 1932-56, retired; *b* 28 Nov. 1891; 2nd *s* of late Wm Dorey, London and Worthing; *m* 1st, 1920, Dorothy Ellen (*d* 1949), *o c* of late Richard Midworth, Bowes Park; one *s* two *d*; *m* 2nd, 1956, Evelyn Josephine, *d* of late John Moffatt, Dublin. *Educ:* Owen's Sch., London; Durham Univ. Apprenticeship at Chatham Royal Dockyard, Whitworth Exhibitioner, 1912; Engineer-Lieut, Royal Navy, 1914-19; Engine and Ship Surveyor; Lloyd's Register of Shipping, 1919; Charles Parsons Memorial lecture and medal, 1942; Past President: Engineering Section, British Assoc.; Inst. of Marine Engineers; Institution of Mechanical Engineers; Inst. of Metals; Inst. of Refrigeration; Whitworth Soc. Hon. Vice-Pres. Royal Institution of Naval Architects; Hon. Fellow NE Coast Inst. of Engineers and Shipbuilders; Foreign Mem. Danish Academy of Technical Sciences. Liveryman of Company of Shipwrights, Freeman of City of London. *Publications:* papers to technical institutions and socs. *Recreation:* rural contemplation. *Address:* 3 Springwood Road, Heathfield, Sussex. *T:* Heathfield 3888. *Club:* Athenæum.

**DORKING, Suffragan Bishop of,** since 1968; **Rt. Rev. Kenneth Dawson Evans;** *b* 7 Nov. 1915; *s* of late Dr Edward Victor Evans, OBE; *m* 1939 Margaret, *d* of J. J. Burton; one *s*. *Educ:* Dulwich Coll.; Clare Coll., Cambridge. Ordained, 1938; Curate of: St Mary, Northampton, 1938-41; All Saints', Northampton, 1941-45; Rector of Ockley, 1945-49; Vicar of Dorking, 1949-63. Hon. Canon of Guildford, 1955-63; Ed., Guildford Diocesan Publications, 1947-61; Archdeacon of Dorking and Canon Residentiary of Guildford Cathedral, 1963-68. Mem., Bishop's Finance Commn, 1957. *Address:* 13 Pilgrims Way, Guildford, Surrey. *T:* Guildford 67978.

**DORKING, Archdeacon of;** *see* Purcell, Ven. W. H. S.

**DORLAND, Arthur Garratt,** BA, MA, PhD; FRSC; Professor of History, 1920; and Head of the History Department, University of Western Ontario, London, Ontario; (appointed first J. B. Smallman Professor of History, 1955), retired 1956; *b* Wellington, Prince Edward County, Ont, 1887; *s* of John T.

Dorland, Jun., of Wellington, and Lavina Hubbs of Bloomfield, Ont; *m* 1912, Ellen Uprichard, *d* of Joseph H. Malone, Dublin; three *s* one *d*. *Educ:* Ashburton House, London, England; Bloomfield Public Sch.; Pickering Coll.; Queen's Univ.; Yale Univ.; Chicago Univ. Teacher of History and English, and Housemaster, Pickering Coll., 1911-14; Currier Fellow in History, Yale, 1914-15; Lecturer in History, Queen's Univ., Kingston, 1916-20; Clerk of Canada Yearly Meeting of the Religious Soc. of Friends, 1924. Pres. Coll. and Secondary Sch. Dept of Ontario Education Assoc., 1949; Pres. Section II Royal Society of Canada, 1949; Associate Ed., The Loyalist Gazette, 1966. Hon. LLD Univ. of Western Ontario, 1963. Canada Centennial Medal, 1967. *Publications:* The Royal Disallowance in Massachusetts, 1917; British North America since (1713), published in Expansion of the Anglo-Saxon Nations, 1920; A History of the Society of Friends (Quakers) in Canada, 1927; The Origins of the Holy Alliance, 1939; Our Canada, A History textbook, 1949; Former Days and Quaker Ways, 1965; The Quakers in Canada, 1968. *Recreations:* gardening, boating. *Address:* Fair Acre, Wellington, Ont., Canada.

**DORMAN, Lt-Col Sir Charles (Geoffrey),** 3rd Bt *cr* 1923; MC 1942; *b* 18 Sept. 1920; *o s* of Sir Bedford Lockwood Dorman, 2nd Bart, CBE and Lady Constance Phelps Dorman (*née* Hay), (*d* 1946); *S* father 1956; *m* 1954, Elizabeth Ann, *d* of late George Gilmour Gilmour-White, OBE; one *d*. *Educ:* Rugby Sch.; Brasenose Coll., Oxford (MA). Commissioned, 1941; served with 3rd The King's Own Hussars at Alamein (MC) and in Italian Campaign; Commissioned to 13th/18th Royal Hussars (QMO), 1947; GSO1, 1961-64; Royal Armoured Corps, 1964-70, retired. *Recreation:* gliding. *Heir: cousin* Richard Dorman [*b* 25 May 1918; *m* 1947, Diana, *d* of late Dr H. E. Barrett; one *s* one *d*.] *Address:* Hunters Quay, 3 Dormer Close, Crowthorne, Berks. *Club:* Cavalry.

**DORMAN, Sir Maurice Henry,** GCMG 1961 (KCMG 1957; CMG 1955); GCVO 1961; MA; Governor-General of Malta since Sept. 1964 (Governor, 1962-64); *b* 7 Aug. 1912; *s* of John Ehrenfried and Madeleine Louise Dorman; *m* 1937, Florence Monica Churchward Smith, DStJ 1968; one *s* three *d*. *Educ:* Sedbergh Sch.; Magdalene Coll., Cambridge. Administrative Officer, Tanganyika Territory, 1935; Clerk of Councils, Tanganyika Territory, 1940-45; Asst to the Lt-Governor, Malta, 1945; Principal Asst Sec., Palestine, 1947; Seconded to Colonial Office as Asst Sec., Social Services Dept, 1948; Dir of Social Welfare, Gold Coast, 1950; Colonial Sec., Trinidad and Tobago, 1952-56; Actg Governor of Trinidad, 1954, 1955; Governor, Comdr-in-Chief and Vice-Adm., Sierra Leone, 1956-61. Sierra Leone became independent within the Commonwealth, 27 April 1961; Governor-Gen. and Comdr-in-Chief, 1961-62. Hon. DCL Durham; Hon. LLD Royal Univ. Malta. KStJ 1957. Gran Croce Al Merito Melitense (Sov. Ordine Militaire di Malta), 1966. *Recreations:* sailing, squash and sometimes golf. *Address:* The Old Manor, Overton, Marlborough, Wilts; The Palace, Malta. *Clubs:* Athenæum, East India and Sports; Casino Maltese (Valletta).

**DORMAN, Richard Bostock;** Counsellor and Head of Chancery, British Embassy, Addis Ababa; *b* 8 Aug. 1925; *s* of John Ehrenfried and Madeleine Louise Dorman; *m* 1950, Anna Illingworth; one *s* two *d*. *Educ:* Sedbergh Sch.; St John's Coll., Cambridge. Army Service (Lieut, S Staffs Regt), 1944-48; Asst Principal, War Office, 1951; Principal, 1955; transferred to Commonwealth Relations Office, 1958; First Sec., British High Commission, Nicosia, 1960-64; Dep. High Commissioner, Freetown, 1964-66; SE Asia Dept, FO, 1967-69. *Address:* 67 Beresford Road, Cheam, Surrey. *T:* 01-642 9627. *Club:* Royal Commonwealth Society.

**DORMAN-SMITH, Col Rt. Hon. Sir Reginald Hugh,** PC 1939; GBE, *cr* 1941; Kt 1937; JP; *b* 1899; *s* of Major E. P. Dorman-Smith, Bellamont Forest, County Cavan, Ireland; *m* 1921, Doreen Agnes Edith, *d* of Sir John Watson, 2nd Bt of Earnock; one *d* (and one *d* decd). *Educ:* Harrow; RMC Sandhurst. 15th Sikhs (IA) and 5th Batt. Queen's Royal Regt (TA); County Alderman, 1931-35, and JP for Surrey; MP (C) Petersfield Div. of Hants, 1935-41; Pres. National Farmers Union, 1936-37; Minister of Agriculture and Fisheries, 1939-40; Liaison Officer between Home Defence Forces and Govt Dept, 1940; Governor of Burma, 1941-46. High Sheriff, Hants, 1952; JP, Hants, 1960. KStJ. *Address:* Hunters Croft, Grayswood, Haslemere, Surrey. *T:* Haslemere 3012.

**DORMAND, John Donkin;** MP (Lab) Easington since 1970; *b* 27 Aug. 1919; *s* of Bernard and Mary Dormand; *m* 1963, Doris Robinson; one step *s* one step *d*. *Educ:* Bede Coll., Durham; Loughborough Coll.; Univs of Oxford and Harvard. Teacher, 1940-48; Education Adviser, 1948-52 and 1957-63; District Education Officer, Easington RDC, 1963-70. *Recreations:* music, sport. *Address:* Lynton, Stockton Road, Easington, Peterlee, Co. Durham.

**DORMER,** family name of **Baron Dormer.**

**DORMER,** 15th Baron (*cr* 1615); **Charles Walter James Dormer,** Bt 1615; Captain Life Guards; *b* 20 Dec. 1903; *s* of 14th Baron and Caroline May (*d* 1951), *y d* of late Col Sir Spencer Clifford; *S* father, 1922; *m* 1944, Lady Maureen Therèse Josephine Noel, *o d* of 4th Earl of Gainsborough, Exton Park, Rutland; two *d*. *Educ:* Oratory Sch. and RMC, Sandhurst. ADC to Governor-Gen. of New Zealand, 1939-41. *Heir: b* Hon. Joseph Spencer Philip Dormer, Lieut Scots Guards, *b* 4 Sept 1914. *Address:* Grove Park, Warwick. *T:* Warwick 43633; 58 Melbury Court, W8.

**DORMER, Sir Cecil Francis Joseph,** KCMG, *cr* 1937; MVO; *b* 14 Feb. 1883; *y s* of late Hon. Hubert Dormer, and *g s* of 11th Baron Dormer; *m* 1915, Lady Mary A. C. Feilding, *e d* of 9th Earl of Denbigh. *Educ:* St Augustine's Coll., Ramsgate. Clerk in Foreign Office, 1905; Acting 2nd Sec. in Diplomatic Service, 1911; Asst Private Sec. to Sec. of State for Foreign Affairs (Viscount Grey, KG, and Mr Balfour) 1915-19; Chargé d'Affaires, Caracas, 1919-21; Sec. of British Legation to the Holy See, Rome, 1921-25; Counsellor of Embassy at Tokio, 1926-29; Envoy Extraordinary and Minister Plenipotentiary Bangkok, 1929; Oslo, 1934; Ambassador to Polish Government in London, 1941-43. Grand Cross, Order of St Olav (Norway), 1940; Norwegian War Medal. *Address:* Windmill Piece, Binfield, Bracknell, Berks. *T:* Bracknell 4610.

**D'ORMESSON, Count Wladimir Olivier Marie François de Paule Le Fèvre;** Grand Croix de la Légion d'Honneur; Grand Croix de l'Ordre National du Mérite (Member Council of the Order); Croix de Guerre; French political essayist and journalist and former ambassador; Member of the French Academy since 1956; President Administration Council, Radiodiffusion-Télévision française, 1964-68; *b* St Petersburg, Russia, 2 Aug. 1888; *s* of

Olivier, Comte d'Ormesson, and la Comtesse d'Ormesson (*née* Marguerite de la Guéronnière); *m* 1913, Conchita de Malo; three *s* three *d*. *Educ:* Lycée Janson-de-Sailly; Ecole des Sciences Politiques, Paris. Leader writer for Figaro; foreign political ed. for Temps, Journal de Genève, etc. French Ambassador to: the Holy See, 1940; the Argentine Republic, 1945-48; the Holy See, 1948-56. Holds numerous foreign decorations. *Publications:* Nos Illusions sur l'Europe Centrale, 1922; La Confiance en l'Allemagne?, 1928; Enfances diplomatiques, 1932; La Révolution allemande, 1934; Qu'est-ce qu'un Française? (Clemenceau, Poincaré, Briand), 1935; La Première Mission officielle de la France aux Etats-Unis, 1936; Adieux, 1937; L'Eternel Problème allemand, 1945; La Ville éternelle; La Papauté: La Ville et les Champs, La Présence française dans la Rome des papes; Les vraies Confidences; Auprès de Lyautey, etc. *Address:* Château d'Ormesson, Ormesson-sur-Marne, Seine-et-Oise, France; 9 rue Salignac-Fénelon, Neuilly sur Seine.

**DORNHORST, Antony Clifford,** MD, FRCP; Professor of Medicine, St George's Hospital Medical School, since 1959; *b* 2 April 1915; *s* of Ernst Dornhorst and Florence, *née* Partridge; *m* 1946, Helen Mary Innes; three *d*. *Educ:* St Clement Danes Sch.; St Thomas's Hosp. Medical Sch. MB BS London 1937; MD London 1939; FRCP 1955. Junior Appointments, st Thomas' Hosp., 1937-39. Served with RAMC, mostly in Mediterranean theatre, 1940-46. Reader in Medicine, St Thomas's Hosp. Medical Sch., 1949-59. *Publications:* papers in various journals on normal and abnormal physiology. *Recreation:* music. *Address:* 8 Albert Place, W8. *T:* 01-937 8782.

**DORRELL, Bt Lieut-Col G. T.,** VC 1914; MBE 1925; *m* Lucy (*d* 1969); one *s* two *d*. Ranks, 1895-1914; served South African War, 1899-1902; Commissioned RHA, 1914; Capt. RFA, 1918; European War, 1914-18 (VC). Retired from Regular Army with rank of Major, 1921; granted commission as Capt. in Territorial RA, 1921; Major, 1924; Bt Lieut-Col 1929; Company Comdr, Home Guard, 1940-45. *Address:* 30 Bray Road, Cobham, Surrey.

**DORSET, Archdeacon of;** *see* Seager, Ven. Edward Leslie.

**DOS SANTOS, Sir Errol Lionel,** Kt, *cr* 1946; CBE 1939; President of Alstons Ltd since 1961 (Director, 1948; Chairman, 1953-61); *b* 1 Sept. 1890; *s* of Solomon and Margaret dos Santos; *m* 1st, 1915; one *s* one *d*; 2nd, 1939, Enid Hilda Jenkin, Bath, England; two *d*. *Educ:* St Mary's Coll., Trinidad. Entered Trinidad Civil Service as a junior clerk in the Treasury; Financial Sec., 1941; Colonial Sec., 1947; retired from Colonial Service, 1948. *Address:* Alstons Ltd, Trinidad. *Clubs:* West Indian; Union, Queen's Park Cricket, Portuguese (Trinidad).

**DOSSOR, Rear-Adm. Frederick,** CB 1963; CBE 1959; Director of Hovercraft, Ministry of Technology, since 1968; *b* 12 March 1913; *s* of John Malcolm Dossor and Edith Kate Brittain; *m* 1951, Pamela Anne Huxley Newton; two *d*. *Educ:* Hymers Coll., Hull; Loughborough Coll. BSc(Eng.) London; FIEE. Post Graduate Apprentice and Junior Engineer, Metropolitan Vickers Electrical Co., Manchester, 1935-39; Dept of Dir of Electrical Engineering, Admiralty, 1939-50; Electrical Specialisation, Royal Navy, 1950-65; Chief Staff Officer (Technical), staff of Comdr-in-Chief, Portsmouth, 1961-63; Polaris Project Officer in the Ministry of Technology, 1963-67. Retired, 1965. *Recreations:* gardening, golf. *Address:* 1a Lynch Road, Farnham, Surrey. *Club:* Royal Commonwealth Society.

**DOTRICE, Roy;** actor (stage, films and television); *b* 26 May 1925; *m* 1946, Kay Newman, actress; three *d*. *Educ:* Dayton and Intermediate Schs, Guernsey, CI. Served War of 1939-45: Air Gunner, RAF, 1940; PoW, 1942-45. Acted in Repertory, 1945-55; formed and directed Guernsey Theatre Co., 1955; Royal Shakespeare Co., 1957-65 (Caliban, Julius Caesar, Hotspur, Firs, Puntila, Edward IV, etc); World War 2½, New Theatre, London, 1966; Brief Lives, Golden Theatre, New York, 1967; Latent Heterosexual and God Bless, Royal Shakespeare Co., Aldwych, 1968; Brief Lives (one-man play), Criterion, 1969 (over 200 perfs, world record for longest-running solo perf.); Peer Gynt, Chichester Festival, 1970. *Films include:* Heroes of Telemark, Twist of Sand, Lock up Your Daughters, Buttercup Chain, Tomorrow; One of Those Things; *Television:* appearances in: Dear Liar, Brief Lives, The Caretaker (Emmy award), Imperial Palace, Misleading Cases, etc. TV Actor of the Year Award, 1968. *Recreations:* fishing, riding. *Address:* Talbot House, St Martins Lane, WC2. *T:* 01-836 7054. *Club:* Garrick.

**DOTT, Norman McOmish,** CBE 1948; FRSE 1936; MB, ChB, FRCS (Ed.), 1923; retired 1962; Professor Emeritus; Hon. Consulting Neurological Surgeon to: Royal Infirmary of Edinburgh; Western General Hospital, Edinburgh; Royal Edinburgh Hospital for Sick Children; *b* 26 Aug. 1897; *m* 1932, Margaret Robertson; one *d*. *Educ:* George Heriot's Sch., Edinburgh; University of Edinburgh. After leaving sch. was apprentice joiner, apprentice engineer; accidental injury to hip, 1913; Edinburgh Univ. Med. Sch., 1914; graduated (MB, ChB), 1919; Asst Surgeon, Deaconess and Chalmers Hosps, 1923; Jun. Assoc. in Neurological Surgery, Peter Bent Brigham Hosp., Boston, USA (with Dr Harvey Cushing), 1923-24; Surgeon in Ordinary, Royal Edinburgh Hosp. for Sick Children, 1925; Neurological surgery in private nursing Homes in Edinburgh, 1924-31; Surgeon in Ordinary, Deaconess Hospital, 1929-31; Neurological Surgeon, Royal Infirmary, Edinburgh, 1931; resigned Deaconess and Chalmers Hospital posts, 1931, and Children's Hospital post, 1935, remaining attached as Neurological Surgeon. Lecturer in Neurological Surgery, University of Edinburgh, 1932; Dir of Neurology and Neurosurgery, Bangour EMS Hosp. (near Edinburgh), 1940. Formerly: Prof. of Neurological Surgery, University of Edinburgh, 1947-62; Neurological Surgeon to: Royal Infirmary, Edinburgh; Western Gen. Hosp., Edinburgh; Royal Edinburgh Hosp. for Sick Children. Mem. GMC, 1966; Chairman: Edinburgh Cttee, British Empire Campaign for Cancer Research, 1963; Epilepsy Soc., Edinburgh and SE Scotland, 1967; President: Scottish Assoc. for Occupational Therapy, 1960; Scottish Soc. for the History of Medicine, 1966-68; Hon. President: Scottish Paraplegia Assoc., 1963; Scottish Spina Bifida Assoc., 1965. Vice-Pres., RCS Edinburgh, 1957-67; Hon. FRSM, 1968; Hon. Mem. numerous European, North and South American, Middle Eastern and Asiatic Surgical and Neurosurgical Socs., etc. Freedom of the City of Edinburgh, 1962. Hon. MD Edinburgh, 1969. *Publications:* numerous surgical and Neurosurgical. *Recreations:* fishing, travel, handicrafts. *Address:* 3 Chalmers Crescent, Edinburgh EH9 1TW. *T:* 031-667 2188.

**DOUBLEDAY, Frederic Nicklin;** Consulting Dental Surgeon to Guy's Hospital; Vice-President Medical Defence Union; formerly Vice-President Royal Society of Medicine; Examiner in Dental Surgery to the Royal College of Surgeons of England; *b* 5 March 1885; *s* of F. W. Doubleday; *m* Esther Jane, 2nd *d* of Rev. J. A. Barrow-Clugh, BA, BD. *Educ:* Privately; Guy's Hosp. University of Berlin. Graduated from Guy's Hosp.; LDS, RCS 1908, LRCP, MRCS 1912; Fellow in Dental Surgery, RCS, 1947; Dental Societies Prizeman, 1907, and Dental Travelling Scholar in Berlin, 1909-10; formerly Ed. of the British Dental Journal; External Examiner to the University of Bristol; Extramural Lecturer to the University of Toronto; Dental Surgeon to King George Vth Hosp. for Treatment of Gunshot Injuries of the Face and Jaws; visiting Prof. of Dental Surgery, Fouad Univ., Cairo, 1948; Wallis Lecturer, Royal Society of Medicine, 1948; Hon. Member: Stomatological Soc. of Greece, 1948; Stomatological Soc. of Piedmont, Italy, 1951; Odontological Section, RSM, London, 1956. Hon. Life Mem. Brit. Dental Assoc., 1959. *Publications:* (part author) Guy's Hospital 1725-1948, 1951; many Papers on Medical and Dental Subjects, Lectures in United States, Canada, and other countries; Ed., The New Rambler, Jl of Johnson Society of London. *Recreations:* travel, walking, swimming. *Address:* Hartland, Moores Road, Dorking, Surrey. *T:* Dorking 3955.

**DOUBLEDAY, Sir Leslie,** Kt 1957; JP; *b* 1887; *s* of Rev. John Doubleday, Sittingbourne, Kent; *m* 1912, Nora, *d* of William Foster, Tunbridge Wells; two *s* two *d*. *Educ:* Taunton; Wye Coll. Served European War, 1914-18, Kent Yeomanry (Capt.). Mem., Kent War Agricultural Executive Cttee, 1940-45. JP 1925 (Chm., Sittingbourne Petty Sessions, 1946-60); County Councillor, 1925, County Alderman, 1941, Kent; High Sheriff of Kent, 1942, 1951; Chm., Dartford Tunnel Joint Cttee. Past Master, Fruiterers' Company. *Address:* Hempstead, Tonge, Sittingbourne, Kent. *T:* Sittingbourne 3981. *Clubs:* City Livery, United Sports.

**DOUGHERTY, Maj.-Gen. Sir Ivan Noel,** Kt 1968; CBE 1946; DSO 1941; ED; Director of Civil Defence for New South Wales since 1955; *b* Leadville, NSW, 6 April 1907; *m* 1936, Emily Phyllis Lofts; two *s* two *d* (and one *d* decd). *Educ:* Leadville Primary Sch.; Mudgee High Sch.; Sydney Teachers' Coll.; Sydney Univ. (BEc). NSW Education Dept: Asst Teacher, 1928-32; Dep. Headmaster, 1933-39; Headmaster, 1946-47; Dist Inspector of Schs, 1948-53; Staff Inspector 1953-55. Commissioned Sydney Univ. Regt, 1927. Capt. 1931; Unattached List, 1932-34; transf. to 33/41 Bn. 1934; Major, 1938; Command, 33rd Bn, 1938; Lieut-Col 1939. Served War of 1939-45 (DSO and Bar, CBE, despatches thrice); Australian Imperial Force, Second-in-Command, 2/2 Inf. Bn, 1939-40; Commanded 2/4 inf. Bn (Libya, Greece, Crete campaigns), 1940-42; Brig. 1942; commanded 23 Bde, 1942; commanded 21 Bde, South-West Pacific, 1942-45. R of O, 1946-47; commanded 8th Bde, Austr. Mil. Forces, 1948-52; Maj.-Gen., 1952; commanded 2nd Div., 1952-54; Citizen Military Forces Member, Australian Mil. Bd, 1954-57; R of O, 1957-64; Retired List, 1964; Hon. Col, Australian Cadet Corps, Eastern Command, 1964-70; Representative Hon. Col, Australian Cadet Corps, 1967-70. Mem. Senate University of Sydney, 1954-; Dep. Chancellor, University of Sydney, 1958-66. *Address:* 4 Leumeah Street, Cronulla, New South Wales, Australia. *T:* 523-5465. *Club:* Imperial Service (Sydney).

**DOUGHTY, Charles John Addison;** QC 1954; Recorder of Brighton since 1955; *b* 21 Sept. 1902; *e s* of late Sir Charles Doughty, QC; *m* 1931, Adelaide Baillieu Shackell (CBE 1964), Australia; one *s* one *d*. *Educ:* Eton; Magdalen Coll., Oxford. Called to Bar, Inner Temple, 1926. Served War of 1939-45, with Coldstream Guards, 1940-45. Contested Aston Div. of Birmingham, Gen. Election, 1950; MP (C) Eastern Division of Surrey, 1951-70. *Recreation:* fishing. *Address:* The Mill House, Buckland Monachorum, S Devon: 2 Harcourt Buildings, Temple, EC4. *Club:* Carlton.

**DOUGHTY, George Henry;** General Secretary, Draughtsmen's & Allied Technicians' Association, since 1952; Member, General Council of the TUC, since 1968; *b* 17 May 1911; British; *m* 1941, Mildred Dawson; two *s*. *Educ:* Handsworth Tech. Sch.; Aston Technical Coll. Draughtsman; trained at General Electric Co., Birmingham, 1927-32; employed as Design Draughtsman: English Electric, Stafford 1932-33; GEC Birmingham, 1934-46. With Draughtsmen's & Allied Technician's Assoc., 1946-. *Publications:* various technical and Trade Union publications. *Recreation:* photography. *Address:* (home) 1 Short Way, Whitton, Twickenham, Middx. *T:* 01-894 0299; (office) Onslow Hall, Little Green, Richmond, Surrey. *T:* 01-940 3341.

**DOUGLAS,** family name of **Viscount Chilston, Baron Douglas of Barloch, Earl of Morton,** and **Marquess of Queensberry.**

**DOUGLAS OF BARLOCH,** 1st Baron, *cr* 1950, of Maxfield, Sussex; **Francis Campbell Ross Douglas,** KCMG, *cr* 1947; MA; LLD (hc), Royal University of Malta; Partner in Douglas & Company, Solicitors; *b* Manitoba, 21 Oct. 1889; *s* of late Francis J. B. Douglas; *m* Minnie Findlay Smith, MA, JP, CStJ (*d* 1969); one *d*. *Educ:* Glasgow Univ. Journalist, Accountant, Solicitor; MP (Lab) for North Battersea, 1940-46; Parliamentary Private Sec. to Parliamentary Sec. of Board of Education, 1940-45; Parliamentary Private Sec. to Home Sec., 1945-46; Temp. Chm., House of Commons and Chm. of Standing Cttees, 1945-46; Chm. of Estimates Cttee, 1945-46; Mem. of Railway Assessment Authority, 1938-46; Mem. of Anglo-Scottish Railway Assessment Authority, 1941-46; Mem. of Public Works Loan Board, 1936-46; Chm. of Finance Cttee of LCC, 1940-46; Governor and Comdr-in-Chief of Malta, 1946-49; Vice-Chm. of Corby Development Corp., 1950-62; Deputy Speaker of House of Lords, 1962-; FRAS; KStJ. *Publications:* Land Value Rating, 1961; numerous pamphlets and articles on land tenure, taxation, soil fertility and nutrition. *Heir:* none. *Address:* 8 Cambridge Road, SW11. *T:* 01-228 2247; Maxfield Manor, Three Oaks, Sussex. *T:* Hastings 51074.

**DOUGLAS, Dr Alexander Edgar,** FRS 1970; FRSC 1954; Director, Division of Physics, National Research Council of Canada, since 1969; *b* 12 April 1916; *s* of Donald Douglas and Jessie F. Douglas (*née* Carwardine); *m* 1945, Phyllis H. Wright; two *s* one *d*. *Educ:* Univ. of Saskatchewan; Pennsylvania State University. BA 1939, MA 1940, Saskatchewan; PhD Penn 1948. Nat. Research Council of Canada: Research Scientist, Acoustics Lab., 1942-46; Spectroscopy Lab., 1948; Assoc. Dir, Div. of Pure Physics, 1967. Fellow, American Physical Soc., 1970. *Publications:* numerous articles on spectroscopy and molecular structure. *Address:* 150 Blenheim Drive, Ottawa, Ont, Canada. *T:* 746-1453.

**DOUGLAS, Prof. Alexander Stuart;** Regius Professor of Medicine, University of Aberdeen, since Oct. 1970; *b* 2 Oct. 1921; *s* of late Dr R. Douglas, MOH for Moray and Nairn; *m* 1954, Christine McClymont Stewart; one *s* one *d*. *Educ:* Elgin Academy, Morayshire. Mil. Service, RAMC, 1945-48 (despatches 1947). Research Fellow, Radcliffe Infirmary, Oxford, and Postgrad. Med. Sch., London, 1951-53; Lectr, Sen. Lectr and Reader in Medicine, Univ. Dept of Med., Royal Infirmary, Glasgow, 1953-64; Hon. Consultant status, 1957; Prof. of Med., Univ. of Glasgow, 1964-70; secondment to Univ. of East Africa with hon. academic rank of Prof., 1965; Hon. Consultant Physician in Administrative Charge of wards, Royal Infirmary, Glasgow, 1968-70. *Publications:* scientific papers on blood coagulation, etc. *Recreations:* curling, travel. *Address:* Department of Medicine, University Medical Buildings, Foresterhill, Aberdeen AB9 2ZD. *T:* Aberdeen 23423 (ext. 2454).

**DOUGLAS, Archibald Vivian Campbell,** MA; JP; DL; *b* 6 Nov. 1902; *s* of late Brig.-Gen. D. C. Douglas, CB, Mains, Milngavie, Dunbartonshire; *m* 1927, Elizabeth Cicely, 2nd *d* of late Sir Maurice de Bunsen, 1st Bt, PC, GCMG, GCVO, CB; two *d*. *Educ:* Eton; Christ Church, Oxford. 2nd Lieut Scots Guards, 1925; Captain 1931; Lt-Col 1943, DL 1953, Dunbartonshire; Mem. of Royal Company of Archers (Queen's Body Guard for Scotland). Vice-Lieutenant of County of Dunbarton, 1957-68. JP Perthshire, 1962. *Address:* Laraich, Aberfoyle, by Stirling. *T:* Aberfoyle 232. *Clubs:* Flyfishers; New (Edinburgh).

**DOUGLAS, Arthur John Alexander,** CMG 1965; OBE 1962; *b* 31 May 1920; *s* of Alexander and Eileen Douglas; *m* 1948, Christine Scott Dyke; two *d*. *Educ:* Dumfries Academy; Edinburgh Univ. Royal Navy, 1940-45. District Officer, Basutoland, 1946; Seconded Colonial Office, 1957; Administration Sec., Bechuanaland, 1959; Government Sec. and Chief Sec. 1962-65; Dep. Commissioner for Bechuanaland, 1965-66; Ministry of Overseas Development, 1967-. *Address:* 57 Lucastes Avenue, Haywards Heath, Sussex. *Club:* Royal Commonwealth Society.

**DOUGLAS, Lord Cecil Charles,** late Lt KOSB and RFC; 2nd *s* of 10th Marquess of Queensberry; *b* 27 Dec. 1898; *m* 1927, Ruby St B. Kirkley, 2nd *d* of De Vere Fenn; one *d*. *Educ:* Lancing; RMC, Sandhurst. Served European War, 1914 (wounded). *Address:* 3 Chesham Street, SW1. *T:* 01-235 5757. *Clubs:* White's, St James'; Puffins (Edinburgh).

**DOUGLAS, Prof. Charles Primrose,** FRCOG; Professor of Obstetrics and Gynæcology, Royal Free Hospital School of Medicine, London, since 1965; *b* 17 Feb. 1921; *s* of Dr C. Douglas, Ayr, Scotland; *m* 1948, Angela Francis; three *s* one *d*. *Educ:* Loretto Sch.; Peterhouse; Edinburgh Univ. Surg. Lieut RNVR, 1944-47. Registrar and Sen. Registrar, Victoria Infirmary, Glasgow, 1950-59; William Waldorf Astor Foundation Fellow, 1957; Visiting Fellow, Duke Univ., NC, 1957; Sen. Lecturer, University of the West Indies, 1959-65. *Publications:* contribs to BMJ, Amer. Heart Jl, Jl of Obst. and Gynæc. of Brit. Commonwealth, etc. *Recreations:* tennis, equestrian events, skin diving. *Address:* Arkley Rise, Barnet Road, Arkley, Herts. *T:* 01-440 4104. *Club:* Royal Naval Volunteer Reserve (Scotland).

**DOUGLAS, David Charles,** MA Oxon; Hon. DLitt Wales; FBA; Docteur *hc*, Caen; Emeritus Professor of History, Bristol University, since 1963; Fellow of the British Academy since 1949; Hon. Fellow, Keble College, Oxford; *b* London, 1898; *o s* of Dr J. J. Douglas and Margaret E. Peake; *m* 1932, Evelyn Helen, *o d* of Dr B. M. Wilson; one *d*. *Educ:* Sedbergh; Keble Coll., Oxford (Louisa Wakeman Scholar). 1st Class Hons in Modern History, Oxford, 1921; University Research Scholar in Medieval History and Thought, Oxford, 1922-24; Lecturer in History, Glasgow Univ., 1924-34; Prof. of History, University Coll. of the South West, 1934-39; Prof. of Medieval History, Leeds Univ., 1939-45; Prof. of History, Bristol Univ., 1945-63; Dean of the Faculty of Arts, 1958-60; Trustee of London Museum since 1945; David Murray Lectr to University of Glasgow, 1946, Sir Walter Raleigh Lectr to Brit. Acad., 1947; Ford's Lectr in English History, Oxford Univ., 1962-63; Lewis Fry Memorial Lectr, Bristol Univ., 1969. Vice-Pres., Royal Historical Soc., 1953-57; Pres., Bristol and Glos Archæological Soc., 1956. *Publications:* The Norman Conquest, 1926; The Social Structure of Medieval East Anglia, 1927; The Age of the Normans, 1928; Feudal Documents from the Abbey of Bury St Edmunds, 1932; The Development of Medieval Europe, 1935; English Scholars, 1939 (James Tait Black Memorial Prize); Domesday Monachorum, 1944; The Rise of Normandy, 1947; William the Conqueror, 1964; The Norman Achievement, 1969. general Ed., Bristol Record Soc., 1945-; English Historical Documents, 1953, etc.; articles in English Historical Review, Times Lit. Supplt, History, Economic History Reveiw, Revue Historique, French Studies, etc. *Recreation:* book-collecting. *Address:* 4 Henleaze Gardens, Bristol. *Club:* Oxford and Cambridge.

**DOUGLAS, Prof. Donald Macleod,** MBE 1943; ChM St Andrews, MS Minn, FRCSEd, FRCS; Surgeon to the Queen in Scotland; Professor of Surgery, University of Dundee (formerly Queen's College), and Surgeon, Royal Infirmary, Dundee, since 1951; Dean of the Faculty of Medicine, University of Dundee, since 1969; President: Association of Surgeons of Great Britain and Ireland, 1964; Surgical Research Society of Great Britain, 1966-69; *b* 28 June 1911; *s* of William Douglas and Christina Broom; *m* 1945, Margaret Diana Whitley; two *s* two *d*. *Educ:* Madras Coll.; Universities of St Andrews and Minnesota. Commonwealth Fellow in Surgery, Mayo Clinic, University of Minnesota, USA, 1937-39; First Asst in Surgery, British Postgraduate Medical Sch., 1939-40; RAMC, 1941-45; Reader in Experimental Surgery, University of Edinburgh, 1945-51; Asst Surgeon, Edinburgh Municipal Hospitals, 1945. Assoc. Asst Surgeon, Royal Infirmary, Edinburgh. *Publications:* contributions to: American Jl of Digestive Diseases, British Jl of Surgery, Lancet, BMJ. *Address:* Department of Surgery, University of Dundee, Dundee, Angus.

**DOUGLAS, Donald Wills;** President Douglas Aircraft Co. Inc., 1928-57, Chairman, 1957-67, Hon. Chairman since 1967; *b* 6 April 1892; *s* of William Edward Douglas and Dorothy Locker; *m* 1954, Marguerite Tucker; four *s* one *d* (by a previous marr.). *Educ:* United States Naval Acad.; MIT (BSc 1914). Asst Instructor in aero-dynamics, Mass. Inst. of Tech., 1914-15; Chief Engineer, G. L. Martin Co., Los Angeles, 1915-16; Chief Civilian Aero Engineer, US Signal Corps, 1916; Chief Engineer, G. L. Martin Co., Cleveland, 1916-20; Pres., Douglas Co., 1920-28. President's Certificate of Merit, 1947; Guggenheim Medal, 1939; Collier Trophy, 1940; Comdr,

Order of Orange-Nassau, 1950; Chevalier, Legion of Honour, 1950. *Recreations:* yachting, fishing, hunting. *Address:* 4 Crest Road East, Rolling Hills, Calif. *Club:* Los Angeles Yacht (Wilmington, Calif.).

**DOUGLAS, Very Rev. George James Cosmo;** Dean of Argyll and The Isles since 1952; Provost of Cumbrae Cathedral and Rector of St Andrew, Millport, since 1949. *Educ:* University of Edinburgh (MA); Edinburgh Theological Coll. Curate, St Paul's Cathedral, Dundee, 1914-16. TCF, 1916-19; Vice-Principal, Dorchester Missionary Coll., 1919-22; Curate, Dundee Cathedral, 1922-29; Priest-in-charge, St Andrew and St George, Rosyth, 1929-36; St John Baptist, Dundee, 1936-50; Canon, St Paul's Cathedral, Dundee, 1942-50 (Hon. Canon, 1966); Exam. Chaplain to the Bishop of Brechin, 1949-; Exam. Chaplain to the Bishop of Argyll, 1952-. *Address:* The College, Millport, Isle of Cumbrae. *T:* Millport 353. *Club:* New (Edinburgh).

**DOUGLAS, Rt. Rev. Hugh Osborne,** CBE 1961; DD; Chaplain to The Queen since Dec. 1959; Minister at Dundee Parish Church (St Mary's), since 1951; Moderator of the General Assembly of the Church of Scotland, May 1970- May 1971 (designation subsequently Very Rev.); *b* Glasgow, 11 Sept. 1911; *s* of Rev. Robert Baillie Douglas, DD, missionary in W India, and Mary Isabella Osborne. *m* 1939, Isabel Crammond, *d* of William Rutherford, Coldstream, Berwicks; one *s* two *d*. *Educ:* Glasgow Academy; Glasgow Univ.; Trinity Coll., Glasgow. MA 1st Cl. Hons (Classics), 1932. Licensed to preach by Presbytery of Glasgow, 1935; Asst, Govan Old Parish Church, 1935-39; Ordained, Glasgow, 1937; Minister: St John's Leven, 1939; North Leith, Edinburgh, 1942. Member: Legal Aid Central Cttee of Law Soc. of Scotland, 1955; Scottish Religious Advisory Cttee of BBC, 1956; Gen. Advisory Council of BBC, 1966; Convener of Gen. Assembly's Special Cttee on Fourth Centenary of the Reformation, 1955-60; Convener of Gen. Assembly's Special Cttee on Religious Education, 1960-64. Centenary Preacher, St Andrew's Church, Brisbane, 1962. Visiting Lectr, Christian Council of Ghana, 1967. Hon. DD St Andrews Univ., 1958. *Publications:* Coping with Life, 1964; various pamphlets and articles. *Recreation:* golf. *Address:* Manse of Dundee, 371 Blackness Road, Dundee. *T:* 69406. *Club:* New (Edinburgh).

**DOUGLAS, Irvine;** *see* Douglas, R. I.

**DOUGLAS, James Albert Sholto,** CMG 1966; Permanent Secretary, Ministry of Education, Guyana, since 1966, seconded as Director, IDA/IBRD Education Implementation Unit, 1969; *b* 23 April 1913; *s* of Dr James Henry Sholto Douglas and Cécile Anne (*née* Brotherson); *m* 1945, Marjorie Lucille (*née* Reynolds); two *s*. *Educ:* Privately in Guyana (Brit. Guiana); Culford Sch., England. Entered Brit. Guyana CS in Commissary's Dept 1932; various posts in Dist Admin, 1933-48; Asst Dist Comr, 1948; Dist Comr, 1953; seconded as a Local Govt Comr, 1957; Dep. Comr of Local Govt, 1960; Permanent Sec., Community Develt and Educn, 1961, Home Affairs 1961-66, Guyana. *Recreations:* swimming, riding. *Address:* 93 Duke Street, Georgetown, Guyana. *T:* 61403. *Clubs:* West Indian, Royal Commonwealth Society (both London).

**DOUGLAS, James Archibald,** MA, DSc; FGS; Professor Emeritus, Geology, in the University of Oxford since 1950; *b* 1 Dec. 1884; *s* of James Herbert Douglas, Ilkley, Yorks; *m* 1914, Hannah Call Weddell (*d* 1966); two *s* two *d*. *Educ:* Haileybury Coll.; Keble Coll., Oxford. Fellow University Coll., Oxford, 1937. Former Sec. and Vice-Pres. Geological Soc. of London; served European War, Capt. 1st Batt. Gordon Highlanders and 172 Tunnelling Co., RE: 1941 Lieut-Col OC 6th Oxon (Oxford City) Bn HG Bolitho Gold Medal, Royal Geol Society, Cornwall, 1939. Foreign Mem., Geol Soc. of Peru, 1952. *Recreation:* yachting. *Address:* Saxonbury, Yarmouth, Isle of Wight. *T:* Yarmouth 380.

**DOUGLAS, Maj.-Gen. John Primrose,** CB 1968; OBE 1945 (MBE 1938); QHS 1965-68; Deputy Director-General Army Medical Services, 1964-68; *b* 22 Feb. 1908; *m* 1934, Anne Fyfe. *Educ:* Perth Acad.; St Andrews Univ. MB, ChB 1930. Joined RAMC, 1933; served in Gibraltar, France, NW Europe, MELF, AFNORTH, BAOR, etc. DDMS, 21 Army Gp, 1944-46; GHQ, MELF, 1946-49; Med. Cons., NATO Coun., 1958-59; Inspector of Med. Services, 1961-63; DDMS, 1 (Br.) Corps, 1963-64. Col Comdt, RAMC, 1969-. CStJ 1967 (OStJ 1945). Order of Merit, German Red Cross, 1938; Legion of Merit, US, 1945; Order of Orange Nassau, Netherlands, 1945; Order of White Lion, Czechoslovakia, 1946; Order of Leopold, Belgium, 1946. *Address:* c/o Glyn Mills & Co., Kirkland House, Whitehall, SW1.

**DOUGLAS, Katharine Greenhill;** Matron, St Mary's Hospital, Paddington, W2, 1949-63, retired; *b* 13 Jan. 1908; *yr d* of Rev. Daniel Greenhill Douglas and of Catherine Eudora Douglas. *Educ:* St Andrews Sch., Bexhill-on-Sea. Student Nurse, Nightingale Training Sch., St Thomas's Hospital, 1932-36; SRN 1936; Staff Nurse, St Thomas's Hospital, 1936-37; Pupil Midwife, Gen. Lying-In Hospital, SE1, 1937-38; SCM 1938; Ward Sister, St Thomas's Hospital, 1938-43; Administrative Sister, 1943-45; Dep. Matron, 1945-49. Chm., Standing Nursing Advisory Cttee, 1951-57; Mem. of Central Health Services Council, 1951-57. *Recreations:* music, needlework, tennis. *Address:* 33 Digdens Rise, Epsom, Surrey. *T:* Epsom 22048.

**DOUGLAS, Kenneth;** Managing Director, Upper Clyde Shipbuilders Ltd, since 1969; *b* 28 Oct. 1920; British; *m* 1942, Doris Lewer; one *s* two *d*. *Educ:* Sunderland Technical Coll. Dep. Shipyard Manager, Vickers Armstrong Naval Yard, Newcastle-upon-Tyne, 1946-53; Dir and Gen. Manager, Wm Gray & Co. Ltd, West Hartlepool, 1954-58; Man. Dir, Austin & Pickersgill Ltd, Sunderland, 1958-69. *Recreations:* fishing, golf. *Address:* Upton, 15 Queen Street, Helensburgh, Dunbartonshire. *Club:* Western (Glasgow).

**DOUGLAS, Lewis Williams,** GBE (Hon.), 1957; Chairman of Executive Committee, Mutual Life Insurance Co. of New York; Hon. Chairman, Southern Arizona Bank & Trust Co., Tucson, Arizona; *b* Bisbee, Arizona, USA, 2 July 1894; *e s* of late James Stuart Douglas and of Josephine Williams; *m* 1921, Peggy, *d* of Fred G. Zinsser and Emma Sharman; two *s* one *d*. *Educ:* Amherst Coll.; Mass. Institute of Technology. BA (Amherst), 1916; Instructor in history, Amherst Coll., 1920; mining, ranching and general business, Arizona, since 1921; Mem. Arizona House of Representatives, 1923-25; Congressman-at-large from Arizona, 1927-33; Dir of Budget, 1933-34; Vice-Pres. and Dir Am. Cyanamid Co., 1934-37; Principal and Vice-Chancellor, McGill Univ. 1938-40; Pres. Mutual Life Ins. Co., NY, 1940-47, Chm., 1947-59; US Ambassador to the Court of St James's, 1947-50. Served European War, 1917-18, 1st Lieut

FA, Cit. Gen. Pershing (Belgian Croix de Guerre); War of 1939-45, Dep. Adm., War Shipping Adm., 1942-44; Mem. Combined Shipping Adjustment Board; Special Adviser Gen. L. D. Clay, German Control Council, 1945. Hon. degrees: LLD: Amherst Coll., Harvard Univ., 1933; Queen's Coll., Princeton, Brown, New York and Wesleyan Univs, 1938; University of Arizona, 1940; Leeds, 1948; Glasgow, Edinburgh, 1950; DCL, Oxford, 1948; LLD University of London, Universities of Bristol and St Andrews, 1949, Birmingham Univ., 1950, University of Calif., McGill Univ., Columbia Univ., Dalhousie Univ. (Halifax), 1951. National Chm. English-Speaking Union of the US, 1951-59 (now Hon.) (Pres. 1946-47); Chm. American Shakespeare Festival Foundation; Governor, Royal Shakespeare Theatre, Stratford-on-Avon; Vice-Pres. Pilgrims of the United States; Member Board of Trustees; Memorial Hosp.; Amherst Coll. (Emer.); Alfred P. Sloan Foundation. American Museum of Natural History, St Luke's Hospital, Phoenix; Director: Union Corporation; International Nickel Co. Inc.; Western Bancorporation; Chairman: Western Bancorporation International Bank; Investment Cttee United States Branch of The Employers' Liability Assurance Company Ltd. Freedom of City of Edinburgh, 1950. Grand Croix de la Légion d'Honneur (France), 1950; Grand Croix de l'Ordre de la Couronne (Belgium), 1951. *Recreations:* fishing, horse-back. *Address:* Sonoita, Arizona; c/o Southern Arizona Bank and Trust Company, Tucson, Arizona. *T:* Main 2-6611; 1740 Broadway, New York City 19. *T:* Judson 6-4000. *Clubs:* Athenæum, White's, Thirty; Metropolitan, Links (Washington); Anglers' (New York); Old Pueblo (Arizona); Union Interalliée (France).

**DOUGLAS, Richard Giles;** MP (Lab and Co-op) Clackmannan and East Stirlingshire, since 1970; *b* 4 Jan. 1932; *m*; two *d*. *Educ:* Co-operative College, Stanford Hall, Loughborough; Univ. of Strathclyde. Engineer (Marine); Mem. AEF. Tutor organiser in Adult Educn, Co-operative movement, 1957; Sectional Educn Officer, Scotland, 1958-61. Contested (Lab): South Angus, 1964, Edinburgh West, 1966, Glasgow Pollok, March 1967. *Address:* House of Commons, SW1.

**DOUGLAS, (Ronald) Irvine;** Journalist; Press Adviser, Bank of NSW, since 1964; *b* Zeehan, Tasmania, 31 May 1899; *s* of Ronald C. G. amd Jean Douglas; *m* 1935, Williamina, *d* of late Alexander and Williamina Murdoch. *Educ:* Selborne Coll., South Africa; Launceston High Sch., Tasmania. Ed. Sydney Sunday-Pictorial, 1927-28; Special representative of Sydney Morning Herald at UNO Conference, San Francisco, 1945; also had assignments to New Guinea, India, New Caledonia, New Zealand, SE Asia, etc.; Commonwealth Government Publicity Officer, 1934-38, also Private Sec. to Australian Prime Minister (Rt Hon. J. A. Lyons), 1936-38; Press Officer for Duke of Gloucester's Australian tour, 1934; Joint Press Officer for Imperial Conf., London, 1937; Manager and Ed., Australian Associated Press, London, 1940-44; London Manager and Ed., Sydney Morning Herald Overseas News Service, 1945-49. Political Correspondent, Sydney Morning Herald, 1949-52; Editorial staff, Mirror Newspapers, Ltd, Sydney, 1952-64; Federal Vice-Pres., Australian Journalists' Association, 1934; Hon. Sec. Overseas Empire Correspondents Association, London, 1940-43, Pres., 1944; Pres. London Association of British Empire Newspapers Overseas, 1947-48; Vice-Pres. Cen. Acclimatisation Soc., NSW, 1956-57. *Publication:* Opportunity in Australia, 1948; 2nd edn, 1958. *Recreations:* fly-fishing, shooting, golf, rowing. *Address:* 1 Stewart Street, Artarmon, NSW 2064, Australia. *Clubs:* Savage (London); NSW Sports, Journalists' (Sydney); Royal Sydney Golf.

**DOUGLAS, Prof. Ronald Walter,** DSc, FInstP, FSGT, FICeram; Professor of Glass Technology, University of Sheffield, since 1955; *b* 28 March 1910; *s* of John H. P. and A. E. Douglas; *m* 1933, Edna Maud Cadle; two *s*. *Educ:* Latymer Upper Sch.; Sir John Cass Coll., London. Mem., Research Staff, research Laboratories of General Electric Company, 1927-55. *Publications:* many papers on the physics of glass and semiconductors. *Recreations:* a little gardening and listening to music. *Address:* Department of Glass Technology, The University, Sheffield S10 2TZ. *T:* Sheffield 78555, ext. 128.

**DOUGLAS, Sir Sholto (Courtenay Mackenzie),** 5th Bt, *cr* 1831; MC 1918; *b* 27 June 1890; *s* of Donald Sholto Mackenzie Douglas (*d* 1928), and Edith Elizabeth Anne (*d* 1933), *y d* of George Robinson, Bagatelle, Mauritius; *S* cousin 1954; *m* 1929, Lorna Tichborne, *d* of Captain Hugh Nangle; two *d*. Served European War, 1914-18 (MC) and War of 1939-45 with Seaforth Highlanders. *Heir:* none. *Address:* 192 Cooden Drive, Cooden, Sussex.

**DOUGLAS, William Orville;** Associate Justice, Supreme Court of United States, Washington, DC, since 1939; *b* 16 Oct. 1898; *s* of William Douglas and Julia Bickford Fiske; *m* 1st, 1923, Mildred Riddle; one *s* one *d*; 2nd, 1954, Mercedes Hester; 3rd, 1963, Joan Martin; 4th, Cathleen Heffernan. *Educ:* Whitman Coll., Washington; Columbia Univ. Law Sch., New York City. Practised Law in New York City, 1925-27; Mem., Columbia Law Sch., Faculty 1925-28 and Yale Law Sch. Faculty, 1928-34; Dir, Protective Cttee Study, Securities and Exchange Comm., 1934-36; Mem., Securities and Exchange Comm., 1936-39, Chm., 1937-39. Fellow Royal Geographical Soc., London. *Publications:* Democracy and Finance, 1940; Being an American, 1948; Of Men and Mountains, 1950; Strange Lands and Friendly People, 1951; Beyond the High Himalayas, 1952; North From Malaya, 1953; Almanac of Liberty, 1954; Russian Journey, 1956; We The Judges, 1956; The Right of People, 1958; Exploring the Himalaya, 1958; West of the Indus, 1958; America Challenged, 1960; My Wilderness–The Pacific West, 1960; A Living Bill of Rights, 1961; Muir of the Mountains, 1961; My Wilderness–East to Katahdin, 1961; Democracy's Manifesto, 1962; Mr Lincoln and the Negroes, 1963; Freedom of the Mind, 1963; The Anatomy of Liberty, 1963; contrib. to various legal periodicals. *Recreations:* fishing, hunting, hiking. *Address:* Supreme Court of the US, Washington, DC, USA. *Clubs:* University (Washington, DC); Yale, Circumnavigators', Explorers', Overseas Press Club (NY City); Himalayan (Delhi, India).

**DOUGLAS, Hon. Sir William (Randolph),** Kt 1969; Chief Justice of Barbados since 1965; *b* Barbados, 24 Sept. 1921; *e s* of William P. Douglas and Emily Frances Douglas (*née* Nurse); *m* 1951, Thelma Ruth (*née* Gilkes); one *s* one *d*. *Educ:* Bannatyne Sch. and Verdun High Sch., Verdun, Que., Canada; McGill Univ. (BA, Hons); London Sch. of Economics (LLB). Private Practice at Barbados Bar, 1948-50; Dep. Registrar, Barbados, 1950; Resident Magistrate, Jamaica, 1955; Asst Attorney-Gen., Jamaica, 1959; Solicitor-Gen., Jamaica, 1962; Puisne Judge, Jamaica, 1962; *Address:* Leland, Pine Gardens, St Michael,

Barbados. *T:* 92030. *Clubs:* Barbados Yacht, Bridgetown, Rockley Golf and Country (Barbados).

**DOUGLAS and CLYDESDALE, Marquess of;** *see* Clydesdale.

**DOUGLAS-HAMILTON,** family name of **Duke of Hamilton** and **Earl of Selkirk.**

**DOUGLAS-HOME,** family name of **Baroness Dacre.**

**DOUGLAS-HOME, Rt. Hon. Sir Alec, (Alexander Frederick),** KT 1962; PC 1951; DL; MP (U) Kinross and West Perthshire Division since Nov. 1963; Secretary of State for Foreign and Commonwealth Affairs since 1970; First Chancellor of Heriot-Watt University, 1966; *b* 2 July 1903; *e s* of 13th Earl of Home (*d* 1951), KT, and Lilian (*d* 1966), *d* of 4th Earl of Durham; *S* father, 1951, but disclaimed his peerages for life, 23 Oct. 1963; *m* 1936, Elizabeth Hester, 2nd *d* of late Very Rev. C. A. Alington, DD; one *s* (styled Lord Dunglass, 1951-63; this being courtesy title while his father held peerages) three *d. Educ:* Eton; Christ Church, Oxford. MP (U) South Lanark, 1931-45; MP (C) Lanark Div. of Lanarkshire, 1950-51; Parliamentary Private Sec. to the Prime Minister, 1937-39; Joint Parliamentary Under-Sec., Foreign Office, May-July 1945; Minister of State, Scottish Office, 1951-April 1955; Sec. of State for Commonwealth Relations, 1955-60; Dep. Leader of the House of Lords, 1956-57; Leader of the House of Lords, and Lord Pres. of the Council, 1957-60; Sec. of State for Foreign Affairs, 1960-63; Prime Minister and First Lord of the Treasury, Oct. 1963-64; Leader of the Opposition, Oct. 1964-July 1965. Brig., Royal Co. of Archers, Queen's Body Guard for Scotland, 1955. Mem., National Farmers' Union, 1964. DL Lanarkshire, 1960. Hon. DCL Oxon., 1960; Hon. Student of Christ Church, Oxford, 1962; Hon. LLD: Harvard, 1961; Edinburgh, 1962; Aberdeen Univ., 1966; Liverpool, 1967; St Andrews, 1968; Hon. DSc, Heriot-Watt Univ., 1966. Hon. Master of the Bench, Inner Temple, 1963; Grand Master, Primrose League, 1966; Pres. of MCC, 1966-67. Freedom of Selkirk, 1963; Freedom of Edinburgh, 1969. Hon. Freeman, Skinners' Co., 1968. *Address:* House of Commons, SW1; The Hirsel, Coldstream, Berwickshire. *T:* Coldstream 2345; Castlemains, Douglas, Lanarkshire. *T:* Douglas, Lanark 241.
*See also Hon. William Douglas-Home, Duke of Sutherland, J. C. V. Wilkes.*

**DOUGLAS-HOME, Hon. William;** *see* Home.

**DOUGLAS-MANN, Bruce Leslie Home;** MP (Lab) North Kensington since 1970; *b* 23 June 1927; *s* of Leslie John Douglas-Mann, MC and Alice Home Douglas-Mann; *m* 1955, Helen Tucker; one *s* one *d. Educ:* Upper Canada Coll., Toronto; Jesus Coll., Oxford. Leading Seaman, RN, 1945-48; Oxford, 1948-51; Solicitor's Articled Clerk, 1951-54; private legal practice, 1954- (started firm of Douglas-Mann & Co., 1964). Contested (Lab): St Albans, 1964; Maldon, 1966. Mem., Kensington or Kensington and Chelsea Borough Council, 1962-68. *Recreation:* boats. *Address:* 26 Queensdale Road, W11. *T:* 01-727 6780.

**DOUGLAS-PENNANT,** family name of **Baron Penrhyn.**

**DOUGLAS-SCOTT-MONTAGU,** family name of **Baron Montagu of Beaulieu.**

**DOUGLAS-WILSON, Ian,** MD, FRCPE; Editor of the Lancet since 1965; *b* 12 May 1912; *o s* of late Dr H. Douglas-Wilson; *m* 1939, Beatrice May, *e d* of late R. P. Bevan; one *s* two *d. Educ:* Marlborough Coll.; Edinburgh Univ. MD (commended) Edinburgh 1938; FRCP Edinburgh 1945. Served with RAMC, 1940-45 (temp. Major). House-physician, Royal Infirmary, Edinburgh, 1937; joined the Lancet staff, 1946; Asst Ed., 1952-62; Dep. Ed., 1962-64. *Publications:* contribs to medical jls. *Address:* 1a Lower Camden, Chislehurst, Kent. *T:* 01-467 1703. *Club:* Athenæum.

**DOUGLAS-WITHERS, Maj.-Gen. John Keppel Ingold,** CBE 1969; MC 1943; GOC South-West District since 1970; *b* 11 Dec. 1919; *s* of late Lt-Col H. H. Douglas-Withers, OBE, MC, FSA, and of Mrs V. G. Douglas-Withers; *m* 1945, Sylvia Beatrice Dean, Croydon, Surrey; one *s* one *d. Educ:* Shrewsbury Sch.; Christ Church, Oxford. Diploma in French, Univ. of Poitiers, 1938; Associate of Inst. of Linguists, in French and German, 1939. Commissioned into RA, 1940; Service in UK, Iraq, Western Desert, N Africa and Italy, 1940-45. Instr in Gunnery, Sch. of Artillery, Larkhill, 1945-47; service in Canal Zone, 1947-48; attended Staff Coll., Camberley, 1950; Staff appt in War Office (Mil. Ops), 1951-53; service in King's Troop, RHA, 1953-55; Instr, Staff Coll., Camberley, 1956-58; Battery Comdr, G Bty, Mercers Troop, RHA, 1959-60; Staff appt in WO (Mil. Sec. Dept), 1961; commanded 49 Field Regt in BAOR and Hong Kong, 1962-64; student at idc, 1965; Comd 6 Inf. Bde in BAOR, 1966-67; Chief of Staff, 1st Brit. Corps, 1968-69. *Recreations:* golf, riding, history, music. *Address:* c/o Australia and New Zealand Bank, 71 Cornhill, EC3. *Clubs:* East India and Sports, MCC.

**DOUGLASS,** family name of **Baron Douglass of Cleveland.**

**DOUGLASS OF CLEVELAND,** Baron *cr* 1967 (Life Peer); **Harry Douglass,** Kt 1964; Chm., Trades Union Congress, 1966-67; General Secretary, Iron and Steel Trades Confederation, 1953-67; Part-time Member: Electricity Council, since 1966; Monopolies Commission, since 1967; *b* 1 Jan. 1902; *m* 1926, Edith Amer; one *d. Educ:* Elementary Sch. and WEA. Mem. Brit. Labour Party Exec. 1948-53; Pres., Internat. Metalworkers Federation, 1950-59; Member: Trades Union Congress, 1953-67; Council, Dept Sci. Indust. Res., 1954-59; Advisory Council, Export Credits Guarantee Dept, 1954-57, 1965-67; Iron and Steel Board, 1960-67; Export Council for Europe, 1961-67; Nat. Econ. Develt Coun., 1962-67; Chairman: TUC Economic Cttee, 1962-67; British Productivity Council, 1962-67. *Address:* 5 The Chase, Stanmore, Middx. *T:* (home) 01-954 2101.

**DOULL, Hon. John;** Judge Supreme Court of Nova Scotia, 1933-61; Permission to retain title Honourable granted upon retirement from Supreme Court; *b* New Glasgow, Nova Scotia, 1 Nov. 1878; *s* of James F. Doull and Christy A. McLellan; *m* 1914, Irene McGregor (*d* 1962); two *s* one *d. Educ:* Dalhousie Univ. and Law Sch., BA 1909; LLB 1910. Accountant Dominion Coal Co. 1903-07; Town Solicitor, Town of Trenton, 1914-30; Mayor, Town of New Glasgow, 1925; Mem. of NS House of Assembly, 1925-33; Mem. of Executive Council, 1928; Provincial Secretary, 1930; Attorney General of Nova Scotia, 1931-33; Chairman Board of Management, NS Hospital for Insane, 1938-41; Chairman National Mobilisation Board (Nova Scotia District), 1940-45; President Halifax Canadian Club, 1941-42; President North British

Society, Halifax, 1942-43; Lecturer on Evidence, Dalhousie Law School, 1937-51; Member Boards of Governors, Dalhousie Univ., 1941-62; Pine Hill Divinity Hall; Hon. President Dalhousie Alumni Assoc., 1962; President, Nova Scotia Historical Society, 1945-48 (now Hon. Member); Hon. Life Member Canadian Bible Society. Hon. LLD St Francis Xavier Univ., NS, 1961. *Publications:* Life of the Rev. Alex McGillivray; Pine Hill Lectures; Sketches of NS Attorney Generals; History NS Bible Society; The McLellans of McLellans Brook. Articles in Canadian Bar Review; Articles in translations of NS Historical Society; Canadian Masonic Research. *Address:* 856 Marlborough Avenue, Halifax, Nova Scotia.

**DOULTON, Alfred John Farre,** OBE 1946; TD 1954; psc 1943; MA Oxon; Headmaster of Highgate School since 1955; *b* 9 July 1911; *s* of H. V. Doulton, Housemaster, Dulwich Coll., and Constance Jessie Farre, Dulwich; *m* 1940, Vera Daphne, *d* of A. R. Wheatley, Esher; four *s* one *d. Educ:* Dulwich Coll.; Brasenose Coll., Oxford (Classical Scholar). Asst Master, Uppingham School, 1934-40. Served War, 1940-46 (despatches twice); DAAG 11 Army Group, 1944; active service, Burma, Malaya, Java, 1945-46; DAQMG 4 Corps, AA&QMG 23 Indian Division, 1945-46. Burma Star, Far East and GS Medal with Java Clasp. Head of Classics and Housemaster of The Lodge, Uppingham Sch., 1946. Vice-Chm., HMC, 1967 (Hon. Treasurer, 1964). Alderman, Haringey, 1968 (Vice-Chm. Educn Cttee). Trustee, Uppingham Sch.; Member of Council, Westfield Coll. *Publication:* The Fighting Cock, 1951. *Recreations:* music, cricket, books, dinghy sailing. *Address:* Highgate School, N6. *T:* 01-340 1224. *Clubs:* Athenæum, MCC.

**DOUNE, Lord; Douglas John Moray Stuart;** *b* 13 Feb. 1928; *e s* of 19th Earl of Moray, *qv; m* 1964, Lady Malvina Murray, *er d* of 7th Earl of Mansfield and Mansfield, *qv*; one *s* (*b* 29 Aug. 1966) one *d. Educ:* Trinity Coll., Cambridge (BA), FLAS 1958. *Address:* Doune Park, Doune, Perthshire. *T:* Doune 333; Darnaway Castle, Forres, Moray, Scotland. *Club:* New (Edinburgh).

**DOURO, Marquess; Arthur Valerian Wellesley,** MVO 1952; OBE 1957; MC; *b* 2 July 1915; *s* of 7th Duke of Wellington (who renounced Spanish title of Duke of Ciudad Rodrigo in favour of *s,* the Marquess Douro, who thus became a Grandee of Spain, 1st class, 1968), *qv; m* 1944, Diana Ruth, *o d* of Maj.-Gen. D. F. McConnel; four *s* one *d. Educ:* Eton; New Coll., Oxford. Served War of 1939-45 in Middle East (MC), CMF and BLA. Lt-Col Comdg Royal Horse Guards, 1954-58; Silver Stick-in-Waiting and Lt-Col Comdg the Household Cavalry, 1959-60; Comdr 22nd Armoured Bde, 1960-61; Comdr RAC 1st (Br.) Corps, 1962-64; Defence Attaché, Madrid, 1964-67, retired. Director: Massey Ferguson Holdings Ltd, 1967; Motor Iberica SA, Spain, 1967. Hampshire CC 1967. Governor of Wellington Coll., 1964-. OStJ. Officier, Légion d'Honneur (France). *Heir: s* Earl of Mornington, *qv. Address:* Park Corner, Heckfield, Basingstoke, Hants; Apsley House, 149 Piccadilly, W1. *Clubs:* Turf, Buck's, White's.

**DOUTHWAITE, Arthur Henry,** MD; FRCP; Consulting Physician Emeritus to Guy's Hospital, London; Hon. Consulting Physician, Horsham Hospital; Vice-President Medical Defence Union; Chairman Permanent Insurance Company; Director: Medical Sickness Annuity and Life Assurance Society; Medical Sickness Finance Corporation; *b* Chefu, China, 1896; *s* of late A. W. Douthwaite, MD, Sheffield, and Constance Groves, Redland, Bristol; *m* Gladys Olivia, *d* of late John Dannhern; three *d. Educ:* Bristol Grammar Sch.; Bristol Univ.; University College, London; Guy's Hospital, London. Civilian Prisoner of War, Ruhleben, Germany, 1914-18; Beaney Prize for Pathology, 1921; Murchison Prize (Medicine) Royal College of Physicians, 1922; Science Scholarships, Middlesex Hospital and Guy's Hospital, 1919. Croonian Lecturer, Royal College of Physicians, 1956. Late Clinical Assistant, Assistant House Surgeon, House Physician, Medical Registrar and Tutor, Chief Assistant in Neurology, Guy's Hospital; Consulting Physician, Mitcham Cottage Hospital and Edenbridge Hospital; Examinder in Medicine and in Therapeutics, University of London, and Conjoint Board, and in Therapeutics, Royal College of Physicians; late Examiner in Medicine, University of Edinburgh; Physician in EMS; late President, Medical Society of London; late Senior Censor, RCP; President British Gastroenterological Society; President, Section of Medicine, Royal Society of Medicine. *Publications:* The Treatment of Rheumatoid Arthritis and Sciatica; The Treatment of Asthma; A Guide to General Practice; late Editor Hale-White's Materia Medica and French's Differential Diagnosis; various articles in Medical Journals. *Address:* Lister House, 11 Wimpole Street, W1. *T:* 01-580 3475; Quarries, Itchingfield, Horsham, Sussex. *T:* Slinfold 247.

**DOVE, Maj.-Gen. Arthur Julian Hadfield,** CB 1948; CBE 1946 (MBE 1937); *b* Marton, New Zealand, 25 Aug. 1902; *s* of late Rev. J. Ll. Dove; *m* 1948, Betty Eyre Godson Bartholomew; one *d. Educ:* Haileybury Coll.; RMA, Woolwich. 2nd Lieut RE, 1922; served Palestine, 1936-38 (MBE, despatches, Bt Major). Served War of 1939-45, France, 1940; Dep. Director HG, 1942; CRE Guards Armoured Div., 1942-43; Chief Engineer, Combined Ops., 1943-44; Dep. Director of Military Ops, 1944-47; WO rep. with Council of Foreign Ministers and at Peace Conference, 1946-47; Dep. Adjutant General, BAOR, 1948-50; Brigadier, General Staff (Staff Duties), GHQ, MELF, 1951-53; Director of Quartering, War Office, 1954-57; Technical Director, FBI, 1957-61; retired 1957. Colonel Comdt RE, 1961-66. *Recreation:* fencing. *Address:* Moors Farm, Reigate Heath, Surrey. *T:* Reigate 45436. *Club:* National.

**DOVE, Sir Clifford (Alfred),** Kt 1967; CBE 1960 (MBE 1944); ERD 1963; MInstT; Chairman, British Transport Docks Board, since 1970; Director-General and Member, Mersey Docks and Harbour Board, Liverpool, 1965-69 (General Manager, 1962); Member: National Ports Council, since 1967; Council Institute of Transport, since 1963 (Vice-President, 1964-65); Chairman Merseyside and District Section, Institute of Transport, since 1964; Council, Dock and Harbour Authorities Assoc., since 1970 (Executive Committee, 1962-69, Vice-President, 1970; *b* 1 Dec. 1904; *e s* of Frederick George Dove and Beatrice Dove (*née* Warren); *m* 1936, Helen Taylor, *d* of James Wilson; no *c. Educ:* Russell Sch.; West Ham Municipal Coll.; London School of Economics. Joined Port of London Authority, 1921; Asst Port Director, Calcutta, 1945-46; Asst to Gen. Manager, Tees Conservancy Comrs, 1947-52; Gen. Manager, Ports, Nigeria and British Cameroons, 1952-54; Chm. and Gen. Manager, Nigeria Ports Authority, 1954-61; Mem. Nigeria Railway Corp., 1955-61; Mem. Nigeria Coal Corp., 1956-61; Comr of St John, Nigeria, 1956-61; Vice-Chm., Nat.

Stadium Board of Nigeria, 1959-61; First Chm., Inst. of Transport, Nigeria Sect., 1959-61 Member: NW Economic Planning Council, 1965-69; Economic Develt Cttee for Movement of Exports, 1965-69; Exec. Cttee, Nat. Assoc. of Port Employers, 1968-69. Served War, 1939-46 (despatches, MBE): enlisted RE as 2nd Lieut, 1939; BEF, 1940; Middle East, 1941-44; Military Dock Supt., Alexandria, 1942-44; Dep. Asst Director of Transportation, MEF, 1944; AQMG (Movements) India and Embarkation Comdt, Calcutta, 1946; Demob., as Lt-Col. Joined Suppl. Reserve, 1947; retd., 1952, as Lt-Col. OStJ 1956. FRSA 1967. *Publication:* (with A. H. J. Bown) Port Operation and Administration, 1950. *Recreation:* golf. *Address:* British Transport Docks Board, Melbury House, Melbury Terrace, NW1. *Club:* East India and Sports.

**DOVE-EDWIN, George Frederick,** CMG 1969; **Hon. Mr Justice Dove-Edwin;** Justice of Appeal, Sierra Leone, since 1961; Judge, Gambia Court of Appeal since 1962, and Acting President of the Court since 1968; Barrister-at-Law; *b* 18 May 1896; *s* of late James Nicol Edwin and Clarice Marion Edwin (*née* Dove); *m* 1935, Ethel Elizabeth Jones; three *d* (*o s* decd). *Educ:* CMS Grammar Sch., Freetown. Telegraphist, 1914-17; Fourah Bay Coll., 1917-18; Lincoln's Inn, 1920-23; called to Bar, 1923. Practised in Freetown, 1923-24; practised in Calabar, Nigeria, 1924-40; Magistrate, 1940-Jan. 1951; Acting Puisne Judge, Aba, Nigeria, Jan.-Feb, 1951; Puisne Judge, Nigeria, 1951-55; Judge of the High Court, Eastern Region of Nigeria, 1955-59; Member Victoria League. *Recreation:* tennis. *Address:* 11 Crescent Road, Wimbledon, SW20. *Club:* Royal Commonwealth Society.

**DOVER, Suffragan Bishop of,** since 1964; **Rt. Rev. Anthony Paul Tremlett;** *b* 14 May 1914; *s* of late Laurence and Nyda Tremlett; unmarried. *Educ:* King's Sch., Bruton; King's Coll., Cambridge; Cuddesdon Theological Coll. Ordained, 1938; Curate of St Barnabas, Northolt Park, Middx. Chaplain to the Forces (Emergency Commission), 1941-46 (despatches). Domestic Chaplain to the Bishop of Trinidad, BWI, 1946-49; Chaplain of Trinity Hall, Cambridge, 1949-58; Vicar of St Stephen with St John, Westminster, 1958-64. *Address:* Upway, St Martin's Hill, Canterbury, Kent. *T:* Canterbury 64537.

**DOVER, Prof. Kenneth James,** FBA 1966; Professor of Greek, University of St Andrews, since 1955; *b* 11 March 1920; *o s* of P. H. J. Dover, London, Civil Servant; *m* 1947, Audrey Ruth Latimer; one *s* one *d*. *Educ:* St Paul's Sch. (Scholar); Balliol Coll. (Domus Scholar). Gaisford Prize, 1939; 1st in Classical Hon. Mods., 1940. Served War of 1939-45; Army (RA), 1940-45; Western Desert, 1941-43, Italy, 1943-45 (despatches). Ireland Scholar, 1946; Cromer Prize (British Academy), 1946; 1st in Litt. Hum., Derby Scholar, Amy Mary Preston Read Scholar, 1947; Harmsworth Sen. Scholar, Merton Coll., 1947; Fellow and Tutor, Balliol Coll., 1948-55. Visiting Lecturer, Harvard, 1960. Dean of the Faculty of Arts, St Andrews, 1960-63. Sather Prof. of Classical Literature, University of California, 1967. *Publications:* Greek Word Order, 1960; Commentaries on Thucydides, Books VI and VII, 1965; ed, Aristophanes' Clouds, 1968; Lysias and the Corpus Lysiacum, 1968; (with A. W. Gomme and A. Andrewes) Historical Commentary on Thucydides, vol. IV, 1970; articles in learned journals; Co-editor, Classical Quarterly, 1962-68. *Recreations:* linguistics, hill walking. *Address:* 49 Hepburn Gardens, St Andrews, Fife. *T:* St Andrews 589.

**DOW, David Rutherford,** MB, ChB (with distinction), MD (with commendation), DPH, FRCPE, FRSE; LLD University of St Andrews, 1959; Professor of Anatomy, University of St Andrews (Queen's College, Dundee), 1925-58, now Emeritus; Master of Queen's College, Dundee, 1954-58; *b* Crail, Fifeshire, 1887; *o s* of late Dr Dow, MA, MD, Crail; *m* 1942, Agnes W. Morton, MA, MB, ChB. *Educ:* Waid Academy, Anstruther; University of St Andrews. Lecturer and Senior Demonstrator of Anatomy, University of St Andrews; Life Member of Anatomical Society of Great Britain and Ireland; Dundee Branch BMA (Pres., 1936-37). Hon. President, Crail Golfing Society. Commission RAMC 1st Southern General Hospital, Birmingham. *Publications:* papers in various journals. *Recreations:* golf, shooting, fishing. *Address:* 13 Marketgate, Crail, Fife. *T:* Crail 302. *Club:* Royal and Ancient (St Andrews).

**DOW, Sir Hugh,** GCIE, *cr* 1947 (CIE 1932); KCSI, *cr* 1940 (CSI 1937); KStJ; *b* 8 May 1886; *s* of Alfred Dow; *m* 1913, Ann (CBE 1947, CStJ, K-i-H Gold Medal) (*d* 1956), *d* of J. Sheffield; one *s* one *d*. *Educ:* Aske's Hatcham Sch.; University Coll. London. Entered ICS, 1909; Secretary, Finance Dept, Bombay, 1923; Financial Adviser, Public Works in Sind, 1925; Financial Adviser, Public Works and Development, Bombay, 1926; Revenue Officer, Lloyd (Sukkur) Barrage, 1927; Member of the Sind Conference, 1932; Chairman of Sind Administrative Cttee, 1933-34; Joint Secretary, Commerce Dept, 1934; Secretary to the Govt of India, Commerce Dept, 1936-39; Director-General of Supply, and President of the War Supply Board, India, 1939-41; Governor of Sind, 1941-46; Governor of Bihar, 1946-47; Consul-General, Jerusalem, 1948-51; Chairman, Ordination Funds Commission, 1952; Chairman Royal Commission on East Africa, 1952-54; Chairman of Council, Royal Central Asian Society, 1957-58. *Address:* 6 Charles Street, W1. *Clubs:* Athenæum, Oriental.

**DOW, James Findlay;** Consultant Physician, St George's Hospital, SW1, since 1947; Physician to King Edward VII Hospital for Officers; *b* 13 May 1911; *s* of John Archibald Dow and Jetta Findlay; *m* 1952, Dr Jean Millbank; two *s* two *d*. *Educ:* Strathallan; St John's Coll., Cambridge; Middlesex Hospital. Resident posts at Middlesex and Brompton Hospitals. MB, BChir Cantab., MRCP 1938, FRCP 1948. Major, RAMC, 1947-49. Examiner in Medicine, Cambridge and London Universities, 1950-63. Member Board of Governors, St George's Hospital, 1962; Member Assoc. of Physicians; Member British Society of Gastro-Enterology. *Publications:* Papers in medical journals on gastro-enterology. *Recreations:* golf, fishing. *Address:* 149 Harley Street, W1. *T:* 01-935 4444. *Clubs:* Caledonian, MCC; Royal Wimbledon Golf.

**DOW, John Christopher Roderick;** Assistant Secretary-General, Organization for Economic Co-operation and Development, Paris, since 1963; *b* 25 Feb. 1916; *s* of Warrender Begernie and Amy Langdon Dow; *m* 1960, Clare Mary Keegan; one *b* three *d*. *Educ:* Bootham Sch., York; Brighton, Hove and Sussex Grammar Sch.; University College London. Economic Adviser, later Senior Economic Adviser, HM Treasury, 1945-54; on staff, and Dep. Dir, National Inst. for Economic and Social Research, 1954-62; Treasury, 1962-63. *Publications:* The Management of the British Economy, 1945-

1960, 1964; Fiscal Policy for a Balanced Economy (jointly), 1968. Various articles in learned jls. *Address:* 96 bis, Rue de Longchamp, 92 Neuilly sur Seine, France. *T:* Paris 722-10-54. *Club:* Reform.

**DOW, R(onald) Graham; His Honour Judge Dow;** County Court Judge (Clerkenwell) since 1961; *b* 7 Dec. 1909; *s* of John Graham Dow and Bessie Graham Dow; *m* 1937, Dorothy May Christie; two *s*. *Educ:* Kelvinside Academy; Uppingham Sch.; University Coll., Oxford. Called to Bar, 1932. Military Service, 1939-45. County Court Judge (Brentford and Uxbridge), 1959-61. *Recreations:* golf and gardening. *Address:* 2 Kirkwick Avenue, Harpenden, Herts. *T:* Harpenden 2006.

**DOWD, Ronald;** freelance singer; *b* Sydney, Australia, 23 Feb. 1914; *s* of Robert Henry Dowd and Henrietta (*née* Jenkins); *m* 1938, Elsie Burnitt Crute (English born); one *s* one *d*. *Educ:* Sydney. Prior to Army service in Australia, New Guinea and the Celebes, was a bank officer. Upon discharge, adopted full-time singing and performed for various opera organisations and Australian Broadcasting Commission in the Commonwealth. Came to UK for Sadler's Wells, 1956, and returned to Australia by arrangement with Elizabethan Theatre Trust; then rejoined Sadler's Wells, 1959, remaining for a year. Since then has been fully engaged in concerts and opera singing with leading conductors and organisations, including Royal Opera House. Toured NZ and Australia for Australian Broadcasting Commission, 1964; toured Continent with Sadler's Wells, 1963 and 1965. *Recreations:* squash and coin collecting. *Address:* Flat 1(b), Vanbrugh Terrace, SE3. *T:* 01-858 3870. *Club:* Savage (London).

**DOWDING,** family name of **Baron Dowding.**

**DOWDING,** 2nd Baron *cr* 1943, of Bentley Priory; **Derek Hugh Tremenheere Dowding;** Wing Commander, RAF, retired; *b* 9 Jan. 1919; *s* of (Air Chief Marshal) 1st Baron Dowding, GCB, GCVO, CMG, and Clarice Maud (*d* 1920), *d* of Captain John Williams, IA; *S* father, 1970; *m* 1st, 1940, Joan Myrle (marr. diss. 1946), *d* of Donald James Stuart, Nairn; 2nd, 1947, Alison Margaret (marr. diss. 1960), *d* of Dr James Bannerman, Norwich and *widow* of Major R. M. H. Peebles; two *s*; 3rd, 1961, Odette, L. M. S. Hughes, *d* of Louis Joseph Houles. *Educ:* Winchester; RAF College, Cranwell. Served War of 1939-45, UK and Middle East; in comd No 49 (B) Sqdn, 1950; Wing Commander, 1951. *Heir: s* Hon. Piers Hugh Tremenheere Dowding, *b* 18 Feb. 1948. *Address:* c/o Lloyds Bank Ltd, 6 Pall Mall, SW1.

**DOWELL, Anthony James;** Senior Principal, Royal Ballet, Covent Garden, since 1967; *b* 16 Feb., 1943; *s* of Catherine Ethel and Arthur Henry Dowell; unmarried. *Educ:* Hampshire Sch., St Saviour's Hall, Knightsbridge; Royal Ballet Sch., White Lodge, Richmond, Surrey; Royal Ballet Sch., Barons Court. Joined Opera Ballet, 1960; 1st Company, for Russian Tour, 1961; created The Dream, 1964; Italian Tour, 1965; promoted Principal Dancer, 1966; Eastern Europe Tour, 1966; created Shadow Play, 1967; American Tours and Metropolitan Opera House, New York, 1968, 1969. Principal role in: La Fête Etrange, 1963; Napoli, 1965; Romeo and Juliet, 1965; Song of the Earth, 1966; Card Game, Giselle, Swan Lake, 1967; The Nutcracker, Cinderella, Monotones, Symphonic Variations, new version of Sleeping Beauty, Enigma Variations, Lilac Garden, 1968; Raymonda Act III, Daphnis and Chloe, 1969. *Recreations:* painting, paper sculpture, theatrical costume design. *Address:* Royal Opera House, Covent Garden, WC2.

**DOWER, Col. Alan Vincent Gandar,** TD; DL; MFH; *b* 1898; *s* of late J. W. G. Dower and Mrs Dower, 17 Sussex Place, NW1; *m* 1928, Aymée Lavender, Jun. Com. (Temp. Sen. Com.) ATS, *d* of Capt. Sir George James Robert Clerk, 9th Bt, and Hon. Lady Clerk (*sister* of 6th Baron Sherborne, DSO); one *d*. *Educ:* RMC, Sandhurst; Oxford Univ. 2nd Lieut RW Surrey Regt, 1915; 2nd Lieut 2nd Dragoon Guards, 1916; served in France during European War, 1916-17; attached Royal Air Force, 1918; Capt. 2nd Dragoon Guards; Reserve of Officers, 1928; Major 35th AA Bn, RE, 1937; Lt-Col comdg 36th AA Bn, 1938-40; Comdg 39th (Lancs. Fus.) SL Regt, 1940; Comdg 84th SL Regt, 1951; Hon. Colonel 609 HAA Regt RA, 1947-55; Hon. Col, 4th Middx Bn Mobile Def. Corps, 1956-; Colonel, 1948, retired, 1954; Member Middx TA Association; MP (C), Stockport, 1931-35, Cumberland (Penrith and Cockermouth Div.), 1935-50; Member of Select Cttee on Estimates, 1938-39; Member Select Cttee of Public Accounts, 1945-. Freeman of City of London; Liveryman, Barbers Company; FRGS; FZS. MFH South Oxfordshire Hunt, 1950-53; Joint Master Old Berkeley Hunt, 1953-; County Pres. for Oxfordshire, St John Ambulance Bde and Association, 1953-. Member Executive and Council, Royal Society of St George; Patron, SSAFA Middlesex Appeals Cttee. DL, Middlesex, 1961-65; DL Greater London, 1965-. KStJ. *Recreations:* hunting, big game shooting, polo, tennis, golf. *Address:* 35 Lowndes Street, SW1. *T:* 01-235 1491; Newington House, Warborough, Oxfordshire. *T:* Warborough 205; High Head Castle, Cumberland. *Clubs:* Carlton, Naval and Military, Princes, Hurlingham, Queen's; Muthaiga (Nairobi).

**DOWER, E. L. G.;** *see* Gandar Dower.

**DOWLING, Geoffrey Barrow,** MD, FRCP; Hon. MD Universities of Utrecht and Pretoria; Consulting Physician to Department for Skin Diseases, St Thomas's Hospital; Consultant in Dermatology to RAF; Late Director, Institute of Dermatology; *b* Cape Town, 9 Aug. 1891; *s* of Thomas Barrow Dowling, Mus.Doc., and Minna Grant; *m* 1923, Mary Elizabeth Kelly (*d* 1965); two *s* two *d*. *Educ:* Dulwich Coll.; Guy's Hospital. Watson Smith Lecturer, RCP, 1955. Hon. Fellow Royal Society of Medicine (Ex-Pres. Section of Dermatology); Hon. Member (Pres. 1956) British Association of Dermatology. Hon. Member French and other foreign Dermatological Societies. *Publications:* papers on medical subjects. *Address:* 52 Ravenscourt Gardens, W6.

*See also* ***P. G. Greenham.***

**DOWN, Alastair Frederick,** OBE 1944 (MBE 1942); MC 1940; TD 1951; Deputy Chairman, The British Petroleum Co. Ltd, since 1969 (and a Managing Director since 1962); *b* 23 July 1914; *e s* of Frederick Edward Down and Margaret Isobel Down (*née* Hutchison); *m* 1947, Maysie Hilda Mellon; two *s* two *d*. *Educ:* Edinburgh Acad.; Marlborough Coll. Commissioned in 7th/9th Bn, The Royal Scots (TA), 1935. CA 1938. Joined British Petroleum Co. Ltd in Palestine, 1938. Served War of 1939-45 (despatches twice, MC, MBE, OBE, Kt Comdr, Order of Orange Nassau, with swords, 1946): Middle East, N Africa, Italy and Holland, with Eighth Army and 1st Canadian Army as Lt-Col and full Col. Rejoined BP, in Iran, 1945-47; Head Office, 1947-54; Canada, 1954-62 (Chief Rep. of BP in Canada, 1954-57; Pres., BP Group in Canada,

1957-62); Pres. BP Oil Corpn, 1969-70. JDipMA (Hon.), 1966. *Recreations:* shooting, golf, fishing. *Address:* Fir Hill, Droxford, Hampshire. *T:* Droxford 521; 17 Derwent House, Stanhope Gardens, SW7. *T:* 01-370 5333. *Clubs:* Bath; Mount Royal (Montreal); York, Toronto (Toronto); Ranchmen's (Calgary).

**DOWN, Barbara Langdon;** *see* Littlewood, Lady (Barbara).

**DOWN, Lt-Gen. Sir Ernest Edward,** KBE 1953 (CBE 1943); CB 1949; late King's Shropshire Light Infantry; *b* 1902. 2nd Lieut Dorset Regt, 1923; transferred to King's Shropshire Light Infantry, from Dorset Regt, 1935; Brigade Major, 1937-39; Colonel, 1944; temp. Maj.-Gen., 1944; Maj.-Gen., 1945; Lt-Gen., 1952; GOC British troops in Greece, 1947-48; Commander British Military Mission to Greece, 1948-49. Commander Mid-West District and 53rd (Welsh) Infantry Division (TA), 1950-52; Gen. Officer Commanding-in-Chief, Southern Command, 1952-55; retired, 1955. Colonel KSLI 1955-57. *Address:* Whistlers Mead, Appleshaw, nr Andover, Hants.

**DOWN, Air Commodore Harold Hunter,** CBE 1945; AFC; late Royal Air Force; *b* 17 May 1895; *s* of Thomas Down, Jersey, Channel Islands; *m* 1931, Noëla Joyce Farrall; one *s*. Army and RFC 1915-18; RAF from 1918; Commandant, Central Flying School, 1940-42; commanded Bomber Operational Base, 1944-45; retired, 1945. *Address:* Stanley Wood, Lockeridge, Marlborough, Wilts. *T:* Lockeridge 247.

**DOWN, Norman Cecil Sommers,** CMG 1955; Senior Principal Inspector of Taxes, Inland Revenue, 1946-Dec. 1956, retired; *b* 9 Sept. 1893; *s* of late James Erskine Down; *m* 1st, 1917, Edith Gertrude (*née* Steddy) (*d* 1961); two *d*; 2nd, 1962, Agnes (*née* Sandham). *Educ:* St Lawrence Coll., Ramsgate. Inland Revenue since 1912; served European War, 1914-19, in 4th Gordon Highlanders, 51st Div. (Captain, despatches, wounded thrice). *Publications:* Temporary Heroes, 1918; Temporary Crusaders, 1919. *Address:* Binnlands, Swan Lane, Edenbridge, Kent. *T:* Edenbridge 3129. *Club:* Civil Service.

**DOWN and CONNOR, Bishop of, (RC),** since 1962; **Most Rev. William J. Philbin,** DD; *b* 26 Jan. 1907; *s* of late James Philbin and Brigid (*née* O Hora). *Educ:* St Nathy's Coll., Ballaghaderreen; St Patrick's, Maynooth. Priest, 1931; DD Maynooth, 1933. Curate, Eastbourne, 1933; Secondary teacher, Ballaghaderreen, 1934; Prof. of Dogmatic Theology, Maynooth, 1936; Bishop of Clonfert, 1953. *Publications:* Does Conscience Decide?, 1969; pamphlets on socio-moral questions; Irish translation of St Patrick's writings. Contributor to The Irish Theological Quarterly, Studies, The Irish Ecclesiastical Record. *Address:* Lisbreen, Somerton Road, Belfast 15. *T:* 76185.

**DOWN and DROMORE, Bishop of,** since 1970; **Rt. Rev. George Alderson Quin.** *Educ:* Trinity College, Dublin (MA). Deacon, 1937, priest 1938, Down; Curate of St Jude, Ballynafeigh, Belfast, 1937-39; Dean's Vicar of St Anne's Cathedral, Belfast, 1939-41; Holywood, 1941-43; Incumbent of Magheralin, 1943-51; Vicar of Ballymacarrett, 1951-58; Canon of St Anne's Cathedral, Belfast, 1955-56; Archdeacon of Down 1956-70; Exam. Chaplain to Bishop of Down and Dromore, 1957-70; Rector of Bangor, Dio. Down, 1958-70. *Address:* The See House, Knockdene Park, S Belfast.

**DOWNE,** 11th Viscount, *cr* 1680; **John Christian George Dawnay;** Bt 1642; Baron Dawnay of Danby (UK) *cr* 1897; *b* Wykeham, 18 Jan. 1935; *s* of 10th Viscount Downe, OBE and Margaret Christine (*d* 1967), *d* of Christian Bahnsen, NJ; *S* father, 1965; *m* 1965, Alison Diana, *d* of I. F. H. Sconce, MBE; one *s* one *d*. *Educ:* Eton Coll.; Christ Church, Oxford. 2nd Lieut, Grenadier Guards, 1954-55. Non-marine broker at Lloyd's, 1957-65. Chairman Kenton Laboratories Ltd, 1960-64; Director Brookdeal Electronics Ltd, 1962-. *Publications:* contributions to various journals. *Recreations:* linear circuit design and motor racing. *Heir:* *s* Hon. Richard Dawnay, *b* 9 April 1967. *Address:* Wykeham Abbey, Scarborough, Yorks. *T:* Wykeham 2404; 5 Douro Place, W8. *T:* 01-937 9449. *Clubs:* Pratt's, Guards'.

**DOWNER, Hon. Sir Alexander (Russell),** KBE 1965; MA; High Commissioner for Australia in the United Kingdom since Oct. 1964; *b* Adelaide, 7 April 1910; *s* of late Hon. Sir John Downer, KCMG, KC, MP, Adelaide, a founder of the Australian Commonwealth and a former Premier of S. Australia; *m* 1947, Mary I., *d* of late Sir James Gosse, Adelaide; one *s* three *d*. *Educ:* Geelong Grammar Sch.; Brasenose Coll., Oxford (MA, Dip. of Economics and Political Science). Called to Bar, Inner Temple, 1934; admitted South Australian Bar, 1935. Served 8th Div. AIF, 1940-45 (Prisoner-of-War, Changi Camp, Singapore, for 3½ years). Member Board Electricity Trust of South Australia, 1946-49; MP (Liberal) Angas, Australia, 1949-64; Australian Minister for Immigration, 1958-63. Member: Australian Parliamentary Foreign Affairs Cttee, 1952-58; Australian Constitution Review Cttee, 1956-59; Commonwealth Parliamentary Delegation to Coronation, 1953; Board of National Gallery, S Australia, 1946-63; Pres. Royal Over-Seas League, S Australia Branch, 1946-62. Freeman, City of London, 1965. FRSA 1968. *Recreations:* travelling, collecting antiques, reading, golf. Address: 45 Hyde Park Gate, SW7; Oare House, Oare, Wiltshire; 10 Mugga Way, Canberra, Australia. *Clubs:* Brooks's, Junior Carlton, (Hon.) Cavalry; Adelaide (Adelaide); Union (Sydney).

**DOWNES, George Robert,** CB 1967; Director, Operations and Overseas, Post Office, since 1967; *b* 25 May 1911; *o s* of late Philip George Downes; *m* Edna Katherine Millar; two *d*. *Educ:* King Edward's Grammar School, Birmingham; Grocers', London. Entered GPO, 1928; Assistant Surveyor, 1937; Asst Principal, 1939. Served War of 1939-45: RNVR, in destroyers, 1942-45. Principal, GPO, 1946; Principal Private Sec. to: Lord President of the Council, 1948-50, Lord Privy Seal, 1951; Assistant Secretary, 1951; Imperial Defence College, 1952; Deputy Regional Director, GPO London, 1955; Dir, London Postal Region, 1960-65; Dir of Postal Services, 1965-67. *Recreations:* music, gardening. *Address:* Muircraig, Gordon Avenue, Stanmore, Middlesex.

**DOWNES, M. P.;** *see* Panter-Downes.

**DOWNES, Ralph (William),** CBE 1969; Organist, Brompton Oratory, since 1936; Organ Professor, Royal College of Music, since 1954; Curator-Organist, Royal Festival Hall, since 1954; *b* 16 Aug. 1904; *s* of James William and Constance Edith Downes; *m* 1929, Agnes Mary (*née* Rix); one *s*. *Educ:* Derby Municipal Secondary Sch. (Scholar); Royal

College of Music, London; Keble Coll., Oxford. ARCM 1925, MA 1931, BMus 1933. Asst Organist, Southwark Cathedral, 1924; Organ Scholar, Keble Coll., 1925-28; Director of Chapel Music and Lecturer, Princeton Univ., USA, 1928-35. Organ Curator to LCC, 1949. Consultant to the Corporation of Croydon, 1960; Designer and Supervisor of organs in: Buckfast Abbey, 1952; Chigwell Sch., 1953; Royal Festival Hall, 1954; Brompton Oratory, 1954; St Clement Danes, 1958; St John's Cathedral, Valletta, Malta, 1961; St Albans Abbey, 1962; Chigwell Church, 1963; Fairfield Halls, 1964; Carmelite Priory, Kensington, 1966; Paisley Abbey, 1968; Trinity Coll., Dublin, 1969. Received into the Catholic Church, 1930. Hon. RAM 1965; Hon. FRCO 1966, KSG 1970. *Publications:* Miscellaneous articles on the organ, compositions for keyboard and chorus. *Address:* c/o Ibbs & Tillett Ltd, 124 Wigmore Street, W1. *T:* 01-486 4021.

**DOWNEY, Air Vice-Marshal John Chegwyn Thomas,** DFC 1945, AFC; Commander Southern Air Region, 18 (Maritime) Group, Strike Command, since 1969, with NATO responsiblities as Air Commander Central Sub-Area, Eastern Atlantic Command, and Plymouth Sub-Area, Channel Command; *b* 26 Nov. 1920; *s* of Thomas Cecil Downey and Mary Evelyn Downey; *m* Diana, (*née* White); one *s* two *d. Educ:* Whitgift Sch. Entered RAF 1939; served War of 1939-45 in Coastal Command (DFC 1945 for his part in anti-U-boat ops). Captained Lincoln Aries III on global flight of 29,000 miles, during which London-Khartoum record was broken. RAF Farnborough 1956-58; commanded Bomber Comd Develt Unit 1959-60; head of NE Defence Secretariat, Cyprus, 1960-62; Comd RAF Farnborough, 1962-64; a Dir, Op. Requirements (RAF) MoD, 1965-67; Imp. Def. Coll., 1968; Comdt, RAF Coll. of Air Warfare, Manby, Jan./Oct. 1969. AFRAeS. *Recreation:* sailing. *Address:* Monckswood, Wembury, Plymouth. *T:* Wembury 234. *Club:* Royal Air Force.

**DOWNEY, William George,** CB 1967; Under-Secretary, Ministry of Technology, since 1967; *b* 3 Jan. 1912; *s* of late William Percy Downey; *m* 1936, Iris, *e d* of late Ernest Frederick Pickering; three *d. Educ:* Southend Grammar Sch. ACWA 1935, ACA 1937, FCA 1960. Ministry of Aircraft Production, 1940; Ministry of Supply, 1946 (Director of Finance and Administration, Royal Ordnance Factories, 1952-57); Ministry of Aviation, 1959; Under-Secretary, 1961. *Address:* Starvelarks, Dawes Heath Rd, Rayleigh, Essex. *T:* Rayleigh 4138.

**DOWNIE, Prof. Allan Watt,** FRS 1955; Professor of Bacteriology, Liverpool University, 1943-66; *b* 5 Sept. 1901; *s* of William Downie, Rosehearty, Aberdeenshire; *m* 1936, Nancy McHardy; one *s* two *d. Educ:* Fraserburgh Academy, Aberdeen Univ. MB, ChB, Aberdeen Univ., 1923; MD, 1929; DSc, 1937. Lecturer Aberdeen Univ., 1924-26, Manchester Univ., 1927-34; Senior Freedom Research Fellow, London Hospital, 1935-39; Member Scientific Staff, Nat. Institute Medical Research, 1939-43. Voluntary Asst, Rockefeller Inst. Med. Research, New York City, USA, 1934-35. Vis. Prof., Medical Sch., Univ. of Colorado, Denver, 1966-69. Hon. LLD Aberdeen Univ., 1956. *Publications:* (Jt) Virus and Rickettsial Diseases of Man, 1950; numerous articles in scientific journals. *Recreations:* golf, fishing, ornithology. *Address:* Canna, College Close, Birkdale, Lancs. *T:* Southport 67269.

**DOWNING, Dr Anthony Leighton;** Director, Water Pollution Research Laboratory, Stevenage, Ministry of Technology, since 1966; *b* 27 March 1926; *s* of Sydney Arthur Downing and Frances Dorothy Downing; *m* 1952, Kathleen Margaret Frost; one *d. Educ:* Arnold Sch., Blackpool; Cambridge and London Universities. BA Cantab. 1946; BSc Special Degree 2 (1) Hons. London, 1950; DSc London 1967. Joined Water Pollution Research Lab., 1946; seconded to Fisheries Research Lab., Lowestoft, 1947-48; granted transfer to Govt Chemist's Lab., 1948; returned to WPRL as Scientific Officer, 1950; subsequently worked mainly in field of biochemical engrg. AMIChemE 1964; Fellow Institute Water Pollution Control, 1965; FIBiol 1965; Hon. FIPHE 1965. *Publications:* papers in scientific and technical journals. *Recreations:* golf, gardening. *Address:* 2 Tewin Close, Tewin Wood, Welwyn, Herts. *T:* Tewin 474. *Club:* Knebworth Golf.

**DOWNING, Henry Julian;** Head of Claims Department, Foreign and Commonwealth Office, since 1969; *b* 22 March 1919; *o s* of Henry Julian Downing and Kate Avery; *m* 1951, Ruth Marguerite Ambler. *Educ:* Boys' High Sch., Trowbridge; Hertford Coll., Oxford. Indian Civil Service (Madras) 1941-47. Joined HM Foreign Service, 1947; 2nd Secretary, Madras and Dacca, 1947-50; Foreign Office, 1950-52; 1st Secretary (Commercial), Istanbul, 1952-56; Foreign Office, 1956-58; 1st Secretary and Head of Chancery, Kabul, 1958-62; Foreign Office, 1963-65; HM Consul-General, Lourenço Marques, 1965-69. *Recreations:* swimming, walking, bird watching. *Address:* 8b Greenaway Gardens, Hampstead, NW3. *T:* 01-435 2593. *Club:* United University.

**DOWNMAN, Prof. Charles Beaumont Benoy,** PhD; Sophia Jex-Blake Professor of Physiology, University of London, at the Royal Free Hospital School of Medicine, since 1960; *b* 1916; *s* of Rev. Leonard Charles and Sarah Alice Downman; *m* 1947, Thais Hélène Barakan; one *s* one *d. Educ:* City of London Sch.; St Thomas's Hospital Medical Sch., MRCSEng, LRCP, 1941; PhD London, 1953. FRSocMed; Member: Physiological Society; Biophysical Society; EEG Society. *Publications:* papers in medical journals. *Address:* Royal Free Hospital School of Medicine, Hunter Street, Brunswick Square, WC1N 1BP; 4 Wendover Drive, New Malden, Surrey.

**DOWNS, Brian Westerdale,** MA Cantab; Fellow (Master, 1950-63) of Christ's College, Cambridge; Professor of Scandinavian Studies, 1950-60; Member of the Court and Council of the University of Hull; *b* 4 July 1893; *s* of late James Downs, OBE, JP; *m* Evelyn Wrangham (*née* Doubble). *Educ:* Abbotsholme Sch.; Christ's Coll., Cambridge (Entrance Scholar). First Class Honours (with distinction), Medieval and Modern Languages Tripos, 1915; Charles Oldham Shakespeare Scholar, 1914, and Allen Scholar, 1918. Lecturer in Modern Languages and English, Christ's Coll., Cambridge, 1918; Fellow, 1919, Tutor, 1928; Member of Council of Senate, University of Cambridge, 1939-44, and 1954-60; Vice-Chancellor of the University of Cambridge, 1955-57. Representative of the British Council in the Netherlands, 1945-46. DLitt (*hc*), Hull. Commander, Royal Swedish Order of the North Star, 1954; Officier de la Légion d'Honneur, 1957. *Publications:* Cambridge Past and Present, 1926; Richardson, 1928; Ibsen, the Intellectual Background, 1946; (with Miss B. M. Mortensen) Strindberg, 1949; A Study of Six

Plays by Ibsen, 1950; Norwegian Literature, 1860-1920, 1966; translations from the French, Dutch and German; editions of Shamela and Richardson's Familiar Letters. *Recreation:* walking. *Address:* Christ's College, Cambridge; 75 Long Road, Cambridge. *Clubs:* Athenæum; Nieuwe of Litteraire Societeit (The Hague).

**DOWNS, Mrs George Wallingford;** *see* Tureck, Rosalyn.

**DOWNS, Leslie Hall,** CBE 1942; MA Cantab; FIMechE; Chairman: Rose, Downs & Thompson Ltd, Old Foundry, Hull; Rose Downs (Holdings) Ltd, Hull; Barnsley Canister Co. Ltd, Barnsley; Blundell-Permaglaze (Holdings) Ltd; *b* 6 June 1900; *s* of late Charles Downs, Hull and Bridlington; *m* 1930, Kathleen Mary Lewis; three *d*. *Educ:* Abbotsholme Sch., Derbys; Christ's Coll., Cambridge (Scholar, BA, 1922, MA, 1927). European War, Artists' Rifles; served engineering apprenticeship and subsequently employed in various positions with Rose, Downs & Thompson Ltd; Past President Hull Chamber of Commerce and Shipping (Treasurer); Custodian Trustee, Hull Trustee Savings Bank; Treasurer and Member of Council, Hull Univ. Hon. DSc Hull Univ. *Recreations:* fly-fishing, cabinet making, reading. *Address:* King's Mill, Driffield, E. Yorks. *T:* Driffield 3204; Rowling End Farm. Newlands, Keswick, Cumberland. *T:* Keswick 335.

**DOWNSHIRE,** 7th Marquess of, *cr* 1789; **Arthur Wills Percy Wellington Blundell Trumbull Sandys Hill;** Viscount Hillsborough, Baron Hill, 1717; Earl of Hillsborough, Viscount Kilwarlin, 1751; Baron Harwich (Great Britain), 1756; Earl of Hillsborough and Viscount Fairford, 1772; Hereditary Constable of Hillsborough Fort; late Lieut Berks Yeomanry; *b* 7 April 1894; *s* of 6th Marquess and Katherine, 2nd *d* of Hon. Hugh Hare, Forest House, Bracknell, Berks, and *g d* of 2nd Earl of Listowel; *S* father, 1918; *m* 1953, Mrs Noreen Gray-Miller, *d* of late William Barraclough. *Heir: nephew* (Arthur) Robin Ian Hill [*b* 10 May 1929; *m* 1957, Hon. Juliet Mary Weld-Forester, *d* of 7th Baron Forester, *qv*; two *s* one *d*]. *Address:* 21 Wilton Crescent, Belgrave Square, SW1; Murlough House, Dundrum, Co. Down; Old Brick Farm, Burwash, Sussex.

**DOWNSIDE, Abbot of;** *see* Passmore, Rt Rev. N. W.

**DOWSE, Maj.-Gen. Sir Maurice Brian,** KCVO, *cr* 1953; CB 1952; CBE 1947 (OBE 1940); retired; *b* 10 Sept. 1899; *s* of late Bishop Charles Dowse, and of Mrs Charles Dowse; unmarried. *Educ:* Wellington Coll.; RMC, Sandhurst. 2nd Lieut 1918; Lieut 1920; Captain, 1927; Major, 1936; Lt-Col, 1941; Brigadier, 1943; Maj.-Gen. 1951. Served Royal Welch Fusiliers and on Staff at home and overseas, 1918-44; on Staff at home and Far East, 1944-53; retired, 1953. *Address:* 39 Hyde Park Gate, SW7. *Club:* Travellers'.

**DOWSETT, Prof. Charles James Frank,** MA, PhD Cantab; Calouste Gulbenkian Professor of Armenian Studies, University of Oxford, and Fellow of Pembroke College, Oxford, since 1965; *b* 2 Jan. 1924; *s* of late Charles Aspinall Dowsett and Louise, *née* Stokes; *m* 1949, Friedel, *y d* of Herr Fritz Lapuner, Kornberg, E Prussia. *Educ:* Owen's Sch.; St Catherine's Society, Oxford, 1942-43; Peterhouse, Cambridge (Thomas Parke scholar), 1947-50 (Mod. and Mediaeval Languages Tripos, Part I, 1st Class Russian, 1st Class German, 1948, Part II, Comparative Philology, 1st Class with distinction, 1949). Treasury Studentship in Foreign Languages and Cultures, 1949-54. Ecole Nationale des Langues Orientales Vivantes, Univ. de Paris, 1950-52 (diplôme d'arménien); Ecole des Langues Orientales Anciennes, Institut Catholique de Paris, 1950-53 (diplôme de géorgien); Lecturer in Armenian, School of Oriental and African Studies, University of London, 1954; Reader in Armenian, 1965. In HM Forces, 1943-47. *Publications:* The History of the Caucasian Albanians by Movses Dasxuranci, 1961; The Penitential of David of Ganjak, 1961; (with J. Carswell) Kütahya Armenian Tiles: vol. 1, The Inscribed Tiles, 1970; articles in Bulletin of the School of Oriental and African Studies, Le Muséon, Revue des Etudes Arméniennes, The Geographical Journal, W. B. Henning Memorial Volume, 1970, etc; translations from Flemish (F. Timmermans' Driekoningentryptiek–"A Christmas Triptych", 1955, E. Claes' De Witte–"Whitey", 1970) and Russian (A. Chekhov's Kashtanka, 1959). *Address:* Pembroke College, Oxford. *Club:* Oxford and Cambridge University.

**DOWSON, Maj.-Gen. Arthur Henley,** CB 1964; CBE 1961 (OBE 1945); Director-General, Ordnance Survey, 1961-65, retired; *b* 7 Dec. 1908; *s* of late Kenneth Dowson and Beatrice Mary (*née* Davis); *m* 1933, Mary Evelyn, *d* of Col. A. J. Savage, DSO; one *d*. *Educ:* Haileybury; RMA; King's Coll., Cambridge (BA). Commissioned in RE, 1928; War Service in NW Europe, N. Africa, Italy. Director of Military Survey, War Office and Air Ministry, 1957. ADC to the Queen, 1958-61; Maj-Gen. 1961. Chm., Norfolk Broads Consortium Cttee, 1966-. FRICS 1949. Bronze Star (USA) 1945. *Address:* Little Saltings, Brancaster, Norfolk. *T:* 373. *Club:* Army and Navy.

**DOWSON, Prof. Duncan;** Professor of Engineering Fluid Mechanics and Tribology, University of Leeds, since 1966, and Director of The Institute of Tribology, Department of Mechanical Engineering, Univ. of Leeds, since Dec. 1967; *b* 31 Aug. 1928; *o s* of Wilfrid and Hannah Dowson, Kirkbymoorside, York; *m* 1951, Mabel, *d* of Mary Jane and Herbert Strickland; one *s* (and one *s* decd). *Educ:* Lady Lumley's Grammar Sch., Pickering, Yorks; Leeds Univ. BSc Mech Eng. Leeds, 1950; PhD Leeds, 1952. Research Engineer, Sir W. G. Armstrong Whitworth Aircraft Co., 1953-54; Univ. of Leeds: Lecturer in Mechanical Engineering, 1954; Sen. Lecturer, 1963; Reader, 1965; Prof. 1966. Chm., Tribology Group Cttee, IMechE, 1967-69. James Clayton Fund Prize (jtly), IMechE, 1963; Thomas Hawksley Gold Medal, IMechE, 1966; Gold Medal, British Soc. of Rheology, 1969. *Publications:* Elastohydrodynamic Lubrication–the fundamentals of roller and gear lubrication (jointly), 1966. Several papers on tribology, published by: Royal Society; Instn of Mech Engineers; Amer. Soc. of Mech. Engineers; Amer. Soc. of Lubrication Engineers. *Recreations:* travel, astronomy, photography. *Address:* 23 Church Lane, Adel, Leeds 16. *T:* Leeds 678933.

**DOWSON, Graham Randall;** Director and Deputy Chief Executive, Rank Organisation, since 1960; *b* 13 Jan. 1923; *o s* of late Cyril James Dowson and late Dorothy Celia (*née* Foster); *m* 1954, Fay Valerie (*née* Weston); two *d*. *Educ:* Alleyn Court Sch.; City of London Sch.; Ecole Alpina, Switzerland. Served War of 1939-45 (1939-43 and Africa Stars, Atlantic and Defence Medals, etc.); RAF, 1941-46 (Pilot, Sqdn.-Ldr). Sales, US

Steel Corporation (Columbia Steel), Los Angeles, 1946-49; Sales and Senior Commentator, Mid South Network (MBS), radio, US, 1949-52; Director, A. C. Nielsen Co., Oxford, 1953-58; Director, Southern Television Ltd, London, 1958-. *Recreation:* sailing. *Address:* 38 South Street, W1. *T:* 01-629 7454. *Clubs:* Carlton, Royal Aero; Royal London Yacht, Royal Cork Yacht, Royal Air Force Yacht.

**DOWTY, Sir George (Herbert),** Kt 1956; DL; Founder and Chairman of the Dowty Group of Companies; *b* 27 April 1901; *y s* of William Dowty and Laura (*née* Masters); *m* 1948, Marguerite Anne Gowans, *d* of late M. J. H. Lockie and Annie B. Lockie, Newmarket, Ont, Canada; one *s* one *d. Educ:* Worcester Royal Grammar Sch. Hon. Freeman of Borough of Cheltenham, 1955; Hon. Freeman of Borough of Tewkesbury, 1964. President of Royal Aeronautical Society, 1952-53; Hon. Fellow, 1967; RAeS Gold Medal for Advancement of Aeronautical Science, 1955. Treasurer, Society of British Aerospace Companies Ltd, 1961-68; President: The Society of British Aircraft Constructors, 1960-61; Gloucestershire and S. Worcestershire Productivity Association; Chairman: Industrial Development Board for Malta, 1960-63; North Gloucestershire Disablement Cttee, 1952-63. Hon. DSc Bath Univ. of Technology, 1966. DL Glos, 1969. *Recreations:* blood-stock breeding, tennis, curling, golf. *Address:* Arle Court, Cheltenham, Glos. *T:* Cheltenham 54382. *Clubs:* Royal Aero, Royal Automobile.

**DOXIADIS, Constantinos Apostolos;** President, Doxiadis Associates International Co. Ltd, Consultants on Development and Ekistics, Athens; Chairman, Board of Directors, Athens Technological Organization; President, Athens Center of Ekistics; Chairman, Doxiadis System Development Center, Washington, DC; *b* 1913; *s* of Apostolos Doxiadis, Pediatrician, and Evanthia (*née* Mezeviri); *m* 1940, Emma Scheepers; one *s* three *d. Educ:* Technical Univ., Athens (Architect-Engineer); Berlin-Charlottenburg Univ. (DrIng). Chief Town Planning Officer, Greater Athens Area, 1937-38; Head, Dept of Regional and Town Planning, Ministry of Public Works, Greece, 1939-44; Lecturer and Acting Professor of Town Planning, Techn. Univ. of Athens, 1939-43; Minister and Permanent Secretary of Housing Reconstruction, Greece, 1945-48; Minister-Co-ordinator of Greek Recovery Program, 1948-51. Member of various delegations and cttees; Consultant to many organizations and governments of numerous countries; Researcher for National Assoc. of Housing and Redevelopment Officials (US) and various Athens Technol Organization projects. Has studied, planned and designed numerous human settlements and their development in many fields throughout the world. Visiting Lecturer at many US universities and Colleges; Hon. LLD: Swarthmore Coll., 1962; Mills Coll., 1964; Univ. of Mich, 1967; Tulane Univ., 1968; Kalamazoo Coll., 1968; Hon. DH Wayne State Univ., 1964; Hon. LHD: N Mich Univ., 1965; Case Western Reserve Univ., 1969; Hon. DS Detroit Inst. of Technology, 1966; Hon. DFA Univ. of RI; Hon. DSc: Univ. of Pittsburgh, 1967; Marietta Coll., 1969. Also various foreign awards including Aspen Award for Humanities, 1966. Greek Military Cross, 1941; Hon. OBE, 1945; Order of Cedar, Lebanon, 1958; Royal Order of the Phoenix, Greece, 1960; Yugoslav Flag Order with Golden Wreath, 1966. *Publications:* Raumordnung im griechischen Städtebau, 1937; A Simple Story, 1945 (in Greek); Ekistic Analysis, 1946; Destruction of Towns and Villages in Greece, 1947; (jointly) A Plan for the Survival of the Greek People (2 vols), 1947; Ekistic Policies for the Reconstruction of the Country with a 20-year Program, 1947; March of the People, 1948; Our Capital and its Future, 1960; Architecture in Transition, 1963; (with T. B. Douglass) The New World of Urban Man, 1965; Urban Renewal and the Future of the American City, 1966; Between Dystopia and Utopia, 1966; Emergence and Growth of an Urban Region, The Developing Urban Detroit Area: vol. I, 1966; vol. II, 1967; vol. III, 1970; Ekistics: An Introduction to the Science of Human Settlements, 1968; several volumes on programs and projects for many areas and cities around the world. *Address:* Doxiadis Associates International, 24 Stratiotikou Syndesmou, Athens 136, Greece.

**DOYLE, Rear-Adm. Alec Broughton,** CBE 1937; Royal Australian Navy; *b* 5 Oct. 1888; *s* of James H. and Rebekah Doyle, Invermien, Scone, NSW; *m* 1917, Charlotte Madge, *d* of Dr Herbert Lillies, Armadale, Victoria, Australia; two *s. Educ:* Scone Grammar Sch., NSW; The King's Sch., Parramatta, NSW; Sydney Univ., NSW. Bachelor of Engineering, 1911; joined Royal Australian Navy, 1912; sea service, 1914-18; Squadron Engineer Officer, 1929-32; Engineer Manager, Royal Australian Naval Dockyard, Garden Island, and General Overseer, Naval Shipbuilding and Repair, Sydney, 1933-42; Engineer Captain, 1934; Director of Engineering (Naval), 1942-43; Engineer Rear-Admiral, 1943; Third Naval Member Australian Commonwealth Naval Board, Navy Office, Melbourne, and Chief of Construction, 1943-48; retired 1948. *Recreations:* pastoral pursuits. *Address:* Invermien, Scone, NSW 2337, Australia. *Clubs:* Union, University, Royal Sydney Golf (Sydney).

**DOYLE, Brian André; Hon. Mr Justice Doyle;** Justice of Appeal, Court of Appeal for Zambia, since 1965; Acting Chief Justice of Zambia, 1969; Chairman, Local Government Service Commission, Zambia, 1964; *b* 10 May 1911; *s* of John Patrick Doyle, ICS and Louise Doyle (*née* Renard); *m* 1937, Nora (*née* Slattery); one *s* one *d. Educ:* Douai Sch.; Trinity Coll., Dublin. Called to Irish Bar, 1932; Magistrate, Trinidad and Tobago, 1937; Resident Magistrate, Uganda, 1942; Solicitor-Gen., Fiji, 1948; Attorney-Gen., Fiji, 1949; KC (Fiji), 1950; N Rhodesia, 1956; Minister of Legal Affairs and Attorney-Gen., Northern Rhodesia (Zambia, 1964), 1959-65, retired. *Recreations:* fishing, golf. *Address:* c/o Court of Appeal for Zambia, PO Box RW 67, Lusaka, Zambia. *Club:* University (Dublin).

**DOYLE, Sir John (Francis Reginald William Hastings),** 5th Bt, *cr* 1828; *b* 3 Jan. 1912; *s* of Col Sir Arthur Havelock James Doyle, 4th Bt, and Joyce Ethelreda (*d* 1961), 2nd *d* of Hon. Greville Howard; *S* father, 1948; *m* 1947, Diana, *d* of Col Steel, Indian Army (now of Milford-on-Sea, Hants); one *d. Educ:* Eton. RMC Sandhurst. Served Palestime, 1938 (medal with clasp); War of 1939-45, in France, Italy, Greece; Major, Cameronians; retired, 1950. *Address:* Glebe House, Camolin, Co. Wexford. *Club:* Kildare Street (Dublin).

**DOYLE, Joseph,** DSc, MRIA; Professor of Botany, University College, Dublin, 1924, Professor Emeritus, since 1961; Vice-President, Royal Dublin Society; *b* 1891; *Educ:* O'Connell Schs, Dublin; University Coll. Dublin. Graduated in the Royal University of Ireland in Biology, 1910; studied in Germany. *Publications:* various technical papers in the Proceedings of the Royal Dublin Society, The

Royal Irish Academy and elsewhere mainly on Conifers. *Address:* 14 St Kevin's Park, Dartry, Dublin 6.

**DOYLE, Brig. Richard Stanislaus,** CBE 1957 (OBE 1954); MBIM; General Manager, Glenrothes New Town, Fife, since Dec. 1962; *b* 6 Oct. 1911; *s* of Richard Joseph Doyle, Dublin; *m* 1940, Rae Phyllis, *d* of H. D. Pascoe, Northampton; two *s* one *d*. *Educ:* O'Connell Sch., Dublin; University Coll., Dublin. Served War of 1939-45 (despatches, 1945): RAOC, Burma, Malaya; Col DDOS, Burma Comd, 1945; Col i/c Admin. Cyprus, 1955-58; Brig., and Dir of Quartering, War Office, 1960-62; retd, 1962. *Recreations:* golf and work. *Address:* Alburne Knowe, Glenrothes, Fife. *T:* Glenrothes 2413. *Club:* Army and Navy.

**D'OYLY, Sir John (Rochfort),** 13th Bt, *cr* 1663; Commander, RN retired; *b* 19 April 1900; *s* of Sir (Hastings) Hadley D'Oyly, 11th Bt, and Beatrice, *d* of late Francis Bingham Clerk, JP; *S* brother, Sir Charles Hastings D'Oyly, 12th Bt, 1962; *m* 1930, Kathleen, *er d* of late Robert Brown Gillespie, Halgolle, Yatiyantota, Ceylon (marr. diss. 1944); two *d* (one *s* decd). *Educ:* Hill Brow, Eastbourne; Eastman's Royal Naval Academy, Southsea; HMS Conway. Served European War, 1916-18, with Grand Fleet; Baltic Operations, 1919. Gonville and Caius Coll., Cambridge, 1920-21. Specialised in physical and recreational training, 1921-22; Mediterranean, 1923-25; Term Officer at Royal Naval Coll., Dartmouth, 1925-27; East Indies, 1928-30; HMS St Vincent Boys' Training Establishment, 1930-32; Fleet Physical and Recreational Training Officer, Mediterranean, 1932-35; Asst Superintendent, RN Sch. of Physical and Recreational Training, Portsmouth, 1936-38. Served European War, 1939-45: Comdr of the Coll., RNC, Greenwich; Atlantic; East Indies; Pacific; retd, 1946. *Heir: half-brother,* Nigel Hadley Miller D'Oyly [*b* 6 July 1914; *m* 1940, Dolores, *d* of R. H. Gregory; one *s* two *d*]. *Address:* c/o Lloyds Bank Ltd, 39 Piccadilly, W1. *Club:* Royal Naval (Portsmouth).

**DRABBLE, John Frederick; His Honour Judge Drabble;** Judge of County Courts, Circuit 33 (Suffolk and Essex), since 1965; *b* 8 May 1906; *s* of late Joseph and Emily Drabble, Conisbrough, Yorks; *m* 1933, Kathleen Marie Bloor; one *s* three *d*. *Educ:* Mexborough Grammar Sch.; Downing Coll., Cambridge (MA). Called to Bar, 1931, Served War of 1939-45. RAF, 1940-45, finally as Sqdn Leader. QC 1953; Recorder of Huddersfield, 1955-57; of Kingston-upon-Hull, 1957-58. *Address:* St Mary's, Martlesham, Woodbridge, Suffolk. *T:* Kesgrave 2615.

*See also Margaret Drabble.*

**DRABBLE, Margaret, (Mrs C. W. Swift);** author; *b* 5 June 1939; 2nd *d* of His Honour Judge Drabble, *qv*; *m* 1960, Clive Walter Swift; two *s* one *d*. *Educ:* The Mount Sch., York; Newnham Coll., Cambridge. Lives in London. *Publications:* A Summer Birdcage, 1963; The Garrick Year, 1964; The Millstone, 1966 (filmed, as A Touch of Love, 1969); Wordsworth, 1966; Jerusalem the Golden, 1967; The Waterfall, 1969.

**DRAKE, Antony Elliot,** CBE 1967 (OBE 1945); *b* 15 June 1907; *s* of Francis Courtney Drake and Mabel Grace (*née* Drake); *m* 1935, Moira Helen Arden Wall; one *s* one *d*. *Educ:* Aldenham Sch.; New Coll., Oxford. Indian Civil Service, 1930; Bihar and Orissa, 1931-37; seconded to Indian Political Service, 1937; served Rajputana, 1937-39; Baluchistan, 1939-43; Mysore (Sec. to Resident), 1943-46; Rajkot (Political Agent, E Kathiawar), 1946-47; appointed to Home Civil Service, HM Treasury, 1947; Asst Sec., 1950; on loan to UK Atomic Energy Authority as Principal Finance Officer, 1957; transferred permanently to UKAEA, 1960; Finance and Programmes Officer, 1964-69; retd, 1969. Mem., Hosp. Management Cttee, Royal Weston Counties Hosp. Group, 1970-. *Recreations:* fishing, golf. *Address:* Winneford Farm House, Awliscombe, Honiton, Devon. *T:* Honiton 2502. *Club:* Flyfishers'.

**DRAKE Sir (Arthur) Eric (Courtney),** Kt 1970; CBE 1952; MA; FCA; Chairman, British Petroleum Co. Ltd, since 1969 (a Managing Director since 1958, Deputy Chairman 1962-69); *b* 29 Nov. 1910; *e s* of Dr A. W. Courtney Drake; *m* 1st, 1935, Rosemary Moore; two *d*; 2nd, 1950, Margaret Elizabeth Wilson; two *s*. *Educ:* Shrewsbury; Pembroke Coll., Cambridge. With The British Petroleum Co. Ltd, 1935-; Gen. Man., Iran and Iraq, 1950-51; Rep. in USA, 1952-54. Director: BP Trading Ltd; BP Tanker Co. Ltd; BP Exploration Co. Ltd; Société Française des Pétroles BP and other subsidiaries. Pres., Chamber of Shipping, 1964 (Mem. of Council, 1958-, Vice-Pres., 1963); Vice-Chm., Gen. Council of British Shipping, 1963; Member: Gen. Cttee, Lloyd's Register of Shipping, 1960-; Cttee on Invisible Exports, 1969-; Comdr, Ordre de la Couronne, Belgium, 1969. Bd of Governors, Pangbourne Nautical Coll., 1958-69; Court of Governors, London Sch. of Economics and Political Science, 1963-; Governing Body of Shrewsbury Sch., 1969-. *Address:* The Old Rectory, Cheriton, Alresford, Hants. *T:* Bramdean 334; 18 Princes Gate, SW7. *T:* 01-584 0077. *Clubs:* Royal Yacht Squadron, Leander, Royal Thames Yacht.

**DRAKE, Donald Henry Charles,** CIE 1933; *b* 23 Aug. 1887; *m* 1915, Dorothy, *d* of Lt-Col Edmund Waller, OBE; one *s*. *Educ:* Blundell's Sch., Tiverton; Christ Church, Oxford. Entered Indian Civil Service 1911; retired, 1937. *Address:* c/o Lloyds Bank, Ltd, Cox & King's Branch, 6 Pall Mall, SW1.

**DRAKE, Sir Eric;** *see* Drake, Sir A. E. C.

**DRAKE, Sir Eugen M.;** *see* Millington-Drake.

**DRAKE, (Frederick) Maurice,** DFC 1944; QC 1968; *b* 15 Feb. 1923; *o s* of Walter Charles Drake and Elizabeth Drake; *m* 1954, Alison May, *d* of W. D. Waterfall, *qv*; two *s* three *d*. *Educ:* St George's Sch., Harpenden; Exeter Coll., Oxford. MA Hons 1948. Called to Bar, Lincoln's Inn, 1950. Dep. Chm., Beds QS, 1966. Chm. Governors, Aldwickbury Prep. Sch. (Trust), 1969-. *Recreations:* music, gardening, countryside. *Address:* The White House, West Common Way, Harpenden, Herts. *T:* Harpenden 2329; 4 Paper Buildings, Temple, EC4.

**DRAKE, Harold William,** CBE 1941; *b* 8 April 1889; *s* of William Henry Drake and Mary Ann Robinson; *m* 1st, 1918, Gertrude Alice Terry; 2nd, 1954, Sarah Louise Johnson (*d* 1964). *Educ:* City of London Sch. Colonial Service, 1914-46, Nigeria, Nyassaland and British Guiana; war service, Royal West African Frontier Force, Cameroons and East Africa, 1914-19. *Address:* c/o Barclay's Bank Ltd, 139/142 North Street, Brighton BN1 1RU. *Club:* East India and Sports.

**DRAKE, Brig. Dame Jean Elizabeth R.;** *see* Rivett-Drake.

**DRAKE, John Collard Bernard,** CSI 1933; CIE 1926; CBE 1930; Indian Civil Service, retired; *b* 7 March 1884; 3rd *s* of late Felix Drake of

East Coker, Yeovil, Somerset. *Educ:* Blundell's Sch.; Balliol Coll., Oxford. Joined Indian Civil Service, 1908; Under-Sec. to Government of Bihar and Orissa, 1912-15; Private Sec. to Lieut-Governor of Bihar and Orissa, 1915-18; Indian Army Reserve of Officers, 1918-19; Under-Sec. to Government of India, 1919-20; Dep. Sec., 1921-24; Sec. to the High Commissioner for India in London, 1924-29; Joint Sec. to the Government of India, Dept of Commerce, 1929-32; Sec., 1932-33; Mem. Pensions Appeal Tribunals, 1944-66. *Address:* c/o Lloyds Bank Ltd, 6 Pall Mall, SW1. *Clubs:* East India and Sports; Bath and County.

**DRAKE, Maurice;** *see* Drake, F. M.

**DRAKELEY, Thomas James,** CBE 1952; DSc, PhD; FRIC, FIRI; *b* Barwell, Leicester, 17 Dec. 1890; *o s* of late Thomas Drakeley; *m* Margaret (*d* 1957), *e d* of late Frank T. Hill. *Educ:* Sir Walter St John's Sch.; University Coll., London. Senior Lecturer in Chemistry, at the Wigan and District Mining and Technical Coll., 1912-19; Head of Dept of Chemistry and Rubber Technology at Northern Polytechnic, 1919-31; Principal, Northern Polytechnic, 1932-55 and 1958-61; Dir, National Coll. of Rubber Technology, Holloway, N7, 1948-55 and 1958-61; Deleg. for UK on International Dairy Federation; Ed. Transactions of Instn of the Rubber Industry, 1925-50; Mem. of Council of Chemical Soc., 1930-33; Mem. of Appeals Tribunal (England and Wales) for further Education and Training Scheme, Ministry of Labour and National Service, 1945-52; Pres. Assoc. of Principals of Technical Institutions, 1946-47; Mem. Regional (London and Home Counties) Advisory Council for Higher Technological Education, 1947-55; Vice-Chm. Regional (London and Home Counties) Academic Board. 1947-52, Chm. 1952-55; Mem. Nat. Advisory Council on Education for Industry and Commerce, Min. of Education, 1948-55; Hancock Medal Institution of the Rubber Industry, 1952; Chm. Northern Group Hosp. Management Cttee, 1956-60; Life Vice-Pres. Institution of the Rubber Industry, 1958-. Chm. of Council, 1962-65, Pres., 1966-68. *Publications:* research contributions. *Address:* 101 Barrington Court, Pages Hill, N10. *T:* 01-883 3667.

**DRAPER, William H.,** Jr, Hon. LLD; Investment Banker; Corporation Executive; *b* NY City, 10 Aug. 1894; *s* of William Henry Draper and Mary Emma (*née* Carey); *m* 1918, Katharine Louise Baum (decd); one *s* two *d*; *m* 1949, Eunice Barzynski. *Educ:* New York Univ. (MA). Served European War, 1917-18, Major, Inf. US Army. With Nat. City Bank, NYC, 1919-21; Asst Treas. Bankers Trust Co., NYC, 1923-27; joined Dillon Read & Co. investment bankers, NYC, 1927, Vice-Pres., 1937-53; Exec. Officer, Chm. Bd, Mexican Light & Power Co., 1954-59; Partner, Draper, Gaither & Anderson, 1959-62; Chm., Combustion Engineering, Inc., 1962-65; Chm., Pension Corp. of America, 1965-67; Chief of Staff, 77th Div., org. Reserve Corps, 1936-40; War of 1939-45, on active duty as Col Inf. with Gen. Staff, US Army, Washington, 1940-41; comd 136th Inf. Regt, 33rd Inf. Div., 1942-44, incl. service in Pacific theater; in charge contract termination for War Dept, Washington, 1944; Brig.-Gen., 1945; Chief, Economic Div., Control Council for Germany, 1945-46; Economic Adviser to C-in-C, European theatre, 1947, with rank of Maj.-Gen.; Mil. Govt Advisor to Sec. of State at Moscow Conf. of Foreign Ministers, 1947; Under-Sec. of War (title after reorganization Under-Sec. of Army), 1947; resigned 1949. Legion of Merit (Army), 1943 and (Navy), 1945: Selective Service Medal, 1946; DSM (US), 1948; Order of Orange Nassau, Netherlands, 1949; Medal for Merit (US), 1953; Grand Cross, Order of Merit (Italy), 1954; Member: President's Advisory Cttee on Selective Service, Washington, 1940; Joint Army and Navy Cttee on Welfare and Recreation, 1941. Trustee The Kosciuszko Foundation; Mem. Council on Foreign Relations; Soc. of Amer. Magicians and Acad. of Political Science; Am. Legion (Westchester County Comdr, 1933-34); US Special Representative in Europe, with the rank of Ambassador, stationed in Paris, Jan. 1952-June 1953, representing US in the North Atlantic Council and OEEC, and supervising the Mutual Security Programme in Europe; Chm., President's Cttee on US Mil. Assistance, 1958-59; formerly Trustee Long Island Rail Road Co. and Chm., Long Island Transit Authority. Mem. Governing Body, Planned Parenthood Fedn; National Chm., Population Crisis Cttee, 1965-69, Hon. Chm. 1969-; US Mem., UN Population Commn, 1969-; Mem. Bd of Dirs, Atlantic Council of US, 1955-. Holds several hon. degrees. Republican. Presbyterian. *Address:* (Home) 2202 Foxboro Place NW, Washington, DC, USA; (Office) 1730 K St NW, Washington, DC. *Clubs:* Recess, Downtown Athletic, The Brook (New York); Army and Navy, Metropolitan (Washington); Pacific-Union (San Francisco).

**DRAWBELL, James Wedgwood;** Managing Editor, and Editorial Consultant, with Geo. Newnes Ltd (1946-64); previously Editor, Sunday Chronicle (1925-46); *b* 15 April 1899. *Educ:* Edinburgh. Worked on newspapers in New York (The World); Montreal (Montreal Star); Edinburgh (Evening Dispatch); served with Royal Scots Fusiliers, European War of 1914-18. *Publications:* Dorothy Thompson's English Journey, 1942; All Change Here, 1943; Night and Day, 1945; Drifts my Boat, 1946; The Long Year, 1958; The Sun Within Us, 1963; Time on My Hands, 1968; A Garden, 1970. *Address:* Mill Hill, Rodmell, near Lewes, Sussex. *T:* Lewes 2912. *Clubs:* Scottish Liberal, Kilspindie Golf.

**DRAYCOTT, Douglas Patrick,** QC 1965; MA Oxon; Recorder of Shrewsbury since 1966; *b* 23 Aug. 1918; *s* of George Draycott and Mary Ann Draycott (*née* Burke); *m* Elizabeth Victoria Hall; two *s* three *d*. *Educ:* Wolstanton Grammar Sch.; Oriel Coll., Oxford (MA). War Service: Royal Tank Regiment and General Staff, 1939-46. Barrister-at-Law, Middle Temple, 1950; joined Oxford Circuit, 1950, and practised from Chambers in Birmingham, 1950-65. *Address:* 10 Pakenham Road, Edgbaston, Birmingham 15. *T:* 021-440 3796; 1 Essex Court, Temple, EC4. *T:* 01-353 6717, 1974.

**DRAYSON, Rear-Adm. Edwin Howard,** CB 1945; CBE 1942 (OBE 1937); retired; *b* 1889; *m* 1914, Hilda Jeannie, *d* of Isaac Harding (son killed in action, 1944). *Address:* Little Orchard, Lustleigh, South Devon.

**DRAYSON, George Burnaby;** MP (C) Skipton Division of West Riding, Yorks, since 1945; *b* 9 March 1913; *s* of late Walter Drayson, Stevenage, Herts, and Dorothy Dyott, *d* of late Captain Hugo Burnaby, RN; *m* 1939, Winifred Heath (marr. diss., 1958); one *d*; *m* 1962, Barbara Radonska-Chrzanowska, Warsaw. *Educ:* Borlasse Sch. Entered City, 1929; Mem. Stock Exchange, 1935-54; Company Director. Commnd Essex Yeomanry, 1931, Captain, 1938; served RA in Western Desert (TD, despatches, prisoner of war, June 1942-Sept. 1943, escaped, walked 500 miles to freedom). Mem. of Inter-Parliamentary Union Delegn to Turkey, 1947; Mem. Royal Agric. Society; Vice-Chm., Parly All Party East/West Trade Cttee. *Recreations:* fishing, walking (completed London to Brighton walk, 1939); foreign travel. *Address:* 12 Harley Road, NW3. *T:* 01-722 4241; Linton House, Linton-in-Craven, Skipton, Yorks. *T:* Grassington 362. *Clubs:* Carlton, Royal Automobile.

**DRAYSON, Robert Quested,** DSC 1943; MA; Headmaster of Stowe since 1964; *b* 5 June 1919; *s* of late Frederick Louis Drayson and of Elsie Mabel Drayson; *m* 1943, Rachel, 2nd *d* of Stephen Spencer Jenkyns; one *s* two *d*. *Educ:* St Lawrence Coll., Ramsgate; Downing Coll., Cambridge. Cambridge: 1938-39, 1946-47; History Tripos, BA 1947, MA 1950. Served, RNVR, 1939-46; Lieut in command HM Motor Torpedo Boats. Asst Master and Housemaster, St Lawrence Coll., 1947-50; Asst Master, Felsted Sch., 1950-55; Headmaster, Reed's Sch., Cobham, 1955-63. FRSA 1968. *Recreations:* hockey (Cambridge Blue, 1946, 1947; Kent XI, 1947-56); cricket. *Address:* Stowe School, Buckingham. *T:* Buckingham 3165. *Club:* Hawks (Cambridge).

**DRENNAN, Alexander Murray,** MD Edinburgh 1924; MB, ChB 1906; FRCPE 1914; FRSE 1932; Professor of Pathology, Edinburgh, 1931-Sept. 1954, retired; Professor Emeritus; *b* Jan. 1884; *s* of late Alexr Drennan, Dunalwyn, Helensburgh; *m* 1909; one *s* two *d*. *Educ:* Larchfield, Helensburgh; Kelvinside Academy Glasgow; Edinburgh Univ. Professor of Pathology, Otago Univ., Dunedin, NZ, 1914-28; Professor of Pathology, Queen's Univ. Belfast, 1928-31; Temporary Acting Lt-Comdr, RNVR (Sp.), 1942-47. *Publications:* various articles on pathological subjects, etc. *Recreations:* fishing, motoring, sailing. *Address:* Lochard Cottage, By Aberfoyle, Perthshire, Scotland. *Club:* Royal Scottish Automobile (Glasgow).

**DRENNAN, Basil St George;** Clerk of Financial and Miscellaneous Committees, House of Commons, 1958-60; *b* 22 Jan. 1903; *s* of Rev. William St George Drennan, MSc, and Kate, *d* of Josiah Lawrence Walker, Banbury; *m* 1960, Joan Madeline Norris, *d* of George Richards, FCH; one *s*. *Educ:* Radley (scholar); Keble Coll., Oxford (exhibitioner, MA). asst Clerk, House of Commons 1926; Sen. Clerk, 1940; attached Select Cttee on National Expenditure, 1940-45; Clerk to Select Cttee on Estimates, 1946; Clerk of Financial Cttees, 1948-52; Clerk of Private Bills and Taxing Officer, House of Commons, and Examiner of Petitions for Private Bills, both Houses of Parliament, 1953-58; (compiled (1961-70) and ed) The Keble College Centenary Register 1870-1970, 1970. *Recreations:* gardening; going abroad; philately (FRPSL, 1962). *Address:* 16 Blandford Avenue, Oxford OX2 8DY. *T:* Oxford 58280.

**DRENNAN, John Cherry,** CBE 1959; JP; Senator, Northern Ireland, since 1961; HM Lieutenant for Co. Londonderry since 1965; *b* 1899; *s* of late John Wallace Drennan, Carse Hall, Limavady, Co. Londonderry; *m* 1926, Margaret, *d* of late Charles Macfarlane, West Hartlepool; two *d* (one *s* decd). *Educ:* Foyle Coll., Londonderry. JP 1923, High Sheriff, 1955, DL 1955, Co. Londonderry. *Address:* Deerpark, Limavady, Co. Londonderry, N Ireland. *T:* Limavady 2321.

**DRESCHFIELD, Ralph Leonard Emmanuel,** CMG 1957; *b* 18 March 1911; *s* of late Henry Theodore and Jessie Mindelle Dreschfield; unmarried. *Educ:* Merchiston Castle Sch.; Trinity Hall, Cambridge (BA). Called to Bar, 1933; entered Colonial Service, 1938, and apptd resident Magistrate, Uganda; served in War of 1939-45, in 4th King's African Rifles; Crown Counsel, Uganda, 1948; Solicitor-Gen., Uganda, 1949; QC 1950; Attorney-Gen., Uganda, 1951-62. Chm. Trustees of Uganda National Parks, 1952-62. Sec., Community Council of Essex, 1963-. *Recreation:* yachting. *Address:* 15 Bridge Street, Writtle, Chelmsford. *T:* Writtle 234. *Clubs:* Royal Ocean Racing, Bar Yacht, Little Ship; West Mersea Yacht.

**DRESDEL, Sonia;** *b* Hornsea, Yorkshire. *Educ:* High Sch. and University, Aberdeen. Repertory prior to 1940, then Old Vic, CEMA, and ENSA tours; Hedda Tesman in Hedda Gabler, Mrs Millamant in Way of the World, Mercury Theatre and tour, 1942; Clotilde in Parisienne, St James's, 1943; Olivia Russell in This Was a Woman, Comedy, 1944; name part in Laura, St Martin's, 1945; Nurse Wayland in The Sacred Flame, Comedy, 1946; Lend me Robin, 1949; The Power of Darkness, 1949; The Third Visitor, 1949; at Edinburgh Festival, 1950 (as Juno in The Queen's Comedy); Message for Margaret (Australia); Lady Starcross in After My Fashion, 1952. Edinburgh Festival, 1955, 1956; Dr Jo, 1955; at Aldwych, 1956; The Best Damn Lie, 1957; toured Africa, 1958; Dir of Productions, Harrogate Opera House, 1959; Christine in Mourning Becomes Electra, Old Vic, 1961; All's Well That Ends Well, Bristol Old Vic; The Possessed, Mermaid, 1963; Oedipus the King and Oedipus at Colonus, Mermaid, 1965; Dandy Dick, Mermaid, 1965. *Films:* While I Live, This Was a Woman, The Fallen Idol, The Third Visitor, Clouded Yellow, Now and Forever, The Secret Tent, Oscar Wilde, The Break. *Television:* The Guardsman, Thérèse Raquin, Mrs Dot, Eternal Triangle, Way of the World, What's your Story, Sorry Wrong Number, Count Albany, Rebecca, Crime on my Hands, the Mayerling Tragedy, Twilight of a Warrior, Judge for Yourself, David Copperfield, The Publican's Story, Mystery of Edwin Drood, The Adventures of Alice, Solitaire (with Françoise Rosay), Saki, Maigret, Jane Eyre. *Recreation:* gardening. *Address:* c/o Eric Glass Ltd, 28 Berkeley Square, W1.

**DREVER, James;** Principal and Vice-Chancellor, University of Dundee, since 1967; Professor of Psychology, University of Edinburgh, 1944-66; *b* 29 Jan. 1910; *s* of late Prof. James Drever; *m* 1936, Joan Isabel Mackay Budge; one *s* one *d*. *Educ:* Royal High Sch., Edinburgh; Universities of Edinburgh (MA Hons Philosophy, 1932) and Cambridge (MA Moral Science Tripos, 1934). FRSE. Asst, Dept of Philosophy, Edinburgh, 1934-38; Lecturer in Philosophy and Psychology, King's Coll., Newcastle, 1938-41; Royal Navy, 1941-45; Visiting Professor, Princeton Univ., 1954-55. Editor, British Journal of Psychology, 1954-58; President: British Psychological Soc., 1960-61; Internat. Union of Scientific Psychology, 1963-66. Member: Cttee on Higher Education, 1961-63; Social Science Research Council, 1965-; Chm., Advisory Council on Social Work, in Scotland, 1970-. *Publications:* papers and reviews. *Address:* The University, Dundee. *Club:* Athenæum.

**DREW, Sir Arthur (Charles Walter),** KCB 1964 (CB 1958); Permanent Under-Secretary of State (Administration), Ministry of Defence; *b* 2 Sept. 1912; *er s* of late Arthur Drew, Mexico City, and Louise Schulte-Ummingen; *m* 1943, Rachel, *er d* of G. W. Lambert, *qv*; one *s* three *d. Educ:* Christ's Hospital; King's Coll., Cambridge. Asst Principal, War Office, 1936; Principal, 1939; Asst Private Sec. to Secretary of State for War, 1944; Principal Private Sec. to successive Secs of State for War, 1945-49; Asst Sec., 1949; IDC, 1949; International Staff, NATO, 1951-53; Asst Under Sec. of State, 1955; Dep. Under Sec. of State, WO, 1957-Nov. 1961; Dep. Under Sec. of State, Home Office, 1961-63; last Permanent Under Sec. of State, War Office, 1963-64. Warden, Drapers' Co., 1970. Coronation Medal, 1953. *Recreation:* following Baedeker. *Address:* 2 Branstone Road, Kew, Surrey. *T:* 01-940 1210. *Club:* Reform.

**DREW, Brig. Cecil Francis,** DSO 1918; *b* 1890; *o s* of late Albert Francis Drew, JP of Foston, Farnham Royal, Bucks; *m* 1915, Elizabeth Seymour Hawker; one *s* (and one *s* decd). *Educ:* Highgate and Royal Milit. Acad.; Joined The Cameronians, 1910; served European War (despatches twice, DSO); temp. Lt-Col, 1917-19; Brevet Lt-Col, 1932; Lt-Col, 1936; Col, 1938; Brigadier, 1939; GSO 3, War Office, 1919-22; GSO 3, Scottish Command, 1924; DAA and QMG Highland Area, 1925-27; DAQMG South China Command, 1927-28; GSO 51st (Highland) Division, 1929-33; commanded 1st Bn The Cameronians, 1936-38; AAG War Office, 1938-39; Comd East Lancs Area, 1939-40; Comd 183 Inf. Brigade, 1940-42; Brigadier i/c Administration, 1st Corps District, 1942; AAG Southern Command, 1943; Gen. Staff, GHQ Home Forces, 1944-45; retired pay, 1945. JP Bucks, 1949. *Address:* Gatehouse Cottages, Framfield, Sussex. *Club:* Army and Navy.

**DREW, Charles Edwin,** MVO 1952; VRD 1960; FRCS; Surgeon, Westminster Hospital since 1951; Thoracic Surgeon, St George's Hospital, since 1955; Civilian Consultant in Thoracic Surgery to the Royal Navy; Hon. Consultant in Thoracic Surgery to Queen Alexandra Hospital, Millbank, since 1960; Hon. Consulting Thoracic Surgeon, King Edward VII Hospital, Midhurst; *b* 1916; *s* of Edwin Frank Drew, Croydon; *m* 1950, Doreen, *d* of Frederick James Pittaway, Stocksfield, Northumberland; one *s* one *d. Educ:* Westminster City Sch.; King's Coll., London, MB, BS London 1941; MRCS, LRCP 1941; FRCS 1946. Served War of 1939-45, RNVR (Surgeon-Comdr 1957). Formerly Chief Asst and Surg. Registrar, Westminster Hosp.; Chief Surgical Asst, Brompton Hosp. Mem. Soc. Thoracic Surgeons: FRSocMed. *Publications:* papers in med. jls. *Address:* 17 Rodway Road, SW15. *T:* 01-788 7030; 97/24 John Islip Street, SW1. *T:* 01-828 4709.

**DREW, Sir Ferdinand (Caire),** Kt 1960; CMG 1951; FASA; Under-Treasurer, South Australia and Chairman State Grants Committee, 1946-60, retired; *b* Adelaide, S Aust., 1 May 1895; *s* of late Charles H. Drew, Adelaide; *m* 1934, Chrissie A., *d* of George M. McGowan; one *s* two *d. Educ:* Rose Park Public Sch.; Muirden Coll. Asst Auditor-Gen., 1936-39; Asst Under-Treasurer, 1939-46. Chm. Supply and Tender Board, 1943-49; Mem. Industries Development Cttee, 1942-49; Mem. Board of State Bank of South Australia, 1948 (Dep. Chm. 1963); Director: Unit Trust of SA; United Insurance Co. Ltd; Chrysler Aust. Ltd; former Director: Cellulose Australia Ltd; Adelaide Steamship Co.; Oil Investments Ltd. Chm. of Board of Electricity Trust, South Australia, 1949-. *Address:* 614 Anzac Highway, Glenelg, South Australia 5045, Australia.

**DREW, Lt-Col Hon. George Alexander,** PC Can. 1953; CC Canada 1967; CD; QC; LLD; Canadian barrister; former High Commissioner for Canada in the UK, and former Premier of Ontario and Minister of Education; Chairman Board, Lake Ontario Cement Ltd; Director of other companies; Governor, University of Toronto; Chancellor, University of Guelph; *b* Guelph, Ontario, 7 May 1894; *s* of late John J. Drew, KC, Guelph; *m* 1st, 1936, Florenza d'Arneiro (*d* 1965), *d* of Edward Johnson, CBE; one *s* one *d*; 2nd, 1966, Phyllis C. McCullagh (*née* Laidlaw), *widow* of C. George McCullagh, Toronto. *Educ:* Guelph Collegiate Inst.; Upper Canada Coll.; University of Toronto. Called to Bar (Ontario), 1920; practised in Guelph, 1920-25; Asst Master Supreme Court, Ont., 1926; Master, 1929; KC 1933. Leader Cons. Party, Ont., 1938; Ontario Legislature, 1939-48; Leader, Opposition of Ontario, 1939-43; Prime Minister, Province of Ontario, 1943, until chosen Leader of Cons. Party of Canada, Oct. 1948; Leader of Opposition of Canada, 1949-56; High Comr for Canada in UK, 1957-64, retd Alderman, City of Guelph, 1921-24; Mayor, 1925. Served European War, 1914-18, 16th Battery, Canadian Expeditionary Force (wounded): comd 64th Battery; comd 11th Field Regt, Royal Canadian Artillery, Guelph, Ont., 1929-36; Pres. Canadian Artillery Assoc., 1932-33. Headed various Canadian Delegations, 1958-62. Holds hon. doctorates. Is an Anglican. *Publications:* Canada's Fighting Airmen; The Truth about the War; Canada's Part in the Great War; Salesmen of Death; Tell Britain; The Truth About War Debts; numerous articles. *Recreations:* golf, fishing, photography. *Address:* Suite 2111, 44 Victoria Street, Toronto 1, Ont, Canada. *T:* 366-3452. *Clubs:* York, Toronto, Toronto Golf, Albany, University (Toronto); Rideau, Ottawa Country (Ottawa); Guelph Country; Caledon Mountain Trout.

**DREW, Prof. George Charles,** MA; London University Professor of Psychology, University College, since 1958; *b* 10 Dec. 1911; *e s* of George Frederick Drew; *m* 1936, Inez Annie, *d* of F. Hulbert Lewis; one *s* one *d. Educ:* St George's Sch., Bristol; Bristol, Cambridge and Harvard Univs. Viscount Haldane of Cloan studentship, Cambridge, 1935-36; Rockefeller Fellowship, Harvard Univ., 1936-38; Rockefeller Research Fellowship, Cambridge, 1938-42; Psychological Adviser, Air Ministry, 1942-46; Lecturer in Psychology, University of Bristol, 1946-49, Reader, 1949-51, Prof. of Psychology, 1951-58. Mem. Science Research Council, 1965-67. Vis. Prof., University of Calif, Berkeley, USA, 1967-68. *Publications:* articles on animal behaviour, learning, vision, and other psychological problems, in various British and American journals. *Address:* University College, Gower Street, WC1.

**DREW, Harry Edward,** CB 1970; Director-General of Quality Assurance, Ministry of Technology, since 1966; *b* 18 Jan. 1909; 2nd *s* of W. H. Drew and F. E. Drew (*née* Brindley), Gillingham, Kent; *m* 1937, Phyllis (*née* Flippance); one *s. Educ:* Wesleyan Sch., Gillingham; RAF Apprentice Sch., Flowerdown, RAF, 1924-37; Air Min. Research Stn, Bawdsey, 1937; Works Man., Radio Prodn Unit, Woolwich, Min. of Supply, 1943; Officer i/c, Research Prototype Unit, W. Howe, Bournemouth, Min. of Aircraft Prodn, 1946; Asst Dir, 1951, Dir, 1959, Electronic Prodn, Min. of Supply, London; Dir of Techn. Costs, Min. of Aviation, London, 1964. Gov., SE London Technical Coll. FIERE (Mem. Charter Council); FIProdE; FIWM (Nat. Chm., 1966-68, Vice-Pres., 1969). Liveryman, Worshipful Co. of Scientific Instrument Makers. *Publications:*

papers on training and quality and reliability. *Recreations:* photography, reading, gardening. *Address:* 25 Celtic Avenue, Shortlands, Kent. *T:* Ravensbourne 3988. *Clubs:* Civil Service, City Livery.

**DREW, Jane Beverly,** FRIBA; FIArb; architect; Partner in firm of Fry Drew and Partners, since 1946; *b* 24 March 1911; *m* 1st; two *d*; 2nd, 1942, Edwin Maxwell Fry, *qv*. *Educ:* Croydon. Was in partnership with J. T. Alliston, 1934-39; independent practice, 1939-45; in partnership with Maxwell Fry, 1945-. Asst Town Planning Adviser to Resident Minister, West African Colonies, 1944-45; Senior Architect to Capital project of Chandigarh, Punjab, India, 1951-54; Beamis Prof. Mass Inst. of Techn., Jan.-June, 1961; Vis. Prof. of Architecture, Harvard, Feb-March 1970. Completed work includes housing, hospitals, schools, and colleges in UK, West Africa, including Univs in Nigeria, Middle East and India; a section of Festival of Britain, 1951; town planning, housing and amenity buildings in Iran, W Africa and India. Current work, office planning, industrial housing, Hospitals, the Open University, in UK. Mem. Council, RIBA; Mem. Council and President, Architectural Association, 1969. LLD (Hon.) Ibadan. *Publications:* (with Maxwell Fry) Architecture for Children, 1944; (with Maxwell Fry and Harry Ford) Village Housing in the Tropics, 1945; (Founder Editor, 1945-) Architects' Year Book; (with Maxwell Fry) Architecture in the Humid Tropics; Tropical Architecture, 1956. *Recreations:* reading, writing, friends. *Address:* 63 Gloucester Place, W1. *T:* 01-935 3318. *Clubs:* Institute of Contemporary Arts, Studio.

**DREW, John Alexander,** CB 1957; Director of Companies; *b* 19 July 1907; *s* of Charles Edward Drew, Okehampton, Devon, and Ethel Margaret Drew; *m* 1930, Edith Waud Marriott; two *s* (and one *s* decd). *Educ:* Gram. Sch., Okehampton. Entered CS, 1928; Secretaries' Office, HM Customs and Excise, 1935-40; employed on special duties, 1940-45; Asst Sec., Cabinet Office, 1945-48; Bd of Trade, 1948-50; Asst Under-Sec. of State, Ministry of Defence, 1951-67, retired, 1967. US Medal of Freedom with Bronze Palm, 1946. *Address:* 28 Montague Avenue, Sanderstead, Surrey. *T:* 01-657 3264. *Club:* Naval and Military.

**DREW, Lt-Gen. Sir Robert;** *see* Drew, Lt-Gen. Sir W. R. M.

**DREW, Lt-Gen. Sir (William) Robert (Macfarlane),** KCB 1965 (CB 1962); CBE 1952 (OBE 1940); FRCP; Deputy Director, British Postgraduate Medical Federation, University of London, since 1970; *b* 4 Oct. 1907; *s* of late William Hughes Drew and Ethel Macfarlane; *m* 1934, Dorothy, *d* of late Alfred E. Dakingsmith, Bowral, NSW; one *s* one *d*. *Educ:* Sydney Gram. Sch.; Sydney Univ. MB, BS, BSc Sydney, 1930; DTM&H (Eng.), 1938; MRCP 1938; FRCP 1945; FRCPEd, 1966; FRACP, 1966. Joined RAMC, 1931; served India, France (Dunkirk), Iraq, MELF; Consulting Physician to the Army, 1959-61; Commandant, Royal Army Medical Coll., 1960-63; Dir of Medical Services, British Army of the Rhine, 1963-64; Dir-Gen., Army Medical Services, 1965-69. QHP, 1959-69. Leishman Prize, Royal Army Medical Coll., 1938; Goulstonian Lecturer, RCP, 1946; Mitchener Medallist, RCS, 1955; Lettsomian Lecturer, Medical Soc., London, 1961. Prof. Medicine, Royal Faculty of Med., Baghdad, 1946-52; Lectr Westminster Med. Sch., 1954-57; Pres. Clin. Section, Royal Society of Medicine, 1968-70. Hon. Sec. and later Councillor: Royal Society of Tropical Medicine and Hygiene; Med. Soc. of London (Pres., 1967-68); Australia and NZ Med. Assoc. (Chm.); Councillor: Royal Society of Medicine; RCP; Hunterian Soc.; Mem. Bd of Governors: Hospital for Sick Children, Gt Ormond Street, London; Royal Sch. for Daughters of Officers of the Army; Member: RCS Working Party on Medical Aid to Developing Countries; Cttee of Management, Postgraduate Medical Sch. of London, 1955-57, 1959-63, 1967-69; Governing Body, Postgrad. Med. Fedn, London Univ., 1954-56, 1967-69; Assoc. Physicians Gt Britain and Ireland; Exec. Cttee, Forces Help Soc., 1968-; Control Bd, Army Benevolent Fund; Bd, Kennedy Inst. of Rheumatology. Comr, The Royal Hosp., Chelsea. Hunterian Orator, Hunterian Soc., 1966. Corr. FACP, 1967; Hon. FRCS 1970. FRSA, 1965. CStJ 1965. Comdr Order of El-Rafidain (Iraq), 1951. *Publications:* in medical journals, 1927-70. *Recreations:* travel, gardening. *Address:* 10 Pembroke Gardens Close, W8. *T:* 01-602 6050. *Clubs:* Athenæum, Army and Navy; Australian, royal Sydney Golf (Sydney).

**DREWE, Basil,** OBE 1943; MC; QC 1945; *b* 1894; *s* of late J. C. Drewe, Castle Drogo, Drewsteignton, Devon; *m* 1919, Ruth (*d* 1945), *d* of F. C. Haselden, East Lymden, Ticehurst; two *s* one *d*. *Educ:* Eton; Christ Church, Oxford. Called to Bar, 1920; Master of Bench, Inner Temple, 1952. Devonshire Regt and RA, 1914-18 (MC and Bar); RAF 1939-45 (OBE). *Address:* Castle Drogo, Drewsteignton, Devon. *T:* Chagford 2206. *Club:* Athenæum.
*See also Sir Cedric Drewe.*

**DREWE, Sir Cedric,** KCVO, *cr* 1953; *b* 26 May 1896; 3rd *s* of late J. C. Drewe, JP, of Castle Drogo, Drewsteignton. Devon; *m* 1918, Beatrice Foster, *o d* of late Campbell Newington, JP of Oakover, Ticehurst, Sussex; three *s* one *d*. *Educ:* Eton; Royal Military Acad., Woolwich. Served with RFA, 1914-19. MP (C) South Molton Division of Devon, 1924-29; Honiton Division, Devon, 1931-55; Parliamentary Private Sec. to Rt Hon. Sir R. Dorman-Smith, 1939-40; to Rt Hon. R. S. Hudson (Ministry of Agriculture), 1940-43; Asst Govt Whip, 1943; Lord Commissioner of Treasury, 1944-45; a Conservative Whip, 1945-49. Deputy Chief Conservative Whip, 1949; Treasurer to the Queen's Household, 1952-55 (to the Household of King George VI, 1951-52). Governor Seale Hayne Agricultural Coll., 1959. *Address:* Broadhembury House, near Honiton, Devon. *T:* Broadhembury 205. *Club:* Carlton.
*See also B. Drewe.*

**DREWE, Geoffrey Grabham,** CIE 1947; CBE 1958 (OBE 1942); Assistant to the Honorary Treasurers of the Conservative Party, 1948-70; Manager, Conservative Party Board of Finance, 1965-70; *b* 3 May 1904; 2nd *s* of late Alfred John Drewe, Bournemouth; *m* 1934, Christine Evelyn Isabel Young; two *d*. *Educ:* Cheltenham Coll.; Pembroke Coll., Oxford. Entered ICS, 1928; served in various parts of Sind and Bombay Provinces; Collector and Dist. Magistrate, Ahmedabad, 1938-43; Home Sec. to Government of Bombay, 1944-47; retired from Indian Civil Service, 1947. *Recreation:* gardening. *Address:* Beech Hanger, Woodhurst Park, Oxted, Surrey. *T:* Oxted 3450. *Club:* East India and Sports.

**DREYER, Adm. Sir Desmond (Parry),** GCB 1967 (KCB 1963; CB 1960); CBE 1957; DSC; Member, National Board for Prices and Incomes, since 1968; *b* 6 April 1910; *yr s* of late Adm. Sir Frederic Dreyer, GBE, KCB; *m* 1st,

1934, Elisabeth (*d* 1958), *d* of late Sir Henry Chilton, GCMG; one *s* one *d* (and one *s* decd); 2nd, 1959, Marjorie Gordon, *widow* of Hon. R. G. Whiteley. Served War of 1939-45 (DSC). Cdre First Class, 1955. Chief of Staff, Mediterranean, 1955-57; Asst Chief of Naval Staff, 1958-59; Flag Officer (Flotillas) Mediterranean, 1960-61; Flag Officer Air (Home), 1961-62; Comdr, Far East Fleet, 1962-65; Second Sea Lord, 1965-67; Chief Adviser (Personnel and Logistics) to Sec. of State for Defence, 1967-68. Rear-Adm., 1958; Vice-Adm., 1961; Adm., 1965. Principal Naval ADC to the Queen, 1965-68. Pres., Royal Naval Benevolent Trust, 1970-; Chm., Royal Navy Club. *Address:* 35 Brompton Square, SW3. *T:* 01-584 1647; Brook Cottage, Cheriton, near Alresford, Hants. *T:* Bramdean 215. *Club:* United Service.

**DRIBERG, Thomas Edward Neil;** MP (Lab) Barking since Oct. 1959; journalist, lecturer and broadcaster; *b* Crowborough, Sussex, 22 May 1905; 3rd *s* of John James Street Driberg and Amy Mary Irving Bell; *m* 1951, Mrs Ena Mary Binfield. *Educ:* Lancing; Christ Church, Oxford. On editorial staff of the Daily Express, 1928-43. Contributor since 1943 to Reynolds News and other periodicals; television and radio critic, New Statesman, 1955-61. War Correspondent, War of 1939-45 and in Korea. Elected to Nat. Exec. Cttee of Labour Party 1949, Chm. 1957-58. MP Maldon Div. of Essex, 1942-55 (Ind. 1942-45; Lab. 1945-55). Chairman: House of Commons Select Cttee on Publications and Debates Reports, 1964-65; Select Cttee on Broadcasting of Proceedings in Parliament, 1965-67; Commonwealth and Colonies Gp, Parly Labour Party, 1965-68; Leader, Parly Delegn to Sarawak and Sabah, 1966. Select Preacher before the University of Oxford, 1965. Mem. Historic Buildings Council, 1966-. Finalist (bronze medal) in first Nat. Crossword Championship, 1970. *Publications:* Colonnade, 1949; The Best of Both Worlds, 1953; Beaverbrook: a Study in Power and Frustration, 1956; Guy Burgess: a Portrait with Background, 1956; The Mystery of Moral Re-Armament: a Study of Frank Buchman and his Movement, 1964. *Address:* House of Commons, SW1.

**DRIDAN, Julian Randal,** CMG 1955; Chairman, Housing Trust, South Australia, since 1967; Member Electricity Trust of South Australia since 1953; *b* 24 Nov. 1901; *s* of Sydney John Dridan and Eliza Gundry Dridan; *m* 1925, Ivy Viola Orr; two *d*. *Educ:* South Australian Sch. of Mines; University of Adelaide (BE). Entered service with Govt of S Australia, 1923; construction of locks and weirs on River Murray, 1923-34; District Engineer, 1934-44; Deputy Engineer-in-Chief, 1946; Engineer-in-Chief 1949-67. Mem. River Murray Commission, 1947-. Coronation Medal, 1953. *Recreations:* bowls, fishing. *Address:* 555 Fullarton Road, Mitcham, South Australia. *Club:* Rotary (Adelaide).

**DRINAN, Adam;** *see* Macleod, Joseph T. G.

**DRING, Lt-Col Sir (Arthur) John,** KBE 1952; CIE 1943; JP; *b* 4 Nov. 1902; *s* of late Sir William Dring, KCIE; *m* 1934, Marjorie Wadham (*d* 1943); two *d*; *m* 1946, Alice Deborah, *widow* of Maj.-Gen. J. S. Marshall, CB, DSO, OBE, and *o d* of late Maj.-Gen. Gerald Cree, CB, CMG. *Educ:* Winchester Coll.; RMC, Sandhurst. Joined Guides Cavalry, 1923; Indian Political Service, 1927; Asst Private Sec. to Viceroy, 1930-32; Deputy Commissioner, Dera Ismail Khan, 1935-36; Sec. to Governor, NWFP, 1937-40; Political Agent, South Waziristan, 1940-42 (despatches); Sec. to NWFP Govt Development Depts; Revenue Commissioner, NWFP; Chief Sec. NWFP, 1947; Prime Minister of Bahawalpur, 1948-52; Adviser to Governor of Gold Coast on Togoland Plebiscite, 1955-56. Adviser to Governor-Gen. of Nigeria and the Governor of the Northern Region for the N & S Cameroons Plebiscite, 1959. JP 1954. *Recreations:* riding and gardening. *Address:* Ava Cottage, Purbrook, Hants. *T:* Waterlooville 3000.

**DRING, (Dennis) William,** RA 1955 (ARA 1944); RWS; *b* 26 Jan. 1904; *s* of William Henry Dring; *m* 1931, Grace Elizabeth Rothwell; one *s* two *d*. *Educ:* Slade Sch. of Fine Art. Portrait and landscape painter; during the war official war artist to Ministry of Information, Admiralty, and Air Ministry. *Address:* Windy Ridge, Compton, Winchester, Hants. *T:* Twyford, Hants 2181. *Clubs:* Arts, Chelsea Arts.

**DRING, Lieut-Col Sir John;** *see* Dring, Lieut-Col Sir A. J.

**DRING, William;** *see* Dring, D. W.

**DRINKALL, John Kenneth;** Head of Western European Department, Foreign and Commonwealth Office, since 1970; *b* 1 Jan. 1922; *s* of J. H. Drinkall; *m* 1961, Patricia Ellis; two *s* two *d*. *Educ:* Haileybury Coll.; Brasenose Coll., Oxford. Indian Army, 1942-45. Entered HM Foreign Service, 1947; 3rd Sec., Nanking, 1948; Vice-Consul, Tamsui, Formosa, 1949-51; Acting Consul, 1951; Foreign Office, 1951-53; 1st Sec., Cairo, 1953-56; Foreign Office, 1957-60; 1st Sec., Brasilia, 1960-62; Foreign Office, 1962-65. Appointed Counsellor, 1964; Counsellor: Nicosia, Cyprus, 1965-67; British Embassy, Brussels, 1967-70. *Recreations:* lawn tennis, golf, racquets and squash. *Address:* c/o Foreign and Commonwealth Office, SW1; 12 Fentiman Road, SW8. *T:* 01-735 8974. *Clubs:* Royal Automobile, All England Lawn Tennis.

**DRIVER, Sir Arthur (John),** Kt 1962; JP; *b* 1900; *s* of Percy John Driver, East Sheen, and Mary Amelie Driver; *m* 1937, Margaret, *d* of Hugh Semple McMeekin, Carnmoney, Northern Ireland; one *s* one *d*. Served in Royal Air Force, 1918. Pres. of Law Soc., 1961-62. Chm. London Council of Social Service, 1963-. JP, South West London. *Address:* Frogmore Cottage, East Clandon, Surrey. *Club:* Reform.

**DRIVER, His Honour Major Arthur Robert,** AMIEA; Director, Resources Development, Victorian Employers' Federation; Company Director, since 1960; *b* Albany, W Australia, 25 Nov. 1909; *s* of late Henry and Mary Driver, Western Australia; *m* 1st, 1936; one *s* one *d*; 2nd, 1949, Marjorie Campbell, *d* of George Leighton, Wodonga, Victoria, Australia; one *d*. *Educ:* Hale Sch., Perth, Western Australia; University of Western Australia. Civil Engineer, PWD of WA, 1928-39. War of 1939-45, AMF; Regimental Officer 2/4 Aust. Pioneer Bn, Bde Major, 23rd Aust. Inf. Bde, GSO II (Ops.), Advanced HQ, AMF, 1940-45. Administrator of the Northern Territory and President of Legislative Council of N Territory, Australia, 1946-51; Australian Chief Migration Officer, Rome, 1951-54; Austria and Germany, 1954-56; Chief of Operations, Inter-Govermental Cttee for European Migration, Geneva, 1956-60. *Recreations:* golf, squash, tennis, fishing. *Address:* 15 William Street, Brighton, Victoria 3186, Australia. *T:* 922952. *Clubs:* Naval and Military, VATC, RACV, Kingston Heath (Melbourne).

**DRIVER, Sir Godfrey (Rolles),** Kt 1968; CBE 1958; MC; MA; FBA 1939; Hon. DD:

Aberdeen, 1946; Manchester 1956; Hon. DLitt: Durham, 1948; Oxford, 1970; Hon. LittD, Cambridge, 1964; Professor of Semitic Philology, Oxford University, 1938-62; Hon. Fellow, Magdalen College, 1962 (Fellow, 1919-62); Hon. Fellow, School of Oriental and African Studies, London, 1963; *b* 20 Aug. 1892; *s* of late Rev. S. R. Driver, DD, Regius Prof. of Hebrew and Canon of Christ Church, Oxford, and Mabel Burr; *m* 1924, Madeleine Mary, *d* of John Goulding, Bridlington; three *d*. *Educ:* Winchester Coll. (Scholar); New Coll., Oxford (Scholar). Junior Hall-Houghton Prize for Septuagint, 1912; Pusey and Ellerton Hebrew Scholarship, 1912; 2nd class Classical Moderations, 1913; Gaisford Prizes for Greek Prose, 1913 and Verse, 1916; BA, 1917, MA, 1919; Senior Kennicott Hebrew Scholarship, 1921. Military service BEF (wounded, despatches, MC), 1915-18; EEF, 1919; MEF, 1940-42; Ministry of Information, 1943-44. Fellow, 1919, Classical Tutor, 1919-28, Librarian, 1923-40, Vice-Pres., 1931-32 of Magdalen Coll.; Lecturer, 1927-28 and Reader, 1928 in Comparative Semitic Philology, Oxford Univ.; Pro-proctor, 1923, Hebrew Lecturer at St John's Coll., 1928-38; Dep. Prof. of Hebrew, 1934, 1953-54, 1959-60; Grinfield Lecturer on the Septuagint, Oxford, 1935-39; Joint Dir of New English Bible, 1965; Visiting Prof. at Chicago Univ., 1925, and at Louvain Univ., 1950; Jt Ed. of the Journal of Theological Studies, 1933-40; Pres., International Organisation for the Study of the Old Testament, 1953-59; Leverhulme Fellow, 1939 (resigned owing to war); Schweich Lecturer at British Academy, 1944; Cadbury Lecturer, Birmingham, 1958; Walker Lecturer, Belfast, 1960, Burkitt Medal for Biblical Studies, 1953. *Publications:* Report on Kurdistan and the Kurds (for EEF), 1919; Letters of the First Babylonian Dynasty, 1925; Grammar of the Colloquial Arabic of Syria and Palestine, 1925; Nestorius, the Bazaar of Heracleides (jointly with the Rev. L. Hodgson), 1925; Assyrian Laws and Babylonian Laws (jointly with Sir J. C. Miles), 1935, 1952, 1955; Problems of the Hebrew Verbal System, 1936; Semitic Writing, 1948, 1954; Aramaic Documents from Egypt, 1953; Canaanite Myths and Legends, 1956; Aramaic Documents of the Fifth Century BC (Editor), 1955; Aramaic Documents, 1957; The Judaean Scrolls, 1965. Articles and reviews in English and foreign publications on Semitic languages and Old Testament. *Recreation:* walking. *Address:* 41 Park Town, Oxford. *T:* Oxford 55165.

**DROGHEDA,** 11th Earl of, *cr* 1661 (Ireland); **Charles Garrett Ponsonby Moore,** KBE 1964 (OBE 1946); Baron Moore of Mellifont, 1616; Viscount Moore, 1621; Baron Moore of Cobham (UK), 1954; Managing Director of the Financial Times Ltd; Chairman, Industrial and Trade Fairs Holdings; Director: S. Pearson Publishers; Economist Newspaper Ltd; Chairman: Royal Opera House, Covent Garden Ltd; Governor, The Royal Ballet; *b* 23 April 1910; *o s* of 10th Earl of Drogheda, PC, KCMG; *S* father, 1957; *m* 1935, Joan, *o d* of late William Henry Carr; one *s*. *Educ:* Eton; Trinity Coll., Cambridge. 2nd Lieut Royal Artillery (TA), 1939; Captain 1940. On staff of Ministry of Production, 1942-45. Chm., Newspaper Publishers' Assoc., to 1970. Commander: Legion of Honour (France), 1960; Ordine al Merito (Italy), 1968. *Heir:* Viscount Moore, *qv*. *Address:* Parkside House, Englefield Green, Surrey. *T:* Egham 2800. *Club:* White's.

*See also Sir Richard Latham, Bt.*

**DROMORE, Bishop of, (RC),** since 1944; **Most Rev. Eugene O'Doherty.** Formerly President of St Columb's College, Londonderry. *Address:* Bishop's House, Newry, Ireland.

**DRONFIELD, John,** MA Cambridge; JP; Headmaster of St Peter's School, York, 1937-67; *b* Heather, Leics, 23 Dec. 1898; *er s* of late Matthew H. Dronfield, Heather, Leics; *m* 1939, Sheila Mary Ross, *e d* of F. W. Williams, Greystones, Co. Wicklow; two *s* two *d*. *Educ:* Ashby-de-la-Zouch; Emmanuel Coll., Cambridge. War Service, 1917-19; 2nd Lieut in 2nd Hampshire Regt 1918; Asst Master and House Tutor at Stanley House Sch., Edgbaston, 1923-26; Asst Master at Worksop Coll., 1926-37; Housemaster of Talbot's House in 1927, and for six years Senior Housemaster and Sixth form Mathematical Master at Worksop; Acting Headmaster of Worksop, Aug.-Dec. 1935. JP City of York, 1942. *Address:* Askham Bryan, York. *T:* York 65757. *Club:* Public Schools.

**DROUGHT, C. C. W.;** *see* Worster-Drought.

**DROWER, Lady; (E. M. S.);** hon. DLitt Oxon; hon. DD Uppsala; hon. Fellow, School of Oriental and African Studies, University of London; writer and lecturer, student of religions, languages and folklore of the Middle East, particularly of the Mandæans; *b* 1 Dec. 1879; *d* of Rev. S. W. Stevens, MA, LLM; *widow of* Sir E. M. Drower, KBE; two *s* one *d*. *Educ:* sch., travel, and long residence in Middle East. In earlier life wrote novels and travel books under name of E. S. Stevens. Awarded Lidzbarski Gold Medal by the Deutsche Morgenländische Gesellschaft, 1964. *Publications: novels:* The Veil, 1909; The Mountain of God, 1910; The Lure, 1911; The Long Engagement, 1911; The Earthen Drum, 1912; Sarah Eden, 1914; Allward, 1915; And What Happened? 1916; The Safety Candle, 1917; Magdalene, 1919; Sophy: a Tale of Baghdad, 1924; The Losing Game, 1926; Ishtar, 1927; *travel books:* My Sudan Year, 1912; By Tigris and Euphrates, 1923; Cedars, Saints and Sinners in Syria, 1926; *orientalia:* Folk Tales of Iraq, 1931 (under name of Stevens); The Mandæans of Iraq and Iran: their Cults, Customs, Magic, Legends, and Folklore, 1937 (reprinted Leiden, 1962); Peacock Angel, 1941; Water into Wine: a study of ritual idiom in the Middle and Near East, 1956; The Secret Adam: a study of Nasoraean Gnosticism, 1960. Translations from the Mandaic: The Book of the Zodiac, 1949; The Diwan Abatur (Studi e Testi 151), 1950; Explanatory Commentary of the Marriage Ceremony of the Great Shishlam (Biblica et Orientalia No. 12), 1950; The Haran Gawaita and The Baptism of Hibil-Ziwa (Studi e Testi 176), 176), 1953; The Canonical Prayer Book of the Mandæans, 1959; A Thousand and Twelve Questions (Deutsche Akademie der Wissenschaften), 1960; The Coronation of the Great Šišlam, 1962; A Pair of Nasoraean Commentaries, 1963; A Mandaic Dictionary (with R. Macuch), 1963. *Address:* The Cottage, 8 Willenhall Avenue, New Barnet, Herts. *T:* 01-449 4351.

**DROWLEY, Air Vice-Marshal Thomas Edward,** CB 1947; CBE 1943 (OBE 1933); Director of Equipment, RAF delegation, Washington, 1941-46; Director-General of Equipment, Air Ministry, 1946-49; retd 1949. Legion of Merit (Commander) USA. *Address:* Cedarwood, Christmas Lane, Farnham Common, Bucks. *T:* Farnham Common 4151.

**DRUCKER, Prof. Peter (Ferdinand);** writer and consultant; Professor of Management, New York University, since 1950; *b* 19 Nov. 1909; *s* of Adolph B. Drucker and Caroline (*née* Bond); *m* 1937, Doris Schmitz; one *s* three *d*.

*Educ:* Austria, Germany, England. Investment banker, London, 1933-36; newspapers, 1937-41; Professor of Philosophy and Politics, Bennington Coll., Bennington, Vt, USA, 1942-49. Management Consultant (internat. practice among businesses and govts) (as well as Professorships), 1948-. Holds hon. doctorates, and medals for his work. Hon. FBIM; FAAAS; Fellow: Amer. Acad. of Management; Internat. Acad. of Management. Order of Sacred Treasure (Japan). *Publications:* End of Economic Man, 1939; Future of Industrial Man, 1942; Concept of Corporation, 1946; The New Society, 1950; Practice of Management, 1954; America's Next Twenty Years, 1959; Landmarks of Tomorrow, 1960; Managing for Results, 1964; The Effective Executive, 1967; The Age of Discontinuity, 1969; Technology, Management and Society, 1970. *Recreations:* mountaineering; Japanese history and paintings. *Address:* 138 North Mountain Avenue, Montclair, NJ 07042, USA. *T:* (201) 746-8123. *Club:* University (New York).

**DRUCQUER, Sir Leonard,** Kt 1968; CEng, FIEE; *b* 4 Feb. 1902; *s* of late William Henry and Sophie Drucquer; *m* 1928, Inez Hildegard Banham. *Educ:* Haberdashers' Aske's Sch.; Polytechnic Coll. of Engineering, Regent Street, W1. Joined British Thomson Houston Ltd, 1920; Manager, Switchgear Sales, 1945; Manager, Home Sales (Plant and Apparatus), 1950; Director, Home Sales, 1956; Dir and Gen. Manager, AEI Heavy Plant Div., 1958; Consultant to Industrial Group, AEI, 1966-68. Pres. Instn of Electrical Engrs, 1965-66; Chm., Council of Engineering Instns, 1967-69; Mem. Council, Loughborough Univ. of Technology, 1967-; Governor, Lanchester Polytechnic, 1969-. *Recreation:* gardening. *Address:* Crick Manor, near Rugby, Warwicks. *T:* Crick 353. *Clubs:* United Service, united Hunts.

**DRUITT, Sir Harvey;** *see* Druitt, Sir W. A. H.

**DRUITT, Sir (William Arthur) Harvey,** KCB 1965 (CB 1951); HM Procurator-General and Treasury Solicitor since 1964; *b* 19 April 1910; *s* of late Arthur Druitt, Gullane, East Lothian; *m* 1940, Joan Holdsworth, *d* of late L. D. P. Swift, Eastbourne; one *s* (and one *d* decd). *Educ:* Edinburgh Acad.; Oriel Coll., Oxford. Entered Dept of HM Procurator-General and Treasury Solicitor, 1937; Deputy Treasury Solicitor, 1956-63. *Address:* 76 Baron's Keep, Baron's Court, W14. *T:* 01-603 6433. *Clubs:* Athenæum, Hurlingham.

**DRUMALBYN,** 1st Baron, *cr* 1963; **Niall Malcolm Stewart Macpherson,** PC 1962; Minister without Portfolio, since Oct. 1970; *b* 3 Aug. 1908; 3rd *s* of late Sir T. Stewart Macpherson, CIE, LLD, and of Lady Macpherson, Newtonmore, Inverness-shire; *m* Margaret Phyllis, *d* of late J. J. Runge and of Mrs N. C. Ross (*see* N. C. Runge); two *d* (and one *d* decd). *Educ:* Edinburgh Academy; Fettes Coll.; Trinity Coll., Oxford (Scholar). First Class Honour Mods. 1929; First Class Litt Hum. 1931; MA; Rugby Football Blue, 1928. Business training with J. & J. Colman Ltd; Manager Turkish branch, 1933-35; Export branch, London, 1936-39. Commissioned QO Cameron Highlanders, TA June 1939: Staff Coll., 1942; Temp. Major 1942; MP (Nat L) 1945-50 (Nat L and U), 1950-63, Dumfriesshire. Scottish Whip, 1945-55; Chm., Commonwealth Producers' Organisation, 1952-55, Pres., 1967-. Member BBC General Advisory Council, 1952-55. Joint Under-Sec. of State for Scotland, 1955-60; Parly Sec., Board of Trade, 1960-62; Minister of Pensions and National Insurance, 1962-63; Minister of State, Board of Trade, 1963-64. Chairman: Advertising Standards Authority, 1965-; Overseas Policy Cttee, Associated British Chambers of Commerce, 1969-. *Heir:* none. *Address:* High Larch, Iver Heath, Bucks. *Clubs:* Carlton, Royal Automobile; New (Edinburgh).

**DRUMMOND,** family name of **Earl of Perth** and of **Baron Strange.**

**DRUMMOND, Lieut-Gen. Sir Alexander;** *see* Drummond, Lieut-Gen. Sir W. A. D.

**DRUMMOND, Maj.-Gen. Anthony John D.;** *see* Deane-Drummond.

**DRUMMOND, Dame (Edith) Margaret,** DBE 1966 (OBE 1960); MA; Director of the Women's Royal Naval Service, 1964-June 1967; *b* 4 Sept. 1917; *d* of Prof. Robert James Drummond and Marion (*née* Street). *Educ:* Park Sch., Glasgow; Aberdeen Univ. Joined WRNS, April 1941 and progressed through various ranks of the Service. *Recreations:* gardening, reading, theatres, concerts and friends. *Address:* Somersham Cottage, Saxlingham, Holt, Norfolk, *Club:* University Women's.

**DRUMMOND, Dame Margaret;** *see* Drummond, Dame E. M.

**DRUMMOND, Lieut-Gen. (Retd) Sir (William) Alexander (Duncan),** KBE 1957 (CBE 1951; OBE 1945); CB 1954; Director-General, Army Medical Services, War Office, 1956-61 (Deputy Director-General, 1954-56); late RAMC; *b* 1901. *Educ:* Dundee Univ. MRCS, LRCP 1924; DLO Eng. 1932; FRCS 1947. Formerly: Registrar, Throat, Nose and Ear Hospital, Golden Square; Registrar, Throat, Nose and Ear Dept, Charing Cross Hosp. Served War of 1939-45 (despatches five times, OBE). Col Comdt RAMC, 1961-66. KStJ, 1959. Hon. LLD: Birmingham, 1959; Punjab, 1960. *Publications:* contributions to medical journals. *Address:* c/o National and Grindlay's Bank, 13 St James's Square, SW1.

**DRUMMOND, Sir William (Hugh Dudley) Williams-,** 6th Bt *cr* 1828; retired; *b* 13 Feb. 1901; *s* of Sir Francis Dudley Williams-Drummond, KBE (4th *s* of 3rd Bt) (*d* 1935) and Marguerite Violet Maud (*d* 1939), *d* of Sir Andrew Agnew, 8th Bt; *S* cousin, Sir James Hamlyn Williams Williams-Drummond, 5th Bt, 1970; unmarried. *Educ:* Eton. *Recreations:* hockey, tennis. *Heir:* none. *Address:* Guessens, Welwyn, Herts. *T:* Welwyn 4049.

**DRUMMOND-WOLFF, Henry;** *b* 16 July 1899; *s* of late Cecil Drummond-Wolff (*s* of Rt Hon. Sir Henry Drummond-Wolff, PC, GCB, GCMG), and Zaida Drummond-Wolff, Caplanne, Billère, Pau, BP, France; *m* 1933, Margaret, *d* of late Gibson Fahnestock, Newport, Rhode Island, USA; one *d*. *Educ:* Radley (Scholar); RMC Sandhurst (Prize Cadet). Served with Royal Flying Corps, 1917; retired from Royal Air Force, 1919; contested Rotherham Feb. 1933; MP (C) Basingstoke Division of Hants, 1934-35. Life Mem., Commonwealth Parliamentary Assoc. Member of: Grand Council of Primrose League; Migration Council, 1951; Cttee of Empire Economic Union, 1934- (Vice-Chm. 1949; President 1952); Council of Empire Industries Association, 1934-; Council of Empire Industries Association and British Empire League. Has travelled extensively in Europe, USA, and British Commonwealth. *Publications:* British Declaration of Independence, 1947; Declaration of Independence and Interdependence, 1948;

Commonwealth, 1949; Sovereignty and Fiscal Freedom, 1952; Commonwealth Development and Defence, 1953; Constructive Conservatism, 1953; The Rule of Reciprocity, 1954; Europe and the Commonwealth, 1961; The Commonwealth, 1962; Commonwealth, 1966. *Recreation:* travel. *Address:* Beau Rivage, Lausanne, Switzerland; Newport, Rhode Island, USA. *Clubs:* Carlton, Pratt's, Royal Air Force, 1900; Clambake (Newport, USA).

**DRUON, Maurice Samuel Roger Charles;** Chevalier de la Légion d'Honneur; author; Member of the French Academy since 1966; *b* Paris 23 April 1918; *s* of René Druon de Reyniac and Léonilla Jenny Samuel-Cros; *m* 1968, Madeleine Marignac. *educ:* Lycée Michelet and Ecole des Sciences Politiques, Paris. Ecole de Cavalerie de Saumur, aspirant, 1940; joined Free French Forces, London, 1942; Attaché Commissariat à l'Intérieur et Direction de l'Information, 1943; War Correspondent, 1944-45; Lieut de réserve de cavalerie. Journalist, 1946-47; awarded Prix Goncourt, 1948, for novel Les Grandes Families; Prix de Monaco, 1966. Officier des Arts et Lettres, 1964. *Publications:* Lettres d'un Européen, 1944; La Dernière Brigade (The Last Detachment), 1946 (publ. in England 1957); Les Grandes Familles, La Chute des Corps, Rendez-Vous aux Enfers, 1948-51 (trilogy publ. in England under title The Curtain falls, 1959); La Volupté d'Etre (Film of Memory), 1954 (publ. in England 1955); Les Rois Maudits (The Accursed Kings), 1955-60 (six vols: The Iron King, The Strangled Queen, The Poisoned Crown, The Royal Succession, The She-Wolf of France, The Lily and the Lion, publ. in England 1956-61); Tistou les pouces verts (Tistou of the green fingers), 1957 (publ. in England 1958); Alexandre le Dieu (Alexander the God), 1958 (publ. in Eng. 1960); Des Seigneurs de la Plaine—(The Black Prince and other stories), 1962 (publ. in Eng. 1962); Les Mémoires de Zeus I (The Memoirs of Zeus), 1963 (in Eng. 1964); Bernard Buffet, 1964; Paris, de César à Saint Louis (The History of Paris from Caesar to St Louis), 1964 (in Eng. 1969); Le Pouvoir, 1965; Les Tambours de la Mémoire, 1965; Le Bonheur des Uns, 1967; Les Mémoires de Zeus II, 1967; L'Avenir en décarroi, 1968; *plays:* Mégarée, 1942; Un Voyageur, 1953; La Contessa, 1962; *song:* Le Chant des Partisans (with Joseph Kessel and Anna Marly), 1943 (London). *Recreations:* riding, travel. *Address:* 73 rue de Varenne, Paris 7e, France. *Club:* Savile.

**DRURY, Sir Alan (Nigel),** Kt 1950; CBE 1944; FRS 1937; MA, MD Cantab; FRCP; MRCS; *b* 3 Nov. 1889; *s* of Henry George and Elizabeth Rose Drury; *m* 1916, Daphne Marguerite Brownsword; one *s* one *d*. *Educ:* Merchant Taylors' Sch., London; Gonville and Caius Coll., Cambridge; St Thomas' Hospital, London. George Henry Lewes Student in Physiology; War service, Major RAMC, DADMS (Sanitary) 9th Secunderabad Div., India; late Fellow of Trinity Hall, Cambridge; late Huddersfield Lecturer in Special Pathology, University of Cambridge; Mem. of Scientific Staff, Medical Research Council, 1921-43; late Dir Lister Institute; Mem. of Scientific Staff, Agricultural Research Council, 1952-60. Hon. Fellow Trinity Hall. *Publications:* in Heart, Journal of Physiology, Quarterly Journal of Experimental Physiology, etc. *Address:* 25 Millington Road, Cambridge. *Club:* Athenæum.

**DRURY, Allen Stuart;** Author; *b* Houston, Texas, 2 Sept. 1918; *s* of Alden M. and Flora A. Drury. *Educ:* Stanford Univ. (BA). Served with US Army, 1942-43. Ed., The Tulare (Calif) Bee, 1939-41; county ed., The Bakersfield Californian, Bakersfield, Calif, 1941-42; United Press Senate Staff, Washington, DC, 1943-45; freelance correspondent, 1946; Nation Ed., Pathfinder Magazine, Washington, DC, 1947-53; National Staff, Washington Evening Star, 1953-54; Senate Staff, New York Times, 1954-59. Sigma Delta Chi Award for Editorial Writing, 1942; hon. LitD, Rollins Coll., Winter Park, Fla, 1961. *Publications:* Advise and Consent, 1959 (Pulitzer Prize for Fiction, 1960); A Shade of Difference, 1962; A Senate Journal, 1963; That Summer, 1965; Three Kids in a Cart, 1965; Capable of Honor, 1966; "A Very Strange Society", 1967; Preserve and Protect, 1968; The Throne of Saturn, 1971. *Address:* Box 972, Maitland, Fla 32751, USA. *Clubs:* Cosmos, University, National Press (Washington, DC); Players' (New York); Bohemian (San Francisco); University (Orlando, Fla).

**DRURY, Charles Mills,** CBE 1946 (MBE 1942); DSO 1944; ED 1956; President of the Treasury Board, Canada, since 1968; *b* 17 May 1912; *s* of Victor Montague Drury, Montreal, and Pansy Jessie Mills, Ottawa; *m* 1939, Jane Ferrier Counsell; two *s* two *d*. *Educ:* Bishops Coll. Sch., Lennoxville, Quebec; Royal Military Coll. of Canada, Kingston, Ontario; McGill Univ., Montreal (BCL); University of Paris, France. Practised at law, 1936-39; served War of 1939-45, Canadian Army (final rank Brig.). Chief of UNNRA Mission to Poland, 1945-46; Dept of External Affairs, Canada, 1947-48; Dep. Minister of National Defence, Canada, 1949-55; Minister, Dept of Defence Production, and Minister of Industry, 1963-68. Chevalier de la Légion d'Honneur (France), 1946; Order of Polonia Restituta (Poland), 1946. *Address:* (home) Ottawa, Ont; (business) Confederation Building, Wellington Street, Ottawa, Ont, Canada. *Clubs:* Rideau (Ottawa); Royal St Lawrence Yacht (Dorval, Que).

**DRURY, Paul Dalou,** PRE 1970 (RE 1932); Etcher and painter; Principal, Goldsmiths' College School of Art, 1967-69, retired; *b* London, 14 Oct. 1903; *s* of late Alfred Drury, RA; *m* 1937, Enid Marie, painter, *o c* of late Victor Solomon; one *s*. *Educ:* King's Coll. Sch.; Bristol Grammar Sch.; Westminster Sch.; Goldsmiths' Coll. Sch. of Art. British Institution Scholarship in Engraving, 1924; has exhibited etchings and paintings at the Royal Academy, and galleries in England, and prints at representative exhibitions of British Art in Paris, Vienna, Florence, Stockholm, Buenos Aires, Tokyo, etc., and in Canada and the USA; etchings and drawings acquired by the Print Room, British Museum, Ashmolean, The Wakefield Collection, Contemporary Art Soc., Boston, USA, and by various museums and galleries in the provinces and abroad. Mem., faculty of Engraving, British Sch. at Rome. Governor, W Surrey Coll. of Art, 1969- . *Recreation:* music. *Address:* Rangers Cottage, Nutley, Uckfield, Sussex. *T:* Nutley 2857. *Club:* Arts.

**DRYDEN, Sir John (Stephen Gyles),** 8th and 11th Bt *cr* 1795 and 1733; *b* 26 Sept. 1943; *s* of Sir Noel Percy Hugh Dryden, 7th and 10th Bt, and of Rosamund Mary, *e d* of late Stephen Scrope; *S* father, 1970; *m* 1970, Diana Constance, *o d* of Cyril Tomlinson, Highland Park, Wellington, NZ. *Educ:* Oratory School. *Address:* c/o Midland Bank Ltd, Redhill, Surrey. *Club:* Public Schools.

**D'SILVA, Prof. John Leonard,** JP; Halliburton Professor of Physiology, King's College, London, since 1959; *b* 27 Oct. 1910; *e c* of Albert Robert and Kathleen Isabelle D'Silva;

*m* 1936, Phyllis Maude Tyler; one *s* one *d*. *Educ:* South India. BSc (Special) Chemistry, King's Coll., London, 1929; PhD Chemistry (Organic), 1931; Sir Halley Stewart Fellow, 1933; Demonstrator in Physiology at St Bartholomew's Medical Coll., 1936-39; DSc, 1940, MB, BS London, 1940-42, MRCP, 1943, FRCP 1969. House Physician, Medical Professorial Unit, St Bartholomew's Hosp., 1942; Chief Asst, St Bartholomew's Hosp., and Asst Physician, EMS, 1942-44; Lecturer in Physiology, 1944-46, Reader in Physiology, 1946-48, St Bartholomew's Hosp. Medical Coll., EC1; Prof. of Physiology, London Hosp. Med. Coll., E1, 1948-59. JP 1964. *Publications:* papers in various medical journals. *Recreations:* gardening, photography. *Address:* 36 Avenue Road, St Albans, Herts. *T:* St Albans 54701.

**D'SOUZA, Most Rev. Albert V.;** *b* Mangalore, India, 5 April 1904. Priest, 1928; nominated Auxiliary Bishop of Mysore, 1959; consecrated Bishop, 1959; nominated Archbishop of Calcutta, Aug. 1962; took possession of Archdiocesan See of Calcutta, Dec. 1962; retired, 1969.

**DUBLIN, Archbishop of, and Primate of Ireland,** since 1969; **Most Rev. Alan Alexander Buchanan;** Bishop of Glendalough and of Kildare; *m* 1935, Audrey Kathryn, *d* of W. A. Crone, Knock, Belfast; two *d*. *Educ:* Trinity College, Dublin. Exhibitioner, Moderator, 1928, TCD Deacon, 1930; Priest, 1931. Assistant Missioner, Church of Ireland Mission, Belfast, 1930-33, Head Missioner, 1933-37; Incumbent of Inver, Larne, 1937-45; Incumbent of St Mary, Belfast, 1945-55; Rural Dean of Mid-Belfast, 1951-55; Rector of Bangor, Co. Down, 1955-58; Canon of St Patrick's Cathedral, Dublin, 1957-58; Bishop of Clogher, 1958-69. Chaplain to the Forces, Emergency Commission, 1942-45. *Address:* The See House, 17 Temple Road, Dublin 6.

**DUBLIN, Archbishop of, and Primate of Ireland, (RC),** since 1940; **Most Rev. John Charles McQuaid,** DD, MA, DLitt, MRIA; FRSAI; *b* Cootehill, Co. Cavan, 28 July 1895; *e s* of late Dr Eugene Ward McQuaid. *Educ:* St Patrick's Diocesan Coll., Cavan; Blackrock Coll.; Clongowes Wood Coll.; National Univ. of Ireland; Rome. Entered Novitiate of Holy Ghost Fathers at Kimmage Manor, 1913; professed, 1914; ordained priest, 1924. Pres., Blackrock Coll., 1931-39; Chm. Catholic Headmasters' Assoc. for many years; represented Ireland at International Education Congresses in Brussels, The Hague, Luxembourg, and Fribourg; Rector of Catholic Univ., Ireland. *Address:* Archbishop's House, Dublin 9.

**DUBLIN, Auxiliary Bishop of, (RC);** *see* Dunne, Most Rev. Patrick.

**DUBLIN,** (Christ Church), **Dean of;** *see* Salmon, Very Rev. T. N. D. C.

**DUBLIN,** (St Patrick's), **Dean of;** *see* Griffin, Very Rev. V. G. B.

**DU BOISROUVRAY, Rt. Rev. Bernard;** Abbot, OSB; *b* Bagnères de Bigorre (Hautes Pyrénées), 1877. *Educ:* Paris; Cadet at the French Military Coll., Saint Cyr, 1897-98. On the staff of the Bank of France, 1900-09; took his degree in Civil Law, 1902; professed at Farnborough Abbey, 1911; priest, 1915; prior, 1920; Abbot-Coadjutor of Farnborough, 1924-37; Abbot, 1937-41; resigned, 1941. *Publication:* Vie de Mgr Gay, 2 vols 1922, which was awarded a prize by the French Academy. *Address:* St John's Convent, Kiln Green, Twyford, Berks. *T:* Wargrave 64.

**DU BOULAY, Prof. Francis Robin Houssemayne;** Professor of Mediæval History in the University of London, at Bedford Coll., since 1960; *b* 19 Dec. 1920; *er s* of Philip Houssemayne Du Boulay and Mercy Tyrrell (*née* Friend); *m* 1948, Cecilia Burnell Matthews; two *s* one *d*. *Educ:* Christ's Hospital; Phillip's Academy, Andover, Mass., USA; Balliol Coll., Oxford. Williams Exhibitioner at Balliol Coll., 1939; Friends' Ambulance Unit and subsequently Royal Artillery, 1940-45; MA 1947; Asst lecturer at Bedford Coll., 1947, Lecturer, 1949; Reader in Mediæval History, in University of London, 1955. FRHistS (Hon. Sec., 1961-65). *Publications:* A Handlist of medieval ecclesiastical terms, 1952; The Register of Archbishop Bourgchier, 1953; Medieval Bexley, 1961; Documents Illustrative of Medieval Kentish Society, 1964; The Lordship of Canterbury, 1966; An Age of Ambition, 1970. Various essays and papers in specialist journals. *Address:* Broadmead, Riverhead, Sevenoaks, Kent.

**du BOULAY, Roger William H.;** *see* Houssemayne du Boulay.

**DuBRIDGE, Lee A(lvin);** Science Adviser to President of the United States, since 1969; *b* 21 Sept. 1901; *s* of Frederick A. and Elizabeth Browne DuBridge; *m* 1925, Doris May Koht; one *s* one *d*. *Educ:* Cornell Coll., Mt Vernon, Ia (BA); University of Wisconsin (MA, PhD). Instructor in Physics, University of Wisconsin, 1925-26; Nat. Research Council Fellow at Calif. Inst. Tech., 1926-28; Asst Prof. Physics, Washington Univ. (St Louis, Mo.), 1928-33; Assoc. Prof., Washington Univ., 1933-34; Prof. of Physics and Dep. Chm., University of Rochester (NY), 1934-46; Dean of Faculty, University of Rochester, 1938-42; on leave from University of Rochester, 1940-45, as Dir of Radiation Lab. of Nat. Def. Research Comm. at MIT, Cambridge; Pres., California Inst. of Techn., Pasadena, 1946-69. Hon. ScD: Cornell Coll.; Mt Vernon, Indiana, 1940; Weslyan Univ., Middletown, Conn., 1946; Polytechnic Inst. of Brooklyn, New York, 1946; University of Brit. Columbia, Can., 1947; Washington, 1948; Occidental Coll., 1952; Maryland, 1955; Columbia, 1957; Indiana, 1957; Wisconsin, 1957; Pennsylvania Mil. Coll., Chester, Pa, 1962; DePauw, Indiana, 1962; Pomona Coll., Claremont, Calif., 1965; Carnegie Inst. of Techn., Pittsburgh, 1965; Hon. LLD: California, 1948; Rochester, 1953; Southern California, 1957; Northwestern, 1958; Loyola, Los Angeles, 1963; Notre Dame, Indiana, 1967; Illinois Inst. Technology, 1968; Hon. LHD: University Judaism, Los Angeles, 1958; Redlands, 1958; Hon. DCL, Union Coll., Schenectady, NY, 1961; Hon. DSc: Rockefeller Institute, NY, 1965; Tufts Univ., 1969; Syracuse Univ., 1969; Rensselaer Polytech. Inst., 1970. King's Medal, 1946; Research Corp. Award, 1947; Medal for Merit of US Govt, 1948, Golden Key Award, 1959; Leif Erikson Award, 1959. Arthur Noble Award, 1961. *Publications:* Photoelectric Phenomena (with A. L. Hughes), 1932; New Theories of Photoelectric Effect (Paris), 1934; Introduction to Space, 1960; articles in various scientific and other journals. *Address:* 2440 Virginia Avenue, Washington, DC 20037, USA. *T:* 293-1216. *Clubs:* California, Sunset (Los Angeles); Bohemian (San Francisco); Cosmos (Washington, DC).

**DUBUFFET, Jean;** artist (exclusively since 1942); *b* Le Havre, 31 July 1901; *s* of George S.

Dubuffet and Jeanne (*née* Paillettle); *m* 1st, 1927, Paulette Bret (marr. diss., 1935); one *d*; 2nd, 1937, Emilie (Lili) Carlu. *Educ:* art schs, Paris. Settled at Vence, 1955, after travels. *Exhibitions include:* Paris, 1944; Pierre Matisse Gall., NY, 1947; Cercle Volney and Galerie Rive Gauche, Paris, 1954. *One-man exhibitions:* ICA, London, 1955; Tooth, London, 1958; Daniel Cordier, Paris, 1960, 1962, 1963; Robert Fraser, London, 1962, 1964, 1966. *Retrospective exhibitions:* Musée des Arts Décoratifs, Paris, 1960; Museum of Modern Art, NY, 1962; Tate Gall., London, 1966. *Address:* 51 rue de Verneuil, Paris 7e, France.

**DU CANE, Comdr Peter,** CBE 1964 (OBE 1942); MRINA; CEng, FIMechE; AFRAeS; FRSA; Royal Navy (emergency list); Deputy Chairman, Vosper Ltd, Shipbuilders, Portsmouth, since 1963 (Managing Director, 1931-63); *b* 18 March 1901; *s* of C. H. C. Du Cane, DL, Braxted Park, Essex, and Dorothy Blenkinsopp (*née* Coulson), Newbrough Park, Northumberland; *m* 1929, Victoria Geraldine Pole Carew; one *s* two *d*. *Educ:* RNC, Osborne, Dartmouth, Keyham and Greenwich. Served as midshipman afloat, European War, 1917-18; Fleet Air Arm as pilot and technical officer, 1940-41. Specialised design and construction high speed craft including Bluebird II, holder of world's unlimited water speed record at 141.7 mph, for which awarded Segrave Medal for year 1939, also John Cobb's Crusader, first boat to exceed 200 mph, 1952. Designs include many Motor Torpedo Boats used by Royal Navy, Royal Barge, and High Speed Rescue Launches for RAF, also Tramontana, winner of Daily Express Internat. Offshore Power Boat Race, 1962. *Publication:* High Speed Small Craft, 1951, 3rd edn, 1964. *Address:* Seamark, Glandore, Co. Cork, Ireland. *T:* Leap 95. *Clubs:* White's; Royal Yacht Squadron (Cowes).

**du CANN, Rt. Hon. Edward Dillon Lott,** PC 1964; MP (C) Taunton Division of Somerset since Feb. 1956; Founder, Unicorn Group of Unit Trusts, 1957; Chairman: Barclays Unicorn Ltd; Dillon Walker & Co. Ltd; Griffin Assurance Co. Ltd; Keyser Ullman Holdings Ltd; Director: Barclays Bank Trust Company Ltd; Barclays Bank Ltd (London Board); Central and District Properties (Chairman designate); Bow Group Publications Ltd; *b* 28 May 1924; *er s* of C. G. L. du Cann, Barrister-at-Law, and Janet (*née* Murchie); *m* 1962, Sallie Innes, *e d* of late James Henry Murchie, Caldy, Cheshire; one *s* two *d*. *Educ:* Colet Court; Woodbridge Sch.; St John's Coll., Oxford (MA, Law). Served with RNVR, 1943-46. Contested West Walthamstow Div., Gen. Election, 1951; Contested Barrow-in-Furness Div., Gen. Election, 1955. Vice-Pres., Somerset and Wilts Trustee Savings Bank, 1956-; Chairman, Association of Unit Trust Managers, 1961. Joint Hon. Sec.: United National Parl. Group, 1961-62; Conservative Parly Finance Group, 1961-62; Mem., Select Cttee on House of Lords Reform, 1962. Economic Sec. to the Treasury, 1962-63; Minister of State, Board of Trade, 1963-64. Chairman, Cons. Party Organisation, 1965-67. Visiting Fellow, Univ. of Lancaster Business School, 1970-. Commodore, House of Commons Yacht Club, 1962. Lecturer, broadcaster. *Publications:* Investing Simplified, 1959; articles on financial and international affairs. *Recreations:* travel, gardening, sailing. *Address:* 19 Lord North Street, SW1. *T:* 01-222 5950; Easterlands, Sampford Arundel, Wellington, Somerset. *Clubs:* Carlton, Somerset County (Taunton).

**DUCAT, David;** Chairman, The Metal Box Co. Ltd., 1967-70, retired (Managing Director 1949-66; Vice-Chairman 1952-66; Deputy Chairman 1966-67); *b* 1 June 1904; *s* of William John and Amy Ducat; *m* 1933, Hilary Mildred Stokes; three *s* one *d*. *Educ:* Merchant Taylors' Sch.; Gonville and Caius Coll., Cambridge (MA). ACIS 1935. Min. of Production, 1942-45. British Tin Box Manufacturers Fedn: Chm., 1952-61; Vice-Chm., 1961-69. Mem. Court of Assts, Merchant Taylors' Co., 1956- (Master, 1964). Vice-Pres., British Inst. of Management (Council Chm., 1966-68); Mem. Coun., City University, 1966-. FCIS 1967. *Address:* Morar, 16 Sandy Lodge Road, Moor Park, Rickmansworth, Herts. *T:* Rickmansworth 73562. *Club:* United University.

**DUCHÊNE, Louis-François;** Director, Institute for Strategic Studies, since 1969; *b* 17 Feb. 1927; *s* of Louis Adrien Duchêne and Marguerite Lucienne Duchêne (*née* Lainé); *m* 1952, Anne Margaret Purves; one *d*. *Educ:* St Paul's Sch.; London Sch. of Economics. Leader writer, Manchester Guardian, 1949-52; Press attaché, High Authority, European Coal and Steel Community, Luxembourg, 1952-55; Correspondent of The Economist, Paris, 1956-58; Dir, Documentation Centre of Action Cttee for United States of Europe (Chm. Jean Monnet), Paris, 1958-63; Editorial writer, The Economist, London, 1963-67. Recipient of Ford Foundation research grant on internat. affairs, 1967-69. *Address:* 3 Powis Villas, Brighton, Sussex, BN1 3HD. *T:* Brighton 29258.

**DUCHESNE, Jacques;** *see* Saint-Denis, Michel Jacques.

**DUCIE,** 6th Earl of *cr* 1837; **Basil Howard Moreton;** Baron Ducie, 1763; Baron Moreton, 1837; *b* 15 Nov. 1917; *s* of Hon. Algernon Howard Moreton (2nd *s* of 4th Earl) (*d* 1951), and Dorothy Edith Annie, *d* of late Robert Bell; *S* uncle 1952; *m* 1950, Alison May, *d* of L. A. Bates, Pialba, Queensland; three *s* one *d*. *Heir: s* Lord Moreton, *qv*. *Address:* Tortworth House, Falfield, Glos.

**DUCKER, Herbert Charles,** BSc London; NDA; Field Officer Groundnut Research, under the Federal Ministry of Agriculture, Rhodesia and Nyasaland, now retired; *b* 13 May 1900; *s* of Charles Richard and Gertrude Louise Ducker; *m* 1925, Marjorie, *y d* of late Charles Tuckfield, AMICE; two *s* one *d*. *Educ:* Kingston Grammar Sch., Kingston-on-Thames; South-Eastern Agricultural Coll., Wye; Imperial Coll. of Science, South Kensington. British Cotton Industry Research Assoc. Laboratories; Asst Cotton Specialist, Nyasaland, 1922; Cotton Specialist, Empire Cotton Growing Corporation, Nyasaland, 1925-56; Superintendent-Curator of the National Botanic Gardens, Salisbury, Southern Rhodesia, under the Federal Ministry of Agriculture, of Rhodesia and Nyasaland, 1957. *Publications:* Annual Reports on Cotton Research work 1925-55, carried out in Nyasaland; articles on Cotton Growing. *Recreation:* fishing. *Address:* c/o P. C. Ducker, Private Bag 603, Sinoia, Rhodesia. *Club:* Royal Over-Seas League.

**DUCKHAM, Prof. Alec Narraway,** CBE 1950 (OBE 1945); Professor of Agriculture, University of Reading, 1955-69; *b* 23 Aug. 1903; *e s* of Alexander Duckham, FCS, and Violet Ethel Duckham (*née* Narraway); *m* 1932, Audrey Mary Polgreen (*d* 1969), St Germans, Cornwall; one *s* two *d*. *Educ:* Oundle Sch.; Clare Coll., Cambridge. MA (Hons) Cantab.: Cambridge Dip. Agric. Sci. (dist. in

Animal Husbandry), 1926; FIBiol; Silver Research Medallist, Royal Agricultural Society, England, 1926. Research and Advisory work on Animal Husbandry at Cambridge, Aberdeen, Belfast, 1927-39. Chm. Home and Overseas Agric. Supplies Cttees and Dir of Supply Plans Div., Min. of Food, 1941-45. Agric. Attaché, Brit. Embassy, Washington, and Agric. Adviser to UK High Comr, Ottawa, 1945-50. Asst Sec. to Min. of Agriculture and Fisheries, 1950-54. Liaison Officer (SE Region), to the Minister of Agriculture, Fisheries and Food, 1965-. Vice-Chm., Alex. Duckham and Co. Ltd, 1945-68. *Publications:* Animal Industry in the British Empire, 1932; American Agriculture, 1952 (HMSO); The Fabric of Farming, 1958; Agricultural Synthesis: The Farming Year, 1963; (with G. B. Masefield) Farming Systems of the World, 1970. *Recreations:* painting and music. *Address:* Studio Cottage, Bessels Way, Didcot Road, Blewbury, Berks. *Clubs:* Farmers', Royal Automobile.

**DUCKMANTON, Talbot Sydney;** General Manager, Australian Broadcasting Commission, since 1965 (Deputy General Manager, 1964-65); *b* 26 Oct. 1921; *s* of Sydney James Duckmanton. Joined Australian Broadcasting Commission, 1939. War Service: AIF and RAAF. *Address:* c/o Australian Broadcasting Commission, 145 Elizabeth Street, Sydney, NSW 2000, Australia. *T:* 310211. *Clubs:* Legacy, Australian, Tattersalls (Sydney).

**DUCKWORTH, Arthur;** *see* Duckworth, G. A. V.

**DUCKWORTH, Frederick Victor,** CMG 1954; *b* 11 Aug. 1901; *s* of Arthur Robbins Duckworth and May Ellen Anderson; *m* 1939, Margaret Wade; one *d* (one *s* decd). *Educ:* North Point; Selwyn Coll., Cambridge. MCS, 1924; Magistrate, Singapore, 1925; Dist Officer, Balik Pulau, 1927; Asst Controller of Labour, Klang, 1928; Contr of Labour, Johore, 1933; Dep. Contr of Labour, FMS, 1938; Chief Press Censor, Malaya, 1940; Malayan Agent in South Africa, 1942; seconded to Kenya, 1943; ALFSEA, 1945; Col, Labour, Brit. Mil. Admin., Malaya, 1945; Comr for Labour, Fedn Malaya, 1950; Mem. for Industrial and Social Relations, 1953; British Adviser, Selangor, 1954-56; retired 1956. Selangor Meritorious Service Medal, 1956. *Recreations:* golf, tennis, trout-fishing. *Address:* Heathfield, Old Heath, Colchester, Essex. *T:* Colchester 5477.

**DUCKWORTH, (George) Arthur (Victor),** JP; *b* 3 Jan. 1901; *e s* of Major A. C. Duckworth of Orchardleigh Park, Frome; *m* 1927, Alice, 3rd *d* of John Henry Hammond, New York; three *d*; *m* 1945, Elizabeth, *o d* of Alfred Ehrenfeld, Bridgeham Farm, Forest Green, Surrey; two *d*; *m* 1968, Mary, *y d* of Archdeacon Edmund Hope, and *widow* of Captain K. Buxton. *Educ:* Eton; Trinity Coll., Cambridge (BA). MP (C) Shrewsbury Div. of Salop, 1929-45; Parliamentary Private Sec. to G. H. Shakespeare, 1932-39. Served War of 1939-45, 36th (Middlesex) AA Bn RA, 1939-41. CC Somerset, 1949-64; JP Somerset, 1957. *Address:* Orchardleigh Park, Frome, Somerset. *T:* Beckington 306. *Clubs:* Travellers', Garrick.

**DUCKWORTH, John Clifford;** Managing Director: National Research Development Corporation, 1959-70; International Computers (Holding) Ltd; Spear & Jackson Ltd; British Ropes Ltd; Member, United Kingdom Atomic Energy Authority, since 1965; Special Adviser to N. M. Rothschild & Sons, since 1970; *b* 27 Dec. 1916; *s* of late H. Duckworth, Wimbledon, and of Mrs A. H. Duckworth (*née* Woods); *m* 1942, Dorothy Nancy Wills; three *s*. *Educ:* KCS, Wimbledon; Wadham Coll., Oxford. Telecommunications Research Establishment, Malvern: Radar Research and Development, 1939-46; National Research Council, Chalk River, Ont., 1946-47; Atomic Energy Research Establishment, Harwell, 1947-50; Ferranti Ltd: Chief Engineer, Wythenshawe Laboratories, 1950-54; Nuclear Power Engineer, Brit. Electricity Authority, 1954-58; Central Electricity Authority, 1957-58; Chief Research and Development Officer, Central Electricity Generating Board, 1958-59. Pres., Institute of Fuel, 1963-64; Vice-Pres., Parliamentary and Scientific Cttee, 1964-67. *Recreations:* tennis, squash, swimming, colour photography, cartography. *Address:* The Old Malt House, St Peter's Street, Marlow, Bucks. *T:* Marlow 2677. *Club:* Athenæum.

**DUCKWORTH, Captain Ralph Campbell Musbury,** CBE 1946 (OBE 1943); CEng; RN, retired; Director, British Water & Effluent Treatment Plant Association; *b* 11 June 1907; 2nd *s* of Major Arthur Campbell Duckworth, DL, JP, orchardleigh Park, Frome, Som; *m* 1945, Ruby Cortez, 2nd Officer WRNS, *o d* of A. W. Ball, Sydenham, London. *Educ:* Royal Naval Colleges, Osborne and Dartmouth. War of 1939-45: served as Lieut-Comdr and Torpedo Officer of HMS Illustrious, 1940-41; Comdr 1941 and staff of C-in-C Mediterranean and C-in-C Levant, 1941-43; OBE for duties in planning and execution of operations for capture of Sicily; Dep. Chief of Staff (acting Capt.) to Vice-Adm. Administration, British Pacific Fleet, 1944-45 (CBE); Captain 1946; Dep. Dir Underwater Weapons Dept, Admiralty, 1946-48; Naval Attaché, British Embassy, Rio de Janeiro, 1949-51; Imperial Defence Coll., 1952; Capt., 1st Destroyer Sqdn, 1953-54; Staff of C-in-C, Mediterranean, 1954-55. Member: Northern Ireland Development Council, 1956-65; Dollar Exports Council, 1956-59; Manager, Industrial Engineering, Morgan Crucible Co. Ltd, 1956-58; Commercial Manager Elliott Bros (London) Ltd, 1959-61; Dir, British Mechanical Engrg Fedn, 1963-68. *Recreations:* gardening and travelling. *Address:* 9 Cadogan Street, SW3. *T:* 01-589 4991. *Club:* United Service.

**DUCKWORTH, Major Sir Richard Dyce,** 3rd Bt, *cr* 1909; *b* 30 Sept. 1918; *s* of Sir Edward Dyce Duckworth, 2nd Bt, and Cecil Gertrude, *y d* of Robert E. Leman; *S* father, 1945; *m* 1942, Violet Alison, *d* of Lieut-Col G. B. Wauchope, DSO; two *s*. *Educ:* Marlborough Coll. Started business in 1937. *Recreations:* sailing, golf, squash, shooting. *Heir: s* Edward Richard Dyce Duckworth, *b* 13 July 1943. *Address:* c/o Bank of Scotland, 30 Bishopsgate, EC2.

**DUCKWORTH-KING, Sir John (Richard),** 7th Bt, *cr* 1792; *b* 11 June 1899; *o surv. s* of Col Sir Dudley Gordon Alan Duckworth-King, 5th Bt and Eva Mary, *d* of Maj.-Gen. Ralph Gore; *S* brother, 1952; *m* 1943, Alice Patricia, *d* of Thomas Rutledge, Fugar House, Ravensworth, Co. Durham. *Educ:* Wellington Coll.; RMC Sandhurst. Lieut Coldstream Guards, 1919-27; served War of 1939-45, Royal Air Force. *Recreations:* Joint Holder of Army Doubles Racquet Championship 1925, 1926 and 1927; Runner-up Army Racquet Singles, 1927. *Heir:* none. *Address:* c/o Commonwealth Trading Bank of Australia, Australia House, WC2. *Club:* Guards.

**DU CROS, Sir (Harvey) Philip,** 2nd Bt, *cr* 1916; *b* 19 June 1898; *s* of Sir Arthur Philip du Cros, 1st Bt and Maude (*d* 1938), *d* of late William

Gooding, Coventry; *S* father 1955; *m* 1st, 1922, Dita Matilda (marr. diss., 1950), *d* of late Sir Claude Coventry Mallet, CMG and late Lady Mallet, CBE; one *s* two *d*; 2nd, 1950, Rosemary Theresa, MBE, *d* of Sir John Rees, 1st Bt, KCIE. *Educ:* Harrow. Served in European War with 3rd (King's Own) Hussars, 1916-19; War of 1939-45 (despatches), RA. Military Pioneer Corps, 1939-44. Dir of St Martin's Le Grand Property Co., etc. *Recreations:* fishing, golf, etc. *Heir: s* Claude Philip Arthur Mallet du Cros [*b* 22 Dec. 1922; *m* 1953, Mrs Christine Nancy Tordoff, *d* of late F. R. Bennett, Spilsby, Lincs; one *s*]. *Address:* Little Bocombe, Parkham, N Devon. *T:* Horns Cross 206. *Clubs:* Bath, Carlton.
*See also Sir Richard Jenks, Bt.*

**DUDBRIDGE, Bryan James,** CMG 1961; retired from HM Overseas Civil Service, Nov. 1961; Deputy Director, formerly Associate Director, British Council of Churches Department of Christian Aid, since 1963; *b* 2 April 1912; *o s* of late W. Dudbridge, OBE, and of Anne Jane Dudbridge; *m* 1943, Audrey Mary, *o d* of late Dr and Mrs Heywood, Newbury; two *s* one *d*. *Educ:* King's Coll. Sch., Wimbledon; Selwyn Coll., Cambridge. Appointed to Colonial Administrative Service as Cadet in Tanganyika, 1935; Asst Dist Officer, 1937; Dist Officer, 1947; Sen. Dist Officer, 1953; Actg Provincial Commr, Southern Province; Administrative Officer (Class IIA), 1955, and Actg Provincial Commissioner (Local Government); Provincial Commissioner, Western Province, 1957; Minister for Provincial Affairs, 1959-60, retd. *Publications:* contrib. Journal of African Administration, and Tanganyika Notes and Records. *Recreations:* natural history, and wildfowl. *Address:* Bridge Farm, High Halden, Ashford, Kent. *T:* High Halden 221. *Club:* Royal Commonwealth Society.

**DUDDING, Sir John (Scarbrough),** Kt 1963; Chairman: Scunthorpe Group of Hospitals Management Committee; Lincolnshire County Committee, Voluntary Service Overseas; Executive Committee, Lincolnshire Association; *b* 28 Nov. 1915; *s* of Col Thomas Scarbrough Dudding, OBE, MRCS, LRCP, RAMC, and Maude Campbell Dudding; *m* 1945, Enid Grace Gardner, The Old Hall, Tacolneston, Norwich; one *s* one *d*. *Educ:* Cheltenham Coll.; Jesus Coll., Cambridge (BA Hons). Entered Colonial Service, posted to Nigeria, 1938. War service with Nigeria Regt of Royal West African Frontier Force, in Nigeria, India and Burma, 1940-45 (Major). Dep. Comr of the Cameroons, 1956-58; Permanent Sec., Federal Nigerian Ministries of Works and Survey, Communications and Aviation, Transport and Aviation, and Communications, 1959-63; retd, 1964. Lindsey CC, 1967. *Recreations:* gardening, local history and book-collecting. *Address:* Scarbrough House, Winteringham, near Scunthorpe, Lincs. *T:* Winterton 393. *Club:* Royal Commonwealth Society.

**DUDGEON, Air Vice-Marshal Antony Greville,** CBE 1955; DFC 1941; MBIM 1968; with McKinsey & Coy Inc., management consultants; *b* 6 Feb. 1916; *s* of late Prof. Herbert William Dudgeon, Guy's Hosp. and Egyptian Government Service; *m* 1942, Phyllis Margaret, *d* of Group Capt. John McFarlane, OBE, MC, AFC, Lowestoft, Suffolk; one *s* one *d*. *Educ:* Eton; RAF Cranwell; Staff Coll., Flying Coll.; Polytechnic London. RAF Service, 1933-68, in UK, Europe, Near, Middle and Far East, USA; personnel work, training, operations, flight safety, organisation of new formations, liaison with civilian firms and youth organisations; NATO Staff; 6 command appointments; 3,500 hours as pilot. *Publications:* A Flying Command (under pen-name Tom Dagger), 1962; several stories contributed to Blackwood's Magazine. *Recreations:* writing, photography, swimming, golf; (languages, French, Egyptian). *Address:* Manager of Professional Staff Services, McKinsey & Coy Inc., 40 Avenue George V, Paris 8ème; 3 Quick Street, Islington, N1. *Clubs:* Royal Air Force, MCC.

**DUDGEON, Henry Alexander;** HM Diplomatic Service; Head of Marine and Transport Department, Foreign and Commonwealth Office, since 1970; *b* 12 Aug. 1924; *er s* of late John Brown Dudgeon and late Alison Dudgeon (*née* Winton); *m* 1952, Marjorie Patricia, *d* of Joseph Harvey, MD; no *c*. *Educ:* Knox Academy, Haddington; Magdalene Coll., Cambridge. Served in HM Forces, 1943-47; entered HM Foreign Service, 1949; served at: FO, 1949-52; Sofia, 1952-54; Amman, 1954-58; FO, 1958-61; 1st Sec. and Head of Chancery, Havana, 1966-69; Civil Service Research Fellow at Glasgow Univ., 1969-70. *Recreation:* bridge. *Address:* 295 Fir Tree Road, Epsom Downs, Surrey. *T:* Burgh Heath 52637.

**DUDLEY,** 4th Earl of, *cr* 1860; **William Humble David Ward;** Baron Ward, 1644; Viscount Ednam, 1860; *b* 5 Jan. 1920; *e s* of 3rd Earl of Dudley, MC, TD, and Rosemary Millicent, RRC (*d* 1930), *o d* of 4th Duke of Sutherland; *S* father, 1969; *m* 1st, 1946, Stella (marr. diss., 1961), *d* of M. A. Carcano, *qv*; one *s* twin *d*; 2nd, 1961, Maureen Swanson; five *d*. *Educ:* Eton; Christ Church, Oxford. Joined 10th Hussars, 1941, Adjt, 1944-45; ADC to Viceroy of India, 1942-43. Served War of 1939-45 (wounded). Chairman: Grecon Systems Ltd; Noise Control Products Ltd. director: Baggeridge Brick Co. Ltd; Tribune Investment Trust Ltd. *Heir: s* Viscount Ednam, *qv*. *Address:* 6 Cottesmore Gardens, W8. *Clubs:* White's, Pratt's; Royal Yacht Squadron.

**DUDLEY,** 13th Baron, *cr* 1439-1440 (called out of abeyance, 1916); **Ferdinando Dudley Henry Lea Smith;** late Lieut 8th Bn Worcs Regt; late Squadron Leader, RAF; *b* 18 June 1910; *s* of 12th Baron and Sybil Augusta (*d* 1958), *d* of Rev. H. W. Coventry, Rector of Severn Stoke, Worcester; *S* father 1936. *Heir: sister,* Hon. Barbara Amy Felicity Wallace [*b* 23 April 1907; *m* 1929, Guy Wallace (*d* 1967); three *s* one *d*]. *Address:* 12a Half Moon Street, W1. *Club:* Royal Air Force.

**DUDLEY, Archdeacon of;** *see* Williams, Ven. J. C.

**DUDLEY, Sir Alan Alves,** KBE 1961; CMG 1948; Director, Electronic Components Board, since 1968; *b* 1907; *s* of Bertram and Ethel Dudley; *m* 1930, Isabel, *d* of David and Margaret Brunton; one *d*. *Educ:* St Christopher's Sch.; London Sch. of Economics; University Coll. of Wales, Aberystwyth. Asst Dir, British Library, New York, 1930-40; Dir, British Press Service and British Information Service, New York, 1940-42; Foreign Office, 1942-49 (Head of Information Policy Dept, 1946-49); Counsellor, UK Deleg. to OEEC, Paris, 1949-50; Head of UN Economic and Social Dept, FO, 1950-53; Dep. Commissioner-Gen. for the UK in South-East Asia, 1953-56; HM Minister at Bucharest, 1956-59; HM Minister in UK Mission to UN, 1959-61; Under-Sec., Dept of Technical Co-operation, 1961-64; Dep. Sec., ODM, 1964-68. *Address:* 42 Rivermead Court, SW6. *T:* 01-736 1443; Plas Derwen, Llansantffraid, Mont. *T:* Llansantffraid 373. *Clubs:* Athenæum, English-Speaking Union.

**DUDLEY, Prof. Donald Reynolds;** Professor of Latin, University of Birmingham, since 1955; Dean, Faculty of Arts, 1958-61; *b* 3 March 1910; *s* of J. J. Dudley; *m* 1938, Eryl Margaret, *d* of W. St Bodfan Griffith, Bangor, N Wales; two adopted *d*. *Educ:* King Edward's Sch., Birmingham; St John's Coll., Cambridge. Henry Fund Fellow, Yale Univ., USA, 1932-33; Fellow, St John's Coll., Cambridge, 1935-37; Lecturer in Classics, Reading Univ., 1937-44; Fereday Fellow, St John's Coll., Oxford, 1938-41; Dir of Extra-Mural Studies, University of Birmingham, 1944-55. Visiting Lectr, Tulane Univ., New Orleans, USA, 1952. Member: Governing Body, King Edward's Foundation (Bailiff, 1963-64); Worcs Educ. Cttee. *Publications:* A History of Cynicism, 1937; Civilization of Rome, 1960; (with Graham Webster) The Rebellion of Boudicca, 1962, The Roman Conquest of Britain, AD 43-57, 1965; The Annals of Tacitus (trans.) 1966; Urbs Roma, 1967; The World of Tacitus, 1968; The Romans, 1970; articles on Roman history; ed (with T. A. Dorey), Studies in Latin Literature and its Influence (6 vols publ. to date). *Recreations:* archæology and travel. *Address:* Blackhill, Malvern, Worcs. *T:* Colwall 202. *Club:* English-Speaking Union.

**DUDLEY, Prof. Norman Alfred,** PhD; Lucas Professor of Engineering Production, University of Birmingham, since 1959; Head of Department of Engineering Production and Director of University Institute for Engineering Production, since 1956; Chartered Engineer; *b* 29 Feb. 1916; *s* of Alfred Dudley; *m* 1940, Hilda Florence, *d* of John Miles; one *s* two *d*. *Educ:* Kings Norton Grammar Sch.; Birmingham Coll. of Technology. BSc London, PhD Birmingham. FIProdE, MBIM; industrial training and appts: H. W. Ward & Co. Ltd, 1932-39; Imperial Typewriter Co. Ltd, 1940-45; Technical Coll. Lectr, 1945-52; Sen. Lectr, Wolverhampton and Staffs, 1948-52; Lectr in Eng. Prod., 1952, Reader, 1956, University of Birmingham. Chm., Manufacturing Processes Div., Birmingham Univ. Inst. for Advanced Studies in Engineering Sciences, 1965-68. Gov., Dudley and Staffs Tech. Coll.; Mem. Council, Birmingham Productivity Assoc.; Dir, Birmingham Productivity Services Ltd; Mem. Council Internat. Univ. Contact for Management Education, 1957; Mem. Council, Instn of Prod. Engineers, 1959-61, Chm., Research Cttee, 1965-66. Member: UK Delegn to UNCSAT Geneva, 1963; W Midlands Economic Planning Council, 1970-. Pres., Midlands Operational Research Soc., 1966-. J. D. Scaife Medal, 1958. *Publications:* Work Measurement: Some Research Studies, 1968; various papers on Engineering Production; Ed., International Journal of Production Research. *Address:* The University, Edgbaston, Birmingham 15. *T:* 021-472 1301.

**DUDLEY-WILLIAMS, Sir Rolf (Dudley),** 1st Bt, *cr* 1964; *b* 17 June 1908; *s* of Arthur Williams, Plymouth; assumed and adopted surname of Dudley-Williams, by Deed Poll, 1964; *m* 1940, Margaret Helen, *er d* of F. E. Robinson, OBE, AMIMechE; two *s*. *Educ:* Plymouth Coll.; Royal Air Force Coll., Cranwell. Gazetted, 1928, Flying Officer, 1930; Central Flying Sch., 1933, invalided from service, 1934. Founded Power Jets Ltd, 1936, to develop Whittle system of jet propulsion; Managing Dir, 1941. Mem. Council Soc. of British Aircraft Constructors, 1944; Companion Royal Aeronautical Society, 1944. Contested (C) Brierley Hill, 1950. PPS to Sec. of State for War, 1958; PPS to Minister of Agriculture, 1960-64. Chm., Western Area of National Union of Conservative Assocs, 1961-64. MP (C) Exexer, 1951-66. *Heir:* *s* Alastair Edgcumbe James Dudley-Williams, *b* 26 Nov. 1943. *Address:* Little Hayne, Plymtree, near Cullompton, Devon. *T:* Plymtree 204. *Clubs:* Carlton, Royal Air Force; Exeter and County.

**DUDMAN, George Edward;** Legal Adviser, Department of Education and Science, since 1965; *b* 2 Dec. 1916; *s* of William James Dudman and Nora Annie (*née* Curtis); *m* 1955, Joan Doris, *d* of late Frederick John Eaton; one *s* one *d*. *Educ:* Merchant Taylors' Sch., London; St John's Coll., Oxford. Royal Artillery, 1940-46; Control Commn, Germany, 1946-49. Called to Bar, Middle Temple, 1950. Law Officers' Dept, 1951; Legal Sec., Law Officers' Dept, 1958. *Recreations:* gardening, cooking. *Address:* 10 Viga Road, Grange Park, N21. *T:* 01-360 5129.

**DUDOK, Willem Marinus;** architect, BNA; Officer of Order of Oranje-Nassau, Holland; Knight of Order of the Lion, Netherlands; *b* 6 July 1884; *s* of Johannes Cornelis Dudok and Cornelia Bertha Holst; *m* 1911, Marie Alette Smit; one *s* one *d*. *Educ:* Royal Military Academy, Breda. Was an officer of the corps of engineers, 1905-13; became an engineer of the city of Leiden, 1913; Dir Public Works in Hilversum, 1915; built many workmen's houses, schools, town hall 1928-31; also country houses, the Columbarium at Westerveld, 1925-26, extended, 1937-38; a quarter with middle class houses, Eindhoven, 1935-39; Stores, Beehive (de Bijenkorf) at Rotterdam, 1929-30 (destroyed during war); Cinema CA, Calcutta, 1936-38; Theatre, Utrecht, 1939-41; Offices for HAV Bank, Schiedam, 1934-35; "The Netherlands of 1845", Arnhem, 1938-39; office for crematorium at Westerveld, 1939-41; Dutch student-home in Cité Universitaire, Paris, 1927-38; Erasmus House, Rotterdam, 1937; town-planning, design for reconstruction of The Hague, Velsen-Ymuiden; Zwolle, Head Office for Royal Dutch Steelworks, Ymuiden, 1949-; Offices "The Netherlands of 1845", Rotterdam, 1952; Flats, Stores and housing in Hilversum, Amsterdam, Bussum, etc. since 1954; Aulas at new cemeteries in Velsen and Hilversum, 1962-64; Town Hall, Velsen, designed 1950, executed 1962-65; Harbour building at Amsterdam, 1960 (with R. M. H. Magnee), etc. Royal Gold Medal of RIBA, Gold Medal AIA, 1955, and other gold medals. Officer, Order of Crown of Belgium. *Publications:* articles on architecture and town planning. *Recreations:* music and drawing. *Address:* Utrechtscheweg 71, Hilversum, Holland. *TA:* Dudok, Hilversum. *T:* 7336.

**DUESBURY, Rev. J. P. T.;** *see* Thornton-Duesbury.

**DUFF, Maj.-Gen. Alan Colquhoun,** CB 1945; OBE 1941; MC 1916; Commander, Legion of Merit (USA), 1946; *b* 11 Nov. 1896; *e s* of J. D. Duff, Fellow of Trinity Coll., Cambridge, and Laura, *d* of Sir William Lenox-Conyngham, KCB; *m* 1935, Diana Francis, *d* of late Col R. P. Crawley, DSO, OBE, MVO; one *s* two *d*. *Educ:* Wellington Coll.; RMA, Woolwich. Commissioned Royal Engineers, 1915; Capt. 1918; Major, 1930; Lieut-Col 1938; Col 1941; Maj.-Gen. 1946. European War, 1915-18 (Gallipoli, Serbia, Macedonia, Palestine); Staff Coll., 1926-27; Nigeria Regt, 1930-35; Campaign in East Africa, 1941 (despatches twice); DQMG, War Office, 1943-44; DQMG, Allied Force HQ, Italy, 1945; Chief Admin. Officer to Field-Marshal Alexander and Actg Lieut-Gen., 1945; Maj.-Gen. i/c Administration Southern Command, 1946-47; retired pay, 1947. Gen. Manager, Stevenage Development Corporation, 1947-57. A Governor of Bryanston Sch. since 1948.

*Publications:* 65 RE, 1920; The Spine, 1929; On Helle's Wave, 1930; The House of the Apricots, 1933 (the three last under nom-de-plume Hugh Imber); Sword and Pen, 1950; Britain's New Towns, 1961. *Address:* Rider's Croft, Little Chesterford, Essex. *Club:* Naval and Military.

**DUFF, Arthur Antony,** CMG 1964; DSO 1944; DSC; HM Diplomatic Service; Deputy High Commissioner, Kuala Lumpur, since 1969; *b* 25 Feb. 1920; *s* of late Adm. Sir Arthur Allen Morison Duff, KCB; *m* 1944, Pauline Marion, *d* of Capt. R. H. Bevan, RN, and *widow* of Flt-Lieut J. A. Sword; two *s* two *d*. *Educ:* RNC, Dartmouth. Served in RN, 1937-46. Mem., Foreign (subseq. Diplomatic) Service, 1946; 3rd Sec., Athens, Oct. 1946; 2nd Sec., 1948; 2nd Sec., Cairo, 1949; 1st Sec., 1952; transferred Foreign Office, Private Sec. to Minister of State, 1952; 1st Sec., Paris, 1954; Foreign Office, 1957; Bonn, 1960; Counsellor, 1962; British Ambassador to Nepal, 1964-65; Commonwealth Office, 1965-68; FCO, 1968-69. *Address:* c/o National Westminster Bank, The Hard, Portsmouth. *Club:* Royal Commonwealth Society.

**DUFF, Sir (Charles) Michael (Robert Vivian),** 3rd Baronet, *cr* 1911; Lord Lieutenant of Caernarvonshire since 1960; *b* 3 May 1907; *s* of 2nd Bt and Lady (Gladys Mary) Juliet Lowther, *o d* of 4th Earl of Lonsdale (Lady Juliet Duff; *d* 1965); *S* father, 1914; *m* 1949, Lady Caroline Paget, *e d* of 6th Marquess of Anglesey, GCVO. *Educ:* Sandhurst. Flying Officer late RAFVR. High Sheriff of Anglesey, 1950-51. KStJ. *Recreations:* shooting and hunting. *Address:* Vaynol Park, Bangor, N Wales. *T:* Bangor 42. *Club:* Turf.

**DUFF, Sir (Charles) Patrick,** KCB, *cr* 1932 (CB 1928); KCVO, *cr* 1937 (CVO 1924); Director, James Oakes & Co.; *b* 1889; *s* of late Harry Duff; *m* 1929, Margaret, *d* of late James Woodcock. *Educ:* Blundell's Sch., Tiverton; Balliol Coll., Oxford. Entered Bd of Trade by open competition (Cl. I), 1912; served European War, 1914-18, Gallipoli, France, Mesopotamia (wounded, despatches twice); Private Sec. to successive Presidents of the Board of Trade, 1919-23; Private Sec. to successive Prime Ministers (Rt Hon. Stanley Baldwin, Rt Hon. J. Ramsay Macdonald, Rt Hon. Stanley Baldwin, Rt Hon. J. Ramsay Macdonald), 1923-33; Sec., Ministry of Works and Public Buildings, 1933-41; Dep. High Comr, Canada, 1941-44; High Commissioner for the UK, New Zealand, 1945-49; a Church Commissioner for England, 1949-54. Chm. of the National Parks Commission, 1949-54; Mem. of Nature Conservancy, 1949-54. *Address:* Eight Bells House, Haddenham, Bucks. *Club:* Oxford and Cambridge.

**DUFF, Sir Michael;** *see* Duff, Sir C. M. R. V.

**DUFF, Sir Patrick;** *see* Duff, Sir C. P.

**DUFF, Patrick William;** Fellow of Trinity College, Cambridge; *b* 21 Feb. 1901; 3rd *s* of J. D. Duff, Fellow of Trinity College, Cambridge, and Laura, *d* of Sir William Lenox-Conyngham, KCB. *Educ:* Winchester; Trinity Coll., Cambridge; Munich Univ.; Harvard Law Sch. 1st Class, Classical Tripos Parts I and II; Craven and Whewell Scholar; Tancred Scholar of Lincoln's Inn; Fellow of Trinity, 1925; Lecturer, 1927; Tutor, 1938; Senior Tutor, 1945; Dean of Coll., 1950; Vice-Master, 1960. Regius Prof. of Civil Law, Cambridge, 1945-68. Barrister-at-Law, 1933. Cambridge Borough Councillor, 1947-51. Fellow of Winchester Coll., 1948; Warden, 1959-62. Pres. Soc. of Public Teachers of Law, 1957-58. Hon. Bencher of Lincoln's Inn, 1959. *Publications:* The Charitable Foundations of Byzantium (in Cambridge Legal Essays presented to Doctor Bond, Prof. Buckland and Prof. Kenny), 1926; The Personality of an Idol (in Cambridge Law Journal), 1927; Delegata Potestas Non Potest Delegari (in Cornell Law Quarterly), 1929; Personality in Roman Private Law, 1938; Roman Law Today (in Tulane Law Review), 1947. *Recreation:* scouting. *Address:* Trinity College, Cambridge.

**DUFF, Col Thomas Robert G.;** *see* Gordon-Duff.

**DUFF GORDON, Sir Andrew (Cosmo Lewis),** 8th Bt, *cr* 1813; *b* 17 Oct. 1933; *o s* of Sir Douglas Duff Gordon, 7th Bt and Gladys Rosemary (*d* 1933), *e d* of late Col Vivien Henry, CB; *S* father, 1964; *m* 1967, Grania Mary, *d* of Fitzgerald Villiers-Stuart, Ireland; one *s*. *Educ:* Repton. Served with Worcs Regiment and 1st Bn Ches Regt, 1952-54. Mem. of Lloyd's. *Recreations:* golf, shooting, riding. *Heir:* *s* Cosmo Henry Villiers Duff Gordon, *b* 18 June 1968. *Address:* Downton House, Walton, Presteigne, Radnorshire. *T:* New Radnor 223. *Clubs:* Kington Golf; Nairobi (Kenya).

**DUFFERIN and AVA,** 5th Marquess of, *cr* 1888; **Sheridan Frederick Terence Hamilton-Temple-Blackwood;** Baron Dufferin and Clandeboye, Ireland, 1800; Baron Clandeboye, UK, 1850; Earl of Dufferin, Viscount Clandeboye, 1871; Earl of Ava, 1888, and a Bt; *b* 9 July 1938; *o s* of 4th Marquess (killed in action, 1945) and Maureen (she *m* 1948, Major Desmond Buchanan, MC, from whom she obtained a divorce, 1954; *m* 1955, John Cyril Maude, *qv*), 2nd *d* of late Hon. (Arthur) Ernest Guiness; *S* father, 1945; *m* 1964, Serena Belinda Rosemary, *d* of Group Capt. (Thomas) Loel Evelyn Bulkeley Guinness, *qv*. *Educ:* Eton Coll. *Address:* 4 Holland Villas Road, W14. *T:* 01-937 3163; Clandeboye, Co. Down, Northern Ireland.

**DUFFIELD, Anne;** Writer of Fiction; *b* Orange, New Jersey; British Canadian; *m* 1921, Edgar Willoughby Duffield, OBE; no *c*. *Educ:* Westburne, Toronto; Mademoiselle Osselins, Paris. *Publications:* Some thirty-eight novels, first being The Lacquer Couch, 1928, and among others Grecian Rhapsody, The Dragon's Tail, The House on the Nile, Bubbling Springs, 1940, The Sweeping Tide, 1940; The Shadow of the Pines, 1940; A Bevy of Maids, 1941; The Inscrutable Nymph, 1942; Old Glory, 1943; Sunrise, 1943; Out of the Shadows, 1944; Tappy Came to Cairo, 1945; Repent at Leisure, 1945; Forever Tomorrow, 1946; Song of the Mocking Bird, 1947; Arkady, 1948; Dusty Dawn, 1949; Beloved Enemy, 1950; Sugar Island, 1951; Tomorrow is Theirs, 1952; Harbour Lights, 1952; The Grand Duchess, 1953; The Golden Summer, 1954; Come back Miranda, 1955; Fiametta, 1956; Castle in Spain, 1958; Violetta, 1960. *Recreations:* travel, ski-ing, Canadian canoe trips, reading, gardening. *Address:* 10 The Green, Aldbourne, Wilts. *TA:* Aldbourne, Wilts. *T:* Aldbourne 336.

**DUFFUS, Hon. Sir Herbert (George Holwell),** Kt 1966; Chief Justice of Jamaica, since 1968; *b* 30 Aug. 1908; *e s* of William Alexander Duffus, JP, and Emily Henrietta Mary (*née* Holwell); *m* 1939, Elsie Mary (*née* Hollinsed); no *c*. *Educ:* Cornwall Coll., Jamaica. Admitted as Solicitor: Jamaica, 1930, England, 1948. Resident Magistrate, Jamaica, 1946-58; Called to the Bar, Lincoln's Inn, 1956; acted as Puisne Judge, Jamaica, 1956-58; Puisne Judge, Jamaica, 1958-62; Judge of Appeal, Jamaica, 1962-64; Pres. Court of Appeal, 1964-67. Chm.

of Commission of Enquiry into Prisons of Jamaica, 1954. Chm. of The Police Service Commission (Jamaica), 1958-68 (Captain of Jamaica Local Forces, 1940-46). Pres., Boy Scouts Assoc., Jamaica, 1967. *Address:* The Supreme Court, Kingston, Jamaica; 62 Lady Musgrave Road, Kingston 10, Jamaica. *T:* 78,265.

**DUFFUS, William Algernon Holwell; Hon. Mr Justice Duffus;** President of the Court of Appeal for East Africa, since 1970; *b* Jamaica, 13 Aug. 1911; *s* of William Alexander Duffus, JP, and of Emily (*née* Holwell); *m* Helen Hollinsed; two *s* one *d*. *Educ:* Cornwall Coll. and Titchfield Sch., Jamaica. Solicitor, Supreme Court, Jamaica, 1933. In private practice in Jamaica. Legal Service, Jamaica, 1935; Magistrate, Jamaica, 1943; Magistrate, Nigeria, 1949, Chief Magistrate, 1953. Called to the Bar, Gray's Inn, 1954; Chief Registrar of the Federal Supreme Court, Nigeria, 1955; Judge of High Ct, W Nigeria, 1957; Justice of Ct of Appeal for E Africa, 1964, Vice-Pres., 1969. *Address:* Box 30187, Court of Appeal for East Africa, Nairobi, Kenya.

**DUFFY, Albert Edward Patrick,** PhD; MP (Lab) Sheffield, Attercliffe, since 1970; *b* 17 June 1920. *Educ:* London Sch. of Economics (BSc(Econ.), PhD); Columbia Univ., Morningside Heights, New York, USA. Served War of 1939-45, Royal Navy, as an Officer (6 years service). Lecturer, University of Leeds, 1950-63, 1967-. Visiting Prof., Drew Univ., NJ, 1966-70. Contested (Lab) Tiverton Division of Devon, 1950, 1951, 1955. MP (Lab) Colne Valley Division of Yorks, 1963-66; Chm., Parly Labour Party Economic and Finance Gp, 1965-66. *Publications:* contrib. to Economic History Review, Victorian Studies, Manchester School, etc. *Address:* 169 Bennetthorpe, Doncaster, Yorks. *Clubs:* RNVR; Trades and Labour (Doncaster).

**DUFTY, Arthur Richard;** Secretary and General Editor Royal Commission on Historical Monuments (England), since 1962 (on staff since 1937), with responsibility also for National Monuments Record (including National Buildings Record) since 1964; Master of the Armouries in HM Tower of London since 1963; *b* 23 June 1911; *o c* of Thomas Ernest Dufty, Nottingham and Flamborough, and Beatrice, *d* of Samuel Henry Holmes, Hull; *m* 1937, Kate Brazley, *o c* of Charles Ainsworth, Bolton, and Mabel, *d* of John Perceval Haslam, Bolton; one *s* two *d*. *Educ:* Rugby; Liverpool School of Architecture. War service in RN, Ord. Seaman to Lieut RNVR. Editor, 1952-56, Vice-Pres., 1960-64, Royal Archaeological Inst; Sec., 1954-64, Vice-Pres. 1964-67, Soc. of Antiquaries; Vice-Pres., 1962-65, Council for Brit. Archaeology. Member: Ancient Monuments Bd for England; Guildford Dio. Adv. Cttee, 1947-; Council for Care of Churches, 1949-60; 2nd Bridges Commn on Redundant Churches, 1961-63; Council of Georgian Gp, 1954-63; Council, Nat. Army Museum, 1963-; Historic Bldgs Adv. Cttee, GLC, 1964-67; Conf. of Dirs of Nat. Museums, 1963-; Management Cttee of Inst. of Archaeology, Univ. of London, 1965-, etc. Vice-Chm., Cathedrals Advisory Cttee, 1965-; Chm. (first) Surrey Local History Council (Council of Social Service for Surrey), 1965-, etc. Directed, for Soc. of Antiquaries, repair and rehabilitation of Kelmscott, William Morris's home in Oxfordshire, 1964-67. ARIBA 1935; FSA 1946. *Publications:* Kelmscott: an illustrated guide, 1970; (with F. H. Cripps-Day) *Fragmenta Armamentaria* IV: Supplementary list of armour preserved in English Churches, 1939. Edited four RCHM Inventories (incl. authorship of accounts of King's College Chapel, Corfe Castle, etc); ed. for MPBW: European Armour in the Tower of London, 1968; Arms and Armour in England (rev. Tower Guide), 1969. Articles in learned jls, etc., on armour, cathedrals, churches, glass, MSS, William Morris, Kelmscott, etc. *Recreations:* viewing sales; taking pleasure in Victoriana and Art Nouveau; whenever possible visiting the Outer Hebrides. *Address:* The Mount, Great Austins, Farnham, Surrey. *T:* Farnham 5720; c/o RCHM (England), Fielden House, Great College Street, SW1. *T:* 01-930 9652. *Clubs:* Athenæum, Arts, RNVR.

**DUGARD, Arthur Claude,** CBE 1969; Chairman, Cooper & Roe Ltd (formerly Joint Managing Director); *b* 1 Dec. 1904; *s* of Arthur Thomas Turner Dugard, Nottingham; *m* 1931, Christine Mary Roe, Nottingham; two *s*. *Educ:* Oundle Sch., Northants. Joined Cooper & Roe Ltd, Knitwear manufacturers, 1923 (Dir, 1936; Chm. and Jt Man. Dir, 1947). President: Nottingham Hosiery Manufrs Assoc., 1952-53; Nat. Hosiery Manufrs Fedn, 1959-61; Nottingham Chamber of Commerce, 1961-62. First Chm., CBI North Midland Regional Coun., 1965-66; Chm. British Hosiery & Knitwear Export Gp, 1966-68; Mem. East Midlands Economic Planning Coun. 1967-. Liveryman, Worshipful Co. of Framework Knitters, 1949-. *Recreation:* golf. *Address:* 72 Lucknow Avenue, Mapperley Park, Nottingham NG3 5BB. *T:* Nottingham 65170.

**DUGDALE,** family name of **Baron Crathorne.**

**DUGDALE, Amy K.;** *see* Browning, A. K.

**DUGDALE, Sir William (Stratford),** 2nd Bt *cr* 1936; MC 1943; *b* 29 March 1922; *er s* of Sir William Francis Stratford Dugdale, 1st Bt, and Margaret, 2nd *d* of Sir Robert Gordon Gilmour, 1st Bt, of Liberton and Craigmillar; *m* 1st, 1952, Lady Belinda Pleydell-Bouverie (*d* 1961), 2nd *d* of 6th Earl of Radnor; one *s* three *d*; 2nd, 1967, Cecilia Mary, *e d* of Sir William Malcolm Mount, 2nd Bt, *qv*; one *d*. *Educ:* Eton; Balliol Coll., Oxford. Served War of 1939-45, Grenadier Guards (Captain), Admitted as Solicitor, 1949. Dir, Phoenix Assurance Co., 1968-. Mem., Warwicks County Council; Chm., Trent River Authority, Governor, lady Katherine Leveson's Hosp., Temple Balsall. JP 1951, DL 1955, Warwicks. *Heir: s* William Matthew Stratford Dugdale, *b* 22 Feb. 1959. *Address:* Blyth Hall, Coleshill, near Birmingham. *T:* Coleshill 62203; Merevale Hall, Atherstone. *T:* Atherstone 3143; 24 Bryanston Mews West, W1. *T:* 01-262 2510. *Clubs:* Brooks's, White's, MCC; Jockey (Newmarket).

**DUGGAN, Rt. Rev. John Coote;** *see* Tuam, Killala and Achonry, Bishop of.

**DUGMORE, Rev. Dr Clifford William,** DD; Professor of Ecclesiastical History in the University of London, at King's College, since Oct. 1958; Editor of The Journal of Ecclesiastical History since 1950; British Member of Editorial Board of Novum Testamentum since 1956; *b* 9 May 1909; *s* of late Rev. Canon William Ernest Dugmore, MA, RD, and late Frances Ethel Dugmore (*née* Westmore); *m* 1938, Ruth Mabel Archbould Prangley; one *d*. *Educ:* King Edward VI Sch., Birmingham (foundation scholar); Exeter Coll., Oxford; Queens' Coll., Cambridge. Oxford: BA (Hons Sch. of Oriental Studies), 1932; MA and James Mew Rabbinical Hebrew Scholar, 1935; BD 1940; DD 1957. Cambridge: BA (by incorporation) 1933; MA 1936; Norrisian Prizeman 1940; Select Preacher 1956; Hulsean Lecturer, 1958-60.

Deacon 1935, Priest 1936; Asst Curate of Holy Trinity, Formby, 1935-37; Sub-Warden St Deiniol's Library, Hawarden, 1937-38; Rector of Ingestre-with-Tixall, 1938-43; Chaplain of Alleyn's Coll. of God's Gift, Dulwich, 1943-44; Rector of Bredfield and Dir of Religious Education, dio. St Edmundsbury and Ipswich, 1945-47; Sen. Lecturer in Ecclasiast. Hist., University of Manchester, 1946-58; Tutor to Faculty of Theology, 1958; Chm. of British Sous-Commission of Commission Internationale d'Histoire Ecclésiastique, 1952-62; Pres. of the Ecclesiastical History Soc., 1963-64; Mem. of the Senate, University of London 1964-; FKC 1965. *Publications:* Eucharistic Doctrine in England from Hooker to Waterland, 1942; The Influence of the Synagogue upon the Divine Office, 1944 (2nd edn 1964); The Interpretation of the Bible (ed.) 1944 (2nd edn 1946); The Mass and the English Reformers, 1958; Ecclesiastical History No Soft Option, 1959. Contributor to: Chambers's Encyclopædia, 1950 (Advisory Editor, 1960-); Weltkirchenlexikon 1960; Studia Patristica IV, 1961; Neotestamentica et Patristica, 1962; The English Prayer Book, 1963; A Companion to the Bible, 2nd revised edn, 1963; Studies in Church History I, 1964 (Ed.); Studies in Church History II, 1965 (contrib.); Eucharistic Theology then and now, 1968; Gen. Ed., Leaders of Religion, 1964-; articles and reviews in Journal of Theological Studies, Journal of Ecclesiastical History, Theology, History, etc. *Recreations:* motoring and philately. *Address:* King's College, Strand, WC2; 77 The Street, Puttenham, Surrey. *T:* Puttenham 460. *Club:* Royal Societies.

**DUGUID, Maj.-Gen. David Robertson,** CB 1945; MBE; MIMechE; AMIEE; FHWC; late REME; *b* 5 Dec. 1888; *s* of Jas. Duguid, Bo'ness, NB; *m* 1918, Mary Paris; three *s*. *Educ:* Bo'ness Academy; Heriot-Watt Coll., Edinburgh. Asst Engineer with Marshall & Duguid, Engineers, Bo'ness, 1912-15; with RAOC as Inspector of Ordnance Machinery, 1915-19; served throughout European War in France, Salonika and South Russia; with Inter-Allied Control Commission in Germany, 1919-24; Ordnance Mechanical Engineer, Western Command, UK, 1924-25; Asst Inspector of Guns and Carriages with CIA Dept, Woolwich Arsenal, 1925-29; OC RAOC Workshops, Woolwich Arsenal, 1929-32; OC Ordnance Workshops, Quetta Arsenal, India, 1932-37; OC RAOC Depot Workshops, Chilwell, 1937-39; OC Advanced Base Workshop, France, 1939-40; Deputy Dir of Mechanical Engineering, War Office, 1941-43; Dir of Mechanical Engineering, India, and Head of Corps of Indian Electrical and Mechanical Engineers, 1943-46; retired, 1946. Fellow, Heriot-Watt Coll., 1951. *Recreation:* golf. *Address:* Eden House, 4 Well Road, Bridge of Allan, Stirlingshire. *T:* 3106.

**DUGUID, Prof. John Bright,** CBE 1966; MD (Aberdeen); Adviser in Histopathology, Institute for Medical Research, Kuala Lumpur, Malaya, Nov. 1960-68, retired; Emeritus Professor of Pathology, University of Durham, Professor, 1948-60; *b* 5 May 1895; *s* of John Duguid, Farmer, Black Dog, Belhelvie, Aberdeenshire; *m* 1925, Agnes Mildred Emslie Benzie, MB, ChB; one *s* one *d*. *Educ:* Friends Sch., Wigton, Cumberland; Gordon's Coll., Aberdeen, MB, ChB (Aberdeen) 1920; MD (Aberdeen), 1925. Asst in dept of Pathology, Aberdeen Univ., 1922; Lecturer in Morbid Anatomy and Histology, Victoria Univ., Manchester, 1925; Lecturer in Pathology, Welsh Nat. Sch. of Medicine, Cardiff, 1926; Prof. of Pathology and Bacteriology, University of Wales, 1932. *Publications:* on arterial diseases and lung pathology. *Recreation:* angling. *Address:* 17 Cairn Road, Bieldside, Aberdeen.

**DU HEAUME, Sir (Francis) Herbert,** Kt, *cr* 1947; CIE 1943; OBE 1932; *b* 27 May 1897; *s* of George Du Heaume, OBE; *m* 1923, Blanche Helen Learmonth Tainsh; two *s*. Served European War, 1914-18, as Capt.; joined Indian Police, 1920; Principal, Police Training Sch., Punjab, 1934-42; Deputy Inspector-Gen. of Police, 1942-47. King's Police Medal; Indian Police Medal. *Address:* c/o National and Grindlay's Bank, 13 St James's Square, SW1.

**DUKE,** family name of **Baron Merrivale.**

**DUKE, Cecil Howard Armitage;** Director of Establishments and Organisation, Ministry of Agriculture, Fisheries and Food, since 1965; *b* 5 May 1912; *s* of John William Duke and Late Gertrude Beatrice (*née* Armitage); *m* 1939, Eleanor Lucy (*née* Harvie); one *s* one *d*. *Educ:* Selhurst Gram. Sch.; LSE RNVR, 1942-45 (Corvettes). Entered Civil Service, 1929; Asst Princ., 1940; Princ., 1945; Private Sec. to Lord Presidents of the Council, 1951-53; Asst Sec., Land Drainage Div. and Meat Div., 1953; Under-Sec., 1965. *Recreations:* walking, gardening, watching Sussex cricket. *Address:* 45 Tongdean Avenue, Hove, Sussex. *T:* Brighton 54051. *Clubs:* Farmers', Civil Service.

**DUKE, Sir Charles (Beresford),** KCMG 1956 (CMG 1954); CIE 1947; OBE 1946; Director-General, Middle East Association, 1964-70; *b* 19 Dec. 1905; *o s* of late Arthur Herbert and Ann Victoria Duke, Bangkok, Siam and Marlow, Bucks; *m* 1938, Morag Craigie, *o d* of Capt. Patrick Grant; two *d*. *Educ:* Charterhouse; Lincoln Coll., Oxford. Entered Indian Civil Service by competitive examination, 1928; appointed to United Provinces of Agra and Oudh, 1929; transferred to Indian Political Service, 1934; Asst Private Sec. to Viceroy, 1934-38; Sec. to Governor, NWFP, 1940-41; Political Agent, Waziristan, 1941-43; External Affairs Dept, Govt of India, New Delhi, 1943-47; transferred to HM Foreign Service, 1947; served in Pakistan, FO, Persia and Egypt, 1947-54; HM Ambassador to Jordan, 1954-56 and to Morocco, 1957-61; retired, 1961. *Recreations:* riding, shooting, tennis, sailing, reading. *Address:* Cadenham Grange, Cadnam, near Southampton; 33 Bury Street, St James's, SW1. *TA:* Hellenist (Piccy). *Club:* Athenæum.

**DUKE, Maj.-Gen. Sir Gerald (William),** KBE 1966 (CBE 1945); CB 1962; DSO 1945; DL; *b* 12 Nov. 1910; *e s* of late Lieut-Col A. A. G. Duke and of Mrs Duke, Farnham, Surrey; *m* 1946, Mary Elizabeth, *er d* of late E. M. Burn, Church Stretton; one *s* one *d*. *Educ:* Dover Coll.; RMA Woolwich; Jesus Coll., Cambridge. Commissioned RE, 1931; served Egypt and Palestine, 1936-39; War of 1939-45, in Western Desert and Italy; BGS Eighth Army, 1944; North West Europe, Brig. Q (Movements), 21st Army Group, 1944; CRE 49th Div., 1945. Chief Engineer, Malaya Comd, 1946; idc 1948; Mil. Attaché, Cairo, 1952-54; Comdt Sch. of Mil. Engineering, 1956-59. Commodore Royal Engineer Yacht Club, 1957-60. DPS, WO, 1959-62; Engineer-in-Chief (Army), 1963-65; retired. Col Comdt, RE, 1966-. Governor of Dover Coll.; Special Comr, Duke of York's Royal Military Sch. FICE. DL Kent, 1970. *Recreations:* sailing, shooting. *Address:* Little Tawsden, Brenchley, Kent. *T:* Brenchley 2310. *Clubs:* Army and Navy, Royal Ocean Racing; Royal Yacht Squadron.

**DUKE, Brigadier (retd) Jesse Pevensey,** DSO 1919; MC; *b* 10 June 1890; *s* of Lieut-Col Olliver Thomas Duke and Blanche Wheeler; *m* 1936, Marion, *widow* of Major G. W. H. Massey. *Educ:* Wellington Coll.; Sandhurst. Gazetted to Royal Warwickshire Regt, 1910; served in international occupation of North Albania, 1914, subsequent to Balkan War; various Staff appointments in European War, 1914-18 (DSO, MC, Bt Majority); GSO 3 North Russia, 1920; Staff Coll., Camberley, 1921-22; GSO 3 and 2 Northern Command, 1923-27; Instructor, RMC Sandhurst, 1929-32; Commanded 1st Bn Royal Warwickshire Regt, 1934-36; 1936-47: Col at War Office; AAG, HQ Eastern Command, 153 Inf. Bde; AAG Scottish Command; Army HQ India, Dir of Organisation, Selection of Personnel, India (temp. Brig.); retired, 1947. British Resident, CCG, 1947-50. *Recreations:* golf, painting. *Address:* c/o Lloyds Bank, 6 Pall Mall, SW1. *Club:* United Service.

**DUKE, Rt. Rev. Michael Geoffrey H.;** *see* Hare Duke.

**DUKE, Neville Frederick,** DSO 1943; OBE 1953; DFC and Two Bars, 1942, 1943, 1944; AFC 1948; MC (Czech) 1946; ARAeS; Managing Director, Duke Aviation Ltd; Technical Adviser and Consultant, and Chief Test Pilot, Miles Aviation Ltd; *b* 11 Jan. 1922; *s* of Frederick and Jane Duke, Tonbridge, Kent; *m* 1947, Gwendoline Dorothy Fellows. *Educ:* Convent of St Mary and Judds Sch., Tonbridge, Kent. Joined Royal Air Force (cadet), 1940, training period, 1940; 92 Fighter Sqdn, Biggin Hill, 1941; Desert Air Force: 112 Fighter Sqdn, Western Desert, 1941-42, 92 Fighter Sqdn, Western Desert, 1943, Chief Flying Instructor, 73 Operational Training Unit, Egypt, 1943-44, Commanding 145 Sqdn Italy (Fighter), 1944, 28 enemy aircraft destroyed. Hawker Aircraft Ltd test flying, 1945; Empire Test Pilots Sch., 1946; RAF high speed flight, 1946 (world speed record); test flying Aircraft and Armament Experimental Estab., Boscombe Down, 1947-48; resigned from RAF as Sqdn Leader, 1948; test flying Hawker Aircraft Ltd, 1948; Commanding 615 (County of Surrey) Sqdn, Royal Auxiliary Air Force, Biggin Hill, 1950; Chief Test Pilot, Hawker Aircraft Ltd, 1951-56 (Asst Chief, 1948-51). World records: London-Rome, 1949; London-Karachi, 1949; London-Cairo, 1950. World Speed Record, Sept. 1953. Closed Circuit World Speed Record, 1953. Gold Medal Royal Danish Aero Club, 1953; Gold Medal, Royal Aero Club, 1954; two De la Vaux Medals, FAI, 1954; Segrave Trophy, 1954; Queen's Commendation, 1955. Member: RAF Escaping Soc.; Royal Aero Club (Associate); Royal Aeronautical Soc. *Publications:* Sound Barrier, 1953; Test Pilot, 1953; Book of Flying, 1954; Book of Flight, 1958; The Crowded Sky (anthology), 1959. *Recreations:* sporting flying, yachting; Pres. Aircraft Golfing Soc., 1956. *Address:* 5 Hunters Close, Aldwick Bay, Bognor Regis, Sussex. *Clubs:* Royal Air Force, Royal Air Force Yacht; Royal Cruising, Royal Naval Sailing.

**DUKE, Most Rev. William Mark;** Titular Archbishop of Seleucia in Isauria since 1964; *b* St John, NB, 1879. *Educ:* University of St Joseph, Memramcook, NB; Grand Seminary, Quebec. Priest, 1905; ministered at Moncton, Shediac, Buctouche; Pastor, Cathedral Parish of St John, New Brunswick, 1912-28; Coadjutor with succession to Archbishop of Vancouver and Titular Archbishop of Fasi, 1928; Archbishop of Vancouver, (RC), 1931-64. Asst at the Pontifical Throne, 1936. *Address:* 1114 Holy Rosary Residence, 1100 Burnaby Street, Vancouver 5, BC, Canada.

**DUKE-ELDER, Sir Stewart,** GCVO 1958 (KCVO 1946); Kt 1933; GCStJ, FRS 1960; MA (first-class Hons.), BSc (Sp. Distinction), DSc, PhD (London), MD (gold medal), ChB (St Andrews); FRCS, FRCP; Extra Surgeon-Oculist to the Queen, since 1965, Surgeon-Oculist, 1952-65 (formerly to King Edward VIII and to King George VI): Counsellor, Order of St John; Hon. Ophthalmic Consultant to the Royal Air Force; Ophthalmic Consultant, London Transport; Director of Research, Institute of Ophthalmology, University of London, 1947-65; President, 1965; Hon. Consulting Ophthalmic Surgeon, St George's Hospital, London and Moorfields Eye Hospital; Fellow University College, London, and Institute of Ophthalmology; Hon. Life President International Council of Ophthalmology; surgeon-oculist in London since 1929; *m* 1928, Phyllis Mary, MB, BS, *d* of W. Edgar, London. *Educ:* St Andrews and London Univs. St Andrews Univ., 1st Foundation Scholar, 1915; British Assocn medallist, 1915; Demr. of Physiology (St Andrews), 1918; University Coll. Scholar, 1919; Demonstrator of Anatomy, 1920; Pres. Students' Union and Representative Council, 1921; Royal Infirmary, Edinburgh, 1922; St George's Hospital London, 1923; Henry George Plimmer Research Fellow, 1925; Sir Francis Laking Research Scholar, 1926-29; Paul Philip Reitlinger Prizeman, 1926; BMA Scholar, 1927; BMA Middlemore Prizeman, 1928; William Mackenzie Memorial Medallist (Glasgow), 1929; Research Associate, UC, London, 1930; Howe Lecturer in Ophthalmology, Harvard Univ., USA, 1930; Nettleship Medal for Research in Ophthalmology, 1933; Howe Medallist (USA), 1946; Research Medallist, American Medical Association, 1947; Donders Medallist (Holland), 1947; Doyne Medallist, Oxford, 1948; Proctor Lect., USA, 1951; Gullstrand Medallist (Sweden), 1952; Craig Prizeman (Belfast), 1952; Medallist, Strasbourg Univ., 1952, Ghent Univ., 1953; Gonin Medallist (International), 1954; Lister Medal, 1956; Bowman Medal, 1957; Ophthalmiatreion Medal, Athens, 1957; Charles Mickle Fellow, Toronto, 1959; Proctor Medal (USA) 1960; Fothergillian Medal, 1962; Lang Medal (Royal Society of Medicine), 1965. Served in Army during War of 1939-45 (Brigadier, RAMC), 1940-46; Consulting Ophthalmic Surgeon to the Army, 1946-61; Examiner in Ophthalmology, Royal Coll. of Surgeons, 1947-51; Editor, Ophthalmic Literature; Chm. Editorial Board, British Journal Ophthalmology. Hon. Life Pres., International Council of Ophthalmology; Past President: Faculty of Ophthalmologists; Ophthalmological Soc., UK; Hon. Member: American, Canadian, Australian, French, Belgian, Danish, Swedish, Dutch, Swiss, Italian, Lombardy, Greek, Pan-American, Mexican, Egyptian, All-Indian and Hyderabad Ophthalmic Socs; National Association for Research in Ophthalmology (USA); Ophthalmic Institute of Australia; Australian Coll. of Ophthalmology; Hon. Life Pres., Greek Ophthalmological Soc.; Hon. Mem. Royal Society Sciences, Upsala; Fellow, Med. Soc. Sweden; Royal Netherlands Acad. of Sciences; Hon. Fellow, Internat. Soc. of Eye Surgeons; Correspondant étranger de l'Académie royale de médecine de Belgique; Member: Med. Acad., Rome; Royal Acad., Athens; Chm., Med. Advisory Cttee, British Empire Soc. for the Blind; Consultant, National Soc., Prevention of Blindness, USA; Canadian Nat. Inst. Blindness; Hon. Fellow American Medical Assoc.; American Acad. Ophthalmology; Pan-American Med. Soc.; Pan-American Surg. Assoc.; Hon. DSc (Northwestern, McGill, Manchester), Hon. MD (Dublin), DM (Utrecht, Strasbourg, Ghent, Athens), LLD (St Andrews); Hon. FRCS Edinburgh; FACS; FRACS; FRCP; Hon. FRSM; Hon. Col RAMC; Bronze Star Medal (USA); Star of Jordan (1st class). Kt Comdr, Royal Order of the Phoenix (Greece); Comdr of Orthodox Crusaders, Order of the Holy Sepulchre (Jerusalem). *Publications:* Text-Book of Ophthalmology, Vols I-VII, 1932-54; System of Ophthalmology, Vol. I-XII, 1958-69; Century of International Ophthalmology, 1958; British Ophthalmological Monographs, III, 1927; IV 1930; Recent Advances in Ophthalmology, 1927, 4th ed. 1951; Diseases of the Eye (16th ed.), 1969; The Practice of Refraction, 8th edition, 1968; numerous scientific and clinical papers in the Proceedings of the Royal Society, Board of Research for Industrial Fatigue, and other British, European and American journals, etc. *Address:* 28 Elm Tree Road, NW8. *T:* 01-286 9491; 63 Harley Street, W1. *T:* 01-580 1264. *Clubs:* Athenæum, Garrick.

**DUKES, Cuthbert Esquire,** OBE; MSc, MD, FRCS, DPH; FCPath; Hon. Consultant Pathologist St Mark's Hospital; Hon. Consultant Pathologist, Institute of Urology, University of London; *b* Bridgwater, 24 July 1890; *s* of late Rev. E. J. Dukes and Edith Mary Dukes, BA; *m* Dr Ethel Dukes; one *s*. *Educ:* Caterham Sch.; Edinburgh Univ.; University Coll., London. Past President: Section of History of Medicine, Royal Society of Medicine, 1959; Section of Urology, Royal Society of Medicine, 1957; Medical Soc. of London, 1952; Assoc. of Clinical Pathologists, 1948-49; Section of Proctology, Royal Society of Medicine, 1944; Hunterian Medal and Triennial Prize, RCS of England, 1949-51; Hunterian Prof., RCS of England, 1952; Lettsomian Lecturer, Medical Soc. of London, 1948; Foundation Lecturer, Assoc. of Clinical Pathologists, 1958; Thomas Vicary Lecturer, RCS of England, 1960. Hon. Fellow: Royal Society of Medicine; Assoc. of Clinical Pathologists; Amer. Assoc. of Clinical Pathologists; Med. Soc. of London; Mem. of Pathological Soc. of Great Britain. *Publications:* Several contributions to medical and scientific journals. *Address:* 22 Albemarle, Wimbledon Park Side, SW19. *T:* 01-788 2699. *Club:* Athenæum.

**DUKES, Dame Marie;** *see* Rambert, Dame Marie.

**DULVERTON,** 2nd Baron, *cr* 1929, of Batsford; **Frederick Anthony Hamilton Wills,** TD; Bt 1897; *b* 19 Dec. 1915; *s* of 1st Baron Dulverton, OBE, and Victoria May, OBE (*d* 1968), 3rd *d* of Rear-Adm. Sir Edward Chichester, 9th Bt, CB, CMG; *S* father, 1956; *m* 1st, 1939, Judith Betty (marr. diss., 1960), *e d* of late Lieut-Col Hon. Ian Leslie Melville, TD; two *s* two *d*; 2nd, 1962, Mrs Ruth Fanshawe. *Educ:* Eton; Magdalen Coll., Oxford. Commissioned Lovat Scouts (TA), 1935; Major, 1943. Joint Master of the Heythrop Hunt. *Heir:* *s* Hon. Gilbert Michael Hamilton Wills, *b* 2 May 1944. *Address:* Batsford Park, Moreton-in-Marsh, Glos. *T:* 2116; Fassfern, Kinlocheil, Fort William, Inverness-shire. *T:* Kinlocheil 211. *Club:* Boodles's.

**DULY, Sidney John,** MA; Consultant on the carriage of goods by sea; a Governor of City of London College; *b* London, 30 Oct. 1891; *s* of Henry Charles Duly; *m* 1916, Florence, *d* of William George Smith. *Educ:* St Olave's Gram. Sch.; Corpus Christi Coll., Cambridge; Berlin Univ. Till 1941 Head of the Dept for the Scientific Study of Commercial Products, City of London Coll. Visited Pacific Coast of N America as Mitchell Research Scholar on the carriage of goods by sea, 1926; further voyages of investigation in 1927, 1929, 1930, 1932, 1933, 1934, 1935, 1936 and 1937. Dir, Cargocaire Ltd, 1946-60. *Address:* 34 Sheldon Court, Bath Road, Worthing, Sussex.

**DUMAS, Sir Lloyd,** Kt 1946; FJI; FRGS; Chairman, 1942-67 (Managing Director, 1938-61, retired), Advertiser Newspapers Ltd, Adelaide; Managing Editor of The Advertiser and associated publications, 1929-53; Director: Advertiser Newspapers Ltd, 1931-67; Elder Smith & Co. 1941-67; Elder Smith-Goldsbrough Mort Ltd, 1962-67; Australian Newsprint Mills Ltd, 1938-66, Australian Associated Press, 1940-61 (Chairman, 1949-51, 1959-61); Herald and Weekly Times Ltd (Melbourne), 1946-67; Reuters, 1950-53; Television Broadcasters Ltd, 1959-67 (Chairman); *b* Mount Barker, S Australia, 15 July 1891; *y s* of C. M. R. Dumas; *m* Daisy (*d* 1962), *y d* of E. Smith Hall, S Australia; three *d*. *Educ:* Teachers' Training Coll., Adelaide. Joined The Advertiser Literary Staff as cadet, 1907; transferred to The Argus, Melbourne; subsequently accompanied Mr W. M. Hughes to Imperial Conference, London, 1918; re-joined The Argus on return, becoming Chief of Staff, 1921-24; Editor of the Sun News-Pictorial, 1924-27; Manager and Editor of Australian Newspapers Cable Service, London, 1927-29. Member Board: SA Nat. Gall., 1945-63 (Chm., 1956-63); Wyatt Benevolent Instn, 1962-70 (Chm., 1967-70). *Recreation:* golf. *Address:* Sunbury House, Dutton Terrace, Medindie, S Australia. *Clubs:* Adelaide (Adelaide); Melbourne (Melbourne).

**DUMAS, Sir Russell (John),** KBE 1964; Kt 1959; CMG 1950; Director of a number of West Australian Companies; *b* 17 Jan. 1887; *s* of late C. M. R. and A. Dumas, Mount Barker, SA; *m* 1920, Muriel Elsie Rogers; one *s* one *d*. *Educ:* Prince Alfred Coll., Adelaide, SA; Adelaide Univ., SA, ME (Adelaide), 1931. Carried out various engineering works in S and W Australia, including locks on River Murray, SA, irrigation works and dams in WA. Designed and supervised construction of Canning Dam (218 ft high) in WA and Stirling Dam, 150 ft high (highest earthen dam in Australia). Formerly Co-ordinator of Works and Industrial Development, State of Western Australia; Chm. State Electricity Commission of Western Australia, 1946-54, retired. MICE (London), 1925; MIEA, 1927. *Publications:* contributed papers to engineering journals. *Recreations:* golf and gardening. *Address:* Lawson Flats, 6 Esplanade, Perth, Western Australia.

**du MAURIER, Dame Daphne,** DBE 1969; (**Lady Browning**); writer; *b* 1907; 2nd *d* of late Sir Gerald du Maurier; *m* 1932, Lieut-Gen. Sir Frederick A. M. Browning, GCVO KBE, CB, DSO (*d* 1965); one *s* two *d*. *Educ:* privately; in Paris. Began writing short stories and articles in 1928; first novel appeared 1931. *Publications:* The Loving Spirit, 1931; I'll Never Be Young Again, 1932; The Progress of Julius, 1933; Gerald, a Portrait, 1934; Jamaica Inn, 1936; The du Mauriers, 1937; Rebecca, 1938; Frenchman's Creek, 1941; Hungry Hill, 1943; The King's General, 1946; The Parasites, 1949; My Cousin Rachel, 1951; The Apple Tree, 1952; Mary Anne, 1954; The Scapegoat, 1957; The Breaking Point, 1959; The Infernal World of Branwell Brontë, 1960; Castle Dor (continuation of MS left by late Sir Arthur Quiller-Couch (Q)), 1962; The Glassblowers, 1963; The Flight of the Falcon, 1965; Vanishing Cornwall, 1967; The House on the Strand, 1969; *drama:* The Years Between, 1945; September Tide, 1948; *Edited:* The

Young George du Maurier, 1951. *Recreations:* walking and sailing. *Address:* Kilmarth, Par, Cornwall.

**DUMBELL, Dr Keith Rodney;** Professor of Virology, University of London at St Mary's Hospital Medical School, since Oct. 1964; *b* 2 Oct. 1922; *s* of late Stanley Dumbell and late Dorothy Ellen (*née* Hewitt); *m* 1950, Brenda Margaret (*née* Heathcote); two *d. Educ:* Wirral Gram. Sch.; University of Liverpool, MB, ChB 1944; MD (Liverpool), 1950. Asst Lecturer, Dept of Bacteriology, University of Liverpool, 1945-47; Mem. of Scientific Staff, MRC, 1947-50; Junior Pathologist, RAF, 1950-52; Asst in Pathology and Microbiology, Rockefeller Inst. for Medical Research (Dr Peyton Rous' laboratory), 1952-53; Lecturer in Bacteriology, University of Liverpool, 1952-58; Senior Lecturer, 1958-64. *Publications:* articles in various medical and scientific journals. *Address:* 19 Hillcroft Crescent, Ealing, W5. *T:* 01-997 5528.

**DUMFRIES, Earl of; John Colum Crichton-Stuart;** *b* 26 April 1958; *s* and *heir* of 6th Marquess of Bute, *qv*.

**DUMINY, Jacobus Petrus;** Principal and Vice-Chancellor, University of Cape Town, 1958-67; *b* 16 Dec. 1897; *s* of Johan Andreas Duminy and Maria Catherina Zeederberg; *m* 1930, Gwendoline Ellen Finnemore; two *s* one *d. Educ:* Cape Town Univ. (MA); Oxford Univ. (Rhodes Scholar) (MA, BSc); the Sorbonne. Lecturer in Mathematics and Astronomy, Transvaal Univ. Coll., 1923; Prof. in Mathematics, University of Pretoria, 1930. Principal, Pretoria Technical Coll., 1942. First Vice-Pres., Rotary International, 1969-70. Coronation Medal, 1953. Hon. LLD: Natal, 1962; Rhodes, 1967. *Publications:* various papers on scientific and educational subjects. *Recreations:* tennis, reading, writing, music, drama. *Address:* 2 Winchcombe, The Cotswolds, Kenilworth, Cape, S Africa. *Clubs:* Vincent's (Oxford); City, Country (Pretoria); Owl, Civil Service, (Cape Town).

**DUMMETT, Michael Anthony Eardley,** FBA 1968; Fellow, All Souls College, Oxford, since 1950; Reader in the Philosophy of Mathematics, University of Oxford, since 1962; *b* 27 June 1925; *s* of George Herbert Dummett and Iris Dummett (*née* Eardley-Wilmot); *m* 1951, Ann, *d* of Arthur and Kitty Chesney; three *s* two *d* (one *s* one *d* decd). *Educ:* Sandroyd Sch.; Winchester Coll. (1st Schol.); Christ Church, Oxford. Major hist. schol. (Ch. Ch.), 1942. Served in Army, 1943-47: in RA and Intell. Corps (India, 1945, Malaya, 1946-47, Sgt). Ch. Ch., Oxford, 1947-50, First Class Hons, PPE, 1950. Asst Lectr in Philosophy, Birmingham Univ., 1950-51; Commonwealth Fund Fellow, Univ. of California, Berkeley, 1955-56. Vis. Lectr, Univ. of Ghana, 1958; Vis. Prof.: Stanford Univ., several occasions, 1960-66; Univ. of Minnesota, 1968. Founder Mem., Oxford Cttee for Racial Integration, 1965 (Chm., Jan.-May 1966); Member: Exec. Cttee, Campaign Against Racial Discrimination, 1966-67; Legal and Civil Affairs Panel, Nat. Cttee for Commonwealth Immigrants, 1966-68; Chm., Jt Council for the Welfare of Immigrants, 1970 (Vice-Chm., 1967-69). *Publications:* Contrib. entry on Frege, to Encyclopedia of Philosophy (ed P. Edwards), 1967; (with Ann Dummett) chapter on Rôle of the Government, in Justice First (ed L. Donnelly), 1969; articles in: Aristotelian Soc. Proceedings, Philos. Review, Econometrica, Jl of Symbolic Logic, Zeitschrift für mathematische Logik, Dublin Review, New Blackfriars, Clergy Review. *Recreations:* listening to the blues, investigating the history of card games, reading science fiction. *Address:* 54 Park Town, Oxford. *T:* Oxford 58698.

**DUMMETT, Robert Bryan;** a Deputy Chairman since 1967, Managing Director since 1957, British Petroleum Co. Ltd; *b* 15 July 1912; 2nd *s* of G. H. Dummett; *m* 1936, Mary, *d* of R. A. Grieve; one *s* one *d. Educ:* Rugby Sch.; Göttingen Univ.; Trinity Coll., Cambridge. Joined Anglo-Iranian Oil Co., 1936. HM Legation, Berne, 1941-45. Managing Dir, BP Marketing Interests in Australia, 1953-57. Grand Officer, Order of Merit (Italy), 1967. *Recreation:* gardening. *Address:* Gulson's, Boxted, Essex. *T:* Boxted 207; 4 Audley Square, W1. *T:* 01-499 2884. *Club:* Australian (Melbourne).

**DUNALLEY,** 6th Baron *cr* 1800; **Henry Desmond Graham Prittie;** Lt-Col (retired) late The Rifle Brigade; *b* 14 Oct. 1912; *er s* of 5th Baron Dunalley, DSO, and Beatrix Evelyn (*d* 1967), *e d* of late James N. Graham of Carfin, Lanarkshire; *S* father, 1948; *m* 1947, Philippa, *o d* of late Hon. Philip Cary; two *s* one *d. Educ:* Stowe; RMC, Sandhurst. Retd 1953. *Recreation:* fishing. *Heir: s* Hon. Henry Francis Cornelius Prittie, *b* 30 May 1948. *Address:* Inglefield, Greystones, Co. Wicklow. *Clubs:* Kildare Street (Dublin); Royal Irish Yacht.

**DUNBABIN, Thomas,** BA Oxon; MA (Tasmania); representative in Canada of Consolidated Press of Sydney, NSW, since 1951; *b* Bream Creek, Tasmania, 6 July 1883; 4th *s* of late Thomas Dunbabin; *m* Beatrice Isabel Beedham, MA (Tasmania); one *d* (one *s* decd). *Educ:* University of Tasmania; Corpus Christi Coll., Oxford. Rhodes Scholar for Tasmania, 1906-9; scholar in geography, Oxford, 1908-9; on staff Mercury, Hobart, 1910-16; Argus, Melbourne, 1916-21; The Sun, Sydney, 1921; News Editor, The Sun, 1926-29; Editor and Manager, Australian Newspaper Cable Service, 1929-31; Editor of Daily Telegraph Sydney, 1931-34; Editor The Sun, 1934-36; Editor and Manager, Australian Newspaper Service, 1936-38; special writer, Daily Telegraph, Sydney, 1939-44; Commonwealth press attaché in Canada, 1944-45; Dir of Australian News Buraeu, London, 1946-47; Dir of Australian News Bureau, New York, 1947-48; news editor of Commonwealth of Australia's short-wave world broadcasts, 1940; special correspondent for London Daily Chronicle on return of Amundsen from South Pole, 1912; Pres. Historical section, Australasian Association for Advancement of Science, Hobart meeting, 1928; mem. World's Geographical Conference, Amsterdam, 1938; representative of Australia and New Zealand Science Assoc. at British Assoc. Meeting, Cambridge 1938; Australian Press Attache, Ottawa, Canada, 1948-50. *Publications:* The Making of Australasia, 1922; Sailing the World's Edge, 1931; Slavers of the South Seas, 1935; A Farm at the World's End, 1954. Tasmanian section of volume on Australasia in the Oxford Survey of the British Empire; contributions to Australian Encyclopædia, Encyclopædia Canadiana, Dictionary of Canadian Biography, and Oxford Junior Encyclopædia; historical and geographical essays and studies. *Address:* 124 Springfield Road, Ottawa, Ont, Canada.

**DUNBAR, Sir Adrian Ivor,** 12th Bt of Mochrum, *cr* 1694; *b* 11 June 1893; *s* of Clement Adrian Dunbar (*d* 1940), and Emily Morgan; *S* kinsman, Sir Richard Sutherland Dunbar, 25 Jan. 1953; *m* 1st, 1917, Emma Marie, *d* of Jean Wittevrongel; one *s*; 2nd, 1930, Esther Naomi, *d* of William Henry Robinson; two *s*. Served European War 1914-19, in France, with

Australian Imperial Force. Naturalized an American citizen, 1939. *Heir: s* Jean Ivor Dunbar [*b* 4 April 1918; *m* 1944, Rose Jeanne, *d* of Henry William Hertach; two *s* one *d*. Served as sergeant, Mountain Engineers, War of 1939-45]. *Address:* (seat) Mochrum Park, Kirkcowan, Wigtownshire.

**DUNBAR, Alexander Arbuthnott;** Director, UK and British Commonwealth Branch, Calouste Gulbenkian Foundation, since 1970; *b* 14 March 1929; *yr s* of late Sir Edward Dunbar; *m* 1965, Elizabeth Susannah, *d* of Rev. Denzil Wright, Vicar of Corringham, Lincs; one *s* one *d*. *Educ:* Wellington Coll., Berks; Pembroke Coll., Cambridge (MA). Mil. Service, Lieut QO Cameron Highlanders, 1947-49. Called to the Bar, Inner Temple, 1953. Joined ICI, 1954: Asst Sec., Wilton Works, 1959-63. Joined North Eastern Assoc. for the Arts, 1963, Sec. 1964, Dir 1967; Dir, Northern Arts Assoc., 1967-69; Sec., Standing Conf. of Regional Arts Assocs, 1967-69. *Publications:* contribs to various jls. *Recreations:* art, theatre, running, ski-ing. *Address:* c/o British Linen Bank, 38 Threadneedle Street, EC2.

**DUNBAR, Alexander Robert,** CBE 1964 (OBE 1956); MInstT; Chairman, British Express Carriers Ltd; *b* 20 Oct. 1904; *s* of Robert MacKay Dunbar and Isabella Dunbar; *m* 1941, Margaret Wilby; one *s* one *d*. *Educ:* Whitehill Sch., Glasgow. Traffic Apprentice, LNER, 1924; various Rly Operating appts. Operating Supt (Eastern) BR, 1948; Asst Gen. Man., N Eastern Region, 1954; Manpower Adviser, British Transport Commission, 1958; Mem., British Railways Board, 1962. Chm., St Margaret's House Settlement; Member: Central Training Council; London University Appointments Board. Past Pres., Inst. of Transport; Past Pres. Rly Students' Assoc.; Lieut-Col, Engineer and Rly Staff Corps, RE (TA). OStJ. *Publications:* various papers, Inst. of Transport. *Recreations:* walking and fishing. *Address:* Garden Cottage, New Lodge, Windsor Forest, Berks. *T:* Winkfield Row 2696; 29 John Street, WC1. *T:* 01-405 5602.

**DUNBAR, Sir Archibald (Ranulph),** 10th Bt *cr* 1700; *b* 8 Aug. 1927; *er s* of Sir (Archibald) Edward Dunbar, 9th Bt and Olivia Douglas Sinclair (*d* 1964), *d* of Maj.-Gen. Sir Edward May, KCB, CMG; *S* father, 1969. *Educ:* Wellington Coll.; Pembroke Coll., Cambridge; Imperial Coll. of Tropical Agriculture, Trinidad. Mil. Service, 2nd Lt, Cameron (att. Gordon) Highlanders, 1945-48. Entered Colonial Agricultural Service, Uganda, as Agricultural Officer, 1953; retired, 1970. *Publications:* A History of Bunyoro-Kitara, 1965; Omukama Chwa II Kabarega, 1965; The Annual Crops of Uganda, 1969; various articles in Uganda Jl. *Recreations:* cross-country running, painting. *Heir: b* Alexander Arbuthnott Dunbar [*b* 14 March 1929; *m* 1965, Elizabeth Susannah, *d* of Rev. Edward Denzil Chetwood Wright; one *s* one *d*]. *Address:* The Old Manse, Duffus, Elgin, Scotland. *T:* Hopeman 270.

**DUNBAR, Charles,** CB 1964; Director, Fighting Vehicles Research and Development Establishment, Ministry of Defence, 1960-67; *b* 12 Jan. 1907; *s* of John Dunbar, Barrow-in-Furness, Lancs; *m* 1933, Mary Alice (*née* Clarke), Barnes, SW; two *d*. *Educ:* Grammar Sch., Barrow-in-Furness; Manchester Univ. (MSc). National Physical Laboratory, Dept of Scientific and Industrial Research, 1929-43; Tank Armament Research Establishment, Min. of Supply, 1943-47; Fighting Vehicles Research and Development Establishments, 1947-67, retired. *Publications:* contribs to learned journals. *Recreations:* golf, fishing. *Address:* Edenwood, Chobham Road, Camberley, Surrey. *T:* Camberley 26592.

**DUNBAR, Maj.-Gen. Charles Whish,** CBE 1968; Director of Infantry, since 1970; *b* 2 June 1919; *s* of Dr J. Dunbar, Auchterarder, Scotland; *m* 1941, Jean Elinor Kerr Morton; two *s* one *d*. *Educ:* Glasgow High Sch.; Glasgow Univ. Commnd 2nd Lieut into Royal Northumberland Fusiliers, 1940; served with Maritime RA, 1940-43; served with Para. Regt 1944-48; transf. to RA 1945; Transf. to Highland Light Inf., 1946; Co. Comdr with a Para. Bn and DAA&QMG Para. Bde Palestine, 1945-48; Staff Coll., 1949; Co. Comdr with HLI, N Africa, Malta and Egypt, 1951-53; Bde Major, Para. Bde, Cyprus; Suez, 1956; Jordan, 1958; comd 1 RHF in Aden, Malta and Libya, 1960-62; comd Inf. Bde Gp, Germany, 1962-65; Imp. Def. Coll., 1966; Brig. Gen. Staff, HQ, MELF, Aden, 1967; GOC North West District, 1968-70; Col, Royal Highland Fusiliers, 1969-. Mem., Royal Company of Archers (Queen's Body Guard for Scotland). *Recreation:* general sport. *Address:* Milton, Auchterarder, Perthshire. *T:* Auchterarder 2242. *Club:* Army and Navy.

**DUNBAR, Maj.-Gen. Claude Ian Hurley,** CB 1961; CBE 1950; DSO 1945; DL; late Foot Guards; *b* 1909; *s* of Col C. MacG. Dunbar, MC, of Pityoulish and Kincardine, Aviemore, NB; *m* 1940, Susan, *d* of Gerald Simonds, Farley Hill, near Reading; one *s* one *d*. *Educ:* Eton; RMC, Sandhurst. Commanded: 1st Bn Scots Guards, 1943; 3rd Armoured Bn Scots Guards, 1943-45; 1st Bn Scots Guards, 1945-47; AQMG, London District, 1948-49; Commanded: 2nd Guards Brigade, 1949-50; 4th Guards Brigade, 1950-52; Scots Guards Regt and Regimental District, 1952-54; Brig. A/Q, Eastern Command, 1954-57; Student, Imperial Defence Coll., 1958; Gen. Officer Commanding 42 (Lancs) Infantry Division TA, 1959-62, and North West District, 1960-62; GOC Berlin, British Sector, 1962; invalided, 1963. Croix de Guerre avec Palme (France), 1944; Silver Star (USA), 1947. DL Inverness-shire, 1965. *Recreations:* shooting and fishing. *Address:* Kincardine, Boat of Garten, Inverness-shire. *T:* Boat of Garten 216. *Clubs:* Guards, mcc.

**DUNBAR, Sir David H.;** *see* Hope-Dunbar.

**DUNBAR, Sir Drummond Cospatrick Ninian,** 9th Bt, *cr* 1697; MC 1943; Major Black Watch, retired; *b* 9 May 1917; *o s* of Sir George Alexander Drummond Dunbar, 8th Bt and Sophie Kathleen (*d* 1936), *d* of late J. Benson Kennedy; *S* father, 1949; *m* 1957, Sheila Barbara Mary, *d* of John B. de Fonblanque, London; one *s*. *Educ:* Radley Coll.; Worcester Coll., Oxford. BA 1938. Served War of 1939-45, Middle East, Sicily, Normandy (wounded twice, MC). Retired pay, 1958. *Heir: s* Robert Drummond Cospatrick Dunbar, *b* 17 June 1958. *Address:* Beaufield House, St Saviour, Jersey, Channel Islands. *Club:* Naval and Military.

**DUNBAR, Sir J(ohn) Greig,** Kt 1962; DL; company director since 1931; *b* 19 Sept. 1906; *s* of John Gillison Dunbar and Anne Gardner Greig; *m* 1931, Elizabeth Hart Roy; two *s* one *d*. *Educ:* Royal High Sch., Edinburgh. Banking Apprenticeship, 1923-27; Company Sec., 1930; Bank Dir, 1963; Director: Royal Bank of Scotland; United Biscuits (Holdings) Ltd. Chm. Transport Users Consultative Cttee for Scotland, 1963-; Mem. Council, Scottish Special Housing Assoc. Ltd, 1964-; Mem. South of Scotland Electricity Bd, 1969-. Lord Provost, City of Edinburgh, 1960-63. DL, City of Edinburgh, 1963. Hon. LLD

(Edinburgh), 1962. *Address:* 23 Corrennie Gardens, Edinburgh 10. *T:* 031-447 3622. *Club:* Caledonian (Edinburgh).

**DUNBAR of Hempriggs, Lady Maureen Daisy Helen,** Btss (8th in line) *cr* 1706 (NS); *b* 19 Aug. 1906; *d* of Courtenay Edward Moore and Janie King Moore (*née* Askins); *m* 1940, Leonard James Blake (assumed the name of Dunbar, in lieu of Blake, on claiming succession to the Hempriggs baronetcy after death of kinsman, Sir George Cospatrick Duff-Sutherland-Dunbar, 7th Bt, in 1963; claim established and title recognised by Lyon Court, 1965); one *s* one *d. Educ:* Headington Sch.; Royal Coll. of Music. LRAM 1928. Music teacher at: Monmouth Sch. for Girls, 1930-33; Oxford High Sch., 1935-40; Malvern Coll., 1957-68. *Heir:* (to mother's Btcy) *s* Richard Francis Dunbar of Hempriggs, younger [*b* 8 Jan. 1945 (assumed the name of Dunbar, 1965); *m* 1969, Elizabeth Margaret Jane Lister]. *Address:* 51 Gloucester Street, Winchcombe, Cheltenham, Glos. *T:* Winchcombe 122; Ackergill Tower, Wick, Caithness. *T:* Wick 2812.

**DUNBAR-NASMITH, Rear-Adm. David Arthur,** CB 1969; DSC 1942; Flag Officer, Scotland and Northern Ireland, since 1970; *b* 21 Feb. 1921; *e s* of late Admiral Sir Martin Dunbar-Nasmith, VC, KCB, KCMG, DL, and of late Justina Dunbar-Nasmith, CBE, DStJ; *m* 1951, Elizabeth Bowlby; two *s* two *d. Educ:* Lockers Park; RNC, Dartmouth. To sea as Midshipman, 1939. War Service, Atlantic and Mediterranean, in HM Ships Barham, Rodney, Kelvin and Petard. In comd: HM Ships Haydon 1943, Peacock 1945-46, Moon 1946, Rowena 1946-48, Enard Bay 1951, Alert 1954-56, Berwick, and 5th Frigate Squadron, 1961-63; Commodore, Amphibious Forces, 1966-67. RN and Joint Service Staff Colls, 1948-49; Staff of Flag Officer 1st Cruiser Squadron, 1949-51; NATO HQ, SACLANT, 1952-54 and SACEUR, 1958-60; Dir of Defence Plans, Min. of Defence, 1963-65; Naval Secretary, 1967-70. Comdr 1951; Capt. 1958; Rear-Adm. 1967. *Recreations:* sailing, ski-ing and shooting. *Address:* Glen Rothes, Rothes, Moray. *T:* Rothes 216. *Clubs:* United Service; Royal Ocean Racing.

**DUNBOYNE,** 28th Baron by Summons, 18th Baron by Patent; **Patrick Theobald Tower Butler;** Barrister-at-Law; Recorder of Hastings, since 1961; Deputy Chairman, Kent Quarter Sessions, since 1963; Commissary General of the Diocese of Canterbury since 1959; *b* 27 Jan. 1917; *e s* of 27th Baron Dunboyne and Dora Isolde Butler, *e d* of Comdr F. F. Tower; *S* father, 1945; *m* 1950, Anne Marie, *d* of late Sir Victor Mallet; one *s* three *d. Educ:* Winchester; Trinity Coll., Cambridge (MA). Pres. of Cambridge Union. Lieut Irish Guards (Suppl. Res.); served European War, 1939-44 (prisoner, then repatriated); Foreign Office, 1945-46. Barrister-at-Law, Middle Temple (Harmsworth Scholar), Inner Temple, South-Eastern Circuit, King's Inns, Dublin. Dep. Chm., Mddx Quarter Sessions, 1963-65. *Publications:* The Trial of J. G. Haigh, 1953; (with others) Cambridge Union, 1815-1939, 1953; Butler Family History, 1966. *Recreations:* rowing, lawn tennis, chess. *Heir: s* Hon. John Fitzwalter Butler, *b* 31 July 1951. *Address:* 36 Ormonde Gate, SW3. *T:* 01-357 1837; (chambers) 5 King's Bench Walk, Temple, EC4. *T:* 01-353 4713. *Clubs:* Irish; International Lawn Tennis Clubs of Great Britain (Dep. Pres.) and of USA; All England Lawn Tennis and Croquet Club (Wimbledon); Pitt, Union (Cambridge).

**DUNCAN, Alfred Charles;** *b* 1886; *s* of Samuel Duncan and Mary (*née* McDowell); *m* 1st, 1913, Elizabeth Oakley; two *s*; 2nd 1930, Gwendoline Davies. *Educ:* Newry; Dublin and London Univs. Banking and business experience in Winnipeg, Canada, 1906-08; company and private secretarial experience in City of London, 1910-11; articled clerk to Messrs Franklin Wild & Co., Chartered Accountants, City of London, 1912-16. Served European War, 1914-18, with Artists Rifles, 1917-18. Qualified as Chartered Accountant, 1919. Odhams Press Ltd: Chief Accountant, 1920; Sec. and Chief Acct, 1921; Exec. Dir and Sec., 1942; Financial Dir, 1946; Financial and Joint Managing Dir, 1947; Chm., 1949-60. *Recreations:* golf, literature, preferably philosophical. *Address:* Stormont, Dinorben Avenue, Fleet, Hants. *T:* Fleet 5575. *Clubs:* Golfers.

**DUNCAN, Prof. Archibald Alexander McBeth;** Professor of Scottish History and Literature, Glasgow University, since Oct. 1962; *b* 17 Oct. 1926; *s* of Charles George Duncan and Christina Helen McBeth; *m* 1954, Ann Hayes Sawyer, *d* of W. E. H. Sawyer, Oxford; two *s* one *d. Educ:* George Heriot's Sch.; Edinburgh Univ.; Balliol Coll., Oxford. Lecturer in History, Queen's Univ., Belfast, 1951-53; Lecturer in History, Edinburgh Univ., 1953-61; Leverhulme Research Fellow, 1961-62. Mem. Royal Commn on the Ancient and Historical Monuments of Scotland, 1969-. *Address:* 17 Campbell Drive, Bearsden, Dunbartonshire.

**DUNCAN, Prof. Archibald Sutherland,** DSC, 1943; FRCSE, FRCPE, FRCOG; Executive Dean of the Faculty of Medicine and Professor of Medical Education, Edinburgh University, since 1966; *b* 17 July 1914; *y s* of late Rev. H. C. Duncan, K-i-H, DD and late Rose Elsie Edwards; *m* 1939, Barbara, *d* of late John Gibson Holliday, JP, Penrith, Cumberland. *Educ:* Merchiston Castle Sch.; Universities of Edinburgh, Neuchâtel and Heidelberg. MB, ChB Edinburgh, 1936. Resident hosp. appts in Edinburgh and London, 1936-41. Served RNVR Surg. Lieut-Comdr (surg. specialist), 1941-45 (DSC). Temp. Cons. in Obst. and Gynæc., Inverness, 1946; Lectr in Univ. and part-time Cons. Obstetr and Gynæcol., Aberdeen, 1946-50; Sen. Lectr, University of Edinburgh and Obstetr. and Gynæcol. to Western Gen. Hosp., Edinburgh 1950-53; Prof. of Obstetrics and Gynæcology in the Welsh National Sch. of Medicine, Univ. of Wales, 1953-66; Cons. Obstetrician and Gynæcologist, United Cardiff Hosps, 1953-66; Advisor in Obstetrics and Gynæcology to Welsh Hosp. Board, 1953-66. Member: Clin. Res. Bd of MRC, 1965-69; RCSE, 1968-; Hon. Pres., Brit. Med. Students Assoc., 1965-66. Fellow, Edinburgh Obstetrical Soc.; FRSocMed, etc. At different times Examiner in Obst. and Gynæc. to: Universities of London, Edinburgh, Cambridge, Manchester, Birmingham, Dublin and Liverpool; to RCS, Edinburgh and RCOG. *Publications:* contribs on scientific and allied subjects in various med. jls. *Recreations:* mountains, photography. *Address:* 1 Walker Street, Edinburgh EH3 7JY. *T:* 031-225 7657. *Clubs:* Naval; New (Edinburgh).

**DUNCAN, Sir Arthur (Bryce),** Kt 1961; Convener Dumfriesshire County Council, 1961-68, retired; Chairman of Directors, Crichton Royal Hospital Board, since 1958; *b* 27 Aug. 1909; 2nd *s* of J. B. Duncan, Newlands, Dumfries; *m* 1936, Isabel Mary Kennedy-Moffat; four *s* one *d. Educ:* Rugby; St John's Coll., Cambridge. Chm., The Nature Conservancy, 1953-61, retd. DL,

Dumfriesshire, 1967-69. Lord Lieutenant 1967-69. *Recreations:* ornithology, entomology and shooting. *Address:* Gilchristland, Closeburn, Thornhill, Dumfries. *T:* Closeburn 204. *Clubs:* Farmers', New (Edinburgh).

**DUNCAN, Brian Arthur Cullum,** CBE 1963 (MBE 1949); Judge Advocate General of the Forces since 1968; *b* 2 Feb. 1908; *yr s* of late Frank Hubert Duncan, LDS, RCS, and late Edith Jane Duncan (*née* Cullum); *m* 1934, Irene Flora Templeman, *o c* of late John Frederick Templeman and late Flora Edith Templeman; two *s* two *d. Educ:* Queens' Coll., Cambridge (MA). Called to the Bar, Lincoln's Inn, 1931. Practised South Eastern Circuit, Central Criminal Court, North London Sessions, and Herts and Essex Sessions. Commissioned RAF, April 1940; relinqd commn, 1950 (Wing Comdr). Joined JAG's Dept, 1945. Dep. Judge Advocate Gen. (Army and RAF): Middle East, 1950-53; Germany, 1954-57; Far East, 1959-62; Vice Judge Advocate Gen. 1967-68. *Recreations:* tennis, swimming. *Address:* Elmside, 101 Green Lane, Northwood, Mddx. *Clubs:* United Service, United University.

**DUNCAN, Colin;** *see* Duncan, (P.) C.

**DUNCAN, Surgeon Rear-Adm. David,** CB 1957; OBE 1946; Retired as Medical Officer in Charge RN Hospital, Chatham and Staff Medical Officer to C-in-C, The Nore (1955-58), QHP 1955; *b* 21 Sept. 1900; *m* 1933, Vera McGeorge Payne, Dumfries; one *s* one *d. Educ:* Aberdeen Univ. MB, ChB, 1924; joined RN, 1924; DPH 1929; MD 1934. Malariologist and hygienist, Singapore, 1930-38; Asst to Med. Dir Gen. of the Navy, 1939-46; staff of Flag Officer, Malaya, 1946-48; Asst to Med. Dir Gen., 1948-50; RN Hosp., Chatham; Senior Medical Officer in Charge of Medical and Hygiene Sections, and Naval MOH on staff of C-in-C, The Nore, 1950-53. Naval MOH to C-in-C, Portsmouth Command, 1953-55. OStJ 1947. *Publications:* various articles on the control of mosquitoes, and the prevention and treatment of malaria. *Recreations:* horticulture, golf. *Address:* Wayside, Thorndon Cross, Okehampton, Devon. *T:* Bridestowe 357.

**DUNCAN, Rev. Denis Macdonald,** MA, BD; Managing Editor, British Weekly, 1957-70; Managing Director: British Weekly Ltd, 1967-70; DPS Publicity Services Ltd; *b* 10 Jan. 1920; *s* of late Rev. Reginald Duncan, BD, BLitt and late Clarice Ethel (*née* Hodgkinson); *m* 1942, Henrietta Watson McKenzie (*née* Houston); one *s* one *d. Educ:* George Watson's Boys' Coll., Edinburgh; Edinburgh Univ.; New Coll., Edinburgh. Minister of: St Margaret's, Juniper Green, Edinburgh, 1943-49; Trinity Duke Street Parish Church, Glasgow, 1949-57; Founder-editor, Rally, 1956-57; broadcaster and scriptwriter, Scottish Television, 1963-68; concert promotion at Edinburgh Festival and elsewhere, 1966-. *Recreations:* cricket, badminton. *Address:* 1 Cranbourne Road, N10. *T:* 01-883 1831. *Club:* Arts.

**DUNCAN, George Alexander;** Fellow Emeritus of Trinity College, Dublin, since 1967; Pro-Chancellor of the University of Dublin since 1965; *b* 15 May 1902; *s* of Alexander Duncan and Elizabeth Linn; *m* 1932, Eileen Stone, MSc, *d* of William Henry Stone and Sarah Copeland; one *d. Educ:* Ballymena Academy; Campbell Coll., Belfast; Trinity Coll., Dublin; University of North Carolina. BA, LLB 1923, MA 1926; Research Fellow on the Laura Spelman Rockefeller Memorial Foundation, 1924-25; Prof. of Political Economy in the University of Dublin, 1934-67; Registrar of TCD, 1951-52, and Bursar, 1952-57. Leverhulme Research Fellow, 1950; Visiting Fellow, Princeton Univ., 1963-64. Mem. of IFS Commissions of Inquiry into Banking, Currency and Credit, 1934-38; Agriculture, 1939; Emigration and Population, 1948. Planning Officer (temp.) in Ministry of Production, London, 1943-45; Economic Adviser to British National Cttee of Internat. Chambers of Commerce, 1941-47. Member, Council Royal Dublin Society; Formerly: Mem. Irish National Productivity Cttee; Council Irish Management Inst.; Exec. Bd, Dublin Economic Research Inst. *Publications:* numerous papers in the economic periodicals. *Recreations:* travel, walking. *Address:* 7 Braemor Park, Churchtown, Dublin 14. *T:* Dublin 905721. *Club:* University (Dublin).

**DUNCAN, Sir James (Alexander Lawson),** 1st Bt, *cr* 1957; *b* 1899; *m* Adrienne (*d* 1966), *d* of late William Brandon St Quintin; *m* 1966, Mrs B. M. M. Blair-Oliphant, *widow* of Major Philip Blair-Oliphant, Ardblair Castle. *Educ:* Marlborough. Served European War, 1917-20, 2nd World War, 1940-45, Scots Guards. MP (U) North Kensington, 1931-45; (L-U) South Angus Div. of Angus and Kincardine, 1950-64. *Address:* Jordanstone, Alyth, Perthshire. *Clubs:* Carlton, Guards.

**DUNCAN, Prof. James Playford,** ME Adelaide, DSc Manchester; Professor of Mechanical Engineering, University of British Columbia, since 1966; *b* 10 Nov. 1919; *s* of late Hugh Sinclair Duncan and of Nellie Gladys Duncan, 49 Victoria Avenue, Dulwich, S Australia; *m* 1942, Jean Marie Booth; three *s* one *d. Educ:* Scotch Coll., Adelaide; University of Adelaide, S Australia. Executive Engineer, Richards Industries Ltd, Keswick, S Australia, 1941-46; Senior Physics Master, Scotch Coll., Adelaide, 1946-47; Lecturer in Mechanical Engineering, University of Adelaide, 1948-49, Senior Lecturer, 1950-51 and 1953-54; Turbine Engineer, Metropolitan Vickers Electrical Co., Trafford Park, Manchester, 1952; Turner and Newall Research Fellow, University of Manchester, 1955; Lecturer in Mechanical Engineering, University of Manchester, 1956; Prof. of Mechanical Engineering, University of Sheffield, 1956-66. *Recreations:* sailing, flautist. *Address:* 25 Oceanview Road, West Vancouver, BC, Canada. *T:* (604) 921-7191.

**DUNCAN, James Stuart,** CMG 1946; Hon. Air Commodore; company director; *b* 1893; *m* 1936, Victoria Martinez Alonso, Cordoba, Spain; one *s* two *d. Educ:* Coll. Rollin, Paris. Joined Massey-Harris Ltd, Berlin, 1909; went to Canada, 1911. Served with UK Forces in 1914-18 War, rising to be Capt. and Adjutant of 180th Brigade 16th Irish Divisional Artillery. Apptd Gen. Manager Massey-Harris Co., 1936; Pres. 1941; Chm. and Pres. 1949 until his resignation in 1956. Apptd Actg Dep. Minister of Defence for Air, 1940, when he took over leadership of Brit. Commonwealth Air Trg Plan; declined invitation of Prime Minister, in summer 1940, to join Federal Cabinet as Minister of Air. Chm., Combined Agricl & Food Cttee of UNRRA, 1941-42; Mem. Nat. Res. Council, Ottawa, during War Years. Past Chm.: Toronto Bd of Trade, Toronto Community Chest, Canadian Council of Internat. Chambers of Commerce, Montreal; Hon. Pres., Toronto section, "Free Fighting French"; Chm. Dollar Sterling Trade Council, 1949-61. First Canadian chosen by Nat. Sales Exec. Organization as "Canadian Businessman of the Year," 1956; Chm., Nat. Conf. on Engrg, Sci. and Tech. Manpower, NB, 1956; Dep. Chm. Canadian Trade Mission to the UK, 1957. On accepting Chairmanship of Hydro-Electric Power Commn of Ont., Nov. 1956, resigned from bd of many Canadian cos incl. Argus Corp. Ltd, Canada Cement, Ltd, Canadian Bank of Commerce, Internat. Nickel of Canada, Ltd, Page-Hersey Tubes; resigned from Chmship Hydro-Electric Power Commn of Ont., 1961. Upon establishing residence in Bermuda, Aug. 1961, resigned from Gov., University Toronto; Chm., Dollar Sterling Trade Coun.; Chm., Australian-Canadian Assoc.; Dir, Industrial Foundn on Educn; Dir, Atomic Energy of Canada, Ltd; Chm., Royal Conservatory of Music Cttee. Hon. LLD, Dartmouth Coll., NH, USA, 1957. Chevalier, French Legion of Honour; Croix de Lorraine; King Haakon VII Cross of Liberation. *Publications:* Russia's Bid for World Supremacy, 1955; The Great Leap Forward, 1959; Russia Revisited, 1960; In The Shadow of the Red Star, 1962; A Businessman Looks At Red China, 1965. *Address:* Somerset House, Paget, Bermuda. *Clubs:* York (Toronto); Athenæum (London, England); Rideau (Ottawa); Mid Ocean, Royal Bermuda Yacht (Bermuda); River (New York).

**DUNCAN, Jane;** Author since 1959; *b* 10 March 1910; *d* of Duncan Cameron and Janet Sandison. *Educ:* Lenzie Academy; Glasgow Univ. (MA). Various posts, mainly secretarial in nature, 1931-39. Served War of 1939-45, WAAF, mainly in Photographic Intelligence; demobilised with rank of Flight Officer. Commercial work, 1945-58. Spent years 1948-58 in Jamaica. *Publications:* My Friends the Miss Boyds, 1959; My Friend Muriel, 1959; My Friend Monica, 1960; My Friend Annie, 1961; My Friend Sandy, 1961; My Friend Martha's Aunt, 1962; My Friend Flora, 1963; My Friend Madame Zora, 1963; My Friend Rose, 1964; My Friend Cousin Emmie, 1964; My Friends the Mrs Millers, 1965; My Friends from Cairnton, 1966; My Friend My Father, 1966; My Friends the Macleans, 1967; My Friends the Hungry Generation, 1968; My Friend, the Swallow, 1970; (as Janet Sandison) Jean in the Morning, 1969; *for children:* Camerons on the Train, 1963; Camerons on the Hills, 1963; Camerons at the Castle, 1964; Camerons Calling, 1966; Camerons Ahoy!, 1968. *Recreations:* reading, needlework, gardening. *Address:* The Old Store, Poyntzfield, By Conon Bridge, Ross. *T:* Poyntzfield 249. *Club:* PEN International (Scottish Section).

**DUNCAN, Sir John Norman Valette;** *see* Duncan, Sir Val.

**DUNCAN, John Spenser Ritchie,** CMG 1967; MBE 1953; Minister, British High Commission in Canberra, since 1969; *b* 26 July 1921; *s* of late Rev. J. H. Duncan, DD; *m* 1950, Sheila Conacher, MB, ChB, DObstRCOG; one *d. Educ:* George Watson's Boys' Coll.; Glasgow Acad.; Dundee High Sch.; Edinburgh Univ. Entered Sudan Political Service, 1941. Served in HM Forces, 1941-43. Private Sec. to Governor-Gen. of the Sudan, 1954; Dep. Adviser to Governor-Gen. on Constitutional and External Affairs, 1955; appointed to Foreign (subseq. Diplomatic) Service, 1956; seconded to Joint Services Staff Coll., 1957; Political Agent, Doha, 1958; Dep. Dir-Gen., British Information Services, New York, 1959-63; Consul-Gen., Muscat, 1963-65; Head of Personnel Dept, Diplomatic Service, 1966-68. *Publications:* The Sudan: A Record of Achievement, 1952; The Sudan's Path to Independence, 1957. *Recreation:* golf. *Address:* c/o Foreign and Commonwealth Office, SW1. *Club:* Travellers'.

**DUNCAN, Maj.-Gen. Nigel William,** CB 1951; CBE 1945; DSO 1945; DL; *b* 27 Nov. 1899; *s* of George William and Edith Duncan, Earlston, Guildford; *m* 1928, Victoria Letitia Troyte, *d* of late Capt. J. E. Acland, Wollaston House, Dorchester, Dorset; three *d. Educ:* Malvern Coll.; RMC Sandhurst. 2nd Bn The Black Watch, 1919; transf. Royal Tank Corps, 1923; Captain, 1931; Major, 1938; Lieut-Col, 1940; Col, 1943; Brig. 30 Armoured Bde, 1943, 2nd Armoured Bde, 1946; Comdr Royal Armoured Corps Centre, 1947; Maj.-Gen., 1949; Dir Royal Armoured Corps, WO, 1949-52; retired pay, 1952. Col Comdt Royal Tank Regt, 1952-58. Lieut-Governor Royal Hospital, Chelsea, 1953-57. DL Dorset, 1959. *Address:* The Old Parsonage, Kimmeridge, Wareham, Dorset. *T:* Kimmeridge 222. *Club:* Army and Navy.

**DUNCAN, (Peter) Colin,** MC 1918; QC 1963; Barrister-at-Law; *b* 3 Oct. 1895; *s* of late Peter Thomas Duncan, MD and late Emma Gertrude, *er d* of late Rev. E. H. Genge. *Educ:* Rugby Sch.; Trinity Coll., Oxford. Barrister-at-Law, 1928; Master of the Bench, Inner Temple, 1960. Recorder of Bury St Edmunds, 1949-63; Recorder of Norwich 1963-68. Served European War, 1914-18, Queen's Royal Regiment, Capt. (despatches, MC), Gallipoli, Egypt, Palestine, France, Flanders; War of 1939-45, staff appointments, Lieut-Col. *Publication:* (with Anthony Hoolahan) Guide to Defamation Practice, 1953 (revised edn, 1958). *Address:* Argyle Cottage, Petersham, Surrey. *T:* 01-940 5716; 1 Brick Court, Temple, EC4. *T:* 01-353 8845.

**DUNCAN, Ronald;** *b* 6 Aug. 1914; *s* of Reginald John and Ethel Duncan; *m* 1941, Rose Marie Hansom; one *s* one *d. Educ:* Switzerland; Cambridge Univ. Poetry Editor, Townsman, 1938-46; founded Devon Festival of the Arts, 1953. The English Stage Company, 1955. This way to the Tomb, first produced 1945 at Mercury Theatre, London; The Eagle has Two Heads, London, Sept. 1946; The Rape of Lucretia, Glyndebourne, 1946; Stratton, Theatre Royal, Brighton, 1949; Nothing Up My Sleeve, Watergate, 1950; Our Lady's Tumbler, Salisbury Cathedral, 1951; Don Juan, 1953; The Death of Satan, 1954; The Catalyst, 1956; Abelard and Heloïse, 1960; Christopher Sly, 1962. Pforzheim Opera House; The Seven Deadly Virtues, 1968. *Publications:* The Dull Ass's Hoof, 1941; Postcards to Pulcenella, 1942; Journal of a Husbandman, 1944; This Way to the Tomb, 1946; The Rape of Lucretia, 1946; Home Made Home, 1947; Ben Jonson, 1947; Songs and Satires of the Earl of Rochester, 1948; Stratton, a play, 1948; Jan's Journal, 1948; The Typewriter, a play, 1948; Beauty and the Beast, 1948; Pope's Letters, 1948; The Cardinal, 1949; The Mongrel and other Poems, 1950; Tobacco growing in England, 1950; Our Lady's Tumbler, 1951; Selected Writings of Mahatma Gandhi, 1951; The Blue Fox, 1951; Don Juan, 1952; Jan at the Blue Fox, 1952; Where I Live, 1953; Jan's Journal; The Death of Satan, 1954; Judas, 1959; The Solitudes and other poems, 1960; Judas, 1960; St Spiv, 1960; Abelard and Heloïse, 1961; Anthology of Classical Songs, 1962; All Men Are Islands (Vol I, autobiog.), 1964; The Catalyst, 1965; O-B-A-F-G, 1965; How to Make Enemies (Vol. ii, autobiog.), 1968; The Perfect Mistress and other stories, 1969; Unpopular Poems, 1969; Man, part I of poem, 1970. *Recreation:* breeding Arab Horses. *Address:* Welcombe, near Bideford, Devon. *T:* Morwenstow 375. *Club:* Garrick.

**DUNCAN, Sir Val, (John Norman Valette),** Kt 1968; OBE 1944; Chairman and Chief Executive, The Rio Tinto-Zinc Corporation Ltd, since 1964; Chairman: Rio Algom Mines Ltd, Toronto; New Broken Hill

Consolodated; Churchill Falls (Labrador) Corp. Ltd; a Director of the Bank of England, since 1969; *b* 18 July 1913; *s* of Norman Duncan, MC; *m* 1950, Lorna Frances (*d* 1963), *d* of late Robert Archer-Houblon, Kelowna, BC, Canada. *Educ:* Harrow; Brasenose Coll., Oxford (MA, Law). Called to English Bar, 1938. Served War of 1939-45: RE, mainly on staffs of Generals Montgomery, Eisenhower and Alexander; despatches (twice); Col. Asst Sec., Control Office for Germany and Austria, 1946-47; Asst Dir Marketing, National Coal Board, 1947-48; joined The Rio Tinto Co. Ltd, 1948; Managing Dir, 1951; Managing Dir and Chief Executive, The Rio Tinto-Zinc Corp. Ltd, 1962. Chm., Review Cttee on Overseas Representation, 1968-69. Awarded (twice) Legion of Merit (US); Comdr Order of Orange Nassau (Holland). *Address:* Edenbridge House, Edenbridge, Kent. *Clubs:* St James'; York (Toronto), Mount Royal (Montreal); Melbourne (Melbourne); Royal Yacht Squadron.

**DUNCAN MILLAR, Ian Alastair,** MC; CEng, MICE; DL, JP; Depute Chairman, North of Scotland Hydro-Electric Board, since 1970 (Member since 1956); Chairman, United Auctions (Scotland) Ltd, Perth, since 1967 (Member since 1963); Member: Macdonald Fraser & Co. Ltd, Perth, since 1961; Governing Body of Hill Farming Research Organisation since 1966; Royal Company of Archers (Queen's Body Guard for Scotland) since 1956; Convener of County of Perth and Chairman of Joint County Council of Perth and Kinross since 1970; *b* 22 Nov. 1914; *s* of late Sir James Duncan Millar and Lady Duncan Millar (*née* Forester Paton); *m* 1945, Louise Reid McCosh; two *s* two *d*. *Educ:* Gresham's Sch., Holt; Trinity Coll., Cambridge (MA). Served with Corps of Royal Engineers, 1940-45 (Major; wounded; despatches): 7th Armoured Div., N Africa and Normandy; 51 (Highland) Div., France and Germany. CC 1947 (Chm. Planning Cttee, 1954-), DL 1963, JP 1952, Perthshire. *Recreations:* studying and catching salmon; shooting, meeting people. *Address:* Remony, Aberfeldy, Perthshire. *T:* Kenmore 209. *Clubs:* Royal Automobile; Royal Golfing Society (Perth).

**DUNCOMBE,** family name of **Baron Feversham.**

**DUNCOMBE, Sir Everard (Philip Digby) Pauncefort-,** 3rd Bt, *cr* 1859; DSO 1918; DL, County of Bucks, 1934; JP, *b* 6 Dec. 1885; *s* of 2nd Bt and Flora, *d* of Sir Alexander Matheson, 1st Bt (she *m* 2nd, Arthur Lucas); *S* father, 1895; *m* 1922, Evelyn Elvira, *d* of Frederick Anthony Denny, Horwood House, Bucks; one *s* one *d*. *Educ:* Eton; Trinity Coll., Cambridge (MA 1911). Hon. Attaché at HM Embassy at Madrid, 1908-09; served European War, 1914-18 (DSO, Croix de Guerre). High Sheriff of Buckinghamshire, 1949-50. *Heir: s* Philip Digby Pauncefort-Duncombe [*b* 18 May 1927; *m* 1951, Rachel Moyra, *yr d* of Major H. G. Aylmer, 44 Eaton Place, SW1; one *s* two *d*]. *Address:* Lane End, Great Brickhill, Bletchley, Bucks.

**DUNDAS,** family name of **Viscount Melville,** and of **Marquess of Zetland.**

**DUNDAS, Lord; Robin Lawrence Dundas;** *b* 5 March 1965; *s* and *heir* of Earl of Ronaldshay, *qv*.

**DUNDAS, Sir Ambrose Dundas Flux,** KCIE 1947 (CIE 1936); CSI 1946; ICS, retired; *b* 14 April 1899; *s* of late Rev. A. W. Flux Dundas; *m* 1931, Mary Forrest, *d* of late Rev. Canon Bracewell; one *d*. *Educ:* Harrow; Royal Military Academy, Woolwich; Christ Church, Oxford. Indian Civil Service, 1922; Foreign and Political Dept, 1925; Political Agent, Tochi, 1928-31; Dep. Commissioner, Peshawar, 1934-36; Chief Sec. to Govt NWFP, 1937-41; Resident in Waziristan, 1941-43; Revenue Commr NW Frontier Province, 1943-45; Sec. Defence Dept, Govt of India, 1946-47; Agent to Governor-Gen., Baluchistan, 1947-48; Governor, North-West Frontier Province, 1948-49; retired, 1949. Lieut-Governor, Isle of Man, 1952-59. Chm. Bracknell Development Corporation, 1959-67 (Gen. Manager, 1950-52). KStJ 1953. *Address:* Southfield, Binfield, Berks. *Club:* Royal Automobile.

**DUNDAS, Robert Giffen,** CBE 1961; HM Diplomatic Service, retired 1969; *b* 4 March 1909; *s* of James Dundas and Grace Haxton Giffen; *m* 1938, Pauleen Gosling; three *s* one *d*. *Educ:* Edinburgh Univ. Entered Levant Consular Service, 1931; Vice-Consul: Beirut, 1931; Cairo, 1932; Third Sec., Ankara, 1934; Vice-Consul: Casablanca, 1936; Alexandria, 1938; Suez, 1939; Baghdad, 1941; Consul, Tangier, 1944; assigned to Foreign Office, 1947; Consul, Kermanshah, 1949; Consul-General: Tabriz, 1950; Salonika, 1952; New Orleans, 1955; Stuttgart, 1958; Alexandria, 1961; HM Counsellor and Consul-Gen., Benghazi, 1963-66; Consul-Gen., Amsterdam, 1966-69. *Address:* The Old Forge, Marstow, near Ross-on-Wye, Herefordshire. *Club:* (Hon. mem.) Royal Automobile.

**DUNDAS, Sir Robert (Whyte-Melville),** 6th Bt, *cr* 1821; JP, Perthshire; *b* 31 Oct. 1881; *o surv s* of Sir George Whyte Melville Dundas, 5th Bt, and Matilda Louisa Mary (*d* 1945), *d* of Minden J. Wilson; *S* father 1934; *m* 1926, Dorothea (*d* 1963), *er d* of late A. W. Wiseman, MA, MusBac, Monmouth; no *c*. *Educ:* Trinity Coll., Glenalmond; Keble Coll., Oxford, MA. Administrative Officer, Nigeria, 1911-30. *Recreation:* cricket. *Address:* Comrie House, Comrie, Perthshire. *T:* Comrie 330. *Club:* New (Edinburgh).

**DUNDAS, Sir Thomas (Calderwood),** 7th Bt *cr* 1898; MBE 1945; Director of Barclays Bank Ltd, 1954-67; *b* 27 Nov. 1906; 5th *s* of Sir Henry Herbert Philip Dundas, 3rd Bt of Arniston, and Lady Beatrix Douglas Home, 2nd *d* of 12th Earl of Home; *S* brother, Sir James Durham Dundas, 6th Bt, OBE, 1967; *m* 1933, Isabel, *o d* of late Charles Goring, Wiston Park, Sussex; two *d*. *Educ:* Loretto, Musselburgh. Entered Barclays Bank, 1924; a Local Dir of Barclays Bank, Brighton District, 1935-67. High Sheriff of Sussex, 1959. Major, Scots Guards; served War of 1939-45 (despatches, MBE). *Recreations:* shooting, gardening. *Heir:* none. *Address:* Hammer Hill, Plummers Plain, Horsham, Sussex. *T:* Handcross 267. *Club:* Guards.

**DUNDEE,** 11th Earl of, *cr* 1660 (Scotland); **Henry James Scrymgeour-Wedderburn,** Viscount Dudhope and Lord Scrymgeour, *cr* 1641 (Scotland); Lord Inverkeithing, *cr* 1660 (Scotland); Lord Glassary, *cr* 1954 (UK); PC; JP, DL; LLD; Hereditary Royal Standard-Bearer for Scotland; *b* 3 May 1902; *s* of Col Henry Scrymgeour-Wedderburn, *de jure* 10th Earl and Edith (*d* 1968), *d* of John Moffat, CE, Ardrossan, and Jessie Fulton Arthur; *S* father 1924 (claim admitted by Cttee for Privileges, House of Lords, as Viscount, 1952, as Earl, 1953); *m* 1946, Patricia Katherine, *widow* of Lieut-Col (Hon.) David Scrymgeour-Wedderburn, and *d* of late Col Lord Herbert Montagu Douglas Scott; one *s* (and two step *d*). *Educ:* Winchester; Balliol Coll., Oxford. Pres. Oxford Union, Oct. 1924; MP (U) Western Renfrew, 1931-45; Parliamentary Under-Sec. of State for Scotland, 1936-39;

served with 7th Black Watch, 1939-41; Additional Parl. Under-Sec. of State, Scottish Office 1941-42. Minister without Portfolio, 1958-61; Minister of State for Foreign Affairs, 1961-64; Asst Dep. Leader, 1960-62, Dep. Leader, 1962-64, House of Lords. Hon. LLD St Andrews, 1954. *Heir:* *s* Lord Scrymgeour, *qv.* *Address:* Birkhill, Cupar, Fife. *TA:* Gauldry. *T:* Gauldry 209. *Clubs:* Carlton, Travellers', White's, Pratt's; New (Edinburgh).

*See also John Moffat, Sir Iain Moncreiffe of that Ilk, Bt, Baron Teynham.*

**DUNDEE, Provost of** (St Paul's Cathedral); *see* Haggart, Very Rev. A. I. M.

**DUNDERDALE, Comdr Wilfred Albert,** CMG 1942; MBE 1920; RNVR; *b* 24 Dec. 1899; *s* of Richard Albert Dunderdale, Shipowner, and Sophie Dunderdale; *m* 1952, Dorothy Brayshaw Hyde. Trained as Naval Architect, 1914-17; served with Mediterranean Fleet, 1918-22 (despatches twice); Lieut RNVR, 1920; transferred to British Embassy, Constantinople, 1922-26; Paris, 1926-40; Comdr, 1939. Russian Order of St Anne; Polonia Restituta; French Legion of Honour (Officer); French Croix de Guerre with palm; United States Legion of Merit (Officer). *Recreations:* yachting, tennis. *Address:* Castlefield, Bletchingley, Surrey. *T:* Bletchingley 421. *Clubs:* Boodle's; Royal Harwich Yacht (Harwich).

**DUNDONALD,** 14th Earl of, *cr* 1669, **Ian Douglas Leonard Cochrane;** Lord Cochrane of Dundonald, 1647; Lord Cochrane of Paisley and Ochiltree, 1669; Chairman, Secure Holdings Ltd, de Jersey & Co. (Finland) Ltd and associated companies; a Representative Peer for Scotland, 1959-63; *b* 6 Dec. 1918; *s* of late Hon. Douglas Robert Hesketh Roger Cochrane (2nd *s* of 12th Earl) and of Hon. Mrs Douglas Cochrane (*d* 1960), Hawkhurst, Kent; *S* uncle 1958; *m* 1960, Aphra Farquhar, *d* of late Comdr George Fetherstonhaugh; one *s* one *d*. *Educ:* Wellington Coll.; RMC, Sandhurst. Joined 1 Battalion The Black Watch, 1938; Adjutant, 16 DLI, 1940-41; Staff Capt. 139 Inf. Bde, 1941-42; Staff Coll., Camberley, 1942 (psc); Asst Mil. Landing Officer, 51 (H) Div., 1943; GSO 3 and GSO 2, HQ Eighth Army, 1943; Company Comdr 6 Bn The Black Watch, 1944-45; Bde Major, 180 Inf. Bde, 1946-47; GSO 2, Army Air Transport Development Centre, 1947-49; Company Comdr 1 Bn The Black Watch, 1949-51; DAQMG, SHAPE, 1951; GSO 2, SD3, War Office and GSO 2, Army Council Secretariat, 1952-53; retired 1953. North American Representative, Atlantic Shipbuilding Co., 1953-54. Mem., UK Delegn to NATO Citizens Convention, Paris, 1962. Chm. Anglo-Chilean Soc., 1958-65. Pres., Ayr and Bute Assoc. of Youth Clubs. Vice-Pres., Royal Caledonian Schs. Mem. Council, Anglo-Finnish Soc. *Recreations:* shooting, sailing, ski-ing, golf. *Heir:* *s* Lord Cochrane, *qv.* *Address:* Lochnell Castle, Ledaig, Argyll; Beacon Hall, Benenden, Kent. *Club:* Carlton.

**DUNEDIN, Bishop of,** since 1969; **Rt. Rev. Walter Wade Robinson;** *b* 10 Dec. 1919; *s* of Walter Maitland Robinson and Jessie Maud Robinson (*née* Wade); *m* 1946, Amy Jean Carnie; three *s*. *Educ:* Cathedral Grammar Sch., Christchurch; Canterbury Univ. College; College House, Christchurch; King's Coll., London. Curate, S Mary's, Timaru, 1943-45; Asst Principal, College House, 1945-46; Curate, S Gabriel's, Cricklewood, London, 1946-49; Vicar of Linwood, Christchurch, 1949-52; Curate, Suva Cathedral, 1952-55; Vicar of Viti Levu West, 1955; priest evangelist, Lambasa, 1956; Superintendent, Indian Mission, Lambasa, 1957-62; Vicar of Hornby, Christchurch, 1962-64; Gen. Secretary, NZ Anglican Board of Missions, 1964-69. *Recreations:* music, photography, gardening. *Address:* Bishop's House, 10 Claremont Street, Roslyn, Dunedin, New Zealand. *T:* 60710.

**DUNGARPUR, Rai-i-Ryan Mahimahendra Maharajadhiraj Maharawal Shri Sir Lakshman Singhji Bahadur,** GCIE 1947; KCSI 1935; *b* 7 March 1908; *S* father, 1918; *m* grand-daughter of Raja Saheb of Bhinga, and *d* of Lieut-Col His late Highness Maharajadhiraj Sir Madan Singh Bahadur, KCSI, KCIE, of Kishengarh; three *s* four *d*. *Educ:* Mayo Coll., Ajmer. Visited England, Scotland, Switzerland, France, and other European Countries, 1927; invested with full ruling powers, 1928; Mem., Standing Cttee of Chamber of Princes, 1931-47; one of the select Princes chosen by his order to meet Cabinet Mission, 1946; elected Mem., Rajya Sabha, 1952-58; Leader, Rajasthan Assembly Swatantra Party and Leader of Opposition, 1962; Leader of Assembly Swatantra Party, Leader of SVD, and Leader of Opposition, 1967; President: Swatantra Party in Rajasthan, 1961-69; All-India Kshatriya Mahasabha, 1962-. Patron: Rajputana Cricket Assoc.; Cricket Club of India; Mem., MCC; captained Rajputana XI against MCC and Australian XI on four occasions. Is a keen naturalist and is interested in agriculture and study of wild life. *Address:* Udai Bilas Palace, Dungarpur, Rajasthan India.

*See also Maharaja of Bikaner, Raja of Suket.*

**DUNGLASS, Lord** (courtesy title used by heirs to Earldom of Home before title was disclaimed); *see under* Douglas-Home, Rt Hon. Sir Alec.

**DUNHAM, Cyril John;** Vice-Chairman, Peterborough New Town Development Corporation; *b* 22 April 1908; *m* 1936, Vera Georgia; one *s* two *d*. *Educ:* Watford Gram. Sch.; Coll. of Estate Management. FRICS 1929. Technical Adviser, War Damage Commn, 1941; Dir, Co-operative Permanent Building Soc., 1944; Mem. Council Building Societies Assoc., Chm., 1961-63; Vice-Pres., Internat. Union of Building Socs. Has also served on: Wembley Borough Council; Nat. House-Builders Registration Council; Town and Country Planning Assoc. *Address:* 15 Turner Close, Hampstead, NW11. *T:* 01-455 8348.

**DUNHAM, Doctor Kingsley Charles,** FRS 1955; PhD Dunelm, 1932; SD Harvard, 1935; DSc *hc*; Dunelm, 1946; Liverpool, 1967; Birmingham, 1970; FGS; MIMM; Director, Institute of Geological Sciences, since 1967; *b* Sturminster Newton, Dorset, 2 Jan. 1910; *s* of Ernest Peddar and Edith Agnes Dunham; *m* 1936, Margaret, *d* of William and Margaret Young, Choppington, Northumberland; one *s*. *Educ:* Durham Johnston Sch.; Hatfield Coll., Durham Univ.; Adams House, Harvard Univ. Temporary Geologist, New Mexico Bureau of Mines, 1934; HM Geological Survey of Great Britain; Geologist, 1935-45; Senior Geologist 1946; Chief Petrographer, 1948; Prof. of Geology, Univ. of Durham, 1950-66, Emeritus, 1968-; Sub-Warden of Durham Colls, 1959-61; Miller Prof., University of Ill., 1956; Member: Council, Royal Society, 1965-66; Council for Scientific Policy (Min. of Ed. & Sci.), 1965-66. President: Instn Mining and Metallurgy, 1963-64 (Gold Medal, 1968); Yorks Geological Soc., 1958-60; Internat. Union of Geological Sciences, 1969-. Pres., Geological Soc. of London, 1966-68; Council 1949-52, 1960-64, Bigsby Medal, 1954;

Murchison Medal 1966. Trustee, British Museum (Natural History), 1963-66. Member Geology-Geophysics Cttee (NERC) 1965-. *Publications:* Geology of the Organ Mountains, 1935; Geology of the Northern Pennine Orefield, 1948; (as Ed.) Symposium on the Geology, Paragenesis and Reserves of the Ores of Lead & Zinc, 2nd ed., 1950; Fluorspar, 1952; Geology of Northern Skye (with F. W. Anderson) 1966. Articles in Quarterly Jl of Geological Soc., Mineralogical Magazine, Geological Magazine, American Mineralogist, etc. *Recreations:* music (organ and pianoforte); gardening. *Address:* 29 Bolton Gardens, SW5. *T:* 01-370 2279; Charleycroft, Quarryheads Lane, Durham. *T:* Durham 3977. *Clubs:* Athenæum; Smeatonian; Geological Society's.

**DUNK, Sir William (Ernest),** Kt 1957; CBE 1954; retired as Chairman Commonwealth of Australia Public Service Commission (1947-62); Commissioner, British Phosphates Commission and Christmas Island Phosphates Commission; Director, General Television Corporation and other companies; *b* S Australia, 11 Dec. 1897; *s* of Albert L. Dunk; *m* 1922, Elma K. Evans; one *s* one *d*. *Educ:* Kapunda High Sch., Australia. Australian Public Service from 1914; Auditor-General's Office, 1914-39, Adelaide, New Guinea, London, Sydney; Treasury, 1939-45, as Asst Sec., Special War Services, Dir Reverse Lend Lease, 1943-45; Permanent Sec., Dept of External Affairs, 1945-46. *Address:* 7 Tintern Avenue, Toorak, Melbourne, Australia. *Clubs:* Commonwealth (Canberra); Melbourne (Melbourne).

**DUNKELD, Bishop of, (RC),** since 1955; **Rt. Rev. Mgr William Andrew Hart;** *b* Dumbarton, 9 Sept. 1904; *s* of Daniel Hart and Margaret Gallagher. *Educ:* St Mungo's Academy, Glasgow; St Mary's Coll., Blairs, Aberdeen; Royal Scots Coll. and Pontifical Univ., Valladolid, Spain. Asst Priest, St Mary's, Hamilton, 1929-33; St John's, Glasgow, 1933-39; Army Chaplain, 1939-45; Asst Priest, St Michael's, Glasgow, 1945-48; Vice-Rector, Royal Scots Coll., Valladolid, 1948-49; Parish Priest, St Nicholas', Glasgow, 1949-51, St Saviour's, Glasgow, 1951-55. Mem., Vatican Ecumenical Council's Secretariat for Promoting Christian Unity, 1964-. *Address:* Bishop's House, 39 Roseangle, Dundee. *T:* 24327.

**DUNKERLEY, Harvey John,** CBE 1953; Controller, Midland Region, BBC, 1948-64, retired; now actively engaged in farming; *b* 10 Oct. 1902; *s* of Joseph Braithwaite Dunkerley and Rose Maria (*née* Harvey); *m* 1st, 1928, Kay Hargreaves (*d* 1958); 2nd, 1961, Thelma Couch; one *s* three *d*. *Educ:* Owen's Sch., London; Magdalen Coll., Oxford (2nd class Hons Mod. Hist.). Announcer, BBC, Savoy Hill, 1924; Asst, BBC Relay Station, Liverpool, 1924; Education Officer, BBC, Manchester, 1928; Programme Dir, BBC Midland Region, 1933; BBC European Service, Sept. 1939, latterly as Dep. to Controller. *Recreation:* country life. *Address:* Gallipot Farm, Broadway, Worcs. Eversham 830395. *Club:* Farmers'.

**DUNKLEY, Sir Herbert Francis,** Kt 1943; *b* 2 July 1886; *s* of Charles Dunkley, JP; *m* 1912, Gwendoline Scott Willows Wilson (*d* 1956); no *c*. *Educ:* Wellingborough Sch.; St John's Coll., Cambridge. Called to Bar, Lincoln's Inn, 1921; Joined Indian Civil Service and posted to Burma, 1910; became a District Judge, 1918; Divisional Judge, 1921; Puisne Judge, High Court, Rangoon, 1930-46; Acting Chief Justice, 1945-46; retired 1947. *Publications:* Digest of Burma Rulings, 1872-1937 (2 vols). *Address:* 209 Grosvenor Square, Rondebosch, Cape Town, South Africa.

**DUNKLEY, Captain James Lewis,** CBE 1970 (OBE 1946); RD 1943; Marine Superintendent, P&O Lines, since 1968; *b* 13 Sept. 1908; *s* of William E. Dunkley, Thurlaston Grange, Warwickshire; *m* 1937, Phyllis Mary Cale; one *d*. *Educ:* Lawrence Sheriff Sch., Rugby; Thames Nautical Training Coll., HMS Worcester. Junior Officer, P&O Line, 1928; Captain, 1954; Cdre, 1964. RNR: Sub-Lt, 1931; Comdr, 1951; Captain, 1956. Master, Honourable Co. of Master Mariners, 1970. *Recreations:* gardening, collecting. *Address:* 4 Lancaster Gardens, Clacton-on-Sea, Essex. *T:* Clacton 23047.

**DUNLAP, Air Marshal Clarence Rupert,** CBE 1944; CD; RCAF retired; *b* 1 Jan. 1908; *s* of late Frank Burns Dunlap, Truro, Nova Scotia; *m* 1935, Hester, *d* of Dr E. A. Cleveland, Vancouver, BC; one *s*. *Educ:* Acadia Univ.; Nova Scotia Technical Coll. Joined RCAF 1928 as Pilot Officer; trained as pilot and specialised in aerial survey; later specialised in armament; Dir of Armament, RCAF HQ Ottawa on outbreak of War; commanded: RCAF Station, Mountain View, Ont., Jan.-Oct. 1942; RCAF Station, Leeming, Yorks, Dec. 1942-May 1943; 331 Wing BNAF, May-Nov. 1943; 139 Wing TAF, Nov. 1943-Feb. 1945; 64 Base, Middleton St George, Feb.-May 1945; Dep., AMAS, AFHQ, Ottawa, 1945-48; Air Mem. for Air Plans, AFHQ, Ottawa, 1948-49; AOC North-West Air Command, Edmonton, Alberta, 1949-51; Commandant of National Defence Coll., Kingston, Ont., 1951-54; Vice Chief of the Air Staff, AFHQ, Ottawa, 1954-58; Dep. Chief of Staff, Operations, SHAPE, Paris, 1958-62; Chief of Air Staff, AFHQ, Ottawa, 1962-64; Dep. C-in-C, N Amer. Air Def. Comd, 1964-67. Hon. DCL Acadia Univ., 1955; Hon. DEng Nova Scotia Technical Coll., 1967. *Address:* Island Park Towers, 195 Clearview Avenue, Ottawa 3, Ontario, Canada. *T:* 728 3637. *Clubs:* Rideau, Royal Ottawa Golf (Ottawa).

**DUNLEATH,** 4th Baron, *cr* 1892; **Charles Edward Henry John Mulholland,** TD; DL; Lieutenant-Colonel (Acting) Commanding North Irish Horse T, until 1969; *b* 23 June 1933; *s* of 3rd Baron Dunleath, CBE, DSO, and of Henrietta Grace, *d* of late Most Rev. C. F. D'Arcy, Archbishop of Armagh; *S* father, 1956; *m* 1959, Dorinda Margery, *d* of late Lieut-Gen. A. E. Percival, CB, DSO and Bar, OBE, MC. *Educ:* Eton; Cambridge Univ. Governor of BBC for N Ireland, 1964-. DL, Co. Down, 1967-. *Recreations:* vintage motoring, mixtures and mutations. *Heir: uncle* Sir Henry George Hill Mulholland, *qv*. *Address:* Ballywalter Park, Co. Down, Northern Ireland. *T:* Ballywalter 203. *Clubs:* Cavalry; Ulster (Belfast).

**DUNLOP, Agnes M. R.;** *see* Kyle, Elisabeth.

**DUNLOP, Mrs Annie Isabella,** OBE 1942; *b* 10 May 1897; *er d* of James Cameron and Mary Sinclair Cameron (*née* Cameron), Glasgow; *m* 1938, George Brown Dunlop, publisher and newspaper proprietor. *Educ:* Glasgow High Sch. for Girls; Glasgow Univ.; Edinburgh Univ. MA Glasgow, 1919; PhD Edinburgh, 1922; Diplomée of the Vatican in Palaeography, 1930; DLitt St Andrews, 1934. Teaching of History, 1920-22; historical research and editing in Edinburgh, 1924-28; research at Vatican and other European Archives as Carnegie Fellow, 1928-31; Mem. staff of Scottish Record Office, 1934-38; part-time war teaching in History, Edinburgh

Univ., 1942-48. Local Dir, Kilmarnock Standard and contributor to it. Mem. of Royal Commission on Ancient Monuments (Scotland); Mem., Advisory Council for Scottish Records. Hon. LLD St Andrews, 1950. *Publications:* King James's Secret (with R. S. Rait). 1927; Warrender Papers, 2 vols, 1931, 1932; Calendar of Scottish Supplications to Rome, 2 vols (first, with Rev. and Hon. E. R. Lindsay), 1934, 1956; The Apostolic Camera and Scottish Benefices, 1934; Life and Times of James Kennedy, Bishop of St Andrews, 1950; Acta Facultatis Arcium Universitatis Sancti-andree (1413-1588), 1965. Contributions to Scottish Historical Review, miscellany vols of Scottish Hist. Soc. and other learned jls. *Address:* Torwood, London Road, Kilmarnock, Ayrshire. *T:* Kilmarnock 22239. *Clubs:* University Women's, Royal Over-Seas League; St Rule (St Andrews).

**DUNLOP, Rear-Adm. Colin Charles Harrison,** CBE 1963; RN; Commander, British Navy Staff, Washington, since 1969, and Chief Naval Supply and Secretariat Officer since 1970; *b* 4 March 1918; *s* of late Engr Rear-Adm. S. H. Dunlop, CB; *m* 1941, Moyra Patricia O'Brien Gorges; two *s* (and one *s* decd). *Educ:* Marlborough Coll. Joined RN, 1935; served War of 1939-45 at sea in HM Ships Kent, Valiant, Diadem and Orion; subseq. HMS Sheffield, 1957-59; Sec. to 1st Sea Lord, 1960-63; comd HMS Pembroke, 1964-66; Programme Evaluation Gp, MoD, 1966-68; Director, Defence Policy (A), MoD, 1968-69. *Recreations:* cricket, shooting, smallholding. *Address:* Chanceford Farm, Sand Lane, Frittenden, near Cranbrook, Kent. *T:* Frittenden 242; 4807 Newport Avenue, Spring Hill, Washington, DC, USA. *Clubs:* Army and Navy; MCC, I Zingari, Free Foresters, Incogniti, RN Cricket.

**DUNLOP, Cdre David Kennedy B.;** *see* Buchanan-Dunlop.

**DUNLOP, Maj.-Gen. Dermott,** CB 1949; CBE 1944; *b* 3 Nov. 1898; *s* of late Lieut-Col A. S. Dunlop, RA, Knowle, Lustleigh, S Devon; *m* 1935, Ethel Whitson Scott; two *s*. *Educ:* Sandroyd; Charterhouse; RMA, Woolwich. Commissioned RA 1916; served European War, 1916-19, France and Flanders, RHA (wounded); service at Home and Abroad in various Regtl Staff and Instructional appts, 1919-39; Bde Comdr UK, 1940-41; Middle East and 8th Army, 1942-45; UK, 1946-47; Comdr 2nd Army Group, RA, Tripolitania, 1947-48; GOC, Singapore District, 1948-51, and MEC, Colony of Singapore, 1948-51; Major, 1938; Temp. Lieut-Col 1939; Temp. Brig. 1941; Temp. Maj.-Gen., 1948; Maj.-Gen. 1949; retired, July 1951. Employed Colonial Office, 1951-66. *Address:* c/o Lloyd's Bank Ltd, Cox's and King's Branch, 6 Pall Mall, SW1.

**DUNLOP, Sir Derrick (Melville),** Kt 1960; BA Oxon; MD; FRCP, FRCPE; Extra Physician to the Queen in Scotland since 1965 (Physician, 1961-65); Professor of Therapeutics and Clinical Medicine, University of Edinburgh and Physician, Royal Infirmary, Edinburgh, 1936-62; Chairman: Seager Evans, since 1969; Medicines Commission, since 1969; *b* 1902; *s* of late George Harry Melville Dunlop, MD; FRCPE; *m* 1936, Marjorie, *d* of late H. E. Richardson, WS; one *s* one *d*. *Educ:* Oxford and Edinburgh Univs. Chm. Ministry of Health's Cttee on Safety of Drugs, 1964-69. Formerly Chm. British Pharmacopœia Commission; Vice-Chm. Regional Hosp. Board, SE of Scotland; Mem. Scottish Sec. of State's Adv. Cttee on Medical Research; Ministry of Health's Cttees on Drug Addiction and on Food Policy; Health Services Council's Cttee on Prescribing; Chm. Ministry of Agriculture's Cttee on Food Additives; Chm. Scottish Post-Graduate Medical Assoc.; Sim's Commonwealth Travelling Prof.; Lumleian and Croonian Lectr, RCP London. Ed. Quarterly Jl of Med. Hon. Fellow, Brasenose Coll., 1968. Hon. FACP. Hon. LLD Edinburgh, 1967; Hon. DSC Birmingham, 1967; Eire. *Publications:* Clinical Chemistry in Practical Medicine; Textbook of Medical Treatment; numerous med. papers. *Recreations:* reading, shooting. *Address:* 28 Saxe-Coburg Place, Edinburgh 3. *T:* 031-332 2170. *Club:* New (Edinburgh).

**DUNLOP, Prof. Douglas Morton;** Professor of History, Columbia University, New York, since 1963; *b* 25 Feb. 1909; *o s* of Rev. H. Morton Dunlop and Helen Oliver, *e d* of W. D. Dunn; *m* 1948, Margaret Sinclair, *y d* of Major A. R. Munro, TD, Hillend, Edinburgh. *Educ:* Glasgow Academy; Glasgow Univ.; University Coll., Oxford. Scholar, 1928-32; Vans Dunlop Scholar in Medicine, Edinburgh Univ., 1933; Trinity Coll., Glasgow, 1934-37; Brown Downie Fellow, 1937; Maclean Scholar, 1937 and 1938; University of Bonn, 1937-39; BA Oxon 1939, MA 1960. Trinity Hall, Cambridge (MA) 1950; DLitt Glasgow, 1955. Travelled in Turkey and Syria, 1938; Syria (Jabal Ansariyah), 1939; Asst to Prof. of Hebrew, Glasgow Univ., 1939-46. NFS 1942-44. Asst to Prof. of Oriental Langs, 1947-48, Lectr in Semitic Langs, 1948-50, St Andrews Univ.; Mem. CCG, 1948; Lectr in Islamic History, Cambridge Univ., 1950-62. Visiting Prof. of History, Columbia Univ., 1962-63. FRAS; FIAL. *Publications:* The History of the Jewish Khazars, 1954; The Fusul al-Madani (Aphorisms of the Statesman) of al-Farabi, 1961; Arabic Science in the West, 1965; Arab Civilization to AD 1500, 1970; original papers and reviews in British and foreign Orientalist publications, and articles in encyclopædias. *Recreations:* hill-walking, Scottish history. *Address:* 423 West 120th Street, New York, NY 10027, USA. *T:* RI 9-6557; 46 Owlstone Road, Cambridge. *T:* 54147.

**DUNLOP, Sir Edward;** *see* Dunlop, Sir Ernest Edward.

**DUNLOP, Sir (Ernest) Edward,** Kt 1969; CMG 1965; OBE 1947; Consultant Surgeon; Senior Hon. Surgeon, Royal Melbourne Hospital, since 1964; *b* Wangaratta, Australia, 12 July 1907; *s* of James Henry and Alice Emily Maud Dunlop; *m* 1945. Helen Raeburn Ferguson, *d* of Mephan Ferguson; two *s*. *Educ:* Benalla High Sch.; Victorian Coll. of Pharmacy, Melbourne; Ormond Coll., Melbourne Univ.; St Bartholomew's, London. Qual. in Pharmacy, Gold Medallist, 1928; MB, BS Melbourne Univ., 1st Cl. Hons and Exhibn 1934; MS Melbourne 1937; FRCS 1938; FRACS 1947; FACS 1964. Membre Titulaire, Internat. Soc. of Surgeons. Ho. Surg. and Registrar, Royal Melbourne Hosp., 1935-36; Royal Children's, Melbourne, 1937; Brit. Post-Grad. Med. Sch., Hammersmith, 1938; Specialist Surgeon, EMS London, St Mary's, Paddington, 1939. Served War, 1939-46 (despatches, OBE); RAAMC (Capt. to Col), Europe. Middle East and Far East. Hon. Surg. Royal Melbourne Hosp., 1946; Hon. Surg. Victorian Eye and Ear Hosp., 1949, Hon. Life Governor, 1967; Cons. Surg., Peter MacCallum Clinic, Cancer and Repatriation Dept. Colombo Plan Adviser, Thailand and Ceylon 1956, India 1960-64; Team Leader, Australian Surgical Team, South Vietnam, 1969. Vice-Pres. Victorian Anti-Cancer Council. Cecil Joll Prize and Lectr, RCS 1960. Pres. Aust.-Asian Assoc., Victoria; Pres. Ex-

POW and Relatives Assoc., Victoria. Hon. Fellow Pharmaceutical Soc. of Victoria. Hon. DSc (Punjab), 1966. *Publications:* Carcinoma of the Oesophagus; Reflections upon Surgical Treatment, 1960; Appendix of Into the Smother, 1963; contribs to med. and surg. jls. *Recreations:* farming, travelling, golf; Rugby Union football (Blue, Aust. Caps 1932-34, British Barbarians 1939); formerly boxing (Blue). *Address:* (home) 605 Toorak Road, Toorak, Victoria 3142, Australia. *T:* 20 4749; (professional) 14 Parliament Place, East Melbourne, Victoria 3002, Australia. *T:* 63 1214. *Clubs:* Melbourne, Naval and Military, Peninsula Golf, Melbourne Cricket (Melbourne); Barbarian Football.

**DUNLOP, Frank;** Administrative Director, The National Theatre of Great Britain, since 1968; Director, The Young Vic, since 1970; *b* 15 Feb. 1927; *s* of Charles Norman Dunlop and Mary Aarons. *Educ:* Kibworth Beauchamp Grammar Sch.; University Coll., London. BA Hons, English. Postgrad. Sch. in Shakespeare, at Shakespeare Inst., Stratford-upon-Avon; Old Vic Sch., London. Served with RAF before going to University. Director of: (own young theatre co.) Piccolo Theatre, Manchester, 1954; The Enchanted, for Bristol Old Vic Co., 1955; Arts Council Midland Theatre Co., 1955; Associate Dir, Bristol Old Vic, 1956; Writer and Dir, Les Freres Jacques' presentation, Adelphi, 1960; Director: Theatre de Poche, Brussels, 1959-60; London première, The Bishop's Bonfire, Mermaid, 1960; Nottingham Playhouse, 1961-63; Schweyk, Mermaid, 1963; New Nottingham Playhouse, 1963-64; The Taming of the Shrew, Univ. Arts Centre, Oklahoma, 1965; Any Wednesday, Apollo, 1965; Too True to be Good, Edinburgh Fest., also Strand and Garrick, 1965; Saturday Night and Sunday Morning, Prince of Wales, 1966; (Founder and Dir) Pop Theatre, 1966; The Winter's Tale and The Trojan Women, Edin. and Venice Festivals, also Cambridge Theatre, London, 1966; The Burglar, Vaudeville, 1967; Getting Married, Strand, 1967; A Midsummer Night's Dream and The Tricks of Scapin, Edin. Fest. and Saville Theatre, London, 1967; (Associate Dir) National Theatre, 1967; Mem., Arts Council Young People's Panel, 1968; Productions for the National Theatre 1968-70: Edward II (Brecht and Marlowe); Home and Beauty; Macrune's Guevara; The White Devil; Dir, The Tricks of Scapino (for The Young Vic), 1970. Governor, Central School of Arts and Crafts, 1970. Hon. Fellow of Shakespeare Inst. *Recreation:* travel. *Address:* c/o The National Theatre of Great Britain, The Archway, 10a Aquinas Street, SE1. *T:* 01-928 2033.

**DUNLOP, Sir John Kinninmont,** KBE 1956 (CBE 1945; OBE 1937); CMG 1952; MC; TD; Military Historian; *b* 6 April 1892; *s* of late Andrew Dunlop, merchant; *m* 1922, Agnes Maitland Walker (*d* 1948); one *s*. *Educ:* Mill Hill Sch.; St John's Coll., Cambridge (History Scholar, MA, LLB); Queen Mary Coll., University of London (PhD). Served European War, 1914-18, with 12th London Regt (Rangers) TF and Machine Gun Corps, France, Flanders and USA (wounded, despatches thrice, MC, Order of St Anne 4th class); rejoined Rangers after war and commanded the Battalion, 1935-37; explored and proved the Korba Coalfield, MP, India, 1924-27. From 1932 devoted energies to work on behalf of the Territorial Army, writing, lecturing, etc. In 1937 became AAG, TA at the War Office. Various A/Q appointments, 1939-43; joined Allied Commission Italy, 1943; Regional Commissioner (Brig.) Sardinia, 1943; Lazio and Umbria, 1944; Southern Italy, 1944; Venezia, 1945. Control Commission for Germany, 1946; Dep. Regional Commissioner, Hamburg, 1947; Land Niedersachsen, 1948; Land Commissioner, Hamburg, 1949; HM Consul-Gen., Hamburg, Sept. 1952-56; retired, 1957. Chm., Sevenoaks Urban District Council, 1964; Chm., Anglo-German Assoc., 1965-66; Pres. Kent Archæolog. Soc., 1967. Hon. Citizen of: Cagliari, Sardinia; Padua; Bolzano; Merano; Brezzanone; Brunico. *Publications:* several booklets on territorial matters, 1933-39; The Development of the British Army, 1899-1914, 1935; The Territorial Army of Today, 1939; Hamburg 800 AD-1945 AD, 1948: A Short History of Germany, 1957 (revised edn 1964); The Pleasant Town of Sevenoaks: A History, 1964. *Recreations:* opera, travel, local history. *Address:* Garden House, Solefields Road, Sevenoaks, Kent. *T:* Sevenoaks 52437. *Club:* Athenæum.

**DUNLOP, Richard B.;** *see* Buchanan-Dunlop.

**DUNLOP, Roy Leslie,** CMG 1965; The Clerk of the Parliament, Queensland, since 1954; *b* 14 April 1899; *s* of E. J. D. Dunlop; *m* 1925, Olive M. F. Black; one *s*. *Educ:* Rockhampton. Parliamentary service, 1920-; 2nd Clerk-Asst, 1920-32; Clerk-Asst and Sergeant-at-Arms, 1933-54. Hon. Sec., Commonwealth Parliamentary Assoc., 1954-. *Address:* 30 Ralston Street, Wilston, Brisbane, Queensland, Australia. *T:* 56-3914.

**DUNLOP, R. O.,** RA 1950 (ARA 1939); RBA; London Group; artist; *b* Dublin 1894; *s* of D. N. Dunlop, Kilmarnock, and E. Fitzpatrick, Dublin. *Educ:* Friends' Sch., Saffron Walden. Studied at Manchester and Wimbledon Schs of Art; one of founders of the Emotionist Group of Painters and Writers; held first one-man-show at Redfern Galleries, 1928; held 1939 exhibition Reid and Lefèvre Galleries; exhibition, Upper Grosvenor Galleries, 1969; pictures purchased by the Chantrey Bequest for Tate Gallery, also purchased by Walker Art Gallery, Liverpool, Contemporary Art Soc., Leeds, Bradford, Hull, New South Wales, Australia, Preston, Southport, Glasgow, Aberdeen, Newcastle, Greenock, Bristol, Cheltenham and Rochdale Art Galleries for permanent collections. *Publications:* Modern Still Life Painting in Oils; Understanding Pictures; Painting for Pleasure; Sketching for Pleasure; Ancient Arundel; Landscape Painting; Struggling with Paint. *Address:* Old Mill Cottage, Barnham, Sussex. *T:* Eastergate 2084.

**DUNLOP, Sir Thomas,** 3rd Bt, *cr* 1916; Partner, Thomas Dunlop & Sons, Ship & Insurance Brokers & Lloyd's Agents, Glasgow, since 1938; *b* 11 April 1912; *s* of Sir Thomas Dunlop, 2nd Bt; *S* father, 1963; *m* 1947, Adda Mary Alison, *d* of T. Arthur Smith, Lindsaylands, Biggar, Lanarks; one *s* two *d*. *Educ:* Shrewsbury; St John's Coll., Cambridge (BA). Chartered Accountant, 1939. Former Chm., Savings Bank of Glasgow. Member: Bd of Management, Royal Hosp. for Sick Children, Glasgow; Cttee of Princess Louise Scottish Hosp., Erskine; Royal Alfred Merchant Seamen's Soc.; Exec. Cttee, Trustee Savings Bank Assoc.; Scottish Cttee, Lloyd's Register of Shipping. Governor, Hutcheson's Educational Trust. OStJ 1965. *Recreations:* hunting, fishing, yachting, golf. *Heir: s* Thomas Dunlop, *b* 22 April 1951. *Address:* The Corrie, Kilmacolm, Renfrewshire. *T:* Kilmacolm 3239. *Clubs:* Western (Glasgow); Royal Clyde Yacht.

**DUNLUCE, Viscount; Alexander Randal Mark McDonnell;** Restorer, the Ulster Museum, since 1969; a Restorer, Tate Gallery, since 1965; *b* 3 Feb. 1935; *er s* and *heir* of 13th Earl of Antrim, *qv*; *m* 1963, Sarah Elizabeth Anne, 2nd *d* of St John Harmsworth, Valley Holme, Horsted Keynes, Sussex; one *s* two *d*. *Educ:* Downside; Christ Church, Oxford; Ruskin Sch. of Art. *Recreations:* painting, vintage cars. *Heir: s* Hon. Randal Alexander McDonnell, *b* 9 July 1967. *Address:* Glenarm Castle, Glenarm, Co. Antrim, N Ireland. *T:* Glenarm 229. *Club:* Brooks's.

**DUNMORE,** 9th Earl of, *cr* 1686; **John Alexander Murray;** Viscount Fincastle, Lord Murray, 1686; Baron Dunmore (UK), 1831; Public Relations Executive, Charles Barker & Sons; *b* 3 April 1939; *g s* of 8th Earl of Dunmore, VC, DSO, MVO; *o s* of Viscount Fincastle (killed in action, 1940) and Hon. Pamela Kate Hermon-Hodge (who *m* 2nd, 1944, Capt. Follett Watson Bell, RA), *e d* of 2nd Baron Wyfold, DSO, MVO; *S* grandfather, 1962; *m* 1967, Anne Augusta, *e d* of T. C. Wallace, Dounby, Orkney; one *d*. *Educ:* Eton. National Service, 1957-59, TA Service, 1959-65, The Queen's Own Cameron Highldrs. PRO, Schweppes (USA) Ltd, New York, 1964-67; MIPR 1968. *Recreation:* hill walking. *Heir: kinsman* Reginald Arthur Murray [*b* 17 July 1911; *m* 1948, Patricia Mary, *d* of Frank Coles; two *d*]. *Address:* 32 Regent Terrace, Edinburgh. *Clubs:* Caledonian; Western (Glasgow).

**DUNN, Lt-Col Sir (Francis) Vivian,** KCVO 1969 (CVO 1954); OBE 1960; Royal Marines (retired, 1968) as Principal Director of Music; *b* 1908; *s* of Captain W. J. Dunn, MVO, Royal Horse Guards; *m* 1938, Margery Kathleen Halliday. *Address:* c/o Royal Marines School of Music, Deal, Kent.

**DUNN, James Anthony;** MP (Lab) Kirkdale Division of Liverpool since 1964; *b* 30 Jan. 1926; *s* of James Richard Dunn and Margaret (*née* McDermott); *m* 1954, Dorothy (*née* Larkey); two *s* two *d*. *Educ:* St Teresa's Sch., Liverpool; London Sch. of Economics and Political Science. Chairman: Newsham Community Council; Lyster Youth Club; St John's Youth Centre, Liverpool. Member: Internat. Playgrounds Assoc.; Episcopal Commn for Justice and Peace; Governors, Kirkdale Community Centre; Liverpool City Council, 1958-66. *Recreation:* youth clubs. *Address:* 45 Lisburn Lane, Liverpool 13, Lancs. *T:* 051-226 6054.

**DUNN, Sir John Henry,** 2nd Bt, *cr* 1917; *b* 12 Dec. 1890; *s* of 1st Bt and Ellen, *d* of John Pawle; *S* father, 1926; *m* Mabel, *d* of Alfred Cook, Canterbury (formerly Mrs Harold Letton, Chicago). *Educ:* Downside. Was in South African Police; served European War, 1914-18 (wounded). *Heir:* none.

**DUNN, Brig. Keith Frederick William,** CBE 1941; DL; retired; *b* 31 July 1891; *s* of Brig.-Gen. R. H. W. Dunn, DL, Althrey, Wrexham, and Constance, *d* of Maj.-Gen. G. E. Erskine; *m* 1st, 1915, Ava (*d* 1938), *d* of Brig.-Gen. H. F. Kays, CB; one *s* one *d* (and one *s* decd); 2nd, 1946, Joan, *d* of Sir Frank Beauchamp, 1st Bt, CBE and *widow* of Major Claude de Lisle Bush. *Educ:* Wellington Coll.; RMA 2nd Lieut RA 1911. Served European War, 1914-19 (despatches). Equitation Sch., Weedon, 1922-25; Adjt RMA, 1926-29; Lieut-Col 1938; served in North West Europe, 1939; Brig. 1939; CRA, 1st Cavalry Div., 1939-40; comd 5th Cavalry Bde, MEF, 1940-41; retd 1942; re-employed, comd Glos Sub-District, 1942-45. Chief Training Officer, Min. of Agriculture and Fisheries, 1946-47. DL Glos, 1960. *Recreations:* hunting, golf. *Address:* Bencombe House, Uley, Dursley, Glos. *T:* Uley 255. *Club:* Army and Navy.

*See also R. H. W. Dunn.*

**DUNN, Air Marshal Sir Patrick Hunter,** KBE 1965 (CBE 1950); CB 1956; DFC 1941; director of property companies; Aviation Consultant, British Steel Coporation; *b* 31 Dec. 1912; *s* of late William Alexander Dunn, Ardentinny, Argyllshire; *m* 1939, Diana Ledward Smith; two *d*. *Educ:* Glasgow Academy; Loretto; Glasgow Univ. Commissioned, 1933, Pre-war service in flying boats; as flying instructor 500 (County of Kent) Sqdn, AAF; with the Long Range Development Unit and as instructor at the Central Flying Sch. War service included command of 80 and 274 Fighter Squadrons and 71 OTU, all in Middle East (1940-42); at Air Ministry, and in Fighter Command, Sector Commander, 1945-46. Post-war service in Air Ministry, 1947-48; Malaya, 1949-50; NATO Defence Coll., 1950-52; Fighter Command, 1953-56; ADC to the Queen, 1953-58. AOC and Commandant, RAF Flying Coll., 1956-58; Deputy Air Sec., 1959-61; AOC No. 1 Group, Bomber Command, 1961-64; AOC-in-Chief, Flying Training Command, 1964-66; retired from RAF, 1967. Director i/c Management Services, British Steel Corp., 1967-68; resigned to become Dep. Chm., British Eagle Internat. Airlines Ltd; Chm., Eagle Aircraft Services, 1969. Mem. Council and Chm., Defence Cttee, Air League, 1968-. A Trustee of Loretto, 1959-. *Recreations:* squash, tennis, sailing, shooting. *Address:* Little Hillbark, Cookham Dean, Berks. *Clubs:* Royal Air Force, Hurlingham.

*See also Sir John Denton Marsden, Bt.*

**DUNN, Sir Philip (Gordon),** 2nd Bt, *cr* 1921; *b* 26 Oct. 1905; *s* of Sir James Dunn, 1st Bt and Gertrude Patterson (*d* 1957), *d* of Herbert Molesworth Price, Montmorency, Quebec; *S* father 1956; *m* 1933, Lady Mary St Clair-Erskine (marr. diss., 1944), *d* of 5th Earl of Rosslyn; two *d*. *Educ:* Eton; Trinity Coll., Cambridge. Served War of 1939-45. *Heir:* none. *Address:* Stowell, Marlborough, Wilts. *T:* Pewsey 3439; 65 Eaton Square, SW1. *T:* 01-235 7744. *Club:* White's.

*See also Baron Rothschild.*

**DUNN, Sir Robin Horace Walford,** Kt 1969; MC 1944; **Hon. Mr Justice Dunn;** Judge of the High Court of Justice (Probate, Divorce and Admiralty Division), since 1969; Deputy Chairman, Somerset Quarter Sessions, since 1965; *b* 16 Jan. 1918; *s* of Brig. K. F. W. Dunn, *qv*, and of late Mrs Dunn; *m* 1941, Judith, *d* of late Sir Gonne Pilcher, MC; one *s* one *d* (and one *d* decd). *Educ:* Wellington; Royal Military Academy, Woolwich (Sword of Honour). First Commissioned, RA, 1938; RHA, 1941; Staff Coll., 1946; retired (hon. Major), 1948. Served War of 1939-45; France and Belgium, 1939-40; Western Desert and Libya, 1941-42; Normandy and NW Europe, 1944-45 (wounded thrice, despatches twice, MC). Called to Bar (Inner Temple), 1948; Master of the Bench, Inner Temple, 1969. Western Circuit, Standing Counsel to Registrar of Restrictive Trading Agreements, 1959-62; QC 1962. Treas., Gen. Council of the Bar, 1967-69 (Mem., 1959-63); Chm. Betting Levy Appeal Tribunal, 1964-69. Mem., Lord Chancellor's Cttee on Legal Educn, 1968-69. *Recreation:* hunting. *Address:* 42 Roland Way, SW7. *T:* 01-373 1319; Lynch, Allerford, Somerset. *T:* Porlock 509. *Club:* Cavalry.

**DUNN, Sir Vivian;** *see* Dunn, Sir F. V.

**DUNNE, Irene (Mrs F. D. Griffin),** Hon Doctor of Music, Hon. LLD; *b* Louisville, Kentucky,

USA, 1904; *d* of Joseph A. Dunne and Adelaide A. Henry; *m* 1927, Dr Francis D. Griffin; one *d*. *Educ:* Loretta Academy, St Louis, Mo., USA; Chicago Musical Coll., Chicago. Acted in the original Show Boat, 1929. Entered motion pictures, 1931; first film Cimarron. Films include: Back Street, Awful Truth, Roberta, Anna and the King of Siam, Life with Father, I Remember Mama, The Mudlark (as Queen Victoria), Never a Dull Moment. Laetare Medal, University of Notre Dame. Mem. Defence Advisory Cttee, US, to advise on welfare matters in the women's services, 1951; Mem. US Delegation to United Nations 12th Gen. Assembly. *Recreation:* golf. *Address:* 461 North Faring Road, Moment. Angeles, California, USA. *T:* Crestview 56226.

**DUNNE, Most Rev. Patrick,** DD; Auxiliary Bishop of Dublin, (RC) and titular Bishop of Nara since 1946; Parish Priest of St Mary's Haddington Road, Dublin; Dean of the Metropolitan Chapter; Vicar-General; *b* Dublin, 3 June 1891. *Educ:* Holy Cross Coll., Clonliffe, Dublin; Irish Coll., Rome. Ordained in Rome, 1913; Sec. to Archbishops of Dublin, 1919-43; Parish Priest, Church of the Holy Family, Aughrim Street, Dublin, 1943-47; Domestic Prelate, 1943. *Address:* St Mary's, Haddington Road, Dublin.

**DUNNETT, Alastair MacTavish;** Editor, The Scotsman, since 1956; Chairman, The Scotsman Publications, Ltd, since 1970 (Managing Director, 1956-70); *b* 26 Dec. 1908; *s* of David Sinclair Dunnett and Isabella Crawford MacTavish; *m* 1946, Dorothy Halliday; two *s*. *Educ:* Overnewton Sch.; Hillhead High Sch., Glasgow. Commercial Bank of Scotland, Ltd, 1925; Co-founder of The Claymore Press, 1933-34; Glasgow Weekly Herald, 1935-36; The Bulletin, 1936-37; Daily Record, 1937-40; Chief Press Officer, Sec. of State for Scotland, 1940-46; Editor, Daily Record, 1946-55; Governor, Pitlochry Festival Theatre. Member: Scottish Tourist Board, 1956-; Press Council, 1959-62; Council of Nat. Trust for Scotland, 1962-; Council of Commonwealth Press Union, 1964-; Edinburgh Univ. Court, 1964-66; Edinburgh Festival Soc. Ltd, 1967-. *Publications:* Treasure at Sonnach, 1935; Heard Tell, 1946; Quest by Canoe, 1950; Highlands and Islands of Scotland, 1951; *plays:* The Original John Mackay, Glasgow Citizens, 1956; Fit to Print, Duke of York's, 1962. *Recreations:* sailing, riding, walking. *Address:* 87 Colinton Road, Edinburgh 10. *T:* 031-337 2107. *Clubs:* Caledonian; Scottish Arts (Edinburgh).

**DUNNETT, Denzil Inglis,** CMG 1967; OBE 1962; HM Diplomatic Service; seconded to Board of Trade since 1967; *b* 21 Oct. 1917; *s* of late Sir James Dunnett, KCIE and late Annie (*née* Sangster); *m* 1946, Ruth Rawcliffe; two *s* one *d*. *Educ:* Edinburgh Acad.; Corpus Christi Coll., Oxford. Served with RA, 1939-45. Diplomatic Service: Foreign Office, 1947-48; Sofia, 1948-50; Foreign Office, 1950-53; UK Delegn to OEEC, Paris, 1953-56; Commercial Sec., Buenos Aires, 1956-60; Consul, Elisabethville, 1961-62; Commercial Counsellor, Madrid, 1962-67. *Recreations:* golf, music. *Address:* 11 Victoria Grove, W8. *T:* 01-584 7523. *Club:* Oxford and Cambridge University.

**DUNNETT, Sir George Sangster,** KBE 1952; CB 1950; Chairman: International Molasses, since 1970; Rionda de Pass, since 1970; *b* 12 May 1907; *e s* of late Sir James Dunnett, KCIE; *m* 1938, Margaret Rosalind, *er d* of David Davies, MD, Tunbridge Wells; one *s* three *d*. *Educ:* Edinburgh Academy; Corpus Christi Coll., Oxford. Bd of Educn, 1930; Treasury, 1931; Min. of Civil Aviation, 1946; Dep. Sec., Min. of Agriculture and Fisheries, 1947-56; Chm., Sugar Board, 1956-70. *Recreations:* cricket, philosophy. *Address:* 25 Bark Place, W2. *T:* 01-727 7963. *Club:* Athenæum.

**DUNNETT, Jack;** MP (Lab) Central Nottingham since 1964; *b* 24 June 1922; *m* 1951; two *s* three *d*. *Educ:* Whitgift Middle Sch., Croydon; Downing Coll., Cambridge (MA, LLB). Served with Cheshire Regt, 1941-46 (Capt.). Admitted Solicitor, 1949. Middlesex CC, 1958-61; Councillor, Enfield Borough Council, 1958-61; Alderman, Enfield Borough Council, 1961-63; Councillor, Greater London Council, 1964-67. Former PPS to: Minister of State, FCO; Minister of Transport. *Recreation:* watching professional football (Chairman, Notts County Football Club). *Address:* 97/99 Park Street, W1. *T:* 01-629 2662/3.

**DUNNETT, Sir James;** *see* Dunnett, Sir L. J.

**DUNNETT, Sir (Ludovic) James,** GCB 1969 (KCB 1960; CB 1957); CMG 1948; Permanent Under-Secretary of State, Ministry of Defence since 1966; *b* 12 Feb. 1914; *s* of late Sir James Dunnett, KCIE; *m* 1944, Olga Adair; no *c*. *Educ:* Edinburgh Acad.; University Coll., Oxford. Entered Air Ministry, 1936; Private Sec. to Permanent Sec., 1937-44; transferred to Ministry of Civil Aviation, 1945; Under Sec., 1948; Under Sec., Min. of Supply, 1951, Deputy Sec., 1953; Deputy Sec., Min. of Transport, 1958; Permanent Secretary: Min. of Transport, 1959-62; Min. of Labour, 1962-66. Visiting Fellow, Nuffield Coll., Oxford, 1964. *Recreation:* golf. *Address:* 2 Warwick Square, SW1. *T:* 01-834 5144.

**DUNNING, John Ernest Patrick;** Director, Ministry of Technology, Rocket Propulsion Establishment, Westcott, since 1955; *b* 19 Sept. 1912; *s* of late Rev. E. M. Dunning, MA, sometime Rector of Cumberworth and Denby Dale, Yorks; *m* 1939, Mary Meikle Robertson. *Educ:* Wheelwright Gram. Sch., Dewsbury; Downing Coll., Cambridge (Exhibr, MA). 1st cl. hons Mech. Scis Tripos, 1935. Blackstone Ltd, Stamford, 1935-37; Bristol Aeroplane Co. Ltd (Engines), 1937-38; Armstrong Whitworth Securities Ltd (Kadenacy Dept), 1938-40; RAE, 1940-50; Asst Dir, Min. of Supply, 1950-55; Dir, Engine Research, Min. of Supply, 1955. FRAeS, FIMechE. *Publications:* scientific and technical papers. *Recreations:* gardening (an enjoyable imposition); chess (when possible). *Address:* Church Farm House, Westcott, Aylesbury, Bucks. *T:* Aylesbury 3796.

**DUNNING, John Ray,** PhD, ScD; LLD; Lindsley Professor of Applied Science, Columbia University, New York; Dean of the Faculty of Engineering and Applied Science since 1950, and Scientific Director and Professor of Physics since 1946, Columbia University; *b* Shelby, Nebraska, USA, 24 Sept. 1907; *s* of Albert Chester Dunning and Josephine Thelen; *m* 1930, Esther Laura Blevins; one *s* one *d*. *Educ:* Nebraska Wesleyan Univ. (AB 1929, highest hons); Columbia Univ. (PhD 1934). Began as Physicist-radio engineer, 1927; with Columbia Univ. since 1929, as Asst in Physics, 1929-32; Univ. Fellow, 1932-33; Instructor in Physics, 1933-35; Cutting Travelling Fellow, 1936; Asst Prof. of Physics, 1935-38; Associate Prof. of Physics, 1938; Official Investigator, Office of Scientific Research and Development, 1941-46; Dir of Research, Division 1, Research Laboratories, Columbia Univ., 1942-45; Dir, Division of War Research, Columbia Univ., 1945-46; Special Rep. Manhattan District,

Operation "Cross-roads", Bikini, July 1946; Medal for Merit, 1946. Chairman: Mayor's Cttee on Atomic Energy, New York Golden Jubilee Anniversary, 1948; ASME National Research Council Cttee on Nuclear Energy Glossary, 1948; Basic Science Foundn; Nuclear Energy Policy Board; National Lecturer, Sigma Xi, 1948; Engineers Jt Council Cttee on Nuclear Engineering and Science; Vice-Pres., New York Academy of Sciences, 1951-; Trustee, Horace Mann Sch. for Boys, 1951-59; Bd of Visitors, US Military Academy, West Point, 1953- (Chm., 1954); Amer. Soc. for Engineering Educ. (Vice-Chm., Physics Div.), 1953-; Chm. NY Adv. Cttee on Scientific Manpower, 1956-; Mem. Scientific Adv. Panel, War Dept, 1956-. Fellow: Amer. Physical Soc.; NY Academy of Science; AAAS; Amer. Nuclear Soc.; Mem., Inst. of Radio Engineers, Optical Soc., Amer. Assoc. of Physics Teachers; Bd of Directors: The Oak Ridge Inst. of Nuclear Studies, 1950-; Fund for Peaceful Atomic Development, 1954-; Congressional Panel on Impact of Peaceful Uses of Atomic Energy, 1955-. Trustee Member: Engineering Index Inc., 1956-; Armstrong Memorial Research Foundn, 1957-; Science Service, 1958-; Mem. Adv. Committee: Nat. Urban League, Tech. Adv. Cttee, 1958-; Thomas A. Edison Foundn; Nat. Rivers and Harbors Congress, 1959-; Mem. Scientific Adv. Cttee, Dept of Defense, 1954-; Adv. Council for the Advancement of Industrial Research and Development in NY State, 1959-; Council for the Advancement of Science Writing, 1959-; NY State Science Advisory Council to the Legislature, 1963- (Chm.); Member: Nat. Acad. of Sciences, 1948; Amer. Inst. of Mining and Metallurgical Engineers; Amer. Soc. of Mechanical Engineers; Newcomen Soc. in N Amer., 1960-; Soc. for Hist. of Technology, 1962-; Nat. Sci. Foundn, Divisional Cttee for Mathematical, Physical and Engineering Sciences, 1958-; Empire State Atomic Development Associates. Chm., President's Cttee on Super Sonic Transport–Sonic Boom, Nat. Acad. of Sciences, 1964-; President: Hall of Science, City of NY, 1965; Inst. for Applied Science, 1969-; Chm., NYC Adv. Coun. on Science and Technology, 1965-. Phi Kappa Tau; Sigma Xi, Phi Kappa Phi; Sigma Pi Sigma; Tau Beta Pi; Theta Tau. Director City Investing Co. 1957; Oak Ridge Associated Univs, 1965-; Science Service, 1958. Stevens Award, 1958; Pupin Medal, 1959; Pegram Medal, 1964; Graduate Faculties Alumni Award, Columbia, 1967. Hon. ScD, Nebraska Wesleyan, 1945; Temple Univ., 1955; Whitman Coll., 1958; Trinity Coll., 1958; Hon. LLD: Adelphi, 1951; Phila Coll. of Osteopathy, 1961; Hon. DScEd, Coll. of Puget Sound, 1957; Hon. ScD: University of Jacksonville, 1965; Marquette Univ., 1967. *Publications:* Matter, Energy and Radiation (with H. C. Paxton), 1940; contrib. to Physics Review, Review of Scientific Instruments, American Journal of Physics, National Academy of Science; many monographs and papers on atoms, atomic transmutations, neutrons and nuclear physics and nuclear energy processes. *Recreations:* general interests: development of scientific teaching, researches in Atomic Transmutations, Nuclear Physics, Nuclear Energy, Atomic Power Systems. *Address:* Columbia University, School of Engineering, New York, NY 10027, USA. *T:* 280-2982; Spring Lake Road, Sherman, Connecticut. *Clubs:* Ambassador's, University, Columbia University, Engineers', Men's Faculty (New York); Cosmos (Washington).

**DUNNING, Sir Simon (William Patrick),** 3rd Bt, *cr* 1930; *b* 14 Dec. 1939; *s* of Sir William Leonard Dunning, 2nd Bt, and Kathleen Lawrie, *d* of J. P. Cuthbert, MC; *S* father, 1961. *Educ:* Eton. *Recreations:* shooting, billiards. *Address:* Barclayhills, Guildtown, Perth. *T:* Scone 51764; 13 Winton Lane, Glasgow W2. *T:* 041-334 5408. *Clubs:* Turf; Western (Glasgow); Royal Perth Golfing Society.

**DUNNING, Rev. Thomas George,** MA, PhD; retired; General Secretary, Temperance Council of the Christian Churches, 1952-59; President, Baptist Union of Great Britain and Ireland, 1958-59; *b* 25 Dec. 1885; *s* of John Dunning; *m* 1923, Mary Bell Anderson (decd); *m* 1955, Doris Mabel Rose, MBE; one *s* (of a former marriage). *Educ:* Glasgow Univ.; Scottish Baptist Theological Coll. Asst Minister, John Knox Street Baptist Church, Glasgow, 1915-17, Minister, 1917-23; Minister, Park Street Baptist Church, Luton, Beds, 1923-28; Dir of Education, Temperance and Social Service for Baptist Union of Great Britain and Ireland, 1928-52. Chairman: Bd of Governors of Stonar Sch., Wilts, 1948-58; British Lessons Council, 1947-59. *Publications:* author of various books on religion, citizenship, etc, 1926-. *Recreations:* golfing and gardening. *Address:* 16 Lyford Road, SW18. *T:* 01-874 8336.

**DUNNINGTON-JEFFERSON, Lt-Col Sir John Alexander,** 1st Bt, *cr* 1958; Kt 1944; DSO 1917; LLD (hon.) Leeds; DUniv. York; DL, JP; Chairman, York County Savings Bank; *b* 10 April 1884; *s* of late Capt. Mervyn Dunnington-Jefferson of Thicket Priory, York; *m* 1938, Isobel, *d* of Col H. A. Cape, DSO; one *s* one *d*. *Educ:* Eton; RMC, Sandhurst. Entered Army (Royal Fusiliers), 1904; retired 1919 with rank of Lieut-Col; served European War, 1914-18 (despatches six times, Bt Major, DSO); St Maurice and St Lazarus (Italy); Couronne and Croix de Guerre (Belgium); Legion of Honour (France). *Heir: s* Mervyn Stewart Dunnington-Jefferson, *b* 5 Aug. 1943. *Address:* Deighton House, Escrick, York. *Clubs:* Travellers'; Yorkshire (York).

**DUNOYER de SEGONZAC, André;** artiste, peintre et graveur; *b* 6 Juillet 1884; *s* of Louis Dunoyer de Segonzac, officier de la Marine de Guerre; célibataire. *Educ:* Lycée Henri IV, Paris. Servit Guerre Européenne, 1914-18 (Chevalier de la Légion d'Honneur, Croix de Guerre, 4 citations); Prix Carnegie, Pittsburgh, 1933; Prix de la Biennale de Venise; Médaille d'Or, 1934; Membre de l'Académie Royale de Florence; Sociétaire du Salon d'Automne et des Peintres Graveurs Français. Mem., Hon. Acad. Roy. de Belgique; Hon. Mem., Nat. Inst. of Arts and Letters of New York, 1955. Hon. RA. *Publications: illustrations:* Croix de Bois, de R. Dorgelès, Treille Muscate, de Colette, Georgiques, de Virgile, Le Lierre de P. Brisson, Sonnets de Ronsard, Sport de J. Giraudoux, etc. *Address:* 13 rue Bonaparte, Paris 6e.

**DUNPHIE, Maj.-Gen. Sir Charles (Anderson Lane),** Kt 1959; CB 1948; CBE 1942; DSO 1943; Director: Vickers Ltd; Royal Exchange Assurance; South West Regional Board, National Westminster Bank Ltd; *b* 20 April 1902; *s* of late Sir Alfred Dunphie, KCVO, Rotherfield Greys, Oxon; *m* 1931, Eileen, *d* of late Lieut-Gen. Sir Walter Campbell, KCB, KCMG, DSO; one *s* one *d*. *Educ:* RN Colls Osborne and Dartmouth; RMA Woolwich. Commissioned into RA, 1921; served War of 1939-45 (wounded, despatches); Brig. RAC, 1941; Comdr 26 Armoured Bde, 1942-43; Dep. Dir RAC, War Office, 1943-45; Temp. Maj.-Gen., Dir Gen. Armoured Fighting Vehicles 1945-48; retired 1948. One of HM's

Honourable Corps of Gentlemen-at-Arms, 1952-62. Mem. Board of Governors, Sherborne Sch. US Legion of Merit (Commander); US Silver Star. *Address:* Elliscome House, Wincanton, Somerset. *Club:* Cavalry.

**DUNPHY, Rev. Thomas Patrick,** SJ; on staff of the Provincial of the Society of Jesus in England, since 1967; *b* Donnybrook, Dublin, 17 Aug. 1913; *o s* of Thomas Joseph Dunphy and Agnes Mary (*née* Rogers), Dublin; unmarried. *Educ:* Wimbledon Coll. Joined Soc. of Jesus, 1932; Priest, 1946. Headmaster of St John's (preparatory sch. of Beaumont Coll.), 1949-64; Rector, Beaumont Coll., 1964-67. *Address:* 114 Mount Street, W1.

**DUNRAVEN and MOUNT-EARL,** 7th Earl of, *cr* 1822; **Thady Windham Thomas Wyndham-Quin;** Baron Adare, 1800; Viscount Mountearl, 1816; Viscount Adare, 1822; Bt 1871; *b* 27 Oct. 1939; *s* of 6th Earl of Dunraven and Mount-Earl, CB, CBE, MC, and Nancy, *d* of Thomas B. Yuille, Halifax County, Va; *S* father 1965; *m* 1969, Geraldine, *d* of Air Commodore Gerard W. McAleer, CBE, MB, BCh, DTM&H, Wokingham. *Educ:* Ludgrove; Le Rosey. *Address:* Adare Manor, Adare, Co. Limerick, Ireland. *Clubs:* White's; Kildare Street (Dublin).

**DUNROSSIL,** 2nd Viscount, *cr* 1959; **John William Morrison;** HM Diplomatic Service; Counsellor and Head of Chancery, British High Commission, Ottawa, since 1970; *b* 22 May 1926; *e s* of William Shepherd Morrison, 1st Viscount Dunrossil, PC, GCMG, MC, QC; *S* father, 1961; *m* 1st, 1951, Mavis (marr. diss. 1969), *d* of A. Ll. Spencer-Payne, LRCP, MRCS, LDS; three *s* one *d*; 2nd, 1969, Diana Mary Cunliffe, *d* of C. M. Vise. *Educ:* Fettes; Oxford. Royal Air Force, 1945-48, Flt-Lieut (Pilot). Joined Commonwealth Relations Office, 1951; Asst Private Sec. to Sec. of State, 1952-54; Second Sec., Canberra, 1954-56; CRO, 1956-58; First Sec. and Acting Deputy High Commissioner, Dacca, East Pakistan, 1958-60; First Sec., Pretoria/Capetown, 1961-64; FO, 1964-68; seconded to Intergovernmental Maritime Consultative Org., 1968-70. *Heir: s* Hon. Andrew William Reginald Morrison, *b* 15 Dec. 1953. *Address:* c/o Foreign and Commonwealth Office, SW1; 1 Temple Gardens, EC4. *Clubs:* Royal Scots (Edinburgh); Country (Pretoria).

**DUNSANY,** 19th Baron of, *cr* 1439; **Randal Arthur Henry Plunkett;** Lieut-Col (retd) Indian Cavalry (Guides); *b* 25 Aug. 1906; *o s* of 18th Baron Dunsany, DL, LittD, and Rt Hon. Beatrice, Lady Dunsany (*d* 1970); *S* father, 1957; *m* 1st, 1938, Mrs Vera Bryce (from whom he obtained a divorce, 1947), *d* of Señor G. De Sã Sottomaior, São Paulo, Brazil; one *s*; 2nd, 1947, Sheila Victoria Katrin, widow of Major John Frederick Foley, Baron de Rutzen, DL, JP, CC, Welsh Guards (killed in action, 1944), *o d* of Sir Henry Philipps, 2nd Bt; one *d*. *Educ:* Eton. Joined the 16th/5th Lancers (SR), 1926; transferred to the Indian Army, 1928, Guides Cavalry, Indian Armoured Corps, retired, 1947. *Heir: s* Hon. Edward John Carlos Plunkett [*b* 10 Sept. 1939. *Educ:* Eton]. *Address:* (Seats) Dunsany Castle, Co. Meath, Ireland. *T:* Dunsany 8; Dunstall Priory, Shoreham, Kent. *Clubs:* Beefsteak, Bath, Cavalry; Kildare Street (Dublin).

**DUNSHEATH, Percy,** CBE 1946; MA Cantab, DSc (Eng) London; Hon. DEng Sheffield; Hon. LLD London; Member of Senate, University of London, 1946-67; *b* 16 Aug. 1886; *s* of late Hugh and Anna Dunsheath, Sheffield; *m* 1st, 1910, Elizabeth Alice, *d* of W. D. F. Vincent, Acton; one *d* decd and one *s* killed on active service; *m* 2nd, 1938, Cissie Providence, *d* of C. Houchen, Hempnall, Norwich. *Educ:* Sheffield Grammar Sch.; Universities of Sheffield, London and Cambridge (Mech. Sci. Tripos). GPO Engineer in Chief's office, 1908-19. Served European War, 1914-18; commissioned; France (despatches twice, OBE). Research Dir, W. T. Henley's, 1919; subs. Chief Engineer; retd, 1946. President, Instn of Electrical Engineers (1945-46). Hon. mem., 1964-; Chm. of Convocation, University of London, 1949-61. Mem. Heyworth Cttee on Univ. appointments Boards, 1964. Pres. Internat. Electrotechnical Commn (1955-58); Pres. British Electrical Development Association (1952-53); Past Chm. Govs Woolwich Polytechnic; Pres. ASLIB (Assoc. Special Libraries Information Bureau), 1949, 1950; Chairman: London Reg. Academic Board Technical Educ., 1947-53; FBI Educ. Cttee, 1951-55; Cambridge Instrument Co., 1956-63 (Dir 1950-64); Special Cttee on Shortage of Science Teachers, 1954. Faraday lecturer, 1947; Royal Institution Christmas Lectures, 1949. Hon. Fellow, University Coll., London, 1967. *Publications:* The Graduate in Industry, 1947; (ed) A century of Technology, 1951; The Electric Current, 1951; Industrial Research, 1956; Convocation in the University of London, 1958; Electricity: How it works, 1960; A History of Electrical Engineering, 1961; Giants of Electricity, 1967; many papers and articles on scientific, technical and educational subjects. *Recreation:* water colour painting. *Address:* Sutton Place, Abinger Hammer, Surrey. *T:* Dorking 730309. *Club:* Athenæum.

**DUNSTAN, (Andrew Harold) Bernard,** RA 1968 (ARA 1959); painter; *b* 19 Jan. 1920; *s* of late Dr A. E. Dunstan; *m* 1949, Diana Maxwell Armfield; three *s*. *Educ:* St Paul's; Byam Shaw Sch.; Slade Sch. Mem. New English Art Club, RWA. *Recreation:* music. *Address:* 10 High Park Road, Kew, Richmond, Surrey. *T:* 01-876 6633.

**DUNSTAN, Bernard;** *see* Dunstan, A. H. B.

**DUNSTAN, Rev. Prof. Gordon Reginald;** F. D. Maurice Professor of Moral and Social Theology, King's College, London, since 1967; *b* 25 April 1917; *yr s* of late Frederick John Menhennet and Winifred Amy Dunstan (*née* Orchard); *m* 1949, Ruby Maud (*née* Fitzer); two *s* one *d*. *Educ:* Plymouth Corp. Gram. Sch.; University of Leeds; College of the Resurrection, Mirfield. BA, 1st cl. Hist., 1938, Rutson Post-Grad. Schol. 1938, MA w dist. 1939, Leeds Univ. FSA 1957. Deacon 1941, priest 1942; Curate, King Cross, Halifax, 1941-45; Huddersfield, 1945-46; Sub Warden, St Deiniol's Library, Hawarden, 1945-49; Vicar of Sutton Courtney with Appleford, 1949-55; Lecturer, Wm Temple Coll., 1947-49; Ripon Hall, Oxford, 1953-55; Minor Canon, St George's Chapel, Windsor Castle, Suffolk IP14 4PQ. westminster Abbey, 1959-67; Canon Theologian, Leicester Cathedral, 1966-. Sec., C of E Council for Social Work, 1955-63; Sec., Church Assembly Jt Bd of Studies, 1963-66; Editor of Crucible, 1962-66; Editor of Theology, 1965-; Dep. Priest in Ordinary to the Queen, 1959-64, Priest in Ordinary, 1964-; Select Preacher: University of Cambridge 1960; Leeds, 1970. Prideaux Lectr, Univ. of Exeter, 1968; Gresham's Prof. in Divinity, 1969-. Mem. Council, Canterbury and York Soc., 1950-. Mem. or Sec. cttees on social and ethical problems; Vice-Pres., 1965-66, and Chm. Brit. Cttee, of Internat. Union of Family Organizations, 1964-66. *Publications:* The Family Is Not Broken, 1962; The Register of Edmund Lacy, Bishop of Exeter 1420-1455: vol. I, 1963; vol. II, 1966; vol. III, 1967; vol. IV, 1971; A Digger Still, 1968; Not Yet the Epitaph, 1968; The Sacred Ministry, 1970. *Recreations:* local history, music, bee-keeping. *Address:* King's College, Strand, WC2R 2LS. *T:* 01-836 5454; 34 Cranes Park, Surbiton, Surrey. *T:* 01-399 9249.

**DUNTZE, Sir George (Edwin Douglas),** 6th Bt, *cr* 1774; CMG 1960; *b* 1 June 1913; *o s* of Sir George Puxley Duntze, 5th Baronet, and Violet May, *d* of late Henry M. Sanderson; *S* father, 1947; *m* 1st, 1941, Joan, *d* of late Major F. E. Bradstock, DSO, MC (marriage dissolved, 1966); one *d*; 2nd, 1966, Nesta, *e d* of late Thomas R. P. Herbert, Newport, Mon. *Educ:* Shrewsbury Sch.; Trinity Coll., Oxford. (MA). Entered Colonial Administrative Service, 1936. Provincial Comr, Uganda, 1952-61. *Heir: kinsman,* John Alexander Duntze [*b* 13 Nov. 1909; *m* 1935, Emily Ellsworth, *d* of Elmer E. Harlow, USA]. *Address:* 25 Ennismore Gardens, SW7. *Clubs:* Royal Automobile; Leander.

**DUNWICH, Suffragan Bishop of,** since 1967; **Rt. Rev. David Rokeby Maddock;** *b* 30 May 1915; *s* of Walter Rokeby Maddock; *m* 1943, Mary Jesse Hoernle, *widow* of Edward Selwyn Hoernle, ICS and *d* of Rev. Selwyn Charles Freer; one *s* one *d*. *Educ:* Clifton Coll.; Bristol Univ.; St Catherine's, Oxford; Wycliffe Hall, Oxford. Curate, Chard, Somerset, 1939-43; Vicar, Wilton, Taunton, 1943-47; Rector, Wareham, 1947-61; Rector of Bradford Peverell and Stratton, 1961-66; Rector of West Stafford with Frome Billet, 1966-67. Rural Dean of Purbeck, 1948-61; Canon of Salisbury, 1956-67; Archdeacon of Sherborne, 1961-67; Archdeacon of Sudbury, 1968-70. Hon. Chaplain Dorset Constabulary, 1964-67. *Recreation:* rough gardening. *Address:* Old Newton House, near Stowmarket, Suffolk IP14 4PQ.

**DUNWOODY, Gwyneth Patricia, (Mrs J. E. O. Dunwoody);** Executive Director, Film Production Association of Great Britain, since 1970; *b* 12 Dec. 1930; *d* of late Morgan Phillips and of Baroness Phillips, *qv*; *m* 1954, Dr John Elliott Orr Dunwoody, *qv*; two *s* one *d*. MP (Lab) Exeter, 1966-70; Parly Sec. to BoT, 1967-70. *Address:* 214 Ashley Gardens, SW1. *T:* 01-828 9201.

**DUNWOODY, Dr John (Elliott Orr);** *b* 3 June 1929; *s* of Dr W. O. and Mrs F. J. Dunwoody; *m* 1954, Gwyneth Patricia (*née* Phillips), *qv*; two *s* one *d*. *Educ:* St Paul's Sch.; King's Coll., London Univ.; Westminster Hosp. Med. Sch. MB, BS London; MRCS, LRCP 1954. House Surgeon, Westminster (Gordon) Hosp., 1954; House Physician, Royal Berks Hosp., 1954-55; Sen. House Physician, Newton Abbot Hosp., 1955-56; Family Doctor and Medical Officer, Totnes District Hosp, 1956-66. MP (Lab) Falmouth and Camborne, 1966-70; Parly Under-Sec., Dept of Health and Social Security, 1969-70. Mem. Exec. Cttee, British Council; Sec. South-West Group of Labour MPs; Pres., Cornwall Fedn of Labour Parties. *Address:* 214 Ashley Gardens, SW1. *T:* 01-828 9201.

**DUNWORTH, John Vernon,** CB 1969; CBE 1955; Director, National Physical Laboratory, since 1964; *b* 24 Feb. 1917; *o c* of late John Dunworth and Susan Ida (*née* Warburton); *m* 1967, Patricia Noel Boston; one *d*. *Educ:* Manchester Grammar Sch. Major Scholar, Clare Coll., Cambridge, 1933; Denman Baynes Research Studentship, 1937. Robins Prize, 1937. War Service: Ministry of Supply on Radar Development, 1939-44; National Research Council of Canada, on Atomic Energy Development, 1944-45. PhD (Cambridge), 1941; Twisden Studentship and elected Fellow, Trinity Coll., Cambridge, 1941. Univ. Demonstrator in Physics, Cambridge, 1945. Joined Atomic Energy Research Establishment, Harwell, 1947; Head of Reactor Division, 1956; Deputy Director, Atomic Energy Establishment, Winfrith Heath, Dorset, 1959-62; Deputy Dir, National Physical Laboratory, 1962-64. Mem. British Science Writers Association, 1957; Alternate United Kingdom Member on Organising Cttee of UN Atoms for Peace Confs in Geneva, 1955 and 1958. FInstP 1955; Mem. Cambridge Univ. Engineering Soc., 1957; FIEE 1960; Fellow Amer. Nuclear Soc. 1960. Chm., British Nuclear Energy Soc., 1964-70; Member: Council of Institute of Physics; Physical Soc., 1963 (Vice-Pres., 1965). Gov., Borough Polytechnic, London, 1964. CEng 1966. Comdr (with Star), Order of Alfonso X el Sabio, Spain, 1960. *Recreations:* music, travel, bridge, chess. *Address:* Bushy House, Teddington, Middlesex. *T:* 01-977 1070. *Club:* Athenæum.

**DUPONT-SOMMER, André;** Member of the Institut de France (Secrétaire Perpétuel de l'Académie des Inscriptions et Belles-Lettres) since 1961; Professor at the Collège de France since 1963; Hon. Professor at the Sorbonne; Director of Studies, Ecole des Hautes Etudes, since 1938; *b* 23 Dec. 1900. Gen. Sec., Collège de France, 1934; Pres., Institut d'Etudes Sémitiques, University of Paris, 1952. Officier de la Légion d'Honneur; Comdr des Palmes académiques. *Publications:* Le Quatrième Livre des Machabées, 1939; La Doctrine gnostique de la lettre "Wâw", 1946; Les Araméens, 1949; Aperçus préliminaires sur les manuscrits de la mer Morte, 1950 (publ. Eng. The Dead Sea Scrolls. A preliminary Study, 1952); Nouveaux Aperçus sur les manuscrits de la mer Morte, 1953 (publ. Eng. The Jewish sect of Qumran and the Essenes, 1954); Le Livre des Hymnes découvert près de la mer Morte, 1957; Les inscriptions araméennes de Sfiré, 1958; Les écrits esséniens découverts près de la mer Morte, 1959 (Eng. trans., The Essene Writings from Qumran); articles in Revue d'Assyriologie, Revue d'Histoire des Religions, Semitica, Syria, Jl of Semitic Studies, Vetus Testamentum, etc. *Address:* 23 quai de Conti, Paris VIe, France. *T:* 362.92.82.

**DUPPA-MILLER, John Bryan Peter;** *see* Miller, J. B. P. D.

**DUPPLIN, Viscount; Charles William Harley Hay;** *b* 20 Dec. 1962; *s* and *heir* of 15th Earl of Kinnoull, *qv*.

**du PRÉ, Jacqueline;** British violoncellist; *b* 1945; *m* 1967, Daniel Barenboim, *qv*. *Educ:* studied with William Pleeth both privately and at Guildhall Sch. of Music, with Paul Tortelier in Paris, and with Rostropovich in Moscow. Concert début at Wigmore Hall at age of sixteen, followed by appearances on the continent and with principal English orchestras and conductors. Soloist in London and at Bath and Edinburgh Festivals. N American début, 1965. Continued studies in Moscow with Rostropovitch, 1966, returning later to USSR as soloist with BBC Symphony Orchestra. Toured N America, and appeared New York and at World Fair, Montreal; subseq. concerts, major musical centres, 1967. Awarded Suggia Gift at age of ten; Gold medal, Guildhall Sch. of Music, and Queen's Prize, 1960. *Address:* c/o Messrs Ibbs & Tillett, 124 Wigmore Street, W1.

**DUPREE, Sir Vernon,** 3rd Bt, *cr* 1921; *b* 23 Dec. 1884; *s* of Sir William Thomas Dupree, 1st Bt, VD, TD, and 1st wife, Mary (*d* 1907), *d* of George Groves, Selsey, Sussex; *S* brother 1953; *m* 1st, 1912, Amy Marcella (*d* 1953), *d* of late John Price, Askeaton, Co. Limerick; one *d* (and one *s* killed in action, 1942); 2nd, 1955, Louise Jennie Hillyard. Formerly Capt. (Hon. Major) 7th Royal Fusiliers: served European War, 1914-18 (wounded). *Heir: b* Victor Dupree [*b* 19 Dec. 1887; *m* 1st, 1910, Gladys (*d* 1922), *d* of Charles Henry Lawson; 2nd, 1922, Margaret Cross; one *s*. Formerly Lieut 3rd Dragoon Guards and Royal Tank Corps (Capt. Reserve of Officers); served European War, 1914-18 (wounded, prisoner)]. *Address:* Downings, Prinsted, near Emsworth, Hampshire.

**DUPUCH, Hon. Sir (Alfred) Etienne (Jerome),** Kt 1965; OBE 1949; KCSG, OTL, CHM; Editor-Proprietor, The Tribune, Nassau, Bahamas; *b* Nassau, 16 Feb. 1899; *m* 1928, Marie Plouse, USA; three *s* three *d*. *Educ:* Boys' Central Sch., Nassau; St John's Univ., Collegeville, Minn., USA. Served War, 1914-18, BWI Regt; Rep. for Inagua, House of Assembly, Bahamas, 1925-42; Eastern District, New Providence, 1949-56; MLC, 1960-64; Mem. Senate, 1964-68. Hon. LittD, Hon. LLD. IAPA Award for breaking down racial discrimination in Bahamas, 1956; IAPA Award for successful defence of Freedom of Press, 1969; Citation from Associated Press N American Editors' Assoc. for outstanding coverage of fire on SS Yarmouth Castle, 1965. Has RSA medal and several decorations from governments of three nations. *Address:* PO Box 207, Nassau, Bahamas.

**DUPUIS, Raymond,** QC (Canada); LLD; Canadian Lawyer and Administrator; Director: The Royal Bank of Canada; Dominion Tar & Chemical Co. Ltd; Burns & Co. Ltd; Canada Life Assurance Co.; Globe Indemnity Co. of Canada; Hudson Bay Insurance Co.; Western Assurance Co.; British America Assurance Co.; Compagnie d'Assurance du Québec; Member Canadian Advisory Board; Royal Insurance Co. Ltd, Liverpool & London & Globe Insurance Co. Ltd; *b* Montreal, 2 Aug. 1907; *s* of late Albert Dupuis, KSG, former Pres. of Dupuis Frères, Ltee, and Henriette Beullac, both of Montreal; *m* 1st 1937, Hélène Saint-Pierre (*d* 1961); one *s* two *d*; 2nd, 1962, Françoise Demezieres. *Educ:* Mont-Saint-Louis Coll. (grad. Scientific Course); Montreal Univ. Read law with Godin, Dussault & Cadotte; called to Bar of Prov. of Quebec, 1930; KC 1945. Elected Dir of firm of Dupuis Frères, 1933; after his father's death in 1945 was elected to succeed him as Pres. of Dupuis Frères, Ltée; retired, 1961. Past Pres., La Chambre de Commerce du District de Montréal (1949-50); Past Nat. Pres., The Canadian Chamber of Commerce (1956-57). Member: Dollar Sterling Trade Advisory Council (Canadian Section); Montreal Board of Trade; Board of Research on Traffic and Transportation Problems of City of Montreal; Centre d'Etudes du Commerce de Paris; Canadian Bar Assoc; Member, Sales Tax Cttee apptd by Federal Govt, 1955; Governor: L'Orchestre Symphonique de Montréal; Notre-Dame and St Justine Hosps; La Comédie Canadienne: Past Pres. and Mem. Exec. Cttee Federation of French Catholic Charities; Director: Province of Quebec Society for Crippled Children Inc.; Pres., Internat. Law Assoc. (Montreal Section), 1964. Roman Catholic. Hon. LLD University of Montreal, 1959. *Recreation:* yachting. *Address:* (home) 21 Messier Street, Saint-Hilaire, Que, Canada; (business) 612 St James Street W, Montreal, Que. *Clubs:* Canadian (Montreal), Cercle Universitaire de Montréal, Laval-sur-le-Lac, Montreal Badminton and Squash, Montreal, Mount Bruno Country, Mount Royal, Palestre Nationale, St Denis.

**DURAND, Brigadier Sir Alan (Algernon Marion),** 3rd Bt, *cr* 1892; MC 1919; Colonel (retired) and Hon. Brigadier RA; *b* 14 Oct. 1893; *s* of Lieut-Col Sir Edward Law Durand, 1st Bt, CB, and Maude Ellen, 4th *d* of Algernon Charles Heber-Percy; *S* brother 1955; *m* 1st, 1924, Vivien Enid (from whom he obtained a divorce, 1936), *d* of late Herbert Chamberlain; one *d*; 2nd, 1944, Evelyn Sherbrooke, *d* of late C. Arnold Crane, Cheltenham, and *widow* of Sir Stanley Tubbs, 1st and last Bt. *Educ:* Cheltenham; RMA. 2nd Lieut RA 1913; served European War, 1914-18 (wounded twice, despatches twice): Capt. 1917; served War, 1939-46; Belgium and France, 1939-40 (despatches); Egypt, 1944-46; Col 1942; retd 1946. DL Glos, 1950; High Sheriff, 1953; Vice-Lieutenant Glos, 1957-69. CC (Glos). *Heir: nephew* Rev. Henry Mortimer Dickon Marion Durand, *b* 19 June 1934. *Address:* Ellerncroft, Wotton-under-Edge, Glos. *Club:* Army and Navy.

**DURAND, Victor,** QC 1958; *s* of Victor and Blanche Durand; *m* 1935, Betty Joan Kirchner; one *s* one *d*. *Educ:* Howard High Sch. (Kitchener Scholar). LLB, BSc, AMInstCE. *Address:* Queen Elizabeth Building, Temple, EC4.

**DURANT, Rear-Adm. Bryan Cecil,** CB 1963; DSO 1953; DSC 1945; DL; Director-General, Navy League, since 1964; *b* 17 June 1910; *o s* of Francis Durant and Dulce, *d* of Fraser Baddeley; *m* 1st, 1939, Pamela (*d* 1963), *yr d* of Brig.-Gen. William Walter Seymour; three *d* (and one *s* decd); 2nd, 1967, Rachel, *d* of late Col Hon. David Bruce, and of Hon. Mrs David Bruce. *Educ:* Radley. Entered Royal Navy, 1929; specialised in navigation, 1935. War of 1939-45; actions in HMS Dorsetshire in Atlantic and Indian Oceans including sinking of Bismarck, 1940-42; sunk by Japanese aircraft, 1942 (despatches); actions in HMS Victorious off North Norway, Sabang, Palembang, Okinawa and Japan, 1942-45; suicide Bomber attacks, 1945 (DSC). Comdr 1945; Capt. 1951; Comd 4th Frigate Sqdn in Korean War, 1952-54 (DSO). Dir, Ops Div., Admlty, 1957; Captain of the Fleet, Home Fleet, 1959; Chief of Staff Far East Station, 1961-63; retired list, 1963. ADC to the Queen, 1960. DL Greater London, 1970. Commendador Henriquina (Portuguese), 1960. *Address:* The Old House, Bighton, near Alresford, Hants. *Clubs:* Army and Navy, Marylebone Cricket.

**DURANT, William James,** BA, MA, PhD; engaged in writing; *b* North Adams, Mass, 5 Nov. 1885; *s* of Joseph Durant and Mary Allors, of French-Canadian stock; *m* 1913, Ida Kaufman; one *s* one *d*. *Educ:* St Peter's Coll., Jersey City, NJ; Columbia Univ., New York. Prof. of Latin and French, Seton Hall Coll., South Orange NJ, 1907-11; Instructor in Philosophy, Columbia Univ., 1917; Dir of Labour Temple Sch., 1914-27. *Publications:* Philosophy and the Social Problem, 1917; The Story of Philosophy, 1926; Transition, 1927; The Mansions of Philosophy, 1929; Adventures in Genius, 1931; Our Oriental Heritage, 1935; The Life of Greece; 1939; Cæsar and Christ, 1944; The Age of Faith, 1950; The Renaissance, 1953; The Reformation, 1957; (With Ariel Durant) The Age of Reason Begins, 1961; The Age of Louis XIV, 1963; The Age of Voltaire, 1965; Rousseau and Revolution, 1967; The Lessons of History, 1968. *Recreations:* none. *Address:* 5608 Briarcliff Road, Los Angeles 28, Calif, USA.

**DURBIN, Prof. James;** Professor of Statistics, University of London (London School of Economics), since 1961; *b* 30 June 1923; *m* 1958, Anne Dearnley Outhwaite; two *s* one *d*. *Educ:* Wade Deacon Grammar Sch., Widnes; St John's Coll., Cambridge. Army Operational Research Group, 1943-45. Boot and Shoe Trade Research Assoc., 1945-47; Dept of Applied Economics, Cambridge, 1948-49; Asst Lectr, then Lecturer, in Statistics, London Sch. of Economics, 1950-53; Reader in Statistics, 1953-61. *Publications:* Articles in statistical journals, *eg* Biometrika, Jl of Royal Statistical Society, etc. *Recreation:* ski-ing. *Address:* 31 Southway, NW11. *T:* 01-458 3037.

**DURBIN, Leslie,** MVO 1943; silversmith; *b* 21 Feb. 1913; *s* of late Harry Durbin and of Lillian A. Durbin; *m* 1940, Phyllis Ethel Durbin (*see* Phyllis E. Ginger); one *s* one *d*. *Educ:* Central Sch. of Arts and Crafts, London. Apprenticed to late Omar Ramsden, 1929-39; full-time schol., 1938-39, travelling schol., 1939-40, both awarded by Worshipful Co. of Goldsmiths. Started working on own account in workshop of Francis Adam, 1940-41. RAF, Allied Central Interpretation Unit, 1941-45. Hon. LLD Cambridge, 1963. *Address:* 62 Rochester Place, NW1. *T:* 01-485 5192.

**DURBRIDGE, Francis (Henry);** playwright and author; *b* 25 Nov. 1912; *s* of late Francis and Gertrude Durbridge; *m* 1940, Norah Elizabeth Lawley; two *s*. *Educ:* Bradford Grammar Sch.; Wylde Green Coll.; Birmingham Univ. After period in stockbroker's office, began to write (as always intended); short stories and plays for BBC; many subseq. radio plays, including Promotion, 1933; created character of Paul Temple. Entered Television with The Broken Horseshoe, 1952 (the first adult television serial); other serials followed; Portrait of Alison, 1954; My Friend Charles, 1955; The Other Man, 1956; The Scarf 1960; The World of Tim Frazer (Exec. Prod.), 1960-61; Melissa, 1962; Bat Out of Hell, 1964. The television serials have been presented in many languages, and are continuing; novels, based on them, have been published in USA, Europe, etc. The European Broadcasting Union asked for a radio serial for an internat. market (La Boutique, 1967, being broadcast in various countries). Films include two for Korda and Romulus, 1954-57. *Publications:* include contribs to newspapers and magazines, at home and abroad. *Recreations:* family, reading, travel. *Address:* The Moat House, Silverdale Avenue, Walton-on-Thames, Surrey. *T:* Walton-on-Thames 20119. *Club:* Royal Automobile.

**DURBIN, Mrs Leslie;** *see* Ginger, P. E.

**DURHAM,** 6th Earl of, *cr* 1833; Baron Durham, 1828; Viscount Lambton, 1833 [Disclaimed his Peerages for life, 1970]; *see under* Lambton, A. C. F.

**DURHAM, Bishop of,** since 1966; **Rt. Rev. Ian Thomas Ramsey;** *b* Kearsley, Bolton, 31 Jan. 1915; *o c* of late Arthur Ramsey and of May Ramsey; *m* 1943, Margretta, *y d* of late John and Janeanna McKay, Coleraine, Co. Londonderry; two *s*. *Educ:* St John's Sch., Farnworth, near Bolton; Farnworth Gram. Sch.; Christ's Coll., Cambridge (Scholar); Ripon Hall, Oxford. First Classes in Mathematical Tripos Part I, 1936, Moral Sciences Tripos Part IIa, 1938, and with distinction in Theological Tripos Part II, Section V (Old Regulations), 1939; Burney Prizeman 1938, Burney Student 1939; MA 1940. Asst Curate of Headington Quarry, Oxford, 1940-43; Chaplain of Christ's Coll., Cambridge, 1943-49; Coll. ARP and Fire Officer, 1943-45; Fellow of Christ's Coll., Cambridge, and Dir of Studies in Theology and Moral Sciences, 1944-51, Tutor, 1949-51; University Lecturer, 1944-51; Stanton Lecturer in Philosophy of Religion, Cambridge, 1947-50, Hulsean Preacher, 1950. Canon Theologian of Leicester Cathedral, 1944-66. Nolloth Prof. of the Philosophy of the Christian Religion in University of Oxford, and Fellow of Oriel Coll., 1951-66; Dir, Lambeth Diploma in Theology, 1964-67. Select Preacher: University of Cambridge, 1944, 1949, 1956; University of Oxford, 1951; Forwood Lecturer, University of Liverpool, 1957; F. D. Maurice Lecturer, KCL, 1961; Whidden Lecturer, McMaster Univ., Hamilton, Ont., 1963; Visiting Prof. Colgate Rochester Div. Sch., New York, and South Calif. Univ., 1963; Riddell Lecturer, Newcastle upon Tyne Univ., 1963; Stephenson Lecturer, Sheffield, 1964; Zenos Lecturer, Chicago, 1966; Hon. Librarian, Faculty of Theology, 1952-65; General Board of Faculties, Oxford, 1953-59. Examining Chaplain to Bishop of Bradford, 1947-55; to Bishop of Portsmouth, 1952-59, 1960-66; to Bishop of Sheffield, 1954-62, 1963-66; to Bishop of Norwich, 1960-66; Governor of Ripon Hall, Oxford, 1946-, Treasurer, 1952-66; Governor of Westminster Coll., Oxford, 1959-66; Governor: Aldenham Sch., 1961-66; William Temple Coll., 1964- (Chm. 1967-); Member: Archbishop's Commission on Divine Healing, 1953-57; Warneford and Park Hosps Management Cttee, 1954-66 (Chm. 1960-66). Church Assembly Board for Social Responsibility, 1958-. Chairman: Archbishops' Commn on Doctrine, 1967-; Commn on Religious Education, 1967-. Chaplain and Sub-Prelate, Order of St John of Jerusalem, 1969. Hon. DD: Oxford, 1966; Durham, 1967; Glasgow, 1968. Hon. Fellow: Oriel Coll., Oxford, 1967; Christ's Coll., Cambridge, 1967. *Publications:* Miracles: an exercise in logical mapwork, 1952; Religious Language, 1957; Freedom and Immortality, 1960; On Being Sure in Religion, 1963; Models and Mystery, 1964; Science and Religion: conflict and synthesis, 1964; Christian Discourse, 1965; ed.: Reasonableness of Christianity (John Locke), 1958; Prospect for Metaphysics, 1961; Biology and Personality, 1965; Christian Ethics and Contemporary Philosophy, 1966. *Recreations:* family and home; reading maps and (once) Bradshaw. *Address:* Auckland Castle, Bishop Auckland, Co. Durham. *T:* Bishop Auckland 2576. *Club:* Athenæum.

**DURHAM, Assistant Bishop of;** *see* Skelton, Rt Rev. K. J. F.

**DURHAM, Dean of;** *see* Wild, Very Rev. J. H. S.

**DURHAM, Archdeacon of;** *see* Perry, Ven. M. C.

**DURIE, Alexander Charles;** Director-General, The Automobile Association, since 1964; Managing Director, Shell-Mex and BP Ltd, 1963-64 (Director, 1962); *b* 15 July 1915; *er s* of late Charles and Margaret Durie (*née* Gardner), Shepton Mallet, Somerset; *m* 1941, Joyce, *o c* of late Lionel and Helen Hargreaves (*née* Hirst), Leeds and Bridlington, Yorks; one *s* one *d*. *Educ:* Queen's Coll., Taunton. Joined Shell-Mex and BP Ltd, 1933. Served War of 1939-45, Royal Artillery; Gunnery Staff Course (IG), 1941; Lieut-Col 1945. Mem. Inst. of Transport, 1953-; Dir Shell Co. of Australia Ltd, 1954-56; Mem. Exec. and Finance Cttees, Motor and Cycle Trades Benevolent Fund,

1959-; Vice-Pres. British Assoc. of Industrial Editors, 1959-; Gen. Commissioner of Income Tax, 1960-; FBIM, 1962, Council mem., 1962-, Vice-Chm. and Chm. Exec. Cttee, 1962-67; Mem., Nat. Road Safety Adv. Council, 1965-68. Mem., Adv. Council on Road Res., 1965-68; Vice-Chm. Brit. Road Fedn Ltd, 1962-; Mem. Council, Internat. Road Fedn Ltd, London, 1962-64; Mem. Council, World Touring & Automobile Organisation, 1965-; Vice-Chm., Alliance Internationale de Tourisme, 1965-; Mem., Marketing Cttee, BTA, 1970-. Chm., Public Schools Appointments Bureau, 1969-; Governor: Ashridge Coll., 1963-; Queen's Coll., Taunton, 1969-. Mem. Cttee, Surrey CCC, 1970-. Freeman of City of London and Liveryman, Worshipful Co. of Paviors, 1965. Hon. MInstHE 1969. *Recreations:* cricket, curling, golf, racing. *Address:* Redwood House, Windlesham, Surrey. *T:* Bagshot 2035. *Clubs:* MCC, Junior Carlton; Royal and Ancient; Berkshire Golf.

**DURLACHER, Adm. Sir Laurence (George),** KCB 1961 (CB 1957); OBE 1943; DSC 1945; retired; *b* 24 July 1904; *s* of late Frederick Henry Keeling Durlacher and V. M. Durlacher (*née* Hanson); *m* 1934, Rimma, *d* of late R. V. Sass-Tissovsky; one *s* one *d*. *Educ:* RNC Osborne and Dartmouth. Lieut 1927; Comdr 1939; Capt. 1945; Cdre 1st Class, 1952; Rear-Adm. 1955; Vice-Adm. 1958; Adm. 1961. On Staff of Adm. of the Fleet Viscount Cunningham of Hyndhope during N Africa, Sicily and Italian Campaigns (despatches); commanded HMS Volage, 1944-45; Admiralty, 1945-47; commanded 3rd Destroyer Flotilla, Mediterranean, 1949-50; commanded Admiralty Signals and Radar Establishments, 1950-52; Chief of Staff to C-in-C Far East Station, 1952-54; Dep. Chief of Naval Personnel (Personal Services), at Admiralty, 1955-57; Flag Officer Commanding Fifth Cruiser Squadron and Flag Officer Second-in-Command, Far East Station, 1957-58; Dep. Chief of Naval Staff and Fifth Sea Lord, 1959-62; retired, 1962. US Legion of Merit, 1945. *Address:* Mas Tournamy, Mougins, A-M, France. *Club:* United Service.

**DURNFORD-SLATER, Adm. Sir Robin (Leonard Francis),** KCB 1957 (CB 1955); *b* 9 July 1902, *s* of Captain L. Slater, Royal Sussex Regiment (killed in action, 1914), and Constance Dorothy Durnford-Slater; *m* 1936, Mary Alice Hilleary, *d* of late Col E. H. Gregson, CMG, CIE; one *s* one *d*. *Educ:* Osborne; Dartmouth. Comdr, 1938; Capt., 1944; Rear-Adm., 1953; Vice-Adm., 1956; Adm., 1959. Served War of 1939-45; Executive officer, HMS Hermes, HMS Vernon; Senior Officer, 42nd and subseq. 7th Escort Grp Western Approaches; Trg Capt. Western Approaches; Dir of Underwater Weapons, Admiralty (Bath). Post War: Senior Officer 1st Escort Flotilla, Far East; Commandant Sch. of Amphibious Warfare; Capt. HMS Gambia; Dep. Controller, Admiralty, 1953-56; Flag Officer, 2nd in Command, Mediterranean Fleet, 1956-58; Commander-in-Chief, The Nore, 1958-61; retd. Flag Officer Naval Brigade, Coronation, 1953. Comdr of the Legion of Honour, 1958. *Recreation:* golf. *Address:* Passfield Place, Liphook, Hants.

**DURRANDS, Kenneth James,** DGS, MSc, CEng, FIMechE, MIEE; Director of The Polytechnic, Queensgate, Huddersfield, since 1970; *b* 24 June 1929; *s* of A. I. Durrands, Croxton, Kerrial; *m* 1956, Betty Cole, BA, *d* of late J. W. Cole, Solihull; one *s*. *Educ:* King's Sch., Grantham; Nottingham Technical Coll.; Birmingham Univ. Min. of Supply Engrg Apprentice, ROF, Nottingham, 1947-52; Techn. Engr, UKAEA, Risley, 1954-58; Lecturer in Mechanical and Nuclear Engrg, Univ. of Birmingham, 1958-61; Head of Gen. Engrg Dept, Reactor Engrg Lab., UKAEA, Risley, 1961-67; Mem. Council, IMechE, 1963-66; Visiting Lecturer, Manchester Univ., 1962-68; Technical Dir, Vickers Ltd, Barrow Engrg Works, 1967-70. Mem., Advisory, and Research and Liaison Tribology Cttees, Min. of Technology, 1969-; Mem. Council and Court, Leeds Univ., 1970; Hon. Treas., Cttee of Directors of Polytechnics, 1970. *Publications:* several technical papers. *Recreations:* motor sport, travel, gardening, squash rackets. *Address:* The Grange, Antrobus, Northwich, Cheshire. *T:* Arley 243.

**DURRANT, Albert Arthur Molteno,** CBE 1945; CEng; FIMechE; MInstT; FRSA; retired from London Transport Board; *b* 11 Sept. 1898; *s* of late Sir Arthur I. Durrant, CBE, MVO; *m* 1922, Kathleen, *d* of Arthur J. Wright; no *c*. *Educ:* Alleyn's Sch., Dulwich. Joined London Gen. Omnibus Co., 1919; Chief Engineer (Buses and Coaches), London Passenger Transport Bd, 1935-40; Director of Tank Design, Ministry of Supply, 1940-45; Chief Mechanical Engineer (Road Services) London Transport, 1945-65. *Address:* 108 Chiltern Court, Baker Street, NW1.

**DURRANT, Maj.-Gen. James Thom,** CB 1945; DFC 1941; *b* 1913; *s* of late J. C. Durrant, Hertford and Johannesburg; *m* 1939, Jean Lucy, *d* of G. Harding, Pretoria. Commanding a group in Air Command, South-East Asia, 1945; formerly Dir-Gen. South African Air Force; retired, 1952. *Address:* 204 Corlett Drive, Johannesburg, South Africa.

**DURRANT, Sir William Henry Estridge,** 7th Bt, *cr* 1784; JP (NSW); *b* 1 April 1901; *s* of Sir William Durrant, 6th Bt; *S* father 1953; *m* 1927, Georgina Beryl Gwendoline, *d* of Alexander Purse, Kircubbin, Co. Down, N Ireland; one *s* one *d*. Served War of 1939-45 (Pacific Area). *Heir:* *s* William Alexander Estridge Durrant [*b* 26 Nov. 1929; *m* 1953, Dorothy (BA), *d* of Ronal Croker, Quirindi, NSW; one *s* one *d*]. *Address:* Havilah Road, Lindfield, NSW, Australia.

**DURRELL, Gerald Malcolm;** Zoologist and Writer since 1946; regular contributor to BBC Sound and TV Services; *b* Jamshedpur, India, 7 Jan. 1925; *s* of Lawrence Samuel Durrell, Civil Engineer, and Louisa Florence Dixie; *m* 1951, Jacqueline Sonia Rasen; no *c*. *Educ:* by Private Tutors, in France, Italy, Switzerland and Greece. Student Keeper, Whipsnade, 1945-46; 1st Animal Collecting Expedition, British Cameroons, 1947-48; 2nd Cameroon Expedition, 1948-49; Collecting trip to British Guiana, 1949-50; began writing, script writing and broadcasting, 1950-53; trip with wife to Argentine and Paraguay, 1953-54; filming in Cyprus, 1955; 3rd Cameroon Expedition with wife, 1957; Trans-Argentine Expedition, 1958-59; Expedition in conjunction with BBC Natural History Unit, Sierra Leone, 1965; collecting trip to Mexico, 1968; Aust. Expedn, 1969-70. Founder and Hon. Director: Jersey Zoological Park, 1958; Jersey Wildlife Preservation Trust (Jersey Zoo Park), 1964. FZS; (Life) FIAL; FRGS; MBOU. *Films for TV:* 1st series, 1956, Two in the Bush, 1962, Catch Me a Colobus, 1966; A Day in the Zoo, 1967, Garden of the Gods, 1967. *Publications:* The Overloaded Ark, 1953, Three Singles to Adventure, 1954; The Bafut Beagles, 1954; The New Noah, 1955; The Drunken Forest, 1956; My Family and Other Animals, 1956; Encounters with Animals, 1958; A Zoo in my Luggage, 1960; The Whispering Land, 1961; Island Zoo, 1961; Look at Zoos, 1961; My

Favourite Animal Stories, 1962; Menagerie Manor, 1964; Two in the Bush, 1966; Rosy is My Relative, 1968; The Donkey Rustlers, 1968; Birds, Beasts and Relatives, 1969; Catch Me A Colobus, 1970. contribs to Zoo Life, etc. *Recreations:* reading, riding, filming, photography, drawing, swimming, study of the History and Maintenance of Zoological Gardens. *Address:* Jersey Zoo Park, Les Augres Manor, Trinity, Jersey, Channel Isles. *T:* North 949.

*See also Lawrence G. Durrell.*

**DURRELL, Lawrence George,** FRSL 1954; lately Director of Public Relations, Government of Cyprus; *b* 27 Feb. 1912; *m* 1937, 1947 and 1960; two *d. Educ:* College of St Joseph, Darjeeling, India; St Edmund's Sch., Canterbury. Formerly: Foreign Service Press Officer, Athens and Cairo; Press Attaché, Alexandria; Dir of Public Relations, Dodecanese Islands; Press Attaché, Belgrade, Yugoslavia; Dir of British Council Institutes of Kalamata, Greece, and Cordoba, Argentina. *Publications:* (novel, under pseudonym Charles Norden) Panic Spring, 1937; The Black Book, 1938 (published in France and USA); (poetry) Private Country, 1943; Prospero's Cell, 1945; (trans) Four Greek Poets, 1946; Cities, Plains and People, 1946; Cefalu, 1947 (republished as The Dark Labyrinth, 1958); On Seeming to Presume, 1948; (trans) Pope Joan, 1948; (verse play) Sappho, 1950; Reflections on a Marine Venus, 1953; The Tree of Idleness, 1955; Selected Poems, 1956; Bitter Lemons, 1957 (Duff Cooper Memorial Prize); (juvenile) White Eagles Over Serbia, 1957; The Alexandria Quartet: Justine, 1957, Balthazar, 1958; Mountolive, 1958, Clea, 1960; Esprit de Corps, 1957; Stiff Upper Lip, 1958; (ed) The Best of Henry Miller, 1960; Collected Poems, 1960, new edn with additions and revisions, 1968; (verse play) An Irish Faustus, 1963; The Ikons, 1966; (novel) Tunc, 1968; Spirit of Place: letters and essays on travel, 1969; (novel) Nunquam, 1970. *Recreation:* travel. *Address:* c/o National and Grindlay's Bank, 13 St James's Square, SW1.

*See also Gerald M. Durrell.*

**DÜRRENMATT, Friedrich;** Swiss author and playwright; *b* Konolfingen, Switzerland, 5 Jan. 1921; *s* of Reinhold Dürrenmatt, pastor, and Hulda (*née* Zimmermann); *m* 1947, Lotti Geissler; three *c. Educ:* Gymnasium, Bern; University of Bern; University of Zürich. Drama Critic for Die Weltwoche, of Zürich. *Publications: Plays:* Es steht geschrieben, 1947; Der Blinde, 1948; Romulus der Grosse, 1949; Die Ehe des Herrn Mississippi (The Marriage of Mr Mississippi), 1952 (produced New York, Fools Are Passing Through, 1958; filmed, 1961); Nächtliches Gespräch mit einem verachteten Menschen, 1952; Ein Engel kommt nach Babylon (An Angel Comes to Babylon), 1953; Der Besuch der alten Dame, 1956 (The Visit, produced New York, 1958, London, 1960) (Eng. trans., by Patrick Bowles, publ. 1962); Frank V-Oper einer Privatbank, 1960; Die Physiker, 1962 (prod. Aldwych Theatre, London as The Physicists, 1963); The Meteor (prod. Aldwych Theatre, London, 1966); The Deadly Game (prod. Savoy Theatre, 1967); *plays for radio:* Stranitzki und der Nationalheid; Herkules und der Stall des Augias; Das Unternehmen der Wega; Abendstunde im Spätherbst; *novels:* Pilatus, 1949; Der Nihilist, 1950; Die Stadt (short stories), 1952; Der Richter und sein Henker, 1952 (Eng. trans. by Therese Pol, The Judge and His Hangman, 1955); Der Verdacht, 1953 (Eng. trans. as The Quarry, by Eva H. Morreale), 1962; Grieche sucht Griechen, 1955; Die Panne, 1956 (Eng. trans. by R. and C. Winston, The Dangerous Game, 1960); Das Versprechen, 1958 (Eng. trans. by R. and C. Winston, The Pledge, 1959). *Recreations:* painting and astronomy. *Address:* Pertuis du Sault 34, Neuchâtel, Switzerland.

**DURST, Alan Lydiat,** ARA 1953; Sculptor; *b* 1883; 2nd *s* of late Rev. Canon William Durst; *m* 1918, Clare Butler (*d* 1967); no *c. Educ:* Marlborough Coll.; Switzerland. Commissioned in RMLI and served for several years, mainly at sea; left the Service to take up art, and studied at Central Sch. of Arts and Crafts, London, and in Chartres; re-joined Marines for both wars, serving during War of 1939-45 at Admiralty. Started to practise as a sculptor in 1920, working almost entirely as a direct carver in stone, wood and ivory. One-man shows at Leicester Galleries, 1930 and 1935. Taught wood carving at RCA, 1925-48 (except war years). Mem. London Group, 1928-51. Represented in Tate Gallery; Glasgow, Manchester, Bradford city galleries; Maritime Museum, Greenwich; Thomas J. Watson Gallery, New York; private collections. Work purchased under terms of the Chantrey Bequest, 1965. Has work on or in many churches and schools, including Canterbury, Winchester, Peterborough, Manchester and Llandaff Cathedrals; RADA, and Merchant Taylors' Sch. *Publication:* Wood Carving (How-to-do-it series), 1938 (2nd edn 1948, new revised edn, 1959, new edn, 1969). *Recreations:* sight-seeing at home and abroad. *Address:* 4 Wychcombe Studios, England's Lane, NW3. *T:* 01-722 0515.

**DURWARD, James,** CMG 1953; retired; *b* 3 Dec. 1892; *m* 1918; two *s. Educ:* Aberdeen Univ. Served European War, 1914-18, Capt., Royal Engineers. First Class Hons in Mathematics and Natural Philosophy, Aberdeen, 1918. Joined Meteorological Office, 1919; served at Sch. of Artillery, Larkhill, 1920-22; Asst-Supt and transf. to Calshot Flying Boat Base, 1922; Supt and transf. to RAF Middle East HQ, 1927; Dir of Iraqi Meteorological Service, 1937; Principal Technical Officer in home establishment, 1940; Asst Dir, 1946; Dep. Dir (Services), 1948. Order of Rafidain, Iraq, 1940. *Publications:* author of numerous Professional Notes in Meteorological Office series. *Recreations:* gardening, golfing and motoring. *Address:* 40 King's Road, Richmond, Surrey. *T:* 01-940 5201.

**du SAUTOY, Peter Francis,** OBE 1964; Vice-Chairman and Joint Managing Director, Faber & Faber Ltd, since 1960; *b* 19 Feb. 1912; *s* of late Col E. F. du Sautoy, OBE, TD, DL; *m* 1937, Phyllis Mary (Mollie), *d* of late Sir Francis Floud, KCB, KCSI, KCMG; two *s. Educ:* Uppingham (Foundn Schol.); Wadham Coll., Oxford (Sen. Class. Schol.). MA, 1st cl. Lit. Hum. Dept of Printed Books, British Museum, 1935-36; Asst Educn Officer, City of Oxford, 1937-40; RAF, 1940-45; joined Faber & Faber Ltd, 1946; Dir, Dec. 1946. Pres., Publishers Assoc., 1967-69, Vice-Pres., 1969-71. Mem. of Board of London companies of following N American Univ. Presses: Yale, Chicago, Columbia, McGill-Queen's. *Recreations:* reading, the theatre, travel, swimming. *Address:* 117 Bedford Court Mansions, Bedford Avenue, WC1. *T:* 01-636 4980. *Club:* Garrick.

**DUTHIE, Prof. Robert Buchan,** MA Oxon, MB, ChM; FRCSE, frcs, FACS; Nuffield Professor of Orthopædic Surgery, Oxford University; Professorial Fellow, Worcester College, Oxford; Surgeon, Nuffield Orthopædic Centre, Oxford; *b* 4 May 1925; 2nd *s* of late James Andrew Duthie and late Elizabeth Jean Duthie, Edinburgh; *m* 1956,

Alison Ann Macpherson Kittermaster, MA; two *s* two *d*. *Educ:* Aberdeen Grammar Sch.; King Edward VI Gram. Sch., Chelmsford; Heriot-Watt Coll., Edinburgh; University of Edinburgh Med. Sch. Robert Jones Prize 1947, MB, ChB 1948, ChM (with dist.) (Gold Medal for Thesis) 1956, University of Edinburgh; FRCSE 1953. Ho. Surg. Royal Infirmary, 1948-49; Ho. Phys., Western Gen. Hosp., Edinburgh, 1949. Active service in Malaya, RAMC, 1949-51. Registrar, Royal Infirmary, Edinburgh, 1951-53; David Wilkie Res. Schol. of University of Edinburgh, 1953-; Res. Fellow of Scottish Hosps Endowment Research Trust, Edinburgh, 1953-56; Res. Fellow, Nat. Cancer Inst., Bethesda, USA, 1956-57; Extern. Mem. of MRC in Inst. of Orthopædics, London and Sen. Registrar, 1957-58; Prof. of Orthopædic Surg., University of Rochester Sch. of Medicine and Dentistry and Orthopædic Surg.-in-Chief, University of Rochester Med. Centre, 1958-66. Fellow Brit. Orthopædic Assoc.; Member: Internat. Soc. for Orthopædic Surgery and Traumatology; Orthopædic Research Soc.; Inter-urban Orthopædic Club: Internat. Orthopædic Club. Amer. Rheumatism Assoc. President's Prize, Soc. Internat. de Chirurgie, 1957. *Publications:* (co-author) Textbook of Orthopædic Surgery, 5th edn, 1964; contribs to med. and surg. jls relating to genetics, histochemistry, transplantation, pathology, neoplasia of musculo-skeletal tissues, and clinical subjects. *Recreations:* sailing, tennis. *Address:* Nuffield Orthopædic Centre, Headington, Oxford; Barna Brow, Harberton Mead, Headington, Oxford.

**DUTHIE, Sir William (Smith),** Kt 1959; OBE 1943; *b* 22 May 1892; *s* of Lewis Duthie, Portessie, Banffshire; *m* 1921, Elizabeth Tyson; one *s* one *d*. *Educ:* Rathven and Buckie Schs. Bank of Scotland, 1908-11; Canadian Bank of Commerce, 1911-20; Canadian Army, 1915-16, Gordon Highlanders, 1916-18 (severely wounded); business in London, 1921 onwards; advised Food Defence Plans Dept Board of Trade on Bread Supplies from Oct. 1938; Chm. London Bread Supplies Cttee, 1939; Area Bread Officer London and SE England, 1940; Dir of Emergency Bread Supplies, Ministry of Food, 1941; Dep. Chief UNRRA Balkans Mission, Jan. 1945. MP (U) Banffshire, 1945-64. Resigned Party Whip, Oct. 1962-May 1964. Chairman: House of Commons Cons. and Unionist Mems. Fisheries Sub-Cttee, 1951-62; House of Commons Scottish Unionist Mems Cttee, 1958; Royal National Mission to Deep Sea Fishermen. *Publication:* ed with C. L. Foster: Letters from the Front, 1914-18, for Canadian Bank of Commerce, 1919. *Recreations:* golf, sailing, archæology. *Address:* Sandings Farm, Lydeard St Lawrence, near Taunton, Somerset. *T:* Lydeard St Lawrence 276; 28a West Hill, Sanderstead, Surrey. *T:* 01-657 3961. *Club:* Caledonian.

**du TOIT, Very Rev. Lionel Meiring Spafford,** MA; Dean of Carlisle since 1960; *b* 1903; 3rd *s* of late Justice A. P. N. du Toit, S Africa; *m* 1933, Gladys Evelyn, 2nd *d* of late J. D. Hatt, Elsfield, Oxford; one *s* (decd). *Educ:* Manchester Grammar Sch.; Merton Coll., Oxford. Deacon 1928, Priest 1929; Asst Curate: Rochdale Parish Church, 1928-31; Swinton Parish Church, 1931-35; Rector, Christ Church, Moss Side, Manchester, 1935-43; Chaplain, Manchester Royal Infirmary, 1935-43; Lecturer, Egerton Hall Theological Coll., 1932-38; Vicar, St Mary's, Windermere, 1943-60. Proctor in Convocation, 1950-59. Member: Archbishops' Commn on Roman Catholic Relations and of Anglican-Presbyterian Conversations; Anglican Methodist Unity Commission. *Recreation:* country life. *Address:* The Deanery, Carlisle. *T:* Carlisle 2-3335.

**DUTT, (Rajani) Palme,** BA Oxon; Editor of Labour Monthly since 1921; *b* Cambridge, 1896; *m* 1922, Salme (*d* 1964), *d* of Ernst Murrik, Walk, Estonia. *Educ:* Perse Sch., Cambridge; Balliol Coll., Oxford (First Classical scholar, first class hons). Imprisoned 1916, 1925; expelled from Oxford for propoganda of Marxism, 1917. Sec., International Section, Labour Research Dept, 1919-22; Chm., Communist Party Reorganisation Commission, 1922; Ed., Workers' Weekly, 1922-24; Ed., Daily Worker, 1936-38; Executive Cttee Mem. of the Communist Party, 1922-65. Contested (Communist) Sparkbrook Div. of Birmingham, 1945, Woolwich East, 1950. Hon. Dr of History, Moscow Univ., 1962. *Publications:* The Two Internationals, 1920; The Labour International Handbook, 1921 (Ed.); articles on Communism and The International in the Encyclopædia Britannica (12th edn); Modern India, 1926; Socialism and the Living Wage, 1927; Lenin, 1933; Fascism and Social Revolution, 1934; World Politics, 1918-36; (new edn with supplement, 1936-60, 1961). The Political and Social Doctrine of Communism, 1938; India To-day, 1940; Britain in The World Front, 1942; Road to Labour Unity, 1943; Britain's Crisis of Empire, 1949; India Today and Tomorrow, 1956; Crisis of Britain and the British Empire, 1957; Problems of Contemporary History, 1963; Rise and Fall of the Daily Herald, 1964; The Internationale, 1964; Whither China?, 1967. *Address:* 8 Highfield Court, NW11.

**DUTTON,** family name of **Baron Sherborne.**

**DUTTON, Alan Hart,** CMG 1958; MVO 1954; British Petroleum Co. Ltd; *b* 13 March 1913; *s* of late Thomas Dutton. Bolton Lancs; *m* 1940, Mollie Gledden, *d* of late Thomas Perry, Streetly End, Cambs; one *s* two *d*. *Educ:* Sedbergh Sch.; Bonn Univ.; Brasenose Coll., Oxford. Colonial Service: Administrative Officer, Nigeria, 1936. RAF, 1940-45. Colonial Office, 1945-47; Senior Asst Sec. and Commissioner, Cyprus, 1947-52; Asst Chief Sec., Aden, 1952-56; Financial Sec., Aden, 1956-59. USA Silver Star, 1945. *Address:* Stubble Hill, Guildown Avenue, Guildford, Surrey. *T:* Guildford 67749. *Club:* East India and Sports.

**DUTTON, Eric Aldhelm Torlogh,** CMG 1946; CBE 1938 (OBE 1930); MA Oxon; Comdr Crown of Belgium; Order of Brilliant Star of Zanzibar; *b* 24 May 1895; 5th *s* of late Rev. Charles and Helen Dutton; *m* 1936, Myrtle Eleonore, *e d* of late Gen. Sir Hubert de la Poer Gough, GCB, GCMG, KCVO; two *s* one *d*. *Educ:* Hurstpierpoint; Keble Coll., Oxford. Joined West Yorks Regt Aug. 1914; Major, 1915; served in Gallipoli (wounded, despatches); passed ICS examination, 1920; Private Sec. to Sir Robert Coryndon, Governor of Uganda and subsequently of Kenya, 1920-25; Private Sec., to Lieut-Col Sir Edward Grigg, Governor of Kenya, 1925-30; Principal Asst Chief Sec., Northern Rhodesia, 1930; Chm. Northern Rhodesian Finance Commission, 1932; Chm., Town Planning Board, 1935; Administrative Sec., Northern Rhodesia, 1938; Colonial Sec., Bermuda, 1938-42; Chief Sec., Zanzibar, 1942-52; Chm., Town Planning Board, Zanzibar, 1943-52, and of Central Development Authority, 1946-52; Delegate to First African Conf., London, 1948; administered Govt in Bermuda and Zanzibar for various periods. *Publications:* The Basuto of Basutoland, 1923; Kenya Mountain,

1929; The Planting of Trees and Shrubs, 1937; Lillibullero, or The Golden Road, 1944. *Recreation:* architecture. *Address:* Villa Luiza, Rua do Pinheiro, Monte Estoril, Portugal. *Clubs:* Bath, Spanish.

**DUTTON, James Macfarlane;** Head of Rhodesia Economic Department, Foreign and Commonwealth Office, since 1970; *b* 3 June 1922; *s* of late H. St J. Dutton and of Mrs E. B. Dutton; *m* 1958, Jean Mary McAvoy; one *s*. *Educ:* Winchester Coll.; Balliol Coll., Oxford. Dominions Office, 1944-46; Private Sec. to Permanent Under Sec., 1945; Dublin, 1946-48; CRO, 1948-50; Asst Private Sec. to Sec. of State, 1948; 2nd Sec., New Delhi, 1950-53; CRO, 1953-55; 1st Sec., Dacca and Karachi, 1955-58, Canberra, 1958-62; Head of Constitutional and Protocol Dept. CRO, 1963-65; Canadian Nat. Defence Coll., 1965-66; Dep. High Comr and Counsellor (Commercial), Colombo, 1966-70. *Recreations:* golf, trout-fishing. *Address:* c/o Foreign and Commonwealth Office, King Charles Street, SW1. *Clubs:* Travellers', Royal Commonwealth Society.

**DUTTON, Ralph Stawell,** FSA; *b* 25 Aug. 1898; *s* of late Henry John Dutton, Hinton Ampner House, Hants. *Educ:* Eton; Christ Church, Oxford. Employed in the Foreign Office, 1939-45. High Sheriff of Hants, 1944. A Trustee of the Wallace Collection, 1948-69. Member: Executive Cttee of National Art Collections Fund; Historic Buildings Cttee of Nat. Trust; Historic Buildings Council. *Publications:* The English Country House, 1935; The English Garden, 1937; The Land of France (with Lord Holden), 1939; The English Interior, 1948; Wessex, 1950; The Age of Wren, 1951; London Homes, 1952; Normandy and Brittany, 1953; The Victorian Home, 1954; The Châteaux of France, 1957; English Court Life, 1963; Hinton Ampner, A Hampshire Manor, 1968; Hampshire, 1970. *Address:* Hinton Ampner House, Alresford, Hants. *T:* Bramdean 222; 95N Eaton Square, SW1. *T:* 01-235 2950. *Club:* Brooks's.

**DUTTON, Reginald David Ley;** Chairman, LPE Ltd, since 1966; Chief Executive, The London Press Exchange Ltd, since 1964; Chairman and Chief Executive, Leo Burnett-LPE International Inc., since 1969; *b* 20 Aug. 1916; *m* 1952, Pamela Jean (*née* Harrison); two *s* one *d*. *Educ:* Magdalen Coll. Sch., Oxford. Joined OUP; subseq. joined leading British advertising agency, London Press Exchange, 1937. During War of 1939-45 served in Royal Navy. Returned to agency after his service; there, he worked on many of major accounts; Dir, 1954; Man. Dir and Chief Exec., 1964. Pres. Inst. Practitioners in Advertising, 1969; FIPA 1960. *Recreation:* deep sea fishing. *Address:* 3 Bournemouth Drive, Herne Bay, Kent. *T:* Herne Bay 5790; Flat 11, 48 St Martin's Lane, WC2. *T:* 01-836 2919. *Club:* American.

**DUVEEN, Claude Henry,** MBE 1946; QC 1953; JP 1955; **His Honour Judge Duveen;** Judge of County Courts, Circuit No 61, since 1962 (Herts and Middlesex Circuit, 1958-62); Chairman, Berks Quarter Sessions, since 1966 (Deputy Chairman, 1958-66); *b* 6 April 1903; *s* of Louis Duveen and Beatrice Salamon; *m* 1930, Eileen Schomberg; one *d*. *Educ:* Eton; New Coll., Oxford. Admitted Middle Temple, 1925; called to Bar, 1927; practised in London and on Midland Circuit, 1927-40, 1945-59. Served RAFVR, 1940-45. *Recreation:* roses. *Address:* Foxleigh Grange, Holyport, Berks. *T:* Maidenhead 27968. *Clubs:* Oxford and Cambridge, Pratt's, MCC.

**DUVEEN, Sir Geoffrey,** Kt 1948; VRD; *b* London, 4 July 1883; *s* of Henry J. and Dora Duveen; *m* 1907; one *s*; *m* 1942, Elise Adolph. *Educ:* Bath Coll.; Merton Coll., Oxford. Served European War, 1914-18, and War of 1939-45, in RNVR (retired as Comdr, RNVR). Barrister-at-Law (Inner Temple); MA (Oxon.). Late Chm. of Royal Ear Hospital (moved Hosp. from Dean Street, Soho, to site adjacent to University Coll. Hosp., 1924); ex-mem. most Cttees of UCH and visitor for King Edward VII Hosp. Fund. Founded a post-grad. travelling lectureship in otology at University of London. Past Master, Worshipful Company of Plumbers. *Publications:* Postage Stamps of Gibraltar, 1932; The History of the Gold Sovereign, 1961 (with H. J. Stride). *Recreations:* salmon fishing, motoring, numismatics. *Address:* Flat 31, Grosvenor House, W1. *Clubs:* Athenæum, Royal Thames Yacht.

**du VIGNEAUD, Prof. Vincent;** Professor of Chemistry, Department of Chemistry, Cornell University, New York, since 1967; Emeritus Professor of Biochemistry, Cornell University Medical College, New York, NY; *b* 18 May 1901; *s* of Alfred Joseph and Mary du Vigneaud; *m* 1924, Zella Zon Ford; one *s* one *d*. *Educ:* University of Illinois (BS 1923, MS 1924); University of Rochester, NY, USA (PhD 1927). Asst Biochemist, Philadelphia Gen. Hosp. and Graduate School of Medicine, University of Pa, 1924-25; Asst Biochemist, Graduate School of Medicine, University of Rochester, NY, USA, 1925-27; Nat. Research Council Fellow, Johns Hopkins Univ. Medical Sch., 1927-28; Kaiser Wilhelm Inst, Germany; University of Edinburgh Medical Sch.; UCH Medical Sch., London, 1928-29; Assoc. Dept of Chemistry, Univ. of Illinois, 1929-30; Asst Prof., 1930-32; Prof. and Head of Dept of Biochemistry, George Washington Univ. Sch. of Medicine, 1932-38. Mem., Bd of Trustees, Rockefeller Univ. Numerous scientific awards, 1936-. Mem. Royal Society of Sciences of Upsala (Sweden), 1950; Chandler Medal, Columbia Univ., 1955; Nobel Laureate in Chemistry, 1955; Willard Gibbs Medal, 1956. Hon. FRSE 1951; Hon. Fellow Chemical Soc. (London), 1955; Hon. FRIC 1959. Hon. ScD: New York Univ., 1955; Yale, 1955; Univ. of Illinois, 1960; Univ. of Rochester, 1965; St Louis Univ., 1965; George Washington Univ., 1968. *Publications:* A Trail of Research in Sulfur Chemistry and Metabolism and Related Fields, 1952; articles in: Jl of Biological Chemistry; JL of Amer. Chemical Soc.; Jl of Medicinal Chemistry; Biochemistry. *Address:* Department of Chemistry, Cornell University, Ithaca, New York 14850, USA; (Home) 200 White Park Road, Ithaca, New York 14850, USA.

**DWORKIN, Prof. Ronald Myles;** Professor of Jurisprudence, Oxford University, since 1969; *b* 11 Dec. 1931; *s* of David Dworkin and Madeline Talamo; *m* 1958, Betsy Celia Ross; one *s* one *d*. *Educ:* Harvard Coll.; Oxford Univ.; Harvard Law Sch. Legal Sec. to Judge Learned Hand, 1957-58; Associate, Sullivan & Cromwell, New York, 1958-62; Yale Law School: Associate Prof. of Law, 1962-65; Prof. of Law, 1965-68; Wesley N. Hohfeld Prof. of Jurisprudence, 1968-69. *Publications:* several articles in legal and philosophical jls. *Address:* University College, Oxford.

**DWYER, Most Rev. George Patrick;** *see* Birmingham, Archbishop of, (RC).

**DWYER, Air Vice-Marshal Michael Harington,** CB 1961; CBE 1955; retired; *b* 18 Sept. 1912; *s* of late M. H. Dwyer, Royal Garrison Artillery; *m* 1936, Barbara, *d* of late S. B. Freeman, CBE;

one *s* one *d. Educ:* Oundle Sch. Entered RAF, 1931; served India, 1933-36; UK and NW Europe, 1939-45; Middle East, 1949-51; Air Officer Commanding No. 62 Group, 1954-56; SASO No. 3 Group, RAF, 1956-57. Student at Imperial Defence Coll., 1958. AOC No. 3 Group, 1959-61. AOA, HQ Bomber Command, 1961-65; Regional Dir of Civil Defence, North-West Region, 1966-68. *Address:* Island House, Rambledown Lane, West Chiltington, Sussex.

**DYALL, Valentine;** Actor; *b* 7 May 1908; *s* of late Franklin Dyall; *m* 1940, Babette Holder, adopted *d* of N. F. Holder; two *s. Educ:* Harrow; Christ Church, Oxford. Began acting career at the Old Vic, 1930 and continued regularly on the West End stage until 1938; subsequently mainly in films and broadcasting. First appeared in films, 1941, and has acted in numerous pictures. Took the role of The Man in Black in a radio series. *Publications:* Unsolved Mysteries, 1954; Famous Sea Tragedies, 1955; Flood of Mutiny, 1957. *Recreations:* fishing, sailing and travelling. *Address:* c/o Essanay Ltd, 60 Wardour Street, W1.

**DYBALL, Maj.-Gen. Antony John,** CBE 1970 (OBE 1966); MC 1945; TD; Chief of Staff and Deputy Director of Operations Northern Ireland, 1969-70; *b* 10 July 1919; *s* of John Francis Dyball; *m* 1941, Elizabeth Margaret Siddle; one *d. Educ:* Downsend; Epsom College. London Irish Rifles (TA); joined Depot RUR, Armagh, 1939; 1st Bn RUR, part of 6th Airborne Div., NW Europe, 1945 (MC); Trng Major, RUR Depot at Ballymena, 1954-56; comd Queen's Univ. OTC, Belfast, 1956-58; Bde Major, 124 Inf. Bde (TA), 1958-60; CO, London Irish Rifles (TA), 1960-62; AAG, Middle East Comd, 1963-65; Bde Comdr, 107 Independent Inf. Bde (TA), 1965-67; Chief of Staff, HQ Northern Ireland, 1967-69. *Recreations:* golf, racing. *Address:* 12 Deramore Park, Belfast 9, Northern Ireland. *T:* Belfast 666190. *Club:* Army and Navy.

**DYDE, John Horsfall,** CBE 1970 (OBE 1957); Chairman, Eastern Gas Board, 1959-69; *b* 4 June 1905; *m* 1930, Ethel May Hewitt; two *s. Educ:* Scarborough High Sch.; University of Leeds. Engineer and Manager, North Middlesex Gas Co., 1937-42; prior to nationalisation was Engineer and Gen. Manager of Uxbridge, Maidenhead, Wycombe & District Gas Co. and Slough Gas & Coke Co.; also Technical Director of group of undertakings of the South Eastern Gas Corp. Ltd; Dep.-Chm., Eastern Gas Board, 1949. President: Western Junior Gas Assoc., 1935-36; Southern Assoc. of Gas Engineers and Managers, 1949-50; Institution of Gas Engineers, 1951-52; British Road Tar Association. Chm., Printar Industries Ltd. MSc; MIChemE; MInstGasE. *Recreations:* golf, sailing. *Address:* Burniston, Sudbury Road, Boxford, Suffolk. *T:* Boxford 732. *Club:* Anglo-Belgian.

**DYE, Maj.-Gen. Jack Bertie,** CBE 1968 (OBE 1965); MC; General Officer Commanding Eastern District since 1969; Major-General late Royal Norfolk Regiment; *b* 1919. Served War of 1939-45 (MC). Brigadier, 1966; psc. Commanded South Arabian Army, 1966-68. Col Comdt, The Queen's Division, 1970-. *Address:* c/o Glyn, Mills & Co., 22 Whitehall, SW1.

**DYER, Charles;** playwright and novelist; actor-director (as Raymond Dyer); *b* 7 July 1928; *s* of James Sidney Dyer and Florence (*née* Stretton); *m* 1959, Fiona Thomson, actress; three *s. Educ:* Queen Elizabeth's Sch., Barnet. Plays: Clubs Are Sometimes Trumps, 1948; Who On Earth!, 1951; Turtle In The Soup, 1953; The Jovial Parasite, 1954; Single Ticket Mars, 1955; Time, Murderer, Please, and Poison In Jest, 1956; Wanted-One Body!, 1958; Prelude To Fury, 1959 (also wrote theme music); Red Cabbage And Kings, (as R. Kraselchik) 1960 (also wrote theme music); (as Charles Dyer) Rattle of A Simple Man, 1962 (also in Berlin, Paris, NY, Rome); Staircase, 1966 (for RSC; also in NY, Paris, Amsterdam, Berlin, Rome); Mother Adam, Paris, Berlin, 1970, London, 1971; screenplays: Rattle, 1964; Insurance Italian Style, 1967; Staircase, 1968; Brother Sun and Sister Moon, 1970. Also directed plays for the stage and television. Acted in: Worm's Eye View, 1948; Room For Two, 1955; Dry Rot, 1958; films: Cuptie Honeymoon, 1947; Britannia Mews, 1949; Road Sense, 1950; Off The Record, 1952; Pickwick Papers, 1952; Dockland Case, 1953; Strange Case of Blondie, 1953; Naval Patrol, 1959; Loneliness of A Long Distance Runner, 1962; Mouse On The Moon, 1962; Knack, 1964; Rattle of A Simple Man, 1964; How I Won The War, 1967; Staircase, 1968. Television series, Hugh and I, 1964. *Publications:* (as Charles Dyer): plays: Wanted-One Body!, 1961; Time, Murderer, Please, 1962; Rattle Of A Simple Man, (Fr.) 1963; Staircase, 1966; Mother Adam, 1970; novels: Rattle Of A Simple Man, 1964; Charlie Always Told Harry Almost Everything, 1969 (USA and Europe, 1970). *Recreations:* amateur music and carpentry. *Address:* Old Wob, Gerrards Cross, Bucks.

**DYER, Henry Peter Francis S.;** *see* Swinnerton Dyer.

**DYER, Sir Leonard Schroeder Swinnerton,** 15th Bt, *cr* 1678; Engineer; Chairman: British Automatic Refrigerators, Ltd; J. D. Insulating Co. Ltd; Linford Estates Ltd; Blandstone Investments Ltd; Brownswood Properties Ltd; Milestone & Staniforth Ltd; Equipment Credit Ltd; Cranleigh Group Ltd; Stamford Finance Ltd; Goulston Discount Co. Ltd; Oxford & Cowley Ironworks Ltd; Estates & General Investments Ltd; *b* 30 March 1898; *s* of Sir Leonard Whitworth Swinnerton Dyer, 14th Bt, and Lucy (*d* 1948), *d* of late Hon. Francis Schroeder, New York; *S* father 1947; *m* 1925, Barbara, *d* of Hereward Brackenbury, CBE; one *s* one *d. Educ:* Repton. Served European War, 1914-18. RFA 1916-19. Pres. British Chess Federation, 1956-59 (Chm., 1951-56); Chm., Shropshire CC. *Recreations:* shooting, chess. *Heir: s* Henry Peter Francis Swinnerton Dyer, *qv. Address:* Westhope Cottage, Craven Arms, Salop. *T:* Seifton 219. *Clubs:* Bath; Shropshire.

**DYER-SMITH, Rear-Adm. John Edward;** Director-General Aircraft (Naval), Ministry of Defence, since 1970; *b* 17 Aug. 1918; *s* of Harold E. Dyer-Smith and Emily Sutton; *m* 1940, Kathleen Powell; four *s* one *d. Educ:* Devonport High Sch.; RN Engineering Coll.; Imperial Coll. of Science. Served War of 1939-45: Engineer Officer, HMS Prince of Wales, 1940-41; Asst Fleet Engr Officer, Eastern Fleet, 1942-43; HMS Illustrious, 1943. Various MAP and Min. of Aviation appts, 1946-54; Head of Naval Air Dept, RAE, 1957-61; Dir of RN Aircraft/Helicopters, Min. of Aviation, 1961-64; Defence and Naval Attaché, Tokyo, 1965-67; Superintendent, RN Aircraft Yard, Belfast, 1968-70. *Recreations:* painting, golf. *Address:* 41 Links Road, Epsom, Surrey. *T:* Epsom 26893. *Club:* Royal Automobile.

**DYKE, Sir Derek William Hart,** 9th Bt *cr* 1676; *b* 4 Dec. 1924; *s* of Sir Oliver Hamilton Augustus Hart Dyke, 8th Bt, and Millicent Zoë, *d* of Dr

Mayston Bond; *S* father, 1969; *m* 1st, 1953, Dorothy Moses, Hamilton, Ont (marr. diss. 1963); one *s* one *d*; 2nd, 1964, Margaret Dickson Elder, Ottawa. *Educ:* Harrow; Millfield. *Heir: s* David William Hart Dyke, *b* 6 Jan. 1955. *Address:* 28 King Street West, Stoney Creek, Ontario, Canada.

**DYKE, Sidney Campbell,** DM, FRCP, FCPath; Curator, Regional Histological Collection, University of Birmingham; Hon. Consultant pathologist, The Royal Hospital, Wolverhampton and General Hospital, Walsall, Staffs; *b* 1886; *s* of John and Martha Dyke; *m* 1918, Janet Mary, *d* of W. D. Smith, Llanelly; one *s* one *d*. *Educ:* University of Toronto and Oxford (Coll. Exon). Journalism, Canada to 1910; Rhodes Scholar, British Columbia, 1910, 1st Class Natural Science, 1913; served European War, 1914-18, with King Edward's Horse and RAMC; Asst Bacteriologist Sch. of Medicine, University of Durham; Pathologist to Clinical Units, St Thomas' Hosp., London; Radcliffe Prize for Advancement of Medicine, 1929; late Chm. of Council, late Pres., late Hon. Sec. Assoc. of Clinical Pathologists; Président d'Honneur Société Internationale de Biologie Clinique; Hon. Member: American Soc. of Clinical Pathologists; Associacion Nacional de Medicos Especialistas de Analisis Clinicos España; Société Française de Biologie Medicale. Fellow, BMA. *Publications:* (ed) Recent Advances in Clinical Pathology, 1946, 1952, 1960, 1964, 1968; contribs to various med. jls. *Recreations:* fishing, walking. *Address:* Upper Green, Tettenhall, Wolverhampton. *T:* Wolverhampton 751394. *Club:* United University.

**DYKES, Hugh John;** MP (C) Harrow (East) since 1970; Partner in Simon & Coates, Stockbrokers, London, since 1968; *b* 17 May 1939; *s* of Richard Dykes and Doreen Ismay Maxwell Dykes; *m* 1965, Susan Margaret Dykes (*née* Smith); one *s*. *Educ:* Weston super Mare Grammar Sch.; Pembroke Coll. Cambridge. Joined firm of Simon & Coates, 1963. Contested (C) Tottenham, Gen. Elec., 1966. PPS to three Parliamentary Under-Secretaries of State for Defence, 1970-. *Publications:* (ed) Westropp's "Invest £100", 1964, and Westropp's "Start your own Business", 1965; many articles and pamphlets on political and financial subjects. *Recreations:* music, theatre, swimming, travel. *Address:* House of Commons, SW1. *T:* 01-930 6240. *Club:* Carlton.

**DYKES BOWER, Sir John,** Kt 1968; CVO 1953; Hon. DMus Oxon, 1944; MA, MusB Cantab; Hon. RAM; FRCM; Hon. FRCO; Hon. FTCL; FRSCM; Hon. Secretary, Royal College of Organists, since 1968; Organist of St Paul's Cathedral, 1936-67; Professor Royal College of Music; *b* 13 Aug. 1905; 3rd *s* of late Ernest Dykes Bower, MD, Glos; unmarried. *Educ:* Cheltenham Coll.; Corpus Christi Coll., Cambridge (Organ Scholar). John Stewart of Rannoch Scholar in Sacred Music, 1922-28; Organist and Master of the Choir of Truro Cathedral, 1926-29; Succentor, 1929; Organist of New Coll., Oxford, 1929-33; of Durham Cathedral, 1933-36; Conductor of the Oxford Harmonic Soc., 1930-33; Lecturer in Music at University of Durham, 1934; Fellow of Corpus Christi Coll., Cambridge, 1934-37; Associate Dir of Royal Sch. of Church Music, 1945-52; Pres., Incorporated Association of Organists, 1949-50; Pres. of the Royal College of Organists, 1960-62. Master, Worshipful Co. of Musicians, 1967-68. RAFVR 1940-45, with rank of Squadron Leader. *Address:* Flat 4z, Artillery Mansions, SW1. *Club:* Athenæum.

**DYKES BOWER, S(tephen) E(rnest),** MA; FRIBA; FSA; Surveyor of the Fabric of Westminster Abbey since 1951; Consulting Architect, Carlisle Cathedral, since 1947; Chelmsford Cathedral since 1949; Norwich Cathedral since 1953; *b* 18 April 1903; 2nd *s* of Ernest Dykes Bower, MD; unmarried. *Educ:* Cheltenham Coll.; Merton Coll., Oxford (Organ Schol.); Architectural Assoc. Sch. of Architecture. Private practice as architect since 1931, work chiefly domestic and ecclesiastical. Architect for: New High Altar, Baldachino and American Memorial Chapel, St Paul's Cathedral (with W. Godfrey Allen); enlargement of Bury St Edmunds Cathedral; Cathedral Library and Bishop's Palace, Exeter; completion of Lancing Coll. Chapel; re-building of Gt Yarmouth Parish Church; St Vedast, Foster Lane, EC; and other churches in London and country; work in Canterbury, Winchester, Norwich, Ely, Gloucester, Wells, Carlisle, Peterborough and other cathedrals, Oxford and Cambridge Colls, Public Schs, etc. *Publications:* papers and addresses on architectural subjects. *Address:* Quendon Court, Quendon, near Saffron Walden, Essex. *T:* Rickling 242; 6 The Little Cloister, Westminster Abbey, SW1. *T:* 01-222 5801. *Clubs:* Athenæum, Oxford and Cambridge.

**DYKSTRA, John;** retired; former Director of Ford Motor Company; Director of other Ford companies; Director, Tecumseh Products; Director and Consultant, Sheller-Globe Inc., Toledo, Ohio; *b* Netherlands, 16 April 1898; *s* of Theodore Dykstra and Nellie (*née* De Vries); came to America 1902; became American citizen, 1919; *m* 1918, Marion S. Hyde; one *s* one *d*. *Educ:* Cass Technical High Sch., Detroit; (courses) La Salle Extension Univ. Started as apprentice die maker, 1914, while taking mechanical engineering courses. Served in Army, European War of 1914-18; returned to Detroit, 1919; associated with Oldsmobile Div. of Gen. Motors Corp. from 1934 (Manuf. Man., 1941-47); joined Ford Motor Company, 1947, as gen. production Asst to Vice-Pres. (manufacturing); Gen. Man. of former gen. manuf. div., 1948; a Ford Vice-Pres., 1950; Manufacturing Group Vice-Pres., 1957; Dir, 1958; Pres., 1961-63. Responsible for company's aircraft Engine Div., Oct. 1950-Sept. 1958; engaged in intensified quality control program for Ford products, as Vice-Pres. Manuf., 1958-61. Mem. Soc. of Automotive Engineers. *Recreations:* golf, fishing. *Address:* 1147 Glengarry Road, Birmingham, Michigan 48010, USA. *T:* Midwest 6-2111. *Clubs:* Athletic, Golf, Recess (all of Detroit).

**DYMENT, Clifford Henry,** FRSL 1951; Author; *b* Alfreton, Derbyshire, 20 Jan. 1914; *e c* of late William Clifford Dyment and Elizabeth Riding, Caerleon, Mon; *m* 1947, Marcella (*d* 1968), *y d* of late Marcell and late Gisella Salzer, Vienna; no *c*. *Educ:* Grammar Sch., Loughborough. Freelance literary journalist and critic, 1934-40; writer of film commentaries and dir of documentary films for Min. of Information, British Council, War Office and other official bodies, 1942-48. Atlantic Award in Literature 1950. Commentaries, BBC television series, The Face of Britain, 1951; Granada television series, Another World, 1964-65; Commentaries, BBC TV, 1968-70. *Publications:* First Day, 1935; Straight or Curly?, 1937; Selected Poems, 1943; The Axe in the Wood, 1944; Matthew Arnold: an Introduction and a Selection, 1948; Thomas Hood: a selection of his serious poems with an introduction, 1949; Poems, 1935-48, 1949; Experiences and Places, 1955; C. Day Lewis (Writers and their Work), 1955; The Railway

Game: An Early Autobiography, 1962; Fur, Feather, and Fin (with Marcella Dyment, co-author, and Hafis Bertschinger, artist), 1968; Collected Poems, 1970. *Recreations:* sampling inexpensive wines, listening to 78 rpm gramophone records, collecting cigarette cards, playing the mouth organ. *Address:* c/o J. M. Dent & Sons Ltd, Aldine House, 10-13 Bedford Street, WC2.

**DYMOND, Charles Edward,** CBE 1967; Counsellor in Charge, British High Commission, Auckland, New Zealand, since 1967; *b* 15 Oct. 1916; *s* of Charles George Dymond and Dora Kate Dymond (*née* Gillingham); *m* 1945, Dorothy Jean Peaker; two *s* two *d. Educ:* Tiverton Grammar Sch.; Exeter Univ. BSc (Econ) London. Royal Artillery, 1939-46; BoT Regional Div., 1946; Trade Commn Service, 1951; Trade Comr, Johannesburg, 1951; Cape Town, 1955; Nairobi, 1957; Sen. Trade Comr, Lagos, 1963-64; Counsellor (Commercial), Lagos, 1965-66. *Recreations:* music, photography. *Address:* St Valery, Silverton, Devon. *T:* Silverton 294.

**DYNEVOR,** 9th Baron *cr* 1780; **Richard Charles Uryan Rhys;** *b* 19 June 1935; *s* of 8th Baron Dynevor, CBE, MC; *S* father, 1962; *m* 1959, Lucy, *d* of Sir John Rotherstein, *qv*; one *s* three *d. Educ:* Eton; Magdalene Coll., Cambridge. *Heir: s* Hon. Hugo Griffith Uryan Rhys, *b* 19 Nov. 1966. *Address:* 18 Brook Green, W6. *T:* 01-603 4720.

**DYSART, Countess of,** *cr* 1643, 10th in Line; **Wenefryde Agatha Greaves;** Baroness Huntingtower, 1643; *b* 13 Nov. 1889; *d* of Charles Norman Lindsay Scott and Lady Agnes Mary Tollemache, *d* of late Lord Huntingtower; *S* uncle 1935; *m* 1913, Major Owain Greaves, late Royal Horse Guards (served RHG, European War of 1914-18) (*d* 1941), two *d* (and one *d* decd). *Heir: d* Lady Rosamund Agnes Greaves, *b* 15 Feb. 1914. *Address:* Stobo Castle, Peeblesshire.

**DYSON, Rev. Anthony Oakley,** BD, MA, DPhil; Principal of Ripon Hall, Oxford, since 1969; *b* 6 Oct. 1935; *s* of Henry Oakley Leslie Dyson and Lilian Dyson; *m* 1960, Edwina Anne Hammett; two *s. Educ:* William Hulme's Grammar Sch., Manchester; Univs of Cambridge and Oxford. 2nd Lieut, West Yorks Regt, 1954-56; Emmanuel Coll., Cambridge, 1956-59; Exeter Coll., Oxford and Ripon Hall, Oxford, 1959-61; Curate of Putney, Dio. Southwark, 1961-63; Chaplain of Ripon Hall, Oxford, 1963-69. Editor, The Teilhard Review. *Publications:* Existentialism, 1965; Who is Jesus Christ?, 1969; contribs to Theology, The Modern Churchman, etc. *Recreations:* literature, sport. *Address:* Principal's House, Ripon Hall, Boars Hill, Oxford OX1 5ET. *T:* Oxford 35579.

**DYSON, Sir Cyril (Douglas),** Kt 1953; Managing Director of Dyson and Sons Ltd since 1948; *b* 6 Dec. 1895; *s* of late Albert Harry Dyson and late Frances Emma Dyson (*née* White); *m* 1923, Sylvia Rix (*née* Lingwood); one *s* one *d. Educ:* Cliftonville Coll., Margate; Northampton Polytechnical Coll. (student of horology and of optics). Service in Berks Yeomanry and in the Tenth Hussars, 1914-19. Mem. of family business of jewellers, watchmakers and opticians since 1919. Mayor of the Royal Borough of New Windsor, 1952, 1953 (Councillor, 1943, Alderman, 1951). FSMC, FBHI 1914 Star; Victory, Civil Defence, Gen. Service and Police medals; Coronation Medal, 1953. *Recreations:* rowing, golf, swimming. *Address:* 11 York Road, Windsor, Berks. *T:* 65572. *Clubs:* Rotary, and many local athletic.

**DYSON, Edith Mary Beatrice,** OBE 1946; RRC 1948, Bar to RRC 1952; *b* 18 June 1900. *Educ:* Greenhead, Huddersfield. Student Nurse, Royal Free Hospital, London, 1919-24; joined Army Nursing Service, 1924, Germany (with the Army of Occupation, 1926), also India, Burma; served War of 1939-45, i/c nursing units Hong Kong; Prisoner of War, 1941-45; War Office, 1946-48; Col, Queen Alexandra's Royal Army Nursing Corps and Deputy Dir Army Nursing Services, 1951-52; retired 1952. *Recreation:* golf. *Address:* Vine Cottage, Higher Trevilla, Feock, Cornwall. *Club:* English-Speaking Union.

**DYSON, Freeman John,** FRS 1952; Professor, School of Mathematics, Institute for Advanced Study, Princeton, New Jersey, since 1953; *b* 15 Dec. 1923; *s* of late Sir George Dyson, KCVO; *m* 1st, 1950, Verena Esther (*née* Huber) (marr. diss. 1958); one *s* one *d*; 2nd, 1958, Imme (*née* Jung); four *d. Educ:* Winchester; Cambridge; Cornell University. Operational research for RAF Bomber Command, 1943-45. Fellow of Trinity Coll., Cambridge, 1946-50; Commonwealth Fund Fellow at Cornell and Princeton, USA, 1947-49; Mem. of Institute for Advanced Study, Princeton, USA, 1949-50; Professor of Physics, Cornell Univ., Ithaca, NY, USA, 1951-53. Mem. of National Academy of Sciences (USA), 1964. Lorentz Medal, Royal Netherlands Acad. of Sciences, 1966; Hughes Medal, Royal Soc., 1968; Max Planck Medal, German Physical Soc., 1969. *Publications:* contrib. to The Physical Review, Annals of Mathematics, etc. *Address:* Institute for Advanced Study, Princeton, NJ 08540, USA.

**DYSON, Dr James,** FRS 1968; Superintendent, Division of Optical Metrology, National Physical Laboratory, since 1963; *b* 10 Dec. 1914; *s* of George Dyson and Mary Grace (*née* Bateson); *m* 1948, Marie Florence Chant (*d* 1967); one *d. Educ:* Queen Elizabeth Sch., Kirby Lonsdale; Christ's Coll., Cambridge. BA 1936; MA 1960; ScD 1960. Student Apprentice, BT-H Co., Rugby, 1936-39; Research Engr, BT-H Co., Rugby, 1939-46; Consultant (Optics), AEI Research Lab., Aldermaston, 1946-63. FInstP 1960; Hon. Fellow Royal Microscopical Soc., 1969. *Publications:* Interferometry, 1969; papers on applied optics in learned jls. *Recreations:* astronomy, mechanical occupations, music, people, deploring the motor-car. *Address:* 19 Hansler Grove, East Molesey, Surrey. *T:* 01-979 6403.

# E

**EABORN, Prof. Colin,** FRS 1970; PhD, DSc (Wales); FRIC; Professor of Chemistry since 1962 and Chairman of Science since 1968, University of Sussex; *b* 15 March 1923; *s* of Tom Stanley and Caroline Eaborn; *m* 1949, Joyce Thomas. *Educ:* Ruabon Grammar Sch., Denbighshire; Univ. Coll. of N Wales, Bangor. Asst Lecturer, 1947, Lecturer, 1950, and Reader 1954, in Chemistry, Univ. of Leicester. Research Associate, Univ. of California at Los Angeles, 1950-51; Robert A. Welch Visiting Scholar, Rice Univ., Texas, 1961-62; Erskine Fellow, Univ. of Canterbury (NZ), 1965. Hon. Sec., Chemical Society, 1964-71; Chm, British Cttee on Chemical Educn, 1967-69. *Publications:* Organosilicon Compounds, 1960; Organometallic Compounds of the Group IV Elements, Vol. 1, Part 1, 1968; numerous publications, mainly in Jl of Chem. Soc. and Jl of Organometallic Chemistry. *Address:* School of Molecular Sciences, University of Sussex, Brighton BNI 9QJ. *T:* Brighton 66755.

**EADES, Sir Thomas,** Kt 1945; Hon. President, formerly Chairman, Automatic Telephone & Electric Co. Ltd, Liverpool; *b* 1888; *s* of William Joseph and Sarah Ellen Eades, Worcs; *m* 1914, Eleanor Rachel Jesper; one *s* one *d.* *Educ:* Wolverley; private. Chm. of Telephone Development Association, 1938, 1939, 1944, 1945, also Chm. of Telecommunication Engineering and Manufacturing Assoc., 1945, 1957. FCIS, FRSA, FBIM. *Publications:* articles to Technical Press. *Address:* Knightons, Keston, Kent.

**EADIE, Alexander,** BEM 1960; JP; MP (Lab) Midlothian since 1966; *b* 23 June 1920; *m* 1941; one *s.* *Educ:* Buckhaven Senior Secondary Sch. Coal-miner from 1934. Chm., Fife County Housing Cttee, 9 yrs; Chm., Fife County Educn Cttee 18 mths; Governor, Moray House Teachers' Training Coll., Edinburgh, 5 yrs; Exec. Committee: Scottish Council of Labour Party, 9 yrs; NUM Scottish Area, 2 yrs; Mem., Eastern Regional Hosp. Bd. (Scotland), 14 yrs. Contested Ayr, 1959 and 1964; Former PPS to Miss M. Herbison, MP, Minister of Social Security, and Mem. of Parly Select Cttee on Scottish Affairs; Vice-Chm., Parly Trade Union Group. JP Fife, 1951-. *Recreations:* motoring, bowling, gardening. *Address:* 9 Hugo Avenue, Coaltown-of-Wemyss, Fife. *T:* Dysart 5836.

**EADIE, Mrs Ellice (Aylmer),** CBE 1966; Parliamentary Counsel since 1968; *b* 30 June 1912; *d* of late Rt Rev. R. T. Hearn, LLD, sometime Bishop of Cork, and of late Dr M. E. T. Hearn, MD, FRCPI; *m* 1946, John Harold Ward Eadie. *Educ:* Cheltenham Ladies' Coll.; St Hugh's Coll., Oxford. Called to Bar, Gray's Inn, 1936. Flt Officer, WAAF, 1941-46. Parliamentary Counsel Office, 1949-. *Address:* Twyfordbury Farmhouse, Bishops Stortford, Herts. *T:* Bishops Stortford 2869.

**EADIE, William Ewing;** Director: The Burmah Oil Company Limited, 1950-67 (Chairman, 1957-64); Chartered Bank, since 1957; Bank of Scotland (London), since 1961; *b* 18 Oct. 1896; *s* of late John Ewing Eadie; *m* 1936, Dorothy Owen Jones. *Educ:* Harris Academy, Dundee. Served European War, 1914-19 (despatches, 1918). Qualified Chartered Accountant, 1921; joined The Burmah Oil Co. Ltd, Rangoon, 1921; seconded to Burmah-Shell, 1928-41; returned to The Burmah Oil Co. Ltd, London, 1941; Chief Accountant, 1948-50; appointed to Board of Directors, 1950; Asst Managing Dir, 1951; Managing Dir, 1955-61. *Recreations:* golf and motoring. *Address:* Woodside, Groombridge, Kent. *T:* Groombridge 260. *Clubs:* City of London, East India and Sports, Royal Commonwealth Society; Oriental, Bengal (Calcutta).

**EADY,** family name of **Baron Swinfen.**

**EAGGER, Brig. Arthur Austin,** CBE 1944 (OBE 1940), TD 1945; Consultant to Slough Industrial Health Service, since 1963; *b* 14 March 1898; *s* of Edward and Elsie Eagger; *m* 1st, 1935, Kate Mortimer Hare (*d* 1946); three *s*; 2nd, 1948, Barbara Noel Hare. *Educ:* Aberdeen Univ. (MB ChB 1922). Lieut 6th Bn Gordon Hldrs. Commissioned RAMC (TA), 1928; late DDMS 1 Airborne Corps. Medical Dir Slough Industrial Health Service, retired 1963. Bronze Star (USA), 1945. *Publications:* Industrial Resettlement (Proc. RSM), 1952; Health in the Factory (Jl Royal Institute of Public Health and Hygiene), 1953; Venture in Industry, 1965. *Address:* Leahurst, Thorverton, Exeter, Devon. *T:* Silverton 469.

**EAGLESHAM, Eric John Ross,** MA, BEd, LLB; Professor of Education, Durham University, 1947-66, retired; Professor Emeritus, 1966; *b* 29 Oct. 1905; 3rd *s* of late Reverend David Eaglesham, Chapelknowe, Canonbie, Dumfriesshire; *m* 1957, Nancy, *yr d* of late J. F. Rintoul; three *s* one *d.* *Educ:* Dumfries Acad.; Edinburgh Univ., 1923-27, 1930-31. Asst Teacher, Gretna Sch., 1927-30; Asst Teacher, Lockerbie Academy, 1931-35; Lecturer, Education Dept, Manchester Univ., 1936-38; Master of Method, Jordanhill Training Centre, Glasgow, 1938-40; RAF, rank Flight Lieut, on planning staff of Air Ministry dealing with questions of International Law, 1941-42; Principal Master of Method, Jordanhill Training Centre, Glasgow, 1942-43; Depute Dir of Studies, Jordanhill Training Centre, 1944-46. *Publications:* From School Board to Local Authority, 1956; Morant on the March (Yearbook of Education), 1957; The Foundations of Twentieth Century Education in England, 1967; articles in various learned journals. *Address:* The Croft, Park Road, Scotby, Cumberland.

**EAGLETON, Guy Tryon;** *b* 1 July 1894; *s* of late John Eagleton and of Violet Marion Eagleton; *m* 1947, Amy Rubina Gothard; no *c.* *Educ:* Aldenham Sch. Solicitor, 1919; Asst Clerk Haberdashers' Company, 1925; Clerk of the Haberdashers' Company, 1931-50, retired. *Recreations:* golf and gardening. *Address:* 31 Hillydeal Road, Otford (Sevenoaks), Kent. *T:* Otford 3220. *Club:* Royal Blackheath Golf (Sen. Past Captain).

**EAKER, Lt-Gen. Ira Clarence,** Hon. KCB 1945; Hon. KBE 1943; DSM, US Army (2 Oak Leaf Clusters), US Navy; DFC (Oak Leaf Cluster); Silver Star; Legion of Merit; Vice-President, Douglas Aircraft Co., Washington, DC, since 1957; *b* Field Creek, Texas, 13 April 1896; *s* of Y. Y. Eaker and Dona Lee; *m* Ruth Huff Apperson; no *c.* *Educ:* South Eastern State Teachers' Coll., Durant, Okla; University of Southern California; Columbia Univ., 2nd Lieut of Infantry, Regular Army, 1917; Capt. 1920; Major, 1935; Lieut-Col (temp.) 1937; Lieut-Col 1940; Col (temp.), 1941; Brig.-Gen. (temp.) Jan. 1942; Maj.-Gen. (temp.) Sept. 1942; Lieut-Gen. (temp.) 1943; permanent Brig.-Gen. RA 1944. Served in Philippines, 1919-22; pilot of one of planes of Pan-American Flight round South America, 1926-27 (DFC); chief pilot of Airplane Question Mark on refuelling endurance flight, 1929, establishing a new world flight endurance record (Oak Leaf Cluster for DFC). In command of VIII Bomber Command in European Theatre of Operations, 1942; commanded Eighth Air Force, 1942-44 and also US Army Air Forces in UK, 1943-44; comd. Mediterranean Allied Air Forces in Italy, 1944; Dep. Comdg Gen. Army Air Forces and Chief of Air Staff, US, 1945-47; retired 1947. Author, syndicated weekly column on subjects in nat. security area, 1962-. French Legion of Honour (Grand Officer) and many other foreign decorations. *Publications:* (with Gen. Arnold); Army Flyer, This Flying Game, Winged Warfare. *Address:* c/o Hughes Aircraft Co., 1612 K Street NW, Washington, DC 20006, USA.

**EARDLEY-WILMOT, Sir John (Assheton),** 5th Bt *cr* 1821; MVO 1956; DSC 1943; AMBIM 1965; Staff of Monopolies Commission since 1967; *b* 2 Jan. 1917; *s* of Commander Frederick Neville Eardley-Wilmot (*d* 1956) (*s* of 3rd Bt) and Dorothy Little (*d* 1959), formerly of Brooksby, Double Bay, Sydney; *S* uncle, 1970;

*m* 1939, Diana Elizabeth, *d* of Commander Aubrey Moore, RN, and Mrs O. Bassett; one *s* one *d*. *Educ:* Stubbington; RNC, Dartmouth. Motor Torpedo Boats, 1939-43; served HMS Apollo, 1944; HMS Fencer, 1945-46; RN Staff Course, 1950; HMS Opossum, 1951-53; Cabinet Office, 1954-57; Admiralty, 1958-67; retired 1967, as Deputy Director Naval Administrative Planning. Norwegian War Medal. *Recreation:* fishing. *Heir:* *s* Michael John Assheton Eardley-Wilmot, *b* 13 Jan. 1941. *Address:* 41 Margravine Gardens, W6. *T:* 01-748 3723. *Clubs:* Naval and Military, Norwegian; XL, Enton Fishing.

**EARL, Christopher Joseph,** MD, FRCP; Physician to: Neurological Department, London Hospital, E1, since 1961; National Hospital, Queen Square, since 1958; Moorfields Eye Hospital, since 1959; Consultant Neurologist, King Edward VII Hospital for Officers, since 1966 and Hospital of St John and St Elizabeth, since 1967; *b* 20 Nov. 1925; *s* of Christopher and Winifred Earl, Ashbourne, Derbyshire; *m* 1951, Alma Patience Hopkins, Reading; two *s* three *d*. *Educ:* Cotton Coll.; Guy's Hosp. House phys. and house surg., Guy's Hosp., and MO, RAF, 1948-50. Lecturer in Chemical Pathology, Guy's Hosp., 1950-52; Research Fellow, Harvard Med. Sch., and Neurological Unit, Boston City Hosp., 1952-54; Resident MO, Nat. Hosp., Queen Square, 1954-56; Chief Asst, Neurological Dept, Guy's Hosp., 1956-58. Hon. Dir of Photography, Royal Society of Medicine. Hon. Sec., Assoc. British Neurologists. Hon. Vice-Pres., Med. Defence Union. *Publications:* Papers in learned jls on Biochemistry and Neurology. *Recreation:* reading history. *Address:* 23 Audley Road, Ealing, W5. *T:* 01-997 0380. *Club:* Garrick.

**EARLE, Air Chief Marshal Sir Alfred,** GBE 1966 (KBE 1961; CBE 1946); CB 1956; *b* 1907; *s* of late Henry Henwood Earle, Beaworthy, Devon, and Mary Winifred Earle; *m* 1st, 1934, Phyllis Beatrice (*d* 1960), *o d* of W. J. Rice, Watford; one *s* one *d*; 2nd, 1961, Rosemary, *widow* of Air Vice-Marshal F. J. St G. Braithwaite, and *d* of late G. Grinling Harris, Clifford's Inn. *Educ:* Shebbear Coll., Beaworthy, Devon. Graduated from Royal Air Force Coll., Cranwell, 1929. Served in Bomber Squadrons in United Kingdom and Iraq and as instructor at RAF Sch. of Photography, 1930-38; psa 1939; Training Command, 1940; Air Ministry, in Directorate of Plans, 1941-42; Comd No 428 RCAF Sqdn and stations in Bomber Comd, 1942-43; Offices of War Cabinet and Minister of Defence (attended Cairo and Yalta Confs), 1943-45; AOC No 300 Transport Grp (Austr.) and No 232 Transport Grp (Far East), 1945-46; Directing Staff, RAF Staff Coll., 1946-49; idc 1950; Comd RAAF Staff Coll., 1951-53; Air Ministry, Dir of Policy (Air Staff), 1954; Asst Chief of Air Staff (Policy), 1955-57; AOC No 13 Group, 1957-59; Deputy Chief of Defence Staff, 1960-62; AOC-in-C, Technical Training Command, 1962-64; Vice-Chief of Defence Staff, 1964-66; retd 1966; Dir Gen. of Intelligence, Min. of Defence, 1966-68. *Recreations:* golf, gardening. *Address:* 16 Park Lane, Southwold, Suffolk. *Club:* Royal Air Force.

**EARLE, Arthur Frederick;** Principal, The London Graduate School of Business Studies, since 1965; Director, Hoover Ltd, since 1961; Director, The British Aluminium Co. Ltd, since 1965; *b* Toronto, 13 Sept. 1921; *s* of Frederick C. Earle and Hilda M. Earle (*née* Brown); *m* 1946, Vera Domini Lithgow; two *s* one *d*. *Educ:* Toronto; London Sch. of Economics (BSc (Econ.), PhD). Royal Canadian Navy (Rating to Lieut Comdr), 1939-46. Canada Packers Ltd, 1946-48; Aluminium Ltd cos in British Guiana, West Indies and Canada, 1948-53; Treas., Alumina Jamaica Ltd, 1953-55; Aluminium Union, London, 1955-58; Vice-Pres., Aluminium Ltd Sales Inc., New York, 1958-61; Dep. Chm., 1961-65, Man. Dir, 1963-65, Hoover Ltd. Member: Commn of Enquiry, Jamaican Match Industry, 1953; Consumer Council, 1963-68; NEDC Cttee on Management Educn, Training and Develt, 1967-69; NEDC for Electrical Engineering Industry. Governor: Ashridge Management Coll., 1962-65; LSE; Nat. Inst. of Economic and Social Research, 1968; Governor and Mem. Council, Ditchley Foundn, 1967. FBIM. Thomas Hawksley Lecture, IMechE, 1968. *Recreation:* hill climbing. *Address:* 1 Sussex Place, Regents Park, NW1. *Club:* Travellers'.

**EARLE, Lt-Col Charles,** DSO 1945; OBE 1943; jssc; psc; Secretary-General, International Cargo Handling Association, 1961; *b* 23 Nov. 1913; *s* of late Col Maxwell Earle, CB, CMG, DSO; *m* 1st, 1939, Marguerite (marr. diss., 1956), 2nd *d* of Herbert Carver; one *s* two *d*; 2nd, 1957, Fenella, *o d* of late H. C. Whitehouse. *Educ:* Wellington; RMC. Grenadier Guards, 1933; Lieut-Col 1953, Retired 1958. Served War of 1939-45 in NW Europe, Africa and Italy. Adjt RMA Sandhurst, 1948. Associate, Inst. of Transport. Croix de Guerre with palm, France, 1943. *Address:* Flat G, 54 Cadogan Square, SW1. *T:* 01-589 6150.

**EARLE, Ven. E(dward) E(rnest) Maples;** Archdeacon of Tonbridge since 1953; Vicar of Shipbourne, Kent, since Nov. 1959; *b* 22 Dec. 1900; 2nd *s* of Ernest William Earle and Lilian Geraldine Earle (*née* Hudson); *m* 1966, Mrs Jocelyn Mary Offer, *widow* of Canon C. J. Offer, Hadlow, Kent. *Educ:* London Coll. of Divinity; St John's Coll., Durham University (LTh, MA). Vicar of: St John, Bexley, 1936-39; Rainham (Kent), 1939-44; Secretary Rochester Diocesan Reorganisation Cttee, 1944-52, Great Appeal Cttee, etc., 1944-49; Hon. Canon, Rochester Cathedral, 1949; Rector of Chatham, 1950-52; Proctor in Convocation, 1950-53. Rector of Wrotham 1952-59. *Recreations:* artistic and architectural interests. *Address:* The Vicarage, Shipbourne, Kent. *T:* Plaxtol 478.

**EARLE, Rev. George Hughes,** SJ; Headmaster of Stonyhurst College since Sept. 1963; *b* 20 Sept. 1925; *s* of Lieut-Col F. W. Earle, DSO, JP, Morestead House, Winchester, and late Marie Blanche Lyne-Stivens. *Educ:* Pilgrims' Sch., Winchester; Westminster Sch.; Peter Symonds' Sch., Winchester; Balliol Coll., Oxford. Served with RAF, 1943-47. Joined Soc. of Jesus, 1950. Taught at Beaumont Coll., 1955-57, and Stonyhurst Coll., 1962-63. *Recreations:* none; wasting time. *Address:* Stonyhurst College, Lancs. *T:* Stonyhurst 247, 345-6.

**EARLE, Sir Hardman Alexander Mort,** 5th Bt, *cr* 1869; TD; *b* 19 Aug. 1902; *s* of Lieut-Col Sir Algernon Earle, 4th Bt, and Edith, *d* of General Disney Leith, CB, of Glenkindie, Aberdeenshire, and *sister* of 7th Lord Burgh; *S* father, 1945; *m* 1931, Maie, *d* of John Drage, The Red House, Chapel Brampton; one *s* one *d*. *Educ:* Eton. *Heir:* *s* Hardman George Algernon Earle [*b* 4 Feb. 1932; *m* 1967, Diana Gillian Bligh, *y d* of late Col F. F. B. St George, CVO; one *s* one *d*]. *Address:* 14 Kensington Gate, W8. *Clubs:* Cavalry, Anglo-Belgian.

**EARLE, Ion,** TD 1946; Deputy Director-General, British National Export Council, since 1965 (Director 1964-65); *b* 12 April 1916; *s* of late Stephen Earle and of E. Beatrice Earle (*née* Blair White); *m* 1946, Elizabeth Stevens, US citizen; one *s* one *d*. *Educ:* Stowe Sch.; University Coll., Oxford; University de Grenoble. Federation of British Industries, Birmingham, 1938-51, London, 1952-60; Chief Executive, Export Council for Europe, 1960-64. Royal Artillery, TA, 1939-46 (Major). *Recreations:* golf, tennis, gardening. *Address:* 5 McKay Road, Wimbledon Common, SW20. *T:* 01-946 5831. *Clubs:* United University, English-Speaking Union; Royal Wimbledon Golf.

**EASON, Henry,** CBE 1967; FIB; JP; Secretary-General of The Institute of Bankers, since 1959, a Vice-President, 1969; *b* 12 April 1910; *s* of late H. Eason and of F. J. Eason; *m* 1939, Isobel, *d* of Wm Stevenson; one *s* two *d*. *Educ:* Yarm (Schol.); King's Coll., University of Durham. Graduated with distinction. Barrister-at-law, Gray's Inn. Served Lloyds Bank until 1939; Asst Sec., Institute of Bankers, 1939. Served War of 1939-45 and until 1946, with Royal Air Force (Wing Commander, despatches twice). Asst Dir, Military Gov. (Banking), NW Europe, 1944-46; United Nations Adviser (Banking) to Pakistan Govt, 1952; Deputy Sec., Institute of Bankers, 1956; Governor, City of London Coll., 1958; Mem., British National Cttee, ICC, 1959. Director: Internat. Banking Summer Sch., 1961 and 1964; Cambridge Banking Seminar, 1968 and 1969. *Publications:* Editor, Journal of Inst. of Bankers, 1959; contributions to professional journals. *Recreations:* golf, walking, conscript gardening. *Address:* High View, Westerham, Kent. *T:* Biggin Hill 3180. *Clubs:* Gresham; Overseas Bankers; Limpsfield Golf.

**EASSIE, Maj.-Gen. William James Fitzpatrick,** CB 1953; CBE 1943 (OBE 1941); DSO 1943; retired; *b* 1899; *s* of late Brig.-Gen. F. Eassie, CB, CMG, DSO; *m* 1930, Margaret Joan, *d* of L. G. P. Thring, Cambridge; two *s* one *d*. *Educ:* St Columba's College, Dublin; RMC Sandhurst. 2nd Lieut Royal Dublin Fusiliers, 1919; transferred to RASC, 1923; Iraq (medal), 1930-31; Col, 1942; Brigadier, 1944; Maj.-Gen., 1952; served War of 1939-45: Middle East, Sicily, NW Europe (despatches four times, OBE, CBE, DSO); Dir of Supplies and Transport Far East Land Forces, 1949-51; Inspector RASC (Maj.-Gen.) 1951-54; ADC to King George VI, 1951; retired 1954. Commander Legion of Merit (US). *Address:* Orchard End, Wargrave, Berks. *T:* 2341. *Club:* Army and Navy.

**EASSON, Rt. Rev. Edward Frederick;** *see* Aberdeen and Orkney, Bishop of.

**EAST, Frederick Henry,** CEng, FIEE, FRAeS; Assistant Chief Scientific Adviser (Projects), Ministry of Defence, since 1969; *b* 15 Sept. 1919; *s* of Frederick Richard East; *m* 1942, Pauline Isabel Veale Horne. *Educ:* Skinners' Company's Sch., Tunbridge Wells; University Coll., Exeter (Visc. St Cyres Schol., Tucker and Franklin Prize, 1939). BSc London 1940; AInstP. Joined Research Dept, Min. of Aircraft Production, 1940; various appts in RAE, 1942-57; Asst Dir of Air Armament Research and Develt, Min. of Supply/Aviation, 1957-62; Head of Weapon Project Gp, RAE, 1962-67; Student, IDC, 1968. *Publications:* contrib. to: Application of Critical Path Techniques, 1968; official reports, and articles in jls. *Address:* Ministry of Defence, Whitehall, SW1; The Patch, Vicarage Hill, Farnham, Surrey. *T:* Farnham 21411. *Clubs:* Royal Aero, Pathfinder, Civil Service.

**EAST, Grahame Richard,** CMG 1961; Special Commissioner of Income Tax since 1962; 2nd *s* of William Robert and Eleanor East; *m* 1937, Cynthia Mildred, *d* of Adam Louis Beck, OBE; two *s* two *d*. *Educ:* Bristol Grammar Sch.; Corpus Christi Coll., Oxford. Scholar; 1st Class Final Hon. Sch. of Mathematics, 1929. Asst Master, Royal Belfast Academical Institution, Belfast, 1929; Inland Revenue Dept, Secretaries Office: Asst Principal, 1930; Principal, 1936; Asst Sec., 1941. *Recreation:* cycling. *Address:* 44 Devonshire Road, Sutton, Surrey. *T:* 01-642 0638.

**EAST, Kenneth Arthur;** Minister, British High Commission, Lagos, since 1970; *b* 9 May 1921; *s* of H. F. East; *m* 1946, Katherine Blackley; two *s* three *d*. *Educ:* Taunton's Sch; Southampton Univ. Served HM Forces, 1942-46. India Office/Commonwealth Relations Office, 1946-50; Asst Private Sec. to Sec. of State; First Secretary: Ottawa, 1950-53; Colombo, 1956-60; Head of East and General Africa Dept, CRO, 1961-63; Head of Personnel Dept, CRO, 1963-64; Counsellor, Diplomatic Service Administration, 1965; Counsellor and Head of Chancery, Oslo, 1965-70. *Address:* c/o Foreign and Commonwealth Office, SW1; British High Commission, Kajola House, 62-64 Campbell Street, Lagos, Nigeria.

**EAST, Sir (Lewis) Ronald,** Kt 1966; CBE 1951; retired as Chairman, State Rivers and Water Supply Commission, Victoria (1936-65) and as Commissioner, River Murray Commission, Australia (1936-65); *b* 17 June 1899; *s* of Lewis Findlay East, ISO, Evansford, Vic., Australia and Annie Eleanor (*née* Burchett) Brunswick, Vic.; *m* 1927, Constance Lilias Keil, MA, Kilwinning, Ayrshire; three *d*. *Educ:* Scotch Coll., Melbourne; Melbourne Univ. BCE (Melbourne) 1922; MCE (Melbourne) 1924. Mem., Snowy Mountains Coun., until 1965; Pres., Instn of Engrs, Austr., 1952-53; Mem. Coun., Instn of Civil Engrs, 1960-62; Vice-Pres., Internat. Commn on Irrigation and Drainage, 1959-62. Hon. Fellow, Instn of Engineers, Australia, 1969. Kernot Memorial Medal, University of Melbourne, 1949; Peter Nicol Russell Memorial Medal, Instn of Engineers, Australia, 1957. *Publications:* River Improvement, Land Drainage and Flood Protection, 1952; many technical papers on water conservation and associated subjects in Proc. Instn Engs, Austr., Proc. Instn Civil Engrs, Amer. Soc. Civil Engrs and other jls. *Recreation:* handicrafts (model engineering). *Address:* 57 Waimarie Drive, Mt Waverley, Victoria 3149, Australia. *T:* Melbourne 277-4315.

**EAST, Sir Ronald;** *see* East, Sir L. R.

**EAST, William Gordon;** Professor of Geography in the University of London at Birkbeck College, 1947-70; *b* 10 Nov. 1902; *s* of George Richard East and Jemima (*née* Nicoll); *m* 1934, Dorothea Small; two *s* two *d*. *Educ:* Sloane Sch., Chelsea; Peterhouse, Cambridge. Open scholarship in History, 1921, and research studentship, 1924, at Peterhouse. BA (Hons), Cambridge Univ., with Class I in Historical Tripos, Part II, 1924. MA 1928; Thirlwall Prizeman of Cambridge Univ., 1927. Asst in historical geography, London Sch. of Economics, 1927; temp. administrative officer in Ministry of Economic Warfare and Foreign Office, 1941-45; Reader in Geography in University of London, 1946. Visiting Professor: University of Minn, 1952; University of Calif, Los Angeles, 1959-60; University of Mich, 1966-67. Myres Memorial Lectr, Oxford Univ., 1970-71. Mem., RGS Council, 1956-59; Pres., Inst. of British Geographers, 1959. *Publications:* The Union of

Moldavia and Wallachia, 1859, 1929; An Historical Geography of Europe, 1935; The Geography Behind History, 1938; Mediterranean Problems, 1940; (Jt Ed.) The Changing Map of Asia, 1950; (Jt) The Spirit and Purpose of Geography, 1951; The Soviet Union, 1963; (Jt Ed.) The Changing World, 1956; (Ed.) The Caxton Atlas, 1960; (Ed.) Regions of The British Isles, 1960-; (Ed.) Hutchinson University Library in Geography; contributions to journals of geography, history and foreign affairs. *Address:* Wildwood, Danes Way, Oxshott, Surrey. *T:* Oxshott 2351.

**EAST AFRICA, Archdiocese of;** divided into two archdioceses of Kenya and Tanzania.

**EASTAUGH, Rt. Rev. Cyril;** *see* Peterborough, Bishop of.

**EASTAUGH, Ven. John (Richard Gordon);** Archdeacon of Middlesex since 1966; Vicar of St Peter, Eaton Square, since 1967; *b* 11 March 1920; *s* of Gordon and Jessie Eastaugh; *m* 1963, Bridget Nicola, *y d* of Sir Hugh Chance, *qv*; two *s* one *d*. *Educ:* Leeds Univ.; Mirfield. Curate of All Saints, Poplar, 1944; Rector: of W. Hackney, 1951; of Poplar, 1956; Commissary of Bp of Polynesia, 1962; Vicar of Heston, 1963. *Recreations:* theatre, music. *Address:* 18 Wilton Street, SW1. *T:* 01-235 3622.

**EASTCOTT, Harry Hubert Grayson,** MS; FRCS; Consultant Surgeon, St Mary's Hospital, and Lecturer in Surgery, St Mary's Hospital Medical School since 1955; Hon. Surgeon, Florence Nightingale Hospital since 1955; Consultant in Surgery and Vascular Surgery to the Royal Navy since 1957; Surgeon, Royal Masonic Hospital since 1964; Consultant Surgeon, King Edward VII Hospital for Officers, since 1965; *b* 17 Oct. 1917; *s* of Harry George and Gladys Eastcott; *m* 1941, Doreen Joy, *e d* of Brenchley Ernest and late Muriel Mittell; four *d*. *Educ:* Latymer Sch.; St Mary's Hosp. Medical School and Middlesex Hospital Medical Sch., University of London; Harvard Med. Sch. War of 1939-45, Junior surgical appts and service as Surgeon Lieut, RNVR up till 1946. Surg. Lieut Comdr RNVR, London Div., until 1957. MRCS; LRCP; MB, BS (Hons), 1941; FRCS 1946; MS (London), 1951. Sen. Registrar, 1950 as Hon. Cons. to St Mary's and Asst Dir Surgical Unit; Research Fellow in Surgery, Harvard Med. Sch., and Peter Bent Brigham Hosp., Boston, Mass, 1949-50; Hunterian Prof., RCS, 1953; recognised teacher, 1953, and Examr, 1959, in surgery, University of London; Hon. Surg., RADA, 1959-; Mem. Court of Examrs, RCS of Eng., 1964-; External Examr in Surgery: Queen's Univ., Belfast, 1964-67; Cambridge Univ., 1968. FRSocMed (Hon. Sec., Section of Surgery, 1963-65, Vice-President, 1966); Fellow Medical Soc. of London (Hon. Sec., 1962-64, Vice-Pres. 1964). Mem., Soc. Apothecaries, 1967. *Publications:* Arterial Surgery, 1969; various articles on gen. and arterial surgery, and on tissue transplantation and preservation, Lancet, Brit. Jl of Surg., etc.; contrib. chap. of peripheral vascular disease, Med. Annual, 1961-69; various chaps in textbooks on these subjects. *Recreations:* music, languages, travel, ski-ing, and a lifelong interest in aeronautics. *Address:* 4 Upper Harley Street, NW1. *T:* 01-935 2020. *Club:* Middlesex County Cricket.

**EASTER, Bertie Harry,** CMG 1944; CBE 1936 (MBE 1927); BA; retired as Resident Tutor, Windward Islands, for University College of the West Indies (Extra-Mural Studies); *b* 4 June 1893; *s* of Samuel and Lucy Elizabeth Easter; *m* 1930, Hazel Marie Swabey; one *s*. *Educ:* Christ's Coll., Finchley. Head Master, St Mary's Coll., St Lucia and Secondary Sch., Grenada; Dir of Education, Grenada; Acting Colonial Sec. (or Administrator), Grenada, Jamaica; Dir of Education, Jamaica, 1932-48; Information Officer and Officer i/c Broadcasting, 1939; served European War, Royal Naval Div. and Scots Guards (Lieut). *Address:* Castries, St Lucia, West Indies. *Club:* Vigie (St Lucia).

**EASTERBROOK, Prof. William Thomas James,** FRSC 1957; Professor of Economics, University of Toronto, Canada, since 1956; Chairman, Department of Political Economy, University of Toronto, since 1961; *b* 4 Dec. 1907; *s* of W. J. Easterbrook and Emily McKerr; *m* 1937, Dorothy Mary Walker; two *s* one *d*. *Educ:* Universities of Manitoba, Toronto, and Harvard. BA (Hon.) Manitoba, 1933; University of Toronto Sch. of Grad. Studies, 1933-36; MA 1935; Harvard Univ., 1936-37; PhD, University of Toronto, 1937. Dept Economics, Univ. of Manitoba, 1938-40 and 1942-47; Guggenheim Fellow, 1940-41; Research Associate, Research Center in Entrepreneurial History, Harvard Univ., 1949 (leave of absence from Toronto). Vice-Pres. Economic History Assoc. (US), 1959-61; Trustee, Business History Inc., 1959-; Mem. Research Cttee on Culture and Communications (Ford Foundation), 1953-55. Pitt Prof. of American History and Institutions, Cambridge Univ., 1955-56; Marshall Lecturer, University of Cambridge, 1956; Professorial Fellow of Jesus Coll. Cambridge, 1955-56; MA Cantab. 1956. Economic Adviser, Ministry of Economic Affairs and Develt Planning, Tanzania, 1966-67. LLD Manitoba, 1963. *Publications:* Agricultural Credit in Canada, 1937; Canadian Economic History (with H. Aitken), 1955; Approaches to Canadian Economic History (with M. H. Watkins), 1968; articles contrib. to Canadian Jl of Economics and Political Science, Jl of Economic History, American Economic Review, etc.; also to Canada (ed George Brown) UN Series, and The Progress of Underdeveloped Countries (ed B. Hoselitz). *Address:* 45 Willowbank Boulevard, Toronto 12, Canada. *T:* 487-2270. *Club:* University Faculty (Toronto).

**EASTHAM, Leonard Ernest Sydney,** MA Cantab, MSc Leeds; Emeritus Professor of Zoology, University of Sheffield (Professor, 1932-58); *b* 8 Feb. 1893; *s* of William Eastham, Penwortham, Preston; *m* K. M. Jackson, Bingley, Yorks; one *s* two *d*. *Educ:* Hutton Grammar Sch., Lancs; Harris Institute, Preston; Leeds Univ. War service Royal Engineers Special Brigade; National Diploma in Agriculture, 1914; graduated in Hons Zoology and in Agriculture, 1921; Lecturer in Zoology in the University of Birmingham, 1921-27; Lecturer in Advanced and Economic Entomology in the University of Cambridge, 1927-31. Pro-Vice-Chancellor, University of Sheffield, 1946-50. *Publications:* Scientific papers on Entomology. *Recreation:* gardening. *Address:* 9 Carrick Way, St Mawes, Cornwall. *T:* St Mawes 332.

**EASTHAM, Michael;** *see* Eastham, T. M.

**EASTHAM, (Thomas) Michael,** QC 1964; Recorder of Deal, since 1968; *b* 26 June 1920; *y s* of late His Hon. Sir Tom Eastham, QC; *m* 1942, Mary Pamela, *o d* of Dr H. C. Billings; two *d*. *Educ:* Harrow; Trinity Hall, Cambridge. Served with Queen's Royal Regiment, 1940-46 (Capt.). Called to the Bar, Lincoln's Inn, 1947. *Address:* Stowe Maries, Westcott, Dorking,

Surrey. *T:* Dorking 5557; 5 Essex Court, Temple, EC4. *T:* 01-3583 2440.

**EASTICK, Brig. Sir Thomas (Charles),** Kt 1970; CMG 1953; DSO 1942; ED 1939; JP (for the State of South Australia); Chairman Standing Committee "Call to the People of Australia", 1951-57; President: El Alamein Group (SA), 1946-60; Chairman of Trustees, Poppy Day Fund (Inc.); President of Australia Day Council, S Australian Branch (Federal President, 1962-65); Chairman of Trustees Services Cemetaries Trust; Deputy Chairman, World War II Fund; *b* 3 May 1900; *s* of Charles William Lone and Agnes Ann Eastick; *m* 1925, Ruby Sybil Bruce; five *s. Educ:* Goodwood Sch., Australia. Senior Cadets, 1914-18; Citizen Forces, 1918 (Artillery); Lieut 1922, Capt. 1926, Major 1930, Lieut-Col 1939. Served War of 1939-45 (despatches, ED, DSO); raised and commanded 2/7 Aust. Fd Regt 1940-43; Middle East, Alamein; Brig., CRA 7 Aust. Div., 1943; CRA 9 Aust. Div., 1944; Comdr Kuching Force, 1945; took Japanese surrender and relieved Kuching Prisoner Compound; administered comd 9 Aust. Div., 1945-Feb. 1946, when Div. disbanded. Hon. ADC to Governor-Gen. of Australia, 1950-53; Mem., Betting Control Board, 1954-65; State Pres. Returned Sailors, Soldiers and Airmen's Imperial League of Australia, S Australia, 1950-54-61-; Comdr HQ Group Central Command, 1950-54. Col Comdt, Royal Australian Artillery, 1955-60. Pres. Engine Reconditioners Assoc. of Austr., 1958-61. Comp. Most Excellent Order of the Star of Sarawak. *Recreation:* photography. *Address:* Astana, 44 Kingston Crescent, Kingston Park, S Australia 5049, Australia. *Clubs:* Naval, Military and Air Force of SA, RSL, (Adelaide).

**EASTMAN, Ven. Derek Ian Tennent,** MC 1945; Archdeacon of Buckingham since 1970; Vicar of Chilton and Dorton since 1970; *b* 22 Jan. 1919; *s* of Archibald Tennent Eastman and Gertrude Towler Eastman (*née* Gambling); *m* 1949, Judith Mary, *e d* of Canon Philip David Bevington Miller; three *s* one *d. Educ:* Winchester; Christ Church, Oxford; Cuddesdon Theol. Coll. BA 1941; MA 1946. Coldstream Guards, 1940-46: Guards Armoured Div., Temp. Major. Cuddesdon Theol. Coll., 1946-48; Deacon 1948; Priest 1949; Asst Curate, Brighouse, 1948-51; Preist-in-Charge, St Andrew's, Cavershan, 1951-56; Vicar: Headington, Oxford, 1956-64; Banbury, 1964-70. Proctor in Convocation for Dio. of Oxford, 1964-70. *Recreations:* sea fishing, painting. *Address:* Chilton Vicarage, Aylesbury, Bucks. *T:* Long Crendon 315.

**EASTON, Rear-Adm. Ian,** DSC 1946; Assistant Chief of the Naval Staff (Policy), 1969-71; *b* 27 Nov. 1917; *s* of Walter Easton and Janet Elizabeth Rickard; *m* 1st, 1943, Shirley Townend White (marr. diss.); one *s* one *d*; 2nd, 1962, Margharetta Elizabeth Martinette Van Duyn de Sparwoude; one *d. Educ:* The Grange, Crowborough; RNC, Dartmouth. Entered Royal Navy, 1931, and, as an actg Sub-Lt, qualified as a pilot, 1939. During War of 1939-45 served as pilot in HM Ships Glorious, Ark Royal and Formidable and as Direction Officer HMS Indefatigable; Comdr, 1952; Naval Staff Coll., 1953; on staff of BJSM, Washington, 1955-57; Staff Direction Officer, on Staff of Flag Officer Aircraft Carriers, 1957-59; JSSC, 1959; Captain, 1960; Asst Dir of Tactical and Weapons Policy Div., 1960-62; two years exchange service with RAN, in command of HMAS Watson, 1962-64; Naval Asst to Naval Member of Templer Cttee, 1965; Dir of Naval Tactical and Weapons Policy Div., 1966-68; Comdg Officer of HMS Triumph, Far East, 1968-69. *Recreations:* boats, books, gardening. *Address:* Causeway Cottage, Freshwater, Isle of Wight. *T:* Freshwater 2775. *Clubs:* United Hunts; Royal Solent Yacht (Yarmouth, IoW).

**EASTON, Air Cdre Sir James (Alfred),** KCMG, 1956; CB 1952; CBE 1945; RAF retired; Research Consultant on Trade Development of Great Lakes Area, USA, since 1968; *b* 11 Feb. 1908; *s* of late W. C. Easton, Winchester; *m* 1939, Anna Mary, *d* of Lieut-Col J. A. McKenna, Ottawa; one *s* one *d. Educ:* Peter Symonds' Sch., Winchester; RAF Coll., Cranwell. Joined RAF 1926; served NWF India, 1929-32, Egypt, 1935-36, and Canada, 1937-39, as Air Armament Adviser to Dept of National Defence; despatches, 1940; Group Capt., 1941; Air Cdre, 1943; Dir in Air Staff Branch, Air Ministry, 1943-45, and then in RAF Delegation, Washington; retired, 1949; attached Foreign Office, 1945-58; HM Consul-Gen., Detroit, 1958-68. Officer Legion of Merit (US). *Recreations:* travel and travel literature, gardening, golf. *Address:* 390 Chalfonte Avenue, Grosse Pointe Farms, Mich 48236, USA; 71 Cornwall Gardens, SW7. *T:* 01-937 0430. *Clubs:* Royal Air Force; Country, Detroit (Detroit).

**EASTON, John Murray,** FRIBA; Partner in Firm of Easton and Robertson Cusdin Preston and Smith, Architects (retired, 1963); *b* 30 Jan. 1889; *y s* of David Easton, Aberdeen; *m* 1927, Ruth Meryon, *d* of H. A. Tinker, Westover, Croyde, North Devon; two *s. Educ:* Aberdeen Grammar Sch. Architectural education Scotland and London; served with London Scottish, France and Belgium, 1914; Godwin Bursar, 1927; Pres. of Architectural Assoc., 1939-40; Vice-Pres. RIBA, 1945-47; RIBA Medals for best building of years 1928 and 1937 in London and 1938 in Cambridge; Royal Gold Medal for Architecture, 1955; Associé de l'Académie Royale de Belgique, 1958. Principal works: in London: Royal Horticultural Society's New Hall; Royal Bank of Canada; Metropolitan Water Board's Laboratories; No. 2-12 Gresham Street; Friend's & Century Insurance Co. (Dorking); in New York: British Pavilion, World's Fair, 1939; in Cambridge: reconstruction of Old Library, Pitt Press, Caius Coll. new buildings, and following Laboratories: Zoological, Anatomy, Engineering, Chemistry, Veterinary Anatomy and Chemical Engineering. Science and other buildings for Universities of London, Durham, Queen's Belfast, Reading and Malaya. Hospitals, including: Children's, Great Ormond Street; Queen Charlotte's Maternity; Children's, Dublin; Regional, Limerick; Royal Victoria, Belfast, Harlow; Hong Kong; Addenbrookes, Cambridge. *Address:* 7 St Hilda's Close, Christchurch Avenue, NW6. *Club:* Arts.

**EASTWOOD, Christopher Gilbert,** CMG 1947; Assistant Under-Secretary of State, Colonial Office, 1947-52, and 1954-66; *b* 21 April 1905; *s* of late W. Seymour Eastwood, West Stoke House, Chichester, and Cecil Emma Eastwood; *m* 1934, Catherine Emma, *d* of late John Douglas Peel, Stonesfield Manor, near Oxford; one *s* three *d. Educ:* Eton (Schol.); Trinity Coll., Oxford. Entered Home Civil Service, 1927; appointed to Colonial Office; Private Sec. to High Commissioner for Palestine, 1932-34; Sec. of International Rubber Regulation Cttee, 1934; Private Sec. to Lord Lloyd and Lord Moyne when Secs of State for Colonies, 1940-41. Prin. Asst Sec. Cabinet Office, 1945-47; Commissioner of Crown Lands, 1952-54. *Address:* Stonesfield Manor, near Oxford. *T:* Stonesfield 222. *Club:* United University.

**EASTWOOD, Eric,** CBE 1962; FRS 1968; Director of Research, General Electric-English Electric Companies, since 1968; Director: Marconi-Elliott Computers, since 1969; Marconi Company, since 1963; Marconi Instruments, since 1962; English Electric Valve, since 1968; Visiting Professor, Department of Electrical Engineering, Imperial College, London University, since 1969; *b* 12 March 1910; *s* of George Eastwood and Eda (*née* Brooks); *m* 1937, Edith (*née* Butterworth); two *s*. *Educ:* Oldham High Sch.; Manchester Univ.; Christ's Coll., Cambridge. PhD 1935; MSc 1932; FIEE 1951; FInstP 1968. Academic work, 1936-41. Sqdn Ldr, RAF, 1941-46 (despatches). Head of Radiation Laboratory, Nelson Research Lab., English Electric Co., 1946-48; Dep. Dir of Research, Marconi Wireless Telegraph Co., 1948-54; Dir, 1954-62. Dir of Research, English Electric, 1962-68. Mem., SRC, 1968-. Hon. DSc Exeter, 1969; Hon. DTech Loughborough, 1970. Wakefield Medal, RAeS, 1961; Glazebrook Medal, Inst. of Physics and Physical Soc., 1970. *Publications:* Radar Ornithology, 1967; various papers on spectroscopy, radar techniques, radar meteorology, radar ornithology in Proc. Physical Soc., Proc. Royal Society, Nature, etc. *Recreation:* music ('cello, flute). *Address:* Greenlanes, Little Baddow, Danbury, Essex. *T:* Danbury 3240.

**EASTWOOD, Frank Sandford,** CBE 1951; MInstT; Major, late The 22nd (Cheshire) Regiment; Chairman of Traffic Commissioners and Licensing Authority, Yorkshire Traffic Area, 1939-65 (Ministry of Transport Appointment); Regional Transport Commissioner, 1939-65; *b* Broughton, Lancs, 1 Dec. 1895; *o s* of S. C. Eastwood, Broughton; *m* 1920, Constance, *o d* of A. Webb, Wrexham; one *s* one *d*. *Educ:* Manchester and Oxford. Served European War, 1915-18; Regimental and Staff Service, to Lieut-Col (wounded); The 22nd (Cheshire) Regt, 1919-21; seconded Criminal Investigation Dept, Royal Ulster Constabulary, 1922-23; Staff Capt., 49th (WR) Div. 1924-25; Staff Capt., 7th Inf. Bde, 1926; Staff Capt. Experimental Mechanised Force and Experimental Armoured Force, 1927-29; retired, 1930; Transport Adviser to large commercial companies, 1931-38; 1939-45 War appointment, Regional Transport Commissioner, North Eastern Region. *Recreations:* riding, tennis, and badminton. *Address:* Ridge Mount House, 59 Cliff Road, Headingley, Leeds 6. *T:* 54914. *Club:* Constitutional.

**EASTWOOD, Major Sir Geoffrey (Hugh),** KCVO 1965 (CVO 1956); CBE 1945; Chief Steward of Hampton Court Palace since 1970; *b* 17 May 1895; *s* of late John Edmund Eastwood. Served 1914-19, 3rd King's Own Hussars. Hon. Attaché, Brit. Emb., Paris, 1919-21; Clerk and Prin. Clerk, House of Lords, 1924-58. Comptroller to Gov.-Gen. of Canada, 1941-46; Comptroller to the Princess Royal, 1959-65; Extra Equerry to the Queen, 1965. *Address:* Wilderness House, Hampton Court Palace, Surrey. *Clubs:* Brooks's, MCC.

**EASTWOOD, Dr Wilfred;** Partner, Husband & Co., consulting engineers; *b* 15 Aug. 1923; *s* of Wilfred Andrew Eastwood and Annice Gertrude Eastwood; *m* 1947, Dorothy Jean Gover; one *s* one *d*. Road Research Laboratory, 1945-46; University of Manchester, 1946-47; University of Aberdeen, 1947-53; University of Sheffield, 1954-70: Head, Dept of Civil Engrg, 1964-70; Dean, Faculty of Engrg, 1967-70. Mem. Council, IStructE, 1960- (Vice-Pres., 1969-71). *Publications:* papers in Proc. ICE and Jl IStructE, etc. *Recreation:* cricket. *Address:* 242 Abbeydale Road South, Sheffield S17 3LL. *T:* 364645. *Clubs:* Athenæum; Yorks County Cricket.

**EATES, Edward Caston,** CMG 1968; MVO 1961; Commissioner, The Royal Hong Kong Police (formerly The Hong Kong Police), 1967-69, retired; *b* London, 8 April 1916; *o s* of late Edward Eates and Elizabeth Lavinia Issac Eates (*née* Caston); *m* 1941, Maureen Teresa McGee; no *c*. *Educ:* Highgate Sch.; King's Coll., London (LLB). Asst Examr, Estate Duty Office, 1935. Army, 1939-46: 22nd (Cheshire) Regt, later Royal Tanks; served with 2nd Derbs Yeomanry, Western Desert and NW Europe, 1941-44; Adjt 1943; Sqdn Ldr 1944; Staff Coll., Quetta (sc), 1945; DAAG Nagpur District. Apptd to Colonial Police Service, Nigeria, 1946; Sen. Supt, Sierra Leone, 1954; Comr, The Gambia, 1957; Asst Comr, 1963, Dep. Comr, 1966, Hong Kong. Colonial Police Medal, 1956; Queen's Police Medal, 1961. *Recreations:* cricket and association football (inactive); travel, motoring. *Address:* Banjul, Toadpit Lane, Ottery St Mary, Devon. *Clubs:* Royal Commonwealth Society, Public Schools; Surrey County Cricket.

**EATHER, Maj.-Gen. Kenneth William,** CB 1947; CBE 1943; DSO 1941; Executive Director, Water Research Foundation of Australia, 1958; *b* 1901. Served War of 1939-45. AMF, Middle East and SW Pacific (despatches, DSO, CBE). *Address:* 7, 82/84 Houston Road, Kingsford, NSW, Australia. *T:* 6631176. *Club:* Imperial Service (Sydney).

**EATON,** family name of **Baron Cheylesmore.**

**EATON, Air Vice-Marshal Brian Alexander,** CB 1969; CBE 1959; DSO and Bar, DFC, American Silver Star; Air Member for Personnel, RAAF, Department of Air, Canberra, since 1969; *b* Launceston, Tas, 15 Dec. 1916; *s* of S. A. Eaton; *m* 1952 Josephine Rumbles; one *s* two *d*. *Educ:* Carey Grammar Sch., Melbourne; RAAF Coll., Pt Cook. Served war of 1939-45: Co 3 Sqdn N Africa–Medit., 1943, CO 239 Wing RAF Italy, 1944-45. UK, 1945-46; OC 81 Fighter Wing, Japan, 1948; OC BCAIR, 1948-49; OC 78 Wing Malta, 1952-54; Dir of Ops, RAAF HQ, 1955; OC Williamtown RAAF and Comdt Sch. of Land-Air Warfare, 1957-58; Dir Joint Service Plans, 1959-60; Imp. Defence Coll., 1961; Dir-Gen. of Operational Requirements, 1962; Deputy Chief of Air Staff, 1966-67; AOC HQ 224 Mobile Group (RAF) Far East Air Force, Singapore, 1967-68; Chief of Staff HQFEAF, 1968-69. *Recreations:* shooting, fishing. *Address:* Department of Air, Russell Offices, Canberra, ACT, Australia. *Club:* Commonwealth (Canberra).

**EATON, Cyrus Stephen;** industrialist and banker; Partner, Otis & Co., bankers; Organizer Republic Steel Corp. and United Light & Power Co.; Chairman Board of Directors: Chesapeake & Ohio Railway; Detroit Steel Corporation; Steep Rock Iron Mines Ltd; Director: Cleveland-Cliffs Iron Co.; Cleveland Electric Illuminating Co.; Kansas City Power & Light Co.; Sherwin-Williams Co.; Baltimore & Ohio Railroad Co.; *b* Nova Scotia, 27 Dec. 1883; *s* of Joseph Howe Eaton and Mary Adelle McPherson; *m* 1st, 1907, Margaret House; two *s* five *d*; 2nd, 1957, Anne Kinder Jones, *d* of Judge Walter Tupper Kinder; one step-*d*. *Educ:* McMaster Univ., Toronto (BA); Acadia Univ. (DCL). Trustee: University of Chicago, Denison Univ., Case Institute of Technology, Harry S. truman Library, Metropolitan Park Board, Cleveland Museum of Natural History; Mem. of Coll. of

Electors, Hall of Fame, Royal Norwegian Academy of Sciences, American Council of Learned Societies; American Historical Assoc., Amer. Philosophical Assoc. FAAS. Initiator Pugwash Intellectual Life Confs (Assoc. of Amer. Colls), 1956; Pugwash Internat. Confs of Nuclear Scientists, 1957; Member: Amer. Shorthorn Breeders' Assoc.; Amer. Acad. of Political and Social Science. Holds several hon. doctorates in Law from American, Canadian and European universities. Received Internat. Lenin Peace Prize, 1960. *Publications:* The Third Term "Tradition," 1940; Financial Democracy, 1941; The Professor Talks to Himself, 1942; Investment Banking-Competition or Decadence, 1944; A New Plan to re-open the US Capital Market, 1945; A Capitalist Looks At Labor, 1947; Is the Globe Big Enough for Capitalism and Communism?, 1958; Canada's Choice, 1959; The Engineer as Philosopher, 1961; and numerous articles and speeches on economics, politics and international affairs. *Recreations:* MFH Summit Hunt, tennis, yachting, ski-ing and skating. *Address:* Acadia Farms, Northfield, Ohio 44067, USA; Terminal Tower, Cleveland, Ohio 44101; Deep Cove Farms, Chester, Nova Scotia, Canada. *Clubs:* Union, Mayfield, Chagrin Valley Hunt, Summit Hunt (Cleveland); Metropolitan (New York); Glenelg Fishing; Royal Nova Scotia Yacht Squadron (NS).

**EATON, Vice-Adm. Sir John (Willson Musgrave),** KBE 1956; CB 1953; DSO 1941; DSC 1941; RN retired; *b* Nov. 1902; 2nd *s* of Dr Walter Musgrave Eaton and Margaret Emily (*née* Ibbetson); *m* 1945, Cynthia Mary Hurlstone, *widow* of Major Gerald Tatchell, The Royal Lincolnshire Regiment; (two *step-d*). *Educ:* Temple Grove, Eastbourne; RNC Osborne and RNC Dartmouth. HMS Barham, Midshipman, 1919-21; HM Destroyers, 1922-25; HM Submarines, 1925-28; HMS Malaya, 1928-30; HM Destroyers, 1930-38; Student RN Staff Coll., 1939; HM Destroyers, 1939-43; HMS Sheffield, 1945; HMS St Vincent, 1946-48; idc, 1948-49; Dir of RN Staff Coll., Greenwich, 1949-51; Flag Officer Commanding HM Australian Fleet, Oct. 1951-53; Flag Officer Commanding Reserve Fleet, 1954-55; C-in-C America and West Indies Station, 1955-56; Dep. Supreme Allied Comdr Atlantic, Oct. 1955-Dec. 1957. *Recreations:* golf, shooting. *Address:* Dolphins, Church Street, Kelvedon, Essex. *T:* Kelvedon 283. *Club:* United Service.

**EAYRS, Prof. John Thomas,** PhD, DSc; Sands Cox Professor of Anatomy, University of Birmingham, since 1968; *b* 23 Jan. 1913; *e s* of late Thomas William Eayrs, AMICE, and Florence May (*née* Clough); *m* 1941, Frances Marjorie Sharp; one *s* two *d*. *Educ:* King Edward's, Birmingham; University of Birmingham. In industry until 1938. War service: Pte Royal Warwicks Regt, 1939-40; 2nd Lieut Manchester Regt, 1940; Lieut 1940; Capt. 1941; Major 1942; Worcester Regt, 1943; sc Staff Coll., Camberley, 1944. University of Birmingham: Peter Thompson Prize, 1947; John Barritt Melson Memorial Gold Medal, 1947; Lectr in Anatomy, 1948; Bertram Windle Prize, 1950; Sen. Lectr 1955; Research Fellow, Calif. Inst. of Technology, 1956-57; Reader in Comparative Neurology, Birmingham, 1958; Henry Head Research Fellow, Royal Society, London, 1957-62; Prof. of Neuroendocrinology, Birmingham, 1961; Fitzmary Prof. of Physiology, London Univ., 1963-68. *Publications:* Scientific Papers dealing with developmental neuroendocrinology and behaviour in Jl Endocrin., Jl Anat. (London), Anim. Behav., etc. *Recreations:* cricket, foreign travel and languages. *Address:* Lake Hall, Edgbaston, Birmingham 15; Penllyn Dyfi, Aberangell, Montgomeryshire.

**EBBELS, Brig. Wilfred Austin,** CBE 1943; late RA; *b* 1 April 1898; *s* of late W. P. Ebbels, Mauritius; *m* 1924, Phyllis (*née* Greenwood-Teale), *widow* of Capt. Arthur Toller, Welch Regt; two *d*. *Educ:* Yardley Court (Tonbridge); Marlborough Coll.; RMA, Woolwich. Commissioned, 1915; France and Flanders, 1916-18; Army of Occupation (Rhine), Jan.-June 1919; Acting Capt. Feb. 1918, Acting Major, Aug. 1918 (wounded, despatches, MC); appointed RHA July 1919; Capt., 1927; seconded Egyptian Army, 1928-34; Major, 1936; Instructor of Gunnery, 1937-40; Acting Lieut-Col Comd 11 (HAC) Regt RHA 1940; Western Desert MEF 1941-44; Brig. (CRA 10 Armoured Div.) 1942; retired pay, 1946. *Recreations:* shooting, fishing. *Address:* Noah's Ark Farmhouse, Ware, Herts. *Club:* Cavalry.

**EBBISHAM,** 2nd Baron, *cr* 1928, of Cobham, Surrey; **Rowland Roberts Blades,** Bt, *cr* 1922; TD; MA; *b* 3 Sept. 1912; *o s* of 1st Baron Ebbisham, GBE, and Margaret (MBE 1943, Officer Legion of Honour, OStJ) (*d* 1965), *d* of Arthur Reiner, Sutton, Surrey; *S* father, 1953; *m* 1949, Flavia Mary, *y d* of Charles Meade, Pen y lan, Meifod, Montgomeryshire; three *d*. *Educ:* Winchester; Christ Church, Oxford (MA). Served War of 1939-45; Lieut 98th (Surrey and Sussex Yeo.) Field Regt, RA. Master, Mercers' Co., 1963; Common Councilman, City of London, 1947-; Chm., City Lands Cttee, and Chief Commoner, Corp. of London, 1967-68. Pres., London Chamber of Commerce, 1958-61; Pres., Assoc. of British Chambers of Commerce, 1968; Mem., Export Council for Europe, 1961. Dir, WLP Ltd. Vice-Pres. The London Record Society. *Address:* The Old Rectory, Blechingley, Surrey. *T:* Blechingley 388. *Clubs:* Bath, MCC.

*See also Rear-Adm. John E. H. McBeath, Adm. Hon. Sir Guy H. E. Russell.*

**EBERHART, Richard (Ghormley);** Professor of English and Poet in Residence, Dartmouth College, USA; *b* Austin, Minn, 5 April 1904; *s* of late Alpha La Rue Eberhart and late Lena Eberhart (*née* Lowenstein); *m* 1941, Helen Elizabeth Butcher, Christ Church, Cambridge, Mass; one *s* one *d*. *Educ:* Dartmouth Coll., USA (AB); St John's Coll., Cambridge Univ., England (MA); Harvard Univ. Grad. Sch. of Arts and Sciences. Taught English, 1933-41, also tutor to son of King Prajadhipok of Siam for a year. Served War in USN Reserve finishing as Lieut-Comdr, 1946; subseq. entered Butcher Polish Co., Boston, Mass, as Asst Man., finishing as Vice-Pres. (now Hon. Vice-Pres. and Mem. Bd of Directors). Founder (and first Pres.) Poet's Theatre Inc., Cambridge, Mass, 1950. Called back to teaching, 1952, and has served as Poet in Residence, Prof., or Lecturer at University of Washington, University of Conn., Wheaton Coll., Princeton, and in 1956 was apptd Prof. of English and Poet in Residence at Dartmouth Coll. Class of 1925 Chair, 1968 (being absent as Consultant in Poetry to the Library of Congress, 1959-61). Visiting Prof., University of Washington, 1967. Shelley Memorial Prize; Bollingen Prize, 1962; Pulitzer Prize, 1966; Fellow, Acad. of Amer. Poets, 1969 (Award of $5000). Advisory Cttee on the Arts, for the National Cultural Center, Washington, 1959; Member: Nat. Inst. of Arts and Letters, 1960; Nat. Acad. of Arts and Sciences, 1967; Elliston Lecturer on Poetry University of Cincinnati, 1961. Apptd Hon. Consultant in American Letters, The Library of Congress, 1963-66, reapptd, 1966-69. Hon.

LittD Dartmouth Coll., 1954; Skidmore Coll., 1966; Coll. of Wooster, 1969; Phi Beta Kappa poem, Harvard, 1967; Hon. Mem., Alpha Chapter, Mass, 1967. *Publications:* (concurrently in England and America): A Bravery of Earth, 1930; Reading the Spirit, 1936; Selected Poems, 1951; Undercliff, Poems, 1946-53, also Great Praises, 1957; Collected Poems, 1930-60, 1960; Collected Verse Plays, 1962 (USA); The Quarry, 1964; Selected Poems, 1930-65, New Directions, 1965; Thirty One Sonnets, 1967 (USA); Shifts of Being, 1968. He contributes book reviews to The New York Times Book Review; critical articles in USA and abroad. Recorded Readings of his Poetry, 1961, 1968. *Recreations:* swimming, cruising, tennis, flying 7-ft kites. *Address:* 5 Webster Terrace, Hanover, New Hampshire 03755, USA. *Clubs:* Century (New York); Buck's Harbor Yacht (S Brooksville, Maine).

**EBERT, Prof. Carl (Anton Charles),** CBE 1960; Opera Director; naturalized American citizen; *b* Berlin, 20 Feb. 1887; *s* of Maria and Wilhelm Ebert; *m* 1st, 1912, Lucie Splisgarth (marr. diss., 1923); one *s* (and one *d* decd); 2nd, 1924, Gertrude Eck; one *s* two *d*. *Educ:* Berlin, Friedrich Werder'sche Oberrealschule; Max Reinhardt's Sch. of Dramatic Art. Actor; Max Reinhardt's Deutsches Theater, Berlin, 1909-14; Schauspielhaus, Frankfurt, 1915-22; Staatstheater, Berlin, 1922-27; Founder and Dir of Schools of Dramatic Art: Frankfurt 1919, Berlin, Hochschule für Musik (Prof.), 1925; Gen.-Intendant (and Producer), Landestheater, Darmstadt, 1927-31; Intendant, Staedtische Oper, Berlin, 1931-33; A Director: Actors' Union, 1919-27; Deutscher Bühnenverein, 1927-33. Guest Producer since 1933 at Zürich, Basel, Maggio Musicale Florence, Verona, Salzburg Festival, Colon, Buenos Aires, Burgtheater and State Opera, Vienna, Cambridge Theatre, London (New London Opera Company), Scala, Milan, Royal Opera, Copenhagen, Metropolitan, New York; Artistic Dir and Producer, Glyndebourne Festival Opera, 1934-59; Producer Edinburgh Festival, 1947-55. Adviser on Theatrical Affairs to Turkish Min. of Educn, Ankara, 1936-47; Founder of Turkish State Sch. for Opera and Drama and of Turkish National Theatre. Prof. and Head of Opera Dept, University of S Calif, Los Angeles, 1948-54; Gen. Dir Guild Opera Co., Los Angeles, 1950-54, Artistic Dir since 1954; Intendant, Staedtische Oper, Berlin, 1954-61; Pres. German Section of International Theatre Institute, 1956-61. Guest Producer: Glyndebourne, 1962, 1963; Opera House, Zürich, 1963, 1965; Wexford Festival, 1965; Deutsche Oper, Berlin, 1967. Master Classes, BBC TV, 1965, 1967. Awarded Ernst Reuter Plakette, City of Berlin, 1957. Hon. MusDoc, Edinburgh, 1954, Hon Doc. of Fine Arts, University of S California, Los Angeles, 1955. Knight, Dannebrog Order, Denmark; Das Grosse Verdienstkreuz mit Stern, Germany; Das Grosse Ehrenzeichen for services to Mozart, Austria, 1959; Hon. Comdr of the Order of the British Empire, 1960; La Grande Médaille d'Argent de la Ville de Paris, 1961; Commendatore, Order of Merit (Italy), 1966; Hon. Member: Deutsche Oper, Berlin, 1961; Landestheater, Darmstadt, 1963; Hon. Life Mem., Bd of Dirs, Opera Guild of S Calif, LA, 1965. *Address:* 809 Enchanted Way, Pacific Palisades, Calif 90272, USA. *T:* 454-6705. *Club:* PEN (Internat.).

**EBERT, Peter;** Producer; Intendant, Stadttheater, Augsburg, since 1968; Director, Opera School, Richard Strauss Academy, Munich, since 1968; Director of Productions, Scottish Opera, since 1965; *b* 6 April 1918; *s* of Carl Ebert, *qv*, and Lucie Oppenheim; *m* 1st, 1944, Kathleen Havinden, two *d*; 2nd, 1951, Silvia Ashmole; five *s* three *d*. *Educ:* Salem Sch., Germany; Gordonstoun, Scotland. BBC Producer, 1948-51; 1st opera production, Mefistofele, Glasgow, 1951; Mozart and Rossini guest productions: Rome, Naples, Venice, 1951, 1952, 1954, 1955: Wexford Festival: 12 prods, 1952-65; 1st Glyndebourne Fest. prod., Ariecchino, 1954, followed by Seraglio, Don Giovanni, etc.; 1st Edinburgh Fest. prod., Forza del Destino, 1955; Chief producer: Hannover State Opera, 1954-60; Düsseldorf Opera, 1960-62; directed opera class, Hannover State Conservatory, 1954-60; Head of Opera studio, Düsseldorf, 1960-62. Guest productions in Europe, USA, Canada. TV productions of Glyndebourne operas, 1955-64; 1st TV studio prod., 1963; Opera Adviser to BBC TV, 1964-65. First drama prod., The Devils, Johannesburg, 1966; first musical, Houdini, London, 1966. Dir, Opera Sch., University of Toronto, 1967-68. *Recreation:* raising a family. *Address:* Arminstr. 24, 8902 Göggingen-Augsburg, Germany. *T:* Augsburg 3244902; Ades House, Chailey, Lewes, Sussex. *T:* Newick 2441.

**EBOO PIRBHAI, Sir;** *see* Pirbhai.

**EBRAHIM, Sir Currimbhoy;** *see* Ebrahim, Sir M. C.

**EBRAHIM, Sir Fazulbhoy Currimbhoy,** Kt, *cr* 1913; CBE 1918; Millowner and Merchant, Bombay; *b* 1873; 2nd *surv s* of Sir (Huscinali) Currimbhoy Ebrahim, 1st Bt; *m* 1889, Sakinabai (*d* 1930), *d* of Datoobhoy Ebrahim, of Cutch Mandvi; five *s*. Formerly Fellow of Bombay Univ. Past Pres., Corporation of Bombay.

**EBRAHIM, Sir (Mahomed) Currimbhoy,** 4th Bt, *cr* 1913; BA, LLB, Advocate, Pakistan; Member, Standing Council of the Baronetage, 1961; *b* 24 June, 1935; *o s* of Sir (Huseinali) Currimbhoy Ebrahim, 3rd Bt, and Alhaja Lady Amina Khanum, *d* of Alhaj Cassumali Jairajbhoy; *S* father 1952; *m* 1958, Dur-e-Mariam, *d* of Minuchehir Ahmud Ghulamaly Nana; one *s*. *Recreations:* tennis (Karachi University No. 1, 1957, No. 2, 1958), cricket, table-tennis, squash, reading (literary), art, poetry writing, debate, quotation writing. *Heir: s* Zulfiqar Ali Currimbhoy Ebrahim, *b* 5 Aug. 1960. *Address:* Bait-ul-Aman, 33 Mirza Kalig Beg Road, Jamshed Quarters, Karachi, Pakistan.

**EBRINGTON, Viscount; Richard Archibald Fortescue,** JP; *b* 14 April 1922; *s* and *heir* of 6th Earl Fortescue, *qv*; *m* 1st, 1949, Penelope Jane (*d* 1959), *d* of late Robert Evelyn Henderson, one *s* one *d*; 2nd, 1961, Margaret Anne, *d* of Michael Stratton; two *d*. *Educ:* Eton; Christ Church, Oxford. Capt. Coldstream Guards (Reserve). JP Oxon, 1964. *Heir: s* Hon. Charles Hugh Richard Fortescue, *b* 10 May 1951. *Address:* The Old Farm, Swinbrook, Burford, Oxon. *T:* Burford 3135. *Club:* White's.

**EBSWORTH, Brig. Wilfrid Algernon,** CB 1950; CBE 1943; *b* 1 Feb. 1897; *s* of Rev. Algernon Frederic Ebsworth and Mary Frances Harcourt-Vernon; *m* 1925, Cynthia, *d* of Edward Charles Bleck, CMG; one *s* one *d*. *Educ:* Tonbridge Sch.; RMC Sandhurst. Served European War, 1914-18, 2nd Lieut The Sherwood Foresters (twice wounded). Regimental and Staff Service, Egypt, Turkey, and India, 1919-27; Staff Coll., 1928-29; Regimental and Staff Service in England, 1930-38; Instructor, Staff Coll., 1938-39; War of 1939-45, commanded 1st Bn The Sherwood Foresters, Palestine, 1939-40; GSO 1, Middle

East, 1940-41 (despatches); Comd 22nd and 30th East African Brigades, Brig. Gen. Staff, East African Command and 15 Indian Corps, Burma, 1942-45; Comdr, British Army Staff, France, 1946-47; Dep. Fortress Comdr, Gibraltar, 1947-50; retd pay, 1950. Légion d'Honneur (Officier), Croix de Guerre avec palme, 1947 (France). *Recreations:* fishing, golf. *Address:* 3 Tekels Park, Camberley, Surrey. *T:* Camberley 23050.

**EBURY,** 6th Baron, *cr* 1857; **Francis Egerton Grosvenor;** *b* 8 Feb. 1934; *s* of 5th Baron Ebury, DSO and Ann Acland-Troyte; *heir-pres.* to 7th Earl of Wilton, *qv*; *S* father 1957; *m* 1st, 1957, Gillian Elfrida (Elfin) (marr. diss. 1962), *d* of Martin Soames, London; one *s*; 2nd, 1963, Kyra, *d* of late L. L. Aslin. *Educ:* Eton. *Recreation:* golf. *Heir:* *s* Hon. Julian Francis Martin Grosvenor, *b* 8 June 1959. *Address:* Flat 22, 36 Grange Road, Toorak, Melbourne, Australia. *Club:* Savage (Melbourne).

**ECCLES,** family name of **Viscount Eccles.**

**ECCLES,** 1st Viscount, *cr* 1964; 1st Baron, *cr* 1962; **David McAdam Eccles,** PC 1951; KCVO 1953; MA Oxon; Paymaster-General since 1970; *b* 18 Sept. 1904; *s* of late W. McAdam Eccles, FRCS and Anna Coralie, *d* of E. B. Anstie, JP; *m* 1928, Sybil, *e d* of Viscount Dawson of Penn, PC, GCVO, KCB, KCMG; two *s* one *d*. *Educ:* Winchester, New Coll., Oxford. Joined Ministry of Economic Warfare, Sept. 1939; Economic Adviser to HM Ambassadors at Madrid and Lisbon, 1940-42; Ministry of Production, 1942-43. MP (C) Chippenham Div. of Wilts, 1943-62. Minister of Works, 1951-54; Minister of Education, 1954-57; Pres. of the Board of Trade, 1957-59; Minister of Education, Oct. 1959-July 1962; Trustee, British Museum, 1963-, Chm. of Trustees, 1968-70; Dir, Courtaulds, 1962-70; Chm., West Cumberland Silk Mills Ltd, 1964-70. chm., Anglo-Hellenic League, 1967-. Hon. Fellow, RIBA. *Publications:* Half-Way to Faith, 1966; Life and Politics: A Moral Diagnosis, 1967; On Collecting, 1968. *Heir:* *s* Hon. John Dawson Eccles [*b* 20 April 1931; *m* 1955, Diana Catherine, *d* of Raymond Sturge, Ashmore, Dorset; one *s* two *d*]. *Address:* Dean Farm, Chute, near Andover, Hants; 6 Barton Street, SW1. *T:* Chute Standen 210. *Clubs:* Brooks's, Roxburghe.

*See also Marquess of Lansdowne.*

**ECCLES, Sir John Carew,** Kt 1958; FRS 1941; FRSNZ; FRACP; FAA; Distinguished Professor and Head of Research Unit of Neurobiology, Health Sciences Faculty, State University of New York at Buffalo, since 1968; *b* 27 Jan. 1903; *s* of William James and Mary Eccles; *m* 1st, 1928, Irene Frances Miller (marr. diss. 1968); four *s* five *d*; 2nd, 1968, Helena Táboříková. *Educ:* Melbourne Univ.; Magdalen Coll., Oxford. Melbourne University: 1st class Hons MB, BS 1925; Victoria Rhodes Scholar, 1925. Univ. of Oxford: Christopher Welch Scholar; 1st class Hons Natural Science (Physiology), 1927; MA 1929; DPhil 1929; Gotch Memorial Prize, 1927; Rolleston Memorial Prize, 1932. Junior Res. Fellow, Exeter Coll., Oxford, 1927-32; Staines Med. Fellow, Exeter Coll., 1932-34; Fellow and Tutor of Magdalen Coll., and Univ. Lectr in Physiology, 1934-37; Dir, Kanematsu Memorial Inst. of Pathology, Sydney, 1937-44; Prof. of Physiology: Univ. of Otago, Dunedin, NZ, 1944-51; ANU, Canberra, 1951-66; Mem., Inst. for Biomedical Res., Chicago, 1966-68. Lectures: Waynflete, Magdalen Coll., Oxford, 1952; Herter, Johns Hopkins Univ., 1955; Ferrier, Royal Soc., 1959. Pres., Australian Acad. of Science, 1957-61. Member: Pontifical Acad. of Science; Deutsche Akademie der Naturforscher Leopoldina. Foreign Hon. Member: Amer. Acad. of Arts and Sciences; Amer. Philosophical Soc.; Amer. Neurological Soc.; Accademia Nazionale dei Lincei. Hon. Life Mem., New York Acad. of Sciences, 1965; Foreign Associate, Nat. Acad. of Sciences. Hon. Fellow: Exeter Coll., Oxford, 1961; Magdalen Coll., Oxford, 1964. Hon. ScD Cantab; Hon. DSc: Tasmania; British Columbia; Gustavus Adolphus Coll., Minnesota; Marquette Univ., Wisconsin; Loyola, Chicago; Yeshiva, NY; Hon. LLD Melbourne; Hon. MD Charles Univ., Prague. (Jointly) Nobel Prize for Medicine, 1963; Baly Medal, RCP, 1961; Royal Medal, Royal Soc., 1962; Cothenius Medal, Deutsche Akademie der Naturforscher Leopoldina, 1963. *Publications:* (jt author) Reflex Activity of Spinal Cord, 1932; Neuro-physiological Basis of Mind, 1953; Physiology of Nerve Cells, 1957; Physiology of Synapses, 1964; (jt author) The Cerebellum as a Neuronal Machine, 1967; The Inhibitory Pathways of the Central Nervous System, 1969; papers in Proc. Royal Soc., Jl of Physiology, Jl of Neurophysiology, Experimental Brain Research. *Recreations:* walking, European travel. *Address:* 100 Lincoln Parkway, Buffalo, NY 14222, USA; Dept of Physiology, Capen Hall, State University of New York, Buffalo, NY 14214, USA.

**ECCLES, Maj.-Gen. Ronald Whalley,** CBE 1968; Assistant Master General of the Ordnance (Quality Assurance, formerly Inspection), Ministry of Defence (Army), 1967-70; *b* 25 Sept. 1912; *s* of W. J. Eccles, Wolverhampton; *m* 1938, Sadie Rodrigues; one *d*. *Educ:* Wolverhampton Sch. Alfred Herbert Ltd, 1931-36; Rolls Royce Ltd, 1936-39; RAOC, 1939-42; REME, 1942. WhSch, CEng, FIMechE. *Recreations:* golf, bridge. *Address:* 9 The Spinney, Stanmore, Mddx. *T:* 01-958 7156.

**ECCLESTON, Harry Norman,** RE 1961 (ARE 1948); ARWS 1964; Artist Designer at the Bank of England Printing Works since 1958; *b* 21 Jan. 1923; *s* of Harry Norman Eccleston and Kate Pritchard, Coseley, Staffs; *m* 1948, Betty Doreen Gripton; two *d*. *Educ:* Sch. of Art, Bilston; Coll. of Art, Birmingham; Royal College of Art. ATD 1947; ARCA (1st Class) 1950. Studied painting until 1942. Served in Royal Navy, 1942-46; Temp. Commn, RNVR, 1943. Engraving Sch., Royal College of Art, 1947-51; engraving, teaching, free-lance graphic design, 1951-58. *Recreation:* reading. *Address:* 110 Priory Road, Harold Hill, Romford, Essex. *T:* Ingrebourne 40275. *Club:* Chelsea Arts.

**ECHLIN, Sir Norman David Fenton,** 10th Bt, *cr* 1721; Captain 14/1st Punjab Regiment, Indian Army; *b* 1 Dec. 1925; *s* of Sir John Frederick Echlin, 9th Bt, and Ellen Patricia, *d* of David Jones, JP, Dublin; *S* father, 1932; *m* 1953, Mary Christine, *d* of John Arthur, Oswestry, Salop. *Educ:* Masonic Boys' School, Dublin. *Heir:* none. *Address:* Nartopa, 36 Marina Avenue, Appley, Ryde, IoW.

**ECKERSLEY, Thomas,** OBE 1948; RDI 1964; FSIA; Head of Graphic Design, London College of Printing; *b* Sept. 1914; *s* of John Eckersley and Eunice Hilton; *m* Daisy Eckersley; three *s*; *m* 1966, Mary Kessell, painter. *Educ:* Salford Sch. of Art. Free-lance Graphic Designer for London Transport, Shell Mex, BBC, GPO and other leading concerns since 1936. Work exhibited in Sweden, USA, Paris, Hamburg, Lausanne, Milan, Amsterdam; work in permanent collection at V&A Museum. Mem. of Alliance Graphique Internationale; Hon. Fellow, Manchester Coll.

of Art and Design. *Publications:* contribs to technical journals, etc. *Recreation:* cricket. *Address:* 71a Fitzjohn's Avenue, NW3. *T:* 01-794 2250.

**ECKMAN, Samuel Jr,** Hon. CBE 1947; Member, Advisory Committee of Royal Naval Film Corporation; *b* New York City. *Educ:* New York Public Schools; College of the City of New York. Entered Motion Picture industry in New York as exhibitor with his father; later elected Vice-Pres. of Goldwyn Distributing Corp.; subsequently on amalgamation with Metro, and formation of Metro-Goldwyn-Mayer, assumed charge of New England, New York, and New Jersey Districts; appointed Man. Dir of Metro-Goldwyn-Mayer Pictures Ltd, London, 1927, and continued as Chairman and Managing Director until 1954, Chm. until 1957. Former Capt. US Army Mil. Intelligence; during War of 1939-45 was Hon. Chm. USO, European Theatre of Operations. Member: the Pilgrims; Motion Picture Pioneers, New York; American Legion Post No. 1; Cinema Veterans, London (ex-Pres.); American Soc. in London (ex-Chm.); Cinematograph Films Council, 1941-44 and 1951-57; Pres., Kinematograph Renters Soc. (London), 1931-34. Mem. various Masonic bodies. *Address:* 945 Fifth Avenue, New York, NY 10021, USA. *Clubs:* American; Variety Clubs of Great Britain, New York and Israel; Army Athletic Association (US).

**EDDEN, Alan John,** CMG 1957; Ambassador to the Lebanon, since 1970; *b* 2 Dec. 1912; *s* of late Thomas Frederick Edden and Nellie Shipway; *m* 1939, Pauline Klay; one *s. Educ:* Latymer Sch., Edmonton; Gonville and Caius Coll., Cambridge (Exhibitioner). Served at HM Legation, Bangkok, 1935; Batavia, 1938; Foreign Office, 1939; HM Legation, Bangkok, 1940; HM Legation, Tehran, 1942; Kermanshah, 1944; with SHAEF, May 1945; Actg Consul-Gen. Amsterdam, June 1945; Foreign Office, Oct. 1945; HM Embassy, Warsaw, 1948; Brit. Information Services, New York, 1951; FO, 1953; Counsellor, Foreign Office, 1954-58; Counsellor, HM Embassy, Beirut, 1958-62; HM Consul-Gen., Durban, 1962-66; Ambassador to: Cameroons, Central African Republic, Gabon and Chad, 1966-70; Equatorial Guinea, 1969-70. *Recreations:* music, travel. *Address:* British Embassy, Beirut, Lebanon. *Club:* Royal Automobile.

**EDDEN, Vice-Adm. Sir (William) Kaye,** KBE 1960 (OBE 1944); CB 1956; *b* 27 Feb. 1905; *s* of late Major H. W. Edden, The Cameronians, and late Mrs H. W. Edden (*née* Neilson); *m* 1936, Isobel Sybil Pitman (*d* 1970), Bath, *g d* of Sir Isaac Pitman; one *s. Educ:* Royal Naval Colls, Osborne and Dartmouth. Comdr, 1938; Admiralty, 1938-40; served War of 1939-45: HMS London, 1941-42; Staff C-in-C, Eastern Fleet, 1942-44 (OBE); Capt. 1944, Admty, 1944-47; RNAS Yeovilton, 1947-49; Capt. (D) 6th Destroyer Sqdn, and HMS Battleaxe, 1949-51; Admiralty, 1951-53; Rear-Adm. 1954; Commandant, Jt-Services Staff Coll., Latimer, 1953-56; Flag Officer Commanding Fifth Cruiser Sqdn and Flag Officer Second-in-Command, Far East Station, 1956-57; Vice-Adm. 1957; Admiral Commanding Reserves, 1958-60, retd 1960. *Address:* Littlecroft, Old Bosham, Sussex. *T:* Bosham 3119. *Clubs:* Army and Navy; Bosham Sailing.

**EDDIE, Sir George (Brand),** Kt 1966; OBE 1948; DL; JP; retired; *b* 14 Nov. 1893; *s* of William and Jessie Eddie, Banchory, Kincardineshire; *m* 1926, Mary, *d* of George Ferguson, Glasgow; one *s* two *d. Educ:* Banchory. Secretary/Agent, Blackburn Trades Council and Labour Party, 1920-60; Vice-Chm. and Chm., NW Regional Council of Labour Party, 1940-; Mem., Blackburn Town Council, 1927- (Leader, 1945-68). Freeman, Blackburn Co. Borough, 1960. JP Blackburn, 1946. DL Lancs, 1968. *Recreations:* golf, bowls, motoring. *Address:* 44 Willow Trees Drive, Blackburn, Lancs. *T:* Blackburn 56088.

**EDDIS, Sir Basil Eden Garth,** Kt 1929; *s* of late W. K. Eddis and Mrs Eddis, Penketh, Harrow; *m* 1930, Yolande, MBE 1944, JP (*d* 1965), *er d* of Michael Faraday, Aldeburgh, Suffolk. *Educ:* Charterhouse; University Coll., Oxford. Formerly partner in firm of Gillanders, Arbuthnot & Co., Calcutta. JP Suffolk, 1937. *Address:* Longcroft, Aldeburgh, Suffolk.

**EDDISON, Rear-Adm. (Retd) Talbot Leadam,** CB 1961; DSC 1945; *b* 10 June 1908; *e s* (*yr twin*) of late Edwin and Mrs Eddison (*née* Leadam); *m* 1932, Doris (*née* Mavrogordato); one *s* one *d. Educ:* Royal Naval Coll., Dartmouth. Entered Dartmouth 1922. Commodore, Royal Naval Barracks, Devonport, 1958-59; Rear-Adm. 1959; served as Vice-Naval Dep. to Supreme Allied Comdr Europe, 1959-62; retired, 1962. *Address:* Dial Dene, Bransgore, Christchurch, Hants BH23 8DJ. *T:* Bransgore 593. *Club:* Royal Commonwealth Society.

**EDDLEMAN, Gen. Clyde Davis;** DSM (US); Silver Star; Legion of Merit; Bronze Star; Philippines Distinguished Service Star; Vice-Chief of Staff, US Army, 1960-62; *b* 17 Jan. 1902; *s* of Rev. W. H. Eddleman and Janie Eddleman (*née* Tureman); *m* 1926, Lorraine Heath; one *s* (and one *s* decd). *Educ:* US Military Academy, West Point, New York. Commissioned 2nd Lieut of Infantry upon graduation from US Military Academy, 1924. Advanced, through the ranks, and reached grade of Gen. 1959. Comdr, Central Army Group (NATO), and C-in-C, US Army, Europe, at Heidelberg, Germany, 1959-60. Knight Commander's Cross, Order of Merit (Germany). *Recreations:* hunting, fishing. *Address:* 4400 33rd Road N, Arlington, Va, USA.

**EDDY, Prof. Alfred Alan;** Professor of Biochemistry, University of Manchester Institute of Science and Technology since 1959; *b* 4 Nov. 1926; Cornish parentage; *s* of Alfred and Ellen Eddy; *m* 1954, Susan Ruth Slade-Jones; two *s. Educ:* Devonport High Sch.; Open scholarship Exeter Coll., Oxford, 1944; BA 1st Class Hons, 1949. ICI Research Fellow, 1950; DPhil 1951. Joined Brewing Industry Research Foundation, Nutfield, 1953. *Publications:* various scientific papers. *Address:* Larchfield, Buxton Road, Disley, Cheshire.

**EDDY, John Percy,** QC 1936; *b* Kidderminster, 19 May 1881; *yr s* of late Edward Eddy; *m* 1st, 1905, Alice Marion Evans (*d* 1968), *d* of late John Brymer; one *s* one *d*; 2nd, 1969, Charlotte Halford Armitstead, *widow* of Leslie Armitstead. Educ: King Charles I Sch., Kidderminster, and privately. Engaged for some years in journalism; was present at the Siege of Sidney Street, Jan. 3, 1911; called to the Bar, Middle Temple, 1911; joined the South Eastern Circuit; Judge, High Court of Judicature, Madras, 1929-30; Recorder of West Ham, 1936-49; Stipendiary Magistrate for East and West Ham, 1949-54. Served as Army Officer and with Min. of Nat. Service, 1917-18, and with Claims Commn, 1941-43; Mem. Gen. Council of the Bar, 1946-48; Divorce Comr, 1947; Mem. Council of Medico-Legal Soc., and of Inst. for the Study and Treatment of Delinquency; lectured at

Yale, Duke, Northwestern (Chicago) and other American Univs, 1952; at McGill Univ., Montreal, and Univ. of Toronto, 1953; at Delhi, Madras and Bombay, 1963; at Karachi, Lahore, Delhi, Calcutta, Madras and Bombay, 1964; at Delhi, Madras, Bombay and Karachi, 1965. Pres., West Ham Hostel for Youths (an approved probation hostel), 1953-56; Chm., The Worcs Assoc., 1953-55. *Publications:* Guide to National Insurance, 1911; The Law of Distress for Rent, Rates and Tithe Rent-charge; (with F. H. Lawton) India's New Constitution, 1935; The Justices' Handbook, 1st edn 1947, 2nd edn 1951, 3rd edn 1953; Professional Negligence (five lectures), 1955; The Law of Copyright, 1957; Scarlet and Ermine: Famous trials as I saw them, 1960; (with L. L. Loewe) The New Law of Betting and Gaming, 1961, 2nd edn 1964; Justice of the Peace, 1963; I Know My Rights: The Citizen's Charter, 1967; (with L. L. Loewe) The New Gaming Act, 1968; India and the Privy Council: The Last Appeal, 1950; and other papers. *Recreation:* golf. *Address:* Francis Taylor Building, Temple, EC4. *T:* 01-353 2182. *Clubs:* Royal Commonwealth Society, MCC; Athenæum (Liverpool).

**EDE, Jeffery Raymond;** Keeper of Public Records since 1970; *b* 10 March 1918; *e s* of late Richard Arthur Ede; *m* 1944, Mercy, *d* of Arthur Redfern Sholl; one *s* one *d*. *Educ:* Plymouth Coll.; King's Coll., Cambridge (MA). Served War of 1939-45, Intell. Corps (despatches); GSO2 HQ 8 Corps District, BAOR, 1945-46. Asst Keeper, Public Record Office, 1947-59; Principal Asst Keeper, 1959-66; Dep. Keeper, 1966-69. Lectr in Archive Admin., Sch. of Librarianship and Archives, University Coll., London, 1956-61; Unesco expert in Tanzania, 1963-64. FRHistS 1969. *Publications:* Guide to the Contents of the Public Record Office, Vol. II (major contributor), 1963; articles in archival and other professional jls. *Recreations:* theatre, countryside. *Address:* 36 North Road, Berkhamsted, Herts. *T:* Berkhamsted 4291. *Club:* Royal Commonwealth Society.

**EDEL, (Joseph) Leon;** Henry James Professor of English and American Letters, New York University, since 1966, and Citizens Professor of English, University of Hawaii, since 1970; *b* 9 Sept. 1907; *e s* of Simon Edel and Fanny (*née* Malamud), Pittsburgh, Pa; *m* 1950, Roberta J. Roberts; no *c*. *Educ:* McGill Univ., Montreal (BA 1927, MA 1928); Univ. of Paris (Docteur-ès-Lettres 1932). Served with US Army in France and Germany, 1943-47: Bronze Star Medal (US), 1945; Chief of Information Control, News Agency, US Zone, 1946-47. Asst Prof., Sir George Williams Coll., Montreal, 1932-34; miscellaneous writing and journalism, 1934-43; Christian Gauss Seminar in Criticism, Princeton Univ., 1951-52; New York University: Vis. Prof., 1952-53; Associate Prof., 1953-55; Prof. of English, 1955-66. Guggenheim Fellow, 1936-38, 1965-66; Alexander Lectures, Toronto, 1956; Vis. Professor: Indiana, 1954; Hawaii, 1955, 1969, 1970; Harvard, 1959-60; Purdue, 1970; Centenary Vis. Prof., Toronto, 1967. Pres., US Center of PEN, 1957-59. Fellow, Amer. Acad. of Arts and Sciences, 1959; Bollingen Fellow, 1959-61. Member: Nat. Inst. of Arts and Letters, 1964- (Sec., 1965-67); Council, Authors' League, 1965-68 (Pres., 1969-70). FRSL 1970. Hon. Mem., W. A. White Psychiatric Inst., 1966. Hon. DLitt: McGill, 1963; Union Coll., Schenectady, 1963. Nat. Inst. of Arts and Letters Award, 1959; US Nat. Book Award for non-fiction, 1963; Pulitzer Prize for biography, 1963. *Publications:* James Joyce: The Last Journey, 1947; (ed) The Complete Plays of Henry James, 1949; (with E. K. Brown) Willa Cather, 1953; The Life of Henry James: The Untried Years, 1953, The Conquest of London, 1962, The Middle Years, 1963, The Treacherous Years, 1969; The Psychological Novel, 1955; (ed) Selected Letters of Henry James, 1956; Literary Biography, 1957; (ed) The Complete Tales of Henry James, 12 vols, 1962-65; (ed) The Diary of Alice James, 1964; (ed) Literary History and Literary Criticism, 1965; Thoreau, 1970. *Recreations:* music, book-collecting. *Address:* Department of English, 19 University Place, New York University, New York, NY 10003, USA. *T:* 598-2871. *Clubs:* Athenæum; Century, Grolier (New York).

**EDELMAN, Maurice;** MP (Lab) Coventry West, 1945-50, North since 1950; author and journalist; *b* 2 March 1911; *s* of S. Edelman, Cardiff; *m* 1933; two *d*. *Educ:* Cardiff High Sch.; Trinity Coll., Cambridge. Exhibitioner in Mod. Langs, Trinity Coll., Cambridge, 1929; BA Cantab 1932; MA Cantab 1941. Engaged in industry and research in application of plastic materials to aircraft construction, 1932-41. Journalist and War Corresp. in N Africa and France. Vice-Pres., Anglo-French Parly Relations Cttee; Delegate to Consultative Assembly of Council of Europe, 1949-51, 1965-70, and Chm., Socialist Gp of WEU, 1968-70; Leader of Parly Delegn to Hungary, 1965; Special Rep. of Colonial Sec., to Cayman Islands and Turks and Caicos Islands, 1965. Vice-Chm., British Council, 1951-67; Mem., Air League Council, 1966-67. Chevalier de la Légion d'Honneur, 1954; Officier, 1960. *Publications:* France: The Birth of the Fourth Republic (Penguin), 1945; David Ben-Gurion, 1964; The Mirror: A Political History, 1966; *novels:* A Trial of Love, 1951; Who Goes Home, 1953; A Dream of Treason, 1953; The Happy Ones, 1957; A Call on Kuprin, 1959; The Minister, 1961; The Fratricides, 1963; The Prime Minister's Daughter, 1964; Shark Island, 1967; All on a Summer's Night, 1969. TV plays include, The Trial of Admiral Byng (BBC 1958). *Recreations:* tennis and painting. *Address:* House of Commons, SW1. *Clubs:* Queen's, Hurlingham.

**EDEN,** family name of **Earl of Avon** and of **Barons Auckland** and **Henley.**

**EDEN, Lt-Col The Viscount; Nicholas Eden,** OBE 1970; TD 1965; *b* 3 Oct. 1930; *o surv s* of 1st Earl of Avon, *qv* and late Mrs Eden (*née* Beckett). *Educ:* Eton. Served with KRRC, 1949-51; ADC to the Governor-Gen. of Canada, 1952-53; served in Queen Victoria's Rifles (TA), 1953-61; on amalgamation, served in Queen's Royal Rifles (TA), 1961-67; 4th (Volunteer) Bn, Royal Green Jackets, 1967-70; Major, Nov. 1959; Lt-Col, 1965. *Recreations:* lawn tennis, Eton fives. *Address:* 17 Bolton Street, W1.

**EDEN, Conrad W.,** TD; BMus Oxon; Organist of Durham Cathedral since 1936; *m* 1943, Barbara L., *d* of late Rev. R. L. Jones, Shepton Mallet. *Educ:* Wells Choir Sch., Rugby; St John's Coll., Oxford. Organist, Wells Cathedral, 1933-36. *Address:* The College, Durham. *T:* 4766.

**EDEN, Sir John (Benedict),** 9th Bt *cr* 1672 and 7th Bt *cr* 1776; MP (C) Bournemouth West since Feb. 1954; Minister for Industry, Department of Trade and Industry, since Oct. 1970; *b* 15 Sept. 1925; s of Sir Timothy Calvert Eden, 8th and 6th Bt and Patricia, *d* of Arthur Prendergast; *S* father, 1963; *m* 1958, Belinda Jane, *o d* of late Sir John Pascoe; two *s* two *d*. Lieut Rifle Bde, seconded to 2nd KEO Goorkha Rifles and Gilgit Scouts, 1943-47. Contested (C) Paddington North, 1953. Mem.

House of Commons Select Cttee on Estimates, 1962-64; Vice-Chm., Conservative Parly Defence Cttee, 1963-66; Chm., Defence Air Sub-Cttee; Hon. Sec., Space Sub-Cttee; Vice-Chm., Aviation Cttee, 1963-64; Additional Opposition Front Bench Spokesman for Defence, 1964-66; Opposition Front Bench Spokesman for Power, 1968-70; Minister of State, Min. of Technology, June-Oct. 1970. jt Vice-Chm., Conservative Parly Trade and Power Cttee, 1966-68; Vice-Chm., Assoc. of Conservative Clubs Ltd, 1964-67, Vice-Pres., 1970-. UK Deleg. to Council of Europe and to Western European Union, 1960-62; Mem., NATO Parliamentarians' Conf., 1962-66. Pres., Independent Schs Assoc., 1969-; a Vice-Pres., Nat. Chamber of Commerce. *Heir:* *s* Robert Frederick Calvert Eden, *b* 30 April 1964. *Address:* 41 Victoria Road, W8; Knoyle Place, East Knoyle, Salisbury, Wilts. *Clubs:* Boodle's, Pratt's.

**EDEY, Prof. Harold Cecil,** BCom (London), FCA; Professor of Accounting, London School of Economics, University of London, since 1962; *b* 23 Feb. 1913; *s* of Cecil Edey and Elsie (*née* Walmsley); *m* 1944, Dilys Mary Pakeman Jones; one *s* one *d*. *Educ:* Croydon High Sch. for Boys; LSE. Chartered Accountant, 1935. Commnd in RNVR, 1940-46. Lectr in Accounting and Finance, LSE, 1949-55; Reader in Accounting, Univ. of London, 1955-62; Pro-Dir, LSE, 1967-70. Mem., UK Adv. Coun. on Educn for Management, 1961-65; Mem., Academic Planning Bd for London Grad. Sch. of Business Studies, and Governor, 1965-; Chm., Arts and Social Studies Cttee, CNAA, and Mem. Coun., 1965-; Chm., Bd of Studies in Econs, University of London, 1966-; Mem. Council, Inst. of Chartered Accountants in England and Wales, 1969-. *Publications:* (with A. T. Peacock) National Income and Social Accounting, 1954; Business Budgets and Accounts, 1959; Introduction to Accounting, 1963; (with B. S. Yamey and H. Thomson) Accounting in England and Scotland 1543-1800, 1963; (with B. V. Carsberg) Modern Financial Management, 1969; articles in various jls. *Address:* 9 Thanescroft Gardens, Croydon CRO 5JR.

**EDGAR, Frederick Percy,** OBE; late Midland Regional Controller, BBC; retired, 1948; *b* 3 March 1884; *s* of Edward and Sarah Lane Edgar; *m* 1914, Elsie Ann, *o d* of Edward and Jane Wright, Wolverhampton; one *s*. *Educ:* Stafford. Concert Platform, 1907-14; organising Camp and Military Hosp. Concerts, 1914-18; Concert Direction, 1919-21; Music Hall and Theatrical Stage, 1921-22; Broadcasting, 1922. *Recreations:* motor boating and sailing. *Address:* Bryony House, Bryony Road, Selly Oak, Birmingham 29.

**EDGAR, Gilbert Harold Samuel,** CBE 1960; Chairman: H. Samuel Group of Companies, since 1935; Priory Gate Estates Ltd, since 1946; Underwriting Member of Lloyd's; *b* 1 Jan. 1898; *er s* of Edgar Samuel Edgar, Liverpool; *m* 1923, Eileen Victoria (*d* 1970), *yr d* of Sir Stuart Samuel, 1st Bt, MP for Tower Hamlets Div., 1900-18; one *d* (and one *d* decd). *Educ:* Charterhouse. Served European War, 1916, Lieut RHA (wounded); War of 1939-45, Sqdn Ldr, RAAF (Actg Wing Comdr). Mem. Coun., Royal Eye Hosp., 1934-60; assisted in foundn of Chair of Ophthalmology, RCS and Royal Eye Hosp., 1943; Gov., King's Coll. Hosp. Gp, 1951-61; on Bldg Cttee, RCOG, 1959-62; Founder, Edgar-Gentilli Memorial Schol. and Prize connected with Cancer Research. Contested (C) Smethwick, Gen. Elec. and By Elec., 1945; Chm. Wycombe Div. Conservative Assoc., 1955-60. CC, 1952-, CA, 1964, Bucks. Lay Sheriff of City of London, 1963-64. Thames Conservancy, 1965-. Trustee, Charterhouse Tercentenary Fund, 1948-63; Governor, Thomas Sutton's Hosp. in Charterhouse; Master, Worshipful Co. of Clockmakers, 1967-68. Hon. Fellow, RCOG, 1964. *Recreations:* farming, golf, shooting, fishing. *Address:* E 5, Albany, W1. *T:* 01-734 7836; Burrow Farm, Hambleden, Henley-on-Thames, Oxon. *T:* Hambleden (Bucks) 256. *Clubs:* Bath, United and Cecil, City Livery; Royal and Ancient (St Andrews); Huntercombe Golf (Oxon).

**EDGAR, Lieut-Gen. Hector Geoffrey,** CB 1960; CBE 1955; General Officer Commanding Eastern Command, Australian Military Forces, 1960-63; *b* 31 Oct. 1903; *s* of Thomas George Edgar, Wedderburn, Vic., Australia; *m* 1929, Margaret A., *d* of Charles Cooper; two *s* one *d*. *Educ:* Albert Park Grammar Sch.; RMC Duntroon, Canberra; idc; psc; pac. Training in India, 1925-26; Military Coll. of Science, Woolwich, 1933-36. Served with Third Australian Div., New Guinea and Bougainville; Chief Instructor, Senior Wing, Australian Staff Coll., 1945; Inspector-Gen., Munitions, 1946-47; Dep. Dir, Staff Duties, Army HQ, 1948-49; IDC, 1950; Comdt, Australian Staff Coll., 1951-53; Dir of Staff Duties, 1954; Dep. Chief of Gen. Staff, and Mem., Military Board, Army Headquarters, 1954-58; GOC Southern Command, 1958-60. First Superintendent, Rocket Range, Woomera, South Australia, 1949. *Address:* 21 Glen Road, Toorak, Victoria 3142, Australia.

**EDGCUMBE,** family name of **Earl of Mount Edgcumbe.**

**EDGCUMBE, (John) Aubrey Pearce,** CMG 1929; CBE 1920; Deputy Comptroller General, Department of Overseas Trade, 1939-46, when he retired; *b* 21 Sept. 1886; 2nd *s* of late Sir Robert Edgcumbe; *m* 1932, Madeleine, *d* of Thomas Jones, Y Gaer, Brecon. *Educ:* Winchester Coll. (Senior Commoner); Magdalene Coll., Cambridge (Scholar); Classical Tripos, Class 1. Entered Board of Trade (Class I competitive examination), 1910; National Health Insurance Commission, 1912; War Trade Statistical Dept, 1916; Dir, 1918; attended Peace Conference, Paris, 1919; Dept of Overseas Trade, 1919; accompanied Special Service Sqdn during Empire Cruise, 1923-24, as Economic Adviser on Staff of Admiral in Command; Colonial Office, 1924; Private Sec. to Rt Hon. L. S. Amery, MP, 1924-29, and subs. to Lord Passfield, Sec. of State for Dominion Affairs and for Colonies. *Address:* Hunsett Mill, Stalham, Norfolk Z/34. *T:* Stalham 449.

**EDGE, Sir Knowles,** 2nd Bt *cr* 1937; JP; *b* 31 Dec. 1905; *s* of Capt. Sir William Edge, 1st Bt, and Ada, *d* of I. Ickringill, Keighley; *S* father, 1948; *m* 1932, Dorothea Eunice, *y d* of Robert Walker, Newhaven, Conn, USA; two *s*. *Educ:* Bolton Sch.; Trinity Hall, Cambridge. Formerly Chm. and Man. Dir William Edge & Sons Ltd and assoc. cos. Contested Hillsborough Div. of Sheffield, 1950. Mem. of Bolton Town Council, 1931-58. Chm., British Federation of Music Festivals. Mem. Cttee of Management, Royal National Lifeboat Institution. *Recreation:* yacht cruising. *Heir:* *s* William Edge [*b* 5 Oct. 1936; *m* 1959, Avril Elizabeth Denson; two *s* one *d*]. *Address:* 1 Seafield Road, Lytham, Lancs. *Club:* Royal Mersey Yacht.

**EDGE, Maj.-Gen. Raymond Cyril Alexander,** CB 1968; MBE 1945; FRICS 1949; Director General, Ordnance Survey, 1965-69, retired; Colonel Commandant, Royal Engineers, since

1970; *b* 21 July 1912; *s* of Raymond Clive Edge and Mary (*née* Masters); *m* 1939, Margaret Patricia, *d* of William Wallace McKee, Tyrone, N Ireland; one *s* one *d*. *Educ:* Cheltenham Coll.; RMA; Caius Coll., Cambridge (BA). Commissioned in RE, 1932. Served in India, Royal Bombay Sappers and Miners and Survey of India, 1936-39. War Service in India, Burma (despatches), and Malaya. Lt-Col 1951; Col 1954; Dir (Brig.) Ordnance Survey, 1961; Maj.-Gen. 1965. Chairman: Assoc. British Geodesists, 1963-65; Geodesy Sub-Ctte Royal Soc., 1968-; Field Survey Assoc., 1968-. Pres., Section E, British Assoc., 1969. Member: Council, RGS, 1966-69; Council, RICS, 1966-. *Publications:* various papers on geodetic subjects in Bulletin Géodesique and other publications. *Recreations:* sailing, tennis. *Address:* Windsor Cottage, Hockering Gardens, Woking, Surrey. *T:* Woking 2182. *Club:* Army and Navy.

**EDGEWORTH, Lt-Col Kenneth Essex,** DSO 1917; MC; FRAS; MIEE; Royal Corps of Signals (retired); *b* 26 Feb. 1880; *e s* of Thomas N. Edgeworth; *m* Isabel Mary, *widow* of Arthur F. Eves, Resident Engineer, Cawnpore, and *e d* of John Trench Pigott. *Educ:* Marlborough (House Schol. and Senior Mathematical Schol.); RMA Woolwich (Pollock Medal and Prizes for Maths and Chemistry). Entered RE, 1898; Captain 1908; Major 1915; Temp. Lt-Col 1916; Lt-Col 1920; served S Africa, 1900-02 (Queen's medal 2 clasps, King's medal 2 clasps); East Africa, 1903-04 (medal with clasp); Sudan, 1908 (Egyptian medal and clasp); European War (despatches thrice, DSO, MC, 3 medals); retired pay, 1926; Chief Engineer, Posts and Telegraphs Dept, Sudan, 1926-31. *Publications:* The Industrial Crisis; The Trade Balance; The Price Level; Unemployment Can be Cured; The Earth, the Planets and the Stars: their Birth and Evolution; papers on theoretical astronomy; biography. *Address:* Cherbury, Booterstown, Co. Dublin. *T:* Dublin 882241.

**EDGEWORTH-JOHNSTONE, Maj.-Gen. Ralph,** CBE 1947; *b* 1893; *m* 1933, Cecily Margaret Thorp. *Educ:* France and Germany. Enlisted Fort Garry Horse, 1914; served European War, 1914-18 (wounded twice); commissioned Royal North'd Fusiliers, 1915. Retired, 1938, to join Public Relations Directorate War Office; Asst Dir, Lieut-Col, 1940; Dep. Dir, Brig., 1944; Dir, Maj.-Gen., 1946-52. *Address:* c/o Lloyds Bank, 6 Pall Mall, SW1.

**EDGEWORTH JOHNSTONE, Prof. Robert;** *see* Johnstone.

**EDIE, Thomas Ker; His Honour Judge Edie;** Deputy Chairman of Middlesex Quarter Sessions, since 1970; *b* 3 Oct. 1916; *s* of H. S. Ker Edie, Kinloss, Morayshire; *m* 1945, Margaret, *d* of Rev. A. E. Shooter, TD; four *s* one *d*. *Educ:* Clifton; London Univ. Called to Bar, Gray's Inn, 1941. Metropolitan Magistrate, 1961-70. *Address:* Worfield Lodge, Pennington Road, Southborough, Kent.

**EDINBURGH, Bishop of,** since 1961; **Rt. Rev. Kenneth Moir Carey,** MA; *b* 6 April 1908; *s* of late Godfrey Mohun Carey and Agnes Charlotte Milligan; unmarried. *Educ:* Marlborough; Exeter Coll., Oxford; Westcott House, Cambridge. Chaplain of Oxford House, Bethnal Green, 1932-36; Curate of St Andrew's, Handsworth, Birmingham, 1936-38; Vicar of Whitworth with Spennymoor, 1939-44; Gen. Sec., Central Advisory Council of Training for the Ministry, 1944-48; Principal of Westcott House, Cambridge, 1947-61; Hon. Canon of Portsmouth Cathedral, 1956-61. Chaplain to the Queen, 1957-61. Hon. DD Edinburgh, 1964. *Publication:* The Historic Episcopate (Ed.), 1955. *Address:* Bishop's House, 4 Lansdowne Crescent, Edinburgh EH12 5EQ. *T:* 031-225 6032.

**EDINBURGH, Dean of;** *see* Clark, Very Rev. R. J. V.

**EDINBURGH, Provost of** (St Mary's Cathedral); *see* Crosfield, Very Rev. G. P. C.

**EDMENSON, Sir Walter Alexander,** Kt 1958; CBE 1944; DL; shipowner; *b* 1892; 2nd *s* of late Robert Robson Edmenson; *m* 1918, Doris Davidson; one *d* (and one *s* killed in action, 1940). Served European War, 1914-18, RFA (despatches). Min. of War Transport Rep., N Ireland, 1939-45. President: The Ulster Steamship Co. Ltd; G. Heyn & Sons Ltd; Chairman: The Belfast Banking Co. Ltd; The North Continental Shipping Co. Ltd; The Belfast Bank Executor & Trustee Co. Ltd; Dir, Commercial Insurance Co. of Ireland Ltd; Member Board: BEA, 1946-63; Gallaher Ltd, 1946-66. Chm., N Ireland Civil Aviation Adv. Cttee, 1946-61; Member: Bd, Ulster Transport Authority, 1948-64; Council, Chamber of Shipping; Lloyd's Register of Shipping. Belfast Harbour Comr, 1940-61; Irish Lights Comr. Amer. Medal of Freedom with Palms, 1945. *Address:* 23 Castlehill Road, Belfast. *T:* Belfast 653763. *Clubs:* St James'; Ulster (Belfast); Kildare Street (Dublin).

**EDMONDS, Cecil John,** CMG 1941; CBE 1930 (OBE 1925); *b* 26 Oct. 1889; *y s* of late Rev. Walter and Laura Edmonds; *m* 1935, Alison, *o c* of late George Hooper, Birmingham; one *s* two *d*; *m* 1947, Phyllis, 2nd *d* of late F. L. Stephenson, Skegness; one *s*. *Educ:* Bedford Sch.; Christ's Hosp.; Pembroke Coll., Cambridge. Student Interpreter in HM Levant Consular Service, 1910; acting Vice-Consul, Bushire, 1913; Asst Political Officer, Mesopotamia, 1915 (Temp. Captain), SW Persia, 1917; Political Officer, British Forces, NW Persia, 1919 (Temp. Major, Special List); Special Duty in S Kurdistan, 1922; Divisional Adviser and Administrative Inspector in the Kirkuk and Sulaimani provinces under Iraq Govt, 1922; Political Officer with military columns in Kurdistan, 1924; Liaison Officer with League of Nations Commission of Inquiry into frontier between Iraq and Turkey, 1925; Asst Adviser, Min. of Interior, Iraq, 1926; Consul, 1928; British Assessor, League of Nations Commn of Inquiry into the frontier between Iraq and Syria, 1932; Mem. of Demarcation Commn of Iraqi-Syrian Frontier, 1933; Adviser, Min. for Foreign Affairs, Iraq, 1933; Mem. of Iraqi Delegation to League of Nations, annually 1932-38; Adviser to the Ministry of the Interior, Iraq, 1935-45; Consul-Gen., 1937. Order of the Rafidain (Cl. II), 1945; UK Perm. Deleg. to Internat. Refugee Organisation, 1947; Minister in HM Foreign Service, 1948; retired, 1950. Lecturer in Kurdish, Sch. of Oriental and African Studies, University of London, 1951-57. Burton Memorial Medal, 1963; Sykes Memorial Medal, 1966. *Publications:* Kurds, Turks and Arabs, 1957; (jt) A Kurdish-English Dictionary, 1966; A Pilgrimage to Lalish, 1967; contributions on Persian, Arabian and Kurdish subjects. *Recreation:* gardening. *Address:* 5 Longslip, Langton Green, near Tunbridge Wells, Kent. *T:* Langton 2771. *Club:* Athenæum.

**EDMONDS, Charles;** *see* Carrington, C. E.

**EDMONDS, Edward Alfred Jubal;** Member, Panel of Chairmen of Medical Appeal Tribunals, since 1969; *b* Newcastle, Natal, 21 Aug. 1907; *s* of late Edward Jubal Edmonds, Solicitor, and of Hilda O'Rorke Edmonds (*née* Stanton); *m* 1937, Maria Pauline du Toit; one *s* two *d*. *Educ:* Hilton Coll., Natal; Houghton Coll., Johannesburg; Natal Univ. Coll. Admitted a Solicitor, 1932; Attorney of Supreme Court of South Africa, 1933; Advocate of High Court of Tanganyika, Nov. 1934; Advocate, Supreme Court of Natal, 1939; entered Colonial Legal Service as a Resident Magistrate, Tanganyika, 1946; Puisne Judge, Kenya, 1955-64; retired from Colonial Service, 1964; called to the Bar, Gray's Inn, 1965; Resident Judge, Sovereign Base Areas, Cyprus, 1965-69. *Address:* Ridgeway. Hogs Back, Seale, Surrey.

**EDMONDS, Edward Reginald,** CMG 1954; *b* 25 Nov. 1901; *y s* of late G. F. Edmonds; *m* 1928, Edna May Dennis (*d* 1955); one *s* one *d*; *m* 1956, Dorothy Edith (*d* 1970) (she *m* 1st, 1923, Ewart G. Sheaves; he *d* 1925), *er d* of late Benjamin George Bishop, Woodford Green, Essex. *Educ:* King's Coll., London Univ. (BA). Entered Colonial Office, 1917; Asst Principal, 1938; Principal, 1941; Asst Sec., 1947; retired, 1961. Served in Uganda, 1926-28. *Address:* Conegar, Whitchurch Canonicorum, Bridport, Dorset. *T:* Chideock 364.

**EDMONDS, John Christopher;** Counsellor, British Embassy, Ankara, since 1968; *b* 23 June 1921; *s* of late Captain A. C. M. Edmonds, OBE, RN, and late Mrs. Edmonds; *m* 1st, 1948, Elena Tornow (marr. diss., 1965); two *s*; 2nd, 1966, Armine Williams. *Educ:* Kelly College. Entered Royal Navy, 1939; psc, 1946. Staff: of NATO Defence Coll., Paris, 1953-55; of C-in-C Home Fleet, 1956-57 (Comdr, 1957); of Chief of Defence Staff, 1958-59. Entered Diplomatic Service, 1959; Foreign Office, 1959-60; 1st Secretary (Commercial), Tokyo, 1960-62; FO, 1963-67; 1st Secretary and Head of Chancery, Ankara, 1967-68. *Recreations:* golf, tennis, travel. *Address:* c/o Foreign and Commonwealth Office, SW1; North Lodge, Sonning, Berks. *T:* Sonning 3651. *Club:* United Service.

**EDMONDS, Robert Humphrey Gordon,** CMG 1969; MBE 1944; HM Minister, Moscow, since 1969; *b* 5 Oct. 1920; *s* of late Air Vice-Marshal C. H. K. Edmonds, CBE, DSO; *m* 1951, Georgina Combe; four *s*. *Educ:* Ampleforth; Brasenose Coll., Oxford. Pres., Oxford Union, 1940. Served Army, 1940-46; Intelligence Officer, Western Desert, N African and Italian Campaigns; attached to Political Div., Allied Commn for Austria, 1945-46. Entered Foreign Service, Dec. 1946; served Cairo, 1947; FO, 1949; Rome, 1953; Warsaw, 1957; FO, 1959 (promoted Counsellor, 1962); Caracas, 1962; Head of American Dept, FO, 1966-67; Head of Mediterranean Dept, CO, 1967-68; Head of Southern European Dept, FCO, 1968-69. *Recreations:* golf, swimming, travel. *Address:* Bay Tree House, Aston Rowant, Oxon. *T:* Kingston Blount 335. *Club:* Turf.

**EDMONDS, Sheila May,** MA, PhD; Fellow and Vice-Principal of Newnham College, Cambridge (Fellow since 1945, Vice-Principal since 1960); Lecturer in Mathematics, Newnham College, since 1945; *b* 1 April 1916; *d* of Harold Montagu Edmonds and Florence Myra Edmonds. *Educ:* Wimbledon High Sch.; Newnham Coll., Cambridge. Research Student of Westfield Coll., 1939-40, and of Newnham Coll., 1940-41; Research Fellow of Newnham Coll., 1941-43; Asst Lecturer, Newnham Coll., 1943-45. *Publications:* papers in mathematical journals. *Address:* Newnham College, Cambridge. *T:* Cambridge 62273.

**EDMONDS, Winston Godward,** CBE 1966; ERD 1945; Managing Director, Manchester Ship Canal Co., since 1961; *b* 27 Nov. 1912; *s* of Wilfred Bell Edmonds and Nina (*née* Godward); *m* 1940, Sheila Mary (*née* Armitage); one *s*. *Educ:* Merchant Taylors'. Joined LNER, first as traffic apprentice and then in various positions, 1930-46; Manchester Ship Canal Co.: Commercial Manager, 1947-58; Manager, 1959-61. *Recreations:* golf, philately. *Address:* Myrtle Cottage, 1 Clark Lane, West Bollington, Macclesfield, Cheshire SK10 5AH. *T:* Bollington 2345. *Club:* St James's (Manchester).

**EDMONDSON,** family name of **Baron Sandford.**

**EDMONDSON, George D'Arcy,** CMG 1953; CVO 1957; OBE 1946; HBM Consul-General at Boston, 1959-62, retired; *b* 18 July 1904; *s* of George D'Arcy Edmondson and Agnes Mary Whitell; *m* 1st, 1935, Gwynfa (marriage dissolved, 1955), *d* of Sir Robert Burton-Chadwick, 1st Bt; no *c*; 2nd, 1955, Rosamond, *d* of late Prof. Robert L. Taylor, Williamstown, Mass, USA; two step *s*. *Educ:* Wimbledon Coll.; University Coll., Oxford (Hons, Jurisprudence). Called to Bar, Inner Temple, 1928; Press Censorship Bureau, 1939; Ministry of Information, 1941; British Information Services, New York; Dir Reference Div., 1942; Actg Controller, 1944; Controller, 1945; Dir-Gen. of British Information Services in the US, and Counsellor, British Embassy, Washington, 1953. *Address:* Blow-Me-Down, Star Route 4, Windsor, Vt 05089, USA. *Clubs:* Achilles, Travellers'; St Botolph (Boston, USA).

**EDMONSTONE, Sir Archibald (Bruce Charles),** 7th Bt *cr* 1774; *b* 3 Aug. 1934; *o surv. s* of Sir Charles Edmonstone, 6th Bt, and Gwendolyn Mary, *d* of late Marshall Field and of Mrs Maldwin Drummond; *S* father, 1954; *m* 1957, Jane (marr. diss. 1967), *er d* of Maj.-Gen. E. C. Colville, *qv*; two *s* one *d*; *m* 1969, Juliet Elizabeth, *d* of Maj.-Gen. C. M. F. Deakin, *qv*. *Educ:* St Peter's Court; Stowe Sch. *Heir:* *s* Archibald Edward Charles Edmonstone, *b* 4 Feb. 1961. *Address:* Duntreath Castle, Blanefield, Stirlingshire.

*See also Sir A. R. J. B. Jardine, Captain Sir C. E. McGrigor.*

**EDMONTON, Archbishop of, (RC),** since 1964; **Most Rev. Anthony Jordan,** OMI; *b* Broxburn, West Lothian, Scotland, 10 Nov. 1901; Priest, July 1929; Consecrated Bishop, Sept. 1945; Vicar Apostolic of Prince Rupert, Canada, and Titular Bishop of Vada, 1945-55; Coadjutor, 1955, translated as Archbishop of Edmonton in 1964. *Address:* Archbishop's Residence, 10044, 113th Street, Edmonton, Alta, Canada.

**EDMONTON, Bishop of,** since 1961; **Rt. Rev. William Gerald Burch,** DD; *m* 1942, Carroll Borrowman; four *d*. *Educ:* University of Toronto (BA); Wycliffe Coll., Toronto. Deacon, 1936; Priest, 1938. Curate, Christ Church, Toronto, 1936-40; Incumbent, Scarborough Junction with Sandown Park, 1940-42; Rector: St Luke, Winnipeg, 1942-52; All Saints, Windsor, 1952-56; Exam. Chaplain to Bishop of Huron, 1955-56; Canon of Huron, 1956; Dean and Rector, All Saints Cathedral, Edmonton, 1956-60; Suffragan Bishop of Edmonton, 1960-61. *Address:* Synod Office, 9707, 107th Street, Edmonton, Alta, Canada. *T:* 424-0791.

**EDMONTON, Suffragan Bishop of,** since 1970; **Rt. Rev. Alan Francis Bright Rogers,** MA; *b* 12

Sept. 1907; *s* of Thomas and Alice Rogers, London, W9; *m* 1932, Millicent Boarder; two *s*. *Educ:* Westminster City Sch.; King's Coll., London; Leeds Univ.; Bishop's Coll., Cheshunt. Curate of St Stephen's, Shepherds Bush, 1930-32; Holy Trinity, Twickenham, 1932-34; Civil Chaplain, Mauritius, 1934-49; Archdeacon of Mauritius, 1946-49; Commissary to Bishop of Mauritius, 1948-59; Vicar of Twickenham, 1949-54; Proctor in Convocation, 1951-59; Vicar of Hampstead, 1954-59; Rural Dean of Hampstead, 1955-59; Bishop of Mauritius, 1959-66; Suffragan Bishop of Fulham, 1966-70. MA Lambeth 1959. *Recreations:* walking, light music. *Address:* 14 Manor Mansions, Belsize Grove, Hampstead, NW3. *T:* 01-586 0757. *Club:* Royal Commonwealth Society.

**EDMUNDS, Christopher Montague,** MusD; Member Corporation, and Examiner, Trinity College of Music, London; *b* 26 Nov. 1899; 2nd *s* of Charles Edmunds; *m* 1923, Kathleen, *d* of Arthur Vaughan-Jones; one *s* one *d*. *Educ:* King Edward VI Sch., Camp Hill, Birmingham; Birmingham Univ.; Manchester Univ.; Birmingham Sch. of Music. 1st Cl. Hons BMus Birmingham, 1922; MusD, Manchester, 1936. Theory Teacher and Dir of opera class, Birmingham Sch. of Music, 1928-45; Principal, Birmingham Sch. of Music, 1945-56; Fellow Birmingham Sch. of Music; Fellow Trinity Coll. of Music. *Publications:* compositions include: The Blue Harlequin (opera); chamber and orchestral music; vocal and instrumental music; Romance, 1946 (pianoforte and orchestral work, commissioned by BBC). *Recreations:* cruising, gardening. *Address:* 247 Mereside Way North, St Bernard's Road, Olton, Solihull, Warwicks. *T:* 021-706 8055.

**EDNAM, Viscount; William Humble David Jeremy Ward;** *b* 27 March 1947; *s* and *heir* of Earl of Dudley, *q v* and of Stella Viscountess Ednam, *d* of M. A. Carcano, *qv*. *Educ:* Eton; Christ Church, Oxford. *Address:* 4 Cumberland Place, NW1.

**EDWARDES,** family name of **Baron Kensington.**

**EDWARDES JONES, Air Marshal (Retd) Sir (John) Humphrey,** KCB 1957 (CB 1954); CBE 1943; DFC 1940; AFC 1941; retired 1961; *b* 15 Aug. 1905; *s* of late G. M. Edwardes Jones, KC and G. R. Johnston; *m* 1935, Margaret Rose Graham; one *s* one *d*. *Educ:* Brighton Coll.; Pembroke Coll., Cambridge. Entered RAF, Sept. 1926; served in Egypt, 4 Flying Training Sch. and 208 Sqdn, 1930-35; Commanded: No. 213 Fighter Sqdn, 1937-40; No. 56 Op. Trg Unit, 1940; Nos 60 and 58 OTU's, 1941; Exeter Fighter Sector, 1942; No. 323 Fighter Wing, Algiers, Nov. 1942; AOC, No. 210 Group, Algiers, 1943; idc 1950; Dir of Plans, Air Ministry, 1951. Commandant, Sch. of Land/Air Warfare, RAF, Old Sarum, Wilts, 1955-57; Comdr-in-Chief, 2nd Tactical Air Force, and Comdr, 2nd Allied Tactical Air Force, 1957-61. Legion of Honour (French), 1946. *Recreation:* golf. *Address:* Old Marks, Holtye, Sussex. *T:* Cowden 317. *Club:* Royal Air Force.

**EDWARDES-KER, Lt-Col Douglas Rous,** OBE; Managing Director, Exe Shellfish Ltd; Principal, Seale Hayne Agricultural College, Newton Abbot, 1919-33; *b* 21 Jan. 1886; *s* of late Dr George Cordy Edwardes-Ker, Woodbridge, Suffolk; *m* 1912, Frances Edith Watts, Rampside, Lancs; two *s*. *Educ:* Woodbridge Sch.; Brasenose Coll., Oxford (Open Scholar). MA Oxon., 1st Class Hons; BSc London, 1st Class Hons. Coll. Warden and Mem. of Staff of South-Eastern Agricultural Coll., Wye, 1909-14; enlisted in Buffs, Aug. 1914; Commission in Royal Engineers, rising to rank of Lt-Col; Asst Dir of Gas Services, BEF, France (OBE, despatches thrice; French Croix de Guerre avec palme). *Recreations:* lawn tennis, for ten years Mem. of Devon County Team, and Vice-Chm. Devon County LTA; fly-fishing. *Address:* Green Hollow, Exmouth, Devon. *TA:* Exmouth. *T:* 2738. *Club:* Oxford University Alembic.

**EDWARDS,** family name of **Baron Chelmer.**

**EDWARDS, Brig. Arthur Bertie Duncan,** CBE 1943; MC; *b* 29 April 1898; *s* of Joseph Arthur Edwards, Portsmouth, and Rosa May Duncan, Isle of Wight; *m* 1925, Clara Elizabeth, 3rd *c* of late Edmund Barkworth, JP, Seaton, Devon; three *s*. *Educ:* RMA Woolwich. 2nd Lieut RE 1916; Capt. 1926; Major 1935; Lt-Col 1942; Temp. Col 1943, Brig. 1943; Col 1945; Brig. 1949. Served France, 1917-18 (BWM and VM); India, 1918-19; Iraq, 1919-20 (MC, BGS with Iraq clasp); India, 1920-22; England, 1922-35; Malta, 1935-39; England, 1939-40; France, 1940 (despatches); Greece, 1940-41; Libya, 1941; CRE Eighth Army Troops Engineers, Libya and Egypt, 1941-42 (despatches twice, OBE, North African Star); Dep. Chief Engineer, N Delta Defences, Egypt, 1942; Chief Engineer, Malta, 1942-43 (CBE); Chief Engineer, British Troops in Egypt, 1943; No. 13 CE Works (Construction), Middle East, 1943-44; Engineer Adviser, AA Command, England, 1944; Dep. Dir Works 21 Army Group BLA and BAOR, 1944-48 (despatches); Chief Engineer, Eastern Command, United Kingdom, 1948-51; retired, 1951. *Address:* c/o Lloyds Bank Ltd, 6 Pall Mall, SW1. *Club:* Royal Commonwealth Society.

**EDWARDS, (Arthur) Trystan,** MA Oxon; FRIBA; MTPI; FRGS; *b* Merthyr Tydfil, 10 Nov. 1884; *s* of late William Edwards, MA, LLD, formerly HMIS and Chief Inspector to the Central Welsh Bd; *m* 1947, Margaret Meredyth (*d* 1967), *d* of late Canon F. C. Smith, FRZS, FLS, Richmond (Surrey) and Hellingly. *Educ:* Clifton Coll.; Hertford Coll., Oxford (hons in maths and lit. hum.). Articled pupil to Sir Reginald Blomfield, RA, 1907-10; Dept of Civic Design, Sch. of Architecture, Liverpool Univ., 1911-12; served European War, 1915-18, Able Seaman Royal Navy, Fourth Destroyer Flotilla; Ministry of Health (Housing Dept), 1919-25. Founded Hundred New Towns Assoc., 1933, and subsequently submitted evidence on its behalf before Royal Commission on the Geographical Distribution of Industrial Population, Lord Justice Scott's Cttee on Land Utilisation, The New Towns Cttee, and Royal Commission on Population. *Publications:* The Things Which Are Seen: A Revaluation of the Visual Arts, 1921, re-issued 1948; Good and Bad Manners in Architecture, 1924, re-issued 1947; Style and Composition in Architecture, 1925, re-issued 1947; Sir William Chambers (Masters of Architecture Series), 1926; Three Rows of Tape, A Social Study of the Royal Navy, 1929, re-issued 1941 and 1970; Architectural Drawing, Perspective and Rendering (with Cyril Farey, FRIBA), 1931, re-issued 1949; A Hundred New Towns for Britain, 1933, re-issued 1935, 1944, 1970; Modern Terrace Houses (publication sponsored by Chadwick Trust), 1946; Merthyr, Rhondda and The Valleys (in Robert Hale's County and Regional series), 1959; Towards Tomorrow's Architecture: The Triple Approach, 1968; World Geography For All, The Comprehensive Wall Map derived from the Twin Globes, 1970; The Planets Earth and Mars in relation to The Solar System, 1970; The Second Battle of Hastings, 1939-45, 1970; Second-Best Boy: The

Autobiography of a Non-Speaker, 1970. *Address:* 7 Courtland Terrace, Merthyr Tydfil, Glam. *T:* Merthyr 2054. *Clubs:* Athenæum; Economic Reform, Victory Ex-Services.

**EDWARDS, Lt-Col (Bt Col) Sir Bartle M.,** Kt 1956; CVO 1961; MC; Vice-Lieutenant of Norfolk since 1958; served in HM hon. Corps of Gentlemen-at-Arms, 1938-61; Standard Bearer, 1956-61; *b* 30 March 1891; *s* of Major Mordaunt Edwards, VC, and Alice, *d* of General Norton; *m* 1921, Daphne, MBE, *d* of late Sir Cyril Kendall Butler, KBE; two *s* (and *e s* killed in action, March 1943) one *d*. *Educ:* Eton; RMC Sandhurst. Joined the Rifle Brigade, 1910; served with that regt and on general staff during European War, 1914-18, in France, Salonika, and Palestine (MC, despatches twice); Commanded Suffolk and Norfolk Yeo. Artillery Brigade, 1931-35; High Sheriff of Norfolk, 1946-47; Alderman, Norfolk County Council, Chm., 1950-66; DL and JP Norfolk. *Address:* Hardingham Hall, Norwich. *T:* Hingham 236. *Club:* Army and Navy.

*See also Maj.-Gen. R. H. Whitworth.*

**EDWARDS, Carl Johannes;** stained glass artist; *b* 15 Feb. 1914; *m* 1941, Kathleen Margaret Selina Morgan; two *d*. *Educ:* studied Art under James Hogan, RDI, and at various London Art Schs. Chief Designer Whitefriars Glass Works, 1948; resigned 1952. Governor Harrow Sch. of Art, 1949; Liveryman, Worshipful Company of Glaziers, 1949. Chief works in: Cairo Cathedral; Liverpool Cathedral; House of Lords; Lambeth Palace Chapel; Temple Church; Royal Air Force Church, St Clement Dane's; Portsmouth Cathedral; St David's Cathedral, Wales; Auckland Cathedral, NZ; Westminster Sch., and several works in concrete and glass for England and abroad. *Recreations:* golf and music. *Address:* Apothecaries Hall, Blackfriars Lane, EC4. *T:* 01-236 5123. *Clubs:* Challoner; Highgate Golf.

**EDWARDS, Sir Christopher (John Churchill),** 5th Bt *cr* 1866; *b* 16 Aug. 1941; *s* of Sir (Henry) Charles (Serrell Priestley) Edwards, 4th Bt and of Lady Daphne Edwards (*née* Birt); *S* father, 1963. *Educ:* Frensham Heights, Surrey; Loughborough, Leics. *Heir:* *b* Peter Henry Edwards, *b* 11 Jan. 1944. *Address:* 47 Redcliffe Gardens, Kensington, SW10. *T:* 01-352 9247.

**EDWARDS, Sir Clive;** *see* Edwards, Sir J. C. L.

**EDWARDS, Corwin D.;** Professor of Economics, University of Oregon, since 1963 (on leave June 1969-Sept. 1970); *b* 1 Nov. 1901; *s* of Granville D. Edwards and Ida May Moore; *m* 1st, 1924, Janet Ward; one *s* one *d*; 2nd, 1948, Gertrud Greig. *Educ:* Univ. of Missouri (BA); Oxford Univ. (BLitt); Cornell Univ. (PhD). Asst Prof. of Economics, New York Univ., 1926-33; Economist and Tech. Dir, Consumers' Advisory Bd, National Recovery Administration, 1933-35; co-ordinator, trade practice studies, Nat. Recovery Admin., 1935; Economist, President's Cttee of Industrial Analysis, 1936; Asst Chief Economist, Federal Trade Commn, 1937-39; Chief of Staff, Amer. Tech. Mission to Brazil, 1942-43; Economist, Chm. Policy Bd, Anti-Trust Div., Dept of Justice, 1939-44; Consultant on Cartels, Dept of State, 1943-48; Prof. of Economics, Northwestern Univ., 1944-48; Head of Mission on Japanese Combines, 1946; Dir, Bureau of Economics, Federal Trade Commn, USA, 1948-53; US Rep., *ad hoc* Cttee on Restrictive Business Practices, 1952-53; Pitt Prof., Cambridge Univ., 1953-54; Prof. of Economics, Univ. of Virginia, 1954-55; Prof. of Business and Government, Graduate Sch. of Business, Univ. of Chicago, 1955-63. Mem., Consumers Adv. Council, 1967-69. *Publications:* Maintaining Competition, 1949; Big Business and the Policy of Competition, 1956; The Price Discrimination Law: A Review of Experience, 1959; Trade Regulation Overseas, the National Laws, 1966; Control of Cartels and Monopolies, an International Comparison, 1967; Co-author: Economic Behavior, 1931; Economic Problems in a Changing World, 1939; A Cartel Policy for the United Nations, 1945; various govt reports and articles in professional jls. *Recreations:* swimming, sailing. *Address:* Dept of Economics, University of Oregon, Eugene, Oregon, USA.

**EDWARDS, Rev. Canon David Lawrence;** Canon of Westminster and Rector of St Margaret's, Westminster, since 1970; *b* 20 Jan. 1929; *s* of Lawrence Wright and Phyllis Boardman Edwards; *m* 1960, Hilary Mary (*née* Phillips); one *s* three *d*. *Educ:* King's Sch., Canterbury; Magdalen Coll., Oxford. Lothian Prize, 1951; 1st cl. hons Mod. Hist., BA 1952; MA 1956. Fellow, All Souls Coll., Oxford, 1952-59. Deacon, 1954; Priest, 1955. On HQ staff of Student Christian Movement of Gt Brit. and Ireland, 1955-66; Editor and Man. Dir, SCM Press Ltd, 1959-66; Gen. Sec. of Movt, 1965-66. Curate of: St John's, Hampstead, 1955-58; St Martin-in-the-Fields, 1958-66; Fellow and Dean of King's College, Cambridge, 1966-70; Exam. Chaplain: to Bp of Manchester, 1965-70; to Bp of Durham, 1968; Asst Lecturer in Divinity, University of Cambridge, 1967-70. Hulsean Lectr, 1967; Six Preacher, Canterbury Cathedral, 1969. Mem. of Administrative Cttee, British Council of Churches, 1969. *Publications:* A History of the King's School, Canterbury, 1957; Not Angels But Anglicans, 1958; This Church of England, 1962; God's Cross in Our World, 1963; Religion and Change, 1969; F. J. Shirley: An Extraordinary Headmaster, 1969; The Last Things Now, 1969; Leaders of the Church of England, 1971; (ed) The Honest to God Debate, 1963. *Address:* 2 Little Cloister, Westminster, SW1. *T:* 01-222 6428.

**EDWARDS, Donald Isaac,** CBE 1965 (OBE 1958); Managing Director, Independent Television News, since 1968; *b* 27 Sept. 1904; *s* of late Isaac Edwards, Bolton, Lancs; *m* 1930, Enid Bent; two *s*. *Educ:* Bolton Sch.; Emmanuel Coll., Cambridge (MA). Tillotsons Newspapers, 1926-28; Daily News, 1928-30; Allied Newspapers, 1930-33; Daily Telegraph, 1933-39; BBC: Asst European News Editor, 1940-42; European News Editor, 1942-45; Correspondent in India, 1946; Dir, European News, 1946-48; Head of External Services, News Dept, 1948-58; Editor, News, 1958-60; News and Current Affairs, 1960-67; Gen. Man., Local Radio Development, 1967-68. *Publications:* The Two Worlds of Donald Edwards (autobiography), 1970; contribs to various books on journalism and broadcasting. *Recreations:* music, golf, walking. *Address:* 2 Burghley Road, Wimbledon, SW19. *T:* 01-946 1245. *Club:* Reform.

**EDWARDS, Edward George,** PhD, BSc, FRIC; Vice-Chancellor and Principal, University of Bradford, since 1966; Principal of Bradford Institute of Technology, 1957-66; *b* 18 Feb. 1914; *m* 1940, Kathleen Hewitt; two *s* two *d*. *Educ:* Cardiff High Sch.; University of South Wales; Cardiff Coll. of Technology. Lecturer in Chemistry, University of Nottingham, 1938-40; Research Chemist (ICI Ltd), 1940-45; Head of Dept of Chemistry and Applied Chemistry, Royal Technical Coll., Salford, 1945-54; Principal, Coll. of Technology, Liverpool, 1954-57. *Publications:* various research papers in chemical jls; articles and papers on higher educn, technological innovation, university planning. *Recreations:* philosophy, music, walking, travel. *Address:* Corner Cottage, Westwood Drive, Ilkley, Yorks. *T:* Ilkley 2137.

**EDWARDS, Geoffrey Francis,** OBE 1968 (MBE 1956); TD; HM Consul-General, Berlin, since Nov. 1966; *b* 28 Sept. 1917; *s* of late Oliver Edwards, Langley, Bucks, and Frances Margaret Edwards; *m* 1st, 1949, Joyce Black (*d* 1953); one *d*; 2nd, 1961, Johanna Elisabeth Franziska Taeger. *Educ:* Brighton Coll. Joined Pixley & Abell, Bullion Brokers, 1936. Commissioned 117 Fd Regt, RA (TA), June 1939; served with 117 Fd Regt and 59 (Newfoundland) Heavy Regt RA in NW Europe, 1939-45; joined Control Commn for Germany, 1945; joined British Military Govt, Berlin, 1949; First Sec. (Economic), 1956; Economic Adviser, British Mil. Govt, Berlin, 1956; established in Diplomatic Service, 1966. *Recreations:* gardening, fishing, golf. *Address:* British Consulate-General, Uhlandstrasse 7/8, Berlin 12, Germany. *T:* 309 52 94.

**EDWARDS, George,** FFARCS; Consulting Anæsthetist: St George's, General Lying-in (St Thomas'), Samaritan (St Mary's) and Queen Charlotte's Hospitals; *b* 14 Jan. 1901; *m* 1934, Jean Lilian Smith, MD; one *s*. *Educ:* Royal Grammar Sch., Worcester; St George's Hospital (Johnson Anatomy Prize). MRCS, LRCP 1926; DA, RCP and S 1936; FFARCS 1948. RAMC, 1941-44; Lt-Col. Adviser in Anæsthetics, BNAF and CMF. Hon. Mem. (Pres. 1945-46), Sect. Anæsthetics, RSocMed. Mem. of Bd of Faculty of Anæsthetists, RCS, 1948-54; first Hewitt Lectr, RCS, 1950; first Snow Memorial Lectr, Assoc. of Anæsthetists, 1958. *Publications:* articles in medical journals. *Address:* 7 Chiltern Hills Road, Beaconsfield, Bucks. *T:* Beaconsfield 3504.

**EDWARDS, Sir George (Robert),** Kt 1957; CBE 1952 (MBE 1945); FRS 1968; Managing Director, British Aircraft Corporation (Holdings) Ltd; Chairman and Managing Director, British Aircraft Corporation Ltd; Pro-Chancellor, University of Surrey, appointed Dec. 1964; *b* 9 July 1908; *m* 1935, Marjorie Annie (*née* Thurgood); one *d*. *Educ:* S West Essex Tech. Coll.; London Univ. (BScEng). Gen. engineering, 1928-35; joined Design Staff, Vickers-Aviation Ltd, Weybridge, 1935; Experimental Manager, Vickers-Armstrongs Ltd, Weybridge Works, 1940. Chief Designer, Weybridge Works, 1945; Dir, Vickers Ltd, 1955-67. Pres., Royal Aeronautical Soc., 1957-58; Mem. of Council: Soc. of British Aerospace Cos, 1965-; Royal Society of Arts. CEng; FBIM; Hon. Fellow: RAeS 1960; Inst. of Aeronautical Sciences (USA); Manchester Coll. of Science and Technology; Hon. FAIAA. Hon. DSc: Southampton; Salford; Cranfield Inst. of Technology, 1970; Hon. ScD(Eng) London, 1970. George Taylor Gold Medal, 1948; British Gold Medal for Aeronautics, 1952; Daniel Guggenheim Medal, 1959; Guild of Air Pilots and Air Navigators Founders Medal, 1969. *Publications:* various papers and lectures in Jl RAeS, Amer. Inst. of Aeronautical Sciences and Amer. Soc. of Automotive Engrs. *Recreations:* golf, sailing. *Address:* Albury Heights, White Lane, Guildford, Surrey. *T:* Guildford 4488. *Clubs:* Royal Aero, Royal Automobile.

**EDWARDS, Gordon,** CBE 1955; *b* 14 July 1899; *s* of Frank George and Emily Maude Edwards, Crouch End, N8; *m* 1929 Marjorie Agnes, *d* of A. J. Hobson, OBE, RCNC; one *s*. *Educ:* Southend High Sch. Served European War, Inns of Court OTC and Royal Tank Corps, 1917-20. Inland Revenue Dept, 1920-45; Asst Sec., Min. of National Insurance, 1946-57; Chief Insurance Officer under the National Insurance and Industrial Injuries and Family Allowances Acts, 1957-62; Under-Sec., Min. of Pensions and National Insurance, 1962-64. *Publications:* Roses for Enjoyment, 1962; Mein Rosengarten, 1967; numerous articles in horticultural press. *Recreations:* growing roses and painting. *Address:* Hobbits, Copyhold Lane, Cuckfield, Sussex. *T:* Haywards Heath 4429. *Clubs:* United Service, St Stephen's.

**EDWARDS, Sir Goronwy;** *see* Edwards, Sir J. G.

**EDWARDS, Harold Clifford,** CBE 1945; MS, FRCS, FACS (Hon.); Honorary Colonel RAMC; Consulting Surgeon to King's College Hospital; Emeritus Lecturer and late Director, Department of Surgery, King's College Hospital Medical School; Surgeon to Royal Masonic Hospital; Consulting Surgeon to King Edward VII Hospital for Officers; St Saviour's Hospital; Consultant Adviser in Surgery to the Minister of Health; Surgeon Emeritus to the Evelina Hospital for Children; *b* 15 Aug. 1899; *s* of William Evans Edwards and Mary Selina Jones; *m* 1926, Ida Margaret Atkinson Phillips; two *s*. *Educ:* University Coll., Cardiff; King's College Hospital, London. Served in Royal Engineers, 1917-19; entered University Coll., Cardiff, 1919; MRCS, LRCP, MB, BS 1923; FRCS 1926; MS London Univ., 1928; Hon. Surgeon to King's Coll. Hosp., 1928, and to Evelina Hosp. for Children, 1931; Robert Jones Gold Medal for an Essay upon Injuries to Muscles and Tendons, 1930, and Jacksonian Prize of RCS for a Dissertation on Diverticula of the Intestine, 1932; Hunterian Prof., RCS, 1934; Consulting Surg. Southern Comd, England, 1942-44; Consulting Surg., Central Mediterranean Forces, 1944-46; late Dean of King's College Hosp. Medical Sch. Past Master, Worshipful Soc. of Apothecaries. Mem. Court of Examiners, and Mem. Council, RCS (past Vice-Pres.). examiner in Surgery, Univs of London, Cambridge, Wales, Birmingham, Dublin and Bristol. President: British Soc. of Gastroenterology; Assoc. of Surgeons of Gt Brit. and Ireland, 1962; Hon. Fellow: American Surgical Assoc.; Assoc. of Surgeons of W Africa; Assoc. of Surgeons of West Indies; Mem. Académie de Chirurgie. Former Editor of GUT the British Jl of Gastro-enterology. *Publications:* Surgical Emergencies in Children, 1935; Diverticula and Diverticulitis of the Intestine, 1939; Recent Advances in Surgery, 1954; papers in BMJ, Lancet, etc. *Recreations:* golf, travel. *Address:* Nickersons, Barton, Cambridge. *T:* Comberton 2367. *Club:* Athenæum.

**EDWARDS, Lt-Col Harold Walter,** DSO 1918; MC; MA; DL; CC, W Riding Yorks, 1949-52; Director, Dewsbury and West Riding Building Society, 1953-62; City Councillor, Bradford, 1954-57; *b* 1887; *y s* of S. E. Edwards, CC; *m* 1913, Celia (*d* 1941), *d* of G. A. Smith, Handsworth; one *s* (and one *s* decd); *m* 1948, Mabel Reina Fox, Bradford. *Educ:* March Grammar Sch.; Christ's Coll., Cambridge. Five years Science Master at King Edward Grammar Sch., Camp Hill, Birmingham; Chief Sec., Birmingham Liberal Association; Private Sec., 1920-21; Principal and Dir of Technical Schs, Cheltenham; Headmaster, Heckmondwike Grammar Sch., Yorks, 1924-48; retired, 1948. Four years' active service in France, Belgium, and Germany, with Royal Warwicks Regt and Signals (despatches twice, DSO, MC, Croix de Guerre (French); OC 41 Bn WR Home Guard, 1940-45. Prospective Parliamentary Candidate, Handsworth Div., Birmingham, 1918; Mem. Council IAHM,

1929, Joint Hon. Sec. 1941, Pres. 1942, Hon. Treas. 1947; Mem. Joint Matric Board, 1945; Mem. Sulgrave Deputation to USA, 1920; Officier d'Académie, 1934. DL West Riding of Yorks, 1947. *Publications:* newspaper articles on the land question, *Recreations:* motoring, gardening. *Address:* 20 Beechwood Avenue, Wibsey, Bradford.

**EDWARDS, (H. C.) Ralph,** CBE 1953; BA; FSA; Adviser on Works of Art to the Ministry of Works and the Historic Buildings Councils, since 1954; Keeper, Department of Woodwork, Victoria and Albert Museum, 1937-54, retired Oct. 1954; *b* 24 June 1894; *s* of late Rev. W. A. Edwards, formerly Rector of Tredington, Shipston-on-Stour, and of Edith Lilian, *e d* of late C. J. Collins Prichard, Pwllywrach, Glamorgan; *m* 1926, Marjorie Ingham Brooke; three *s*. *Educ:* privately; Hertford Coll., Oxon. BA (War Degree). European War 2nd Lieut, 1917-18, twice invalided; Middle Temple, Final Bar Exam. 2nd Cl.; Mem. of Editorial staff of Country Life, 1921-26; Asst, Dept of Woodwork, Victoria and Albert Museum, 1926-28; Asst Keeper, 1st Class, 1928; Keeper, 2nd Class, 1937, 1st Class, 1945. Member: The Court of Govs, and Council, Nat. Museum of Wales and of Cttees of Art and Archæology (Chm., 1958-61); Cttee, Slade Sch. of Art. *Publications:* (with late Percy Macquoid) The Dictionary of English Furniture, 3 vols, 1924-27 (2nd edn, rev. and enl., 1953; one volume edn 1963); Georgian Cabinet-makers (with Margaret Jourdain) (3rd edn 1955); Early Conversation Pictures, 1954; Introd. to Cat. for RA Exhibn, English Taste in the Eighteenth Century, 1955-56 and for exhibns for Arts Council and GLC; Co-Editor the Connoisseur Period Guides, 1956-58; various official publications and many articles on English pictures and decorative art. *Address:* Suffolk House, Chiswick Mall, W4. *T:* 01-994 3381; Pontesgob Mill Cottage, Fforest, Abergavenny, Mon. *Club:* Athenæum.
*See also R. N. Edwards.*

**EDWARDS, Air Cdre Hughie Idwal,** VC 1941; CB 1959; DSO 1942; OBE 1947; DFC 1941; Selection Trust Representative in Australia since 1964; *b* W Australia, 1 Aug. 1914; *s* of late Hugh Edwards; *m* 1942, Cherry Kyrle (*d* 1966), *widow* of Flight Lieut H. R. A. Beresford; one *s* one *d*. *Educ:* Fremantle, W Australia. Joined Regular Australian Army, 1934; transferred to RAAF, 1935, to RAF, 1936. Served War of 1939-45, in European, Middle and Far East theatres (despatches, DFC, VC, DSO). Commandant, Central Fighter Establishment, 1958-60; ADC to the Queen, 1960-63; idc 1961; Dir of Estabts, Air Ministry, 1962-63, retd. *Recreations:* squash, cricket. *Address:* c/o Australian Selection (Pty) Ltd, 22-30 Bridge Street, Sydney, NSW 2000, Australia. *Clubs:* Royal Air Force, MCC; Union, Imperial Service (Sydney).

**EDWARDS, Iorwerth Eiddon Stephen,** CBE 1968; MA, LittD; FBA 1962; Keeper of Egyptian Antiquities, British Museum, since 1955; *b* 21 July 1909; *s* of late Edward Edwards and Ellen Jane (*née* Higgs); *m* 1938, Elizabeth, *y d* of late Charles Edwards Lisle; one *d* (one *s* decd). *Educ:* Merchant Taylors'; Gonville and Caius Coll., Cambridge (Major Scholar). Merchant Taylors' Sch. Exhibitioner and John Stewart of Rannoch Univ. Scholar, Cambridge, 1928; 1st Cl. Oriental Languages Tripos, Parts I and II, 1930-31; Mason Prize, Tyrwhitt Scholarship and Wright Studentship, 1932. Entered Dept of Egyptian and Assyrian Antiquities, British Museum, 1934; seconded to Foreign Office; attached to British Embassies, Cairo and Baghdad, and to Secretariat, Jerusalem, 1942-45. Visiting Prof., Brown Univ., Providence, RI, USA, 1953-54. T. E. Peet Prize, Liverpool Univ., 1947. Vice-Pres. Egypt Exploration Soc. Mem. of German Archæological Inst. *Publications:* Hieroglyphic Texts in the British Museum, Vol. VIII, 1939; The Pyramids of Egypt, 1947, 2nd edn 1961; Hieratic Papyri in the British Museum, 4th Series (Oracular Amuletic Decrees of the Late New Kingdom), 1960; The Early Dynastic Period in Egypt, 1964; Joint Editor of The Cambridge Ancient History (3rd edn), 1970; articles in Journal of Egyptian Archæology and other scientific periodicals. *Recreations:* golf, gardening. *Address:* Morden Lodge, Morden, Surrey. *T:* 01-648 6023. *Club:* Athenæum.

**EDWARDS, Very Rev. Irven David;** Dean of Wells, since 1963; *b* 19 Nov. 1907; *s* of Rev. J. Edwards, Prebendary of Lichfield Cathedral; *m* 1938, Diana Vernon Douglas, 2nd *d* of Rt Rev. D. H. Crick, *qv*; one *s* three *d*. *Educ:* Repton; Christ's Coll., Cambridge. Chaplain of Christ's Coll., Cambridge, 1935-40; Gen. Sec. of Central Advisory Council of Training for the Ministry, 1935-44; Rector of Milton, Hampshire, 1940-47; Vicar of Norton, Co. Durham, 1947-56; Archdeacon of Leicester and Vicar of All Saints', City and Diocese of Leicester, 1956-63. Examining Chaplain to Bishops of: Portsmouth, 1936-47; Manchester, 1938-40; Chester, 1940-50; Durham, 1949-52; Leicester, 1956-63. *Address:* The Dean's Lodging, Wells, Somerset. *T:* Wells 2192.

**EDWARDS, James Keith O'Neill; (Jimmy Edwards),** DFC 1945; MA (Cantab); *b* 23 March 1920; *s* of late Prof. R. W. K. Edwards and late Mrs P. K. Edwards; *m* 1958, Valerie Seymour (marr. diss. 1969). *Educ:* St Paul's Cathedral Choir Sch.; King's Coll. Sch., Wimbledon; St John's Coll., Cambridge. Served War of 1939-45, in RAF, 1940-46. Windmill Theatre, London, 1946; Adelphi Theatre, 1950-51, 1952-54, 1954-55 and 1960-61; Take It From Here, BBC, 1948-59; Whack-O!, BBC Television, 1957-61; Seven Faces of Jim, 1961-62; Six More Faces of Jim, 1962-63; Bold as Brass, 1964; John Jorrocks, Esq., BBC-2, 1966; Fosset Saga, ATV, 1969. *Films:* Three Men in a Boat, 1957; Bottoms Up, 1960; Nearly a Nasty Accident, 1961. *Stage:* Big Bad Mouse, Shaftesbury, 1966-68; Halfway up the Tree, Queen's, 1968. Lord Rector of Aberdeen Univ., 1951-54. *Publication:* Take It From Me, 1952. *Recreations:* foxhunting, polo, flying, squash, brass bands. *Address:* c/o O'Neill Productions Ltd, Atheralls Farm, Fletching, Uckfield, Sussex. *T:* Newick 2258. *Club:* Savile.

**EDWARDS, John;** Editor, Yorkshire Post, since 1969; *b* 2 Jan. 1932; *s* of late Arthur Leonard Edwards; *m* 1954, Nancy Woodcock; one *s* one *d*. *Educ:* Wolverhampton Municipal Grammar School. Entered journalism, Wolverhampton Chronicle; subseq. worked on newspapers and magazines in Fleet Street and provinces; from 1961, Yorkshire Post: Dep. Night Editor, Business Editor, Asst Editor and Dep. Editor. *Address:* Wensley House, Wensley Drive, Leeds 7. *T:* 689639. *Club:* Authors'.

**EDWARDS, Sir John (Arthur),** Kt 1970; CBE 1953; President, London Rent Assessment Panel, since 1968 (Vice-President, 1965-68); *b* 1 June 1901; *s* of late John Edwards, JP, and Mary Elizabeth Cromar, Rossett; *m* 1932, Dorothy Margaret, *y d* of late Sir Richard Williams, OBE, DL, JP, Bangor, North Wales; two *s*. *Educ:* Grove Park Sch., Wrexham. FRICS; FAI. Chartered Surveyor. Articles and various appointments as a Chartered Surveyor and Land Agent, 1919-28; joined Valuation Office, 1929; Dep. Chief Valuer, Valuation Office, Bd of Inland Revenue, 1950-65. *Recreation:* golf. *Address:* 16 Oakridge Avenue, Radlett, Herts. *T:* 6550. *Club:* Reform.

**EDWARDS, Sir (John) Clive (Leighton),** 2nd Bt *cr* 1921; *b* 1916; *s* of 1st Bt and Kathleen Ermyntrude, *d* of late John Corfield, JP; *S* father, 1922. *Educ:* Winchester Coll. Volunteered and served in the Army, 1940-46. *Recreations:* motoring, gardening, very early motor cars. *Heir:* none. *Address:* Milntown, Lezayre, near Ramsey, Isle of Man.

**EDWARDS, Sir (John) Goronwy,** Kt 1960; MA; DLitt Oxon; Hon. DLitt Wales and Reading; Hon. LittD Leeds and Manchester; FBA 1943; FSA 1959; Director of the Institute of Historical Research and Professor of History, University of London, 1948-60, Professor Emeritus, 1960; Hon. Fellow of Jesus College, Oxford, 1949; Chairman, Royal Commission on Ancient Monuments in Wales and Monmouthshire, 1955-67; Member, Ancient Monuments Board for Wales, 1959; Member, Royal Commission on Historical Manuscripts, 1953; *b* 14 May 1891; *s* of John William and Emma Edwards; *m* 1925, Gwladys, *e d* of Rev. William Williams. *Educ:* Holywell Grammar Sch.; Jesus Coll., Oxford (Scholar); Manchester Univ. (Research Scholar). 1st Class Modern History, 1913; 2nd Lieut Royal Welch Fusiliers, 1915: served in France; retired with rank of Capt., 1919; Fellow and Tutor of Jesus Coll., Oxford, 1919-48; Librarian, 1920-25; Junior Bursar, 1926-29; Senior Tutor, 1931-46; Vice-Principal, 1945-48; Examiner, Sch. of Modern History, Oxford, 1926-28, 1941-43; University Lecturer in Modern History, 1928-36, 1947-48; Proctor, 1932-33; Pres. of the Dafydd ap Gwilym Soc., 1919-48; Joint Editor of the English Historical Review, 1938-59. Member: Cttee on House of Commons Personnel and Politics 1264-1832, 1929-31; Grigg Cttee on Departmental Records, 1952-54; British Acad. Cttee on Research in Humanities and Social Sciences, 1958-60; UGC Cttee on Libraries, 1963-66. Rhys Memorial Lecturer, British Academy, 1944; David Murray Lecturer, University of Glasgow, 1955; Raleigh Lecturer, Brit. Acad., 1956; Creighton Lecturer, University of London, 1957; Ford's Lecturer, University of Oxford, 1960-61; President, Royal Historical Society, 1961-64. Cymmrodorion Medal, 1970. *Publications:* Flint Pleas, 1283-85, 1922; Calendar of Ancient Correspondence concerning Wales, 1935; Littere Wallie, 1940; articles in English Historical Review and other historical journals. *Address:* 35 Westmorland Road, SW13. *T:* 01-748 7197.

**EDWARDS, Joseph Robert,** CBE 1963; JP; Member, Commission on Industrial Relations, since 1969; Chairman, Harland & Wolff Ltd, since 1970 (Deputy Chairman, 1968-70); Director: Associated Engineering, since 1969; Joseph Lucas Industries; Carrier Engineering Ltd, and other companies; British Airports Authority, *b* 5 July 1908; *y s* of late Walter Smith Edwards and Annie Edwards, Gt Yarmouth; *m* 1936, Frances Mabel Haddon Bourne; three *s* one *d*. *Educ:* High Sch., Great Yarmouth. Joined Austin Motor Co., Birmingham, 1928; Hercules factory, 1939; rejoined Austin Motor Co., 1941; Gen. Works Manager, 1951; Local Dir, 1953; Works Dir, 1954; Dir of Manufacturing, British Motor Corp., 1955; Managing Director: British Motor Corp., 1966-68; Pressed Steel/Fisher Ltd, 1966-67. Pres., Motor Industry Research Assoc. JP Oxford, 1964. Hon. MA Oxon, 1968. *Recreation:* golf. *Address:* Yatscombe, Boars Hill, Oxford. *T:* Oxford 35261. *Club:* Royal Motor Yacht.

**EDWARDS, Prof. Kenneth Charles,** CBE 1970; Professor of Geography in the University of Nottingham (first holder of the Chair) since 1948; *b* 2 March 1904; *s* of C. W. Edwards, Southampton; *m* 1937, Barbara Joyce West, Southsea; no *c*. *Educ:* Itchen Grammar Sch.; University Coll., Southampton. Asst Lectr in Geography and Demonstrator in Geology, University Coll., Nottingham, 1927; Indep. Lecturer in Geography and Head of Dept of Geography, University Coll., Nottingham, 1934; Reader in Geography, 1939; seconded to Ministry of Town and Country Planning, as Regional Research Officer for East Midlands, 1944-46; Temp. appt as Acting-Head of Dept of Geography, University Coll., Auckland, NZ, 1951; Dean of Faculty of Law and Social Sciences, Univ. of Nottingham, 1958. chm., Editorial Cttee of the East Midland Geographer, 1954. Pres., Section E British Assoc. for the Advancement of Science, 1959; Pres., Inst. of British Geographers, 1960; Pres., Geographical Assoc., 1963. Visiting Prof., Makerere Univ. Coll., Uganda, 1963; Murchison Grant, RGS, 1964. Mem., East Midlands Economic Planning Council, Dept of Economic Affairs, 1966. Order of the Crown of Oak, Grand Duchy of Luxembourg; Cross of the Order of the Restitution of Poland. *Publications:* Sweden; Dalarna Studies, 1940; The Land of Britain; Nottinghamshire, 1944; Studies in Regional Planning (ed G. H. J. Daysh); The East Midlands, 1949; (with F. A. Wells) A Survey of the Chesterfield Region, 1950; (with H. H. Swinnerton and R. H. Hall) The Peak District, 1962; Nottingham and its Region (ed), 1966; various contribs and research papers to geog. periodicals. *Recreations:* walking, including field excursions at home and abroad; music. *Address:* 24 Bramcote Drive, Beeston, Notts. *T:* 25-7309.

**EDWARDS, Rt. Rev. Lewis Mervyn Charles-;** *see* Charles-Edwards.

**EDWARDS, Rev. Maldwyn Lloyd,** PhD; Methodist Chairman in South Wales since 1957 (Cardiff and Swansea District of Methodist Church); President, Methodist Conference, July 1961-62; *b* 18 May 1903; *s* of John Lloyd and F. B. Edwards, Liverpool; *m* 1931, Eleanor M. L. Broadbelt; two *d*. *Educ:* Liverpool Collegiate Sch.; Universities of Wales, Cambridge and London. MA Wales and Cambridge; BD Cantab; PhD London. Asst Tutor, Handsworth Coll., 1929-30; Methodist Minister in Central Halls in six industrial centres. Sec., Christian Citizenship Dept of Methodist Church, 1945-48. Hon. DD Wofford Coll., N Carolina, USA, 1956. *Publications:* many books including several on various phases of Methodism, and on sociology, including The Signs of Our Times (Cato Lecture); also some devotional books and a number of papers and pamphlets on social subjects. *Recreations:* Methodist history and sociology. *Address:* 12 Llwyn-y-Grant Road, Cardiff CF3 7ET. *T:* Cardiff 34751.

**EDWARDS, Nicholas;** *see* Edwards, R. N.

**EDWARDS, Ralph;** *see* Edwards, H. C. R.

**EDWARDS, Richard Lionel,** QC 1952; *b* 1 Aug. 1907; *s* of late Lionel T. Edwards, BA, JP, Weston Underwood, Olney, Bucks; *m* 1944, Eleanor Middleton, *d* of late Sir Henry Japp, KBE; no *c*. *Educ:* Rugby Sch.; Oriel Coll., Oxford. Called to English Bar, 1930; Bencher of Lincoln's Inn, 1957. *Recreations:* gardening,

Italian painting and fishing. *Address:* Weston Underwood, Olney, Bucks. *T:* Olney 312. *Club:* English-Speaking Union.

**EDWARDS, Robert;** MP (Lab and Co-op) Bilston since 1955; General Secretary, Chemical Workers' Union, since 1947; *b* 1906. *Educ:* Council Schs and Technical Coll. Served with Republicans in Spain during Spanish civil war. Chm. delegns to Russia, 1926 and 1934. Mem. Liverpool City Council, 1929-32; Nat. Chm., ILP, 1943-48; Founder Pres., Socialist Movement for United States of Europe. Contested (ILP) Chorley 1935, Stretford 1939 and Newport 1945. Vice-President: British Section European League for Economic Co-operation; Economic Research Council; Council of Europe, 1969; Dep. Leader, British Delgn to Council of Europe, and Chm., Defence Cttee, WEU Assembly, 1968-; Leader, British Delegn, N Atlantic Assembly, 1968-69. Editor, The Chemical Worker. Dir, Corton Beach (Holdings) Ltd, 1969-. *Publications:* Chemicals–Servant or Master; A Study of a Master Spy, etc. *Address:* House of Commons, SW1.

**EDWARDS, Robert John;** Editor, The People, since 1966; *b* 26 Oct. 1925; *m* 1952, Laura Ellwood; two *s* two *d*. *Educ:* Ranelagh Sch., Bracknell. Editor, Tribune, 1951-54; Dep. Editor, Sunday Express, 1957-59; Man. Editor, Daily Express, 1959-61; Editor, Evening Citizen, Glasgow, 1962-63; Editor, Daily Express, 1963-65. Member, Variety Club of Great Britain. Broadcaster. *Address:* Old Thatch, Altwood Road, Maidenhead, Berks. *T:* Maidenhead 23963. *Club:* Kennel.

**EDWARDS, Sir Robert Meredydd W.;** *see* Wynne-Edwards.

**EDWARDS, Robert Septimus Friar,** CVO 1964; CBE 1963; Director-General, Mersey Docks and Harbour Board, since 1969 (General Manager, 1967-69); *b* 21 Oct. 1910; *y s* of late Augustus C. Edwards and of Amy Edwards; *m* 1946, Janet Mabel Wrigley; one *s* two *d*. *Educ:* Hereford Cathedral Sch. Chief Engineering Asst, Hereford, until 1936; Min. of Transport, Highway Engineering, 1936-43; Principal, Min. of War Transport, 1943; Mem. British Merchant Shipping Mission, Washington, DC, 1944-46. Sec. Gen. Internat. Conf. on Safety of Life at Sea, 1948; Principal Private Sec. to Minister of Transport, 1949-51; Shipping Attaché, British Embassy, Washington, DC, 1951-54; Dir of Sea Transport, 1954-57; Gen. Manager, London Airports, 1957-63. Called to the Bar, Middle Temple, 1941. *Recreations:* golf (for fun); gardening (*force majeure*). *Address:* Dock Office, Liverpool 3; Heatherlea, 9 Priory Road, West Kirby, Cheshire. *T:* 051-625 5863.

**EDWARDS, Captain Roderick Latimer Mackenzie,** CBE 1944; Royal Navy retired; *b* 1900; *s* of late Lt-Col C. and E. K. Mackenzie-Edwards; *m* 1929, Beryl Gertrude, *d* of late F. P. Clements, Maiden Newton, Dorset; one *d* (one *s* lost in sinking of HM Submarine Affray). *Educ:* Aldwick Preparatory Sch.; Osborne and Dartmouth. Served European War, 1916-18; specialised submarines, 1919; War of 1939-45; Capt.-in-Charge, Portland, 1947-49; retired list, 1950. Foreign decorations: Commander, Order of Orange Nassau, (Netherlands), 1945; Chevalier, Legion of Honour, 1945; Croix de Guerre with Palms (France), 1945. *Address:* Summerleaze, Maiden Newton, Dorchester, Dorset. *T:* Maiden Newton 244. *Clubs:* United Service; Royal Dorset Yacht.

**EDWARDS, (Roger) Nicholas;** MP (C) Pembroke since 1970; Managing Director, Wm Brandt's Sons & Co. (Insurance) Ltd, since 1963; *b* 25 Feb. 1934; *s* of (H. C.) Ralph Edwards, *q v*; *m* 1963, Ankaret Healing; one *s* one *d*. *Educ:* Westminster Sch.; Trinity Coll., Cambridge. Served as 2nd Lt, Royal Welch Fusiliers, 1952-54; Trinity Coll., Cambridge, 1954-57; read History: BA 1957, MA, 1968. Member of Lloyds, 1965-. Vice-Chm., Barons Court Conservative Assoc., 1967. *Publications:* articles and reviews in The Connoisseur and other jls. *Recreations:* fishing, gardening, collecting English drawings. *Address:* Warwick House, 2 Montpelier Row, Twickenham, Mddx. *T:* 01-892 3918; Pant-y-Bryn, St Davids, Pembrokeshire; Pontescob Mill, Fforest, Breconshire. *Club:* City University.

**EDWARDS, Dr Roger Snowden,** CBE 1964; Chairman, Gas Industry Training Board, since 1965; *b* 19 Dec. 1904; *s* of late Herbert George Edwards and late Margaret Alice Edwards; *m* 1935, Eveline Brunton; two *s* one *d*. *Educ:* Enfield Grammar Sch.; Imperial Coll. of Science. Junior Staff, Imperial Coll. of Science, 1925-28; Physicist, British Xylonite Co., 1928-29; Physicist, Boot Trade Research Association, 1929-39; Dir, Co-operative Wholesale Soc., 1939-49. Chairman: Council of Industrial Design, 1947-52 (Mem., 1944-47); NE Gas Board, 1949-66; Mem., Gas Council, 1966-70. JP Harrogate, 1960; Surrey, 1966. *Recreation:* golf. *Address:* Wood End, Warren Drive, Kingswood, Surrey.

**EDWARDS, Prof. Sir Ronald Stanley,** KBE 1963; Chairman, Beecham Group Ltd, since 1968; Director, ICI Ltd, since 1969; Professor of Economics, with special reference to Industrial Organisation, in the University of London since 1949; *b* 1 May 1910; *er s* of Charles and Alice Edwards; *m* 1936, Myrtle Violet Poplar; two *d*. *Educ:* Southgate County Sch. BCom (London), DSc (Econ.). Certified accountant. In professional accountancy, 1926-35; Asst Lectr and later Lectr in Business Administration with special reference to Accounting, London Sch. of Economics, 1935-40; Finance Mem. and Gen. Sec., Birmingham War Factories Jt Cttee, Dep. Dir of Labour and Asst Sec., Min. of Aircraft Production, 1940-45; Sir Ernest Cassel Reader in Commerce with special reference to Industrial Administration in University of London, 1946-49; Dep. Chm., Electricity Council, 1957-61, Chm., 1962-68. Member: Interdepartmental Cttee on Further Education and Training, 1944; Ministry of Fuel and Power Cttee on Electricity Peak Load in relation to Non-Industrial Consumers, 1948; Advisory Council, Dept of Scientific and Industrial Research, 1949-54; Min. of Fuel and Power Cttee of Inquiry into the Organisation and Efficiency of Electricity Supply Industry, 1954-55; University Grants Cttee, 1955-64; NEDC 1964-68. Governor: Admin. Staff Coll., Henley, 1962-; London Graduate Sch. of Business Studies, 1964-. Independent Chm., British Clock and Watch Manufacturers Assoc. (Watch Section), 1946-59, Hon. Pres., 1959-; Pres., Market Research Soc., 1965-69; Chm., Govt Cttee of Inquiry into Civil Air Transport Industry, 1967-69. Hon. LLD Edinburgh, 1966; Hon. DSc Bath, 1966. *Publications:* Co-operative Industrial Research, 1950; Industrial Research in Switzerland, 1951; Business Enterprise, 1958; (with H. Townsend) Studies in Business Organisation, 1961; (with H. Townsend) Business Growth 1966; contribs to Studies in Accounting (ed Baxter), Studies in Costing (ed Solomons), and to learned jls on economic, industrial and accounting questions.

*Recreation:* sailing. *Address:* 49 Lowndes Square, SW1. *T:* 01-235 4253; Nothe House, Weymouth, Dorset. *T:* Weymouth 923.

**EDWARDS, Rev. Rowland Alexander,** MA; Canon Residentiary of Norwich, 1948-68, Canon Emeritus, 1968 (Vice-Dean, 1954-68); *b* 20 Aug. 1890; *s* of late Philip Harris Edwards, solicitor, and late Emily, *d* of Alexander Gribbon, Belfast; *m* 1923, Monica Winterburn, Buckingham; two *s* two *d*. *Educ:* Campbell Coll., Belfast; St John's Coll., Oxford (Casberd Scholar). Graduated History, 2nd class. Ordained Dec. 1913; Chaplain, Christ's Hosp. Served European War, 1914-18; RAMC, Mesopotamia, 1916-19. Curate of Buckingham, 1920, of St Edmund's, Northampton, 1924; Vicar of St Faith's, Stepney, 1926, of Wisborough Green, Sussex, 1931; Rector of Dartington, Devon, 1940; Rural Dean of Totnes, 1943; Senior Examining Chaplain to Bishop of Norwich, 1948. Editor, St Martin's Review, 1938-39. *Publications:* Plain Tales from the Slums, 1933; Jack, Jill and God, 1936; World Adrift, 1937; Is the Church Worth While?, 1938; City of God, 1939; The Upper Room, 1941; The Church and the Modern World, 1944; contributor to Am I My Brother's Keeper?, 1946; (play) The Fighting Bishop, 1950; Church and Chapel, 1952; The Gospel According to St John, 1954; contributor to journals, etc. *Recreation:* writing. *Address:* 60 The Close, Norwich. *T:* Norwich 24726.

**EDWARDS, Prof. Samuel Frederick,** FRS 1966; Professor of Theoretical Physics, University of Manchester, since 1963; *b* 1 Feb. 1928; *s* of Richard and Mary Jane Edwards, Manselton, Swansea; *m* 1953, Merriell E. M. Bland; one *s* three *d*. *Educ:* Swansea Grammar Sch.; Caius Coll., Cambridge (MA, PhD); Harvard University. Inst. for Advanced Study, Princeton, 1952; Univ. of Birmingham, 1953; Univ. of Manchester, 1958. Vice-Pres., Institute of Physics, 1970- (Men. Council, 1967-); Member: Physics and Polymer Cttees, SRC, 1968-; Council, European Physical Soc., 1969- (Chm., Condensed Matter Div., 1969-). FInstP; FIMA. *Publications:* contribs to learned jls. *Address:* The University, Manchester M13 9PL.

**EDWARDS, Stewart Leslie,** CMG 1967; Under-Secretary, Board of Trade, since 1970; *b* 6 Nov. 1914; *s* of late Walter James and Lilian Emma Edwards; *m* 1940, Dominica Jeanne Lavie, *d* of Joseph Lavie and Jeanne Jauréguiberry; two *s*. *Educ:* King's Sch., Canterbury; Corpus Christi Coll., Cambridge (Foundn Scholar). BA 1936; MA 1943. Appointed to War Office, 1937; Asst Private Sec. to Sec. of State, 1939-40; Private Sec. to Civil Mem. of Army Council, 1940-42. Military service, 1942-44. Called to the Bar, Inner Temple, 1947. Seconded from War Office to OEEC, 1948-51; Board of Trade, 1951-65; Minister (Economic), Bonn, 1965-70. *Recreations:* music, reading, hill-walking. *Address:* Wildshaw House, West Heath, Limpsfield, Surrey. *T:* Oxted 4753. *Club:* Oxford and Cambridge University.

**EDWARDS, Trystan;** *see* Edwards, A. T.

**EDWARDS, Vero C. W.;** *see* Wynne-Edwards.

**EDWARDS, Lieut-Col Walter Manoel;** *b* 17 Feb. 1885; *s* of late Major E. G. Edwards, RA; *m* 1947, Rosa Charlotte Pennick, *d* of Ireton and Ethel Jones; one *s* one *d*. *Educ:* Rugby; RMA Woolwich; Exeter Coll., Oxford. Commission in Royal Garrison Artillery, 1904; War Service, 1914-18 (despatches, MC); retired as Major, 1921; BA Oxon 1925, MA 1927; Fellow, Merton Coll., Oxford, 1925; Professor of Greek Language and Literature, University of Leeds, 1928-50; Lieut-Col (Reserve). *Publications:* contributions to: New Chapters in Greek Literature, 1930; Oxford Latin Dictionary, 1950-69; articles in classical and other periodicals. *Recreation:* reading. *Address:* 43 Cumnor Hill, Oxford.

**EDWARDS, William (Henry);** MP (Lab) Merioneth since 1966; solicitor; *b* 6 Jan. 1938; *s* of Owen Henry Edwards and S. Edwards; *m* 1961, Ann Eleri Rogers; two *d*. *Educ:* Sir Thomas Jones' Comprehensive Sch.; Liverpool Univ. *Recreations:* golf, Association football (from the terraces). *Address:* Bryniau Golau, Bala, Merioneth.

**EDWARDS, William Philip Neville,** CBE 1949; Associate Director, Business International; Director, Public Relations (Industrial) Ltd; *b* 5 Aug. 1904; *s* of late Neville P. Edwards, Orford, Littlehampton, Sussex; *m* 1931, Hon. Sheila Cary, 2nd *d* of 13th Viscount Falkland; two *s*. *Educ:* Rugby Sch.; Corpus Christi Coll., Cambridge; Princeton Univ., USA (Davison Scholar). Joined Underground Electric group of companies, 1927; shortly afterwards appointed Sec. to Lord Ashfield, Chm. of Board; First Sec. of Standing Jt Cttee of Main Line Railway Companies and of LPTB, 1933; Officer of Board as Personal Asst to Gen. Manager of Railways, 1937; Outdoor Supt of Railways, 1938; Public Relations Officer of Board, 1939; Asst to Chm. of Supply Council of Min. of Supply, 1941-42; Head of Industrial Information Div. of Min. of Production and Alternate Dir of Information of British Supply Council in N America, 1943-45; First Dir of Overseas Information Div. of Board of Trade, 1945-46; Head of British Information Services in USA, 1946-49. A Dir, Confedn of British Industry (previously FBI), 1949-66; Man. Dir, British Overseas Fairs Ltd, 1959-66, Chm., 1966-68. Chevalier (1st class) of Order of Dannebrog (Denmark), 1955; Commander of Order of Vasa (Sweden), 1962. *Recreations:* golf, gardening. *Address:* (residence) Baddiley House, Church Hill, Merstham, Surrey; (office) 5 Plough Place, Fetter Lane, EC4. *Club:* Carlton.

**EDWARDS-JONES, Ian,** QC 1967; *b* 17 April 1923; *o s* of late Col H. V. Edwards-Jones, MC, DL, Swansea, Glam; *m* 1950, Susan Vera Catharine McClintock, *o d* of E. S. McClintock and of Mrs A. MacRossie; three *s*. *Educ:* Rugby Sch.; Trinity Coll., Cambridge (BA). Capt., RA, N Africa, Italy, Palestine, 1942-47. Called to Bar, Middle Temple, Lincoln's Inn, 1948. *Recreations:* fishing, shooting, photography. *Address:* 7 Stone Buildings, Lincoln's Inn, WC2. *T:* 01-405 3886/7. *Clubs:* Oxford and Cambridge University; Bar Yacht.

**EDWARDS-MOSS, Sir John (Herbert Theodore),** 4th Bt *cr* 1868; *b* 24 June 1913; *s* of late Major John Edwards-Moss and Dorothy Kate Gwyllyam, *e d* of late Ven. Henry William Watkins, DD; *S* uncle, Sir Thomas Edwards-Moss, 3rd Bt, 1960; *m* 1951, Jane Rebie, *d* of Carteret John Kempson; five *s* one *d*. *Educ:* Downhouse, Rottingdean. *Heir: s* David John Edwards-Moss, *b* 2 Feb. 1955. *Address:* Ruffold Farm, Cranleigh, Surrey.

**EDWIN, G. F. D.;** *see* Dove-Edwin.

**EELES, Air Cdre Henry,** CB 1956; CBE 1943; retired as Director of Administrative Plans, Air Ministry, 1959; *b* 12 May 1910; *yr s* of Henry Eeles, Newcastle upon Tyne; *m* 1st, 1940, Janet (*d* 1960), *d* of Major J. H. Norton; two *s* one *d*; 2nd, 1963, Pamela Clarice, *d* of Comdr G. A. Matthew, Royal Navy. *Educ:*

Harrow. Entered RAF Coll., 1929; Commnd Dec. 1930; Sqdn Ldr 1938; Group Capt. 1949; Air Cdre 1955. Comdt RAF Coll. and AOC RAF Cranwell, 1952-56. *Address:* The Cottage, Sutton Veny, Warminster, Wilts. *Clubs:* Brooks's, United Service.

**EFFINGHAM,** 6th Earl of, *cr* 1837; **Mowbray Henry Gordon Howard;** 15th Baron Howard of Effingham, *cr* 1554; *b* 29 Nov. 1905; *er s* of 5th Earl and Rosamond Margaret, *d* of late E. H. Hudson; *S* father, 1946; *m* 1st, 1938, Manci Maria Malvina (marr. diss. 1946), *d* of Ferenz Joseph Gertler, Hungary; 2nd, 1952, Gladys Irene Kerry, *d* of late William Freeman, Captain in Merchant Navy. *Heir: b* Hon. John Algernon Frederick Charles Howard [*b* 1907; *m* 1st, 1938 (marr. diss. 1942); one *s*; 2nd, 1946, Naida Frances, *d* of H. Guest; one *s*]. *Address:* House of Lords, SW1.

**EGELAND, Leif;** *b* 19 Jan. 1903; *s* of late J. J. Egeland, Consul for Norway in Natal, and Ragnhild Konsmo; *m* 1942, Marguerite Doreen, *d* of late W. J. de Zwann, Waterkloof, Pretoria; one *d*. *Educ:* Durban High Sch.; Natal University Coll.; Oxford Univ. MA English Lang. and Literature, Natal Univ. Coll.; MA, Hons BA, Jurisprudence, BCL Oxon; Rhodes Scholar (Natal), Trinity Coll., Oxford, 1924-27; official Fellow in Law and Classics, Brasenose Coll., 1927-30; Harmsworth Scholar, Middle Temple, 1927-30; Barrister, Middle Temple, 1930, bencher, 1948; Hon. LLD Cambridge, 1948. Admitted as Advocate of Supreme Court of S Africa, 1931; Vice-Consul for Norway, Natal, 1931-44; MP (House of Assembly) for Durban (Berea), 1933-38, for Zululand, 1940-43; SA Minister to Sweden, 1943, to Holland and Belgium, 1946. Served War of 1939-45, as AJAG, in UDF, 1940-43; Middle East with 6th Armoured Div. of UDF, 1943. SA Delegate to San Francisco Conf., 1945, to 1st Gen. Assembly of UN, London, 1946, to Final Assembly of League of Comr 1946; SA delegate and Pres. of Commn on Italian Political and Territorial Questions at Peace Conf., Paris, 1946. High Comr in London for the Union of South Africa, 1948-50; Chairman, Cape Asbestos Insulations Pty Ltd; Director: Johannesburg Consolidated Investment Co.; South African Breweries Ltd; Rhodesian Breweries Ltd; Standard Bank Investment Corp.; Goodyear Tyre & Rubber Co. (SA) Ltd; Johannesburg Local Board of Natal Building Soc.; African Pension Trustees Ltd; Standard General Insurance Co. Ltd; Nat. Chm., South Africa Inst. of Internat. Affairs; Chm., Smuts Memorial Trust. FRSA 1948. *Recreation:* tennis. *Address:* 97 Fourth Road, Hyde Park, Johannesburg, S Africa. *Clubs:* Durban, Rand (S Africa).

**EGERTON,** family name of **Duke of Sutherland** and **Earl of Wilton.**

**EGERTON, Lady Alice,** CVO 1957; Woman of the Bedchamber to The Queen since 1953; *b* 7 Aug. 1923; 6th *d* of 4th Earl of Ellesmere, MVO. *Educ:* privately. Lady-in-Waiting to Princess Elizabeth, Duchess of Edinburgh, 1949-52. Served Red Cross Transport, 1941-45. *Address:* Stetchworth Park, Newmarket, Suffolk. *T:* Stetchworth 281; 26 Hans Crescent, SW1. *T:* 01-584 9432. *See also Duke of Sutherland.*

**EGERTON, Maj.-Gen. David Boswell,** CB 1968; OBE 1956; MC 1940; President of the Ordnance Board, 1969-70; *b* 24 July 1914; *s* of Vice-Admiral W. de M. Egerton, DSO, and of Anita Adolphine (*née* David); *m* 1946, Margaret Gillian, *d* of Canon C. C. Inge; one *s* two *d*. *Educ:* Stowe; RMA Woolwich. Commissioned Royal Artillery, Aug. 1934; served in India, 1935-39, including ops in Waziristan, 1937; France and Belgium, 1940 (MC); Egypt 1942, Italy 1944 (wounded). Attended first Technical Staff course, RMCS, 1946; BJSM, Washington, DC, 1950-52; Asst Chief Engineer in charge of ammunition development, Royal Armament R&D Estabt, 1955-58; idc 1959; Army Mem., Defence Research Policy Staff, 1959-62; Comdt, Trials Estabt Guided Weapons, RA, 1962-63; Army Mem., Air Defence Working Party, 1963-64; Dir-Gen. of Artillery, Ministry of Defence, Army Dept, 1964-67; Vice-Pres., Ordnance Board, 1967-69. Col Comdt, RA, 1970-. *Recreations:* swimming, sailing. *Address:* Pendrys, West Clandon, Surrey. *T:* Clandon 640. *Club:* United Service.

**EGERTON, Vice-Adm. (Henry) Jack,** CB 1946; DL, JP; *b* 29 March 1892; *s* of late Charles Augustus Egerton, Mountfield, Robertsbridge, and Lady Mabelle Egerton, *d* of late Earl Brassey, GCB; *m* 1919, Marion, *d* of Hon. Sir Gervase Beckett, 1st Bt; one *s* (*er s* killed in action, 1942). *Educ:* RNC Dartmouth, RN: Captain, 1934; Rear-Adm. 1944; Vice-Adm., 1948. Senior British Naval Officer, North Russia, 1944-45; Flag Officer, Malayan Area, 1946-47; retired list, 1948. DL North Riding, 1951-. *Recreations:* hunting and shooting. *Address:* Colville House, Coxwold, York. *Club:* United Service.

**EGERTON, Vice-Adm. Jack;** *see* Egerton, Vice-Adm. (Henry) Jack.

**EGERTON, Sir Philip John Caledon G.;** *see* Grey Egerton.

**EGERTON, Sir Seymour John Louis,** KCVO 1970; Chairman Coutts & Co., Bankers, since Nov. 1951; *b* 24 Sept. 1915; *s* of late Louis Egerton and Jane, *e d* of Rev. Lord Victor Seymour; unmarried. *Educ:* Eton. Served War of 1939-45, in Grenadier Guards. Director: Romney Trust Ltd; Phoenix Assurance Co. Ltd (Dep. Chm.); Alexanders Discount Co. Ltd; Local Dir, National Westminster Bank. governor, St George's Hosp., 1958. Treasurer, Boy Scouts' Assoc., 1953-64; Vice-Pres., Corporation of the Church House. Sheriff of Greater London, 1968. *Address:* Flat A, 51 Eaton Square, SW1. *T:* 01-235 2164. *Clubs:* Boodle's, Beefsteak, Pratt's.

**EGGERS, Henry Howard,** CMG 1950; OBE 1945; Director, Cable & Wireless Ltd, 1954-69 (Managing Director, 1955-69); *b* 13 Nov. 1903; *yr s* of late H. A. F. Eggers, London; *m* 1936, Sheila (marr. diss. 1949), *d* of late F. R. Addie, Dunblane; one *s* one *d*. *Educ:* Dulwich Coll.; Magdalen Coll., Oxford. Central and South American merchant, 1924-39; Ministry of Economic Warfare, 1940-45; HM Treasury, 1945-54. Order of Istiqlal (Jordan), 1965. *Address:* The Barn, Ockenden Lane, Cuckfield, Sussex. *T:* Haywards Heath 4363.

**EGGLESTON, Anthony Francis,** OBE 1968; Headmaster, Felsted School, since 1968; *b* 26 Jan. 1928; *s* of late J. F. Eggleston and Mrs J. M. Eggleston, Harrow, Middx; *m* 1957, Jane Morison Buxton, JP, *d* of late W. L. Buxton, MBE and Mrs F. M. M. Buxton, Stanmore, Middx; one *s* two *d*. *Educ:* Merchant Taylors' Sch., Northwood (Schol.); St John's Coll., Oxford (Sir Thomas White Schol.). BA 1949, MA 1953; 2nd cl. hons Chemistry. National Service, 1950-52; 2nd Lieut, RA, Suez Canal Zone. Asst Master, Cheltenham Coll., 1952-54; Sen. Science Master, English High Sch., Istanbul, 1954-56; Asst Master, Merchant Taylors' Sch., Northwood, 1956-62; Princ., English Sch., Nicosia, 1962-68. *Recreations:* archaeology, architecture. *Address:* School

House, Felsted, Dunmow, Essex. *T:* Felsted 258.

**EGGLESTON, Prof. Harold Gordon;** Professor of Pure Mathematics in London University and Head of Department of Mathematics, at Royal Holloway College, since 1966; *b* 27 Nov. 1921; 2nd *s* of H. T. and E. M. Eggleston, Bents Green, Sheffield; *m* 1955, Elizabeth, *o d* of F. R. and C. A. W. Daglish, Beamish, County Durham; two *s* one *d*. *Educ:* High Storrs Grammmar Sch., Sheffield; Trinity Coll., Cambridge. Lecturer and Senior Lecturer, University Coll. of Swansea, 1948-53; Lecturer, University of Cambridge, 1953-58; Prof. of Mathematics, University of London at Bedford Coll., 1958-66. *Publications:* Problems in Euclidean Space, 1957; Convexity, 1958; Elementary Real Analysis, 1962. *Address:* Royal Holloway College, Englefield Green, Surrey.

**EGLINTON and WINTON,** 18th Earl of, *cr* 1507; **Archibald George Montgomerie;** Lord Montgomerie, 1448; Baron Seton and Tranent, 1859; Baron Kilwinning, 1615; Baron Ardrossan (UK), 1806; Earl of Winton (UK), 1859; Hereditary Sheriff of Renfrewshire; *b* 27 Aug. 1939; *s* of 17th Earl of Eglinton and Winton and Ursula, *er d* of Hon. Ronald Watson, Edinburgh; *S* father, 1966; *m* 1964, Marion Carolina, *o d* of John Dunn-Yarker; two *s*. *Educ:* Eton. *Heir: s* Lord Montgomerie, *qv*. *Address:* The Dutch House, West Green, Hartley Wintney, Hants. *Club:* Boodle's.

**EGMONT,** 11th Earl of, *cr* 1733; **Frederick George Moore Perceval;** Bt 1661; Baron Perceval, 1715; Viscount Perceval, 1722; Baron Lovell and Holland (Great Britain), 1762; Baron Arden, 1770; Baron Arden (United Kingdom), 1802; *b* 14 April 1914; *o s* of 10th Earl and Cecilia (*d* 1916), *d* of James Burns Moore, Montreal; *S* father, 1932; *m* 1932, Ann Geraldine, *d* of D. G. Moodie; two *s* one *d*. *Heir: s* Viscount Perceval, *qv*. *Address:* Two-dot Ranch, Nanton, Alberta, Canada.

**EGREMONT,** 1st Baron *cr* 1963, and **LECONFIELD,** 6th Baron *cr* 1859; **John Edward Reginald Wyndham,** MBE 1945; JP; *b* 5 June 1920; *s* of 5th Baron Leconfield, DSO and Gladys Mary, *o d* of F. J. W. Farquhar; *S* father 1967, as 6th Baron Leconfield, but prefers to be known as Lord Egremont; *m* 1947, Pamela, *d* of Captain the Hon. Valentine Wyndham-Quin; two *s* one *d*. *Educ:* Eton; Trinity College, Cambridge. Civil Servant, 1940-46; Conservative Research Dept, 1947-52. Private Secretary to the Prime Minister (Rt. Hon. Harold Macmillan), 1957-63 (when he was created 1st Baron Egremont). Trustee of the Wallace Collection, 1953-. JP West Sussex, 1953. High Sheriff of Sussex, 1960. *Publication:* Wyndham and Children First, 1968. *Heir: s* Hon. John Max Henry Scawen Wyndham, *b* 21 April 1948. *Address:* Petworth House, Sussex. *T:* Petworth 3147; Cockermouth Castle, Cumberland. *T:* Cockermouth 3118; 62 Chester Square, SW1. *T:* 01-730 2003. *Clubs:* Turf, White's, Beefsteak, Pratt's, Other, Sussex; Puffins (Edinburgh).

**EHRENBERG, Victor Leopold,** PhD; ancient historian; *b* 22 Nov. 1891; *s* of late Otto Maximilian Ehrenberg and Emilie Gabriele (*née* Fischel); *m* 1919, Eva Dorothea Sommer; two *s*. *Educ:* Univs of Göttingen, Berlin and Tübingen. PhD 1920; Privatdozent, Univ. of Frankfurt, 1922; Prof., German Univ. at Prague, 1929; Prof. Emeritus, 1954. Emigration, 1939; naturalised in Great Britain, 1947. Classics Master, Carlisle Grammar Sch., 1941; Lectr, King's Coll., Newcastle on Tyne, 1941-45; Senior Classics Master, Bootham Sch., 1945-46; Lecturer, Bedford Coll., University of London, 1946; Reader in Ancient History in the University of London, 1949-57. Visiting Prof., Brandeis Univ., USA, 1958; Martin Lecturer, Oberlin (Ohio), 1962; Hon. Res. Fellow, Bedford Coll., Univ. of London, 1966. Hon. LittD Cambridge, 1966. Jt Editor, Historia; Jt Founder of London Classical Soc., 1947; Sec. to Internat. Congress of Class. Studies, London, 1959. Corresponding Mem. Heidelberger and Österreichischen Akademien der Wissenschaften. Gold Medal Pro Meritis of University of Graz, 1961. Great Cross of Merit of the German Federal Republic, 1966. *Publications:* Die Rechtsidee im frühen Griechentum, 1921; Neugründer des Staats, 1925; Alexander und Aegypten, 1926; Der griechische und der hellenistische Staat, 1932; Ost und West, 1935; Alexander and the Greeks, 1938; The People of Aristophanes, 1943, 3rd edn (Paperback) 1962; L'Atene di Aristofane, 1957; Aristophanes und das Volk von Athen, 1968; Aspects of the Ancient World, 1946; (with Prof. A. H. M. Jones) Documents Illustrating the Reigns of Augustus and Tiberius, 1949, 2nd edn 1955; Sophocles and Pericles, 1954 (German edn 1956, Italian edn 1959); Der Staat der Griechen I, 1957, II, 1958, 2nd edn 1965 (The Greek State, 1961, Paperback, 1964, 2nd edn 1969, Lo Stato dei Greci, 1967); Von den Grundformen griechischer Staatsordnung, 1961; Society and Civilization in Greece and Rome, 1964; Polis und Imperium, 1965; The Hellenistic Age (Encyclop. Britannica), 1965; From Solon to Socrates, 1968; many articles in English, American and German learned jls; appreciation and full bibliography: Historia X, 1961; Ancient Society and Institutions, Studies presented to VE, 1966. *Address:* 1/112 Fitzjohn's Avenue, NW3. *T:* 01-435 2456.
*See also G. R. Elton.*

**EHRMAN, John Patrick William,** FBA 1970; historian; *b* 17 March 1920; *o s* of Albert and Rina Ehrman; *m* 1948, Elizabeth Susan Anne, *d* of late Vice-Adm. Sir Geoffrey Blake; four *s*. *Educ:* Charterhouse; Trinity Coll., Cambridge (MA). Served Royal Navy, 1940-45. Fellow of Trinity Coll., Cambridge, 1947-52; Historian, Cabinet Office, 1948-56; Lees Knowles Lectr, Cambridge, 1957-58. Hon. Treas., Friends of the National Libraries; Mem., Reviewing Cttee on Export of Works of Art. FSA 1958; FRHistS. *Publications:* The Navy in the War of William III, 1953; Grand Strategy, 1943-5 (2 vols, UK Official Military Histories of the Second World War), 1956; Cabinet Government and War, 1890-1940, 1958; The British Government and Commercial Negotiations with Europe, 1783-1793, 1962; The Younger Pitt: the years of acclaim, 1969. *Address:* Sloane House, 149 Old Church Street, SW3; Clobb Copse, Buckler's Hard, Beaulieu, Hants. *Clubs:* Athenæum, Garrick.

**EIGEN, Manfred;** Director of Max-Planck-Institut für physikalische Chemie, Göttingen, since 1964; *b* 9 May 1927; *s* of Ernst and Hedwig Eigen; *m* 1952, Elfriede Müller; one *s* one *d*. *Educ:* Göttingen Univ. Dr rer. nat. (Phys. Chem.) 1951. Research Asst, Inst. für physikal. Chemie, Göttingen Univ., 1951-53; Asst, Max-Planck-Institut für physikal. Chemie, 1953; Research Fellow, Max-Planck-Gesellschaft, 1958; Head of separate dept of Kinetic Chemistry, Max-Planck-Inst., 1962. Andrew D. White Prof. at Large, Cornell Univ., 1965; Hon. Prof., Technische Hochschule Braunschweig, 1965. For. Hon. Mem., Amer. Acad. of Arts and Sciences, 1964; Mem. Leopoldina, Deutsche Akad. der Naturforscher, Halle, 1964; Mem., Akad. der Wissenschaften, Göttingen, 1965; Hon. Mem.,

Amer. Assoc. Biol Chemists, 1966; For. Assoc., Nat. Acad. of Scis, Washington, 1966. Dr of Science *hc*, Washington, Harvard and Chicago Univs, 1966. Has won prizes, medals and awards including Nobel Prize for Chemistry (jointly), 1967. *Publications:* numerous papers in Z. Elektrochem., Jl Phys. Chem., Trans Faraday Soc., Proc. Royal Soc., Canad. Jl Chem., ICSU Rev., and other learned jls. *Address:* Max-Planck-Institut für physikalische Chemie, Bünsenstr. 10, 34 Göttingen, Germany. *T:* 0551/44051.

**EILON, Prof. Samuel;** Professor of Industrial Management (formerly Industrial and Management Engineering), and Head of Management Engineering Section, Imperial College of Science and Technology, University of London, since 1963; *b* 13 Oct. 1923; *s* of Abraham and Rachel Eilon; *m* 1946, Hannah Ruth (*née* Samuel); two *s* two *d*. *Educ:* Reali Sch., Haifa; Technion, Israel Inst. of Technology, Haifa; Imperial Coll., London. PhD 1955, DScEng 1963, London. FIMechE, FIProdE. Engr, Palestine Electric Co. Ltd, Haifa, 1946-48; Officer, Israel Defence Forces, 1948-52; CO of an Ordnance and workshop base depot (Major); Res. Asst, Imperial Coll., 1952-55; Lectr in Production Engrg, Imperial Coll., 1955-57; Associate Prof. in Industrial Engrg, Technion, Haifa, 1957-59; Reader, Imperial Coll., 1959-63. Professorial Research Fellow, Case-Western-Reserve Univ., Cleveland, Ohio, 1967-68. Mem. and Past Mem. of several cttees of IProdE and Dept of Educn and Science. Mem. Coun., Operational Res. Soc., 1965-67. Editor, Management Studies Series; Dep. Editor, Management Science. Two Joseph Whitworth Prizes for papers, IMechE, 1960. *Publications:* Elements of Production Planning and Control, 1962; Industrial Engineering Tables, 1962; (jtly) Exercises in Industrial Management, 1966; (jtly) Industrial Scheduling Abstracts, 1967; (jtly) Inventory Control Abstracts, 1968; numerous scientific papers. *Recreations:* theatre, tennis, walking. *Address:* 1 Meadway Close, NW11; Imperial College, Exhibition Road, SW7. *T:* 01-589 5111.

**EINZIG, Paul,** DSc Pol. & Econ. (Paris); London Correspondent of the Commercial and Financial Chronicle, New York, since 1945; *b* Brasov (Transylvania), 25 Aug. 1897; *s* of late Bernard Einzig, Brasov, and late Giselle Weisz; *m* 1931, Eileen Ruth, *d* of late J. Telford Quick, St Mawes, Cornwall; one *s* one *d*. *Educ:* Brasov; Oriental Academy of Budapest; University of Paris. Paris Correspondent of the Financial News, 1921; Foreign Ed., 1923; Political Correspondent, 1939-45; Political Correspondent, Financial Times, 1945-56. British subject by naturalisation, 1929. *Publications:* Le Mouvement des Prix, 1923; International Gold Movements, 1929; The Bank for International Settlements, 1930; The Fight for Financial Supremacy, 1931; The World Economic Crisis, 1931; Behind the Scenes of International Finance, 1931; The Tragedy of the Pound, 1932; Finance and Politics, 1932; Montagu Norman, 1932; The Comedy of the Pound, 1933; The Economic Foundations of Fascism, 1933; The Sterling-Dollar-Franc Tangle, 1933; Germany's Default, 1934; The Economics of Rearmament, 1934; Exchange Control, 1934; France's Crisis, 1934; The Future of Gold, 1934; World Finance since 1914, 1935; Bankers, Statesmen and Economists, 1935; Exchange Clearing, 1935; Monetary Reform in Theory and Practice, 1936; The Theory of Forward Exchange, 1937; World Finance 1935-37, 1937; Will Gold Depreciate?, 1937; Foreign Balances, 1938; World Finance, 1937-38, 1938; Bloodless Invasion, 1938; Economic Problems of the Next War, 1939; World Finance, 1938-39, 1939; Economic Warfare, 1940; World Finance, 1939-40, 1940; Europe in Chains, 1940; Hitler's "New Order" in Europe, 1941; Economic Warfare, 1939-40, 1941; Appeasement Before, During, and After the War, 1941; Can We Win the Peace?, 1942; The Japanese "New Order" in Asia, 1943; Currency After the War, 1944; Freedom from Want, 1944; Primitive Money in its Ethnological, Historical and Economic Aspects, 1949; Inflation, 1952; How Money is Managed, 1954; The Economic Consequences of Automation, 1956; The Control of the Purse, 1959; In the Centre of Things: An Autobiography, 1960; A Dynamic Theory of Forward Exchange, 1961; The History of Foreign Exchange, 1962; The Euro-Dollar System, 1964; Monetary Policy: Ends and Means, 1964; Foreign Dollar Loans in Europe, 1965; A Textbook on Foreign Exchange, 1966; Foreign Exchange Crises, 1968; Leads and Lags, 1968; Decline and Fall? Britain's Crisis in the Sixties, 1969; The Euro-Bond Market, 1969; The Case against Floating Exchanges, 1970. *Recreations:* music, reading, walking. *Address:* 120 Clifford's Inn, EC4. *T:* 01-405 1444; Suffolks, Ashurst Wood, East Grinstead, Sussex. *T:* Forest Row 3386.

**EISENBERG, Maurice;** violoncellist; Concert-Artist, HMV Records; Director Founder, International 'Cello Centre in London; Professor of Violoncello of Juilliard School of Music, NYC; US Representative, International Juries, Pablo Casals 'Cello Competitions, Paris, Mexico, Israel, Budapest; *b* Königsberg, 24 Feb. 1902; *s* of Rev. Samuel Eisenberg and Fannie Eisenberg; *m* 1921, Paula Halpert; one *s* one *d*. *Educ:* Peabody Conservatory, Baltimore; studied with Klengel in Leipzig, Becker in Berlin, and at the Ecole Normale de Musique in Paris under Alexanian; under Casals in Spain for six years, Summer Master Classes, Internat. Summer Courses in Estoril, Portugal. *Publication:* Violoncello Playing of Today, 1956 (2nd edn). *Address:* 119 Cypress Street, Millburn, New Jersey 07041, USA.

**EISENHOWER, Milton Stover;** President, The Johns Hopkins University, 1956-67; *b* 15 Sept. 1899; *s* of David Jacob and Ida Stover Eisenhower; *m* 1927, Helen Elsie Eakin (decd); one *s* one *d*. *Educ:* Kansas State Univ. (BS); Univ. of Edinburgh. City Ed., Abilene (Kan.) Daily Reflector, 1918 and 1920-21; Asst Prof. Journalism, Kansas State Univ., 1924; Amer. Vice-Consul, Edinburgh, 1924-26; Asst to Sec. of Agric., 1926-28; Dir Inf., US Dept of Agric., 1928-41, Land Use Co-ordinator, 1937-42; Dir, War Relocation Authority, 1942; Assoc. Dir, Office of War Inf., 1942-43; Pres., Kansas State Univ., 1943-50; Pres., Pennsylvania State Univ., 1950-56. Mem. Fact-finding Board in Gen. Motors labor-management dispute, 1945; Famine Emergency Relief Ctee, 1946; Exec. Bd Unesco, 1946; President's Cttee on Government Organisation, 1953-60; Nat. Advisory Cttee on Inter-American Affairs, 1960; Special Ambassador and Personal Rep. of US Pres., on Latin Amer. Affairs, 1953, 1957, 1958, 1959, 1960; Chm., US Nat. Commn for Unesco, 1946-48; Deleg., Unesco Confs, 1946-47-48-49. Mem., President's Commn on Higher Educn, 1946; Problems and Policies Cttee, Amer. Council on Educn, 1950-53; Exec. Cttee, Assoc. Land-Grant Colls and Univs, 1944-47, 1950-53, Chm., 1946-47, 1952-53; Pres. Assoc., 1951-52. Chm. Nat. Cttee for The People Act, 1951-53; Director: Fund for Adult Educn, 1953-61; Freedoms Foundn Inc., 1951-; The Geisinger Memorial Hosp., 1952-; Mem., Atlantic-Pacific Interoceanic Canal Study Commn,

1965-; Chm., President's Commn on Causes and Prevention of Violence, 1968-69. Also trusteeships, etc both past and present. Holds thirty-five hon. degrees (including LLD Johns Hopkins), foreign orders, etc. *Publications:* The Wine is Bitter, 1963; Ed. many publications for US Dept of Agric.; articles for Scholar, Sat. Evening Post, Colliers, Country Gentlemen, etc. *Address:* Evergreen House, 4545 North Charles, Baltimore, Md 21210, USA. *T:* Hopkins 7-3300. *Clubs:* Maryland, Johns Hopkins (Baltimore); Mill Reef (Antiqua).

**EKIN, Maj.-Gen. Roger Gillies,** CIE 1946; IA, retired; *b* 18 Nov. 1895; *yr s* of Col T. C. Ekin, MInstCE; *m* 1923, Phyllis Marian (*d* 1967), *er d* of Maj.-Gen. Sir Henry Croker, KCB, CMG; one *s* two *d. Educ:* Westminster; RMC Sandhurst. First Commissioned, 1914; Palestine campaign, 1916-19; on Operations in Waziristan, 1920-21; Operations NWFP, 1930; Brevet Lt-Col 1936; Comdt 5th Bn FF Rifles, 1937-40; Comd Kohat Bde Ahmedzal Ops, 1940; Col 1939; Temp. Maj.-Gen. 1946; Comdt Tactical Sch., India, 1940-41; Comd 46 Inf. Bde, Burma campaign, 1942; Comd Nowshera Bde, 1942-45; Comd Kohat (Independent) Bde, 1945-46. Despatches five times. GOC Bihar and Orissa Area, India, 1946-47; retired, 1947; Sec., Hereford Diocesan Board of Finance, 1947-61. *Address:* Aynhoe Park, near Banbury, Oxon. *T:* Goughton 641. *Club:* United Service.

**EKING, Maj.-Gen. (Retd) Harold Cecil William,** CB 1959; CBE 1954; DSO 1945; retired Jan. 1960; *b* 17 Nov. 1903; *s* of Harold Turney Eking; *m* 1st 1933, Eileen (*née* Brewer); one *s*; 2nd, 1943, Betty (*née* Stokes); one *d. Educ:* Rugby Sch.; RMA Woolwich. Commissioned Royal Engineers, 1924; Staff Coll., 1940; GSO1, 4 Div., 1941; 46 Div., 1942-43; CRE, 78 Div., 1943-44; CE, 13 Corps, 1944; Comd Engr Gp, Italy and Burma, 1945-46; CRE, Bde Comd and 2 i/c 10 Indian Div., 1946-47; Col GS, SME, 1948-50; Col AQ, Hong Kong, 1950; DDPS, War Office, 1951-54; Comdt, Sch. of Military Engineering, 1954-56; Chief Engineer, HQ Northern Army Group, 1956-60. *Address:* Pugg's Meadow, Kington Magna, Gillingham, Dorset. *Club:* Royal Automobile.

**EKLUND, Dr (Arne) Sigvard;** Director General, International Atomic Energy Agency, Vienna, since Dec. 1961; *b* Kiruna, Sweden, 1911; *m* 1941, Anna-Greta Johansson; one *s* two *d. Educ:* Uppsala Univ., Sweden (DSc). Assoc. Prof. in Nuclear Physics, Royal Inst. of Technology, Stockholm, 1946-56; Dir of Research, later Reactor development Div., AB Atomenergi, 1950-61. Conference Sec.-Gen., 2nd Internat. UN Conf. on Peaceful Uses of Atomic Energy, 1957-58. Fellow, Amer. Nuclear Soc., 1961; Mem., Royal Swedish Acad. of Engineering Sciences, 1953; Hon. Mem., British Nuclear Energy Soc., 1963. Dr hc Univ. of Graz, 1968. (Jointly) Atoms for Peace Award, 1968. *Publications:* Studies in Nuclear Physics, 1946 (Sweden). *Address:* International Atomic Energy Agency, Kärntnerring 11, 1010 Vienna I, Austria. *T:* Vienna 52 45 25.

**ELAM, Henry; His Honour Judge Elam;** Deputy Chairman of the Court of Quarter Sessions, Inner London, since 1954; barrister-at-law; *b* 29 Nov. 1903; *o s* of Thomas Henry Elam, 33 Sackville Street, W1; *m* 1930, Eunice, *yr d* of J. G. Matthews, 41 Redington Road, NW3; one *d. Educ:* Charterhouse; Lincoln Coll., Oxford (MA). Called to Bar, Inner Temple, 1927; Western Circuit; Junior Prosecuting Counsel to the Treasury, Central Criminal Court, 1937; late Dep. Judge Advocate, RAF; Recorder of Poole, 1941-46; 2nd Junior Prosecuting Counsel, 1942-45; 1st Junior, 1945-50; 3rd Senior, Jan.-March 1950; 2nd Senior, 1950-53; Recorder of Exeter, 1946-53; Dep. Chm., West Kent QS, 1947-53. Mem. of Tin Plate Workers' Co. *Recreation:* flyfishing. *Address:* White Gates, Burwash Common, Sussex. *T:* West Burwash 275; 5 Paper Buildings, Temple, EC4. *T:* 01-353 7811.

**ELATH, Eliahu,** PhD; President Emeritus, Hebrew University, Jerusalem; Israeli diplomatist; Chairman, Board of Governors, Israel Afro-Asian Institute; *b* 30 July 1903; *s* of Menachem and Rivka Epstein (Elath); *m* 1931, Zehava Zalel, *Educ:* Hebrew Univ., Jerusalem; American Univ., Beirut, Lebanon. Mem. Political Dept of Jewish Agency for Palestine in Jerusalem, 1934-45; Dir Political Office of Jewish Agency for Palestine in Washington, 1945-48; Special Representative of Provisional Govt of Israel in USA, 1947; Ambassador of Israel to USA, 1948-50; Minister of Israel, 1950-52, Ambassador, 1952-59, to the Court of St James's. Pres., Israel Oriental Soc. *Publications:* The Bedouin, Their Customs and Manners, 1933; Trans-Jordan, 1934; Israel and her Neighbours, 1960; The Political Struggle for Inclusion of Elath in the Jewish State, 1967; contribs to Quarterly of Palestine Exploration Fund, Jl of Royal Central Asian Society. *Address:* 17 Bialik Street, Beth Hakerem, Jerusalem, Israel.

**ELBORNE, Sydney Lipscomb,** MBE 1918; Chairman of Hunts Quarter Sessions, 1947-63; *b* 6 July 1890; *e s* of late William Elborne, MA, Wootton House, Peterborough; *m* 1925, Cavil Grace Mary, *d* of late George E. Monckton, Fineshade Abbey, Northants; one *s* one *d. Educ:* King's Sch., Peterborough; Trinity Coll. Cambridge (MA). Asst Inspector of High Explosives (Technical), The Royal Arsenal, Woolwich, 1914-18; called to Bar, Inner Temple, 1919; Mem. Midland Circuit; Mem. Gen. Council of the Bar, 1940-47; Mem. Hunts CC, 1930-45; JP Hunts, 1932. Pres. Soc. of Chairmen and Dep. Chm. of Quarter Sessions, 1955. Mem. Mr Justice Austen Jones's Cttee on County Court procedure, 1947; a Trustee and Mem. Council, Northants Record Soc.; formerly Trustee of Peterborough Museum Soc. and Maxwell Art Gallery; Mem. Area Cttee (No 11) Legal Aid, 1950-69. Contested (C) Leicester (Bosworth Div.), 1929 and Manchester (Ardwick), by-election, 1931. FRSA; formerly FGS, ARIC. *Address:* 5 Pump Court, Temple, EC4. *T:* 01-353 2628; Water Newton, near Peterborough. *T:* Castor 223. *Club:* Carlton.

**ELDER, Hugh,** MA; *b* 1905; *s* of late Rev. Hugh Elder, MA, Edinburgh; *m* 1939, Winifred Mary, *o d* of late Col M. Stagg, OBE, RE; one *s* (and one *s* decd). *Educ:* Edinburgh Academy; Edinburgh Univ. (Scholar); Corpus Christi Coll., Oxford. MA Hons Classics, Edinburgh, 1927; BA, Lit. Hum. 1929, MA 1934, Oxford. Asst Master at Sherborne Sch., 1929-35; Asst Master at Fettes Coll., 1935-38; Headmaster of Dean Close Sch., Cheltenham, 1938-46; Headmaster of Merchant Taylors' Sch., 1946-65. *Recreations:* music, golf. *Address:* Millbrook, Huish Episcopi, Langport, Somerset.

**ELDER, Sir (William) Stewart D.;** *see* Duke-Elder.

**ELDER-JONES, Thomas; His Honour Judge Elder-Jones;** Judge of County Courts, Circuit No 52 (Somerset, Wilts, etc); *b* 4 Oct. 1904; *o s* of late David Jones, JP, Foxcote Grange, Andoversford, shipowner, and late Anne Amelia (Roberts); *m* 1948, Hon. Diana

Katherine Taylor (*née* Russell), *o d* of 25th Baron de Clifford; one adopted *d* one step *s*. *Educ:* Shrewsbury; Trinity Coll., Oxford (MA). Barrister-at-law, Inner Temple, 1927. Served 1939-43, 2nd Royal Gloucestershire Hussars, retired, rank of Hon. Major. Sec. National Reference Tribunal for Coal Mining Industry, 1943-53; Judge of County Courts Circuit No. 34 (Brentford and Uxbridge), 1953-57. At Bar practised in Common Law and Coal Mining matters. *Recreation:* fox-hunting. *Address:* Somerford Keynes House, Cirencester, Glos. *T:* Ashton Keynes 296. *Clubs:* Oxford and Cambridge University, Cavalry.

**ELDON,** 4th Earl of, *cr* 1821; **John Scott;** Baron Eldon, 1799; Viscount Encombe, 1821; GCVO 1963 (KCVO 1952); Flight Lieutenant AAF; late Scots Guards; a Lord-in-Waiting to the Queen, 1952-68 (to King George VI, 1937-52); *b* 29 March 1899; *s* of late Viscount Encombe and Mary Laura Fraser (*d* 1946), *d* of 15th Baron Lovat; *S* Grandfather, 1926; *m* 1934, Hon. Magdalen Fraser, OBE 1953 (*d* 1969), *d* of 16th Baron Lovat; two *s*. *Educ:* Ampleforth Coll.; Magdalen Coll., Oxford. Served European War, 1918. Grand Officier, Légion d'Honneur. Owns about 10,000 acres. *Heir: s* Viscount Encombe, *qv*. *Address:* Cardrona House, Innerleithen, Peeblesshire. *T:* Innerleithen, 2426; 174 Cranmer Court, SW3. *T:* 01-589 0811. *Club:* White's.

**ELDRIDGE, Eric William,** CB 1965; OBE 1948; Public Trustee since 1963; *b* 15 April 1906; *o s* of late William Eldridge; *m* 1936, Doris Margaret Kerr; one *s* one *d*. *Educ:* Millfields Central Sch.; City of London Coll. Admitted Solicitor (Hons), 1934. Chief Administrative Officer, Public Trustee Office, 1955-60; Asst Public Trustee, 1960-63. *Address:* Old Stocks, Gorelands Lane, Chalfont St Giles, Bucks. *T:* Chalfont St Giles 2159.

**ELDRIDGE, Lt-Gen. Sir (William) John,** KBE 1954 (CBE 1941); CB 1944; DSO 1919; MC; Chairman, Kearney and Trecker, CVA Ltd, 1957-68; *b* 2 March 1898; *s* of late William Henry Eldridge; *m* 1954, Violet Elizabeth (*d* 1956), *e d* of John Cane, Wrexham. 2nd Lieut RA 1915; served European War, France and Belgium, 1916-18 (wounded, despatches twice, DSO, MC); Iraq Operations, 1919-20; War of 1939-45 (despatches, CBE, Bar to DSO). Dir-Gen. of Artillery, Ministry of Supply, 1945-48; Comdt Mil. Coll. of Science, 1948-51; GOC Aldershot District, 1951-53; Controller of Munitions, Min. of Supply, 1953-57, retired. Col Comdt: RA, 1951-61; Glider Pilot Regt, Glider Pilot and Parachute Corps, 1951-57. *Address:* Fir Acre, Ash Vale, Surrey. *Club:* Royal Air Force.

**ELEK, Prof. Stephen Dyonis,** MD, DSc; Professor of Medical Microbiology in the University of London since 1957; Consultant Bacteriologist, St George's Hospital, SW1, since 1948; *b* 24 March 1914; *s* of Dezso and Anna Elek; *m* Sarah Joanna Hall; three *d*. *Educ:* Lutheran High Sch., Budapest, Hungary; St George's Hosp. Med. Sch., Univ. of London. MB, BS 1940; MD 1943; PhD 1948; DPH 1943; DSc 1958; MRCP 1960; FCPath 1964. Clinical Pathologist, Maida Vale Hosp. for Nervous Diseases, 1946-47; Laking-Dakin Fellow, 1942-43; Fulbright Fellow, Harvard Medical Sch., 1956. Member: Royal Society of Medicine; Pathological Soc. of Great Britain; American Society for Microbiology; New York Academy of Sciences; Soc. of Gen. Microbiology, etc. *Publications:* Staphylococcus pyogenes and its Relation to Disease, 1959; scientific papers in Lancet, BMJ, Jl Path. and Bact., Brit. Jl Exper. Path., etc. *Recreations:* sculpting, walking. *Address:* 7 Fife Road, East Sheen, SW14. *T:* 01-878 1799; St George's Hospital, SW1. *T:* 01-235 5835. *Club:* Athenæum.

**ELEY, Prof. Daniel Douglas,** OBE 1961; FRS 1964; ScD, PhD Cantab; MSc, PhD Manchester; Professor of Physical Chemistry, University of Nottingham, since 1954; Dean of Faculty of Pure Science, 1959-62; *b* 1 Oct. 1914; *s* of Daniel Eley and Fanny Allen Ross; *m* 1942, Brenda May Williams, MA, MB, BChir (Cantab), 2nd *d* of B. T. Williams, Skewen, Glam; one *s*. *Educ:* Christ's Coll., Finchley; Manchester Univ.; St John's Coll., Cambridge. Manchester Univ.: Mercer Schol. 1934, Darbishire Fellow 1936, PhD 1937; PhD, 1940, ScD 1954, Cambridge. Bristol Univ.: Lectr in Colloid Chemistry, 1945; Reader in Biophysical Chemistry, 1961. Reilly Lectr, Univ. of Notre Dame (USA), 1950. Medal of Liege Univ., 1950; Mem. Council of Faraday Soc., 1951-54, 1960-63; Vice-Pres., 1963-. Meetings Sec., British Biophysical Soc., 1961-, Hon. Sec., 1963-65. Scientific Assessor to Sub-Cttee on Coastal Pollutions, House of Commons Select Cttee on Science and Technology, 1967-68. *Publications:* Ed., Adhesion, 1961; papers in Trans Faraday Soc., Proc. Royal Soc., Jl Chem. Soc., Biochem. Jl, etc. *Recreations:* hill walking, lawn tennis, skiing. *Address:* Chemistry Department, Nottingham University, University Park, Nottingham.

**ELEY, Sir Geoffrey (Cecil Ryves),** Kt 1964; CBE 1947; Chairman: Thomas Tilling Ltd; Heinemann Group of Publishers Ltd; Vice-Chairman, The British Oxygen Co. Ltd; Deputy Chairman, British Bank of the Middle East; Director, Equity & Law Life Assurance Society; Member Committee, Royal United Kingdom Benevolent Association; Vice-President, Middle East Association; *b* 18 July 1904; *s* of late Charles Cuthbert Eley, JP, VMH, East Bergholt Place, Suffolk, and of Ethel Maxwell Eley (*née* Ryves); *m* 1937, Penelope Hughes, *d* of late Adm. Sir Frederick Wake-Walker, KCB, CBE, and of Lady Wake-Walker, East Bergholt Lodge, Suffolk; two *s* two *d*. *Educ:* Eton; Trinity Coll., Cambridge; Harvard Univ. (Davison Scholar). On Editorial Staff of Financial News, 1926-28; banking, finance and brokerage in England, France, Switzerland and the USA, 1928-32; London Manager of Post and Flagg, members of New York Stock Exchange, 1932-39; Naval Intelligence Div., Admiralty, 1939-40; Capital Issues Cttee, 1940-41; Min. of Supply as Dir of Contracts in charge of Capital Assistance to Industry, 1941-46; Min. of Supply as Dir of Overseas Disposals, 1946-47; Chm., British Drug Houses Ltd, 1948-65; Dep. Chm. and Chm., Brush Group, 1953-58; Chairman: Richard Thomas & Baldwin's Ltd, 1959-64; Richard Crittall Holdings Ltd, 1948-68; Dir, Bank of England, 1949-66; High Sheriff, Co. of London, 1954-55; High Sheriff of Greater London, 1966. *Recreations:* gardening, the arts, foreign travel. *Address:* 13 Holland Villas Road, W14. *T:* 01-603 6265; The Change House, Great Yeldham, Essex. *T:* Great Yeldham 260. *Clubs:* United University, Beefsteak; Royal Harwich Yacht (Woolverstone).

**ELEY, John L.;** *see* Lloyd-Eley.

**ELGIN,** 11th Earl of, *cr* 1633, and **KINCARDINE,** 15th Earl of, *cr* 1647; **Andrew Douglas Alexander Thomas Bruce,** DL; JP; Baron Bruce of Kinloss, 1604, Baron Bruce of Torry, 1647; Baron Elgin (UK), 1849; late Scots Guards; member of Royal Company of Archers, HM Body Guard for Scotland; *b* 17 Feb. 1924; *e s* of 10th Earl of Elgin, KT, CMG,

TD and Hon. Katherine Elizabeth Cochrane (DBE 1938), *er d* of 1st Baron Cochrane of Cults; *S* father, 1968; *m* 1959, Victoria, *o d* of Dudley Usher, MBE and Mrs Usher of Larach Bhan, Kilchrennan, Argyll; two *s* two *d*. *Educ:* Eton; Balliol College, Oxford (BA Hons, MA Hons). Served War of 1939-45 (wounded). Director: Dominion Ins. Co.; Gurr, Johns & Co.; Wine Traders Consortium (Scotland) Ltd; United Dominions Trust, Scottish Local Board; Scottish Amicable Life Assurance Soc., 1970-. County Cadet Commandant, Fife, 1952-65. DL County Fife. Grand Master Mason of Scotland, 1961-65. Brigade Pres. of the Boys' Brigade. Freeman, City of Bridgetown, Barbados. *Heir: s* Lord Bruce, *qv*. *Address:* Broomhall, Dunfermline. *T:* Limekilns 222; Flat 15, 35 Bryanston Square, W1. *Clubs:* Beefsteak, Guards, Pratt's; New (Edinburgh); Royal Scottish Automobile (Pres.) (Glasgow).

**ELGOOD, Captain Leonard Alsager,** OBE 1919; MC 1915; DL; JP; FRSE; Director, The Distillers Co. Ltd, 1943-60; Chairman, United Glass Ltd, 1951-61; Director, Royal Bank of Scotland, 1946-66, Extraordinary Director, since 1966; Chairman of Committee on Natural Resources of Scotland (Scottish Council for Development and Industry), 1958-62; *b* 13 Dec. 1892; *s* of late William Alsager Elgood, Dundee, and late Mrs Elgood; *m* 1917, Jenny Coventry Wood, *d* of late R. A. Harper Wood and late Mrs Wood, Perth; two *s*. *Educ:* Dundee High Sch. Served with the Black Watch (Capt.), 1914-19 (despatches thrice); retd, 1919. Chartered Accountant, 1919; Sec., John Dewar & Sons Ltd, Perth, 1936; Sec., The Distillers Co. Ltd, 1939. DL 1948, JP 1943, County of the City of Edinburgh. *Address:* 16 Cumlodden Avenue, Edinburgh EH12 6DR. *T:* 031-337 6919.

**ELIBANK,** 13th Baron *cr* 1643 (Scotland); **James Alastair Frederick Campbell Erskine-Murray;** Bt of Nova Scotia, 1628; *b* 23 June 1902; *s* of James Robert Erskine-Murray, DSc, Sqdn Ldr RAF, and Alleine F. F., *d* of Maj.-Gen. G. F. Gildea, CB; *S* to Barony and Btcy of kinsman, 3rd and last Viscount Elibank, 1962. *Educ:* Harrow; RMC Sandhurst. MA (2nd Class Hons in History), Glasgow, 1952. Commissioned 2nd Lieut, 1922; joined 2nd HLI, 1922; Lieut 1924; RARO, 1933; Capt. 1939; Major 1944. Served War of 1939-45. France, Dep. Asst Provost Marshal, Medical Base Sub-Area, Dieppe, Sept. 1939, and Le Havre, May 1940; OC Provost Co. 51 Div., June-Dec. 1940; Dep. Asst Provost Marshal, Port Said, 1941; attached Physical Trng, MEF, 1941-45; Asst Camp Comdt, GHQ, MEF, March-June 1945; UK 1945. Student Univ. of Glasgow, 1947. Cttee Scottish Centre of Outdoor Training, Scottish Council of Physical Recreation, 1950; Scottish HQ Commissioner for Rover Scouts, 1951-62; Hon. Adviser in Recreational Training to Scottish HQ, Boy Scouts Assoc., 1963. Convener, Murray Clan Association. Mem. Soc. of Scottish Artists; FSAScot. *Recreations:* piping, sketching, mountaineering. *Heir: cousin* Alan D'Ardis Erskine-Murray [*b* 31 Dec. 1923; *m* 1962, Valerie Sylvia, *d* of Herbert William Dennis; two *s*]. *Address:* 3 Duncan Street, Edinburgh 9. *T:* 031-667 3983. *Club:* Royal Over-Seas League.

**ELIOT,** family name of **Earl of St Germans.**

**ELIOT, Lord; Peregrine Nicholas Eliot;** *b* 2 Jan. 1941; *o s* of 9th Earl of St Germans, *qv*, and of late Helen Mary, *d* of late Lieut-Col Charles Walter Villiers, CBE, DSO, and Lady Kathleen Villiers; *m* 1964, Hon. Jacquetta Jean Frederika Lampson, *d* of 1st Baron Killearn and Jacqueline Aldine Lesley (*née* Castellani); two *s*. *Educ:* Eton, *Recreation:* mucking about. *Heir: s* Hon. Jago Nicholas Eliot, *b* 24 March 1966. *Address:* Port Eliot, St Germans, Cornwall. *Clubs:* Bath; Cornish.

**ELIOT, Ven. Peter Charles,** MBE 1945; TD 1945; Archdeacon of Worcester since 1961; Residentiary Canon, Worcester Cathedral, since 1965; *b* 30 Oct. 1910; *s* of late Hon. Edward Granville Eliot and late Mrs Eliot; *m* 1934, Lady Alethea Constance Dorothy Sydney Buxton, *d* of 1st and last Earl Buxton, PC, GCMG, and late Countess Buxton; no *c*. *Educ:* Wellington Coll.; Magdalene Coll., Cambridge. Commissioned in Kent Yeomanry (Lt-Col Comdg, 1949-52), 1933. Admitted Solicitor, 1934; Partner in City firm until 1953. Studied at Westcott House, Cambridge, 1953-54; made Deacon to serve in Parish of St Martin-in-the-Fields, London, 1954; Priest, 1955; Vicar of Cockermouth, 1957-61; Rural Dean of Cockermouth and Workington, 1960-61; Vicar of Cropthorne with Charlton, 1961-65. *Recreations:* amateur acting (Canterbury Old Stagers); sketching; sight-seeing. *Address:* 12 College Green, Worcester. *T:* Worcester 23538. *Club:* Travellers'.

**ELIOTT of Stobs, Sir Arthur Francis Augustus Boswell,** 11th Bt *cr* 1666; Chief of the Clan Elliot; *b* 2 Jan. 1915; *s* of Sir Gilbert Alexander Boswell, 10th Bt, and Dora Flournoy Adams, *o d* of late Alexander Stephens Hopkins, Atlanta, Georgia, USA; *S* father, 1958; *m* 1947, Frances Aileen, *e d* of late Sir Francis McClean, AFC; one *d*. *Educ:* Harrow; King's Coll., Cambridge. BA 1936, MA 1949. 2nd Lieut, King's Own Scottish Borderers (TA), 1939, Major, 1944. Served in East Africa and Burma with King's African Rifles, 1941-45. Member of Queen's Body Guard for Scotland, Royal Company of Archers. *Address:* 17 Montagu Square, W1. *T:* 01-935 3542; Redheugh, Newcastleton, Roxburghshire. *T:* Liddesdale 213. *Clubs:* Carlton; New (Edinburgh); Leander.

**ELIOTT LOCKHART, Sir Allan (Robert),** Kt 1953; CIE 1943; *b* 3 Aug. 1905; *s* of late Col R. H. Eliott Lockhart, Royal Scots Greys, and M. C., *d* of William Eliott Lockhart, Cleghorn, Lanark; *m* 1939, Roslyn Maurice (marr. diss., 1947), *d* of Maurice Barton, Sydney, NSW; two *s*; *m* 1947, Sonia, *widow* of Major Hugh Lyons-Montgomery, *d* of B. C. J. Oldrini, Chilwell, Beeston, Notts; one *s*. *Educ:* Harrow. Lanarkshire Yeomanry, 1923-30. gladstone Lyall & Co. Ltd, Calcutta, 1926-58, Managing Dir, 1948-58; Stewarts & Lloyds Ltd, 1958-67. Director: Taylor Forge Ltd; Stewarts & Lloyds of India Ltd. Chm., Calcutta Branch of European Assoc., 1937-39; Mem. of All India Council, 1932-39; MLC Bengal, 1931-37; Dept of Supply, Govt of India, 1940-46; Dir-Gen. of Munitions Production, 1945-46; Pres. Associated Chambers of Commerce and Bengal Chamber of Commerce and Industry, 1951-52; Pres., UK Citizen's Assoc. of India, 1954-55. *Recreation:* shooting. *Address:* Willows, Darby Green, Camberley, Surrey. *T:* Yateley 2172; Cleghorn, Lanark. *T:* Lanark 2318. *Clubs:* Oriental; Bengal, Tollygunge, etc (Calcutta).

**ELKES, Prof. Joel,** MD, ChB; FACP, FAPA; Henry Phipps Professor and Director, Department of Psychiatry and Behavioral Sciences, The Johns Hopkins University School of Medicine, since 1963; Psychiatrist-in-Chief, The Johns Hopkins Hospital, Baltimore, Maryland, since 1963; *b* 12 Nov. 1913; *s* of Dr Elkanan Elkes and Miriam (*née* Malbin); *m* 1943, Dr Olwyn Charmian Bourne;

one *d*. *Educ:* private schools; Lithuania and Switzerland; Univ. of Birmingham Med. Sch. (MB, ChB 1947; MD Hons 1949). MRCS, LRCP 1941. University of Birmingham: Sir Halley Stewart Research Fellow, 1942-45; Lectr, Dept of Pharmacology, 1945-48; Senior Lectr and Actg Head of Dept, 1948-50; Prof. and Chm., Dept of Experimental Psychiatry, 1951-57; Clinical Professor of Psychiatry, George Washington Univ. Med. Sch., Washington, 1957-63; Chief of Clinical Neuropharmacology Research Center, Nat. Inst of Mental Health, Washington, 1957-63; Dir, Behavioral and Clinical Studies Center St Elizabeth's Hosp., Washington, 1957-63; Dir, Foundns Fund for Research in Psychiatry, 1964-68; Consultant, WHO, 1957-. Vis. Fellow, New York Univ. and New England Med. Center, Boston, 1950. President: (first) Amer. Coll. of Neuropsychopharmacology, 1962; Amer. Psychopathological Assoc., 1968. Formerly Member: Council, Internat. Collegium N Psychopharm; Central Council, Internat. Brain Research Organisation, UNESCO (Chm., Sub-Cttee on Educn). Fellow, Amer. Acad. of Arts and Sciences. Member: RSM; RMPA; Physiological Soc., Gt Britain; Pharmacological Soc., Gt Britain; British Psychological Soc.; British Electro Encephalographic Soc.; Soc. for Study of Drug Addiction; Amer. Soc. for Pharmacology and Experimental Therapeutics; Soc. of Biological Psychiatry; Acad. of Medicine, Washington; New York Acad. of Science; Sigma Xi; Scientific Assoc.; Acad. of Psychoanalysis. *Publications:* papers to various jls and symposia. *Recreations:* sleep, painting. *Address:* 3925 Canterbury Road, Baltimore, Md 21218, USA. *Clubs:* Cosmos (Washington); West Hamilton Street (Baltimore).

**EL-KHALIFA, Sir-El-Khatim,** (Hon.) GCMG 1965; Sudanese Ambassador to the Court of St James's, 1965-69; *b* 1 Jan. 1919; Sudanese parentage; *m* 1964, Zahra El-Fadil Mahmoud; one *s* one *d*. *Educ:* Old Gordon Memorial Coll., Khartoum; Teachers' Section, Gordon Coll.; Univ. Coll. of the South West, Exeter. *Recreations:* reading, swimming. *Address:* c/o Ministry of Foreign Affairs, Khartoum, Sudan.

**ELKIN, Adolphus Peter,** CMG 1966; PhD; retired as Professor of Anthropology, University of Sydney (1933-56), now Emeritus Professor; *b* 27 March 1891; *s* of Reuben and Ellen Elkin; *m* 1922, Sara Thompson; two *s*. *Educ:* East Maitland High Sch.; St Paul's Coll., Sydney; University of Sydney (MA); University of London (PhD). C of E Clergyman (Parishes), 1915-25; Australian Nat. Research Council Fellow, 1927-31. Editor (Hon.) of Oceania (Internat. Jl of Anthropology), 1933-; Founder (1966) and Editor (hon.), Jl of Archæology and Physical Anthropology in Oceania. Pres., Royal Soc. of New South Wales, 1941; Vice-Chm., Aborigines' Welfare Board of New South Wales, 1941-69; Chm., Aust. Nat. Research Council, 1953-55. Crown Trustee, 1946-, and Pres. 1961-68, the Australian Museum; Fellow of Senate, Univ. of Sydney, 1959-69; Mem. Council (Chm. Finance Cttee) Internat. House (Univ. of Sydney), 1966-. Macrossan Memorial Lectr, Univ. of Queensland, 1944; David Lectr (Aust. and NZ Assoc. for the Advancement of Science), 1949; Centenary Oration, Royal Soc. of NSW, 1966. Hon. Life Fellow, Pacific Science Assoc., 1961. DLitt *hc* Sydney, 1970. Medal of Royal Society of NSW, 1949; James Cook Medal, 1955; Mueller Medal, 1957; H. E. Gregory Medal, 1961. *Publications:* The Australian Aborigines: How to Understand Them, 1938 (4th edn 1964); Our Opinions and the National Effort, 1941; Society, the Individual and Change, 1941; Wanted–a Charter for the Peoples of the South-West Pacific, 1943; Citizenship for the Aborigines, 1944; Social Anthropology in Melanesia, 1953; The Diocese of Newcastle: A History, 1955; Aboriginal Men of High Degree, 1946; Pacific Science Association: Its History and Role in International Cooperation, 1961.; contribs to Oceania, American Anthropologist, etc. *Recreations:* music; formerly cricket and tennis. *Address:* 15 Norwood Avenue, Lindfield, NSW 2070, Australia. *T:* Sydney 46.4521. *Club:* University of Sydney Staff.

**ELKINGTON, Reginald Geoffrey,** CB 1962; Establishment Officer (part-time), Monopolies Commission; *b* 24 Dec. 1907; *s* of Harold and Millicent Elkington; *m* 1935, Bertha Phyllis, *d* of William and Bertha Dyason; one adopted *s* one adopted *d*. *Educ:* Battersea Grammar Sch.; Fitzwilliam Coll., Cambridge. Inland Revenue, 1929-42; Min. of Supply, 1942-57 (Under-Sec., 1954); DSIR, 1957-65; Principal Establishment Officer, Min. of Technology, 1964-67; retired from Civil Service, 1967. Sec., AERE Harwell, 1948-51. *Recreations:* gardening, motoring. *Address:* Maranwood, Highfield Road, West Byfleet, Surrey. *T:* Byfleet 43766.

**ELKINGTON, Reginald Lawrence,** CBE 1957; retired as Controller of Export Licensing, Board of Trade (1947-58); *b* 25 May 1898; *s* of Edwin and Sarah Elkington; *m* 1925, Doris May Humphreys; one *s*. *Educ:* King Edward VI Grammar Sch., Totnes. Commissioned, 1917; served in France with West Yorkshire Regt and Tank Corps. Entered Customs and Excise Dept, 1919. Board of Trade, 1939; Asst Sec. 1952. *Recreations:* bowls, gardening, travel, bridge, etc. *Address:* 30 Blenheim Road, SW20. *T:* 01-542 1912.

**ELKINS, Sir Anthony (Joseph),** Kt 1952; CBE 1944; Chairman: British Match Corp. Ltd; Gestetner Ltd; Vice-Chairman, Army & Navy Stores Ltd; *b* 30 May 1904; *s* of late Dr and Mrs F. A. Elkins, Herts; *m* 1930, Mabel Brenda Barker (decd); three *s* one *d*; *m* 1944, Ines Erna Miller (*née* Neele) (marr. diss.); *m* 1969, Nora Christianne Elliot (*née* Rowe). *Educ:* Haileybury Coll. With Gillanders Arbuthnot & Co. Ltd in India, 1924-54 (Chm., 1945-54); Chm., Darjeeling-Himalayan Railway Co. Ltd, 1945-54. Controller of Supplies (Bengal Circle), 1941-45; President: Bengal Chamber of Commerce, 1949; Associated Chambers of Commerce of India, 1949; UK Citizens' Assoc. of India, 1953; Inst. of Export, 1967-70; Vice-Pres., Imperial Bank of India (Bengal Circle), 1949. Chm. of Bryant & May Ltd, 1955-64. Chairman: London and South-Eastern Resettlement Cttee, Regular Forces Resettlement Service; London Regional Industrial Cttee, Nat. Savings Movement. *Address:* 59 Moscow Road, Bayswater, W2. *T:* 01-229 2117. *Clubs:* Oriental; Bengal, Royal Calcutta Turf (Calcutta), etc.

*See also Sir Robert Elkins.*

**ELKINS, Vice-Adm. (Retd) Sir Robert (Francis),** KCB 1958 (CB 1954); CVO 1952; OBE 1942; *b* 12 Jan. 1903; *er s* of Dr F. A. Elkins, Leavesden, Kings Langley; *m* 1940, Gwendolen Hurst Flint. *Educ:* RNC, Osborne and Dartmouth. Qualified as Interpreter (German), 1928; specialised in Gunnery, 1929; Commander, 1937; in comd HMS Bideford, 1939-40; Prisoner of War, 1940; Comdr, HMS Renown, 1940; Capt. Dec. 1942; in comd HMS Dido, 1944-45; idc 1949; in comd HMS Ocean, 1949-50; in comd HMS Excellent, 1950-52; ADC to King George VI, 1952; ADC to the

Queen until July 1952; Rear-Adm. 1952; Vice-Adm. 1955; Flag Officer, 2nd in Comd, Far East Station, 1955-56; Admiral, British Joint Staff Mission, Washington, 1956-58, retired 1959. *Recreations:* all outdoor sports. *Address:* Branlea, Foreland Road, Bembridge, IoW. *T:* Bembridge 2522. *Club:* United Service.
*See also Sir Anthony Elkins.*

**ELLACOMBE, Air Cdre John Lawrence Wemyss,** CB 1970; DFC 1942 (Bar 1944). Director of Operations (Air Defence and Overseas) Ministry of Defence (Air) since 1970; *b* Livingstone, N. Rhodesia, 28 Feb. 1920; *s* of Dr Gilbert H. W. Ellacombe; *m* 1951, Wing Officer Mary Hibbert, OBE, WRAF; one *s* two *d*. *Educ:* Diocesan Coll., Rondebosch, Cape. War of 1939-45: RAF, 1939; Fighter Command and Two ATA Force, 1940-45 (Pilot, Battle of Britain). Aden, 1946-48; RAF Staff Coll., 1948-49; Fighter Command, 1949-57; BJSM, Washington, 1959. JSSC, 1959-60; Gp Capt., Co, RAF Linton on Ouse, to Nov 1962; CFE, to Aug. 1965; Defence Operational Analysis Estabt, West Byfleet, 1965-68; Air Cdre, Commander Air Forces Gulf, 1968-70. *Recreations:* photography, golf, cricket. *Address:* c/o Lloyds Bank, 6 Pall Mall, SW1. *Club:* Royal Air Force.

**ELLENBERGER, Lt-Col Jules,** CMG 1925; ISO 1922; *b* 16 Jan. 1871; 5th *s* of late Rev. D. F. Ellenberger, Basutoland; *m* 1895, Fanny Sarah, *d* of late Eugene Casalis, MD, Paris; one *s*. *Educ:* Lovedale, South Africa; Lycée St Louis, Paris. Joined Bechuanaland Protectorate Service, 1890; Actg Asst Comr, Northern District, 1892, 1894; Interpreter: (English-Sechuana) to Bechuanaland Protectorate Concessions Commn, 1893; Sir Sidney Shippard's Boundary Commn (Bechuanaland Protectorate), 1894; Asst Resident Magistrate, 1898. Served South African War: Advanced Armoured Train from Rhodesia; with Plumer's Column to Relief of Mafeking. Comr for Oath of Allegiance, 1901; Asst Comr, Southern Protectorate, 1902; Mem., Sir Ralph Williams' special mission to Ngamiland, 1906; Special Comr, Ngamiland and Resident Magistrate, Northern Protectorate, 1908; Govt Sec., 1916; Actg Resident Comr, 1920, 1921, 1923; Special Duty, Ngamiland and Ghanzi Districts, 1920-21; Resident Comr, Bechuanaland Protectorate, 1923 (in command of Police with local rank of Lt-Col); retired, 1927. Represented: Bechuanaland Protectorate Govt at fixing of N-Eastern and N-Western beacons of Caprivi Zipfel; Northern Rhodesia, N-Western beacon, Angola-Caprivi Boundary, 1930; Chief Cordon Officer, Foot and Mouth Disease, Bechuanaland Protectorate, 1933; acted for Bechuanaland Govt, Commn to settle estate of Linchwe, late Chief of Bakgatla Tribe, 1935. JP Bechuanaland, 1891. *Address:* c/o PO Box 790, Salisbury, Rhodesia.

**ELLENBOROUGH,** 8th Baron *cr* 1802; **Richard Edward Cecil Law;** Partner, McAnally, Montgomery & Co. (Stockbrokers); Director, Towry Law & Co.; *b* 14 Jan. 1926; *s* of 7th Baron and Helen Dorothy, *o d* of late H. W. Lovatt; *S* father, 1945; *m* 1953, Rachel Mary, *o d* of late Major Ivor Hedley; three *s*. *Educ:* Eton Coll.; Magdalene Coll., Cambridge. Pres., National Union of Ratepayers, 1954-. *Heir:* *s* Hon. Rupert Edward Henry Law, *b* 28 March 1955. *Address:* Broadfield House, Wadhurst, Sussex. *T:* Wadhurst 2426. *Clubs:* Gresham, Turf.

**ELLERMAN, Sir John Reeves,** 2nd Bt *cr* 1905; Director of Ellerman Lines Ltd; *b* 21 Dec. 1909; *o s* of Sir John Ellerman, 1st Bt, CH, and Hannah (*d* 1939), *d* of George Glover; *S* father, 1933; *m* 1933, Esther, *d* of late Clarence De Sola, Montreal. *Heir:* none. *Address:* 19-21 Moorgate, EC2.

**ELLERTON, Air Commodore Alban Spenser,** CBE 1944 (OBE 1919); RAF; Air ADC to the King, 1944 (ADC, 1949); *b* 3 Oct. 1894; 6th *s* of Alfred Ellerton, Hampstead; *m* 1919, Maureen Gilliland, *o c* of T. F. Husband, ISO; two *s*. *Educ:* privately; Germany. Enlisted Coldstream Guards, Aug. 1914, on return from Germany; commission RFC 1916; Major HQ RFC 1917 (despatches twice); permanent commission RAF 1918; retd 1949. *Address:* 4 Mermaid Street, Rye, Sussex. *Club:* Royal Air Force.

**ELLERTON, Geoffrey James,** CMG 1963; MBE 1956; Director, Elder Dempster Lines; *b* 25 April 1920; *er s* of late Sir Cecil Ellerton; *m* 1946, Peggy Eleanor, *d* of late F. G. Watson; three *s*. *Educ:* Highgate Sch.; Hertford Coll., Oxford (MA). Military Service, 1940-45. Apptd Colonial Administrative Service as District Officer, Kenya, 1945. Acting Minister for Defence, 1960 and 1962. Retired as Permanent Sec., Prime Minister's Office and Sec. to the Cabinet, at time of Kenya's Independence, Dec. 1963. Sec. to the Maud and Mallaby Cttees on Management and Staffing in Local Government, 1964. *Recreation:* reading. *Address:* Cedar Court, Wood Lane, Parkgate, Cheshire. *T:* Neston 4413. *Clubs:* Reform, MCC; Nairobi.

**ELLICOTT, Langford Pannell,** CBE 1959; Chief Housing and Planning Inspector, Ministry of Housing and Local Government, 1961-68; *b* 29 April 1903; *s* of Ernest Albert Ellicott, Wells, Som, and Mary Ellen Ellicott (*née* Hartnett); *m* 1935, Florence Louise, *d* of Charles Farraghan, Wadebridge, Cornwall; one *d*. *Educ:* Sedbergh Sch., Yorks; University Coll., London. ARIBA, RIBA Distinction in Town Planning, MTPI. Housing and Planning Inspector, Ministry of Health, 1937; Sen. Planning Officer, London Region, Min. of Town and Country Planning, 1944-45; Regional Controller, W Midlands, 1946; Dep. Chief Planner, Min. of Town and Country Planning, later Min. of Housing and Local Govt, 1947-58; Chief Planner, 1959-60. *Recreations:* gardening, painting. *Address:* The Gate Cottage, Monken Hadley, Barnet, Herts. *T:* 01-449 3233.

**ELLINGTON, Hon. Edward Kennedy, (Duke);** pianist, composer and band leader; *b* Washington, DC, 29 April 1899. *Educ:* Armstrong High Sch.; studied music with Henry Grant. First professional appearance, 1916; New York, 1922; engaged Cotton Club, NYC, 1927-32; tours include: Europe, 1933, 1938, 1948, 1950, 1958, 1963, 1964, 1965, 1966, 1967, 1969; for US State Dept: Near and Middle East, 1963; Japan, 1964; Dakar, 1966; S America and Mexico, 1968; Scores for: Chocolate Kiddies, 1924; Jump for Joy, 1940; Beggar's Holiday, 1947; A Drum is a Woman, 1957; Anatomy of a Murder, 1959; Paris Blues, 1961; Turcaret, 1962; My People, 1963; Timon of Athens, 1963; Sugar City, 1964; Murder in the Cathedral, 1966. Major works include: Black Brown and Beige; Liberian Suite; Perfume Suite; Deep South Suite; Harlem; Shakespeare Suite (Such Sweet Thunder); Night Creature; Suite Thursday; Far East Suite; The Golden Broom and the Green Apple; First Sacred Concert, 1965; Second Sacred Concert, 1968. Member: Nat. Council on the Arts, 1968; Nat. Institute of Arts and Letters, 1970; American Academy of Arts and Sciences, 1970. Hon. degrees: Dr of Music: Wilberforce Univ., Ohio; Yale Univ.; Brown Univ., 1969; Dr of Humanities, Milton Coll.,

Wis.; Dr of Fine Arts, California Coll. of Arts and Crafts. President's Gold Medal, 1966; The Medal of Freedom, 1969. *Address:* 333 Riverside Drive, New York, NY 10025, USA.

**ELLINGWORTH, Richard Henry;** Head of Oil Department, Foreign and Commonwealth Office, since 1969; *b* 9 March 1926; *s* of Vincent Ellingworth; *m* 1952, Joan Mary Waterfield; one *s* three *d*. *Educ:* Uppingham; Aberdeen Univ.; Magdalen Coll., Oxford (Demy). Served War of 1939-45: RA, and Intelligence Corps, 1944-47. Oxford, 1947-50 (first Lit. Hum.); HM Embassy, Japan, 1951-55; FO, 1955-59; HM Embassy: Belgrade, 1959-63; Japan, 1963-68 (Olympic Attaché, 1964). *Publication:* An Anthology of Oratory (with A. N. Gilkes), 1946. *Recreations:* gardening, music, languages. *Address:* The Mount, Sparepenny Lane, Farningham, Kent. *T:* Farningham 3709. *Club:* Travellers'.

**ELLIOT;** *see* Scott-Elliot.

**ELLIOT,** family name of **Baroness Elliot of Harwood** and **Earl of Minto.**

**ELLIOT OF HARWOOD,** Baroness *cr* 1958 (Life Peer); **Katharine Elliot,** DBE 1958 (CBE 1946); JP; *b* 15 Jan. 1903; *d* of Sir Charles Tennant, 1st Bt, Innerleithen, Peeblesshire, and late Mrs Geoffrey Lubbock; *m* 1934, Rt Hon. Walter Elliot, PC, CH, MC, FRS, LLD, MP (*d* 1958); no *c*. *Educ:* Abbot's Hill, Hemel Hempstead; Paris. Chairman: Nat. Assoc. of Mixed Clubs and Girls' Clubs, 1939-49; Adv. Cttee on Child Care for Scotland, 1956-65; Women's Nat. Adv. Cttee of Conservative Party, 1954-57; Nat. Union of Conservative and Unionist Assocs, 1956-67; Carnegie UK Trust, 1965- (Trustee, 1937-); Consumer Council, 1963-68; Lawrie & Symington Ltd, Lanark. Member: Women's Consultative Cttee, Dept of Employment and Productivity (formerly Min. of Labour), 1941-51, 1958-70; Home Office Adv. Cttee on Treatment of Offenders, 1946-62; King George V Jubilee Trust, 1936-68; NFU. UK Delegate to Gen. Assembly of UN, New York, 1954, 1956 and 1957. Contested (C) Kelvingrove Div. of Glasgow, March 1958. Roxburghshire: CC 1946-; JP Roxburghshire, 1968-. Farms in Roxburghshire. FRSA 1964. Hon. LLD Glasgow, 1959. Grand Silver Cross, Austrian Order of Merit, 1963. *Recreations:* foxhunting, golf, music. *Address:* Harwood, Bonchester Bridge, Hawick, Roxburghshire; 17 Lord North Street, Westminster, SW1. *T:* 01-222 3230. *Club:* Queen's (Edinburgh).

**ELLIOT, Lt-Col Henry Hawes,** CIE 1941; MBE 1923; MC 1917; IMS, retd; *b* 22 May 1891; 6th *s* of late John Elliot, Binks, Roxburghshire. *Educ:* Monkton Combe Sch.; Durham; Edinburgh; Guy's Hospital. MB, BS Dunelm 1914; MRCS, LRCP 1915; FRCSE 1921; DMRE Cambridge 1926. commissioned RAMC, 1915; attached 8th Welch Regt and 2nd Rifle Bde, Gallipoli and France, 1915-18 (twice wounded); entered IMS 1921; Waziristan Field Force, 1922-24; transferred Foreign and Political Dept 1929; Surgeon British Legation, Kabul, 1930-35; Surgeon to the Viceroy, 1936-43; Chief Medical Officer, Baluchistan, 1944; retired, 1946. *Address:* Springbank, Melrose, Roxburghshire. *Clubs:* East India and Sports; New (Edinburgh).

**ELLIOT, James Robert McDowell,** CMG 1949; OBE 1945; *b* 1 Jan. 1896; *e s* of late Lieut-Col R. H. Elliot, IMS (and Ophthalmic Surgeon), and late Mrs E. C. I. Elliot; *m* 1922, Joan Helen Caudery, *d* of late Capt. A. S. Littlejohns, CMG, RN, and late Mrs Littlejohns; one *s* one *d*. *Educ:* Lancing Coll., Sussex. Served European War, 1914-19, in 2/4th Bn Wilts Regt, and Machine Gun Corps, Capt. (Actg Major). Cadet, Uganda, 1920; ADC 1922; District Officer, 1931; Senior District Officer, 1944; Provincial Commissioner, Uganda, 1945. Retired from Colonial Civil Service, Jan. 1950. Compiled labour enquiry reports, 1936 and 1937. *Address:* c/o National and Grindlay's Bank Ltd, 13 St James's Square, SW1; Flat A, 263 Goldhurst Terrace, NW6. *T:* 01-624 4393.

**ELLIOT, Sir John,** Kt 1954; industrialist, transport man, author; Sheriff of Greater London, 1970-71; Chairman, London & Provincial Poster Group Ltd; Director, Cie Internationale des Wagons-Lits; *b* London, 1898; *m* 1924, Elizabeth, *e d* of late Dr A. S. Cobbledick; one *s* one *d*. *Educ:* Marlborough; Sandhurst. European War in 3rd Hussars; after four years in journalism joined former Southern Rly, 1925, in charge public relations (first in UK) and advertising. Visited USA, Canada, frequently; Deputy General Manager, Southern Rly, 1937, Gen. Manager, 1947; Chief Regional Officer, Southern Region, British Railways, 1948-49. London Midland Region, Euston, 1950-51; Chairman: Railway Exec., 1951-53; London Transport, 1953-59; Pullman Car Co., 1959-63; Thos. Cook & Son Ltd, 1959-67; Willing & Co. Ltd, 1959-70. director: Commonwealth Development Corp., 1959-66; Railway Air Service Ltd, 1933-48; Thomas Tilling Ltd, 1959-70; British Airports Authority, 1965-69. Vice-Pres., Internat. Union of Railways (UIC), 1947 and 1951-53. Formerly Col. (Comdg) Engineer and Railway Staff Corps, Royal Engineers, 1956-63. Visited Australia, 1949, at invitation of Govt of Victoria, to report on rail and road transport and E Africa, 1969, on transport study (World Bank), 1968. MInstT (Pres., 1953-54). Mem. Société de l'histoire de Paris, 1958. Officier, Légion d'Honneur; American Medal of Freedom. *Publications:* The Way of the Tumbrils (Paris during the Revolution); Where our Fathers Died; regular newspaper feature, Speaking of That . . .; book reviews; many papers on transport. *Recreations:* gardening, shooting, cricket, reading history. *Address:* Stonyfield, Great Easton, Dunmow, Essex. *Clubs:* Cavalry, MCC.

**ELLIOT, Captain Walter,** DSC 1944; RN Retd; MP (C) Carshalton and Banstead since 1960; *b* 17 Feb. 1910; *s* of John White Elliot and Frances Hampson; *m* 1936, Thelma Pirie Thomson; four *d*. *Educ:* HMS Conway; Royal Naval Coll. Joined RN, 1929; specialised in Naval Aviation. Served War of 1939-45 (DSC, despatches); retired, 1958. Took Economics Degree, London Univ., 1958 (BSc Econ). In business, 1958-60. *Recreations:* fencing, fishing, tennis. *Address:* House of Commons, SW1.

**ELLIOT, Air Chief Marshal Sir William,** GCVO 1953; KCB 1951 (CB 1944); KBE 1946 (CBE 1942); DFC 1918; *b* 1896; *s* of late Gilbert John Elliot; *m* 1951, Rosemary, *d* of Sir John Chancellor, GCMG, GCVO, GBE, DSO; one *s* one *d*. *Educ:* Switzerland; Tonbridge Sch. Served European War, 1914-18 (despatches, DFC and bar), South Russia, 1919; Asst Sec. to Cttee of Imperial Defence, 1937-39, and to War Cabinet, 1939-41; Fighter Command, 1941-42; Director of Plans, Air Ministry, 1942-44; AOC RAF, Gibraltar, Feb.-June 1944; AOC Balkan Air Force, 1944-45; Asst Chief Exec., Ministry of Aircraft Production, 1945-46; Asst Chief of Air Staff (Policy), 1946-47; C-in-C, Fighter Command, 1947-49; Chief Staff Officer to Minister of Defence and Dep. Sec. (Mil.) to Cabinet, 1949-51; Chm. of British Joint Services Mission, Washington, and UK Representative on the Standing

Group of the Military Cttee of the North Atlantic Treaty Organisation, 1951-54. ADC to King George VI, 1950-52; ADC to the Queen, 1952-54. Chm. of Council, Royal Institute of International Affairs, Chatham House, 1954-58. *Address:* Stourpaine House, near Blandford, Dorset. *Clubs:* Brooks's, Buck's.

**ELLIOT-SMITH, Alan Guy,** CBE 1957; *b* 30 June 1904; *s* of late F. Elliot-Smith; *m* 1939, Ruth Kittermaster; no *c. Educ:* Charterhouse; Oriel Coll., Oxford. Hons Mod. Lang. Sch., 1925; Asst Master, Harrow Sch., 1925-40; Headmaster, Cheltenham Coll., 1940-51; Mem., Harrow UDC, 1933-36; Deleg. to Inst. of Pacific Relations Conf., Calif., 1936; lectured to German teachers on Education, 1947 and 1948; lectured to Service units in the Middle East, 1949; Head-master of Victoria Coll., Cairo, 1952-56; Representative in Nigeria of the West Africa Cttee, 1957-58; Headmaster, Markham Coll., Lima, Peru, 1960-63. *Recreations:* travel, reading. *Address:* Bevois Mount, Rowsley Road, Eastbourne, Sussex.

**ELLIOTT, Albert George,** CBE 1941; retired as Executive Vice-Chairman, 1955 (Joint Managing Director, 1951-55 and Chief Engineer, 1937-55), Rolls-Royce Ltd; *b* 3 Dec. 1889; *m* 1st, 1921, Cecilia, *d* of late Rennie Gray, Aberdeen; one *d* (decd); 2nd, 1962, Ann, *d* of late George Wrightson, Kirk Ireton, Derbs. *Educ:* Northampton Engineering Coll.; London Univ. Responsible for engine design with Napier Co.; joined Rolls-Royce Co. in 1912 to take charge of Engine Drawing Office, was attached to Sir H. Royce's personal staff and worked with him for 20 years; Chief Designer, 1929, responsible for both Car and Aero Engine Design; Chief Engineer of Aero Div., 1937; Chief Engineer and appointed to Board, 1945. Tech. Dir, Rotol Ltd, Cheltenham, 1946-55; Mem., Air Registration Bd, 1947-58; Gov., Loughborough Coll., 1950-62; Mem., Air Safety Bd, 1955-65; CEng; FRAeS; MIMechE; FRSA; Brit. Gold Medal, RAeS, 1954. *Recreations:* motoring, art, yachting. *Address:* Flat 3, Oceania, West Parade, Bexhill-on-Sea, Sussex. *Club:* Royal Automobile.

**ELLIOTT, Rt. Rev. Anthony Blacker,** DD; Warden, Church of South India Retreat House, Alir, since 1959; *b* 1887; *s* of Canon A. L. Elliott. *Educ:* Trent Coll., Derbs; Trinity Coll., Dublin (MA, DD). Curate, Aston, Birmingham, 1910-12; Missionary, Church Missionary Society, India, from 1913; Archdeacon of the Deccan, 1930; Asst Bishop in Dornakal Diocese, 1935; Bishop of Dornakal, 1945-47; Bishop in Dornakal, 1947-55, in Krishna-Godavarl, 1955-59, Church of South India. *Publication:* Hebrews. *Recreations:* birds, stars. *Address:* CSI, Alir S. C. Railway, Nalgonda District, AP, India.

**ELLIOTT, Sir Claude (Aurelius),** Kt 1958; OBE 1920; Hon. DCL (Durham); Fellow of Jesus College, Cambridge, since 1910; *b* 1888; *y s* of late Sir Charles Elliott, KCSI, Lieut-Governor of Bengal; *m* 1913, Gillian (*d* 1966), *d* of late F. T. Bloxam, Chief Chancery Registrar; one *s. Educ:* Eton; Trinity Coll., Cambridge. Tutor, Jesus Coll., 1914; Red Cross Unit in Flanders, 1915; then temporary work at Admiralty till 1919; sometime Univ. Lecturer in History, and Mem. of Univ. Financial Board, Gen. Board, and Council of Senate; Head Master of Eton Coll., 1933-49; Provost of Eton Coll., 1949-64; Pres. Alpine Club, 1950-52. *Address:* Lower Gatesgarth, Buttermere, Cockermouth, Cumberland. *Clubs:* Travellers', Alpine; Leander.

**ELLIOTT, Denholm Mitchell;** actor, stage and films; *b* 31 May 1922; *m* 1954, Virginia McKenna (marr. diss. 1957; she *m* 1957, Bill Travers); *m* 1962, Susan Darby Robinson; one *s* one *d. Educ:* Malvern. *Plays:* The Guinea-Pig, Criterion, 1946; Venus Observed, St James's, 1949; Ring Round the Moon, Martin Beck, New York, 1950; Sleep of Prisoners, St Thomas's, Regent Street, 1950; Third Person, Criterion, 1951; Confidential Clerk, Lyric, 1954; South, Arts, 1955; Who Cares, Fortune, 1956; Camino Real, Phœnix, 1957; Traveller Without Luggage, Arts, 1958; The Ark, Westminster, 1959; Stratford-on-Avon Season, 1960; Write Me a Murder, Belasco Theatre, New York, 1961; The Seagull, The Crucible, Ring Round the Moon, Nat. Repertory Co., New York, 1963-64; Come as You Are, New, 1970. *Films:* Sound Barrier, 1949; The Cruel Sea, 1952; They Who Dare, 1953; Pacific Destiny, 1955; Scent of Mystery, 1959; Station Six Sahara, 1962; Nothing But the Best, 1963; King Rat, 1964; The High Bright Sun, 1964; You Must Be Joking, 1965; Alfie, 1966; Here we go round the Mulberry Bush, 1967; The Seagull, 1968; Too Late the Hero, 1969, etc. Has awards, London and New York. *Recreations:* ski-ing, golf. *Address:* 75 Albert Street, Regents Park, NW1. *Club:* Garrick.

**ELLIOTT, Frank Abercrombie,** MD, FRCP; Professor of Neurology, University of Pennsylvania, Philadelphia, since 1959; *b* 18 Dec. 1910; *s* of Arthur Abercrombie Elliott and Kathleen Gosselin; *m* 1940, Betty Kathleen Elkington; two *d*; *m* 1970; Mrs Josiah Marcel (*née* Hopkins). *Educ:* Rondebosch; Univ. of Cape Town. Univ. entrance schol., 1928; Lewis Memorial schol., 1930-34; MB, ChB Cape Town, with Hons and Gold Medal; Hiddingh Travelling Fellowship, 1936-39. House Surg. and House Phys. to professorial units, Cape Town; House Physician, British Postgrad. Sch. of Medicine and Nat. Hosp. for Nervous Diseases, London; Resident MO, Nat. Heart Hosp. RAMC, 1943-48, Lt-Col; Adviser in Neurology, India and War Office. FRCP 1948. Physician to Charing Cross Hosp., 1947-58; to Moorfields Eye Hospital, 1949-58, Lecturer and Examiner, London Univ. Member: Assoc. of British Neurologists; Assoc. of British Physicians; Internat. Soc. of Internal Medicine; Am. Acad. of Neurology; Philadelphia Neurological Soc. *Publications:* (ed) Clinical Neurology, 1952; Clinical Neurology, 1964; papers on neurological subjects in scientific journals. *Address:* Pennsylvania Hospital, Philadelphia, Pa, USA.

**ELLIOTT, Harold William,** CBE 1967; Managing Director, Pickfords Ltd, since 1963; *b* 24 Nov. 1905; *s* of late W. J. Elliott and Ellen Elliott; *m* Betty, *d* of late C. J. Thumling and Mrs V. A. Thumling; two *s* one *d. Educ:* Brighton Coll. Apprenticed to Adolf Saurer, AG Arbon, Switz., 1924; joined Pickfords Ltd, 1926. Mem., Road and Rail Central Conf., 1938; Transport Adv. Cttee, Food Defence Plans Dept, BoT, 1939; Asst Divisional Food Officer (Transport), London, 1940; Controller of Road Transport, Min. of Supply, 1941; Mem., Salvage Bd; Dir of Transport, Middle East Supply Centre, Cairo, 1943; Mem., Road Haulage Central Wages Bd and Vice-Chm., Meat Transport Organisation Ltd, 1945; Gen. Man., Hay's Wharf Cartage Co. Ltd, Pickfords Ltd and Carter Paterson & Co. Ltd, 1947; Chief Officer (Freight), Road Transport Exec.; Mem., Coastal Shipping Adv. Cttee, 1948; Mem. Bd of Management, Brit. Road Services, and Dir, Atlantic Steam Navigation Co. Ltd, 1959; Dir, Containerway & Roadferry Ltd; Mem. Coun., Nat. Freight Fedn (NFC) Ltd; a Vice-Pres., Inst. of

Transport; Mem. Nat. Exec. Coun., Road Haulage Assoc. Governor, Brighton Coll., 1955. Liveryman, Worshipful Co. of Carmen. MInstT. *Address:* Stumbleholt, near Dorking, Surrey. *T:* Dorking 6514. *Clubs:* Anglo-Belgian, No 10.

**ELLIOTT, Sir Hugh (Francis Ivo),** 3rd Bt *cr* 1917; OBE 1953; Secretary, Ecology Commission, International Union for Conservation of Nature, since 1966 (posted in London); *b* 10 March 1913; *er s* of Sir Ivo Elliott, 2nd Bt; *S* father, 1961; *m* 1939, Elizabeth Margaret, *er d* of A. G. Phillipson; one *s* two *d. Educ:* Dragon Sch.; Eastbourne Coll.; University Coll., Oxford. Tanganyika Administration, 1937; Administrator, Tristan da Cunha, 1950-52; Permanent Sec., Min. of Natural Resources, Tanganyika, 1958; retired, 1961. Commonwealth Liaison Officer for International Union for Conservation of Nature, 1961-66; acting Sec.-Gen., 1962-64, Sec.-Gen., 1964-66. Hon. Sec., British Ornithologists' Union, 1962-66, Vice-Pres. 1970. *Publications:* contributor to Ibis, British Birds, Tanganyika Notes and Records, Corona. *Recreations:* ornithology, travel. *Heir: s* Clive Christopher Hugh Elliott, *b* 12 Aug. 1945. *Address:* 173 Woodstock Road, Oxford. *T:* Oxford 55469.

*See also T. A. K. Elliott.*

**ELLIOTT, Hugh Percival,** CMG 1959; retired, 1967; *b* 29 May 1911; *s* of late Major P. W. Elliott, IA; *m* 1951, Bridget Rosalie, *d* of late Rev. A. F. Peterson. *Educ:* St Lawrence Coll., Ramsgate; Hertford Coll., Oxford. Joined Colonial Administrative Service, Nigeria, 1934; seconded Colonial Office, 1946; Supervisor, Colonial Service Courses, London, 1948-50; Senior District Officer, 1954; Permanent Sec., 1956; Adviser, Govt of Eastern Nigeria, 1962-67. CON, 1964 (Comdr, Order of the Niger, Nigeria). *Address:* 14 Eldon Avenue, Shirley, Croydon, Surrey. *Club:* Royal Commonwealth Society.

**ELLIOTT, Maj.-Gen. James Gordon,** CIE 1947; retd; *b* 6 April 1898; *s* of late Dr William Elliott, Welshpool, Montgomeryshire; *m* 1931, Barbara Eleanor, *y d* of William Douglas, Malvern; one *s* one *d. Educ:* Blundell's Sch. Commissioned, Indian Army, 1916; 1st Punjab Regt, 1922; GSO2 Staff Coll., Quetta, 1935-37; Dir Military Training, India, 1942-43; Bde Comdr, 1943-44; Dep. Welfare Gen., India, 1945-46; Dep. Sec. (Mil.), Defence Cttee, India, 1947-48; retired 1948. *Publications:* Administrative Aspect of Tactics and Training, 1938; The Story of the Indian Army, 1939-45, 1965; The Frontier 1839-1947, 1968. *Recreations:* gardening, fishing. *Club:* United Service.

**ELLIOTT, Vice-Adm. Sir Maurice (Herbert),** KCB 1956 (CB 1954); CBE 1952 (OBE 1938; MBE 1919); *b* 19 Feb. 1897; *s* of late Rev. Dr R. Elliott; *m* 1925, Margaret, *d* of late A. E. Ward, solicitor; no *c. Educ:* Dulwich Coll. Joined Navy, 1914; served throughout European War, 1914-18, in Grand Fleet; offices of Commanders-in-Chief, China and Portsmouth, 1919-26; Sec. to Vice-Adm. A. E. F. Bedford in various appts, 1926-37; served War of 1939-45, HMS Nelson, Admiralty, Newfoundland and Canada; Dep. Dir-Gen. Supply and Secretariat Branch, 1946-49; Command Supply Officer (Air), 1951-54; Dir-Gen. Supply and Secretariat Branch, 1954-57. *Recreation:* golf. *Address:* Pillar Box Cottage, Littleton, near Guildford. *T:* Guildford 69103. *Club:* Army and Navy.

**ELLIOTT, Sir Norman (Randall),** Kt 1967; CBE 1957 (OBE 1946); MA; Chairman of the Electricity Council, since 1968; Chairman, British National Committee, Union Internationale des Producteurs et Distributeurs d'Energie Electrique; *b* 19 July 1903; *s* of William Randall Elliott and Catherine Dunsmore; *m* 1963, Phyllis Clarke. *Educ:* privately; St Catharine's Coll., Cambridge. Called to the Bar, Middle Temple, 1932 (J. J. Powell Prizeman, A. J. Powell Exhibitioner). London Passenger Transport Board; London and Home Counties Joint Electricity Authority; Yorkshire Electric Power Co.; 21 Army Group: first as CRE (Royal Engineers) then, as Col, Deputy Dir of Works, 21 Army Group (OBE); Chief Engineer and Manager, Wimbledon Borough Council; Gen. Manager and Chief Engineer, London and Home Counties Joint Electricity Authority and sometime Chm. and Dir, Isle of Thanet Electric Supply Co., and Dir, James Howden & Co. Ltd; Chairman: S-E Electricity Bd, 1948-62; S of Scotland Electricity Bd, 1962-67; Member: Brit. Electricity Authority, 1950 and 1951; Central Electricity Authority, 1956 and 1957; Electricity Council, 1958-62; N of Scotland Hydro-Electric Bd, 1965-69. *Publication:* Electricity Statutes, Orders and Regulations, 1947, rev. edn 1951. *Recreations:* ball games and the theatre. *Address:* 30 Millbank, SW1. *Clubs:* Athenæum; Western (Glasgow); Royal Northern Yacht.

**ELLIOTT, Ralph Edward;** a Deputy Chairman, National Westminster Bank Ltd, since 1970 (Joint Chief Executive, 1968-70); *b* 7 May 1908; *y s* of late Frederick Worsley Elliott, Ruckinge, Kent; *m* 1934, Phyllis, 2nd *d* of late William Douglas Craig, Kingsnorth, Kent; two *s* one *d. Educ:* Ashford Gram. Sch. Entered Westminster Bank Ltd, Rochester, 1926; Jt Gen. Man., 1958; Dep. Chief Gen. Man., 1965; Chief Gen. Man., 1966-68. Fellow, Inst. of Bankers. *Address:* Little Hendra, Shire Lane, Chorleywood, Herts. *T:* Chorleywood 2223.

**ELLIOTT, Rt. Rev. Robert Cyril Hamilton,** DD; Hon. CF; *b* 18 Nov. 1890; *s* of Canon A. L. Elliott, MA, Rector of Killiney, County Dublin; unmarried. *Educ:* Trent College, Derbyshire; Trinity College, Dublin (MA). DD 1957. Deacon, 1914; priest, 1915; CF, 1917-19 (despatches twice). Rector of All Saints, Belfast, 1922-30; Vicar of Ballymacarrett, 1930-38; Dean of Down and Rector of Downpatrick, Co. Down, 1938-45; Incumbent of Belfast and Dean of St Anne's Cathedral, 1945-56; Bishop of Connor, 1956-69. Sub-Prelate, OStJ, 1969. *Recreation:* golf. *Address:* 9 Mount Aboo Park, Finaghy, Belfast 10. *Club:* Ulster (Belfast).

**ELLIOTT, Air Vice-Marshal Robert D.;** *see* Deacon Elliott.

**ELLIOTT, Robert William;** MP (C) Newcastle upon Tyne North since March 1957; Vice-Chairman, Conservative Party Organisation, since 1970; *b* 11 Dec. 1920; *s* of Richard Elliott; *m* 1956, Jane Morpeth; one *s* four *d* (of whom two are twin *d*). *Educ:* Morpeth Grammar Sch. Farmer, 1939-, at Low Heighley, Morpeth, Northumberland. Parliamentary Private Secretary: to joint Parliamentary Secs, Ministry of Transport and Civil Aviation, April 1958-Oct. 1959; to Under-Sec., Home Office, Nov. 1959-60; to Minister of State, Home Office, Nov. 1960-61; to Sec. for Technical Co-operation, 1961-63; Asst Govt Whip (unpaid), 1963-64; Opposition Whip, 1964-70; Comptroller of the Household, June-Sept. 1970. *Address:* Low Heighley, Morpeth, Northumberland. *T:* Morpeth 247; 29 Palace Street, SW1. *Clubs:* Carlton, Farmers'; Northern Counties Conservative (Newcastle upon Tyne).

**ELLIOTT, Sydney Robert;** Editor of the Daily Herald, 1953-57; *b* 31 Aug. 1902; *o surv. s* of Robert Scott Elliott and Helen Golden; *m* 1927, Janet Robb Johnston; two *s* one *d* (one *s* decd). *Educ:* Govan High Sch., Glasgow. Managing Editor, Reynolds News, 1929; Editor, Evening Standard, 1943; Political Adviser, Daily Mirror, 1945; Managing Dir, The Argus and Australian Post, Melbourne, 1949; Gen. Manager, Daily Herald, 1952. *Publications:* Life of Sir William Maxwell, 1922; Co-operative Storekeeping; Eighty Years of Constructive Revolution, 1925; England, Cradle of Co-operation, 1937. *Address:* 5 Frognal Close, Hampstead, NW3. *T:* 01-435 4149.

**ELLIOTT, Thomas Anthony Keith,** CMG 1968; HM Diplomatic Service: Minister and Head of Chancery, British Embassy, Washington, since 1970; *b* Burford, Oxon, 27 May 1921; *s* of Sir Ivo Elliott, 2nd Bt, ICS, Oxford, and of Margery (*née* Carey); *m* 1951, Alethea, *d* of late Major Alistair B. H. Richardson, King's Dragoon Guards, Richmond, Surrey; one *s* three *d*. *Educ:* Dragon Sch., Oxford; Eton (King's Schol.); Balliol Coll., Oxford. MA Oxon 1946. Served War of 1939-45: King's Shropshire LI, 1941-46; Capt.; served with East African Forces in Ethiopia and Somaliland. Joined HM Foreign Service, 1947; Third Sec., Belgrade, 1949-52; First Sec., Foreign Office, 1953; Head of Chancery, Peking, 1957-59; Athens, 1960-61; Foreign Office, 1961-65; Political Adviser, Govt of Hong Kong, 1965-68; Counsellor, Washington, 1968. *Address:* British Embassy, Washington, DC, USA; c/o Foreign and Commonwealth Office, SW1.
*See also Sir Hugh Elliott, Bt.*

**ELLIOTT, Walter Archibald,** MC 1943; QC (Scotland) 1963; *b* 6 Sept. 1922; 2nd *s* of late Prof. T. R. Elliott, CBE, DSO, FRS, Broughton Place, Broughton, Peeblesshire; *m* 1954, Susan Isobel MacKenzie Ross, Kaimend, North Berwick; two *s*. *Educ:* Eton; Trinity Coll., Cambridge; Edinburgh Univ. Active service in Italy and North West Europe with 2nd Bn Scots Guards, 1943-45; captured and escaped, Salerno landings (MC); demobilised, Staff Capt., 1947. Barrister-at-law, Inner Temple, 1950; Advocate at Scottish Bar, 1950. Standing Junior Counsel to Accountant of Court and later to Minister of Aviation. Member: Legal Aid Central Cttee, 1966-; Council, Nat. Trust for Scotland, 1966-. Contested (C) Dunfermline Burghs, 1959, and Leith, 1966. Mem., Royal Company of Archers (Queen's Body Guard for Scotland). *Publications:* articles in legal periodicals. *Recreations:* gardening, ski-ing, shooting. *Address:* Morton House, Fairmilehead, Edinburgh. *T:* 031-445 2548. *Club:* New (Edinburgh).

**ELLIOTT, William Rowcliffe,** CB 1969; Senior Chief Inspector, Department of Education and Science, since 1968; *b* 10 April 1910; *s* of Thomas Herbert Elliott and Ada Elliott (*née* Rowcliffe); *m* 1937, Karin Tess, *d* of Ernest and Lilly Classen; one *s*. *Educ:* St Paul's Sch.; The Queen's Coll., Oxford. Schoolmaster, 1933-36; HM Inspector of Schools: in Leeds, 1936-39; in Leicestershire, 1940-44; in Liverpool, 1944-48; Staff Inspector: for Adult Education, 1948-55; for Secondary Modern Education, 1955-57; Chief Inspector for Educational Developments, 1957-59; for Secondary Educn, 1959-66; Dep. Sen. Chief Insp., 1966-67. *Publication:* Monemvasia, The Gibraltar of Greece, 1970. *Recreations:* Village life; photography; rose-growing; travel; translation from Scandinavian languages. *Address:* Astwick House, Farthinghoe, Brackley, Northants. *T:* Middleton Cheney 388. *Clubs:* Anglo-Belgian, English-Speaking Union.

**ELLIOTT-BINNS, Edward Ussher Elliott;** Under-Secretary, Scottish Home and Health Department, since 1966; *b* 24 Aug. 1918; *e s* of Leonard and Anna Elliott-Binns; *m* 1942, Katharine Mary McLeod, *d* of late Dr J. M. Caie; one *d*. *Educ:* Harrow; King's Coll., Cambridge. Served with Army, 1939-46; Leics Regt and Special Forces (Major). Asst Principal, Scottish Home Dept, 1946; Principal, 1948; Asst Sec., Royal Commn on Capital Punishment, 1949-53; Private Sec. to Minister of State, Scottish Office, 1956-57; Asst Sec., 1957. *Address:* 22 Wilton Road, Edinburgh EH16 5NX. *T:* 031-667 2464. *Club:* Special Forces.

**ELLIS;** *see* Scott-Ellis.

**ELLIS, Amabel W.;** *see* Williams-Ellis.

**ELLIS, Arthur Robert Malcolm;** Barrister-at-law; *b* 27 June 1912; *s* of David and Anne Amelia Ellis, Nottingham; *m* 1938, Brenda Sewell; one *d*. *Educ:* Nottingham High Sch. Admitted Solicitor, 1934; called to the Bar, Inner Temple, 1953. Chm., Nottingham Council of Social Service, 1950-55; Dep. Chm., E Midland Traffic Area, 1955-; Chm., Ministry of Pensions and National Insurance Tribunal, Sutton-in-Ashfield, Notts, 1961-64, resigned; Chm., Min. of Pensions and Nat. Insce Tribunal, Notts, 1964-. Chm., Notts QS, 1963- (Dep.-Chm., 1962-63); Chm., Derbyshire QS, 1966- (Dep.-Chm., 1965-66). *Recreations:* golf, bridge. *Address:* Eldon Chambers, Wheeler Gate, Nottingham. *T:* Nottingham 43844; Overfields, 104 Cropwell Road, Radcliffe-on-Trent, Notts. *T:* Radcliffe-on-Trent 664. *Clubs:* United Services, Borough (Nottingham); Royal Overseas League (Nottingham Branch).

**ELLIS, Sir Charles Drummond,** Kt 1946; FRS 1929; BA, PhD; Scientific Adviser to: British American Tobacco Co. Ltd; Gas Council; Battelle Memorial Institute; Tobacco Research Council; Governor, Harrow; *b* 11 Aug. 1895; *s* of A. C. Ellis; *m* 1925, Paula Warzcewska. *Educ:* Harrow; RMA Woolwich; Trinity Coll., Cambridge. Fellow and Lectr of Trinity Coll., Cambridge; Lectr in Dept of Physics in Univ. of Cambridge; Wheatstone Prof. of Physics, King's Coll., London, 1936-46; Scientific Adviser to Army Council, 1943-46; Mem. Advisory Council on Scientific Research and Technical Development to Ministry of Supply, 1943-46; Scientific Mem. of National Coal Board, 1946-55; Pres. British Coal Utilisation Research Association, 1946-55; Mem. Advisory Council to Ministry of Fuel and Power, 1947-55; Mem. of Court of Governors, Administrative Staff Coll.; Senior Scientific Adviser Civil Defence London Region, 1947-65; Mem. Gas Council's Research Advisory Cttee, 1955-. *Publications:* (with Sir Ernest Rutherford and James Chadwick) Radiations from Radioactive Substances, 1930; various papers on radioactivity and connected problems. *Address:* Seawards, Cookham Dean, Berks. *T:* Marlow 3166. *Club:* Athenæum.

**ELLIS, Charles Howard,** CMG 1953; CBE 1941 (OBE 1919); TD 1953; retired from Foreign Office; *b* 13 Feb. 1895; *s* of William Edward Ellis, Exeter, Devon, and Sydney, Australia, and Lillian Mary Hobday; *m* 1st, 1933, Barbara Mary Burgess-Smith (marr. diss., 1947); one *s* one *d*; 2nd, 1954, Alexandra Wood (*née* Surtees). *Educ:* Melbourne Univ; Oxford Univ.; Sorbonne. Served European War, 1914-

18; Middlesex Regt; France, Egypt, India, Persia, S Russia; Afghan War, 1919; Caucasus and Black Sea, 1919-20; Foreign Office and Consular posts in Turkey, Berlin, Far East and USA, 1921-39; War of 1939-45; Col on staff of missions in USA and Egypt and Far East. Foreign Office and posts in Far East, 1946-53; retired, 1953. US Legion of Merit, 1946. *Publications:* The Transcaspian Episode, 1963; The Expansion of Russia, 1965; The New Left in Britain, 1968. *Recreations:* music, drama, travel. *Address:* 28 Freeman Avenue, Hampden Park, Eastbourne, Sussex. *Clubs:* Travellers', Royal Automobile.

**ELLIS, Clough W.;** *see* Williams-Ellis.

**ELLIS, Rt. Rev. Edward;** *see* Nottingham, Bishop of, (RC).

**ELLIS, Prof. Harold,** MA, MCh, DM, FRCS; Professor of Surgery, University of London; Hon. Consultant Surgeon, Westminster Hospital, since 1962; *b* 13 Jan. 1926; *s* of Samuel and Ada Ellis; *m* 1958, Wendy Mae Levine; one *s* one *d*. *Educ:* Queen's Coll. (State scholar and Open Scholar in Natural Sciences), Oxford; Radcliffe Infirmary, Oxford. BM, BCh, 1948; FRCS, MA, 1951; MCh 1956; DM 1962. House Surgeon, Radcliffe Infirmary, 1948-49; Hallett Prize, RCS, 1949. RAMC, 1949-51. Res. Surgical Officer, Sheffield Royal Infirm., 1952-54; Registrar, Westminster Hosp., 1955; Sen. Registrar and Surgical Tutor, Radcliffe Infirm., Oxford, 1956-61; Sen. Lectr in Surgery, Westminster Hosp., 1961-62. Member: Association of Surgeons; British Soc. of Gastroenterol.; Surgical Research Soc. *Publications:* Clinical Anatomy, 1960; Anatomy for Anaesthetists, 1963; Lecture Notes on General Surgery, 1965; Principles of Resuscitation, 1967; History of the Bladder Stone, 1970; numerous articles on surgical topics in medical journals. *Recreation:* medical history. *Address:* 16 Bancroft Avenue, N2. *T:* 01-348 2720. *Club:* Oxford and Cambridge University.

**ELLIS, Harold Owen,** CMG 1958; OBE 1952; CEng; FIEE; *b* 11 April 1906; *s* of Owen Percy Ellis, accountant, and Kate Beatrice Ellis, Plymouth; *m* 1932, Phyllis Margaret Stevenson (decd); *m* 1954, Ella Stewart Mathieson. *Educ:* Sutton Secondary Sch., Plymouth. Apprentice, Devonport Dockyard. Engineering Inspector, Post Office, 1926; Executive Engineer, 1940. Served Army, 1944-47, Col. Asst Controller-Gen., Posts and Telegraphs, Control Commn, Germany, 1947; Postmaster-Gen., Nyasaland, 1949; Dir of Posts and Telegraphs, Federation of Nigeria, 1954; Postmaster-Gen., E Africa, 1958; retd Colonial Service, 1962; Administrative Consultant, 1962-66. Has attended many internat. conferences on telecommunications, sometimes representing Britain. AMIEE 1936; MIEE 1944; MIERE 1950. *Publications:* technical articles and papers. *Recreations:* sailing, swimming, photography. *Address:* Ruwenzori, Milltimber, Aberdeen AB1 ODJ.

**ELLIS, Rev. Canon Henry;** Canon Residentiary and Precentor of Liverpool Cathedral since 1962; Rural Dean of Toxteth, since 1966; *b* 1909; *s* of William and Maud Ellis, Abbeywood, Breadsall, near Derby; *m* 1934, Marjorie Thelma (*née* Dobie); one *s* three *d* (and one *s* decd). *Educ:* St John's Coll., Durham. LRAM 1928; MA 1930. Deacon 1932; Priest 1933. Curate of Holy Trinity, St Helens, 1932-34; Curate of Prescot, 1934-38; Vicar of St Catharine's, Wigan, 1938-47; Rector of Wavertree, 1947-57; Vicar of Prescot, 1957-62. Hon. Chaplain and Divinity Lecturer, St Edmund's Coll., Liverpool, 1953-61; Canon Diocesan, 1960-62. *Address:* The Cathedral, Liverpool L1 7AZ. *T:* 051-709 6271; 20 Garth Drive, Liverpool L18 6HW. *T:* 051-724 4532.

**ELLIS, Humphry Francis,** MBE 1945; MA; writer; *b* 1907; 2nd *s* of late Dr John Constable Ellis, Metheringham, Lincs and Alice Marion Raven; *m* 1933, Barbara Pauline Hasseldine; one *s* one *d*. *Educ:* Tonbridge Sch.; Magdalen Coll., Oxford (Demy). 1st cl. Hon. Mods, 1928; 1st cl. Lit. Hum., 1930. Asst Master, Marlborough Coll., 1930-31. Contributor to Punch, 1931-68; Editorial staff, 1933; Literary and Dep. Ed., 1949-53. Privilege Mem., RFU Cttee, 1952-. Served War of 1939-45 in RA (AA Command). *Publications:* So This is Science, 1932; The Papers of A. J. Wentworth, 1949; Why the Whistle Went (on the laws of Rugby Football), 1947; Co-Editor, The Royal Artillery Commemoration Book, 1950; Editor, Manual of Rugby Union Football, 1952; Twenty Five Years Hard, 1960; Mediatrics, 1961; A. J. Wentworth, BA (Retd), 1962; The World of A. J. Wentworth, 1964; contribs to Countryman and The New Yorker. *Recreation:* fishing. *Address:* Hill Croft, Kingston St Mary, Taunton, Somerset. *T:* Kingston St Mary 264. *Clubs:* Garrick, MCC.

**ELLIS, John;** *b* Hexthorpe, Doncaster, 22 Oct. 1930; *s* of George and Hilda Ellis; *m* 1953, Rita Butters; one *s* two *d*. *Educ:* Rastrick Gram. Sch., Brighouse. Laboratory technician, Meteorological Office, 1947-63. Vice-Chm., Staff side, Air Min. Whitley Council, 1961-63; Mem., Easthampstead RDC, 1962-66. Contested (Lab) Wokingham, 1964; MP (Lab) Bristol North-West, 1966-70. JP, North Riding Yorks, 1960-61. *Recreations:* gardening, cricket. *Address:* 15 Churchleaze, Shirehampton, Bristol.

**ELLIS, John Rogers,** MBE 1943; MA, MD, FRCP; Physician to the London Hospital since 1951; Dean, London Hospital Medical College, since 1968; Secretary, Association for the Study of Medical Education, since 1957; Member, WHO Expert Advisory Cttee on Education and Training of Medical and Ancillary Personnel, since 1963; Editor, British Journal of Medical Education; *b* 15 June 1916; 3rd *s* of late Frederick William Ellis, MD, FRCS; *m* 1942, Joan, *d* of late C. J. C. Davenport; two *s* two *d*. *Educ:* Oundle Sch.; Trinity Hall, Cambridge; London Hosp. Served RNVR, 1942-46, Mediterranean and Far East, Surg.-Lt Gen. Practice, Plymouth, 1946; Sen. Lectr, Med. Unit, London Hosp., 1948-51; Sub-Dean, London Hosp. Med. Coll., 1948-58; Asst Registrar, RCP, 1957-61; Physician to Prince of Wales Gen. Hosp., 1958-68; PMO (part-time), Min. of Health, 1964-68. Mem., UGC's Med. Sub-cttee, 1959-69; formerly Member: Porrit (Med. Services) Cttee; Royal Commn on Med. Educn. Goulstonian Lectr, RCP, 1956; Wood-Jones Lectr, Univ. of Manchester, 1960; Porter Lectr, Univ. of Kansas, 1960; Sir Charles Hastings Lectr, BMA, 1964; Anders Lectr, Coll. of Physicians, Pa, 1965; Adams Lectr, RCSI, 1965; Shattuck Lectr, Massachusetts Med. Soc., 1969; Vis. Lecturer: Teaching Inst., Assoc. of Amer. Med. Colls, 1957, 1960 and 1963; Ghana Acad. of Sciences, 1967. Corr. Mem., Royal Flemish Acad. of Medicine; Hon. Consultant, Nat. Bd of Med. Examiners, USA. Member Bd of Governors: London Hosp., 1968-; Queen Mary Coll., 1968-; Mem. Governing Body, Brit. Post-graduate Med. Fedn; formerly Member Bd of Governors: Inst. of Psychiatry; Bethlem Royal and Maudsley Hosps. *Publications:* articles on medical education in medical and scientific journals. *Recreations:* painting, gardening.

*Address:* Little Monkhams, Woodford Green, Essex. *T:* 01-504 2292.

**ELLIS, Prof. John Romaine;** Professor of Automobile Engineering and Director of the Advanced School of Automobile Engineering, Cranfield, since 1960; *b* 30 Sept. 1922; *m* 1947, Madelaine Della Blaker; one *s* one *d*. *Educ:* Tiffin Sch., Kingston-on-Thames. Royal Aircraft Establishment, 1944-56; Fairey Aviation Company, 1946-48; Royal Military Coll. of Science, Shrivenham, near Swindon, Wilts, 1949-60. *Recreations:* golf, tennis, music. *Address:* Advanced School of Automobile Engineering, Cranfield Institute of Technology, Cranfield, Bedford. *T:* Bedford 51551.

**ELLIS, Joseph Stanley,** CMG 1967; OBE 1962; Head of News Department, Commonwealth Office, 1967; retired; *b* 29 Nov. 1907; *m* 1933, Gladys Harcombe; one *s*. *Educ:* Woodhouse Grove, Bradford; University Coll., University of London. Journalist, Manchester Evening News, 1930-40; Publications Div., Min. of Inf., 1941-45; Seconded to Dominions Office for service in Australia until 1949. Central Office of Information, 1949-51; Regional Information Officer, Karachi, 1952; Dir, British Information Services: Pakistan, 1953-55; Canberra, Australia, 1955-58; Kuala Lumpur, Malaya, 1958-62; Head, Information Services Dept, Commonwealth Office, 1962-66. *Recreation:* cricket. *Address:* 14 Lodge Close, Stoke D'Abernon, Surrey. *T:* Cobham 3985.

**ELLIS, Hon. Sir Kevin,** KBE 1969; MLA; Speaker, Parliament of New South Wales, since 1965; *b* 15 May 1908; *s* of J. P. Ellis, Liverpool, England; *m* 1941, Bettie, *d* of C. Maunsell; one *s* one *d*. *Educ:* Fort Street Boys' High Sch.; Univ. of Sydney. LLB Sydney, 1931, 1st class Hons, Univ. medal, 2 schols; BEc Sydney, 1937. Served War of 1939-45: Middle East and Medit.; Flt Lt, RAAF on attachment to RAF. Supreme Court of NSW, Solicitor, 1932-. MLA (Coogee), 1948-53, 1956-62, 1965-. Director: Nat. Heart Foundation of Australia (NSW Div.) (also Hon. Sec.), 1958-; Prince of Wales Hosp., 1961-; Prince Henry Hosp., 1962-; Eastern Suburbs Hosp., 1968-; Nat. Heart Foundn of Australia, Canberra, 1965-; Medical Foundn of Univ. of NSW, 1965-; Unisearch Ltd, 1970-. mem. Council, Univ. of NSW, 1965-; Past Fellow, Senate of Univ. of Sydney. *Recreations:* bowls, boating, and deep sea fishing. *Address:* 4 Wolseley Crescent, Point Piper, NSW 2027, Australia. *T:* 36.4076 (Sydney). *Clubs:* American National, Automobile (Sydney).

**ELLIS, Malcolm Henry,** CMG 1956; Hon. DLit Newcastle, Australia; historian; *b* Narine, Queensland, 21 Aug. 1890; *e s* of Thomas James Ellis and Constance Ruegg; *m* 1st, Melicent Jane, *d* of Major J. W. Ayscough, Brisbane; one *d*; 2nd, Gwendoline Mary, *y d* of Harry and Sarah Wheeler. *Educ:* Brisbane Grammar Sch. Chief Special Correspondent of Sydney Daily Telegraph, 1922-28; Mem. of Australian Meat Council's Delegate Cttee to British Ports, 1926; in command Daily Telegraph motor expedition across Australia, 1924 (first complete double crossing of the continent by motor car) and of semi-official British motor expedition, London-Delhi, 1927; Dir, Electrical Development Assoc. of NSW, 1929-31; Mem., Govt Cttee of Inquiry into Municipal Trading in Electrical Appliances, 1930; Staff of Sydney Bulletin, 1933-65; Mem., Australian editorial delegation to Korea, 1951-52. Life Member: NSW United Service Instn; Australian Pioneers' Club; Hon. Mem., Australian Humanities Research Council. Hon. Sec., NSW and Canberra Group, Order of St Michael and St George; Macrossan Lectr, Univ. of Queensland, 1942; Harbison-Higinbotham Research Award (Melbourne Univ.), 1948. *Publications:* The Long Lead, 1927; Express to Hindustan, 1929; The Red Road, 1932; The Beef Shorthorn in Australia, 1932; The Defence of Australia, 1933; Lachlan Macquarie (Macrossan Lectures), 1942; The Life and Times of Lachlan Macquarie, 1947; The Life of Francis Greenway, 1948; The Garden Path, 1949; John Macarthur, 1955; The Torch, 1957; The Drama of Coal, 1959; various historical papers. A Prior Prize for best manuscript of the year (Australia), 1940, for Life of Lachlan Macquarie. *Address:* 18 Reed Street, Cremorne, Australia. *T:* 90-6261. *Clubs:* Australian (Sydney); Savage (Melbourne).

**ELLIS, Mary;** actress; singer; *b* New York City, 15 June 1901; *m* 1st, L. A. Bernheimer (decd); 2nd (marr. diss.); 3rd, Basil Sydney (marr. diss.); 4th, J. Muir Stewart Roberts (decd). *Educ:* New York. Studied art for three years; studied singing with Madame Ashforth. First Stage appearance, Metropolitan Opera House, New York, in Sœur Angelica, 1918; with Metropolitan Opera House, 1918-22; first appearance dramatic stage, as Nerissa in Merchant of Venice, Lyceum, New York, 1922; was the original Rose Marie (in the musical play, Rose Marie), Imperial, 1924; The Dybbuk, New York, 1925-26; Taming of the Shrew, 1927, and many New York leads followed; first appearance on London stage, as Laetitia in Knave and Quean, Ambassadors', 1930; in following years alternated between London and US. From 1932-39: London: Strange Interlude, 1932; Double Harness, 1933; Music in the Air, 1934; Glamorous Night, Drury Lane, 1935; 2 years, Hollywood, 1936-37; Dancing Years, Drury Lane, 1939. From 1939-43: doing hospital welfare work and giving concerts for troops. Re-appeared on stage as Marie Foret in Arc de Triomphe, Phœnix, London, 1943; Old Vic (at Liverpool Playhouse), 1944 (Ella Rentheim in John Gabriel Borkman; Linda Valaine in Point Valaine; Lady Teazle in The School for Scandal); Maria Fitzherbert in The Gay Pavilion, Piccadilly, 1945; Season at Embassy: Mrs Dane's Defence, also tour and première of Ian Hay's Hattie Stowe, 1946-47; post-war successes include: Playbill, Phœnix, 1949. Stratford-on-Avon Season, 1952: Volumnia in Coriolanus. London: After the Ball (Oscar Wilde-Noel Coward), Globe, 1954-55; Mourning Becomes Electra, Arts, 1955-56; Dark Halo, Arts, 1959; Look Homeward Angel, Pembroke Theatre, Croydon, 1960; Phœnix, 1962. First appeared in films, in Bella Donna, 1934; films, 1935-38; (Hollywood) Paris in the Spring: The King's Horses; Fatal Lady; Glamorous Night; Gulliver's Travels, 1961; Silver Cord (revival), Yvonne Arnaud, Guildford, 1968; Mrs Warren's Profession, Yvonne Arnaud, Guildford, 1970. Has made several major television appearances; Television plays, 1956-: Shaw's Great Catherine, Van Druten's Distaff Side and numerous others. In 1965 designed small house in hills behind Nice where she paints and studies. *Recreations:* painting, travel, writing. *Address:* c/o Chase Manhattan Bank, 1 Mount Street, W1.

**ELLIS, Maxwell (Philip),** MD, MS, FRCS; Dean of the Institute of Laryngology and Otology, University of London, since 1965; Surgeon, Royal National Throat, Nose and Ear Hospital, since 1936; Ear, Nose and Throat Surgeon, Central Middlesex Hospital since 1937; *b* 28 Feb. 1906; *s* of Louis Ellis; *m* 1935, Barbara Gertrude Chapman. *Educ:* University

Coll., London (Exhibitioner); University Coll. Hosp. Liston and Alexander Bruce Gold Medals, Surgery and Pathology, UCH, 1927-29. MB, BS (London), Hons Medicine, 1930; MD 1931; FRCS 1932; MS 1937; Geoffrey Duveen Trav. Student, Univ. of London, 1934-36; Leslie Pearce Gould Trav. Schol., 1934, Perceval Alleyn Schol. (Surg. research), 1936, UCH; Hunterian Prof., RCS, 1938. RAFVR, 1940-45 (Wing-Comdr). FRSM, also Mem. Council; Past Pres., Section of Otology; Editorial Rep., Section of Otology; Library Rep., Section of Laryngology; Pres., Med. Soc. London (also Hon. Treas., Mem. Council, Hon. Sec. 1961-63; Hon. Member: Assoc. of Otolaryngologists of India; Salonika Soc. of Otolaryngology; Corresp. Mem., Société Française d'Oto-Rhino-Laryngologie; Hon. Corresp. Mem., Argentine Soc. of Otolaryngology. Lectr on Diseases of Ear, Nose and Throat, Univ. of London, 1952-. *Publications:* Modern Trends in Diseases of the Ear, Nose and Throat (Ed. and part author), 1954, 2nd edn 1971; Operative Surgeon (Rob and Smith), Vol. 8 on Diseases of the Ear, Nose and Throat (Ed. and part author), 1958; 2nd edn 1969; Clinical Surgery (Rob and Smith), Vol. 11, Diseases of the Ear, Nose and Throat (Ed. and part author), 1966; Sections in Diseases of the Ear, Nose and Throat (Ed. Scott-Brown), 1952, new edn 1965; Sections in Cancer, Vol. 4 (Ed. Raven), 1958; Section in Modern Trends in Surgical Materials (Ed. Gillis), 1958; papers in various medical and scientific jls. *Recreations:* golf, gardening; formerly bridge and squash rackets. *Address:* 149 Harley Street, W1. *T:* 01-935 4444; 48 Townshend Road, NW8. *T:* 01-722 2252. *Clubs:* Royal Automobile; Sunningdale Golf; Royal St George's Golf (Sandwich).

**ELLIS, Robert Thomas;** MP (Lab) Wrexham since 1970; *b* 15 March 1924; *s* of Robert and Edith Ann Ellis; *m* 1949, Nona Harcourt Williams; three *s* one *d*. *Educ:* Universities of Wales and Nottingham. Works Chemist, ICI, 1944-47; Coal Miner, 1947-55; Mining Engineer, 1955-70; Manager, Bersham Colliery, N Wales, 1957-70. *Recreations:* golf, reading, music. *Address:* Whitehurst House, Whitehurst, Chirk, Wrexham. *T:* Chirk 3462.

**ELLIS, Roger Henry,** MA; FSA; FRHistS; Secretary, Royal Commission on Historical Manuscripts, since 1957; *b* 9 June 1910; *e s* of late Francis Henry Ellis, Debdale Hall, Mansfield; *m* 1939, Audrey Honor, *o d* of late H. Arthur Baker, DL; two *d*. *Educ:* Sedbergh (scholar); King's College, Cambridge (scholar, Augustus Austen Leigh Student). 1st Cl. Class. Tripos, 1933. Asst Keeper, Public Record Office, 1934; Principal Asst Keeper, 1956. Served War of 1939-45: Private, 1939; Commnd R Northumb Fus, 1940, Maj. 1944; on staff, with 2 Bn RNF (Africa, Italy), and as Monuments, Fine Arts and Archives Officer in Italy and Germany. Lectr in Archive Admin., Sch. of Librarianship and Archives, University Coll. London, 1947-57. Mem. London Council, British Inst. in Florence, 1947-55; Hon. Editor, British Records Assoc., and (first) Editor of Archives, 1947-57, Chm. Council, 1967-. Vice-Pres., Business Archives Council, 1958-; Pres., Soc. of Archivists, 1964-. *Publications:* opuscula and articles in British and foreign jls on care and use of archives and MSS. *Recreations:* poetry, travel, the arts, gardening (unskilled). *Address:* Cloth Hill, 6 The Mount, Hampstead, NW3; Clappers, Goose Green, West Harting, near Petersfield, Hants. *Club:* Athenæum.

**ELLIS, Roger Wykeham;** Headmaster of Rossall School since Sept. 1967; *b* 3 Oct. 1929; *s* of Cecil Ellis, solicitor, and Pamela Unwin; *m* 1964, Margaret Jean Stevenson; one *s* two *d*. *Educ:* St Peter's Sch., Seaford; Winchester Coll.; Trinity Coll., Oxford (Schol., MA). Royal Navy, 1947-49. Asst Master, Harrow Sch., 1952-67, and Housemaster of the Head Master's House, 1961-67. Mem., Harrow Borough Education Cttee, 1956-60. *Recreations:* golf, fishing. *Address:* Rossall School, Fleetwood, Lancs.

**ELLIS, Sir Thomas Hobart,** Kt, *cr* 1953; *b* 11 Oct. 1894; *s* of late Rev. Herbert Ellis. *Educ:* Manchester Grammar Sch.; Queen's Coll., Oxford. Entered Indian Civil Service, 1919; Additional Judge of High Court, Calcutta, 1944-47; Judge of High Court of East Bengal, 1947-53; Chief Justice, 1953-54. Acting Governor of East Bengal, Sept.-Dec. 1954. Officer on Special Duty, Government of Pakistan, 1955-57. *Recreations:* photography, trekking. *Address:* c/o National and Grindlay's Bank, 13 St James's Square, SW1

**ELLIS, Vivian;** Lt-Comdr RNVR; composer, author; Vice-Chairman, Performing Right Society; *s* of Harry Ellis and Maud Isaacson. *Educ:* Cheltenham Coll. (Musical Exhibition). Commenced his career as concert pianist after studying under Myra Hess; studied composition at the Royal Academy of Music; first song published when fifteen; his first work for the theatre was the composition of additional numbers for The Curate's Egg, 1922; contributed to The Little Revue and The Punch Bowl Revue, 1924; to Yoicks, Still Dancing, and Mercenary Mary, and composer of By the Way, 1925; to Just a Kiss, Kid Boots, Cochran's Revue, My Son John, Merely Molly and composer of Palladium Pleasures, 1926; to Blue Skies, The Girl Friend, and Clowns in Clover, 1927; to Charlot, 1928; and composer of Peg o' Mine, Will o' The Whispers, Vogues and Vanities, 1928; to A Yankee at the Court of King Arthur, The House that Jack Built, and (with Richard Myers) composer of Mister Cinders, 1929; part-composer of Cochran's 1930 Revue, and composer of Follow a Star and Little Tommy Tucker, 1930; part-composer of Stand Up and Sing, and Song of the Drum (with Herman Finck), and composer of Folly to be Wise, and Blue Roses, 1931; part-composer of Out of the Bottle, 1932; composer of Cochran's revue Streamline, 1934; Jill Darling, 1935; music and lyrics of Charlot Revue, The Town Talks, 1936; Hide and Seek, 1937; The Fleet's Lit Up, Running Riot, Under Your Hat, 1938; composer (to Sir A. P. Herbert's libretto) Cochran light operas: Big Ben, 1946; Bless the Bride, 1947; Tough at the Top, 1949; Water Gipsies, 1955; music and lyrics of And So To Bed, 1951; music for The Sleeping Prince, 1953; music and lyrics of Listen to the Wind, 1954; Half in Earnest (musical adaptation of The Importance of Being Earnest), 1958; composer of popular songs; many dance items; Coronation Scot; also music for the films Jack's the Boy, Water Gipsies, 1932; Falling for You, 1933; Public Nuisance No. 1, 1935; Piccadilly Incident, 1946, etc. *Publications: novels:* Zelma; Faint Harmony; Day Out; Chicanery; *travel:* Ellis in Wonderland; *autobiography:* I'm on a See-Saw; *humour:* How to Make your Fortune on the Stock Exchange; How to Enjoy Your Operation; How to Bury Yourself in the Country; How to be a Man-about-Town; Good-Bye, Dollie; *children:* Hilary's Tune; Hilary's Holidays; The Magic Baton. *Recreation:* gardening. *Club:* Garrick.

**ELLIS, Very Rev. Vorley Spencer;** Dean of St Asaph, 1938-57; late Hon. Canon, Liverpool; *b* 1882; *s* of Rev. R. Ellis, LLD, Llangollen. *Educ:* Ruthin Grammar Sch.; Oxford. Asst Master at Worksop; Curate of Chesterfield;

Vicar of Christ Church, Liverpool; of St Stephen's, Liverpool; of St Paul's, Stanley, 1937-38. *Recreation:* motoring. *Address:* Rectory Lane, Hawarden, Chester.

**ELLIS-REES, Sir Hugh,** KCMG 1953 (CMG 1943); CB 1951; *b* 19 April 1900; *s* of Hugh Rees, Chelsea; *m* Eileen Frances Anne, *d* of Reginald Clench, Highgate; one *s*. *Educ:* Tollington Sch.; London Univ. Served with RAF, 1918-19; Inland Revenue, 1919-38; Asst Controller, Clearing Office, 1938-39; HM Treasury, 1940-48; Asst Sec., 1943; Under-Sec., 1948; Financial Adviser to British Embassy, Madrid, 1940-44; Mem. of UK Delegation to OEEC, with rank of Minister, 1948; Vice-Chm., Managing Bd of European Payments Union, 1950-51; Permanent Delegate, 1952, rank of Ambassador, 1954-60; Official Chm. of OEEC, 1952-60, retired. Head of World Bank Mission to Spain, 1961-62: Chm., Egyptian Grants Cttee and Egyptian Loans Advisory Bd, 1963-70; Administrator, Catholic Fund for Overseas Develt, 1963-69; Chm., Anglo-Spanish Soc., 1967-70. Dir, Tharsis Sulphur & Copper Co., 1963-. Grand Cross, Isabel la Catolica, 1967. *Address:* 14 St George's Court, Gloucester Road, SW7. *Clubs:* Carlton, Hurlingham.

**ELLISON, Ven. Charles Ottley;** Archdeacon of Leeds, 1950-69, Emeritus since 1969; Honorary Canon of Ripon Cathedral, 1953-62; *b* 8 Feb. 1898; *s* of late S. Ellison, Leeds; *m* 1926, Lavinia (*d* 1970), *d* of late J. E. MacGregor, Flers-Breucq, Nord, France; one *d*. *Educ:* Wrekin Coll.; University of Leeds (BSc); Ripon Hall, Oxford. Curate of St Chad, Far Headingley, Leeds, 1932-37; Vicar of Kippax, 1937-46; Surrogate, 1942-; Rural Dean of Whitkirk, 1944-46; Vicar of Wetherby, 1946-55; Vicar of St John's, Briggate, Leeds, 1955-65. Pres., Yorks Assoc. of Change-Ringers, 1947-66; Chm., C of E Council for Social Aid, 1967-69; Mem., C of E Pensions Board, 1962-. *Recreation:* numismatics. *Address:* 1 Weetwood Avenue, Leeds 16. *T:* Leeds 52191. *Club:* Leeds (Leeds).

**ELLISON, Rt. Rev. Gerald Alexander;** *see* Chester, Bishop of.

**ELLISON, Randall Erskine,** CMG 1960; ED 1946; *b* 6 March 1904; 2nd *s* of late Rev. Preb. J. H. J. Ellison, CVO, Rector of St Michael's, Cornhill, EC, and Mrs Ellison; unmarried. *Educ:* Repton Sch.; New Coll., Oxford (MA). Superintendent of Education, Northern Provinces, Nigeria, 1928; seconded to British Somaliland as Dir of Education, 1938-43; Military Service with British Somaliland and Nigerian Forces, 1940-43; Asst Dir of Education, Tanganyika, 1945; Deputy Dir, 1946; Deputy Dir of Education, Northern Region, Nigeria, 1955; Dir of Education, 1956; Adviser on Education, 1957. Chm., Public Service Commission, Northern Region, Nigeria, 1958, retired 1961. Asst Sec., Church Assembly, Dean's Yard, SW1, 1962-63. Chm., Africa Cttee of CMS, 1969; Mem. Council, Westfield Coll., London Univ., 1964 (Chm., 1967-68; Hon. Treasurer, 1969). *Publication:* An English-Kanuri Sentence Book, 1937. *Recreations:* choral singing, chamber music. *Address:* 32 Oppidans Road, Hampstead, NW3. *Clubs:* Oxford and Cambridge University, Royal Commonwealth Society.

**ELLISON, Prof. William,** BSc, PhD (Dunelm); JP; Professor of Agriculture (Crop Husbandry), University College of Wales, Aberystwyth, since 1946; Vice-Principal of the College, 1966-68; *b* 28 June 1911; *o s* of late William Ellison, Eden Hall, Horden, Co. Durham; *m* 1937, Florence Elizabeth, *yr d* of late J. W. Robinson; two *d*. *Educ:* St Cuthbert's Gram. Sch.; King's Coll., Newcastle upon Tyne, Durham Univ. Asst Lectr, Agricultural Botany, UCW Aberystwyth, 1934. Seconded as Chief Technical Adviser to Montgomeryshire WAEC, 1940-46. Hill Farming Research Organization, 1958-66. Member: UGC Agric. Cttee, 1965-; NERC Land Use Research Cttee. Pres., Section M, Brit. Assoc. for Advancement of Science, 1966. JP County of Cardigan, 1957. *Publications:* Marginal Land in Britain, 1953; numerous contribs to scientific and agric. jls, on land reclamation, land use, grassland and crop production. *Recreations:* tennis, cricket. *Address:* Institute of Rural Science, Penglais, Aberystwyth. *T:* 3111. *Club:* Farmers'.

**ELLMAN-BROWN, Hon. Geoffrey,** CMG 1959; OBE 1945; FCA 1950 (ACA 1934); *b* 20 Dec. 1910; *s* of John and Violet Ellman-Brown; *m* 1936, Hilda Rosamond Fairbrother; two *s* one *d*. *Educ:* Plumtree Sch., S Rhodesia. Articled to firm of Chartered Accountants in London, 1929-34; final Chartered Accountant exam. and admitted as Mem. Inst. of Chartered Accountants of England and Wales, 1934. In Rhodesia Air Force (rising to rank of Group Capt.), 1939-46. Resumed practice as Chartered Accountant, 1946-53. Entered S Rhodesia Parliament holding ministerial office (Portfolios of Roads, Irrigation, Local Government and Housing), 1953-58. Re-entered Parliament, 1962, Minister of Finance; re-elected, 1962-65, in Opposition Party. Pres. Rhodesia Cricket Union, 1950-52; Mem. S African Cricket Board of Control, 1951-52. Chairman: Rothmans of Pall Mall (Rhodesia) Ltd; The Rhodesia Sugar Assoc.; Sugar Sales (Private) Ltd; Discount Co. of Rhodesia Ltd; Industrial Promotion Corp. Central Africa Ltd; Salisbury Portland Cement Ltd; Bowring, Duncan, Lowndes, Beddall (Private) Ltd; Director: Barclays Bank in Rhodesia; Rhodesian Milling Co. Ltd; Rhodesian Acceptances Ltd; Hippo Valley Estates Ltd; Rhodesian Castings Ltd; Colonial Mutual Life Assurance Soc. Ltd; Parry, Leon & Hayhoe (Rhodesia) Ltd; City Engineering & Carron Ltd. *Recreations:* cricket, golf, shooting, fishing. *Address:* PO Box 8426, Salisbury, Rhodesia. *T:* 28511. *Clubs:* Salisbury, Royal Salisbury Golf (Salisbury, Rhodesia); Ruwa Country.

**ELLMANN, Richard,** PhD; Goldsmiths' Professor of English Literature, Oxford University, since 1970; *b* Highland Park, Michigan, 15 March 1918; *s* of James Isaac Ellmann and Jeanette (*née* Barsook); *m* 1949, Mary Donahue; one *s* two *d*. *Educ:* Highland Park High Sch.; Yale Univ. (MA, PhD); Trinity Coll., Dublin (LittB). Served War of 1939-45, Office of Strategic Services, USNR, 1943-46. Instructor at Harvard, 1942-43, 1947-48; Briggs-Copeland Asst Prof. of Eng. Composition, Harvard, 1948-51; Prof. of English, Northwestern Univ., Evanston, Ill., 1951, Franklin Bliss Snyder Prof., 1963-68; Prof. of English, Yale, 1968-70. Rockefeller Fellow, 1946-47; Guggenheim Fellow, 1950, 1957, 1970; Kenyon Review Fellow Criticism, 1955-56; Consultant, Ford Foundation, 1958; Fellow, Sch. of Letters, Indiana Univ., 1956, 1960; Senior Fellow, 1966-; Frederick Ives Carpenter Vis. Prof., Univ. of Chicago, 1959. Mem. Editorial Committee: Publications of the Modern Language Assoc., 1968-; American Scholar, 1968-. Fellow, Amer. Acad. of Arts and Sciences. National Book Award, 1960. *Publications:* Yeats: The Man and the Masks, 1948; The Identity of Yeats, 1954; James Joyce: a biography, 1959; Eminent Domain, 1967; Edited: Selected Writings of Henri

Michaux (trans.), 1951; My Brother's Keeper, by Stanislaus Joyce, 1958; (with others) Masters of British Literature, 1958; Arthur Symons: The Symbolist Movement in Literature, 1958; (with Ellsworth Mason) The Critical Writings of James Joyce, 1959; Edwardians and late Victorians, 1959; (with Charles Feidelson, Jr), The Modern Tradition, 1965; Letters of James Joyce (Vols II and III), 1966; James Joyce, Giacomo Joyce, 1968; The Critic as Artist: Critical Writings of Oscar Wilde, 1970; Selected Letters of James Joyce, 1971. *Address:* New College, Oxford. *Clubs:* The Signet (Harvard); Elizabethan (Yale).

**ELLSWORTH, Robert** ; Ambassador, and Permanent Representative of United States on North Atlantic Council, since 1969; *b* 11 June 1926; *s* of Willoughby Fred Ellsworth and Lucille Rarig Ellsworth; *m* 1956, Vivian Esther Sies; one *s* one *d*. *Educ:* Univs of Kansas (BSME) and Michigan (JD). Active service, US Navy, 1944-46, 1950-53 (Lt-Comdr). Mem. United States Congress, 1961-66; Asst to President of US, 1969. Hon. LLD: Ottawa, 1969; Boston, 1970. *Recreations:* tennis, skiing, swimming. *Address:* US Mission to NATO, B-1110 Brussels, Belgium. *T:* Brussels 41-00-40.

**ELLWOOD, Air Marshal Sir Aubrey (Beauclerk),** KCB 1949 (CB 1944); DSC; DL; *b* 3 July 1897; *s* of late Rev. C. E. Ellwood, Rector of Cottesmore, Rutland, 1888-1926; *m* 1920, Lesley Mary Joan Matthews; one *s* one *d* (and one *s* decd). *Educ:* Cheam Sch.; Marlborough Coll. Joined Royal Naval Air Service, 1916; permanent commission RAF 1919. Served India 1919-23 and 1931-36 in RAF; RAF Staff Coll., Air Min., Army Co-operation Comd variously, 1938-42; AOC No. 18 Group RAF, 1943-44; Temp. Air Vice-Marshal, 1943; SASO HQ Coastal Comd RAF, 1944-45; Actg Air Marshal, 1947; a Dir-Gen. of Personnel, Air Ministry, 1945-47. Air Marshal, 1949; AOC-in-C, Bomber Command, 1947-50; AOC-in-C, Transport Command, 1950-52; retired, 1952. Governor and Commandant, The Church Lads' Brigade, 1954. DL, Somerset, 1960. *Recreations:* riding, fishing, music. *Address:* The Old House, North Perrott, Crewkerne, Somerset. *Clubs:* United Service, United Hunts.

*See also M. O. D. Ellwood.*

**ELLWOOD, Captain Michael Oliver Dundas,** DSO 1940; *b* 13 July 1894; *s* of late Rev. C. E. Ellwood, Cottesmore, Rutland. *Educ:* Cheam Sch., Surrey; RN Colls, Osborne and Dartmouth. Entered Royal Navy, 1907; retired as Comdr, 1934; rejoined as Capt. on retired list, 1939; reverted to retired list, Sept. 1946. *Club:* Army and Navy.

*See also Sir Aubrey Ellwood.*

**ELMHIRST, Leonard Knight,** MA Cantab; BSc Cornell; Chairman, Dartington Hall Trust; 2nd *s* of Rev. William Heaton Elmhirst, BA Cantab and Mary Knight; *m* 1925, Dorothy Whitney Straight (*d* 1968); one *s* one *d*. *Educ:* Repton Sch.; Trinity Coll., Cambridge; New York State Coll. of Agriculture; Cornell Univ. Dir, Inst. of Rural Reconstruction Visva Bharati, Bolpur, Bengal, India, 1921-24; purchased Dartington Hall for the founding of experiment in Rural Industry, Research and Education, 1925; joint British-American agricultural mission to Middle East, 1942; Pres., Internat. Conf. of Agricultural Economists, 1930-61; Founder Pres., Internat. Assoc. of Agricultural Economists; Chm., Political and Economic Planning (PEP), 1939-53; Agricultural Adviser Govt of Bengal, 1944-45; Devon CC, 1937-52; Mem., Hobhouse Cttee on National Parks, 1945-47; Vice-Chm., Cttee on Footpaths and Access. Pres. Royal Forestry Soc. of England and Wales, 1946-48; Pres., Agricultural Economics Soc., 1949; a Development Comr, 1949-65; Council Mem., Festival of Britain, 1951; Mem., Indian Govt Cttee on Higher Education for Rural Areas, 1954-55; Mem. Council, Exeter Univ., 1955-. Hon. Dr Pol Science, Freiburg Univ.; Hon. DLitt, Visva Bharati, 1960; Hon. DCL: Durham, 1962; Oxford, 1970. *Publications:* Robbery of the Soil, 1922; Rural Reconstruction, 1923; The Application of Economic Research to a Village in Bengal, 1930; Trip to Russia, 1933; Social Trends in Rural Areas, 1938; Collected Notes on Agricultural Problems in Bengal, 1945; Rabindranath Tagore and Sriniketan, 1958; Rabindranath Tagore, Pioneer in Education, 1961. *Recreation:* care of trees. *Address:* Dartington Hall, Totnes, S Devon.

*See also Sir Thomas Elmhurst.*

*See also M. A. Ash.*

**ELMHIRST, Air Marshal Sir Thomas (Walker),** KBE 1946 (CBE 1943); CB 1945; AFC 1918; RAF retired; Lieutenant-Governor and Commander-in-Chief of Guernsey, 1953-Oct. 1958; *b* 15 Dec. 1895; 4th *s* of late Rev. W. H. Elmhirst, Elmhirst, near Barnsley, Yorks; *m* 1st, 1930, Katharine Gordon (*d* 1965), 4th *d* of William Black, Chapel, Fife; one *s* one *d*; 2nd, 1968, Marian Louisa, *widow* of Col Andrew Ferguson and *d* of late Lt-Col Lord Herbert Montagu-Douglas-Scott. *Educ:* RN Colls, Osborne and Dartmouth. RN, 1908-15, Dardanelles and Dogger Bank in HMS Indomitable; RN Air Service, 1915-18; RAF as Major, Comdg Naval Airship Patrol Station, Anglesey, 1918 (AFC); RAF Staff Coll., 1925; commanded No. 15 Bomber Squadron and Abingdon Wing, 1935-37; 1st British Air Attaché to HM Embassy, Ankara, 1937-39; Dep. Dir Intelligence Air Ministry and Air Cdre HQ Fighter Comd, 1940 (Battle of Britain); RAF mem. of British Mission for Staff conversations with Turkish Gen. Staff, Ankara, 1941; AOC RAF Egypt, 1941 (despatches twice); 2nd in Comd Desert Air Force (Alamein campaigns), 1942 (CBE); Air Officer i/c Administration NW Africa, TAF, 1943 (despatches, CB, Tunis and Sicily campaigns); 2nd in Comd British Air Forces in NW Europe, Normandy-Germany campaign (KBE, despatches), 1944-45; Asst Chief of Air Staff (Intelligence), 1945-47; Chief of Inter-Service Administration in India, 1947; C-in-C Indian Air Force, 1947-50; retd, 1950. Hon. Air Marshal in the Indian Air Force, 1950. Fife County Councillor, 1950; Civil Defence Controller Eastern Zone, Scotland, 1952-53. DL, County of Fife, 1960-70. US Legion of Merit; Grand Officer, Crown of Belgium and Croix de Guerre; Legion of Honour and French Croix de Guerre. KStJ 1954. *Recreations:* forestry and fishing. *Address:* The Cottage, Dummer, Basingstoke, Hants. *Clubs:* United Service, Royal Air Force.

*See also L. K. Elmhurst.*

**ELMSLIE, Maj.-Gen. Alexander Frederic Joseph,** CB 1959; CBE 1955; psc; *b* 31 Oct. 1905. Commissioned in Royal Army Service Corps, and subsequently served in Shanghai; Captain 1935; served War of 1939-45; Substantive Major, 1942; Lt-Col 1948; Temp. Brig. 1950; Brig. 1953; Maj.-Gen. 1958. Dep. Dir of Supplies and Transport, War Office, 1953-55; Dir of Supplies and Transport, GHQ Far East Land Forces, 1956-57; Inspector, RASC, War Office, 1957-60, retired. Chm., Traffic Commissioners, NW Traffic Area, 1962-. Hon. Col 43 (Wessex) Inf. Div. Coln, RASC, TA, 1960-64; Col Comdt, RASC, 1964-65; Col Comdt, Royal Corps of Transport, 1965-.

AMIMechE 1934. *Address:* c/o Ministry of Defence (Army), Chessington, Surrey.

**ELPHINSTONE,** family name of **Baron Elphinstone.**

**ELPHINSTONE,** 17th Baron *cr* 1509; **John Alexander Elphinstone,** DL; Baron Elphinstone (UK), 1885; *b* 22 March 1914; *e s* of 16th Baron Elphinstone, KT and Lady Mary Bowes Lyon, DCVO (*d* 1961), *d* of 14th Earl of Strathmore, KG, KT, GCVO; *S* father, 1955. *Educ:* Eton; Christ Church, Oxford. Served War of 1939-45, Black Watch. Lieut, Queen's Body Guard for Scotland (Royal Company of Archers). DL Angus, 1955. Dir, Bank of Scotland and Scottish Provident Institution. President: Scottish Assoc. Boys' Clubs; Royal Zoological Society, Scotland; Hon. Pres., Scottish Football Assoc. Chm. of Council, Scottish Branch, BRCS. *Heir: b* Rev. the Hon. Andrew Charles Victor Elphinstone (*b* 10 Nov. 1918; *m* 1946, Jean Frances (*see* Hon. Mrs Andrew Elphinstone); one *s* one *d*]. *Address:* Drumkilbo, Meigle, Perthshire. *T:* Meigle 216; Glenmazeran, Tomatin, Inverness-shire.

**ELPHINSTONE of Glack, Sir Alexander Logie,** 10th Bt of Logie Elphinstone and Nova Scotia, *cr* 1701; *b* 8 March 1880; *e s* of John Elphinston, HEICS, Bombay, and Emma Eliza, 2nd *d* of George R. Betham; *m* 1st, 1911, Agnes Gertrude Blanche Durell (*d* 1961), *e d* of Capt. T. E. Charles King, West Yorks Regt; 2nd, 1962, Mrs Muriel Eileen Patterson Sayles, *widow* of James Patterson Sayles, N Ireland and 2nd *d* of late John MacComish, N Ireland; proved his right (as 10th Bt), 1927 (title had remained dormant since death of 4th Bt in 1743); claimant, Barony of New Glasgow, Nova Scotia, 1625. Entered Army (Univ. candidate, Pembroke Coll., Cambridge), 1899; retired 1930; served South African War, 1899-1902 (Queen's medal 6 bars, King's medal 2 bars); European War, 1914-19 (Star, Victory and Allies medals); War of 1939-45, attached to BRC. Coronation Medals (1902 and 1937), Silver Jubilee (1935); Freeman of City of London; Liveryman of Needle Makers' Company. *Heir: nephew* John Elphinston [*b* 12 Aug. 1924; *m* 1953, Margaret Doreen, *e d* of Edric Tasker, Cheltenham; four *s*]. *Address:* Kingsway, 5 Bath Road, Worthing, Sussex. *Club:* Royal Over-Seas League.

**ELPHINSTONE, Hon. Mrs Andrew (Jean Frances),** CVO 1953; *b* 22 Feb. 1923; *d* of late Capt. A. V. Hambro; *m* 1st, 1942, Capt. Hon. Vicary Paul Gibbs, Grenadier Guards (killed in action, 1944), *er s* of 4th Baron Aldenham; one *d* (and one *d* decd); 2nd, 1946, Rev. Hon. Andrew Charles Victor Elphinstone, 2nd *s* of 16th Baron Elphinstone, KT and *heir-pres.* to 17th Baron Elphinstone, *qv*; one *s* one *d*. Lady-in-Waiting to the Queen as Princess Elizabeth, 1945; Extra Woman of the Bedchamber to the Queen, 1952-. *Address:* Maryland, Worplesdon, Surrey. *T:* Worplesdon 2629.

**ELPHINSTONE, Sir Howard (Graham)**; 4th Bt *cr* 1816; *b* 28 Dec. 1898; *o s* of Graham Warburton Elphinstone, ICS, 2nd *s* of 3rd Bt and Susan Sophy, *d* of late Henry C. R. Harley, Madanapalle, India (she *m* 2nd, George Middleton); *S* grandfather, 1917; *m* 1924, Alice Mary Emerton, *er d* of P. J. Emerton Brown; two *d. Educ:* Sedbergh Sch. Enlisted army, 1917-20; appointed Administrative Service, Kenya Colony, 1921. *Heir: cousin* Maurice Douglas Warburton Elphinstone, TD [*b* 13 April 1909; *s* of Rev. Maurice Curteis Elphinstone; *m* 1943, Helen Barbara, *d* of late George Ramsay Main; one *s* one *d*]. Address: Los Colones, La Jara, Sanlucar de Barrameda, Cadiz, Spain.

**ELSDEN, Sidney Reuben,** BA, PhD (Cambridge); Director, ARC Food Research Institute, since 1965; Professor of Biology, University of East Anglia, since 1965; *b* 13 April 1915; *er s* of late Reuben Charles Elsden, Cambridge; *m* 1st, 1942, Frances Scott Wilson (*d* 1943); 2nd, 1948, Erica Barbara Scott, *er d* of late Grahame Scott Gardiner, Wisbech, Cambs; twin *s. Educ:* Cambridge and County High Sch. for Boys; Fitzwilliam House, Cambridge. Lecturer, Biochemistry, University of Edinburgh, 1937-42; Mem. Scientific Staff of ARC Unit for Animal Physiology, 1943-48; Sen. Lectr in Microbiology, Univ. of Sheffield, 1948-59; Hon. Dir, ARC Unit for Microbiology, Univ. of Sheffield, 1952-65. Visiting Prof. of Microbiology, Univ. of Illinois, Urbana, Ill, USA, 1956. *Publications:* contribs to scientific jls on metabolism of micro-organisms. *Recreations:* gardening, angling. *Address:* 26a The Street, Costessey, Norwich NOR 51X; Agricultural Research Council, Food Research Institute, Colney Lane, Norwich, NOR 70F. *Club:* National Liberal.

**ELSTUB, Sir St John de Holt,** Kt 1970; CBE 1954; BSc, CEng, FIMechE, FInstP; Managing Director, Imperial Metal Industries Ltd, since 1962; Director: Royal Insurance Co.; British Engine Boiler & Electrical Insurance Co.; Alcoa (Great Britain) Ltd; Nuclear Developments Ltd; Local Director (Midlands), Hill Samuel & Co. Ltd; *b* 16 June 1915; *s* of Ernest Elstub and Mary Gertrude (*née* Whitaker); *m* 1939, Patricia Arnold; two *d. Educ:* Rugby Sch.; Manchester Univ. Joined ICI, Billingham, 1936. Served War of 1939-45 as RAF Bomber Pilot; Supt, Rocket Propulsion Dept, Ministry of Supply, 1945. Joined ICI Metals Div., 1947, Prod. Dir, 1950, Man. Dir, 1957, Chm., 1961. Vice-President: IMechE; British Non-Ferrous Metals Federation. Chm., Jt Government/Industry Cttee on Aircraft Industry, 1967-69; Member: Plowden Cttee on Aircraft Industry, 1964-65; Engrg Industry Trng Bd, 1964-; Midlands Electricity Bd, 1966-. Governor, Administrative Staff Coll., Henley; Vice-Chm. of Council, Univ. of Aston in Birmingham; Life Governor, Univ. of Birmingham. *Recreations:* gardening, travel, motor sport. *Address:* Perry House, Hartlebury, Worcs. *T:* Hartlebury 327.

**ELTON,** family name of **Baron Elton.**

**ELTON,** 1st Baron *cr* 1934, of Headington; **Godfrey Elton;** *b* 29 March 1892; *e s* of late Edward Fiennes Elton, Ovington Park, Hants, and Burleigh Court, Glos; *m* 1921, Dedi, *d* of Gustav Hartmann, Oslo, Norway; one *s* two *d. Educ:* Rugby Sch. (Head of Sch., 1910-11); Balliol Coll., Oxford. First Class Classical Mods, 1913. 2nd Lieut 4th Hants Regt, Sept. 1914; Captain 1918; served in Mesopotamia, Siege of Kut-el-Amara, 1915-16 (slightly wounded); Prisoner of war in Asiatic Turkey, 1916-18; Fellow of Queen's Coll., Oxford, and Lecturer in Modern History, 1919-39; Dean, 1921-23; Tutor, 1927-34; Supernumerary Fellow, 1939-. Contested (Lab) Thornbury Div. of Glos, 1924, 1929; resigned prospective candidature and was expelled from Labour Party as supporter of Mr MacDonald, Sept. 1931; Hon. Political Sec., National Labour Cttee, 1932; Hon. Ed. the News-Letter, 1932-38; Mem., Ullswater Cttee on the future of Broadcasting, 1935; Chm., Executive Cttee, Road Accidents Emergency Council, 1936-41; Chm., Commonwealth Youth Sunday Cttee, 1941-62; Pres., Metropolitan Assoc. of

Building Socs, 1943-61; Mem., Archbishops' Commn on Evangelism, 1944; Gen. Sec., Rhodes Trust, 1939-59; Pres., Christian Service Union, 1941-63; Mem. of Royal Commission for Exhibition of 1851, 1943-64. Dir, Cape Asbestos Group, 1950-65; has done much broadcasting, "It occurs to me", etc. Is Independent in politics. *Publications:* Schoolboys and Exiles (verse), 1920; The Revolutionary Idea in France, 1789-1878, 1923 (fourth impression of second edn, 1959); Years of Peace (verse), 1925; The Testament of Dominic Burleigh, 1926; Against the Sun, 1928; The Stranger, 1930; England Arise! a study of the pioneering days of the Labour Party, 1931; Towards the New Labour Party, 1932; Among Others, 1938; Life of James Ramsay MacDonald, Vol. I 1866-1919, 1939; It Occurs to Me, 1939; Notebook in Wartime, 1941; Saint George or the Dragon, 1942; Imperial Commonwealth, 1945; Such is the Kingdom, 1947; The Two Villages, 1949; General Gordon, 1954; Edward King and our times, 1958; General Gordon's Khartoum Journal (ed), 1961; Simon Peter, a study of discipleship, 1965; The Unarmed Invasion, 1965; contributor to DNB and many newspapers and journals. *Heir: s* Hon. Rodney Elton [*b* 2 March 1930; *m* 1958, Anne Frances, *d* of Robert Tilney, The Hall, Sutton Bonington, Leics; one *s* three *d. Educ:* Eton; New Coll., Oxford]. *Address:* Adderbury, near Banbury, Oxon. *T:* Adderbury 205. *Club:* Athenæum.

**ELTON, Sir Arthur Hallam Rice,** 10th Bt *cr* 1717; Chairman: Clevedon Printing Co. Ltd; Film Centre (International) Ltd; Publisher, North Somerset Mercury; Director, Canadian Film Institute; *b* 10 Feb. 1906; *er s* of Sir Ambrose Elton, 9th Bt, and Dorothy Wynne (*d* 1957), *o d* of Arthur Wiggin, Oddington Estate, Ceylon; *S* father, 1951; *m* 1948, Margaret Ann Bjornson; one *s* two *d. Educ:* Marlborough Coll.; Jesus Coll., Cambridge. Joined script dept, Gainsborough Pictures Ltd, 1927, rep. company in Germany, 1929; joined Empire Marketing Bd Film Unit, 1931, and transferred to GPO Film Unit. With John Grierson and others helped to found theory and practice of documentary film and founded Film Centre Ltd, 1938; Supervisor of Films, MOI, 1941-45; Founder Pres., Scientific Film Assoc., 1943-46, 1953-56 (Chm., 1963-67); Film Adviser: Danish Govt, 1945-46; CCG, 1947-48. Governor, British Film Institute, 1949-50. Member: Council Nat. Film Archive, 1956; Assoc. of Cine and Television Technicians, 1928-; Experimental Production Cttee of British Film Inst., 1957-; joined Shell Internat. Petroleum Co. 1957, in charge of films, television, until 1960; Gen. Manager Publicity, Associated Electrical Industries Ltd, 1961-63; Film Adviser, Shell Internat. Petroleum Co., 1963-. Chairman: Film Centre (International) Ltd; Centre for Study of the History of Technology, Bath Univ.; British Industrial and Scientific Film Assoc., 1967-; President: Friends of Nat. Film Archive, 1962-66; Brit. Nat. Film Catalogue, 1964-67; Internat. Scientific Film Assoc., 1968-; Somerset Archaeological Soc., 1963. Member: BBC Adv. Council, 1966-68; Working Party on Preservation of Technological Material, 1970. *Publications:* (with Robert Fairthorne) Why Aeroplanes Fly, 1936; How Motorcars Run, 1939; British Railways, 1946; (with Peter Brinson) The Film Industry in Six European Countries, UNESCO, 1950; The Film as Source Material for History, Aslib. Proc. Vol. VII No. 4, 1955; Gas for Light and Heat, A History of Technology Vol. IV, 1958; Editor, new enl. edn of Klingender, Art and the Industrial Revolution, 1968. *Recreation:* history of technology and industrial archæology. *Heir: s* Charles Abraham Grierson Elton, *b* 23 May 1953. *Address:* Clevedon Court, Som. *T:* Clevedon 2768; 73 Clarence Gate Gardens, NW1. *T:* 01-723 5588. *Club:* Athenæum.

**ELTON, Charles Sutherland,** FRS 1953; Director, Bureau of Animal Population, Department of Zoological Field Studies, 1932-67, and Reader in Animal Ecology, Oxford University, 1936-67; Senior Research Fellow, Corpus Christi College, Oxford, 1936-67, Hon. Fellow since Oct. 1967; *b* 29 March 1900; *s* of late Oliver Elton; *m* 1st, 1928, Rose Montague; no *c*; 2nd, 1937, Edith Joy, *d* of Rev. Canon F. G. Scovell; one *s* one *d. Educ:* Liverpool Coll.; New Coll., Oxford. First Class Hons Zoology, Oxford, 1922; served as Ecologist on Oxford Univ. Expedition to Spitsbergen, 1921, Merton Coll. Arctic Expedition, 1923, Oxford Univ. Arctic Expedition, 1924 and Oxford Univ. Lapland Expedition, 1930. Mem. Nature Conservancy, 1949-56. Foreign Hon. Mem., Amer. Acad. of Arts and Sciences, 1968. Linnean Soc. Gold Medal, 1967. *Publications:* Animal Ecology, 1927; Animal Ecology and Evolution, 1930; The Ecology of Animals, 1933; Exploring the Animal World, 1933; Voles, Mice and Lemmings, 1942; The Ecology of Invasions by Animals and Plants, 1958; The Pattern of Animal Communities, 1966. *Recreations:* natural history, reading. *Address:* 61 Park Town, Oxford OX2 6SL. *T:* Oxford 57644.

**ELTON, Geoffrey Rudolph,** LittD; PhD; FBA 1967; Professor of English Constitutional History, Cambridge, since 1967; *b* 17 Aug. 1921; changed name to Elton under Army Council Instruction, 1944; *e s* of Victor Ehrenberg, *qv*; *m* 1952, Sheila Lambert; no *c*. *Educ:* Prague; Rydal Sch. London External BA (1st Cl. Hons) 1943; Derby Student, University Coll. London, 1946-48; PhD 1949. Asst Master, Rydal Sch., 1940-43. Service in E Surrey Regt and Int. Corps (Sgt), 1944-46. Asst in History, Glasgow Univ., 1948-49; Univ. Asst Lectr, Cambridge, 1949-53, Lectr, 1953-63, Reader in Tudor Studies, 1963-67. Visiting Amundson Prof., Univ. of Pittsburgh, Sept.-Dec. 1963. FRHistS 1954; Fellow of Clare Coll., Cambridge, 1954-; LittD 1960. *Publications:* The Tudor Revolution in Government, 1953; England under the Tudors, 1955; (ed) New Cambridge Modern History, vol. 2, 1958; Star Chamber Stories, 1958; The Tudor Constitution, 1960; Henry VIII: an essay in revision, 1962; Renaissance and Reformation (Ideas and Institutions in Western Civilization), 1963; Reformation Europe, 1963; The Practice of History, 1967; The Future of the Past, 1968; The Sources of History: England 1200-1640, 1969; Political History: Principles and Practice, 1970; contribs to English Hist. Review, Econ. Hist. Rev., History, Hist. Jl, Times Lit. Supplement, Listener, etc. *Recreations:* squash rackets, joinery, and beer. *Address:* Clare College, Cambridge; Faculty of History, West Road, Cambridge. *T:* Cambridge 61661.

**ELTON, John;** *see* Elton, P. J.

**ELTON, John Bullen;** Master of the Supreme Court, Queen's Bench Division, since 1966; *b* 18 Jan. 1916; *s* of Percy Maden Elton, company director; *m* 1939, Sonia; three *d. Educ:* Bishop's Stortford Coll.; Brasenose Coll., Oxford. Called to the Bar, Inner Temple, 1938. RNVR, 1943-46. *Recreation:* sailing. *Address:* 3 Ailsa Road, St Margaret's, Twickenham, Middx. *Club:* Royal Victoria Yacht.

**ELTON, Air Vice-Marshal John Goodenough,** CB 1955; CBE 1945; DFC 1940; AFC 1935; Managing Director, Capitol Radio Engineering Institute; *b* 5 May 1905; *s* of late Rev. George G. Elton, MA Oxon; *m* 1st, 1927, Helen Whitfield (marr. diss.); one *s*; 2nd, 1949, Francesca Cavallero. *Educ:* St John's, Leatherhead. Entered RAF, 1926; service in UK, 1926-31; Singapore, 1932-35 (AFC); Irak, 1939. Served War of 1939-45 (despatches twice, DFC, CBE); CO 47 Sqdn, Sudan, 1940; HQ, ME, Cairo, 1941; comd in succession Nos 242, 238 and 248 Wings, N Africa, 1942; CO RAF Turnberry, Scotland, 1943; CO RAF Silloth, Cumberland, 1944; AOA, HQ Mediterranean Allied Coastal Air Force, 1945-46; idc 1947; Dep. Dir, Air Min., 1948; RAF Mem., UK Delegn, Western Union Military Cttee, 1949-50; Comdt, Sch. of Tech. Training, Halton, 1951; Air Attaché, Paris, 1952; Air Officer i/c Administration, HQ Bomber Comd, 1953-56; Chief of Staff to the Head of British Jt Services Mission, Washington, DC, 1956-59; retired, 1959. *Address:* c/o Lloyds Bank, Cox's and King's Branch, 6 Pall Mall, SW1. *Club:* Royal Air Force.

**ELTON, (Peter) John,** MC 1944; Managing Director, Alcan Aluminium (UK) Ltd; Chairman and Managing Director, Alcan Booth Industries Ltd; Chairman, Alcan (UK) Ltd; director of other companies; *b* 14 March 1924; 2nd *s* of Sydney George Elton; *m* 1948, Patricia Ann Stephens; two *d*. *Educ:* Eastbourne Coll.; Clare Coll., Cambridge. Indian Army: 14th Punjab Regt, 1942-45 (twice wounded). Hons Degree, Econs and Law, Cambridge. *Recreations:* sailing, swimming, golf. *Address:* Wildwood House, Bucklers Hard, Beaulieu, Hants. *T:* Bucklers Hard 206. *Clubs:* Bath; New Zealand Golf (West Byfleet).

**ELTON-BARRATT, Major Stanley George Reeves;** late 16/5th Lancers (R of O); Director of Barratt & Co., Ltd, London, 1923-67; *b* 10 Feb. 1900; *o surv. s* of late Sir Albert Barratt; granted Royal Licence and authority to use additional surname of Elton, 1970; *m* 1926, Mary Katherine Gloria, *e d* and *co-heir* of late Brig.-Gen. F. A. G. Y. Elton, RA; two *s* one *d*. *Educ:* Highgate. Served European War, 1918-19, Lieut 1st Res. Regt of Cavalry; attached Inns of Court Cav., 1924-25; Transfd 16/5 Lancers (R of O), 1935; re-employed, 1939, Remount Service, Capt.; served on Staff with Special Forces, 1940-44, Major 1942, retd 1945. Joint Master, Romney Marsh Hounds, 1929-30; Master or Jt-Master Old Berkeley Foxhounds, 1931-44; Master, Old Berkeley (East) Foxhounds, 1944-48; Jt Master, Coollattin Foxhounds, 1950-52. CC Herts, 1933-46; formerly Lord of the Manor of Loddington, Northants. OStJ 1931; Gold Staff Officer at Coronations, 1937 and 1953. *Recreation:* fox hunting. *Address:* Blackwell Hall, Chesham, Bucks. *T:* Little Chalfont 3483. *Clubs:* Special Forces, Royal Automobile.

**ELVEDEN, Viscount; Arthur Edward Rory Guinness;** *b* 10 Aug. 1969; *s* and *heir* of Earl of Iveagh, *qv*.

**ELVEY, Lewis Edgar,** CMG 1967; company director; *b* 18 Oct. 1908; *s* of Robert Montgomery Elvey and Kate (*née* Smith); *m* 1938, Mary, *d* of Thomas Regan and Mary (*née* Kilmartin); one *s* one *d*. *Educ:* Sch. of Mines, Western Australia. Mining Engineer. Chairman: Hadwa Ltd (formerly Hadfields (WA) 1934 Ltd), 1966-; North Kalgurli (1912) Ltd, 1966-; Westralian Sands Ltd; Director: Great Boulder Gold Mines Ltd, 1965- (Gen. Man., 1951-66); The Griffin Coal Mining Co. Ltd, 1964-; Bell Bros Holdings Ltd. President: Chamber of Mines WA, 1960-67; Australasian Inst. of Mining and Metallurgy, 1964. *Recreation:* golf. *Address:* 38 Pearse Street, Cottesloe, W Australia. *T:* 3-1039. *Club:* Hannans (Kalgoorlie, WA).

**ELVIN, Herbert Lionel;** Director of the University of London Institute of Education, since 1958 (Professor of Education in Tropical Areas, 1956); Director, Department of Education, UNESCO, Paris, 1950-56; *b* 7 Aug. 1905; *e s* of late Herbert Henry Elvin; *m* 1934, Mona Bedortha, *d* of Dr C. S. S. Dutton, San Francisco; one *s*. *Educ:* elementary schs; Southend High Sch.; Trinity Hall, Cambridge (1st Class Hons, History and English). Commonwealth Fellow, Yale Univ., USA. Fellow of Trinity Hall, Cambridge, 1930-44; Temporary Civil Servant (Air Min., 1940-42, MOI, 1943-45); Principal, Ruskin Coll., Oxford, 1944-50. Parliamentary candidate (Lab), Cambridge Univ., 1935; Pres., English New Education Fellowship; Pres., Council for Education in World Citizenship; Chm., Commonwealth Educn Liaison Cttee. Formerly Member: Cttee on Higher Education; Govt of India Educn Commn; University Grants Cttee, 1946-50; Central Advisory Council for Education (England) and Secondary School Examinations Council. *Publications:* Men of America (Pelican Books), 1941; An Introduction to the Study of Literature (Poetry), 1949; Education and Contemporary Society, 1965. *Recreations:* most games indifferently; formerly athletics (half-mile, Cambridge *v* Oxford, 1927). *Address:* University of London Institute of Education, Malet Street, WC1.

**ELVIN, Violetta, (Violetta Prokhorova) (Signora Fernando Savarese);** ballerina; a prima ballerina of Sadler's Wells Ballet, Royal Opera House, London (now The Royal Ballet), 1951-56; *b* Moscow, 3 Nov. 1925; *d* of Vassilie Prokhorov, engineer, and Irena Grimouzinskaya, former actress; *m* 1st, 1944, Harold Elvin (divorced 1952), of British Embassy, Moscow; 2nd, 1953, Siegbert J. Weinberger, New York; 3rd, 1959, Fernando Savarese, lawyer; one *s*. *Educ:* Bolshoi Theatre Sch., Moscow. Trained for ballet since age of 8 by: E. P. Gerdt, A. Vaganova, M. A. Kojuchova. Grad, 1942, as soloist; made mem. Bolshoi Theatre Ballet; evacuated to Tashkent, 1943; ballerina Tashkent State Theatre; rejoined Bolshoi Theatre at Kuibishev again as soloist, 1944; left for London, 1945. Joined Sadler's Wells Ballet at Covent Garden as guest-soloist, 1946; later became regular mem. Has danced all principal rôles, notably, Le Lac des Cygnes, Sleeping Beauty, Giselle, Cinderella, Sylvia, Ballet Imperial, etc. Danced four-act Le Lac des Cygnes, first time, 1943; guest-artist Stanislavsky Theatre, Moscow, 1944, Sadler's Wells Theatre, 1947; guest-prima ballerina, La Scala, Milan, Nov. 1952-Feb. 1953 (Macbeth, La Gioconda, Swan Lake, Petrouchka); guest artist, Cannes, July 1954; Copenhagen, Dec. 1954; Teatro Municipal, Rio de Janeiro, May 1955 (Giselle, Swan Lake, Les Sylphides, Nutcracker, Don Quixote and The Dying Swan); Festival Ballet, Festival Hall, 1955; guest-prima ballerina in Giselle, Royal Opera House, Stockholm (Anna Pavlova Memorial), 1956; concluded stage career when appeared in Sleeping Beauty, Royal Opera House, Covent Garden, June 1956. *Appeared in films:* The Queen of Spades, Twice Upon a Time, Melba. Television appearances in Russia and England. Has toured with Sadler's Wells Ballet, France, Italy, Portugal, United States and Canada. *Recreations:* chess, tennis, swimming. *Address:*

c/o British Consulate-General, Via Crispi, Naples, Italy.

**ELWES, Simon,** RA 1967 (ARA 1956); RP 1933; portrait painter; *b* 29 June 1902; *s* of late Gervase Elwes, DL, JP, Knight of Malta, Billing Hall, Northampton, and Roxby, Lincs and late Lady Winefride Feilding, 3rd *d* of Rudolph, 8th Earl of Denbigh and Desmond; *m* 1926, Hon. Gloria Rodd, 2nd *d* of 1st Lord Rennell of Rodd, PC, GCB, GCMG, GCVO; three *s*. *Educ:* The Oratory. Studied at the Slade Sch., 1919 and in Paris until 1926; Vice-Pres. Royal Society of Portrait Painters, 1953-. Created Knight of Malta, 1929. Served war of 1939-45, 10th Royal Hussars; Lt-Col 1944 (Public Relations). *Recreation:* painting landscape. *Address:* Old Place, Amberley, Sussex. *Clubs:* White's, Beefsteak, Chelsea Arts.

**ELWORTHY, Marshal of the Royal Air Force Sir (Samuel) Charles,** GCB 1962 (KCB 1961; CB 1960); CBE 1946; DSO 1941; MVO 1953; DFC 1941; AFC 1941; Constable and Governor of Windsor Castle, since 1971; *b* 23 March 1911; *e s* of late Percy Elworthy, late Capt., 1st Life Guards, Gordon's Valley, Timaru, New Zealand; *m* 1936, Audrey Hutchinson; three *s* one *d*. *Educ:* Marlborough; Trinity Coll., Cambridge. Commissioned in RAFO 1933, transferred to Auxiliary Air Force, 1934; called to Bar, Lincoln's Inn, 1935, Hon. Bencher 1970; permanent commission in RAF, 1935; War Service in Bomber Comd; Acting Group Capt., 1942; Acting Air Cdre, 1944; Group Capt., 1949; Air Cdre, 1956; Air Vice-Marshal, 1957; Actg Air Marshal, 1959; Air Marshal, 1960; Air Chief Marshal, 1962; Marshal of the RAF, 1967. Comdt RAF Staff Coll., Bracknell, 1957-59; DCAS, 1959-60; C-in-C, Middle East, 1960-63; CAS, 1963-67; Chief of the Defence Staff, 1967-71. Governor, Wellington Coll., 1970-. *Address:* Ministry of Defence, Whitehall, SW1; Perseverance Cottage, Harpsden, Henley-on-Thames, Oxon. *Clubs:* Bath; Leander.

**ELY,** 8th Marquess of, *cr* 1801; **Charles John Tottenham;** Bt 1780; Baron Loftus, 1785; Viscount Loftus, 1789; Earl of Ely, 1794; Baron Loftus (UK), 1801; Headmaster, Boulden House, Trinity College School, Port Hope, Ontario, since 1941; *b* 30 May 1913; *s* of G. L. Tottenham, BA (Oxon), and Cécile Elizabeth, *d* of J. S. Burra, Bockhanger, Kennington, Kent; *g s* of C. R. W. Tottenham, MA (Oxon), Woodstock, Newtown Mount Kennedy, Co. Wicklow, and Plâs Berwyn, Llangollen, N Wales; *S* cousin, 1969; *m* 1938, Katherine Elizabeth, *d* of Col W. H. Craig, Kingston, Ont; three *s* one *d*. *Educ:* Collège de Genève, Internat. Sch., Geneva; Queen's Univ., Kingston, Ont (BA). Career as Schoolmaster. *Recreation:* fishing. *Heir: e s* Viscount Loftus, *qv*. *Address:* Trinity College School, Port Hope, Ontario, Canada. *T:* 885 5209. *Clubs:* Kildare Street (Dublin); University (Toronto).

**ELY, Bishop of,** since 1964; **Rt. Rev. Edward James Keymer Roberts;** *b* 18 April 1908; *s* of Rev. Arthur Henry Roberts; *m* 1941, Dorothy Frances, *d* of Canon Edwin David Bowser, Deal; three *s* one *d*. *Educ:* Marlborough; Corpus Christi Coll., Cambridge; Cuddesdon Theological Coll. BA 2nd class Theological Tripos, 1930; MA 1935. DD (*hc*) Cambridge, 1965. Deacon, 1931; priest, 1932; Curate of All Saints, Margaret Street, 1931-35; Vice-Principal Cuddesdon Coll., 1935-39; Examining Chaplain to Bishop of Portsmouth and Commissary, Johannesburg, 1936-39; Vicar of St Matthew, Southsea, 1940-45; Curate-in-charge of St Bartholomew, Southsea, 1941-45; Examining Chaplain to Bishop of Portsmouth, 1942-56; Proctor in Convocation, Portsmouth, 1944-49; Commissary, Northern Rhodesia, 1946-51; Hon. Canon of Portsmouth, 1947-49; Archdeacon of Isle of Wight, Vicar of Brading, Rector of Yaverland, 1949-52; Archdeacon of Portsmouth, 1952-56; Suffragan Bishop of Malmesbury, 1956-62; Examining Chaplain to Bishop of Bristol, 1959-62; Suffragan Bishop of Kensington, 1962-64. Hon. Fellow, Corpus Christi Coll., Cambridge, 1964-. Select Preacher, University of Cambridge, 1966. *Address:* The Bishop's House, Ely, Cambs. *T:* Ely 2749.

**ELY, Dean of;** *see* Carey, Very Rev. M. S.

**ELY, Archdeacon of;** *see* Long, Ven. J. S.

**ELY, Paul;** Général d'Armée; Président du Comité d'Orientation et de Perfectionnement du Haut Enseignement de Défense; Grand Croix, Légion d'Honneur; Médaille Militaire; Croix de Guerre (1914-18, 3 citations), Croix de Guerre (1939-45, 2 citations), France; Croix de Guerre TOE (1 citation Indochine); *b* 17 Dec. 1897; *m* Graziella Ortoli. *Educ:* Lycée de Brest; Ecole Spéciale Militaire de Saint-Cyr; Ecole Supérieure de Guerre. Sous-Lt, 1918; CO 10th Bn de Chasseurs, 1941-42; Rep. of Allied High Command with Resistance, 1944; Gén. de Bde, 1945; Dir of Inf., 1945; Gén. de Div., 1946; Mil. Cab. Dir Min. of Nat., 1946; Cmdr 7th Mil. Region, 1947; Chief of Staff to Inspector Gen. of Armed Forces, 1948; Général de Corps d'Armée, 1949; French Rep., to Western Union, 1948-49, and to Standing Group, NATO, 1950-53; Général d'Armée, 1953; Général Chef d'Etat Major Général des Forces Armées, 1953-54; C-in-C and Gen. Comr in Indo-China 1954-55; Chef d'Etat-Major Général des Forces Armées, 1956-58; Chef d'Etat-Major Général de la Défense Nationale, 1959-61. Hon. GBE (UK) and other foreign Grand Crosses etc., of Orders. *Publications:* L'Armée dans la Nature, 1961; L'Indochine dans la Tourmente, 1964. *Address:* 4 rue Puvis de Chavannes, Paris.

**ELYAN, Sir (Isadore) Victor,** Kt 1970; Chief Justice of Swaziland, 1965-70, retired; *b* 5 Sept. 1909; *s* of Jacob Elyan, PC, JP and Olga Elyan; *m* 1939, Ivy Ethel Mabel Stuart-Weir (*d* 1965); no *c*; *m* 1966, Rosaleen Jeanette O'Shea. *Educ:* St Stephen's Green Sch., Dublin; Trinity Coll., Dublin Univ. BA 1929, LLB 1931, MA 1932, TCD. Admitted a Solicitor of Supreme Court of Judicature, Ireland, 1930; Barrister-at-Law, King's Inns 1949, Middle Temple, 1952. Resident Magistrate, HM Colonial Legal Service, Gold Coast, 1946-54; Senior Magistrate, 1954-55; Judge of Appeal of the Court of Appeal for Basutoland, the Bechuanaland Protectorate and Swaziland, 1955-66; Puisne Judge, High Courts of Basutoland and the Bechuanaland Protectorate, 1955-65; on occasions acted as Judge between 1953 and 1955, Gold Coast; as Justice of Appeal, West African Court of Appeal; and as Chief Justice of Basutoland, the Bechuanaland Protectorate and Swaziland, also Pres. Court of Appeal, during 1956, 1961 and 1964; Judge of Appeal: Court of Appeal for Botswana, 1966-; Court of Appeal for Swaziland, 1967-; Court of Appeal, Lesotho, 1968-. Served War, 1942-46; attached to Indian Army, 1944-46; GSO2 Military Secretary's Branch (DAMS), 1945-46 in rank of Major. Mem., Internat. Adv. Bd, The African Law Reports, 1969. *Publications:* Editor, High Commission Territories Law Reports, 1956, 1957, 1958, 1959, 1960. *Recreation:* sailing. *Address:* PO Box 31, Brighton Beach, Natal, South Africa.

**EMANUEL, Aaron,** CMG 1957; Assistant Under-Secretary of State, Ministry of Housing and Local Government; Chairman, West Midlands Economic Planning Board, since 1968; *b* 11 Feb. 1912; *s* of Jack Emanuel and Jane (*née* Schaverien); *m* 1936, Ursula Pagel; two *s* one *d*. *Educ:* Henry Thornton Sch., Clapham; London Sch. of Economics (BSc Econ.). Economist at International Institute of Agriculture, Rome, 1935-38; Board of Trade, 1938; Ministry of Food, 1940; Colonial Office, 1943; Ministry of Health, 1961; Dept. of Economic Affairs, 1965. *Address:* 17 Court Lane Gardens, SE21. *T:* 01-693 6505; 35 Warwick Crest, Arthur Road, Edgbaston, Birmingham 15. *T:* 021-454 5695.

**EMANUEL, Richard Wolff,** MA, DM Oxon, FRCP; Physician to Department of Cardiology, Middlesex Hospital, since 1963; Lecturer in Cardiology, Middlesex Hospital Medical School since 1963; Physician to National Heart Hospital since 1963; Lecturer to Institute of Cardiology since 1963; *b* 13 Jan. 1923; *s* of Prof. and Mrs J. G. Emanuel, Birmingham; *m* 1950, Lavinia Hoffmann; three *s*. *Educ:* Bradfield Coll.; Oriel Coll., Oxford; Middlesex Hospital. House Appts at Middx Hospital, 1948 and 1950. Captain RAMC, 1948-50; Med. Registrar, Middx Hosp., 1951-52; Sen. Med. Registrar, Middx Hosp., 1953-55; Sen. Med. Registrar, Nat. Heart Hosp., 1956-58; Fellow in Med., Vanderbilt Univ., 1956-57; Sen. Med. Registrar, Dept of Cardiology, Brompton Hosp., 1958-61; Asst Dir, Inst. of Cardiology and Hon. Asst Physician to Nat. Heart Hosp., 1961-63. Vis. Lecturer: Univ. of Med. Sciences and Chulalongkorn Univ., Thailand; Univ. of the Philippines; Univ. of Singapore; Univ. of Malaya; St Cyre's Lectr, London, 1968; Ricardo Molina Lectr, Philippines, 1969. Has addressed numerous Heart Socs in SE Asia. Asst Sec., British Cardiac Soc., 1966-68, Sec., 1968-70; Fellow: American Coll. of Cardiology; Scientific Council of Internat. Coll. of Angiology; Hon. Fellow, Philippine Coll. of Cardiology. Member: Brit. Acad. of Forensic Sciences (Med.); Cardiological Cttee, RCP. Asst Editor, British Heart Journal. *Publications:* various articles on diseases of the heart in British and American jls. *Recreations:* XVIIIth century glass, fishing, sailing. *Address:* 6 Upper Wimpole Street, W1M 7TD. *T:* 01-935 3243; 6 Lansdowne Walk, W11. *T:* 01-727 6688; Canute Cottage, Old Bosham, near Chichester, Sussex. *T:* Bosham 3318. *Club:* Bath.

**EMBERTON, John James,** CMG 1944; MC 1918; *b* 26 Feb. 1893; *m* 1933, Sybil Challoner (author of Shrub Gardening for Flower Arrangement, 1965, and Garden Foliage for Flower Arrangement, 1968), *d* of late Dr David Ewart, OBE, Chichester; two *s*. *Educ:* Newcastle-under-Lyme. Hon. Artillery Co. and Royal Artillery, 1914-19 (MC); Nigeria Administrative Service, 1920-46 (retired); late Senior Resident, Plateau Province, Nigeria. Subsequently employed in CO and in CCG. *Recreations:* golf, gardening. *Address:* Little Close, Linkside East, Hindhead, Surrey. *T:* Hindhead 701.

**EMBLING, John Francis,** CB 1967; Deputy Under-Secretary of State, Department of Education and Science, since 1966; *b* 16 July 1909; *m* 1940, Margaret Gillespie Anderson; one *s*. *Educ:* University of Bristol. Teaching: Dean Close, 1930; Frensham Heights, 1931; Lecturer: Leipzig Univ., 1936; SW Essex Technical Coll., 1938 (Head of Dept, 1942); Administrative Asst, Essex LEA, 1944; Ministry of Education: Principal, 1946; Asst Secretary, 1949; Under-Secretary of State for Finance and Accountant-General, Dept of Education and Science, 1960-66. *Address:* The Old Rectory, Wixoe, Suffolk. *T:* Ridgewell 241. *Clubs:* Athenæum, English-Speaking Union.

**EMBRY, Air Chief Marshal Sir Basil Edward,** GCB, *cr* 1956 (KCB, *cr* 1953; CB 1945); KBE, *cr* 1945; DSO 1938; DFC 1945; AFC 1926; retired as Commander, Allied Air Forces, Central Europe, North Atlantic Treaty Organisation, 1956; *b* 28 Feb. 1902; *s* of late James Embry, MA Cantab; *m* 1928, Hope, *d* of late Captain C. S. Elliot, RN; three *s* one *d*. *Educ:* Bromsgrove Sch. First Commission, 1921; served Iraq, 1922-27 (AFC) (ops in Kurdistan and Southern Desert); served Central Flying Sch. (A1 flying instructor), 1929-32; RAF Staff Coll.; psa, 1933; India, 1934-39; Mohmand Operations, 1935 (despatches); Waziristan, 1937-38 (DSO); War of 1939-45 (despatches thrice, three Bars to DSO, CB, DFC, KBE); served in Bomber and Fighter Commands, Western Desert and 2nd TAF; Comd of No 2 Group Ops over Norway, NW Europe, Great Britain, 1939-41; Western Desert, 1941-42; NW Europe, 1943-45. ADC to the King, 1941-43; Asst Chief of Air Staff (Training), Air Ministry, 1945-48; Air Officer Commanding-in-Chief, Fighter Command, 1949-53; Knight Commander, 1st Class, Order of Dannebrog; Grand Officer Order of Orange Nassau, with swords; Comdr of Legion of Honour; Croix de Guerre. Hon. Freedom of Borough and Cinque Port of Dover; Freeman City of London; Hon. Liveryman, Worshipful Company of Glass-Sellers. *Publication:* Mission Completed, 1957. *Recreations:* farming, shooting, fishing. *Address:* Ardua, Cape Riche, via Albany, Western Australia 6330, Australia. *T:* Mettler 526.

**EMDEN, Alfred Brotherston,** MA; Hon. DLitt; FBA; FSA; Principal of St Edmund Hall, Oxford, 1929-51; Hon. Fellow of Lincoln College and St Edmund Hall; *b* 22 Oct. 1888; *e s* of His Honour Judge Alfred Emden. *Educ:* King's Sch., Canterbury; Lincoln Coll., Oxford (Scholar); Inner Temple. Head of Edghill House, Sydenham, 1913-15; AB (RNVR), 1915-19, serving in HMS Parker; Tutor and Bursar, St Edmund Hall, 1919; Vice-Principal, 1920; Member of the Hebdomadal Council, 1935-47; Lieut-Commander RNVR (Sp.), 1942-44. Corr. Fellow, Mediaeval Academy of America. Hon. LittD Cambridge. *Publications:* An Oxford Hall in Medieval Times, 1927; Joint Editor (with Prof. Sir F. M. Powicke) of Rashdall's Medieval Universities, 1936; Biographical Register of the University of Oxford to AD 1500, in 3 vols, 1957-59; Biographical Register of the University of Cambridge to 1500, 1963; A Survey of Dominicans in England, 1967. *Address:* Dunstan Cottage, Old Headington, Oxford.

**EMELEUS, Prof. Harry Julius,** CBE 1958; FRS 1946; MA, DSc; Professor of Inorganic Chemistry, University of Cambridge, 1945-70; now Professor Emeritus; Fellow of Sidney Sussex College, Cambridge; Fellow of Imperial College, London; *b* 22 June 1903; *s* of Karl Henry Emeleus and Ellen Biggs; *m* 1931, Mary Catherine Horton; two *s* two *d*. *Educ:* Hastings Grammar Sch.; Imperial Coll., London. 1851 Exhibition Senior Student, Imperial Coll. and Technische Hochschule, Karlsruhe, 1926-29; Commonwealth Fund Fellow, Princeton Univ., 1929-31; Member of Staff of Imperial Coll., 1931-45. President: Chemical Society, 1958; Royal Institute of Chemistry, 1963-65. Trustee, British Museum, 1963-. Hon. Fellow, Manchester Institute of Science and Technology. Hon. Member: Austrian, Finnish and French Chemical Societies; Finnish Scientific Academy; Royal Academy of Belgium; Akad. Naturf. Halle; Akad. Wiss. Gottingen; Spanish Royal Society for Physics and Chemistry. Hon. Doctor: Ghent; Kiel; Lille; Paris; Tech. Hoch. Aachen. Lavoisier Medal, French Chem. Society; Stock Medal, Gesellschaft Deutsche Chemiker; Davy Medal, Royal Society, 1962. *Publications:* scientific papers in chemical journals. *Recreation:* fishing. *Address:* 149 Shelford Road, Trumpington, Cambridge CB2 2ND. *T:* Trumpington 2374.

**EMELEUS, Karl George,** CBE 1965; MA, PhD ScD, DSc, MRIA; Professor of Physics, Queen's University, Belfast, 1933-66, now Emeritus; *b* 4 Aug. 1901; *s* of Karl Henry Emeleus and Ellen Biggs; *m* 1928, Florence Mary Chambers; three *s* one *d. Educ:* Hastings Grammar Sch.; St John's Coll., Cambridge. *Address:* c/o Queen's University of Belfast, Belfast BT7 1NN.

**EMERTON, Rev. John Adney;** Regius Professor of Hebrew, Cambridge, since 1968; *b* 5 June 1928; *s* of Adney Spencer Emerton and Helena Mary Emerton; *m* 1954, Norma Elizabeth Bennington; one *s* two *d. Educ:* Minchenden Grammar Sch., Southgate; Corpus Christi Coll., Oxford; Wycliffe Hall, Oxford. BA (1st class hons Theology), 1950; 1st class hons Oriental Studies, 1952; MA 1954. Canon Hall Jun. Greek Testament Prize, 1950; Hall-Houghton Jun. Septuagint Prize, 1951, Senior Prize, 1954; Houghton Syriac Prize, 1953; Liddon Student, 1950; Kennicott Hebrew Fellow, 1952. Corpus Christi Coll., Cambridge, MA (by incorporation), 1955; BD 1960. Deacon, 1952; Priest, 1953. Curate of Birmingham Cathedral, 1952-53; Asst Lecturer in Theology, Birmingham Univ., 1952-53; Lecturer in Hebrew and Aramaic, Durham Univ., 1953-55; Lecturer in Divinity, Cambridge Univ., 1955-62; Reader in Semitic Philology and Fellow of St Peter's Coll., Oxford, 1962-68. Visiting Prof. of Old Testament and Near Eastern Studies, Trinity Coll., Toronto Univ., 1960. *Publications:* The Peshitta of the Wisdom of Solomon, 1959; The Old Testament in Syriac: Song of Songs, 1966; articles in Journal of Semitic Studies, Journal of Theological Studies, Theology, Vetus Testamentum, Zeitschrift für die Alttestamentliche Wissenschaft. *Address:* 34 Gough Way, Cambridge CB3 9LN.

**EMERY, Rt. Rev. Anthony Joseph;** Auxiliary Bishop of Birmingham (RC), since 1968; Titular Bishop of Tamallula; *b* Burton-on-Trent, 17 May 1928. Ordained, 1953. *Address:* 84 St Bernard's Road, Olton, Solihull, Warwickshire.

**EMERY, Douglas,** CB 1967; Under-Secretary, Ministry of Health, 1960-67, retired; *b* 4 Nov. 1915; *s* of late Frederick and Mary Emery; *m* 1945, Margaret Wickham Pennington; one *s* two *d. Educ:* Hull Grammar Sch.; Christ's Coll., Cambridge. 1st Class Hons History Tripos, 1936; 1st Class Hons Modern and Medieval Langs Tripos, 1937. Entered Ministry of Health as Asst Principal, 1938; Principal, 1946; Asst Secretary, 1953. *Recreation:* entering competitions. *Address:* La Conchée, Perelle, St Saviour's, Guernsey. *T:* Guernsey 64582.

**EMERY, Eleanor Jean;** Head of Pacific and Indian Ocean Department, Foreign and Commonwealth Office, since 1969; *b* 23 Dec. 1918; *d* of Robert Paton Emery and Nellie Nicol Wilson. *Educ:* Western Canada High Sch., Calgary, Alberta; Glasgow Univ. MA Hons in History, 1941. Dominions Office, 1941-45; Asst Private Sec. to Sec. of State, 1942-45; British High Commn, Ottawa, 1945-48; CRO, 1948-52; Principal Private Sec. to Sec. of State, 1950-52; First Sec., British High Commn, New Delhi, 1952-55; CRO, 1955-58; First Sec., British High Commn, Pretoria/Cape Town, 1958-62; Head of South Asia Dept, CRO, 1962-64; Counsellor, British High Commn, Ottawa, 1964-68. *Recreations:* walking, swimming, reading. *Address:* 68 College Road, Dulwich, SE21. *T:* 01-693 1094. *Club:* Oxford and Cambridge University.

**EMERY, Sir (James) Frederick,** Kt 1957; JP; Company Director; *b* 17 Dec. 1886; *s* of William Joseph and Ruth Emery; *m* 1912, Florence Beatrice Gradwell; one *s* one *d. Educ:* Manchester Univ. MP (U) West Salford, 1935-45; Member of Salford City Council, 1921-35 (Councillor 1921-33, Alderman, 1933-35); Pres. North Fylde Conservative Association; Mayor of Salford, 1932-33. *Address:* Illawalla, Thornton-le-Fylde, Lancs. *T:* Thornton 2976. *Club:* Constitutional.

**EMERY, Peter;** MP (C) Honiton, since 1967 (Reading, 1959-66); Director: Phillips Petroleum–UK Ltd; Phillips Petroleum Products Ltd; *b* 27 Feb. 1926; *s* of late F. G. Emery, Highgate; *m* 1954, Elizabeth Nicholson; one *s* one *d. Educ:* Scotch Plains, New Jersey, USA; Oriel Coll., Oxford. Joint Founder and First Secretary of the Bow Group. Parliamentary Private Secretary: to Rt Hon. David Ormsby-Gore, Minister of State for Foreign Affairs, 1960-61; to Rt Hon. Joseph Godber, when Minister of State for Foreign Affairs, 1961-63, when Secretary of State for War, 1963, and when Minister of Labour, 1963-64; Jt Hon. Secretary, 1922 Cttee, 1964-65; Opposition Front Bench Spokesman for Treasury, Economics and Trade, 1964-66; Jt Vice-Chairman, Conservative Power Cttee. Member, Delegation to CPA Conference, Westminster, 1961; Member CPA Delegation to Canada, 1962; Delegate, Council of Europe and Western European Union, 1962-64. Director: Property Growth Insurance; Institute of Purchasing and Supply; Secretary-General, European Federation of Purchasing; Chairman, Consultative Council of Professional Management Organisations. *Recreations:* sliding down mountains, tennis, cricket and golf. *Address:* Tytherleigh Manor, near Axminster, Devon. *T:* South Chard 309; 15 Tufton Court, Tufton Street, SW1. *T:* 01-222 6666. *Clubs:* East India and Sports, Carlton.

**EMERY, Prof. Walter Bryan,** CBE 1969 (MBE 1943); MA Liverpool 1939; DLitt London 1959; FBA 1959; FSA 1941; Edwards Professor of Egyptology, University of London (University College), 1951-70; Field Director of the Egypt Exploration Society since 1952; *b* 2 July 1903; *s* of Walter Thomas Emery and Beatrice Mary Benbow; *m* 1928, Mary Cowhey; no *c. Educ:* St Francis Xavier's Coll., Liverpool. Student Institute of Archæology, University of Liverpool, 1921-23; Asst on Egypt Exploration Society's expedition to Tell-el-Amarna, 1923-24; Director of Mond Excavations of University of Liverpool at Luxor and Armant, 1924-28; Egyptian Govt Service of Antiquities: Director Archæological Survey of Nubia, 1929-35; Director Excavation at North Sakkara, 1935-39. British Army service retiring with hon. rank of Lt-Col, 1939-46. HBM's Embassy, Cairo: Attaché, 1947-50; First Secretary, 1950-51. Norton Lecturer of Archæological Institute of America, 1954-55. Member: German Archæological Institute; L'Institut d'Egypte. *Publications:* Excavations and Survey between Wadi-es-Sebua and Adindan (with L. P. Kirwan), 1937; The Royal Tombs of Ballana and Qustol, 1938; The Tomb of Hemaka, 1939; Hor-Aha, 1940; Nubian Treasure, 1949; Great Tombs of the First Dynasty, Vol. I, 1949, Vol. II, 1954, Vol. III, 1958; Archaic Egypt, 1961; De Buck Memorial Lecture: A Funerary Repast in an Egyptian Tomb of the Archaic Period, 1962; Egypt in Nubia, 1965. *Address:* 1 Alleyn Road, West Dulwich, SE21; *T:* 01-670 4770. *Clubs:* Athenæum; Turf (Cairo).

**EMETT, Rowland**; artist and inventor. His humorous mechanical models have been displayed all over the world. *Address:* Wild Goose Cottage, Ditchling, Sussex. *T:* Hassocks 2459.

**EMLYN, Viscount; Colin Robert Vaughan Campbell;** *b* 30 June 1962; *s* and *heir* of Earl Cawdor, *qv.*

**EMLYN WILLIAMS, Arthur;** *see* Williams.

**EMMERSON, Mrs. C. L.;** *see* Peto, G. E.

**EMMERSON, Sir Harold Corti,** GCB 1956 (KCB 1947; CB 1942); KCVO 1953; *b* 1896; *m* 1931, Lucy Kathleen Humphreys; two *s* three *d. Educ:* Warrington Secondary Sch. Served War of 1914-18 in Royal Marine Artillery. Ministry of Labour, 1920; Secretary Government Mission on Industrial Conditions in Canada and United States, 1926-27; Secretary Royal Commn on Unemployment Insurance, 1930-32; Principal Private Secretary to Ministers of Labour, 1933-35; Secretary Department of Commissioner for Special Areas, 1938-39; Principal Officer, Civil Defence, Northern Region, 1939-40; Under-Secretary Ministry of Home Security, 1940-42; Chief Industrial Commissioner, Ministry of Labour, 1942-44; Deputy-Secretary and Director General of Man Power, 1944-46; Permanent Secretary: Ministry of Works, 1946-56; Ministry of Labour, 1956-59. Member: Security Inquiry Cttee, 1961; Council on Prices, Productivity and Incomes, 1960-62; War Works Commission, 1960-64; Council on Tribunals, 1961-64. Chairman, London Government Staff Commn, 1963-65. Hon. MA Liverpool. *Publication:* The Ministry of Works, 1956. *Address:* 26 Millfield, Berkhamsted, Herts. *Clubs:* Athenæum, Arts.

**EMMET,** family name of **Baroness Emmet of Amberley.**

**EMMET OF AMBERLEY,** Baroness *cr* 1964 (Life Peeress); **Evelyn Violet Elizabeth Emmet,** JP; CA West Sussex; *b* Cairo, 18 March 1899; *er d* of 1st Baron Rennell of Rodd, PC, GCB, GCMG, GCVO (*d* 1941), and Lilias Guthrie (*d* 1951); *m* 1923, T. A. Emmet, late Royal Navy (*d* 1934), Amberley Castle, Sussex; two *s* two *d. Educ:* St Margaret's Sch., Bushey, and abroad; Lady Margaret Hall, Oxford (MA). JP Sussex, 1936. Member LCC, 1925-34 (Chairman several cttees); Member W Sussex CC, 1946-67; Alderman, 1952-66 (Chairman numerous cttees). Co. Organiser, WVS, 1938-45. Chairman: Conservative Women's National Advisory Cttee, 1951-54; Nat. Union of Conservatives, 1955-56; Legal Aid Advisory Cttee, 1966-. Full British Delegate to Assembly of United Nations in New York, 1952, and 1953. MP (C) East Grinstead Division East Sussex, 1955-64. A Dep. Speaker and a Dep. Chm. of Cttees, House of Lords, 1968-. *Recreation:* gardening. *Address:* Amberley Castle, Amberley, Sussex. *T:* Bury (Sussex) 319; 3 Grosvenor Cottages, Eaton Terrace, SW1. *T:* 01-730 4627.

**EMMET, Dorothy Mary,** MA Oxon and Manchester; *b* 1904; *d* of late Rev. C. W. Emmet, Fellow of University Coll., Oxford, and of Gertrude Julia Emmet (*née* Weir). *Educ:* St Mary's Hall, Brighton; Lady Margaret Hall, Oxford. Classical Exhibitioner, Lady Margaret Hall, Oxford, 1923; Hon. Mods Class I, 1925; Lit. Hum. Class I, 1927. Tutor, Maesyrhaf Settlement, Rhondda Valley, 1927-28 and 1931-32; Commonwealth Fellow, Radcliffe Coll., Cambridge, Mass, USA, 1928-30; Research Fellow, Somerville Coll., Oxford, 1930-31; lecturer in Philosophy, Armstrong (now King's) Coll., Newcastle upon Tyne, 1932-38; lecturer in Philosophy of Religion, University of Manchester, 1938-45; Reader in Philosophy, 1945-46; Prof. of Philosophy, University of Manchester, 1946-66; Prof. Emeritus, 1966. Stanton Lecturer in Philosophy of Religion, University of Cambridge, 1950-53. Vis. Prof., Barnard Coll., Columbia Univ., New York, 1960-61. President Aristotelian Society, 1953-54. Dean of the Faculty of Arts, University of Manchester, 1962-64. Hon. Fellow, Lady Margaret Hall, Oxford. Fellow, Lucy Cavendish Coll., Cambridge. *Publications:* Whitehead's Philosophy of Organism, 1932; Philosophy and Faith, 1936; The Nature of Metaphysical Thinking, 1945; Function, Purpose and Powers, 1958; Rules, Roles and Relations, 1966; (ed with Alastair MacIntyre) Sociological Theory and Philosophical Analysis, 1970; contributions to philosophical journals. *Recreations:* walking, reading. *Address:* 11 Millington Road, Cambridge. *See also Prof. R. C. Wilson.*

**EMMINGER, Otmar,** Dr oec. publ.; Vice-President, Monetary Committee of EEC (Common Market) since 1958; Chairman, Working Party III, OECD, since 1969; Deputy Governor, Deutsche Bundesbank (Federal Bank), since 1970; *b* Augsburg, 2 March 1911; *s* of Erich Emminger, Senatspräsident (Reichsminister der Justiz, 1923-24) and Maria Scharff; *m* 1966, Dr *rer. pol.* Gisela Boden; two *s. Educ:* in Law and Economics, at Univs of Berlin, Munich, Edinburgh, and London Sch. of Economics. Mem. and Div. Chief, Inst. for Business Research (Institut für Konjunkturforschung), Berlin, 1935-39. Served War of 1939-45. Div. Chief, Bavarian Min. of Economics, 1947-50; Mem. German Delegn to OEEC, Paris, 1949-50; Dir, Research and Statistics Dept, Bank deutscher Länder, 1951-53; Mem. Bd of Governors, Deutsche Bundesbank (Federal Bank), 1953-69; Exec. Dir, IMF, Washington, 1953-59; Chm., Deputies of Group of Ten, 1964-67. *Publications:* Die englischen Währungsexperimente der Nachkriegszeit, 1934; Die bayrische Industrie, 1947; Deutschlands Stellung in der Weltwirtschaft, 1953; Währungspolotik im Wandel der Zeit, 1966; The Price of Gold, 1967; Zwanzig Jahre deutsche Geldpolitik, 1968. *Recreations:* ski-ing, hiking. *Address:* Frankfurt am Main, Hasselhorstweg 36, West Germany. *T:* 268219.

**EMMS, David Acfield,** MA; Headmaster of Sherborne School, since 1970; *b* 16 Feb. 1925; *s* of Archibald George Emms and Winifred Gladys (*née* Richards); *m* 1950, Pamela Baker Speed; three *s* one *d. Educ:* Tonbridge Sch.; Brasenose Coll., Oxford. BA Hons Mod. Langs Oxford, 1950, Diploma in Education, 1951; MA 1954. Served War of 1939-45, RA, 1943-47. Undergraduate, 1947-51; Asst Master, Uppingham Sch. (Head of Mod. Languages Dept, CO, CCF Contingent), 1951-60; Headmaster of Cranleigh School, 1960-70. Dep. Chm., Public Schools Appointments Bureau. *Recreations:* Rugby football (Oxford *v* Cambridge, 1949, 1950); travel, ski-ing.

*Address:* Abbey Grange, Sherborne, Dorset. *Club:* Public Schools.

**EMMS, Mrs S. A. G.;** *see* Charques, Dorothy.

**EMPSON, Sir Charles,** KCMG 1956 (CMG 1943); Foreign Service, retired; *b* 24 April 1898; *s* of late Arthur Reginald Empson, Yokefleet, East Yorks; *m* 1931, Monica, *d* of late Canon J. W. S. Tomlin; one *s* one *d*. *Educ:* Harrow; Magdalene Coll., Cambridge. War Service, 1917-19 (Mesopotamia); joined staff of Civil Commissioner, Bagdad, 1920, and remained on staff of High Commissioner, Bagdad, until 1934 (Consul, 1924-32, Commercial Secretary, 1932-34); Commercial Agent for Palestine, 1934-38; Commercial Secretary HM Embassy, Rome, 1938-39; Commercial Counsellor, HM Embassy, Cairo, 1939-46; Minister (Economic), Special Commission in SE Asia, 1946-47; Minister (Commercial) HM Embassy, Rome, 1947-50; Minister (Commercial) HM Embassy, Washington, 1950-55; Ambassador to Chile, 1955-58. Rural District Councillor, Bridge-Blean, 1960-. *Address:* Seatonden, Ickham, Canterbury, Kent. *Club:* English-Speaking Union.

**EMPSON, Vice-Adm. Leslie Derek,** CB 1969; Commander, Far East Fleet, 1969-71; *b* 29 Oct. 1918; *s* of Frank Harold Empson amd Madeleine Norah Empson (*née* Burge); *m* 1958, Diana Elizabeth Kelly; one *s* one *d*. *Educ:* Eastbourne Coll.; Clare Coll., Cambridge (Class. Exhibn). Athletics Blue, 1939; BA 1940. Joined Royal Navy for pilot duties, 1940; commd as Sub-Lieut (A) RNVR, 1940; flew as Fleet Air Arm pilot, 1940-45; perm. commn in RN, 1944; Comdr 1952; Captain 1957; Naval Asst to First Sea Lord, 1957-59; Comd HMS Eagle, 1963-65; Imp. Def. Coll., 1966; Rear-Adm. 1967; Flag Officer, Aircraft Carriers, 1967-68; Asst Chief of Naval Staff (Operations and Air), 1968-69; Vice-Adm. 1970. *Recreations:* gardening, travel, his children. *Address:* Deep Field, West Street, Hambledon, Hants. *T:* Hambledon 451. *Clubs:* MCC; Hawks (Cambridge), Achilles.

**EMPSON, William;** Professor of English Literature, Sheffield University, since 1953; *b* 27 Sept. 1906; *s* of A. R. Empson, Yokefleet Hall, Howden, Yorks, and Laura (*née* Micklethwait); *m* 1941, Hester Henrietta Crouse; two *s*. *Educ:* Winchester; Magdalene Coll., Cambridge. Chair of English Literature, Bunrika Daigaku, Tokyo, 1931-34; Professorship in English Literature, Peking National University, then part of the South-Western Combined Universities, in Hunan and Yunnan, 1937-39; BBC Chinese Editor, 1941-46, after a year in BBC Monitoring Dept; returned to Peking National Univ., 1947, Prof., Western Languages Department. *Publications:* Seven Types of Ambiguity, 1930; Poems, 1935; Some Versions of Pastoral, 1935; The Gathering Storm (verse), 1940; The Structure of Complex Words, 1951; Collected Poems, 1955; Milton's God, 1961. *Address:* Studio House, Hampstead Hill Gardens, NW3; The University, Sheffield.

**EMSLIE, Hon. Lord; George Carlyle Emslie,** MBE 1946; Senator of the College of Justice in Scotland and Lord of Session, since 1970; *b* 6 Dec. 1919; *s* of Alexander and Jessie Blair Emslie; *m* 1942, Lilias Ann Mailer Hannington; three *s*. *Educ:* The High School of Glasgow; The University of Glasgow (MA, LLB). Commissioned A&SH, 1940; served War of 1939-45 (despatches): North Africa, Italy, Greece, Austria, 1942-46; psc Haifa, 1944; Brigade Major (Infantry), 1944-46. Advocate, 1948; Advocate Depute (Sheriff Courts), 1955; QC (Scotland) 1957; Sheriff of Perth and Angus, 1963-66; Dean of Faculty of Advocates, 1965-70. Chm., Scottish Agricultural Wages Bd, 1969-; Member: Council on Tribunals (Scottish Cttee), 1962-70; Rules Council of Court of Session, 1956-70; Sheriff Court Rules Council, 1963-70. *Recreation:* golf. *Address:* 47 Heriot Row, Edinburgh. *T:* 031-225 3657. *Clubs:* New (Edinburgh); The Honourable Company of Edinburgh Golfers.

**EMSLIE, George Carlyle;** *see* Emslie, Hon. Lord.

**EMSLIE, Prof. John William;** Professor Emeritus of Veterinary Pathology, University of Glasgow; *b* 28 March 1901; *s* of John R. Emslie and Isabella Cassie; *m* 1932, Margaret Noble, MA, Aberdeen, *d* of Andrew Noble and Margaret Trail; one *s*. *Educ:* Robert Gordon's Coll., Aberdeen; University of Aberdeen; Royal Dick Veterinary Coll., Edinburgh. Assistant, Dept of Pathology, Royal Dick Veterinary Coll., Edinburgh, 1926-28; Head, Dept of Pathology, Glasgow Veterinary Coll., 1929-49; Prof. of Veterinary Pathology, Univ. of Glasgow, 1951-68. *Publications:* papers in professional journals. *Recreations:* gardening, wood-work. *Address:* 19 Lady Margaret Drive, Troon, Ayrshire. *T:* Troon 2346.

**EMSLIE, Rosalie,** RBA; artist (painter); *b* Jan. 1891; *d* of A. E. Emslie, RWS, and Rosalie M. Emslie, RMS; unmarried; (one adopted *s* decd). *Educ:* privately. Studied at Royal Academy Schools, London, Paris, Florence and Madrid. Exhibitor at RA, RBA, NEAC, London Group, etc.; also Paris Salon, Venice International, Carnegie Institute (Pittsburgh). Hon. Mention, Pittsburgh, 1925. Pictures at Buffalo Art Gallery, USA, Toronto Art Gallery, and in private collections. Member Contemporary Art Society. *Recreations:* reading and travel. *Address:* 28 Rushworth Road, Reigate, Surrey.

**EMSON, Air Marshal Sir Reginald (Herbert Embleton),** KBE 1966 (CBE 1946); CB 1959; AFC 1941; Inspector-General of the Royal Air Force, since 1967; *b* 11 Jan. 1912; *s* of Francis Reginald Emson, Hitcham, Buckinghamshire; *m* 1934, Doreen Marjory, *d* of Hugh Duke, Holyport, Maidenhead, Berkshire; two *s* two *d*. *Educ:* Christ's Hospital; RAF Coll., Cranwell. Joined RAF, 1931; served War of 1939-45 in Aeroplane Armament Establishment Gunnery Research Unit, Exeter; Fighter Command Headquarters and Central Fighter Establishment. Director, Armament Research and Development (Air), Ministry of Supply, 1950-59; Commander RAF Staff and Air Attaché, British Defence Staffs, Washington, 1961-63; Asst Chief of Air Staff (Operational Requirements), 1963-66; Dep. Chief Air Staff, 1966-67. Group Captain, 1943; Air Commodore, 1958; Air Vice-Marshal, 1962; Air Marshal (Acting), 1966. *Address:* Vor Cottage, Holyport, Maidenhead, Berks. *T:* Maidenhead 21992. *Club:* Royal Air Force.

**ENCOMBE, Viscount; John Joseph Nicholas Scott;** *b* 24 April 1937; *s* of 4th Earl of Eldon, *qv*; *m* 1961, Comtesse Claudine de Montjoye-Vaufrey et de la Roche, Vienna; one *s* two *d*. *Educ:* Ampleforth; Trinity Coll., Oxford. 2nd Lieut Scots Guards (National Service). Lieut AER. *Heir:* *s* Hon. John Francis Thomas Scott, *b* 9 July 1962. *Address:* The Coach House, 32 Somerset Road, Wimbledon, SW19.

**ENDERS, Dr John Franklin;** Chief, Research Division of Infectious Diseases, Children's Medical Center, Boston, Mass, since 1946;

University Professor Emeritus, Harvard University, USA; *b* 10 Feb. 1897; *s* of John Ostrom Enders and Harriet Goulden Whitmore; *m* 1927, Sarah Frances Bennett (*d* 1943); one *s* one *d*; 1951, Carolyn Bernice Keane; one step *s*. *Educ:* St Paul's Sch., Concord, NH; Yale Univ. (BA 1919); Harvard Univ. (MA 1922, PhD 1930). USNR Flying Corps, 1917-20. Teaching and research in field of infectious diseases of man, 1927-. Member Faculty Harvard Medical Sch., 1929-; Civ. Cons. to Secretary of War on Epidemic Diseases in Army, 1942-46; Member Commn on Virus Dis, US Army, 1949-68; Member WHO Expert Advisory Panel on Virus Diseases, 1958. Passano Award, 1953; Lasker Award, 1954; Nobel Laureate, 1954, in Physiology and Medicine; Cameron Prize, 1960; Ricketts Award, 1962; Robert Koch Medal, 1963; US Presidential Medal of Freedom, 1963. Commander of the Republic of Upper Volta, 1965. Member: National Academy of Sciences (US); American Philosophical Society; Academie Nat. de Med. (France); Deut. Akad. d. Naturforsch. (Leopoldina); Hon. Member: RSM (England); Acad. Roy. de Med. (Belgium); Foreign Mem., Royal Soc. (England). Fellow American Academy of Arts and Sciences. Hon. FACS. Holds several honorary degrees. *Publications:* (joint) Immunity: Principles and Application in Medicine and Public Health, 1939; papers in scientific journals. *Recreations:* fishing, sailing. *Address:* Children's Medical Center, 300 Longwood Avenue, Boston, Mass 02115, USA; (home) 64 Colbourne Crescent, Brookline, Mass 02147. *T:* Longwood 6-3539. *Clubs:* Country (Brookline); Harvard (Boston, Mass).

**ENERGLYN,** Baron *cr* 1968 (Life Peer), of Caerphilly; **William David Evans,** MSc, DSc, PhD; Professor of Geology, University of Nottingham, since 1949; formerly Dean of the Faculty of Pure Science; *b* 25 Dec. 1912; *s* of Councillor D. G. Evans; *m* 1941, Jean Thompson Miller; no *c*. *Educ:* Caerphilly Grammar Sch.; University Coll., Cardiff. Geologist to HM Geological Survey of Great Britain, 1939; Member of Regional Survey Board of Ministry of Fuel and Power for South Wales Coalfield, 1945; Senior Lecturer in Geology, University College of South Wales and Monmouthshire, 1947. FGS 1939; FRGS 1944; FLS 1945; MIME 1952; MIMM 1949. MSc Wales, 1938; PhD London, 1940. *Publications:* Research papers in Trans and Proc. of Geol Society of London, Royal Geog. Society, Institute of Mining and Metallurgy, etc, on geology of older rocks of Wales, and Cornwall, and cause of dust diseases among coalminers and metalliferous miners at home and abroad. *Address:* 14 Village Close, Edwalton, West Bridgford, Nottinghamshire. *Club:* Reform.

**ENFIELD, Viscount; Thomas Edmund Byng;** *b* 26 Sept. 1936; *s* and *heir* of 7th Earl of Strafford, *qv*; *m* 1963, Jennifer Mary, *er d* of late Rt Hon. W. M. May, PC, FCA, MP, and of Mrs May, Mertoun Hall, Holywood, Co. Down; two *s* two *d*. *Educ:* Eton; Clare Coll., Cambridge. Lieut, Royal Sussex Regt (National Service). *Recreation:* gardening. *Heir:* *s* Hon. William Robert Byng, *b* 10 May 1964. *Address:* Abbots Worthy House, Abbots Worthy, Winchester, Hants. *T:* Winchester 4110.

**ENFIELD, Sir Ralph Roscoe,** Kt 1947; CB 1944; MA; BSc; *b* 22 Dec. 1885; *s* of Ernest William Enfield, The Grove, Burton Joyce, Notts; *m* 1921, Doris Edith (*d* 1951), *d* of Edmund Hussey; one *s* one *d*. *Educ:* Bedales; High Sch., Nottingham; Christ Church, Oxford (scholar, exhibitioner, and Dixon Research Scholar). Entered Civil Service, 1913; Board of Trade, 1913-14; Ministry of Munitions, 1914-18; Ministry of Agriculture and Fisheries, 1919-52; Asst Secretary, 1936; UK Representative International Institute of Agriculture, 1934-38; Principal Asst Secretary, 1942; Chief Economic Adviser to Ministry of Agriculture and Fisheries, 1945-52; UK representative on Council of FAO of the UN, 1947-52. Pres., Agricultural Economic Soc., 1935-36. *Publications:* The Agricultural Crisis, 1920-23, 1924; various reports, articles, etc. *Address:* 12 Dunstan Road, NW11. *T:* 01-455 1805. *Club:* Reform.

**ENGELHARD, Charles William;** Chairman: Engelhard Minerals & Chemicals Corporation; Engelhard Hanovia Incorporated; American-South African Investment Company Ltd; SA Forest Investment Ltd; Executive Committee, Eurofund Incorporated; Director of other companies; Commissioner, Port of New York Authority; *b* NY City, 15 Feb. 1917; *s* of late Charles Engelhard; *m* Jane Reis-Brian; five *d*. *Educ:* St Paul's Sch., NH; Princeton Univ. (BA). Served with US Army Air Corps, 1941-45; Pte; bomber pilot; Captain. Personal rep. of President at: Independence Day Ceremonies, Gabon, 1962; Coronation of Pope Paul VI and 1st Anniversary celebration of Algerian independence, 1963; Independence Day Ceremonies (and Head of US Delegation), Zambia, 1964; Member, Community Relations Service, 1964; Member, President's Cttee to study East West Trade, 1965. Trustee: American Heritage Foundation; American Museum of Immigration (Vice-Pres.); Bernardsville Library Assoc.; Cttee for Economic Development; Foxcroft Sch.; John F. Kennedy Memorial Library; Seton Hall Univ.; Atlantic Council of US Inc.; Foreign Policy Assoc.; NJ State Chamber of Commerce; NY Zoological Society; US Cttee for Refugees; World Wildlife Fund; Member: Citizens Cttee for Higher Education in NJ; Democratic State Cttee of NJ; Eleanor Roosevelt Mem. Foundation; Foundation for Advance of Graduate Study in Engineering, Newark; Newcomen Society in N America; Pres., Newark Mus.; Vice-Pres., Greater Newark Development Council; NJ Industrialist of Year, 1965; Brotherhood Award NJ Region, Nat. Conference of Christians and Jews, 1966. *Address:* (business) Engelhard Minerals & Chemicals Corporation, Engelhard Industries Div., 113 Astor Street, Newark, NJ 07114, USA; (home) Cragwood, Far Hills, NJ, USA. *Clubs:* Racquet and Tennis (NY); Ivy (Princeton); Monmouth Jockey (NJ); Rand (Johannesburg); Travellers' (Paris); Tarratine (Dark Harbor, Maine).

**ENGHOLM, Sir Basil Charles,** KCB 1968 (CB 1964); Permanent Secretary, Ministry of Agriculture, Fisheries and Food since Jan. 1968; *b* 2 Aug. 1912; *o s* of late C. F. G. Engholm; *m* 1936, Nancy, *er d* of Lifford Hewitt, St Anthony, Rye; one *d*. *Educ:* Tonbridge Sch.; Sorbonne, Paris; Sidney Sussex Coll., Cambridge (Law Tripos, MA). Member of Gray's Inn; Metal business, New York, 1933-34; entered Ministry of Agriculture and Fisheries, 1935; War of 1939-45: part-time NFS; Principal Private Secretary to Minister of Agriculture and Fisheries, 1943-45; Asst Secretary, 1945; Under-Secretary, 1954; Fisheries Secretary, 1960-62; Dep. Secretary, 1964-67. *Recreations:* reading, riding, and painting in oils. *Address:* 93 Meadway, NW11. *T:* 01-455 3975. *Clubs:* United University, Farmers', Arts.

**ENGINEER, Sir Noshirwan Phirozha,** Kt 1945; Lawyer; practising in India; *b* 22 Jan. 1884; *m* 1916, Jerbai Jamsetji Kanga; one *s* two *d*. *Educ:* Elphinstone Coll., Bombay. Dakshina Fellow, Elphinstone Coll.; a solicitor of Bombay High Court, 1910-21; an Advocate (original side) of Bombay High Court from 1921; Additional Judge Bombay High Court, 1936-38; Advocate-General of Bombay, 1942-45; Advocate-General of India, 1945-50. *Address:* Sakar Apartment, Pochkhanawala Road, Worli, Bombay 18, India. *Clubs:* Willingdon Sports (Bombay); Delhi Gymkhana.

**ENGLAND, E(ric) C. Gordon;** Business Consultant; Chairman, Lots Farm Ltd; *b* 5 April 1891; *s* of George England and Amy Attlee; *m* 1913, Doris Isabel Troughton; one *s* two *d*. *Educ:* New Coll., Eastbourne; Framlingham Coll., Suffolk. Trained as mechanical engineer Great Northern Railway works, Doncaster. Entered aviation in 1909. Holds pilot's certificate 68, became test pilot and aircraft designer. Manager of F. Sage & Co., Aircraft Manufacturing Works, 1916-18; engaged in Automobile Industry, 1919-30. Became successful racing motorist. Designer of Gordon England motor-car body. Chairman and Managing Director, Gordon England, Ltd; President, Motor Agents Association, 1929; joined Vacuum Oil Co. Ltd, 1930-35, and became a Director; Managing Director, General Aircraft Ltd, 1935-42; Deputy Chairman, Aero Engines Ltd, 1936-43; Member of Gorell Cttee on Civil Aviation, 1932-33; Chairman, Engineering Industries Association, 1940-44; General Manager, Eugene Ltd, 1945-50. Life Member Council British Automobile Racing Club; Founder Member of Railway Conversion League. Member, Economic Research Council. FIMI, FRAeS, MIProdE. *Recreations:* motor racing, ecological research. *Address:* Flat 7, Lynwood, Rise Road, Sunninghill, Berks. *T:* Ascot 20565. *Club:* Royal Automobile.

**ENGLAND, Rear-Adm. Hugh Turnour,** CB 1947; DSO 1943 (Bar 1944); *b* 1884; *s* of late Captain W. G. England, RN; *m* Alice Marian (*d* 1968), *d* of late Rev. Claypon Bellingham, Dunany, Co. Louth, Ireland; one *s* two *d* (and one *s* killed on active service, Fleet Air Arm, War of 1939-45). *Educ:* Eastman's; HMS Britannia. Joined RN 1900. Served S African War; European War, 1914-19, Dardanelles and E Mediterranean (despatches, severely wounded); War of 1939-45, Commodore of Convoy, Principal Sea Transport Officer, Middle East, 1941-43; Commodore-in-Charge, Hamburg, and in command German Minesweeping Administration, 1945-47 (Croix de Guerre, France). ADC to the King, 1934; Rear-Adm. 1935; retired, 1935. *Address:* Dunany, Togher, Drogheda, Co. Louth, Eire. *T:* Togher 7. *Club:* United Service.

**ENGLEDOW, Sir Frank Leonard,** Kt 1944; CMG 1935; FRS 1946; MA, BSc; Fellow of St John's College, Cambridge; Drapers' Professor of Agriculture, Cambridge University, 1930-57; *b* 1890; *m* Mildred (*d* 1956); four *d*. *Educ:* St John's Coll., Cambridge. The Queen's Own (Royal West Kent Regt), 1914-18; Adjutant, 5th Batt. Mesopotamian Expeditionary Force; retiring rank Lt-Col; asst Director of Agriculture, Mesopotamia, 1918-19. *Address:* Hadleigh, Huntingdon Road, Girton, Cambridge CB3 0LH.

**ENGLISH, Cyril Rupert;** Director-General, City and Guilds of London Institute, since 1968; *b* 19 April 1913; *s* of William James and Edith English; *m* 1936, Eva Moore; two *s*. *Educ:* Northgate Sch., Ipswich. BScEng Ext. London, 1934. Technical teacher, 1935-39. Served Royal Navy, 1939-46, Lieut-Commander (E). HM Inspector of Schools, 1946-55; Staff Inspector (Engineering), 1955-58; Chief Inspector of Further Education, in connection with Industry and Commerce, 1958-65; Senior Chief Inspector, Dept of Education and Science, 1965-67. Member, Anglo-American Productivity Team, 1951; attended Commonwealth Education Conferences, Delhi, 1962, Ottawa, 1964. Pres., Assoc. for Liberal Educn, 1969-; Chairman: British Assoc. for Commercial and Industrial Educn, 1970-71; RAF Educn Adv. Cttee; Nuffield/Schools Council Humanities Curriculum Project Consultative Cttee; Member: Services Colleges Cttee, 1965-66; Adv. Bd, RAF Coll., Cranwell; Academic Adv. Council, Royal Defence Acad.; Bd of Dirs, Industrial Training Service; Central Training Council; CTC Gen. Political Cttee; CTC Research Cttee; Nat. Adv. Council for Educn in Industry and Commerce; Council for Tech. Educn and Training for Overseas Countries; Reg. Adv. Council for Technol. Educn (London and Home Counties); Schools Science and Technology Cttee; Educn Cttee, IMechE; Associated Examining Bd. FIMechE; FIProdE; AMIMarE. Hon. DTech Brunel, 1970. *Recreations:* music, gardening. *Address:* 76 Portland Place, W1N 4AA.

**ENGLISH, Gerald;** Professor, Royal College of Music, since 1960; *b* 6 Nov. 1925; *m* 1954, Jennifer Ryan; two *s* two *d*. *Educ:* King's Sch., Rochester. After War service studied at Royal College of Music and then began career as lyric tenor; subsequently travelled in USA and Europe, appeared at Sadler's Wells, Covent Garden and Glyndebourne and recorded for major gramophone companies. *Address:* 63 Springfield Road, NW8. *T:* 01-328 0401.

**ENGLISH, Joseph Sandys,** BA, MD, BCh, BAO Dublin University; LM Rotunda; FRCOG; Hon. Consultant Obstetrician and Gynæcologist, North Down Group of Hospitals; *b* 3 Oct. 1890; *s* of Thomas James English, Lisburn, N Ireland; *m* 1925, Elizabeth Hamilton (*d* 1969), *d* of H. W. Mann, MD, Nairn; one *s* one *d*. *Educ:* Campbell Coll., Belfast; Trinity Coll., Dublin. Captain RAMC 1914 (1914-15 Star, Victory and General Service medals); External Maternity Assistant, Rotunda Hospital, Dublin, 1918; Assistant Master, Rotunda Hospital, Dublin, 1919-21; Professor of Midwifery and Gynæcology, King Edward VII College of Medicine, Singapore, 1922-48; formerly Gynæcologist to the General Hospital, Singapore; Obstetrician to the Maternity Hospital, Singapore; Consulting Gynæcologist to St Andrews Hospital, Singapore; Chairman Central Midwives Board, Straits Settlements; Representative of Malaya at 4th Conference of Child Welfare, 1925; President, Malaya Branch BMA, 1939-40. Interned Singapore, Feb. 1942-Aug. 1945. *Recreation:* golf. *Address:* Culmore, Park Close, Milford-on-Sea, Hants. *T:* Milford-on-Sea 2535.

**ENGLISH, Michael;** MP (Lab) Nottingham (West) since 1964; *b* 24 Dec. 1930; *s* of late William Agnew English; unmarried. *Educ:* King George V Grammar Sch., Southport; Liverpool Univ. (LLB). Joined Labour Party, 1949; Rochdale County Borough Council,

1953-65 (Chairman Finance Cttee until 1964); contested (Lab) Shipley Div., WR Yorks, 1959. Member, official parliamentary panel NUGMW. Employed until 1964 as Asst Manager of department concerned with organisation and methods in subsidiary of large public company. Parliamentary Private Secretary, Board of Trade, 1966-67. *Recreations:* reading history, and the more usual pleasures of the majority of bachelors. *Address:* House of Commons, SW1. *T:* 01-930 6240 (ext. 1058).

**ENGLISH, Commander Reginald Wastell,** DSO 1940; Royal Navy; *b* 12 April 1894; *s* of late Marcus Valentine English, Orton Longueville, Peterborough, and Emmeline Fanny Whytehead, Acomb, York; *m* 1916, Olive Taylor (*d* 1964), Ermington, Devon; one *s* two *d. Educ:* Orleton Sch., Scarborough; Osborne and Dartmouth Colleges. Served RN, 1907-20, 1939-44. A/S Trawlers, home, USA, S Africa (DSO Dover). *Address:* Oxley House, Lenham, Kent.

**ENGLISH, William John,** MBE 1951; JP; Chairman, South Western Regional Hospital Board, since 1966; Part-time Member, South Western Electricity Board, since 1960; *b* 23 Nov. 1903; 4th *s* of William Mirl English, Aylburton, nr Lydney, Glos; *m* 1929, Edith May Moss, Collingbourne Ducis, Wilts; two *s* one *d. Educ:* Aylburton C. of E. Sch. Apprenticed Fairfield Shipbuilding Co., Boiler Maker, Chepstow, 1918-21; Engineer, West Gloucestershire Power Co., 1922-38; District Secretary, Transport and General Workers Union, 1938-60. Chairman, S. Western Federal Laundry, 1956-; Governor, various schools; Chairman, Yeovil Technical Coll. Mayor of Yeovil, 1957, 1958, 1959; JP Somerset, 1947 (Chairman of Bench, 1953-). *Recreations:* gardening, walking. *Address:* 91 Mudford Road, Yeovil, Somerset. *T:* Yeovil 4193.

**ENNALS, Rt. Hon. David Hedley,** PC 1970; *b* 19 Aug. 1922; *s* of A. F. Ennals, 8 Victoria Terrace, Walsall, Staffs; *m* 1950, Eleanor Maud Caddick; three *s* one *d. Educ:* Queen Mary's Grammar School, Walsall; Loomis Inst., Windsor, Conn, USA. Served with HM Forces, 1941-46: Captain, RAC. Secretary, Council for Education in World Citizenship, 1947-52; Secretary, United Nations Association, 1952-57; Overseas Sec., Labour Party, 1957-64. MP (Lab) Dover, 1964-70; PPS to: Minister of Overseas Development, 1964; Minister of Transport, 1966; Parly. Under-Sec. of State, Army, 1966-67; Parly. Under-Sec., Home Office, 1967-68; Minister of State, Dept of Health and Social Security, 1968-70. Dep. Chm., Ockenden Venture, 1968-. *Publications:* Strengthening the United Nations, 1957; Middle East Issues, 1958; United Nations Peace Force, 1960; United Nations on Trial, 1962. *Recreation:* camping. *Address:* 26 Beverley Road, SW13. *T:* 01-876 7953.

**ENNISKILLEN,** 6th Earl of, *cr* 1789; **David Lowry Cole,** MBE 1955; Baron Mountflorence, 1760; Viscount Enniskillen, 1776; Baron Grinstead (UK), 1815; company director; farmer, Kenya and N Ireland; *b* 10 Sept. 1918; *er s* of Hon. Galbraith Lowry Egerton Cole (*d* 1929) (3rd *s* of 4th Earl of Enniskillen) and of Lady Eleanor Cole, *d* of 2nd Earl of Balfour; *S* uncle, 1963; *m* 1st, 1940, Sonia Mary Syers (from whom he obtained a divorce, 1955); one *s* one *d*; 2nd, 1955, Nancy Henderson MacLennan, former American Vice Consul. *Educ:* Eton; Trinity Coll., Cambridge. BA Agric. 1940. Served War of 1939-45, Captain Irish Guards: Kenya Emergency, 1953-55, Provincial Comdt, Kenya Police Reserve (MBE). MLC for North Kenya, 1961-63. Formerly: Member Kenya Meat Commn; Member Exec., Kenya National Farmers Union; Vice-Chairman Kenya Stockowners Council; Member Exec., Kenya Board of Agriculture; Member Board: Land and Agric. Bank of Kenya; East African Diatomite Syndicate Ltd. *Recreations:* shooting, golf, fishing. *Heir: s* Viscount Cole, *qv. Address:* PO Box 7345, Nairobi, Kenya; Florence Court, Enniskillen, N Ireland. *T:* Florencecourt 229. *Clubs:* Carlton; Woking Golf; Muthaiga Country (Nairobi); Rift Valley Sports (Nakuru); Fly Fishers (Kenya).

**ENNISMORE, Viscount; Francis Michael Hare;** *b* 28 June 1964; *s* and *heir* of 5th Earl of Listowel, *qv.*

**ENNOR, Sir Arnold Hughes, (Hugh),** Kt 1965; CBE 1963; Secretary, Commonwealth Department of Education and Science, since 1967; *b* 10 Oct. 1912; *s* of Arnold Martin and Charlotte van de Leur Ennor; *m* 1939, Violet Phyllis Argall; one *s* one *d. Educ:* Melbourne Univ. DSc Melbourne, 1943. Research Biochemist, Baker Institute of Medical Research, Melbourne, 1938-42; Research with Ministry of Munitions and Armed Forces, 1942-46; Wellcome Research Fellow, Dept of Biochemistry, Oxford Univ., 1946-48; Professor of Biochemistry, Australian National University, Canberra, 1948-67; Dean of John Curtin School of Medical Research, 1953-67; Deputy Vice-Chancellor, Australian National Univ., 1964-67. Hon. DSc NSW, 1968; Hon. MD Monash, 1969. *Publications:* numerous contributions to Biochemical Journal, Journal of Biological Chemistry, etc. *Recreation:* tennis. *Address:* 3a Vancouver Street, Red Hill, Canberra, ACT 2603, Australia. *T:* 95 9426. *Clubs:* Commonwealth (Canberra); Athenæum (Melbourne).

**ENRICI, Most Rev. Domenico,** JCD; Apostolic Delegate to Great Britain and Gibraltar since 1969; *b* 9 April 1909; *s* of late Domenico Enrici and of Maria Dalmasso Enrici. *Educ:* Diocesan Seminary, Cuneo; Pontifical Gregorian Univ. and Pontifical Ecclesiastical Academy, Rome. Ordained, 1933; parochial work in Dio. Cuneo, 1933-35. Served at various Apostolic Nunciatures and Delegations: Ireland, 1938-45; Egypt, 1946-48; Palestine and Jordan, 1948-53; Formosa, Free China, 1953-55; apptd Titular Archbp of Ancusa, 1955; Apostolic Internuncio to Indonesia, 1955-58; Apostolic Nuncio to Haiti and Apostolic Delegate to West Indies, 1958-60; Apostolic Internuncio to Japan, 1960-62; Apostolic Delegate to Australia, New Zealand and Oceania, 1962-69. *Address:* Apostolic Delegation, 54 Parkside, Wimbledon, SW19. *T:* 01-946 1410.

**ENRIGHT, Dennis Joseph;** freelance writer and teacher; Joint Editor of Encounter since 1970; *b* 11 March 1920; *s* of late George Enright; *m* 1949, Madeleine Harders; one *d. Educ:* Leamington Coll.; Downing Coll., Cambridge. MA Cantab; DLitt Alexandria. Lecturer in English, University of Alexandria, 1947-50; Organising Tutor, University of Birmingham Extra-Mural Dept, 1950-53; Vis. Prof., Kōnan Univ., Japan, 1953-56; Vis. Lecturer, Free University of Berlin, 1956-57; British Council Professor, Chulalongkorn Univ., Bangkok, 1957-59; Prof. of English, Univ. of Singapore, 1960-70. FRSL 1961. *Publications: poetry:* The Laughing Hyena, 1953; Bread Rather Than Blossoms, 1956; Some Men Are Brothers, 1960; Addictions, 1962; The Old Adam, 1965; Unlawful Assembly, 1968; Selected Poems, 1969; *novels:* Academic Year, 1955; Heaven Knows Where, 1957; Insufficient Poppy, 1960; Figures of Speech, 1965; *criticism:* The

Apothecary's Shop, 1957; English Critical Texts (co-editor), 1962; Conspirators and Poets, 1966; Shakespeare and the Students, 1970; *travel:* The World of Dew: Japan, 1955; Memoirs of a Mendicant Professor, 1969; *translation:* The Poetry of Living Japan (co-editor), 1957; contributor to: Scrutiny, Encounter, etc. *Recreations:* reading, writing, films, listening to music. *Address:* c/o Chatto & Windus, 40-42 William IV Street, WC2.

**ENSOR, (Alick Charles) David;** journalist and author; *b* 27 Nov. 1906; *s* of Charles William Ensor, MRCS, LRCP, and Helen Margaret Creighton Ensor; *m* 1st, 1932, Norah Russell (marr. diss.); one *s* two *d*; 2nd, 1944, Frances Vivienne Mason. *Educ:* Westminster Sch. Solicitor, 1928; Prosecuting Solicitor, Newcastle upon Tyne, 1932; Prosecuting Solicitor, Metropolitan Police, 1935; Law Lecturer, Police Coll., Hendon, 1935; Deputy Clerk of Peace, Middlesex, 1937; Clerk of Peace, London, 1938. War service with Army in France, Africa, Far East, 1939-44. Practised as Solicitor in Brussels, 1945-47. Retired from Law and farmed in Dorset, 1948. MP (Lab) Bury and Radcliffe, 1964-70; Member Select Cttee on Estimates, 1964-68; Chm., House of Commons Catering Cttee, 1969-70. Has broadcast regularly for radio and television since 1957. Films include: The Trials of Oscar Wilde; The Pot Carriers; Death and the Sky Above. *Publications:* Thirty Acres and a Cow, 1955; I was a Public Prosecutor, 1958; Verdict Afterwards, 1960; With Lord Roberts through the Khyber Pass, 1963; contributions to Local Government Law in England and Wales, Journal of Criminal Law. *Recreations:* gardening, travelling. *Address:* St Margarets, Boxgrove, Chichester, Sussex. *T:* Halnaker 287.

**ENSOR, Arthur Hinton;** Director: Lloyds Bank Ltd, 1954-70 (Chief General Manager, 1946-54; Vice-Chairman, 1955-63); Legal & General Assurance Society Ltd, 1954-67; Bank of London & South America Ltd, 1950-66 (Deputy Chairman, 1955); National Bank of New Zealand Ltd, 1953 (Chairman 1955-65 and 1969); Regis Property Co. Ltd, 1955; *b* 14 Sept. 1891; *s* of John J. Ensor, Handsworth, Birmingham; *m* 1921, Sylvia Lockerbie; one *s* two *d*. *Educ:* King Edward's High Sch., Birmingham. FRSA 1948. Pres., Institute of Bankers, 1952-53, 1953-54; Dir, National Cash Register Co. Ltd, 1954-64. Master of Worshipful Co. of Tallow-chandlers, 1958-59. *Recreations:* golf, gardening. *Address:* Chenies House, Chenies, Rickmansworth, Herts. *T:* Chorleywood 2660. *Club:* Boodle's.

**ENSOR, David;** *see* Ensor, A. C. D.

**ENSOR WALTERS, P. H. B.;** *see* Walters.

**ENTERS, Angna;** mime; dancer; painter; sculptor; author; dramatist; composer; choreographer; scene and costume designer for the theatre; *b* NYC, US, 28 April 1907; *o c* of Edward Enters and Henriette Gasseur-Styleau; *m* Louis Kalonyme. *Educ:* privately and self-educated in US; Europe; Egypt; Greece. Theatre début New York, 1924, presenting in solo performance a new theatre form in which she combined for the first time the arts of mime, dance, music, costume, scenic design; originated phrase dance-mime now in Amer. dictionaries; first performer to be presented in a theatrical performance, 1943, by Metropolitan Museum of Art, NYC; presented for her 25th Broadway (NY) season, 1959; a nationwide television broadcast, in US, presented a composite portrait of her work in theatre, painting, writing, 1959. London début, St Martin's Theatre, 1928; many subseq. British seasons including television. Paris début, 1929; Am. Rep. in Internat. Theatre Season presented by C. B. Cochran, Queen's Theatre, 1931. Rep. Am. Nat. Theatre and Acad., at Internat. Arts Festival, Berlin, and tour of W Germany. Guggenheim Foundation Fellowships, 1934 and 1935 (research in Greece, Egypt, Near East). Début exhibn of painting, NY, 1933, many subseq. Début exhibn of paintings in London, Eng., 1934 and subseq. Début exhibn of sculpture, New York, 1945; subseq. one-woman shows of painting and sculpture in US and Canada. Works are in Metropolitan Museum of Art, New York, etc. Painted mural, modern Penthouse Theatre of University of Washington, Seattle, 1950. Rep. in Exhibns, NY Museum of Modern Art, 1953. First work in Ceramics exhibited in New York and Los Angeles, 1953. Lecture tours US, 1954-. Prof. of Acting, Baylor Univ., Waco, Texas, and Director of plays, Dallas Theatre Center, Dallas, Texas, 1961-62. Fellow: Center for Advanced Studies, Wesleyan Univ., Middletown, Conn, 1962-; Pennsylvania State Univ., 1970. Films based on her original stories: Lost Angel, Tenth Avenue Angel, Silly Girl, 1944-47; You Belong to Me, 1950. Created and staged Commedia dell'Arte (play within play seq.) in film Scaramouche, 1951; Dir, also designer of stage settings and costumes, for play, Yerma, by G. Lorca (Broadway, NY, etc.), 1958. Plays produced: Love Possessed Juana, 1946; The Unknown Lover–A Modern Psyche, 1947. *Publications:* First Person Plural (self-illustr.), 1937; Love Possessed Juana (self-scored and illustr. play), 1939; Silly Girl (self-illustr. autobiog.), 1944; A Thing of Beauty (novel), 1948; The Flowering Bud (novel), 1955 (publ. London, 1956, as Among the Daughters); Artist's Life (self-illustrated), 1957; Artist's Life (publ. London, 1959); (trans.) Chantecler, by E. Rostand, 1960; Mime for Actors, 1961; The Loved and the Unloved (novel), 1961; Angna Enters on Mime, 1965; also illustrated Best American Short Stories of 1945; article on Pantomime, Encyclopædia Britannica. *Address:* 35 West 57th Street, NY 10019, USA.

**ENTHOVEN, Roderick Eustace,** FRIBA; FSA; *b* 30 May 1900; *o surv. s* of late Ernest James Enthoven, Great Ote Hall, Wivelsfield, Sussex, and Rosaline Mary Eustace Smith; *m* 1933, Cecilia Mary Le Mesurier; three *s*. *Educ:* Clifton College. Received architectural education at Architectural Association Sch., 1919-24, qualifying with SADG Medal, Architectural Association Diploma; Engaged in architectural practice at 4 Raymond Buildings, Gray's Inn, WC1; Partner in Enthoven & Mock; Partner in Pakington & Enthoven until war of 1939-45. Civil Camouflage Officer to Air Ministry, 1940-44; served in Italy as Monuments, Fine Arts and Archives Officer, 1944-45. Pres. Architectural Association, 1948-49; Vice-Pres. RIBA, 1951-53. *Publications:* contributor to various architectural journals. *Recreations:* theatre, foreign travel. *Address:* 3 Berkeley Gardens, Kensington Church Street, W8. *T:* 01-229 1482. *Club:* Athenæum.

**ENTWISTLE, Major Sir Cyril Fullard,** Kt 1937; MC 1918; QC 1931; LLB: Director, Decca Ltd; *b* 23 Sept. 1887; *s* of Joe Entwistle of St Annes; *m* 1940, Ethel M. Towlson, Skerryvore, Hale, Cheshire. *Educ:* Bolton Sch.; Victoria Univ., Manchester, 1st class hons LLB, Dauntsey Legal Scholar, Graduate Legal Scholar; Clement's Inn Prizeman, Daniel Reardon Prizeman, Travers Smith Scholar; called to Bar, 1919. Served European War (despatches, MC); commanded 235 Siege Battery, RGA; MP (L) South-West Hull, Dec.

1918-Nov. 1924; Dep. Chm. of Cttees, Feb.-Nov. 1924; MP (U) Bolton, 1931-45; formerly one of the two House of Commons assessors, appointed under the Parliament Act 1911; Chm. of Standing Cttees and Temp. Chm. of House of Commons; introduced as Private Member's Bill, Matrimonial Causes Act 1923. *Recreations:* golf, painting, fly-fishing, shooting. *Address:* 12 Durley Chine Court, West Cliff Road, Bournemouth, Hants. *T:* 26049.

**ENTWISTLE, Sir (John Nuttall) Maxwell,** Kt 1963; Practising Solicitor and Notary; Director of companies; Under-writing Member of Lloyd's since 1964; *b* 8 Jan. 1910; *s* of Isaac and Hannah Entwistle; *m* 1940, Jean Cunliffe McAlpine, *d* of late Dr John and Amy Margaret Penman; two *s. Educ:* Merchant Taylors' Sch., Great Crosby. Solicitor, 1931; Notary Public, 1955. Liverpool City: Councillor, 1938; Alderman, 1960; Leader of Liverpool City Council, when initiated preparation of develt plan for City centre. Chm., Merseyside Development Cttee; Chm., Mersey Tunnel Cttee, 1961-63. Mem., Liverpool Univ. Court and Council, 1955-64. Pres. Edge Hill Liverpool Conservative Assoc. Merchant Taylors' School: Chm., Appeal Cttee; Pres., Old Boys' Assoc.; Governor. *Recreations:* gardening, shooting. *Address:* The Dunes, Victoria Road, Freshfield, Liverpool. *T:* Formby 72236. *Clubs:* Old Hall, Exchange, Palatine (Liverpool).

**ERDELYI, Prof. Arthur;** Professor of Mathematics, University of Edinburgh, since 1964; *b* 2 Oct. 1908; *s* of Ignac Diamant and Friderike (*née* Roth); *m* 1942, Eva Neuburg; no *c. Educ:* Madách Imre Fögimnázium, Budapest; Deutsche Technische Hochscule, Brno; Universities of Prague and Edinburgh. Cand. Ing. (Brno) 1928; Dr rer. nat. (Prague) 1938; DSc (Edinburgh) 1940. Asst Lectr, then Sen. Lectr, University of Edinburgh, 1941-49; Vis. Prof. of Maths, Calif Inst. of Technology, 1947-48; Prof. of Maths, Calif Inst. of Techn., 1949-64; Vis. Professor: Hebrew Univ., Jerusalem, 1956-57; Univ. of Melbourne, 1970. Scientific Cons. to Admty during War of 1939-45. FRSE 1945; For. Mem., Acad. of Sciences, Turin, 1953. *Publications:* (jtly) Higher Transcendental Functions, 3 vols, 1953-55; (jtly) Tables of Integral Transforms, 2 vols, 1954; Asymptotic Expansions, 1956; Operational Calculus and Generalized Functions, 1962; past and present jt editor of several math. periodicals; contrib. research papers and reviews to encycls and math. jls. *Recreations:* music, walking. *Address:* Mathematical Institute of the University, 20 Chambers Street, Edinburgh EH1 1HZ. *T:* 031-667 1011, Ext. 2551.

**ERHARD, Prof. Ludwig;** *b* Fürth, Bavaria, W Germany, 4 Feb. 1897. *Educ:* Handelshochschule, Nuremberg (Dipl.-Kfm.); University of Frankfurt am Main (Dr rer. pol.). Asst and finally Head, Inst. für Wirtschaftsbeobachtung, Nuremberg, 1928-42; Head of Inst. für Industrieforschung, Nuremberg, 1943-45; State Minister for Econ. Affairs, Bavaria, Oct. 1945-Dec. 1946; Hon. Prof., Ludwig-Maximilian-Univ., Munich, Nov. 1947; Chm. Sonderstelle Geld und Kredit (for currency reform), Bad Homburg, 1947; Dir, Dept of Economics, in United Economic Region, Frankfurt am Main, 1948; elected to 1st Bundestag (CDU), 1949; Minister of Economic Affairs, 1949-63; Vice-Chancellor, Federal Republic of Germany, 1957-63; Chancellor, 1963-66. Hon. Prof. (Rhineland) Friedrich-Wilhelm Univ., Bonn, 1950; German Governor, World Bank, 1952. Pres. Internat. Freedom Academy, 1969-. Holds foreign decorations, also hon. doctorates from several universities, both in Germany and abroad. *Publications:* Deutschlands Rückkehr zum Weltmarkt; Wohlstand für Alle; Deutsche Wirtschaftspolitik (all publ. Düsseldorf); The Economics of Success; numerous analyses, expertises, speeches, discourses, discussions, etc. *Recreations:* music (classical), discussions (serious themes, especially Economic Science). *Address:* 8 Johanniterstrasse, 53 Bonn, Germany.

**ERITH, Raymond Charles,** RA, FRIBA; Architect; *b* 7 Aug. 1904; *e s* of Henry Charles Erith; *m* 1934, Pamela, *y d* of Arthur Spencer Jackson; four *d.* RIBA Howard Colls Student, 1922. ARIBA 1927; FRIBA 1946; ARA 1959; RA 1964. In private practice, 1928-. Works include: reconstruction of 10, 11 and 12 Downing Street; Library and Wolfson Buildings, Lady Margaret Hall, Oxford; Jack Straw's Castle, Hampstead. Mem. Royal Fine Art Commn, 1960-. *Address:* Dedham House, Dedham, Essex. *T:* Dedham 3186. *Club:* Athenæum.

**ERKIN, Feridun Cemal;** Minister of Foreign Affairs, Turkey, 1962-65; *m* Madame Mukaddes Feridun Erkin (*d* 1955). *Educ:* Galatasaray Lyceum, Istanbul; Faculty of Law, University of Paris. First Sec., London, 1928-29; Chief of Section, Ankara, 1930-33; Counsellor and Chargé d'Affaires, Berlin, 1934-35; Consul-Gen., Beirut, 1935-37; Dir-Gen., Econ. Dept, Min. of Foreign Affairs, 1937; Dir-Gen., Polit. Dept, 1939; Asst Sec.-Gen., 1942; Deleg, UN Conf. San Francisco, 1945; Sec.-Gen. of Min., 1945; Chm. Turkish Delegn, final session of League of Nations, 1946; Ambassador to Italy, 1947-48; to USA, 1948-55; to Spain, 1955-57; to France, 1957-60; to the Court of St James's, 1960-62. Turkish Governor to Internat. Banks, 1954; Mem. Internat. Diplomatic Academy, 1949-; Mem. Inst. of France, 1959-. Holds Grand Cross of several foreign Orders, including Grand Cross of the Legion of Honour of France. *Recreation:* classical music. *Address:* Ankara, Turkey.

**ERLANGER, L. F. A.;** *see* d'Erlanger.

**ERLEIGH, Viscount; Simon Charles Henry Rufus Isaacs;** stockbroker; *b* 18 May 1942; *e s* and *heir* of 3rd Marquess of Reading, *qv. Educ:* Eton. Formerly Lieut in 1st Queen's Dragoon Guards. *Address:* Staplefield Grange, Staplefield, near Haywards Heath, Sussex. *T:* Handcross 253. *Club:* Cavalry.

**ERNE,** 6th Earl of, *cr* 1789; **Henry George Victor John Crichton;** Baron Erne 1768; Viscount Erne (Ireland), 1781; Baron Fermanagh (UK), 1876; Lieutenant North Irish Horse (TA); *b* 9 July 1937; *s* of 5th Earl and Lady Katharine Cynthia Mary Millicent (Davina) Lytton (who *m* 1945, Hon. C. M. Woodhouse, *qv*), *yr d* of 2nd Earl of Lytton, KG, PC, GCSI, GCIE; *S* father, 1940; *m* 1958, Camilla Marguerite, *er d* of late Wing-Comdr Owen G. E. Roberts, and of Mrs Roberts, 30 Groom Place, Belgrave Square, SW1; four *d. Educ:* Eton. Joined RN as Ord. Seaman, 1956. Page of Honour to the Queen, 1952-54 (to King George VI, 1952). Member: Royal Ulster Agricultural Society; Royal Forestry Society. *Recreations:* sailing, shooting. *Heir: cousin,* David George Crichton [*b* 31 July 1914; *m* 1941, Joan Fenella, *o d* of Lieut-Col Douglas Cleaver; one *s* one *d*]. *Address:* Crom Castle, Newtown Butler, Co. Fermanagh. *T:* Newton-butler 208; 16 Chesham Mews, Belgrave Square, SW1. *Clubs:* St James', Turf; Royal Yacht Squadron (Cowes); Ulster (Belfast).

*See also Duke of Abercorn.*

**ERNST, Max;** painter and sculptor; a founder of Dadaism and a pioneer Surrealist; *b* Brühl, cologne, 2 April 1891; US citizen, 1948, French citizen, 1958; *s* of Philipp Ernst and Louise (*née* Kopp); *m* 1st, 1918, Louise Strauss (marr. diss.); one *s*; 2nd, 1927, Marie-Berthe Aurenche (marr. diss.); 3rd, 1941, Peggy Guggenheim (marr. diss.); 4th, 1946, Dorothea Tanning. *Educ:* Bonn Gymnasium (Baccalauréat) and University. Served European War of 1914-18 as Artillery Officer (wounded twice). Taught himself to paint. First exhibition, Bonn, 1912; subseq. exhibns in Paris, Berlin, New York, Chicago, New Orleans, London, etc. *Retrospective exhibitions:* Copley Galleries, Beverly Hills, 1948; La Hune bookstore, Paris, 1949; Galerie René Drouin, Paris, 1950; Brühl, 1951; Knocke-le-Zoute, Belgium, 1953; Kunsthalle, Berne, 1956; Musée d'Art Moderne, Paris, 1959; Museum of Modern Art, New York, 1961; Art Inst. of Chicago, 1961; Tate Gallery, London, 1962; Kunsthaus, Zurich, 1963; Walraff-Richartz Mus., Cologne, 1963. Represented at Dunn Internat. Exhibn, London, 1963. Grand Prize, Venice Biennale, 1954. *Publications:* La Femme 100 Têtes, 1929; Beyond Painting, and Other Writings by the Artist and His Friends, 1948, etc. *Relevant publication:* Max Ernst, by Patrick Waldberg, 1958. *Address:* c/o Musée d'Art Moderne, Paris, France; Le Pin Perdu, Huismes, France.

**ERNST, Morris Leopold;** Lawyer; *b* Uniontown, Ala, 23 Aug. 1888; *s* of Carl Ernst and Sarah (*née* Bernheim); *m* 1923, Margaret Samuels; one *s* two *d*. *Educ:* Public Sch. and Horace Mann High Sch.; Williams Coll. (AB 1909); New York Law Sch. (LLB 1912). Manufacturer of shirts, 1909-11; retail furniture, 1911-15; Mem. law firm Greenbaum, Wolff & Ernst, New York, 1915-; served as Arbiter for Mayor La Guardia in taxicab strike, 1934; Mem., Mission to Virgin Islands, 1935; drafted Legislation for Governor Lehman on insurance and banking; Special Asst to Attorney-General on election fraud matters; Personal Representative to Pres. Roosevelt during Second World War on various missions to England; Mem., Governmental Mission to Germany, 1946. Special Counsel: Amer. Newspaper Guild; War Production Bd; Counsel: NY State Legislative Commn for Hard of Hearing; Dramatists' Guild; Authors' League of America. Representative of British and Amer. authors, particularly on censorship cases such as: The Well of Loneliness; Joyce's Ulysses; Marie Stopes' books; other volumes attacked in England and USA. Lectr, clubs and colls. Member: Pa Anthracite Coal Commn; NY State Banking Bd, 1933-45; Pres. Truman's Civil Rights Commn; Pres. Truman's Adv. Bd for PO; Bar Assoc., City of NY (Lawyer of the Year, 1960); NY County Lawyers' Assoc.; Phi Gamma Delta; Amer. Political Science Assoc.; Gargoyle Soc., Williams Coll. Hon. Member: Phi Beta Kappa; Nat. Hon. Fraternity of Alpha Kappa Delta; Gamma Chapter, NY Univ.; Williams Coll., 1961; Soc. of Anthroplogy, Sociology and Research, 1965. Hon. JD Nasson Coll., 1963; Hon. DHL Lincoln, 1964. French Legion of Honour. *Publications:* (with William Seagle) To the Pure, 1928; (with Pare Lorentz) Censored, 1930; America's Primer, 1931; (with A. Lindey) Hold Your Tongue, 1932; (jtly) Sex Life of the Unmarried Adult, 1934; Ultimate Power, 1937; (with A. Lindey) The Censor Marches On, 1939; Too Big, 1940; The Best is Yet, 1945; The First Freedom, 1946; So Far So Good, 1948; (with David Loth) American Sexual Behavior and the Kinsey Report, 1948; For Better or Worse, 1952; Report on the American Communist, 1952; Utopia 1976, 1955; Touch Wood, 1960; (with Alan U. Schwartz) Privacy: The Right to be Let Alone, 1962; Untitled: The Diary of my 72nd Year, 1962; (with Alan U. Schwartz) Censorship: The Search for the Obscene, 1964; (with David Loth) How High is Up, 1964; (with Alan U. Schwartz) Lawyers and What They Do, 1964; (ed) The Teacher, 1967; (with Judith Posner) Comparative International Almanac, 1967; A Love Affair with the Law, 1968. Contribs to magazines and encyclopedias; weekly column in The Villager. *Recreations:* cruising, carpentry, boating. *Address:* (home) 2 Fifth Avenue, New York, NY 10011, USA; (office) 437 Madison Avenue, New York, NY 10022. *Clubs:* PEN, City (past Trustee), Williams, Players, NY University Faculty (New York).

**ERRINGTON, Viscount; Evelyn Rowland Esmond Baring;** *b* 3 June 1946; *e s* of 3rd Earl of Cromer, *qv*. *Educ:* Eton. *Address:* French Street Farm, Westerham, Kent. *T:* Westerham 2141.

**ERRINGTON, Sir Eric,** 1st Bt *cr* 1963; Kt 1952; MA, JP; Barrister-at-law; *b* 17 March 1900; *m* 1924, Marjorie Grant Bennett; two *s* one *d*. *Educ:* Mill Hill Sch.; Liverpool Coll.; Trinity Coll., Oxford. 2nd Lieut Gordon Highlanders, 1918; called to Bar 1923 and practises on Northern Circuit; MP (U) Bootle Div. of Lancs, 1935-45; contested: Hanley Div. of Stoke-on-Trent 1929; Scotland Div. of Liverpool 1931; Bootle 1945; Edge Hill Div. of Liverpool, 1950; MP (C) Aldershot Div. of Hants, 1954-70. Chm. N-W Area of Conservative Assoc., 1946-51; Chm. National Executive Cttee of Conservative and Unionist Assoc., 1952-57; Pres. Wessex Area of Conservative Assocs, 1962-65; Vice-Pres. of Liverpool Constitutional Assoc.; Mem., UK Delegation to Council of Europe and Western European Union, 1962-66; Chm., Sub-Cttee of Estimates Cttee of House of Commons, 1963-70. pres. National Federation of Property Owners, 1956-60; Pres. Hire Purchase Trade Assoc., 1965. Member: Exec. Cttee Nat. Assoc. Boys Clubs, 1953; Liverpool City Council, 1934-35. JP City of Liverpool. pres. of Liverpool Philomathic Soc., 1936-37; Chm. United Club, 1944-51. Pilot Officer AAF (Balloon Barrage), 1939; Wing Comdr, 1944. *Recreations:* golf, travelling. *Heir: s* Geoffrey Frederick Errington, Lt-Col, The King's Regt [*b* 15 Feb. 1926; *m* 1955, Diana, *o d* of E. Barry Davenport; three *s*]. *Address:* Lombard Chambers, Bixteth Street, Liverpool 3. *T:* 051-236 4328; Ynys Dwna, Trearddur Bay, near Holyhead. *T:* Trearddur Bay 408. *Clubs:* United University, United and Cecil; Liverpool Racquet (Liverpool).

**ERRINGTON, Lancelot,** CB 1962; Assistant Under-Secretary of State, Department of Health and Social Security, since 1968; *b* 14 Jan. 1917; *e s* of late Major L. Errington; *m* 1939, Katharine Reine, *o d* of late T. C. Macaulay; two *s* two *d*. *Educ:* Wellington Coll.; Trinity Coll., Cambridge. Entered Home Office, 1939. Served RNVR, 1939-45. Transferred to Ministry of National Insurance, 1945; Principal Private Sec. to Minister of National Insurance, 1951; Asst Sec., 1953; Under-Sec., 1957-65; Cabinet Office, 1965-68; Min. of Social Security, 1968. *Recreation:* sailing. *Address:* The Paddock, Portmore Park Road, Weybridge, Surrey. *T:* Weybridge 47346. *Club:* Oxford and Cambridge University.

**ERRINGTON, Richard Percy,** CMG 1955; Chartered Accountant (FCA); *b* 17 May 1904; 2nd *s* of Robert George Errington and Edna Mary Errington (*née* Warr); *m* 1935, Ursula, *d* of Henry Joseph Laws Curtis and Grace

Barton Curtis (*née* Macgregor); one *d. Educ:* Sidcot Sch. Asst Treasurer, Nigeria Government, 1929-37; Colonial Administrative Service: Nigeria, 1937-46; Nyasaland, 1946-48; Financial Sec. to Govt of Aden Colony (also Mem. Bd of Trustees of Port of Aden), 1948-51; Chm., Aden Port Trust, 1951-60. Mem. Governor's Exec. Council, Aden, 1948-58. Unofficial Mem. Aden Colony Legislative Council, 1951-60 (Offical Mem., 1948-51). Chairman: Aden Soc. for the Blind, 1951-60; Aden Lab. Advisory Bd, 1951-57. Area Comr, St John Amb. Bde, 1964. SBStJ, 1965. *Recreations:* golf, tennis, swimming, walking. *Address:* Whitecliffs, Wodehouse Road, Old Hunstanton, Norfolk. *T:* 2356.

**ERROCK, Michael Warden;** Counsellor, HM Diplomatic Service, since 1964; *b* 4 July 1921, *s* of Frederick James and Olive Amy Errock; *m* 1952, Marie Norah Ileana, *d* of Sir Hugh Stonehewer Bird, *qv*; one *s* two *d. Educ:* Abbotscholme Sch.; Ecole des Roches; Peterhouse, Cambridge (Scholar). Served in HM Forces, 1941-46: 2nd Lt 13/18 Royal Hussars (QMO); later Capt. and Adjt, Hodson's Horse, IA. HM Foreign Service, 1946: Middle East Centre for Arabic Studies; Baghdad; Jedda; Jerusalem; Tehran; Copenhagen; FO; UK Mission to the United Nations, New York; Kuwait; MOD (Head of Internat. Dept); Rawalpindi (Economic Counsellor); Middle East Centre, Cambridge Univ. Member: RIIA; RCAS. *Recreations:* walking, bridge. *Address:* 1 Park Parade, Cambridge. *T:* Cambridge 58181. *Club:* Travellers'.

**ERROLL,** Countess of, 23rd in line, *cr* 1452; **Diana Denyse Hay;** Lady Hay, 1429; Baroness of Slains, 1452; 27th Hereditary Lord High Constable of Scotland, *cr* 1314; Celtic title, Mac Garaidh Mhor; 32nd Chief of the Hays since 1171; Senior Great Officer, Royal Household in Scotland; OStJ 1949; *b* 5 Jan. 1926; *d* of 22nd Earl and Lady Idina Sackville (*d* 1955), *d* of 8th Earl De La Warr; *S* father 1941; *m* 1st, 1946, Sir Ian Moncreiffe of that Ilk, 11th Bt (marr. diss. 1964), *qv*; two *s* one *d*; 2nd, 1964, Major R. A. Carnegie; one *s. Heir: s* Lord Hay, *qv. Address:* Crimonmogate, Lonmay, Aberdeenshire. *T:* Lonmay 202.
*See also Earl De La Warr, Baron Kilmarnock.*

**ERROLL OF HALE,** 1st Baron, *cr* 1964; **Frederick James Erroll,** PC 1960; MA, FIEE; FIMechE; *b* 27 May 1914; *s* of George Murison Erroll, engineer, and Kathleen Donovan Edington, both of Glasgow and London; *m* 1950, Elizabeth, *o d* of R. Sowton Barrow, Exmouth, Devon. *Educ:* Oundle Sch.; Trinity Coll., Cambridge. Engineering Apprenticeship, 1931-32; Cambridge Univ., 1932-35; Engineer at Metropolitan-Vickers Electrical Co. Ltd, Manchester, 1936-38; Commissioned into 4th County of London Yeomanry (Sharpshooters), TA, 1939; technical appointments in connection with Tank Construction and Testing, 1940-43; service in India and Burma, 1944-45; Col 1945. MP (C) Altrincham and Sale, 1945-64; Dep. Chm. Parliamentary and Scientific Cttee, 1948-52; Vice-Pres., 1952-55; Member: Select Cttee on Delegated Legislation, 1953; Jt Select Cttee on Private Bill Procedure, 1954. A Director of Engineering and Mining Companies until April 1955; Parliamentary Sec., Ministry of Supply, April 1955-Nov. 1956; Parliamentary Sec., Board of Trade, 1956-58; Economic Sec. to the Treasury, Oct. 1958-59; Minister of State, Board of Trade, 1959-61; Pres., Board of Trade, 1961-63; Minister of Power, 1963-64. Chairman: ASEA (Great Britain) Ltd; Stal-Laval (Great Britain) Ltd; Stal-Levin Ltd; Whessoe Ltd; SF Air Treatment Ltd; Deputy Chairman, BPB Industries Ltd; Director: Consolidated Gold Fields Ltd; Norwest Holst Ltd; Nuclear Power Group Ltd. Member: Council Inst. Directors, 1949-55, and 1965-; NEDC, 1962-63. President: London Chamber of Commerce, 1966-69; Hispanic and Luso-Brazilian Councils, 1969-; British Export Houses Assoc., 1969. Dep. Chm., Decimal Currency Board, 1966-. *Heir:* none. *Address:* 21 Ilchester Place, W14. *T:* 01-937 2707. *Club:* Carlton.

**ERROLL, Master of;** *see under* Hay, Lord.

**ERSKINE;** *see* St Clair-Erskine.

**ERSKINE,** family name of **Earls of Buchan** and **Mar and Kellie,** and of **Baron Erskine of Rerrick.**

**ERSKINE OF RERRICK,** 1st Baron, *cr* 1964; **John Maxwell Erskine,** Bt 1961; GBE 1956 (CBE 1946); Kt 1949; DL, JP; LLD; FRSE; Governor of Northern Ireland, 1964-68; General Manager, 1932-53, and Director, 1951-69, The Commercial Bank of Scotland Ltd, subsequently National Commercial Bank of Scotland, now absorbed in Royal Bank of Scotland; Member Queen's Body Guard for Scotland (Royal Company of Archers), since 1935; Chairman, Securicor (Scotland) Ltd; formerly Director, Caledonian Insurance Co., Guardian Assurance Co., and other companies; President, Scottish Savings Committee (Chairman, 1945-58); Chairman Scottish Hospital Endowments Research Trust (Hospital Endowments Scotland Act, 1953); Vice-President, Trustee Savings Banks Association; Foundation Member and Member Council, The Thistle Foundation; *b* 14 Dec. 1893; *s* of late John Erskine, Kirkcudbright; *m* 1922, Henrietta, CStJ, *d* of late William Dunnett, East Canisbay, Caithness; one *s* one *d. Educ:* Kirkcudbright Acad.; Edinburgh Univ. Admitted Solicitor; Pres. Inst. of Bankers in Scotland, 1937-40; Pres. Edinburgh Chamber of Commerce and Manufactures, 1941-44 (Hon. Life Mem., 1968); Chm. Central Cttee of Scottish Chambers of Commerce, 1942-44; Mem. Hetherington Deptl Cttee on Hospital Policy in Scotland, 1942; Chm. King George and Queen Elizabeth Officers' club, Edinburgh, for Overseas Personnel under Empire Societies War Hosp. Cttee (War 1939-45), latterly Chm. Scottish Cttee (CBE); Mem. Postmaster General's Adv. Coun., 1945-49; Mem. Scottish Cttee on Scottish Financial and Trade Statistics (Catto Cttee), 1950-52; Chm. Transp. Users' Consultative Cttee for Scotland, 1954-57; Mem. Central Transp. Consultative Cttee, 1954-57; Mem. Scottish Transp. Council, 1955-56; Pres. Scottish Council of Social Service, 1949-57 (Chm. 1945-49); Pres. Edinburgh Union of Boys' Clubs, 1945-56; Trustee and Mem. Exec. Cttee Carnegie Trust for Scottish Univs, 1944-57; Mem. Cttee of Management, Royal Victoria Hosp. Tuberculosis Trust, 1944-56; Mem. Nat. Ref. Tribunal for Coal Mining Industry, 1956-59; Member: War Works Commn, 1945-59; N of Scotland Hydro-Electric Bd, 1948-59 (Dep. Chm. 1960, 1961). Hon. Life Mem., N Ireland Chamber of Commerce and Industry, 1968; Hon. Mem., Company of Merchants of City of Edinburgh, 1970. Freeman, Royal Burgh of Kirkcudbright, 1967. Hon. LLD: Glasgow, 1962; Queen's Univ., Belfast, 1968. KStJ. 1965. *Heir: s* Major Hon. Iain Maxwell Erskine, Grenadier Guards, retd [*b* 22 Jan. 1926. Chevalier, Legion of Honour, OStJ]. *Address:* 20 Great Stuart Street, Edinburgh EH3 7TH. *T:* 031-225 5455. *Clubs:* New, Caledonian United Service & Northern

(Edinburgh) (Hon. Life Mem.). *See also Sir Robert George Erskine.*

**ERSKINE, Lord; James Thorne Erskine;** *b* 10 March 1949; *s* and *heir* of 13th Earl of Mar and 15th Earl of Kellie, *qv. Educ:* Eton. Community Service Volunteer, York, 1967-68. *Address:* Claremont House, Alloa, Clackmannanshire. *T:* Alloa 2020. *Clubs:* Royal Over-Seas League; Puffins (Edinburgh).

**ERSKINE, Sir David;** *see* Erskine, Sir T. D.

**ERSKINE, Sir Derek (Quicke),** Kt 1964; *b* 12 Feb. 1905; *s* of late Sir James Monteith Erskine; *m* 1927, Elisabeth Mary, *d* of late Major R. S. Spurrier, King's Dragoon Guards; two *s* one *d. Educ:* Eton Coll.; RMC Sandhurst. King's Dragoon Guards, 1924-27, resigned. Settled in Kenya, Oct. 1927. DAQMG East Africa Command, 1942-45. MLC Kenya, 1948-51; MP and Chief Whip, Kenya African Nat. Union Parly Gp, 1961-64. Vice-Pres., Kenya Nat. Chamber of Commerce and Industry, 1967. Pres., Kenya Amateur Athletic Assoc., 1952-65. *Recreations:* polo and racing. *Address:* Riverside, PO Box 132, Nairobi, Kenya. *Clubs:* Cavalry; United Kenya, Muthaiga Country (Nairobi).

**ERSKINE, Hon. Francis Walter;** *b* 9 Jan. 1899; *y s* of the 12th Earl of Mar and 14th Earl of Kellie, KT; *m* 1925, Phyllis Burstall, Quebec; two *d. Educ:* Eton. Lieut, Scots Guards, 1917-25; Aide-de-Camp to Governor-Gen. of Canada (Lord Byng), 1921-25. Formerly Mem. of London Stock Exchange. Capt. Scots Guards, 1939-45. *Address:* 36 Hurlingham Court, SW6. *Clubs:* Guards, Pratt's.

**ERSKINE, Sir George;** *see* Erskine, Sir R. G.

**ERSKINE, Maj.-Gen. (Hon.) Ian David,** CB 1949; CBE 1947; DSO 1941; *b* 17 March 1898; *s* of late A. D. Erskine, OBE; *m* 1945, Mariora Hankey. *Educ:* Winchester; Sandhurst; Staff Coll., Camberley. Regtl Adjutant, Scots Guards, 1930-33; Staff Coll., Camberley, 1933-35; Brigade Major 1st Guards Brigade, 1935-39; Comdt Middle East Tactical Sch., 1939; Commanded 2nd Bn Scots Guards, 1940; Commanded 22nd Guards Brigade, 1941; Brig. Gen. Staff, Sudan, 1942; Brig. Comdr 148 Pre OCTU Training Establishments, 1943-45; Provost Marshal and Maj.-Gen., 1945-48; (Local Maj.-Gen.); retired 1949; hon. Maj.-Gen., 1951. *Recreations:* cricket, golf. *Address:* St Clement's House, Sandwich, Kent. *T:* Sandwich 2288. *Clubs:* Guards, Pratt's.

**ERSKINE, Keith David;** Chairman: Metal Closures Group; Associated Hotels; Kensington Palace Hotel; Managing Director, Securicor; Director, London Board, Norwich Union Group; Solicitor; Senior Partner, Hextall Erskine & Co.; *b* 11 June 1907; *m* 1944, Audrey Skinner, 2nd Officer in WRNS; one *s* five *d. Educ:* Westminster Sch. (Scholar). Qualified as Solicitor, 1933. War of 1939-45: Captain, RA, Middle East and Italy, 8th Army (despatches twice, 1944). *Recreations:* ski-ing, fishing, gardening, swimming, working. *Address:* Beech Hurst, Waterhouse Lane, Kingswood, Surrey. *T:* Mogador 2738. *Club:* City of London.

**ERSKINE, Ralph;** architect; own practice since 1939 (in Sweden since 1939, both on land and on a Thames Barge at Drottningholm; also at Byka, Newcastle upon Tyne); *b* 24 Feb. 1914; *s* of late George and Mildred Erskine; *m* 1939, Ruth Monica Francis; one *s* two *d. Educ:* Friends' Sch., Saffron Walden, Essex; Regent Street Polytechnic (architecture). ARIBA 1936; AMTPI 1938; SAR 1965. Won number of prizes in arch. comps in Sweden; one year's study at Academy for Fine Arts, Sweden, 1945. *Work executed:* town plans; workers' houses; co-operative housing and industrial housing; flats; hostels; factories; ski-hotel; shopping centre; school; town hall; hall of residence at Clare Coll., Cambridge; churches; housing estates at Newmarket and Killingworth; slum clearance scheme, Byka, Newcastle upon Tyne. Lecturing: in America, Canada, Japan and many countries in Europe. Hon Fellow of AIA, 1966. *Publications:* for several arch. magazines, on building in northern climates, etc. *Recreations:* ski-ing, skating, swimming, yachting, ice yachting, gardening, carpentry on sailing boat Verona, etc. *Address:* Gustav III's väg, Drottningholm, Sweden. *T:* 7720352.

**ERSKINE, Sir (Robert) George,** Kt 1948; CBE 1945; Member of Directors' Advisory Committee of Morgan Grenfell & Co. Limited; Director: Investment Trust Corporation Ltd; London & Provincial Trust Ltd (Chairman); London Maritime Investment Co. Ltd; Metropolitan Trust Co. Ltd; Member of London Advisory Committee, Scottish Council (Development and Industry); Member Council, RAF Benevolent Fund; *b* 5 Nov. 1896; *s* of late John Erskine, Kirkcudbright; unmarried. *Educ:* Kirkcudbright Academy; Edinburgh Univ. (BL). On staff of National Bank of Scotland, 1913-29, when joined Morgan Grenfell; Director, 1945-67. Served European War, 1914-18. Dep. Chm. NAAFI, 1941-52; Pres. Institute of Bankers, 1954-56; Master of Glaziers' Company, 1960-61; Mem. Jenkins Cttee on Company Law, 1959-62. High Sheriff of Surrey, 1963-64. *Address:* Busbridge Wood, Godalming, Surrey. *T:* Hascombe 378. *Clubs:* Caledonian, City of London. *See also Baron Erskine of Rerrick.*

**ERSKINE, Sir (Thomas) David,** 5th Bt, *cr* 1821; JP; DL; Convener, Fife County Council, since 1970; *b* 31 July 1912; *o surv. s* of Sir Thomas Wilfred Hargreaves John Erskine, 4th Bt, and late Magdalen Janet, *d* of Sir Ralph Anstruther, 6th Bt of Balcaskie; *S* father, 1944; *m* 1947, Ann, *er d* of late Lt-Col Neil Fraser-Tytler, CBE, DSO, MC, and of Christian Helen Fraser-Tytler, *qv*; two *s* one *d. Educ:* Eton; Magdalene Coll., Cambridge. Employed by Butterfield & Swire, London and China, in 1934 and served with them in China, 1935-41. Joined HM Forces in India and commissioned into Indian Corps of Engineers. Served with them in Mid-East, India and Malaya, being demobilised in 1945 with rank of Major. JP Fife, 1951; DL Fife, 1955. *Heir: s* Thomas Peter Neil Erskine, *b* 28 March 1950. *Address:* Cambo, Kingsbarns, Fife. *T:* Crail 313. *Club:* New (Edinburgh).

**ERSKINE CRUM, Maj.-Gen. Vernon Forbes,** CIE 1947; MC 1944; GOC Northern Ireland, since 1971; *b* 11 Dec. 1918; *yr s* of late Sir Walter Erskine Crum, OBE; *m* 1948, Rosemary Aimée Douglas, *d* of late Brig.-Gen. Sir Douglas Dawson, GCVO, KCB, CMG; one *s. Educ:* Eton; New Coll., Oxford. Commissioned Scots Guards, 1940. Served War of 1939-45, North-West Europe, 1944 (MC); Conference Sec. to Viceroy and Gov.-Gen. of India, 1947-48 (CIE); Regtl Adjt Scots Guards, 1948-51; Adjt RMA Sandhurst, 1951-54; Bde Major, Household Bde, 1954-57; Commandant Guards Depot, 1957-60; AAG London Dist, 1960-62; Sec. Jt Planning Staff, 1962-63; Comdr 4th Guards Bde, 1963-65; GOC 4th Div., BAOR, 1967-69; Chief Army Instructor, IDC, 1970. *Address:* Pear Tree

Cottage, Windlesham, Surrey. *T:* Bagshot 3143. *Clubs:* Guards, Leander.

**ERSKINE-HILL, Sir Robert,** 2nd Bt, *cr* 1945; Member of the Royal Company of Archers, Queen's Body Guard for Scotland; Chartered Accountant; partner in firm of Chiene and Tait, Chartered Accountants, Edinburgh; *b* 6 Feb. 1917; *er s* of Sir Alexander Galloway Erskine-Hill, 1st Bt, KC, DL, and Christian Hendrie, MBE (*d* 1947), *o d* of John Colville, MP, Cleland, Lanarkshire; *S* father, 1947; *m* 1942, Christine Alison, *o d* of late Capt. (A) Henry James Johnstone of Alva, RN; two *s* two *d*. *Educ:* Eton; Trinity Coll., Cambridge (BA). Served War of 1939-45, in RNVR. *Heir: s* Alexander Roger Erskine-Hill, *b* 15 Aug. 1949. *Address:* Quothquhan Lodge, Biggar, Lanarkshire. *T:* Tinto 332. *Club:* New (Edinburgh).

**ERSKINE-LINDOP, Audrey Beatrice Noël;** novelist; *b* London; *d* of late Lt-Col A. H. Erskine-Lindop, MC, and of Ivy Monck-Mason; *m* 1945, Dudley Gordon Leslie, scriptwriter and playwright. *Educ:* Convent of Our Lady of Lourdes, Hatch End, Middx; Blackdown Sch., Wellington, Somerset. Started career in Worthing Repertory Company; became scriptwriter (England and Hollywood). Books have been published in numerous countries. *Plays:* Beware of Angels (in collaboration with Dudley Leslie), prod Westminster Theatre, 1959; Let's Talk Turkey, prod 1955. Freeman of City of London, 1954. *Publications:* In Me My Enemy, 1948; Soldiers' Daughters Never Cry, 1949; The Tall Headlines, 1950; Out of the Whirlwind, 1951; The Singer Not the Song, 1953 (Book Society choice; filmed, 1961); Details of Jeremy Stretton, 1955; The Judas Figures, 1956; I Thank a Fool, 1958; The Way to the Lantern, 1961; Nicola, 1964; I Start Counting, 1966 (Prix Roman Policier, France, 1968); Sight Unseen, 1969. *Recreations:* history (particularly collecting relics of favourite historical characters); anything to do with caged birds and cats; very fond of the wilder type of countryside. *Address:* Seaton Cottage, 3 Holland Park Avenue, W11. *T:* 01-727 6997; Kestorway, Chagford, South Devon. *T:* Chagford 2157. *Clubs:* Ghost, Pen.

**ERSKINE-MURRAY,** family name of **Baron Elibank.**

**ERSKINE-WYSE, Marjorie Anne, (Mrs Michael Erskine-Wyse);** National Secretary, National Union of Townswomen's Guilds, since 1965; *b* 14 Oct. 1914; *d* of late Robert Brooks Lester Thomas and Annie (*née* Moller), Melbourne, Australia; *m* 1943, Michael Erskine-Wyse. *Educ:* Box Hill Technical Coll., Melbourne (Dip. DSc). ABC Public Relations Officer, 1939. Programme and Presentation Officer, Far Eastern Bureau, Foreign Office, attached All-India Radio, New Delhi, 1944-45. Asst Editor, Home and Country, London, 1946; Sub-editor, Arab News Agency, Cairo, 1947-49; Freelance journalist SE Asia, 1950; Asst to Basil Dean in compilation of autobiography and Fest. of Brit. production of Flecker's Hassan, Cambridge Theatre, 1950-51; Admin. Officer, Nutrition Div. UN Food and Agric. Orgn, Rome, 1952-56; Conf. Sec. and Dep. Nat. Sec., NUTG, 1957-60; Features Editor, Beirut (Eng. Lang. daily), Lebanon, 1960-61; Editor, The Townswoman, and Public Relations Officer, NUTG, 1962-65. *Recreations:* music, theatre, chess, swimming, riding, tennis. *Address:* 18 Gate Hill Court, W11. *T:* (home) 01-727 9433, (office) 01-589 8817.

**ERTZ, Susan,** FRSL; writer; *d* of Charles Edward Ertz and Mary Gertrude Le Viness of New York; *m* 1932, Major J. Ronald McCrindle, *qv*. *Publications:* Novels: Madam Claire. Nina; Afternoon; Now East, Now West; The Galaxy; Julian Probert, Face to Face (short stories); The Proselyte, 1933; Now We Set Out, 1934; Woman Alive, 1935; No Hearts to Break, 1937; Big Frogs and Little Frogs (short stories), 1938; Black, White, and Caroline (for children), 1938; One Fight More, 1940; Anger in the Sky, 1943; Two Names upon the Shore, 1947; The Prodigal Heart, 1950; The Undefended Gate, 1953; Charmed Circle, 1956; In the Cool of the Day, 1961; contributions to various periodicals. *Address:* 17 Sloane Court West, SW3. *T:* 01-730 6361; Lossenham Manor, Newenden, Hawkhurst, Kent. *T:* Northiam 2196.

**ERVINE, St John Greer,** FRSL; Dramatist and Novelist; Hon. LLD (St Andrews); Hon. DLitt Queen's University, Belfast; *b* Belfast, 28 Dec. 1888; *s* of late William Ervine, Belfast; *m* 1911, Leonora Mary (*d* 1965), *d* of late G. W. Davis, Birmingham. Trooper Household Battalion, Oct. 1916-April 1917; Lieut 1st Batt. Royal Dublin Fusiliers in France, Oct. 1917-May 1918, when wounded. Manager, Abbey Theatre, Dublin, 1915; Prof. of Dramatic Literature, Royal Society of Literature, 1933-36; Mem. of the Irish Academy; wrote The Magnanimous Lover (one-act play), 1907, produced at the Abbey Theatre, Dublin, 1913; Mixed Marriage (four-act play), 1910, Abbey Theatre, 1911; Jane Clegg (three-act play), 1911, Gaiety Theatre, Manchester, 1912; John Ferguson (four-act play), 1914, Abbey Theatre, 1916; The Ship (three-act play); Mary, Mary, Quite Contrary (four-act play); The Lady of Belmont (five-act play); Anthony and Anna (three-act play); The First Mrs Fraser, 1928 (three-act play); People of our Class, 1934 (three-act play); Boyd's Shop (four-act play), 1935; Robert's Wife (three-act play), 1937; The Christies (three-act play), 1939; Friends and Relations, 1940; Private Enterprise, 1947; My Brother Tom, 1952; Ballyfarland's Festival, 1953 and with H. G. Wells, The Wonderful Visit (five-act play); Esperanza, 1957. *Publications:* All the plays named above; Some Impressions of my Elders (essays), 1923; A Journey to Jerusalem, 1936; The Mountain, and other stories, 1928; and seven novels: Mrs Martin's Man; Alice and a Family; Changing Winds; The Foolish Lovers; The Wayward Man; the First Mrs Fraser; and Sophia; three political studies: Sir Edward Carson and the Ulster Movement, Parnell, If I Were Dictator; three books on Theatre Craft: The Organised Theatre, How to Write a Play, and the Theatre in my Time; God's Soldier (a life of Gen. Booth); Craigavon: Ulsterman; Oscar Wilde: a Present-Time Appraisal; Bernard Shaw: His Life, Work and Friends. *Address:* c/o Lloyds Bank, Seaton, Devon. *Club:* Garrick.

**ERVINE-ANDREWS, Lieut-Col Harold Marcus,** VC 1940; East Lancashire Regiment, retired; *b* 29 July 1911; *s* of late C. C. Ervine-Andrews, New Ross, Wexford, Southern Ireland; *m* 1939, Betty, *er d* of R. I. Torrie; one *s* one *d*. *Educ:* Stonyhurst Coll.; Royal Military Coll., Sandhurst. 2nd Lieut East Lancs Regt, 1932; Captain 1940; Temp. Major, 1940; War Subst. Major, 1942; Temp. Lieut-Col 1942; served with RAF during North-West Frontier of India Operations, 1936-37 (medal and two clasps, despatches) and NW Frontier, 1938-39; served in France with BEF (VC); attached to RAF in UK, 1940; on loan to Australian Military Forces, 1941; attached RAAF, 1942; GSO 1 Air HQ Allied Land Forces in South-West Pacific Area, 1943; commanding No. 61

Carrier-Borne Army Liaison Section, 1944; SALO in 21st Aircraft Carrier Squadron (East Indies), 1945; Lieut-Col Commanding No. 18 Infantry Holding Bn, 1946; attached to The Army Mobile Information Unit, 1948; Asst Dir of Public Relations to BAOR, 1951, as a Lieut-Col; retired pay, 1952. *Address:* The Old Mill, Dunmere, Bodmin, Cornwall. *T:* Bodmin 3408.

**ESCOMBE, Capt. William Malcolm Lingard,** CBE 1960; DSO 1915; late 20th Battalion London Regiment (The Queen's Own) TA; *b* 1891; *m* 1st, 1915, Eileen M., 4th *d* of Dr W. Love, Hoddesdon, Herts; one *s*; 2nd, 1948, Elizabeth M., *d* of late Rev. W. D. Lindley and of Mrs Lindley, Wheathampstead, Herts. Entered army (TF), 1911; served European War, 1914-19 (despatches, DSO); Chm. and Managing Dir of Escombe McGrath, Co. Ltd, 1955-64. Master N Herts Beagles, 1929-32; Pres. Assoc. of Masters of Harriers and Beagles, 1938; Master of Merchant Taylors' Company, 1941-42 and 1957-58; late Supt Herts Spec. Constabulary. Chm. St Albans (Parliamentary) Div. Conservative and Unionist Assn, 1946-52, and Pres., 1951-58; Pres. Old Bradfieldian Soc., 1945-49. *Recreation:* following hounds. *Address:* Junipers, Wheathampstead, Herts. *Club:* City of London.

**ESCRITT, Charles Ewart,** OBE 1970; MA; Secretary, Oxford University Appointments Committee, 1947-70; Fellow, Keble College, Oxford, 1965-70; *b* 26 Aug. 1905; *s* of late Rev. Charles Escritt; *m* 1939, Ruth Mary, *d* of T. C. Metcalf; two *s* one *d*. *Educ:* Christ's Hospital; Keble Coll., Oxford. Asst Master, Bromsgrove Sch., 1928; Staff of Tootal Broadhurst Lee Co. Ltd, 1933-46. Served War of 1939-45: 42 Div. RASC (TA), 1939; 18 Div. RASC, Capt. 1940; POW, Singapore and Thailand, 1942-45. *Address:* 16 Northmoor Road, Oxford. *T:* Oxford 59304.

**ESCRITT, Maj.-Gen. Frederick Knowles,** CB 1953; OBE 1943; MRCS; late RAMC, retired Nov. 1953; QHS, since 1952; *b* 29 Nov. 1893; *s* of Harold Teal Escritt; *M* 1931, Elsa Alfrida, *d* of Director Larssen, Stockholm; one *d*. *Educ:* Dulwich Coll.; Guy's Hosp. MRCS, LRCP, 1918. Joined RAMC, Nov. 1918 (1914-15 Star, British War and Victory Medals). Served War of 1939-45 (Gen. Service Iraq, 1939-45 Star, Burma Star, Defence and War Medals, 1939-45). ADMS Eastern and 14 Armies, 1942-45; DDMS 1 Corps Dist, BAOR, 1945-47; Inspector of Training, AMS, 1950-51; DDMS, Eastern Command, 1951-53. Order of St John (Officer Brother), 1952. *Address:* 31 Pine Bank, Hindhead, Surrey. *Club:* Royal Automobile.

**ESDAILE, Philippa Chichele,** DSc, FLS; Reader in Biology, University of London, and Head of Biology Department, King's College of Household and Social Science, 1921-51; *b* 1888; *y d* of late George Esdaile, Manchester and late Georgina, *d* of George Doswell, Somerset. *Educ:* Manchester High Sch. for Girls. Graduated Univ. of Manchester, 1910; Research Fellow of University of Manchester and University Coll., Reading; Acting Head of Zoology Dept, Bedford Coll., University of London, 1915-20; Senior Lecturer in Zoology, Birkbeck Coll., University of London, 1920-21; Vice-Pres. of Linnean Soc. of London, 1932-33; Member: Makerere-Khartoum Education Commission, 1937; Advisory Committee on Education, Colonial Office, 1933-38; Committee on Nutrition in the Colonial Empire, Econ. Adv. Coun., 1933; Federation of Univ. Women; Crosby Hall. Formerly Mem. of Coun. of Girls' Public Day Sch. Trust, Ltd. Vice-Chm. of Governing Body of Hatfield Sch., Herts. *Publications:* Economic Biology for Students of Social Science, Parts 1 and 2; various scientific papers. *Address:* Mansard Gables, Burnham Green Road, Tewin, Herts.

**ESHER,** 4th Viscount, *cr* 1897; Baron *cr* 1885; **Lionel Gordon Baliol Brett,** CBE 1970; MA; PPRIBA; FILA; DisTP; Rector and Vice-Provost, Royal College of Art, from July 1971; Architect in private practice (Messrs Brett & Pollen); *b* 18 July 1913; *o s* of 3rd Viscount Esher, GBE; *S* father, 1963; *m* 1935, Christian, *e d* of late Col Ebenezer Pike, CBE, MC; five *s* one *d*. *Educ:* Eton (Scholar); New Coll., Oxford (Scholar). BA (1st Class), 1935; RIBA Ashpitel Prizeman, 1939. Served War in RA, 1940-45; France and Germany, 1944-45 (despatches); Major. Architect Planner, Hatfield New Town, 1949-59; major housing projects: Hatfield, Stevenage, Basildon, Southampton; consultant architect: Downside Abbey; Maidenhead Town Centre; St John's Coll. Estate, Oxford; Cadogan Estate, London; Portsmouth City Centre; historic core of York. Lecture tours: USA 1953; India, 1954; Australia, 1959. Mem. Royal Fine Art Commn, 1951-69; Governor, Museum of London; Mem., Advisory Council, Victoria and Albert Museum; Vice-Pres., RIBA, 1958-59, 1962-63, 1964-65; Pres., 1965-67. Hon. DLitt Strathclyde Univ.; Hon. DUniv York, 1970. hon. Fellow, Amer. Inst. of Architects. *Publications:* Houses, 1947; The World of Architecture, 1963; Landscape in Distress, 1965; York: a study in conservation, 1969; Parameters and Images, 1970; many articles on Architecture. *Recreations:* writing and painting. *Heir:* *s* Hon. Christopher Lionel Baliol Brett [*b* 23 Dec. 1936; *m* 1962, Camilla Charlotte, *d* of Sir (Horace) Anthony Rumbold, 10th Bt, *qv*; one *s* two *d*]. *Address:* Christmas Common Tower, Watlington, Oxford. *T:* Watlington 604. *Clubs:* Athenæum, Garrick.

*See also Sir Martyn G. Beckett, Sir Evelyn Shuckburgh.*

**ESKDAILL, Lord; Richard Walter John Montagu Douglas Scott;** *b* 14 Feb. 1954; *s* of Earl of Dalkeith, *qv*.

**ESMONDE, Sir Anthony Charles,** 15th Bt, *cr* 1629; Deputy, Dail Eireann, since 1951; *b* 18 Jan. 1899; 3rd *s* of Dr John Esmonde, MP; *S* brother (Capt. Sir John Lymbrick Esmonde, Bt) 1958; *m* 1927, Eithne Moira Grattan, *y d* of Sir Thomas Grattan Esmonde, 11th Bt; three *s* three *d*. *Educ:* Clongowes Wood Coll.; Germany. Surgeon Lieut, RN, 1921-25; LRCS & P Ireland, 1921. Consultative Assembly, Council of Europe, 1954 (Cttees of Agriculture and Non-represented nations); Mem. Irish National Health Council, 1956. Mem. Catholic Truth Soc. of Ireland, 1936. Mem. Royal Dublin Soc., 1938. Knight of Honour and Devotion, Order of Malta, 1957. *Recreations:* agriculturist; fishing, shooting, etc. *Heir:* *e s* John Henry Grattan Esmonde, Barrister-at-Law [*b* 27 June 1928; *m* 1957, Pamela Mary, *d* of late Francis Stephen Bourke, FRCPI; two *s* one *d*]. *Address:* Ballynastragh, Gorey, Co. Wexford, Eire. *T:* Gorey 52.

**'ESPINASSE, Prof. Paul Gilbert;** Emeritus Professor of Zoology, The University, Hull; *b* 10 June 1900; *s* of late Rev. Richard Talbot 'Espinasse; *m* 1934, Margaret Patricia MacPherson Wattie; two *d*. *Educ:* privately; St Edmund Hall, Oxford. *Publications:* papers in learned journals. *Address:* 46 Marlborough Avenue, Hull. *T:* Hull 43908.

**ESPLEN, Sir William Graham,** 2nd Bt, *cr* 1921; Shipowner; *b* 29 Dec. 1899; *s* of 1st Bt and Laura Louise (*d* 1936), *d* of late John Dickinson, Sunderland; *S* father, 1930; *m* 1928, Aline Octavia (marr. diss. 1951), *y d* of late A. Octavius Hedley; one *s*. *Educ:* Harrow; Cambridge. Joined Royal Naval College, Keyham, 1918; retired, 1922. *Recreation:* fishing. *Heir: s* John Graham Esplen [*b* 4 Aug. 1932; *m* 1956, Valerie Joan, *yr d* of Maj.-Gen. A. P. Lambooy, *qv*; one *s* three *d*]. *Club:* Formby Golf.
*See also Sir Peter Hoare.*

**ESPLEY, Arthur James,** CBE 1951 (OBE 1918); JP; PhC: *s* of late Thomas Espley, Audley, Staffs; *m* 1912, Elsie (*d* 1965), *d* of late William Thornber; four *s*. *Educ:* Accrington Technical Sch.; Birmingham Univ. Served European War, 1915-18 (OBE, despatches twice); Managing Dir and Vice-Chm., Timothy Whites & Taylors Ltd until 1944. Ministry of Aircraft Production; Dir-Gen. of Equipment, 1940-41; Member: Industrial Court of Arbitration; Railways Staff National Tribunal; Court of Inquiry, Dockyard, Malta, 1949; Court of Inquiry, Sugar Industry, Trinidad, 1955. Pres., Postgraduate Institute of Obstetrics and Gynæcology, London University; Ex-Chm. Queen Charlotte's and Chelsea Hospital for Women. *Address:* Thornbers, Nash Street, Golden Cross, Hailsham, Sussex. *T:* Chiddingly 262. *Club:* Constitutional.

**ESPLIN, Air Vice-Marshal Ian (George),** CB 1963; OBE 1946; DFC 1943; retired (voluntarily) 1965; *b* 26 Feb. 1914; *s* of late Donald Thomas Esplin and Emily Freame Esplin; *m* 1944, Patricia Kaleen Barlow; one *s* one *d*. *Educ:* Sydney Univ.; Oxford Univ. BEc 1936; MA 1939. NSW Rhodes Schol., 1937. Entered RAF from Oxford, 1939. Served War of 1939-45, as Pilot in Night-Fighters; destroyed three enemy aircraft at night; also served at CFS and in HQ, SEAC; Air Min. (Policy), 1945; Comd Desford, 1947; Dep. Senior Personnel Staff Officer, HQ Reserve Comd, 1948; Directing Staff, RAF Staff Coll., 1950-51; Comd first Jet All Weather Wing, Germany (No. 148), 1952-54; Flying Coll. Course, 1954; Dep. Dir of Operational Requirements, Air Min., 1955-58; Comd RAF Wartling, 1958-60; Dir of Operational Reqts, 1960-62; Comdr, RAF Staff and Air Attaché, Washington, DC, 1963-65. *Recreations:* golf, tennis, swimming, ski-ing. *Address:* c/o National Westminster Bank Ltd, West End Office, 1 St James's Square, SW1. *Clubs:* Vincent's (Oxford); Leander (Henley-on-Thames).

**ESSAAFI, M'hamed,** Commander, Order of Tunisian Republic, 1963; Secretary General, Ministry of Foreign Affairs, Tunis, since 1970; Tunisian Ambassador to the Court of St James's, 1964-69; *b* 26 May 1930; *m* 1956, Hedwige Klat; one *s* one *d*. *Educ:* Sadiki Coll., Tunis; Sorbonne, Paris. Secretariat of State for For. Affairs, 1956; 1st Sec., Tunisian Embassy, London, 1956; 1st Sec., Tunisian Embassy, Washington, 1957; Secretariat of State for For. Affairs, Tunis: Dir of Amer. Dept, 1960; America and Internat. Confs Dept, 1962. *Recreation:* shooting. *Address:* Ministry of Foreign Affairs, Tunis.

**ESSAME, Enid Mary,** MA Cantab; JP; Headmistress of Queenswood School since 1943; 2nd *d* of Oliver Essame. *Educ:* Wyggeston Gram. Sch., Leicester; Girls' High Sch., Newark; Newnham Coll., Cambridge (Hist. Tripos, 1928); King's Coll., University of London (Certificate of Education, 1929). Mary Ewart Travelling Scholar, Newnham Coll., 1934-35; AM in Education, American Univ., Washington, DC, USA, 1935. Asst Headmistress Queenswood Sch., 1935-43. British Council lecturer, India and Pakistan, 1953, Nigeria, 1961. Hon. Mem. Council, English New Education Fellowship, 1954; Governor, Chorleywood Coll. for Girls with Little or No Sight, 1957; Trustee of The New Coll. of Speech and Drama, 1962. Hon. Sec. Assoc. of Headmistresses of Boarding Schools, Pres. 1962-64. Chm., Assoc. of Ind. and Direct Grant Schools, 1966-68. Member British Federation of Univ. Women. *Address:* Queenswood, Hatfield, Herts. *T:* Potters Bar 54285. *Club:* Arts Theatre.

**ESSAME, Maj.-Gen. Hubert,** CBE 1945; DSO 1944; MC 1918; Military Lecturer, Broadcaster, Journalist and TV Advisor; *b* 24 Dec. 1896; *s* of late Ernest H. Essame, Wokingham, Berks; *m* 1st, 1926, Hilda Mary (decd), *d* of late T. J. Kennedy, ICS; two *s* one *d*; 2nd, 1964, Dorothy Mary, *er d* of late Sir Frank and Lady Fox, Sydney, Australia. *Educ:* Nottingham High Sch.; Staff Coll. Served BEF, 1916-18, with 2nd Northants Regt (wounded twice). Gen. Staff, WO, 1934-36; Major, 1938; CO 1st East Lancs Regt, 1941-42; Brig., 214 Independent Inf. Bde, 1942-43; 43rd Wessex Inf. Div., NW Europe, 1944-45; Maj.-Gen. 1947. Pres. Regular Commissions Board; retd 1949. Governor, Royal School, Bath. *Publications:* The 43rd Wessex Division at War, 1952; The North West Europe Campaign, 1944-45, 1962; (with E. M. G. Belfield) Battle for Normandy, 1965; The Battle for Germany, 1969; Normandy Bridgehead, 1970. *Recreations:* Military Historical Research; golf. *Address:* The Courtyard, West Wittering, near Chichester, Sussex. *T:* West Wittering 2289. *Club:* United Service.

**ESSEN, Louis,** OBE 1959; FRS 1960; DSc, PhD; Deputy Chief Scientific Officer, National Physical Laboratory, since 1960; *b* 6 Sept. 1908; *s* of Fred Essen and Ada (*née* Edson); *m* 1937, Joan Margery Greenhalgh; four *d*. *Educ:* High Pavement Sch., Nottingham; London Univ. (Ext.). BSc 1928, PhD 1941, DSc 1948, London. Joined the National Physical Laboratory, 1929; Senior Principal Scientific Officer, 1956-60. Charles Vernon Boys Prize, Phys. Soc. 1957; Tompion Gold Medal, Clockmakers' Company, 1957; Wolfe Award, 1959; A. S. Popov Gold Medal, USSR Acad. of Sciences, 1959. *Publications:* Velocity of Light and Radio Waves, 1969; scientific papers. *Recreations:* walking, gardening, music. *Address:* High Hallgarth, 41 Durleston Park Drive, Great Bookham, Surrey. *T:* Bookham 4103.

**ESSENDON,** 2nd Baron, *cr* 1932, of Essendon; **Brian Edmund Lewis;** 2nd Bt, *cr* 1918; *b* 7 Dec. 1903; *s* of 1st Baron and Eleanor (*d* 1967), *d* of R. H. Harrison of West Hartlepool; *S* father, 1944; *m* 1938, Mary, *widow* of Albert Duffil and *d* of late G. W. Booker, Los Angeles. *Educ:* Malvern; Pembroke Coll., Cambridge. *Recreation:* golf. *Address:* Essendon Manor, Essendon, Herts. *T:* Essendon 259. *Club:* Bath.

**ESSEX,** 9th Earl of, *cr* 1661; **Reginald George de Vere Capell,** TD; Baron Capel, 1641; Viscount Malden, 1661; Hon. Colonel 47 Signals Regiment (Middlesex Yeomanry), TA; *b* 9 Oct. 1906; *o s* of 8th Earl of Essex and Mary Eveline (*d* 1955), *d* of late W. R. Stewart Freeman; *S* father, 1966; *m* 1st, 1937, Mrs Mary Reeve Strutt (marr. diss. 1957), *d* of Gibson Ward, Bermuda; 2nd, 1957, Nona Isobel (*née* Miller), Christchurch, NZ (widow of Frank Smythe). *Educ:* Eton; Cambridge. Lt-Col 1947, Hon. Col 1957 ( Signal Regt), Mddx Yeo. *Heir:*

*kinsman* Robert Edward de Vere Capell [*b* 13 Jan. 1920; *m* 1942, Doris Margaret, *d* of G. F. Tomlinson; one *s*]. *Address:* Floyds Farm, Wingrave, Aylesbury, Bucks. *T:* Aston Abbotts 220. *Clubs:* Bath, MCC.

**ESSEX, Francis William,** CMG 1959; Temporary Principal, Ministry of Overseas Development, since 1968; *b* 29 June 1916; *s* of Frank Essex; *m* 1947, Marjorie Muriel Joyce Lewis; two *s*. *Educ:* Royal Grammar Sch., High Wycombe; Reading Univ.; Exeter Coll., Oxford. Joined Colonial Administrative Service, Sierra Leone, 1939; Asst District Commissioner, 1942; District Commissioner, 1948; HM Treasury, 1951; Dep. Financial Sec., Sierra Leone, 1953; Financial Sec., British Guiana, 1956-60; Financial Sec. to High Comr for Basutoland, Bechuanaland and Swaziland, 1960-64; Counsellor, British Embassy, South Africa, 1964-65; Sec. for Finance and Development, later Permanent Sec., Min. of Finance, Commerce and Industry, Swaziland, 1965-68. *Address:* c/o Ministry of Overseas Development, Eland House, Stag Place, SW1.

**ESSEX, Rosamund Sibyl,** MA; Editor of the Church Times, 1950-60; Member of Staff, Christian Aid, British Council of Churches, since 1960; *b* 26 July 1900; *d* of late Rev. Herbert J. Essex and late Rachel Watson; unmarried; one adopted *s*. *Educ:* Bournemouth High Sch. for Girls; St Hilda's Coll., Oxford. Editorial staff of the Church Times, 1929-47; Asst Ed., 1947-50. Chm. Religious Press Group, 1952-53 and 1957-58. Commissioned and licensed a Reader in the Church of England, dio. St Albans, 12 July 1969. *Publications:* (with Sidney Dark) The War Against God, 1937; Into the Forest, 1963. *Recreation:* photography. *Address:* 32 Holywell Hill, St Albans, Herts. *T:* St Albans 53424. *Club:* Royal Commonwealth Society.

**ESSLEMONT, Mary,** CBE 1955; MA, BSc, MB, ChB, DPH, LLD, JP; *d* of late George Birnie Esslemont, MP for South Aberdeen. *Educ:* Aberdeen High Sch. for Girls; Aberdeen Univ. Asst, Botany Dept, University of Aberdeen, 1915-17; Science Lecturer, Stockwell Training Coll., London, 1917-19; Asst MOH, Keighley, Yorks, 1924-29; Gen. Practitioner, Aberdeen, 1929, now retired. Fellow: BMA, 1959; RCGP, 1969. Mem., Aberdeen Univ. Court, 1947. Hon. LLD, University of Aberdeen, 1954. JP for County of City of Aberdeen. *Recreation:* travel. *Address:* Mile End House, Beechgrove Terrace, Aberdeen, Scotland. *T:* 53601. *Club:* Soroptimist Headquarters.

**ESSLIN, Martin J.;** Head of Drama (Radio), BBC, since 1963; *b* 8 June 1918; *s* of Paul Pereszlenyi and Charlotte Pereszlenyi (*née* Schiffer); *m* 1947, Renate Gerstenberg; one *d*. *Educ:* Gymnasium, Vienna; Vienna Univ.; Reinhardt Seminar of Dramatic Art, Vienna. Naturalized, 1947. Joined BBC, 1940; Producer and Scriptwriter, BBC European Services, 1941-55; Asst Head, BBC European Productions Dept, 1955; Asst Head, Drama (Sound), BBC, 1961. Mem. Drama Panel, Arts Council of Great Britain. Awarded title Professor by Pres. of Austria, 1967. *Publications:* Brecht, A Choice of Evils, 1959; The Theatre of the Absurd, 1962; (ed) Beckett (anthology of critical essays), 1965; Harold Pinter, 1967; The Genius of the German Theatre, 1968; Reflections, Essays on Modern Theatre, 1969 (UK, as Brief Chronicles, 1970); The Peopled Wound: the plays of Harold Pinter, 1970. *Recreations:* reading, book collecting. *Address:* 64 Loudoun Road, NW8. *T:* 01-722 4243; Ballader's Plat, Winchelsea, Sussex. *T:* Winchelsea 392. *Club:* Garrick.

**ESTCOURT, Maj.-Gen. Edward Noel Keith,** DSO 1944; OBE 1945; psc; *b* 17 Dec. 1905; *s* of E. A. Estcourt, Gloucester and B. M. Carr-Calthorp, Norfolk; *m* 1938, Pamela Wellesley; two *s* one *d*. *Educ:* Cheltenham Coll.; RMA Woolwich. Commissioned RA, 1925. Served War of 1939-45: N Africa, Italy and Greece. Staff Coll., Camberley, 1940; GSO1 1st Inf. Div., 1944-45; GSO1 4th Inf. Div., 1945-46. Dep. Dir Mil. Ops, War Office, 1951-55; Dep. Comdt, NATO Defence Coll., 1955-57; Commandant, NATO Defence Coll., Paris, 1958. Principal, Ashridge Coll., 1958-62. Bronze Star, USA, 1945. *Recreations:* shooting, fishing, golf. *Address:* The Vyne, Sherborne St John, Basingstoke, Hants.

**ETCHELLS, Frederick,** FRIBA; (Retired) Architect and Artist; *s* of late John Charles Etchells; *m* 1932, Hester Margaret (*d* 1967), *d* of late Harrington Sainsbury, MD, OBE; one *d*. *Educ:* Classical and Architectural; Royal Coll. of Art; Paris. Has practised as an architect before and continuously since the war of 1914-18; works include: domestic and other buildings, and much church work, throughout the country. *Publications:* Translated Le Corbusier's Vers Une Architecture, and Urbanisme; various papers and articles on architectural subjects; (with Canon G. W. O. Addleshaw) The Architectural Setting of Anglican Worship, 1948. *Recreations:* rural. *Address:* West Challow, Wantage, Berks. *T:* Wantage 3440.

**ETHERINGTON-SMITH, (Raymond) Gordon (Antony),** CMG 1962; HM Diplomatic Service; Ambassador to the Democratic Republic of the Sudan, since 1970; *b* 1 Feb. 1914; *o s* of late T. B. Etherington-Smith and Henriette de Pitner; *m* 1950, Mary Elizabeth Besly; one *s* three *d*. *Educ:* Downside; Magdalen Coll., Oxford. Entered FO, 1936. Served at: Berlin, 1939; Copenhagen, 1939-40; Washington, 1940-42; Chungking, 1943-45; Kashgar, 1945-46; Moscow, 1947; Foreign Office, 1947-52; Holy See, 1952-54; Counsellor, saigon, 1954-57; The Hague, 1958-61; Office of UK Commissioner-Gen. for South-East Asia, Singapore, 1961-63; Ambassador to Vietnam, 1963-66; Minister, and Dep. Commandant, Berlin, 1966-70. *Recreations:* fishing, squash rackets, travel. *Address:* c/o Foreign and Commonwealth Office, King Charles Street, SW1. *T:* 01-930 8440. *Club:* St James'.

**ETHERTON, Ralph,** MA; Barrister-at-Law; *b* 11 Feb. 1904; *o s* of late Louis Etherton and Bertha Mary, *d* of late John Bagge; *m* 1944, Johanne Patricia, *y d* of late Gerald Cloherty, Galway, Ireland; one *s* one *d*. *Educ:* Charterhouse; Trinity Hall, Cambridge. Called to Bar, Inner Temple, 1926, and joined Northern Circuit, practised at Common Law Bar until 1939; Municipal Reform Candidate LCC election, N Camberwell 1931, and W. Fulham 1937; served in RAFVR (Special Duties), Flt Lt, 1940-42; MP (Nat. C) for Stretford div. of Lancs, 1939-45; contested (Nat. C) Liverpool (Everton div.), 1935, Stretford div. of Lancs, 1945; engaged in commerce, 1945-. Chm. of Coningsby Club, 1933-34; Mem. of Parliamentary Delegation to Australia and New Zealand, 1944. *Recreations:* travel, riding, shooting. *Address:* Greentree Hall, Balcombe, Sussex. *T:* Balcombe 319. *Clubs:* Carlton, Pratt's.

**ETHIOPIA, Emperor of; HIM Haile Sellassie I,** KG 1954; GCB (Hon.); GCMG (Hon.); Royal Victorian Chain; Field Marshal (Hon.) of the British Army; LLD (Hon.), Cambridge, 1924, Columbia, Howard, McGill, Montreal, Michigan, Athens, Laval, 1954; Banaras, Moscow, Charles; DCL (Hon.) Oxford, 1954;

Doc. Ag. (Hon.) Bonn, 1954; *b* 23 July 1892; 2nd *s* of HH Ras Makonnen, a great-grandson of Sahle Sellassie, King of Shoa; his mother belonged to the nobility of the Wollo; *m* 1911, Woyzero Menen (*d* 1962), a *g d* of King Mikael of Wollo; one *s* one *d* (and two *s* and two *d* decd). On the accession of the Empress Zauditu, 1916, proclaimed heir-apparent and Prince Regent, and invested with the Grand Cordon of the Order of Solomon; took Ethiopia to the League of Nations, 1923; proclaimed abolition of slavery, 1924; visited the principal European Capitals 1924; crowned King of Ethiopia, 7 Oct. 1928; succeeded to the Imperial Throne 2 April and crowned Emperor 2 Nov. 1930; proclaimed, by his own free will, constitution with two legislative chambers, 1931. As a result of Italian aggression in 1935 and unsupported by the League of Nations he was forced to quit his capital on 2 May 1936; took refuge in Great Britain during his period of exile; re-entered his capital after victorious campaign and the eventual driving out of the enemy, 5 May 1941. Amongst reforms initiated since his return were the abolition of serfdom on 2 Nov. 1941, and of the legal status of slavery on 26 Aug. 1942; created history by giving Revised Constitution, 1955, granting free democratic elections based on adult franchise for both men and women, without any popular demand at all; first elections successfully concluded, Sept. 1957. Entered into diplomatic relations with most of the important nations of the world and visited them officially; secured reintegration of Eritrea, 1952. Is a devoted student; has founded several educational, medical and other institutions in Addis Ababa and other cities of Ethiopia; has also, in pursuit of the same objects, despatched young Ethiopians to study in America, Europe, India, Japan and Egypt; gave own ancestral Palace, in Addis Ababa, as seat of University, Dec. 1961. Grand Cross of the Order of the Légion d'Honneur; of the Annunsiata; of Leopold, Belgium; of the Lion d'or de la Maison de Nassau, Luxemburg; of the Lion of the Netherlands; of Mohammed Ali, Egypt; of the Saviour, Greece; of the Seraphines, Sweden, etc. *Recreations:* gardening, tennis, ancient and modern history, comparative religion, riding, and walking. *Address:* The Imperial Palace, Addis Ababa, Ethiopia.

**ETIANG, Paul Orono,** BA London; High Commissioner for Uganda in London, since 1969; *b* 15 Aug. 1938; *s* of late Kezironi Orono and Adacat Ilera Orono; *m* 1967, Zahra Ali Foun; two *s*. *Educ:* Makerere Univ. Coll., Uganda. Admin. Officer, 1962-64; Asst Sec., Foreign Affairs, 1964-65; 3rd Sec., 1965-66, 2nd Sec., 1966-67, Uganda Embassy, Moscow; 1st Sec., Uganda Mission to UN, New York, 1968; Counsellor, Uganda High Commission, London, 1968-69. *Recreations:* chess, classical music, billiards. *Address:* Uganda House, 58/59 Trafalgar Square, WC2. *T:* 01-839 1963.

**ETON, Robert;** *see* Meynell, L. W.

**ETTLINGER, Prof. Leopold David;** Professor of History of Art, University of California, Berkeley, since Oct. 1970; *b* 20 April 1913; *s* of Dr Emil Ettlinger, University Librarian, and Dora (*née* Beer); *m* 1st, 1939, Amrei (*née* Jacoby); she *d* 1955; 2nd, 1959, Madeline (*née* Noirot). *Educ:* Stadtgymnasium Halle; Universities of Halle and Marburg. Social Worker for Refugee Children from Germany, 1938-41; Asst Master, King Edward VI Grammar Sch., Five Ways, Birmingham, 1941-48; Asst Curator, Photographic Collection, Warburg Institute, University of London, 1948-51; Curator of Photographic Collection, 1951-56; Lectr, Warburg Inst., 1956-59; Durning Lawrence Prof. of History of Art, Univ. of London, 1959-70. Fellowship, Inst. for Advanced Study, Princeton, 1956; Vis. Professor: Yale Univ., 1963-64; University of Calif, Berkeley, 1969. FSA 1962-. British Academy award, 1963. *Publications:* (with R. G. Holloway) Compliments of the Season, 1947; The Art of the Renaissance in Northern Europe, in New Cambridge Modern History, Vol. I, 1957; Kandinsky's "At Rest", 1961; Art History Today, 1961; The Sistine Chapel before Michelangelo: Religious Imagery and Papal Politics, 1965; contribs to Journal of Warburg and Courtauld Insts, Burlington Magazine, Architectural Review, Connoisseur, Italian Studies. *Address:* Department of Art, University of California, Berkeley, Calif 94720, USA; 172 Burbage Road, Dulwich Village, SE21. *T:* 01-274 3516.

**ETZDORF, Hasso von;** *b* 2 March 1900; *s* of Rüdiger von Etzdorf-Neumark and Agnes Maria Lorentz; *m* Katharina Otto-Margonin. *Educ:* Universities of Berlin, Göttingen, Halle (LLD). German Foreign Office, 1928; served in Berlin, Tokyo, Rome, Genoa (Consul-Gen.). FO Bonn, 1950-53; Head of German Delegn at Interim Cttee for Eur. Def. Community in Paris, rank of Minister, 1953; Dep. Sec.-Gen., WEU, London, 1955; Ambassador of German Federal Republic to Canada, 1956-58; Dep. Under-Sec. and Head of Western Dept, FO, Bonn, 1958-61; Ambassador of German Fed. Rep. to Court of St James's, 1961-65. Vice-Pres., Inter Nuclear SA, Brussels. GCVO (Hon.) 1964. *Address:* 8019 Eichtling, Post Moosach, bei Grafing, Obb, Germany. *T:* Glonn (08107) 402. *Club:* Travellers'.

**ETZEL, Franz;** Grand Cross of Order of The Federal Republic (Germany), 1958; Partner of Bankhaus Friedrich Simon, Düsseldorf, since Nov. 1961; lawyer; *b* 12 Aug. 1902; *s* of Franz Etzel and Hélène (*née* Roepling); *m* 1932, Hilde (*née* Lehnen); two *s* one *d*. *Educ:* studied law at Frankfort, Münich and Munster. First Law Exam., Hamm, 1925; final, Berlin, 1930. Barrister, Duisburg District and Municipal Court, 1930-52; Notary public at Duisburg, 1939-62. War of 1939-45, German Army (last rank First Lieut). Chm. Duisburg District Gp of Christian Democratic Union (CDU), 1945-48; Mem. Exec. Cttee Rhineland Section, CDU, 1946-53; Chm. CDU's Economic Policy Cttee for Brit. Zone of Germany, 1947-49; Chm. CDU's Economic Policy Cttee for whole of Germany, 1949-; Mem. First German Bundestag and Chm. Bundestag's Economic Policy Cttee, 1949-53; First Vice-Pres. of High Authority of European Coal and Steel Community, 1952-57; Federal Minister of Finance, German Federal Republic, 1957-61. Holds Grand Cross of various foreign orders, etc. *Address:* Wittlaer, bei Düsseldorf, Am Töllershof 10, Federal Republic of Germany. *T:* Düsseldorf 401076. *Club:* Rotary (Luxemburg).

**EUGSTER, Lt-Gen. Sir Basil,** KCB 1970 (CB 1966); KCVO 1968; CBE 1962; DSO 1945; MC 1938, and Bar, 1940; GOC-in-C, Southern Command, since 1971; *b* 15 Aug. 1914; *er s* of late Oscar Louis Eugster, DSO, Kempston Hoo, near Bedford; *m* 1939, Marcia Elaine, *er d* of Air Commodore Sir Percy Smyth-Osbourne, CMG, CBE; two *s*. *Educ:* Beaumont; Christ Church, Oxford (MA). 2nd Lieut Irish Guards, 1935. Served War of 1939-45 in Narvik, Italy and NW Europe; Bde Maj., HQ 140 Inf. Bde, 1943-44; GSO 2 (Ops); HQ 5 Corps CMF, Oct-Nov., 1944; OC 3rd Bn IG, Jan.-Feb., 1945; GSO 1, Guards Div., Dec. 1945-Jan. 1947; OC 2nd Bn, Irish Guards, 1947; JSSC, 1950; OC 1st Bn, Irish Guards,

1951-54; AAG War Office, 1954-56; Comdt, Eaton Hall Officer Cadet Sch., 1956-58; Comdt Mons Officer Cadet Sch., 1958; IDC 1959; Comd, 3rd Inf. Bde Gp, and Dhekelia Area, Cyprus, 1959-62; Comdt Sch. of Infantry, Warminster, 1962-63; GOC 4 Div., BAOR, 1963-65; GOC London Dist, and Maj.-Gen. Comdg Household Bde, 1965-68; Commander, British Forces, Hong Kong, 1968-70. *Address:* c/o Barclays Bank, Bedford. *Clubs:* White's, Guards', Pratts', Leander.

**EURICH, Richard Ernst,** RA 1953 (ARA 1942); Artist (Painter); *b* Bradford, 14 March 1903; *s* of late Professor Frederick Wm Eurich; *m* 1934, Mavis Llewellyn Pope; one *s* two *d. Educ:* St George's Sch., Harpenden; Bradford Grammar Sch. Studied art at Bradford Sch. of Arts and Crafts, and Slade Sch., London; held One Man Show of drawings at Goupil Gallery in 1929, and several exhibitions of paintings at Redfern Gallery; exhibited at Royal Academy, New English Art Club and London Group; works purchased by Contemporary Art Soc. and Chantrey Bequest; Painting, Dunkirk Beach 1940, purchased for Canadian Government; Official War Artist, 1941-45; representative works in various public galleries. *Recreations:* music and gardening. *Address:* Appletreewick, Dibden Purlieu, Southampton. *T:* Hythe (Hants) 2291; Arthur Tooth & Sons Ltd, 31 Bruton Street, W1.

**EUSTACE, Edward Arthur Rawlins,** CIE 1947; OBE 1941; *b* 18 Nov. 1899; 2nd *s* of late Lieut-Col Edward Eustace and Mary, *d* of Maj.-Gen. Rawlins; unmarried. *Educ:* Wellington Coll.; RMC Sandhurst. 4th Gurkha Rifles, 1918-22; ICS, 1923-47. *Address:* Newstown, Tullow, Co. Carlow, S Ireland. *Club:* Athenæum.

**EUSTACE, John Curtis Wernher,** CIE 1945; MA; *b* 22 Nov. 1906; *o s* of late Maj.-Gen. A. H. Eustace, CB, CBE, DSO, 2nd Sikhs Punjab Frontier Force; *m* 1st, 1937, Pamela Mary (marriage dissolved, 1954), *o d* of late Sir Harold Glover; three *s*; 2nd, 1961, Alys, *o d* of late Donald S. Wedderburn Ogilvy, RNVR; four *d. Educ:* Wellington Coll.; Brentwood Coll., Vancouver Island; Exeter Coll., Oxford. BA 1928; Indian Civil Service, Punjab commn, 1929; Dep. Comr: Jhelum, 1933, Kangra, 1939, Lahore 1939 and 1947; Cooperative Dept, 1934-38. Prov. organiser National War Front and dep. Home Sec., 1942-46; retired 1947. With Guest, Keen & Nettlefolds (Midlands) Ltd, Birmingham, 1948-67. *Address:* Denton Lodge, Shute End, Wokingham, Berks.

**EUSTON, Earl of; Hugh Denis Charles FitzRoy;** Captain Grenadier Guards; *b* 3 April 1919; *e s* of 10th Duke of Grafton, *qv*; *m* 1946, Fortune (*see* Countess of Euston); two *s* three *d. Educ:* Eton; Magdalene Coll., Cambridge. ADC to the Viceroy of India, 1943-47. Mem. Historic Buildings Coun. for England, 1953-; Chairman: Society for the Protection of Ancient Buildings; Jt Cttee, Soc. for Protection of Ancient Buildings, Georgian Gp, Victorian Soc., and Civic Trust; International Students Trust; Coun. of British Soc. of Master Glass Painters; National Trust East Anglian Regional Cttee. Member: Advisory Cttee to Minister of Housing and Local Government; Cathedrals Advisory Cttee; Council for the Care of Churches. Trustee and Chm. Exec. Cttee, historic Churches Preservation Trust; Trustee: London Museum; Nat. Portrait Gallery; Sir John Soane's Museum. *Heir: s* Viscount Ipswich, *qv. Address:* North Leys, Much Hadham, Herts. *T:* Much Hadham 2530. *Club:* Boodle's.

**EUSTON, Countess of; (Ann) Fortune Fitzroy,** DCVO 1970 (CVO 1965); JP; Mistress of The Robes to The Queen since 1967; *o d* of Captain Eric Smith, MC, Lower Ashfold, Slaugham; *m* 1946, Earl of Euston, *qv*; two *s* three *d.* Lady of the Bedchamber to The Queen, 1953-66. Mem. Bd of Governors, The Hospital for Sick Children, Great Ormond Street, 1952-66. JP, County of London, 1949. *Address:* North Leys, Much Hadham, Herts. *T:* Much Hadham 2530.

**EUWE, Dr Machgielis;** Officer, Order of Oranje Nassau, 1936; Ordinary Professor, University of Tilburg, since 1965 (Extraordinary Professor in Automation at University, Rotterdam, 1964); *b* 20 May 1901; *m* 1926, Carolina Elizabeth Bergman; three *d. Educ:* Amsterdam Univ. Mathematical; University, 1918; Final proof, 1923; Dissertation (doctor-degree), 1926; Chess: Champion of Holland, 1921, Amateur Champion of the World, 1928, World Champion (Universal) being still amateur, by winning a match against Alekhine (15½-14½), 1935, lost the title in the return match against Alekhine (9½-15½), 1937; several wins in tournament, especially in British tournaments. Chm. Cttee installed by Euratom which studied process of human thinking with particular relation to chess, 1961-63. Dir Netherlands Automatic Information Processing Research Centre, 1959-64. *Publications:* Dutch: Practische Schaaklessen, 1927; Schaakopeningen, 1937; Eindspelen, 1940; Positiespel en Combinatiespel, 1949; Middenspelen, 1951; English: Strategy and Tactics, 1936; From my Games, 1938; Judgment and Planning, 1953; The Logical Approach to Chess (with U. Blaine and J. F. S. Rumble), 1958; A Guide to Chess Endings (with David Hooper), 1959; Master against Amateur, Road to Mastery (with Prof. W. Meiden), 1963; The Development of Chess Style, 1966; several publications on automatic data processing. *Address:* Mensinge 40, Amsterdam-Buitenveldert, Netherlands.

**EVAN-COOK, John Edward,** JP; *b* 25 Oct. 1902; 2nd *s* of late Evan Cook, JP, of London; *m* 1928, Winifred Elizabeth, *d* of Joseph Samuel Pointon; no *c. Educ:* Westminster City Sch. Served War, 1940-46, Major, RAOC. Adviser on Packaging, War Office, 1940-46. Vice-Chm. London District Rotary, 1950-52; Pres. Rotary Club of Camberwell, 1948. Chairman: Visiting Cttee HM Prison, Brixton; Evan-Cook Group (retd); Inst. of Packaging (Nat. Chm., 1954, President, 1954-57); Min. of Labour & Nat. Service Local Disablement Cttee, 1959-67. Chief Scouts' Medal of Merit, 1962; Silver Acorn, 1968. Past Master, Worshipful Company of Paviors; Liveryman: Worshipful Co. of Carmen; Worshipful Co. of Farmers. Sheriff of London, 1958-59; Common Councilman, City of London, 1960-66. JP City of London, 1950. Order of Homayoun, 3rd Class (Iran); Grand Cross of Merit, Order of Merit (Federal Republic of Germany). *Address:* 25 Pond Mead, Dulwich, SE21. *T:* 01-693 4396; Old Deaks, Cuckfield, Sussex. *T:* Haywards Heath 3220. *Clubs:* City Livery (Pres., 1964-65), United Wards, Royal Automobile.

**EVANG, Karl;** Norwegian physician; Director-General, Norwegian Health Services, since 1939; *b* 19 Oct. 1902; *s* of Jens Ingolf Evang and Beate, *née* Wexelsen; *m* 1929, Gerda Sophie Landmark Moe; one *s* three *d. Educ:* Oslo Univ. (MD). On Staff, Oslo Municipal Hosp., 1932-34; MO, State Factor, Inspection Office, 1937-38; represented Norway at UNRRA, FAO, and WHO, 1943-. Pres., 2nd World Health Assembly, 1949; Chm., WHO Exec. Bd,

1966; Member: WHO Panel on Public Health Administration; Norwegian Soc. of Hygiene. Hon. FRSM. Hon. Fellow, Amer. Public Health Assoc. Léon Bernard Medal and Prize, WHO, 1966. *Publications:* Birth Control, 1930; Norwegian Medical Dictionary, 1933; Race Policy and Reaction, 1934; Education to Peace, 1947; The Rehabilitation of Public Health in Norway, 1947; The Public Health Services, 1948; Sexual Education, 1951; Health Service, Society and Medicine, 1958; Health Services in Norway, 1960; Use and Abuse of Drugs, 1966; Current Narcotic Problems, 1967. *Address:* Måltrostveien 11B, Oslo 3, Norway; Helsedirecktoratet, Oslo, Norway.

**EVANS,** family name of **Barons Energlyn, Evans of Hungershall** and **Mountevans.**

**EVANS OF HUNGERSHALL,** Baron *cr* 1967 (Life Peer), of Borough of Royal Tunbridge Wells; **Benjamin Ifor Evans,** Kt 1955; MA, DLit London; FRSL; *b* London, 19 Aug. 1899; *y s* of Benjamin Evans; *m* 1923, Marjorie Ruth, *d* of late John Measures, Ifield; one *d. Educ:* Stationers' Company's Sch.; University Coll., London. Prof. of English at Southampton, Sheffield and London; Principal, Queen Mary Coll. (University of London), 1944-51; Provost, University Coll., London, 1951-66. Educational Dir of the British Council, 1940-44; Vice-Chm. of Arts Council, 1946-51; Chairman: National Insurance Advisory Cttee; Educational Advisory Council, Thames Television; Linguaphone Adv. Cttee. Consultant to the Wates Foundation. Fellow: UCL; Queen Mary Coll. Hon. Dr of Letters, University of Paris; Hon. LLD, University of Manchester. Officer of the Legion of Honour; Chevalier, Order of the Crown of Belgium; Comdr, Order of Orange Nassau; Comdr, Order of Dannebrog. *Publications:* Encounters, 1926; English Poetry in the Later Nineteenth Century, 1933; The Limits of Literary Criticism, 1933; Keats, 1934; edns, with W. W. Greg, of The Commody of Susanna, and Jack Juggler, 1937; Tradition and Romanticism, 1940; A Short History of English Literature, 1940; English Literature (for British Council), 1944; in Search of Stephen Vane, 1946; The Shop on the King's Road, 1947; Literature Between the Wars, 1948; A Short History of English Drama, 1948; The Church in the Markets, 1948; (with Mary Glasgow) The Arts in England, 1948; The Use of English, 1949; (with Marjorie R. Evans) A Victorian Anthology, 1949; The Language of Shakespeare's Plays, 1951; Science and Literature, 1954; English Literature: Values and Traditions, 1962. *Address:* 1317 Minster House, St James Court, Buckingham Gate, SW1. *Club:* Athenæum.

**EVANS, A. Briant;** Gynæcological Surgeon, Westminster Hospital; Surgeon, Chelsea Hospital for Women; Consulting Obstetric Surgeon, Queen Charlotte's Maternity Hospital; *b* 26 June 1909; *e s* of late Arthur Evans, OBE, MD, MS, FRCS; *m* 1939, Audrey Marie, *er d* of late Roland Eveleigh Holloway; three *s. Educ:* Westminster Sch.; Gonville and Caius Coll., Cambridge; Westminster Hosp. MA, MB, BCh Cantab; FRCS; FRCOG. Examiner in Obstetrics to Univs of Cambridge and London and to Royal College of Obstetricians and Gynæcologists. Temp. Lieut-Col RAMC, served in Egypt, Italy and Austria; OC No. 9 Field Surgical Unit. *Publications:* (in collaboration) Queen Charlotte's Textbook of Midwifery; Midwifery by Ten Teachers; Diseases of Women by Ten Teachers. *Address:* 69 Harley Street, W1. *T:* 01-935 3221; Bere Farm, Boarhunt, near Fareham, Hants. *T:* Wickham 2169.

**EVANS, Albert;** MP (Lab) West Islington, Sept. 1947-Feb. 1950, South-West Islington, 1950-70; retired; Mem. of the London County Council, 1946-49. *Address:* The Garden House, Peacock Lane, Holt, Norfolk.

**EVANS, Alfred Thomas, (Fred Evans);** BA; MP (Lab) Caerphilly, since July 1968; *b* 24 Feb. 1914; *s* of Alfred Evans, Miner, and Sarah Jane Evans; *m* 1939, Mary (*née* O'Marah); one *s* two *d. Educ:* Primary and Grammar Schs; University of Wales. Head of Dept, Grammar Sch., Bargoed, Glam, 1937-49; Headmaster, Bedlinog Secondary Sch., Glam, 1949-66; Headmaster, Lewis Boys Grammar Sch., Pengam, Mon, 1966-68. Contested (Lab) Leominster, 1955, Stroud, 1959; Organising Agent, Caerphilly Constituency Labour Party, 1962-66. *Address:* Menai, Dilwyn Avenue, Ystradmynach, Hengoed, Glam. *Clubs:* Aneurin Labour (Caerphilly); Labour (Bargoed).

**EVANS, Alun S.;** *see* Sylvester-Evans.

**EVANS, Sir Anthony (Adney),** 2nd Bt, *cr* 1920; *b* 5 Aug. 1922; *s* of Sir Walter Harry Evans, 1st Bt, and Margaret Mary, *y d* of late Thomas Adney Dickens; *S* father 1954; married; two *s* one *d. Educ:* Shrewsbury; Merton Coll., Oxford. *Address:* c/o National Provincial Bank Ltd, 11 Waterloo Street, Birmingham 2. *Club:* Leander (Henley).

**EVANS, Rev. Arthur Norman,** MA Oxon; Perpetual Curate, St Andrew's, Waterloo Street, Hove, since 1961; *b* 18 Dec. 1900; *s* of Rev. Edward Foley Evans and Mary Walker; *m* 1925, Madge Cassienet Palmer; one *s* three *d. Educ:* St John's Sch., Leatherhead; Keble Coll., Oxford (Classical Exhibitioner). 2nd Class Hons Moderations, 3rd Class Literae Humaniores; Asst-master, St John's Sch., Leatherhead, 1923-24; Christ's Hosp., 1924-27; Headmaster of the Preparatory Dept. Christ's Hosp., 1927-34; Headmaster, Colet Court, Hammersmith, 1934-44. Headmaster of Bishop's Stortford Coll., 1944-57; ordained, Chichester Cathedral, 1958; Asst Curate, All Saints, Hove, 1958-61; MRST. *Address:* 50 Wilbury Road, Hove, Sussex BN3 3PA. *T:* Brighton 733106.

**EVANS, Sir Arthur Trevor,** Kt 1954; Controller of Death Duties, 1951-57; *b* 7 Nov. 1895; *er s* of Benjamin Evans; *m* 1925, Mary Dagmar, *d* of J. H. Powell, JP, Aberdare, Glam; one *s* one *d. Educ:* Stationers' Company's Sch.; King's Coll., London. LLB. Asst Controller of Death Duties, 1944. Dep. Controller, 1947. *Address:* Flat 1, Cliff Court, Rottingdean, Sussex.

**EVANS, Sir Athol (Donald),** KBE 1963 (CBE 1954; MBE 1939); retired as Secretary for Home Affairs, Government of the Federation of Rhodesia and Nyasaland (Sept. 1953-Dec. 1963); *b* 16 Dec. 1904; *s* of Henry Evans; *m* 1931, Catherine Millar Greig; one *s* two *d. Educ:* Graeme Coll. and Rhodes Univ., Grahamstown, S Africa (BA, LLB). Joined S Rhodesia Public Service, 1928: consecutively Law Officer, Legal Adviser, Mem. of Public Services Board, and Sec. for Internal Affairs. Chairman of: Board of Trustees Rhodes National Gallery; Rhodesia National Trust; Member: National Parks Advisory Board; Welcome to Rhodesia Assoc. Gold Cross of St Mark (Greece), 1962. *Recreations:* tennis, shooting. *Address:* 8 Harvey Brown Avenue, Salisbury, Rhodesia. *T:* 82171. *Club:* Salisbury (Rhodesia).

**EVANS, Sir Bernard,** Kt 1962; DSO 1941; ED 1944; FRAIA; FRVIA; architect; Governing Director, Bernard Evans & Partners Pty Ltd, since 1946; Director, Sun Alliance & London Insurance Group, Victoria; Managing Director, Withalit Pty Ltd; *b* 13 May 1905; *s* of Isaac Evans and Lucy (*née* Tunnicliffe); *m* 1929, Dorothy May Evans (*née* Ellis), *d* of William and Mary Ellis; one *s* two *d*. *Educ:* private sch.; Melbourne Technical Coll. Raised 2/23rd Bn, AIF, War of 1939-45; 24th Bde 9th Div.; served Tobruk, El Alamein (Brig.), Lae and Finschaven (despatches thrice, DSO, ED). Lord Mayor of Melbourne, 1959-61 (Councillor, Gipps Ward, 1949-). Comr Melb. and Metropolitan Bd of Works; Pres. Royal Melbourne Institute of Technology, 1958-60; Pres. Princes Hill Village, 1958-; Pres. Royal Commonwealth Society, Victorian Br., 1960-; Past Nat. Pres. Royal Commonwealth Society. Mem. Inst. of Dirs, London. *Recreation:* artist in oils. *Address:* Warrawee, 205 Orrong Road, Toorak, Victoria 3142, Australia. *T:* 24-5591. *Clubs:* Athenæum, Naval and Military (Melbourne); VRC, VATC, RACV, Kelvin, West Brighton (all Melbourne, Australia).

**EVANS, Briant;** *see* Evans, A. B.

**EVANS, Carey;** *see* Evans, D. C. R. J.

**EVANS, Sir Charles;** *see* Evans, Sir R. C.

**EVANS, Vice-Adm. Sir Charles (Leo Glandore),** KCB 1962 (CB 1958); CBE 1953; DSO 1941; DSC 1940; Chairman, various companies mostly in export field; Director-General, British Film Producers' Association, 1964; Vice-President, Film Production Association of Great Britain, and Chairman, Central Casting Ltd, 1967-68; *b* 2 Aug. 1908; *o s* of Major S. G. Evans, MC; *g s* of Gen. Leopold Evans and Col John Crosbie; *m* 1942, Kyriakoula, 3rd *d* of Gen. Doulcaris, Athens, Greece. Entered Royal Naval Coll., 1922; specialised as a pilot, 1930; served as fighter pilot in Aircraft Carriers in Norwegian, Dunkirk, Mediterranean and Middle East campaigns and in North Sea, Mediterranean and Pacific theatres in War of 1939-45 (despatches thrice, DSC, DSO); Naval Air Attaché in USA, 1946 and 1947; Dir of Air Warfare Division, Naval Staff, The Admiralty, 1950-51; Commanding HMS Ocean (CBE) in Mediterranean and Korea, 1951 and 1952; student Imperial Defence Coll., 1953; Commodore, RN Barracks, Portsmouth, 1954 and 1955; Flag Officer, Flying Training, 1956-57; Deputy Chief of Naval Personnel and Head of Directorate of Officer Appointments, 1957-59; Flag Officer, Aircraft Carriers, 1959-60; NATO Deputy Supreme Allied Commander, Atlantic, 1960-62; retired list, 1962. Pres., Fleet Air Arm Officers Assoc. 1963. *Address:* 18 Lowndes Square, SW1. *Club:* Army and Navy.

**EVANS, Charles Tunstall,** CMG 1948; Registrar, Order of St John of Jerusalem; *b* 16 May 1903; *e s* of late Frank Alfred and Beatrice Evans, Birmingham; *m* 1938, Kathleen, *e d* of late Ernest Armstrong, Hankham Place, Pevensey; two *s* one *d*. *Educ:* King Edward's Sch., Birmingham; Christ's Coll., Cambridge. Colonial Administrative Service: Administrative Officer, Palestine, 1925; Deputy Dist Comr, 1939; Principal Asst Sec. 1942; Senior Dist Comr (Galilee), 1945; retired on termination of British Mandate, 1948. Seconded to Colonial Office, 1935-37; called to Bar (Middle Temple), 1941. Admitted solicitor, 1949. Asst Sec.-Gen., Order of St John of Jerusalem, 1950-51, Sec.-Gen., 1951-68. Councillor, Cuckfield UDC, 1953-68, Chm., 1962-65. Gen. Comr of Income Tax. *Address:* Ash Lodge, 3 Calbourne, Muster Green, Haywards Heath, Sussex. *T:* Haywards Heath 51435. *Club:* East India and Sports.

*See also Bishop of Crediton, Prof. C. F. Evans, Sir Reginald Payne.*

**EVANS, Rev. Prof. Christopher Francis,** MA; Professor of New Testament Studies, King's College, London, since 1962; *b* 7 Nov. 1909; 2nd *s* of Frank and Beatrice Evans; *m* 1941, Elna Mary, *d* of Walter and Elizabeth Burt; one *s*. *Educ:* King Edward's Sch., Birmingham; Corpus Christi Coll., Cambridge. Asst Curate, St Barnabas, Southampton, 1934-38; Tutor Schol. Canc. Linc., 1938-44; Chaplain and Divinity Lecturer, Lincoln Training Coll., 1944-48; Chaplain, Fellow and Lecturer in Divinity, Corpus Christi Coll., Oxford, 1948-58; Lightfoot Prof. of Divinity in the University of Durham and Canon of Durham Cathedral, 1959-62. Select Preacher, University of Oxford, 1955-57; Proctor in Convocation for University of Oxford, 1955-58; Exam. Chaplain: to Bishop of Bristol, 1948-58; to Bishop of Durham, 1958-62; to Archbishop of Canterbury, 1962-; to Bishop of Lichfield, 1969-. FKC, 1970. *Publications:* contributions to Journal of Theological Studies, Theology and Religious Studies, to Studies in the Gospels and to Christian Faith and Communist Faith; Christology and Theology; The Lord's Prayer; The Beginning of the Gospel; Resurrection and the New Testament; (ed jtly) The Cambridge History of the Bible: vol. I, From the Beginnings to Jerome, 1970. *Recreation:* fishing. *Address:* 55 Carlisle Mansions, SW1.

*See also C. T. Evans, Bishop of Crediton.*

**EVANS, Collis William,** CB 1958; CBE 1949; Under Secretary, Ministry of Civil Aviation, 1948-59; *b* 27 May 1895; *s* of late W. J. Evans, Folkestone; *m* 1st, 1938, Annie Urquhart (*d* 1957); 2nd, 1970, Hilda Stewart. Served European War, 1914-18, Yeomanry and RFA, Middle East, Macedonia and France. Exchequer and Audit Dept, 1914; Principal, Air Ministry, 1938; Financial Adviser to HQ RAF, Middle East and North Africa, 1938-43; Adviser on Administration and Finance, Transport Command, 1943; Asst Sec., Dept of Civil Aviation, 1944. *Address:* Ringle Crouch, Nash, near Bletchley, Bucks. *T:* Whaddon 285.

**EVANS, David Carey Rees Jones,** MA, BCL Oxon; **His Honour Judge Carey Evans;** Judge of County Courts Circuit No 32 (Norfolk) since 1946; Deputy Chairman, Quarter Sessions, Norfolk; *b* 3 March 1899; *s* of late Sir David W. Evans; *m* 1937, Margaret Willoughby Gale; one *d*. *Educ:* Sherborne Preparatory Sch.; Sherborne Sch.; Jesus Coll., Oxford (Scholar); Gray's Inn (Holt Scholar). Called to Bar, 1923; S Wales and Chester Circuit, practising at Cardiff; formerly part-time Lecturer in Law at University Coll. of S Wales and Mon, Cardiff. Chm. of Ministry of Labour Tribunals for Breconshire and Merthyr, 1937-46; Recorder of Merthyr Tydfil, 1945-46. 2nd Lieut RGA 1918-19. *Address:* 16 Cross Street, Hoxne, Diss, Norfolk. *Club:* Norfolk (Norwich).

**EVANS, Ven. David Eifion;** Archdeacon of Cardigan since 1967; *b* 22 Jan. 1911; *e s* of John Morris Evans, Borth, Cards; *m* 1941, Iris Elizabeth Gravelle; one *s*. *Educ:* Ardwyn, Aberystwyth; UCW, Aberystwyth; St Michael's Coll., Llandaff. BA 1932; MA 1951. Deacon, 1934; Priest, 1935. Curate: Llanfihangel-ar-Arth, 1934-36; Llanbadarn Fawr, 1936-40; Chaplain to the Forces, 1940-45; Vicar, Llandeloy with Llanrheithan, 1945-48; Penrhyncoch, 1948, with Elerch, 1952-57; St Michael, Aberystwyth, 1957-67; Rural Dean, Llanbadarn Fawr, 1957-67; Chaplain, Anglican Students, 1966-67; Canon of St David's Cathedral (Caerfai), 1963-67; Vicar: Llanafan with Llanwnnws, 1967-69; Newcastle

Emlyn, 1969-. Mem. Governing Body of Church in Wales, 1956-; Mem. Court of Governors, and Mem. Council, UCW, Aberystwyth, 1958-. *Publications:* contribs to Jl of Hist. Soc. of Church in Wales and other Welsh Church periodicals. *Recreations:* reading, walking. *Address:* The Vicarage, Newcastle Emlyn, Carmarthenshire. *T:* Newcastle Emlyn 385.

**EVANS, His Honour David Eifion (Puleston),** QC 1954; Member Foreign Compensation Commission since 1963; *b* 8 Dec. 1902; *s* of late John Owain Evans, CBE and Margaret Anne Evans; *m* 1933, Roberta (*d* 1966), *y d* of Sir Robert McAlpine, 1st Bt. *Educ:* Towyn Sch.; University Coll. of Wales, Aberystwyth; Downing Coll., Cambridge (Foundation Schol., MA, LLB). Barrister, Gray's Inn, 1926, practised London, Wales and Chester Circuit; commissioned RASC 1940; Office of Judge Advocate Gen., 1941-45, Major; resumed practice, 1945; Mem. General Council of the Bar, 1955-56; Chm., Radnorshire Quarter Sessions, 1959-62; Deputy Chm., Brecknock Quarter Sessions, 1960-62; County Court Judge, Circuit No. 28 (Mid-Wales and Shropshire), 1956-62. *Club:* Oxford and Cambridge.

**EVANS, Prof. David Gwynne,** CBE 1969; FRS 1960; Professor of Bacteriology and Immunology, London School of Hygiene and Tropical Medicine, since 1961; Member Medical Research Council since 1965; *b* 6 Sept. 1909; *s* of Frederick George Evans, Atherton, Manchester; *m* 1937, Mary (*née* Darby); one *s* one *d*. *Educ:* Leigh Grammar Sch.; University of Manchester. BSc, 1933; MSc, 1934; PhD, 1938; DSc, 1948. Demonstrator and Asst Lecturer in Chemistry, Dept of Bacteriology, University of Manchester, 1934; Mem. of Scientific Staff, Dept of Biological Standards, Nat. Inst. for Medical Research, London, 1940; Reader in Chemical Bacteriology, Dept of Bacteriology, University of Manchester, 1947; Head of Biological Standards Control Laboratory, Nat. Inst. for Medical Research, London, 1955-58; Dir, Dept of Biological Standards, 1958-61. Mem. Northumberland Cttee on Foot-and-Mouth Disease, 1968. *Publications:* numerous scientific papers, mainly on bacteriology and immunology. *Recreations:* various. *Address:* Highthwaite, Stony Lane, Little Kingshill, Great Missenden, Bucks. *T:* Great Missenden 3278. *Club:* Athenæum.

**EVANS, Sir David (Lewis),** Kt 1958; OBE 1947; BA, BLitt, Hon. DLitt Wales; Keeper of Public Records, Jan. 1959-Oct. 1960, retired (Deputy Keeper of the Records, 1954-58); Commissioner, Historical MSS Commission, since 1954; *b* 14 Aug. 1893; *s* of Rev. David Evans and Margaret Lewis; *m* 1923, Marie Christine (*d* 1966), *d* of Edwin Austin, JP; two *d*. *Educ:* Bridgend County Sch.; University Coll. of Wales, Aberystwyth; Jesus Coll., Oxford. Lieut, Duke of Wellington's Regt, 1915-19, France and Belgium (despatches). Entered Public Record Office, 1921; Principal Asst Keeper, 1947. Lectr, Administrative History and Archive Administration, Sch. of Librarianship and Archives, University Coll. London, 1947-54. FRHistS (Vice-Pres. 1956-60); Council, Hon. Soc. of Cymmrodorion; Member: Advisory Council on Public Records, 1959-65; History and Law Cttee, Bd of Celtic Studies; Exec Committee: Internat. Council on Archives, 1953-68 (Vice-Pres. 1956-60); Pres. 4th Internat. Congress of Archivists, Stockholm, 1960; Governor: British Film Institute, 1961-64; Nat. Library of Wales, 1961- (Council, 1962-); Nat. Museum of Wales, 1965. *Publications:* Flintshire Ministers' Accounts, 1328-1352, 1929; History of Carmarthenshire: Chapter on Later Middle Ages, 1935; (part author) Notebook of John Smibert, Painter, Mass Hist. Soc., 1969; articles, reviews, in Cymmrodorion Transactions, Eng. Hist. Review, Nat. Lib. of Wales Jl, Virginia Hist. Soc. Trans, etc. *Address:* 2 Bay Court, Doctors Commons Road, Berkhamsted, Herts. *T:* Berkhamsted 3636. *Club:* National Liberal.

**EVANS, David Meurig; His Honour Judge Meurig Evans;** County Court Judge, North Wales Circuit, since 1957; Chairman: Cardigan Quarter Sessions; Denbigh Quarter Sessions; Deputy Chairman, Anglesey and Caernarvon Quarter Sessions; *b* 9 Sept. 1906; *s* of H. T. Evans, Aberayron, Cards; *m* 1933, Joyce Diedericke Sander (decd), St Albans; two *s* two *d*; *m* 1969, Mrs Anne Blackmore. *Educ:* Cardiff High Sch.; Aberayron County Sch.; Cardiff Technical Coll. Journalist on staff of Western Mail and The Economist, 1925-31. Called to Bar, Gray's Inn, 1931; practised on Wales and Chester Circuit, 1932-57. Served 1940-45, Lieut-Comdr RNVR. Chm., Medical Appeal Tribunal for Wales, 1952-57. *Recreations:* golf and yachting. *Address:* Bryn-Owen, Menai Bridge, Anglesey. *T:* Menai Bridge 253. *Clubs:* Naval; Royal Ocean Racing, etc.

**EVANS, David Milne;** Assistant Under-Secretary of State, Ministry of Defence, since 1967; *b* 8 Aug. 1917; *s* of Walter Herbert Evans, MSc and Florence Mary Evans (*née* Milne); *m* 1946, Gwynneth May (*née* Griffiths). *Educ:* Charterhouse; Gonville and Caius Coll., Cambridge (Schol.; Wrangler, Math. Tripos). Administrative Class, Home Civil Service (War Office), 1939. Served in Army (Major, RA), 1940-45. Asst Sec., 1954; Imp. Def. Coll., 1954. *Address:* 13 Copse Hill, Purley, Surrey. *T:* 01-660 4372. *Club:* Royal Automobile.

**EVANS, David Morgan;** Barrister, Wales and Chester Circuit; *b* 12 April 1892; *e s* of late Evan Price Evans and Sarah Anne Evans, Glasallt Isaf, Llangadock, Carmns; *m* 1924, Mary Gwynydd, 2nd *d* of late Thomas Lloyd, Havenholme, Hadley Wood and Mrs J. T. Lewis, 9 Dawson Place, Bayswater, W2; two *s* one *d* (and one *s* decd). *Educ:* Llangadock Sch.; Llandovery Coll.; Jesus Coll., Oxford (Classical Exhibn). MA Oxon. Barrister-at-law, Gray's Inn (Arden Prize). Legal Chm. Appellate Tribunal (Prescriptions) for South Wales under 1945 National Health Act; retd as Gen. Commissioner and Land Tax Commissioner; Deputy Chm. Cardiganshire Quarter Sessions, 1953-64. Formerly local Chm., Cardiff City's Rent Tribunal. Parish Councillor; Chm. Cardiff Mothercraft Clinic; Hon. Treasurer Oxford Soc., E Glam and Mon Br.; former Barr. Mem. Legal Aid Executive Cttee No 5 Area. Served 1915-19; Infantry; Artists' Rifles; Lieut 5th Bn (TF), The Welch Regt; 159 Bde Staff EEF Palestine, Egypt and Syria. *Recreations:* reading, gardening, fishing. *Address:* 33 Park Place, Cardiff; 3 New Square, Lincoln's Inn; Brynderi, Hollybush Road, Cyncoed, Cardiff. *T:* Cardiff 33313; Cardiff 752148; Llanarth, Cards 383.

**EVANS, David M.;** *see* Moule-Evans.

**EVANS, Air Chief Marshal Sir Donald Randell,** KBE 1964 (CBE 1944); CB 1955; DFC 1942; Commandant of the Imperial Defence College, 1968-69; retired, 1970; *b* 31 Jan. 1912; *o s* of late Col Percy Evans, CMG; *m* 1st, 1939, Pauline Mary Breach (marr. diss., 1950); one *s* (one *d* decd); 2nd, 1951, Eleanor Margaret (*née* Christie), *widow* of S/Ldr Philip Hunter, DSO; one *s*. *Educ:* Wellington Coll., RAF Coll., Cranwell, 1930-32; Acting Group Capt., 1942;

Group Capt., 1949; Actg Air Cdre, 1952; Air Cdre, 1956; Actg Air Vice-Marshal, 1957; Air Vice-Marshal, 1958; SASO, Fighter Command, 1957-58; Comdt, Sch. of Land/Air Warfare, 1959-61; Asst Chief of the Defence Staff, 1961-63; Chm., Chiefs of Staff working party on Defence Re-organisation, Ministry of Defence, 1963; Air Marshal, 1964; AOC-in-C, Technical Training Comd, 1964-66; Air Sec., MoD, 1966-67; Air Chief Marshal, 1967. American Bronze Star, 1944. *Address:* c/o Lloyds Bank (Cox's and King's Branch), 6 Pall Mall, SW1. *Club:* Royal Air Force.

**EVANS, Dame Edith,** DBE, *cr* 1946; (**Dame Edith Mary Booth**); Actress; *b* London; *o d* of late Edward and Ellen Evans; *m* 1925, George Booth (*d* 1935). *Educ:* St Michael's Sch., Chester Square. Made first appearance at King's Hall, Covent Garden, Dec. 1912, as Cressida in Troylus and Cressida (Elizabethan Stage Soc., Dir William Poel); played in George Moore's Elizabeth Cooper, 1913; became mem. Vedrenne and Eadie Co., 1914, at Royalty; toured with Ellen Terry in Variety Theatres, 1918, as Mistress Ford (Basket Sc., Merry Wives of Windsor) also as Nerissa (Trial Sc., Merchant of Venice); part of Nerissa in its entirety, Court Theatre, 1919; Caroline in The Three Daughters of M Dupont, and Lady Utterwood in Heartbreak House (first prod.), etc., 1920; Mistress Page in Merry Wives of Windsor and Mrs Millamant in The Way of the World, Lyric, Hammersmith, 1922; The Serpent and The She-Ancient in Back to Methuselah: Birmingham Rep. Theatre (first prod.), 1923, Court Theatre, 1924; Helena in A Midsummer Night's Dream, Drury Lane, 1924; Joined Old Vic Co. for 1925-26 Season; returned to West End, 1926; Mrs Sullen in The Beaux Strategem, Lyric, Hammersmith, 1927; later went into jt management with Leon M. Lion at Wyndham's; again played in Back to Methuselah and as Josephine in Napoleon's Josephine, 1928; Florence Nightingale in The Lady With a Lamp (first prod.), Arts, then Garrick, 1929 (also in New York); Malvern Festival, 1929; Orinthia in The Apple Cart (first prod.), (also in London); Diana in The Humours of the Court. Went to Prince of Wales' under her own management, 1930. Later appearances include: Irela in Evensong, Queen's, 1932, and New York, 1933; Gwenny in The Late Christopher Bean, St James's, 1933; Duchess of Marlborough in Viceroy Sarah, Arts, 1934; Nurse in Romeo and Juliet, New York, 1934, and New, 1935; Agatha Payne in The Old Ladies, New, 1935; Arcadina in The Seagull, New, 1936; Country Wife, As You Like It, Witch of Edmonton, at Old Vic; As You Like It, Taming Of The Shrew, at New; Robert's Wife, Lady Bracknell in The Importance of Being Earnest, Cousin Muriel, at Globe; Kit Markham in Old Acquaintance, Apollo. Joined Company going to Gibraltar to entertain troops, 1942; Hesione Hushabye in Heartbreak House, Cambridge Theatre, 1943; tour of RAF camps, playing one night stands; Garrison Theatre, Salisbury, 1944; took Company to India for ENSA, 1945. Mrs Malaprop in The Rivals, Criterion, 1945-46; Katerina Ivanovna in Crime and Punishment, New, 1946; Cleopatra in Antony and Cleopatra, Piccadilly, 1946-47; Lady Wishfort in The Way of the World, and Madame Ranevsky in The Cherry Orchard, New, 1948; Lady Pitts in Daphne Laureola, Wyndham's, 1949, (also in New York); Helen Lancaster in Waters of the Moon, Haymarket, 1951-53; Countess Rosmarin Ostenburg in The Dark is Light Enough, Aldwych, 1954; Mrs St Maugham in The Chalk Garden, Haymarket, 1956; Queen Katherine in Henry VIII, Old Vic, 1958 (also in Paris). Stratford-upon-Avon: Countess of Rousillion in All's Well That Ends Well, Volumnia in Coriolanus, 1959; Margaret in Richard III, Nurse in Romeo and Juliet, 1961; Violet in Gentle Jack, Queen's, 1963; Judith Bliss in Hay Fever, National Theatre, 1964; Mrs Forrest in The Chinese Prime Minister, Globe, 1965; Narrator in The Black Girl in Search of God, Mermaid, 1968. *Began film career in* The Queen of Spades, 1948; The Last Days of Dolwyn, 1948; The Importance of Being Earnest, 1951; Look Back in Anger, 1959; The Nun's Story, 1959; Tom Jones, 1963; The Chalk Garden, 1963; Young Cassidy, 1965; Fitzwilly Strikes Back, 1966; Prudence and the Pill, 1967; The Whisperers, 1967 (prize for best actress, Berlin Film Festival, 1967); Crooks and Coronets, 1969; The Madwoman of Chaillot, 1969; David Copperfield, 1970; Scrooge, 1970. Hon. DLit London, 1950; Hon. LittD Cambridge, 1951; Hon. DLitt: Oxford, 1954; Hull, 1968. Awards: Brit. Film Acad.; NY Film Critics; Hollywood Foreign Press; Variety Club of Great Britain. *Address:* Albany, Piccadilly, W1.

**EVANS, Rt. Rev. Edward Lewis;** *see* Barbados, Bishop of.

**EVANS, Edward Walter,** CMG 1931; formerly Lecturer in Colonial history and administration, Bristol University, 1946; *b* 1890; 2nd *s* of late Arthur Evans; *m* 1923, Margaret, *d* of late J. K. Young, Barrister-at-Law; two *s* one *d*. *Educ:* Marlborough Coll.; Corpus Christi Coll., Oxford (Classical Scholar). 1st Class Classical Mods, 1st Class Lit. Hum.; appointed to Colonial service, 1914; served in various dependencies in East Africa and Caribbean area before retiring from post of Colonial Sec., Mauritius, in 1939, after administering the Government of Mauritius on various occasions; during 1939-45 War served in Gibraltar and on Overseas Services of BBC; served on Control Commission for Germany, 1945-46; employed in History Dept Bristol Univ., 1946-55. *Publications:* Britannia Overseas, 1946; The British Yoke, 1949. *Recreation:* writing. *Address:* 2 Arlesey Close, Lytton Grove, SW15.

**EVANS, Ven. Eifion;** *see* Evans, Ven. D. E.

**EVANS, Prof. Emyr Estyn,** CBE 1970; Director, Institute of Irish Studies, Queen's University of Belfast, 1965-70; Leverhulme Emeritus Fellow, 1970-71; *b* 29 May 1905; 4th *s* of Rev. G. O. and Elizabeth Evans, Shrewsbury; *m* 1931, Gwyneth Lyon, *e d* of Prof. Abel Jones, Aberystwyth; four *s*. *Educ:* Welshpool County Sch.; University Coll., of Wales, Aberystwyth. BA Geography and Anthropology, 1925, MA 1931, DSc 1939. Hon. ScD; FSA, MRIA, Hon. MTPI. Independent Lecturer in Geography, QUB, 1928-44; Reader, 1944-45; Prof., 1945-68; Dean of the Faculty of Arts, 1951-54; Mem. of Senate. Tallman Visiting Professor: Bowdoin Coll., Maine, 1948-49; Visiting Professor: Indiana Univ., 1964; Louisiana State Univ., 1969. Chm., Ancient Monuments Advisory Council (NI) and Mem. Adv. Council, Republic of Ireland; President: Ulster Folk Life Soc. and Ulster Archæological Soc.; Ulster Architectural Heritage Soc.; Trustee: Ulster Folk Museum; Ulster Museum; Vice-Pres., Montgomeryshire Soc.; Hon. Mem. and former Vice-Pres., Prehistoric Soc. Former Member: Executive Cttee, NI Council of Social Service; NI Tourist Bd; Pres. Sect. E 1958 and Sect. H 1960, Brit. Assoc. for the Advancement of Science (first Chm. NI Area Cttee); Sir James Frazer Memorial Lectr, 1961; Sir Everard im Thurn Memorial Lectr, 1966; Chm., Northern Ireland Government Cttee on Itinerants; Vice-Chm., Cttee on Nature Conservation. FSA; MRIA; Hon. MTPI. Hon. ScD; Hon.

LittD. *Publications:* France, A Geographical Introduction, 1937; (joint) Preliminary Survey of the Ancient Monuments of Northern Ireland, 1940; Irish Heritage, 1942; A Portrait of Northern Ireland (Festival of Britain) 1951; Mourne Country, 1951; Lyles Hill: A Late Neolithic Site in County Antrim, 1953; Irish Folk Ways, 1957; Prehistoric and Early Christian Ireland, 1966; papers in scientific journals. *Address:* 100 Malone Road, Belfast. *T:* 668510.

**EVANS, Ven. Eric Herbert;** Archdeacon of Warrington, 1959-70, Emeritus since 1970; *b* 31 Jan 1902; *s* of late Captain E. B. Evans. *Educ:* Liverpool Institute; Bishop Wilson Theological Coll., Isle of Man. Rector of North Meols, Diocese of Liverpool, 1948-68. *Recreation:* travelling. *Address:* 36 Salford Road, Ainsdale, Southport, Lancs. *T:* Southport 78715.

**EVANS, Evan Stanley,** CBE 1951; FRCS; Medical Superintendent, Lord Mayor Treloar Hospital, Alton, since 1946; Chairman, Queen Elizabeth's Training College, Leatherhead, since 1942; *b* 2 July 1904; *e s* of David Evans; *m* 1934, Muriel Gordon, *y d* of Peter Henderson; five *s*. *Educ:* St Bartholomew's Hospital. MRCS, LRCP, 1927; FRCS 1931; MB, BS London 1932; House Surg. and House Surg. (orthop.), St Bartholomew's Hosp., 1928; Medical Supt, Heatherwood Hosp., Ascot, 1932; Medical Supt, Queen Mary's Hosp., Carshalton, 1942. Cons. Orthop. Surg. to Morland Clinics, and to Farnham Hosp. Fellow Brit. Orthop. Assoc. and rep. on Joint Tuberculosis Council; Founder Mem. Exec. Cttee of British Council of Rehabilitation; Vice-Chm. Exec. Cttee and Chm. Development Cttee of Central Council for Care of Cripples; Chm. Jt Examination Board for orthopædic nursing. *Publications:* articles on non-pulmonary tuberculosis and cerebral palsy, in medical journals and books. *Address:* Alton Park, Alton, Hants. *T:* Alton 2068.

**EVANS, Sir Francis (Edward),** GBE 1957; KCMG, *cr* 1946 (CMG 1944); DL; Agent for the Government of N Ireland in Great Britain, 1962-66; *b* 4 April 1897; *s* of late Thomas Edward Evans, Belfast; *m* 1920, Mary, *d* of late Rev. Prof. James Dick, MA, DD, Belfast; no *c*. *Educ:* Royal Academy, Belfast; London Sch. of Economics. Served European War, Lieut Royal Irish Rifles, 1915-19; Consular Service, 1920; Vice-Consul in New York, 1920-26, Boston, 1926-29, Colon, Panama, 1929-32, and Boston, 1932-34; Consul at Los Angeles, 1934-39; in Foreign Office, 1939-43; Consul at New York, 1943; Consul-Gen., 1944-50; Asst Under-Sec. of State, FO, 1951; British Ambassador to Israel, 1952-54 (Minister, 1951-52); British Ambassador to the Argentine, 1954-57. Dep. Chm. Northern Ireland Development Coun., 1957-65. Hon. Col, 6th (T) Bn Royal Ulster Rifles, 1961-67, (T&AVR), 1967-. LLD (Hon.) Queen's Univ., Belfast; DCL (Hon.) Ripon Coll., Wisconsin. DL Belfast, 1959. KStJ. *Address:* Helen's Bay, Co. Down. *Clubs:* Travellers'; Ulster (Belfast).

**EVANS, Frankis Tilney,** MB, BS; FRCS, FFARCS; Consulting Anæsthetist, St Bartholomew's Hospital, since 1924, St Mark's Hospital for Diseases of the Rectum, since 1932, Royal Masonic Hospital, since 1944; *b* 9 March 1900; *s* of Edwin Evans and Alice (*née* Motterway), both of London; *m* 1931, Viola Hamilton (*d* 1960), *o d* of Dr Robert Quennell, Brentwood, Essex; one *s* one *d*. *Educ:* Forest Sch., Snaresbrook, Essex; St Bartholomew's Hosp. MB, BS London, 1921. Surg. Sub-Lieut RNVR, 1918. Resident Anæsth., St Bart.'s, 1921; House Surg. St Bart.'s, 1922; Sen. Res. Anæsth., St Bart.'s, 1923-24. Formerly: Anæsthetist, Brompton Hosp.; Consulting Anæsthetist, King George Hosp., Ilford, Gerrard's Cross Hosp. Pres. Anæsth. Sect., Royal Society of Medicine, 1945; Examiner Fellow Fac. Anæsth., RCS; Examiner, Diploma Anæsth, Eng., 1952-56; Ext. Examr Diploma Anæsth., Ireland, 1954; Dean of Faculty of Anæsthetists, Royal College Surg. Eng., 1955-58; Mem. Council, RCS, 1955-58. *Publications:* (ed and contrib.) Modern Practice in Anæsthesia, 1949 and 1954; (co-ed) Modern Trends in Anæsthesia, 1958; (co-ed and contrib.) General Anæsthesia, 1959; (contrib.) Operative Surgery, (Rob and Smith, 1958; various articles in Lancet and BMJ. *Recreations:* music and sailing. *Address:* 40 Harley Street, W1. *T:* 01-935 2511; 3 St James's Close, Birdham, Chichester, Sussex. *Clubs:* Royal Thames, Savage, Royal Cruising.

**EVANS, Fred;** *see* Evans, Alfred T.

**EVANS, Frederick Anthony;** General Secretary, The Duke of Edinburgh's Award Scheme; *b* 17 Nov. 1907; *s* of Herbert Anthony Evans, mining engineer, and Pauline (*née* Allen); *m* 1934, Nancy (*née* Meakin); two *s* one *d*. *Educ:* Charterhouse; Corpus Christi, Cambridge. Manager Doondu Coffee Plantation, Kenya, 1927-31; Colonial Service, 1934; Asst District Officer, Nigeria, 1935-39; Provincial Commissioner and Asst Colonial Sec., Gambia, 1940-47; Colonial Sec., Nassau, Bahamas, 1947-51; Acting Governor, 1950; Permanent Sec., Gold Coast (later Ghana), 1951-57. Dir, Anglo-Gambian Archæological Expedition, 1965-66. *Recreations:* golf, ski-ing. *Address:* St Katherine's, Froyle, Hants; 11 Iverna Gardens, Kensington, W8. *Club:* Royal Commonwealth Society.

**EVANS, Lt-Gen. Sir Geoffrey (Charles),** KBE 1954 (CBE 1945); CB 1946; DSO 1941 (bars 1942, 1944); retired, 1957; *b* 13 March 1901; *s* of late Col C. R. Evans, DSO; *m* 1928, Ida Louise, *d* of late H. R. Sidney; no *c*. *Educ:* Aldenham Sch.; Royal Military Coll., Sandhurst. 2nd Lieut The Royal Warwickshire Regt, 1920; Adjutant: 1st Bn, 1926-29; 7th Bn (TA), 1934-35; Staff Coll., 1936-37. Served War of 1939-45 (despatches five times): Bde Major, N Africa and Eritrea, 1940-41; OC 1st Bn Royal Sussex Regt, N Africa, 1941-42; Comdt Staff Coll., Quetta, 1942; Brig. Comd., India, 1943; Brig., Gen. Staff 4 Corps, Burma, 1943-44; Bde Commander, Burma, 1944; GOC 5 and 7 Indian Divs, Burma, 1944-45; GOC Allied Land Forces, Siam, 1945-46; GOC 42 (Lancs) Div. and North-West District, 1947-48; Dir of Military Training War Office, 1948-49; GOC 40 Div., Hong Kong, 1949-51; Temp. Comd. (Lt-Gen.), British Forces, Hong Kong, 1951-52; Asst Chief of Staff (Org. and Trng), Supreme HQ, Allied Powers, Europe, 1952-53; GOC-in-C, Northern Command, 1953-57; retired. Hon. Col 7th Bn The Royal Warwickshire Regt, 1959-64. A Vice-Pres., Nat. Playing Fields Assoc.; Chairman: London and Middlesex Playing Fields Association, 1959-70; Anglo-Thai Soc., 1967-. Comr, Royal Hosp., Chelsea, 1968-. *Publications:* The Desert and the Jungle, 1959; (with A. Brett-James) Imphal, 1962; The Johnnies, 1964; Slim as Military Commander, 1969; articles and reviews. *Recreation:* fishing. *Address:* 11 Wellington Square, SW3. *Club:* United Service.

**EVANS, Rear-Adm. George Hammond,** CB 1968; retired; *b* 15 Jan. 1917; *er s* of late W. A. Evans, Liverpool and Mrs Evans (*née* Hammond), Hale, Lancs; *m* 1949, Margaret Ruth, *yr d* of Capt. C. C. Bell, DSO, RN (retired); one *s*. *Educ:* Bristol Grammar Sch. Cadet, Merchant

Navy, 1933-37; transferred to Royal Navy, 1938; commanded: HMS Eggesford, 1943-45; HMS Nepal, 1949-50; Naval Mem., Jt Intelligence Staff, Far East Station, 1951-52; Trng Comdr, RN Barracks, Chatham, 1952-54; commanded: HMS Modeste, 1954-56; HMS Temeraire, 1957-58; Senior British Naval Officer, Ceylon, 1958-60; Deputy Asst Chief of Staff, SHAPE, 1960-62; Dir of Naval Recruiting, 1962-64; Capt. of Dockyard, Rosyth, 1964-66; Naval Deputy, Allied Forces, Northern Europe, 1966-69. Commander 1951; Capt. 1957; Rear-Adm. 1966; psc 1946; jssc 1957. Royal Humane Society Medal for Lifesaving, 1942. *Recreations:* golf, sailing. *Address:* Vale Cottage, North Berwick, East Lothian. *T:* North Berwick 2365. *Club:* Army and Navy.

**EVANS, Sir Geraint Llewellyn,** Kt 1969; CBE 1959; Opera Singer; Principal Baritone, Royal Opera House, Covent Garden, and Glyndeborne Festival Opera; *b* 16 Feb. 1922; *m* 1948, Brenda Evans Davies; two *s*. *Educ:* Guildhall Sch. of Music. Royal Opera House, Covent Garden, 1948-; Glyndebourne Festival Opera, 1950; Mem. Royal Opera House, Covent Garden; Mem. Vienna State Opera. Has sung at La Scala (Milan), Metropolitan (New York), Teatre Colon (Buenos Aires), San Francisco, Chicago, Salzburg, Promenade Concerts and on Radio, and made frequent Television appearances. Hon. DMus: Wales, 1965; Leicester, 1969. Hon. RAM 1969; FGSM. *Recreations:* photography, Rugby football. *Address:* Lone Pool, 34 Birchwood Road, Petts Wood, Kent. *T:* Orpington 20529.

**EVANS, Godfrey;** *see* Evans, T. G.

**EVANS, Professor Emeritus, Griffith Conrad;** Professor, Department of Mathematics, University of California, Berkeley, Calif, USA, 1934-55, retired; *b* Boston, Mass, 11 May 1887; *s* of George William Evans and Mary Taylor; *m* 1917, Isabel John; three *s*. *Educ:* Harvard Coll.; Harvard Univ.; University of Rome, Italy (Sheldon Fellow). BA Harvard Coll, 1907; PhD Harvard Univ., 1910; Instructor (part-time) Harvard, 1906, 1906-07, 1909-10; Asst Prof. and Prof., Rice Institute, 1912-34; Visiting Prof., summer, Calif, 1921, 1928, Chicago 1925, Minn 1931, Washington (Walker Ames Prof.) 1941, Rice Inst., Spring 1959; lectured in France and Belgium, 1929-30, and in Rome, Jan.-Feb., 1961. Capt., Signal Corps and Air Service, 1918-19; Technical Consultant and Scientific Expert, War Dept, Ordnance, 1943-47; Distinguished Assistance Award, 1946; Presidential Citation of Merit, 1948; National Research Council, 1927-30, 1940-43, and 1950-53; Member: American Acad. of Arts and Sciences, Boston; American Philosophical Soc., Philadelphia; Nat. Acad. of Sciences, Washington, DC; American Mathematical Soc. (Vice-Pres. 1924-26, Pres. 1938-40); Mathematical Assoc. of America (Vice-Pres. 1932); AAAS (Vice-Pres. for Economics, 1931, for Maths, 1936). LLD (hon.) University of Calif, 1956. *Publications:* Functionals and their Applications, 1918 (rev. 1964); Logarithmic Potential, 1927 (rev. 1969); Mathematical Introduction to Economics, 1930; Stabilité et Dynamique de la Production dans l'Economie Politique, 1932; technical and popular articles. *Recreation:* mostly writing. *Address:* Department of Mathematics, University of California, Berkeley, Calif 94720, USA. *Clubs:* Faculty, Arts (Berkeley); Sierra (Norden, Calif); University (San Francisco).

**EVANS, Gwynfor;** President, Plaid Cymru, since 1945 (Vice-Pres. 1943-45); *b* 1 Sept. 1912; *s* of Dan Evans and Catherine Mary Richard; *m* 1941, Rhiannon Prys Thomas; four *s* three *d*. *Educ:* Gladstone Road Elementary Sch.; County Sch., Barry; University of Wales, Aberystwyth; St John's Coll., Oxford. Qual. Solicitor, 1939. Hon. Sec. Heddychwyr Cymru (Welsh Pacifist movement), 1939-45; Chm. Union of Welsh Independents, 1954. MP (Plaid Cymru) Carmarthen, July 1966-1970. Member: Carmarthen CC, 1949-; Ct of Nat. Museum of Wales; Ct of Govs, University of Wales and UC, Aberystwyth; Council Univ. of Wales, and UC Aberystwyth. Past Mem. Welsh Broadcasting Council. *Publications:* Plaid Cymru and Wales, 1950; Rhagom i Ryddid, 1964. *Address:* Talar Wen, Llangadog, Sir Gaerfyrddin, Wales. *T:* Llangadog 252.

**EVANS, Sir Harold,** 1st Bt, *cr* 1963; CMG 1957; OBE 1945; Adviser on Public Relations to the Vickers Board since 1966; *b* 29 April 1911; *s* of Sidney Evans and Gladys Mary Lythgoe; *m* 1945, Elizabeth Jaffray; one *d* (one *s* decd). *Educ:* King Edward's Sch., Stourbridge. Editorial staff of newspapers in Worcs and Sheffield, 1930-39; Freelance Journalism, 1939-40; British Volunteers in Finland, 1940; Staff of British Legation, Helsinki, 1940-42; Min. of Information Rep. in W Africa (Staff of Resident Minister), 1942-45; Dep. Public Relations Officer, Colonial Office, 1945-53; Chief Information Officer, Colonial Office, 1953-57; Public Relations Adviser to the Prime Minister, 1957-64; Head of Information and Research, Independent Television Authority, 1964-66. *Publications:* Men in the Tropics, Anthology, 1949; various contributions. *Address:* 3 Challoners Close, Rottingdean, Sussex. *T:* Brighton 33397.

**EVANS, Harold Matthew;** Editor, Sunday Times, since 1967; *b* 28 June 1928; *s* of Frederick and Mary Evans; *m* 1953, Enid, *d* of late John Parker and of Susan Parker; one *s* two *d*. *Educ:* St Mary's Road Central Sch., Manchester; Durham Univ. BA 1952, MA Dunelm 1966. Ashton-under-Lyne, Lancs, Reporter Newspapers, 1944-46 and 1949; RAF, 1946-49; Durham Univ., 1949-52; Manchester Evening News, 1952; Commonwealth Fund Fellow in Journalism, Chicago and Stanford Univs, USA, 1956-57; Asst Ed, Manchester Evening News, 1958-61; Ed., Northern Echo, 1961-66; Editor-in-Chief, North of England Newspaper Co., 1963-66; Chief Asst to Editor, Sunday Times, 1966; Managing Editor, Sunday Times, 1966. Mem., Exec. Bd, Times Newspapers Ltd, 1968-; Dir, The Sunday Times Ltd, 1968-. *Publications:* The Active Newsroom, 1961; The Suez Crisis: A Study in Press Performance, 1967; Editing and Design, 1971. *Recreations:* music, table-tennis, chess. *Address:* The Sunday Times, Thomson House, 200 Gray's Inn Road, WC1. *T:* 01-837 1234. *Club:* Royal Automobile.

**EVANS, Lt-Col Harrie Smalley,** CMG 1918; *b* 1887; *m* 1920, Marjorie Nightingale, *o d* of Millin Selby, of Lille, France, and Knocke, Belgium. Served European War, 1914-18, Australian Army Pay Corps (despatches, CMG).

**EVANS, (Harry) Lindley,** CMG 1963; Pianist; Composer; Professor of Pianoforte, NSW State Conservatorium of Music, Sydney, Australia, 1928-66, a Governor, since 1966; *b* 18 Nov. 1895; British; *m* 1926, Marie Florence Stewart. *Educ:* St George's Grammar Sch., Capetown, South Africa. Pianist with Dame Nellie Melba, 1922-31. Celebrated a 40-year partnership in giving two-piano recitals, 1964. Melody Man in Children's Hour (ABC) since its inception, 1940. Pres., Musical Assoc. of NSW (life Mem.); Past Pres., Fellowship of Australian Composers. *Publications:* many musical compositions. *Recreations:* bowls, yachting. *Address:* 9 Werambie Street, Woolwich. NSW, Australia. *T:* 89-1874. *Clubs:* Savage (Sydney) (Life Mem.; Pres. 13 yrs); Hunter's Hill Bowling.

**EVANS, Haydn T.;** *see* Tudor Evans.

**EVANS, Maj.-Gen. Henry Holland;** Director of Army Education since 1969; *b* Harrogate, 18 Nov. 1914; *o s* of Major H. Evans; *m* 1939, Norah Mary, *d* of F. R. Lawson, Wolstanton, Staffs; one *s* one *d*. *Educ:* King James Grammar Sch., Almondbury, near Huddersfield; Manchester Univ. Commissioned Duke of Wellington's Regt (TA), 1936; Regular Army Commission in AEC, 1939; Officer Instructor, Duke of York's Royal Mil. Sch., 1939-41; Staff Officer: 43 (Wessex) Div., 1942-45; War Office, 1945-48; Chief Educn Officer, Malta and Libya, 1948-51; various RAEC appts, incl. Headmaster DYRMS and Chief Inspector of Army children's schools, to 1963; CEO, Northern Comd, 1963-65; CEO, BAOR, 1965-68. *Recreations:* gardening, golf. *Address:* 136 Richmond Hill, Richmond, Surrey. *T:* 01-940 4126. *Club:* Army and Navy.

**EVANS, Herbert Edgar,** CMG 1957; QC (NZ) 1946; *b* Sudbury, Suffolk, 21 Nov. 1884; *s* of Captain E. J. Evans (Shaw Savill Line) and Ada E. G. Evans (*née* Green); *m* 1912, Ella Mary Harman, West Acton, London; two *s*. *Educ:* Whitgift Grammar Sch., Croydon; Victoria University Coll., Wellington, NZ. BA 1906, LLM 1910. University of New Zealand. Arrived in New Zealand (Wellington), 1902. Entered Office of Bell, Gully, Bell and Myers (Barristers and Solicitors), 1903; admitted Barrister and Solicitor, 1910; Partner in successors to that firm, 1922-45; Solicitor-Gen. for New Zealand, 1945-57; Chancellor of Anglican Diocese of Wellington, 1946-64. *Recreation:* Gardening. *Address:* Flat 110, Lichfield, Selwyn Village, Point Chevalier, Auckland, New Zealand. *T:* 80.119.

**EVANS, Herbert McLean,** BS, MD, DMed *hc* Freiburg and Santiago, ScD San Marcos, Docteur hc (Paris); retired, 1953; Professor of Anatomy, University of California, 1915-52, Professor Emeritus, since 1952; Herzstein Professor of Biology and Director of the Institute of Experimental Biology, University of California, 1930-52. Professor Emeritus and Director Emeritus, since 1952; *b* 23 Sept. 1882; *s* of Dr C. W. Evans, Modesto, Calif; *m* 1st, 1905; one *d*; 2nd, 1932; one *d*; 3rd, 1945, Dorothy Frances Atkinson (*d* 1969). *Educ:* University of Calif; Johns Hopkins Univ., Baltimore, Md. Asst, Instructor, Associate and Assoc. Prof. of Anatomy, Johns Hopkins Univ., 1908-15; Research Associate Carnegie Institution of Washington, 1913-15. MD *hc*; Albert Ludwigs-Universität, Freiburg i. Br., 1930; Universidad Catholica of Chile, 1941; Docteur *hc*; Universidad Nacional of San Marcos de Lima, 1941; University of Paris, 1946; Universidad Central del Ecuador, 1954; ScD: University of Birmingham, 1950; Johns Hopkins Univ., 1957; LLD, University of California, 1955; Docteur ès Sciences, *hc* Université de Genève, 1956. John Scott Medal, 1928; gold medal (first award) for Scientific Exhibit, Am. Med. Assoc., San Francisco, 1946; Banting Medal, 1949; Squibb Award, Assoc. for Study of Internal Secretion, 1949; Charles Mickle Fellow, University of Toronto, 1949; Passano Award, Baltimore, 1952; F. H. A. Marshall Medal, 1967. Foreign Member of the Royal Society, 1951. Many lectureships in USA. Demonstrated origin of body vascular trunks from capillary plexes, 1909; explained physiological behaviour of vital stains of benzidine series, 1915; introduced use of certain azo dyes, especially Evans' Blue for estimation of blood volume, 1917; charted 48 chromosomes in man, 1918, 1929; (with J. A. Long) first description of oestrous cycle in rat, 1921, of essential value in isolation of female sex hormones; produced gigantism and other specific endocrine effects from anterior-hypophyseal hormones administered parenterally, 1922, and established separation of pituitary growth promoting substance of hormone, 1939, and finally purified this (with C. H. Li), 1944; production of permanent diabetes by chronic administration of anterior pituitary extracts, 1932; first detected criterion of vitamin A deficiency in continuous vaginal cornification, 1922; discovered vitamin E, essential for reproduction in higher animals, 1922, and (with O. H. and G. A. Emerson) first purified and determined empirical constitution of same, 1935; (with C. H. Li) was first to purify the anterior hypophyseal adrenocorticotropic hormone, 1942. Joint Editor of Am. Anatomical Memoirs, 1918-38, and Journal of Nutrition, 1928-33. Delegate to Third Internat. Conf. on Standardisation of Hormones, Geneva, 1938; delegate to Second Pan-American Congress of Endocrinology, Montevideo, 1941. *Publications:* over 600 scientific papers on anatomy, histology, embryology, cytology, physiology, biochemistry, nutrition, and endocrinology. *Recreations:* botany of Sierra Nevada arctic alpine zone, mountain climbing; book collecting (especially in field of history of medicine and science and of Western American exploration and pioneer life). *Address:* 511 Coventry Road, Berkeley, Calif, USA; University of California, Berkeley 4, Calif. *T:* (home) Landscape 5-9010; (university) 642-3535. *Clubs:* University of California Faculty (California); Roxburghe, Bohemian (San Francisco).

**EVANS, Hubert John Filmer,** CMG 1958; LLD; HM Diplomatic Service; Central Asian Research Centre; *b* 21 Nov. 1904; *y s* of late Harry Evans and late Edith Gwendoline Rees; *m* 1948, Marjory Maureen Filmer (*née* Carrick), *widow* of Col R. A. M. Tweedy. *Educ:* City of London Sch.; Jesus Coll., Oxford (Classical Scholar); Montpellier. Studied oriental languages with Ross, Minorsky, and in the East. Entered Indian Civil Service, 1928; served as Magistrate in various districts of United Provinces, 1929-37; Deputy Commissioner of Delhi, 1938-42; Sec. Delhi Provincial Administration, 1942-45; Collector of Agra, 1945-47; appointed to Foreign Service, 1947; at the Foreign Office, 1948-50; Financial Adviser to Persian Gulf Residency, 1950-51; Consul-Gen. at Meshed, 1951; in Latin America, 1952-54; Consul-Gen., Rotterdam, 1955-56; HM Ambassador to Korea, 1957-61. Hon. Sec., Royal Central Asian Soc. and Chm. Ed. Board 1965-. Hon. MRAS Korea; Hon. LLD Korea, 1960; Freedom of Seoul, 1960. *Publications:* various in oriental jls. *Recreations:* The Persian Poets, and travel. *Address:* c/o The Foreign and Commonwealth Office, SW1; Manoir d'Arlette, Fatouville, Eure, Normandy, France. *Club:* Athenæum.

**EVANS, Hywel Eifion;** Welsh Secretary, Ministry of Agriculture, Fisheries and Food, since 1968; *b* 24 Jan. 1910; *s* of late Gruffydd Thomas and Winnifred Evans, Felin Rhydhir, Pwllheli, Caernarvonshire; *m* 1939, Mary Elizabeth, *d* of late Richard and Hannah Jones, Gilfach, Glanywydden, Llandudno; one *s* one *d*. *Educ:* Pwllheli Grammar Sch.; University Coll. of North Wales, Bangor. BSc (Hons) (Agric.). Research Asst, Dept of Agricultural Economics, UCW, Aberystwyth, 1934-40;

Dist and Dep. Exec. Officer, Leicester WAEC, 1940-46; County Advisory Officer: Radnor AEC, 1946-47; Carmarthen AEC, 1947-57; Dep. Regional Dir, Nat. Agric. Advisory Service, Wales, 1957-59; Regional Dir, Nat. Agricl Adv. Service (Wales), 1959-66; Dep. Dir, Nat. Agricl Adv. Service (London), 1967-68. *Publications:* articles on agricultural economic and sociological topics in Welsh Jl of Agriculture, Agriculture, and other jls. *Recreations:* idling, fishing, shooting. *Address:* Fflur y Main, Maeshendre, Waunfawr, Aberystwyth, Wales. *T:* Aberystwyth 3828. *Club:* Farmers'.

**EVANS, Hywel Wynn;** Assistant Under-Secretary of State, Welsh Office, since 1968; *b* 30 May 1920; *s* of late Dr T. Hopkin Evans, MusDoc; *m* 1949, Jessie Margaret Templeton; one *d*. *Educ:* Liverpool Collegiate Sch.; Liverpool Univ. RA and Intell. Corps, 1940-46. Joined Min. of Labour, as Asst Principal, 1947; Commonwealth Fellow, 1957-58; Private Sec. to Minister of Labour, 1959-60; Sec., NEDC, 1964-68. *Publication:* Governmental Regulation of Industrial Relations, 1960 (USA). *Address:* Coed-yr-Iarll, St Fagans, near Cardiff, S Wales. *T:* Cardiff 565214. *Clubs:* Reform; Cardiff and County (Cardiff).

**EVANS, Sir Ian William G.;** *see* Gwynne-Evans.

**EVANS, Ioan (Lyonel);** JP; Director, International Defence and Aid Fund, since 1970; *b* 1927; *m* 1949, Maria (*née* Griffiths); one *s* one *d*. *Educ:* Llanelly Grammar Sch.; University Coll., Swansea. Has held various Co-op. (incl. Sec. Birm. and Dist Co-op. Party) and Labour Party offices. Co-opted Mem., W Bromwich Educn Cttee; Gov., West Bromwich Grammar Sch.; Lecturer for WEA and NCLC. MP (Lab and Co-op) Birmingham Yardley, 1964-70; Subseq. PPS to Postmaster-Gen.; Asst Govt Whip, 1966-68; Comptroller of HM Household, 1968-70. Vice-Chm. West Midlands Parly Labour Group of MP's; UK Parly deleg. to Consultative Assembly of Council of Europe; Mem., UK Delegn to Assembly of WEU. JP, Birmingham. *Address:* 169 Eastcote Road, Ruislip, Mddx. *T:* Ruislip 32545.

**EVANS, Col J(ames) Ellis,** OBE 1952; TD 1947; JP; Vice-Lieutenant of Flintshire since 1970; *b* 6 Aug. 1910; *s* of James William Evans and Eleanor Evans, MBE, JP; unmarried. *Educ:* Epworth Coll., Rhyl. Chartered Accountant (FCA). Joined TA, 1937; served War of 1939-45, RA: France, 1940; N Africa, 1941-44; Italy, 1944-45; comd 384 Light Regt RA (RWF), TA, 1947-52; Dep. CRA, 53 (Welsh) Div., 1953-57; Chm. Denbigh and Flint TA Assoc., 1961-68; Vice-Chm., Wales and Mon TA&VRA, 1968-. Mem., Prestatyn UDC, 1939- (Chm. 1947). Flintshire: JP 1951; DL 1953; High Sheriff, 1970-71. *Recreations:* lawn tennis, gardening. *Address:* Trafford Mount, Gronant Road, Prestatyn, Flintshire. *T:* Prestatyn 4119. *Clubs:* City (Chester); Racquets (Liverpool); Cardiff and County (Cardiff).

**EVANS, Major James John Pugh,** MBE; MC; *b* 13 May 1885; 3rd *s* of late Sir Griffith Evans, KCIE, DL, JP, and Lady Evans of Lovesgrove, Cardiganshire; *m* 1916, Viola Murielle, *e d* of late Lionel Robinson, DL, Old Buckenham Hall, Norfolk; one *s* (and one *s* decd). *Educ:* Eton; Sandhurst. Joined Royal Welch Fusiliers, 1905; Welsh Guards, 1915; served, France, 1915-19; Major, 1919; Brigade Major 1st Guards' Brigade, Aldershot, 1920-21. DL 1950, JP 1926-65. High Sheriff, 1927, Cardiganshire; DL Carmarthenshire, 1943-65; Mem. County Agric. Exec. Cttee, 1948. *Recreation:* painting. *Address:* Pentre, Capel Bangor, Aberystwyth. *T:* Capel Bangor 628.

**EVANS, Joan,** DLitt, DLit; Hon. LLD; Hon. LittD; FSA, FRHistS; Hon. ARIBA; Hon. Vice-President, Society of Antiquaries; Hon. Fellow of St Hugh's College, Oxford, 1936; Fellow of University College, London, 1950; *d* of late Sir John Evans, KCB, FRS. *Educ:* Berkhamsted Girls' Sch.; St Hugh's College, Oxford; University Coll., London. DLit London 1930; DLitt Oxford, 1932; Hon. LLD, Edinburgh, 1952; Hon. LittD, Cambridge, 1956; Librarian, St Hugh's Coll., 1917-22; Susette Taylor Fellow, Lady Margaret Hall, 1933-35; External Examiner in History of Art, London University, 1938-46; President, Royal Archæological Inst., 1948-51 (Treasurer, 1958-62); Pres. Soc. of Antiquaries, 1959-64 (Vice-Pres., 1948-52), Dir, 1954-59; Trustee: London Museum, 1951-69; British Museum, 1963-67; Mem. Adv. Coun. V. & A. Mus., 1953-67; Mem. Exec. Cttee, Friends of the National Libraries, 1955-67; Vice-Pres., Friends of the Ashmolean Museum, 1969. Supernumerary Fellow, St Hugh's Coll., Oxford, 1951-58, Mem. of Council 1922-58; Hon. Mem., former Chm. Council and President, Bristol and Glos Archæological Soc.; Membre d'honneur Académie de Mâcon; Corresponding Fellow and Hon. Research Associate, Mediæval Academy of America; Hon. Fellow Huguenot Soc. of London; Membre honoraire, Société Nationale des Antiquaires de France, 1967; membre de la Société de l'histoire de l'art français. Chevalier de la Légion d'Honneur. *Publications:* English Jewellery, 1921; Magical Jewels of the Middle Ages and the Renaissance, 1922; Anglo-Norman Lapidaries (with Prof. Studer), 1924; Life in Mediæval France, 1925 (reprinted 1957); St Joan of Orleans, 1926; The Unconquered Knight, a Chronicle of the deeds of Don Pero Niño, 1928; Pattern, a study of Ornament in Western Europe from 1180 to 1900, 1931; Monastic Life at Cluny, 1931; English Posies and Posy Rings, 1932; English Mediæval Lapidaries (with Dr Mary Serjeantson), 1933; Nature in Design, 1934; Index to Sir Arthur Evans' Palace of Minos, 1936; Joinville's History of St Louis, 1937; The Romanesque Architecture of the Order of Cluny, 1938; Taste and Temperament, 1939; Chateaubriand, 1939; Time and Chance, the story of Arthur Evans and his forebears, 1943; The Pursuit of Happiness, 1946; The Unselfish Egoist, 1947; Art in Mediæval France, 1948; English Art, 1307-1461 (Oxford History of English Art), 1949; Cluniac Art of the Romanesque Period, 1950; Style in Ornament, 1950; Dress in Mediæval France, 1952; A History of Jewellery, 1100-1870, 1953; John Ruskin, 1954; (ed) An Adventure, 1955; The Endless Web, Messrs John Dickinson & Co., 1804-1954, 1956; History of the Society of Antiquaries, 1956; The Diaries of John Ruskin, 1956, 1958, 1959; The Lamp of Beauty, 1959; Madame Royale, 1959; Monastic Architecture in France from the Renaissance to the Revolution, 1964; Prelude and Fugue (autobiography), 1965; The Victorians, 1966; (ed) Flowering of the Middle Ages, 1966; The Conways, 1966; articles in archæological periodicals. *Address:* Thousand Acres, Wotton-under-Edge, Glos. *T:* Wotton 3224; 72 Campden Hill Court, W8. *T:* 01-937 3831. *Club:* University Women's.

**EVANS, Prof. John Davies;** Professor of Prehistoric Archæology, London University, since 1956; *b* 22 Jan. 1925; *o s* of Harry Evans and Edith Haycocks; *m* 1957, Evelyn Sladdin. *Educ:* Liverpool Institute High Sch. (open schol. in English to Pemb. Coll.); Pembroke

Coll., Cambridge. War Service, 1943-47. BA 1948, MA 1950, PhD 1956. Fellow of British Institute of Archæology at Ankara, 1951-52; Research Fellow of Pembroke Coll., Cambridge, 1953-56. *Publications:* Malta (Ancient Peoples and Places Series), 1959; (with Dr A. C. Renfrew) Excavations at Saliagos, near Antiparos, 1968; The Prehistoric Antiquities of the Maltese Islands, 1970; papers and reports in archæological journals. *Recreations:* walking, listening to music. *Address:* Institute of Archæology, Gordon Square, WC1.

**EVANS, Sir John (Harold),** KBE 1958; CB 1948; Member, delegacy, King's College, London; *b* 16 Feb. 1904; *s* of William Evans, Lowestoft; *m* 1936, Phyllis (formerly Bathurst); one *s. Educ:* Lowestoft Secondary Sch.; University of London, King's Coll. Entered Civil Service, 1925. Dep. Chm., Bd of Inland Revenue, 1954-65. FKC 1959. *Address:* Whitehill Cottage, Meopham, Kent. *T:* Meopham 2284. *Club:* National Liberal.

**EVANS, John Marten Llewellyn,** CBE 1956 (MBE 1945); JP; Official Solicitor to the Supreme Court of Judicature, 1950-70; *b* 9 June 1909; *s* of late Marten Llewellyn Evans, Solicitor, and Edith Helena (*née* Lile); *m* 1943, Winifred Emily, *y d* of late Austin Reed; one *s* one *d. Educ:* Rugby Sch.; Trinity Coll., Oxford. Admitted Solicitor, 1935; Legal Asst to the Official Solicitor, 1937. Served War of 1939-45, Major RA. Senior Legal Asst to the Official Solicitor, 1947; Asst Master in Lunacy, 1950. Vice-Chm., Austin Reed Group Ltd, 1969. Master of Worshipful Company of Cutlers, 1967-68. JP City of London, 1969. *Recreations:* the theatre, cricket, golf, tennis. *Address:* The Paddock, Waltham St Laurence, Reading, Berks. *Clubs:* Garrick, MCC.

**EVANS, Ven. John Mascal;** Archdeacon of Surrey since 1968; *b* 17 May 1915; *s* of Rev. Edward Foley Evans and Mary Evans; *m* 1941, Mary Elizabeth (*née* Rathbone); three *s* two *d. Educ:* St John's Sch., Leatherhead; Brasenose Coll., Oxford; Wells Theological Coll. Asst Curate, St Martin's, Epsom, 1938; Perpetual Curate, Stoneleigh, Epsom, 1942, All Saints, Fleet, 1952; Vicar, St Mary, Walton-on-Thames, 1960-68; Hon. Canon of Guildford, 1963-. *Recreations:* outdoor sports, fishing. *Address:* Hilgay, 50 Warren Road, Guildford, Surrey.

**EVANS, Rt. Rev. Kenneth Dawson;** *see* Dorking, Suffragan Bishop of.

**EVANS, Laurence James;** Consul-General at Geneva since 1969; *b* 16 Dec. 1917; *s* of Albert Victor and Margaret Evans; *m* 1940, Clare Mary (*née* Kolb); one *d. Educ:* Alsop High Sch., Liverpool; Univ. of Liverpool (BA Hons, French); Univ. of Rennes (Diploma). Reader in the Faculté des Lettres, Univ. of Rennes, 1938-39. HM Forces (Intell. Corps), 1939-45. Foreign Office, Asst Principal, 1946-47; Bd of Inland Revenue (HM Inspector of Taxes), 1947-49; rejoined Foreign Service and apptd to Brussels, 1950-51; HM Vice-Consul, Khorramshahr, 1951-52; FO, 1952-54; Second Sec. and Vice-Consul, Ciudad Trujillo, Dominican Republic, 1954-57 (Chargé d'Affaires, 1955 and 1957); FO, 1957-63 (Asst Head of Communications, 1959); HM Consul, New York, 1963-66; Asst Head of Personnel Dept (Ops), DSAO, 1966-69. *Recreations:* swimming, music. *Address:* c/o Foreign and Commonwealth Office, SW1. *Club:* Royal Commonwealth Society.

**EVANS, L(eonard) G(lyde) Lavington,** CIE 1935; ICS; *b* 9 Nov. 1888; *s* of Frederick Lavington Evans; *m* 1925, Barbara Joan, *e d* of A. Durant Watson, Mill House, Mitcham Common; two *s. Educ:* Harrow; New Coll., Oxford. Entered ICS 1912; served in Bihar and Orissa until selected for Political Dept Govt of India; served as Political Officer in Mesopotamia 1918-20; thereafter in Indian States; officiating Agent to the Governor-Gen. Eastern States, 1935; officiated Resident, Mysore and Chief Commissioner, Coorg, 1935-36; retired, 1938. *Address:* Blake's House, Halse, Taunton, Somerset. *T:* Bishop's Lydeard 235.

**EVANS, Lindley;** *see* Evans, (Harry) Lindley.

**EVANS, Dr Luther Harris;** Director, International Collections, Columbia University New York, since 1962; *b* near Sayersville, Bastrop County, Texas, USA, 13 Oct. 1902; *s* of George Washington and Lillie Johnson Evans; *m* 1925, Helen Murphy; one *s. Educ:* University of Texas; Leland Stanford Univ., USA. AB 1923, MA 1924 Texas; PhD Stanford, 1927; Doctor of Humane Letters, Yale, 1946; LLD Pa Mil. Coll., 1948, British Columbia Univ., 1948; DL Loyola Coll, 1950; Denison Univ., 1961; DLitt Brown Univ., 1953; LLD Columbia, 1953; LLD Dartmouth Coll., 1956; Doctor of the Humanities Washington Univ., 1959; Marietta Coll. 1962; Dr of Literature Adelphi Coll., 1960. Instructor in freshman orientation course in problems of citizenship, Stanford Univ., 1924-27; Instructor in Government, New York Univ., 1927-28; Instructor in Political Science, Dartmouth Coll., 1928-30; Asst Prof. of Politics, Princeton Univ., 1930-35; Dir, Historical Records Survey of Work Projects Administration, 1935-39; Dir of Legislative Reference Service, Library of Congress, 1939-40; Chief Asst Librarian, on occasion Acting Librarian of Congress, 1940-45; Librarian of Congress, 1945-53. Member: UNESCO Executive Board, 1949-53; US Nat. Commission for UNESCO, 1946-52 (Chm. 1952); (adviser, London Conference on an international educational and cultural organisation, 1945; deleg. or adviser, General Conf., UNESCO, 1947-53); Dir-Gen. United Nations Educational, Scientific and Cultural Organisation, 1953-58; Mem. US National Commission for UNESCO, 1959-63; Senior Staff Mem. Brookings Instn, Washington, DC, 1959-61; Dir Nat. Educn Assoc. Project on Educational Implications of Automation, Washington, DC, 1961-62; Chm., Washington Area Cttee on Refugees, 1960-62; Chm., US Cttee for Refugees (life mem.); Member Nat. Board: UNA of USA, 1964-69; Amer. Civil Liberties Union, 1964-69; Chm. Exec. Cttee, Commn to Study Organisation of Peace, 1966-. Hon. Vice-Pres. Library Association (Eng.); Hon. Mem., Association of Special Libraries and Information Bureaux (Eng.); Member: American Library Assoc. (life-mem.); Nat. Education Assoc.; American Political Science Assoc.; Soc. for Internat. Development. Decorations awarded by: Brazil, France, Japan, Lebanon and Peru. *Publications:* The Virgin Islands, from naval base to new deal, 1945; Survey of Federal (US) Departmental Libraries, 1961; The Decade of Development: problems and issues (with others), 1966; articles and book reviews in professional journals. *Address:* 25 Claremont Avenue, New York, NY 10027, USA. *Club:* Cosmos (Washington, DC).

**EVANS, Maurice;** Actor-manager; *s* of Alfred Herbert Evans, JP (Dorset). *Educ:* Grocers' Company Sch. Commenced theatrical career at Festival Theatre, Cambridge; later in a series of plays at Wyndham's, London; made his first successes in John van Druten's

Diversion and R. C. Sherriff's Journey's End; following several years of appearances in West End became leading man at the Old Vic, where he was seen as Hamlet, Richard II, Petruchio, Benedick, etc.; went to America, 1936, to play Romeo to Katharine Cornell's Juliet; also appeared as the Dauphin in St Joan, Napoleon in St Helena. Produced and played title role Richard II, New York City, 1937; uncut Hamlet, 1938-39; produced and played Falstaff in Henry IV (Part 1), 1939; appeared as Malvolio in Twelth Night with Helen Hayes, 1940-41; produced and played title role in Macbeth, New York City, 1941-42; in each play toured provinces extensively. Went on a lecture tour in aid of British War Relief, 1941. Captain US Army, 1942; disch. with rank of Major, 1945. Played Hamlet in own GI version, 1945-46, New York; 1946-47, in provinces (acting version published Doubleday & Co., 1947). Produced and starred in Man and Superman, New York, 1947-48, establishing record New York run for play of Bernard Shaw; toured provinces, 1948-49; produced, and co-starred with Edna Best in Terence Rattigan's Browning Version, 1949; starred in Shaw's The Devil's Disciple, New York, and toured provinces, 1950; revived Richard II at NY City Center, 1951; starred in Dial 'M' for Murder, New York, 1952-54, and toured provinces, 1954; starred in Shaw's The Apple Cart, New York and provinces, 1956-57; produced and starred in Shaw's Heartbreak House, New York, 1959-60; starred in Tenderloin (musical), New York, 1960-61; The Aspern Papers, New York; 1961-62; with Helen Hayes in Shakespeare Revisited, A Program For Two Players, at Stratford (USA) and on tour, 1962-63; produced The Teahouse of the August Moon (Pulitzer-Critics' prize), 1953; No Time for Sergeants, 1955; Artistic Supervisor, New York City Center Theatre Company, 1949-51. Made first American picture 1950, co-starring with Ethel Barrymore in Kind Lady; also made Androcles and the Lion, Warlord, Jack of Diamonds, Planet of the Apes, Rosemary's Baby, Thin Air, Beneath the Planet of the Apes, and, in England, Gilbert and Sullivan, 1952 and Macbeth, 1960. Became United States citizen, 1941. *Address:* c/o Lloyd V. Almirall, 1 Chase Manhattan Plaza, New York, NY 10005, USA. *Club:* Players (New York).

**EVANS, Merlyn Oliver;** Artist; *b* Cardiff, 1910; *s* of Pryce Oliver Evans and Minnie Veronica Evans (*née* Edwards); *m* 1950, Margerie Few; one *s* one *d*. *Educ:* Allan Glen's Sch., Glasgow; Glasgow Sch. of Art; Royal College of Art, London. Haldane travelling scholarship and Royal Exhibition prize. Began exhibiting, International Surrealist Exhibition, London, 1936; Salon de Mai, Paris, 1937. Lived in Natal, SA, 1938-41, and held 1st One-man Show in City Art Gall., Durban, 1939. War of 1939-45 (Italy Star, and war medals); served in N. Africa, Middle East (8th Army) and Italy, 1942-46 (demob, London). Since 1949 has held regular One-man Exhibns in London, also Philadelphia, 1964. Retrospective Exhibn of paintings, etchings and drawings: Whitechapel Art Gall., 1956; Chicago Art Inst., 1967; Exhibition of paintings 1930-68, Marlborough New London Gall., 1968. Paintings and engravings have been included in many internat. exhibns, incl. São Paulo Biennials, 1953-54 and 1961; Brit. Pavilion, 30th Venice Biennale, 1960; Pittsburg International, 1964; Profile 3, Bochum, Germany, 1964; exhibns at Tate Gall. Work in public collections: Tate Gall.; Victoria and Albert Mus.; Nat. Mus. of Wales; Glasgow Mus. and Art Gall; State Galls of NSW and Victoria; Nat. collections in NZ and S Africa; Mus. of Modern Art, New York; Art Institute of Chicago, 1967, etc. Work reprod in: Surrealism (by Herbert Read), British Painting (by Herbert Read); The Modern Movement in Art (by R. H. Wilenski). Gold Medal for Fine Art, National Eisteddfod of Wales, 1966. *Address:* 40a Downshire Hill, NW3. *Club:* Savile.

**EVANS, Meurig;** *see* Evans, David Meurig.

**EVANS, Michael Nordon,** CMG 1964; Permanent Secretary, Ministry of Health and Housing, Kenya, 1960-64, retired; now British Vice-Consul, Cape Town; *b* 27 April 1915; *s* of Christmas and Lilian Margaret Louise Evans, Tunbridge Wells; *m* 1st, 1939, Mary Stockwood; one *d*; 2nd, 1951, Mary Josephine Suzette van Vloten; one *d*. *Educ:* Eastbourne Coll.; Queens' Coll., Cambridge. Apptd District Officer in Colonial Administrative Service, Kenya, 1939; African Courts Officer, Kenya, 1953; Dep. Commissioner for Local Government, 1954; Permanent Sec., 1958. *Recreations:* judo, tennis, golf, photography. *Address:* Glengariff, Stellenbosch Road, Somerset West, Cape Province, South Africa. *Clubs:* Hawks (Cambridge); Nairobi; City (Cape Town).

**EVANS, Lady Olwen Elizabeth C.;** *see* Carey Evans.

**EVANS, Prof. Peter Angus,** DMus; FRCO; Professor of Music, University of Southampton, since Oct. 1961; *b* 7 Nov. 1929; *y s* of Rev. James Mackie Evans and Elizabeth Mary Fraser; *m* 1953, June Margaret Vickery. *Educ:* West Hartlepool Grammar Sch.; St Cuthbert's Soc., University of Durham. BA (1st cl. hons Music), 1950; BMus, MA 1953; DMus 1958; FRCO 1952. Music Master, Bishop Wordsworth's Sch., Salisbury, 1951-52. Lecturer in Music, University of Durham, 1953-61. Conductor, Palatine Opera Group, 1956-61; Opera Conductor, Hovingham Festival, 1959; Conductor, Southampton Philharmonic Soc., 1965-. *Publications:* Sonata for Oboe and Piano, 1953; Three Preludes for Organ, 1955; Edns of 17th Century Chamber Music, 1956-58; contributor to Die Musik, in Geschichte und Gegenwart, since 1955, to A Concise Encyclopædia of Music, 1958, and to the New Oxford History of Music; Writer and reviewer, especially on 17th century and contemporary music. *Address:* 9 Bassett Close, Southampton. *T:* Southampton 68125.

**EVANS, Dr Philip Rainsford,** CBE 1968; Children's Physician and Director of Department of Paediatrics, Guy's Hospital, since 1946; Physician, The Hospital for Sick Children, Great Ormond Street, since 1946; *b* 14 April 1910; 2nd *s* of Charles Irwin Evans, headmaster of Leighton Park Sch., and Katharine Evans; *m* 1935, Barbara Dorothy Fordyce Hay-Cooper; three *s* one *d*. *Educ:* Sidcot Sch., Winscombe, Som; Leighton Park Sch., Reading; Manchester University. BSc 1930, MSc 1941, MB, ChB 1933, MD 1941, Manchester; MRCP 1935, FRCP 1945, London. Rockefeller Travelling Research Fellow, 1937-38; Asst Pædiatrician, Johns Hopkins Hosp., Baltimore, 1938-39; Asst Physician to Children's Dept, King's Coll. Hosp., London, 1939-46. Served War of 1939-45, RAMC, N Africa and Italy, 1942-46 (despatches); Hon. Col AMS. Editor, Archives of Disease in Childhood, 1947-54. Mem., British, French and American Pædiatric Socs. Member, Cttee on Milk Composition, 1957-59, Ministry of Agriculture, Fisheries and Food. FRSM (Pres., Section of Pædiatrics, 1968-69); Hon. Sec. British Pædiatric Assoc., 1954-59; Hon. Consultant to the Army in Pædiatrics, 1962-66; Visiting Prof., Faculty of Medicine, Saigon, 1967-68; late Examr

Universities of Bristol, Leeds, Birmingham, Cambridge, and RCP; Mem. Council, RCP, 1962-65. (Jointly) Dawson Williams Prize, BMA, 1969. *Publications:* (joint) Infant Feeding and Feeding Difficulties, 1954; Jt Editor, Garrod, Batten and Thursfield's Diseases of Children, 1953; original papers in med. journals and chapters in textbooks. *Address:* 24 Abbey Road, NW8. *T:* 01-624 1668.

**EVANS, Phyllis Mary Carlyon,** MA; Headmistress, St Swithun's School, Winchester, since 1952; *b* 17 April 1913; *d* of L. L. C. Evans, late Headmaster of Swanbourne House Sch., Bletchley, Bucks, and of Mrs M. Evans (*née* Gore-Browne), Carlyon Cottage, Kingsgate Road, Winchester. *Educ:* Wycombe Abbey Sch., Bucks; St Hugh's Coll., Oxford. Lit Hum, 1935. Classics mistress, St Mary's, Calne, 1935-39; Yates Theology Scholar St Hugh's Coll., Oxford, 1939-40; Degree in Theology, 1940; MA 1940. Senior Classics mistress, The Alice Ottley Sch., Worcester, 1940-45; Head Mistress, Wellington Diocesan Sch. for Girls, Marton, New Zealand, 1946-51. Member: Women's Cttee NZ Nat. Council of Churches, 1948-51; Education Cttee, NZNCC, 1950-51; Representative of Winchester Diocese in Church Assembly, 1957-70; Mem. Winchester Dio. Bd of Finance; Mem. Dio. Ordination Candidates' Cttee; Vice-Chm., Dio. Educn Coun.; Pres., Assoc. of Heads of Girls Boarding Schools, 1970. *Publications:* articles on religious education in Studies (published by NZ Nat. Council of Churches), 1949, 1950, 1951. *Recreation:* cooking. *Address:* St Swithun's School, Winchester. *T:* Winchester 61316. *Club:* English-Speaking Union.

**EVANS, Very Rev. Raymond Ellis;** Dean of Monmouth, since 1953, and Vicar of St Woolos, Newport, Mon, since 1953; *m* 1944, Alice Craigie, *d* of John and Alice Logan, Stirling, Scotland; two *c*. *Educ:* St David's Coll., Lampeter; St John's Coll., Oxford (MA). Deacon, 1934; Priest, 1935; Curate of Penmaen, 1934-36, of St John the Evangelist, Newport, 1936-44; Vicar of St Andrew's, Newport, 1944-47; Examining Chaplain to Bishop of Monmouth, 1946; Vicar of Blackwood, 1947-52; Sec. Monmouth Diocesan Conf., 1951; Vicar of St Mark, Newport, 1952-53. *Address:* The Deanery, Stow Hill, Newport, Mon. *T:* Newport 63338.

**EVANS, Raymond John Morda,** MA, PhD; JP; Headmaster, Silcoates School, since 1960; *b* 1 Oct. 1917; 2nd *s* of late Rev. J. Morda Evans, Congregational Minister; *m* 1942, Catherine Mair Gernos Davies, *er d* of late Rev. J. Gernos Davies, Congregational Minister; one *s* two *d* (and one *s* decd). *Educ:* Silcoates Sch., near Wakefield; (Casberd Scholar) St John's Coll., Oxford. BA Oxon (Mod. Langs), 1939, MA 1942; MA, PhD London (Russian Lang. and Lit.), 1959. Dauntsey's Sch., 1939-40; Intelligence Corps (Captain), 1940-46; Leeds Grammar School, 1946-52; Head of Dept of Modern Languages, Royal Naval Coll., Greenwich, 1952-60. *Publications:* contrib. to Slavonic and Eastern European Review, and to Mariners' Mirror. *Recreation:* swimming. *Address:* Headmaster's House, Silcoates School, near Wakefield, Yorks. *T:* Wakefield 76915.

**EVANS, Prof. Rhydwyn Harding,** CBE 1958; MSc, DSc Manchester, PhD Leeds; FICE, FIMechE, FIStructE, MSocCE France, FICE, Hon. MIPlantE; Professor of Civil Engineering and Administrative Head of Engineering Departments, University of Leeds, 1946-68, Emeritus Professor, 1968; *b* 9 Oct. 1900; *s* of late David Evans, Tygwyn, Pontardulais, Glam; *m* 1929, Dilys Elizabeth, *o c* of late George Rees, Welsh Poet and Hymnologist, and Kate Ann Rees, London; one *s*. *Educ:* Llanelly Grammar Sch.; University of Manchester. Mercantile Marine, 1918-20. BSc Graduate Prizeman, 1923; MSc 1928; PhD 1932; DSc 1943: Hon. DesSc Ghent, 1953; Demonstrator, Asst Lecturer, Lecturer, Senior Lecturer and later Reader in Civil Engineering, University of Leeds, 1926-46. Dean, Faculty of Tech. University of Leeds, 1948-51. Pro-Vice-Chancellor, University of Leeds, 1961-65. Chm., Yorks Branch of Instn of Structural Engineers, 1940-41, 1955-56 and 1958-59. Chm. Yorks Assoc. of Instn of Civil Engineers, 1942-43 and 1952-53; Vice-Pres. Instn of Structural Engineers, 1948-49; Mem. Council Instn Civil Engineers, 1949-52. Hon. Mem., Concrete Soc., 1970. Hon. DTech Bradford, 1970. telford Premiums, 1942-43-44; George Stephenson Gold Medal, 1956; Institution of Water Engineers, Instn Premium, 1953; Reinforced Concrete Assoc. Medal, 1961; Research Diploma, 1965, and Certif. of Commendation, 1970, Instn of Struct. Engrs. *Publications:* Prestressed Concrete (with E. W. Bennett), 1962; Concrete Plain, Reinforced Prestressed, Shell (with C. B. Wilby), 1963; papers on elasticity and plasticity of concrete and other building materials; strain and stress distribution in reinforced concrete beams and arches; pre-stressed concrete; extensibility, cracking and tensile stress-strain of concrete; bond stresses; shear stresses; combined bending and shear stresses; torsional stresses; preflexed pre-stressed concrete beams; lightweight aggregate concrete; vibration and pressure moulding of concrete in Journals of Institutions of Civil, Struct. and Water Engineers, Concrete Soc., Philosophical Magazine, Engineer, Engineering, Civil Engineering and Public Works. *Recreations:* motoring, travel, gardening. *Address:* The University, Leeds. *T:* 31751.

**EVANS, Sir (Robert) Charles,** Kt 1969; MA, FRCS; Principal, University College of North Wales; Vice-Chancellor, University of Wales, 1965-67; *b* 19 Oct 1918; *o s* of late R. C. Evans and of Mrs Charles Evans; *m* 1957, Denise Nea Morin; three *s*. *Educ:* Shrewsbury Sch.; University Coll., Oxford. BM, BCh Oxon 1943; MA Oxon 1947; FRCS 1949. RAMC, 1943-46 (despatches). Surgical Registrar, United Liverpool Hosps, and Liverpool Regional Hosps, 1947-57. Hunterian Prof., Royal College Surg. Eng., 1953. Dep. Leader, Mt Everest Expedition, 1953; Leader, Kangchenjunga Expedition, 1955; Pres., Alpine Club, 1967-70; Mem. Council, Royal Geog. Society, 1960-61. Hon. DSc Wales, 1956. Cullum Medal, American Geog. Soc., 1954; Livingstone Medal, Scottish Geog. Soc., 1955; Founder's Medal, Royal Geog. Society, 1956. *Publications:* Eye on Everest, 1955; On Climbing, 1956; Kangchenjunga–The Untrodden Peak, 1956; articles in Alpine Journal, Geographical Journal, etc. *Recreations:* mountaineering, sailing. *Address:* Bryn Haul, Bangor, N Wales. *T:* Bangor 2144. *Club:* Alpine.

**EVANS, Very Rev. Seiriol John Arthur,** CBE 1969; Dean of Gloucester since 1953; *b* 22 Nov. 1894; *er s* of Rev. John Arthur Evans, DD, Sible Hedingham, Essex, and Amelia Annie Price; *m* 1928, Selina Georgiana, *d* of Rev. Charles Francis Townley, CBE, Fulbourn Manor, Cambridge; no *c*. *Educ:* King's Sch., Worcester; King's Coll., Cambridge; Salisbury Theological Coll. Asst Master at Felsted Sch., 1917-19; Deacon, 1920; Priest, 1921; Curate of St Mary and All Saints, Kidderminster, 1920-

22; Minor Canon and Sacrist of Gloucester Cathedral and Assistant Master at King's Sch., Gloucester, 1922-23; Precentor of Ely Cathedral and Headmaster of the Choir Sch., 1923-29; Rector of Upwell-Christchurch 1929-47. Chaplain RNVR, 1940-45. FSA 1935; FRHistSoc 1940; Proctor in Convocation for Diocese of Ely, 1940-47; Archdeacon of Wisbech, 1945-53; Rector of Upwell-St Peter, 1947-53. Chm., Council for the Care of Churches, 1954. Mem. of the Royal Commission on Historical Manuscripts, 1957; Church Commissioner, 1958-68; Trustee, National Portrait Gallery, 1963-70. *Publications:* A Short History of Ely Cathedral, 1925; Ely Chapter Ordinances (Camden Misc.: Vol. XVII), 1940. *Recreation:* fishing. *Address:* The Deanery, Gloucester. *Club:* United Service.

**EVANS, Sir Sidney Harold;** *see* Evans, Sir Harold.

**EVANS, Rev. Canon Sydney Hall;** Dean of King's College, London, since 1956; Hon. Canon of Southwark since 1959; *b* 23 July 1915; *s* of William and Winifred Evans; *m* 1941, Eileen Mary (*née* Evans); two *s* one *d*. *Educ:* Bristol Grammar Sch.; St Chad's Coll., Durham. MA 1940, BD 1945, Durham. Deacon 1939, priest 1940; Curate of Bishop Auckland, Co. Durham, 1939-41; Curate of Ferryhill, Co. Durham, 1941-43. Chaplain RAFVR, 1943-45. Chaplain and Lecturer, King's Coll., London, 1945-48; Warden of King's Coll. post-graduate coll. at Warminster, 1948-56. Preacher of Gray's Inn, 1960-; Exam. Chaplain to Bishops of Southwark, Chelmsford, Truro, Durham. FKC 1955. *Recreations:* walking and bird-watching. *Address:* 72 Vincent Square, Westminster, SW1. *T:* 01-834 3650.

**EVANS, (Thomas) Godfrey,** CBE 1960; *b* Finchley, 1920; *s* of A. G. L. Evans; *m* Jean Tritton. *Educ:* Kent Coll., Canterbury. Joined Kent County Staff at age of 16. First kept wicket for England in Test *v* India, 1946; first overseas Test tour, Australia and New Zealand, 1946-47; has also played in Test matches in W Indies and S Africa. Has played in 91 Test matches (a world record); dismissed 218 batsmen in Test cricket from behind the stumps, 88 more than Oldfield, the previous record-holder; the only wicket-keeper to have dismissed more than 200 victims and scored over 2000 runs in Test cricket; holds world record for not conceding a bye while 1,054 runs were scored in a Test series (Australia, 1946); holds record for longest Test innings without scoring (95 minutes *v* Australia, Adelaide, 1947); holds jointly, with Charles Barnett, record for fastest score before lunch in a Test match (98 *v* India, Lord's, 1952); in making 47 in 29 minutes was three runs off the fastest 50 in Test cricket (*v* Australia, Old Trafford, 1956); the only Englishman to have toured Australia with MCC four times since War of 1939-45. *Publications:* Behind the Stumps, 1951; Action in Cricket, 1956; The Gloves Are Off, 1960. *Recreations:* golf, squash. *Address:* The Jolly Drover, Hillbrow, East Liss, near Petersfield, Hants.

**EVANS, Thomas Henry,** CBE 1957; DL; LLM; Clerk of the Peace, Clerk of the County Council, and Clerk to Lieutenancy for Staffordshire, since 1942; Clerk of Staffordshire Magistrates Courts Committee, since 1952; Clerk of Staffordshire County and Stoke-on-Trent Police Authority, since 1968; *b* 1907; *s* of late Henry Evans, Bootle, Lancs. *Educ:* Merchant Taylors' Sch., Crosby, Lancs; University of Liverpool (LLM). Admitted Solicitor, 1930. Asst Solicitor with Surrey County Council, 1930-35; Asst County Solicitor and later Dep. Clerk of Staffs County Council, 1935-42. Member: Cttee on Consolidation of Highway Law, 1958; Interdepartmental Cttee (Streatfeild) on business of Criminal Courts, 1958; Nat. Advisory Coun. on Training of Magistrates, 1964-. DL Staffs, 1947. *Publication:* contributor to Macmillan's Local Government Law and Administration. *Address:* 8 High Park, Newport Road, Stafford.

**EVANS, Trefor Ellis,** CMG 1956; OBE 1948; Professor of International Politics, University of Wales, Aberystwyth, since 1969; *b* 4 March 1913; *s* of late John and Mary Evans; *m* Nest Margaret, *d* of late Trefor Williams, OBE and of Margaret Williams; two *d*. *Educ:* Cowbridge; Balliol Coll., Oxford; Hamburg. BA Oxon, 1934; DrPhil Hamburg, 1937. Appointed HM Consular Service, 1937; Vice-Consul, Beirut, 1937-39, Alexandria, 1939-41; Asst Oriental Sec. and Private Sec. to the Ambassador, with local rank of 3rd Sec. in Diplomatic Service, at HM Embassy, Cairo, 1941; local rank of 2nd Sec., 1942; Vice-Consul and Actg Consul, Damascus, 1945; Actg Consul, Aleppo, 1946; Actg 1st Sec., HM Legation, Beirut, 1946; 1st Sec. HM Foreign Service, 1946; Chargé d'Affaires, Beirut, 1947 and 1948; Head of Middle East Secretariat, FO, 1949-52; Oriental Couns., HM Embassy, Cairo, 1952-56; Counsellor Berne, 1957-59; Consul-Gen., Algiers, 1959-62; HM Ambassador to: Algeria, 1962-64; Syria, 1964-67; Iraq, 1968-69. Coronation Medal, 1953. *Recreation:* tennis. *Address:* 20 New Street, Aberystwyth, Cardiganshire; Plas Maes-y-Groes, Talybont, Bangor. *Club:* Royal Automobile.

**EVANS, Sir Trevor (Maldwyn),** Kt 1967; CBE 1963; Director, Beaverbrook Newspapers Ltd, 1954-69; Industrial Consultant, Beaverbrook Group, since 1967; *b* 21 Feb. 1902; *s* of late Samuel Evans and late Margaret Evans, Abertridwr, Glam; *m* 1930, Margaret, *d* of late J. B. Gribbin and late S. J. Gribbin, Heaton Moor, Ches; one *s* one *d*. *Educ:* Pontypridd Gram. Sch. Journalist, Glamorgan Free Press, Pontypridd, 1922-24; South Wales News, 1924-26; Daily Dispatch, 1926-28; Daily Mail, 1928-30; Daily Express, 1930- (Industrial Correspondent, 1930-67). Mem. Press Council, 1964-. *Publications:* Strange Fighters, We British, 1943; Ernest Bevin, biography, 1946; The Great Bohunkus, biography of Ian Mackay, 1953. *Recreations:* watching Rugby and cricket; listening to discussion groups. *Address:* 17 Wolsey Close, Kingston Hill, Surrey. *T:* 01-942 6016. *Clubs:* Reform, Press.

*See also D. E. Butler.*

**EVANS, Ulick Richardson,** FRS 1949; ScD Cambridge 1932; ScD *hc* Dublin 1947; scientific writer and consultant; Emeritus Reader in Science of Metallic Corrosion, Cambridge University (Reader, 1945-54); Hon. Fellow, King's College, Cambridge; *b* 31 March 1889; unmarried. *Educ:* Marlborough Coll.; King's Coll., Cambridge. Served European War, 1914-18, Army (Signal Service), 1914-19. Engaged in research, writing and teaching at Cambridge Univ., 1921-55 (main subjects: Metallic Corrosion and the growth of thin Films on Metals). Hon. Dr of Metallurgy, Sheffield Univ., 1961. Palladium Medallist, Electrochemical Soc., 1955; Hothersall Medallist, 1957; Gold Medallist, Inst. of Metal Finishing, 1961. *Publications:* Metals and Metallic Compounds (4 vols), 1923; Corrosion of Metals, 1924 and 1926; Metallic Corrosion, Passivity and Protection, 1937 and 1946; Introduction to Metallic Corrosion, 1948 (and 1963); The Corrosion and Oxidation of Metals, 1960, and 1968; papers in Proc. Royal Society, Trans. Faraday Soc., J. Chem. Soc., J. Iron Steel Inst., J. Inst. Met., etc. *Recreation:* swimming. *Address:* 19 Manor Court, Grange Road, Cambridge. *T:* Cambridge 55005. *Club:* Oxford and Cambridge.

**EVANS, Sir Vincent;** *see* Evans, Sir W. V. J.

**EVANS, William,** MD, DSc, FRCP; Consulting Physician: to Cardiac Department, London Hospital; to National Heart Hospital; and to Institute of Cardiology; Consulting Cardiologist to Royal Navy, 1946-67; Hon. Cardiologist to Royal Society of Musicians; *b* 24 Nov. 1895; *s* of late Eben Evans, Tregaron, Cardiganshire; *m* 1936, Christina (*d* 1964), *d* of late John Lessels Downie, Kirkcaldy. *Educ:* University Coll. of Wales, Aberystwyth; London Hospital; London Univ., MB, BS (London) 1925, hons in Surgery; MD (London) 1927; FRCP 1937; DSc (London) 1944; K. E. D. Payne Prize in Pathology, 1927; Hutchinson Triennial Prize in Clinical Surgery, 1929; Liddle Triennial Prize in Pathology, 1931; Sydney Body Gold Medal, 1954; Strickland Goodall Lect., 1942; Finlayson Lect., 1947; St Cyres Lect., 1952; Gerrish Milliken Lect., University of Philadelphia, 1954; First Rufus Stolp Memorial Lect., University of Evanston, Ill., 1954; Carbutt Memorial Lect., 1957; Schorstein Lect., 1961; Wiltshire Lect., 1961. First Leonard Abrahamson Memorial Lecture, Royal College of Surgeons in Ireland, Dublin, 1963; Sir Thomas and Lady Dixon Lecture, Belfast, 1965. Formerly Asst Dir to Medical Unit, Paterson Medical Officer and Chief Asst to Cardiac Dept, London Hosp. Served European War, 1914-18, Combatant Officer, Lancs Fusiliers, and Battalion Education Officer. Hon. DSc (Wales), 1961. Mem. American Heart Assoc.; Hon. Mem. British Cardiac Soc.; Hon. Mem. Soc. of Phys. in Wales. Guest Lecturer at Centenary Meetings of Royal Melbourne Hospital, 1948. High Sheriff of Cardiganshire, 1959. Hon. Mem. Order of Druids, 1960. *Publications:* Student's Handbook of Electrocardiography, 1934; Cardiography (2nd edn, 1954); Cardiology (2nd edn, 1956); Cardioscopy, 1952; Diseases of the Heart and Arteries, 1964; Journey to Harley Street, 1969; various papers on medical and cardiological subjects in Quarterly Jl of Med., Lancet, BMJ and Brit. Heart Jl. *Recreations:* fishing, gardening. *Address:* Bryndomen, Tregaron, Cardiganshire, West Wales.

**EVANS, William Edis Webster;** *b* London, 26 Aug. 1908; *yr s* of late Rev. William Evans, Rector of Brondesbury; *m* 1956, Jean Hilda, *widow* of Andrew Allan and *d* of late Robert Smith Marshall, Forfar, Angus. *Educ:* Merchant Taylors' Sch., London. Editorial staff, John o' London's Weekly, 1928-39; Dep. Editor, 1951; Editor, 1953-54. Asst Editor, PTO, 1939; Gen. Editor, Country Life Books, 1954-67. Served RAF, 1940-47; Middle East, Italy, Germany; Wing Comdr (despatches). *Publications:* Editor (with Tom Scott) of In Praise of Golf, 1949; The Golfers' Year, 1950 and 1951; Rubs of the Green, 1969; The Encyclopaedia of Golf, 1971. *Recreations:* golf, reading. *Address:* 16 Chatterton Court, Kew Road, Richmond, Surrey. *T:* 01-940 7789. *Club:* Royal Mid-Surrey Golf.

**EVANS, William Ewart;** Acting Chief Justice, High Court of Lesotho, since 1968; a former Judge of High Court of Northern Rhodesia and of the Rhodesia and Nyasaland Court of Appeal, retired in 1962; *b* 24 May 1899; *s* of late John William Evans and Catherine Evans, Swansea, S Wales; *m* 1919, Agnes May Wilson; one *s* four *d*. *Educ:* Swansea Grammar Sch. Served European War, 1917-19, in King's Royal Rifle Corps and Royal Army Service Corps. Called to Bar, 1934; practised on South Wales Circuit; Colonial Legal Service, 1938; acted in various judicial capacities; Resident Magistrate, Lusaka, Livingstone, N'Dola, Broken Hill, and Luanshya, 1940; Acting Judge High Court, 1951, 1953. Judge, High Court of Lesotho, 1967-68. *Recreation:* gardening. *Address:* 7 Guest Avenue, Alexandra Park, Salisbury, Rhodesia.

**EVANS, William John;** retired as General Secretary of Associated Society of Locomotive Engineers and Firemen (Oct. 1960-July 1963); Civil Representative, National Association for Employment of Regular Sailors, Soldiers and Airmen, since 1962; *b* 4 Oct. 1899; *m* 1919; one *s*. *Educ:* Eccles Grammar Sch. Joined LNW Railway, 1916. Royal Navy Service, 1916-21. Great War and Victory Medals; Mine Clearance Service Medal. Served as Executive Cttee Mem. of Trade Union, 1934-39; Pres. of Executive Cttee, 1937-38-39; Organising Sec., 1939-56; Asst Gen. Sec., 1956-60. Mem., Eastern Region Railways Board, 1963-66. Mem., Eccles Town Council, 1932-34. *Recreations:* boxing, bowling, and Association football. *Address:* 16 Hollies Drive, Bayston Hill, Shrewsbury, Salop.

**EVANS, Sir William Shirley W. W.;** *see* Worthington-Evans.

**EVANS, Sir (William) Vincent (John),** KCMG 1970 (CMG 1959); MBE 1945; Legal Adviser, Foreign and Commonwealth Office, since 1968; *b* 20 Oct. 1915; *s* of Charles Herbert Evans and Elizabeth (*née* Jenkins); *m* 1947, Joan Mary Symons; one *s* two *d*. *Educ:* Merchant Taylors' Sch.; Wadham Coll., Oxford. 1st Class Hons, Jurisprudence, 1937; BCL, 1938; MA, 1941; elected Cassel Scholar, Lincoln's Inn, 1937; called to Bar, Lincoln's Inn, 1939. Served in HM Forces, 1939-46. Legal Adviser (Lt-Col) to British Military Administration, Cyrenaica, 1945-46; Asst Legal Adviser, Foreign Office, 1947-54; Legal Counsellor, UK Permanent Mission to the United Nations, 1954-59; Legal Counsellor, FO, 1959-60; Dep. Legal Adviser, FO, 1960-68. Chm., European Cttee on Legal Cooperation, Council of Europe, 1969-. *Recreation:* gardening. *Address:* 4 Bedford Road, Moor Park, Northwood, Mddx. *T:* Northwood 24085.

**EVANS-ANFOM, Emmanuel,** FRCSE 1955; Vice-Chancellor, University of Science and Technology, Kumasi, Ghana; *b* 7 Oct. 1919; *m* 1952, Leonora Francetta Evans; three *s* one *d*. *Educ:* Achimota School; Edinburgh University (MB; ChB; DTM&H). House Surgeon, Dewsbury Infirmary, 1948-49; Medical Officer, Gold Coast Medical Service, 1950-56, Specialist Surgeon, 1956-67; Senior Lecturer, Ghana Medical School, 1966-67. *Publication:* Aetiology and Management of Intestinal Perforations, Ghana Med. Jl, 1963. *Recreations:* hockey, music, art. *Address:* University of Science and Technology, Kumasi, Ghana. *T:* 3201.

**EVANS BEVAN, Sir David (Martyn),** 1st Bt, *cr* 1958, of Cadoxton-Juxta-Neath; Chairman, Evans & Bevan Ltd; Director, Whitbread Wales Ltd; *b* 4 March 1902; *s* of Evan and Caroline Evans Bevan; *m* 1929, Eira Winifred Glanley; one *s* one *d*. *Educ:* Uppingham. Director of: Barclays Bank Ltd; Phœnix Assurance Co. Ltd. Governor of London House; Mem., Shipwrights Company. JP 1932-

67; DL Glamorganshire; High Sheriff of Breconshire, 1929-30, of Glamorganshire, 1951-52; Freeman of Neath, 1949; Freeman of Port Talbot, 1952; KStJ; Sub-Prior, Order of St John for Wales. *Recreations:* shooting and fishing. *Heir:* *s* Martyn E. Evans Bevan [*b* 1 April 1932; *m* 1957, Jennifer Marion, *d* of Robert Hugh Stevens, Eardisley, Herefordshire; three *s*]. *Address:* Twyn-yr-Hydd, Margam, Port Talbot, Glam. *T:* Port Talbot 3712. *Club:* Carlton.

*See also Lord Leslie.*

**EVANS LOMBE, Vice-Adm. Sir Edward (Malcolm),** KCB 1954 (CB 1946); DL, JP; RN retired; *b* 15 Oct. 1901; *s* of Major A. Evans Lombe, 40 Elm Park Gardens, SW10; *m* 1931, Diana Vivien Katharine Mackeson; one *s* one *d*. *Educ:* RN Coll., Dartmouth. Naval Asst to 3rd Sea Lord and Controller, Sept. 1939-April 1942; Commanding Officer HMS Glasgow, 1942-43; Director of Gunnery Div., Admiralty, 1943-44; Chief of Staff, Eastern Fleet, Aug.-Dec. 1944; Chief of Staff, British Pacific Fleet, 1944-46; Naval ADC to the King, 1948-49; Flag Officer, Training Sqdn, 1949-50; a Lord Commissioner of the Admiralty and Dep. Chief of Naval Staff, 1950-53; Comdr, Allied Naval Forces in Northern Europe, 1953-55; retired, 1955. JP Norfolk, 1960, DL 1961; High Sheriff, Norfolk, 1962. *Address:* Marlingford Hall, Norwich. *T:* Honingham 319. *Club:* Naval and Military.

**EVANS-PRITCHARD, E. E.,** MA Oxon; PhD London; FBA 1956; Professor of Social Anthropology, University of Oxford, 1946-70; Fellow of All Souls (Sub-Warden, 1963-65); *b* 1902; 2nd *s* of late Rev. Thomas John Evans-Pritchard; *m* 1939, Ioma (*d* 1959), *d* of late Rt Hon. G. Heaton Nicholls; three *s* two *d*. *Educ:* Winchester Coll. (Commoner); Exeter Coll., Oxford (Hon. Scholar). Six major and several minor anthropological expeditions to Central, East and North Africa, 1926-39; Prof. of Sociology, Egyptian Univ., Cairo, 1931-34; Leverhulme Fellow, 1935-36; Research Lecturer, Oxford, 1935-40; Hon. Research Asst University Coll., London; Active Service (despatches), 1940-45; Reader, Cambridge, 1945. Pres., Royal Anthropological Inst., 1949-51; Life Pres., Assoc. of Social Anthropologists. Mem., Amer. Philosophical Soc., 1968. Hon. Fellow, SOAS University of London, 1963. Mem. Hon., Inst. Française de Sociologie, 1950; For. Hon. Mem., Amer. Acad. of Arts and Sciences, 1958. Hon. DSc: University of Chicago, 1967; Bristol, 1969; Hon. DLitt Manchester, 1969. *Publications:* Witchcraft, Oracles and Magic among the Azande, 1937; The Nuer, 1940; The Sanusi of Cyrenaica, 1949; Kinship and Marriage among the Nuer, 1951; Social Anthropology, 1951; Nuer Religion, 1956; Essays in Social Anthropology, 1962; The Position of Women in Primitive Societies, 1965; Theories of Primitive Religion, 1965; The Zande Trickster, 1967; and numerous papers in scientific journals. *Recreations:* gardening, bird watching. *Address:* The Ark, Jack Straws Lane, Headington, Oxford.

**EVE,** family name of **Baron Silsoe.**

**EVELEIGH, Sir Edward Walter,** Kt 1968; ERD; MA; **Hon. Mr Justice Eveleigh;** Judge of the High Court of Justice, Queen's Bench Division, since 1968; Chairman, Court of Quarter Sessions, County of Oxford, since 1968 (Deputy Chairman, 1963-68); *b* 8 Oct. 1917; *s* of Walter William and Daisy Emily Eveleigh; *m* 1940, Vilma Bodnar; *m* 1953, Patricia Helen Margaret Bury; two *s* (and one *s* decd). *Educ:* Peter Symonds Sch., Winchester; Brasenose Coll., Oxford. Commissioned in the Royal Artillery (Supplementary Reserve), 1936; served War of 1939-45 (despatches, 1940). Called to Bar, Lincoln's Inn, 1945, Bencher 1968; QC 1961. Recorder of Burton-on-Trent, 1961-64, of Gloucester, 1964-68. *Address:* 128 Home Park Road, Wimbledon, SW19. *T:* 01-947 2314.

**EVELEIGH, Air Vice-Marshal Geoffrey Charles,** CB 1964; OBE 1945; RAF retired; *b* 25 Oct. 1912; *s* of Ernest Charles Eveleigh, Henley-on-Thames; *m* 1939, Anthea Josephine, *d* of F. H. Fraser, Ceylon; one *s* one *d*. *Educ:* Brighton Coll.; RAF Coll., Cranwell. Joined RAF, 1932; served War of 1939-45 in Bomber Command and No 2 Group; Dep. Chief of Air Staff, Royal New Zealand Air Force, 1955-57; Air Commodore, 1957; Dir-Gen. of Signals, Air Ministry, 1959-61; Air Vice-Marshal, 1961; Air Officer, Administration, Fighter Command, 1961-64; retd 1965. *Address:* Kingfishers, Mill Lane, Henley-on-Thames, Oxon. *Club:* Royal Air Force.

**EVELEIGH-DE-MOLEYNS,** family name of **Baron Ventry.**

**EVELING, Walter Raphael Taylor,** CBE 1960; Chartered Surveyor, retired, 1968; Dep. Chief Valuer, Inland Revenue, 1965-68 (Asst Chief Valuer, 1951); *b* 8 March 1908; *s* of late Raphael Eveling, Hampstead Garden Suburb; *m* 1935, Annie Ferguson Newman, Belfast; one *s*. *Educ:* Paradise House Sch., Stoke Newington. Joined the Valuation Office, Inland Revenue, 1935. FRICS, FAI. *Address:* 11 Thornhill Close, Lezayre, near Ramsey, Isle of Man.

**EVERALL, John Harold;** Hon. Treasurer, Royal Agricultural Society of the Commonwealth, since 1966; *b* 12 Oct. 1908; *s* of late William and Annie Haines Everall, Shrawardine Castle, Shrewsbury; *m* 1935, Breda, *d* of late Gerald J. Sherlock, Town Clerk of Dublin; one *s* one *d*. *Educ:* Malvern Coll. Former Chartered Surveyor and Pedigree Cattle Breeder (retired). War of 1939-45, Intelligence Officer (Captain), 4 Salop Bn, HG. Member original Artificial Insemination Supervisory Cttee set up by Min. of Agric., 1943. Past President: Hereford Herd Book Soc.; Nat. Cattle Breeders' Assoc.; Shropshire and Montgomeryshire Agric. Valuers' Assoc., Shropshire Chamber of Agric.; Vice-Pres., Shropshire and W Midland Agric. Soc., 1964-. Former Mem. Exec. Cttee: Farmers' Club; Royal Smithfield Club; Vice-Chm., Shrewsbury Div. Conservative Assoc., 1946-50; former Hon. Sec., Shropshire, Herefordshire and Mid-Wales branch, RICS. Mem. Council, Royal Agric. Soc. of Eng., 1949-; Vice-Chm., Livestock Cttee of Brit. Agric. Export Council, 1967- (rep. BAEC at Santarem, Portugal, Fairs, 1967 and 1969). Rep. UK: World Confs of Pedigree Hereford Cattle Breeders, Hereford 1951, Kansas City, USA, 1960 and Dublin 1964; Royal Agric. Soc. of the Commonwealth Confs (as one of three delegs) at Sydney 1963, Toronto 1967, Nairobi 1969. Mem., Stapledon Trust Memorial Cttee, 1969-. Internat. Judge of Pedigree Hereford Cattle and former owner of Shrine herd (dispersed 1968). Judged: Palermo, Argentina, 1944 and 1963; Sydney, 1963; Nairobi (Borans), 1969; also at Royal of England, Royal Highland, Royal Welsh and Royal Dublin Shows. Director, QMP Ltd, 1958-65. Freeman of Kansas City, USA, and City of London (Liveryman). *Recreations:* shooting, fishing, gardening, beagling; formerly fox-hunting (Mem. S Shropshire Hunt Cttee, 1953-68). *Address:* Ravens Hill, Owslebury, Winchester, Hants. *T:* Owslebury 341. *Clubs:* Travellers'; Cowdray Park Polo.

**EVERARD, Maj.-Gen. Sir Christopher E. W.;** *see* Welby-Everard.

**EVERARD, Lt-Col Sir Nugent Henry,** 3rd Bt, *cr* 1911; late The Duke of Wellington's Regiment (W Riding); *b* 28 Feb. 1905; *er s* of 2nd Bt and Louisa Cole, *d* of R. H. Metge, MP, Athlumney, Navan; *S* father, 1929; *m* 1933, Frances Audrey, *y d* of J. C. Jesson; one *s* one *d*. Retired with the hon. rank of Lt-Col, 1958. *Heir: s* Robin Charles Everard [*b* 5 Oct. 1939; *m* 1963, Ariel Ingrid, *e d* of Col Peter Cleasby-Thompson, The Manor House, Cley-next-the-Sea; two *d*].

**EVEREST, Arthur Ernest,** DSc, PhD, FRIC; Fellow of the Society of Dyers and Colourists; retired; *b* 1888; *m* 1914, Annie Kathleen Broome; two *d*. *Educ:* Wrekin Coll.; University of Birmingham and on the Continent. Formerly Managing Director John W. Leitch & Co. Ltd and associated companies; Vice-Pres. of Royal Institute of Chemistry, 1936-39, Mem. of Council, 1933-36 and 1945-48; Mem. of Council of Assoc. of Brit. Chemical Manufacturers, 1934-54; Mem. of Governing Council Wrekin Coll. *Publications:* two books and various memoirs on Chemical and allied subjects. *Address:* Harborne, Cliddesden Road, Basingstoke, Hants. *T:* Basingstoke 4158.

**EVERETT, Rear-Adm. Douglas Henry,** CB 1950; CBE 1946 (MBE 1919); DSO 1940; *b* 16 June 1900; *s* of Douglas and Blanche Everett, Park House, Broadlands, Romsey; *m* 1932, Margery Annette Yeldham; three *s* one *d*. *Educ:* Oakham Sch.; Cadet HMS Conway, 1913; RN Coll., Dartmouth. Served European War, 1916-18; War of 1939-45 (despatches twice); Flag Officer, Ground Training, 1949-51; Pres. Admiralty Interview Board, 1951-52; retired list, 1952. Chilean Order of Merit, 1939. *Address:* Gillinghams, Milford-on-Sea, Lymington, Hants. *T:* Milford-on-Sea 2368.

**EVERETT, Douglas Hugh,** MBE 1946; Leverhulme Professor of Physical Chemistry, University of Bristol, since 1954; Dean of Faculty of Science, 1966-68; *b* 26 Dec. 1916; *e s* of Charles Everett and Jessie Caroline; *m* 1942, Frances Elizabeth Jessop; two *d*. *Educ:* Grammar Sch., Hampton-on-Thames; University of Reading; Balliol Coll., Oxford. Wantage Scholar, Reading Univ., 1935-38; Kitchener Scholar, 1936-39; BSc, 1938; Ramsay Fellow, 1939-41; DPhil 1942. Special Scientific Duties, WO, 1942-45. ICI Fellow, Oxford Univ., 1945-47; Chemistry Lecturer, Dundee Univ. Coll., 1947; MA 1947; Fellow, Lecturer and Tutor, Exeter Coll., Oxford, 1947-48; Prof. of Chemistry, Dundee Univ. Coll., University of St Andrews, 1948-54. FRSE 1950; DSc 1956. Mem., Building Research Board, DSIR, 1954-61; a Vice-Pres., Faraday Soc., 1958-61, 1963-65, 1968-70; Mem. Chemical Soc. Council, 1961-64. *Publications:* Introduction to Chemical Thermodynamics, 1959; papers on Physical Chemistry in scientific jls. *Address:* School of Chemistry, The University, Bristol.

**EVERETT, Richard Marven Hale,** QC 1952; JP; Recorder of Maidstone since 1968; *b* 26 June 1909; *s* of B. R. Everett, Solicitor; *m* 1935, Kathleen Lucy Eve; one *s*. *Educ:* Repton. Called to Bar, Gray's Inn, 1933; Master of the Bench, Gray's Inn, 1959. Recorder of Deal, 1959-68; Leader, SE Circuit, 1968. Served War of 1939-45, in Army, 1941-43. JP Herts, 1953. *Publications:* Joint Ed. 4 edns of Willis' Workmen's Compensation Acts. *Recreations:* gardening, shooting, golf. *Address:* 54 Ashley Gardens, SW1. *T:* 01-828 3811; Shaw Wood Cottage, Farnham Green, Bishop's Stortford, Herts. *T:* Albury 385; (professional) 5 Paper Buildings, Temple, EC4. *T:* 01-353 2711. *Club:* Royal Automobile.

**EVERINGTON, Geoffrey Devas,** QC 1968; Barrister-at-Law; *b* 4 May 1915; *s* of late Herbert Devas Everington, MB and Muriel Frances Everington, Sanderstead; *m* 1951, Laila Nissen Hovind; four *s* three *d*. *Educ:* Westminster. Called to Bar, Gray's Inn, 1939; commenced practice at Bar, 1945. *Recreations:* music, tennis. *Address:* South Gable, Granville Road, Limpsfield, Oxted, Surrey. *T:* Oxted 4000.

**EVERS, Claude Ronald;** MA; Warden of Pendley Residential Centre of Adult Education, since 1967; *b* 17 Jan. 1908; *s* of late C. P. Evers (formerly housemaster at Rugby Sch.); *m* 1935, Marjorie Janet Ironside Bruce; four *s*. *Educ:* Rugby; Trinity Coll., Oxford. Asst Master, Wellington Coll., 1931-35; Asst Master, Rugby Sch., 1936-40; Headmaster of Berkhamsted Sch., 1946-53; Headmaster of Sutton Valence Sch., 1953-67; War service (Royal Warwicks Regt), 1940-45. Chm., Pendley Shakespeare Festival. *Publication:* Rugby (Blackie's Public School Series), 1939. *Address:* Pendley Manor, Tring, Herts.

**EVERS, H(enry) Harvey,** MS, FRCS, FRCOG; Professor of Obstetrics and Gynæcology, University of Durham, 1950-58 (now Emeritus) also Obstetrician and Gynæcologist in charge of the Department at Royal Victoria Infirmary and Princess Mary Maternity Hospital, Newcastle upon Tyne, 1950-58 (now Hon. Obstetrician and Gynæcologist); Pastoral Visitor, Newcastle Regional Hospital Board; *b* 28 May 1893; 2nd *s* of Charles Henry Evers, Medical Practitioner; *m* 1923, Marian Isabel Graham; two *s*. *Educ:* Royal Grammar Sch., Newcastle upon Tyne; University of Durham. Co. of Northumberland, Sch. and Univ. Schol., 1911; Gibson, Outterson-Wood, etc. Schols, 1914; MB, BS (1st Cl. Hons), Durham, 1916; MS Durham (Hons), 1921; MRCS, LRCP, 1916; FRCS 1921. Surg. Prob. (RNVR), 1914-15; Capt., RAMC, 1916-20. Foundation Mem. Royal College of Obstetrics and Gynæcology, 1933; FRCOG 1937. Pastoral Visitor, Regional Adviser and Assessor, Newcastle upon Tyne, 1948; External Examiner, Univs of London, Liverpool, Manchester, Sheffield, Wales; Examiner Conjoint Bd, RCOG, Central Midwives Bd, etc.; Past Pres. North of England Obst. and Gyn. Soc. Formerly: House Surg. (General, Eye and Throat, Nose and Ear), Royal Victoria Infirmary, Newcastle upon Tyne, 1915; Hon. Asst Surg., Hosp. for Sick Children; Demonstrator in Anatomy and Operative Surgery, 1920; Lectr in Obstetrics and Gynæcology, 1930. *Publications:* various medical. *Recreations:* fishing, golf. *Address:* Oakwood Lodge, Clayton Road, Newcastle upon Tyne 2. *T:* Newcastle upon Tyne 81-4441.

**EVERSON, Sir Frederick (Charles),** KCMG 1968 (CMG 1956); Director, BPB Industries Ltd; economics consultant; *b* 6 Sept. 1910; *s* of Frederick Percival Everson; *m* 1937, Linda Mary Clark; three *s* one *d*. *Educ:* Tottenham County Sch., Middlesex. BSc (Econ.) London. Entered Civil Service, July 1928; Consular Service, Dec. 1934. Chief Administrative Officer, British Embassy, Bonn, Germany, 1953-56; Ambassador to El Salvador, 1956-60; Commercial Counsellor, British Embassy, Stockholm, 1960-63; Minister (Economic), British Embassy, Paris, 1963-68. Chairman, The Dulwich Soc. *Address:* 11 Peckarman's Wood, Dulwich, SE26. *T:* 01-693 8125.

**EVERY, Sir John (Simon),** 12th Bt, *cr* 1641; *b* 24 April 1914; *er s* of Sir Edward Oswald Every, 11th Bt and Lady Ivy Linton Every; *S* father, 1959; *m* 1st, 1938, Annette Constance (marr. diss., 1942), *o c* of late Major F. W. M. Drew, Drewscourt, Co. Cork; 2nd, 1943, Janet Marion, *d* of John Page, Blakeney, Norfolk; one *s* two *d*. *Educ:* Harrow. Served War of 1939-45. Capt., Sherwood Foresters. Business Co. Dir, 1945-60, Dir of private companies. *Recreations:* cricket, tennis, shooting. *Heir: s* Henry John Michael Every; *b* 6 April 1947. *Address:* Egginton, near Derby. *T:* Etwall 245. *Club:* MCC.

**EVETTS, Lieut-Gen. Sir John (Fullerton),** Kt 1951; CB 1939; CBE 1937; MC; *b* 30 June 1891; *s* of late Lieut-Col J. M. Evetts, Tackley Park, Oxon.; *m* 1916, Helen Phyllis, *d* of late Captain C. A. G. Becher, Burghfields, Bourton on the Water, Glos; one *s*. *Educ:* Temple Grove; Lancing; Royal Military Coll., Sandhurst; Staff Coll., Camberley. Entered Army, 1911; joined The Cameronians (Scottish Rifles); served European War, 1914-18 (MC, despatches); Lieut 1913; Captain 1915; temp. Major Machine Gun Corps, 1916; Bt-Major 1929; Substantive, 1929; Bt Lt-Col 1931; Substantive Lt-Col Royal Ulster Rifles, 1934; Col 1935; Maj.-Gen. 1941; employed with Iraq Army, 1925; DAAG War Office, 1932; Commander British Troops in Palestine, 1935; GSO1 Palestine, 1936; Brig. Comd. 16th Inf. Bde, Palestine and Trans-Jordan, 1936-39 (despatches); BGS, HQ, Northern Command, India, 1939-40; Comdr Western (Indept) Dist, India, 1940-41; Divl Comdr, 1941 (despatches); Asst CIGS, 1942; Senior Military Adviser to Minister of Supply, 1944-46; retired pay, 1946; Head of British Ministry of Supply Staff in Australia, 1946-51, and Chief Executive Officer Joint UK-Australian Long Range Weapons, Board of Administration, 1946-49. Managing Dir, 1951-58, Chm., 1958-60, Rotol Ltd and Brit, Messier. Pres., Western Division, YMCA; Chm. of Council, Glos Outward Bound Association; Fellow, Corp. of SS Mary and Nicolas (Woodard Schs). OStJ. Legion of Merit (US), 1943. *Address:* Pepper Cottage, Kemerton, near Tewkesbury, Glos. *Club:* Naval and Military.

**EVILL, Air Chief Marshal Sir Douglas Claude Strathern,** GBE 1946; KCB 1943 (CB 1940); DSC 1916; AFC 1919; *b* 1892; *m* 1920, Henrietta Hortense, *d* of Sir Alexander Drake Kleinwort, 1st Bt; one *s* two *d*. *Educ:* Royal Naval Colleges, Osborne and Dartmouth. Served European War, 1914-19 (DSC, AFC); War of 1939-45 (despatches twice, CB, KCB). Head of Royal Air Force Delegation in Washington, 1942; Vice-Chief of the Air Staff, and addtl Mem. of the Air Council, 1943-46; Air Chief Marshal, 1946; retired 1947. *Address:* South Lawn, Cheriton Close, Winchester, Hants. *Clubs:* United Service, Lansdowne.

**EVOE;** *see* Knox, Edmund G. V.

**EWALD, Paul P.,** FRS 1958; DrPhil; Professor Emeritus of Physics, Polytechnic Institute of Brooklyn, since 1957; Professor of Physics and Head of Department, Polytechnic Institute of Brooklyn, 1949-57; *b* Berlin, Germany, 23 Jan. 1888; *s* of Paul Ewald, Historian (Univ. Berlin), and Clara Ewald, Portrait-Painter; *m* 1913, Ella (Elise Berta) (*née* Philippson); two *s* two *d*. *Educ:* Victoria Gymnasium, Potsdam; Univs of Cambridge, Göttingen and Munich (DrPhil). Lecturer in Theoretical Physics, Univ. of Munich, 1918; Prof. of Theoretical Physics, TH Stuttgart, 1921-37; Lecturer, later Prof. of Mathematical Physics, The Queen's Univ., Belfast, 1939-49. Corresp. Mem. Acad. Göttingen, 1937; Fellow Nat. Acad. Arts and Sci., US, 1954; Membre d'honneur Société Française de Minéralogie et de Cristallographie, 1955; Ehrenmitglied, Deutsche Mineralog. Ges., 1958. Mem. Exec. Cttee, Internat. Union of Crystallography, 1948-66, Pres., 1960-1963. Corresp. Mem. Bavarian Acad. Sci., 1962; Fellow, Deut. Akad. d. Naturforscher (Leopoldina), 1966; Dr *hc;* TH Stuttgart, 1954; Univ. de Paris, 1958; Adelphi Univ., 1966; Univ. Munich, 1968. *Publications:* Kristalle und Rontgenstrahlen, 1923 (Germany); 50 Years of X-ray Diffraction, 1962 (Oosthoek, Holland). Contrib. Thermodynamics and Physics of Matter, 1955 (USA), etc. Editor: Zeitschrift für Kristallographie, 1923-37; Acta Crystallographica, 1948-59. *Address:* 19 Fordyce Road, New Milford, Conn 06776, USA. *T:* (203) 354-3582; Polytechnic Institute, Brooklyn, NY 11201, USA.

**EWART, Sir Ivan;** *see* Ewart, Sir W. I. C.

**EWART, Sir (William) Ivan (Cecil),** 6th Bt, *cr* 1887; DSC 1945; JP; Chairman, William Ewart & Son Ltd, Linen Manufacturers, Belfast; *b* 18 July 1919; *s* of late Major William Basil Ewart (*y s* of late Frederick William Ewart, 7th *s* of 1st Bt); *S* kinsman (Sir Talbot Ewart, 5th Bt), 1959; *m* 1948, Pauline Chevallier (*d* 1964), *e d* of Wing Comdr Raphael Chevallier Preston, OBE, AFC, JP, Derry Hill, Downpatrick, Co. Down; one *s* two *d*. *Educ:* Radley. Joined Ulster Div., RNVR, 1938. Served War of 1939-45; Lieut, RNVR; service in Coastal Forces (Motor Torpedo-Boats), 1939-42; POW, Germany, 1942-45 (DSC). A Northern Ireland Delegate to the Duke of Edinburgh's Study Conf. on the Human Problems of Industrial Communities within the Commonwealth and Empire, Oxford, 1956; Pres., Church of Ireland's Young Men's Soc., 1951-61; Chm. Flax Spinners Assoc., 1961-66; Pres., Oldpark Unionist Assoc., 1950-68. Belfast Harbour Comr, 1968. *Recreations:* travel and photography. *Heir: s* William Michael Ewart, *b* 10 June 1953. *Address:* Derryvolgie, Lisburn, Co. Antrim, N Ireland. *T:* Lisburn 3113. *Clubs:* Naval; Ulster (Belfast).

**EWART-BIGGS, Christopher Thomas Ewart,** CMG 1969; OBE 1963; HM Diplomatic Service; Counsellor, British Embassy, Brussels, since 1969; *b* 5 Aug. 1921; *s* of Lt-Col Henry Ewart-Biggs and Mollie Hilda Madelene Ewart-Biggs (*née* Brice); *m* 1st, 1952, Gavrelle Verschoyle (*d* 1959); 2nd, 1960, Felicity Jane Randall; one *s* two *d*. *Educ:* Wellington Coll.; University Coll., Oxford. History Scholar of University Coll., Oxford, 1939; BA Oxon 1945. Commissioned in Queen's Own Royal West Kent Regt, 1942; British Military Administration, Tripolitania, Civil Affairs Officer, Jefren, 1943; Arab Affairs Officer, 1945; Deputy Chief Sec. (Lt-Col), 1946; British Administration, Cyrenaica, 1947; Public Information Officer, Cyrenaica, 1948. Appointed Second Sec., HM Foreign Service, 1949. Middle East Centre for Arab Studies, 1950; Political Officer, Qatar, 1951; Eastern Dept, FO, 1953; First Sec., HM Embassy, Manila, 1956; NATO Defence Coll., 1958; Asst, African Dept, FO, 1959; Algiers: Consul, 1961; Head of Chancery, 1962; Counsellor, 1963; Counsellor, FO, 1965-69. *Address:* 31 Radnor Walk, Chelsea, SW3. *T:* 01-352 4275. *Clubs:* Brooks's, Hurlingham.

**EWBANK, Maj.-Gen. Sir Robert Withers,** KBE 1964 (CBE 1954); CB 1957; DSO 1945; MA; late Royal Engineers; retired; President: Officers' Christian Union of GB; Fellowship of National Officers' Christian Union; *b* 20 July 1907; *s* of late Brig.-Gen. W. Ewbank, CB,

CIE, RE and Mrs Ewbank, *d* of late Col Barrow, IMS; *m* 1932, Isobel Joyce Forster; one *s* two *d*. *Educ:* Weymouth Coll.; Royal Military Academy, Woolwich (King's and Pollock Medals, Armstrong Memorial Prize for Science); Christ's Coll., Cambridge (Scholar; MA 1st Class Hons Mech. Sciences Tripos). Garrison Engineer, Trincomalee, Ceylon, 1934-36; Adjt, Kent Fortress RE TA, 1936-39; GSO2 War Office, 1939-41; Instructor Staff Coll., Camberley, 1941-42; GSO1 War Office, 1942-44; Comdr, Royal Engineers, 50 Northumbrian Division, BLA, 1944-46; Col Q (Movements) War Office, 1946-49; Student Imperial Defence Coll., 1950; Sec. Chiefs of Staff Cttee, Ministry of Defence, 1951-53; Chief of Staff, British Army Staff, Washington, USA, 1954-56; Dir of Movements, War Office, 1956-58; Chief of Staff, HQ Northern Army Group, 1958-60; Commandant, Royal Military Coll. of Science, 1961-64; retd 1964. *Recreations:* photography, climbing, travel, ski-ing. *Address:* 5 Petworth Court, Overstrand, Rustington, Sussex. *Club:* Ski of Great Britain.

**EWEN, Peter;** Chartered Accountant; Partner, Allan Charlesworth & Co., EC3; *b* 4 June 1903; *s* of Alexander H. and Elizabeth Ewen, Liverpool; *m* 1932, Janet Howat (*née* Allan); two *d*. *Educ:* Merchant Taylors, Crosby. Qualified as Chartered Accountant, 1927; after 4 years in India joined Allan Charlesworth & Co., 1931; Partner, 1938; Senior Partner, 1953. Dir of companies; Chm., Westinghouse Brake and Signal Co. Ltd. *Address:* 64 North Gate, NW8. *T:* 01-722 0717. *Club:* Oriental.

**EWER, Prof. Tom Keightley,** HDA; BVSc; PhD; MRCVS; Professor of Animal Husbandry, Bristol University, since 1961; *b* 21 Sept. 1911; *s* of William Edward Frederick Ewer and Maria Louisa Wales; *m* 1st, 1937, Iva Rosalind Biddle; three *s*; 2nd, 1959, Margaret June Fischer; three *d* one step *s* two step *d*. *Educ:* Fowey Grammar Sch.; Sydney Univ. (BVSc); Cambridge Univ. (PhD). Veterinary research with NZ Govt, 1938-45; Senior Lecturer, Univ. of NZ, 1945-47; Wellcome Research Fellow, University of Cambridge, 1947-50; Prof. of Animal Husbandry, University of Queensland, 1950-61. *Publications:* contrib. to scientific publications, on animal nutrition and veterinary education. *Recreation:* music. *Address:* Langford House, Langford, near Bristol. *T:* Churchill 581.

**EWING;** *see* Orr Ewing.

**EWING, Vice-Adm. Sir Alastair;** *see* Ewing, Vice-Adm. Sir R. A.

**EWING, Sir Alexander (William Gordon),** Kt 1959; MA (Edinburgh), PhD (Manchester); Emeritus Professor of Audiology and Education of the Deaf and Director (1944-64) of Audiology and Education of the Deaf in the University of Manchester; *b* 6 Dec. 1896; *s* of late Rev. A. Gordon C. Ewing, MA, formerly Rector of St Vincent's Episcopal Church, Edinburgh; *m* 1st, 1922, Irene R. Goldsack (*d* 1959); no *c*; 2nd, 1961, Ethel Constance Goldsack. *Educ:* St Clare Preparatory Sch., Walmer, Kent; Dean Close Sch., Cheltenham; University of Edinburgh; University of Manchester. Service in HM Forces, 1918-19. Directed private clinic for deaf children and held hon. special lectureship in Dept of Educ. of the Deaf, University of Manchester, 1922-44. Norman Gamble Prize of the Royal Society of Medicine and Actonian Prize of Royal Institution, 1943 (with Dr Irene Ewing); Hon. Mem. Amer. Otological Soc., 1946-; Hon. Fellow Manchester Med. Soc., 1964-; (with Dr Irene Ewing) visited schs for the deaf in Canada, and in Australia and New Zealand at invitation of Govts concerned, to inspect and advise about their provision of education for the deaf, and conducted post-grad. courses during a summer session at North-Western Univ., Ill, 1946-50. Mem. Med. Research Council's Cttee on the Physiology of Hearing and Cttee on the Educational Treatment of Deafness, 1932-52; Pres. Brit. Association of the Hard of Hearing, 1956-; Vice-Pres., National Coll. of Teachers of the Deaf, 1965-; Vice-Pres., Health Visitors' Assoc., 1966-. Hon. LittD, Ithaca, NY; Hon. LLD Manchester. *Publications:* Aphasia in Children, 1930; The Handicap of Deafness, 1938; (with I. R. Ewing) Opportunity and the Deaf Child, 1947; Speech and the Deaf Child, 1954 (with I. R. Ewing); Educational Guidance and the Deaf Child, 1957 (with others); New Opportunities for Deaf Children, 1961 (with I. R. Ewing); Teaching Deaf Children to Talk, 1964 (with E. C. Ewing); Hearing Aids, Lipreading and Clear Speech, 1967 (with E. C. Ewing); articles and papers in the Journal of Laryngology and Otology, Lancet, Practitioner, Proc. Royal Society of Medicine, Teacher of the Deaf. *Recreations:* gardening, travel. *Address:* Horseshoe Cottage, Alderley Edge, Cheshire. *T:* Alderley Edge 3258.

**EWING, Alfred Cyril,** FBA 1941; LittD, MA; retired as Reader in Philosophy, University of Cambridge (1954-66); Fellow, Jesus College, Cambridge, 1962 (Hon. Fellow, 1966); *b* 1899; *s* of H. F. and E. M. Ewing; unmarried. *Educ:* Wyggeston Grammar Sch., Leicester; University Coll., Oxford (open exhibitioner). First class hons in Classical Moderations and Finals (Lit Hum); Bishop Fraser Scholar Oriel Coll., 1920; Senior Demy Magdalen Coll., 1921; John Locke Scholarship in Mental Philosophy, 1921; DPhil Oxon, 1923; Green Prize in Moral Philosophy, 1926; Temporary Lecturer at Michigan Univ., and Armstrong Coll., Newcastle; Asst Lecturer in Philosophy at University Coll., Swansea, 1927-31; Lectr in Moral Science, University of Cambridge, 1931-54. LittD Cantab, 1933; President of Aristotelian Soc., 1941-42. Visiting Professor: Princeton and Northwestern Univs, USA, 1949; South America and Univ. of South California, 1961; Univ. of Colorado, 1963; State Coll. of San Francisco, 1967. British delegate to Indian Silver Jubilee Congress of Philosophy in Calcutta, 1950; Hon. Treas. Internat. Fed. of Philosophical Socs, 1953-; Chairman: Faculty Board of Moral Science, Cambridge Univ., 1957-59 and 1964-66; Philosophy Section, British Academy, 1953-61. *Publications:* Kant's Treatment of Causality, 1924; The Morality of Punishment (with some suggestions for a General Theory of Ethics), 1929; Idealism, A Critical Survey, 1934; A Short Commentary on Kant's Critique of Pure Reason, 1938; Reason and Intuition (British Academy Lecture), 1941; The Individual, The State, and World Government, 1947; The Definition of Good, 1947; The Fundamental Questions of Philosophy, 1951; Ethics (Teach Yourself Series), 1953; The Idealist Tradition (sels) ed 1957; Second Thoughts in Moral Philosophy, 1959; Non-Linguistic Philosophy, 1968. Articles in Mind, Philosophy, Procs of Aristotelian Soc., Philosophy and Phenomenological Research, Review of Metaphysics, Theoria, Revue Internationale de Philosophie, Philosophical Studies, Hibbert Journal, Monist, Ethics, Analysis, Personalist, Philosophical Quarterly, Religious Studies, Proc. Internat. Congresses of Philosophy, Indian Jl of Philosophy. *Recreations:* reading, walking. *Address:* 10 Lyndhurst Road, Manchester 20. *T:* 061-445

5121; Matterdale End, Penrith, Cumberland. *T:* Glenridding 282.

**EWING, James,** Comp. TI; FCIS; FBIM; Chairman, The Bradford Dyers' Association Ltd, 1947-62 (Joint Managing Director 1946-58); *b* 25 Aug. 1884; *s* of late Archibald and Jean Ewing, Edinburgh; *m* 1911, Margaret Nimmo; one *s* two *d. Educ:* Secondary Sch., Edinburgh; Heriot-Watt Coll., Edinburgh. With Bradford Dyers Assoc. Ltd, 1909, Mem. Bd, 1926-62. *Address:* Flat 6 Woodhurst South, Raymead Road, Maidenhead, Berks.
*See also J. R. McK. Willis.*

**EWING, Vice-Adm. Sir (Robert) Alastair,** KBE 1962; CB 1959; DSC 1942; *b* 10 April 1909; *s* of Major Ian Ewing and Muriel Adèle Child; *m* 1940, Diana Smeed, *d* of Major Harry Archer, DSO; one *s. Educ:* Royal Naval Coll., Dartmouth. In command of Destroyers during War of 1939-45; NATO Standing Group Staff, 1950-51; Imperial Defence Coll., 1952; in command of HMS Vanguard, 1953-54; Dir of Naval Staff Coll., Greenwich, 1954-56; Naval Sec. to First Lord of the Admiralty, 1956-58; Flag Officer Flotillas (Mediterranean), 1958-60; Adm. Commanding Reserves and Inspector of Recruiting, 1960-62; retd list, 1962. *Address:* 328 Chilean Avenue, Palm Beach, Florida, USA. *Clubs:* Naval and Military, United Hunts.

**EWING, Air Vice-Marshal Vyvyan Stewart,** CB 1954; CBE 1951; RAF Medical Branch, retired; Principal Medical Officer, Home Command, 1953-55. MB, ChB (St Andrews); Diploma in Public Health. Air Vice-Marshal, 1951; retired, 1955. CStJ. *Address:* Sunset Cottage, 10 Staunton Avenue, Hayling Island, Hants. *T:* Hayling Island 3159.

**EWING, Mrs Winifred Margaret;** *b* 10 July 1929; *d* of George Woodburn and Christina Bell Anderson; *m* 1956, Stewart Martin Ewing; two *s* one *d. Educ:* Queen's Park Sen. Sec. Sch.; University of Glasgow (MA, LLB). Qual. as Solicitor, 1952. Lectr in Law, Scottish Coll. of Commerce, 1954-56; Solicitor, practising on own account, 1956-. Sec., Glasgow Bar Assoc., 1961-67. MP (Scottish Nationalist) for Hamilton, Nov. 1967-70. Vice-Pres. and Mem. Nat. Exec., Scottish National Party. Pres., Glasgow Central Soroptimist Club, 1966-67. *Address:* 52 Queen's Drive, Glasgow S2. *T:* 041-423 1765.

**EXETER,** 6th Marquess of, *cr* 1801, **David George Brownlow Cecil,** KCMG 1943; Baron Burghley, 1571; Earl of Exeter, 1605; DL; Hereditary Grand Almoner; Lord Paramount of the Soke of Peterborough; *b* 9 Feb. 1905; *e s* of 5th Marquess of Exeter, KG, CMG; *S* father, 1956; *m* 1st, 1929, Lady Mary Theresa Montagu-Douglas-Scott (marr. diss. 1946), 4th *d* of 7th Duke of Buccleuch; three *d*; 2nd, 1946, Diana Mary Forbes, *widow* of Col David Forbes and *er d* of late Hon Arnold Henderson; one *d. Educ:* Eton; Magdalene Coll., Cambridge. Lieut Grenadier Guards, retired 1929, re-employed 1939; served War of 1939-45: Staff Captain, 1940; Major, Dep. Asst Dir, 1941, Lt-Col, Asst Dir, Tank Supply, 1942; Controller of Aircraft Repairs and Overseas Supplies, Min. of Aircraft Production, 1942-43; Hon. Colonel: 5th Bn Northants Regt, 1939-48; Bermuda Militia, 1935-46. MP (U) Peterborough Div., Northants, 1931-43; Parly Private Secretary to: late Lord Hailsham for World Economic Conf.; Parly Sec. at Min. of Supply, 1939-41; Governor and C-in-C of Bermuda, 1943-45. Leader, UK Industrial Mission to Pakistan, 1950, and to Burma, 1954. Rector of St Andrews Univ., 1949-52. Mayor of Stamford, 1961. President: Amateur Athletic Assoc., 1936-; Internat. Amateur Athletic Fedn, 1946-; British Olympic Assoc., 1966- (Chm., 1936-66); Mem., Internat. Olympic Cttee, 1933-, Vice-Pres., 1952-66, now Doyen. Chairman: Propoganda Cttee, Nat. Fitness Council, 1938; Organising and Exec. Cttee for 1948 Olympic Games in London. President: Young Britons Assoc., 1933-37; Junior Imperial League, 1939 (Chm., 1933-37); Council, Radio Industry, 1952; Fedn of Chambers of Commerce of British Commonwealth, 1952-54; BTA, 1966-. Director: National Westminster Bank Ltd; Lands Improvement Co.; Firestone Tyre & Rubber Co. Ltd; Birmid-Qualcast (Chm.); London Bd, Royal Insurance Co. (Dep. Chm.). Mem. Exec. Cttee, King George VI Nat. Memorial Fund. Pres., CUAC, 1926-27; Winner of: Oxford v Cambridge 120 yards hurdles and 220 yards hurdles, 1925, 1926, 1927; eight British Championships, 1928; Olympic 400 metres hurdles, 1928; 5th, 110 metre hurdles, 4th, 400 metre hurdles, and 2nd, 4x400 metres, Olympic Games, 1932; 1st three times, Empire Games, 1930; many other races at home and abroad. Hunted own private pack of foxhounds, 1935-39; Joint-Master: E Sussex, 1939-53; Old Berkshire Hunt, 1953-57; Burghley Hunt, 1957-67; Pres., BHS, 1963. DL Northants, 1937-46, Huntingdon and Peterborough, 1965-. Hon. FRCS. Hon. LLD St Andrews, 1942. KStJ. *Recreations:* hunting, shooting, fishing, athletics. *Heir: b* Lord (William) Martin Alleyne Cecil, *qv. Address:* Burghley House, Stamford, Lincs. *Clubs:* Pratt's, Junior Carlton (Pres., 1956-).
*See also Baron Barnard, Lt-Col Hon. P. E. Brassey, Sir J. D. Floyd, Bt, Baron Hotham.*

**EXETER, Bishop of,** since 1949; **Rt. Rev. Robert Cecil Mortimer;** *b* Bristol, 6 Dec. 1902; *y s* of Rev. E. Mortimer; *m* 1933, Mary Hope, *d* of J. R. Walker, Barrister-at-Law; two *s* two *d. Educ:* S Edward's Sch., Oxford; Keble Coll., Oxford; Wells Theological Coll. 1st Class Hon. Mods 1923; 1st Class Lit Hum 1925; BA 1925, MA 1929, BD 1939; DD 1947; Curate S Mary Redcliffe, Bristol, 1926-29; Deacon, 1926; Priest, 1927; Lecturer Christ Church, Oxford, 1929; Student and Tutor, 1930-44; University Lecturer in Early Canon Law, 1935-43; Junior Censor of Christ Church, 1940-44; Canon of Christ Church, Oxford, and Regius Prof. of Moral and Pastoral Theology, 1944-49. Examining Chaplain to the Bishop of Ripon, 1931-46, to Bishops of Salisbury and Bristol, 1946-49; Proctor of University of Oxford in the Convocation of Canterbury, 1943-49; Select Preacher to University of Oxford, 1939-41; Select Preacher to Cambridge University, 1947; Provost of Denstone, 1948; Chancellor of the Diocese of Blackburn, 1948. Hon. Fellow, Keble Coll., 1951; Hon. Student, Christ Church, Oxford, 1968. *Publications:* Gambling, 1933; Origins of Private Penance, 1939; The Elements of Moral Theology, 1947; Marriage in Church and State (Revised and Supplemented), 1947; Christian Ethics, 1950; The Duties of a Churchman, 1951; Western Canon Law, 1953. *Recreations:* hockey (played for West of England, 1927-29) and other games. *Address:* The Palace, Exeter. *T:* 72362. *Club:* Athenæum.

**EXETER, Dean of;** *see* Knight, Very Rev. Marcus.

**EXETER, Archdeacon of;** *see* Ward, Ven. A. F.

**EXHAM, Maj.-Gen. Kenneth Godfrey,** CB 1954; DSO 1945; retired as General Officer Comanding Nigerian Military Forces (1956-59); *b* 17 Sept. 1903; *er s* of late Col Frank Simeon Exham, DSO; *m* 1927, Joan Eleanor Stewart, *d* of Allan Ball Hamilton; no *c. Educ:*

Radley Coll.; RMC Sandhurst. Commissioned, Duke of Wellington's Regt, 1923; served War of 1939-45; despatches 1946; Brit. Mil. Mission to USSR, 1941-43; Comd 56 Inf. Brigade, 1945; comd 151 Inf. Bde (TA), 1946-47; Dep. Dir Mil. Trg, 1948-51; idc, 1952; ADC to King George VI and to the Queen, 1950-53; Chief of Staff, HQ, Western Command, 1953-56; Comdt Queen's Own Nigeria Regt, 1956-59; Col The Duke of Wellington's Regt, 1958-65; Hon. Col 6/7 Bn The Royal Welch Fusiliers, TA, 1964-65. *Recreations:* shooting, fishing. *Address:* Brynglas Hall, Llanfair Caereinion, Montgomery. *Clubs:* Army and Navy; MCC.

**EXHAM, Maj.-Gen. Robert Kenah,** CB 1952; CBE 1949 (OBE 1946); MC 1940; Director Land/Air Warfare, War Office, 1957-60, retired; *b* 25 Jan. 1907; *s* of late Col Frank Simeon Exham, DSO; *m* 1940, Avril Mary, *d* of late Major F. Langley Price; two *s*. *Educ:* Radley Coll. Served North-West Frontier of India, 1935 (despatches twice, medal with clasp); War of 1939-45 (despatches, MC). Maj.-Gen. late Duke of Wellington's Regt (West Riding). *Address:* Eagle Lodge, Mile Path, Woking, Surrey. *T:* Woking 60129. *Club:* Army and Navy.

**EXMOUTH,** 9th Viscount, *cr* 1816; **Pownoll Irving Edward Pellew;** Bt 1796; Baron, 1814; *b* 28 May 1908; *s* of 8th Viscount and Frances, *d* of Alfred W. Edwards; *S* father, 1951; *m* 1938, Maria Luisa, Marquesa de Olias (Spain, *cr* 1652; *S* 1940), *d* of Luis de Urquijo, Marques de Amurrio and Marquesa de Zarreal, Madrid; two *s* two *d*. *Educ:* Oundle. *Heir: s* Hon. Paul Edward Pellew [*b* 8 Oct. 1940; *m* 1964, Maria Krystina, *d* of late R. Garay, Madrid; one *d*]. *Address:* Canonteign, near Exeter, Devon. *T:* Christow 333.

*See also Earl of Iddesleigh.*

**EXTON, Clive;** Playwright since 1959; *b* 11 April 1930; *s* of J. E. M. Brooks and Marie Brooks (*née* Rolfe); *m* 1st, 1952, Patricia Fletcher Ferguson (marr. diss.); two *d*; 2nd, 1957, Margaret Josephine Reid; one *s* two *d*. *Educ:* Christ's Hospital. Worked in advertising, 1946-48; served with HM Forces as Private, 1948-50; unsuccessful actor, stage manager and occasional waiter, 1950-59. *TV plays:* No Fixed Abode, 1959; The Silk Purse; Where I Live; Some Talk of Alexander; Hold My Hand, Soldier; I'll Have You to Remember; The Big Eat; The Trial of Doctor Fancy; Land of my Dreams; The Close Prisoner; The Bone Yard; Are You Ready for the Music?; Rainbird. *Stage plays:* Have You Any Dirty Washing, Mother Dear?; The Changing of the Guard, 1970. *films:* Night Must Fall; Isadora; Entertaining Mr Sloane; Ten Rillington Place, 1970. *Publications:* No Fixed Abode (in Six Granada Plays, anthol.), 1960; Have You Any Dirty Washing, Mother Dear? (in Plays of the Year, vol. 37), 1970. *Address:* 4 Elms Avenue, N10. *T:* 01-444 9152.

**EYRE, Hon. Dean Jack;** New Zealand High Commissioner to Canada, since 1968; *b* Westport, NZ, 1914; *m*; two *s* one *d*. *Educ:* Hamilton High Sch.; Auckland University Coll. Served War of 1939-45, Lieut in RNVR. Electrical importer and manufacturer. MP (Nat) North Shore, 1949-66; Minister of Customs, Industries and Commerce, Social Security, Defence, Police, War Pensions, Housing, State Advances, Tourist and Health Resorts, New Zealand, 1954-57; Minister in Charge of Police, 1960-63; Minister of Defence, 1960-66; Minister i/c Tourism, 1961-66. Pres. of the Junior National League, Remuera, New Zealand, 1938. *Recreations:* yachting, fishing. *Address:* 3 Crescent Road, Rockcliffe, Ottawa, Canada. *Clubs:* Royal New Zealand Yacht Squadron, Northern, Officers (Auckland); Wellington, United Services (Wellington).

**EYRE, Graham Newman,** QC 1970; *b* 9 Jan. 1931; *s* of Newman Eyre; *m* 1954, Jean Dalrymple Walker; one *s* three *d*. *Educ:* Marlborough Coll.; Trinity Coll., Cambridge. BA 1953, LLB 1954, MA 1958. Council Prize, 1954. Called to Bar, Middle Temple, 1954; Harmsworth Law Schol., Middle Temple, 1955. *Publication:* Rating Law and Valuation, 1963. *Recreations:* painting, bridge, golf. *Address:* Wilmer House, Ham Common, Surrey. *T:* 01-940 9000. *Clubs:* Athenæum; Sotogrande (Spain).

**EYRE, Sir Oliver E. C.;** *see* Crosthwaite-Eyre.

**EYRE, Reginald Edwin;** MP (C) Birmingham (Hall Green) since May 1965; Comptroller of HM Household, since 1970; *b* 28 May 1924; *s* of late Edwin Eyre. *Educ:* King Edward's Camp Hill Sch., Birmingham; Emmanuel Coll., Cambridge (MA). Midshipman and Sub-Lieut, RNVR, War of 1939-45. Admitted a Solicitor, 1950, and founded firm of Eyre & Co., solicitors, Birmingham. Hon. Consultant, Poor Man's Lawyer, 1948-58. Contested (C) Birmingham (Northfield) 1959; Conservative Political Centre: Chm., W Midlands Area, 1960-63; Chm., National Advisory Cttee, 1964-66; Opposition Whip, 1966-70; a Lord Comr of the Treasury, June-Sept. 1970. *Recreations:* walking and history. *Address:* Fulbrook House, Upper Fulbrook, Stratford-on-Avon, Warwicks. *T:* Snitterfield 304; Fountain Court, Steelhouse Lane, Birmingham 4. *T:* 021-236 3002. *Clubs:* Carlton; Conservative (Birmingham).

**EYRES-MONSELL,** family name of **Viscount Monsell.**

**EYSENCK, Prof. Hans Jurgen,** PhD; Professor of Psychology, University of London, Institute of Psychiatry, since 1955; Director, Psychological Department, Maudsley Hospital, since 1946; *b* 4 March 1916; *s* of Eduard Anton and Ruth Eysenck; *m* 1st, 1938, Margaret Malcolm Davies; one *s*; 2nd, 1950, Sybil Bianca Giuletta Rostal; three *s* one *d*. *Educ:* Schools in Germany, France and England; Univ. of London. Senior Research Psychologist, Mill Hill Emergency Hosp., 1942-46; Reader in Psychology, Univ. of London (Inst. of Psychiatry), 1950-54; Visiting Prof., Univ. of Pennsylvania, 1949-50; Visiting Prof., Univ. of California, Berkeley, 1954. *Publications:* Dimensions of Personality, 1947; The Scientific Study of Personality, 1952; The Structure of Human Personality, 1953; Uses and Abuses of Psychology, 1953; The Psychology of Politics, 1954; Sense and Nonsense in Psychology, 1957; Dynamics of Anxiety and Hysteria, 1957; Perceptual Processes and Mental Illness, 1957; (ed) Handbook of Abnormal Psychology 1960; (ed) Behaviour Therapy and the Neuroses, 1960; (ed) Experiments in Personality, 1960; (ed) Experiments with Drugs, 1963; (ed) Experiments in Behaviour Therapy, 1964; (ed) Experiments in Motivation, 1964; Crime and Personality, 1964; Causes and Cures of Neurosis, 1965; Fact and Fiction in Psychology, 1965; Smoking, Health and Personality, 1965; The Biological Basis of Personality, 1968; Description and Measurement of Personality, 1969; (co-author) Personality Structure and Measurement, 1970; Editor-in-Chief, Behaviour Research and Therapy; (ed) International Monographs of Experimental Psychology; some 300 articles in British, American, German, Spanish and French Jls of

Psychology. *Recreations:* walking, tennis, chess, detective stories, driving. *Address:* 10 Dorchester Drive, SE24.

**EYSTON, Capt. George Edward Thomas,** OBE 1948; MC; MIMechE; MSAE; *b* 28 June 1897; *s* of E. R. J. Eyston; *m* 1924; two *d. Educ:* Stonyhurst; Trinity Coll., Cambridge. Served in European War, 1914-18, Lieut 3 Battalion Dorset Regt, and Staff Capt. Royal Artillery (despatches twice, wounded). Holder of Land Speed Record three times in America and many other World's Records Motoring. Awarded Segrave Trophy, 1937, Gold Medal of AIACR; Chevalier of Legion of Honour. *Publications:* Flat Out; (with Barre Lyndon) Motor Racing and Record Breaking, 1935; (with W. F. Bradley) Speed on Salt, 1936; Editor, Fastest on Earth, 1939. *Address:* 524 Hillside Terrace, West Orange, New Jersey, USA. *Clubs:* Royal Automobile, Hawks, Leander, MCC; Royal Yacht Squadron.

**EYTON, Mrs Selena Frances W.;** *see* Wynne-Eyton.

**EZARD, Bernard John Bycroft,** CBE 1957; *b* 13 Dec. 1900; *s* of late Edward Henry Ezard, MD, DSc Edinburgh. MA Cantab and late Jessie Hogg Ezard (*née* Glegg); *m* 1927, Mabel Elsie Burton (*d* 1970); one *s. Educ:* Perse Sch.; Trinity Hall, Cambridge (MA, LLB). Called to the Bar (Middle Temple), 1922. Asst solicitor, Ministry of Labour and National Service, 1948-59; Solicitor to Ministry of Labour, 1959-62. *Recreations:* archæology, literature, walking. *Address:* Parkgate, 30 Upper South View, Farnham, Surrey. *T:* Farnham 6023.

**EZARD, Clarence Norbury,** CBE 1954 (OBE 1942); Retired as Ambassador to Costa Rica; *b* 6 Oct. 1896; *m* 1936, Olive Lillian Vaneus. *Educ:* Carlisle Grammar Sch.; Emmanuel Coll., Cambridge. Probationer Vice-Consul in General Consular Service, 1924; Acting Vice-Consul, Havana, 1926; Chargé d'Affaires, May-Oct. 1928; Sec. to Special Mission at Inauguration of Pres. of Republic of Cuba, with Temp. rank of 3rd Sec. in Diplomatic Service, 1929; Subst. rank of Vice-Consul, 1929; Vice-Consul at Bogotá, 1930; local rank of 2nd Sec. in Dipl. Service, 1930; in charge of Consulate at Havana, March-June 1931, of Legation April-June 1931. Transferred to New York, 1932, to Piræus, 1934. Acting Consul at Athens, 1935 and 1936; Consul at Beira, 1938; Montevideo, 1945, with rank of Consul and 1st Sec.; Consul-Gen., Gdansk, 1946; Consul-Gen., Haifa, 1949; Minister to Costa Rica, 1953; Ambassador to Costa Rica, 1956; retired, 1957. *Address:* Three Fields, Mayfield, Sussex. *Club:* Junior Carlton.

**EZRA, Sir Alwyn,** Kt 1936; FRGS, FRSA, FRES, FZS, JP, 1928; *b* 1900; *s* of Joseph Elias Ezra, Bombay. *Educ:* Bombay. Government Nominee on Bombay Municipal Corporation, 1929-32; Bombay Chamber of Commerce Representative on Corporation, 1932-35; represented Corporation on Board of Trustees of Prince of Wales Museum of Western India, and on Executive Cttee of Bombay Presidency Infant Welfare Soc.; Chairman: Central Cine Corp.; J. Curtis & Co. Ltd; MEMA Ltd; Patel (India) Ltd. Hon. Presidency Magistrate (Single Sitting) Bombay, 1931; Hon. Special Magistrate, Matheran, 1933; Mem., Executive Cttee St John Ambulance Association Indian Council, Advisory Cttee Jamsetji Jeejeebhoy and Allied Hospitals; and other cttees. Donor, Sir Alwyn Ezra Holiday Home for British Troops, Kashmir, and two Mobile Canteens for the Services. *Address:* Buckley Court, 25 Wodehouse Road, Bombay 1, India. *Clubs:* Willingdon, Orient, Turf (Bombay).

**EZRA, Derek,** MBE 1945; Member of National Coal Board since 1965, Deputy Chairman since 1967; *b* 23 Feb. 1919; *s* of David and Lillie Ezra; *m* 1950, Julia Elizabeth Wilkins. *Educ:* Monmouth Sch.; Magdalene Coll., Cambridge (MA). Army, 1939-47. Representative of NCB at Cttees of OEEC and ECE, 1948-52; Mem. of UK Delegation to High Authority of European Coal and Steel Community, 1952-56; Regional Sales Manager, NCB, 1958-60; Dir-Gen. of Marketing, NCB, 1960-65. *Address:* 43 Eaton Terrace, SW1. *T:* 01-730 5006.

# F

**FABER, Richard Stanley;** Counsellor, HM Embassy, The Hague, since 1969; *b* 6 Dec. 1924; *er s* of late Sir Geoffrey Faber and of Enid, *d* of Sir Henry Erle Richards, KCSI, KC; unmarried. *Educ:* Westminster Sch.; Christ Church, Oxford (MA). RNVR, 1943-46. 1st cl. Lit. Hum. Oxon; Pres., Oxford Union Soc., 1949. Joined HM Foreign (subseq. Diplomatic) Service, 1950; service in FO and in Baghdad, Paris, Abidjan, Washington; Head of Rhodesia Political Dept, FCO, 1967-69. *Publications:* Beaconsfield and Bolingbroke, 1961; The Vision and the Need: Late Victorian Imperialist Aims, 1966; Proper Stations: Class in Victorian Fiction, 1971. *Address:* Flat 9, 14 Ennismore Gardens, SW7. *T:* 01-589 0654. *Club:* Travellers'.

**FADDEN, Rt. Hon. Sir Arthur William,** PC 1942; GCMG 1958 (KCMG 1951); Treasurer, Commonwealth of Australia, 1940-41 and 1949-58, also Deputy Prime Minister, 1949-58; Member Australian House of Representatives for Darling Downs, Qld, 1936-49 and for McPherson, Qld, 1949-58; *b* 13 April 1895; *s* of Richard Fadden, Ingham, North Qld; *m* 1916, Ilma Thornber; two *s* two *d.* Asst Treasurer and Asst Minister for Supply and Development, Australia, March 1940; Minister for Air and for Civil Aviation, Aug.-Oct. 1940; Prime Minister, Aug.-Oct. 1941; Leader of Opposition, 1941-43; of Country Party, 1941-58. Mem. of Advisory War Council, 1940-45. Acting Prime Minister 8 times, 1950-56. *Address:* Box 575J, GPO, Brisbane, Qld, Australia.

**FAGAN, Brian Walter,** CBE 1949; MC 1918; *b* 13 Feb. 1893; *s* of late Sir Patrick Fagan, KCIE, CSI; *m* 1918, Mary Gwendoline Margaret, *er d* of late William Moir; two *s. Educ:* Rugby Sch. (Scholar); Queen's Coll., Oxford (Scholar). BA 1918. Served European War, 6th Batt. Oxford and Bucks Lt Inf., 1914-18; GSO3, 3rd Army, 1918 (despatches twice, wounded twice). Dir of Edward Arnold (Publishers) Ltd, retired 1960. Pres. of Publishers' Association, 1945-47. *Address:* The Wellington Hotel, Mount Ephraim, Tunbridge Wells, Kent. *T:* Tunbridge Wells 20286.

**FAGE, Arthur,** CBE 1953; FRS 1942; FRAeS, ARCS; formerly Superintendent of the Aerodynamics Division of National Physical Laboratory; *b* 4 March 1890; *s* of William John and Annie Fage; *m* 1920, Winifred Eliza Donnelly (*d* 1951); one *s* one *d. Educ:* Portsmouth Royal Dockyard Sch.; Royal College of Science (Royal Exhibitioner). *Publications:* numerous scientific papers, mostly on aero- and hydro-dynamics in Proc. Royal Society, etc. *Address:* 65 High Point, Richmond Hill Road, Edgbaston, Birmingham

**FAGG, Bernard Evelyn Buller,** MBE 1962; FSA; Curator, Pitt Rivers Museum, Oxford; *b* 8 Dec. 1915; *s* of late W. P. Fagg and of Mrs W. P. Fagg; *m* 1942, Mary Catherine, *d* of G. W. Davidson; two *s* two *d* (and one *s* decd). *Educ:* Dulwich Coll.; Downing Coll., Cambridge. Nigerian Admin. Service, 1939-47. War service with West African Engineers, East African Campaign, 1939-43. Dept of Antiquities, Republic of Nigeria, 1947-64 (Dir, 1957-64); Curator, Pitt Rivers Museum, since Oct. 1963 (assumed duty, 1964); Lincoln Coll., Oxford, 1964; Fellow of Linacre Coll., 1965; Leverhulme Fellowship, 1965. *Publications:* contribs to learned jls. *Address:* 45 Woodstock Road, Oxford. *T:* 54875.

**FAGG, William Buller,** CMG 1967; Keeper, Department of Ethnography, British Museum, since 1969 (Deputy Keeper, 1955-69); *b* 28 April 1914; *s* of late William Percy Fagg and of Lilian Fagg. *Educ:* Dulwich Coll.; Magdalene Coll., Cambridge. Sir Wm Browne's Medal for Latin Epigram; Montagu Butler Prize for Latin Hexameters; BA Classics, 1936; Archaeology and Anthropology, 1937; MA 1939. Asst Keeper Dept of Ethnography, BM, 1938; seconded to Bd of Trade, Industries and Manufactures Dept, 1940-45. Royal Anthropological Institute: Hon. Sec., 1939-56; Mem. Council, 1966-69; Vice-Pres., 1969-; Patron's Medal, 1966; Hon. Editor, Man: A Monthly Record of Anthropological Science, 1947-65; Chm., UK Cttee for First World Festival of Negro Arts, Dakar, 1966; Consulting Fellow in African Art, Museum of Primitive Art, NY, 1957-. Fieldwork: Nigeria and Congo, 1949-50; Nigeria, 1953, 1958-59; Cameroon, 1966; Mali, 1969. Organised and arranged many loan exhibns including: Nigerian Art (Arts Council), London, Manchester, Bristol, 1960, Munich, Basel, 1961; African Art, Berlin Festival, 1964, Musée des Arts Décoratifs, Paris, 1964-65; African Sculpture, Nat. Gall. of Art, Washington, DC, Kansas City Art Gall., and Brooklyn Museum, 1970. FRSA (Silver-Medalist, 1951). Member: Reindeer Council of UK; Royal African Soc.; RIIA; Internat. African Inst.; Museums Assoc.; ICA. *Publications:* The Webster Plass Collection of African Art, British Museum, 1953; (with E. Elisofon) The Sculpture of Africa, 1958; Afro-Portuguese Ivories, 1959; Nigerian Images, 1963 (awarded P. A. Talbot Prize, 1964, and grand prize for best work on African art at World Festival of Negro Arts, Dakar, 1966); (with Margaret Plass) African Sculpture: An Anthology, 1964; Tribes and Forms in African Art, 1966; African Tribal Sculptures, 2 vols, 1967; Arts of Western Africa, Arts of Central Africa (UNESCO), 1967; African Tribal Images (The Katherine White Reswick Collection of African Art), 1968; African Sculpture (Washington, DC), 1970; Miniature Woodcarvings from Africa, 1970. Numerous exhibn catalogues, articles in Man, etc. *Recreations:* photography (esp. of art), listening to music, cycling, travel. *Address:* 6 Galata Road, Barnes, SW13. *T:* 01-748 6620.

**FAGGE, Sir John William Frederick,** 11th Bt, *cr* 1660; *b* 28 Sept. 1910; *s* of late William Archibald Theodore Fagge (*b* of 9th Bt) and Nellie (*d* 1924), *d* of H. T. D. Wise; *S* uncle, 1940; *m* 1940, Ivy Gertrude, *d* of William Edward Frier, 15 Church Lane, Newington, Kent; one *s. Heir: s* John Christopher Fagge, *b* 30 April 1942. *Address:* 26 The Mall, Faversham, Kent.

**FAIR, Hon. Sir Arthur,** Kt 1951; MC; QC (New Zealand); Judge of the Supreme Court of New Zealand, 1934-55, retired; *s* of J. W. Fair and Teresa Fair of Westport, New Zealand. *Educ:* Nelson Coll.; Victoria University Coll., NZ. LLB, barrister and solicitor, 1907; Crown Solicitor, 1921; Principal Law Officer of Crown, 1923; KC 1925; Solicitor-Gen. of NZ, 1925-34; served 1914-19, Inns of Court Officers' Training Corps, 8th Batt. Suffolk Regt, 1/5th Batt. Suffolk Regt (TF), Egypt and Palestine (temporary Capt. and Adjutant; MC 1918). *Publication:* History 1/5th Batt. Suffolk Regt (with E. C. Wolton). *Recreations:* golf, motoring. *Address:* 19 Upland Road, Kelburne, Wellington, NZ. *Club:* Wellington (Wellington, NZ).

**FAIRBAIRN, Douglas Chisholm,** CIE 1945; CBE 1956; MA; JP; Director, Thomas Hamling & Co. Ltd, St Andrew's Dock, Hull; *b* 1904; *s* of late Rev. R. T. and Mrs Fairbairn; *m* 1938, Agnes, *d* of late Rev. William amd Mrs Arnott; two *s. Educ:* George Heriot's, Edinburgh; Edinburgh Univ. (MA). Formerly: Secretary Bengal Chamber of Commerce and Industry, Calcutta, 1938-56, also in that capacity Sec. Associated Chambers of Commerce of India; Chm., Hull Fishing Vessel Owners and Hull Fishing Industry Associations, 1957-62. JP for City and County of Kingston-upon-Hull, 1966. *Recreations:* golf, gardening. *Address:* Fir Croft, Kemp Road, Swanland, East Yorks. *T:* Hull 631580. *Clubs:* Oriental, Bengal, Royal Calcutta Golf (Calcutta).

**FAIRBAIRN, Robert Duncan,** JP; Director and General Manager, Clydesdale Bank Ltd; *b* 25 Sept. 1910; *s* of late Robert Fairbairn and Christina Fairbairn; *m* 1939, Sylvia Lucinda, *d* of late Rev. Henry Coulter; two *s* one *d. Educ:* Perth Academy. Joined service of The Clydesdale Bank at Perth, 1927; Beckett & Whitehead Prizeman, Inst. of Bankers, 1934; Midland Bank, 1934. Lt-Comdr (S) RNVR, 1939-46. Asst Gen. Manager, Clydesdale & North of Scotland Bank, 1950. Mem. Scottish Council (Develt and Industry), Vice-Pres., 1967-68; Mem. Scottish Cttee, Council of Industrial Design; Pres., Scottish Economic Soc., 1966-69; Director: Commercial Union Assurance Group (Local Board); Scottish Amicable Life Assurance Soc. (Pres., 1969); Scottish Agricultural Securities Corp. (Chm. 1970); Midland Bank Finance Corp. Ltd, 1967-; Clydesdale Bank Finance Corp. Ltd, 1967-; Glasgow Chamber of Commerce (Vice-Pres., 1969). Pres. Inst. of Bankers in Scotland, 1961-63; Chm., Cttee of Scottish Bank General Managers, 1963-66; Vice-Pres., British Bankers Assoc. FIB. FRSA. *Recreations:* golf, fishing. *Address:* The Grange, Hazelwood Road, Bridge of Weir, Renfrewshire. *T:* Bridge of Weir 2102. *Clubs:* Caledonian, MCC; Western (Glasgow); Corinthian Casuals; Royal and Ancient (St Andrews).

**FAIRBAIRN, Thomas Charles;** Hon. RCM; Dramatist and Producer of Opera and Pageants; *s* of Charles Fairbairn and Emma Bastow; *m* 1904, Antonie Seiter, a singer of opera; two *s. Educ:* New Holland; Maxton, Scotland. Began as Engineer; later, Operatic vocalist and stage manager, Moody Manners Opera Co.; produced in Covent Garden and Drury Lane for Beecham Opera Cos; ran own opera cos in Surrey Theatre; produced opera in India and Burma; produced own dramatic version of Hiawatha, with the Royal Choral Society, Royal Albert Hall, 1924 (an annual event); founded Fairbairn Pageant Choir for Elijah in 1934; same year produced Hiawatha, Open Air Theatre, Scarborough, and other works, including Faust and Tannhäuser, all in Pageant form; Elijah, a Passion Pageant, and Faust with the Fairbairn Pageant Choir, Royal Albert Hall, 1936, 1937, 1938, and 1939. Produced Hiawatha in the Exhibition Building, Melbourne, Australia, 1939.

*Publication:* Robert Burns, A Folk song opera, produced by the Peoples Theatre, Dumbarton, 1939. *Recreations:* writing, and endeavouring to restore the past glories of Glastonbury. *Address:* 41 Essex Park, W Finchley, N3.

**FAIRBAIRN, Sir William Albert,** 5th Bt of Ardwick, *cr* 1869; *b* 6 April 1902; *o surv. s* of 4th Bt and Jennie Cora, *d* of Albert Davis, Boston; *S* father, 1931; *m* 1925, Christine Renée Cotton, *y d* of late Rev. Canon Croft, Kelvedon Vicarage, Essex; two *s* one *d* (and one *d* decd). *Educ:* privately. *Heir: s* James Brooke Fairbairn [*b* 10 Dec. 1930; *m* 1960, Mary Russell Scott, *d* of Dr W. R. Scott, MB, ChB, FFARCS, Weymouth; two *s* one *d*]. *Address:* Loom House, Radlett, Herts. *T:* Radlett 6446.

**FAIRBANK, Alfred John,** CBE 1951; FRSA; calligrapher; *b* 12 July 1895; *er s* of Alfred John and Emma Fairbank; *m* 1919, Elsie Kneeshaw; one *s* (one *d* decd). Entered Civil Service, 1911; Senior Executive Officer, Admiralty, 1949-55; retired from Civil Service, 1955. Pres. Soc. of Scribes and Illuminators, 1951-63; Vice-Pres. of Soc. for Italic Handwriting; Member: Soc. of Designer Craftsmen; Art Workers Guild; The Double Crown Club. Leverhulme Research Awards, 1956 and 1957. Designer and responsible for production of The Books of Remembrance of the Royal Air Force, Church of St Clement Danes. *Publications:* A Handwriting Manual, 1932; A Book of Scripts, 1949; Editor and calligrapher of Beacon Writing Books I-VI, 1958; (with Berthold Wolpe) Renaissance Handwriting, 1960; (with Dr R. W. Hunt) Humanistic Script of the Fifteenth and sixteenth Centuries, 1960; A Roman Script for Schools, 1961; (with Prof. Bruce Dickins) The Italic Hand in Tudor Cambridge, 1962; The Story of Handwriting, 1970. *Relevant publication:* Calligraphy and Palæography: Essays presented to Alfred Fairbank on his seventieth birthday, 1965. *Address:* 27 Granville Road, Hove, Sussex. *T:* Brighton 733431.

**FAIRBANKS, Maj.-Gen. Cecil Benfield,** CB 1950; CBE 1946 (MBE 1940); retired 1958; Administrative Secretary, National Council of Social Service, 1958-65; *b* 12 June 1903; *s* of F. C. Fairbanks, Montreal, Canada; *m* 1936, Rosamonde Beryl Fisher; one *s* one *d*. *Educ:* Marlborough Coll.; Keble Coll., Oxford. Commissioned with The Sherwood Foresters, Jan. 1924; Adjutant 1st Foresters, 1935-38; Adjutant 5th Foresters TA, 1938-40. Served UK, 1924-35; West Indies, 1935-38; War of 1939-45, France, 1939-40; Middle East, 1941-45 (Irak, 1943, Italy, 1945); France and Germany, 1945-46. OC 14th Foresters, 1943; Comd Inf. Bde, 1944-46; BGS 1947; idc 1948; Dir of Inf., 1948-49; GOC Nigeria Dist, 1949-52; Chief Army Instructor, Imperial Defence Coll., 1953-54; GOC Rhine District, British Army of the Rhine, 1955-58, retd. Col The Sherwood Foresters, 1958-65. *Recreations:* hunting, golf, tennis. *Address:* c/o Bank of Montreal, 9 Waterloo Place, SW1, *Club:* Army and Navy.

**FAIRBANKS, Douglas (Elton), (Jr),** KBE (Hon.) 1949; DSC 1944; Captain, USNR, retired; company director, producer, actor; Chairman: Douglas Fairbanks Ltd; Dougfair Corporation; Fairbanks International, Inc. (US); Boltons Trading Corp. Inc., etc., and of associated companies, in US and UK, since 1946; International Investments, Inc.; Thomas Holmes, Inc.; Director: Scripto Pens Ltd (US and UK); Rambagh Palace Hotel, Ltd (Jaipur, India); Cavalcade Film Co. Ltd (UK); *b* New York City, 9 Dec. 1909; *s* of Douglas Elton Fairbanks, Denver, Colorado, and Anna Beth Sully, Providence, RI; *m* 1939, Mary Lee Epling, Keystone, W Virginia; three *d*. *Educ:* Bovée Sch., Knickerbocker Greys, Collegiate Mil. Sch., NY; Pasadena Polytechnic, Harvard Mil. Sch., Los Angeles; tutored privately in London and Paris. Began career as film actor, 1923, on stage 1927. Organised own producing company, UK, 1935. Studied painting and sculpture, Paris, 1922-24; began writing, professionally, 1928; articles and essays on public affairs, etc., 1936-. Vice-Pres. Franco-British War Relief and National Vice-Pres. Cttee "Defend America by Aiding the Allies", 1939-40; Presidential Envoy, Special Mission to Latin America, 1940-41; one-time Consultant to Office of the Presidency (Washington, DC); Lieut (jg), USNR, 1941; promoted through grades to Capt., 1954. National Chm., CARE Cttee, 1947-50; Nat. Vice-Pres. Amer. Assoc. for the UN, 1946-60; Pres. Brit.-Amer. Alumni Assoc. 1950; Bd Mem., English-Speaking Union of the US, 1949-60; Nat. Chm., Amer. Relief for Korea, 1950-54; Trustee, Edwina Mountbatten Trust; Mem. Council, American Museum in Brit.; a Governor: Royal Shakespeare Theatre; Ditchley Foundations; Mem. Bd, Music Theater, Lincoln Center (NY), etc; Mem. Guild of St Bride's Church, Fleet Street, EC; Mem., Council on Foreign Relations (NY); Vis. Fellow, St Cross Coll., Oxford; MA Oxon; Senior Churchill Fellow, Westminster Coll., Fulton, Mo; Hon. DFA Westminster Coll., Fulton, Mo, USA; Silver Star Medal (US); Legion of Merit (Valor clasp) (US), Special Naval Commendation (US), KJStJ 1950, etc; Officer Legion of Honour (Fr.), Croix de Guerre with Palm (Fr.); Knight Comdr Order of George I (Greece); Knight Grand Officer, Order del Merito (Chile); Comdr Order of Orange Nassau (Neth.); Officer of: Orders of Crown (Belg.), of Star of Italy (It.), Cross of Mil. Valour (It.), Southern Cross (Brazil), Hon. Citizen and National Medal of Korea, etc. *Publications:* short stories, poems, articles, to periodicals. *Relevant publication:* Knight Errant, by Brian Connell. *Recreations:* swimming, tennis, golf, travel. *Address:* 28 The Boltons, SW10; The Blackstone, 50 East 58th Street, New York, NY 10022, USA (offices) 10 Park Place, St James's, SW1; 711 Fifth Avenue, New York, NY 10022; 6772 Hollywood Boulevard, Los Angeles, Calif 90028, USA. *Clubs:* White's, Buck's, Naval and Military; Puffin's (Edinburgh); Knickerbocker, Century (NY); Metropolitan (Washington, DC); Travellers' (Paris).

**FAIRBURN, Harold,** CMG 1935; *b* 1884. Appointed Assistant Commissioner of Police, Federated Malay States, 1904; Deputy Commissioner, 1921; Inspector General of Police, Straits Settlements, 1925; retired, 1938. JP Hants, 1942. *Address:* 75 Sea Mills Lane, Bristol 9. *T:* 683952.

**FAIRCLOUGH, Anthony John;** Head of West Indian Department, Foreign and Commonwealth Office, since 1968; *b* 30 Aug. 1924; *m* 1957, Patricia Monks; two *s*. Ministry of Aircraft Production and Ministry of Supply, 1944-48; Colonial Office, 1948; Secretary, Nyasaland Commn of Inquiry, 1959; Private Secretary to Minister of State for Commonwealth Relations and for the Colonies, 1963-64; Assistant Secretary, 1964; Head of Pacific and Indian Ocean Dept, Commonwealth Office (formerly Colonial Office), 1964-68; Senior UK Commissioner at Sessions of South Pacific Commn, 1965-67. *Address:* 5 Fabye House, Cumberland Road, Kew, Richmond, Surrey.

**FAIRCLOUGH, Hon. Ellen Louks,** PC (Can.) 1957; FCA 1965; Secretary and Director, Hamilton Trust and Savings Corporation; President, Hamilton Office Service Ltd, Hamilton, Ont; Member of Progressive Conservative Party, Canada; *b* Hamilton, Ont, 28 Jan. 1905; *d* of Norman Ellsworth Cook and Nellie Bell Louks; *m* 1931, David Henry Gordon Fairclough; one *s*. *Educ:* Hamilton Public and Secondary Schs. Certified Public Accountant, public practice, 1935-57. Hamilton City Council, Alderman, 1946-49; Controller, 1950. Elected to House of Commons as Progressive Conservative mem. for Hamilton West, 1950; re-elected at gen. elections, 1953, 1957, 1958, 1962, defeated in 1963 election. Sec. of State for Canada, 1957-58; Minister of Citizenship and Immigration, 1958-62; Postmaster-Gen., 1962-63. *Recreations:* music, reading and photography. *Address:* 25 Stanley Avenue, Hamilton, Ont, Canada. *T:* Hamilton 522-5248.

**FAIRCLOUGH, Wilfred,** RE; RWS; ARCA (London); Assistant Director, Kingston Polytechnic, and Head of the Division of Design, since 1970; Principal of Kingston College of Art, Surrey, 1962-70; *b* 13 June 1907; *s* of Herbert Fairclough and Edith Amy Milton; *m* 1936, Joan Cryer; one *s* one *d*. *Educ:* Royal College of Art, London, 1931-34 (Diploma 1933); British Sch. at Rome, Italy, 1934-37; Rome Scholar in Engraving, 1934-37. Army and Royal Air Force, 1942-46. Rome Scholarships, Faculty of Engraving, 1951 (Chm., 1954); Leverhulme Research Award, 1961. RE 1946 (ARE 1934); RWS 1968 (1961). Chairman: Assoc. of Art Instns, 1965; Assessors, Vocational Courses of Surrey CC. *Work in public and private collections: paintings:* Min. of Supply; Min. of Works; Surrey CC; Scottish Modern Art Assoc.; Beaumont Coll.; *drawings:* British Museum; V&A Museum; Arts Council; Contemporary Art Soc.; Wye Coll., London Univ.; English Electric Co.; Art Galls at Blackburn, Kingston-upon-Thames, Worthing; Graves Art Gall., Sheffield; Atkinson Art Gall., Southport; *prints:* British Museum, V&A Museum; Ashmolean Museum, Oxford; Contemporary Art Soc.; British Sch. at Rome; South London Art Gall.; Stoke Educn Authority; Wye Coll., London Univ.; Gottenburg Museum; Print Collectors Club. *Publications:* work reproduced: Recording Britain; Londoners' England; Royal Academy Illustrated; Studio; Fine Prints of the Year; Print Collectors Quarterly; illustrated article, Leisure Painter, 1969; paintings, drawings and prints. *Address:* 12 Manorgate Road, Kingston-upon-Thames, Surrey. *Club:* Arts.

**FAIRFAX,** family name of **Baron Fairfax of Cameron.**

**FAIRFAX OF CAMERON,** 14th Baron, *cr* 1627; **Nicholas John Albert Fairfax;** *b* 4 Jan. 1956; *e s* of 13th Baron and Sonia, *yr d* of late Capt. Cecil Gunston, MC; *S* father, 1964. *Heir: b* Hon. Hugh Nigel Thomas Fairfax, *b* 29 March 1958. *Address:* Gays House, Holyport, near Maidenhead, Berks. *T:* Maidenhead 27956.

**FAIRFAX, James Griffyth;** *b* 15 July 1886; *e s* of C. B. Fairfax, Sydney, NSW; *m* 1922, Rosetta Mary, *o d* of late Sir John Glover, GCMG, RN; one *d*. *Educ:* Winchester Coll.; New Coll., Oxford, 3rd Class Hon. Mods, 1st Class Hon. Sch. English Language. Called to Bar, Inner Temple, 1912; Bar of NSW, Australia, 1920; MP (C) Norwich, 1924-29; contested the Div., 1929; served European War, 1914-19 (Mesopotamia) (despatches four times); Capt. RASC attached 15th Indian Div.; mem. Exec. Council Assoc. Chambers of Commerce, 1928-45. *Publications:* Poems, 1908; Troubled Pool, 1911; Horns of Taurus, 1912; Temple of Janus, 1917; Mesopotamia, Carmina Rapta, 1919; The Fifth Element, 1937; and numerous contributions to the Press. *Address:* Villa Sous la Madone, Roquebrune, France A-M. *TA:* Barclosea Monte Carlo. *T:* Roquebrune 829092. *Clubs:* Athenæum, Hurlingham.

**FAIRFAX, Vincent Charles,** CMG 1960; Company Director and Pastoralist, Australia; *b* 26 Dec. 1909; *s* of late J. H. F. Fairfax; *m* 1939, Nancy, *d* of Dr C. B. Heald, *qv*; two *s* two *d*. *Educ:* Geelong Church of England Grammar Sch., Australia; Brasenose Coll., Oxford Univ. (BA). Staff, John Fairfax & Sons Pty Ltd, 1933; Advertising Manager, 1937-38. Major, Australian Imperial Forces, 1940-46. Director: John Fairfax & Sons Pty Ltd, 1946-53; John Fairfax Ltd (Publishers, Sydney Morning Herald), 1956; Chm. Australian Sectn, Commonwealth Press Union, 1950; Chm. Stanbroke Pastoral Co. Pty Ltd, 1964; Director: Bank of NSW, 1953; Australian Mutual Provident Soc., 1956 (Chm. 1966); Australis Investment Co. Ltd, 1959; Chief Comr Boy Scouts Assoc., for NSW, 1958-68, for Australia, 1969; Dep. Pres., Royal Agric. Society of Commonwealth, 1966; Mem. C of E Property Trust, 1950; Mem. Council: Art Gall. Soc. of NSW, 1953; Royal Flying Doctor Service, 1954; Royal Agric. Society of NSW, 1956 (Pres., 1970). *Recreations:* tennis, golf, trout fishing. *Address:* Elaine, 550 New South Head Road, Double Bay, Sydney, NSW 2000, Australia. *T:* 36 1416. *Clubs:* Bath, Leander; Union, University, Imperial Service, Royal Sydney Golf (Sydney).

**FAIRFAX, Sir Warwick (Oswald),** Kt 1967; MA; Chairman of: John Fairfax & Sons Ltd (The Sydney Morning Herald, The Sun Herald, The Sun, The Australian Financial Review, and other publications); Associated Newspapers Ltd; Member Board Australian Elizabethan Theatre Trust; Member Council Australian National University; owns Harrington Park, and poll Hereford stud; *b* 1901; *o s* of Sir James Oswald Fairfax, a Proprietor and Dir of John Fairfax and Sons, Ltd, and Mabel, *d* of Capt. Francis Hixson, RN; *m* 1928, Marcie Elizabeth, *o d* of David Wilson, Barrister of Sydney; one *s* one *d*; *m* 1948, Hanne Anderson, 2nd *d* of Emil Bendixsen, Copenhagen; one *d*; *m* 1959, Mary, *o d* of Kevin Wein; one *s*. *Educ:* Geelong Grammar Sch., St Paul's Coll., Sydney Univ.; Balliol Coll., Oxford. 2nd Class Hons in Sch. of Philosophy, Politics and Economics; joined staff of John Fairfax and Sons, Ltd, 1925; Dir, 1927; Managing Dir 1930; Chairman of Dirs, 1956. Plays: A Victorian Marriage, Vintage for Heroes, The Bishop's Wife, performed Sydney, 1951, 1952, 1956. *Publications:* Men, Parties, and Policies, 1943; The Triple Abyss: Towards a Modern Synthesis, 1965; ed A Century of Journalism (The Sydney Morning Herald), 1931. *Recreations:* the arts, philosophy, cattle breeding, motoring and vintage cars. *Address:* John Fairfax & Sons Ltd, Box 506, GPO Sydney, Australia; Harrington Park, Narellan, NSW 2567; Fairwater, 560 New South Head Road, Double Bay, Sydney, NSW 2028, Australia. *Clubs:* Carlton, Oriental, Australian, Union, Pioneers (Sydney).

**FAIRFAX-CHOLMELEY, Francis William Alfred,** CBE 1960; Director: Barclays Bank Ltd, since 1957; Barclays Bank SA, France, since 1968 (Chairman, 1968-70); Barclays Export Finance Co. Ltd; Banque de Bruxelles, Belgium; *b* 20 Sept. 1904; *e s* of Hugh Charles Fairfax-Cholmeley, JP of Brandsby, York, and of Alice Jane (*née* Moverley); *m* 1940, Janet Meta, *e d* of Sir John Ogilvy-Wedderburn, 11th and 5th Bt; two *d* (one *s* decd). *Educ:* Eton; Magdalene Coll., Cambridge (MA). Joined Barclays Bank Ltd, 1926; Local Dir, 54 Lombard Street, 1939-48; Resident Dir in Paris, Barclays Bank (France) Ltd, 1948-64, Chm., 1964-68; Local Dir, Foreign Branches, 1964-66, and Pall Mall East, 1966-68. Served RA, 1939-45 (Major). *Address:* Balendoch, Meigle, Perthshire. *T:* Meigle 318. *Clubs:* St James'; Cercle Interallié (Paris).

**FAIRFAX-LUCY, Major Sir Brian Fulke Cameron-Ramsay-,** 5th Bt, *cr* 1836; *b* 18 Dec. 1898; *s* of Col Sir Henry William Cameron-Ramsay-Fairfax-Lucy, 3rd Bt, CB, and Ada Christina, *d* of Henry Spencer Lucy, Charlecote, Warwicks; *S* brother, 1965; *m* 1933, Hon. Alice Caroline Helen Buchan, *o d* of 1st Baron Tweedsmuir, PC, GCMG, GCVO, CH; one *s* one *d*. *Educ:* Eton; RMC. Queen's Own Cameron Highlanders: served European War, 1916-18 (wounded); NW Frontier, India, 1919-25 (ADC to GOC Madras District, 1922-25); Army of Occupation, Germany, 1926; Adjutant 2nd Cameron Highlanders, 1927-30; ADC to Lord High Commissioner to Gen. Assembly of Church of Scotland, 1931-34; retired, 1933; War of 1939-45 (Major). National Greyhound Racing Club: Steward, 1928-33; Stipendiary Steward, 1933-36. *Publications:* Author of a number of children's books, including: Horses in the Valley; The Horse from India; The Cat Did It; The Children of the House. *Recreations:* riding, breeding racehorses, shooting, fishing, gardening. *Heir: s* Edmund John William Hugh Cameron-Ramsay-Fairfax-Lucy, *b* 4 May 1945. *Address:* The Mill, Fossebridge, Glos. *T:* Fossebridge 261; Charlecote Park, Warwicks. *T:* Wellesbourne 277. *Club:* Lansdowne.

**FAIRFIELD, (Josephine) Letitia Denny,** CBE 1919, MD, ChB Edinburgh; DPH London; Barrister-at-Law of the Middle Temple; *e d* of late C. Fairfield. *Educ:* Richmond High Sch.; Edinburgh Univ.; University Coll., London. Bathgate Memorial Prize of Royal College of Surgeons, Edinburgh, 1904; MB, ChB, Edinburgh, 1907; MD, 1911; Area Medical Controller QMAAC 1917; and transferred to the RAF Medical Service, 1918; RAMC, 1940-42; Lieut-Col (retired) RAMC; Senior Medical Officer, London County Council, 1911-48. Pres., Medico-Legal Soc., 1957 and 1958. Papal Medal, Pro Ecclesia et Pontifice, 1966. *Publications:* Trial of John Henry Straffen, 1954; Epilepsy, 1954. *Address:* 60 Beaufort Mansions, Beaufort Street, SW3. *T:* 01-352 3917.

**FAIRFIELD, Sir Ronald (McLeod),** Kt 1970; CBE 1966; BScEng CEng, FIEE, MIMechE; Deputy Chairman and Managing Director, British Insulated Callender's Cables, Ltd, since 1964; *b* Newcastle upon Tyne, 25 May 1911; *er s* of late Geoffrey Fairfield and Inez Helen Thorneycroft McLeod; *m* 1939, Mary Moore (marr diss. 1952); no *c*. *Educ:* Llandaff Cathedral Sch.; King Edward's Sch., Bath; Erith Tech. Coll.; London Univ. Trainee Apprentice, Callender's Cable & Con. Co. Ltd, 1929; Research Engr, 1932; Mullard Radio Valve Co., 1934; rejoined Callender Co., 1937 as Tech. Man. Leigh Works, and Erith Works, 1942; on amal. of Brit. Ins. Cables Ltd and Callender Co. in 1945 to form BICC, became Chief Engr (Designs and Processes) of new Co.; Director and General Manager: former St Helens Cable & Rubber Co. Ltd, 1948-51; W. T. Glover & Co. Ltd, 1952; BIC (Sub. Cables) Ltd, 1953 (later Dep. Chm.); apptd BICC Bd, 1954 as Dir (Prod. and Engrg); Dir (Home Ops), 1958; Asst Man. Dir, 1960; Jt Man. Dir, 1962; Chm., BIC Con. Co. Ltd, 1964-68; Director: RTZ-BICC Aluminium Holdings Ltd; Anglesey Aluminium; Chm., Automatic Light Controlling Co. Ltd; Dep. Chm., Submarine Cables Ltd, 1961-66; Chm., European Cables Ltd, 1962-. Wartime Mem., Cablemakers Tech. Cttee; Mem. Cttee, Transmission Sect. (later Supply Sect.), IEE, 1943-45; IEE Premium for 1956-57; Mem., NEDC for Elec. Engrg Industry, 1964-; Member Council, BEAMA (Pres., 1968-69); FRSA. *Publications:* various Tech. papers. *Recreations:* game shooting, forestry. *Address:* 66 Whitehall Court, SW1. *T:* 01-930 3160; Owlswood, Tennyson's Lane, Haslemere, Surrey. *T:* Haslemere 3465. *Clubs:* Savage, National Sporting.

**FAIRHALL, Hon. Sir Allen,** KBE 1970; Member, House of Representatives, 1949-69; *b* 24 Nov. 1909; *s* of Charles Edward and Maude Fairhall; *m* 1936, Monica Clelland, *d* of James and Ellen Ballantyne; one *s*. *Educ:* East Maitland Primary and High Sch.; Newcastle Tech. Inst. Founded commercial broadcasting stn 2KO, 1931; Supervising Engr, Radio and Signals Supplies Div., Min. of Munitions, 1942-45; Pres., Austr. Fedn of Commercial Broadcasting Stns, 1942-43. Mem. Australian Delegn to UN Gen. Assembly, 1954; Minister for Interior and Works, 1956-58; Minister for Supply, 1961-66; Minister for Defence, 1966-69. Mem. Newcastle CC, 1941. Hon. DSc Univ. of Newcastle, 1968. *Recreations:* amateur radio; deep sea fishing. *Address:* 7 Parkway Avenue, Newcastle, NSW 2300, Australia. *T:* 2.2295. *Clubs:* Tattersall's, National (Sydney); Newcastle (Newcastle); Commonwealth (Canberra).

**FAIRHAVEN,** 2nd Baron, *cr* 1929 (UK) and 1961 (UK) (new creation); **Henry Rogers Broughton;** Major, retired; *b* 1 Jan. 1900; 2nd *s* of late Urban Hanlon Broughton (who would have been granted a barony in 1929 had he lived) and *yr b* of 1st Baron Fairhaven (2nd *cr* 1961); *S* brother, 1966; *m* 1st, 1932, Hon. Diana Rosamond (*d* 1937), *o d* of late Capt. Hon. Coulson Fellowes; one *s*; 2nd, 1953, Joyce Irene, *widow* of Lieut G. H. C. Dickens, RN. *Educ:* Harrow; Royal Military College, Sandhurst. Joined Royal Horse Guards, 1919; Capt., 1926; retired, 1933; rejoined, 1939-45. *Heir: s* Hon. Ailwyn Henry George Broughton [*b* 16 Nov. 1936; *m* 1960, Patricia, *d* of Col J. H. Magill; two *s* two *d*]. *Address:* 56 Eaton Place, SW1. *T:* 01-235 4174; South Walsham Hall, near Norwich, Norfolk. *T:* South Walsham 202. *Clubs:* Boodle's, Buck's.

**FAIRHURST, William Albert,** CBE 1961; Senior Partner since 1940, W. A. Fairhurst & Partners, Glasgow (formerly F. A. Macdonald & Partners), Consulting Civil Engineers; *b* 21 Aug. 1903; *s* of John Robert Fairhurst and Elizabeth Ann Massey, Alderley Edge, Cheshire; *m* 1937, Elizabeth Robertson Jardine; one *s* one *d*. *Educ:* Cavendish Road Sch., W Didsbury; Manchester Coll. of Technology. FICE; FIStructE; MInstHE: Mem. Assoc. Cons. Engrs; Mem. Soc. Civil Engrs, France. Designer of many bridges, including Queen's Bridge, Perth, Howford Bridge, Ayrshire, Kingston Bridge, Glasgow, and new Tay Road Bridge. Mem. of Royal Fine Art Commission for Scotland, 1963. Pres. of Scottish Chess Assoc., 1957-69; British Chess Champion, 1937; eleven times Scottish Chess Champion and seventeen times West of Scotland Chess Champion; awarded title of International Chess Master by Internat. Federation of Chess, 1951. Chess Correspondent, Glasgow Herald, 1959-69. Hon. LLD St Andrews, 1968. *Publications:* Arch Design Simplified; (jointly) Design and Construction of Reinforced Concrete Bridges;

numerous papers on bridges and structural engineering to engineering institutions. *Recreations:* bridge, art, chess. *Address:* Torr Hall, Bridge of Weir, Renfrewshire. *T:* Bridge of Weir 2486. *Clubs:* Royal Automobile, Golfers'; Glasgow Art, Royal Scottish Automobile (Glasgow).

**FAIRLEY, Prof. Barker,** MA Leeds, PhD Jena; Hon. LittD: Leeds; Waterloo (Canada); Toronto; Carleton; Hon. LLD Alberta; FRSC; Emeritus Professor of German in University College, University of Toronto; *b* Barnsley, Yorks, 21 May 1887; *s* of Barker and Charlotte Fairley; *m* 1914, Margaret Adele Keeling (*d* 1968), Bradford, Yorks; one *s* one *d*. *Educ:* Universities of Leeds and Jena. Lektor in English at University of Jena, 1907-10; Lecturer in German at University of Alberta, 1910; Henry Simon Prof. of German Language and Literature, Manchester Univ., 1932-36. *Publications:* Charles M. Doughty, 1927; Goethe as revealed in his Poetry, 1932; A Study of Goethe, 1947; Goethe's Faust, 1953; Heinrich Heine, An Interpretation, 1954; Wilhelm Raabe, an Introduction to his Novels, 1961; (trans.) Goethe, Faust, 1970. *Address:* The University, Toronto 5, Ontario, Canada.

**FAIRLIE-CUNINGHAME, Sir William Alan;** *see* Cuninghame.

**FAIRMAN, Prof. Herbert Walter;** Brunner Professor of Egyptology, University of Liverpool, since 1948; Special Lecturer in Egyptology, University of Manchester, 1948-69; *b* 9 March, 1907; *s* of Rev. W. T. Fairman, DD; *m* 1937, Olive Winnifred Nicholls; one *s* one *d*. *Educ:* Goudhurst Sch. for Boys, Goudhurst, Kent; University of Liverpool. Excavations of the Egypt Exploration Soc. at Armant and Tell el Amarna (Egypt), 1929-36, and Sesebi and Amarah West (Sudan), 1936-48. Field Dir, Egypt Exploration Society's Nubian Expedition, 1937-48. *Publications:* chapters on the inscriptions in: Mond and Myers, The Bucheum, 1934; Frankfort and Pendlebury, The City of Akhenaten II, 1933; (also editor) Pendlebury, The City of Akhenaten III, 1950; articles in Journal of Egyptian Archaeology, Annales du Service des Antiquités de l'Egypte and Bulletin de l'Institut français d'archéologie orientale. *Recreations:* swimming, walking. *Address:* 6 Garth Drive, Mossley Hill, Liverpool L18 6HW. *T:* 051-724 2875.

**FAIRN, (Richard) Duncan;** Training Officer, Lord Chancellor's Office, since 1970 (Part-time Officer, 1967-70); *b* 1 June 1906; *s* of Percy Frederick and Mary Fairn; *m* 1930, Marion Cristina, *d* of James M. Sturrock; one *s*. *Educ:* Elementary Sch.; Battersea County (now Henry Thornton) Sch.; London Sch. of Economics, BSc (Econ). Voluntary prison teacher and visitor, 1926-30. Education Officer, Pettit Farm Settlement, Dagenham, 1929-30; Joint Warden, The Settlement, York, 1930-38; Dep. Governor, Manchester Prison, 1938-39; Dep. Governor, Wakefield Prison, 1939-42; Governor, Rochester Borstal, 1942-45; First Principal, Prison Service Staff Coll., Wakefield, 1945-48; Asst Comr of Prisons, 1948-55; a Comr of Prisons, 1955-63, when Prison Commn was dissolved; Dir of Prison Administration, 1952-60; Chief Dir, Prison Dept, Home Office, 1960-64, Asst Under-Sec. of State, 1964-67. Visited various parts of Commonwealth to advise on prison administration, 1955-69; Chm. Cttee on Detention Camps in Kenya, 1959. Swarthmore Lectr, Society of Friends, 1951; Vis. Lectr, UN Inst. at Fuchū, Tokyo, 1967. Pres., Pinner Branch of UNA, 1970-; Vice-Pres., Nat. Assoc. of Prison Visitors, 1970-; Member: Council of National Book League, 1951-; European Cttee on Crime Problems (Strasbourg), 1964-67; Internat. Penal and Penitentiary Foundn, 1965-67; UK delegn to UN Social Develt Commn, 1967-; Consultative Panel for Social Develt (Min. of Overseas Develt), 1967-; Parole Bd, 1967-71; UN Adv. Cttee of Experts on Prevention of Crime and Treatment of Offenders (Kyoto), 1970. Chm. Management Cttee E London Family Service Unit, 1958-; Chm., Bd of Governors, Bedales Sch., 1963-65; Governor, Leighton Park Sch., 1961-. *Publications:* Quakerism, a faith for ordinary men, 1951; The Disinherited Prisoner (Eleanor Rathbone Memorial Lecture), 1962. *Recreations:* reading, walking, music and people. *Address:* Lavender Cottage, 82 Paines Lane, Pinner, Mddx HA5 3BL. *T:* 01-866 9650. *Club:* Authors'.

**FAIRWEATHER, Brig. Claude Cyril,** CB 1967; CBE 1965 (OBE 1944); TD 1944; DL, JP; Chairman, North of England TA&VRA, since 1968; *b* 17 March 1906; *s* of Nicholas Fairweather, Middlesborough; *m* 1930, Alice Mary, *e d* of late Sir William Crosthwaite; one *s* one *d*. *Educ:* St Peter's Sch., York. 2nd Lieut, Royal Corps of Signals, 1928; Lt-Col 1941; Col 1943; Brig. 1945. Chm., North Riding T & AFA, 1950-53 and 1962-68; Member: TA Advisory Cttee; TA Exec. Cttee. Co. Comr, NR Yorks. St John Amb. Bde; Hon. Col, 34 (N) Signal Regt (V); Chairman: N Riding Co. Cadet Cttee, 1947-52; St Luke's Hosp. Man. Cttee, Middlesborough. Retd Company Dir. DL 1949, JP 1963, NR Yorks. OStJ 1967. *Recreations:* golf, cricket, Rugby football. *Address:* The White Lodge, Hutton Rudby, Yarm, Yorks. *T:* Hutton Rudby 598. *Clubs:* Army and Navy, Airborne; Cleveland (Middlesborough); Royal and Ancient (St Andrews).

**FAISAL, King;** *see* Saudi Arabia, HM the King of.

**FALCON, Michael;** *b* 1888; *s* of late Michael Falcon; *m* 1920, Kathleen, *o d* of late Captain Gascoigne, Seaforth Highlanders, and Mrs Gascoigne; one *s* three *d*. *Educ:* Harrow; Pembroke Coll., Cambridge. BA; LLB; Barrister-at-Law, Inner Temple; MP (U) East Norfolk, 1918-23; High Sheriff of Norfolk, 1943-44. *Address:* 10 Cathedral Close, Norwich NOR 16P. *T:* Norwich 23984.

**FALCON, Norman Leslie,** FRS 1960; Geological Adviser, British Petroleum Company Ltd (formerly Chief Geologist, 1955-65); *b* 29 May 1904; 2nd *s* of late Thomas Adolphus Falcon, MA, RBA; *m* 1938, Dorothy Muriel, 2nd *d* of late F. G. Freeman, HM Consular Service; two *s* one *d*. *Educ:* Exeter Sch.; Trinity Coll., Cambridge. MA Cantab. Joined Anglo-Persian Oil Company as geologist, 1927; FGS, FRGS, 1927; Geological Exploration in Persia, UK and elsewhere, 1927-40. Served War of 1939-45, Intelligence Corps, 1940-45. Rejoined Anglo-Iranian Oil Company as Geologist on Head Office staff, 1945. FInstPet, 1959; Geological Soc. of London: Mem. Council, 1954-58, 1967-; Foreign Sec. 1967-70; Murchison Medal, 1963; Member: Council, RGS, 1966-69; Natural Environment Research Council, 1968-. Bronze Star Medal (USA), 1945. *Publications:* geological papers. *Recreations:* outdoor pursuits. *Address:* The Downs, Chiddingfold, Surrey. *T:* Wormley 3101.

**FALCONER, Prof. Alexander Frederick,** VRD; BLitt, MA; Professor of English in the University of St Andrews since 1955; *s* of Alexander W. Falconer and Emily Henrietta

Carlow Kirk. *Educ:* Universities of Glasgow and St Andrews; Magdalen Coll., Oxford. Lecturer, St Salvator's Coll., St Andrews, 1935-39. Served in Home and Eastern Fleets, rank of Lieut, and Lt-Comdr RNVR, 1940-45. Senior Lecturer in Univ. of St Andrews, 1946. Mem. of group of editors for Boswell's correspondence at Yale, 1952-. Folger Fellow, 1958. Jt Gen. Editor, Percy Letters Series, 1964. Divl Officer, St Andrews Univ. RNR Div. Trustee, Nat. Library of Scotland, 1956-. *Publications:* A. Spir, Right and Wrong (trans.), 1954; The Percy Letters, Vol. IV, 1954, Vol. VI, 1960; Shakespeare and the Sea, 1964; A Glossary of Shakespeare's Sea and Naval Terms, 1965; articles and reviews. *Address:* 6 Alexandra Place, St Andrews. *T:* St Andrews 3457. *Club:* Naval.

**FALCONER, Douglas William,** MBE 1946; QC 1967; *b* 20 Sept. 1914; *s* of late William Falconer, S Shields; *m* 1941, Joan Beryl Argent, *d* of late A. S. Bishop, Hagley, Worcs; one *s* one *d*. *Educ:* South Shields; Durham Univ.; BSc (Hons) Physics. Served War of 1939-45 (Hon. Major): commissioned E Yorks Regt, 1939. Called to Bar, Middle Temple, 1950. Apptd 1970 to exercise appellate jurisdiction of BoT under Trade Marks Act. *Publications:* (Jt Editor) Terrell on the Law of Patents (11th edn), 1965. *Recreations:* music, theatre. *Address:* 6 Pump Court, Temple, EC4. *T:* 01-353 8588; Ridgewell House, West Street, Reigate, Surrey. *T:* Reigate 44374. *Club:* Royal Automobile.

**FALCONER, Lieut-Col Sir George Arthur,** KBE 1947; CIE 1942; DL; *b* 3 June 1894; *s* of late E. J. Falconer; *m* 1925, Esther, *d* of late Major M. Boyd-Bredon. 2nd Lieut 1916; Indian Army, Cavalry, 1917; Capt. 1921; Major, 1935; Lt-Col 1943; Asst Consul-Gen. Meshed, 1919-21; Indian Political Service, 1923; Under Sec. Persian Gulf Residency, 1924-26; Asst Resident, Aden, 1927-29, Kashmir, 1929-31; Sec. to Resident, Kolhapur, 1932-33, Baroda, 1933-35; HM Consul, Kerman (Persia), 1937-42; Pol. Agent, Bhopal, 1942-44; HM Minister in Nepal, 1944-47; United Kingdom Ambassador to Nepal, 1947-51; retired 1951. CC, W Suffolk, 1955 (Vice-Chm., 1965-70; CA, 1966); DL, High Sheriff, Suffolk, 1964. Mem. Church Assembly, 1955-70. OStJ. *Address:* The Old Rectory, Whatfield, near Ipswich, Suffolk. *T:* Hadleigh, Suffolk 3174. *Club:* United Service.

**FALCONER, James Fyfe,** MBE 1944; JP; Town Clerk of Glasgow since 1965; *b* 18 Nov. 1911; *m* 1938, Jessie Elizabeth Paterson; two *s* two *d*. *Educ:* Queen's Park Secondary Sch.; Glasgow University. Law Apprentice, 1926-32; Solicitor, 1932-48; Town Clerk Depute, 1948-59; Senior Town Clerk Depute, 1959-65. JP Glasgow, 1962. *Recreations:* gardening, angling. *Address:* 101 St Andrew's Drive, Glasgow S1. *T:* 041-423 0681.

**FALCONER, Murray Alexander,** MCh (NZ), FRCS, FRACS; Director, Guy's-Maudsley Neuro-surgical Unit, London, SE5, since 1950; Hon. Consultant Neurosurgeon, King's College Hospital; *b* 15 May 1910; *s* of Alexander R. Falconer, CBE, and Agnes J. Falconer; *m* 1939, Valda H. Falconer; two *d*. *Educ:* Otago University, Dunedin, NZ. Major RAMC, 1941-43. Assoc. Prof. of Neurosurgery, Otago Univ., 1943-50; Fellow, Mayo Foundation, Rochester, Minn., 1937-38; Nuffield Dominions Fellow in Surgery, University of Oxford, 1938-40; Hon. Consulting Neurological Surgeon, Johns Hopkins Hosp., Baltimore, Md, 1959-; Visiting Prof. of Surgery, Univ. of Calif., Los Angeles, 1960, 1966. Comdr, Order of Cedars, Lebanon, 1959. *Publications:* several in medical journals. *Recreation:* golf. *Address:* 48 Durham Avenue, Bromley BR2 0QG. *T:* 01-460 5575. *Club:* Athenæum.

**FALK, Oswald Toynbee,** CBE 1920; Partner in Falk and Partners; *b* 1879; *s* of late H. John Falk, West Kirby, Cheshire and Rachel *d* of Joseph Toynbee. *Educ:* Rugby; Balliol Coll., Oxford. Treasury, 1917-19; Treasury Delegate, Paris Peace Conference, 1919. *Address:* Tall Trees, Boar's Hill, Oxford. *T:* Oxford 35649.

**FALK, Sir Roger (Salis),** Kt 1969; OBE 1945; Director: P. E. Holdings Ltd; Gordon & Gotch Holdings; Hygienex Ltd (Chairman); Provincial Insurance (Chairman, London Board); *b* 22 June 1910; *s* of Lionel David Falk; *m* 1938, Margaret Helen (*née* Stroud) (*d* 1958); one *s* two *d*. *Educ:* Haileybury; Geneva Univ. Gen. Manager's Office, Rhodesia Railways, Bulawayo, 1931; D. J. Keymer & Co: Manager in Bombay and Calcutta, 1932-35; Dir, 1935-49; Managing Dir, 1945-49; Vice-Chm., 1950. Shoreditch Borough Council, 1937-45; Parly Candidate SE Southwark, 1938, resigned 1939. Dir-Gen. British Export Trade Research Organisation (BETRO) from 1949 until disbandment. Chairman: Furniture Development Council, 1963-; Central Council for Agric. and Hort. Cooperation, 1967-. Member: Council of Industrial Design, 1958-67; Monopolies Commn, 1965-; Council, RSA, 1968-. Served War of 1939-45, RAFVR; Wing-Comdr, 1942. *Publication:* The Business of Management, 1961. *Recreations:* writing, music, reading. *Address:* 603 Beatty House, Dolphin Square, SW1. *T:* 01-828 3752; Old Barn Cottage, Little Marlow, Bucks. *Club:* Garrick.

**FALKINER, Lt-Col Sir Terence (Edmond Patrick),** 8th Bt of Annmount, Cork, *cr* 1778; DL; late Coldstream Guards; retired 1956; *b* 17 March 1903; *s* of 7th Bt and Kathleen (*d* 1948), *e d* of Hon. Henry Robert Orde-Powlett, 2nd *s* of 3rd Baron Bolton; *S* father, 1917; *m* 1925, Mildred, *y d* of Sir John Cotterell, 4th Bt; two *s*. three *d*. *Educ:* St Anthony's, Eastbourne; The Oratory Sch., Edgbaston. DL, Herefordshire, 1965. KStJ. *Heir: s* Edmond Charles Falkiner [*b* 24 June 1938; *m* 1960, Janet Iris, *d* of Arthur E. B. Darby, Bromyard, Herefordshire; two *s*]. *Address:* Kingsthorne House, Hereford. *T:* Wormelow 343.

**FALKINGHAM, Very Rev. John Norman;** Dean of Newcastle, New South Wales, since 1961; Warden, Community of the Holy Name, since 1969; *b* 9 Feb. 1917; 2nd *s* of Alfred Richard Falkingham and Amy Grant (*née* Macallister); *m* 1947, Jean Dorothy Thoren; two *d*. *Educ:* Geelong Gram. Sch., Corio, Vic.; Trinity Coll., University of Melbourne. BA (Hons) Melbourne 1940; ThL (1st Cl. Hons) Australian Coll. of Theol.; prizes for Divinity and Biblical Greek. Deacon, 1941; Priest, 1942. Curate of Holy Trinity, Surrey Hills, Vic., 1941-44; Chaplain, Trinity Coll., Univ. of Melbourne, 1944-50; Incumbent, St Paul's, Caulfield, Vic., 1950-61. Exam. Chaplain to Archbishop of Melbourne, 1947-61; Lectr in Theol. Faculty, Trinity Coll., Melbourne, 1950-60; Canon of St Paul's Cath., Melbourne, 1959-61. Sec., Liturgical Commn of Gen. Synod, 1966-; Mem.: Bd of Delegates, Aust. Coll. of Theology, 1962-. *Publications:* articles in various jls. *Recreation:* walking. *Address:* The Deanery, 46 Newcomen Street, Newcastle, NSW 2300, Australia. *T:* 22052. *Club:* Newcastle.

**FALKLAND,** 14th Viscount and 14th Lord Cary, *cr* 1620; **Lucius Henry Charles Plantagenet Cary;** *b* 25 Jan. 1905; *e s* of 13th Viscount

Falkland and Ella Louise (*d* 1954), *e d* of E. W. Catford; *S* father, 1961; *m* 1st, 1926, Joan Sylvia (who obtained a divorce, 1933), *d* of Capt. Charles Bonham Southey, of Frinton-on-Sea; two *d*; 2nd, 1933, Constance Mary, *d* of late Capt. Edward Berry; one *s*; 3rd, 1958, Charlotte Anne, *e d* of late Bevil Granville, Chadley, Wellesbourne, Warwick. *Educ:* Eton. Flying Officer RAFVR, 1941-45 (invalided). *Heir: s* Master of Falkland, *qv. Address:* 18 Tower Park, Fowey, Cornwall. *T:* Fowey 3211. *Clubs:* Carlton, Royal Commonwealth Society; Royal Fowey Yacht.
*See also Sir W. V. H. Nelson, Bt.*

**FALKLAND, Master of; Hon. Lucius Edward William Plantagenet Cary;** *b* 8 May 1935; *s* and *heir* of 14th Viscount Falkland, *qv*; *m* 1962, Caroline Anne, *o d* of late Lt-Comdr Gerald Butler, DSC, RN, and Mrs Ian Skimming, Newton Valence, Hants; one *s* one *d. Educ:* Wellington Coll.; Alliance Française, Paris. Late 2nd Lieut 8th Hussars. *Recreations:* racing, cinema. *Address:* 69 Limerston Street, SW10. *Club:* Hurlingham.

**FALKNER, Sir (Donald) Keith,** Kt 1967; Hon. DMus Oxon, 1969; FRCM; Hon. RAM; Hon. GSM; Hon. FTCL; Hon. FLCM; Director, Royal College of Music, since 1960; Professional Singer; *b* Sawston, Cambs, 1900; *y s* of late John Charles Falkner; *m* 1930, Christabel Margaret, *o d* of Thomas Fletcher Fullard, MA; two *d. Educ:* New Coll. Sch.; Perse Sch.; Royal College of Music; Berlin, Vienna, Paris. Has sung at all principal festivals in England, and many European cities; toured USA eight times, including concerts with Boston Symphony, New York Philharmonic, Cincinnati, St Louis, and Philadelphia Orchestras; toured South Africa, 1935, 1939, 1955, 1962; Canada in 1953; New Zealand in 1956. British Council Music Officer for Italy, 1946-50. Prof. of the Dept of Music at Cornell Univ., USA, 1950-60. Served European War, 1914-18, in RNAS, 1917-19; War of 1939-45, RAFVR, 1940-45. *Recreations:* cricket, golf, lawn tennis, squash rackets, walking. *Address:* Royal College of Music, SW7. *Clubs:* Athenæum, Royal Automobile, MCC.

**FALKNER, Sir Keith;** *see* Falkner, Sir D. K.

**FALLA, Paul Stephen;** *b* 25 Oct. 1913; *s* of Norris Stephen Falla and Audrey Frances Stock, Dunedin, New Zealand; *m* 1958, Elizabeth Shearer; one *d. Educ:* Wellington and Christ's Colls, NZ; Balliol Coll., Oxford (Scholar). Appointed to Foreign Office, 1936; served HM Embassies, Warsaw, 1938-39, Ankara, 1939-43, Tehran, 1943; Foreign Office, 1943-46; UK Delegation to UN, New York, 1946-49; Foreign Office, 1949-67 (Dep. Dir of Research, 1958-67). *Recreations:* reading (history, philosophy, poetry); languages and linguistics. *Address:* 63 Freelands Road, Bromley, Kent. *T:* 01-460 4995. *Club:* Travellers'.

**FALLA, Robert Alexander,** CMG 1959; FRSNZ; Director, Dominion Museum, Wellington, NZ, 1947-66; *b* 21 July 1901; *s* of G. Falla; *m* 1928, Elayne M., *d* of A. Burton, Te Aroha; one *s* two *d. Educ:* Auckland Grammar Sch.; Auckland Univ. (MA, DSc). Lecturer, Auckland Teachers' Training Coll., 1925-30; Asst Zoologist, British, Australian and New Zealand Antarctic Research Expedition, 1929-31; Ornithologist, Auckland War Memorial Museum, 1931-35; Asst Dir, 1936-37; Dir, Cant Museum, 1937-47. Served War of 1939-45. Delegate, First Gen. Conference, New Zealand Nat. Commission, UNESCO, 1946; Mem. Ross Sea Cttee, 1955. Polar Medal (bronze). *Publications:* Scientific papers and reports on Antarctic birds of Mawson expedition. *Address:* Kotari Road, Day's Bay, Wellington, New Zealand.

**FALLE, Samuel,** CMG 1964; DSC 1945; High Commissioner in Singapore, since 1970; *b* 19 Feb. 1919; *s* of Theodore and Hilda Falle; *m* 1945, Merete Rosen; one *s* three *d. Educ:* Victoria Coll., Jersey, CI. Served Royal Navy, 1937-48; joined Foreign (subseq. Diplomatic) Service, 1948; British Consulate, Shiraz, Iran, 1949-51; British Embassy, Tehran, 1952; British Embassy, Beirut, 1952-55; FO, 1955-57; British Embassy, Baghdad, 1957-61; Consul-Gen., Gothenburg, 1961-63; Head of UN Dept, FO, 1963-67; with Lord Shackleton's mission to Aden 1967; Deputy High Comr, Kuala Lumpur, 1967-69; Ambassador to Kuwait, 1969-70. *Recreation:* swimming. *Address:* c/o Foreign and Commonwealth Office, SW1; 4 Lewes Crescent, Brighton, Sussex. *T:* 63940.

**FALLOWS, Rt. Rev. William Gordon;** *see* Pontefract, Bishop Suffragan of.

**FALLS, Capt. Cyril Bentham,** CBE 1967; *b* 1888; *e s* of late Sir Charles Fausset Falls; *m* 1915, Elizabeth Heath; two *d. Educ:* Bradfield Coll.; Portora Royal Sch., Enniskillen; London Univ.; abroad. Late Royal Inniskilling Fusiliers; served European War, with regiment, General Staff 36th and 62nd Divisions, Liaison Officer with French (despatches twice, French Croix de Guerre, two citations); employed, 1923-39, in Historical Section (Military Branch) Cttee of Imperial Defence. Military Correspondent of the Times, 1939-53; Chichele Prof. of the History of War, Oxford, and Fellow of All Souls Coll., 1946-53, Emeritus Prof., Oxford, since 1953. *Publications:* Official: the official military histories of the British Campaigns in Egypt and Palestine (first volume with Lieut-Gen. Sir George MacMunn), Macedonia and France (1917, first volume); Unofficial: Rudyard Kipling, A Critical Study; The History of the 36th (Ulster) Division; The Critic's Armoury (essays); War Books, a Critical Guide; The Birth of Ulster; Marshal Foch (Order of Merit Series); The Nature of Modern Warfare, 1941; Ordeal by Battle, 1943; The Man for the Job (fiction); A Short History of the Second World War; Elizabeth's Irish Wars; A Hundred Years of War; Mountjoy–Elizabethan General; The Gordon Highlanders in the First World War; The First World War; The Art of War from the Age of Napoleon to the Present Day; Armageddon: 1918, 1964; Caporetto, 1917, 1966. *Recreations:* formerly yachting, shooting, and riding; now chiefly in recollection. *Address:* 16 Archery Close, W2. *T:* 01-262 1524. *Club:* Turf.

**FALMOUTH,** 9th Viscount, *cr* 1720; **George Hugh Boscawen,** DL; 26th Baron Le Despencer, 1264; Baron Boscawen-Rose, 1720; *b* 31 Oct. 1919; 2nd but *e surv. s* of 8th Viscount; *S* father, 1962; *m* 1953, Elizabeth Price Browne; four *s. Educ:* Eton Coll.; Trinity Coll., Cambridge. Served War, 1939-46, Italy. Capt., Coldstream Guards. DL Cornwall, 1968. *Heir: s* Hon. Evelyn Arthur Hugh Boscawen, *b* 13 May 1955. *Address:* Tregothnan, Truro, Cornwall; Graythwaite, Mereworth, Kent. *Club:* Athenæum.
*See also Hon. R. T. Boscawen.*

**FALSHAW, Sir Donald,** Kt 1967; retired; *b* 22 Jan. 1905; *s* of James and Martha Falshaw; *m* 1937, Jessie Louise Taylor; no *c. Educ:* Lancaster Royal Gram. Sch.; Sidney Sussex Coll., Cambridge. Indian Civil Service (Punjab), 1928-66: District and Sessions

Judge, 1932-46; Judge, Lahore High Court, 1946-47; Judge, Punjab High Court, India, after partition, 1947-66, Chief Justice, Dec. 1961-May 1966. *Recreations:* cricket, racing. *Address:* 125 Kenilworth Court, Putney, SW15. *T:* 01-788 8058. *Club:* East India and Sports.

**FANE,** family name of **Earl of Westmorland.**

**FANE, Harry Frank Brien,** CMG 1967; OBE 1957 (MBE 1945); Department of Employment and Productivity, retired 1968; *b* 21 Aug. 1915; *s* of late Harry Lawson Fane and Edith (*née* Stovold); *m* 1947, Stella, yr d of John Hopwood; two *d. Educ:* William Ellis Sch.; Birkbeck Coll., London. Joined Ministry of Labour, 1933. HM Forces, 1940-45: Major, Royal Corps of Signals (despatches); served in N Africa, Italy and Austria. British Embassy, Washington: First Sec. (Labour), 1950-56; Counsellor (Labour), 1960-66. Regional Controller, Dept of Employment and Productivity (formerly Min. of Labour), Birmingham, 1966-68. *Address:* 40 Winterbourne Road, Solihull, Warwicks.

**FANE TREFUSIS,** family name of **Baron Clinton.**

**FANNER, John Lewis,** MA; Headmaster of Alleyn's School, since 1967; *b* 7 Dec. 1921; *s* of H. L. Fanner, Croydon; *m* 1947, Jill Carne, *o d* of J. O. Corin, Illogan, Cornwall; two *d. Educ:* Whitgift Sch.; Brasenose Coll., Oxford (1st cl. Nat. Sci.). MA Oxon 1947. War service, RAF Technical Branch, 1942-45. Asst Master: Shrewsbury Sch., 1947-52; Harrow Sch., 1952-60; Headmaster, Lewes County Gram. Sch. for Boys, 1960-67. *Recreations:* reading, sailing. *Address:* 8 Dulwich Village, SE21. *T:* 01-693 2983; Gerrans, near Truro, Cornwall. *Club:* Percuil Sailing.

**FANSHAWE, Maj.-Gen. Sir Evelyn Dalrymple,** Kt 1961; CB 1946; CBE 1942; *b* 25 May 1895; *e s* of late Gen. Sir Hew Dalrymple Fanshawe, KCB, KCMG; *m* 1920, Marie, *e d* of late Sir Victor Harari, CMG; no *c. Educ:* King's Sch., Canterbury; Royal Military Coll., Sandhurst. 2nd Lieut The Queen's Bays. 1914; served European War, 1914-18, France, Egypt, Palestine, Mesopotamia, Persia, Russia, Syria (1914 star, Allied and Victory medals); ADC, GOC Cavalry Corps, 1915; seconded to RFC 1915-19; returned to Regt and made Adjutant, 1919; Lieut-Col The Queen's Bays, 1935; Col, 1938; Brig. to Comd. 20th Mech. Cav. Bde 1939; Comd. 20 Armd Bde 1940-41; Maj.-Gen. Armd Training and Comdr RAC Training Establishment, 1942-45; retired pay, 1945. UNRRA Dir in British Zone of Germany, 1945-48. Dir of the International Refugee Organisation in British Zone of Germany, 1948-52; Mission to Dominion Countries on behalf of UNO, 1952. Chm., Pre-Services Cttee, Northants TA Assoc., 1953-65; Pres., Northants Spastic Assoc.; Pres. Northants Outward Bound Cttee; Vice-President: Northants County Amateur Athletic Assoc.; Northants County Cricket Club. Hon. Treas. East Midlands Area, Conservative and Unionist Associations, 1952-67; Chm., Kettering Div., Conservative and Unionist Assoc., 1953-65 (Pres. 1965); Chm. of Stallion Cttee, Hunters Improvement Soc. (President 1965); President: Ponies of Britian Club, 1962; National Pony Soc., 1966. High Sheriff, Northants, 1960. King's Coronation Medal, 1937. *Recreations:* hunting, polo, yachting, shooting and fishing, racing, flying. *Address:* Guilsborough House, Northampton. *T:* Guilsborough 258. *Clubs:* Cavalry, Hurlingham; Royal Armoured Corps Yacht, Travellers' (Paris).

**FANSHAWE, Maj.-Gen. George Drew,** CB 1954; DSO 1944; OBE 1944; *b* 27 Sept. 1901; *s* of Lt-Col Edward Cardwell Fanshawe; *m* 1934, Dorothy Elizabeth Norman-Walker; one *s* one *d. Educ:* Tonbridge. 2nd Lieut, RFA, 1922, Lieut 1924. RHA 1928; Capt. 1935; Adjt Herts Yeomanry, 1935; Brigade-Maj., RA, 1939, CO 1942; CRA, 3 Div., 1945; 5th Anti-Aircraft Bde, 1949; Comdr 1st Anti-Aircraft Group, 1952-55; retired 1955. BRA Southern Comd, 1950. Col. Comdt, Royal Artillery, 1956-66 (Representative Col Comdt, 1961-62). High Sheriff, Wilts, 1961-62; Alderman, Wilts CC. CStJ. Order of Merit (US). *Address:* Farley Farm, Farley, Wilts. *T:* Farley 202. *Club:* Army and Navy.

**FAREED, Sir Razik,** Kt, *cr* 1951; OBE 1948; Member of Ceylonese Parliament since 1952; Member of Senate, Ceylon, 1947-52; member, State Council of Ceylon until Ceylon Independence Act, 1947; Founder, only Muslim Ladies' College in Ceylon; Founder and President, Moors' Islamic Cultural Home (Inc.); Chairman Orchid Circle of Ceylon. Is a Ceylon Moor by race and a Muslim by religion. *Address:* Hajara Villa, Fareed Place, Colombo 4, Ceylon. *T:* 8357 and 91098. *Clubs:* Ceylon Turf, Ceylon Poultry (Vice-Pres.), Young Moors' Sports (Pres.).

**FAREY-JONES, Frederick William;** Chairman of Farey-Jones (Insurance) Ltd, Insurance Brokers; *b* 21 May 1904; *s* of Evan Francis and Gladys Gertrude Jones; *m* Lilian Ada (*née* Farey); one *s* one *d. Educ:* Queen Elizabeth's Grammar Sch., Carmarthen; Paris, Liége, Geneva. Founder of the Conference of International Air Traffic Operators; also founder of the revived Air Transport Association. Contested (C) Goole, 1950 and Pembroke, 1951; MP (C) Watford, 1955-64. Director: Australian Estates Ltd; National Group of Unit Trusts Ltd. Master, Worshipful Co. of Horners, 1970. FRSA. Knight Commander of Order of Civil Merit (Spain), 1958. *Address:* Ruffetts Wood, Chipstead, Surrey; 46 Chancery Lane, WC2. *Clubs:* Royal Aero, City Livery; Knights of the Round Table.

**FARGHER, John Adrian,** CMG 1957; The South Australian Railways Commissioner, 1953-66; *b* 13 Jan. 1901; *s* of Philip and Matilda Maud Fargher; *m* 1926, Elsie Pearl, *d* of Charles French; one *s* one *d* (and one *d* decd). *Educ:* Melbourne Univ (MCE). *Publications:* has contributed a number of Papers to Journal of The Institution of Engineers, Australia. *Recreation:* golf. *Address:* 8 Cambridge Terrace, Brighton, South Australia 5048, Australia.

**FARIDKOT, Col HH Farzand-i-Saadat Nishan Hazrrat-i-Kaisar-i-Hind, Raja Sir Har Indar Singh Brar Bans Bahadur, Ruler of,** KCSI, *cr* 1941; *b* 29 Jan. 1915; *S* father as Raja, 1919; *m* 1933. *Educ:* Aitchison Chiefs Coll., Lahore. Full Ruling Powers, 1934; is one of Ruling Princes of India; Hon. Col Sikh LI; Hon. Col Bengal Engineer Group; MLA Pepsu LA. Salute, 11 guns. Formerly Mem. National Defence Council of India and of Standing Cttee of Chamber of Princes. *Address:* Faridkot, Punjab, India.

**FARINGDON,** 2nd Baron *cr* 1916; **Alexander Gavin Henderson,** Bt *cr* 1902; *b* 20 March 1902; *e s* of late Lt-Col Hon. H. G. Henderson, CVO, and Lady Violet Dalzell, *sister* of 15th Earl of Carnwath; *S* grandfather, 1934. *Educ:* Eton; McGill Univ., Montreal; Christ Church, Oxford (MA). Diploma of Internat. Exhibn of Brussels, 1935. Auxiliary Fire Service, 1940; Column Officer, NFS, 1941; Staff 15 FF.

Treasurer, Cttee of Inquiry into Non-Intervention in Spain, 1936; Pres., Swindon Branch, Labour League of Youth, 1936; Treasurer, Nat. Council for Civil Liberties, 1940-45; co-opted Mem. of Exec. Cttee, Inter-Parly Union (British Group), 1948; Mem., Colonial Economic and Develt Council, 1948-51; Mem., Parly Cttee of Labour Party, 1957-60. Fabian Society: elected and co-opted Mem. of Exec. Cttee, 1942-66; Vice-Chm., 1959-60; Chm., 1960-61. London County Council: co-opted Mem., Mental Hospitals Cttee, 1937-38; Mem. for W Woolwich, 1958-61; Alderman, 1961-65. Adv. Expert, GLC Historic Buildings Bd. President: Assoc. of Friends of City Churches, 1943; Theatres Adv. Council, 1964; British Fire Services Assoc., 1960-69. Chm., Cttee on Appearance of Local Authorities' Housing Estates. Member: Council, Nat. Buildings Record, 1942; Central Housing Adv. Cttee, 1946; No Conscription Council, 1946; Colonial Social Welfare Adv. Cttee, 1947-52; Central Adv. Water Cttee, 1949-52; Treatment, Offenders Cttee, CO, 1951; Historic Buildings Council, MPBW, 1964. Trustee, Wallace Collection, 1946-53, 1966-. FRSA 1936. Master, Worshipful Co. of Plumbers, 1968-69. *Heir: n* Charles Michael Henderson [*b* 3 July 1937; *m* 1959, Sarah Caroline, *d* of Major J. M. E. Askew, *qv*; two *s* one *d*]. *Address:* Buscot Park, Faringdon, Berks. *Clubs:* St James', Canning, Reform.

**FARLEY, Dr Francis James Macdonald;** Dean, Royal Military College of Science, Shrivenham, since 1967; *b* 13 Oct. 1920; *er s* of late Brig. Edward Lionel Farley, CBE, MC; *m* 1945, Josephine Maisie Hayden; three *s* one *d*. *Educ:* Clifton Coll.; Clare Coll., Cambridge. MA 1945; PhD 1950; ScD Cantab 1967. Air Defence Research and Development Establishment, 1941-45; Chalk River Laboratories, 1945-46; Research Student, Cavendish Lab., Cambridge, 1946-49; Auckland Univ. Coll., NZ, 1950-57; attached AERE, 1955; CERN, Geneva, 1957-67. Vis. Lectr, Univ. of Bristol, 1965-66. Rep. NZ at UN Conf. on Atomic Energy for Peaceful Purposes, 1955. FInstP; Fellow, British Computer Soc. *Publications:* Elements of Pulse Circuits, 1955; Progress in Nuclear Techniques and Instrumentation, Vol. I, 1966, Vol. II, 1967, Vol. III 1968; scientific papers on nuclear physics, electronics and high energy particle physics. *Recreations:* gliding (FAI gold and diamond); ski-ing. *Address:* 2 Lake Road, Shrivenham, Swindon, Wilts. *T:* Shrivenham 434. *Club:* Athenæum.

**FARMAR, Hugh William;** Clerk to the Drapers' Company, since 1952; Governor (Treasurer) Queen Mary College, University of London, Hon. Fellow, 1967; Member Executive Committee, Field Studies Council; *b* 6 June 1908; *o s* of late Col H. M. Farmar, CMG, DSO, and of Violet, *y d* of late Sir William Dalby; *m* 1944, Constantia, *o d* of late Rt Hon. Sir Horace Rumbold, 9th Bt, GCB, and late Etheldred, Lady Rumbold, CBE; two *s*. *Educ:* Eton; Balliol Coll., Oxford. 2nd class clerk, Charity Commn, 1937; RAFVR, 1939-46 (on staff, Resident Minister, Accra, 1942-43; Asst Private Sec. to Sec. of State for Air 1945-46). Principal clerk, Charity Commn, 1946. Hon. LLD William and Mary Coll., Virginia, 1968. *Publications:* The Cottage in the Forest, 1949; A Regency Elopement, 1969; articles and broadcasts on travel and country subjects. *Recreations:* country pursuits. *Address:* Drapers' Hall, EC2. *T:* 01-588 5002. *Clubs:* Brooks's, Pratt's.

*See also Sir H. Anthony Rumbold, Bt, Lord Swinfen.*

**FARMER, Prof. Edward Desmond;** Louis Cohen Professor of Dental Surgery, since 1957, and Pro-Vice-Chancellor, 1967-70, University of Liverpool; *b* 15 April 1917; *s* of late S. R. and M. L. Farmer; *m* 1942, Mary Elwood Little; one *s* two *d*. *Educ:* Newcastle-under-Lyme High Sch.; Univ. of Liverpool (1936-41); Queens' Coll., Cambridge (1948-50). MA Cantab, 1955; MDS Liverpool, 1951; FDSRCS 1952; MRCPath 1967, FRCPath 1968. RNVR, Surgeon Lieut (D), 1942-45; Lectr in Parodontal Diseases, Univ. of Liverpool, 1950-57; Nuffield Fellow, 1948-50. Hon. Cons. Dent. Surg. to Bd of Govs of United Liverpool Hosps and to Liverpool Regional Hosp. Bd, 1957-. Member Council: Brit. Soc. of Periodontology, 1954-59 (Pres. 1957-58); RSM, Odonto. Sect., 1965-68. Member: Central Cttee and Exec., Hosp. Dental Service, 1964-; Bd of Govs, United Liverpool Hosps, 1968-71; UGC Dental Sect., 1968-. Pres. NW Br. Brit. Dental Assoc., 1967-68. *Publications:* (with F. E. Lawton) Stones' Oral and Dental Diseases, 5th edn, 1966; papers in Proceedings Royal Society Med., Jl of Gen. Microbiology, Brit. Med. Jl, Dental Practitioner. *Recreations:* gardening, painting and enjoyment of the countryside. *Address:* Highlands, Tower Road North, Heswall, Cheshire L60 6RT. *T:* 051-342 3179.

**FARMER, Sir George;** *see* Farmer, Sir L. G. T.

**FARMER, Rev. Herbert Henry,** MA Cantab, Hon. DD Glasgow; Emeritus Professor of Systematic Theology 1935-60, in Westminster College, Cambridge; *b* 27 Nov. 1892; *s* of William Charles Farmer and Mary Ann Buck; *m* 1923, Gladys Sylvie Offord; one *s* two *d*. *Educ:* Owen's Sch., Islington; Peterhouse, Cambridge (1st cl. Moral Sciences Tripos; Burney Studentship in the Philosophy of Religion, University of Cambridge); Westminster Coll., Cambridge. Minister of Presbyterian Church, Stafford, 1919-22; Minister of St Augustine's Presbyterian Church, New Barnet, 1922-31; Carew Lecturer, Hartford Seminary Foundation, USA, 1930; Riley Prof. of Christian Doctrine, Hartford Seminary Foundation, USA, 1931-35; Barbour Prof. of Systematic Theology, Westminster Coll. (Presbyterian), Cambridge, 1935-60; Norris-Hulse Prof. of Divinity, Cambridge University, 1949-60; Fellow of Peterhouse, Cambridge, 1950-60. Stanton Lecturer in the Philosophy of Religion, University of Cambridge, 1937-40; Warrack Lecturer, 1940; Lyman Beecher Lecturer, Yale Univ., 1946; Gifford Lecturer, Glasgow Univ., 1950-51. *Publications:* Things Not Seen, 1927; Experience of God, 1929; The World and God, 1935; The Healing Cross, 1938; The Servant of the Word, 1941; Towards Belief in God, 1942; God and Men, 1948; Revelation and Religion, 1954; The Word of Reconciliation, 1967. *Address:* 24 Woodland Drive, Hove 4, Sussex. *T:* 504901.

**FARMER, Hugh Robert Macdonald,** CB 1967; Clerk/Administrator, House of Commons, since 1965; *b* 3 Dec. 1907; *s* of late Charles Edward Farmer and late Emily (*née* Randolph); *m* 1st, 1934, Penelope Frances (*d* 1963), *d* of late Capt. Evelyn Boothby, RN; one *s* three *d*; 2nd, 1966, Jean, *widow* of Peter Bluett Winch. *Educ:* Cheam Sch.; Eton Coll.; New Coll., Oxford. House of Commons: Asst Clerk, 1931; Sen. Clerk, 1943; Clerk of Private Bills and Taxing Officer, and Examr of Petitions for Private Bills, 1958-60; Clerk of Cttees, 1960-65. *Recreations:* golf, gardening. *Address:* Brook Lawn, Whitmoor Vale, Hindhead, Surrey. *T:* Hindhead 5791. *Club:* MCC.

**FARMER, Sir (Lovedin) George (Thomas),** Kt 1968; MA, FCA, JDipMA; Chairman, Rover Co. Ltd, since 1963; 2nd Vice-Chairman and Member of Advisory Committee, Metalurgica de Santa Ana, SA, Madrid; Director: British Leyland Motor Corporation; ATV Network Ltd; Empresa Nacional de Automcamiones, SA, Madrid; Pro-Chancellor, Birmingham University, since 1966 (Deputy Pro-Chancellor 1965-66); *b* 13 May 1908; *m* 1938, Editha Mary Fisher; no *c*. *Educ:* Oxford High Sch. President: Birmingham Chamber of Commerce, 1960-61; Soc. of Motor Manufrs and Traders, 1962-64 (Dep. Pres., 1964-65; Chm., Exec. Cttee, 1968-); Past Mem., Advisory Council, ECGD (Board of Trade); Member of: Export Council for Europe; UK Committee of Federation of Commonwealth and British Chambers of Commerce; Vice-Pres., West Midlands Engineering Employers' Assoc.; Governor, Chm. Executive Council (1966-), and Chm. Finance Cttee, Royal Shakespeare Theatre; Pres., Loft Theatre, Leamington Spa. Mem. Court, Worshipful Co. of Coach and Coach Harness Makers. *Recreations:* theatre, golf, fishing. *Address:* Sicca Lodge, Long Marston, Stratford-on-Avon, Warwicks. *T:* Pebworth 282. *Clubs:* Bath, Kennel, Fly-Fishers', Coventry Aeroplane.

**FARMER, Norman William,** CBE 1955; Director, S. W. Farmer & Son Ltd; *b* 11 Oct. 1901; *s* of Sydney William and Anna Emily Farmer; *m* 1925, Brenda Modwyn Briselden; one *s* one *d*. *Educ:* Hither Green Sch.; Addey and Stanhope Sch. Constructional Engineer in family business (established 1898). Deputy Chairman, London County Council, 1960-61; Chm., North Lewisham Conservative Assoc., 1946-64; Chm. London Conservative Union, 1959-60. Mem. of LCC for North Lewisham, 1945-65. Liveryman, Founders' Company; Life Deacon, Lewisham Congregational Church. *Address:* Avonhurst, Camden Park Road, Chislehurst, Kent. *Clubs:* Royal Automobile, City Livery, United Wards, Guild of Freemen.

**FARNCOMB, Rear-Adm. Harold Bruce,** CB 1945; DSO 1943; MVO 1935; RAN retired; Solicitor; *b* Sydney, Australia, 28 Feb. 1899; *s* of Frank Farncomb and Helen Sampson; *m* 1927, Jean Ross Nott; no *c*. *Educ:* Royal Australian Naval Coll. Joined Royal Australian Navy, 1913; Grand Fleet, 1917-18; RN Staff Coll., 1923-24; Imperial Defence Coll., 1930; Comdr, 1932; HMAS Australia, 1933-35, return of Duke of Gloucester (MVO); Admiralty (NID), 1935-37; One of RAN representatives at the funeral of King George V; Attached to the Delegation from the Argentine Republic at the Coronation of King George VI; Capt., 1937; Commodore, 1st class, Dec. 1944. Commanded HMA Ships Perth, Canberra, Australia (1939-44), HMS Attacker (1944), HMA Squadron (1944-45), Commodore Superintendent of Training (1945-46), Commodore (later Rear-Adm.) Comdg Australian Squadron (DSO, CB, despatches thrice); Rear-Adm., 1947. Called to Bar, Supreme Court of NSW, 1958; transferred to Solicitor, 1963. Commander United States Legion of Merit; US Navy Cross. *Recreation:* lawn tennis. *Address:* 10 Wyldefel Gardens, Pott's Point, Sydney, Australia. *Clubs:* United Service; Australian (Sydney).

**FARNHAM,** 12th Baron, *cr* 1756; **Barry Owen Somerset Maxwell;** Bt (Nova Scotia) 1627; Director, Brown, Shipley & Co. Ltd (Merchant Bankers), since 1959; *b* 7 July 1931; *s* of Hon. Somerset Arthur Maxwell, MP (died of wounds received in action, 1942), and Angela Susan (*d* 1953), *o d* of late Capt. Marshall Owen Roberts; *S* grandfather 1957; *m* 1959, Diana Marion, *er d* of Nigel Gunnis; two adopted *d*. *Educ:* Eton; Harvard Univ. *Heir:* *b* Hon. Simon Kenlis Maxwell [*b* 12 Dec. 1933; *m* 1964, Karol Anne, *d* of Maj.-Gen. G. E. Prior-Palmer, *qv*; two *s* one *d* (of whom one *s* one *d* are twins)]. *Address:* 11 Earl's Court Gardens, SW5; Farnham, Co. Cavan. *Clubs:* Boodle's; Kildare Street (Dublin).

**FARNHILL, Rear-Adm. Kenneth Haydn,** CB 1968; OBE 1945; Director of Management and Support of Intelligence, Ministry of Defence, 1966-69, retired; *b* 13 April 1913; *s* of late H. Haydn Farnhill, Bedford; *m* 1938, Helen May, *d* of late W. Houghton, Southsea; one *s* one *d*. *Educ:* Bedford. Joined RN, 1930. Served 1939-45: Home Fleet, Admty, Eastern Fleet. Sec. to Controller of Navy, 1953-56; Capt., RN Supply Sch., 1958-59; IDC 1960. Comdr 1948; Capt. 1957; Rear-Adm. 1966. *Address:* 1 Christchurch Gardens, Widley, Portsmouth, Hants. *T:* Cosham 77187. *Club:* Royal Naval (Portsmouth).

**FARNSWORTH, John Windsor;** Chairman, East Midlands Economic Planning Board, since 1965; *b* 5 May 1912; *yr s* of late Arthur Claude and Annie Farnsworth, Derby; *m* 1938, Betty Mary Bristow; two *s*. *Educ:* Hanley High Sch.; Balliol Coll., Oxford; Univ. of Birmingham. Asst Comr, Nat. Savings Cttee, 1935; transf. to Min. of Nat. Insurance, 1948; Regional Controller, N Midland Region, Min. of Pensions and Nat. Insurance, 1961; transf. to Dept of Economic Affairs, 1965; Min. of Housing and Local Govt, 1969. Pres., Nottingham and E Mids Group, Royal Inst. of Public Administration, 1966-68. *Address:* 143 Melton Road, West Bridgford, Nottingham. *T:* Nottingham 231937.

**FARQUHAR, Lt-Col Sir Peter (Walter),** 6th Bt, *cr* 1796; DSO 1943 (and Bar 1944); JP; 16th/5th Lancers; RAC Reserve of Officers, retired; *b* 8 Oct. 1904; *s* of 5th Bt and Violet (*d* 1959), *d* of Col Charles Seymour Corkran, late Grenadier Guards; *S* father, 1918; *m* 1937, Elizabeth Evelyn, *d* of late Francis Cecil Albert Hurt; three *s*. *Educ:* Eton; RMC, Sandhurst. Served War of 1939-45, France, Middle East and Italy (wounded thrice, DSO and Bar). Joint-Master of Portman Hounds, 1947-59. JP Dorset, 1955. *Heir:* *s* Michael Fitzroy Henry Farquhar [*b* 29 June 1938; *m* 1963, Veronica Geraldine, *e d* of Patrick Hornidge, Newton Ferrers, and of Mrs M. F. L. Beebee, Walton, Radnorshire; two *s*]. *Address:* West Kington House, Chippenham, Wiltshire. *T:* Castle Coombe 331. *Club:* White's.

**FARQUHARSON, Eric L(eslie),** MD, VPRCSEd, FRCS; Surgeon in charge, Royal Infirmary Edinburgh; Member Council and Examiner, Royal College of Surgeons, Edinburgh; Member, Council, Royal College of Surgeons, England; *b* 13 Dec. 1905; *s* of W. A. Farquharson, SSC and Agnes N. Cowie; *m* 1940, Dr Elizabeth MacWatt, *yr d* of late Dr John MacWatt, Duns, Berwickshire; two *d*. *Educ:* Edinburgh Academy; Univ. of Edinburgh. Lt-Col, RAMC, 1939-45; active service in Africa, Ceylon and India. *Publications:* Illustrations of Surgical Treatment, 1939; Textbook of Operative Surgery, 4th edn 1969; numerous contributions to Medical and Surgical Journals. *Recreations:* golf, photography. *Address:* 6 Chamberlain Road, Edinburgh 10.

**FARQUHARSON, Sir James (Robbie),** KBE 1960 (CBE 1948; OBE 1944); retired, and is now farming; *b* 1 Nov. 1903; *s* of Frank

Farquharson, Cortachy, Angus, Scotland, and Agnes Jane Robbie; *m* 1933, Agnes Binny Graham; two *s. Educ:* Royal Technical College, Glasgow; Glasgow Univ. BSc Glasgow 1923. Asst Engineer, LMS Railway, 1923-25; Asst Engineer, Kenya and Uganda Railway, 1925-33; Senior Asst Engineer, Kenya and Uganda Railway, 1933-37; Asst to Gen. Manager, Tanganyika Railways, 1937-41; Chief Engineer, Tanganyika Railways, 1941-45; General Manager, Tanganyika Railways, 1945-48; Deputy General Manager, East African Railways, 1948-52; Gen. Manager, Sudan Railways, 1952-57; Gen. Manager, East African Railways and Harbours, 1957-61; Asst Crown Agent and Engineer-in-Chief of Crown Agents for Overseas Governments and Administrations, 1961-65. Dir (non-exec.): English Electric–AEI Traction Ltd; Millbank Technical Services Ltd; Consultant to: African Development Bank; Associated Railway Consultants. *Publication:* Tanganyika Transport, 1944. *Recreation:* cricket. *Address:* Kinclune, By Kirriemuir, Angus, Scotland. *T:* Kingoldrum 210. *Club:* Nairobi (Kenya).

**FARR, John Arnold;** MP (C) Harborough Division of Leicestershire since 1959; Member of Lloyd's; *b* 25 Sept. 1922; *er s* of late Capt. John Farr, JP, and Mrs M. A. Farr, JP; *m* 1960, Susan Ann, *d* of Sir Leonard Milburn, 3rd Bt, and of Joan Lady Milburn, Guyzance Hall, Acklington, Northumberland; two *s. Educ:* Harrow. RN, 1940-46; now in Reserve. Executive Dir, Home Brewery and Apollo Productions Ltd, 1950-55. Pres. Worksop Boys Club, 1951-55. Contested Ilkeston, General Election, 1955. Past Member: East Midlands Land Tribunal and Council of Notts Branch of Country Landowners Association. *Recreations:* cricket and shooting. *Address:* Shortwood House, Lamport, Northants. *T:* Maidwell 260; 11 Vincent Square, Westminster, SW1; Tanrago, Beltra, Co. Sligo. *T:* Beltra 6. *Clubs:* Boodle's, MCC.

**FARR, Air Vice-Marshal Peter Gerald Desmond,** CB 1968; OBE 1952; DFC 1942; Air Officer-in-Charge Administration, Strike Command, since 1969; *b* 26 Sept. 1917; *s* of late Gerald Farr and Mrs Farr (*née* Miers); *m* 1949, Rosemarie, *d* of late R. S. Haward; two *s* one *d. Educ:* Tonbridge Sch. Commnd. in RAF, 1937; flying duties, Middle East, 1938-39; served War of 1939-45, Middle East, India and Burma; OC, No. 358 Sqdn, 1944-45; OC, RAF Pegu, 1945-46; Air Min., 1947-50; OC, 120 Sqdn, 1950-51; Dep. Dir, Jt Anti-Submarine sch., 1952-54; OC, RAF Idris, 1954-55; Air Min., Policy and Plans, 1956-58; Directing Staff, Jt Services Staff Coll., 1959; SASO, Malta, 1960-63; OC, RAF Kinloss, 1963-64; Air Officer Administration, RAF Germany, 1964-68; HQ Strike Command, 1968-69. *Recreations:* golf, fishing, music. *Address:* c/o Lloyds Bank, Stanmore, Middx. *Club:* Royal Air Force.

**FARRANT, Maj.-Gen. Ralph Henry,** CB 1964; retd; *b* 2 Feb. 1909; *s* of late Henry Farrant, MICE, Rye, Sussex; *m* 1932, Laura Bonella, *d* of late Lieut-Col G. Clifford M. Hall, CMG, DSO; two *d. Educ:* Rugby; RMA, Woolwich. 2nd Lieut, RA 1929; Field and Mountain Artillery till 1938. War of 1939-45: Tech. Appts in Min. of Defence (1) and HQ, MEF, 3rd British Inf. Div., 1944. Lieut-Col 1950, Min. of Supply; Col 1954; Brig. 1957; Dir of Munitions, Brit. Jt Services Mission, Washington, 1955-58; Sen. Mil. Officer, Armament R&D Estabt, 1958-61; Maj.-Gen. 1961; Vice-Pres., Ordnance Board, 1961-63; Pres. of Ordnance Bd, War Office, 1963-64. *Recreation:* sailing. *Address:* King's Acre, Stoborough, Wareham, Dorset. *Clubs:* Army and Navy, Royal Yacht Squadron, Royal Ocean Racing, Royal Artillery Yacht.

**FARRAR-HOCKLEY, Maj.-Gen. Anthony Heritage,** DSO 1953 and bar 1964; MBE 1957; MC 1944; author (Military History); Commander, Land Forces, Northern Ireland, since 1970; *b* 8 April 1924; *s* of late Arthur Farrar-Hockley; *m* 1945, Margaret Bernadette Wells; two *s* (and one *s* decd). *Educ:* Exeter Sch. War of 1939-45 (despatches, MC): enlisted under-age in ranks of The Gloucestershire Regt and served until Nov. 1942; commissioned into newly forming 1st Airborne Div., campaigning in Greece, Italy, S France, to 1945. Palestine, 1945-46; Korea, 1950-53; despatches, 1954; Cyprus and Port Said, 1956; Jordan, 1958; College Chief Instructor, RMA Sandhurst, 1959-61; commanded parachute bn in Persian Gulf and Radfan campaign, 1962-65; Principal Staff Officer to Dir of Borneo Ops, 1965-66; Comdr, 16 Parachute Bde, 1966-68; Defence Fellowship, Exeter Coll., Oxford, 1968-70; DPR (Army), 1970. *Publications:* The Edge of the Sword, 1954; (ed) The Commander, 1957; The Somme, 1964; Death of an Army, 1968; Airborne Carpet, 1969; War in the Desert, 1969. *Recreations:* cricket, badminton, walking. *Address:* Headquarters Northern Ireland, Lisburn, Co. Antrim, N Ireland. *Club:* Savage.

**FARRELL, Arthur Acheson,** CB 1962; *b* Portadown, 29 July 1898; *s* of late Arthur T. Farrell, Portadown, solicitor, and of Ellen Moorcroft, *d* of late Hugh Anderson, Belfast; *m* 1st, 1925, Margaret Kerr (*d* 1945), *d* of Archibald Irwin, JP, Belfast; three *s*; 2nd, 1954, Wilhelmina (*sister* of 1st wife). *Educ:* Campbell Coll., Belfast; Trinity Coll., Dublin. Royal Artillery, 1917-19. Chartered Accountant, 1922; Registrar of Claims Tribunal, 1923; Civil Service, Northern Ireland: Ministry of: Finance, Asst Principal, 1924; Home Affairs, Dep. Principal, 1928, Principal, 1935, Asst Sec., 1939; Public Security, 1940; Commerce, 1945-58. Comptroller and Auditor-Gen. for Northern Ireland, 1959-63, retired. *Recreations:* photography, bowls, carpentry. *Address:* 61 Lisburn Road, Belfast BT9 7AE. *T:* Belfast 22196.

**FARRELL, Arthur Denis,** CMG 1970; *b* 27 Jan. 1906; *s* of Joseph Jessop Farrell, CBE; *m* 1953, Margaret Madeline (*née* Cox); one *s. Educ:* St Paul's Sch.; Balliol Coll., Oxford. Sixth Form (Classical) Master, Sedbergh Sch., 1929-30, Bradford Grammar Sch., 1930-36; called to the Bar, Middle Temple, 1937; Sixth Form (Classical) Master, Bedford Sch., 1939-41; served RAF, 1941-46. Squadron-Leader; Crown Counsel, Singapore, 1947-51: Legal Draftsman, Fedn of Malaya, 1951-56; Solicitor-Gen., Fedn of Malaya, 1956-58; QC 1957; Puisne Judge, Kenya, 1958-69 (Acting Chief Justice, 1968). Coronation Medal, 1953. *Recreations:* golf, photography, music. *Address:* 64 East Avenue, Bournemouth, Hants. *Club:* Oxford and Cambridge University.

**FARRELL, James T.;** Novelist and Critic; *b* Chicago, Ill, 27 Feb. 1904; *m* Dorothy Butler (divorced); *m* Hortense Alden (divorced, 1955); one *s*; re-married Dorothy Butler (separated). *Educ:* De Paul [now Depaul] Univ., Chicago; Univ. of Chicago; New York Univ., no degrees. Worked for express company, in gasoline filling station, as salesman, etc.; received John Simon Guggenheim Memorial Foundation Fellowship in Creative Literature, 1926-37; Nat. Inst. Arts and Letters, NYC. Formerly

Adjunct Prof., St Peter's Coll., Jersey City, NJ; in residence, Richmond Coll., Richmond, Va, Sept. 1969-Feb. 1970. Hon. Dr of Letters Miami Univ., Oxford, Ohio, 1968. *Publications:* Studs Lonigan; A Note on Literary Criticism; Fellow Countrymen (in US as The Collected Short Stories of James T. Farrell); A World Never Made; Gas House McGinty (in US only); No Star is Lost; Tommy Gallagher's Crusade, 1939; Father and Son, 1940 (in England, 1943); Ellen Rogers, 1941 (in England. 1942); $1000 a Week and Other Stories, 1942; My Days of Anger, 1943 (England 1945); To Whom it may Concern, 1944; The League of Frightened Philistines and other Papers; Bernard Clare, 1946 (England 1948); When Boyhood Dreams Come True, 1946; More Fellow-Countrymen, 1946; Literature and Morality, 1947; The Life Adventurous, 1947; A Misunderstanding, 1948; The Road Between, 1949; (under pseudonym of Jonathan Lituleson Fogarty) The Name is Fogarty; An American Dream Girl, 1950; This Man and This Woman, 1951; Yet Other Waters, 1952; The Face of Time (England), 1953; Reflections at Fifty (England), 1954; French Girls are Vicious, 1955; A Baseball Diary, also A Dangerous Woman and Other Stories, 1957; It Has Come to Pass, 1958; Boarding House Blues (novel), 1961; Side Street (stories), 1961; Sound of the City (stories), 1962; The Silence of History (novel), 1963; What Time Collects (novel), 1967; The Collected Poems of James T. Farrell, 1965; Lonely For the Future (novel), 1966; When Time Was Born (prose poem), 1966; New Year's Eve, 1929 (novel), 1967; A Brand New Life (novel), 1968; Childhood Is Not Forever and other Stories, 1969; Judith (novel), 1969; Invisible Swords (novel), 1970. *Address:* c/o Doubleday & Co., 277 Park Avenue, New York, NY 10017, USA.

**FARRELL, M. J.;** *see* Keane, Mrs Robert.

**FARREN, Most Rev. Neil;** *see* Derry, Bishop of, (RC).

**FARRER, Hon. Dame Frances (Margaret),** DBE, *cr* 1950; Director, Abinger Hall Estate Co., since 1942; *b* 17 March 1895; *d* of 2nd Baron Farrer. *Educ:* St Leonard's Sch., St Andrews; Newnham Coll., Cambridge. Hon. Sec. Leith Hill Musical Festival, 1919-39; Gen. Sec., National Federation of Women's Institutes, 1929-59; Member: ITA, 1957-61; Post Office Advisory Council, 1957-64. Cttee on Rural Bus Services, 1959-61. *Address:* West Hackhurst, Abinger Hammer, Surrey.

**FARRER, Sir Leslie;** *see* Farrer, Sir W. L.

**FARRER, Sir (Walter) Leslie,** KCVO, *cr* 1948; solicitor (retired); *b* 30 Jan. 1900; 2nd *s* of late Bryan Farrer, Binnegar Hall, Wareham, Dorset; *m* 1926, Hon. Marjorie Laura Pollock, *d* of 1st Viscount Hanworth; one *s* one *d. Educ:* Rugby; Balliol. Admitted a Solicitor, 1926; Partner Messrs Farrer & Co., 1927-64; Mem. Council of Law Soc., 1945-52; Mem. Disciplinary Cttee under Solicitors Acts, 1953-63. Private Solicitor to King George VI and to the Queen, 1937-64. Pres., London Life Assoc. Ltd; Dir, Mercantile and General Reinsurance Co. Ltd; Pres. Selden Soc., 1955. Prime Warden, Fishmongers' Co., 1968-69. *Recreations:* reading and sight-seeing. *Address:* Charlwood Place Farm, Charlwood, Surrey. *T:* Norwood Hill 413. *Club:* Travellers'.

**FARRER-BROWN, Leslie,** CBE 1960; Consultant; Director, Nuffield Foundation, 1944-64; *b* 2 April 1904; *er s* of late Sydney and Annie Brown; *m* 1928, Doris Evelyn, *o d* of late Herbert Jamieson; two *s. Educ:* LSE (BSc Econ.); Gray's Inn (Barrister-at-Law, 1932). Asst Registrar, LSE, 1927-28; on Administrative Staff, Univ. of London, 1928-36; Sec., Central Midwives Bd, 1936-45; seconded to Min. of Health, 1941-44. Dir, Alliance Building Soc., 1969-; Pres., Surrey and Sussex Rent Assessment Panel, 1965-. Vice-President, Inst. of Race Relations, 1968-; Royal Commonwealth Soc., 1969-. Sec., Interdepartmental Cttee on Med. Schs, 1942-44. Chairman: Malta Med. Services Commn, 1956; Highgate Juvenile Court, 1952-61; Highgate Court, 1961-65; Nat. Council of Social Service; Centre for Educational Television Overseas, 1962-70; Overseas Visual Aid Centre, 1958-70; Voluntary Cttee on Overseas Aid and Develt; Centre for Information on Language Teaching; Cttee for Res. and Develt in Modern Languages, 1964-70; Rhodesia Med. Sch. Cttee; Univ. of London Inst. of Child Health. Member: Colonial Adv. Med. Cttee, 1946-61; Colonial Social Science Res. Council, 1954-61; Med. Educn Cttee of UGC, 1945-52; Rating of Charities Cttee, 1958-59; Adv. Council, BBC, 1956-65; Court of Governors, LSE; Council, Univ. of Sussex (Vice-Chm.). Trustee, Nuffield Provincial Hospitals Trust, 1955-67; UK Trustee, Commonwealth Foundn, 1966-. JP: Middx, 1947-65; East Sussex, 1966-. Hon. FDSRCS. Hon. LLD: Birmingham; Witwatersrand; Hon. DSc Keele. *Publication:* (jt) A Short Textbook on Public Health and Social Services. *Recreations:* travel, painting. *Address:* Dale House, Keere Street, Lewes, Sussex. *Club:* Athenæum.

**FARRINGTON, Benjamin;** *b* 10 July 1891; *s* of Thomas Farrington and Mary Emily Foreman; *m* 1935, Ruth Hedwig Schechter (*d* 1942); *m* 1943, Cecily Barbara Sell; one *d. Educ:* University Coll., Cork; Trinity Coll., Dublin. Asst in Classics, Queen's Univ., Belfast, 1916-20; Lecturer in Greek, University of Capetown, 1920-22; Senior Lecturer in Classics, 1922-30; Prof. of Latin, 1930-35; Lecturer in Classics, University of Bristol, 1935-36; Prof. of Classics, University Coll., Swansea, 1936-56. *Publications:* Primum Graius Homo; Samuel Butler and the Odyssey; Science in Antiquity, rev. edn 1969; Science and Politics in the Ancient World, 1939; Greek Science: Its Meaning for Us, Vol. I. 1944, Vol. II, 1948, revised edn in one Vol., 1953; Head and Hand in Ancient Greece, 1947; Francis Bacon, Philosopher of Industrial Science (New York), 1949; The Philosophy of Francis Bacon, 1962; Aristotle: The Founder of Scientific Philosophy, 1965; What Darwin Really Said, 1965; The Faith of Epicurus, 1967; etc. *Address:* 8 Daniell's Walk, Lymington, Hants. *T:* Lymington 2059.

**FARRINGTON, Sir Henry Francis Colden,** 7th Bt, *cr* 1818; RA retired; *b* 25 April 1914; *s* of Sir Henry Anthony Farrington, 6th Bt, and Dorothy Maria (*d* 1969), *o d* of Frank Farrington; *S* father, 1944; *m* 1947, Anne, *e d* of late Major W. A. Gillam, DSO; one *s* one *d. Educ:* Haileybury. Retired from Army, 1960 (Major). *Heir: s* Henry William Farrington, *b* 27 March 1951. *Address:* Quarry Cleeve, Wiveliscombe, Taunton, Somerset. *T:* Wiveliscombe 219.

**FARRIS, Hon. John Wallace de Beque,** QC; DCL, LLD (British Columbia); Barrister; Member of Senate of Canada since 1937; *b* 3 Dec. 1878; *s* of Hon. L. P. and Mary Louise Hay Farris; *m* 1905, Evlyn F. Keirstead; three *s* one *d. Educ:* Acadia University; University of Pennsylvania. Attorney-Gen. British Columbia, 1917-22; Past Treasurer Law Soc. of British Columbia; Pres. Canadian Bar Association, 1937-38; Hon. member: American

Bar Assoc.; Vancouver Bar Assoc.; Hon. Bencher BC Law Soc. *Address:* 3351 Granville Street, Vancouver, BC, Canada. *Clubs:* Union (Victoria); Vancouver (Vancouver); Rideau (Ottawa).

**FARROW, G. Martin,** CBE 1934; JP; FICS; *b* 10 April 1896; *s* of George Frederick and Ruth Jane Eleanor Farrow; *m* 1923, Dorothy Elaine Drysdale; two *d. Educ:* Sydney, New South Wales. Served with the 18th Bn AIF in Egypt, Gallipoli, and France (wounded at Anzac and Pozieres); Chm., War Pensions Inquiry, 1931; Federal Pres., Limbless Soldiers Assoc., 1924-38; Trustee of the Anzac Memorial, 1926-37; Mem. of War Pensions Entitlement Appeal Tribunal, 1937-38. *Address:* 8 Esther Road, Balmoral Beach, NSW, Australia. *T:* Sydney 96-8351. *Club:* Legacy (Sydney).

**FARROW, Leslie William,** CBE 1947; FCA, FID, FRSA; chartered accountant; *b* 7 Oct. 1888; *s* of late Albert Lee Farrow and Elfleda Susan Taylor; *m* 1915, Elsie Beatrice Allman; three *d. Educ:* Alleyn's, Dulwich; London Sch. of Economics. Formerly: dir of public companies, mem. of the Bacon Development Board; Deputy Controller of Paper, 1939-40; Dir for Commercial Relations, 1940-42; Deputy Chm. Rubber Control Board, 1942; Deputy Dir-Gen. (raw materials), Ministry of Supply, 1942; Chm. National Brick Advisory Council, Ministry of Works and Planning, 1942; Chm. Paper Economy Cttee, Ministry of Production, 1942; Mem. of Board of Referees, 1948. Commandeur de l'Ordre de la Couronne (Belge), 1957. Paper Trade Gold Medal Award, 1957. *Address:* Dengie Manor, near Southminster, Essex. *T:* Tillingham 216. *Club:* City of London.

**FARWELL, Rt. Rev. Gerard Victor;** Abbot of Worth since 1965; Abbot President of English Benedictine Congregation since 1967; *b* 15 Oct. 1913; 3rd *s* of late Frederick Arthur Farwell and Monica Mary Quin. *Educ:* St Benedict's, Ealing. Entered Downside Abbey, 1932; Housemaster at Downside Sch., 1946-48; Bursar at Worth, 1950-57; Prior of Worth, 1957-65. *Address:* Worth Abbey, Crawley, Sussex.

**FATT, Dr Paul,** FRS 1969; Reader, Department of Biophysics, University College, London, since 1956; *b* 13 Jan. 1924; *s* of David Fatt and Annie Fatt (*née* Arkin); *m* 1st, 1953, Ione Copplestone (marr. diss. 1960); one *s* two *d*; 2nd, 1961, Gertrude Falk; one *d. Educ:* Los Angeles City Coll.; University of California (Berkeley). Served in US Army, 1943-46. University Coll., London, 1948-52; Australian National Univ., 1952-55. *Publications:* papers in: Jl of Physiology, Jl of Neurophysiology, Proc. Royal Soc., etc. *Recreation:* walking. *Address:* 5b Hampstead Hill Gardens, NW3.

**FAULDS, Andrew M. W.;** MP (Lab) Smethwick since 1966; *b* 1 March 1923; *s* of late Rev. Matthew Faulds, MA, and of Doris Faulds; *m* 1945, Bunty Whitfield; one *d. Educ:* George Watson's, Edinburgh; King Edward VI Grammar Sch., Louth; Daniel Stewart's, Edinburgh; High Sch., Stirling; Glasgow Univ. Three seasons with Shakespeare Memorial Co., Stratford-upon-Avon; BBC Repertory Co.: Jet Morgan in Journey into Space (BBC). Has appeared in over 30 films and many TV and radio performances. Parliamentary Private Secretary: to Minister of State for Aviation, Min. of Technology, 1967-68; to Postmaster General, 1968-69. *Recreation:* cosseting his constituents. *Address:* 14 Albemarle Street, W1. *T:* 01-499 7589.

**FAULKNER, Rt. Hon. (Arthur) Brian (Deane),** PC (Northern Ireland) 1959; MP (Northern Ireland) for East Down, since 1949; Minister of Development Northern Ireland, since 1969; *b* 18 Feb. 1921; *er s* of James Alexander Faulkner, OBE, and Nora Lilian Faulkner; *m* 1951, Lucy Barbara Ethel, *o d* of William Forsythe, JP, and Ethel Forsythe; two *s* one *d. Educ:* Elm Park, Co. Armagh, Northern Ireland; College of St Columba, Rathfarnham, Co. Dublin. Dir, Belfast Collar Co. Ltd, 1941-63. Govt Chief Whip and Parly Sec., Min. of Finance, N Ire., 1956-59; Minister of Home Affairs, 1959-63; Minister of Commerce, 1963-69. *Recreations:* hunting (Jt Master Iveagh Hunt); sailing. *Address:* Highlands, Seaforde, Co. Down, Northern Ireland. *T:* Seaforde 663. *Clubs:* Ulster Reform (Belfast); Royal North of Ireland Yacht.

**FAULKNER, Eric Odin,** MBE 1945; Chairman: Lloyds Bank Ltd, since 1969; Director: Hudson's Bay Company; Vickers Ltd; Bank of London and South America; National and Commercial Banking Group Ltd; *b* 21 April 1914; *s* of late Sir Alfred Faulkner, CB, CBE; *m* 1939, Joan Mary, *d* of Lt-Col F. A. M. Webster; one *s* one *d. Educ:* Bradfield; Corpus Christi Coll., Cambridge. Joined Glyn, Mills & Co., 1936. Served War of 1939-45, Royal Artillery and Leics Yeomanry; Staff Coll.; Bde Major RA and GSO2; commanded 91 Field Regt RA. Rejoined Glyn, Mills & Co., 1946; Local Dir, 1947-50; Exec. Dir, 1950-68; Dep. Chm., 1959-63; Chm., 1963-68. Warden of Bradfield Coll., 1965. *Recreations;* fishing and walking; formerly cricket and Association football (CUAFC XI 1935). *Address:* Chart Cottage, Seal Chart, Kent. *T:* Sevenoaks 61210. *Club:* Boodle's.

**FAULKNER, Capt. George Haines,** CB 1947; DSC 1916; Royal Navy; *b* 27 April 1893; *s* of Rev. Thomas George Faulkner and Kate Nicholls; *m* 1st, 1924, Kathleen (*d* 1947), *d* of Dr Henry Wilson, Cheadle, Cheshire; no *c*; 2nd, 1959, Marjorie Lucy Rowland, Lustleigh, Devon. *Educ:* Lickey Hills Sch., Worcs; RN Colleges, Osborne and Dartmouth. Osborne, 1906; Midshipman, 1910. Served European War, 1914-18, in destroyers (despatches) Battle of Heligoland Bight, special promotion to Lieut; commanded HMS Mystic, Thruster and Patriot, 1918-19; psc 1922-23; served in HMS Hood on Special Service Squadron World Cruise, 1923-24; commanded HMS Voyager, 1926-28; Comdr 1928; Capt. 1935; commanded HMS Bideford, 1937-38; Chief of Staff and Capt. on Staff of C-in-C the Nore, 1939-41; in command of HMS Berwick, 1941-43; Chief of Staff to C-in-C South Atlantic, with rank of Commodore 2nd class and stationed at Capetown, 1943-45; retired list, 1945; re-appointed. First Naval Mem. of New Zealand Naval Board and Chief of Naval Staff, NZ, with rank of Commodore 2nd Class, 1945-47; reverted to retired list, 1947. *Address:* Lynnfield, Lustleigh, Devon. *T:* 215.

**FAULKNER, Harry,** CMG 1949; Retired as Director Telecommunications Engineering and Manufacturing Association, 1954-62; *b* 17 April 1892; *s* of Harry Faulkner, Nottingham; *m* 1915, Elsie Emma Bray, Norwich; three *s. Educ:* High Pavement Secondary Sch. and University Coll., Nottingham. Laurence Scott & Co., Norwich, 1911-14; appointed Asst Engineer in GPO, 1914; served in Royal Engineers (Signals), 1916-19; Engineer-in-charge Rugby Radio Station, 1925; Suptdg Engineer, N Wales District, 1935; Dep. Regional Dir, Wales and Border Counties, 1939; Controller of Factories, 1941-44; Asst Engineer-in-Chief, GPO, 1944-47; Deputy Engineer-in-Chief, GPO, 1947-54. Mem. of

Council, IEE, 1945-48; Chm. South Midland Section, IEE, 1938-39; Chm. London meeting of Internat. Consultative Radio Cttee, 1953; leader of UK delegn to several Internat. Radio Confs. *Publications:* papers read before IEE, Instn of PO Electrical Engrs, etc. *Recreation:* golf. *Address:* 36 Park Gate, Somerhill Road, Hove 2, Sussex. *T:* Hove 71871.

**FAULKNER, Most Rev. Leonard Anthony;** *see* Townsville, Bishop of, (RC).

**FAULKNER, Sir Percy,** KBE 1964; CB 1950; Controller of HM Stationery Office and Queen's Printer of Acts of Parliament, 1961-67; *b* 11 May 1907; *s* of late Thomas Faulkner and Margaret A. Hood; *m* 1933, Joyce Rosemary Lois MacDonogh; one *s* one *d*. *Educ:* Royal Academical Institution, Belfast; Trinity Coll., Dublin. Entered Ministry of Transport, 1930; Private Sec. to Permanent Sec., 1935-37; Asst Sec., 1942; Under-Sec., 1947; Dep. Sec. (Inland Transport), 1957; Dep. Sec. (Shipping), 1958-61; Chm. British Cttee on Prevention of Pollution of the Sea by Oil, 1953-57; rep. UK at various international conferences on shipping matters, 1947-60. *Address:* St Columbs, Watford Road, Northwood, Mddx. *T:* Northwood 21700. *Club:* Athenæum.

**FAULKNER, Vincent Clements;** Editorial Consultant, The Foundry Trade Journal; *b* 27 Dec. 1888; *s* of Isaac and Hannah Faulkner; *m* 1929, Alice MacGregor; one *d*. *Educ:* Wesley Coll.; Sheffield Univ. Pioneer in making Steel by electricity; 1st metallurgist to make electric steel in Spain, 1916; Pres. Institute of British Foundrymen, 1926; Council of British Cast Iron Research Association, 1927; and of National Ironfounding Employers Federation, 1933; Oliver Stubbs Medallist, 1934; Vice-Pres. Institute of Vitreous Enamellers, and mem. of the University of Sheffield Advisory Cttee on Degree Course in Foundry Practice 1935; hon. mem. Czecho-Slovak Foundrymen's Association, 1946; Pres. International Cttee of Foundry Technical Associations, 1948; hon. mem. Institute of British Foundrymen, 1949; Livery of Founders' Company, 1949. Chm., Borough Polytechnic Foundry Advisory Cttee, 1953; Co-opted to Governing Bd Borough Polytechnic, 1956; Hon. Mem. German Foundrymen's Assoc. Prix d'Honneur, International Cttee of Foundry Technical Assocs, 1955; Hon. Mem. Nat. Soc. of Master Patternmakers. Hon. Mem. French Foundrymen's Assoc., 1959. Levy Medallist, 1961. *Publications:* Articles in Times, Sheffield Independent, Die Giesserei; Scientific Papers in Proceedings of Iron and Steel Inst., American Foundrymen's Soc., etc. *Address:* 15 Crescent Court, Surbiton, Surrey. *T:* 01-399 1496.

**FAULKS, Hon. Sir Neville (Major Ginner),** Kt 1963; MBE 1944; TD 1946; **Hon. Mr Justice Faulks;** Judge of the High Court of Justice, Probate, Divorce and Admiralty Division, since 1963; *b* 27 Jan. 1908; *s* of M. J. Faulks, MA and Ada Mabel Faulks; *m* 1st, 1940, Bridget Marigold Bodley (*d* 1963); two *s* one *d*; 2nd, 1967, Elizabeth, *widow* of Rt Rev. A. G. Parham, MC; one step *s* four step *d*. *Educ:* Uppingham Sch. (scholar); Sidney Sussex Coll., Cambridge (Exhibitioner). Called to the Bar, LLB, 1930; QC 1959. Joined TA; served War of 1939-45 (despatches twice), Alamein. Prosecuting Counsel to Bd of Trade and other ministries at Central Criminal Court, etc., 1946-59. Recorder of Deal, 1957-59; Recorder of Norwich, 1959-63. *Publications:* Fraser on Libel (ed, with late Mr Justice Slade); Investigation into the Affairs of H. Jasper and Company Limited, 1961. *Recreation:* lawn tennis. *Address:* June Farm, Reigate Heath, Surrey. *T:* Reigate 42547; Royal Courts of Justice, WC2; 38 Donne Place, SW3. *T:* 01-584 2693. *Club:* MCC.

**FAUSSETT, Brig. Bryan T. G.;** *see* Godfrey-Faussett.

**FAUTEUX, Rt. Hon. (Joseph Honoré) Gérald,** PC (Can.) 1970; **Rt. Hon. Mr Justice Fauteux;** Chief Justice of Canada, since 1970; Judge, Supreme Court of Canada, since Dec. 1949; *b* St Hyacinthe, PQ, 22 Oct. 1900; *s* of Homère Fauteux and Héva Mercier; *m* 1929, Yvette Mathieu, Montreal; two *s* three *d*. *Educ:* Collège Ste-Marie, Montreal; University of Montreal (law degree). Practised law in Montreal; Crown Attorney, 1929; KC Canada 1933; QC Canada 1952; Asst Chief Crown Counsel, 1930-36; Chief Crown Counsel, 1939-44. Life mem. Canadian Bar Assoc., Hon. Sec. of that Assoc. for several years; legal adviser to the Royal Canadian Mounted Police for several years. Prof., 1936-50, Dean, 1949, Law Faculty of McGill Univ.; Univ. of Ottawa: Dean of Law Faculty, 1953-62; Chm. Bd of Govs (of reorganized Univ.) 1965-67. Judge of the Superior Court in Montreal, 1947. Acted as legal adviser to Royal Commission appointed to investigate spying activities in Canada. Hon. LLD: University of Ottawa, 1953; Laval Univ., Quebec, 1957; University of Sudbury, 1958; University of Montreal, 1962; Hon. DCL McGill Univ., Montreal, 1955. *Recreations:* outdoor sports. *Address:* (home), 50 Goulburn Avenue, Ottawa, Ont, Canada. *T:* CE3-4200; (office) Supreme Court of Canada, Ottawa, Ont. *T:* 99-25388. *Clubs:* L'Alliance Française, Cercle Universitaire, Country (Ottawa), Rideau (Ottawa).

**FAVILLE, Air Vice-Marshal Roy,** CBE 1945; *b* Aug. 1908; *s* of late L. W. Faville, Hamilton, New Zealand; *m* 1936, Beatrice Marie Louise, *d* of late Major (retired) J. E. Orr; one *s* one *d*. *Educ:* Canterbury Coll., University of New Zealand (BEng.). Commissioned, RAF, 1932; OC 42 (TB) Sqdn, 1940-41; OC 140 Wing, 1946-47; Air Force Staff at British Joint Services Mission, USA, 1950-52; Imperial Defence Coll., 1953; OC, RAF, St Eval, 1954. RAF Staff Coll., Bracknell; Asst Comdt, 1955-56; Commandant Aug. 1956; Air Officer Commanding No. 22 Group, RAF, Buntingsdale Hall, Market Drayton, Shropshire, 1957-60, retired 1960. Gen. Manager, Libya, Richard Costain (Middle East) Ltd, 1960-64. Sec., Torch Trophy Trust, 1968. *Recreation:* fishing. *Address:* 103 Collingwood House, Dolphin Square, SW1. *Clubs:* United Service, Royal Air Force.

**FAWCETT, Colin,** QC 1970; *b* 22 Nov. 1923; *s* of Frank Fawcett, Penrith; *m* 1952, Elizabeth Anne Dickson; one *s* one *d*. *Educ:* Sedbergh. Commnd Border Regt, 1943. Called to Bar, Inner Temple, 1952. *Recreations:* fishing, music. *Address:* Fairings, Valley Way, Gerrards Cross, Bucks. *T:* Gerrards Cross 83999.

**FAWCETT, James Edmund Sandford,** DSC 1942; Director of Studies and Stevenson Research Fellow, Royal Institute of International Affairs, since 1969; *b* 16 April 1913; *s* of Rev. Joseph Fawcett and Edith Fawcett; *m* 1937, Frances Beatrice, 2nd *d* of late Dr E. A. Lowe; one *s* four *d*. *Educ:* Rugby Sch.; New Coll., Oxford. Practised at the Bar, 1937-39 and 1950-55. Fellow of All Souls Coll., Oxford, 1938. Served War of 1939-45, Royal Navy. Asst Legal Adviser to FO, 1945-50 (to UK Delegn to UN and British Embassy, Washington, 1948-50); Gen. Counsel, IMF,

1955-60; Fellow of All Souls Coll., Oxford, 1960-69. Associate, Inst. of Internat. Law, 1961-; Member: European Commn of Human Rights, 1962- (Vice-Pres., 1969-); Legislative Cttee of Internat. Union for the Conservation of Nature, 1969; Governing Bd, Lanchester Polytechnic, 1970-. *Publications:* British Commonwealth in International Law, 1963; International Law and the Uses of Outer Space, 1968; The Law of Nations (Penguin), 1968; The Application of the European Convention on Human Rights, 1969; numerous articles. *Recreations:* astronomy, piano. *Address:* 15 Cavendish Avenue, NW8. *T:* 01-286 4719.

**FAWCUS, Louis Reginald,** CSI 1946; CIE 1939; *b* 7 Nov. 1887; *m* 1914, Irene d'A. Lesser; one *s* one *d*. *Educ:* Uppingham; Trinity Coll., Cambridge; University Coll., London. Entered ICS 1911; Mem. Board of Revenue, Bengal, 1940; Adviser to Governor of Bengal, 1945-46. *Address:* c/o National and Grindlay's Bank, 13 St James's Square, SW1; Apartment 2, 830 Lake Street, San Francisco, Calif 94118, USA. *T:* Bayview 1.1823. *Club:* East India and Sports.

**FAWCUS, Sir Peter;** *see* Fawcus, Sir (Robert) Peter.

**FAWCUS, Sir (Robert) Peter,** KBE 1964 (OBE 1957); CMG 1960; Overseas Civil Service, retd; *b* 30 Sept. 1915; *s* of late A. F. Fawcus, OBE; *m* 1943, Isabel Constance (*née* Ethelston); one *s* one *d*. *Educ:* Charterhouse; Clare Coll., Cambridge. Served RNVR, 1939-46. Joined Colonial Service (District Officer, Basutoland), 1946; Bechuanaland Protectorate: Govt Sec., 1954; Resident Commissioner, 1959; HM Commissioner, 1963-65; retd 1965. *Address:* Dochart House, Killin, Perthshire.

**FAY, Rt. Rev. Mgr. Cyril Damian,** CBE 1960 (OBE 1953); Parish priest of St John's, Alton, Staffs, since 1963; Domestic Prelate to the Pope, since 1957; Conventual Chaplain, Sovereign and Military Order of the Knights of Malta, 1959; Principal Roman Catholic Chaplain, Royal Navy, and Vicar General to Archbishop David Mathew for the Royal Navy, 1956-63, retired; *b* St Helens, Lancs 1903; *s* of John Fay and Mary Elizabeth (*née* Flynn). *Educ:* Up Holland Coll., Lancs; Ecclesiastical Studies in Latin Patriarchal Seminary, Palestine. Ordained Jerusalem, 1927; served on Mission at Es-Salt and Amman, Transjordan; English Sec. to Latin Patriarch of Jerusalem, and Chaplain to English Speaking Community, 1929-33; short service commn in RAF as Chaplain, 1933; commissioned in RN, 1936; apptd to 1st Cruiser Squadron, Mediterranean Fleet, in HMS Devonshire, 1937; detached in HMS Shropshire to S Atlantic, Sept. 1939; HMS Assegai, Durban, S Africa, 1943-44; with Naval Forces, Germany, May 1945-48; RN Barracks, Portsmouth, 1948; Admiralty, 1956. Hon. Canon, Collegiate Church of St Lawrence, Vittoriosa, Malta, 1961. *Address:* The Priest's House, Alton, Stoke-on-Trent, Staffs. *Club:* Army and Navy.

**FAY, Edgar Stewart,** QC 1956; Recorder of Plymouth, since 1964; a Deputy Chairman, Hampshire Quarter Sessions, since 1960; *b* 8 Oct. 1908; *s* of late Sir Sam Fay; *m* 1930, Kathleen Margaret (*d* 1970), *e d* of late C. H. Buell, Montreal, PQ, and Brockville, Ont; three *s*. *Educ:* Courtenay Lodge Sch.; McGill Univ.; Pembroke Coll., Cambridge (MA). Called to Bar, Inner Temple, 1932; Master of the Bench, 1962. Recorder: of Andover, 1954-61; of Bournemouth, 1961-64. Mem., Bar Council, 1955-59, 1966-70. *Publications:* Why Piccadilly?, 1935; Londoner's New York, 1936; Discoveries in the Statute Book, 1937; The Life of Mr Justice Swift, 1939. *Address:* 3 Paper Buildings, Temple, EC4. *T:* 01-353 8192; 4 Studio Place, Kinnerton Street, SW1. *T:* 01-235 3450. *Clubs:* Reform; Hampshire (Winchester).

**FAYLE, Lindley Robert Edmundson,** CBE 1957 (OBE 1946); DSO 1945; Brigadier, retired; Rating Secretary, Royal Ocean Racing Club, since 1957; Chief Measurer to Offshore Rating Council of International Yacht Racing Union, since 1969; *b* 31 July 1903; *s* of late Lieut-Col R. J. L. Fayle, DSO, RAMC and of Mrs Fayle; *m* 1928, Cicily Rosamonde Annette, *d* of late C. F. Bigge and late Mrs Bigge; one *s* one *d*. *Educ:* Avondale Sch., Clifton; Clifton Coll.; RMA, Woolwich. 2nd Lieut, RE, 1923; Lieut 1925; India (Royal Bombay Sappers and Miners), 1925-30; Asst Instr, SME, 1932-36; Capt. 1934; Ministry of Supply, 1938-40; Major 1940; Actg Lieut-Col 1941; Temp. Lieut-Col 1942; War Office, 1940-42; CRE Kent Corps Troops (later 15 (Kent) GHQ Troops), 1942-45, UK and NW Europe; CRE 5th Inf. Div., 1945-46; Temp. Col 1946. Min. of Supply, 1946-49; subs. Lieut-Col 1948; subs. Col 1949; Min. of Supply, 1949-53; Brig. 1953; Dir MEXE, 1953-57; Retired 1957. MIEE 1968 (AMIEE 1938); MIMechE 1968 (AMIMechE 1939); Associate, RINA, 1970. *Address:* Woodmansterne, 46 Foxholes Road, Southbourne, Bournemouth, Hants. *T:* Bournemouth 44694. *Club:* Royal Ocean Racing.

**FAYRER, Sir Joseph Herbert Spens,** 3rd Bt, *cr* 1896; DSC 1941; Lieut-Comdr RNVR; *b* 20 Oct. 1899; *s* of Sir Joseph Fayrer, 2nd Bt, CBE, and Ella, *d* of late Col W. A. J. Mayhew, Bengal Army; *S* father, 1937; *m* 1st, 1926, Elizabeth (whom he divorced, 1936), *d* of late Capt. William Barker-Mill, Mottisfont Abbey; 2nd, 1939, Helen Diana Scott (*d* 1961), *o d* of late John and Jean Lang; one *s* one *d*; 3rd, 1964, Noreen, *d* of late Rev. John Yuill Walker. *Educ:* Wellington Coll. *Heir:* *s* John Lang Macpherson Fayrer, *b* 18 Oct. 1944. *Address:* Overhailes, Haddington, E Lothian, Scotland. *T:* East Linton 258.

**FAZAN, Sidney Herbert,** CMG 1946; CBE 1934 (OBE 1930); *b* 27 June 1888; *s* of Dr C. H. Fazan, Wadhurst, Sussex; *m* 1924, Sylvia (marr. diss., 1946), *d* of Brian Hook, Churt, Surrey; one *s* four *d*; *m* 1949, Phyllis, *d* of John Jeffery; one *s* one *d*. *Educ:* Epsom Coll.; Christ Church, Oxford. Provincial Commissioner, Kenya, and mem. of Legislative Council, 1936-42; Liaison Officer with East African Forces, 1943-46. *Address:* 110 Dorset Road, Bexhill-on-Sea, Sussex.

**FEA, William Wallace;** a Deputy Chairman, Guest, Keen & Nettlefolds Ltd, since 1968; *b* Cordova, Argentina, 3 Feb. 1907; *s* of Herbert Reginald Fea and Hilda Florence Fea (*née* Norton); *m* 1935, Norah Anne, *d* of Richard Festing; two *s*. *Educ:* Cheltenham Coll.; Brasenose Coll., Oxford (BA). ACA 1932; FCA. Member Council: Inst. of Chartered Accountants, 1953-; BIM, 1969-. *Recreations:* squash racquets, ski-ing, shooting, lawn tennis, listening to music. *Address:* The Lowe, Worfield, near Bridgnorth, Shropshire. *T:* Worfield 241. *Clubs:* Lansdowne; Edgbaston Priory (Birmingham).

**FEARN, John Martin;** Under-Secretary, Scottish Education Department, since 1968; *b* 24 June 1916; *s* of William Laing Fearn and Margaret Kerr Fearn; *m* 1947, Isobel Mary Begbie, MA, MB, ChB; one *d*. *Educ:* High Sch.

of Dundee; Univ. of St Andrews (MA); Worcester Coll., Oxford. Indian Civil Service, Punjab, 1940-47; District Magistrate, Lahore, 1946; Scottish Home Dept, 1947; Asst Sec., 1956; Under-Sec., 1966. *Recreation:* golf. *Address:* 29 Liberton Brae, Edinburgh EH16 6AG. *T:* 031-664 3765. *Club:* Royal Commonwealth Society.

**FEARNLEY, John Thorn;** HM Consul-General, Frankfurt-am-Main, since 1969; *b* 9 Feb. 1921; *o s* of Tom Fearnley and Grace Gertrude (*née* Thorn); *m* 1947, Margaret Ann Davies; two *s* three *d*. *Educ:* Manchester Gram. Sch.; Caius Coll., Cambridge (Scholar). Served with RN, 1942-46. Joined Foreign Service, 1947; FO, 1947-48; New York (UN), 1948-50; Tehran, 1950-52; FO, Civil Service Selection Bd, 1953; Tehran, 1953-56; Berlin, 1956-58; FO, 1958-60; Lagos, 1960-62; Paris, 1962-65. Head of Oil Dept, FO, 1965-69; Senior Officers' War Course, RN Coll., Greenwich, 1969. *Address:* c/o Foreign and Commonwealth Office, SW1; British Consulate-General, Bockenheimer Landstrasse 51-53, Frankfurt-am-Main. *Clubs:* Oxford and Cambridge University; Frankfurter Gesellschaft (Frankfurt).

**FEARNLEY SCARR, J. G.;** *see* Scarr.

**FEATHER, Norman,** FRS 1945; FRSE 1946; PhD Cantab; Professor of Natural Philosophy, University of Edinburgh, since 1945; *b* Crimsworth, WR Yorks, 16 Nov. 1904; *s* of Samson and Lucy Feather; *m* 1932, Kathleen Grace Burke; one *s* twin *d*. *Educ:* Bridlington Sch., E Yorks; Trinity Coll., Cambridge (Scholar). BA Cantab, BSc London, 1926; PhD Cantab, 1930; Fellow of Trinity Coll., 1929-33; Associate in Physics, Johns Hopkins Univ., Baltimore, Md, 1929-30; University Demonstrator in Physics, Cambridge, 1933-35; Leverhulme Fellow and Lecturer, University of Liverpool, 1935-36; Fellow and Lecturer in Natural Sciences, Trinity Coll., Cambridge; University Lecturer in Physics, 1936-45. Gen. Sec., 1956-66, and Pres., 1967-70, RSE. *Publications:* An Introduction to Nuclear Physics, 1936; Lord Rutherford, 1940; Nuclear Stability Rules, 1952; An Introduction to the Physics of Mass, Length and Time, 1959; An Introduction to the Physics of Vibrations and Waves, 1961; Electricity and Matter: an introductory survey, 1968; Matter and Motion, 1970; numerous papers on radioactivity and nuclear physics in Proc. Royal Society and other jls. *Recreations:* cricket, lawn tennis. *Address:* Department of Natural Philosophy, University of Edinburgh; 9 Priestfield Road, Edinburgh EH16 5HJ. *T:* 031-667 2631.

**FEATHER, Victor (Grayson Hardie),** CBE 1961; General Secretary of Trades Union Congress, since 1969 (Assistant General Secretary, 1960-69); *b* Bradford, 10 April 1908; *s* of Harry and Edith Feather; *m* 1930, Alice Helena Fernyhough Ellison; one *s* one *d*. *Educ:* Hanson, Bradford. Co-op. employee, 1923-37; joined TUC staff, 1937; Asst Sec., 1947-60. Sec. TUC delegn to USSR, 1943; assisted re-org. Greek trade unions, 1945, Berlin trade unions, 1949; India and Pakistan, 1959; settlement Japan rail strike, 1958; lectured on trade unions in USA, 1954, SE Asia, 1957. Member: Govt Cttee of Inquiry into Overseas Information Services, 1952; Internat. Confedn of Free Trade Unions (Vice-Chm.); Cttee on the Pay of Postmen, 1964; Kennedy National Memorial Cttee; Exec. Cttee Brit. Council; BBC's Gen. Advisory Council; Royal Commn on Local Govt in England, 1968-69; Advertising Standards Authority, 1962-70; Consumers Assoc. (Vice-Chm.); British Productivity Council; Court of Univ. of Birmingham; Board of Trustees, Civic Trust; Exec. Cttee, Overseas Development Institute; NEDC; BNEC. Dir, Nat. Building Agency. Vice-President: Workers' Educational Assoc.; Inst. Manpower Studies; a Vice-Chm., Nat. Savings Cttee, 1970-; Governor, Nat. Inst. Economic and Social Research. FRSA. *Publications:* Trade Unions, True or False, 1951; How Do the Communists Work?, 1953; Essence of Trade Unionism, 1963. *Recreations:* painting, reading, cricket. *Address:* 43 Shelley Crescent, Heston, Middx. *T:* 01-570 6241.

**FEDDEN, Sir (Alfred Hubert) Roy,** Kt 1942; MBE; Hon. DSc; Hon. FRAeS; Hon. FAIAA; Hon. FSE; FRSA; FIMechE; Member Lilienthal Society; Liveryman, Guild of Pilots; Fellow British Interplanetary Society; *b* 6 June 1885; *s* of Henry Fedden, JP; *m* 1948, Norah Lilian, 3rd *d* of Edgar Crew, Clifton. *Educ:* Clifton Coll.; Bristol Merchant Venturers Technical Coll. Drawing Office of Brazil Straker and Co., Fishponds, Bristol, 1906-08; Works Manager and Chief Engineer of Brazil Straker and Co., 1909-14; Technical Dir of Brazil Straker and Co., 1914; during European war remained Technical Dir and Chief Engineer of Fishponds Works which were employed in manufacture of Rolls-Royce and Renault aero engines and shells; founded Engine Dept, British Aeroplane Co., 1920; Chief Engineer, Bristol Aeroplane Co., Ltd, 1920-42; responsible for design and development of all Bristol Aero Engines until 1945; Special Technical Adviser to Minister of Aircraft Production, 1942-45; research work for Ministry of Supply, 1945-47; Aeronautical Adviser to NATO, 1952-53; Aircraft Consultant to Dowty Group, 1953-60. Hon. DSc, Bristol Univ. Belgian Bronze Medal, 1930; Royal Aeronautical Society Silver Medal, 1933; Manly Gold Medal, 1933; Simms Gold Medal, 1934, 1954; Guggenheim Trophy, 1938; Lilienthal Ring, 1938; Pres. Royal Aeronautical Society, 1938, 1939, 1945 (hon. fellow, diploma, 1954); Board of Governors, College of Aeronautics, Cranfield 1946-. *Publication:* Britain's Air Survival, 1957. *Recreations:* writing on aeronautical matters and fly-fishing. *Address:* Buckland Old Mill, Bwlch, Breconshire, S Wales. *T:* Bwlch 274. *Clubs:* Royal Thames Yacht; Bristol Yacht (Bristol).

**FEDDEN, (Henry) Robin Romilly;** Deputy Director-General and Historic Buildings Secretary, The National Trust for Places of Historic Interest or Natural Beauty; author; *b* 26 Nov. 1908; *s* of Arthur Romilly Fedden and Katharine Waldo Douglas, Chantemesle, Seine-et-Oise, France; *m* 1942, Renée Catzeflis; two *d*. *Educ:* Clifton; Magdalene Coll., Cambridge; and abroad. *Publications:* As the Unicorn (novel), 1933; Suicide: a social and historical study, 1938; The Land of Egypt, 1939; St Anthony's Monastery, 1939; Syria, 1946; Crusader Castles, 1950; Alpine Ski Tour, 1956; Ski-ing in the Alps, 1958; The Enchanted Mountains, 1962; Chantemesle, 1964; The Continuing Purpose: A History of the National Trust, Its Aims and Work, 1968; The White Country (verse), 1968; Churchill at Chartwell, 1969. Co-editor of Personal Landscape, 1941-44. *Recreations:* travel, mountaineering, ski-ing. *Address:* 20 Eldon Road, W8. *Club:* St James', Beefsteak, Alpine.

**FEIBUSCH, Hans;** Painter, Mural Painter, Lithographer, Writer; *b* 15 Aug. 1898; *s* of Dr Carl Feibusch and Marianne Ickelheimer; *m* 1935, Sidonie (*d* 1963), *e d* of D. Gestetner. *Educ:* Frankfurt a/M and Munich Univs. Studied at the Berlin Academy, at Paris Art Schs, in Florence and Rome; received German State award and grant in 1931; pictures in

German Public Galleries; work banned and destroyed by Nazis in 1933; since then in London; large mural paintings in churches: St Wilfred's, Brighton; St Elizabeth's, Eastbourne; St Martin's, Dagenham; St John's, Waterloo Road, SE1; St Ethelburga's, Bishopsgate; St Alban's, Holborn; Town Hall, Dudley; Civic Centre, Newport, Mon; Chichester Cathedral; Chichester Palace; Parish Churches, Egham, Goring, Wellingborough, Welling, Preston, Plumstead, Eltham, Portsmouth, Bexley Heath, Wembley, Merton, Southwark, Harrow, Exeter, Battersea, Rotherhithe, Plymouth, Coventry, Christchurch Priory, Bournemouth, Christ Church, St Laurence, Sydney. 4 one-man exhibns. German Cross of Merit, 1967. *Publications:* Mural Painting, 1946; The Revelation of Saint John, 1946. *Recreations:* music and poetry. *Address:* 30 Wadham Gardens, NW3. *Club:* Athenæum.

**FEILDEN, Bernard Melchior,** OBE 1969; FRIBA 1968 (ARIBA 1949); Partner, Feilden and Mawson, Chartered Architects; *b* 11 Sept. 1919; *s* of Robert Humphrey Feilden, MC, and Olive Feilden (*née* Binyon); *m* 1949, Ruth Mildred Bainbridge; two *s* two *d*. *Educ:* Bedford Sch. Exhibr, Bartlett Sch. of Architecture, 1938. Served War of 1939-45: Bengal Sappers and Miners. AA Diploma (Hons), 1949; Bratt Colbran Schol., 1949. Architect, Norwich Cathedral, 1963-; Surveyor to the Fabric: York Minster, 1965-; St Paul's Cathedral, 1969-. FSA 1969. *Recreations:* painting, sailing, fishing, photography. *Address:* 6 The Close, Norwich NOR 16P. *T:* 26623. *Clubs:* Athenæum; Norfolk (Norwich).
*See also G. B. R. Feilden.*

**FEILDEN, Geoffrey Bertram Robert,** CBE 1966; FRS 1959; MA Cantab, MIMechE; Director-General, British Standards Institution, since 1970 (Deputy Director-General, 1968-70); *b* 20 Feb. 1917; *s* of Major R. H. Feilden, MC, RFA, and Olive (*née* Binyon); *m* 1945, Elizabeth Ann Gorton; one *s* two *d*. *Educ:* Bedford Sch.; King's Coll., Cambridge. Lever Bros. and Unilever Ltd, 1939-40; Power Jets Ltd, 1940-46; Ruston and Hornsby Ltd, 1946-59; Chief Engineer, Turbine Dept, 1949; Engineering Dir, 1954; Man. Dir, Hawker Siddeley Brush Turbines Ltd, and Dir of Hawker Siddeley Industries Ltd, 1959-61; Gp Technical Dir, Davy-Ashmore Ltd, 1961-68. Member: Cttees and Sub-Cttees of Aeronautical Research Council, 1947-62; BTC Res. Adv. Council, 1956-61; Council for Sci. and Indust. Res. of DSIR, 1961-65; Council of Industrial Design, 1966-; Central Adv. Council for Science and Technology, 1970-. DSIR Visitor to Prod. Engineering Res. Assoc. of Gt Brit., 1957-65, and to Machine Tool Industry Res. Assoc., 1961-65. Member Council: Royal Society (a Vice-Pres., 1967-69); IMechE, 1955-61, 1969-. *Publications:* Gas Turbine Principles and Practice (contributor), 1955; First Bulleid Memorial Lecture (Nottingham Univ.), 1959; numerous papers and articles on engineering subjects. *Recreations:* sailing, ski-ing. *Address:* Greys End, Rotherfield Greys, Henley-on-Thames, Oxon. *T:* Rotherfield Greys 211; 2 Park Street, W1. *T:* 01-629 9000. *Club:* Athenæum.
*See also B. M. Feilden.*

**FEILDEN, Maj.-Gen. Sir Randle Guy,** KCVO, *cr* 1953; CB 1946; CBE 1944 (OBE 1943); *b* 14 June 1904; *e s* of Major P. H. G. Feilden; *m* 1929, Mary Joyce, *d* of Sir John Ramsden, 6th Bt; two *s* (and one *s* decd). *Educ:* Eton; Magdalene Coll., Cambridge. Coldstream Guards, 1925; ADC GOC London Dist, 1933-36; Regimental Adjutant, 1936-39; Staff Capt. 7 Gds Bde 1939-40; DAQMG 3 Div. April-Sept. 1940; AQMG 5 Corps, 1940-41; AA and QMG Guards Armoured Division, 1941-42; DQMG Home Forces, Feb.-Aug. 1943; DQMG 21 Army Group, Aug. 1943-45; DQMG Rhine Army, Aug. 1945-March 1946; VQMG, War Office, 1947-49; retired pay, 1949. A Steward of the Jockey Club, 1952, senior Steward, 1954, 1961, 1965, 1966, 1967, 1968, 1969; Chm., Turf Board, 1965, 1966, 1967, 1968, 1969. *Recreations:* cricket, shooting, racing. *Address:* Old Manor House, Minster Lovell, Oxford. *T:* Asthall Leigh 228; 3 Kingston House South, SW7. *T:* 01-589 7135. *Clubs:* Turf, Pratt's, White's.

**FEILDEN, Sir William Morton Buller,** 5th Bt, *cr* 1846; of Feniscowles, Lancs; MC; *b* 20 May 1893; *o s* of Sir W. H. Feilden, 4th Bt; *S* father 1946; *m* 1st, 1922, Margery Hannah (*d* 1925), *o d* of Robert Knowles, JP, Ednaston, Derby; 2nd, 1927, Reva, *d* of late Martin Morrison, Faceby, Yorks, and *widow* of Major Guy Winterbottom. Joined Derbyshire Yeomanry, 1912; served European War, 1914-18, Comd Derbyshire Yeomanry, Gallipoli Evacuation (despatches twice, MC, Italian Silver Medal, wounded 1916); District Remount Officer, Western Command, 1919-37; Commandant No. 6 Group Royal Observer Corps, 1938-45. *Heir: cousin,* Henry Wemyss Feilden, [*b* 1916; *e s* of late Colonel Wemyss Gawne Cunningham Feilden, CMG (3rd *s* of 3rd Bt); *m* 1943, Ethel Atkinson, Newcastle; one *s* two *d*]. *Address:* The Yelt Farm, Doveridge, Derby. *TA:* Doveridge, Derby. *T:* Uttoxeter 2074. *Club:* Boodle's.

**FEILDING,** family name of **Earl of Denbigh.**

**FEILING, Anthony,** BA, MD, BCh Cambridge, FRCP; Consulting Physician to St George's Hospital, National Hospitals for Nervous Diseases, Royal National Orthopædic Hospital, and Epsom College; Emeritus Lecturer in Medicine, St George's Hospital; Fellow (late President and late Lettsomian Lecturer) of Medical Society of London; Fellow (late President, Section of Neurology, and late Member of Council) Royal Society of Medicine; President Association of British Neurologists, 1954; Member, Association of Physicians of Great Britain; Corresponding Member, Société de Neurologie de Paris; Vice-President International Congress of Neurologists, Paris, 1949; Member American Academy of Neurology; *b* Leatherhead, Surrey, 30 Sept. 1885; 2nd *s* of late Ernest Feiling and late Joan Barbara Hawkins; *m* 1919, Helga Isabel Hope, *d* of late Geoffrey Grahame Hawkins and late Inga Olsen; one *s*. *Educ:* Marlborough Coll.; Pembroke Coll., Cambridge. BA, Hons Nat. Sci. Tripos, 1906; MRCS, LRCP, 1909; MB, ChB Cambridge 1911; MD Cambridge 1914; FRCP 1921; late Casualty Physician and Temporary Asst Physician, St Bartholomew's Hospital; Physician to Metropolitan Hospital and to Western Ophthalmic Hospital; Dean of Medical School, St George's Hospital, 1926-36; Temp. Major RAMC (despatches); late Censor and Senior Censor, late Gouldstonian Lecturer, Royal Coll. of Physicians; Examiner in Medicine to Royal Coll. of Physicians, Universities of Cambridge, London, and Birmingham; Neurologist to Air Ministry; Gold Staff Officer at Coronation of King George VI; late Sector Hospital Officer, EMS, 1939-45. *Publications:* Modern Medical Treatment (jointly); Article, Multiple Neuritis, Oxford System of Medicine; numerous papers in medical journals. *Recreation:* travel. *Address:* Wychwood House, Good Easter, near Chelmsford, Essex.

**FEILING, Sir Keith (Grahame),** Kt 1958; OBE 1918; DLitt, MA; Professor Emeritus in the University of Oxford since 1950; *b* 1884; *s* of late Ernest Feiling and late Joan Barbara Hawkins; *m* 1912, Caroline, *d* of late Dearman Janson and late Rachel Louisa Lloyd; one *s* two *d*. *Educ:* Marlborough; Balliol Coll., Oxford; Prize Fellow of All Souls Coll., 1906-11; Lecturer at University of Toronto, 1907-09; Lecturer at Christ Church, 1909; Student and Tutor, 1911-46; Chichele Prof. of Mod. Hist., Oxford, 1946-50; 2nd Lieut 3rd Black Watch, 1915; Sec. to Central Recruiting Bd, India, 1917-19; University Lecturer in Modern History, 1928-36; Ford's Lecturer in English History, 1931-32. Hon. Student of Christ Church, 1952. Hon. Mem. Mass Hist. Soc. *Publications:* History of the Tory Party (1640-1714), 1924; England under the Tudors and Stuarts (Home University Library), 1926; British Foreign Policy, 1660-1672, 1930; Sketches in Nineteenth Century Biography, 1930; The Second Tory Party, (1714-1832), 1938; The Life of Neville Chamberlain, 1946; A History of England, 1950; Warren Hastings, 1954 (James Tait Black Memorial Prize); In Christ Church Hall, 1960. *Address:* Christ Church, Oxford.

**FELDBERG, Wilhelm Siegmund,** CBE 1963; FRS 1947; MD Berlin; MA; Professor Emeritus; Head, Laboratory of Neuropharmacology, National Institute for Medical Research, London, since Sept. 1966; Hon. Lecturer, University of London, since 1950; *b* 19 Nov. 1900; *m* 1925, Katherine, *d* of late Karl Scheffler; one *d* (and one *s* decd). Reader in Physiology, Cambridge Univ., until 1949; Head of Physiology and Pharmacology Division, National Institute for Medical Research, London, 1949-65 (Hon. Head of Division, 1965-66). Dunham Lecturer, Harvard Univ., 1953; Evarts Graham Memorial Lectr., Washington Univ., St Louis, USA, 1961; Aschoff Memorial Lectr, Freiburg Univ., Germany, 1961; Dixon Memorial Lectr, RSM, 1964; William Withering Lectr, 1966. Hon. Member: Br. Pharmacol. Soc.; RSM; Physiol. Soc.; Soc. française d'allergie; Deutsche Phys. Gesell.; Deutsche Pharm. Gesell. Hon. MD: Freiburg, Berlin, Cologne, Liège. Grand Cross, Order of Merit of German Federal Republic, 1961. Baly Medal, 1963; Schmiedeberg Plakette, 1969; Stöhr Medal, 1970. *Publications:* Histamin (with E. Schilf); A Pharmacological Approach to the Brain from its Inner and Outer Surface, 1963; articles in med. and scientific jls. *Address:* Lavenham, Marsh Lane, Mill Hill, NW7. *T:* 01-959 5545.

**FELGATE, Air Vice-Marshal Frank Westerman,** CB 1958; CBE 1946; *b* 1901; *s* of John Wyncoll Felgate, South Africa; *m* 1931, May, *d* of Major J. W. Osborne, OBE, RAMC, retd. *Educ:* Rondesbosch, South Africa. Served as Cadet with British India Steam Navigation Company, 1918, and later as navigation officer. Joined RAF, 1925; served War of 1939-45; Air Ministry; Rhodesian Air Training Group. Dir Equipment, HQ, MEAF, 1949-50; AOC 206 Group, MEAF, 1951; Dir of Movements, Air Ministry, 1952-55; Dir of Equipment (C), Air Ministry, 1956; Senior Air Staff Officer, Maintenance Command, Andover, 1956-59, retired. Wing Commander, 1942; Air Commodore, 1949; Air Vice-Marshal, 1956. *Address:* Heatherlea, Downton, Lymington, Hants.

**FELL, Anthony;** MP (C) Yarmouth Division of Norfolk, 1951-66 and since 1970; *b* 18 May 1914; *s* of Comdr David Mark Fell, RN; *m* 1939; one *s* one *d*. *Educ:* Bedford Grammar Sch.; New Zealand. Contested (C) Brigg, 1948, South Hammersmith, 1949 and 1950. *Address:* 58 Park Street, W1.

**FELL, Charles Percival,** LLD; Director and Hon. Chairman, Empire Life Assurance Co., Kingston, Ont.; Director, Canadian Surety Co.; Director and Member Toronto Advisory Board, Royal Trust Co.; Governor, McMaster University (Chancellor, 1960-65); *b* Toronto, 1894; *s* of I. C. Fell and Sarah (Branton) Fell, both of Toronto, Ont.; *m* Grace E. Matthews; three *s* one *d*. *Educ:* Winchester Public Sch.; University of Toronto Schs; McMaster Univ. Associated with Dillon, Read & Co., NY, 1921-24; Dominion Securities Corp., Toronto, 1925-29; Chm. Canadian group, Investment Bankers Assoc. of America, 1928. Mem. Bd of Referees (Excess Profits Tax Act, Canada), Ottawa, 1940-45. Pres., Art Gall. of Toronto, 1950-53; Chm., Bd of Trustees, Nat. Gall. of Canada, 1953-59. Coronation Medal, Canada, 1953. Hon. LLD McMaster Univ., 1957. *Address:* 52 Park Lane Circle, Don Mills, Ont., Canada. *T:* 447-7523. *Clubs:* York; Toronto; Rosedale Golf.

**FELL, Dame Honor Bridget,** DBE 1963; FRS 1952; Director, Strangeways Research Laboratory, Cambridge, 1929-70; Foulerton Research Fellow, Royal Society, since 1941; Fellow of Girton College, Cambridge, 1955; *b* 22 May 1900; *d* of Col William Edwin Fell and Alice Fell (*née* Pickersgill-Cunliffe). *Educ:* Wychwood Sch., Oxford; Madras Coll., St Andrews; Edinburgh Univ. BSc (Edinburgh) 1922; PhD (Edinburgh) 1924; DSc (Edinburgh) 1930; MA (Cantab) 1955. Research Student, DSIR, 1922; Research Asst, MRC, 1924; Junior Beit Fellow, 1924; 4th Year Beit Fellow, 1927; Senior Beit Fellow, 1928; Messel Research Fellow, Royal Society, 1931; Royal Society Research Professor, 1963-67. Hon. LLD: Edinburgh, 1959; Glasgow, 1970; Hon. DSc: Oxon, 1964; London, 1967; Hon. ScD: Smith Coll., USA, 1962; Harvard, 1964; Cambridge, 1969; For. Mem., Royal Netherlands Academy, 1964; Hon. Fellow, Somerville Coll., Oxford, 1964; Fellow, King's Coll., London, 1967. Prix Charles-Leopold Mayer, French Academy of Science, 1965. *Publications:* various communications to biological journals. *Recreation:* travel. *Address:* 42b Queen Edith's Way, Cambridge. *T:* Cambridge 47022.

**FELL, Vice-Adm. Michael Frampton,** CB 1969; DSO 1943; DSC 1944 (Bar, 1952); Flag Officer, Naval Air Command, since Nov. 1970; *b* 17 Jan. 1918; *yr s* of Herbert Leigh Fell and Winifred Adeline Fell; *m* 1948, Joan McLauchlan-Slater; no *c*. *Educ:* Harrow. Joined Royal Navy, 1938; Fleet Air Arm pilot, 1939-45: Norwegian campaign and Gibraltar, 1940; fighter squadron, Western Desert, 1941-42; Salerno landings, 1943; attack on battleship Tirpitz (DSO) and other Norwegian operations, 1943; Southern France landings and ops in Aegean Sea (DSC), 1944; various instructional flying appts, Gen. Service, and Naval Staff Course, 1945-50; Air Gp Comdr HMAS Sydney, 1950-52; served in Korea (bar to DSC); Comdr (Air) HMS Ark Royal, 1954-56; comd HMS Puma, 1957-58; Capt. 1958; comd RN Air Stn, Lossiemouth, 1958-61; Capt. (F), 3rd Frigate Sqdn Far East Fleet, comd HMS Loch Killisport, 1961-63; Chief of Staff to C-in-C Portsmouth, 1963-65; comd HMS Ark Royal, 1965-66; Flag Officer: Gibraltar, Nov. 1966-68; Carriers and Amphibious Ships, also NATO Cmdr, 2nd Carrier Striking Force, 1968-70. *Recreations:* fishing, shooting, boats, flying, gliding. *Address:* Jeremys, Stoughton, Chichester, Sussex. *T:* Compton 351. *Clubs:* (Naval Mem.)

Royal Yacht Squadron, Royal Naval Sailing Association.

**FELL, Sheila Mary,** ARA 1969; artist since 1950; *b* 20 July 1931; *d* of John and Anne Fell, Aspatria, Cumberland. *Educ:* Thomlinson Grammar Sch., Wigton, Cumberland; Carlisle Sch. of Art; St Martin's Sch. of Art, London. One Man Exhibitions: Beaux Arts Gallery, London, 1955, 1958, 1960, 1962, 1964; Derwent Centre, Cockermouth, Cumberland, 1961; Middlesbrough Art Gall., 1962; Maryport Educational Settlement, Cumberland, 1964; Abbot Hall Art Gall., Kendal, 1965; Queen Square Gall., Leeds, 1965; Stone Gall., Newcastle upon Tyne, 1967, 1969. Paintings in Public Collections: Arts Council; Contemporary Art Soc.; Tate Gallery; Municipal Galleries of Carlisle, Liverpool, Middlesbrough, Southport, Sunderland, Swindon and Newcastle upon Tyne; Abbot Hall Art Gall., Kendal. Works in many private Collections. 2nd prize, Junior Section, John Moore's Liverpool Competition, 1957; Boise Travelling Scholarship, 1958; awarded £500 (Arts Council purchase award scheme), 1967; Austin Abbey Award for Research into Mural Painting, 1970. *Publication:* chapter in Breakthrough, ed Ronald Goldmann, 1968. *Recreations:* travelling, reading, visiting friends. *Address:* c/o The Stone Gallery, St Mary's Place, Newcastle upon Tyne.

**FELL, Capt. William Richmond,** CMG 1957; CBE 1947; DSC 1941; RN retd; Admiralty Marine Salvage Officer, Grade I, 1948-60; *b* 31 Jan. 1897; *s* of Walter Fell, MD Oxon, and Margaret Richmond; *m* 1921, Phyllis (*née* Munday); two *s*. *Educ:* Wellington Coll., New Zealand. Joined RN 1915; Midshipman HMS Warspite, 1916-17 (Jutland); Dover Patrol, 1917-18. Served in submarines, 1918-39; first comd, 1925. War of 1939-45 (despatches, DSC): "Q" boat ops, 1940; Norway, 1941; Combined ops, 1941-42; rejoined submarines, 1942; Comd Human Torpedo ops, 1942-43. Training officer, midget submarines, 1943; Comd of HMS Bonaventure, in rank of Capt. (midget submarines), 1943-47, home and Pacific waters. Boom Defence and Salvage Officer, 1948 (Malta and Med.); retired with rank of Capt., 1948, and joined Admty Salvage; Ship Target Trials home and abroad, 1949-50; Salvage ops at home, 1951-56; Suez, as Principal Salvage Officer, 1956-57. Legion of Merit, Officers' Class, 1947 (US). *Publications:* short stories contributed to Blackwood's, 1945-49; The Sea Surrenders, 1960; The Sea our Shield, 1966. *Recreations:* yachting, fishing. *Address:* Mahina Bay, Eastbourne, Wellington, NZ.

**FELLINI, Federico;** film director since 1942; *b* 20 Jan. 1920; *s* of late Urbano Fellini and Ida Barbiani; *m* 1943, Giulietta Masina. *Educ:* Bologna, Italy. Journalist, 1937-39; radio-author, scenario writer, etc, 1939-42. Has gained many prizes and awards in every part of the world including three "Oscars" (1957, 1958, 1964) for films La Strada, Cabiria, and 8½. Films include: La Dolce Vita, 1960; 8½, 1963 (foreign awards); Giulietta Degli Spiriti, 1965; Satyricon, 1968. *Address:* 141-A Via Archimede, Rome. *T:* 879.203.

**FELLOWES,** family name of **Barons Ailwyn** and **De Ramsey.**

**FELLOWES, Sir Edward (Abdy),** KCB 1955 (CB 1945); CMG 1953; MC 1917; Chairman: General Advisory Council, BBC, 1962-67; Council of Hansard Society for Parliamentary Government, 1962-67; *b* 23 June 1895; *e s* of late W. G. Fellowes, barrister-at-law; *m* 1921, Ella Mary, *d* of late Lieut-Col MacRae-Gilstrap, Eilean Donan, Ross-shire; three *d*. *Educ:* Marlborough Coll. Served European War, 1914-18, Queen's Royal Regt, Capt. 1917 (despatches, MC). Asst Clerk, House of Commons, 1919; 2nd Clerk-Asst, 1937-48, Clerk-Asst, 1948-54, Clerk, 1954-61, retired. FRSA 1964. *Publications:* Finance of Government (with late J. W. Hills, MP), 1931; Sir Thomas Erskine May's Treatise on the Law, Privileges, Proceedings and Usage of Parliament (ed. with T. G. B. Cocks), 1957. *Recreations:* golf, bowls. *Address:* Paddocks, Scole, Norfolk. *T:* Scole 241. *Clubs:* Athenæum, Oxford and Cambridge University, MCC.

**FELLOWES, Maj.-Gen. Halford David,** CB 1957; DSO 1945; *b* 1906; *er s* of late Major Halford Le M. Fellowes, 47th Sikhs (retd), Tenterden; *m* 1st, 1932, Angela Mary (marr. diss. 1941), *d* of P. E. Cammiade, ICS (retd); one *d*; 2nd, 1942, Rosemary, *er d* of late Brig.-Gen. Sir Terence Keyes, KCIE, CSI, CMG. *Educ:* St Paul's Sch., London. Royal Marines: 2nd Lieut 1924; Lieut 1927; Capt. 1936; A/Maj. 1940; A/Lt-Col 1940; Bt Major 1941; A/Col 1945; T/Brig. 1945; Major 1946; A/Lieut-Col 1947; Lieut-Col 1948; A/Col 1952; Col 1952; Maj.-Gen. 1954. Served HM Ships Berwick, Resolution, Sheffield, Base Defences Mediterranean, 1935-36; RM Siege Regt, 1940-42; GSO1, Special Service Group, 1943-44; 42 Commando RM (SE Asia), 1944-45 (wounded in Arakan, 1945); HQ 3 Commando Bde, 1945-46; GSO1 (Trg), RM office, 1947-49; Commando Sch., RM, 1949-52; Depot, RM Deal, 1952-54; psc 1943; jssc 1947. Commander Plymouth Group, Royal Marines, 1954-57, retired. *Recreation:* golf. *Address:* Pastures, Rolvenden, Kent. *T:* Rolvenden 332. *Clubs:* Army and Navy; Rye Golf.

**FELLOWES, Brig. Reginald William Lyon,** CBE 1943; *b* 6 Aug. 1895; *s* of late Frederick William Fellowes and late Mrs Fellowes, The Grange, Hitchin; *m* 1921, Dulcie M. B. H. Peel; two *s*; *m* 1947, M. G. Joan Beard. *Educ:* Wellington Coll.; Royal Military Academy, Woolwich. 2nd Lieut RFA August 1914; served in France, Belgium, and Italy, 1914-19 (MC and Bar, despatches); psc; retired with rank of Major, 1938; mobilised Sept. 1939, France, Iraq and Persia, Sicily and Italy (CBE, despatches, Legion of Honour); released Aug. 1945, hon. rank Brig. *Address:* Cladich, Dalmally, Argyll. *T:* Dalmally 246. *Club:* United Service.

**FELLOWES, Sir William (Albemarle),** KCVO 1964 (CVO 1952); DL; Agent to the Queen, Sandringham Estate, 1936-64, retired; Member, firm of Alfred Savill & Sons (Land Agents and Valuers) since 1964; *b* 10 Sept. 1899; 2nd *surv. s* of Charles Arthur Fellowes and Mary Fellowes; *m* 1934, Jane Charlotte, *d* of Brig.-Gen. A. F. H. Ferguson; two *s* two *d*. *Educ:* Winchester Coll.; Oriel Coll., Oxford. Agent to: Major W. S. Gosling, Hassobury Estate, Essex, 1925-30; Old Warden Estates, Beds, 1930-36. Became Agent to King George VI, 1936. Served with Scots Guards, 1940-45. DL Norfolk, 1965. FLAS 1927, Professional Associate of the Chartered Surveyors, 1923. FRICS 1964. *Recreations:* shooting and fishing. *Address:* Flitcham House, Flitcham, King's Lynn, Norfolk. *T:* Hillington 346. *Clubs:* Kennel; Norfolk (Norwich).

**FELTIN, His Eminence Cardinal Maurice;** Archbishop of Paris, 1949-66; Officier de la Légion d'Honneur, Médaille Militaire, Croix de Guerre; *b* Delle, near Belfort, 15 May 1883. *Educ:* Collège St-Ignace, Dijon; Grand Séminaire St Sulpice, Paris. Bishop of Troyes,

1928; Archbishop of Sens, 1932; Archbishop of Bordeaux, 1935. Cardinal, 1953. *Address:* 32 rue Barbet de Jouy, Paris 7e, France.

**FENBY, Charles;** Editorial Consultant, Westminster Press Ltd, since 1970 (Editorial Director, 1957-70); *b* 21 May 1905; *s* of Skelton Fenby; *m* 1941, June Head; one *s* one *d. Educ:* Royal Grammar School, Guildford; Wadham Coll., Oxford. Joined editorial staff of Westminster Gazette, 1926, transferred to Daily News, 1927; helped to launch Oxford Mail, 1928, Ed. until 1940. Joined Hulton Press, 1940, as Asst Ed., Picture Post; Ed., Leader Magazine, 1944-48. Returned to Westminster Press as Ed., Birmingham Gazette, 1949; Ed.-in-Chief and Dir, The Birmingham Gazette and Despatch Ltd, 1953-57; Chairman: British Cttee Internat. Press Inst.; Training and Educn of Journalists Cttee, Commonwealth Press Union. *Publication:* (with C. Day Lewis) Anatomy of Oxford, 1938; Gray's Oxford, 1970. *Address:* 9 Holly Lodge Gardens, N6. *Club:* United University.

**FENBY, Prof. Eric William,** OBE 1962; Professor of Harmony, Royal Academy of Music, since 1964; *b* 22 April 1906; *s* of Herbert Henry and Ada Fenby; *m* 1944, Rowena Clara Teresa Marshall; one *s* one *d. Educ:* Municipal Sch., Scarborough; privately. Amanuensis to Frederick Delius, 1928-34; Mus. Adv. Boosey & Hawkes, 1936-39; dêbut as composer, BBC Promenade Concerts, 1942. Captain, RAEC Sch. of Educn, Cuerdon Hall, 1942-45. Mus. Dir, N Riding Coll. of Educn, 1948-62; Artistic Dir, Delius Centenary Festival, 1962; Pres. Delius Soc., 1964-; Chm., Composers' Guild of Great Britain, 1968. Visiting Prof. of Music and Composer in Residence, Jacksonville Univ., Fla, USA, 1968. Hon. Mem., RAM, 1965. *Publications:* Delius as I Knew Him, 1936, rev. edn 1966; Menuhin's House of Music, 1969; Delius, 1970. *Recreations:* walking, chess. *Address:* 35 Brookfield, Highgate West Hill, N6. *T:* 01-340 5122. *Club:* Royal Academy of Music.

**FENDER, Percy George Herbert;** Chairman: Herbert Fender & Co. Ltd; Crescens Robinson & Co. Ltd; London Wine Exchange; *b* 22 Aug. 1892; *s* of Percy Robert Fender and Lily Herbert; *m* 1924, Ruth Marion Clapham (*d* 1937); one *s* one *d*; *m* 1962, Susan (Victoria Gordon) (*d* 1967), *er d* of Capt. and Mrs J. T. Kyffin, South Brent. *Educ:* St George's Coll., Weybridge; St Paul's Sch. Cricket for Sussex, 1910-13, for Surrey, 1914-36, toured Australia for MCC, 1920-21; also South Africa, 1922-23; toured Australia for Star as First Special Cricket Correspondent for any newspaper, 1928-29; Capt. Surrey, 1921-32; Special Cricket Correspondent for Evening News, Tests of 1934-38. Contributor to Field, Sporting and Dramatic, Observer, etc; Cricket for England Home and Abroad, 1920-24, etc; Football for Casuals, Corinthians and Fulham. Began in Lancs Paper Mill then same in Belgium, etc; Secretariat Concours Hippique Brussels Cinquantenaire, 1912; created Herbert Fender & Co., 1920; served Royal Fusiliers, 1914-15, Royal Flying Corps, 1915 and Royal Air Force, 1915-18; rejoined RAF, 1940-46 (despatches, Invasion of Europe). Mem. LCC for Norwood Div. of Lambeth, 1952-55 and 1955-58. DL County of London, 1958; Greater London, 1965. Freeman, City of London. Pres., Horsham and District Football Assoc., 1963-. *Publications:* Defending the Ashes, 1921; Turn of the Wheel, 1929; The Tests of 1930, 1930; Kissing the Rod, 1934; Lonsdale Library on Cricket; ABC of Cricket, 1937, BBC and Television Cricket, etc. *Recreations:* cricket, football, billiards, golf, writing, shooting. *Clubs:* MCC, Canning, Royal Air Force.

**FENN, Harold Robert Backwell;** Professor Emeritus in the University of London since 1960, when retired from Guy's; Hon. Consultant, Guy's Hospital; late Locum Consultant to King's College Dental School and Royal Dental Hospital; *b* 14 Jan. 1894; *s* of S. Backwell Fenn, LRCP, MRCS, and Annie Smith; *m* 1926, Margaret Winter; two *d. Educ:* private sch.; Neuchatel, Switzerland. LDS Liverpool, 1919; DDS Pennsylvania, USA, 1920; FDS, RCS, 1948. Hon. Dental Surgeon, Liverpool Heart Hosp., 1926-29; Liverpool Dental Hosp., 1929-35; Lecturer in Dental Prosthetics and Mechanics, University of Liverpool, 1931-35; Examiner in Dental Prosthetics and Mechanics, University of Liverpool, 1931-35; Prof. of Prosthetic Dental Surgery, University of London, at Guy's Hosp., 1935-60; Internal Examiner, Dental Prosthetics, University of London; External Examiner, Dental Prosthetics, Universities of Manchester, Liverpool and Durham, 1944-. *Publication:* (part author) Clinical Dental Prosthetics. *Recreation:* gardening. *Address:* Madryn, Morley's Road, Weald, Sevenoaks, Kent. *T:* Weald 254.

**FENNELL, John Lister Illingworth,** MA, PhD Cantab; Professor of Russian, Oxford University, since Oct. 1967; *b* 30 May 1918; *s* of Dr C. H. Fennell and Sylvia Mitchell; *m* 1947, Marina Lopukhin; one *s* one *d. Educ:* Radley Coll.; Trinity Coll., Cambridge. Served with Army, 1939-45. Asst Lectr, Dept of Slavonic Studies, Cambridge Univ., 1947-52; Reader in Russian and Head of Dept of Slavonic Languages, Nottingham Univ., 1952-56; Lectr in Russian, Oxford Univ., 1956-67, Fellow and Praelector in Russian, University coll., Oxford, 1964-67. Vis. Lectr, Harvard Univ., 1963-64. Joint Editor, Oxford Slavonic Papers. *Publications:* The Correspondence between Prince A. M. Kurbsky and Ivan IV, 1955; Ivan the Great of Moscow, 1961; The Penguin Russian Course, 1961; Pushkin, 1964; Kurbsky's History of Ivan IV, 1965; The Emergence of Moscow, 1968; (ed jtly) Historical Russian Reader; Cambridge Modern History, Vol. II, Chap. 19; articles in Slavonic and East European Review, Jahrbücher für Geschichte Osteuropas, etc. *Recreation:* music. *Address:* 8 Canterbury Road, Oxford. *T:* Oxford 56149.

**FENNER, Mrs Bernard;** *see* Fenner, Mrs Peggy.

**FENNER, Tan Sri Sir Claude Harry,** KBE 1965 (MBE 1946); CMG 1963; Special Representative in Malaysia of the Rubber Growers' Assoc.; *b* 16 Jan. 1916; *s* of late Major C. H. Fenner, MBE, Indian Army; *m* 1941, Joan Margaret, *d* of late J. Fenner, Brisbane, Queensland; one *d. Educ:* Highgate Sch. Probationary Asst Supt, Federated Malay States Police, 1936; Supt, 1950; Asst Commissioner, 1953; Senior Asst Commissioner (Head of Special Branch), 1954; Dep. Sec. (Security and Intelligence), Prime Minister's Dept, March 1958; Commissioner of Police, Sept. 1958; Dir of Police Affairs, 1962; Inspector Gen. of Police, Malaysia, 1963-66. War Service with Special Forces (Force 136), 1942-45, Lieut-Col. Colonial Police Medal, 1950; Queen's Police Medal, 1957. Panglima Mangku Negara, Fedn of Malaya, 1961; National Order of Vietnam, 3rd cl., 1965; Dato Paduka Makhota Brunei, 1966. *Recreations:* all forms of sport. *Address:* 1a Girdle Road, Kuala Lumpur, Malaysia. *T:* KL 27354. *Club:* Special Forces.

**FENNER, Prof. Frank John,** MBE 1944; FRS 1958; FAA 1954; FRCP 1967; Professor of Microbiology, Australian National University, since 1949; Director, John Curtin School of Medical Research, Australian National University, since 1967; *b* 21 Dec. 1914; *s* of Charles and Emma L. Fenner; *m* 1944, Ellen Margaret Bobbie Roberts; one *d* (and one *d* decd). *Educ:* Thebarton Technical High Sch.; Adelaide High Sch.; Univ. of Adelaide. MB, BS (Adelaide) 1938; MD (Adelaide) 1942; DTM (Sydney) 1940. Served as Medical Officer, Hospital Pathologist, and Malariologist, AIF, 1940-46; Francis Haley Research Fellow, Walter and Eliza Hall Inst. for Medical Research, Melbourne, 1946-48; Rockefeller Foundation Travelling Fellow, 1948-49; Overseas Fellow, Churchill Coll., Cambridge, 1962-63. David Syme Prize, Univ. of Melbourne, 1949; Harvey Lecture, Harvey Soc. of New York, 1957; Leeuwenhoek Lecture, Royal Society, 1961; Matthew Flinders Lecture, Australian Acad. of Science, 1967; Mueller Medal, Australian and New Zealand Assoc. for the Advancement of Science, 1964. Hon. MD Monash, 1966. Britannica Australia Award for Medicine, 1967. *Publications:* The Production of Antibodies (with F. M. Burnet), 1949; Myxomatosis (with F. N. Ratcliffe), 1965; The Biology of Animal Viruses, 1968; Medical Virology (with D. O. White), 1970; numerous scientific papers, dealing with virology, epidemiology and bacteriology. *Recreations:* gardening, tennis, fishing. *Address:* 8 Monaro Crescent, Red Hill, Canberra, ACT 2603, Australia. *T:* 95-9176.

**FENNER, Mrs Peggy; (Mrs B. Fenner)**; MP (C) Rochester and Chatham since 1970; *m* 1940, Bernard Fenner; one *d*. *Educ:* LCC School, Brockley; Ide Hill, Sevenoaks. Member, Sevenoaks Urban District Council, 1957- (Chairman, 1962 and 1963). *Recreations:* reading, travel, theatre, gardening. *Address:* Tylers, St Nicholas Drive, Sevenoaks, Kent.

**FENNESSY, Group Captain Edward,** CBE 1957 (OBE 1944); BSc; FIEE, FIN; Managing Director (Telecommunications), and Member of Board, Post Office Corporation, since 1969; *b* 17 Jan. 1912; *m* 1937, Marion Banks; one *s* one *d*. *Educ:* Univ. of London. Telecommunications Research, Standard Telephones and Cables, 1934-38; Radar Research, Air Min. Research Station, Bawdsey Manor, 1938. War of 1939-45: commissioned RAFVR, 1940; Group Captain, 1945; staff No 60 Group, RAF, 1940-45; resp. for planning and construction radar systems for defence of UK, and Bomber Ops. Joined Bd of The Decca Navigator Co., 1946; Managing Director: Decca Radar Ltd, 1950-65; The Plessey Electronics Group, 1965-69. Chairman: British Telecommunications Research Ltd, 1966-69; Electronic Engineering Assoc., 1967-68. *Recreations:* sailing, golf. *Address:* Northbrook, Littleford Lane, Shamley Green, Surrey. *T:* Bramley 2444. *Clubs:* Royal Air Force; Island Sailing.

**FENTON, Air Cdre Harold Arthur,** CBE 1946; DSO 1943; DFC 1942; BA; AFRAeS; *b* Gallegos, Patagonia, Argentine, 9 Feb. 1909; *s* of Dr E. G. Fenton, FRCSI, DPH, Co. Sligo and J. Ormsby, Glen Lodge, Ballina, Co. Mayo; *m* 1935, H. de Carteret; no *c*. *Educ:* Sandford Park Sch.; Trinity Coll., Dublin (BA 1927). Joined RAF 1928. Served India, 1930-33. Flying Instructor at Air Service Training Ltd, Hamble, until outbreak of war. During war commanded: Fighter Sqdn, Battle of Britain; Fighter Wing, and Fighter Group, Western Desert and Libya; Fighter Sector, London Area. Finished war as Senior Staff Officer, Germany (83 Group) (despatches thrice). Managing Dir, Deccan Airways Ltd, Hyderabad, Deccan, until 1947; Gen. Manager of Airways Training Ltd, 1947-48; Operations Manager, BOAC, 1949-52; Managing Dir, Peter Jones, 1952-58. *Recreations:* gardening, sailing. *Address:* Le Vallon, St Brelade, Jersey, Channel Islands. *T:* 41172.

**FENTON, James Stevenson,** CMG 1941; OBE 1935; *b* 9 Feb. 1891; *e s* of Rev. James Fenton, Dundee; *m* 1928, Margaret, *yr d* of Rev. Joseph E. Richers, BD, Blairgowrie; three *d*. *Educ:* Dundee High Sch.; Edinburgh Univ. (MA). Asst Dist Comr, Sierra Leone, 1915; Chief Comr, 1946; retd, 1947. Chief Electoral Comr, 1961-63. *Address:* 20 Moorgarth Avenue, York.

**FENTON, Roy Pentelow,** CMG 1960; Chief, Overseas Department, Bank of England, since 1965; *b* 1 July 1918; *s* of late Heber Fenton, Salford; *m* 1941, Daphne, *d* of late E. Cheason; one *s*. *Educ:* Salford Grammar Sch. Served, 1939-46; commissioned Lancs Fusiliers. United Kingdom Alternate Mem., Management Board of European Payments Union, 1954-57; Governor, Central Bank of Nigeria, 1958-63; Dep. Chief of Central Banking Information Dept, Bank of England, 1963-65. UK Mem., Man. Bd of European Monetary Agreement, 1967, Vice-Chm., 1968. *Address:* Furzewood, Speldhurst, Kent. *T:* 155. *Clubs:* East India and Sports, Overseas Bankers.

**FENTON, Wilfrid David Drysdale,** CBE 1963; FRSE; BSc, MIEE; Chairman, London Electricity Board since Nov. 1968; *b* 27 March 1908; *s* of late David Fenton, Edinburgh; *m* 1955, Isobel Stewart, *d* of late Dr Mowat, Edinburgh; no *c*. *Educ:* George Watson's Coll., Edinburgh; Edinburgh Univ. Called to Bar, Middle Temple, 1937. Kennedy and Donkin, Cons. Engrs, London, 1931-33; Central Electricity Bd, London, 1933-38; Personal Asst to Gen. Manager, Midland Counties Electric Supply Co., 1938-44; Commercial Engr, 1944-48, Sec. and Commercial Engr, 1948-55, N of Scotland Hydro-Electric Bd; Chm., 1955-62, Uganda Electricity Bd; Chm., S Wales Electricity Bd, 1962-68; Dir, Uganda Development Corp., 1955-57; Hon. Treas., 1956-57, Vice-Chm., 1957-62, Makarere Univ. Coll.; Chm. Mulago Hosp. (Kampala) Autonomy Cttee, 1961. *Recreation:* golf. *Address:* 31 Cadogan Lane, SW1. *Clubs:* Reform, Royal Commonwealth Society.

**FENTON, Col Sir William (Charles),** Kt 1954; MC; JP; Chairman of BBA Group Ltd, Cleckheaton, Yorks, 1954-69; *b* 29 Sept. 1891; *s* of John Fenton, Cleckheaton; *m* 1921, Margaret, *d* of Robert Hirst, Cleckheaton; three *s* one *d*. *Educ:* Heckmondwike Grammar Sch. Served European War, 1914-19; Major 4 Bn, Duke of Wellington's Regt (TF), 1918; Commanded Bradford Sector Home Guard, 1940-42 (Col). JP West Riding of Yorks, 1932. *Recreation:* fishing. *Address:* Fieldhead, Cleckheaton, Yorks. *T:* Cleckheaton 2783.

**FENWICK, Robert George;** HM Inspector of Constabulary since 1967; *b* 1913; *s* of late George R. F. Fenwick, Horton Grange, Northumberland; *m* 1943, Eileen Winifreda, *d* of late James Carstairs Dodds, Buenos Aires. *Educ:* Dame Allan's Sch. Barrister-at-Law, Gray's Inn, 1951. Metropolitan Police, 1934-59; seconded to Foreign Office for duties in São Paulo, Brazil, 1957-58; Directing Staff, Police Coll., 1959-60; Asst Chief Constable, Glos, 1960-62; Chief Constable, Salop, 1962-67. QPM 1969. *Address:* Ebor House, Kingsland, Shrewsbury, Salop. *T:* Shrewsbury

4158. *Clubs:* Public Schools; Shropshire County (Shrewsbury).

**FERENS, Sir Thomas (Robinson),** Kt 1957; CBE 1952; *b* 4 Jan. 1903; *e s* of late J. J. T. Ferens, Hull; *m* 1934, Jessie, *d* of P. G. Sanderson, Hull and Scarborough; two *d. Educ:* Rydal; Leeds Univ. (BSc Eng). Hon Treasurer: Hull Seaman's and General Orphanage, 1933-48; Hull Conservative Federation, 1945-52 (Dep. Chm., 1951-62). *Recreation:* fly-fishing. *Address:* Sunderlandwick, Driffield, E Yorks. *T:* Driffield 2323.

**FERGUS, Most Rev. James;** *see* Achonry, Bishop of, (RC).

**FERGUSON, Ernest Alexander;** Assistant Under-Secretary of State, Department of Employment and Productivity, since 1969; *b* 26 July 1917; *s* of William Henry and Lilian Ferguson; *m* 1949, Mary Josephine Wadsworth; two *s. Educ:* Priory Sch., Shrewsbury; Pembroke Coll., Cambridge. Scholar, Pembroke Coll., 1935-39; MA 1944. Served War, RA (Captain), 1940-45. Entered Ministry of Labour, 1945; Principal, 1948; Asst Sec., 1962. Chm., Central Youth Employment Executive, 1967-69. *Recreations:* sport, mountaineering, reading. *Address:* 25 Balcombe Road, Horley, Surrey. *T:* Horley 5254. *Club:* Army and Navy.

**FERGUSON, Major Sir John (Frederick),** Kt 1953; CBE 1948; DL; Chief Constable of Kent, Aug. 1946-Oct. 1958, retd; *b* 23 Aug. 1891; *e s* of Major J. E. Ferguson, IA; *m* 1929, Vera Millicent, *d* of late Brig.-Gen. F. C. Lloyd, CB; one *s. Educ:* Aberdeen Univ.; RMC Sandhurst. Joined Durham Light Infantry, 1912; served NW Frontier, India, 1912-16; served Palestine and Mesopotamia, 1916-18; Adjt 1st DLI, 1919-22; Staff Coll., 1926; Gen. Staff, Shanghai Defence Force, 1927; Brig. Major 2nd Rhine Bde and 14th Inf. Bde, 1928-31; Brevet Major, 1930; Subst. Major, 1931; Naval Staff Coll., 1932; retired, 1933. Chief Constable, Met. Police, 1933; Dep. Asst Commissioner, Met. Police, 1935-40; Commandant, Met. Police Coll., 1938-39; rejoined Army Feb. 1940; GSO1, War Office; rejoined Met. Police Sept. 1940; Chief Constable Sussex Joint Police Force, 1943-45; Asst Commissioner of Police of the Metropolis, 1945-46. DL Kent, 1958. Queen's Police Medal, 1957. CStJ 1961. *Recreation:* golf. *Address:* 24 Watchbell Street, Rye, Sussex. *Club:* Army and Navy.

**FERGUSON, Sir Neil Edward J.;** *see* Johnson-Ferguson.

**FERGUSON, Samuel Fergus,** CBE 1952; Director, The Australian Association of British Manufacturers, 1927-62, now part-time consultant; *b* Melbourne, Australia, 27 Feb. 1897; *s* of Rev. Andrew Fergus Ferguson, late of Glasgow, and Catherine Oatt (*née* Brown); *m* 1st, 1929, Kathleen (*d* 1967), *d* of John and Annie Revell, late of Heathcote, Australia; 2nd, 1968, Elizabeth Isabel, *d* of late H. P. P. Daniel, and *widow* of Mr Justice Roper, NSW; no *c. Educ:* State Schs; privately; Melbourne Univ. National Bank of Australasia Ltd, 1913. Served European War, 1914-18, in AIF, 1916-19. British Phosphate Commission, Nauru, Central Pacific, 1922; AICA 1920; Licensed Company Auditor, 1926; practised as public accountant, 1926-27. *Publications:* Postwar World Trade, 1943; John Bull Gets Tough, 1944; contribs to daily press, England and Australia. *Recreations:* golf, swimming, reading. *Address:* 3/17 Wentworth Street, Point Piper, NSW 2027, Australia. *T:* 36.4863. *Club:* Athenæum (Melbourne).

**FERGUSON, Dr Thomas,** CBE 1954; Emeritus Professor of Public Health, University of Glasgow; *b* 23 May 1900; *s* of Alexander Gray Ferguson and Agnes Ferguson; *m* 1927, A. Elizabeth Webster; no *c. Educ:* Edinburgh Univ. Late HM Medical Inspector of Factories; late Dept Chief Med. Officer, Dept Health, Scotland. Mem., MRC Cttee on Social Medicine and Chm. of Cttee on Carcinogenic Action of Mineral Oils; formerly Chm. Gen. Nursing Council, Scotland. Hon Consult. Physician: Glasgow Western Infirmary, Falkirk Royal Infirmary. *Publications:* The Dawn of Scottish Social Welfare, 1948; A Scottish Experiment in the Employment of Severely Disabled Men, 1948; The Young Wage Earner, 1951; The Young Delinquent in his Social Setting, 1952; Hospital and Community, 1954, 1962; Scottish Social Welfare, 1864-1914, 1958; Handicapped Youth, 1960; Children in Care and After, 1966; papers on public health and social medicine. *Recreations:* football, writing. *Address:* Chowrassie, Lezayre Road, Ramsey, IOM. *T:* Ramsey 3167. *Club:* Athenæum.

**FERGUSON, William Alexander,** OBE 1965; Secretary, British Museum (Natural History), 1959-65; *b* 13 Jan. 1902; *m* 1930, Jessie Miller Whitelaw: one *s. Educ:* Bellahouston Academy; Royal Technical Coll., Glasgow. Production Manager and Sec., Strand Films Ltd, 1937-41; Films Contracts Assessor, Min. of Information, then British Council, 1941-47; Studio Manager, Gainsborough Pictures, 1947-49; Principal Administrative Officer, Crown Film Unit, 1949-53; Finance Officer, British Museum, 1953-59. Founder and Pres., Robert Ross of Tarbert Soc. *Address:* Holmes Cottages, Betchworth, Surrey. *T:* Betchworth 3106.

**FERGUSON DAVIE, Rev. Sir (Arthur) Patrick,** 5th Bt *cr* 1641 and *re-created* 1847 for General Henry Ferguson, husband of Juliana, *d* of Sir John Davie, 8th Bt of Creedy; TD 1954; Hon. Chaplain to Bishop of Exeter since 1949; *b* 17 March 1909; *s* of late Lt-Col Arthur Francis Ferguson-Davie, CIE, DSO (3rd *s* of 3rd Bt), and late Eleanor Blanche Daphne, *d* of late C. T. Naylor (she *m* 1918, Major J. H. W. Knight-Bruce, who *d* 1951; she *d* 1964); *S* uncle, 1947; *m* 1949, Iris Dawn Cable-Buller, *o d* of Capt. and Hon. Mrs Buller, Downes, Crediton; one *s. Educ:* Wellington Coll.; Lincoln Coll., Oxford (MA). Ely Theological Coll., 1932-34; Deacon, 1934, Priest, 1935. Asst Curate, Littleham-cum-Exmouth, 1934-37; St Augustine's, Kilburn, NW6, 1938-39; CF (TA), 1937-45; Hon. CF 1945. Served with 4th Bn Devonshire Regt in UK and Gibraltar, 1939-43; CMF, N Africa and Italy, 1943-45; Vicar of St John's Torquay, 1945-48. *Publication:* The Bishop in Church, 1961. *Recreation:* shooting. *Heir: s* Antony Francis Ferguson Davie, *b* 23 March 1952. *Address:* Creedy Park, Crediton, Devon. *T:* Crediton 2809; Skalatos, Klepini, Kyrenia, Cyprus.

**FERGUSON DAVIE, Rev. Sir Patrick;** *see* Ferguson Davie, Rev. Sir A. P.

**FERGUSSON, Brig. Sir Bernard (Edward),** GCMG 1962; GCVO 1963; DSO 1943; OBE 1950; Governor-General and Commander-in-Chief of New Zealand, 1962-67; Chairman, London Board, Bank of New Zealand, since 1968; *b* 6 May 1911; *y s* of Gen. Sir Charles Fergusson of Kilkerran, 7th Bt, GCB, GCMG, DSO, MVO, and of Lady Alice Boyle (*d* 1958), *d* of 7th Earl of Glasgow; *m* 1950, Laura Margaret, *y d* of Lieut-Col A. M. Grenfell, DSO; one *s. Educ:* Eton; RMC Sandhurst. Joined The Black Watch, 1931; Lieut 1934, Capt. 1939; ADC to Maj.-Gen.

(later F.-M.) Wavell, 2nd Div. Aldershot, 1935-37; served Palestine, 1937 (medal and clasp); Instructor RMC, 1938-39; served War of 1939-45 (wounded, despatches twice, DSO); Staff Coll., 1940; Bde Major 46th Inf. Bde, 1940; Middle East, 1941; GSO1 Joint Plans India, 1942; Wingate Expeditions into Burma, 1943-44; comd 16th Inf. Bde in 1944 expedition; Dir of Combined Ops (Military), 1945-46. Asst Inspector-Gen., Palestine Police, 1946-47; commanded 1st Bn The Black Watch, 1948-51; Col Intelligence, Supreme HQ, Allied Powers, Europe, 1951-53; idc 1954; Comdr, 153rd Highland Bde, TA, 1955-56; Allied Force HQ Port Said Operations, 1956; Comdr, 29th Infantry Bde, 1957-58, retd. Internat. Observer Team, Nigeria, Oct. 1968-March 1969. Col The Black Watch (Royal Highland Regt), 1969-. Hon. DCL, Canterbury; DUniv Waikato. *Publications:* Eton Portrait, 1937; Beyond the Chindwin, 1945; Lowland Soldier (verse), 1945; The Wild Green Earth, 1946; The Black Watch and the King's Enemies, 1950; Rupert of the Rhine, 1952; The Rare Adventure, 1954; The Watery Maze: The Story of Combined Operations, 1961; Wavell: Portrait of a Soldier, 1961; Return to Burma, 1962; The Trumpet in the Hall, 1970. *Address:* Auchairne, Ballantrae, Ayrshire. *T:* 344. *Clubs:* White's; New (Edinburgh).

**FERGUSSON, Sir Ewen (MacGregor Field),** Kt 1953; Director: Gopeng Consolidated; Kinta Tin Mines; Kinta Kellas Tin Dredging; Renong Tin Dredging; Tronoh Mines Ltd; Chairman and Managing Director, The Straits Trading Co. Ltd, 1946-65; *b* 16 Oct. 1897; *m* 1931, Winifred Evelyn Bagnall; two *s* one *d*. *Educ:* Coatbridge Sch., Lanarks. Capt. Royal Engineers, 1914-20. The Straits Trading Co. Ltd, 1920-65. Singapore: Chm. Chamber of Commerce, 1946-53; Adv. Council, 1946-47; Exec. Council, 1947-54; Mem. (for Chamber of Commerce) Legislative Council, 1947-54; MLA Singapore, 1959-60. Dir of Public Companies. Dept War Organisation of Industry, Aust., 1942-44. *Recreations:* golf, tennis. *Address:* c/o Chartered Bank, 38 Bishopsgate, EC2. *Clubs:* Singapore (Singapore); Royal Selangor Golf.

**FERGUSSON, Ian Victor Lyon;** Director, Carless, Capel & Leonard; *b* 22 Jan. 1901; *y s* of late Rev. Dr John Moore Fergusson; *m* 1927, Hannah Grace (*née* Gourlay); three *s* one *d*. *Educ:* Berkhamsted Sch. Joined Evans Medical Ltd. (then Evans Sons Lescher & Webb Ltd), 1919; Dir, 1927; Man. Dir, 1941; Chm. and Man. Dir, Evans Medical Ltd, 1943-62; Dir, Glaxo Group Ltd, 1961-62. Pres., Chemists Federation, 1940-41; Chm., Assoc. British Pharmaceutical Industry, 1946-47. Mem., Liverpool Regional Hospital Board, 1958-61. *Recreations:* fishing, gardening. *Address:* Orchard Lodge, Avon Dassett, via Leamington Spa, Warwickshire. *T:* Farnborough 228.

**FERGUSSON of Kilkerran, Sir James,** 8th Bt *cr* 1703; LLD (Glasgow); FRSE; Lord Lieutenant of Ayrshire, since 1969; Member: Queen's Body Guard for Scotland (Royal Company of Archers); Royal Commission on Historical Manuscripts; Scottish Cttee on the History of Parliament; *b* 18 Sept. 1904; *e s* of 7th Bt and Lady Alice Boyle (*d* 1958), 2nd *d* of 7th Earl of Glasgow; *S* father, 1951; *m* 1930, Louise Frances Balfour, *o d* of Edgar Trevelyan Stratford Dugdale; two *s* one *d* (and one *d* decd). *Educ:* Eton; Balliol Coll., Oxford (BA 1925). Worked as bookseller and publisher, 1927-33; talks producer, BBC, Edinburgh, 1934-40, Overseas service, London, 1940-41; broadcast nightly as commentator on Nazi propaganda, Overseas service, 1941-44; civilian lecturer with Middle East Forces, 1944-45; leader-writer, Glasgow Herald, 1945-49; Board of Trustees, National Galleries of Scotland, 1947-49; Keeper of the Records of Scotland, 1949-69. Andrew Lang Lecturer, St Andrews, 1956-57. *Publications:* Letters of George Dempster to Sir Adam Fergusson, 1756-1813, 1934; Alexander the Third, 1937; William Wallace, 1938; The Green Garden (anthology), 1946; John Fergusson, 1727-1750, 1948; Lowland Lairds, 1949; Argyll in the Forty-Five, 1951; The Fergussons, 1956; The Kennedys, 1958; The Sixteen Peers of Scotland, 1960; The White Hind, 1963; The Curragh Incident, 1964; The Man behind Macbeth, 1969; The Declaration of Arbroath, 1970; various articles on Scottish history and literature. *Heir: s* Charles Fergusson [*b* 10 May 1931; *m* 1961, Hon. Amanda Mary Noel-Paton, *e d* of Lord Ferrier, *qv*; two *s*]. *Address:* Kilkerran, by Maybole, Ayrshire. *T:* Crosshill 207. *Club:* New (Edinburgh).

*See also Brig. Sir Bernard Fergusson.*

**FERGUSSON, Sir James H. H.;** *see* Colyer-Fergusson.

**FERGUSSON, John Douglas,** FRCS; Surgeon, St Peter's, St Paul's and St Philip's Hospitals; Surgeon and Urologist, Central Middlesex Hospital; Director of Teaching and Research, Institute of Urology, London University; *b* 5 Dec. 1909; *s* of John Newbery Fraser Fergusson and Mildred Gladys (*née* Mercer); *m* 1st, 1936, Alice Alyne (*d* 1968), *d* of Hon. Mr Justice Maartensz; two *s*; 2nd, 1969, Myrtle, *d* of Maj.-Gen. K. M. Body, *qv*. *Educ:* St Peter's, York; Cambridge Univ.; St Thomas' Hosp. 1st Class Hons Nat. Science Tripos, 1931; Coll. Prizeman and Scholar, St John's Coll., Cambridge; Open Univ. Scholar, St Thos Hosp.; Sutton Sams Prize, 1934, and Cheselden Medal for Surgery, 1936, St Thos Hosp.; MA 1945, MD 1946 Cantab; FRCS 1936; Hunterian Prof., RCS, 1945-46; Fellow and late Mem. of Council, Assoc. of Surgeons of Gt Britain and Ireland; Vice-Pres., British Assoc. of Urological Surgeons; Member: Internat. Soc. of Urology; Bd of Governors, St Peter's, St Paul's and St Philip's Hospitals; FRSocMed (Pres. of Section of Urology, 1962-63). Hon. Editor, British Journal of Urology. Associate Examiner in Surgery, Univ. of London. *Publications:* various contribs to surgical and urological journals. *Recreation:* fishing. *Address:* 149 Harley Street, W1. *T:* 01-935 8273. *Club:* Royal Automobile.

**FERMOR, Patrick Michael Leigh,** DSO 1944; OBE 1943; author: Hon. Citizen of Herakleion, Crete, 1947, Gytheion, Laconia, 1966, and of Kardamyli, Messenia, 1967; *b* 11 Feb. 1915; *s* of late Sir Lewis Leigh Fermor, OBE, FRS, DSc, and Eileen, *d* of Charles Taaffe Ambler; *m* 1968, Hon. Mrs Joan Rayner, *d* of 1st Viscount Monsell, PC, GBE. *Educ:* King's Sch., Canterbury. After travelling for four years in Central Europe, Balkans and Greece, enlisted in Irish Guards at outbreak of War of 1939-45; 2nd Lieut, "I" Corps, 1940; Lieut, British Mil. Mission, Greece, 1940; Liaison Officer, Greek GHQ, Albania; campaigns of Greece and Crete; 2 years in German occupied Crete with Cretan guerillas, entering island by sea, 1942, 1944, by parachute, 1944; Captain 1941; commanded some minor guerilla operations in Crete; Major 1943; at end of war team-commander in Special Allied Airborne Reconnaissance Force, N Germany; demobilised, 1945. Dep.-Dir British Institute, Athens, till middle 1946; travelled in Caribbean and Central American republics, 1947-48. *Publications:* The Traveller's Tree (Heinemann Foundation

Prize for Literature, 1950, and Kemsley Prize, 1951); A Time to Keep Silence, 1953; The Violins of Saint Jacques, 1953; Mani, 1958 (Duff Cooper Prize; Book Society's Choice); (trans.) The Cretan Runner (George Psychoundakis), 1955; Roumeli, 1966. *Recreation:* travel. *Address:* c/o Messrs John Murray, 50 Albemarle Street, W1. *Clubs:* Travellers', White's, Pratt's, Special Forces; Cercle Huysmans (Paris).

**FERMOR-HESKETH,** family name of **Baron Hesketh.**

**FERMOY,** 5th Baron *cr* 1856; **Edmund James Burke Roche;** with World Wildlife Fund, since 1967; *b* 20 March 1939; *s* of 4th Baron Fermoy and Ruth Sylvia (*see* Dowager Lady Fermoy); *S* father, 1955; *m* 1964, Lavinia Frances Elizabeth, *o d* of late Capt. John Pitman and of Mrs Pitman, Foxley House, Malmesbury, Wilts; one *s* one *d. Educ:* Eton; Sandhurst; RAC, Cirencester. Capt., Royal Horse Guards (The Blues), retd 1967. *Recreations:* polo, racing. *Heir: s* Hon. Patrick Maurice Burke Roche, *b* 11 Oct. 1967. *Address:* 80 Chelsea Park Gardens, SW3. *T:* 01-352 7835; Eddington House, Hungerford, Berks. *T:* Hungerford 2540. *Clubs:* White's, Turf.

**FERMOY, Dowager Lady; Ruth Sylvia; (Rt. Hon. Ruth Lady Fermoy),** CVO 1966; OBE 1952; JP; Woman of the Bedchamber to Queen Elizabeth the Queen Mother since 1960 (an extra Woman of the Bedchamber, 1956-60); *b* 2 Oct. 1908; *y d* of late W. S. Gill, CB, Dalhebity, Bieldside, Aberdeenshire; *m* 1931, Edmund Maurice Burke Roche, 4th Baron Fermoy (*d* 1955); one *s* (*see* 5th Baron Fermoy) two *d.* JP Norfolk, 1944. Freedom of King's Lynn, 1963. Hon. RAM 1968. *Address:* 107 Eaton Square, SW1; La Vieille Maison, St Paul (AM), France.

**FERNALD, John Bailey;** Professor in the Department of Theatre, New York State University; West End of London stage producer; *b* 21 Nov. 1905; *s* of C. B. Fernald and Josephine Harker; *m* 1942, Jenny Laird; one *d. Educ:* Marlborough Coll.; Trinity Coll., Oxford. Pres., OUDS, 1927; Dramatic Editor, The Pall Mall Magazine, 1929; first professional production, Arts Theatre, 1929; subsequently produced plays continuously in London till 1936, when became Associate Producer for Associated British Pictures Corporation; returned to theatre, 1938; on teaching staff of Royal Academy of Dramatic Art, 1934-40. Joined RNVR, 1940 and served almost continuously at sea until 1945; left service with rank of Lieut-Comdr. Dir of Productions, Reunion Theatre, 1946; Dir of the Liverpool Playhouse, 1946-49; subsequently produced: The Love of Four Colonels, Wyndham's; The White Sheep of the Family, Piccadilly; The First Born, Winter Garden; Nightmare Abbey and Dial M for Murder, Westminster; Escapade, Strand; The Devil's General, Savoy; Crime and Punishment (Television); Saint Joan, St Martin's; The Remarkable Mr Pennypacker, New; The House by the Lake, Duke of York's; Jubilee Production of Peter Pan; Tea and Sympathy, Comedy; Hedda Gabler, Nye Teater, Oslo; The Love of Four Colonels, Kansanteatteri, Helsinki; Ghosts, Old Vic; The Tchekov Centenary Production of The Seagull, Edinburgh Festival and Old Vic; The Affair, Henry Miller Theatre, New York; The Schoolmistress, Savoy; The Enchanted, Arts Theatre; Ivanov, Uncle Vanya, The Seagull, and various plays at Arts Theatre and elsewhere; 1st production in England of Bertolt Brecht's The Caucasian Chalk Circle, Vanbrugh Theatre, Royal Academy of Dramatic Art; Anton Tchekov's The Cherry Orchard at the National Theatre, Pretoria and Johannesburg. Shute Lectr on the Art of the Theatre, Liverpool Univ., 1948. Principal, Royal Academy of Dramatic Art, 1955-65; Dir, John Fernald Co., Meadowbrook Theatre, Rochester, Mich, and Prof. of Dramatic Art, Oakland Univ., Rochester, Mich, 1966-70. *Publications:* The Play Produced: a Manual of Stage Production, 1933; Destroyer from America, 1942; Sense of Direction, 1968. *Recreations:* sailing, navigation, looking at cats, and producing the plays of Anton Tchekov. *Address:* 2 Daleham Mews, NW3. *T:* 01-435 2992. *Club:* Garrick.

**FERNANDEL, (Fernand Joseph Désiré Contandin);** French comedian; *b* Marseille, 8 May 1903; *s* of Denis Charles Contandin and Désirée (*née* Bedouin); *m* Henriette Manse; two *s* two *d.* On leaving school worked in a bank, soap factory, etc; first appeared as Fernandel, Nice, 1922; since 1930 has appeared in over 134 films, including The Little World of Don Camillo, 1953, and The Sheep has Five Legs, 1953; has also appeared in music hall, reviews, television, radio, and made records. Chevalier de la Légion d'Honneur, Officier des Palmes Académiques, Chevalier de l'Ordre des Arts et des Lettres. *Relevant Publication:* Fernandel, by Carlo Rim, 1952. *Address:* (business) 44 Avenue Foch, Paris 16e; (home) Villa Les Milleroses, Route des Trois-Lucs, Marseilles; l'Oustaü de la Mar, Carry-le-Rouet (BDR), France.

**FERNANDES, Most Rev. Angelo;** *see* Delhi, Archbishop of, (RC).

**FERNANDO, Hugh Norman Gregory; Hon. Chief Justice Fernando,** OBE 1952; Chief Justice of Ceylon since 1966; *b* 17 Nov. 1910; *s* of late V. M. Fernando, Puisne Justice, Ceylon; *m* 1935, Doris Pieris; four *s. Educ:* St Joseph's Coll., Colombo; Balliol Coll., Oxford (BA, BCL). Called to Bar, Gray's Inn, 1933; Advocate, Ceylon, 1934; Asst Legal Draftsman, 1936; Legal Draftsman, Ceylon, 1949; Puisne Justice, 1955; Chief Justice and Chm., Judicial Service Commn, 1966. Officer Administering the Govt of Ceylon in Oct. 1967 and Feb. 1970. *Recreations:* bridge, billiards. *Address:* 129 Macarthy Road, Colombo 7, Ceylon. *Club:* Orient (Colombo).

**FERNS, Prof. Henry Stanley,** MA, PhD Cantab; Professor of Political Science and Dean of Faculty of Commerce and Social Science, University of Birmingham, 1961-65; *b* Calgary, Alberta, 16 Dec. 1913; *er s* of Stanley and Janie Ferns; *m* 1940, Helen Maureen, *d* of John and Eleanor Jack; three *s* one *d. Educ:* St John's High Sch., Winnipeg; Univ. of Manitoba; Trinity Coll., Cambridge. Research Scholar, Trinity Coll., Cambridge, 1938. Secretarial staff of Prime Minister of Canada, 1940; Asst Prof. of History and Government, Univ. of Manitoba, 1945; Fellow, Canadian Social Science Research Council, 1949; Lectr in Modern History and Government, Univ. of Birmingham, 1950; successively Sen. Lectr, Head of Dept and Prof. of Political Science. Pres., Bd of Dirs, Winnipeg Citizens' Cooperative Publishing Co. Ltd, 1946-48; Member of various Conciliation Boards appointed by Minister of Labour of Govt of Manitoba, 1947-49. Vice-Chm., Sparkbrook Assoc., Birmingham. Mem., Planning Bd, Independent Univ. *Publications:* (with B. Ostry) The Age of McKenzie King: The Rise of the Leader, 1955 (Toronto and London); Britain and Argentina in the Nineteenth Century, 1960 (Oxford); Towards an Independent University, 1969; Argentina, 1969; articles in learned jls. *Recreations:* journalism, idling and pottering about.

*Address:* 1 Kesteven Close, Sir Harry's Road, Birmingham 15. *T:* 021-440 1016.

**FERNYHOUGH, Rt. Hon. Ernest,** PC 1970; MP (Lab) Jarrow since May 1947; *b* 24 Dec. 1908; British; *m* 1934, Ethel Edwards; one *s* one *d* (and one *s* decd). *Educ:* Wood Lane Council Sch. Full-time official, Nat. Union of Distributive and Allied Workers, 1936-47. PPS to the Prime Minister, 1964-67; Jt Parly Under-Sec. of State, Dept of Employment and Productivity (formerly Min. of Labour), 1967-69. *Address:* House of Commons, SW1.

**FERNYHOUGH, Brigadier Hugh Edward,** CBE 1956; DSO 1945; retired; Deputy Director Officers' Association Resettlement and Employment Department, Victoria Street, Westminster; *b* 15 April 1904; *s* of late Col Hugh Clifford Fernyhough and Mrs Beatrice Fernyhough; *m* 1943, Mary, *d* of late T. D. and Mrs Moore, Mill Down, Clyst St Mary, Exeter; one *s*. *Educ:* Wellington Coll., Berks; RMA Woolwich. 2nd Lieut 1924; Lieut 1927; Capt. 1937; grad. Staff Coll., Camberley, 1939; GSO2, 12 Corps, 1940; GSO2, Instr, Staff Coll., Camberley, 1941; Comdt (Col) NZ Staff Coll., 1942-43; OC 53 (London) Medium Regt, 1944-45; Comdt (Col) RA, OCTU, 1945-46; CRA (Col) HQ, E Africa, 1947-48; Col i/c Admin., E Africa, 1948-49; AAG, RA, War Office, 1949-52; CRA 40 Inf. Div. (Hong Kong), 1952-53; Dep. Dir, RA, 1954-56; retd 1956. Col Comdt, Royal Artillery, 1957-62. *Address:* Sylvan Lodge, Puttenham, near Guildford, Surrey. *T:* Puttenham 368. *Club:* Army and Navy.

**FEROZE, Rustam Moolan,** FRCS, FRCOG; Consulting Obstetrician and Gynæcologist, King's College Hospital and SE Metropolitan Regional Hospital Board; Consulting Obstetrician, Queen Charlotte's Maternity Hospital; Surgeon, Chelsea Hospital for Women; *b* 4 Aug. 1920; *s* of Dr J. Moolan-Feroze; *m* 1947, Margaret Dowsett. *Educ:* Sutton Valence Sch.; King's Coll. Hospital, London. MRCS, LRCP 1943; MB, BS 1946; MRCOG 1948; MD (Obst. & Dis. Wom.) London 1952; FRCS 1952; FRCOG 1962. Dean, Inst. of Obstetrics and Gynæcology, Univ. of London, 1954-67. Senr Registrar: Chelsea Hosp. for Women, and Queen Charlotte's Maternity Hosp., London, 1953-54; Hosp. for Women, Soho Square, and Middlesex Hosp., 1950-53; Resident Medical Officer, Samaritan Hosp. for Women, 1948. *Publications:* contribs to medical jls and to Queen Charlotte's Textbook of Obstetrics. *Address:* 127 Harley Street, W1. *T:* 01-935 9108. *Club:* Naval.

**FERRANTI;** *see* de Ferranti.

**FERRAR, Lieut-Col Michael Lloyd,** CSI 1927; CIE 1922; OBE 1919; JP Essex; *b* 16 April 1876; *s* of M. L. Ferrar, ICS; *m* 1st, 1903, Maud Evelyn (*d* 1906), *d* of W. B. Oldham, CIE, ICS; 2nd, 1912, Nancy (*d* 1962), *d* of John Grey Russell; two *s* two *d*. *Educ:* St Coumba's Coll.; Rugby Sch.; Sandhurst. Served in Indian Army and Punjab Commission; Tirah Campaign, 1897-98 (medal 3 clasps); commanded Baluch Levy, D. G. Khan, 1902-06; Asst Colonisation Officer, Lyallpur, 1907-11; Postal Censor, Bombay, 1914-19 (OBE); Deputy Comr, Lahore, 1919-23 (CIE); Chief Comr, Andaman and Nicobar Islands, 1923-31 (CSI); retired, 1931. Examiner in Urdu, Cambridge Univ., 1932-62. Major, Home Guard, 1940-41. *Address:* 7 Newton Hall, Dunmow, Essex. *T:* Gt Dunmow 2434.

**FERRAR, William Leonard;** Principal, Hertford College, Oxford, 1959-64; *b* 21 Oct. 1893; *s* of George William Parsons and Maria Susannah Ferrar; *m* 1923, Edna O'Hara; one *s*. *Educ:* Queen Elizabeth's Hospital, Bristol; Bristol Grammar Sch.; Queen's Coll., Oxford. Open Mathematical Schol., Queen's, 1912; Univ. Junior Math. Schol., 1914; Sen. Schol., 1922; MA Oxon 1920; DSc Oxon 1947. Served European War, 1914-18, in ranks, Artillery and Intelligence, 1914-19. Lecturer, University Coll. of N Wales, Bangor, 1920-24; Sen. Lecturer, Edinburgh, 1924-25; Fellow, Hertford Coll., Oxford, 1925-59, Bursar, 1937-59. Formerly mem. Hebdomadal Council, Gen. Board and the Chest, Oxford Univ.; Sec., London Math. Soc., 1933-38. *Publications:* Convergence, 1938; Algebra, 1941; Higher Algebra for Schools, 1945, Part II, 1948; Finite Matrices, 1951; Differential Calculus, 1956; Integral Calculus, 1958; Mathematics for Science, 1965; Calculus for Beginners, 1967; Advanced Mathematics for Science, 1969; various research papers, 1924-37. *Recreations:* gardening; a little music. *Address:* 21 Sunderland Avenue, Oxford.

**FERRARI, Enzo;** President and Managing Director of Ferrari Automobili SpA Sefac; *b* Modena, 20 Feb. 1898; *s* of Alfredo Ferrari and Adalgisa Bisbini; *m* 1923, Laura Garello; one *s* decd. *Educ:* State sch.; Professional Institute of Technology. Started as tester, Turin, 1918; later with CMN, Milan; tester, driver, sales executive, Alfa Romeo, 1920-39; subsequently Dir, Alfa Corse; Pres. and Managing Dir of Scuderia Ferrari, later of Auto Avio Construzione Ferrari, 1940-60. Builder of racing, sports and gran turismo cars in factory built at Maranello in 1943 and reconstructed in 1946. Commendatore, 1928; Cavaliere del Lavoro, 1952. Holds an hon. doctorate in engineering (1960). *Publication:* Le mie giole terribili (autobiog.). *Address:* viale Trento Trieste 31, Modena, Italy. *T:* 24081-24082; (office) Maranello, Modena, Italy. *T:* 91161-91162.

**FERRARO, Prof. Vincenzo Consolato Antonino,** PhD, DIC, FRAS; Professor of Mathematics, University of London (Queen Mary College), since 1952; *b* 10 April 1907; *s* of late Filippo Ferraro and Amalia Ferraro; *m* 1937, Maria Giovanna Giordano; one *s*. *Educ:* Holborn Estate Grammar Sch., London; Imperial Coll. of Science and Technology, London (scholar). Demonstrator in Mathematics, Imperial Coll., London, 1930-33; Asst Lecturer and Lecturer, King's Coll., London, 1933-47; Prof. of Applied Mathematics, University Coll. of the South West, Exeter, 1947-52. Member: Meteor Research Cttee, 1960-62; Sub-cttee for Geomagnetism and Aeronomy; Nat. Cttee for Geodesy and Geophysics; UGC Mathematical Sciences Sub-Cttee; Visiting Investigator, Dept of Terrestrial Magnetism, Carnegie Institution of Washington, USA, 1948: Visiting Prof., Yerkes Observatory, University of Chicago, USA, 1953; George A. Miller Visiting Prof. of Astronomy, University of Illinois, 1963. *Publications:* Electromagnetic Theory, 1954; Magneto-Fluid Mechanics (with C. Plumpton), 2nd edn 1966; papers on geomagnetism and astrophysics in scientific jls. *Recreations:* pictorial arts and music. *Address:* Queen Mary College, Mile End Road, E1; 266 Ballards Lane, N12.

**FERRER, José Vicente;** actor, director and producer, USA; *b* 8 Jan. 1912; *s* of Rafael Ferrer and Maria Providencia (*née* Cintron); *m* 1st, 1938, Uta Hagen (marr. diss. 1948); one *d*; 2nd, 1948, Phyllis Hill (marr. diss. 1953); 3rd, 1953, Rosemary Clooney (marr. diss. 1967); three *s* two *d*. *Educ:* Princeton Univ. AB (architecture), 1933. First appearance, The

Periwinkle, Long Island show-boat, 1934; Asst Stage Manager Summer Theatre Stock Co., NY, 1935; first appearance NY stage, 1935; A Slight Case of Murder, 1935; Boy Meets Girl, 1935; Spring Dance, Brother Rat, 1936; In Clover, 1937; Dir Princeton Univ. Triangle Club's Fol-de-Rol, 1937; How To Get Tough About It, Missouri Legend, 1938; Mamba's Daughters, Key Largo, 1939; first star rôle, Lord Fancourt Babberley, Charley's Aunt, 1940; producer and dir, The Admiral Had A Wife, 1941; staged and co-starred, Vickie, 1942; Let's Face It, 1943; played Iago to Paul Robeson's Othello, Theatre Guild, 1943, 1944, 1945; producer and dir Strange Fruit, 1945; Play's The Thing, Richard III, Green Goddess, 1946; producer and star, Cyrano, 1946; Design For Living, Goodbye Again, 1947; Gen. dir to NY Theatre Co., City Centre, 1948; Silver Whistle, Theatre Guild, 1948; produced, directed and appeared in Twentieth Century, 1950; produced, directed, Stalag 17; The Fourposter, 1951; producer, dir and appeared in The Shrike, 1952; The Chase, 1952; staged My 3 Angels, 1953; dir and co-author, Oh Captain, 1958; producer, dir, and starred in, Edwin Booth, 1959; dir, The Andersonville Trial, 1960; starred in, The Girl Who Came to Supper, 1963-64. *Films include:* Joan of Arc, 1947; Whirlpool, 1949; Crisis, Cyrano, 1950; Anything Can Happen, 1951; Moulin Rouge, 1952; Miss Sadie Thompson (Rain), Caine Mutiny, 1953; Deep in My Heart, 1955; Cockleshell Heroes, The Great Man, Bay the Moon, 1957; The High Cost of Loving, I Accuse, The Shrike (Dir, starred), 1958; Return to Peyton Place (Dir), 1962; State Fair (Dir), 1963; Nine Hours to Rama, Lawrence of Arabia, 1963; Cyrano et D'Artagnan, Train 349 From Berlin, The Greatest Story Ever Told, 1964. Holds hon. degrees. Various awards for acting, etc, since 1944, include American Academy of Arts and Letters Gold Medal, 1949; Academy Award, 1950 (Best Actor, Cyrano). *Recreation:* tennis. *Address:* (home) Pinesbridge Road, Ossining, NY; (business) 375 Park Avenue, New York, NY 10022, USA. *T:* MU 8-4530.

**FERRERS,** 13th Earl *cr* 1711; **Robert Washington Shirley;** Viscount Tamworth 1711; Bt 1611; *b* 8 June 1929; *o s* of 12th Earl Ferrers and Hermione Morley (*d* 1969); *S* father, 1954; *m* 1951, Annabel Mary, *d* of Brig. W. G. Carr, *qv*; two *s* three *d. Educ:* Winchester Coll.; Magdalene Coll., Cambridge. MA (Agric.). Lieut Coldstream Guards, 1950 (as National Service). A Lord-in-Waiting, 1962-64. Trustee, East Anglian Trustee Savings Bank; Mem. of Council, Hurstpierpoint Coll., 1959-68. *Heir: s* Viscount Tamworth, *qv. Address:* Hedenham Hall, Norfolk. *T:* Woodton 250.

**FERRIER,** Baron *cr* 1958, of Culter (Life Peer); **Victor Ferrier Noel-Paton,** ED; DL; *b* Edinburgh, 1900; *s* of late F. Noel-Paton, Dir-Gen. of Commercial Intelligence to the Govt of India; *m* 1932, Joane Mary, *d* of late Sir Gilbert Wiles, KCIE, CSI; one *s* three *d. Educ:* The Edinburgh Academy. Merchant/Managing Agents firm, Bombay, 1920-51; Dir and Chm. of a number of Cos; Dir, Imperial Bank of India; Trustee, Port of Bombay; Pres., Bombay Chamber of Commerce; Vice-Pres. of Associated Chambers of Commerce; Pres., Fedn of Electrical Undertakings, and Bombay Branch of Indian Roads and Transport Development Assoc. Mem. Church of Scotland Trust. Served RE, 1918-19, IAF (Major, ED), 1920-46, and IARO. Mem. of Royal Company of Archers. DL, Lanarks, 1960. *Recreations:* shooting, angling, golf. *Address:* Culter House, Biggar, Lanarks. *Clubs:* Cavalry, Beefsteak; New (Edinburgh).

*See also Sir James Fergusson, Bt.*

**FERRIER, Sir Grant;** *see* Ferrier, Sir H. G.

**FERRIER, Sir (Harold) Grant,** Kt 1969; CMG 1964; Chairman, Associated Portland Cement Manufacturers (Australia) Ltd; *b* 26 Aug. 1905; *m* 1949, Margaret James; one *d. Educ:* Sydney Grammar Sch. CEng, MIMarE. President: Metal Trades Employers' Assoc., 1949-51; Australian Metal Industries Assoc., 1951-52; Chamber of Manufactures of NSW, 1963-65; Associated Chambers of Manufactures of Aust., 1963-65; Chm. of Directors, The Commonwealth Portland Cement Co. Ltd and subsids, 1952-. Chairman: State Develt Corp. of NSW, 1966-69; Heavy Engineering Industry Adv. Cttee to Commonwealth Govt, 1957-67; Nat. Employers Policy Cttee, 1962-64; Dep. Employer Mem., Gov. Body, ILO. Pres., Internat. Organisation of Employers, Geneva, 1966-67. *Recreations:* yachting and fly-fishing. *Address:* Lyndhurst Gardens, 3 Rosemount Avenue, Woollahra, NSW 2025, Australia. *T:* 32-4487. *Clubs:* Commonwealth (Canberra); Royal Sydney Yacht Squadron, Royal Sydney Golf, Rugby Union.

**FERRIS, Paul Frederick;** author and journalist; *b* 15 Feb. 1929; *o c* of late Frederick Morgan Ferris and of Olga Ferris; *m* 1953, Gloria Moreton; one *s* one *d. Educ:* Swansea Gram. Sch. Staff of South Wales Evening Post, 1949-52; Womans Own, 1953; Observer Foreign News Service, 1953-54. *Publications: novels:* A Changed Man, 1958; Then We Fall, 1960; A Family Affair, 1963; The Destroyer, 1965; The Dam, 1967; *reportage:* The City, 1960; The Church of England, 1962; The Doctors, 1965; The Nameless: abortion in Britain today, 1966; Men and Money: financial Europe today, 1968; contribs to The Observer; radio and TV programmes. *Address:* c/o Curtis Brown Ltd, 13 King Street, Covent Garden, WC2. *T:* 01-240 2488.

**FERRIS, Sir Robert G.;** *see* Grant-Ferris.

**FERRYMAN, Col E. E. M.;** *see* Mockler-Ferryman.

**FESSEY, Mereth Cecil;** Director, Business Statistics Office, since 1969; *b* Windsor, Berks, 19 May 1917; *s* of late Morton Fessey and Ethel Fessey (*née* Blake), Bristol; *m* 1945, Grace Lilian, *d* of William Bray, Earlsfield, London; one *s* two *d. Educ:* Westminster City Sch.; LSE, Univ. of London. London Transport, 1934; Army, 1940; Min. of Transport, 1947; Board of Trade, 1948; Statistician, 1956; Chief Statistician, 1965. Chm. of Council, Inst. of Statisticians. *Publications:* articles and papers in: Economic Trends; The Statistician; Annales de Sciences Economiques Appliquées, Louvain; etc. *Recreations:* chess, walking. *Address:* 3 Park Close, Moor Park, Herts WD3 1QH. *T:* Northwood 22228. *Club:* Civil Service.

**FESTING, Field Marshal Sir Francis Wogan,** GCB 1957 (KCB 1956; CB 1946); KBE 1952 (CBE 1945); DSO 1942; DL; Chief of the Imperial General Staff, 1958-61; ADC General to the Queen, 1958-60; *b* 28 Aug. 1902; *o s* of late Brig.-Gen. F. L. Festing, CB, CMG; *m* 1937, Mary Cecilia, *er d* of late Cuthbert David Giffard Riddell, Swinburne Castle, Northumberland; four *s. Educ:* Winchester; RMC Sandhurst. 2nd Lieut Rifle Bde, 1921; psc 1934; Bt Major 1938; Lt-Col 1939; Instr Staff Coll., 1939; comd 2nd Bn East Lancs Regt, 1939; comd a Bde in Madagascar, 1941; comd 86th Div. in Burma, 1942-45; GOC Land

Forces, Hong Kong, 1945-46; Maj.-Gen. 1942; Dir of Weapons and Development, War Office, 1947-49; Commander British Forces, Hong Kong, during 1949 (temp. Lieut-Gen.); Pres., Regular Commissions Board, 1950-51; Asst Chief of Staff (Organization and Training), Supreme Headquarters, Allied Powers in Europe, 1951-52; Lieut-Gen. 1952; GOC British Troops in Egypt, 1952-54; GOC-in-C, Eastern Comd, 1954-56; Gen. 1956; C-in-C FARELF, 1956-58; Col Comdt, The Rifle Bde, 1958; Field Marshal, 1960. Col Royal Northumberland Fusiliers, 1953-65. DL Co. Northumberland, 1962. Pres., Corps of Commissionaires, 1963-. Comdr, Legion of Merit (USA); Comdr of the Cloud and Banner (China). DCL (*hc*) Newcastle upon Tyne, 1964. Kt of Malta, 1965. *Recreations:* hunting, yachting. *Address:* Birks, Tarset, Northumberland. *TA and T:* Greenhaugh 221. *Clubs:* Boodle's, Northern Counties; Royal Yacht Squadron.

**FETHERS, Hon. Col (retired) Wilfrid Kent,** DSO 1917; VD; FIIA; formerly Manager for Australia, Royal Insurance Co. Ltd, and Associated Companies; *b* Victoria, 26 Nov. 1885; *s* of William Fethers, *s* of James Fethers of Liverpool, England, who came out to Australia, 1852; *m* Phyllis Doyne, Sydney; one *s* two *d. Educ:* Caulfield Grammar Sch., Victoria. Commission in Victorian Volunteer Forces, 1905; served Gallipoli, Egypt, and France, 1914-18 (despatches). Took Australian contingent to New York to assist in Liberty Loan flotation in May 1918; Pres., Melbourne Metropolitan Fire Brigades Board, 1942; Pres., Council of Fire and Accident Underwriters of Australia, 1936 and 1944; Pres., Incorporated Australian Insurance Institute, 1941-42; Pres., Council of Marine Underwriters of the Commonwealth of Australia, 1941-42. Member: Board of Management, Alfred Hospital; Melba Trust for Limbless Soldiers. Trustee, Ed. Wilson Estate. *Address:* 41 The Ridge, Canterbury, Victoria 3126, Australia. *Clubs:* Australian, Naval and Military (Melbourne).

**FETHERSTON-DILKE, Mary Stella,** CBE 1968; RRC 1966; Matron-in-Chief, Queen Alexandra's Royal Naval Nursing Service, 1966-70, retired; *b* 21 Sept. 1918; *d* of late B. A. Fetherston-Dilke, MBE. *Educ:* Kingsley Sch., Leamington Spa; St George's Hospital, London (SRN). Joined QARNNS, 1942. OStJ 1966. *Recreations:* archery, antiques. *Address:* 12 Clareville Court, Clareville Grove, SW7.

**FETHERSTON-GODLEY, Brig. Sir Francis William Crewe,** Kt 1937; OBE 1918; DL Glos; *b* 25 Jan. 1893; *s* of late Major H. C. Godley, DSO, 48th Regt; *m* 1919, Kathleen May Jenner Davies (marr. diss. 1940; she *d* 1955); one *s*; 2nd, 1941, Reine Cecilia Siddons Faulder (*d* 1958); 3rd, 1961, Alice Kathleen Llewhellin. *Educ:* Cheltenham; Royal Military Coll., Sandhurst. Served European War, 1914-19; Expedition NWF, 1920; War of 1939-45 (despatches, Croix de guerre). Assumed by royal licence additional name of Fetherston, 1923; National Vice-Chm., British Legion, 1932-34; National Chm., 1934-39; Provincial Comdt, Kenya Police Reserve, 1950-54; Queen's Colonial Police Medal; Commander of Légion d'Honneur and other foreign decorations. *Recreations:* yachting, shooting. *Address:* Les Varvots, St Lawrence, Jersey, Channel Islands. *Club:* United Service.

**FEUILLÈRE, Edwige;** Chevalier de la Légion d'Honneur; Commandeur des Arts et Lettres; French actress; *b* 29 Oct.; *m* (divorced). *Educ:* Dijon; Paris. *Plays include:* La Dame aux camélias; Sodome et Gomorrhe; L'Aigle a deux têtes; Partage de midi; Pour Lucrèce; La Parisienne; Phèdre; Lucy Crown; Constance; Rodogune; La Folle de Chaillot; Delicate Balance. *Films include:* L'Idiot; Olivia; Le Blé en herbe; L'Aigle a deux têtes; En cas de malheur; La vie à deux; Les amours célèbres; Le crime ne paye pas. *Address:* 19 Rue Eugène Manuel, Paris XVIe.

**FEVERSHAM,** 6th Baron *cr* 1826; **Charles Antony Peter Duncombe;** free-lance journalist; *b* 3 Jan. 1945; *s* of Col Antony John Duncombe-Anderson and G. G. V. McNalty; *S* (to barony of) *kinsman,* 3rd Earl of Feversham (the earldom having become extinct), 1963; *m* 1966, Shannon, *d* of Sir Thomas Foy, CSI, CIE; one *s. Educ:* Eton; Middle Temple. Chairman: Yorkshire Arts Assoc., 1969; Standing Conf. of Regional Arts Assocs, 1969. Governor, Leeds Polytechnic, 1969. *Publication: novel:* A Wolf in Tooth, 1967. *Heir: s* Hon. Jasper Orlando Slingsby Duncombe, *b* 14 March 1968. *Address:* Beckdale House, Helmsley, York.

**FEYNMAN, Prof. Richard (Phillips);** Professor of Physics, California Institute of Technology, Pasadena, Calif, since 1951; *b* 11 May 1918; *s* of Melville Feynman and Lucille (*née* Phillips); *m* 1960, Gweneth Howarth, Ripponden, Yorks; one *s* one *d. Educ:* MIT; Princeton Univ. Los Alamos, N Mex. Atomic Bomb Project, 1943-46; Cornell Univ., 1946-51. Nobel Prize for Physics (jointly), 1965. Mem. Brazilian Acad. of Sciences; Fellow (Foreign), Royal Soc., London. *Publications:* The Feynman Lectures in Physics, 1963; The Character of Physical Law, 1965; papers in Physical Review on quantum electro-dynamics, liquid helium, theory of beta-decay. *Recreations:* Mayan Hieroglyphics, opening safes, playing bongo drums, drawing, biology experiments (none done well). *Address:* 2475 Boulder Road, Altadena, Calif 91001, USA. *T:* 213-797-1262.

**FFOLKES, Sir Robert (Francis Alexander),** 7th Bt *cr* 1774; *b* 2 Dec. 1943; *o s* of Capt. Sir (Edward John) Patrick (Boschetti) ffolkes, 6th Bt (*s* of Sir Francis ffolkes, 5th Bt, MVO), and of Geraldine (*d* of late William Roffey, Writtle, Essex); *S* father, 1960. *Educ:* Stowe Sch.; Christ Church, Oxford. *Address:* Starlings, Yoxford, Saxmundham, Suffolk. *T:* Yoxford 387. *Club:* Turf.

**FFORDE, Sir Arthur (Frederic Brownlow),** GBE 1964; Kt 1946; MA Oxon; *b* 23 Aug. 1900; *s* of late Arthur Brownlow fforde, Indian Civil Service, and Mary Alice Storer Branson; *m* 1926, Mary Alison, *yr d* of late James MacLehose, printer to University of Glasgow; two *s* one *d. Educ:* Rugby Sch.; Trinity Coll., Oxford. Admitted Solicitor, 1925; Partner in firm of Linklaters & Paines, London, 1928-48; Mem. of Council of Law Soc., London, 1937-48; Deputy Dir-Gen., Ministry of Supply, (Finance) 1940, (Contracts) 1941; Under-Sec., Contracts Finance, Ministry of Supply, 1943; Under-Sec., HM Treasury, 1944-45; Head Master of Rugby Sch., 1948-57; Chm., the British Broadcasting Corporation, 1957-64; Mem., central Board of Finance of Church of England, 1957-70 (Vice-Chm., 1957-60, Chm., 1960-65); Director, 1957-70: Equity & Law Life Assurance Society Ltd; National Westminster Bank Ltd, and other cos. Hon. LLD University of Wales. *Address:* Wall's End, Wonersh, near Guildford, Surrey. *Club:* Athenæum.

*See also M. W. McCrum.*

**FFORDE, John Standish;** an Executive Director of the Bank of England, since 1970; *b* 16 Nov. 1921; 4th *s* of late Francis Creswell Fforde and late Cicely Creswell; *m* 1951, Marya, *d* of late Joseph Retinger; three *s* one *d. Educ:* Rossall

Sch.; Christ Church, Oxford (1st cl. Hons PPE). Served RAF, 1940-46. Prime Minister's Statistical Branch, 1951-53; Fellow, Nuffield Coll., Oxford, 1953-56; entered Bank of England, 1957; Dep. Chief, Central Banking Information Dept, 1959-64; Adviser to the Governors, 1964-66; Chief Cashier, 1966-69. *Publications:* The Federal Reserve System, 1945-49, 1953; An International Trade in Managerial Skills, 1957. *Recreations:* travel, walking. *Address:* 21 Hollycroft Avenue, NW3. *T:* 01-435 7918.

**FFRANGCON-DAVIES, Gwen;** Actress; *d* of David Ffrangcon-Davies, the famous singer, and Annie Frances Rayner. *Educ:* South Hampstead High Sch.; abroad. First London success The Immortal Hour, 1922; created the part of Eve in Shaw's Back to Methuselah; principal successes, Tess, in Tess of the Durbevilles, Elizabeth Barrett, in The Barretts of Wimpole Street, Anne of Bohemia, in Richard of Bordeaux. Played Lady Macbeth to Macbeth of John Gielgud, Piccadilly, 1942. Appeared, in association with Marda Vanne, in leading parts in various plays in S Africa, 1943-46. Returned to England, 1949; played in Adventure Story, St James's, 1949; Stratford Festival, 1950, as Katherine in King Henry VIII; Portia in Julius Cæsar, Regan in King Lear (again Katherine, Old Vic. 1953); Madame Ranevsky in The Cherry Orchard, Lyric, 1954; Aunt Cleofe in Summertime, Apollo, 1955; Rose Padley in The Mulberry Bush, Royal Court, 1956; Agatha in The Family Reunion, Phoenix, 1956; Miss Madrigal in The Chalk Garden, Haymarket, 1957; Mrs Callifer in The Potting Shed, Globe Theatre, 1958; Mary Tyrone in Long Day's Journey into Night, Edinburgh Fest. and Globe, 1958; Queen Isolde in Ondine, Aldwych, 1961; Queen Mother in Becket, Aldwych, 1961; Hester Bellboys in A Penny for a Song, Aldwych, 1962; Beatrice in Season of Goodwill, Queen's, 1964; Amanda in The Glass Menagerie, Haymarket, 1965. *Films:* The Burning, 1967; Leo the Last, 1969. *Recreation:* gardening. *Address:* c/o Larry Dalzell, Bond Street House, 14 Clifford Street, W1.

**FFRENCH,** family name of **Baron ffrench.**

**FFRENCH,** 7th Baron, *cr* 1798; **Peter Martin Joseph Charles John Mary ffrench;** *b* 2 May 1926; *s* of Capt. Hon. John Martin Valentine ffrench (*d* 1946), *s* of 5th Baron, and of Sophia, *d* of late Signor Giovanni Brambilla, Villa Sucota, Como, Italy; *S* uncle 1955; *m* 1954, Sonia Katherine, *d* of Major Digby Cayley; one *s* two *d*. *Heir: s* Hon. Robuck John Peter Charles Mario ffrench, *b* 14 March 1956. *Address:* Castle ffrench, Ballinasloe, Co. Galway.

**FFRENCH-BLAKE, A. O'B.;** *see* Blake.

**FICKLING, Benjamin William,** FRCS, FDS, RCS; Senior Dental Surgeon, St George's Hospital, SW1, since 1936; Dental Surgeon, Royal Dental Hospital of London, since 1935; Senior Dental Surgeon, Mount Vernon Centre for Plastic and Jaw Surgery (formerly Hill End), since 1941; Civilian Dental Consultant to Royal Navy since 1954; *b* 14 July 1909; *s* of Robert Marshall Fickling and Florence (*née* Newson); *m* 1943, Shirley Dona, *er d* of Albert Latimer Walker, FRCS; two *s* one *d*. *Educ:* Framlingham; St George's Hosp. Royal Dental Hospital. William Brown Senior Exhibition, St George's Hosp., 1929; LDS RCS, 1932; MRCS, LRCP, 1934; FRCS 1938; FDS, RCS 1947. Charles Tomes Lecturer, RCS 1956. Examr in Dental Surgery, RCS; formerly Examr, Univ. of London and Univ. of Edinburgh. Dean of Faculty of Dental Surgery, and Mem. Council, Royal College of Surgeons, 1968- (Vice-dean, 1965); Fellow Royal Society of Medicine (Pres. Odontological Section, 1964-65); Pres., British Assoc. of Oral Surgeons, 1967-68. Dir, Med. Sickness Annuity and Life Assurance Soc. Ltd. *Publications:* (joint) Injuries of the Jaws and Face, 1940; (joint) Chapter on Faciomaxillary Injuries and Deformities in British Surgical Practice, 1951. *Address:* 129 Harley Street, W1. *T:* 01-935 1882. Linksview, Linksway, Northwood, Middx. *T:* Northwood 22035. *Club:* Ski Club of Great Britain.

**FIDDAMENT, Air Vice-Marshal Arthur Leonard,** CB 1948; CBE 1944; DFC; RAF (Retd); *b* 1 July 1896; *s* of late A. W. Fiddament, Norwich; *m* 1924, Doris Ward, Lincoln; two *d*. *Educ:* Norwich. Norfolk Regt, 1914-15; RE (Special Brigade), 1915-17; RFC 1917; India, 1920-24; RAF Staff Coll. (student), 1926; Air Ministry (intelligence), 1927-31; commanded 17 Squadron, 1931-32; RAF Staff Coll. (Directing Staff), 1932-35; commanded 30 Squadron, Iraq, 1935-36; idc 1937; Air Ministry (Plans), 1938-39; Air Ministry (Dominions Liaison), 1940; RAF Delegation, Washington, 1941; Dir of Personal Services, Air Ministry, 1942; Asst Comdt, RAF Staff Coll., 1943; AOC No. 46 Group, 1944; Senior Air Staff Officer, Transport Command, 1944-46; AOC No. 38 Group, RAF, 1946; retired, 1949. Officier de la Légion d'Honneur. *Address:* Greenlawn, Rectory Road, Burnham on Sea, Som. *T:* Burnham on Sea 2415.

**FIDDES, James Raffan,** QC (Scot.) 1965; *b* 1 Feb. 1919; *er s* of late Sir James Raffan Fiddes, CBE; *m* 1954, Edith Margaret, 2nd *d* of late Charles E. Lippe, KC. *Educ:* Aberdeen Gram. Sch.; Glasgow Univ. (MA, 1942; LLB 1948); Balliol Coll., Oxford, (BA 1944). Advocate, 1948. *Address:* 23 South Learmonth Gardens, Edinburgh 4. *T:* 031-332 1431. *Clubs:* New, Scottish Arts (Edinburgh).

**FIDGE, Sir (Harold) Roy,** Kt 1967; Commissioner since 1956, Chairman since 1963, Geelong Harbor Trust; *b* Warracknabeal, Vic., 24 Dec. 1904; *s* of Edward Fidge, Beulah, Vic.; *m* 1st, 1934, Mavis Melba Jane (*d* 1948), *d* of James Robert Burke, Warracknabeal; one *s* one *d*; 2nd, 1949, Nance, *d* of George Davidson, Sydney, NSW. *Educ:* Geelong High Sch.; Geelong Coll.; Ormond Coll., University of Melbourne (LLB). Admitted Barrister and Solicitor, Supreme Court of Victoria, 1929. Royal Australian Navy, 1940-45; Lt-Comdr RANR. Councillor, City of Geelong, 1939-40, and 1946-; Mayor of City of Geelong, 1954-56 and 1964-68. Hon. Nat. Sec.-Treas, Assoc. of Apex Clubs, 1934-40, 1946-47; President: East Geelong Br., Aust. Red Cross Soc., 1961-67; Geelong E Techn. Sch. Coun. 1960-65; Geelong Law Assoc., 1959-60 (Hon. Sec.-Treas., 1934-40, 1945-54). Victorian Employers' Fedn Community Service Award, 1967. *Recreations:* gardening, woodwork. *Address:* 23 Meakin Street, Geelong, Victoria 3219, Australia. *T:* Geelong 95304. *Clubs:* Geelong, RSL, Ex-Navalmen's Assoc., Legacy, United Services, Victoria League (all Australia).

**FIDLER, Alwyn G. Sheppard,** CBE 1963; MA, BArch, DipCD, FRIBA, MPTI; in private practice as architect and town planning consultant (A. G. Sheppard Fidler and Associates), 1964; *b* 8 May 1909; *e s* of late W. E. Sheppard Fidler and Phoebe M. Williams; *m* 1936, Margaret, *d* of Capt. J. R. Kidner, Newcastle upon Tyne; one *s*. *Educ:* Holywell Gram. Sch.; University of Liverpool; British Sch. at Rome. Tite Finalist, 1930; studied in

USA, 1931; Victory Schol., 1933; Rome Schol. in Architecture, 1933-35. Chief Architect: Land Settlement Assoc., 1937; Barclays Bank Ltd, 1938; Sen. Tech. Intelligence Officer, Min. of Home Security, 1940-46; Chief Archt, Crawley New Town, 1947-52 (Housing Medals of Min. of Housing and Local Govt in 1951, 1952 and 1954); City Archt of Birmingham, 1952-64 (Distinction in Town Planning, 1955, for work at Crawley and Birmingham Redevelopment Areas). Coun. Mem., 1953-62, 1963-, Vice-Pres., 1958-60, Chm. Practice Cttee, 1958-62. External Examr in Architecture, 1958-, RIBA. pres. City and Borough Architects Soc., 1956-58; Chm. Fac. of Architecture, British Sch. at Rome, 1958- (Mem. Finance Sub-Cttee); Chm. ARC of UK, 1960-63; Mem. Jt Consultative Cttee of Architects, Quantity Surveyors and Builders, 1958-61; Mem. Birmingham and Five Counties Architectual Assoc. (Mem. Council, 1956-, Vice-Pres., 1960-62, Pres., 1962-64); Chm. Assoc. of Building Centres, 1964-; Gov., Coll. of Estate Management, 1965-; Mem. SE Regional Adv. Cttee to Land Commn. Mem. or past Mem., of many other councils and cttees. *Publications:* Contrib. to professional jls. *Recreations:* travel and gardening. *Address:* Woodlands, Alma Road, Reigate, Surrey. *T:* Reigate 43849. *Club:* Union (Birmingham).

**FIDLER, Alderman Michael M.,** JP; MP (C) Bury and Radcliffe since 1970; President, Board of Deputies of British Jews, since 1967; Vice-Chairman, World Conference of Jewish Organisations, since 1967; President, Holy Law Congregation, Manchester, since 1967; business consultant; Managing Director: H. & L. Fidler Ltd, since 1941; Michael Lewis Ltd, since 1942; Wibye Ltd, since 1968; *b* 10 Feb. 1916; *s* of Louis Fidler and Goldie Fidler (*née* Sherr); *m* 1939, Maidie (*née* Davis); one *s* one *d*. *Educ:* Salford Gram. Sch.; Salford Royal Tech. Coll. Cllr, Borough of Prestwich, 1951-63; Mayor, 1957-58; Alderman, 1963-. Pres., Middleton, Prestwich and Whitefield Div. Conservative Assoc., 1965-69; Chm., Divl Educn Exec. (Prestwich, Whitefield and Radcliffe), Lancs CC, 1967-69. Lectr, Extra Mural Dept, Manchester Univ., 1966-. Member: Grand Council, CBI, 1965-67. Nat. Exec. Nat. Assoc. of British Manufacturers 1953-65. President: Fedn of Jewish Youth Socs of Gt Britain and Ireland, 1951-; Manchester Union of Jewish Socs, 1964-; Vice-Pres. Children and Youth Aliyah Cttee for Gt Britain, 1968-; Life Vice-President: Manchester Jewish Bd of Guardians, 1967-; Manchester Jewish Social Services, 1967-; Mem. Exec. Cttee, Council of Christians and Jews, Manchester Branch, 1966-. Governor: Strand Grammar Schools, 1955-; St Peter's RC Grammar Sch., 1968-. JP, Co. Lancs, 1958-. FRGS, FRAS, FREconS, FIAI. *Publications:* One Hundred Years of the Holy Law Congregation, 1964; articles. *Recreations:* politics, travel, reading, filming, foreign affairs, education. *Address:* 51 Tavistock Court, Tavistock Square, WC1. *T:* 01-387 4925; San Remo, Sedgley Park Road, Prestwich, Manchester M25 8AL. *T:* 061-773 1471; Woburn House, Upper Woburn Place, WC1. *T:* 01-387 3952. *Clubs:* Embassy; Milverton Lodge (Manchester).

**FIELD, Edward,** DSO 1918; Retired; Rag Merchant; President, Dewsbury Chamber of Commerce, 1954-57; *b* 22 May 1898; *s* of late Joseph Field and Louisa Wardell; *m* 1924, Florrie, *d* of Alderman F. Greenwood, Dewsbury; one *d*. *Educ:* The Wheelwright Grammar Sch., Dewsbury. Artists' Rifles, 1916; 2nd Lieut, MG Corps, 1917 (DSO, despatches); Asst Officer in charge of Salvage Inspectorate, 1918; Managing Dir and Chm., Joseph Field, Ltd; Pres. British Woollen Rag Merchants Association, 1945-48; Technical Officer Wool Control (Salvage Section), 1940-45; Waste (MR) Wages Council; CO 2nd Cadet Battalion KOYLI (Major), 1942-46. Chm. Dewsbury and District Employment Cttee, 1956-68. FInstD, 1955-68. *Publications:* various articles on Social Credit 1930-46. *Recreations:* contract bridge (Yorks Individual Champion, 1960, Yorks Pairs Championship, 1961), motoring. *Address:* Southlands, Staincliffe, Batley, Yorks. *T:* Dewsbury 61247. *Club:* Dewsbury (Dewsbury).

**FIELD, Sir Ernest (Wensley Lapthorn),** Kt 1953; CBE 1947; JP; The Director, Scottish Engineering Employers' Association, 1944-58, retired; *b* Alverstoke, 4 Feb. 1889; *s* of Frederick Ernest and Lily Mary Field; *m* 1916, Edith Maude Lillicrap, Plymouth (*d* 1969); no *c*. *Educ:* Froebel House Sch. Devonport; Queen Elizabeth Grammar Sch., Bideford; RN Engineering Coll., Keyham. Engineer Cadet, Royal Navy, 1905-09; various managerial positions in engineering works of John Brown & Co., Clydebank, 1909-34, and personal asst to Engineering-Dir, 1934-44. Was chm. of various Scottish cttees in connection with industry, etc.; an Office Bearer of various Scottish benevolent institutions. JP Co. of City of Glasgow. Has given several lectures on Industrial Relations, FIMechE, FRINA. *Recreations:* motoring, reading. *Address:* Green's Hotel, Woodlands Terrace, Glasgow C3. *Club:* Royal Scottish Automobile (Glasgow).

**FIELD, Frank Eustace; Hon. Mr Justice Field;** Chief Justice of the Supreme Court of the Windward Islands and Leeward Islands, 1963; *b* 11 April 1911; *s* of Hugh Alfred and Lilian S. Field; *m* 1939, Rosario Ramirez; one *s*. *Educ:* Harrison College, Barbados. Puisne Judge, Supreme Court, Barbados, 1957-63; Solicitor-Gen., Barbados, 1954-57. *Clubs:* West Indian; Royal Barbados Yacht.

**FIELD, George David,** CBE 1944; MVO (4th class) 1936, (5th class) 1928; *b* 16 May 1887; *s* of Burns Field and Jane E. Rolfe, Horringer, Suffolk; *m* 1923, Edith (LRAM), *d* of late C. F. Howell; one *s* one *d*. *Educ:* Horringer Sch., Suffolk; Archbishop Tenison's Grammar Sch. Junior Clerk in Office of Paymaster of HM's Household, 1901-3; Clerk to Paymaster, 1903-20; Accountant (Pay Office) Buckingham Palace, 1920-32; Chief Accountant and Paymaster (HM's Household), 1932-49; Assessor and Collector of Income Tax (HM's Household), 1924-49; Sergeant at Arms to King George V, 1935; Sergeant at Arms to King George VI, 1937-49; retired, 1949. *Address:* Gossamer, 11 Hawley Road, Rustington, Sussex. *T:* Rustington 5982.

**FIELD, John,** CBE 1967; Co-Director, Royal Ballet Company, since 1970; *b* 22 Oct. 1921; *m* 1958, Anne Heaton. *Educ:* Wheatley Boys' Sch., Doncaster. Sadlers Wells Ballet Co., 1939; RAF, 1942-46; Principal, Sadlers Wells Ballet Co., 1947-56; Resident Dir, Sadlers Wells Theatre Ballet, 1956-57; Asst Dir, Royal Ballet, 1957-70. *Address:* Royal Opera House, Covent Garden, WC2. *T:* 01-240 1200.

**FIELD, Sir John (Osbaldiston),** KBE 1967; Kt 1962; CMG 1959; Resident Commissioner, Gilbert and Ellice Islands Colony, since 1970; *b* 30 Oct. 1913; *s* of late Frank Osbaldiston Field; *m* 1951, Irene Margaret, 2nd *d* of late Harold Godfrey Judd, CBE. *Educ:* Stellenbosch Boys' High Sch. S Africa; Magdalene Coll., Cambridge (MA). Colonial Administrative Service, Nigeria, 1936; Senior District Officer, 1951; Resident, 1954; Commissioner of the

Cameroons, 1956; UK Special Representative for British Cameroons at UN Trusteeship Council, 1956-61; Commissioner of Southern Cameroons, 1960-61; Governor and C-in-C of St Helena, 1962-68; Staff Liaison Officer, HM Overseas Civil Service, 1968-69; acting Administrator, Montserrat, 1969. *Recreation:* fishing. *Address:* The Residency, Tarawa, Gilbert and Ellice Islands Colony, Western Pacific. *Club:* Oxford and Cambridge University.

**FIELD, John William,** CMG 1951; JMN 1964; MD; DSc; Colonial Medical Service, retired; *b* 5 Aug. 1899; *s* of late Walter Field, Birmingham, England; *m* 1921, Elsie Mary, *d* of late William Dodd, Cardiff; one *s* three *d*. *Educ:* Oldbury Secondary Sch.; Birmingham Univ. Served European War, 1917-19. MB, ChB (Birmingham), 1924; Medical Officer, Malayan Medical Service, 1925; MD (Birmingham, Hons), 1929; Malaria Research Officer, Inst. for Med. Research, Federation of Malaya, 1931. Chalmers Memorial Medal for research in tropical medicine, Royal Society of Tropical Medicine, 1941. Interned by Japanese in Singapore, 1942-45. Dir, Institute for Medical Research, Federation of Malaya, 1949-56. Hon. DSc (Malaya), 1959. *Publications:* various papers on tropical medicine. *Address:* The Knoll, Whitchurch, Ross-on-Wye, Herefordshire.

**FIELD, Brig. Leonard Frank,** CB 1953; CBE 1945; *b* 6 March 1898; *s* of Major Joseph Thomas Field and Amelia Phillips; *m* 1923, Genevieve Bowyer; one *s*. *Educ:* Bedford; RMC, Sandhurst. Served European War: commissioned 2nd Lieut, 1916; War of 1939-45: DDMI (Far East), 1941; Dir of Intelligence, SW Pacific Command, 1942; Chief Chinese Liaison Officer, Burma, 1942; Military Attaché: China, 1945-49; Indo-China, 1951-52. Brig. 1952; retired Nov. 1952. Knight Comdr, Order of Orange Nassau (with Swords), 1945. *Address:* c/o Lloyds Bank Ltd (Cox's & King's), 6 Pall Mall, SW1.

**FIELD, Group Capt. Roger Martin,** CBE 1941; late RAF; *b* 27 Nov. 1890; *s* of Henry Field, Solicitor, The Quarry, Leamington Spa, and Margaret A. W. Bickmore; *m* 1932, Kathleen Mildred, *widow* of his Hon. Judge Dobb, and *e d* of late H. Caldwell Lipsett; no *c*. *Educ:* Rugby Sch.; Birmingham Univ. Enlisted RFA, 5 Aug. 1914; Flight Sub-Lt RNAS, Oct. 1914; Major RAF, 1918; seconded as Air Adviser to Govt of Finland 1925-28 (Order of White Rose); Air Attaché, Paris, Brussels, The Hague, Lisbon, Madrid, 1933-36; Inter-Services Mission to Portugal, 1937; France, 1939-40 (despatches); retired, 1943; holds Spanish Naval Order of Merit. *Recreations:* fishing, ski-ing, yachting. *Address:* Oakshott Hanger, Hawkley, Liss, Hants. *T:* Hawkley 297. *Club:* United Hunts.

**FIELD, William James;** *b* 22 May 1909; *s* of late Frederick William Field, Solicitor; unmarried. *Educ:* Richmond County Sch.; London Univ; abroad. Joined Labour Party, 1935; Parliamentary Private Sec. to Sec. of State for War, May-Oct. 1951 (to Under-Sec. for War, 1950-51); Chm. South Hammersmith Divisional Labour Party, 1945-46; contested Hampstead Div., General Election, 1945; MP (Lab) North Paddington, Nov. 1946-Oct. 1953. Mem. Hammersmith Borough Council, 1945-53, and Leader of that Council, 1946-49; a Vice-Pres. of Assoc. of Municipal Corporations, 1952-53; for several years, mem. Metropolitan Boroughs' Standing Joint Cttee and of many local govt bodies. Volunteered for Army, Sept. 1939 and served in ranks and as officer in Intelligence Corps and RASC.

**FIELD-FISHER, Thomas Gilbert,** QC 1969; TD 1950; Deputy Chairman, Cornwall Quarter Sessions, since 1968; *b* 16 May 1915; *s* of Caryl Field-Fisher, Torquay; *m* 1945, Ebba, *d* of Max Larsen, Linwood, USA. *Educ:* King's Sch., Bruton; Peterhouse, Cambridge. BA 1937, MA 1942. Called to Bar, Middle Temple, 1942. Served Queen Victoria's Rifles, KRRC, 1939-47. Vice-Chm., London Council of Social Service, 1966-; Dep.-Chm., SW Agricultural Land Tribunal, 1967-. *Publications:* Animals and the Law, 1964; Rent Regulation and Control, 1967; contribs to Halsbury's Laws of England, Law Jl, and other legal publications. *Recreations:* tennis, dogs, social welfare. *Address:* 38 Hurlingham Court, SW6. *T:* 01-736 4627. *Clubs:* Hurlingham, International Lawn Tennis of Great Britain.

**FIELDEN, Lieut-Col Edward Anthony,** MC; DL; JP; *b* 30 March 1886; *e s* of late E. B. Fielden, MP; *m* 1914, Phœbe, *d* of late Adm. Hon. T. S. Brand; three *s*. *Educ:* Eton; RMC, Sandhurst. 10th Hussars, 1906-21 (retired as Major); Brigade-Major, 6th and 8th Cavalry Brigades, BEF, 1917-18; re-employed 2nd in command OCTU, 1939-42; Lt-Col Home Guard, 1942; High Sheriff of Salop, 1954. Pres., Ludlow Div., Conservative Assoc., 1960-68. MFH, South Salop Hounds, 1925-29, and North Cotswold Hounds, 1929-32. JP 1946, DL 1952, Salop. *Recreations:* hunting, fishing. *Address:* Court of Hill, Ludlow, Salop. *T:* Cleehillstone 300. *Club:* Cavalry.

**FIELDEN, Air Vice-Marshal Sir Edward Hedley,** GCVO 1968 (KCVO 1952; CVO 1943; MVO 1936); CB 1946; DFC 1943; AFC 1929; Senior Air Equerry to the Queen 1962-69, an Extra Equerry since 1970; Captain of Queen's Flight, 1952-62 (of King George VI's Flight, 1936-52); *b* 4 Dec. 1903; *e s* of Edward Fielden, MB, and Maud Fielden, Bracknell, Berks; *m* 1940, Mary Angela, *y d* of late Lieut-Col Henry Ramsden Jodrell, CMG; one *d* (and one *s* decd). *Educ:* Malvern. RAF 1924-29; Royal Air Force Reserve, 1929; Pilot to Prince of Wales, 1929; Extra Equerry, 1932: Equerry to King George VI, 1937; Extra Equerry to the King, 1946, to the Queen, 1952. *Recreations:* shooting, fishing. *Address:* Scraces Farm, Pangbourne, Berks. *T:* Pangbourne 3244. *Clubs:* Pratt's, Royal Aero.

**FIELDEN, Prof. Frank,** MA (Dunelm), FRIBA; Secretary, Royal Fine Art Commission, since 1969; *b* 3 Oct. 1915; *s* of Ernest and Emma Fielden, Greenfield, Yorks; *m* 1939, Margery Keeler; two *d*. *Educ:* University of Manchester. Graduated, 1938. Served 1939-45 with Royal Engineers (Special Forces), France, N Africa, Italy, Germany. Town Planning Officer to Nigerian Government, 1945-46; Lecturer and Sen. Lectr, University of Durham, 1946-59; Prof. of Architecture, Univ. of Strathclyde, 1959-69. Mem., Royal Fine Art Commn for Scotland, 1965. RIBA Athens Bursar, 1950, Bronze Medallist 1960. Chm., Soc. of Architectural Historians of Great Britain, 1965-67. *Publications:* articles in professional journals and national press. *Recreations:* music, gardening, travel, food and wine. *Address:* 15 Portland Terrace, The Green, Richmond, Surrey. *T:* 01-948 0395. *Club:* Special Forces.

**FIELDEN, Lionel,** CIE 1941; *b* 15 May 1896; *s* of late Joshua Fielden, Kineton, Warwickshire. *Educ:* Eton; Brasenose Coll., Oxford. Artists Rifles, 1914; RGA, 1915-19; Gallipoli, Palestine (capt.); League of Nations Secretariat, 1920-22; representative of High Commissioner for refugees in Greece and the Levant, 1922-23; sec. to Lord Pres. of Council, 1924; BBC 1927; Head of General Talks Dept,

1930-35; Controller of Broadcasting in India, 1935-40; Indian Editor, BBC, April-Nov. 1940; Ministry of Food; Ministry of Aircraft Production, 1941-42; editorial staff Observer, 1942; major SOII CA Italy, 1943; Dir of Public Relations, Allied Control Commission, Italy, 1944-45. *Publications:* Beggar my Neighbour, 1943; The Natural Bent, 1960. *Recreation:* trying to avoid being organised. *Address:* La Spinetta, Arsina, 55100 Lucca, Italy.

**FIELDEN, Thomas Perceval,** MA; BMus Oxon, DMus Edinburgh; FRCM; Pianist and Composer; late Director of the Rhodesian Academy of Music, Bulawayo (1952-58); 2nd *s* of late John Fielden, Chichester, Sussex; *m* 1st, Edith, *d* of Richard Stapley, Wolverton; one *s* (one *d* decd); 2nd, Ethel, *d* of Major George Olden, OBE, MC, Braunton, Devon. *Educ:* Prebendal Sch., Chichester; Royal College of Music (Open Schol. Composition) 1902; Jesus Coll., Oxford (Organ Exhibner), 1905. Formerly: Dir of Music, Hurstpierpoint Coll., Sussex; Dir. of Music, Fettes Coll., Edinburgh; Organist to the Foundling Hospital; prof. and lecturer, Ladies' Coll., Cheltenham; Dir of Music, Charterhouse Sch., 1928-47; Prof. of Pianoforte, Royal College of Music, 1921-52. Has given pianoforte recitals in London, Berlin, Paris, Hanover, and in all the British Colonies. Lieut RFA, 1915; Lieut RNVR, 1943-45. *Publications:* The Science of Pianoforte Technique, 1927; Music and Character, 1929; Marks and Remarks, a study of examination problems, 1937; Piano Pieces and Part-songs (some Part-songs sung by Fleet Street Choir, etc); article on the Pianoforte, in Chambers's Encyclopædia; contrib. Proc. Royal Musical Assoc.; and to Music and Letters; editor (Associated Board) Chopin's Works. *Recreations:* tennis, sailing. *Address:* The Corner Cottage, Forest Green, Nailsworth, Glos. *T:* Nailsworth 2952. *Club:* *Naval.*

**FIELDGATE, Alan Frederic Edmond,** CMG 1945; *b* 20 Nov. 1889; *m* 1915, Dorothy Alice Thomas. *Educ:* Worcester Coll., Oxford (BA). Asst District Commissioner, Gold Coast Colony, 1915; District Commissioner, 1922; Provincial Commissioner, 1934-46. *Address:* Olde Court, Higher Lincombe Road, Torquay, Devon.

**FIELDHOUSE, Sir Harold,** KBE 1949 (OBE 1934): CB 1947; Secretary, National Assistance Board, 1946-59, retired; Member of Letchworth Garden City, Welwyn Garden City and Hatfield Corporations, retired; *b* Leeds, Yorks; *e s* of Frank and Mary Ellen Fieldhouse; *m* 1922, Mabel Elaine Elliott, Conisborough, Yorks; two *s*. *Educ:* Armley Higher Grade Sch., Leeds. Asst Clerk, Leeds Board of Guardians, 1909-30; Public Assistance Officer, City of Leeds, 1930-34; Regional Officer, Asst Sec. and Under-Sec. Assistance Board, 1934-46. *Recreations:* golf, bridge, music, reading. *Address:* 10 Gayton Court, Harrow, Mddx. *T:* 01-427 0918. *Clubs:* City Livery; Grim's Dyke Golf, West Hill Golf.

**FIELDING, Fenella Marion;** actress; *b* London 17 Nov. 1934. *Educ:* North London Collegiate Sch. Cockles and Champagne, and Ray the Piper, Saville, 1954; Luba in Jubilee Girl, Victoria Palace, 1956; Lady Parvula de Panzoust in Valmouth, Lyric, Hammersmith, 1958, and Saville, 1959; Pieces of Eight, Apollo, 1959; Five Plus One, Lyceum, Edinburgh Fest., 1961; Phoebe in As You Like It, also Lydia Languish in The Rivals, Pembroke Th., Croydon, 1961; Twists (Best Revue Performance of the Year in Variety, 1962), Arts; Annie Wood in Doctors of Philosophy, New Arts, 1962; Ellen in Luv, New Arts, 1963; So Much to RememberThe Life Story of a Great Lady, The Establishment, and Vaudeville, 1963; Cyprienne in Let's Get a Divorce, Mermaid, and Comedy, 1966; Mrs Sullen in The Beaux Stratagem, and Baroness de Champigny in The Italian Straw Hat, Chichester Fest. Th., 1967; Mrs Gracedew in The High Bid, Mermaid, 1967; Lysistrata in Lysistrata, Univ. of Oklahoma, 1968; Arkadina in The Seagull, Nottingham Playhouse, 1968; Hedda in Hedda Gabler, Phoenix, Leicester, 1969; Nora in A Doll's House, Univ. of Sussex, 1970; Colette in Colette, Ellen Stewart Th. (first appearance in New York), 1970. *Recreation:* reading. *Address:* c/o BKM (Personal Agency Ltd), 27 Curzon Street, W1.

**FIELDING, Gabriel, (Alan Gabriel Barnsley);** Professor of English, Washington State University, since 1967; *b* 25 March 1916; *s* of late George Barnsley, Clerk in Holy Orders, and Katherine Mary (*née* Fielding-Smith), a descendant of Henry Fielding, the novelist; *m* 1943, Edwina Eleanora Cook, Storrington, Sussex; three *s* two *d*. *Educ:* The Grange Sch., Eastbourne; St Edward's Sch., Oxford; Trinity Coll., Dublin; St George's Hospital, London. BA, TCD, 1939. MRCS (Eng.), LRCP (London) 1942. Served with RAMC, 1943-46 (Capt.). Dep. Medical Officer, HM Training Establishment, Maidstone, Kent, 1954-64. Appointed Author in Residence (Prof. of English) to Washington State Univ., USA, 1966-67. Hon. DLitt Gonzaga Univ., Spokane, Washington, 1967. *Publications:* The Frog Prince and Other Poems, 1952; Brotherly Love (novel), 1954; Twenty-Eight Poems, 1955; In the Time of Greenbloom (Novel), 1956; Eight Days (Novel), 1958; Through Streets Broad and Narrow (Novel), 1960; The Birthday King (novel), 1963 (W. H. Smith Prize for Literature, 1964); Gentlemen in Their Season (novel), 1966. *Recreations:* televised news; competitions, space; theology; walking. *Address:* 1811 Monroe Street, Pullman, Washington, USA.

**FIELDS, Gracie,** CBE 1938; MA; actress; *b* Rochdale, 9 Jan. 1898; *d* of Fred Stansfield and late Sarah Jane Bamford; *m* 1st, Archie Pitt (Selinger) from whom she obtained a divorce 1940 (he *d* 1940); 2nd, 1940, Monty Banks (Mario Bianchi) (*d* 1950), Film Director; 3rd, 1952, Boris Alperovici, Capri. *Educ:* Rochdale. Eight Command Performances, 1928, 1931, 1937, 1947, 1950, 1951, 1952, 1957. Received hon. freedom of Rochdale, 1937; Order of St John of Jerusalem. *Publication:* Sing as We Go, 1960. *Address:* Canzone del Mare, 80073, Capri, Italy.

**FIENNES, Gerard F. G.** and **John S. W.;** *see* Twisleton-Wykeham-Fiennes.

**FIENNES,** family name of **Baron Saye and Sele.**

**FIENNES, Sir Maurice (Alberic Twisleton-Wykeham-),** Kt 1965; CEng; MIMechE; Chairman and Managing Director of Davy-Ashmore Ltd, 1961-69; *b* 1 March 1907; *s* of Alberic Arthur Twisleton-Wykeham-Fiennes and Gertrude Theodosia Pomeroy Colley; *m* 1st, 1932, Sylvia Mabel Joan (marr. diss., 1964), *d* of late Major David Finlay, 7th Dragoon Guards. two *s* three *d*; 2nd, 1967, Fräulein Erika Hueller von Huellenried, *d* of Dr Herbert Hueller. *Educ:* Repton; Armstrong Coll., Newcastle upon Tyne. Apprenticeship with Ransomes and Rapier Ltd, Ipswich; joined Sir W. G. Armstrong, Whitworth & Co Ltd (Engineers), Newcastle-upon-Tyne, 1930; with The United Steel Companies Ltd, 1937, first as Commercial Asst to Managing Dir, then in charge Gun Forgings and Gun Dept at Steel Peech & Tozer; Gen. Works Dir, Brush Electrical Engineering Co. Ltd, 1942; Managing Dir, Davy and United Engineering Co. Ltd, 1945; Managing Dir, Davy-Ashmore Ltd, 1960. Mem. Economic Develt Cttee for Mech. Eng, 1964-67; Pres. of Iron and Steel Institute, 1962-63; Chairman: Athlone Fellowships Cttee, 1966; Overseas Scholarships Bd, CBI, 1970; Governor, Yehudi Menuhin School, 1969. *Recreations:* music, grandchildren. *Address:* Hill Top Farm, Dronfield, Sheffield. *T:* Dronfield 2274; 90 Eaton Square, SW1. *T:* 01-235 2313. *Club:* Bath.

**FIENNES, Very Rev. Hon. Oliver William Twistleton-Wykeham-;** Dean of Lincoln since 1968; *b* 17 May 1926; *yr s* of 20th Baron Saye and Sele, OBE, MC, and Hersey Cecilia Hester, *d* of late Captain Sir Thomas Dacres Butler, KCVO; *m* 1956, Juliet, *d* of Dr Trevor Braby Heaton, *qv*; two *s* two *d*. *Educ:* Eton; New College, Oxford; Cuddesdon College. Asst Curate, New Milton, Hants, 1954; Chaplain, Clifton College, Bristol, 1958; Rector of Lambeth, 1963. *Address:* The Deanery, Lincoln. *Clubs:* Brooks's, MCC; Vincent's (Oxford).

**FIENNES, Sir Ranulph Twisleton-Wykeham-,** 3rd Bt, *cr* 1916; *b* 7 March 1944; *s* of Lieut-Col Sir Ranulph Twisleton-Wykeham-Fiennes, DSO, 2nd Bt (died of wounds, 1943) and Audrey Joan, *yr d* of Sir Percy Newson, 1st Bt; *S* father 1944; *m* 1970, Virginia Pepper. *Educ:* Eton. Liveryman, Vintners' Company, 1960. French Parachutist Wings, 1965. Lieut, Royal Scots Greys, 1966, Captain 1968 (retd 1970). Attached 22 SAS Regt, 1966, Sultan of Muscat's Armed Forces, 1968; Dhofar Campaign Medal, 1969; Sultan's Bravery Medal, 1970. *Publication:* A Talent for Trouble, 1970. *Recreations:* alpinism, langlauf, photography. *Heir:* none. *Address:* St Peter's Well, Lodsworth, Petworth, Sussex. *T:* Lodsworth 302.

**FIFE,** 3rd Duke of, *cr* 1900; **James George Alexander Bannerman Carnegie;** Master of Southesk; *b* 23 Sept. 1929; *o s* of 11th Earl of Southesk, *qv*, and Princess Maud (*d* 1945); *S* aunt, Princess Arthur of Connaught (Dukedom of Fife), 1959; *m* 1956, Hon. Caroline Cicely Dewar (marr. diss. 1966), *er d* of 3rd Baron Forteviot, *qv*; one *s* one *d*. *Educ:* Gordonstoun. Nat. Service, Scots Guards (Malaya). Royal Agricultural College. Liveryman Cloth-workers' Company, and Freeman City of London, 1954. Pres. of ABA, 1959-. *Recreation:* shooting. *Heir: s* Earl of Macduff, *qv*. *Address:* Elsick House, Stonehaven, Kincardineshire AB3 2NT. *Clubs:* Turf, Pratt's, MCC; Royal Northern (Aberdeen).

**FIFE, Charles Morrison,** CB 1950; *s* of Alexander John Fife and Margaret Anne Morrison; *m* 1940, Evelyn Mary Thicthener (*d* 1970); no *c*. *Educ:* King Edward's High Sch., Birmingham; Christ's Coll., Cambridge. Senior Scholar, Christ's Coll., 1922; John Stewart of Rannoch (Univ.) Scholar, 1923; 1st Cl. Classical Trip. Pt I, 1924; Browne (Univ.) Scholar, 1925; 1st Cl. Div. I Classical Trip. Pt II, 1925; 2nd Cl. Hons Economics Trip. Pt II, 1926. Entered Civil service, War Office, 1926; Private Sec. to Sir Reginald Paterson (Dep. Under Sec. of State), 1934-35; Asst Under-Sec. of State, WO, 1948-64, Ministry of Defence, 1964, retired. Conservator of Wimbledon Common, 1961-68. *Recreation:* golf. *Address:* 4 Cokers Lane, Croxted Road, SE21. *Club:* Oxford and Cambridge University.

**FIFE, Ian Braham,** MC 1945; TD (2 bars) 1946; **His Honour Judge Fife;** County Court Judge since 1965; an Acting Deputy Chairman, Greater London Sessions; *b* 10 July 1911; *o s* of late Donald Fulford Fife and Muriel Alice Fife (*née* Pitt); *m* 1947, Pauline, *e d* of late T. R. Parsons and of Ald. Mrs Winifred Parsons, Cambridge; two *s* two *d*. *Educ:* Monkton Combe Sch. Served, Royal Fusiliers, 1939-47. Called to Bar, Inner Temple, 1948. *Publications:* Ed. (with E. A. Machin) Redgrave's Factories Acts (20th & 21st edns) and Redgrave's Offices and Shops. Contrib. Halsbury's Laws of England, 3rd edn. *Address:* 2 Castello Avenue, Putney, SW15. *T:* 01-788 6475. *Club:* Savage.

**FIFOOT, Cecil Herbert Stuart,** MA; FBA 1954; Fellow of Hertford College, Oxford, 1925-59, Hon. Fellow, 1963; *b* 1899; *s* of Sydney Fifoot and Maria Trevor; *m* 1924, Hjördis Baars, *yr d* of Dr Eriksen, Kongsberg, Norway; one *s*. *Educ:* Berkhamsted Sch.; Exeter Coll., Oxford (History Scholar). 2nd Lieut RFA 1917-18 (wounded, July 1918); 1st Class Law Sch., 1921; Barrister-at-law, Middle Temple, 1922; Bursar, Hertford Coll., 1926-34; Dean, 1940-44; Univ. Lecturer in Law, 1930-45; Senior Proctor, 1936; All Souls Reader in English Law, 1945-59; Reader in Common Law to the Inns of Court, 1954-67. *Publications:* English Law and its Background, 1932; Lord Mansfield, 1936; The law of Contract (with Dr G. C. Cheshire), 1945, 7th edn, 1969; Cases on the Law of Contract (with Dr G. C Cheshire), 1945, 5th edn 1969; History and Sources of the Common Law, 1949; Judge and Jurist in the Reign of Victoria, 1959; Letters of F. W. Maitland (Selden Soc.), 1965. *Address:* 203 Braid Road, Edinburgh 10.

**FIGG, Leonard Clifford William;** Regional Export Director, Board of Trade Eastern Region and London, since 1970; *b* 17 Aug. 1923; *s* of late Sir Clifford Figg and late Lady (Eileen) Figg (*née* Crabb); *m* 1955, Jane Brown; two *s*. *Educ:* Charterhouse; Trinity Coll., Oxford. RAF, 1942-46 (Flt-Lt). HM Diplomatic Service, 1947; served In: Addis Ababa, 1949-52; FO, 1952-58; Amman, 1958-61; FO, 1961-67; Counsellor, 1965; Deputy Consul-General, Chicago, 1967-69. *Recreations:* field sports. *Address:* Court Field House, Little Hampden, Great Missenden, Bucks. *T:* Hampden Row 205. *Club:* Brooks's.

**FIGGESS, Sir John (George),** KBE 1969; CMG 1960; OBE 1949; Commissioner General for Britain, World Exposition, Osaka, Japan, 1970, since 1968; *b* 15 Nov. 1909; *e s* of Percival Watts Figgess and Leonora (*née* McCanlis); *m* 1948, Alette, *d* of Dr P. J. A. Idenburg, The Hague; two *d*. *Educ:* Whitgift Sch. In business in Japan, 1933-38. Commissioned, Intelligence Corps, 1939; Staff Coll., 1941; served with Intelligence Corps, India/Burma Theatre, 1942-45. Attached to UK Liaison Mission, Japan, 1945; Asst Mil Adviser (Lt-Col), UKLM, Tokyo, 1947-52; GSO1, War Office (MI Directorate), 1953-56; Military Attaché, Tokyo, 1956-61; Information Counsellor, British Embassy, Tokyo, 1961-68. *Publications:* (with Fujio Koyama) Two Thousand Years of Oriental Ceramics, 1960; contrib. to Oriental Art, Far Eastern Ceramic Bulletin, etc. *Recreations:* Chinese and Japanese art; sailing. *Address:* The Manor House, Burghfield, Berks. *Club:* Army and Navy.

**FIGGURES, Sir Frank (Edward),** KCB 1970 (CB 1966); CMG 1959; Second Secretary, HM Treasury, since 1968; *b* 5 March 1910; *s* of Frank and Alice Figgures; *m* 1941, Aline, *d* of Prof. Hugo Frey; one *s* one *d*. *Educ:* Rutlish

Sch.; New Coll., Oxford. Harmsworth Senior Scholar, Merton Coll., Oxford, 1931; Henry Fellow, Yale Law Sch., 1933; Called to Bar, Lincoln's Inn, 1936; Military Service (RA), 1940-46; Joined HM Treasury, 1946; Dir of Trade and Finance, OEEC, 1948-51; Under-Sec., HM Treasury, 1955-60; Sec.-Gen. to EFTA, 1960-65; Third Secretary, Treasury, 1965-68. *Address:* 42 Southway, NW11. *Club:* Reform.

**FILDES, Sir Paul,** Kt 1946; OBE 1919; ScD; FRS 1934; late Director of Chemical Bacteriology (Medical Research Council); *b* 10 Feb. 1882; *s* of late Sir Luke Fildes, KCVO, RA. *Educ:* Winchester; Trinity Coll., Cambridge; London Hospital. MA, MB, BCh, Cantab., 1909; Asst Bacteriologist, London Hospital, 1909-34; Pathologist, RN Hospital, Haslar, 1915-19; Surgeon Lt-Comdr RNVR, 1917; founder of British Journal of Experimental Pathology, 1920; Examiner in Pathology, University of Cambridge, 1933; Pres. of Pathological Section, Royal Society of Medicine, 1934; Mem. of the Scientific Staff, Medical Research Council, 1934-49; Examiner in Pathology, University of Oxford, 1937. Mem. Advisory Board, Beit Memorial Research Fund, 1939-54; Mem. Governing Body, Lister Institute, 1942-56. Hon. ScD (Cantab.), 1948; Hon. ScD (Reading), 1959; Royal Medal, Royal Society, 1953; Copley Medal, Royal Society, 1963; Hon. Fellow Royal Society of Medicine, 1962. *Publications:* Haemophilia (with W. Bulloch) in Treasury of Human Inheritance, 1911; Syphilis from the Modern Standpoint (with J. McIntosh), 1911; various monographs and papers on pathological subjects. *Address:* 48 Melton Court, SW7. *Club:* Athenæum.

**FILER, Albert Jack,** CB 1954; President Brick Development Association Ltd; *b* 14 Aug. 1898; 2nd *s* of Albert James Shephard Filer and Jessie (*née* Marrison); *m* 1923, Violet D., *o d* of late Edward T. Booth, Bexhill, Sussex; one *d*. *Educ:* County Secondary Sch., Holloway, N. Entered Civil Service, 1914, Office of Works. Served European War of 1914-18 in Civil Service Rifles. Principal, 1940, Min. of Works, Asst Sec., 1943, Under Sec., 1948; Gen. Manager, Directorate Gen. of Works, 1958-60, retired from Civil Service, 1960. *Recreation:* golf. *Address:* 1 Heatherwood, Midhurst, Sussex. *T:* Midhurst 2816.

**FILON, Sidney Philip Lawrence,** TD; Librarian and Secretary to the Trustees, National Central Library, since 1958; *b* 20 Sept. 1905; *s* of late Prof. L. N. G. Filon, FRS and late Anne Godet; *m* 1st, 1939, Doris Schelling; one *d*; 2nd, 1959, Liselotte Florstedt; one *d*. *Educ:* Whitgift Sch.; University Coll., London (BSc). Sch. of Librarianship, University Coll., London, 1929-30; FLA 1931. National Central Library, 1930-39. Military service, 1939-45. Dep. Librarian, National Central Library, 1946-58. Mem., Library Advisory Council (England). *Address:* 107 Littleheath Road, Selsdon, Surrey.

**FILSON, Alexander Warnock;** Director, Film Production Association of Great Britain, 1967-70; *b* 23 Aug. 1913; *s* of late J. T. W. Filson, Indian Police; *m* 1941, Judith Henrietta, *d* of late major R. H. Greig, DSO, and of Mrs Rokeling; one *s* two *d*. *Educ:* Clifton Coll., (Schol.); The Queen's Coll., Oxford (Schol.) (MA). Served War of 1939-45 in Army; Asst Sec., Parliamentary Labour Party, 1945-47; Sec. Fabian Soc., 1947-49; Mem. of Kensington Borough Council, 1937-49; Contested (Lab) Brentford and Chiswick, 1955. *Publications:* (asst to Prof. G. D. H. Cole) British Trade Unionism Today, 1939; ed (with Prof. G. D. H. Cole) British Working Class Movements, 1789-1875: Select Documents, 1951. *Recreations:* reading and sightseeing. *Address:* 99 Queen's Road, Richmond, Surrey.

**FINBERG, Prof. Herbert Patrick Reginald,** MA, DLitt (Oxon); FSA; FRHistS; Visiting Fellow of Clare Hall, Cambridge; general editor of the Agrarian History of England and Wales; *b* 21 March 1900; *e s* of A. J. Finberg; *m* 1933, Joscelyne Henrietta Prideaux Payne; two *s*. *Educ:* Merchant Taylors' School; St John's Coll., Oxford. Founded and directed The Alcuin Press, 1928-36; Dir of The Broadwater Press Ltd, 1936-44; Typographical Adviser to the Ministry of Works, 1944-48, and to HM Printers (Eyre and Spottiswoode Ltd), 1944-58. Designer of Twickenham edn of Alexander Pope, London Shakespeare, Latin-English Missal, Coronation Service. Editorial Dir of Burns Oates & Washbourne Ltd, 1944-49. Editor of the Agricultural History Review, 1953-64. Head of Dept of English Local History, University of Leicester, as Reader, 1952-63, Prof. 1963-65; Prof. Emeritus, 1966. Pres., British Agricultural Hist. Soc., 1965-68. Mem. Internat. Cttee on English in the Liturgy. Prix Graphica Belgica, 1965. *Publications:* Axel (from the French of Villiers de l'Isle-Adam), 1925; The Missal in Latin and English (with Rev. J. O'Connell), 1949; Tavistock Abbey, 1951; Devonshire Studies (with W. G. Hoskins), 1952; The Early Charters of Devon and Cornwall, 1953; Gloucestershire (in the "Making of the English Landscape" series), 1955; The Gostwicks of Willington, 1956; Gloucestershire Studies, 1957; The Early Charters of the West Midlands, 1961; The Early Charters of Wessex, 1964; Lucerna, 1964; Local History: Objective and Pursuit, 1967; West-Country Historical Studies, 1969. *Address:* 151 Park Road, Chiswick, W4. *T:* 01-994 8987. *Club:* Royal Societies.

**FINCH;** *see* Finch-Knightley.

**FINCH, George Ingle,** MBE 1917; FRS 1938; DTechChem (Zürich), FInstP, FNI; Hon. DSc (Brussels); Hon. ACGI; Professor Emeritus of Applied Physical Chemistry, University of London, since 1952; Director of the National Chemical Laboratory of India, 1952-Sept. 1957, retired; *b* Orange, New South Wales, 4 Aug. 1888; *e s* of late C. E. Finch, Chm. of the Land Court of NSW; *m* 1921, Agnes Isobel Johnston; three *d*. *Educ:* Wolaroi Coll., NSW; Ecole de Médecine (Paris); Swiss Federal High Sch., Zürich; Geneva Univ. Research Chemist at Royal Arsenal, 1912-13; Demonstrator, Imperial Coll., 1913-14; served European War, 1914-19, with RFA and RAOD, France, Egypt, Macedonia (despatches, MBE); Demonstrator, Imperial Coll., 1919; lecturer (Electro-Chemistry), 1921; Asst Prof., 1927; Prof. of Applied Physical Chemistry in the Univ. of London at Imperial Coll., 1936-52; Francqui Prof., Brussels, 1937-38; Scientific Adviser, Ministry of Home Security, 1941-45; Pres. Physical Soc., 1947-49; Pres. Alpine Club, 1959-61; Fellow Imperial Coll. of Science and Technology, 1962. Mem., 1922 Everest Expedition and led 2nd climbing party to 27,300 ft. Hughes Medal, Royal Society, 1944; Physical Soc. Guthrie Lecturer, 1950; Joykissen–Mookerjee Gold Medal, 1957. Commandeur de L'Ordre de Léopold II, 1938; Chevalier de la Légion d'Honneur, 1952. *Publications:* La Diffraction des Electrons et la Structure des Surfaces (Liége), 1938; Scientific Papers in Proc. Royal Society, etc; The Making of a Mountaineer, 1924; articles in Alpine Journal, Jahrbuch des Schweizer Alpen Club, etc. *Recreations:* mountain climbing, yacht cruising, wildfowling. *Address:* c/o The Grange, East Hanney, near Wantage, Berks. *Clubs:* Athenæum, Alpine.

**FINCH, Harold Josiah;** Compensation Secretary, South Wales Area, National Union of Mineworkers, since 1939; Secretary Miners' Parliamentary Group; *b* 2 May 1898; *s* of late Josiah Coleman Finch and Emmie Keedwell; *m*; one *s* one *d*. *Educ:* Barry Elementary Sch.; Cardiff Evening Schs. Left Sch. at 14; Railway Clerk with Barry Rly Co. (now no longer existent); Sec. Tredegar Valley District of Miners' at Blackwood (Mon.), 1919; Mem. of Mynyddislwyn UDC, 1922-33, Chm., 1932; Asst Compensation Sec., then Sec. South Wales Miners Federation at Cardiff 1934-39. MP (Lab) Bedwellty, 1950-70; Parly Under-Sec. of State, Welsh Office, 1964-66; former Mem., Council of Europe. *Publications:* Guide to Workmen's Compensation Acts; Industrial Injuries Act Explained. *Recreation:* gardening. *Address:* 34 Elim Way, Pontllanfraith, Mon; 56 Kenwyn Road, Clapham, SW4. *T:* 01-622 6806.

**FINCH, Col John Charles W.;** *see* Wynne Finch.

**FINCH, Maj.-Gen. Lionel Hugh Knightley,** CB 1941; DSO 1916, Bar 1917; OBE; FLS; *b* 18 July 1888; *o s* of late Capt. E. H. Franklyn Finch, 30th Regt; *m* 1919, Hildegard, *d* of Mrs J. C. A. Sepp-Clésius, Nijmegen, Holland; one *d*. *Educ:* Cheltenham Coll.; Birmingham Univ.; London Univ. Served European War, 1914-18 (DSO and bar, OBE, despatches, BT Major); Staff Coll., Camberley, 1924-25; GSO3 at HQ, Northern Command, 1926-27; DAA and QMG at HQ Northumbrian Area, 1928-29; commanded Depot, Cheshire Regt, 1930-33; DAQMG at Army HQ India, 1934; comd 1st Bn Lancs Fusiliers, 1934-36; Asst Adjutant-Gen., War Office, 1936-39; Dep. Dir of Recruiting and Organisation, War Office, 1939; Dir of Recruiting and Organisation, War Office, 1939-40; Dep. Adjutant-Gen., War Office, 1940; Divisional Comdr, 1940; Chm., War Office Committees, 1940-41; District Comdr, Home Forces, 1941-42; retired, 1943; late The Lancs Fusiliers, The Cheshire Regt, and The Royal Sussex Regt. *Address:* National Westminster Bank, Petworth, Sussex.

**FINCH, Peter;** actor; *b* London, 28 Sept. 1916 (**Peter Ingle-Finch**); *m* 1943, Tamara Tchinarova (marr. diss. 1959); one *d*; *m* 1959, Yolande Turner (marr. diss. 1966); one *s* one *d*. *Educ:* North Sydney Inter High Sch., Australia. First appeared on stage, New South Wales and Qld, in While Parents Sleep, 1935; first part on London stage in Daphne Laureola, 1949. Chief stage appearances in: Captain Carvallo, St James's, 1950; Othello, (Iago), St James's, 1951; The Happy Time, St James's, 1952; Romeo and Juliet (Mercutio), Old Vic, 1952; An Italian Straw Hat, Old Vic, 1952; Two for the See-Saw, Haymarket, 1959; The Seagull, Queen's, 1964. Has appeared in numerous films since 1936, including the Battle of the River Plate, A Town Like Alice, The Shiralee, Robbery under Arms, Windom's Way, The Nun's Story, Kidnapped, The Sins of Rachel Cade, The Trials of Oscar Wilde, No Love for Johnnie, I Thank a Fool, In the Cool of the Day, Girl with Green Eyes, The Pumpkin Eater, Judith, Flight of the Phoenix, 10.30 One Summer Evening, Far From the Madding Crowd, Lylah Claire, The Red Tent. Gained British Film Academy Award, 1956, 1961. *Address:* c/o International Famous Agency Ltd, 11-12 Hanover Street, W1. *T:* 01-629 8080. *Club:* Garrick.

**FINCH HATTON,** family name of **Earl of Winchilsea and Nottingham.**

**FINCH-KNIGHTLEY,** family name of **Earl of Aylesford.**

**FINCHAM, Prof. John Robert Stanley,** FRS 1969; Professor of Genetics, University of Leeds, since 1966; *b* 11 Aug. 1926; *s* of Robert Fincham and Winifred Emily Fincham (*née* Western); *m* 1950, Ann Katherine Emerson; one *s* three *d*. *Educ:* Hertford Grammar Sch.; Peterhouse, Cambridge. BA 1946, PhD 1950, ScD 1964. Bye-Fellow of Peterhouse, 1949-50; Lectr in Botany, University Coll., Leicester, 1950-54; Reader in Genetics, Univ. of Leicester, 1954-60; Head of Dept of Genetics, John Innes Inst., 1960-66; Vis. Associate Prof. of Genetics, Massachusetts Inst. of Technology, 1960-61. *Publications:* Fungal Genetics (with P. R. Day), 1963; Microbial and Molecular Genetics, 1965; Genetic Complementation, 1966; papers in Biochemical Jl, Jl Gen. Microbiol., Jl Biol. Chem., Heredity, Jl Molecular Biol., Genet. Res. *Recreations:* mountaineering and hill walking, squash, watching Rugby League. *Address:* 35 Gledhow Wood Road, Leeds 2. *T:* Leeds 657740.

**FINDLAY, Alexander John,** CMG 1937; *b* 1886; *s* of late James Smith Findlay, Aberdeen; *m* 1913, Primrose Alice, *d* of Arthur Aiken, Aberdeen. *Educ:* Aberdeen Grammar Sch.; Aberdeen Univ.; North of Scotland Coll of Agriculture; MA, BSc (Agric.), NDA, NDD. Entered Colonial Agricultural Service 1912; served in Dept of Agriculture, Nigeria, 1912-31; Dir of Agriculture, Zanzibar, 1931-37; Retired 1937; Commissioner for the Colonial Exhibit., World's Fair, New York, 1939 and 1940; served Cameroons, 1915, with West African Frontier Force. *Address:* 24 Carden Place, Aberdeen.

**FINDLAY, Comdr James Buchanan,** CBE 1957; RN (Retd); Deputy Governor of Bank of Scotland since 1966, Director since 1933, and also of companies; *b* 7 Jan. 1895; *m* 1923, Mary Sancroft Findlay-Hamilton; three *s* one *d*. *Educ:* Royal Naval Colls, Osborne and Dartmouth. Retired from RN after European War of 1914-18; served in War of 1939-45. *Recreations:* shooting, golf, gardening. *Address:* Carnell, Hurlford, Ayrshire. *Club:* Lansdowne.

**FINDLAY, Prof. John Niemeyer;** Clark Professor of Moral Philosophy and Metaphysics, Yale University, since 1967; *b* 25 Nov. 1903; 2nd *s* of J. H. L. Findlay, Pretoria, South Africa; *m* 1941, Aileen May, *d* of G. S. Davidson, Wellington, NZ; one *s* one *d* (and one *d* decd). *Educ:* Boys' High Sch., Pretoria; Transvaal Univ. Coll.; Balliol Coll., Oxford (Rhodes Scholar, 1st Lit. hum.); University of Graz. Lecturer in Philosophy, Transvaal University Coll., 1927-33; Prof. of Philosophy, University of Otago, NZ, 1934-44; Prof. of Philosophy, Rhodes University Coll., Grahamstown, S Africa, 1945; Prof. of Philosophy, Natal University Coll., 1946-48; Prof. of Philosophy, King's Coll., Newcastle upon Tyne, University of Durham, 1948-51; University Prof. of Philosophy, King's Coll., University of London, 1951-66. Gifford Lecturer, University of St Andrews, 1964-66. Prof. of Philosophy, University of Texas, 1966-67. FBA 1956. FKC 1970. *Publications:* Meinong's Theory of Objects and Values, 1933, new edn, 1963; Hegel: A Re-Examination, 1958; Values and intentions, 1961; Language, Mind and Value, 1963; The Discipline of the Cave, 1965; The Transcendence of The Cave, 1967; trans. Husserl, Logische Untersuchungen, 1969; articles in Mind, Philosophy, Philosophy and Phenomenological Research, Proc. of the

Aristotelian Soc., etc. *Address:* 14 Lambolle Road, NW3; 470 Whitney Avenue, New Haven, Conn., USA.

**FINDLAY, Lt-Col Sir Roland Lewis,** 3rd Bt *cr* 1925; Lieutenant-Colonel (retired) 2nd Dragoons (Royals Scots Greys); *b* 14 July 1903; 2nd *s* of Sir John Ritchie Findlay, 1st Bt, KBE, DL, JP; *S* brother, Sir (John) Edmund Ritchie Findlay, 1962; *m* 1927, Barbara Joan, JP, Northants, *d* of late Major H. S. Garrard, Welton Place, Daventry, Northants; one *d*; 1964, Mrs M. M. Cripps. *Educ:* Harrow; Royal Military Coll., Sandhurst. Lieut Royal Scots Greys, 1924, Capt., 1934. Served War of 1939-45, with Royal Scots Greys, 1939-43, Lieut-Col 21st Army Group, 1944; Col, ALFSEA, 1945-46. High Sheriff of Northants, 1956-57; DL Northants 1958-60. *Address:* Chapel Farm, Burley, Oakham, Rutland. *Clubs:* Cavalry, White's.

*See also Sir Hugh Munro-Lucas-Tooth, Bt, Earl of Westmorland.*

**FINER, Morris,** QC 1963; *b* 12 Dec. 1917; *s* of Charles and Ray Finer; *m* 1943, Edith (*née* Rubner); two *s*. *Educ:* Kilburn Grammar Sch.; London Sch. of Economics and Political Science. Scholar, London Univ., 1936-39; LLB (Hons), 1939; called to the Bar, Gray's Inn, 1943. Governor, London Sch. of Economics and Political Science, 1964- (Vice-Chm., 1970-). Board of Trade Inspector, Rolls Razor Ltd, 1964. Chm., Cinematograph Films Council, 1966-. *Publications:* Company Law, 1948. *Recreations:* reading, walking. *Address:* 10 Clorane Gardens, Hampstead, NW3. *T:* 01-435 7270. *Club:* Reform.

**FINER, Prof. Samuel Edward;** Professor of Government, University of Manchester, since 1966; *b* 22 Sept. 1915; *y s* of Max and Fanny Finer, 210a Green Lanes, N4; *m* 1949, Margaret Ann, 2nd *d* of Sir Andrew McFadyean, *qv*; two *s* one *d*. *Educ:* Holloway Sch., London; Trinity Coll., Oxford. BA (Oxon.) 1st Class Hons Mod. Greats, 1937; 1st Cl. Hons Mod. Hist., 1938; MA (Oxon.) 1946; Sen. George Webb-Medley Schol., 1938-40. Served War, 1940-46; Capt. Royal Signals, 1945. Lecturer in Politics, Balliol Coll., Oxford, 1946-49; Junior Research Fellow, Balliol Coll., Oxford, 1949-50; Prof. of Political Institutions, University of Keele, 1950-66; Dep. Vice-Chancellor, University of Keele, 1962-64. Visiting Prof. and Faculty Mem., Institute of Social Studies, The Hague, Netherlands, 1957-59. Visiting Prof. in Government: Cornell Univ., 1962; Hebrew Univ., Jerusalem, 1969. Chm. Political Studies Assoc. of UK, 1965-69; Vice-Pres. Internat. Political Science Assoc. FRHistSoc. *Publications:* A Primer of Public Administration, 1950; The Life and Times of Sir Edwin Chadwick, 1952; (with Sir John Maud) Local Government in England and Wales, 1953; Anonymous Empire–a Study of the Lobby in Britain, 1958, 2nd edn 1966; Private Industry and Political Power, 1958; (with D. J. Bartholomew and H. B. Berrington) Backbench Opinion in the House of Commons, 1955-59, 1961; The Man on Horseback: The Rôle of The Military in Politics, 1962; Great Britain, in Modern Political Systems: Europe, ed. Macridis and Ward, 1963, 1968; (ed) Sieyès: What is the Third Estate, 1963; Pareto: Sociological Writings, 1966; Comparative Government, 1970. *Recreation:* oil-painting. *Address:* The Mount, Legh Road, Knutsford, Cheshire. *T:* Knutsford 3032.

**FINESTEIN, Israel,** MA; QC 1970; *b* 29 April 1921; *y c* of late Jeremiah Finestein, Hull; *m* 1946, Marion Phyllis, *er d* of Simon Oster, Hendon, Mddx. *Educ:* Kingston High School, Hull; Trinity Coll., Cambridge (Major Scholar and Prizeman). MA 1946. Called to the Bar, Lincoln's Inn, 1953. *Publications:* Short History of the Jews of England, 1956; Sir George Jessel, 1959, etc. *Recreation:* reading history. *Address:* 4 Fairhazel Mansions, Fairhazel Gardens, NW6. *T:* 01-624 3980; Lamb Building, Temple, EC4. *T:* 01-353 0774.

**FINGALL,** 12th Earl of *cr* 1628; **Oliver James Horace Plunkett,** MC; Baron Killeen, 1436; Baron Fingall (UK) 1831; Major, late 17th/21st Lancers; *b* 17 June 1896; *er s* of 11th Earl and Elizabeth Mary Margaret (*d* 1944), *e d* of George Burke, JP, Danesfield, Co. Galway; *S* father, 1929; *m* 1926, Jessica (*d* 1965), *yr d* of late Allan Hughes, Lynch, Allerford, Somerset; *m* 1966, Mrs Clair Richardson, *widow* of Frank Richardson, Geelong, Vic., Aust. *Educ:* Downside. Served European War (MC); retired pay, 1931; in army again, 1939-45. Roman Catholic. *Recreations:* hunting, racing. *Heir:* (to barony of Killeen only) *kinsman*, Baron Dunsany, *qv*. *Address:* The Commons, Dunsany, Co. Meath. *TA:* Fingall, Dunsany. *T:* An Uaimh 2 5193. *Clubs:* Cavalry; Kildare Street (Dublin).

**FINGLAND, Stanley James Gunn,** CMG 1966; HM Diplomatic Service; Assistant Under-Secretary of State, Foreign and Commonwealth Office, since 1969; *b* 19 Dec. 1919; *s* of Samuel Gunn Fingland and Agnes Christina (*née* Watson); *m* 1946, Nellie (*née* Lister); one *s* one *d*. *Educ:* Royal High Sch., Edinburgh. TA 1938. War service, 1939-46 as Major, Royal Signals; served N Africa, Sicily, Italy, Egypt. Commonwealth Relations Office, 1948-; British High Commission, India, 1948-51; Australia, 1953-56; Adviser on Commonwealth and External Affairs to Governor-Gen., Nigeria, 1958-60; British High Commission, Nigeria, 1960; Adviser on Commonwealth and External Affairs to Governor-Gen., Fedn of The W Indies, 1960-61, and to the Governor of Trinidad and Tobago, 1962; British Dep. High Commissioner: Trinidad and Tobago, 1962-63; Rhodesia, 1964-66; High Comr, Sierra Leone, 1966-69. *Recreations:* tennis, fishing, golf. *Address:* Foreign and Commonwealth Office, Downing Street, SW1. *Club:* Royal Over-Seas League.

**FINLAISON, Brig. (retd) Alexander Montagu,** CBE 1957; DSO 1944; *b* 14 March 1904; *s* of Maj.-Gen. J. B. Finlaison, CMG, late Royal Marines, Dedham, Essex; *m* 1935, Monica Mary Louisa, *d* of T. W. Donald, Grendon, Stirling; two *d*. *Educ:* RN Colls Osborne and Dartmouth; RMC Sandhurst. Commissioned Cameronians (Scottish Rifles), 1924; seconded Sudan Defence Force, 1932-38; served War of 1939-45; Greece, Crete, Sicily, Italy; commanded 2nd Wiltshires, 2nd Cameronians, 17 Infantry Brigade, Italy, 1943-44; BGS, HQ Scottish Command, 1954-57; ADC to the Queen, 1955-57; retired, 1957; Commandant, Queen Victoria Sch., Dunblane, 1957-64. *Address:* Gledenholm, Parkgate, Dumfries. *T:* Parkgate 242.

**FINLAY, Bernard,** QC 1967; *b* 4 July 1913. LLB (Hons I); Bar final (Hons I) (certificate of honour); L. J. Holker Scholar. Called to the Bar, Gray's Inn, 1945, Middle Temple, 1966; practises on South-Eastern Circuit. Participates in the Legal Aid Scheme. *Address:* 1 Essex Court, Temple, EC4. *T:* 01-353 5724.

**FINLAY, Maj.-Gen. Charles Hector,** CB 1966; CBE 1958 (OBE 1942); retired; *b* 6 Oct. 1910; 3rd *s* of Frank J. Finlay and Margaret A. Stephenson; *m* 1935, Helen M., *d* of Arthur P.

and Edith M. Adams; two *s. Educ:* Sydney; RMC Duntroon, Australia. Graduated RMC, 1931; Light Horse and Cavalry service, 1931-39; ADC to Gov.-Gen., 1932-35; with 14th/20th Hussars, India, 1935-36. Served War of 1939-45; Western Desert, Syria, New Guinea, Philippines, Borneo; Comd 2/24 Inf. Bn, 1942-43. Exchange duty, Canada, 1946-49; DMI, 1950-53; Comd Aust Component BCFK, 1953-54; attended Imperial Def. Coll., 1955; Aust. Army Rep., London, 1956-57; Quartermaster Gen. AMF, 1957-62; Commandant Royal Military Coll., Duntroon, Australia, 1962-67. *Recreation:* cricket. *Address:* Amungula, via Queanbeyan, NSW, Australia. *Club:* Naval and Military (Melbourne).

**FINLAY, Sir George Panton,** Kt 1955; Senior Puisne Judge, Supreme Court, New Zealand, 1943-58; *b* 7 Aug. 1886; *m* 1912, Mabel Florence (*née* Duder); one *d. Educ:* Thames High Sch., NZ. *Address:* 103 Mountain Road, Epsom, Auckland, New Zealand. *T:* 61.292. *Clubs:* Northern, Auckland (Auckland, NZ).

**FINLAY, Sir Graeme (Bell),** 1st Bt, *cr* 1964; ERD; barrister-at-law; a Deputy Judge of County Courts, since 1967; *b* 29 Oct. 1917; *yr s* of late James Bell Pettigrew Finlay and late Margaret Helena, *d* of John Euston Davies, JP, Portskewett House, nr Chepstow, Mon.; *m* 1953, June Evangeline, *y d* of Col Francis Collingwood Drake, OBE, MC, DL, late 10th Royal Hussars, Harlow, Essex; one *s* two *d. Educ:* Marlborough; University College, London. Served War of 1939-45, 2nd Lieut S. Wales Borderers (suppl. res.), 1939; seconded to 5th Royal Gurkha Rifles (Frontier Force), 1942-45; Martial Law Officer, Upper Sind Force (Hur Rebellion), 1943; Acting Major and DAAG, HQ, NW Army, 1945. Hon. Captain, The Royal Regt of Wales. Called to Bar, Gray's Inn, 1946 (Lord Justice Holker Sen. Exhibr); pupil of Rt Hon. Quintin Hogg, QC, MP; President of Hardwicke Society, 1950-51. Presided over first televised joint debate between Oxford and Cambridge Union Societies, 1950. Contested (C) Ebbw Vale, General Election, 1950; MP (C) Epping Division of Essex, 1951-64; Parliamentary Private Secretary to Rt Hon. Iain Macleod, Minister of Health, 1952-55; Asst Whip, 1957-59; Lord Commissioner of the Treasury, 1959-60; Vice-Chamberlain of the Household, 1960-64. Mem., Parly Delegn to USSR, 1960. *Publications:* frequent contributor to Justice of the Peace and Local Government Review. *Recreations:* whippets, walking, riding and painting. *Heir:* *s* David Ronald James Bell Finlay, *b* 16 Nov. 1963. *Address:* 3 Verulam Buildings, Gray's Inn, WC1. *T:* 01-242 3850; 4 Paper Buildings, Temple, EC4. *T:* 01-353 3366; Hurdle Hall, Cowlinge, nr Newmarket, Suffolk. *T:* Wickhambrook 386. *Club:* Carlton.
*See also J. E. B. Finlay.*

**FINLAY, Ian;** *see* Finlay, W. I. R.

**FINLAY, John Euston Bell,** CB 1959; OBE 1946; TD 1947; consultant on indirect taxation, since 1968; *b* 11 Sept. 1908; *e s* of late James Bell Pettigrew Finlay and late Margaret Helena Finlay, Douro Court, Cheltenham; *m* 1942, Zoë Josephine, *d* of late Brigadier Edward Lees, DSO, Whyte Cottage, Selsey, Sussex; one *s* one *d. Educ:* Marlborough; Geneva Univ. Junior Legal Asst, Board of Customs, 1933; Senior Legal Asst, 1945. Principal, 1948, Asst Secretary, 1949; Under-Sec., 1954-68; Commissioner and Director of Estab. and Org., 1954-65; Comr i/c Internat. and Tariff Divs, Bd of Customs and Excise, 1965-68; retired. Chairman, Finance Cttee, Customs Co-operation Council, Brussels, 1967-68. Governor St Dunstan's Educational Foundation, 1964-. Member Management Cttee, CS Benevolent Fund, 1958-68. Commnd from Inns of Court Regt to 1st (Rifle) Bn The Mon. Regt TA, 1934. Served, 1939-42, with 38 Div., 53 Div. and at Western Command (ADC to GOC-in-C and GSO2) (ops); psc Staff Coll., Camberley, 1942; seconded 1943-45, AIF; served New Guinea, Moluccas, Philippines and Borneo as GSO2 and GSO1 (special ops) (OBE). Hon. Lieut-Colonel FRGS. *Recreation:* gardening. *Address:* 30 Lower Belgrave Street, SW1. *T:* 01-730 1137; Selsey House, 22 Lavant Road, Chichester, Sussex. *T:* Chichester 7369. *Clubs:* Travellers', Royal Automobile.
*See also Sir Graeme Finlay, Bt.*

**FINLAY, Thomas Victor William,** CMG 1948; *b* 14 Nov. 1899; *e s* of Thomas Finlay, Armagh, N. Ireland; *m* 1927, Eileen, *d* of John O'Connor, Solicitor, Crossmaglen, Co. Armagh; two *s. Educ:* King's Hospital, Dublin. Army (Inns of Court OTC), 1918-19; Royal Irish and Royal Ulster Special Constabulary, 1920-25; Nigeria Police, 1925; Commissioner of Police, Nigeria, 1946; retired. King's Police Medal, Colonial Police Medal, Coronation Medal, 1939-45 War Medal. *Recreations:* golf and bridge. *Address:* Arigideen, Rostrevor, Co. Down.

**FINLAY, (William) Ian (Robertson),** CBE 1965; MA; Director of the Royal Scottish Museum, since 1961 (Keeper of the Department of Art and Ethnography, 1955-61); *b* Auckland, New Zealand, 2 Dec. 1906; *s* of William R. Finlay and Annie M. Somerville; *m* 1933, Mary Scott, *d* of late W. Henderson Pringle; two *s* one *d. Educ:* Edinburgh Academy; Edinburgh Univ. Joined staff of Royal Scottish Museum, 1932; Deputy Regional Officer for Scotland, Ministry of Information, 1942-44; Vice-Chairman, Scottish Arts Council, 1967; Secretary, Royal Fine Art Commission for Scotland, 1953-61. Guest of State Department in US, 1960. Freeman of City of London; Member of Livery, Worshipful Company of Goldsmiths, London; Member: Holyrood (Amenity) Trust; British Nat. Cttee of ICOM. *Publications:* Scotland, World To-Day Series, 1945; Scottish Art (for British Council), 1945; Art in Scotland, 1948; Scottish Crafts, 1948; The Scottish Tradition in Silver (Saltire booklet), 1948; Scottish Architecture (for schools), 1951; Treasures in Edinburgh, 1951; Scotland, Young Traveller Series, 1953; A History of Scottish Gold and Silver Work, 1956; Scotland, 1957; The Lothians, 1960; The Highlands, 1963; The Young Robert Louis Stevenson, 1965; The Lowlands, 1967; articles, reviews and broadcast talks on art and general subjects. *Address:* Currie Riggs, Balerno, Midlothian. *T:* Balerno 3249. *Club:* Scottish Arts (Edinburgh).

**FINLAYSON;** *see* Gordon-Finlayson.

**FINLAYSON, Maj.-Gen. Forbes;** *see* Finlayson, Maj.-Gen. W. F.

**FINLAYSON, Maj.-Gen. (William) Forbes,** OBE 1955; Director, Army Dental Service, 1966-70; *b* 12 Oct. 1911; *s* of late Lieut-Colonel W. T. Finlayson, OBE, Army Dental Corps, Edinburgh; *m* Anne McEwen, *d* of Walter Stables Smith, Peebles; one *s* one *d. Educ:* George Heriot's Sch., Edinburgh; Royal College of Surgeons, Edinburgh. LDS 1933. Lieut, Army Dental Corps, 1935; Captain 1936; Major 1945; Lieut-Colonel 1952; Colonel 1959; Maj.-General 1966. Served in: UK, 1935-39, 1945-50, 1955-59, 1963-; Far East, 1939-45 (POW); BAOR, 1950-52, 1959-63; MELF, 1952-55. QHDS, 1966-70. *Recreations:* Rugby football, golf, tennis, walking. *Address:* c/o Glyn, Mills, & Company, Whitehall, SW1.

**FINLETTER, Hon. Thomas K.**; US Ambassador to NATO, 1960-65; *b* 11 Nov. 1893; *m* 1920, Margaret Blaine Damrosch; two *d*. *Educ:* Episcopal Academy, Philadelphia, Pa.; University of Pennsylvania, Philadelphia, Pa. Special Assistant to US Secretary of State, Washington, DC, 1941-44; Consultant to US Delegation to UNO Conference at San Francisco, 1945; Chairman President's Air Policy Commission, Washington, DC, 1947. Partner, Coudert Brothers (lawyers), New York, 1926-41, 1944-48; returned to firm, 1965; retired, 1970. Minister in charge of ECA Mission to the United Kingdom, 1948-49; Secretary of the Air Force, United States, 1950-53. Hon. LLD University of Pennsylvania, 1950; University of Rochester, 1950; Syracuse Univ., 1950; College of St Joseph, SJ, 1951; Rutgers Univ., 1959. *Publications:* Principles of Corporate Reorganization, 1937; Cases of Corporate Reorganization, 1938; Law of Bankruptcy Reorganization, 1939; Can Representative Government Do The Job?, 1945; Power and Policy, 1954; Foreign Policy: The Next Phase, 1958; Interim Report on the American Search for a Substitute for Isolation, 1968. *Recreations:* tennis and gardening. *Address:* 151 East 79 Street, NY City, USA. *Clubs:* Athenæum (London); Knickerbocker, Century Association, (New York); Metropolitan (Washington).

**FINLEY, David Edward**; Director, National Gallery of Art, Washington, DC, 1938-56, retired; Chairman, Commission of Fine Arts, 1950-63; *b* 13 Sept. 1890; *s* of David Edward Finley and Elizabeth Lewis Gist; *m* 1931, Margaret Morton Eustis. *Educ:* University of South Carolina; George Washington Law Sch. AB (University of S. Carolina), 1910; LLB (George Washington Law Sch.), 1913; Doctor of Fine Arts (Yale), 1946; Doctor of Literature (S. Carolina), 1950; LLD George Washington Univ., 1960; Doctorate, Georgetown Univ., 1960; practised law, Philadelphia, 1915-17; European War, 1917-18, 2nd Lieut US Army; Asst Counsel War Finance Corp., 1921-22; Member War Loan Staff, US Treasury, 1922-27; special Asst to Secretary of Treasury, 1927-32; Adviser American delegation, London Financial Conference, 1931; Hon. Counselor American Embassy, London, 1932-33; practised law, Washington, 1933-37; President American Assoc. of Museums, 1945-49; Vice-President International Council of Museums, 1946-49; Chairman US National Cttee on International Co-operation among Museums, 1945-49; Chairman National Trust for Historic Preservation, 1949-62; Vice-Chairman American Commission for Protection and Salvage of Artistic and Historic Monuments in War Areas, 1943-46; Trustee, Corcoran Gallery of Art, 1957-; member Smithsonian Art Commission, Assoc. of Art Museum Directors. National Portrait Gallery Commission, 1963. Theodore Roosevelt Distinguished Service Medal for outstanding service by a private citizen, 1957; Joseph Henry Medal, Smithsonian Institute, 1967. *Address:* 3318 O Street, Washington, DC 20007, USA. *Clubs:* Metropolitan, Alibi, Chevy Chase (Washington, DC); Century (New York, NY).

**FINLEY, Michael John**; Chief Editorial Executive, Kent Messenger Group, since 1969; *b* 22 Sept. 1932; *s* of late Walter Finley and of Grace Marie Butler; *m* 1955, Sheila Elizabeth Cole; four *s*. *Educ:* King Edward VII Sch., Sheffield. Reporter and Sub-Editor, 1951-56, News Editor, 1960-63, Asst Editor, 1963-64, Editor, 1964-69, Sheffield Morning Telegraph (formerly Sheffield Telegraph); Daily Herald, Manchester, 1956-59. National Councillor, Guild of British Newspaper Editors, Editor Guild Jl. Mem., BBC Region Adv. Council, 1967-. Broadcasts on radio and TV. *Publication:* contrib. Advertising and the Community, 1968. *Recreations:* golf, sailing, squash, watching Association football. *Address:* c/o Kent Messenger, 123 Week Street, Maidstone, Kent. *Clubs:* Wig and Pen; Maidstone (Maidstone).

**FINLEY, Dr Moses I.**; Professor of Ancient History, Cambridge University, since 1970; Fellow of Jesus College, since 1957; *b* 20 May 1912; became British subject, 1962; *m* 1932, Mary F. Thiers; no *c*. *Educ:* Syracuse Univ., USA; Columbia Univ., USA. BA Syracuse 1927 (*magna cum laude*) (*Phi Beta Kappa*); MA Columbia, 1929 and PhD 1950. Held various teaching, research, editorial and consulting posts with: Encyclopaedia of the Social Sciences, 1930-33; Inst. of Social Research (then affiliated with Columbia Univ.), 1937-39; City Coll. of New York, 1934-42; Columbia Univ., 1933-34, 1948-54; exec. posts with war relief agencies, 1942-47. Fellow in History, Columbia Univ., 1934-35; Fellow, Amer. Council of Learned Socs, 1948; Lectr, then Asst Prof. of History, Newark Colls of Rutgers Univ., 1948-52; Faculty Fellow, Fund for the Advancement of Educn, 1951-52. Lectr in Classics, Cambridge Univ., 1955-64; Reader in Ancient, Social and Economic History, Cambridge University, 1964-70; Librarian, Jesus Coll., 1960-64; Chm., Faculty Bd of Classics, Cambridge Univ. 1967-69. Sec., Cambridge Philological Soc., 1959-65; Convener of Ancient Hist. section, Internat. Economic Hist. Conf., Aix-en-Provence, 1962, Munich, 1965; Chm., sub-cttee on Ancient Hist., Jt Assoc. of Classical Teachers, 1964-. Editor: Views and Controversies in Classical Antiquity, 1960-; Ancient Culture and Society, 1969-. *Publications:* Studies in Land and Credit in Ancient Athens, 1952; The World of Odysseus, 1954; The Greek Historians (ed), 1958; Slavery in Classical Antiquity (ed), 1960; The Ancient Greeks, 1963; Josephus (ed), 1965; Aspects of Antiquity, 1968; Ancient Sicily, 1968; Early Greece: the Bronze and Archaic Ages, 1970; articles and reviews in classical, historical and legal jls, and in literary weeklies and monthlies in Britain and the US. *Recreations:* conversation, listening to music, travel. *Address:* 12 Adams Road, Cambridge. *T:* Cambridge 57784, (Jesus College) 56360.

**FINN, Donovan Bartley**, CMG 1946; FRSC, FCIC, Director of Fisheries, Food and Agriculture Organization of the United Nations, 1946-64, retired; *b* Hendon, 1 March 1900; *s* of Edwin Bartley Finn and Eleanor Penton; *m* 1946, Florence Stewart Daly. *Educ:* University of Manitoba (BSc, MSc); Cambridge Univ. (PhD). Director Fisheries Expt. Station, Prince Rupert, BC, of the Fisheries Research Board of Canada, 1925; Director Fisheries Expt. Station, Halifax, NS, of Fisheries Research Board of Canada, 1934; Chairman Salt Fish Board of Canada, 1939; Deputy Minister of Fisheries, Dominion of Canada, 1940-46; Member Economic Advisory Cttee, Dominion of Canada, 1941; Chairman Food Requirements Cttee, 1943-46. Represented Canada as delegate and adviser at various international bodies and conferences during war with respect to fisheries and food matters. *Publications:* scientific journals, on physics and chemistry of food proteins. *Recreations:* mountaineering, music. *Address:* Castello di Sterpeto, Sterpeto d'Assisi,

Perugia, Italy. *Clubs:* Rideau, University (Ottawa).

**FINNEMORE, Sir Donald Leslie,** Kt 1947; Judge of High Court (Queen's Bench Division), 1948-64, retired (Probate, Divorce, and Admiralty, 1947-48); Chairman Warwickshire Quarter Sessions since 1950; JP Warwickshire; *b* 13 June 1889; *s* of late William and Kate Finnemore, and *g s* of late J. S. Wright, MP, Birmingham; unmarried. *Educ:* King Edward's Sch.; Pembroke Coll., Oxford (Scholar). First Class in Jurisprudence and Proxime Accessit for Vinerian Law Scholarship at Oxford; called by Inner Temple (Prize for Constitutional Law and Legal History) in 1914; Midland Circuit; served in France as BRCS Officer, 1916-19; Hon. Legal Adviser to Midland Regional Commissioner for Civil Defence, 1940-45; County Court Judge (North Staffs and Birmingham), 1940-44, (Wolverhampton, etc.), 1944-46; (Birmingham), 1946-47; Chairman Midland Conscientious Objectors Tribunal, 1940-47; Member of Matrimonial (Trial in Provinces) Cttee, 1942-43; Member, Criminal Law Revision Cttee, 1965-; contested (L) Sparkbrook, 1923, and Stourbridge, 1929, 1931, 1935; Life Governor of Birmingham Univ., 1945 (Hon. LLD 1966); Governor King Edward's Sch., 1946; Hon. Fellow Pembroke Coll., 1948; President Baptist Union of Great Britain, 1966-67. *Publication:* Boys!, 1925. *Recreations:* travel and The Boys' Brigade. *Address:* 2 Charles Road, Handsworth, Birmingham 20. *Club:* Reform.

**FINNEY, Albert;** actor, stage and film; film director; *m* 1957, Jane Wenham, actress (marr. diss.); one *s*; *m* 1970, Anouk Aimée. First London appearance in The Party, New, 1958; Cassio in Othello, and Lysander, Stratford-on-Avon, 1959; subsequently in: The Lily White Boys, Royal Court, 1960; Billy Liar, Cambridge Theatre, 1960; Luther, in Luther: Royal Court Theatre and Phoenix Theatre, 1961-62; New York, 1963; Armstrong in Armstrong's Last Goodnight; Miss Julie and Black Comedy, Chichester, 1965, Old Vic, 1966; Love for Love, National Theatre, 1965; Much Ado About Nothing, National Theatre, 1965; A Flea in Her Ear, National Theatre, 1966; A Day in the Death of Joe Egg, NY, 1968. Films include: Saturday Night and Sunday Morning; Tom Jones; Night Must Fall; Two for the Road; Charlie Bubbles (also Director); Scrooge. Hon. LittD (Sussex), 1965. Holds stage and film awards. *Address:* London International, 11 Hanover Street, W1.

**FINNEY, Prof. David John,** FRS 1955; FRSE; MA, ScD (Cantab); Professor of Statistics, University of Edinburgh, since 1966; Director Agricultural Research Council Unit of Statistics; *b* Latchford, Warrington, 3 Jan. 1917; *e s* of late Robert G. S. Finney and of Bessie E. Whitlow; *m* 1950, Mary Elizabeth Connolly; one *s* two *d*. *Educ:* Lymm and Manchester Grammar Schools; Clare Coll., Cambridge. Asst Statistician, Rothamsted Experimental Station, 1939-45; Lecturer in the Design and Analysis of Scientific Experiment, University of Oxford, 1945-54; Reader in Statistics, University of Aberdeen, 1954-63, Professor, 1963-66. Consultant in Statistics, Nat. Foundation for Educational Research, 1951-57; United Nations FAO expert attached to Indian Council of Agricultural Research, 1952-53. Scientific Consultant, Cotton Research Corporation, 1959-. Chm., Computer Bd for Univs and Research Councils, 1970- (Mem., 1966-); Member: Adverse Reactions Sub-Cttee, Cttee on Safety of Drugs, 1963-; Visiting Prof. of Biomathematics, Harvard Univ., 1962-63; President of Biometric Society, 1964-65 (Vice-President, 1963, 1966); Fellow: Royal Statistical Society; American Statistical Assoc.; Member: International Statistical Institute; FAO Statistics Advisory Cttee, 1967-; Hon. Fellow Eugenics Society; Hon. Mem., Société Adolphe Quetelet. Weldon Memorial Prize, 1956. Dr *hc*, Faculté des Sciences Agronomiques de l'Etat à Gembloux, Belgium. *Publications:* Probit Analysis; A Statistical Treatment of the Sigmoid Response Curve, 1947 (2nd edn 1952); Biological Standardization (with J. H. Burn, L. G. Goodwin), 1950; Statistical Method in Biological Assay, 1952 (2nd edn 1964); An Introduction to Statistical Science in Agriculture, 1953 (3rd edn 1964); Experimental Design and its Statistical Basis, 1955; Tecnica y Teoria en el diseño de Experimentos, 1957; An Introduction to the Theory of Experimental Design, 1960; Statistics for Mathematicians: An Introduction, 1968. Numerous papers in statistical and biological journals. *Recreations:* travel (active), music (passive), and the 3 R's. *Address:* Statistics Department, University EH10 of Edinburgh, 21 Buccleuch Place, Edinburgh EH8 9LN. *T:* 031-667 1011; 43 Cluny Drive, Edinburgh EH10 6DU. *T:* 031-447 2332.

**FINNISTON, Harold Montague,** BSc, PhD; FRS 1969; Deputy Chairman (Technical), British Steel Corporation, since 1967; *b* 15 Aug. 1912; *s* of late Robert and Esther Finniston; *m* 1936, Miriam Singer; one *s* one *d*. *Educ:* Allan Glen's Sch., Glasgow; Glasgow Univ.; Royal College of Science and Technology, Glasgow. Lecturer in Metallurgy Royal College of Science and Technology, 1933-35; Metallurgist, Stewart & Lloyds, 1935-37; Chief Research Officer, Scottish Coke Research Cttee, 1937-40; Metallurgist, RN Scientific Service, 1940-46; seconded to Ministry of Supply, Chalk River, Canada, 1946-47; Chief Metallurgist, UKAEA, Harwell, 1948-58. Man. Director, International Research and Development Co., and Technical Director, C. A. Parsons & Co. Ltd, 1959-67; Chairman: Cryosystems Ltd; System Computors Ltd; Electronics Association of the North-East; Director, C. A. Parsons & Co. Ltd; Member: Board of Thorn-Parsons Co. Ltd and Northern Economic Planning Council, 1963-67; Council British Non-Ferrous Metals Research Assoc. (Vice-Chm. 1969-; Chm. Research Board), 1965-; NRDC, 1963-; Advisory Council, R&D, Ministry of Power, 1966-; Ministry of Technology SRC, University Science and Technology Board, 1965-67; NPL Steering Cttee, 1966-68; Exec. Cttee, PEP, 1968-; Iron and Steel Adv. Cttee, 1969-; Academic Adv. Cttee, Cranfield Inst. of Technology, 1970-; Pres., Inst. of Metals, 1967-68; Vice-Pres., Iron and Steel Inst., 1968-; Gen. Sec., British Assoc. for Advancement of Science, 1970-. Lectures: Dunn Meml, 1968; 19th Hatfield Meml, 1968; 18th Coal Science, BCURA, 1969; Edward Williams, 1970; Andrew Laing, 1970. Vis. Fellow, Univ. of Lancaster, 1970-. ARTC; FIM; FInstP. Hon. DSc, Strathclyde; Hon. DUniv, Surrey, 1969. *Publications:* Editor: Metallurgy of the Rare Metals; Progress in Nuclear Energy; Structural Characteristics of Materials; Various scientific papers. *Recreations:* reading, writing and spectator interest in sport. *Address:* Flat 72, 33 Prince Albert Road, St John's Wood, NW8. *T:* 01-722 8197. *Club:* Athenæum.

**FINSBERG, Geoffrey,** MBE 1959; MP (C) Hampstead since 1970; JP; Controller of Personnel, Great Universal Stores, since 1968; *b* 13 June 1926; *o s* of Monte Finsberg, MC, and May Finsberg (*née* Grossman); *m* 1969,

Pamela Benbow Noel. *Educ:* City of London Sch. National Chm., Young Conservatives, 1954-57; Member: Nat. Exec. Cttee, Conservative Party, 1954-70; Greater London Area Exec., Conservative Party, 1949-. Borough Councillor: Hampstead, 1949-65; Camden, 1964- (Leader, 1968-70). Director, London Trustee Savings Bank, 1963-. Dep. Chm., Assoc. of Municipal Corporations, 1969-; Mem., Post Office Users Nat. Council, 1970-. JP (Inner London) 1962-. *Recreations:* bridge, reading, walking. *Address:* 80 Westbere Road, NW2. *T:* 01-435 5320. *Club:* Carlton.

**FIRBANK, Maj.-Gen. Cecil Llewellyn,** CB 1953; CBE 1951; DSO 1944 and Bar 1945; DL (Somerset); Director of Civil Defence for Wales since 1960; *b* 18 March 1903; *m* 1st, 1934, Audrey Hobhouse (marr. diss. 1952); one *s*; 2nd, 1952, Marye Brenda Fleetwood-Wilson. *Educ:* Cheltenham Coll.; RMC Sandhurst. Gazetted to 1st Somerset LI, 1924; served Egypt, 1926-29; seconded to Royal West African Frontier Force, 1929-34; served with Somerset LI, 1934-42; on active service, North West Europe, 1944-45; Comd 71 Infantry Bde, 1945-46; Staff Coll., 1947-48; Commandant School of Infantry, Warminster, 1948-51; GOC SW District and 43rd Wessex Division (TA), 1951-54; Director of Infantry, War Office, 1955-58; retired pay, 1959. Colonel Commandant, Aden Protectorate Levies, 1958; Colonel, Somerset and Cornwall Light Infantry, 1963-68; Dep. Colonel, The Light Infantry (Somerset and Cornwall), 1968-70. Hon. Colonel: 4/5th Somerset LI (TA), 1955-60; North Somerset Yeomanry (44th Royal Tank Regt), 1959-64. *Recreations:* cricket, field sports. *Address:* The Owls, Charlton Horethorne, near Sherborne, Dorset. *T:* Corton Denham 279. *Club:* Army and Navy.

**FIREBRACE, Comdr Sir Aylmer Newton George,** Kt 1945; CBE 1941; RN (retired); *b* 17 June 1886; *s* of Lt-Col George Firebrace, Royal Artillery; *m* 1912, Dorothy Vernon (*d* 1952), *d* of Douglas Grey; one *s* one *d*. *Educ:* HMS Britannia. Commander, 1917; Principal Officer, London Fire Brigade, 1919; Chief Officer of London Fire Brigade, 1938; Regional Fire Officer, London Region, 1939; Chief of the Fire Staff and Inspector-in-Chief of the Fire Services, 1941-47; retired 1947. King's Police and Fire Brigades Medal, 1936; Bronze Medal, Royal Humane Society, 1918; Commander of Order of St Olav (Norway), 1947. *Publications:* Fire Service Memories, 1948; If thou criest after Knowledge, 1952; Light on the Gospel of John, 1957; the Revelation to John, 1963. *Address:* 17 Lincoln House, Basil Street, SW3. *T:* 01-584 2826.

**FIRTH, Maj.-Gen. Charles Edward Anson,** CB 1951; CBE 1945; DSO 1943; *b* 9 Oct. 1902; *s* of late Major E. W. A. Firth, Indian Army; *m* 1933, Mary Kathleen, *d* of late Commander W. St J. Fraser, RN; two *s*. *Educ:* Wellington Coll., Berks; RMC Sandhurst. 2nd Lieut The Gloucestershire Regt, 1923; Lieut, 1925; Captain, 1935; Staff Coll., 1936-37; War Office, 1938-40; Major, 1940; Middle East: Temp. Lieut-Colonel; AA and QMG 50 Div., 1941-42; OC 1st Royal Sussex Regt in Middle East, 1942-43; Temp. Brigadier, 4 Indian Infantry Bde, 1943; Comd 167 Infantry Bde, 1943-44 (Italy); Comd 21 Tank Bde, 1944 (N. Africa); Comd 2 Infantry Bde, 1944 (Italy); Comdr and Dep. Comdr British Military Mission to Greece, 1944-45. Colonel 1946; War Office, 1946-48; Comd Area Troops, Berlin (British Sector), 1948-50; Maj.-General, 1950; Comd East Anglian Dist, 1950; GOC Salisbury Plain Dist, 1951-53; Director of Personal Services, War Office, 1953-56. Colonel The Gloucestershire Regt, 1954-64; first Colonel Comdt, Military Provost Staff Corps, 1956-61. Governor, Dauntsey's Sch., 1961- (Vice-Chairman, 1965-). Grand Commander Order of the Phoenix (Greek), 1946. *Recreations:* tennis, golf, fishing. *Address:* Crofton Lodge, Burbage, Marlborough, Wilts. *T:* Great Bedwyn 270. *Club:* Army and Navy.

**FIRTH, Edward Michael Tyndall,** CB 1951; *b* 17 Feb. 1903; *s* of Edward H. Firth, Sheffield; *m* 1929, Eileen Marie, *d* of Edward Newman, Hove; two *s*. *Educ:* King Edward VII Sch., Sheffield; University College, Oxford. Classical Scholar, 1922-26. Inland Revenue, 1926; Ministry of Health, 1945; Under Secretary, 1947-58; Registrar General, 1958-63. *Address:* 65 Middle Way, Oxford. *Club:* Athenæum.

**FIRTH, Raymond William,** MA; PhD; FBA; Professor of Anthropology, University of London, 1944-68, now Emeritus; *b* 25 March 1901; *s* of Wesley Hugh Bourne Firth and Marie Elizabeth Jane Cartmill; *m* 1936, Rosemary, *d* of late Sir Gilbert Upcott, KCB; one *s*. *Educ:* Auckland Grammar Sch.; Auckland University College; London School of Economics. Anthropological research in British Solomon Islands, including one year on Tikopia, 1928-29; Lecturer in Anthropology, University of Sydney, 1930-31; Acting Professor of Anthropology, University of Sydney, 1931-32; Lecturer in Anthropology, London School of Economics, 1932-35; Reader, 1935-44; Hon. Secretary Royal Anthropological Institute, 1936-39 (President 1953-55); Research in peasant economics and anthropology in Malaya, as Leverhulme Research Fellow, 1939-40; served with Naval Intelligence Division, Admiralty, 1941-44; Secretary of Colonial Social Science Research Council, Colonial Office, 1944-45; Fellow, Center for Advanced Study in the Behavioral Sciences, Stanford, 1958-59; Prof. of Pacific Anthropology, Univ. of Hawaii, 1968-69. Foreign Hon. Member American Academy of Arts and Sciences, 1963; Hon. Member Royal Society, NZ, 1964; Foreign Member: American Philosophical Society, 1965; Royal Danish Academy of Sciences and Letters, 1966. Social research surveys: W Africa, 1945; Malaya, 1947; New Guinea, 1951; Tikopia, 1952, 1966; Malaya, 1963. Hon. degrees: DPh Oslo, 1965; LLD Michigan, 1967; LittD East Anglia, 1968, ANU, 1969; DHumLett Chicago, 1968; 1968; PSc British Columbia 1970. *Publications:* The Kauri Gum Industry, 1924; Primitive Economics of the New Zealand Maori, 1929; Art and Life In New Guinea, 1936; We, The Tikopia: A Sociological Study of Kinship in Primitive Polynesia, 1936; Human Types, 1938; Primitive Polynesian Economy, 1939; The Work of the Gods in Tikopia, 1940 (new edn, 1967); Malay Fishermen: Their Peasant Economy, 1946 (enlarged edn, 1966); Elements of Social Organization, 1951; Two Studies of Kinship in London (ed.), 1956; Man and Culture: An Evaluation of the Work of Malinowski (ed.), 1957; Economics of the New Zealand Maori, 1959; Social Change in Tikopia, 1959; History and Traditions of Tikopia, 1961; Essays on Social Organization and Values, 1964; Tikopia Ritual and Belief, 1967; Rank and Religion in Tikopia, 1970. *Recreation:* viewing Romanesque art. *Address:* 33 Southwood Avenue, N6. *Club:* Athenæum.

**FISCHER, Annie;** Hungarian Pianist; *b* Budapest, 1914. *Educ:* Franz Liszt Landemusikhochschule, Budapest. Studied under Arnold Szekule and Ernst von Dohnanyi. Concert Début, Budapest, at age of eight (performed Beethoven's C Major Concerto), 1922; began international career as a concert pianist, Zurich, 1926; toured and played in most European Music centres, 1926-39. Concert pianist, Sweden, during War of 1939-45. Returned to Hungary after War and has made concert tours to all parts of the world. Awarded 1st prize, Internat. Liszt Competition, Budapest, 1933; Kossuth Prizes 1949, 1955, 1965. *Address:* Szent Istvan Ter. 14, Budapest XIII, Hungary.

**FISCHER, John;** Contributing Editor, Harper's Magazine; Editor-in-Chief, 1953-67; *b* 21 April 1910; *s* of John Simpson and Georgie Caperton Fischer; *m* 1936, Elizabeth Wilson; two *d*. *Educ:* Oklahoma Univ.; Oxford, England (Rhodes Scholar, 1933 and 1934-35). Reporter, Daily Oklahoman, 1932-33; US Dept of Agriculture, 1936; Washington Correspondent for Associated Press, 1937; Board of Economic Warfare, Intelligence Division, 1939; in India as Chief of Economic Intelligence, and Lend-lease, for Foreign Econ. Admin., 1943; Assoc. Editor, Harper's Magazine, 1944-47; Editor-in-Chief, General Book Dept of Harper & Row, Publishers, Inc.; leave of absence from Harper's to join Relief and Rehabilitation mission to the Ukraine, 1946. Member, National Advisory Commn on Rural Poverty. Trustee, Brookings Institution, National Educational Television Network. Regents Prof., Univ. of Calif, 1969; Vis. Fellow, Yale Univ. Hon. Doctor: Kenyon Coll., 1953; Bucknell Univ., 1954; University of Massachusetts, 1956. *Publications:* Why They Behave Like Russians, 1947 (English title: Scared Men in the Kremlin); Master Plan USA, 1951; The Stupidity Problem, 1964; articles in Harper's, Life, New Yorker, Reader's Digest. *Recreations:* gardening, music, carpentry, travel. *Address:* Two, Park Avenue, New York, NY 10016, USA. *Clubs:* Century Association, Council on Foreign Relations, American Association of Rhodes Scholars (New York City).

**FISCHER-DIESKAU, Dietrich;** First Baritone of the Städtische Oper, Berlin, since 1948; Member of Vienna State Opera since 1957; *b* Berlin, 28 May 1925; *s* of Dr Albert Fischer-Dieskau; *m* 1949, Irmgard Poppen (*d* 1963); three *s*; *m* 1965, Ruth Leuwerik; *m* 1969, Kristina Pugell. *Educ:* High Sch., Berlin; Music Academy, Berlin. Extensive Concert Tours of Europe and USA; Permanent soloist in Festivals at Edinburgh, Salzburg, Bayreuth, Vienna, Berlin, Munich, Holland, Luzern, Prades, etc. Opera roles include: Wolfram, Jochanaan, Almaviva, Marquis Posa, Don Giovanni, Falstaff, Mandryka, Wozzeck, Danton, Macbeth. Many recordings. Member of Academy of Arts, Berlin, Kunstpreis der Stadt Berlin, 1950; Internationaler Schallplattenpreis, 1955, 1957, 1958, 1960, 1961; Orfeo d'oro, 1955 and 1966; Bayerischer Kammersänger, 1959; Edison Prize, 1961, 1964, 1966, 1970; Naras Award, USA, 1962; Ehrenmitgliedschaft Wiener Konzerthausgesellschaft, 1962; Mozart-Medaille, Wien, 1963; Berliner Kammersänger, 1963. Distinguished Services Medal (1st Class) of the German Federal Republic.

**FISH, Sir (Eric) Wilfred,** Kt 1954; CBE 1947; MD; DSc; FDSRCS; FRCS; Hon. Consulting Dental Surgeon to: St Mary's Hospital, Paddington; Royal Dental Hospital; late Hon. Director Department of Dental Science, Royal College of Surgeons; *b* 30 Jan. 1894; *s* of Rev. George M. C. Fish; *m* 1916, Hilda Gertrude, *e d* of Rev. S. J. Russell; one *s* one *d*; *m* 1950, Myfanwy Hazel Bruce Hodge (*née* Dunlop). *Educ:* Kingswood; Owen's Coll., Manchester; University College, London. LDS Manchester 1914; ChB 1916; Dumville Surgical Prizeman, 1916; MD 1924; DSc London 1933; FDSRCS England 1947; FRCS 1961. Late Captain RAMC (SR); Temp. Surgical Specialist, Bombay Brigade; late Hon. Research Associate in Physiology, University College, London; Hon. Fellow Royal Society of Medicine, 1955; Hon. Member: British Dental Assoc., 1951; Dental Associations of: Vienna, 1931; Spain, 1932; Australia, 1938; Netherlands, 1939; Sweden, 1950; American Academy of Dentistry, 1957. Late Member Physiological Society. postgraduate lecturer, by invitation, to Dental Board of Victoria and South Australia, 1935. President XIth International Dental Congress, London, 1952; Chairman Dental Board, UK, 1944-56; Dean, Faculty of Dental Surgery, RCS, 1956-59; Hon. Consulting Dental Surgeon to the Army, 1959-64; President, General Dental Council, 1956-64; Vice-Pres. d'Honneur, Internat. Dental Fedn. Hon. degrees: DDSc Melbourne, 1935; HDD Glasgow, 1955; DDSc Dunelm, 1959; ScD Trinity Coll., Dublin, 1960; FDSRCS Edinburgh, 1962; FFD, RCSI 1964; FDSRCP & S. Glasgow, 1967. John Tomes Prizeman, RCS, 1933; Howard Mummery Prizeman (1st award), 1933; Colyer Gold Medal, RCS, 1962; Wilfred Fish Research Fellowship, founded RCS, 1970. *Publications:* Principles of Full Denture Prosthesis; Experimental Investigation of the Enamel Dentine and Dental Pulp; Parodontal Disease; Surgical Pathology of the Mouth; papers in Proc. Royal Society, etc. *Recreations:* formerly stalking, now gardening. *Address:* Hurst Lodge, Sandgate Lane, Storrington, Sussex.

**FISH, Sir Wilfred;** *see* Fish, Sir Eric W.

**FISHENDEN, Margaret White,** DSc, FInstP; Formerly Reader in Applied Heat at Imperial College (University of London), (Mechanical Engineering Department); *y d* of late R. W. White; one *s*. *Educ:* University of Manchester, 1st class Honours in Physics, 1909; Higginbottom Scholar, 1907, Graduate Scholar, 1909; Beyer Fellow, 1910-11; Lecturer, University of Manchester, 1910-15; in charge of research work for Air Pollution Advisory Board of the Manchester Corporation, 1916-22; research work on Atmospheric Conditions, Humidity and Ventilation in Spinning Mills and Weaving Sheds, Domestic Heating, Heat Transfer, etc. *Publications:* House Heating, 1925; The Calculation of Heat Transmission, 1932; An Introduction to Heat Transfer, 1950; scientific and technical papers. *Recreations:* gardening, hunting rare wild flowers. *Address:* 2 Cleevemede House, Cleeve Road, Goring, Reading.

**FISHER,** family name of **Barons Fisher** and **Fisher of Lambeth.**

**FISHER,** 3rd Baron, *cr* 1909, of Kilverstone; **John Vavasseur Fisher,** DSC 1944; DL; *b* 24 July 1921; *s* of 2nd Baron and Jane (*d* 1955), *d* of Randal Morgan, Philadelphia, USA; *S* father, 1955; *m* 1st, 1949, Elizabeth Ann Penelope (marr. diss. 1969), *yr d* of Herbert P. Holt, *qv*; two *s* two *d*; 2nd, 1970, Hon. Mrs Rosamund Anne Fairbairn. *Educ:* Stowe; Trinity Coll., Cambridge. Mem., Eastern Gas Bd, 1962-. DL Norfolk, 1968. *Heir: s* Hon. Patrick Vavasseur Fisher, *b* 14 June 1953. *Address:* Kilverstone Hall, Thetford, Norfolk. *T:* Thetford 2222. *Clubs:* Buck's, RNVR.
*See also Baron Clifford of Chudleigh.*

**FISHER OF LAMBETH,** Baron *cr* 1961, of Lambeth (Life Peer); **Most Rev. and Rt. Hon. Geoffrey Francis Fisher;** PC 1939; GCVO *cr*

1953; Royal Victorian Chain, 1949; Hon. DD, LLD, and DCL; MA; *b* 5 May 1887; *y s* of late Rev. H. Fisher, Rector of Higham-on-the-Hill, Nuneaton; *m* 1917, Rosamond Chevallier, *d* of late Rev. A. F. E. Forman, and *g d* of Dr S. A. Pears, once Headmaster of Repton; six *s*. *Educ:* Marlborough Coll., Exeter Coll., Oxford (open scholar); First Class Honours in Moderations, 1908; Lit Hum 1910; Theology, 1911; Liddon Scholarship, 1911; Wells Theological Coll., 1911. Deacon, 1912; Priest, 1913. Hon. Fellow, Exeter Coll., Oxford, 1939; Asst Master, Marlborough Coll., 1911-14; Headmaster of Repton Sch., 1914-32; Bishop of Chester, 1932-39; Bishop of London, 1939-45; Archbishop of Canterbury, 1945-61. Dean of the Chapels Royal, 1939-45; Prelate of Order of British Empire, 1939-45; Prelate, 1946, and Bailiff Grand Cross, 1947, of Order of S John of Jerusalem; President of the World Council of Churches, 1946-54. Select Preacher, Oxford Univ., 1925-27, Cambridge Univ., 1937 and 1940; Freeman of Cities of London and Canterbury, 1952; of Croydon, 1961. Hon. Doctor of Laws (Universities of Pennsylvania and Columbia, 1946, Yale and British Columbia, 1954); Hon. DD; Oxford, 1933; Cambridge and Princeton, 1946, Edinburgh, 1953; Montreal, 1962; TCD 1963; Hon LLD: Pennsylvania and Columbia, 1946; London 1948; Manchester, 1950; Yale and BC, 1954; Rikkyo, Japan, 1959; Yonsel, Korea, 1959; Hon. DCL (Roman Catholic) University of the Assumption, Windsor, Canada; Hon. STD, Northwestern, Evanston, 1954; Doctor of Theology, General Theological Seminary, New York, 1957. Grand Cross of Greek Order of the Redeemer, 1947; Grand Cross of St Olav (Norway), 1947; Czechoslovak Order of the White Lion (II Class), 1948. *Address:* Trent Rectory, Sherborne, Dorset. *T:* Marston Magna 441.

*See also Hon. Sir H. A. P. and Hon. F. F. Fisher.*

**FISHER, Alan Wainwright;** General Secretary, National Union of Public Employees, since 1968; Member: TUC General Council, since 1968; BOAC, since 1970; *b* 20 June 1922; *s* of Thomas Wainwright Fisher and Ethel Agnes Fisher; *m* 1958, Joyce Tinniswood; two *s* one *d*. *Educ:* Primary and Secondary Schools in Birmingham. National Union of Public Employees: Junior Clerk, 1939; Midlands Divisional Officer, 1953; Asst General Secretary, 1962. Member: Nat. Jt Council for Local Authorities, Services, 1956-; Ancillary Staffs Council (Sec. 1965-) and Gen. Council (Chm. 1966-69) of Whitley Councils for Health Services; Potato Marketing Bd, 1969-70; Bd, Centre for Educnl Develt Overseas (Governor 1970-). *Recreation:* seismography. *Address:* 114 Riefield Road, Eltham, SE9. *T:* 01-850 4363.

**FISHER, Allan George Barnard;** *b* Christchurch, New Zealand, 1895; *m* Airini Pope; one *s* one *d*. *Educ:* University of Melbourne; London School of Economics, University of Otago, Dunedin, 1924-35; Professor of Economics, University of Western Australia, 1936-37; Price Professor of International Economics, RIIA, 1938-46; (temporary appointment) Economist to Bank of New South Wales, Sydney, 1934; (temporary appointment) Counsellor, NZ Legation, Washington, 1944. Chief Editor, International Monetary Fund, retired 1960. *Publications:* Some Problems of Wages and their Regulation in Great Britain since 1918, 1926; Moscow Impressions, 1932; The Clash of Progress and Security, 1935; World Economic Affairs (in Survey of International Affairs, 1937, 1938); Economic Progress and Social Security, 1945; International Implications of Full Employment in Great Britain, 1946; (with H. S. Fisher) Slavery and Muslim Society in Africa, 1970. *Address:* Kempsford House, Brize Norton, Oxon.

**FISHER, Anne;** *see* Fisher, Phyllis Anne.

**FISHER, Brig. Arthur Francis,** CBE 1945; DSO 1943; Farmer; *b* 11 July 1899; *s* of Major J. F. Fisher, RA, and Eleanor Mary (*née* Stanier); *m* 1926, Margaret Charlotte, *d* of General Sir George Kirkpatrick, KCB, KCSI; two *s* one *d*. *Educ:* Wellington Coll.; RMA Woolwich. Commissioned 2nd Lieut, RA, 1918; served European War, 1914-18 (despatches); transferred as Captain 12 R. Lancers, 1929; Staff Coll., 1935-36; Major, 1938; War Office, GSO2 1938; GSO1 1939; Comdg E. Riding Yeomanry, 1940-41; Brigadier 1941; Comdg various Brigades Home and Middle East; Acting Maj.-General. 1942; Brigadier RAC, 2nd Army, 1943-44; Dep. Director RAC, War Office, 1944-46; Ministry of Supply, 1946-52. Medal of Freedom with Bronze Palm (USA), 1945. *Recreation:* shooting. *Address:* Coopers Farm, Winterslow, Salisbury, Wilts. *T:* Winterslow 297. *Club:* Cavalry.

*See also R. A. Sykes.*

**FISHER, Lieut-General Sir Bertie Drew,** KCB, *cr* 1938 (CB 1929), CMG 1919; DSO 1915; Colonel 17th-21st Lancers, 1938-47; *b* 13 July 1878; *m* 1918, Marjorie Frances, *d* of Lady Burdett, Foremarke Hall, Derbyshire; two *s*. *Educ:* Marlborough; New Coll., Oxford. Entered Army, 1900; Commissioned 17th Lancers, 1900; Captain, 1905; Major, 1914; Bt Lieut-Colonel 1916, Lieut-Colonel 1919; Colonel 1920; Maj.-General 1931; Lt-Gen. 1937; served South African War, 1900-02 (Queen's Medal 3 clasps, King's Medal 2 clasps); GSO3 (Military Aeronautics Dept), 1913-14. European War, 1914-18 (despatches four times, twice wounded, CMG, DSO and Bar, Bt Lieut-Colonel, Croix d'Officier Legion of Honour); ADC to the King, 1926-31; commanded 2nd Cavalry Brigade, 1923-27; Commandant Senior Officers' Sch., 1927-30; Brigadier, General Staff, Aldershot Command, 1930-31; Director of Recruiting and Organisation, War Office, 1932-34; Commadant RMC, Sandhurst, 1934-37; retired pay, 1938; GOC-in-Chief, Southern Command, Salisbury, 1939-40. *Address:* Hartley House, Turgis Green, Basingstoke, Hants. *T:* Turgis Green 277. *Club:* Cavalry.

**FISHER, Prof. Charles Alfred,** MA Cantab; Professor of Geography, School of Oriental and African Studies, University of London, since Oct. 1964; *b* 23 April 1916; *er s* of Rev. Charles Fisher and Bertha Fisher (*née* Anderson); *m* 1945, Irene Mary Clarke, ARCM; GRSM; one *s* one *d*. *Educ:* Strand Sch., London; St Catharine's Coll., Cambridge (Exhibr 1935, Scholar 1938, Junior Librarian 1938-40). Geog. Tripos, Parts I and II (First Class Hons), 1937, 1938; University Bartle Frere Exhirb, 1938, 1939; MA 1942. Served War of 1939-45 with RE Malaya Comd HQ. Asst Lecturer in Geography, University College of Leicester, 1946; Lecturer in Geography, University College of Wales, Aberystwyth, 1946-49; Senior Research Officer, Institute of Colonial Studies, Oxford, 1950-51; Lecturer in Geography, University (Coll.) of Leicester, 1951-58, Reader, 1958-59; Professor and Head of the Department of Geography, 1959-64, and Director of Centre of Japanese Studies, 1962-64, University of Sheffield. RGS Travelling Fellowship, 1947; Visiting Lecturer in Geography and Visiting Fellow of Trumbull Coll., Yale Univ., 1952-54. Chairman Assoc. of British Orientalists, 1962-63. Editor, Modern Asian Studies. *Publications:* Geographical Essays on British

Tropical Lands, 1956 (Joint Editor); South-East Asia: a Social Economic and Political Geography, 1964; Essays in Political Geography, 1968 (Editor); articles, mostly on political geography of Asia, in Geog. Journal, Econ. Geog., International Affairs, Politique Etrangère, etc. *Recreations:* music and foreign travel. *Address:* School of Oriental and African Studies, University of London, WC1. *Club:* National Liberal.

**FISHER, Major (Hon.) Charles Howard Kerridge,** MC 1918; DL, JP; Director of a small property company since 1960; *b* 21 Dec. 1895; *s* of late Charles Henry Fisher, Westbury, Wilts.; *m* 1923, Ethel Mary (*d* 1958), *d* of Sidney Redcliffe Chope, JP, Bideford, Devon; one *s* one *d*; *m* 1967, Gertrude Elizabeth, *widow* of William Walter Symper, Harrow. *Educ:* Trowbridge High Sch., Wiltshire. Served European War, 1914-18 (MC); with Hon. Artillery Company and RA in Belgium and France; War of 1939-45: Home Guard and Army Welfare Officer; Hon. Major 1958. Manufacturer ladies' clothing, 1923-59, when retired (Company Dir). Member Acton Borough Council, 1940-45 (Educn Cttee, 1945-65). JP 1947, DL 1961. Middlesex (now London). First High Sheriff of Greater London, 1965. Lord Lieutenant's Representative for Acton, 1958 (now London Borough of Ealing, 1965); Member, National Assistance Board (now Ministry of Social Security), 1962; Dep. Chairman, Willesden Petty Sessional Division, 1962. General Comr of Income Tax, 1965. Freeman, City of London, 1947; Liveryman, Haberdashers' Company, 1948; Trustee, Acton Methodist Church, etc; President: Boy Scouts Assoc.; Harlesden Branch, British Legion, Vice-President: Acton Branch, British Legion; NW County Met. Area British Legion. Member, War Pension Cttee, Ealing, 1940 (Vice-Chairman 1960). *Recreations:* local social activities. *Address:* Beverley, 56 Twyford Avenue, Acton, W3. *T:* 01-992 2481. *Clubs:* City Livery, Royal Automobile.

**FISHER, Desmond (Michael);** Deputy Head of News, Radio Telefis Eireann, Dublin, since 1967; *b* 9 Sept. 1920; *e s* of Michael Louis Fisher and Evelyn Kate Shier; *m* 1948, Margaret Elizabeth Smyth; three *s* one *d*. *Educ:* St Columb's Coll., Derry; Good Counsel Coll., New Ross, Co. Wexford; University Coll., Dublin (BA (NUI)). Asst Editor, Nationalist and Leinster Times, Carlow, 1945-48; Foreign Editor, Irish Press, Dublin, 1948-51; Economic Correspondent, Irish News Agency, Dublin, 1951-54; London Editor, Irish Press, 1954-62; Editor, Catholic Herald, 1962-66. *Publications:* The Church in Transition, 1967; Contributor to The Statist, The Furrow, Irish Digest and to various Irish, US and foreign magazines. *Address:* Louvain 22, Dublin. *T:* 981434.

**FISHER, Doris G.;** *b* 1907; *d* of Gathorne John Fisher, Pontypool. *Educ:* Farringtons, Chislehurst; Royal Holloway Coll., University of London (BA Hons (English) 1929, (French) 1931); Sorbonne. Senior English Mistress, Maidenhead County Gram. Sch. 1934-39; Second Mistress, Dover County Grammar Sch., 1945; Headmistress of Farringtons, Chislehurst, Kent, 1946-57, retired. Lecturer at Westminster Training Coll., 1957-59; Lecturer at Avery Hill Training Coll., 1959-62. *Address:* 245 Latymer Court, W6.

**FISHER, Doris Mary Gertrude;** MP (Lab) Ladywood division, Birmingham, since 1970; *b* 13 Sept. 1919; *d* of late Frederick J. Satchwell; *m* 1939; two *d*. *Educ:* Tinker's Farm Girls' Sch.; Fircroft Coll.; Bournville Day Continuation Coll. JP 1961-; Member: Birmingham City Council; Labour Party, 1945-; UNESCO study group; Nat. Pres. Co-operative Guild, 1961-62. Contested Ladywood, Birmingham, 1969 by-election. *Recreations:* swimming, walking. *Address:* House of Commons, SW1.

**FISHER, Rt. Rev. Edward George Knapp-;** *see* Pretoria, Bishop of.

**FISHER, Hon. Francis Forman,** MC 1944; Master of Wellington College since Sept. 1966; *b* 25 Sept. 1919; 2nd *s* of Most Rev. and Rt Hon. Lord Fisher of Lambeth, *qv*; unmarried. *Educ:* Repton; Clare Coll., Cambridge (MA). Commissioned, The Sherwood Foresters, 1940; served War of 1939-45, Middle East, and Western Desert (POW Tobruk, 1942); escaped and returned to England, 1943; demobilised, rank of Capt., 1946; returned to Cambridge, 1946; Asst Master, Repton Sch., 1947-54; Housemaster, 1948-54; Warden of St Edward's Sch., Oxford, 1954-66. Incorporated MA Oxford Univ. through Christ Church, 1955. *Recreations:* cricket, hockey (rep. CUHC *v* Oxford, 1947), and other games. *Address:* Wellington College, Berks. *T:* Crowthorne 2261. *Clubs:* Public Schools; Hawks (Cambridge).

*See also Hon. Sir Henry A. P. Fisher.*

**FISHER, Francis George Robson,** MA Oxon; Headmaster of Bryanston School, Blandford, since 1959; *b* 9 April 1921; *s* of late John Henry Fisher and of Hannah Clayton Fisher; *m* 1965, Sheila Vernon, *o d* of late D. Dunsire and of Mrs H. E. Butt; one *s*. *Educ:* Liverpool Coll. (Schol.); Worcester Coll., Oxford (Classical Exhibitioner). Served War of 1939-45; Capt. in Ayrshire Yeomanry, North Africa and Italy, 1942-45. Housemaster and Senior English Master, Kingswood Sch., Bath, 1950-59. *Recreations:* music, lawn tennis, sailing. *Address:* Bryanston School, Blandford, Dorset. *T:* Blandford 2411.

**FISHER, Prof. Frederick Jack,** MA (London); Professor of Economic History, University of London, since 1954; *b* 22 July 1908; *s* of A. H. Fisher, Southend-on-Sea; *m* 1943, Barbara Vivienne, *d* of J. E. Whisstock, Southend-on-Sea; one *s* one *d*. *Educ:* Southend High Sch.; London Sch. of Economics. Asst Lecturer and Lecturer in Economic History, London Sch. of Economics, 1935-47. Served RAF, 1941-46. Reader in Economic History, University of London, 1947-54. *Publications:* contributions to Economic History Review. *Address:* 22 Lyndale Avenue, NW2.

**FISHER, Sir George Read,** Kt 1967; CMG 1961; Mining Engineer; Chairman of Directors, Mount Isa Mines Ltd, since 1953; *b* 23 March 1903; *s* of George Alexander and Ellen Harriett Fisher; *m* 1927, Eileen Elaine Triggs; one *s* three *d*. *Educ:* Prince Alfred Coll., Adelaide; Adelaide Univ. (BE). Formerly Gen. Manager of Operations for Zinc Corporation Ltd, Broken Hill, NSW. *Recreations:* shooting and bowling. *Address:* Mount Isa Mines Ltd, Mount Isa, Qld, Australia. *T:* Mount Isa 6 and 55. *Clubs:* Athenæum (Melbourne); Brisbane (Brisbane).

**FISHER, Harold Wallace;** Director, 1959-69, and Vice-President, 1962-69, Standard Oil Company (New Jersey) New York, retired; *b* 27 Oct. 1904; *s* of Dean Wallace Fisher and Grace Cheney Fisher; *m* 1930, Hope Elisabeth Case; one *s*. *Educ:* Massachusetts Institute of Technology (BSc). Joined Standard Oil Company (NJ), 1927; Dir Esso Standard Oil Co. and Pres. Enjay Co. Inc., 1945. Resided in London, 1954-59. UK Rep. for Standard Oil

Co. (NJ) and Chm. of its Coordination Cttee for Europe, 1954-57; Joint Managing Dir, Iraq Petroleum Co. Ltd and Associated Companies, 1957-59. Hon. DSc 1960, Clarkson Coll. of Technology, Nat. Acad. of Engrg. *Publications:* various patents and technical articles relating to the Petroleum Industry. *Recreations:* golf, photography, horology. *Address:* Suite 1250, 1 Rockefeller Plaza, New York, NY 10020, USA; (Home) Park Drive South, Rye, NY. *Clubs:* Pilgrims, American; University (New York), Westchester Country, Apawamis (Rye, NY).

**FISHER, Hon. Sir Henry (Arthur Pears),** Kt 1968; a Director of J. Henry Schroder Wagg & Co., since 1970; *b* 20 Jan. 1918; *e s* of Most Rev. and Rt Hon. Lord Fisher of Lambeth, *qv*; *m* 1948, Felicity, *d* of late Eric Sutton; one *s* three *d*. *Educ:* Marlborough; Christ Church, Oxford (Schol.); Gaisford Greek Prose Prize, 1937; 1st Cl. Hon. Mods 1938; BA 1942; MA 1943. Served Leics Regt, 1940-46; Staff Coll., Quetta, 1943; GSO2, 1943-44. GSO1 HQ 14th Army, 1945. Hon. Lieut-Col 1946 (despatches). Fellow of All Souls Coll., 1946-, Estates Bursar, 1961-66, Sub-Warden, 1965-67. Barrister, Inner Temple, 1947, Bencher, 1966; QC 1960; Recorder of Canterbury, 1962-68; a Judge of the High Court of Justice, Queen's Bench Div., 1968-70. Mem., Gen. Council of the Bar, 1959-63, 1964-68, Vice-Chm., 1965-66, Chm., 1966-68; Vice-Pres., Senate of the Four Inns of Court, 1966-68. Member: Private Internat. Law Cttee, 1961-63; Coun. on Tribunals, 1962-65; Law Reform Cttee, 1963-66; Council, Marlborough Coll.; a Trustee of the Pilgrim Trust, 1965-. *Recreation:* music. *Address:* Linchmere House, near Haslemere, Surrey. *T:* Liphook 2343; 37 Bury Street, St James's, SW1. *T:* 01-930 4096. *Clubs:* Travellers', Royal Automobile.
*See also Hon. F. F. Fisher.*

**FISHER, Rev. Canon James Atherton;** Canon of St George's, Windsor, since 1958; *b* 1 May 1909; *s* of Rev. Legh Atherton Fisher and Beatrice Edith Fisher; *m* 1938, Joan Gardiner Budden; two *s* one *d*. *Educ:* Haileybury; Sidney Sussex Coll., Cambridge; Cuddesdon Theological Coll. BA 1932, MA 1945; Deacon 1933; Priest, 1934; Asst Curate: St Matthew's, Oxhey, 1933-36; The Priory Church, Dunstable, 1936-39; Chaplain of Bedford Sch., 1939-43; Vicar of St Paul's, Peterborough, 1943-53; Religious Broadcasting Asst, BBC, 1953-58; Chaplain of St Christopher's Coll., Blackheath, 1954-58; Chaplain of Heathfield Sch., Ascot, 1959-64. *Recreations:* driving, reading and collecting useless information. *Address:* 6 The Cloisters, Windsor Castle. *T:* Windsor 66313.

**FISHER, Sir John,** Kt 1942; *b* 1892; Shipowner; *s* of James Fisher, Barrow-in-Furness; *m* 1947, Maria Elsner, *d* of Richard Elsner, Vienna, Austria. *Educ:* Sedbergh; Malvern. Chairman: James Fisher & Sons, Ltd, Barrow-in-Furness; Seaway Coasters, Ltd; Fisher Line Ltd; Director: Barrow Housing Co. Ltd; Fisher and Duforest Ltd; Louis Duforest Ltd; Sidney Cater & Co Ltd; Barrow Quarries Ltd; Holyhead Shipping Agency Ltd; Maritima Midway SA; Member Council of Chamber of Shipping of United Kingdom and of Coasting and Home Trade Tramp Section, Chamber of Shipping of UK (Chairman 1935-39); Chm. Coastal Shipping Advisory Cttee appointed by Ministry of Transport; Mem. Transport Advisory Council, 1934-39; Dir Coasting and Short Sea Shipping, Min. of Transport, 1939-46; Chm. United Maritime Authority, European Area, 1945-46; Pres. Baltic and International Maritime Conf., 1951-53; FICS Comdr Order of Orange-Nassau (Netherlands); Officer Order of Merite Maritime of France. Served European War, 1914-18, with King's Own RL Regt (Staff Capt. 154 Inf. Brigade, 51st Div., 1915-16). *Address:* Blakeholme Wray, Newby Bridge, N Lancs. *T:* 345. *Clubs:* City of London; Windermere Royal Yacht (Windermere).

**FISHER, John Lenox,** CMG 1956; *b* 9 Oct. 1899; *s* of George Henry Fisher; *m* 1929, Kathleen Maysie Mackie; one *s* one *d*. *Educ:* Liverpool University. RFC/RAF, 1917-19 (Pilot, 2nd Lieut). Joined Bank of England, Oct. 1921; Asst Adviser, 1938; Dir of Operations, International Monetary Fund, Washington, DC, 1946-47; Dep. Chief Cashier, Bank of England, 1948-50; Adviser to Governors, Bank of England, 1950-59. *Recreations:* golf, swimming. *Address:* 2 Orchards, Lower Street, Pulborough, Sussex. *T:* Pulborough 2812. *Clubs:* Oriental; West Sussex golf.

**FISHER, John Mortimer,** CMG 1962; HM Diplomatic Service, retired; HBM Consul-General at Düsseldorf, 1966-70; *b* 20 May 1915; *yr s* of late Capt. Mortimer Fisher (W Yorks Regt) and Mrs M. S. Fisher (*née* Bailey); *m* 1949, Helen Bridget Emily Caillard; two *s*. *Educ:* Wellington; Trinity Coll., Cambridge. Entered Consular (subseq. Diplomatic) Service, 1937; Probationer Vice-Consul, Bangkok, 1938. Served at Casablanca, 1942, Naples, 1943; 1st Sec. in Foreign Office, 1946, Mexico City, 1949; Detroit, Mich., USA, 1952; Counsellor in charge of British Information Services, Bonn, 1955; an Inspector in HM Foreign Service, 1959; Counsellor and Consul-Gen. at Bangkok, 1962. *Address:* The North Garden, Treyford, Midhurst, West Sussex. *T:* Harting 448.

**FISHER, Ven. Leslie Gravatt;** Archdeacon of Chester and Canon Residentiary of Chester Cathedral since Nov. 1965; *b* 18 Aug. 1906; *m* 1935, Dorothy Minnie, *née* Nash; two *d*. *Educ:* Hertford Grammar Sch.; London Coll. of Divinity. ALCD 1933. Deacon, 1933; Priest 1934. Curate of Emmanuel, Northwood, 1933-36; Vicar of St Michael and All Angels, Blackheath Park, 1936-39; Rector of Bermondsey, 1939-47; Curate-in-charge, Christ Church, Bermondsey, 1942-47; Chap., Bermondsey Med. Mission Hosp., 1946-47; Home Sec., CMS, and Licensed Preacher, Diocese of Southwark, 1947-; License to Officiate, Bromley, Dio. of Rochester, 1948-. *Recreations:* music and photography. *Address:* 5 Abbey Street, Chester.

**FISHER, Nancy Kathleen;** *see under* Trenaman, N. K.

**FISHER, Mrs Nigel, (Patricia);** *b* 5 April 1921; *d* of late Lieut-Col Sir W. D. Smiles, CIE, DSO, DL, MP for N Down; *m* 1st, 1941, Capt. Neville M. Ford (marr. diss., 1956), 2nd *s* of late Dr Lionel Ford, sometime Headmaster of Harrow and Dean of York; two *d*; 2nd, 1956, Nigel T. L. Fisher, *qv*. *Educ:* privately and abroad. MP (UU) North Down (unopposed return), April 1953-55 (as Mrs Patricia Ford). *Recreations:* sailing, travel. *Address:* 16 North Court, Great Peter Street, SW1; Portavo Point, Donaghadee, Co. Down, N Ireland. *T:* 2596.

**FISHER, Nigel Thomas Loveridge,** MC 1945; MA (Cambridge); MP (C) Hitchin Division of Herts, 1950-55, Surbiton since 1955; *b* 14 July 1913; *s* of late Comdr Sir Thomas Fisher, KBE, Royal Navy and of late Lady Shakespeare; step *s* of Rt Hon. Sir Geoffrey Shakespeare, Bt, *qv*; *m* 1935, Lady Gloria Vaughan (marr. diss. 1952), *e d* of 7th Earl of Lisburne; one *s* one *d*; *m* 1956, Patricia, *o d* of late Lieut-Col Sir Walter Smiles, CIE, DSO, DL, MP (*see* Mrs Nigel Fisher). *Educ:* Eton; Trinity Coll., Cambridge. Hons Degree, Law, Cambridge, 1934. Served War of 1939-45; volunteered Welsh Guards and commissioned as 2nd Lieut 1939; Hook of Holland, Boulogne, 1940 (despatches); Capt., 1940; Major, 1944; N West Europe, 1945 (wounded, MC). A former mem. of National Executive Cttee of Conservative Party; contested Chislehurst (N Kent), Gen. Election, 1945. Mem. British Parl. Deleg. to Sweden, 1950, W Indies 1955, Malta 1966, Canada 1966, Uganda 1967, St Kitts, Anguilla, 1967. Parl. Private Sec. to Minister of Food, 1951-54, to Home Sec., 1954-57; Parl. Under-Sec. of State for the Colonies, July 1962-Oct. 1963; Parl Under-Sec. of State for Commonwealth Relations and for the Colonies, 1963-64; Opposition Spokesman for Commonwealth Affairs, 1964-66. Treasurer, CPA, 1966-68. Mem. Exec., 1922 Cttee, 1960-62, 1969-. *Recreations:* tennis, riding, walking. *Address:* 16 North Court, Great Peter Street, Westminster, SW1. *T:* 01-222 3532; Portavo Point, Donaghadee, Co. Down, N Ireland. *T:* 2596; St George's Court, St George's Bay, Malta, GC. *Club:* MCC.

**FISHER, Norman George;** Chairman, Butterworth & Co. (Publishers) Ltd, since 1968; *b* 9 July 1910; *s* of late Thomas Daniel and Kate Fisher; *m* 1934, Jenny, *d* of late John and Barbara Cole; three *s* (one *d* decd). *Educ:* Cardiff High Sch.; St Edmund Hall, Oxford (MA). Asst to Education Sec., Cambs, 1938-46; Dep. Educ. Officer, Lancs, 1946-49; Chief Educ. Officer, Manchester, 1949-55; Principal, the Staff Coll. of the National Coal Board, 1955-61. War Service: RASC, RAEC, Commandant, Army Sch. of Education (ABCA), 1943; Command Educ. Officer, ALFSEA, 1945-46. Chairman: North Regional Advisory Council, BBC, 1953-55; The Fifty-One Soc., 1951-55; Seminar of the Caribbean Countries on Adult Education (at Jamaica), 1953; Gen. Advisory Council, BBC, 1955-62; OECD Project, Management training; Printing and Publishing Industry Training Bd, 1968-; Council of Technical Examining Bodies. Reference Cttee, Dept of Educn and Science. Member: Cttee on Proceedings before Examining Magistrates, 1957; Cttee on Awards to University Students, 1958-60; Council BIM, 1962-66 (Fellow 1964-); Exec. Governor, Royal Shakespeare Theatre, 1963-; Drama Advisory Cttee, British Council. Chairman: Butterworth (Australia); Butterworth (New Zealand); Ginn & Co. Ltd; Iliffe Books Ltd; Director: The Hamlyn Publishing Group Ltd; IPC Books Ltd; Triton Publishing Co. Ltd; Provident Clothing & Supply Co. Ltd. *Recreations:* reading, music, open-air pursuits. *Address:* 88 Kingsway, WC2. *Club:* Athenæum.

**FISHER, Mrs O. H.;** *see* Anderson, Marian.

**FISHER, Patricia;** *see* Fisher, Mrs Nigel.

**FISHER, (Phyllis) Anne;** Headmistress, Wycombe Abbey School, since 1962; *b* 8 March 1913; *d* of Rev. L. A. Fisher, Rector of Higham on the Hill, Nuneaton, and Beatrice Fisher (*née* Eustace). *Educ:* Sch. of St Mary and St Anne, Abbots Bromley; Bristol Univ. BA History Hons, 1938. Senior History Mistress: St Helen's, Northwood, 1938-41; St Anne's Coll., Natal, SA, 1941-44; Headmistress, St Winifred's Sch., George, SA, 1944-45; Joint Headmistress, St George's, Ascot, 1946-49; Headmistress, Limuru Girls' Sch., Limuru, Kenya Colony, 1949-57; Headmistress, Arundel Sch., Salisbury, S Rhodesia, 1957-61. *Recreations:* study of old churches, the history of painting. *Address:* Wycombe Abbey School, High Wycombe, Bucks. *Club:* Royal Commonwealth Society.

**FISHER, Rear-Adm. Ralph Lindsay,** CB 1957; DSO 1940; OBE 1941; DSC 1943; *b* 18 June 1903; *s* of F. Lindsay Fisher, CBE, one-time Pres. Inst. of Chartered Accountants, and Ethel Owen Pugh, Caernarvon; *m* 1934, Ursula Carver, Torquay; five *d*. *Educ:* Osborne and Dartmouth. First went to sea, 1920; Commanded: HMS Wakeful, 1940 (Dunkirk, DSO); Musketeer, 1943-45 (sinking of Scharnhorst, DSC); Solebay, 1947-48; Indefatigable, 1952-54. Naval Staff Course, 1934; Jt Services Staff Coll., 1949; Flag Officer Ground Trng (Home Air Comd), 1954-57. Retd, 1957. *Recreation:* sailing. *Address:* Dalnacreoch, Gartmore, by Stirling. *Clubs:* United Service; Royal Cruising.

**FISHER, Prof. Reginald Brettauer,** CBE 1966; Professor of Biochemistry, University of Edinburgh; *b* 13 Feb. 1907; *s* of Joseph Sudbury and Louie Fisher; *m* 1929, Mary, *d* of late C. W. Saleeby; one *s* three *d*. *Educ:* King Edward VII Sch., Sheffield; St John's Coll., Oxford. MA, DPhil (Oxon.), 1933. University Demonstrator in Biochemistry, Oxford, 1933; Rockefeller Travelling Fellow, 1939; Research Officer, Min. of Home Security, 1942; Air Ministry, 1943-45; Consultant, US War Dept, 1945. Member: Biochemical Soc.; Physiological Soc.; Royal Society of Medicine. *Publications:* Protein Metabolism, 1954. Contributions to: Biochem. Jl; Jl Physiol.; Jl Biol. Chem.; Am. Jl Physiol., etc. *Address:* Department of Biochemistry, University of Edinburgh Medical School, Teviot Place, Edinburgh EH8 9AG.

**FISHER, Sir Samuel,** Kt 1967; JP; Vice-President, London Diamond Bourse; Senior Vice-President, Board of Deputies of British Jews, since 1967; *b* 20 Jan. 1905; *m* 1930, Millie Gluckstein; one *d* (and one *d* decd). *Educ:* London. Mayor of Stoke Newington, 1953-54; first Mayor of London Borough of Camden, 1965-66. Chairman: London Labour Mayors' Assoc.; Betting and Licensing Bench, West Central Div.; Governor: University Coll., Hosp.; University Coll. Sch. *Recreations:* writing book reviews; reading autobiographies. *Address:* 15 Highpoint, Highgate, N6. *T:* 01-340 8631.

**FISHER, Sydney Humbert,** CVO 1948; *b* 9 Feb. 1887; *s* of late Edward Fisher, Aspley Guise, Beds; *m* 1915, Doris Mary, *d* of late Dr Adam Oakley; two *d*. *Educ:* Repton. Joined London North Western Railway, 1904; Chief Operating Manager: LMS Rly, 1944, London Midland Region, Br. Rlys, 1948; late Dep. Chief Regional Officer, London Midland Region, Railway Executive. Medal of Freedom with Bronze Palm (USA). *Address:* 6 The Mead, Cirencester, Glos.

**FISHER, Sylvia Gwendoline Victoria; (Signora U. Gardini);** Principal Soprano, Royal Opera House, London; *d* of John Fisher and Margaret Fisher (*née* Frawley); *m* 1954, Ubaldo Gardini. *Educ:* St Joseph's Coll., Kilmore, Australia; Conservatorium of Music, Melbourne. Won "Sun" Aria Competition, Melbourne, 1936; International Celebrity Concert in Australia, 1947; tour of Australia, 1955. Operatic Debut in Cadmus and Hermione, 1932; Covent Garden Debut in Fidelio (Leonora), 1948. Appeared in: Rome (Sieglinde), 1952; Cagliari (Isolde), 1954; Bologna (Gutrune), 1955; Covent Garden (Brunnhilde), 1956; Frankfurt Opera House (in Der Rosenkavalier), 1957, etc. *Recreations:* gardening and rare books on singing. *Address:* 24 Dawson Place, W2. *T:* 01-229 0175.

**FISHER, Thomas Gilbert F.;** *see* Field Fisher.

**FISHER, Vardis;** author; *b* 31 March 1895; *s* of Joseph Oliver Fisher and Temperance Thornton; *m* 1st, 1918, late Leona McMurtrey; two *s*; 2nd, 1928, Margaret Trusler; one *s*; 3rd, 1940, Opal Laurel Holmes. *Educ:* University of Utah; University of Chicago. Asst Prof. of English, University of Utah, 1925-28; New York Univ., 1928-31; Corporal, European War. *Publications:* include: various until 1941, subseq. The Mothers, 1943; Darkness and the Deep, 1943; The Golden Rooms, 1944; Intimations of Eve, 1945; Adam and the Serpent, 1947; The Divine Passion, 1948; The Valley of Vision, 1951; The Island of the Innocent, 1952; God or Caesar, 1953; Jesus Came Again: A Parable, 1956; Pemmican, 1956; A Goat for Azazel, 1956; Peace Like a River, 1957; Tale of Valor, 1958; My Holy Satan, 1958; Love and Death, 1959; Orphans in Gethsemane, 1960; Suicide or Murder, 1962; Thomas Wolfe as I Knew Him, and other Essays, 1963; Mountain Man, 1965; Gold Rushes and Mining Camps of the Early American West, 1968. *Recreations:* horticulture, photography. *Address:* Hagerman, Idaho, USA.

**FISHER, V. O.;** *see* Cressy-Marcks, V. O.

**FISHER, Prof. William Bayne,** Dr University of Paris; Professor of Geography, University of Durham, since 1956; first Principal of the Graduate Society, Durham University, since 1965; *b* 24 Sept. 1916; unmarried. *Educ:* Darwen Gram. Sch.; Universities of Manchester, Louvain, Paris. Research Scholar, University of Manchester, 1937; RAF 1940; Liaison Officer to French in Syria and Lebanon, 1944; Asst Lectr, University of Manchester, 1946; Lectr University of Aberdeen, 1947; Carnegie Fellow, 1951; Reader, University of Durham, 1954; Dir, Centre of Middle Eastern and Islamic Studies, Durham Univ., 1963-65. *Publications:* Les Mouvements de population en Normandie, 1940; The Middle East, a Physical Social and Regional Geography, 1951; (with H. Bowen-Jones) Spain, a geographical background; (with H. Bowen-Jones and J. C. Dewdney) Malta, 1961; (Ed) The Cambridge History of Iran, Vol. I (The Land of Iran), 1968. Various articles in periodicals and works of reference. *Recreations:* music, travel, geographical gastronomy. *Address:* 38 Old Elvet, Durham; Abbey View, 42 South Street, Durham. *T:* Durham 4350 and 4291. *Club:* County (Durham).

**FISHER, Sir Woolf,** Kt 1964; Chairman and Managing Director of Fisher & Paykel Ltd; Chairman, New Zealand Steel Ltd, since 1965; *b* 1912; *s* of Michael Fisher; *m* 1935, Joyce, *d* of George Paykel. *Educ:* Mt Albert Grammar Sch., Auckland. Co-founder of Fisher & Paykel Ltd, 1934; Member: Council Auckland Chamber of Commerce, 1956-62; Cttee Auckland Racing Club, 1958-; Council NZ Thoroughbred Breeders Assoc., 1948-; Pres. Auckland Polo Club, 1957-62; Mem. Auckland Rotary, 1952-; Chairman: New Zealand Steel Investigating Co., 1960-65; New Zealand Steel Ltd, 1965-; Pres. Outward Bound Trust of New Zealand, 1961-63; Trustee, New Zealand Inst. of Economic Research, 1958-62; Leader, New Zealand Trade Mission to Australia, 1959; Trade Promotion Council, 1962-63; Director: New Zealand Insurance Co. Ltd, 1963-; BNZ Finance Co. Ltd, 1966-; Pacific Steel Ltd, 1966-. *Recreations:* shooting, fishing. *Address:* Ra Ora, Waiouru Road, East Tamaki, Auckland, New Zealand. *T:* 598-935. *Clubs:* Northern, Professional (Auckland).

**FISK, James B(rown);** President, Bell Telephone Laboratories, Inc., NJ, USA, since 1959; *b* 30 Aug. 1910; *s* of Henry James and Bertha Brown Fisk; *m* 1938, Cynthia Hoar; three *s*. *Educ:* Mass. Inst Technology (BS, PhD); Trinity Coll., Cambridge (Proctor Travelling Fellow), Soc. of Fellows, Harvard Univ., 1936-38; Associate Prof. of Physics, University of North Carolina, 1938-39; Gordon McKay Prof. and Senior Fellow, Harvard Univ., 1948-49; Dir of Research, US Atomic Energy Commn, 1947-48; Bell Telephone Laboratories: 1939-47 and 1949-; Vice-Pres. Research, 1954-55; Executive Vice-Pres., 1955-59. President's Science Advisory Cttee, 1952-60; Consultant, 1960-; Gen. Advisory Cttee, Atomic Energy Commission, 1952-58; Chm. Geneva Technical Discussions on Nuclear Tests, 1958. Presidental Certificate of Merit, 1946. Industrial Research Inst. Medal, 1963; Fellow: Amer. Acad. of Arts and Sciences; Amer. Phys. Soc.; IEEE; Member: Nat. Acad. of Sciences; Amer. Philosoph. Soc.; Nat. Acad. of Engrg. Washington Award, Western Soc. of Engineers, 1968; Midwest Res. Inst. Citation, 1968. Holds several Hon. Degrees. *Publications:* various scientific and technical articles in: Proceedings Royal Society, Bell System Technical Journal, Physical Review. *Recreations:* gardening, mountain climbing, golf. *Address:* Bell Telephone Laboratories, Murray Hill, New Jersey 07974, USA. *T:* 201-582-4471 (Murray Hill, (NJ). *Clubs:* Harvard (NY City); Ausable (NY); Cosmos (Washington); Somerset Hills (NJ).

**FISKE,** family name of **Baron Fiske.**

**FISKE,** Baron *cr* 1967, of Brent (Life Peer); **William Geoffrey Fiske;** Kt 1965; CBE 1956; DL; Chairman, Decimal Currency Board, since 1966; Vice-Chairman, The Centre for Environmental Studies, since 1966; *b* 3 July 1905; *s* of William George Fiske and Clementina (*née* Gage). *Educ:* Berkhamsted Sch. Bank of England, 1923-35; Civil Service, 1940-45. Parliamentary Candidate Hornsey, 1945. Mem. London County Council, 1946-65; Chm. Town Planning Cttee, LCC, 1949-55; Chm., Housing Cttee, LCC, 1955-60. Majority Party Chief Whip, LCC, 1960; Leader, Greater London Council, 1964-67. Chm., Consultative Council for LEB, 1965-67. Mem. South Bank Theatre and Opera House Board, 1965-. Vice-Chm. Sutton Dwellings Trust, 1957-67. Hon. AMTPI. DL Greater London, 1967. *Recreations:* music, gardening, study of architecture. *Address:* House of Lords, SW1.

**FISKEN, Archibald Clyde Wanliss,** CMG 1963; OBE 1958; MC 1918; Chairman of Melbourne Board, Commercial Union Assurance Company of Australia, since 1959; Chairman of Dennys Lascelles Ltd; *b* Ballarat, Aust., 11 March 1897; *s* of A. J. Fisken, Lal Lal Estate, Yendon, Vic.; *m* 1924, Elspeth A., *d* of E. N. Cameron; one *s* three *d*. *Educ:* Ballarat Coll.; Geelong Grammar Sch. Served European War, 1914-18: Lieut, 281st (London) Brigade, RFA, 1916-18 (MC). MHR for Ballarat, 1934-37; Councillor, Shire of Buninyong, 1921- (Pres., 1930, 1947, 1958, 1967); Trustee, Royal Agricultural Society of Vic. and Graziers' Assoc. of Vic.; Chm., Australian Meat Board, 1936-46. *Recreation:* watching cricket. *Address:* Lal Lal Estate, Yendon, Victoria 3332, Australia. *Clubs:* Australian, Naval and Military (Melbourne); Ballarat; Geelong.

**FISON, Sir (Frank Guy) Clavering,** Kt 1957; DL; JP; *b* 1892; *er surv s* of late J. O. Fison, of Stutton Hall, Ipswich; *m* 1922, Evelyn Alice (OBE 1964), *er d* of late F. L. Bland Rookwood, Copdock, Ipswich; two *d*. *Educ:*

Charterhouse; Christ Church, Oxford. MP (U) Woodbridge Div. of Suffolk, 1929-31. Hon. Life Pres., Fisons Ltd. JP East Suffolk, 1942-; High Sheriff of Suffolk, 1942; DL Suffolk, 1958. *Address:* Crepping Hall, Stutton, Suffolk.

**FISON, Sir Guy;** *see* Fison, Sir R. G.

**FISON, Rt. Rev. Joseph Edward;** *see* Salisbury, Bishop of.

**FISON, Sir (Richard) Guy,** 4th Bt *cr* 1905; DSC 1944; Director: Charles Kinloch & Co. Ltd since 1962; Saccone & Speed Ltd since 1952; *b* 9 Jan. 1917; *er s* of Sir William Guy Fison, 3rd Bt; *S* father, 1964; *m* 1952, Elyn Hartmann; one *s* one *d*. *Educ:* Eton; New Coll., Oxford. Served RNVR, 1939-45. Entered Wine Trade, 1948. Master of Wine, 1954. *Recreations:* fishing, gardening, swimming in the Mediterranean. *Heir: s* Charles William Fison, *b* 6 Feb. 1954. *Address:* 4 Queens Ride, Barnes, SW13. *T:* 01-788 2542. *Club:* RNVR.
*See also Maj.-Gen. W. R. Beddington.*

**FISTOULARI, Anatole;** Founder and Principal Conductor of London International Orchestra since 1946; Principal Conductor of London Philharmonic Orchestra, 1943, now guest conductor; *b* Kiev, Russia, 20 Aug. 1907; obtained British nationality, 1948; *s* of Gregor and late Sophie Fistoulari; *m* 1942, Anna Mahler (marr. diss., 1956); one *d*; 1957, Mary Elizabeth, *y d* of late James Lockhart, Edinburgh. *Educ:* Kiev, Berlin, and Paris. Conducted first concert at age of 7 at Opera House in Kiev and later all over Russia; at 13 gave concerts in Germany and Holland; at 24 conducted Grand Opera Russe in Paris at the Châtelet Theatre with Colonne Orchestra and Chaliapine with whom he then toured France and Spain; then conducted the Ballet de Monte-Carlo with Massine in Drury Lane and Covent Garden before the War; toured with same company all over America, France, and Italy; in England in 1941 started opera production of Sorotchinsky Fair by Moussorgsky; March 1942 gave first Symphony Concert with London Symphony Orchestra and later conducted it regularly at Cambridge Theatre; first concert with London Philharmonic Orchestra in Bristol, Jan. 1943; concert engagements in numerous countries, from 1949. Guest conductor for Sadler's Wells Ballet, Royal Opera House, Covent Garden and NY Metropolitan Opera House, 1955; on tour with London Philharmonic Orchestra, to Moscow, Leningrad, Paris, 1956. Has made recordings for several firms. *Recreation:* listening to good concerts. *Address:* 65 Redington Road, NW3. *Club:* Savage.

**FITCH, Alan;** *see* Fitch, Ernest Alan.

**FITCH, (Ernest) Alan,** JP 1958; MP (Lab) Wigan Division, since June 1958; Opposition Whip, since 1970; *b* 10 March 1915; *e s* of Rev. and Mrs E. W. Fitch; *m* 1950, Nancy Maude, *y d* of late R. Kennard Davis; one *s* one *d*. *Educ:* Kingswood Sch., Bath. Was formerly Mineworker. Asst Whip (paid), 1964-66; a Lord Comr of the Treasury, 1966-69; Vice-Chamberlain, HM Household, Oct. 1969-June 1970. Chm., North West Regional Council of the Labour Party. *Recreations:* reading, walking. *Address:* 117 The Avenue, Leigh, Lancs. *T:* Leigh 73992.

**FITT, Gerard;** MP (Repub Lab) Belfast West since 1966; MP (Eire Lab) Parliament of Northern Ireland, for Dock Division of Belfast, since 1962; *b* 9 April 1926; *s* of George Patrick and Mary Ann Fitt; *m* 1947, Susan Gertrude Doherty; five *d* (and one *d* decd). *Educ:* Christian Brothers' Sch., Belfast. Merchant Seaman, 1941-53; various positions, 1953-. Councillor for Dock Ward, Belfast Corp., 1958. *Recreation:* full-time politics. *Address:* 85 Antrim Road, Belfast 15, N Ireland. *T:* 743094.

**FITTON, James,** RA 1954 (ARA 1944); painter; *b* Oldham, Lancs; *s* of James Fitton and Janet Chadwick; *m* 1929, Margaret Cook; one *s* one *d*. Mem. of the London Group, 1933. First one-man show, Arthur Tooth & Sons, Bond Street, Jan.-Feb. 1933. Work represented in exhibition of British Art since Whistler, National Gallery, 1939. Works purchased by: Contemporary Art Soc.; Chantry Bequest. Work in collections of: British Museum; Victoria & Albert Museum; Tate Gallery; Manchester; Bristol; Nottingham; Cardiff, etc. Trustee: Royal Academy; British Museum. Served on: Arts Council (Art Panel); Royal College of Art Council; Mem., Nat. Council for Art Educn; Chief Assessor to Min. of Educn for Nat. Diploma of Design (Pictorial); Chm., HM Stamp Advisory Cttee; Governor: Chelsea Coll. of Art; Central Sch. of Art and Design; Dulwich Coll. Prep. Sch. Trust. FSIA. *Publications:* The First Six Months are the Worst, 1939. *Address:* 10 Pond Cottages, College Road, Dulwich Village, SE21. *T:* 01-670 0958.

**FITTS, Sir Clive (Hamilton),** Kt 1963; MD Melbourne, FRCP, FRACP, DTM Sydney; Consulting Physician to: Royal Melbourne Hospital; Royal Women's Hospital; Austin Hospital for Chronic Diseases; Victorian Tuberculosis Service; *b* 14 July 1900; *s* of Hamilton Fitts and Katherine Fitts (*née* Pardey); *m* 1939, Yrsa E., *d* of Prof. W. A. Osborne; two *s* three *d*. *Educ:* Scotch Coll. and Melbourne Church of England Gram. Sch., Melbourne; Trinity Coll., University of Melbourne. Post-Graduate: England, Switzerland, USA. Mem. Brit. Cardiac Soc.; Mem. Brit. Thoracic Soc.; Pres. Cardiac Soc. of Aust. and NZ, 1960; Vice-Pres. RACP, 1958; Mem. Coun., University of Melbourne; Mem. Coun., Melbourne C of E Gram. Sch.; Vice-Pres. and Mem. Exec. Cttee, Nat. Heart Foundn, 1960-65; Chm. Felton Bequest Cttee; First Pres., Nat. Gall. Soc. Major AAMC Reserve. Mem. Commonwealth Drug Evaluation Cttee. *Publications:* various papers on diseases of heart and lungs in medical journals. *Recreations:* mountaineering, tennis (represented University of Melbourne, and Victoria), fly fishing. *Address:* (residence) 21 Kooyongkoot Road, Hawthorn, Victoria 3122, Australia. *T:* 81.2208; 14 Parliament Place, Melbourne, Victoria 3002, Australia. *T:* 63.1225. *Clubs:* Beefsteak; Melbourne, Beefsteak (Melbourne).

**FITZALAN-HOWARD,** family name of **Baroness Beaumont, Baron Howard of Glossop,** and **Duke of Norfolk.**

**FITZALAN-HOWARD, Maj.-Gen. Hon. Michael,** CB 1968; CBE 1962; MVO 1952; MC 1944; GOC London District, and Major-General commanding The Household Brigade, since 1968; *b* 22 Oct. 1916; 2nd *s* of 3rd Baron Howard of Glossop, *qv*, and Baroness Beaumont (11th in line), *qv*; *m* 1st, 1946, Jean (*d* 1947), *d* of Sir Hew Hamilton-Dalrymple, 9th Bt; one *d*; 2nd, 1950, Margaret, *d* of Capt. W. P. Meade-Newman; four *s* one *d*. *Educ:* Ampleforth Coll.; Trinity Coll., Cambridge. Joined Scots Guards, 1938. Served in: North West Europe, 1944-45; Palestine, 1945-46; Malaya, 1948-49; Egypt, 1952-53; Germany, 1956-57 and 1961-66; Commanding Allied Command Europe Mobile Forces (Land), 1964-66; Chief of Staff, Southern Command,

1967-68. Col: The Lancs Regt (Prince of Wales's Volunteers), 1966-70; The Queen's Lancashire Regiment, 1970-. Joint Hon. Col, Cambridge Univ. OTC, 1968-. *Address:* Horton Lodge, Horton, Colnbrook, Bucks. *T:* Colnbrook 2136. *Clubs:* Guards, Turf.
*See also Maj.-Gen. Hon. M. F. Fitzalan-Howard.*

**FITZALAN-HOWARD, Maj.-Gen. Hon. Miles Francis,** CB 1966; CBE 1960; MC 1944; a Director, Robert Fleming and Co., since 1969; *b* 21 July 1915; *s* and *heir* of 3rd Baron Howard of Glossop, *qv*, and Baroness Beaumont (11th in line), *qv*; *m* 1949, Anne Mary Teresa, *e d* of late Wing Commander Gerald Joseph Constable Maxwell, MC, DFC, AFC; two *s* three *d*. *Educ:* Ampleforth Coll.; Christ Church, Oxford (BA). 2nd Lieut, Grenadier Guards, 1937. Served War of 1939-45, France, Sicily, Italy (despatches, MC), NW Europe. Appointed Head of British Military Mission to Russian Forces in Germany, 1957; Commanded 70 Bde KAR, 1961-63; GOC, 1 Div., 1963-65; Dir, Management and Support Intelligence, MoD, 1965-66; Director, Service Intelligence, MoD 1966-67; rtd 1967. Knight of the Sovereign Order of Malta. *Address:* Bacres House, Hambleden, Henley-on-Thames, Oxfordshire. *T:* Hambleden 350; 2 Lexham Walk, W8. *T:* 01-370 4722.
*See also Maj.-Gen. Hon. Michael Fitzalan-Howard.*

**FITZCLARENCE,** family name of **Earl of Munster.**

**FITZER, Herbert Clyde,** OBE 1958; Head of Royal Naval Engineering Service, 1970-71, Director of Engineering (Ships), Navy Department, Ministry of Defence, 1968-71, retired; *b* 3 Nov. 1910; *s* of Herbert John Fitzer; *m* 1938, Queenie Stent; one *d*. *Educ:* Portsmouth Royal Dockyard Sch.; RNC Greenwich; London Univ. 1st cl. hons BSc (Eng) London, 1932; Greenwich Professional Certif. in Electrical Engrg, 1933. CEng, FIEE 1959. Asst Elec. Engr, Admty, 1936; Sheerness Dockyard, 1938; Elec. Engr, Submarine Design, Admty, 1939; Shore Estabs, 1945; Suptg Elec. Engr, Submarine Design, 1950; Asst Dir of Elec. Engrg, Ships Power Systems, 1961; Polaris Project, 1963; Dep. Dir of Elec. Engrg, 1966. Licensed Lay Reader, Dio. Bath and Wells. *Publication:* Christian Flarepath, 1956. *Address:* Meadowcroft, 54 High Street, Saltford, Bristol. *T:* Saltford 2262.

**FitzGEORGE-BALFOUR, Gen. Sir (Robert George) Victor,** KCB 1968 (CB 1965); CBE 1945; DSO 1950; MC 1939; UK Military Representative to NATO since 1971; *b* 15 Sept. 1913; *s* of Robert S. Balfour and Iris (*née* FitzGeorge), 47 Wilton Crescent, SW1; *m* 1943, Mary (Diana), *er d* of Rear-Adm. Arthur Christian, 3 Sloane Gardens, SW3; one *s* one *d*. *Educ:* Eton; King's Coll., Cambridge (BA). Commissioned 2nd Lieut Coldstream Guards, 1934; Palestine, 1936; Middle East, 1937-43; France and NW Germany, 1944-46; commanded 2nd Bn Coldstream Guards, Malaya, 1948-52; idc 1955; Chief of Staff to Governor of Cyprus, 1956; Commanded 1st Guards Brigade, 1957; Chief of Staff, HQ Southern Comd, 1962-63; Dir of Military Operations, Ministry of Defence, 1964-66; Senior Army Instructor, IDC, 1966-68; Vice-Chief of the General Staff, 1968-70. Knight Commander of the Order of Orange Nassau with swords (Netherlands), 1946. *Address:* The Old Rectory, West Chiltington, Sussex. *T:* West Chiltington 2255. *Club:* Guards.

**FITZGERALD,** family name of **Duke of Leinster.**

**FITZGERALD, Sir (Adolf) Alexander,** Kt 1955; OBE 1953; Chairman, Commonwealth Grants Commission, 1946-60; Commissioner, State Electricity Commission of Victoria, 1955-69; Member of firm of Fitzgerald Gunn and Partners, Chartered Accountants, 1916-66; President, Graduate Union, University of Melbourne, 1961-65; Professor of Accounting, University of Melbourne, 1955-58; *b* 26 Oct. 1890; *s* of Michael and Mary Ann Fitzgerald; *m* 1916, Ivy Alice Brunstein; three *d*. *Educ:* Victorian State Sch.; Box Hill Grammar Sch.; University of Melbourne. In practice as a public accountant, 1916-66; Lectr in Accountancy, University of Melbourne, 1925-51; BCom. (Melbourne) 1926. Gen. Pres., Commonwealth Inst. of Accountants, 1940-41 (Victorian State Pres., 1928-30 and 1934-37); Victorian State Pres., Australasian Inst. of Secs, 1940. Mem. Royal Commission on Country Water Supply, Vic, 1936-37; Dep. Dir, Dept of War Organisation of Industry, 1942-46. Editor, Australian Accountant, 1936-54. Dir or Chm. of public and private cos. Melbourne Rotary Vocational Service Award, 1967; Aust. Inst. Management John Storey Medal Award, 1967. *Publications:* Statistical Methods as Applied to Accounting Reports, 1940; Analysis and Interpretation of Financial and Operating Statements, 1946; (jointly) Form and Contents of Published Financial Statements, 1948; Current Accounting Trends, 1952; (jointly) Classification in Accounting, 1952; (ed) Fitzgerald's Accounting; numerous articles in Australian Accountant, etc. *Recreations:* reading, writing, bowls. *Address:* 572 Whitehorse Road, Surrey Hills, Vic 3127, Australia. *T:* 89. 1736. *Clubs:* Melbourne, Melbourne Savage, University House, Australian-American (Melbourne).

**FITZGERALD, Sir Alexander;** *see* Fitzgerald, Sir A. A.

**FitzGERALD, Brian S. V.;** *see* Vesey FitzGerald.

**FITZGERALD, Charles Patrick;** Professor of Far Eastern History, Australian National University, 1953-67, now Emeritus; Visiting Fellow, Department International Relations, Australian National University, 1968-69; *b* 5 March 1902; *s* of Dr H. Sauer; *m* 1941, Pamela Knollys; three *d*. *Educ:* Clifton. China, 1923-27, 1930-32, 1936-38, 1946-50. Leverhulme Fellowship for Anthropological Research in South-West China. DLitt ANU 1968. *Publications:* Son of Heaven, 1932; China, a Cultural History, 1935; The Tower of Five Glories, 1941; (with George Yeh) Introducing China, 1948; Revolution in China, 1951 (revised version (Penguin) as The Birth of Communist China, 1965); The Empress Wu, 1955; Flood Tide in China, 1958; Barbarian Beds: the origin of the chair in China, 1965; A Concise History of Eastern Asia, 1965; The Third China, Chinese Communities in SE Asia, 1965; Des Mantchous â Mao Tse-tong, 1968; History of China, 1969; Communism Takes China, 1970. *Address:* c/o Hongkong and Shanghai Bank, 9 Gracechurch Street, EC3; 20 Shiel Street, North Melbourne, Victoria 3051, Australia. *Club:* Savile.

**FITZ-GERALD, Desmond John Villiers** (29th Knight of Glin); Assistant Keeper, Department of Furniture and Woodwork, Victoria and Albert Museum, since 1965; *b* 13 July 1937; *s* of Desmond Windham Otho Fitz-Gerald, 28th Knight of Glin (*d* 1949), and Veronica (who *m* 2nd, 1954, Ray Milner, CC (Canada), QC, LLB, DCL, BA, of Edmonton, Alta, and of Qualicum Beach, Vancouver Island, Brit. Columbia), 2nd *d* of late Ernest Villiers, MP, and of Hon. Elaine Augusta

Guest, *d* of 1st Baron Wimborne; *m* 1966, Louise Vava Lucia (marr. diss. 1970), *d* of Comte Alain de la Falaise, Paris; *m* 1970, Olda Willes. *Educ:* King's Mead Sch., Seaford, Sussex; Stowe Sch.; University of British Columbia (BA 1959); Harvard Univ. (MA 1961). FSA 1970. Vice-Pres., Irish Georgian Soc. Adviser on Irish Decorative Arts to Ulster Museum, Belfast, 1967. Member: Council, Royal Archæological Institute, 1968; Furniture History Soc. (Friends of Leighton Ho.), 1968. *Publications:* (ed) Georgian Furniture, 1969; (with Maurice Craig) Ireland Observed, a handbook to the buildings and antiquities, 1970; Catalogues: Irish Houses and Landscapes (jointly), 1963; Irish Architectural Drawings (jointly), 1965; Irish Portraits 1660-1860 (jointly), 1969; articles and reviews on architecture and the decorative arts in Bulletin of Irish Georgian Soc., Burlington Magazine, Connoisseur, Victoria and Albert Museum Bulletin, Apollo, Spectator, etc. *Recreations:* architecture, collecting. *Address:* 5 Milbourne Grove, SW10. *T:* 01-373 3396; Glin Castle, Glin, Co. Limerick, Ireland. *TA:* Knight Glin. *T:* Glin 3. *Clubs:* Beefsteak, Turf; Kildare Street (Dublin).

**FITZGERALD, Edward,** CBE 1918; *b* 9 Nov. 1874; *s* of Charles Lionel John FitzGerald, Turlough Park, County Mayo; *m* Kate, *d* of John Bulmer, Montreal; one *s* one *d*. *Educ:* Model Sch., Ottawa. *Address:* Heather Hospital, Rawdon, PQ, Canada.

**FITZGERALD, Rev. (Sir) Edward Thomas,** 3rd Bt *cr* 1903; a Roman Catholic priest; *b* 7 March 1912; *S* father, Sir John Joseph Fitzgerald, 2nd Bt, 1957, but does not use title. *Heir: b* Rev. Daniel Patrick Fitzgerald, *b* 28 June 1916.

**FITZGERALD, Garrett Ernest,** CMG 1965; *b* 30 June 1894; *s* of Michael Fitzgerald, Melbourne, Victoria; *m* 1st, 1915; one *s*; 2nd, 1931, Maude, *d* of Eugene de Pelsenaire; one *s* one *d*. *Educ:* Victorian State Schs; Melbourne Univ. Lieut 1st AIF, 1916; Lieut-Col 4th Australian Div., 1942. Councillor, City of Heidelberg (Austr.), 1938-48 and 1950-52; Mayor, 1945-46. Comr, Melbourne and Metrop. Bd of Works, 1945-48. Victorian Div. Councillor, Commonwealth Inst. of Accountants, 1942-52 (State Pres., 1946-48; Australian Pres., 1951-52); Victorian Div. and Gen. Coun., Australian Soc. of Accountants, 1953-66 (Australian Pres., 1955-57; Victorian Pres., 1964-65). Mem. of Tribunals on salaries and allowances of Victorian State Parliament, 1954, 1964, and 1968, Federal Parliament, 1955 and 1959; Chm. Cttee of Inquiry, Victorian Housing Commn, 1956; Gen. Councillor, Australasian Inst. of Cost Accountants, 1957-66. Lectr in Accountancy, University of Melbourne, 1927-47. *Publications:* (jtly) Holding Companies in Australia and New Zealand, 1946 (5th edn 1963); (jtly) Form and Content of Published Financial Statements, 1947 (3rd edn 1963). *Recreation:* gardening. *Address:* 81 Relowe Crescent, Box Hill North, Victoria 3129, Australia. *T:* 89.5928. *Clubs:* Kelvin, Royal Automobile, Melbourne Cricket (all Melbourne).

**FitzGERALD, Sir George (Peter Maurice),** 5th Bt *cr* 1880; 23rd Knight of Kerry; MC 1944; Major, Army, retired; *b* 27 Feb. 1917; *s* of Sir Arthur Henry Brinsley FitzGerald, 4th Bt, and Mary Eleanor (*d* 1967), *d* of late Capt. Francis Forester; *S* father 1967; *m* 1939, Angela Dora Mitchell; one *s* one *d*. *Educ:* Harrow; RMC, Sandhurst. Commnd into Irish Guards, 1937; 2nd in comd, 1st Bn, 1944; 2nd in comd, 2nd Bn, 1946; retired, 1948. *Heir: s* Adrian James Andrew Denis FitzGerald, *b* 24 June 1940. *Address:* Cedar Court, Alderton, near Woodbridge, Suffolk. *T:* Shottisham 331. *Clubs:* White's, Pratt's, Royal Automobile.

**FITZGERALD, Brig. (retd) Gerald Loftus,** CBE 1956; DSO 1945; *b* 5 May 1907; *s* of late Col D. C. V. FitzGerald, MC, Nairobi Kenya; *m* 1937, Mary Stuart, *d* of Charles E. Mills, Holbrook, Suffolk; one *s* one *d*. *Educ:* Wellington Coll.; Royal Military Academy, Woolwich. Commissioned 2nd Lieut RA, 1926; Regimental duty UK and overseas, 1926-39; staff and regimental duty in UK and NW Europe during War of 1939-45. Brit. Mil. Mission to Greece, 1946-48; Chief Instructor, Officer Cadet Sch., 1949-50; Brit. Joint Services Mission, Washington, USA, 1951-52; Comdr Trg Bde, RA, 1953-55; Dep. Dir, War Office, 1956-58; retired pay, 1959. Order of Leopold (with Palm), Belgium, 1945; Croix de Guerre (with Palm), 1945. *Recreations:* field sports, travel. *Club:* Army and Navy.

**FITZ-GERALD, Sir Patrick (Herbert),** Kt 1955; OBE 1944; *b* 1899; *s* of Gerald and Florence Fitz-Gerald; *m* 1947, Dorothy Preece (marr. diss., 1957; she died 1960). *Educ:* Tonbridge Sch. Served European War, 1914-18 in Irish Guards, and War of 1939-45 as Lieut-Col Sherwood Foresters; despatches twice. *Recreations:* polo and cricket. *Club:* Golfers'.

**FITZGERALD, Prof. Patrick John;** Professor of Law, The University of Kent at Canterbury, since Oct. 1966; *b* 30 Sept. 1928; *s* of Dr Thomas Walter and Norah Josephine Fitzgerald; *m* 1959, Brigid Aileen Judge; two *s* one *d*. *Educ:* Queen Mary's Grammar Sch., Walsall; University Coll., Oxford. Called to the Bar, Lincoln's Inn, 1951; Fellow, Trinity Coll., Oxford, 1956-60. Professor of Law, Leeds Univ., 1960-66. Visiting Prof., University of Louisville, 1962-63. *Publications:* Criminal Law and Punishment, 1962; Salmond on Jurisprudence (12th edn), 1966. *Recreations:* music, golf, bridge. *Address:* The Curraghs, St Thomas's Hill, Canterbury, Kent. *T:* Canterbury 60937. *Club:* National Liberal.

**FITZGERALD, Terence;** Assistant Under-Secretary of State, Immigration and Nationality Department, Home Office, since 1966; *b* 20 March 1919. *Educ:* Allhallows Sch.; Exeter Coll., Oxford; Middle Temple. Served with Royal Artillery, 1940-46; attached Royal Indian Artillery, 1941-45. Joined Home Office as Asst Principal, 1948; Principal, 1948; Asst Sec., 1957; Imperial Defence Coll., 1962; HM Treasury (Overseas Finance), 1963-64; Asst Under-Sec. of State, Home Office, 1964. *Address:* Home Office, Whitehall, SW1.

**FITZGERALD, Walter, (Walter Fitzgerald Bond);** Actor; *b* 18 May 1896; *s* of Rev. Richard James Bond, BD, and Julia Caroline Theresa (*née* Prynne); *m* 1st, Rosalie Constance Gray; one *s*; 2nd, Angela Dorothea Radford-Rowe (*d* 1970), *d* of Rev. Preb. P. T. R.-R. Kirk; three *s* one *d*. *Educ:* King's Coll., Taunton. Studied at Royal Academy of Dramatic Art. Toured with Mrs Patrick Campbell, 1923-24; first London appearance as Alf Cope in The Likes of 'Er, Century, 1924, with Lena Ashwell Players and remained with them until 1927; understudy to Sir Gerald du Maurier. St James's, 1928-29; toured in Canada with Sir John Martin-Harvey, 1929-30; London, 1930-31; toured Canada, 1932; Malvern Festival, July-Aug. 1932; went to America, 1933; London from 1933 (went to S Africa with Sir Seymour Hicks, 1936); toured 1938 and 1942; Mr Bolfrey in play of that name, Playhouse, 1943; Stephen Marlowe in Zero Hour, Lyric; Mr

Darling and Capt. Hook in Peter Pan, Stoll; Charles in The Astonished Ostrich, St James's. At the Edinburgh Festival, 1950, Jupiter in The Queen's Comedy. Recent London stage appearances; Sir Robert Rawley in The Paragon, Fortune; Relling in The Wild Duck, St Martin's; Charles Perrier in Marriage Story, Strand: Mr Owen in The Green Bay Tree, Playhouse; Captain Shotover in Heartbreak House, Arts; the King in Hamlet, New; toured India and Pakistan for British Council, 1950-51, playing Shylock, Brutus, Jacques, Iago; Henry Vining in The Day's Mischief, Duke of York's; Father Brown in The Living Room, Wyndham's (subseq. Henry Miller Theatre, New York); Ulysses in Tiger at the Gates, Apollo, and Plymouth Theatre, NY; The Best DAmn Lie, Winter Garden; Gilt and Gingerbread, Duke of York's; Maj.-Gen. FitzAdam in The Amorous Prawn, Saville; Sir William Gascony in The Judge's Story, Ashcroft Theatre, Croydon; Twelve Angry Men, Queen's. *Films:* include: San Demetrio, London (Chief Engineer), 1942; Treasure Island (Squire Trelawney) (Walt Disney prod.), 1949; Mr Wardle in film of Pickwick Papers; Appointment in London; The Net; The Cruel Sea; Personal Affair (film of The Day's Mischief); Newspaper Story; Man in the Sky; Round the World in 80 days; Something of Value; Darby O'Gill and The Little People as Lord Fitzpatrick (Walt Disney prod.); Banner in the Sky (Walt Disney prod.). Has appeared on television frequently (Simon Peter in Paul of Tarsus, BBC Series), including programmes in New York and Hollywood. *Recreations:* work, family, home. *Address:* c/o Lloyds Bank Ltd, 179 Earls Court Road, SW5. *Club:* Garrick.

**FitzGERALD, Sir William James,** Kt 1944; MC; QC 1936; *b* Cappawhite, Co. Tipperary, May 1894; *s* of late Joseph FitzGerald, MB, Cappawhite; *m* 1st, 1933, Erica (marr. diss., 1946), *d* of F. J. Clarke, Chikupi Ranch, Northern Rhodesia; one *s*; 2nd, Cynthia Mary, *d* of late W. Foster, Jerusalem. *Educ:* Blackrock Coll.; Trinity Coll., Dublin. Served European War, Durham Light Infantry and XV Corps Mounted Troops (MC and Croix de Guerre); BA 1919; Barrister-at-Law, King's Inns, Dublin, 1922, and Middle Temple; Nigerian Administrative Service, 1920; Police Magistrate, Lagos, 1921; Crown Counsel, Nigeria, 1924; Solicitor-Gen., N Rhodesia, 1932; Attorney-Gen., N Rhodesia, 1933; Palestine, 1937-43; Chief of Justice of Palestine, 1944-48. Pres. Lands Tribunal, 1950-65. Hon. LLD 1960. *Address:* 15 De Vere Gardens, W8. *Club:* Athenæum.

**FITZGERALD, William Knight,** JP; Lord Provost of Dundee, and Lord Lieutenant of the County of the City of Dundee, since 1970; *b* 19 March 1909; *e s* of John Alexander Fitzgerald and Janet Fitzgerald; *m* 1938, Elizabeth, *d* of Alexander Grant; three *s*. *Educ:* Robertson Grammar Sch., S Africa. Assessor, Dundee Repertory Theatre, 1967-; Member: Tayside Economic Consultative Group, 1970-; Dundee Harbour Trust, 1970-; University Court, Dundee, 1970-; Dundee Town Council, 1956; City Treasurer, 1967-70; Chairman: Tay Road Bridge Joint Board, 1970-; Dundee High Sch. Directors, 1970-; Vice-Chm., Dundee Coll. of Art and Technology, 1970-. JP Dundee, 1958. *Recreations:* gardening, reading. *Address:* 1 Law Steps, Dundee DD3 6DX, Scotland. *T:* 68475. *Club:* University (Dundee).

**FITZGERALD, Most Rev. William Michael,** OP; *b* 4 June 1906; *s* of John and Ellen Fitzgerald, Tralee, Co. Kerry. *Educ:* Christian Schools, Tralee; St Mary's, Tallaght, Co. Dublin; Pontificio Ateneo Angelicum, Rome. Served in several Trinidad parishes; Vicar General of Archdiocese of Port of Spain, 1948; retired from Archdiocese, 1968; Apostolic Administrator, 1966-68. *Address:* St Dominic's, Ennismore, Cork.

**FitzGIBBON, Constantine;** *see* FitzGibbon, R. L. C. L.-D.

**FITZGIBBON, (Robert Louis) Constantine (Lee-Dillon);** writer; *b* 8 June 1919; *s* of Comdr Francis Lee-Dillon FitzGibbon, RN, and Georgette Folsom, Lenox, Mass, USA; *m* 1967, Marjorie (*née* Steele); one *d*; (by a previous marr. to Marion (*née* Gutmann) one *s*., *b* 1961). *Educ:* Munich Univ.; Sorbonne; Exeter Coll., Oxford. Served War of 1939-45, British Army (Oxford and Bucks Light Infantry), 1939-42; US Army, 1942-46. Schoolmaster, Saltus Gram. Sch., Bermuda, 1946-47; now independent writer. Mem. Irish Acad. of Letters. FRSL; Fellow, Guggenheim Memorial Foundn, 1966. *Publications:* The Arabian Bird, 1949; The Iron Hoop, 1950; Dear Emily 1952: Miss Finnigan's Fault, Norman Douglas, The Holiday, 1953; The Little Tour, 1954; The Shirt of Nessus, 1955; In Love and War, 1956; The Blitz, 1957; Paradise Lost and More, 1959; When the Kissing had to Stop, 1960; Going to the River, 1963; Random Thoughts of a Fascist Hyena, 1963; The Life of Dylan Thomas, 1965; (ed) Selected Letters of Dylan Thomas, 1966; Through the Minefield, 1967; Denazification, 1969; High Heroic, 1969; Out of the Lion's Paw, 1969; and trans from French, German and Italian. Contributor to several newspapers and periodicals in Britain, America and elsewhere. *Address:* St Anne's, Killiney Hill Road, Co. Dublin. *Clubs:* Beefsteak; Kildare Street (Dublin).

**FitzHARRIS, Viscount; James Carleton Harris;** *b* 19 June 1946; *o s* and *heir* of 6th Earl of Malmesbury, *qv*; *m* 1969, Sally Ann, *yr d* of Sir Richard Newton Rycroft, *qv*; one *s*. *Educ:* Eton; Queen's Coll., St Andrews (MA). *Heir: s* Hon. James Hugh Harris, *b* 29 April 1970. *Address:* 21 West Street, Titchfield, Fareham, Hants. *T:* Titchfield 3074. *Club:* Royal Yacht Squadron.

**FITZHERBERT,** family name of **Baron Stafford.**

**FITZHERBERT, Cuthbert;** a Director of Barclays Bank Ltd (Vice-Chairman of the Board, 1948-64); Director: of Barclays Bank DCO; of the Atlas Assurance Co. Ltd; of London Montrose Investment Trust; *b* 24 May 1899; British; 4th *s* of William Joseph Fitzherbert-Brockholes, CBE, and Blanche Winifred Mary, 2nd *d* of late Maj.-Gen. Hon. Sir Henry Hugh Clifford, VC, KCMG, CB; *m* 1930, Barbara, *e d* of Henry Scrope, Danby; three *s* three *d*. *Educ:* Oratory Sch.; New Coll., Oxford (BA). Commissioned Coldstream Guards, 1917; served European War, 1914-18, in 1st Bn Coldstream Guards (wounded). Joined Barclays Bank Ltd, 1922; Union Bank of Manchester, 1923-26; Local Dir, Barclays Bank Ltd, Darlington, 1926; Local Dir, Barclays Bank Ltd, Birmingham, 1939. Served War of 1939-45, with Coldstream Guards, 1940-44. Returned as Gen. Man. (Staff), Barclays Bank Ltd, 1944. *Recreation:* shooting. *Address:* Street House, Mortimer, Berks. *T:* Mortimer 2312. *Clubs:* Brooks's, Guards.

**FITZHERBERT, Maj.-Gen. Edward Herbert,** CBE 1943; DSO 1918; MC; *b* 3 Dec. 1885; *s* of late Col E. H. Fitzherbert, King's Own Royal Lancaster Regt. *Educ:* Rossall Sch.; RMC Camberley. 2nd Lieut, ASC, 1905; Lieut, 1907;

Capt., 1914; T/Major, 1914; a/Lieut-Col, 1917; Major, 1924; Lieut-Col, 1931; Col, 1935; Brigadier, 1939; Maj.-Gen., 1941; DAQMG, 1915-17; Asst Dir of Supplies and Transport, War Office, 1937-39; Asst Inspector, RASC, 1939; Inspector, RASC, 1940-43; retired pay, 1943; served European War, 1914-18 (despatches thrice, DSO, MC); served War of 1939-45, 1939-43. Col Commandant RASC, 1947-50. *Recreations:* golf and shooting. *Address:* c/o Lloyds Bank, Ltd, Cox & King's Branch, 6 Pall Mall, SW1. *Clubs:* United Service, MCC.

**FitzHERBERT, Sir John (Richard Frederick),** 8th Bt, *cr* 1784; TD; Partner in firm of Land Agents and Surveyors (John German & Son, Ashby-de-la-Zouch), since 1950; *b* 15 Sept. 1913; *s* of Ven. Henry E. FitzHerbert, sometime Archdeacon of Derby, and Hon. Margaret Elinor (*d* 1957), *d* of 3rd Baron Heytesbury; *S* uncle, Sir William FitzHerbert, 7th Bt, 1963; *m* 1957, Kathleen Anna Rees; no *c. Educ:* Charterhouse; Royal Agricultural Coll., Cirencester. Served War of 1939-45, Sherwood Foresters (TA). FLAS 1950. *Recreation:* shooting. *Heir: b* Rev. David Henry FitzHerbert, MC [*b* 9 Sept. 1918; *m* 1962, Charmian Hyacinthe, *yr d* of Samuel Ranulph Allsopp, *qv*; one *s* three *d* (including twin *d*)]. *Address:* Tissington Hall, Ashbourne, Derbyshire. *T:* Parwich 246. *Club:* Derby County (Derby).

**FITZ-MAURICE,** family name of **Earl of Orkney.**

**FITZMAURICE;** *see* Petty-Fitzmaurice.

**FITZMAURICE, Lt-Col Sir Desmond FitzJohn,** Kt 1946; CIE 1941; late RE; *b* 17 Aug. 1893; *s* of John Day Stokes Fitzmaurice, ICS, Tralee, Co. Kerry; *m* 1926, Nancy, *d* of Rev. John Sherlock Leake, Grayswood, Surrey; one *s* three *d. Educ:* Bradfield; RMA, Woolwich; Cambridge Univ. Joined RE, 1914. Served in France, Belgium and Italy, European War, 1914-18 (despatches); Instructor, RMA Woolwich, 1918-20; Cambridge Univ., 1920-22; Instructor, Sch. of Military Engineering, Chatham, 1923, 1924; hp list, 1925; Deputy Mint Master, Bombay, 1929-30; Calcutta, 1931-32; Deputy Master, Security Printing, India, 1932; Master Security Printing and Controller of Stamps, India, 1934; retired. *Address:* Mount Rivers, Killorglin, Co. Kerry.

**FITZMAURICE, Sir Gerald (Gray),** GCMG 1960 (KCMG 1954; CMG 1946); QC; Senior Judge of the International Court of Justice since 1966 (Judge 1960-66); *b* 24 Oct. 1901; *s* of late Vice-Admiral Sir Maurice Fitzmaurice, KCVO, CB, CMG, and Mabel Gertrude, *y d* of late S. W. Gray; *m* 1933, Alice Evelina Alexandra Sandberg; two *s. Educ:* Malvern; Gonville and Caius Coll., Cambridge (BA, LLB 1924). Called to Bar, Gray's Inn, 1925; Bencher, 1961; practised, 1925-29; QC 1957; 3rd Legal Adviser to Foreign Office, 1929; seconded as Legal Adviser to Ministry of Economic Warfare, 1939-43; 2nd Legal Adviser, FO, 1945-53; Legal Adviser, FO, 1953-60. Legal Adviser to UK Delegations, San Francisco UN Charter Conference, 1945; Paris Peace Conference, 1946. UN Assembly, 1946, 1948-59, Japanese Peace Conference, San Francisco, 1951, and Berlin and Manila Confs, 1954; Counsel for HM Govt in several cases before the International Court of Justice at the Hague; Member: Permanent Court of Arbitration, 1964-; UN Internat. Law Commission, 1955-60 (Pres. 1959); Mem. Inst. International Law (Pres., 1967-69); Pres. Grotius Soc., 1956-60. Hon. Fellow, Gonville and Caius Coll., Cambridge, 1961. *Publications:* articles in British Year Book of International Law, 1931-58, Hague Recueil, 1948 and 1957 and in other legal journals. *Address:* West House, Crockham Hill, Edenbridge, Kent; 3 Gray's Inn Square, WC1; International Court of Justice and 76 Riouwstraat, The Hague, Netherlands. *Clubs:* Athenæum, United University.

**FitzPATRICK, Air Cdre David Beatty,** CB 1970; OBE 1953; AFC 1949 and Bar, 1958; Director, Guided Weapons (Trials and Ranges), Ministry of Technology, since 1969; *b* 31 Jan. 1920; *s* of late Comdr D. T. FitzPatrick, RN and Beatrice Anne Ward; *m* 1941, Kathleen Mary Miles; one *d. Educ:* Kenilworth Coll., Exeter; Midhurst. Commnd RAF, 1938; served War of 1939-45, Atlantic, Mediterranean and Far East theatres; comd No 209 Sqdn (Far East), 1944; (GD Pilot) Sqdn flying duty, 1945-52; cfs, pfc and GW Specialist, RAF Henlow, 1952-57; Base Comdr Christmas Island, 1959-60 (British Nuclear Trials); NATO Def. Coll., and jssc, 1960-61; Dep. Dir (Ops) Air Staff, 1961-64; comd RAF Akrotiri and Nicosia, 1964-66; Dir of (Q) RAF, MoD, 1966-69; attached NBPI for special duty, 1969. *Recreations:* swimming (Pres. Royal Air Force Swimming Assoc.), deep-sea fishing, cricket. *Address:* Whistledown, 38 Courts Mount Road, Haslemere, Surrey. *T:* Haslemere 4589. *Clubs:* Royal Air Force; Naval, Military and Air Force (Adelaide).

**FITZPATRICK, Gen. Sir (Geoffrey Richard) Desmond,** KCB 1965 (CB 1961); DSO 1945; MBE 1943; MC 1939; Deputy Supreme Allied Commander, Europe, since 1970; Deputy Colonel, The Blues and The Royals, since 1969; ADC (General) to the Queen since 1970; *b* 14 Dec. 1912; *o s* of late Brig.-Gen. Sir Richard Fitzpatrick, CBE, DSO, and Lady (G. E.) Fitzpatrick; *m* 1944, Mary Sara, *o d* of Sir Charles Campbell, 12th Bt; one *s* one *d. Educ:* Eton; RMC Sandhurst. Commissioned The Royal Dragoons, 1932. Served in Palestine, 1938-39 (MC); War of 1939-45 (despatches, MBE, DSO); in Middle East, Italy, NW Europe. Bt. Lieut-Col 1951; Col 1953; ADC to the Queen, 1959; Maj.-Gen. 1959; Asst Chief of Defence Staff, Ministry of Defence, 1959-61; Dir Mil. Ops, War Office, 1962-64; Chief of Staff, BAOR, 1964-65; Lt-Gen. 1965; GOC-in-C, N Ire., 1965-66; Vice-Chief of Gen. Staff, 1966-68; Gen. 1968; C-in-C, BAOR, and Commander N Army Gp 1968-70. Col, The Royal Dragoons, 1964-69. *Address:* c/o Lloyds Bank, 6 Pall Mall, SW1. *Clubs:* Cavalry; Royal Yacht Sqdn; Bembridge Sailing.

**FITZ ROY,** family name of **Viscount Daventry.**

**FITZROY,** family name of **Duke of Grafton** and of **Southampton Barony.**

**FITZROY, Charles;** late 2nd Lieutenant Royal Horse Guards and Pioneer Corps; *b* 3 Jan. 1904; *o s* of 4th Baron Southampton, OBE, and late Lady Hilda Mary Dundas, *d* of 1st Marquess of Zetland; *S* father, 1958, as 5th Baron Southampton, but disclaimed his title for life, 16 March 1964; *m* 1st, 1927, Margaret (*d* 1931), *d* of Prebendary H. Mackworth Drake, Vicar of Paignton; one *s*; 2nd, 1940, Mrs Joan Leslie (marr. diss., 1944); 3rd, 1951, Rachel Christine, *d* of Charles Zaman, Lille, France. *Educ:* Harrow. Served Royal Horse Guards, 1923-25; re-employed, 1940, with RA, Pioneer Corps, 1941. Joint-master, Grove Fox-hounds, 1930-32. *Heir:* (*to disclaimed barony*): *s* Hon. Charles James FitzRoy [*b* 12 Aug. 1928; *m* 1951, Pamela Anne, *d* of E. Henniker, Maidenhead, Berks; two *s* one *d*]. *Address:* East Lodge, Fernbank Road, Ascot,

Berks.
*See also Brig. W. M. Sale.*

**FITZSIMMONS, Rt. Hon. William Kennedy,** PC (N Ireland) 1965; MP (N Ireland Parliament) Duncairn Division of Belfast since 1956; JP; Minister of Health and Social Services for Northern Ireland since 1969; *b* 31 Jan. 1909; *m* 1935, May Elizabeth Lynd; two *d. Educ:* Skegoniell National Sch.; Belfast Jun. Techn. Sch. Mem., Belfast City and Dist Water Comrs, 1948-57 (Chm. 1954-55); Pres., Duncairn Unionist Assoc.; N Ireland Parliament: Dep. Govt Whip, 1961-63; Parl. Secretary: Min. of Commerce, 1961-65; Min. of Home Affairs, 1963-64; Min. of Develt, 1964-65; Min. of Education, 1965-66; Minister of Development, 1966-67. MRSH; JP Belfast, 1951. *Address:* Sandown, Chichester Park, Belfast, N Ireland BT15 5DU. *T:* Belfast 77692.

**FITZSIMONS, Robert Allen,** FRCS; Hon. Consulting Surgeon to Charing Cross Hospital and to The Metropolitan Hospital; *b* 16 March 1892; *s* of James Fitzsimons and Mary L. McDonald, Sligo; *m* 1927, Mary Patricia, *d* of Thomas McKelvey, Cardiff; one *s* one *d. Educ:* Summerhill Coll., Sligo; Birkbeck Coll., King's Coll., and Charing Cross Hospital Medical Sch., University of London. BSc London 1920; MB, BS London 1930; MRCS, LRCP, 1926; FRCS 1932. Formerly: Analyst to HM Govt Laboratory; House Surgeon and Surgical Registrar to Charing Cross Hosp.; Registrar to Royal National Orthopædic Hospital. Fellow of the Assoc. of Surgeons, Great Britain and Ireland. *Address:* 16 Lansdowne Road, W11. *T:* 01-727 5759.

**FITZWALTER,** 21st Baron, *cr* 1295; **(Fitzwalter) Brook Plumptre,** JP; Hon. Captain, The Buffs; *b* 15 Jan. 1914; *s* of late George Beresford Plumptre, Goodnestone, Canterbury, Kent; *S* uncle, 1943 (Barony called out of abeyance in his favour, 1953); *m* 1951, Margaret Melesina, *yr d* of (Herbert) William Deedes, JP, Galt, Hythe, Kent; five *s. Educ:* Diocesan Coll., Rondebosch, Cape; Jesus Coll., Cambridge. Served War of 1939-45, with the Buffs (Royal East Kent Regt) in France, Belgium, UK and India; attached RIASC, as Capt. JP, Kent, 1949-. Landowner and farmer; succeeded to family estate, 1943. *Heir: s* Hon. Julian Brook Plumptre, *b* 18 Oct. 1952. *Address:* Goodnestone Park, Canterbury, Kent. *T:* Nonington 218.

**FITZWILLIAM, Wentworth-,** family name of **Earl Fitzwilliam.**

**FITZWILLIAM,** 10th Earl *cr* 1716; **William Thomas George Wentworth-Fitzwilliam,** Baron Fitzwilliam, 1620; Earl Fitzwilliam and Viscount Milton, 1716 (Irish honours); Baron Milton (Great Britain), 1742; Earl Fitzwilliam and Viscount Milton, 1746; DL; JP; CA Huntingdon and Peterborough; Chairman, Milton (Peterborough) Estates Co.; Director: Modport Group Ltd; Neanco Holdings Ltd; Limestone Products Ltd; Bewac Motor Corporation Ltd; Fitzwilliam (Peterborough) Properties Ltd; SYCW (Realizations) Ltd; *b* 28 May 1904; *s* of late George Charles Wentworth-Fitzwilliam (*g g s* of 5th Earl) and Evelyn, *o d* of Charles Stephen Lyster; *S* cousin, 1952; *m* 1956, Joyce (who *m* 1922, Hon. Henry Fitzalan-Howard, later 2nd Visc. Fitz Alan of Derwent (marr. diss., 1955; he *d* 1962); *two d*), *e d* of Col Philip Langdale, OBE, Houghton Hall, Yorks. *Educ:* Eton; Magdalene Coll., Cambridge. Joint Master Fitzwilliam Hunt, 1935-; JP for Peterborough and County Alderman for the Soke of Peterborough; Chm. Peterborough Divisional Conservative Assoc. Served War of 1939-45; American Bronze Star Medal. *Recreation:* shooting. *Heir:* none. *Address:* Milton, Peterborough. *T:* Castor 202; Wentworth Woodhouse, Rotherham. *Clubs:* Boodle's, Pratt's, White's.

**FLACK, Bertram Anthony;** Diplomatic Service Inspector since 1968; *b* 3 Feb. 1924; *y s* of Dr F. H. Flack and Alice Cockshut, Nelson, Lancs; *m* 1948, Jean W. Mellor; two *s* two *d. Educ:* Epsom Coll.; Liverpool Univ. (LLM Hons). Enlisted Gren. Gds, 1942; commissioned E Lancashire Regt, 1943; served in NW Europe (Captain). Joined Foreign Service, 1948; served Karachi, 1948-50; Alexandria, 1950-52; Stockholm, 1955-58; Accra, 1958-61; Johannesburg, 1964-67; Dep. High Comr, E Pakistan, 1967-68. *Recreations:* cricket, golf. *Address:* Drakelow, Christchurch Road, Virginia Water, Surrey. *T:* Wentworth 3772. *Club:* Travellers'.

**FLAHIFF, His Eminence Cardinal George Bernard;** *see* Winnipeg, Archbishop of, (RC).

**FLANDERS, Allan David,** MA Oxon; Full-time Member, Commission on Industrial Relations, since 1969; Visiting Professor of Industrial Relations, University of Manchester, since 1969; *b* 27 July 1910; *s* of Frederick William Flanders and Emily Louisa (*née* Shaw); *m* 1951, Annemarie Klara Laura (*née* Tracinski). *Educ:* Latymer Upper Sch.; Landerziehungsheim Walkemuhle, Germany. Research Asst, TUC, 1943-46; Head of Political Branch, Brit. CCG, 1946-47; Sen. Lectr in Industrial Relations, Univ. of Oxford, 1949-69; Faculty Fellow, Nuffield Coll., 1964-69. Mem., Sec. of State's Colonial Adv. Cttee, 1954-62; Industrial Relations Adviser to Nat. Bd for Prices and Incomes, 1965-68. *Publications:* Trade Unions, 1952 (7th rev. edn, 1968); The System of Industrial Relations in Great Britain (with H. A. Clegg), 1954; The Fawley Productivity Agreements, 1964; Industrial Relations: What is Wrong with the System?, 1965; Collective Bargaining: Prescription for Change, 1967; Experiment in Industrial Democracy (with R. Pomeranz and J. Woodward), 1968; (ed) Collective Bargaining (Modern Management Readings), 1969; Management and Unions, 1970. *Recreations:* gardening, walking. *Address:* Chapel Lane, Northmoor, Oxford. *T:* Standlake 331.

**FLANDERS, Dennis;** ARWS; RBA; Artist: townscapes and landscapes in pencil and water-colour; Vice-President, Royal Drawing Society, since 1954; *b* 2 July 1915; *s* of late Bernard C. Flanders, ARAM (pianist), and late Jessie Marguerite Flanders, ARMS (artist); *m* 1952, Dalma J. Darnley, *o d* of late J. Darnley Taylor and of Mrs Joan Darnley Taylor; one *s* one *d. Educ:* Merchant Taylors' Sch.; Regent Street Polytechnic; St Martin's Art Sch.; Central Sch. of Arts and Crafts. Princess Louise Gold Medal at age of 7. Mem. of St Paul's Watch, 1940-42; Royal Engineers, 1942-46. Occasional drawings for Daily Telegraph and other journals; series of drawings for Yorkshire Post, 1949; Birmingham Post, 1950-51; "Famous Streets," Sunday Times, 1952-53; Special artist to the Illustrated London News, 1956-64. Water-colours (reproduced as prints) of:

RMA Sandhurst; Police Coll., Bramshill; St Edward's Sch., Oxford. Drawings in private collections and Nat. War Collection (1939-45), Guildhall Library and Museums at Exeter, York, Lincoln, Kensington, St Marylebone, Walthamstow and Wolverhampton, also Bank of England. Exhibitor: RA and in provinces: one-man shows: London, 1947, 1951, 1953, 1955, 1964, 1967; Bedford, 1965, 1966; Boston (Lincs), 1966; Southport, 1969. Member: Art Workers Guild; The Sette of Odd Volumes; Cttee, Soc. for Protection of Ancient Buildings. Freeman: City of London, 1970; Painter Stainers' Co., 1970. Hon. RDS. Lord Mayor's Art Award, 1966. *Publications:* Bolton Abbey (illustrations), 1947; Chelsea by Richard Edmonds (illustrations), 1956; Soho for East Anglia by Michael Brander, 1963. *Recreations:* walking, riding, reading Who's Who. *Address:* 51 Great Ormond Street, WC1. *T:* 01-405 9317; Baker's Cross House, Cranbrook, Kent. *T:* 2018.

**FLANDERS, Michael,** OBE 1964; actor and writer; *b* London, 1 March 1922; *s* of Peter Henry Flanders and Rosa Laura (Laurie O'Beirne, violinist); *m* 1959, Claudia, *er d* of Prof. Robert Gorham Davis, Columbia Univ., USA; two *d. Educ:* Westminster Sch.; Christ Church, Oxford (BA). Acted with OUDS, ETC and professionally at Playhouse, 1941. AB on destroyer, 1942; Sub-Lieut RNVR, Coastal Forces; contracted poliomyelitis, 1943; discharged hospital but confined to wheel-chair, 1946. First broadcast, 1948; since then he has broadcast regularly, on radio and TV, mainly as poetry reader and narrator; gave weekly Current Affairs talk (BBC European Service), 1951-58; first televised, 1953; Commentator TV Newsreel, 1953-54; Science Review, 1953-56; Chm. of The Brains Trust, 1958, etc. From 1948 wrote for many revues. Main author Penny Plain, 1951; Airs on a Shoestring, 1953; Pay the Piper, 1954; Fresh Airs, 1956. Also wrote opera libretti, Three's Company, 1953, and A Christmas Story, 1954 (Anthony Hopkins), both televised. Trans. The Soldier's Tale (Stravinsky) with Kitty Black, for Edinburgh Fest., 1954; trans. radiophonic opera Orestes (Henk Badings) for Radio-Unie (Hilversum), 1955, in which he took a leading role. With Donald Swann presented their two-man revue At the Drop of a Hat, New Lindsay Theatre, Dec. 1956; transferred to Fortune Theatre, Jan. 1957-May 1959; Edinburgh Fest., Aug. 1959; New York, Oct. 1959-May 1960; toured USA and Canada, Oct. 1960-March 1961; Geneva, May 1961; GB and Canada, Oct. 1962-March 1963. Joined Royal Shakespeare Co. in The Caucasian Chalk Circle, 1962; (with Donald Swann) At the Drop of Another Hat (Haymarket), Oct. 1963-March 1964; toured Australia and New Zealand, Aug.-Dec. 1964; Hong Kong, Jan. 1965; (Globe) Oct. 1965-Feb. 1966; toured USA and Canada, 1966; New York, 1966, 1967; 10 Years Hard (Revue), Mayfair, 1970. *Film:* The Raging Moon, 1970. *Publications:* Creatures Great and Small, 1964; Captain Noah and His Floating Zoo, 1971. *Address:* 57 Campbell Court, Queen's Gate Gardens, SW7. *T:* 01-584 7747.

**FLAVELL, Geoffrey,** FRCS; MRCP; Surgeon, Department of Thoracic Surgery, The London Hospital, since 1950; Consultant Thoracic Surgeon, Royal Masonic Hospital, since 1957; Senior Thoracic Surgeon, Broomfield Hospital, since 1947; Consultant in Thoracic Surgery to Whipps Cross, Wanstead, Hart, Oldchurch, St Margaret's and Harold Wood Hospitals; *b* 23 Feb. 1913; *o* surviving *s* of late W. A. Flavell, JP, of Wellington, NZ; *m* 1943, Joan Margaret, *o d* of S. Ewart Adams, Hawkwell, Essex; no *c. Educ:* Waitaki; Otago; University of New Zealand; St Bartholomew's Hospital, London. Qualified in medicine, 1937; House appts, St Bartholomew's Hosp., 1937-39; Resident Surgical Officer, Brompton Hosp., 1940-41. Surgeon Specialist, RAF, 1942, O/C Surgical Divs RAF Gen. Hosps, Carthage and Algiers, 1943; RAF Gen. Hosp., Cairo; Adviser in Surgery RAF Med. and Middle East Command, 1944; retired rank of Wing Comdr, 1958. Consultant Thoracic Surgeon, British Legion Hosp., and to LCC, 1946. Senior Registrar to London Hosp., 1947. *Publications:* Introduction to Chest Surgery, 1957; Basic Surgery (Thoracic section), 1958; The Oesophagus, 1963; many contribs to surgical textbooks and med. jls; various articles on travel, wine and food, in lay periodicals. *Recreations:* history; architecture; sailing; ski-ing; indulging the senses. *Address:* 148 Harley Street, W1. *T:* 01-935 1207; 22 Downshire Hill, NW3. *T:* 01-435 7099; The Mill Cottage, Stow Maries, Essex. *T:* Purleigh 265.

**FLAVELLE, Sir (Joseph) Ellsworth,** 2nd Bt, *cr* 1917; *b* 25 May, 1892; *s* of Sir Joseph Wesley Flavelle, 1st Bt, and Clara, *d* of Rev. Oren Ellsworth; *S* father 1939; *m* 1917, Muriel McEachren; two *s* one *d. Educ:* St Andrew's Coll., University of Toronto. Trustee, Toronto General Hosp.; Mem. of Board, Community Welfare Council of Ontario; Mem. Advisory Council Knights of the Round Table. *Recreations:* yachting, photography. *Heir: s* Joseph David Ellsworth Flavelle [*b* 9 Nov. 1921; *m* 1942, Muriel Barbara, *d* of Reginald Morton; three *d*]. *Address:* Kingswold, RR2, King, Ontario, Canada; 780 Eglington Avenue, Toronto, Ont., Canada. *Clubs:* York, Royal Canadian Yacht (Toronto).

**FLAXMAN, Brigadier Sir Hubert (James Marlowe),** Kt 1962; CMG 1954; retired as Chief Justice of Gibraltar (Dec. 1955-Sept. 1965); *b* 22 July 1893; *s* of James and Florence Flaxman; *m* 1st, 1920, Muriel Kathleen Bateman (*d* 1961); one *s*; 2nd, 1961, Vivien Aderna Barton. *Educ:* The Drapers' Sch., Purley. Political Officer, Mesopotamia, 1918; joined Sudan Civil Service, 1924, as District Commissioner; District Judge, 1926; Judge of the High Court, 1933. Called to the Bar, Middle Temple, 1934. Chief Justice of the Sudan, 1940; British Judge, Joint Court, New Hebrides, 1949; Resident Commissioner, New Hebrides, 1950-55; Acting Attorney-Gen., Gibraltar, Oct.-Dec. 1955. Served in the Army, 1914-21 and 1944-49 (despatches). Order of the Nile (4th Class), 1934. *Recreation:* gardening. *Address:* Ashton Cottage, Yaxley, near Eye, Suffolk. *Club:* East India and Sports.

**FLEETWOOD-HESKETH, Charles Peter F.;** *see* Hesketh.

**FLEMING, Amy M.,** MD, DSc, FRCOG; Hon. Consulting Obstetrician and Gynæcologist: St Mary's Hospital, Harrow Road; St Mary Abbot's Hospital, Kensington; Teacher in Queen Charlotte's Hospital, and Institute of Obstetrics and Gynæcology, University of London; *d* of Charles Friskin Fleming and Margaret Burns Elphinstone Waddell. *Educ:* Universities of Glasgow, Vienna, Tübingen. Formerly Prof. of Obstetrics and Gynæcology, University of London; Senior Asst Surgeon Royal Samaritan Hospital for Women, Glasgow, and Royal Maternity and Women's

Hospital, Glasgow. *Publications:* papers in Transactions of the Royal Society of Edinburgh, and other medical monographs. *Recreation:* gardening. *Address:* Bowerhouse, 2 Gallow Hill, Peebles, Scotland. *T:* Peebles 3018.

**FLEMING, Dr Charles Alexander,** OBE 1964; FRS 1967; Chief Palæontologist, New Zealand Geological Survey, Department of Scientific and Industrial Research, since 1953; *b* 9 Sept. 1916; *s* of Geo. H. Fleming, Auckland, NZ; *m* 1941, Margaret Alison, *d* of S. G. Chambers, Auckland; three *d. Educ:* King's Coll., Auckland; University of Auckland. Boyhood interest in birds and shell-collecting led to participation in Auckland Mus. expedns, 1933-35; student fieldwork on birds of NZ and Chatham Is (basis of papers publ. 1939); Asst Geologist, NZ Geol Survey, 1940; subseq. Palæontologist and Sen. Palæontologist. Overseas service as coastwatcher, Auckland Is, 1942-43. Pres., Ornithol. Soc. NZ, 1948-49; NZ Delegate: Internat. Geol Congresses, 1948, 1960; British Commonwealth Conf. on Geology and Mineral Resources, 1948; Mem. Bd of Trustees: Nat. Art Gall. and Dominion Mus.; NZ Fauna Protection Adv. Coun.; NZ Nat. Commn for Unesco, 1966. President: Internat. Paleont. Union (Oceania Filial), 1964-68; Aust. and NZ Soc. for Advancement of Science, 1968-70. Fellow, Royal Society of NZ, 1952 (Pres. 1962-66); Fellow, Art Galls and Museums Assoc. of NZ, 1956; Corresp. Fellow, American Ornithologists' Union, 1962; Commonwealth and Foreign Fellow, Geol. Soc. London, 1967. Several scientific prizes and awards. *Publications:* (ed.) Checklist of New Zealand Birds, 1953; geol and palæontol bulletins; about 200 research papers on mollusca, birds, geology, palæontology, biogeography. *Recreations:* recorded music, natural history. *Address:* Balivean, 42 Wadestown Road, Wellington, NZ. *T:* Wellington 46-653.

**FLEMING, Prof. Charles Mann,** CBE 1964; Dean of the Faculty of Medicine since 1959 and Professor of Administrative Medicine since 1960 in University of Glasgow; *b* 1 March 1904; *y s* of John Somerville Fleming and Christina Taylor Gerard, Glasgow; *m* 1930, Margaret Hamilton Barrie, *er d* of George Simpson, Newfoundland; one *d. Educ:* Hillhead High Sch; Glasgow Univ. MA 1924, MB, ChB 1929, MD 1933 (Glasgow); MRCPEd 1945, FRCPEd 1952, FRFPS (G.) 1959, FRCP (Glasgow) 1962. Hon. FRCGP 1964. Regional MO, 1937-39, Hospital Officer (Eastern Dist, Scotland), 1939-46, Principal MO, 1946-59, Dept of Health for Scotland. Convener Post-Grad. Med. Board, and Dir, Post-Grad. Med. Educn, University of Glasgow; Chairman: Scottish Central Medical Recruitment Cttee; Jt Adv. Cttee on Training Senior Registrars; Member: General Medical Council; WHO Expert Advisory Panel on Organisation of Medical Care; Med. Adv. Cttee, ODM; Royal Commission on Med. Educn, 1966-68; Western Regional Hosp. Bd; Central Cttee on Postgraduate Med. Educn (GB); Manpower and Training Cttee, Inter-Univ. Council for Higher Educn Overseas; Scottish Council for Postgraduate Med. Educn. Addtl Mem. Gen. Dental Council. *Publications:* contributions to medical journals. *Recreation:* golf. *Address:* 8 Thorn Road, Bearsden, Glasgow. *T:* Bearsden 2810.

**FLEMING, Hon. Donald Methuen,** PC (Canada) 1957; QC (Ontario) 1944; *b* Exeter, Ont., 23 May 1905; *s* of Louis Charles and Maud Margaret Wright Fleming; *m* 1933, Alice Mildred Watson, Toronto; two *s* one *d. Educ:* public schools and Collegiate Inst., Galt; Univ. of Toronto (BA, LLB); Osgoode Hall Law Sch. Called to Bar, Ontario, 1928; subsequently practised in Toronto; Counsel to Blake, Cassels and Graydon, Barristers and Solicitors, Toronto, 1963-67. MP for Toronto-Eglinton, 1945-63; Minister of Finance and Receiver-General, 1957-62; Minister of Justice and Attorney-General of Canada, 1962-63. A Governor, Internat. Bank and IMF, 1957-63; Chairman: Commonwealth Finance Ministers' Conf., Mont Tremblant, Province of Quebec, 1957; Commonwealth Trade and Economic Conf., Montreal, 1958; OECD, 1961, 1962; Leader: delegn of Canadian Ministers to meetings of US-Canada Jt Trade and Economic Cttee, Washington, 1957, 1960, 1961 (Chm. Ottawa meeting, 1959, 1962); Canadian delegn to OEEC Confs, Paris, 1960; Canadian delegate: NATO Conf. of Heads of Govt, Paris, 1957; NATO Ministerial Confs, 1958, 1959, 1961; Commonwealth Parly Confs, London, 1948, Ottawa, 1952, Nairobi, 1954. Has taken part in numerous parly, political, municipal and civic welfare activities and in church affairs. Man. Dir, Bank of Nova Scotia Trust Cos; General Counsel to Bank of Nova Scotia in Bahamas, etc; Director: Gore Mutual Insurance Co.; Empresas Consolidadas Sudamericanos SA; Kroehler Mfg Co. Ltd; Jersey External Trust Ltd; Sceptre Trust Ltd; Scythes & Co. Ltd; British Commercial Property Investments (Canada) Ltd. Past Pres., Toronto YMCA. Hon. Mem., Canadian Legion; Hon. Life Mem., Canadian Bar Assoc. DCL hc Bishop's Univ., 1960; LLD hc Waterloo Lutheran Univ., 1967. *Publications:* numerous works and articles on legal subjects; contribs to legal periodicals including Canadian Encyclopedic Digest, Canadian Bar Review, Canadian Abridgement, etc. *Recreations:* all branches of sport. *Address:* Bayview, PO Box 1355, Nassau, Bahamas. *Clubs:* Canadian (Pres., 1964), Empire, Granite, National, Raredale Golf, Toronto Cricket (Toronto); Rideau, Country (Ottawa); Lyford Cay, Nassau East Hill, Nassau City (Bahamas).

**FLEMING, Ian,** RSA 1956 (ARSA 1947); RSW 1947; Head, Gray's School of Art, Aberdeen, since 1954; *b* 19 Nov. 1906; *s* of John and Catherine Fleming; *m* 1943, Catherine Margaret Weetch; one *s* two *d. Educ:* Hyndland Sch., Glasgow; Glasgow Sch. of Art. Lectr, Glasgow Sch. of Art, 1931-48; Warden, Patrick Allen-Fraser Art Coll., Hospitalfield, Arbroath, 1948-54. *Recreation:* anything Scottish. *Address:* 15 Fonthill Road, Aberdeen. *T:* 20680. *Clubs:* Art (Glasgow); Rotary (Aberdeen).

**FLEMING, Rev. James George Grant,** DSO 1917; MC 1917; TD 1939; retired; *b* 2 April 1895; *s* of late James Fleming, Glenfarg, Craigleith, Edinburgh; *m* 1st, 1919, Daisy (*d* 1924), *s* of late Maj. W. J. Trotter, RAMC, Readstown, Co. Meath, Ireland; one *d*; 2nd, 1930, Saidie Caroline, *d* of late W. J. Stewart, MP, Crawfordsburn, Co. Down, Ireland; one *s. Educ:* Stewart's Coll., Edinburgh; Edinburgh Univ. (MA 1928). Army 1914-23. Served European War, 1914-18 (wounded; despatches; DSO; MC); Waziristan FF, 1919-21. Ordained 1930; Minister: Lasswade Old Parish Church, 1930-35; East Church of St Nicholas, Aberdeen, 1935-41; Banchory-St Ternan East Church, Banchory, Kincardineshire, 1952-65. Served 1939-47: SCF 9th (Highland) Div., 1939; SCF 51st (Highland) Div., 1940-42; DACG 1942; Senior

Staff Chaplain, India, 1942-44; Asst Chaplain-Gen., L of C and Burma, 1944-46 (despatches twice); Hon. CF (1st class), 1947; C of S Chaplain, CCG and UK High Commission, Germany, 1948-52. *Publications:* various. *Recreations:* philately, painting. *Address:* Dunard, Banchory, Kincardineshire. *T:* Banchory 2828. *Club:* Royal Northern (Aberdeen).

**FLEMING, Instructor Rear-Adm. Sir John,** KBE 1960; DSC 1944; Director of the Naval Education Service, 1956-60; *b* 2 May 1904; *s* of late James Fleming; *m* 1930, Jean Law, *d* of late James Stuart Gillitt, South Shields; no *c*. *Educ:* Jarrow Grammar Sch.; St John's Coll., Cambridge. BA 1925, MA 1957. Entered RN as Instructor Lieut, 1925; Instr Lieut-Comdr, 1931; Instr Comdr, 1939; Instr Capt., 1950; Instr Rear-Adm., 1956. Asst Dir Naval Weather Service, 1945, Dep. Dir, 1947; Fleet Instructor Officer and Fleet Meteorological Officer, Home Fleet, 1950; Command Instructor Officer, The Nore, 1951; Education Dept, Admiralty, 1952. *Recreation:* gardening. *Address:* Blackdown Cottage, Denbigh Road, Haslemere, Surrey. *T:* Haselmere 2412.

**FLEMING, John Marcus,** CMG 1950; MA Edinburgh; Deputy Director, Research Department, International Monetary Fund, 1964; *b* 13 March 1911; *s* of John and Helen Fleming, Bathgate, West Lothian; *m* 1936, Etta (marr. diss., 1958), *d* of Kapitän Leist, Vienna, Austria; two *d*; *m* 1959, Gloria, *d* of Wayne Hile, Detroit, Michigan, USA. *Educ:* Bathgate Academy; Edinburgh Univ. Mem. of Financial Section, League of Nations, 1935-37; Travelling Fellow of Rockefeller Foundation, 1937-39; Ministry of Economic Warfare, 1939-42; Cabinet Offices, Economic Section, 1942, Deputy Dir, 1947-51; Visiting Prof., Columbia Univ., New York, 1951-54; Chief, Special Studies Div., IMF, 1954; Adviser, IMF, 1959. Mem. of UK delegation to San Francisco Conference of 1945, and to meetings of Economic and Social Council, etc.; UK Rep. on Economic and Employment Commission of UN, 1950-51. *Publications:* contrib. to learned journals in UK and USA on questions of economic theory and policy. *Recreations:* theatre, philosophy. *Address:* c/o International Monetary Fund, 19th and H Street NW, Washington, DC 20431, USA.

**FLEMING, Prof. Marston Greig,** BSc; PhD; MIMM; Professor of Mineral Technology, since 1961 and Head of Department of Mining and Mineral Technology, since 1967, Imperial College, London University; Dean of the Royal School of Mines, since 1968; *b* 1913; *s* of late Alexander Greig Fleming, Montreal; *m* 1951, E. Box, painter; two *s* one *d* (by a previous marriage). *Educ:* Westmount High Sch.; Queen's Univ., Canada. Metallurgist with Canadian goldmining companies, 1936-41. RCAF navigator, 1941-46; Flight Lieut, 1943. Imperial Coll., Royal Sch. of Mines: Lecturer, 1946-51, Senior Lecturer, 1951-58, Reader, 1958-61. Mineral processing consultant to governments, mining companies and to DSIR, at various times, 1946-. Chm., Mineral Processing Cttee, DSIR and Min. of Technology, 1959-66; Mem., Steering Cttee, Warren Spring Lab., 1966-68. Chm. Advisory Panel, BCURA, 1961-66; IMM Council, 1962-, Vice-Pres., 1968-. British rep., Scientific Cttee, Internat. Mineral Processing Congress, France, 1963, USA, 1964, USSR, 1968, Czechoslovakia, 1970; Canadian Rep., Council of Commonwealth Mining and Metall. Instns, 1969-. Dir, UNESCO Regional Course, Benares, 1964; Chm., Brighton Conf. on the Technologist in the Mineral Ind. of the Future, 1969. Hon. ARSM, 1966. *Publications:* Identification of Mineral Grains (with M. P. Jones), 1965; papers in a number of scientific and technical journals, etc. *Address:* Zoffany House, 65 Strand-on-the-Green, W4. *Club:* Garrick.

**FLEMING, Patrick Lyons;** Director of companies; Member of Council of Institute of Directors and of Aims of Industry; *b* Aberdeen, 3 April 1905; *er s* of late Col Frank Fleming, DSO; *m* 1929, Eleanor (*d* 1970), *d* of late H. G. Tapper; two *d*. *Educ:* Shrewsbury; Lincoln Coll., Oxford (Schol., MA). Chm. of Epsom Division Conservative Assoc., 1949-50. *Recreation:* fishing. *Address:* Sutton Boxes, Sutton Park, near Guildford, Surrey.

**FLEMING, Peter;** *see* Fleming, R. P.

**FLEMING, Major Philip,** DL, JP, N Bucks; *b* 15 Aug. 1889; *s* of Robert Fleming, LLD, JP; *m* 1924, Joan Cecil, *d* of late Sir Philip Hunloke, GCVO; one *s* two *d*. *Educ:* Eton; Magdalen Coll., Oxford. Stroked Leander VIII winners Olympic Games, 1912. Served European War, 1914-18, in Queen's Own Oxfordshire Hussars. Dir Robert Fleming & Co. Ltd, Merchant Bankers. High Sheriff of Oxon., 1948-49. *Recreations:* hunting, stalking, fishing. *Address:* Barton Abbey, Steeple Aston, Oxon. *T:* 227. *Club:* Carlton.

**FLEMING, Richard Evelyn,** MC; TD; Merchant Banker; Chairman: Robert Fleming & Co.; Sun Alliance and London Insurance Ltd, since 1968; Director, Barclays Bank and other companies; *b* 23 Feb. 1911; *s* of Major Valentine Fleming, DSO, MP, and Evelyn Ste Croix Fleming; *m* 1938, Hon. Dorothy Charmian Hermon Hodge, 3rd *d* of 2nd Baron Wyfold; five *s* three *d*. *Educ:* Eton; Magdalen Coll., Oxford. Served War of 1939-45, with Lovat Scouts and 5th (Sutherland) Bn, Seaforth Highlanders. Trustee of Pilgrim Trust (Chm., 1968-). *Recreations:* most country pursuits. *Address:* Leygore Manor, Northleach, Glos. *T:* Northleach 234. *Clubs:* Brooks's; New (Edinburgh).
*See also Baron Wyfold.*

**FLEMING, (Robert) Peter,** OBE 1945; DL; *b* 31 May 1907; *e s* of late Major Valentine Fleming, DSO, MP, and Evelyn Beatrice Ste Croix Rose; *m* 1935, Celia (*see* Celia Johnson), *yr d* of Dr J. R. Johnson; one *s* two *d*. *Educ:* Eton; Christ Church, Oxford. 1st class English Literature, 1929; at one time travelled widely, generally as a Special Correspondent of The Times; Commissioned Grenadier Guards (Supp. R of O), 1930; served War of 1939-45, Norway, 1940 (mention); Greece, 1941 (wounded); SEAC 1942-45. Order of the Cloud and Banner (Chinese) for War Services. Commanded 4th Bn Oxford and Bucks Light Infantry (TA), 1951-54; promoted Bt Col and transferred to TARO, 1954. High Sheriff of Oxon., 1952. Pres. Oxfordshire Branch of Country Landowners Association, 1960-; DL Oxon. *Publications include:* Brazilian Adventure; One's Company, News from Tartary; Invasion, 1940; The Siege at Peking; Bayonets to Lhasa; The Fate of Admiral Kolchak; Translated from French: Tibetan Marches by A. Migot. *Recreations:* shooting, riding. *Address:* Merrimoles House, Nettlebed, Oxon. *T:* Nettlebed 304. *Club:* Garrick.

**FLEMING, William Arnot,** MA, LLB; Hon. LLD Edinburgh; Advocate; *b* 1879; *s* of Alexander Fleming, SSC, Edinburgh; *m* 1909, Mollie M'Leod, *d* of John Adam Bryden, Edinburgh; two *s* one *d*. *Educ:* George Watson's Coll., and University, Edinburgh; University of Paris. Thow Scholar, Lorimer Scholar. Scottish Bar, 1904; Capt. 8th Bn The Royal Scots, 1915-19; on active service in France, 1917-18; Pres. of the Pensions Appeal Tribunals for Scotland, 1919-24; Sec. to the University of Edinburgh, 1924-45, mem. of Edinburgh Univ. Court, 1949-52. *Publication:* University Court Ordinances, 1925-47. *Recreation:* golf. *Address:* 22 India Street, Edinburgh. *Club:* Caledonian United Service (Edinburgh).

**FLEMING, Rt. Rev. William L. S.;** *see* Norwich, Bishop of.

**FLEMINGTON, Rev. William Frederick,** MA Oxon, BD Cantab; Principal of Wesley House, Cambridge, 1955-67; held Greenhalgh Chair of New Testament Language and Literature, Wesley House, Cambridge, 1937-67, retired; *b* 24 May 1901; *er s* of Rev. William Frederick Flemington and Annie Mary Geden Bate; *m* 1930, Ethel Phyllis Goodenough, *er d* of Rev. John Henry Doddrell; one *s* one *d*. *Educ:* Liverpool Coll.; Jesus Coll., Oxford (Exhibitioner, 2nd Cl. Classical Hon. Mods, 2nd Cl. Lit. Hum.); Jesus Coll., Fitzwilliam Coll. and Wesley House, Cambridge (Carus Greek Testament Prize; 1st Cl. Theological Tripos, Pt II, Sect. 2, New Testament). Entered Wesleyan Methodist Ministry, 1925; Asst Tutor, Handsworth Coll., Birmingham, 1926-30; Minister in Stourbridge Circuit (Cradley), 1930-33; West Bromwich Circuit, 1933-37; Tutor, Wesley House, 1937-55. Select Preacher, Cambridge Univ., 1944, 1950, 1954. Pres. of Cambridge Theological Soc., 1963-65. *Publications:* The New Testament Doctrine of Baptism, 1948; contributor to Prayer and Worship, 1945; articles and reviews in Expository Times and Jl of Theological Studies. *Recreations:* walking and cycling. *Address:* 204 Chesterton Road, Cambridge.

**FLEMMING, Cecil Wood,** CBE 1964 (OBE 1944); FRCS, MCh; Consultant Orthopædic Surgeon, University College Hospital, London, 1933-65; retired; *b* 20 Aug. 1902; *s* of Percy and Elizabeth Flemming; *m* 1931, Elizabeth, *d* of W. Nelson Haden, JP; two *s* one *d*. *Educ:* Rugby; Trinity Coll., Oxford. FRCS, 1928; MCh Oxford, 1929. Served War of 1939-45, in RAF (Volunteer Reserve), Air Commodore (OBE). *Publications:* contrib. to learned journals on surgical subjects. *Address:* 14 Northampton Park, Canonbury, N1. *T:* 01-226 3125. *Club:* Reform.

**FLEMMING, Sir Gilbert Nicolson,** KCB 1953 (CB 1948); *b* 13 Oct. 1897; *s* of Percy Flemming, FRCS, and E. E. Flemming, MD; *m* 1935, Virginia Coit; two *s* two *d*. *Educ:* Rugby; Trinity Coll., Oxford. Ministry of Education (Board of Education), 1921-59; Permanent Sec. to the Ministry of Education, 1952-59. Mem., Restrictive Practices Court, 1960-64. *Address:* 13H John Spencer Square, N1.

**FLETCHER,** family name of **Baron Fletcher.**

**FLETCHER,** Baron *cr* 1970 (Life Peer), of Islington; **Eric George Molyneux Fletcher,** PC 1967; Kt 1964; LLD London; Solicitor, Senior partner of Denton, Hall & Burgin, Gray's Inn and Paris; *b* 26 March 1903; *s* of late Clarence George Eugene Fletcher, Town Clerk of Islington; *m* 1929, Bessie Winifred, *d* of late James Butt, Enfield; two *s* one *d*. *Educ:* Radley; University of London, LLB London, 1923; Admitted Solicitor, 1924; BA London, 1926; LLD, London, 1932, FSA; FRHistS. MP (Lab) East Islington, 1945-70; Minister without Portfolio, 1964-66; Chairman of Ways and Means and Deputy Speaker, House of Commons, 1966-68. Mem. LCC for South Islington, 1934-49 (Chm. Finance Cttee); formerly Mem. Exec. Cttee Fabian Soc.; Commissioner for Public Works Loans, 1946-55; Senator of London Univ.; Mem. Exec. Cttee Grotius Soc.; Pres. of Seldon Soc., 1967-70; Governor Birkbeck Coll., 1934-62, and London Sch. of Economics; Member: Evershed Cttee on Practice and Proceudre of Supreme Court; Church Assembly, 1962; Commission on Church and State, 1951; Advisory Council on Public Records; Royal Commission on Historical Manuscripts, 1966-; Statute Law Cttee, 1951-. A Trustee of the British Museum, 1968-. Chm., Advisory Bd for Redundant Churches, 1969-. Pres. British Archæological Assoc., 1960-63. *Publications:* The Students' Conflict of Laws, 1928 (with late E. Leslie Burgin; The Carrier's Liability, 1932; miscellaneous articles on legal historical, and archæological subjects. *Recreations:* golf, swimming. *Address:* 3 Gray's Inn Place, WC1. *T:* 01-242 7485; 9 Robin Grove, Highgate, N6. *Club:* Athenæum.

**FLETCHER;** *see* Aubrey-Fletcher.

**FLETCHER, Prof. Basil Alais,** MA, BSc; Emeritus Professor, University of Leeds; *b* 10 April 1900; *s* of Walter Henry and Julia Fletcher; *m* 1928, Gerrardine Mary, *d* of William Daly; one *s* one *d*. *Educ:* Ilford Sch., Essex; University Coll., London. Physics Master, Gresham's Sch., Holt, Norfolk, 1922-26; Fellow Commoner, Sidney Sussex Coll., Cambridge, 1926-27; Senior Science Master, Gresham's Sch., Holt, 1927-30; Albert Kahn Fellow for Great Britain, 1930-31; Headmaster, Chippenham Sch., Wilts, 1932-35; Prof. of Education, Dalhousie Univ., Halifax, Canada, 1935-39; Prof. of Education, University Coll., Southampton, 1939-41; Prof. of Education, Bristol Univ., 1941-45; Vice-Principal of the University Coll. of Rhodesia and Nyasaland, Salisbury, 1956-60. *Publications:* Laboratory Physics (with H. W. Heckstall-Smith), 1926; Youth Looks at the World, 1932; Education and Colonial Policy, 1936; Child Psychology for Parents, 1938; The Next Step in Canadian Education, 1939; Education and Crisis, 1946; A Philosophy for the Teacher, 1961; Universities in the Modern World, 1968. *Address:* Camerton Lodge, Camerton, Bath.

**FLETCHER, Edward Joseph;** MP (Lab) Darlington since 1964; *b* 25 Feb. 1911; *m*; two *d*. *Educ:* St Mary's Sch., Handsworth; Fircroft Coll., Bourneville, Birmingham. Joined Labour Party, 1926; has held many offices. Member: AEU, 1932 (Mem. Birmingham Dist Cttee); Clerical and Admin. Workers' Union, 1950 (Northern Area Sec., 1949-64); Newcastle City Council, 1952 (Chm. Finance Cttee, Dep. Ldr Labour Gp). Chm. N Eastern Assoc. for the Arts, 1961-65. *Address:* 46 Neville Road, Darlington, Co. Durham.

**FLETCHER, Prof. Frank Thomas Herbert,** DLitt; retired as James Barrow Professor of French in the University of Liverpool (1946-65); *b* 6 Jan. 1898; *s* of George Fletcher and Kate Rhoda (*née* Gaunt); *m* 1933, Hilda Patricia, *d* of Henry and Martha Gibson-Jackson; three *d*. *Educ:* Birmingham and

Nancy Univs. BA (Birmingham) 1922, MA 1923, Docteur de l'Université (Nancy) 1924, DLitt 1934, Officier d'Académie, 1948. Asst Lectr in French, University Coll. of Wales, Aberystwyth, 1924-25; Lectr, University of Birmingham, 1925-27; Assoc. Prof. of French, University of Toronto, 1927-32; Lectr, Goldsmith's Coll., University of London, 1932-36; Senior Lectr, University of Liverpool, 1936-46. Pres. Assoc. of Univ. Teachers, 1951-52; Sec.-Gen. Internat. Assoc. of Univ. Profs and Lectrs, 1952-61; Chm., Assoc. of Univ. Profs of French, 1963-65. *Publications:* La Langue des Vœux du Paon, 1924; Basic French Composition, 1934; Tour de France en auto, 1937; Montesquieu and English Politics, 1939; Pascal and the Christian Mystical Tradition, 1953. Numerous Textbooks; contribs to Modern Languages Review, French Studies, Modern Languages, Revue de Littérature Comparée, etc. *Recreation:* travel. *Address:* Torwood, Abbey Road, West Kirby, Cheshire. *T:* 051-625 8328.

**FLETCHER, Geoffrey Bernard Abbott,** MA Cantab; *b* Hampstead, 28 Nov. 1903; *s* of J. Alexander Fletcher and Ursula Constance, *d* of William Richard Rickett and *cousin* of Rt Honourable Sir Joseph Compton-Rickett, MP. *Educ:* Rugby Sch.; King's Coll., Cambridge (Senior Scholar), First Class, Classical Tripos, Part I, 1924; First Class Classical Tripos, Part 2, 1926; Prendergast Student, 1926; Asst Lectr in Classics, University of Leeds, 1927-28; Lectr in Greek, University of Liverpool, 1928-36; Prof. of Classics in the University of Durham, King's Coll., Newcastle upon Tyne, 1937-46, Prof. of Latin, 1946-63; Prof. of Latin, University of Newcastle upon Tyne, 1963-69, now Emeritus Prof. Examiner in Greek, University of Leeds, 1940-42; Examiner in Latin, Queen's Univ., Belfast, 1949-51, University of Wales, 1954-56, Bristol, 1961-63; Dean of Faculty of Arts, University of Durham, 1945-47; Public Orator, University of Durham, 1956-58. *Publications:* an appendix on Housman's Poetry in Housman, 1897-1936, by Grant Richards, 1941; Annotations on Tacitus, 1964; many contributions to classical and other periodicals, British and foreign, and to co-operative works. *Recreations:* music, reading, art-galleries, walking, travel. *Address:* Thirlmere Lodge, Elmfield Road, Gosforth, Northumberland. *T:* Gosforth 852873. *Club:* Athenæum.

**FLETCHER, Geoffrey Scowcroft;** artist and author; *b* 3 April 1923; *o s* of Herbert Fletcher and Annie Talence Fletcher; *m* 1953, Mary Jean Timothy. *Educ:* University Coll., London Univ. (Dip. in Fine Art). Abbey Major Schol., British Sch. at Rome, 1948. Drawings appeared in Manchester Guardian, 1950; London drawings and articles featured in The Daily Telegraph, 1958-. Author of television features on unusual aspects of London; has been instrumental in saving a number of metropolitan buildings from demolition. Drawings and paintings in various public and private collections in England and abroad. *Publications:* The London Nobody Knows (filmed, 1968), 1962; Down Among the Meths Men, 1966; Geoffrey Fletcher's London, 1968; City Sights, 1963; Pearly Kingdom, 1965; London's River, 1966; Elements of Sketching, 1966 (Amer. edn, 1968); London's Pavement Pounders, 1967; London After Dark, 1969; Changing London (Drawings from The Daily Telegraph), 1969; The London Dickens Knew, 1970. *Address:* c/o The Daily Telegraph, Fleet Street, EC4.

**FLETCHER, Harold Roy,** PhD, DSc, FRSE, VMH; Regius Keeper of the Royal Botanic Garden, Edinburgh, 1958-70; Her Majesty's Botanist in Scotland since 1967; Hon. Professor of Botany, University of Edinburgh, since 1968; *b* 14 April 1907; *s* of James Fletcher, Glossop, Derbs; *m* 1941, Evelyn Betty Veronica, *d* of Rev. Dr Andrew David Sloan, St Andrews; one *s* one *d*. *Educ:* Grammar Sch., Glossop; Victoria Univ., Manchester. Asst Lecturer in Botany, University of Aberdeen, 1929-34; Botanist, Royal Botanic Garden, Edinburgh, 1934-51; Dir, Royal Horticultural Society's Gardens, Wisley, Ripley, Woking, Surrey, 1951-54. Asst Regius Keeper, Royal Botanic Garden, Edinburgh, 1954-56. Sec., Internat. Commn for: Horticultural Nomenclature and Registration, 1956-66; Nomenclature of Cultivated Plants, 1956-66; Vice-Pres., Royal Society, Edinburgh, 1961-65; Pres., Botanical Soc., Edinburgh, 1959-60; Pres., Internat. Assoc. of Botanic Gardens, 1964-69; Gen. Sec., 10th Internat. Botanical Congress, 1964. *Publications:* The Story of the Royal Horticultural Society, 1969; The Royal Botanic Garden, Edinburgh, 1670-1970, 1970; numerous scientific papers chiefly on flora of Asia in Trans. Royal Society, Edinburgh, Trans. Botanical Soc., Edinburgh, Kew Bulletin; also numerous articles in horticultural and gardening journals. *Recreations:* systematic botany; music, and art appreciation. *Address:* Royal Botanic Garden, Edinburgh.

**FLETCHER, Sir James,** Kt 1946; Founder President, Fletcher Holdings Ltd; *b* 29 March 1886; *s* of John Shearer Fletcher; *m* Charlotte Muir Cameron; two *s* one *d*. *Educ:* Allan Glen's Coll., Glasgow. Arrived in New Zealand, 1908. Started in business in Dunedin, 1909, as a Building Contractor. Formed, with his brother William, Fletcher Bros Ltd in 1912 and The Fletcher Construction Company in 1919; the Company became Fletcher Holdings Ltd, 1940, and now owns and controls the following subsidiary companies: The Fletcher Construction Co. Ltd; The Fletcher Steel and Engineering Cos Ltd; The Fletcher Industries Ltd; The Fletcher Timber Co. Ltd; The Fletcher Merchants Ltd; The Fletcher Group Services Ltd; The Fletcher Trust and Investment Co. Ltd, all of New Zealand, and The Fletcher Construction Co. (Pty) Ltd, of Sydney. *Address:* 5 Omana Avenue, Auckland 3, New Zealand. *Club:* Northern (Auckland).

**FLETCHER, James Thomas,** CBE 1967; Chairman, North Riding of Yorkshire County Council, since 1957; *b* 3 Dec. 1898; *s* of Thomas Fletcher; *m* 1933, A. Walburn; two *s* one *d*. *Educ:* St John's Sch., Whitby. Mayor of Borough of Redcar, 1944; Chm., S Tees-side Hosp. Man. Cttee, 1958-; Mem., N Riding Yorks. CC, 1934-. *Address:* Burndale House, Ingham Close, Sleights, Whitby, Yorks. *T:* Sleights 488.

**FLETCHER, Leonard Ralph;** Secretary, University Grants Committee, since 1970; *b* 11 June 1917; *o s* of late L. R. and Mrs K. M. Fletcher, Atherton, Lancs; *m* 1948, Sheila Margaret Lerpinière; three *d*. *Educ:* Charterhouse; Balliol Coll., Oxford. 1st cl. Hon. Mods, 1st cl. Litt Hum. Temp. Asst Principal, Ministry of Agriculture and Fisheries, 1940-46; Asst Principal, Ministry of Education, 1946, Principal 1947, Asst Sec. 1956, Under-Sec. 1961; Asst Under-Sec. of

State, Dept of Educn and Science, 1964-69. *Address:* Marlin Way, Cross Oak Road, Berkhamsted, Herts. *T:* Berkhamsted 3273.

**FLETCHER, (Leopold) Raymond;** MP (Lab) Ilkeston since 1964; Journalist; *b* 3 Dec. 1921; *s* of Leopold Raymond Fletcher, Ruddington, Notts; *m* 1947, Johanna Klara Elisabeth, *d* of Karl Ising, Berlin. *Educ:* University Coll., Nottingham. Served 1941-48 with Indian Army Ordnance Corps. Columnist on The Guardian and contributor to other journals at home and abroad. Mem., T&GWU, and NUJ. *Publication:* Sixty Pounds a Second on Defence, 1963. *Recreation:* theatre. *Address:* 65 Elsley Road, SW11. *T:* 01-223 5971.

**FLETCHER, Leslie;** General Manager (Chief Executive Officer) Williams Deacon's Bank Ltd, 1964-70, Director, 1966-70, retired; *b* 30 Jan. 1906; *s* of late Edward Henry and Edith Howard Fletcher; *m* 1934, Helen, *d* of Frank Turton; one *s* one *d*. *Educ:* City Gram. Sch., Chester; Manchester Univ. (BA Com). Entered Williams Deacon's Bank Ltd 1922; Asst Gen. Man., 1957; Dep. Gen. Man., 1961. Fellow and Mem. Council, Inst. of Bankers. *Recreations:* lawn tennis, golf. *Address:* March, Macclesfield Road, Wilmslow, Cheshire. *T:* Wilmslow 22559. *Clubs:* Royal Automobile; St James's (Manchester).

**FLETCHER, Nora Kathleen,** CBE 1919; *b* Sydney, Australia; 2nd *d* of late J. W. Fletcher, MA Oxon, and Ann, *d* of late Capt. Joseph Hines-Clarke, Indian Mutiny. *Educ:* Katoomba Coll. On British Red Cross Commission for France and Belgium, 1914-19, despatches, Royal Red Cross 1st Class, 1915; Hon. Serving Sister Order of St John of Jerusalem, 1916; Order of Elizabeth 1st Class and Certificate, Belgium; Médaille de la Reconnaissance in gold and Certificate, France; 1914 Star, British War and Victory Medals. *Address:* c/o National and Grindlay's Bank Ltd, 13 St James's Square, SW1.

**FLETCHER, Hon. Sir Patrick Bisset,** KBE 1958; CMG 1953; sometime MP for Matopo (SR); *b* 1901; 3rd *s* of late Hon. R. A. Fletcher, CBE, JP, Bulawayo, S Rhodesia; *m* 1929, Dorothy Maud, *d* of late Col W. Napier, CMG, Bulawayo, S Rhodesia; one *s* two *d*. *Educ:* Rondebosch Boys' High Sch.; Rhodes Univ., Grahamstown. Civil Service, 1923-30; Gold Mine Owner and Farmer; elected to S African Parliament, 1936; Mem., War Supplies and Price Advisory Bds, 1940-44. Minister of Agriculture and Lands, 1945-51 (Southern Rhodesia); Minister of Native Affairs, 1951-58; Minister of Lands, 1956-58; Minister of Irrigation and Surveys, 1957-58. Represented S Rhodesia, Coronation, 1953. President: Rhodesia Assoc. for prevention of Tuberculosis; Central African Trade Fair. *Recreation:* golf. *Address:* Box 37, Sinoia, Rhodesia. *Club:* Bulawayo (Rhodesia).

**FLETCHER, Air Marshal Sir Peter Carteret,** KCB 1968 (CB 1965); OBE 1945; DFC 1943; AFC 1952; Controller of Aircraft, Ministry of Aviation Supply (formerly Ministry of Technology), since 1970; *b* 7 Oct. 1916; *s* of F. T. W. Fletcher, Oxford (sometime tobacco farmer, Southern Rhodesia), and Dora Clulee, New Zealand; *m* 1940, Marjorie Isobel Kotze; two *d*. *Educ:* St George's Coll., Southern Rhodesia; Rhodes Univ., S Africa. SR Law Dept, 1937. Served War of 1939-45: SR Air Force, 1939; trans. to RAF, 1941; commanded 135 and 258 Fighter Sqdns and RAF Station Belvedere. Directing Staffs at: RAF Staff Coll., 1945-46; Jt Services Staff Coll., 1946-48; Imp. Defence Coll., 1956-58; Mem. Jt Planning Staff, 1951-53; comdg RAF Abingdon, 1958-60; Dep. Dir Jt Planning Staff, 1960-61; Dir of Opl Requirements (B), Air Min., 1961-63; Asst Chief of Air Staff (Policy and Plans), 1964-66; AOC, No 38 Group, Transport Command, 1966-67; VCAS, 1967-70. *Recreations:* books, travel. *Address:* 108 Coleherne Court, SW5. *T:* 01-373 8806.

**FLETCHER, Raymond;** *see* Fletcher, L. R.

**FLETCHER, Richard Cawthorne,** MA; JP; Headmaster, Worcester College for the Blind, since Sept. 1959; *b* 30 Aug. 1916; *s* of late Philip C. Fletcher, MC, and of Edith Maud (*née* Okell); *m* 1946, Joan Fairlie Woodcock; one *s* one *d*. *Educ:* Marlborough; University Coll., Oxford. Served Army (Emergency Commn), 1939-46. Asst Master, Charterhouse, 1946-Aug. 1959. *Recreations:* music and games. *Address:* The Gables, Whittington Road, Worcester.

**FLÈTCHER-COOKE, Charles Fletcher,** QC 1958; MP (C) Darwen Division of Lancashire since 1951; MA Cantab; *b* 5 May 1914; *yr s* of late Capt. C. A. and of Gwendolen May Fletcher-Cooke; *m* 1959, Diana Lady Avebury (whom he divorced, 1967), *d* of late Capt. Edward King and of Mrs J. St Vincent Hand; no *surv. c.* *Educ:* Malvern Coll. (Scholar); Peterhouse, Cambridge (Scholar). Pres., Cambridge Union, 1936; Editor, The Granta, 1936. Called to Bar through Lincoln's Inn, 1938 (1st Class Hons, Bar Final Examination; Studentship and Certificate of Honour). Served War of 1939-45, in Naval Intelligence Div. and on Joint Intelligence Staff, with rank of Lieut-Comdr, RNVR. Contested (Lab) East Dorset Div., 1945, re-adopted, 1946, but resigned from Labour Party shortly afterwards. Legal Adviser to British Delegation, Danube Conf., Belgrade, 1948; Deleg. to Consultative Assembly of Council of Europe, 1954-55. Mem. of Statute Law Cttee, 1955-61. Joint Parliamentary Under-Sec. of State, Home Office, 1961-63. Bencher, Lincoln's Inn, 1969. *Publications:* (with others) The Rule of Law; (with M. J. Albery) Monopolies and Restrictive Trade Practices. *Address:* 4 North Court, Great Peter Street, SW1. *T:* 01-799 5859; 2 Paper Buildings, Temple, EC4. *T:* 01-353 1853. *Clubs:* Garrick, Pratt's.

*See also Sir John Fletcher-Cooke.*

**FLETCHER-COOKE, Sir John,** Kt 1962; CMG 1952; MA Oxon; *b* 8 Aug. 1911; *er s* of late Charles Arthur and Gwendolen May Fletcher-Cooke; *m* 1949, Alice Elizabeth, *d* of Russell Forest Egner, Mineapolis, USA; two *s* one *d*. *Educ:* Malvern Coll. (Barham Schol.); University of Paris (Diplomé, degré supérieure); Oxford Univ. (Kitchener Scholar, Senior Exhibitioner, St Edmund Hall). First Cl. Hons Politics, Philosophy and Economics; economic research, Oxford Univ., 1933; Asst Principal, Colonial Office, 1934; Private Sec. to successive Permanent Under-Secs of State for the Colonies, 1937; Officer Malayan CS, 1937; Asst Sec., FMS, 1938; special duty, FMS, 1939; Magistrate, Singapore, 1939; Sec., Foreign Exchange Control, Malaya, 1939; Dist Officer, FMS, 1940. Served with RAF as intelligence officer, FO, 1942-46; Prisoner of War in Japan, 1942-45. Attached to Colonial Office for special duty and accompanied Constitutional Comr to Malta, 1946; Under-Sec. to Govt of Palestine, 1946-48; Mem. Exec. Council, Palestine, 1947; Special Rep. for Palestine at UN discussions on Palestine, 1948; UK rep. on Special Cttee and later on Trusteeship Council UN, Geneva and Lake Success, 1948-50; Counsellor (Colonial Affairs), Perm. UK Deleg. to UN, New York, 1949-51; Colonial Adviser to UK Deleg. to UN

Gen. Assembly, 1948-50 and alternate UK deleg. to UN Gen. Assembly 1949; Colonial Sec., Cyprus, 1951-55. Acted as Governor of Cyprus for various periods, 1951-55. Attached Colonial Office for Special Duty (temp.), 1956; Minister for Constitutional Affairs, Tanganyika, 1956-59; Chief Sec. to the Govt of Tanganyika, 1959-60. Special Rep. of Tanganyika at Ghana Independence Celebrations, 1957, at Economic Commission for Africa, Addis Ababa, 1959, and at Trusteeship Council, UN, New York, 1957, 1958, 1959, 1960 and 1961. Acted as Governor of Tanganyika for various periods, 1959-61; Dep. Governor, Tanganyika, 1960-61. Visiting Prof. (African Affairs) University of Colorado, Boulder, USA, 1961-62 and 1966; Fellow, African Studies Assoc., NY, 1961-. Mem. Constituencies Delimitation Commn for Kenya, 1962; Mem. Exec. Cttee, Overseas Employers' Federation, 1963-67. Contested (C) Luton, Nov. 1963. MP (C) Test Div. of Southampton, 1964-66. Mem. Councils of Royal Commonwealth Society and of United Society for Propogation of the Gospel, 1964-67. Vice-Chm., Internat. Team to review structure and organisation of FAO, Rome, 1967. Dir, Programmes in Diplomacy, Carnegie Endowment for International Peace, New York, 1967-69. Mem., Mission for British Govt to Anglo-French Condominium of New Hebrides, 1969. *Publications:* contrib. to Parliament as an Export, 1966, and to many periodicals. *Recreation:* golf. *Address:* c/o Lloyds Bank, 3 Broad Street Place, EC2. *Club:* Travellers'.

*See also Charles Fletcher-Cooke.*

**FLETCHER-VANE,** family name of **Baron Inglewood.**

**FLETT, Sir Martin (Teall),** KCB 1965 (CB 1953); Second Permanent Under-Secretary of State (Equipment), Ministry of Defence; *b* 30 July 1911; *s* of late Sir John Smith Flett, KBE, FRS, and of Lady (Mary Jane) Flett (*née* Meason); *m* 1936, Mary, *er d* of Sir Alec Martin, *qv*; two *s* one *d. Educ:* George Watson's Coll.; St Paul's Sch.; St John's Coll., Oxford. 1st Class Modern History, 1933; Home Civil Service, Dominions Office, 1933; HM Treasury, 1934; War Cabinet Office, Ministry of Reconstruction and Lord President's Office, 1944-46; Under-Sec., HM Treasury, 1949-56; Alternate UK Dir, International Bank and Financial Counsellor, British Embassy, Washington, 1953-56; Dep. Sec., Ministry of Power, 1956-61; Dep. Under-Sec. of State, 1961-63, Permanent Under-Sec. of State, 1963-64, Air Ministry; Second Permanent Under-Sec. of State (RAF), MoD, 1964-68. *Address:* 45 Campden Hill Road, W8. *T:* 01-937 9498. *Club:* Athenæum.

**FLEW, John Douglas Score,** MRCS, LRCP, 1928; MB, BS (London) 1930; MD 1933; MRCOG 1933; FRCOG 1949; Obstetrical and Gynæcological Surgeon, University College Hospital, 1947-67, retired; Dean of the Medical School, 1954-60; Fellow of University College, London, since 1958; *b* 8 Feb. 1902; *s* of J. P. Flew, JP, and P. E. Flew; *m* 1935, Annie Cantrell Taylor, MA, MB, BCh (Cantab.); three *s* one *d. Educ:* St Paul's; University Coll., and University Coll. Hosp., London. House appointments UCH and Queen Charlotte's Hosp., 1928-32; 1st Asst to Obst. and Gynæc. Unit, UCH, 1933-37; Ante-natal Phys., Queen Charlotte's, 1933-; Visiting Obst. Surg., Queen Mary's Maternity Hosp., Hampstead, 1933-47. Examiner Universities London and Oxford; Central Midwives' Board. *Publications:* articles in BMJ, Jl Obst. and Gynæc., etc. *Recreations:* gardening, fishing. *Address:* 28 Weymouth Street, W1. *T:* 01-580 1723, 01-946 1281.

**FLINN, Major William Henry,** CMG 1941; OBE 1919; *b* 1895; *o s* of late S. J. Flinn; *m* Olive, *y d* of late G. E. T. P. Thompson, JP; one *s.* Royal Irish Regt and Staff, 1914-27; Colonial Sec., Barbados, 1938-42; Acting Governor, Barbados, 1939, 1940, and 1941; Colonial Sec., Jamaica, 1942-45; Acting Governor, Jamaica, 1943; Mem. Commission of Govt of Newfoundland, 1945-49. *Recreations:* salmon and trout fishing. *Address:* Kells Grange, Kells, Kilkenny.

**FLINT, Abraham John,** DL; **His Honour Judge Flint;** Judge of Circuit No 18 (Nottingham) since 1957; Major, RA retired; *b* 1903; *s* of Abram Reginald Flint, solicitor, Derby; *m* 1930, Eleanor Mary; two *d. Educ:* Oundle. Called to the Bar, Inner Temple, 1929; MP (Nat Lab) Ilkeston Div. of Derbyshire, 1931-35. DL Notts, 1970. *Address:* The Cottage, Newton, Notts. *T:* East Bridgford 486.

**FLINT, Prof. David,** TD, MA, BL, CA; Johnstone Smith Professor of Accountancy, University of Glasgow, Oct. 1964; Partner Mann Judd Gordon & Co. Chartered Accountants, Glasgow, London, Aberdeen and Dundee, since 1951; *b* 24 Feb. 1919; *s* of David Flint, JP, and Agnes Strang Lambie; *m* 1953, Dorothy Mary Maclachlan Jardine; two *s* one *d. Educ:* Glasgow High Sch.; University of Glasgow. Served with Royal Signals, 1939-46, Major (despatches). Awarded distinction final examination of Institute of Chartered Accountants of Scotland, 1948. Lecturer, University of Glasgow, 1950-60. Hon. Pres. Glasgow Chartered Accountants Students Soc., 1959-60. Mem. Council, Scottish Economic Soc. *Recreations:* golf. *Address:* 3 Merrylee Road, Newlands, Glasgow S3. *T:* 041-637 3060. *Club:* Western (Glasgow).

**FLINT, Henry Thomas,** PhD, DSc, MRCS, LRCP, DMRE (Cambridge); Hildred Carlile Professor of Physics, University of London, Bedford College, 1944-56; Professor Emeritus since 1956; *b* 4 Dec. 1890; *s* of Robert and Mary Jane Flint, Pillerton Hersey, Warwick; *m* 1933, Ruth Lieck; one *d. Educ:* Wyggeston Sch., Leicester; Universities of Birmingham and London. Asst Lecturer in Physics, Cardiff, 1919; Lecturer, Reading Univ. Coll., 1920; Lecturer, King's Coll., 1920-26; Reader in Physics, University of London, King's Coll., 1926-44. Clinical Asst in Radiology Dept., Westminster Hosp., 1930-33; Consultant Physicist to Westminster Hosp. and KCH Fellow of King's Coll., London, 1956. *Publications:* (with B. L. Worsnop) Advanced Practical Physics, 1923; Wave Mechanics, 1967; Geometrical Optics, 1936; The Quantum Equation and the Theory of Fields, 1966. *Recreations:* walking and riding. *Address:* Pillerton Hersey, Warwick. *T:* Ettington 262. *Club:* Athenæum.

**FLORENCE, Philip Sargant,** Hon. CBE 1952; MA (Cantab.), PhD (Columbia); Hon. LittD (Hum) (Columbia); Hon. DSocSc (Birmingham); Professor of Commerce, 1929-55, Dean of the Faculty of Commerce and Social Science, 1947-50, University of Birmingham; *b* 25 June 1890; *s* of late Henry Smythe Florence and late Mary Sargant-Florence; *m* 1917, Lella Faye Secor (*d* 1966); two *s. Educ:* Rugby Sch.; Caius Coll., Cambridge (History Scholar); 1st Class Economics, 1914, Columbia Univ., New York (Garth Fellow). Organising Sec., British Assoc. Cttee on Fatigue from the Economic Standpoint, 1913-15; Investigator to the Health of Munition Workers' Cttee, 1915-16;

Investigator (Associate Sanitarian), US Public Health Service, 1917-21; Lecturer, Bureau of Industrial Research and Bureau of Personnel Administration, New York, 1919-21; University Lecturer in Economics, Cambridge Univ., 1921-29; Staff Lecturer in Economics, Magdalene Coll., Cambridge, 1924-29; Chm., Social Study Cttee, Birmingham Univ., 1930-46; Council, Royal Economic Society, 1930-61; Pres. Section F (Economics) British Assoc. for the Advancement of Science, 1937; Visiting Prof. University of Cairo, 1940; Consultunt US National Resources Planning Board, 1940-41; Retail Trade Cttee, Board of Trade, 1941; Chm., Greater Birmingham Employment Cttee, 1957-63. Visiting Prof., Johns Hopkins Univ., 1959; Consultant, Jordan Development Bd, 1960-61; Leverhulme Lecturer, University of Malta, 1962; Visiting Prof., University of Rhode Island, 1967. *Publications:* Use of Factory Statistics in the Investigation of Industrial Fatigue, 1918; US Public Health Bulletin No. 106, Comparison of an Eight-Hour Plant and a Ten-Hour Plant (in collaboration), 1920; Economics of Fatigue and Unrest, 1924; Over-Population, Theory and Statistics, 1926; Economics and Human Behaviour, 1927; The Statistical Method in Economics and Political Science, 1929; Uplift in Economics, 1930; The Logic of Industrial Organisation, 1933; (joint) Consumers Cooperation in Great Britain, 1938; (joint) County Town, 1946; Investment Location and Size of Plant, 1947; Labour, 1948; The Logic of British and American Industry, 1953; Industry and the State, 1957; Ownership, Control and Success of Large Companies, 1961; Post-War Investment, Location and Size of Plant, 1962; Economics and Sociology of Industry, 1964; Analytical Atlas of Economic Structure and Policies, 1967; articles, etc. in Economic, Sociological, Statistical and Psychological Journals. *Address:* Highfield, Selly Park Road, Birmingham. *T:* 021-472 0498.

**FLOWER,** family name of **Viscount Ashbrook.**

**FLOWER, Group Capt. Arthur Hyde,** CBE 1939; *b* Bemboka, NSW, 13 Dec. 1892; *s* of late Thomas Flower; *m* 1924, Nina Joan Castleden, Whitby; no *c. Educ:* Tilba, NSW. Served with AIF, Egypt and France, 1915-16; Transferred to Royal Flying Corps, 1917; served in No. 42 Squadron, France and Italy, 1917-1918 (French Croix de Guerre with palm); Egypt and Turkey, 1920-23; Egypt, 1926-31 and 1934-36; Palestine, 1937-38 (CBE, despatches); France, Sept. 1939-May 1940; England, 1940-42; SWP Area, Aug. 1942-Nov. 1944; retired May 1945. Comdr Order of Leopold (Belgium). *Recreations:* shooting, golf. *Address:* Heathfield, Mount Lofty, S Australia. *Club:* Royal Air Force.

**FLOWER, Desmond John Newman,** MC 1944; Chairman, Cassell & Co. Ltd, since 1958; President, Cassell Australia Ltd, 1965; *b* London, 25 Aug. 1907; *o s* of late Sir Newman Flower; *m* 1st, 1931, Margaret Cameron Coss (marr. diss., 1952); one *s*; 2nd, 1952, Anne Elizabeth Smith; one *s* two *d. Educ:* Lancing; King's Coll., Cambridge. Entered Cassell & Co. 1930; Dir, 1931; Literary Dir, 1938; Dep.-Chm., 1952; Chm. Cassell & Co. (Holdings) Ltd, 1958-70. Served War of 1939-45 (despatches, MC); commissioned 1941, 5 Bn Argyll and Sutherland Highlanders later 91 (A&SH) A/T-Regt. chm., the Folio Society; President des Comités d'Alliance Française en Grande Bretagne, 1963. Chevalier de la légion d'honneur, 1950. DLitt (*hc*) University of Caen, 1957. *Publications:* founder and editor (with A. J. A. Symons) Book Collector's quarterly, 1930-34; ed, Complete Poetical Works of Ernest Christopher Dowson, 1934; compiled (with Francis Meynell and A. J. A. Symons) The Nonesuch Century, 1936; The Pursuit of Poetry, 1939; (with A. N. L. Munby) English Poetical Autographs, 1938; Voltaire's England, 1950; History of 5 Bn Argyll and Sutherland Highlanders, 1950; (with James Reeves) The War, 1939-1945, 1960. *Recreations:* golf, book collecting. *Address:* 187 Clarence Gate Gardens, NW1. *T:* 01-262 4690. *Clubs:* Brooks'; Royal and Ancient (St Andrews).

**FLOWERDEW, Richard Edward,** CIE 1937; MB, ChB Aberdeen; DTM&H London; Lieutenant-Colonel IMS (retired); *b* 26 Sept. 1886; 9th *s* of late Arthur J. B. Flowerdew, Billingford Hall, Scole, Norfolk; *m* 1912, Caroline Jane, (*d* 1957), *g d* of Col Sir Digby Mackworth, Bt; one *s. Educ:* Framlingham Coll., Suffolk; Aberdeen Univ. Indian Medical Service, 1909; served European War, 1914-21 (despatches twice); served Suez Canal Defences, Mesopotamia and North-West Frontier, India; Burma Jail Dept, 1922-30; Inspector-Gen. of Prisons, Bengal, 1931; retired, 1939. *Address:* PO Box 5948, Nairobi, Kenya, East Africa.

**FLOWERS, Prof. Sir Brian Hilton,** Kt 1969; FRS 1961; Chairman of Science Research Council since 1967, and Langworthy Professor of Physics, University of Manchester, since 1961; *b* 13 Sept. 1924; *o s* of Rev. Harold J. Flowers, Swansea; *m* 1951, Mary Frances, *er d* of Sir Leonard Behrens, *qv*; two step *s. Educ:* Bishop Gore Gram. Sch., Swansea; Gonville and Caius Coll. (Exhibitioner), Cambridge (MA); University of Birmingham (DSc). Anglo-Canadian Atomic Energy Project (Tube Alloys), Montreal and Chalk River, Ont., Canada, 1944-46; Research work in nuclear physics and atomic energy at Atomic Energy Research Establishment, Harwell, 1946-50; Dept of Mathematical Physics, University of Birmingham, 1950-52; Visiting Prof., Mass. Institute of Technology and University of Calif., 1955. Head of Theoretical Physics Div., AERE, Harwell, 1952-58, and Chief Research Scientist, 1958; Prof. of Theoretical Physics, Manchester Univ., 1958-61. Member of Council of the Physical Society, 1956-60; Mem. of Council of Inst of Physics and Physical Soc., 1960, and Vice-Pres. 1962-66; Nuffield Vis. Professorship at Universities of Vancouver and Alberta, July-Aug., 1960; Visiting Prof., Cairo Univ., Jan., 1963. Member: Advisory Council on Scientific Policy, 1962-64; Council for Scientific Policy, 1965-67; Governing Board, National Institute for Research in Nuclear Science, 1962-65; Bd of Governors, Weizmann Inst. of Science, Israel, 1969-. Chairman: joint working group on computers for research, 1965; Computer Bd for Univs and Research Councils, 1966-70. Editor: Advances in Physics, 1959-63; Cambridge Monographs, 1962-66. Rutherford Medal and Prize, IPPS, 1968. FInstP 1961. Hon. DSc Sussex, 1968. *Publications:* various contribs to scientific periodicals, on the structure of the atomic nucleus, on nuclear reactions, and on science policy. *Recreations:* music, walking. *Address:* 36 Douglas Road, N1. *T:* 01-226 9939; Science Research Council, State House, High Holborn, WC1. Schuster Laboratory, University of Manchester. *Club:* Athenæum.

**FLOWERS, John,** QC 1929; *b* 1882; *s* of George Arthur Flowers; *m* 1914, Kathleen Vera, *d* of W. Gordon-Powell; two *s. Educ:* New College, Eastbourne; Trinity Coll., Oxford. Served War of 1914-18, Lieut RASC. Barrister, Inner Temple, 1908, KC 1929, Bencher, 1937; Recorder of Guildford, 1928-38, of Southend-on-Sea, 1938-57. *Address:* 3 Temple Gardens,

EC4. *T:* 01-353 2163; 01-353 1700. *Clubs:* MCC, New (Brighton).

**FLOYD, Dr Alfred Ernest,** OBE 1948; Organist of St Paul's Cathedral, Melbourne, Australia, 1915-47; *b* Birmingham, 5 Jan. 1877; *s* of Rev. C. H. and A. M. Floyd; *m* 1913, Frances Mary Griffiths, *d* of Dr W. Aylmer Lewis, Frankton Grange, Salop; two *s. Educ:* Bradford Grammar Sch.; the Leys Sch., Cambridge. Dep. Organist Winchester Cathedral; Organist Llangollen and Oswestry Parish Churches; Mus. Bac. Oxon., 1912; ARCM 1913; Mus. Doc. Cantuar, 1917; lecturer, writer, adjudicator, composer, broadcaster. *Publications:* Church music, part-songs, organ pieces, school songs. *Recreation:* walking. *Address:* 21 Selborne Road, Toorak, Victoria 3142, Australia.

**FLOYD, Charles Murray,** OBE 1945; FRICS; FLAS; Member, Wiltshire County Council, since 1965; Chairman: Avon Rubber Co. Ltd, 1955-68; George Spencer Moulton & Co. Ltd, 1956-68; *b* 12 Sept. 1905; *s* of Sir Henry R. P. Floyd, 4th Bt (*d* 1915), RN, and late Dowager Lady Floyd; *m* 1948, Mary Elizabeth, *o d* of late Major R. F. Fuller, and *widow* of Lieut-Col P. J. S. Boyle, Royal Scots Fusiliers; three *s. Educ:* Eton; Trinity Coll., Cambridge (MA). Partner Powlett & Floyd, Chartered Surveyors and Land Agents, Bath, 1935-55. Served throughout War of 1939-45; BEF France, 1939-40, 21 Army Group, Normandy, Belgium and Germany, 1944-45; Lieut-Col RE (despatches, OBE). Mem. Cttee for England: HM Forestry Commn, 1954; Nature Conservancy, 1955; Mem., Nature Conservancy, 1958; Pres. Royal Forestry Society of England and Wales, 1954-56; Member: Royal Commission on Common Land, 1955-58; MPBW Cttee on Field Monuments, 1966-68. High Sheriff of Wilts, 1962-63. FLS. *Recreation:* natural history. *Address:* Great Chalfield, Melksham, Wilts. *T:* North Trowbridge 239. *Clubs:* Travellers'; University Estate Management (Cambridge) (Pres., 1956-57).

**FLOYD, Sir John (Duckett),** 6th Bt *cr* 1816; TD; Solicitor, retired 1968; *b* 1 Nov. 1903; 2nd *s* of Sir Henry Floyd, 4th Bt and Edith Ann (*d* 1955), *d* of late Major John Kincaid Smith, Polmont House, Stirlingshire; *S* brother, 1968; *m* 1929, Jocelin Evadne (JP Hants, 1947), *d* of late Sir Edmund Wyldbore Smith; two *s* (and one *s* decd). *Educ:* Eton; Trinity Coll., Cambridge (BA). Admitted a Solicitor, 1929; lately senior partner, Frere Cholmeley & Co., 28 Lincolns Inn Fields, WC2. Joined Hampshire Yeomanry, 1923; Adjutant, 1939; in comd same (as HAA), 1949-52. Served NW Europe, 1944. *Recreations:* hunting (Chairman, Hampshire Hunt Club); fishing. *Heir: er surv. s* Giles Henry Charles Floyd [*b* 27 Feb. 1932; *m* 1954, Lady Gillian Moira Katherine, 2nd *d* of Marquess of Exeter, *qv*; two *s*]. *Address:* Lovington House, Alresford, Hants. *T:* Itchen Abbas 371. *Club:* Cavalry.

**FLOYER-ACLAND, Lt-Gen. Arthur Nugent,** CB 1940; DSO; MC; DL; *b* 1885; *s* of late Capt. J. E. Acland and N. L. N. Bankes, Wollaston House, Dorchester, Dorset; *m* 1913, Evelyn Stafford, *d* of Stafford Still, Lincoln's Inn; one *s. Educ:* Blundell's Sch., Tiverton. Gazetted to the Duke of Cornwall's Light Infantry, 1907; served European War, France and Italy (DSO, MC, French Croix de Guerre (2 awards), Bt Major, 1917; despatches six times); graduated at Staff Coll., Camberley, 1921; Bt Lieut-Col 1927; Lieut-Col 1931; commanded 1st Bn The Duke of Cornwall's Light Infantry, 1931-34; Col 1934; AAG War Office, 1934-36; Comdr 3rd (Jhelum) Infantry Bde, India, 1936-38; served operations Waziristan NWFP, India, 1937-38 (despatches); Comdr 43rd (Wessex) Div. TA, 1938-39; Military Sec. to Sec. of State for War, 1940-42; Lt-Gen. 1941. High Sheriff, Dorset, 1953; DL Dorset, 1957. Assumed name of Floyer in addition to own name on succeeding to the estate of George Floyer of Stafford House, near Dorchester, 1927. *Address:* The Paddock, West Stafford, Dorchester, Dorset. *Club:* Army and Navy.

**FOAD, Roland Walter,** CBE 1968; UK Administrator, Roulston & Company Inc.; Director, Cleveland Offshore Fund NV; *b* 7 April 1908; *er s* of late Walter James Foad and late Frances Mary Foad (*née* Inge); *m* 1st, 1934, Isabel Sarah Stewart McKeen (*d* 1962); one *s* one *d*; 2nd, 1966, Maria-Isabel, Marquesa de Piedrabuena. *Educ:* Manwood's Sch., Sandwich. ACA 1929; FCA 1953 (Mem. Council, 1964-). Dep. Controller, Raw Materials Accountancy, 1941-45; Chief Accountant, Industrial and Commercial Finance Corporation, 1946-48; Partner, McClelland Ker & Co., Chartered Accountants, 1949-53; Dir of Finance, Iron and Steel Board, 1954-62, Exec. Mem., 1962-67; UK Chm., Steel Cttee, Council of Assoc., ECSC, 1962-67. *Address:* 11 Roxburghe Mansion, Kensington Court, W8. *T:* 01-937 1337. *Club:* United Service.

**FODEN, Air Vice-Marshal Arthur,** CB 1964; CBE 1960; CEng; FIEE; Director (C), Government Communications Headquarters, since 1969; *b* 19 April 1914; *s* of Henry Foden, Macclesfield, Cheshire; *m* 1938, Constance Muriel Foden (*née* Corkill); one *s* one *d. Educ:* Manchester Univ. (BSc). Electronic Engineer, 1935-37; Education Officer, Royal Air Force, 1937-39; Signals Officer, Royal Air Force, 1939; Dep. Dir, Signals Staff, Min. of Def., 1964-67; Asst Chief of Defence Staff (Signals), 1967-69, retired. *Recreations:* gardening, music. *Address:* Ravenglass, Wargrave, Berks. *T:* Wargrave 2589.

**FODEN, William Bertram,** CB 1945; formerly Assistant Under-Secretary of State, Air Ministry; retired; *b* 19 Sept. 1892; *s* of late W. G. Foden, Newcastle, Staffs; *m* 1920, Zélie, *d* of late G. K. Lemmy, Lewisham; one *s* one *d. Educ:* High Sch., Newcastle, Staffs; St John's Coll., Cambridge (scholar). BA 1914; RGA and RE, 1916-18; Research Dept., Woolwich Arsenal, 1918; Air Ministry, 1919-53. *Address:* 2 Westwood Close, Threshers, Crediton, Devon EX17 3NJ. *T:* Crediton 2709.

**FOGARTY, Christopher Winthrop;** Treasury representative in S Asia and the Far East since 1967; *b* 18 Sept. 1921; *s* of late Philip Christopher Fogarty, ICS, and late Hilda Spenser Fogarty; *m* 1961, Elizabeth Margaret Ince. *Educ:* Ampleforth Coll.; Christ Church, Oxford. War Service (Lieut RA), 1942-45. Asst Principal, 1946, Principal, 1949, HM Treasury. Permanent Sec., Min. of Finance of Eastern Nigeria, 1956. Asst Sec., HM Treasury, 1959, Under-Sec., 1966. *Address:* Huntly Cottage, 29 The Downs, Wimbledon, SW20; British High Commission, Kuala Lumpur, Malaysia. *T:* 01-947 1738. *Club:* Royal Commonwealth Society.
*See also M. P. Fogarty.*

**FOGARTY, Air Chief Marshal Sir Francis,** GBE 1957 (KBE 1950); KCB 1953 (CB 1946); DFC; AFC; *b* 16 Jan. 1899; *s* of Michael Fogarty, Cork, Eire; *m* 1939, Fenella Evelyn, *d* of Capt. Forsyth Grant, Ecclesgreig, Kincardineshire; one *s* one *d. Educ:* Farran Ferris Coll., Cork. Served 98 Squadron, 1918; 84 Sqdn, 1920-23, 1923-30; Commanded 84 Squadron, 1935-37; Adjt County of Mddx Sqdn AAF, 1930-34; Comd 37 Bomber Sqdn, 1938-40; RAF

Mission, Ottawa, 1943; SASO, No. 4 Group, Bomber Comd, 1944; Air Officer i/c Administration Mediterranean Allied Air Forces, 1945; AOC, RAF, Italy, 1946; AOA, RAF, Mediterranean and Middle East, 1946-47; SASO, Flying Training Comd, RAF, 1947-49; C-in-C, Far East Air Force, 1949-52; Air Council Member for Personnel, 1952-56; Air ADC to the Queen, 1956-57; retired 1957. Pres., British Airport Construction and Equipment Association, 1970-; Dep. Pres., Air League. Dir, Racal Electronics. *Address:* Wey Cottage, Elstead, Surrey. *Club:* Royal Air Force.

**FOGARTY, Michael Patrick;** Director, Economic and Social Research Institute, Dublin; *b* 3 Oct. 1916; *s* of late Philip Christopher Fogarty, ICS, and Mary Belle Pye, Galway; *m* 1939, Phyllis Clark; two *s* two *d*. *Educ:* Ampleforth Coll.; Christ Church, Oxford. Lieut RA, 1940 (wounded, Dunkirk). Nuffield Coll., 1941-51 (Fellow, 1944); Montague Burton Prof. of Industrial Relations, University Coll. of S Wales and Mon, 1951-66. Also held posts in Oxford Institute of Statistics, Nat. Institute of Economic and Social Research, Ministry of Town and Country Planning, and as Asst Editor, The Economist. Chm., Cttee on Industrial Relations in the Electricity Supply Bd (Ireland), 1968-69; Mem., Commn on the Status of Women (Ireland), 1970-. Pres., Newman Assoc., 1957-59; Chm., Catholic Social Guild, 1959-63; Vice-Pres. Assoc. of University Teachers, 1964-66. Prospective Parly. candidate (Lab) Tamworth, 1938-44; Parliamentary Candidate (L) Devizes, 1964 and 1966. Vice-Pres. of the Liberal Party, 1964-66. Hon. Dr of Political and Social Science, Louvain, 1963. *Publications:* Prospects of the Industrial Areas of Great Britain, 1945; Plan Your Own Industries, 1947; (ed) Further Studies in Industrial Organisation, 1948; Town and Country Planning, 1948; Economic Control, 1955; Personality and Group Relations in Industry, 1956; Christian Democracy in Western Europe, 1820-1953, 1957; The Just Wage, 1961; Under-Governed and Over-Governed, 1962; The Rules of Work, 1963; Company and Corporation–One Law?, 1965; Companies Beyond Jenkins, 1965; Wider Business Objectives, 1966; A Companies Act 1970?, 1967; (with R. and R. Rapoport) Women and Top Jobs, 1967. *Recreations:* gardening and walking. *Address:* Brook Lodge, Ballywaltrim, Bray, Co. Wicklow, Ireland. *Clubs:* National Liberal; Stephen's Green (Dublin). *See also C. W. Fogarty.*

**FOGG, Albert,** DSc, CEng, FIMechE, MSAE, FInstPet; Chairman, Leyland Gas Turbines Ltd; Director: the British Leyland Motor Corporation Ltd; ENASA (Spain). *b* 25 Feb. 1909; *o s* of late James Fogg, Bolton. *Educ:* Manchester Univ. Scientific staff, National Physical Laboratory, 1930; First Dir, Motor Industry Research Assoc., 1946. Member: Min. of Technology Adv. Cttee for Mechanical Engineering; Nat. Engineering Laboratory Adv. Bd. Inst. of Mechanical Engineers: T. Bernard Hall Prize, 1945 and 1955; Starley Premium, 1956; James Clayton Prize, 1962. Viva Shield and Gold Medal, Worshipful Company of Carmen, 1962. *Publications:* numerous papers in jls of scientific socs and professional instns. *Recreations:* sport and travel. *Address:* 7 Hilton Court, South Promenade, St Anne's-on-Sea, Lancs FY8 1LZ. *T:* St Anne's 28582. *Club:* Royal Automobile.

**FOGG, Cyril Percival;** Deputy Controller of Electronics, Ministry of Technology, since 1967; *b* 28 Nov. 1914; *s* of Henry Fogg and Mabel Mary (*née* Orton); *m* 1939, Margaret Amie Millican; two *d*. *Educ:* Herbert Strutt Sch., Belper; Gonville and Caius Coll., Cambridge (BA, 1st cl. Mechanical Sciences Tripos). Research Staff, General Electric Co., 1936-37; various positions in Scientific Civil Service from 1937 with Air Ministry, Ministries of Aircraft Production, Supply, Aviation and Technology. Head of Ground Radar Dept, RRE Malvern, 1956-58; Dir Electronics R&D (Ground), 1959-63; Imperial Defence Coll., 1961; Dir of Guided Weapons Research, 1963-64; Dir-Gen. of Electronics R&D, Min. of Aviation, 1964-67. *Address:* Towan, 14 Woodlands Park, Merrow, Guildford, Surrey. *T:* Guildford 66950.

**FOGG, Prof. Gordon Elliott,** FRS 1965; Professor of Botany in the University of London at Westfield College, 1960-Oct. 1971; Professor and Head of the Department of Marine Biology, University College of North Wales, Bangor, from Oct. 1971; *b* 26 April 1919; *s* of Rev. L. C. Fogg; *m* 1945, Elizabeth Beryl Llechid-Jones; one *s* one *d*. *Educ:* Dulwich Coll.; Queen Mary Coll., London; St John's Coll., Cambridge. BSc (London), 1939; PhD (Cambridge), 1943; ScD (Cambridge), 1966. Sea-weed Survey of British Isles, 1942; Plant Physiologist, Pest Control Ltd, 1943-45; successively Asst Lectr, Lectr and Reader in Botany, University Coll., London, 1945-60; Rockefeller Fellow, 1954. Royal Soc. Leverhulme Vis. Prof., Kerala, 1969-70. Botanical Sec., Soc. for Experimental Biology, 1957-60; Pres. British Phycological Soc., 1961-62; Pres. International Phycological Soc., 1964; Joint Organizing Sec., X International Botanical Congress. Visiting research worker, British Antarctic Survey, 1966; Biological Gen. Sec., British Assoc., 1967. *Publications:* The Metabolism of Algae, 1953; The Growth of Plants, 1963; Algal Cultures and Phytoplankton Ecology, 1965; Photosynthesis, 1968; papers in learned jls. *Recreations:* water colour painting; far eastern studies. *Address:* 27 Grovewood Close, Chorleywood, Rickmansworth, Herts. *T:* Chorleywood 2940; (from Oct. 1971) Marine Science Laboratory, Menai Bridge, Anglesey.

**FOGGIN, Myers;** *see* Foggin, W. M.

**FOGGIN, (Wilhelm) Myers;** Principal, Trinity College of Music, London, since 1965; *b* 23 Dec. 1908; *m* 1952, Lotte Breitmeyer; one *s* one *d*. *Educ:* Dr Erlich's Sch., Newcastle upon Tyne; Royal Academy of Music. Concert Pianist; Prof. of Piano, RAM, 1936; Conductor, People's Palace Choral and Orchestral Soc., 1936-49. Intelligence Officer, RAF, 1940-45. Guest Conductor, Carl Rosa Opera, Sadler's Wells Opera and BBC; Dir of Opera, RAM, 1948-65; Conductor, Croydon Philharmonic Soc., 1957-; Warden, RAM, 1949-65. Dir of Music, Queenswood Sch., 1966-; Pres., Nat. Fedn of Music Socs, 1967-; Chm., Royal Philharmonic Soc., 1968-. Hon. FTCL, FRAM, Hon. RCM, Hon. GSM. *Recreation:* golf. *Address:* 43 Northway, NW11. *T:* 01-455 7527. *Club:* Athenæum.

**FOGGON, George,** CMG 1961; OBE 1949 (MBE 1945); Overseas Labour Adviser, Foreign and Commonwealth Office (formerly Foreign Office), and Ministry of Overseas Development, since 1966; *b* 13 Sept. 1913; *s* of Thomas Foggon, Newcastle upon Tyne; *m* 1st, 1938, Agnes McIntosh (*d* 1968); one *s*; 2nd, 1969, Audrey Blanch. Joined Min. of Labour, 1930. Served War of 1939-45 (MBE), Wing-Comdr, RAFVR, 1941-46. Seconded to FO, 1946; on staff of Mil. Gov., Berlin, 1946-49; Principal, CO, 1949; Asst Sec., W African

Inter-Territorial Secretariat, Gold Coast (now Ghana), 1951-53; Comr of Labour, Nigeria, 1954-58; Labour Adviser: to Sec. of State for Colonies, 1958-61; to Sec. for Techn. Co-op., 1962-64; to Min. of Overseas Development, 1965-66. *Recreations:* walking, photography. *Address:* 8 Churton Place, SW1. *T:* 01-828 1492. *Club:* Travellers'.

**FOGH, Prof. Torkel W.**; *see* Weis-Fogh.

**FOLDES, Andor**; international concert pianist since 1933; Head of Piano Master Class, Conservatory, Saarbrücken, 1957-65; *b* Budapest, Hungary, 21 Dec. 1913; *s* of Emil Foldes and Valerie Foldes (*née* Ipolyi); *m* 1940, Lili Rendy (writer); no *c*. *Educ:* Franz Liszt Academy of Music, Budapest. Started piano playing at 5; first appeared with Budapest Philh. Orch. at 8; studied with Ernest von Dohnanyi, received Master Diploma (Fr. Liszt Acad. of Music, Budapest), 1932. Concerts all over Europe, 1933-39; US debut (NBC Orch.), 1940; toured US extensively, 1940-48. US citizen since 1948. Concerts, since, all over the world. Grand Prix du Disque, Paris, for Bartok Complete Works (piano solo), 1957. Beethoven concerts, Bonn Festival and throughout Europe. Recordings of all Beethoven Sonatas. Order of Merit, First Class, 1956, Gr. Cross, 1964 (Germany); Commandeur, Mérite Culturel et Artistique (City of Paris), 1968. *Publications:* Keys to the Keyboard, 1950; Cadenzas to Mozart Piano Concertos (W Germany); Is there a Contemporary Style of Beethoven-playing?, 1963; various piano compositions. *Relevant publication:* Wolf-Eberhard von Lewinski, Andor Foldes, 1970. *Recreations:* collecting art, reading, writing on musical subjects; swimming, hiking. *Address:* Herrliberg near Zürich, Switzerland.

**FOLETTA, George Gotardo,** CMG 1962; Governing Director since 1948 and Chairman since 1943, Prestige Ltd (Parent Co.) and all major subsidiaries in Australia and NZ; Director of other companies; *b* 30 Jan. 1892; *s* of late H. G. Foletta, Ivanhoe, Vic., Australia; *m* 1915, A. Myra Cooper; four *s*. *Educ:* Prince's Hill State Sch.; South Melbourne Coll. Joined H. G. Foletta & Co., Merchants & Importers, 1909; Co-founder and Man., Atlas Knitting and Spinning Mills Pty Ltd, 1920 (which became Prestige Ltd, 1922); Man. Dir, Prestige Group of Cos, 1937-48, retd; Co-founder and first Pres., 1951-56, Aust. Industries Development Assoc. (AIDA); FAIM. Member: Austr. Inst. Polit. Science; Economic Soc. of Aust. and NZ; Aust. and NZ Assoc. for Advancement of Science (ANZAAS). Trustee, Cttee for Econ. Devlt of Australia (CEDA). *Recreations:* fly fishing, political science. *Address:* 6 Redesdale Road, Ivanhoe, Victoria 3079, Australia. *T:* 49.1320. *Club:* Athenæum (Melbourne).

**FOLEY,** family name of **Baron Foley.**

**FOLEY,** 8th Baron *cr* 1776; **Adrian Gerald Foley;** *b* 9 Aug. 1923; *s* of 7th Baron and Minoru (*d* 1968), *d* of late H. Greenstone, South Africa; *S* father, 1927; *m* 1958, Patricia Meek; one *s* one *d*. *Heir:* *s* Hon. Thomas Henry Foley, *b* 1 April 1961. *Address:* c/o Westminster Bank Ltd, 329 High Holborn, WC1. *Club:* Turf.

**FOLEY, Rt. Rev. Brian C.**; *see* Lancaster, Bishop of, (RC).

**FOLEY, Maurice (Anthony)**; MP (Lab) West Bromwich since July 1963; *b* 9 Oct. 1925; *s* of Jeremiah and Agnes Foley; *m* 1952, Catherine, *d* of Patrick and Nora O'Riordan; three *s* one *d*. *Educ:* St Mary's Coll., Middlesbrough. Formerly: electrical fitter, youth organiser, social worker. Member: ETU, 1941-46; Transport and General Workers Union, 1948-; Royal Arsenal Co-operative Soc.; Joint Parliamentary Under-Sec. of State, Dept of Economic Affairs, 1964-66; Parly Under-Secretary: Home Office, 1966-67; Royal Navy, MoD, 1967-68; FCO, 1968-69; Royal Navy, MoD, 1969-70. *Address:* House of Commons, SW1.

**FOLEY-BERKELEY,** family name of **Baroness Berkeley.**

**FOLJAMBE,** family name of **Earl of Liverpool.**

**FOLKESTONE, Viscount; William Pleydell-Bouverie;** *b* 5 Jan. 1955; *s* and *heir* of 8th Earl of Radnor, *qv*.

**FOLL, Hon. Hattil Spencer;** retired; *b* 31 May 1890; *s* of John Hattil and Kate Elizabeth Foll; *m* 1915; four *d* (one *s* decd). *Educ:* Clapham Collegiate Sch. Served AIF, European War, 1914-15; Home Forces, 1942-43; Minister for Repatriation and War Service Homes, Australia, 1937-39, and Minister for Health, 1938-39; Minister for the Interior, Commonwealth of Australia, 1939-41, and Minister of Information, 1940-41; Senator for Queensland, 1917-47; has served on numerous select cttees especially relating to returned soldier problems. Formerly pastoralist. *Recreations:* bowls, swimming. *Address:* 6 Arncliffe Avenue, Port Macquarie, NSW 2444, Australia. *T:* 83-1356. *Club:* Port Macquarie Bowling.

**FOLLETT, Sir David (Henry),** Kt 1967; MA Oxon, PhD London; FInstP; FMA; Director, Science Museum, since 1960; *b* 5 Sept. 1907; *er s* of Septimus and Rose Annie Follett; *m* 1932, Helen Alison Wilson; three *s* decd. *Educ:* Rutlish Sch.; Brasenose Coll. (Hulme Exhibitioner); Birkbeck Coll. (post-graduate). Joined Adam Hilger Ltd, optical instrument manufacturers, 1929. Asst Keeper, Dept of Physics, Science Museum, 1937. Meteorological Branch, RAFVR, 1939. Returned to Science Museum, 1945; Deputy Keeper, Dept of Physics, 1949; Keeper of Dept of Electrical Engineering and Communications, 1957-60. Governor Imperial Coll. of Science and Technology; Trustee Imperial War Museum; Vice-Pres., Institute of Physics and Physical Soc., 1965-69; Mem., Ancient Monuments Board for England, 1966-. *Publications:* papers in scientific jls. *Recreations:* gardening, sailing. *Address:* 3 Elm Bank Gardens, Barnes, SW13. *T:* 01-876 8302. *Club:* Athenæum.

**FOLLETT, Samuel Frank,** CMG 1959; BSc, CEng, FIEE, FRAeS; Scientific Adviser to the Board of Trade since 1966; *b* 21 March 1904; *o s* of Samuel Charles Follett and Kate Bell; *m* 1932, Kathleen Matilda Tupper. *Educ:* Farnham Gram. Sch.; Univ. of London. Electrical Research Assoc., 1924-27; Electrical Engineering Dept, RAE Farnborough, 1927-45; Asst Dir of Instrument R&D (Electrics), Min. of Supply, 1946-50; Dir of Instrument R&D, 1950-54; Dep. Dir-Gen. Aircraft, Equipment, R&D, 1954-56; Dir.-Gen., Min. of Supply Staff, Brit. Jt Services Mission, Washington, DC, 1956-59; Dep. Dir, RAE Farnborough, 1959-63; Dep. Controller of Guided Weapons, Min. of Aviation, 1963-66. *Address:* Darby Cottage, St Johns Road, Farnham, Surrey. *T:* Farnham 6610.

**FOLLOWS, Sir (Charles) Geoffry (Shield),** Kt, *cr* 1951; CMG 1945; Northern Rhodesia representative on Federal Interim Public Service Commission, 1953-59; *b* 4 July 1896; *m*

1922, Claire Camille, *d* of late Julien Lemarchand. *Educ:* Wellington Sch., Som. 2nd Lieut The King's (Liverpool) Regt 1914; served in France, 1915-18, and in various Staff appts until 1920; Colonial Service, Seychelles, 1920-24; attached Colonial Office, 1925; Gibraltar, 1925-36; N Rhodesia, 1936-45; Chief Financial Adviser to Mil. Admin, Hong Kong, 1945-46; Fin. Sec., Hong Kong, 1946-52; Chm. N Rhodesia Salaries Commn, 1952; Mem. Preparatory Commn on Federation of Rhodesias and Nyasaland, 1952. *Address:* 12 Lanark Road, Salisbury, Rhodesia.

**FOLLOWS, Denis,** CBE 1967 (MBE 1950); Secretary of the Football Association since 1962; *b* 13 April 1908; *s* of Amos Follows; *m* 1938, Mary Elizabeth Milner; two *d*. *Educ:* City Sch., Lincoln; Nottingham Univ. (BA). Pres., National Union of Students, 1930-32; Pres., Internat. Confedn of Students, 1932-34; Vice-Pres., 1933, Chm., 1948, Universities Athletic Union. Asst Master, Chiswick Grammar Sch. for Boys, 1932-40. Royal Air Force, Flight Lieut, 1940-46. Sec., British Airline Pilots Assoc., 1946-62. Chm., Nat. Jt Council for Civil Air Transport, 1951-52. *Recreation:* cricket. *Address:* 70 Barrowgate Road, Chiswick, W4. *T:* 01-994 5782. *Club:* Royal Aero.

**FONDA, Henry;** actor, USA; *b* Grand Island, Nebraska, USA, 16 May 1905; *s* of William Brace Fonda and Herberta Jaynes; *m* 1965, Shirlee Adams; one *s* two *d* of previous *m*. *Educ:* University of Minnesota, Minneapolis, Minn. Began acting at Omaha Community Playhouse, Nebraska; subseq. played many parts with touring companies. Made first appearance on New York stage, Guild Theatre, 1929; since then has played parts in many plays including: The Farmer Takes a Wife, 46th Street, 1934; Mister Roberts, Alvin, 1948; Point of No Return, Alvin, 1951; Caine Mutiny Court Martial, Plymouth, 1954; Two for the Seesaw, 1958; Critics' Choice; Silent Night, Lonely Night; A Gift of Time, 1962; Generation, 1965; Our Town. Entered films, 1935 and has appeared in numerous films including: Jesse James, Grapes of Wrath, Mister Roberts, The Wrong Man, 12 Angry Men (also produced), Warlock, The Best Man, A Big Hand for the Little Lady, Trail of the Lonesome Pine, You Only Live Once, Young Mr Lincoln, The Lady Eve, The Ox Bow Incident, The Male Animal, My Darling Clementine, The Rounders, Madigan, Yours, Mine and Ours, The Boston Strangler, Once upon a Time. . . in the West, Too Late the Hero, There Was a Crooked Man, The Cheyenne Social Club, Sometimes a Great Notion. Served USN, 1942-45. Hon. DHL, Ursinus Coll., 1966. *Address:* c/o John Springer, 667 Madison Avenue, NYC, USA.

**FONTANNE, Lynn;** actress; *m* Alfred Lunt, *qv*. Began as child in pantomime in Drury Lane; walked on in various London companies with Lewis Waller, Beerbohm Tree, Lena Ashwell; played in touring company with Weedon Grossmith for few seasons, playing name part in Young Lady of 17 and other small parts in various curtain raisers; on tour in Milestones, then revival in London; small parts in My Lady's Dress; then America; many plays with Laurette Taylor; name part in Dulcy, followed by many leads including Goat Song, Strange Interlude, Second Man, Caprice, At Mrs Beams, Pygmalion, The Guardsman, Meteor, Design for Living, Point Valaine, Taming of the Shrew, Idiot's Delight, Amphytrion 38, There Shall Be No Night, Love in Idleness (O Mistress Mine, in New York), Quadrille, The Great Sebastians, The Visit, The Sea Gull. Presidential Medal of Freedom, 1964; Antoinette Perry Award; Emmy Award. Holds hon. degrees from 12 universities and colleges.

**FONTEYN, Dame Margot;** *see* Arias, Dame Margot Fonteyn de.

**FOOKES, Janet Evelyn;** MP (C) Merton and Morden since 1970; *b* 21 Feb. 1936; *d* of Lewis Aylmer Fookes and Evelyn Margery Fookes (*née* Holmes). *Educ:* Hastings and St Leonard Ladies' Coll.; High Sch. for Girls, Hastings; Royal Holloway Coll., Univ. of London (BA Hons). Teacher, 1958-70. Councillor for County Borough of Hastings, 1960-61 and 1963-70 (Chm. Educn Cttee, 1967-70). Mem., Nat. Art Collections Fund. *Recreations:* riding, dancing. *Address:* House of Commons, SW1; Delphia, 11 Branksome Road, St Leonards-on-Sea, Sussex. *T:* Hastings 4108. *Club:* VAD Ladies'.

**FOOKS, Sir Raymond (Hatherell),** Kt 1954; CBE 1949; KPM 1945; Chief Constable of Lincolnshire, 1934-54; *b* 23 June 1888; *s* of late W. H. Fooks, Cerne Abbas, Dorset, and Leigh-on-Sea, Essex; *m* 1st, 1922, Mary Gwendoline (*d* 1926), *d* of late Francis William Baily, Bishopstoke, Hants; one *s* one *d*; 2nd, 1935, Madeline Player (*d* 1953), *widow* of Lieut-Col R. D. Crosby, OBE, MC, The Royal Lincolnshire Regt; 3rd, 1954, Hon. Mrs Mary Josephine Bruce, *widow* of E. H. Bruce, Indian Police Service, and *e d* of 1st Baron Riverdale, GBE, LLD, JP. *Educ:* King Edward VI Sch., and University Coll., Southampton; Exeter Coll., Oxford. BA (London), 1908; MA (Oxford), 1933. Joined Indian Police Service, 1908; Supt, Punjab, 1919-31; served on NW Frontier of India in European War, 1914-19 (despatches); Deputy Inspector-Gen., 1931-33; retired, 1933. Barrister, Inner Temple, 1933. Deputy Pres. of the North Lincs Branch, British Red Cross Soc., 1959-60 (County Dir, 1954-58); DL County of Lincoln, 1956-59. *Recreations:* gardening and study. *Address:* Broom Hill Copse, Boar's Hill, Oxford. *T:* 35401. *Clubs:* Athenæum, Lansdowne.

**FOORD-KELCEY, Air Vice-Marshal Alick,** CBE 1956; AFC 1943; Executive Director, Federation of World Health Foundations, Geneva; *b* Viking, Alta, Canada, 6 April 1913; *s* of William Foord-Kelcey, MC (killed War of 1914-18); *m* 1st, 1944 (marr. diss.); two *s*; 2nd, 1951, Diane, *d* of Lloyd and Ethel Fenwick, Berkeley, Calif. *Educ:* King's Sch., Canterbury; Corpus Christi Coll., Cambridge. Mem., CUAS. commissioned RAF, Oct. 1935; 1935-39: fighter pilot and flying instructor, UK and Egypt; 1939-44: flying, flying instructor, and Air Staff duties, Egypt, Aden, Western Desert and UK; 1944-46: Jt Planning Staff, War Cabinet Offices; 1947-57: Flying Comd, Air Staff duties, UK, Germany (Berlin airlift), BJSM Washington, France (Fontainebleau). RAF Staff Coll., 1943; Imperial Defence Coll., 1958. AOC No 11 Group, Fighter Comd, 1959-60; ACAS (Intell.), 1961-64, retd at own request. dep. Dir Foreign Office Arms Control and Disarmament Research Unit, 1965-66. *Address:* 7 rue Robert-de-Traz, 1206 Geneva, Switzerland.

**FOOT,** family name of **Baron Caradon** and **Baron Foot.**

**FOOT,** Baron *cr* 1967 (Life Peer), of Buckland Monachorum; **John Mackintosh Foot;** Senior Partner, Foot & Bowden, Solicitors, Plymouth; Member, Commission on the Constitution, since 1969; Chairman, United Kingdom Immigrants Advisory Service, since 1970; *b* 17 Feb. 1909; 3rd *s* of late Rt Hon. Isaac Foot, PC and Eva Mackintosh; *m* 1936, Anne, *d* of Dr Clifford Bailey Farr, Bryn Mawr, Pa; one *s* one *d*. *Educ:* Forres Sch., Swanage; Bembridge Sch., IoW; Balliol Coll., Oxford. Pres., Oxford Union, 1931; Pres., OU Liberal Club, 1931; BA Oxon (2nd cl. hons Jurisprudence), 1931. Admitted Solicitor, 1934. Served in Army, 1939-45 (Hon. Major); jsc 1944. Contested (L); Basingstoke, 1934 and 1935; Bodmin, 1945 and 1950. Mem., Dartmoor National Park Cttee, 1963-. *Recreations:* chess, crosswords, defending Dartmoor. *Address:* Yew Tree, Crapstone, Yelverton, Devon. *T:* Yelverton 3417. *Clubs:* English-Speaking Union; Royal Western Yacht.

*See also Baron Caradon, Rt Hon. Sir Dingle Foot, Michael Foot.*

**FOOT, Rt. Hon. Sir Dingle (Mackintosh),** PC 1967; Kt 1964; QC 1954; *e s* of late Rt. Hon. Isaac Foot; *b* Plymouth, 1905; *m* 1933, Dorothy Mary, *er d* of late William Rowley Elliston, TD, LLB. *Educ:* Bembridge Sch., Isle of Wight; Balliol Coll., Oxford. MA Oxon 1960. Pres., Oxford Univ. Liberal Club, 1927; Pres., Oxford Union Soc., 1928; contested Tiverton Div. of Devon, 1929; Dundee, 1945; North Cornwall, 1950 and 1951; MP (L) Dundee, 1931-45; Parliamentary Sec., Min. of Economic Warfare, 1940-45; joined the Labour Party, July 1956; MP (Lab) Ipswich, Oct. 1957-70; Solicitor-Gen., 1964-67. Led British Economic Warfare Delegn to Switzerland, 1945; Mem. of British Delegn to San Francisco Conf., 1945. Called to Bar, Gray's Inn, 1930; Bencher, 1952; Treasurer, 1968; Vice-Treasurer, 1969. Western Circuit. Admitted to Gold Coast Roll of Legal Practitioners, 1948; to Ceylon Roll of Advocates, 1951; to Nigerian Bar, 1955; to Northern Rhodesian Bar, 1956; to Sierra Leone Bar, 1959; to Supreme Court of India (as a Senior Advocate), 1960; to Bahrain Roll of Legal Practitioners, 1962; to Malaya Roll of Legal Practitioners, 1964; to S Rhodesia Roll of Legal Practitioners, 1964, to Northern Ireland Bar. Has also appeared in courts of Kenya, Uganda, Tanganyika, Nyasaland, Pakistan, Hong Kong. Chm., Observer Trust, 1953-55. Chm., Soc. of Labour Lawyers, 1960-64. *Recreation:* football fan. *Address:* 2 Paper Buildings, Temple, EC4. *T:* 01-353 9119. *Clubs:* Garrick, Beefsteak.

*See also Baron Caradon, Baron Foot, Michael Foot.*

**FOOT, Michael;** MP (Lab) Ebbw Vale Division of Monmouthshire since Nov. 1960; Managing Director, Tribune; *b* 23 July 1913; *s* of late Rt Hon. Isaac Foot, PC; *m* 1949, Jill Craigie. *Educ:* Forres Sch., Swanage; Leighton Park Sch., Reading; Wadham Coll., Oxford (Exhibitioner). Pres. Oxford Union, 1933; contested (Lab) Mon, 1935; MP (Lab) Devonport Div. of Plymouth, 1945-55. Asst Editor, Tribune, 1937-38; Acting Editor, Evening Standard, 1942; Editor, Tribune, 1948-52, 1955-60; political columnist on the Daily Herald, 1944-64; Book Critic, Evening Standard, 1964-. Hon. Fellow, Wadham Coll., 1969. *Publications:* Armistice 1918-39, 1940; Trial of Mussolini, 1943; Brendan and Beverley, 1944; Still at Large, 1950; Full Speed Ahead, 1950; Guilty Men (with Mervyn Jones), 1957; The Pen and the Sword, 1957; Parliament in Danger, 1959; Aneurin Bevan: Vol. I, 1897-1945, 1962. *Recreations:* Plymouth Argyle supporter, chess, reading, walking. *Address:* c/o Tribune, 24 St John Street, EC1.

*See also Baron Caradon, Baron Foot, Rt Hon. Sir Dingle Foot.*

**FOOT, Prof. Michael Richard Daniell;** historian; Professor of Modern History, Manchester, since 1967; *b* 14 Dec. 1919; *s* of late R. C. Foot and Nina (*née* Raymond); *m* twice; one *s* one *d*. *Educ:* Winchester (scholar); New Coll., Oxford (scholar). Served in Army, 1939-45 (Major RA, parachutist, wounded). Taught at Oxford, 1947-59; research, 1959-67. French Croix de Guerre, 1945. *Publications:* Gladstone and Liberalism (with J. L. Hammond), 1952; British Foreign Policy since 1898, 1956; Men in Uniform, 1961; SOE in France, 1966; (ed) The Gladstone Diaries: vols I and II, 1825-1839, 1968. *Recreations:* reading, walking. *Address:* Department of History, University of Manchester, Manchester M13 9PL. *T:* 061-273 3333. *Club:* Savile.

**FOOT, Robert William,** OBE 1919; MC 1916; Member of Livery of Haberdashers' Company, since 1918, and Member of Court of Assistants, 1958-70; *b* 7 June 1889; *m*; two *s* one *d*. *Educ:* Winchester. Admitted a Solicitor, 1912; with Orr, Dignam & Co., Solicitors, in Calcutta, 1913-14. Served 1914-18, with RFA in Belgium and France, Staff Capt. 21st Divisional Artillery, Staff Capt. RA and DAQMG 1st Corps (despatches twice, OBE, MC); joined Gas Light and Coke Co., 1919; General Manager, 1928-41; acted at request of Govt, as Adviser to the BBC on War-Time Organisation; Joint Dir-Gen., BBC, 1942-43, Dir-Gen., 1943-44; Chm. of Mining Assoc. of Great Britain, 1944-47; President: British Coal Utilization Research Assoc., 1944-47. Coal Utilization Joint Council, 1945-47; Mining Assoc. of Great Britain, 1947-52; Dep.-Chm. and Man. Dir, Powell Duffryn Ltd, and Chm. Powell Duffryn Technical Services Ltd, 1947-52; Dir Barclays Bank Ltd, 1947-53; Dir Australia and New Zealand Bank Ltd, 1949-52; Chm. Wankie Colliery Co. Ltd, 1949-53. *Publication:* A Plan for Coal, 1945. *Address:* 18 Flag Court, Kingsway, Hove, Sussex. *T:* Brighton 70407.

**FOOT, Maj.-Gen. William,** CB 1947; MC 1915; MB; *b* 2 Dec. 1889; *s* of A. R. Foot, DL, Dublin; *m* 1921, Aileen Katherina Curling, The Castle, Newcastle West, Co. Limerick; one *d*. *Educ:* Shrewsbury Sch.; Trinity Coll., Dublin. BA (Trinity Coll., Dublin), 1910; MB, BCh, BAO, LM (*Rot*), 1914; House Surg. Victoria Hospital, Blackpool; European War, 1914-18, joined RAMC 1914; served in France, 1914-18 (MC and bar); Afghan War, Indian Frontier, 1919; War of 1939-45, France, 1940; ADMS Division, DDMS, Persia and Iraq, 1943-45; DMS, MELF, 1946-47; Maj.-Gen.; late Deputy Dir of Medical Services, Eastern Command, UK; retired pay, 1949. KHP 1947. Hereditary Freeman of the City of Dublin; played hockey for Ireland, 1909, 1911, 1912. *Recreations:* sports and games; music. *Address:* Ashbourne, 49 Woodlands Park, Blackrock, Co. Dublin, Eire.

**FOOTE, Maj.-Gen. Henry Robert Bowreman,** VC 1944; CB 1952; DSO 1942; *b* 5 Dec. 1904; *s* of Lieut-Col H. B. Foote, late RA; *m* 1944, Anita Flint Howard. *Educ:* Bedford Sch. Royal Tank Corps; 2nd Lieut, 1925; Lieut, 1927; Capt., 1936; Staff Coll., 1939; GSO3, WO, 1939; GSO2, WO, 1940; GSO2, Staff Coll., 1940-41; GSO1, 10th Armd Div., 1941-42; OC 7th Royal Tank Regt, 1942; Subst. Major, 1942; GSO1, AFHQ, Italy, 1944; 2i/c, 9th Armd Bde, 1945; Brig. RAC, MELF, 1945-47; Subst. Lieut-Col, 1946; Subst. Col, 1948; OC 2nd Royal Tank Regt, 1947-48; OC Automotive Wing, Fighting Vehicles Proving Establishment, Ministry of Supply, 1948-49; Comd 7th Armd Bde, 1949-50; Maj.-Gen. 1951; Comd 11th Armoured Div., 1950-53; Dir-Gen. of Fighting Vehicles, Min. of Supply, 1953-55; Dir, Royal Armoured Corps, at the War Office, 1955-58; retd. *Address:* Furzfield, West Chiltington

Common, Pulborough, Sussex. *Club:* Army and Navy.

**FOOTE, Rev. John Weir,** VC 1946; DD, LLD University of Western Ontario, 1947; Minister of Reform Institutions, Government of Ontario, since Nov. 1950; *b* 5 May 1904; *s* of Gordon Foote, Madoc, Ontario; *m* 1929. *Educ:* University of Western Ontario, London, Ont; Presbyterian Coll. (McGill). Minister St Paul's Presbyterian Church, Port Hope, Ont. Canadian Army from 1939, Asst Principal Chaplain (P). *Recreations:* golf, fishing. *Address:* Parliament Buildings, Toronto, Ont, Canada.

**FOOTE, Prof. Peter Godfrey;** Professor of Old Scandinavian and Director of Scandinavian Studies, University College, London, since 1963; *b* 26 May 1924; 4th *s* of late T. Foote and Ellen Foote, Swanage, Dorset; *m* 1951, Eleanor Jessie McCaig, *d* of late J. M. McCaig and of Margaret H. McCaig; one *s* two *d*. *Educ:* Grammar Sch., Swanage; University Coll., Exeter; Univ. of Oslo; University Coll., London. BA London 1948; MA London 1951. Served with RNVR, 1943-46. Asst Lectr, Lectr and Reader in Old Scandinavian, University Coll., London, 1950-63. Jt Sec., Viking Soc., 1956-. Member: Royal Gustav Adolfs Academy, Uppsala, Sweden, 1967; Kungl. Humanistiska Vetenskapssamfundet, Uppsala, 1968; Vísindafélag Islands, 1969; Hon. Mem., Isl. Bókmenntafélag, 1965. Crabtree Orator, 1968. Chevalier, Icelandic Order of the Falcon, 1963. *Publications:* Gunnlaugs saga ormstungu, 1957; Pseudo-Turpin Chronicle in Iceland, 1959; Laing's Heimskringla, 1961; Lives of Saints: Icelandic manuscripts in fascimile IV, 1962; (with G. Johnston) The Saga of Gisli, 1963; (with D. M. Wilson) The Viking Achievement, 1970; Jt Editor, Saga Book of Viking Society and Mediæval Scandinavia; Mem. of Ed. Board, Scandinavica; papers in Saga-Book, Arv, Studia Islandica, Islenzk Tunga, etc. *Recreations:* bell-ringing, walking. *Address:* 18 Talbot Road, N6. *T:* 01-340 1860. *Club:* Athenæum.

**FOOTMAN, Charles Worthington Fowden,** CMG 1952; *b* 3 Sept. 1905; *s* of Rev. William Llewellyn and Mary Elizabeth Footman; *m* 1947, Joyce Marcelle Law; one *s* two *d*. *Educ:* Rossall Sch.; Keble Coll., Oxford. Colonial Administrative Service, Zanzibar, 1930; seconded to East African Governors' Conference, 1942; seconded to Colonial Office, 1943-46; Financial Sec., Nyasaland, 1947; Chief Sec., Nyasaland, 1951-60. Retired from HM Overseas Civil Service, 1960. Chm., Public Service Commissions, Tanganyika and Zanzibar, 1960-61; Commonwealth Relations Office, 1962-64; Min. of Overseas Development, 1964-. *Recreations:* golf and tennis. *Address:* c/o National Westminster Bank, Worthing, Sussex. *Club:* East India and Sports.

**FOOTMAN, David John,** CMG 1950; MC 1916; MA 1953; *b* 17 Sept. 1895; *s* of Rev. John Footman and Ella Mary (*née* Kennard); *m* 1927, Joan Isabel (marr. diss. 1936; she *d* 1960), *d* of Edmund Footman; no *c*. *Educ:* Marlborough; New Coll., Oxford. European War, 1914-19, Royal Berks Regt. Levant Consular Service, 1919-29; Foreign Office, 1935-53; Fellow of St Antony's Coll., Oxford, 1953-63, Emeritus Fellow, 1963-. *Publications:* Half-way East, 1935; Pig and Pepper, 1936; Pemberton, 1943; Red Prelude, 1944; The Primrose Path, 1946; Civil War in Russia, 1961; The Russian Revolutions, 1962; Editor: St Antony's Papers; Soviet Affairs: vols 1-3, 1956, 1959, 1962; International Communism, 1960; etc. *Address:* 11a Collingham Gardens, SW5. *Club:* Naval and Military.

**FORBES,** family name of **Baron Forbes** and of **Earl of Granard.**

**FORBES,** 22nd Baron *cr* 1442 or before; **Nigel Ivan Forbes,** KBE 1960; JP; DL; Premier Baron of Scotland; Representative Peer of Scotland, 1955-63; Major (retired) Grenadier Guards; Director: Grampian Television Ltd; Aberdeen Salmon Co. Ltd; Davell & Rufford Ltd; Deputy Chairman, Tennent Caledonian Breweries Ltd; *b* 19 Feb. 1918; *o s* of 21st Baron and Lady Mabel Anson, *d* of 3rd Earl of Lichfield; *S* father, 1953; *m* 1942, Hon. Rosemary Katharine Hamilton-Russell, *o d* of 9th Viscount Boyne; two *s* one *d*. *Educ:* Harrow; RMC Sandhurst. Served War of 1939-45 (wounded); Adjt, Grenadier Guards, Staff Coll. Military Asst to High Comr for Palestine, 1947-48. Minister of State, Scottish Office, Oct. 1958-59. Mem. Inter-Parly Union Delegn to Denmark, 1956; Commonwealth Parly Assoc. Delegn to Canada, 1961; Parly Delegn to Pakistan, 1962; Inter-Parly Union Delegn to Hungary, 1965. Mem., Aberdeen and District Milk Marketing Bd; Mem. Alford District Council, 1955-58; DL Aberdeenshire, 1958. Pres. Royal Highland and Agricultural Society of Scotland, 1958-59. Chairman: River Don District Bd; Scottish Br., Nat. Playing Fields Assoc.; Member: Sports Council for Scotland; Institute of Directors. *Heir: s* Master of Forbes, *qv*. *Address:* Balforbes, Alford, Aberdeenshire. *T:* Whitehouse 216. *Club:* Guards.

**FORBES, Master of; Hon. Malcolm Nigel Forbes;** journalist; with Scottish Daily Express; *b* 6 May 1946; *s* and *heir* of 22nd Baron Forbes, *qv*; *m* 1969, Carole Jennifer Andrée, *d* of N. S. Whitehead, Aberdeen; one *s*. *Educ:* Eton; Aberdeen Univ. Chm., Impulse Publications Ltd, 1968-. *Address:* 25 Burnbrae Avenue, Bearsden, Dunbartonshire. *T:* 041-942 1748.

**FORBES, Hon. Sir Alastair (Granville),** Kt 1960; President, Courts of Appeal for Seychelles, St Helena, Falkland Islands and British Antarctic Territories, 1965; a Chairman, Pensions Appeal Tribunals for England and Wales, since 1965; Panel of Chairmen of Industrial Tribunals (England and Wales), 1965; *b* 3 Jan. 1908; *s* of Granville Forbes and Constance Margaret (*née* Davis); *m* 1936, Constance Irene Mary Hughes–White; two *d*. *Educ:* Blundell's Sch.; Clare Coll., Cambridge. Called to the Bar, Gray's Inn, 1932; Magistrate and Govt Officer, Dominica, BWI, 1936; Crown Attorney, Dominica, 1939; Resident Magistrate, Fiji, 1940; Crown Counsel, Fiji, 1942; Solicitor-Gen., Fiji, and Asst Legal Adviser, Western Pacific High Commission, 1945; Legal Draftsman, Federation of Malaya, 1947; Solicitor-Gen., Northern Rhodesia, 1950; Permanent Sec., Ministry of Justice, and Solicitor-Gen., Gold Coast, 1951; Puisne Judge, Kenya, 1956; Justice of Appeal, Court of Appeal for Eastern Africa, 1957; Vice-Pres., Court of Appeal for Eastern Africa, 1958; Federal Justice, Federal Supreme Court of Rhodesia and Nyasaland, 1963-64. Chairman: Constituencies Delimitation Commissions, N Rhodesia, 1962 and 1963, and Bechuanaland, 1964; Gibraltar Riot Inquiry, 1968. *Publications:* Index of the Laws, Dominica, 1940; Revised Edition of Laws of Fiji, 1944. *Recreations:* fishing, shooting. *Address:* Beeches, Marnhull, Sturminster Newton, Dorset. *T:* Marnhull 458. *Club:* East India and Sports.

**FORBES, Sir Archibald (Finlayson),** GBE 1957; Kt 1943; Chartered Accountant; Chairman:

Midland Bank Ltd and Midland and International Banks Ltd since 1964; President, Spillers Ltd, since 1969; Director of other companies; *b* 6 March 1903; *s* of late Charles Forbes, Johnstone, Renfrewshire; *m* 1943, Angela Gertrude (*d* 1969), *o d* of late Horace Ely, Arlington House, SW1; one *s* two *d*. *Educ:* Paisley; Glasgow Univ. Formerly Mem. of firm of Thomson McLintock & Co., Chartered Accountants. Joined Spillers Ltd as Executive Dir, 1935. Mem. of various Reorganisation Commns and Cttees appointed by Minister of Agriculture, 1932-39; Dir of Capital Finance, Air Min., 1940; Deputy Sec., Min. of Aircraft Production, 1940-43; Controller of Repair, Equipment and Overseas Supplies, 1943-45; Mem. of Aircraft Supply Council, 1943-45; Chairman: First Iron and Steel Board from its formation, 1946, to dissolution 1949; Iron and Steel Board from its inception under the Iron and Steel Act, 1953, until 1959; British Millers' Mutual Pool Ltd, 1952-62 (Dep. Chm. 1940-52); Central Mining and Investment Corp., 1959-64; Spillers Ltd, 1965-68. Pres., FBI, 1951-53; Dep. Chm., Cttee of London Clearing Bankers, 1968-70; Pres., British Bankers' Assoc., 1970 (Vice-Pres. 1969-70). Member: Cttee to enquire into Financial Structure of Colonial Develt Corp., 1959; Review Body on Doctors' and Dentists' Remuneration, 1962-65. *Recreations:* golf and fishing. *Address:* 26 Orchard Court, Portman Square, W1. *T:* 01-935 9304; Mattingley Green Cottage, Mattingley, Hants. *T:* Heckfield 247. *Clubs:* Brooks's, Royal Thames Yacht, Pratt's, Beefsteak.

**FORBES, Bryan;** Managing Director and Head of Production, ABPC Studios, since 1969; Managing Director and Chief Executive, EMI-MGM, Elstree Studios, since 1970; *b* 22 July 1926; *m* 1955, Nanette Newman, actress; two *d*. *Educ:* West Ham Secondary Sch. Studies at RADA, 1941; entered acting profession, 1942, and (apart from war service) was on West End stage, then in films here and in Hollywood, 1948-60. Formed Beaver Films with Richard Attenborough, 1959; wrote and co-produced The Angry Silence, 1960. Subseq. wrote, dir. and prod. numerous films; *films include:* The League of Gentlemen; Only Two Can Play; Whistle Down the Wind; The L-Shaped Room; Séance on a Wet Afternoon; King Rat (in Hollywood); The Wrong Box; The Whisperers; The Madwoman of Chaillot; The Raging Moon. Won British Academy Award, 1960; Writers' Guild Award (twice); numerous internat. awards. Mem. BBC Gen. Adv. Council, 1966-69; Trustee, Writers' Guild of GB. *Publications:* Truth Lies Sleeping, 1950 (paperback, 1961); contribs to: The Spectator, New Statesman, Queen, and other periodicals. *Recreations:* running a bookshop, reading, landscape gardening. *Address:* ABPC Studios, Boreham Wood, Elstree, Herts.

**FORBES of Pitsligo, Sir Charles Edward Stuart-,** 12th Bt *cr* 1626; Building contractor from 1945; *b* 6 Aug. 1903; *s* of Sir Charles Hay Hepburn Stuart-Forbes, 10th Bt, and Ellen, *d* of Capt. Huntley; *S* brother, 1937; *m* 1966, Ijah Leah MacCabe, Wellington, NZ. *Educ:* Ocean Bay Coll. *Recreations:* motoring, football, cricket, hockey, swimming, deep sea fishing, hunting, rowing, launching, tennis. *Heir:* *n* William Daniel Stuart-Forbes [*b* 21 Aug. 1935; *m* 1956, Jannette MacDonald; three *s* two *d*]. *Address:* PO Box 6165, Te Aro, Wellington, NZ.

**FORBES, Charles Harington Gordon,** CBE 1965 (OBE 1941); Registrar, Principal Probate Registry, Somerset House, 1946-64; *b* 20 Feb. 1896; *s* of Harington G. Forbes, OBE; *m* 1927, Jean J. Beith; one *d*. *Educ:* Malvern Coll. Entered service of Principal Probate Registry, 1914. Served European War, 1914-18, with The Honourable Artillery Company. *Address:* Chetwynd, Watermill Lane, Bexhill-on-Sea, Sussex.

**FORBES, Donald James,** MA; Headmaster, Merchiston Castle School, since 1969; *b* 6 Feb. 1921; *s* of Andrew Forbes, Hythe, Hants; *m* 1945, Patricia Muriel Yeo; two *s* one *d*. *Educ:* Oundle; Clare Coll., Cambridge (Mod. Lang. Tripos). Capt. Scots Guards, 1941-46; 1st Bn Scots Guards, 1942-46, N Africa, Italy. Asst Master, Dulwich Coll., 1946-55; Master i/c cricket, 1951-55; Headmaster, Dauntsey's Sch., 1956-69. Diploma in Spanish, Univ. of Santander, 1954; Lectr in Spanish, West Norwood Tech. Coll., 1954-55. *Recreations:* cricket, Rugby football, tennis, Rugby fives; history, literature; instrumental and choral music. *Address:* Merchiston Castle School, Colinton, Edinburgh, 13; Breachacha Castle, Isle of Coll. *Clubs:* MCC; Hawks (Cambridge).

**FORBES, Sir Douglas (Stuart),** Kt 1964; Managing Director since 1940, Chairman of Directors since 1955, The Millaquin Sugar Co. Ltd; *b* 6 Feb. 1890; *s* of William Forbes, Brisbane, formerly of Aberdeen, Scotland; *m* 1916, Grace Isobel Fallon; one *d*. Banker and Company Director. Gen. Manager, Queensland National Bank Ltd, 1937-48; Dir, National Bank of Australasia Ltd, and Chm. of its Queensland Board of Advice, 1948-67; Dir, Castlemaine Perkins Ltd (Brewers), 1944- (Chm. of Dirs, 1958-): Chm. of Dirs, Queensland National Pastoral Co. Ltd, 1940-62; Dir, Qld Trustees Ltd, 1949-66; Dir, Brisbane Television Co. Ltd, 1958-; Chm. of Dirs, QOR Road Services Pty Ltd, 1966-. *Recreations:* golf and surfing. *Address:* 10 Ludlow Street, Hamilton, Brisbane, Qld, Australia. *T:* 68.2807. *Clubs:* Queensland, Tattersalls, Queensland Turf (Brisbane).

**FORBES OF BRUX, Hon. Sir Ewan,** 11th Bt *cr* 1630, of Craigievar; landowner and farmer; *b* 6 Sept. 1912; 2nd *s* of Sir John Forbes-Sempill, 9th Bt (Forbes) of Craigievar, 18th Lord Sempill; *S* (to Btcy) brother, 1965; *m* 1952, Isabella, *d* of A. Mitchell, Glenrinnes, Banffshire. *Educ:* Dresden; Univ. of Munich; Univ. of Aberdeen. MB, ChB 1944. Senior Casualty Officer, Aberdeen Royal Infirmary, 1944-45; Medical Practitioner, Alford, Aberdeenshire, 1945-55. *Recreations:* shooting, fishing, ski-ing and skating. *Heir:* *kinsman* John Alexander Cumnock Forbes-Sempill [*b* 29 Aug. 1927; *m* 1st, 1958, Penelope Margaret Ann (marr. diss. 1964), *d* of A. G. Grey-Pennington; 2nd, 1966, Jane Carolyn, *o d* of C. Gordon Evans]. *Address:* Brux, Alford, Aberdeenshire. *T:* Kildrummy 223.

*See also Lady Sempill.*

**FORBES, Dr Gilbert;** Regius Professor of Forensic Medicine, University of Glasgow, since 1964; *b* 5 Aug. 1908; *s* of late George and of Jane Gilbert Forbes; *m* 1938, Marian Margaret Macrae Guthrie, Springfield, Fife; one *d*. *Educ:* Hillhead High Sch., Glasgow; Glasgow Univ. (BSc). MB, ChB Glasgow, 1933; Brunton Memorial Prize, 1933; FRFPSG 1935; FRCSE 1935; MD 1945. House posts at Western Infirmary, Glasgow, 1933-34; Demonstrator in Anatomy, University of Glasgow, 1934-36; Lecturer in Anatomy, University of Aberdeen, 1936-37; Police Surgeon to City of Sheffield and Lecturer in Forensic Medicine, University of Sheffield, 1937-48; Senior Lectr in Forensic Medicine, Univ. of Sheffield, 1948-56; Reader in Forensic Medicine, Univ. of Sheffield, 1956-64. Asst Deputy Coroner to City of Sheffield, 1945-59. At various times external examiner in forensic medicine in Univs of Manchester, Birmingham, Leeds, Glasgow, Aberdeen and Edinburgh. *Publications:* original papers on medico-legal subjects in medical and scientific journals. *Recreation:* motoring. *Address:* Department of Forensic Medicine, The University, Glasgow, W2. *T:* 041-339 8855.

**FORBES, Hon. Sir Hugh (Harry Valentine),** Kt 1970; **Hon. Mr Justice Forbes;** a Judge of the High Court, Queen's Bench Division, since 1970; *b* 14 Feb. 1917; *e s* of late Rev. H. N. Forbes, sometime Rector of Castle Bromwich; *m* 1st, 1940, Julia Margaret (marr. diss. 1970), *yr d* of Frank Gilbert Weller; one *s* two *d*; 2nd, 1970, Janet Moir, *o d* of Campbell Andrews, MD, Harrow. *Educ:* Rossall; Trinity Hall, Cambridge (1st cl. Law). Served War of 1939-45: Major, Gordon Highlanders; GSO2 War Office and GHQ India. Called to Bar, Middle Temple, 1946; QC 1966; Bencher, 1970. Chm., Lincs (Kesteven) QS, 1967- (Dep. Chm., 1961-67); Dep. Chm., Hunts and Peterborough QS, 1965-. Chancellor: Dio. of Ely, 1965-69; Dio. of Chelmsford, 1969. *Publication:* Real Property Law, 1950. *Recreations:* sailing, listening to music. *Address:* 28 Chepstow Place, W2; Royal Courts of Justice, WC2. *Clubs:* Royal Thames Yacht; Union (Birmingham).

**FORBES, Ian,** QPM 1966; Deputy Assistant Commissioner, Metropolitan Police and National Co-ordinator, Regional Crime Squads (England and Wales), since 1970; *b* 30 March 1914; *y s* of John and Betsy Forbes, Auchlossan, Lumphanan, Aberdeenshire; *m* 1941, Lilian Edith Miller, Edgware, Mddx; two *s*. *Educ:* Lumphanan School, Aberdeenshire. Joined Metropolitan Police, 1939; served in East End, Central London Flying Squad, New Scotland Yard; Detective Superintendent, 1964; served on New Scotland Yard Murder Squad, 1966-69; Commander, No 9 Regional Crime Squad (London area), 1969. *Recreations:* gardening, motoring, reading. *Address:* 20 Greenbank Avenue, Wembley, Mddx. *T:* 01-902 8614.

**FORBES, Col Sir John Stewart,** 6th Bt of Newe *cr* 1823; DSO; DL, JP; RE; *b* 8 Jan. 1901; *o surv. s* of 5th Bt and late Emma Theodora, *d* of Robert Maxwell; *S* father, 1927; *m* 1933, Agnes Jessie, *er d* of late Lt-Col D. L. Wilson-Farquharson, DSO; five *d*. *Educ:* Wellington Coll.; RMA, Woolwich. 2nd Lieut RE, 1920; Capt., 1933; Major, 1938; Lieut-Col 1946; Temp. Col 1947; Temp. Brig. 1948; Col 1949; served Norway Campaign, 1940 (DSO, despatches); Burma, 1944-45 (despatches); retired 1953. Hon. Col 51st (H) Div. Engineers, TA, 1960-67. DL Aberdeenshire. *Heir: cousin* Major Hamish Stewart Forbes, MBE, MC [*b* 15 Feb. 1916; *m* 1945, Jacynthe Elizabeth Mary, *o d* of late Eric Gordon Underwood; one *s* three *d*]. *Address:* Allargue, Corgarff, Aberdeenshire. *Clubs:* St James'; Royal Northern (Aberdeen).

**FORBES, Air Chief Comdt Dame Katherine (Jane Trefusis);** *see* Watson-Watt, Air Chief Comdt Dame Katherine.

**FORBES, Mrs Muriel Rose,** CBE 1963; JP; Chairman: St Charles's Group Hospital Management Committee, 1968-69; Paddington Group Hospital Management Committee, 1963-68; Member, Greater London Council, 1964-67 (Vice-Chairman, 1964-66); Member, Middlesex CC, 1934-65 (Chairman, 1960-61); *b* 20 April 1894; *yr d* of John Henry Cheeseright; *m* 1923, Charles Gilbert Forbes (*d* 1957); two *d*. *Educ:* Gateshead Grammar Sch.; Southlands Teacher Training Coll. Mem. of Willesden Borough Council, 1936-47; Mem. of Central Middx Hospital Management Cttee, 1948-63 (Vice-Chm., 1952-63). JP County of Middx, 1946. Hon. DTech Brunel Univ., 1966. *Address:* 7 Hamilton Road, Willesden, NW10. *T:* 01-452 7761.

**FORBES-COCKELL, Seton;** Chairman, Forbes Group of Companies, since 1953; *b* 14 Aug. 1927; *s* of Cedric Forbes-Cockell and Adelina Forbes-Cockell (*née* Reese); *m* 1951, Ann McVicker Forbes-Cockell (*née* Redfern); two *s* one *d*. *Educ:* Eton Coll. Mem. Stock Exchange, London, 1948-; Chm., Fulham Conservative Assoc., 1959-69 (Pres., 1969-); elected to GLC (Kensington and Chelsea), 1964 (re-elected, 1967, 1970); Leader of Opposition, Inner London Educn Authority, 1964-67; Chm., Thamesmead Cttee of GLC, 1967- (Mem. or Past Mem. various cttees of GLC). Alderman, Hammersmith Borough Council, 1968- (Dep. Leader, 1968-69, 1970-71); Chm., Borough Develt Group Cttee, 1968-69; Mayor of the London Borough of Hammersmith, 1969-70. Mem. Bd, PLA, 1967-; Mem., Lord Chancellor's Adv. Cttee on Justices of the Peace, Inner London Commn Area, 1970-. Mem. Court, Univ. of London, 1966-67; Chm., Nat. Educn Assoc., 1965-69. Freeman of City of London, 1955; Liveryman, Worshipful Co. of Carmen, 1955. *Publication:* The Conservation of Wealth, 1950. *Recreations:* shooting, riding, polo, reading. *Address:* 102 Rivermead Court, SW6. *T:* 01-736 4707; Lavender Farm, Ascot, Berkshire. *T:* Winkfield Row 4545. *Clubs:* City of London, City Livery, Junior Carlton, Hurlingham, Roehampton; Guards Polo (Windsor); Henley Royal Regatta (Henley); Surrey County Cricket.

**FORBES-LEITH of Fyvie, Sir (Robert) Ian (Algernon),** 2nd Bt *cr* 1923; MBE 1946; JP Co. of Aberdeen; Lord Lieutenant of the County of Aberdeen since 1959 (Vice-Lieutenant, 1953); Member, Aberdeen CC, 1938 (Vice-Convener, 1950; Convener, 1955-58); Member of Queen's Body Guard for Scotland, The Royal Company of Archers; Major RA; Governor: North of Scotland College of Agriculture; Rowett Research Institute; *b* 27 Dec. 1902; *o surv. s* of Col Sir Charles R. Forbes-Leith, 1st Bt, and Hon. Ethel Louise Forbes-Leith, OBE (*d* 1930), *o d* of Baron Leith of Fyvie; *S* father, 1930; *m* 1927, Ruth Avis, *d* of Edward George Barnett, Halton, Corbridge, Northumberland; one *s* two *d* (and one *s* killed on active service). *Educ:* Eton. Served War of 1939-45 (despatches, MBE). Hon. LLD, Aberdeen, 1967. *Heir: s* Andrew George Forbes-Leith [*b* 20 Oct. 1929; *m* 1962, Jane Kate (*d* 1969), *o d* of late David McCall-McCowan and Mrs McCall-McCowan, Dalwhat, Moniaive, Dumfriesshire; two *s* two *d*]. *Address:* Kinharrachie, Ellon, Aberdeenshire. *Clubs:* White's; Royal Northern (Aberdeen); Leander.

**FORBES-SEMPILL,** family name of **Baron Sempill.**

**FORD,** *see* St Clair-Ford.

**FORD, Benjamin Thomas;** MP (Lab) Bradford North since 1964; *b* 1 April 1925; *s* of Benjamin Charles Ford and May Ethel (*née* Moorton); *m* 1950, Vera Ada (*née* Fawcett-Fancet); two *s* one *d*. *Educ:* Rowan Road Central Sch., Surrey. Apprenticed as compositor, 1941. War Service, 1943-47, Fleet Air Arm (Petty Officer). Electronic Fitter/Wireman, 1951-64; Convener of Shop Stewards, 1955-64. Pres., Harwich Constituency Labour Party, 1955-63; Clacton UDC, 1959-62; Alderman Essex CC, 1959-65; JP Essex, 1962-67. *Publication:*

Piecework, 1960. *Recreations:* music, swimming, shooting, family. *Address:* House of Commons, SW1. *Club:* Royal Automobile.

**FORD, Prof. Boris,** MA; Professor of Education and Dean of the School of Cultural and Community Studies, University of Sussex, since Oct. 1963; *b* 1 July 1917; *s* of late Brig. G. N. Ford, CB, DSO; *m* 1950, Noreen Auty (*née* Collins); one *s* three *d*. *Educ:* Gresham's Sch., Holt, Norfolk; Downing Coll., Cambridge. Army Education, finally OC Middle East School of Artistic Studies, 1940-46. Chief Ed. and finally Dir, Bureau of Current Affairs, 1946-51; Information Officer, Technical Assistance Bd, UN (NY and Geneva), 1951-53; Sec., Nat. Enquiry into Liberalising Technical Educn, 1953-55; Sec., Children's Play Activities, 1955-57; Editor, Journal of Education, 1955-58; first Head of Sch. Broadcasting, Associated-Rediffusion, 1957-58; Educn Sec., Cambridge Univ. Press, 1958-60; Ed., Universities Quarterly, 1955-. Prof. of Education and Dir of the Inst. of Education, Univ. of Sheffield, 1960-63. Chairman: Nat. Assoc. for the Teaching of English, 1963-65; Educational Dir, Pictorial Knowledge; Editorial Dir, Pergamon English Library, 1966. *Publications:* Discussion Method, 1949; Teachers' Handbook to Human Rights, 1950; Liberal Education in a Technical Age, 1955; Young Readers: Young Writers, 1960; (Gen. Ed.) Pelican Guide to English Literature, 1954-61. *Recreation:* music. *Address:* Arts Building, University of Sussex, Falmer, Brighton.

**FORD, Brinsley;** Trustee of the Watts Gallery, Compton, since 1955; Member, Executive Committee, National Art Collections Fund; *b* 10 June 1908; *e s* of late Capt. Richard Ford, Rifle Brigade, and Rosamund, *d* of Sir John Ramsden, 5th Bt; *m* 1937, Joan, *d* of late Capt. Geoffrey Vyvyan; two *s* one *d*. *Educ:* Eton; Trinity Coll., Oxford. Joined TA 1939; served for one year as Troop Sergeant Major, RA; commissioned 1941, and transferred to Intelligence Corps (Major 1945). Selected works for Arts Council Festival of Britain and Coronation Exhibitions; a Trustee of the National Gallery, 1954-61; great-grandson of Richard Ford (1796-1858) who wrote the Handbook for Spain; owner of the Ford Collection of Richard Wilsons. Officer, Belgian Order of Leopold II; US Bronze Star; Médaille d'Argent de la Reconnaissance Française. *Publications:* The Drawings of Richard Wilson, 1951; contributor to the Burlington Magazine. *Address:* 14 Wyndham Place, Bryanston Square, W1. *T:* 01-723 0826. *Club:* Brooks's.

**FORD, Charles Edmund,** FRS 1965; DSc London, FLS, FIBiol; Head of Cytogenetics Group, Medical Research Council, Radiobiological Unit, Harwell, since 1949; *b* 24 Oct. 1912; *s* of late Charles Ford and Ethel Eubornia Ford (*née* Fawcett); *m* 1940, Jean Ella Dowling; four *s*. *Educ:* Slough Grammar Sch.; King's Coll., University of London. Demonstrator, Dept of Botany, King's Coll., University of London, 1936-38; Geneticist, Rubber Research Scheme, Ceylon, 1938-41 and 1944-45. Lieut Royal Artillery, 1942-43. PSO Dept of Atomic Energy, Min. of Supply, at Chalk River Laboratories, Ont, Canada, 1946-49. *Publications:* papers on cytogenetics in scientific journals. *Recreations:* travel, friends. *Address:* 156 Oxford Road, Abingdon, Berks. *T:* Abingdon 1.

**FORD, Cdre Charles Musgrave,** CBE 1946; RD; Commodore (retired) Royal Naval Reserve; Commodore of Cunard White Star Fleet, retired; *b* 1887; *m* 1959, Vera Gordon Evans. Joined Cunard Co. Ltd, 1912. Royal Naval Reserve ADC to the King, 1941-42. Served European War, 1914-18; War of 1939-45: Commodore of Ocean Convoys, 1940-42. Commanded several Cunard vessels, including SS Queen Mary and SS Queen Elizabeth. Order of St Anne, 3rd Class, 1915 (Russian); Commander Legion of Merit, 1949 (USA). *Address:* 3 Exeter Park Mansions, Bournemouth, Hants. *T:* Bournemouth 21934.

**FORD, Edmund Brisco,** FRS 1946; MA, DSc Oxon, Hon. DSc Liverpool; Fellow, All Souls College, Oxford; Professor of Ecological Genetics, 1963-69, and Director of Genetics Laboratory, Zoology Department, 1952-69, Oxford; Emeritus Professor since 1969; *b* 23 April 1901; unmarried; *s* of Harold Dodsworth Ford and Gertrude Emma Bennett. *Educ:* Wadham Coll., Oxford. Research worker, Univ. Lectr and Demonstrator in Zoology and Comparative Anatomy, Univ. Reader in Genetics, Oxford; Pres., Genetical Soc. of Great Britain, 1946-49; Mem. of Nature Conservancy, 1949-59; Mem. various scientific (chiefly zoological) societies. Wild Life Conservation Cttee of Ministry of Town and Country Planning, 1945-47 (Cmd Rept 7122). Formerly represented British Empire on Permanent Internat. Cttee of Genetics. Has travelled in USA, NZ, Australia, Near and Far East. Darwin Medallist, Royal Society, 1954. Delivered Galton Lecture of London Univ., 1939; Woodhall Lectr of the Royal Institution, 1957; Woodward Lectr, Yale Univ., 1959. Weldon Memorial Prize, Oxford Univ., 1959. Medallist of Helsinki Univ., 1967. Foreign Mem., Finnish Acad. Commemorated by E. B. Ford Lectures of Manchester Univ. Pres. Somerset Archæological Soc., 1960-61. *Publications:* Mendelism and Evolution, 1931 (8th edn 1965); The Study of Heredity (Home University Library) 1938 (2nd edn 1950); Genetics for Medical Students, 1942 (6th edn 1967); Butterflies (Vol. I of New Naturalist Series), 1945 (4th edn 1967); British Butterflies (King Penguin Series), 1951; Moths (New Naturalist Series), 1955 (2nd edn 1967); Ecological Genetics, 1964 (2nd edn 1965); Genetic Polymorphism (All Souls Monographs), 1965; Mimicry (with G. D. Hale Carpenter), 1933; numerous contribs to scientific jls, on genetical and zoological subjects. *Recreations:* archæology, literature, riding, travel. *Address:* 5 Apsley Road, Oxford; University Museum, Oxford; All Souls College, Oxford. *TA:* and *T:* Oxford 58147.

**FORD, Sir Edward,** Kt 1960; OBE 1945; Professor of Preventive Medicine and Director of the School of Public Health and Tropical Medicine, University of Sydney, since 1947; *b* 15 April 1902; *s* of Edward John and Mary Ford, South Yarra, Victoria. *Educ:* Universities of Melbourne, Sydney and London. RMO, Melbourne Hospital, 1930; Lecturer in Anatomy, Melbourne Univ., 1933; Sen. Lectr in Anatomy and Histology, Melbourne Univ., 1934-36; Lectr, Sch. of Public Health and Tropical Medicine, Sydney, 1937-39. Served War of 1939-45: in Australian Army Middle East, New Guinea, Burma; Senior Malariologist, AIF, and late Dir of Hygiene and Pathology, Aust. Army; Col AAMC, 1940-45. Rockefeller Fellow, 1946; Dean of Faculty of Medicine and Fellow of Senate, Sydney Univ., 1953-57. *Address:* University of Sydney, Sydney, NSW, Australia. *T:* MW 1307. *Club:* Australian (Sydney).

**FORD, Sir Edward (William Spencer),** KCB 1967 (CB 1952); KCVO 1957 (MVO 1949); MA; Secretary to the Pilgrim Trust since 1967; Assistant Private Secretary to the Queen,

1952-67 (to King George VI, 1946-52); *b* 24 July 1910; 4th (twin) *s* of late Very Rev. Lionel G. B. J. Ford, Headmaster of Repton and Harrow and Dean of York, and of Mary Catherine, *d* of Rt Rev. E. S. Talbot, Bishop of Winchester and Hon. Mrs Talbot; *m* 1949, Virginia, *er d* of 1st and last Baron Brand, CMG, and *widow* of John Metcalfe, Polk, NY; two *s*. *Educ:* Eton (King's Schol.); New Coll., Oxford (Open Scholar). 1st Class Hon. Mods; 2nd Class Lit. Hum. (Greats). law Student (Harmsworth Scholar) Middle Temple, 1934-35. Called to Bar, Middle Temple, 1937 and practised 1937-39; 2nd Lieut (Supplementary Reserve of Officers) Grenadier Guards, 1936; Lieut 1939; served in France and Belgium, 1939-40 (despatches), and in Tunisia and Italy, 1943-44 (despatches), Brigade Major 10th Infantry and 24th Guards Brigades; Instructor at Staff Coll., Haifa, 1944-45. psc†. Extra Equerry to the Queen, 1955. Dir, London Life Assoc. High Sheriff, Northants, 1970. Member Council: Ditchley Foundn Ltd; Royal Coll. of Art. *Address:* 18 Hale House, 34 De Vere Gardens, W8. *T:* 01-937 2818; Eydon Hall, Eydon, near Rugby. *T:* Byfield 282. *Clubs:* White's, Beefsteak, MCC.

**FORD, Elbur;** *see* Hibbert, Eleanor.

**FORD, Ven. Frank Edward;** Archdeacon of the East Riding, 1957-70; Rector of Cherry-Burton, 1965-70; *b* 9 July 1902; *s* of Frank Chubb Ford, MD, Wimbledon; *m* 1st, 1934, Mary Katherine Eve, *d* of Robert Hamilton Welchman, MA, Oxford; 2nd, 1953, Marjorie, *d* of Francis Benjamin Chatterton, Scarborough, and *widow* of John Stanley Snowball, Scarborough; one *s* one *d*. *Educ:* Lancing; Hertford Coll., Oxford; Westcott House, Cambridge. BA 1924, MA 1928. Rector of Bainton, 1957-65. *Recreations:* housework, gardening and crosswords. *Address:* Barnyard, Sinnington, York YO6 6RY. *T:* Kirkbymoorside 797. *Club:* Royal Over-Seas League.

**FORD, Harold Frank;** Sheriff Substitute of Perth and Angus at Forfar since 1951; *b* 17 May 1915; *s* of Sir Patrick Ford, 1st Bt, and *b* of Sir Henry Ford, *qv*; *m* 1948, Lucy Mary, *d* of late Sheriff J. R. Wardlaw Burnet, KC; one *s* three *d*. *Educ:* Winchester Coll.; University Coll., Oxford; Edinburgh Univ. War service with Lothians and Border Yeomanry (Prisoner of War, 1940-45): Hon. Capt. Scottish Bar, 1945; Legal Adviser to UNRRA and IRO in British Zone of Germany, 1947. *Recreations:* golf, gardening, shooting. *Address:* Murlingden, by Brechin, Angus, Scotland. *T:* Brechin 2371. *Clubs:* New (Edinburgh); Honourable Company of Edinburgh Golfers.

**FORD, Henry, II;** Chairman and Chief Executive Officer, Ford Motor Company, Dearborn, Michigan; *b* Detroit, 4 Sept. 1917; *s* of Edsel B. and Eleanor (Clay) Ford; *m* 1st, 1940, Anne McDonnell (marr. diss.); one *s* two *d*; 2nd, 1965, Maria Christina Vettore Austin. *Educ:* Hotchkiss Sch., Lakeville, Conn.; Yale Univ. With Ford Motor Co. from 1940: Dir, 1938; Vice-Pres., 1943; Executive Vice-Pres., 1944; Pres., 1945; Chm., 1960. Trustee, The Ford Foundation; Chairman: Nat. Center for Voluntary Action, 1970; Nat. Alliance of Businessmen, 1968-69; Mem., Business Council, President's Advisory Cttee on Labour-Management Policy. *Address:* Grosse Pointe Farms, Michigan, USA.

**FORD, Sir Henry Russell,** 2nd Bt *cr* 1929; TD; JP; *b* 30 April 1911; *s* of Sir Patrick Ford, 1st Bt, and Jessie Hamilton (*d* 1962), *d* of Henry Field, WS, Moreland, Kinross-shire, and Middlebluf, Manitoba; *S* father, 1945; *m* 1936, Mary Elizabeth, *y d* of late Godfrey F. Wright, Whiddon, Bovey Tracy; one *s* three *d*. *Educ:* Winchester; New Coll., Oxford. War of 1939-45 served in UK, North Africa and Italy (despatches). Chm., Berwick and E Lothian Unionist Assoc., 1948-50, 1958-60. JP 1951. TD 1960. *Recreations:* golf, gardening. *Heir:* *s* Andrew Russell Ford [*b* 29 June 1943; *m* 1968, Penelope Anne, *d* of Harry Relph; one *d*]. *Address:* Seaforth, Gullane, East Lothian. *T:* Gullane 2214. *Club:* Hon. Company of Edinburgh Golfers (Muirfield).

*See also Harold Frank Ford.*

**FORD, Air Vice-Marshal Howard,** CB 1959; CBE 1954; AFC 1944; RAF (retd); *b* 18 Dec. 1905; *s* of late Lewis Ford and Beatrice Leal; *m* 1936, Marie, *d* of late Daniel O'Reilly, Cork, and Agnes Mayne, New York. *Educ:* Blundell's Sch.; Pembroke Coll., Cambridge (BA). Represented Cambridge at ski-ing and athletics, also England and Great Britain at athletics; British Olympic Athletic Team, 1928. Joined Royal Air Force, 1930; served War of 1939-45 (AFC). Transferred to Technical Branch, 1951; Dir, Air Armament R&D, Min. of Supply, 1952-55; Senior Technical Staff Officer, Flying Training Command, 1956-59; Vice-Pres. Ordnance Board, 1960-61, Pres., 1962; retired from RAF, 1963. Group Capt., 1947; Air Cdre, 1953; Air Vice-Marshal, 1960. *Club:* Royal Automobile.

**FORD, Prof. Hugh,** FRS 1967; Professor of Mechanical Engineering, University of London (Imperial College of Science and Technology), since 1969; Head of the Dept of Mechanical Engineering, since 1965; Technical Director, Davy-Ashmore Group, since 1968; *b* 16 July 1913; *s* of Arthur and Constance Ford; *m* 1942, Wynward, *d* of Major F. B. Scholfield; two *d*. *Educ:* Northampton Sch.; City and Guilds Coll., Univ. of London. Practical trng at GWR Locomotive Works, 1931-36; researches into heat transfer, 1936-39; R and Eng, Imperial Chemical Industries, Northwich, 1939-42; Chief Engr, Technical Dept, British Iron and Steel Fedn, 1942-45, then Head of Mechanical Working Div., British Iron and Steel Research Assoc., 1945-47; Reader in Applied Mechanics, Univ. of London, 1948-51, Prof., 1951-69. Pres., Inst. of metals, 1963; Member: Council, IMechE; SRC, 1968- (Chm. Engineering Bd). DSc (Eng) (London), PhD; FIMechE; MICE; Whitworth Schol.; FIM; FCGI; Thomas Hawksley Gold Medallist, IMechE, 1948, for researches into rolling of metals; Robertson Medal, Inst. of Metals. *Publications:* Advanced Mechanics of Materials, 1963; papers to Royal Soc., IMechE, Iron and Steel Inst., Inst. of Metals, foreign societies, etc. *Recreations:* gardening, music. *Address:* 18 Shrewsbury House, Cheyne Walk, SW3. *T:* 01-352 3804; Shamley Cottage, Stroud Lane, Shamley Green, Surrey. *T:* Bramley 2366. *Club:* Athenæum.

**FORD, James Allan,** MC 1946; Director of Establishments, Scottish Office, since 1969; *b* 10 June 1920; 2nd *s* of Douglas Ford and Margaret Duncan (*née* Allan); *m* 1948, Isobel Dunnett; one *s* one *d*. *Educ:* Royal High School, Edinburgh; University of Edinburgh. Served 1940-46, Capt. Royal Scots. Entered Civil Service, 1938; Asst Sec., Dept of Agriculture and Fisheries for Scotland, 1958; Registrar Gen. for Scotland, 1966-69. *Publications:* The Brave White Flag, 1961; Season of Escape, 1963; A Statue for a Public Place, 1965; A Judge of Men, 1968. *Address:* 29 Lady Road, Edinburgh EH16 5PA. *T:* 031-667 4489. *Clubs:* Royal Commonwealth Society; Royal Scots (Edinburgh).

**FORD, John Archibald,** CMG 1967; MC 1945; Assistant Under-Secretary, Foreign and Commonwealth Office, since 1970; *b* 19 Feb. 1922; *s* of Ronald Mylne Ford and Margaret Jesse Coghill, Newcastle-under-Lyme, Staffs; *m* 1956, Emaline Burnett, Leesville, Virginia; two *d*. *Educ:* St Michael's Coll., Tenbury; Sedbergh Sch., Yorks; Oriel Coll., Oxford. Served in Royal Artillery, 1942-46 (temp. Major); demobilised, 1947. Joined Foreign (subseq. Diplomatic) Service, 1947. Third Sec., British Legation, Budapest, 1947-49; Third Sec. and a Resident Clerk, FO, 1949-52; Private Sec. to Permanent Under-Sec. of State, FO, 1952-54; HM Consul, San Francisco, 1954-56; seconded to HM Treasury, 1956-59; attended Course at Administrative Staff Coll., 1959; First Sec. and Head of Chancery, British Residency, Bahrain, 1959-61; Asst, FO Personnel Dept, 1961-63; Asst, FO Establishment and Organisation Dept, 1963; Head of Diplomatic Service Establishment and Organisation Dept, 1964-66; Counsellor (Commercial), Rome, 1966-70. *Recreations:* walking, gardening, sailing. *Address:* Loquats, Guildown, Guildford, Surrey. *Clubs:* Travellers', Little Ship; Yvonne Arnaud Theatre (Guildford).

**FORD, (John) Peter,** CBE 1969; Director, Plessey Overseas Ltd, since 1963; *b* 20 Feb. 1912; *s* of Ernest and Muriel Ford; *m* 1939, Phoebe Seys, *d* of Herbert McGregor Wood, FRIBA; one *s* two *d*. *Educ:* Wrekin Coll.; Gonville and Caius Coll., Cambridge. BA (Hons Nat. Sci. Tripos) 1934; MA Cantab 1937. Cambridge Univ. Air Sqdn, 1932-35 (Pilot's A Licence, 1933-). Air Ministry (subsequently FO, RAFVR), 1939-40; Coventry Gauge and Tool Co. Ltd (Asst to Chm.), 1941-45; Gen. Man., Brit. Engineers Small Tools and Equipment Co. Ltd, and Gen. Man. Scientific Exports (Gt Brit.) Ltd, 1945-48; Man. Dir, Brush Export Ltd, Associated British Oil Engines (Export) Ltd and National Oil Engines (Export) Ltd, and Dir of other associated cos of The Brush Group, 1949-55; Dir, Associated British Engineering Ltd and subsidiaries, 1957-58; Man. Dir, Coventry Climax International Ltd, 1958-63. Chm. Institute of Export, 1954-56, 1965-67; Vice-Pres., Soc. of Commercial Accountants, 1956-; Member: Council, London Chamber of Commerce, 1951- (Dep. Chm., 1970-); FBI, Overseas Trade Policy Cttee, 1952-63; Council British Internal Combustion Engine Manufacturers Assoc., 1953-55; BNEC Cttee for Exports to Latin America, 1964-67, Chm. 1968-. Freeman of City of London, 1945; Freeman Worshipful Company of Ironmongers, 1945; Gov., Wrekin Coll., 1953-57; Gov., Oversea Service Coll., 1966-. CEng, CIMechE, CIMarE, MIEE, FIPE. *Publications:* contributor to technical press and broadcaster on international trade subjects. *Recreations:* Athletics (Cambridge Univ. and Internat. Teams, 1932-35; held various county championships, 1932-37; Hon. Treas. Achilles Club, 1947-58; Pres., London Athletic Club, 1964-66). *Address:* 40 Fairacres, Roehampton Lane, SW15. *T:* 01-876 2146. *Clubs:* Oxford and Cambridge University, City of London, MCC, Roehampton; Hawks (Cambridge); Royal Wimbledon Golf.

**FORD, John, (Sean O'Feeney);** director of motion pictures, USA; *b* Cape Elizabeth, Me, 1 Feb. 1895; *s* of Sean O'Feeney and Barbara Curran; *m* 1920, Mary McBryde Smith; one *s* one *d*. Began as property man, Universal City, Calif., 1914; later became dir; has directed more than 80 pictures for Universal-Fox, Metro-Goldwyn Mayer, United Artists, Radio-RKO. Served as Lieut-Comdr, Comdr, Capt., US Navy, War of 1939-45; discharged as Rear-Adm. after service in Korea. NY Critics Award, 1935-39, 1940-41; Academy Motion Picture Arts and Sciences directorial Award, 1935, 1940, 1941, 1952. *Films include:* Arrowsmith, Stagecoach, Quiet Man, Long Voyage Home, Grapes of Wrath, How Green Was My Valley, The Informer, The Searchers, Gideon's Day, Donovan's Reef, The Man Who Shot Liberty Valance, Cheyenne Autumn, Seven Women. Received Academy Awards for two documentaries made for Government while in Navy, midway, Dec. 7th. Dr Fine Arts (Hon.) Univ. of Maine, 1939; MA (Hon.) Bowdoin Coll., Brunswick, Me, 1947; DHL, Brandeis Univ. Legion of Merit (Combat); Purple Heart; Air Medal; Commendation; Chevalier Crown of Belgium; Knight Comdr, Italian Republic; Legion of Honour; Croix de Guerre; Knight of Malta, etc. Catholic. *Address:* (studio) 321 South Beverly Drive, Beverly Hills, Calif 90212, USA.

**FORD, Joseph Francis,** CMG 1960; OBE 1949; Director of Research Department, Foreign and Commonwealth Office (formerly Joint Research Department, FO/CO), 1967-70, retired; *b* 11 Oct. 1912; *s* of J. W. Ford, Chesterfield, Derbs; *m* 1938, Mary Margaret Ford (*née* Taylor); two *s*. *Educ:* Chesterfield Grammar Sch.; Emmanuel Coll., Cambridge (BA). Appointed probationer Vice-Consul to Peking, Nov. 1935; served at Shanghai, Chungking, Washington, Peking, Hanoi, New Orleans and Saigon. *Address:* 10 Raymond Road, Wimbledon, SW19.

**FORD, Sir Leslie (Ewart),** Kt 1956; OBE 1945; General Manager, Port of London Authority, 1948-64; *b* 27 July 1897; *e s* of late Elias Ford, OBE; *m* 1925, Mary Mabel, *e d* of late Walter Powles, Acocks Green, Warwicks; one *d*. *Educ:* Cardiff High Sch. Joined GW Railway Co., 1912. Served European War, 1914-18, with Welch Regt and 2nd Bn Monmouthshire Regt. Stationed various South Wales Ports, 1923-39; Chief Docks Manager, 1944. Major, Home Guard, 1941-45. Col Engineer and Railway Staff Corps RE (TA), 1957. CStJ. Commander: Royal Order of North Star (Sweden); Military Order of Christ (Portugal); Order of Dannebrog (Denmark). *Recreation:* golf. *Address:* 26 Bedford Gardens, Campden Hill, W8. *T:* 01-727 5595.

**FORD, Percy;** Professor Emeritus, The University of Southampton; *b* 19 Feb. 1894; 4th *s* of George Horace Ford, Brighton; *m* 1921, Grace Lister, Long Eaton; one *s* one *d*. *Educ:* Varndean Sch.; London Sch. of Economics, University of London (Gerstenberg Scholar). Resident Lecturer, Ruskin Coll.; Lecturer, Amherst Coll., Mass, USA; Lecturer in Dept of Economics, and Sec. of University Extension Board and Tutorial Classes Joint Cttee, King's Coll., Univ. of Durham, 1923-26; Head of Dept and Prof. of Economics, University of Southampton, 1926-59; Sen. Research Fellow, 1959-61. National Service, Ministry of Supply, 1939-46. *Publications:* Economics and Modern Industry, 1930; Work and Wealth in a Modern Port, 1934; Incomes, Means Tests and Personal Responsibility, 1939; Economics of Collective Bargaining, 1958; Social Theory and Social Practice, 1969; Parliamentary Papers Series, 1951-62 (with G. Ford): Breviate of Parliamentary Papers, Vol. I, 1900-16; Vol. II, 1917-39, Vol. III, 1940-54; Select List of British Parliamentary Papers, 1833-1899; Hansard's and Catalogue and Breviate of Parliamentary Papers, 1696-1834; Guide to Parliamentary Papers; Luke Graves Hansard's Diary, 1814-41; (with J. Bound) Coastwise Shipping and the Small Ports, 1951; (with G. Ford and D. Marshallsay) Select List of

Parliamentary Papers 1955-64, 1970; (with C. J. Thomas) Industrial Prospects of Southampton, 1951, Shops and Planning, 1953, Housing, 1953, Problem Families, 1955; Ed., Southampton Civic Survey, 1931; Contributor, Britain in Depression, 1935; articles in journals of economics. *Address:* Lane End, Sullington, Sussex; 34 Orchards Way, Southampton.

**FORD, Peter;** *see* Ford, J. P.

**FORD, Raymond Eustace,** CBE 1963; MD, MRCP; retired as Principal Medical Officer i/c Regional Medical Service, Ministry of Health (1946-63); *b* 24 April 1898; *s* of Rev. George Ford; *m* 1924, Elsie (*née* Tipping); two *s* one *d*. *Educ:* Sheffield Univ. *Recreations:* golf, gardening. *Address:* St John's Road, Hythe, Kent.

**FORD, Robert Webster;** HM Consul-General, Luanda, since 1970; *b* 27 March 1923; *s* of Robert Ford; *m* 1956, Monica Florence Tebbett; two *s*. *Educ:* Alleyne's Sch. Served RAF, 1939-45. Served with British Mission, Lhasa, Tibet and Political Agency in Sikkim and Bhutan, 1945-47; joined Tibetan Govt Service, 1947; advised on and installed Tibet's first radio communication system and broadcasting stn; travelled extensively in Northern and Eastern Tibet, 1947-50; taken prisoner during Chinese Occupation of Tibet, 1950; imprisoned in China, 1950-55; free-lance writer and broadcaster on Chinese and Tibetan affairs, 1955; entered Foreign Service, 1956; 2nd Sec., Saigon, 1957-58; 1st Sec. (Information), Djakarta, 1959; Washington, 1960-62; FO, 1962-67; Consul-Gen., Tangier, 1967-70. *Publication:* Captured in Tibet, 1956. *Recreations:* ski-ing, gardening, travelling. *Address:* HM Consulate-General, Rua Diogo Cão 4, Caixa Postal No 1244, Luanda, Angola. *Clubs:* Royal Commonwealth Society, Royal Geographical Society.

**FORD, Sir Sidney (William George),** Kt 1967; MBE 1944; President, National Union of Mineworkers, since 1960; *b* 29 Aug. 1909; *s* of George and Harriet Ford; *m* 1st, 1936, Ivy Elizabeth Lewis (*d* 1964); one *s* two *d*; 2nd, 1965, Sheila Simon. *Educ:* Silver Street Elementary Sch. Joined Staff of Miners' Federation of Great Britain (later NUM), 1925. Mem., Central Transport Consultative Cttee for GB, 1970-. *Address:* 18 Woodland Way, Winchmore Hill, N21. *T:* 01-886 8837.

**FORD ROBERTSON, Francis Calder,** OBE 1959; Director-Editor, Multilingual Forestry Terminology Project, at Commonwealth Forestry Institute, Oxford and Washington, DC, USA, 1964-70; *b* 19 March 1901; 3rd *s* of Dr W. Ford Robertson, MD, and Marion Elam; *m* 1928, Cynthia Mary de Courcy Ireland; two *s*. *Educ:* Edinburgh Academy; Edinburgh Univ. Appointed to Indian Forest Service as probationer, 1923; IFS, 1924-47; Director: Commonwealth Forestry Bureau, Oxford, 1947-65. Hon. MA Oxford, 1952. *Publications:* Our Forests, 1934, and sundry scientific, mainly bibliographical, articles. *Recreations:* choral singing, gardening, local history and archaeology. *Address:* 54 Staunton Road, Headington, Oxford. *T:* Oxford 62073.

**FORDE, Daryll,** PhD London, FBA; Professor of Anthropology, University of London, 1945-69, and Fellow of University College since 1945; Director, International African Institute since 1944; Member: International Social Science Council; Council, International Congress of Africanists; Council International Congress, Anthropological Sciences; *b* 16 March 1902; *o s* of Rev. J. P. D. Forde; *m* 1930, Joyce Marion (*née* Stock) (marr. diss., 1947); two *s*; *m* 1948, Evelyn Harty, *y d* of late David Singer, former Chm. of Rowe Swann Ltd. *Educ:* Middlesex County Sch., Tottenham; University Coll., London. Lecturer, Dept of Geography, University Coll., 1923-28; Franks Student of the Soc. of Antiquaries, 1924; Commonwealth Fellow in Anthropology, University of Calif., USA, 1928-30; Gregynog Prof. of Geography and Anthropology, Univ. of Wales, 1930-45; Leverhulme Research Fellow, 1935; Anthropological Field Expeditions, Arizona and Northern Mexico, 1928-29; New Mexico, 1929; Nigeria, 1935 and 1939; Gambia, 1945; Dep. Head, US Sect., FO Res. Dept (formerly FRPS), 1941-43. Visiting Prof., Univ. of Calif, 1949 and 1956, Yale Univ., 1951, Harvard Univ., 1963. Wellcome and Rivers Medallist, Past Pres., and Vice-Pres., Royal Anthropological Institute. Past Pres., Anthrop. Section, Brit. Assoc. Adv. Science. Frazer Lecturer, University of Liverpool, 1958; Munro Lecturer, University of Edinburgh, 1956; Lugard Memorial Lecturer, 1967. Wellcome Medallist, Royal African Soc., 1970. *Publications:* Ancient Mariners, 1928; Early Cultures of Atlantic Europe, 1930; Ethnography of the Yuma Indians, 1931; Hopi Agriculture and Land Ownership, 1932; Habitat, Economy and Society, 1934, 12th edn 1967; Marriage and the Family in South-Eastern Nigeria, 1941; The Native Economies of Nigeria, 1946; African Worlds (ed and contrib.), 1953; Yakö Studies, 1964; West African Chiefs in the Nineteenth Century (ed), 1967, etc; editor of Ethnographic Survey of Africa, 1946-, of Africa, 1944-, and of African Abstracts, 1948-. *Address:* 8 The Boltons, SW10. *T:* 01-373 9805. *Club:* Athenæum.

**FORDE, Rt. Hon. Francis Michael,** PC 1944; Australian High Commissioner in Canada, 1946-53; Dean of the Diplomatic Corps, Ottawa, Canada, 1952-53; *m* 1925, Veronica Catherine O'Reilly; one *s* three *d*. *Educ:* Christian Brothers Coll., Toowoomba, Qld, Aust. School teacher; electrical engineer; Mem. of Qld State Parliament, 1917-22; elected to House of Representatives for Capricornia, Qld Gen. Elections, 1922, 1925, 1928, 1929, 1931, 1934, 1937, 1940, 1943; Mem. Jt Select Cttee on Motion Picture Industry in Australia, 1927, and of Royal Commission on same, 1927-28; Mem. of Joint Cttee on Public Accounts, 1929; Acting Minister for Trade and Customs, Australia, 1929-30; Acting Minister for Markets and Transport, 1930-31; Minister for Trade and Customs, 1930-31, 1932; Dep. Leader Federal Parliamentary Labour Party, 1932-46, and Dep. Leader of the Opposition, 1932-41; Dep. Prime Minister, Minister for Army, Mem. and Vice-Chm. of War Cabinet, Australia, 1941-46; Minister for Defence, 1946; Acting Prime Minister, April-July 1944 and Oct. 1944-Jan. 1945; Prime Minister for short period, 1945; Actg Prime Minister (about two months), 1946. Leader of Australian Delegn to UN Conf., San Francisco, April 25 1945. Mem. for Flinders, Qld Parliament, By-Election, March 1955; re-elected, Gen. Election, May 1956. Represented Australia at Gen. Douglas MacArthur's funeral in USA, 1964. LLD (Hon.); Ottawa Univ., 1950; Montreal Univ., 1952; Laval Univ., 1952. *Recreations:* tennis, golf, bowls. *Address:* 44 Highland Terrace, St Lucia, Brisbane 4067, Australia.

**FORDER, Ven. Charles Robert;** Archdeacon of York, Canon and Prebendary of Fenton in York Minster, since 1957; *b* 6 Jan. 1907; *s* of late Henry Forder, Worstead, Norfolk; *m* 1933, Myra, *d* of late Harry Peat, Leeds; no *c*. *Educ:* Paston Sch., North Walsham; Christ's

Coll. and Ridley Hall, Cambridge. Exhibitioner of Christ's Coll. and Prizeman, 1926; 1st Cl. Math. Trip. Part I, 1926, BA (Sen. Opt. Part II) 1928, MA 1932; Ridley Hall, 1928. Curate: St Peter's, Hunslet Moor, 1930-33; Burley, 1933-34; Vicar: Holy Trinity, Wibsey, 1934-40; St Clement's, Bradford, 1940-47; Organising Sec., Bradford Church Forward Movement Appeal, 1945-47; Vicar of Drypool, 1947-55; Rector of Routh and Vicar of Wawne, 1955-57; Rector of Sutton-on-Derwent, 1957-63; Rector of Holy Trinity, Micklegate, York, 1963-66. Chaplain to HM Prison, Hull, 1950-53; Proctor in Convocation, 1954-57; Organising Sec., Diocesan Appeal, 1955; Church Comr, 1958-. *Publications:* A History of the Paston Grammar School, 1934; The Parish Priest at Work, 1947; Synods in Action, 1970. Contrib. to Encyclopædia Britannica. *Recreations:* reading and writing. *Address:* 14 St George's Place, York. *T:* York 23775.
*See also Prof. H. G. Forder.*

**FORDER, Prof. Henry George;** Professor of Mathematics, Auckland University, 1934-55; Professor Emeritus since 1955; *b* 27 Sept. 1889; *s* of Henry Forder, Worstead, Norwich; *m* 1921, Dorothy (*d* 1970), *d* of William Whincup, Bingham, Notts; no *c. Educ:* Paston Grammar Sch., N Walsham; Sidney Sussex Coll., Cambridge. Wrangler, 1910. Mathematical Master at Hulme Grammar Sch., Oldham; High Sch., Cardiff; St Olave's Sch.; Hymers Coll. Hector Medal, Royal Society NZ, 1946. Hon. DSc 1959. *Publications:* Foundations of Euclidean Geometry, 1927 (Dover Reprint, 1958); School Geometry, 1930; Higher Course Geometry, 1931; The Calculus of Extension, 1941 (Chelsea Reprint, 1960); Geometry (Hutchinson's University Library), 1950, Turkish translation, 1965; various articles. *Recreations:* walking and talking. *Address:* The University, Auckland, NZ.
*See also Ven. C. R. Forder.*

**FORDHAM, Sir (Alfred) Stanley,** KBE 1964; CMG 1951; JP; *b* 2 Sept. 1907; *e s* of late Alfred Russell Fordham, JP, Melbourn Bury, Cambs, and Caroline Augusta Stanley; *m* 1934, Isabel, *y d* of Juan Ward, Lima, Peru; one *s* one *d. Educ:* Eton; Trinity Coll., Cambridge. Vice-Consul, San Francisco, 1930-33; Lima, 1933-36; Guatemala, 1936-43; Los Angeles, 1943-44; Consul and Chargé d'Affaires, San Salvador, 1944-45; Consul, St Louis, 1945-48; transferred to Foreign Office, 1948, and promoted Counsellor (Head of American Dept), 1949; Warsaw, 1951-52; Stockholm, 1952-54; Minister, HM Embassy, Buenos Aires, 1954-56; HM Ambassador in Havana, 1956-60; HM Ambassador to Colombia, 1960-64; retired from Foreign Service, 1964. Grand Cross of San Carlos (Colombia). *Recreations:* golf, shooting. *Address:* Melbourn Bury, Royston, Herts. *T:* Melbourn (Cambs) 206. *Clubs:* MCC; Cambridge County.

**FORDHAM, Lieut-Col Reginald Sydney Walter,** QC 1933; LLB; ED; Acting Chairman, Tax Appeal Board, Ottawa, since 1962; Barrister-at-Law; *b* London, England, 9 May 1897; *m* 1925, Margaret Casson, *d* of Dr E. T. Kellam, Niagara Falls, Canada; one *d. Educ:* privately; Univ. of Toronto; Osgoode Hall Law Sch. Called to Bar of Ont., 1921; served European War, France, with Canadian Infantry, as Lieut 1916; Capt. 1917 (wounded and prisoner, despatches); Alderman in Niagara Falls City Council four years; Mem., Court of Revision and Public Library Board; Bde Major, 5th Inf. Bde, 1934-36; Lieut-Col 1936; commanded Lincoln and Welland Regt, 1936-40; comd Welland Canal Force during last four months of 1939 until its dissolution; Comr of Refugee Camps, Dept of Sec. of State, Ottawa, and Home Office representative, 1941-43; Dir of Labour Projects (P of W), Dept of Labour, Canada, 1943. KStJ 1970 (CStJ 1964; OStJ 1941). *Publication:* Tax Appeal Board Practice, 1958. *Recreations:* riding, lawn-bowling, bridge, reading. *Address:* Strathcona Apts, Ottawa, Ont, Canada. *Clubs:* Rideau, Country (Ottawa); Ottawa Valley Hunt.

**FORDHAM, Sir Stanley;** *see* Fordham, Sir A. S.

**FORDHAM, Wilfrid Gurney,** QC 1967; *b* 9 Dec. 1902; *s* of Edward Wilfrid Fordham and Sybil Harriet (*née* Langdon-Davies); *m* 1930, Peta Marshall Freeman; one *s. Educ:* St George's, Harpenden; Magdalene Coll., Cambridge. Called to Bar, Inner Temple, 1929. Contested: (L) Bromley, Kent, 1929, 1930; (Lab) Wycombe, Bucks, 1959. *Publications:* various legal books. *Recreations:* travel, country life. *Address:* 4 Paper Buildings, Temple, EC4. *T:* 01-353 2739; The Summer House, East Hill, Otford, Kent. *Club:* Garrick.

**FORDYCE, Catherine Mary,** MA (London and Oxford); *b* Wareham, Dorset, 18 Dec. 1898; *d* of Ernest Chilcott, MA, Vicar of Elberton, Glos; *m* 1929, Christian James Fordyce, *qv. Educ:* St Mary's Hall, Brighton; Bedford Coll. for Women. London BA Classical Hons Cl. I, 1920; Gilchrist Studentship, 1921; MA (with distinction), 1922; Fellow and Classical Tutor of Lady Margaret Hall, Oxford, 1922-29. *Publications:* articles in Classical Quarterly, 1923; Essay, Myth and Reality, in Adventure, 1927. *Address:* 3 The College, Glasgow W2.

**FORDYCE, Christian James,** MA; Professor of Humanity, University of Glasgow, since 1934; *b* Fraserburgh, 25 Sept. 1901; *s* of James Wilson Fordyce, MA, and Helen Wilson McAllan; *m* 1929, Catherine Mary Chilcott (*see* C. M. Fordyce). *Educ:* University of Glasgow; Balliol Coll., Oxford (Scholar and Snell Exhibitioner). First Class Hons in Classics, Glasgow Univ., 1920; Gaisford Prize (Greek Prose), 1921; First Class, Classical Mods, 1922; Hertford Scholar, 1922; Craven Scholar, 1922; Chancellor's Prize (Latin Prose), 1923; First class, Literæ Humaniores, 1924; War Memorial Research Student in Classics, Balliol Coll., 1925; Lecturer in Greek in the University of St Andrews, 1925-26; Lecturer in Humanity in the University of Edinburgh, 1926; Fellow, Classical Tutor, and Librarian of Jesus Coll., Oxford, 1927-34. Hon. LLD St Andrews, 1962. Comdr, Order of St Olav, 1961. *Publications:* Commentary on Catullus, 1961; articles in classical journals; Editor of the Classical Review. *Address:* 3 The College, Glasgow W2. *T:* 041-339 3985.

**FOREMAN, Carl;** screen writer; producer; director; Managing Director and Executive Producer of Open Road Films Ltd; *b* Chicago, USA, 23 July 1914. *Educ:* Crane Coll.; Univ. of Illinois; Northwestern Univ., USA. *Film scripts:* So This is New York, 1948; Champion, 1949; Home of the Brave, 1949; The Men, 1950; Cyrano de Bergerac, 1950; (writer-prod.) High Noon, 1951; The Bridge on the River Kwai, 1957; (writer-prod.) The Key, 1959; (exec. prod.) The Mouse that Roared, 1960; The Guns of Navarone, 1961; (film writer-prod.-dir) The Victors, 1963; (exec. prod.) Born Free, 1965; (writer-prod.) Mackenna's Gold, 1967; (exec. prod.) Otley, and The Virgin Soldiers, 1968. Mem. Bd of Governors, British Film Inst., 1966-; Mem. Exec. Council, Film Production Assoc., 1967-; Pres., Writers' Guild of GB, 1968- (Dist. Service Award, 1968); Writers' Guild of Amer. Laurel Award, 1969. FRSA 1969. Comdr, Order of the

Phoenix (Greece), 1962. *Publication:* A Cast of Lions, 1966. *Address:* 25 Jermyn Street, SW1. *T:* 01-437 4534. *Clubs:* Savile, Royal Automobile.

**FOREST SMITH, John,** FRCP; Physician-in-charge, Children's Department, St Thomas's Hospital; Physician, Grosvenor Hospital for Women. *Educ:* St Thomas's Hosp. MRCS, LRCP 1916; FRCP 1931. Formerly Senior Censor, RCP, Physician and John and Temple Research Fellow, St Thomas's Hosp.; Examiner in Medicine, RCP, Univ. of Birmingham and Conjoint Board. Mem., Assoc. of Physicians. *Address:* 2K Portman Mansions, W1. *T:* 01-935 6452; 149 Harley Street, W1. *T:* 01-935 4444.

**FORESTER, WELD-,** family name of **Baron Forester.**

**FORESTER,** 7th Baron (UK) *cr* 1821; **Col Cecil George Wilfrid Weld-Forester;** *b* 12 July 1899; *o s* of 6th Baron and Christine Isabel (*d* 1948), *d* of Duncan Davidson of Tulloch; *S* father, 1932; *m* 1931, Marie Louise Priscilla, CStJ, *d* of late Col Sir Herbert Perrott, Bt, CH, CB; one *s* four *d. Educ:* Durham Univ. Joined Royal Horse Guards, 1918; served in France, 1918; Capt., 1921; ADC to Gov.-Gen. and Comdr-in-Chief, S Africa, 1924-27; Major, 1930; Bt Lieut-col 1934; Lieut-Col 1938; Lieut-Col commanding Royal Horse Guards, 1938-41; Acting Col CMF 1943 (despatches); served in BLA, 1944; retd pay with rank of Col, 1945; Mayor of the Borough of Wenlock, 1936-37 and 1961-62; Alderman, Borough of Wenlock, 1940; Alderman, Salop CC, 1960. Freeman, Borough of Wenlock, 1963. JP. Owns about 10,000 acres. *Heir: s* Hon (George Cecil) Brooke Weld-Forester [*b* 20 Feb. 1938; *m* 1967, Hon. Catherine Lyttelton, 2nd *d* of Viscount Cobham, *qv*; two *d*]. *Address:* Willey Park, Broseley, Salop. *T:* Ironbridge 2146. *Club:* Turf.

*See also Sir Brian W. de S. Barttelot, Baron Bolton, Marquess of Downshire.*

**FORESTIER-WALKER, Sir George F.;** *see* Walker.

**FORFAR, Prof. John Oldroyd,** MC 1944; Professor of Child Life and Health, University of Edinburgh, since 1964; *b* 16 Nov. 1916; *s* of Rev. David Forfar, MA and Elizabeth Edith Campbell; *m* 1942, Isobel Mary Langlands Fernback, MB, ChB, DPH; two *s* one *d. Educ:* Perth Acad.; St Andrews Univ. BSc 1938, MB, ChB 1941, St Andrews; MRCP 1947; MRCPE 1948; DCH (London) 1948; FRCPE 1953; MD (Commendation) St Andrews, 1958; FRCP 1964. House Officer, Perth Royal Infirmary, 1941; RAMC, 1942-46: Med. Off., 47 Royal Marine Commando, 1943-45 (despatches, 1945); Registrar and Sen. Registrar, Dundee Royal Infirmary, 1946-48; Sen. Lectr in Child Health, St Andrews Univ., 1948-50; Sen. Paediatric Phys., Edinburgh Northern Gp of Hosps, and Sen. Lectr in Child Life and Health, Edinburgh Univ., 1950-64. *Publications:* contribs to general medical and to paediatric jls and books. *Recreations:* walking, mountaineering, canoeing. *Address:* 110 Ravelston Dykes, Edinburgh 12. *T:* 031-337 7081.

**FORGAN, Robert,** MC; MA, MD, DPH; *b* 1891; *s* of late Rev. Robert Forgan, DD, Edinburgh; *m* 1st, Winifred Mary, *d* of Robert Cran, Ballater; one *d*; 2nd, Winifred Jan, *d* of Henry Rees, Kenton; one *s* two *d. Educ:* Aberdeen Grammar Sch.; Universities of Aberdeen and Cambridge. Served in RAMC, 1915-19 (MC); Specialist Medical Officer, Lanarks County Council, 1921-29; Mem. of Glasgow City Council, 1926-29; MP (Lab) West Renfrew Div., 1929-31. *Address:* Meadow Place, Hookend, Kelvedon Common, near Brentwood, Essex. *T:* Blackmore 267.

**FORMAN, Rev. Adam,** CBE 1919; *b* 1876; *s* of J. T. Forman, Las Palmas; *m* 1908, Flora (*d* 1961), *d* of James Smith, Craigielands, Beattock; four *s* one *d* (and one *d* decd). *Educ:* Loretto; Pembroke Coll., Cambridge (MA). Cambridge Rugby XV, 1904-05 and 1905-06. Chaplain, Loretto Sch., Edinburgh, 1907-11; Curate of St Andrew's, Bishop Auckland, 1913-14; Sec. for Sphagnum Moss, Scotland, Red Cross, 1915-18. District Comr, Boy Scouts Assoc., 1936-. Silver Wolf Medal, 1961. Inspector Dumfriesshire Special Constabulary Moffat and Beattock District, 1939-45. *Recreations:* scouting, reading, music. *Address:* Dumcrieff, Moffat, Scotland. *T:* Moffat 60. *Club:* New (Edinburgh).

*See also J. D. Forman, M. B. Forman.*

**FORMAN, John (Calder),** JP; Insurance Agent. Member, Glasgow Town Council, 1928-45; Chairman Glasgow Co-operative Conference Assoc.; Member, Amalgamated Engineering Union, 1906; MP (Lab-Co-op) Springburn Div. of Glasgow, 1945-64. *Address:* 168 Knightswood Road, Glasgow W3.

**FORMAN, John Denis,** OBE 1956; Joint Managing Director, Granada Group; *b* 13 Oct. 1917; *s* of Adam Forman, *qv*; *m* 1948, Helen de Mouilpied; two *s. Educ:* at home; Loretto; Pembroke Coll., Cambridge. Served War, 1940-45: Argyll and Sutherland Highlanders; Commandant, Orkney and Shetland Defensive Battle Sch., 1942 (wounded, Cassino, 1944). Chief Production Officer, Central Office of Information Films, 1947; Dir, Brit. Film Inst., 1948. Ufficiale dell'ordine Al Merito della Repubblica Italiana. *Publication:* Mozart's Piano Concertos, 1971. *Recreations:* fishing, eighteenth century music, shooting. *Address:* Little Garnetts, Dunmow, Essex. *T:* Good Easter 250. *Club:* Savile.

*See also M. B. Forman.*

**FORMAN, Louis,** MD London; FRCP; Consultant Dermatologist Emeritus, Guy's Hospital and St John's Hospital for Diseases of the Skin; Hon. Consultant, London Jewish Hospital. *Educ:* Guy's Hosp., Univ. of London. MRCS, LRCP 1923; MB, BS 1924; MRCP 1925; FRCP 1939. Formerly Dermatologist SE Group, London CC; Medical Registrar, Guy's Hosp. *Publications:* various articles in med. jls. *Address:* 22 Harley House, Regents Park, NW1. *T:* 01-580 3262.

**FORMAN, Michael Bertram,** TD 1945; Personnel Director, Steel Tube Division, Tube Investments Ltd, since 1968; *b* 28 March 1921; *s* of Rev. A. Forman, *qv*; *m* 1947, Mary Railston-Brown; four *d. Educ:* Loretto Sch., Musselburgh; Manchester Coll. of Technology. TA commn, 7th KOSB, 1939. War Service in Inf. and Airborne Forces, 1939-46: UK, Holland, Germany (POW), India. Labour Management, Courtaulds Ltd, 1946-53; Dir, Inst. of Personnel Management, 1953-56; Head of Staff Planning, NCB, 1956-59; Chief Staff Officer, SW Div., NCB, 1959-62; Personnel Relations Adviser and Dep. Dir of Personnel, Tube Investments Ltd, 1962-68. Mem. NBPI, 1968-70. FIPM, 1963. *Publications:* contribs IPM Jl and Brit. Jl of Industrial Relations. *Recreations:* reading, gardening, fishing, shooting. *Address:* The Priory, Stoke Prior, Bromsgrove, Worcs. *T:* Bromsgrove 2196. *Club:* Savile.

*See also J. D. Forman.*

**FORMBY, Myles Landseer,** CBE 1962; TD 1946; Consulting Otolaryngologist, retired: University College Hospital, 1933-66, now Hon. Consulting Surgeon; Royal Masonic Hospital, 1948-66; *b* 13 March 1901; *s* of Arthur Formby, South Australia; *m* 1931, Dorothy Hussey Essex (marr. diss. 1952); one *s* one *d*. *Educ:* St Peter's Coll., Adelaide, South Australia; Univ. of Adelaide; Magdalen Coll., Oxford. Elder Scholarship, Univ. of Adelaide, 1920 and 1921, Everard Scholarship, 1924; MB, BS, Adelaide, 1924; Rhodes Scholar for S Australia, 1925; BA Oxford, 1927; BSc Oxford, 1928; FRCS 1930; MA Oxford, 1953. Hon. Asst Surg., Ear, Nose and Throat Hosp., Golden Square, 1931; Hon. Surg., Ear, Nose and Throat, Miller Gen. Hosp., 1932; Hon. Asst Surg., Ear, Nose and Throat Dept, University Coll. Hosp., 1933; Hon. Surg., 1940; Hon. Surg., Ear, Nose and Throat Dept, Royal Masonic Hosp., 1948. RAMC TA, Lieut, 1932; Capt., 1933; Major, 1939; Lieut-Col, 1941; Brig. Consulting Oto-Rhino-Laryngologist to the Army, 1943; served in the Middle East, Italy, North West Europe and India, in War of 1939-45. Hon. Civilian Consultant to War Office, 1946. Mem. Court of Examiners, Royal College of Surgeons, 1947-53; Mem. Council, 1952-57; Hon. Dir of Photography, Royal Society of Medicine, 1958-61; Pres., Section of Laryngology, RSM, 1959-60; Hon. Treas. RSM 1962-68; Hon. Laryngologist to Royal Academy of Music; Pres., British Assoc. of Otolaryngologists. Bronze Star, USA, 1945. *Publications:* Dental Infection in the Aetiology of Maxillary Sinusitis, 1934; Treatment of Otitis Media, 1938; Nasal Allergy, 1943; chapters in Diseases of the Ear, Nose and Throat, 1952; The Maxillary Sinus, 1960; Ultrasonic Destruction of the Labyrinth, 1963. *Recreations:* rowing, lacrosse, golf. *Address:* 5 Harcourt House, 19a Cavendish Square, W1M 9AD. *T:* 01-636 0724. *Clubs:* Royal Automobile; Leander.

**FORMSTON, Prof. Clifford;** Vice-Principal, Royal Veterinary College; Professor of Veterinary Surgery in the University of London, since 1943; *b* 15 Jan. 1907; *s* of Alfred and Annie Formston; *m* 1934, Irene Pembleton, *d* of Capt. Roland Wood; one *s* one *d*. *Educ:* Chester City Grammar Sch.; Royal Veterinary College, London. MRCVS 1928; FRCVS 1944. Mem. of Royal Veterinary Coll. staff, 1928-; Mem. of Council, RCVS, 1954-62; Past Pres. Royal Counties Veterinary Assoc. and Central Veterinary Soc. External Examiner in veterinary surgery to Univs of Bristol, Cambridge, Dublin, Glasgow, Liverpool, Edinburgh and Khartoum; Hon. Cons. Veterinary Surg. to Childe-Beale Trust. *Recreations:* golf, gardening, reading. *Address:* Crondall, 55 Old Park View, Enfield, Mddx. *T:* 01-363 4520.

**FORRES,** 3rd Baron *cr* 1922, of Glenogil; **John Archibald Harford Williamson;** Bt, 1909; *b* 30 Oct. 1922; *s* of 2nd Baron and Jessie, *er d* of late William Alfred Harford, JP, Petty France, Badminton, Glos; *S* father, 1954; *m* 1st, 1945, Gillian Ann Maclean (marr. diss. 1967), *d* of Major J. Maclean Grant, RA retd; one *s* two *d*; 2nd, 1969, Cecily Josephine, *e d* of Sir Alexander Gordon Cumming, 5th Bt, and of Countess Cawdor, and *widow* of 2nd Earl of Woolton. *Educ:* Eton; Trinity Coll., Cambridge. Served War of 1939-45: with Black Watch 51st (Highland) Div., North Africa, Sicily, Normandy (despatches), with 6th (British) Armoured Div., Italy, as ADC to Comdr, 1944-45. *Heir: s* Hon. Alastair Stephen Grant Williamson [*b* 16 May 1946; *m* 1969, Margaret, *d* of late G. J. Mallam, New South Wales]. *Address:* Glenogil, By Forfar, Angus. *T:* Fern 226. *Club:* Brooks's.

**FORREST, Prof. Andrew Patrick McEwen,** BSc, MD, ChM; FRCS, FRCSE, FRCSGlas; Regius Professor of Clinical Surgery, University of Edinburgh, since 1970; *b* 25 March 1923; *s* of Rev. Andrew James Forrest, BD, and Isabella Pearson; *m* 1955, Margaret Beryl Hall (*d* 1961); one *s* one *d*; *m* 1964, Margaret Anne Steward. *Educ:* Dundee High Sch.; Univ. of St Andrews. BSc 1942; MB, ChB 1945; ChM hons, University Gold Medal, 1954; MD hons, Rutherford Gold Medal, 1958; FRCSE 1950; FRCS 1952; FRCSGlas 1962. Surg.-Lt RNVR, 1946-48. Mayo Foundation Fellow, 1952-53; Lectr and Sen. Lectr, Univ. of Glasgow, 1955-62; Prof. of Surgery, Welsh Nat. Sch. of Medicine, 1962-70. McIlrath Vis. Prof., Royal Prince Alfred Hosp., Sydney, 1969; Lectures: Lister Meml, Canadian Med. Assoc., 1970; Inaugural Bruce, Wellesley Hosp., Toronto, 1970; Michael Williams', RSM, 1970. Member: Medical sub-cttee, UGC, 1967-; Grants Cttee, MRC, 1968-. Asst Editor and Editor, Scottish Med. Jl, 1957-61; Hon. Secretary: Scottish Soc. for Experimental Medicine, 1959-62; Surgical Research Soc., 1963-66. Fellow, Assoc. of Surgeons of GB and Ireland; Member: Moynihan Chirurgical Club; Internat. Surgical Gp; Surgical Research Soc.; British Soc. of Gastroenterology; British Assoc. for Cancer Research. *Publications:* (ed jtly) Prognostic Factors in Breast Cancer, 1968; various papers in surgical jls, mainly on gastro-intestinal disease and breast cancer. *Address:* Department of Clinical Surgery, University of Edinburgh. *T:* 031-667 1011. *Club:* RNVR (Glasgow).

**FORREST, Geoffrey;** Senior Officer of Forestry Commission in Scotland, 1965-69; *b* 31 Oct. 1909; *er s* of late George Forrest, CA, Rossie Lodge, Inverness; *m* 1951, Marjorie, *d* of late W. S. Ridehalgh, Broughton Lodge, Cartmel; two *s*. *Educ:* Marlborough Coll. Chartered Land Agent (FLAS 1952). Served War of 1939-45, in Lovat Scouts. Joined Forestry Commn, 1946; Chief Land Agent for Forestry Commn in Wales, 1958-64; Chief Land Agent for Forestry Commn in Scotland, 1964-65. *Publications:* papers on land use and estate management in professional jls. *Recreations:* fishing, shooting, lawn tennis. *Address:* Hallyne House, near Peebles, Scotland. *T:* Kirkton Manor 200. *Club:* New (Edinburgh).

**FORREST, Cdre (Retd) Geoffrey Cornish;** Master of P & O vessel Arcadia from her completion in Jan. 1954 until Oct. 1956; Commodore P & O Fleet, 1955-56; *b* 1898; *s* of late William Forrest, an Examiner of Master and Mates; *m* 1941, Monica Clemens. *Educ:* Thames Nautical Training Coll. (the Worcester). Cadet, P & O, 1915; Chief Officer of the Stratheden, 1939. Comdr, Naval Reserve, 1940-45. Master of P & O ships Pinjarra, Chitral and Stratheden, 1946-53. *Recreations:* sailing, photography, chess, bridge. *Address:* 3 Narla Road, Bayview, New South Wales, Australia.

**FORREST, Gilbert Alexander;** His Honour Judge Forrest; County Court Judge, London, since 1970; *b* 27 July 1912; *s* of G. C. Forrest and Janet Forrest, Heaton Moor, Stockport; *m* 1937, Emily Maureen, *d* of Joseph Armstrong, Co. Fermanagh and Stockport; two *s* two *d*. *Educ:* Stockport Grammar Sch.; Manchester Univ.; St Edmund Hall, Oxford. Barrister, Gray's Inn, 1937; practised, Western Circuit, 1937-70. Lectr in Law, Bristol Univ., 1937-70. Dep. Chm., Somerset QS, 1966. Army, 1940, British Military Mission to N America, 1943-45; Captain, RAOC. *Publications:* articles in legal jls. *Recreations:* bird-watching, gardening.

*Address:* 43 Canynge Road, Bristol 8. *Club:* Bristol (Bristol).

**FORREST, Sir James (Alexander),** Kt 1967; Chairman: Australian Consolidated Industries Ltd, since 1953; National Bank of Australasia Ltd, since 1959; Chase NBA Group Ltd, since 1969; Alcoa of Australia Ltd, since 1970; Director: Australian Mutual Provident Society, since 1961 (Chairman, Victoria Branch Board, since 1957); Western Mining Corporation Ltd, since 1970; Partner, Hedderwick Fookes & Alston, Solicitors, 1933-70, Consultant since 1970; *b* 10 March 1905; *s* of John and Mary Gray Forrest; *m* 1939, Mary Christina Forrest (*née* Armit); three *s*. *Educ:* Caulfield Grammar Sch.; Melbourne Univ. RAAF and Dept Aircraft Production, 1942-45. Mem. Council: Monash Univ.; Royal Children's Hosp. Research Foundn. *Recreations:* golf, fishing. *Address:* (business) 19th Floor, AMP Tower, 535 Bourke Street, Melbourne, Victoria 3000, Australia. *T:* 62-6192; (home) 11 Russell Street, Toorak, Victoria 3142, Australia. *T:* 20-5227. *Clubs:* Melbourne, Australian, Naval and Military (Melbourne); Union (Sydney).

**FORREST, John Samuel,** MA, DSc; FRS 1966; FInstP, CEng, FIEE; Director, Central Electricity Research Laboratories, since 1940; *b* 20 Aug. 1907; *m* 1940, Ivy May Olding; one *s*. *Educ:* Hamilton Acad.; Glasgow Univ. Physicist, Central Electricity Board: Glasgow, 1930; London, 1931; i/c of CEB Research Lab., 1934-40; Dir and founder, Central Electricity Research Labs, Leatherhead, 1940; Sec., Electricity Supply Research Coun., 1949-. Vis. Prof. of Electrical Engrg, University of Strathclyde, 1964-; Hunter Memorial Lectr, 1961; Baird Memorial Lectr, 1963; Faraday Lectures, 1963-64. Mem. Bd, Inst. of Physics, 1945-49; Chm., London Br. Inst. of Physics, 1954-58; Chm., Supply Sect. of IEE, 1961-62; Vice-Chm., British Nat. Cttee, Conference Internationale des Grands Réseaux Electriques; Pres., Sect. A, Brit. Assoc., 1963; Member Council: IEE; Royal Meteorological Society, 1945-47; Research Associations. Hon. DSc Strathclyde 1969. Coopers Hill War Memorial Prize and Medal, 1941; Willans Medal, 1958. *Publications:* papers on electrical power transmission and insulation. *Address:* Central Electricity Research Laboratories, Kelvin Avenue, Leatherhead, Surrey. *T:* Leatherhead 4488; Arbores, Portsmouth Road, Thames Ditton, Surrey. *Club:* Royal Automobile.

**FORREST, Richard Haddow,** QC 1953; Judge of the Court of Appeal, Jersey, and of the Court of Appeal, Guernsey, since 1965; Presiding Judge, Liverpool Court of Passage, since 1964; Leader of the Northern Circuit since 1968; Lieut Bailiff of Jersey since 1970; *b* 13 Sept. 1908; *o s* of John Duggan and Marie Josephine Forrest; *m* 1936, Monica Constance Neville; two *s* two *d*. *Educ:* Merchant Taylors' Sch., Crosby; Pembroke Coll., Oxford (MA). Called to the Bar, Gray's Inn, 1932; Bencher, 1960. Recorder of Salford, 1956-64. King's Regiment, 1930-45 (SR, 1930-39). *Address:* High Wood, Firle Road, Seaford, Sussex. *Clubs:* United Service and Sports; Racquets (Liverpool).

**FORREST, Surgeon Rear-Adm. (D) William Ivon Norman,** CB 1970; QHDS; Director of Naval Dental Services, Ministry of Defence, since 1968; *b* 8 June 1914; *m* 1942, Mary Margaret McMordie Black; three *s*. *Educ:* Christ's Hospital. Guy's Hospital, 1931-36. LDS, RCS. Dental House Surgeon, Guy's Hosp., 1936-37. Royal Navy: Surg. Lieut (D), 1937; Surg. Lt-Comdr (D), 1943; Surg. Comdr (D), 1950; Surg. Capt. (D), 1960; Surg. Rear-Adm. (D), 1968. Consultant in Dental Surgery, 1963. *Recreations:* golf, gardening, photography. *Address:* 8 Queen's Road, Waterlooville, Hants. *T:* Waterlooville 3139; 63 Fitz George Avenue, W14. *T:* 01-603 0668.

**FORRESTER, Charles,** K-i-H 1944; BSc, FHWC; FRIC, PhD (Edinburgh), AMIChemE, FInstF, FRSE; scientific consultant; *y s* of Wm Fordie Forrester, HM Sasines Office, Edinburgh; *m* Joyce Annie, *o d* of Horace Purver Gripton; one *s* one *d*. *Educ:* Heriot-Watt Coll., Edinburgh. Prof. of Chemistry, Indian Sch. of Mines, Government of India, 1926, Vice-Principal, 1932, Principal, 1936-49; Chief Scientist's Div., Min. of Power, 1949-60, Dep. Chief Fuel Engr, later Senior Principal Scientific Officer; Brit. Coal Utilisation Res. Assoc., 1960-63; Royal Inst. of Chemistry, Council, 1948-52, 1960-63, Chm. Indian Sect., 1945-48; Institute of Fuel Council, 1932; Mem. of Mining, Geological and Metallurgical Inst. of India (Council, 1932-35 and 1942-48, Vice-Pres., 1938-39); Mem., Basic Chemicals Cttee (Supply Development Council, India), 1942-43; Mem., Fuel Research Cttee, CSIR, Govt of India. Founded, 1938, Blood Bank, Dhanbad, Bihar; social service at Leprosy Hospital, Sijua; advised CID Bihar on forensic laboratory, 1938; Kaisar-i-Hind Medal for public service in India, 1944. Editor, the Plant Engineer, 1953-55. Hon. Fellow, Heriot-Watt Coll. *Publications:* Trans Min. Geol. and Met. Inst. India (bronze, silver, and gold medals and twice Govt of India Prize, Rs 500); Journal of the Institute of Fuel, Proc. Indian Science Congr., Proc. Nat. Inst. Sciences, India; Fuel Research Report No. 1, CSIR (India); Editor and part-contributor, The Efficient Use of Fuel (HMSO), 1958. *Recreations:* gardening, Scottish country dancing, organ and classical music. *Address:* 1 Hampton Grove, Ewell, Surrey. *T:* 01-393 1004.

**FORRESTER, John Stuart;** MP (Lab) Stoke-on-Trent, North, since 1966; *b* 17 June 1924; *s* of Harry and Nellie Forrester; *m* 1945, Gertrude H. Weaver. *Educ:* Eastwood Council Sch.; City Sch. of Commerce, Stoke-on-Trent; Alsager Teachers' Training Coll. Teacher, 1946-66. Sec., Constituency Labour Party, 1961-66; Mem., Executive Cttee, Stoke-on-Trent City Labour Party, 1958-66. *Recreations:* sport, gardening, do-it-yourself. *Address:* House of Commons, SW1; 13 Newmill Street, Milton, Stoke-on-Trent, Staffs. *T:* Stoke-on-Trent 54305.

**FORRESTER, Maj.-Gen. Michael,** CB 1969; CBE 1963 (OBE 1960); DSO 1943 and Bar, 1944; MC 1939 and Bar, 1941; Director of Infantry, Ministry of Defence, 1968-70; *b* 31 Aug. 1917; 2nd *s* of late James Forrester, Chilworth, Hants, and Elsie (*née* Mathwin); *m* 1947, Pauline Margaret Clara (marr. diss. 1960), *d* of late James Fisher, Crossmichael; two *s*. *Educ:* Haileybury. 2nd Lieut, Queen's Royal Regt, 1938; served in Palestine (Arab Rebellion), 1938-39; served War of 1939-45 in Palestine, Egypt, Greece, Crete, Western Desert, Syria, N Africa, Italy and France; GSO3 (Ops), HQ Western Desert Force and HQ 13 Corps, 1941-42; Staff Coll., Haifa, 1942; Bde Major, 132 Inf. Bde, 1942 (despatches); GSO2 (Ops), HQ 13 Corps and HQ 18 Army Gp, 1943; Comdr, 1st/6th Bn, Queen's Royal Regt, 1943-44; wounded, Normandy; GSO1 (Ops), HQ 13 Corps, 1945-46; Mil. Asst to Supreme Allied Comdr Mediterranean, 1947; Mil. Asst to Comdr Brit. Army Staff and Army Mem., Brit. Jt Services Mission, Washington, DC, 1947-50; Co. Comdr, 2nd Bn Parachute Regt, Cyprus and Canal Zone, 1951-52; Dirg

Staff, Staff Coll., Camberley, 1953-55; GSO1 (Ops), GHQ East Africa, 1955-57; transf. to Parachute Regt, 1957; Comdr, 3rd Bn Parachute Regt, 1957-60; Col., Military Operations (4), War Office, 1960-61; Comdr, 16 Parachute Bde Gp, 1961-63; Imp. Def. Coll., 1964; GOC 4th Div., BAOR, 1965-67. Col Comdt, The Queen's Division, 1968-70. *Address:* Pullens, West Worldham, near Alton, Hants. *T:* Alton 84470. *Club:* United Service.

**FORRESTER, Rev. William Roxburgh;** Professor of Practical Theology and Christian Ethics, St Mary's College, St Andrews University, 1934-58; Emeritus Professor; *b* 19 Feb. 1892; *s* of Rev. David Marshall Forrester, DD, and Annie Roxburgh; *m* 1922, Isobel Margaret Stewart McColl; five *c*. *Educ:* Glasgow Acad.; Glasgow and Edinburgh Univs. MA (Hons) Edinburgh, 1914; European War: France, Mesopotamia, Persia and India in RFA, 1914-19; Studies at New Coll., Edinburgh; France and Germany, 1919-22; BD, 1924; Minister at Roslin, 1922-28; Minister at Cairns Memorial Church, Edinburgh, 1928-34; Interim Gen. Sec. Scottish National YMCA, 1940-44; DD (Edinburgh) 1939. Cunningham Lecturer, New Coll., Edinburgh, 1947-48-49; LLD St Andrews, 1959. Associate Minister, St Andrew's Presbyterian Church, Nairobi, Nov. 1961-Nov. 1962. *Publications:* Christian Vocation, Studies in Faith and its Relation to Work, 1951; Conversion, 1937, Concern, 1963; The Pen and the Panga, two Addresses on Education and Religion (East Africa), 1965; Your Life and Mine, 1967. *Recreations:* fishing, gardening. *Address:* 7 Newbattle Terrace, Edinburgh E10 4RU. *T:* 031-447 2870.

**FORRESTER-PATON, Douglas Shaw,** QC 1965; **His Honour Judge Forrester-Paton;** a Judge of County Courts, since 1970; *b* 1921; 3rd *s* of late Alexander Forrester-Paton, JP; *m* 1948, Agnete, *d* of Holger Tuxen; one *s* two *d*. *Educ:* Gresham's Sch., Holt; Queen's Coll., Oxford (BA). Called to Bar, Middle Temple, 1947; North East Circuit. Served RAF, 1941-45. Recorder: Middlesbrough, 1963-68; Teesside, 1968-70. *Address:* 27 Heaton Grove, Bradford 9, Yorks; 5 King's Bench Walk, Temple, EC4. *T:* 01-353 2882.

**FORSBERG, (Charles) Gerald,** OBE 1955; Comdr RN (Retd); Deputy Director of Marine Services, Ministry of Defence (Navy Dept), since 1958; *b* Vancouver, 18 June 1912; *s* of Charles G. Forsberg and Nellie (*née* Wallman); *m* 1952, Joyce Whewell Hogarth, *d* of Dr F. W. Hogarth; one *s* one *d*. *Educ:* Polytechnic School; Training Ship Mercury; Sir John Cass Coll. Merchant Navy: Cadet to Chief Officer, 1928-38; qual. Master Mariner; transf. RN, 1938. Norwegian campaign, 1940; Malta Convoys, Matapan, Tobruk, Crete, etc, 1940-42; comd HMS Vega as Convoy Escort Comdr, 1943-45 (despatches). Comd HMS Mameluke and HMS Chaplet, 1945-49; comd Salvage Sqdn off Elba in recovery of crashed Comet aircraft in 100 fathoms, 1954. Swam Channel (England-France) in record time, 1957; first person to swim Lough Neagh and Loch Lomond, 1959; British long-distance champion, 1957-58-59; swam Bristol Channel in record time, 1964; many long-distance championships and records, 1951-. Younger Brother of Trinity House, 1958; Civil Service, 1962. Pres. Channel Swimming Assoc., 1963; Master of Navy Lodge, 1966; Liveryman, Hon. Co. of Master Mariners. Freeman, City of London, 1968. *Publications:* Long Distance Swimming, 1957; First Strokes in Swimming, 1961; Swimming (part author), 1961; Modern Long Distance Swimming, 1963; many short stories, articles, papers, and book reviews for general periodicals, technical jls and encyclopædia; regular monthly contribs to Swimming Times. *Recreations:* motoring, Association football refereeing, books. *Address:* c/o Barclays Bank DCO, Goodenough House, 33 Old Broad St, EC2. *Clubs:* Royal Automobile; Otter Swimming.

**FORSBERG, Gerald;** *see* Forsberg, C. G.

**FORSDYKE, Sir (Edgar) John,** KCB 1937; MA; Hon. ARIBA; Director and Principal Librarian of British Museum, 1936-50; 2nd *s* of F. P. Forsdyke, Hasketon, Suffolk; *b* 12 Sept. 1883; *m* 1942, Dea Gombrich, violinist, *e d* of Dr Karl Gombrich of Vienna; two *d*. *Educ:* Christ's Hospital; Keble Coll., Oxford (Scholar and Hon. Fellow). Entered British Museum, 1907; Keeper of Greek and Roman Antiquities in the British Museum, 1932-36. military service, 1914-19, France, Macedonia, Egypt, Palestine; Capt., RFA. editor Journal of Hellenic Studies, 1912-23; Hon. Sec. Hellenic Soc.; Hon. Member: Archæological Soc. of Athens; Archæological Inst. of America. *Publication:* Greece before Homer, 1956. *Address:* 13 Sandringham Road, NW11.

**FORSEY, Prof. George Frank,** MA; Professor of Classics in University of Southampton, 1926-54; *b* 15 May 1889; *s* of George and Sarah Colbert Forsey; *m* 1924, Caroline Alice Homeyer, *d* of Rev. George Homeyer; no *c*. *Educ:* University Coll., London. Lecturer in charge of Latin classes, Goldsmiths' Coll. (University of London), 1912-19. Served, 1915-19, in commissioned service in Mesopotamia with Machine Gun Corps, 1917-19. Lecturer in charge of Classics in University Coll., Southampton, 1919; subsequently Reader. Vice-Principal Southampton Univ., 1939-52, Deputy Vice-Chancellor, 1952-54. Has been at various times Member of Council of Classical Assoc. and Roman Soc., and co-opted mem. of Dorset Educn Cttee. For a number of years Examiner in Latin for Final and Higher Degrees in University of London. Fellow of University Coll., London 1953. *Publications:* occasional reviews or contributions in learned journals. *Address:* 12 Highfield Close, Southampton. *T:* Southampton 57002.

**FORSHAW, John Henry,** CB 1954; MC, FRIBA; retired; Chief Architect and Housing Consultant, Ministry of Housing and Local Government, 1951-59, and of Ministry of Health, 1946-59; *b* 6 Sept. 1895; *y s* of late Henry Forshaw and Ellen, *d* of James Haselden; *m* 1923, Alice Holland, *o d* of H. W. Rigby-Jones, JP, Lathom; one *s* one *d*. *Educ:* Ormskirk Grammar Sch.; Liverpool Univ. (BArch, MA; Lever Prize, Dept of Civic Design). Formerly: Architect to the London County Council and Superintending Architect of Metropolitan Buildings, 1941-46, Deputy Architect, 1939-41; Dir, War Debris Survey, London Civil Defence Region, and Head of London (Heavy) Rescue Service, 1940-45; Chief Architect, Miners' Welfare Commn, 1926-39. Mem. Council, London Soc., Hon. Vice-Pres. Inst. of Landscape Architects; Member: Official Cttee, Festival of Britain, 1951; Min. of Housing Bailey Cttee Report, 1953; Anglo-French Soc. of Architects; Member: WVS Housing Assoc.; National Playing Fields Assoc., London; National Playing Fields Joint Advisory Cttee, Polytechnic; Hon. Mem. Institute of Architects of Brazil. Served European War, 1915-19, Inns of Court Regt; Royal Engineers; Adjt 55th Divisional RE, capt. (MC). County of London Plan, 1943, prepared with Sir Patrick Abercrombie; LCC reconstruction and housing schemes; pithead baths, welfare centres; experimental and demonstration housing. *Publications:* Lancaster Regional Planning Scheme, 1926; County of London Plan, 1943 (joint report); contribs to RIBA Jl. *Address:* Park Fell, Skelwith, near Ambleside, Westmorland. *T:* Ambleside 2354. *Club:* Reform.

**FORSHAW, Thomas;** Chairman and Director of Burtonwood Brewery Co. (Forshaw's) Ltd, Burtonwood Manor Estates Ltd and Bangor Hotels Ltd; *b* 29 June 1888; *e s* of Richard Forshaw, County Councillor, Burtonwood, Lancs; *m* 1927, Margaret Jean, *o d* of Edgar Francis Snoad, Great Bookham, Surrey; two *d. Educ:* Sir Thomas Boteler Grammar Sch., Warrington. High Sheriff, Anglesey, 1944-45. *Recreations:* Mem. of Lancs and Cheshire Antiquarian Soc., Chatham Soc., Record Soc., Historic Soc. *Address:* Burtonwood House, Burtonwood, Warrington, Lancs. *T:* Newton-le-Willows 4197; Penmorfa, Pentraeth, Anglesey. *T:* Pentraeth 205.

**FORSSMANN, Werner (Theodor Otto),** MD; surgeon and urologist; Chief of the Surgical Department, Evangelisches Hospital, Düsseldorf; general practitioner from 1945; *b* 29 Aug. 1904; *s* of late Julius Forssmann and Emmy Forssmann (*née* Hindenberg); *m* 1933, Dr Elsbeth Forssmann (*née* Engel); six c. *Educ:* Askanisches Gymnasium; Univ. of Berlin (MD). First discovered technique of cardiac catheterisation when working at Eberswalde Surgical Clinic, near Berlin, 1929; worked with Dr Ferdinand Sauerbruch, 1931-32; subsequently Chief of Surgical Dept, City Hospital, Dresden. Served War of 1939-45 (POW); Honorarprofessor für Chirurgie und Urologie, Universitat Mainz, 1956; Honorarprofessor der Universität Düsseldorf, 1964. Prof. Hon. der Universidad Nacional de Córdoba/Argentinien, 1961. Mem., Perspektives in Biology and Medicine, 1968. For. Corres. Mem., BMA; Hon. Fellow Indian Acad. of Sciences, 1967. Leibniz-Medaille, der Deutschen Akademie der Wissenschaften, 1954; Gold Medal, Società Medico Chirurgica di Ferrara, 1968; Ordentliches Mitglied der Rheinisch-Westfälishcen Akad. der Wissenschaften des Landes Nordrhein Westfalen, 1968. Grosses Bundesverdienst Kreuz, 1958, mit Schulterband und Stern, 1964. Awarded (jointly) Nobel Prize for Medicine and Physiology, 1956. *Publications:* many articles in German medical journals. *Address:* Chir. Klinik des Evangelischen Krankenhauses, Düsseldorf, West Germany; (private) 4041 Holzbüttgen über Neuss, Feldstrasse 6. *T:* Neuss 6.58.40.

**FORSTER,** family name of **Baron Forster of Harraby.**

**FORSTER OF HARRABY,** 1st Baron *cr* 1959, of Beckenham; **John Forster,** KBE 1948; Kt 1939; QC 1946; Barrister-at-Law; Chairman of National Arbitration Tribunal since 1944; Judge, Administrative Tribunal, International Labour Organisation, 1957-60; *b* Carlisle, Cumberland; *yr s* of John J. Forster; *m* 1917, Muriel, *er d* of late Samuel Vosper, Devonport; one *d. Educ:* Sedbergh. Called to Bar, Gray's Inn, 1919; served throughout European War (RA); presided over the Trinidad Labour Riots Commission, 1937, Court of Inquiry into London Bus Dispute, and other industrial inquiries. Deputy Umpire under Unemployment Insurance Act, 1935. Chairman, Railway Staff National Tribunal, 1940-60; Pres. of the Industrial Court, 1946-60. *Recreations:* fishing, gardening. *Address:* Broome, 84 Albemarle Rd, Beckenham, Kent. *T:* 01-460 2092; 1 Brick Court, Temple, EC4. *T:* 01-353 1687.

**FORSTER, Charles Ian Kennerley,** CBE 1964; Director of Statistics, Ministry of Technology (formerly Ministry of Power), since 1965; *b* 18 July 1911; *s* of Douglas Wakefield Forster; *m* 1942, Thelma Primrose Horton; one *s* one *d. Educ:* Rossall Sch. FIA 1936. Served RA, 1939-45. Statistics Branch, Admty, 1946-54; Ministry of Power, 1954 (Chief Statistician, 1955-65), Min. of Technology, 1969. *Publications:* contribs to Jls of Inst. of Actuaries and Inst. of Actuaries Students Soc., Trans VII World Power Conf., Trans Manchester Statistical Soc., Statistical News. *Recreations:* gardening, stamps. *Address:* Brook End, Blackbrook, Dorking, Surrey; *T:* Dorking 6114. *Club:* Royal Automobile.

**FORSTER, Rear-Adm. Herbert Acheson,** MVO 1925; RN, retired; *o surv. s* of Paul Forster, Malverleys, Newbury; *m* Violet (*d* 1961), *d* of Major H. B. Dodgson, DSO; three *d. Educ:* HMS Britannia, Dartmouth. Served in HM Ships Agincourt and Resolution during 1914-18; Comdr HMS Southampton, Flagship, E Indies Station, 1921-23; HM Yacht Victoria and Albert, 1924-26; in comd RAN College, Jervis Bay, NSW, 1927-29; HMS Frobisher, 1929-30 and 1932-34; Naval Asst to Adm. Comdg Reserves, 1931-32; HMAS Australia, 1935-37; Rear-Adm., 1937; retired list, 1937. Served during 1939-45 as NOIC Isle of Man and in command of HMS St George, 1939-42 and as Naval Attaché, Buenos Aires, 1942-45. *Recreation:* shooting. *Address:* Barton Cottage, Barton Stacey, Winchester, Hants. *Club:* United Service.

*See also Sir Patrick William Donner.*

**FORSTER, Prof. Leonard Wilson;** Schröder Professor of German, University of Cambridge since 1961; *b* 30 March 1913; *o s* of Edward James Forster, merchant, and Linda Charlotte (*née* Rogers), St John's Wood, NW8; *m* 1939, Jeanne Marie Louise, *e d* of Dr Charles Otto Billeter, Basel; one *s* two *d. Educ:* Marlborough Coll.; Trinity Hall, Cambridge. Thomas Carlyle Student, 1934-35; English Lektor: Univ. of Leipzig, 1934; Univ. of Königsberg, 1935-36; Univ. of Basel, 1936-38; study at Univ. of Bonn, 1935. Fellow and Lectr, Selwyn Coll., Cambridge, 1937; Faculty Asst Lectr, Univ. of Cambridge, 1937; Dr phil., Basel, 1938. Naval Staff Admiralty, 1939-41; Foreign Office, 1941-45; Lt-Comdr RNVR (Sp.), 1945-46. Univ. Lectr in German, Cambridge, 1947-50; Dean and Asst Tutor, Selwyn Coll., 1946-50; Prof. of German, University Coll., London, 1950-61. Corr. Mem. Deutsche Akademie für Sprache und Dichtung, 1957; Member: Maatschappij der Nederlandse Letterkunde, Leiden, 1966; Provinciaal Utrechts Genootschap van Kunsten en Letteren, 1968; Royal Netherlands Acad. of Sciences and Letters, 1968. Visiting Professor: Univ. of Toronto, 1957; Univ. of Heidelberg, 1964; McGill Univ., 1967-68; Univ. of Otago, 1968. Gold Medal, Goethe-Institut, Munich, 1966. *Publications:* G. R. Weckherlin, zur Kenntnis seines Lebens in England, 1944; Conrad Celtis, 1948; German Poetry, 1944-48, 1949; The Temper of Seventeenth Century German Literature, 1952; Penguin Book of German Verse, 1957; Poetry of Significant Nonsense, 1962; Lipsius, Von der Bestendigkeit, 1965; Die Niederlande und die Anfänge der deutschen Barocklyrik, 1967; Janus Gruter's English Years, 1967; The Icy Fire, 1969; German Life and Letters (co-ed); articles in British and foreign jls. *Recreation:* foreign travel. *Address:* 51 Maids Causeway, Cambridge. *T:* 57513; Selwyn College, Cambridge. *Club:* Athenæum.

**FORSTER, Oliver Grantham,** MVO 1961; Counsellor, British High Commission, New Delhi, since 1970; *b* 2 Sept. 1925; 2nd *s* of Norman Milward Forster and Olive Christina Forster (*née* Cockrell); *m* 1953, Beryl Myfanwy Evans; two *d. Educ:* Hurstpierpoint; King's Coll., Cambridge. Served in RAF, 1944-48. Joined Commonwealth Relations Office, 1951. Private Sec. to Parly Under-Sec., 1953-54; Second Sec., Karachi, 1954-56; Principal, CRO, 1956-59; First Sec., Madras, 1959-62; First Sec., Washington, 1962-65; Private Sec. to Sec. of State for Commonwealth Relations, 1965-67; Counsellor, Manila, 1967-70. *Address:* c/o Foreign and Commonwealth Office, King Charles Street, SW1.

**FORSTER, Sir (Samuel Alexander) Sadler,** Kt 1966; CBE 1956; Hon. DCL Durham; Chairman: English Industrial Estates Corporation, since 1960; Malta Development Corporation, since 1968; *b* 1900; *o s* of Fred J. Forster, JP, FCA, Middlesbrough; *m* 1st, 1928, Edna (*d* 1930), *o d* of Wm Henry Potts, Middlesbrough; one *d*; 2nd, 1932, Kathleen, *d* of Harold Bulmer, Great Ayton, North Yorks; one *s. Educ:* Middlesbrough High Sch. Chartered Accountant (not in practice since 1935); Industrial Man., Welwyn Garden City Ltd, 1936-41; Board of Trade (Dir for Industrial Estates in the Development Areas, 1945-48), 1941-48; Chm., North Eastern Trading Estates Ltd, 1948-60. Mem. Peterlee (New Town) Development Corp., 1950-59; Mem. Exec. Council, NE Industrial and Development Assoc., 1952-61, and Vice-Pres., 1957-61; Mem., Northern Economic Planning, 1965-69. Pres., National Assoc. for Advancement of Education for Commerce, 1954. Mem. Appointments Board, Universities of Newcastle and Durham, 1955-; Mem. Newcastle Regional Hospital Board, 1959-62; Chm. North of England Industrial Health Service, 1959-; Mem. Northern Adv. Cttee for Civil Aviation, 1964-; Chm., Tyneside Productivity Assoc., 1966-. Pres., NE Div., YMCA, 1969-. Comdr Order of St Olav, 1962. *Publications:* Location of Industry Policy in Britain (for ECSC), 1965; numerous articles on industrial estates. *Recreations:* gardening, swimming, travel. *Address:* Welwyn Cottage, 29 Osbaldeston Gardens, Newcastle upon Tyne NE3 4JE. *T:* Gosforth 858485.

**FORSTER, Walter Leslie,** CBE 1942; Legion of Merit (USA), 1944; BSc; FInstPet; Director: Petrofina Canada Ltd; Gen Star Ltd, and other cos; *b* 30 June 1903; *s* of John Mark Forster, Leeds; *m* 1936, Lorna, *d* of T. L. Bonstow, Coulsdon, Surrey; one *s. Educ:* Leeds Univ. *Address:* 61 Summit Crescent, Westmount, Montreal, Canada. *Clubs:* University, St James's, Mount Royal, Montreal (Montreal).

**FORSYTH, William Douglass,** OBE 1955; Australian Ambassador to Lebanon, 1967-68; *b* Casterton, Australia, 5 Jan. 1909; of Australian parents; *m* 1935, Thelma Joyce (*née* Sherry); one *s* two *d. Educ:* Ballarat High Sch.; Melbourne Univ. (MA, DipEd); Balliol Coll., Oxford (BLitt). Teacher of History, 1931-35; Rockefeller Fellow, Social Studies, Europe, 1936-37 and 1939; Research Fellow, Melbourne Univ., 1940; Editor Austral-Asiatic Bulletin, Melbourne, 1940; Research Sec., Aust. Inst. International Affairs, 1940-41; Australian Dept of Information, 1941-42; Australian Dept of External Affairs, 1942-: First Sec., 1946; Counsellor, Aust. Embassy, Washington, 1947-48; Aust. rep. Trusteeship Council, 1948 and 1952-55; Sec.-Gen., South Pacific Commission, 1948-51. Australian Member UN Population Commission, 1946-47; Mem., Australian Delegns to UN General Assembly, 1946-48 and 1951-58; San Francisco UN Confs, 1945 and 1955; Minister, Australian Mission to UN, 1951-55; Asst-Sec., Dept of External Affairs, Canberra, 1956-59, 1961-63; Australian Minister to Laos, 1959-60; Australian Ambassador to Viet-Nam, 1959-61; Sec.-Gen., South Pacific Commn, Nouméa, 1963-66. *Publications:* Governor Arthur's Convict System, 1935; The Myth of Open Spaces, 1942; Captain Cook's Australian Landfalls, 1970; articles in Economic Record, etc. *Address:* 88 Banks Street, Yarralumla, Canberra, ACT 2600, Australia. *Club:* Commonwealth (Canberra).

**FORT, Mrs Jean;** Headmistress of Roedean School, Brighton, 1961-70; *b* 1915; *d* of G. B. Rae; *m* 1943, Richard Fort (*d* 1959), MP Clitheroe Division of Lancs; four *s* one *d. Educ:* Benenden Sch.; Lady Margaret Hall, Oxford (MA, DipEd). Asst Mistress, Dartford County Sch. for Girls, 1937-39; WVS Headquarters staff, 1939-40; Junior Civil Asst, War Office, 1940-41; Personal Asst to Sir Ernest Gowers, Sen. Regional Comr for Civil Def., London, 1941-44. Mem., Advertising Standards Authority, 1965-. *Address:* Ruscombe House, Twyford, near Reading, Berks.

**FORTE, Sir Charles,** Kt 1970; FRSA; Chairman: Forte's & Co. Ltd; Forte's (Holdings) Ltd; Deputy Chairman, Trust Houses Forte Ltd, since 1970; *b* 26 Nov. 1908; *m* 1943, Irene Mary Chierico; one *s* five *d. Educ:* Alloa Academy; Dumfries Coll.; Maminni, Rome. Fellow and Mem. Exec. Cttee, Catering Inst., 1949; Mem. Small Consultative Advisory Cttee to Min. of Food, 1946; Pres. Italian Chamber of Commerce for Great Britain and Ireland, 1952; Mem. Council: BTA; London Tourist Board. Hon. Consul Gen. for Republic of San Marino. Grand Officier, Ordine al Merito della Repubblica Italiana; Cavaliere di Gran Croce della Repubblica Italiana. *Publications:* articles for catering trade papers. *Recreations:* golf, fishing, shooting, fencing, music. *Address:* Chester House, Upper Belgrave Street, SW1. *Clubs:* Royal Automobile, Arts; National Sporting (President).

**FORTES, Prof. Meyer,** MA, PhD; FBA 1967; William Wyse Professor of Social Anthropology, University of Cambridge, since 1950; Fellow of King's College; *b* Britstown, Cape, 25 April 1906; *e s* of late Nathan and late Mrs Bertha Fortes, Cape Town, S Africa; *m* 1928, Sonia (*d* 1956), *d* of late N Donen, Worcester, Cape, SA; one *d*; *m* 1960, Doris Y. Mayer, MD, *d* of late D. S. Yankauer, NY. *Educ:* South African Coll. High Sch., Cape Town; University of Cape Town; University of London. Univ. of Cape Town: Roderick Noble Schol., 1926, Willem Hiddingh Schol., 1927-30; London Sch. of Economics: Ratan Tata Student, 1930-31, Rockefeller Fellow, 1933-34; Fellow, International African Institute, 1934-38; Lectr, LSE, 1938-39; Research Lectr, University of Oxford, 1939-41; National Service, West Africa, 1942-44; Head of Sociological Dept, West African Insitute, Accra, Gold Coast, 1944-46; Reader in Social Anthropology, Oxford, 1946-50; Josiah Mason Lecturer, University of Birmingham, 1949; Rivers Medal, Royal Anthropological Institute, 1946; Pres. Section H, Brit. Assoc. for the Advancement of Science, 1953; Frazer Lectr, Glasgow, 1956; Henry Myers Lectr, Royal Anthrop. Inst., 1960; Lewis Henry Morgan Lectr, Univ. of Rochester, USA, 1963. Foreign Hon. Mem. Amer. Acad. of Arts and Sciences, 1964. Field Research: Northern Territories, Gold Coast, 1934-37; Nigeria, 1941-42; Ashanti Gold Coast, 1945-46;

Bechuanaland, 1948. Pres., Royal Anthropological Institute; Hon. Editor, Jl Royal Anthropological Inst., 1947-53; Mem. Exec. Council, International African Institute; Mem. Exec. Cttee, British Sociological Assoc., 1952-55. Visiting Prof., Chicago Univ., 1954. Fellow, Center for Advanced Study in Behavioral Science, Stanford, 1958-59, and 1967-68. *Publications:* The Dynamics of Clanship among the Tallensi, 1945; The Web of Kinship among the Tallensi, 1949; Social Anthropology at Cambridge since 1900, 1953; Oedipus and Job in West African Religion, 1959; Kinship and the Social Order, 1969; various papers in psychological and anthropological journals. *Address:* King's College, Cambridge.

**FORTESCUE,** family name of **Earl Fortescue.**

**FORTESCUE,** 6th Earl *cr* 1789; **Denzil George Fortescue,** MC 1918; TD; Viscount Ebrington, 1789; Baron Fortescue, 1751; *b* 13 June 1893; *s* of 4th Earl Fortescue, KCB, TD, and Hon. Emily Ormsby Gore, *d* of 2nd Baron Harlech; *S* brother 1958; *m* 1st, 1920, Marjorie (*d* 1964), OBE, *d* of late Col C. W. Trotter, CB, TD, and of Hon. Mrs Trotter, OBE; two *s* one *d*; 2nd, 1941, Sybil, *d* of 3rd Viscount Hardinge, CB; one *s*. *Educ:* Eton; New Coll., Oxford (MA). 2nd Lieut, Royal North Devon Hussars, 1913; Lieut-Col 96th Royal Devon Yeo. Regt, RA, 1935-41; Lieut-Col 1st Heavy Regt, RA, 1942-44. *Heir: s* Viscount Ebrington, *qv*. *Address:* Ebrington Manor, Chipping Campden, Glos. *T:* Paxford 230; 40 Cranmer Court, Sloane Avenue, SW3. *T:* 01-584 6199. *Club:* Boodle's.

**FORTESCUE, Trevor Victor Norman;** MP (C) Liverpool Garston since 1966; an Assistant Government Whip, since 1970; *b* 28 Aug. 1916; *s* of Frank Fortescue; *m* 1939, Margery Stratford, *d* of Dr G. H. Hunt; two *s* one *d*. *Educ:* Uppingham Sch.; King's Coll., Cambridge. BA 1938; MA 1945. Colonial Administrative Service, Hong Kong, 1939-47 and Kenya, 1949-51 (interned, 1941-45); FAO, UN, Washington, DC, 1947-49 and Rome, 1951-54; Chief Marketing Officer, Milk Marketing Bd of England and Wales, 1954-59; Manager, Nestlé Gp of Cos, Vevey, Switz., 1959-63 and London, 1963-66. *Recreations:* golf, Napoleon. *Address:* 20 Upbrook Mews, W2. *T:* 01-262 2383; 1a Park Avenue, Liverpool 8. *T:* 051-724 4749. *Club:* Racquet (Liverpool).

**FORTEVIOT,** 3rd Baron *cr* 1916; **Henry Evelyn Alexander Dewar,** Bt, *cr* 1907; MBE 1943; DL; Chairman John Dewar & Sons Ltd, since 1954; Director, Distillers Co. Ltd; *b* 23 Feb. 1906; 2nd *s* of 1st Baron Forteviot and Margaret Elizabeth, *d* of late Henry Holland; *S* half-brother 1947; *m* 1933, Cynthia Monica, *e d* of late Cecil Starkie, Hethe Place, Cowden, Kent; two *s* two *d*. *Educ:* Eton; St John's Coll., Oxford (BA). Served War of 1939-45, with Black Watch (RHR) (MBE). DL Perth, 1961. *Heir: s* Hon. John James Evelyn Dewar [*b* 5 April 1938; *m* 1963, Lady Elisabeth Waldegrave, 3rd *d* of 12th Earl Waldegrave, *qv*; three *d*]. *Address:* Dupplin Castle, Perth, Perthshire. *Club:* Brooks's; Royal (Perth).
*See also Duke of Fife.*

**FORTIER, Most Rev. John Mary;** *see* Sherbrooke, Archbishop of, (RC).

**FORTUNE, Allan Stewart,** CBE 1956; TD 1935; Chief Inspector, Department of Agriculture for Scotland, 1951-60; *b* 22 Sept. 1895; *s* of Allan Fortune, JP, Portsoy, Banffshire, Scotland, and Agnes Ballantyne Stewart, Meiklerig, East Lothian; *m* 1926, Margaret Donaldson, *d* of Thomas Smith, Blackpark, Stranraer; one *d*. *Educ:* Fordyce Academy, Banffshire; Edinburgh Univ. BSc (Agric.) Edinburgh, 1922. Dept of Agric. for Scotland: Inspector, 1922; Chief Inspector, 1951. Army Service: The Gordon Highlanders, 1914-36; commanded 6th Bn The Gordon Highlanders, 1931-36; retired with rank of Lt-Col-Bt-Col 1936; Reserve of Officers, TA, 1936-39. *Address:* 23 Hillpark Avenue, Edinburgh 4. *T:* 031-336 4150.

**FORTY, Francis John,** OBE 1952; BSc, FICE, FSA, FRSH, FIMunE; City Engineer, Corporation of London, 1938-64; *b* Hull, Yorks, 11 Feb. 1900; *s* of J. E. Forty, MA Oxon, headmaster, Hull Grammar Sch., and Maud C. Forty; *m* 1st, 1926, Doris Marcon Francis (*d* 1958), *d* of Dr A. G. Francis, BA Cantab, FRCS; one *s* two *d*; 2nd, 1965, Elizabeth Joyce Tofield. *Educ:* Hymers Coll., Hull; Glasgow Univ. (BSc 1923). RNAS, RAF, 1918-19 (Commnd Pilot). Engineering Asst, Hull; Engineering Asst, York; Chief Engineering Asst, Willesden. Deputy Borough Surveyor, Ealing; Borough Engineer and Surveyor, Ealing, 1934-38. Works include: (with Sir Albert Richardson) St Paul's Garden, 1951; (in consultation with Prof. W. F. Grimes) exposure and preservation of section of Town Wall of London, 1951-53; London Wall new route between Moorgate and Aldersgate Street, with car park underneath, 1959; Blackfriars Bridgehead Improvement with underpass, 1962-; multi-storey car park, Upper Thames Street, 1962; (with Sir Hugh Casson) Walbrook Wharf Public Cleansing Depot and Wharf 1963. Formerly Member: London Regional Bldg Cttee; Nat. Soc. for Clean Air; Roman and Mediaeval London Excavation Council; Festival of Britain Council for Architecture, Town Planning and Bldg Research; Minister of Transport's Parking Survey Cttee for Inner London; Minister of Housing and Local Govt's Thames Flooding Technical Panel; Sussex Archaeological Trust. Liveryman of the Worshipful Company of Painter-Stainers, of the City of London. *Publications:* Bituminous Emulsions for Use in Road Works (with F. Wilkinson), 1932; Swimming Bath Water Purification from a Public Health Point of View (with F. W. Wilkinson), various contribs technical and other jls; notably contrib. on exposure and preservation of Roman and Mediæval work in the Town Wall of London. *Recreations:* gardening, photography, reading. *Address:* Little Oakley, Wilmington, near Polegate, Sussex. *T:* Alfriston 268. *Club:* Athenæum.

**FORWOOD, Sir Dudley (Richard),** 3rd Bt *cr* 1895; Member of Lloyd's; *b* 6 June 1912; *s* of Sir Dudley Baines Forwood, 2nd Bt, CMG, and Norah Isabella (*née* Lockett) (*d* 1962); *S* father, 1961; *m* 1952, Mary Gwendoline (who *m* 1st, Viscount Ratendone, now Marquis of Willingdon; 2nd, Robert Cullingford), *d* of Basil S. Foster. *Educ:* Stowe Sch. Attaché, British Legation, Vienna, 1934-37; Equerry to the Duke of Windsor, 1937-39. Served War of 1939-45, Scots Guards (Major). Master, New forest Buckhounds, 1956-65. *Recreation:* hunting. *Heir: cousin* Peter Noel Forwood [*b* 1925; *m* 1950, Roy Murphy; six *d*]. *Address:* 43 Addison Road, W14. *T:* 01-603 3620; The Old House, Burley, near Ringwood, Hants. *T:* Burley 2345.

**FOSKETT, Rt. Rev. Reginald,** PhD, MA; *b* 1909; *o s* of A. E. and E. E. Foskett, Retford, Notts; *m* 1937, *o d* of Lt-Col J. W. C. and M. A. Kirk, Gedling, Notts; two *d*. *Educ:* Derby School; Keble College, Oxford; Cuddesdon College, Oxford. BA 2nd Class Hons Theol. 1931, MA 1935, Oxon; PhD Nottingham, 1957. Deacon,

1932; Priest, 1933; Curate of All Hallow's, Gedling, 1932-35; Curate of Mansfield, 1935-37; Curate in charge, Rainworth Conventional Dist, 1937-43; Rector of Ordsall, Notts, 1943-47; Surrogate, 1943-47 and 1948-57; Lecturer Notts County Training Coll. for Teachers, 1946-50; Vicar of Ilkeston, Derbys, 1948-57; Rural Dean of Ilkeston, 1950-57; Hon. Canon of Derby Cathedral, 1954-57; Exam. Chap. to Bp of Derby, 1954-57; Provost of St Mary's Cathedral, Edinburgh, 1957-67; Examining Chaplain to the Bishop of Edinburgh, 1959-67; Bishop Suffragan of Penrith, 1967-70. *Publications:* Some Scottish Links with the American Episcopal Church 1685-1785, 1962; (ed) The Zambesi Journal of Dr John Kirk, 1964; Zambesi Doctors (correspondence of Dr David Livingstone and Dr John Kirk), 1964. *Recreations:* reading and research. *Address:* The Old Vicarage, Field Broughton, Grange-over-Sands, Lancashire. *T:* Cartmel 414. *Clubs:* Overseas; County Club (Carlisle).

**FOSTER;** *see* Hylton-Foster.

**FOSTER, Sir (Albert) Ridgeby,** Kt 1964; Hon. Adviser to India, Pakistan, Burma Association since 1964; *b* 12 June 1907; *s* of Albert John Foster; *m* 1937, Nancy Leigh; two *s. Educ:* Reading Sch.; Reading and Cambridge Univs; Imperial College of Tropical Agriculture, Trinidad. Imperial Chemical Industries (India) Ltd, 1933-64; Chairman, ICI (India), and associated companies, Alkali & Chemical Corp. of India, Indian Explosives, Atic Industries, Chemicals & Fibres of India, 1961-64. Past Pres., Bengal Chamber of Commerce and Industry and of Associated Chambers of Commerce of India. Governor, India Institute of Technology, Delhi and Doon Sch. *Recreations:* shooting, photography. *Address:* Symnells, Aldington, Kent. *Clubs:* Oriental; Bengal, Royal Calcutta Turf, Tollygunge (Calcutta).

**FOSTER, Prof. Allan (Bentham);** Professor of Chemistry, University of London, since 1966; Head of Department of Chemistry, Chester Beatty Research Institute, Institute of Cancer Research: Royal Cancer Hospital, since 1966; *b* 21 July 1926; *s* of late Herbert and Martha Alice Foster; *m* 1949, Monica Binns; two *s. Educ:* Nelson Grammar Sch., Lancs; University of Birmingham. Frankland Medal and Prize, 1947; PhD, 1950; DSc, 1957. University Res. Fellow, University of Birmingham, 1950-53; Fellow of Rockefeller Foundn, Ohio State Univ., 1953-54; University of Birmingham: ICI Res. Fellow, 1954-55; Lectr, 1955-62; Sen. Lectr, 1962-64; Reader in Organic Chemistry, 1964-66. FChemSoc (Mem. Coun., 1962-65, 1967-); FRIC; MACS; Mem. Cttee of Management, Inst. of Cancer Res.; Regional Editor, Carbohydrate Research. *Publications:* numerous scientific papers mainly in Jl Chem. Soc. and Carbohydrate Research. *Recreations:* golf, gardening, foreign travel. *Address:* Chester Beatty Research Institute, Institute of Cancer Research: Royal Cancer Hospital, Fulham Road, SW3. *T:* 01-352 8133. *Club:* Banstead Downs.

**FOSTER, Rev. Canon Charles,** PhD, BSc (London), MA (Bristol); Senior Lecturer in Divinity, King Alfred's College, Winchester, since 1968; Canon Emeritus, Portsmouth Cathedral, since 1968; *b* Willesden, 29 Sept. 1907; *o c* of Chas S. Foster, schoolmaster, and Gertrude Baker; *m* 1932, Marian Constance Mills, *y d* of Frederick Mills and Sarah Eleanor Marshall, Wednesfield, Staffs; one *s. Educ:* Latymer Upper Sch., Hammersmith; King's Coll., London; Bristol Univ.; St Augustine's Coll., Canterbury. First degree Physics and Maths, research degrees in Education. Asst Master, Midsomer Norton County Sch., 1931-35; Aylesbury Grammar Sch., 1936-41; Acting Headmaster, Royal Latin Sch., Buckingham, 1942-45; HM Inspector of Schs, 1946-54; Asst Curate, St Mary's, Alverstoke, 1955-59; Hon. Canon of Portsmouth, 1959-64; Canon Residentiary of Portsmouth Cathedral, 1964-68 and Diocesan Dir of Religious Education, 1959-68. *Publications:* articles on science teaching, education and religion. *Recreations:* gardening, collecting porcelain douters. *Address:* Four Winds, Sleepers Hill, Winchester, Hants. *T:* Winchester 5381.

**FOSTER, Christopher David,** MA; Head of the Unit for Research in Urban Economics, LSE, since 1970; *b* 30 Oct. 1930; *s* of George Cecil Foster; *m* 1958, Kay Sheridan Bullock; two *s* three *d. Educ:* Merchant Taylors' Sch.; King's Coll., Cambridge (Scholar). Economics Tripos 1954; MA 1959. Hallsworth Research Fellow, Manchester Univ., 1957-59; Senior Research Fellow, Jesus Coll., Oxford, 1959-64; Official Fellow and Tutor, Jesus Coll., 1964-66; Dir-Gen. of Economic Planning, MoT, 1966-70. Governor, Centre for Environmental Studies, 1967-70. Vis. Prof. of Economics, MIT, 1970. *Publications:* The Transport Problem, 1963; papers in various economic and other journals. *Address:* 59 Elsham Road, W14. *T:* 01-602 1027. *Club:* Reform.

**FOSTER, E(rnest) Marshall;** Taxing Master of the Supreme Court, 1952-70; *b* 6 Sept. 1907; *s* of Ernest Henry Foster, JP, The Rookery, Horsforth, near Leeds; *m* 1941, Mrs Stella Stones, Headingley, Leeds; one step *s. Educ:* Clifton Coll.; Hertford Coll. (Exhibitioner), Oxford (BA). 2nd Cl. Hons Hon. Mods and Final Honour Sch. of Jurisprudence; Solicitor (Hons) 1933; Partner in firm of W. J. Cousins Fletcher & Foster, solicitors, Leeds, 1933-43. Mem. of Management Cttee, Hospital for Women, Leeds, 1935-45; Sec. Yorks Regional Council, Nuffield Provincial Hosps Trust, 1941-45. County Court Registrar and District Registrar of the High Court: Leeds, Barnsley and Pontefract, 1943-45; Cambridge group, 1945-51. Registrar, Willesden County Court, 1951. Hon. Pres., British Limbless Ex-servicemen's Assoc., Cambridge, 1947-51. Mem. of Herbert Cttee on hours of work in the Law Courts, 1952-53. *Address:* Flat 1, 1 Palace Gate, Kensington, W8. *T:* 01-584 8947. *Clubs:* National Liberal, Kennel.

**FOSTER, F(ermian) Le Neve;** *b* 3 Feb. 1888; *s* of late Herbert Le Neve Foster, Great Barr, Staffs; *m* 1915, Katie May Dorothy (*d* 1968), *d* of late C. W. Troughton, Blackheath, SE; three *s* (and two *s* decd). *Educ:* Shrewsbury. Admitted a Solicitor, 1910; Travers-Smith Law Scholar, 1910. Served European War, 1914-18, Capt. Inns of Court OTC (TA). Partner in Warren Murton & Co., Solicitors, 1919-53; Director: Industrial Public Companies, 1926-; Stanton Ironworks Co. Ltd, 1936-62; Crompton Parkinson Ltd, 1938-46; Stewarts & Lloyds Ltd, 1941-67; Chairman: British Van Heusen Co. Ltd, 1952-58; Smith's Potato Crisps Ltd, 1952-63; Smith's Potato Estates Ltd, 1952-66; Chm. (1926-61) and Man. Dir or Joint Man. Dir (1940-56), Davis & Timmins Ltd. A Governor of Shrewsbury Sch., 1952-65. *Recreations:* fishing and bridge. *Address:* Farlands, Chalfont St Giles, Bucks. *T:* Chalfont St Giles 2156.

**FOSTER, Francis;** *see* Foster, Major R. F.

**FOSTER, Geoffrey Norman;** Director of Companies; *b* 16 Oct. 1884; *s* of Rev. Henry Foster and Sophia M. Harper; *m* 1915, Vera H.

Prest; one *s* one *d. Educ:* Malvern Coll.; Worcester Coll., Oxford. Retired; represented Oxford *v* Cambridge at cricket, 1905-6-7-8, Association football, 1905-6-7-8, golf, 1906-7, raquets, 1906-7-8; has played representative football and cricket; Sec. of the Corinthians FC, 1919-24. *Publications:* contributor to papers on sporting matters. *Recreations:* all games and gardening. *Address:* 63 Chesterfield House, W1.

**FOSTER, George Arthur C.;** *see* Carey-Foster.

**FOSTER, Idris Llewelyn,** MA Wales and Oxon; FSA; Jesus Professor of Celtic in the University of Oxford and Fellow of Jesus College since 1947; Member Royal Commssion on Ancient Monuments in Wales and Monmouthshire; Treasurer, National Library of Wales, since 1964; Member Standing Commssion on Museums and Galleries; *b* 23 July 1911; *e s* of Harold L. Foster and Ann J. (Roberts), Carneddi, near Bangor, Caerns; unmarried. *Educ:* County Sch., Bethesda; University Coll. of North Wales, Bangor; National Univ. of Ireland, Dublin. BA (Wales) with First Class Hons, 1932; University Research Student, 1933-35; MA (Wales) with distinction, 1935; Fellow of University of Wales, 1935; Head of Dept of Celtic, University of Liverpool, 1936-47; Warden of Derby Hall, University of Liverpool, 1946-47; served in Intelligence Div., Naval Staff, Admiralty, 1942-45; Sir John Rhys Memorial Lectr, Br. Acad., 1950; O'Donnell Lectr, Univ. of Edinburgh, 1960; President: Soc. for Study of Mediæval Languages and Literature, 1953-58; Cambrian Archaeological Assoc., 1968-69; Vice-Chm., Council of Nat. Eisteddfod of Wales. Hon. Treasurer, Irish Texts Soc; Hon. Editor, Trans and publications, Cymmrodorian Soc. *Publications:* (ed with L. Alcock) Culture and Environment, 1963; (ed with Glyn Daniel) Prehistoric and Early Wales, 1965; papers and reviews. *Recreation:* music. *Address:* Jesus College, Oxford; Cae'ronnen, Bethesda, near Bangor, Caerns. *Club:* Athenæum.

**FOSTER, Rev. Prof. John,** DD; Professor of Ecclesiastical History, University of Glasgow, 1949, Emeritus, 1969; Dean, Faculty of Divinity, 1957-60; *b* 2 Oct. 1898; *s* of Bateman and Kate Foster, Bradford, Yorks; *m* 1926, Amy Dorothy Whittaker; two *s* one *d. Educ:* Bradford Grammar Sch.; Birmingham Univ.; Handsworth Theological Coll. RNVR, 1917-19: active service in armed trawlers in Home Waters. Ordained to ministry of Methodist Church, 1922, and to S China under Methodist Missionary Soc; Prof. of Church History: Union Theological Coll., Canton, 1926-37; Selly Oak Colleges, Birmingham, 1937-47. Delegate to Internat. Missionary Council, Madras, 1938, and Willingen, 1952; Consultant at First Assembly, World Council of Churches, Amsterdam, 1948. Examr to University of Wales, 1948-52, of Aberdeen, 1951-54, and of St Andrews, 1957-61; Visiting Prof., theol colls of India, 1954, and Nigeria, 1965. Frequent broadcaster, 1943-, and on TV, 1956-. Hon. DD Aberdeen, 1945. *Publications:* books on China, 1928-39; Then and Now, the Historic Church and the Younger Churches, 1942; After the Apostles, 1952; Beginning from Jerusalem, 1956; To All Nations, 1960; Five Minutes a Saint, 1964; They Converted our Ancestors, 1965; Men of Vision, 1965; God has no Favourites, 1968. *Recreation:* the countryside. *Address:* The Old Quarry, Kilcreggan, Dunbartonshire.

**FOSTER, John Frederick,** CMG 1964; Secretary-General, Association of Commonwealth Universities, London, 1964-70 (Secretary, Association of Universities of the British Commonwealth, 1947-64); *b* 28 March 1903; *s* of Frederick W. and Annie Foster, Melbourne, Vic.; *m* 1st, 1934, Winifred Betty Bedggood (*d* 1967); one *s* two *d*; 2nd, 1968, Margaret Sarah Bate, Vice-Principal, St Gabriel's Coll. of Educn, London. *Educ:* Wesley Coll., Melbourne; Queen's Coll., Univ. of Melbourne; London Sch. of Economics, MA, LLM (Melbourne) 1925; called to Victorian Bar, 1928; Vice-Master, Queen's Coll., Melbourne, 1928-34; Registrar, Univ. of Melbourne, 1937-47; Secretary: Australian Vice-Chancellor's Cttee, 1936-47; Cttee of Vice-Chancellors and Principals of Univs of UK, 1947-64. Exec. Sec., Marshall Aid Commemoration Commn, 1953-70; Sec., Commonwealth Scholarship Commn in the UK, 1959-70. Mem., Commonwealth Educn Confs, 1959 (Oxford), 1961 (New Delhi), and 1968 (Lagos); Sec., Kennedy Memorial Trust, 1966-70. MRI; Freeman, Drapers' Co. and of City of London; Trustee, British Inst. in Paris. Hon. LLD, Laval Univ., Quebec, 1949; Hon. MA, Oxford, 1953; Hon. DSc, Salford, 1969. *Publications:* Editor, Commonwealth Universities Yearbook, 1947-62; Joint Editor, 1963-70. *Recreations:* gardening, photography. *Address:* Farthingale, Worlingworth, near Woodbridge, Suffolk; 21 Mecklenburgh Square, WC1N 2AD. *T:* 01-837 4033. *Clubs:* Athenæum, Royal Commonwealth Society; Melbourne Cricket.

**FOSTER, Sir John (Galway),** KBE 1964; QC 1950; MP (C) Northwich Division of Cheshire since 1945; Barrister-at-Law; *s* of late General Hubert John Foster. *Educ:* Eton; New Coll., Oxford. Fellow of All Souls, 1924; Lectr in Private International Law, Oxford, 1934-39; First Sec., British Embassy, Washington, 1939; Brigadier, General Service, 1944. Recorder of Dudley, 1936-38; Recorder of Oxford, 1938-51 and 1956-64. Parliamentary Under-Secretary of State, CRO, 1951-Oct. 1954. Legion of Honour; American Legion of Merit; Croix de Guerre. *Publications:* lectures and articles on constitutional and private international law. *Address:* Parsonage House, Stanton Harcourt, Oxon. *T:* Standlake 231. *Clubs:* Brooks's, Pratt's, Carlton.

**FOSTER, Sir John (Gregory),** 3rd Bt *cr* 1930; Consultant Physician, George, Cape Province; *b* 26 Feb. 1927; *s* of Sir Thomas Saxby Gregory Foster, 2nd Bt, and Beryl, *d* of late Dr Alfred Ireland; *S* father, 1957; *m* 1956, Jean Millicent Watts; one *s* three *d. Educ:* Michaelhouse Coll., Natal. South African Artillery, 1944-46; Witwatersrand Univ., 1946-51; MB, BCh 1951; Post-graduate course, MRCPE 1955; Medical Registrar, 1955-56; Medical Officer, Cape Town, 1957. DIH London, 1962. *Recreation:* outdoor sport. *Heir: s* Saxby Gregory Foster, *b* 3 Sept. 1957. *Address:* 122 York Street, George, Cape Province, South Africa. *T:* George 3251. *Club:* Johannesburg Country (S Africa).

**FOSTER, Very Rev. John William,** BEM 1946; Dean of Hong Kong since 1963; *b* 5 Aug. 1921; *m* 1943, Nancy Margaret Allen; one *s. Educ:* St Aidan's Coll., Birkenhead. Served Leicestershire Yeomanry, 1939-46; Chaplain, Hong Kong Defence Force, 1958-. Reserve of Officers, Hong Kong Defence Force, 1967-. Priest 1955; Curate of Loughborough, 1954-57; Chaplain, St John's Cathedral, Hong Kong, 1957-60, Precentor, 1960-63. *Address:* St John's Cathedral, Hong Kong.

**FOSTER, Leslie Thomas,** CB 1966; *b* 24 Sept. 1905; *e s* of Thomas Henry and Elizabeth Foster; *m* 1933, Winifred Marie, *d* of Henry Stinchcombe. *Educ:* Reading Sch. Entered

Office of Comr of Police of the Metropolis, 1930; Private Sec. to Comr (Air Vice-Marshal Sir Philip Game), 1940-41; transferred to Min. of Works, 1942, Principal, 1946; Asst Sec., 1952. Under-Sec., 1958; Dir of Establishments, Ministry of Public Building and Works, 1964-67. *Address:* 11 Waldens Park Road, Horsell, Woking, Surrey. *T:* Woking 2777. *Club:* Devonshire.

**FOSTER, Maj.-Gen. Norman Leslie,** CB 1961; DSO 1945; Director of Security (Army), Ministry of Defence, since 1965; *b* 26 Aug. 1909; *s* of late Col A. L. Foster, Wimbledon; *m* 1937, Joan Constance, *d* of late Canon T. W. E. Drury; two *s*. *Educ:* Westminster; RMA Woolwich. 2nd Lieut, RA, 1929; Served War of 1939-45 in Egypt and Italy; CRA 11th Armoured Division, 1955-56; Deputy Military Sec., War Office, 1958-59; Maj.-Gen., 1959; GOC Royal Nigerian Army, 1959-62; Pres., Regular Commissions Board, 1962-65; retired, 1965. Col Comdt, Royal Regt of Artillery, 1966-. *Address:* Besborough, Heath End, Farnham, Surrey. *Club:* Army and Navy.

**FOSTER, Hon. Sir Peter Harry Batson Woodroffe,** Kt 1969; MBE 1943; TD 1946; QC 1957; **Hon. Mr Justice Foster;** a Judge of the Chancery Division of the High Court of Justice since 1969; *b* 5 Dec. 1912; *s* of late Frank Foster; *m* 1937, Jane Hillcoat Easdale, *d* of late James Easdale, Troon, Ayrshire; one *s* three *d*. *Educ:* Rugby Sch.; Corpus Christi Coll., Cambridge (BA, LLB). Called to the Bar, Inner Temple, 1936; Bencher, Lincoln's Inn, 1963. Fife and Forfar Yeomanry, 1939; War of 1939-45: Dunkirk, 8th Armd Div., Alamein, Tripoli, Col, 21 Army Group, North Western Europe (despatches thrice, MBE). Resumed practice, 1945. Mem., Gen. Council of the Bar, 1956-60; Mem., Senate, 1966-69. Chm., Chancery Bar Assoc., 1963-68; formerly Member Council: Officers' Assoc.; Royal Albert Hall; Steward British Boxing Board of Control. Church Commissioner for England, 1965-69. Reserve Chm., Conscientious Objectors Tribunal, 1965-69; Chm., Performing Right Tribunal, 1969. *Recreations:* golf, tennis. *Address:* 70 Elizabeth Street, SW1. *T:* 01-730 1984; Otley Hall, Suffolk. *T:* Helmingham 264. *Clubs:* White's; Royal and Ancient Golf (St Andrews); Hawks (Cambridge).

**FOSTER, Peter Martin;** Counsellor and Consul-General, HM Embassy, Tel Aviv, since 1970; *b* 25 May 1924; *s* of Frederick Arthur Peace Foster and Marjorie Kathleen Sandford; *m* 1947, Angela Hope Cross; one *s* one *d*. *Educ:* Sherborne; Corpus Christi Coll., Cambridge. Army (Horse Guards), 1943-47; joined Foreign (now Diplomatic) Service, 1948; served in Vienna, Warsaw, Pretoria/Cape Town, Bonn, Kampala. *Recreations:* a diminishing number of common or garden pastimes of no special interest. *Address:* Rew Cottage, Abinger Lane, Abinger Common, Surrey. *T:* Dorking 740114.

**FOSTER, Major Reginald Francis;** IA officer, retired; priest and author (pen name, Francis Foster); *b* 13 April 1896; *s* of late B. H. Foster, Buxted, Sussex; *m* 1951, Joan Elizabeth, *d* of Sir A. Harold Bibby, 1st Bt; one *d*; (three *s* two *d* by former *m*). *Educ:* Sloane Sch., Chelsea; privately; Community of the Resurrection, Mirfield. Served in Artists' Rifles, 1915, and (with rank of Lieut) in East Lancs Regt in France, 1915-17; transferred to Indian Army, 1918; served (with rank of Capt.) in 70th Burma Rifles and 38th Dogras in India, Palestine and Egypt, 1918-21; Adjutant of 91st Punjabis, and served (with rank of Major) in Waziristan Campaigns of 1919-21, 1921-24; retired from Indian Army, 1923; entered journalism and authorship, 1924; Chief Literary Adviser, Elkin Mathews and Marrot Ltd, 1925-27. Received into 3rd Order of Friars Minor, 1927. Ordained priest in Syro-Chaldean Church, 1933. Superior of the Order of the Divine Mission, 1934-40. Returned to Army during national crisis, 1940, and joined Queen's Royal Regt; seconded to Provost Service in Jan. 1941, and given command of 55th Divisional Provost Company, Corps of Military Police; re-posted, after sustaining an injury, to Queen's Royal Regt, Dec. 1941; formed and assumed command of No. 1 Independent Company, Queen's Royal Regt, Oct. 1943; Commandant of invasion troops marshalling camps, Portsmouth and Winchester, 1944; retd with rank of Major. *Publications:* The Missing Gates, 1925; The Lift Murder, 1925; Anthony Ravenhill, 1926; How to Write Short Stories, 1926; The Captive King, 1927; The Trail of the Thugs, 1927; Confession, 1928; The Music Gallery Murder, 1928; The Secret Places, 1929; The Moat House Mystery, 1929; Murder from Beyond, 1930; The Dark Night, 1930; Joyous Pilgrimage, 1930; Something Wrong at Chillery, 1931; The Wayside Book (part author), 1932; Famous Short Stories Analysed, 1932; Separate Star (autobiography), 1938; Longshanks and I, 1939; The Island, 1946; The Ancient Way, 1949; Modern Punctuation Handbook, 1947; Desert Journey, 1965; contrib. Promise of Greatness (a Great War Symposium), 1968; The Perennial Religion, 1969; many short stories, essays, plays, etc. *Recreations:* philosophy, meteorology and drawing. *Address:* Charlwood Cottage, Ropley, Alresford, Hants.

**FOSTER, Sir Ridgeby;** *see* Foster, Sir A. R.

**FOSTER, Robert,** CBE 1963 (OBE 1949); General Manager, London Trustee Savings Bank, 1943-63, retired; *b* 4 March 1898; *s* of Robert Foster; *m* 1927, Edith Kathleen (*née* Blackburn); two *d*. *Educ:* Rutherford Coll., Newcastle upon Tyne. RNVR, 1915-19. Newcastle-on-Tyne Savings Bank, 1919-24; London Trustee Savings Banks, 1924-63; Mem. Nat. Savings Cttee, 1957-62. Dir, City & Metropolitan Building Soc. mem. Court, Worshipful Company of Plumbers, 1959- (Master, 1965). *Recreations:* golf, gardening. *Address:* Larchfield, Highercombe Road, Haslemere, Surrey. *T:* Haslemere 4353. *Club:* City Livery.

**FOSTER, Air Chief Marshal Sir Robert Mordaunt,** KCB 1950 (CB 1945); CBE 1944; DFC; DL; *b* 3 Sept. 1898; 3rd *s* of Col M. G. Foster; *m* 1940, Ruth Elliott, Broomswell, Suffolk; one *s* one *d*. *Educ:* Winchester. Joined Royal Flying Corps as pilot, June 1916; served in France, 1916-18 (despatches twice, DFC); India, 1919-23 (India Gen. Service Medal and 3 clasps); RAF Staff Coll., 1925-26; Iraq, 1926-32 (Gen. Service Medal and 2 clasps, Iraqi Campaign Medal). Served in Bomber Command, 1939-41; Near East, N Africa and Italy, 1941-45 (despatches, CBE, CB, Commander of Legion of Merit, USA); AOC Malta, 1944; AOC Desert Air Force, Italy, 1944-45; Chief of Air Div., Control Commn, Austria, 1945-46; AOC No 3 Group Bomber Comd, 1946-47; Asst Chief of Air Staff (Policy), 1947-49; AOC-in-C, Reserve Comd (now Home Command), 1949-51; C-in-C, 2nd (British) Tactical Air Force, 1951-53, 2nd Allied TAF, 1952-53; retired, 1954. DL Suffolk, 1968. *Recreations:* riding, shooting. *Club:* Royal Air Force.

**FOSTER, Sir Robert (Sidney),** GCMG 1970 (KCMG 1964; CMG 1961); KCVO 1970;

Governor-General of Fiji, since 1970 (Governor and C-in-C, 1968-70); *b* 11 Aug. 1913; *s* of Sidney Charles Foster and late Jessie Edith (*née* Fry); *m* 1947, Margaret (*née* Walker); no *c*. *Educ:* Eastbourne Coll.; Peterhouse, Cambridge. Appointed Cadet, Administrative Service, Northern Rhodesia, 1936; District Officer, N Rhodesia, 1938. War Service, 2nd Bn Northern Rhodesia Regt, 1940-43, Major. Provincial Commissioner, N Rhodesia, 1957; Sec., Ministry of Native Affairs, N Rhodesia, 1960; Chief Sec., Nyasaland, 1961-63; Dep. Governor, Nyasaland, 1963-64; High Comr for W Pacific, 1964-68. KStJ 1969. Officer of the Legion of Honour, 1966. *Recreation:* fishing. *Address:* Government House, Suva, Fiji. *Clubs:* Public Schools, Royal Commonwealth Society; Leander (Henley).

**FOSTER, Air Vice-Marshal William Foster MacNeece,** CB 1933; CBE 1922; DSO 1917; DFC 1918; MA Oxon (hon.), 1941; Deputy Lord Mayor of Oxford, 1967 (Lord Mayor, 1966); *b* 21 Aug. 1889; *e s* of Col T. F. MacNeece, Castle Cary, Co. Donegal; *m* 1928, Jean, *d* of Ralph W. Bruce, Langtons, South Weald, Essex: two *d*. *Educ:* Cheltenham Coll.; Sandhurst. Served European War, 1914-18, promoted Lieut-Col RFC, Dec. 1916 (wounded, despatches, DSO, DFC); Chief Staff Officer Royal Air Force in Iraq, March 1921-Oct. 1922 (CBE, Gen. Service Medal and clasp); British Air Representative to Council of League of Nations, 1926-29; commanded No. 1 Air Defence Group Headquarters, 1929-34; retired list, 1937; British Commission for Exchange of Prisoners in Spain, 1938-39; Air Officer Commanding No. 6 Group RAF, 1939; Dep. Head of RAF Delegation, Washington, April 1942-Sept. 1943; Mem. of Combined Chiefs of Staff Cttee, Dec. 1942-May 1943; Head of Inter-Service Liaison Cttee, Washington, Oct. 1943-March 1944; Head of RAF Training Mission to China, Sept. 1944-April 1946; reverted to retired list Oct. 1946. Mem. Oxford City Council, 1950-. Sheriff of Oxford, 1963-64. Comdr of Legion of Merit (USA), Orders Cloud and Banner, and Loshu decoration (China). Assumed surname of Foster by Royal Licence, Aug. 1927. *Publications:* occasional verses in The Times, Spectator, etc, of which An Airman's Te Deum was printed in 1936 to music by Sir Walford Davies and in 1937 to music by Dr Martin Shaw. *Address:* 26 Northmoor Road, Oxford. *T:* 55588; The Corner House, Aldeburgh, Suffolk. *T:* 2568. *Clubs:* Army and Navy, Royal Air Force.

**FOSTER-BROWN, Rear-Adm. Roy Stephenson,** CB 1958; RN Retired; *b* 16 Jan. 1904; *s* of Robert Allen Brown and Agnes Wilfreda Stephenson; *m* 1933, Joan Wentworth Foster; two *s*. *Educ:* RNC, Osborne and Dartmouth. Specialised in Submarines, 1924-28; specialised in Signals, 1930. Fleet Signal Officer, Home Fleet, 1939-40; Staff Signal Officer, Western Approaches, 1940-44; Comdr HMS Ajax, 1944-46; Capt., 1946; Capt. Sixth Frigate Sqdn, 1951; Dir Signal Div., Admiralty, 1952-53; Capt. HMS Ceylon, 1954; Rear-Adm. 1955; Flag Officer, Gibraltar, 1956-59; retd 1959. *Recreations:* sailing, shooting, golf, tennis. *Club:* United Service.

**FOSTER-SUTTON, Sir Stafford William Powell,** KBE 1957 (OBE 1944); Kt 1951; CMG 1948; QC (Jamaica, 1938, Fedn Malaya, 1948); President, Pensions Appeal Tribunals for England and Wales, since 1958; *b* 24 Dec. 1898; *s* of late G. Foster Sutton and Mrs Foster Sutton; *m* 1919, Linda Dorothy, *d* of late John Humber Allwood, OBE, and of Mrs Allwood, Enfield, St Ann, Jamaica; one *d* (one *s* decd). *Educ:* St Mary Magdalen Sch.; private tutor. HM Army, 1914-26; served European War, 1914-18, Infantry, RFC and RAF, active service. Called to the Bar, Gray's Inn, 1926; private practice, 1926-36; Solicitor Gen., Jamaica, 1936; Attorney-Gen., Cyprus, 1940; Col Comdg Cyprus Volunteer Force and Inspector Cyprus Forces, 1941-44; Mem. for Law and Order and Attorney-Gen., Kenya, 1944-48; actg Governor, Aug. and Sept. 1947; Attorney-Gen., Malaya, 1948-50; Officer Administering Govt, Malaya, Sept., Dec. 1950; Chief Justice, Fedn of Malaya, 1950-51; Dir of Man-Power, Kenya, 1944-45; Chm. Labour Advisory Board, Kenya, and Kenya European Service Advisory Board, 1944-48; Pres. of the West African Court of Appeal, 1951-55; Chief Justice, Fedn of Nigeria, 1955-58; Actg Governor-Gen., Nigeria, May-June 1957. Chairman: Zanzibar Commn of Inquiry, 1961; Kenya Regional and Electorial Commns, 1962-; Referendum Observers, Malta, 1964. *Recreations:* tennis, golf. *Address:* 7 London Road, Saffron Walden, Essex. *Club:* East India and Sports.

**FOU TS'ONG;** concert pianist; *b* 10 March 1934; *m* 1960, Zarmira Menuhin (marr. diss. 1970); one *s*. *Educ:* Shanghai and Warsaw. Debut, Shanghai, 1953. Concerts all over Eastern Europe including USSR up to 1958. Arrived in Great Britain, Dec. 1958; London debut, Feb. 1959, followed by concerts in England, Scotland and Ireland; subsequently has toured all five Continents. *Recreations:* many different ones. *Address:* c/o Harold Holt Ltd, 124 Wigmore Street, W1.

**FOUCHÉ, Jacobus Johannes;** State President of the Republic of South Africa since 1968; *b* Wepener, OFS, 6 June 1898; *s* of late J. J. Fouché; *m* 1920, Letta Rhoda, *d* of late T. P. McDonald, Zastron, OFS; one *s*. *Educ:* Victoria Coll., Stellenbosch. MP for Smithfield, 1941-50 and for Bloemfontein West, 1960-68; Administrator of the OFS, 1951-59; Minister of Defence, 1959-66, of Agricultural Technical Services and of Water Affairs, 1966-68. DPhil (*hc*) Univ. of Stellenbosch, 1966. Hon. Col, Regt President Steyn, Bloemfontein. Freeman of several cities and towns in Republic of S Africa. *Recreation:* farming. *Address:* State President's Residence, Pretoria (or Cape Town), Republic of South Africa.

**FOULIS, Sir Ian P. L.;** *see* Liston-Foulis.

**FOULKES, Maj.-Gen. Thomas Herbert Fischer,** CB 1962; OBE 1945; civil engineering consultant; *b* 29 May 1908; *e s* of late Maj.-Gen. C. H. Foulkes, CB, CMG, DSO; *m* 1947, Delphine Elizabeth Smith; two *s*. *Educ:* Clifton Coll., Bristol; RMA Woolwich; St Catharine's Coll., Cambridge. BA 1930, MA Cantab 1954. Commissioned into RE, 1928; served in India and Burma, 1931-46 (CRE 39 Indian Div., also CRE 17 Indian Div. during Burma campaign); Comdr Corps RE (Brig.) 1 Br. Corps in BAOR, 1956-57; Chief Engr (Brig.) Middle East, 1957-58; Chief Engr (Brig.) Southern Command, UK, 1958-60; Engineer-in-Chief, War Office, 1960-63. Col Comdt, Royal Engineers, 1963-. Hon. Col, RE Resources Units, AER, 1964-67; Hon. Col, RE Volunteers (Sponsored Units), T & AVR, 1967-. Governor, Clifton Coll., 1964. Liveryman, Worshipful Co. of Plumbers of City of London, 1960. Pres., Instn of Royal Engrs; CEng, FICE. *Recreations:* shooting, travel, fishing, photography. *Address:* The Warren, Fitzroy Road, Fleet, Hants. *T:* Fleet (Hants) 6650. *Club:* United Service.

**FOURNIER, Pierre;** 'cellist; Officier Légion d'Honneur; *b* 24 June 1906; *m* 1936, Lydia Antik; one *s. Educ:* University and Conservatoire, Paris. Formerly teacher at the National Conservatoire, Paris. Concert soloist every season in the European Capitals as well as in USA, South America and Far East; also soloist playing with chief orchestras. *Address:* 14 Parc Château Banquet, Geneva, Switzerland.

**FOWDEN, Leslie,** FRS 1964; Professor of Plant Chemistry, and Dean of Faculty of Science, University College, London, WC1, since 1964; *b* Rochdale, Lancs, 13 Oct. 1925; *s* of Herbert and Amy D. Fowden; *m* 1949, Margaret Oakes; one *s* one *d. Educ:* University Coll., London. PhD Univ. of London, 1948. Scientific Staff of Human Nutrition Research Unit of the MRC, 1947-50; Lecturer in Plant Chemistry, University Coll., 1950-55, Reader, 1956-64. Rockefeller Fellow at Cornell Univ., 1955; Visiting Prof. at Univ. of California, 1963; Royal Society Visiting Prof., Univ. of Hong Kong, 1967. Mem. Advisory Board, Tropical Product Inst., 1966-70. *Publications:* contribs to scientific journals on topics in plant biochemistry. *Address:* 36a Douglas Road, Canonbury, N1. *T:* 01-226 6332.

**FOWKE, Sir Frederick (Woollaston Rawdon),** 4th Bt *cr* 1814; *b* 14 Dec. 1910; *e s* of Sir Frederick Ferrers Conant Fowke, 3rd Bt, and Edith Frances Daubeney (*d* 1958), *d* of late Canon J. H. Rawdon; *S* father, 1948; *m* 1948, Barbara, *d* of late E. Townsend; two *d. Educ:* Uppingham. Served War of 1939-45, in Derbs Yeomanry, 1939-43 (wounded). *Recreation:* shooting. *Heir: n* David Frederick Gustavus Fowke, *b* 28 Aug. 1950. *Address:* Lower Woolstone Farm, Bishops Tawton, Barnstaple, N Devon.

**FOWLE, Brig. John Le Clerc,** CB 1946; CIE 1943; *b* 13 Sept. 1893; *e s* of late Col Sir (Henry) Walter Hamilton Fowle, KBE; *m* 1932, Kathleen Sylvestre (Anne), Kaisar-i-Hind Medal (Silver), 1946, ROI 1968, Gold Medallist, Paris Salon, *d* of late Gerald Sichel, FRCS, Sevenoaks, Kent. Indian Army, 1912-46; joined 15th Lancers (CM), 1913; last appt Comdr Jubbulpore Area, India. Served European War, 1914-19, Mesopotamia, S Persia (despatches); Waziristan, 1920-21 (despatches); War of 1939-45; Eastern Army and Fourteenth Army (despatches). *Recreations:* polo, racing, golf. *Address:* Kingswood, Derby Road, SW14. *T:* 01-876 7324. *Clubs:* United Service, Cavalry.

**FOWLER, Christopher B.;** *see* Brocklebank-Fowler.

**FOWLER, Gerald Teasdale;** Visiting Professor in the Department of Administration, Strathclyde University, since 1970; *b* 1 Jan. 1935; *s* of James A. Fowler, Long Buckby, Northants, and Alfreda (*née* Teasdale); *m* 1968, Julie Marguerite, *d* of Wilfrid Brining, Slough. *Educ:* Northampton Grammar Sch.; Lincoln Coll., Oxford; University of Frankfurt-am-Main. Craven Fellowship, Oxford Univ., 1957-59; part-time Lectr, Pembroke Coll., Oxford, 1958-59; Lectr, Hertford and Lincoln Colls, Oxford, 1959-65; Lectr, Univ. of Lancaster, 1965-66. Oxford City Councillor, 1960-64. Contested (Lab) Banbury, 1964. MP (Lab) The Wrekin, 1966-70; Jt Parly Sec., Min. of Technology, 1967-69; Minister of State, Dept of Educn and Science, Oct. 1969-June 1970. *Address:* 1 St Chad's Close, Wellington, Salop. *T:* Wellington 2347.

**FOWLER, Henry Hamill;** Partner, Goldman, Sachs & Co., New York, since 1969; *b* 5 Sept. 1908; *s* of Mack Johnson Fowler and Bertha Browning Fowler; *m* 1938, Trudye Pamela Hathcote; two *d* (one *s* decd). *Educ:* Roanoke Coll., Salem, Va; Yale Law Sch. Counsel, Tennessee Valley Authority, 1934-38, Asst Gen. Counsel, 1939; Special Asst to Attorney-Gen. as Chief Counsel to Sub-Cttee, Senate Cttee, Educn and Labor, 1939-40; Special Counsel, Fed. Power Commn, 1941; Asst Gen. Counsel, Office of Production Management, 1941, War Production Board, 1942-44; Econ. Adviser, US Mission Econ. Affairs, London, 1944; Special Asst to Administrator, For. Econ. Administration, 1945; Dep. Administrator, National Production Authority, 1951, Administrator, 1952; Administrator, Defense Prodn Administration, 1952-53; Dir Office of Defense Mobilization, Mem. Nat. Security Coun., 1952-53; Under-Sec. of the Treasury, 1961-64; Secretary of the US Treasury, 1965-68. Sen. Mem. of Fowler, Leva, Hawes & Symington, Washington, 1946-51, 1953-61, 1964-65. Hon. Degrees: Roanoke Coll., 1961; Wesleyan Univ., 1966; Univ. of William and Mary, 1966. *Recreation:* tennis. *Address:* 55 Broad Street, New York, NY, USA. *Clubs:* Links, Recess, Pinnacle (NYC); Metropolitan (Washington).

**FOWLER, Prof. John Francis,** MSc, PhD; FInstP; Director of Cancer Research Campaign's Research Unit in Radiobiology at Mount Vernon Hospital, Northwood, since 1970; *b* 3 Feb. 1925; *er s* of Norman V. Fowler, Bridport, Dorset; *m* 1953, Kathleen Hardcastle Sutton, MB, BS; two *s* five *d. Educ:* Bridport Grammar Sch.; University Coll. of the South-West, Exeter. BSc 1st class Hons (London) 1944; MSc (London) 1946; PhD (London) 1955; FInstP 1957. Research Physicist: Newalls Insulation Co. Ltd, 1944; Metropolitan Vickers Electrical Co. Ltd, 1947; Newcastle upon Tyne Regional Hosp. Board (Radiotherapy service), 1950; Principal Physicist at King's Coll. Hosp., SE5, 1956; Head of Physics Dept in Medical Research Council Radiotherapeutic Res. Unit, Hammersmith Hosp., 1959 (later the Cyclotron Unit); Reader in Physics, London Univ. at Med. Coll. of St Bartholomew's Hosp., 1962; Prof. of Med. Physics, Royal Postgraduate Med. Sch., London Univ., Hammersmith Hosp., 1963-70, Vice-Dean, 1967-70. Mem., Internat. Commn on Radiological Units, 1965-69. Pres., Hosp. Physicists Assoc., 1966-67. Roentgen Award of the British Inst. of Radiology, 1965. *Publications:* (ed) The Scope of Physics in Medicine (publ. Hosp. Physicists' Assoc.), 1962; contributor: Current Topics in Radiation Research, 1966; Vol. II Radiation Dosimetry, 1967; Modern Trends in Radiotherapy, 1967; papers on radiation dosimetry, radio-biology, radioisotopes, in Proc. Royal Soc., Brit. Jl Radiology, Lancet, Nature, Physics in Medicine and Biology, Radiology, etc. *Recreations:* theatre; getting into the countryside. *Address:* CRC RUR, Mount Vernon Hospital, Northwood, Mddx. *T:* Northwood 26111.

**FOWLER, Norman;** *see* Fowler, P.N.

**FOWLER, Peter Howard,** FRS 1964; DSc; Royal Society Research Professor, Physics Department, University of Bristol, since 1964; *b* 27 Feb. 1923; *s* of Sir Ralph Howard Fowler, FRS, and Eileen, *o c* of 1st and last Baron Rutherford; *m* 1949, Rosemary Hempson (*née* Brown); three *d. Educ:* Winchester Coll.; Bristol Univ. BSc 1948, DSc 1958. Flying Officer in RAF, 1942-46 as a Radar Technical Officer. Asst Lectr in Physics, 1948, Lectr, 1951, Reader, 1961, Bristol Univ. Visiting Prof., Univ. of Minnesota, 1956-57.

*Publication:* (with Prof. C. F. Powell and Dr D. H. Perkins) The Study of Elementary Particles by the Photographic Method, 1959. *Recreations:* gardening, meteorology. *Address:* 320 Canford Lane, Westbury on Trym, Bristol.

**FOWLER, (Peter) Norman;** MP (C) South Nottingham since 1970; *b* 2 Feb. 1938; *s* of late N. F. Fowler and Katherine Fowler; *m* 1968, Linda Christmas. *Educ:* King Edward VI Sch., Chelmsford; Trinity Hall, Cambridge (MA). Nat. Service commn, Essex Regt, 1956-58; Cambridge, 1958-61; Chm., Cambridge Univ. Conservative Assoc., 1960. Joined staff of The Times, 1961; Special Corresp., 1962-66; Home Affairs Corresp., 1966-70; reported Middle East War, 1967. Mem. Council, Bow Group, 1967-69; Editorial Board, Crossbow, 1962-69; Vice-Cham., North Kensington Conservative Assoc., 1967-68; Chm., E. Midlands Area, Cons. Political Centre, 1970-. *Publications:* political pamphlets on Home Office subjects including the police. *Recreation:* travel. *Address:* 44 Doria Road, Parsons Green, SW6. *T:* 01-736 3059; Culag, Newstead Abbey Park, Ravenshead, Nottingham. *T:* Blidworth 3742.

**FOWLER, Rees John,** CBE 1954; *b* 14 Oct. 1894; *s* of late Thomas and Sarah Ann Fowler; *m* 1924, Lillian Elizabeth Stockton; no *c*. *Educ:* Port Talbot Grammar Sch.; Aberystwyth Univ.; London Sch. of Economics. Vice-Consul, Mexico City, 1921; Caracas, 1923; Beira, 1925; Tunis, 1927; Acting Consul-Gen. at Tunis in 1927, 1928, 1929 and 1930; Vice-Consul, Frankfurt, 1930, Acting Consul-General there in 1931 and 1932; Vice-Consul, Hamburg, 1933, Acting Consul-Gen. there in 1933, 1934 and 1935; Acting Consul-Gen. at Danzig, 1935; Consul, Antofagasta, Chile, 1936; Chargé d'Affaires, La Paz in 1937 and 1938; Acting Commercial Sec. at Santiago, Chile, in 1938 and 1939; returned to Antofagasta, 1939; HBM Minister and Consul-Gen. to Republic of Honduras, 1945-50; Consul-Gen., Genoa, Italy, 1950-55, retired 1955. *Address:* Via Mameli 34/18, 16035 Rapallo, Italy.

**FOWLER, Robert MacLaren,** SM 1967; President Canadian Pulp & Paper Association, since 1945; associated in practice of law with Gowling, Mactavish, Osborne, and Henderson, Ottawa, since 1945; Member, Economic Council of Canada, since 1963; *b* 7 Dec. 1906; *s* of late Edward Bruce Fowler and Genevieve Amey Fowler, Peterborough, Ont.; *m* 1934, Sheila Gordon Ramsay, *d* of A. Gordon Ramsay, Toronto, Ont.; three *s* two *d*. *Educ:* University of Toronto; Osgoode Hall Law Sch., Toronto, Ont. Practised Law, Toronto, Ont., with McMaster, Montgomery, Fleury and Co., 1931-37; Legal Sec. to Chm., Rowell-Sirois Commn on Dominion-Provincial Relations, 1937-39; practised law, Toronto, Ont., with McCarthy and McCarthy, 1939-45; Sec. and Gen. Counsel, of War-time Prices and Trade Board, Ottawa, 1942-45. Pres., Canadian Institute of International Affairs, 1945-50; Chm. Exec. Council, Canadian Chamber of Commerce, 1953-54; Chm.: Royal Commission on Broadcasting, 1956-57; Cttee on Broadcasting, 1964-65. Hon. LLD Montreal, 1960. *Address:* 36 Summit Circle, Westmount, PQ, Canada. *T:* Wellington 5-4500. *Clubs:* Mount Royal, St James's (Montreal); University (Toronto).

**FOWLER, Sir Robert (William Doughty),** KCMG 1966 (CMG 1962); Ambassador to Sudan from Oct. 1966 until break in relations in June 1967; reappointed Ambassador, 1968-70 (during the break, Administrator of Gibraltar Referendum and Under-Secretary of State, Commonwealth Office); *b* 6 March 1914; *s* of William and Martha Louise Fowler; *m* Margaret MacFarquhar (*née* MacLeod); one *s* one *d* (twins). *Educ:* Queen Elizabeth's Grammar Sch., Mansfield; Emmanuel Coll., Cambridge. Burma CS, 1937-48; Burma Army (Military Administration), 1944-46; Additional Sec. to Governor of Burma, 1947; Commonwealth Relations Office from 1948; seconded to Foreign Service for UK Delegn to UN, 1950-53; Fedn of Rhodesia and Nyasaland and High Commn Territories Dept, CRO, 1954-56; Brit. Dep. High Comr: Pakistan, 1956-58; Canada, 1960-62; Nigeria, 1963-64. Attended IDC, 1959. British High Comr to Tanzania, Aug. 1964, until diplomatic relations broken off in Dec. 1965. *Recreations:* tennis, sailing, painting, photography. *Address:* c/o Foreign and Commonwealth Office, King Charles Street, SW1. *Club:* Oxford and Cambridge University.

**FOWLER, Ronald Frederick,** CBE 1950; Director of Statistical Research, Department of Employment and Productivity, since 1968; *b* 21 April 1910; *e s* of late Charles Frederick Fowler; *m* 1937, Brenda Kathleen Smith. *Educ:* Bancroft's Sch.; LSE, University of London; Universities of Lille and Brussels. BCom (hons) London, 1931. Sir Ernest Cassel Travelling Scholar, 1929-30; Asst, later Lectr in Commerce, LSE, 1932-40; Central Statistical Office, 1940-50; Dir of Statistics, Min. of Labour, 1950-68. *Publications:* The Depreciation of Capital, 1934; The Duration of Unemployment, 1968; Some Problems of Index Number Construction, 1970; articles in British and US economic jls. *Address:* 10 Silverdale Road, Petts Wood, Kent. *T:* Orpington 23895. *Club:* Reform.

**FOWLER-HOWITT, William;** *see* Howitt, W. F.

**FOWWEATHER, Frank Scott,** MSc, MD (Liverpool) 1925; FRCP 1943; FRIC, DPH 1924; Professor of Chemical Pathology, Leeds University, 1946-56, Professor Emeritus, 1956; late Chemical Pathologist, Leeds General Infirmary; *b* 13 Aug. 1892; *e s* of W. T. Fowweather, engineer, late of Bolton, Lancs; *m* 1922, Nellie, *d* of A. N. Godwin Chester, and *g d* of late J. P. Birch, surgeon, Cotton Hall, Denbigh; no *c*. *Educ:* Municipal Secondary Sch., Bolton; Liverpool Univ. BSc, First Class Hons in Chemistry, and awarded Willox Exhibition and Isaac Roberts Scholarship, 1914, and MSc, 1915. chemist with Evans, Sons, Lescher & Webb Ltd, Runcorn, 1915-16; chemist with British Dyes Ltd, Huddersfield, 1916-17; practised as analytical and consulting chemist at 62 Dale Street, Liverpool, 1917-22; MB, ChB, 1922; in general medical practice at Wallasey and at Ellesmere Port, 1922-24; Lecturer in Chemical Pathology, University of Leeds, 1924-30; Reader, 1930-46. *Publications:* A Handbook of Clinical Chemical Pathology; contributions to scientific journals. *Recreations:* gardening, bookbinding. *Address:* 40 Queensbury, West Kirby, Wirral, Cheshire L48 6EP. *T:* 051-625 8535.

**FOX, Rev. Adam;** Canon of Westminster, 1942-63; Canon Emeritus of Chichester; *b* 15 July 1883; *s* of late W. H. Fox; unmarried. *Educ:* Winchester Coll.; University Coll., Oxford (Exhibitioner). BA 1906; MA 1909; Hon. DD, St Andrews, 1947; Holy Orders, 1911; Asst Master at Lancing, 1906-18; Warden of Radley Coll., 1918-24; Asst Master Diocesan Coll., Rondebosch, 1925-29; Fellow of Magdalen Coll., Oxford, 1929-42; Prof. of Poetry, Oxford Univ., 1938-43; Select Preacher,

Oxford, 1932-33, 1957-58; Cambridge, 1938 and 1949; Sacred Poem Prize, 1929; Exam. Chap. to Bishop of Southwark, 1933-47. Master of the Skinners' Company, 1947-48. *Publications:* Dominus Virtutum, 1936; Old King Coel, 1937; Plato for Pleasure, 1946; English Hymns and Hymn Writers (Britain in Pictures), 1947; Meet the Greek Testament, 1952; John Mill and Richard Bentley, 1954; Plato and the Christians, 1957; God Is an Artist, 1957; Dean Inge, (James Tait Black Memorial Prize), 1960; English Well Used, an Anthology (with Sir Andrew Claye), 1968. *Address:* 4 Little Cloister, Westminster Abbey, SW1.

**FOX, Ven. (Benjamin) George (Burton),** MC 1944; TD 1950; Archdeacon of Wisbech since 1965; Hon. Canon, Ely Cathedral, since 1968; *b* 28 July 1913; *s* of J. B. Fox, Manor Farm, Erpingham, Norfolk; *m* 1943, Hon. Margaret Joan Davidson, *d* of Viscount Davidson, *qv*; one *s* four *d*. *Educ:* Norwich Sch.; University of London. Curate: Emmanuel, Guildford, 1936-38; St Andrew's, Bath, 1938-39. Chaplain, HM Forces, 1939-45. Vicar, Potten End, 1945-46, St Andrew's, Bedford, 1946-50, Dio. St Albans; Rector, Montego Bay, Jamaica, 1950-55; Archdeacon of Cornwall, Jamaica, 1950-55; Vicar, St Etheldreda's, Fulham, 1956-65; Vicar of Haddenham, Dio. Ely, 1965-. *Recreations:* cricket, boxing. *Address:* The Vicarage, Haddenham, Ely, Cambs. *T:* Haddenham 309.

**FOX, Bernard Joshua,** CBE 1964; QC; Recorder of Belfast, 1944-60, retired; *b* 3 Feb. 1885; *s* of Herman and Dora Fox; *m* 1908, Elizabeth Myers; two *s*. *Educ:* Belfast Royal Academy; Royal University of Ireland. Called to Irish Bar, 1914. Auditor, Law Students Soc. of Ireland, 1913-14. Called to Inner Bar of Northern Ireland, 1939; Legal Adviser to Govt of Northern Ireland, 1939-44; Chairman: Price Regulation Cttee for Northern Ireland, 1940-44; Northern Ireland Teachers' Salaries Cttee, 1957; Northern Ireland Coal Inquiry Cttee, 1961. Hon. LLD Queen's Univ. of Belfast. *Recreations:* golf, bridge. *Address:* No 5 Flat, 693 Antrim Road, Belfast. *T:* Belfast 76058. *Club:* Ulster Reform (Belfast).

**FOX, Captain Charles,** CBE 1943; Merchant Navy; Orient Steam Navigation Co., London, 1919-51, retired 1951; *b* 26 Sept. 1890; *s* of Frederick Fox, Withernwick, Holderness, E Yorks; *m* 1926, Irene Lillian (marr. diss.), *d* of J. Cadden, Colleray, Sydney, NSW; one *d*; *m* 1948, Marjory Elsie Inglis, Loughton, Essex. *Educ:* Trinity House Navigation Sch., Kingston-upon-Hull, Yorks. Went to sea, 1906, Merchant Navy; served European War, 1914-18, Lieut RNR; Lloyd's War Medal, 1944. Commodore of Orient Line Fleet, 1949-51. *Address:* 8 The Avenue, Betchworth, Surrey.

**FOX, Sir David S.;** *see* Scott Fox.

**FOX, Douglas Gerard Arthur,** OBE 1958; MA, BMus Oxon, FRCO, ARCM; Hon. ARCM; MusD Edinburgh; Hon. RAM; Hon. DMus Bristol; Organist Emeritus, Great St Mary's Church, Cambridge (Organist, 1957-63); *s* of Gerard E. Fox, Clifton, Bristol. *Educ:* Clifton Coll. (Music Scholar); Royal College of Music (Organ Scholar); Keble Coll., Oxford (Organ Scholar). La Fontaine Prize, 1911; Lieut 4th Gloucester Regt; lost right arm, France, Aug. 1917; Pres., Oxford Univ. Musical Club, 1918; Dir of Music, Bradfield Coll., 1918-30; composed music for Bradfield Greek Play (Agamemnon), 1925, and Antigone, 1931; Conductor, Newbury Amateur Orchestral Union, 1923-30; Dir of Music, Clifton Coll., 1931-57; Pres. of the Incorporated Soc. of Musicians, 1958-59; Pres. Cambridge Philharmonic Soc., 1960-68; Co-Pres., Bristol Music Club, 1964. La Fontaine Prize, RCO. *Address:* 1 Grange Road, Clifton, Bristol. *T:* Bristol 35940. *Club:* Savile.

**FOX, Francis Gordon Ward L.;** *see* F. G. W. Lane Fox.

**FOX, Ven. George;** *see* Fox, Ven. B. G. B.

**FOX, Sir John,** Kt, *cr* 1943; OBE 1919; *b* London, 27 May 1882; *e s* of late Sir John Charles Fox and Mary Louisa, 2nd *d* of John Sutherland Valentine, CE; *m* 1st, 1908, Edith Gertrude Olive (*d* 1940), *yr d* of Henry Wait Sharp; one *s*; 2nd, 1942, Lilian (*d* 1959), *d* of John Lawler; 3rd, 1963, Pearl (*née* Gallantry), *widow* of J. F. Shuter. *Educ:* Trinity Coll., Glenalmond. Solicitor, 1905; Legal Asst to Chief Registrar of Friendly Socs, 1905; Asst Registrar of Friendly Socs, 1912; Dep. Industrial Assurance Comr, 1923; Chief Registrar of Friendly Socs and Industrial Assce Comr, 1937-47; Member: Trustee Savings Bank inspection Cttee, 1928-30, 1950-65; Perm. Consultative Cttee on Official Statistics, 1926-37; Nat. Savings Cttee, 1937-47; a Comr under Crown Estates Paving Act, 1851, 1948; Member: Council Trinity Coll., Glenalmond, 1938-48; Public Schs Govng Bodies Assoc., 1942-48; a Vice-Pres., Bldg Socs Assoc. Formerly Dir and later Chairman: King's Lynn Docks and Railway Co.; Minworth Metals Ltd; Britannic Alloys Ltd; Peerless & Ericson Ltd. Served European War, 1915-19 (despatches twice, OBE). *Address:* 18 Millers Close, Goring-on-Thames, Reading, Berks. *T:* Goring 2780.

**FOX, John Marcus,** MBE 1963; MP (C) Shipley, since 1970; company director and owner of textile finishing firm; *b* 11 June 1927; *s* of late Alfred Hirst Fox; *m* 1954, Ann, *d* of F. W. J. Tindall; one *s* one *d*. *Educ:* Wheelright Grammar Sch., Dewsbury. Mem. Dewsbury Borough Council, 1957-65; contested (C): Dewsbury, 1959; Huddersfield West, 1966. *Recreations:* reading, tennis. *Address:* House of Commons, SW1.

**FOX, Rt. Rev. Langton Douglas,** DD; Auxiliary Bishop of Menevia (RC) since 1965; *b* 21 Feb. 1917; *s* of Claude Douglas Fox and Ethel Helen (*née* Cox). *Educ:* Mark Cross, Wonersh and Maynooth. BA 1938; DD 1945. Priest 1942. Lectr, St John's Seminary, Womersh, 1942-55; Mem., Catholic Missionary Soc., 1955-59; Parish Priest, Chichester, 1959-65. *Recreations:* sailing, swimming. *Address:* Our Lady of Peace, Waunlanyrafon, Llanelli, Carms. *T:* Llanelli 4070.

**FOX, Leslie,** DSc Oxon; Professor of Numerical Analysis, Oxford University, and Professorial Fellow, Balliol College, since 1963; Director, Oxford University Computing Laboratory, since 1957; *b* 30 Sept. 1918; *m* 1943, Paulene Dennis. *Educ:* Wheelwright Grammar Sch., Dewsbury; Christ Church, Oxford. Admiralty Computing Service, 1943-45; Mathematics Div., Nat. Physical Laboratory, 1945-56; Associate Prof., Univ. of California, Berkeley, 1956-57; Research Prof., Univ. of Illinois, 1961-62. *Publications:* Numerical Solution of Boundary-value Problems in Ordinary Differential Equations, 1957; (Ed.) Numerical Solution of Ordinary and Partial Differential Equations, 1962; An Introduction to Numerical Linear Algebra, 1964; (Ed.) Advances in Programming and Non-Numerical Computation, 1966; Chebyshev Polynomials in Numerical Analysis (with I. J. Parker), 1968; Computing Methods for Scientists and

Engineers (with D. F. Mayers), 1968; numerous papers in learned journals. *Recreations:* sport, music, literature. *Address:* 24 Sandfield Road, Headington, Oxford. *T:* Oxford 62421; University Computing Laboratory, 19 Parks Road, Oxford. *T:* Oxford 54409.

**FOX, Michael John,** QC 1968; *b* 8 Oct. 1921; *s* of late Michael Fox; *m* 1954, Hazel Mary Stuart; three *s* one *d. Educ:* Drayton Manor Sch., Hanwell; Magdalen Coll., Oxford (BCL, MA). Admiralty, 1942-45. Called to the Bar, Lincoln's Inn, 1949. *Address:* 3 New Square, Lincoln's Inn, WC2. *T:* 01-405 5577.

**FOX, Patrick Loftus B.;** *see* Bushe-Fox.

**FOX, Paul Leonard;** Controller, BBC 1, BBC Television, since 1967; *b* 27 Oct. 1925; *o s* of late Dr Walter Fox and Mrs Hilda Fox; *m* 1948, Betty Ruth (*née* Nathan); two *s. Educ:* Bournemouth Grammar Sch.; abroad. Parachute Regt, 1943. Reporter: Kentish Times, 1946; The People, 1947; Scriptwriter, Pathé News, 1947; BBC Television: Scriptwriter, 1950; Ed., Sportsview, 1953; Ed., Panorama, 1961; Head, Public Affairs Dept, 1963; Head, Current Affairs Group, 1965. *Publications:* various Sportsview books, 1957-60. *Recreations:* television, attending race meetings. *Address:* BBC Television Centre, W12. *T:* 01-743 8000.

**FOX, Sir (Robert) David (John) S.;** *see* Scott Fox.

**FOX, Roy,** OBE 1967; British Deputy High Commissioner in East Pakistan, since 1968; *b* 1 Sept. 1920; *s* of J. S. and A. Fox; *m* 1943, Sybil Verity; two *s* one *d. Educ:* Wheelwright Grammar Sch., Dewsbury; Bradford Technical Coll. Served in RNVR, 1940-46. Bd of Trade, 1947-58; British Trade Commissioner: Nairobi, 1958-60; Montreal, 1960-62; Winnipeg, 1962-64; Dep. Controller, Bd of Trade Office for Scotland, 1964-65. First Sec. Commercial, Karachi, 1965-68. *Recreations:* golf, reading. *Address:* c/o Foreign and Commonwealth Office, SW1. *Clubs:* Oriental; Services Gymkhana (Dacca).

**FOX, Sir Theodore,** Kt 1962; MA, MD Cambridge, LLD Glasgow, DLitt Birmingham; FRCP; *b* 1899; 3rd *s* of late R. Fortescue Fox; *m* Margaret (*d* 1970), *e d* of late W. S. McDougall, Wallington, Surrey; four *s. Educ:* Leighton Park Sch.; Pembroke Coll., Cambridge (scholar); London Hosp. (house physician). Mem. of Friends' Ambulance Unit, BEF, 1918; Ship Surg., 1925; joined staff of The Lancet, 1925; served in RAMC, 1939-42 (late temp. Major); Ed., The Lancet, 1944-64. Dir, Family Planning Assoc., 1965-67. Croonian Lectr, RCP, 1951; Heath Clark Lectr, Univ. of London, 1963; Harveian Orator, RCP, 1965; Maurice Bloch Lectr, Univ. of Glasgow, 1966. Hon. Fellow, Royal Australian Coll. of Gen. Practitioners. *Publication:* Crisis in Communication, 1965. *Address:* Green House, Rotherfield, Sussex. *T:* Rotherfield 270. *Club:* Athenæum.

**FOX, Rt. Rev. Thomas Martin,** DD; *b* Broken Hill, NSW, 6 May 1893; *s* of Martin and Mary J. Fox. *Educ:* Marist Brothers' Coll., Adelaide, S Australia; St Columba's Coll., Springwood, NSW; St Patrick's Coll., Manly, NSW; Collegio Urbano de Propoganda Fide, Rome. Bishop of Wilcannia-Forbes, NSW, 1931-67. *Address:* c/o Bishop's House, Broken Hill, NSW, Australia.

**FOX, Uffa,** CBE 1959; RDI; Owner and Managing Director of Uffa Fox Ltd, Cowes, designers and builders of small-class racers, including International 14-footer Avenger (52 firsts, 2 seconds, 3 thirds, in 57 starts 1928) and sliding-seat canoe East Anglian, winner of principal Canoe Cups in this country and in America and Canada in 1933; *b* Cowes, 15 Jan. 1898; *m* 1956, Mme Yvonne Bernard, Paris. Apprenticed with S. E. Saunders. Served European War, 1914-18, RNAS. In sliding-seat canoes, won Championship of America for paddling and sailing, and New York International Canoe Trophy, 1933. During War of 1939-45 designed and built craft for Admiralty, War Office and Air Ministry, amongst which was parachuted self-baling and self-righting Airborne Lifeboat, with engine and fuel for 1,000 miles, and food and clothing on board for a month, and capable of carrying 25 men over thousands of miles of stormy ocean. RDI (Royal Society of Arts), 1955. *Publications:* Sailing, Seamanship, and Yacht Construction; Uffa Fox's Second Book; Sail and Power; Racing, Cruising, and Design; Thoughts on Yachts and Yachting; Beauty of Sail; Crest of the Wave; Sailing Boats; Seamanlike Sense in Powercraft, 1968. *Address:* Uffa Fox Ltd, Cowes, Isle of Wight.

**FOX, William Sherwood,** MA, PhD, DLitt, LLD, Docteur en Droit, FRSC 1922; President and Vice-Chancellor, University of Western Ontario, London, Ontario, 1927-47; *b* Throopsville, NY, 17 June 1878; *s* of Edward Theophilus and Emma Fox, both of Toronto, Ontario; *m* 1906, Julia McKinnon; two *d. Educ:* Harbord Street Collegiate Institute, Toronto; McMaster Univ., Toronto; University of Geneva; Johns Hopkins Univ., Baltimore. Instructor in Classics, Brandon Coll., Brandon, Manitoba, 1900-09; Fellow in Classical Archæology, Johns Hopkins Univ., Baltimore, 1909-11; Asst Prof. in Classics, Princeton Univ., Princeton, NJ, 1911-17; Prof. of Classics, Western Univ., London, Ontario, 1917-27; Dean of Faculty of Arts, Western Univ., London, 1919-27. Dir Royal Botanical Gardens, Hamilton, Ontario. Baptist. OStJ. *Publications:* Johns Hopkins Tabellae Defixionum, Baltimore, 1912; The Mythology of Greece and Rome (vol. I in The Mythology of All Races series), Boston, 1916, 1928; Trans. of Greek and Latin passages relating to Zoroaster (Jl of K. R. Cama, Oriental Inst., Bombay); A Century of Service, London, Ont., 1945; Letters of William Davies, Toronto, 1854-1861, Toronto, 1946; 'T Ain't Runnin' No More, London, Ont., 1946 (fourth impression, 1958 with a sequel 'T Ain't Runnin' No More–Twenty Years After); St Ignace, Canadian Altar of Martyrdom, Toronto, 1949; The Bruce Beckons, Toronto, 1952 (1962, paperback edn with appendix, etc); Silken Lines and Silver Hooks, Toronto, 1954; Sherwood Fox of Western, Toronto, 1964; contribs to Trans Royal Can. Inst. on Carolinian Native Trees and Shrubs of Ontario (with Dr James H. Soper), Toronto, 1952, 1953, 1954; numerous articles in classical, botanical and archæological jls and in literary periodicals. *Recreations:* fishing and botanizing. *Address:* 14 Harrison Crescent, London, Ont, Canada. *T:* General 4-4747. *Clubs:* London, Rotary, London Hunt (all London, Ont).

**FOX, Winifred Marjorie, (Mrs E. Gray Debros);** Under-Secretary, Ministry of Housing and Local Government, since 1963; *d* of Frederick Charles Fox and Charlotte Marion Ogborn; *m* 1953, Eustachy Gray Debros (*d* 1954); one *d. Educ:* Streatham County Sch.; St Hugh's Coll., Oxford. 1st Cl. Hons Eng. Lang. and Lit. 1937. Entered Administrative Class of Home Civil Service, in Unemployment Assistance Board, 1937; Cabinet Office, 1942; Ministry of Town and Country Planning, 1944; Ministry of Housing and Local Govt, 1952. *Address:* Vale House, Westcott, Surrey.

**FOX-ANDREWS, James Roland Blake,** QC 1968; *b* 22 March 1922; step *s* of Norman Roy Fox-Andrews, *qv*; *m* 1950, Angela Bridget Swift; two *s. Educ:* Stowe; Pembroke Coll., Cambridge. Called to the Bar, Gray's Inn, 1949. Dep. Chm., Devon QS, 1970-. *Recreation:* book-collecting. *Address:* 20 Cheyne Gardens, SW3. *T:* 01-352 9484; Lepe House, Exbury, Hants. *Clubs:* MCC; Hampshire (Winchester).

**FOX-ANDREWS, Norman Roy,** QC; Recorder, retired; *b* 15 April 1894; *s* of Stephen and Emily Fox-Andrews; *m* 1st, 1921, Olive Dunn; one *d*; 2nd, 1931, Mary Butler (*d* 1970). *Educ:* Leys Sch.; Trinity Hall, Cambridge. Law Tripos Parts I and II. DCLI 1914-18. Called to Bar, Lincoln's Inn, 1921; Bencher Lincoln's Inn, 1951; KC 1945; QC 1952; Recorder of Bridgwater, 1945; Royal Commission on Capital Punishment, 1949; Recorder of Bournemouth, 1945-61, Bristol, 1961-64. RAF 1939-40. *Recreations:* golf, gardening, philately. *Address:* Yew Tree Cottage, Barfreston, Kent. *T:* Shepherdswell 204. *See also J. R. B. Fox-Andrews.*

**FOX-PITT, Maj.-Gen. William Augustus Fitzgerald Lane,** CVO 1966 (MVO 1936); DSO 1940; MC 1916; retired; DL; Member of HM Bodyguard of Hon. Corps of Gentleman-at-Arms, 1947-66; Lieutenant, 1963-66; (Standard Bearer, 1961-63); *b* 28 Jan. 1896; *s* of late Lieut-Col W. A. Fox-Pitt, Presaddfed, Anglesey; *m* 1931, Mary Stewart, *d* of A. H. H. Sinclair, MD, FRCSE; two *s* one *d. Educ:* Charterhouse. ADC to the King, 1945-47; joined Cheshire Regt 1914; served with Welsh Gds, 1915-39; Comd, 1st Bn, 1934-37; OC Welsh Guards Regt, 1937-40; Comd Gds Bde BEF, 1940, Armd Bde, 1941-43; Comdr, East Kent Dist as Maj.-Gen., 1943; retired with hon. rank of Maj.-Gen. 1947. Mem. Dorset CC 1952; DL Dorset, 1957. *Recreations:* hunting, shooting, golf. *Address:* Marsh Court, Sherborne, Dorset. *T:* Bishops Caundle 230. *Club:* Turf.

**FOX-STRANGWAYS,** family name of **Earl of Ilchester.**

**FOXELL, Rev. Maurice Frederic,** KCVO 1965 (CVO 1953; MVO 1942); MA; Extra Chaplain to the Queen since 1965; Honorary Minor Canon St Paul's Cathedral; *b* 15 Aug. 1888; 4th *s* of late Rev. W. J. Foxell, PhD, and Annie Harte; *m* 1914, Mariana, 2nd *d* of late John Morton Fountain, Hillingdon, Middx; two *s* two *d. Educ:* Christ's Hospital; Queen's Coll., Oxford. Asst Curate St Paul's, Hammersmith, 1911-15; Friern Barnet, 1915-17; Minor Canon St George's Chapel, Windsor Castle, 1917-21; Minor Canon and Succentor, St Paul's Cathedral, 1921-39; Rector of St James's, Garlickhythe, EC4, 1939-64. Sub-Dean of HM Chapels Royal, Sub-Almoner, Deputy Clerk of the Closet, and Domestic Chaplain to the Queen, 1952-65 (to King George VI, 1948-52). *Publication:* Wren's Craftsmen at St Paul's, 1934. *Recreations:* water-colour, wood-engraving, piano. *Address:* Jay Cottage, Lamberhurst, Kent. *T:* Lamberhurst 350. *Club:* Athenæum.

**FOXLEY-NORRIS, Air Marshal Sir Christopher (Neil),** KCB 1969 (CB 1966); DSO 1945; OBE 1956; Chief of Personnel and Logistics, Ministry of Defence, since 1971; *b* 16 March 1917; *s* of Major J. P. Foxley-Norris and Dorothy Brabant Smith; *m* 1948, Joan Lovell Hughes; no *c. Educ:* Winchester; Trinity Coll., Oxford; Middle Temple. Commissioned RAFO, 1936; France, 1940; Battle of Britain, 1940; various operational tours of duty in wartime, MA 1946; Directing Staff, RAF Staff Coll., 1951-53; idc 1961; Dir of Organization and Admin. Plans, Air Min., 1962; ACDS, 1963; AOC No. 224 Gp, FEAF, 1964-67; Dir-Gen., RAF Organization, MoD, 1967-68; C-in-C, RAF Germany and Comdr, NATO 2nd Tactical Air Force, 1968-70. *Publications:* various in RUSI and other service jls. *Recreations:* golf, sailing. *Address:* Dower House, Elvaston Place, SW7. *T:* 01-584 2549. *Clubs:* Royal Air Force; Ashdown Forest.

**FOXON, Prof. George Eric Howard,** MA, MSc; Professor of Biology, University of London, since 1955; Head of Biology Department, Guy's Hospital Medical School, since 1948; *b* 1908; *s* of George Thomas Foxon, OBE, and Edith Maud (*née* Lewis); *m* 1932, Joan Burlinson; one *s* one *d* (and one *s* decd). *Educ:* King's Coll. Sch., Wimbledon; Queens' Coll., Cambridge. BA 1930, 1st Cl. Hons Nat. Sci. Tripos Pt II, 1931; MA 1934; MSc (Wales) 1943. Asst in Zoology, University of Glasgow, 1932-37; Asst Lectr and Lectr in Zoology, University Coll., Cardiff, 1937-48; Reader in Biology, University of London, 1948-55. Chm. of the British Univs Film Council, 1959-63, 1967-69. Fellow Cambridge Philosophical Soc., FLS; FIBiol; FZS. *Publications:* various scientific papers, mainly dealing with the comparative study of the heart and blood system of vertebrate animals. *Address:* Thorpe Cloud, Woodfield Lane, Ashtead, Surrey. *T:* Ashtead 72306.

**FOXTON, Maj.-Gen. Edwin Frederick,** CB 1969; OBE 1959; MA; Fellow and Domestic Bursar, Emmanuel College, Cambridge, since 1969; *b* 28 Feb. 1914; *y s* of F. Foxton and T. Wilson; unmarried. *Educ:* Worksop Coll.; St Edmund Hall, Oxford. Commissioner from General List TA, 1937; served: India, 1939-42; Middle East, 1942-45; India, 1945-47 (Chief Educn Officer, Southern Comd, India); War Office, 1948-52; Chief Instructor, Army Sch. of Educn, 1952-55; Dist Educn Officer, HQ Northumbrian District, 1955-57; War Office, 1957-60; Commandant, Army Sch. of Educn, 1961-63; War Office, 1963-65; Chief Educn Officer, FARELF, 1965; Dir of Army Educn, 1965-69. *Recreation:* mountaineering. *Address:* Emmanuel College, Cambridge. *Club:* Oxford and Cambridge University.

**FOY, Sir Thomas Arthur Wyness,** Kt 1956; CSI 1947; CIE 1945; MICE; *b* 1895; *s* of late Dr Frederick Arthur Foy, London. *Educ:* Truro Coll.; Birmingham Univ. Chief Engineer and Sec., Punjab Public Works Dept (Irrigation Branch), 1945-47; Chief Engineer and Sec., Lower Sind Barrage, Govt of Sind, 1947-55. *Address:* c/o National and Grindlay's Bank Ltd, 13 St James's Square, SW1. *See also Baron Feversham.*

**FOYLAN, Rt. Rev. Michael;** *see* Aberdeen, Bishop of, (RC).

**FOYLE, Christina Agnes Lilian, (Mrs Ronald Batty);** Managing Director, W. & G. Foyle Ltd; *d* of late William Alfred Foyle; *m* 1938, Ronald Batty. *Educ:* Aux Villas Unspunnen, Wilderswil, Switzerland. Began Foyle's Literary Luncheons, 1930, where book lovers have been able to see and hear great personalities. *Recreations:* ski-ing, sailing, music. *Address:* Goldbeaters House, Manette Street, W1.

**FOYLE, Gilbert Samuel;** Founder Director, W. & G. Foyle Ltd (Booksellers); *b* 9 March 1886; *s* of William and Deborah Foyle; *m* 1911, Ethel

Ellen Cook; two *s.* *Educ:* Owen's Sch., Islington; King's Coll., University of London. Served European War, 1914-18, France, 1916-17. With brother William, founded firm of W. & G. Foyle, Booksellers, 1903; Founder of Gilbert Foyle Educational Trust, administered by LCC. Freeman, City of London, 1935; Mem. of Eastbourne Town Council, 1952-62, resigned for health reasons. *Recreations:* reading, social work. *Address:* 4 Ashbourne Court, Eastbourne, Sussex. *T:* Eastbourne 3518.

**FRAENKEL, Heinrich;** freelance author and regular contributor to, inter alia, the New Statesman; *b* 28 Sept. 1897; *s* of Benno Fraenkel and Alwina (*née* Taendler); *m* 1936, Gretel Levy-Ries; two *s.* *Educ:* German schools and universities. Began career in film trade journalism, Berlin; as screen-writer, went to Hollywood for two years but returned to Germany; continued to write screen plays but increasingly interested in politics; emigrated to avoid arrest in night of Reichstag fire, 1933; went to Paris, then London; still made living writing screen-plays but wrote political books, lectured on German history, the roots of Nazism, etc. At war's end, determined to return to Germany; disillusioned by many long trips made for the New Statesman; sought British nationality, 1949. Has written chess column in New Statesman (as Assiac) since 1949. Order of Merit (1st class) of Fed. Rep. of Germany, 1967. *Publications:* The German People Versus Hitler, 1940; Help Us Germans to Beat the Nazis, 1941; The Winning of the Peace, 1942; The Other Germany, 1943; A Nation Divided, 1949; The Boy Between, 1956; Farewell to Germany, 1958; with Roger Manvell: Dr Goebbels, 1959; Hermann Goering, 1962; The July Plot, 1964; Heinrich Himmler, 1965; The Incomparable Crime, 1967; The Canaris Conspiracy, 1969; History of the German Cinema, 1970; Rudolf Hess, 1971. As Assiac: Adventure in Chess, 1950; Delights of Chess, 1960. *Address:* Christopher Cottage, Thaxted (Dunmow), Essex. *T:* Thaxted 293. *Club:* Authors'.

**FRAME, Rt. Rev. John Timothy;** *see* Yukon, Bishop of.

**FRAMPTON, Algernon de Kewer,** CMG 1952; *b* 30 Jan. 1904; *s* of Heathfield James and Elizabeth Frampton, Devon, England; *m* 1st, 1935, Marion May (*d* 1953), *d* of Col G. H. May, Inspector-Gen. of Police, Trinidad, BWI; 2nd, 1954, Emma Huggins (*née* Pereira) (*d* 1970); no *c.* *Educ:* Christ's Hosp.; Seale Hayne Agricultural Coll., Devon; School of Rural Economics, Oxford University; Wye Coll., Kent; Imperial Coll. of Tropical Agriculture, Trinidad, BWI. Joined Colonial Agricultural Service; Dept of Agriculture: Nigeria, 1927-29, British Guiana, 1929-35, Malaya, 1935-. Served War of 1939-45 (despatches); Capt., Volunteer Force (4th Malacca Bn), 1940; POW Singapore, 1942-45. Seconded from Malaya, 1946; Prof. of Agriculture, Imperial Coll. of Tropical Agriculture, Trinidad, BWI, 1946-49; Agricultural Adviser to Comptroller, Colonial Development and Welfare, BWI, 1949-58; Dir of Agriculture, Barbados, 1959-64; retd from Colonial Service, 1965; now living in the Canary Islands. *Address:* c/o 17 Forde Park, Newton Abbot, Devon.

**FRAMPTON, Henry James,** CSI 1947; CIE 1941; MC; MA; *b* 14 Aug. 1897; *s* of Henry Manwell Frampton; *m* 1st, Alys Ann Mary, *d* of C. H. Holmes; 2nd, Hilda Mary, *d* of Rev. Alex. Brown; three *s* one *d.* *Educ:* Christ's Hospital; St John's Coll., Oxford. Joined Indian Civil Service, 1921; retired 1947. *Address:* 65 Park Road, Woking, Surrey. *T:* Woking 60221.

**FRAMPTON, Meredith,** RA 1942 (ARA 1934); *b* 1894; *s* of Sir George Frampton, RA; *m* 1951, Hilda Norman, *d* of late James B. Dunn, RSA, FRIBA, and of Mrs Dunn, Edinburgh. *Educ:* Westminster. *Address:* Hill Barn, Monkton Deverill, Warminster, Wilts. *Club:* Athenæum.

**FRAMPTON, Walter Bennett,** OBE 1945; Metropolitan Magistrate, Marylebone Magistrates' Court, 1952-67, retired; *b* 1 Oct. 1903; *er s* of late Walter Frampton, Recorder of Chichester, and Catherine Bennett; *m* 1928, Gwyneth Davies; one *s* one *d.* *Educ:* Westminster Sch.; London Univ. Called to Bar, Middle Temple, 1925; joined ROC 1939; RAFVR, 1940-45; Wing-Commander, 1941; Senior Administrative Officer, Nos 16 and 19 Groups, RAF (despatches, OBE). Metropolitan Magistrate, 1947. *Recreation:* cricket. *Address:* Cranford, Peppard Common, Henley-on-Thames, Oxon. *T:* Rotherfield Greys 328.

**FRANCE, Sir Arnold William,** KCB 1965 (CB 1957); Chairman, Board of Inland Revenue, since 1968; *b* 20 April 1911; *s* of late W. E. France; *m* 1940, Frances Margaret Linton, *d* of late Dr C. J. L. Palmer; four *d.* *Educ:* Bishop's Stortford Coll. District Bank, Ltd, 1929-40. Served War of 1939-45, Army, 1940-43; Deputy Economic and Financial Adviser to Minister of State in Middle East, 1943; HM Treasury, 1945; Asst Sec., 1948; Under Sec., 1952; Third Sec., 1960; Ministry of Health: Dep. Sec., 1963-64; Permanent Sec., 1964-68. Mem., Economic Planning Board, 1960. *Address:* Thornton Cottage, Lingfield, Surrey. *T:* Lingfield 278. *Club:* Reform.

**FRANCIS, (Alan) David,** CBE 1959; MVO 1957; *b* 2 Dec. 1900; *m* 1932, Norah Turpin; two *s.* *Educ:* Winchester; Magdalen Coll., Oxford (MA); Corpus Christi Coll., Cambridge (BA). Passed into General Consular Service, 1923; after course in Economics at Cambridge, appointed Vice-Consul, Antwerp, 1925; served as Vice-Consul at Rotterdam, Panama, Bogota and Prague; was also LLoyds Agent at Prague; served in FO, 1936, appointed Vice-Consul, Brussels, and Consul there, 1937. Attached to Costarican Delegation to Coronation of King George VI. Seconded as Principal in Aliens Dept, Home Office, 1940; Consul at Lisbon, 1941; Barcelona, 1942; First Sec. and Consul, Caracas, 1944; Chargé d'Affaires there, 1946; served in FO, 1947; Consul-Gen. at Danzig, 1949, New Orleans, 1951; Consul-Gen., Oporto, 1955-58; retired, 1958. Mem., Lord Chancellor's Advisory Council on Public Records, 1962-67. FRHistS. *Publications:* The Methuens and Portugal, 1966; articles in learned periodicals. *Recreation:* walking. *Address:* 21 Cadogan Street, SW3. *Club:* Travellers'.

**FRANCIS, Sir Brooke;** *see* Francis, Sir C. G. B.

**FRANCIS, Sir (Cyril Gerard) Brooke,** Kt 1938; QC (Tanganyika) 1934; Chief Justice of Bermuda and President Legislative Council, 1941, retired 1952; *b* 26 Nov. 1883; *m* 1909, Mavis Rodd, *y d* of late Richard Windeyer Robertson, NSW; no *c.* *Educ:* private tutor. Barrister-at-Law, Inner Temple, 1907; Fiji Civil Service in various administrative and legal appointments until transferred to British Honduras as Attorney-Gen. in 1921; Attorney-Gen., Zanzibar, 1924; Attorney-Gen., Tanganyika Territory, 1929; Chief Justice of Northern Rhodesia, 1934-39, and Member Rhodesian Court of Appeal, 1939; retired

1939; Major, second in command of Fiji Defence Force, 4 Aug. 1914 (mentioned by Army Council for services in connection defence Fiji); E Surrey Regt, 1915, and KAR, East Africa, 1916-19. *Address:* 39 Hans Place, SW1. *T:* 01-584 7745. *Club:* Lansdowne.

**FRANCIS, David;** *see* Francis, A. D.

**FRANCIS, Sir Frank (Chalton),** KCB 1960 (CB 1958); FSA; FMA; Director and Principal Librarian, British Museum, 1959-68; *b* Liverpool, 5 Oct. 1901; *o s* of late F. W. Francis and Elizabeth Chalton; *m* 1927, Katrina McClennon, Liverpool; two *s* one *d*. *Educ:* Liverpool Inst.; Liverpool Univ.; Emmanuel Coll., Cambridge. Asst Master, Holyhead Co. Sch., 1925-26; British Museum: entered Library, 1926; Sec., 1946-47; Keeper, Dept of Printed Books, 1948-59. Lectr in Bibliography, Sch. of Librarianship and Archives, University Coll., London, 1945-59. David Murray Lectr, Univ. of Glasgow, 1957. Editor, The Library, 1936-53; Jt Editor, Jl of Documentation, 1947-68. Museums Association: Mem. Council, 1960-; Vice-Pres., 1964-65; Pres., 1965-66. Bibliographical Society: Jt Hon. Sec. (with late R. B. McKerrow), 1938-40; Hon. Sec. 1940-64; Pres., 1964-66. Library Association: Council, 1948-59; Chm. Exec. Cttee, 1954-57; Pres., 1965. President: ASLIB, 1957-58; Internat. Fedn of Library Assocs, 1963-69; Chm. Trustees, Nat. Central Library. Vice-Pres., Unesco Internat. Adv. Cttee on Bibliography, 1954-60. Chairman: Circle of State Librarians, 1947-50; Internat. Cttee of Library Experts, UN, 1948; Council, British Nat. Bibliography, 1949-59; Unesco Provisional Internat. Cttee on Bibliography, 1952; Academic Libraries Section, Internat. Fedn of Library Assocs; Anglo-Swedish Soc., 1964-68. Trustee, Imp. War Museum; Governor, Birkbeck Coll. Correspondant, Institut de France; Mem., Bibliographical Soc. of America, and other bibliographical socs; Corresp. Mem., Massachusetts Historical Soc.; Hon. Mem., Kungl. Gustav Adolfs Akademien; Foreign Hon. Mem., Amer. Acad. of Arts and Sciences. Hon. Fellow: Emmanuel Coll., Cambridge; Pierpont Morgan Library, NY; Hon. FLA. Hon. LittD: Liverpool; TCD; Cambridge; Hon. DLitt: British Columbia; Exeter; Leeds; Oxford; New Brunswick; Wales. *Publications:* Historical Bibliography in Year's Work in Librarianship, 1929-38; (ed) The Bibliographical Society, 1892-1942: Studies in Retrospect, 1945; (ed) Facsimile of The Compleat Catalogue 1680, 1956; Robert Copland: Sixteenth Century Printer and Translator, 1961; translations from German, including W. Cohn, Chinese Art, 1930; articles and reviews in The Library, TLS, etc. *Recreations:* golf, walking, bibliography. *Address:* The Vine, Nether Winchendon, Aylesbury, Bucks. *Clubs:* Athenæum; Grolier (New York); Cosmos (Washington, DC).

**FRANCIS, Hugh Elvet,** QC 1960; practising at Chancery Bar, 1932-39, and since 1945; Chancellor of the County Palatine of Durham, since 1969; *b* 28 March 1907; *s* of Maurice Evan Francis, JP, Cemmes, Montgomeryshire and Ellen Francis (*née* Jones); *m* 1932, Emma Frances Wienholt, *d* of J. G. W. Bowen, Tyddyn, Llanidloes; three *s* one *d* (and one *s* decd). *Educ:* Machynlleth County Sch.; UCW Aberystwyth; St John's Coll., Cambridge. LLB Wales 1st Cl. Hons, 1929; Schol. St John's Coll., Cambridge, 1930; LLB Cantab 1st Cl. Hons, Macmahon Law studentship, 1931; Arden Schol. and Lord Justice Holker Sen. Schol., Gray's Inn, Certificate of Honour, Bar Final Exams, 1931; Barrister, Gray's Inn, 1932; Bencher, Gray's Inn, 1956. Served War of 1939-45 in RA and JAG Dept (despatches). Pres., Iron and Steel Arbitration Tribunal; Chm., Performing Right Tribunal. Hon. Treas., Bar Council, 1961-64. *Publication:* Jt Ed. Lindley on Partnership, 1950. *Recreations:* fishing, gardening and country pursuits. *Address:* 2 Ringwood Avenue, East Finchley, N2. *T:* 01-883 4371; Tyddyn, Llanidloes, Mont. *T:* Llanidloes 448.

**FRANCIS, Lieut-Col John Clement Wolstan,** MBE; Vice-Lieutenant of Cambridgeshire, since 1958; *b* 2 Aug. 1888; *s* of late Major Wolstan Francis, Cambridgeshire; *m* 1918, Evelyn Maud, JP, *d* of Augustus William Benyon, Windsor; one *s*. *Educ:* Wellington; Pembroke Coll., Cambridge. Served European War, 1914-18. Major 1920, Lt-Col 1930; retired 1935. DL 1945, High Sheriff, 1954, Cambridgeshire. *Recreations:* horses and shooting. *Address:* Quy Hall, Cambridgeshire. *T:* Bottisham 205. *Clubs:* Cavalry, Royal Automobile.

**FRANCIS, John Gordon Loveband,** CBE 1964; Director of Finance, British Broadcasting Corporation, since 1969; *b* 4 Feb. 1907; *s* of late Dr J. E. Francis, Westward Ho!, N Devon; *m* 1935, Ann, *d* of late O. A. Sherrard, Lyme Regis, Dorset; four *d*. *Educ:* Blundell's Sch., Tiverton. Articled Clerk, E. C. Price, Son & Reid, 1926-32; Asst in Cost Office, Harris, Lebus & Co., Mass Production Furniture Manufacturers, 1933-34; Accountant, later Sec., Brickwood & Co., Brewers, Portsmouth, 1934-39. BBC: Asst Chief Accountant, 1939-43; Chief Accountant, 1943-59; Controller, Finance, 1959-69. FCA, ACWA. *Address:* Lingwood Grove, Blackheath, Guildford, Surrey. *T:* Bramley 2081.

**FRANCIS, Norman;** *see* Francis, W. N.

**FRANCIS, Owen,** CB 1960; Deputy Chairman of Central Electricity Generating Board since 1965 (Member, 1962-64); *b* 4 Oct. 1912; *yr s* of Sidney and Margaret Francis, The White House, Austwick, Yorks; *m* 1938, Joan St Leger (*née* Norman); two *d*. *Educ:* Giggleswick Sch., Yorks. Entered Civil Service as Asst Auditor, Exchequer and Audit Dept, 1931; Asst Principal, Mines Dept, 1937; Principal, 1940; Asst Sec., Ministry of Fuel and Power, 1943; Under-Sec., Ministry of Power, 1954-61. *Recreations:* golf and sailing. *Address:* Low Felling, Clare Hill, Esher, Surrey. *T:* Esher 65126. *Clubs:* Reform; St George's Hill Golf (Weybridge); Seaview Yacht.

**FRANCIS, William Lancelot,** CBE 1961; Secretary, Science Research Council, since 1965; Director, Grants and Information Divisions, Department of Scientific and Industrial Research, 1958-65; *b* 16 Sept. 1906; *s* of G. J. Francis and Ethel, *d* of L. G. Reed, Durham; *m* 1st, 1937, Ursula Mary Matthew (*d* 1966); two *s* three *d*; 2nd, 1968, Margaret Morris. *Educ:* Latymer Upper Sch., Hammersmith; King's Coll., Cambridge (Exhibitioner). BA Cambridge (Natural Sciences Tripos) 1928; BSc London 1928; MA, PhD in Physical Chemistry, Cambridge 1931. DSIR Sen. Research Award, Cambridge, 1931-33; Rockefeller Foundn Fellowship in Experimental Zoology, Rockefeller Institute, New York, 1933-34; Science Master, Repton Sch., 1935-40; Radar research and administration in Ministries of Supply and Aircraft Production (TRE Malvern), 1940-45. DSIR Headquarters, 1945-65. *Publications:* papers on physical chemistry and experimental zoology in scientific jls, 1931-37. *Recreations:* gardening, travel. *Address:* 269 Sheen Lane, SW14. *T:* 01-876 3029. *Club:* Athenæum.

**FRANCIS, (William) Norman; His Honour Judge Francis;** Judge of County Courts, since 1969; *b* 19 March 1921; *s* of Llewellyn Francis; *m* 1951, Anthea Constance (*née* Kerry); one *s* one *d*. *Educ:* Bradfield; Lincoln Coll., Oxford (BCL, MA). Served War of 1939-45, RA. Called to Bar, Gray's Inn, 1946. Dep. Chm., Brecknock QS, 1962. *Recreations:* hockey, cricket. *Address:* 2 The Woodlands, Lisvane, near Cardiff. *T:* Cardiff 753070.

**FRANCKENSTEIN, Baroness Joseph von;** *see* Boyle, Kay.

**FRANCKLIN, Comdr (Mavourn Baldwin) Philip,** DSC 1940; RN; JP; Vice-Lieutenant for Nottinghamshire since 1968; *b* 15 Jan. 1913; *s* of Capt. Philip Francklin, MVO, RN (killed in action, 1914); *m* 1949, Xenia Alexandra, *d* of Alex. Davidson, Co. Wicklow; two *s* one *d*. *Educ:* RNC Dartmouth. Joined RN, 1926. Served War of 1939-45: Norway, N and S Atlantic, Indian Ocean (despatches twice); Asst to 5th Sea Lord, 1947-49; Comdr 1950; Asst Naval Attaché, Paris, 1952-53. DL, 1963, JP 1958, Notts; High Sheriff of Notts, 1965. Croix de Guerre (France). *Address:* Gonalston Hall, Nottingham. *T:* Lowdham 3635. *Club:* Boodle's.

**FRANCO BAHAMONDE, General Don Francisco;** Head of Spanish State and Generalissimo of National Armies since 1936; *b* 1892; *m* 1923, Doña Carmen Polo y Martinez-Valdés; one *d*. *Educ:* Infantry Academy. Took part in campaign, Morocco, 1912-17; with Oviedo garrison, 1917-20; Dep. Comdr, Foreign Legion, Morocco, 1920-23; Comdr, 1923-27; Dir.-Gen., Military Academy, Saragossa, 1927-31; Capt.-Gen., Balearic Islands, 1933; C-in-C Moroccan Army, 1935; Chief of Gen. Staff, 1935; C-in-C Canary Islands, 1936. Capt. 1914; Major 1916; Lieut-Col 1922; Col 1924; Maj.-Gen. 1934. Gran Cruz Laureada de San Fernando: Medalla Militar Individual; Gran Cruz de San Hermenegildo, etc. Also holds many foreign decorations. *Address:* Madrid, Spain.

**FRANÇOIS-PONCET, André,** de l'Académie Française, 1952 et de l'Académie des Sciences morales et politiques; LLD; Grand Croix de la Légion d'Honneur; politician, diplomat and writer; Chancellor of the French Institute, 1961-64; *b* Provins, France, 13 June 1887. Served European War, 1914-16, Lieut 304 Infantry Regt (Croix de Guerre). Mem. International Economic Mission, US, 1919; Govt delegate Conference of Genoa and in Ruhr. Founder and Dir, Bulletin de la Société d'Etudes et d'Informations économiques, 1920-24; Mem. Cttee Republican Party; Deputy, 1924-31; Under-Sec. of State, 1928-31; Ambassador to Germany, 1931-38; Ambassador to Italy, 1938-40; Mem. National Council, 1941; arrested by the Gestapo, 1943; liberated by the Allies, May 1945. President of the French Red Cross. Pres. Permanent Commission of International Red Cross, 1949-; French High Commissioner, Allied High Commission, Germany, 1949-55; French Ambassador to Western Germany, May-Sept. 1955. *Publications:* Les Affinités électives de Goethe, 1910; Ce que pense la jeunesse allemande, 1913; La France et le problème des réparations; Discours français; Réflexions d'un républicain moderne; Souvenire d'une Ambassade à Berlin, 1946; De Versailles à Potsdam, 1948; Carnets d'un Captif, 1952; Discours de Réception à l'Académie Française, Au Palais Farnese, 1961. *Address:* 92 rue du Ranelagh, Paris 16e.

**FRANGULIS, A. F.;** Ambassador, Permanent Secretary-General of Académie Diplomatique Internationale; *b* the Piraeus, Greece, 8 Nov. 1888. *Educ:* Lycée in Athens and Constantinople; Universities of Athens, Geneva, Lausanne, Berlin and Paris. In 1920 and 1921, Mem. Greek Delegn to Supreme Council in London for negotiating terms of Peace with Turkey; rep. Greece in Council of League of Nations, with rank of Minister, with responsibility for negotiations respecting Northern Epirus, 1921; later was deleg. of Greece to Conf. of Ambassadors, with special ref. to settlement of territorial questions relating to delimitation of frontiers of that country; attended 1st, 2nd and 3rd Assembly of League of Nations as Delegate of Greece; in 1926 founded, in assoc. with MM Adatchi, Poullet, Guerrero, Franklin Roosevelt, Beneš, Titulesco, etc, the Académie Diplomatique Internationale; in 1933 and 1934, as deleg. to League of Nations at time of persecution of Jews in Germany, in a resolution which made a great impression, he asked the Assembly of Geneva to give international jurisdictional protection of human rights and individual liberties; that resolution was written into the Charter of United Nations at San Francisco in 1945. He spoke at Assemblies of League of Nations, 1933-39, on behalf of refugees and secured a resolution advocating the "chèque compensation" with a view to promoting exchanges between various nations. Delegate to League of Nations, 1920-44. *Publications:* Dictionnaire Diplomatique, vols I-VII; La Conception Nouvelle de la Neutralité: Une ligue des Nations comme garantie d'une Paix durable; Wilson, sa vie et son œuvre; Les Précurseurs de la SDN; La Norvège et le droit des Gens; Le Principe des Nationalités et le droit de libre disposition; Les SAnctions contre les responsables de la Guerre; l'Albanie et l'Epire du Nord; La Question du Proche Orient; La Grèce et la Crise Mondiale (I-II vols); Le Pacte général de renonciation à la Guerre; La Garantie Juridictionnelle des Droits de l'Homme; Théorie et Pratique des Traités Internationaux; La Grèce, son Histoire Diplomatique, son Statut International (Vols I-II), etc. *Address:* 4 bis, Avenue Hoche, Paris.

**FRANK, Mrs Alan;** *see* Tate, Phyllis M. D.

**FRANK, Air Vice-Marshal Alan Donald,** CB 1967; CBE 1962; DSO 1943; DFC 1941; Bursar, Worcester College, Oxford, since 1970; *b* 1917; *s* of late Major N. G. Frank and late M. H. Frank (*née* Donald); *m* 1941, Jessica Ann Tyrrell; two *s* two *d*. *Educ:* Eton; Magdalen Coll., Oxford. Commanded 51 Squadron Bomber Command, 1943; RAF Staff Coll., 1944; OC 83 Sqdn, 1957; OC RAF Honington, 1958-60; Group Captain Ops, Bomber Comd, 1960-62; Dir Operational Requirements, MoD, 1962-65; Air Attaché and OC, RAF Staff, Washington, 1965-68. SASO, RAF Air Support Command, 1968-70. *Recreations:* ski-ing, squash, tennis. *Address:* c/o Barclays Bank, 50 High Street, Crawley, Sussex.

**FRANK, Douglas George Horace,** QC 1964; *b* 16 April 1916; *s* of late George Maurice Frank and late Agnes Winifred Frank; *m* 1963, Sheila Frances (*née* Beauchamp); three *d* (and one *s* two *d* by a former marr.; two *step s*). *Educ:* City of London Sch. and privately. War service in Royal Artillery. Called to the Bar, Gray's Inn, 1946. Asst Commissioner, Boundary Commission for England. Mem., Cttee Public Participation in Planning (Min. Housing and Local Govt), 1968; Chm., Gen. Council of the Bar's Cttee on Administrative Law, 1967-. *Publications:* various legal. *Recreations:* theatre, ski-ing, sailing. *Address:* Little Northover, Akeley, Bucks. *T:* Lillingstone

Dayrell 233. *Clubs:* Reform; Northampton and County (Northampton).

**FRANK, Prof. Frederick Charles,** OBE 1946; FRS 1954; DPhil; Henry Overton Wills Professor of Physics and Director of the H. H. Wills Physics Laboratory, University of Bristol, since 1969 (Professor in Physics, 1954-69); *b* 6 March 1911; *e s* of Frederick and Medora Frank; *m* 1940, Maia Maita Asché, *y d* of late Prof. B. M. Asché; no *c. Educ:* Thetford Grammar Sch.; Ipswich Sch.; Lincoln Coll., Oxford. BA, BSc, Oxon. 1933; DPhil Oxon. 1937; Hon. Fellow, Lincoln Coll., 1968. Research: Dyson Perrins Laboratory and Engineering Laboratory, Oxford, 1933-36; Kaiser Wilhelm Institut für Physik, Berlin, 1936-38; Colloid Science Laboratory, Cambridge, 1939-40; Scientific Civil Service (temp.), 1940-46; Chemical Defence Research Establishment, 1940, Air Ministry, 1940-46; Research, H. H. Wills Physical Laboratory, Bristol Univ., 1946-; Research Fellow in Theoretical Physics, 1948; Reader in Physics, 1951-54; a Vice-Pres., Royal Society, 1967-69. Hon. DSc, Ghent, 1955. *Publications:* articles in various learned journals, mostly dealing either with dielectrics or the physics of solids in particular crystal dislocations and crystal growth. *Recreations:* hill walking, digging. *Address:* Orchard Cottage, Grove Road, Coombe Dingle, Bristol 9. *T:* Bristol 68-1708. *Club:* Athenæum.

**FRANK, Ilya Mikhailovich;** Professor, Moscow University, since 1944; working at Lebedev Institute of Physics under USSR Academy of Sciences, since 1934, where he heads atomic nuclear physics laboratory; *b* Leningrad, 23 Oct. 1908; *yr s* of Mikhail Lyudvigovich Frank, Prof. of mathematics, and Dr Yelizaveta Mikhailovna Gratsianova; *m* 1937, Ella Abramovna Beilikhis, historian; one *s. Educ:* Moscow University (under S. I. Vavilov's guidance). Engaged by State Optical Inst. in Leningrad after graduation and worked at Prof. A. H. Terenin's laboratory, 1931-34; DSc 1935. Subsequently taught at Moscow Univ. Elected Corr. Mem. USSR Acad. of Sciences, 1946. Has participated from beginning in investigations dealing with Vavilov-Cerenkov radiation; carried out many theoretical investigations into Vavilov-Cerenkov effects and in related problems (The Doppler effect in a refractive medium, transition, radiation, etc.) and continues this research. Awarded Nobel Prize for Physics (jointly with P. A. Cerenkov and I. E. Tamm) for discovery and interpretation of Cerenkov effect, 1958. *Address:* PN Lebedev Institute of Physics, Academy of Sciences of the USSR, Moscow, USSR.

**FRANK, Sir Robert John,** 3rd Bt, *cr* 1920; ARICS, FAI; late Flying Officer, RAFVR; Director, Ashdale Land and Property Co. Ltd, since 1963; *b* 16 March 1925; *s* of Sir Howard Frank, 1st Bt, GBE, KCB, and Nancy Muriel (she *m* 2nd, 1932, Air-Marshal Sir Arthur Coningham, KCB, KBE, DSO), *e d* of John Brooks; *S* brother, killed in action, 1944; *m* 1st, 1950, Angela Elizabeth (marriage diss., 1959), *e d* of Sir Kenelm Cayley, 10th Bt, *qv*; two *d*; 2nd, 1960, Margaret Joyce Truesdale; one *s. Heir: s* Robert Andrew Frank, *b* 16 May 1964. *Address:* Ruscombe End, Waltham St Lawrence, near Reading, Berks. *Club:* Bath.

**FRANKEL, Benjamin;** composer; *b* 31 Jan. 1906; *s* of late Charles (Polish birth) and late Golda Dora (Austrian birth); *m* 1st, 1932, Joyce Stanmore Rayner (marriage dissolved, 1945); two *s* (one *d* decd); 2nd, 1945, Phyllis (Anna) Leat (*d* 1967). *Educ:* Latymer Sch., Hammersmith. Began as watchmaker's asst; studied piano, Cologne and Berlin with Victor Benham; earned living as jazz violinist in night clubs while continuing further studies at Guildhall Sch. of Music under Orlando Morgan; composition scholarship, Worshipful Co. of Musicians. Conducted in theatre for C. B. Cochran, Noel Coward and others; more than 100 original scores for films. Since 1958 resident in Switzerland. FGSM 1951. *Publications:* Quartets, Trios, other Chamber works, 7 Symphonies, Instrumental Mass, Songs, etc. (publ. England). *Recreations:* walking, claret. *Address:* Via ai Monti 11, Locarno, Switzerland. *T:* (093) 7.13.27.

**FRANKEL, Dan;** *b* 18 Aug. 1900; *s* of Harris Frankel, Mile End; *m* 1921, Lily, *d* of Joseph Marks, Stepney; one *s*. Mem. LCC for Mile End Division of Stepney, 1931-46; MP (Lab) Mile End Division of Stepney, 1935-45. *Address:* 670a Finchley Road, NW11.

**FRANKEL, Sir Otto (Herzberg),** Kt 1966; FRS 1953; DSc; DAgr; FRSNZ; FAA; Senior Research Fellow, Division of Plant Industry, CSIRO, Canberra, Australia, since 1966; Vice-President, International Biological Programme, since 1966; *b* 4 Nov. 1900; *m* 1939, Margaret Anderson. *Educ:* Vienna; Berlin; Cambridge. Plant Geneticist, 1929-42, and Chief Executive Officer, 1942-49, Wheat Research Institute, NZ; Dir, Crop Research Division, Dept of Scientific and Industrial Research, New Zealand, 1949-51; Chief, Division of Plant Industry, CSIRO, Australia, 1951-62; Member of Executive, Commonwealth Scientific and Industrial Research Organization, Melbourne, Aust, 1962-66. *Publications:* numerous articles in British, NZ and Australian scientific journals. *Recreations:* ski-ing, gardening, angling. *Address:* 4 Cobby Street, Campbell, Canberra, ACT 2601, Australia. *T:* 479460.

**FRANKEL, Prof. Sally Herbert,** MA Rand, PhD London, DScEcon London, MA Oxon; Professor in the Economics of Underdeveloped Countries; Professorial Fellow, Nuffield College; *b* 22 Nov. 1903; *e s* of Jacob Frankel; *m* 1928, Ilse Jeanette Frankel; one *s* one *d*. *Educ:* St John's Coll., Johannesburg; University of the Witwatersrand; London Sch. of Economics. Prof. of Economics, University of Witwatersrand, Johannesburg, 1931-46; responsible for calculations of National Income of S Africa for the Treasury, 1941-48; Jt Editor of South African Journal of Economics from its inception to 1946; Mem. of Union of South Africa Treasury Advisory Council on Economic and Financial Policy, 1941-45; Mem. of Union of South Africa Miners' Phthisis Commission, 1941-42; Commissioner appointed by Govts of Southern and Northern Rhodesia and the Bechuanaland Protectorate to report upon Rhodesia Railways Ltd, 1942-43; Chm. Commission of Enquiry into Mining Industry of Southern Rhodesia, 1945; Mem. East Africa Royal Commission, 1953-55; Consultant Adviser, Urban African Affairs Commn, Govt of S Rhodesia, 1957-58. *Publications:* Co-operation and Competition in the Marketing of Maize in South Africa, 1926; The Railway Policy of South Africa, 1928; Coming of Age: Studies in South African Citizenship and Politics (with Mr J. H. Hofmeyr and others), 1930; Capital Investment in Africa: Its Course and Effects, 1938; The Economic Impact on Underdeveloped Societies: Essays on International Investment and Social Change, 1953; Investment and the Return to Equity Capital in the South African Gold Mining Industry 1887-1965: An International Comparison, 1967; Gold and International Equity Investment (Hobart Paper 45), 1969.

*Recreation:* gardening. *Address:* The Knoll House, Hinksey Hill, Oxford. *T:* Oxford 35345. *Club:* Reform.

**FRANKEL, William,** CBE 1970; Editor, Jewish Chronicle, since 1958; *b* 3 Feb. 1917; *s* of Isaac and Anna Frankel, London; *m* 1939, Gertrude Freda Reed; one *s* one *d*. *Educ:* elementary and secondary schs in London; London Univ. (LLB Hons). Called to Bar, Middle Temple, 1944; practised on South-Eastern circuit, 1944-55. General Manager, Jewish Chronicle, 1955-58. Director: Jewish Chronicle Ltd; Vallentine Mitchell & Co. Ltd; Jewish Gazette Ltd. Vis. Prof., Jewish Theological Seminary of America, 1968-69. *Address:* 25 Furnival Street, EC4. *T:* 01-405 9252. *Clubs:* Athenæum, MCC.

**FRANKEN, Rose, (Mrs W. B. Meloney);** Novelist; Playwright; *b* Texas, 28 Dec. 1898; *m* 1915, Dr S. W. A. Franken (*decd*); three *s*; *m* 1938, William Brown Meloney. *Educ:* Ethical Culture Sch., NYC. *Publications: novels:* Pattern, 1925; Twice Born, 1935, new edn 1970; Of Great Riches, 1937 (as Gold Pennies, UK, 1938); Claudia: the story of a marriage, 1939; Claudia and David, 1940; Another Claudia, 1943; Young Claudia, 1946; The Marriage of Claudia, 1948; From Claudia to David, 1949; The Fragile Years (as Those Fragile Years, UK), 1952; Rendezvous (as The Quiet Heart, UK), 1954; Return of Claudia, 1957; Antic Years, 1958; (with W. B. Meloney): Call Back Love, 1937; Strange Victory, 1939; American Bred, 1941; When Doctors Disagree, 1941; (autobiography) When All is Said and Done, 1963; You're Well Out of Hospital, 1966; *plays:* Another Language, 1932; (with J. Lewin) Mr Dooley, Jr: a comedy for children, 1932; Claudia, 1941; Outrageous Fortune, 1944; Soldier's Wife, 1945; Hallams, 1948; also short stories. *Address:* New Canaan, Conn, USA.

**FRANKLAND,** family name of **Baron Zouche.**

**FRANKLAND, (Anthony) Noble,** DFC 1944; MA, DPhil; Director of Imperial War Museum since 1960; *b* 4 July 1922; *s* of late Edward Frankland, Ravenstonedale, Westmorland; *m* 1944, Diana Madeline Fovargue, *d* of late G. V. Tavernor, of Madras and Southern Mahratta Rly, India; one *s* one *d*. *Educ:* Sedbergh; Trinity Coll., Oxford. Served Royal Air Force, 1941-45 (Bomber Command, 1943-45). Air Historical Branch Air Ministry, 1948-51; Official Military Historian, Cabinet Office, 1951-58. Rockefeller Fellow, 1953. Deputy Dir of Studies, Royal Institute of International Affairs, 1956-60. Lees Knowles Lecturer, Trinity Coll., Cambridge, 1963. *Publications:* Documents on International Affairs: for 1955, 1958; for 1956, 1959; for 1957, 1960; Crown of Tragedy, Nicholas II, 1960; The Strategic Air Offensive Against Germany, 1939-1945 (4 vols) jointly with Sir Charles Webster, 1961; The Bombing Offensive against Germany, Outlines and Perspectives, 1965; Bomber Offensive: the devastation of Europe, 1970. Historical Chapter in Manual of Air Force Law, 1956; other articles. *Address:* Thames House, Eynsham, Oxford. *T:* Eynsham 327. *Club:* Athenæum.

**FRANKLAND, Noble;** *see* Frankland, A. N.

**FRANKLIN, Albert Andrew Ernst,** CVO 1965; CBE 1961 (OBE 1950); HM Consul-General, Los Angeles, USA, since 1966; *b* 28 Nov. 1914; *s* of Albert John Henry Franklin; *m* 1944, Henrietta Irene Barry; two *d*. *Educ:* Merchant Taylors' Sch.; St John's Coll., Oxford. Joined HM Consular Service, 1937; served in Peking, Kunming, Chungking, Calcutta, Algiers, Marseilles, Kabul, Basle, Tientsin, Formosa, Düsseldorf and in the FO. Member of Kitchener Association. *Recreation:* Chinese ceramics. *Address:* British Consulate-General, 3324 Wilshire Boulevard, Los Angeles, Calif 90005, USA.

**FRANKLIN, Alfred White,** FRCP; Physician in charge of Department of Child Health, Saint Bartholomew's Hospital; Pædiatrician, Queen Charlotte's Maternity Hospital; *b* 1905; *yr s* of Philip Franklin, FRCS; *m* 1943, Ann Grizel, *er d* of late Rev. Francis Dent Vaisey; two *s* two *d*. *Educ:* Epsom Coll.; Clare Coll., Cambridge (scholar); St Bartholomew's Hospital. MB, BCh, 1933, FRCP, 1942. Lawrence Scholarship and Gold Medal, 1933 and 1934, St Bartholomew's Hosp.; Temple Cross Research Fellow, Johns Hopkins Hosp., 1934-35. Pædiatrician to Sector III, EMS. Formerly Chm., Invalid Chidren's Aid Assoc.; Co-founder and Treasurer, The Osler Club, London. Past Pres., British Pædiatric Assoc.; Treasurer, British Soc. for Medical History. *Publications:* (Ed.) Selected Writings of Sir D'Arcy Power, 1931, and of Sir William Osler, 1951; (Ed.) The Care of Invalid and Crippled Children, 1960; contrib. to books and jls on medical, historical and bibliographical subjects. *Address:* 149 Harley Street, W1. *T:* 01-935 4444; The Cottage, Northaw, Herts. *T:* Potters Bar (PR) 52184. *Club:* Athenæum.

**FRANKLIN, Sir Eric (Alexander),** Kt 1954; CBE 1952; *b* 3 July 1910; *s* of late William John Franklin; *m* 1936, Joy Stella, *d* of late George Oakes Lucas, Cambridge. *Educ:* The English Sch., Maymyo; Emmanuel Coll., Cambridge. Appointed to ICS in 1935 and posted to Burma; Subdivisional Officer, 1936-39. Deputy Registrar, High Court of Judicature at Rangoon, 1939-40; District and Sessions Judge, Arakan, 1941-42; Deputy Sec. to Government of Burma at Simla, 1942-45; Registrar, High Court of Judicature at Rangoon, 1946-47; retired prematurely from ICS, 1948. Appointed on contract as Deputy Sec. to Government of Pakistan. Cabinet Secretariat, 1949; Joint Sec., Cabinet Secretariat, 1952; Establishment Officer and Head of Central Organisation and Methods Office, 1953; Establishment Sec. to Governmnet of Pakistan, 1956-58; Chm. Sudan Government Commission on terms of service, 1958-59; Civil Service Adviser to Government of Hashemite Kingdom of Jordan, 1960-63; acting Resident Representative, UN Technical Assistance Board, Jordan, 1961; Senior UN Administrative Adviser to Government of Nepal, 1964-66. Chm., Cambridgeshire Soc. for the Blind. *Recreations:* walking, hill-climbing, music, and caring for dogs. *Address:* The Birches, 16 Cavendish Avenue, Cambridge.

**FRANKLIN, George Frederic;** formerly Headmaster, Lincoln School, retired Dec. 1957; *b* Greenwich, 28 Dec. 1897; *s* of John and Alice Franklin; *m* 1926, Edith Kate Young; one *s* one *d*. *Educ:* Roan Sch.; King's Coll., Cambridge. Asst Master, Merchant Taylors' Sch., Crosby; Senior Mod. Langs Master, Christ's Hosp. *Publications:* French and German school texts. *Address:* Wilburton, Ely, Cambs.

**FRANKLIN, Henry William Fernehough;** Headmaster Epsom College, 1940-1962; *b* 30 June 1901; *s* of Henry Franklin, Schoolmaster; *m* 1931, Phyllis Denham; one *d*. *Educ:* Christ's Hosp.; Christ Church, Oxford. Asst Master, Radley Coll., 1924-27; Asst Master, Rugby Sch., 1927-39. Chm. of Home Office Departmental Cttee on Punishments in

Prisons, Borstals, etc., 1948. Mem., Advertising Standards Authority, 1962-67. *Publications:* Fifty Latin Lyrics, 1955; (with J. A. G. Bruce) Latin Prose Composition, 1937; Latin Reader, 1939. *Recreations:* formerly various games: cricket (OU XI 1924; Essex County XI); Rugby football (OU XV 1923; Barbarian FC), hockey, fives, etc.; also music and change-ringing; nowadays mostly teaching and change-ringing. *Address:* The Cottage, Westward Lane, West Chiltington, Pulborough, Sussex. *T:* W Chiltington 2282. *Club:* MCC.

**FRANKLIN, John Lewis,** MA, MD Cambridge; FRCP; Consulting Dermatologist: Westminster Hospital; Princess Beatrice Hospital; Edenbridge Cottage Hospital; *b* 13 Feb. 1904; *e s* of late Philip Franklin, FRCS; *m* 1937, Katharine Mary Raeburn Balmer (marr. diss. 1947); one *s* one *d*; *m* 1968, Dorothy Balderston. *Educ:* Epsom Coll.; Pembroke Coll., Cambridge; St George's Hosp. Medical Sch. Represented Cambridge Univ. versus Oxford at fencing with the épée, 1925. *Publications:* Diseases of the Skin (with Dr S. E. Dore), 1934; numerous papers on dermatological subjects. *Recreation:* fishing. *Address:* 100 Harley Street, W1. *T:* 01-935 6377.

**FRANKLIN, Michael David Milroy;** Under-Secretary (External Relations), Ministry of Agriculture, Fisheries and Food, since 1968; *b* 24 Aug. 1927; *o s* of late Milroy Franklin; *m* 1951, Dorothy Joan Fraser; two *s* one *d*. *Educ:* Taunton Sch.; Peterhouse, Cambridge. Asst Principal, Min. of Agric. and Fisheries, 1950; Economic Section, Cabinet Office (subseq. Treasury), 1952-55; Principal, Min. of Agric., Fisheries and Food, 1956; UK Delegn to OEEC (subseq. OECD), 1959-61; Private Sec. to Minister of Agric., Fisheries and Food, 1961-64; Asst Sec., Head of Sugar and Tropical Foodstuffs Div., 1965. *Address:* 15 Galley Lane, Barnet, Herts. *T:* 01-440 4460. *Club:* United University.

**FRANKLIN, Norman Laurence,** OBE 1963; MSc, PhD; Member for Production, UK Atomic Energy Authority, since 1969; *b* 1 Sept. 1924; *s* of William Alexander and Beatrice Franklin; *m* 1949, Bessie Coupland; one *s* one *d*. *Educ:* Batley Grammar School; University of Leeds. British Coke Res. Assoc., 1945-48; Lecturer in Chemical Engineering, Univ. of Leeds, 1948-55; UK Atomic Energy Authority, 1955-. *Publications:* Statistical Analysis in Chemistry and the Chemical Industry, 1954; The Transport Properties of Fluids, Vol. 4, Chemical Engineering Practice, 1957; Heat Transfer by Conduction, Vol. 7, Chemical Engineering Practice, 1963; papers in Trans Instn of Chemical Engineers, 1953-66. *Recreation:* walking. *Address:* 9 Fir Tree Avenue, Knutsford, Cheshire. *T:* Knutsford 3045. *Club:* East India and Sports.

**FRANKLIN, Olga Heather,** CBE 1950 (MBE 1919); RRC 1946 (ARRC 1942); *b* 20 Sept. 1895; *e c* of late Robert Francis Franklin, OBE. *Educ:* St Michael's Lodge, Stoke, Devonport, VAD, 1915-17; WRNS, 1917-19; King's Coll. Hosp., 1923; Queen Alexandra's Royal Naval Nursing Service, 1927-50; Matron-in-Chief, 1947-50; King's Hon. Nursing Sister (the first appointed), 1947-50; retired, 1950. Prisoner of war, Hongkong, 1941-45. *Address:* Hillcroft, Rottingdean, Sussex. *T:* Brighton 32202. *Club:* Naval and Military.

**FRANKLIN, Richard Harrington;** Surgeon: Royal Postgraduate Medical School since 1945; Kingston Hospital since 1946; St Anthony's Hospital, Cheam, since 1959; Consulting Surgeon to the Royal Navy, since 1961; Hon. Consulting Surgeon, Star and Garter Home, Richmond, since 1957; *b* 3 April 1906; *s* of late P. C. Franklin; *m* 1933, Helen Margaret Kimber, *d* of Sir Henry D. Kimber, Bt; two *s*. *Educ:* Merchant Taylors' Sch.; St Thomas's Hosp., London Univ. MRCS, LRCP 1930; MB, BS 1930; FRCS 1934. First Asst, Brit. Postgrad. Med. Sch., 1936; Surgeon EMS, 1940-45; Hunterian Prof., RCS, 1947. Fellow, Med. Soc. of London. Mem. Ct of Examrs, RCS, 1956-66; Examr in Surgery, Cambridge Univ., 1958-69. Vice-Pres. 1960, Pres. 1969-70, Sect. of Surgery, RSM; Mem. Coun., RCS, 1965-; Mem. Coun., Imperial Cancer Research Fund, 1967. *Publications:* Surgery of the Oesophagus, 1952; articles in various med. jls and text books. *Recreation:* sailing. *Address:* 148 Harley Street, W1. *T:* 01-935 1207; Wolsey House, 4 Montpelier Row, Twickenham, Middx. *Clubs:* Ranelagh Sailing, Aldeburgh Yacht.

**FRANKLYN, Charles Aubrey Hamilton,** MD Lausanne, MB, BS London, MA *hc* Malaya 1951; MRCS, LRCP 1923; FLS; FSA Scot.; Physician and Genealogical historian; *b* Brentwood, Co. Essex, 25 Aug. 1896; *er s* of late Aubrey Hamilton Franklyn and Ethel Mary, *d* of late Walter Gray. *Educ:* Tonbridge Sch.; St Thomas's Hosp.; Universities of London, Lausanne, Oxford (Exeter Coll.), France, 1916-19. Lieut RA (SR), 1915-20; in practice as physician from 1925; temp. MO, P & O Line, 1933; MO (part-time) HM Prison, Lincoln, 1934-37; in EMS (Grade III) from 1939. Mem. of Standing Cttee, University of London, 1927-61 (Senior mem., 1954-61); Bedell of Convocation, University of London, from 1932; a Provincial Supervisor in Charge of Final Degree Examns (June) 1941-56. Mem. BMA, 1923-48; Life Mem. Oxford Soc.; Fellow Philosophical Soc. of England; Mem. Amer. Institute for Philosophical Studies. Hon. Asst to Editor Burke's Landed Gentry, Centenary (15th) edn, 1937, and to Editor Armorial Families, 7th edn, 1929-30 (2 vols). Authority on Academical Dress, University Degrees and Ceremonies, Modern Heraldry and Genealogy, etc. Designer of Official Robes and Academical Dress for Universities: Malaya, Australian National, Southampton, Hull; designed: armorial ensigns and 3 badges, British Transport Commn, 1956; Arms of Borough of Bridgnorth, 1959; Arms of St Peter's Hall (now College), Oxford. *Publications:* The Bearing of Coat-Armour by Ladies, 1923; English and Scottish Heraldry compared and contrasted (Scots. Mag. Jan. 1925); University Hoods and Robes (25 cards), 1926; The Genealogy of the Chavasse Family, 1929; A Genealogical History of The Family of Tiarks of Foxbury, 1929, 2nd edition, rev. and enlarged 1966 (priv. printed); A Genealogical and Heraldic History of Four Families (privately printed), 1932; A Genealogical History of the families of Paulet (or Pawlett), Berewe (or Barrow), Lawrence, and Parker (privately printed), 1964, Supplement, Morgan of Llanfabon, Turner of Oldland in Keymer, etc, 1969; A Genealogical History of the Families of Montgomerie of Garboldisham, Hunter of Knap, and Montgomerie of Fittleworth (privately printed), 1968; Academical Dress from the Middle Ages to the Present Day, including Lambeth Degrees, 1970. Cuckfield Rural Dist. Official Local Guide (new edn), 1947; A Dedication Service for the Parish Church of St John the Baptist, Mexborough, 1967; contribs to Enc. Brit., to 5th edn of Grove's Dic. of Music and Musicians, to Pears Cyclopædia, to Chambers's Enc., etc. *Recreations:* music, cats, motoring, travelling, lecturing, and writing, etc. *Address:* Wickham Hill House, Hassocks, Sussex; c/o Westminster Bank, Ltd, 1 Lee Road, Blackheath, SE3; Exeter College, Oxford. *T:* Hurstpierpoint 2100.

**FRANKS,** family name of **Baron Franks.**

**FRANKS,** Baron *cr* 1962, of Headington (Life Peer); **Oliver Shewell Franks,** PC 1949; GCMG, 1952; KCB 1946; CBE 1942; FBA 1960; Provost of Worcester College, Oxford, since 1962; Chancellor of East Anglia University since 1965; *b* 16 Feb. 1905; *s* of late Rev. R. S. Franks; *m* 1931, Barbara Mary Tanner; two *d.* *Educ:* Bristol Grammar Sch.; Queen's Coll., Oxford (MA). Fellow and Praelector in Philosophy, Queen's College, Oxford, 1927-37; University Lecturer in Philosophy, 1935-37; Visiting Prof., Univ. of Chicago, 1935; Prof. of Moral Philosophy, University of Glasgow, 1937-45; temp. Civil Servant, Ministry of Supply, 1939-46; Permanent Sec. Ministry of Supply, 1945-46; Provost of Queen's Coll., Oxford, 1946-48. British Ambassador at Washington, 1948-52; Director: Lloyds Bank Ltd, (Chm., 1954-62); Schroders; Chm., Friends' Provident & Century Life Office, 1955-62; Cttee of London Clearing Bankers, 1960-62; Mem. of Rhodes Trust 1957-; Chairman: Bd of Govs, United Oxford Hosps, 1958-64; Wellcome Trust, 1965- (Trustee, 1963-65); Pres., Kennedy Memorial Cttee, 1963; Commission of Inquiry into Oxford Univ., 1964-66. Mem., National Economic Development Council, 1962-64. Trustee: Pilgrim Trust, 1947-; Rockefeller Foundn, 1961-70. Hon. Fellow: Queen's Coll., Oxford, 1948; St Catharine's Coll., Cambridge, 1966; Wolfson Coll., Oxford, 1967; Visiting Fellow, Nuffield Coll., 1959. Hon. DCL, Oxford, and other Honorary Doctorates. *Address:* The Provost's Lodgings, Worcester College, Oxford. *Club:* Athenæum.

**FRANKS, Arthur Temple,** CMG 1967; HM Diplomatic Service; Foreign Office since 1966; *b* 13 July 1920; *s* of Arthur Franks, Hove; *m* 1945, Rachel Marianne, *d* of late Rev. A. E. S. Ward, Thame, Oxon; one *s* two *d.* *Educ:* Rugby; Queen's Coll., Oxford. HM Forces, 1940-46 (despatches). Entered Foreign Service, 1949; British Middle East Office, 1952; Tehran, 1953; Bonn, 1962. *Address:* South Corner, Pachesham Park, Leatherhead, Surrey. *T:* Oxshott 2038. *Clubs:* Travellers'; Sunningdale Golf.

**FRANKS, Mrs David;** *see* Glauert, Audrey Marion.

**FRANKS, Air Vice-Marshal John Gerald,** CB 1954; CBE 1949; RAF retired, 1960; *b* 23 May 1905; *e s* of late James Gordon Franks, and of Margaret, *y d* of Lord Chief Justice Fitz-Gibbon, Dublin; *m* 1936, Jessica Rae West; two *d.* *Educ:* Cheltenham Coll.; RAF Coll., Cranwell. RAF; commissioned from Cranwell, 1924; Mediterranean, 1928-29; India, 1930-35; Middle East, 1936; RAF Staff Coll., 1939; Air Armament Sch., Manby, 1941; Experimental Establishment, Boscombe Down, 1944; Dir Armament Research and Development, 1945-48; idc 1951; Comdt RAF Technical Coll., Henlow, 1952; Air Officer Commanding No 24 Group, Royal Air Force, 1952-55; Pres. of Ordnance Board, 1959-60. Comdr American Legion of Merit, 1948. *Recreations:* golf, fishing, shooting. *Address:* The Old Glebe, Templeshanbo, Ferns, Co. Wexford, Republic of Ireland.

**FRASER,** family name of **Barons Fraser of Lonsdale, Fraser of North Cape,** also of **Barons Lovat, Saltoun** and **Strathalmond.**

**FRASER OF ALLANDER;** Barony of (*cr* 1964); title disclaimed by 2nd Baron; *see under* Fraser, Sir Hugh, 2nd Bt.

**FRASER OF LONSDALE,** Baron *cr* 1958 (Life Peer); **William Jocelyn Ian Fraser,** CH 1953; Kt 1934; CBE 1922; Chairman of the Council of St Dunstan's since 1921; Life President, St Dunstan's, South Africa; National President British Legion, 1947-58; Vice-President Royal National Institute for the Blind; Trustee, South Africa Foundation; Chairman: Frasers Ltd, South Africa; Bass Charrington Vintners Ltd; Sun Alliance Insurance Group (West End); Director, Canada Dry (UK) Ltd; *b* Eastbourne, 1897; *o s* of late William Percy Fraser and Ethel Maude, *d* of J. P. Cooke, Johannesburg; *m* Irene Gladys, CBE, *d* of George Mace, Chipping Norton; one *d.* *Educ:* Marlborough; RMC, Sandhurst. Served European War, 1915-16, 1st Batt. King's (Shropshire) Light Infantry, attached 1/4th Glosters; Mem. London County Council (North St Pancras Div.), 1922-25; MP (U) North St Pancras Div., 1924-29 and 1931-36, resigned; MP (U), Lonsdale Div. of Lancaster, 1940-50, Morecambe and Lonsdale Div. of Lancaster, 1950-58. Mem. Broadcasting Cttee of Inquiry, 1925-26; Governor, British Broadcasting Corporation, 1937-39 and 1941-46. Barrister-at-Law, Inner Temple, 1932. *Publication:* Whereas I Was Blind, 1942; My Story of St Dunstan's, 1961. *Recreation:* fishing. *Address:* St John's Lodge, Inner Circle, Regent's Park, NW1. *T:* 01-935 8232; Low Wood House, Haverthwaite, Ulverston, Lancs; Fraser House, Wepener, Orange Free State, South Africa. *Clubs:* Bath, Flyfishers'; Rand (Johannesburg).

**FRASER OF NORTH CAPE,** 1st Baron, *cr* 1946, of Molesey; **Admiral of the Fleet Bruce Austin Fraser,** GCB, *cr* 1944 (KCB 1943; CB 1939); KBE 1941; (OBE 1919); Hon. DCL Oxon; *b* 1888; *s* of late Gen. Alex. Fraser, RE, CB. *Educ:* Bradfield. Was Flag Captain, East Indies; commanded Glorious; Chief of Staff, Mediterranean Fleet; Third Sea Lord and Controller, 1939-42; 2nd-in-Command, Home Fleet, 1942; C-in-C Home Fleet, 1943-44; Adm. 1944; C-in-C Eastern Fleet, 1944; C-in-C British Pacific Fleet, 1945-46; C-in-C Portsmouth, 1947-48; Adm. of the Fleet, 1948; First Sea Lord and Chief of Naval Staff, 1948-51. Hon. Degrees Oxford, Edinburgh and Wales Univs. *Heir:* none. *Address:* 18 Wolsey Road, E Molesey, Surrey. *T:* 01-979 1136. *Club:* United Service.

**FRASER, Hon. Lord; Walter Ian Reid Fraser;** one of the Senators of HM College of Justice in Scotland since 1964; Member of the Queen's Body Guard for Scotland (Royal Company of Archers); *b* 3 Feb. 1911; *o s* of late Alexander Reid Fraser, stockbroker, Glasgow; *m* 1943, (Mary Ursula) Cynthia (Gwendolen), *o d* of Col I. H. Macdonell, DSO (late HLI); one *s.* *Educ:* Repton; Balliol Coll., Oxford (scholar). BA Oxon 1932; LLB Glasgow 1935; Advocate, 1936; QC Scotland 1953. Lecturer in Constitutional Law, Glasgow Univ., 1936; and at Edinburgh Univ., 1948. Served Army (RA and staff), 1939-45; UK; Burma. Contested (U) East Edinburgh constituency, Gen. Election, 1955. Mem. Royal Commission on Police, 1960. Dean of the Faculty of Advocates, 1959-64. *Publication:* Outline of Constitutional Law, 1938 (2nd edn, 1948). *Recreations:* shooting, walking. *Address:* 20 Moray Place, Edinburgh. *T:* 031-225 3509; Tullybelton House, Bankfoot, Perthshire. *T:* Bankfoot 312. *Clubs:* New (Edinburgh); Western (Glasgow).

**FRASER, Lady Antonia;** writer; *b* 27 Aug. 1932; *er d* of 7th Earl of Longford, *qv*, and of Countess of Longford, *qv*; *m* 1956, Rt Hon. Hugh Charles Patrick Joseph Fraser, *qv*; three *s* three *d*. *Educ:* Dragon School, Oxford; St Mary's Convent, Ascot; Lady Margaret Hall, Oxford. Has lectured, broadcast and appeared on television. Member, Arts Council, 1970-. *Publications:* King Arthur and the Knights of the Round Table, 1954 (reissued, 1970); Robin Hood, 1955; Dolls, 1963; A History of Toys, 1966; Mary Queen of Scots (James Tait Black Memorial Prize, 1969), 1969. *Recreation:* family life. *Address:* 52 Campden Hill Square, W8; Eilean Aigas, Beauly, Invernesshire.

**FRASER, Sir (Arthur) Ronald,** KBE, *cr* 1949 (MBE 1930); CMG 1934; *b* 3 Nov. 1888; *s* of late John and Louisa Fraser; *m* 1915, Sylvia Blanche Powell; two *s* two *d*. *Educ:* St Paul's. Served European War, Flanders and France, 1914-16 (wounded and disabled for further active service); civil servant; acted as Gen. Sec. during the Anglo-Argentine negotiations of 1933, and as Board of Trade Representative and adviser to HM Ambassador, Buenos Aires, during the subsequent tariff negotiations, 1933; Minister (Commercial), HM Embassy, Paris, 1944-49, and Resident Government Dir, Suez Canal Co.; Pres. Caledonian Soc. of France, 1946-53. Companion Order of Orange Nassau. *Publications:* under the name of Ronald Fraser: The Flying Draper, 1924; Landscape with Figures, 1925 and 1952; Flower Phantoms, 1926; The Vista, 1928; Rose Anstey, 1930; Marriage in Heaven, 1932; Tropical Waters, 1933; The Ninth of July, 1934; Surprising Results, 1935; A House in the Park, 1937; Bird under Glass, 1938; Miss Lucifer, 1939; Financial Times, 1942; The Fiery Gate, 1943; Circular Tour, 1946; Maia, 1948; Sun in Scorpio, 1949; Beetle's Career, 1951; Glimpses of the Sun, 1952; Latin America: A Personal Survey, 1953; Bell From a Distant Temple, 1954; Flight of Wild Geese, 1955; Lord of the East, 1956; The Wine of Illusion, 1957; A Visit from Venus, 1958; Jupiter in the Chair, 1958; Trout's Testament, 1959; City of the Sun, 1961; Her-Bak Egyptian Initiate (translation from the French), 1967. *Address:* Swanlands, Chinnor Hill, Oxford. *T:* Kingston Blount 405.

**FRASER, Sir Basil (Malcolm),** 2nd Bt, *cr* 1921; *b* 2 Jan. 1920; *s* of Sir (John) Malcolm Fraser, 1st Bt, GBE, and of Irene, *d* of C. E. Brightman of South Kensington; *S* father, 1949. *Educ:* Northaw, Pluckley, Kent; Eton Coll.; Queen's Coll., Cambridge. Served War of 1939-45, RE, 1940-42; Madras Sappers and Miners, 1942-46 (despatches). Mem. AA and RAC. *Recreations:* motoring, music, electronic reproduction of sound. *Heir:* none. *Address:* 175 Beach Street, Deal, Kent. *Clubs:* Bath, Roadfarers'.

**FRASER, Sir Bruce (Donald),** KCB 1961 (CB 1956); Comptroller and Auditor-General, Exchequer and Audit Department, since 1966; *b* 18 Nov. 1910; *s* of late Maj.-Gen. Sir Theodore Fraser, KCB and late Constance Ruth Fraser (*née* Stevenson); *m* 1939, Audrey, *d* of late Lieut-Col E. L. Croslegh; one *d* (one *s* decd). *Educ:* Bedford Sch.; Trinity Coll., Cambridge (Scholar); First Class in Classical Tripos Part I, 1930 and in English Tripos Part II, 1932; BA 1932, MA 1964. Ed. the Granta, 1932. Entered Civil Service as Asst Principal, Scottish Office, 1933; transf. to HM Treasury, 1936; Private Sec. to Financial Sec., 1937, and to Permanent Sec., 1941; Asst Sec., 1945; Under Sec., 1951; Third Sec., 1956-60; Dep. Sec., Ministry of Aviation, Jan.-April 1960; Permanent Sec., Ministry of Health, 1960-64; Joint Permanent Under-Sec. of State, Dept of Education and Science, 1964-65; Permanent Sec., Ministry of Land and Natural Resources, 1965-66. *Address:* 72 Queen's Gate, SW7. *T:* 01-370 4900. *Club:* Athenæum.

**FRASER, Colin Neil,** QC Scotland 1958; Counsel to Secretary of State under Private Legislation (Scotland) Procedure since 1958; *b* 21 Sept. 1905; *s* of late Robert Dick Fraser, CA; *m* 1937, Alix Leslie, *d* of late Alexander Stephen, shipbuilder, Glasgow; one *s* two *d*. *Educ:* Glenalmond; Glasgow Univ. (MA, LLB). Advocate, 1931; RA (Capt.), 1939-46; Pres., Pensions Appeal Tribunal (Scotland), 1946-58. *Recreations:* ski-ing, golf. *Address:* Catherine Lodge, Inveresk, Musselburgh. *T:* 031-665 2683. *Clubs:* New (Edinburgh); Honourable Company of Edinburgh Golfers.

**FRASER, Maj.-Gen. David William,** OBE 1962; GOC 4 Division, since 1969; *b* 30 Dec. 1920; *s* of Brig. Hon. William Fraser, DSO, MC, *y s* of 18th Lord Saltoun and Pamela, *d* of Cyril Maude and *widow* of Major W. La T. Congreve, VC, DSO, MC; *m* 1st, 1947, Anne Balfour; one *d*; 2nd, 1957, Julia de la Hey; two *s* two *d*. *Educ:* Eton; Christ Church, Oxford. Commnd into Grenadier Guards, 1941; served NW Europe; comd 1st Bn Grenadier Guards, 1960-62; comd 19th Inf. Bde, 1963-65; Dir, Defence Policy, MoD, 1966-69. *Recreation:* shooting. *Address:* Vallenders, Isington, Alton, Hants. *T:* Bentley 3166. *Clubs:* Turf, Pratt's.

**FRASER, Donald Blake,** FRCS; FRCOG; Gynæcologist and Obstetrician, St Bartholomew's Hospital, since 1946; *b* 9 June 1910; *o s* of Dr Thomas B. Fraser, Hatfield Point, NB, Canada; *m* 1939, Betsy, *d* of late Sir James Henderson, KBE; one *s* one *d*. *Educ:* University of New Brunswick; Christ Church, Oxford. Rhodes Scholar, 1930; BA 1st Cl. Hons, 1932, BM, BCh Oxon 1936; MRCS, LRCP, LMCC, 1936; FRCS, 1939; MRCOG, 1940, FRCOG, 1952. Examiner: Central Midwives Bd; Universities of Oxford and London; Conjoint Bd; Royal College of Obstetricians and Gynæcologists. *Publications:* (joint) Midwifery (textbook), 1956. Articles in medical journals. *Recreation:* philately. *Address:* 73 Harley Street, W1N 1DE. *T:* 01-935 6042.

**FRASER, Sir Douglas (Were),** Kt 1966; ISO 1962; President, Queensland Ambulance Transport Brigade Council; Adviser, Civil Defence activities in Queensland; Member: Queensland University Senate; Advisory Council, Queensland Conservatorium of Music; *b* 24 Oct. 1899; *s* of late Robert John Fraser and late Edith Harriet (*née* Shepherd); *m* 1927, Violet Pryke (*d* 1968); three *s*. *Educ:* State High Sch., Gympie, Qld. Entered Qld State Public Service, 1916; Public Service Board and Public Service Comr's Dept; Sec. to Public Service Comr, 1939; Sen. Public Service Inspector, 1947; Dep. Public Service Comr, 1952; Public Service Comr, 1956; retired 1965; War-time Asst Dir of Civil Defence, Sec., Public Safety Adv. Cttee. *Recreations:* gardening, fishing, music, reading. *Address:* 76 Prince Edward Parade, Redcliffe, Qld 4020, Australia. *T:* 84 5538.

**FRASER, Very Rev. Dr Duncan;** Moderator of the General Assembly of the Church of Scotland, May, 1964-65; Minister of the Church of Scotland, Invergordon, 1929-67 (Minister of the United Free Church of Scotland, Invergordon, 1927-29); *b* 7 Aug. 1903; *s* of Rev. Duncan Fraser, Bracadale, Isle of Skye; *m* 1935, Helen Louise, 2nd *d* of ex-Provost John Macdonald, Invergordon. *Educ:* Portree High Sch.; University of Edinburgh; New Coll., Edinburgh. MA Edinburgh, 1924; Hons Diploma in Theology, and Junior

Cunningham Fellow, New Coll., Edinburgh, 1927; PhD Edinburgh, 1944; Hon DD, Edinburgh, 1958. Officiating Minister, RN, 1927-47; Officiating Chaplain, Army and RAF, 1939-45. Member: Ross-shire Educ. Cttee, 1946-49; Invergordon Town Council, 1954-55; Governor, Highlands and Islands Educ. Trust, 1961-70. JP, Ross and Cromarty, 1946-67. *Publications:* Life and Writings of James Fraser of Brea, 1944; Story of Invergordon Church, 1946; contribs to theological jls in UK and USA. *Recreations:* reading, motoring. *Address:* 14 Orchard Road South, Edinburgh 4. *T:* 031-332 5771.

**FRASER, Francis Charles,** CBE 1962; FRS 1966; DSc; FIBiol; Deputy Chief Scientific Officer, British Museum (Natural History), 1960-65; re-employed, Principal Scientific Officer, 1965-69, retired 1969; *b* 16 June 1903; *y s* of James and Barbara Anne Fraser, Dingwall, Ross & Cromarty; *m* 1938, Anne Nuttall. *Educ:* Dingwall; Glasgow Univ. Demonstrator, Dept of Geology, University of Glasgow, 1924-25. "Discovery" investigations, 1925-33, with service in Discovery, William Scoresby, Discovery II and at shore station, S Georgia. Danish Atlantide Expedition, W Africa, 1945-46. British Museum (Natural History): Asst Keeper, Mammalian Osteology, 1933-48; Dep. Keeper of Zoology, 1948-57; Keeper of Zoology, 1957-64. Polar Medal, 1942. *Publications:* (with late J. R. Norman) Giant Fishes, Whales and Dolphins, 1937. Technical papers mainly on subjects relating to whales and dolphins. Reports on Cetaceans stranded on the British Coast, 1926-32, 1933-37, 1938-47. *Recreation:* gardening. *Address:* 78 Hayes Road, Bromley, Kent BR2 9AB. *T:* 01-460 3668. *Club:* Athenæum.

**FRASER, Air Marshal Sir (Henry) Paterson,** KBE 1961 (CBE 1945); CB 1953; AFC 1937; RAF, retired; Chairman, Isle of Man Potteries Ltd; *b* 15 July 1907; *s* of late Harry Fraser, Johannesburg, South Africa; *m* 1933, Avis Gertrude Haswell; two *s*. *Educ:* St Andrews Coll., Grahamstown, South Africa; Pembroke Coll., Cambridge (BA) RAFO, and Pres. University Air Sqdn, Cambridge; joined RAF, 1929; served in India; RAF Engineering Course, Henlow, 1933-34; Aerodynamic Flight, RAE, Farnborough, 1934-38; RAF Staff Coll., 1938; Directorate of War Organization, Air Ministry, 1939-40; commanded Experimental Flying Section, RAE, Farnborough, 1941; Mem. RAF Element, Combined Chiefs of Staff, Washington DC, 1942; Dep. Dir of War Organization, Air Ministry, 1943; Senior Administrative Planner, 2nd Tactical Air Force, 1943-44, and Dep. Air Officer in Charge of Administration, 2nd TAF, 1944-45; commanded Aircraft and Armament Experimental Establishment, Boscombe Down, 1945-46; Dep. Dir (Air Staff) Policy, Air Ministry, 1947-48; Defence Research Policy Staff, Ministry of Defence, 1948-51; idc 1951; Senior Air Staff Officer, Headquarters Fighter Command, 1952-53; Chief of Staff, Headquarters Allied Air Forces, Central Europe, 1954-56; AOC No. 12 Group, Fighter Command, 1956-58; Dir, RAF Exercise Planning, 1959; UK Representative on Permanent Military Deputies Group of Cento, 1959-62; Inspector-Gen., RAF, 1962-64. Taylor Gold Medal of RAeS, 1937; FRAeS. *Address:* Denizli, Ballajora, Maughold, Isle of Man. *Club:* Royal Automobile.

**FRASER, Sir Hugh,** 2nd Bt *cr* 1961, of Dineiddwg; Chairman (since 1966); House of Fraser Ltd (Dep. Chm. 1965; Dir 1958); Harrods Ltd (Managing Director since 1970); John Barker & Co. Ltd; Binns Ltd; J. J. Allen Ltd; Scottish and Universal Investments Ltd; George Outram & Co. Ltd; House of Fraser (Northern Management) Ltd (since 1962); Director: Highland Tourist (Cairngorm Development) Ltd; Noble Grossart Ltd; *b* 18 Dec. 1936; *s* of 1st Baron Fraser of Allander, DL, LLD, JP (Bt 1961) and of Kate Hutcheon, *d* of late Sir Andrew Lewis, LLD, JP; *S* to father's Btcy, and disclaimed Barony, 1966; *m* 1962, Patricia Mary, *e d* of John Bowie; three *d*. *Educ:* St Mary's, Melrose; Kelvinside Academy. *Recreations:* farming, water-skiing. *Address:* Dineiddwg, Mugdock, near Milngavie, Stirlingshire. *T:* Milngavie 1182.

**FRASER, Rt. Hon. Hugh Charles Patrick Joseph,** PC 1962; MBE; MP (C) Stone Div. of Staffs, 1945-50, Stafford and Stone Division of Staffs, since 1950; *b* 23 Jan. 1918; *s* of 16th Baron Lovat; *m* 1956, Lady Antonia Pakenham (*see* Lady Antonia Fraser); three *s* three *d*. *Educ:* Ampleforth Coll.; Balliol Coll., Oxford; The Sorbonne, Paris. Roman Catholic. Ex-Pres. Oxford Union; war service with Lovat Scouts, Phantom and Special Air Service. Parliamentary Private Sec. to Sec. of State for the Colonies, 1951-54; Parl. Under-Sec. of State and Financial Sec., War Office 1958-60. Parliamentary Under-Sec. of State for the Colonies, 1960-62; Sec. of State for Air, 1962-64. Pres., West Midlands Conservative and Unionist Assoc., 1967. Director: Sun Alliance; Ionian Bank; industrial cos. Order of Orange Nassau, Order of Leopold with palm, Belgian Croix de guerre. *Address:* 52 Campden Hill Square, W8; Eilan Aigas, Beauly, Scotland. *Clubs:* Beefsteak, White's.

**FRASER, Col Hugh Vincent,** CMG 1957; OBE 1946; TD 1947; retired 1960; *b* 20 Sept. 1908; *yr s* of William Neilson and Maude Fraser; *m* 1941, Noreen, *d* of Col M O'C Tandy; one *s* one *d*. *Educ:* Sherborne Sch. Commissioned into Royal Tank Regt; served War of 1939-45, India and Burma, with 14th Army. Military Attaché, Cairo, 1954-56; NATO, Washington DC, 1957-60. *Recreations:* hunting, shooting; Master Aldershot Command Beagles, 1939. *Address:* Green End, Steeple Morden, Cambs. *Club:* Army and Navy.

**FRASER, Sir Ian,** Kt 1963; DSO 1943; OBE 1940; DL; FRSE, FRCS, FRCSI, FACS; Senior Surgeon: Royal Victoria Hospital, Belfast; Royal Belfast Hospital for Sick Children; Surgeon in Ordinary to the Governor of Northern Ireland; Hon. Consulting Surgeon to the Army in Northern Ireland; Director, Provincial Bank of Ireland; *b* 9 Feb. 1901; *s* of Robert Moore Fraser, BA, MD, Belfast; *m* 1931, Eleanor Margaret Mitchell; one *s* one *d*. *Educ:* Royal Academical Institution, Belfast; Queen's Univ., Belfast. MB, BCh 1st Cl. Hons 1923; MD 1932; MCh 1927; FRCSI 1926; FRCS 1927; FRSE 1938; FACS 1945. War Service, 1939-45 (OBE, DSO): W Africa, N Africa, Sicily, Italy, France and India; Brig. 1945. Formerly Examiner in Surgery: Liverpool, Cambridge, Manchester, Glasgow, National Univ. of Ireland. President: Surgical Section, RSM; NI Branch, LEPRA; Past President: RCSI (1954-56); Assoc. of Surgeons GB and Ireland (1957-58); BMA (1962); Irish Med. Graduates Assoc., London; Queen's Univ. Assoc., London; Ulster Med. Soc. Hon. Life Governor, Royal Victoria Hosp., Belfast; Governor for GB, Amer. Coll. Surgeons; Lieut, Commandery of Ards, St John, Ulster; Hon. Col, RAMC, T&AVR. Hon. DSc Oxon, 1963. KStJ 1940; DL Belfast, 1955; Commandeur de l'Ordre de la Couronne (Belgium), 1963; Order of Orange Nassau, 1969. *Publications:* various monographs on surgical subjects. *Address:* 19 Upper Malone

Road, Belfast. *T:* Belfast 668235. *Clubs:* Ulster, Malone Golf (Belfast); Royal North of Ireland Yacht.

**FRASER, Ian Edward,** VC 1945; DSC 1943; Joint Managing Director North Sea Diving Services Ltd, since 1965; Chairman, Universal Divers Ltd, since 1965 (Managing Director, 1947-65); *b* 18 Dec., 1920; *s* of S. Fraser, Bourne End, Bucks; *m* 1943, Melba Estelle Hughes; four *s* one *d*. *Educ:* Royal Grammar Sch., High Wycombe; HMS Conway. Merchant Navy, 1937-39; Royal Navy, 1939-47; Lt-Comdr, RNR 1951. Officer, American Legion of Merit. *Publication:* Frogman VC, 1957. *Address:* Clarecourt, 39 Warren Drive, Wallasey, Cheshire. *T:* 051-638 3355.

**FRASER, Ian James,** MC 1945; Director-General, Panel on Take-overs and Mergers, since 1969; *b* 7 Aug. 1923; 2nd *s* of late Hon. Alastair Thomas Joseph Fraser and Lady Sibyl Fraser (*née* Grimston); *m* 1958, Evelyn Elizabeth Anne Grant; two *s* two *d*. *Educ:* Ampleforth Coll.; Magdalen Coll., Oxford. Served War of 1939-45: Lieut, Scots Guards, 1942-45 (despatches, MC). Reuter Correspondent, 1946-56; S. G. Warburg & Co. Ltd, 1956-69. *Recreations:* fishing, gardening, Scottish history. *Address:* Westmead House, Westmead, Roehampton, SW15. *T:* 01-788 9650. *Club:* White's.

**FRASER, Ian Montagu,** MC 1945; an executive Director, GUS Export Corporation; *b* 14 Oct. 1916; *e s* of Col Herbert Cecil Fraser, DSO, OBE, TD, and Sybil Mary Statter; *m* 1st, 1945, Mary Stanley (*d* 1964); one *s* one *d*; 2nd, 1967, Angela Meston, one *s*. *Educ:* Shrewsbury Sch.; Christ Church, Oxford. 1st Cl. Class. Hon. Mods, 1937; 1st Cl. Lit Hum 1939. Regular Commn in Frontier Force Rifles, IA, 1939, and served War of 1939-45, NW Frontier, Iraq, Syria and Western Desert (MC, despatches twice, POW); retired 1948. Executive, Guthrie and Co. Ltd, 1948; Gen. Sec., The John Lewis Partnership, 1956-59, Consultant, 1959-64. RARO, Rifle Bde, 1948-. MP (C) Sutton Div. of Plymouth, 1959-66; PPS to Sec. of State for the Colonies, 1962; Asst Govt Whip, 1962-64; Opposition Whip, 1964-66; Conservative Research Dept, 1966-67. *Recreations:* flyfishing, sailing. *Address:* How Hatch, Chipstead, Surrey. *T:* Downland 51944. *Clubs:* Carlton; Royal Western Yacht (Plymouth).

**FRASER, Sir James (David),** 2nd Bt, *cr* 1943; Professor of Surgery, University of Southampton, since 1970, and Hon. Consultant Surgeon, Southampton Hospital Group; *b* 19 July 1924; *o s* of Sir John Fraser, 1st Bt, KCVO, MC, and Agnes Govane Herald, The Manse, Duns, Berwickshire; *S* father 1947; *m* 1950, Maureen, *d* of Rev. John Reay, MC, Bingham Rectory, Nottingham; two *s*. *Educ:* Edinburgh Academy; Magdalen Coll., Oxford (BA); Edinburgh Univ. (MB, ChB); ChM 1961; FRCSE 1953. RAMC (Major), 1948-51; Senior Lectr in Clinical Surgery, Univ. of Edinburgh and Hon. Cons. Surgeon, Royal Infirmary, Edinburgh, 1951-70. *Recreations:* golf, swimming. *Heir:* *s* Ian Michael Fraser, *b* 27 June 1951. *Address:* The Keep, Heatherlands Road, Chilworth, Southampton.

**FRASER, Very Rev. John Annand,** MBE 1940; TD 1945; DD; Moderator of the General Assembly of the Church of Scotland, May 1958-May 1959; Extra Chaplain to The Queen, in Scotland, since 1964 (Chaplain, 1952-64); Minister of Aberdalgie and Dupplin, Perth, since 1960; *b* 21 June 1894; *er s* of Rev. Charles Fraser, BD, Minister of Croy, Inverness-shire, and Elizabeth Annand; *m* 1925, Leila, *d* of Col Ewen Campbell; one *s* one *d*. *Educ:* Robert Gordon's Coll., Aberdeen; Inverness Royal Academy; Universities of Aberdeen and Edinburgh. MA Aberdeen 1919. Served European War, 1914-18: in ranks 4th Bn Gordon Highlanders, 1915, Commd 7th Bn 1917. CF (TA) 1935; SCF, 52nd (Lowland) Div., 1940; Dep. Asst Chaplain Gen., West Scotland Dist, 1942. Asst Minister, St Matthew's, Edinburgh, 1921; Minister of Humble, East Lothian, 1923; Minister of Hamilton, Second Charge, 1931, First Charge, 1949. Convener of Maintenance of Ministry Cttee of Church of Scotland, 1950-54; Convener of Business Cttee, 1962-67; Convener of Gen. Administration Cttee, 1062-66; Chm. of Judicial Commn, 1962-66; Chm. of Church of Scotland Trust, 1962-66; Mem. Broadcasting Council for Scotland, 1963-67. Hon. DD Aberdeen, 1951. *Recreations:* fishing, gardening. *Address:* The Manse, Aberdalgie, Perth. *T:* Perth 21462. *Club:* Scottish Conservative (Edinburgh).

**FRASER, John Denis;** MP (Lab) Norwood since 1966; *b* 30 June 1934; *s* of Archibald and Frances Fraser; *m* 1960, Ann Hathaway; two *s* one *d*. *Educ:* Sloane Grammar Sch., Chelsea; Co-operative Coll., Loughborough; Law Soc. Sch. of Law (John Mackrell Prize). Entered Australia & New Zealand Bank Ltd, 1950; Army service, 1952-54, as Sergt, RAEC (educnl and resettlement work). Solicitor, 1960; practised with Lewis Silkin and Partners. Mem. Lambeth Borough Coun., 1962-68 (Chm. Town Planning Cttee; Chm. Labour Gp). PPS to First Sec. of State (Rt Hon. Barbara Castle), 1968-70. *Recreations:* athletics, walking. *Address:* 55 Lancaster Avenue, West Norwood, SE27. *T:* 01-670 6539. *Club:* York (West Norwood).

**FRASER, Rear-Adm. John Stewart Gordon,** CBE 1946; DSO 1917; RN retired; *b* 1883; *m* 1915; one *s* two *d*. Served European War, 1914-18 (despatches, DSO); retired list, 1935. Called up and served in war of 1939-45 (despatches, CBE). *Address:* 41 Elizabeth Avenue, St Brelade, Jersey, Channel Islands. *Clubs:* United Service; La Moye Golf (Jersey).

**FRASER, Sir Keith Charles Adolphus,** 6th Bt, *cr* 1806; *b* 14 Sept. 1911; *s* of Major Sir Keith Fraser, 5th Bt, and Lady Dorothy Coventry (*d* 1965), 2nd *d* of 9th Earl of Coventry; *S* father 1935; *m* 1934, Blanca de Undurraga y Sandiford (from whom he obtained a divorce, 1946), *d* of Julio de Undurraga; *m* 1947, Mrs Sybil Craven, *d* of George Savage. *Educ:* Eton; Cambridge. *Heir:* none. *Address:* c/o Brown Shipley & Co. Ltd, Founders Court, EC2.

**FRASER, Kenneth Wharton,** CMG 1962; OBE 1945; Manager, Advertising and Public Relations, General Motors New Zealand Ltd, 1946-70; retired as Dominion President, New Zealand Returned Services' Association; *b* 1 Nov. 1905; *s* of late William Fraser, Edinburgh, Scotland; *m* 1926, Ione May, *d* of late William James Moor, Auckland, NZ; two *s* three *d*. *Educ:* Auckland, NZ. Asst Advertising Man., Farmers' Trading Co., Ltd, Auckland, 1928-39. War service: 1940-45, 2nd NZEF, Lt-Col; Cmdg Officer, 5 Field Regt, NZ Artillery, 1940-41 (then POW to 1945). Dominion Executive, New Zealand Returned Services' Assoc., 1946-48; Dominion Vice-Pres. (NZRSA), 1949-54; Dominion Pres., 1955-62, retired. *Address:* Waikanae, Wellington, New Zealand. *T:* 188R. *Clubs:* Officers' (Auckland); United Services Officers', Wellesley, Civil Service (Wellington).

**FRASER, Louis Nathaniel B.;** *see* Blache-Fraser.

**FRASER, Sir Michael;** *see* Fraser, Sir R. M.

**FRASER, Air Marshal Sir Paterson;** *see* Fraser, Air Marshal Sir H. P.

**FRASER, Peter Marshall,** MC 1944; MA; FBA 1960; Director, British School of Archaeology at Athens, since 1968; Fellow of All Souls College, Oxford, since 1954; Lecturer in Hellenistic History, 1948-64, Reader since 1964; *b* 6 April 1918; *y s* of late Archibald Fraser; *m* 1st, 1940, Catharine, *d* of late Prebendary Heaton-Renshaw (marr. diss.); one *s* three *d*; 2nd, 1955, Ruth Elsbeth, *d* of late F. Renfer, Bern, Switzerland; two *s*. *Educ:* City of London Sch.; Brasenose Coll., Oxford. Seaforth Highlanders, 1941-45; Military Mission to Greece, 1943-45. Sen. Scholar, Christ Church, Oxford, 1946-47; Junior Proctor, Oxford Univ., 1960-61; Domestic Bursar, All Souls Coll., 1962-65. *Publications:* (with G. E. Bean) The Rhodian Peraea and Islands, 1954; (with T. Rönne) Boeotian and West Greek Tombstones, 1957; Rostovtzeff, Social and Economic History of the Roman Empire, 2nd edn, revised, 1957; Samothrace, The Inscriptions, (Vol. ii, Excavations of Samothrace), 1960; E. Löfstedt, Roman Literary Portraits, trans. from the Swedish (Romare), 1958; The Wares of Autolycus; Selected Literary Essays of Alice Meynell (ed.), 1965; E. Kjellberg and G. Säflund, Greek and Roman Art, trans. from the Swedish (Grekisk och romersk konst), 1968; articles in learned journals. *Address:* British School of Archaeology, Athens, Greece; All Souls College, Oxford. *Club:* Athenæum.

**FRASER, Sir (Richard) Michael,** Kt 1962; CBE 1955 (MBE 1945); Deputy Chairman of the Conservative Party Organisation, since Oct. 1964; Chairman, Conservative Research Department, since Sept. 1970; Deputy Chairman, Conservative Party's Advisory Committee on Policy, since Aug. 1970; *b* 28 Oct. 1915; *yr s* of late Dr Thomas Fraser, CBE, DSO, TD, DL, LLD, Aberdeen; *m* 1944, Elizabeth Chloë, *er d* of Brig. C. A. F. Drummond, OBE; one *s* (and one *s* decd). *Educ:* Fettes; King's Coll., Cambridge. Begg Exhibition, 1934; James Essay Prize, 1935; BA Hons History, 1937; MA 1945. Served War of 1939-45 (RA); 2nd Lieut 1939; War Gunnery Staff Course, 1940; Capt. Feb. 1941; Major, June 1941; Lieut-Col (GSO1) 1945. Joined Conservative Research Dept, 1946; Head of Home Affairs Sect., 1950-51; Dir, Conservative Research Dept, Aug. 1951-Oct. 1964 (Joint Dir, 1951-59); Sec. to Conserv. Party's Adv. Cttee on Policy, Aug. 1951-Oct. 1964; Sec. to the Conservative Leader's Consultative Cttee (Shadow Cabinet), Oct. 1964-June 1970. Smith-Mundt Fellowship, USA, 1952. *Recreations:* reading, music, opera, ballet, travel; collecting and recollecting. *Address:* 18 Drayton Court, Drayton Gardens, SW10. *T:* 01-370 1543. *Clubs:* Carlton, St James'.

*See also T. C. Fraser.*

**FRASER, Sir Robert;** *see* Fraser, Sir W. R.

**FRASER, Sir Robert Brown,** Kt 1949; OBE 1944; Director-General, Independent Television Authority, 1954-70; *b* 26 Sept. 1904; *s* of Reginald and Thusnelda Fraser, Adelaide, South Australia; *m* 1931, Betty Harris; one *d*. *Educ:* St Peter's Sch., Adelaide; Trinity Coll., Univ. of Melbourne (BA); Univ. of London (BSc Econ.). Leader Writer Daily Herald, 1930-39; Empire Div., Ministry of Information, 1939-41; Dir, Publications Div., Ministry of Information, 1941-45; Controller of Production, Ministry of Information, 1945-46; Dir-Gen., Central Office of Information, 1946-54. Hon. Fellow, LSE, 1965. Gold Medal, Royal Television Soc., 1970. *Address:* Flat 5M, Portman Mansions, Chiltern Street, W1. *Club:* Athenæum.

**FRASER, Ronald;** *see* Fraser, Sir A. R.

**FRASER, Ronald Petrie;** Under-Secretary, Ministry of Agriculture, Fisheries and Food, since 1968; *b* 2 June 1917; *yr s* of late T. Petrie Fraser, Elgin; *m* 1962, Ruth Wright Anderson, Edinburgh; one *d*. *Educ:* Daniel Stewart's Coll., Edinburgh; University of Edinburgh; The Queen's Coll., Oxford. Joined Dept of Health for Scotland for work on emergency hosp. service, 1940; Asst Private Sec. to Sec. of State for Scotland, 1944; Cabinet Office, 1947; Sec., Scottish Hosp. Endowments Commn, 1950; Asst Sec., Dept of Health for Scotland, 1954; Asst Sec., Scottish Education Dept, 1961; Under-Sec., 1963. *Recreations:* walking, music. *Address:* 36 Ross Court, Putney Hill, SW15. *T:* 01-789 4365. *Club:* Scottish Arts (Edinburgh).

**FRASER, Rt. Hon. Thomas,** PC 1964; Chairman, North of Scotland Hydro-Electric Board, since 1967; Member, Highlands and Islands Development Board, since 1967; *b* 18 Feb. 1911; *s* of Thomas and Mary Fraser, Kirkmuirhill, Lanarks; *m* 1935, Janet M. Scanlon, Lesmahagow, Lanarks; one *s* one *d*. *Educ:* Lesmahagow Higher Grade Sch. Left school 1925 and started work in a coal-mine (underground); worked underground, 1925-43; Miners' Union Branch Official, 1938-43; Sec., Lanark Constituency Labour Party, 1939-43; MP (Lab) Hamilton Div. of Lanarks, 1943-67; Joint Parliamentary Under-Sec. of State, Scottish Office, 1945-51; Minister of Transport, 1964-65. Mem., Royal Commn on Local Govt in Scotland, 1966-69. *Address:* 15 Broompark Drive, Lesmahagow, Lanarks.

**FRASER, Thomas Cameron,** CB 1966; MBE 1945; TD 1951; Chairman, Economic Development Committee for the Wool Textile Industry, since 1970; *b* 21 Jan. 1909; *er s* of late Dr Thomas Fraser, CBE, DSO, TD, DL, LLD, Aberdeen; *m* 1934, Dorothy Graham (*d* 1966), *y d* of late Graham Partridge, East Grinstead; two *s* two *d*. *Educ:* Fettes; University Coll., Oxford. BA Hons PPE 1931, MA 1935. Lloyds Bank Ltd, 1931-39. Served RA (TA), 1939-45; Major (GSO2) War Office, 1942; Lt-Col (GSO1) HQ, AA Command, 1943-45. Board of Trade (Central Price Regulation Cttee), 1946. Sec. Wool Textile Delegation, and Wool (and Allied) Textile Employers' Council, Bradford, 1947; appointment changed to Dir, 1958; Industrial Dir, NEDC, 1962-70. Mem. British Delegation to International Labour Conferences, Geneva, 1953, 1954, 1956, 1957, 1959, and European Regional Conf., ILO, 1955. Mem., BBC North Regional Advisory Council, 1960-62. *Recreations:* golf, walking. *Address:* 25 Bedford Gardens, W8. *T:* 01-727 0674. *Clubs:* United University, Royal Automobile.

*See also Sir R. M. Fraser.*

**FRASER, Prof. Thomas Russell Cumming,** MD, FRCP; Professor of Clinical Endocrinology in the University of London, Royal Postgraduate Medical School, since 1957. *Educ:* Otago Univ. Medical School. MB, ChB (distinction) 1932; MRCP 1936; DPM (Eng.) 1937; MD (NZ) 1945; FRCP 1948. Hallett Prize, 1935; NZ University Travel Fellowship, 1935; Rockefeller Travel Fellowship, 1938. Formerly Asst Med. Officer, Maudsley Hosp.; Research Fellow in Medicine, Harvard Univ.; Reader in Medicine, Harvard Univ.; Reader in Medicine, Postgrad. Med. Sch., London. Member: Assoc. Physicians of Gt Brit.; Med.

Research Soc. *Publications:* contribs to medical journals. *Address:* Hammersmith Hospital, Du Cane Road, W12. *T:* 01-743 2030.

**FRASER, Veronica Mary;** Headmistress, Godolphin School, Salisbury, since 1968; *b* 19 April 1933; *o d* of late Archibald Fraser. *Educ:* Richmond County Sch. for Girls; St Hugh's Coll., Oxford. Head of English Department: The Alice Ottley Sch., Worcester, 1962-65; Guildford County Sch. for Girls, 1965-67 (also Librarian). *Recreations:* choral singing, cooking, walking. *Address:* Godolphin School, Salisbury, Wilts. *T:* 3059.

**FRASER, Walter Ian Reid;** *see* Fraser, Hon. Lord.

**FRASER, Sir (William) Robert,** KCB 1952 (CB 1939); KBE 1944; MA; *b* Hemingford Grey, St Ives, Hunts, 9 Oct. 1891; *e s* of Garden William Fraser (W. F. Garden) and Ethel Mary Syson; *g g s* of Francis Fraser, Findrack, Aberdeenshire; *m* 1915, Phyllis (*d* 1970), *d* of William Smith, London; three *s* one *d*. *Educ:* Christ's Hosp.; University Coll., Oxford (MA). First Mods 1912; First Lit. Hum. 1914; entered Treasury, 1914; Principal, 1919; Asst Sec., 1932; Princ. Asst Sec., 1934-39; Sec., Dept of Health for Scotland, 1939-43; Sec. War Damage Commn, 1943, and Central Land Bd, 1947; Dep. Chm. and Permanent Sec., 1949-59; Chm. (part-time), 1959-62. Hon. Treasurer and Vice-Pres., Lawn Tennis Assoc. (Chm., 1958); Vice-Pres. Civil Service Sports Council; Pres., Civil Service Lawn Tennis Assoc. *Recreations:* gardening, lawn tennis, motoring. *Address:* 33 Hollycroft Avenue, NW3. *T:* 01-435 3566. *Clubs:* Oxford and Cambridge University, All-England Lawn Tennis.

**FRASER DARLING, Sir Frank,** Kt 1970; DSc, PhD, LLD, FIBiol, FRSE; Vice-President, Conservation Foundation, Washington, DC; Hon. Trustee, National Parks of Kenya; Member: Nature Conservancy, since 1969; Royal Commission on Environmental Pollution, since 1970; *b* 23 June 1903; *m* 1st, 1925, Marian Fraser; one *s*; 2nd, 1948, Averil Morley (*d* 1957); two *s* one *d*; 3rd, 1960, Christina Macinnes Brotchie. *Educ:* Midland Agricultural Coll.; University of Edinburgh. On Agricultural Staff, Bucks County Council, 1924-27; Research Student, Inst. of Animal Genetics, Univ. of Edinburgh, 1928-30; Chief Officer, Imperial Bureau of Animal Genetics, 1930-34; Leverhulme Research Fellow, 1933-36; Carnegie Research Fellow, 1936-39; Dir, West Highland Survey, 1944-50; Rockefeller Special Research Fellow, 1950. Senior Lectr in Ecology and Conservation, Univ. of Edinburgh, 1953-58. Reith Lectr, 1969. Mungo Park Medallist, Royal Scottish Geographical Society, 1947. *Publications:* Biology of the Fleece of the Scottish Mountain Blackface Breed of Sheep, 1932; Animal Breeding in the British Empire, 1934; Wild Life Conservation, 1934; A Herd of Red Deer, 1937; Bird Flocks and the Breeding Cycle, 1938; Wild Country, 1938; A Naturalist on Rona, 1939; The Seasons and the Farmer, 1939; Island Years, 1940; The Seasons and the Fisherman, 1941; The Story of Scotland, 1942; Wild Life of Britain, 1943; Island Farm, 1943; The Care of Farm Animals, 1943; Crofting Agriculture, 1945; Natural History in the Highlands and Islands, 1947; Report of the West Highland Survey, 1952; (with A. S. Leopold) Alaska: an Ecological Reconnaissance, 1953; West Highland Survey, 1955; Pelican in the Wilderness; Odyssey of a Naturalist, 1956; Wild Life in an African Territory, 1960; An Ecological Rennaissance of the Mara Plains in Kenya Colony, 1960; The Unity of Ecology, 1963; The Nature of a National Park, 1968; Impacts of Man on the Biosphere, 1969; Wilderness and Plenty, 1970; many scientific papers. *Recreations:* watching animals, English literature. *Address:* Shefford-Woodlands House, by Newbury, Berks. *T:* Great Shefford 220. *Clubs:* Athenæum; New (Edinburgh); Highland (Inverness); Cosmos (Washington).

**FRASER McLUSKEY, Rev. James;** *see* McLuskey.

**FRASER ROBERTS, John Alexander;** *see* Roberts.

**FRASER-TYTLER, Christian Helen,** CBE 1941; JP; Senior Controller ATS, retired; *b* 23 Aug. 1897; *d* of John Campbell Shairp, Houstoun; *m* 1919, Col Neil Fraser-Tytler, DSO, Croix de Guerre (*d* 1937); two *d*. *Educ:* Home. Foreign Office, 1917-19; War Office, 1939-43; AA Command until 1945; (TD). JP Inverness-shire, 1958. *Recreation:* fishing. *Address:* 43 Sussex Square, W2. *T:* 01-723 2565; Old Clune House, Aldourie, Inverness. *T:* Dores 216.
*See also Sir Thomas David Erskine.*

**FRAYN, Michael;** writer; *b* 8 Sept. 1933; *s* of late Thomas Allen Frayn and of Violet Alice Lawson; *m* 1960, Gillian Palmer; three *d*. *Educ:* Kingston Gram. Sch.; Emmanuel Coll., Cambridge. Reporter, Guardian, 1957-59; Columnist, Guardian, 1959-62; Columnist, Observer, 1962-68. TV plays: Jamie, 1968; Birthday, 1969; stage play: The Two of Us, 1970. Somerset Maugham Award, 1966; Hawthornden Prize, 1967. *Publications: collections of columns:* The Day of the Dog, 1962; The Book of Fub, 1963; On the Outskirts, 1964; At Bay in Gear Street, 1967; *novels:* The Tin Men, 1965; The Russian Interpreter, 1966; Towards the End of the Morning, 1967; A Very Private Life, 1968. *Address:* c/o Elaine Greene Ltd, 42 Great Russell Street, WC1.

**FREARS, John Newton,** CBE 1955; MA; JP; Chairman Frears & Blacks Ltd since 1937; Pro Chancellor, Leicester University, since 1962; *b* 29 June 1906; *s* of John Russell Frears and Minnie Keighley Frears (*née* Cape); *m* 1931, Elaine Pochin; one *s* one *d*. *Educ:* Gresham's Sch., Holt; Trinity Coll., Cambridge. Frears & Blacks Ltd, 1928-; Dir, Nabisco-Frears Biscuits Ltd, 1964-. Dir of Bakeries for UK, Min. of Food, 1941-45. Hon. LLD Leicester, 1967. *Address:* Narborough House, Narborough, Leics. *T:* Narborough 3259.

**FREDERICK, Sir Charles Boscawen,** 10th Bt *cr* 1723; *b* 11 April 1919; *s* of Sir Edward Boscawen Frederick, 9th Bt, CVO and Edith Katherine (Kathleen) Cortlandt, *d* of late Col W. H. Mulloy, RE; *S* father, 1956; *m* 1949, Rosemary, *er d* of late Lt-Col R. J. H. Baddeley, MC; two *s* two *d*. *Educ:* Eton. 2nd Lieut Grenadier Guards, 1942; served N Africa and Italy, 1943-45 (despatches); Capt. 1945; Palestine, 1946-47 (despatches); Malaya, 1948-49; Egypt, 1952-53; Major, 1953. Mem. London Stock Exchange, 1954-62; Mem. Provincial Brokers Stock Exchange, 1962 (Mem. Coun., 1966). JP County of Bucks, 1960-61. General Commissioner of Income Tax, 1966. *Recreations:* sailing, fishing. *Heir: s* Christopher St John Frederick, *b* 28 June 1950. *Address:* Place Farm, Nether Wallop, Stockbridge, Hants. *T:* Wallop 332. *Clubs:* Hampshire (Winchester); Royal Southampton Yacht; Royal Fowey Yacht.

**FREDERICTON, Archbishop of,** and Metropolitan of the Province of Canada, since 1963; **Most Rev. Alexander Henry O'Neil,** MA, DD; *m* 1931, Marguerite (*née* Roc); one *s*.

*Educ:* University of Western Ontario, London, Ont; Huron Coll., London, Ont; Univ. of W Ontario: BA 1928, BD 1936, MA 1943, DD (Hon.) 1945; Huron Coll., London, LTh 1929; DD (Hon.) Wycliffe Coll., Toronto, 1954; DD (Hon.) King's Coll., Halifax, 1958; LLD (Hon.) Univ. of Western Ontario, 1962; DCL (Hon.) Bishop's Univ., Lennoxville, 1964. Deacon, 1929; Priest, 1930; Principal, Huron Coll., London, Ont., 1941-52; Gen. Sec., British and Foreign Bible Soc. in Canada, 1952-57; Bishop of Fredericton, 1957-63. Hon. LLD, St Thomas Univ., Fredericton, 1970. *Address:* Bishop's Court, 791 Brunswick Street, Fredericton, New Brunswick, Canada.

**FREEBODY, Air Vice-Marshal Wilfred Leslie,** CB 1951; CBE 1943; AFC; RAF Technical Branch; Director of Work Study, at Air Ministry. Squadron Leader, 1937; Acting Air Commodore commanding 226 Group, Air Cdre, 1949; Actg Air Vice-Marshal, 1956; Air Vice-Marshal, 1957. Has Order of Polonia Restituta 3rd class, of Poland.

**FREEDMAN, Prof. Maurice,** MA, PhD; Professor of Anthropology, University of Oxford, since 1970; *b* 11 Dec. 1920; *s* of Harry Freedman and Minnie (*née* Glazer); *m* 1946, Judith Djamour; no *c. Educ:* Hackney Downs; King's Coll. London; London Sch. of Economics. RA (in ranks, subseq. commnd), 1941-45. Research Fellow, CSSRC, Singapore, 1949-50; Lectr, LSE, 1951-57; Reader, LSE, 1957-65. Consultant, WHO (in Indonesia), 1964. Vis. Assoc. Prof., Yale Univ., 1960-61; Vis. Prof., Cornell Univ., 1965. Prof. of Anthropology, LSE, 1965-70. Governor, LSE, 1966-70; Mem. Senate, Univ. of London, 1967-70. Pres., Royal Anthropological Inst., 1967-69. Chm., London-Cornell Project, 1965-69. Man. Ed., Jewish Jl of Sociology, 1959-. Malinowski Memorial Lectr, 1962. *Publications:* (Ed.) A Minority in Britain, 1955; Chinese Family and Marriage in Singapore, 1957; Lineage Organization in Southeastern China, 1958; Chinese Lineage and Society, 1966; (Ed.) Social Organization, Essays Presented to Raymond Firth, 1967; (ed) Family and Kinship in Chinese Society, 1970; articles in Brit. Jl Sociology, Jl Asian Studies, Jl Royal Anthropological Inst., etc. *Address:* Institute of Social Anthropology, 51 Banbury Road, Oxford. *T:* Oxford 55971; 187 Gloucester Place, St Marylebone, NW1.

**FREELAND, Lt-Gen. Sir Ian Henry,** KCB 1968 (CB 1964); DSO 1944; *b* 14 Sept. 1912; *s* of late Maj.-Gen. Sir H. F. E. Freeland, KCIE, CB, DSO, MVO, RE; *m* 1940, Mary, *d* of General Sir C. C. Armitage, *qv*; two *s* one *d. Educ:* Wellington Coll.; RMC, Sandhurst. Commissioned into the Norfolk Regt, 1932; Adjt, 1940; Bde Major 7 Inf. Bde, 1942; GSO2 War Office (MT2), 1943; OC 7 Royal Norfolk, 1944; OC 1/5 Queen's, 1944-45; Col GS, HQ 8 Corps Dist, 1945-46; 2nd i/c 4th Armoured Brigade, 1946; GSO1 (SD), HQ BAOR, 1946-47; GSO1, BOAR Trg Centre, 1947-48; Comdt All Arms Training Centre, 1948-49; GSO1, War Office (Western Union), 1949-50; GSO1, Staff Coll., Camberley, 1951-53; OC 2 R Inniskilling Fusiliers, 1954-56; Comdr, 12 Inf. Bde, 1956-57; Imperial Defence Coll., 1958; Brigadier Q (Ops) War Office, 1959-61; GOC 54 (E Anglian) Div./Dist, 1961-63; GOC, E Africa Comd, 1963; British Land Forces, Kenya, and Kenya Army, 1963-64; Vice Adj.-Gen., Min. of Def., 1965-68 Deputy CGS, 1968; GOC and Director of Operations, N Ireland, 1969-70; retired Feb. 1971. Dep. Col, Royal Anglian Regt, 1966. Croix de Guerre, 1940, with Palm (Belgium); Chevalier, Order of Crown, with Palm (Belgium). *Recreations:* shooting, cricket, golf, tennis. *Address:* Foxley Lodge, near Dereham, Norfolk. *T:* Bawdeswell 237. *Clubs:* Army and Navy; MCC; I Zingari; Free Foresters.

**FREELAND, John Redvers;** HM Diplomatic Service; Counsellor (Legal Adviser), UK Mission to the United Nations, New York, since 1970; *b* 16 July 1927; *o s* of C. Redvers Freeland and Freda Freeland (*née* Walker); *m* 1952, Sarah Mary, *er d* of late S. Pascoe Hayward, QC; one *s* one *d. Educ:* Stowe; Corpus Christi Coll., Cambridge. Royal Navy, 1945 and 1948-51. Called to Bar, Lincoln's Inn, 1952; Mem. *ad eundem,* Middle Temple. Asst Legal Adviser, FO, 1954-63, and 1965-67; Legal Adviser, HM Embassy, Bonn, 1963-65; Legal Counsellor, FCO (formerly FO), 1967-70. *Address:* 1155 Park Avenue, New York, NY 10028, USA. *Club:* Travellers'.

**FREELING, Nicolas;** writer since 1960; *b* 1927, of English parents; *m* 1954, Cornelia Termes; four *s* one *d. Educ:* primary and secondary schs. Hotel-restaurant cook, throughout Europe, 1945-60; novelist, 1960-. *Publications:* (numerous trans.) Love in Amsterdam, 1961; Because of the Cats, 1962; Gun before Butter, 1962; Valparaiso, 1963; Double Barrel, 1963; Criminal Conversation, 1964; King of the Rainy Country, 1965; Dresden Green, 1966; Strike Out Where Not Applicable, 1967; This is the Castle, 1968; Tsing-Boum, 1969; Kitchen Book, 1970. *Address:* Grandfontaine, 67 Schirmeck, Bas Rhin, France.

**FREEMAN, Anthony;** *see* Freeman, Philip Anthony M.

**FREEMAN, Sir Bernard;** *see* Freeman, Sir N. B.

**FREEMAN, George Robert,** CBE 1957; Nominal partner, formerly Senior partner, Gane, Jackson, Nelson & Freeman, Chartered Accountants, City-Gate House, Finsbury Square, EC2; *b* 31 July 1875; *yr s* of John Freeman, Winnipeg; *m* 1st, 1900, Lilian M. Rossiter (*d* 1920); one *s* two *d*; 2nd, 1923, Frieda E. de Buriatte; one *d. Educ:* Upper Canada Coll., Toronto; St John's Coll., Winnipeg. Articled to present firm, 1891; Chartered Accountant, 1897; Partner, 1903; FCA, 1909, elected to Council, 1915, Vice-Pres., 1924-25, Pres., 1925-26, Chm. Exam. Cttee, 1922-31, Chm. of Parliamentary and Law Cttee, 1936-44; nominated Rep. of Inst. on Trustees Savings Banks Inspection Cttee, 1921-60, Chm. 1938-60; resigned from most of his hon. appts 1957. Council of London Chamber of Commerce, 1922, Chm. of Journal Cttee, Mem. of Commercial Educn, Parliamentary and Commercial Law and Taxation Cttees; Royal Society of Arts Exams Cttee; Bd of Governors, City of London Coll. Pres. Chartered Accountants Benevolent Assoc. and a Vice-Pres. of London Chartered Accountant Students Soc.; Delegate from Inst. to Conf. Amer. Inst. of Accountants, St Louis, 1924, and to Dominion Assoc. of Chartered Accountants, Toronto, 1936, and Saskatoon, 1939. Officier d'Académie avec palmes (France), 1930. *Address:* Orillia, Greenhill Road, Otford, Kent. *T:* Otford 3200.

**FREEMAN, Harold Webber;** Author; *b* 1899; *s* of Charles Albert Freeman and Emma Mary Ann Mills; *m* Elizabeth Boedecker. *Educ:* City of London Sch.; Christ Church, Oxford (classical scholar). 1st class Hon. Mods, 2nd class Lit. Hum. Main background was work on the land, mostly organic gardening; travelled in Europe (foot and bicycle); casual work as linguist (translation, monitoring, travel trade). Has lived mostly in Suffolk, but also, for long periods, in Italy. *Publications:* Joseph and His Brethren, 1928; Down in the Valley, 1930;

Fathers of Their People, 1932; Pond Hall's Progress, 1933; Hester and Her Family, 1936; Andrew to the Lions, 1938; Chaffinch's, 1941; Blenheim Orange, 1949; The Poor Scholar's Tale, 1954; Round the Island: Sardinia Re-explored, 1956. *Address:* c/o Westminster Bank Ltd, Princes Street, Ipswich.

**FREEMAN, Ifan Charles Harold,** CMG 1964; TD 1961; Registrar, University of Malawi, since 1965; *b* 11 Sept. 1910; *s* of late C. E. D. W. Freeman; *m* 1937, Enid, *d* of late Edward Hallum; two *d. Educ:* Friars Sch., Bangor; Univ. of Wales (MA). Served with Royal Artillery, 1939-46 (Major; despatches). Colonial Service: Kenya, 1946-58; Nyasaland, 1958-65. *Recreation:* gardening. *Address:* University of Malawi, Limbe, Malawi. *Clubs:* Royal Commonwealth; Mombasa (Kenya).

**FREEMAN, Rt. Hon. John,** PC 1966; MBE 1943; British Ambassador in Washington since 1969; journalist and broadcaster; *b* 19 Feb. 1915; *e s* of Horace Freeman, barrister-at-law, New Square, Lincoln's Inn; *m* 1st, 1938, Elizabeth Allen Johnston (marr. diss., 1948); 2nd, 1948, Margaret Ista Mabel Kerr (*d* 1957); 3rd, 1962, Catherine Dove; two *s* one *d* and one adopted *d. Educ:* Westminster Sch.; Brasenose Coll., Oxford (Hon. Fellow, 1968). Advertising Consultant, 1937-40. Active Service, 1940-45. MP (Lab) Watford Div. of Herts, 1945-50, Borough of Watford, 1950-55; PPS to Sec. of State for War, 1945-46; Financial Sec., War Office, 1946; Parliamentary Under Sec. of State for War, April 1947; Leader, UK Defence Mission to Burma, 1947; Parliamentary Sec., Ministry of Supply, 1947-51, resigned. Asst Editor, New Statesman, 1951-58; Deputy Editor, 1958-60; Editor, 1961-65. British High Commissioner in India, 1965-68. *Address:* c/o Foreign and Commonwealth Office, SW1. *Club:* Garrick.

**FREEMAN, Sir (John) Keith (Noel),** 2nd Bt *cr* 1945; *b* 28 July 1923; *o s* of Air Chief Marshal Sir Wilfrid Rhodes Freeman, 1st Bt, GCB, DSO, MC, and Gladys, *d* of J. Mews; *S* father 1953; *m* 1946, Patricia Denison, *yr d* of late C. W. Thomas, Sandown, IoW; one *s* one *d. Educ:* Rugby; Christ Church, Oxford. Served War of 1939-45: Flight-Lieut RAF, Europe and Middle East. *Heir: s* James Robin Freeman, *b* 21 July 1955. *Address:* Delly End Farm, Hailey, Witney, Oxon. *T:* Ramsden 360. *Clubs:* Travellers'; Hurlingham, Cheltenham Steeplechasing.

**FREEMAN, Sir Keith;** *see* Freeman, Sir J. K. N.

**FREEMAN, Sir (Nathaniel) Bernard,** Kt 1967; CBE 1956; Chairman, Metro-Goldwyn-Mayer Pty Ltd, 1967-68, retired; *b* 1 Sept. 1896; *s* of Adolph and Malvina Freeman; *m* 1926, Marjorie Arabel (*née* Bloom); one *s* one *d. Educ:* Public Sch. and Xavier Coll., Melbourne. Served European War, 1914-18: 38th Bn, 3rd Div., First AIF, and Austr. Flying Corps; inaugurated free films to Austr. Troops, 1939-45. Founded Metro-Goldwyn-Mayer Austr., NZ and S Pacific, 1925; Man. Dir, Metro-Goldwyn-Mayer, 1925-66. First Mem. Chm., Motion Picture Distributors' Assoc. of Austr., 1939-41, also 1963. Chm. various cttees, appeals and trusts, 1945-; National Chm., UNICEF, 1952; Chm., World Refugee Year, NSW, 1960; Chm. of Trustees and Internat. Houses Appeal, Univs of Sydney and NSW; Mem. Exec., Sydney Opera House Trust, 1962-69; mem. of many other cttees; Life Mem., RSL State Br., 1945-; Life Governor: Royal NSW Instn for Deaf and Blind Children; Vic. Ear and Eye Hosp.; Vic. Sch. for Deaf Children. *Recreations:* swimming, bowls. *Address:* The Penthouse, Santina, 85 Yarranabbe Road, Darling Point, NSW 2027, Australia. *Clubs:* Journalists', Australian-American Assoc., American National, Australian Flying Corps Assoc., City Bowling, Rose Bay Bowling (all Sydney).

**FREEMAN, Paul,** ARCS, DSc (London), FRES, FIBiol; Keeper of Entomology, British Museum (Natural History), since 1968; *b* 26 May 1916; *s* of Samuel Mellor Freeman and Kate Burgis; *m* 1942, Audrey Margaret Long; two *d. Educ:* Brentwood Sch., Essex; Imperial Coll., London. Demonstrator in Entomology, Imperial Coll., 1938. Captain, RA and Army Operational Research Group, 1940-45. Lecturer in Entomology, Imperial Coll., 1945-47. Asst Keeper, Dept of Entomology, British Museum (Nat. Hist.), 1947-64, Dep. Keeper, 1964-68, Keeper, 1968. Hon. Sec., Royal Entomological Soc. of London, 1958-62 (Vice-Pres., 1956, 1957); Sec., XIIth Internat. Congress of Entomology, London, 1964. *Publications:* Diptera of Patagonia and South Chile, Pt III–Mycetophilidae, 1951; Simuliidae of the Ethiopian Region (with Botha de Meillon), 1953; numerous papers in learned jls, on taxonomy of Hemiptera and Diptera. *Recreations:* gardening, natural history. *Address:* Briardene, 75 Towncourt Crescent, Petts Wood, Orpington, Kent BR5 1PH. *T:* Orpington 27296.

**FREEMAN, (Philip) Anthony Mallows,** MBE; FSA; MA; *b* 10 Nov. 1892; *o s* of Ann and late George Mallows Freeman, KC, JP, Grey Friars, Winchelsea; *m* 1928, Enid Campbell Adam (*d* 1949); no *c. Educ:* Eton; Oxford. Served European War, France, 1914-15, RA staff, 1917-18; Mayor of Winchelsea, 1930, 1931, 1944, 1945, 1946, 1952, 1953, 1957, 1962; High Sheriff of Sussex, 1939; Baron of the Cinque Ports, 1953. *Recreations:* fishing, shooting. *Address:* Wickham Manor, Winchelsea, Sussex. *T:* Winchelsea 216. *Clubs:* Bath, MCC.

**FREEMAN, Sir Ralph,** Kt 1970; CVO 1964; CBE 1952 (MBE 1945); FICE, FASCE; Senior Partner, Freeman, Fox & Partners, Consulting Engineers, since 1962 (Partner since 1947); Consulting Engineer to the Queen for Sandringham Estate since 1949; *b* 3 Feb. 1911; *s* of late Sir Ralph Freeman and late Mary (*née* Lines); *m* 1939, Joan Elizabeth, *er d* of Col J. G. Rose, DSO, VD, FRIC, Wynberg, Cape, S Africa; two *s* one *d. Educ:* Uppingham Sch.; Worcester Coll., Oxford (MA). Under J. L. Hill, Pretoria, 1932-34; Construction Engineer: Dorman Long & Co., Rhodesia and Denmark, 1934-36 and 1937-39; Braithwaite & Co., 1936-37; on staff of Freeman, Fox & Partners, 1939-46, Admty and other war work; served RE, 1943-45 (Temp. Major) at Exp. Bridging Estab. and later seconded as bridging adviser to CE 21 Army Gp HQ, NW Europe campaign. Past Pres., Instn of Civil Engrs (Mem. Council, 1951-55 and 1957-61, Vice-Pres., 1962-66; Pres., 1966-67); Member: Governing body, SE London Techn Coll., 1952-58; Nat. Cons. Coun. to Min. of Works, 1952-56; Bd of Govs, Westminster Hosp., 1963-69; Coun., Worcester Coll. Soc., 1964-; Adv. Coun. on Scientific Res. and Develt (MoD), 1966-69; Defence Scientific Adv. Council, 1969-; Royal Fine Art Commn, 1968-; Council, Assoc. of Consulting Engrs, 1969-; Societé des Ingénieurs Civils de France; Chm., Limpsfield Common Cttee, 1957-. Col, Engr and Rly Staff Corps RE (T&AVR), 1963-, Col comdg 1970-. Hon. Fellow, Rhodesian Instn of Engrs, 1969; FRSA. Kt, Order of Orange Nassau (Netherlands), 1945. *Publications:* several papers in Proc. ICE. *Recreations:* golf, carpentry, sailing. *Address:* c/o Freeman, Fox & Partners, 25 Victoria Street (South block),

SW1. *T:* 01-799 1290. *Clubs:* Athenæum, United Service; Leander (Henley-on-Thames).

**FREEMAN, Richard Gavin; His Honour Judge Freeman;** County Court Judge since 1968; *b* 18 Oct. 1910; *s* of John Freeman, MD, and Violet Alice Leslie Hadden; *m* 1937, Marjorie Pear; one *s* two *d*; *m* 1961, Winifred Ann Bell. *Educ:* Charterhouse; Hertford Coll., Oxford. Called to Bar, Gray's Inn, 1947. Deputy Chairman, Warwicks Quarter Sessions, 1963-. Hon. Major, RA. *Recreations:* cricket, gardening. *Address:* 10 Rees Street, N1. *Club:* Streatley Cricket.

**FREEMAN, Capt. Spencer,** CBE 1942; Director: Hospitals Trust (1940) Ltd, Dublin; Donegal Carpets Ltd; *b* Swansea, S Wales, 10 Dec. 1892; *s* of late A. Freeman; *m* 1924, Hilda Kathleen, *d* of Charles Simpkin Toler; one *s*. *Educ:* Johannesburg Coll., S Africa; Technical Institute, York, Pa, USA. Up to 1914, Automotive Industry USA, organised entire Mechanical Transport Salvage in France, European War, and subsequently Consulting Business Engineer; Emergency Services Organisation, for restoration of production in all munitions factories, Ministry of Aircraft Production: Dir 1940-41; Princ. Dir, 1941-44; Business Mem. Industrial and Export Council, Board of Trade, 1944-45. Member: Radio Board (a Cttee of British War Cabinet); Radio Planning and Production Cttee; Radio Production Executive, 1944-45. Served European War, 1914-19, non-commissioned ranks to Capt. (despatches, Mons Medal). MSAE. *Publication:* Production under Fire, 1967. *Recreations:* all sports. *Address:* Knocklyon House, Templeogue, Co. Dublin, Eire. *T:* Dublin 900234. *Clubs:* Royal Aero; Kildare Street (Dublin).

**FREEMAN-GRENVILLE,** family name of **Baroness Kinloss.**

**FREEMAN-THOMAS,** family name of **Marquess of Willingdon.**

**FREER, Charles Edward Jesse,** DL, JP (Leics); Chairman Leicestershire Quarter Sessions since 1949; *b* 4 March 1901; *s* of late Canon S. Thorold Winckley, FSA and Elizabeth (*née* Freer); changed name to Freer by Deed Poll, 1922; *m* 1st, 1927, Violet Muriel (*d* 1944), *d* of H. P. Gee, CBE, Leicester; two *s* two *d*; 2nd, 1945, Cynthia Lilian, *d* of Leonard R. Braithwaite, FRCS, Leeds; two *d*. *Educ:* Radley Coll. Solicitor, 1924; served RA (TA) in France, 1940; DJAG in Iceland, 1941-42; at SHAEF, 1943-44, Lt-Col. Chm. Leicester Diocesan Board of Finance, 1946-56; Chm. Mental Health Tribunal, Sheffield Regional Board, 1961. A Chm. of Industrial Tribunals, 1966. *Recreation:* sailing. *Address:* Shoal House, 48 Pearce Avenue, Parkstone, Dorset. *T:* Parkstone 1393. *Clubs:* Public Schools; Parkstone Yacht.

**FREER, Air Commodore Robert William George,** CBE 1966; ADC; Deputy Commandant, RAF Staff College, Bracknell, since 1969; *b* Darjeeling, 1st Sept. 1923; *s* of William Freer, Fair View, Chedworth, near Cheltenham, Glos; *m* 1950, Margaret, 2nd *d* of late J. W. Elkington and of Mrs M. Elkington, Ruskington Manor, near Sleaford, Lincs; one *s* one *d*. *Educ:* Gosport Grammar Sch. Flying Instructor, S Africa and UK, 1944-47; RAF Coll., Cranwell, 1947-50; served 54 and 614 Fighter Sqdns, 1950-52; Central Fighter Estabt, 1952-54; commanded 92 Fighter Sqdn, 1955-57 (Queen's Commendation, 1955); Directing Staff, USAF Acad., 1958-60; Staff of Chief of Defence Staff, 1961-63; Station Comdr, RAF Seletar, 1963-66; DD Defence Plans (Air), MoD, 1966-67. Air ADC to the Queen, 1969; psa, 1957; pfc, 1960; IDC, 1968. Mem., RUSI. *Recreations:* golf, tennis, squash. *Address:* The Flat, RAF Staff College, Bracknell, Berkshire. *T:* Bracknell 4593 (ext. 206). *Clubs:* Royal Air Force; Wentworth (Sunningdale).

**FREESON, Reginald;** MP (Lab) Willesden East since 1964; *b* 24 Feb. 1926. *Educ:* Jewish Orphanage, West Norwood. Served in Army, 1944-47. Middle East magazines and newspapers, 1946-48. Joined Labour Party on return to United Kingdom, 1948. Journalist, 1948-64. Magazines: John Bull, Illustrated, Today, Education. Free-lance for Everybody's Weekly, Tribune, News Chronicle, Daily Mirror, Reader's Digest, Associated Rediffusion TV. Asst Press Officer with Min. of Works, British Railways Board. Has written also for various publications and ghosted books and pamphlets. British rep. of Internat. News Service, HQ Geneva, 1960-62; Editor of Searchlight, against fascism and racialism. Radio and television: housing, race relations and foreign affairs. Elected Willesden Borough Council, 1952; Alderman, 1955; Leader of Council, 1958-65; Chm. of new London Borough of Brent, 1964-65 (Alderman, 1964-68). PPS to Minister of Transport, 1964-67; Parly Secretary: Min. of Power, 1967-69; Min. of Housing and Local Govt, 1969-70. Dep. Chm., Iron and Steel Adv. Cttee, 1967-. Mem., Internat. Voluntary Service and UNA International Service. Sponsor, Willesden Housing Assocs. Founder-Chairman: Willesden (now Brent) Coun. of Social Service, 1960-62; Willesden Social Action, 1961-63; Willesden and Brent Friendship Coun., 1959-63 (Vice-Pres., 1967); Chm., Warsaw Memorial Cttee, 1964-67. *Address:* 49 Chatsworth Road, NW2. *T:* 01-459 3007.

**FREETH, Andrew;** *see* Freeth, H. A.

**FREETH, Denzil Kingson;** Member of London Stock Exchange; *b* 10 July 1924; *s* of Walter Kingson and late Vera Freeth. *Educ:* Highfield Sch., Liphook, Hants; Sherborne Sch. (Scholar); Trinity Hall, Cambridge (Scholar). Served War, 1943-46: RAF (Flying Officer). Pres. Union Soc., Cambridge, 1949; Chm. Cambridge Univ. Conservative Assoc. 1949; debating tour of America, 1949, also debated in Ireland; Mem. Exec. Cttee Nat. Union, 1955. MP (C) Basingstoke Division of Hants, 1955-64. PPS to Minister of State, Bd of Trade, 1956, to Pres. of the Bd of Trade, 1957-59, to Minister of Educn, 1959-60; Parly Sec. for Science, 1961-63. Mem. Parliamentary Cttee of Trustee Savings Bank Assoc., 1956-61. Mem. Select Cttee on Procedure, 1958-59. Worked for stockbroking firms, 1950-61 and 1964-; Mem. of London Stock Exchange, 1959-61, 1965-. *Recreations:* good food, wine and conversation. *Address:* 66a Warwick Way, SW1. *T:* 01-834 8656. *Clubs:* Carlton; Pitt (Cambridge).

**FREETH, Hon. Gordon;** Ambassador of Australia to Japan, since 1970; *b* 6 Aug. 1914; *s* of Rt Rev. Robert Evelyn Freeth, *qv*; *m* 1939, Joan Celia Carew Baker; one *s* two *d*. *Educ:* Sydney Church of England Grammar Sch.; Guildford Grammar Sch.; Univ. of Western Australia. Admitted as Barrister and Solicitor, WA, 1938; practised Law at Katanning, WA, 1939-49. Served as Pilot, RAAF, 1942-45. Elected to House of Representatives as Member for Forrest, 1949; MP 1949-69; Minister: for Interior, 1958-63; for Shipping and Transport, 1963-68; Assisting Attorney-Gen., 1962-64; for Air, and Minister Assisting the Treasurer, 1968; for External Affairs, 1969. *Recreations:* squash, golf. *Address:*

Australian Embassy, 1-14 2 Chome Mita, Minato-ku, Tokyo, Japan.

**FREETH, H. Andrew,** RA 1965 (ARA 1955); RE 1946; RWS 1955; RBA 1949; RP 1966; Portrait Painter and Etcher; on staff of St Martin's School of Art, London; *b* Birmingham, 29 Dec. 1912; *s* of John Stewart Freeth and Charlotte Eleanor Stace, Hastings; *m* 1940, Roseen Marguerite Preston, Beaconsfield; three *s* one *d. Educ:* College of Art, Birmingham; British School at Rome, 1936-39 (Rome Scholarship in Engraving). ARE 1938. Served in Intelligence Corps (Major), 1940-46, in Mediterranean theatre; loaned to RAF Middle East as Official War Artist, 1943. Drawings and etchings have been purchased by Contemporary Art Society for British Museum, by Fitzwilliam Museum, by British Council, Bristol, Birmingham and Sunderland Art Galleries, by numerous Oxford and Cambridge Colls, etc; represented in Nat. Portrait Gall., Ashmolean Museum, Imperial War Museum, and Victoria and Albert Museum; reproduced in various publications. Best known works: (Portraits): Sir Alec Douglas-Home, J. Enoch Powell, W. Somerset Maugham, G. E. Moore, Walter de la Mare, Sir Samuel Gurney-Dixon, Lord Avon, Sir Bernard Lovell, also of Bishops (some past) of Dover, London, Peterborough, Derby, Gloucester, St Albans. *Address:* 37 Eastbury Road, Northwood, Middx. *T:* Northwood 21350. *Club:* Athenæum.

**FREETH, Rt. Rev. Robert Evelyn,** MA Cantab, ThD ACT; *b* 7 April 1886; *s* of Sir Evelyn Freeth and Florence Oakes; *m* 1913, Gladys Mary Snashall; two *s* one *d. Educ:* King's Coll. Sch., Wimbledon; Selwyn Coll., Cambridge (scholar), 1905; BA 2nd Cl. Classical Tripos, 1908. Ridley Hall, Cambridge, 1908; MA 1912; Derbyshire Prize, 1915. Deacon, 1909; Priest, 1910; Melanesian Mission, 1909-13; Curate, Christ Church, North Adelaide, South Australia, 1913-14; priest in charge, Angaston, 1914-15; Asst Chaplain, King's Sch., Parramatta, NSW, 1915-16; Precentor, St Andrews Cathedral, Sydney, and Principal of Choir Sch., 1916-18; Chaplain and House Master, King's Sch., Parramatta, 1918-20; Sydney Church of England Grammar Sch., 1920-27; Headmaster, Guildford Grammar Sch., Western Australia, 1928, resigned Dec. 1949. Canon of St George's Cathedral, Perth, WA, 1941-50. Archdeacon of Perth, WA, 1953-61; Asst Bishop of Perth, WA, 1957-62; retd, 1963. *Recreation:* gardening. *Address:* 142 Victoria Avenue, Dalkeith, Western Australia 6009, Australia.

*See also G. Freeth.*

**FREKE, Cecil George,** CIE 1937; MA Cantab, BSc London; Indian Civil Service (retired); *b* 8 Oct. 1887; *m* Judith Mary Marston; one *s* one *d. Educ:* Merchant Taylors' School, London; St John's Coll., Cambridge. Under-Sec., Government of India, Commerce and Industries Dept, 1919; Dir-Gen. of Commercial Intelligence and Statistics, India, 1921-26; Financial Sec. to the Govt of Bombay, 1930-37. Vice-Pres., All-India Lawn Tennis Assoc., 1933-37. Sec., Iraq Currency Board, 1943-49; Dir, British National Cttee, International chamber of Commerce, 1946-54. A Vice-Pres. Royal National Life-Boat Instn. *Address:* c/o National and Grindlay's Bank, 23 Fenchurch Street, EC3. *Club:* United Service.

**FREMANTLE,** family name of **Baron Cottesloe.**

**FRENCH,** family name of **Baron De Freyne** and **Earl of Ypres.**

**FRENCH, Major Arthur Cecil,** CBE 1952 (OBE 1947); Secretary, Council of Territorial and Auxiliary Forces Associations, 1947-61; *b* 11 Nov. 1896; *s* of Rev. W. A. French, Little Blakenham, Ipswich; *m* 1927, Audrey Frances, *d* of W. F. Paul, Ipswich; one *s* one *d. Educ:* Felsted; RMC, Sandhurst. Suffolk Regt, 1915. Brigade Major 6th Inf. Brigade, 1935-37; Brevet Major, 1937; retired, 1938. Sec. Cambs and Isle of Ely T&AFA, 1938-47; GSO2, 66 Div., 1939-40; psc 1931. *Recreations:* fishing and fruit growing. *Address:* Longacre, Stapleford, Cambs. *T:* Shelford 2135. *Club:* Army and Navy.

**FRENCH, Christopher James Saunders,** QC 1966; Deputy Chairman, Bucks Quarter Sessions, since 1966; *b* 14 Oct. 1925; 2nd *s* of late Rev. Reginald French, MC, MA, Hon. Chaplain to the Queen, and Gertrude Emily Mary (*née* Haworth); *m* 1957, Philippa, *d* of Philip Godfrey Price, Abergavenny; one *s* one *d. Educ:* Denstone Coll.; Brasenose Coll., Oxford. Coldstream Guards, 1943-48 (Capt.). Called to the Bar, Inner Temple, 1950. *Recreations:* walking, hunting, music, painting. *Address:* 59 Blenheim Terrace, St Johns Wood, NW8. *T:* 01-624 2734. *Club:* Garrick.

**FRENCH, Lt-Col Hon. (Edward) Gerald,** DSO 1918; 2nd *s* of 1st Earl of Ypres; *u* and *heir-pres* to 3rd Earl of Ypres, *qv*; *b* 11 Dec. 1883; *m* 1906, Leila (*d* 1959), *d* of R. King, JP; two *d. Educ:* Wellington Coll. Joined Cape Colonial Forces, 1904; served during Zulu Rebellion, 1906 (medal); British North Borneo Constabulary, 1910-14 (severely wounded, commended by Government and awarded grant); Adjutant 11th Batt. Yorks Regt 1914; 2nd in comd 11th Batt. Cheshire Regt Sept. 1915, and proceeded to France; served European War in inf. and as Asst Provost Marshal (despatches twice, DSO, slightly wounded and gassed, 1917; horse killed, 1918); relinquished commn, 1920; R of O, The Green Howards; Deputy Gov., Dartmoor Prison, 1921-23; specially employed under Colonial Office to advise Government as to reorganisation of Bahamas Police Force, 1923-24; Gov. of Newcastle Prison, 1924. Expeditionary Force, 1940; Lt-Col 1942; retd, 1944. *Publications:* The Life of Field-Marshal Sir John French, First Earl of Ypres, 1931; French Replies to Haig, 1936; edited Some War Diaries, Addresses and Correspondence of Field-Marshal the Earl of Ypres, 1937; Lord Chelmsford and the Zulu War, 1939; John Jorrocks and other characters from the works of Robert Surtees, 1947; The Corner Stone of English Cricket, 1948; Good-bye to Boot and Saddle, 1951; Gordon Pasha of the Sudan, 1958; It's Not Cricket (An Analysis of the Game's Unwritten Laws), 1960; The Kitchener-French Dispute (A Last Word), 1961; The Martyrdom of Admiral Byng, 1961; The Hanslope Park Tragedy, 1968; Leila, 1969. *Recreations:* cricket (represented Devon in Minor Counties Championship); racing (rode on the flat in Far East); rifle-shooting (rep. Br. N Borneo in Empire rifle-shooting competition for Daily Mail Cup); squash rackets (rep. MCC in Bath Club Cup Competition and against American touring team; originated old public schoolboys' competition for Londonderry Cup). *Address:* c/o Glyn, Mills & Co. (Holt's Branch), Kirkland House, Whitehall, SW1. *Clubs:* MCC, I Zingari, Free Foresters.

**FRENCH, Lieut-Col Hon. Gerald;** *see* French, Lieut-Col Hon. E. G.

**FRENCH, Henry William,** BSc (London); CEng, FIEE, FInstP; Chief Inspector for Further

Education for Industry and Commerce, Department of Education and Science, since 1965; *b* 14 Feb. 1910; *s* of Henry Moxey French and Alice French (*née* Applegate); *m* 1936, Hazel Anne Mary Ainley; two *s*. *Educ:* Varndean School, Brighton; Woolwich Polytechnic. Engineering Technician, 1925-27; Armed Forces (Royal Corps of Signals, Army Educational Corps), 1927-38; Lecturer, Radar Engineering, Mil. Coll. of Science, 1938-46; Dep. Dir, Educn and Training, Electric and Musical Industries, 1946-48; HM Inspector of Schools (Further Education), 1948-56; Regional Staff Inspector (NW), 1956-59; Staff Inspector (Engineering), 1956-65. Hon. DSc, Loughborough Univ. of Technology, 1966. *Recreations:* polyphonic music, opera, physics of music, travel. *Address:* 26 Crossways, Sutton, Surrey. *T:* 01-642 5277.

**FRENCH, Maj.-Gen. John,** CB 1960; retired 1961; Chief of Industrial Section, Armament Control Agency, Western European Union since 1962; *b* 16 May 1906; *s* of Frederick Featherstonhaugh French and Edith l'Anson (*née* Watson). *m* 1935, Ursula Daphne (*née* Hutton); two *s* one *d*. *Educ:* Oundle; Corpus Christi, Cambridge (BA). Commissioned RTC, 1929; pac Military Coll. of Science, 1938; Instructor of Ballistics, Military Coll. of Science, 1939; Admiralty Research Laboratory, 1941; WTSFF 21 Army Gp, 1945; Dept of Artillery, Min. of Supply, 1946; Mem. of the Ordnance Board, 1949; British Joint Services Mission, Washington, 1952; Department of Artillery, Min. of Supply, 1955; Vice-Pres., Ordnance Board, 1958-60, Pres., 1960-61. *Recreation:* ocean racing. *Address:* WEU, 43 Avenue du Président Wilson, Paris XVIe. *Clubs:* Royal Ocean Racing, RA Yacht (hon.); RAC Yacht.

**FRENCH, Leslie Richard;** Actor; *b* Kent, 23 April 1904; *s* of Robert Gilbert French and Jetty Sands Leahy; unmarried. *Educ:* London Coll. of Choristers. Began stage work 1914; early Shakespearean training with Sir Philip Ben Greet; recent parts include Hansel in Hansel and Gretel, Bert in Derby Day; Shakespearean parts include Puck, Ariel, Feste, Costard, etc; The Spirit in Comus; played Feste in the ballet Twelfth Night with the International Ballet at His Majesty's Theatre. Joined the Royal Corps of Signals, 1942; Lord Fancourt Babberly in Charley's Aunt, Christmas 1943. Produced Much Ado About Nothing and The Tempest for OUDS; Everyman as a ballet for the International Ballet Co., Lyric Theatre, 1943; Comus for the International Ballet, London Coliseum, 1946. Recent productions include: Charles and Mary, Cheltenham Festival, 1948; The Servant of Two Masters; Aladdin (Widow Twanky); Mother Goose (Mother Goose); She Stoops to Conquer for Edinburgh Festival (Tony Lumpkin), 1949; pantomime, Cinderella, 1950; The Dish Ran Away, Whitehall, 1950; Midsummer Night's Dream (Puck), Open Air Theatre during Cheltenham Festival; Open Air Theatre, Regent's Park, 1951; pantomime, Nottingham, 1951-52; The Ghost Train, Huddersfield, 1952; Pisanio in Cymbeline, Attendant Spirit in Comus, Open Air Theatre, 1952. Dyrkin in Out of the Whirlwind, Westminster Abbey, 1953. Open Air Theatre, Cape Town: The Taming of the Shrew, 1956; Midsummer Night's Dream, 1957; As You Like It (Touchstone), 1958. Johannesburg: The Tempest, 1956; Hamlet, 1957. Shakespearean seasons in Cape Town, 1959, 1960, 1961, 1962, 1963, 1966, 1969; Tempest, E. Oppenheimer Theatre, OFS, 1968; The Tell Tale Heart, 1969; An Evening with Shakespeare (tour), 1969; Twelfth Night, Port Elizabeth, 1970; The Way of the World, S Africa, 1970. Co-dir, Open Air Theatre, Regent's Park, 1958. Prod., Twelfth Night (in Great Hall of Hampton Ct Palace), 1965; Le Streghe (for Visconti), 1966. *Films:* Orders to Kill (M Lafitte), 1957; The Scapegoat (M Lacoste), 1958; The Singer not the Song (Father Gomez); The Leopard (Chevalley), 1963; The Witches, 1966; Happy Ever After, 1966; Joseph of Coppertino, 1966; Murder in Venice (Visconti), 1970. Several TV appearances incl. Villette (serial), 1970. First Exhibition of Paintings–oil and water colour, Parsons Gall. Presented with Key to City of Cape Town, Jan. 1963. *Recreations:* gardening and painting. *Address:* Leith Grove Cottage, Hedgerley Green, Bucks. *T:* Gerrard's Cross 82501. *Club:* Garrick.

**FRENCH, William Innes,** DSO 1945; OBE 1950; TD; DL; CA; Partner of French & Cowan, Chartered Accountants, Glasgow, since 1934; *b* 4 Oct. 1910; *e s* of James Andrew French, CA, Glasgow, and Christina Helen Youl. *Educ:* Kelvinside Academy, Glasgow. Joined 9th (GH) Bn HLI, TA, 1928. Served War of 1939-45: 15th (Scottish), 76th (Norfolk) and 52nd (Lowland) Divs in regimental and staff appointments; psc (Camberley) 1942; GSO2, War Office, 1943. Commanded 1st Bn Glasgow Highlanders (52nd Division) in BLA, 1944-45 (DSO, despatches) and in TA, 1947-49 (OBE, Substantive Col 1949). Chartered Accountant, 1934. Mem. Council, Inst. of Chartered Accountants of Scotland, 1953-57. Pres., Glasgow Chamber of Commerce, 1958-60. Chairman: Sir William Arrol & Co. Ltd, Engineers, Glasgow, 1961-69; Scotcros Ltd; Dir, Scottish Life Assurance Co. Ltd, and other cos. Member: Scottish Industrial Estates Corp., 1960-; Council on Tribunals, 1962-. DL City of Glasgow, 1962. *Recreations:* reading, walking. *Address:* (home) 5 Whittingehame Drive, Glasgow W2. *T:* 041-339 3382; (office) 144 St Vincent Street, Glasgow C2. *T:* 041-221 2984. *Clubs:* Caledonian, East India and Sports; Western (Glasgow).

**FREND, Charles Herbert;** Film Director since 1941; *b* 21 Nov. 1909; *s* of Edward Charles and Bertha Maud Frend; *m* 1940, Sonja Petra Baade Thornburn. *Educ:* King's Sch., Canterbury; Trinity Coll., Oxford. Entered cutting rooms at British Internat. Pictures, Elstree, 1931; became film editor, 1933; film editor for: Gaumont-British Picture Corp., 1934-37; Metro-Goldwyn-Mayer British Studios, 1937-39; Pascal Productions, 1940; became film dir for Ealing Studios, 1941; directed: The Big Blockade and The Foreman went to France, 1941; San Demetrio, London, 1943; The Return of the Vikings, Johnny Frenchman, 1944; The Loves of Joanna Godden, 1946; Scott of the Antarctic, 1947-48; A Run for your Money, 1949; The Magnet, 1950; The Cruel Sea, 1952; Lease of Life, 1954; The Long Arm, 1955; Barnacle Bill, 1957; Cone of Silence, 1960; Girl on Approval, 1961; While the Storm Lasts, 1962; The Sky-Bike, 1967. Mem. Order of Knighthood (First Class) of St Olav, 1953. *Recreation:* the cinema. *Address:* Flat 10, 111 Westbourne Terrace, W2. *T:* 01-723 0326. *Club:* Den Norske.

**FREND, Prof. William Hugh Clifford,** TD 1959 (Clasp, 1966); DD, FSA; Professor of Ecclesiastical History, Glasgow University, since Oct. 1969; *b* 11 Jan. 1916; 2nd *s* of late Rev. E. G. C. Frend, Shottermill, Surrey and late Edith (*née* Bacon); *m* 1951, Mary Grace, *d* of E. A. Crook, *qv*; one *s* one *d*. *Educ:* Fernden Sch.; Haileybury Coll. (Schol.); Keble Coll., Oxford (Schol.). 1st cl. hons Mod. Hist., 1937; Craven Fellow, 1937; DPhil 1940; BD Cantab 1964; DD Oxon 1966. Asst Princ., War Office,

1940; seconded Cabinet Office, 1941; FO, 1942; service in N Africa, Italy and Austria, 1943-46; Ed. Bd, German Foreign Min. Documents, 1947-51; Res. Fellow, Nottingham Univ., 1951; S. A. Cook Bye-Fellow, 1952, Fellow, 1956-69, Gonville and Caius Coll.; University Asst Lectr, 1953, Lectr in Divinity, 1958-69; Birkbeck Lectr in Ecclesiastical History, 1967-68. Assoc. Dir, Egypt Exploration Soc. excavations at Q'asr Ibrim, Nubia, 1963-64; Guest Scholar at Rhodes Univ., 1964 and Peter Ainslie Mem. Lecturer. Licensed Lay Reader, 1956; Ed., Modern Churchman, 1963. Commission Queen's Royal Regt (TA), 1947-67. FSA 1952; FRHistSoc 1954. *Publications:* The Donatist Church, 1952; Martyrdom and Persecution in the Early Church, 1965; The Early Church, 1965; (contrib.) The Layman in Christian History, 1963; (contrib.) Religion in the Middle East, 1968; articles in Jl Theol Studies, Jl Roman Studies, Jl Eccles. History, etc. *Recreations:* archæology, occasional golf and tennis, writing, collecting old coins and stamps. *Address:* Marbrae, Balmaha, Stirlingshire. *T:* Balmaha 227. *Club:* Authors'.

**FRERE, Alexander Stewart,** CBE 1946; MA Cantab; *b* 23 Nov. 1896; *m* 1933, Patricia Marion Caldecott, *d* of late Edgar Wallace; two *s* one *d*. *Educ:* Christ's Coll., Cambridge. Served Royal East Kent Yeomanry, seconded Royal Flying Corps. European War, 1914-18; edited the Granta, Cambridge, 1920-21; on staff of London Evening News, 1922-23; joined William Heinemann Ltd, Publishers, 1923; Dir, 1926; Man. Dir, 1932-40; Chm., 1945-61; Pres., 1961-62; Mem. of council Publishers Assoc., 1938-39. Assisted organise National Service Campaign, Ministry of Labour and National Service, Jan.-June 1939; Dir of Public Relations, Min. of Labour and National Service, 1940-44. Adviser to HM Govt Delegn to ILO Conf., Columbia Univ., New York, 1941. Chevalier de la Légion d'Honneur, 1953. *Address:* H5/6 Albany, W1; Knoll Hill House, Aldington, Kent. *Clubs:* White's, Garrick, Royal Thames Yacht; Century (NY); Travellers' (Paris).

**FRERE, James Arnold,** FSA; an Officer of Supreme Court of Judicature since 1966; *b* 20 April 1920; *e s* of late John Geoffrey Frere; one adopted *s*. *Educ:* Eton Coll.; Trinity Coll., Cambridge. Lieut Intelligence Corps, 1944-47. Regular Army R of O, 1949-67. Bluemantle Pursuivant of Arms, 1948-56; Chester Herald of Arms, 1956-60. Member: of the Surrey Archæological Soc. (Council, 1949-53, 1954-58 and 1959-63; Soc. of Authors and American Soc. of Authors; Soc. for the Protection of Ancient Buildings; Council of the Harleian Soc., 1951-66; Hon. Mem. Heraldry Soc. of Southern Africa, 1953-; a Vice-Pres. of Museum of Costume, 1952-60. Press Sec., New Gallery Clinic, 1967-70. Liveryman, Worshipful Co. of Scriveners. *Publications:* The British Monarchy at Home, 1963; (jointly with the Duchess of Bedford) Now . . . The Duchesses, 1964. *Recreations:* walking, painting, archæology. *Address:* c/o Society of Antiquaries, Burlington House, W1. *Club:* Civil Service.

**FRERE, Brigadier Jasper Gray,** DSO 1919; OBE 1946; MC; psc; BA; retired; *b* Kurow, New Zealand, 2 Jan. 1894; 5th *s* of late Ven. Hugh Corrie Frere and Florence, *d* of Robert Gray, first Bishop Metropolitan of Cape Town; *m* 1929, Cynthia Keble, *d* of late Rev. Arthur Keble White of Chevington, Suffolk; two *s*. *Educ:* Trinity Coll., Glenalmond; Keble Coll., Oxford; BA 1921. Served European War, 1914-18 (despatches four times, MC, DSO); operations in Waziristan, 1920-21; War of 1939-45 (OBE, Special Class Syrian Order of Merit); retired pay, 1946, Brig. (hon.). General Sec., Catholic Marriage Advisory Council, 1948-50; Mem. Home Office Marriage Guidance Training Board, 1949-51; Chm., British Cttee and Mem. of General Council Internat. Union of Family Organisations, 1952-57, Vice-Pres., 1957-63. *Publications:* Frere of Suffolk and Norfolk, 1275-1965; sundry political and economic papers on the Middle East. *Address:* Redthorne, Yateley, Hants.

**FRERE, Prof. Sheppard Sunderland;** Professor of the Archæology of the Roman Empire, Oxford University, since 1966; *b* 23 Aug. 1916; *e s* of late N. G. Frere, CMG; *m* 1961, Janet Cecily Hoare; one *s* one *d*. *Educ:* Lancing Coll.; Magdalene Coll., Cambridge. BA 1938, MA 1944. Master, Epsom Coll., 1938-40. National Fire Service, 1940-45. Master, Lancing Coll., 1945-54; Lecturer in Archæology, Manchester Univ., 1954-55; Reader in Archæology of Roman Provinces, London Univ. Inst. of Archæology, 1955-62; Prof. of the Archæology of the Roman Provinces, London Univ., 1963-66. Dir, Canterbury Excavations, 1946-60; Dir, Verulamium Excavations, 1955-61. Vice-Pres., Soc. of Antiquaries, 1962-66; Hon. Corr. Mem. German Archæological Inst., 1964, Fellow, 1967; Member: Royal Commn on Hist. Monuments (England), 1966-; Ancient Monuments Board (England), 1966-. *Publications:* (Ed.) Problems of the Iron Age in Southern Britain, 1961; Britannia, a history of Roman Britain, 1967; papers in learned jls. *Recreation:* gardening. *Address:* All Souls College, Oxford.

**FRESNAY, Pierre, (Pierre Laudenbach);** French actor; *b* Paris, 4 April 1897. *Educ:* Lycée Henri-IV; Conservatoire de Paris. *Plays include:* Classiques, Marius, Vient de paraître, Léocadia, L'Hermine, Noë, Trois Valses, Du côté de chez Proust, Auprès de ma blonde, Les Œufs de l'autruche, Hyménée, Mon Faust, Le Neveu de Rameau, La Guerre civile, L'Idée fixe, Machiavel et Montesquieu, La Tour d'Einstein, On ne sait jamais, etc. *Films:* Marius, Fanny, La Dame aux Camélias, Koenigsmark, La Grande Illusion, Le Corbeau, Le Voyageur sans bagages, Monsieur Vincent, Barry, Dieu a besoin des hommes, Il est minuit, Docteur Schweitzer, Le Défroqué, The Aristocrats, Le Grand-patron, L'Homme aux clefs d'or, La Millième fenêtre, Les Vieux de la vieille, etc. Television: Le Neveu de Rameau, L'Idée fixe, Mon Faust, Tête d'horloge. Prize, Best Actor, Venice Biennale, 1947; Prix Féminin du Cinema, 1949. *Address:* 4 Rue de la Michodière, Paris 2, France; 8 bis, Rue Saint-James, Neuilly-sur-Seine (Seine), France.

**FRESSANGES, Air Marshal Sir Francis J.,** KBE 1955; CB 1945; idc, psa; RAF retired; *b* 27 Feb. 1902; *s* of Capt. G. Fressanges; *m* Margaret Gordon Thomson. *Educ:* Royal Air Force Coll., Cranwell. Commissioned RAF 1923; Squadron Leader, 1936; Wing Commander, 1939; commanded Flying Boat Squadron in Battle of Atlantic, Jan. 1940-March 1941 (despatches); Group Capt. 1941; attached US Fleet, March-Sept. 1941 (US Legion of Merit); Dep. Dir of Overseas Operations, 1941-43; Air Commodore, 1943; Dir of Overseas Operations, 1943; AOC 47 Group, RAF, 1944-45; Dir of Operations, Air Ministry, 1946-48; idc 1949; Air Officer Commanding British Forces, Aden, 1950-52; Asst Chief of the Air Staff (Intelligence), 1952-54; Air Marshal, 1955; C-in-C FEAF and British Mil. Adviser to SEATO, 1954-57; retired; *Recreations:* tennis, golf, riding, fencing. *Address:* Blue Hayes, Bahati, Box 136, Nakuru, Kenya; c/o Coutts

& Co., 1 Cadogan Place, SW1. *Clubs:* Royal Air Force, United Hunts; Jockey Club of Kenya.

**FRETWELL, Elizabeth;** operatic and dramatic soprano; *b* Melbourne, Australia; *m* Robert Simmons; one *s* one *d*. *Educ:* privately. Joined National Theatre, Melbourne, 1950; came to Britain, 1955; joined Sadler's Wells, 1956; Australia, Elizabethan Opera Co., 1963; tour of W Germany, 1963; USA, Canada and Covent Garden, 1964; tour of Europe, 1965. Rôles include Violetta in La Traviata, Leonora in Fidelio, Ariadne in Ariadne auf Naxos, Senta in The Flying Dutchman, Minnie in The Girl of the Golden West, Leonora in Il Trovatore, Aida, Ellen Orford in Peter Grimes. Has sung in BBC Promenade Concerts and on TV. *Recreation:* rose-growing. *Address:* 5 Higher Drive, Purley, Surrey.

**FRETWELL, Sir George (Herbert),** KBE 1953; CB 1950; Director General of Works, Air Ministry, 1947-59, retired; *b* 21 March 1900; *s* of late Herbert Fretwell, Ripley, Derbyshire; *m* 1930, Constance Mabel, *d* of late George Ratcliffe, Woodford Green, Essex; no *c*. *Educ:* Heanor Grammar Sch., Derbs. Entered Air Ministry as Asst Civil Engineer, 1928; Civil Engineer, 1934; Superintending Engineer, 1937; Chief Engineer, 1940; Dep. Dir of Works, 1945, Dir, 1946. *Address:* North Lodge, 2 North Street, Sheringham, Norfolk. *T:* Sheringham 2336.

**FREUD, Anna,** CBE 1967; Psycho-Analyst; Director of Hampstead Child Therapy Course and Clinic, since 1952; *b* 3 Dec. 1895; *d* of Professor Sigmund Freud and Martha Freud (*née* Bernays). *Educ:* Cottage Lyceum, Vienna. Chm., Vienna Inst. of Psycho-Analysis until 1938; Mem., London Inst. of Psycho-Analysis since then. Hon. degrees: LLD: Clark Univ., USA, 1950; Univ. of Sheffield, 1966; ScD: Jefferson Med. Coll., USA, 1964; Univ. of Chicago, 1966; Yale 1968. *Publications:* The Ego and the Mechanisms of Defence, 1937; Normality and Pathology in Childhood, 1965 (New York); annual: Psychoanalytic Study of the Child; contribs to Internat. Jl of Psycho-Analysis. *Address:* 20 Maresfield Gardens, NW3. *T:* 01-435 2002.

**FREUD, Clement Raphael;** writer, broadcaster, caterer; Director, Genevieve Restaurants, London; Director and Trustee, Playboy Club of London Ltd; Berkeley Hotel, Southampton; Consultant, New Mauritius Hotels Ltd, Curepipe; *b* 24 April 1924; *s* of late Ernst and Lucie Freud; *m* 1950, Jill, 2nd *d* of H. W. Flewett, MA; three *s* two *d*. Apprenticed, Dorchester Hotel, London. Served War, Royal Ulster Rifles; Liaison Officer, Nuremberg, 1946. Trained, Martinez Hotel, Cannes. Proprietor, Royal Court Theatre Club, 1952-62. Sports writer, Observer, 1956-64; Cookery Editor: Time and Tide, 1961-63; Observer Magazine, 1964-68; Daily Telegraph Magazine, 1968-. Sports Columnist, Sun, 1964-69; Columnist: Sunday Telegraph, 1963-65; News of the World, 1965; Financial Times, 1964-. Writer and performer Sweet and Sour (Southern), 1962-64; Freud on Food (Tyne Tees), 1968-70; BBC: Frost Shows; Braden Shows; Jackanory; ITV: (talk shows): Eamon Andrews, Simon Dee; David Jacobs, Late Late Show (Telefis Eireann); Carson Show (NBC, USA), etc. Award winning petfood commercial: San Francisco, Tokyo, Berlin, 1967. BBC (sound) Just a Minute, 1968-. *Publications:* Grimble, 1968; contributor to: Punch, Queen, Town, Which, New Yorker, etc. *Recreations:* racing, cricket, backgammon, golf; also other forms of gambling. *Address:* 7 Boundary Road, NW8. *T:* 01-722 1877. *Clubs:* Savile, MCC, Lord's Taverners'.

*See also Lucian Freud.*

**FREUD, Lucian;** painter; teacher at Slade School, London University; *b* 8 Dec. 1922; *s* of Ernst and Lucie Freud; *m* 1953, Lady Caroline Maureen Blackwood (marr. diss. at Juarez, Mexico, 1957), *d* of 4th Marquess of Dufferin and Ava. *Educ:* Central Sch. of Art; Goldsmiths' Coll. Held his first one-man exhibn, 1944; other one-man shows, 1946, 1950, 1952, 1958, 1963, 1968. After War of 1939-45 was painting in Paris and Greece. Painting bought by Museum of Modern Art, New York, 1947; Melbourne National Gallery, 1950; in Arts Council Festival of Britain Exhibn (by invitation), Sixty Paintings for '51, his picture Interior near Paddington was one of five bought by the Council for £500 each on the recommendation of a selection jury. Represented by three works in the Tate Gallery. *Address:* Slade School of Fine Art, Gower Street, WC1.

*See also C. R. Freud.*

**FREUND, Otto K.;** *see* Kahn-Freund.

**FREW, Air Vice-Marshal Sir Matthew Brown,** KBE 1948; CB 1943; DSO 1918; MC; *b* 7 April 1895; *s* of Henry Lorimer Frew and Annie Brown; *m* 1921, Gertrude Fairley; one *s*. *Educ:* Hutcheson's Grammar Sch., Glasgow. Joined HLI, 1914; transferred RFC, 1916; Capt., 1917; Squadron Leader, 1927; Wing Comdr, 1934; Group Capt., 1938; Acting Air Vice-Marshal, 1942; Temp. Air Vice-Marshal, 1943; Air Commodore, 1943; Air Vice-Marshal, 1945; retired, 1948. Served European War, 1914-18 (DSO, MC and bar, Air Force Cross, Italian Silver Medal for Military Valour); Northern Kurdistan, 1931-32 (Bar to DSO). Comdr Royal Order of George I of Greece with swords, 1943; Belgian Military Cross, 1st Class, 1945. *Recreation:* golf. *Club:* Pretoria (Pretoria, SA).

**FREW, Engineer Rear-Adm. Sir Sydney (Oswell),** KBE, *cr* 1949; CB 1946. Joined Royal Navy, 1905; Engineer Captain, 1939; Engineer Rear-Admiral, 1945; retired list, 1950. Served European War, 1914-19. Grand Officer Order of Orange Nassau with Swords (Netherlands). *Address:* 3 Goldhurst Mansions, Goldhurst Terrace, NW6.

**FREWEN, Adm. Sir John Byng,** GCB 1969 (KCB 1964; CB 1961); idc; Commander-in-Chief, Naval Home Command, 1969-70; *b* 28 March 1911; *s* of Capt. E. L. Frewen, RN, Northiam, Sussex; *m* 1937, June Gwendolen Cazenove. Rear-Adm. 1959. Chief of Staff to the C-in-C, Home Fleet, Aug. 1959-April 1961; Flag Officer 2nd-in-Comd, Far East Station, 1961-62; Vice-Chief of the Naval Staff, 1963-65. C-in-C, Home Fleet and NATO C-in-C, Allied Forces, Eastern Atlantic, 1965-67; Nato C-in-C, Channel, 1966-67; C-in-C Portsmouth, 1967-69. Principal Naval ADC to the Queen, 1968-70. *Address:* Clench Green, Northiam, Sussex. *T:* Northiam 2279.

**FREWER, Rt. Rev. John,** CBE 1957; *b* Fulletby Rectory, Horncastle, Lincs, 1 Nov. 1883; 3rd *s* of late Rev. Canon G. E. Frewer; unmarried. *Educ:* King's Sch., Canterbury; Lincoln Theological Coll. Deacon, 1908; Priest, 1909; Curate of St Nicholas, Skirbeck, 1908-11; Domestic Chaplain to Bishop of Bunbury, West Australia, 1911-16; Priest-in-Charge, Yarloop, 1912-13; Rector of St David's, South Bunbury, 1913-16; Priest of Brotherhood of St Boniface, Williams, Diocese of Bunbury, 1916-29; Warden of the Brotherhood, 1919-29; Hon.

Chaplain to Bishop of Bunbury, 1918-29; Canon of Bunbury, 1922-29; Bishop of North-West Australia, 1929-65. *Address:* Flat 4, Riley House, 20 Excelsior Street, Shenton Park, Western Australia 6008, Australia. *Club:* Royal Over-Seas League.

**FREYBERG,** family name of **Baron Freyberg.**

**FREYBERG,** 2nd Baron, *cr* 1951, of Wellington, New Zealand, and of Munstead in the Co. of Surrey; **Paul Richard Freyberg,** OBE 1965; MC 1945; Lieut-Col, Grenadier Guards; Defence Policy Staff, Ministry of Defence, since 1968; *b* 27 May 1923; *s* of 1st Baron Freyberg, VC, GCMG, KCB, KBE, DSO (and 3 bars), and Barbara (*née* Jekyll) (*see* Lady Freyberg); *S* father, 1963; *m* 1960, Ivy Perronelle Katharine Guild, Aspall Hall, Debenham, Suffolk; three *d. Educ:* Eton Coll. Joined NZ Army, 1940; served with 2nd NZEF: Greece, 1941; Western Desert, 1941-42; transferred to British Army, 1942; North Africa, 1943; Italy, 1943-45 (MC); Palestine, 1947-48; Cyprus, 1956-58; British Cameroons, 1961; Comd HAC Infantry Battalion, 1965-68. Staff Coll., 1952; jssc 1958. *Address:* Munstead House, Godalming, Surrey. *T:* 6004. *Clubs:* Guards, Royal Automobile.

**FREYBERG, Lady,** GBE 1953 (OBE 1943), (**Barbara Freyberg**); *d* of late Sir Herbert Jekyll, KCMG, and Lady Jekyll, DBE; *m* 1st, 1911, Hon. Francis McLaren, MP (killed in action, 1917); two *s*; 2nd, 1922, 1st Baron Freyberg, VC, GCMG, KCB, KBE, DSO (*d* 1963); one *s* (*see* 2nd Baron Freyberg). *Educ:* at home. Served during War of 1939-45 with Welfare Branch of New Zealand Div. in Egypt, Italy and London; Africa Star; 1939-45 Medal; Defence Medal; New Zealand War Medal; despatches, 1943. DGStJ. *Address:* 65 Chelsea Square, SW3. *T:* 01-352 5168. *Club:* Bath. *See also Martin McLaren.*

**FRICKER, Peter Racine,** FRCO, ARCM; Resident Composer at Santa Barbara, University of California, 1965 (Professor of Music, University of California, 1964-65); Director of Music, Morley College, 1952-64; *b* 5 Sept. 1920; *s* of late Edward Racine Fricker; *m* 1943, Audrey Helen Clench. *Educ:* St Paul's Sch. Royal College of Music, 1937-40. Served War, 1940-46, in Royal Air Force, working in Signals and Intelligence. Has worked as Composer, Conductor, and Music Administrator since 1946. Hon. DMus (Leeds), 1958. Order of Merit, West Germany, 1965. Hon. RAM, 1966. *Publications:* Four Fughettas for Two Pianos, 1946; Wind Quintet, 1947; Three Sonnets of Cecco Angiolieri da Siena, for Tenor and Seven Instruments, 1947; String Quartet in One Movement, 1948; Symphony No 1, 1948-49; Prelude, Elegy and Finale, for String Orchestra, 1949; Concerto for Violin and Orchestra, 1949-50; Sonata for Violin and Piano, 1950; Concertante for Cor Anglais and String Orchestra, 1950; Symphony No 2, 1950; Concertante for Three Pianos, Strings and Timpani, 1951; Four Impromptus for Piano; Concerto for Viola and Orchestra, 1951-53; Concerto for Piano and Orchestra, 1952-54; String Quartet No 2, 1952-53; Rapsodia Concertante, for Violin and Orchestra, 1953-54; Dance Scene for Orchestra, 1954; Musick's Empire, for Chorus and Small Orchestra, 1955; Litany for Double String Orchestra, 1955; 'Cello Sonata, 1956; Oratorio, The Vision of Judgement, 1956-58; Octet, 1958; Toccata for Piano and Orchestra, 1958-59; Serenade No 1, 1959; Serenade No 2, 1959; Symphony No 3, 1960; Studies for Piano, 1961; Cantata for Tenor and Chamber Ensemble, 1962; O Longs Désirs: Song-cycle for Soprano and Orchestra, 1963; Ricercare for Organ, 1965; Four Dialogues for Oboe and Piano, 1965; Four Songs for High Voice and Orchestra, 1965; Fourth Symphony, 1966; Fantasy for Viola and Piano, 1966; Three Scenes for Orchestra, 1966; The Day and the Spirits, for Soprano and Harp, 1967; Seven Counterpoints for Orchestra, 1967; Magnificat, 1968; Episodes, for Piano, 1968; Concertante No 4, 1968; Toccata for Organ, 1968; Saxophone Quartet, 1969; Praeludium for Organ, 1969; Paseo for Guitar, 1970; also music for film, stage and radio. *Recreation:* travel. *Address:* Department of Music, University of California, Santa Barbara, Calif 93106, USA.

**FRIEL, Brian;** writer; *b* 9 Jan. 1929; *s* of Patrick Friel and Christina Friel (*née* MacLoone); *m* 1954, Anne Morrison; one *s* four *d. Educ:* St Columb's Coll., Derry; St Patrick's Coll., Maynooth; St Joseph's Trng Coll., Belfast. Taught in various schools, 1950-60; writing full-time from 1960. Lived in Minnesota during first season of Tyrone Guthrie Theater, Minneapolis. *Publications: collected stories:* The Saucer of Larks, 1962; The Gold in the Sea, 1966; *plays:* Philadelphia, Here I Come!, 1965; The Loves of Cass McGuire, 1967; Lovers, 1968; Crystal and Fox, 1969; The Mundy Scheme, 1969. *Recreations:* reading, trout-fishing, slow tennis. *Address:* Ardmore, Muff, Lifford, Co. Donegal, Ireland. *T:* Muff 30.

**FRIEND, Archibald Gordon; His Honour Judge Friend;** Deputy Chairman, Middlesex Area Sessions, since 1969 (Inner London Sessions, 1965-69); *b* 6 July 1912; *m* 1940, Patricia Margaret Smith; no *c*. Called to Bar, Inner Temple, 1933. Dep. Chm., Herts Quarter Sessions, 1963. *Recreation:* gardening. *Address:* Guildhall, Westminster, SW1. *T:* 01-839 3924.

**FRIML, Rudolf;** pianist and composer; *b* Prague, Czechoslovakia, 7 Dec. 1884. *Educ:* Prague Conservatoire of Music. Studied Piano with Prof. Jiranek, composition with Antonin Dvořák. Went to America 1904 for concert tour, playing his own piano concerto with New York Symphony Orchestra, Walter Damrosch, conducting. Composed and published several thousand piano, violin, 'cello, organ compositions. Among many musical comedies and operettas are: Firefly, High Jinks, Katinka, You're in Love, Gloriana, Tumble In, Sometimes, Blue Kitten, White Eagle, June Love, Little Whopper, Luanna, Peasant Girl, Annina, Bird of Paradise, Kitty Darling, Rose Marie, Vagabond King, Three Musketeers. His latest compositions are: Chinese Suite, Arabian Suite (Chinese operetta Sing Song Girl, two piano concertos and Round the World Symphony in manuscripts). When not travelling, resides in Hollywood. *Address:* American Society of Composers, Authors and Publishers, 575 Madison Avenue, New York.

**FRINK, Elisabeth,** CBE 1969; *b* 14 Nov. 1930; British; *m* 1st, 1955, Michel Jammet (marr. diss. 1963); one *s*; 2nd, Edward Pool, MC. *Educ:* Convent of The Holy Family, Exmouth. Guildford Sch. of Art, 1947-49; Chelsea Sch. of Art, 1949-53. Exhibitions: Beaux Arts Gallery, 1952; St George's Gallery, 1955; exhibits regularly at Waddington Gallery, London. Represented in collections in USA, Australia, Holland, Sweden, Germany and Tate Gallery, London. *Address:* c/o Waddington Gallery, 2 Cork Street, W1; Le Village, Corbès, 30 Anduze, France.

**FRIPP, Alfred Thomas,** BM; FRCS; Member, Pensions Appeal Tribunal; *b* 3 July 1899; *s* of late Sir Alfred Fripp, KCVO, and late Lady M. S. Fripp, *d* of late T. B. Haywood; *m* 1931, Kathleen Kimpton; one *s* two *d*. *Educ:* Winchester; Christ Church, Oxford. 2nd Lieut 1st Life Guards, 1917-18. Christ Church, Oxford, 1919-21; Guy's Hospital, 1921; Surg., Royal National Orthopædic Hospital, 1934-64. FRCS 1927. Pres. Orthopædic Section, RSocMed, 1950-51. *Recreations:* gardening, rowing. *Address:* Mascalls Farm, Banks Road, North Chailey, Sussex. *T:* Newick 2866. *Clubs:* Bath; Leander (Henley-on-Thames).

**FRISBY, Maj.-Gen. Richard George Fellowes,** CB 1963; CBE 1958; DSO 1944; MC 1939; *b* 17 Dec. 1911; *er s* of late Col H. G. F. Frisby, Royal Hants Regt, and late Mrs R. M. Frisby, Bacton Grange, Herefordshire; *m* 1938, Elizabeth Mary, 2nd *d* of late Col W. G. Murray, 3rd King's Own Hussars, Twyford House, Winchester, and late Mrs M. Murray, Pretoria, South Africa; two *s*. *Educ:* Haileybury Coll.; Royal Military College, Sandhurst. Commissioned Hants Regt, 1931; Mohmand Campaign, 1935; British Army Staff, Washington, 1941-42. Commanded: 4 Bn Welch Regt, 1944-45; 1 Bn Hants Regt, 1945-46; 14 Bn Parachute Regt, 1949-51; 1 Bn R Hants Regt, 1951-53; Tactical Wing Sch. of Infantry, 1953-54; 1 Commonwealth Div., Korea, 1955-56; 24 Independent Brigade, 1957-58; Gen. Staff, HQ Eastern Command, 1959-60; GOC 53 Infantry Div. (TA), 1961-63; Maj.-Gen., 1961; Chief of Staff to the C-in-C, Allied Forces, Northern Europe, Dec. 1963-65; retd. *Address:* Dunderry House, Navan, Co. Meath, Eire. *Club:* Army and Navy; Kildare Street (Dublin).

**FRISBY, Roger Harry Kilbourne,** QC 1969; *b* 11 Dec. 1921; 2nd *s* of late Herbert Frisby and Hylda Mary Frisby; *m* 1961, Audrey Mary (*née* Jennings); two *s* one *d* (and one *s* one *d* by previous marriage). *Educ:* Bablake Sch.; Christ Church, Oxford; King's Coll., Univ. of London. Called to the Bar, Lincoln's Inn, 1950. *Address:* 3 King's Bench Walk, Temple, EC4. *T:* 01-353 0431. *Clubs:* Oxford and Cambridge University, Hurlingham.

**FRISCH, Otto Robert,** OBE 1946; DSc; FRS 1948; Jacksonian Professor of Natural Philosophy, University of Cambridge, since 1947; *b* Vienna, Austria, 1 Oct. 1904; *o s* of late Dr Justinian Frisch and Auguste Meitner; *m* 1951, Ursula, *o d* of Karl Blau; one *s* one *d*. *Educ:* Vienna Univ. (Dr phil 1926). Scientific research in Berlin, Hamburg, London, Copenhagen, Birmingham, Liverpool, Oxford, Los Alamos, Harwell, Cambridge. *Publications:* Meet the Atoms, 1947 (London); Atomic Physics Today, 1961 (New York); Working with Atoms, 1965 (Leicester); The Nature of Matter, 1970; numerous papers on various topics in atomic and nuclear physics, in scientific periodicals. *Recreation:* music (piano and violin). *Address:* Trinity Coll., Cambridge.

**FRISCH, Prof. Ragnar Anton Kittil;** Norwegian economist; Director of Research, Economic Institute, Oslo University (Professor of Economics since 1931); *b* 3 March 1895. *m* 1st, Marie Smedal (decd); one *d*; 2nd, 1953, Astrid Johannessen. *Educ:* Univ. of Oslo. Visiting Professor: Yale Univ., 1930; Sorbonne, 1933. Fellow and one of Founders of Econometric Soc., 1931. Chief Ed. of Econometrica, 1933-35. Chm., first session of Econ. and Employment Commn of UN. Member: Internat. Statistical Inst., 1937-; Norske Videnskapsakademi i Oslo; Kungl. Humanistiska Vetenskapssamfundet i Lund; Kungl. Svenska Vetenskapsakademien; Accademia Naz. dei Lincei, Rome (Antonio Feltrinelli Prize, 1961); Hon. Member: Amer. Acad. of Arts and Sciences; Amer. Economic Assoc.; Corresp. Mem., Royal Economic Soc.; Advising Mem., Acad. of Human Rights, Rome; Fellow, Inst. of Math. Statistics, USA; Corresp. Fellow, British Academy; Hon. Fellow, Royal Statistical Soc. Schumpeter Prize, Harvard, 1955; (jointly) Prize in Economics to the memory of Alfred Nobel, 1969. Hon. Doctorates: Handelshögskolan i Stockholm; Copenhagen; Stockholm Univ.; Hon. DSc Cambridge, 1967. *Address:* Slemdalsveien 98, Vinderen, Oslo 3, Norway.

**FRODSHAM, Anthony Freer;** Managing Director, P-E Consulting Group Ltd, since 1963; *b* Peking, China, 8 Sept. 1919; *er s* of George William Frodsham and Constance Violet Frodsham (*née* Neild); *m* 1953, Patricia Myfanwy Wynne-Edwards; two *s*. *Educ:* Ecole Lacordaire, Paris; Faraday House Engineering Coll., London, DFH, CEng, FIMechE, FIMC, FRSA. Served War, 1939-46: Engineer Officer, RN, Asst Fleet Engr on staff of C-in-C Mediterranean, 1944-46 (despatches, 1945). P-E Consulting Group Ltd, 1947-; Manager, Midlands Area, 1954; Dir, in charge of Midlands Area and Continent of Europe, 1956-63. Mem. Council, Inst. of Management Consultants (Pres., 1967-68); Mem. Council: Management Consultants Assoc. (Chm., 1968-70); Fédération Européene des Conseils en Organisation; Mem. BNEC Canada Cttee (Chm., Machinery Sub-Gp); Dir, principal subsidiaries of P-E Consulting Gp, incl. those in S Africa and Australia. *Publications:* contrib. to technical jls; lectures and broadcasts on management subjects. *Recreations:* swimming, boating, modern languages. *Address:* (home) 1 The Grange, Wimbledon Common, SW19; *T:* 01-946 3413; (office) 12 Grosvenor Place, SW1. *T:* 01-235 5444. *Clubs:* Royal Automobile, Naval.

**FRÖHLICH, Herbert,** FRS 1951; DPhil; Professor of Theoretical Physics, The University of Liverpool, since 1948; *b* 9 Dec. 1905; *m* 1950, Fanchon Aungst. *Educ:* Munich. Studied Theoretical Physics at University of Munich; DPhil 1930; Subsequently Privatdozent at Freiburg Univ. Left Germany in 1933. Research Physicist, Lecturer, and Reader in Theoretical Physics, University of Bristol, 1935-48. Hon. Dr of Science, Rennes, 1955; Hon. LLD Alberta, 1968; Hon. ScD Dublin, 1969. *Publications:* various scientific papers and books. *Address:* University of Liverpool, Liverpool L69 3BX.

**FROME, Sir Norman (Frederick),** Kt 1947; CIE 1945; DFC 1918; MSc, FIEE; late Consultant, Messrs Preece, Cardew & Rider, Consulting Engineers; formerly Indian Posts and Telegraphs Department; *b* 23 Sept. 1899; *s* of late John Frome, Bristol; *m* 1928, Edith S. Guyan. *Educ:* Fairfield Grammar Sch.; University of Bristol. Served European War, 1914-18, in RFC and RAF, 1917-18. Joined Indian Posts and Telegraphs Dept, 1923; Dir of Telegraphs, 1937; Postmaster-Gen., 1941; Chief Engineer, 1946. *Publications:* articles on telecommunications, 1928-60. *Recreations:* astronomy, ornithology. *Address:* Elmwood, Gussage All Saints, near Wimborne, Dorset BH21 5ET. *Club:* Royal Commonwealth Society.

**FROOD, Hester;** *b* 1882; *d* of James N. Frood, Topsham, Devon; *m* 1921, F. Gwynne Evans. *Educ:* Exeter High Sch. Studied Art at Exeter and Paris; exhibited at the RA, New English Art Club, International, etc; Etchings, Drypoints and Water Colour Drawings in: British Museum (presented additionally 12 drawings and one etching, 1966); South Kensington; Ashmolean Museum, Oxford; and various Municipal Galls. One-man shows at Colnaghi's: 1925, 1930, 1943, 1946, 1949; at Royal Memorial Museum, Exeter, 1957; also (from 1925) in the USA, Scotland, provinces, etc. *Address:* Bradfield Place, Bradfield, near Manningtree, Essex.

**FROST, David (Paradine),** OBE 1970; author, producer, columnist; star of "The Frost Report", "The Frost Programme", "Frost on Friday", "The David Frost Show", etc; Joint Founder, London Weekend Television; Chairman and Chief Executive, David Paradine Ltd; *b* 7 April 1939; *s* of late Rev. W. J. Paradine Frost, Beccles, Suffolk. *Educ:* Gillingham Grammar Sch.; Wellingborough Grammar Sch.; Gonville and Caius Coll., Cambridge (MA). Sec., The Footlights; Editor, Granta. LLD, Emerson Coll., USA. BBC Television series: That Was the Week That Was, 1962-63 (in USA, 1963-64); Not So Much a Programme, More a Way of Life, 1964-65; The Frost Report, 1966-67; Frost Over England, 1967; Frost Over America, 1970. David Frost at the Phonograph (BBC Sound), 1966. Rediffusion series: The Frost Programme, 1966-67, 1967-68; Frost on Friday, 1968-69, 1969-70. Other programmes include: David Frost's Night Out in London, (USA), 1966-67; The Next President, (USA), 1968; Robert Kennedy the Man, (USA), 1968; The David Frost Show, (USA), 1969-70. Golden Rose, Montreux, for Frost Over England, 1967; Royal Television Society's Silver Medal, 1967; Richard Dimbleby Award, 1967; Emmy Award (USA), 1970; Religious Heritage of America Award, 1970. *Stage:* An Evening with David Frost (Edinburgh Fest.), 1966. *Publications:* That Was the Week That Was, 1963; How to Live under Labour, 1964; Talking with Frost, 1967; To England With Love, 1967; The Presidential Debate 1968, 1968; The Americans, 1970. *Address:* 46 Egerton Crescent, SW3.

**FROST, Edward Granville Gordon,** CBE 1953; JP; MA (Hon.); *b* 18 Feb. 1886; *s* of late Col H. Frost; *m* 1920, Dorothy Alice (*d* 1963), *d* of late Rev. J. A. Fletcher, Fransham, Norfolk; one *d. Educ:* Felsted Sch.; Pembroke Coll., Cambridge. 2nd Lieut 2 Volunteer Bn Cambs Regt, retired 1920; Commandant Red Cross to 1920. CC 1928, CA 1937-, Cambridge; Chm. Ely Dioc. Bd of Finance, 1937-63; JP Cambs, 1924-; Vice-Chm. Cambs Quarter Sessions, 1948-61; Chm. Cambridge County Council, 1949-May 1952; High Sheriff of Hunts and Cambs, 1957-58. Fellow, Corporation of SS Mary and Nicholas (Woodard Schs), 1969-. Defence Medal. *Recreations:* music, gardening. *Address:* 29 Barrow Road, Cambridge. *T:* 50543. *Clubs:* Cambridge County, University Union (Cambridge).

**FROST, Maj.-Gen. John Dutton,** CB 1964; DSO 1943 and Bar, 1945; MC 1942; *b* 31 Dec. 1912; *s* of late Brig.-Gen. F. D. Frost, CBE, MC; *m* 1947, Jean MacGregor Lyle; one *s* one *d. Educ:* Wellington Coll.; RMC Sandhurst. Commissioned The Cameronians, Sept. 1932; Capt., Iraq Levies, 1938-41; Major and Lt-Col, Parachute Regt, 1941-45; Staff Coll., Camberley, 1946; GSO2, HQ Lowland Dist, 1948-49; GSO2, Senior Officers' Sch., 1949-52; AA and QMG, 17 Gurkha Div., 1952-53; GSO1, 17 Gurkha Div., 1953-55; Comd, Netheravon, 1955-57; Comd, 44 Parachute Bde, 1958-61; Comdr 52nd Lowland Div./District, 1961-64; GOC Troops in Malta and Libya, 1964-66; Comdr Malta Land Force, 1965; retired, 1967. Cross of Grand Officer, SMO, Malta, 1966. *Recreations:* field sports, polo, golf. *Address:* Northend Farm, Milland, Liphook, Hants. *Club:* Army and Navy.

**FROST, Norman,** CBE 1959; KPM; *b* 18 March 1899; *s* of William Frost and Maud Frost (*née* Strickland); *m* 1927, Ivy Edna (*née* Bush); two *s. Educ:* March, Cambs. Royal Engineers (Signals), 1917-20. Peterborough Police, 1926-44; Boston Police, 1944-47; seconded Home Office; Commandant Police Training Sch., 1945-47; Eastbourne Police, 1947-54; Chief Constable of Bristol, 1954-64. OStJ. *Recreation:* collecting antiques. *Address:* Westovers, Wedmore, Somerset. *T:* Wedmore 568. *Club:* St John House.

**FROST, Terence, (Terry Frost);** Artist; *b* Oct. 1915; *m* 1945; five *s* one *d. Educ:* Leamington Spa Central Sch. Exhibitions: Leicester Galls, 1952-58; Waddington Galls, 1958-62, 1966; B. Schaeffer Gallery, New York, 1960-62. Oil paintings acquired by Tate Gallery, National Gallery of Canada, National Gallery of NSW; also drawing acquired by Victoria and Albert Museum. Other work in public collections; Canada, USA, Germany, Australia, and in Edinburgh, Dublin, Leeds, Hull, Manchester, Birmingham, Liverpool, Bristol, etc. Gregory Fellow in Painting, Univ. of Leeds, 1954-56. *Address:* 2 Old Parr Road, Banbury, Oxon. *T:* Banbury 4180.

**FROWEN, Brig. John Harold,** DSO 1941; OBE 1941; RA; retired; *b* 14 Sept. 1898; *s* of Fraser Frowen and Elizabeth Mary, *d* of late Sir John Heffernan, KCB, RN. *Educ:* privately; RMA Woolwich. 2nd Lieut RA, 1916; Capt. 1929; Major 1938; Temp. Lieut-Col 1940; Col, 1946; Brig., 1949; served in France and Flanders, 1917-19; India, 1919-26; Home, 1926-29; employed in mission to Egyptian Army, 1939-40; served Western Desert campaigns, Greece, Crete, etc (prisoner); repatriated UK 1943; BRA Southern Army, India Command, 1943-44; Comdt Artillery Sch., India, 1944-47; Comdr AA Bde, UK, 1947-51; loaned Pakistan Army, 1951-52; retd 1952. Sec. RA Institution, 1952-58; Sec. RA Printing Press, 1958-64. *Recreation:* played in Wimbledon lawn tennis tournament, 1929, 1930, 1931. *Address:* 29 Morden Road, SE3. *T:* 01-852 5308. *Club:* Army and Navy.

**FRY, Christopher;** dramatist; *b* 18 Dec. 1907; *s* of Charles John Harris and Emma Marguerite Hammond, *d* of Emma Louisa Fry; *m* 1936, Phyllis Marjorie Hart; one *s. Educ:* Bedford Modern Sch. Actor at Citizen House, Bath, 1927; Schoolmaster at Hazlewood Preparatory Sch., Limpsfield, Surrey, 1928-31; Dir of Tunbridge Wells Repertory Players, 1932-35; life too complicated for tabulation, 1935-39; The Tower, a pageant-play produced at Tewkesbury Fest., 1939; Dir of Oxford Repertory Players, 1940 and 1944-46, directing at Arts Theatre, London, 1945; Staff dramatist, Arts, 1947. FRSL. Queen's Gold Medal (for Poetry), 1962. *Plays:* A Phoenix Too Frequent, Mercury, 1946; The Lady's Not for Burning, Arts, 1948, Globe, 1949; The Firstborn, Edinburgh Festival, 1948; Thor, with Angels, Canterbury Festival, 1949; Venus Observed, St James's, 1950; The Boy with a Cart, Lyric, Hammersmith, 1950; Ring Round the Moon (translated from French of Jean Anouilh), Globe, 1950; A Sleep of Prisoners, produced St Thomas' Church, Regent Street, W1, 1951; The Dark is Light Enough, Aldwych, 1954; The Lark (trans. from French of Jean Anouilh), Lyric, Hammersmith, 1955; Tiger at the Gates (trans. from French of Jean Giraudoux), Apollo, 1955; Duel of Angels (trans. from Pour Lucrèce, of Jean Giraudoux), Apollo, 1958; Curtmantle, Edinburgh Festival, 1962; Judith (trans. from Giraudoux), Her Majesty's, 1962; A Yard of Sun, National, 1970. *Film Commentary* for The Queen is Crowned (Coronation film, 1953);

*Film scripts* (participation): Ben Hur; Barabbas; The Bible. *Publications:* The Boy with a Cart, 1939; The Firstborn, 1946; A Phoenix Too Frequent, 1946; The Lady's Not for Burning, 1949; Thor, with Angels, 1949; Venus Observed, 1950; A Sleep of Prisoners, 1951; The Dark is Light Enough, 1954; Curtmantle, 1961 (Heinemann Award of RSL); A Yard of Sun, 1970; (trans.) Peer Gynt, 1970. *Address:* 37 Blomfield Road, W9.

**FRY, Prof. Dennis Butler;** Professor of Experimental Phonetics since 1958, and Head of Department of Phonetics since 1949, University College, London; *b* 3 Nov. 1907; *s* of late F. C. B. Fry and Jane Ann (*née* Butler), Stockbridge, Hants; *m* 1937, Chrystabel, *er d* of late Charles Smith, JP, Brighton; one *s* two *d*. *Educ:* Gosport Grammar Sch.; University of London. Asst Master, Tewkesbury Grammar Sch., 1929-31; Asst Master, Kilburn Grammar Sch., 1931-34; Asst Lecturer in Phonetics, University Coll., London, 1934-37; Lecturer and Superintendent of Phonetics Laboratory, 1937-49. Served as Squadron Leader, RAFVR, 1940-45; in charge of Acoustics Laboratory, Central Medical Establishment, RAF, 1941-45. Reader in Experimental Phonetics, University of London, 1948. Editor of Language and Speech. pres. Permanent Internat. Council for Phonetic Sciences, 1961; Hon. Fellow, College of Speech Therapists, 1964; Fellow, Acoustical Soc. of America, 1966; Governor: Sadler's Wells Foundation, 1966; British Inst. of Recorded Sound, 1966. Trustee, Inst. for Cultural Research. *Publications:* (with E. M. Whetnall) The Deaf Child, 1963; Learning to Hear, 1970; papers on speech and hearing in scientific and linguistic journals. *Recreation:* music, especially singing. *Address:* 18 Lauriston Road, SW19. *T:* 01-946 3046.

**FRY, Donald William,** CBE 1970; Director, Atomic Energy Establishment, Winfrith, since 1959; *b* 30 Nov. 1910; *m* 1934, Jessie Florence (*née* Wright); three *s*. *Educ:* Weymouth Gram. Sch.; King's Coll., London. Research Physicist, GEC Laboratories, 1932; RAE Farnborough (Radio Dept), 1936; Air Min. Research Establishment (later the Telecommunications Research Establishment, TRE) Swanage, 1940; moved with the Estab. to Malvern, 1942; joined staff of AERE (still at Malvern), 1946; demonstrated with other mems of group a new Principle for accelerating particles: the travelling wave linear accelerator, 1947. Awarded Duddell Medal of Physical Soc., 1950; Head of Gen. Physics Div. at AERE Harwell, 1950; Chief Physicist, 1954, Dep. Dir, 1958, AERE Harwell. Member, Inst. of Physics and Physical Soc., 1950; FIEE; FIEEE 1960; CEng. Hon. Freeman of Weymouth, 1958. FKC London, 1959. *Publications:* papers in learned journals. *Address:* Coveway Lodge, Overcombe, near Weymouth, Dorset. *T:* Preston (Weymouth) 3276. *Clubs:* Athenæum; Royal Dorset Yacht.

**FRY, Prof. E. Maxwell,** CBE 1953; ARA 1966; BArch; FRIBA, MTPI; Dist Town Planning; in private practice as architect and town planner; Professor of Architecture, Royal Academy; *b* 2 Aug. 1899; *s* of Ambrose Fry and Lydia Thompson; *m* 1927, Ethel Speakman (marr. diss.); one *d*; *m* 1942, Jane B. Drew, *qv*. *Educ:* Liverpool Inst.; Liverpool Univ. Sch. of Architecture. Practised with Walter Gropius as Gropius and Fry, 1934-36; as Maxwell Fry and Jane Drew, 1945-50, as Fry, Drew, Drake, & Lasdun, 1951-58; now as Fry, Drew & Partners. Work includes schools, hospitals, working-class and other flats, houses in England and educational buildings in Ghana and Nigeria. Served with Royal Engineers, 1939-44. Town Planning Adviser to Resident Minister for West Africa, 1943-45; Senior Architect to New Capital Chandigarh, Punjab, 1951-54. Ex-Mem. Royal Fine Art Commission: Corr. Mem. Académie Flamande, 1956; Hon. FAIA 1963; Council Mem. RIBA (Vice-Pres. 1961-62) and RSA; Royal Gold Medal for Architecture, 1964. Hon. LLD Ibadan Univ., 1966. *Publications:* Fine Building; (jointly with Jane B. Drew) Architecture for Children; Architecture in the Humid Tropics; Art in a Machine Age; contribs to architectural and other papers. *Address:* 63 Gloucester Place, W1H 4DJ. *T:* 01-935 3318. *Club:* Garrick.

**FRY, Henry Kenneth,** DSO 1917; BSc, MD (Adelaide); BSc, DPH, Diploma Anth. (Oxon); FRACP; Medical Officer of Health, City of Adelaide, from 1938; *b* 25 May 1886; *s* of Henry Thomas Fry; *g s* of Rev. Henry Fry; *m* Dorothy Editha Deeley; one *s* one *d*. *Educ:* Prince Alfred Coll.; Univ. of Adelaide; Rhodes Scholar, Balliol Coll., Oxford. AAMC, AIF, 1914-19. Lecturer in Materia Medica and Therapeutics, University of Adelaide, 1920-39; Hon. Physician, Adelaide Hospital, 1935-46. *Publications:* An Introduction to General Therapeutics, 1935; Medical and Anthropological papers to various jls. *Address:* Waverley Ridge, Crafers, South Australia.

**FRY, Sir Leslie Alfred Charles,** KCMG 1957 (CMG 1955); OBE 1947 (MBE 1944); *b* 17 April 1908; *o s* of late Capt. and Mrs A. A. Fry; *m* 1st, 1935; one *s* one *d*; 2nd, Marian Elizabeth Penelope Bentley, *o d* of late Norman Bentley, Pannal Hall, Pannal, Yorks. *Educ:* Royal Masonic Sch.; Royal Military College, Sandhurst. First commission, 1928; served with 4th PWO Gurkha Rifles; transferred Indian Political Service, 1933; Under-Sec., External Affairs Dept, Govt of India, 1941; Dep. Sec. 1946; retired from IPS and entered HM Foreign Service, 1947; 1st Sec., UK High Commission in India, 1947-48; Foreign Office, 1949-51; Counsellor, HM Embassy, Lisbon, 1951-53; Counsellor, Eastern Dept, FO, 1953-55; Minister to Hungary, 1955-59; Ambassador to Indonesia, 1959-63; Ambassador to Brazil, 1963-66. Grand Cross, Order of Southern Cross, Brazil, 1968. *Address:* Gorehill House, Gorehill, near Petworth, Sussex. *T:* Petworth 3150. *Club:* United Service.

**FRY, Maxwell;** *see* Fry, E. Maxwell.

**FRY, Sir Penrose;** *see* Fry, Sir T. P.

**FRY, Peter Derek;** MP (C) Wellingborough since Dec. 1969; Insurance Broker since 1963; *b* 26 May 1931; *s* of Harry Walter Fry and late Edith Fry; *m* 1958, Edna Roberts; one *s* one *d*. *Educ:* Royal Grammar School, High Wycombe; Worcester College, Oxford (MA). Tillotsons (Liverpool) Ltd, 1954-56; Northern Assurance Co., 1956-61; Political Education Officer, Conservative Central Office, 1961-63. Member Bucks County Council, 1961-67. Contested (C) North Nottingham, 1964, East Willesden, 1966. Played Rugby for Bucks County, 1956-58, Hon. Secretary, 1958-61. *Recreations:* watching Rugby football; reading history and biographies. *Address:* 63 Wordsworth Road, High Wycombe, Bucks. *T:* High Wycombe 24273.

**FRY, Richard Henry,** CBE 1965; Financial Editor of The Guardian, 1939-65; *b* 23 Sept. 1900; *m* 1929, Katherine (*née* Maritz) no *c*. *Educ:* Berlin and Heidelberg Univs. *Address:* 8 Montagu Mews West, W1. *T:* 01-262 0817. *Clubs:* Reform, Royal Automobile.

**FRY, Sir (Theodore) Penrose,** 3rd Bt *cr* 1894; *b* 6 April 1892; *e s* of Sir John Pease Fry, 2nd Bt and Margaret Theodora (*d* 1941), *d* of Francis Edward Fox, JP; *S* father, 1957; *m* 1924, Sheila Kaye-Smith (*d* 1956); no *c*. *Educ:* Winchester; King's Coll., Cambridge. Commission in 5th Durham LI (T), 1914-18; Anglican Clergyman, 1921-29; became RC, 1929. Served in National Fire Service, War of 1939-45. *Publications:* The Church Surprising, 1932; The Making of a Layman, 1938. *Heir: b* John Nicholas Pease Fry [*b* 23 Oct. 1897; *m* 1927, Helen Murray, *d* of late William Gibson Bott, MRCS, JP; one *d* (and one *d* decd)]. *Address:* c/o Barclay's Bank Ltd, High Street, Battle, Sussex.
*See also M. C. Burkitt.*

**FRY, William Norman Hillier-;** *see* Hillier-Fry.

**FRYARS, Sir Robert (Furness),** Kt 1952; *b* 1887; *s* of William Fryars and Mary Emma (*née* Wilsdon); *m* 1915, Doris, *yr d* of William Magall, Newcastle on Tyne; one *s* two *d*. *Educ:* various schools and colls overseas. Freeman City of London; Hon. Mem. Court Worshipful Company of Blacksmiths. Freeman, City of Fort William (Canada). Chm., Man. Dir or Dir various public companies, 1930-55; Mem. Nat. Adv. Council for Motor Manfg Industry, 1946-52; Mem. of Council Soc. Motor Mfrs & Traders, 1945; Chm. British Transport Vehicle Mfrs Assoc., 1946-52; Hon. Pres. Asturian Omnibus Co. ALSA (Spain), 1962. FCIS, FREcons. Cross and Kt Comdr, Order of Civil Merit (Spain), 1965. *Recreations:* travel, reading, music, gardening, conversation. *Address:* El Toboso, 14 Clifton Crescent, Falmouth, Cornwall.

**FRYBERG, Sir Abraham,** Kt 1968; MBE 1941; retired; *b* 26 May 1901; *s* of Henry and Rose Fryberg; *m* 1939, Vivian Greensil Barnard; one *s*. *Educ:* Wesley Coll., Melbourne; Queen's Coll., University of Melbourne. MB, BS (Melbourne) 1928; DPH, DTM (Sydney) 1936, MD (Qld). Served with 9 Australian Div. (Tobruk, Alamein), 1940-45. Resident Med. Officer, then Registrar, Brisbane Hosp. and Brisbane Children's Hosp., 1929-33; GP, Hughenden, 1934; Health Officer, Qld Health Dept, 1936-46 (except for war service); Dep. Dir-Gen., 1946, Dir-Gen. of Health and Medical Services, Qld, 1947-67, retired. Hon. Col, RAAMC Northern Comd, 1962-67. SBStJ 1958. *Recreations:* racing, bowls. *Address:* 19 Dublin Street, Clayfield, Qld 4011, Australia. *T:* Brisbane 62-2549. *Clubs:* United Service, University of Queensland (Brisbane).

**FRYE, Jack;** Chairman: B. Elliott & Co. Ltd, since 1955 (Managing Director since 1949); B. Elliott Group of Companies; Rotaflex (Gt Britain) Ltd and subsidiary cos, since 1962; Goldfields Industrial Corporation of South Africa and subsidiaries, since 1967; Iron and Steel Consumers' Council, since 1967; *b* 2 Oct. 1914; 3rd *s* of late Hugo Frye and Beatrice Elliott; *m* 1937, Daphne Aron (marr. diss. 1956), *d* of late Eugene Aron; two *s* two *d*. *Educ:* Institute Rhenania, Schaffhausen, Switzerland; Badingham Coll., Leatherhead; Loughborough Univ. of Technology. Joined B. Elliott & Co. Ltd, 1932; started Victoria Milling Machine Co. Ltd (now Elliott Milling Machines Ltd), 1937, and built up whole of B. Elliott manufacturing organisation. Officer, Ordre du Mérite Français d'Outre Mer, 1965. *Recreations:* machine tools, sailing, fishing, shooting, tennis, squash, ski-ing. *Address:* 9 Swan Walk, SW3; Shelleys, Guestling, Sussex. *Clubs:* Royal Aero, Royal Automobile; Royal Corinthian Yacht.

**FRYER, Maj.-Gen. (retd), Wilfred George,** CB 1956; CBE 1951 (OBE 1941); *b* 1 May 1900; *s* of James and Marion Fryer, Kington, Herefordshire; *m* 1931, Jean Eleanore Graham Binny, Edinburgh; three *s*. *Educ:* Christ Coll., Brecon; RMA Woolwich. Commissioned 2nd Lieut RE, 1919, Regular Army; served in India, Royal Bombay Sappers and Miners, 1933-38; Major RE, Instructor, Sch. of Mil. Engineering, Chatham, 1938. Served War of 1939-45: Lt-Col RE, ADWE & M, GHQ, Middle East, 1941; SO1 to Chief Engineer, Eighth Army, Western Desert Campaign (OBE), 1941; Col DDWE & M, GHQ, Middle East, 1942; GSO1 to Scientific Adviser to Army Council, 1944; ADWE & M, GHQ and Dep. Chief Engineer, 8 Corps, NW Europe Campaign (despatches), 1944-45; Brig.-Chief Engr, Brit. Army Staff, Washington, DC, 1945; Col E (Equipment), War Office, 1946-48; Brig.-Chief Engr, Singapore Dist, 1948-51; Brig.-Chief Engr, Southern Comd, UK, 1951-53; Maj.-Gen. 1954; Chief Engineer, Middle East Land Forces, 1954-57. "A" Licence air pilot, 1942. MIEE 1952. Chm., Warminster Press Ltd. Nat. Champion, Wayfarer Dinghy, 1960. *Recreations:* ocean racing (Transatlantic Race, 1931), ski-ing, tennis. *Address:* Critchells Green Farmhouse, Lockerley, Romsey, Hants SO5 OJD. *Clubs:* Army and Navy, Royal Ocean Racing, Hurlingham.

**FUCHS, Sir Vivian (Ernest),** Kt 1958; MA, PhD; Director of the British Antarctic Survey, since 1958; Leader Commonwealth Trans-Antarctic Expedition, 1955-58; *b* 11 Feb. 1908; *s* of late E. Fuchs, Farnham, Surrey, and late Violet Anne Fuchs (*née* Watson); *m* 1933, Joyce, 2nd *d* of late John Connell; one *s* one *d* (and one *d* decd). *Educ:* Brighton Coll.; St John's Coll., Cambridge. Geologist with: Cambridge East Greenland Expedn, 1929; Cambridge Expdn to E African Lakes, 1930-31; E African Archæological Expdn, 1931-32; Leader Lake Rudolf Rift Valley Expedn, 1933-34; Royal Geog. Society Cuthbert Peek Grant, 1936; Leader Lake Rukwa Expedn, 1937-38. 2nd Lieut Cambs Regt, TA, 1939; served in W Africa, 1942-43; Staff Coll., Camberley, 1943; served NW Europe (despatches), 1944-46; demobilized (Major), 1946. Leader Falkland Islands Dependencies Survey (Antarctica), 1947-50; Dir FIDSc Bureau, 1950-55. Founder's Gold Medal, Royal Geog. Soc., 1951; Silver Medal RSA, 1952; Polar Medal, 1953, and Clasp, 1958; Special Gold Medal, Royal Geog. Soc., 1958; Gold Medal Royal Scottish Geog. Society 1958; Gold Medal Geog. Society (Paris), 1958; Richthofen Medal (Berlin), 1958; Kirchenpauer Medal (Hamburg), 1958; Plancius Medal (Amsterdam), 1959; Egede Medal (Copenhagen), 1959; Hubbard Medal, Nat. Geog. Soc. (Washington), 1959; Explorers Club Medal (New York), 1959; Geog. Soc. (Chicago) Gold Medal, 1959; Geol. Soc. of London Prestwich Medal, 1960. Hon. Fellow, University Coll., Cambridge, 1970. Hon. LLD Edinburgh 1958; Hon. DSc Durham 1958; Hon. DSc Cantab 1959. *Publications:* The Crossing of Antarctica (Fuchs and Hillary), 1958; geographical and geological reports and papers in scientific jls. *Recreations:* squash racquets, swimming. *Address:* 78 Barton Road, Cambridge. *T:* Cambridge 59238. *Club:* Athenæum.

**FULBRIGHT, J. William;** US Senator (Democrat) for Arkansas since 1945; *b* Sumner, Mo, 9 April 1905; *s* of Jay Fulbright and Roberta (*née* Waugh); *m* 1932, Elizabeth Kremer Williams; two *d*. *Educ:* public schools of Fayetteville, Arkansas; University of Arkansas (AB); (Rhodes Scholar) Pembroke Coll., Oxford Univ. (BA, MA); George Washington Univ. Sch. of Law (LLB). Special Attorney, Dept. of Justice, 1934-35; Lectr in

Law, George Washington Univ., 1935-36; Mem. Law Sch. Faculty, University of Arkansas, 1936-39, and Pres. of University, 1939-41. Elected to Congress for 3rd Dist of Arkansas, 1942; Mem. Foreign Affairs Cttee. Elected to Senate, 1945, and subsequently; Mem. US Delegn to Gen. Assembly, UN, 1954; Chm. Banking and Currency Cttee of Senate, 1955-59, resigning to become Chm. Senate Cttee on Foreign Relations, also Mem. Finance Cttee and Jt Economic Cttee. Hon. Fellow, Pembroke Coll., Oxford, 1949; Fellow, Amer. Acad. of Arts and Sciences (Boston), 1950; Award by Nat. Inst. of Arts and Letters, 1954. Holds several hon. degrees, including DCL Oxford, 1953. *Publications:* Old Myths and New Realities, 1964; Prospects for the West, 1965; The Arrogance of Power, 1967. *Address:* Fayetteville, Arkansas, USA; 2527 Belmont Road NW, Washington, DC, USA.

**FULCHER, Derick Harold,** DSC 1944; Assistant Under-Secretary of State, Department of Health and Social Security, since 1969; *b* 4 Nov. 1917; *s* of Percy Frederick Fulcher and Gertrude Lilian Fulcher; *m* 1943, Florence Ellen May Anderson; one *s* one *d*. *Educ:* St Olave's Grammar School. Served in Royal Navy, 1940-46 (Lieut, RNVR). Entered Civil Service (War Office), 1936; Asst Principal, Ministry of National Insurance, 1947; Principal, 1950; Asst Sec. 1959. Seconded to HM Treasury, 1957-59; served on an ILO mission in Trinidad and Tobago, 1967-69. *Recreations:* walking, motoring, travel. *Address:* 100 Downs Road, Coulsdon, Surrey, CR3 1AF. *T:* Downland 54231.

**FULFORD, Robert John;** Keeper, Department of Printed Books, British Museum, since 1967; *b* 16 Aug. 1923; *s* of John Fulford, Southampton; *m* 1950, Alison Margaret Rees; one *s* one *d*. *Educ:* King Edward VI Sch., Southampton; King's Coll., Cambridge; Charles Univ., Prague. Asst Keeper, Dept of Printed Books, British Museum, 1945-65; Dep. Keeper, 1965-67 (Head of Slavonic Div., 1961-67); Keeper, 1967-. *Address:* 5 Fosse Bank Close, Tonbridge, Kent. *T:* Tonbridge 4310.

**FULFORD, Roger Thomas Baldwin,** CVO 1970; *b* 24 Nov. 1902; *o surv s* of late Canon Fulford; *m* 1937, Sibell, *widow* of Rev. Hon. C. F. Lyttelton and *d* of late Charles Adeane, CB. *Educ:* St Ronans; Lancing; Worcester Coll., Oxford. Pres. of Union, 1927; called to Bar, 1931; Liberal Candidate for Woodbridge Div. of Suffolk, 1929; for Holderness Div. of Yorks, 1945; for Rochdale, 1950; joined editorial staff of The Times, 1933; Part-time Lecturer in English, King's Coll., London, 1937-48; Asst Censor, 1939-40; Civil Asst War Office, 1940-42; Asst Private Sec. to Sec. of State for Air, 1942-45. Pres., Liberal Party, 1964-65. *Publications:* Royal Dukes, 1933; George IV, 1935; The Right Honourable Gentleman, 1945; The Prince Consort, 1949; Queen Victoria, 1951; History of Glyn's, 1953; Votes for Women, 1957; The Liberal Case, 1959; Hanover to Windsor, 1960; ed (with late Lytton Strachey) The Greville Memoirs, 1937; ed, The Autobiography of Miss Knight, 1960; ed, Letters Between Queen Victoria and the Princess Royal: Dearest Child, 1964; Dearest Mama, 1968; C. H. Wilkinson, 1965; Samuel Whitbread, 1967; The Trial of Queen Caroline, 1967. *Address:* Barbon Manor, Carnforth, Lancs. *Clubs:* Boodle's, National Liberal.

*See also Lord Shuttleworth.*

**FULHAM, Suffragan Bishop of,** with oversight of the diocese of Gibraltar, since 1970; **Rt. Rev. John Richard Satterthwaite;** General Secretary, Church of England Council on Foreign Relations, since 1959 (Asst General Secretary, 1955-59); Guild Vicar, St Dunstan-in-the-West, City of London, since 1959; *b* 17 Nov. 1925; *s* of William and Clara Elisabeth Satterthwaite. *Educ:* Millom Grammar Sch.; Leeds Univ. (BA); Coll. of the Resurrection, Mirfield. History Master, St Luke's Sch., Haifa, 1946-48; Curate: St Barnabas, Carlisle, 1950-53; St Aidan, Carlisle, 1953-54; St Michael Paternoster Royal, London, 1955-59, Curate-in-Charge 1959-65. Gen. Sec., Archbp's Commn on Roman Catholic Relations, 1965-; Hon. Canon of Canterbury, 1963-; Asst Chaplain, Order of St John of Jerusalem, 1963-; Hon. Canon of Utrecht, Old Catholic Church of the Netherlands, 1969. Holds decoration from various foreign churches. *Recreations:* fell walking, music. *Address:* 50 Walcot Square, SE11. *T:* 01-735 4067. *Club:* Athenæum.

**FULLARD, Air Commodore Philip Fletcher,** CBE 1941; DSO 1917; MC; AFC 1919; psa; *o s* of T. Fletcher Fullard, Hatfield, Herts; *b* 27 May 1897. *Educ:* Privately; Norwich. Enlisted in Inns of Court OTC, 1915, commissioned in Royal Irish Fusiliers, 1916; transferred Royal Flying Corps, 1916; served France, 1917, No. 1 Squadron RFC (DSO, MC and Bar, Croix de Guerre); Permanent Commission in Royal Air Force, 1919; served in USA, Germany, Poland, Austria, Turkey and Iraq since European War; served Mohmand Operations, 1935 (despatches). Retired list, 1946. *Recreations:* ski-ing, travelling.

**FULLBROOK-LEGGATT, Maj.-Gen. Charles St Quentin Outen;** *see* Leggatt.

**FULLER, Buckminster;** *see* Fuller, R. B.

**FULLER, Sir Gerard;** *see* Fuller, Sir J. G. H. F.

**FULLER, Major Sir (John) Gerard (Henry Fleetwood),** 2nd Bt, *cr* 1910; late Life Guards; *b* 8 July 1906; *s* of 1st Bt and Norah Jacintha (who married secondly Col R. Forestier Walker, DSO, and died 1935), *d* of late C. Nicholas Paul Phipps of Charlcot, Westbury, Wilts; *S* father, 1915; *m* 1st, 1931, Lady Fiona Pratt (marriage dissolved, 1944), *yr d* of 4th Marquess Camden, GCVO; two *s*; 2nd, 1945, Kathleen Elizabeth, MBE, DStJ (*d* 1964), 5th *d* of late Sir George Farrar, Bt, Chichely Hall, Newport Pagnell, Bucks; 3rd, 1966, Mrs Mary Leventon. *Educ:* Uppingham. 2nd Lieut Life Guards, 1930; Captain 1938; Major, 1941; retired, 1946; served War of 1939-45 (despatches). JP Wilts, 1946; Mem. Wilts CC 1947-; County Alderman, 1961; Joint Master Avon Vale Fox Hounds, 1947-61, and 1962-64. *Heir: s* John William Fleetwood Fuller [*b* 18 Dec. 1936; *m* 1968, Lorna Marian, *o d* of F. R. Kemp-Potter, Findon, Sussex; one *s*. Major, The Life Guards, 1968]. *Address:* Neston Park, Corsham, Wilts. *T:* Hawthorn 211; Balmore, Cannich, Inverness-shire. *T:* Cannich 262.

*See also Col M. E. M. C. Maitland.*

**FULLER, Leonard J.,** ROI 1932; RCA 1939; Artist, Portrait Painter; Principal, St Ives School of Painting; Founder Member and First Chairman of Penwith Society of Arts in Cornwall; St Ives Society of Artists; *b* 11 Oct. 1891; *yr s* of late John Haire and Mary A. Fuller; *m* 1917, Marjorie Florence, 2nd *d* of late Tom Mostyn, ROI; one *s*. *Educ:* Dulwich Coll.; Royal Academy Schs (British Institution Scholar). Exhibited first picture Royal Academy, 1919; most prominent works include Silver and Blue, 1922, My Son John, 1923, Silver and Gold, 1929, Diana Fishwich, 1931, Jack Hobbs, 1934; Autumn Sunshine, 1933, purchased for permanent collection by city of Newport (Mon); We Want The King, RA 1938; Studio Haphazard (RA 1943), purchased by City of Newport; Moffat Lindner, RWS (RA 1943); Mr Gall (RA 1944); The Colourful Years (RA 1945), etc.; Very Rev. W. R. Matthews, 1957, purchased by the Dean and Chapter for the Chapter House, St Paul's; On the Verandah, 1960, by Plymouth Corporation Art Gallery; Sirens, by Education Cttee for Cornwall, 1963. Mrs Guthrie Smith for St Mary's Hosp., London; Col Sir Herbert Shiner, for Sussex CC; Lord Tredegar, Ald. Kt, for Newark Town Hall, Paris Salon, Artistes Français, Médaille d'argent 1927, Mention honorable 1931; Teacher of painting, St John's Wood Art Sch., 1922-32; Asst Art Master, Dulwich Coll., 1927-38; served European War, 1914-18, 10th Bn Royal Fusiliers, service in France, commissioned to East Surrey Regt 1915, transferring to Machine Gun Corps, rising to temporary rank of Captain; Home Guard, 1940-44. Rotarian. *Address:* 3 Seagull House, The Wharf, St Ives, Cornwall. *T:* St Ives 6826. *TA:* St Ives, Cornwall. *Club:* Chelsea Arts.

**FULLER, Richard Buckminster;** engineer, US; Distinguished University Professor, Southern Illinois University, since 1956; *b* Milton, Mass, 12 July 1895; *s* of Richard Buckminster Fuller and Caroline Wolcott Fuller (*née* Andrews); *m* 1917, Anne Hewlett; one *d* (and one *d* decd). *Educ:* Milton Acad.; Harvard Univ. Apprentice machine fitter, 1914; US Navy, 1917-19; Pres. Stockade Building System, 1922-27; Founder, Pres., 4-D Co., Chicago, 1927-32; Founder, Dir and Chief Engr, Dymaxion Corp., Bridgeport, 1932-36; Asst to Dir, Res. and Devclt, Phelps Dodge Corp., 1936-38; Tech. Consultant, Fortune Mag., 1938-40; Vice-Pres., Chief Engr, Dymaxion Co. Inc., Delaware, 1941-42; Chief Mech. Engr, US Bd of Econ. Warfare, 1942-44; Special Asst to Dep. Dir, US Foreign Econ. Administration, 1944; Chm. Bd and Admin. Engr, Dymaxion Dwelling Machines, 1944-46; Chm. Bd of Trustees, Fuller Research Foundn, Wichita, Kansas, 1946-54; Pres. Synergetics Inc., Raleigh, NC, 1954-59; Pres. Geodesics Inc., Cambridge, Mass, 1954-; Pres. Plydomes Inc., Des Moines, 1957-; Chm. Bd, Tetrahelix Corp., Hamilton, 1959-. Charles Eliot Norton Prof. of Poetry, Harvard Univ., 1961-62; Harvey Cushing Orator, Amer. Assoc. of Neuro-Surgeons, 1967; Jahawarlal Nehru Lectr, New Delhi, 1969; Hoyt Fellow, Yale Univ., 1969. Holds many patents in architecture and building; inventions include Dymaxion house, car, bathroom. Discovered energetic/synergetic geometry, 1917; geodesic structures, 1947. Architect of US geodesic pavilion for Montreal World Fair, 1967; over 3000 geodesic domes erected in 50 different countries; architect: Samuel Beckett Theatre, St Peter's Coll., Oxford, 1969-; geodesic auditorium, Kfar Menachem Kibutzin, Israel, 1969; Tri-centennial Pavilion of S Carolina, Greenfield, 1970. Mem. many professional instns; Hon. Fellow, St Peter's Coll., Oxford, 1970; holds hon. degrees from 21 univs/colleges; awards include Industrial Designers Soc. of Amer. (first) Award of Excellence, 1966; Gold Medal, Architecture, Nat. Inst. of Arts and Letters, 1968; Royal Gold Medal for Architecture, RIBA, 1968; Humanist of the Year Award, Amer. Assoc. of Humanists, 1969; Master Designer Award, McGraw Hill, 1969; Gold Medal, Amer. Inst. Architects, 1970. *Publications:* 4D Timelock, 1927; Nine Chains to the Moon, 1938; Education Automation, 1963; No More Second Hand God, 1963; Ideas and Integrities, 1963; The Unfinished Epic of Industrialization, 1963; Operating Manual for Space Ship Earth, 1969; World Resources Inventory (6 documents), 1963-67; Utopia or Oblivion, 1969; Buckminster Fuller Reader, 1970; I Seem to be a Verb, 1970; many contribs to jls etc. *Address:* PO Box 909, Carbondale, Illinois 62901, USA.

**FULLER, Roy Broadbent,** CBE 1970; MA Oxon (by Decree); FRSL; poet and author; solicitor; Professor of Poetry, University of Oxford, since 1968; *b* 11 Feb. 1912; *e s* of late Leopold Charles Fuller, Oldham; *m* 1936, Kathleen Smith; one *s*. *Educ:* Blackpool High Sch. Admitted a solicitor, 1934; served Royal Navy, 1941-46; Lieut, RNVR, 1944; Asst Solicitor to Woolwich Equitable Building Soc., 1938-58, Solicitor, 1958-69, Director, 1969-. Vice-Pres., Bldg Socs Assoc., 1969- (Chm. Legal Adv. Panel, 1958-69). Dir, Poetry Book Soc. *Publications:* Poems, 1939; The Middle of a War, 1942; A Lost Season, 1944; Savage Gold, 1946; With My Little Eye; Byron for Today, 1948; Questions and Answers in Building Soc. Law and Practice; Epitaphs and Occasions, 1949; The Second Curtain, 1953; Counterparts; Fantasy and Fugue, 1954; Image of a Society, 1956; Brutus's Orchard, 1957; The Ruined Boys, 1959; The Father's Comedy, 1961; Collected Poems, 1962; The Perfect Fool, 1963; Buff, 1965; My Child, My Sister, 1965; Catspaw, 1966; New Poems, 1968 (Duff Cooper Memorial Prize 1968); Off Course, 1969; The Carnal Island, 1970. (Edited) The Building Societies Acts. *Address:* 37 Langton Way, Blackheath, SE3. *T:* 01-858 2334.

**FULLER-ACLAND-HOOD;** family name of **Baron St Audries.**

**FULLER-GOOD, Air Vice-Marshal James Laurence Fuller,** CB 1957; CVO 1953; CBE 1951; RAF retired; Air Officer Commanding, Air Headquarters, Malaya, 1951 (CBE); Director of Personal Services (Air), Air Ministry, 1952-53; Air Officer Commanding No. 22 Group, Technical Training Command, 1953-57; Commandant-Gen. of the Royal Air Force Regt and Inspector of Ground Combat Trg 1957-58, retd. Air Vice-Marshal, 1954. *Club:* Royal Air Force.

**FULLERTON, Brigadier John Parke,** DSO 1932; *b* Cawnpore, 8 Sept. 1894; *s* of late Major T. W. A. Fullerton, IMS; *g s* of Rev. Alexander Fullerton; *m* 1st, 1917, Georgina (*d* 1942), *d* of J. Hunter, Sligo; 2nd, 1945, Elizabeth, *d* of Lt-Col R. J. Marks, IMS; one *s* one *d*. *Educ:* Wellington Coll.; RMC, Sandhurst. KIC Commissioned 1914; entered 41st Dogras, now 3rd Bn The Dogra Regt; served Egypt and Mesopotamia, 1915-16 (wounded, despatches 1919, for services in India); Afghanistan, 1919; Mahsud, 1920; Waziristan, 1919-21; NWF, 1930-31 (DSO, despatches); NWF, 1938-39 (wounded, despatches); Area Commander Jullundur, 1941-44; Services Resettlement Liaison Officer, Punjab, etc., 1944-46; chief Civil Liaison Officer, Northern Area, 1946; Dir of Resettlement, GHQ, India, 1946-47; retired, 1947. *Address:* Bridge House, Hele, near Taunton, Somerset. *T:* Bradford-on-Tone 296.

**FULTHORPE, Henry Joseph;** General Manager, HM Dockyard, Portsmouth (Dep. Director of Naval Construction), since 1967; *b* Portsmouth, 2 July 1916; *s* of Joseph Henry and Clarissa Fulthorpe; *m* 1939, Bette May Forshew; two *s* one *d*. *Educ:* Royal Naval Coll., Greenwich. Principal (Ship) Overseer, Vickers, Barrow-in-Furness, 1943-46; Dep. Manager, HM Dockyard, Malta, 1946-49; Sec., Radiological Defence Panel, 1949-52; Staff Constr, first British atom bomb, Montebello Is, 1952-53; Constr i/c Minesweeper Design,

Admty, Bath, 1953-54; Chief Constr, Maintenance, Bath, 1954-56; Dep. Manager, HM Dockyard, Portsmouth, 1956-58; Chief Constructor: HM Dockyard, Singapore, 1958-61; Dockyard Dept, Bath, 1961-63; Asst Dir of Naval Construction, Bath, 1963-64; Production Manager, HM Dockyard, Chatham, 1964-67; Manager, Constructive Dept, HM Dockyard, Portsmouth, 1967. President: Civil Service Sports Assoc. (Portsmouth); Dockyard Football Assoc. (Portsmouth). Mem., RCNC; MRINA. *Address:* General Manager's Residence, The Parade, HM Dockyard, Portsmouth, Hants. *T:* Portsmouth 22351 (ext. 22465 or (home) 23194). *Club:* Royal Naval (Portsmouth) and its affiliations elsewhere.

**FULTON,** family name of **Baron Fulton.**

**FULTON,** Baron, *cr* 1966, of Falmer (Life Peer); **John Scott Fulton,** Kt 1964; Chairman of the British Council since 1968 (Member Executive Committee, since 1964); a Governor of the BBC since 1965 (Vice-Chm. 1965-67 and since 1968); *b* 27 May 1902; *y s* of the late Principal A. R. Fulton, Dundee; *m* 1939, Jacqueline, *d* of K. E. T. Wilkinson, York; three *s* one *d. Educ:* Dundee High Sch.; St Andrews Univ; Balliol Coll., Oxford (Exhibitioner). Asst in Logic and Scientific Method, London Sch. of Economics, 1926-28; Fellow, 1928-47, Balliol Coll. Oxford; Tutor in Philosophy, 1928-35; Tutor in Politics, 1935-47; Jowett Lecturer, 1935-38; Jowett Fellow, 1945-47; Rockefeller Fellow, 1936-37; Faculty Fellow, Nuffield Coll., 1939-47; Principal, University Coll. of Swansea, 1947-59; Vice-Chancellor: University of Wales, 1952-54 and 1958-59; University of Sussex, 1959-67. Principal and Asst Sec., Mines Dept, 1940-42; Principal Asst Sec. Min. of Fuel and Power, 1942-44. Dir Wales and Mon Industrial Estates Ltd, 1948-54. Chairman: Board for Mining Qualifications, 1950-62; Universities Council for Adult Educ., 1952-55; Council of Nat. Inst. of Adult Educ., 1952-55; Commn on educational requirements of Sierra Leone, 1954; Selection Cttee for Miners' Welfare Nat. Scholarships, 1949-59; Nat. Adv. Coun. on the Training and Supply of Teachers, 1959-63; Univs Central Coun. on Admissions, 1961-64; Commn on establishment of a second University in Hong Kong, 1962; Inter Univ. Coun. for Higher Educn Overseas, 1964-68 (Vice-Chm., 1968-); BBC Liaison Advisory Cttee on Adult Education Programmes, 1962-65; BBC Further Education Adv. Coun. for the UK, 1965; Institute of Development Studies, 1966-67; Cttee on the Civil Service, 1966-68; ITA Adult Educn Adv. Cttee, 1962-65; Coun. of Inst. of Educn, University of London, 1967-; Coun. of Tavistock Inst. of Human Relations, 1968-. Member: Commn. on Royal University of Malta, 1957 (Chm. 1962-); National Reference Tribunal for Coal Industry of Great Britain, 1957-; Cttee on University Teaching Methods, 1961-64. Pres., Soc. for Research into Higher Education, 1964-67; Pres., Morley College, 1969. Hon. Fellow, Balliol Coll., Oxford Univ., 1969. Hon. LLD: Chinese Univ. of Hong Kong, 1964; California, 1966; Yale, 1967; Sussex, 1967; Wales, 1968; Dundee, 1968; Hon. DLitt, Ife, 1967: Royal Univ. of Malta, 1967. *Publications:* (with C. R. Morris) In Defence of Democracy, 1935; various articles. *Recreation:* golf. *Address:* Brook House, Priestman's Lane, Thornton-le-Dale, Pickering, Yorks. *T:* Thornton-le-Dale 221. *Club:* Athenæum.

**FULTON, Alexander Strathern,** CBE 1953; DLitt 1941; MA; Keeper, Department of Oriental Printed Books and Manuscripts, British Museum, 1940-53, retd; *b* Beith, Ayrshire, 18 Feb. 1888; *y s* of late James Graham Fulton, Craigellan, Beith, and Eleanor Strathern. *Educ:* Spier's Sch.; Glasgow Univ. MA (First Class Hons in Semitic Langs), 1910; Cleland and Rae-Wilson Gold Medallist; John Clark scholar; Asst Prof. of Semitic Langs, Edinburgh Univ., 1910-11; entered British Museum, 1911; Dep. Keeper, Dept of Oriental Printed Books and Manuscripts, 1936. At various times Examiner in Arabic and Hebrew for Glasgow and Edinburgh Univs, in Arabic for London and Manchester Univs, and Additional Lecturer in Arabic at the School of Oriental Studies, London Univ.; Fellow of Royal Asiatic Society. *Publications:* Supplementary Catalogue of Arabic Printed Books in the British Museum (with A. G. Ellis), 1926; Seond Supplementary Vol. (with Dr M. Lings), 1959; Vol. III of the Catalogue of Arabic Printed Books in the British Museum (Indexes), 1935; Facsimile of al-Kitab-al-Bari, edited with introduction, 1933; History of Hayy Ibn Yaqzan, Ockley's translation, revised and partly rewritten, with an introduction, 1929; articles in various periodicals. *Recreation:* golf. *Address:* 102 The Promenade, Peacehaven, Sussex.

**FULTON, Hon. Edmund Davie,** PC (Canada) 1957; QC (BC) 1957; Barrister, Solicitor; *b* 10 March 1916; *s* of Frederick John Fulton, KC, and Winifred M. Davie; *m* 1946, Patricia Mary, *d* of J. M. Macrae and Christine Macrae (*née* Carmichael), Winnipeg; three *d. Educ:* St Michael's Sch., Victoria, BC; Kamloops High Sch.; University of British Columbia; St John's Coll., Oxford. BA (BC), BA Oxon (Rhodes Scholar, elected 1936). Admitted to Bar of British Columbia, 1940. Served in Canadian Army Overseas as Company Comdr with Seaforth Highlanders of Canada and as DAAG 1st Canadian Inf. Div., 1940-45, including both Italian and Northwest Europe campaigns (despatches); transferred to R of O with rank of Major, 1945. Partner in legal firm of Fulton, Rogers, Kelly, Reilly and Dohm, Kamloops, BC. Elected to House of Commons of Canada, 1945; re-elected in 1949, 1953, 1957, 1958, 1962, 1965. Mem. Senate, University of British Columbia, 1948-57; Pres. Young Progressive Conservatives of Canada, 1946-49. Acting Minister of Citizenship and Immigration, June 1957-May 1958; Minister of Justice and Attorney Gen., Canada, June 1957-Aug. 1962; Minister of Public Works, Aug. 1962-April, 1963. Hon. Col, Rocky Mountain Rangers, 1959. Mem. Bar of Ontario. Hon LLD: Ottawa, 1960; Queen's, 1963. *Clubs:* Vancouver (Vancouver); Golf and Country (Kamloops); Rideau (Ottawa).

**FULTON, Prof. Forrest;** Professor of Virology in the University of London at The London School of Hygiene and Tropical Medicine since 1959; *b* 13 Aug. 1913; *o s* of late Leonard Jessopp Fulton, solicitor. *Educ:* Westminster; Pembroke Coll., Oxford. Read Law Oxford, 1931-33 then chose scientific career and studied Animal Physiology for remaining two years; BA 1935, MA 1939 (Oxon.); clinical work at London Hosp. BM, BCh, 1939, DM 1945 (Oxon.). Emergency Public Health Service, Oxford, 1939; worked for Med. Research Council on Typhus vaccines, London, 1942; after short period at Yale Univ., returned to London Univ. as Reader in Bacteriology and Immunology, 1949. FCPath, 1967. *Publications:* contrib. to Advances in Virus Research, Vol. V and many papers in journals concerned with microbiology and immunology. *Address:* London School of Hygiene and Tropical Medicine, Keppel Street, WC1.

**FUNSTON, G(eorge) Keith;** Chairman, Olin Corporation, since 1967; *b* Waterloo, Iowa, USA, 12 Oct. 1910; *s* of George Edwin and Genevieve (Keith) Funston; *m* 1939, Elizabeth Kennedy; one *s* two *d*. *Educ:* Trinity Coll., Hartford, Conn.; Harvard. AB, Trinity Coll., 1932; MBA (*cum laude*), Harvard, 1934. Mem. Research Staff, Harvard Business Sch., 1934-35; Asst to VP Sales, then Asst to Treas., American Radiator & Standard Sanitary, 1935-40; Dir, Purchases & Supplies, Sylvania Electronics, 1940-44; Special Asst to Chm., War Production Bd, 1941-44; Lt-Comdr, US Navy, 1944-46; Pres., Trinity Coll., Hartford, 1944-51; Pres. and Governor, New York Stock Exchange, 1951-67. Director: IBM; Metropolitan Life; Republic Steel; AVCO Corp.; Illinois Central Industries; Chemical Bank; Putnam Trust; Hartford Steam Boiler & Insurance Co.; National Aviation; Winn-Dixie Stores. Holds numerous hon. doctorates. *Recreations:* riding, reading, ski-ing, tennis. *Address:* (home) Vineyard Lane, Greenwich, Conn., USA. *T:* Townsend 9-5524. *Clubs:* Round Hill (Greenwich, Conn.); University, The Century Assoc., The Links, (New York).

**FÜRER-HAIMENDORF, Prof. Christoph von,** DPhil Vienna; Professor of Asian Anthropology, School of Oriental and African Studies, University of London, since 1951; *b* 27 July 1909; *s* of Rudolf Fürer von Haimendorf und Wolkersdorf; *m* 1938, Elizabeth Barnardo; one *s*. *Educ:* Theresianische Akademie, Vienna; Vienna Univ. Asst Lecturer, Vienna Univ., 1931-34; Rockefeller Foundation Fellowship, 1935-37; Lecturer, Vienna University, 1938; Anthropological Fieldwork in Hyderabad and Orissa, 1939-43; Special Officer Subansiri, External Affairs Dept, Govt of India, 1944-45; Adviser to HEH the Nizam's Govt and Prof. of Anthropology in the Osmania Univ., 1945-49; Reader in Anthropology with special reference to India, University of London, 1949-51. Anthropological Research: in India and Nepal, 1953; in Nepal, 1957-58, 1962, 1966; in the Philippines, 1968; in India, 1970. Munro Lectr, Edinburgh Univ., 1959; Visiting Prof., Colegio de Mexico, 1964, 1966. Corresponding Member: Austrian Academy of Science, 1964; Anthropological Soc. of Vienna, 1970. Rivers Memorial Medal of Royal Anthropological Institute, 1949; SC Royal Gold Medal, Asiatic Soc., Calcutta, 1964; Sir Percy Sykes Memorial Medal, Royal Central Asian Soc., 1965. *Publications:* The Naked Nagas, 1939; The Chenchus, 1943; The Reddis of the Bison Hills, 1945; The Raj Gonds of Adilabad, 1948; Himalayan Barbary, 1955; The Apa Tanis, 1962; (joint author) Mount Everest, 1963; The Sherpas of Nepal, 1964; (ed and jt author) Caste and Kin in Nepal, India and Ceylon, 1966; Morals and Merit, 1967; The Konyak Nagas, 1969. Articles in Journal of Royal Anthropological Inst., Man, Anthropos, Geographical Jl, Man in India. *Recreation:* music. *Address:* 32 Clarendon Road, W11. *T:* 01-727 4520, 01-636 2737.

**FURLONG, Hon. Robert Stafford,** MBE 1945; Chief Justice of Newfoundland since 1959; *b* 9 Dec. 1904; *o s* of Martin Williams Furlong, KC, and Mary Furlong (*née* McGrath). *Educ:* St Bonaventure's Coll., St John's, Newfoundland. Called to the Bar, 1926, appointed KC 1944. Temp. Actg Lt-Comdr (S) RNVR. OStJ 1937; Knight of St Gregory 1958. *Recreations:* golf and motoring. *Address:* Judges' Chambers, Court House, St John's, Newfoundland; (home) 8 Winter Avenue, St John's, Newfoundland. *T:* 2310. *Clubs:* Royal Naval Volunteer Reserve (London); Bally Haly Golf and Country, City, Murray's Pond, Crow's Nest (all in St John's).

**FURLONG, Ronald (John),** FRCS; Orthopædic Surgeon to St Thomas's Hospital since 1946; Hon. Consulting Orthopædic Surgeon to the Army since 1951; *b* 3 March 1909; *s* of Frank Owen Furlong and Elsie Muriel Taffs, Woolwich; *m* 1st, 1936, Elva Mary Ruth Lefeaux (marr. diss., 1947); one *s* three *d*; 2nd, 1948, Nora Christine Pattinson (marr. diss. 1970); one *d*; 3rd, 1970, Eileen Mary Watford. *Educ:* Eltham Coll.; St Thomas's Hosp. MB, BS London 1931; MRCS, LRCP, 1931; FRCS 1934. Served with Royal Army Medical Corps, 1941-46. Home Commands, North Africa and Italy; Brigadier, Consulting Orthopædic Surgeon to the Army, 1946. *Publication:* Injuries of the Hand, 1957. *Recreations:* reading, history and archæology. *Address:* 149 Harley Street, W1. *T:* 01-935 4444. *Club:* Athenæum.

**FURLONGE, Sir Geoffrey (Warren),** KBE 1960 (OBE 1942); CMG 1951; *b* 16 Oct. 1903; *s* of Robert Shekleton Furlonge and Agnes Mary (*née* Hatch); *m* 1952, Anne, *d* of late E. A. Goldsack. *Educ:* St Paul's Sch.; Emmanuel Coll., Cambridge. Entered Levant Consular Service, 1926; served at Casablanca, 1928-31; Jedda, 1931-34; Beirut, 1934-46; Political Officer with HM Forces in the Levant States, 1941-46. At Imperial Defence Coll., 1947; served in FO, 1948 (Head of Commonwealth Liaison Dept, 1948-50, Head of Eastern Dept, 1950-51); Minister (later Ambassador) to Jordan, 1952-54; HM Minister at Sofia, 1954-56; HM Ambassador to Ethiopia, 1956-59. *Publications:* The Lands of Barbary, 1966; Palestine is my Country, 1969. *Recreations:* mountaineering, chess. *Address:* 57 Princes Gate, SW7.

**FURNEAUX, Viscount; Frederick William Robin Smith;** *b* 17 April 1936; *o s* of 2nd Earl of Birkenhead, *qv*. *Educ:* Eton; Christ Church, Oxford. *Publication:* The Amazon, 1969. *Address:* 25 Wilton Street, SW1. *T:* 01-235 7126; The Cottage, Charlton, Banbury, Oxon. *T:* Kings Sutton 224. *Clubs:* Buck's, White's, St James'.

**FURNESS,** family name of **Viscount Furness.**

**FURNESS,** 2nd Viscount, *cr* 1918; **William Anthony Furness;** Baron Furness, *cr* 1910, of Grantley; Chairman and Managing Director, United & General Trust Ltd; Director other private companies; Theatrical and Film Producer; *b* 31 March 1929; *s* of 1st Viscount and Thelma (*d* 1970), *d* of late Harry Hays Morgan, American Consul-Gen. at Buenos Aires; *S* father, 1940. *Educ:* Downside; USA. Served as Guardsman, Welsh Guards (invalided, 1947). Delegate to Inter-Parliamentary Union Conferences, Washington, 1953, Vienna, 1954, Helsinki, 1955, Warsaw, 1959, Brussels, 1961, Belgrade, 1963. Vice-Chm. University of London Catholic Chaplaincy Assoc., 1953-; Mem. Council, Hansard Soc. for Parliamentary Govt, 1955-67. Pres., Employment Agents Federation of GB; Founder Chm., Anglo-Mongolian Soc., 1963; Chm. Council, Soc. of St Augustine of Canterbury. CStJ 1964. SMO of Malta: (Sec. Assoc. of Brit. Members, 1956-65, Sec.-Gen. 1965-; Mem. Sovereign Council, 1960-62; Grand Officer of Merit, 1965). Grand Officer, Order of Merit, Italy, 1961; KCSG 1966. *Heir:* none. *Address:* 60 St James's Street, SW1. *T:* 01-629 8953; 508 North Alpine Drive, Beverly Hills, Calif, USA. *Clubs:* Carlton, American; Travellers' (Paris).

**FURNESS, Sir Christopher,** 2nd Bt, *cr* 1913; *s* of 1st Bt and Eleanor (*d* 1936), *d* of Matthew Forster, CE, of Mount Brown, South Australia; *b* 18 Oct. 1900; *S* father, 1914; *m*

1930, Flower (OBE 1970), *d* of late Col G. C. Roberts; three *s* one *d*. *Educ:* Charterhouse; Pembroke Coll., Cambridge. Vice-Pres. Royal Northumberland Yacht Club. Served RNVR European War, 1914-18, 1918-19, and War of 1939-45, 1940-45. *Heir:* *s* Stephen Roberts Furness [*b* 10 Oct. 1933; *m* 1961, Mary, *d* of Jack Fitzroy Cann, Cullompton, Devon; one *s* one *d*. Lieut, Royal Navy, retd]. *Recreation:* walking. *Address:* Netherbyres, Eyemouth, Berwickshire. *T:* 337; Glebe Cottage, Longformacus, Duns, Berwickshire. *T:* Longformacus 256. *Clubs:* Royal Over-Seas League; Caledonian (Edinburgh).

**FURNESS, Stephen Noel,** Barrister-at-Law; MA; *b* 18 Dec. 1902; 2nd *s* of late Sir Stephen W. Furness, Bart., and Eleanor Lady Furness. *Educ:* Charterhouse; Oriel Coll., Oxford. Called to Bar, Middle Temple, 1927; Contested Hartlepools (Liberal) 1929, Sunderland (L Nat) 1945; MP (L Nat) Sunderland, 1935-45; Parliamentary Private Sec. to Sir J. Simon, 1936-37; Asst Government Whip, 1937-38; Junior Lord of the Treasury, 1938-40; 1st Bn London Irish Rifles, Major; late Chairman, Furness Shipbuilding Co. Ltd. *Address:* Otterington Hall, Northallerton, Yorks. *Club:* Brooks's.

**FURNESS-SMITH, Sir Cecil,** Kt 1949; QC (Tanganyika Territory); JP; Chief Justice, Trinidad and Tobago, 1946-53; *b* 20 March 1890; *s* of Rev. George Furness-Smith, late of Riverdale Road, Twickenham Park, and Elizabeth Hayes, Edmondstown Park, Rathfarnham, Co. Dublin; *m* 1921, Mary Kathleen, *d* of John Price Hargreaves, The Moorlands, Oxton, Birkenhead; one *s*. *Educ:* Birkenhead Sch.; St John's Coll., Cambrdige. Colonial Administrative Service, Gold Coast 1914; called to Bar, Inner Temple, 1923; Colonial Legal Service, Crown Counsel, Gold Coast, 1925; Solicitor-Gen., Tanganyika Territory, 1932; Attorney-Gen., Zanzibar, 1936; Attorney-Gen., Tanganyika Territory, 1940. JP County of Devon, 1953. *Recreations:* golf and bridge. *Address:* Drummetts Lodge, Torrington, N Devon. *TA:* Torrington, Devon. *T:* Torrington 2165.

**FURNIVAL JONES, Sir (Edward) Martin,** Kt 1967; CBE 1957; *b* 7 May 1912; *s* of Edward Furnival Jones, FCA; *m* 1955, Elizabeth Margaret, *d* of Bartholomew Snowball; one *d*. *Educ:* Highgate Sch.; Gonville and Caius Coll., Cambridge. BA 1934, MA 1938. Admitted a Solicitor, 1937. Served War of 1939-45: General Staff Officer at Supreme Headquarters, Allied Expeditionary Force, and War Office (despatches, American Bronze Star Medal).

**FURNIVALL, Barony** *cr* 1295; in abeyance. *Co-heiresses:* Hon. Rosamond Mary Dent (Sister Ancilla, OSB); *b* 3 June 1933; Hon. Patricia Mary Dent [*b* 4 April 1935; *m* 1956, Captain Thomas Hornsby (marr. diss., 1963; he *d* 1967); one *s* one *d*; she resumed surname of Dent, 1964].

**FURNIVALL, Maj.-Gen. Lewis Trevor,** CB 1964; DSO 1943; Dir of Medical Services, Far East Land Forces, 1965-66; retired 1967; *b* 6 Sept. 1907; *er s* of late Lt-Col C. H. Furnivall, CMG, and late Mrs D. Furnivall (*née* Macbean); *m* 1941, Audrey Elizabeth Furnivall (*née* Gibbins); three *s* one *d*. *Educ:* Blundell's Sch.; St Mary's Hosp., London. MRCS, LRCP 1931; House Surg., Worcester Gen. Infirmary, 1931; Lieut, RAMC 1931; NW Frontier of India (Mohmand), 1933 (medal and clasp); Capt. 1934; Major 1941; Lieut-Col 1947; Col 1953; Brig. 1960; Maj.-Gen. 1961. Service in India, 1932-38; DADMS, 1939-. War Service, 1939-45 (UK, MELF, Italy, France, Germany); ADMS, 1944-48 (despatches, 1946); DDMS, HQ, BAOR, 1949-52; ADMS, HQ, Land Forces, Hong Kong, 1953-54; ADMS, HQ, Northumbrian Dist, 1955-57; Dep. Chief Med. Officer, SHAPE, 1957-60; Inspector of Training, Army Med. Services, 1960; Deputy Dir Medical Services, Eastern Command, 1961-65. QHS 1961-67. La Médaille d'Honneur du Service de Santé, 1960. *Recreations:* Rugby football, golf, tennis, cricket, swimming, ski-ing. *Address:* Marlingford, Greenhill Road, Farnham, Surrey. *T:* Farnham 5771. *Clubs:* Farnham Conservative, Hankley Common Golf.

**FURSE, Rear-Adm. John Paul Wellington,** CB 1958; OBE 1946; CEng; FIMechE; FLS; retired; *b* 13 Oct. 1904; *s* of late Charles Furse, artist, and late Dame Katharine, GBE, RRC, Dir, WRNS; *m* 1929, Cicely Rathbone; one *s*. *Educ:* Osborne; Dartmouth; RN Engineering Coll., Keyham. Service in Submarines, etc, 1927-39; Asst Naval Attaché, Europe and the Americas, 1940-43; 5th and 4th Submarine Flotillas, 1943-46; Admiralty, 1947, Dir of Aircraft Maintenance and Repair, Admiralty, 1955-58; Dir-Gen. of the Aircraft Dept, Admiralty, 1958-59; retired, 1959. Botanical expeditions in Turkey and Iran, 1960, 1962; Afghanistan, 1964, 1966. VMH 1965. *Recreations:* mountains, ski-ing, botany, painting. *Address:* Hegg Hill, Smarden, Kent. *T:* Smarden 229. *Club:* Army and Navy.

**FURSE, Major Sir Ralph Dolignon,** KCMG 1941 (CMG 1935); DSO 1918; Hon. DCL Oxford 1949; King Edward's Horse; *b* 1887; *s* of John Henry Monsell Furse; *m* 1914, Margaret Cecilia, *d* of late Sir Henry Newbolt, CH; two *s* one *d* (and one *d* decd). *Educ:* Eton; Balliol Coll., Oxford (MA). Asst Private Sec., Colonial Office, to Mr Harcourt, 1910-14; served European War, 1914-18 (despatches twice, DSO and bar); Asst Private Sec at the Colonial Office to Viscount Milner, 1919, Mr Churchill, 1921, the Duke of Devonshire, 1922; Private Sec. to Mr J. H. Thomas, 1924; to Mr Amery, 1924; to Lord Passfield, 1929. Dir of Recruitment, Colonial Service, 1931-48; Adviser to Sec. of State for Colonies on Training Courses for Colonial Service, 1948-50. *Publication:* Aucuparius: Recollections of a Recruiting Officer, 1962. *Address:* Halsdon, Dolton, Winkleigh, N Devon. *T:* Dolton 214. *Club:* Savile.

*See also Laurence Whistler.*

**FURSE, Roger Kemble,** RDI 1949; freelance theatre and film designer; painter; illustrator; *b* 11 Sept. 1903; *s* of late Lieut-Gen. Sir William Furse, KCB, KCMG; *m* 1936, Alice Margaret (*née* Watts) (marriage dissolved, 1951); no *c*; *m* 1952, Ines Sylvia Perg. *Educ:* St George's Choir Sch., Windsor Castle; Eton; Slade Sch. of Fine Arts. Worked in Paris, 1924-27, in USA, 1927-31 (commercial work, portraits, etc.); returned to London, 1931, since when has been designing for Theatre; and later, 1943, for films. *Films include:* Henry V, 1944; Odd Man Out, 1946; Hamlet, 1948; Ivanhoe, 1952; Knights of the Round Table, 1953; Helen of Troy, 1954; Richard III; The Prince and the Showgirl, 1956; St Joan; Bonjour Tristesse, 1957; Spartacus (in Hollywood), 1958-59; The Roman Spring of Mrs Stone, 1961; The Road to Hong Kong, 1961. *Plays* for which he has designed settings and costumes include: Victoria Regina, Gate, 1936; Othello, Old Vic, 1938; Spring Meeting, Ambassadors, 1938; Hamlet (mod. dress), Old Vic, 1938; Goodness How Sad!, Vaudeville, 1938; The Taming of the Shrew and Romeo and Juliet, Old Vic, 1939; Rebecca, Queen's, 1940; King Lear, Old Vic, 1940; Arsenic and Old Lace, Strand, 1942;

Uncle Vanya, Westminster, 1943; The Duchess of Malfi, Haymarket, 1945; Henry IV (I and II), Old Vic Co., New, 1945; Portrait in Black, Piccadilly, 1946; (décor of) Venus Observed, St James's, 1949; Twelfth Night for Old Vic season, 1950-51; settings for Antony and Cleopatra, and Caesar and Cleopatra, St James's, 1951; Verdi's Don Carlos opera, Sadler's Wells, 1951; The Mortimer Touch, Duke of York's, 1952; settings for: Romeo and Juliet, for Old Vic, Edinburgh, 1952; The Italian Straw Hat, The Merchant of Venice, for Old Vic, 1952; The Mouse Trap, Ambassadors; Macbeth, Stratford Season, 1955; The Egg, Saville Theatre, 1957; Duel of Angels, 1958; Once More with Feeling, 1959; Look after Lulu, 1960; The Tumbler, New York, 1960; The Broken Heart, Chichester Festival Theatre, 1962; The Workhouse Donkey, Chichester Festival Theatre, 1963. Served War of 1939-45; joined Navy 1940; commnd in RNVR, 1941. *Recreation:* friends. *Address:* c/o Westminster Bank Ltd, Tavistock Square, WC1.

**FURTADO, Robert Audley,** CB 1970; Special Commissioner of Income Tax since 1946, Presiding Commissioner since 1963; *b* 20 August 1912; *yr s* of Montague C. Furtado; *m* 1945, Marcelle Elizabeth, *d* of W. Randall Whitteridge; one *s* one *d. Educ:* Whitgift Sch.; University Coll., London. LLB London Univ., 1933; called to Bar, Gray's Inn, 1934. Served War of 1939-45, in Army in India and Burma (Despatches); demobilised rank of Lieut-Col, 1945. *Recreation:* bricolage. *Address:* 17 Fitzjames Avenue, Croydon CRO 5DL. *T:* 01-654 4623; 39 Strand Court, Topsham, Devon. *Club:* Athenæum.

*See also J. E. Pater, Prof. David Whitteridge and Sir Gordon Whitteridge.*

**FUSSELL, Edward Coldham,** CMG 1954; Governor, Reserve Bank of New Zealand, 1948-62; *b* Auckland, 16 July 1901; *s* of Rev. James Coldham Fussell; *m* 1935, Eileen, *d* of C. S. Plank; three *s* two *d. Educ:* King's Coll., Auckland; Victoria University Coll. (BA). With National Bank of NZ, 1919-34; Head Office, 1930. Rep. Associated Banks at Monetary Commn, 1934. With Reserve Bank of NZ, 1934-62; Asst to Governors, 1939; Dep.-Gov., 1941-48; rep. Reserve Bank on Royal Commn, 1955. Has attended financial confs in UK and USA, including Bretton Woods Conf., 1944. Served HG, War of 1939-45. Mem., Senate and Grants Cttee, University of NZ, 1951-60; Hon. Treas, University of NZ, 1954-60. *Recreation:* golf. *Address:* 5 Taumaru Avenue, Lowry Bay, Wellington, New Zealand. *T:* 63-838. *Clubs:* Wellington, Rotary International; Heretaunga Golf, Wellington Racing.

**FYERS, FitzRoy Hubert;** *b* 13 March 1899; *s* of late Major Hubert Alcock Nepean Fyers, MVO, and Evangeline Blanche, *e d* of late Captain Hon. Francis A. J. Chichester and Lady Emily Chichester; *m* 1949, Bryda Hope Collison, *d* of late Octavius Weir. *Educ:* Eton; RMC, Sandhurst. Entered Rifle Brigade, 1917; served in European War, France, 1918; seconded to Machine Gun Corps, 1920; ADC to Gen. Sir Alex. Godley, British Army of the Rhine, 1922-24, and to Gen. Sir John Du Cane, 1924-25; retired from Army, 1926; Sec. to Sir H. Hesketh Bell, on special mission to Yugoslavia, 1929; Extra-Equerry to the Duke of Connaught, 1929-30; Equerry to The Duke of Connaught, 1930-39, and Comptroller, 1938-41. Rejoined Rifle Brigade on outbreak of War, Sept. 1939; transferred to King's Own Scottish Borderers, Nov. 1939; on Staff of Lt-Gen. Sir Wm Dobbie, Malta, as Military Asst, 1940 (despatches); Major, 1940; Military Liaison Officer to Rear-Adm., Alexandria, 1942-43; Asst Sergeant-at-Arms, House of Commons, 1945-48. OStJ. *Address:* Craigburn, Fortrose, Ross-shire. *Clubs:* Travellers'; New (Edinburgh); Royal Scottish Automobile (Glasgow).

**FYFE, Prof. William Sefton,** FRS 1969; Royal Society Research Professor (Geochemistry), University of Manchester, since 1967; *b* 4 June 1927; *s* of Colin and Isabella Fyfe; *m* 1968, Elisabeth Stumpfl; two *s* one *d. Educ:* Otago Univ., New Zealand. BSc 1948, MSc 1949, PhD 1952. Univ. of California, Berkeley, Calif; Lecturer in Chemistry, 1952, Reader, 1958; Prof. of Geology, 1939. Hon. Fellow, Geological Soc. Amer. Mineralogical Soc. of Amer. Award, 1964. *Publications:* Metamorphic Reactions and Metamorphic Facies, 1958; The Geochemistry of Solids, 1964; also numerous scientific papers. *Address:* Geology Department, Manchester University.

**FYFFE, Lt-Gen. Sir Richard (Alan),** KBE 1969 (OBE 1950); CB 1964; DSO 1945; MC 1943; Deputy Chief of the Defence Staff (Intelligence), Ministry of Defence, 1968-71; *b* 12 Aug. 1912; *s* of late Alan Herbert Fyffe and Veronica Fyffe; *m* 1937, Diana Gwyneth, *d* of Major and Mrs J. G. Moore-Gwyn, Clayton Court, Liss, Hants; three *d. Educ:* Winchester Coll.; RMC Sandhurst. 2nd Lieut The Rifle Bde, 1932, Lieut 1935; seconded for service with RAF, 1938-40; GSO3, War Office, 1940 (Captain); Student, Staff Coll., 1941; GSO2, HQ Army Co-op. Comd 1941 (Major); Regimental duty with The Rifle Bde in N Africa and Italy, 1942-45; GSO1 (DS), Staff Coll., 1945; Jt Services Staff Coll., 1947; GSO1 (Plans) FAR ELF, 1948; AAG War Office, 1950 (Bt Lieut-Col); Regtl Duty with The Rifle Bde, 1952, comdg 1st Bn, 1953 (Lieut-Col); Comdg 11 Inf. Bde (BAOR), 1955 (Brig.); Dep. Mil. Sec., War Office, 1957; IDC, 1959; Brig. Army Air Corps, 1960; DPR, War Office, 1961-62; GOC 54 (E Anglian) Div./Dist, 1963-65; Comdr Brit. Army Staff, Mil. Mem. Brit. Defence Staff, and Mil. Attaché, Washington, 1965-67; Dir, Service Intelligence, MoD, 1967-68. Colonel Commandant: 3rd Bn The Royal Green Jackets, 1968-; Intelligence Corps, 1969-. *Address:* Green Hailey Farm House, Princes Risborough, Aylesbury, Bucks. *T:* Princes Risborough 3894. *Club:* United Service.

**FYLER, Maj.-Gen. Arthur Roderic,** CB 1964; OBE 1954; *b* 28 June 1911; *s* of late Adm. H. A. S. Fyler, CB, DSO, and late Mrs H. A. S. Fyler; *m* 1940, Anthea Mary de Fontaine Stratton, *d* of late Lt-Col F. C. G. Stratton, TD, Nairobi, Kenya; two *s* two *d. Educ:* Charterhouse. 2/Lieut (Sup. Res.) The Buffs, 1931-34; 2/Lieut Queen's Own Royal West Kent Regt, 1934. Served War of 1939-45: E Africa, British Somaliland, Abyssinia (King's African Rifles), NW Europe; despatches 1940 and 1954. AQMG, HQ Land Forces, Hong Kong, 1950-52; OC 1st Bn Queen's Own Royal West Kent Regt, 1953-55; Comd 130 (West Country) Infantry Bde (TA), 1955-58; Dep. Adjt Gen., GHQ, FARELF, 1958-61; Dir of Army Personnel Administration, 1961-64, War Office and MoD (A); retired 1964. *Recreations:* cricket, tennis, squash. *Address:* Starlings, Beechwood Road, Beaconsfield, Bucks. *T:* Beaconsfield 3321. *Clubs:* Naval and Military; Middlesex County Cricket; Devon Dumplings Cricket.

**FYNES-CLINTON, David Osbert;** *b* 25 Jan. 1909; *s* of late Prof. O. H. Fynes-Clinton, University Coll. of North Wales, Bangor; *m* 1947, Betty Lawrence; one *s. Educ:* Clifton; St John's Coll., Oxford. Entered Consular

Service, 1931; Genoa, 1931; Cairo, 1933; Colon, Panama, 1935; La Paz, Bolivia, 1938; Rio de Janeiro, 1940; Luanda, Angola, 1947; Basle, 1949; Consul-Gen. at Tananarive, Madagascar, 1952; Zagreb 1956; retired 1957. Joined Staff of UN, 1958. *Address:* c/o United Nations, Geneva, Switzerland.

**FYSH, Sir (Wilmot) Hudson,** KBE 1953; DFC 1917; FRAeS, MInstT, FRGSA; Chairman Qantas Empire Airways Ltd, 1947-66 (Chairman and Managing Director, 1947-55; Managing Director Qantas Ltd, 1922-34, and Qantas Empire Airways Ltd, 1934-47); Past Member Executive Committee, IATA (President, 1961); Fellow British Interplanetary Society; *b* 7 Jan. 1895; *s* of Frederic Wilmot Fysh and Mary Reed; *m* 1924, Eleanor Elizabeth Dove; one *s* one *d*. *Educ:* Geelong Church of England Grammar Sch. Served European War, 1914-18; Trooper in 3rd Aust. LH Regt; Lieut 1st Aust MG Section, Lieut No. 1 Sqdn AFC (despatches, DFC). A founder of Qantas Ltd, 1920. Surveyed (jointly) original air route across Australia from Longreach to Darwin for Ross Smith Flight, 1919; Pilot 1st official air mail service in Eastern Australia; formerly: Dep. Chm., Australian National Travel Assoc.; Chm. Qantas Wentworth Holdings Ltd. *Publications:* Taming the North, 1934; Qantas Rising, 1965; Qantas at War, 1966; Round the Bend in the Stream, 1968; general writer on Air Transport. *Recreations:* dry fly fishing and country pursuits. *Address:* Lyndhurst Gardens, 3 Rosemount Avenue, Woollahra, Sydney, Australia. *T:* FB1586. *Clubs:* Royal Air Force; Australian, Royal Sydney golf, Rotary (Sydney); Queensland (Brisbane); Royal Aero (NSW).

# G

**GABB, W. H.,** MVO 1961; Organist, Choirmaster and Composer at HM Chapels Royal, since 1953; Sub-Organist, St Paul's Cathedral, London, since 1946; Professor and Examiner of Organ Playing at The Trinity College of Music, London; Special Commissioner for Royal School of Church Music; Member, Council of the Royal College of Organists; Adjudicator and Recitalist; *m* 1936, Helen Burnaford Mutton. *Educ:* Scholarship at Royal Coll. of Music for Organ and Composition, ARCO 1928; FRCO 1930; ARCM Solo Organ, 1931; Organist, St Jude's, West Norwood, 1925; Organist and Choirmaster, Christ Church, Gypsy Hill, 1928; Sub-Organist, Exeter Cathedral, also Organist, Church of St Leonard's, Exeter and Heavitree Parish Church, 1929-37; Organist and Master of the Choristers, Llandaff Cathedral, 1937; Lecturer St Michael's Theological Coll., Llandaff; Royal Armoured Corps, War of 1939-45. Returned from Army to Llandaff, Jan. 1946. Played organ at the Coronation of Elizabeth II and at many Royal Weddings and Baptisms. Hon. Fellow Trinity Coll. of Music, 1954. *Address:* Flat 4, St Augustine's House, 4 New Change, EC4. *T:* 01-236 8477. *Club:* Athenæum.

**GABIN, Jean, (Alexis Jean Montgorge);** Médaille Militaire; Croix de Guerre; French film actor; *b* 17 May 1904; *m* 1949, Dominique Fournier; one *s* two *d*. *Educ:* Paris. *Films include:* Pépé le Moko, Bandera, Belle Equipe, Bête humaine, Bas Fonds, Grande Illusion, French Can-Can, Quai des brumes, Jour se lève, Gueule d'amour, Remorques, Marie du port, Au Delà des grilles, Minute de Vérité, Touchez pas au Grisbi, La Nuit est mon royaume, Crime and Punishment, Chnouf, En cas de Malheur; The Case of Dr Laurent; Maigret Tend Un Piège: Le Clochard; Un Singe en Hiver; Les Grandes Familles; Le Président; The Big Snatch; The Sicilian Clan. *Recreation:* stock-breeder. *Address:* 55 Avenue George V, Paris, France.

**GABOR, Prof. Dennis,** CBE 1970; FRS 1956; DSc London 1964; DrIng Berlin, FInstP, FIEE; Professor Emeritus of Applied Electron Physics in the University of London, at Imperial College of Science and Technology (Reader in Electronics, 1949-58; Professor, 1958-67); Senior Research Fellow since 1967; *b* 5 June 1900; *s* of Bertalan Gabor and Ady (*née* Kálmán); *m* 1936, Marjorie Louise Butler, Rugby. *Educ:* Technical Univ., Budapest; Technische Hochschule, Berlin-Charlottenburg. Asst, TH, Berlin, 1924-26; Research associate, German Res. Assoc. for High Voltage Plants, 1926-27; Research engineer, Siemens & Halske AG, Berlin-Siemensstadt, 1927-33; Research engineer, British Thomson-Houston Co., Rugby, 1934-48. Inventor of holography. Hon. Member Hungarian Academy of Sciences, 1964. Thomas Young Medal and Prize, RPS, 1967; Cristoforo Colombo Prize, Genoa, 1967; Rumford Medal, Royal Soc., 1968; Medal of Honor, IEEE, 1970. Hon. DSc Southampton, 1970. *Publications:* The Electron Microscope, 1946; Electronic Inventions and their Impact on Civilisation. 1959; Inventing the Future, 1963; Innovations, Scientific, Technological and Social, 1970. About 100 scientific papers on electrical transients, gas discharges, electron dynamics, communication theory and physical optics. *Recreations:* swimming, writing on social problems. *Address:* (summer) La Margioretta, 00040 Anzio, Lavinio, Viale dei Gigli, Italy; (winter) 91 Vicarage Court, Kensington Church Street, W8. *Club:* Athenæum.

**GABRIEL, William Bashall,** MS London; FRCS; Honorary Consultant Surgeon; Royal Northern Hospital; St Mark's Hospital. *Educ:* Epsom Coll.; Middlesex Hosp., London Univ., MRCS, LRCP, 1916; MB, BS, 1916; FRCS, 1918; MS London, 1919. Formerly House Surg., St Mark's Hosp.; (temp.) Surgeon-Lieut, RN. FRSocMed. *Publications.* Principles and Practice of Rectal Surgery (5th edn), 1963; articles in med. jls. *Address:* Fenside, Ludham, Great Yarmouth, Norfolk.

**GADD, Maj.-Gen. Alfred Lockwood,** CBE 1962 (OBE 1955); Director of Army Education, The War Office, 1962-65; *b* 10 July 1912; *s* of late Charles A. Gadd; *m* 1st, 1936, Gwenrudd Eluned (*d* 1965), *d* of late Morgan Edwards; one *s* one *d*; 2nd, 1965, Anna Louisa Margaret, *d* of Carl-August Koehler. *Educ:* Harvey Grammar Sch., Folkestone; Peterhouse, Cambridge (Open Scholar, MA). Asst Master: Bedford Sch., 1934-35; King's Sch., Rochester, 1935-39; Marlborough Coll., 1939-40. Commissioned Intelligence Corps, 1941; GSO3 War Office, 1942; Major, 1942; Lt-Col 1944; Chief Instructor 5 Formation Coll., 1945; Comdt No 1 Army Coll., 1946; Chief Education Officer, Far ELF, 1947; SO1 (Education): HQAA Command, 1950; The War Office (AE2), 1952; HQ Lübbecke District, 1956; HQ1 (Br.) Corps, 1957. Chief Education Officer, HQ Southern Command, 1959. *Recreations:* travel, archæology. *Address:* Lane End, Norton St Philip, near Bath. *T:* Faulkland 343.

**GADSBY, Gordon Neville;** Director, Chemical Defence Establishment, Porton, Wilts, since

1968; *b* 29 Jan. 1914; *s* of William George and Margaret Sarah Gadsby; *m* 1938, Jeanne (*née* Harris); two *s* one *d*. *Educ:* King Edward VI Sch., Stratford-upon-Avon; University of Birmingham. BSc 1935, DipEd 1937, Cadbury Prizeman 1937, Birmingham; FRIC 1967. Sen. Chemistry Master, Waverley Gram. Sch., Birmingham, 1937-40; Captain Royal Warwicks Regt, and Sen. Instructor, Applied Chem., RMCS, 1941-46; Princ. Lectr, RMCS, 1946-51; Supt, Special Weapons and Logistics Divs, Army Operational Research Gp, 1951-55; Dep. Sci. Adviser to Army Coun., 1955-59; idc 1960; Dir of Army Operational Science and Research, 1961; Dir, Army Operational Res. Estab., 1961-64; Dir of Biol. and Chem. Defence, Army Dept, MoD, 1965-67; Dep. Chief Scientist (Army), MoD, 1967-68. *Publications:* Lubrication, 1949; An Introduction to Plastics, 1950. *Recreations:* oil painting, photography. *Address:* Beech Gate, Hurdle Way, Compton Down, Winchester, Hants. *T:* Twyford (Hants) 2231.

**GADSDEN, Peter Drury,** MA; JP; Company Director; Underwriting Member of Lloyd's; Mineral Marketing Consultant since 1969; *b* Canada, 28 June 1929; *er s* of late Basil Claude Gadsden, ACT, ThL, and late Mabel Florence Gadsden (*née* Drury); *m* 1955, Belinda Ann, *e d* of Captain Sir (Hugh) Carnaby de Marie Haggerston, 11th Bt, *qv*; four *d*. *Educ:* Rockport, Belfast; The Elms, Colwall; Wrekin Coll., Wellington; Jesus Coll., Cambridge (MA). 2nd Lieut King's Shropshire LI, attached Oxf. and Bucks LI and Durham LI, Germany, 1948-49; Cambridge, 1949-52; Fergusson Wild & Co. Ltd, 1952-61; Dir, Fergusson Wild (Metals) Ltd, 1962-63; Man. Dir, London subsid. of Australian Mineral Sands Producer, 1964-70. Marketing Economist (Mineral Sands) to UN Industrial Development Organisation, 1969. Director: J. H. Little Metals Ltd, 1970-; St Piran Mining Co. Ltd, 1970-; Siamese Tin Syndicate Ltd, 1967-; South Crofty Ltd, 1969-; Bangrin Tin Dredging Co. Ltd, 1969-; Thomas Hill-Jones Ltd, 1964-; Klockner Steel Co. Ltd, 1970-; Guthrie & Co. (UK) Ltd (Alt.), 1970-; Stoney Creek Exploration Pty Ltd, 1970-; Tractor Distributors Pty Ltd, 1967-. Sheriff, City of London, 1970-71; Common Councilman (Cripplegate Within and Without), 1969-; Liveryman, Clothworkers' Co., 1965-; Member: Guild of Freemen; Royal Soc. of St George (City of London Br.). Governor, Lady Eleanor Holles Sch., 1968-. JP Inner London Area of Greater London, 1969. *Publications:* articles on titanium, zirconium, and hafnium in Mining Jl Annual Reviews. *Recreations:* ski-ing, sailing, photography. *Address:* (home) 606 Gilbert House, Barbican, EC2Y 8BD. *T:* 01-638 9968; (office) Iando House, Bartholomew Close, EC1. *T:* 01-606 0081. *Clubs:* City of London, City Livery, United Wards, Mining, Australia, Canada.

**GADSDON, Sir Laurence Percival,** Kt 1960; Managing Director, Wilson Gray & Co. Pty, Ltd, Perth, WA; Mayor of Cottesloe, WA, 1945-61; *b* Ongar, Essex, 24 March 1897; *s* of Frank Benjamin and Mary Gertrude Gadsdon; *m* 1929, Hilda Mary, *d* of John and Eily Hedges; one *d*. *Educ:* Haberdashers' Aske's Hatcham Boys' Sch., London. Migrated to W Australia, 1913. Served AIF 1914-18 (Gallipoli Star, Gen. Service Medal). Sec., later Vice-Pres., Perth Branch Returned Soldiers Assoc., 1916-20; joined Wilson Gray & Co., 1919. Sec., Treas, Pres., N Cottesloe Surf Life Saving Club, 1918-35, now Life Member; Treas., 1925, Sec. and Pres., Surf Life Saving Assoc. of Australia (WA State Centre), now Life Mem. Councillor of Cottesloe, 1922. Pres. Local Government Assoc. of WA, 1950-60. Hon. Dir of Communications, Civil Defence, and mem. Civil Defence Council, 1939-45. *Recreations:* tennis, surfing and golf. *Address:* 14 Dean Street, Cottesloe, W Australia. *T:* 3, 2807.

**GAFFNEY, Maj.-Gen. (Hon.) Edward Sebastian B.;** *see* Burke-Gaffney.

**GAGE,** family name of **Viscount Gage.**

**GAGE,** 6th Viscount, *cr* 1720; **Henry Rainald Gage,** KCVO 1939; Bt 1622; Baron Gage (Ireland), 1720; B Gage (Great Britain), 1790; Vice-Lieutenant of Sussex since 1957; *b* 30 Dec. 1895; *o s* of 5th Viscount and Leila (*d* 1916), 2nd *d* of Rev. Frederick Peel, MA, and Hon. Adelaide, *d* of 3rd Baron Sudeley; *S* father, 1912; *m* 1931, Hon. Alexandra Imogen Clare Grenfell (*d* 1969), *yr d* of 1st Baron Desborough, KG, GCVO; two *s* one *d*. *Educ:* Eton; Christchurch, Oxford. Served European War, 1914-18 (wounded); War of 1939-45, Coldstream Guards and Staff; Lord-in-Waiting, 1925-29 and 1931-39; Parliamentary Private Sec. to Sec. of State for India, 1925-29. Patron, National Federation of Housing Societies and various Sussex County Organisations; Alderman, E Sussex CC. *Heir: s* Hon. George John St Clere Gage, *b* 8 July 1932. *Address:* Firle, Lewes, Sussex. *T:* Glynde 256. *Clubs:* Brooks's, White's.

**GAGE, Sir Berkeley (Everard Foley),** KCMG 1955 (CMG 1949); Retired; *b* 27 Feb. 1904; *s* of late Brig.-Gen. M. F. Gage, DSO; *m* 1931, Maria von Chappuis (marriage dissolved, 1954), Liegnitz, Silesia; two *s*; *m* 1954, Mrs Lillian Riggs Miller. *Educ:* Eton Coll.; Trinity Coll., Cambridge. 3rd Sec. Foreign Office or Diplomatic Service, 1928; appointed to Rome, 1928; transferred to Foreign Office, 1931; 2nd Sec., 1933; Private Sec. to Parl. Under-Sec. of State, 1934; served Peking, 1935; FO 1938; acting 1st Sec., 1939; China, 1941; FO 1944; UK Deleg. Dumbarton Oaks Conf., 1944; Adviser on UK Deleg., San Francisco Conf., April-June 1945; Foreign Service Officer, Grade 5, 1950; Counsellor, British Embassy, The Hague, 1947-50; Chargé d'Affaires, The Hague, in 1947 and 1948; Consul-Gen., Chicago, 1950-54; Foreign Service Officer, Grade IV, 1954; Ambassador to Siam, 1954-57; Ambassador to Peru, 1958-63. Chairman: Latin America Cttee, Brit. Nat. Export Council, 1964-66; Anglo-Peruvian Soc., 1969-; Member: Council for Volunteers Overseas, 1964-66; Council of Fauna Preservation Soc., 1969-. Grand Cross, Order of the Sun (Peru), 1964. *Recreations:* shooting, tennis. *Address:* 24 Ovington Gardens, SW3. *T:* 01-589 0361. *Clubs:* Boodle's, Beefsteak; Tavern (Chicago).

**GAGE, Conolly Hugh; His Honour Judge Gage;** Judge of County Courts (Cambridgeshire Circuit No. 35, since Oct. 1962; No. 62, Oct. 1958-62); Barrister-at-law; Chancellor, Diocese of Coventry and Diocese of Lichfield; Chairman Huntingdonshire and Peterborough Quarter Sessions, 1963; Deputy Chairman Essex Quarter Sessions, 1955; Fellow Commoner, Sidney Sussex College, Cambridge, 1962; *b* 10 Nov. 1905; *s* of William Charles Gage and May Guerney Holmes, *d* of Rt Hon. Lord Justice Holmes; *m* 1932, Elinor Nancy Martyn; one *s* one *d*. *Educ:* Repton; Sidney Sussex Coll., Cambridge. Called to Bar, Inner Temple, 1930; enlisted as Gunner in RA, TA, April 1939; served with First Canadian Army as ADJAG (Br.) (despatches). MP (UU) S Belfast, 1945-52; Recorder of Maldon and Saffron Walden, 1950-52. *Recreations:* fishing, shooting, gardening. *Address:* Fruit Hill, Widdington, Saffron Walden, Essex. *T:* Newport 401. *Clubs:* Carlton, Ulster (Belfast).

**GAGGERO, Sir George,** Kt 1941; OBE 1934; JP; *b* 5 April 1897; *e s* of late Joseph Gaggero and Mary Dassoy; *m* 1925, Mabel, *o d* of late James Andrews-Speed, CBE, JP, and Mrs Speed; two *s* two *d*. *Educ:* in Gibraltar, Germany and England. Chairman, M. H. Bland & Co. Ltd (Managing Director, 1915-65), and Bland Group of cos incl. Rock Hotel Ltd, Bland Cable Cars Ltd, Bland Line, Thomas Mosley & Co. Ltd, and M. H. Bland & Co. (UK) Ltd. Chairman: Gibraltar Stevedoring Co. Ltd, 1948-59; Stevedoring & Cargo Handling Co. Ltd, 1959-65; Gibraltar Shipping Assoc., 1956-60. President: Gibraltar Airways Ltd. (Chm. 1937-66); Gibraltar Employers Fedn, 1928-40. Director: Gibraltar Transporters Ltd, 1930-66; Mackintosh & Co. (Gibraltar) Ltd, 1943-67; Gibraltar Chamber of Comm., 1918-22; Rock Fire Assurance Co. Ltd, 1927-52. City Councillor, 1921-24; Unofficial Mem. Exec. Council, 1924-30 and 1936-43; Chief ARP Warden, Gibraltar, 1938-40; Chairman: Bench of Justices, 1949-59; Bd Dist Comrs, 1940-43; Merchant Navy Welfare Cttee, 1942-47; Member: Public Service Commn, 1956-58; Merchant Navy Club Cttee; served on many local cttees apptd by the Governor in connection with public matters. Swedish Consul, 1939, Swedish Consul-Gen., 1954-66. FRSA; Coronation Medals, 1937 and 1953; Chevalier (1st Class), Royal Swedish Order of Vasa, 1947. *Address:* 75 Prince Edward's Road, Gibraltar. *Clubs:* Royal Automobile, Royal Thames Yacht; Royal Gibraltar Yacht.

**GAHAN, Frank,** QC 1952; Lieutenant Bailiff and Magistrate, Guernsey, 1957-64; *b* 7 July 1890; *y s* of Henry Beresford Gahan and Mary Jane (*née* Burriss), London, Ontario; *m* 1st, 1919, Adelaide Hildegarde Grenside (*d* 1931); 2nd, 1934, Madge Sturgeon; no *c*. *Educ:* Trinity Coll., Toronto; Trinity Coll., Oxford. Served in Overseas Military Forces of Canada, 1916-19. LLB London 1919; BCL Oxon 1920; MA Oxon 1920. Yarborough-Anderson Scholar, Inner Temple, 1920-25; barrister-at-law, Inner Temple, 1921. Vice-Principal, Working Men's Coll., 1936-45; Hon. Fellow, 1957. *Publications:* Law of Damages, 1935; ed 10th edn Mayne on Damages, 1927; articles in 14th edn Encyc. Brit. *Address:* Sausmarez Place, Les Gravées, St Peter Port, Guernsey.

**GAILEY, Thomas William Hamilton,** CBE 1968; Chief Executive, National Bus Company, since 1968; *b* 7 Oct. 1906; *s* of late Thomas Andrew Gailey, ISO, and late Mabel Gailey; *m* 1937, Beryl, *er d* of late Harold Kirkconnel; one *d*. *Educ:* King's Sch., Rochester; University Coll., Oxford (MA). Served with companies in Tilling Bus Group, 1932-59. Served War of 1939-45, with RAF: Wing Comdr, RAF Transp. Comd and psc, 1943. Vice-Chm., Bristol Wing, Air Trng Corps, 1945-56. Mem., Tilling Gp Management Bd, 1960-64; Chm., Tilling Bus Gp, 1965-68; Dir, Passenger Planning, Transp. Holding Co., 1967-68; Mem., Nat. Council for Omnibus Industry, 1960-69; Dir, Bristol Commercial Vehicles and Eastern Coach Works, 1962-; Director: Leyland National Co. Ltd; Park Royal Vehicles Ltd, 1969-. Corporate Mem. Inst. of Transp. (Vice-Pres., 1966-68); Chm., Public Transp. Assoc., 1967-69. Vice-Chm., Road Operators' Safety Council, 1964-68. Freeman of City of London; Liveryman, Worshipful Co. of Carmen; Governor, British Transp. Staff Coll.; Mem., Scottish Transp. Gp, 1968-. *Publications:* various papers for professional institutes and societies. *Address:* Greystones, Bentley, Hants. *T:* 2208. *Clubs:* Travellers'; Royal Automobile; Bristol Savages (Bristol).

**GAINFORD,** 2nd Baron of Headlam, *cr* 1917; **Joseph Pease;** TD; retired Major, Lovat Scouts; *b* 8 March 1889; *o s* of 1st Baron and Ethel (*d* 1941), *o d* of Sir Henry Havelock-Allan, 1st Bt; *S* father, 1943; *m* 1921, Veronica, *o c* of Sir George Noble, 2nd Bt; three *s*. *Educ:* Eton. *Heir: s* Hon. Joseph Edward Pease [*b* 25 Dec. 1921; *m* 1953, Margaret Theophila Radcliffe, *d* of late H. E. G. Tyndale, Winchester Coll. and of Mrs Tyndale, 60 Lansdowne Road, W11; two *d*]. *Address:* Duntaynish, Tayvallich, Argyll. *T:* Tayvallich 215.

**GAINHAM, Sarah Rachel, (Mrs Kenneth Ames);** Author; *b* 1 Oct. 1922; *d* of Tom Stainer and May Genevieve Gainham; *m* 1964, Kenneth Ames. *Educ:* Newbury High Sch. for Girls; afterwards largely self educated. From 1947 onwards, travelled extensively in Central and E Europe; Central Europe Correspondent of The Spectator, 1956-66. Mem. PEN, England. *Publications:* Time Right Deadly, 1956; Cold Dark Night, 1957; The Mythmaker, 1957; Stone Roses, 1959; Silent Hostage, 1960; Night Falls on the City, 1967 (Book Soc. Choice and US Book of Month Club); A Place in the Country, 1968; Takeover Bid, 1970; contrib. to Encounter, Atlantic Monthly, BBC, etc. *Recreations:* theatre, opera. *Address:* c/o George Weidenfeld & Nicholson Ltd, 5 Winsley Street, W1.

**GAINSBOROUGH,** 5th Earl of, second *cr* 1841; **Anthony Gerard Edward Noel,** Bt 1781; Baron Barham, 1805; Viscount Campden, Baron Noel, 1841; *b* 24 Oct. 1923; *s* of 4th Earl and Alice Mary (*d* 1970), *e d* of Edward Eyre, Gloucester House, Park Lane, W1; *S* father 1927; *m* 1947, Mary, *er d* of Hon. J. J. Stourton (and of Mrs Kathleen Stourton, Withington, Glos), *qv*; four *s* three *d*. *Educ:* Georgetown, Garrett Park, Maryland, USA. JP Co. Rutland, 1957; Chairman: Oakham RDC, 1952-67; Executive Council RDC's Association of England and Wales, 1963 (Vice-Chairman 1962, Pres., 1965); Vice-Chm. Rutland CC, 1958-70, Chm., 1970-. Alderman, 1967; Mem. Court of Assistants, Worshipful Co. of Gardeners of London, 1960 (Upper Warden, 1966; Master, 1967). Hon. FIMunE 1969. Knight of Malta, 1948; Bailiff Grand Cross Order of Malta, 1958; Pres. Br. Assoc., SMO, Malta, 1968-. KStJ 1970. *Recreations:* shooting, sailing. *Heir: s* Viscount Campden, *qv*. *Address:* Exton Park, Oakham, Rutland. *T:* Cottesmore 209; 10 St Albans Mansions, W8. *T:* 01-937 7605. *Clubs:* Boodle's, Brooks's; Royal Solent Yacht, Bembridge Sailing, Royal Yacht Squadron.

*See also Baron Dormer, Earl of Liverpool.*

**GAINSBOROUGH, George Fotheringham,** PhD, FIEE; Barrister-at-law; Secretary, Institution of Electrical Engineers, since 1962; *b* 28 May 1915; *o s* of Rev. William Anthony Gainsborough and Alice Edith (*née* Fennell); *m* 1937, Gwendoline, *e d* of John and Anne Berry; two *s*. *Educ:* Christ's Hospital; King's Coll., London; Gray's Inn. Scientific Staff, Nat. Physical Laboratory, 1938-46; Radio Physicist, British Commonwealth Scientific Office, Washington, DC, USA, 1944-45; Administrative Civil Service (Ministries of Supply and Aviation), 1946-62. Imperial Defence College, 1960. Secretary, Commonwealth Engineering Conf., 1962-69; Sec.-General, World Fedn of Engineering Organizations, 1968-. *Publications:* papers in Proc. Instn of Electrical Engineers. *Address:* 46 Acacia Road, Hampton, Middlesex. *T:* 01-979 1478. *Club:* Athenæum.

**GAINSBOROUGH, Hugh,** MD, FRCP; Consulting Physician to St George's Hospital, since 1959. *Educ:* Cambridge Univ.; St George's Hosp. Medical Sch. MA Cambridge 1919; MB, ChB, 1921, MD 1928; MRCS 1917; FRCP 1929. Late Examiner in Medicine, Conjoint Board and University of London. Formerly: Physician St George's Hosp., and London Jewish Hospital; Dir of Medical Unit, St George's Hosp. Medical Sch. Fellow Royal Soc. Med.; Member: Biochemical Soc.; Association of Physicians. *Publications:* Principles of Hospital Design (with John Gainsborough), 1964; articles in Quar. Jl Med., Lancet, BM Jl, Biochem. Jl, The Architects' Jl. *Address:* 37 Clifton Hill, NW8. *T:* 01-624 5722.

**GAIRDNER, Gen. Sir Charles Henry,** GBE 1969 (KBE 1960; CBE 1941); KCMG 1948; KCVO 1954; CB 1946; Governor of Tasmania, 1963-68; *b* 20 March 1898; *e surv s* of late C. A. Gairdner, Lisbeg House, County Galway; *m* 1925, Hon. Evelyn Constance Handcock, CStJ, *o d* of 5th Baron Castlemaine, Moydrum Castle, Co. Westmeath; no *c. Educ:* Repton; RMA, Woolwich. Entered Army in 1916, served in France and Flanders (wounded); Staff Coll., Camberley, 1933-35; commanded 10th Royal Hussars, 1937-40; GSO 1st grade 7 Armoured Division, 1940-41; Deputy Dir of Plans, Middle East, 1941; GOC 6th Armoured Division, 1942; Commandant, Higher Commanders Sch., 1943. GOC 8th Armoured Division, 1943; CGS North Africa, 1943; Maj.-Gen. Armoured Fighting Vehicles, India, 1944; Maj.-Gen., 1941; Lt-Gen., 1944; Head, UK Liaison Mission, Japan, 1945-46. Prime Minister's Special Representative in Far East, 1945-48. Gov., State of W Australia, 1951-63. Col 10th Royal Hussars, 1949-52; Hon. Col 10th Light Horse, 1952-68; Hon. Col Royal Tasmanian Regt, 1964-68. Hon. Air Commodore, RAAF. KStJ 1951; Hon. DLitt W Australia, 1956; Hon. LLD, University of Tasmania, 1967. American Medal of Freedom with Silver Palm. *Recreations:* hunting, polo, golf, yachting. *Address:* 24 The Esplanade, Peppermint Grove, W Australia. *Clubs:* Cavalry; Weld, West Australian (Perth), Royal Perth Yacht.

**GAISFORD, Lt-Col Sir Philip,** Kt 1946; CIE 1942; *b* 28 Nov. 1891; *s* of Lt-Col Gilbert Gaisford, Indian Political Dept; *m* 1918, Sheila Mary, *d* of Lt-Col H. O'Reilly; three *s* one *d. Educ:* Wellington; RMC, Sandhurst. Royal Irish Fusiliers, 1911; entered Indian Army, 1912; served European War, Mesopotamia and Salonika, 1914-18; Resident for Kolhapur and the Deccan States, 1940-42; Resident for the States of Western India, 1942-44; Resident in Mysore, 1944-46; retired 1946. *Address:* Standard Bank of South Africa, Salisbury, Rhodesia.

**GAISFORD, Prof. Wilfrid Fletcher,** MD London, MSc Manchester, FRCP; Czechoslovak Military Medal of Merit, 1st class, 1945; First Professor of Child Health and Pædiatrics and Director of the Department of Child Health, University of Manchester, 1947-67, now Emeritus; *b* 6 April 1902; *s* of Captain Harold Gaisford, RN, and Annie, *d* of Captain Wm Fletcher, RIN; *m* 1933, Mary, *d* of Captain Wm Guppy; one *s* four *d. Educ:* Bristol Grammar Sch.; St Bartholomew's Hosp., London, MB London, 1925; MD London, 1928; Post-graduate study in St Louis Children's Hosp., University of Washington, USA, 1928-29; FRCP, 1940; MSc Manchester, 1951. Hon. Asst Physician, East London Children's Hosp., 1932; Member: British Pædiatric Assoc., 1933; Assoc. of Physicians of Gt Britain and Ireland, 1940; Physn, Dudley Road Hosp., Birmingham, 1935-42; Cons. Pædiatrician, Warwicks CC, 1942-47; Leonard Parsons Memorial Lecturer, University of Birmingham, 1954-55; Catherine Chisholm Memorial Lecturer, 1965. Hon. Physician, Royal Manchester Children's Hosp. and St Mary's Hosp., Manchester; Hon. Cons. Pædiatrician, United Manchester Hosp., 1967. Regional Adviser in Child Health, 1948. Hon. Member: Canadian Pædiatric Association, 1949; Swedish Pædiatric Association, 1960; Finnish Pædiatric Association, 1965; Hon. Fellow, American Acad. of Pediatrics, 1962; Pres., British Paediatric Assoc., 1964-65. Extraord. Mem., Swiss Paediatric Soc., 1965; Pres., Paediatric Section, Manchester Med. Soc., 1966-67. *Publications:* contrib. to the Encyclopædia of British Medical Practice, Lancet, BMJ, Practitioner, Archives of Disease in Childhood, Jl Paediatrics, etc. Joint Editor, Pædiatrics for the Practitioner (Gaisford and Lightwood). *Recreation:* gardening. *Address:* Treloyhan, Restronguet Point, Feock, Truro. *T:* Truro 55620.

**GAITSKELL,** Baroness, *cr* 1963, of Egremont (Life Peeress); **Anna Dora Gaitskell;** *d* of Leon Creditor; *m* 1937, Rt Hon. Hugh Todd Naylor Gaitskell, PC, CBE, MP. (*d* 1963), *s* of late Arthur Gaitskell, Indian Civil Service; two *d* (and one *s* by a former marriage). *Address:* 18 Frognal Gardens, NW3.

*See also Sir Arthur Gaitskell.*

**GAITSKELL, Sir Arthur,** Kt 1970; CMG 1949; Member, Commonwealth (formerly Colonial) Development Corporation, since 1954; *b* Oct. 1900; *s* of late Arthur Gaitskell, ICS; *m* 1939, Jeanne Stephanie, *d* of Col E. C. Townsend, ICS; one *s* two *d. Educ:* Winchester Coll.; New Coll., Oxford. Manager, Sudan Plantations Syndicate, 1945-50; Chm. and Managing Dir, Sudan Gezira Board, 1950-52. Consultant, 1952-53; Member: Royal Commission on East Africa, 1953-54; Tanganyika Agricultural Corp., 1955. Research Fellow, Nuffield Coll., Oxford, 1955-58; Nominee of International Bank on Food and Agriculture Commn, Pakistan, 1959-60; Consultant: to Mitchell Cotts, Ethiopia, to Kenya African National Union, Kenya, and to Ford Foundation, Nigeria, 1961-62. Lecturer at Economic Development Institute, International Bank, Washington, 1963. Consultant to: Euphrates Project Authority, 1965; Sir Alex Gibb and Partners on Indus Basin Survey, 1965-66; World Food Program, Mexico, 1966; FAO for Philippines, 1967, for Thailand, 1968. Member: Coun., Overseas Develt Inst., 1965; Adv. Bd, Mekong River, 1968; ILO Mission to Colombia, 1970. *Publication:* Gezira, 1959. *Address:* Bicknoller, Taunton, Somerset.

*See also Baroness Gaitskell.*

**GAJE GHALE,** VC 1943; Subedar 2/5 Royal Gurkha Rifles FF; *b* 1 July 1922; *s* of Bikram Ghale; *m* 1939, Dhansuba; no *c. Educ:* IA 2nd class certificate of education. Enlisted as a Recruit Boy 2nd Bn 5th Royal Gurkha Rifles FF, Feb. 1935; transferred to the ranks, Aug. 1935; Naik, 1941; Acting Havildar, May 1942; War Subst. Havildar, Nov. 1942; Bn Havildar Major June 1943; Jemadar, Aug. 1943. Waziristan operations, 1936-37 (medal with clasp); Burma, 1942-43 (1939-45 Star, VC). *Recreations:* football, basketball, badminton and draughts. *Address:* Barpak, Gorkha, No 2 West, Nepal.

**GALANTE, Mme P. P.;** *see* de Havilland, Olivia M.

**GALBRAITH,** family name of **Baron Strathclyde.**

**GALBRAITH, James Hunter;** Assistant Under Secretary of State, Department of Employment and Productivity (Research and

Planning Division), since 1968; *b* 16 July 1925; *o s* of Prof. V. H. Galbraith, *qv*, and Dr G. R. Galbraith; *m* 1954, Isobel Gibson Graham; two *s*. *Educ:* Edinburgh Academy; Balliol Coll., Oxford. Fleet Air Arm, 1944-46. Entered Ministry of Labour, 1950; Private Sec. to Permanent Sec., 1953-55; Jun. Civilian Instructor, IDC, 1958-61; Private Sec. to Minister of Labour, 1962-64; Chm. Central Youth Employment Exec., 1964-67; Sen. Simon Research Fellow, Manchester Univ., 1967-68. *Recreations:* golf, fishing. *Address:* White Posts, Walkwood End, Beaconsfield, Bucks. *T:* Beaconsfield 4828. *Club:* Oxford and Cambridge University.

**GALBRAITH, Prof. John Kenneth;** Paul M. Warburg Professor of Economics, Harvard University, since 1949; *b* Ontario, Canada, 15 Oct. 1908; *s* of Willliam Archibald and Catherine Galbraith; *m* 1937, Catherine M. Atwater; three *s*. *Educ:* Toronto Univ.; California Univ. BS, MS, PhD. Tutor, Harvard Univ., 1934-39; Social Science Research Fellow, Cambridge Univ., 1937; Asst Prof. of Economics, Princeton Univ., 1939; Asst Administrator, Office of Price Administration, 1941; Deputy Administrator, 1942-43; Dir, State Dept Office of Economic Security Policy, 1945; Mem. Bd of Editors, Fortune Magazine, 1943-48. United States Ambassador to India, 1961-63 (on leave from Professorship). Reith Lecturer, 1966; Vis. Fellow, Trinity Coll., Cambridge, 1970-71. Chm., Americans for Democratic Action, 1961-. LLD Bard, 1958; Miami Univ., 1959; University of Toronto, 1961; Brandeis Univ., 1963; University of Mass, 1963; University of Saskatchewan, 1965; Rhode Island Coll., 1966; Boston Coll., 1967; Hobart and William Smith Colls, 1967; President's Certificate of Merit; Medal of Freedom. *Publications:* American Capitalism, the Concept of Countervailing Power, 1951; The Great Crash, 1929, 1955; The Affluent Society, 1958; Journey to Poland and Yugoslavia, 1958; The Liberal Hour, 1960; Made to Last, 1964; The New Industrial State, 1967; Ambassador's Journal, 1969; contribs to learned jls. *Address:* 30 Francis Avenue, Cambridge, Mass, USA. *Clubs:* Century (NY); Federal City (Washington).

**GALBRAITH, Neil;** HM Inspector of Constabulary since 1964; *b* 25 May 1911; *s* of late Peter and Isabella Galbraith; *m* 1942, Catherine Margaret Thornton; one *s* one *d*. *Educ:* Kilmarnock Academy. Constable to Inspector, Lancs Constabulary, 1931-46. Chief Supt, Herts Constabulary, 1946-51; Asst Chief Constable, Monmouthshire Constabulary, 1951-55; Chief Constable, Leicester City Police, 1956; Chief Constable, Monmouthshire Constabulary, 1957-64. *Recreation:* reading. *Address:* Neath House, Trostrey, Usk, Mon. *T:* Usk 2779.

**GALBRAITH, Hon. Thomas Galloway Dunlop;** MP (U) for Hillhead Division of Glasgow since 1948; Member of Queen's Body Guard for Scotland (Royal Company of Archers); a Governor of Wellington College; *b* 10 March 1917; *e s* and *heir* of 1st Baron Strathclyde, *qv*; *m* 1956, Simone, *e d* of late Jean du Roy de Blicquy, Bois d'Hautmont, Brabant; two *s* one *d*. *Educ:* Aytoun House, Glasgow; Wellington Coll.; Christ Church, Oxford (MA); Glasgow Univ. (LLB). Served War of 1939-45, in RNVR (Lieut). 1939-46. Contested (U) Paisley, July 1945; East Edinburgh, Oct. 1945; Asst Conservative Whip, 1950; Scottish Unionist Whip, 1950-57; a Lord Commissioner of the Treasury, 1951-54; Comptroller of HM Household, 1954-55; Treasurer of HM Household, 1955-57; Civil Lord of the Admiralty, 1957-59; Joint Parliamentary Under-Sec. of State, Scottish Office, 1959-62; Joint Parliamentary Sec., Ministry of Transport, 1963-64. Chm., Cttee on Nuclear propulsion for Merchant Ships, 1957-59. Pres. Scottish Georgian Soc., 1970. *Address:* Barskimming, Mauchline, Ayrshire. *T:* Mauchline 334. *Clubs:* Carlton; Conservative (Glasgow); New (Edinburgh).

**GALBRAITH, Vivian Hunter,** MA, FBA; Hon. DLit Belfast; Hon. LittD Manchester and Emory, Atlanta, USA; Hon. DLitt Edinburgh and Exeter; *b* 15 Dec. 1889; *s* of David Galbraith and Eliza Davidson McIntosh; *m* 1921, Georgina Rosalie Cole Baker; one *s* two *d*. *Educ:* Highgate Sch.; Manchester Univ.; Balliol Coll., Oxford (scholar). Lieut The Queen's (Royal West Surrey) Regt, 1915-18; Asst Lectr Manchester Univ., 1920-21; Asst Keeper of the Public Records, 1921-28; Fellow and Tutor in Modern History, Balliol Coll., Oxford and University Reader in Diplomatic, 1928-37; Prof. of History, Edinburgh Univ., 1937-44; Dir of Inst. of Historical Research in University of London, 1944-48; Regius Prof. of Modern History in University of Oxford, 1947-57; late Lecturer in Palaeography and Archives to the Sch. of Librarianship, London; Ford's Lecturer in English History, Oxford, 1940-41; David Murray Lectureship (Glasgow Univ.), 1943-44; James Bryce Memorial Lecturer, Somerville Coll., 1944; Creighton Lecturer (University of London), 1949; Purington Lectr Mount Holyoke Coll. (Mass), 1965; Penrose Lect (Amer. Phil. Soc.), 1966. Mem. American Philosophical Soc.; Hon. Fellow of Balliol Coll., Oxford, 1957; Hon. Fellow of Oriel Coll., Oxford, 1958. *Publications:* articles (Eng. Hist. Review); The Anonimalle Chronicle of St Mary's Abbey, York, 1927; An Introduction to the Use of the Public Records, 1934; The Literacy of the Medieval English Kings, 1935; The St Albans Chronicle, 1406-1420, 1937; Roger Wendover and Matthew Paris, 1944; Studies in the Public Records, 1949; Hereford Domesday (Pipe Roll Soc., 1950, with late James Tait); Historical Research in Medieval England, 1951; The Making of Domesday Book, 1961; The Historian at Work, 1962; An Introduction to the Study of History, 1964. *Recreation:* golf. *Address:* 20a Bradmore Road, Oxford OX2 6QP.

*See also J. H. Galbraith.*

**GALE, Arthur James Victor,** MA; *b* 10 Feb. 1895; *s* of James Webb and Emma Gale; *m* 1929, Gwendoline Veysey; one *s* one *d*. *Educ:* Latymer Upper Sch.; Selwyn Coll., Cambridge (Scholar). Special Brigade, RE, 1915-18; Asst Editor of Nature, 1920-38; Joint Editor, 1939-61. FPhysSoc.; Mem. Brit. Soc. Hist. Sci.; Pres., Selwyn Coll. Assoc., 1967-68. *Address:* 36 Elmwood Road, W4.

**GALE, Ernest Frederick,** FRS 1953; BSc London; BA, PhD, ScD Cantab; Professor of Chemical Microbiology, University of Cambridge, since 1960; Fellow of St John's College, Cambridge; *b* 15 July 1914; *s* of Nellie Annie and Ernest Francis Edward Gale; *m* 1937, Eiry Mair Jones; one *s*. *Educ:* St John's Coll. Cambridge (Scholar). Research in biochemistry, Cambridge, from 1936; Senior Student, Royal Commn for Exhibition of 1851, 1939; Beit Memorial Fellow, 1941; Scientific Staff of Med. Research Council, 1943; Reader in chemical Microbiology, University of Cambridge, 1948-60; Dir, Medical Research Council Unit for Chemical Microbiology, 1948-62. Herter Lecturer, Johns Hopkins Hosp., Baltimore, USA, 1948; Commonwealth Travelling Fellow, Hanna Lecturer, Western Reserve Univ., 1951; Harvey Lectr, New York, 1955; Leeuwenhoek Lectr Royal

Society, London, 1956; Visiting Fellow, Australian National Univ., 1964-65. Malcolm Lectr, Syracuse Univ., 1967. Meetings Sec., Society for General Microbiology, 1954-58, International Representative, 1963-67 (Pres., 1967-69); Mem. Food Investigation Board, 1954-58; Mem. International Union of Biochemistry Commission on Enzymes, 1957-61. *Publications:* Chemical Activities of Bacteria, 1947. Scientific papers in Biochem. Journal, Journal of General Microbiology, Advances in Enzymology, Advances in Protein Chemistry, etc. *Recreations:* photography, disliking gardening. *Address:* Department of Biochemistry, University of Cambridge. *T:* Cambridge 51781; 25 Luard Road, Cambridge. *T:* Cambridge 47585.

**GALE, Lt-Gen. Sir Humfrey Myddelton,** KBE 1943 (CBE 1940); CB 1942; CVO 1943; MC; *b* 4 Oct. 1890; *e s* of Ernest Sewell Gale, Architect, Tile Cottage, Liphook; *m* 1917, Winifred (*d* 1936), 2nd *d* of William Cross; two *d*; *m* 1945, Minnie Grace (*d* 1970), widow of Charles Louis, Prince de Beauvau Craon (*d* 1942), and *d* of Count Gregorini-Bingham of Bologna. *Educ:* St Paul's Sch.; RMC, Sandhurst. Commissioned ASC 1911; served European War, 1914-18; GSO2, Staff Coll., Camberley, 1934-37; Col, 1937; Maj.-Gen., 1941; Temp. Lt-Gen. 1944; Dep. Chief of Staff and Chief Admin. Officer under Gen. Eisenhower, 1942-45; Personal Rep. in Europe of Dir.-Gen., UNRRA, 1945-47; retired pay, 1947. Chm., Basildon New Town Develt Corp., 1954-64. Col Comdt RASC, 1944-54; Col Comdt Army Catering Corps, 1946-58. Chief Commander Legion of Merit and DSM (USA); Officer, Legion of Honour. *Address:* 1 l'Avenue de Sully, La Tour de Peilz, Vaud, Switzerland. *Club:* United Service.

**GALE, Malcolm,** CBE 1964 (MBE 1948); HM Diplomatic Service, retired; Representative of N. M. Rothschild & Sons for Argentine and Chile, since 1970; *b* 31 Aug. 1909; *s* of late George Alfred Gale and late Agnes Logan Gale (*née* Ruthven); *m* 1st, 1932, Doris Frances Wells; 2nd, 1936, Ilse Strauss; one *s* one *d*. *Educ:* Sedbergh; Madrid Univ. Market Officer, Santiago, 1945; Third Sec., Dec. 1947; Second Sec. (Commercial), Caracas, 1948; First Sec. (Commercial), 1952; First Sec. (Commercial), Ankara, 1953; Actg Counsellor (Commercial), 1954; First Sec. (Commercial), Bahrein, 1955; Consul (Commercial), Milan, 1958; Acting Consul-Gen., Milan, 1958 and 1959; Counsellor, 1959; Counsellor (Commercial): Washington, 1960-64; Lisbon, 1964-67; Minister (Commercial) Buenos Aires, 1967-69. *Recreations:* golf, photography. *Address:* Casilla 5130, Correo Central, Buenos Aires, Argentine.

**GALE, General Sir Richard Nelson,** GCB 1954 (KCB 1953; CB 1945); KBE 1950 (OBE 1940); DSO 1944; MC 1918; *b* 25 July 1896; *s* of late Wilfred Gale and Helen Webber Ann, *d* of Joseph Nelson, Townsville, Qld, Australia; *m* 1st, 1924, Ethel Maude Larnack (*d* 1952), *d* of Mrs Jessie Keene, Hove; no *c*; 2nd, 1953, Daphne Mabelle Eveline, *d* of late Francis Blick, Stroud, Glos. *Educ:* Aldenham; RMC, Sandhurst. 2nd Lieut Worcestershire Regt, 1915; Captain DCLI 1930; Major, Royal Inniskilling Fusiliers, 1938; Lt-Col Sept. 1939; Brig. 1941; Maj.-Gen. 1946; act. Lt-Gen. 1945; Lt-Gen. 1947; Gen. 1952; raised and commanded the 1st Parachute Brigade; commanded 6th British Airborne Div.; Deputy Commander 1st Allied Airborne Army, 1945; Commander 1st British Airborne Corps, 1945; 1st Inf. Div. 1946-47; GOC British Troops, Egypt and Mediterranean Command, 1948-49; Dir-Gen. of Military Training, War Office, 1949-52; Commander-in-Chief, Northern Army Group, Allied Land Forces Europe and British Army of the Rhine, 1952-57; retired 1957; re-employed NATO 1958; Dep. Supreme Allied Comdr, Europe, 1958-60. ADC (General) to the Queen, 1954-57; Col, The Worcestershire Regt, 1950-61; Col Comdt, The Parachute Regt, 1956-61. Comdr Legion of Merit (US); Comdr Legion of Honour, Croix de Guerre with palm (France). *Publications:* With the 6th Airborne Division in Normandy; Call to Arms; Great Battles of Biblical History; The Worcestershire Regiment, 1970. *Recreations:* yachting; principal interest Eastern and Central Asian affairs. *Address:* 6 Meadow Way, Seaford, Sussex. *Club:* Army and Navy.

**GALEA, Hon. Prof. Robert V.,** OBE 1936; (Hon.) LLD Bristol; DSc; Vice-Chancellor and Rector Magnificus of the Royal University of Malta, 1934-48; Architect and Civil Engineer; *b* Malta, 11 Jan. 1882; *s* of late Annetto Galea, *m* 1908, Mary, *d* of late Chevalier Francesco d'Ancona; one *s* two *d*. *Educ:* Malta. Matriculated with honours; completed a theoretical course of Engineering and Architecture, 1904; has practical experience in England and on the Continent, 1905, 1906; Lecturer on Engineering and Architecture, and Teacher of Architectural, Topographical and Industrial Drawing, Malta Univ. 1905-15; Professor of Engineering and Architecture and Mem. of General Council of the Univ., 1915-34; acted as Rector of the Univ. and Dir of the Museum, 1923; MLA Valletta District, 1924-33; Minister for Health, Malta, 1927-32, and also Minister for the Treasury, 1929-32; Malta Delegate at the Conference of the Empire Parliamentary Association held in Canada in 1928; acting Prime Minister, June-Nov. 1930; elected for Legistlative Assembly and for the Senate, 1932; Leader of the Opposition in the Legislative Assembly, 1932-33; Leader of the Constitutional Party, 1950-53; MLA, elected in 1950 and 1951; Mem. (later Chm.), Nat. Service Appeals Cttee, 1940-45; Chm. Deleg. from Royal Univ. of Malta to Congress of Universities of the Commonwealth, Oxford, 1948; Chm. of Technical Reconstruction Board in charge of Reconstruction Dept, 1943-46; Mem. of Inter-University Council for Higher Education in the Colonies, 1946-48; holds title of Honourable for Life; King's Jubilee Medal, 1935; Coronation Medal, 1937. Officier d'Académie, 1948. *Address:* 3 Balluta Buildings, St Julian's, Malta. *Clubs:* Royal Commonwealth Society; Royal Over-Seas League; Casino Maltese (Malta).

**GALIPEAULT, Hon. Antonin,** QC 1910; BA, LLL, LLD; resigned as Judge, Province of Quebec, 1961; now practising as counsel-lawyer; late head of the firm Galipeault, Lapointe & Boisvert, advocates, 80 St Peter Street, Quebec; Batonnier of the Quebec Bar, 1921, 1922, 1923 and 1924, and Batonnier General of the Province of Quebec, 1923 and 1924; Dir, Quebec Technical Sch., of the Quebec Land Company, of the Limoilou Land Company, of the Sun Trust Company, of the Montmagny Electric Power Company; President of la Traverse de Levis Limitée; Dir Brasserie Champlain Limited; *b* Maskinongé, 7 Aug. 1879; *s* of Louis Edouard Galipeault, Notary, and Caroline Ratelle; *m* 1903, Ernestine, *d* of Elzéar Lamontagne, Montreal; three *s* one *d*. *Educ:* College of Joliette; Laval Univ. Called to Bar, Province of Quebec, 1900; began business as member of the firm of Lane & Galipeault; head of firm Galipeault, St-Laurent, Gagné, Métayer & Devlin, 1909-30; Contested (L) Legislative Assembly, County of Maskinongé, 1904; Alderman of Quebec, 1906 and 1908; MLA Bellechasse 1909-30;

Deputy Speaker of the Legislative Assembly, 1914; Chm. of Cttees, 1914; Speaker of the Legislative Assembly, 1916; Minister of Public Works and Labour, 1919-30. Judge of Court of Appeals, Quebec, from 1930; Chief Justice of Queen's Bench, Province of Quebec, with title and quality of Chief Justice for Prov. Quebec, 1950-61; also apptd Administrator for Govt of Quebec. Roman Catholic. *Address:* 565 Grande Allée, East Quebec City, Quebec, Canada. *Clubs:* Garrison, Reform (Quebec); Reform, Canadian (Montreal); Laurentide Fish and Game.

**GALLAGHER, Francis George Kenna,** CMG 1963; HM Diplomatic Service; Assistant Under-Secretary of State, Foreign and Commonwealth Office, since 1968; *b* 25 May 1917; *er s* of George and Johanna Gallagher. *Educ:* St Joseph's Coll.; King's Coll., University of London (LLB (Hons)). Clerical officer, Min. of Agric., 1935-38; Asst Examr, Estate Duty Office, 1938-44; served in HM Forces, 1941-45; Examr, Estate Duty Office, 1944-45; apptd a Mem., HM Foreign (subseq. Diplomatic) Service, 1945; Vice-Consul Marseilles, 1946-48; Acting Consul-Gen., there, in 1947; HM Embassy, Paris, 1948-50; FO, 1950-53; First Sec., HM Embassy, Damascus, 1953-55; acted as Chargé d'Affaires, 1953, 1954 and 1955; FO, 1955; appointed Counsellor and Head of European Economic Organisations Dept, 1960; Counsellor (Commercial), HM Embassy, Berne, 1963-65; acted as Chargé d'Affaires (Berne) in 1963 and 1964; Head of Western Economic Dept, CO, 1965-67, of Common Market Dept, 1967-68. *Recreations:* music, chess. *Address:* 26 Kensington Court, W8. *T:* 01-937 7930; The Old Courthouse, Kirkwhelpington, Northumberland. *Club:* Travellers'.

**GALLAGHER, Francis Heath; Hon. Mr Justice Gallagher,** CMG 1957; Coal Industry Tribunal (Australia) since 1947; Presidential Mem. Commonwealth Conciliation and Arbitration Commn since 1957; *b* 10 Feb. 1905; *s* of James Gallagher; *m* 1938, Heather Elizabeth Clark; no *c. Educ:* Sydney Grammar Sch.; University of Sydney. BA 1929, LLB 1933, University of Sydney. Admitted as solicitor, Supreme Court of NSW, 1933. Mem. of Industrial Commn of NSW 1955-57. *Recreations:* reading, gardening, sailing, surfing. *Address:* 2 Foam Crest Avenue, Newport Beach, NSW, Australia. *T:* XX 1724. *Clubs:* Royal Prince Alfred Yacht, Turf (Sydney).

**GALLAGHER, Prof. John Andrew;** Vere Harmsworth Professor of Imperial and Naval History, University of Cambridge, since 1970; *b* 1 April 1919; *o c* of Joseph and Mary Adeline Gallagher; unmarried. *Educ:* Birkenhead Institute; Trinity Coll., Cambridge (MA). Major Schol., Trinity Coll., Cambridge, 1937. Royal Tank Regt, 1939-45. Fellow of Trinity Coll., Cambridge, 1948-63 (Dean of Coll., 1960-63); University Lectr in History, Cambridge, 1953-63; Beit Prof. of History of British Commonwealth, Oxford, and Fellow of Balliol Coll., 1963-70. Rockefeller Foundn Fellow, 1957. *Publications:* Africa and the Victorians (with R. E. Robinson), 1961; chapters in New Cambridge Modern History, volumes VII and XI; articles in learned jls. *Address:* Department of History, Cambridge.

**GALLAHER, Patrick Edmund;** Chairman, Wales Gas Board, since 1970; *b* 17 June 1917; *s* of late Cormac Brenden Gallaher and of Agnes Mary Wyer; *m* 1947, Louise Hatfield (*d* 1965); one *s* two *d. Educ:* St Philip's Grammar School and College of Technology, Birmingham. Chemist and Engineer, City of Birmingham Gas Dept, 1934-46; Asst Engineer, Redditch Gas Co., 1946-49. With West Midlands Gas Board: Engineer and Manager, Redditch, 1949-53; Divisional Engineer, 1953-62; Regional Distribution Engineer, 1962-64; Distribution Controller, 1964-66; Area Construction Engineer, 1966-67; Area Distribution Engineer, 1967-68. Dep. Chairman, Wales Gas Board, 1968-70. *Recreations:* sailing, gardening, travel. *Address:* 1 Windsor Road, Radyr, Cardiff. *T:* Cardiff 842403.

**GALLEGHAN, Brig. Sir Frederick (Gallagher),** Kt 1969; DSO 1942; OBE 1946; ISO 1959; ED 1937; Chairman NSW Services Canteens Trust Fund, since 1963; *b* 11 Jan. 1897; *s* of Alexander Galleghan; *m* 1st, 1922, Vera Florence Dawson (decd); 2nd, 1969, Persia Elspbeth Porter, *née* Blaiklock. *Educ:* Cooks Hill High Sch., Newcastle, NSW. Commissioned Aust. Cadet Corps, 1913. Served in AIF, 34th Bn, European War, 1914-18. Comd 2nd Bn, 1932-35, and 2/35 Bn, 1935-37, Newcastle, NSW; Comd 17 Bn, N Sydney, 1937-40. Served War of 1939-45: Comd 2/30 Bn 1940-42; first Aust. unit to engage Japanese, Malaya (DSO); POW, 1942-45: Comd AIF P's W, Malaya, and Dep. Comdr Allied P's W, Malaya, 1942-45; Comd Changi POW Camp, 1944-45 (OBE). Promoted Brig., 1945 (as from 1942), on return to Australia; Head, Aust. Mil. Mission to Germany, 1947-50 (Temp. Maj.-Gen.); retired 1959. Hon. Col 34 Bn, 1957-60; Hon. Col Aust. Cadet Corps, 1959-64. *Recreations:* reading, lawn bowls. *Address:* 68 Avenue Road, Mosman, NSW 2088, Australia. *T:* 969-6865. *Club:* Imperial Service (Sydney).

**GALLEY, Robert Albert Ernest,** PhD; FRIC; Director, Shell Research Ltd, Woodstock Agricultural Research Centre, Sittingbourne, Kent, 1960-69; *b* 23 Oct. 1909; *s* of John and Jane A. Galley; *m* 1933, Elsie Marjorie Walton; one *s* two *d. Educ:* Colfe's Gram. Sch.; Imperial Coll., London. BSc 1930, PhD 1932, FRIC 1944. Research Chemist, Wool Industries Research Assoc., 1932-34; Chemist, Dept of War Department Chemist, 1934-37; Lectr, Sir John Cass Coll., 1937-39; Prin. Exper. Officer, Min. of Supply, Chemical Inspectorate, 1939-45, Flax Establishment, 1945-46; Sen. Prin. Scientific Officer, Agric. Research Council (Sec. Interdepartmental Insecticides Cttees), 1946-50; seconded to Scientific Secretariat, Office of Lord Pres. of Council, 1950-52; Dir, Tropical Products Institute, Dept of Scientific and Industrial Research (formerly Colonial Products Laboratory), 1953-60. *Publications:* papers in Journal of Chem. Soc., Chemistry and Industry, World Crops, etc. *Recreations:* tennis, gardening, sailing. *Address:* Swanton Old House, Bredgar, near Sittingbourne, Kent. *Club:* Farmers'.

**GALLICO, Paul W(illiam);** author and journalist; fiction writer, novelist, screen writer; *b* New York City, 26 July 1897; *s* of Paolo Gallico, Mantua, Lombardy, and Hortense Erlich, Vienna; *m* 1st, 1921, Alva Thoits Taylor (marr. diss., 1934); two *s* (and one *s* decd); 2nd, 1935, Elaine St John (marr. diss., 1936); 3rd, 1939, Pauline Gariboldi (marr. diss., 1954); 4th, 1963, Baroness Virginia Falz-Fein. *Educ:* Columbia Univ. (BS). Served European War, 1914-18; Gunner's Mate, USNR Force, 1918 (Victory Medal, 1918); served War of 1939-45: Amer. Expeditionary Force, European Theatre (Ribbon with battle star, 1945); War Correspondent, Cosmopolitan Magazine, 1944. Sports Editor, Columnist, Assistant Managing Editor, New York Daily News, New York, 1922-36. Film scripts include: Never Take No for an Answer (from the book The Small Miracle); Pride of the Yankees; The

Clock; Lili. *Publications:* Adventures of Hiram Holliday, 1939; The Snow Goose, 1941; The Lonely, 1947; Jennie, 1950; Trial by Terror, 1952; The Small Miracle, 1952; Snowflake, 1952; The Foolish Immortals, 1953; Love of Seven Dolls, 1954; Ludmila, 1955; Thomasina, 1957; The Steadfast Man (a life of St Patrick), 1958; Flowers For Mrs Harris, 1958; The Hurricane Story, 1959; Mrs Harris Goes to New York, 1960; Too Many Ghosts, 1961; Confessions of a Story-Teller, 1961; Scruffy, 1962; Coronation, 1962; The Day the Guinea Pig Talked, 1963; Love, Let Me Not Hunger, 1963; The Hand of Mary Constable, 1964; Mrs Harris, MP, 1965; The Day Jean-Pierre Went Round the World, 1965; The Man Who was Magic, 1966; The Story of Silent Night, 1967; Manxmouse, 1968; The Poseidon Adventure, 1969; The Day Jean-Pierre joined the Circus, 1969; Matilda, 1970. *Recreation:* fencing. *Address:* 69 Great Russell Street, WC1. *Clubs:* Lansdowne, Epée, Buck's.

**GALLIE, Prof. Walter Bryce;** Professor of Political Science, and Fellow of Peterhouse, Cambridge University, since Oct. 1967; *b* 5 Oct. 1912; 3rd *s* of Walter S. Gallie, structural engineer, The Tower, Lenzie, Dunbartonshire; *m* 1940, Menna Humphreys; one *s* one *d*. *Educ:* Sedbergh Sch.; Balliol Coll., Oxford (Classical Exhibitioner). BA (1st Cl. PPE), 1934, BLitt 1937, MA Oxon, 1947. University Coll. of Swansea; Asst Lectr, Philosophy, 1935; Lectr, 1938; Sen. Lectr, 1948; Prof. of Philosophy, University Coll. of North Staffordshire 1950; Prof. of Logic and Metaphysics, Queen's Univ., Belfast, 1954-67. Visiting Prof., New York Univ., 1962-63; Lewis Fry Memorial Lecturer, Bristol Univ., 1964. Served War, 1940-45, ending with rank of Major, Croix de Guerre, 1945. *Publications:* An English School, 1949; Peirce and Pragmatism, 1952; Free Will and Determinism Yet Again (Inaugural Lecture), 1957; A New University: A. D. Lindsay and the Keele Experiment, 1960; Philosophy and the Historical Understanding, 1964; articles in Mind, Aristotelian Soc. Proc., Philosophy, French Studies, etc. *Recreations:* travelling and reading. *Address:* 38 Parkside, Cambridge.

**GALLOWAY,** 12th Earl of, *cr* 1623; **Randolph Algernon Ronald Stewart;** Lord Garlies, 1607; Bt 1627; Baron Stewart of Garlies (Great Britain), 1796; *s* of 11th Earl and Amy Mary Pauline (*d* 1942), *d* of Anthony John Cliffe of Bellevue, Co. Wexford; *b* 21 Nov. 1892. *S* father, 1920; *m* 1924, Philippa Fendall, *d* of late J. Wendell, New York; one *s* one *d*. *Educ:* Harrow; RMC, Sandhurst. Gazetted Scots Guards, 1913; served European War, 1914-15 (prisoner); Hon. Attaché, HM Legation at Berne, 1918; ADC to Military Governor at Cologne, 1919; Lt-Col commanding 7th (Galloway) Bn KOSB, 1939-40, now Hon. Col; JP Kirkcudbrightshire; Lord-Lieutenant of Kirkcudbrightshire since 1932. Grand Master Mason of Scotland, 1945-49. *Heir: s* Lord Garlies, *qv*. *Address:* Cumloden, Newton-Stewart, Kirkcudbrightshire. *Clubs:* St James', Carlton; New (Edinburgh).
*See also Sir Mark Dalrymple.*

**GALLOWAY, Bishop of, (RC),** since 1952; **Rt. Rev. Joseph McGee;** *b* 13 Dec. 1904; *s* of Denis McGee and Sarah McGlinchey. *Educ:* St Dominic's Sch. and Morrison's Academy, Crieff; Blair's Coll., Aberdeen; Royal Scots Coll., Valladolid. Formerly Vicar-General and Canon (Penitentiary) of Dunkeld. *Address:* Candida Casa, 8 Corsehill Road, Ayr. *T:* Ayr 66750.

**GALLOWAY, Lt-Gen. Sir Alexander,** KBE 1949 (CBE 1941); CB 1946; DSO 1941; MC 1918; retired; *b* 3 Nov. 1895; *yr s* of late Rev. A. and Mrs Galloway, Minto Manse, Harwick and Broadstone, Dunbar, Scotland; *m* 1920, Dorothy Hadden White; three *s*. *Educ:* King William's Coll. Served European War, 1914-18, Gallipoli, Egypt, Palestine, France, Belgium, 1914-19 (despatches, MC, 1914-15 Star, two medals); War of 1939-45, Middle East, Italy, North-West Europe (despatches twice, CBE, DSO, CB); GOC 30th Corps BAOR, 1946; GOC-in-C Malaya Command, 1946-47; High Commissioner and C-in-C, British Troops in Austria, 1947-50; retired, 1950. Chm., Jordan Development Bank, 1951-52; subsequently joined firm of Richard Costain Ltd, Building & Civil Engineering Contractors. 1st cl. Mil. Cross of Greece and of Czechoslovakia, Orders of Merit and White Lion of Czechoslovakia, Order of Orange-Nassau (Netherlands). *Address:* Whitsome Lea, Berwickshire, Scotland.

**GALLOWAY, Lt-Col Arnold Crawshaw,** CIE 1946; OBE 1941; *b* 1901; *o s* of late Percy Christopher Galloway; *m* 1946, Mary, *d* of Arthur William Odgers, Oxford; three *s*. *Educ:* City of London Sch.; RMC. Entered Indian Political Service, 1928; Under-Sec. Rajputana, 1929-30; Vice-Consul, Ahwaz, Persia, 1930-31; Vice-Consul, Zahidan, Persia, 1932-33; Under-Sec. to Resident, Persian Gulf, 1934; Sec., British Legation, Kabul, Afghanistan, 1935-36; Sec. to Polit. Resident, Persian Gulf, 1937-38; Polit. Agent, Kuwait, Persian Gulf, 1939-41; Polit. Advr to British Forces in Iraq and Persia, 1941-43 (despatches); Consul-Gen., Ahwaz, 1943-44; Polit. Agent, Muscat, 1944-45; Polit. Resident, Persian Gulf, 1945; Polit. Agent, Bahrein, 1945-47; Consul-Gen., Bushire, 1947; Polit. Agent, Kuwait, 1948-49; UK Repres. of Bahrain Petroleum Company Ltd, 1950-68; Chm., Middle East Navigation Aids Service, 1958-68. *Address:* Yeo House, Long Load, near Langport, Somerset. *T:* Long Sutton 329. *Club:* Flyfishers'.

**GALLOWAY, Maj.-Gen. Rudolf William,** CB 1944; CBE 1943; DSO 1919; MB, ChB; late RAMC; retired, 1950; *b* 22 July 1891; *s* of late Dr Alexander Rudolf Galloway, OBE, Aberdeen; *m* 1930, Lois Mary Kerr, *yr d* of Lt-Col A. Leaning, DSO; one *d* (one *s* decd). *Educ:* Aberdeen Grammar Sch.; Aberdeen Univ. Served European War, 1914-19 (despatches twice, DSO); Iraq, 1923; War of 1939-45 (despatches twice, CBE, CB). Hon. Surg. to King George VI (KHS). *Publication:* Anatomy and Physiology of Physical Training, 1937. *Recreation:* writing. *Address:* 29 Brae Court, Kingston Hill, Surrey. *T:* Kingston 5363.

**GALLWEY, Sir Philip (Frankland) Payne-,** 6th Bt, *cr* 1812; *b* 15 March 1935; *s* of late Lt-Col Lowry Philip Payne-Gallwey, OBE, MC and of Janet, *d* of late Albert Philip Payne-Gallwey; *S* cousin, 1964. *Educ:* Eton; Royal Military Academy, Sandhurst. Lieut, 11th Hussars, 1957. *Recreations:* hunting, shooting, golf. *Heir: kinsman* Lt-Col (retd) Peter Payne-Gallwey, DSO, 11th Hussars [*b* 27 July 1906; *m* 1953, Ann Josephine, *d* of Roger John Kinloch Barber-Starkey; one *d*]. *Address:* The Little House, Boxford, Newbury, Berks. *T:* Boxford 315. *Club:* Cavalry.

**GALPERN, Sir Myer,** Kt 1960; DL; JP; MP (Lab) Shettleston Division of Glasgow since Oct. 1959; house furnisher; *b* 1903. *Educ:* Glasgow Univ. Mem. of Glasgow Corporation; JP for Glasgow. Lord Provost of Glasgow and Lord Lieut for the County of the City of Glasgow, 1958-59. Mem. of the Court of Glasgow Univ.; Mem., Advisory Cttee on Education in Scotland. DL, Co. of City of

Glasgow, 1962. *Address:* House of Commons, SW1; 219 Nithsdale Road, Glasgow S1.

**GALPIN, Sir Albert James,** KCVO 1968 (MVO, 4th class 1958; 5th class 1945); CBE 1963 (OBE 1953); Secretary, Lord Chamberlain's Office, 1955-68; Serjeant-at-Arms to the Queen, 1955-68; *b* 1903; *s* of C. A. Galpin; *m* 1930, Vera, *d* of J. Tiller; one *s* one *d.* Entered Lord Chamberlain's Office, 1936; Asst Sec., 1941. *Recreation:* scouting. *Address:* Alderman's Cottage, Knowl Hill, Reading, Berks. *T:* Littlewick Green 2637.

**GALSWORTHY, Sir Arthur (Norman),** KCMG 1967 (CMG 1953); British High Commissioner in New Zealand since 1969, in Tonga and Western Samoa (non-resident), since 1970; *b* 1 July 1916; *s* of late Captain Arthur Galsworthy and late Violet Gertrude Harrison; *m* 1940, Margaret Agnes Hiscocks; two *s. Educ:* Emanuel Sch.; Corpus Christi Coll., Cambridge. Entered Colonial Office as Asst Principal, Administrative Grade, Oct. 1938. On active service, Dec. 1939-Dec. 1945: enlisted Royal Fusiliers, Sept. 1939; commnd in DCLI, 1940; attached Intelligence Corps, 1941; N Africa (First Army), 1942-43; Captain 1942; Sicily and Italy (Eighth Army), 1943-44; Major 1943; GSO1 with HQ, 21 Army Gp, 1944-45. Returned to Colonial Office, Dec. 1945; Asst Sec. in charge of International Relations Dept of Colonial Office, 1947-51; Chief Sec., West African Inter-Territorial Secretariat, Accra, 1951-54; in charge of Colonial Office Finance Dept, 1954-56; Asst Under-Sec. of State, 1956-65; Dep. Under-Sec. of State, Colonial Office, 1965-66, Commonwealth Office, 1966-68, Foreign and Commonwealth Office, 1968-69. *Recreations:* fishing, bird-watching. *Address:* British High Commission, PO Box 1812, Wellington, New Zealand. *Club:* Oxford and Cambridge University.

*See also J. E. Galsworthy.*

**GALSWORTHY, John Edgar,** CMG 1968; Minister, European Economic Affairs, Paris, since 1970; *b* 19 June 1919; *s* of Arthur Galsworthy; *m* 1942, Jennifer Ruth Johnstone; one *s* three *d. Educ:* Emanuel Sch.; Corpus Christi Coll., Cambridge. HM Forces 1939-41; Foreign Office, 1941-46; Third Sec., Madrid, 1946; Second Sec., Vienna, 1949; First Sec., Athens, 1951; Foreign Office, 1954; Bangkok, 1958; Counsellor, Brussels (UK Delegation to EEC) 1962; Counsellor (Economic), Bonn, 1964-67, Paris, 1967-70. *Recreation:* fishing. *Address:* c/o Foreign and Commonwealth Office, SW1. *Club:* Oxford and Cambridge University.

*See also Sir Arthur Galsworthy.*

**GALWAY,** 9th Viscount, *cr* 1727; **Simon George Robert Monckton-Arundell,** Baron Killard 1727; Baron Monckton (UK) 1887; DL; *b* 11 Nov. 1929; *o s* of 8th Viscount and Hon. Lucia White, *yr d* of 3rd Baron Annaly; *S* father, 1943; *m* 1953, Hon. Teresa Jane Fox-Strangways, *o d* of 7th Earl of Ilchester; one *d. Educ:* Eton. Commissioned in The Life Guards 1948; retd; Major 1960. DL Nottinghamshire, 1963. *Heir: kinsman* William Arundell Monckton, *b* 1894. *Address:* Bishopfield House, Bawtry, Doncaster, Yorks. *T:* Ranskill 224. *Clubs:* White's, Buck's.

**GALWAY and KILMACDUAGH, Bishop of, (RC),** since 1937; **Most Rev. Michael Browne,** DD, DCL, Apostolic Administrator of Kilfenora; *s* of Michael Browne, Westport, Co. Mayo. *Educ:* St Jarlath's Coll., Tuam; St Patrick's Coll., Maynooth. BA Hons Classics, National Univ. of Ireland, 1916; ordained, 1920; DD Rome, 1921; DCL 1924; Prof. of Theology Maynooth, from 1921; Sec. Maynooth Union, 1929-37; Mem. of Senate, Nat. University of Ireland, 1934; Chm. of State Commission on Vocational Organisation. *Publications:* various articles in Irish Ecclesiastical Record on Theological subjects. *Address:* Mount St Mary's, Galway.

**GAMAGE, Sir Leslie,** Kt 1959; MA; MC; FCIS; Chairman and Managing Director General Electric Co. Ltd, 1957-60; *b* 5 May 1887; 2nd *s* of A. W. Gamage; *m* 1919, Hon. Muriel Elsie Hirst, DStJ (*d* 1969), *er d* of late Baron Hirst; no *c. Educ:* Marlborough; Exeter Coll., Oxford (Senior Scholar, Hons Degree). MA 1910; training for Law, 1910-14; Hons in Solicitors' Final Exam.; served in European War, 1914-18; Captain and Adjt 24th London Regt (MC, twice wounded and finally prisoner); with Gen. Electric Co. Ltd, 1919-60, first as Sec., then Dir, Gen. Manager, and Managing Dir; specialised in export and travelled widely in Empire; Pres.: Chartered Institute of Secretaries in its Jubilee Year, 1941; Institute of Export, 1942-58; Master Company of Glaziers, 1942; Royal Pinner Foundn (formerly Royal Commercial Travellers' Schs), 1950-70; Chief Business Adviser, Min. of Civil Aviation, 1947-60; Pres. of British Electrical and Allied Manufacturers' Association (BEAMA), 1959-60. CStJ. *Recreation:* golf. *Address:* Springmead, Ascot, Berks. *T:* Ascot 23619. *Club:* Buck's.

**GAMBIER-PARRY, Maj.-Gen. Michael Denman,** MC 1916; retired; *b* 21 Aug. 1891; *e s* of late Sidney Gambier-Parry and of Grace Gambier-Parry (*née* Denman), Duntisbourne Rous, Cirencester, Glos; *m* 1918, Barbara Evelyn, *e d* of late Captain H. M. Tufnell, Fairfields, Hatfield Peverell, Essex; one *s* two *d. Educ:* Eton; RMC, Sandhurst. Commissioned Royal Welch Fusiliers, 1911; Captain 1914; served European War, 1914-18, Gallipoli and Mesopotamia (6 mentions), Bt Major, 1917; temp. Lt-Col, 1917; psc, 1924; transferred Royal Tank Corps, 1924; Major, 1925; Bt Lt-Col, 1929; Lt-Col, 1935; War of 1939-45: Brig., Malaya Inf. Bde, 1938-40; ADC to King George VI, 1939-40; Maj.-Gen. 1940; Head of Military Mission to Greek Army (temp.), 1940; GOC, 2 Armoured Div., 1941; POW, Italy, 1941-43; retired 1944. DL Wilts, 1952-54; Mem. of Council Royal College of Music, 1951; FRCM 1961. *Address:* Forest Gate, Poundgate, near Crowborough, Sussex. *Club:* United Service.

*See also Edgar T. Williams.*

**GAMBLE, Rev. Arthur Mellor;** Rector of Cley-next-the-Sea with Wiveton, since 1958, of Letheringsett with Glandford, since 1969; Head Master of Denstone College, 1941-57, retired; *b* 6 Feb. 1899; *s* of late P. A. Gamble, Morton; *m* 1924, Doris Mary, 2nd *d* of late Percy Evershed, The Plantation, Norwich; one *s* two *s. Educ:* Shrewsbury Sch. (Schol.); Oriel Coll., Oxford. Served European War in Royal Engineers in France and Belgium, 1917-19; Asst Master, Gresham's Sch., Holt, 1922; Housemaster, 1930. Ordained Deacon, March 1958, Priest, Sept. 1958. Mem. Diocesan Council for Education. *Recreations:* usual; OUAFC and Corinthians FC 1921. *Address:* Wiveton Rectory, Holt, Norfolk.

**GAMBLE, Sir David Arthur Josias,** 4th Bt *cr* 1897; *b* 9 Dec. 1907; *e s* of Sir David Gamble, 3rd Bt and Eveline Frances Josephine (*d* 1952), 2nd *d* of late Rev. Arthur R. Cole; *S* father, 1943; *m* 1st, 1932, Elinor Mary (Molly) (*d* 1961), *o d* of Henry E. Cole, Summers, Long Sutton, Hants; one *s*; 2nd, 1965, Evelyn Gamble. *Educ:* Shrewsbury; Wadham Coll., Oxford. BA 1930, MA 1945. Colonial Service,

1930-32; Farmer, 1932-49. Chm. Cirencester RDC, 1958-59. *Heir:* *s* David Gamble [*b* 5 June 1933; *m* 1956, Dawn Adrienne Stuart; one *s* two *d*]. *Address:* Wood End, Tregony, nr Truro, Cornwall.

**GAMBLE, Sir (Frederick) Herbert,** KBE 1964; CMG 1955; HM Ambassador to Bolivia, 1964-67; *b* 21 May 1907; *s* of Frederick West Gamble and Edith (*née* Moore); *m* 1942, Janine Corbisier de Cobreville; two *d*. *Educ:* Portora Royal School, Enniskillen; Trinity Coll., Dublin. Entered Levant Consular Service, Nov. 1930; HM Consul, Suez, 1945-46; Commercial Counsellor, Bagdad, 1948-52; Commercial Counsellor, Athens, 1952-55; Ambassador to Ecuador, 1955-59; HM Consul-Gen., Los Angeles, 1959-64. *Recreations:* tennis, golf. *Address:* Santana, Delgany, Co. Wicklow, Ireland. *Club:* Travellers'.

**GAMBLE, Sir Herbert;** *see* Gamble, Sir F. H.

**GAMES, Abram,** OBE 1958; RDI 1959; graphic designer; *b* 29 July 1914; *s* of Joseph and Sarah Games; *m* 1945, Marianne Salfeld; one *s* two *d*. *Educ:* Grocers' Company Sch., Hackney Downs. Studio, 1932-36; freelance designer, 1936-40. Infantry, 1940-41; War Office Poster Designer, 1941-46. Freelance, 1946-; Lecturer Royal College of Art, 1947-53. Postage Stamps for Great Britain and Israel, Festival of Britain, BBC Television, Queen's Award to Industry Emblems. One-man shows of graphic design: London, New York, Chicago, Brussels, Stockholm, Jerusalem, Tel Aviv, São Paulo. Rep. Gt Brit. at Museum of Modern Art, New York; first prizes, Poster Competitions: Helsinki, 1957; Lisbon, 1959; New York, 1960; Stockholm, 1962, Barcelona, 1964; Design Medal, Soc. of Industrial Artists, 1960. Silver Medal, Royal Society of Arts, 1962. Inventor of Imagic Copying Processes. *Publication:* Over my Shoulder, 1960. *Recreations:* painting, travel, carpentry. *Address:* 41 The Vale, NW11. *T:* 01-458 2811.

**GAMINARA, Albert William,** CMG 1963; HMOCS (retired); *b* 1 Dec. 1913; *s* of late Albert Sidney Gaminara and late Katherine Helen Copeman; *m* 1947, Monica (*née* Watson); one *s* three *d*. *Educ:* City of London Sch.; St John's Coll., Cambridge; Oriel Coll., Oxford. MA Cantab 1943. Appointed to Sierra Leone as Administrative Cadet, 1936; seconded to Colonial Office as Principal, 1947-50; Transferred as Administrative Officer to N Rhodesia, 1950; Mem. of Legislative Council, 1963; Admin. Sec. to Govt of Northern Rhodesia (now Zambia), 1961-63; Sec. to the Cabinet, 1964, Adviser, Cabinet Office, Zambia, 1965. *Recreation:* riding. *Address:* Stratton House, Over Stratton, South Petherton, Somerset. *Clubs:* Royal Commonwealth Society, East India and Sports; Hawks (Cambridge).

**GAMMANS, Lady; (Ann Muriel);** FRSA; *d* of late Frank Paul, Warblington, Hants; *m* 1917, David Gammans, 1st and last Bt, *cr* 1955 (*d* 1957). *Educ:* Portsmouth High Sch. Travelled widely in the Far East, Europe and North America. Spent many years of her married life in Malaya and Japan. MP (C) Hornsey, 1957-66. Retired March 1966. *Recreation:* travel. *Address:* 19 Buckingham Palace Mansions, SW1. *T:* 01-730 4463. *Clubs:* Royal Commonwealth Society, (Assoc. Lady Member) Naval and Military.

**GAMMELL, Lt-Gen. Sir James (Andrew Harcourt),** KCB 1944 (CB 1940); DSO 1917; MC; *e s* of late Sir Sydney J. Gammell, Countesswells, Aberdeenshire; *b* 1892; *m* 1st, 1919, Gertrude (*d* 1960), *e d* of late Gilbert W. Don; two *s* two *d*; 2nd, 1964, Mrs Mary Kirkwood, *widow of* Comdr David Kirkwood, RN. *Educ:* Winchester; Pembroke Coll., Cambridge (BA, 2nd class Hons Hist. Trip.). Commission, Royal Field Artillery, Dec. 1912; served European War, 1914-18 (despatches 7 times, DSO, MC); promoted Major and transferred to QO Cameron Highlanders, 1927; Bt Lt-Col 1931; Instructor Staff Coll., Camberley, 1930-33; Lt-Col 1935; comd 1st Bn Queen's Own Cameron Highlanders, 1935-38; Col 1938; idc 1938; comd 4th Infantry Bde, 1938-40; Maj.-Gen. 1941; acting Lt-Gen., 1941; Temp. Lt-Gen., 1942; GOC-in-C Eastern Comd, 1942-43; Chief of Staff to Supreme Allied Comdr, Mediterranean Theatre, 1944; Lt-Gen. 1944; Representative of British Chiefs of Staff with USSR and Head of British Military Mission in Moscow, 1945; retd pay, 1946. DL Co. Angus, 1946. *Address:* Alrick, Glenisla, by Alyth, Perthshire. *T:* Glenisla 257. *Clubs:* Naval and Military; New (Edinburgh).

*See also C. M. Dalley, J. F. Gammell, J. C. Stormonth Darling.*

**GAMMELL, John Frederick,** MC 1943; MA; Headmaster of Repton School since 1968; *b* 31 Dec. 1921; 2nd *s* of Lieut-Gen. Sir James A. H. Gammell, *qv*; *m* 1947, Margaret Anne, *d* of Ralph Juckes, Fiddington Manor, Tewkesbury; two *s* one *d*. *Educ:* Winchester Coll.; Trinity Coll., Cambridge. MA 1953. Asst Master, Horris Hill, Newbury, 1940-41. War Service with KRRC, 1941-44; wounded, 1943; invalided out, 1944. Trinity Coll., Cambridge, 1946-47 (BA); Asst Master, Winchester Coll., 1944-45 and 1947-68; Exchange with Sen. Class. Master, Geelong Gram. Sch., Australia, 1949-50; Housemaster of Turner's, Winchester Coll., 1958-68. *Recreation:* friends. *Address:* The Hall, Repton, Derby DE6 6FH. *T:* (office) Repton 2375, (private) Repton 2187.

**GAMMON, John Charles,** OBE 1919; ACGI, MIStructE; President and Founder of Civil Engineering Companies; Gammon India Ltd, 1919; Gammon Malaya Ltd, 1924 (now Gammon South East Asia Berhad); Gammon Pakistan Ltd, 1947; Gammon East Pakistan Ltd, 1954; Gammon Gulf Ltd, 1958; *b* 2 June 1887; *m* 1954, Angela Duncan; two *s* one *d* (and one *s* two *d* by previous marr.). *Educ:* Felsted Sch.; Imperial Coll. of Technology, London Univ. (BSc 1st Class Hons). Advanced Workshop Student, Woolwich Arsenal, 1908-09; PWD India, 1910-14; Indian Army, 1914-19, serving 4 years in France with 3rd Sappers and Miners, with 1st Indian Field Sqdn, and on staff of Chief Engineer, 3rd Army in charge of Workshops, Stores and Bridging. *Publication:* Re-inforced Concrete Design Simplified, 1910. *Recreations;* directing and developing Trevose Golf Club; cricket, bridge. *Address:* 80 Eaton Square, SW1. *Clubs:* East India and Sports; Royal Yacht, Willingdon (Bombay); Sind (Karachi).

**GANDAR DOWER, Eric Leslie,** MA (Law); owner of Aberdeen Airport; Chairman and Managing Director, Allied Airways (Gandar Dower) Ltd, Aberdeen Flying School Ltd, Aberdeen Flying Club Ltd, and Aberdeen Aerodrome Fuel Supplies Ltd; 3rd *s* of late Joseph Wilson Gandar-Dower and late Amelia Frances Germaine. *Educ:* Brighton Coll.; Jesus Coll., Cambridge. Trained for stage at RADA. Toured with Alan Stevenson, Cecil Barth and Harold V. Neilson's Companies in Kick In, Betty at Bay, The Witness for the Defence, and The Marriage of Kitty. Played wide range of parts on tour with Sir Philip Ben Greet's Shakespeare Company, including Horatio in Hamlet, Antonio in Merchant of Venice,

Sicinius Velutus in Coriolanus, Don Pedro in Much Ado About Nothing and Oliver in As You Like It, also in London Shakespeare for Schools LCC Educational Scheme. Wrote and produced The Silent Husband. Toured under own management as Lord Stevenage in Young Person in Pink. Competed King's Cup Air Race 5 years. Holder of FAI Aviators Certificate. Built Dyce (Aberdeen) Airport. Founded Allied Airways (Gandar Dower) Ltd, 1934; Mem. Exec. Council Aerodrome Owners Assoc., 1934-45; Founder Mem. Air Registration Bd; Pioneered Scottish Air Lines Aberdeen/Edinburgh, Aberdeen/Glasgow, Aberdeen/Wick/Thurso/Kirkwall/Stromness and Shetland, which operated throughout 1939-45 War. Pioneered first British/Norwegian Air Line, 1937, Newcastle to Stavanger. Founded, May 1939, 102nd Aberdeen Airport Air Training Corps. Served as Flight Lieut RAFVR, 1940-43. First Chm. and Founder, Assoc. of Brit. Aircraft Operators, 1944. MP (C) Caithness and Sutherland, 1945-50. Attached Mau Mau Campaign, Kenya, 1952-53. *Publication:* Visit to Kenya, 1963. *Recreations:* ski-ing, squash, tennis, lawn tennis, swimming, poetry, flying, motoring. *Address:* Westerings, Clos des Fosses, St Martin, Guernsey, Channel Islands. *T:* Guernsey 38637. *Clubs:* Arts, Royal Aero, Royal Automobile; Hawks, Amateur Dramatic, Footlights (Cambridge); Sussex Motor Yacht (Brighton); Automobile de France.

**GANDEE, John Stephen,** CMG 1967; OBE 1958; HM Diplomatic Service, retired; British High Commissioner in Botswana, 1966-69; *b* 8 Dec. 1909; *s* of John Stephen and Constance Garfield Gandee; *m* 1st, May Degenhardt (*d* 1954); one *s* two *d*; 2nd, Junia Henman (*née* Devine); two *d* (and one step *s* one step *d*). *Educ:* Dorking High Sch. Post Office, Dorking, 1923-30; India Office, 1930-47; Private Sec. to Parly Under-Sec. of State, 1946-47; and 1947-49; Asst Private Sec. to Sec. of State, 1947; First Sec., Ottawa, 1952-54; seconded to Bechuanaland Protectorate, 1958-60 and 1961; seconded to Office of High Comr for Basutoland, Bechuanaland Protectorate and Swaziland, 1960-61; Head of Administration Dept, CRO, 1961-64; Head of Office Services and Supply Dept, Diplomatic Service Administration, 1965-66. *Recreations:* walking, gardening, badminton. *Address:* South View, Holmwood, Dorking, Surrey. *T:* Dorking 6513.

**GANDELL, Captain Wilfrid Pearse,** CBE 1940; Royal Navy; *b* 1 Nov. 1886; *s* of T. Pearse Gandell, 16 Earl's Court Square, SW5; *m* 1923, Lilian A. M., *d* of Maj.-Gen. Maxwell Campbell, RE; one *d* (one *s* decd). *Educ:* Stoke House; HMS Britannia. Went to sea as Midshipman in 1902; specialised in torpedo; present at battle of Jutland in HMS St Vincent; retired in 1929; recalled Sept. 1939; served as Principal Sea Transport Officer, French Ports, from declaration of war till fall of France (despatches, CBE), then as PSTO Clyde till 1941, both with rank of Commodore; Chief Staff Officer, Plymouth, 1941-44 (US Legion of Merit); Senior Officer Reserve Fleet, Forth Area, 1944-46; reverted to retired list, April 1946. Member: West Sussex CC, 1958-64; Horsham RDC, 1952-64; Asst Chief Warden CD, Horsham Area, 1952-65. RHS medal, 1918. *Address:* Hayes Warren, Slinfold, Horsham, Sussex. *T:* Slinfold 246. *Club:* United Service.

**GANDER, L(eonard) Marsland;** journalist, war correspondent, author; Television and Radio Correspondent and Critic of The Daily Telegraph 1946-70; *b* London, 27 June 1902; *s* of James Gander and Ellen Marsland; *m* 1931, Hilda Mabel Ellen Rowley; two *s*. *Educ:* Higher Elementary Sch., Stratford; City of London Coll. Reporter, Stratford Express, West Ham, 1919-24; Chief Reporter, Times of India, Bombay, 1924-26; Acting Editor, Illustrated Weekly of India, 1925; Radio Correspondent of the Daily Telegraph, 1926, Television Critic and Correspondent, 1935; War Correspondent of The Daily Telegraph, 1941-45; covered campaigns in Dodecanese, Italy, Southern France, Greece, 1943-44; with 6th Airborne Div. and 1st Canadian Army, Europe, 1945. Chm., Press Club, 1959; Fellow of the Television Soc., 1961 (Mem. Council, 1965). Toured United States for Ford Fund for Advancement of Education, 1963. *Publications:* Atlantic Battle, 1941; Long Road to Leros, 1945; After These Many Quests, autobiography, 1950; Television for All, 1950. *Recreations:* desultory chess, tennis, swimming, gardening, washing-up. *Address:* 8 Paddock Green, East Preston, Sussex. *T:* Rustington 2966. *Clubs:* Press, Savage, Roehampton, Lord's Taverners'.

**GANDHI, Mrs Indira Priyadarshini;** Prime Minister of India since 1966; Leader of the Congress Party since 1966; *b* 19 Nov. 1917; *d* of late Pandit Jawaharlal Nehru and Kamala Kaul; *m* 1942, Feroze Gandhi (*d* 1960); two *s*. *Educ:* Visva-Bharati. Founded Vanar Sena (Congress children's organisation), 1929; joined Indian National Congress, 1938; Mem., Working Cttee, 1955; Pres., Congress Party, 1959-60; Chm., Citizens' Central Council, 1962; Mem., Rajya Sabha, 1964-; Minister of Information and Broadcasting, 1964-66. Dep. Chm., Internat. Union of Child Welfare; Vice-Pres., Indian Coun. of Child Welfare. *Address:* Office of the Prime Minister, New Delhi, India; 1 Safdar Jung Road, New Delhi 3, India.

**GANDHI, Manmohan Purushottam,** MA, FREconS, FSS; JP; Editor, Major Industries of India Annual and Textile Industry Annual; Member: All-India Council of Technical Education; Governing Body, Seksaria Technological Institute, Indore; Advisory Council on Trade; All-India Board of Studies in Commerce; Senate, University of Bombay; Director: East India Cotton Association Ltd; Saru Engineering Corporation Ltd; Indian Link Chain Manufacturers Ltd; Hon. Presidency Magistrate, Bombay; *b* 5 Nov. 1901; *s* of late Purushottam Kahanji Gandhi, of Limbdi (Kathiawad); *m* 1926, Rambhagauri, BA (Indian Women's Univ.), *d* of Sukhlal Chhaganlal Shah of Wadhwan. *Educ:* Bahauddin Coll., Junagad; Gujerat Coll., Ahmedabad; Hindu Univ., Benares. BA (History and Econs), Bombay Univ., 1923; MA (Political Econ. and Political Philosophy), Benares Hindu Univ., 1925; Ashburner Prize of Bombay Univ., 1925. statistical Asst, Govt of Bombay, Labour Office, 1926; Asst Sec., Indian Currency League, Bombay, 1926; Sec., Indian Chamber of Commerce, Calcutta, 1926-36; Sec., Indian Sugar Mills Assoc., 1932-36; Officer-in-Charge, Credit Dept, National City Bank of New York, Calcutta, 1936-37; Chief Commercial Manager, Rohtas Industries Ltd; Dalmia Cement Ltd, 1937-39; Dir, Indian Sugar Syndicate Ltd, 1937-39; Controller of Supplies, Bengal and Bombay, 1941-43; Sec., Indian Nat. Cttee, Internat. Chamber of Commerce, Calcutta, 1929-31; Sec., Fedn of Indian Chambers of Commerce and Industry, 1927-28. Mem. East Indian Railway Adv. Cttee, 1939-40; Bihar Labour Enquiry Cttee, 1937-39; UP and Bihar Power Alcohol Cttee, 1938; UP and Bihar Sugar Control Board, 1938; Western Railway Adv. Cttee, Bombay, 1950-52; Technical Adviser, Indian Tariff Board, 1947. Hon. Prof.,

Sydenham Coll. of Commerce, 1943-49. *Publications:* How to Compete with Foreign Cloth, 1931; The Indian Sugar Industry: Its Past, Present and Future, 1934; The Indian Cotton Textile Industry–Its Past, Present and Future, 1937; The Indian Sugar Industry (annually, 1935-64); The Indian Cotton Textile Industry, (annually, 1937-); Centenary Volume of the Indian Cotton Textile Industry, 1851-1950; Major Industries of India (Annually, 1951-); Problems of Sugar Industry in India, 1946; Monograph on Handloom Weaving in India, 1953; Some Impressions of Japan, 1955. *Recreations:* tennis, badminton, billiards, bridge, swimming. *Address:* Nanabhay Mansions, Pherozeshah Mehta Road, Fort, Bombay. *T:* (home) 358805, (office) 261047 and 264839. *TA:* Gandhi care Keen, Bombay. *Clubs:* Radio, National Sports (Bombay).

**GANDY, Christopher Thomas;** HM Diplomatic Service, retired; *b* 21 April 1917; *s* of Dr Thomas H. Gandy and Mrs Ida Gandy (authoress of A Wiltshire Childhood, Around the Little Steeple, etc); unmarried. *Educ:* Marlborough; King's Coll., Cambridge. On active service with Army and RAF, 1939-45. Entered Foreign Office, Nov. 1945; Tehran, 1948-51; Cairo, 1951-52; FO, 1952-54; Lisbon, 1954-56; Libya, 1956-59; FO, 1960-62; apptd HM Minister to The Yemen, 1962, subsequently Counsellor, Kuwait; Minister (Commercial) Rio de Janeiro, 1966-68. *Recreations:* music, photography, walking. *Address:* 60 Ambleside Drive, Headington, Oxford.

**GANE, Sir Irving (Blanchard),** KCVO 1954; Chamberlain of London, 1945-62; *b* 15 April 1892; *o c* of Douglas Montagu Gane and Florence Kate Blanchard; *m* 1916, Florence Montgomery (*d* 1951), *d* of Thomas Coulter, Bowmanville, Ontario; three *d*; *m* 1954, Mrs Valerie Woolland, *d* of Sir Donald Cory, 2nd Bt, and of Gertrude Lady Cory. *Educ:* Merchant Taylors' Sch. Admitted a Solicitor, 1914; Private First Bn, HAC, France, 1914-15; Gazetted to 2/22nd Bn London Regt (The Queens), France 1916, Salonika 1917, Palestine 1917-19; Adjt, Gen. Staff, GHQ, Palestine, 1918; Gen. Staff, War Office, 1940; retired, 1945, Major. A Vice-Pres., Royal Society of St George; a Vice-Pres., Ex-Services Mental Welfare Soc.; Chm., City of London Centre, St John Ambulance Assoc.; Hon. Sec., Tristan Da Cunha Fund; Mem. Court of Common Council for Ward of Farringdon Without, 1934-45; Mem. Court of Assts Merchant Taylors' Company, 1951, Master, 1959. KStJ. *Address:* Newmans, Pirbright, Woking, Surrey. *T:* Brookwood 2072.

**GANGULY, Most Rev. Theotonius A.;** *see* Dacca, Archbishop of, (RC).

**GANILAU, Ratu Penaia Kanatabatu,** CMG 1968; CVO 1970; DSO 1956; OBE 1960; Minister for Fijian Affairs and Local Government since 1965; *b* 28 July 1918; Fijian; *m* 1949, Adi Laisa Delaisomosomo Yavaca; five *s* two *d*. *Educ:* Provincial Sch. Northern, Queen Victoria Mem. Sch., Fiji. Devonshire Course for Admin. Officers, Wadham Coll., Oxford Univ., 1946-48. Served with FIR, 1940; demobilised, retained rank of Capt. 1946. Colonial Admin. Service, 1947; District Officer, 1948-53; Mem. Commn on Fijian Post Primary Educn in the Colony, 1953. Service with Fiji Mil. Forces, 1953-56; demobilised, retained rank of Temp. Lt-Col, 1956. Seconded to post of Fijian Econ. Devel Officer and Roko Tui Cakaudrove conjoint, 1956; Tour Manager and Govt Rep., Fiji Rugby football tour of NZ, 1957; Dep. Sec. for Fijian Affairs, 1961; Sec. for Fijian Affairs (now Min. for Fijian Affairs and Local Govt), 1965. Mem., Council of Ministers; Offical Mem., Legislative Coun.; Chairman: Fijian Affairs Bd; Fijian Develt Fund Bd; Native Land Trust Bd; Great Council of Chiefs. *Recreation:* Rugby football (rep. Fiji against Maori All Black, 1938 and during Rugby tour of NZ, 1939). *Address:* Ministry of Fijian Affairs and Local Government, Suva, Fiji. *T:* 22971. *Clubs:* Oxford and Cambridge University; Fiji, Defence (Suva, Fiji).

**GANNON, Brig. Jack Rose Compton,** CBE 1945 (OBE 1942); MVO 1922; *b* 1882; *s* of John Gannon, St John's Coll., Cambridge; *m* 1910, Dorothy, *d* of George Robertson, Melbourne; one *d*. *Educ:* Sutton Valence; RMC Sandhurst. South Staffords, 1902-06; 23rd and PAVO Cavalry, 1906-26; Commanded Sam Browne's Cavalry, 1927-32; ADC to Lord Willingdon when Governor of Bombay; Personal Military Sec. to Gen. Lord Rawlinson, C-in-C India, 1920-25; served European War, 1914-18; Afghan War, 1919; Mahsud and Waziristan Expeditions, 1919-20 (despatches twice); Asst Military Sec., GHQ Home Forces, 1939-43; Dep. Military Sec., 21 Army Group, 1943-45; Dep. Mil. Sec., BAOR, 1945-46 (despatches twice); retd, 1946. Manager, Hurlingham Club, 1934-39; Hon. Sec., Hurlingham Polo Assoc., 1934-; Pres., Arab Horse Soc., 1951; Pres., Nat. Pony Soc., 1954-. British Horse Society's Medal of Honour, 1970. Comdr of Legion of Merit (US), Knight Comdr of Order of Orange Nassau, Chevalier of Legion of Honour (France), Croix de Guerre (France). *Recreations:* formerly: polo, cricket, shooting. *Address:* Little Park House, Brimpton, Berks. *T:* Woolhampton 2487. *Club:* Cavalry.

**GANZONI,** family name of **Baron Belstead.**

**GARBETT, Sir Colin (Campbell),** KCIE 1941 (CIE 1917); CSI 1935; CMG 1922; FRGS; FRSA; OStJ 1938; *b* 22 May 1881; *s* of late Hubert Garbett, MICE, Castletown, Isle of Man; *m* 1st, 1911, Abra Faith Hughes-Garbett (*d* 1911); 2nd, 1919, Marjorie Josephine, *d* of late Lt-Col Maynard, IMS; one *d*. *Educ:* King William's Coll., Isle of Man (Sch. Capt. of Football; Victor Ludorum; Cricket XI); Jesus Coll., Cambridge (rowing, football and athletic colours, Victor Ludorum, Sen. Schol.). MA; BA (1st Class Hons Classics) 1903; LLB (2nd Class) 1904. ICS 1904; Asst-Censor, 1915; Revenue Comr, Mesopotamia, and also Administrator Agricultural Development Scheme (Military), 1917 (despatches twice); Secretariat Turkish Peace Treaty Delegn, 1919-20; Asst-Sec., India Office, 1919-20; Sec. High Comr, Iraq, 1920-22; returned to India, 1922; Dep. Comr, Attock; Campbellpur, 1925-29; Rawalpindi, 1929; Chief Sec. to Govt, Punjab, 1931; Comr, Multan Div., 1935; Financial Comr Punjab, 1937; Chm., Punjab Govt Forest Commn, 1937; Financial Comr, Punjab, 1939; Chm. Provincial Transport Authority and of Land Reclamation Board, Punjab; retired Dec. 1941 and became Chm. Interview Board Emergency Commissions (Defence Dept) till 1943; Senior Mem. Govt of India Commn on land schemes for demobilised soldiers; Regional Food Comr, Northern India; Minister for Agriculture, Bhopal, 1944-46; retired, 1946. Missions to Pakistan and India for Raw Cotton Commn, 1948 and 1949. Classics Master, Hilton Coll., Natal, SA, 1951-52. *Publications:* Friend of Friend, 1943; The Hundred Years, 1944; Sun of Tabriz, 1956; The Ringing Radiance, 1968. *Address:* c/o National and Grindlay's Bank Ltd, 13 St James's Square, SW1; 16 Bel Air, Whiteriver, Transvaal, S Africa. *Clubs:* Royal

Commonwealth Society, East India and Sports, Royal Over-Seas League; Royal Bombay Yacht.

**GARBETT, Captain Leonard Gillilan,** CBE 1942; RN (retired); *b* 1 March 1879; *y s* of Rev. Charles Garbett, Vicar of Tongham, Surrey; *m* 1919, Millicent, *e d* of Canon Dunfield, St John's, Newfoundland; one *s* two *d. Educ:* HMS Worcester. Served afloat continuously and in European War, 1914-18, operations on Belgian Coast, 1914, and against German Cruiser Königsberg in Rufiji River, 1915; comd HMS Mersey, 1917-19, HM Surveying Ship, Merlin, 1920-21; Supt Naval Div., Meteorological Office, Air Min., 1921-37; Chief Supt Naval Met. Branch, Admty, 1937-39; Dir, Naval Meteorological Service, 1939-47. FRMetS; FRSA. Younger Brother of Trinity House. USA Legion of Merit, 1946. *Publications:* several professional papers. *Recreations:* fishing, riding. *Address:* The Cottage, Ashford Carbonell, Ludlow, Shropshire. *T:* Richard's Castle 250. *Club:* Army and Navy.

**GARBO, Greta, (Greta Lovisa Gustafsson);** film actress; *b* Stockholm, 18 Sept. 1905; *d* of Sven and Louvisa Gustafsson. *Educ:* Dramatic Sch. attached to Royal Theatre, Stockholm. Began stage career as dancer in Sweden. First film appearance in The Atonement of Gosta Berling, 1924; went to US, 1925; became an American Citizen, 1951. Films include: The Torrent, 1926; The Temptress, 1926; Flesh and the Devil, 1927; Love, 1927; The Divine Woman, 1928; The Mysterious Lady, 1928; A Woman of Affairs, 1929; Wild Orchids, 1929; The Single Standard, 1929; The Kiss, 1929; Anna Christie, 1930 (first talking rôle); Susan Lenox, Her Fall and Rise, 1931; Mata Hari, 1931; Grand Hotel, 1932; As You Desire Me, 1932; Queen Christina, 1933; Anna Karenina, 1935; Camille, 1936; Conquest, 1937; Ninotchka, 1939; Two-Faced Woman, 1941. *Address:* 450 East 52nd Street, New York, USA; 622 North Bedford Drive, Beverly Hills, Hollywood, Calif, USA.

**GARDAM, David Hill,** QC 1968; *b* 14 Aug. 1922; *s* of late Harry H. Gardam, Hove, Sussex; *m* 1954, Jane Mary, *d* of William Pearson, Redcar, Yorks; two *s* one *d. Educ:* Oundle Sch.; Christ Church, Oxford. MA 1948. War Service, RNVR, 1941-46 (Temp. Lieut). Called to the Bar, 1949. *Recreations:* painting, bee-keeping. *Address:* 22 Old Buildings, Lincoln's Inn, WC2. *T:* 01-405 2072; 53 Ridgway Place, SW19.

**GARDENER, Sir (Alfred) John,** KCMG 1954 (CMG 1949); CBE 1944; JP; *b* 6 Feb. 1897; *s* of late G. Northcote Gardener, Exeter; *m* 1st, 1929, Dorothy Caroline (*d* 1967), *d* of late Emile Purgold, Liverpool; no *c*; 2nd, 1968, Marion May, *d* of Linden E. W. Huish, Exeter. *Educ:* Heles Sch., Exeter; Trinity Hall, Cambridge. Served in Army in France and Belgium, 1916-18. Joined Consular Service, 1920, and served in various posts in S Persia, Morocco, Syria and USA. In June 1941 served as Political Officer during Syrian Campaign with rank of Lieut-Col (subsequently Col). Served in Foreign Office, 1946-49; British Ambassador to Afghanistan, 1949-51, and to Syria, 1953-56; retired, 1957. JP Devon, 1959. *Address:* c/o Barclay's Bank, Exeter, Devon.

**GARDHAM, Arthur John,** MS, FRCS; formerly Senior Surgeon to University College Hospital and Examiner in Surgery to University of London; *b* Leytonstone, Essex, Nov. 1899; 2nd *s* of Arthur and Elizabeth Gardham; *m* 1936, Audrey Glenton, 3rd *d* of late Francis Carr, CBE; one *s* two *d. Educ:* Bancroft's Sch.; University College and University College Hospital, London. MRCS, LRCP 1921; MB, BS (London), 1923; FRCS 1924; MS (London), 1926. Served RNVR, 1917-18. Qualified 1921; House appts at UCH; Pearce Gould Scholar, 1925; Asst to Prof. Clairmont at Kantonsspital, Zürich, 1925; Surgical Registrar and later Asst Dir of Surgical Unit, UCH. Surgeon to Hampstead Gen. Hosp. (Royal Free Hosp. Group). Served RAMC, 1940-45; Consulting Surgeon to 14th Army and Eastern Comd, India (despatches). Mem. Court of Examiners of RCS, 1945-51; Examiner in Surgery: to Univ. of Cambridge, 1951-57; to Univ. of Edinburgh, 1957-60; to Univ. of London, 1958-62; associated with Emergency Bed Service of King Edward's Hosp. Fund for London since its foundation in 1938; Hunterian Prof., RCS; Fellow; Royal Society of Medicine (Pres. of Surgical Sect., 1963-64); University Coll., London; Assoc. of Surgeons (Mem. Council, 1957-60). Jt Hon. Sec., Devon and Somerset Stag-hounds, 1967-70. *Publications:* (with Davies) The Operations of Surgery, 1963, Vol. 2, 1969; Sections of Grey Turner's Modern Operative Surgery; various papers on surgical subjects. *Recreations:* field sports. *Address:* Castle Green, Oare, Brendon, nr Lynton, Devon. *T:* Brendon 205.

**GARDHAM, Air Vice-Marshal Marcus Maxwell,** CBE 1965; Air Officer in charge of Administration, RAF Training Command, since 1969; *b* 5 Nov. 1916; *s* of late Arthur Gardham, High Wycombe; *m* 1954, Rosemary Hilda (*née* Wilkins); one *s. Educ:* Royal Grammar Sch., High Wycombe. Commissioned RAF (Accountant Br), 1939; RAF Ferry Command, 1941; HQ AEAF, 1944. BJSM, Washington, 1946 (SOA); RAPO, 1949; No 16 MU, 1953; 2nd TAF (Org. Staff), 1955; Air Ministry (Personnel Staff), 1957; Technical Trng Command (Org. Staff), 1959; FEAF (Command Accountant), 1965; Dir of Personal Services, MoD (Air), 1966; psc 1952; jssc 1957; AIWSP, 1961. *Recreations:* gardening, golf. *Address:* c/o Lloyds Bank, High Street, High Wycombe, Bucks. *Club:* Royal Air Force.

**GARDINER,** family name of **Baron Gardiner.**

**GARDINER,** Baron *cr* 1963, of Kittisford (Life Peer); **Gerald Austin Gardiner,** PC 1964; *b* 30 May 1900; *s* of late Sir Robert Gardiner; *m* 1st, 1925, Lesly (*d* 1966), *o d* of Edwin Trounson, JP; one *d*; 2nd, 1970, Mrs Muriel Box. *Educ:* Harrow Sch.; Magdalen Coll., Oxford. 2nd Lieut Coldstream Guards, 1918; Pres. Oxford Union and OUDS, 1924; called to the Bar, 1925; KC 1948. Friends Ambulance Unit, 1943-45. Mem. Cttee on Supreme Court Practice and Procedure, 1947-53; Mem. of Lord Chancellor's Law Reform Cttee, 1952-63. A Master of the Bench of the Inner Temple, 1955; Chm. Gen. Council of the Bar, 1958 and 1959. Chm (Jt), National Campaign for Abolition of Capital Punishment. Alderman, London County Council, 1961-63. Lord High Chancellor of Great Britain, 1964-70. Hon. LLD: Southampton, 1965; London, 1968; Manitoba, 1969; Law Soc. of Upper Canada, 1969; DUniv, York, 1966. *Publications:* Capital Punishment as a Deterrent, 1956; (Jt Ed.) Law Reform Now, 1963. *Recreations:* law reform and the theatre. *Address:* 1 Harcourt Buildings, Temple, EC4Y 9DA. *Club:* Garrick.

**GARDINER, Lt-Col Christopher John,** DSO 1940; OBE 1945; TD 1942; DL; RE; Chairman of Gardiner, Sons and Co. Ltd, Bristol, merchants; *b* 2 June 1907; *s* of Edward John Lucas Gardiner, Clifton, Bristol; *m* 1938,

Bridget Mary Taplin; three *s* one *d*. *Educ:* Clifton Coll., Bristol. Commissioned in South Midland RE, TA, in 1926; CRE 48 Div., 59 Div., and 12 Corps Tps RE (despatches thrice). Nat. Pres., Soc. of Builders Merchants. Governor: Clifton Coll., Avonhurst Sch. DL Glos. *Recreations:* Rugby (played for Clifton Coll), fishing. *Address:* 7 Beaufort Road, Clifton, Bristol 8. *T:* 35187. *Club:* Constitutional.

**GARDINER, Ernest David,** CMG 1968; CBE 1967; Head of Science Department, Melbourne Grammar School, since 1948; Chairman, Commonwealth Government's Advisory Committee on Standards for Science Facilities in Independent Secondary Schools, since 1964; *b* 14 July 1909; 2nd *s* of Ernest Edward Gardiner and Isabella Gardiner (*née* Notman), Gisborne, Vic.; *m* 1940, Minnie Amanda Neill; one *s* one *d*. *Educ:* Kyneton High Sch.; Melbourne Univ. BSc 1931, BEd 1936, Melbourne; FACE 1968. Secondary Teacher with Educn Dept of Vic., 1932-45; Melbourne Grammar Sch., 1946-. *Publications:* Practical Physics (2 vols), 1948; Practical Problems in Physics, 1959. *Recreations:* music, theatre, swimming. *Address:* 122 Ferguson Street, Williamstown, Vic. 3016, Australia. *T:* 397 6132.

**GARDINER, Frederick Keith,** JP; President, Neepsend Steel and Tool Corporation, Ltd; Director, Sheffield Wednesday Football Club; *b* Plumstead, Kent; *s* of Frederick Gardiner and Edith Mann; *m* 1929, Ruth Dixon; two *s*. Various editorial positions with newspaper companies in the South of England and at Darlington, York, Oxford and Sheffield; formerly Ed. and Dir, The Sheffield Telegraph; Pres. Inst. of Journalists, 1950; FJI. JP Sheffield. *Recreation:* golf. *Address:* 5 Chorley Road, Fulwood, Sheffield 10. *T.A.:* Nepco, Sheffield. *T:* 23231. *Clubs:* St James'; The Club (Sheffield); Hallamshire Golf (Sheffield).

**GARDINER, Dame Helen (Louisa),** DBE 1961 (CBE 1952); MVO 1937; *b* 24 April 1901; *y d* of late Henry Gardiner, Bristol. *Educ:* Clifton High School. Formerly in Private Secretary's Office, Buckingham Palace; Chief Clerk, 1946-61. *Recreations:* reading, gardening. *Address:* Courlands Cottage, Lostwithiel, Cornwall.

**GARDINER, Peter Dod Robin;** Headmaster of St Peter's School, York, since Sept. 1967; *b* 23 Dec. 1927; *s* of Brig. R. Gardiner, *qv*; *m* 1959, Juliet Wright; one *s* one *d*. *Educ:* Radley College; Trinity Coll., Cambridge. Asst Master, Charterhouse, 1952-67, and Housemaster, Charterhouse, 1965-67. *Publications:* (ed) Twentieth-Century Travel, 1963; (with B. W. M. Young) Intelligent Reading, 1964; (with G. A. Gibson) The Design of Prose, 1970. *Recreations:* reading, writing, walking, acting. *Address:* St Peter's School, York YO3 6AB.

**GARDINER, Brig. Richard,** CB 1954; CBE 1946 (OBE 1944); *b* 28 Oct. 1900; *s* of Major Alec Gardiner, RE; *m* 1924, Catherine Dod (*née* Oliver); two *s*. *Educ:* Uppingham Sch.; Royal Military Academy. Commissioned into RFA, 1920; transferred to RE, 1924; Asst Executive Engineer, E Indian Rly, 1927; Sec. to Agent, E Indian Rly, 1930; Exec. Engineer, 1934; Govt Inspector of Rlys, Burma, 1938; reverted to military duty, 1940; Dir of Transportation, India, 1942; reverted to Home Establishment, 1945; Dir of Transportation, War Office, 1948; Dir of Engineer Stores, War Office, 1950; retired Dec. 1953; Man. Dir, Peruvian Corp., Lima, 1954-63. MInstT, 1949. ADC to King George VI, 1951-52, to the Queen, 1952-53. *Recreations:* music, gardening. *Address:* Bridgham Farmhouse, Shamley Green, Surrey. *Club:* United Service. *See also P. D. R. Gardiner.*

**GARDINER, Robert (Kweku Atta);** Executive Secretary, Economic Commission for Africa, since 1962; *b* Kumasi, Ghana, 29 Sept. 1914; *s* of Philip A. D. Gardiner and Nancy Torraine Ferguson; *m* 1943, Linda Charlotte Edwards; one *s* two *d*. *Educ:* Adisadel Coll., Cape Coast; Ghana; Fourah Bay Coll., Sierra Leone; Selwyn Coll., Cambridge (BA); New Coll., Oxford. Lectr in Economics at Fourah Bay Coll., 1943; UN Trusteeship Dept, 1947; Dir, Extra-Mural Studies, University Coll., Ibadan, 1949; Dir, Dept of Social Welfare and Community Development, Gold Coast, 1953; Perm. Sec., Min. of Housing; later Head of Ghana's Civil Service, 1957; Dep. Exec. Sec., Economic Commn for Africa, 1959-60; Mem. Secretariat Mission to the Congo, 1961; Officer-in-Charge, UN Operation in the Congo, Jan. 1962-May 1963; Dir Public Admin. Div., UN Dept of Economic and Social Affairs, 1961. Chm., Commonwealth Foundation, 1970-. Reith Lectures, 1965. David Livingstone Vis. Prof. of Economics, Strathclyde, 1970-. Hon. Fellow: Univ. of Ibadan; Selwyn Coll., Cambridge. Hon. DCL: East Anglia, 1966; Sierra Leone, 1969; Hon. LLD: Bristol, 1966; Ibadan, 1968; E Africa, 1968; Hon. PhD Uppsala 1966; Hon. DSc Kumasi, 1968. *Publications:* (with Helen Judd) The Development of Social Administration, 1951 (publ. Eng.); A World of Peoples (BBC Reith Lectures), 1965. *Recreations:* golf, music. *Address:* The Economic Commission for Africa, PO Box 3001, Addis Ababa, Ethiopia.

**GARDINER-HILL, Harold,** MBE, MA, MD (Cantab), FRCP; Consultant Physician, St Thomas's Hospital; Consulting Physician, Queen Victoria Cottage Hospital, East Grinstead; Fellow Royal Society Medicine; President Section of Endocrinology, 1949-50; Member Association of Physicians, Great Britain; *b* London, 14 Feb. 1891; *e s* of late Hugh Gardiner-Hill, MD; *m* Margaret Helen, *e d* of Sir E. Farquhar Buzzard, 1st Bt, KCVO; three *s*. *Educ:* Westminster Sch.; Pembroke Coll., Cambridge; St Thomas's Hosp. Mem. Cambridge Univ. Golf Team, 1911-12; Medical Registrar, St Thomas's Hospital, 1920; Royal Army Medical Corps, 1915-18; Royal Air Force Medical Service, 1918-19 (despatches); CO RAF Central Hosp., Finchley, 1919; Asst Medical Unit, St Thomas's Hosp., 1925-28; Asst Physician, Royal Free Hosp., 1928-30; Oliver Sharpe Lectr RCP, 1937. *Publications:* Modern Trends in Endocrinology, 1957; Clinical Involvements, 1958; articles in the Quarterly Jl of Medicine, British Jl of Obstetrics and Gynaecology, Lancet, BMJ, Proc. Royal Soc. Medicine, Practitioner and Jl of Mental Science chiefly on endocrine diseases. *Recreations:* golf (Chm. of Rules of Golf Cttee, Royal and Ancient, 1949-52; Captain, Royal and Ancient, 1956), and other games. *Address:* 149 Harley Street, W1. *T:* 01-935 4444; 30 Stanhope Gardens, SW7. *T:* 01-373 2272. *Clubs:* Carlton; Royal and Ancient (St Andrews); Swinley Forest Golf.

**GARDINER SCOTT, Rev. William;** *see* Scott.

**GARDINI, Signora U.;** *see* Fisher, Sylvia.

**GARDNER, Antony John;** *b* 27 Dec. 1927; *s* of David Gardner, head gardener, and Lillian Gardner; *m* 1956, Eveline A. Burden. *Educ:* Elem. school; Co-operative Coll.; Southampton Univ. Pres. Union, Southampton, 1958-59; BSc (Econ) 1959. Apprentice toolmaker, 1941-45; National

Service, RASC, 1946-48; building trade, 1948-53. Tutor Organiser, Co-operative Union, 1959-60; Member and Education Officer, Co-operative Union, 1961-66. Contested (Lab) SW Wolverhampton, 1964; MP (Lab) Rushcliffe, 1966-70. *Recreations:* angling, gardening and the countryside generally. *Address:* 30 Brookside Avenue, East Leake, Loughborough, Leics. *T:* East Leake 2454. *Club:* Parkstone Trades and Labour (Poole).

**GARDNER, Arthur Duncan,** MA, DM, FRCS, FRCP; Hon. Fellow of University College, Oxford, 1950; Professor Emeritus, Oxford, 1954; *b* 28 March 1884; *s* of late James William Gardner, The Stone House, Rugeley, Staffs; *m* Violet Mary, *d* of late John Fowler Newsam, The Hollies, Broxbourne, Herts; one *s* one *d* (and one *s* decd). *Educ:* Rugby; University Coll., Oxford. Member of Oxford hockey eleven, 1906; St Thomas's Hospital, 1908-15; Beaney Prize, House Surgeon, Casualty Officer, Lectr in Pathology, Research Asst. Radcliffe Travelling Fellowship, Oxford, 1914, Radcliffe Prize, 1923. Served in BEF as British Red Cross Surgeon, 1914; Dir of Standards Lab. (MRC) at Oxford, 1915-36; Reader in Bacteriology with title of Professor, 1936; Rede Lectr, Cambridge, 1953; Litchfield Lectr, Oxford, 1954; late Fellow of University Coll., Oxford; Regius Prof. of Medicine, Univ. of Oxford, 1948-54; Student of Christ Church, 1948-54; Hon. Consultant, Oxford United Hospitals, 1954. *Publications:* Microbes and Ultramicrobes, 1931; Bacteriology for Medical Students and Practitioners, 1933 (4th edn 1953); Penicillin as a chemotherapeutic agent (with E. Chain, Sir H. W. Florey and others), 1940; numerous contribs to medical scientific jls from 1914. *Address:* Chilswell Edge, Hinksey Hill, Oxford. *T:* Oxford 35397.

**GARDNER, Sir Douglas Bruce B.;** *see* Bruce-Gardner.

**GARDNER, Edward Lucas,** QC 1960; MP (C) South Fylde, since 1970; Deputy Chairman: East Kent Quarter Sessions, since 1961; County of Kent Quarter Sessions, since 1962; Essex Quarter Sessions, since 1968; *b* 10 May 1912; *s* of Edward Walker Gardner, Fulwood, Preston, Lancs; *m* 1st, 1950, Noreen Margaret (marr. diss. 1962), *d* of John Collins, Moseley, Birmingham; one *s* one *d;* 2nd, 1963, Joan Elizabeth, *d* of late B. B. Belcher, Bedford; one *s.* one *d. Educ:* Hutton Grammar Sch. Served War of 1939-45: joined RNVR as ordinary seaman, 1940; served in cruisers, Mediterranean; commnd RNVR; Chief of Naval Information, E Indies, 1945. Journalist (free-lance; Lancashire Daily Post, then Daily Mail) prior to 1940; broadcasting and free-lance journalism, 1946-49; called to Bar, Gray's Inn, 1947; Master of the Bench of Gray's Inn, 1968; admitted to Nigerian and British Guianan Bars, 1962; has also appeared in Courts of Goa, High Court of Singapore, and Supreme Court of India. Contested (C) Erith and Crayford, April 1955; MP (C) Billericay Div. of Essex, 1959-66; PPS to Attorney-General, 1962-63; Chairman: Justice Working Party on Bail and Remands in Custody, 1966; Bar Council Cttee on Parly Privilege, 1967; Exec. Cttee, Soc. of Cons. Lawyers, 1967 (Vice-Chm., 1969-; Chm., Cttee responsible for pamphlet, Rough Justice, on future of the Law, 1968); Exec. Cttee, Justice, 1968. Member: Departmental Cttee on Jury Service, 1963; Cttee on Appeals in Criminal Cases, 1964. A Governor, Thomas Coram Foundn for Children, 1962-. *Publication:* (part author) A Case for Trial (pamphlet recommending procedural reforms for committal proceedings implemented by Criminal Justice Act, 1967). *Recreations:* walking, history, music. *Address:* 4 Raymond Buildings, Gray's Inn, WC1. *T:* 01-242 4719; Sparrows, Hatfield Broad Oak, Essex; Outlane Head Cottage, Chipping, Lancs. *Clubs:* Carlton, Garrick, United and Cecil.

**GARDNER, Dr Frances,** FRCP; Physician, Royal Free Hospital, London, since 1946; Consulting Physician, Hospital for Women, Soho Square, London; Physician, The Mothers' Hospital, London; Physician, Thorpe Coombe Maternity Hospital, London; Dean, Royal Free Hospital School of Medicine; Examiner, Conjoint Board; late Examiner, MB, BS, University of London; Representative of General Medical Schools on Senate of University of London, 1967; *b* 28 Feb. 1913; *d* of late Sir Ernest and Lady Gardner; *m* 1958, George Qvist, *qv. Educ:* Headington Sch., Oxford; Westfield Coll., Univ. of London; Royal Free Hospital School of Medicine. BSc London, 1935; MB, BS London, 1940; MD London, 1943; MRCP 1943, FRCP 1952. Medical Registrar, Royal Free Hosp., 1943; Clinical Asst, Nuffield Dept of Medicine, Oxford, 1945; Fellow in Medicine, Harvard Univ., USA, 1946; Chief Asst, National Hosp. for Diseases of the Heart, 1947; late Physician, Royal National Throat, Nose and Ear Hospt., London. Commonwealth Travelling Fellow, 1962. *Publications:* papers on cardiovascular and other medical subjects in BMJ, Lancet, and British Heart Jl. *Address:* 72 Harley Street, W1. *T:* 01-935 6053.

**GARDNER, Francis William;** *b* 15 Jan. 1891; *s* of Frederick J. Gardner, Liverpool; *m* 1920, Gladys Robathan. *Educ:* Queens' Coll., Cambridge. Joined C. A. Parsons & Co. Ltd., Newcastle upon Tyne, 1912. Served in RNAS (subsequently RAF), 1915-19. Returned to C. A. Parsons & Co. Ltd, holding office of Chief Engineer then General Manager; Director, 1939; retired from executive office, 1956; Chairman, 1959-60, now retired. *Address:* Lindfield, North Weirs, Brockenhurst, Hants. *T:* Brockenhurst 3146.

**GARDNER, Frank Matthias,** CBE 1967; Borough Librarian, Luton, since 1938; *b* 13 Jan. 1908; *s* of Ernest Frank Gardner and Lily Gardner, Sheffield; *m* 1936, Lysobel Margaret Watt Smith (*d* 1966); one *s* one *d. Educ:* Firth Park Grammar Sch., Sheffield. FLA 1932. Unesco Consultant, India, 1950-51; Leader, Seminar on Public Libraries in Asia, Delhi, 1954; Pres., Library Assoc., 1964; Mem., Library Adv. Council, 1965-; Chm., Books and Libraries Panel, British Council, 1966-; Chm., Public Libraries Section, Internat. Fedn of Library Assocs, 1969-. CStJ 1962. *Publications:* (ed) Sequels, 1947, 1955, 1967; Letters to a Younger Librarian, 1948; Delhi Public Library, Evaluation Report (Unesco), 1955; (with M. J. Lewis) Reading Round the World, 1969; Public Library Legislation: a comparative study (Unesco), 1971. *Recreations:* reading, travel, enjoying church architecture and pictures, contract bridge. *Address:* 14 The Larches, Luton, Beds. *T:* Luton 23066.

**GARDNER, Sir George William Hoggan,** KBE 1959 (CBE 1951); CB 1955; consultant; Director: John Brown & Co. Ltd, since 1963; Constructors John Brown Ltd, since 1967; John Brown Engineering (Clydebank) Ltd, since 1970 (Chairman, 1966-70); *b* 4 May 1903; *m* 1st, 1932, Lorna Marian Boyd (*d* 1962); two *d;* 2nd, 1963, Helen Isabel Burgess. *Educ:* Campbell Coll., Belfast; Queen's Univ., Belfast. BSc, Queen's Univ., 1925. Dir of the Royal Aircraft Establishment, 1955-59; Controller of Aircraft, Min. of Aviation, 1959-

63. FIMechE 1947; Hon. FRAeS 1962. Hon. DSc Queen's Univ., Belfast, 1957. *Address:* The Lawn, Pirbright Rd, Farnborough, Hants. *T:* Farnborough, Hants, 42984. *Club:* Athenæum.

**GARDNER, Dame Helen (Louise),** DBE 1967 (CBE 1962); FBA 1958; FRSL 1962; DLitt: Merton Professor of English Literature, University of Oxford, and Fellow of Lady Margaret Hall, since 1966; Fellow of St Hilda's College, 1942-66, Hon. Fellow, 1966; Delegate, Oxford University Press, since 1959; *b* 13 Feb. 1908; *d* of late C. H. Gardner and Mrs H. M. R. Gardner. *Educ:* North London Collegiate Sch.; St Hilda's Coll., Oxford. BA Oxford (1st class Hons Sch. of English Lang. and Lit.), 1929; MA 1935; DLitt 1963. Asst Lectr, Royal Holloway Coll., Univ. of London, 1931-34; Lectr, Univ. of Birmingham, 1934-41; Tutor in English Literature, St Hilda's Coll., 1941-54; Reader in Renaissance English Literature, Univ. of Oxford, 1954-66; Vis. Prof., Univ. of California, Los Angeles, 1954; Riddell Memorial Lectr, Univ. of Durham, 1956; Alexander Lectr, Univ. of Toronto, 1962; Messenger Lectr, Cornell Univ., 1967; T. S. Eliot Memorial Lectr, Univ. of Kent, 1968. Mem., Robbins Cttee on Higher Education, 1961-63; Mem., Council for National Academic Awards, 1964-67; Trustee, National Portrait Gallery, 1967. Hon. DLitt: Durham, 1960; East Anglia, 1967; London, 1969; Birmingham, 1970; Hon. LLD Aberdeen, 1967. *Publications:* The Art of T. S. Eliot, 1949; The Divine Poems of John Donne, 1952; The Metaphysical Poets (Penguin), 1957; (ed with G. M. Story) The Sonnets of William Alabaster, 1960; The Business of Criticism, 1960; The Elegies and Songs and Sonnets of John Donne, 1965; A Reading of Paradise Lost, 1965; John Donne: Selected Prose (co-ed with T. Healey), 1967; (ed) Shakespearian and Other Studies by F. P. Wilson, 1969; Religion and Literature, 1971. *Recreations:* gardening, foreign travel. *Address:* Myrtle House, Eynsham, Oxford; Lady Margaret Hall, Oxford. *T:* Eynsham 497.

**GARDNER, Hugh,** CB 1966; CBE 1953; Under-Secretary, Ministry of Agriculture, Fisheries and Food, 1953-70; *b* 28 March 1910; *yr s* of C. H. Gardner; *m* 1934, Margaret Evelyn Carvalho; one *s* two *d. Educ:* University College Sch.; Merton Coll., Oxford. Entered Min. of Agriculture and Fisheries as Asst Principal, 1933; Chm., Assoc. of First Div. Civil Servants, 1945-48. *Publication:* Tales from the Marble Mountain, 1967. *Recreations:* golf, gardening, writing. *Address:* The Cobb, North Road, Berkhamsted, Herts. *T:* Berkhamsted 5677. *Club:* United University.

**GARDNER, James,** CBE 1959; RDI 1947; FSIA; Major RE; industrial designer and consultant; *b* 29 Dec. 1907; *s* of Frederic James Gardner; *m* 1935, Mary Williams; two *s. Educ:* Chiswick and Westminster Schools of Art. Jewellery Designer, Cartier Ltd, 1924-31; Publicity Designer, Carlton Studios, 1933-40. Served War of 1939-45, Chief Development Officer, Army Camouflage, 1941-46. Designer, Britain Can Make It Exhibition, 1946; Chief Designer, Festival Gardens, Battersea, 1950; British Pavilion, Brussels, 1959; The New Commonwealth Institute, 1962; responsible for St Helens Glass Museum, 1964; Designer: the Evoluon Museum, Eindhoven, Netherlands; Britain Today section, British Pavilion, Expo '67, Montreal; and responsible for visual design of the Queen Elizabeth 2, 1968. *Address:* The Studio, 140 Haverstock Hill, Hampstead, NW3. *Club:* Arts.

**GARDNER, John Linton;** composer; *b* 2 March 1917; *s* of late Dr Alfred Gardner, Ilfracombe, and Muriel (*née* Pullein-Thompson); *m* 1955, Jane, *d* of N. J. Abercrombie, *qv*; one *s* two *d. Educ:* Eagle House, Sandhurst; Wellington Coll.; Exeter Coll., Oxford (BMus). Served War of 1939-45: RAF, 1940-46. Chief Music Master, Repton Sch., 1939-40. Staff, Covent Garden Opera, 1946-52; Tutor: Morley Coll., 1952- (Dir of Music, 1965-69); Bagot Stack Coll., 1955-62; London Univ. (extra-mural) 1959-60; Dir of Music, St Paul's Girls' Sch., 1962-; Prof. of Harmony and Composition, Royal Acad. of Music, 1956-. Conductor: Haslemere Musical Soc., 1953-62; Dorian Singers, 1961-62; European Summer Sch. for Young Musicians, 1966-. Brit. Council Lecturer: Levant, 1954; Belgium, 1960; Iberia, 1963; Yugoslavia, 1967. Member: Arts Council Music Panel, 1958-62; Council, Composers' Guild, 1961- (Chm., 1963; Delegate to USSR, 1964); Cttee of Management, Royal Philharmonic Soc., 1965-68; Brit. Council Music Cttee, 1968-. Dir, Performing Right Soc., 1965-. Worshipful Co. of Musicians: Collard Fellow, 1962-64; elected to Freedom and Livery, 1965. Hon. RAM 1959. Bax Society's Prize, 1958. *Works include:* Symphony no 1, 1947; A Nativity Opera (libretto by Tyrone Guthrie and A. V. Coton), 1950; *Cantiones Sacrae*, for sop., chor. and orch.; Variations on a Waltz of Carl Nielsen, for orch.; Reflection, ballet (with John Cranko), 1952; The Moon and Sixpence, opera (libretto, based on Somerset Maugham's novel, by Patrick Terry); Piano Concerto No 1, 1957; *Jubilate Deo*, for unacc. chor., 1957; The Ballad of the White Horse (poem by Chesterton), for bar., chor. and orch., 1959; *Sinfonia Piccola* for Strings, 1960; Vile Bodies, musical (script based on Waugh's novel, by Patrick Terry, with lyrics by Paul Jennings); Herrick Cantata, for ten. chor. and orch., 1961; A Latter-Day Athenian Speaks, motet (poem by C. H. O. Scaife), 1962; The Noble Heart, a tribute to Shakespeare for the Quatercentenary Celebrations at Stratford (text arr. by Ormerod Greenwood) for sop., bass, chor, and orch., 1963; *Cantor popularis vocis*, motet for 18th Schuetz Festival, Berlin (poem by Philip Vellacott), 1964; Mass in C for unacc. chor., 1965; Cantata for Christmas, for chor. and cham. orch., 1966; Proverbs of Hell (text arr. from Blake by Ormerod Greenwood), for unacc. chor., 1967; Concerto da Camera for 4 insts, Occasional Suite (for Aldeburgh Festival); Partita for solo 'cello, 1968; An English Ballad for orch., 1969; Chamber Concerto, for organ and 11 insts, 1969; Cantata for Easter, for soli, chor., organ and percussion, 1970; Three Ridings, for orchestra, 1970. Many smaller pieces and music for films, Old Vic and Royal Shakespeare Theatres, BBC. Contributor to: Dublin Review, Musical Times, Tempo, Composer, Music in Education. *Recreations:* loco-spotting and tesseraphily. *Address:* 10 Lynton Road, New Malden, Surrey. *T:* 01-942 7322.

**GARDNER, John William;** Consultant, Carnegie Corporation, since 1968; Chairman, Urban Coalition, since 1968; *b* 8 Oct. 1912; *s* of William Frederick and Marie (Flora) Gardner; *m* 1934, Aida Marroquin, two *d. Educ:* Stanford Univ. (AB 1935, AM 1936); Univ. of Calif. (PhD 1938). 1st Lt-Captain, US Marine Corps, 1943-46. Teaching Asst in Psychology, Univ. of Calif., 1936-38; Instructor in Psychology, Connecticut Coll., 1938-40; Asst Prof. in Psychology, Mt Holyoke Coll., 1940-42; Head of Latin Amer. Section, Federal Communications Commn, 1942-43. Carnegie Corporation of New York: Staff Mem., 1946-47; Exec. Associate, 1947-49; Vice-Pres., 1949-

55; Pres., 1955-67; Pres., Carnegie Foundn for Advancement of Teaching, 1955-67. Chairman: US Adv. Commn on Internat. Educational and Cultural Affairs, 1962-64; Pres. Johnson's Task Force on Educn, 1964; White House Conf. on Educn, 1965. Dir, Amer. Assoc. for Advancement of Science, 1963-65. Member: Divisional Cttee for Social Sciences, Nat. Science Foundn, 1959-62; President's Gen. Adv. Cttee on Foreign Assistance Programs, 1965. Director: New York Telephone Co., 1962-65; Shell Oil Co., 1962-65; Time Inc., 1968-; American Airlines, 1968-. Trustee: Educational Testing Service, 1955-64; System Develt Corpn, 1957-61; Woodrow Wilson Foundn, 1960-63; Metropolitan Museum of Art, 1961-65. Benjamin Franklin Fellow, RSA, 1964. Holds hon. degrees from various colleges and univs. USAF Exceptional Service Award, 1956; Presidential Medal of Freedom, 1964; Public Welfare Medal, Nat. Acad. of Science, 1967. *Publications:* Excellence, 1961; (ed) Pres. John F. Kennedy's book, To Turn the Tide, 1961; Self-Renewal, 1964; No Easy Victories, 1968; The Recovery of Confidence, 1970. *Address:* 5325 Kenwood Avenue, Chevy Chase, Maryland 20015, USA. *Clubs:* Century Association, Coffee House (New York); Cosmos (Washington); Bohemian (San Francisco).

**GARDNER, Kenneth Burslam;** Principal Keeper of Printed Books, British Museum, since 1970; *b* 5 June 1924; *s* of D. V. Gardner; *m* 1949, Cleone Winifred Adams; two *s* two *d*. *Educ:* Alleyne's Grammar Sch., Stevenage; University College, London; School of Oriental and African Studies, Univ. of London (BA Hons Japanese). War service, Intelligence Corps (Captain), 1943-47. Assistant Librarian, School of Oriental and African Studies, 1949-54; Assistant Keeper, Department of Oriental Printed Books and MSS, British Museum, 1955-57, Keeper, 1957-70. *Publications:* contrib. to jls of oriental studies, art and librarianship. *Address:* 1 Duncombe Road, Bengeo, Hertford.

**GARDNER, W(alter) Frank,** CBE 1953; Director, The Prudential Assurance Co. Ltd, since 1961 (Deputy Chairman, 1965-69); *b* 6 Nov. 1900; *s* of late Walter Gardner and late Emma Mabel Gardner, Streatham Hill, SW2; *m* 1st, 1925, Constance Gladys (*d* 1945), *d* of late Ellen Haydon and late Frederick William Haydon, Norwich; one *d*; 2nd, 1949, Kathleen Lilian, *y d* of late Florence Charlotte and late George William Smith, Hampton Hill, and *widow* of Dr Frederick Lishman, Bexhill. *Educ:* Dulwich College; Institute of Actuaries. Actuary, Prudential Assurance Co. Ltd, 1945-50; General Manager, 1950-60. Fellow (FIA), 1924; President, 1952-54. FSS 1952. *Publications:* contributions to Journal of Institute of Actuaries. *Recreations:* golf, cine-photography. *Address:* 8c South Cliff Tower, Eastbourne, Sussex. *Clubs:* Junior Carlton; Devonshire (Eastbourne).

**GARDNER, William Henry,** CMG 1948; *b* 20 April 1895; *s* of William John Gardner, Walthamstow, Essex; *m*. 1st, 1920, Dorothy Margaret (*d* 1950), *e d* of John William Freeman; one *s*; 2nd, 1964, Elsie Stephenson (*d* 1967), Edinburgh, *d* of Henry Stephenson, Co. Durham. *Educ:* Maynard Road Elementary Sch. and Sir George Monoux Grammar Sch., Walthamstow; King's Coll., London. Entered Civil Service as boy clerk, 1910; second division clerk, 1913; Staff Clerk, 1929; Principal, WO, 1940; Asst Secretary, WO, 1942; Asst Under-Secretary of State, 1952-55; retired from War Office, 1955. Served European War, 1914-18, In Queen's Westminster Rifles, 1915-19; Lieut WO Home Guard, 1940-45. Lay Reader in diocese of Chelmsford 1922- and in diocese of Edinburgh, 1965; Hon. Secretary Chelmsford Diocesan Union, Church of England Men's Society, 1925-32, 1958-62; Vice-Chairman, 1962-66, Vice-President, 1966. Deputy Leader, UK delegation to Geneva Conference on Protection of War Victims, 1949. Hon. Member, Florence Nightingale International Nurses' Association, 1967. *Recreations:* walking, reading. *Address:* 3 Lonsdale Terrace, Edinburgh 3. *T:* 031-229 7443. *Clubs:* Royal Commonwealth Society; Essex County Cricket.

**GARDNER, William Maving;** Designer and craftsman in private practice; *b* 25 May 1914; *s* of late Robert Haswell Gardner, MIMarE, and Lucy Maving; *m* 1940, Joan Margaret Pollard; two *s* one *d*. *Educ:* privately; RCA School of Design, Travelling Scholar, Scandinavia, 1939. Sometime Visiting Lecturer, Department of Graphic Art, LCC Central School of Arts and Crafts, Cambridgeshire College of Arts and Technology; Visitor to Hastings School of Art, 1956-; Visiting Lecturer, Hampstead Garden Suburb Institute, 1959-; Examiner in Craft Subjects, Associated Examining Board of City and Guilds of London, 1957-60; Visiting Professor, Department of Science and Arts, Colorado State University, 1963, also Fine Arts Program Lecturer, with Exhibitions of work at Fort Collins and Denver, Colorado. ARCA 1938; Member Royal Mint Panel of Artists, 1939; Hon. Mem., Royal Numismatic Soc. of NZ, 1966. FRSA 1955; FSIA 1964 (MSIA 1957). Churchill Fellowship (Polynesia, New Zealand, Australia), 1966; Leverhulme (Research) Fellowship, 1969. *Official commissions include:* design and engraving of coinage reverses for: Hashemite Kingdom of Jordan, 1950; UK, 1953; Cyprus, 1955; Republic of Cyprus, 1963; Republic of Algeria, 1964; Republic of Guyana, 1967, 1969; Government of New Zealand, 1967; Government of Ceylon, 1968; Dominican Republic, 1969; Seal for HM Secretaries of State (the Greater and Lesser Signets), 1955; Colonial Seal, 1955; HM Privy Council Seal, 1955; Badges of Honour for Sarawak, Singapore and North Borneo; King George VI Medal for Courage in the Cause of Freedom; RCA Silver Medal of Merit; Seal of BMA, 1957; stained glass commemorative window for Tercentenary of the Royal Society, 1960; Seal of the RSA, 1966; Seal of the University of Aston, Birmingham, 1966; Winston Churchill Memorial Trust Foundn Medal, 1969; *calligraphic work includes:* inscription of Rolls of Honour (War of 1939-45) for: Life Guards, Royal Horse Guards, Grenadier, Coldstream, Scots, Irish and Welsh Guards, completed 1956; House of Commons, 1949; London Transport, 1954; Royal Marines Commandos Book of Remembrance, 1960. *Publications:* (jointly), Calligrapher's Handbook, 1956; contributions to The Penrose Annual, Spinks Numismatic Chronicle, Jl of RSA, and other journals. *Address:* Chequertree, Wittersham, Tenterden, Kent.

**GARDNER, Air Commodore William Steven,** CB 1958; OBE 1945; DFC 1940 and bar 1941; AFC 1943; *b* 16 Dec. 1909; *s* of late Campbell Gardner, JP, Groomsport, Co. Down, Northern Ireland; *m* 1937, Theodora, *d* of W. G. Bradley, Castlerock, Co. Derry; one *s* one *d* (and one *d* decd). *Educ:* Campbell Coll., Belfast. Joined RAF 1935; served in 106, 44 and 144 Squadrons, Bomber Command, 1939-45. Group Capt. 1951; Air Commodore, 1956; Head of Plans and Operations, CENTO, 1957-59; Acting Air Vice-Marshal, 1963; Provost

Marshal, 1960-63; Director-General of Personal Services, 1963. *Recreation:* sailing. *Address:* Corner Cottage, Shipton Green, Itchenor, Sussex. *Clubs:* United Hunts; Royal Ulster Yacht.

**GARDNER-BROWN, Anthony Geoffrey Hopwood,** CMG 1958; *b* 1 Oct. 1913; *yr s* of late Rev. F. S. G. Gardner-Brown; *m* 1939, Margaret, *yr d* of H. Sparrow; three *d. Educ:* Marlborough; Pembroke Coll., Cambridge. Cadet, Colonial Administrative Service, Northern Rhodesia, 1936; District Officer, 1938; served 1st Bn Northern Rhodesia Regt, East Africa and Ceylon, 1940-43; Supervisor Colonial Service Courses, Cambridge Univ., 1949-51; Assistant Secretary (Native Affairs), Northern Rhodesia, 1952; Colonial Secretary, Bahamas, 1952-56; Deputy Chief Secretary, Federation of Nigeria, 1956-58; Secretary for Defence and External Affairs, Federation of Nigeria, 1958-59. Deputy Governor-General, Federation of Nigeria, Nov. 1959-Oct. 1960; retired, 1961. Organiser, Community Council of Devon, 1961-63; Chairman, Salaries Commn, Windward and Leeward Islands, 1965; Comr on Anomalies, Western Pacific High Commn, 1965; Salaries Comr, Barbados, Mauritius, 1966, Swaziland, 1967, Bermuda, 1969. Chairman, Somerset County Scout Council, 1967. *Recreation:* fishing. *Address:* The Old Rectory, Stawley, Wellington, Somerset. *T:* Greenham 205. *Club:* Royal Societies.

**GARDNER-MEDWIN, Robert Joseph,** FRIBA, MTPI; Roscoe Professor of Architecture, Liverpool University, since 1952; *b* 10 April 1907; *s* of late Dr and Mrs F. M. Gardner-Medwin; *m* 1935, Margaret, *d* of late Mr Justice and Mrs Kilgour, Winnipeg; four *s. Educ:* Rossall Sch., Lancashire; School of Architecture, Liverpool Univ. (BArch, Dipl Civ Des). Commonwealth Fund Fellowship in City Planning and Landscape Design, Harvard Univ., 1933-35; private practice, and architectural teaching at Architectural Association and Regent Street Polytechnic, 1936-40. Served War of 1939-45, with Royal Engineers (Major, RE), 1940-43. Adviser in Town Planning and Housing to Comptroller of Development and Welfare in the British West Indies, 1944-47, Chief Architect and Planning Officer to Department of Health for Scotland, 1947-52. President, Liverpool Architectural Society, 1966. *Publications:* (with H. Myles Wright, MA, FRIBA) Design of Nursery and Elementary Schools, 1938; contributions to Town Planning Review, Architects' Journal, Journals of the RIBA and the TPI, etc. *Address:* 6 Kirby Mount, West Kirby, Cheshire.

**GARDYNE, John B.;** *see* Bruce-Gardyne.

**GARING, Air Commodore William Henry,** CBE 1943; DFC 1940; Executive Director, Rothmans National Sport Foundation, Sydney, Australia, since 1964; *b* Corryong, Victoria, 26 July 1910; *s* of late George Garing, retired grazier, and late Amy Evelyn Garing; *m* 1st, 1940 (marr. diss. 1951); one *s* one *d*; 2nd, 1954, Marjorie Irene Smith, Preston, England; two *d. Educ:* Corryong Higher Elementary School; Melbourne Technical Coll.; Royal Military Coll., Duntroon, ACT. Began career as Electrical and Mechanical Engineer, 1928; entered RMC, Duntroon, 1929, as specially selected RAAF Cadet; Flying Training in Australia. 1931-32, in UK 1934-35; Seaplane Flying Instructor and Chief Navigation Instructor, Point Cook, Victoria, 1936; commanded Seaplane Squadron, Point Cook; conducted first Specialist Air Navigation Course in Australia, 1938; posted to United Kingdom in 1939; served with No 10 Squadron, RAAF, as Flt Commander in Coastal Command, RAF, 1939; operations in N Atlantic, France and Mediterranean (DFC); flew Lord Lloyd to France for discussions with Pétain Government prior to collapse of France, 1940, and subsequently was pilot to the late Duke of Kent and to Mr Eden (Now Lord Avon), and others (despatches). Arrived Australia, 1941; Senior Air Staff Officer, HQ Northern Area (extended from Neth. Indies through New Guinea, British Solomons to New Caledonia), 1941; commanded No 9 (Ops) Group RAAF, New Guinea, 1942; Milne Bay Campaign, 1942; Buna Campaign, 1942-43 (American DSC); 1943 (CBE); commanded No 1 Operational Training Unit, 1943 (1939-43 star); Director Operational Requirements, 1944; SASO to RAAF Rep., Washington, 1945-46; OC Western Area, 1947; Joint Services Staff Coll., 1948; Commandant School Land/Air Warfare, NSW, 1950; OC Amberley, Qld, 1951; Imperial Defence Coll., London, 1952. AOC Overseas HQ, London, 1953; AOC RAAF, Richmond, NSW, 1953-55; AOC RAAF and Commandant RAAF Staff Coll., Point Cook, Victoria, 1955-60; Air Officer, South Australia, and OC, RAAF, Edinburgh Field, Salisbury, SA, 1960-64, retired. Holds No 1 Air Navigators' Certificate (Australia); Air Master Navigator (RAF). FAIM 1964. *Recreations:* Alpine ski-ing, water ski-ing, yachting, golf, shooting. *Address:* c/o Rothmans National Sport Foundation, 45 Macquarie Street, Sydney, NSW 2000, Australia; (home) Bryn Mawr, 25 Bangalla Street, Warrawee, NSW 2074, Australia. *Clubs:* Imperial Service, NSW Leagues, Royal Prince Alfred Yacht (Sydney).

**GARLAKE, Maj.-Gen. Storr,** CBE 1949; *b* 11 April 1904; *yr s* of John Storr Inglesby and Dorothy Eleanor Garlake, Cradock, CP; *m* 1932, Catherine Ellen, *er d* of James Wightman, Cape Town; one *s* one *d. Educ:* St Andrew's Prep. Sch., Grahamstown; RN Colleges, Osborne and Dartmouth. Joined BSAP, 1925; commissioned 1929; transferred to S Rhodesia Staff Corps, 1933; Maj.-Gen. 1953. Served War of 1939-45, ME and India, 1942-45; Commander Military Forces, S Rhodesia, 1947-53; Imp. Defence Coll., 1949; Chief of General Staff, Federation of Rhodesia and Nyasaland, 1953-59. Additional ADC to the Queen, 1952-54. *Address:* Froghill, PO Box HG 47, Highlands, Salisbury, Rhodesia. *Club:* Salisbury (Salisbury, Rhodesia).

**GARLAND, Ailsa Mary, (Mrs John Rollit Mason);** Fashion Coordinator, IPC Magazines Ltd; *d* of James Francis Garland and Elsie Elizabeth Langley; *m* 1948, John Rollit Mason; one *s. Educ:* La Retraite, Clapham Park; St Mary's, Woodford Green, Essex. Fashion Editor, Vogue Export Book, 1947-50; Editor, Shopping Magazine, 1952-53; Woman's Editor, Daily Mirror, 1953-59, Assistant Editor, 1959-60; Editor of Vogue, 1960-63; Director, Condé Nast Publications Ltd, 1961-63; Editor in Chief, Woman's Jl, 1963-68; Editor of Fashion, 1967-68; Dir, Fleetway Publications Ltd, 1963-68. Governor, London College of Fashion, 1961-68. Mem. Consultative Cttee, Coll. of Fashion and Clothing Technology. Broadcaster on Radio and TV. *Publication:* Lion's Share (autobiog.), 1970. *Recreations:* gardening, reading, theatre. *Address:* 30 Bramham Gardens, SW5. *T:* 01-373 5598; Lion Cottage, Prentice Street, Lavenham, Suffolk.

**GARLAND, (Frederick) Peter (Collison),** CVO 1969; Chief Constable of Norfolk since 1956; *b* 4 Sept. 1912; *s* of late Percy Frederick Garland,

Southsea, Hants; *m* 1945, Gwendolen Mary, *d* of late Henry James Powell, Putney; three *d*. *Educ:* Bradfield Coll. Joined Metropolitan Police, 1934. Served in RAF (Air Crew), 1941-45. Asst Chief Constable of Norfolk, 1952-56. CStJ 1961; Queen's Police Medal, 1965. *Address:* 2 Eaton Road, Norwich. *T:* Norwich 53043; Norfolk Joint Police Headquarters, Norwich. *T:* Norwich 21234. *Clubs:* Royal Air Force; Norfolk County (Norwich).

**GARLAND, Prof. Henry Burnard,** JP; MA, PhD; Professor of German in the University of Exeter since 1948; *b* 30 Aug. 1907; *s* of late William Garland, Dover, and Alice Mary (*née* Jarry); *m* 1949, Hertha Marie Louise (*née* Wiesener); two *d*. *Educ:* Dover County Sch.; Emmanuel Coll., Cambridge. BA, Mod. & Med. Langs. Tripos, 1st Class with Distinction, 1930; Patterson Prizeman, 1930; Tiarks German Scholar, 1931; Faculty Assistant Lecturer, Cambridge, 1934; MA 1934, PhD (Cantab) 1935; University Lecturer, Cambridge, 1937. Served War of 1939-45; Cambridge STC, 1940-43; RA, 1943-46, UK, Belgium, Germany (Colonel). Controller and Chief Editor, Die Welt, Hamburg, 1946; Head German Department, University College, Exeter, 1947; Chairman Arts Faculty, 1947-53; Vice-Principal, 1953-55; Acting Principal, 1953-54; Elector, Schröder Chair of German, Cambridge Univ., 1954-; Deputy Vice-Chancellor, Exeter Univ., 1955-57; Public Orator, 1956-65. JP Exeter, 1961; Member, State Studentship Selection Cttee, Department of Education and Science, 1965-68, Panel Chairman, 1966-68. Governor, Blundell's Sch., 1969-. Bronze Medal, Univ. of Rennes, 1970. *Publications:* Lessing: The Founder of Modern German Literature, 1937; Schiller, 1949; Storm and Stress, 1952; Schiller Revisited, 1959; Schiller the Dramatic Writer, 1969; Editions of works by Schiller (3), Lessing, Fontane and H. v. Kleist; Essays on Schiller, Fontane and Schnitzler; contributions to Cassell's Encyclopædia of Literature, Collier's Encyclopædia. *Recreations:* music, gardening, bird-watching. *Address:* 5 Rosebarn Avenue, Exeter. *T:* Exeter 55009.

**GARLAND, Peter;** *see* Garland, F. P. C.

**GARLICK, Prof. George Frederick John,** BSc, PhD, DSc, FInstP; Professor of Physics, University of Hull, since 1956; *b* 21 Feb. 1919; *s* of George Robert Henry Garlick and Martha Elizabeth (*née* Davies); *m* 1943, Dorothy Mabel Bowsher; one *d*. *Educ:* Wednesbury High Sch.; Univ. of Birmingham (BSc 1940, PhD 1943, DSc 1955). War service: Scientific Officer (Radar Research). In Charge Luminescence Laboratory, Birmingham Univ., 1946-56 (Research Physicist, 1946-49, Lecturer in Physics, 1949-56). FInstP, 1949. *Publications:* Luminescent Materials, 1949; numerous papers in learned scientific journals. *Recreation:* music (organ). *Address:* 98 Fairfax Avenue, Hull, Yorks. *T:* Hull 408890.

**GARLICK, John;** Under-Secretary, Ministry of Transport, since 1966; *b* 17 May 1921; *m* 1945, Frances Esther Munday; three *d*. *Educ:* Westcliff High Sch., Essex; University of London. Entered Post Office Engineering Dept, 1937; Ministry of Transport, 1948; Private Secretary to Rt Hon. Ernest Marples, 1959-60; Assistant Secretary, 1960; National Economic Development Office, 1962-64. *Address:* 16 Astons Road, Moor Park, Northwood, Middlesex. *T:* Northwood 24628.

**GARLICK, Rev. Canon Wilfrid;** Vicar of St George, Stockport, since 1948 and Rural Dean of Stockport since 1964; Hon. Canon of Chester since 1958; Hon. Chaplain to the Queen since 1964; *b* 12 Oct. 1910; *s* of Arthur and Clemence Garlick; *m* 1936, Edith, *d* of late H. Goddard; one *s*. *Educ:* Oldham Hulme Grammar Sch.; Manchester Univ. (MA *hc* 1968); Egerton Hall Theological Coll. BSc 1931, Manchester. Curate St Andrew, Ancoats, Manchester, 1933-35; Curate St Clement, Chorlton-cum-Hardy, 1935-38; Rector St Nicholas, Burnage, Manchester, 1938-44; Officiating Chaplain to Forces, 1938-44; Vicar of St George, Sheffield, 1944-48. *Recreations:* golf, travel. *Address:* St George's Vicarage, Stockport, Cheshire. *T:* Stockport 2453. *Club:* Royal Commonwealth Society.

**GARLIES, Lord; Randolph Keith Reginald Stewart;** *b* 14 Oct. 1928; *s* and *heir* of 12th Earl of Galloway, *qv*. *Educ:* Harrow. *Address:* Cumloden, Newton Stewart, Wigtownshire, Scotland.

**GARMOYLE, Viscount; Simon Dallas Cairns;** *b* 27 May 1939; *er s* and *heir* of 5th Earl Cairns, *qv*; *m* 1964, Amanda Mary, *d* of late Major E. F. Heathcoat Amory, and of Mrs Roderick Heathcoat Amory, Oswaldkirk Hall, York; three *s*. *Educ:* Eton; Trinity Coll., Cambridge. *Heir:* *s* Hon. Hugh Sebastian Cairns, *b* 26 March 1965. *Address:* 43 Bedford Gardens, W8. *T:* 01-727 0673. *Club:* Turf.

**GARNER,** family name of **Baron Garner.**

**GARNER,** Baron *cr* 1969 (Life Peer), of Chiddingly; **(Joseph John) Saville Garner,** GCMG 1965 (KCMG 1954; CMG 1948); Chairman, Board of Governors, Commonwealth Institute, and Chairman, Commonwealth Scholarship Commission in the UK, since 1968; *b* 14 Feb. 1908; *s* of Joseph and Helena Maria Garner, Highgate, N; *m* 1938, Margaret Beckman, Cedar Lake, Ind, USA; two *s* one *d*. *Educ:* Highgate Sch.; Jesus Coll., Cambridge. Appointed Dominions Office, 1930; Private Sec. to successive Secretaries of State, 1940-43; Senior Sec., office of UK High Comr Ottawa, 1943-46; Dep. High Comr for the UK, Ottawa, Canada, 1946-48; Asst Under-Sec., Commonwealth Relations Office, 1948-51; Deputy High Commissioner for the UK in India, 1951-53; Deputy Under-Secretary, Commonwealth Relations Office, 1952-56; British High Commissioner in Canada, 1956-61; Permanent Under-Secretary of State, Commonwealth Relations Office, 1962-65, Commonwealth Office, 1965-68; Head of HM Diplomatic Service, 1965-68. Secretary, Order of St Michael and St George, 1966-68 (Registrar, 1962-66). London Dir, Bank of Adelaide, 1969-. Member: Council, Voluntary Service Overseas, 1969-; Security Commission, 1968-. Bd of Govs, SOAS, Univ. of London, 1968-; Governor, Highgate School, 1962-. Hon. LLD: Univ. of Brit. Columbia, 1958; Univ. of Toronto, 1959; Hon. Fellow, Jesus College, Cambridge, 1967. President, Old Cholmeleian Society, 1964. *Publications:* The Books of the Emperor Wu Ti (transl. from German), 1930. *Recreations:* gardening, travel. *Address:* 23 Kennington Palace Court, SE11. *T:* 01-735 7408; Highdown Farmhouse, Horam, Sussex. *T:* Chiddingly 432. *Clubs:* Travellers', Royal Automobile.

**GARNER, Frank Harold;** Principal, Royal Agricultural College, Cirencester, Gloucestershire, 1958-Sept. 1971; *b* 4 Dec. 1904; *m* 1929, Hilda May Sheppard; one *d*. *Educ:* Swindon Technical Sch.; Universities of Cambridge, Oxford, Reading and Minnesota, USA. MA (Cantab), MA (Oxon), MSc (Minnesota, USA). Assistant to Director of Cambridge University Farm, 1924; University

Demonstrator in Agriculture at Cambridge, 1927; University Lecturer (Animal Husbandry) at Cambridge, 1929; Assistant to Executive Officer, Cambridgeshire War Agriculture Executive Cttee, 1939; County Agricultural Organiser, East Suffolk, 1940; General Manager of Frederick Hiam Ltd, 1944. Liveryman, Farmers' Livery Co. *Publications:* British Dairy Farming; Cattle of Britain; The Farmers Animals; (with E. T. Halnan and A. Eden) Principles and Practice of Feeding Farm Animals. *Recreation:* swimming. *Address:* Royal Agricultural College, Cirencester, Glos. *T:* Cirencester 2531; (after Sept. 1971) Culverton Farm, Princes Risborough, Bucks. *Club:* Farmers'.

**GARNER, Frederic Francis,** CMG 1959; Ambassador to Costa Rica, 1961-67; retired; *b* 9 July 1910; *m* 1946, Muriel (*née* Merrick). *Educ:* Rugby Sch.; Worcester Coll., Oxford. Joined HM Consular Service in China, 1932; served at Peking, Canton, Shanghai, POW in Japan, 1942-45. Consul, Tangier, 1947-50; First Secretary, Bogota, 1950-54; Consul-General, Shanghai, 1954-56; Head of Consular Department, Foreign Office, 1956-58; Ambassador at Phnom Penh, 1958-61. *Address:* 44 Belgrave Mews South, SW1. *T:* 01-235 7507.

**GARNER, Sir Harry Mason,** KBE 1951; CB 1948; FRAeS; Chief Scientist to Ministry of Supply, 1949-53; *b* 3 Nov. 1891; *s* of William Garner, Wymeswold, Loughborough; *m* 1921, Hilda Annie Green; one *s* one *d*. *Educ:* Market Bosworth Grammar Sch.; St John's Coll., Cambridge. Senior Scientific Officer, Royal Aircraft Establishment, 1927; Chief Technical Officer, Marine Aircraft Experimental Establishment, Felixstowe, 1929; Deputy Director Scientific Research, Ministry of Aircraft Production, 1943; Principal Director, Scientific Research (Air), Ministry of Supply, 1946-49. *Publications:* Oriental Blue and White, 1954; Chinese and Japanese Cloisonné Enamels, 1962; scientific on aerodynamics and on oriental art. *Recreations:* music, oriental art. *Address:* 79 Downs Hill, Beckenham, Kent. *T:* 01-650 3364. *Club:* Athenæum.

**GARNER, Maurice Richard;** Under-Secretary, Electricity Division, Ministry of Technology, since 1969; *b* 31 May 1915; *o s* of Jesse H. Garner; *m* 1943, Joyce W. Chapman; one *s* one *d*. *Educ:* Glendale County Sch.; London Sch. of Economics and Political Science. Royal Armoured Corps, 1942-45 (despatches). Inland Revenue (Tax Inspectorate), 1938-46; BoT, Asst Principal and Principal, 1947; Commercial Sec. and UK Trade Comr in Ottawa, 1948-55; transf. to Min. of Power, 1957; Asst Sec. 1960. *Recreations:* sailing, reading, oenology. *Address:* 12 Greenbrook Avenue, Hadley Wood, Herts. *T:* 01-449 7495.

**GARNER, Robert Livingston;** *b* Bolton, Mississippi, 7 Aug. 1894; *s* of late Robert Vincent Garner and Lillian Hardgrave Garner; *m* 1926, Ellen Wright Garner (decd); one *d*. *Educ:* Columbia Military Acad.; Vanderbilt Univ., Nashville, Tennessee (BS); Columbia University School of Journalism, New York. Captain of Infantry, 77th Division, War, 1917-18. Guaranty Trust Company: Educational Department, 1919-20; Buying Department, 1920-25; Investment Department Continental Insurance Co., 1925-26; Guaranty Trust Co. as Asst Treasurer and subseq. Treasurer and Vice-President, 1926-43; Financial Vice-President and Director of General Foods Corp., 1943-47; Vice-President, International Bank for Reconstruction and Development, 1947-56; President, International Finance Corporation, 1956-61. Trustee, Vanderbilt Univ. Director, American Security & Trust Co., Washington. *Recreations:* golfing, fishing, shooting. *Address:* 730 15th Street, NW, Washington 5, DC, USA. *T:* Sterling 3-6000, ext. 245. *Clubs:* University, The Links (NY); Chevy Chase, Metropolitan, Burning Tree (Washington).

**GARNETT, Bernard John,** CMG 1962; OBE 1950; Minister in UK Delegation to 18 Nation Disarmament Conference in Geneva, since 1966; *b* 20 June 1913; *o s* of late James Holden and Bertha Garnett; *m* 1950, Gwyneth May Jones; one *d*. *Educ:* Pembroke Dock County Sch.; The Leys; Emmanuel Coll., Cambridge. Entered HM Consular Service, 1936; has served at Bangkok, Lourenço Marques, Funchal, Algiers, Naples, and as a Foreign Service Inspector; Counsellor in British Military Government, Berlin, 1957-59; Counsellor (Commercial), Athens, 1960-63 (also Consul-General, 1960-62); Chief Inspector, HM Foreign Service, 1963-64, Diplomatic Service, 1965-66. *Address:* c/o Foreign and Commonwealth Office, SW1. *Club:* Travellers'.

**GARNETT, David,** CBE 1952; author; *b* 1892; *s* of late Edward and Constance Garnett; *m* 1st, Rachel Alice (*d* 1940), *d* of W. C. Marshall, architect; two *s*; 2nd, 1942, Angelica Vanessa, *o d* of late Clive Bell; four *d*. *Educ:* Royal College of Science, South Kensington. Fellow, Imperial College of Science and Technology, 1956. *Publications:* The Kitchen Garden and its Management; Lady into Fox (Hawthornden and Tait-Black Prizes for 1923); A Man in the Zoo; The Sailor's Return; Go She Must!; The Old Dovecote, 1928; No Love, 1929; The Grasshoppers Come, 1931; A Rabbit in the Air, 1932; Pocahontas, 1933; Beany-Eye, 1935; War in the Air, 1941; The Golden Echo, 1953; Flowers of the Forest, 1955; Aspects of Love, 1955; A Shot in the Dark, 1958; A Net for Venus, 1959; The Familiar Faces, 1962; Two by Two, 1963; Ulterior Motives, 1966; A Clean Slate, 1971. Edited: The Letters of T. E. Lawrence, 1938; The Novels of Thomas Love Peacock, 1948; The Essential T. E. Lawrence, 1951; The White-Garnett Letters, 1968; Carrington: Letters and extracts from her diaries, 1970. *Recreation:* travel. *Address:* Le Verger de Charry, Montcuq, Lot 46, France. *Club:* Reform.

**GARNETT, John;** *see* Garnett, W. J. P. M.

**GARNETT, Thomas Ronald,** MA; Headmaster of Geelong Church of England Grammar School, Australia, since Sept. 1961; *b* 1 Jan. 1915; *s* of E. N. Garnett; *m* 1946, Penelope, *d* of Philip Frere; three *s* two *d*. *Educ:* Charterhouse (Scholar); Magdalene Coll., Cambridge (Scholar). BA 1936, MA 1946. Assistant master: Westminster School, 1936-38; Charterhouse, 1938-52; Master of Marlborough College, 1952-61. Served War of 1939-45, RAF, India and Burma, 1941-46, Squadron Leader (despatches). Cricket for Somerset, 1939. *Recreation:* country life. *Address:* Geelong Church of England Grammar School, Corio, Victoria, Australia. *T:* Geelong 79452.

**GARNETT, (William) John (Poulton Maxwell),** CBE 1970; MA; Director, Industrial Society, since 1962; *b* 6 Aug. 1921; *s* of Dr Maxwell Garnett, CBE, and Margaret Lucy Poulton; *m* 1943, Barbara Rutherford-Smith; two *s* two *d*. *Educ:* Rugby Sch.; Kent Sch., USA; Trinity Coll., Cambridge. Royal Navy, 1941-46 (commnd, 1942). ICI Ltd, 1947-62. *Publications:* The Manager's Responsibility for Communication, 1964; Targets for Leaders in Industry, 1965. *Recreations:* sailing, rowing. *Address:* 31 Charlwood Road, Putney, SW15.

*T:* 01-788 5248. *Clubs:* Athenæum; Leander (Henley).

**GARNHAM, Prof. Percy Cyril Claude,** CMG 1964; FRS 1964; MD; Professor of Medical Protozoology (now Emeritus Professor), London University, and Head of Department of Parasitology, London School of Hygiene and Tropical Medicine, 1952-68; Senior Research Fellow, Imperial College Field Station, Ashurst Lodge, Ascot, Berks, since 1968; *b* 15 Jan. 1901; *s* of late Lieut P. C. Garnham, RN Division, and late Edith Masham; *m* 1924, Esther Long Price, Talley, Carms; two *s* four *d*. *Educ:* privately; St Bartholomew's Hospital. MRCS, LRCP, 1923, MB, BS London, 1923, DPH Eng. 1924, MD London, 1928 (University Gold Medal); Dipl. de Méd. Malariol., University of Paris, 1931. Colonial Medical Service, 1925-47; since 1947 on staff of London School of Hygiene and Tropical Medicine, first as reader, then as professor. Heath Clark Lectr, Univ. of London, 1968. Member, Expert Panels of Parasitic Diseases, of WHO; Pres., British Soc. of Parasitologists; Past President, Royal Society of Tropical Medicine and Hygiene; Vice-President: World Federation of Parasitologists; International Association against Filariasis; Corresponding Member: Academie Royale des Sciences d'Outre Mer, Belgium; Accad. Lancisiana, Rome; Hon. Member: Société Belge de Médicine Tropicale; Brazilian Soc. Tropical Medicine; Soc. of Protozoologists; Société de Pathologie Exotique; Mexican Soc. of Parasitologists; Polish Soc. of Parasitologists; British Soc. of Parasitologists. Hon. FRCP Edinburgh, 1967; FRCP 1967; FIBiol, 1962. Freedom, City of London in Farriers Co., 1964. DSc London, 1952; DUniv Bordeaux, 1965; Academician of Pontifical Acad. of Sciences, 1970. Darling Medal and Prize, 1951; Bernhard Nocht Medal, 1957; Gaspar Vianna Medal, 1962; Manson Medal, 1965. *Publications:* Malaria Parasites; Progress in Parasitology; numerous papers on parasitology in medical journals. *Recreations:* chamber music and European travel. *Address:* Southernwood, Farnham Common, Bucks. *T:* 3863. *Club:* Nairobi (Kenya).

**GARNOCK, Viscount; David Lindesay-Bethune;** *b* 9 Feb. 1926; *er s* of 14th Earl of Lindsay, *qv*; *m* 1953, Hon. Mary Clare Douglas-Scott-Montagu (marr. diss., 1968), *y d* of 2nd Baron Montagu of Beaulieu; one *s* one *d*.; *m* 1969, Penelope, *er d* of late Anthony Crossley, MP. *Educ:* Eton; Magdalene Coll., Cambridge. Scots Guards, 1943-45. US and Canadian Railroads, 1948-50; Director: John Crossley, Carpet Trades Holdings Ltd, Halifax; Crossley-Karastan Carpet Mills Ltd, Canada; Festiniog Railway Co. Ltd; John Howson Ltd; Abbey Life Insurance Co. of Canada. Mem., Queen's Body Guard for Scotland (Royal Company of Archers), 1960. *Heir: s* Master of Garnock, *qv*. *Address:* Kilconquhar House, Fife. *T:* Colinsburgh 212; The Slack, Heptonstall, Hebden Bridge, Yorks. *T:* Hebden Bridge 2201. *Club:* Bath.

**GARNOCK, Master of; Hon. James Randolph Lindesay-Bethune;** *b* 19 Nov. 1955; *s* and *heir* of Viscount Garnock, *qv*.

**GARNONS WILLIAMS, Basil Hugh;** Headmaster of Berkhamsted School since 1953; *b* 1 July 1906; 5th *s* of Rev. A. Garnons Williams, Rector of New Radnor; *m* 1943, Margaret Olive Shearme; one *s* two *d*. *Educ:* Winchester Coll. (Scholar); Hertford Coll., Oxford (Scholar). 1st Hon. Classical Moderations 1927; 2nd Lit Hum 1929; BA 1929; BLitt 1933; MA 1938; Classical VI Form Master, Sedbergh Sch., 1930-35; Marlborough Coll., 1935-45; Headmaster of Plymouth Coll., 1945-53. *Publications:* articles in Classical Quarterly and Greece and Rome; contributor to History of the World (ed by W. N. Weech), 1944. *Address:* Wilson House, Berkhamsted School, Herts. *T:* Berkhamsted 4827.

**GARNONS WILLIAMS, Captain Nevill Glennie,** MBE 1919; Royal Navy (Retired); Lord Lieutenant of Brecknockshire since 1964 (Vice-Lieutenant, 1959-64); *b* 1899; *s* of late Rev. Arthur Garnons Williams, Abercamlais, Brecon; *m* 1928, Violet, *d* of late B. G. Tours, CMG; one *d*. *Educ:* RN Colls, Osborne and Dartmouth; Caius Coll., Cambridge. Joined Royal Navy, 1912; served European War, 1914-18, Jutland (despatches); and War of 1939-45; retired as Capt., 1946. DL 1948, JP 1956, Brecknockshire. Mem. of Gov. Body, Rep. Body and Liturgical Commn of Church in Wales; Governor, Christ Coll., Brecon. Croix de Guerre (avec Palmes), 1916. CStJ 1966. *Recreations:* forestry, fishing, cricket, scouting. *Address:* Abercamlais, Brecon, S Wales. *T:* Sennybridge 206. *Clubs:* United Service, MCC.

**GARNSEY, Rt. Rev. David Arthur;** *see* Gippsland, Bishop of.

**GARNSWORTHY,** Baron *cr* 1967 (Life Peer) of Reigate; **Charles James Garnsworthy,** OBE 1965; JP; *b* 10 Dec. 1906; *s* of Charles Edward Garnsworthy and Helen Garnsworthy (*née* Edyvean); *m* 1943, Joyce Kingsley Morgan. *Educ:* Wellington Sch., Som. Bldg Industry, 1925; Insce Agency, 1931; Royal Corps of Signals, 1940-45. Member: Banstead UDC, 1937-47; Surrey CC, 1952- (Alderman, 1966-); Union of Shop Distributive and Allied Workers; (Coopted Mem.), LCC Children's Cttee, 1949-54; Chairman: De Burgh and Nork Park Schs, Banstead; Epsom Sch. of Art; Governors, Royal Alexandra and Albert Sch. Contested (Lab) Reigate, 1945, 1950, 1951, 1955, 1960 and 1964. JP Surrey, 1959. *Recreations:* walking, travel, theatre. *Address:* Little Dormers, Smith Lane, Lower Kingswood, Surrey. *T:* Mogador 2680.

**GARRAN, Sir (Isham) Peter,** KCMG 1961 (CMG 1954); HM Diplomatic Service, retired; Ambassador to the Netherlands, 1964-69; *b* 15 Jan. 1910; *s* of late Sir Robert Randolph Garran, GCMG, QC; *m* 1935, Mary Elisabeth, *d* of late Sir Richard Rawdon Stawell, KBE, MD; two *s* one *d*. *Educ:* Melbourne Grammar Sch.; Trinity Coll., Melbourne Univ. (BA). Joined Foreign Office as Third Sec., 1934; Second Sec., 1939; First Sec., 1944; Counsellor, 1947. Previous posts: Belgrade, 1937-41; Lisbon, 1941-44; Berlin (seconded to CCG as Chief of Political Div.), 1947-50; The Hague, 1950-52; Inspector in HM Foreign Service, 1952-54; Minister (Commercial), Washington, 1955-60; Ambassador to Mexico, 1960-64. Director: Lend-Lease Corp., NSW; Property Holdings International (Bermuda); UK Branch, Australian Mutual Provident Soc.; National Industrial Conference Bd, NY (Dir for UK). *Recreations:* golf, sailing. *Address:* Roanoke, Bosham Hoe, Sussex. *T:* Bosham 2347. *Club:* Boodle's.

**GARRARD, Henry John; His Honour Judge Garrard;** County Court Judge, Circuit No 26, since 1967 (Circuit No 25, 1965-67); *b* 15 Jan. 1912; *s* of late C. G. Garrard; *m* 1945, Muriel, *d* of late A. H. S. Draycott, Stratford-on-Avon; one *s* one *d*. *Educ:* Framlingham Coll., Suffolk. Called to the Bar, Middle Temple, Nov. 1937; Mem. of Oxford Circuit. Served 1939-45, Staffs Yeomanry (QORR) and Worcestershire Regt, East and North Africa, rank of Lieut;

prisoner-of-war, 1942-45. Mem. of Mental Health Review Tribunal for Birmingham Area, 1963-65; Recorder of Burton-on-Trent, 1964-65. *Recreations:* family and dogs. *Address:* The General's Farmhouse, Chartley, Stafford. *T:* Dapple Heath 268.

**GARRARD, Rev. Lancelot Austin,** LLD; BD, MA; Professor of Philosophy and Religion, Emerson College, Boston, USA, since 1965; *b* 31 May 1904; *s* of late Rev. W. A. Garrard; *m* 1932, Muriel Walsh; two *s*. *Educ:* Felsted (Scholar); Wadham Coll., Oxford (exhibitioner); Manchester Coll., Oxford; Marburg (Hibbert scholar). 2nd Class, Classical Mods; 2nd Class Lit Hum; Abbot Scholar; BD, MA (Oxon). Asst Master: Edinburgh Acad., 1927; St Paul's Sch., 1928; Unitarian Minister, Dover, 1932-33; Tutor and Bursar, Manchester Coll., Oxford, 1933-43; Minister, Lewins Mead Meeting, Bristol, 1941-43; Liverpool, Ancient Chapel of Toxteth, 1943-52; Tutor, Unitarian Coll., Manchester, 1945-51; Manchester Coll., Oxford, 1952-56; Principal of Manchester Coll., Oxford, 1956-65; Editor of The Hibbert Journal, 1951-62. Hon. Chief, Chickasaw Nation. Hon. LLD (Emerson Coll, Boston). *Publications:* Duty and the Will of God, 1935; The Interpreted Bible, 1946; The Gospels Today, 1953; The Historical Jesus: Schweitzer's Quest and Ours, 1956; Athens or Jerusalem?, 1965. *Recreation:* cycling. *Address:* Emerson College, 130 Beacon Street, Boston, Mass 02116, USA. *Club:* Athenæum.

**GARRATT, Gerald Reginald Mansel,** MA, CEng, FIEE; FRAeS; Keeper, Department of Aeronautics and Marine Transport, Science Museum, South Kensington, since 1966; *b* 10 Dec. 1906; *s* of Reginald R. and Florence Garratt; *m* 1931, Ellen Georgina Brooks, Antwerp, Belgium; two *d*. *Educ:* Marlborough Coll.; Caius Coll., Cambridge. International Telephone & Telegraph Laboratories, 1929-30; RAE, Farnborough, 1930-34; Asst Keeper: Dept of Textiles and Printing, Science Museum, 1934; Dept of Telecommunications, 1936; Dep. Keeper 1949. Served RAF 1939-46 (Wing Comdr). Founder Mem., Cambridge Univ. Air Squadron, 1926. Commissioned RAF Reserve of Officers, 1928; retired 1966 (Wing Comdr). *Publications:* One Hundred Years of Submarine Cables, 1950; numerous articles on history of telecommunications. *Recreations:* sailing, amateur radio. *Address:* Littlefield, Parkwood Avenue, Esher, Surrey. *T:* 01-398 1582. *Club:* Royal Automobile.

**GARRETT, Alexander Adnett,** MBE 1934; *b* London, 1886; *e s* of late Adnett William Garrett and Marion Walker Bruce; *m* 1928, Mildred, *g d* of L. S. Starrett, Athol, Mass. *Educ:* Owen's Sch., London; London Sch. of Economics (BSc); King's Coll., London (Gilbart Prizeman); Christ's Coll., Cambridge (Economics Tripos). FCIS; attended the 20th Convention of the American Institute of Accountants, St Louis, USA, 1924; Internat. Congresses on Accounting, Amsterdam, 1926, New York, 1929, and Berlin, 1938; Asst Sec., 4th Internat. Congress on Accounting, London, 1933; sometime Hon. Mem., former Soc. of Incorporated Accountants (Sec. 1919-49, retired 1949; Asst Sec., 1913); visited Accountancy Bodies in Canada, USA, Australia, New Zealand, South Africa, 1947-50. Dept of Applied Economics, Cambridge, 1950-59. Hon. Mem., Australian Soc. of Accountants, 1956. Served Royal Naval Reserve, 1915-31; Comdr (S), RNR (retired). *Publication:* History of the Society of Incorporated Accountants, 1885-1957, 1961. *Address:* 7 King's Bench Walk, Temple, EC4. *T:* 01-353 7880; Ayot St Lawrence, Herts. *T:* Codicote 269. *Clubs:* Athenæum, Reform.

**GARRETT, Lieut-Gen. Sir (Alwyn) Ragnar,** KBE 1959 (CBE 1944); CB 1957. Formerly Chief of the General Staff, Australian Military Forces (1958-60); *b* 12 Feb. 1900; *o s* of Alwyn and Marie Garrett; *m* 1925, Shirley Lorraine Hunter; one *s* one *d*. *Educ:* Guildford Gram. Sch.; Royal Military Coll., Duntroon. Attached Queen's Bays, India, 1922-23; served with Austr. Mil. Forces, 1923-37; Staff Coll., Camberley, 1938-39; AIF, 1939-46; Comdt, Austr. Staff Coll., 1946; Principal Administrative Officer and Comdt Austr. Component, BCOF, Japan, 1947-49; Comdt Austr. Staff Coll., 1950-51; GOC, Western Command, 1951-52; DCGS Australia, 1953; Adjutant-Gen., 1954; GOC Southern Command, 1954-58; Principal of the Australian Administrative Staff Coll., 1960-65. Chm., Australian Shipping Service, 1966. *Recreations:* golf, tennis. *Address:* 129 Forest Street, Peppermint Grove, Perth, Western Australia. *Clubs:* Melbourne, Naval and Military (Melbourne).

**GARRETT, Sir Hugh;** *see* Garrett, Sir J. H.

**GARRETT, Sir (Joseph) Hugh,** KCIE, *cr* 1939; CSI 1931; ICS (retired); BA (Cantab.); Capt. 10th Devon Bn Home Guard; *b* 22 June 1880; *s* of J. P. Garrett, Highgate; *m* Dilys M. Silvanus; one *d*; *m* 1967, Mrs F. M. Lipson-Ward. *Educ:* Highgate Sch.; Gonville and Caius Coll., Cambridge. Served in various districts of the Bombay Presidency as District Officer in later years chiefly in Gujarat; officiated on several occasions as Chief Sec. to Government of Bombay; Acting Governor of Sind, 1938. *Address:* Hesketh Cottage, Torquay, Devon. *Club:* East India and Sports.

**GARRETT, Philip Leslie;** Editor of The Ironmonger, 1934-53; *b* 11 Nov. 1888; *s* of late Joseph Payne Garrett, Highgate and Eleanor Adelaide Hope; *m* 1914, Phyllis Kathleen, *d* of late Lewis Medland; two *s* one *d*. *Educ:* Highgate Sch. Admitted a solicitor, 1911; practised in partnership with father; joined editorial staff of The Ironmonger, 1914; Asst Ed., 1926; Mem. of Law Soc. and for many years of Board of Management of Royal Metal Trades Pension and Benevolent Soc.; Hon. Mem. Nat. Federation of Ironmongers and first Hon. Mem. and Governor, Nat. Inst. of Hardware. *Publications:* Literary contributions to various newspapers and periodicals. *Recreations:* ornithology, reading. *Address:* Hilltop, Ballinger, Great Missenden, Bucks. *T:* The Lee 253.

**GARRETT, Lieut-Gen. Sir Ragnar;** *see* Garrett, Lieut-Gen. Sir A. R.

**GARRETT, Sir Ronald (Thornbury),** Kt, *cr* 1944; *b* 5 Nov. 1888; 3rd *s* of late Samuel Garrett, Aldeburgh, Suffolk, late Pres. of Law Soc.; *m* 1912, Catriona Marion Stewart Robertson (*d* 1961); one *s* one *d*. *Educ:* Rugby Sch. Articled to his father, 1909; gave up the law, 1912; entered employment of Anderson, Anderson & Co., joint managers of Orient Steam Navigation Co. Ltd. Served in the Army, Aug. 1914-Jan. 1919, retiring with rank of Capt. Member of Council of Chamber of Shipping, retd 1958; first Chm. of Nat. Dock Labour Corp; Chm. (1942-43) of London Gen. Shipowners' Soc.; mem. Port of London Authority, 1934-47; Underwriting Mem. of Lloyd's, 1952-; Chm., Lloyd's Register of Shipping, 1946-57; Dir, Anderson Green & Co. (Managers of Orient Line), 1924-58, retd. Pres. Inst. of Marine Engineers, 1957; Chm. Central Transport Consultative Cttee for

Great Britain, 1958-62. Prime Warden, Worshipful Co. of Shipwrights, 1956. *Recreations:* gardening, yachting, golf. *Address:* Brockley Place, Bury St Edmunds, Suffolk. *T:* Hartest 278. *Club:* Royal Cruising.

**GARRETT, Dr Stephen Denis,** FRS 1967; Reader in Mycology since 1961 and Director of Sub-department of Mycology since 1952, University of Cambridge; Fellow of Magdalene College, Cambridge, since 1963; *b* 1 Nov. 1906; *s* of Stephen and Mary Garrett, Leiston, Suffolk; *m* 1934, Ruth Jane Perkins; three *d. Educ:* Eastbourne Coll.; Cambridge Univ.; Imperial Coll., London. Asst Plant Pathologist, Waite Agric. Res. Inst., Univ. of Adelaide, 1929-33; Research Student, Imperial Coll., 1934-35; Mycologist, Rothamsted Experimental Stn, 1936-48; Lectr, later Reader, Botany Sch., University of Cambridge, 1949-. *Publications:* Root Disease Fungi, 1944; Biology of Root-infecting Fungi, 1956; Soil Fungi and Soil Fertility, 1963; Pathogenic Root-infecting Fungi, 1970; numerous papers. *Address:* Botany School, Downing Street, Cambridge. *T:* 61414; 179 Hills Road, Cambridge. *T:* 47865.

**GARRETT, William Edward;** MP (Lab) Wallsend since 1964; *b* 21 March 1920; *s* of John Garrett, coal miner, and Frances (*née* Barwise); *m* 1946, Beatrice Kelly; one *s. Educ:* Prudhoe Elementary Sch.; London Sch. of Economics. Commenced work in coal mines, 1934; served engineering apprenticeship, 1936-41; employed by ICI, 1943-64; Union Organiser at ICI, 1944-64; Mem. of AEU. Member: Prudhoe UDC, 1946-64; Northumberland County Council, 1955-64. Mem. of Labour Party, 1939-; Labour Candidate for Hexham 1953-55, Doncaster 1957-64. Mem., Select Cttee on Agriculture, 1966-69. *Recreations:* gardening, walking, reading. *Address:* 84 Broomhill Road, Prudhoe-on-Tyne, Northumberland. *T:* Prudhoe 2580. *Clubs:* Prudhoe Working Men's, Prudhoe Golf (Prudhoe).

**GARRETT, Sir William (Herbert),** Kt 1958; MBE 1944; retired as President, British Employers' Confederation, 1958-60; *b* 13 March 1900; *s* of William Henry Garrett and Mary Elizabeth (*née* Odgers); *m* 1925, Marion Birchall (*d* 1967), *yr d* of Joseph Henry Houghton; one *s* one *d. Educ:* Grove Park Sch.; Liverpool Univ. Served RFC and RAF 1917-19. BSc Hons, 1921, PhD, 1923, Liverpool Univ. Mem. Civil Service Arbitration Tribunal, 1960-65; Chm., Association of British Chemical Manufacturers, 1959-61. *Publications:* The Human Side of Industry, 1950; papers to several technical journals, 1946-. *Recreations:* golf, music. *Address:* 7c South Cliff Tower, Eastbourne, Sussex. *Club:* Junior Carlton.

**GARRINGTON, Mrs J. L. St C.;** *see* Chamberlain, Rev. Elsie D.

**GARRO JONES;** formerly family name of **Baron Trefgarne** (surname now changed to **Trefgarne**).

**GARROD, Geoffrey,** MA Oxon; Barrister-at-Law; *b* 31 Oct. 1886; *e s* of Herbert Baring Garrod, MA Oxon, Barrister-at-Law, and Lucy Florence Colchester; *g s* of Sir Alfred Baring Garrod, FRS, FRCP; *m* 1914, Margaret Langford (*d* 1953), *d* of Benjamin Duke, MD; one *s* three *d. Educ:* Winchester Coll. (Scholar); New Coll., Oxford (Scholar). Second Class in Class. Mods, 1907, and in Final Hons, 1909; BA 1909; MA 1912; literary and musical criticism in The Times, The Academy, The Onlooker, Colour, etc; Called to Bar, Inner Temple, 1912; Master St Paul's Preparatory Sch., 1914; City of London Sch., 1915-19; Headmaster of Sevenoaks School, Kent, 1919-25; Principal, Royal Academical Institution, Belfast, 1925-40; Lectr in Classics, University Coll., Exeter, for three years; Dir of Anglo-Brazilian Cultural Soc., Curitiba, Brazil, 1943-47; Senior Classical Master, Fernden Sch., 1950-65. *Publications:* ed (with mother), of Goethe, Dante's Faust and other Essays, by Herbert Baring Garrod; various articles on literary and musical subjects. *Recreations:* music (especially singing), stamp collecting, yachting, walking, lawn tennis, boating, swimming. *Address:* 30 Rectory Gardens, Worthing, Sussex. *T:* Worthing 30380. *Club:* Oxford and Cambridge Musical.

*See also P. A. G. Dixey.*

**GARROD, Lawrence Paul,** MD (Cambridge); FRCP; Emeritus Professor of Bacteriology, University of London; Hon. Consultant in Chemotherapy, Royal Postgraduate Medical School; Fellow of Royal Society of Medicine (Ex-President, Section Pathology); Editor, British Journal Experimental Pathology, 1951-57; *b* 7 Dec. 1895; *s* of late Cubitt Garrod and Gertrude Dwelley Davey; *m* 1922, Marjorie, *d* of late Bedford Pierce, MD, FRCP; three *s* one *d. Educ:* Sidcot Sch.; King's Coll., Cambridge; St Bartholomew's Hosp. Surg.-Sub-Lieut RNVR 1917-18; Brackenbury Scholar in Medicine, St Bartholomew's Hosp., 1919; Gillson Scholar, Society of Apothecaries, 1923-25; Studied clinical medicine for five years after qualification; from 1925-61 held appointments on staff of Dept of Pathology, St Bartholomew's Hosp.; late Bacteriologist to St Bartholomew's Hosp. and to City of London; late Consultant in Antibiotics to the Army; late Examiner in Pathology, Universities of London, Oxford and Cambridge; formerly Pres. Institute of Medical Laboratory Technology. Hon. LLD (Glasgow), 1965. Hon. Alumnus Medical Faculty, University of Louvain. *Publications:* Hospital Infection, 1960-66; Antibiotic and Chemotherapy (jointly), 1963, 3rd edn 1970; various papers, mainly on bacteriology and chemotherapy. *Recreations:* music, gardening, golf. *Address:* 2 Cross Path, Radlett, Herts. *T:* Radlett 6873.

**GARROW, Sir Nicholas,** Kt 1965; OBE 1956; JP; retired, 1960; *b* 21 May 1895; *m* 1919; two *s* one *d.* Chm., Northumberland CC, 1952-67 (CC 1925; CA 1937); JP Nothumberland, 1936-; Representative County Councils Assoc., 1946- (Vice-Pres., 1970-); Chairman: Nat. Joint Council Workshops for Blind; CC Assoc. Health and Welfare Cttee; Northumberland Playing Fields Assoc., 1954-; Northumberland Old People's Voluntary Welfare Cttee, 1954-. Member: Royal National Institute for Blind, 1936-; Royal Commonwealth Society for the Blind; Church of Christ, 1917-, Senior Elder, 1950-. *Recreation:* work. *Address:* 21 Russell Terrace, Bedlington, Northumberland. *T:* Bedlington 3221.

**GARRY, Robert Campbell;** Regius Professor of Physiology, University of Glasgow, 1947-70, retired; *b* April 1900; *s* of Robert and Mary Campbell Garry; *m* 1928, Flora Macdonald, *d* of Archibald and Helen Campbell; one *s. Educ:* Glasgow Univ. MB, ChB with Hons, Glasgow Univ., 1922; Brunton Memorial Prize; DSc, Glasgow Univ., 1933; Continued studies in Freiburg im B, Germany; University Coll., London; Medical Sch., Leeds; Asst and then Lectr, Institute of Physiology, Glasgow Univ.; Head of Physiology Dept, Rowett Research Institute, Aberdeen, 1933-35; Lectr on the Physiology of Nutrition, University of Aberdeen, 1933-35; Prof. of Physiology,

University Coll., Dundee, The University of St Andrews, 1935-47; FRSE. *Publications:* Papers in scientific periodicals, dealing especially with gastrointestinal physiology and nutrition. *Recreations:* gardening, reading. *Address:* Laich Dyke, Dalginross, Comrie, Perthshire.

**GARSIDE, Air Vice-Marshal Kenneth Vernon,** CB 1962; DFC 1942; Managing Director, BXL Plastics Materials Group Ltd; *b* 13 Aug. 1913; *s* of late Dyson Garside, Maidenhead, Berks; *m* 1940, Margery June, *d* of late William Henry Miller, Tanworth-in-Arden; one *s* one *d*. *Educ:* Bradfield Coll.; St John's Coll., Oxford (MA). First commissioned RAF, 1937. Served War of 1939-45 (despatches twice, DFC); Sqdn and War Service in Far East, Mediterranean and Indian Ocean theatres, 1938-44; European theatre, 1944-45. Command and staff appts in UK and USA, 1945-57; Air Cdre 1957; AOC No 16 Group, 1957; Dep. COS, Logistics and Admin., Allied Forces Central Europe, 1958; Dir of Quartering, Air MIn., 1959; Air Vice-Marshal 1960; Senior Air Staff Officer, HQ Coastal Command, RAF, 1961-63; AOC No 18 Group, Coastal Command, and Air Officer, Scotland and Northern Ireland, 1963-65. Liveryman, Worshipful Co. of Horners; Freeman of City of London; Mem., Inst. of Directors. *Recreations:* rowing (Blue 1936), swimming (Blue 1935). *Address:* Beltons, Cookham Dean, Berks. *Clubs:* Oxford and Cambridge University, Royal Air Force; Vincent's (Oxford); Leander (Henley).

**GARSON, Greer;** Actress; *b* Northern Ireland, 29 Sept. 1908; *d* of George Garson and Nina Sophia Greer; *m* 1st, Edward A. Shelson (marr. diss.); 2nd, 1943, Richard Ney (marr. diss.); 3rd, 1949, Col E. E. Fogelson, Texas. *Educ:* London and Grenoble Univs. BA Hons London. Birmingham Repertory Theatre, 1932 and 1933. First London appearance, Open Air Theatre, Regent's Park, 1934, as Iris, in The Tempest. Entered films, 1938; Good-Bye Mr Chips, Pride and Prejudice, When Ladies Meet, Mrs Miniver, Madame Curie, Mrs Parkington, The Forsyte Saga (Royal Command Performance), The Miniver Story, The Law and the Lady, Her Twelve Men, Sunrise at Campobello, etc. *Address:* c/o MGM Studios, Culver City, Calif.

**GARSTANG, Cecil,** CBE 1969; Director since 1964 and General Manager since 1960 of Thos Cook & Son Ltd and subsidiary companies; Director and Chairman since 1966 of Hernu, Peron & Stockwell Ltd, and England's & Perrott's Ltd; Chairman, Sir Henry Lunn Ltd, and subsidiary companies, since 1968; *b* 1 Dec. 1904; *s* of Arthur Harold Garstang and Lilian Emma (*née* Meacock); *m* 1930, Winifred Eva Purkiss; two *s*. *Educ:* Salisbury Cath. Sch.; Merchant Taylors' Sch. Joined Thos Cook & Son Ltd, 1924. Served War of 1939-45, Econ. Adv. Br. of FO and at Supreme HQ of AEF (Lt-Col). Vice-Chm. 1958-59, Chm. 1960-62, Assoc. of British Travel Agents. MTAI, MBIM. Cavaliere Ufficiale, Order of Merit, Republic of Italy; Hon. Citizen of New Orleans. *Publications:* various papers on travel and tourism. *Recreations:* travel, reading, gardening. *Address:* (home) 66 Chiltern Avenue, Bushey, Herts. *T:* Bushey Heath 2014; (business) Thos Cook & Son Ltd, Berkeley Street, W1. *T:* 01-499 4000. *Clubs:* Travel Luncheon, Skal.

**GARSTANG, Walter Lucian,** BSc, MA; Headmaster of the Roan School, Greenwich, 1959-68, retired 1968; *b* 2 Sept. 1908; *o s* of late Walter Garstang, MA, DSc; *m* 1933, Barbara Mary, *d* of late Dr S. E. Denyer, CMG, MD; one *s* two *d*. (and one *s* decd). *Educ:* Oundle Sch.; Oxford. Scholar of Trinity Coll., Oxford, 1927-31. Research chemist, The Gas Light and Coke Co., 1931-37; asst master, Oundle Sch., 1937-44; asst master, Merchant Taylors' Sch., 1944-46; senior science master, Maidstone Grammar Sch., 1946-48; Headmaster, Owen's Sch., 1949-54; Headmaster, Loughborough Grammar Sch., 1955-58. *Address:* 1/8 The Paragon, Blackheath, SE3.

**GARSTIN, Lieut-Col William Arthur MacDonell,** CBE 1930 (OBE 1922); late Government of India Foreign and Political Department; *b* 14 May 1882; *s* of John Henry Garstin, CSI; *m* 1915, Mary, *d* of James Ramsay-Smith, WS, Peebles; one *d*. *Educ:* Sherborne Sch.; Sandhurst. Indian Army (7th Gurkha Rifles). Transferred Political Dept, 1907. Dep. Comr Bannu, N-WFP, 1920-23; Divisional and Sessions Judge, Peshawar Div., 1925-28; Political Agent, Khyber Pass, 1928-30; Resident, Gwalior, and Resident, Udaipur, 1932-35; Agent to the Governor-Gen., Madras States (Travancore and Cochin), 1935-37; retired, 1937. Frontier medals: Afghanistan, 1919; Waziristan, 1921-24; NWFP, 1931-32. *Address:* 65 Campden Hill Court, W8. *T:* 01-937 2074. *Club:* United Service.

**GARTHWAITE, Brig. Clive Charlton,** CBE 1961; *b* 22 Oct. 1909; *er s* of late Major Alan Garthwaite, DSO, MC, The West Garth, Guisborough, Yorks; *m* 1945, Hon. Elisabeth Clegg-Hill (*née* Smyth-Osbourne) (*d* 1967); one *d*. *Educ:* Wellington Coll., Berks; Royal Military Academy, Woolwich. 2/Lieut Royal Artillery, 1929; Hong Kong 1932-37; Major, 1939. Served in Western Desert, 1941-42 (despatches); GSO1, 1949; Col 1955; Brig. 1959; Comdr 5 Army Group RA, 1956-58; Comdt Sch. of Artillery, Manorbier, 1958-60; Comdr Woolwich Garrison, 1960-63. Retired 1963. ADC 1960-63. With British Aircraft Corpn, 1966-. *Recreations:* cricket, golf, ski-ing, shooting. *Address:* Larkfield, Bacombe Lane, Wendover, Bucks. *T:* Wendover 2206. *Clubs:* MCC; Forty.

**GARTHWAITE, Sir William,** 2nd Bt, *cr* 1919; DSC 1941 and Bar, 1942; Director of Sir William Garthwaite (Insurance) Co. Ltd; *b* 3 Jan. 1906; *o s* of Sir William Garthwaite, 1st Bt and Francesca Margherita, *d* of James Parfett; *S* father 1956; *m* 1st, 1931, Hon. Dorothy Duveen (marr. diss., 1937), *d* of 1st Baron Duveen; 2nd, 1945, Patricia Leonard (marr. diss., 1952); one *s*; 3rd, 1957, Patricia Merriel, *d* of Sir Philip d'Ambrumenil; three *s* (one *d* decd). *Educ:* Bradfield Coll., Berks; Hertford Coll., Oxford. Lloyd's Underwriter and Insur. Broker at Lloyd's, 1927-. Contested (C): Hemsworth Div. of W Riding of Yorks, 1931; Isle of Ely, 1935; E Div. of Wolverhampton, 1945. Served War of 1939-45 as pilot, Fleet Air Arm (DSC and bar, despatches thrice, Air Crew Europe Star, Atlantic Star, Africa Star, 1939-45 Star, Defence Medal). Coronation Medal, 1953. *Recreations:* flying, ski-ing, golf and sailing. *Heir:* *s* William Mark Charles Garthwaite, *b* 4 Nov. 1946. *Address:* Garthwaite House, 39 Bell Lane, E1 7LX; Matfield House, Matfield, Kent. *T:* Brenchley 2454. *Clubs:* Bath, Portland, RNVR, Royal Automobile, Royal Aero, Royal Thames.

**GARTLAN, Maj.-Gen. Gerald Ion,** CBE 1940; DSO 1919; MC; DL; JP; *b* 24 June 1889; *s* of late Alexander Gartlan of Cabra House, Co. Down and Emily Hamill; *m* 1933, Dorothy Macafee; two *d*. *Educ:* Downside Sch.; Sandhurst. 2nd Lieut Royal Irish Rifles, 1909; Capt. 1915; Bt-Major, 1918; Major, 1924; Bt Lieut-Col 1932; Lieut-Col 1933; Col 1937; served European War, 1914-18 (wounded twice, DSO, MC, Bt Majority, despatches);

served on Staff in France, Germany, Upper Silesia, Egypt, and at War Office; commanded Depot, Royal Ulster Rifles, 1929-33; commanded 2nd Bn The Royal Ulster Rifles, 1933-36; Brigadier 5th Infantry Brigade, 1938; War of 1939-45, France 1939-1940 (CBE, despatches); retired pay, 1944; idc; psc; High Sheriff of County Down, 1954. Hon Col 6th Bn Royal Ulster Rifles, 1950-56. *Recreations:* polo, tennis, golf, hockey, fishing, shooting. *Address:* Castle Park, Ardglass, Co. Down.

**GARTON, John William,** JP; FCWA; Chairman: Brown Bayley Ltd, 1957-69; Brown Bayley Steels Ltd, 1947-69; The Hoffmann Manufacturing Company Ltd, 1952-69; *b* 29 Sept. 1895; *s* of late William Garton and Mary Ann Garton, Sheffield; *m* 1922, Edris Irene, *er d* of late Kennard Riley and Jane Riley, Llandudno; one *s*. *Educ:* Sheffield. Served European War, 1914-19. Joined steel industry as a boy being third successive generation in same works. Served on Council of Institute of Costs and Works Accountants, 1945-46; part-time mem. Iron and Steel Corporation of Great Britain, 1951-53. JP Essex, 1954. Mem. Advisory Cttee for Essex of Gen. Comrs of Income Tax, 1961-68. *Recreations:* gardening, walking, fishing. *Address:* Birchfield, Nethy Bridge, Inverness-shire. *Club:* Devonshire.

**GARTON, Prof. William Reginald Stephen,** FRS 1969; Professor of Spectroscopy, University of London, Imperial College, since 1964; *b* Chelsea, SW3, 7 March 1912; *s* of William and Gertrude Emma Caroline Garton; *m* 1940, Margarita Fraser (*née* Callingham); four *d*. *Educ:* Sloane Sch., SW10; Chelsea Polytechnic, SW3; Imperial Coll., SW7. BSc, ARCS 1936; DSc 1958. Demonstrator in Physics, Imperial Coll., 1936-39. Served in RAF, 1939-45. Imperial Coll.: Lectr in Physics, 1946-54; Sen. Lectr, 1954-57; Reader, 1957-64. Associate, Harvard Coll. Observatory, 1963-. *Publications:* contrib. on Spectroscopy in Advances in Atomic and Molecular Physics (ed D. R. Bates), 1966 (New York); numerous papers on Spectroscopy and Atomic Physics. *Recreations:* speliology, Oriental history. *Address:* Department of Physics, Imperial College, SW7. *T:* 01-589 5111.

**GARTRELL, Rt. Rev. Frederick Roy;** *see* Columbia, British, Bishop of.

**GARVAGH,** 5th Baron *cr* 1818; **Alexander Leopold Ivor George Canning;** President, Disaster Relief Association; *b* 6 Oct. 1920; *s* of 4th Baron and Gladys Dora May, *d* of William Bayley Parker; *S* father 1956; *m* 1947, Christine Edith, *d* of Jack Cooper, Little Bridley, Worplesdon, Surrey; one *s* two *d*. *Educ:* Eton; Christ Church, Oxford. Commissioned Corps of Guides Cavalry, Indian Army, 1940; served Burma (despatches). Chm., Lord Garvagh & Associates Ltd; Dir, campden Research & Sales Ltd; Elgico Agencies Ltd. Formerly Director: International Business Services. Member: Brit. Inst. of Management; Inst. of Export; Assoc. Mem., Amer. Inst. of Management, New York. FInstD. *Publications:* contrib. to The Manufacturing Optician, 1949. *Recreations:* travel, motoring, and motor sport; tennis, squash, ski-ing; writing articles, short stories, etc. *Heir:* *s* Hon. Spencer George Stratford de Redcliffe Canning, *b* 12 Feb. 1953. *Address:* 12a Eaton Square, SW1. *T:* 01-245 9393; Little Barley Mow, Headley, near Bordon, Hants. *Clubs:* Steering Wheel, No 10 (Inst. of Directors).

**GARVEY, Sir Ronald Herbert,** KCMG 1950 (CMG 1947); KCVO 1953; MBE 1941; Secretary, Soil Association, since 1967; *b* 4 July 1903; *s* of Rev. H. R. Garvey, MA, and Alice M. Lofthouse; *m* 1934, Patricia Dorothy Edge, *d* of Dr V. W. T. McGusty, *qv*; one *s* three *d*. *Educ:* Trent Coll.; Emmanuel Coll., Cambridge. MA 1930; appointed to Colonial Service, 1926, and attached to Western Pacific High Commission, Suva, Fiji; District Officer British Solomon Islands, 1927-32; Asst Sec. Western Pacific High Commission, 1932-40; acted on various occasions as Res. Comr, Gilbert and Ellice Islands Colony; Asst to Res. Comr New Hebrides Condominium, 1940-41; acted as British Res. Comr, New Hebrides, on various occasions; Nyasaland Protectorate, District Officer, 1942-44; Administrator, St Vincent, Windward Islands, BWI, 1944-48; acted as Governor of Windward Is, 1946, 1948; Governor and C-in-C, British Honduras, 1948-52; Governor and C-in-C, Fiji, Governor, Pitcairn Is, Consul-Gen. for Western Pacific, and Senior Commissioner for UK on South Pacific Commission, 1952-58; Lieut-Gov. of the Isle of Man, 1959-66. Director: Raymond Kerry Enterprises Ltd, 1966-; Garvey (London) SA Ltd, 1966-. Fellow, British Interplanetary Soc. KStJ. *Recreations:* golf, deep-sea fishing, gardening. *Address:* New Bells Farm, Haughley, Stowmarket, Suffolk; The Priory, Brandeston, Woodbridge, Suffolk.

**GARVEY, Sir Terence Willcocks,** KCMG 1969 (CMG 1955); British Ambassador to Yugoslavia, since 1968; *b* Dublin, 7 Dec. 1915; *s* of Francis Willcocks Garvey and Ethel Margaret Ray; *m* 1st, 1941, Barbara Hales Tomlinson (marr. diss.); two *s* one *d*; 2nd, 1957, Rosemary, *d* of late Dr Harold Pritchard. *Educ:* Felsted; University Coll., Oxford (Scholar). BA Oxon (1st Class Philosophy, Politics and Economics), 1938; Laming Fellow of The Queen's Coll., Oxford, 1938. Entered Foreign (subsequently Diplomatic) Service, 1938; has served in USA, Chile, Germany, Egypt and at Foreign Office; Counsellor, HM Embassy, Belgrade, 1958-62; HM Chargé d'Affaires, Peking, 1962-65 and Ambassador to Mongolia, 1963-65; Asst Under-Sec. of State, Foreign Office, 1965-68. *Recreation:* fishing. *Address:* British Embassy, Belgrade, Yugoslavia. *Club:* Travellers'.

**GARY, Romain,** Officier de la Légion d'Honneur; Compagnon de la Libération; Croix de Guerre; author; *b* Tiflis, Georgia, 1914; *s* of parents named Kacewgary (Kassevgari being the spelling later used); *m* 1st, Lesley Blanch (marr. diss. 1963), *qv*; 2nd, 1963, Jean Seberg; one *s*. *Educ:* Lycée de Nice; Aix-en-Provence; Universities of Paris and Warsaw. Served with French Air Force, 1937-40; RAF and Free French Air Force in Africa, Palestine and Russia, 1940-45. Joined French Foreign Service, serving at embassies in UK, Bulgaria and Switzerland; 1st Sec., French delegation to United Nations; Consul-Gen. for France at Los Angeles, USA, 1956-60. Directed film, Les Oiseaux vont mourir au Pérou, 1968. *Publications:* Education Européenne, 1943 (Eng. trans. Forest of Anger; revised as Nothing Important Ever Dies, 1961); Tulipe, 1946; Le Grand Vestiaire, 1949 (Eng. trans. The Company of Men, 1950); Les Couleurs du Jour, 1952 (Eng. trans. Colours of the Day, 1953); Les Racines du Ciel, 1956 (Prix Goncourt, Eng. trans. The Roots of Heaven, 1958); Promesses de l'Aube, 1959 (Eng. trans. Promise at Dawn, 1962); Lady L., 1959 (filmed 1965); Le Mangeur d'Etoiles (Eng. trans. The Talent Scout, 1961); Hissing Tales, 1964; The Dance of Genghis Cohn, 1969. *Address:* c/o Editions Gallimard, 5 rue Sebastien-Bottin, Paris 7e, France.

**GASCOIGNE, Maj.-Gen. Sir Julian (Alvery),** KCMG 1962; KCVO 1953; CB 1949; DSO 1943; DL; *b* 25 Oct. 1903; *e s* of late Brig.-Gen. Sir Frederick Gascoigne, KCVO, CMG, DSO, and of Lady Gascoigne, Ashtead Lodge, Ashtead, Surrey; *m* 1928, Joyce Alfreda, *d* of late Robert Lydston Newman and of Mrs Newman; one *s* one *d. Educ:* Eton; Sandhurst. 2nd Lieut Grenadier Guards, 1923; Staff Coll., Camberley, 1938-39; served War of 1939-45, commanding 1st Bn Grenadier Guards, 1941-42; commanding 201 Guards Brigade, 1942-43; North Africa and Italy, 1943 (wounded). Imperial Defence Coll., 1946; Dep. Comdr British Jt Services Mission (Army Staff), Washington, 1947-49. GOC London District and Maj.-Gen. commanding Household Brigade, 1950-53; retired pay, 1953; Mem. of Stock Exchange and Partner in Grievson Grant & Co., 1955-59; Governor and C-in-C Bermuda, 1959-64; Col Commandant, Hon. Artillery Co., 1954-59. Pres. Union Jack Services Clubs, 1964 (Vice-Pres., 1955-64); a Commr of the Royal Hospital, Chelsea, 1958-59; Chm. Devon and Cornwall Cttee, The National Trust, 1965-. JP 1966; DL Devon, 1966. KStJ, 1959. *Address:* Sanders, Stoke Fleming, Dartmouth, S Devon. *Clubs:* Guards; Royal Bermuda Yacht.

**GASCOYNE-CECIL, Victor Alexander;** b 1891; *s* of Right Rev. Lord William Gascoyne-Cecil, late Bishop of Exeter, and Lady Florence Cecil; *m* 1915; Fairlie Estelle Caroline, *d* of Lieut-Col Arthur Watson, Suffolk Regt; two *s. Educ:* Westminster Sch.; Sandhurst. Hants Regt 1911; served European War, 1914-18, 1st Bn (wounded twice); Tank Corps, 1921-22; NW Frontier, India, 1922; retired, 1923; War of 1939-45, HM Forces, 1939-44. 1914 Star and War Medal, Indian Gen. Service, 1939-44, Defence and War Medal. JP Essex, 1936; High Sheriff, Essex, 1949; DL Essex, 1951-68. *Address:* Gold Hanger, Rettendon Common, Chelmsford, Essex. *T:* Hanningfield 371. *Club:* Farmers'.

**GASH, Prof. Norman,** FBA 1963; FRHistS; Professor of History, St Salvator's College, University of St Andrews, since 1955; *b* 16 Jan. 1912; *s* of Frederick and Kate Gash; *m* 1935, Dorothy Whitehorn; two *d. Educ:* Reading Sch.; St John's Coll., Oxford. Scholar, St John's Coll.; 1st cl. Hons Mod. Hist., 1933; BLitt, 1934; MA 1938. Temp. Lectr in Modern European History, Edinburgh, 1935-36; Asst Lectr in Modern History, University Coll., London, 1936-40. Served War, 1940-46: Intelligence Corps; Capt. 1942; Major (Gen. Staff), 1945. Lectr in Modern British and American History, St Salvator's Coll., University of St Andrews, 1946-53; Prof. of Modern History, University of Leeds, 1953-55. Fellow Royal Historical Society; 1953; Hinkley Prof. of English History, Johns Hopkins Univ., 1962; Ford's Lectr in English History, Oxford Univ., 1963-64. Vice-Principal, St Andrews Univ., 1967-. Vice-Pres., Hist. Assoc. of Scotland 1963-64. *Publications:* Politics in the Age of Peel, 1953: Mr Secretary Peel, 1961; The Age of Peel, 1968; Reaction and Reconstruction in English Politics, 1832-1852, 1966; articles and reviews in Eng. Hist. Review, Trans. Royal Historical Society, and other learned jls. *Recreations:* gardening, swimming. *Address:* Gowrie Cottage, Hepburn Gardens, St Andrews.

**GASKAIN, John Stuart Hinton,** CBE 1968 (MBE 1950); Commandant of the Police College, Bramshill, Hants, 1966-68; HM Inspector of Constabulary, 1962-68, retired; *b* 11 May 1910; *s* of William Francis Gaskain and Gladys Therese Gaskain; *m* 1938, Nancy Evelyn Swan; one *s* one *d. Educ:* Haileybury Coll. Metropolitan Police, 1936-42; Hendon Police Coll., 1936-37. Barrister-at-Law, 1944. Asst Chief Constable of Norfolk, 1942-52; seconded as Commandant of Police Training Centre, Eynsham Hall, Witney, Oxfordshire, 1946-50; Chief Constable: Cumberland and Westmorland, 1952-59; Glos, 1959-62. Queen's Police Medal, 1960. OStJ 1962. *Recreation:* golf. *Address:* 10e Sussex Heights, St Margarets Place, Brighton, Sussex. *Club:* Royal Commonwealth Society.

**GASKILL, William;** Artistic Director, English Stage Company, since 1965; *b* 24 June 1930; *s* of Joseph Linnaeus Gaskill and Maggie Simpson. *Educ:* Salt High Sch., Shipley; Hertford Coll., Oxford. Asst Artistic Dir, English Stage Co., 1957-59; freelance Dir with Royal Shakespeare Co., 1961-62; Assoc. Dir, National Theatre, 1963-65. *Address:* Royal Court Theatre, Sloane Square, SW1. *T:* 01-730 2273.

**GASKIN, Catherine;** author; *b* Co. Louth, Eire, 2 April 1929; *m* 1955, Sol Cornberg. *Educ:* Holy Cross Coll., Sydney, Australia. Brought up in Australia; lived in London, 1948-55, New York, 1955-67. *Publications:* This Other Eden, 1946; With Every Year, 1947; Dust In Sunlight, 1950; All Else Is Folly, 1951; Daughter of the House, 1952; Sara Dane, 1955; Blake's Reach, 1958; Corporation Wife, 1960; I Know My Love, 1962; The Tilsit Inheritance, 1963; The File on Devlin, 1965; Edge of Glass, 1967; Fiona, 1970. *Recreations:* music, cinema. *Address:* Ballymacahara, Wicklow, Co. Wicklow, Ireland.

**GASS, Sir Michael David Irving,** KCMG 1969 (CMG 1960); High Commissioner for the Western Pacific, since 1969; *b* 24 April 1916; *e s* of late George Irving Gass and late Norah Elizabeth Mustard; unmarried. *Educ:* King's Sch., Bruton; Christ Church, Oxford (MA); Queens' Coll., Cambridge (BA). Appointed Colonial Administrative Service, Gold Coast, 1939. Served War of 1939-45 (despatches twice) with The Gold Coast Regt, RWAFF; East Africa, Burma; Major. District Commissioner, Gold Coast, 1945; Asst Regional Officer, Ashanti, 1953-56; Permanent Sec., Ministry of the Interior, Ghana, 1956-58; Chief Sec. to the Western Pacific High Commission, 1958-65; Acting High Commissioner for the Western Pacific for periods in 1959, 1961, 1963 and 1964; Colonial Secretary, Hong Kong, 1965-69. Actg Governor, Hong Kong, for periods in 1966, 1967, and 1968. *Recreation:* ornithology. *Address:* Government House, Honiara, British Solomon Islands; Broadway, Butleigh Wootton, Glastonbury, Somerset. *T:* Street 2856. *Clubs:* East India and Sports; Hong Kong (Hong Kong).

**GASSON, Sir Lionel Bell,** Kt, *cr* 1944; *b* 9 Aug. 1889; *s* of George Henry Gasson and Estelle Mary Bell; *m* 1916, Katherine Grace Moberly; no *c. Educ:* Dulwich Coll. Joined Indian Police Service, 1910; King's Police Medal, 1928; Indian Police Medal, 1934; Dep. Inspector-Gen. of Police, 1936; Commissioner of Police, Madras City, 1939; Inspector-Gen. of Police, Madras Presidency, 1942; retired, 1944. *Recreations:* hunting, golf, fishing. *Address:* Longacre, Fleet, Hants. *T:* Fleet 814. *Club:* East India and Sports.

**GASYONGA II, Sir Charles Godfrey,** Kt 1962; Omugabe (Hereditary Ruler) of Ankole, Uganda, since 1944. Ankole is a Federal State in Uganda and its government has separate legislative powers since the Independence of Uganda on 9th Oct. 1962. *Address:* c/o Native

Government, PO Box 102, Mbarara, Ankole, Uganda.

**GATACRE, Rear-Adm. Galfry George Ormond,** CBE 1960; DSO 1952; DSC 1941 (and Bar 1942); Company Director; *b* Wooroolin, Australia, 11 June 1907; *s* of R. H. W. Gatacre, Bath, Somerset, and Wooroolin, and of C. E. Gordon, Banchory, Scotland; *m* 1933, Wendy May, *d* of E. A. Palmer, Sydney, Australia; one *s* one *d*. *Educ:* Brisbane Boys' Coll.; Royal Australian Naval Coll. Service at sea has been in HM and HMA ships around the world. Lieut 1930; Lieut-Comdr 1938; Comdr 1942; Capt. 1948; Rear-Adm. 1958. Australian Naval Attaché in USA, 1953-55; Command of HMAS Melbourne, 1955-56; Dep. Chief of Naval Staff, 1957-58; Flag Officer Comdg HM Australian Fleet, 1959; Head, Australian Joint Services Staff in USA, 1960-61; Flag Officer East Australian Area, 1962-64. *Recreations:* golf, tennis. *Address:* 76 Newcastle Street, Rose Bay, Sydney, Australia. *Clubs:* Royal Sydney Golf, American National (Sydney).

**GATEHOUSE, Robert Alexander,** QC 1969; *b* 30 Jan. 1924; *s* of late Major-Gen. A. H. Gatehouse, DSO, MC; *m* 1st, 1951, Henrietta Swann; 2nd, 1966, Pamela Fawcett. *Educ:* Wellington Coll.; Trinity Hall, Cambridge. Served War of 1939-45: commissioned into Royal Dragoons; NW Europe. Called to the Bar, Lincoln's Inn, 1950. Governor, Wellington Coll., 1970-. *Recreation:* golf. *Address:* 1 Brick Court, Temple, EC4. *T:* 01-353 0777. *Club:* Royal Automobile.

**GATES, Ernest Everard,** MA; Company Director; *b* 29 May 1903; *o c* of Ernest Henry Gates, Old Buckenham Hall, Norfolk, and Eva, *y d* of George Siggs, JP, Streatham; *m* 1931, Stella, *y d* of Henry Knox Simms. *Educ:* Repton; Corpus Christi Coll., Cambridge. Formerly a director, Manchester Chamber of Commerce (1945-51), and various other companies. Gazetted Lieut RA Sept. 1939; Major, 1941. MP (C) Middleton and Prestwich Div. of Lancs, May 1940-Oct. 1951. PPS to Rt Hon. W. S. Morrison, Min. of Town and Country Planning, 1943-45. *Recreations:* shooting, fishing, stalking, ski-ing, golf, travel. *Address:* 15 Grosvenor Square, W1. *T:* 01-629 3030; Pride's Crossing, Ascot, Berks. *T:* Ascot 2330; Round Hill, Jamaica, W1. *Clubs:* St James', Portland, MCC.

**GATES, Sidney Barrington,** OBE 1943; FRS 1950; Consultant, Ministry of Aviation, 1959-66; *b* 1893; *s* of Ernest Edwin Gates, Norwich; *m* 1915, Edith Annie Tofts, Cambridge; one *s* one *d* (and one *d* decd). *Educ:* City of Norwich Sch.; Corpus Christi Coll., Cambridge. Wrangler, 1914. Research work on stability and control of aircraft, Royal Aircraft Establishment, Farnborough, since 1915. Ed., of Scientific War Records of Min. of Supply (Air), 1944-46. Dep. Chief Scientific Officer, Min. of Supply (Air) 1950-52, Chief Scientific Officer, 1952-59. Hon. Fellow Royal Aeronautical Society, 1959 (FRAeS 1948). Literary Critic: The Nation, 1923; New Statesman, 1925; Times Literary Supplement, 1928-. *Publications:* Poems, 1925; The Mulligatawny Medallion, 1926; numerous papers on aeronautical theory in Reports and Memoranda of Aeronautical Research Council. *Recreations:* walking, gardening. *Address:* Firgrove, Ash Vale, Aldershot, Hants. *T:* Aldershot 25262.

**GATES, Sylvester Govett,** CBE 1944; Chairman: International Commercial Bank, since 1967; Tecalemit Ltd; Deputy Chairman: National Westminster Bank, since 1968; Standard Bank; Director, Standard & Chartered Banking Group Ltd; *b* 2 Sept. 1901; *s* of late Walter George Gates, CB, and Beatrice Helen Govett; *m* 1936, Pauline (*d* 1968), *d* of Algernon Newton, RA; one *s*. *Educ:* Winchester; New Coll., Oxford. First Class Hon. Mods, 1922; First Class Lit Hum, 1924; Commonwealth Fund Fellow (Private International Law), Harvard Univ., USA, 1925-27. Called to Bar, Inner Temple, 1928; practised London and Western Circuit, 1928-39; Controller of Home Publicity, Ministry of Information, 1941-44; attached to Office of Minister of Reconstruction, 1944; Mem. of Royal Commission on Taxation, 1953; Chm. Brit. Film Institute, 1956-64; Mem. Port of London Authority, 1958-64. *Address:* 29 Eaton Square, SW1; Manningford Abbas, Pewsey, Wilts.

**GATES, Thomas S(overeign) Jr;** Chairman, Executive Committee, Morgan Guaranty Trust Co., 1961-62, 1965-68 and since 1969 (President, 1962-65); Secretary of Defense, USA, Dec. 1959-Jan. 1961; *b* Philadelphia, 10 April 1906; *s* of Thomas Sovereign Gates and Marie (*née* Rogers); *m* 1928, Millicent Anne Brengle; three *d* (one *s* decd). *Educ:* Chestnut Hill Acad.; University of Pennsylvania (AB). Joined Drexel & Co., Philadelphia, 1928; Partner, 1940-. War Service, 1942-45 (Bronze Star, Gold Star): US Naval Reserve (Capt.). Under-Sec. of Navy, 1953-57; Sec. of the Navy, 1957-59; Dep. Sec. of Defense, 1959. Director: Beaver Coal Corp.; Bethlehem Steel Corp.; General Electric Co.; Campbell Soup Co.; Cities Service Co.; Insurance Co. of N America; Scott Paper Co.; Smith, Kline & French Laboratories; Life Trustee, University of Pennsylvania. Hon. LLD: University of Pa, 1956; Yale Univ. 1961; Columbia Univ. 1961. *Address:* Mill Race Farm, Devon, Pennsylvania, USA; 1 East 66 Street, NYC, USA. *Clubs:* Philadelphia, Racquet (Philadelphia); The Links (NYC); Chevy Chase, Metropolitan (Washington, DC); Gulph Mills Golf.

**GATES, William Thomas George,** CBE 1967; Chairman: West Africa Committee, London, since 1961; Liverpool Porterage Rates Panel, since 1969; Director, edinburgh & Overseas Investment Trust Ltd, Edinburgh; *b* 21 Jan. 1908; *s* of Thomas George and Katherine Gates; *m* 1938, Rhoda (*née* Sellars), *d* of Mrs W. E. Loveless; two *s*. *Educ:* Ilford County High Sch., National Bank of New Zealand, London, 1925-30; John Holt & Co. (Liverpool) Ltd, resident Nigeria, 1930-46; Gen. Manager: Nigeria, 1940; Gold Coast, 1947; Liverpool, 1947; Man. Dir, 1956; Dep. Chm., 1964; retired, 1967. MLC, Nigeria, 1940-46; Director: W African Airways Corp, 1941-46; Edward Bates & Sons (Holdings) Ltd, 1964-70. dist Scout Comr, Northern Nigeria 1940-42; Mem. Liverpool Dist Cttee, Royal National Life-Boat Instn, 1956; Mem. Bd of Govs, United Liverpool Hosps, 1958-70; Gen. Comr of Income Tax, 1967. *Recreations:* golf, fishing, cricket, gardening. *Address:* Banks Farm, Caldy, Wirral, Cheshire. *T:* 051-625 7006; West Africa Committee, 23 Lawrence Lane, EC2. *T:* 01-638 9491. *Clubs:* Travellers', Golfers'; Royal Liverpool Golf (Hoylake).

**GATHORNE-HARDY,** family name of **Earl of Cranbrook.**

**GATHORNE-HARDY, Geoffrey Malcolm;** *b* 28 Jan. 1878; *s* of late Hon. A. E. Gathorne-Hardy, Donnington Priory, Newbury; *m* 1914, Kathleen, *d* of late Henry Goschen; no *c*. *Educ:* Eton; New Coll., Oxford. Pres. Oxford Union, 1899. Called to Bar, Inner Temple, 1903; Served South African War, and European War, 1914-18 (MC, Belgian Croix de Guerre); Hon.

Sec. Royal Institute of International Affairs, 1920-35; Asst Librarian, House of Lords, 1923-28. Hon. PhD (Oslo). Comdr Order of St Olav (Norwegian). *Publications:* The Norse Discoverers of America, 1921; Norway (Modern World series), 1925; A Short History of International Affairs, 1920-34, 1934; Final edn, 1949; War Poems of Nordahl Grieg, 1944; A Royal Impostor, 1956. *Recreations:* shooting and fishing. *Address:* Donnington Priory, Newbury, Berks. *T:* Newbury 241. *Club:* Junior Carlton.

**GATHORNE-HARDY, Hon. Robert;** *b* 31 July 1902; *s* of 3rd Earl of Cranbrook and Lady Dorothy Boyle. *Educ:* Eton; Christ Church, Oxford. As a schoolboy, was an amateur geologist, collected flint implements and discovered a doubtfully palæolithic chalk carving in Suffolk; went to northern Labrador, thence to Oxford; studied for Medicine and took degree in Law; worked for a time on a monthly paper and afterwards at antiquarian bookselling, until the beginning of 1931; worked for many years in association with Logan Pearsall Smith. During War of 1939-45 was employed in Civil Defence, and finally as a builder's labourer on bomb damage in London. For many years shared in a private press. Mem. of Bradfield RDC, 1932-69 (Chm. 1953-61, Vice-Chm. 1961-62). Fellow of the Linnæan Soc., 1960. *Publications:* A Bibliography of the Works of Jeremy Taylor (in The Golden Grove by Logan Pearsall Smith), 1930; Lacebury Manor, 1930; Village Symphony, and other poems, 1931; The House by the Bay, 1932; Other Seas, 1933; Coronation Baby, 1935; The Wind and the Waterfall, 1938; Wild Flowers in Britain, 1938; Three Acres and a Mill, 1939; Garden Flowers, 1948; Recollections of Logan Pearsall Smith, 1949; The Tranquil Gardener, 1958; The Native Garden, 1962; Traveller's Trio, 1963; Amalfi: Aspects of the City and Her Ancient Territories, 1968. Editor: The Golden Shakespeare, selections chosen by Logan Pearsall Smith, 1949; A Religious Rebel, letters of Hannah Whitall Smith, 1949; Ottoline, memoirs of Lady Ottoline Morrell, 1963. *Recreations:* sight-seeing, bibliography, botany. *Address:* The Mill House, Stanford Dingley, near Reading, Berks. *T:* Bradfield 378.

**GATTIE, Maj.-Gen. Kenneth Francis Drake,** DSO 1917; MC; DL; *b* 22 April 1890; *s* of late Walter Montagu Gattie and Catherine Anne, *d* of late Rev. T. R. Drake. *Educ:* Tonbridge Sch. Commissioned 3rd Monmouthshire Regt, 1910; served on Western front, 1915-Armistice; Adjutant, 3rd Monmouthshire Regt, 1915; Brigade Major, 75th Infantry Brigade, 1916; Capt., South Wales Borderers, 1917; Gen. Staff, GHQ, 1918 (MC, DSO, despatches five times); Brigade Major, Rhine Army, 1919; served in India, 1919-22 and in 1924; psc, Camberley, 1923; Gen. Staff Officer, War Office, 1924; Brevet Major, 1926; Brigade Major, Rhine Army, 1927; Instructor in Tactics, Sch. of Artillery, 1929; DAA and QMG, Highland Area, 1931; Brevet Lieut-Col, 1931; Major, 1934; GSOII, 43rd (Wessex) Division, 1935-37; Lieut-Col 1937; Commanded 1st Bn Queen's Royal Regt (West Surrey) 1937-38; Col, 1938; Commander 2nd (Rawalpindi) Infantry Brigade, India, 1938; acting Maj.-Gen., 1941; temp. Maj.-Gen.; District Commander, India, 1941; retired pay, 1945. DL Brecknock, 1954. *Address:* Tymawr, Llyswen, Breconshire. *Club:* United Service.

**GAULT, Charles Alexander,** CBE 1959 (OBE 1947, MBE 1941); retired from HM Foreign Service, 1959; *b* 15 June 1908; *o s* of late Robert Gault, Belfast, and late Sophia Ranken Clark; *m* 1947, Madge, *d* of late William Walter Adams, Blundellsands; no *c*. *Educ:* Harrow; Magdalene Coll., Cambridge. Entered Levant Consular Service, 1931; served in Egypt, Persia, Saudi Arabia, at Foreign Office, India (on secondment to Commonwealth Relations Office), Libya, Israel, Bahrain (HM Political Agent, 1954-59). *Recreation:* walking. *Address:* 103 Old Bath Road, Cheltenham, Glos. *Club:* Oriental.

**GAULT, Brig. Sir James (Frederick),** KCMG 1952; MVO 1943; OBE 1946; *b* 26 June 1902; *y s* of late Leslie Hamilton Gault; *m* 1st, 1936, Margaret Ella Campbell (marr. diss. 1960), *y d* of Brig.-Gen. Douglas Campbell Douglas, CB, Mains, Milngavie, Scotland, and Hon. Mrs Douglas; no *c*; 2nd, 1960, Elizabeth Marchioness Townshend (who *m* first 7th Marquess Townshend, whom she divorced, 1960), *d* of Lieut-Col Thomas Luby, Indian Civil Service, Judicial Commissioner. *Educ:* Eton; Trinity Coll., Cambridge (BA). Joined Scots Guards, 1939; served War of 1939-45, in Middle East, North Africa, Sicily, Italy, N West Europe; Col 1944; RARO 1949; re-employed, 1951; Brigadier 1951; Military Asst, Supreme Commander Allied Powers in Europe, 1951-53. Order of Legion of Merit (USA). *Address:* Hemingstone Hall, near Ipswich, Suffolk. *T:* Coddenham 304; 51 Eaton Square, SW1. *T:* 01-235 7589. *Clubs:* Guards, White's.

**GAUNT, Rev. Howard Charles Adie;** Precentor, Winchester Cathedral, since 1967; Sacrist, 1963 and Hon. Canon, 1966; *b* 13 Nov. 1902; *s* of C. F. Gaunt, Edgbaston; *m* 1927, Mabel Valery, *d* of A. E. Bond, Wannerton, near Kidderminster; two *s*. *Educ:* Tonbridge Sch.; King's Coll., Cambridge. Asst Master: King Edward's Sch., Birmingham, 1928-29; Rugby Sch., 1929-37; Headmaster, Malvern Coll., 1937-53; Chaplain, Winchester Coll., 1953-63. Select Preacher, Universities of Oxford and Cambridge. *Publications:* Two Exiles: a school in Wartime; School: A Book for Parents. *Address:* 57 Canon Street, Winchester.

**GAUNT, William;** Author and Painter; *b* Hull, 1900; *s* of William and Harriet Gaunt; *m* 1935, Mary Catherine O'Reilly (*née* Connolly). *Educ:* Hull Gram. Sch.; Worcester Coll., Oxford. BA Oxon 1922; MA 1926; AICA; Editor of numerous illustrated works, mainly on the Fine Arts. Exhibitions of paintings and drawings at Redfern Gallery, 1930; Leger Gallery, 1932; Reid and Lefevre Galls, 1936; Walker Galls., 1947. Art critic, Evening Standard, 1946; Special Correspondent to The Times on Art Subjects, 1957-. *Publications:* principal: London Promenade, 1930; Bandits in a Landscape, 1936; The Pre-Raphaelite Tragedy, 1942; The Aesthetic Adventure, 1945; British Painting from Hogarth's Day to Ours, 1945; The March of the Moderns, 1948-49; Victorian Olympus, 1952; Arrows of Desire: A Study of William Blake, 1956; (novel) The Lady in the Castle, 1956. *Topography:* Chelsea, 1954; London in Colour, 1957; Kensington, 1958; London, 1961; Oxford, 1965. Introductions to Selected Writings of William Morris, 1948; Renoir (Phaidon), 1952; Editor, History of Painting, 1955; The Study of Sculpture, 1957; The Observer's Books: of Painting and Graphic Art, 1958; Modern Art, 1964; Sculpture, 1966; Everyman's Dictionary of Pictorial Art, 1962; Concise History of English Painting, 1964; A Companion to Painting, 1967; The City of Westminster, 1968; Flemish Cities, Their Art and History, 1969; Impressionism: a visual history, 1970. *Address:* 35b Lansdowne Road, W11. *T:* 01-727 6762.

**GAUNT SUDDARDS, H.;** *see* Suddards.

**GAUNTLETT, Major Eric Gerald,** CBE 1919; DSO 1918; *b* 1 Nov. 1885; *s* of late T. L. Gauntlett, Putney, SW; *m* 1919, Hilda Mary Gerrard, RRC; one *s* (and two *s* decd). *Educ:* King's Coll. Sch.; King's Coll. Hospital. MB, BS (gold medal), London; FRCS; LRCP; Surgical Registrar and Tutor, King's Coll. Hospital; Asst Surgeon Paddington Green children's Hospital; late Lieut-Col RAMC and Consulting Surgeon to the Salonica Forces (CBE, DSO, despatches four times); Major South Africa Medical Corps, 1942-46; retired, 1966. Hon. Associate of St John of Jerusalem, 1921. *Publications:* contributions to medical journals. *Address:* 3 Vint Crescent, Colchester, Essex.

**GAUSSEN, Maj.-Gen. Charles de Lisle,** CB 1949; MC 1918; psc †; late RE; *b* 1 Aug. 1896; *m*; one *d*; 2nd Lieut, 1915; Lieut, 1916; Adjutant, 1916-18; Capt., 1918; Adj., 1926-28; Major, 1930; Lieut-Col, 1938; Temp. Col, 1940; Actg Brig., 1941; Brig., 1948; Hon. Maj.-Gen., 1950. Served European War, 1914-18, France and Belgium, 1915-18 (wounded, despatches twice, 1914-15 Star, British War Medal, Victory Medal, MC); GSO3, France, 1918-19; Staff Capt., France, 1919; Waziristan, 1921-24 (Medal and clasp); GSO3 India (temp.), 1921-23; Staff Capt., School of Military Engineering, 1931-32; GSO3, WO, 1932-35; Brig. Major, India, 1937-38; War of 1939-45 (despatches). Chief Eng. Northern Comd, India, 1946-47; E-in-C, India, 1947; Dep. E-in-C, WO, 1948-49; retired, 1950. *Address:* Tumble Top, Weedon, Aylesbury, Bucks. *Club:* Royal Over-Seas League.

**GAUTREY, Peter,** CVO 1961; British High Commissioner in Swaziland, since 1968; *b* 17 Sept. 1918; *s* of late Robert Harry Gautrey, Hindhead, Surrey, and Hilda Morris; *m* 1947, Marguerite Etta Uncles; one *s* one *d*. *Educ:* Abbotsholme Sch., Derbys. Joined Home Office, 1936. Served in Royal Artillery, (Capt.), Sept. 1939-March 1946. Re-joined Home Office; Commonwealth Relations Office, 1948; served in British Embassy, Dublin, 1950-53; UK High Commission, New Delhi, 1955-57 and 1960-63; British Deputy High Commissioner, Bombay, 1963-65; Corps of Diplomatic Service Inspectors, 1965-68. *Recreations:* golf, music, art. *Address:* 24 Fort Road, Guildford, Surrey. *Club:* Royal Automobile.

**GAVEY, Clarence John,** MD, FRCP; Physician and Physician i/c Cardiographic Department, Westminster Hospital; Teacher and Staff Examiner in Medicine, University of London; Physician Moorfields Eye Hospital; Physician Edenbridge and District War Memorial Hospital; *b* 20 June 1911; 2nd *s* of late Walter John Gavey, Jurat of Royal Court, Guernsey; *m* 1937, Marjorie, *d* of late John Guille, Guernsey; three *d*. *Educ:* Elizabeth College, Guernsey; London Hospital Medical Sch., Buxton Prize in Anat. and Phys.; MRCS LRCP 1934; MB, BS, London 1934. Formerly Emergency Officer, Ho. Phys., Ho. Phys. to Cardiac Dept, Paterson Schol. and Chief Asst, Cardiac Dept, London Hosp.; Chief Med. Asst, Westminster Hosp. MD London 1936, MRCP 1936, FRCP 1948. Goulstonian Lecturer, Royal College of Physicians London, 1949; Buckston Brown Medal, Harveian Soc. London 1950; FRSM; Mem. Assoc. of Physicians of Gt Britain and Ireland; Mem. Internat. Soc. of Internal Medicine; Mem. British Cardiac Soc.; Mem. London Cardiological Club; Mem. Harveian Soc. of London; Mem. Ophthalmic Soc. of UK. Hon. Lieut-Col RAMC; served MEF, 1942-46. *Publications:* The Management of the "Hopeless" Case, 1952; cardiac articles in French's Differential Diagnosis of Main Symptoms, 1967; various papers in Lancet, Brit. Med. Jl, Brit. Heart Jl, etc. *Address:* 106 Harley Street, W1. *T:* 01-935 7655; Tissington House, Castlemaine Avenue, S Croydon. *T:* 01-688 4051.

**GAVIN, Maj.-Gen. James Merricks Lewis,** CB 1967; CBE 1963 (OBE 1953); Director, British Standards Institution, since 1968; *b* Antofagasta, Chile, 28 July 1911; *s* of Joseph Merricks Gavin; *m* 1942, Barbara Anne Elizabeth, *d* of Group Capt. C. G. Murray, CBE; one *s* two *d*. *Educ:* Uppingham Sch.; Royal Military Academy; Trinity Coll., Cambridge. 2nd Lieut Royal Engineers, 1931. Mem. Mt Everest Expedn, 1936. Instructor, Royal Military Academy, 1938; Capt. 1939; served War of 1939-45 in Far East, Middle East, Italy, France, including special operations; Brit. Jt Services Mission, Washington, 1948-51; Commanding Officer, 1951-53; Col Staff Coll., Camberley, 1953-55; BAOR, 1956-58; Comdt (Brig.) Intelligence Centre, Maresfield, 1958-61; Maj.-Gen. 1964; Asst Chief of Staff (Intelligence), SHAPE, 1964-67. Col Comdt, Corps of Royal Engineers, 1968-. FRSA. *Recreations:* mountaineering, sailing, ski-ing. *Address:* Littlewick Meadow, Knaphill, Surrey. *Clubs:* Army and Navy, Royal Ocean Racing, Alpine.

**GAVIN, Malcolm Ross,** CBE 1966 (MBE 1945); MA, DSc, CEng, FIEE, FInstP, FIMA; Principal, Chelsea College of Science and Technology, University of London, since 1966; Director, Fulmer Research Institute, since 1968; *b* 27 April 1908; 3rd *s* of James Gavin; *m* 1935, Jessie Isobel Hutchinson; one *s* one *d*. *Educ:* Hamilton Acad.; Glasgow Univ. Mathematics Teacher, Dalziel High Sch., Motherwell, 1931-36; Physicist, GEC Res. Labs, Wembley, 1936-47; HMI, Scottish Education Dept, 1947-50; Head of Dept of Physics and Mathematics and Vice-Principal, College of Technology, Birmingham, 1950-55; Prof. of Electronic Engrg and Head of Sch. of Engrg Sci, University Coll. of N Wales, 1955-65. Member: Electronics Res. Coun., Min. of Aviation, 1960-64; Res. Grants Cttee of DSIR (Chm., Electrical and Systems Sub-Cttee, 1964-65); Science Research Council (Mem. Univ. Sci. and Tech. Bd and Chm. Electrical Sub-Cttee, 1965-69, Mem. Control Engineering Cttee, 1969-; Mem. Engineering Bd, 1969-); Inter-Univ. Council for Higher Education Overseas, 1967-; Univ. Grants Cttee, Hong Kong; Council, European Physical Soc., 1968-; Pres. Inst. of Physics and Physical Soc., 1968- (Vice-Pres., 1964-67). Hon. ACT, Birmingham, 1956; Hon. DSc (Ife), 1970. *Publications:* Principles of Electronics (with Dr J. E. Houldin), 1959. Numerous in Jl of IEE, Brit. Jl of Applied Physics, Wireless Engineer, Jl of Electronics, etc. *Recreations:* gardening, walking. *Address:* c/o Chelsea College of Science and Technology, Manresa Road, SW3. *T:* 01-352 6421. *Club:* Athenæum.

**GAWNE, Ewan Moore,** CSI 1945; CIE 1942; *b* 26 March 1889; *m* 1946, Muriel Henderson (*d* 1947), Camberley. *Educ:* Wellington; Brasenose Coll., Oxford. Entered ICS, 1913; Mem., Board of Revenue, Madras. *Address:* Vine Cottage, South Warnborough, Basingstoke, Hants.

**GAWTHORPE, Brig. John Bernard,** CBE 1939; TD; Major (Hon. Brig.) (retired pay), late The West Yorkshire Regiment (Prince of Wales' Own); *b* Ossett, Yorks, 12 Nov. 1891; *e s* of late John H. Gawthorpe, Roundhay, Leeds; *m* 1915, Clarice Turner (*d* 1956), Roundhay; one *d. Educ:* Wakefield; Leeds. Territorial Army: 2nd Lieut 1911; Lieut 1913; Capt. 1915; Regular Army: Capt. (West Yorks Regt) 1917; Temp. Major (Machine Gun Corps), 1917-21; Bt Major, 1919; retd, 1931; Territorial Army: Lieut-Col Comdg 7th (Leeds Rifles) Bn West Yorks Regt 1934; Bt. Col 1938; Col 1938; served European War, France and Belgium, 1915, 1917, 1918 (wounded); North Russia, 1919; Instructor: Machine Gun Sch., 1916 and 1919-21; Technical Officer, 1921-24; Infantry Brigade Commander (temp. Brig.), 1939-40; Active Service France and Belgium 1940, including evacuation of Dunkirk (despatches); Commander, Cambridge Sub-Dist, 1943-44; Hon. Col 12th (Yorks) Bn Parachute Regt (TA), 1949-56. *Recreation:* oil-painting. *Address:* The Brow, Creskeld Lane, Bramhope, near Leeds. *T:* Leeds 673081; Bayview, Castle Bay, Isle of Barra, Outer Hebrides. *T:* Castle Bay 209.

**GAY, Rear-Adm. George Wilsmore,** CB 1969; MBE 1946; DSC 1943; Director-General of Naval Training, 1967-69; *b* 1913; *s* of late Engr Comdr G. M. Gay and Mrs O. T. Gay (*née* Allen); *m* 1941, Nancy Agnes Clark; two *s* one *d. Educ:* Eastman's Sch., Southsea; Nautical Coll., Pangbourne. Entered RN, 1930; Cadet Trng, 1930-32; RNEC, Keyham, 1932-35; HMS Glorious, 1935-37; Engr. Off., HMS Porpoise, 1939-41, HMS Clyde, 1941-43; HMS Dolphin, 1938 and 1943-46; HM Dockyard, Portsmouth, 1946-47; HMS Euryalus, 1947-49; Sqdn Engr Off., 1st Submarine Sqdn, HMS Forth, 1949-50; Trng Comdr, HMS Raleigh, 1951-53; Admiralty Engr Overseer, Vickers Armstrong Ltd, 1953-55; HMS Dolphin, 1956-58; Senior Officer, War Course, Royal Naval Coll., Greenwich, 1958; HM Dockyard, Malta, 1959-60; CO, HMS Sultan, Gosport 1960-63; Chief Staff Off. Material to Flag Off. Submarines, 1963-66; Admty Interview Bd, 1966. Comdr 1947; Capt. 1958; Rear-Adm. 1967. MIMechE 1958. *Recreations:* fishing, sailing, gardening. *Address:* 29 Whiteford Road, Mannamead, Plymouth, Devon. *T:* Plymouth 64486. *Clubs:* Army and Navy; Royal Western Yacht.

**GAYDON, Prof. Alfred Gordon,** FRS 1953; Professor of Molecular Spectroscopy, Imperial College of Science and Technology, London, since 1961; Warren Research Fellow of Royal Society since 1945; *b* 26 Sept. 1911; *s* of Alfred Bert Gaydon and Rosetta Juliet Gordon; *m* 1940, Phyllis Maude Gaze; one *s* one *d. Educ:* Kingston Grammar Sch., Kingston-on-Thames; Imperial Coll., London. BSc (Physics) Imperial Coll., 1932; worked on molecular spectra, and on measurement of high temperatures, on spectra and structure of flames, and shock waves, 1939-; DSc (London) 1942; Hon. Dr (University of Dijon), 1957. Rumford Medal, Royal Society, 1960; Bernard Lewis Gold Medal, Combustion Inst., 1960. *Publications:* Identification of Molecular Spectra (with Dr R. W. B. Pearse), 1941, 1950, 1963, 1965; Spectroscopy and Combustion Theory, 1942, 1948; Dissociation Energies and Spectra of Diatomic Molecules, 1947, 1953, 1968; Flames, their Structure, Radiation and Temperature (with Dr H. G. Wolfhard), 1953, 1960, 1970; The Spectroscopy of Flames, 1957; The Shock Tube in High-temperature Chemical Physics (with Dr I. Hurle), 1963. *Recreations:* wild-life photography; formerly rowing. *Address:* 43 Surbiton Hill Park, Surbiton, Surrey. *T:* 01-399 6098; Imperial College, SW7. *T:* 01-589 5111.

**GAYRE of Gayre and Nigg, Robert;** Lieutenant-Colonel (late Reserve of Officers); ethnologist and armorist; Editor of The Armorial since 1959, The Mankind Quarterly since 1960, etc; Director of several companies; *b* 6 Aug. 1907; *s* of Robert Gayre of Gayre and Nigg, and Clara Hull; *m* 1933, Nina Mary, *d* of Rev. Louis Thomas Terry, MA and Margaret Nina Hill; one *s. Educ:* University of Edinburgh (MA); Exeter Coll., Oxford. BEF France, 1939; Staff Officer Airborne HQ, 1942; Educl Adviser, Allied Mil. Govt, Italy, 1943-44; Dir of Educn, Allied Control Commn for Italy, 1944; Chief of Educn and Religious Affairs, German Planning Unit, SHAEF, 1944; Prof. of Anthropology and head of Dept of Anthropo-geography, University of Saugor, India, 1954-56; Falkland Pursuivant Extraord., 1958; Consultore pro lingua Anglica, Coll. of Heralds, Rome, 1954-; Chamberlain to the Prince of Lippe, 1958-; Grand Bailiff and Comr-Gen. of the English Tongue, Order of St Lazarus of Jerusalem, 1961-69; Grand Referendary, 1969-; Grand Almoner, 1969-; Sec.-Gen., VIth Internat. Congress of Genealogy, Edinburgh, 1962. Chm., The Seventeen Forty-Five Association. President: Scottish Rhodesia Soc., to 1968; Aberdeenshire and Banffshire Friends of Rhodesia Assoc., 1969-; St Andrew Soc. of Malta, 1968; Life Pres., Heraldic Soc. of Malta, 1970. Sec.-Gen., Internat. Orders' Commn; Mem. Coun. Internat. Inst. of Ethnology and Eugenics, New York. Mem. Cttee of Honour, Cercle Internat. Généalogique, Paris, Mem. Nat. Acad. Sc. of India; Fellow Collegio Araldico, Rome; F Ist Ital di Geneal. e Arald., Rome, FInstD. Hon. or corr. mem. of heraldic and other socs of many countries. Grand Cross of Merit, SMO Malta, 1963 (Kt Comdr, 1957). Holds knighthoods in international and foreign orders, hon. Doctorates from Italian Univs, and heraldic societies' medals, etc. Hon. Lt-Col, ADC to Governor, Georgia, USA, 1969-. *Publications:* Teuton and Slav on the Polish Frontier, 1944; Italy in Transition, 1946; Wassail! In Mazers of Mead, 1948; The Heraldry of the Knights of St John, 1956; Heraldic Standards and other Ensigns, 1959; The Nature of Arms, 1961; Heraldic Cadency, 1961, Gayre's Booke, 4 vols 1948-59; Who is Who in Clan Gayre, 1962; A Case for Monarchy, 1962; The Armorial Who is Who, 1961-62, 1963-65, and 1966-68; Roll of Scottish Arms (Pt I Vol. I, 1964, Pt I Vol. II, 1969); Ethnological Elements of Africa, 1966; The Zimbabwean Culture of Rhodesia, 1971; contribs Mankind Quarterly, contrib. Encyc. Brit., etc. *Recreations:* yachting, ocean cruising. *Address:* c/o 1 Darnaway Street, Edinburgh 3. *T:* 031-225 1896; Villa Lochore, 115 The Strand, Gzira, Malta; *T:* Malta 34563; Lochore House, Sandown, Johannesburg, South Africa; (owns as feudal baron of Lochoreshyre) Lochore Castle, Fife. *Clubs:* Army and Navy, Royal Thames Yacht; Caledonian (Edinburgh); Pretoria (Pretoria, SA); Casino Maltese (Valletta); Malta Union (Sliema); Royal Forth Yacht, Royal Highland Yacht, Royal Malta Yacht, etc.

**GEACH, Gertrude Elizabeth Margaret;** *see* Anscombe, G. E. M.

**GEACH, Prof. Peter Thomas,** FBA 1965; Professor of Logic, University of Leeds, since Oct. 1966; *b* 29 March 1916; *o s* of Prof. George Hender Geach, IES, and Eleonora Frederyka Adolfina Sgonina; *m* 1941, Gertrude Elizabeth Margaret Anscombe, *qv*; three *s* four *d. Educ:* Balliol Coll., Oxford (Domus Schol.). 2nd cl. Class, Hon. Mods, 1936; 1st cl. Lit. Hum., 1938. Gladstone Research Student, St Deiniol's Library, Hawarden, 1938-39; philosophical research, Cambridge, 1945-51; University of Birmingham: Asst Lectr in Philosophy, 1951; Lectr, 1952; Sen. Lectr, 1959; Reader in Logic, 1961. *Publications:*

Mental Acts, 1957; Reference and Generality, 1962; (with G. E. M. Anscombe) Three Philosophers, 1961; God and the Soul, 1969; articles in Mind, Philosophical Review, Analysis, Ratio, etc. *Recreation:* reading stories of detection, mystery and horror. *Address:* Department of Philosophy, The University, Leeds; 3 Richmond Road, Cambridge. *T:* 53950. *Club:* Union Society (Oxford).

**GEAKE, Maj.-Gen. Clifford Henry,** CB 1945; CBE 1944; Hon. Maj.-Gen. (retired) RAOC; *b* 3 June 1894; *s* of Thomas Henry Geake; *m* 1915, Brenda Mary, *d* of Dr A. W. F. Sayres; two *s*. Served European War, 1914-18, France and Belgium (wounded, despatches); War of 1939-45, Middle East and Italy (despatches, CBE, CB); retired pay, 1946.

**GEAR, William,** DA (Edinburgh) 1936; RBSA 1966; Painter; Head of Faculty of Fine Art, College of Art and Design, Birmingham, since Sept. 1964; Member London Group, 1953; *b* Methil, Fife, 2 Aug. 1915; *s* of Porteous Gordon Gear; *m* 1949, Charlotte Chertok; two *s*. *Educ:* Buckhaven High Sch.; Edinburgh Coll. of Art; Edinburgh Univ.; Moray House Training Coll.; Edinburgh Coll. of Art: Post-grad. schol., 1936-37; Travelling schol., 1937-38; Académie Fernand Leger, Paris, 1937; study in France, Italy, Balkans; Moray House Trg Coll., 1938-39. War Service with Royal Corps of Signals, 1940-46, in Middle East, Italy and Germany. Staff Officer, Monuments, Fine Arts and Archives Br., CCG, 1946-47; worked in Paris, 1947-50; Curator, Towner Art Gallery, Eastbourne, 1958-64. Guest lecturer, Nat. Gall. of Victoria, Melbourne, and University of Western Australia, 1966. One-man exhibitions since 1944 in various European cities, N and S America, Japan, etc.; London; Gimpel Fils Gall., 1948-; S London Art Gall. (retrospective), 1954; Edinburgh Fest., 1966; (retrospective) Arts Council, N Ireland, 1969; (retrospective) Scottish Arts Council 1969. Works shown in many exhibitions of contemporary art, also at Royal Acad., 1960, 1961, 1967, 1968. Awarded £500 Purchase prize, Fest. of Britain, 1951; David Cargill Award, Royal Glasgow Institute, 1967. FIAL, 1960. *Works in permanent collections:* Tate Gallery; Arts Council; Brit. Council; Contemp. Art Soc.; Scottish National Gallery of Modern Art; Arts Council (Scottish Cttee); Victoria & Albert Museum; Laing Art Gall., Newcastle; Nat. Gall. of Canada; Bishop Suter Art Gall., NZ; Art Gall., Toronto; City Art Gall., Toledo, Ohio; Museum of Art, Tel Aviv; New Coll., Oxford; Cincinnati Art Gall., Ohio; Nat. Gall. of NSW; Bishop Otter Coll., Chichester; City Art Gall., Manchester; Albright Art Gallery, Buffalo, NY; Musée des Beaux Arts, Liège; Inst. of Contemp. Art, Lima, Peru; Towner Art Gall., Eastbourne; Brighton Art Gall.; Pembroke Coll., Cambridge; Chelsea Coll. of Physical Educn; Southampton Art Gallery; University of Glasgow; Arts Council of Northern Ireland, Whitworth Art Gallery, Manchester; Aberdeen, Dundee and Glasgow Art Galleries, and in numerous private collections in Gt Britain, USA, Canada, Italy, France, etc. Furnishing textiles designed for various firms. *Recreations:* cinema, music, gardening. *Address:* 46 George Road, Birmingham 15.

**GEARY, Major Benjamin Handley,** VC 1915; MA Oxon; Sergeant-at-Arms, Ontario Legislature, 1947; historian for the Legislature; retd; *b* 29 June 1891; *s* of late Rev. Henry Geary and Mrs Geary (*née* Alport); *m* 1st, 1922, Ruth Christiana (from whom he obtained a divorce, 1935; she *m* 2nd, 1935, James Courtenay Sherren), *d* of late C. E. Woakes; two *s*; 2nd, 1935, Constance Joan, *d* of late Mr and Mrs F. H. Henderson-Cleland. *Educ:* Dulwich Coll. Preparatory School; St Edmund's Sch., Canterbury; Keble Coll., Oxford; Wycliffe Hall, Oxford. Master at Forest Sch., Essex, 1913. Served European War, 1914-18 (VC); retired Capt., East Surrey Regt; Curate of West Ham, 1921; Temp. CF, 1923; Chaplain to the Forces, 1926-27; resigned with rank of Capt. Travelling Sec. World Alliance for Internat. Friendship, 1928; Continental Life Insurance Co., 1930; Toronto Better Business Bureau, 1935; Canadian Nat. Inst. for the Blind, 1937; Past-Pres. and Hon. Life Mem. Imperial Officers' Assoc. of Canada; Governor Canadian Corps of Commissionaires; Dir, Kingsley Hall (Toronto) for Men. Hon. Member: University Club of Toronto, Empire Club, Civilian Club, Royal Canadian Military Institute, Royal Society of St George; Life-mem. St George's Soc. Royal Canadian Legion (ex-Pres. Woodbridge Branch), etc. Served War of 1939-45 with Canadian Army, 1940-46, Major. Canadian Centennial Medal, 1967. *Recreations:* formerly: outdoor athletics, Rugby football (Surrey County cap), etc. *Address:* 329 Victoria Street, Niagara-on-the-Lake, Ont., Canada.

**GEDDES,** family name of **Baron Geddes** and of **Baron Geddes of Epsom,**

**GEDDES,** 2nd Baron, *cr* 1942; **Ross Campbell Geddes,** KBE 1970 (CBE 1958); DL; Director: Peninsular and Oriental Steam Navigation Company; Trident Tankers Ltd (Chairman); Limmer Holdings Ltd (Chairman); Clerical, Medical and General Life Assurance Society (Chairman); Monks Investment Trust Ltd (Chairman); Brixton Estate Ltd; Foseco Minsep Ltd; Minerals Separation Ltd; The Electronic Trust Ltd; Technology Investments Ltd; Tanker Adviser to the P & O Group; Chairman, Westminster Medical School Council, since 1968, and Member, Governing Body, Westminster Hospital; *b* 20 July 1907; *s* of 1st Baron Geddes, PC, GCMG, KCB, and Isabella Gamble (*d* 1962), 3rd *d* of W. A. Ross, NY; *S* father 1954; *m* 1931, Enid Mary, *d* of late Clarance H. Butler, Tenterden, Kent and late of Shanghai; one *s* one *d* (and one *s* decd). *Educ:* Rugby; Caius Coll., Cambridge (MA). Shell Group of Oil Companies, 1931-46; British Merchant Shipping Mission, Washington, 1942-44; Deputy-Director Tanker Division, Ministry of War Transport, 1944-45. Chairman: Navy Dept Fuels and Lubricants Adv. Cttee, 1951-57; BTA, 1964-70; Min. of Transport Cttee of Enquiry into Carriers' Licensing, 1963-65. President: Inst. of Petroleum, 1956-57; Chamber of Shipping of the UK, 1968. DL Midlothian, 1957. *Recreations:* gardening and yachting. *Heir: s* Hon. Euan Michael Ross Geddes [*b* 3 Sept. 1937; *m* 1966, Gillian, *yr d* of W. A. Butler; one *s* one *d*]. *Address:* 40 Wimpole Street, W1; Nagshead Field, Lymington, Hants. *T:* Lymington 3333. *Clubs:* United Service; New (Edinburgh); Royal Yacht Squadron, Royal Lymington Yacht.

**GEDDES OF EPSOM,** Baron *cr* 1958, of Epsom (Life Peer); **Charles John Geddes,** Kt 1957; CBE 1950; Director, General Signal and Time Systems Ltd; Chairman, Telenova Ltd; *b* 1 March 1897; *s* of Thomas Varney Geddes and Florence Louisa Mills. *m* 1920, Julia Burke; one *d*. *Educ:* Blackheath Central Sch. Post Office: boy messenger, telegraph learner, telegraphist. Served European War, 1914-18. RFC. Lieut, 1916-19, Pilot, 1918-19. Formerly: General Sec. of the Union of Post Office Workers; Member of the General Council of the Trades Union Congress (Pres. of the TUC, 1954-55); Retired, 1957.

*Recreations:* television, reading, gardening. *Address:* 28 Parkhill Court, Addiscombe Road, Croydon, Surrey CR0 5PJ. *T:* 01-681 1188.

**GEDDES, Air Cdre Andrew James Wray,** CBE 1946 (OBE 1941); DSO 1943; *b* 31 July 1906; *s* of late Major Malcolm Henry Burdett Geddes, Indian Army, and late Mrs Geddes, Seaford, Sussex; *m* 1929, Anstice Wynter, *d* of late Rev. A. W. Leach, Rector of Leasingham, Lincs; one *s* one *d. Educ:* Oakley Hall, Cirencester, Glos; Wellington Coll., Berks; Royal Military Academy Woolwich. 2nd Lt Royal Artillery, 1926; seconded Flying Officer RAF 1928-32; Lieut RA 1929; seconded Flight Lieut RAF 1935-38; Capt. RA 1939; served War of 1939-45 (despatches twice, OBE, DSO, CBE, Commander Legion of Merit, USA); seconded Squadron Leader RAF 1939; Acting Wing Commander RAF 1940; Acting Group Capt., 1942; Acting Air Commodore, 1943; War Subst. Group Capt., 1943; Major RA 1943; Air Commodore Operations and Plans, HQ 2nd TAF for the Invasion. Transferred from RA to RAF, 1945; Air Cdre Dir of Organisation (Establishments), Air Ministry, 1945-47; Group Capt. (subst.), 1947; graduated Imperial Defence Coll., London, 1948; Commanding No. 4 Flying Training Sch. and RAF Station, Heany, S Rhodesia, 1949-51; Dep. Dir of Organisation, Plans, Air Ministry, 1951-54, retd with rank of Air Cdre, 1954; Asst County Civil Defence Officer (Plans), East Sussex County Council, 1957-65; Deputy Civil Defence Officer, Brighton County Borough, 1965-66. *Address:* c/o Midland Bank Ltd, Farnham, Surrey.

**GEDDES, Sir (Anthony) Reay (Mackay),** KBE 1968 (OBE 1943); Chairman, The Dunlop Company Ltd, since 1968; *b* 7 May 1912; *s* of late Rt Hon. Sir Eric Geddes, PC, GCB, GBE, Kt Bach.; *m* 1938, Imogen, *d* of late Captain Hay Matthey, Brixham; two *s* three *d. Educ:* Rugby; Cambridge. Bank of England, 1932; Dunlop Rubber Company Ltd, 1935. Served RAFVR, 1939-45. Pres., Soc. of Motor Manufacturers and Traders, 1958-59; Part-time Mem., UK AEA, 1960-65; Mem. Nat. Economic Devel. Council, 1962-65; Chm., Shipbuilding Inquiry Cttee, 1965-66. Director: Midland Bank Ltd, 1967-; Shell Transport and Trading Co. Ltd, 1968-. Governor, Nat. Inst. of Econ. and Social Research; Mem., Governing Body, London Graduate Sch. of Business Studies. Hon. DSc, Aston, 1967; Hon. LLD Leicester, 1969; Hon. DTech Loughborough, 1970. *Address:* Thornby Grange, Northampton; (office) Dunlop House, Ryder Street, St James's, SW1.

**GEDDES, Ford Irvine,** MBE 1943; a Deputy Chairman and Managing Director P & O Steam Navigation Company, since 1968; *b* 17 Jan. 1913; *e s* of Irvine Campbell Geddes and Dorothy Jefford Geddes (*née* Fowler); *m* 1945, Barbara Gertrude Vere Parry-Okeden; one *s* four *d. Educ:* Loretto Sch.; Gonville and Caius Coll., Cambridge (BA). Joined Anderson Green & Co. Ltd, London, 1934. Served War RE, 1939-45 (Major). Director: Bank of NSW (London Adv. Bd), 1950; Equitable Life Assce Soc., 1955 (Pres.); Hall-Thermotank Ltd, 1960; R. & H. Green & Silley Weir Ltd, 1961; British India Steam Navigation Co. Ltd, 1964; Hain-Nourse Ltd, 1968; Chm., Container Fleets Ltd, 1967. Chm., British Shipping Federation, 1965-68; Pres., Internat. Shipping Fedn, 1967-69. CIMarE. *Address:* Havenfields, Great Missenden, Bucks. *T:* Great Missenden 2461. *Clubs:* City of London; Union (Sydney).

**GEDDES, Sir Reay;** *see* Geddes, Sir A. R. M.

**GEDDIS, Alderman Sir William (Duncan),** Kt 1969; JP; clothing manufacturer; *b* 9 July 1896; *m* 1924, Ethel, *d* of Joseph Barron Wiley, Templepatrick; one *s. Educ:* Skerries Coll., Belfast. Served in RAOC, 1940-48, with rank of Major. Mem., Belfast Corporation, 1938-; Lord Mayor of Belfast, May 1966-69. *Recreation:* golf. *Address:* 7 Waterloo Park, Belfast 15. *T:* 76531. *Clubs:* Ulster Reform (Belfast); Fortwilliam Golf.

**GEDLING, Raymond,** CB 1969; Third Secretary, HM Treasury, since 1968; *b* 3 Sept. 1917; *s* of late John and late Mary Gedling; *m* 1956, Joan Evelyn Chapple; one *s. Educ:* Grangefield Grammar Sch., Stockton-on-Tees. Entered Civil Service as Executive Officer, Min. of Health, 1936; Asst Principal, 1942, Principal, 1947. Cabinet Office, 1951-52; Principal Private Sec. to Minister of Health, 1952-55; Asst Sec., 1955; Under-Sec., 1961; Asst Under-Sec. of State, Dept of Educn and Science, 1966-68. *Recreations:* walking, chess. *Address:* 27 Wallace Fields, Epsom, Surrey. *T:* 01-393 9060.

**GEE, Geoffrey,** CBE 1958; FRS 1951; Sir Samuel Hall Professor of Chemistry, University of Manchester, since 1955 (Professor of Physical Chemistry from 1953-55); Pro-Vice-Chancellor, University of Manchester, 1966-68; *b* 6 June 1910; *s* of Thomas and Mary Ann Gee; *m* 1934, Marion (*née* Bowden); one *s* two *d. Educ:* New Mills Grammar Sch.; Universities of Manchester and Cambridge. BSc 1931, MSc 1932, Manchester; PhD 1936, ScD 1947, Cambridge. ICI (Dyestuffs Group) Research Chemist, 1933-38; British Rubber Producers' Research Association: Research Chemist, 1938-47; Dir, 1947-53. Pres., Faraday Soc., 1969 and 1970. *Publications:* numerous scientific papers in Transactions of the Faraday Soc., and other journals. *Recreation:* photography. *Address:* 8 Holmfield Drive, Cheadle Hulme, Cheshire. *T:* 061-485 3713.

**GELDER, Prof. Michael Graham;** W. A. Handley Professor of Psychiatry, University of Oxford, since 1969; Fellow of Merton College, Oxford; *b* 2 July 1929; *s* of Philip Graham Gelder and Margaret Gelder (*née* Graham); *m* 1954, Margaret (*née* Anderson); one *s* two *d. Educ:* Bradford Grammar Sch.; Queen's Coll., Oxford. Scholar and first class Hons, Physiology finals, 1950; MA, DM Oxon, FRCP, DPM. Goldsmit Schol., UCH London, 1951; MRC Fellow in Clinical Research, 1962-63; Gold Medallist, Royal Medico-Psychological Assoc., 1962; Sen. Lectr, Inst. of Psychiatry, 1965-67 (Vice-Dean, 1967-68); Physician, Bethlem Royal and Maudsley Hosps, 1967-68. *Publications:* articles in medical jls. *Recreations:* theatre, gardening. *Address:* St Mary's, Jack Straw's Lane, Oxford OX3 0DN.

**GELL, Prof. Philip George Houtham,** FRS 1969; Professor and Head of Department of Experimental Pathology, Birmingham University, since 1968; *b* 20 Oct. 1914; *s* of late Major P. F. Gell, DSO, and of Mrs E. Lewis Hall; *m* 1941, Albinia Susan Roope Gordon; one *s* one *d. Educ:* Stowe Sch.; Trinity Coll., Cambridge; University Coll. Hosp. MRCS, LRCP, 1939; MB, BCh, 1940; FCPath, 1969. Ho. Phys. to Med. Unit, UCH, 1939; Emergency Public Health Laboratory Service, 1940-43. On staff of Nat. Inst. for Med. Research, 1943-48; Reader in Dept of Exptl Pathology, Birmingham Univ., 1948-60; Prof. (Personal) of Immunological Pathology, Dept of Exptl Pathology, 1960-68. *Publications:* (ed with R. R. A. Coombs) Clinical Aspects of Immunology (2nd edn), 1969. Contribs to Jl of Experimental Med., Immunology, etc.

*Recreations:* gardening, painting. *Address:* Chadwich Manor, Bromsgrove, Worcs. *T:* 021-453 3521.

*See also D. F. Allen.*

**GELL-MANN, Murray;** Robert Andrews Millikan Professor of Theoretical Physics at the California Institute of Technology since 1967; *b* 15 Sept. 1929; *s* of Arthur and Pauline Gell-Mann; *m* 1955, J. Margaret Dow; one *s* one *d*. *Educ:* Yale Univ.; Massachusetts Inst. of Technology. Mem., Inst. for Advanced Study, Princeton, 1951; Instructor, Asst Prof., and Assoc. Prof., Univ. of Chicago, 1952-55; Assoc. Prof. 1955-56, Prof. 1956-66, California Inst. of Technology. Vis. Prof., Collège de France and Univ. of Paris, 1959-60. Overseas Fellow, Churchill Coll., Cambridge, 1966. Dannie Heineman Prize (Amer. Phys. Soc.), 1959; Ernest O. Lawrence Award, 1966; Franklin Medal (Franklin Inst., Philadelphia), 1967; John J. Carty Medal (Nat. Acad. Scis), 1968; Research Corp. Award, 1969; Nobel Prize in Physics, 1969. Hon. ScD: Yale, 1959; Chicago, 1967; Illinois, 1968; Wesleyan, 1968; Hon. Dr, Turin, 1969. *Publications:* (with Yuval Ne'eman) The Eightfold Way, 1964; various articles in learned jls on topics referring to classification and description of elementary particles of physics. *Recreations:* walking in wild country, study of natural history, languages. *Address:* 1024 Armada Drive, Pasadena, Calif 91103, USA. *T:* 213-792-4740. *Clubs:* Cosmos (Washington); Athenæum (Pasedena).

**GELLERT, Leon;** journalist; special writer, Daily Telegraph, Sydney; *b* Adelaide, 17 May 1892; *s* of J. W. Gellert; *m* 1918, Kathleen Patricia (decd), *y d* of late William Saunders; (one *d* decd). *Educ:* Adelaide High Sch. and Adelaide Univ. (Bundey Prize for English Verse). Served with the original 10th Bn which landed on Gallipoli, 25 April 1915. Co-Editor (with late Sydney Ure Smith), Art in Australia Publications, 1921; later Dir, Art in Australia; Literary Editor and Feature Writer, Sydney Morning Herald, 1942-61. *Publications:* Songs of a Campaign, 1917, illustrd by Norman Lindsay; Isle of San, Illustrd by Norman Lindsay, 1919; Desperate Measures, 1929; These Beastly Australians, Illustrd by Bernard Hesling, 1944; Week after Week, 1953; Year after Year, 1956. *Address:* 22 Burran Avenue, Mosman, NSW 2088, Australia. *T:* 969 4176.

**GELLHORN, Peter;** Director, BBC Chorus, 1961; Conductor and Chorus Master, Glyndebourne Festival Opera, 1954; *b* 24 Oct. 1912; *s* of Dr Alfred Gellhorn, and of late Mrs Else Gellhorn; *m* 1943, Olive Shirley (*née* Layton), 3rd *d* of 1st Baron Layton, CH, CBE; two *s* two *d*. *Educ:* Schiller Realgymnasium, Charlottenburg; University of Berlin; Berlin Music Acad. After passing final exams (with dist.) as pianist and conductor, left Germany 1935. Musical Dir, Toynbee Hall, London, E1, 1935-39; Asst Conductor, Sadler's Wells Opera, 1941-43. On industrial war service, 1943-45. Conductor, Royal Carl Rosa Opera (115 perfs), 1945-46. Conductor and Head of Music Staff, Royal Opera House, Covent Garden (over 260 perfs), 1946-53. Has also been working at National Sch. of Opera, annually at Summer Sch. of Music at Dartington Hall; broadcasting frequently as conductor or pianist; composes; writes or arranges music for silhouette and puppet films of Lotte Reiniger (at intervals, 1933-). Lectures on Courses arranged by Oxford Univ. Extra-Mural Delegacy, the WEA, and various County Councils. Musical Dir, Opera Barga, Italy, from foundn in 1967. *Recreations:* reading, walking and going to plays. *Address:* 33 Leinster Avenue, East Sheen, SW14. *T:* 01-876 3949. *Club:* BBC.

**GEMMELL, Prof. Alan Robertson,** JP; Professor of Biology, University of Keele since 1950; *b* 10 May 1913; *s* of Alexander Nicol Gemmell and Mary Robertson; *m* 1942, Janet Ada Boyd Duncanson; two *s*. *Educ:* Ayr Academy; University of Glasgow. BSc (Hons) Glasgow. Commonwealth Fund Fellow, University of Minnesota, 1935-37 (MS); Agricultural Research at West of Scotland Agricultural Coll., 1937-41; PhD Glasgow, 1939. Lecturer in Botany, Glasgow Univ., 1942-44; Biologist at West Midland Forensic Science Laboratory, 1944-45; Lecturer in Botany, Manchester Univ., 1945-50. Regular broadcaster since 1950. President: Staffs Assoc. of Village Produce Guilds; Nantwich Liberal Assoc. JP 1961. *Publications:* Science in the Garden, 1963; Gardeners Question Time Books, 1965, 1967; Developmental Plant Anatomy, 1969; (Associate Editor) Chronica Botanica, Vol. I, 1935; many contributions to scientific journals. *Recreations:* golf, gardening, popular science, reading. *Address:* Highfield House, Aston, Nantwich, Cheshire. *T:* Aston (Nantwich) 408.

**GENEVOIX, Maurice (Charles Louis);** Grand Croix de la Légion d'Honneur; man of letters; Member of the French Academy since 1946 and Permanent Secretary since 1958; *b* 29 Nov. 1890; *m* Suzanne Neyrolles; two *d*. *Educ:* Lycées d'Orléans, Lakanal; Ecole normale supérieure. Served European War, 1914-18 (Croix de Guerre). Prix Goncourt, 1925. *Publications:* Sous Verdun, 1914; Nuits de guerre, 1917; Au seuil des guitounes, 1918; Jeanne Robelin, 1920; La Boue, 1921; Rémi des Rauches, 1922; Les Eparges, 1923; La Joie, 1924; Euthymos, vainqueur olympique, 1924; Raboliot, 1925; La Boîte à pêche, 1926; Les Mains vides, 1928; Cyrille, 1928; L'Assassin, 1930; Rrou, 1931; HOE, 1931; Gai l'amour, 1932; Forêt voisine, 1933; Marcheloup, 1934; Tête baissée, 1935; Bernard, 1937; La Dernière Harde, 1938; Les Compagnons de l'Aubépin, 1938; L'Hirondelle qui fit le printemps, 1941; Laframboise et Bellehumeur, 1942; Eva Charlebois, 1944; Canada, 1945; Sanglar, 1946; L'Ecureuil du bois bourru, 1947; Afrique blanche, Afrique noire, 1949; Ceux de 14, 1950; L'Aventure est en nous, 1952; Fatou Cissé, 1954; Images pour un Jardin sans murs, 1955; Vlaminck, 1956; le Roman de Renard, 1958; Routes de l'Aventure, 1959; Au cadran de mon clocher, 1960; Vaincre à Olympie, 1960; Jeux de Glaces, 1961; La Loire, Agnès et les Garçons, 1962; Derrière les Collines, 1963; Christian Caillard, 1965; Beau-François, 1965. La Forêt perdue, 1967; Jardins sans murs, 1968; Tendre bestiaire, 1968; Bestiaire enchanté, 1969. *Address:* (winter) 1 Rue de Seine, Paris 6eme. *T:* Médicis 02-47; (summer) Les Vernelles, St Denis de l'Hotel, Loiret, France.

**GENN, Leo John;** Actor and Barrister-at-Law; *b* 9 Aug. 1905; *s* of William Genn and Rachel (*née* Asserson); *m* 1933, Marguerite, *d* of Edward van Praag and Catherine (*née* Bonnar); no *c*. *Educ:* City of London Sch.; St Catharine's Coll., Cambridge (MA). Called to Bar, Middle Temple, 1928. Actor as well as Barrister-at-Law since 1930. First appearance on professional stage, 1930, in A Marriage Has Been Disarranged, Nov., at Eastbourne, Dec. at Royalty, London; various parts at Royalty, 1931-32; Garrick, Gaiety, Wyndham's, 1932-33-34; joined Old Vic Company, appearing in numerous parts in Shakespeare, Shaw, Ibsen, Sheridan, Sept. 1934-March 1936; Daly's, 1936; Old Vic: Feb.-April 1937 (in June, Horatio, at Elsinore); The Flashing Stream,

The Lyric, 1938. First appearance in New York, April 1939, in same play. Joined Officers' Emergency Reserve, 1938; 2nd Lieut RA 1940; Capt. 1941; Maj. 1942; Lieut-Col 1943; comd No. 1 War Crimes Investigation Team, responsible for Belsen Concentration Camp Investigation; Asst Prosecutor Belsen Trial, 1945. Croix de Guerre, 1945. Resumed career in the theatre. Another Part of the Forest, New York, 1946; Jonathan, Aldwych, 1948; The Seventh Veil, Prince's, 1951; Henry VIII, Old Vic, 1953; The Bombshell, Westminster, 1954; Small War on Murray Hill, New York, 1957; The Hidden River, Cambridge, 1959; The Devil's Advocate, NY, 1961; Fair Game for Lovers, NY, 1964; 12 Angry Men, Queen's, 1964; The Sacred Flame, Duke of York's, 1967; The Only Game in Town, New York, 1968; Caesar and Cleopatra, US, 1968; Dr Faustus, US, 1969. First film, Jump for Glory, 1937. *Films include:* The Drum, Ten Days in Paris, Henry V, Desert Victory (Commentary), Theirs was the Glory (Commentary), Green for Danger, Mourning Becomes Electra, The Snake Pit, The Velvet Touch, The Wooden Horse, Quo Vadis, Plymouth Adventure, Red Beret, Personal Affair, The Green Scarf, Moby Dick, L'Amant de Lady Chatterley (in French), Beyond Mombasa, The Steel Bayonet, I Accuse, No Time To Die; Too Hot To Handle; It Was Night in Rome; The Longest Day; 55 Days at Peking; Ten Little Indians; Circus of Fear; Connecting Rooms; The Bloody Judge. TV since 1951; broadcasts since 1933; narrator: Coronation Programme, 1937, 1953. King George VI Memorial Programme, 1952; UN opening (from USA), 1947, etc. Distinguished Vis. Prof. of Theatre Arts, Pennsylvania State Univ., 1968, Univ. of Utah, 1969. Governor, Mermaid Theatre; Trustee and Assessor, Yvonne Arnaud Theatre, Guildford; Councillor, Arts Educational Trust. *Publications:* magazine and newspaper articles. *Recreations:* ball games, books and The Bar. *Address:* Locketts Farm, Itchingfield, Sussex. *T:* Slinfold 344. *Clubs:* Garrick; Stage Golfing; West Sussex Golf (Pulborough); Travellers' (Paris).

**GENTLEMAN, David William,** ARCA; RDI 1970; freelance graphic designer and painter; *b* 11 March 1930; *s* of Tom Gentleman, FSIA; *m*; one *d*; 2nd, 1968, Susan Griselda, *d* of George Ewart Evans; one *d*. *Educ:* Hertford Gram. Sch. Studied at Royal Coll. of Art, London, in Sch. of Graphic Design, 1950-53; held teaching post there, 1953-55. Since then has worked entirely as freelance designer and illustrator. Designs include: fabric prints, wallpapers, book jackets, posters and murals, designs for many sets of British commemorative postage stamps (incl. Shakespeare, Churchill, Battle of Britain, Battle of Hastings, Concorde, British Ships, Prince of Wales Investiture, GPO Develts, Philympia 1970); also for stampbook covers and air-letter forms; symbols and house styles, inc. BSC 1969; lithographs (Curwen Prints), 1967, 1970. Illustrations, include drawings for: books, magazines, newspapers. Paints in watercolours; engraves on wood. Visited India as guest of Govt, 1967; Exhibn of Watercolours of India, Mercury Gall., 1970; Exhibn of Stamps, Nat. Postal Museum, 1970. Mem. College Court, RCA. Phillips Gold Medal for Stamp Design, 1969. *Publications:* Fenella in Ireland, 1967; Fenella in Greece, 1967; Fenella in the South of France, 1967; Fenella in Spain, 1967; *Illustrations only for:* What About Wine, 1953; Plats du Jour, 1957; Italian Journey, 1958; Bristol Fashion, 1960; The Magic Wishbone, 1960; The Griffin and the Minor Canon, 1960; Bridges on the Backs, 1961; House into Home, 1962; Swiss Family Robinson, 1963; Hill Towns of Italy, 1963; The Shell Book of Roads, 1964; The Shepheard's Calendar, 1964; The Dramatic Experience, 1965; Gypsies, 1965; Poems of John Keats, 1966; Pattern under the plough, 1966; Poems to Compare, 1966; The Jungle Book, 1968; The Departed Village, 1968; The Midnight Skaters, 1968; covers for New Penguin Shakespeare, 1968-70; King Solomon's Mines, 1970; The Solitary Song, 1970; Where Beards Wag All, 1970; contribs to New Statesman. *Relevant Publications:* Artists of a certain line; Motif; Who's Who in Graphic Art; Illustrators at Work; Stanley Gibbons Magazine. *Recreation:* travel. *Address:* 51 Gloucester Crescent, Regent's Park, NW1. *T:* 01-485 8824.

**GENTNER, Dr Wolfgang;** Director of the Max-Planck-Institute for Nuclear Physics, Heidelberg, since 1958; Professor of Physics, University of Heidelberg, since 1958; *b* Frankfurt-am-Main, 23 July 1906; *s* of Carl G. Gentner, manufacturer; *m* 1931, Alice Pfaehler; one *s* one *d*. *Educ:* Universities of Erlangen and Frankfurt (PhD). Fellowship at Institut du Radium, Lab. Curie, Paris Univ. (Mme P. Curie), 1933-35; Scientific Asst at Inst. of Physics of Kaiser-Wilhelm-Institut for Med. Research, 1936-46; Lectr in Physics, Univ. of Frankfurt, 1937-41; Fellow, Radiation Lab., Univ. of California (Berkeley), 1938-39; Lectr in Physics, Univ. of Heidelberg, 1941-45, Prof. 1945; Prof. of Physics, Freiburg Univ., 1946-58; Dir of CERN, Geneva, 1955-59. Member: Comité des directives scientifiques, CERN, 1959-; Heidelberger Akad. der Wissenschaften (Pres. 1964-); Bayerische Akad. der Wissenschaften; Akad. Leopoldina; Pontifical Acad. of Science, 1970; Hon. Fellow, Weizmann Inst., Israel, 1965. Officier, Légion d'Honneur, 1965. *Publications:* on biophysics, radioactivity, nuclear physics; (co-author) Atlas of typical expansion chamber photographs, 1954. *Address:* Max-Planck-Institute for Nuclear Physics, Saupfercheckweg, 69 Heidelberg I, Germany; Im Bäckerfeld 6, Heidelberg, Germany. *T:* 42467.

**GENTRY, Jack Sydney Bates,** CIE 1946; CBE 1965 (OBE 1942); ERD 1964; JP; General Manager Tees Conservancy Commission, 1946-66; retired; *b* 4 Oct. 1899; *s* of Frederick and Emma Gentry; *m* 1931, Beatrice Colleen Cundy Wren. *Educ:* Christ's Hosp. Port of London Authority, 1916, Commercial Superintendent, 1945; commission, Hants Regt, 1918; RE, 1938; served War of 1939-45 (despatches twice); Major, 1939; Lieut-Col, Asst Dir of Docks, 1940; Col, Dep. Dir of Movements, 1942. Dep. Regional Port Dir, Calcutta, 1944-45. JP Co. Durham, 1949. MIT, 1947. *Recreations:* cricket (played for Hants, Surrey, Essex, 1919-26); golf, tennis. *Address:* Pancake Cottage, Loxwood, near Billingshurst, Sussex. *T:* Loxwood 289. *Clubs:* MCC, Public Schools; Christ's Hospital.

**GENTRY, Maj.-Gen. (retd) Sir William George,** KBE 1958 (CBE 1950); CB 1954; DSO 1942, and Bar 1945; *b* 20 Feb. 1899; *e s* of late Major F. C. Gentry, MBE and late Mrs F. C. Gentry; *m* 1926, Alexandra Nina Caverhill; one *s* one *d*. *Educ:* Wellington Coll., NZ; RMC of Australia. Commissioned NZ Army, Dec. 1919; attached Indian Army and served in Waziristan, 1921, and Malabar, 1921. Served War of 1939-45 with 2nd NZ Div. (Middle East and Italy): GSO 2 and AA and QMG, 1940; GSO 1, 1941-42; Comd 6 NZ Inf. Bde, 1942-43; DCGS, Army HQ, NZ, 1943-44; Comd 9 NZ Inf. Bde (Italy), 1945. Adjutant Gen., NZ Army, 1949-52; Chief of the Gen. Staff, NZ Army, 1952; retired, 1955. Mem. Licensing Control Commn, 1957-67. Hon. Pres. NZ Boy Scouts Assoc., 1957-67. Greek Military Cross,

1941; United States Bronze Star, 1945. *Address:* 52 Kings Crescent, Lower Hutt, New Zealand. *T:* 60208. *Clubs:* Wellington, United Services (Wellington, NZ).

**GEORGE;** *see* Lloyd George.

**GEORGE, Bishop of,** since 1966; **Rt. Rev. Patrick Harold Falkiner Barron;** *b* 13 Nov. 1911; *s* of Albert Harold and Mary Isabel Barron; *m* 1942, Kathleen May Larter; two *s* one *d. Educ:* King Edward VII Sch., Johannesburg; Leeds Univ. (BA); College of the Resurrection, Mirfield. Curate: Holy Redeemer, Clerkenwell, London, 1938-40; Boksburg, S Africa, 1940-41; CF (S African), 1941-46; Rector: Zeerust, S Africa, 1946-50; Potchefstroom, 1950-51; Blyvooruitzicht, 1951-55. St Cyprian's Mission, Johannesburg, 1956-59; Archdeacon of Germiston, 1957-58; Dean of Johannesburg, 1959-64; Bishop Suffragan of Cape Town, 1965-66. *Recreation:* gardening. *Address:* Bishop's Lea, George, CP, S Africa. *T:* 2267.

**GEORGE, Ven. Christopher Owen;** Rector of Sproughton and Archdeacon of Suffolk, 1947-62; Archdeacon Emeritus, St Edmundsbury and Ipswich, since 1962; *b* 30 Sept. 1891; *s* of late Thomas and Emily Marion George; *m* 1921, Kathleen Iris Maude (*d* 1970), *d* of late Walter Herbert Back; four *d. Educ:* Ipswich Sch.; Selwyn Coll., Cambridge. BA 1913, MA 1917; Deacon 1914, Priest 1915, Diocese of Norwich; Curate, Great Yarmouth, 1914-19; Associate Sec. Dr Barnardo's Homes, 1919-23: Asst Master, Ipswich Sch. 1923-27; Curate, St Mary-le-Tower, 1923-25, St Clement, 1925-27, Vicar, St Augustine, 1927-34 and Rector, St Mary Stoke, Ipswich, 1934-37. *Recreation:* reading. *Address:* The Old Rectory Flat, Harkstead, Ipswich, Suffolk IP9 1DE. *T:* Holbrook 201.

**GEORGE, Frank Bernard;** retired as Managing Director, Consett Iron Company Ltd (1957-64); President, Iron and Steel Institute, 1963-64 (Vice-President 1962); *b* 20 July 1899; *s* of Sir Edward George and Eleanor Dagnall; *m* 1927, Winifred Mary George; three *s. Educ:* Caldicott Sch., Hitchin; The Leys Sch., Cambridge; Armstrong Coll., Durham Univ. Consett Iron Co. Ltd, 1925-64. Pres. Cleveland Institution of Engineers, 1956-57. *Publications:* contrib. Iron and Steel Institute Journal. *Address:* 2 Fir Tree Close, Bolton-le-Sands, Lancs. *T:* Hest Bank 3274.

**GEORGE, Griffith Owen,** JP; TD; DL; Chairman, Glamorgan Quarter Sessions, since 1966; *b* 5 Dec. 1902; *s* of late John and Emiah Owen George, Hirwaun, Glam; *m* 1937, Anne Elinor, *e d* of late Charles and Anne Edwards, Llandaff; one *s. Educ:* Westminster Sch.; Christ Church, Oxford (MA). Beit Prize Essay, 1923; Barrister, Gray's Inn, 1927, Wales and Chester Circuit. Served War of 1939-45, 2nd Lieut RA, 1939; Capt. 1941; Major 1943; on JAG's staff, N Africa, Italy, Middle East, 1943-45. Contested Llanelly (Nat. Con.), 1945. Commissioner in Wales under the National Insurance Acts, 1950-67. Dep. Chm., Glamorgan Quarter Sessions, 1956-66; Chm., Glamorgan Probation Cttee. JP Glamorgan, 1952; DL Glamorgan, 1970. *Address:* The Mount, Peterston super Ely, Glamorgan. *T:* Peterston 358. *Club:* Cardiff and County (Cardiff).

**GEORGE, Herbert Horace,** CB 1944; MC; *b* 1890; *s* of John George, Clapham; *m* 1913, Emily Rose (*d* 1952), *d* of Thomas Eaton, Clapham; no *c. Educ:* Westminster City Sch.; Trinity Coll., Cambridge. Entered Civil Service, 1913. Served in RA in European War, 1914-19. Under-Sec. for Finance and Accountant-Gen., Ministry of Health, 1946-50; retired, 1950. *Address:* Fouryews, Telham, Battle, Sussex. *T:* Battle 2927.

**GEORGE, Hywel,** CMG 1968; OBE 1963; Governor, St Vincent, since 1969 (Administrator, 1967-69); *b* 10 May 1924; *s* of Rev. W. M. George and Catherine M. George; *m* 1955, Edith Pirchl; three *d. Educ:* Llanelli Gram. Sch.; UCW Aberystwyth; Pembroke Coll., Cambridge. RAF, 1943-46. Cadet, Colonial Admin. Service, N Borneo, 1949-52; District Officer, 1952-58; Secretariat, 1959-62; Resident, Sabah, Malaysia, 1963-66. Panglima Darjah Kinabalu (with title of Dato), Sabah, 1964; JMN, Malaysia, 1966. CStJ 1969. *Recreations:* tennis, cricket. *Address:* Government House, Kingstown, St Vincent.

**GEORGE, Sir John (Clarke),** KBE 1963 (CBE 1952); CEng; Director: National Carbonising Co. Ltd; Chairman: Joy Manufacturing Co. (UK) Ltd, of Greenock; Scottish Rexco Ltd; Preswick Precision Products Ltd; *b* 16 Oct. 1901; *s* of John Clarke George, Gracemount, Aberdour, Fife; *m* 1929, Euphamia, *d* of Robert G. Donaldson, Priory, Ballingry, Fife. *Educ:* Ballingry Public Sch., Fife. Entered coal mine at age of 14. Managing Director: New Cumnock Collieries, Ayrshire, 1938-46; Alloa Glass Works Co. Ltd, 1946-55. Mem. Alloa Town Council, 1951-56; CC Clackmannanshire, 1949-56. Contested (C) S Div. of Ayrshire, 1950; MP (U) Pollok Div. of Glasgow, 1955-64; Parly Sec., Min. of Power, 1959-62; Chm., Unionist Party in Scotland, 1963-65. CStJ. *Address:* Seton Lodge, Ayr, Scotland. *T:* 62541. *Club:* Caledonian.

**GEORGE, Mary Dorothy,** OBE 1954; MA, LittD, FRHistSoc; Hon. Fellow of Girton College; *d* of late Alexander Gordon, barrister-at-law, and of late Harriet Emily, *d* of Rev. R. S. Tabor; *m* 1913, Eric Beardsworth George (*d* 1961), painter. *Educ:* St Leonards Sch., St Andrews; Girton Coll., Cambridge (1st Cl. Historical Tripos); London Sch. of Economics (research scholar). War Office, (MI5), 1915-19 (mentioned for valuable services). *Publications:* English Social Life in the Eighteenth Century, 1923; London Life in the XVIII Century, 1925, 1951, paperback 1966; England in Johnson's Day, 1928; England in Transition, 1931, 1952, 1964; British Museum Catalogue of Political and Personal Satires (caricatures), in continuation of that by F. G. Stephens, vols V-XI (1771-1832), 1935-54; English Political Caricature to 1792: a study of Opinion and Propaganda, 1960; English Political Caricature, 1793-1832, 1960; Hogarth to Cruikshank: Social Change in Graphic Satire, 1967. Contributions to Johnson's England, 1933, English Historical Review, Economic Journal, History, etc. *Address:* 51 Paulton's Square, SW3. *T:* 01-352 6228. *Club:* English-Speaking Union.

**GEORGE, Thomas Neville,** FRS 1963; FRSE, FGS, DSc (Wales), PhD Cantab; Professor of Geology in the University of Glasgow since 1947; *b* 13 May 1904; *s* of T. Rupert George, Swansea; *m* 1932, Dr Sarah Davies; no *c. Educ:* Dynevor Sch.; Swansea Grammar Sch.; Universities of Wales (Swansea Coll.), Cambridge (St John's Coll.) and London (Birkbeck Coll.). Fellow of the University of Wales, 1926. Geologist on HM Geological Survey, 1930; Prof. of Geology and Head of the Dept of Geology and Geography, University Coll. of Swansea, 1933; Woodward Lectr, Yale Univ., 1956; Sen. Foreign Fellow (Nat. Sci. Foundation), Northwestern Univ., 1964; Vis. Prof., Universities of the Witwatersrand, Cape Town, and Natal, 1967.

Pres. Geology Section of British Assoc. (Liverpool), 1953. Chairman: Newbattle Abbey Coll. Exec. Cttee; Brit. Assoc. Glasgow Cttee; Mineral Resources Panel (Scottish Council); Geological Conservation Council; Scot. Field Studies Assoc.; Vice-Pres., RSE, 1959-61. President: Geol. Soc. London, 1968-70; Assoc. University Teachers, 1959-60; Palæontological Assoc., 1962-64; Teachers' Geol Assoc. Member: Nature Conservancy; Minerals Resources Consultative Cttee (Dept of Education and Science); Geology and Geophysics Cttee (NERC); Oceanography and Fisheries Cttee (NERC); National Broadcasting Council (Scotland). Hon. LLD Wales 1970; Hon. D-ès-Sc (Rennes). Lyell Medal, Geological Soc. London, 1963. *Publications:* Evolution in Outline, 1951; British Regional Geology: North Wales, 1961; South Wales, 1969; Aspects of the Variscan Fold Belt (in part), 1962; The British Caledonides (in part), 1963; The Geology of Scotland (in part), 1964; University Instruction in Geology, 1965; contributions on geology and palæontology to technical journals. *Address:* Dept of Geology, University of Glasgow, Glasgow W2. *T:* 041-339 8855.

**GEORGE-BROWN,** Baron *cr* 1970 (Life Peer), of Jevington, Sussex; **George Alfred George-Brown,** PC 1951; Industrial Counsellor, Courtaulds Ltd, since 1968; Vice-Chairman and Deputy Leader, Labour Party, 1960-70; *b* 2 Sept. 1914; *s* of George Brown; name changed to George-Brown by deed poll, 1970; *m* 1937, Sophie Levene; two *d.* MP (Lab) Belper Div. of Derbyshire, 1945-70; Parliamentary Private Secretary to Minister of Labour and National Service, 1945-47, to Chancellor of the Exchequer, 1947; Joint Parliamentary Secretary, Ministry of Agriculture and Fisheries, 1947-51; Min. of Works, April-Oct. 1951; First Secretary of State and Secretary of State for Economic Affairs, Oct. 1964-Aug. 1966; Secretary of State for Foreign Affairs, 1966-68. *Address:* c/o House of Lords, SW1.

*See also R. W. Brown.*

**GEORGES-PICOT, Jacques,** KBE (Hon.) 1963; Commandeur, Légion d'Honneur; Chairman of the Board, Suez Finance Company, since 1957; *b* 16 Dec. 1900; *s* of Charles Georges-Picot and Marthe Fouquet; *m* 1925, Angeline Pelle; five *s. Educ:* Lycée Janson de Sailly, Paris. Inspector of Finance, 1925; Chef de Cabinet, Minister of Budget, 1931; Dir Min. of Finance, 1934; Agent Superieur in Egypt, of Suez Canal Co., 1937; Asst Dir-Gen. of Suez Canal Co., 1946; Dir-Gen., 1953; Pres., 1957. Dir, Fondation des Sciences Politiques, Paris. *Recreation:* tennis. *Address:* 2 Square Mignot, Paris 16e. *T:* Passy 79-68. *Clubs:* Circle Interallié (Paris); Links (NYC).

**GEORGETOWN, Bishop of, (RC),** since 1956; **Rt. Rev. Richard Lester Guilly,** SJ; OBE 1945; *b* 6 July 1905; *s* of late Richard Guilly. *Educ:* Stonyhurst Coll.; Campion Hall, Oxford (Hons Mod. Hist.; BA, MA); Heythrop Coll. Entered Soc. of Jesus, 1924; Asst Master, Beaumont Coll., 1933-35; ordained 1938. Served War of 1939-45, Chaplain to the Forces: BEF (France), 1939-40; CF 3rd Cl. 1940; Senior RC Chaplain, N Ireland, 1 Corps District, AA Cmd, 2nd Army, 1940-45 (OBE, despatches). Superior of Soc. of Jesus in British Guiana and Barbados, 1946-54; Titular Bishop of Adraa and Vicar Apostolic of British Guiana and Barbados, 1954-56. *Publications:* various articles on Church History, Christian Social Doctrine and Church in Guyana. *Address:* Bishop's House, 27 Brickdam, Georgetown, Guyana.

**GERAGHTY, William,** CB 1962; Deputy Secretary, Ministry of Aviation Supply, since 1970 (ministry of Technology, 1967-70); *b* 12 Feb. 1917; *e s* of Patrick and Elizabeth Geraghty; *m* 1946, Lilian Irene Travis; no *c. Educ:* Emanuel Sch.; Brasenose Coll., Oxford. 1st Cl. Hon. Mods 1937, 1st Cl. Lit Hum 1939. Appointed War Office, 1939. Served RA and RHA, 1940-45. Private Sec. to Secretaries of State for War, 1949-51. Imperial Defence Coll., 1955. Asst Under-Sec. of State, WO, 1958-60; Under-Sec., Cabinet Office, 1960-62; Dep. Under-Sec. of State: WO, 1962-64; (1) Army Dept, Min. of Defence, 1964-65; (Air), Min. of Defence, 1965; Administration, 1965-66; Dep. Sec., Min. of Aviation, 1966-67. *Address:* 11 Kelvin Grove, Chessington, Surrey. *T:* 01-397 3721. *Club:* Oxford and Cambridge.

**GERAHTY, Sir Charles Cyril,** Kt 1939; QC, Trinidad, 1931; *b* 1888; *s* of Charles Echlin Gerahty; *m* 1st, 1915, Ethel Marian (*d* 1942), *d* of late Dr James Murray, MB, ChB; one *s* (younger killed in action April 1945); 2nd, 1948, Arminell Morshead (*d* 1966); 3rd, 1967, Mary Violet, *widow* of Gerald Watson, late of Pyrford, Woking. *Educ:* Trent Coll. Called to Bar, Middle Temple, 1909; Maj. (retd). 3rd Bn East Lancs Regt; Asst Resident, Nigeria, 1911; on active service, European War, 1914-18; Legal Asst, War Office, 1919; Pres., District Court, Cyprus, 1920; Attorney-Gen., Cyprus, 1926; Attorney-Gen., Trinidad, 1929; Puisne Judge, Straits Settlements (Singapore), 1932; Legal Adviser to Governor of Malta, 1935; Legal Sec. to Government of Malta, 1936; Chief Justice of Trinidad and Tobago and Pres. West Indian Court of Appeal, 1937-43; retired, 1943. Chm. of a Pensions Appeal Tribunal, England, April 1944. Dir-Gen. MGC Branch, Legal Div., CCG, Dec. 1944-July 1946; Acting Attorney-Gen. in Gibraltar, May-Aug. 1949; JP, 1951-55; Dep. Chm. Essex Court of Quarter Sessions, 1951-55. *Address:* Flat 4, Ruscote, Cross Oak Road, Berkhamsted, Herts. *Club:* Royal Societies.

**GERARD,** family name of **Baron Gerard.**

**GERARD,** 4th Baron, *cr* 1876, Bt 1611, **Robert William Frederick Alwyn Gerard,** *b* 23 May 1918; *o s* of 3rd Baron Gerard, MC, and late Mary Frances Emma, *d* of Sir Martin Le Marchant Hadsley Gosselin, GCVO, KCMG, CB; *S* father, 1953. *Heir: cousin* Bt Col Charles Gerard, *qv. Address:* Blakesware, Ware, Herts. *T:* 3665.

**GERARD, Bt Col Charles (Robert Tolver Michael),** DSO 1917; OBE 1944; late Grenadier Guards; late Commanding TA Battalion; JP Lancs; *b* 28 Feb. 1894; *s* of late Hon. R. J. Gerard-Dicconson; *heir-pres* to 4th Baron Gerard, *qv*; *m* 1st, 1915, Aimée (who obtained a divorce, 1930), *d* of Sir R. T. H. Clarke, 2nd Bt; two *s*; 2nd, 1930, Norma, *d* of Mrs Frankford Rogers. *Educ:* Eton; Sandhurst. Served European War (France), 1914-18 (despatches, DSO); Dep. Provost Marshal, London, 1939-45. *Address:* Doone, Sunningdale, Berks. *T:* Ascot 194. *Clubs:* Turf, White's.

**GERARD, Geoffrey;** *see* Gerard, W. G.

**GERARD, Rt. Rev. George Vincent,** CBE 1944; Assistant Bishop of Sheffield since 1947; Residentiary Canon of Sheffield Cathedral, 1960-69; Chairman, House of Clergy, Church Assembly since 1965; *b* 24 Nov. 1898; *e s* of late George and late Frederikke Marie Gerard, Snowdon, Canterbury, New Zealand; *m* 1920, Elizabeth Mary Buckley; one *s* one *d. Educ:* Waihi Sch., Winchester, NZ; Christ's Coll.,

Christchurch, NZ; Brasenose Coll., Oxford. Inns of Court, OTC 1917; 2nd Lieut The Buffs, 1918, Lieut 1918 (MC); demobilised, 1919; BA (Oxon.), 1921; MA 1925; deacon, 1922; priest, 1923; Vicar of Pahiatua, 1929-32; Petone, 1932-36; St Matthew, Auckland, 1936-38; Bishop of Waiapu, 1938-44; served as Senior Chaplain to the NZ Forces, 1940-41 (prisoner, but repatriated to England, 1943). Senior NZ Chaplain South Pacific, 1944; Hospital Ship, 1945. Vicar and Rural Dean of Rotherham, 1945-60; Hon. Canon of Sheffield, 1947-60. Proctor in Convocation of York, 1950 and 1952-70. *Address:* 10 Claremont Place, Sheffield S10 2TB.

**GERARD, (William) Geoffrey,** CMG 1963; Managing Director, Gerard Industries Pty Ltd, S Australia, since 1930; Director Gerard and Goodman Pty Ltd, SA; *b* 16 June 1907; *s* of late A. E. Gerard; *m* 1932, Elsie Lesetta, *d* of late A. Lowe; one *s* one *d*. *Educ:* Adelaide Technical High Sch. Pres., SA Chamber of Manufactures, 1953-54; Pres., Associated Chambers of Manufactures of Aust., 1955; Pres., SA Metal Industries Assoc., 1952 and 1957; Pres., Aust. Metal Industries Assoc., 1962-64; Vice-Chm., Standards Assoc. of Aust., 1956-; Pres., Aust.-Amer. Assoc. in SA Incorp., 1961-63; Chm., Nat. Employers' Assoc., 1964-66; Pres., Liberal and Country League (SA Div. of Liberal Party of Aust.), 1961-64; Mem. Commonwealth Immigration Planning Coun., 1956-; Mem. Commonwealth Manufg Industries Advisory Coun., 1958-62. Past Pres., Electrical Devel. Assoc. of SA and Electrical Manufrs' Assoc. of SA. *Recreations:* golf, tennis. *Address:* 9 Robe Terrace, Medindie, South Australia. *T:* 65 2560. *Clubs:* CTA, Commonwealth (Adelaide).

**GERAUD, Charles Joseph André; (Pertinax);** Officer Legion of Honour, France, 1936; diplomatic correspondent, France-Soir, Paris; contributor to: Daily Telegraph (London), Foreign Affairs (N York); *b* St Louis de Montferrand (Gironde), 18 Oct. 1882; *s* of O. Géraud and Marthe Faux; *m* 1914, Louise Banniard; no *c*. *Educ:* Bordeaux Univ. (Licencié-ès-lettres). London correspondent of L'Echo de Paris, 1908-14; foreign ed. of L'Echo de Paris (Pertinax), 1917-38; ed. of L'Europe Nouvelle, 1938-40; contributor to: New York Times, Baltimore Sun and several other newspapers and reviews. *Publications:* Le Partage de Rome, a study of the Lateran Treaties, 1929; Les Fossoyeurs (Gamelin, Daladier, Reynaud, Pétain, Laval): French edn, 2 vols, N York, 1943; new edn, N York, 1945; English language edn, (The Gravediggers), N York, 1944, Paris edn, 1st vol., 1946. *Address:* 91 rue de l'Université, Paris 7e; Segur-le Château (Corrèze); 58 W 10th Street, New York City.

**GERHARDIE, William Alexander,** OBE 1920; MA, BLitt (Oxon); Author; *b* St Petersburg, 21 Nov. 1895; *y s* of late Charles Alfred Gerhardie, an English industrialist settled at St Petersburg, and Clara Wadsworth. *Educ:* The St Annen Schule, and Reformierte Schule, St Petersburg; Worcester Coll., Oxford. Served European War, 5th Reserve Cavalry (2nd Dragoons, Royal Scots Greys), 1915-16; with Military Attaché, British Embassy, Petrograd, 1917-18; attached 3rd Bn Scots Guards; British Military Mission to Siberia, 1918-20 (Order of St Stanislav, of Imperial Russia; Russia; Czecho-Slovak War Cross; despatches, OBE); demobilized, retaining rank of Capt., 1920; joined Officers' Emergency Reserve, 1940; BBC (European Div.), 1942-45. First Ed. of English by Radio. *Publications:* Futility: A Novel on Russian Themes, 1922; Anton Chehov: A Critical Study, 1923; The Polyglots, a Novel, 1925; A Bad End, 1926; The Vanity-Bag; Donna Quixote: a Comedy in Three Acts; Pretty Creatures: Short Novels, 1927; Doom, a Novel, 1928; Pending Heaven, a Novel, 1930; Memoirs of a Polyglot, (autobiography), 1931; The Memoirs of Satan (with Brian Lunn), 1932; The Casanova Fable (with Hugh Kingsmill), 1934; Resurrection, a Novel, 1934; Meet Yourself: character studies through self-analysis (with Prince Leopold Loewenstein), 1936; Of Mortal Love, a Novel, 1936; My Wife's the Least of It, a Novel, 1938; The Romanoffs: An Historical Biography, 1940, rev. edn 1970; My Literary Credo: an Introduction to the Collected Uniform Revised Edition of the Works, 1947; I Was A King in BabylonAnd You May Very Well Be Right, an implausible comedy, produced by Jerome Kilty, 1948 (Boston, USA); Highlights of Russian History, 1949; Analyze Yourself, an American adaptation of Meet Yourself, 1955; Rasputin, the ironical tragedy, prod. Vanburgh Theatre, London, 1960; The Fool of the Family (with Lord Snow, a play), 1964; Donna Quixote, a lyrical comedy, prod. Little Theatre, London, 1968; Works, 2nd Coll. edn, 10 vols, 1970; essays; articles; broadcasts (inc. TV). *Address:* 19 Rossetti House, Hallam Street, Portland Place, W1. *T:* 01-580 4878.

**GERIN, Winifred, (Mrs John Lock),** MA Cantab; FRSL; author; 2nd *d* of F. C. Bourne and Katharine (*née* Hill); *m* 1st, Eugene Gérin (*d* 1945), of Brussels; 2nd, 1954, John Lock; no *c*. *Educ:* Sydenham High Sch. for Girls; Newnham Coll., Cambridge. War of 1939-45 in Political Intelligence Dept of Foreign Office. James Tait Black Mem. Prize, 1967; RSL Heinemann Prize, 1968; Rose Mary Crawshay Prize, 1968. FRSL 1968. *Plays:* My Dear Master, Arts Theatre, Leeds, 1955; Juniper Hall, BBC TV, 1956. *Publications:* Anne Brontë, 1959; Branwell Brontë, 1961; The Young Fanny Burney, 1961; Charlotte Brontë, 1967; Horatio Nelson, 1970; contribs to Keats/Shelley Mem. Bulletin; also editorial work. *Recreations:* music, country life, travelling. *Address:* 60 West Cromwell Road, SW5; 3 The Green, Stanford-in-the-Vale, Berks.

**GERMAN, Sir Ronald (Ernest),** KCB 1965; Kt 1959; CMG 1953; Director: Securicor Ltd since 1967; National Post Office Building Society since 1966; *b* 19 Oct. 1905; *m* 1931, Dorothy Sparks; no *c*. *Educ:* HM Dockyard Sch., Devonport. Entered GPO 1925; Asst Dir Posts & Telegraphs Dept, Sudan, 1942; British Post Office, 1945; Postmaster-Gen., East Africa, 1950-58; Dep. Dir Gen. of the Post Office, UK, 1959-60, Dir Gen., 1960-66. Chm. Makerere Coll. Council, 1957-58 (Vice-Chm. 1954). CStJ, 1963. *Recreation:* golf. *Address:* 65 Upper Ratton Drive, Eastbourne, Sussex.

**GERNSHEIM, Helmut;** photo-historian and author; *b* Munich, 1 March 1913; 3rd *s* of Karl Gernsheim, historian of literature at Munich Univ., and Hermine Gernsheim (*née* Scholz); *m* 1942, Alison Eames, London (*d* 1969); no *c*. *Educ:* St Anne's Coll., Augsburg; State Sch. of Photography, Munich. Settled in England as free-lance photographer, 1957; became British subject, 1946; during War of 1939-45 made photogr. surveys of historic bldgs and monuments for Warburg Inst. (London Univ.); exhibns of these at Courtauld Inst., 1945 and 1946, Nat. Gall., 1946; one-man show at Royal Photogr. Society 1948; since 1945 has built up Gernsheim photo-historical collection, since 1964 at University of Texas, Austin; selections were shown at art museums, Europe and America. Co-ed. Photography Yearbook, 1953-55; British Representative World Exhibition of Photography, Lucerne,

1952, Biennale and Unesco Conference on Photography, Paris, 1955, etc. Editorial Adviser, photography, Encyclopædia Britannica. First German cultural prize for photography, 1959. Order of Merit, Germany, 1970. *Publications include:* New Photo Vision. 1942; Julia Margaret Cameron. 1948; Lewis Carroll-Photographer, 1949; Beautiful London, 1950; Masterpieces of Victorian Photography, 1951; Those Impossible English, 1952; Churchill, His Life in Photographs, 1955; Creative Photography, 1962; (with Alison Gernsheim): Roger Fenton, 1954; The History of Photography, 1955; L. J. M. Daguerre, 1956; Queen Victoria, a Biography in Word and Picture, 1959; Historic Events, 1960; Edward VII and Queen Alexandra, 1962; Concise History of Photography, 1965, etc. Numerous articles in art and photographic journals in many countries. *Recreations:* travelling, fishing for old photographs, hunting in antique shops, collecting African art. *Address:* Residenza Tamporiva 1, Via Tamporiva, 6976 Castagnola, Ticino, Switzerland. *T:* Lugano 091 515904.

**GERRARD, Prof. Alfred Horace;** Professor of Sculpture in University of London at University College Slade School of Fine Art, 1948-68, now Emeritus; *b* 7 May 1899; *m* 1933, Katherine Leigh-Pemberton (*d* 1970). *Educ:* Hartford County Council Sch.; Manchester Sch. of Art; Slade Sch. of Fine Art, University Coll., London. Head of Dept of Sculpture, Slade Sch., UCL, 1925-48. Served European War, 1914-18, Cameron Highlanders, 1916-17; RFC, 1917-19; War of 1939-45, Staff Capt. Royal Engineers, 1939-43; war artist, 1944-45. RBS Silver Medal, 1960. Fellow, University Coll. London, 1969. *Recreation:* gardening. *Address:* Dairy House, Leyswood, Groombridge, Tunbridge Wells, Kent. *T:* Groombridge 268.

**GERRARD, Basil Harding;** Barrister-at-law; Recorder of Barrow-in-Furness since 1969; *b* 10 July 1919; *s* of Lawrence Allen Gerrard and Mary (*née* Harding); *m* Sheila Mary Patricia (*née* Coggins), *widow* of Walter Dring, DSO, DFC (killed in action, 1945); one *s* two *d* and one step *d*. *Educ:* Bryanston Sch.; Caius Coll., Cambridge (BA). Royal Navy, 1940-46; called to Bar, Gray's Inn, 1947. *Recreations:* golf, gardening. *Address:* Broadway, Broad Oak Park, Worsley, Lancs. *T:* Swinton 4409. *Clubs:* St James's (Manchester); Worsley Golf.

**GERRARD, Major Frederick Wernham,** CIE 1920; *b* 25 Nov. 1887; *s* of M. G. Gerrard; *m* 1928, Dorothy Ursula, *d* of G. H. Teague. Joined Indian Police Service, 1908. IARO: served with 116 Mahrattas, North West Frontier, India, 1915; with 114 Mahrattas, Mesopotamia, 1916-23 (despatches, 1918); with Civil Administration, Iraq, as Deputy Inspector-Gen. of Police, Baghdad, 1921-23; retired from Indian Police Service, 1933; Commissioner of Police Foreign Settlement of Shanghai; retired 1938. *Address:* 1601 Ross Street, Victoria, BC, Canada.

**GERSHEVITCH, Dr Ilya,** FBA 1967; Reader in Iranian Studies, University of Cambridge, since 1965; *b* Zurich, 24 Oct. 1914; *o s* of Arkadi and Mila Gershevitch, Smolensk, Russia; *m* 1951, Lisbeth, *d* of Josef Syfrig, Lucerne; one *d*. *Educ:* Swiss schools at Locarno and Lugano; Univ. of Rome (classics); Univ. of London (Oriental studies). Dottore in Lettere, Univ. of Rome, 1937; PhD, Univ. of London, 1943. Monitored foreign broadcasts, London, 1942-47; Lecturer in Iranian Studies, Univ. of Cambridge, 1948; MA Cambridge, 1948. First European to penetrate into certain areas of Western Makran (dialect field-work), 1956; Vis. Prof. at Columbia Univ., New York, 1960-61 and 1965-66; Fellow of Jesus Coll., Cambridge, 1962; Univ. Exchange Visitor, USSR, 1965; Ratanbai Katrak Lecturer, Univ. of Oxford, 1968. *Publications:* A Grammar of Manichean Sogdian, 1954; The Avestan Hymn to Mithra, 1959; articles in specialist jls, encyclopaedias and collective books. *Recreation:* music. *Address:* 54 Owlstone Road, Cambridge. *T:* Cambridge 57996.

**GERVERS, Brig. Francis Richard Soutter,** CIE 1919; CBE 1929; late Royal Engineers; *b* Kimberley, 10 July 1873; *s* of late F. T. Gervers; *m* 1904, Beryl Firebrace; no *c*. *Educ:* United Services Coll., Westward Ho; RM Academy, Woolwich. Employed, 1901, Gold Coast Survey; served Mohmand, Malakand, and Tirah, 1897-98 (medal with two clasps); India, 1914-19 (medal); Afghanistan, 1919 (medal with clasp); European War (medal); retired, 1928; FRGS. *Recreations:* shooting, fishing. *Address:* Sloane House, Littleworth Avenue, Esher, Surrey. *Club:* United Service.

**GERVIS-MEYRICK, Sir George David Elliott Tapps-;** *see* Meyrick.

**GERY;** *see* Wade-Gery.

**GETHIN, Lt-Col (Retd) Sir Richard Patrick St Lawrence,** 9th Bt, *cr* 1665; late REME; *b* 15 May 1911; *s* of Col Sir Richard Walter St Lawrence Gethin, 8th Bt, and Helen (*d* 1957), *d* of W. B. Thornhill; *S* father 1946; *m* 1946, Fara, *y d* of late J. H. Bartlett; one *s* four *d*. *Educ:* Oundle Sch. Lieut RAOC, 1935; Lieut-Col REME, 1943; Officer Commanding No 11 Vehicle Depot Workshops, until 1957, retired. *Heir:* *s* Richard Joseph St Lawrence Gethin, *b* 29 Sept. 1949. *Address:* Easter Cottage, Bredon, near Tewkesbury, Glos. *T:* Bredon 354.

**GETHING, Air Commodore Richard Templeton,** CB 1960; OBE 1945; AFC 1939; Secretary, Gliding Federation of Australia; *b* 11 Aug. 1911; *s* of George A. Gething, Wilmslow, Cheshire; *m* 1940, Margaret Helen, *d* of late Sir Herbert Gepp, Melbourne, Australia; one *s* one *d*. *Educ:* Malvern; Sydney Sussex Coll., Cambridge. Joined RAF, 1933. Served War of 1939-45: Canada; UK; India; Burma. Actg Group Capt., 1943; Group Capt., 1950; Actg Air Commodore, 1956; Dir Operations, Maritime Navigation and Air Traffic, Air Ministry, 1958-60, retired. FIN 1956. *Recreation:* gliding. *Address:* Garden Hill, Kangaroo Ground, Victoria 3097, Australia. *Club:* Royal Air Force.

**GETTY, J(ean) Paul;** President: Getty Oil Co. since 1947; Mission Corporation since 1947; Trustee and Founder of the J. Paul Getty Museum, Malibu, Calif.; *b* Minneapolis, USA, 15 Dec. 1892; *s* of George Franklin Getty and Sarah Catherine McPherson Risher; *m* 1923 (marr. diss.); one *s*; *m* 1926 (marr. diss.); *m* 1928 (marr. diss.); one *s*; *m* 1932 (marr. diss.); two *s*; *m* 1939 (marr. diss.); one *s* decd. *Educ:* University of Southern California; University of California; Oxford Univ. (non-collegiate Diploma in Economics and Political Science). Pres. and Gen. Manager, George F. Getty Inc., 1930-33; Director: Petroleum Corporation, 1932-34; Tidewater Associated Oil Co., 1932-36; Pres. of other companies. Officier, Légion d'Honneur; Grande Médaille (silver), City of Paris. Hon. LLD, Ohio Northern Univ. *Publications:* A History of the Oil Business of George Franklin and J. Paul Getty, 1903-1939, 1940; Europe in the Eighteenth Century, 1941; (with Ethel Levane) Collector's Choice, 1955; My Life and Fortunes, 1963; How to be Rich, 1965; Joys of

Collecting, 1965; The Golden Age, 1968. *Recreation:* collecting art. *Address:* 17985 Pacific Coast Highway, Malibu, Calif., USA; Sutton Place, near Guildford, Surrey. *Clubs:* Explorers (New York); Beach (Santa Monica, Calif.); Los Angeles Athletic (Los Angeles); Nouveau Cercle (Paris).

**GHALE, Jemadar Gaje;** *see* Gaje Ghale.

**GIAUQUE, William (Francis);** Professor of Chemistry, University of California, Berkeley, since 1934; *b* (as US citizen) Niagara Falls, Ont., Canada, 12 May 1895; *s* of William T. S. Giauque and Isabella Jane (*née* Duncan); *m* 1932, Muriel Frances Ashley, BS, PhD; two *s*. *Educ:* High Sch., Niagara Falls; University of Calif. BS 1920, PhD 1922. Faculty of Chemistry, University of Calif.: Instructor, 1922-27; Asst Prof., 1927-30; Assoc. Prof., 1930-34. Government work during War of 1939-45. Member: National Academy of Sciences; Amer. Philosophical Soc.; Amer. Acad. of Arts and Sciences. Hon. DSc Columbia; Hon. LLD Univ. Calif. Nobel prize for Chemistry, 1949; and other awards. *Publications:* over 100 papers in scientific journals. *Address:* 2643 Benvenue Avenue, Berkeley, Calif 94704, USA; University of California, Berkeley, Calif, USA.

**GIBB, Andrew Dewar,** QC (Scotland), 1947; Hon. LLD: Aberdeen and Glasgow; Regius Professor of Law in the University of Glasgow, 1934-58; *s* of late Dr W. F. Gibb, Paisley; *m* 1923, Margaret Isabel, *d* of late Dr Walker Downie, Glasgow; one *s* two *d*. *Educ:* Glenalmond; Glasgow Univ., LLB (distinction), 1913; called to Scottish Bar, 1914; English Bar, 1917; served European War, 1914-19, Royal Scots Fusiliers and Staff; in practice English Bar since 1919; Lecturer on Law of England, University of Edinburgh, 1929; Lecturer on Law of Scotland, University of Cambridge, 1931; contested (U) Hamilton Div. of Lanarks, 1924; Greenock, 1929; (Scottish Nat.) Scottish Universities, 1935, 1936 and 1938; Chm. of Scottish National Party, 1936-40; Chm. of Saltire Soc., 1955-57; Pres., Scottish Covenant Assoc., 1957-. *Publications:* Law of Collisions on Land; Scottish Judicial Dictionary; A Preface to Scots Law; International Law of Jurisdiction; Select Cases in Law of Scotland; Scotland in Eclipse; With Winston Churchill at the Front; Scottish Empire; Scotland Resurgent; Law from over the Border. *Recreation:* sailing. *Address:* 15 Kirklee Road, Glasgow, W2.

**GIBB, Sir Hamilton Alexander Rosskeen,** Kt 1954; FBA 1944; MA; Hon. LLD Edinburgh; Hon. LittD Harvard; Hon. Dr Algiers; Commander of Order of Orange-Nassau; Chevalier of the Legion of Honour; Director, Center for Middle Eastern Studies, 1957-66; Hon. Fellow, St John's Coll., Oxford, 1955; Foundation Member, Fuad I Academy of Arabic Language, Cairo; Hon. Mem. Amer. Acad. of Arts and Sciences; Fellow Danish Acad.; Mem. Amer. Philosophical Society; Associate Member Institut d'Egypte; Chairman, Permanent Committee on Geographical Names, 1947-55; *b* 2 Jan. 1895; *s* of A. C. Gibb, Alexandria, Egypt; *m* Helen (*d* 1969), *d* of John Stark, DL, JP, Edinburgh; one *s* one *d*. *Educ:* Royal High Sch., Edinburgh; Edinburgh Univ.; London Univ. Served European War in RFA, 1914-19; Lecturer, Sch. of Oriental Studies (University of London), 1921; Reader, 1929; Prof. of Arabic in The University of London, 1930; Laudian Prof. of Arabic, University of Oxford, 1937; Haskell Lecturer, Chicago, 1945; University Prof. and J. R. Jewett Prof. of Arabic, Harvard Univ., 1955-64. Triennial Gold Medal, Royal Asiatic Soc., 1969. *Publications:* The Arab Conquests in Central Asia; Arabic Literature (2nd edn enlarged, 1963); Translation of Barthold's Turkestan; Travels of Ibn Battuta; Studies in Contemporary Arabic Literature; The Damascus Chronicle of the Crusades; Modern Trends in Islam; Mohammedanism; (with Harold Bowen) Islamic Society and the West; (Ed.) Whither Islam. *Address:* 86 Norreys Road, Cumnor, Oxford.

**GIBB, Thomas George;** Managing Director, Freightliners Ltd, since 1969; *b* 21 Feb. 1915; 2nd *s* of late Paul and Phyllis Gibb, Aldeburgh, Suffolk; *m* 1944, Angela, *d* of late Canon and of Mrs G. E. H. Theophilus; three *s* one *d*. *Educ:* St Edward's Sch., Oxford. Joined LNER as Traffic Apprentice, 1933. Commissioned LNER Co. (Supp. Reserve) RE, 1938; Capt. 1939; seconded Min. of Supply, 1941-45. Joined Currie and Co. (Newcastle) Ltd 1945, Dir and Gen. Man., 1947; British Road Services, 1949, appointments including Divisional Manager, NE Div., 1956; Chairman, British Road Services, 1959; Vice-Chm. and Man. Dir, BRS Federation Ltd, 1963-67; Dir, Transport Holding Co., 1967-68. Mem., Road Transport Industry Training Board, 1966-69. Mem., Inst. of Transport (Vice-Pres., 1967-69). *Recreations:* sailing, cricket, golf. *Address:* The Old Kennels, Satwell, Henley-on-Thames, Oxon. *T:* Rotherfield Greys 302. *Clubs:* Royal Thames Yacht; Clyde Cruising (Glasgow).

**GIBB, Walter Frame,** DSO 1945; DFC 1943; Product Support Manager, British Aircraft Corporation Limited, Filton Division; *b* 26 March 1919; British; *m* 1944, Pauline Sylvia Reed; three *d*. *Educ:* Clifton Coll. Apprentice, Bristol Aero Engines, 1937. RAF, 1940-46. Test Pilot, Bristol Aircraft Ltd, 1946; Asst Chief Test Pilot, 1953; Chief Test Pilot, Bristol Aeroplane Co. Ltd, 1956-60. World Altitude Height Record 63,668 feet in Olympus-Canberra, 1953, and second record 65,890 ft in same machine, 1955. AFRAeS. *Recreation:* sailing. *Address:* Greystones, Olveston, near Bristol. *T:* Almondsbury 3279. *Club:* Royal Air Force.

**GIBB, William Eric,** MA, DM Oxon; FRCP; Physician: St Bartholomew's Hospital since 1947; The Metropolitan Hospital since 1952; *b* 30 April 1911; *s* of late James Glenny Gibb, MD, FRCS, and Georgina Henman; *m* 1952, Mary Edith Gertrude Feetham; three *s*. *Educ:* Rugby Sch.; Oriel Coll., Oxford; St Bartholomew's Hosp. BA Oxon 1st Cl. Hons Final Sch. of Nat. Science; Prox. Access. Theodore Williams Scholarship (Anatomy); BM, BCh Oxon 1936; MRCP 1940; DM Oxon 1947; FRCP 1949; George Herbert Hunt Travelling Schol. (University of Oxford), 1938. Res. House appts, St Bart's Hosp. and Brompton Chest Hosp.; Cattlin Research Scholar, 1947. War service with RAFVR Medical Branch, 1941-46; Actg Wing Comdr i/c a Medical Div. Examiner in Medicine, University of Oxford, 1952-59 and Examiner in Medicine, Examg Bd of England. Fellow, Royal Soc. Med. and Med. Soc. London; Mem. Internat. Soc. of Internal Medicine. *Publications:* various articles in medical journals. *Recreation:* gardening. *Address:* 95 Harley Street, W1. *T:* 01-935 6267.

**GIBBENS, (Edward) Brian,** MA Oxon; QC 1962; Recorder of Oxford since 1965 (West Bromwich, 1959-65); *b* 26 Sept. 1912; *s* of Rev. George Percy Gibbens and Dr Fanny Gibbens; *m* 1939, Kathleen Joan Rosier; two *s* one *d*. *Educ:* Newcastle-under-Lyme High Sch.; St Catherine's Society, Oxford. Called to the Bar, Gray's Inn, 1934; Bencher of Gray's Inn, 1967; practised on Oxford Circuit from 1934.

Served in RA and as staff officer, Nov. 1939-45. Major in Army Officers Emergency Reserve, 1946-. Mem. Gen. Council of the Bar, 1947-52, 1964-68, 1969-; Dep. Chm. QS, Oxon., 1964-; Leader of the Oxford Circuit, 1966-; conducted Home Office inquiry into corporal punishments at Court Lees approved sch., 1967; conducted public inquiry into automatic level crossings after railway accident at Hixon, Staffs, 1968. *Address:* 11 Zetland House, Marloes Road, W8. *T:* 01-937 0429; (professional) 3 Pump Court, Temple, EC4.

**GIBBERD, Sir Frederick,** Kt 1967; CBE 1954; RA 1969 (ARA 1961); FRIBA, MTPI, FILA; FSIA; practising as an Architect, Town Planning Consultant and Landscape Architect; *b* 7 Jan. 1908; *e s* of late Frederick Gibberd, Kenilworth, Warwicks; *m* 1938, Dorothy, *d* of late J. H. Phillips, Hampstead; one *s* two *d*. *Educ:* King Henry VIII Sch., Coventry. Private practice in London since 1930. Principal buildings include: Pullman Court, Streatham; London Airport, Terminal Buildings and Chapel; Bath Technical College; St Neots Bridge; Hinkley Point and Didcot Power Stations; Metropolitan Cathedral, Liverpool (won in open competition); New Monastery, Douai Abbey; Longmans Green Offices, Harlow; Doncaster Law Courts (with L. J. Tucker); Designs for: Central London Mosque (won in open competition); Duke of Norfolk's Strand Estate; Coutts Bank, Strand and Hotel, Hyde Park Corner. Principal Town Designs: Harlow New Town, Architect-Planner, Memorial Univ., Newfoundland, Master Plan. Civic Centres for: Doncaster; Harlow; Leamington Spa; Nuneaton and St Albans. Shopping Centres: Lansbury Market; Redcar and Stratford-upon-Avon. Principal Landscape and Garden Designs: Harlow, overall landscape design and Water Gardens; Queen's Gardens, Hull; Llyn Celyn and Derwent Reservoirs and Potash Mine at Boulby. Member: Royal Fine Art Commission, 1950-70; Council RIBA, 1959- (Vice-President 1960-); Concrete Society Council; President, Building Centre; Past Principal, Architectural Association School of Architecture; Hon. LLD, Liverpool, 1969. RIBA Bronze Medal; Two Festival of Britain Awards; Three Housing Medals; Four Civic Trust Awards. *Publications:* The Architecture of England, 1938; Town Design, 1953; Metropolitan Cathedral of Christ the King, Liverpool, 1968. *Recreation:* gardening. *Address:* 49 Downshire Hill, NW3; 8 Percy Street, W1; The House, Marsh Lane, Harlow, Essex. *Club:* Athenæum.

**GIBBERD, George Frederick,** CBE 1962; Consulting Obstetric Surgeon Emeritus: Guy's Hospital; Queen Charlotte's Maternity Hospital; Honorary Consulting Gynæcologist, Samaritan Hospital for Women; *s* of George William Gibberd and Jessie Waters; *m* 1930, Margaret Erica, *y d* of Leslie Hugh Taffs, Langley, Bucks; two *s* one *d*. *Educ:* Aske's Haberdashers'; Guy's Hosp. MB, MS London; FRCS; FRCOG; Sometime Examiner in Obstetrics and Gynæcology for Universities of Cambridge, London, Wales, Manchester and Leeds, for Conjoint Examining Board of RCS and RCP, and for RCOG; Vice-Pres. RCOG, 1958-61 (hon. Sec., 1938-47; Mem. Council, 1936-61); Sims-Black Travelling Prof., RCOG, 1952; Mem. of Gynæcological Visiting Society of Great Britain. Temp. Lieut-Col, RAMC. Served War of 1939-45, in North Africa and Italy. Consulting Gynæcological Surg., St John's Hosp., Lewisham. Member: Medical Adv. Cttee, UGC, 1947-59; Maternity Services (Cranbrook) Cttee, 1956-59; Bd of Govs, Guy's Hosp. Med. Sch., 1956-67, and Guy's Hosp., 1957-69. *Publications:* A Short Text-Book of Midwifery; (in collaboration) Queen Charlotte's Text-Book of Midwifery; contributions to medical literature. *Address:* 5 Tollgate Drive, College Road, Dulwich, SE21. *Club:* Athenæum.

**GIBBINS, Elizabeth Mary,** BA; Headmistress, St Mary's School, Calne, Wilts; *b* 2 May 1911; *d* of late Kenneth Mayoh Gibbins, MB, BS. *Educ:* Sandecotes Sch., Parkstone; Westfield Coll., University of London; Cambridge Univ. Training Coll. for Women (Postgraduate). History Mistress, St Brandons Clergy Daughters' Sch., Bristol, 1935-38; Headmistress, Diocesan Girls' Sch., Hongkong, 1939-45. *Address:* St Mary's School, Calne, Wilts. *T:* Calne 3329.

**GIBBON, Maj.-Gen. John Houghton,** CB 1970; OBE 1944; Director of Army Staff Duties, Ministry of Defence, since 1969; *b* 21 Sept. 1917; *er s* of Brigadier J. H. Gibbon, The Manor House, Little Stretton, Salop; *m* 1951, Brigid Rosamund, *d* of Dr D. A. Bannerman, *qv*; one *s*. *Educ:* Eton; Trinity Coll., Cambridge. Commissioned into Royal Artillery, 1939. Served with 2nd Regt RHA: France, 1939-40; Western Desert, 1940-41; Greece, 1941; on staff of HQ 30 Corps; Western Desert, 1941-43; Sicily, 1943; GSO 1, RA, HQ 21 Army Gp, 1944-45; 6 Airborne Div., Palestine, 1946-47; Instructor and Chief Instructor, RMA Sandhurst, 1947-51; GSO 2, War Office, 1951-53; Battery Comdr, 1953-54; AQMG, War Office, 1955-58; CO Field Regt, BAOR, 1959-60; Bde Comdr, Cyprus, 1962; Dir of Defence Plans, Min. of Def., 1962-64; Sec., Chiefs of Staff Cttee, and Dir, Defence Operations Staff, 1966-69. *Recreations:* rowing, shooting, fishing. *Address:* Moth House, Brown Candover, Alresford, Hants. *T:* Preston Candover 260. *Club:* Flyfishers'.

**GIBBON, Monk;** *see* Gibbon, W. M.

**GIBBON, (William) Monk,** PhD (Dublin); FRSL; poet and writer; *b* Dublin, 15 Dec. 1896; *o s* of late Canon William Monk Gibbon, MA, Rural Dean, Taney, Dundrum, Co. Dublin, and Isabel Agnes Pollock (*née* Meredith); *m* 1928, Mabel Winifred, *d* of Rev. Walter Molyneux Dingwall, MA, and Mabel Sophia Spender; two *s* four *d*. *Educ:* St Columba's Coll., Rathfarnham; Keble Coll., Oxford (Open History Exhibn). Served European War, 1914-18, as Officer, RASC; France, 1916-17; Invalided out, 1918. Taught in Switzerland; master at Oldfield Sch., Swanage (12 yrs). Silver Medal for Poetry, Tailteann Games, 1928. Tredegar Memorial Lecture, Royal Society of Literature, 1952; Tagore Centenary Lecture, Abbey Theatre, Dublin, 1961. Mem. Irish Acad. of Letters, 1960 (Vice-Pres., 1967). *Publications: poetry:* The Tremulous String, 1926; The Branch of Hawthorn Tree, 1927; For Daws to Peck At, 1929; Seventeen Sonnets, 1932; This Insubstantial Pageant (collected poems), 1951; *autobiography:* The Seals, 1935; Mount Ida, 1948; Inglorious Soldier, 1968; The Brahms Waltz, 1970; *biography:* Netta (Hon. Mrs Franklin), 1960; *novel:* The Climate of Love, 1961; *ballet and film criticism:* The Red Shoes Ballet, 1948; The Tales of Hoffmann, 1951; An Intruder at The Ballet, 1952; *travel:* Swiss Enchantment, 1950; Austria, 1953; In Search of Winter Sport, 1953; Western Germany, 1955; The Rhine and its Castles, 1957; Great Houses of Europe, 1962; Great Palaces of Europe, 1964; *literary criticism:* The Masterpiece and the Man, 1959. The Living Torch (an anthology), 1937. *Recreations:* watching ballet and good films. *Address:* 24

Sandycove Road, Sandycove, Co. Dublin, Eire. *T:* 805120.

**GIBBONS, Brig. Edward John,** CMG 1956; CBE 1947; *b* 30 Aug. 1906; *s* of Edward Gibbons, Coventry; *m* 1946, Gabrielle Maria, *widow* of Capt. P. A. Strakosh; one step *d. Educ:* King Henry VIII Sch., Coventry; Gonville and Caius Coll., Cambridge. Nigerian Administrative Service, 1929. Army Service, 1941-46: Dir of Civil Affairs, South East Asia Command; Brig. Sec. Eastern Provinces, Nigeria, 1948; Commissioner of the Cameroons (under UK Trusteeship), 1949-56; Dept of Technical Cooperation, 1962-64; Min. of Overseas Develt, 1964-68. *Recreation:* wood engraving. *Address:* 6 Grove House, The Grove, Epsom, Surrey. *T:* Epsom 26657. *Club:* Royal Automobile.

**GIBBONS, Sir John Edward,** 8th Bt *cr* 1752; Captain (Dorset Regiment); independent; *b* 14 Nov. 1914; *s* of Sir Alexander Doran Gibbons, 7th Bt and Gladys Constance (*d* 1945), *d* of late Rev. Charles Watkins; *S* father 1956; *m* 1937, Mersa Wentworth Foster (marriage dissolved, 1951), Warmwell House, near Dorchester; one *s* two *d. Educ:* Charterhouse. Asst Regional Dir (Nottingham) of Arts Council of Great Britain, 1946-50. Dorset Regt, 1939-45; Staff Officer, 1942-43, Iran and Syria. *Heir: s* William Doran Gibbons, *b* 13 Jan. 1948. *Address:* 2 Malt Cottages, Preston, Weymouth, Dorset. *Clubs:* United Service, MCC.

**GIBBONS, Stella Dorothea,** FRSL; Poet and Novelist; *b* London, 5 Jan. 1902; *d* of C. J. P. T. Gibbons, MD; *m* 1933, Allan Bourne Webb (*d* 1959); one *d. Educ:* N London Collegiate Sch.; University Coll., London. Journalist, 1923-33; BUP, Evening Standard, The Lady. *Publications:* The Mountain Beast (Poems), 1930; Cold Comfort Farm, 1932 (Femina Vie Heureuse Prize, 1933); Bassett, 1934; The Priestess (Poems), 1934; Enbury Heath, 1935; The Untidy Gnome, 1935; Miss Linsey and Pa, 1936; Roaring Tower (Short Stories), 1937; Nightingale Wood, 1938; The Lowland Venus (Poems), 1938; My American, 1939; Christmas at Cold Comfort Farm (Short Stories), 1940; The Rich House, 1941; Ticky, 1943; The Bachelor, 1944; Westwood, 1946; The Matchmaker, 1949; Conference at Cold Comfort Farm, 1949; Collected Poems, 1950; The Swiss Summer, 1951; Fort of the Bear, 1953; Beside the Pearly Water (short stories), 1954; The Shadow of a Sorcerer, 1955; Here Be Dragons, 1956; White Sand and Grey Sand, 1958; A Pink Front Door, 1959; The Weather at Tregulla, 1962; The Wolves were in the Sledge, 1964; The Charmers, 1965; Starlight, 1967; The Snow Woman, 1969; The Woods in Winter, 1970. *Recreations:* reading, listening to music. *Address:* 19 Oakeshott Avenue, Highgate, N6.

**GIBBONS, Col William Ernest,** OBE 1944; *b* 24 April 1898; *s* of W. P. Gibbons, JP, Wombourne, Staffs; *m* 1922, Alma Pfister, OBE, JP (*d* 1955); one *d*; *m* 1964, Verity Anne Parson. *Educ:* Bromsgrove Sch. CO 1/6 S Staffs Regt 1939-42; NI Infantry Sch., 1942-44. Served European War, France and Italy, 1917-18; War of 1939-45, France, 1940. MP (Nat. C) Bilston, Staffs, 1944-45. *Recreation:* fishing. *Address:* Old Farm House, Bilbrook, near Wolverhampton. *T:* Wolverhampton 51159.

**GIBBS,** family name of **Barons Aldenham** and **Wraxall.**

**GIBBS, Dame Anstice (Rosa),** DCVO 1967; CBE 1960; retired as Chief Commissioner and Chairman Girl Guides' Association (British Commonwealth) (1956-66); *b* 2 Jan. 1905; *d* of late Archdeacon The Hon. Kenneth Gibbs and late Mrs Gibbs. *Educ:* privately in England and France. Worked with Girl Guides from 1922; Dep. Chief Commissioner, 1954. Mem. Cttee of World Association of Girl Guides and Girl Scouts, 1952-60, Vice-Chm., 1954-60. *Address:* Blacknest Lodge, Brimpton Common, near Reading, Berks. *T:* Tadley 4365.

**GIBBS, Dennis Raleigh,** CMG 1962; CVO 1966; DSO 1944; Administrator of Montserrat, WI, since 1964; *b* 3 March 1922; *e s* of late Gerard Yardley Gibbs, Epping, and of Carol Gibbs (*née* Francis), London, W2; *m* 1952, Barbara Erica Batty; two *s* one *d. Educ:* Bradfield Coll. RAF, 1940-46; CO 82 Sqdn, 1942-44; Wing Comdr Air Staff, Air HQ, Burma, 1945. Seconded FO, 1946; Colonial Admin. Service, 1946-56, then E Nigerian Public Service, 1956-64 (Perm. Sec., Min. of Works, 1958, Adv. to Min. of Economic Planning, 1962-64). CON (Hon.) 1964. *Recreations:* fishing, shooting, sailing. *Address:* Plymouth, Montserrat, West Indies; Ballahowin, St Marks, Isle of Man. *T:* Marown 251.

**GIBBS, Sir Frank Stannard,** KBE, *cr* 1954 (OBE 1939); CMG 1949; *b* 3 July 1895; *m* 1944, Sylvia Madeleine Knight; one *s* one *d.* Probationer Vice-Consul, Genoa, 1920; served Madrid, Rio de Janeiro, Paris, Marseilles, Beira, Milan; Vice-Consul, 1923; transferred to China Consular Service with Consular rank, 1935; Actg Consul-Gen., Canton, 1937, Addis Ababa, 1939; served Rosario and Tunis: Consul-Gen., 1946; Foreign Service Officer, Grade 5, 1947; Consul-Gen., Saigon, 1947-51, with personal rank of Minister, 1950-51; Ambassador to the Republic of the Philippines, 1954-55 (Minister, 1951-54), retired 1955. *Address:* El Rincón, Maitland Close, West Byfleet, Surrey. *T:* Byfleet 46414.

**GIBBS, Hon. Sir Geoffrey Cokayne,** KCMG 1955 (CMG 1945); Chairman: Antony Gibbs & Sons Limited, merchant bankers; Barclays Overseas Development Corporation; Director: Barclays Bank DCO (formerly Dep. Chm.); Australia and New Zealand Bank Ltd (Chm. 1951-67), and of other companies; Past Chm. Adv. Council Export Credits Guarantee Dept; Chairman: Managing Trustees of the Nuffield Foundation; Imperial Relations Trust; National Corporation for the care of the Aged; A member of the Court of the Grocers' Company (Master, 1938-39); *b* 20 July 1901; 2nd *s* of 1st Baron Hunsdon and Anna Maria, *d* of Richard Durant; *m* 1926, Helen Margaret, CBE 1961, *d* of C. F. H. Leslie; five *s* one *d. Educ:* Eton; Christ Church, Oxford. Min. of Economic Warfare, 1939-45. Hon. DCL, Oxford, 1966. *Address:* The Manor House, Clifton Hampden, Abingdon-on-Thames. *T:* Clifton Hampden 220. *Clubs:* City of London, Brooks's.

*See also Rt. Hon. Sir H. V. Gibbs.*

**GIBBS, Air Marshal Sir Gerald Ernest,** KBE, *cr* 1954 (CBE 1945); CIE 1946; MC; *b* 3 Sept. 1896; *s* of Ernest William Cecil and Fanny Wilmina Gibbs; *m* 1938, Margaret Jean Bradshaw; one *s* one *d.* Served European War, 1914-18; transferred from Army to RFC 1916, and RAF 1918 (MC and 2 bars, Légion d'Honneur, Croix de Guerre). Served various overseas periods with RAF in Iraq, Palestine, Sudan and Kenya between the two wars. Senior Air Staff Officer of No. 11 Group, Fighter Command, 1940-41; Dir of Overseas Operations, Air Ministry, 1942-43; Senior Air Staff Officer, HQ 3rd Tactical Air Force, South-East Asia, 1943-44; Chief Air Staff Officer, Supreme HQ, SEAC, 1945-46; Senior

Air Staff Officer, HQ, RAF Transport Command, 1946-48; Head of Service Advisers to UK Delegation and Chm. UK Members of Military Staff Cttee, UN, 1948-51; Chief of Air Staff and Commander-in-Chief, Indian Air Force, 1951-54, retired 1954. *Publication:* Survivor's Story, 1956. *Recreations:* golf, ski-ing, sailing. *Address:* Lone Oak, 170 Coombe Lane West, Kingston-upon-Thames, Surrey. *Clubs:* Royal Air Force; Royal Wimbledon Golf (Wimbledon); Walton Heath Golf (Tadworth); Trevose Golf (Cornwall).

**GIBBS, Rt. Hon. Sir Humphrey Vicary,** PC 1969; GCVO 1969 (KCVO 1965); KCMG 1960; OBE 1959; Governor of Rhodesia (lately S Rhodesia), 1959-69; *b* 22 Nov. 1902; 3rd *s* of 1st Baron Hunsdon; *m* 1934, Molly Peel Nelson (*see* Molly Peel Gibbs); five *s*. *Educ:* Eton; Trinity Coll., Cambridge. Started farming near Bulawayo, 1928. Hon. LLD Birmingham, 1969; Hon. DCL East Anglia, 1969. *Address:* Bonisa Farm, Redbank, Bulawayo, Rhodesia. *Clubs:* Athenæum; Bulawayo (Bulawayo, Rhodesia); Salisbury (Salisbury, Rhodesia).

*See also Hon. Sir G. C. Gibbs.*

**GIBBS, Martin St John Valentine,** CB 1958; DSO 1942; TD; JP; *b* 14 Feb. 1917; *er s* of late Major G. M. Gibbs, Parkleaze, Ewen, Cirencester; *m* 1947, Mary Margaret (*widow* of late Captain M. D. H. Wills, MC), *er d* of late Col Philip Mitford; two *d*. *Educ:* Eton. 2nd Lieut, Royal Wilts Yeomanry, 1937; served War of 1939-45 with Royal Wilts Yeo., Major 1942, Lieut-Col 1951, Brevet-Col 1955, Col 1958. High Sheriff Glos, 1958. *Recreations:* country pursuits. *Address:* Ewen Manor, Ewen, Cirencester, Glos. *T:* Kemble 206. *Club:* Cavalry.

*See also R. C. Gibbs.*

**GIBBS, Molly Peel, (Hon. Lady Gibbs),** DBE 1969; *b* 13 July 1912; 2nd *d* of John Peel Nelson; *m* 1934, Rt Hon. Sir Humphrey Vicary Gibbs, *qv*; five *s*. *Educ:* Girls' High School, Barnato Park, Johannesburg. *Address:* Bonisa, Private Bag 52.L, Bulawayo, Rhodesia. *T:* Bulawayo 62555.

**GIBBS, Prof. Norman Henry,** MA, DPhil; Chichele Professor of the History of War in the University of Oxford since 1953; *b* 17 April 1910; *m* 1941, Joan Frances Leslie-Melville; two *d*; *m* 1955, Kathleen Phebe Emmett. Open Exhibitioner, Magdalen Coll., Oxford, 1928; Senior Demy, 1931; Asst Lecturer, University Coll., London, 1934-36; Fellow and Tutor in Modern History, Merton Coll., Oxford, 1936. 1st King's Dragoon Guards, 1939; Historical Section, War Cabinet Office, 1943. Member: Naval Education Advisory Cttee; Internat. Council of Institute for Strategic Studies, 1965-; Research Associate, Center for Internat. Studies, Princeton, 1965-66. *Publications:* 2nd edition, Keith, British Cabinet System, 1952; The Origins of the Committee of Imperial Defence, 1955; contribs to: Cambridge Modern History (new edn); L'Europe du XIXme et du XXme siècles, (Milan) 1966; (ed) The Soviet System and Democratic Society, 1967. *Address:* All Souls College, Oxford; Flexneys House, Stanton Harcourt, Oxon.

**GIBBS, Maj.-Gen. Roland Christopher,** CBE 1968; DSO 1945; MC 1943; Commander British Forces, Gulf, since 1969; *b* 22 June 1921; *yr s* of late Maj. G. M. Gibbs, Parkleaze, Ewen, Cirencester; *m* 1955, Davina Jean Merry; two *s* one *d*. *Educ:* Eton Coll.; RMC Sandhurst. Commnd into 60th Rifles, 1940; served War of 1939-45 in N Africa, Italy and NW Europe. Comd 3rd Bn Parachute Regt, 1960-62; GSO1, Brit. Army Staff, Washington, 1962-63; Comdr 16 Para. Bde, 1963-66; Chief of Staff, HQ Middle East, 1966-67; IDC 1968. *Recreation:* out-of-door sports. *Address:* Shalden Lodge, Alton, Hants. *T:* Alton 2391. *Club:* Turf.

*See also M. St J. V. Gibbs.*

**GIBBS-SMITH, Charles Harvard;** Keeper Emeritus, Victoria and Albert Museum, since 1971; aeronautical historian; *b* 22 March 1909; *y s* of late Dr E. G. Gibbs-Smith. *Educ:* Westminster; Harvard Univ., USA (Research Fellow and MA). Asst-Keeper, Victoria and Albert Museum, 1932-39, Keeper of Public Relations and Educn Dept, 1947-70; loaned to Ministry of Information, 1939 (Asst-Dir of Photograph Div., 1943, Dir, 1945). Organised photograph libraries of Ministry of Information; Press Censorship; Admiralty Press Div.; USA Office of War Information, London; Radio Times-Hulton Picture Library. Served in ROC 1941-44 (Hon. Mem., 1945). Hon. Companion, and Cttee Mem. History Group, Royal Aeronautical Society; Cttee Mem., British Theatre Museum; FRSA 1948; FMA 1952; Mem. Bd of Governors, ESU 1956-59. Chevalier, Danish Order of the Dannebrog. *Publications:* V. & A. Museum Costume Bibliography, 1936; Basic Aircraft Recognition, 1942; German Aircraft, 1943; Aircraft Recognition Manual, 1944 (new edn 1945); Ballooning, 1948; The Great Exhibition of 1851, 1950; Air League Recognition Manual, 1952; A History of Flying, 1953; Balloons, 1956; The Fashionable Lady in the 19th Century, 1960; The Invention of the Aeroplane, 1966. Science Museum *monographs:* The Aeroplane: an historical Survey, 1960 (2nd edn as Aviation, etc 1970); Sir George Cayley's Aeronautics, 1962; The Wright Brothers, 1963; The World's First Flights, 1965; A Directory and Nomenclature of the First Aeroplanes, 1966; Leonardo da Vinci's Aeronautics, 1967; Clément Ader, his Flight Claims, 1967; A Brief History of Flying, 1968; The Birth of European Aviation, 1971. *Novels:* Operation Caroline, 1953; Yankee Poodle, 1955; Escape and be Secret, 1957; articles and broadcasts on art, crime, aircraft and tank recognition, aeronautical history, etc. *Recreations:* fencing, classification, travel. *Address:* Residence C, Victoria and Albert Museum, SW7. *T:* 01-589 6371. *Clubs:* Royal Aero, Harvard.

**GIBRALTAR, Diocese of;** *see under* Fulham, Bishop of.

**GIBRALTAR, Bishop of, (RC),** since 1956; **Rt. Rev. John F. Healy,** DD, DCL; *b* 3 Dec. 1900; *s* of Edward Lee Healy and Louisa A. Healy (*née* Edwards). *Educ:* Wimbledon Choir Sch.; St John's Seminary, Wonersh; English Coll., Valladolid. Ordained, 1927; DD 1928; DCL 1930. Secretary to the Catholic Bishop of Southwark, 1930-37; Sec. and Treas., Southwark Catholic Rescue Soc., 1937-48; Parish Priest of Sacred Heart, Camberwell, 1948-56. *Address:* Bishop's House, Gibraltar. *T:* 3120.

**GIBSON,** family name of **Baron Ashbourne.**

**GIBSON, Sir Ackroyd (Herbert),** 3rd Bt *cr* 1926; *b* 5 Aug. 1893; *s* of Sir Herbert Gibson, 1st Bt, and Lilian, *d* of Capt. Neilson Thomas, Sketty, Glam.; *S* brother, 1967; *m* 1918, Maud Lilian, *d* of E. C. Arnold, FRCS, and Fredrikke Wedel von Jarlsberg; one *s* two *d* (and one *s* decd). *Educ:* Stone House, Broadstairs; Malvern Coll. Woodworker and Designer. Served with RAF and 3rd Bn, Essex Regt, 1914-18. *Publications:* various articles. *Recreations:* gardening, literature, archæology, philosophy. *Heir:* *s* Rev. Father David Gibson, *b* 18 July 1922.

**GIBSON, Alexander Boyce;** Professor of Philosophy in the University of Melbourne, Australia, 1935-66, retired, 1966; *b* 10 March 1900; *s* of late William Ralph Boyce Gibson and Lucy Judge Peacock; *m* 1925, Kathleen Grace Derham, Melbourne; one *d*. *Educ:* Melbourne Grammar Sch; University of Melbourne; Balliol Coll., Oxford. Temporary Asst to the Professors of Moral Philosophy and Logic in the University of Glasgow, 1923-25; Staff Tutor to the Joint Tutorial Classes Cttee of the University of Oxford in North Staffs, 1925-27; Lecturer in Philosophy in the University of Birmingham, 1927-35. Hon. LittD, Cantab., 1948. *Publications:* The Philosophy of Descartes, 1932; Should Philosophers be Kings, 1939; (with A. A. Phillips) Thinkers at Work, 1946; Towards an Australian Philosophy of Education, 1962; Muse and Thinker, 1969; Theism and Empiricism, 1970. Articles in philosophical periodicals. *Recreations:* travel, listening to music. *Address:* 747 Canterbury Road, Mont Albert, Victoria 3127, Australia.

**GIBSON, Alexander (Drummond),** CBE 1967; Principal Conductor and Musical Director, Scottish National Orchestra, since 1959; Artistic Director, Scottish Opera Company, since 1962; *b* 11 Feb. 1926; *m* 1959, Ann Veronica Waggett; three *s* one *d*. *Educ:* Dalziel; Glasgow Univ.; Royal College of Music; Mozarteum, Salzburg, Austria; Accademia Chigiano, Siena, Italy. Served with Royal Signals, 1944-48. Repetiteur and Asst Conductor, Sadler's Wells Opera, 1951-52; Asst Conductor, BBC Scottish Orchestra, Glasgow, 1952-54; Staff Conductor, Sadler's Wells Opera, 1954-57; Musical Dir, Sadler's Wells Opera, 1957-59. Hon. RAM 1969. Hon. LLD Aberdeen, 1968. *Recreations:* motoring, tennis, reading. *Address:* 15 Cleveden Gardens, Glasgow W2. *T:* 041-339 6668. *Clubs:* Garrick, Oriental.

**GIBSON, Charles William,** JP County of London; *b* Fulham, 1889; *m* 1915, Jessie Alice Davison; two *s* one *d*. *Educ:* Elementary Schools; WEA; Morley Working Men's Coll. Mem. LCC for Kennington, 1928-49; Vice-Chm. LCC, 1941-42; Lambeth-Vauxhall, 1949-56; Chm. LCC Housing Cttee, 1943-50; Alderman, LCC, 1960; Mem. Central Housing Advisory Cttee, 1945-51. MP (Lab.) Kennington Div. of Lambeth, 1945-50, Clapham Div. of Wandsworth, 1950-Sept. 1959. On staff of Transport and General Workers Union. Retired. Hon. Mem. Institute of Housing. *Address:* 25 Dalmore Road, West Dulwich, SE21. *T:* 01-670 1068.

**GIBSON, Sir Christopher (Herbert),** 3rd Bt *cr* 1931; employed with Industrias Kaiser, Argentina, since 1964; *b* 2 Feb. 1921; *s* of Sir Christopher H. Gibson, 2nd Bt, and Lady Dorothy E. O. Gibson (*née* Bruce); *S* father, 1962; *m* 1941, Lilian Lake Young, *d* of Dr George Byron Young, Colchester; one *s* three *d*. *Educ:* St Cyprian's, Eastbourne; St George's Coll., Argentina. Served, 1941-45 (5 war medals and stars): 28th Canadian Armd Regt (BCR), Lieut. Plantation Manager, Leach's Argentine Estates, 1946-51; Manager, Encyclopædia Britannica, 1952-55; Design Draughtsman, Babcock & Wilcox, 1956-57; Plantation Manager, Liebig's, 1958-60; Ranch Manager, Liebig's Extract of Meat Co., 1961-64. *Recreations:* shooting, fishing, tennis, cricket, architecture. *Heir:* *s* Christopher Herbert Gibson, *b* Argentina, 17 July 1948. *Address:* Candlemas Manor, Casilla Correo No 139, Alta Gracia, Sierras de Cordoba, Provincia de Cordoba, Argentina, South America.

**GIBSON, Rear-Adm. Cuthbert Walter Sumner,** CB 1945; *b* 9 Dec. 1890; *s* of late Walter S. Gibson, MA, Oxford; *m* 1920, Grace Campbell (*d* 1968), *o d* of late Major L. H. Baldwin, 8th Gurkhas; one *s* one *d* (and *er s* killed in Kenya, 1953). *Educ:* RN Colls, Osborne and Dartmouth. Joined RNC Osborne as Naval Cadet, 1903; specialised in Engineering as Lieut 1913; Capt. (E) 1937. Served European War as Lieut (E) in Grand Fleet, Mediterranean and Submarines; War of 1939-45, Admiralty; Squadron Engineer Officer, Mediterranean; Staff Engineer Officer, Western Desert Ports; Fleet Engineer Officer, Levant; Rear-Adm. (E), 1943; Rear-Adm. (E) on Staff of C-in-C, Plymouth, 1944-47; retired list, 1947. *Address:* Tighnamara, Kilmelford, Argyll.

**GIBSON, Vice-Adm. Sir Donald Cameron Ernest Forbes,** KCB 1968 (CB 1965); DSC 1941; Flag Officer, Naval Air Command, 1965-68, retired; *b* 17 March 1916; *s* of late Capt. W. L. D. Gibson, Queen's Own Cameron Highlanders, and of Elizabeth Gibson; *m* 1939, Marjorie Alice, *d* of H. C. Harding, Horley, Surrey; one *s*. *Educ:* Woodbridge Sch., Suffolk. Cadet, Brit. India SN Co. and Midshipman, Royal Naval Reserve, 1933-37; transf. to Royal Navy, 1937; specialised as Pilot, 1938. Served War of 1939-45: HMS Glorious, Ark Royal, Formidable, Audacity; trng Pilots in USA; Empire Central Flying Sch., 1942; Chief Flying Instr, Advanced Flying Sch., 1946-47; HMS Illustrious, 1947-48; Air Gp Comdr, HMS Theseus, 1948-49; Comdr (Air), RNAS Culdrose, 1950-52; RN Staff Course, 1952-53; Comdr (Air) HMS Indomitable and Glory, 1953-54; Capt. RNAS Brawdy, 1954-56, HMS Dainty, 1956-58; Dep. Dir Air Warfare, 1958-60; Canadian Nat. Defence Coll., 1960-61; Capt., HMS Ark Royal, 1961-63; Rear-Adm. 1963; Flag Officer: Aircraft Carriers, 1963-64; Naval Flying Trg, 1964-65; Vice-Adm. 1967. *Recreations:* fishing, shooting, painting. *Address:* Lower Bealy Court, Chulmleigh, North Devon. *T:* Chulmleigh 264. *Clubs:* United Service; Royal Western Yacht.

**GIBSON, Sir Donald (Evelyn Edward),** Kt 1962; CBE 1951; DCL; MA, FRIBA (Distinction Town Planning), MTPI; Controller General, Ministry of Public Building and Works, 1967-69, now Consultant; Member, Agrément Board, since 1969; *b* 11 Oct. 1908; *s* of late Prof. Arnold Hartley Gibson; *m* 1936, Winifred Mary (*née* McGowan); three *s* one *d*. *Educ:* Manchester Gram. Sch.; Manchester Univ. BA Hons Architecture; MA. Work in USA, 1931; private practice, 1933; professional Civil Service (Building Research), 1935; Dep. County Architect, Isle of Ely, 1937; City Architect and Town Planning Officer, County and City of Coventry, 1939; County Architect, Notts, 1955; Dir-Gen. of Works, War Office, 1958-62; Dir-Gen. R. and D., Ministry of Public Building and Works, 1962-67; Hoffmann Wood Prof. of Architecture, University of Leeds, 1967-68. Mem. Central Housing Advisory Cttee, 1951, 1953 and 1954. Pres., RIBA, 1964-65. *Publications:* various publications dealing with housing, planning and architecture in RIBA and TPI Journals. *Recreation:* fishing. *Address:* Bryn Castell, Llanddona, Anglesey. *T:* Beaumaris 399.

**GIBSON, Sir Edmund Currey,** KCIE, *cr* 1941 (CIE 1933); *b* 6 July 1886; *s* of late Rev. Thomas William and Frances Georgina Gibson; unmarried. *Educ:* Merchant Taylors' Sch.; St John's Coll., Oxford. Joined Indian Civil Service in 1910; held various posts in the Central Provinces; Government of India Foreign and Political Dept, 1921; Commissioner, Ajmer-Merwara, 1924 and

1927; Political Agent, Eastern Rajputana States, 1925; Agent to the Governor-Gen., Eastern States, 1933-34; Resident at Gwalior, 1934-37; Resident, States of Western India, 1937-42; China Relations Officer, Calcutta, 1944-46. *Address:* Ramgarh, Clement Town, Dehra Dun, UP, India. *Club:* Royal Societies.

**GIBSON, Sir John (Hinshelwood),** Kt 1969; CB 1962; TD 1944; QC (Scotland) 1961; Counsel to Scottish Law Commission, since 1969; *b* 20 May 1907; *y s* of late William John Gibson, Solicitor, Falkirk, Stirlingshire; *m* 1948, Jane, *o d* of late Captain James Watt (RNR retd), Greenwich, Conn; one *s* one *d*. *Educ:* Fettes Coll.; University of Edinburgh. MA 1928; LLB 1931. Admitted to Faculty of Advocates, and called to Bar (Scot.), 1932. Entered Lord Advocate's Dept, 1945; Legal Sec. to Lord Advocate, and Parly Draftsman for Scotland, 1961-69. Mem. Editorial Bd, Statutes in Force (official rev. edn), 1968-. Served in TA (Royal Artillery), 1931-45 (War service, 1939-45); hon. Major. *Address:* Law Commission's Chambers, Old College, South Bridge, Edinburgh EH8 9BD. *T:* 031-667 3437. *Clubs:* Royal Automobile; New (Edinburgh).

**GIBSON, John Walter;** Assistant Chief Scientific Adviser (Studies), Ministry of Defence, since 1969; *b* 15 Jan. 1922; *s* of late Thomas John Gibson and Catherine Gibson (*née* Gregory), Bamburgh, Northumberland; *m* 1951, Julia, *d* of George Leslie Butler, Buxton, Derbyshire; two *s* one *d*. *Educ:* A. J. Dawson Sch., Durham; Sheffield Univ.; University Coll., London. RNVR, 1942-46. Sheffield Univ., 1940-42, 1946-47 (BSc); University Coll., London, 1947-48; Safety-in-Mines Research Estabt, 1948-53; BJSM, Washington, DC, 1953-56; Royal Armament Research and Develt Estabt, 1957-60; Head of Statistics Div., Ordnance Bd, 1961-64; Supt, Assessment Br., Royal Armament Research and Develt Estabt, 1964-66, Prin. Supt, Systems Div., 1966-69. FSS 1953. *Address:* 17 Lyndhurst Drive, Sevenoaks, Kent. *T:* Sevenoaks 54589.

**GIBSON, Hon. Sir Marcus (George),** Kt 1970; *b* 11 Jan. 1898; *e s* of late Clyde Gibson, Oatlands, Tasmania, and Lucy Isabel (*née* Stanfield); *m* 1929, Iris Lavinia, *d* of A. E. Shone, East Risdon, Tas; one *s* one *d*. *Educ:* Leslie House Sch., Hobart; Univ. of Tasmania. LLB (Tas) 1921; LLM (Tas) 1924. Served European War: Gunner, AIF, 1917-19. Admitted to bar of Supreme Court, Tasmania, 1921; private practice, 1921-29; Solicitor to the Public Trust Office, 1929-38; Police Magistrate, 1939-42; Asst Solicitor-General, 1942-46; KC 1946; Solicitor-General, 1946-51; Puisne Judge, Supreme Court of Tasmania, 1951-68. *Recreations:* theatre, bushwalking. *Address:* 296 Sandy Bay Road, Hobart, Tasmania, Australia. *T:* Hobart 235624. *Club:* Tasmanian (Hobart).

**GIBSON, Very Rev. Matthew Sayer;** Dean of the Diocese of Brechin since 1964; Canon of St Paul's Cathedral, Dundee, since 1956; Rector of St Mary Magdalene, Dundee, Diocese of Brechin since 1952. *Educ:* Edinburgh Theological Coll.; University of Durham (LTh 1940). Deacon, 1940; priest, Brechin, 1941; Curate of St Mary Magdalene, Dundee, 1940-43; Curate-in-charge, St Ninian, Dundee, 1943-52. Chaplain to the Bishop of Brechin, 1952-59; Synod Clerk, Diocese of Brechin, 1957-64. *Address:* 14 Albany Terrace, Dundee, Angus. *T:* Dundee 23510.

**GIBSON, Hon. Maurice White; Hon. Mr. Justice Gibson;** Puisne Judge of the High Court of Justice in Northern Ireland since 1968; *b* 1 May 1913; 2nd *s* of late William James Gibson, Montpelier House, Belfast, and of Edith Mary Gibson; *m* 1945, Cecily Winifred, *e d* of late Mr and Mrs Dudley Roy Johnson, Cordova, Bexhill-on-Sea, Sussex; one *s* one *d*. *Educ:* Royal Belfast Academical Institution; Queen's Univ., Belfast (LLB, BA). English Bar Final Exam. First Cl. and Certif. of Honour, 1937; Called to Bar of N Ire. with Special Prize awarded by Inn of Court of N Ire., 1938; called to Inner Bar, N Ire., 1956. Apptd Mem. several Govt Cttees on Law Reform in N Ire.; Mem. Incorp. Council of Law Reporting for N Ire.; Chm., N Ire. Legal Quarterly. *Recreation:* yachting. *Address:* 15 Kensington Road, Belfast 5. *T:* Belfast 656310. *Clubs:* Ulster (Belfast); Royal Belfast Golf; Royal North of Ireland Yacht; Strangford Lough Yacht.

**GIBSON, Rear-Adm. Peter Cecil,** CB 1968; Manager, Aids Centre, Disabled Living Foundation, since 1970; *b* 31 May 1913; 2nd *s* of Alexander Horace Cecil Gibson and Phyllis Zeline Cecil Gibson (*née* Baume); *m* 1938, Phyllis Anna Mary Hume, *d* of late Major N. H. Hume, IMS, Brecon; two *s* one *d*. *Educ:* Ealing Priory; RN Engrg Coll., Keyham. RN, 1931; HMS Norfolk, EI, 1936-38; maintenance test pilot, RN Aircraft Yard, Donibristle, 1940-41; Air Engr Officer, RNAS, St Merryn, 1941-42; Staff of RANAS, Indian Ocean, E Africa, 1942-43, Ceylon, 1943-44; Staff Air Engr. Off., British Pacific Fleet, 1945-46; Aircraft Maintenance and Repair Dept, 1946-49; loan service RAN, 1950-52; Trng Off., RNAS, Arbroath, 1952-54; Engr Off., HMS Gambia, 1954-56 and as Fleet Engr. Off, E Indies, 1955-56; Staff Engr. Off., Flag Off. Flying Trng, 1957-60; Dep. Dir Service Conditions, 1960-61; Dir Engr Officers' Appts, 1961-63; Supt RN Aircraft Yard, Fleetlands, 1963-65; Dep. Controller Aircraft (RN), Min. of Aviation, 1966-67, Min. of Technology, 1967-69, retired, 1969. ADC, 1965-66. Comdr 1946; Capt. 1957; Rear-Adm. 1966. Chm. United Services Catholic Assoc., 1966-69. *Recreations:* painting, sailing, bridge. *Address:* 15 Melton Court, SW7. *T:* 01-589 2414. *Club:* Army and Navy.

**GIBSON, Prof. Quentin Howieson,** FRS 1969; Professor of Biochemistry and Molecular Biology, Cornell University, Ithaca, NY, since 1966; *b* 9 Dec. 1918; *s* of William Howieson Gibson, OBE, DSc; *m* 1951, Audrey Jane, *yr d* of G. H. S. Pinsent, *qv*; one *s* three *d*. *Educ:* Repton. MB, ChB, BAO, Belfast, 1941, MD 1944, PhD 1946, DSc 1951. Demonstrator in Physiology, Belfast, 1941-44; Lecturer in Physiology: Belfast, 1944-46; Sheffield Univ., 1946-55; Professor of Biochem., Sheffield Univ., 1955-63; Prof. of Biophys. Chem., Johnson Research Foundn, University of Pennsylvania, 1963-66. *Recreation:* sailing. *Address:* 98 Dodge Road, Ithaca, NY 14850, USA.

**GIBSON, Ralph Brian,** QC 1968; *b* 17 Oct. 1922; 2nd *s* of Roy and Emily Gibson; *m* 1949, Ann Chapman Ruether, Chicago; one *s* two *d*. *Educ:* Glengorse Prep. Sch.; Charterhouse; Brasenose Coll., Oxford. MA Oxon 1948. Called to Bar, Middle Temple, 1948. Bigelow Teaching Fellow, University of Chicago, 1948-49. Army Service, 1941-45: Lieut, 1st KDG; Captain, TJFF. *Recreation:* sailing. *Address:* 3 The Orchard, Bedford Park, W4. *T:* 01-994 7004. *Club:* Emsworth Sailing.

**GIBSON, Richard Patrick Tallentyre;** Chairman: Pearson Longman Ltd (formerly S. Pearson Publishers Ltd) since 1967; *b* 5 Feb. 1916; *s* of Thornely Carbutt Gibson and Elizabeth Anne Augusta Gibson; *m* 1945, Elisabeth Dione Pearson; four *s*. *Educ:* Eton Coll.; Magdalen

Coll., Oxford. London Stock Exchange, 1937. Served with Middx Yeo, 1939-46; N Africa, 1940-41; POW, 1941-43; Special Ops Exec., 1943-45; Political Intell. Dept, FO, 1945-46. Westminster Press Provincial Newspapers Ltd, 1947 (Dir, 1948); Director: Whitehall Securities Corp. Ltd, 1948-60; Financial Times and Economist, 1957; S. Pearson & Son Ltd, 1960; Royal Exchange Assce, 1961. Hon. Treas, Commonwealth Press Union, 1957-67; Trustee and Hon. Treas., Historic Churches Preservation Trust, 1958; Member: Exec. Cttee, National Trust, 1963; Council, Nat. Trust, 1966; Adv. Council, V & A Museum, 1968 (Chm. 1970); UK Arts Adv. Commn, Calouste Gulbenkian Foundn, 1969; Redundant Churches Fund, 1970; Exec. Cttee, Nat. Art Collections Fund, 1970; Trustee, Glyndebourne Fest. Opera, 1965. *Recreations:* music, gardening, architecture. *Address:* Penns in the Rocks, Groombridge, Sussex. *T:* Groombridge 244. *Clubs:* Garrick, Brooks's.

**GIBSON, Prof. Robert Donald Davidson,** PhD; Professor of French, University of Kent at Canterbury since 1965; *b* Hackney, London, 21 Aug. 1927; *o s* of Nicol and Ann Gibson, Leyton, London; *m* 1953, Sheila Elaine, *o d* of Bertie and Ada Goldsworthy, Exeter, Devon; three *s*. *Educ:* Leyton County High Sch. for Boys; King's Coll., London; Magdalene Coll., Cambridge; Ecole Normale Superieure, Paris. BA (First Class Hons. French) London, 1948; PhD Cantab. 1953. Asst Lecturer, St Salvator's Coll., University of St Andrews, 1954-55; Lecturer, Queen's Coll., Dundee, 1955-58; Lecturer, Aberdeen Univ., 1958-61; Prof., Queen's Univ. of Belfast, 1961-65. *Publications:* The Quest of Alain-Fournier, 1953; Modern French Poets on Poetry, 1961; Le Bestiaire Inattendu (Edn) 1961; Roger Martin du Gard, 1961; La Mésentente Cordiale, 1963; Brouart et le Désordre (Edn), 1964; Provinciales (Edn) 1965; Le Grand Meaulnes (Edn), 1968; reviews and articles in: French Studies, The London Magazine, Times Literary Supplement, Encyclopædia Britannica, Collier's Encyclopædia. *Recreations:* ball games and playing harmonica. *Address:* 97a St Stephen's Road, Canterbury, Kent.

**GIBSON, Dr Ronald George,** CBE 1970 (OBE 1961); MA Cantab; FRCS, FRCGP; Chairman of Council, British Medical Association, since 1966; *b* 28 Nov. 1909; *s* of George Edward Gibson and Gladys Muriel, *d* of William George Prince, JP, CC, Romsey, Hants; *m* 1934, Dorothy Elisabeth Alberta, *d* of Thomas Alfred Rainey, Southampton; two *d*. *Educ:* Mill Hill Sch., St John's Coll., Cambridge; St Bartholomew's Hosp., London. Gen. Practitioner; MO, Winchester Coll. and St Swithun's Sch., Winchester. Lieut-Col RAMC (Emergency Reserve), PMO Italian Somaliland, 1944-45. Mem. Council: BMA, 1950- (Chm., Representative Body, 1963-66); RCS, 1962-67; FRCS 1968. Mem., Adv. Cttee on Drug Dependence. First Provost, SE Eng. Faculty, Royal College of General Practitioners, 1954 (James Mackenzie Lectr, 1967; FRCGP 1967). Delegate, General Assembly, World Medical Assoc. Liveryman, Worshipful Soc. of Apothecaries of London, 1964. Gold Medallist, BMA, 1970. Hon. LLD (Wales), 1965. *Publications:* Care of the Elderly in General Practice (Butterworth Gold Medal), 1956; Chap. on Geriatrics, Encyclopaedia of General Practice, 1964. Contrib. Lancet, BMJ, etc. *Recreations:* medicine, music, cricket, gardening. *Address:* 21 St Thomas' Street, Winchester, Hants. *T:* Winchester 4582. *Club:* Athenæum.

**GIBSON, Air Vice-Marshal William Norman,** CBE 1956; DFC; Royal Australian Air Force, retired; Senior Air Staff Officer, Operational Comd, RAAF, 1963-64 and 1966; *b* 1915; *s* of late Hamilton Ross Gibson; *m* 1938, Grace Doreen, *d* of John Walter Downton, Sydney; one *d*. *Educ:* NZ; Parramatta High Sch.; Point Cook. RAN, 1936-39; RAAF: CO, Port Moresby, 1942; SASO, RAAF Command, 1943-44; SASO, 1st Tactical Air Force, 1947-48; CO, RAAF East Sale, 1953-54; Dir of Training, 1955-56; Air Cdre, Plans, 1957; CO, RAAF Amberley, 1959-62; SASO, HQ Far East Air Force, 1964-66. Legion of Merit (USA). *Address:* 20 Seaview Avenue, Newport, NSW, Australia. *Club:* Imperial Service (Sydney).

**GIBSON, Sir William Waymouth,** Kt, *cr* 1939; BA, LLM Cantab; DCL Dunelm (*h c*); Past President of Law Society; Solicitor; *b* 30 Aug. 1873; *e s* of William and Annie Gibson, Newcastle upon Tyne; *m* 1st, 1900, Anna Mary Penman; one *s*; 2nd, 1940, Alice (*d* 1958; she *m* 1st, George Sisson, Newcastle upon Tyne). *Educ:* Uppingham; Queens' College, Cambridge. *Address:* Kingmead, Riding Mill, Northumberland; 7 Grey Street, Newcastle upon Tyne. *T:* Riding Mill 286; Newcastle upon Tyne 20761. *Clubs:* Oxford and Cambridge University; Union (Newcastle upon Tyne).

**GIBSON-CRAIG-CARMICHAEL, Sir David Peter William,** 15th Bt *cr* 1702 (Gibson Carmichael) and 8th Bt *cr* 1831; *b* 21 July 1946; *s* of Sir Archibald Henry William Gibson-Craig-Carmichael, 14th Bt and of Rosemary Anita, *d* of George Duncan Crew, Santiago, Chile; *S* father, 1969. *Heir:* *b* Alasdair John Gibson-Craig-Carmichael, *b* 28 Feb. 1948. *Address:* Casilla 2461, Santiago, Chile.

**GIBSON-WATT, D.;** *see* Gibson-Watt, J. D.

**GIBSON-WATT, (James) David,** MC 1943 and 2 Bars; DL; MP (C) Hereford since Feb. 1956; Minister of State, Welsh Office, since 1970; *b* 11 Sept. 1918; *er s* of late Major James Miller Gibson-Watt, DL, JP; *m* 1942, Diana, 2nd *d* of Sir Charles Hambro; two *s* two *d* (and one *s* decd). *Educ:* Eton; Trinity Coll (BA). Welsh Guards, 1939-46; N African and Italian campaigns. Contested (C) Brecon and Radnor constituency, 1950 and 1951. Radnor CC 1946-. A Lord Commissioner of the Treasury, 1959-61. DL Radnorshire, 1968. *Address:* Doldowlod, Llandrindod Wells, Radnorshire. *T:* Newbridge-on-Wye 208. *Clubs:* Boodle's, Farmers'.

**GICK, Rear-Adm. Philip David,** CB 1963; OBE 1946; DSC and Bar, 1942; Director: Emsworth Shipyard Ltd; Emsworth Yacht Harbour Ltd; A. R. Savage, Ltd; Deacon's Boatyard Ltd; *b* 22 Feb. 1913; *s* of late Sir William John Gick, CB, CBE; *m* 1938, Aylmer Roberta Kirkby Rowntree; one *s* three *d*. *Educ:* St Lawrence Coll., Ramsgate. Joined RN, 1931; qualified as Pilot, 1936. Capt. 1952; Comd HMS Daring, RNAS, Lossiemouth, HMS Bulwark, 1952-58; subseq. course IDC; Pres., Second Admiralty Interview Board; Rear-Adm. 1961; Flag Officer, Naval Flying Training, 1961-64, retd. *Recreation:* sailing. *Address:* Furzefield, Bosham Hoe, Sussex. *T:* Bosham 2219. *Clubs:* Royal Yacht Squadron, Royal Ocean Racing; Royal Naval Sailing Association; Bosham Sailing.

**GIDDEN, Barry Owen Barton,** CMG 1962; Assistant Secretary, Department of Health and Social Security; *b* Southampton, 4 July 1915; *s* of late Harry William Gidden, MA, PhD. *Educ:* King Edward VI Sch.,

Southampton; Jesus Coll., Cambridge (Scholar; Class. Tripos Pts 1 and 2; BA). Apptd Asst Principal, HM Office of Works, 1939. Served War of 1939-45: BEF, 1939-40, Major 1943. Principal, Min. of Works, 1946; Private Sec. to Minister of Works (Rt Hon. George Tomlinson and later Rt Hon. Charles Key), 1946-48; Principal, Colonial Office, 1949, Asst Sec 1951; Counsellor, UK Mission to UN, New York, 1954-58; Establishment Officer, Colonial Office, 1958-65. *Recreation:* golf. *Address:* 15 Chesham Street, SW1. *T:* 01-235 4185. *Club:* Walton Heath Golf.

**GIDDINGS, Air Vice-Marshal Kenneth Charles Michael,** OBE 1953; DFC 1945; AFC 1950 and Bar 1955; Assistant Chief of Air Staff (Operational Requirements), since 1968; *b* 27 Aug. 1920; *s* of Charles Giddings and Grace Giddings (*née* Gregory); *m* 1946, Elizabeth McConnell; two *s* two *d*. *Educ:* Ealing Grammar Sch. Conscripted, RAF, 1940; Comd, 129 Sqdn, 1944; Empire Test Pilots Sch., 1946; Test pilot, RAE, 1947-50; HQ Fighter Command, 1950-52; RAF Staff Coll., 1953; OC, Flying Wing, Waterbeach, 1954-56; CFE, 1956-58; OC, 57 Sqdn, 1958-60; Group Captain Ops, Bomber Command, 1960-62; Supt of Flying, A&AEE, 1962-64; Dir Aircraft Projects, MoD, 1964-66; AOC, Central Reconnaissance Estabt, 1967. *Recreations:* tennis, gardening, music. *Address:* 64 Chazey Road, Caversham, Reading, Berks. *T:* Reading 73341. *Club:* Royal Air Force.

**GIELGUD, Sir (Arthur) John,** Kt 1953; Hon. LLD St Andrews 1950; Hon. DLitt Oxon 1953; Actor; *b* 14 April 1904; *s* of late Frank Gielgud and Kate Terry Lewis; unmarried. *Educ:* Westminster. First appearance on stage at Old Vic, 1921; among parts played are Lewis Dodd in Constant Nymph, Inigo Jollifant in The Good Companions, Richard II in Richard of Bordeaux, Hamlet, and Romeo; Valentine in Love for Love, Ernest Worthing in The Importance of Being Earnest, Macbeth and King Lear. Directed Macbeth, Piccadilly, 1942. Raskolnikoff in Crime and Punishment, Jason in The Medea, New York, 1947. Eustace in The Return of the Prodigal, Globe, 1948; directed The Heiress, Haymarket, 1949; directed and played Thomas Mendip, The Lady's not for Burning, Globe, 1949; Shakespeare Festival, Stratford-on-Avon, 1950; Angelo in Measure for Measure, Cassius in Julius Caesar, Benedick in Much Ado About Nothing, the name part in King Lear; directed Much Ado About Nothing and King Lear; Shakespeare season at Phoenix, 1951-52; Leontes in The Winter's Tale, Phoenix, 1951, directed Much Ado About Nothing and played Benedick, 1952. Season at Lyric, Hammersmith, 1953; directed Richard II and The Way of the World (played Mirabel); played Jaffeir in Venice Preserved; directed A Day by the Sea, and played Julian Anson, Haymarket, Nov. 1953-54; also directed Charley's Aunt, New Theatre, Dec. 1953, and directed The Cherry Orchard, Lyric, May, 1954, and Twelfth Night, Stratford, 1955; played in King Lear and Much Ado About Nothing (also produced Much Ado), for Shakespeare Memorial Theatre Company (London, provinces and continental tour), 1955; directed The Chalk Garden, Haymarket, 1956; produced (with Noel Coward) Nude with Violin, and played Sebastien, Globe, 1956-57; produced The Trojans, Covent Garden, 1957; played Prospero, Stratford, and Drury Lane, 1957; played James Callifer in The Potting Shed, Globe, 1958 and Wolsey in Henry VIII, Old Vic, 1958; directed Variation on A Theme, 1958; produced The Complaisant Lover, Globe, 1959; (Shakespeare's) Ages of Man, Queen's, 1959 (recital, based on Shakespeare anthology of G. Rylands); previous recitals at Edinburgh Fest. and in US, also subseq. in US, at Haymarket, 1960 and tour of Australia and NZ, 1963-64; Gothenburg, Copenhagen, Warsaw, Helsinki, Leningrad, Moscow and Dublin, 1964; produced Much Ado About Nothing, at Cambridge, Mass, Festival, and subseq. in New York, 1959; prod. Five Finger Exercise, Comedy, 1958, NY, 1959; acted in The Last Joke, Phœnix, 1960; prod. Britten's A Midsummer Night's Dream, Royal Opera House, 1961; prod Big Fish Little Fish, New York, 1961; prod Dazzling Prospect, Globe, 1961. Stratford-on-Avon Season, 1961: took part of Othello, also of Gaieff in The Cherry Orchard; Gaieff in The Cherry Orchard, Aldwych, 1962; produced The School for Scandal, Haymarket, 1962; prod The School for Scandal, and played Joseph Surface, USA tour, and New York, 1962-63; dir. The Ides of March, and played Julius Caesar, Haymarket, 1963; dir. Hamlet, Canada and USA, 1964; Julian in Tiny Alice, New York, 1965; played Ivanov and directed Ivanov, Phœnix, 1965, United States and Canada, 1966; played Orgon in Tartuffe, Nat. Theatre, 1967; directed Halfway up the Tree, Queen's, 1967; played Oedipus in Oedipus, Nat. Theatre, 1968; produced Don Giovanni, Coliseum, 1968; played Headmaster in 40 Years On, Apollo, 1968; played Sir Gideon in The Battle of Shrivings, Lyric, 1970; Home, Royal Court, 1970. *Films include:* (GB and US) The Good Companions, 1932; The Secret Agent, 1937; The Prime Minister (Disraeli), 1940; Julius Caesar (Cassius), 1952; Richard III (Duke of Clarence), 1955; The Barretts of Wimpole Street (Mr Moulton Barrett), 1957; St Joan (Warwick), 1957; Becket (Louis VII), 1964; The Loved One, 1965; Chimes at Midnight, 1966; Mister Sebastian, 1967; The Charge of the Light Brigade, 1968; Shoes of the Fisherman, 1968; Oh What a Lovely War, 1968; Julius Caesar, 1970. President, Shakespeare Reading Soc., 1958-. Has appeared on Television, including Great Acting, 1967. Companion, Legion of Honour, 1960. *Publications:* Early Stages, 1938; Stage Directions, 1963. *Recreations:* music, painting. *Address:* 16 Cowley Street, Westminster, SW1.

**GIELGUD, Val Henry,** CBE 1958 (OBE 1942); retired as Head of Sound Drama, BBC, after 35 years; *b* 28 Apr 1900; *s* of late Frank and Kate Terry Gielgud; *m* 1921, Natalie Mamontoff (marr. diss., 1925); *m* 1928, Barbara Druce (marr. diss.); one *s*; *m* 1946, Rita Vale (marriage dissolved); *m* 1955, Monica Grey (marriage dissolved); *m* 1960, June Vivienne Bailey. *Educ:* Rugby Sch.; Trinity Coll., Oxford. Had a somewhat variegated early career, including some time as sec. to an MP, as sub-editor of a comic paper, and as an actor; joined the Radio Times, 1928, and was appointed BBC Dramatic Dir, 1929; since then has written novels, stage plays, broadcast plays, and collaborated in several film scenarios, Death at Broadcasting House, Royal Cavalcade, Café Colette, Talleyrand, and Marlborough. *Publications:* Black Gallantry, 1928; Gathering of Eagles, 1929; Imperial Treasure, 1930; The Broken Men, 1931; Gravelhanger, 1932; Outrage in Manchukuo, 1937; The Red Account, 1939; Beyond Dover, 1940; Confident Morning, 1943; Years of the Locust, autobiog., 1946; How to Write Broadcast Plays; Radio Theatre 1946; Fall of a Sparrow, 1948; Special Delivery, 1949; One Year of Grace, 1950; The High Jump, 1953; Cat, 1956; British Radio Drama, 1922-1956, A Survey, 1957; Gallows' Foot, 1958; To Bed at Noon, 1960; And Died So?, 1961; The Goggle-Box Affair, 1963; Years in a Mirror, 1965; Cats: a personal Anthology, 1966; Conduct of a Member, 1967; A

Necessary End, 1969; The Candle-Holders, 1970; *plays:* Away from it All; Chinese White; Party Manners; Iron Curtain; The Bombshell; Mediterranean Blue; Not Enough Tragedy; Gorgeous George; (with Holt Marvell) Under London; Death at Broadcasting House; Death as an Extra; Death in Budapest; The Television Murder (with Eric Maschwitz). *Recreations:* reading, especially Milit. History, enjoying the society of Siamese cats, talking and travel. *Address:* Wychwood, Barcombe, near Lewes, Sussex. *Club:* Savile.

**GIFFARD,** family name of **Earl of Halsbury.**

**GIFFARD, (Charles) Sydney (Rycroft);** Head of Eastern European and Soviet Department, Foreign and Commonwealth Office, since Dec. 1968; *b* 30 Oct. 1926; *m* 1951, Wendy Patricia Vidal; one *s* one *d.* Third Secretary, Tokyo, 1952; Vice-Consul, Osaka, 1953; Second Secretary, Tokyo, 1956; Foreign Office, 1957; First Secretary (Commercial), Berne, 1961 and Tokyo, 1964-67; Counsellor, 1968. *Address:* c/o Foreign and Commonwealth Office, SW1.

**GIFFORD,** family name of **Baron Gifford.**

**GIFFORD, Earl of; Edward Douglas John Hay;** *b* 6 Aug. 1947; *s* and *heir* of 12th Marquis of Tweeddale, *qv*, and of Sonia Mary Peake. *Educ:* Milton Abbey, Blandford, Dorset; Trinity Coll., Oxford. *Address:* Tavool, Isle of Mull. *T:* Tiroran 207; Wychwood Lodge, Ramsden, Oxon. *T:* Ramsden 230.

**GIFFORD,** 6th Baron, *cr* 1824; **Anthony Maurice Gifford;** Barrister at Law, practising since 1966; *b* 1 May 1940; *s* of 5th Baron Gifford and Lady Gifford (*née* Margaret Allen), Sydney, NSW; *S* father 1961; *m* 1965, Katherine Ann, *o d* of Dr Mundy; one *s* one *d.* *Educ:* Winchester Coll. (scholar); King's Coll., Cambridge (scholar). Student at Middle Temple, 1959-62, called to the Bar, 1962. BA Cantab, 1961. Chm., Cttee for Freedom in Mozambique, Angola and Guiné, 1968-; Hon. Sec., N Kensington Neighbourhood Law Centre, 1970-. *Heir: s* Hon. Thomas Adam Gifford, *b* 1 Dec. 1967. *Address:* 31, Bassett Road, W10. *T:* 01-969 2567.

**GILBERT, Carl Joyce;** Special Representative for Trade Negotiations, Washington, DC, in the Executive Office of the President, with rank of Ambassador; *b* 3 April 1906; *s* of Seymour Parker Gilbert and Carrie Jennings Gilbert (*née* Cooper); *m* 1936, Helen Amory Homans; one *s.* *Educ:* University of Virginia; Harvard. AB University of Virginia, 1928; LLB Harvard, 1931. Admitted to Mass bar, 1931; Associate Ropes, Gray, Boyden & Perkins, 1931-38; member firm (name changed to Ropes, Gray, Best, Coolidge & Rugg), 1938-48; Treasurer-Vice-Pres., The Gillette Company (formerly Gillette Safety Razor Company), Boston, 1948-56; Pres., 1956-57; Chm. of Board and Chief Exec. Officer, 1957-66; Chm. Exec. Cttee, 1966-68. Hon. LLD Boston Coll., Mass, 1958. *Address:* (business) 1800 G Street NW, Washington, DC 20506, USA. *T:* 202-395-5115; (home) Strawberry Hill Street, Dover, Mass. *T:* State 5-0311. *Clubs:* Metropolitan (Washington); Somerset, Dedham Country and Polo (Boston).

**GILBERT, Prof. Edmund William;** BLitt, MA; Emeritus Professor of Geography in the University of Oxford, and Fellow Emeritus of Hertford College, Oxford, since 1967; *b* 16 Oct. 1900; *o c* of late Rev. R. H. Gilbert, Hemsworth, Yorks, and Mabel (*née* Billinton); *m* 1927, Barbara Maud, *y d* of late Rev. A. W. Flux Dundas; no *c.* *Educ:* St Peter's Sch., York; Hertford Coll., Oxford (Exhibitioner); Univ. of Basel. Herbertson Prizeman, 1924. Junior Lecturer in Geography, Bedford Coll. for Women (University of London), 1923-26; Lecturer in Historical Geography, University of Reading, 1926-29; Indep. Lecturer in Geography in Faculty of Letters, University of Reading, 1929-36; Research Lecturer in Human Geography, University of Oxford, 1936-43; Lecturer in Geography, Hertford Coll., Oxford, 1939-53; Prof. of Geography, Oxford Univ., and Fellow of Hertford Coll., Oxford, 1953-67. served in Intelligence Div., Naval Staff, Admiralty, 1940-45; Reader in Human Geography in University of Oxford, 1943-53. Council of: RGS, 1948-51, 1954-56, 1959-62; Hakluyt Soc., 1936-41, 1946-50, 1952-56. Corresp. for Gt Brit. of Amer. Soc. for Professional Geographers, 1948-51; Trustee Oxford Preservation Trust, 1954-57. Hon. Mem., Gesellschaft für Erdkunde (Berlin), 1958. Herbertson Memorial Lecturer, 1960; Mackinder Centenary Lecturer (LSE), 1961; Murchison Grant (RGS), 1967; Tyneside Geographical Soc. Lecturer, 1967. *Publications:* The Exploration of Western America, 1800-50, 1933; An Historical Geography of England before AD 1800 (Contributor), 1936; A Survey of the Social Services in the Oxford District (Contributor), 1938; How the Map has Changed, 1938-40, 1941: Geography in the Twentieth Century (Contributor), 1951; Brighton: Old Ocean's Bauble, 1954; Geography as a Humane Study, 1955; The University Town in England and West Germany, 1961; University Towns (University of Sussex), 1962; numerous papers on geographical subjects in Geographical Jl, Scottish Geographical Magazine, etc. *Recreations:* travel, photography, theatre, Staffordshire pottery. *Address:* Old Cottage, Appleton, Abingdon, Berks. *T:* Cumnor 2197.

**GILBERT, Frederick;** Retired as Special Commissioner of Income Tax; *b* North Cornwall, 15 Nov. 1899; *s* of William Gilbert, farmer, and Jessie Cleave; *m* 1st, Ethel (decd), *d* of William Baily, Launceston; three *d;* 2nd, Blanche, *d* of William Banyard, Cambridge. *Recreations:* gardening, bowls, painting. *Address:* 11 Firle Close, Seaford, Sussex. *T:* Seaford 4262.

**GILBERT, Maj.-Gen. Glyn Charles Anglim,** MC 1944; GOC 3rd Division, since June 1970; *b* 15 Aug. 1920; *s* of C. G. G. Gilbert, OBE, MC, and H. M. Gilbert, MBE; *m* 1943, Heather Mary Green; three *s* one *d.* *Educ:* Eastbourne Coll.; RMC Sandhurst. Commnd 1939; served with 2nd Lincolns, 1940-47, NW Europe and Palestine; Instructor, Sch. of Infantry, 1948-50; 3rd Bn Para. Regt, 1951; psc 1952; staff and regimental appts in MoD, Airborne Forces, Royal Lincolns and Para. Regt, 1952-66, Cyprus, Egypt and Malaya; idc 1966; comd Sch. of Infantry, 1967-70. *Recreations:* golf, sailing, tennis. *Address:* c/o Lloyds Bank, Cox's & King's Branch (F Section), 6 Pall Mall, SW1. *Club:* Army and Navy.

**GILBERT, Sir Ian A. J.;** *see* Johnson-Gilbert.

**GILBERT, Prof. John Cannon;** Professor of Economics in the University of Sheffield since Oct. 1957; Dean of Faculty of Economic and Social Studies, 1959-62; *b* 28 Sept. 1908; *s* of James and Elizabeth Louisa Gilbert; *m* 1938, Elizabeth Hadley Crook; two *s.* *Educ:* Bancroft's Sch.; The London Sch. of Economics and Political Science, University of London. Student of the Handels-Hochschule, Berlin (Sir Ernest Cassel Travelling Schol.), 1927-28; BCom Hons London, 1929. Asst on teaching staff, LSE, 1929-31; Lecturer in Economics, Sch. of Economics, Dundee, 1931-

41. Ministry of Supply, 1941-45. Lecturer in Economics, University of Manchester, 1945-48; Senior Lecturer in Economics, University of Sheffield, 1948-56, Reader, 1956-57. Mem. Editorial Bd Yorkshire Bulletin of Economic and Social Research, 1949-. *Publications:* A History of Investment Trusts in Dundee, 1873-1938, 1939; articles in Economica, Review of Economic Studies, etc. *Recreations:* walking, hill climbing. *Address:* 81 High Storrs Drive, Ecclesall, Sheffield S11 7LN. *T:* Sheffield 63544.

**GILBERT, John Orman,** CMG 1958; retired; *b* London, 21 Oct. 1907; *s* of Rev. T. H. Gilbert, late of Chedgrave Manor, Norfolk; *m* 1935, Winifred Mary Harris, Dublin; two *s* two *d*. *Educ:* Felsted Sch., Essex; Pembroke Coll., Oxford. Joined Sarawak Civil Service, 1928; various posts, from Cadet, to District Officer in 1940. During War of 1939-45 served in Bengal Sappers and Miners stationed in India and attained rank of Major. Came back to Sarawak with BM Administration, 1946; Resident, 4th Div., Sarawak, 1946-53; British Resident, Brunei, 1953-58; retd 1959. Coronation Medal, 1953. *Recreations:* sailing, shooting and fishing. *Address:* Moonrising, PO Box 100, Somerset West, Cape, South Africa.

**GILBERT, Dr John William;** MP (Lab) Dudley since 1970; *b* April 1927; *m* 1963, Jean Olive Ross Skinner; two *d*. *Educ:* Merchant Taylors' Sch.; St John's Coll., Oxford; New York Univ. (PhD in Internat. Economics, Graduate Sch. of Business Administration). Chartered Accountant, Canada. Contested (Lab): Ludlow, 1966; Dudley, March 1968. Member: Fabian Soc.; Royal Inst. of Internat. Affairs; Nat. Council for Civil Liberties; Cooperative Members' Assoc. (Secretary); NUGMW. *Address:* House of Commons, SW1. *Club:* Reform.

**GILBERT, Sir (Joseph) Trounsell,** Kt 1955; CBE 1949 (OBE 1933); QC (Bermuda) 1949; Chief Justice of Bermuda and Pres. of Legislative Council, Jan. 1952-July 1958, when retired; *b* 30 Aug. 1888; *s* of late Joseph Trounsell Gilbert and Grace Elizabeth Gilbert (*née* Gosling); *m* 1939, Frances Evelyn Steen; no *c*. *Educ:* Saltus Gram. Sch., Bermuda; Bedford Sch.; Brasenose Coll., Oxford. Barrister-at-Law, Lincoln's Inn, 1914. Asst-Collector, Zanzibar, 1912; 2nd Asst-Sec., 1915; 1st Asst-Sec., 1924; Asst-Chief Sec., 1928; invalided, 1933; private practice as barrister in Bermuda, 1935-38; Attorney-Gen. and Mem. of Executive Council, Bermuda, Jan. 1938-Jan. 1952. Brilliant Star of Zanzibar. *Recreations:* tennis, billiards. *Address:* Huntly, Paget, Bermuda. *T:* 3997. *Club:* Oxford and Cambridge University.

**GILBERT, Keith Reginald,** MA, DIC; Keeper of Mechanical and Civil Engineering, Science Museum, London, since 1962; *b* 19 Dec. 1914; *e s* of late Harry Reginald Gilbert, Edgbaston, Birmingham; *m* 1941, Lucie Marie, *d* of late Dr jur. Oscar Auerbach, Vienna. *Educ:* King Edward VI Sch., Birmingham; St John's Coll., Cambridge. Research Asst, Imperial Coll. of Science and Technology, 1937. Served War of 1939-45: Flg Officer, 1939, Flt Lieut, 1943, RAFVR. Asst Chief Res. Engr, CAV Ltd, 1945; entered Science Museum as an Asst Keeper, 1948, and took charge of collections of textile machinery, hand and machine tools, and fire fighting appliances; Dep. Keeper, 1955. Hon. Sec. of Newcomen Soc. (for study of Hist. of Engineering and Technology), 1957-66; Vice-Pres., 1963. *Publications:* Machine Tools in A History of Technology, Vol. IV, 1958; Science Museum Monograph: The Portsmouth Block-making Machinery, 1965; Science Museum Catalogues: The Machine Tool Collection, 1966; The Fire Fighting Appliances Collection, 1969; Science Museum Illustrated Booklets: Fire Engines, 1966; Sewing Machines, 1970. *Address:* The Science Museum, South Kensington, SW7.

**GILBERT, Martin (John),** MA; historian; Fellow of Merton College, Oxford, since 1962; Official Biographer of Sir Winston Churchill since 1968; *b* 25 Oct. 1936; *s* of Peter and Miriam Gilbert; *m* 1963, Helen Constance, *yr d* of late Joseph Robinson, CBE; one *d*. *Educ:* Highgate Sch.; Magdalen Coll., Oxford. Nat. Service (Army), 1955-57; Sen. Research Scholar, St Antony's Coll., Oxford, 1960-62; Res. Asst (sometime Sen. Res. Asst) to Hon. Randolph S. Churchill, 1962-67; Vis. Prof., Univ. of S Carolina, 1965; Recent Hist. Correspt for Sunday Times, 1967; Res. Asst (Brit. Empire) for BBC, 1968; has lectured on historical subjects at Univs throughout Europe and USA. *Publications:* The Appeasers, 1963 (with Richard Gott) (trans. several langs); Britain and Germany Between the Wars, 1964; The European Powers, 1900-1945, 1965 (trans. Italian, Spanish); Plough My Own Furrow: The Life of Lord Allen of Hurtwood, 1965; Servant of India: A Study of Imperial Rule 1905-1910, 1966; The Roots of Appeasement, 1966; Recent History Atlas, 1966; Winston Churchill (Clarendon Biogs, for young people), 1966; British History Atlas, 1968; American History Atlas, 1968; Jewish History Atlas, 1969; First World War Atlas, 1970; Russian History Atlas, 1971. Editor: A Century of Conflict: Essays Presented to A. J. P. Taylor, 1966; Churchill, 1968, and Lloyd George, 1969 (Spectrum Books). Contributor of historical articles and reviews to jls (incl. Purnell's History of the Twentieth Century). *Recreation:* drawing maps. *Address:* The Map House, Harcourt Hill, Oxford. *T:* Oxford 46307. *Club:* Reform.

**GILBERT, Michael Francis,** TD 1950; Partner, Trower Still & Keeling, Solicitors; crime writer; *b* 17 July 1912; *s* of Bernard Samuel Gilbert and Berwyn Minna Cuthbert; *m* 1947, Roberta Mary, *d* of Col R. M. W. Marsden; two *s* five *d*. *Educ:* Blundell's Sch.; London University. LLB 1937. Served War of 1939-45, Hon. Artillery Co., 12th Regt RHA, N Africa and Italy (despatches 1943). Joined Trower Still & Keeling, 1947. Legal Adviser to Govt of Bahrain, 1960. Mem., Arts Council Cttee on Public Lending Rights, 1968; Mem., Royal Literary Fund, 1969; Founder Mem., Crime Writers' Assoc.; Mem., Mystery Writers of America. *Publications: novels:* Close Quarters, 1947; They Never Looked Inside, 1948; The Doors Open, 1949; Smallbone Deceased, 1950; Death has Deep Roots, 1951; Death in Captivity, 1952; Fear to Tread, 1953; Sky High, 1955; Be Shot for Sixpence, 1956; The Tichborne Claimant, 1957; Blood and Judgement, 1958; After the Fine Weather, 1963; The Crack in the Tea Cup, 1965; The Dust and the Heat, 1967; The Etruscan Net, 1969; *short stories:* Game Without Rules; Stay of Execution; *plays:* A Clean Kill; The Bargain; Windfall; The Shot in Question; *edited:* Crime in Good Company, 1959; has also written radio and TV scripts. *Recreations:* walking, archery, contract bridge. *Address:* Luddesdown Old Rectory, Cobham, Kent. *T:* Cobham (Kent) 272. *Club:* Garrick.

**GILBERT, Sir Trounsell;** *see* Gilbert, Sir J. T.

**GILBEY,** family name of **Baron Vaux of Harrowden.**

**GILBEY, Sir (Walter) Derek,** 3rd Bt, *cr* 1893; Director of W. & A. Gilbey Ltd; Lieut 2nd Bn

Black Watch; *b* 11 March 1913; *s* of Walter Ewart Gilbey and Dorothy Coysgarne Sim; *S* grandfather, 1945; *m* 1948, Elizabeth Mary, *d* of Col Keith Campbell and Marjorie Syfret; one *s* one *d*. *Educ:* Eton. Served War of 1939-45 (prisoner). *Heir: s* Walter Gavin Gilbey, *b* 14 April 1949. *Address:* Culross, Faygate, near Horsham, Sussex. *T:* Faygate 331. *Clubs:* Portland, St James'.

**GILCHRIST, Sir Andrew (Graham),** KCMG 1964 (CMG 1956); Chairman, Highlands and Islands Development Board, since Nov. 1970; *b* 19 April 1910; *e s* of late James Graham Gilchrist, Kerse, Lesmahagow; *m* 1946, Freda Grace, *d* of late Alfred Slack; two *s* one *d*. *Educ:* Edinburgh Acad.; Exeter Coll., Oxford. Diplomatic career, 1933-70, included junior posts in Bangkok, Paris, Marseilles, Rabat, Stuttgart, Singapore, Chicago, also in FO; subseq. Ambassador at Reykjavik, Djakarta and Dublin, retired. War Service as Major, Force 136 in SE Asia (despatches). *Publication:* Bangkok Top Secret, 1970. *Address:* Arthur's Crag, Hazelbank, by Lanark, Scotland. *T:* Crossford 263. *Clubs:* Travellers', Special Forces.

**GILCHRIST, (Andrew) Rae,** CBE 1961; MD Edinburgh, FRCPE, FRCP, Hon. FRACP, Hon. FRFPS Glasgow; Consulting Physician Royal Infirmiry, Edinburgh; *b* 7 July 1899; *o s* of late Rev. Andrew Gilchrist, BA, Edinburgh; *m* 1931, Emily Faulds (*d* 1967), *yr d* of late W. Work Slater, Edinburgh and Innerleithen, Peeblesshire; one *s* one *d*. *Educ:* Belfast, Edinburgh, New York. RFA 1917-18; MB, ChB Edinburgh, 1921; Lauder-Brunton Prizeman, Milner-Fothergill Medallist, McCunn Medical Res. Scholar, Edinburgh Univ., 1924; MD (gold medal) 1933; resident hospital appointments at Addenbrooke's Hosp., Cambridge, Princess Elizabeth Hosp. for Children, London, E1, and at Royal Infirmary, Edinburgh, 1922-24; Resident Asst Physician Rockefeller Hosp. for Medical Research, New York, USA, 1926-27; Asst Physician, 1930; Physician, Royal Infirmary, Edinburgh, 1939-64; Gibson Lecturer RCP Edinburgh, 1944; Lecturer: Canadian Heart Assoc., 1955; Litchfield Lecture, Oxford Univ., 1956; Californian Heart Assoc., 1957; St Cyres Lecturer, National Heart Hosp., London, 1957; Hall Overseas Lecturer, Australia and NZ, 1959; Carey Coombs Memorial Lecture, Bristol Univ., 1960; Gwladys and Olwen Williams Lecture in Medicine, Liverpool Univ., 1961; Orford Lectr, College of Physicians of S Africa, 1962. William Cullen Prize, 1962 (shared). Pres. of the Royal College of Physicians of Edinburgh, 1957-60. Examr in Med. in Univs of Edinburgh, Glasgow, Aberdeen, St Andrews, East Africa (Makerere Coll.), and Baghdad. Mem. Assoc. of Physicians of Gt Brit., of Brit. Cardiac Soc. Hon. Mem. Cardiac Soc. of Australia and NZ. *Publications:* numerous contributions on disorders of heart and circulation, in British and American medical journals. *Recreation:* fishing. *Address:* Grovedale, Winton Terrace, Edinburgh EH10 7AP. *T:* 031-445 1119. *Clubs:* Flyfishers'; New (Edinburgh).

**GILCHRIST, James Finlay Elder,** OBE 1946; Chairman: Harrisons & Crosfield Ltd, since 1962; Harcros Investment Trust Ltd; Director: Overseas Marketing Corporation Ltd; various Plantation Companies; *b* 13 Aug. 1903; *s* of late Thomas Dunlop Gilchrist and Agnes Crawford Elder; *m* 1933, Dorothy Joan Narizzano; two *s* one *d*. *Educ:* Glasgow Academy. *Address:* 58 Queen's Grove, St John's Wood, NW8. *T:* 01-722 0952. *Club:* East India and Sports.

**GILCHRIST, Rae;** *see* Gilchrist, A. R.

**GILCHRIST, Robert Niven,** CIE 1934; Indian Educational Service (retired); *b* 1888; *m* 1917, Winifred Buyers, MA (Aberdeen) (*d* 1964). *Educ:* Aberdeen Grammar School; University of Aberdeen. MA Aberdeen; Triple Honours (Economic Science, History, Philosophy). Appointed to the Indian Educational Service, 1910; Prof., Presidency Coll., Calcutta, 1911-16; University Lecturer in Sociology, Acting Asst Dir of Public Instruction, 1914; Principal and Prof. of Political Economy and Political Philosophy, Krishnagar Coll., Bengal, 1916-21; Controller Labour Bureau, Government of India, 1921-22; Labour Intelligence Officer and Labour Commissioner, Bengal, 1922-34; Adviser to Government Delegations, Seventh, Eighth, and Ninth International Labour Conferences, Geneva, 1925 and 1926; Reforms Officer, Bengal, 1932; Reforms Commissioner and Joint-Sec. to the Government of Bengal, 1934-41; Mem. of the Bengal Legislative Council, 1927-37; retired, 1941. India Office (Principal), 1940-48. Mem. Board of Management, Aberdeen Gen. Hosps, 1951-57. Fellow of the Royal Economic and Royal Statistical Societies; late Fellow of Calcutta Univ. *Publications:* Indian Nationality, 1920; Principles of Political Science, 1921 (7th edn, 1952); Conciliation and Arbitration, 1922; The Executive and Judicial, 1923; The Payment of Wages and Profit Sharing, 1924; Report of the Reforms Office, Bengal, 1932-37; reviews and articles. *Address:* 4 Westholme Avenue, Aberdeen. *T:* Aberdeen 37039. *Clubs:* East India and Sports; University (Aberdeen).

**GILDING, Henry Percy,** MA, BM, BCh Oxon, MD Birmingham; Emeritus Professor of Physiology, University of Birmingham, 1961; Bowman Professor of Physiology, University of Birmingham, 1933-60; Late Consulting Physiologist to Birmingham United Hospital; Hon. Treasurer Physiological Society, 1945-54; Hon. Treasurer British Abstracts of Medical Sciences, 1954-66; Mem. Pneumoconiosis Med. Panel, Ministry of Pensions; *b* 4 March 1895; 3rd *s* of Arthur and Rose Gilding; *m* Violet Mary Frances, *yr d* of James and Mina Hazlitt-Brett; five *d*. *Educ:* St John's Coll., Oxford; St Bartholomew's Hosp. (Kirke's Scholar and Gold Medallist in Clinical Medicine). Demonstrator in Physiology, 1923-26; Senior Demonstrator, 1926-27, St Bartholomew's Hosp.; Asst in Pathology and Bacteriology and Fellow of the Rockefeller Institute, New York, 1927-29; Thomas Young Lecturer in Applied Physiology, St George's Hosp., London; Senior Lecturer in Physiology, University Coll., London, 1930-32; Reader in Experimental Physiology, 1932-33; Examiner in Physiology for Trinity Coll., Dublin; late Examiner in Physiology for Universities of Durham, Oxford, Bristol, Leeds, London, St Andrews and Wales, for Royal College of Surgeons, and Royal College of Surgeons, Dublin; Mem. of Council, British Assoc., 1950-55. Pres., Section I, British Assoc., 1951. Mem. Medical Reforms Commission, Government of Pakistan, 1960. Ranker in Northumberland Fusiliers (Tyneside Scottish), 1916-19. *Publications:* papers in Physiology and Pathology in the Journal of Experimental Medicine, and Proceedings of the Society of Experimental Biology, Journal of Physiology, etc. *Address:* Toll Gate House, 98 Priory Road, Birmingham 15. *T:* 021-440 2626.

**'GILES';** *see* Giles, C. R.

**GILES, Very Rev. Alan Stanley,** CB 1958; CBE 1953 (OBE 1946); MA; Dean of Jersey and Rector of St Helier since 1959; Canon of

Winchester Cathedral since 1959; Canon and Prebendary of St Botolph in Lincoln Cathedral, 1953-59; *b* 28 May 1902; *s* of late Rev. Alfred Albert Giles and late Frances Giles; *m* 1934, Myrtle Catherine, *d* of late B. B. Osmaston, CIE; two *s* one *d*. *Educ:* Manchester Gram. Sch.; The Queen's Coll., Oxford (MA); Clifton Theological Coll. Ordained 1932; Curate, St Ebbes, Oxford, and Chaplain, Christ Church, Oxford, 1932-34; Chaplain, RAF: Cranwell, 1934-37; Singapore, 1937-42; Java, 1942-45; Home Estab., 1945-47; Asst Chaplain-in-Chief, 1947-53; Chaplain-in-Chief, 1953-59, retired. Hon. Chaplain to King George VI, 1950-52, to the Queen, 1953-59. *Recreations:* cricket, gardening. *Address:* The Deanery, Jersey, Channel Islands. *T:* 23078.

**GILES, Sir Alexander (Falconer),** KBE 1965 (MBE 1946); CMG 1960; HM Colonial Service retired; *b* 1915; *o s* of late A. F. Giles, MA, LLD; *m* 1953, Mrs M. E. Watson, *d* of late Lieut-Col R. F. D. Burnett, MC, and *widow* of Lieut-Col J. L. Watson; two *step s* one *step d*. *Educ:* The Edinburgh Academy; Edinburgh Univ.; Balliol Coll., Oxford (BA). Pres. Oxford Union Soc., 1939. 2nd Lieut the Royal Scots, 1940; attached RWAFF, 1941; 81 (WA) Div., 1943; Lieut-Col comdg 5 GCR, 1945 (MBE, despatches). Cadet Colonial Service, Tanganyika, 1947; Administrator, St Vincent, 1955-62; Resident Commissioner, Basutoland, 1962-65; British Govt Representative, Basutoland, 1965-66. Chairman: Victoria League in Scotland, 1968-70; Scottish Council, Royal Over-Seas League, 1969-70. Dir, Toc H, 1968-. *Publications:* articles in service journal. *Recreations:* the printed word; gentle swimming; rough shooting. *Address:* 14 Belgrave Place, Edinburgh 4. *Club:* United Service.

**GILES, Carl Ronald,** OBE 1959; Cartoonist, Daily and Sunday Express, since 1943; *b* 29 Sept. 1916; *m* 1942, Sylvia Joan Clarke. *Educ:* various schools. Trained as animated cartoonist; Animator for Alexander Korda, 1935; Cartoonist: Reynolds News, 1937-43; Daily and Sunday Express, 1943-. Cartoons extensively reproduced in US and syndicated throughout world. Produced and animated Documentary Films for Min. of Information, also War Correspondent-cartoonist in France, Belgium, Holland and Germany, War of 1939-45. *Publications:* "Giles" Annual, 1945-70. Various overseas collections. *Recreations:* yachting, engineering, farming. *Address:* Hillbrow Farm, Witnesham, Suffolk. *T:* Witnesham 239. *Clubs:* Savage, British Racing Drivers', Royal Harwich Yacht, Press.

**GILES, G. C. T.;** Headmaster of the Acton County School for Boys, 1926-56, retired. *Educ:* Eton; King's Coll., Cambridge. Formerly Professor of English at the Public Commercial Sch., Athens; Brice Mackinnon Master at Geelong Grammar Sch., Victoria, Australia; and Senior Latin Master at the Latymer Upper Sch., Hammersmith; Executive Mem. of National Union of Teachers, 1937-49, Pres., 1944. *Address:* 29 Burlington Road, W4.

**GILES, Sir (Henry) Norman,** Kt 1969; OBE 1966; Chairman, Elder Smith Goldsbrough Mort Ltd, Australia, since 1967; Deputy Chairman of the Board, Commonwealth Banking Corporation, since 1967 (and 1959-62); Chairman: Commonwealth Development Bank Executive Committee, since 1959; P&O Australian Holdings Pty Ltd; Director: Babcock & Wilcox Australia Ltd; Elder's Trustee and Executor Co. Ltd; Lensworth Finance Ltd; The Squatting Investment Co. Ltd; Gove Alumina Ltd; *b* Northam, WA, 3 May 1905; *s* of late J. O. Giles, Claremont, WA; *m* 1929, Eleanor, *d* of late S. J. Barker; one *s* one *d*. *Educ:* Christ Church Grammar Sch., WA. Served War of 1939-45: RAAF, 1941-44; Flt-Lt (Aust. and New Guinea). Mem., 1965-70, Mem. Exec. Cttee, 1966, Dep. Chm. Board, 1966-70, Commonwealth Banking Corpn; Member: Council Aust. Admin. Staff Coll., 1956-; SA Industrial Develt Adv. Council, 1968-70; Netherlands Aust. Trade & Industrial Develt Council, 1965-; SA State Cttee, CSIRO, 1962-; Aust. Japan Business Co-op. Cttee, 1966-; Pacific Basin Economic Co-op. Cttee, 1968-; Council, Duke of Edinburgh's Third Commonwealth Study Conf., Aust., 1966-68; Industry Forum, Aust. Acad. of Science, 1967-. Aust. Wool Industry Adv. Cttee, 1970-. Joined Elder Smith & Co. Ltd, 1922; Asst Manager for WA, 1944-47; Manager for WA, 1948-52; Gen. Manager, 1952-55; Man. Dir, 1955-62; Gen. Manager, Elder Smith Goldsbrough Mort Ltd, 1962-67. Mem. Exec., Nat. Council of Wool Selling Brokers of Australia, WA, 1947-53, SA, 1953-62; Vice-Pres. and Member, WA Chamber of Commerce, 1947-50; Mem. Council for C of E Schools, WA, 1933-53. *Recreations:* bowls, gardening. *Address:* (private) Greengates, 2 Brougham Place, North Adelaide, SA 5006, Australia; (business) c/o Elder Smith Goldsbrough Mort Ltd, 256 Stanley Street, North Adelaide, SA 5006, Australia. *Clubs:* Weld (WA); Union (NSW); Commonwealth (Canberra); Adelaide, Naval, Military and Air Force, Stock Exchange, Royal Adelaide Golf, Adelaide Oval Bowling (all in SA).

**GILES, Rear-Adm. Morgan Charles M.;** *see* Morgan-Giles.

**GILES, Sir Norman;** *see* Giles, Sir H. N.

**GILES, Air Commandant Dame Pauline,** DBE 1967; RRC; Matron-in-Chief, Princess Mary's Royal Air Force Nursing Service, 1966-70; *b* 17 Sept. 1912. *Educ:* Sheffield. Joined PMRAFNS, Nov. 1937; later appointments included Principal Matron for Royal Air Force Command in Britain and Western Europe; became Matron-in-Chief, PMRAFNS, Sept. 1966. *Club:* Royal Air Force.

**GILHAM, Harold Sidney,** CB 1956; Asst Comptroller of the Patent Office, Board of Trade, 1955-59, retired. Formerly a Superintending Examiner at the Patent Office. *Address:* 49 Stanley Road, Northwood, Middlesex.

**GILKES, Antony Newcombe;** High Master of St Paul's School, Jan. 1954-Sept. 1962; Director, Public Schools Appointments Bureau, since Sept. 1962; *b* 2 Aug. 1900; *s* of Arthur Herman Gilkes (late Master of Dulwich Coll.) and Millicent Mary Gilkes; *m* 1930, Agatha Ruby, *d* of Bishop Shaw; four *s*. *Educ:* Dulwich Coll.; Christ Church, Oxford (Scholar). Asst Master St Paul's Sch., 1923-28; Uppingham Sch., 1928-46. Housemaster of Meadhurst, 1935-46; Master of Classical VIth, 1939-46; Headmaster of Dean Close Sch., 1946-53; OC Rutland Army Cadet Force, 1942-44. Mem. of Governing Body: Charlotte Mason Schs, 1944-69; Dulwich Coll. Preparatory Sch.; Highgate Sch., 1962-69; Reed's Sch., Cobham, 1962-69; Overstone Sch.; Burgess Hill Sch., 1944-69; Mem. Council, Atlantic Coll., 1960-70; Council, City Univ., 1966-70; Mem. Cttee, Clergy Orphan Corporation. *Publications:* Selections from the Old Testament, 1944; Selections from the New Testament, 1946; An anthology of Oratory, 1955; Independent Education, 1957; Faith for Modern Man, 1960; The Impact of the Dead Sea Scrolls, 1963; Einstein or Frankenstein, 1970. *Recreations:*

music, cricket, travel. *Address:* Compton Cottage, Compton Pauncefoot, near Yeovil, Somerset. *T:* North Cadbury 221.

**GILKS, John Langton,** CMG 1933; MRCS, LRCP, FRCSE; Vice-President, British Medical Association; *b* 29 Aug. 1880; *s* of William John Gilks and Elizabeth Langton; *m* 1911, Margaret Annie (*d* 1957), *d* of Thomas Joseph Messom; one *s*. *Educ:* Merchant Taylors' Sch.; St Thomas's Hospital. Medical Officer, East Africa Protectorate, 1909; PMO, Kenya Colony and Protectorate, 1921; Dir of Medical and Sanitary Services, 1926-33; Mem. of Executive and Legislative Councils, Kenya, 1920-33; retired 1933; Governor of St Thomas's Hosp., 1926-48; Ed., East African Medical Journal, 1929-33; Capt. East Africa Medical Service, 1914; Major, 1915; Mem. of Council of British Medical Assoc., 1935-46. *Recreations:* fishing, shooting, golf. *Address:* 9 Grindleton Road, West Bradford, near Clitheroe, Lancs. *T:* Clitheroe 4234. *Clubs:* East India and Sports.

**GILL, Sir Archibald (Joseph),** Kt *cr* 1949; BSc (Eng), CEng, FIEE, FIEEE; *b* 13 May 1889; *s* of William James Gill; *m* 1914, Irene Bassindale; one *s* one *d*. *Educ:* Regent Street Polytechnic; Paisley Technical Coll.; Glasgow Technical Coll.; London Univ. Pupil of Messrs Yarrow & Co. Ltd, engineers and shipbuilders; Draughtsman British Thomson Houston Co. Ltd, Rugby; entered PO Engineering Dept, 1913; Staff Engineer, radio branch, 1932; Asst Engineer-in-Chief, 1938; Dep. Engineer-in-Chief, 1944; Engineer-in-Chief, 1947-51; Chm. Radio Section Inst. of Electrical Engineers, 1938-39; Vice-Pres. IEE, 1945-50, Pres., 1950-51. *Address:* 24 Acacia Road, Hampton, Middlesex. *T:* 01-979 2689. *Club:* Athenæum.

**GILL, Austin,** CBE 1955; MA, Licencié-ès-lettres; Marshall Professor of French, University of Glasgow, since 1966; *b* 3 Sept. 1906; *m* 1939, Madeleine Monier. *Educ:* Bury Municipal Secondary Sch.; Universities of Manchester, Grenoble, Paris. Manchester Univ. (Research Fellow, 1929-30, Faulkner Fellow, 1930-31, and Langton Fellow, 1931-33). asst Lecturer in French, Edinburgh Univ., 1933-34; Lecturer in French, Edinburgh Univ., 1934-43; British Council Representative in French North Africa, 1943-44; British Council Actg Rep. in France, 1944-45; Official Fellow, Tutor in Modern Langs, Magdalen Coll., Oxford, 1945-50 and 1954-66. Dir of Brit. Inst. in Paris, 1950-54. *Publications:* (ed) Les Ramonneurs, 1957; (ed) Life and Letters in France, 1970; articles and reviews in literary and philological journals. *Address:* The University, Glasgow; 15 Beaumont Gate, Glasgow W2.

**GILL, Cecil G. H.;** *see* Hope Gill.

**GILL, Cyril James,** CB 1965; Senior Lecturer in Education, University of Keele, since 1968 (Gulbenkian Lecturer in Education, 1965-68); *b* 29 March 1904; *s* of William Gill, Carnforth, Lancs; *m* 1939, Phyllis Mary, *d* of Joseph Windsor, Ramsey, Isle of Man. *Educ:* Ulverston Grammar Sch.; Liverpool Univ. Sch. Master, Ramsey, IOM and Archbishop Tenison's, London, 1926-42; Head Master, Salford Grammar Sch., 1942-45. HM Inspectorate of Schools, 1945-65; Midland Divisional Inspector, 1954-61; Chief Inspector (Teacher Training), 1961-65. *Recreations:* gardening, walking, photography, theatre. *Address:* Institute of Education, University of Keele, Keele, Staffs. *T:* Keele Park 371. *Club:* Royal Over-Seas League.

**GILL, Cyril James;** Chairman, Grading Commission, Nigerian Ministry of Communications, since 1970; *b* 24 Dec. 1907; *s* of William and Alice Gill; *m* 1931, Dae M. (*née* Bingley); one *s* one *d*. *Educ:* Mundella Gram. Sch., Nottingham. Engrg Dept, GPO, 1929-48; Telephone Man., Sheffield, 1949; Princ., Post Office HQ, 1950; Princ. Private Sec. to PMG, 1957; Dep. Dir, External Telecommunications Exec., 1958; Controller of Supplies, 1959; Vice-Dir, ETE, 1964; Dir, External Telecomm. Exec., GPO, 1967-69; Dir, Cable and Wireless Ltd, 1967-69; Chm. Commonwealth Telecomm. Council, 1968-69. *Recreations:* gardening, golf, travel. *Address:* 65 Longton Avenue, Upper Sydenham, SE26. *T:* 01-699 2745.

**GILL, Evan W. T.;** Canadian Ambassador to Ireland, 1965-68; *b* 2 Nov. 1902; *s* of Robert Gill; *m* 1930, Dorothy Laurie; two *s* one *d*. *Educ:* RMC, Kingston, Ont.; McGill Univ., Montreal, PQ. Began career with industrial and commercial organs; served Canadian Army, 1940-46; Cabinet Secretariat, 1946-50; External Affairs, 1950; Canada House, 1950-51; High Comr for Canada to Union of S Africa, 1954-57; High Comr for Canada to Ghana, 1957-59; Asst Under-Sec. of State for External Affairs, 1959-62; High Commissioner for Canada in Australia, 1962-64. *Recreations:* golf and fishing. *Address:* St Andrews, New Brunswick, Canada. *Clubs:* Rideau, Country, Royal Ottawa Golf (all in Ottawa).

**GILL, Maj.-Gen. Ian Gordon,** OBE 1959 (MBE 1949); MC 1940, Bar 1945; idc, psc; Assistant Chief of the General Staff (Operational Requirements), since 1970; *b* Rochester, 9 Nov. 1919; *s* of late Brig. Gordon Harry Gill, CMG, DSO and Mrs Doris Gill, Rochester, Kent; *m* 1963, Elizabeth Vivian Rohr, MD, MRCP, *o d* of late A. R. Rohr; no *c*. *Educ:* Edinburgh House, Hants; Repton School. Commnd from SRO into 4th/7th Roy. Dragoon Guards, 1938; served with Regt in: BEF, France, 1939-40; BLA, NW Europe, 1944-45 (despatches, 1945); Palestine, 1946-48; Tripolitania, 1951-52; Instructor, Armoured Sch., 1948-50; Staff Coll., Camberley, 1952; Bde Maj., HQ Inf. Bde, 1953-55; comdg 4th/7th RDG, 1957-59; Asst Mil. Sec., HQ, BAOR, 1959-61; Coll. Comdt RMA Sandhurst, 1961-62; Imp. Def. Coll., 1963; Comdr, 7th Armoured Bde, 1964-66; Dep. Mil. Sec. 1, MoD (Army), 1966-68; Head, British Defence Liaison Staff, Dept of Defence, Canberra, 1968-70. *Recreations:* equitation, ski-ing, cricket, squash rackets. *Address:* c/o Glyn, Mills & Co., Whitehall, SW1. *Clubs:* Cavalry, MCC.

**GILL, Major-General John Galbraith,** CBE 1943 (OBE 1919); DSO 1918; MC; late RAMC (retired); *b* 6 April 1889; *s* of late R. P. Gill, of Guntur, India; *m* 1915, Madge, *d* of late Rev. George Davidson, BSc, of Edinburgh; no *c*. *Educ:* Brentwood School, Essex; Edinburgh University. MB, ChB, 1912; DPH (Scot. Conjoint), 1923; DTM&H (Cantab), 1924. Retired pay, 1946. *Address:* c/o Glyn, Mills & Co., Kirkland House, Whitehall, SW1.

**GILL, Air Vice-Marshal Leonard William George,** DSO 1945; Director-General of Manning (RAF), Ministry of Defence, since 1968; *b* 31 March 1918; *s* of L. W. Gill, Hornchurch, Essex, and Marguerite Gill; *m* 1943, Joan Favill Appleyard; two *s* two *d*. *Educ:* University Coll. Sch., London. Joined RAF, 1937; served in Far East until 1942; then UK as night fighter pilot; comd No. 68 Sqdn for last 6 months of war; subseq. served in various appts incl. comd of Nos 85 and 87 night fighter Sqdns and tour on directing staff at RAF Staff

Coll.; Stn Comdr No. 1 Flying Trng Sch., Linton-on-Ouse, 1957-60; Dir of Overseas Ops, 1960-62; Nat. Def. Coll. of Canada, 1962-63; Dir of Organisation (Estabs), 1963-66; SASO, RAF Germany, 1966-68. MIPM. *Recreations:* shooting, cricket, amateur woodwork. *Address:* 8 Lucks Lane, Buckden, Hunts. *T:* Buckden 349. *Club:* Royal Air Force.

**GILL, Dr Stanley;** Chairman, Software Sciences Holdings, since 1969; *b* 26 March 1926; *s* of Walter Campbell Gill and Rhoda Harriett Gill (*née* Mitchell); *m* 1949, Audrey Eileen Lee; two *s* one *d*. *Educ:* Worthing High Sch.; St John's Coll., Cambridge (PhD). Fellow of St John's Coll., Cambridge, 1952-55; various positions, Computer Dept of Ferranti Ltd, 1955-63; Part-time Prof. of Automatic Data Processing, College of Science and Technology, University of Manchester, and ICT Ltd, 1963-64; Prof. of Computing Science, 1964-70, and Dir, Centre for Computing and Automation, 1966-70, Imperial Coll., Univ. of London. Pres., British Computer Soc., 1967-68. *Address:* 21 Speer Road, Thames Ditton, Surrey. *T:* 01-398 5507. *Club:* Oxford and Cambridge University.

**GILL-CAREY, Chapple,** FRCS; Consulting Surgeon, Royal National Throat, Nose and Ear Hospital; Consulting Ear, Nose and Throat Surgeon: Hospital of St John and St Elizabeth; Surbiton Hospital; Former Member, Council, Royal College of Surgeons; MRCS Eng, LRCP London 1918; FRCS Ed. 1923; FRCS Eng 1948. Formerly: Surgeon, Ear, Nose and Throat Department, Hospital of St John and St Elizabeth; Chief Clinical Assistant, Ear, Nose and Throat Department, Guy's Hospital; Assistant Surgeon, Central London Throat, Nose and Ear Hospital; Dean of the Institute of Laryngology and Otology. Fellow Royal Society of Medicine. Ex-President British Association of Otolaryngologists. *Publications:* contributions to medical journals, etc. *Address:* 106 Harley Street, W1.

**GILL-DAVIES, Derek George,** DSO 1940; TD; TARO; *b* 30 June 1913; *s* of late Ernest George and Beatrice Jane Davies. *Educ:* Ardingly Coll. Brown-Firth Research Laboratories of Thos Firth & John Brown Ltd, 1932; in service of Firth-Vickers, 1934-62, Overseas Sales Manager, Firth-Vickers Stainless Steels Ltd; Director, Grängesberg-Nyby Stainless Steels (UK) Ltd, EC3 (Sales Co. in UK for Nyby Bruks AB, Sweden). Broadcast as a narrator for the BBC, 1938 and 1939. Commnd in 49th W Riding Div. RE, TA, 1934; Staff Coll., 1939, served abroad during War of 1939-45 (Lieut-Col) Norway, Iceland, SEAC (Burma and Malaya), China (despatches), 1st Bn Herts Regt TA, 1947-51, comdg 1949-51. Councillor Welwyn Rural District Council, 1948-51. *Recreations:* stalking, shooting and sailing. *Address:* 5 Park Close, Hatfield, Herts. *Clubs:* Naval and Military, Special Forces; Royal Engineer Yacht.

**GILLAM, Group Captain Denys Edgar,** DSO (and 2 bars); DFC (and bar), 1940; AFC 1938; DL; Deputy Chairman, Homfray & Co. Ltd; Managing Director, British Furtex Ltd; *b* 18 Nov. 1915; *s* of Maj. T. H. J. and D. Gillam; *m* 1945, Nancye Joan Short; one *s* two *d*. *Educ:* Bramcote, Scarborough; Wrekin Coll., Salop. Joined RAF, 1935; trained No 1 FTS Netheravon; served 29 Fighter Sqdn, Middle East, 1937-39, Meteorological Flight Aldergrove. Award Air Force Cross, 1938. 616 Sqdn (Fighter), 1939-40 (DFC, after Battle of Britain); 312 Sqdn (F), 1940-41; HQ 9 Group till March 1941, rank Sqdn Ldr; commanded 306 Sqdn (Polish), then 615 Sqdn (F) (bar DFC and DSO for shipping attacks in Channel); RAF Staff Coll.; then commanded first Typhoon Wing (despatches); graduated US Command and Gen. Staff Coll.; commanded Tangmere Wing (Typhoons), Jan.-March 1944 (bar, DSO for attacks on V-weapon sites); promoted Group Capt., commanded 20 Sector 2nd TAF, then 146 Wing 2 TAF (Typhoon) till March 1945 (2nd bar DSO); then Group Capt. Ops 84 Group (Main) 2nd TAF. DL for West Riding of Yorks and the City and County of York, 1959. *Recreations:* fishing, shooting, sailing. *Address:* The Glebe, Brawby, Malton, Yorks. *T:* Kirbymoorside 530. *Club:* Royal Ocean Racing.

**GILLAM, Stanley George,** BLitt; MA; Librarian, The London Library, since 1956; *b* 11 Aug. 1915; *s* of Harry Cosier Gillam, Oxford; *m* 1950, Pauline, *d* of Henry G. Bennett, Oxford; one *s*. *Educ:* Southfield Sch.; Saint Catherine's Coll., Oxford. Bodleian Library, Oxford, 1931-40 and 1946-54. Oxfordshire and Bucks Light Infantry (1st Bucks Bn), 1940-46. Asst Sec. and Sub-Librarian, The London Library, 1954-56. *Publications:* The Building Accounts of the Radcliffe Camera, 1958; articles in The Bodleian Library Record and other periodicals. *Address:* 47 Woodland Way, West Wickham, Kent. *T:* 01-777 1054. *Club:* Oxford and Cambridge.

**GILLAN, Lt-Col Sir George V. B.,** KCIE 1944 (CIE 1934); late Indian Army, Indian Political Department; *b* 3 Sept. 1890; *o s* of Sir Robert Gillan, KCSI; *m* 1918, Sibell (Kaiser-i-Hind Medal), *y d* of late A. Bulloch Graham, Auldhouse, Crieff; no *c*. *Educ:* Fettes Coll., Edinburgh; Pembroke Coll., Cambridge. Entered Army, 1913; attached 1st Seaforth Highlanders, 1913-14; Lieut 9th Gurkha Rifles, 1914; Adjutant, 1915; Capt., 1916; served Mesopotamia Expeditionary Force (despatches, brevet of Major); Political Officer, Baghdad, 1918; Military Governor, Basrah, 1920-21; Iraq Administration, 1922-23; Under Sec. to the Govt of India, Foreign and Political Dept, 1924; HBM Consul-Gen. in Chinese Turkestan, 1925-27; First Asst Resident in Kashmir, 1928-31; Political Agent, Gilgit, 1931-34; Resident Jodhpur, 1937-39; Resident, Gwalior, 1940-42; Resident for Rajputana, 1942-46. CC Kirkcudbright, 1947-58. *Recreations:* shooting and fishing. *Address:* Blackford, Haugh of Urr, Castle Douglas, Kirkcudbrightshire. *T:* Haugh of Urr 256. *Club:* Army and Navy.

**GILLAN, Sir (James) Angus,** KBE *cr* 1939; CMG 1935; *b* 11 Oct. 1885; *s* of late Rev. James Gillan, DD, and Margaret, *d* of John Wilson; *m* 1917, Margaret Douglas, *d* of late M. A. Ord-Mackenzie; one *s*. *Educ:* Edinburgh Acad.; Magdalen Coll., Oxford. Rowed for Oxford 1907, 1909; won Stewards and Olympic IVs (Magdalen) 1908; Grand (Magdalen) 1911; Olympic VIIIs (Leander) 1912; Entered Sudan Political Service, 1909; Asst Political and Intelligence Officer, Sudan Western Frontier Force, 1916 (despatches twice, Order of Nile, 4th Class); Governor Kordofan Province, 1928; Asst Civil Sec., 1932; Civil Sec., 1934, retired 1939; Principal Officer, North Midland Civil Defence Region, Nottingham, 1940-41; Controller, Commonwealth and Empire Div., British Council, 1941-49; British Council Representative in Australia, 1949-51. Fellow, King's Coll., University of London (Treasurer, 1955-70). Pres., Royal Over-Seas League; Past Chairman: Conservative Commonwealth Council; Royal Over-Seas League; Sudan Govt British Pensioners' Assoc.; Anglo-Sudanese Assoc., etc. Order of

Nile, 2nd Class, 1935. *Publications:* articles in various journals on the Sudan, Commonwealth affairs and cultural relations. *Recreations:* shooting, unskilled gardening and carpentering. *Address:* Sheep Cote Cottage, Leigh, Surrey. *T:* Norwood Hill 432. *Clubs:* Athenæum, Leander, Royal Over-Seas League.

**GILLANDERS, Jeannie Kathleen,** CBE 1953; RRC 1st Cl. 1945; *b* 14 April 1896; *d* of late W. J. Gillanders and late A. J. Gillanders. General Training at Liverpool Royal Infirmary and Leeds Maternity Hospital. Joined Queen Alexandra's Royal Naval Nursing Service, 1924; Hon. Nursing Sister to King George VI, 1950-52; Matron-in-Chief Queen Alexandra's Royal Naval Nursing Service, 1950-53; Hon. Nursing Sister to the Queen, 1952-53. Officer Sister, Order of St John, 1952. *Recreations:* walking, interested in antique furniture. *Address:* 28 Manor Close, Henfield, Sussex. *T:* Henfield 2463. *Club:* Naval and Military.

**GILLARD, Francis George,** CBE 1961 (OBE 1946); Managing Director, Radio, BBC, since 1969 (Director of Sound Broadcasting, 1963-68); Consultant to EMI since 1970; *b* 1 Dec. 1908; *s* of late Francis Henry Gillard and of late Emily Jane Gillard, Stockleigh Lodge, Exford; unmarried. *Educ:* Wellington Sch., Som.; St Luke's Coll., Exeter (BSc London). Schoolmaster, 1932-41; Freelance broadcaster, 1936-; joined BBC as Talks Producer, 1941; BBC War Correspondent, 1941. BBC Head of West Regional Programmes, 1945-55; Chief Asst to Dir of Sound Broadcasting with Controller rank, 1955-56; Controller, West Region, BBC, 1956-63. *Address:* 49 Hallam Street, W1. *T:* 01-580 3960; Trevor House, Poole, Wellington, Somerset. *T:* Wellington 2890.

**GILLEN, Stanley (James);** Chairman and Chief Executive Officer, Ford of Europe Inc., since 1969; Vice-President, Ford Motor Co. USA, since 1967; Director, Ford of Britain since 1965; *b* 10 Aug. 1911; *s* of Bernard J. Gillen, Ohio, and Johanna P. Spillane, Wayne Co., USA; *m* 1935, Mary Elizabeth Marks; three *d*. *Educ:* St Frederick's High Sch., Pontiac, Mich.; University of Detroit. Fisher Body Div., Gen. Motors Corp., 1933-47; Ford Motor Co., USA: Contract Administrator, Defence Products, 1947-48; Controller, Steel Div., 1948-55; Controller, Tractor and Implement Div., 1955-56; Asst Gen. Man., Steel Div., 1956-60; Gen. Man., Steel Div., 1960-61; Gen. Man., Gen. Parts Div., 1961-65; Man. Dir and Chief Exec. Officer, Ford of Britain, 1965-67; Vice-Pres., Manufacturing Ford of Europe Inc., 1967-69. Chm., Autolite Motor Products Ltd, 1962-65; Dir, Ford Credit Co. Ltd, 1965-67; Dir, Henry Ford & Son Ltd, Cork, 1965-67; Dir, Amer. Chamber of Commerce (UK), 1967; Member: British Manufacturers' Exec. Cttee, SMMT, 1965-67; National Advisory Council for Motor Manufacturing Industry (NACMMI), 1966-67. *Recreations:* golf, ski-ing, shooting, horology. *Address:* St Leonards, Ingatestone, Essex. *T:* Ingatestone 21.

**GILLES, Prof. Dennis Cyril;** Professor of Computing Science, University of Glasgow, since 1966; *b* 7 April 1925; *s* of George Cyril Gilles and Gladys Alice Gilles (*née* Batchelor); *m* 1955, Valerie Mary Gilles; two *s* two *d*. *Educ:* Sidcup Gram. Sch.; Imperial Coll., University of London. Demonstrator, Asst Lectr, Imperial Coll., 1945-47; Asst Lectr, University of Liverpool, 1947-49; Mathematician, Scientific Computing Service, 1949-55; Research Asst, University of Manchester, 1955-57; Dir of Computing Lab., University of Glasgow, 1957-66. *Publications:* contribs to Proc. Royal Society and other scientific jls. *Address:* 21 Bruce Road, Glasgow S1. *T:* 041-429 2473.

**GILLESPIE, Brig. Dame Helen (Shiels),** DBE, *cr* 1954 (MBE 1945); RRC 1943; QARANC (retired); *b* 26 March 1898; *d* of John Gillespie and Isabella (*née* Dunlop), Edinburgh. *Educ:* George Watson's Ladies' Coll., Edinburgh. Professional Training, Western Infirmary, Glasgow, 1921-25. Joined Queen Alexandra's Imperial Military Nursing Service (QAIMNS), 1926. Service in: India, 1927-32, 1934-39; Middle East 1939-42; South East Asia Command, 1944-46; War Office, 1946-49; BAOR, 1949-51; Commandant Depot and Training Establishment, QARANC, 1951-52; Matron-in-Chief and Dir of Army Nursing Services, War Office, 1952-56; QHNS 1952-56; retired pay, 1956. Col Comdt QARANC, 1956-61. *Recreations:* music, drama, sports. *Address:* 6 Buckstone Gardens, Edinburgh 10.

**GILLESPIE, Robert,** CBE 1951; MInstT; *b* 24 Nov. 1897; *s* of late James Gillespie and Ann Wilson Gillespie; *m* 1928, Isabella Brown, *d* of late Dr Donald Murray, MP; one *s* one *d*. *Educ:* Queen's Park Sch., Glasgow. Joined Brit. Tanker Co. Ltd, 1922; Asst Manager, 1936; Gen. Manager, 1944; Dir and Gen. Manager, 1946; Managing Dir, 1950-56; a Dir, 1956-67; a Managing Dir of The British Petroleum Co. Ltd, 1956-58, retired; Mem., Council, Chamber of Shipping of UK, 1943-. Served European War in Army, 1914-19; in ranks with Cameronians (Scottish Rifles) TF in UK; commnd KOSB, served UK, Palestine and France. War of 1939-45, served as Asst Dir, Tanker Div. of Ministry of War Transport, 1942-43. *Recreations:* golf, ornithology, shooting. *Address:* Craigrathan, Kippford, Dalbeattie, Kirkcudbrightshire. *T:* Kippford 653.

**GILLESPIE, William Hewitt,** MD, FRCP; Physician, Maudsley Hospital, since 1936; Lecturer, Institute of Psychiatry, since 1944; *b* 6 Aug. 1905; *s* of Rev. W. H. Gillespie, Manchuria and Co. Down, and of Isabella B. Gillespie (*née* Grills), Co. Down, N Ireland; *m* 1932, Dr Helen Turover; one *s* one *d*. *Educ:* George Watson's Coll.; Universities of Edinburgh and Vienna. University Edinburgh: 1st pl. Open Bursary Exam., 1924, MB, ChB (hons), 1929, Dip. in Psychiatry, 1931, MD 1934; MRCP 1936; FRCP 1962; McCosh Travelling Scholarship, in Vienna, 1930-31. LCC Mental Hosps Service, 1931-36. Dir, London Clinic of Psychoanalysis, 1944-47; Trg Sec., Inst. of Psychoanalysis, 1947-50; Pres. Brit. Psychoanalytical Soc., 1950-53; Chm., Inst of Psychoanalysis, 1954-56; Pres., Internat. Psychoanalytic Assoc., 1957-61. FRSocMed. *Publications:* contrib to: Recent Advances in Psychiatry, 1944; Psychiatrie sociale de l'enfant, 1951; Psychoanalysis and the Occult, 1953; The Sexual Perversions, 1956; The Pathology and Treatment of Sexual Deviation, 1964; Foundations of Child Psychiatry, 1968. Various articles in medical, psychiatric and psychoanalytic jls. *Recreations:* music, reading, walking. *Address:* 22a East Heath Road, NW3. *T:* 01-794 6901.

**GILLETT, Sir Edward (Bailey),** Kt, *cr* 1948; Chartered Surveyor; *b* 2 Aug. 1888; 4th and *y s* of William Edward and Florence Gillett; *m* 1916, Bertha Helen (*d* 1957), *d* of William Henry Moss; two *d*. *Educ:* Marlborough Coll. Served European War, 1914-18, Capt. East Surrey Regt in Belgium, France and Italy. Pres. of Royal Institution of Chartered Surveyors, 1945-46. Crown Estate Commissioner, 1957-65. *Address:* Stables

Cottage, Lydwicke, Slinfold, Horsham, Sussex.

**GILLETT, Eric;** Under-Secretary, and Head of Police, Fire and Civil Law Sections, Scottish Home and Health Department, since 1969; *b* 22 July 1920; *m* 1945, Dorothy; one *s. Educ:* public primary and secondary schs; Downing Coll., Cambridge. Royal Artillery, 1942; Dept of Health for Scotland, 1946. *Recreations:* amateur chamber and orchestral music, hill walking. *Address:* 66 Caiystane Terrace, Edinburgh 10. *T:* 031-445 1184. *Club:* Royal Commonwealth Society.

**GILLETT, Eric Walkey,** MA; FRSL; on staff of Royal College of Music since 1961; *b* Bowdon, 24 Aug. 1893; *s* of Samuel Walkey Gillett and Edith Suzette Barlow; *m* 1st, 1926, Joan Edwards (decd); one *s* (one *d* decd); 2nd, 1962, Nancy Miller. *Educ:* Radley; Lincoln Coll., Oxford. Lectr to the Oxford Univ. Extension Delegacy, 1921; Lectr to the Extension Delegacies of the Universities of Cambridge and London, 1935; Warden of Chancellor's Hall and Lecturer in English Literature, University of Birmingham, 1922-27; Johore Prof. of English Language and Literature, Raffles Coll., Singapore, 1927-32; Literary editing, publishing and broadcasting work, 1932-58; Gen. Ed., Royal National Institute for the Blind, 1958-61. London Dramatic Critic, Yorks Post, 1960-65. 2nd Lieut, 7th Batt. Lancs Fusiliers (TF), 1914; wounded 3rd battle of Ypres, Aug. 1917; invalided out with rank of Capt., 1919. *Publications:* Hush (in collaboration), 1920; Books and Writers, 1930; An Anthology of Verse for Children, 1930; Poets of Our Time, 1932; Maria Jane Jewsbury, 1932; Normal English Prose (with late T. Earle Welby), 1934; The Literature of England; AD 500 to 1942 (with W. J. Entwistle), 1943; revised edn, The Literature of England, AD 500 to 1946, 1947; The Literature of England, AD 500-1950, 1952; The Literature of England, AD 500 to 1960, 1961; Elizabeth Ham: By Herself (ed) 1945; J. B. Priestley's All About Ourselves (ed), 1956; Junior Film Annual, 1946-47 (ed), 1946; Eric Gillett's Film Book, 1947; Film Fairyland, 1948; Collins' Film Books, 1948, 1949, 1950, 1951; pamphlets, contributions to various periodicals. *Recreations:* reading, travelling, theatre and broadcasting. *Address:* Flat 4, 29 Brunswick Square, Hove 2, Sussex. *T:* Brighton 731820; Royal College of Music, Prince Consort Road, SW7. *T:* 01-589 3643. *Clubs:* United University, Royal Automobile, MCC; Vincent's (Oxford).

**GILLETT, Sir Harold;** *see* Gillett, Sir S. H.

**GILLETT, Sir Michael Cavenagh,** KBE 1962; CMG 1951; retired from Foreign Service, 1963; *b* 12 July 1907; *s* of late Adm. Owen Francis Gillett, CB, and of Mabel Alice (*née* Cavenagh-Mainwaring); *m* 1952, Margaret Murray (*née* Hobbs); one *s* two *d. Educ:* Western Provinces Preparatory Sch.; Cheam; RN Colls, Osborne and Dartmouth; Manchester Univ. Student interpreter, HBM Consular Service in China, 1929; commissioned, 1931; served at Peking, Canton, Hankow, Nanking, Kashgar, Tengyueh, Chungking and Shanghai; Counsellor (Chinese Affairs), HBM Embassy, Peking, Dec. 1950-53; HM Consul-Gen. at Los Angeles, 1954-57; HM Ambassador to Afghanistan, 1957-63. *Publications:* Notes on Blue Turkish, and other contributions to Journal of Royal Asiatic Society (N China Branch). *Recreation:* Central Asia (FRGS, FRAS). *Address:* Beechmead, Alton Pancras, Dorchester, Dorset. *Club:* Junior Carlton.

**GILLETT, Maj.-Gen. Peter Bernard,** CB 1966; OBE 1955; Secretary of the Central Chancery of the Orders of Knighthood, since 1968; *b* 8 Dec. 1913; *s* of Bernard George Gillett, OBE, Milford on Sea, Hants; *m* 1952, Pamela Graham, *widow* of Col R. J. Lloyd Price and *d* of Col Spencer Graham Walker, Winsley, Wilts. *Educ:* Marlborough Coll.; RMA, Woolwich. Commissioned RA, 1934; apptd to RHA, 1945; service in UK and India to 1944; War Office, 1944; BAOR, 1944-45; Staff Coll., 1946; staff appts in UK and E Africa to 1955; Comd 5 RHA, 1955; SHAPE, 1958; CRA 3 Inf. Div., 1959; IDC, 1962; Chief of Staff, HQ Eastern Comd, 1962-65; GOC, 48th Div. TA, W Midland District, 1965-68. Col 1957, Brig. 1961, Maj.-Gen. 1962. Col Comdt, Royal Regt of Artillery, 1968-. *Recreations:* riding, sailing, shooting and travel. *Address:* c/o Lloyds Bank Ltd, 6 Pall Mall, SW1. *T:* (office) 01-834 2837. *Clubs:* Army and Navy, Royal Ocean Racing, United Hunts.

**GILLETT, Sir Stuart,** Kt 1959; CMG 1952; *b* 1 June 1903; 2nd *s* of late T. G. Gillett, Faversham, Kent; *m* 1931, Irene Mary Holm; two *s. Educ:* Bedford Sch.; Wye Coll., Kent. Asst Agricultural Officer, Kenya, 1928; Agric. Officer and Experimentalist, Kenya, 1931; Senior Coffee Officer, Kenya, 1946; Commissioner of European Settlement, Kenya, 1947; Dir of Agriculture and Chm. European Settlement Board, Kenya, 1948; Chm. Overseas Food Corp., 1951-55; Chm., Tanganyika Agricultural Corporation, 1955-58; London Representative, Kenya Coffee Industry, 1958-66, retired. *Publications:* contributions to EA Agric. Journal and Kenya Coffee Board Bulletin. *Address:* Karibu, off Transfiguration Avenue, Lija, Malta. *Clubs:* Farmers'; Nairobi (Nairobi); Malta Union, United Services Sports, Marsa (Malta).

**GILLETT, Sir (Sydney) Harold,** 1st Bt, *cr* 1959; Kt 1953; MC 1916; Consultant, Dixon Wilson, Tubbs & Gillett, Chartered Accountants; Lord Mayor of London, 1958-59; *b* 27 Nov. 1890; *s* of William Henry Gillett, Highgate, Mx; *m* 1919, Audrey Isabel Penrose Wardlaw (*d* 1962); one *s. Educ:* Marlborough. Qualified as a Chartered Accountant, 1914; served European War, 1914-18. 1/7 Mx Regt (TA) (despatches, MC); War of 1939-45, 2nd i/c 17 Bn Essex HG, Certificate of Merit. Common Councilman, 1930, Alderman, 1948-69 (Ward of Bassishaw); Sheriff of City of London, 1952-53; Chm. London Chamber of Commerce, 1956-58 (now a Vice-Pres.). Dir numerous public cos; Chm. Baden-Powell House Cttee, Boy Scouts' Assoc.; Hon. Col 8th Essex (517 Light Anti-Aircraft) Cadet Regt; Past Prime Warden Worshipful Co. of Basketmakers; Governor, National Corporation for Care of Old People. KStJ 1959 (CStJ 1951); Order of Homayoun (Iran), 1959; Gold Medal of Madrid, 1959. *Recreation:* riding. *Heir: s* Robin Danvers Penrose Gillett [*b* 9 Nov. 1925; *m* 1950, Elizabeth Marion Grace, *d* of late John Findlay, JP, Busby House, Busby, Lanarks; two *s*]. *Address:* 12 Kingston House East, SW7; Outlook, 3rd Avenue, Frinton-on-Sea, Essex; Gillett House, 55 Basinghall Street, EC2. *T:* 01-628 4321. *Clubs:* City of London, City Livery.

**GILLIAT, Lieut-Col Sir Martin (John),** KCVO 1962 (CVO 1954); MBE 1946; DL; Private Secretary to Queen Elizabeth the Queen Mother since 1956; *b* 8 Feb. 1913; *s* of late Lieut-Col John Babington Gilliat and Muriel Helen Lycette Gilliat; unmarried. *Educ:* Eton; RMC, Sandhurst. Joined KRRC, 1933. Served War of 1939-45 (despatches, Prisoner of War). Dep. Military Sec. to Viceroy and Governor-Gen. of India, 1947-48; Comptroller to

Commissioner-Gen. for UK in South-East Asia, 1948-51; Mil. Sec. to Governor-Gen. of Australia, 1953-55. DL Herts, 1963. *Address:* Appletrees, Welwyn, Herts. *T:* Welwyn 4675. *Clubs:* Travellers', Buck's, Brooks's.

**GILLIAT-SMITH, Bernard Joseph;** HBM Consul-Gen. (retired); *b* 20 Oct. 1883; *s* of late Frederick Ernest Gilliat-Smith, The Oaks, Woodmansterne, Surrey, and of late Ellinor Marie Cockerell; *m* 1911, Ida Marie Szymonska-Lubicz; one *d* (and one *d* decd). *Educ:* private tuition in Belgium, Germany, and Spain. Levant Consular Service; served at Constantinople, Sofia, Beirut, Varna, Copenhagen, Foreign Office (London), Tabriz, Sarajevo, Leningrad, Bucharest, New Orleans, Smyrna; retired, 1943. *Publications:* linguistic articles in Journal of Gypsy Lore Society. *Recreations:* riding, swimming, walking, languages, botany. *Address:* 1 Pine Ridge Drive, Lower Bourne, Farnham, Surrey; The Poplars, Newbury, Berks.

**GILLIATT, Prof. Roger William,** DM; FRCP; Professor of Clinical Neurology, University of London, since 1962; Physician, National Hospital, Queen Square, and Middlesex Hospital; *m* 1963, Mary Elizabeth, *er d* of A. J. W. Green; one *s* two *d*. BA 1st Cl. Hons Nat. Sci. (MA), BM, BCh Oxon 1949; MRCP 1951, FRCP 1961; DM 1955. Member: Association of British Neurologists; Physiological Soc. *Publications:* contributions to Journal of Neurology, Neurosurgery and Psychiatry; also to Proc. Royal Society Med. *Address:* Institute of Neurology, Queen Square, WC1N 3BG. *T:* 01-837 3611.

**GILLICK, Rev. John,** SJ, MA Oxon; Director, Fons Vitae (Pastoral Institute for Religious), Johannesburg, since 1970; *b* Wallasey, 27 March 1916; 2nd *s* of Laurence Gillick and Catherine Devine. *Educ:* St Francis Xavier's Coll., Liverpool; Heythrop and Campion Hall, Oxford (1st Cl. Hons Mod. History). Asst Master at Mount St Mary's and Beaumont. Two years writing and photography in Italy and Africa. Headmaster, Beaumont Coll., 1964-67; studied Pastoral Counselling at Loyola Univ., Chicago, 1967-68; Dir, Laboratories for the Training of Religious Superiors in S Africa, 1969. *Publications:* Teaching the Mass, 1961; Baptism, 1962; followed by Teaching the Mass: African, 1963; Teaching the Sacraments: African, 1964; Teaching Confirmation: African, 1964, etc; *illustrations for:* The Breaking of Bread, 1950; The Pilgrim Years, 1956; Our Faith, 1956; The Holy Mass, 1958; Christ Our Life, 1960. *Address:* Jesuit House, 2 Sherwood Road, Forest Town, Johannesburg, South Africa; c/o 114 Mount Street, W1Y 6AH.

**GILLIE, Dame Annis Calder, (Mrs Peter Smith),** DBE 1968 (OBE 1961); MB, BS London, FRCP; formerly in general medical practice (1925-63); *b* 3 Aug. 1900; *d* of late Rev. Dr Robert Calder Gillie and Emily Japp; *m* 1930, Peter Chandler Smith, MA, FRIBA; one *s* one *d*. *Educ:* Wycombe Abbey Sch.; University Coll. and University Coll. Hosp., London. Member: BMA Council, 1950-64; Council of Medical Protection Soc., 1946-; Medical Practices Cttee, 1948-60; Med. Women's Federation (Pres. London Assoc., 1942-45, Pres. 1954); Foundn Mem., Royal College of General Practitioners (Chm., 1959-62, Pres., 1964-67); Mem., Central Health Services Advisory Council, 1956-; North West Regional Hosp. Bd, 1958-63; Mem., Oxford Regional Hosp. Bd, 1964-. Fellow, UCL, 1969. Hon. MD Edinburgh. *Publications:* contributions to medical jls. *Recreations:* reading, listening. *Address:* Bledington, Kingham, Oxford. *T:* Kingham 360.

**GILLIE, (Francis) Blaise,** CB 1958; UN Adviser to National Institute for Physical Planning and Construction Research, Ireland (An Foras Forbartha), since 1967; *b* 29 Feb. 1908; *s* of Rev. R. C. Gillie, Presbyterian Minister, and Emily Japp; *m* 1939, Mary Besly; three *s* one *d*. *Educ:* Gresham's Sch., Holt; Trinity Hall, Cambridge. Entered Ministry of Health, 1930. Asst Gen. Inspector, 1936, Principal, 1937; transf. to Min. of Works and Planning, 1942; Asst Sec., 1943; transf. to Min. of Town and Country Planning, 1943; Imperial Defence Coll., 1948; transf. to Min. of Local Govt and Planning, 1951 (now Min. of Housing and Local Govt); Under-Sec., 1954; Welsh Sec., 1957-63. OECD Consultant on Regional Planning, Turkish Govt, 1963-65; UN appointment, Afghanistan, 1965-67. *Publications:* (pt-author with P. L. Hughes) Some Principles of Land Planning, 1950; Basic Thinking in Regional Planning, 1967. *Recreations:* history, landscape. *Address:* 15 Phillimore Gardens, W8.

**GILLIES, Sir Alexander,** Kt 1959; FRCSEd, FRACS; MChOrth; Consulting Orthopædic Surgeon, Wellington, Nelson and Dannevirke Hospitals, New Zealand; *b* 1891; *s* of Gilbert Gillies; *m* 1920, Effie Lovica, *d* of James Pearson Shaw, Kamloops, BC; one *d* (and one *d* decd). *Educ:* Otago Boys' High Sch.; Edinburgh Univ. MB, ChB. Ed 1923; DMRE Liverpool 1925; FRCSEd 1926; FRACS 1931; MChOrth Liverpool 1936. Fellow, Mayo Clinic, Rochester, Minnesota, 1928. Sen. Orthop. Surg., Wellington Hosp., NZ, 1929-50. President: NZ Red Cross Soc., 1953-61; NZ Crippled Children Soc.; Counsellor of Honour NZ Red Cross Soc., 1961. Emeritus Fellow, Brit. Orthopædic Assoc., 1966. *Publications:* contrib. med. jls. *Recreations:* golf, Rotary. *Address:* 35 Pitt Street, Wellington, New Zealand.

**GILLIES, Prof. Alexander;** Professor of German Language and Literature, University of Leeds, since 1945; *b* Sheffield, 26 May 1907; *s* of late A. Gillies and M. Gillies; *m* 1944, Camilla Hill Hay, MA, D de l'Univ. *Educ:* King Edward VII Sch., Sheffield; Universities of Sheffield and Göttingen. 1st cl. Hons Mod. Langs 1927, MA 1928 (Sheffield), DPhil 1933 (Göttingen). Asst Lecturer in German, University of Manchester, 1930-34, Head of Dept of German, University Coll., Hull, 1934-45; Visiting Lecturer on German Lit., Harvard Univ., USA, 1946-47, on leave of absence from Leeds; Dean of the Faculty of Arts, University of Leeds, 1951-53; Chm., Joint Matriculation Board, 1958-61 (Vice-Chm., 1955-58); Chm., Conference of University Teachers of German in Gt Britain and Ireland, 1966-67; Editor, Mod. Language Review, 1943-, and General Editor, 1956-60; co-editor, Year's Work in Modern Language Studies, 1937-40; Hon. Life Mem. Modern Humanities Research Assoc.; past or present External Examiner to the Univs of Belfast, Dublin, Glasgow, Hull, Liverpool, Nottingham, Oxford, St Andrews, Sheffield, Southampton, Reading. General Editor, Blackwell's German Texts. *Publications:* Herder und Ossian (Berlin), 1933; Herder, 1945; (ed) J. G. Herder, Journal meiner Reise im Jahre 1769, 1947, 2nd rev. edn 1969; (ed) Herzensergiessungen eines Kunstliebenden Klosterbruders, by W. H. Wackenroder and L. Tieck, 1948, 2nd rev. edn, 1966; Herder, der Mensch und sein Werk, (Hamburg) 1949; Goethe's Faust: an Interpretation, 1957; A Hebridean in Goethe's Weimar: The Reverend James Macdonald and the Cultural Relations between Scotland and

Germany, 1969; (ed) J. G. Herder, Über die neuere deutsche Literatur, 1969; numerous contributions to Encyclopædia Britannica, etc; articles and reviews on German and comparative literature in various European and N American periodicals. *Recreations:* foreign travel, gardening, golf. *Address:* Gates House, Ripley Road, Knaresborough, Yorks. *T:* Knaresborough 2374. *Clubs:* Authors'; Harrogate Golf.

**GILLIES, Hugh,** CBE 1967; JP; PhD; Convener of County Council of Dunbarton since 1961; *b* 16 Nov. 1903; *s* of Dugald Gillies and Hannah (*née* Greenhalgh); *m* 1933, Marion Rose (*née* Oswald); two *s* one *d*. *Educ:* Glasgow. Provost, Burgh of Kirkintilloch, 1952-58 (2 terms); Vice-Convener, Dunbarton CC, 1958-61. Mem., Cumbernauld New Town Develt Bd; Mem., Police Council for Gt Britain; Chm., Hosps Bd, Kirkintilloch and Council Hosps. Professional Linguist (knowledge 23 langs). JP Co. of Dunbarton. Freeman of City of London and Mem. Guild of Freemen. *Recreations:* local government, gardening; speaker on foreign affairs and literature in general. *Address:* 14b Lochlea Road, Cumbernauld, Dunbartonshire. *T:* Cumbernauld 22560; (business) 041-221 0201. *Clubs:* Edinburgh Liberal; Glasgow Rotary.

**GILLIES, Dr John,** CVO 1949; MC 1917; J. Y. Simpson Reader in Anæsthetics, University of Edinburgh, 1946-60, retd; *b* 6 Feb. 1895; *s* of late Archibald George Gillies and late Jessie Jane Shier; *m* 1924, Agnes McGilchrist Anderson; two *s* two *d*. *Educ:* Broughton Sch., Edinburgh; Edinburgh Univ. Served European War, 1914-18, with HLI, attaining rank of Capt. Graduated MB, ChB Edinburgh, 1923, DAEng, 1935, FRCSE, 1946, FFARCSEng, 1948, MRCPE 1950, FRCPE 1956, FFARACS (Hon.), 1956, FFARCSI (Hon.), 1960. Pres., Association of Anæsthetists of Great Britain and Ireland, 1947, 1948, 1949. Vice-Dean, Faculty of Anæsthetists, RCS, 1956-58. *Publications:* Textbook of Anæsthetics, 7th Edition, 1948; various papers to medical journals. *Recreation:* golf. *Address:* 18a Mortonhall Road, Edinburgh EH9 2HW. *T:* 031-667 4142.

**GILLIES, Prof. Marshall Macdonald,** MA Cantab; PhD (Edinburgh); retired as Professor of Classics, The University of Hull, now Professor Emeritus; Pro-Vice-Chancellor, 1962-68; *b* 27 April 1901; *s* of late Rev. J. Gillies, DD, Parish Minister of Lesmahagow. *Educ:* Eton; King's Coll., Cambridge; Edinburgh Univ.; New Coll., Oxford; Vienna University. Asst Lecturer in Greek, Liverpool Univ., 1924-28. Head of Dept of Classics on opening of University Coll., Hull, 1928; subsequently Prof. *Publications:* Apollonius Rhodius, *Argonautica*, Book III, 1928; sundry articles, etc., in classical journals. *Recreation:* Siamese cats. *Address:* 131 Westbourne Avenue, Hull, Yorks. *T:* 42085.

**GILLIES, Maurice Gordon,** TD and Bar 1948; QC (Scotland) 1958; Sheriff-Substitute of Lanarkshire, at Lanark, since 1958; *b* 17 Oct. 1916; *s* of James Brown Gillies, Advocate in Aberdeen, and Rhoda Ledingham; *m* 1954, Anne Bethea McCall-Smith. *Educ:* Aberdeen Grammar Sch.; Merchiston Castle; Edinburgh Univ. Advocate, 1946; Advocate Depute, 1953-58. *Recreation:* golf. *Address:* The Old Manse, Elsrickle, near Biggar, Lanarkshire. *T:* Dunsyre 220. *Clubs:* New (Edinburgh); Hon. Company of Edinburgh Golfers.

**GILLIES, Sir William George,** Kt 1970; CBE 1957; ARA 1964; RSA 1947 (ARSA 1940); PRSW; Principal, College of Art, Edinburgh, 1961-66; *b* 1898; unmarried. FEIS 1966; Hon. DLitt (Edinburgh) 1966. *Address:* Temple Cottage, Temple, by Gorebridge, Midlothian.

**GILLIGAN, Arthur Edward Robert;** President of MCC, 1967-68; *b* 23 Dec. 1894; *s* of W. A. Gilligan, JP; *m* 1934, Katherine Margaret Fox. *Educ:* Dulwich Coll.; Pembroke Coll., Cambridge. Cambridge XI, 1919-20. Capt. of MCC: Australian Tour, 1924-25; India and Ceylon, 1926-27. *Publications:* Collins Men, 1926; Sussex Cricket, 1932. *Recreation:* golf (Past President: English Golf Union, 1959; County Cricketers' Golfing Soc.; Capt., Sussex County Golf Union, 1952-). *Address:* Cherry Trees, Mare Hill, Pulborough, Sussex. *T:* Pulborough 2611. *Clubs:* MCC, Royal Air Force; Surrey, Sussex, Yorkshire and Lancashire County Cricket Clubs.

**GILLILAND, David Jervois Thetford;** Member, Independent Television Authority, since 1965; Chairman, Northern Ireland Advisory Committee of ITA, since 1965; also practising solicitor, farmer and boatbuilder; *b* 14 July 1932; *s* of late Major W. H. Gilliland and of Mrs N. H. Gilliland; *m* 1958, Patricia, *o d* of late J. S. Wilson and late Mrs Wilson; two *s* three *d*. *Educ:* Rockport Prep. Sch.; Wrekin Coll.; Trinity Coll., Dublin. BA 1954, LLB 1955. Qualified as solicitor, 1957, own practice. Mem. Council, Internat. Dendrology Soc., 1966-; etc. *Recreations:* gardening, sailing, fishing. *Address:* Brook Hall, Londonderry, Northern Ireland. *T:* Brookhall 297. *Clubs:* Royal Over-Seas League, RNVR; Northern Counties (Londonderry).

**GILLINGHAM, Francis John,** MBE 1944; FRSEd 1970; Professor of Neurological Surgery, University of Edinburgh, since 1963; Director, Departments of Surgical Neurology, Royal Infirmary of Edinburgh and Western General Hospital, Edinburgh, since 1963; Consultant Neuro-Surgeon to the Army in Scotland since 1966; *b* 15 March 1916; *s* of John H. Gillingham, Upwey, Dorset; *m* 1945, Irene Judy Jude; four *s*. *Educ:* Hardye's Sch., Dorset; St Bartholomew's Hosp. Medical Coll., London. Matthews Duncan Gold Medal, 1939, MRCS, LRCP Oct. 1939; MB, BS (London) Nov. 1939; FRCS 1947; FRCSE (*ad eundem*) 1955; FRCPE (*ad eundem*) 1967. Hunterian Prof., RCS, 1957; Morison Lectr, RCP of Edinburgh, 1960; Colles Lectr, College of Surgeons of Ireland, 1962; Elsberg Lectr, College of Physicians and Surgeons, NY, 1967; Penfield Lectr, Middle East Med. Assembly, 1970. Hon. Mem., Soc. de Neurochirurgie de Langue Française, 1964; Hon. Mem., Soc. of Neurol. Surgeons (USA), 1965; Hon. Mem., Royal Academy of Medicine of Valencia, 1967; Hon. and Corresp. Mem. of a number of foreign neuro-surgical societies. Past-Pres. Medico-Chirurgical Soc. of Edinburgh (1965-67). *Publications:* Clinical Surgery: Neurological Surgery, 1969; papers on surgical management of cerebral vascular disease, head and spinal injuries, Parkinsonism and the dyskinesias, epilepsy and other neurosurgical subjects. *Recreations:* sailing, travel, photography. *Address:* Boraston House, Ravelston Dykes Road, Edinburgh 4. *T:* 031-336 3528; Casa Carmen, Jesus Pobre, Alicante, Spain. *Clubs:* English-Speaking Union; Edinburgh University Staff (Edinburgh).

**GILLINGHAM, Rev. Canon Peter Llewellyn,** MVO 1955; MA 1940; QHC since 1952; Vicar of St Mary the Virgin, Horsham, Sussex, since 1960; Hon. Canon of Chichester Cathedral (Wisborough Prebendary), since 1969; *b* 3 May 1914; *s* of late Rev. Canon Frank Hay Gillingham; *m* 1947, Diana, *d* of Lieut-Gen. Sir

Alexander Hood; two *s* two *d*. *Educ:* Cheam; Marlborough; Oriel Coll., Oxford. Curate, Tonbridge Parish Church, 1937-40; Curate-in-Charge, St George's Church, Oakdale, Poole, 1940-43. Served War of 1939-45, Chaplain, RNVR, 1943-46; Chaplain, Blundell's Sch., Tiverton, 1946-49; Hon. Chaplain to King George VI, 1949-52; Chaplain to Royal Chapel of All Saints, Windsor Great Park, 1949-55; Vicar of St Mildred's, Addiscombe, 1955. *Recreations:* cricket, sailing. *Address:* The Vicarage, The Causeway, Horsham, Sussex. *T:* Horsham 3762.

**GILLIS, Bernard (Benjamin),** QC 1954; MA Cantab; **His Honour Judge Gillis;** Additional Judge, Central Criminal Court, since 1964. *Educ:* Downing Coll., Cambridge. Squadron Leader, RAF, 1940-45. Called to the Bar, Lincoln's Inn, 1927, Bencher 1960; North Eastern Circuit and Central Criminal Court. Commr, Central Criminal Court, 1959; Commissioner of Assize: Lancaster, 1960; Chelmsford, 1961; Bodmin, 1963. Recorder of Bradford, 1958-64. *Address:* Central Criminal Court, EC4. *Club:* Royal Air Force.

**GILLMORE, Air Vice-Marshal Alan David,** CB 1955; CBE 1944; RAF (retired); *b* 17 Oct. 1905; *s* of late Rev. David Sandeman Gillmore and Allis Emily Widmer; *m* 1931, Kathleen Victoria Morris; three *s*. *Educ:* St Dunstan's Sch., Burnham-on-Sea; King's Sch., Ely. RAF Cadet Coll., Cranwell, Lincs, 1923-25; Commission in RAF, 1925. Commandant RAF Staff Coll., Bracknell, 1951-53; Senior Air Staff Officer, Far East Air Force, 1953-56; Senior Air Staff Officer, Home Command, 1956-59; retired 1959. *Address:* Mullenders, Swan Lane, Burford, Oxon. *Clubs:* Royal Air Force, United Hunts.

**GILMAN, Horace James,** CBE 1944 (OBE 1942); DSO 1942; TD 1945; Director (1957) Wm Cory & Son Ltd and many subsidiary companies; also Director: John Kelly Ltd, Belfast; Rea Ltd, Liverpool; *b* 7 June 1907; *s* of late Owen H. Gilman, Liverpool; *m* 1937, Barbara, *d* of late W. H. Law, West Kirby, Wirral; no *c*. *Educ:* Liverpool Coll. Joined RASC (TA), 1930; Major, 1939; served in: France, 1940; Western Desert, 1941-43; Italy, 1944-45; Brig., 1944-45; Hon. Brig., TARO, 1946. Chief of Fuel and Power Division, CCG, 1946-48. Hon. Freeman of Company of Watermen and Lightermen of the River Thames (Master, 1970); Past Pres. Assoc. of Master Lightermen and Barge Owners of Port of London. *Address:* 6 Zetland House, Marloes Road, W8. *T:* 01-937 6557. *Clubs:* Swedish; Castle (Rochester).

**GILMOUR, Andrew,** CMG 1949; Malayan Civil Service, retired; Secretary, British European Association, Singapore, since Oct. 1956; also Secretary, Tanglin Trust Ltd, Raeburn Park School Ltd; Editor, BEAM; *b* 18 July 1898; *s* of late James Parlane Gilmour, Solicitor, Burntisland, and late Mima Simpson; *m* Nelle Twigg; two *s* three *d* (and one *s* killed in action). *Educ:* Royal High Sch., Edinburgh; Edinburgh Univ. (MA Hons Classics, 1920). Served European War, 1914-18, Argyll and Sutherland Highlanders, 1915-17. Appointed to Malayan Civil Service, 1921; Asst Controller of Labour, 1923-26; Head of Preventive Service, Singapore, 1927; Resident, Labuan, 1928-29; District Officer, Jasin, 1929-30, Ulu Kelantan, 1930-36; Asst Colonial Sec., SS, 1936-38; Registrar-Gen. of Statistics, SS and FMS, 1938-39; Shipping Controller, Singapore, 1939-41; Defence Intelligence Officer, Hong Kong, Dec. 1941; interned Hong Kong 1942-45; Sec. for Economic Affairs, Singapore, 1946-52; Staff Grade, MCS, 1947; Chm. N Borneo Rubber Commn, 1949; MEC and MLC Singapore (nominated official); acted as Colonial Sec., Singapore, June-Aug. 1948 and March-April 1952; ret. from Colonial Service, 1953; Planning Economist, UN Technical Assistance Mission, Cambodia, 1953-55; Economic Survey Commissioner, British Honduras, 1956. *Recreations:* cricket (Hon. Life Pres., Singapore Cricket Club); philately (Patron, Singapore Stamp Club). *Address:* PO Box 2474, Singapore. *T:* 77247; 103 Ngee Ann Building, Singapore 9. *T:* 39135. *Clubs:* Singapore Cricket (Hon. Life Pres.); various other Singapore.

**GILMOUR, Ian (Hedworth John Little);** MP (C) Central Norfolk since Nov. 1962; Parliamentary Under-Secretary of State, Ministry of Defence, since 1970; *b* 8 July 1926; *er s* of Lt-Col Sir John Little Gilmour, 2nd Baronet, *qv*; *m* 1951, Lady Caroline Margaret Montagu-Douglas-Scott, *yr d* of 8th Duke of Buccleuch and Queensberry, *qv*; four *s* one *d*. *Educ:* Eton; Balliol Coll., Oxford. Served with Grenadier Guards, 1944-47; 2nd Lieut 1945. Called to the Bar, Inner Temple, 1952. Editor, The Spectator, 1954-59. 1952. *Publication:* The Body Politic, 1969. *Address:* The Ferry House, Old Isleworth, Mddx. *T:* 01-560 6769; Thwaite House, Aldborough, Norfolk. *T:* Hanworth 341. *Clubs:* White's; Norfolk (Norwich).

**GILMOUR, Col Sir John (Edward),** 3rd Bt, *cr* 1897; DSO 1945; TD; DL; JP; MP (C) East Fife since 1961; Fife and Forfar Yeomanry; Chairman, Conservative and Unionist Party in Scotland, 1965-67; *b* 24 Oct. 1912; *o s* of Col Rt Hon. Sir John Gilmour, 2nd Bt, GCVO, DSO, MP, and Mary Louise (*d* 1919), *e d* of late E. T. Lambert, Telham Court, Battle, Sussex; *S* father, 1940; *m* 1941, Ursula Mabyn, *yr d* of F. O. Wills, Cote Lodge, Westbury-on-Trym, Bristol; two *s*. *Educ:* Eton; Trinity Hall, Cambridge. Served War of 1939-45 (DSO). Bt Col 1950; Brig., Royal Company of Archers (Queen's Body Guard for Scotland). DL Fife, 1953. *Heir:* *s* John Gilmour [*b* 15 July 1944; *m* 1967, Valerie, *yr d* of late G. W. Russell, and of Mrs William Wilson]. *Address:* Montrave, Leven, Fife. *TA:* Leven. *T:* Leven 2159. *Clubs:* Cavalry, Leander; New (Edinburgh); Conservative (Edinburgh and Glasgow).
*See also Dame Anne Bryans, Viscount Younger.*

**GILMOUR, Sir John (Little),** of Liberton and Craigmillar, 2nd Bt, *cr* 1926; a stockbroker; late Lieut-Col Grenadier Guards; RARO; *b* 5 June 1899; *e s* of Sir Robert Gilmour, 1st Bt, CB, CVO, DSO, and Lady Susan Lygon (*d* 1962, as Lady Susan Gilmour, DBE), 2nd *d* of 6th Earl Beauchamp; *S* father, 1939; *m* 1st, 1922, Hon. Victoria Cadogan (who obtained a divorce, 1929), *y d* of late Visc. Chelsea and Hon. Lady Meux; one *s* one *d*.; 2nd, 1930, Lady Mary Kenyon Slaney, *d* of 3rd Duke of Abercorn, KG; one *s*. *Educ:* Eton. *Recreations:* shooting, fishing, golf. *Heir:* *s* Ian Hedworth John Gilmour, *qv*. *Address:* Carolside, Earlston, Berwickshire. *T:* Earlston 272. *Clubs:* White's, Buck's; New (Edinburgh).
*See also Sir J. G. S. Beith, Sir William Dugdale, Sir H. M. Knatchbull-Hugessen, Baron Rankeillour.*

**GILMOUR, John Scott Lennox,** MA, FLS; Director, University Botanic Garden, and Fellow of Clare College, Cambridge, since 1951; *b* London, 28 Sept. 1906; *s* of late T. L. Gilmour, CBE, and Elizabeth, *o d* of late Sir John S. Keltie; *m* 1935, Molly, *y d* of late Rev. M. Berkley; three *d*. *Educ:* Uppingham Sch.; Clare Coll., Cambridge. Curator of the Herbarium and Botanical Museum, Cambridge, 1930-31; Asst Dir of Royal

Botanic Gardens, Kew, 1931-46; seconded to Petroleum Div., Min. of Fuel and Power, as Principal Officer, 1940-45. Dir, Royal Horticultural Society's Garden, Wisley, Surrey, 1946-51. Sec., Systematics Assoc., 1937-46, Chm., 1952-55; Pres., Botanical Soc. of the British Isles, 1947-51; Chm. Internat. Commn on Horticultural Nomenclature, 1952-66, and International Cttee on Nomenclatural Stabilization, 1954; Rapporteur, Internat. Commission on the Nomenclature of Cultivated Plants, 1956-65, Chm., 1965-; Brit. Rep., Council of Internat. Soc. Hort. Sci., 1960-. Royal Horticultural Society: Victoria Medal of Honour in Horticulture, 1957; Mem. Council, 1957-61, 1962-66, 1968-; Chm., Orchid Cttee, 1964-; Veitch Gold Medal, 1966. Cons., new Botanic Garden at Ramat Hanadiv, Israel, 1964-68; Sec.-Treas. the Classification Society, 1964-68, Vice-Pres., 1968-; Mem. Adv. Cttee Hunt Bot. Library, Pittsburgh, 1961-; Mem. Council, Bibliogr. Soc., 1963-68. First Chm., Cambridge Humanists, 1955-57; Dir, Rationalist Press Assoc., 1961-. *Publications:* British Botanists, 1944; Wild Flowers of the Chalk, 1947; Wild Flowers (in New Naturalist Series with S. M. Walters), 1954; contributions to botanical, bibliographical, and rationalist jls, Jt Editor the New Naturalist, since 1943. *Recreations:* music, book-collecting. *Address:* Cory Lodge, Botanic Garden, Cambridge. *T:* Cambridge 55776. *Club:* Oxford and Cambridge University.

**GILMOUR, Michael Hugh Barrie;** solicitor, retired; Chief Legal Adviser and Solicitor to British Railway Board, 1963-Jan. 1970 (Secretary to Board, Oct. 1965-Jan. 1968); *b* 1 Dec. 1904; *e surv s* of late Thomas Lennox Gilmour, CBE, Barrister, and Elizabeth Hervey, *o c* of late Sir John Scott Keltie, LLD; *m* 1937, Elisabeth, *o d* of late Francis Edward Cuming; one *d*. *Educ:* Leighton Park; abroad. Solicitors Office, Great Western Railway Company, 1929; Solicitor to Company, 1945-47; Solicitor to Railway Executive in Western Region, 1948-49; Chief Solicitor (1949) and Chief Legal Adviser (1951), British Transport Commission, until 1962. Served War of 1939-45, RAFVR, July 1940-Sept. 1941 (Squadron Leader). *Recreations:* walking, reading. *Address:* 55 Strand-on-the-Green, Chiswick, W4. *Club:* Garrick.

**GILPIN, John;** ballet dancer; *b* 10 Feb. 1930; twin *s* of J. and L. M. Gilpin; *m* 1960, Sally Judd. *Educ:* Cone-Ripman Coll. Michael, in Peter Pan, 1942, 1943; and other rôles (stage, films, and broadcasting) until 1945, when he decided to devote himself exclusively to dancing. Awarded Adeline Genée Gold Medal, 1943. With Ballet Rambert, 1945-48; Roland Petit's Ballets de Paris, 1948-49; Grand Ballet du Marquis de Cuevas, 1949-50; Leading dancer, Festival Ballet, 1950-60; guest dancer, Covent Garden, 1961-. Prix Vaslav Nijinsky, of French Academy of Music and Dance, 1957; Paris International Dance Festival Gold Medal, 1964. *Relevant publication:* John Gilpin by Cyril Swinson. *Recreation:* music. *Address:* c/o Covent Garden Opera House, WC2.

**GILPIN, Rt. Rev. William Percy;** *b* 26 July 1902; *e s* of late Percy William and Ethel Annie Gilpin. *Educ:* King Edward's, Birmingham; Keble Coll., Oxford. BA 1st class, Theology, 1925; MA 1928. Curate of Solihull, Warwicks, 1925-28; Vice-Principal of St Paul's Coll., Burgh, 1928-30; Chaplain of Chichester Theological Coll., 1930-33; Vicar of Manaccan with St Anthony, 1933-36; Vicar of St Mary, Penzance, 1936-44; Dir of Religious Education, Gloucester, 1944-51; Canon Missioner of Gloucester, 1946-52; Archdeacon of Southwark, 1952-55; Bishop Suffragan of Kingston-upon-Thames, 1952-70. Examining Chaplain to: Bishop of Truro, 1934-44, Bishop of Gloucester, 1945-52. *Recreation:* general railway matters. *Address:* 50 Lower Broad Street, Ludlow, Salop. *T:* Ludlow 3376.

**GILRAY, Colin Macdonald,** OBE 1951; MC; Principal, Scotch College, Melbourne, Australia, 1934-53; *b* 17 March 1885; 3rd *s* of Prof. Thomas Gilray, MA, LLD (Edinburgh) and Annie Macdonald; *m* 1917, Ethel Muriel, *d* of Arthur Standish, New Plymouth, NZ; one *d*. *Educ:* Otago Boys' High Sch. and Otago Univ. (BA), NZ Rhodes Scholar 1907, University Coll., Oxford, BA 1910, MA 1923 (2nd cl. Greats), Rugger Blue, Scottish and NZ International. Asst Master Mill Hill Sch., 1910-13; called to Bar, Middle Temple, 1913; 2nd Lieut XIIIth Rifle Brigade 1916; A/Capt. 1917 (MC); Capt. 21st OCB, 1918; engaged in legal practice, 1919-22, Otago, NZ; Headmaster John McGlashan Coll., Dunedin, NZ, 1922-34. Member: Otago Univ. Council, 1925-34; New Zealand Univ. Senate, 1927-34; NZ Rhodes Scholarship Selection Cttee, 1922-34; School Board (Melbourne), 1936-52; Council of University of Melbourne, 1939-63 (Dep.-Chancellor, 1954-57, 1959-61 and Mem. Council of Internat. House, 1959-70); Chm. Headmasters' Conference of Australia, 1949-51 (Sec., 1954-65); Mem. Prime Minister's Cttee on Tertiary Education, 1961-65. FACE 1960. Hon. MA 1936 and Hon. LLD 1956, Melbourne Univ. *Recreation:* reading. *Address:* Yarra Braes Road, Eltham, Victoria, Australia. *Clubs:* Melbourne (Melbourne); Dunedin (Dunedin).

**GILROY, John T. Y.,** ARCA, FRSA; Artist; Portrait painter; Landscape painter; *b* 30 May 1898; *s* of John William Gilroy, artist; *m* 1924, Gwendoline Peri-Short; one *s*; *m* 1950, Elizabeth Outram Thwaite. *Educ:* King's Coll., Newcastle on Tyne; Royal College of Art, London. Served European War, 1916-18, Army. British Institute Scholar, 1921; RCA Travelling Scholar, 1922. Exhibition, Upper Grosvenor Galls, 1970. Creator of Guinness posters, also of Royle's publications of humour. *Publications:* (Illustrated) McGill, The Story of a University, 1960; Rough Island Story (News Reel of Depression), 1931-35. *Recreations:* golf, travel. *Address:* 10 Holland Park Road, Kensington, W14. *T:* 01-937 8954. *Clubs:* Garrick, Green Room.

**GILROY, His Eminence Sir Norman (Thomas), Cardinal;** *see* Sydney, Archbishop of, (RC).

**GILSON, Etienne,** DLitt, PhD, LLD; Philosopher and Historian; *b* 1884. *Educ:* Sorbonne. Prof. University of Lille, 1913; University of Strasbourg, 1919; Prof. of Medieval Philosophy, Sorbonne, 1921-32; Dir of Medieval Studies, University of Toronto, 1929; Prof. Coll. de France, 1932; retired, 1951. Corresp. Mem. British Acad.; Fellow French Acad. Holds numerous hon. degrees. Commandeur de la Légion d'Honneur; Croix de Guerre; Orden Pour le Mérite. *Publications:* Le Thomisme, 1922; La Philosophie de St Bonaventure, 1924; Introduction à l'étude de St Augustin, 1929; L'esprit de la philosophie médiévale, 1932; La théologie mystique de St Bernard, 1934 (Eng. trans. 1955); Le réalisme méthodique, 1935; Christianisme et philosophie, 1936; The Unity of Philosophical Experience, 1937; Héloïse et Abélard (Eng. trans. 1953); Reason and Revelation in the Middle Ages, 1938; Dante et la Philosophie, 1939; God and Philosophy, 1940; La philosophie au moyen âge, 1945; Being and Some Philosophers, 1949; L'école des muses, 1950 (Eng. trans., Choir of Muses, 1954); Jean

Duns Scot, 1952; History of Christian Philosophy in the Middle Ages, 1954; Painting and Reality, 1957; Elements of Christian Philosophy, 1959; The Philosopher and Theology, 1962; Modern Philosophy, 1963; Introduction aux arts du beau, 1963; Matières et formes, 1964; The Spirit of Thomism, 1964; Recent Philosophy, 1966. *Address:* 6 rue Collet, Vermenton (Yonne), France; 8 Elmsley Hall, Toronto, Ont., Canada, *T:* WA 4.3845.

**GILSON, John Cary,** CBE 1967 (OBE 1945); Director, Medical Research Council's Pneumoconiosis Research Unit, since 1952; *b* 9 Aug. 1912; 2nd *s* of late Robert Cary Gilson, MA and Marianne C. Gilson, MA (*née* Dunstall); *m* 1945, Margaret Evelyn Worthington, MA, *d* of late Robert A. Worthington, OBE, FRCS; two *s* one *d*. *Educ:* Haileybury Sch.; Gonville and Caius Coll., Cambridge. MB, BChir Cantab 1937; MRCP 1940; FRCP 1956. 1st Asst, London Hosp.; Staff of RAF Inst. of Aviation Medicine, 1940-46; Mem. Scientific Staff of MRC, 1946-, at Pneumoconiosis Research Unit, Asst Ed., Brit. Jl Industr. Med., 1955-64, and on Ed. Bd of various other jls; Pres., British Occupational Hygiene Soc., 1960-61; Hon. Life Mem., NY Acad. of Sciences, 1966. *Publications:* papers on pulmonary physiology and industrial medicine in scientific jls. *Recreations:* domestic engineering; clouds. *Address:* Oakleigh, The Common, Dinas Powis, Glamorgan CF6 4DL. *T:* Dinas Powis 2281.

**GIMSON, Christopher,** CIE 1943; BA; Indian Civil Service (retired); *b* 24 Dec. 1886; *s* of Josiah Mentor Gimson; unmarried. *Educ:* Oundle; Emmanuel Coll., Cambridge. Entered ICS 1911; late Political Agent in Manipur; retired, 1948. *Recreations:* walking, ball games, music. *Address:* Glenalmond, Knighton Grange Road, Leicester. *Clubs:* East India and Sports; Leicestershire Golf (Leicester).

**GIMSON, Sir Franklin Charles,** KCMG 1946 (CMG 1945); BA Oxon; *b* 10 Sept. 1890; *s* of late Rev. C. K. Gimson; *m* 1922, Margaret Dorothy, MBE, *d* of late Canon Ward; two *d*. *Educ:* Balliol Coll., Oxford. Cadet, Ceylon Civil Service, 1914; Controller of Labour, Ceylon, 1937; Colonial Sec., Hong Kong, 1941; Governor and C-in-C, Singapore, 1946-52. Freeman of City of Singapore, 1952; Hon. Doctor of Laws, University of Malaya, 1952. KStJ. *Recreations:* golf and walking. *Address:* Applegarth, Thornton-le-Dale, Pickering, Yorks. *Clubs:* United University, Royal Commonwealth Society.

**GIMSON, George Stanley,** QC (Scotland) 1961; *b* 1915. *Educ:* High School of Glasgow; Glasgow Univ. Advocate, 1949; Standing Junior Counsel, Department of Agriculture for Scotland and Forestry Commission, 1956-61. Mem., Board of Management: Edinburgh Central Hosps, 1960-70; Edinburgh Royal Victoria Hosps, 1970; Dir, Scottish Nat. Orchestra Soc. Ltd, 1962-; Trustee, Nat. Library of Scotland, 1963-. *Address:* 11 Royal Circus, Edinburgh. *T:* 031-225 8055. *Clubs:* Caledonian United Service, Northern (Edinburgh).

**GIMSON, Col Thomas William;** *b* 9 July 1904; 2nd *s* of late Thomas Wallis Gimson and Rosina Skerratt Forsyth; *m* 1958, Heather Mary, *d* of late Capt. P. D. C. Eliot, 14th Lancers, Indian Army, and of the Countess of Powis. *Educ:* Brighton Coll.; St John's Coll., Oxford. Commissioned North Staffs Regt; transferred Irish Guards, 1933; Internat. Force HQ, Saar Plebiscite, 1934; Palestine, 1938; Dunkirk, 1940; Combined Ops, 1943; NW Europe, 1944; Military Mission, Moscow, 1945; Military Attaché, Warsaw, 1946-48; Regtl Lt-Col comd Irish Guards, 1948-50; retd pay, 1950. *Address:* Les Pierrugues, Cavalaire, Var, France. *Clubs:* Guards, Turf.

**GINGER, Phyllis Ethel, (Mrs Leslie Durbin),** RWS 1958 (ARWS 1952); Free Lance artist since 1940; *b* 19 Oct. 1907; *m* 1940, Leslie Durbin, *qv*; one *s* one *d*. *Educ:* Tiffin's Girls' Sch., Kingston on Thames. LCC three years' scholarship at Central School of Arts and Crafts, 1937-39. Water colours for Pilgrim Trust Recording Britain Scheme, 1941-42; Royal Academy Exhibitor; Mem. of Senefelder Group (Artist Lithographers), 1940. Drawings and Lithographs purchased by: Washington State Library, 1941; Victoria and Albert Museum, 1952; London Museum, 1954; South London Art Gallery, 1960. *Publications:* Alexander the Circus Pony, 1941; illustrations to various books, including London by Mrs Robert Henrey, 1948. *Address:* 298 Kew Road, Kew, Richmond, Surrey. *T:* 01-940 2221.

**GINGOLD, Hermione Ferdinanda;** Actress; *b* 9 Dec.; *d* of James and Kate Gingold; *m* 1st, Michael Joseph (marr. diss.); one *s* (and one *s* decd); 2nd, Eric Maschwitz (marr. diss.). *Educ:* privately. Started as child actress at His Majesty's Theatre with Sir Herbert Tree in Pinkie and the Fairies. Played in Shakespeare at Old Vic and Stratford on Avon. Five years in intimate revue. O Dad, Poor Dad, Piccadilly, 1965; Highly Confidential, Cambridge, 1965. *Films:* Bell, Book and Candle, 1958; Gigi, 1959; Jules Verne's Rocket to the Moon, 1967. Many US television appearances. Has recorded Façade and Lysistrata. *Publications:* The World is Square, 1945; articles and short stories. *Address:* 400 East 59th Street, New York City 22, New York, USA.

**GINSBURG, David;** MP (Lab) Dewsbury since 1959; *b* 18 March 1921; *o s* of late N. Ginsburg; *m* 1954, Louise, *er d* of late S. P. Cassy. *Educ:* University Coll. Sch.; Balliol Coll., Oxford. Chm. OU Democratic Socialist Club, 1941; 2nd Cl, Hons Sch. of Politics, Philosophy and Economics, 1941. Commissioned Oxford and Bucks LI, 1942; Capt. Intelligence duties, 1944-45. Senior Research Officer, Govt Social Survey, 1946-52; Sec. of Research Dept of Labour Party and Sec. of Home Policy Sub-Cttee of National Executive Cttee, 1952-59; Market Research Consultant; Chm., Parly. and Scientific Cttee, 1968-. Broadcaster. *Publications:* miscellaneous articles and book reviews in contemporary publications. *Recreations:* walking, swimming, opera. *Address:* 3 Bell Moor, East Heath Road, NW3.

**GINSBURY, Norman;** playwright; *b* Nov. 1902; *s* of late J. S. and Rachel Cecily Ginsbury; *m* 1945, Dorothy Jennings. *Educ:* London University. Plays produced: Viceroy Sarah, Arts Theatre, 1934, Whitehall Theatre, 1935; Walk in the Sun, "Q", and Embassy, 1939; Take Back Your Freedom (with late Winifred Holtby), Neighbourhood, 1940; The Firstcomers, Bradford Civic Playhouse, 1944; The First Gentleman (written, 1935), New and Savoy, 1945; Belasco, New York, 1956; The Gambler (from the story of Dostoievsky), Embassy, 1946; The Happy Man, New, 1948; Portrait by Lawrence (with M. Moiseiwitsch), Theatre Royal, Stratford, 1949; School for Rivals, Bath Assembly and Old Vic, Bristol, 1949. Also following adaptations of plays by Henrik Ibsen: Ghosts, Vaudeville, 1937; Enemy of the People, Old Vic, 1939; Peer Gynt, Old Vic Season at New Theatre, 1944; A Doll's House, Winter Garden, 1946; John Gabriel Borkman, Mermaid, 1961. A new version of Strindberg's Dance of Death at Tyrone Guthrie Theatre, Minneapolis; and at Yvonne Arnaud Theatre, Guildford, 1966; for the Mayflower 350th anniv., The Forefathers, Athenaeum Theatre, Plymouth, 1970. *Publications:* Viceroy Sarah, 1934; Take Back Your Freedom (collab.), 1939; The First Gentleman, 1946; The Fabulous Moneymaker (prod TV 1959); and the following versions of plays by Ibsen: Ghosts, 1938; Enemy of the People, 1939; Peer Gynt, 1945; A Doll's House, 1950; John Gabriel Borkman, 1960; Rosmersholm, 1961; Pillars of Society, 1962. The Old Lags' League (from a story by W. Pett Ridge) published in The Best One-Act Plays of 1960-61; The Shoemaker And The Devil (from a story by Tchehov) published in the Best Short Plays of 1968 (New York). *Address:* Barum Lodge, 25 Prideaux Road, Eastbourne, Sussex. *T:* Eastbourne 29603.

**GIPPSLAND, Bishop of,** since 1959; **Rt. Rev. David Arthur Garnsey;** *b* 31 July 1909; *s* of Canon Arthur Henry Garnsey and Bertha Edith Frances Garnsey (*née* Benn); *m* 1934, Evangeline Eleanor Wood; two *s* two *d*. *Educ:* Trinity and Sydney Grammar Schs; St Paul's Coll., University of Sydney; New Coll., Oxford. University of Sydney, BA (1st cl. Latin and Greek) 1930; Travelling Sec. Australian SCM, 1930-31; NSW Rhodes Scholar, 1931, New Coll. Oxford, BA (2nd cl. Lit. Hum.) 1933, 2nd cl. Theol. 1934, MA 1937; Ripon Hall, Oxford, 1933. Deacon, 1934; Priest, 1935; Curate, St Mary the Virgin (University Church), and Inter-Collegiate Sec. of SCM, Oxford, 1934-38; St Saviour's Cathedral, Goulburn, NSW, 1938-41; Rector of Young, NSW, 1941-45; Gen. Sec. Australian SCM, 1945-48; Exam. Chap. to Bp of Goulburn, 1939-45, 1948-58; Head Master Canberra Grammar Sch., 1948-58; Canon of St Saviour's Cathedral, Goulburn, 1949-58. Hon. Doctor of Theology (ThD), Australian Coll. of Theology, 1955. Coronation Medal, 1953. *Publications:* booklets for study. *Recreation:* tennis. *Address:* Bishopscourt, PO Box 383, Sale, Victoria 3850, Australia. *T:* Sale 2046.

**GIPSON, Lawrence Henry,** PhD; Professor Emeritus, Lehigh University; *b* 7 Dec. 1880; *s* of Albert Eugene and Lina Maria Gipson (*née* West); *m* 1909, Jeannette Reed; no *c*. *Educ:* College of Idaho; University of Idaho; University of Oxford; Yale Univ. AB Idaho, 1903: Rhodes Schol., University of Oxford, 1904-07; BA 1907, MA 1951, PhD Yale, 1918. Prof. of History, College of Idaho, 1907-10; Farnham Fellow, Yale Univ. 1910-11; Prof. of History, Wabash Coll., 1911-17; Prof. of History and Political Science, Wabash Coll., 1917-24; Bulkley Fellow, Yale, 1917-18; Prof. of History and Govt and Head of Dept, 1924-46; Research Prof. of History, 1946-52, Professor Emeritus 1952-, Lehigh Univ.; Harold Vyvyan Harmsworth Prof. of Amer. History, University of Oxford, 1951-52; Fellow Queen's Coll., Oxford, 1951-52; Hon. Fellow, Lincoln Coll., 1965; Hon. Consultant in Amer. Hist. Library of Congress, 1965-67. Co-founder and past Pres. of Conference on British Studies; Mem., various hist. socs; past Pres. Pa Hist. Assoc.; past Mem. Bd of Eds, Amer. Historical Rev.; past Mem. Council of Inst. Early Amer. Hist. and Culture; holder of various grants in aid from: Amer. Council of Learned Societies, Amer. Soc. Sc., Res. Council, Lehigh Univ. Inst. of Res., and Rockefeller Foundation. Hon. Mem. Pa Hist. Junto, 1955; Phi Beta Kappa. Hon. DLitt, 1949; LHD 1951; LLD 1953; LHD 1955; LHD 1961; LLD 1962; LLD 1963; DLitt 1969. Porter Prize, Yale, 1918; Winsor Prize, Amer. Hist. Assoc., 1921; Loubat Prize, 1948; Bancroft Prize, 1950; Athenæum (Philadelphia) Award, 1953; Pulitzer Prize in History, 1962. *Publications:* Jared Ingersoll: A Study of American Loyalism in Relation to British Colonial Government, 1920; The Moravian White River Indian Mission, 1938; Lewis Evans, 1939; Vols I-XV The British Empire before the American Revolution, 1936-70, Vols. I-III, Rev., 1958-60; Some Reflections upon the American Revolution and Other Essays in American Colonial History, 1942; The American Revolution as an Aftermath of the Great War for the Empire and Other Essays in American Colonial History, 1950; The British Empire in the Eighteenth Century, 1952; The Coming of the Revolution, 1763-1775, 1954; contrb. to various jls. *Address:* 825 Delaware Avenue, Bethlehem, Pa 18015, USA. *T:* 868-1649; (professional address) The Library, Lehigh University, Bethlehem, Pa 18015, USA. *Club:* Franklin Inn (Philadelphia).

**GIRDLESTONE, Cuthbert Morton,** Chevalier de la Légion d'Honneur; Professor of French, King's College, Newcastle upon Tyne (University of Durham), 1926-60, retired; *b* Bovey-Tracey, Devon, 17 Sept. 1895; *s* of James Hammond le Breton Girdlestone and Edith Margaret Coles; *m* 1923, Anne Marie Micheletti; two *d*. *Educ:* Southey Hall, Worthing; Immaculée Conception, Pau; Lycée de Pau; Sorbonne, Paris; Trinity Coll., Cambridge (Senior Scholar, 1920). Bachelier-ès-lettres, 1913; Licencié-ès-lettres, 1915; BA Cantab, 1921; MA Cantab, 1924. Lecturer in French, University of Cambridge, 1922. *Publications:* Dreamer and Striver: The Poetry of Frédéric Mistral, 1937; Mozart et ses concertos pour piano, 1939; Jean-Philippe Rameau: his life and work, 1957; Louis-François Ramond: sa vie et son œuvre littéraire, 1968; articles on music, architecture, French literature. *Address:* 1 Parc de la Bérengère, Saint Cloud, France.

**GIRDWOOD, John Graham,** CBE 1946; CA; *b* 1890; 2nd *s* of late David Girdwood, Glasgow; *m* 1924, Janet Ellis Kerr, *d* of late John Hood, Port Glasgow; no *c*. Controller of Canteens, Ministry of Supply, 1941-46; Controller of Admiralty Canteens, 1943-46; Chm. Min. of Health House Building Costs Cttee for England and Wales, 1947-53; Chm. of Aerated Bread Co. Ltd, 1948-58; Chm. of Wm Beardmore & Co. Ltd, 1954-57. Mem. of Council of Inst. of Chartered Accountants of Scotland, 1952-55. *Recreation;* golf. *Address:* 17 High Sheldon, Sheldon Avenue, N6. *T:* 01-348 2364. *Clubs:* Junior Carlton, Royal Automobile; Royal and Ancient (St Andrews).

**GIRDWOOD, Ronald Haxton,** MD, PhD, FRCP, FRCPE, FRCPath; Professor of Therapeutics, University of Edinburgh, since 1962; Physician to Royal Infirmary of Edinburgh since 1951; *b* 19 March 1917; *s* of late Thomas Girdwood; *m* 1945, Mary Elizabeth, *d* of late Reginald Williams, Calstock, Cornwall; one *s* one *d*. *Educ:* Daniel Stewart's Coll., Edinburgh; University of Edinburgh; University of Michigan. MB, ChB (Hons) Edinburgh 1939; Ettles Schol., Leslie Gold Medallist, Royal Victoria Hosp.; Tuberculosis Trust Gold Medallist, Wightman, Beaney and Keith Memorial Prize Winner, 1939; MD (Gold Medal for thesis), 1954. Pres. Edinburgh Univ. Church of Scotland Soc., 1938-39. Served RAMC, 1942-46; Nutrition Research Officer and Officer i/c Med. Div. in India and Burma. Lectr in Medicine, University of Edinburgh, 1946; Rockefeller Research Fellow, University of Michigan, 1948-49; Cons. Phys., Chalmers Hosp., Edinburgh, 1950-51; Sen. Lectr in Med. and Cons. Phys., Royal Infirmary, 1951; Vis.

Lectr, Dept of Pharmacology, Yale Univ., 1956; Reader in Med., University of Edinburgh, 1958; Examiner for RCPE; sometime External Examiner for Universities of London, Sheffield, St Andrews, Dundee and Glasgow; Member: Council, RCPE, 1966-70; South-Eastern Reg. Hosp. Board (Scotland), 1965-69; Board of Management, Royal Infirmary, Edinburgh, 1958-64; Chairman: Scottish Group of Hæmophilia Soc., 1954-60; Non-Professorial Medical Teachers and Research Workers Gp Cttee (Scot.) of BMA, 1956-62; Scottish Gp of Nutrition Soc., 1961-62; Pres. Brit. Soc. for Hæmatology, 1963-64; Member: Coun. Brit. Soc. of Gastroenterology, 1964-68; Coun. of Nutrition Soc., 1957-60 and 1961-64; numerous Med. Socs; Lay Mem., Scottish Soc. of Artists; Chm. Bd of Management, Scottish Med. Jl and Mem. of Editorial Bds of Blood, Brit. Jl of Hæmatology and of Pharmakotherapia; Mem. Editorial Bd, Brit. Jl of Nutrition, 1960-65; British Council visitor to W African Hosps, 1963; Visiting Prof. and WHO Consultant, India, 1965. Cullen Prize, RCPE, 1970. *Publications:* numerous, particularly in relation to nutrition, hæmatology and gastroenterology. Contrib. Davidson's Principles and Practice of Medicine, 1968; (ed) (with A. N. Smith) Malabsorption, 1969; (ed) (with Alstead and Macgregor) Textbook of Medical Treatment, 1971. *Recreations:* photography, painting. *Address:* 2 Hermitage Drive, Edinburgh EH10 6DD. *T:* (home) 031-447 5137, (hospital) 031-229 2477 (ext. 165). *Clubs:* Royal Societies; University Staff (Edinburgh).

**GIRI, Varahagiri Venkata;** President of India since 1969; *b* Berhampore, 10 Aug. 1894. *Educ:* Nat. Univ. of Ireland. Barrister-at-law. During early career as Trade Union leader, appts include: Gen. Sec. and Pres., All India Railwaymen's Fedn; Pres. (twice) All India TUC; Indian workers' deleg. to Internat. Labour Conf., Geneva; workers' rep., Second Round Table Conf., London, 1931. Member, Central Legislative Assembly for several years. Minister of Labour, Industries, Cooperation and Commerce, Madras Ministry, 1937-39; Minister in Madras Govt, 1946; High Commissioner for India in Ceylon, 1947-51; Minister of Labour, Govt of India, 1952-54. Governor: Uttar Pradesh, 1957-60; Kerala, 1960-65; Mysore, 1965-67. Vice-Pres. of India, 1967-69. *Address:* Rashtrapati Bhavan, New Delhi, India.

**GISBOROUGH,** 3rd Baron, *cr* 1917; **Thomas Richard John Long Chaloner;** *b* 1 July 1927; *s* of 2nd Baron and Esther Isabella Madaleine (*d* 1970), *yr d* of late Charles O. Hall, Eddlethorpe; *S* father 1951; *m* 1960, Shane, *e d* of Sidney Newton, London, W8 and *g d* of Sir Louis Newton, 1st Bt; two *s. Educ:* Eton. 16th/5th Lancers, 1948-52; Captain Northumberland Hussars, 1955-61; Lt-Col Green Howards (Territorials), 1967-69. CC Guisborough, 1964-. *Recreations:* all sports. *Heir: s* Hon. Thomas Peregrine Long Chaloner, *b* 17 Jan. 1961. *Address:* Gisborough House, Guisborough, North Yorks. *T:* Guisborough 2002. *Club:* Northern Counties (Newcastle upon Tyne).

**GISCARD d'ESTAING, Valéry;** Croix de Guerre (1939-45); Minister of Finance, France, since June 1969; *b* Coblence, 2 Feb. 1926; *s* of Edmond Giscard d'Estaing and May Bardoux; *m* 1952, Anne-Aymone de Brantes; two *s* two *d. Educ:* Lycée Janson-de-Sailly, Paris; Ecole Polytechnique; Ecole Nationale d'Administration. Inspection of Finances: Deputy, 1952; Inspector, 1954; Dep. Dir, Cabinet of Président du Conseil, June-Dec. 1954. Elected Deputy for Puy-de-Dôme, 1956; re-elected for Clermont N and SW, Nov. 1958, for Puy-de Dôme, Nov-Dec. 1962, for Clermont N and SW, March 1967 and June 1968; Sec. of State for Finance, 1959; Minister of Finance, Jan.-April 1962; Minister of Finance and Economic Affairs, April-Nov. 1962 and Dec. 1962-Jan. 1966. Pres., Nat. Fedn of Indep. Republicans, 1966- (also a Founder); Pres., comm. des finances, de l'économie générale et du plan de l'Assemblée nationale, 1967-68. Mayor of Chamalières, 1967-69. Deleg. to Assembly of UN, 1956, 1957, 1958. Co-founder, Soc. Infi-Press, 1968. *Address:* (private) 11 rue Bénouville, Paris 16e.

**GISH, Lillian Diana;** Actress; *b* 14 Oct. 1899. *Educ:* privately. Began acting in theatre at five years of age and at twelve entered motion pictures. Last played Katrina in Crime and Punishment (with John Gielgud), 1948. The Curious Savage, 1950, Miss Mabel, 1951 (USA). Acting mainly on television, 1952; in play, The Trip to Bountiful (for the Theatre Guild), 1953-54; The Chalk Garden, 1957; The Family Reunion, 1958; directed, The Beggar's Opera, 1958; All the Way House, 1960-61 (won Drama Critics and Pulitzer prize as best play); A Passage to India, play (Chicago), 1962-63; Too True to be Good (G. B. Shaw's play) (New York), 1963; Romeo and Juliet (Stratford Festival Theatre), 1965; Anya (musical), 1967; I Never Sang for my Father, 1968. Lillian Gish and the Movies: the art of film, 1900-28 (concert programmes), Moscow, Paris, London and USA, 1969-70. *Early films include:* Birth of a Nation; Intolerance; Souls Triumphant; Hearts of the World; The Great Love; Broken Blossoms; Way Down East; The Orphans of the Storm; The White Sister; Romola; *later films include:* The Night of the Hunter, 1954; The Cobweb, 1955; Orders to Kill, 1957; The Unforgiven, 1959; Follow Me Boys, 1966; Warning Shot, 1966; The Comedians, 1967. Frequent appearances on television; three TV plays, 1962; TV plays, 1963; Arsenic and Old Lace, TV, 1969. Hon. degree of Doctor of Fine Arts, Rollins Coll., Fla; Hon. Doctor of the Humanities, Holyoke Coll. *Publications:* Lillian Gish: an autobiography, 1968; Lillian Gish, The Movies, Mr Griffith and Me, 1969. *Recreation:* travel. *Address:* 430 East 57th Street, New York, NY 10022, USA.

**GISHFORD, Anthony Joseph,** CBE 1964; MA Oxon; Chairman of English Opera Group Ltd; Director, Faber Music Ltd; *b* 1908; *y s* of Edward Alexander Gishford and Florence Hawkes; unmarried. *Educ:* Westminster Sch.; Handelshochschule, St Gallen, Switzerland; Wadham Coll., Oxford. Served War of 1939-45, Intelligence Corps, 1939-42; Grenadier Guards, 1942-45. Editor of Tempo, 1947-58. Mem. executive cttee (Hon. Sec., 1952-64) The Pilgrims; a Vice-Pres., Youth and Music. A Governor, Bridewell Royal Hospital and King Edward's School, Witley. *Publications:* The Correspondence of Richard Strauss and Hans von Bülow (trans.); Tribute to Benjamin Britten (ed). *Recreation:* gardening. *Address:* 4 The Grove, Highgate Village, N6. *T:* 01-340 2266. *Clubs:* Brooks's, Garrick, Pratt's; Century (new York).

**GITTINGS, Robert (William Victor),** CBE 1970; LittD Cantab, 1970; poet; biographer; playwright; *b* 1 Feb. 1911; *s* of late Surg.-Capt. Fred Claude Bromley Gittings, RN (retd) and late Dora Mary Brayshaw; *m* 1st, 1934, Katherine Edith Cambell (marriage dissolved); two *s*; 2nd, 1949, Joan Grenville Manton; one *d. Educ:* St Edward's Sch., Oxford; Jesus Coll., Cambridge (Scholar). 1st Cl. Historical Tripos, 1933. Research Student, and Research

Fellow, Jesus Coll., 1933-38. Supervisor in History, 1938-40; writer and producer for broadcasting, 1940-63; Professor: Vanderbilt University, Tennessee, 1966; Boston Univ., 1970. *Publications: poetry and verse-plays:* The Roman Road, 1932; The Story of Psyche, 1936; Wentworth Place, 1950; The Makers of Violence (Canterbury Festival), 1951; Through a Glass Lightly, 1952; Famous Meeting, 1953; Out of This Wood (sequence of plays), 1955; This Tower My Prison, 1961; Matters of Love and Death, 1968; Conflict at Canterbury, 1970; *biography and criticism:* John Keats: The Living Year, 1954; The Mask of Keats, 1956; Shakespeare's Rival, 1960; (ed) The Living Shakespeare, 1960; (ed with E. Hardy) Some Recollections by Emma Hardy, 1961; (with Jo Manton) The Story of John Keats, 1962; The Keats Inheritance, 1964; (ed) Selected Poems and Letters of John Keats, 1966; John Keats, 1968 (W. H. Smith Literary Award, 1969); John Keats: Selected Letters, 1970; The Odes of Keats, 1970; contrib. to Keats-Shelley Memorial Bulletin, Keats-Shelley Journal, etc. *Recreations:* most outdoor pursuits except blood-sports. *Address:* Dodds, East Dean, Chichester, Sussex. *T:* Singleton 243.

**GIULINI, Carlo Maria;** conductor; *b* 9 May 1914; *m*; three *s*. *Educ:* Accademia Santa Cecilia, Rome; played viola in Santa Cecilia orchestra, and under Bruno Walter and Klemperer. Début as conductor, Rome, 1944; formed Orchestra of Milan Radio, 1951; Principal Conductor, La Scala, Milan, 1953-55; début in Great Britain, conducting Verdi's Falstaff, Edinburgh Festival, 1955. Has conducted notable revivals of Don Carlos and Il Barbiere di Siviglia, Covent Garden. Closely associated with Philharmonia Orchestra, with whom he frequently appears: London, Edinburgh, Lucerne, Vienna and Leeds Festivals. Has also conducted in Holland, Israel and USA. *Recreation:* sailing.

**GIVEN, Edward Ferguson,** CMG 1968; Counsellor, HM Embassy, Beirut, since 1969; *b* 13 April 1919; *o s* of James K. Given, West Kilbride, Ayrshire; *m* 1st, 1946, Philida Naomi Bullwinkle; one *s*; 2nd, 1954, Kathleen Margaret Helena Kelly. *Educ:* Sutton County Sch.; University Coll., London. Served RA, 1939-46. Entered HM Foreign Service, 1946; 2nd Sec., Paris, 1949; 1st Sec., Rangoon, 1951; FO, 1953; Bahrain, 1957; HM Consul, Bordeaux, 1960; 1st Sec., FO, 1961; Counsellor, Office of Political Adviser to C-in-C Far East, Singapore, 1963; Counsellor, Moscow, 1967. *Recreation:* sailing. *Address:* c/o Foreign and Commonwealth Office, SW1.

**GIVEN, Rear-Adm. John Garnett Cranston,** CB 1955; CBE 1945 (OBE 1943); MIMechE, MIMarE; retired from Royal Navy, June 1955; *b* 21 Sept. 1902; *s* of late J. C. M. Given, MD, FRCP, and Mrs May Given, Liverpool; *m* 1931, Elizabeth Joyce (*née* Payne), Brenchley, Kent, and Durban, Natal; one *s* two *d*. *Educ:* King William's Coll., IOM; Charterhouse, Godalming. RNEC Keyham, 1922-25; HMS Hood, 1926; RNC Greenwich, 1928; Admiralty, 1930; HMS Berwick, China Station, 1933; HMS Neptune, 1940; Admiralty, 1942; HMS Howe, East Indies, 1944; Fleet Train, British Pacific Fleet, 1945; Asst Engineer-in-Chief, Admiralty, 1947; Commanding Officer Royal Naval Engineering Coll., Plymouth, 1948-51; idc 1952; Staff of Comdr-in-Chief, The Nore, 1953-55; Managing Dir, Parsons Marine Turbine Co., Wallsend, 1955-62. *Recreations:* fishing and walking. *Address:* c/o Westminster Bank, 26 The Haymarket, SW1. *Club:* United Service.

**GLADDING, Donald,** CIE 1936; ICS (retired); *b* 22 Aug. 1888; *s* of Rev. Thomas Gladding; *m* 1915, Evelyn Avis McArthur (*d* 1951); no *c*. *Educ:* St Olave's, London; Brasenose Coll., Oxford. ICS 1913; Magistrate and Collector, Bengal, 1928; Deputy Sec. to Govt of India, Home Dept, 1931; Finance Sec., Govt of Bengal, 1933-39; Agent, Calcutta Electric Supply Corporation, Ltd, 1940-49. *Recreation:* golf. *Address:* Red Gables, Fleet, Hants.

**GLADSTONE, Sir (Erskine) William,** 7th Bt *cr* 1846; DL; Head Master of Lancing College, 1961-69; *b* 29 Oct. 1925; *s* of Charles Andrew Gladstone, (6th Bt), and Isla Margaret, *d* of late Sir Walter Erskine Crum; *S* father, 1968; *m* 1962, Rosamund Anne, *yr d* of late Major A. Hambro and Mrs Hambro, 12 Sprimont Place, SW3; two *s* one *d*. *Educ:* Eton; Christ Church, Oxford. Served RNVR, 1943-46. Asst Master at Shrewsbury, 1949-50, and at Eton, 1951-61. DL Flintshire, 1969; Alderman, Flintshire CC, 1970. *Publications:* various school textbooks. *Recreations:* reading history, shooting, gardening. *Heir: s* Charles Angus Gladstone, *b* 11 April 1964. *Address:* Hawarden Castle, Deeside, Flintshire. *T:* Hawarden 2210; Fasque, Laurencekirk, Kincardineshire. *T:* Fettercairn 201.

**GLADSTONE, Adm. Sir Gerald Vaughan,** GBE 1960; KCB 1957 (CB 1954); *b* 3 Oct. 1901; *yr s* of J. E. Gladstone, Llandaff and Braunton; *m* 1925, Marjorie (Justine), (*d* 1964), *e d* of J. Goring Johnston, NZ; two *s* one *d*; *m* 1966, Mrs Dora Brown, *widow* of Capt. (E) W. D. Brown, DSC, RN. *Educ:* RN Colls Osborne and Dartmouth. Midshipman, HMS Tiger, 1917; Rear-Adm. 1952; Vice-Controller of the Navy, 1952-53; Flag Officer Second in Command Far Eastern Station and Flag Officer Comdg 5th Cruiser Sqdn, 1953-55; Vice-Adm. 1955; Comdr, Allied Naval Forces, Northern Europe, 1955-57; Admiral, 1958; Comdr-in-Chief, Far East Station, 1957-60, retired 1960. *Address:* Forsters, Bradpole, Bridport, Dorset. *Club:* United Service.

**GLADSTONE, Sir William;** *see* Gladstone, Sir E. W.

**GLADWYN,** 1st Baron *cr* 1960; **Hubert Miles Gladwyn Jebb,** GCMG 1954 (KCMG 1949; CMG 1942); GCVO 1957; CB 1947; Grand Croix de la Légion d'Honneur, 1957; *b* 25 April 1900; *s* of late Sydney Jebb, Firbeck Hall, Yorks; *m* 1929, Cynthia, *d* of Sir Saxton Noble, 3rd Bart; one *s* two *d*. *Educ:* Eton; Magdalen Coll., Oxon. 1st in History, Oxford, 1922. Entered Diplomatic Service, 1924; served in Tehran, Rome, and Foreign Office; Private Sec. to Parliamentary Under-Sec. of State, 1929-31; Private Sec. to Permanent Under-Sec. of State, 1937-40; appointed to Ministry of Economic Warfare with temp. rank of Asst Under-Sec., Aug. 1940; Acting Counsellor in Foreign Office, 1941; Head of Reconstruction Dept, 1942; Counsellor, 1943, in that capacity attended the Conferences of Quebec, Cairo, Tehran, Dunbarton Oaks, Yalta, San Francisco and Potsdam. Executive Sec. of Preparatory Commission of the United Nations (Aug. 1945) with temp. rank of Minister; Acting Sec.-Gen. of UN, Feb. 1946; Deputy to Foreign Sec. on Conference of Foreign Ministers, March 1946; Assistant Under-Sec. of State and United Nations Adviser, 1946-47; UK rep. on Brussels Treaty Permanent Commission with personal rank of Ambassador, April 1948; Dep. Under-Sec., 1949-50; Permanent Representative of the UK to the United Nations, 1950-54; British Ambassador to France, 1954-60, retired. Dep. Leader of Liberal Party in House of Lords, and Liberal Spokesman on Foreign Affairs and

Defence. Vice-President: Atlantic Treaty Assoc.; Atlantic Institute; Chairman: Britain in Europe; Campaign for European Political Community; Mem., Parly Delegns to Council of Europe and WEU Assemblies. Hon. DCL: Oxford; Syracuse, NY 1954; Hon. Fellow Magdalen Coll. *Publications:* Is Tension Necessary?, 1959; Peaceful Co-existence, 1962; The European Idea, 1966; Half-way to 1984, 1967; De Gaulle's Europe, or, Why the General says No, 1969. *Recreations:* gardening, broadcasting and other forms of sport. *Heir:* s Hon. Miles Alvery Gladwyn Jebb [*b* 3 March 1930. *Educ:* Eton and Oxford]. *Address:* Bramfield Hall, Halesworth, Suffolk. *T:* Bramfield 241; 62 Whitehall Court, SW1. *T:* 01-930 3160. *Clubs:* Turf, Beefsteak, Garrick.
*See also H. S. Thomas.*

**GLAISTER, John;** Emeritus Professor of Forensic Medicine, The University of Glasgow, 1931-62, retired; Medico-Legal Examiner to the Crown (retired except in special cases); Medical Referee under Cremation Act; *b* Glasgow, 1892; 2nd *s* of late Emeritus Prof. John Glaister, MD, LLD; *m* 1918, Isobel Rachel, *o d* of late Sir John Lindsay, KBE, DL, Town Clerk of Glasgow; two *d. Educ:* High Sch., and University, Glasgow. Bachelor of Medicine and Bachelor of Surgery, 1916; Doctor of Medicine with Hons, 1925; Dr of Science, 1927; FRSE; Fellow of Royal College of Physicians, Glasgow. Barrister-at-Law of Inner Temple, 1925. Asst in Forensic Medicine, Glasgow Univ., 1919-25, Lecturer Forensic Medicine, 1925-28; Lecturer on Forensic Medicine to the Police Force of the City of Glasgow, 1920-28; Medico-Legal Examiner and Adviser to the Corporation of Glasgow, 1920-28; Prof. of Forensic Medicine, the Faculty of Medicine, the University of Egypt, Cairo, and Medico-Legal Consultant to the Government of Egypt, 1928-32. Commissioned service with RAMC, 1916-19. Formerly External Examiner in Forensic Medicine, Universities of Edinburgh, Birmingham, Liverpool, Leeds, Aberdeen, St Andrews, and Sheffield. Formerly JP Co. of City of Glasgow. *Publications:* Text-Book of Medical Jurisprudence and Toxicology, 12th edn 1966; Recent Advances in Forensic Medicine, 1939; (joint) Hairs of Mammalia, with a special study of Human Hair, considered from the Medico-Legal Aspect; Medico-Legal Aspects of the Ruxton Case (joint); The Power of Poison, 1954; Final Diagnosis, 1964; numerous papers and monographs. *Address:* 3 Hatfield Drive, Glasgow W2.

**GLANDINE, Viscount; Richard James Graham-Toler;** *b* 5 March 1967; *s* and *heir* of 6th Earl of Norbury, *qv.*

**GLANUSK,** 4th Baron, *cr* 1899; **David Russell Bailey;** Bt, *cr* 1852; Lieutenant-Commander RN (retired); *b* 19 Nov. 1917; *o s* of late Hon. Herbert Crawshay Bailey, 4th *s* of 1st Baron Glanusk and late Kathleen Mary, *d* of Sir Shirley Harris Salt, 3rd Bt; *S* cousin 1948; *m* 1941, Lorna Dorothy, *o d* of late Capt. E. C. H. N. Andrews, MBE, RA; one *s* one *d. Educ:* Orley Farm Sch., Harrow; Eton. RN, 1935-51. Managing Dir, Wandel & Goltermann (UK) Ltd, 1966-. *Heir:* *s* Hon. Christopher Russell Bailey, *b* 18 March 1942. *Address:* c/o National Provincial Bank Ltd, Crickhowell, Breconshire.

**GLANVILLE, Brian Lester;** author; and journalist since 1949; *b* 24 Sept. 1931; *s* of James Arthur Glanville and Florence Glanville (*née* Manches); *m* 1959, Elizabeth Pamela de Boer (*née* Manasse), *d* of Fritz Manasse and Grace Manasse (*née* Howden); two *s* two *d. Educ:* Charterhouse. Joined Sunday Times (football correspondent), 1958. *Publications:* The Reluctant Dictator, 1952; Henry Sows the Wind, 1954; Along the Arno, 1956; The Bankrupts, 1958; After Rome, Africa, 1959; A Bad Streak, 1961; Diamond, 1962; The Director's Wife, 1963; The King of Hackney Marshes, 1965; A Second Home, 1965; A Roman Marriage, 1966; The Artist Type, 1967; The Olympian, 1969; A Cry of Crickets, 1970; etc. *Recreation:* playing football. *Address:* 160 Holland Park Avenue, W11. *T:* 01-603 6908. *Club:* Chelsea Casuals.

**GLANVILLE, Sir William (Henry),** Kt 1960; CB 1953; CBE 1944; DSC, PhD; MICE; MIStructE; FRS 1958; Consulting Engineer; Director of Road Research, Department of Scientific and Industrial Research, 1939-65; *b* 1900; *m* 1930, Millicent Patience, *d* of late E. John Carr; one *s* one *d.* Chairman: Advisory Cttee on Overseas (formerly Colonial) Road Research; Overseas Round Table Conf. on Highways; Internat. Cttee of Highway Research Bd, USA; Organising Cttee, Internat. Soc. of Soil Mechanics, 1957; Internat. Road Safety Research Conf., 1960; Co-Chm. First, Internat. Skid-Prevention Conf., 1958; Member: Informal Interdisciplinary Working Party of Engineering, Technology and Science Socs; Coun., Construction Industry Research and Information Assoc. (Chm., Information Cttee); Ministry of Transport Cttee on Road Safety, 1945-65; Royal Engineers Advisory Board, 1950-65; Cttee of Permanent International Assoc. of Road Congresses (Vice-Pres. Brit. Branch); Cttee of Internat. Assoc of Bridge and Structural Engrg; Brit. Standards Codes of Practice Cttee, 1940-65; Bd, Brit. Nuclear Energy Conf., 1953-58; Colonial Research Council, 1954-59; Past Pres. of Inst. of Civil Engineers (1950-51); Cantor Lecturer, Royal Society of Arts, 1950, 1954; Visiting Lecturer, Cape Town Univ., 1956; James Forrest Lecturer, Inst. of Civil Engineers, 1959. Fellow and Governor, Queen Mary Coll., London Univ.; Almoner and Governor, Christ's Hospital. Pres., Civil Service Motoring Assoc. Gold Medal (1961), Inst. of Struct. Engrs; Ewing Gold Medal (1962), Inst. of Civil Engrs. Viva Shield and Gold Medal, Worshipful Co. of Carmen, 1965. Hon. MIMunE, Hon. MInstHE, Hon. MACI; Hon. Mem. RE Inst; Hon. Mem. Concrete Soc. *Publications:* various scientific and technical books and papers. *Address:* Langthwaite, Kewferry Drive, Northwood, Mddx. *Clubs:* Athenæum, Royal Automobile.

**GLASER, Prof. Donald Arthur;** Professor of Physics and Molecular Biology, University of California, since 1960; *b* 21 Sept. 1926; *s* of William Joseph and Lena Glaser; *m* 1960, Ruth Louise Thompson; one *s* one *d. Educ:* Case Institute of Technology; California Inst. of Technology. Prof., University of Michigan, 1949-59. Henry Russel Award, 1955; Charles Vernon Boys Prize, 1958; Hon. ScD (Case Inst.), 1959; Amer. Phys. Soc. Prize, 1959; Nobel Prize, 1960. National Science Foundation Fellow, 1961; Guggenheim Fellow, 1961-62; Research Biophysicist (Miller Research Professorship, University of Calif., 1962-64); Mem. National Academy of Sciences (USA), 1962; Fellow Amer. Physical Soc.; Fellow Amer. Assoc. for Advancement of Science; Mem. NY Acad. of Science. *Publications:* articles in Physical Review, Bulletin of Amer. Phys. Soc., Nuovo Cimento, Proc. 5th and 7th Annual Rochester Confs, Proc. CERN, Proc. NY Acad. Sci., Symposium on High Energy Accelerators and Pion Physics, 1956, Proc. 2nd UN Geneva Conf., 1958, Handbuch der Physik, Proc. Kiev

Conf., 1959, Jl Molecular Biol., etc. Contributor to Yearbook of the Physical Society, London, 1958. *Address:* 229 Molecular Biology-Virus Laboratory, University of California, Berkeley, Calif 94720, USA.

**GLASER, Mrs O. C.;** *see* Wrinch, Dorothy.

**GLASGOW,** 9th Earl of, *cr* 1703; **David William Maurice Boyle,** CB 1963; DSC 1941; Baron Boyle, 1699; Viscount of Kelburn, 1703; Baron Fairlie (UK), 1897; Rear-Admiral, retired; *b* 24 July 1910; *e s* of 8th Earl of Glasgow, DSO; *S* father, 1963; *m* 1st, 1937, Dorothea (marriage dissolved, 1962), *o d* of Sir Archibald Lyle, 2nd Bart; one *s* two *d*; 2nd, 1962, Vanda, the Hon. Lady Wrixon-Becher, 2nd *d* of 4th Baron Vivian. *Educ:* Eton. Served War of 1939-45 in Atlantic, Channel, Arctic and Far East (despatches, DSC). Comdr, 1945; Capt., 1952; Capt. of the Fleet, Home Fleet, 1957-59; Commodore, RN Barracks, Portsmouth, 1959-61; Rear-Adm., 1961; Flag Officer, Malta, 1961-63; retd Sept. 1963. Mem. of the Royal Co. of Archers (Queen's Body Guard for Scotland). *Recreations:* shooting, golf, travel. *Heir:* *s* Viscount of Kelburn, *qv.* *Address:* Kelburn Castle, Fairlie, Ayrshire. *T:* Fairlie 204. *Clubs:* St James', United Service.
*See also Viscount Caldecote, Baron Cochrane, Earl of Cranbrook, Sir James Fergusson.*

**GLASGOW, Archbishop of,** (RC), since 1964; **Most Rev. Mgr James Donald Scanlan,** Hon. DD University of Glasgow, 1967; DCL, BL; *b* 24 Jan. 1899; 2nd *s* of late Dr Joseph Scanlan, Glasgow. *Educ:* St Mungo's Academy and St Aloysius' Coll., Glasgow; University of Glasgow; RMC Sandhurst; St Edmund's Coll., Ware; Institut Catholique, Paris; Apollinare, Rome. Lieut 1st Highland LI. Active Service in German East Africa and Egypt. Studied medicine and law before ordination by late Cardinal Bourne, 1929; *Officialis* of Westminster, 1936; Vice-Chancellor, 1937; Privy Chamberlain to Pope Pius XI, 1937; Chancellor of Westminster, 1944; Vicar Delegate for US Forces in Britain, 1945; Titular Bishop of Cyme and Co-Adjutor Bishop of Dunkeld with right of succession, 1946; Bishop of Dunkeld, 1949-55; Bishop of Motherwell, 1955-64. *Address:* Archbishop's House, 19 Park Circus, Glasgow C3. *T:* 041-332 1680. *Club:* United Service.

**GLASGOW and GALLOWAY, Bishop of,** since 1952; **Most Rev. Francis Hamilton Moncreiff,** Primus of the Episcopal Church in Scotland since 1962; *b* North Berwick, 29 Sept. 1906; *s* of late James Hamilton Moncrieff. *Educ:* Shrewsbury Sch.; St John's Coll., Cambridge; Cuddesdon Theological Coll. Ordained, 1931; Curate at St Giles, Cambridge, 1931-35, at St Augustine's, Kilburn, 1935-41; Priest-in-charge, St Salvador's, Edinburgh, 1941, Rector, 1947-51; Chaplain at HM Prison, Edinburgh, 1942-51; Canon of St Mary's Cathedral, Edinburgh, 1950; Diocesan Missioner in diocese of Edinburgh, 1951-52. Went on a Mission to European parishes in Northern Rhodesia, 1948 and 1951, to Pretoria and Johannesburg, 1953. Hon. DD Glasgow, 1967. *Address:* 14 Cleveden Crescent, Glasgow W2. *T:* 041-339 0554. *Club:* New (Edinburgh).

**GLASGOW, Auxiliary Bishop of,** (RC); *see* Ward, Rt Rev. James.

**GLASGOW and GALLOWAY, Dean of;** *see* Goldie, Very Rev. Frederick.

**GLASGOW, Provost of** (St Mary's Cathedral); *see* McIntosh, Very Rev. Hugh.

**GLASGOW, Mary Cecilia,** CBE 1949 (MBE 1942); BA; Chairman, Mary Glasgow Publications Ltd, Educational Publishers; *b* 24 May 1905; *d* of late Edwin Glasgow. *Educ:* Lady Margaret Hall, Oxford (Hons Sch. of French Language and Literature). Inspector of Schs, Bd of Education, 1933-39; Sec.-Gen., The Arts Council of Great Britain (formerly CEMA), 1939-51. Chm., The Opera Players. Chevalier, l'Ordre National du Mérite, 1968. *Address:* 5 Justice Walk, Chelsea, SW3. *T:* 01-352 7457; Entrechaux (Vaucluse), France. *Club:* United University.

**GLASS, Prof. David V.,** FBA 1964; Professor of Sociology, University of London, at London School of Economics, since 1948; *b* 2 Jan. 1911; *m* 1942, Ruth Durant (*see* Mrs Ruth Glass); one *s* one *d*. *Educ:* Elementary Sch.; Raine's Grammar Sch.; London Sch. of Economics, London Univ. Chairman: Research Cttee, International Sociological Assoc.; Population Investigation Cttee; UN Working Group on Social Demography of Europe; Hon. Pres., International Union for Scientific Study of Population; Mem., International Statistical Institute. Hon. DSc University of Michigan, 1967. *Publications:* The Town in a Changing World, 1935; The Struggle for Population, 1936; Population Policies and Movements in Europe, 1940; (ed) Introduction to Malthus, 1953; (ed) Social Mobility in Britain, 1954; (with E. Grebenik) The Trend and Pattern of Fertility in Great Britain, 1954; (ed) The University Teaching of Social Sciences: Demography, 1957; Latin American Seminar on Population: Report, 1958; Society: Approaches and Problems for Study, 1962 (co-ed); Differential Fertility, Ability and Educational Objectives, 1962; (ed jtly), Population in History, 1965; papers in Population Studies (Jt Editor), British Journal of Sociology (Jt Editor), Eugenics Review, etc. *Address:* 10 Palace Gardens Terrace, W8.

**GLASS, Sir Leslie (Charles),** KCMG 1967 (CMG 1958); British High Commissioner in Nigeria, since 1969; *b* 28 May 1911; *s* of Ernest Leslie and Kate Glass; *m* 1st, 1942, Pamela Mary Gage; two *s* one *d*; 2nd, 1957, Betty Lindsay Hoyer-Millar; two step *d*. *Educ:* Bradfield Coll.; Trinity Coll., Oxford; Sch. of Oriental Studies, London Univ. Indian Civil Service, 1934; Asst Warden, Burma Oilfields, 1937; Settlement Officer, Mandalay, 1939; Far Eastern Bureau Min. of Inf., 1942; Lt-Col Head of Burma Section, Psychological Warfare Div., SEAC; Head of Information Div., Burma Mil. Admin, 1943; Sec. Information Dept, Govt of Burma, 1945; Comr of Settlements and Land Records, Govt of Burma, 1946; joined Foreign Office as 1st Sec. (Oriental Sec.), HM Embassy, Rangoon, 1947; Foreign Office, 1949-50; Head of Chancery, HM Legation Budapest (Chargé d'Affaires, 1951-52), 1950-53; Head of Information Div., British Middle East Office, 1953; seconded to Staff of Governor of Cyprus, 1955-56; Counsellor and Consul-Gen., British Embassy, Washington, 1957-58; Dir-Gen. of British Information Services in the US and Information Minister, British Embassy, Washington 1959-61; Minister employed in the Foreign Office, 1961; Asst Under-Sec. of State, Foreign Office, 1962-65; Ambassador to Rumania, 1965-67; Ambassador and Dep. Permanent UK Representative to UN, 1967-69. *Recreation:* fishing. *Address:* c/o Foreign and Commonwealth Office, SW1. *Club:* Public Schools.

**GLASS, Mrs Ruth,** MA; Director of Research, Centre for Urban Studies, University College, London, since 1958; *d* of Eli and Lilly Lazarus;

*m* 1st, 1935, Henry Durant (marr. diss. 1941); 2nd, 1942, David V. Glass, *qv*; one *s* one *d*. *Educ:* Geneva and Berlin Univs; London Sch. of Economics; Columbia Univ., NY. Sen. Research Officer, Bureau of Applied Social Research, Columbia Univ., 1940-42; Res. Off., Min. of Town and Country Planning, 1948-50; Hon. Res. Associate, UC London, 1951-; Dir, Social Research Unit, Dept of Town Planning, UC London, 1951-58; Chm., Urban Sociology Research Cttee, Internat. Sociological Assoc., 1958-. *Publications:* Watling, A Social Survey, 1939; (ed) The Social Background of a Plan, 1948; Urban Sociology in Great Britain, 1955; Newcomers, The West Indians in London, 1960; London's Housing Needs, 1965; Jt Editor, Studies in Society (book series). Contributor to: Town Planning Review; Architectural Review; Planning; Population Studies; Internat. Social Science Jl; Trans. World Congresses of Sociology, etc. *Recreations:* walking, travelling, feminine paraphernalia. *Address:* 10 Palace Gardens Terrace, W8; Eastway Cottage, Walberswick, Suffolk. *Club:* Architectural Association.

**GLASSE, Alfred Onslow,** CMG 1969; OBE 1952; MC 1917; CEng, FIEE, FNZIE; electrical engineer, New Zealand, retired; *b* 1889; *s* of William Stacey Glasse; *m* 1920, Ellen Emma Griffiths (*d* 1966); two *d*. *Educ:* Otago High Sch. Auckland Electric Power Bd, 1922-57 (Chief Engr, 1925-54, Cons. Engr 1954-57); Cons. Engr other Bds, etc, 1956-66. Member: Auckland City Council, 1956- (Dep. Mayor, 1962); Nat. Roads Bd, 1960-63; Auck. Harbour Bridge Authority, 1963-; Auck. Metrop. Drainage Bd, 1957-64; Auck. Regional Planning Authority; Auck. War Memorial Mus. Council; Auck. Techn. Inst. Bd; St John Assoc. Past Pres., NZ Instn of Engrs. Also, as Pres. or on Council, numerous other Bds and Cttees. *Publications:* technical papers to various engineering jls. *Address:* 9 Eastbourne Road, Auckland 5, New Zealand. *Club:* Officers' (Auckland).

**GLASSE, Thomas Henry,** CMG 1961; MVO 1955; MBE 1946; retired as Counsellor in HM Diplomatic Service, and Head of Protocol Department, Foreign Office (1957-61); *b* 14 July 1898; *s* of late Thomas and Harriette Glasse; *m* 1935, Elsie May Dyter (*d* 1965); no *c*; *m* 1966, Ethel Alice Needham. *Educ:* Latymer Foundation Upper Sch., Hammersmith. Entered Civil Service as a Boy Clerk, 1914. Army Service, 1/10th Bn Mx Regt, 1917-19. Joined the Foreign Office, 1921. Delegate of United Kingdom to Vienna Conference on Diplomatic Relations, 1961. *Recreations:* books, music, garden, travel. *Address:* 72 Lynch Road, Farnham, Surrey. *T:* Farnham 6662. *Club:* Travellers'.

**GLASSEY, Alec Ewart,** JP; Chief Commissioner of Reconstruction of Congregational Union, 1942-57; *b* Normanton, Yorks, 29 Dec. 1887; *s* of late Rev. William Glassey and late Elizabeth Glassey; *m* 1910, Mary Eleanor Longbottom; three *d*. *Educ:* Penistone Grammar Sch. Served European War, 1914-18 (despatches); Mem. of Council of Congregational Union of England and Wales; contested East Dorset, 1924; MP (L) East Dorset, 1929-31; a Lord Commissioner of the Treasury, 1931; Chm. of Congregational Union of England and Wales, 1941-42; Chm. of Commonwealth Missionary Soc., 1945-47 and 1961-62; Co-Treas., Congregational Union of England and Wales, 1953-57; Dir of Congregational Insurance Co. Ltd; JP, Poole, Dorset. *Recreation:* gardening. *Address:* The Homestead, Penn Hill Avenue, Parkstone, Dorset. *T:* Parkstone 286. *Clubs:* National Liberal, Eighty.

**GLAUERT, Audrey Marion, (Mrs David Franks);** Head of Electron Microscopy Department, Strangeways Research Laboratory, Cambridge, since 1956; *b* 21 Dec. 1925; *d* of late Hermann Glauert, FRS and Muriel Glauert (*née* Barker); *m* 1959, David Franks, PhD; no *c*. *Educ:* Perse Sch. for Girls, Cambridge; Bedford Coll., Univ. of London. BSc 1946, MSc 1947, London; MA Cantab 1967. Asst Lectr in Physics, Royal Holloway Coll., Univ. of London, 1947-50; Mem. Scientific Staff, Strangeways Res. Lab., Cambridge, Sir Halley Stewart Research Fellow, 1950-. Fellow of Clare Hall, Cambridge, 1966. Chm., British Joint Cttee for Electron Microscopy, 1968-; Pres., Royal Microscopical Soc., 1970-. *Publications:* papers on cell and molecular biology in scientific jls. *Recreation:* sailing. *Address:* 29 Cow Lane, Fulbourn, Cambridge. *T:* Fulbourn 463; Strangeways Research Laboratory, Wort's Causeway, Cambridge. *T:* Cambridge 47583.

**GLAVES-SMITH, Frank William;** Under-Secretary, Department of Employment and Productivity, since 1969; *b* 27 Sept. 1919; *s* of James Smith and Blanche (*née* Rastall); *m* 1941, Audrey Glaves; one *s* one *d*. *Educ:* Malet Lambert High Sch., Hull. Inland Revenue, 1938; served with Army, 1940-46. Called to Bar, Middle Temple, 1947. Board of Trade, 1947; Princ. Private Sec. to Pres. of Bd of Trade, 1952-57; Asst Secretary: HM Treasury, 1957-60; Cabinet Office, 1960-62; Bd of Trade, 1962-65; Under-Sec., BoT, 1965-69. *Recreations:* croquet, gardening, sailing. *Address:* Leckhampstead West, Reigate Road, Reigate, Surrey. *T:* Reigate 44070. *Club:* Reform.

**GLAZEBROOK, Francis Kirkland; His Honour Judge Glazebrook;** Judge of the County Courts, Circuit No 63 (Kent), since 1952; *b* 18 Feb. 1903; 3rd *s* of late William Rimington Glazebrook; *m* 1930, Winifred Mary Elizabeth Davison; one *s* two *d*. *Educ:* Marlborough Coll.; Trinity Coll., Cambridge; Harvard Univ., USA. Called to the Bar, Inner Temple, 1928; Practised in the Common Law; Judge of the County Courts, Circuit No 58 (Ilford, etc), 1950-52. Served War in Army, 1939-45. Croix de Guerre (France); Bronze Star (USA). *Recreations:* fishing, gardening, golf. *Address:* Rectory Park, Horsmonden, Kent.

**GLAZEBROOK, Mark;** *see* Glazebrook, R. M.

**GLAZEBROOK, Reginald Field;** Director: Liverpool & London & Globe Insurance Co. Ltd; Liverpool Warehousing Co. Ltd; Liverpool Grain Storage & Transit Co. Ltd; Gandy Belt Ltd; *b* 23 April 1899; *s* of late William Rimington Glazebrook; *m* 1928. Daisy Isabel Broad; four *s*. *Educ:* Marlborough. Served European War, Lieut RFC, 1916-18. Cotton Merchant; Past Pres. Liverpool Cotton Assoc. *Recreations:* fishing, shooting, gardening. *Address:* Bryn Bella, St Asaph, N Wales.

*See also R. M. Glazebrook.*

**GLAZEBROOK, (Reginald) Mark;** Director, Whitechapel Art Gallery, since 1969; *b* 25 June 1936; *s* of Reginald Field Glazebrook, *qv*; *m* 1965, Elizabeth Lea Claridge (marr. diss., 1969); one *d*. *Educ:* Eton; Pembroke Coll., Cambridge (MA); Slade School of Fine Art. Worked at Arts Council, 1961-64; Lectr at Maidstone Coll. of Art, 1965-67; Art Critic, London Magazine, 1967-68. *Publications:* articles in: Studio International, London Magazine. *Recreations:* travelling, theatre, tennis, swimming. *Address:* 5 Priory Gardens, Bedford Park, W4. *T:* 01-994 8749.

**GLAZIER, Dr Edward Victor Denis,** CB 1970; Director, Royal Radar Establishment, Malvern, Ministry of Technology, since 1967; *b* 27 July 1912; *s* of Albert Glazier; *m* 1940, Marjorie May Burgess; one *s*. *Educ:* Northgate Sch.; London Univ. BSc 1935; PhD 1940. GPO Research Dept, 1934; Signals Research and Development Estab., 1942; Dir, Scientific Research (Electronics), Min. of Aviation, 1956; Royal Radar Estab., 1959. *Publications:* Services Textbook of Radio, Transmission and Propagation, 1958; Telecommunications (Vol. 1), 1962; papers on radio and radar. *Recreation:* sailing. *Address:* Royal Radar Establishment, Malvern, Worcs. *T:* Malvern 2733.

**GLEADELL, Maj.-Gen. Paul,** CB 1959; CBE 1951; DSO 1945; Clerk to the Governors, Rookesbury Park School, since 1966; *b* 23 Feb. 1910; *s* of late Captain William Henry and Katherine Gleadell; *m* 1937, Mary Montgomerie Lind, *d* of late Col Alexander Gordon Lind, DSO, and Mrs Lind; two *s* two *d*. *Educ:* Downside Sch.; Sandhurst. Commissioned in The Devonshire Regt, 1930 (Adjutant 1936-39); DAAG, Rawalpindi Dist, 1940; Staff Coll. (Quetta), 1941; Brigade Major 80th Indian Bde, 1942; Commanded 12th Bn The Devonshire Regt (6th Airborne Div.), 1944-45; Secretariat, Offices of the Cabinet and Ministry of Defence, 1945-48; Joint Services Staff Coll., 1948; Col (G S Intelligence), GHQ Far East Land Forces, 1949-51; comd 1st Bn The Devonshire Regt (3rd Inf. Div.), 1951-53; Senior Army Instructor, Joint Services Staff Coll., 1953-55; Brigade Comdr, 24th Independent Infantry Brigade, 1955-56; Imperial Defence Coll., 1957; Chief of Staff to Dir of Operations, Cyprus, 1958-59; in command 44th Div. (TA) and Home Counties District, and Dep. Constable of Dover Castle, 1959-62; Dir of Infantry, 1962-65. French Croix de Guerre with Palm, 1944. *Address:* Botley House, Botley, Hants. *Club:* United Service.

**GLEDHILL, Alan,** MA Cantab, LLD London; Professor Emeritus of Oriental Laws, University of London; Fellow and Temporary Lecturer, School of Oriental and African Studies; *b* 28 Oct. 1895; *s* of late O. Gledhill, Redroofs, Wells Road, Wolverhampton; *m* 1st, 1922, Mercy (*d* 1963), *d* of Victor Harvey, Calcutta; two *s* one *d*; 2nd, 1967, Marion Glover, *d* of late C. W. Watson, Santa Cruz, Argentine. *Educ:* Fishguard Grammar Sch.; Rugby; Corpus Christi Coll., Cambridge; Gray's Inn. Served European War, 1914-18, Lieut Monmouthshire Regt 1915-16; joined ICS 1920; District and Sessions Judge, 1927; Special Judge, Tharrawaddy, 1930-33; Capt. Army in India R of O 1931-34; War of 1939-45: Burma Campaign, 1942; Dep. Comr, Cachar, Assam, 1942-43; Actg Lieut-Col, Army in Burma R of O, Dep. Chief Judicial Officer, British Military Administration, Burma, 1944-45 (despatches); Actg Judge High Court Rangoon, Oct. 1945; Puisne Judge, 1946-48; Lecturer in Indian and Burmese Law, Sch. of Oriental and African Studies, 1948-54; Reader in Oriental Laws, 1954-55; Prof. of Oriental Laws, University of London, 1955-63; Lectr in Hindu Law, Inns of Court Sch. of Law, 1955-67. *Publications:* The British Commonwealth: The Development of its Laws and Constitutions, Vol 6, The Republic of India, 1951 (2nd edn, 1964). Vol. 8, The Islamic Republic of Pakistan, 1957 (2nd edn, 1967); Fundamental Rights in India, 1955; The Penal Codes of Northern Nigeria and the Sudan, 1963. *Recreations:* swimming, walking. *Address:* 24 Chichester Court, Church Farm Garden Estate, Rustington, Sussex. *Club:* Royal Commonwealth Society.

**GLEDHILL, Anthony John;** GC 1967; Police Constable, Metropolitan Police, since 1957; *b* 10 March 1938; *s* of Harold Victor and Marjorie Edith Gledhill; *m* 1958, Marie Lilian Hughes; one *s* one *d*. *Educ:* Doncaster Technical High Sch., Yorks. Accounts Clerk, Officers' Mess, RAF Bruggen, Germany, 1953-56. Metropolitan Police Cadet, 1956-57. *Recreations:* football, carpentry. *Address:* 91 Bourne Vale, Hayes, Bromley, Kent. *T:* 01-462 4033. *Club:* No 4 District Metropolitan Police (Hayes, Kent).

**GLEDSTANES, Elsie,** RBA 1929 (ARBA 1923); portrait, figure and landscape painter; *d* of late Francis Garner Gledstanes, late mem. Stock Exchange Cttee. *Educ:* Eastbourne; Paris. Studied art at Paris, Slade Sch. and Byam Shaw, and Vicat Cole Sch. of Art; served in WRNS, 1917-18; London Auxiliary Ambulance Driver, 1939-45; WVS Transport, 1941-42; Driver Women's Legion, 1942-45; exhibited works in RA, RBA, RPS, NPS, International Soc. and in the Provinces; works in Imperial War Museum, etc.; mem. of Pastel Soc., Campden Hill Club; Fellow Royal Society of Arts. *Address:* 61 Campden Street, W8. *T:* 01-727 8663; Glan-y-Gors, Prenteg, Portmadoc. *T:* Portmadoc 2510.

**GLEESON, Most Rev. James William,** CMG 1958; DD 1957; Coadjutor Archbishop of Adelaide, (RC), and Titular Archbishop of Aurusuliana since 1964; *b* 24 Dec. 1920; *s* of John Joseph and Margaret Mary Gleeson. *Educ:* St Joseph's Sch., Balaklava, SA; Sacred Heart Coll., Gleneig, SA. Priest, 1945; Inspector of Catholic Schs, 1947-52; Dir of Catholic Education for South Australia, 1952-58; Auxiliary Bishop to the Archbishop of Adelaide, and Titular Bishop of Sesta, 1957-64; Episcopal Chm. the Young Catholic Students' Movement of Australia, 1958-65. FACE 1967. *Address:* Archbishop's House, 91 West Terrace, Adelaide, SA 5000, Australia. *T:* 51.3551.

**GLEGG, Alexander Lindsay,** ACGI; AMIEE; Chairman of Hosa Research Laboratories, Sunbury-on-Thames; *b* London, 1882; *s* of late Sir Alexander Glegg, Aberdeen; *m* 1910, Lilian Grace Kilvington Olney (*d* 1951); twin *s*. *Educ:* Dulwich Coll.; City and Guilds Central Technical Coll., S Kensington. Twice Pres. of the National Sunday Sch. Union and twice Pres. of the London Christian Endeavour; Pres. Christian Endeavour Union of Great Britain and Ireland; Pres. and Chm. Bible Testimony Fellowship; Pres., Chm. and Treas. of Advent Testimony and Preparation Movement; Pres., Movement for World Evangelisation; Pres. British Soc. for the Propagation of the Gospel among the Jews; Vice-Pres. of the Crusaders, and The Young Life Campaign; Hon. Trustee of Down Lodge Hall Mission, and Pres. of Landsowne Place Medical Mission, Bermondsey; Vice-Pres. of many other philanthropic bodies. *Publications:* Life with a Capital L; Youth with a Capital Why; Conquering the Capital I; How to run life at a profit; Four Score–and more; Walking on Two Feet. *Recreation:* golf (handicap 16). *Address:* Birchstone, Coombe Park, Kingston Hill, Surrey. *T:* Kingston 5983.

**GLEN, Sir Alexander,** KBE, *cr* 1956; CB 1950; MC 1918; Secretary Department of Agriculture for Scotland, 1953-58; *b* 22 Nov. 1893; *m* 1924, Helen Gordon, *d* of late J. J. Kirk, St Andrews; one *s* one *d*. *Educ:* St Andrews and Oxford. Served in Army, 1915-19 (Black Watch). Entered Civil Service (Treasury), 1920; Dept of Agriculture for Scotland, 1935; Dep. Sec., 1945. *Address:* 17

Merchiston Gardens, Edinburgh 10. *T:* 031-337 5581.

**GLEN, Sir Alexander (Richard),** KBE 1967 (CBE 1964); DSC 1942 (and Bar, 1945); Chairman of H. Clarkson & Co. Ltd, etc; Chairman, British Tourist Authority, since 1969; Director, BICC; *b* 18 April 1912; *s* of late R. Bartlett Glen, Glasgow; *m* 1947, Baroness Zora de Collaert. *Educ:* Fettes Coll.; Balliol Coll., Oxford. BA, Hons Geography. Travelled on Arctic Expeditions, 1932-36; Leader, Oxford Univ. Arctic Expedition, 1935-36; Banking, New York and London, 1936-39. RNVR, 1939-59, Capt. 1955. Export Council for Europe; Dep. Chm., 1960-64; Chm., 1964-66. Member: British National Export Council, 1966-; Board of BEA, 1964-70; Nat. Ports Council, 1966-70. Awarded Cuthbert Peek Grant by Royal Geog. Society, 1933; Bruce Medal by Royal Society of Edinburgh, 1938; Andrée Plaque by Royal Swedish Soc. for Anthropology and Geography, 1939; Patron's Gold Medal by Royal Geog. Society, 1940; Polar Medal (clasp Arctic 1935-36), 1942; Norwegian War Cross, 1943; Chevalier (1st Class), Order of St Olav, 1944; Czechoslovak War Cross, 1946. *Publications:* Young Men in the Arctic, 1935; Under the Pole Star, 1937. *Recreations:* travel, ski-ing, sailing. *Address:* 46 Wilton Crescent, SW1; Croziers, Shalford, Essex. *T:* 01-235 1576, 01-588 4222. *Clubs:* Travellers', City of London; Explorers (NY).

**GLEN, John Mackenzie,** CB 1945; *b* 12 April 1885; 2nd *s* of David James Glen, Edinburgh; *m* 1912, Jessie, *d* of late Alexander McKercher, Edinburgh; one *s*. *Educ:* Daniel Stewart's Coll., Edinburgh; Edinburgh Univ. (MA 1st Class Hons). Entered first Div. of Civil Service, 1907. Served European War, 1914-18. Called to Bar, Lincoln's Inn, 1920. Principal Asst Sec., Ministry of Labour, 1937; Under-Sec., Ministry of Labour and National Service, 1945; retired. *Address:* c/o Westminster Bank, Caxton House, Westminster, SW1.

**GLENAPP, Viscount; Kenneth Peter Lyle Mackay;** *b* 23 Jan. 1943; *er s and heir* of 3rd Earl of Inchcape, *qv*; *m* 1966, Georgina, *d* of S. C. Nisbet and of Mrs G. R. Sutton. *Educ:* Eton. Late 2nd Lieut 9/12th Royal Lancers; business career. *Address:* 2 Bramerton Street, Chelsea, SW3.

**GLENARTHUR,** 3rd Baron, *cr* 1918; **Matthew Arthur,** OBE 1945 (MBE 1943); Bt, *cr* 1903; late Major (temporary Lieutenant-Colonel) Royal Scots Greys; *b* 12 May 1909; *o s* of 2nd Baron and Evelyn, *e d* of late Henry March-Phillipps, Tiverton; *S* father, 1942; *m* 1st, 1931, Audrey Lees-Milne (marriage dissolved, 1939); one *d*; 2nd, 1939, Margaret, *o d* of late Capt. H. J. J. Howie; two *s* one *d*. *Educ:* Winchester; Magdalen Coll., Oxford. DL (Ayrshire) 1948. *Recreations:* hunting and fishing. *Heir: s* Captain Hon. Simon Mark Arthur [*b* 7 Oct. 1944; *m* 1969, Susan, *yr d* of Comdr Hubert Barry, Stockbridge, Hants. Lieut, 10th Royal Hussars, 1966, Captain 1970]. *Address:* Stairaird, Mauchline, Ayrshire. *T:* Mauchline 211.

**GLENAVY,** 3rd Baron, *cr* 1921; **Patrick Gordon Campbell,** Bt 1916; Author (as Patrick Campbell); Columnist, Sunday Times, since 1961; *b* 6 June 1913; *s* of 2nd Baron and Beatrice (*née* Elvery); *S* father, 1963; *m* 1st, 1941, Sylvia Willoughby Lee (marriage dissolved, 1947); 2nd, 1947, Cherry Lowson Monro (marriage dissolved, 1966); one *d*; 3rd, 1966, Mrs Vivienne Orme. *Educ:* Rossall; Pembroke, Oxford. Irish Marine Service, 1941-44. Columnist: Irish Times, 1944-47; Sunday Dispatch, 1947-59; Asst Editor, Lilliput Mag., 1947-53. Writes for TV and Screen. *Publications:* A Long Drink of Cold Water, 1950; A Short Trot with a Cultured Mind, 1952; Life in Thin Slices, 1954; Patrick Campbell's Omnibus, 1956; Come Here Till I Tell You, 1960; Constantly in Pursuit, 1962; How to become a Scratch Golfer, 1963; Brewing Up in the Basement, 1963; Rough Husbandry, 1965; My Life and Easy Times, 1967; A Bunch of New Roses, 1967; The Coarse of Events, 1968. *Recreations:* golf and pleasure. *Heir: b* Hon. Michael Campbell, *b* 25 Oct. 1924. *Address:* 65/66 Eccleston Square, SW1.

**GLENCONNER,** 2nd Baron, *cr* 1911; **Christopher Grey Tennant;** Bt *cr* 1885; *b* 14 June 1899; *s* of 1st Baron and Pamela (*d* 1928), *d* of late Hon. Percy Scawen Wyndham (she *m* 2nd, 1922, 1st Viscount Grey); *S* father, 1920; *m* 1st, 1925, Pamela (who obtained a divorce, 1935), 2nd *d* of Sir Richard Paget, 2nd Bt; two *s*; 2nd, 1935, Elizabeth Mary, *er d* of late Lieut-Col E. G. H. Powell; one *s* two *d*. *Heir: s* Hon. Colin Christopher Paget Tennant [*b* 1 Dec. 1926; *m* 1956, Lady Anne Coke, *e d* of 5th Earl of Leicester, *qv*; three *s*]. *Address:* Rovinia, Liapades, Corfu, Greece; (seat) Glen, Innerleithen, Peebles. *Club:* White's.

**GLENDAY, D. Nonita;** MA Oxon; Headmistress, Clifton High School for Girls, 1933-62; President, Association of Headmistresses, 1958-60. *Educ:* Girls' Gram. Sch., Bury Lancs; St Hugh's Coll., Oxford. Hons Degree in English Language and Literature. Senior English Mistress at Francis Holland Church of England Sch., Graham Street, London, 1921-26. International hockey player. Headmistress of Rugby High Sch., 1926-33. Pres. West of England Branch of Assoc. of Headmistresses, 1946-48; Chm. of Assoc. of Independent and Direct-Grant Schs, 1949-51. *Address:* 1 Hayward Road, Oxford. *Club:* English-Speaking Union.

**GLENDENNING, Raymond Carl;** Sports Commentator, Journalist and Publicity Consultant; Managing Director, Glenray Promotions, since 1968; *b* 25 Sept. 1907; *s* of late Robert James and Mathilde Glendenning, Newport, Monmouthshire; *m* 1945, Sheilagh Dundee Millar. *Educ:* Newport High Sch.; London Univ. (BCom). Chartered Accountant, 1931. Joined BBC as Children's Hour Organiser (Cardiff 5WA), 1932; Outside Broadcasts Asst, Belfast, 1935; recalled to London Outside Broadcasts Staff, 1939; Asst Dir Outside Broadcasts, London, 1942; left permanent staff BBC, for full-time sports commentating and reporting, 1945; main BBC sports commentator on football, boxing, racing, tennis, etc., 1939-63. Television, film work, etc. Dir, Reading Standard Group Ltd, 1961-67; Editorial Dir, Golf News, 1963-67. Mem., Livery Co. of Carmen, 1952-. *Publications:* Just a Word in your Ear (autobiography), 1953; R. G.'s Boys' Book of Sport, 1950 to 1962. *Recreations:* water-colour painting, golf and snooker. *Address:* The Old Forge, Skirmett, near Henley-on-Thames, Oxon. *T:* Turville Heath 337. *Club:* Constitutional.

**GLENDEVON,** 1st Baron, *cr* 1964; **John Adrian Hope;** PC 1959; Chairman, Geigy (UK) Ltd, since 1967; Director: Standard Telephones & Cables; Colonial Mutual Life Assurance Society Ltd; British Electric Traction Omnibus Services Ltd; *b* 7 April 1912; *yr twin s* of 2nd Marquess of Linlithgow, KG, KT, PC; *m* 1948, Elizabeth Mary, *d* of late (William) Somerset Maugham, CH; two *s*. *Educ:* Eton; Christ Church, Oxford (MA 1936). psct; served War of 1939-45 (Scots Guards) at

Narvik, Salerno and Anzio (despatches twice). MP (C) Northern Midlothian and Peebles, 1945-50, Pentlands Div. of Edinburgh, 1950-64; (Joint) Parliamentary Under-Sec. of State for Foreign Affairs, Oct. 1954-Nov. 1956; Parliamentary Under-Sec. of State for Commonwealth Relations, Nov. 1956-Jan. 1957; Jt Parl Under-Sec. of State for Scotland, 1957-Oct. 1959; Minister of Works, Oct. 1959-July 1962. Chm., Royal Commonwealth Society, 1963-66. Fellow of Eton, 1956-67. FRSA 1962. *Heir:* *s* Hon. Julian Somerset Hope, *b* 6 March 1950. *Address:* Greys, Greys Green, Henley-on-Thames, Oxon.

**GLENDINING, Rev. Alan;** Rector of the Sandringham Group of Parishes, and Domestic Chaplain to the Queen, since 1970; *b* 17 March 1924; *s* of Vincent Glendining, MS, FRCS and Freda Alice; *m* 1948, Margaret Locke, *d* of Lt-Col C. M. Hawes, DSO and Frances Cooper Richmond; one *s* two *d*. *Educ:* Radley; Westcott House, Cambridge. Newspaper publishing, 1945-58. Deacon, 1960; Priest, 1961. Asst Curate, South Ormsby Group of Parishes, 1960-63; Rector of Raveningham Group of Parishes, 1963-70. *Recreations:* collecting, shooting. *Address:* Sandringham Rectory, Kings Lynn, Norfolk. *T:* Dersingham 587.

**GLENDYNE,** 3rd Baron, *cr* 1922; **Robert Nivison,** Bt 1914; Senior Partner in the firm of R. Nivison & Co., Stockbrokers; *b* 27 Oct. 1926; *o s* of 2nd Baron and Ivy May Rose; *S* father, 1967; *m* 1953, Elizabeth, *y d* of late Sir Cecil Armitage, CBE; one *s* two *d*. *Educ:* Harrow. Grenadier Guards, 1944-47. *Recreations:* shooting, cricket, water-skiing. *Heir:* *s* Hon. John Nivison, *b* 18 Aug. 1960. *Address:* Red Court, Haslemere, Surrey. *Clubs:* City of London, MCC.

**GLENN, Sir Archibald;** *see* Glenn, Sir J. R. A.

**GLENN, Col John H(erschel), Jr;** American Astronaut; Consultant to National Aeronautics and Space Administration, in Manned Space-flight Program; Member Board of Directors, Corporate Development (Vice-President); *b* Cambridge, Ohio, 18 July 1921; *s* of John H. and Clara Glenn; *m* 1943, Anna Castor; one *s* one *d*. *Educ:* Muskingum Coll., New Concord, Ohio. Joined US Marine Corps, 1943; Served War (2DFC's, 10 Air Medals); Pacific Theater, 1944; home-based, Capt., 1945-46; Far East, 1947-49; Major, 1952; served Korea (5 DFC's, Air Medal with 18 clusters), 1953. Non-stop supersonic flight, Los Angeles-New York (DFC), 1957; Lieut-Col, 1959. In Jan. 1964, declared candidacy for US Senate from Ohio, but withdrew owing to an injury; recovered and promoted Col USMC, Oct. 1964; retired from USMC, Dec. 1964. Became one of 7 volunteer Astronauts, man-in-space program, 1959; made 3-orbit flight in Mercury capsule, Friendship 7, 20 Feb. 1962 (boosted by rocket; time 4 hrs 56 mins; distance 81,000 miles; altitude 160 miles; recovered by destroyer off Puerto Rico in Atlantic). Awarded DSM (Nat. Aeronautics and Space Admin.), Astronaut Wings (Navy), Astronaut Medal (Marine Corps), etc, 1962; Galabert Internat. Astronautical Prize (jointly with Lieut-Col Yuri Gargarin), 1963; also many other awards and citations from various countries and organizations. *Address:* c/o National Aeronautics and Space Administration, Manned Spacecraft Center, Houston, Texas, USA; (home) 203 Sleepy Hollow Court, Seabrook, Texas, USA.

**GLENN, Sir (Joseph Robert) Archibald,** Kt 1966; OBE 1965; BCE; MIChemE, MIE (Aust.); Chairman and Managing Director, Imperial Chemical Industries of Australia and New Zealand Ltd, Australia, since 1963; Director, Imperial Chemical Industries Ltd, since 1970; *b* 24 May 1911; *s* of late J. R. Glenn, Sale, Vic., Aust.; *m* 1939, Elizabeth M. M., *d* of late J. S. Balderstone; one *s* three *d*. *Educ:* Scotch Coll. (Melbourne); University of Melbourne; Harvard (USA). Design and Construction Engr, ICIANZ Ltd, 1935-44. Explosives Dept, ICI (UK), 1945-46. ICIANZ Ltd: Chief Engineer, 1947-48; Controller, Nobel Group, 1948-50; General Manager, 1950-52; Managing Director, 1953-63; Chairman: Fibremakers Ltd; Catoleum Pty Ltd; Director, Bank of NSW, 1967-; Chancellor, La Trobe Univ.; Chm., Council of Scotch Coll.; Member: Manufacturing Industry Advisory Council; Industrial Design Council; Royal Melbourne Hospital Bd of Management, 1960-70; Melbourne Univ. Appointments Bd. *Recreations:* golf, tennis, rowing, Royal tennis. *Address:* 3 Heyington Place, Toorak, Melbourne, Vic. 3142, Australia. *T:* 20 4453. *Clubs:* Australian, Melbourne, Royal Melbourne Golf, Frankston Golf, Victoria Racing, Melbourne Univ. Boat (all in Melbourne); Australian (Sydney).

**GLENN, William James,** CB 1968; BA, BAI, FICE; Chief Engineer, Ministry of Housing and Local Government, since 1968; *b* 26 June 1911; *s* of late John Glenn, Londonderry; *m* 1937, Wilhelmina Jane Gibson, MA, *d* of late John Gibson, Dublin; two *s*. *Educ:* Trinity Coll., Dublin Univ. Entered Air Min. as Asst Civil Engr, Directorate Gen. of Works, 1937; Sen. Civil Engr, Air HQ, W Africa, 1944-45; service in Airfield Construction Br, RAF, BAFO Germany, 1948-50; Chief Engr Flying Trng Comd, RAF, 1952-54; Dep. Dir of Works, 1956-57; Chief Engr, Far East Air Force, 1957-59; Dir of Works, 1962-65; Chief Civil Engr, MPBW, 1965-68. *Recreation:* golf. *Address:* Dromore, Wellington Road, Wokingham, Berks. *T:* Wokingham 302. *Club:* East Berkshire Golf.

**GLENNIE, Alan Forbes Bourne,** CMG 1956; *b* 11 April 1903; *s* of late Vice-Adm. R. W. Glennie, CMG; *m* 1931, Dorothy Sybil, *d* of late J. A. H. Johnston, DSc; one *s* one *d*. *Educ:* RN Colls Osborne and Dartmouth; Trinity Coll., Cambridge. Joined Provincial Administration, N Rhodesia, 1924; Provincial Commissioner, 1945; Resident Commissioner, Barotseland Protectorate, Northern Rhodesia, 1953-57, retired; Government Sec., St Helena, 1963-65, retired. *Address:* 47 Highsett, Hills Road, Cambridge. *Club:* Royal Over-Seas League.

**GLENNIE, Brig. Edward Aubrey,** CIE 1942; DSO 1917; FRAS, FRES, FRGS (Gold Medallist), FGS, FZS; FZS Scientific; Foundation FNI; Fellow, Conchological Society; late RE; *b* 18 July 1889; *s* of late Col E. Glennie; *m* 1923, Agnes Christina, *d* of W. Whigham, late Indian State Railways (one *s* killed on active service, 1944). *Educ:* Haileybury. Entered Army, 1910; Capt. 1916; Major, 1926; Lieut Col, 1934; Col, 1937; late Dir Survey of India; retired 1948; served Mesopotamia, 1916-18 (despatches twice, DSO). *Address:* 15 Shrublands Road, Berkhamsted, Herts.

**GLENNIE, Adm. Sir Irvine Gordon,** KCB, *cr* 1945 (CB 1943); *b* 22 July 1892; *o surv s* of Capt. Gordon Glennie RN, and Edith, *d* of late Gen. J. Mitchell, RMLI; *m* 1928, Gwen, *d* of Edmund Evans; two *s*. *Educ:* RN Colls, Osborne and Dartmouth. Comdr 1928; Capt. 1933; Rear-Adm. 1941; Vice-Adm. 1944; served Home Fleet and China, 1910-14; in Destroyers, Grand Fleet, 1915-18; RNC, Dartmouth, 1922-24; commanding Destroyers, 1925-27 and 1932-34; Staff Coll.,

1929; Admiralty, 1930-32; Imperial Defence Coll., 1935; commanding HMS Achilles, New Zealand Sqdn, 1936-39; commanding HMS Hood, 1939-41; Rear-Adm. Destroyers, Mediterranean, 1941-42; commanded Home Fleet Destroyers, 1943-44; Comdr-in-Chief, America and West Indies, 1945-46; retired list, 1947. *Address:* Wychwood, Fairfield Close, Lymington, Hants SO4 9NP. *T:* Lymington 2554.

**GLENTANAR,** 2nd Baron, *cr* 1916; **Thomas Coats;** KBE, *cr* 1956; DL, JP, Aberdeenshire; Commander of the Order of St Olav; *b* 4 Dec. 1894; *o s* of 1st Baron and Margaret Lothian (*d* 1935), *d* of late James Tait Black of Underscar, Keswick; *S* father, 1918; *m* 1927, Grethe Dagbjört (*d* 1940), 2nd *d* of Thor Thoresen, of Oslo; one *d. Educ:* Eton; Christ Church, Oxford; abroad. Late Lieut 2/6 Black Watch and Signal Service, RE; served in France, European War (despatches); Chm. of British Legion (Scotland), 1923-29; Commissioner for Scotland, Boy Scouts Assoc., 1923-53; Chm. ATC Advisory Council for Scotland, 1941-45; Chm. ATC Scottish Welfare Council, 1942-45; Mem. Queen's Body Guard for Scotland (Royal Co. of Archers); Hon. Bencher, Middle Temple, 1950. Hon. LLD Aberdeen, 1966; Hon. FRCM, 1966. *Heir:* none. *Address:* Glen Tanar, Aboyne, Aberdeenshire. *T:* Aboyne 2450. *Clubs:* Carlton, Beefsteak; New (Edinburgh); Royal Yacht Squadron (Cowes).
*See also Lord Aberdare.*

**GLENTORAN,** 2nd Baron, *cr* 1939, of Ballyalloly; **Daniel Stewart Thomas Bingham Dixon,** 4th Bt, *cr* 1903; PC (Northern Ireland) 1953; Minister in Senate, Northern Ireland, since 1961; Speaker of Senate, since 1964; HM Lieutenant City of Belfast since 1950; *b* 19 Jan. 1912; *s* of 1st Baron, PC, OBE and Hon. Emily Ina Florence Bingham (*d* 1957), *d* of 5th Baron Clanmorris; *S* father 1950; *m* 1933, Lady Diana Mary Wellesley, *d* of 3rd Earl Cowley; two *s* one *d. Educ:* Eton; RMC Sandhurst. Reg. Army, Grenadier Guards; served War of 1939-45 (despatches); retired 1946 (with hon. rank of Lieut-Col); psc. MP (U) Bloomfield Division of Belfast, Northern Ireland Parliament, Oct. 1950-Feb. 1961; Parliamentary Sec., Ministry of Commerce, N Ireland, 1952-53; Minister of Commerce, 1953-61. Hon. Col 6th Battalion Royal Ulster Rifles, 1956-61, retd rank of Hon. Col. *Heir: s* Hon. Thomas Robin Valerian Dixon, [*b* 21 April 1935; *m* 1959, Rona, *d* of Capt. G. C. Colville, Mill House, Bishop's Waltham, Hants; three *s*]. *Address:* Drumadarragh House, Doagh, Co. Antrim, Northern Ireland. *T:* Doagh 222. *Club:* Ulster (Belfast).

**GLENTWORTH, Viscount; Edmund Christopher Pery;** *b* 10 Feb. 1963; *s* and *heir* of 6th Earl of Limerick, *qv.*

**GLERAWLY, Viscount; Patrick Annesley;** *b* 12 August 1924; *e s* and *heir* of 9th Earl Annesley, *qv; m* 1947, Catherine, *d* of John Burgess, Edinburgh; four *d. Educ:* Strode's Grammar Sch., Egham. *Address:* 35 Spring Rise, Egham, Surrey.

**GLIDEWELL, Iain Derek Laing,** QC 1969; Barrister-at-law; *b* 8 June 1924; *s* of Charles Norman Glidewell; *m* 1950, Hilary, *d* of Clinton D. Winant; one *s* two *d. Educ:* Bromsgrove Sch.; Worcester Coll., Oxford. Called to the Bar, Gray's Inn, 1949. *Recreations:* beagling, walking, spasmodic interest in the Arts. *Address:* Oldfield, Knutsford, Cheshire. *T:* Knutsford 3073. *Club:* Manchester (Manchester).

**GLIN, Knight of;** *see* Fitz-Gerald, D. J. V.

**GLOAG, John (Edwards);** author; *b* 10 Aug. 1896; *s* of Robert McCowan Gloag and Lillian Morgan; *m* 1922, Gertrude Mary, *d* of late Ven. G. H. Ward; one *s* one *d. Educ:* Battersea Grammar Sch.; largely self-educated. Studied architecture at Regent Street Polytechnic, 1911-13; with studio Thornton-Smith Ltd, 1913-16; served in Essex Regt, 1916; Household Brigade Cadet Battalion, 1917; 2nd Lieut Welsh Guards, 1918; served with 1st Bn BEF, May-Aug. 1918, and invalided home; Technical and Art Ed. of the Cabinet Maker, 1922; Ed., 1927; Dir, Pritchard, Wood & Partners Ltd, 1928-61; Public Rel. Dir, Timber Development Assoc., 1936-38. FSA; Hon. ARIBA; Hon. FSIA; RSA Silver Medal, 1943, Bicentenary Gold Medal, 1958. Member: Utility Furniture Advisory Cttee (Board of Trade), 1943-47; Council of Industrial Design, 1949-55; Council of Royal Society of Arts, 1948-56, 1958-63 (Vice-Pres., 1952-54); Chairman: Internat. Conf. on Industrial Design, 1951; Council of Building Centre, 1950-64; Pres. of the Soc. of Architectural Historians of Great Britain, 1960-64. Broadcast talks and short stories, 1933 onwards; Mem. team in: Men Talking; Design in Modern Life; Brains Trust (occasionally Question Master); a few appearances on TV, before and after 1939-45 war. *Publications: fiction:* To-Morrow's Yesterday, 1932; The New Pleasure, 1933; Winter's Youth, 1934; Sweet Racket, 1936; Ripe for Development, 1936; Sacred Edifice, 1937 (new edn, with foreword by Sir Basil Spence, 1954); It Makes a Nice Change, 1938; Documents Marked Secret, 1938; Manna, 1940; Unwilling Adventurer, 1940; I Want an Audience, 1941; Mr Buckby is Not at Home, 1942; Ninety-nine per cent, 1944; In Camera, 1945; First One and Twenty (omnibus), 1946; Kind Uncle Buckby, 1947; All England at Home, 1949; Take One a Week, 1950; Not in the Newspapers, 1953; Slow, 1954; Unlawful Justice, 1962; Rising Suns, 1964; Ceasar of the Narrow Seas, 1969; *verse:* Board Room Ballads, 1933; *architecture and design:* Colour and Comfort, 1924; Men and Buildings, 1931 (illustr. edn, 1950); Artifex or the Future of Craftsmanship, 1926; English Furniture (Library of English Art), 1934 (5th edn, 1965); Design in Modern Life (ed.), 1934; Industrial Art Explained, 1934; The Place of Glass in Building (ed), 1942; The Missing Technician in Industrial Production, 1944; The Englishman's Castle, 1944; Plastics and Industrial Design, 1945; House out of Factory (with Grey Wornum, FRIBA), 1945; British Furniture Makers, 1945; Self-training for Industrial Designers, 1947; The English Tradition in Design, 1947 (revised and enlarged edn, 1959); A History of Cast Iron in Architecture (with D. L. Bridgewater, FRIBA), 1948; How to write Technical Books, 1951; A Short Dictionary of Furniture, 1952 (revd edn, 1965, abridged edn, 1966, enl. rev. edn, 1969); Georgian Grace, 1956 (revd edn, 1967); Guide to Western Architecture, 1958, Rev. edn 1969; Introduction to Catalogue of Irwin Untermyer Coll. of Eng. Furniture for Metropolitan Museum of Art, NY, 1958; Victorian Comfort, 1961; Victorian Taste, 1962; The English Tradition in Architecture, 1963; Architecture (Arts of Man), 1963; The Englishman's Chair, 1964; Enjoying Architecture, 1965; Introduction to Early English Decorative Detail, 1965; (with Maureen Stafford) Guide to Furniture Styles, English and French, 1971; *social history:* Home Life in History, 1927, with C. Thompson Walker; Time, Taste and Furniture, 1925; Word Warfare, 1939; The American Nation, 1942 (revised, enlarged edn, with Julian Gloag, 1954); What About Business?, 1943 (enlarged edn entitled What About Enterprise?, 1948); 2000 Years of England, 1952; Advertising in

Modern Life, 1959; A Social History of Furniture Design, 1966; *biography:* Mr Loudon's England, 1970. *Recreation:* reading. *Address:* 3 The Mall, East Sheen, SW14. *T:* 01-876 4530. *Clubs:* Arts, Garrick.

**GLOCK, Sir William (Frederick),** Kt 1970; CBE 1964; Controller of Music, British Broadcasting Corporation, since 1959; *b* London, 3 May 1908. *Educ:* Christ's Hospital; Caius Coll., Cambridge. Studied pianoforte under Artur Schnabel. Joined The Observer, 1934; Chief music critic, 1939-45. Served in RAF, 1941-46. Dir, Summer Sch. of Music, Bryanston, 1948, since 1953 at Dartington Hall. Editor of music magazine The Score, 1949-; adjudicated at Canadian music festivals, 1951; has lectured on music throughout England and Canada. Music Critic, New Statesman, 1958-59; Mem. Bd of Dirs, Royal Opera House, 1968-. Hon. DMus Nottingham Univ., 1968. *Address:* c/o British Broadcasting Corporation, Broadcasting House, W1.

**GLOSSOP, Clifford William Hudson;** agriculturist; Hon. (Life) Vice-President, South African Timber Growers Association; formerly Director of Yorks Electric Power Co., Electrical Distribution of Yorks Ltd, Thorne and District Water Co. (Chm.) and other companies; *b* 30 June 1901; *s* of late Major W. Glossop of Bramwith Hall, near Doncaster; unmarried. *Educ:* Harrow. Formerly Mem. of the Councils of the Royal Agricultural Society of England, The Yorkshire Agricultural Society, The Water Companies Association (Chm.), Yorks Institution for the Deaf; Pres. Elect British Friesian Cattle Soc., 1946 and 1947. MP (C) Penistone Division of Yorks, 1931-35; Mem. of Empire Parliamentary Association's delegation to Uganda and Tanganyika, 1934; Prospective Nat. C. candidate for Berwick-on-Tweed Division of Northumberland, 1936-38; prospective Nat. C. candidate for Howdenshire Division of Yorks, 1939-40 (resigned on appointment as Civil Servant; re-adopted candidate, 1944); Area Meat and Livestock Officer, Ministry of Food, for North-East England, 1940-44; MP (C) Howdenshire Division of Yorks, 1945-47; applied for Chiltern Hundreds, Oct. 1947. Formerly Divisional Comdr Doncaster Div. WR Special Constabulary; has travelled extensively throughout Europe, USA, Canada, West Indies, the Near East, New Zealand, Australia. *Address:* The Stables, 5 Chaceley Place, Durban, S Africa. *T:* Durban 47522. *Clubs:* Carlton, Junior Carlton; Victoria (Pietermaritzburg).

**GLOSSOP, Peter;** Principal Baritone, Royal Opera House, Covent Garden, until 1967, now Guest Artist; *b* 6 July 1928; *s* of Cyril and Violet Elizabeth Glossop; *m* 1955, Joyce Elizabeth Blackham; no *c. Educ:* High Storrs Grammar Sch., Sheffield. Began singing professionally in chorus of Sadler's Wells Opera, 1952, previously a bank clerk; promoted to principal after one season; Covent Garden Opera, 1962-67. Début in Italy, 1964; La Scala, Milan, début, Rigoletto, 1965. Sang Otello and Rigoletto with Metropolitan Opera Company at Newport USA Festival, Aug. 1967; Rigoletto and Nabucco with Mexican National Opera Company, Sept. 1967. Guest Artist (Falstaff, Rigoletto, Tosca) with American National Opera Company, Oct. 1967. Has sung in opera houses of Bologna, Parma Catania, Vienna, 1967-68, and Berlin and Buenos Aires. Is a recording artist. Hon. DMus, Sheffield, 1970. Winner of 1st Prize and Gold Medal in First International Competition for Young Opera Singers, Sofia, Bulgaria, 1961; Gold Medal for finest performance (in Macbeth) of 1968-69 season, Barcelona. *Recreation:* New Orleans jazz music. *Address:* Kenlade, 11 The Bishop's Avenue, East Finchley, N2.

**GLOUCESTER, Bishop of,** since 1962; **Rt. Rev. Basil Tudor Guy,** MA; *b* 9 March 1910; *s* of late Basil Guy and Edith Walrond Guy; *m* 1939, Mary Lilian Joan Ritson; two *s* one *d. Educ:* Forest Sch.; Keble Coll., Oxford; Wells Theological Coll. Ordained, 1934; Asst Curate, Wanstead, 1934-41; Vicar of Bradninch, Devon, 1941-46; Vicar of Tavistock, Devon, 1946-56; Prebendary of Exeter Cathedral, 1952-56; Archdeacon of Bedford, 1956-58; Examining Chaplain: to Bp of Exeter, 1952-56; to Bp of St Albans, 1956, Bishop Suffragan of Bedford, 1957-62. *Recreations:* cricket, golf, fishing, drama. *Address:* Palace House, Pitt Street, Gloucester GL1 2BQ. *T:* Gloucester 24598. *Club:* United University.

**GLOUCESTER, Dean of;** *see* Evans, Very Rev. S. J. A.

**GLOUCESTER, Archdeacon of;** *see* Wardle, Ven. W. T.

**GLOVER, Derek Harding,** CBE 1967; Financial Director, BOAC, since 1962; *b* 17 April 1916; *s* of Harold Harding Glover and Dora McRae; *m* 1947, Joan Marjorie Piper; two *s. Educ:* Hillcrest Prep. Sch., Frinton-on-Sea; Leys Sch., Cambridge. ACA 1937. Services, 1939-46; BOAC, 1946-. *Recreations:* golf, gardening, good food. *Address:* Burr Cottage, Burwood Park, Walton-on-Thames, Surrey. *T:* Walton-on-Thames 24495. *Clubs:* Stock Exchange Sailing, Burhill Golf, St George's Hill Tennis.

**GLOVER, Sir Douglas,** Kt 1960; TD 1945; *b* 13 Feb. 1908; *s* of S. Barnish Glover, Rochdale; *m* 1934, Agnes May, *d* of William Brown, JP, Netherlaw, Kirkcudbright, and Longfield, Heaton Mersey; no *c. Educ:* Giggleswick. TA 1939; 7th Manchester Rgt, 52 Div., NW Europe; Lieut-Col comdg Princess Louise Kensington Regt, 49 Div., 1945; despatches, 1946; comdg 9th Manchester Regt TA 1947-50; Bt-Col 1950; TARO 1950. Contested (C) Blackburn, 1945, Stalybridge and Hyde, 1950 and 1951; MP (C) Ormskirk, 1953-70. Chairman Young Conservatives, North-West Area, 1946; Treasurer, North-West, 1951-54; Mem., Nat. Exec. of Conservative Party, 1951-69; Chm. N Western Area, 1956-60; Chm., Nat. Union of Conservative Assocs, 1961-62. Delegate 10th Commonwealth Parl. Conf., Canberra, 1959. Mem. Mr Speaker's Panel of Chm., 1961; Chm. United and Cecil Club, 1962-65; Deleg. 17th Gen. Assembly of the UN, New York, 1962; Vice-Chm., Lancs and Ches Mems Cttee, 1966; Chm., Anti-Slavery Soc., 1965; Mem. Coun., Nat. Fedn of Housing Assocs, 1966. Governor, Giggleswick School, 1970-. Knight Officer, Order of Orange Nassau, 1946. *Address:* 48 Carrwood Road, Wilmslow, Cheshire. *T:* Wilmslow 23972; 37 Smith Square, SW1. *T:* 01-222 5135. *Clubs:* Carlton, Constitutional; St James's (Manchester).

**GLOVER, Harold;** Deputy Master of the Royal Mint, since 1970; *b* 29 Jan. 1917; 4th *s* of late George Glover, Wallasey, Ches; *m* 1949, Olive, *d* of late E. B. Robotham, Sawbridgeworth, Herts; two *s. Educ:* Wallasey Gram. Sch. Joined Customs and Excise, 1933; joined Min. of Works, 1949 (later MPBW); Controller of Supplies, 1957; Under-Secretary, 1967-70. Served RAF, 1940-46 (Flt Lieut Signals). Bicentenary Medal, RSA, 1967. FRSA. *Recreation:* music. *Address:* 23 Walnut Tree Crescent, Sawbridgeworth, Herts. *T:* Sawbridgeworth 3256. *Club:* Reform.

**GLOVER, John Neville,** CMG 1963; *b* 12 July 1913; *s* of John Robert Glover and Sybil Glover (*née* Cureton); *m* 1st, 1940, Margot Burdick; one *s*; 2nd, 1956, June Patricia Bruce Gaskell. *Educ:* Tonbridge Sch. Commissioned 6th Bn Devonshire Regt (TA), 1933; RAF (Gen. Duties Branch), 1934. Served RAF, 1934-46; RAFRO, 1946-59 (retained rank of Group Capt.). Called to Bar, Gray's Inn, 1949. Appointed to Colonial Legal Service, 1951; served: Ghana (Crown Counsel and Senior Crown Counsel), 1951-57; Western Pacific High Commission (Legal Adviser and Attorney-General, British Solomon Islands Protectorate), 1957-63. QC (Western Pacific), 1962. Retired from HM Overseas Civil Service, 1963. Comr to examine Human Rights Laws in the Bahamas, 1964-65. Legal Draftsman in the Bahamas, 1965-66. Law Revision Comr for certain overseas territories, 1967-. *Recreation:* fishing. *Address:* Clam End, Trebullet, near Launceston, Cornwall. *T:* Coad's Green 347. *Club:* Royal Air Force.

**GLOVER, Maj.-Gen. Malcolm;** CB 1947; OBE 1942; retired; *b* 25 July 1897; *m* Jean *d* of late Col. J. Will, RAMC; two *s* one *d*. *Educ:* Birkenhead Sch.; Staff Coll. Served European War, 1914-19, with South Lancashire Regt; transferred Indian Army; 14 Punjab Regt. War of 1939-45, AMGO GHQ India, 1940; BGS HQ North Western Army, 1941; Commander 3 Indian Infantry Brigade, 1943; Director of Organisation GHQ India (Maj.-Gen.) 1944; Deputy Adjutant General, 1946; retired 1948. *Address:* 5 The Lawn, Budleigh Salterton, Devon.

**GLOVER, Myles Howard;** Clerk of the Skinners' Company since 1959; Hon. Secretary, Governing Bodies' Association since 1967; Member, City & Guilds Art School Committee; *b* 18 Dec. 1928; *yr s* of Cedric Howard Glover and Winifred Mary (*née* Crewdson); *m* 1969, Wendy Gillian, *er d* of C. Coleman; one *s*. *Coleman. Educ:* Rugby; Balliol Coll., Oxford (MA). Called to the Bar, Lincoln's Inn, 1954. *Recreation:* music. *Address:* 9 Malvern Terrace, N1. *T:* 01-607 5790. *Clubs:* Savile, City of London, MCC.

**GLOVER, Maj.-Gen. Peter James,** CB 1966; OBE 1948; Director of Education Services, London Borough of Haringey, since 1970; *b* 16 Jan. 1913; *s* of late G. H. Glover, CBE, Sheephatch House, Tilford, Surrey, and late Mrs G. H. Glover; *m* 1946, Wendy Archer; one *s* two *d*. *Educ:* Uppingham; Cambridge (MA). 2nd Lieut RA, 1934; served War of 1939-45, BEF France and Far East; Lieut-Col 1956; Brig. 1961; Comdt, Sch. of Artillery, Larkhill, 1960-62; Maj.-Gen. 1962; GOC 49 Infantry Division TA and North Midland District, 1962-63; Head of British Defence Supplies Liaison Staff, Delhi, 1963-66; Director, Royal Artillery, 1966-69, retd. *Recreations:* field sports. *Address:* Sheephatch House, Tilford, Surrey. *Club:* Army and Navy.

**GLOVER, Robert Finlay,** TD 1954; Headmaster, Monmouth School, since 1959; *b* 28 June 1917; *yr s* of T. R. Glover, Public Orator in University of Cambridge, and Alice, *d* of H. G. Few; *m* 1941, Jean, *d* of late N. G. Muir, Lincoln; one *s* two *d*. *Educ:* The Leys Sch.; Corpus Christi Coll., Oxford. Served in Royal Artillery (TA), 1939-46; Staff Coll., Camberley, 1944; Major, 1944. Asst Master, Ampleforth Coll., 1946-50; Head of Classics Dept, King's Sch., Canterbury, 1950-53; Headmaster, Adams' Grammar Sch., Newport, Salop, 1953-59. *Publications:* Notes on Latin, 1954; (with R. W. Harris) Latin for Historians, 1954. *Recreations:* watching cricket, rugby football, music. *Address:* Headmaster's House, Monmouth School, Monmouth NP5 3XP. *T:* Monmouth 3143. *Club:* Royal Societies'.

**GLOVER, Ronald Everett,** CBE 1966; MA, DSc, FRCVS; retired as Principal and Dean of the Royal Veterinary College (University of London) (1955-65). Formerly Professor of Veterinary Pathology, University of Liverpool. *Address:* c/o Royal Veterinary College, Royal College Street, NW1. *T:* 01-387 2898.

**GLOVER, William James,** QC 1969; *b* 8 May 1924; *s* of late H. P. Glover, KC and Martha Glover; *m* 1956, Rosemary D. Long; two *s*. *Educ:* Harrow; Pembroke Coll., Cambridge. Served with Royal West African Frontier Force in West Africa and Burma, 1944-47. Called to Bar, Inner Temple, 1950. Second Junior Counsel to Inland Revenue (Rating Valuation), 1963-69. *Recreation:* golf. *Address:* Fairlawn, Ashwood Road, Woking, Surrey. *T:* Woking 61850. *Club:* Oxford and Cambridge University.

**GLUBB, Lt-Gen. Sir John Bagot,** KCB 1956; CMG 1946; DSO 1941; OBE 1925; MC; Chief of General Staff, the Arab Legion, Amman, Jordan, 1939-56; *b* 16 April 1897; *s* of late Maj.-Gen. Sir F. M. Glubb, KCMG, CB, DSO; *m* 1938, Muriel Rosemary, *d* of Dr J. G. Forbes; two *s* two *d*. *Educ:* Cheltenham; Royal Military Academy, Woolwich, Aug. 1914; 2nd Lieut RE, 1915; served in France (wounded thrice, MC); to Iraq as Lieut RE, 1920; resigned commission, 1926, and became Administrative Inspector, Iraq Govt; transferred Transjordan, 1930; Officer Commanding Desert Area, 1932; Officer Commanding Arab Legion, Transjordan, 1939. *Publications:* Story of the Arab Legion, 1948; A Soldier with the Arabs, 1957; Britain and the Arabs, 1959; War in the Desert, 1960; The Great Arab Conquests, 1963; The Empire of the Arabs, 1963; The Course of Empire, 1965; The Lost Centuries, 1967; The Middle East Crisis - A Personal Interpretation, 1967; Syria, Lebanon, Jordan, 1967; A Short History of The Arab Peoples, 1969; The Life and Times of Muhammad, 1970. *Club:* East India and Sports.

**GLUCKMAN, Prof. Max,** BA Rand, MA, DPhil Oxon, MA Manchester; FBA 1968; Professor of Social Anthropology, University of Manchester, since 1949; *b* Johannesburg, South Africa, 26 Jan. 1911; 2nd *s* of late Emmanuel Gluckman and of Kate Gluckman; *m* 1939, Mary Brignoli; three *s*. *Educ:* King Edward VII Sch., Johannesburg; Univ. of Witwatersrand; Exeter Coll., Oxford. Johannesburg Municipal Schol., 1928-30; Transvaal Rhodes Schol., 1934; Research for Nat. Bureau of Educnl and Social Research, S Africa, 1936-38; Asst Anthropologist, Rhodes-Livingstone Inst., Northern Rhodesia, 1939-41; Dir, 1941-47; Univ. Lectr in Social Anthropology, Oxford, 1947-49. Field Research: Zululand, 1936-38; Barotseland, 1939-47; Tonga of N Rhodesia, 1944; Lamba, 1946. Wellcome Medal, Royal Anthropological Inst., 1945; Frazer Memorial Lecture, Glasgow Univ., 1952; Rivers Memorial Medal, 1954; Josiah Mason Lectures, Birmingham Univ., 1955-56; Munro Foundn Lectures, Edinburgh Univ., 1958 and 1960; Storrs Lectures, Yale Law Sch., 1963; Marett Lecture, Exeter Coll., Oxford, 1964, 1965; Vis. Fellow, Aust. Nat. Univ., 1960; Vis. Professor: Delhi Univ., 1960; MS Univ. of Baroda, 1960; Vis. Lectr, Yale Law Sch., 1966, 1968; Fellow, Center for Advanced Studies in the Behavioral Sciences, Palo Alto, 1967; Member: Human Sciences Cttee, DSIR, 1958-

63; Exec. Council, Internat. African Inst., 1959- (and Consultative Dir, 1968-); Social Anthropology Sub-cttee, Social Science Research Council, 1966-69; Social Studies Sub-cttee, University Grants Cttee, 1966-. Served N Rhodesia Defence Force, 1940-45. Chm. Assoc. of Social Anthropologists of the British Commonwealth, 1962-66. Foreign Hon. Mem., Amer. Acad. of Arts and Sciences, 1970. Dr *hc* Soc. Sc., Univ. de Bruxelles, 1965. *Publications:* Economy of the Central and Barotse Plain, 1941; Essays on Lozi Land and Royal Property, 1943; The Barotse Native Authorities, 1943; (with others) Land holding and Land-usage among the Tonga of Mazabuka District, 1945; The Judicial Process among the Barotse of Northern Rhodesia, 1955 (rev. Edn 1967); Rituals of Rebellion in South-East Africa, 1954; Custom and Conflict in Africa, 1955; (ed jtly and contrib.) Seven Tribes of British Central Africa, 1951; Order and Rebellion in Tribal Africa, 1963; Politics, Law and Ritual in Tribal Society, 1965; The Ideas in Barotse Jurisprudence, 1965; (ed and conyrib.) Essays on the Ritual of Social Relations, 1962, Closed Systems and Open Minds, 1964; (ed) Ideas and Procedures in African Customary Law, 1969; various papers in symposia, and in anthropological journals. *Recreations:* golf, sailing, cricket, watching Association football, reading. *Address:* Sheen, Ladybrook Road, Bramhall, Cheshire. *Club:* Royal Commonwealth Society.

**GLUCKMANN, Grigory;** Artist-painter; *b* Russia, 25 Oct. 1898; *m*; American citizen. *Educ:* Ecole des Beaux Arts, Moscow. In Paris from 1924, left for US, 1941. Exhibited at the Salon des Tuileries, Salon d'Automne (Sociétaire), Salon National des Beaux-Arts (Sociétaire), from 1925. Numerous one-man shows in Paris, London, New York, Los Angeles, Chicago, etc; from 1924, represented in Musée du Luxembourg, Paris (2 paintings), Petit Palais, Paris (2), Art Institute of Chicago and various other galleries and collections. Watson F. Blair Prize at the International Water Colour Exhibn, 1938, and at 56th Annual Exhibn, 1945, the Art Inst. of Chicago. FRSA 1948; FIAL 1965. Illustrated: Nuits Florentines by Heinrich Heine; Salvator Rosa by Hoffmann; Manon Lescaut by l'Abbé Prévost. *Relevant publication:* Grigory Gluckmann, by Arthur Millier. *Address:* 155 North Hamel Drive, Beverly Hills, Calif, USA. *T:* Olympia 20482.

**GLUCKSTEIN, Isidore Montague;** President, J. Lyons & Co. Ltd, 1961-68, retired (Chairman, 1956-60); *b* 2 Nov. 1890; *s* of Montague and Matilda Gluckstein; *m* 1920, Rosalind Sophie, *d* of Rev. Michael Adler, DSO, CF, BA, and Sophie Adler; one *s* died of wounds, one *d* decd. *Educ:* St Paul's Sch.; Sidney Sussex Coll., Cambridge (MA). Served European War, 1914-18; Capt., London Regt (wounded, despatches). Called to the Bar, Inner Temple, 1919. Vice-Pres., Anglers' Co-Operative Association. *Recreation:* fishing. *Address:* 35 Cumberland Terrace, Regent's Park, NW1. *Clubs:* Flyfishers' (Pres.), Buck's.

**GLUCKSTEIN, Sir Louis Halle,** GBE 1969 (CBE 1964); Kt 1953; TD 1950; QC 1945; DL; Colonel 5th Suffolk Regiment TA; Director, British Transport Hotels Ltd, since 1963; *b* London, 23 Feb. 1897; *s* of late Joseph Gluckstein, OBE, and Francesca (*née* Halle), MBE, JP; *m* 1925, Doreen, *d* of Alexander Klean, London; two *s* one *d*. *Educ:* St Paul's Sch. (Schol.); Lincoln Coll., Oxford (Schol., MA; Hon. Fellow, 1968). Served European War, 1915-18, Lieut Suffolk Regt (wounded, despatches); served War of 1939-45: France, 1940 (despatches); Italy, 1944. Called to Bar, Lincoln's Inn, 1922, Bencher, 1952, Treasurer, 1970. MP (U) East Nottingham, 1931-45; contested East Nottingham, 1929, 1945 and 1950; contested Holborn and St Pancras South, 1951; DL County of London, 1952; Mem., LCC for St Marylebone, 1955-64; Mem., GLC for City of Westminster, 1964-67; Alderman, 1967-; Chm., Finance and Supplies Commn, 1967-68; Chm., GLC, 1968-69. Chairman: Board of Army Kinema Corp., 1956-68; Services Kinema Corp., 1969-. pres., Royal Albert Hall, 1965 (Vice-Pres., 1961-65); Vice-Pres., Old Pauline Club, 1958, Pres., 1966-69. Pres., St Marylebone Conservative Assoc., 1967-. A Governor of St Paul's Sch., London, 1968. Commendatore, Italian Order of Merit, 1969. *Recreations:* golf, shooting. *Address:* 39 Elm Tree Road, NW8. *T:* 01-286 7169. *Clubs:* Carlton, Savage; Leander.

**GLUECKAUF, Eugen,** DrIng, DSc, FRS 1969; Head of Physical and Radiochemistry Branch, Chemistry Division, Atomic Energy Research Establishment, Harwell, Berks; *b* 9 April 1906; *m* 1934, Irma E. A. Glueckauf (*née* Tepper); one *d*. *Educ:* Technische Hochschule, Berlin. Research Asst to Prof. F. A. Paneth, Imperial Coll., London, 1934-39; Res. Associate, Durham Colls, 1939-47; Mackinnon Res. Student of Royal Society, 1942-44. Group-leader and later Branch-head in Chem. Div., AERE, Harwell, 1947-. *Publications:* Atomic Energy Waste, 1961; contribs in fields of: microgasanalysis of atmospheric gases, theory of ion exchange and chromatography, radio chemistry, electrolyte solution chemistry. *Recreations:* gardening, music, travel. *Address:* Bankside, Chilton, Berks. *T:* Rowstock 296.

**GLYN,** family name of **Baron Wolverton.**

**GLYN, Dr Alan,** ERD; MP (C) Windsor since 1970; *b* 26 Sept. 1918; *s* of John Paul Glyn, Barrister-at-Law, Middle Temple, and Margaret Johnston, Edinburgh; *m* 1962, Lady Rosula Caroline Windsor Clive, *y d* of 2nd Earl of Plymouth, PC, GCStJ (*d* 1943), St Fagan's, Cardiff, S Wales; two *d*. *Educ:* Westminster; Caius Coll., Cambridge; St Bartholomew:s and St George's Hosps. BA (Hons) Cantab 1939. Qualified medical practitioner, 1948. Served War of 1939-45; Far East, 1942-46; psc 1945; Bde Major, 1946; Capt. (Hon. Major) Royal Horse Guards (ER); att. French Foreign Legion, 1960. Called to Bar, Middle Temple, 1955. Co-opted Mem. LCC Education Cttee, 1956-58. MP (C) Clapham Div. of Wandsworth, 1959-64. Member: Chelsea Borough Coun., 1959-62; No 1 Divisional Health Cttee (London), 1959-61; Inner London Local Med. Cttee, 1967-; Governing Body, Brit. Postgrad. Med. Fedn; Greater London Cent. Valuation Panel. Governor, Henry Thornton and Aristotle Schs; Manager, Macaulay C. of E. Sch., Richard Atkins, Henry Cavendish, Telfescot, Glenbrook and Boneville Primary Schs in Clapham. One of Earl Marshal's Green Staff Officers at Investiture of HRH Prince of Wales, Caernarvon, 1969. Freeman, Worshipful Soc. of the Art and Mystery of Apothecaries of the City of London, 1961. Pro-Hungaria Medal of SMO Malta, 1959. *Publication:* Witness to Viet Nam (the containment of communism in South East Asia), 1968. *Address:* 17 Cadogan Place, Belgrave Square, SW1. *T:* 01-235 2957. *Club:* Carlton.

**GLYN, Sir Anthony (Geoffrey Leo Simon),** 2nd Bt, *cr* 1927; author; *b* 13 March 1922; *s* of Sir Edward Davson, 1st Bt, and Margot, OBE (*d* 1966), *er d* of late Clayton Glyn and late Mrs Elinor Glyn; *S* father, Sir Edward Rae Davson, KCMG, 1937; assumed by deed poll, 1957, the surname of Glyn in lieu of his patronymic, and the additional forename of Anthony; *m* 1946, Susan Eleanor, barrister-at-law, 1950, *er d* of Sir Rhys Rhys-Williams, 1st Bt, DSO, QC, and Dame Juliet Rhys-Williams, DBE; two *d*. *Educ:* Eton. Jnd Welsh Guards, 1941; served Guards Armoured Div., 1942-45; Staff Capt, 1945. *Publications:* Romanza, 1953; The Jungle of Eden, 1954; Elinor Glyn, a biography, 1955 (Book Society Non-Fiction Choice); The Ram in the Thicket, 1957 (Dollar Book Club Choice); I Can Take it All, 1959 (Book Society Choice); Kick Turn, 1963; The Terminal, 1965; The Seine, 1966; The Dragon Variation, 1969; The Blood of a Britishman, 1970. *Recreations:* mountaineering, chess, music. *Heir:* *b* Christopher Michael Edward Davson, ACA, late Capt. Welsh Guards [*b* 26 May 1927; *m* 1962, Evelyn Mary, *o d* of late James Wardrop; one *s*]. *Address:* 6 Rue St Louis en l'Ile, Paris 4me. *T:* Odeon 0961; Orchard Cottage, Chawton, Alton, Hants. *Clubs:* Savile, Pratt's.

**GLYN, John Patrick Riversdale;** Chairman: Agricultural Mortgage Corporation Ltd; Alexanders Discount Co. Ltd; Yorkshire Bank Ltd; Deputy Chairman, John Govett & Co Ltd; Director, Exchange Telegraph (Holdings) Co.; a Development Commissioner since 1965; *b* 17 April 1913; *s* of Maurice G. C. Glyn and Hon. Maud Grosvenor; *m* 1937, Audrey Margaret Stubbs; two *s* two *d*. *Educ:* Eton; New Coll., Oxford. Major, Grenadier Guards. A Man. Dir, Glyn, Mills & Co., 1950-70. *Recreations:* fishing, shooting. *Address:* The Dower House, Chute Standen, near Andover, Hants. *T:* Chute Standen 228. *Clubs:* Boodle's, Pratt's.

**GLYN, Col Sir Richard Hamilton,** 5th Bt *cr* 1800, and 9th Bt *cr* 1759; OBE 1955; TD 1941; DL; *b* 12 Oct. 1907; *e s* of Sir Richard Fitzgerald Glyn, 4th and 8th Bt, DSO; *S* father, 1960; *m* 1st, 1939, Lyndsay Mary Baker (marr. diss. 1969); two *s* one *d*; 2nd, 1970, Mrs Barbara Henwood. *Educ:* Worcester Coll., Oxford. 2nd Lieut QO Dorset Yeo. Fd Regt, RA, TA, 1930; comd 141 Dorset Yeo. Fd Regt, RA, TA, 1944-45; comd 294 QO Dorset Yeo. Fd Regt, RA, TA, 1952-55; Hon. Col 1959; ADC, 1958-62. Called to Bar, Lincoln's Inn, 1935. Dep. Chm., Dorset QS, 1952-57. MP (C) North Dorset, 1957-70. Mem., Chelsea Borough Council, 1948-50 (Vice-Chm., Housing Cttee); Mem., Shaftesbury RDC, 1957. PPS to Sir D. Eccles (Pres. Board of Trade), june-Oct. 1958. Vice-Chm., Cons. Agric. Cttee, 1959-; Chm., Cons. Army Cttee, Vice-Chm., Cons. Defence Cttee, 1961-; Mem., Select Cttee on Estimates (Defence and Overseas), 1964-; Comr, Commonwealth War Graves Commn, 1965-. Chairman: Cruft's Dog Show, 1963-; United and Cecil Club, 1960-64; Pres., Soc. of Dorset Men, 1963-70. DL Dorset 1960. *Publications:* Bull Terriers and How to Breed Them, 1937 (6th edn 1953); A Short Account of the Queen's Own Dorset Yeomanry, 1943; Champion Dogs of the World, 1967; The World's Finest Horses and Ponies, 1971. *Recreations:* sport, travel and pedigree livestock. *Heir:* *s* Richard Lindsay Glyn [*b* 3 Aug. 1943. *Educ:* Eton]. *Address:* Bugley Court, Gillingham, Dorset. *T:* Gillingham 3242. *Clubs:* Carlton, Kennel.

**GLYN HUGHES, Hugh Llewelyn;** *see* Hughes, H. L. G.

**GLYN-JONES, Sir Hildreth,** Kt 1953; TD 1950; Judge of the High Court of Justice, Queen's Bench Division, 1953-68; *b* 19 March 1895; *s* of late Sir William Samuel Glyn-Jones and Mary Evans; *m* 1921, Kathleen, *d* of Thomas Melville; three *d*. *Educ:* City of London Sch. Military service, 1914-19 and 1939-44 (Middx Regt, Machine Gun Corps and Judge Advocate-General's Office). Qualified pharmacist, 1920; called to Bar, Middle Temple, 1921; QC 1943; Wales and Chester circuit; Recorder of Merthyr Tydfil, 1944-45; Recorder of Cardiff, 1945-53; Bencher, Middle Temple, 1951. JP (Berks), 1951; Deputy Chm., Berks Quarter Sessions, 1951-62. *Address:* Stone House, Bramley, near Guildford, Surrey. *Club:* Reform.

**GLYNN, Ian Michael,** PhD, FRS 1970; Reader in Membrane Physiology, University of Cambridge, since Oct. 1970; *b* 3 June 1928; 2nd *s* of Hyman and Charlotte Glynn; *m* 1959, Jenifer Muriel, 2nd *d* of Ellis and Muriel Franklin; one *s* two *d*. *Educ:* City of London Sch.; Trinity Coll., Cambridge; University Coll. Hosp. 1st cl. in Pts I and II of Nat. Sci. Tripos; Sen. Schol., Trin. Coll.; BA (Cantab) 1949; MB, BChir, 1952. House Phys., Central Mddx Hosp., 1952-53; Med. Res. Council Scholar at Physiol. Lab., Cambridge; PhD 1956. Nat. Service in RAF Med. Br., 1956-57; Trin. Coll. Res. Fellow, 1955-59, Staff Fellow and Dir of Med. Studies, 1961-; Cambridge Univ. Demonstrator in Physiology, 1958-63, Lecturer, 1963-70. Vis. Prof., Yale Univ., 1969. Chm., Editorial Bd, Jl of Physiology, 1968-70. *Publications:* scientific papers dealing with transport of ions across living membranes, mostly in Jl of Physiology. *Address:* Physiological Laboratory, Cambridge; Daylesford, Conduit Head Road, Cambridge. *T:* Cambridge 53079.

**GLYNN GRYLLS, Rosalie;** *see* Mander, Lady (Rosalie).

**GOAD, Edward Colin Viner;** Secretary-General, Intergovernmental Maritime Consultative Organization, since Jan. 1968 (Deputy Secretary-General, 1963-68); *b* 21 Dec. 1914; *s* of Maurice George Viner Goad and Caroline (*née* Masters); *m* 1939, Joan Olive Bradley; one *s*. *Educ:* Cirencester Grammar Sch.; Gonville and Caius Coll., Cambridge (Scholar, BA, First Class Hons). Ministry of Transport: Asst Principal, 1937; Principal, 1942; Asst Sec., 1948; Imperial Defence Coll., 1953; Under-Sec., 1963. *Recreations:* gardening, reading, eighteenth-century furniture. *Address:* 4 Woodland Court, Epsom, Surrey. *T:* Epsom 20020; The Paddock, Ampney Crucis, Glos. *Club:* Anglo-Belgian.

**GOADBY, Hector Kenneth,** FRCP; retired; Hon. Consulting Physician, St Thomas's Hospital, London; *b* 16 May 1902; *s* of late Sir Kenneth Goadby, KBE; *m* 1937, Margaret Evelyn (*née* Boggon); one *s* two *d*. *Educ:* Winchester; Trinity Coll., Cambridge (MA, MD). MRCS, LRCP 1926; FRCP 1936. Physician, St Thomas's Hosp., 1934-67; Cons. Physician, Southern Army and Eastern Comd, India, 1945; Physician, St Peter's Hosp., Chertsey, 1948. *Publications:* contribs to Jl of Physiology, Lancet, Acta Medica Scandinavica. *Recreations:* sailing, golf. *Address:* 103 Worple Road, Wimbledon, SW20. *T:* 01-946 7820. *Clubs:* Royal Cruising; Rye Golf.

**GOBBI, Tito;** opera singer, baritone; *b* 24 Oct. 1915; *s* of Giovanni and Enrica Weiss; *m* 1937, Tilde de Rensis; one *d*. *Educ:* Padua Univ. Scholarship, Scala Opera House, 1938-39. Appeared Rome Opera House, 1939. Repertoire of 99 operas. Has sung in all the major opera houses and concert halls throughout the world. Notably Salzburg Festival: Don Giovanni (under Fürtwangler), 1950; Falstaff (under von Karajan), 1957. Has recorded 21 Complete Operas and made numerous other records; has made many films and appeared on television in England, USA and Italy. Started as Stage Director, Lyric Opera of Chicago, Oct. 1965; then Royal Opera House, Covent Garden, Master classes in Italy, USA and England. London. Mem., The Friends of Covent Garden. Disco d'Oro (Golden Record), 1959; Leopardo d'Oro, 1962. Hon. Officer, NY Police. Commendatore al Merito della Repubblica Italiana, 1958; Officer of San Jago, Portugal. *Recreations:* painting, driving, shooting, moulding. *Address:* via Asmara 10, Rome. *T:* 837350. *Clubs:* Arts (London) (Hon. Mem.); Societa Dante Alighieri; (Patron) Verdi Soc. (Liverpool); Roma Libera (Rome); Lyons (Hon. Mem.).

**GODBER,** family name of **Baron Godber.**

**GODBER,** 1st Baron *cr* 1956, of Mayfield; **Frederick Godber,** Kt 1942; Grand Officer in Order of Orange Nassau, 1947; Chairman, Commonwealth Development Finance Co. Ltd, 1953-68; *b* 6 Nov. 1888; *s* of Edward and Marion Louise Godber; *m* 1914, Violet Ethel Beatrice Lovesy; two *d.* Spent 10 years in the United States, 1919-29; Pres., Rhoxana Corp., 1922-28; Dir, Shell Union Oil Corp., 1922-46; Chm., Shell Union Oil Corp., 1937-46; one of Managing Dirs of Royal Dutch/Shell Group, 1929-46; Chm. and Man. Dir, Shell Transport & Trading Co. Ltd, 1946-61; Chm., Shell Petroleum Co. Ltd, 1946-61. During war of 1939-45, Chm. of Overseas Supplies Cttee of Petroleum Board and served on number of Govt Missions. Hon. Bencher, Middle Temple, 1954. Hon. Liveryman, Leathersellers' Co., 1962. Hon. FInstPet, 1965. Cadman Medal, 1957. A Trustee of Churchill Coll. Trust Fund, Cambridge, 1958-. Pres., Festivals of Films for Industry, 1957-60. *Recreations:* gardening and farming. *Address:* 50 Kingston House, Prince's Gate, SW7. *T:* 01-589 4722; Cranesden, Mayfield, Sussex. *T:* Mayfield 3271.

**GODBER, Geoffrey Chapham,** CBE 1961; Clerk of the Peace and Clerk to the West Sussex County Council since 1966; Clerk to the Lieutenancy of Sussex, since 1968; *b* 22 Sept. 1912; *s* of late Isaac Godber, Willington Manor, near Bedford; *m* 1937, Norah Enid (*née* Finney); three *s. Educ:* Bedford Sch. LLB (London) 1935; Solicitor, 1936. Deputy Clerk of the Peace, Northants, 1938-44; Clerk of the Peace, Clerk of the County Council and Clerk of the Lieutenancy, Salop, 1944-66; Hon. Sec., Soc. of Clerks of the Peace of Counties, 1953-61 (Chm., 1961-64). Member: Probation Adv. and Trg Bd, 1949-55; Child Care Adv. Council, 1953-56; Cttee of Inquiry into Inland Waterways, 1956-58; Redevelopment Adv. Cttee, Inland Waterways, 1959-62; Waterways Sub-Commn, Brit. Transport, 1959-62; Central Adv. Water Cttee, 1961; Minister of Health's Long Term Study Group, 1965-69; S-E Economic Planning Council, 1969-. *Recreations:* sailing, shooting. *Address:* Pricklows, Singleton, Chichester, Sussex. *T:* Singleton 238. *Club:* United Service.
*See also Rt Hon J. B. Godber.*

**GODBER, Sir George (Edward),** KCB 1962 (CB 1958); Chief Medical Officer, Department of Health and Social Security, Department of Education and Science, and Home Office; *b* 4 Aug. 1908; *s* of late I. Godber, Willington Manor, Bedford; *m* 1935, Norma Hathorne Rainey; three *s* one *d* (and one *s* two *d* decd). *Educ:* Bedford Sch.; New Coll., Oxford; London Hospital; London Sch. of Hygiene. BA Oxon 1930; DM Oxon 1939; FRCP 1947; DPH London 1936. Medical Officer, Min. of Health, 1939; Dep. Chief Medical Officer, Min. of Health, 1950-60. QHP, 1953-56. Hon. Fellow: American Hospital Assoc., and American Public Health Assoc., 1961; British Orthopaedic Assoc.; Mem. Dietetic Assoc., 1961; Hon. Member: Faculty of Radiologists, 1959; British Pædiatric Assoc. Hon. LLD Manchester, 1964, 150th Anniversary Medal, Swedish Med. Soc., 1966. *Publications:* (with Sir L. Parsons and Mr Clayton Fryers) Survey of Hospitals in the Sheffield Region, 1944; papers in Lancet, BMJ, Public Health. Lectures: Thomas and Edith Dixon Belfast, 1962; Bartholomew, Rotunda, Dublin, 1963; Woolmer, Bio-Engineering Soc., 1964; Monkton Copeman, Soc. of Apothecaries, 1968; Michael M. Davis, Chicago, 1969; Harold Diehl, Amer. Public Health Assoc., 1969; Rhys Williams, 1969. *Recreation:* golf. *Address:* The Cedars, Roxton, Bedford. *T:* Great Barford 260. *Club:* United University.

**GODBER, Rt. Hon. Joseph Bradshaw,** PC 1963; MP (C) Grantham Division of Lincs since 1951; Minister of State, Foreign and Commonwealth Office, since 1970; *b* 17 March 1914; 5th *s* of late Isaac Godber and B. M. Godber (*née* Chapman), Willington Manor; *m* 1936, Miriam Sanders; two *s. Educ:* Bedford Sch. Entered family business, 1932. County Councillor, Beds, 1946-52. Asst Govt Whip, 1955-57; Joint Parliamentary Sec., Min. of Agriculture, Fisheries and Food, 1957-60; Parliamentary Under-Sec. of State, Foreign Office, 1960-61; Minister of State, 1961-63; Minister of Labour, 1963-64; Leader, British Delegn to: United Nations General Assembly, 1961-62; 18-Power Disarmament Conference, 1962-63; Commonwealth Parly Assoc., 1970-; Sec. of State for War, June-Oct. 1963; Chief Opposition Spokesman on Agriculture, 1965-70. *Recreations:* gardening, shooting. *Address:* Willington Manor, near Bedford. *T:* Cardington 284. *Club:* Constitutional.
*See also G. C. Godber.*

**GODDARD,** Baron (Life Peer), *cr* 1944, of Aldbourne; **Rayner Goddard;** PC 1938; GCB 1958; Kt 1932; Lord Chief Justice of England, 1946-58, retired; *b* 1877; *m* 1906, Mary Linda (*d* 1928), *d* of Sir Felix Schuster, 1st Bt; three *d. Educ:* Marlborough; Trinity Coll., Oxford. BA 1898; MA 1931. Hon. Fellow, Trinity Coll., Oxford, 1940; Hon. DCL, Oxford, Montreal and New York Univs; Hon. LLD, Cambridge and Sheffield Univs. KC 1923. Recorder of Poole, 1917-25, of Bath, 1925-28, of Plymouth, 1928-32; Judge of High Court, King's Bench Division, 1932-38; Lord Justice of Appeal, 1938-44; a Lord of Appeal in Ordinary, 1944-46. *Address:* Queen Elizabeth Building, Temple, EC4. *T:* 01-353 5480.
*See also Rt Hon. Sir Eric Sachs.*

**GODDARD, Lt-Gen. Eric Norman,** CB 1947; CIE 1944; CBE 1942 (OBE 1919); MVO 1936; MC; IA, retired; *b* 6 July 1897; 3rd *s* of late Arthur Goddard, Chartered Acct, London; *m* 1939, Elizabeth Lynch, *d* of late Major Lynch Hamilton, MBE, and late Frances Prioleau; one *s. Educ:* Dulwich Coll. Commission into Indian Army, 1915; service in Mesopotamia, Persia and Kurdistan, 1916-19 (despatches twice, OBE, MC); GSO3 AHQ India, 1923-25; Staff Coll., Quetta, 1928-29; Bde Major, Nowshera Bde, 1932-34; Chitral Relief Operations, 1932 (despatches, bar to MC); Mohmand operations, 1933 (despatches); Bt Major, 1933; GSO2 Eastern Comd, 1934-36; Officer i/c King's Indian Orderly Officers, 1936 (MVO 4th class); Comdt 4th Bn 15 Punjab Regt, 1936; Col 1939 and Col i/c Administration, Burma Army; Brigade Commander, Oct. 1940; Maj.-Gen. i/c Administration Army in Burma, Dec. 1941; served in Burma and on Eastern front, Dec. 1941-Dec. 1944, including Maj.-Gen. i/c Admin 11th Army Group and Allied Land

Forces SE Asia, 1943-44 (despatches four times, CIE, CBE); GOC-in-C Southern Comd, India, 1947-48; Subst. Maj.-Gen. 1944; Actg Lieut-Gen. 1947; retired Nov. 1948 with hon. rank of Lieut-Gen. Special appointment CC Germany, 1949-53; Dir of Civil Defence, North-Western Region (Manchester), 1955-63; Pres., East Lancs Br., British Red Cross, 1964-66. *Address:* Muddles Cottage, Sparrows Green, Wadhurst, Sussex. *Club:* United Service.

**GODDARD, Maj.-Gen. John Desmond,** MC 1944; Director, Military Assistance Office, Ministry of Defence, since 1969; *b* 13 Jan. 1919; *s* of late Major J. Goddard, HAC, Bombay and Gerrards Cross, Bucks; *m* 1948, Sheila Noel Vera, *d* of C. W. H. P. Waud, Bombay and St John, Jersey; three *s* one *d*. *Educ:* Sherborne; RMA Woolwich. 2 Lieut, RA, 1939. Served War of 1939-45: France, 1939-40; N Africa, 1943; Italy, 1943-45. Brevet Lt-Col 1957; JSSC 1957; CO, 2 Fd Regt, RA, 1960-62; IDC 1964; CRA, 3 Div., 1965-66; BGS, Directorate Mil. Ops, MoD, 1966-69. *Recreations:* yachting, riding, shooting, golf, carpentry, gardening. *Address:* Cranford, Pinewood Hill, Fleet, Hants. *T:* Fleet 4825. *Clubs:* Army and Navy; Royal Lymington Yacht (Lymington).

**GODDARD, Air Marshal (retired) Sir (Robert) Victor,** KCB 1947 (CB 1943); CBE 1940; MA Cantab; *b* 1897; *s* of late Charles Ernest Goddard, OBE, TD, MD; *m* 1924, Mildred Catherine Jane, *d* of Alfred Markham Inglis; two *s* one *d*. *Educ:* RN Colls Osborne and Dartmouth; Jesus Coll., Cambridge; Imperial Coll. of Science, London. Served European War, 1914-19, with RN, RNAS, RFC and RAF; War of 1939-45 (despatches, CBE, CB, American DSM); Dep. Dir of Intelligence, Air Min., 1938-39; AOA, GHQ, BEF, France, 1939, SASO 1940; Dir of Military Co-operation, Air Ministry, 1940-41; Chief of the Air Staff, New Zealand, and Commander Royal NZ Air Forces, South Pacific, 1941-43; Air Officer i/c Administration, Air Command, South-East Asia, 1943-46; RAF Representative at Washington, USA, 1946-48; Mem. of Air Council for Technical Services, 1948-51; retd 1951. Principal of the Coll. of Aeronautics, 1951-54. Governor (Chm. 1948-57), St George's Sch., Harpenden, 1948-64; Governor, Bryanston Sch., 1957-. Occasional broadcaster, 1934-. *Publication:* The Enigma of Menace, 1959. *Address:* Meadowgate, Brasted, near Westerham, Kent.

**GODDARD, Air Marshal Sir Victor;** *see* Goddard, Air Marshal Sir (Robert) V.

**GODDEN, Rumer;** *see* Haynes Dixon, Margaret Rumer.

**GODDEN, Tony Richard Hillier;** Under-Secretary, Scottish Development Department, since 1969; *b* 13 Nov. 1927; *o s* of late Richard Godden and of Gladys Eleanor Godden; *m* 1953, Marjorie Florence Snell; one *s* two *d*. *Educ:* Barnstaple Grammar Sch.; London Sch. of Economics. Commissioned, RAF Education Branch, 1950. Entered Colonial Office as Asst Principal, 1951; Private Sec. to Parly Under-Sec. of State, 1954-55; Principal, 1956; Cabinet Office, 1957-59; transferred to Scottish Home Dept, 1961; Asst Sec., Scottish Development Dept, 1964. *Recreations:* philately, photography, music. *Address:* 9 Ross Road, Edinburgh 9. *T:* 031-667 6556. *Club:* Royal Commonwealth Society.

**GÖDEL, Prof. Kurt;** Professor, School of Mathematics, Institute for Advanced Study, Princeton, NJ, since 1953; *b* 28 April 1906; *s* of Rudolf and Marianne Gödel; *m* 1938, Adele Porkert; no *c*. *Educ:* Univ. of Vienna, Austria. Dozent, Univ. of Vienna, 1933-38; Mem., Inst. for Advanced Study, 1933, 1935, 1938-52. Einstein Award, 1951; holds hon. doctorates from Univs in USA, 1951-. Member: Nat. Acad. Sci. (USA); Amer. Phil. Soc.; Amer. Acad. Arts and Sci.; Hon. Mem., London Math. Soc., 1967; For. Mem., Royal Soc., London, 1968. *Publications:* The Consistency of the Continuum Hypothesis, 1940; Contribs to: Monatsh. für Math. und Phys.; Proc. Nat. Acad. Sci.; Reviews of Mod. Phys.; Internat. Cong. Math., 1950; Dialectica, etc. *Address:* Institute for Advanced Study, Princeton, NJ, USA. *T:* WA4-4400.

**GODFREY, Sir John (Albert),** Kt, *cr* 1950; *b* 17 Feb. 1889; *s* of Robert Arthur Godfrey; *m* 1924, Teresa Christine Kilgallin. *Educ:* Tollington Central Sch.; Civil Service Department of King's Coll., London. Entered Customs and Excise Dept, 1911; Superintending Inspector, 1944; Deputy Chief Inspector, 1946; Chief Inspector, 1947-54. *Recreations:* tennis, motoring. *Address:* 258 Fir Tree Road, Epsom Downs, Surrey. *T:* Burgh Heath 51839.

**GODFREY, Adm. John Henry,** CB 1939; *b* 10 July 1888; *s* of Godfrey Henry Godfrey; *m* 1921, Bertha Margaret, *d* of Donald Hope; three *d*. *Educ:* King Edward's Sch., Birmingham; Bradfield Coll.; HMS Britannia. Capt. 1928; Rear-Adm. 1939; Vice-Adm. 1942; Adm. (retd) 1945; specialised in navigation. Served in HMS Euryalus, Dardanelles, 1915: present at re-occupation of Sollum, bombardment of Smyrna and Red Sea ops in support of Arab forces; on staff of C-in-C Mediterranean, 1916-19; Dep. Dir, Royal Naval Staff Coll., 1929-31; comd HM Ships Kent and Suffolk, 1931-33; Deputy Dir, Plans Division, Admiralty, 1933-35; commanded HMS Repulse, 1936-39. Dir of Naval Intelligence, 1939-42; Flag Officer Commanding Royal Indian Navy, 1943-46 Chm., Chelsea Hosp. Management Cttee, 1949-60; formerly Mem. Bd of Governors: Queen Charlotte's Hosp., Chelsea Hosp. for Women; Mem. Council: Roedean Sch.; King Edward's Hosp. Fund for London. Founder, Centre for Spastic Children, Chelsea. Order of the Nile; Chevalier, Legion of Honour. *Address:* White Stacks, Wilmington, near Polegate, Sussex. *T:* Alfriston 313. *Clubs:* Athenæum, Garrick, United Service, Chelsea Arts.

*See also Prof. J. B. Kinmonth.*

**GODFREY, Air Commodore Kenneth Walter,** CB 1955; CBE 1954; retired; *b* 23 Jan. 1907; *s* of late Walter Godfrey; *m* 1932, Norah Josephine, *d* of J. Fleeman; one *s*. Granted commission in RAFVR, 1939; Gen. Duties Br., 1940; 22 (Torpedo) Bomber Sqdn; joined RAF Regt on formation, 1942. Served War, 1939-45 (Croix de Guerre with Palm; despatches twice). Comd RAF Regt Wing, Germany, 1945; Directorate of Comd and Staff Training, Air Min., 1946-48; comd RAF Station, Dumfries, 1951; apptd Senior Ground Defence Staff Officer, Technical Training Command, 1952; Group Capt. 1952; comd Aden Protectorate Levies, 1953-55; Dep. Dir of Ground Defence, Air Ministry, 1955-59; ADC to the Queen, 1958-61; Air Cdre 1959; Dir of Ground Defence, Air Ministry, 1959-62; Actg Air Vice-Marshal, June 1962; Comdt-Gen. RAF Regt, and Inspector of Ground Defence, Air Min., 1962-63. *Recreations:* gardening, golf. *Club:* Royal Air Force.

**GODFREY, Sir Walter,** KBE 1964 (CBE 1952); *b* 14 Dec. 1907; *s* of late Frank Godfrey; *m* 1943,

Elizabeth Houston; three *s. Educ:* Battersea Grammar Sch.; Jesus Coll., Cambridge. Joined Dept of Overseas Trade, 1929; Trade Comr Service in India, Calcutta, 1930-38; Commercial Sec., British Embassy, Paris, 1938-40; Secretariat of Willingdon Mission to S America, Nov. 1940-Feb. 1941; Commercial Sec., British Embassy, Washington, 1941; Private Sec. to Sec. for Overseas Trade, 1942-43; Commercial Sec., Office of British Reptn to French Cttee for National Liberation, Algiers, 1944; Commercial Sec., British Embassy, Paris, 1944-46; UK Trade Comr, Calcutta, 1946; Actg Senior UK Trade Comr, Delhi, 1947; UK Senior Trade Comr in Pakistan, Karachi, 1947-50; Minister (Commercial), British Embassy, Rio de Janeiro, 1952; Minister (Commercial), British Embassy, Cairo, 1954-56; Senior Inspector of Foreign Service Establishments, 1957-60; Ambassador to Korea, 1961-66. *Address:* 109 Albemarle Road, Beckenham, Kent. *T:* 01-460 3958. *Club:* Royal Automobile.

**GODFREY, Sir William Maurice,** 7th Bt *cr* 1785, of Bushfield, Co. Kerry; *b* 8 March 1909; *s* of 6th Bt and Eileen Mary, *d* of late J. E. Currey, MD, Lismore; *S* father, 1935; *m* 1933, Caroline Iris, *d* of late Alban George Robins, Tunbridge Wells; three *d. Educ:* Clifton. Dir W. M. Godfrey & Partners Ltd. *Recreations:* fishing and gardening. *Address:* Ballinagroun, Annascaul, Tralee, Co. Kerry, Ireland.

**GODFREY-FAUSSETT, Brig. Bryan Trevor,** CB 1945; DSO 1944; OBE 1940; MC 1917; *b* 28 Nov. 1896; *s* of Richard Fermor Godfrey-Faussett; *m* 1925, Katherine Monica, *d* of J. H. Paterson, Harviestoun House, Gorebridge, Midlothian; one *s* one *d. Educ:* RN College, Osborne; Wellington Coll.; RMA, Woolwich; Jesus Coll., Cambridge. Commissioned RE 1915; European War, France and Flanders, 1915-18 (despatches); Major, 1932; Brevet Lieut-Col 1938; Col 1941; Brig. 1941; Operations in France and Belgium, 1940; N Africa and Italy, 1943-45 (despatches); Chief Engineer 8th Army, 1944; Chief Engineer 15th Army Group, 1945; Commandant Sch. of Military Engineering, 1946-48. ADC to the King, 1946. Bronze Star Medal (USA). *Address:* The Old Rectory, Badlesmere, near Faversham, Kent.

**GODLEY,** family name of **Baron Kilbracken.**

**GODLEY, Brig. Sir Francis W. C. F.;** *see* Fetherston-Godley.

**GODLEY, Hon. Wynne Alexander Hugh;** Director of Department of Applied Economics, University of Cambridge, since 1970; *b* 2 Sept. 1926; *yr s* of Hugh John, 2nd Baron Kilbracken, CB, KC and Elizabeth Helen Monteith, *d* of Vereker Monteith Hamilton; *m* 1955, Kathleen Eleonora, *d* of Sir Jacob Epstein, KBE; one *d. Educ:* Rugby; New Coll., Oxford; Conservatoire de Musique, Paris. Professional oboist, 1950. Joined Economic Section, HM Treasury, 1956; Dep. Dir, Economic Sect., HM Treasury, 1967-70. *Publications:* articles, mainly in National Institute Review. *Address:* Manor Farm House, Brede, Rye, Sussex. *T:* Brede 297.

**GODMAN, Col John,** CBE 1957; *b* 1886; *s* of E. T. Godman, DL; unmarried. *Educ:* Eton. 15/19 Hussars, 1905-30; commanded, 1926-30. Glos County Council, 1931 (Chm., 1946-56). Mem., Severn River Board (Chm., 1950-67). JP and DL, Glos; High Sheriff, 1946. *Recreations:* shooting and fishing. *Address:* Banks Fee, Moreton-in-Marsh, Glos. *T:* Stow-on-the-Wold 5. *Club:* Cavalry.

**GODWIN, Dame (Beatrice) Anne,** DBE 1962 (OBE); a Governor of the BBC, 1962-68; a full-time Member of the Industrial Court, 1963-69; *b* 1897. Gen. Sec., Clerical and Administrative Workers' Union, 1956-62. Chm. of the TUC, 1961-62. *Recreations:* talking, gardening, reading. *Club:* English-Speaking Union.

**GODWIN, Prof. Sir Harry,** Kt 1970; FRS 1945; FGS; FLS; MA, ScD; Professor of Botany, University of Cambridge, 1960-68, Emeritus 1968; Fellow of Clare College, Cambridge; *b* 9 May 1901; *m* 1927, Margaret Elizabeth Daniels; one *s.* University Reader in Quaternary Research, Cambridge, Oct. 1948-60. Croonian Lectr, Royal Soc., London, 1960. Pres., Xth International Botanical Congress, 1964. Foreign Member: Royal Danish Acad. of Science and Letters; Royal Scientific Soc. of Uppsala; German Acad. of Science Leopoldina; Hon. Mem., Royal Soc. of New Zealand. Hon. ScD, Trinity Coll., Dublin, 1960. Hon. DSc Lancaster, 1968. Prestwick Medal, Geol. Soc., London, 1951; Gold Medal, Linnean Soc., London, 1966. *Publications:* Plant Biology, 1930; History of the British Flora, 1956. *Address:* 30 Barton Road, Cambridge; Clare College, Cambridge. *T:* Cambridge 50883.

**GOEHR, Alexander;** composer; *b* 10 Aug. 1932; *s* of Walter and Laelia Goehr; *m* 1954, Audrey Baker; three *d. Educ:* Berkhamstead; Royal Manchester Coll. of Music; Paris Conservatoire. Lectr, Morley Coll., 1955-57; Music Asst, BBC, 1960-67; Winston Churchill Trust Fellowship, 1968; Composer-in-residence, New England Conservatory, Boston, Mass, 1968-69; Associate Professor of Music, Yale University, 1969-70. Hon. FRMCM. *Publications:* Fantasia Op. 4; Violin Concerto; Little Symphony; Pastorals; Romanza for 'cello; Symphony in One Movement, Opus 29, 1970. chamber music; Konzertstück; *opera:* Arden must die; *cantatas:* Sutter's Gold; The Deluge; Naboth's Vineyard. *Address:* c/o Schott & Co Ltd, 48 Great Marlborough Street, W1.

**GOENKA, Rai Bahadur Sir Badridas,** Kt 1934; CIE 1928; *b* Calcutta, 29 July 1883. *Educ:* Presidency Coll., Calcutta; Calcutta Univ. (BA). Director: Reserve Bank of India, 1935-41; State Bank of India, 1955-57; Rallis India Ltd, 1940-65; Imperial Bank of India, 1932-35, 1941-55; President: Federation of Indian Chambers of Commerce and Industry, 1945-46; Marwari Assoc., 1928-30; Indian Chamber of Commerce, 1941-42; Trustee: Calcutta Improvement Trust, 1928-40; Victoria Memorial Hall, Calcutta; Chairman: Famine Relief Cttee, Bengal, 1942; Bengal Textile Assoc., 1945; Member: Bengal Legislative Council, 1923-35; Bengal Banking Enquiry Commn, 1929; Sheriff of Calcutta, 1932-33. Made Rai Bahadur, 1925. *Address:* Goenka Nivas, 19 Belvedere Road, Calcutta 27, India. *T:* 45-1202.

**GOEPPERT MAYER, Prof. Maria;** *see* Mayer.

**GOFF, Very Rev. E. N. Porter;** Provost of Portsmouth; *b* 24 Dec. 1902; *s* of John Richards Goff, Canon of Kildare and Rector of Portarlington, Ireland, and Alice Weir; *m* 1926, Barbara Denman Hodgson; two *s. Educ:* Trinity Coll., Dublin (Scholar). BA (Senior Moderatorship and Gold Medal), 1924; MA 1929; Deacon 1926; Priest 1927; Curate of Immanuel, Streatham, 1926-29; Christ Church, Westminster, 1929-31; St Michael's, Chester Square, 1931-33; Vicar of Immanuel, Streatham, 1933-39; Proctor in Convocation, 1939-; Church Comr, 1948-. Chm., Select Preacher: Univ. of Oxford, 1952-54; Dublin,

1956, 1959. *Address:* Provost's House, Portsmouth, Hants. *T:* Portsmouth 23300. *Clubs:* National Liberal; Royal Naval (Portsmouth).

**GOFF, Sir Ernest (William) Davis-,** 3rd Bt *cr* 1905; *b* 11 June 1904; *s* of 2nd Bt and Margaret Aimée, *d* of late Rt Hon. Sir C. S. Scott, GCB; *S* father, 1923; *m* 1941, Alice Cynthia Sainthill Woodhouse (marr. diss. 1960); one *s* three *d*. *Heir: s* Robert William Davis-Goff, *b* 12 Sept. 1955. *Address:* Ardbrack Cottage, Kinsale, Co. Cork, Eire. *Club:* Kildare Street (Dublin).

**GOFF, Martyn;** Director of the National Book League since 1970; *b* 7 June 1923; *s* of Jacob and Janey Goff. *Educ:* Clifton College. Served in Royal Air Force, 1941-46. Film business, 1946-48; Bookseller, 1948-70. Has lectured on: music; English fiction; teenager morality; the book trade, 1946-70; Book and Record Reviewer, 1946-70. FIAL 1958. *Publications:* The Plaster Fabric, 1957; A Short Guide to Long Play, 1957; A Season with Mammon, 1958; A Further Guide to Long Play, 1958; A Sort of Peace, 1960; LP Collecting, 1960; The Youngest Director, 1961; Red on the Door, 1962; The Flint Inheritance, 1965; Indecent Assault, 1967; Why Conform?, 1968. *Recreations:* travel, collecting paintings and sculptures, fast cars, music. *Address:* 13 Tracery, Banstead, Surrey. *T:* Burgh Heath 53260. *Clubs:* Savile, Savage.

**GOFF, Hon. Sir Reginald (William),** Kt 1966; **Hon. Mr. Justice Goff;** Judge of the High Court of Justice (Chancery Division) since 1965; *b* 22 March 1907; *s* of late William Kingsley Goff, East India and China Tea Merchant, and late Louisa Goff; *m* 1944, Marjorie Morwenna Curnow, *d* of late Rev. A. Garfield Curnow, Wallington; two *d*. *Educ:* Sutton County Grammar Sch.; King's Coll. and University Coll., London. LLB (London) First Class Hons, 1928, and Certificate of Hon in the Bar examination, 1928. Called to the Bar, Lincoln's Inn, 1929; Bencher, 1959. War of 1939-45: Auxiliary Fire Service, 1939-42; RAF, 1942-46 (AJAG, 1945-46). Elected to Gen. Council of Bar, 1958. Fellow, UCL, 1968-; FKC, 1970. *Address:* Kingsley Croft, Downs Way, Tadworth, Surrey. *T:* Tadworth 3636.

**GOFF, Robert Lionel Archibald,** QC 1967; *b* 12 Nov. 1926; *s* of Lt-Col L. T. Goff and Mrs Goff (*née* Denroche-Smith); *m* 1953, Sarah, *er d* of Capt. G. R. Cousins, DSC, RN; one *s* two *d* (and one *s* decd). *Educ:* Eton Coll.; New Coll., Oxford. Served in Scots Guards, 1945-48 (commnd 1945). 1st cl hons Jurisprudence, Oxon, 1950. Called to the Bar, Inner Temple, 1951. Fellow and Tutor, Lincoln Coll., Oxford, 1951-55; in practice at the Bar, 1956-. *Publications:* (with Dr Gareth Jones) The Law of Restitution, 1966; articles in Modern Law Review. *Address:* 5 Holland Villas Road, Kensington, W14. *T:* 01-603 3186; Higher Boswarthen, Ding Dong, near Penzance, Cornwall.

**GOHEEN, Robert Francis;** President, Princeton University, USA, and Professor of Classics, since 1957; *b* Venguria, India, 15 Aug. 1919; *s* of Dr Robert H. H. Goheen and Anne Ewing; *m* 1941, Margaret M. Skelly; two *s* four *d*. *Educ:* Princeton Univ. AB 1940; PhD 1948. Instructor, Dept of Classics, Princeton, 1948-50; Asst Prof., 1950-57; Sen. Fellow in Classics, Amer. Academy in Rome, 1952-53; Dir Nat. Woodrow Wilson Fellowship Program, 1953-56. Mem. Board: Education and World Affairs; Carnegie Foundn for Advancement of Teaching; Rockefeller Foundation; Woodrow Wilson Foundn; US Cttee Dag Hammarskjold Foundation; Equitable Life Assurance Soc.; African-American Inst.; Educl Testing Service; Albert Parvin Foundn. Member: American Philological and Archæological Socs; American Academy of Arts and Sciences; Phi Beta Kappa. Hon. degrees: Harvard, Rutgers, Yale, Temple, Brown, Columbia, New York, Madras, Pennsylvania, Hamilton, Middlebury, Saint Mary's (Calif), State of New York, Denver, Notre Dame, N Carolina, Hofstra; Trinity Coll., USA; Coll. of Wooster; Jewish Theological Seminary of America; Ripon Coll.; Rider Coll.; Lowrie House. *Publications:* The imagery of Sophocles' Antigone; articles. *Recreations:* tennis and golf. *Address:* Princeton, New Jersey, USA. *T:* 452-3000. *Clubs:* Princeton, (Hon.) University Century Association (New York); (Hon.) University, Cosmos (Washington); (Hon.) Nassau.

**GOITEIN, Hugh,** LLD; Barrister-at-Law; *b* 7 June 1896; *s* of late Kalman Goitein and Elizabeth Barnett; *m* 1938, Freda, *o d* of late Col Albert William Goodman, MP, Old Dean Hall, Camberley, Surrey; one *s* one *d*. *Educ:* City of London Sch.; University Coll., London. Barstow Law Scholar; called to Bar, 1923; joined the South Eastern Circuit; Mem. of the International Law Assoc. and the Grotius Soc.; Prof. of Commercial Law in the Univ. of Birmingham, 1930-62. *Publications:* The Law as to CIF Contracts, 2nd edn, 1926; Official edn in Polish Umowy CIF, 1929; contribs to the 14th edn of the Encyclopædia Britannica; Company Law, 1960; other works include Primitive Ordeal and Modern Law and More's Utopia (ed. for Broadway Translations). *Recreations:* travel, walking. *Address:* Top Farm, Broadway, Worcs.

**GOLD, Ernest,** CB 1942; DSO 1916; OBE; FRS 1918; MA; *b* 1881; *s* of late John Gold, and Ellen (*née* Peckett), Rowington, Warwicks; *m* 1907, Catherine L., *d* of late John Harlow, and Mary (*née* Bowie), Edinburgh; one *d*. *Educ:* Coleshill Grammar Sch.; Mason's Coll., Birmingham; St John's Coll., Cambridge. Third Wrangler, 1903; Nat. Sci. Tripos, Part II, 1904; Fellow of St John's Coll., Cambridge, 1906; Schuster Reader in Dynamical Meteorology, 1907-10; discovered in 1908 a rational physical explanation of the Isothermal Condition of the Upper Atmosphere or Stratosphere; Pres., Royal Meteorological Society, 1934-36 (Symons Medallist, 1926), Hon. Mem., 1958; Hon. Mem. Amer. Meteorological Soc., 1959; Pres. International Commission for Synoptic Weather Information, 1919-47, and of Meteorological Sub-Commn of International Commn for Aerial Navigation, 1922-46; served European War, 1915-19 (despatches, DSO); in Meteorological Office, 1910-47; US Medal of Freedom with Silver Palms, 1946; Internat. Meteorological Organisation (IMO) Prize and Medal, 1958. *Publications:* Physical and Meteorological Papers and Reports in Proc. Royal Soc., Jl of Royal Meteorological Soc., Reports of British Assoc., Proc. Vienna Academy, and in Memoirs of Meteorological Office, London. *Recreations:* gardening, golf. *Address:* 8 Hurst Close, Hampstead Garden Suburb, NW11. *T:* 01-455 1209.

**GOLD, James Herbert;** *b* 21 Jan. 1885; *s* of Joseph and Aphra Gold of Birmingham; *m* 1909, Kathleen (*d* 1955), *d* of A. E. Cutter of Knutsford, Cheshire; two *s* one *d*. *Educ:* King Edward's Sch., Birmingham; University Coll., London. Solicitor; Bachelor of Laws and University Law Scholar of Univ. of London, 1904; Scott Scholar of the Law Soc., 1907. joint MFH Ludlow, 1928-30; County Councillor for Cheshire (Northwich Div.), 1928-30; Principal (temp.) Ministry of Works and Ministry of Fuel and Power (Open Cast Coal Production), 1941-45; formerly a Dir of Brunner Mond & Co. Ltd, and other companies. *Recreations:* hunting, shooting, golf. *Address:* Brookfield Farm, Warfield, Berks. *T:* Winkfield Row 2281.

**GOLD, John (Joseph Manson);** Editor, London Evening News, since 1967; Director, Harmsworth Publications Ltd, since 1967; *b* 2 Aug. 1925; *m* 1953, Berta Cordeiro; one *d*. *Educ:* Clayesmore Sch., Dorset. Yorkshire Evening News, 1944-47; London Evening News, 1947-52; Australian Associated Press (New York), 1952-55; New York Corresp., London Evening News, 1955-66. *Address:* Flat 3, 36 Wilton Crescent, SW1.

**GOLD, Stephen Charles,** MA, MD, FRCP; Physician to the Skin Department, St George's Hospital; Physician to St John's Hospital for Diseases of the Skin; Hon. Consultant in Dermatology to the Army; *b* Bishops Stortford, Herts, 10 Aug. 1915; *yr s* of late Philip Gold, Stansted, Essex, and late Amy Frances, *er d* of James and Mary Perry; *m* 1941, Betty Margaret, *o d* of late Dr T. P. Sheedy, OBE; three *s* one *d*. *Educ:* Radley Coll.; Gonville and Caius Coll., Cambridge; St George's Hosp. (Entrance Exhibnr); Zurich and Philadelphia. BA 1937; MRCS, LRCP 1940; MA, MB, BChir 1941; MRCP 1947; MD 1952; FRCP 1958. Served RAMC, 1941-46 (Major). Postgrad. Travelling Fellowship, 1948; late House Surg., S Middlesex Hosp., House Physician, St George's Hosp., Med. First Asst to Out-Patients, St George's Hosp., Senior Registrar, Skin Dept, St George's Hosp., Sen. Registrar, St John's Hosp. for Diseases of the Skin; Lectr in Dermatology, Royal Postgraduate Med. Sch., 1949-69; late Ed., Transactions of St John's Hosp. Dermatological Soc.: Dir, Inst. of Dermatology, 1956-58. Sec., Brit. Assoc. of Dermatology, 1965-70; Mem. Bd of Governors, St George's Hosp. Fellow Royal Society Med. (late Sec. Dermatological Section); Fellow St John's Hosp. Dermatological Soc. (Pres., 1965-66). *Publications:* sundry articles in medical jls, largely on dermatological subjects. *Recreations:* ski-ing, music. *Address:* 149 Harley Street, W1N 2DE. *T:* 01-935 4444; Park House, Debden, Essex. *T:* Newport (Essex) 336. *Clubs:* Bath, MCC.

**GOLD, Thomas,** FRS 1964; Director since 1959, and Assistant Vice-President for Research since 1969, Center for Radio-Physics and Space Research, Cornell University; *b* 22 May 1920; *s* of Max and Josefine Gold; *m* 1947, Merle E. Gold (*née* Tuberg); three *d*. BA Mechanical Sciences (Cambridge), 1942; MA Mechanical Sciences, Cambridge, 1946; ScD, Cambridge, 1969. Fellow Trinity Coll., Cambridge, 1947. British Admiralty, 1942-46; Cavendish Laboratory, Cambridge, 1946-47 and 1949-52; Med. Research Council, Zoological Lab., Cambridge, 1947-49; Sen. Principal Scientific Officer (Chief Asst), Royal Greenwich Observatory, 1952-56; Prof. of Astronomy, 1957-58, Robert Wheeler Willson Prof. of Applied Astronomy, 1958-59, Harvard Univ. Hon. MA (Harvard), 1957. Mem. Nat. Acad. of Sciences; Fellow, Amer. Acad. of Arts and Sciences. *Publications:* contribs to learned journals on astronomy, physics, biophysics. *Recreations:* ski-ing, travelling. *Address:* Center for Radiophysics and Space Research, Space Sciences Building, Cornell University, Ithaca, NY 14850, USA.

**GOLDBERG, Prof. Abraham;** Regius Professor of Materia Medica, University of Glasgow; Consultant Physician, Stobhill General Hospital, Glasgow; *b* 7 Dec. 1923; *s* of late Julius Goldberg and Rachel Goldberg (*née* Varinofsky); *m* 1957, Clarice Cussin; two *s* one *d*. *Educ:* George Heriot's Sch., Edinburgh; Edinburgh University. MB, ChB 1946, MD (Gold Medal for thesis) 1956, Edinburgh; DSc Glasgow 1966; FRCP, FRCPE, FRCPGlas. Nuffield Research Fellow, UCH Med. Sch., London, 1952-54; Eli Lilly Trav. Fellow in Medicine (MRC) in Dept of Medicine, Univ. of Utah; Lectr in Medicine 1956, Titular Prof. 1967, Univ. of Glasgow. Editor, Scottish Medical Jl, 1962-63. Sydney Watson Smith Lectr, RCPE, 1964. Watson Prize, RCPGlas, 1959; Alexander Fleck Award, Univ. of Glasgow, 1967. *Publications:* (jtly) Diseases of Porphyrin Metabolism, 1962; papers on clinical and investigative medicine. *Recreations:* swimming, writing. *Address:* 16 Birnam Crescent, Bearsden, Glasgow. *T:* 041-942 7770.

**GOLDBERG, Arthur J(oseph),** DJur; politician and lawyer, USA; US Ambassador to United Nations, 1965-68; Chairman, UNA of USA, since 1968; *b* Chicago, Ill., 8 Aug. 1908; *s* of Joseph Goldberg and Rebecca (*née* Perlstein); one *s* one *d*. *Educ:* City Coll., Chicago; Northwestern Univ. (JD). Admitted to Bar of Ill., 1929, US Supreme Ct Bar, 1937. Private practice, 1929-48. Gen. Counsel: Congress of Industrial Workers, 1948-55; United Steel workers, 1948-61; Industrial Union Dept, AFL-CIO, 1955-61; Special Counsel, Amer. Fedn of Labor-Congress of Indust. Orgns, 1955-61. Member firm: Goldberg, Devoe, Shadur & Mikva, Chicago, 1945-61; Goldberg, Feller & Bredhoff, Washington, 1952-61. Sec. of Labor, 1961-62. Associate Judge, US Supreme Court, Washington, 1962-65. Is a Democrat. *Publications:* Civil Rights in Labor-Management Relations: a Labor Viewpoint, 1951; AFL-CIOLabor United, 1956; Unions and the Anti-Trust Laws, 1956; Management's Reserved Rights, 1956; Ethical Practices, 1958; A Trade Union Point of View, 1959; Suggestions for a New Labor Policy, 1960; The Role of the Labor Union in an Age of Bigness, 1960; The Defenses of Freedom: The Public Papers of Arthur J. Goldberg, 1964. *Address:* c/o United Nations Association of the USA, 345 E 46th Street, New York, NY 10017, USA.

**GOLDBY, Prof. Frank;** Professor of Anatomy, London University, St Mary's Hospital Medical School, 1945-70, retired; *b* Enfield, Middlesex, 25 May 1903; *s* of Frank and Ellen Maud Goldby; *m* 1932, Helen Rosa Tomlin; five *s* one *d*. *Educ:* Mercers' School, Holborn; Gonville and Caius College, Cambridge; King's College Hospital; MRCS, LRCP 1926; MRCP 1928; MD (Cambridge), 1936; FRCP, 1963; Resident appointments King's Coll. Hospital, 1926-28; Asst Clinical Pathologist, King's College Hospital, 1929-30; Senior Demonstrator in Anatomy, University College, London, 1931; Lecturer in charge of Anatomy Dept, Hong Kong, 1932-33; Lecturer in Anatomy, University of Cambridge and Fellow of Queens' College, 1934-37; Prof. of Anatomy, Univ. of Adelaide, 1937-45. *Publications:* papers on Embryology and on the Pathology and Comparative Anatomy of the Nervous System. *Address:* 7 Blomfield Road, W9.

**GOLDEN, Grace Lydia,** ARCA (London); *d* of H. F. Golden. *Educ:* City of London Sch. for Girls. Art Training at Chelsea Art Sch. and Royal College of Art; further studies at Regent Street Polytechnic; Black and White Illustrator, Posters, Panoramas, watercolour artist and wood-engraver; Exhibitor at Royal Academy, 1936, 1937, 1938 and 1940;

watercolour, Summer Evening, Embankment Gardens, and oil-painting, Free Speech, purchased by Chantry Trustees. *Publication:* Old Bankside, 1951. *Recreation:* singing. *Address:* 37 Laurier Road, NW5.

**GOLDEN, Lieut-Col Harold Arthur,** CBE 1960; *b* 1896; *s* of Arthur Golden, Norwich; *m* 1929, Freda Mary, *d* of Ernest W. Lightfoot, Carlisle; one *d*. *Educ:* Norwich Sch.; St John's Coll., Cambridge. Barrister, Gray's Inn, 1935. Served European War, with RE, 1915-19. Major 1935; retired 1935; re-empld, 1943-45. Chief Constable, Salop, 1935-46; Chief Constable of Wilts, 1946-63. County Dir, Wilts Branch British Red Cross Society, 1964-66. *Recreations:* fishing, gardening. *Address:* Bridge Cottage, Winterbourne Stoke, Salisbury, Wilts. *T:* Shrewton 376. *Club:* Army and Navy.

**GOLDIE, Very Rev. Frederick,** MA; BD; Dean of Glasgow and Galloway since 1963; Rector of St Margaret's, Glasgow, since 1963; *b* 1 Sept. 1914; *s* of John and Maria Goldie, Glasgow; *m* 1940, Margaret Baker McCrae, MA; one *s* one *d*. *Educ:* Strathbungo Academy, Glasgow; Hatfield Coll., Durham; New Coll. and Coates Hall, Edinburgh. Open Exhibnr, Hatfield Schol., LTh, BA 1938, Durham; BD Edinburgh, 1939; MA Durham, 1946. Curate at Govan, 1938; Rector at Hillington, Glasgow, 1939-49; Lecturer at Theological Coll., Edinburgh, 1940-63; Rector at Dumbarton, 1949-63; Canon of St Mary's Cathedral, Glasgow, 1956. *Publication:* A History of the Episcopal Church in Scotland, 1950. *Recreations:* reading, walking. *Address:* Rectory, 22 Monreith Road, Glasgow S3. *T:* 041-632 3292.

**GOLDIE, Robert George,** CBE 1949; *b* 4 Oct. 1893; *e s* of Charles Goldie and Lilian (*née* Steggall); *m* 1st, 1924, Ann Mary Laptew (*d* 1930); 2nd, 1933, Helen MacLean Homan; one *s* three *d*. *Educ:* Victoria Coll., Jersey, CI. Served European War, 1914-18, in 28th London Regt (Artists' Rifles) and Loyal North Lancs Regt (despatches 1918). Entered Consular Service, 1919; Vice-Consul: at Hamburg, 1920-21 and 1924-27; at Naples, 1921-24; at Colon (Panama), 1927-39; at Boston (USA), 1929-30; Chargé d'Affaires and Consul at Santo Domingo, 1930-32 and at San Salvador, 1932-35; Consul at Gothenburg (Sweden), 1935-39, and at Málaga (Spain), 1939-45; Consul-Gen. at Milan, 1945-50, at Antwerp, 1950-53; retired Oct. 1953. *Recreation:* gardening. *Address:* 2 Friar's Road, Winchelsea, Sussex.

**GOLDING, Dame (Cecilie) Monica,** DBE 1958; RRC 1950 (ARRC 1940); *b* 6 Aug. 1902; *o d* of Ben Johnson and Clara (*née* Beames); *m* 1961, Rev. Harry Golding, CBE (*d* 1969). *Educ:* Croydon Secondary Sch. Professional training: Royal Surrey County Hospital, Guildford, 1922-25; Louise Margaret Hosp., Aldershot and Queen Victoria's Institute of District Nursing. Joined Army Nursing Services, 1925; India, 1929-34; France, 1939-40; Middle East, 1940-43 and 1948-49; Southern Comd, 1943-44 and 1950-52; WO, 1945-46; India and SE Asia, 1946-48; Far East, 1952-55; Eastern Comd, 1955-56; Matron-in-Chief and Dir of Army Nursing Services, 1956-60, retired (with rank of Brig.), 1960. QHNS 1956-60; Col Commandant, Queen Alexandra's Royal Army Nursing Corps, 1961-66. OStJ 1955. *Recreations:* motoring; amateur bird watching and nature study. *Address:* 9 Sandford Court, 32 Belle Vue Road, Southbourne, Bournemouth, Hants. *T:* 44122. *Club:* United Nursing Services.

**GOLDING, F(rederick) Campbell,** MB, ChM, FRCP, DMRE, FFR; retired; Director, X-Ray Diagnostic Department, Middlesex Hospital, 1956-67; Lecturer in Radiology, Middlesex Hospital Medical School; Hon. Consultant Radiologist, Royal National Orthopædic Hospital; Civilian Consultant in Radiology, RN and RAF; Consultant Radiologist, Arthur Stanley Institute for Rheumatic Diseases; Consultant Radiologist, Chelsea Hospital for Women; *b* 4 June 1901; *o s* of late Frederick Golding, Sydney, Australia, and Nell Campbell, Castlemaine, Victoria; *m* 1942, Barbara Hubbard, *d* of late Charles Hubbard, Nassau and of Mrs Hubbard, 15 Grosvenor Square, W1; two *s*. *Educ:* Scots Coll., Melbourne; St Andrews Coll., University of Sydney. Late Dir, X-Ray Diagnostic Dept, Royal Marsden Hosp.; Examiner in Radiology, Royal College of Physicians, 1954-57. Watson-Jones Lecturer, Royal College of Surgeons, 1964; Mackenzie Davidson Lecturer, British Institute of Radiology, 1961. *Publications:* (contrib.) Textbook of X-Ray Diagnosis by British Authors: (contrib.) Textbook of Rheumatic Diseases; (Jt) Survey of Radiology of the Chest, British Encyclopædia of Medical Practice, 1956; various other medical publications. *Recreation:* fishing in north of Scotland. *Address:* Fisherton de la Mere House, Wylye, Wilts. *T:* Wylye 232.

**GOLDING, John;** MP (Lab) Newcastle-under-Lyme since Oct. 1969; *b* Birmingham, 9 March 1931; *m* 1958, Thelma Gwillym; two *s*. *Educ:* Chester Grammar Sch.; London Univ.; Keele Univ. BA History, Politics, Economics, 1956. Education Officer, Post Office Engineering Union, 1960-. PPS to Minister of Technology, Feb.-June 1970. *Publications:* co-author Fabian Pamphlets; Productivity Bargaining; Trade Unionson to 1980. *Address:* House of Commons, SW1.

**GOLDING, Dame Monica;** *see* Golding, Dame C. M.

**GOLDING, William (Gerald),** CBE 1966; author; *b* 19 Sept. 1911; *s* of Alec A. and Mildred A. Golding; *m* 1939, Ann, *e d* of late E. W. Brookfield, The Homestead, Bedford Place, Maidstone; one *s* one *d*. *Educ:* Marlborough Grammar Sch.; Brasenose Coll., Oxford. MA Oxon 1961. FRSL 1955. Hon. Fellow, Brasenose Coll., Oxford, 1966. Hon. DLitt, Sussex, 1970. *Publications:* Lord of the Flies, 1954 (filmed 1963); The Inheritors, 1955; Pincher Martin, 1956; Brass Butterfly (play), 1958; Free Fall, 1959; The Spire, 1964; The Hot Gates, 1965; The Pyramid, 1967. *Recreations:* music, sailing; Greek. *Address:* Ebble Thatch, Bowerchalke, Wilts. *T:* Broad Chalke 275. *Clubs:* Savile; Royal Southampton Yacht.

**GOLDMAN, Sir Samuel,** KCB 1969 (CB 1964); Second Secretary, HM Treasury; *b* 10 March 1912; *y s* of late Philip and late Sarah Goldman; *m* 1st, 1934, Pearl Marre (*d* 1941); one *s*; 2nd, 1943, Patricia Rosemary Hodges. *Educ:* Davenant Foundation Sch.; Raine's Sch.; London Sch. of Economics, London Univ. Inter-Collegiate Scholar. BSc (Econ.), First Class Hons in Economics and Gladstone Memorial Prize, 1931; MSc (Econ.), 1933. Hutchinson Silver Medallist. Moody's Economist Services, 1934-38; Joseph Sebag & Co., 1938-39; Bank of England, 1940-47. Entered Civil Service, 1947, as Statistician in Central Statistical Office; transferred to Treasury, Sept. 1947; Chief Statistician, 1948; Asst Sec., 1952; Under-Sec., 1960-62; Third Sec., 1962-68. UK Alternate Executive Dir, International Bank, 1961-62. Hon. Fellow

LSE, 1970. *Recreation:* gardening. *Address:* The Old Orchard, Danes Hill, Oxshott, Surrey. *T:* Oxshott 2052. *Club:* Reform.

**GOLDMANN, Dr Nahum;** President of the World Jewish Congress since 1951; *b* 10 July 1895; *s* of Solomon and Rebecca Goldmann; *m* 1934, Alice (*née* Gottschalk); two *s*. *Educ:* Berlin, Marburg, Heidelberg, Germany. Editor of Encyclopædia Judaica in Berlin, 1922-34; Rep. of Jewish Agency for Palestine with League of Nations, Geneva, 1934-40; Pres., Cttee of Jewish Delegations, 1936-; Mem. Exec. Cttee, Jewish Agency for Palestine, 1934-; Chm. Exec. Cttee, World Jewish Congress, 1936-; Rep., Jewish Agency in USA, 1940-; Chm. Admin. Cttee, World Jewish Congress, 1945-; Chm., Jewish Agency, 1951 (Pres., 1956-68); Pres., Conf. on Jewish material claims against Germany, 1950-; Pres., Memorial Foundation for Jewish Culture, 1965. *Address:* 12 Avenue Montaigne, Paris, France. *T:* Alma 22.99; 18 Ahad Haam, Jerusalem. *T:* 38195.

**GOLDNEY, Maj.-Gen. Claude Le Bas,** CB 1943; CBE 1940; MC; *b* 4 Dec. 1887; *s* of late Col W. H. Goldney, RE; *m* 1938, Nora (*d* 1968), *yr d* of late Surg. Maj.-Gen. Sir Gerald Bomford, KCIE; no *c*. *Educ:* Dover Coll.; Portsmouth Grammar Sch.; RMA Woolwich. Commnd in Glos Regt 1906; Transf. ASC 1910; served European War, France, 1914-18 (despatches, MC); Col 1937; ADS & T, Egypt, 1938; ADS & T, Aldershot, 1939; served War of 1939-45; DDS & T, 1st Corps, with BEF, to France, 1939; DDS & T, 3rd Corps, until evacuation Dunkirk, 1940 (CBE, CB, despatches thrice); Acting Maj.-Gen. 1941; Dir of Supplies and Transport, GHQ, Middle East Force, 1941-44; ADC to HM the King, 1942-44, retired 1944. *Recreation:* fishing. *Address:* 38 Mount Hermon Road, Woking, Surrey. *Club:* United Service.

**GOLDNEY, Sir Henry Hastings,** 4th Bt, *cr* 1880; MC; *b* 3 July 1886; *s* of Sir Frederick Hastings Goldney, 3rd Bt; S father, 1940; *m* Violetta (*d* 1965), *o d* of W. C. Barnes. *Educ:* Harrow; Trinity Coll., Cambridge. Served European War as Lieut, Royal Engineers, 1914-17 (despatches, MC). *Club:* Carlton.

**GOLDS, Anthony Arthur,** MVO 1961; British Ambassador to the Federal Republic of Cameroon, the Republic of Gabon, the Republic of Equatorial Guinea since 1970; *b* 31 Oct. 1919; *s* of late Arthur Oswald Golds and Florence Golds (*née* Massey); *m* 1944, Suzanne Macdonald Young; one *s* one *d*. *Educ:* King's Sch., Macclesfield; New Coll., Oxford (Scholar). HM Forces (Royal Armoured Corps), 1939-46; CRO, 1948; 1st Sec., Calcutta and Delhi, 1951-53; Commonwealth Office, 1953-56; Head of Chancery, British Embassy, Ankara, 1957-59; Karachi, 1959-61; Counsellor in Commonwealth Office and Foreign Office, 1962-65; Head of Joint Malaysia/Indonesia Dept, 1964-65; Counsellor, HM Embassy, Rome, 1965-70. *Recreations:* music, cricket, golf, literature. *Address:* British Embassy, Yaounde, Cameroon. *Club:* Authors'.

**GOLDSMID;** *see* d'Avigdor-Goldsmid.

**GOLDSMITH, Sir Allen John Bridson,** KCVO 1970 (CVO 1962); FRCS; Surgeon-Oculist to the Queen since 1965; Surgeon-Oculist to HM Household, 1952-65; Ophthalmic Surgeon, Middlesex Hospital since 1946; Hon. Consultant Surgeon, Moorfields Eye Hospital since 1958; Ophthalmic Surgeon, Royal National Orthopædic Hospital since 1946; *b* 27 Nov. 1909; *s* of Bridson K. Goldsmith; *m* 1936, Mabel Rosemary Elise, *d* of Herdman Porter, MD; one *s* two *d*. *Educ:* King William's Coll., Isle of Man; Middlesex Hosp. MRCS, LRCP 1931; FRCS 1934; MB, BS London (Distinctions Medicine and Pathology), 1931. Demonstrator in Physiology, Senior Broderip Scholar, Lyell Gold Medallist, House Physician, House Surg., Asst Pathologist, Middlesex Hosp., 1928-35; House Surg., Resident Surgical Officer, 1935-37, Pathologist, 1937-40, Moorfields Eye Hosp.; Surgeon and Pathologist, Central London Eye Hosp., 1937; Ophthalmic Surgeon, Paddington Green Children's Hosp., 1937-46; Ophthalmic Surg., EMS, 1939-45; Surg., Moorfields Eye Hosp., 1948-58. FRSM 1934 (Hon. Sec. Ophthalmological Section, 1941-43); Member: Ophthalmological Soc. UK, 1940 (Hon. Sec., 1950-52); Royal Institution, 1943; French Ophthalmological Soc., 1946; Lectr in Ophthalmology, Univ. of London, 1938; Examiner in ophthalmology, RCP and RCS, 1948. *Publications:* (jointly) Recent Advances in Ophthalmology, 5th edn; various papers in ophthalmic and medical jls. *Recreations:* golf, fishing, reading. *Address:* 63 Harley Street. W1. *T:* 01-636 7153 and 01-580 4631. *Club:* Athenæum.

**GOLDSMITH, John Thorburn,** CBE 1959; Member, North West Regional Hospital Board, since 1964; Member, Board of Governors, Middlesex Hospital, since 1964; a Manager of the Royal Institution, 1964-67 and since 1968; Part-time Mem. NW Area Gas Board, 1955-65; *b* 30 May 1903; *s* of the late Lieut-Col Sidney Goldschmidt, Ollerton House, Knutsford; *m* 1932, Monica, *d* of late Capt. Harry Simon; one *d*. *Educ:* Marlborough; Magdalen Coll., Oxford. Entered family firm of Goldschmidt, Hahlo and Co. Ltd, Export Shippers, Manchester, 1924; Chairman, 1949-55. War of 1939-45, Fire Staff Officer, Grade I, National Fire Service; attached to SHAEF as Adviser on Fire Prevention, 1943; Principal, Min. of Production, 1944; Dep. Chm., Civil Service Selection Bd, 1945. Chm., Civil Service Selection Board, and a Civil Service Commissioner, 1951-63. Haakon Cross for Services to Norway, 1945; Order of Orange Nassau for Services to Holland, 1945. *Publications:* Hildebrand (Children's Stories), 1931, 1949; Three's Company, 1932. *Recreation:* fly-fishing. *Address:* 31 Marsham Court, Marsham Street, SW1. *T:* 01-828 1958. *Clubs:* Savile, Royal Automobile.

**GOLDSMITH, Robert;** Under Secretary, Board of Trade, since 1968; *b* 28 Nov. 1924; *e s* of late Stanley Thomas Goldsmith and Ida Goldsmith (*née* Rawlinson); *m* 1957, Eileen Bernadette McCormack; one *d*. *Educ:* King James Grammar Sch., Almondbury; Manchester Univ.; St Catherine's Society, Oxford. War Service, 1943-45. Hons Sch. of Philosophy, Politics and Economics (1st Class Hons, 1947), Oxford. Entered Bd of Trade, 1948; UK Treasury and Supply Delegn, Washington (First Sec.), 1953-57; Private Sec. to successive Ministers of State, Bd of Trade, 1958-61. Asst Sec., 1964; Under Sec., 1968. *Recreation:* cricket. *Address:* Weycroft, Wey Manor Road, New Haw, Weybridge, Surrey. *T:* Weybridge 47078. *Club:* United University.

**GOLDSMITH, Maj.-Gen. (Retd) Robert Frederick Kinglake,** CB 1955; CBE 1952; *b* 21 June 1907; *s* of late Col Harry Dundas Goldsmith, CBE, DSO; *m* 1935, Brenda, *d* of Frank Bartlett, late Ceylon Civil Service; one *s*. *Educ:* Wellington Coll., Berks. Commnd Duke of Cornwall's LI, 1927; served War of 1939-45, in N Africa, Italy, NW Europe; Dep. Chief of Staff, First Allied Airborne Army, 1944-45; comd 131 Inf. Bde (TA), 1950-51;

Chief of Staff, British Troops in Egypt, 1951-54, and of HQ Western Command, 1956-59; GOC Yorks District, 1959-62; Col, Duke of Cornwall's LI, 1958-59; Col Somerset and Cornwall LI, 1960-63. Ed., The Army Quarterly, 1966-. Comdr, Legion of Merit (US) 1945. *Address:* Warren Garth, Courtenay Road, Winchester, Hants. *Clubs:* Army and Navy, MCC.

**GOLDSMITH, Dr William Noel;** Consulting Dermatologist: University College Hospital; St John's Hospital, Lewisham; West Herts Hospital, Hemel Hempstead; Italian Hospital; Consulting Physician, St John's Hospital for Diseases of the Skin; Emeritus Consultant Dermatologist, West End Hospital for Neurology; *b* 26 Dec. 1893; *s* of Ernest Goldschmidt and Bertha Feist; *m* 1969, Irene Sharp. *Educ:* Rugby Sch.; Pembroke Coll., Cambridge; UCH Medical Sch., London. Qualified MRCS, LRCP 1918; RAMC, 1918-20; MRCP 1922; Radcliffe Crocker Travelling Scholarship, 1924 (Vienna and Breslau); MD Cambridge 1927; Physician Skin Dept, University Coll. Hosp., 1932-59; FRCP 1937; Chief Ed., British Jl of Dermatology, 1939-48. Pres., St John's Hosp. Dermatological Soc., 1936-38; Pres., Dermatological Section of RSocMed, 1949-51; Pres., British Assoc. of Dermatology, 1957. Mem. Panel on External Radiotherapy, of Cttee on Radiological Hazards to Patients (Adrian Cttee), 1957-60. Hon. Member: British Assoc. of Dermatology; Dermatogical Section, RSM; Austrian, German, Danish and Berlin Dermatological Socs; Amer. Dermatological Assoc.; Corresp. Member: Hungarian, Swedish and French Dermatological Socs. *Publications:* Recent Advances in Dermatology, 1936, 2nd edn (with Dr F. F. Hellier), 1954; articles chiefly in British Jl of Dermatology. *Recreations:* music, photography. *Address:* Flat 18, 2 Mansfield Street, W1M 9FE. *Clubs:* Hurlingham, National Liberal.

**GOLDSTEIN, Sydney,** FRS 1937; MA; PhD; Gordon McKay Professor of Applied Mathematics, Harvard University, Emeritus; *b* 3 Dec. 1903; *o s* of Joseph and Hilda Goldstein, Hull; *m* 1926, Rosa R. Sass, Johannesburg; one *s* one *d*. *Educ:* Bede Collegiate Sch., Sunderland; University of Leeds; St John's Coll., Cambridge. Mathematical Tripos, 1925; Smith's Prize, 1927; PhD, 1928; Rockefeller Research Fellow, University of Göttingen, 1928-29; Lectr in Mathematics, Manchester Univ., 1929-31; Lect-rer in Mathematics in the Univ. of Cambridge, 1931-45; Fellow of St John's Coll., Cambridge, 1929-32, 1933-45; Leverhulme Research Fellow, Calif. Inst. of Technology, 1938-39; Beyer Prof. of Applied Mathematics, Manchester Univ., 1945-50; Prof. of Applied Mathematics, 1950-55; and Chm. Aeronautical Engineering Dept, 1950-54, Institute of Technology, Haifa, Israel, and Vice-Pres. of the Institute, 1951-54. Worked at Aerodynamics Div., National Physical Laboratory, 1939-45; Adams Prize, 1935. Chm., Aeronautical Research Council, 1946-49. Foreign Mem. of Royal Netherlands Acad. of Sciences and Letters (Section for Sciences), 1950. Hon. Fellow St John's Coll., Cambridge, 1965. Hon. DEng, Purdue Univ., 1967; Hon. DSc: Case Inst. of Technology, 1967; The Technion, Israel Inst. of Technology, Haifa, Israel, 1969. Timoshenko Medal of Amer. Soc. of Mech. Engrs (for distinguished contribs to Applied Mechanics), 1965. *Publications:* (ed) Modern Developments in Fluid Dynamics, 1938; Lectures on Fluid Mechanics, 1960; papers on mathematics and mathematical physics, especially hydrodynamics and aerodynamics. *Address:* 28 Elizabeth Road, Belmont, Mass 02178, USA. *Club:* Athenæum.

**GOLDSWORTHY, Capt. Ivan Ernest Goodman,** RD; RNR retired; formerly Commodore of the Orient Line; *b* 8 May 1894; *s* of John and Ellen Goldsworthy; *m* 1924, Enid Picton Thomas; one *s* one *d*. *Educ:* Jersey Modern Sch. Commenced sea career in a sailing ship, 1909; joined RNR, 1915; served European War, 1914-18 as Sub-Lieut and Lieut with Grand Fleet, until 1918; then in Baltic Sea, 1919; joined Orient Line, 1921. Took part in evacuation, Norway and St Nazaire, 1940; Commodore of Convoys 1941-45. *Recreation:* gardening. *Address:* Highmead, Steeple Lane, St Ives, Cornwall. *T:* St Ives 5969.

**GOLDWATER, Barry M(orris);** US Senator from Arizona, 1953-64, and since 1969; *b* Phoenix, Arizona, 1 Jan. 1909; *s* of late Baron Goldwater and Josephine Williams; *m* 1934, Margaret Johnson; two *s* two *d*. *Educ:* Staunton Mil. Acad., Virginia; University of Arizona. 2nd Lieut, Army Reserve, 1930; transferred to USAAF, 1941; served as ferry-command and fighter pilot instructor, Asia, 1941-45 (Lieut-Col); Chief of Staff, Arizona Nat. Guard, 1945-52 (Col); Maj.-Gen., USAF Reserves. Joined Goldwater's Inc., 1929 (Pres., 1937-53). City Councilman, Phoenix, 1949-52; Republican Candidate for the Presidency of the USA, 1964. Member: Advisory Cttee on Indian Affairs, Dept of Interior, 1948-50; Armed Services Cttee; Labor and Public Welfare Cttee; Director: Assoc. on American Indian Affairs; American Inst. of Foreign Trade; Heard Museum; Museum of Northern Arizona; St Joseph's Hosp.; Member: Veterans of Foreign Wars; American Legion; Royal Photographic Society, etc. US Junior Chamber of Commerce Award, 1937; Man of the Year, Phoenix, 1949. *Publications:* Arizona Portraits (2 vols), 1940; Journey Down the River of Canyons, 1940; Speeches of Henry Ashurst: The Conscience of a Conservative, 1960; Why Not Victory?, 1962; Where I Stand, 1964. *Address:* Phoenix, Arizona, USA.

**GOLDWYN, Samuel;** Motion Picture Producer; General Partner, Samuel Goldwyn Productions; *b* Warsaw, Poland, 27 Aug. 1882; *s* of Abraham and Hannah Goldfish; *m* 1st, 1910, Blanche Lasky (divorced, 1915); one *d*; 2nd, 1925, Frances Howard; one *s*. *Educ:* night schs, New York. Emigrated to United States, 1896; naturalised US, 1902; organised Jesse Lasky Feature Photoplay Co., 1913; organised Goldwyn Pictures Corp. (later Metro-Goldwyn-Mayer), 1916; has produced own films independently since 1923. *Address:* Samuel Goldwyn Productions, 1041 N Formosa Avenue, Los Angeles 54, Calif.

**GOLIGHER, Prof. John Cedric,** ChM, FRCS; Professor of Surgery, Leeds University, since Oct. 1954, and Surgeon, Leeds General Infirmary; *b* Londonderry, N Ireland, 13 March 1912; *s* of John Hunter Goligher, Londonderry; *m* 1952, Gwenllian Nancy, *d* of Norman R. Williams, Melbourne, Aust.; one *s* two *d*. *Educ:* Foyle Coll., Londonderry; Edinburgh Univ. MB, CHB 1934; ChM 1938, edinburgh; FRCS, FRCSE 1938; Demonstrator of Anatomy, Edinburgh Univ., 1935-36; House Surg., Edinburgh Royal Infirmary; Res. Surg. Officer, St Mark's Hosp., London; served War 1940-46, RAMC, as Surgical Specialist; then Surgical Registrar, St Mary's Hosp., London; Hon. Asst Surg. (subsequently Surg.), St Mary's Hosp., and St Mark's Hosp. for Diseases of the Rectum and Colon, 1947. FRSocMed; Fellow, Assoc. Surgeons of Gt Brit. and Ire.; Mem. Surg.

Research Soc.; Mem. Brit. Soc. of Gastroenterology. *Publications:* Surgery of the Anus, Rectum and Colon, 2nd edn 1967; (jointly) Ulcerative Colitis, 1968; contribs to books and med. journals, dealing mainly with gastric, colonic and rectal surgery. *Recreations:* reading and travel. *Address:* Department of Surgery, Leeds General Infirmary, Leeds; Ladywood, Linton, Wetherby, Yorks.

**GOLOMBEK, Harry,** OBE 1966; Chess Correspondent, The Times, since 1945, and Chess Correspondent, The Observer, since 1955; writer on chess; *b* London, 1 March 1911; *s* of Barnet and Emma Golombek; unmarried. *Educ:* Wilson's Gram. Sch.; London Univ. Ed. British Chess Magazine, 1938, 1939, 1940. Served in RA, 1940-42, Foreign Office, 1942-45. Joint Ed., British Chess Magazine, 1949-; British Chess Champion, 1947, 1949, and 1955 (prize-winner 14 times); 1st prize in 4 international chess tournaments. Recognized as international master by Federation Internationale des Echecs, 1948. Represented Great Britain in 9 Chess Olympiads and capt. Brit. team, Helsinki, 1952, Amsterdam, 1954, Munich, 1958, Leipzig, 1960, Varna, 1962. *Publications:* 50 Great Games of Modern Chess, 1942; Capablanca's 100 Best Games of Chess, 1947; World Chess Championship, 1948, 1949; Pocket Guide to Chess Openings, 1949; Hastings Tournament, 1948-49, 1949; Southsea Tournament, 1949, 1949; Prague, 1946, 1950, Budapest, 1952, 1952; Reti's Best Games of Chess, 1954; World Chess Championship, 1954, 1954; The Game of Chess (Penguin), 1954; 22nd USSR Chess Championship, 1956; World Chess Championship, 1957, 1957; Modern Opening Chess Strategy, 1959. *Recreations:* music and the theatre. *Address:* Albury, Albion Crescent, Chalfont St Giles, Bucks. *T:* Chalfont 2808. *Clubs:* Athenæum; Surrey County Cricket.

**GOLT, Sidney,** CB 1964; Second Secretary, Board of Trade, since 1968; *b* West Hartlepool, 31 March 1910; *s* of late Wolf and Fanny Golt; *m* 1947, Jean, *d* of Ralph Oliver, CC; two *d*. *Educ:* Portsmouth Grammar Sch.; Christ Church, Oxford. PPE 1931; James Mew Scholar, Oxford, 1934; Statistician, Tin Producers' Assoc., 1936-40; joined Central Price Regulation Cttee, 1941; Asst Sec., Bd of Trade, 1945-60, sec., Central Price Regulation Cttee, 1945-46; Under-Sec., Bd of Trade, 1960-68, and Adviser on Commercial Policy, 1964-68. UK Mem., Preparatory Cttee for European Free Trade Assoc., Geneva, 1960; Leader, UK Delegns to UN Conf. on Trade and Development, New Delhi, 1968, and to Trade and Development Bd, 1965-68. *Publication:* Ed., Tin, and Tin World Statistics, 1936-40. *Recreations:* travel, reading, bridge. *Address:* The Gore Cottage, Burnham, Bucks. *T:* 4948; 37 Rowan Road, W6. *T:* 01-602 1410. *Club:* Reform.

**GOMBRICH, Prof. Ernst Hans Josef,** CBE 1966; FBA 1960; FSA 1961; PhD (Vienna); MA Oxon and Cantab; Director of the Warburg Institute and Professor of the History of the Classical Tradition in the University of London since Oct. 1959; *b* Vienna, 30 March 1909; *s* of Dr Karl B. Gombrich, Vice-Pres. of Disciplinary Council of Lawyer's Chamber, Vienna, and Prof. Leonie Gombrich (*née* Hock), pianist; *m* 1936, Ilse Heller; one *s*. *Educ:* Theresianum, Vienna; Vienna Univ. Research Asst, Warburg Inst., 1936-39. Served War of 1939-45 with BBC Monitoring Service. Senior Research Fellow, 1946-48, Lectr, 1948-54, Reader, 1954-56, Special Lectr, 1956-59, Warburg Inst., Univ. of London; Durning-Lawrence Prof. of the History of Art, London Univ., at University Coll., 1956-59; Slade Prof. of Fine Art in the University of Oxford, 1950-53; Visiting Prof. of Fine Art, Harvard Univ., 1959; Slade Prof. of Fine Art, Cambridge Univ., 1961-63; Lethaby Prof., RCA, 1967-68. Hon. Fellow, Jesus Coll., Cambridge, 1963; FRSL 1969; Foreign Hon. Mem., American Academy of Arts and Sciences, 1964; For. Mem., Amer. Philosophical Soc., 1968. Corresponding Member: Accademia delle Scienze di Torino, 1962; Royal Acad. of Arts and Sciences, Uppsala, 1970. Hon. DLit Belfast, 1963; Hon. LLD St Andrews, 1965; Hon. DLitt: Leeds, 1965; Oxford, 1969; Cambridge, 1970. W. H. Smith Literary Award, 1964. *Publications:* Weltgeschichte für Kinder, 1936; (with E. Kris) Caricature, 1940; The Story of Art, 1950; Art and Illusion (The A. W. Mellon Lectures in the Fine Arts, 1956), 1960; Meditations on a Hobby Horse, 1963; Norm and Form, 1966; Aby Warburg, an intellectual biography, 1970. contributions to learned journals. *Address:* 19 Briardale Gardens, NW3. *T:* 01-435 6639.

**GOMES, Sir Stanley Eugene,** Kt 1959; Retired Chief Justice, West Indies Federation; *b* Georgetown, British Guiana, 24 March 1901; *s* of late Mr and Mrs M. Gomes; *m* 1936, Elaine Vera (*née* Wight). *Educ:* St Joseph's Coll., Dumfries, Scotland; Jesus Coll., Cambridge. BA Cantab, 1923; called to Bar, Gray's Inn, 1924. British Guiana: Magistrate, 1929; Asst Attorney-Gen., 1933; Attorney-Gen., Leeward Islands, 1944; QC 1946; Puisne Judge, Trinidad, 1948. Chief Justice: Barbados, 1957-58; Trinidad, 1958; WI Fedn, 1961. Pres., Brit. Caribbean Court of Appeal, 1962. Retd Dec. 1962. *Recreations:* fishing, golf. *Address:* Royal Bank of Canada, Cockspur Street, SW1. *Club:* West Indian.

**GONARD, Prof. Samuel Alexandre;** President, International Committee of the Red Cross since Oct. 1964 (Member 1961-); *b* 8 June 1896; *m* 1944, Manon Bosshardt; one *s* one *d*. *Educ:* Univ. of Neuchâtel (Bachelor of Law). Chief of personal Staff to C-in-C Swiss Army, 1939; Brig. 1943; Vice-Chief, Gen. Staff of Swiss Army, 1943; Comdr, 14th Div.; Comdr, 9th Div., 1944; Prof., Mil. Sect., Fed. Polytech. High Sch., Zürich, 1946-53; Comdr 3rd Army Corps, 1951; Comdr, 1st Army Corps, 1954; Expert on Fed. Commn for the study of UN Charter; Mem. Fed. Commn for Nat. Defence, 1951-61; Prof. Grad. Inst. of Internat. Studies, University of Geneva, 1961. *Publications:* La Recherche operationnelle et la Décision. Has contrib. to numerous mil. and internat. affairs reviews. *Recreations:* literature, the arts, travelling. *Address:* Les Gonelles, Corseaux sur Vevey, Vaud, Switzerland. *T:* (021) 51.33.33.

**GONZÁLEZ, Marco Tulio;** Condecoración de la Cruz de Boyacá, 1950; Ambassador of Ecuador to the Court of St James's, 1967-69; *b* July 1917; *s* of Dr Raúl González and Rosa C. de González; *m* 1946, Mariana Tobar; two *s* one *d*. *Educ:* Central Univ., Quito, Ecuador. Lawyer, 1942. Sec. of Central Univ., 1944-45; Gen. Sec. of Public Administration, 1945-46; Minister of Educn, 1946-47; Consul-Gen. of Ecuador in New Orleans, 1947-48; MP, ecuador, 1950-52; Pres., Chamber of Agriculture 1957-62; Senator, 1959-63; Nat. Economics Coun., 1962-63; Minister of Industries, 1966; Dir of Monetary Bd, 1966. Pres of Ecuadorean Airline, 1957-67. Hon. Citizen of New Orleans, 1947. *Recreations:* tennis, riding. *Clubs:* Hurlingham; Lawyers' (Quito); Quito Tennis and Golf.

**GONZI, Most Rev. Michael;** *see* Malta, Archbishop of, (RC).

**GOOCH, George Gordon,** CMG 1958; JP 1926; pastoralist; *b* 1893; *s* of George Joseph Gooch and Fanny Grace Archer Snook; *m* 1923, Doris Hilda Irene Campbell; one *s* three *d. Educ:* Scotch Coll., Swanbourne, WA. Lifelong pastoral career in W Australia; early training in S Australia. Retired from active pastoral life, in 1943, to live in Perth. Former Director: Elder, Smith & Co. Ltd; Caris Holdings Ltd; Caris Bros Pty Ltd; Pastoral Labour Bureau Ltd; WA Trustee Co. Ltd; WA Newspapers Ltd; Perth Newspapers Ltd; Bays Transport Service Ltd; Past Pres., Royal Agricultural Society of WA. *Publication:* Lure of the North, 1952. *Address:* 45 Birdwood Parade, Dalkeith, Western Australia. *T:* 86-4939. *Clubs:* Weld, West Australian (Perth); Carnarvon (Carnarvon).

**GOOCH, Brig. Richard Frank Sherlock,** DSO 1945; MC 1940; Gentleman Usher to the Queen, 1964-69, Extra Gentleman Usher, 1962-64, and since 1969; *b* 8 Nov. 1906; 3rd *s* of Sir Thomas V. S. Gooch, 10th Bt; *m* 1939, Barbara Susan Hoare; two *s. Educ:* Harrow; Caius Coll., Cambridge (MA). Joined Coldstream Guards, 1927; Adjutant, 1934-37; ADC to the Viceroy of India, 1937-39; psc 1942; Bde Major, 5th Guards Armoured Bde, 1942-43. Comd 1st Coldstream, 1944-45; AA and QMG, Guards Div., 1945-46; Comd 2nd Coldstream, 1946-49; AAG, HQ London Dist, 1949-51; Comd 32 Guards Bde, 1951. City Marshal to the City of London, July-Dec. 1957; Private Sec. to the Lord Mayor of London, 1957-62. Croix de Guerre (with Palm), France, 1944; Chevalier of Order of Crown, Belgium, 1945; Croix de Guerre (with Palm), Belgium, 1945. *Recreation:* shooting. *Address:* Oakhill Farm, Earl Soham, Woodbridge, Suffolk. *T:* Earl Soham 251. *Clubs:* Boodle's, Pratt's.

*See also Col Sir Robert Gooch.*

**GOOCH, Sir Robert Douglas,** 4th Bt, *cr* 1866; *b* 19 Sept. 1905; *s* of 3rd Bt and Mary Winifred (*d* 1921), *d* of late Edward William Monro; *S* father 1926; *m* 1st, 1928, Moyra Katharine (who obtained a divorce, 1930), *d* of Dr C. Howard Saunders; 2nd, 1930, Mary Eileen, *widow* of Major H. L. Gifford; one *d. Heir: kinsman,* Trevor Sherlock Gooch; [*b* 15 June 1915; *m* 1956, Denys Anne Venables; one *s* three *d*].

**GOOCH, Col Sir Robert Eric Sherlock,** 11th Bt, *cr* 1746; DSO 1941; DL, JP; Member of HM Body Guard of the Honourable Corps of Gentlemen-at-Arms, 1950; Lieutenant sinc 1968 (Clerk of the Cheque and Adjutant, 1963-67, Standard Bearer, 1967-68); *b* 6 May 1903; *e s* of Sir T. V. S. Gooch, 10th Bt, and Florence Meta (*d* 1932), *y d* of late James Draper, St Heliers; *S* father, 1946; *m* 1926, Katharine C., *er d* of late Maj.-Gen. Sir E. W. C. Chaytor, KCMG, KCVO, CB; two *s* one *d. Educ:* Eton. Served War of 1939-45 (despatches twice, DSO); OC The Life Guards, 1943-46; commanded 1st Household Cavalry Regt, 1942-44. Col commanding The Household Cavalry, 1944-46; retd pay, 1946. Mem. of East Suffolk County Council, 1946- (Chm., 1957-67); County Alderman, 1951; High Sheriff of Suffolk, 1950. Mem. of House of Laity of Church Assembly, 1948-55. Mem. Council, Royal Agricultural Soc. of England, 1950 (Dep. Pres., 1960; Pres., 1961; Vice-Pres., 1961; Chm., 1963-67; Trustee, 1964); Liaison Officer to the Minister of Agriculture, 1952-62. Chm. Suffolk Agricultural Exec. Cttee, 1954-62; Pres., The Royal Smithfield Club, 1966. Hon. Col 4th Bn The Suffolk Regt (TA), 1953-61; Hon. Col Suffolk and Cambs Regt (TA), 1961-67. *Heir: s* Richard John Sherlock Gooch, *b* 22 March 1930. *Address:* Benacre Hall, Wrentham, Beccles, Suffolk. *Clubs:* Turf, Buck's.

*See also Brig. R. F. S. Gooch.*

**GOOD, Donal Bernard Waters,** CMG 1962; JMN (Malaysia), 1965; Commissioner of Law Revision, Malaysia, since 1963; *b* 13 April 1907; *er s* of William John and Kathleen Mary Good, Dublin; *m* 1930, Kathryn, *er d* of Frank Lucas Stanley and Helena Kathleen Stanley, Dublin; one *s* one *d. Educ:* The High Sch., and Trinity Coll., Dublin. Scholar and Moderator in Classics, TCD, 1927-29; MA 1932; LLB 1933; Barrister, King's Inns, Dublin (Benchers' Prizeman), 1935; Barrister, Gray's Inn, 1948. Resident Magistrate, Kenya, 1940-45; Malayan Planning Unit, 1945; Crown Counsel, Malayan Union, 1946-48; Legal Adviser: Negri Sembilan and Malacca, 1948-49; Johore, 1949-50; Legal Draftsman, Sierra Leone, 1951-52; Legal Adviser, Selangor, 1952; Senior Federal Counsel, Federation of Malaya, 1952-55; Actg Solicitor-Gen., 1953 and 1955; Actg Judge of Supreme Court, 1953; Judge of Supreme Court, 1955-59; Judge of the Court of Appeal, Federation of Malaya, 1959-62. Chm. Detainees Review Commn, 1955-60; Pres. Industrial Court, 1956-57; Chm. Detained Persons Advisory Board, 1960-. Coronation Medal, 1953. *Recreations:* orchid-growing, bridge. *Address:* Attorney-General's Chambers, Kuala Lumpur, Malaysia. *T:* 83551. *Clubs:* University (Dublin); Selangor, Lake and Ipoh (Malaysia).

**GOOD, Air Vice-Marshal J. L. F. F.;** *see* Fuller-Good.

**GOOD, Prof. Ronald D'Oyley,** ScD; Head of Department of Botany, University of Hull, 1928-59, Professor Emeritus, 1959; *b* 5 March 1896; 2nd *s* of William Ernest and Mary Gray Good; *m* 1927, Patty Gwynneth Griffith; one *d. Educ:* Weymouth Coll.; Downing Coll., Cambridge (Senior Scholar). MA, ScD Cantab. Served European War, 1914-18, 4th Bn Dorset Regt, and 2/5th Bn Lincolnshire Regt (France); Staff of Botany Department, British Museum (Nat. Hist.), 1922-28. Trustee, Dorset County Museum. *Publications:* Plants and Human Economics, 1933; The Old Roads of Dorset, 1940, 1966; Weyland, 1945; The Geography of the Flowering Plants, 1947, 1953, 1964; A Geographical Handbook of the Dorset Flora, 1948; Features of Evolution in the Flowering Plants, 1956; contributions to scientific journals. *Address:* 8 Durlston Road, Parkstone, Poole, Dorset. *T:* Parkstone 5132.

**GOODACRE, Kenneth,** TD 1952; DL; Partner with Gillhams, Solicitors, since 1969; Deputy Clerk to GLC, 1964-68; Clerk and Solicitor of Middlesex CC, 1955-65; Clerk of the Peace for Middlesex, 1959-65; *b* 29 Oct. 1910; *s* of Clifford and Florence Goodacre; *m* 1936, Dorothy, *d* of Harold Kendall, Solicitor, Leeds; one *s. Educ:* Doncaster Grammar Sch. Admitted Solicitor, 1934; Asst Solicitor: Doncaster Corp., 1934-35; Barrow-in-Furness Corp., 1935-36; Sen. Solicitor, Blackburn Corp., 1936-39; served War of 1939-45, TA with E Lancs Regt and Staff 53 Div. (Major), and 2nd Army (Lieut-Col); released from Army Service, 1945, and granted hon. rank of Major; Dep. Town Clerk: Blackburn, 1945-49, Leicester, 1949-52; Town Clerk, Leicester, 1952-55. DL, Greater London (DL Middlesex, 1960-65), 1965. *Address:* Flat 2, 25 Onslow Square, SW7. *T:* 01-589 6202; 6 Lovat Lane, EC3. *T:* 01-623 7251. *Club:* Army and Navy.

**GOODALE, Sir Ernest (William),** Kt, *cr* 1952; CBE 1946; MC 1917; Director, 1928, Managing Director, 1930-61, and Chairman since 1949, Warner & Sons Ltd, textile manufacturers: *b* 6 Dec. 1896; *s* of Wm Thos Goodale, Charter Town Clerk of Barnes, Surrey, and Frances Mary Wheatley; *m* 1924, Gwendolen Branscombe, *yr d* of late Sir Frank Warner, KBE, Woodcroft, Mottingham, Kent; one *s* one *d*. *Educ:* St Catherine's Coll., Richmond, Surrey; Surrey County Sch., Richmond; King's Coll., London Univ. London Univ. OTC, 1914-15; served European War, 2nd Lieut and Lieut Royal Warwicks Regt, 1916-19, Mesopotamia, Persia, Caucasus, etc. Admitted Solicitor, 1920; Partner, Minet, Pering, Smith & Co., London, retired 1928. Member of: Council for Art and Industry, 1934-39; Council of Industrial Design, 1945-49; Ramsden Cttee on Exhibitions and Fairs, 1945; Bd of Trade Advisory Cttees on Exhibitions and Fairs, 1948-65; Chm. Sub-Cttee on BIF ("Goodale Report"), 1953; Chm. BIF Ltd, 1954-56; Inst. of Export (Vice-Pres., 1956-66); Douglas Cttee on Purchase Tax, 1951; Council, Royal College of Art, 1950-53; Hon. Fellow, Society of Industrial Artists and Designers, 1960; Textile Inst., 1937- (Pres. 1939-40 and 1957-59); Silk and Rayon Controller (Min. of Supply), 1939; Pres., Silk and Man-Made Fibres (formerly Rayon) Users' Assoc. (Inc.), 1945-70; Vice-President: International Silk Assoc., 1949-68; British Man-Made (formerly Rayon and Synthetic) Fibres Federation, 1943-; Chairman: Furnishing Fabric Fedn, 1945-68; Furnishing Fabrics Export Group, 1940-68; Hon. Pres., Furnishing Fabric Manufacturers' Assoc.; a Vice-Pres. and Mem. Grand Council and Cttees, FBI (Chm. Industrial Art Cttee, 1949-62); Mem. Council, CBI; Mem. Council Royal Society Arts, 1935- (Chm., 1949-52, now a Vice-Pres.); Pres. British Colour Council, 1953-70; Mem. Bd of National Film Finance Corp., 1957- (apptd by Pres. of Bd of Trade); Mem. Min. of Educn Adv. Council on Art Educn, 1959-66; Mem. for Dorking (North), Surrey CC, 1961-70, Alderman, 1970-. Liveryman, Worshipful Co. of Weavers, 1929- (Court of Assistants, 1946-. Renter Bailiff, 1956-57, Upper Bailiff, 1957-58); Mem. of Law Soc. *Publications:* contributions to trade literature. *Address:* Branscombe, Nutcombe Lane, Dorking, Surrey. *Clubs:* Royal Automobile; English-Speaking Union.

**GOODALL, Anthony Charles,** MC 1942; **His Honour Judge Goodall;** Judge of County Courts (Circuit No. 40, Bow), since 1968; *b* 23 July 1916; *er s* of late Charles Henry and Mary Helen Goodall, The Manor House, Sutton Veny, Wilts; *m* 1947, Anne Valerie, *yr d* of late John Reginald Chichester and of Audrey Geraldine Chichester, Lurley Manor, Tiverton, Devon; one *s* two *d*. *Educ:* Eton; King's Coll., Cambridge. Called to Bar, Inner Temple, 1939 (Certif. of Hon.). Served War of 1939-45, 1st Royal Dragoons; taken prisoner (twice), 1944. Practised at Bar, 1946-67. *Publications:* (ed jtly) Faraday on Rating; contrib. to Encycl. Court Forms and Precedents. *Address:* 11 Moore Street, SW3. *T:* 01-589 3604; Mardon, Moretonhampstead, Devon. *T:* Moretonhampstead 239.

**GOODALL, David William,** PhD (London); DSc (Melbourne); ARCS, DIC, FLS; FIBiol; Professor of Botany and Range Science, Utah State University, since 1969; *b* 4 April 1914; *s* of Henry William Goodall; *m* 1st, 1940, Audrey Veronica Kirwin (marriage dissolved, 1949); one *s*; 2nd, 1949, Muriel Grace King; two *s* one *d*. *Educ:* St Paul's Sch.; Imperial Coll. of Science and Technology (BSc). Research under Research Inst. of Plant Physiology, on secondment to Cheshunt and East Malling Research Stns, 1935-46; Plant Physiologist, W African Cacao Research Inst., 1946-48; Sen. Lectr in Botany, University of Melbourne, 1948-52; Reader in Botany, University Coll. of the Gold Coast, 1952-54; Prof. of Agricultural Botany, University of Reading, 1954-56; Dir, CSIRO Tobacco Research Institute, Mareeba, Qld, 1956-61; Senior Principal Research Officer, CSIRO Div. of Mathematical Statistics, Perth, Australia, 1961-67; Hon. Reader in Botany, Univ. of Western Australia, 1965-67; Prof. of Biological Science, Univ. of California Irvine, 1966-68. *Publications:* Chemical Composition of Plants as an Index of their Nutritional Status (with F. G. Gregory), 1947; numerous papers in botanical journals. *Address:* Ecology Center, Utah State University, Logan, Utah 84321, USA.

**GOODBODY, Gen. Sir Richard (Wakefield),** GCB 1963 (CB 1953); KBE 1958; DSO 1943; Bath King at Arms since 1965; *b* 12 April 1903; *s* of Gerald E. Goodbody, Woodsdown, Co. Limerick; *m* 1929, Mary Eveline Talbot, Provost's House, Edgmond, Newport, Salop; three *s* one *d*. *Educ:* Rugby; RMA Woolwich. Commissioned RA, 1923; apptd to RHA, 1927; Adjt, HAC, 1936; Bde Major 1st Support Group, 1940; CO 11 RHA, 1942; Comdr 2 Armd Bde, 1943; CRA 7th Armd Div., 1946; Comd 15 Inf. Bde, 1947; Dep. DMT War Office, 1948; Comdt Sch. of Artillery, 1949; GOC 56 (London) Armoured Div., TA, 1951; Dir of Royal Artillery, War Office, 1954; GOC-in-C Northern Comd, 1957-60; Adjt-Gen. to the Forces, 1960-63. Col Commandant: Royal Artillery, 1957-68; Hon. Artillery Co., 1959-66; Royal Horse Artillery, 1960-68; ADC Gen. to the Queen, 1961-63. Retd from the Army, 1963. Governor, The Royal Sch., Bath; a Vice-Pres., Assoc. for Employment of Regular Sailors, Soldiers and Airmen; Mem., Council of St Dunstan's. *Recreations:* shooting, fishing, gardening. *Address:* Broadlea Farm, Sutton Waldron, Blandford, Dorset. *Club:* Naval and Military.

**GOODCHILD, Rt. Rev. Ronald Cedric Osbourne;** *see* Kensington, Suffragan Bishop of.

**GOODDEN, Abington,** CBE 1956; retired, as a Consul-General, from HM Diplomatic Service, 1960; *b* 7 Dec. 1901; *s* of late Dr Wyndham C. Goodden and Clara Joan (*née* Smith); *m* 1930, Johanna Arnolda Jordaan (*d* 1962), South Africa; one *s*. *Educ:* Eton (King's Scholar, 1915); King's Coll., Cambridge. Vice-Consul: Hamburg, 1926-27; Lourenço Marques, 1928-30; Naples, 1931-33; Vice-Consul and Third Sec. of Embassy, Santiago (Chile), 1933-37; attached to Special Representative of Cuba at Coronation of HM King George VI, 1937; Vice-Consul, New York, 1937-38; Consul: Valencia, 1939; Madrid, 1939-41; Chargé d'Affaires *ad interim*, Managua (Nicaragua), 1941-42; Consul, Ponta Delgada (Azores), 1943-45; rep. of CCG (British Element) at Frankfurt, 1945-46; Consul and First Sec. of Embassy, Madrid, 1946-47; Dep. Consul-Gen., Batavia (now Djakarta), 1947-49; Commercial Counsellor, HM Embassy, Oslo, 1950-53; Consul-Gen., Seville, 1953-60. Coronation Medal, 1937; Portuguese Life-Saving Society's Medal, 1946. *Club:* Oxford and Cambridge University.

**GOODDEN, Robert Yorke,** CBE 1956; RDI 1947; Architect and Designer; Professor, School of Silversmithing and Jewellery since 1948, and Pro-Rector since 1967, Royal College of Art; *b* 7 May 1909; 2nd *s* of Lieut-Col R. B. Goodden, OBE and Gwendolen Goodden; *m* 1st, 1936, Kathleen Teresa

Burrow; 2nd, 1946, Lesley Macbeth Mitchell; two *s* two *d*. *Educ:* Harrow Sch. Trained AA Sch. of Architecture, 1926-31; AA Diploma 1932; ARIBA 1933; private practice as architect and designer, 1932-39; served RAFVR, 1940-41; RNVR, 1941-45; resumed private practice, 1946. Designer of Sports Section, Britain Can Make It Exhibition, 1946; joint architect and designer: Lion and Unicorn Pavilion, South Bank Exhibition, 1951; Western Sculpture Rooms, British Museum, 1969; designer of: Coronation hangings for Westminster Abbey, 1953; gold and silver plate for Corp. of London, Worshipful Co. of Goldsmiths, Royal Society of Arts, Royal Pavilion, South Bank Exhibition, Downing Coll., Cambridge, The Steel Co. of Wales, British American Tobacco Co., SS Canberra, Royal Coll. of Art, and others; of glass for King's Coll., Cambridge, Grosvenor House, Min. of Works, and others; of china for Grosvenor House, SS Oriana and Josiah Wedgwood & Sons; of metal foil mural decorations in SS Canberra, 1961. Consulting Architect to Board of Trade for BIF, Olympia, 1947, Earls Ct, 1949, Olympia, 1950 and 1951. Member: Council of Industrial Design, 1955; National Council for Diplomas in Art and Design, 1961. FSIA, 1947; Hon. Des. RCA 1952. Master of Faculty, RDI, 1959-61. Liveryman, Worshipful Co. of Goldsmiths. *Recreation:* crossing the Stour. *Address:* Prospect, Higham, Colchester, Essex. *T:* Higham 278.

**GOODE, Sir William (Allmond Codrington),** GCMG 1963 (KCMG 1957; CMG 1952); Chairman, Water Resources Board, since 1964; *b* 8 June 1907; *e s* of late Sir Richard Goode, CMG, CBE; *m* 1st, 1938, Mary Armstrong Harding (*d* 1947); 2nd, 1950, Ena Mary McLaren; one *d*. *Educ:* Oakham Sch.; Worcester Coll., Oxford (Classical exhibitioner). Barrister-at-Law, Gray's Inn, 1936. Joined Malayan Civil Service, 1931; District Officer, Raub, 1936-39; Asst Commissioner for Civil Defence, Singapore, 1940. Mobilised in 1st Bn Singapore Volunteer Corps as Lance-Corporal, 1941 (prisoner of war, Singapore, 1942; moved to Thailand for work on the Burma Railway; released 1945). Dep. Economic Sec., Federation of Malaya, 1948; Chief Sec., Aden, 1949-53; Acting Governor, Aden, 1950-51; Chief Sec., Singapore, 1953-57; Governor of Singapore, Dec. 1957-2nd June 1959; Yang di-Pertuan Negara of the State of Singapore and UK Commissioner, Singapore, 1959; Governor and C-in-C, North Borneo, 1960-63. KStJ 1958. *Recreation:* sailing. *Address:* East Streatley House, Streatley-on-Thames, Berks. *Club:* East India and Sports.

**GOODENOUGH, Cecilia Phyllis,** MA; STh; Assistant to Diocesan Missioner, Diocese of Southwark, since 1954; *b* 9 Sept. 1905; *d* of late Adm. Sir William Goodenough, GCB, MVO. *Educ:* Rochester Gram. Sch.; Liverpool Coll., Huyton; St Hugh's Coll., Oxford, LCC Care Cttee Sec., 1927-30; Sunday Sch. and Evangelistic work, Diocese of Caledonia, Fort St John, BC, Canada, 1931-36; Head of Talbot Settlement, 14 Bromley Hill, Bromley, Kent, 1937-45. *Publications:* Christ's Challenges, 1937; Religion and the Guide Law, 1938; articles in RGS Journal, 1934, in Geographical Magazine, Jan. 1937. *Address:* 4 Champion Grove, Camberwell, SE5. *T:* 01-274 8328.

**GOODENOUGH, Kenneth Mackenzie,** CMG 1949; MC 1918; *b* Bristol, 30 Oct. 1891; 3rd *s* of late W. T. Goodenough, Bristol; *m* 1916, Florence Alda Bolwell; two *s*. *Educ:* Fairfield Sch., Bristol. Entered surveying profession and qualified as a Professional Associate of the Surveyors' Institution. Served European War, 1914-18 in Royal Artillery, commissioned 1917 (MC). Took up business appointment in S Rhodesia, 1928. Pres. Bulawayo Chamber of Commerce, 1942 and 1943; Dep. Mayor of Bulawayo, 1944. High Comr for S Rhodesia, 1946-Jan. 1953. Freeman of City of London; Liveryman of Worshipful Co. of Needlemakers. *Address:* 34 St Martin's House, Clarence Parade, Southsea, Hants. *Club:* Bulawayo (Bulawayo).

**GOODENOUGH, Sir Richard (Edmund),** 2nd Bt, *cr* 1943; *b* 9 June 1925; *e s* of Sir William (Macnamara) Goodenough, 1st Bt, and of Dorothea (Louisa), *er d* of late Ven. and Hon. K. F. Gibbs, DD; *S* father 1951; *m* 1951, Jane, *d* of late H. S. P. McLernon and of Mrs McLernon, Gisborne, NZ; one *s* two *d*. *Educ:* Eton Coll.; Christ Church, Oxford. Military service, 1943-45, invalided. Christ Church, Oxford, 1945-47. *Heir:* *s* William McLernon Goodenough, *b* 5 Aug. 1954. *Address:* Nyewood House West, Rogate, Sussex.

**GOODERHAM, Very Rev. Hector Bransby,** MA; retired; *b* 11 Oct. 1901; *o s* of Edward Bransby Gooderham and Louisa Elizabeth Gooderham, Richmond, Surrey; *m* 1928, Esther Beatrice, *d* of William Orr, JP, Edinburgh; one *s* one *d*. *Educ:* George Heriot's Sch.; Edinburgh Univ.; Westcott House, Cambridge. MA 1st Cl. Hons, Edinburgh, 1923 (Vans Dunlop Scholar in Logic and Metaphysics). Curate: St Mary's Cathedral, Glasgow, 1924; St John's, Edinburgh, 1925; Rector: St John's, Selkirk, 1929-37; St Baldred's, North Berwick, 1937-49; Provost of the Cathedral Church of St Mary, Edinburgh, 1949-56; Vicar of St Peter's, Cranley Gardens, South Kensington, London, 1957-63. Formerly also: Lecturer, Edinburgh Theological Coll., 1934-43; Canon of St Mary's Cathedral, Edinburgh, 1948. *Recreations:* walking, motoring. *Address:* c/o National Bank of Scotland, 115 Regent Street, W1.

**GOODEVE, Sir Charles Frederick,** Kt 1946; OBE 1941; FRS 1940; FRIC; FIM; MInstT; MSc Manitoba; DSc London; Comdr RNVR (retired); Consultant, British Steel Corporation, since 1969; Director: Industrial and Commercial Finance Corporation since 1965; Technical Development Capital Ltd since 1966; National Industrial Fuel Efficiency Service, since 1969; *b* 21 Feb. 1904; *s* of Canon F. W. Goodeve, Winnipeg, Canada; *m* 1932, Janet I. Wallace, PhD; two *s*. *Educ:* Univ. of Manitoba; University Coll., London. Asst Lectr, Univ. of Manitoba; 1851 Exhibition Scholar, 1927; Lectr and later Reader in Physical Chemistry, University Coll., London; Dep. Dir, Dept of Miscellaneous Weapon Development, Admiralty, 1940-42; Asst and later Dep. Controller for R&D, Admiralty, 1942-45; Dir, BISRA, The Inter-Group Laboratories of the British Steel Corp., formerly British Iron and Steel Research Assoc., 1945-69. Fellow, UCL. Pres., Faraday Soc., 1950-52; Chm., Operational Research Club, 1947-51; Vice-Pres., Parliamentary and Scientific Cttee, 1950-62; Mem., Lord President's Advisory Council on Scientific Policy, 1953-56; Pres. Chemical Section, British Assoc., 1956; Master, Worshipful Co. of Salters, 1958-59; Pres., Iron and Steel Inst., 1961-62; a Vice-Pres., Royal Soc., 1968-70. Scientific Adviser, British Transport Commn, 1948-58. Governor, Imperial Coll., London, 1961-; Fellow, 1967-. Mem., Council of Tavistock Inst. of Human Relations. Fellow, Metallurgical Soc. AIME, 1967. Hon. DSc: Manitoba, 1946; Sheffield, 1956; Birmingham, 1962; Newcastle-upon-Tyne 1970. US Medal of Freedom with Silver Palm; Bessemer Gold

Medallist, 1962; Carl Lueg Gold Medallist, 1962; Silver Medal, Operational Research Soc., 1964. *Publications:* (part author) Iron and Steel Productivity Report; numerous in scientific journals. *Recreation:* ice-skating. *Address:* 38 Middleway, NW11. *T:* 01-455 7308. *Club:* Athenæum.

**GOODFELLOW, Maj.-Gen. Howard Courtney,** CB 1952; CBE 1946 (OBE 1943); retired 1954; *b* 28 July 1898; *yr s* of late Thomas Goodfellow, Plymouth; *m* 1928, Vera St John, *yr d* of late H. St J. Hewitt, Salisbury. *Educ:* Plymouth Coll.; RMC Sandhurst. Commissioned into ASC, 1916; served European War, 1914-18, in France and Italy; seconded to Iraq Army, 1928-32; War of 1939-45, served in Italy and NW Europe, rank of Brig. Order of Rafidain, Class IV (Iraq), 1931. *Address:* Chapel Lodge, Greywell, Hants. *T:* Odiham 2076.

**GOODFELLOW, Keith Frank,** QC 1967; Practising Member of the Bar since 1952; *b* 26 March 1926; *s* of late L. T. Goodfellow and E. M. Goodfellow (*née* Dendy); *m* 1949, Rosalind Erica (*née* Griffith-Jones); two *s* one *d*. *Educ:* St Dunstan's Coll., Catford, SE6; Sydney Sussex Coll., Cambridge. BA 1949; LLB 1950; MA 1952. Called to Bar, Middle Temple, 1951. *Publication:* Outline of the Law of Rating (with W. Scrivens), 1955. *Recreation:* exercising children and dogs. *Address:* Harlyn, Sandy Way, Cobham, Surrey. *T:* Oxshott 3142.

**GOODFELLOW, Sir William,** Kt, 1953; Director: Amalgamated Dairies Ltd; Refrigeration Engineering Co. Ltd; Sulphur & Chemical Importing Co. Ltd; Avalon Investment Trust Ltd; Challenge Investment Co. Ltd; *b* 26 May 1880; *s* of Thomas and Jane G. Goodfellow; *m* 1913, Irene C. Chamberlin; four *s* one *d* (and one *s* killed on active service as Fleet Air Arm Pilot). *Educ:* Mt Eden Primary Sch.; Auckland Grammar Sch. Freeman of City of London, 1951. Hon. LLD, Auckland, 1963. *Recreations:* yachting, trout fishing, gardening. *Address:* 40 Selwyn Avenue, Mission Bay, Auckland, NZ. *T:* 585-367. *Club:* Northern (Auckland, NZ).

**GOODHART, Arthur Lehman,** (Hon.) KBE 1948; QC 1943; FBA 1952; MA, LLM, LLD, DCL; Master of University College, Oxford, 1951-63, retired; Professor Emeritus since 1951; Editor, Law Quarterly Review; Professor of Jurisprudence, Oxford, 1931-51; *b* NY City, 1 March 1891; *s* of late Philip J. Goodhart and Harriet Lehman; *m* 1924, Cecily, *d* of Eric M. Carter, Beaulieu, Hants; three *s*. *Educ:* Hotchkiss Sch.; Yale Univ.; Trinity Coll., Cambridge. Asst Corp. Council for NY City, 1915-17; Capt., Ord. USA, 1917-19. University Lectr in Law, Cambridge, 1919-31; Counsel to Amer. Mission to Poland, 1919; Officier d'Académie de France, 1920; Sec. to Vice-Chancellor of Cambridge Univ., 1921-23; Ed., Cambridge Law Journal, 1921-25. Hon. Bencher, Lincoln's Inn, 1938; Hon. Fellow of Trinity Coll., Corpus Christi Coll., Trinity Hall, Cambridge; Hon. Fellow of Nuffield Coll., University Coll., Oxford; Associate Fellow of Jonathan Edwards Coll., Yale Univ.; Chm. Southern Price Regulation Cttee, 1940-51; Member: Royal Commission on the Police; Monopolies Commission; Law Revision Cttee; Supreme Court Procedure Cttee; Company Law Revision Cttee; Alternative Remedies Cttee; Law Reports Cttee; Amer. Law Inst.; Chm. Internat. Law Assoc.; Curator, Bodleian Library; Deleg., OUP; Pres., Selden Soc., 1964; Pres., Public Teachers of Law, 1950; Vice-Pres., British Academy, 1962; Vice-Pres., Pilgrims, 1963; Pres., American Soc., 1951; Pres., International Assoc. of University Professors, 1948; Pres., Pedestrians' Assoc. for Road Safety, 1951-63; Vice-Président de l'Institut International de Philosophie du Droit; Hon. Mem. American Academy of Arts and Sciences; Visiting Professor: Yale Univ., 1928-29; Harvard Law Sch., 1964; University of Virginia Law School, 1965; McGill Univ. Law Sch., 1966; Tulane Univ. of Louisiana, 1967; Univ. of Arizona, 1967; Scholar-in-Residence, NYC Bar Assoc., 1966. Hon. LLD: Edinburgh Univ., Queen's Univ., Belfast, Yale Univ., Wesleyan Univ., California Univ., Columbia Univ., London Univ., New York Univ., Williams Coll., Princeton Univ., Harvard Univ., Dartmouth Coll., Pennsylvania Univ., Dalhousie Univ., Melbourne Univ., Tulane Univ. of Louisiana, Cincinnati Univ.; Hon. DLitt, Cambridge. *Publications:* Poland and the Minority Races, 1920; Essays in Jurisprudence and the Common Law, 1931; Precedent in English and Continental Law, 1934; The Government of Great Britain, 1946; English Contributions to the Philosophy of Law, 1949; Five Jewish Lawyers of the Common Law, 1950; Ed. Pollock's Jurisprudence and Essays, 1961; English Law and the Moral Law, 1953; Law of the Land, 1966; and legal articles and essays. *Address:* University College, Oxford; Whitebarn, Boars Hill, Oxford. *T:* Oxford 35294. *Clubs:* Athenæum, Oxford and Cambridge University, Savile, Pilgrims'; Century, Yale, Alpha Delta Phi, University.
*See also P. C. Goodhart.*

**GOODHART, Rear-Adm. Hilary Charles Nicholas;** Military Deputy to Head of Defence Sales, Ministry of Defence, since 1970; *b* 28 Sept. 1919; *s* of G. C. Goodhart; *m* 1958, Lydia Sward; no *c*. *Educ:* RNC Dartmouth; RNEC Keyham. Joined RN, 1933; served in Mediterranean in HM Ships Formidable and Dido, 1941-43; trained as pilot, 1944; served as fighter pilot in Burma Campaign, 1945; trained as test pilot, 1946; served on British Naval Staff, Washington, 1953-55; idc 1965; Rear-Adm. 1970. Freedom of London, 1945; Liveryman of Grocers' Co., 1952. US Legion of Merit, 1958. *Publications:* numerous articles on gliding. *Recreations:* gliding (British Gliding Champion, 1962 and 1967); gardening. *Address:* Downwind, Dukes Covert, Bagshot, Surrey. *T:* Bagshot 2477. *Club:* Royal Aero.

**GOODHART, Sir John (Gordon),** 3rd Bt *cr* 1911; MA, MB, BChir; General Practitioner since 1947; *b* 14 Dec. 1916; *s* of Gordon Wilkinson Goodhart, MD, FRCP; *S* uncle, 1961; *m* 1944, Margaret Mary Eileen, *d* of late Morgan Morgan, Cray, Brecon; one *s* one *d*. *Educ:* Rugby; Trinity Hall, Cambridge; Guy's Hospital Med. Sch. MRCS, LRCP, 1941. Served as Surg-Lieut, RNVR, 1942-46. *Recreation:* golf. *Heir:* *s* Robert Anthony Gordon Goodhart, *b* 15 Dec. 1948. *Address:* 1 Garden Road, Sundridge Park, Bromley, Kent.

**GOODHART, Philip Carter;** MP (C) Beckenham Division since March 1957; *b* 3 Nov. 1925; *s* of Prof. Arthur Goodhart, *qv*; *m* 1950, Valerie Winant; three *s* four *d*. *Educ:* Hotchkiss Sch., USA; Trinity Coll., Cambridge. Served KRRC and Parachute Regt, 1943-47. Editorial staff, Daily Telegraph, 1950-55; Editorial staff, Sunday Times, 1955-57. Contested (C) Consett, Co. Durham, Gen. Election, 1950; Mem. LCC Educn Cttee, 1956-57; PPS to Julian Amery at War Office and Colonial Office, 1958-60; Member: British Delegn to Council of Europe and WEU, 1961-63; British Delegation to UN Gen. Assembly, 1963; NATO Parly Assembly (Chm. Arms Standardization Sub-Cttee), 1966-69. Joint Hon. Sec., 1922 Cttee, 1960-. Chm. of Cons. Parly Cttee on Military

Matters, 1964-65; Sec., Cons. Parly Defence Cttee, 1967-; Mem. Council, Consumers' Assoc., 1959-68. *Publications:* The Hunt for Kimathi (with Ian Henderson, GM), 1958; In the Shadow of the Sword, 1964; Fifty Ships that Saved the World, 1965; War without Weapons (with Christopher Chataway), 1968; various pamphlets. *Recreation:* skiing (Chm., Develt Cttee, Nat. Ski Fedn of GB). *Address:* 27 Phillimore Gardens, W8. *T:* 01-937 0822. *Clubs:* Athenæum, Beefsteak, Carlton, Garrick, Savile.

**GOODHEW, Victor Henry;** MP (C) St Albans Division of Herts since Oct. 1959; a Lord Commissioner, HM Treasury, since Oct. 1970; *b* 30 Nov. 1919; *s* of Rudolph Goodhew, Mannings Heath, Sussex; *m* 1st, 1940, Sylvia Johnson (marr. diss.); one *s* one *d*; 2nd, 1951, Suzanne, *d* of Wing-Comdr Cyril Gordon-Burge, OBE, Shepperton, Mddx. *Educ:* King's Coll. Sch. Served War of 1939-45: RAF, 1939-46; comd Airborne Radar Unit, attached 6th Airborne Div.; Sqdn Ldr 1945. Mem. Westminster City Council, 1953-59. Contested (C) Paddington North, 1955. Mem. LCC, 1958-61. PPS to Mr C. I. Orr-Ewing, OBE, MP (when Civil Lord of the Admiralty), May 1962-63; PPS to Hon. Thomas Galbraith, MP (Jt Parly Sec., Min. of Transport), 1963-64; Asst Govt Whip, June-Oct. 1970. *Recreations:* gardening, sailing, ski-ing. *Address:* 61E Eaton Square, SW1; Keeper's Cottage, Water End, Wheathampstead, Herts. *Club:* Carlton.

**GOODING, Air Vice-Marshal Keith Horace,** CB 1966; OBE 1951; Director-General of Equipment (RAF), Ministry of Defence, since 1968; *b* 2 Sept. 1913; *s* of Horace Milford Gooding, Romsey, Hants; *m* 1st, 1943, Peggy Eileen (*d* 1962), *d* of Albert William Gatfield, Guildford, Surrey; one *s*; 2nd, 1968, Jean, *d* of Maurice Stanley Underwood, Andover, Hants; one *s*. *Educ:* King Edward VI Sch., Southampton. Joined RAF 1938; served Aden, Fighter Comd, 1939-45; Germany, 1945-47; NATO Defence Coll., 1953-54; NATO, Oslo, 1954-55; Bomber Comd, 1958-61; AOA Maintenance Comd, 1965-68. *Recreations:* tennis, squash, sailing. *Address:* c/o Lloyds Bank Ltd, Surbiton, Surrey. *Club:* Royal Air Force.

**GOODINGS, Alfred Cecil,** MBE 1946; MSc, PhD; Director of Textile Research, Ontario Research Foundation, 1930-67; *yr s* of late William George Goodings; *b* Leith, Scotland, 10 Sept. 1902; *m* 1931, *yr d* of late Rev. F. W. Ambery Smith; two *s*. *Educ:* Leeds Univ. PhD for research in textiles. *Publications:* papers in scientific periodicals relating to textile Fibres and technology. *Address:* 101 Collegeview Avenue, Forest Hill Village, Toronto, Canada.

**GOODISON, Robin Reynolds,** CB 1964; Second Secretary, Board of Trade, since 1969; *b* 13 Aug. 1912; *s* of Arthur Leathley Goodison; *m* 1936, Betty Lydia, *d* of Comdr L. Robinson, OBE, Royal Navy (retired); three *d*. *Educ:* Finchley Grammar Sch.; University Coll., London Univ. (MA). Joined Ministry of Labour, 1935, transferred to Ministry of Transport, 1936; Principal, 1940; Asst Sec., 1946; Imperial Defence Coll., 1950; Under-Sec., Ministry of Transport and Civil Aviation, 1957, Ministry of Aviation, 1959, Board of Trade, 1966. *Recreation:* sailing. *Address:* Clansthal, Coldharbour Lane, Bushey, Herts. *T:* Bushey Heath 1911.

**GOODMAN,** family name of **Baron Goodman.**

**GOODMAN,** Baron, *cr* 1965, of the City of Westminster (Life Peer); **Arnold Abraham Goodman,** MA, LLM; Senior Partner, Goodman Derrick and Co., Solicitors; Chairman: Arts Council of Great Britain since 1965; Newspaper Publishers' Association, since 1970; Member, Industrial Reorganization Corporation, 1969-71; *b* 21 Aug. 1913; *s* of Joseph and Bertha Goodman; unmarried. *Educ:* University Coll., London; Downing Coll., Cambridge (Hon. Fellow, 1968). Chm. cttee (on behalf of Arts Council) on London orchestras, 1964, reporting 1965; Member: Royal Commission on the Working of the Tribunals of Enquiry (Evidence) Act, 1921, 1966-; British Council, 1967; South Bank Theatre Board, 1968-; Chm., Observer Trust, 1967-. Chm., British Lion Films Ltd; Dir of various cos. Fellow UCL. *Address:* Goodman Derrick & Co., 4 Little Essex Street, WC2.

**GOODMAN, Rt. Rev. Morse Lamb;** *see* Calgary, Bishop of.

**GOODMAN, Neville Marriott,** CB 1961; MA, MD Cantab; PhD London; DPH London; FRCP; retired as Deputy Chief MO, Ministry of Health (1960-April 1963); *b* 22 April 1898; *o c* of Roger Neville Goodman, MD, and Louisa Harvey Marriott; *m* 1928, Beatrix Warr Edwards (*d* 1970). *Educ:* Mill Hill Sch.; RMC Sandhurst; Pembroke Coll., Cambridge; London Hospital. House physician, surgeon, Receiving Room Officer, Ear, Nose and Throat Dept, London Hosp. Served European War, 1914-18, with 4th Bn The Worcs Regt, 1917-19; retd with rank of Capt. General practice, Lymington, Hants, 1925-32; Asst County MOH, Surrey CC, 1933-34; Min. of Health, 1934-63. Mem., Health Cttee, League of Nations, 1938-45; Br. Delegate Office Internat. d'Hygiène publique, Paris, 1938-45; Dir of Health, European Regional Office, UNRRA, 1945-47; Dir of Field Services, WHO, 1947-49; Chm., UK Cttee for WHO. Lectr in Internat. Health at London Sch. of Hygiene and Tropical Medicine. OStJ 1936; Méd. de la Reconnaissance française. *Publications:* International Health Organisations and their Work, 1952; Wilson Jameson: Architect of National Health, 1970; articles on medicine and public health. *Recreation:* gardening. *Address:* 6 The Grove, Highgate Village, N6. *T:* 01-340 2662. *Club:* Athenæum.

**GOODMAN, Maj.-Gen. Walter Rutherfoord,** CB 1954; DSO 1945; MC 1918; retired; *b* 7 Feb. 1899; *s* of Walter James Goodman, JP, Trim, Co. Meath; *m* 1932, Mary, *d* of Lt-Col C. C. Barnes; two *d*. *Educ:* Ellesmere Coll., Salop. 2nd Lieut, Special Reserve, Jan. 1917, Regular, Feb. 1918, Royal Artillery; served European War, 1914-18, and War of 1939-45. Retired, 1955. Col Comdt, RA, 1955-64. *Address:* Bealings Holt, Little Bealings, Suffolk. *Club:* Army and Navy.

**GOODPASTER, Gen. Andrew Jackson;** United States Army; DSC (US); DSM (US) (2 Oak Leaf Clusters); Silver Star; Legion of Merit (Oak Leaf Cluster); Purple Heart (Oak Leaf Cluster); Supreme Allied Commander Europe since July 1969; Commander-in-Chief, United States European Command, since May 1969; *b* 12 Feb. 1915; *s* of Andrew Jackson Goodpaster and Teresa Mary Goodpaster (*née* Mrovka); *m* 1939, Dorothy Anderson Goodpaster (*née* Anderson); two *d*. *Educ:* McKendree Coll., Lebanon, Ill; US Mil. Academy, 1935-39 (BS); Princeton Univ., 1945-50 (MSE, MA, PhD). 11th Eng. Panama, 1939-42; Ex O, 390th Eng. Gen. Svc Regt, Camp Claiborne, La, 1942-43; Comd and Gen. Staff Sch., Ft Leavenworth, Kansas, Feb.-April 1943; CO, 48th Eng. Combat Bn, II Corps, Fifth Army, 1943-44; Ops Div., Gen. Staff, War Dept (incl. Jt War

Plans Cttee, JCS, 1945-46), 1944-47; Student, Civil Eng. Course and Polit. Sc. Grad. Sch., Princeton Univ., 1947-50; Army Mem., Jt Advanced Study Cttee, JCS, 1950-51; Special Asst to Chief of Staff, SHAPE, 1951-54; Dist Eng., San Francisco Dist, Calif, July-Oct. 1954; Def. Liaison Officer and Staff Sec. to President of US, 1954-61; Asst Div. Comdr, 3rd Inf. Div., April-Oct. 1961, and CG, 8th Inf. Div., Oct. 1961-Oct. 1962, USAREUR; Sp. Asst (Policy) to Chm., JCS, Washington, DC, Nov. 1962-Jan. 1964; Asst to Chm., JCS, Washington, DC, Jan. 1964-July 1966; Dir Joint Staff, JCS, Washington, DC, Aug. 1966-Mar. 1967; Dir of Sp. Studies, Office Chief of Staff, USA, Washington, DC, April 1967-July 1967; Senior US Army Mem., Mil. Staff UN, May 1967-July 1968; Comdt, Nat. War Coll., Washington, DC, Aug. 1967-July 1968; Mem. US Delegn for Negotiations with N Vietnam, Paris (addl duty), April 1968-July 1968; Dep. Comdr, US Mil. Assistance Comd, Vietnam, July 1968-April 1969. *Recreations:* golf, swimming, photography, music. *Address:* Supreme Headquarters, Allied Powers Europe (SHAPE B.7010), Belgium. *T:* (065) 44113.

**GOODRICH, Carter;** Andrew Mellon Professor of History, University of Pittsburgh, USA, 1963-71; *b* 10 May 1897; *s* of Charles Lyman Goodrich and Jeannette (Margaret) Carter; *m* 1921, Florence (Perry) Nielsen; one *s* two *d*. *Educ:* Amherst Coll., AB 1918; University of Chicago, PhD, 1921. Scholar and Fellow of Amherst Coll., 1919 (research on British Labour problems), 1921-22, 1923-24 (research on Amer. coal industry); Instructor in Economics, Amherst Coll., 1922-23; Economics Dept, University of Michigan, 1924-27 (Asst Prof.), 1927-29 (Assoc. Prof.), 1929-31 (Prof.); Prof. of Economics, Columbia Univ., 1931-63; Prof. Emeritus, 1963-. Fellow of Social Science Research Council, 1927 (research on Australian and New Zealand labour movements); Dir, Study of Population Redistribution (Wharton Sch., Univ. of Pennsylvania), 1934-36; United States Labour Comr, Geneva, Switzerland, 1936-37 and 1938-40; Special Asst, American Ambassador to Great Britain, 1941; US Government Member of Governing Body, International Labour Office, 1936-46, Chm. 1939-45; Executive Officer, Economics Dept, Columbia Univ., 1946-49; Chm., Preparatory Cttee, UN Resources Conference, 1948-49; Consultant, United Nations, 1947-51; UN special Rep. to Bolivia, 1952-53; Chief, UN Economic Survey Mission to Viet Nam, 1955-56. Rep. Columbia Univ. Sch. of Business to University of Buenos Aires, 1961-62. President, Economic History Association, 1954-56. Mem. Amer. Philosophical Soc., Century (New York); Fellow, American Acad. of Arts and Sciences. Hon. LHD Amherst Coll., 1958. Order of the Condor of the Andes, Bolivia, 1953. *Publications:* The Frontier of Control, 1921; The Miner's Freedom, 1925; Government Promotion of American Canals and Railroads, 1960; as senior author, Migration and Economic Opportunity, 1936; Canals and American Economic Development, 1961; as editor, The Government and the Economy, 1783-1861, 1967. *Address:* 4601 Bayard Street, Pittsburgh, Pa 15213, USA.

**GOODRICH, Dame Matilda,** DBE, *cr* 1947; RRC; retired; *d* of Henry Portry Goodrich, Methwold, Norfolk. Matron-in-Chief, Queen Alexandra's Royal Naval Nursing Service, 1944-47. Retired, 1947. *Address:* Bow-Wood Gardens, Bow-Wood Road, Claremont, Cape Town, South Africa.

**GOODSELL, Sir John William,** Kt 1968; CMG 1954; FASA; Chairman, New South Wales Public Service Board, since Sept. 1960; Member: Prince Henry Hospital Board, since 1960 (Chairman, 1960-61); Prince of Wales Hospital Board, since 1961; Eastern Suburbs Hospital Board, since 1968; State Cancer Council since 1962; Council, University of New South Wales, since 1948; Appointments Board, University of Sydney, since 1963; Convocation, Macquarie University, since 1965; Director: Unisearch Ltd; Winston Churchill Fellowship Trust; *b* 6 July 1906; *s* of late Major S. P. Goodsell, VD, Croix de Guerre (avec Palme), and of late Mrs L. A. Goodsell; *m* 1932, Myrtle Thelma, *d* of late R. H. Austin; three *d*. *Educ:* Canterbury High Sch., NSW. Member: Public Library Bd, 1948-55; Public Accountants Registration Bd, 1948-55; Under-Sec. and Comptroller of Accounts, New South Wales Treasury, 1948-55; Pres. Metropolitan Water Sewerage and Drainage Board, Sydney, April 1955-Sept. 1960; Member, Council, Australian Soc. of Accountants, 1959-61; Mem., Sydney Harbour Transport Board, 1951-55; Chm., Tax Agents Board, 1948-55; Custodian Trustee, Legislative Assembly Members Superannuation Fund, 1948-55; Trustee, Kuring-gai Chase Trust, 1962-64. Coronation Medal, 1953. *Recreations:* tennis and fishing. *Address:* 22 King Street, Ashbury, New South Wales, Australia. *T:* 798 4826.

**GOODSON, Lt-Col Sir Alfred Lassam,** 2nd Bt *cr* 1922; *b* 1893; *er s* of 1st Bt; *S* father, 1940; *m* 1920, Joan (*d* 1939), *d* of C. J. Leyland, Haggerston Castle, Beal, Northumberland; *m* 1941, Enid Clayton Leyland, *d* of late Robert Clayton Swan, Barrowby Grange, Grantham. *Educ:* Radley. Served European War, 1914-19, capt. City of London Yeomanry, TF, 1916; commanded No. 1 Bn Northumberland Home Guard, 1940-45. Master, College Valley foxhounds, 1924-. *Heir: n* Mark Weston Lassam Goodson [*b* 1925; *m* 1949, Barbara Mary Constantine, *d* of Surg.-Capt. R. J. McAuliffe Andrews, RN; one *s* three *d*]. *Address:* Corbet Tower, Kelso, Roxburghshire. *T:* Morebattle 203.

**GOODSTEIN, Prof. Reuben Louis,** PhD, DLit (London); Professor of Mathematics, University of Leicester, since 1948; *b* 15 Dec. 1912; 2nd *s* of late Alexander and Sophia Goodstein; *m* 1938, Louba, *d* of late Samuel Atkin; one *s* one *d*. *Educ:* St Paul's Sch.; Magdalene Coll., Cambridge (BA, MSc). Scholar and Research Scholar, Magdalene Coll., 1931-35; Lectr in Mathematics, Univ. of Reading, 1935-47; Dean of the Faculty of Science, 1954-57; Pro-Vice-Chancellor, 1966-69, Univ. of Leicester. Librarian, Mathematical Assoc., 1955-; Editor, Mathematical Gazette, 1956-62. Mem. Council, Assoc. for Symbolic Logic, 1965-69. *Publications:* Mathematical Analysis, 1948; Constructive Formalism, 1951, 2nd edn, 1965; The Foundations of Mathematics, 1952; Axiomatic Projective Geometry, 1953, 2nd edn 1962; Mathematical Logic, 1957, 2nd edn 1962; Recursive Number Theory, 1957; Recursive Analysis, 1961; Fundamental Concepts of Mathematics, 1962; Boolean Algebra, 1963; Essays in the Philosophy of Mathematics, 1965; Complex Functions, 1965; articles in British, continental and American jls. *Address:* Clarendon Croft, Clarendon Park Road, Leicester. *T:* Leicester 706725.

**GOODWIN, Prof. Albert,** MA; Professor of Modern History in the University of Manchester, 1953-69 (Dean of the Faculty of Arts, 1966-68), now Emeritus Professor; *b* 2 Aug. 1906; 3rd *s* of Albert and Edith Ellen Goodwin; *m* 1935, Mary Ethelwyn, *e d* of late Capt. W. Millner, Tettenhall, Staffs; two *s* one *d. Educ:* King Edward VII School, Sheffield; Jesus Coll., Oxford; Sorbonne. Scholar; Gladstone Memorial Prizeman (Oxford), 1926; 1st Cl. Mod. Hist., 1928; Laming Travelling Fellow, The Queen's Coll., Oxford, 1928-29. Asst Lectr in European History, Univ. of Liverpool, 1929-31; Lectr in Mod. Hist. and Economics, 1931, Fellow and Tutor, Jesus Coll., Oxford, 1933; Junior Dean, Librarian and Dean of Degrees, 1931-39; Univ. Lectr in Mod. French Hist., 1938. Staff Officer (Sqdn Ldr) in RAFVR in Air Ministry War Room, 1940-43; Historical Branch, Air Ministry, 1944-45. Senior Tutor, 1947-48, and Vice-Principal of Jesus Coll., Oxford, 1949-51. Examiner in Final Hon. Sch. of Mod. Hist. (Oxford) 1948-49, Chm., 1950; Senior Univ. Lectr in Revolutionary and Napoleonic Period, 1948-53; Vis. Fellow, All Souls Coll., Oxford, 1969-70. Member: Council of Royal Historical Soc. (Vice-Pres.); Royal Commn on Historical MSS; Governor of John Rylands Library, Manchester. *Publications:* The Abbey of St Edmundsbury, 1931; The Battle of Britain (Air Ministry Pamphlet 156), 1943; The French Revolution, 1953; The European Nobility in the Eighteenth Century (contrib. and ed), 1953; A select list of works on Europe and Europe Overseas, 1715-1815 (co-editor contributor), 1956; (ed and contrib.) Vol. VIII New Cambridge Modern History; articles in Eng. Hist. Review, History, Encyclopædia Britannica, etc. *Recreations:* golf, cricket, antiques. *Address:* 2 Windsor Court, 12 Hound Street, Sherborne, Dorset. *T:* Sherborne 2280.

**GOODWIN, Air Vice-Marshal Edwin Spencer,** CB 1944; CBE 1941; AFC. Served European War, 1914-19; Flt Sub-Lieut RNAS, 1916; War of 1939-45 (CBE, CB). Group Capt. 1939; Air Commodore, 1941; Air Vice-Marshal, 1948. Air Officer i/c Administration, HQ Bomber Command, 1945; retired, 1948.

**GOODWIN, Prof. Geoffrey Lawrence,** BSc (Econ.); Montague Burton Professor of International Relations in the University of London (tenable at London School of Economics) since 1962; *b* 14 June 1916; *s* of Rev. J. H. Goodwin and Mrs E. M. Goodwin; *m* 1951, Janet Audrey (*née* Sewell); one *s* two *d. Educ:* Marlborough Coll.; RMC, Sandhurst; London Sch. of Economics. Regular Army Officer, 1936-43 (The Suffolk Regt; Army Physical Training Staff; Combined Ops; Major, comdg Indep. Company, Gibraltar). Foreign Office, 1945-48; London Sch. of Economics, 1948-. Mem. Council, Royal Inst. of Internat. Affairs; Comr on Internat. Affairs, World Council of Churches. *Publications:* Britain and the United Nations, 1958; (ed.) The University Teaching of International Relations, 1951; articles in International Affairs, International Organization, Political Studies, etc. *Recreations:* painting, sketching. *Address:* 20 Worple Road, Epsom, Surrey. *T:* Epsom 21337.

**GOODWIN, Prof. John Forrest,** MD, FRCP; Professor of Clinical Cardiology, Royal Postgraduate Medical School, London, since 1963; Consulting Physician, Hammersmith Hospital, since 1949; *b* 1 Dec. 1918; *s* of late Col William Richard Power Goodwin, DSO, RAMC, and late Myrtle Dale Goodwin (*née* Forrest); *m* 1943, Barbara Cameron Robertson; one *s* one *d. Educ:* Cheltenham Coll.; St Mary's Hosp. Medical Sch. (Univ. of London). FRSocMed 1943; MD London 1946; FRCP 1957. Med. Registrar, St Mary's Hosp., 1943-44; Physician, Anglo-Iranian Oil Co., Abadan, 1944-45; Med. 1st Asst, Royal Infirmary, Sheffield, 1946-49; Lectr in Medicine and Cons. Physician, Postgraduate Med. Sch., London, 1949-59; Sen. Lecturer, 1959-63. Member: Brit. Cardiac Soc., 1950 (Treas. 1958); Assoc. of Physicians of Great Britain and Ireland, 1953; Council, Brit. Heart Foundation, 1964; Asst Editor, Brit. Heart Journal, 1959; Mem. Editorial Bd Amer. Jl of Cardiology, 1964; Member: Societã Italiana di Cardiologia, 1964; Thoracic Soc., 1967; European Soc. of Pædiatric Cardiologists, 1967; Venezuelan Soc. of Cardiology, 1969; Fellow Amer. Coll. of Cardiology, 1967; Fellow, Council on Clinical Cardiology, Amer. Heart Assoc., 1970. SPk 1968. *Publications:* (jt ed. with R. Daley and R. E. Steiner) Clinical Disorders of the Pulmonary Circulation, 1960; (with W. Cleland, L. McDonald, D. Ross) Medical and Surgical Cardiology, 1969; papers on diagnosis and treatment of congenital and acquired heart disease in British and foreign cardiac and other journals. *Recreations:* photography, history, travel. *Address:* 18 Augustus Road, Wimbledon Park, SW19. *T:* 01-788 1497. *Club:* Royal Society of Medicine.

**GOODWIN, Leonard George;** Director, Nuffield Institute of Comparative Medicine of the Zoological Society of London, since 1964; Director of Science, Zoological Society of London, since 1966; *b* 11 July 1915; *s* of Harry George and Lois Goodwin; *m* 1940, Marie Evelyn Coates; no *c. Educ:* William Ellis Sch., London; University Coll., London; School of Pharmacy, London; University Coll. Hospital. BPharm 1935, BSc 1937, MB, BS 1950, (London). MRCP 1966. Demonstrator, Sch. of Pharmacy, London, 1935-39; Head of Wellcome Labs of Tropical Medicine, 1958-63 (Protozoologist, 1939-63). Jt Hon. Sec., Royal Soc. of Tropical Medicine and Hygiene, 1968-. *Publications:* (pt author) Biological Standardization, 1950; (contrib.) Biochemistry and Physiology of Protozoa, 1955; (jointly) A New Tropical Hygiene, 1960; (contrib.) Recent Advances in Pharmacology, 1962; many contribs to scientific jls, mainly on pharmacology and chemotherapy of tropical diseases, especially malaria, trypanosomiasis and helminth infections. *Recreations:* Dabbling in arts and crafts especially pottery (slipware), gardening and passive participation in music and opera. *Address:* Shepperlands Farm, Park Lane, Finchampstead, Berks. *T:* Eversley 2153.

**GOODWIN, Michael Felix James;** Secretary and Treasurer, International Association for Cultural Freedom; *b* 31 Jan. 1916; *e s* of late F. W. Goodwin; *m* 1944, Alison, *y d* of Capt. Lionel Trower and Ethel Matheson of Achany; one *s* one *d. Educ:* privately. Joined BBC, 1935; North Reg. Drama Dir, 1938; West Reg. Drama Dir, 1939. Served War of 1939-45, in Royal Artillery, 1939-43. Returned to BBC in Features Dept and Overseas News Service, 1943-47. Dramatic critic, The Weekly Review, 1945-46; succeeded Helen Waddell as Asst Editor, The Nineteenth Century and After, 1945-47; Editor, The Twentieth Century (formerly The Nineteenth Century and After), 1947-52; toured US at invitation of State Dept, 1952; Editor, Bellman Books, 1952-55; Dir, Contact Publications, 1955-60. Dir, Newman Neame Ltd, 1960-65. *Publications:* Nineteenth Century Opinion, 1949 (Penguin); Building Victorian London, 1964; Artist and Colourman, 1966; Concise Dictionary of Antique Terms, 1967; Illustrated History of the Industrial Revolution, 1970. *Address:* 42 avenue de Suffren, Paris VIIe, France. *T:* Fontenoy 1911. *Club:* Travellers'.

**GOODWIN, Sir Reginald (Eustace),** Kt 1968; CBE 1960; DL; Leader of the Labour Party, Greater London Council, since 1967; General Secretary, National Association of Boys'

Clubs, since 1945; *b* 3 July 1908; *s* of late Thomas William Goodwin, Streatham, London; *m* 1943, Penelope Mary, *d* of late Capt. R. T. Thornton, MBE, MC, Chepstow, Mon; two *s* one *d*. *Educ:* Strand Sch., London. Tea Buyer in City of London, 1928-34; Asst Gen. Sec., Nat. Assoc. of Boys' Clubs, 1934-45. Served War of 1939-45. Mem., Bermondsey Borough Council, 1937-65 (Leader of Council, 1947-65); Hon. Freeman of the Borough, 1963; Mem. LCC, 1946-65; Alderman, 1961 (Chm. Gen. Purposes Cttee, 1954-58; Establishment Cttee, 1958-60; Housing Cttee, 1960-61; Finance Cttee, 1961-65); Mem., GLC, 1964-(Chm. Finance Cttee, 1964-67; Chm. Inner London Educn Authority Finance Sub-Cttee, 1964-67, 1970-). DL County of London, 1958-. *Recreations:* local government; gardening. *Address:* Twitten Cottage, Marehill, Pulborough, Sussex. *T:* Pulborough 2202.

**GOODWIN, Lt-Gen. Sir Richard (Elton),** KCB 1963 (CB 1959); CBE 1954; DSO 1944; Lieutenent of the Tower of London, since 1969; *b* 17 Aug. 1908; *s* of late Col W. R. P. Goodwin, DSO, and Mrs Goodwin; *m* 1940, Anthea Mary Sampson; three *s*. *Educ:* Cheltenham Coll.; Royal Military Coll., Sandhurst. Commissioned into Suffolk Regt, 1928; served in India, 1930-38; ADC to Governor of Madras, 1935; Adjutant 2nd Suffolk, 1935-38; 2nd i/c 9th Royal Warwickshire, 1941-42; CO 1st Suffolk, 1943-45; College Comdr, RMA Sandhurst, 1947-49; Comdt, Sch. of Infantry, 1951-54; Comdr, 6th Infty Bde, 1954-57; GOC 49th Infty Div. (TA) and N Midland Dist, 1957-60; GOC, E Africa Comd, 1960-63; Comdr 1st (British) Corps, 1963-66; Military Secretary, MoD (Army), 1966-69. Col 1st E Anglian Regt (Royal Norfolk and Suffolk), 1962-64; Dep. Col The Royal Anglian Regt, 1964-66, Col, 1966-. *Recreations:* hunting and other field sports. *Address:* Barrow House, Barrow, Bury St Edmunds, Suffolk. *Club:* Army and Navy.

**GOODWIN, Prof. Trevor Walworth,** FRS 1968; Johnston Professor of Biochemistry, University of Liverpool, since 1966; *b* 22 June 1916; British; *m* 1944, Kathleen Sarah Hill; three *d*. *Educ:* Birkenhead Inst.; Univ. of Liverpool. Lectr 1944, Sen. Lectr 1949, in Biochemistry, University of Liverpool; Prof. of Biochemistry and Agricultural Biochemistry, UCW, Aberystwyth, 1959. *Publications:* Comparative Biochemistry of Carotenoids, 1952; Recent Advances in Biochemistry, 1960; Biosynthesis of Vitamins, 1964; numerous articles in Biochem. Jl, Phytochemistry, etc. *Recreation:* gardening. *Address:* The Beeches, Storeton Road, Birkenhead, Cheshire. *T:* 051-608 2021.

**GOODWIN HUDSON, Rt. Rev. Arthur William;** *see* Hudson.

**GOODY, Most Rev. L.;** *see* Perth (Aust.), Archbishop of, (RC).

**GOOLD, Sir George (Leonard),** 7th Bt *cr* 1801; *b* 26 Aug. 1923; *s* of Sir George Ignatius Goold, 6th Bt, and Rhoda Goold; *S* father, 1967; *m* 1945, Joy Cecelia, *d* of William Cutler, Melbourne; one *s* four *d*. *Educ:* Port Pirie, S Australia. *Heir:* *s* George William Goold, *b* 25 March 1950. *Address:* 5 Afford Road, Port Pirie South, SA 5540, Australia. *T:* Pirie 937.

**GOOLD-ADAMS, Richard John Moreton,** MA; Chairman, Institute for Strategic Studies, since 1963; Director, Ryman Conran Ltd; *b* Brisbane, Australia, 24 Jan. 1916; *s* of Sir Hamilton Goold-Adams, Governor of Qld, and Elsie Riordon, Montreal; *m* 1939, Deenagh Blennerhassett. *Educ:* Winchester; New Coll., Oxford. Served 1939-46 in Army, Major, in Middle East and Italy. The Economist, latterly as an Asst Editor, 1947-55. Councillor: National Inst. of Industrial Psychology, 1956-; Royal Inst. of Internat. Affairs, 1957-; Soc. for Nautical Research, 1970-; Chm., British Atlantic Cttee, 1959-62, Vice-Pres., 1963-. Governor: Atlantic Inst. in Paris, 1962-; Academic Council, Wilton Park, 1963-. A Founder and Vice-Chm., Inst. for Strategic Studies, 1958-62. Dep. Chm., Guthrie Estates Agency Ltd, 1962-63, resigned; re-elected to board, 1964; merged into The Guthrie Corp., 1965; Dir, 1965-69. Chm., SS Great Britain Project, 1968-70. Formerly broadcasting and television on current affairs, and lecturing. *Publications:* South Africa To-day and Tomorrow, 1936; Middle East Journey, 1947; The Time of Powera Reappraisal of John Foster Dulles, 1962; numerous articles, etc in Sunday Times and other journals. *Recreations:* travelling, mowing. *Address:* 25 Porchester Place, W2; Highfield House, Binley, Andover, Hants. *Club:* Travellers'.

**GOOLDEN, Barbara;** novelist; *b* 5 June 1900; *d* of Charles Goolden and Isabel Goolden (*née* Armit); one adopted *s*. *Educ:* Community of the Holy Family; two private schools. Has appeared on TV and spoken on radio. *Publications:* The Knot of Reluctance, 1926; The Sleeping Sword, 1928; Children of Peace, 1928; The Conquering Star, 1929; The Waking Bird, 1929; The Ancient Wheel, 1930; Toils of Law, 1931; Thin Ice, 1931; Sugared Grief, 1932; Eros, 1933; Separate Paths, 1933; Slings and Arrows, 1934; Victory to the Vanquished, 1935; Wise Generations, 1936; The Primrose Path, 1936; Morning Tells the Day, 1937; The Wind My Posthorse, 1937; Within a Dream, 1938; Young Ambition, 1938; Call the Tune, 1939; The Asses Bridge, 1940; The Best Laid Schemes, 1941; Crown of Life, 1941; Men as Trees, 1942; Swings and Roundabouts, 1943; Community Singing, 1944; Ichabod, 1945; Daughters of Earth, 1947; Jig-saw Puzzle, 1948; From the Sublime to the Ridiculous, 1949; Strange Strife, 1952; Venetia, 1952; The China Pig, 1953; Truth is Fallen in the Street, 1953; Return Journey, 1954; Who is my Neighbour?, 1954; Bread to the Wise, 1955; The World His Oyster, 1955; At the Foot of the Hills, 1956; To Have and to Hold, 1956; The Singing and the Gold, 1956; The Nettle and the Flower, 1957; Through the Sword Gates, 1957; The Linnet in the Cage, 1958; The Ships of Youth, 1958; Sweet Fields, 1958; A Pilgrim and his Pack, 1959; For Richer, For Pooere, 1959; Falling in Love, 1960; New Wine, 1960; Where is Love?, 1960; To Love and to Cherish, 1961; One Autumn Face, 1961; Against the Grain, 1961; The Little City, 1962; The Pebble in the Pond, 1962; Marriages are Made in Heaven, 1963; Love-in-a-Mist, 1963; Battledore and Suttlecock, 1963; Fools' Paradise, 1964; The Gentle Heart, 1964; The Gift, 1964; Blight on the Blossom, 1965; A Finger in the Pie, 1965; The Lesser Love, 1965; Anvil of Youth, 1966; Nobody's Business, 1966; Nobody's Business, 1966; A Time to Love, 1966; Second Fiddle, 1967; A Time to Build, 1967; All to Love, 1968; The Eleventh Hour, 1968; The Reluctant Wife, 1968; A Marriage of Convenience, 1969; Today Belongs to Us, 1969; The Snare, 1970; A Question of Conscience, 1970; *for children:* Minty, 1959; Five Pairs of Hands, 1961; Minty and the Missing Picture, 1963; Minty and the Secret Room, 1964; Trouble for the Tabors, 1966; Top Secret, 1969. *Recreations:* reading, enjoying unspoilt country. *Address:* Top End, Felcourt, East Grinstead, Sussex.

**GOOLDEN, Richard Percy Herbert;** Actor and Broadcaster since 1923; *b* 23 Feb. 1895; *s* of

Percy Pugh Goolden Goolden, MA, Barrister-at-Law, and Margarida da Costa Ricci. *Educ:* Charterhouse; New Coll., Oxford. BA 1923, Honour Sch. of Modern Languages (French). Secretary, 1923, OUDS with whom he visited Scandinavia in Loyalties and Mr Pim Passes By, also appeared as Dolon in Doctor Cyril Bailey's production (in Greek) of The Rhesus of Euripides. First professional appearance in 1923 with late J. B. Fagan's newly formed Repertory Company at The (old) Oxford Playhouse, as Mazzini Dunn in Heartbreak House; Shakespearean Season at The (old) Memorial Theatre, Stratford-on-Avon, 1925; from 1926 worked for some time at The Lyric, Hammersmith, under late Sir Nigel Playfair. Varied career in London and Provinces (also Malta and Canada), in diversity of parts ranging from traditional classical repertoire to Farce, Opera Bouffe, Revue, Single Act Variety and Seaside Piers; among several hundred parts played Mole in Toad of Toad Hall (annually for five years 1930-34, Lyric, Savoy, and Royalty Theatres); Prince Paul in Offenbach's The Grand Duchess, Daly's, 1937; Lord Fancourt Babberley in Charley's Aunt, Haymarket, 1938; Professor Cunninghame in Grouse in June, Criterion, 1939; The Fool in King Lear (with Donald Wolfit), St James's, 1943; in Captain Carvallo, St James's, 1950; in Sir Laurence Olivier's Festival Productions of Caesar and Cleopatra, and Antony and Cleopatra, St James's, 1951; Lord Hector in Anouilh's Leocadia (Time Remembered), Lyric Hammersmith and New, 1954-55; Platina in Montherlant's Malatesta, Lyric, Hammersmith, 1957; Nagg in End Game, Royal Court, 1958; The Mayor in Look After Lulu, Royal Court and New, 1959; The White Rabbit in Alice in Wonderland, Winter Garden, 1959-60; Mr Jones in The Cupboard, Arts Theatre Club, 1961; Politic in Lock Up Your Daughters, Mermaid, 1962 and Her Majesty's, 1962-63; has played Mole in Toad of Toad Hall: Westminster, 1960-61; Saville, 1961-62; Comedy (also directed), 1963-64; Queen's, 1964-65; Comedy, 1965-66, 1966-67; Fortune, 1967-68; Duke of York's, 1968-69; Strand, 1969-70; In Regent's Park Open Air Theatre: Shallow in Merry Wives of Windsor, 1968; Old Gobbo in Merchant of Venice, 1969. Verges in Much Ado About Nothing, 1970. Created popular Radio Characters, Mr Chips (the first presentation of this famous character in any medium), Mr Pim, Mr Penny, Old Ebenezer, and The Little Man in Dr L. du Garde Peach's Children's Hour Historical Playlets; has also appeared in films and television plays. Served European War, 1914-18, in France as a private in RAMC; performed continuously throughout War of 1939-45 at Troop Concerts and in shelters and refugee centres (in French), etc. Favourite parts: Mr Pim, Mole, and The Fool in King Lear. *Recreations:* household repairs and decoration; arguing; and singing Edwardian music-hall songs. *Address:* 15 Oakley Street, SW3. *T:* 01-352 7123. *Club:* Oxford and Cambridge University.

**GOONERATNE, Tilak Eranga;** High Commissioner from Ceylon, since 1970; *b* 27 March 1919; *m* 1948, Pamela J. Rodrigo; two *d*. *Educ:* Ceylon Univ. (BA); Ceylon Law Coll. Joined Ceylon Civil Service, 1943; Asst Sec., Min. of External Affairs, 1947-51; Govt Agent: Trincomalee, 1951-54; Matra, 1954-56; Registrar Gen., Marriages, Births and Deaths, 1956-58; Dir-Gen. of Broadcasting and Dir of Information, Ceylon, 1958-60; Comr Co-operative Develt, 1960-63; Acting Permanent Sec., Min. of Commerce and Trade, 1963; Dir of Economic Affairs, 1963; Dep. Sec. to Treasury, 1963-65; Pres., Colombo Plan Council for Technical Co-operation in S and SE Asia, 1964-65; Ceylon deleg. to UN Gen. Assembly, 1964-65; Dep. Sec.-Gen., Commonwealth Secretariat, London, 1965-70. *Publications:* An Historical Outline of the Development of the Marriage and Divorce Laws of Ceylon; An Historical Outline of the Development of the Marriage and Divorce Laws Applicable to Muslims in Ceylon; Fifty Years of Co-operative Development in Ceylon. *Address:* 37 The Water Gardens, Burwood Place, W2. *T:* 01-723 0757.

**GOONETILLEKE, Sir Oliver Ernest,** GCMG 1954 (KCMG 1948; CMG 1941); KCVO 1954; KBE 1944; BA London; LLD Ceylon; FRSA; FRES; Underwriting Member of Lloyd's, London, since 1964; Chairman and Director: Rangalla Consolidated Ltd, since 1966; The Keppitigalla Rubber Estates Ltd; Deviturai Rubber Estates Ltd; Chairman and Managing Director, The Bandarapola Ceylon Company; *b* 1892; *s* of A. E. Goonetilleke; *m* 1920, Esther Jayawardena (*d* 1931); one *s* two *d*; *m* 1968, Phyllis Millar. Asst Auditor for Railways, Ceylon, 1921; Asst Colonial Auditor, 1924; Colonial Auditor June 1931; Auditor-Gen., July 1931; Civil Defence and Food Commissioner, Ceylon, 1942; Mem., Ceylon War Council, 1942; Financial Sec., 1945-47; Min. of Home Affairs and Rural Development, Ceylon, 1947-48; Ceylon High Comr in London, 1948-51; Min. of Home Affairs and Rural Development, Ceylon, 1951-52; of Agriculture and Food, 1952-53, also Leader of the Senate; of Civil Defence, 1953; Min. of Finance, Ceylon, Oct. 1953-54; Governor-Gen. of Ceylon, 1954-62. Ceylon Government Deleg. to Internat. Railway Congress, Cairo, 1933; Chm. Retrenchment Commn, 1938; Chm., Salaries Commn, 1945. Director: The South Wanarajah Tea Estates Ltd; Bentota Holdings Ltd; Elpitiya Rubber Estates; Elpitiya Rubber Holdings; Panagula Rubber Estates; Woolf's Travel Agency Ltd; Planting & Mining Agencies Ltd; DATA Securities Ltd; Colombo Gas Co. Ltd. Chairman: War Fund of Social and Sports Clubs of Ceylon; Royal Society of Internat. Affairs; Royal Empire Society; Royal India, Pakistan and Ceylon Society; Nat. Small-Bore Rifle Assoc.; Empire Day Movement; Mem. Royal Indian Assoc. KStJ. *Address:* 14 Albion Gate, Hyde Park Place, W2. *T:* 01-723 5814. *Club:* National Liberal.

**GOOSSENS, Leon Jean,** CBE 1950; FRCM; Hon. RAM; Solo Oboist; *b* Liverpool, 12 June 1897; *s* of late Eugène Goossens, musician and conductor; *m* 1st, 1926, one *d*; 2nd, 1933, Leslie, *d* of Brig. A. Burrowes; two *d*. *Educ:* Christian Brothers Catholic Institute, Liverpool; Liverpool Coll. of Music. Started oboe studies at 10yrs of age with Charles Reynolds; at 14 studied at RCM, London, and at 16 joined (temp.) London Symphony Orchestra on tour with Nikisch; same year toured Wales with Sir Henry Wood and Queen's Hall Orchestra as temp. principal oboist, the following year accepting post as permanency. Served in European War, 1915-18 (wounded). Principal oboe, Royal Philharmonic Orchestra, also at Covent Garden Opera House, Prof. at RCM and RAM. First Recital tour in USA, 1927. Rep. British Music in most European capitals, also at NY World Fair, with Sir Adrian Boult; and Washington with Dr Clarence Raybould; also lecture recitals for BBC, TV, schools, colleges, music clubs. Has produced in England a new school of oboe-playing and has promoted the oboe to the ranks of solo instruments for which leading composers of the day have written and dedicated music, such as concertos, sonatas and chamber works. Cobbett Medal for services to Chamber

Music, 1954. Toured Australia and New Zealand, also played in Singapore, 1954. Visited Persia and Turkey, also Austria, 1955. Toured Jugoslavia, 1954. Toured USSR with Music Delegation headed by Master of The Queen's Musick, 1956; Coast to Coast Tour Canada, 1957; toured Scandinavia and Portugal, 1959. *Recreations:* agriculture and sailing. *Address:* Park Cottage, 7a Ravenscourt Square, W6. *Clubs:* Garrick, Chelsea Arts, London Corinthian Sailing; Royal Malta Yacht, Malta Union.

**GOPAL, Dr Sarvepalli;** Reader in South Asian History and Fellow of St Antony's College, Oxford, since 1966; *b* 23 April 1923; *y c* and *o s* of Sir Sarvepalli Radhakrishnan, *qv. Educ:* Mill Hill School; Madras Univ.; Oxford Univ. MA (Madras and Oxon), BL (Madras), DPhil (Oxon), DLitt (Oxon). Lecturer and Reader in History, Andhra Univ., Waltair, 1948-52; Asst Dir, Nat. Archives of India, 1952-54; Dir, Historical Div., Min. of Extl Affairs, New Delhi, 1954-66 (now Hon. Historical Adviser); Commonwealth Fellow, Trin. Coll., Cambridge, 1963-64. FRHistS. *Publications:* The Permanent Settlement in Bengal, 1949; The Viceroyalty of Lord Ripon, 1953; The Viceroyalty of Lord Irwin, 1957; British Policy in India, 1965; Modern India, 1967; contribs articles to historical jls. *Recreation:* travel. *Address:* St Antony's College, Oxford; 30 Edward Elliot Road, Mylapore, Madras 4, India. *Club:* Oxford and Cambridge University.

**GOPALLAWA, William,** MBE 1953; Governor-General of Ceylon since 1962; Chancellor: University of Ceylon, Peradeniya; Vidyodaya University of Ceylon, Nugegoda; Vidyalankara University of Ceylon, Kelaniya; *b* Dullewe, Matale, 16 Sept. 1897; *s* of Tikiri Banda Gopallawa, and Dullewa Gopallawa Kumarihamy; *m* 1928, Seelawathie Rambukwella; two *s* two *d. Educ:* Dharmaraja Coll. and St Anthony's Coll., Kandy, Ceylon; Law Coll., Colombo. Teacher, 1918-20; enrolled as Proctor of Supreme Court of Ceylon, 1924; practised in Matale, 1924-39; Mem., Urban Council, Matale, 1927-39 (Chm., 1928-32); Municipal Comr, Kandy, 1939; Municipal Comr, Colombo, 1952; retired, 1957. Ambassador for Ceylon: in China, 1958; in USA, 1961 (concurrently Ambassador to Cuba and Mexico with residence in Washington). Chm., Arts Council's Panel for folk-songs and folk-dancing, 1954-56; A Founder, Dodandeniya Buddhist Schs, Matale; Founder Member: Vidyartha Coll., Kandy; Social Service League, Matale. Past Pres., Kandy Rotary Club; Hon. Mem., Rotary Club of Colombo. Hon. LLD: University of Ceylon (Peradeniya), 1962; Vidyalankara University, 1962; Hon. DLitt, Vidyodaya Univ., 1962. Religion: Buddhist. *Recreations:* cricket, tennis, golf. *Address:* Queen's House, Colombo, Ceylon. *T:* 27821. *Club:* Young Men's Buddhist Assoc.

**GORARD, Anthony John;** Managing Director, Harlech Television Ltd, since 1967; *b* 15 July 1927; *s* of William James and Rose Mary Gorard; *m* 1954, Barbara Kathleen Hampton; one *s* three *d. Educ:* Ealing Grammar School. Chartered Accountant, 1951; Manufacturing Industry, 1952-58; Anglia Television Ltd, 1959-67, Executive Director and Member of Management Cttee; Director, Independent Television Publications Ltd, 1968-; Chairman, British Regional Television Association, 1970-71. *Recreations:* tennis, rambling. *Address:* The Beeches, Chew Magna, Somerset. *T:* Chew Magna 593.

**GORDIMER, Nadine;** Author; *b* 20 Nov. 1923; *d* of Isidore Gordimer; *m* Reinhold Cassirer; one *s* one *d. Educ:* Convent Sch., Witwatersrand. *Publications:* The Soft Voice of the Serpent (stories), 1953; The Lying Days (novel), 1953; Six Feet of the Country (stories), 1956; A World of Strangers (novel), 1958; Friday's Footprint (stories), 1960; Occasion for Loving (novel), 1963; Not for Publication (stories), 1965; The Late Bourgeois World (novel), 1966; South African Writing Today (jt ed.), 1967. Won W. H. Smith Literary Award, 1961. *Address:* 7 Frere Road, Parktown West, Johannesburg, South Africa.

**GORDINE, Dora, (Hon. Mrs Richard Hare);** FRBS; FRSA; sculptor and painter; *b* 1906; *d* of late Mark Gordin, St Petersburg, Russia; *m* 1936, Hon. Richard Hare (*d* 1966). Studied sculpture, Paris. First exhibited in the Salon des Tuileries, Paris, 1932. One-man exhibitions: Leicester Galleries, London, 1928, 1933, 1938, 1945, 1949; Flechtheim Gallery, Berlin, 1929. Commissioned to decorate with bronzes new Town Hall in Singapore, 1930-35; built studio and sculpture gallery in London according to her own designs (1936). Spent a year in America, executing commissions in Hollywood and delivering lectures on art (1947). Also represented by Sculpture in American, Asiatic, African and Australian collections. In England 3 works are in Tate Gallery; other bronzes in: Senate House, London Univ.; RIBA; Westminster Infant Welfare Centre; Maternity Ward in Holloway Prison; Esso Petroleum Refinery, Milford Haven; Royal Marsden Hospital, Surrey; Herron Museum of Art, Indianapolis; schs, institutions and many private collections. *Publications:* articles in Journal of Royal Asiatic Society. *Address:* Dorich House, Kingston Vale, SW15.

**GORDON,** family name of **Marquis of Aberdeen and Temair** and **Marquess of Huntly.**

**GORDON, Lord Adam (Granville),** KCVO 1970 (CVO 1961); MBE 1945; Comptroller to Queen Elizabeth the Queen Mother since 1953; *b* 1 March 1909; *s* of late Lt-Col Douglas Gordon, CVO, DSO, and *brother* of 12th Marquess of Huntly, *qv*; *m* 1947, Pamela, *d* of Col A. H. Bowhill, CBE, Inchmarlo, Banchory, Kincardineshire; two *s. Educ:* Eton. Asst Sec., Hurlingham Club, 1936-39. Served War of 1939-45 (despatches, MBE); Hants Yeomanry in GB, N Africa and Italy; retired 1945, with rank of Major. Sec., Brooks's Club, 1946-53. Mem. Queen's Body Guard for Scotland (Royal Co. of Archers). *Address:* 18 Pont Street, SW1; Hethersett, Littleworth Cross, Seale, Surrey. *Clubs:* Brooks's, MCC.

**GORDON, (Alexander) Esme,** RSA, FRIBA, FRIAS; Architect in private practice since 1936; *b* 12 Sept. 1910; *s* of Alexander Shand Gordon, WS and Elizabeth Catherine (*née* Logan); *m* 1937, Betsy, *d* of James and Bessie McCurry, Belfast; two *s* one *d. Educ:* Edinburgh Acad.; School of Arch., Edinburgh Coll. of Art. RIBA. Owen Jones Schol., 1934. War Service with RE in Europe. Resumed practice, 1946, as Sen. Partner, Gordon and Dey. RSA 1967 (ARSA 1956). Pres., Edinburgh AA, 1955-57; Coun. RIBA, 1955-57; Bd of Management, Edinburgh Coll. of Art, 1955-57; Mem. Scottish Cttee, Arts Coun. of Gt Brit., 1959-65; Mem. Convocation, Heriot-Watt Univ., 1966-. *Work includes:* Third Extension, and other work for Heriot-Watt Coll.; Head Office for Scottish Life Assce Co. Ltd; Head Office and Showroom for S of Scotland Elec. Bd; in High Kirk of St Giles: East End treatment for National Service in Coronation year, War

Memorial Chapel, and (in Chapel of Order of Thistle) Memorial to HM King George VI. *Publications:* A Short History of St Giles Cathedral; The Principles of Church Building, Furnishing, Equipment and Decoration. *Address:* 36 Heriot Row, Edinburgh. *T:* 031-225 7055; 10a Greenhill Park, Edinburgh. *T:* 031-447 7530.

**GORDON, Sir Andrew C. L. D.;** *see* Duff Gordon.

**GORDON, Sir Archibald McDonald,** Kt, *cr* 1952; CMG 1946; LLB; Barrister-at-Law; formerly Counsellor and Labour Attaché, British Embassy, Washington, DC, USA; *b* 29 Oct. 1892; *s* of Archibald McDonald Gordon, OBE, JP, and Miriam M. Gordon, Seaton Lodge, N16; *m* 1924, Dorothy Katharine (*d* 1959), *d* of late Charles Silvester Horne, MP and Hon. Mrs Silvester Horne, *g d* of Lord Cozens Hardy, former Master of Rolls; two *s* one *d*. *Educ:* King's Coll., London, WC1; London Sch. of Economics. Entered Civil Service 1912. Regional Industrial Commissioner London and South Eastern Region, 1942; Asst Sec., Ministry of Labour and National Service, 1944; First Sec. and Labour Attaché, British Embassy, Washington, 1942; Counsellor, 1943-54. Mem. UN Delegations to: UN (San Francisco, New York), ILO (New York, London, Paris, Geneva, Montreal, San Francisco), 1945-51; Chm. Arbitration Tribunal for Jamaican Sugar Industry, 1951; Pres., United Nations League of Lawyers; Mem. Industrial Disputes Tribunal, 1956; Mem. of Panel of Independent Chairmen of National Conciliation Board for the Co-operative Service; National Conciliation Board for the Co-operative Insurance Society's service; and Scottish Co-operative Wholesale Society's Conciliation Board. Dir-Gen., UK Council of European Movement, 1957-61; Chairman: Royal Mutual Benefit Building Society; British-American Associates; Bd of Govs, St George's Sch., Harpenden, 1956-64; Mem. Exec. Council, Hospital Saving Association, 1963, Chm., 1967; Pres., Brit. Hosps Contributary Schemes Assoc. (1948), 1967. Trustee, Liverpool Victoria Friendly Soc. Barrister-at-Law, Gray's Inn. *Address:* Bridge House, Gerrards Cross, Bucks. *T:* Gerrards Cross 82131; 5 King's Bench Walk, Temple, EC4. *T:* 01-353 2882. *Clubs:* Brooks's, Reform, MCC.

**GORDON, Brig. Barbara (Masson),** RRC 1964; QHNS 1968; Matron-in-Chief and Director Army Nursing Service since 1968; *b* 28 Jan. 1913 (Scottish); *d* of Major R. G. Gordon, DSO, MC, MB, ChB, RGA (killed on active service, 1918) and late Mrs B. M. Gordon. *Educ:* St Leonards Sch., St Andrews, Scotland. Trained Edinburgh Royal Infirmary, 1933-37, Oxford Radcliffe Infirmary, 1937. Joined QAIMNS, 1939. Served BEF, MELF and in Germany, 1939-45; in UK, Malta, Egypt and Far East, 1945-68. OStJ 1966. *Recreations:* golf, walking. *Address:* Lettoch, St Andrews, Fife. *T:* St Andrews 214. *Clubs:* United Nursing Services, Vanity Fair; St Rule (St Andrews).

**GORDON, Brian William;** HM Consul-General, Bilbao, since 1969; *b* 24 Oct. 1926; *s* of William and Doris Margaret Gordon; *m* 1951, Sheila Graham Young; two *s* one *d*. *Educ:* Tynemouth Grammar School. HM Forces (Lieut in IA), 1944-47; HM Foreign Service (now Diplomatic Service), 1949-. Served in: Saigon; Libya; Second Sec. in Ethiopia, 1954-58 and in Peru, 1959-61; HM Consul in Leopoldville, Congo, 1962-64, in New York, 1965-67, and in Puerto Rico, 1967-69. *Recreations:* golf, walking. *Address:* c/o Foreign and Commonwealth Office, SW1.

**GORDON, Mrs Charles;** *see* Nerina, Nadia.

**GORDON, Charles Addison Somerville Snowden,** CB 1970; Principal Clerk of the Table Office, House of Commons, since 1967; *b* 25 July 1918; *s* of late C. G. S. Gordon, Liverpool, and of Mrs E. A. Gordon, Emberton, Bucks; *m* 1943, Janet Margaret Beattie; one *s* one *d*. *Educ:* Winchester; Balliol Coll., Oxford. Served in Fleet Air Arm throughout War of 1939-45. Apptd Asst Clerk in House of Commons, 1946; Senior Clerk, 1947; Fourth Clerk at the Table, 1962; Sec., Soc. of Clerks-at-the-Table in Commonwealth Parliaments, and co-Editor of its journal, The Table, 1952-62. *Publications:* Parliament as an Export (jointly), 1966; contribs to: The Table; The Parliamentarian. *Address:* 279 Lonsdale Road, Barnes, SW13. *T:* 01-748 6735.

**GORDON, Christopher Martin P.;** *see* Pirie-Gordon.

**GORDON, Cyrus H.;** Joseph Foster Professor of Near Eastern Studies, and Chairman Department of Mediterranean Studies, Brandeis University, since 1956; *b* 29 June 1908; *s* of Dr Benj. L. and Dorothy Cohen Gordon; *m* 1946, Joan Elizabeth Kendall; two *s* three *d*. *Educ:* University of Pa (AB, MA, PhD). Harrison Schol., University of Pa, 1928-29, and Harrison Fellow, 1929-30; US Army Officer on active duty, 1942-46 (Col, US Air Force Reserve, retired). Instructor of Hebrew and Assyrian, University of Penn., 1930-31; Fellow and Epigrapher, American Schs of Oriental Research in Jerusalem and Baghdad, 1931-35; Fellow, Amer. Coun. of Learned Socs, 1932-33; Teaching Fellow, Oriental Seminary, Johns Hopkins Univ., 1935-38; Lecturer in Hebrew and Ancient History, Smith Coll., 1938-39 and 1940-41; Fellow, Amer.-Scandinavian Foundn, 1939; Mem., Institute for Advanced Study, Princeton, NJ, 1939-40 and 1941-42; Professor of Assyriology and Egyptology, Dropsie Coll., 1946-56; Dean of Graduate Sch. and Associate Dean of Faculty, Brandeis Univ., 1957-58. Mem. Managing Cttee, Amer. Sch. of Classical Studies, Athens, 1958-; Vis. Fellow in Humanities, University of Colorado, March 1967. Fellow: Amer. Acad. of Arts and Sciences, 1968; Explorers Club, 1968. Member: American Oriental Society; Society of Biblical Literature; Archæological Institute of America; American Historical Association; American Philological Association; American Association of University Professors. Corresp. Mem., Inst. for Antiquity and Christianity, Claremont Graduate Sch. and University Center, 1967-. Trustee, Boston Hebrew Coll., 1965-. *Publications:* Nouns in the Nuzi Tablets, 1936; Lands of the Cross and Crescent, 1948; Ugaritic Literature, 1949; Smith College Tablets, 1952; Ugaritic Manual, 1955; Adventures in the Nearest East, 1957; Hammurapi's Code, 1957; World of the Old Testament, 1958 (rev. edn: The Ancient Near East, 1965); Before the Bible, 1962 (rev. edn: The Common Background of Greek and Hebrew Civilizations, 1965); Ugaritic Textbook, 1965, rev. edn 1967; Ugarit and Minoan Crete, 1966; Evidence for the Minoan Language, 1966; Forgotten Scripts: How they were deciphered and their Impact on Contemporary Culture, 1968; Links Between the Old World and Ancient America, 1971; some works translated other languages; numerous articles in learned jls dealing with Near East, Mediterranean, and pre-Columbian contacts between the Old and New Worlds.

*Address:* (home) 130 Dean Road, Brookline, Mass 02146, USA. *T:* Regent 4-3046.

**GORDON, Maj.-Gen. Desmond Spencer,** CB 1961; CBE 1952; DSO 1943; JP; *b* 25 Dec. 1911; *s* of late Harold Eastly Gordon and Gwendoline (*née* Blackett); *m* 1940, Sybil Mary Thompson; one *s* one *d*. *Educ:* Haileybury Coll.; RMC Sandhurst. Commissioned into Green Howards, 1932; India, 1933-38: Adjutant, Regimental Depot, 1938-40; War of 1939-45 (despatches 1944): Norway with Green Howards, 1940; Bde Major, 69 Inf. Bde, 1941-42; Student Staff Coll., Quetta, 1942; Comd 1/7 Queens, 1943; Comd 151 (Durham) Inf. Bde, 146 Inf. Bde, 131 Lorried Inf Bde, 1944-46; Col. GSHQ BAOR, 1946-49; Student Joint Service Staff Coll., 1949; GSO1 inf. Directorate, War Office, 1950; Dep. Dir Inf., War Office, 1951-52; Comd 16 Indep. Para. Bde Gp, 1952-55; Asst Comd RMA Sandhurst, 1956-57; Student, Imperial Defence Coll., 1958; DA & QMG HQ I (BR) Corps, 1959; GOC 4th Division, 1959-61; Chief Army Instructor, Imperial Defence Coll., 1962-64; Asst Chief of Defence Staff (G), 1964-66: Col The Green Howards, 1965-68. JP Hants, 1966. Knight Commander, Order of Orange Nassau with swords (Holland), 1947. *Recreations:* fishing, gardening. *Address:* Southfield, Greywell, Basingstoke, Hants. *Club:* Army and Navy.

**GORDON, Professor Donald James,** MA Edinburgh, PhD Cantab; FRHistSoc; Professor of English in the University of Reading since 1949; *b* 19 July 1915; *s* of Thomas and Sarah Gordon. *Educ:* Dumfries Academy; University of Edinburgh; Trinity Coll., Cambridge. Lecturer in English, University of Liverpool, 1942-46; Lecturer in English, University of Reading, 1946-49. Corresp. Mem., Accademia Olimpico of Vicenza, Italy. *Publications:* (with Jean Robertson) A Calendar of Dramatic Records in the Books of the Livery Companies of London, 1485-1640, 1955; (ed.) Fritz Saxl: Memorial Essays, 1957; Images of a Poet: W. B. Yeats, 1961; papers on problems connected with Renaissance Imagery, and on connexions between literature and visual arts in late nineteenth century. *Address:* Department of English, University of Reading, Berks.; 8 Alexandra Road, Reading. *T:* Reading 65433.

**GORDON, Donald McDonald,** CMG 1970; Head of South East Asia Department, Foreign and Commonwealth Office, since 1969; *b* 14 Aug. 1921; *s* of late Donald McDonald Gordon and late Anabella Gordon (*née* Wesley); *m* 1948, Molly Denise, *o d* of Maurice Norman, Paris; three *s*. *Educ:* Robert Gordon's Coll., Aberdeen; Aberdeen Univ. Served in RA, 1941-47 (despatches). Entered Foreign (later Diplomatic) Service, 1947; FO, 1947; 2nd Sec. (Commercial), Lima, 1950; 2nd, later 1st Sec. (Commercial), Vienna, 1952; FO, 1956; 1st Sec. and Head of Chancery, Rangoon, 1960; 1st Sec., later Counsellor and Head of Chancery, Pretoria/Cape Town, 1962; Imp. Def. Coll., 1966; Counsellor and Consul-Gen., Saigon, 1967-69. *Address:* c/o Foreign and Commonwealth Office, King Charles Street, SW1.

**GORDON, Rt. Rev. Eric;** *see* Gordon, Rt Rev. G. E.

**GORDON, Esmé;** *see* Gordon, A. E.

**GORDON, Sir Eyre,** Kt 1939; CSI 1935; CIE 1931; ICS, retired; *b* 28 Feb. 1884; *s* of Alexander H. Gordon, D.L., Delamont, Killyleagh, Co. Down; *m* 1912, Lilias Edith (*d* 1933), *d* of Capt. A. Lenox Napier, OBE, Merchiston, Manor Road, Sidcup; one *d* (one *s* died on active service). *Educ:* Rossall; Queen's Coll., Oxford, BA. Entered Indian Civil Service, 1908, Chief Sec. to CP Government, 1931; Mem. of Executive Council Central Provinces, 1933-36; Chm. Indian Public Service Commission, 1936-42; Divisional Food Officer for SE Division, 1942; for Midland Division, 1944-46; Chm. NI Joint Electricity Cttee, 1948-55. *Address:* Clonsheen, Tullybrannigan Road, Newcastle, Co. Down, Northern Ireland.

**GORDON, Sir Garnet (Hamilton),** Kt 1962; CBE 1951 (OBE 1945); QC 1957; Chairman Geest Industries (WI), since 1962; *b* 16 Sept. 1904; 2nd *s* of George Stevenson Emmanuel Gordon and Nancy Gordon (*née* Hepburn); *m* 1937, Sheila Perot Christiani (*d* 1969), *e d* of Henry P. Christiani, MBE, and Lilian (*née* Newsum); two *s*. *Educ:* St Mary's Coll., St Lucia; The Middle Temple. Practised at the Bar, 1927-54, resumed practice, 1962. Mem. Castries Town Board, 1940-47 (Chm. 1947); MLC, St Lucia, 1935-51, MEC, 1942-51. Mem. British Section, Caribbean Commission, 1946-50; Mem. Standing Closer Assoc. Cttee, 1948-49; Man. Dir, The Voice Publishing Co. Ltd, and Ed., The Voice of St Lucia, 1940-54; Mem. Council, University Coll. of the West Indies, 1947-54; Trade Comr in the UK for the BWI, Brit. Guiana and Brit. Honduras, 1954-58; Comr in the UK for the West Indies, Brit. Guiana and Brit. Honduras, 1958-62. MHA St Lucia, 1964-69. Pres., St Lucia Bar Assoc., 1964-; Chm., Caribbean Cttee of Fedn of Commonwealth and British Chambers of Commerce; Vice-Pres., Inc. Commonwealth Chambers of Industry and Commerce of Caribbean. *Address:* La Rosière, Castries, St Lucia, West Indies. *Clubs:* Athenæum, West Indian.

**GORDON, Rt. Rev. (George) Eric;** *see* Sodor and Man, Bishop of.

**GORDON, Dr Hugh Walker,** MC 1917; MA; MB; FRCP; Consulting Physician to Department of Skin Diseases, St George's Hospital; Consulting Dermatologist to Royal Marsden Hospital and West London Hospital; Fellow Royal Society Medicine (Past President of Section of Dermatology); Member (Past President) British Association of Dermatology; Member of St John's Dermatological Society; *b* Maxwellton, Kirkcudbright, 5 Aug. 1897; *er s* of late H. Sharpe Gordon, OBE, JP, Dumfries, Scotland and of late John Ann, *d* of Hugh Gilmour, London; *m* 1929, Jean Helen, *d* of late H. W. Robertson, Butterfield and Swire, London; one *s* one *d*. *Educ;* Marlborough Coll.; Pembroke Coll., Cambridge (History Exhibitioner); St George's Hospital (entrance scholar); Paris; Vienna, MB, BCh Cambridge, 1926; MRCS 1925; FRCP 1940. Late Vice-Dean, St George's Hosp. Med. Sch., 1946-51, Actg Dean, 1944-46; Dermatologist EMS Sector VII, 1939-46; Med. Officer i/c St George's Hosp., EMS, 1939-45; late Dermatologist to St John's Hosp., Lewisham, Shadwell Children's Hosp. and East Ham Memorial Hosp. Late Resident Med. Officer, St George's Hosp., and House Surg. and House Physician. Served European War, 1914-18, RFA, 1916-18, invalided out of Army. *Publications:* chapters in Modern Practice of Dermatology, 1950; articles on dermatology in med. journals. *Recreations:* country pursuits. *Address:* 24 Wimpole Street, W1. *T:* 01-935 1000; Yateley Place, Yateley, Hants. *T:* Yateley 2236. *Club:* Buck's.

**GORDON, Prof. Ian Alistair,** MA, PhD, DLitt, LLD; Professor of English Language and

Literature, University of Wellington, NZ, since 1936; *b* Edinburgh, 1908; *e s* of Alexander and Ann Gordon; *m* 1936, Mary Ann McLean Fullarton, Ayr; one *s* three *d*. *Educ:* Royal High Sch., Edinburgh; University of Edinburgh. Bruce of Grangehill Bursar, Sloan Prizeman, Gray Prizeman, Scott Travelling Scholar (Italy), Dickson Travelling Scholar (Germany), Elliot Prizeman in English Literature, Pitt Scholar in Classical and English Literature; MA (Hons Classics) 1930, (Hons English) 1932; PhD 1936; Hon. LLD (Bristol) 1948; Hon. DLitt (NZ), 1961; Asst Lecturer in English language and lit., University of Edinburgh, 1932; Sub-Ed., Scot. Nat. Dictionary, 1930-36; Dean: Faculty of Arts, Victoria Univ. Coll., 1944-47, 1952, 1957-61; Faculty of Languages, 1965-68; Vice-Chancellor University of New Zealand, 1947-52; Visiting Professor: King's Coll., University of London, 1954; University of Edinburgh, 1962; Research Associate, University Coll., London, 1969. mem. Copyright Cttee and Tribunal, 1958; Mem., University Grants Cttee; Chairman: English Language Institute; New Zealand Literary Fund; Exec. Council, Assoc. of Univs of Br. Commonwealth, 1949-50. Army Educ. Service, 2 NZEF, Hon. Major. *Publications:* John Skelton, Poet Laureate, 1943; New Zealand New Writing, 1943-45; The Teaching of English, a study in secondary education, 1947; English Prose Technique 1948; Shenstone's Miscellany, 1759-1763, 1952; Katherine Mansfield, 1954; The Movement of English Prose, 1966; John Galt's The Entail, 1970; part-author: Edinburgh Essays in Scottish Literature, 1933; Essays in Literature, 1934; The University and the Community, 1946; articles in Research journals and other periodicals. *Address:* 91 Messines Road, Wellington, NZ. *Clubs:* PEN; Aorangi Ski, New Zealand (Vice-Patron).

**GORDON, Maj.-Gen. James Leslie,** OBE 1944; Deputy Medical Officer of Health, City of Canterbury, since 1965; *b* 10 Sept. 1909; *s* of Dr James Leslie Gordon and Annie Laycock; *m* 1939, Dorothy Roberson. *Educ:* Epsom Coll.; Middlesex Hosp. MRCS LRCP 1935, DPH London 1948. Commandant, Army Sch. of Health, 1956. Prof. of Army Health, Royal Army Medical Coll., 1958; Dir of Army Health, War Office, 1962-64 (Ministry of Defence, April-May 1964). *Address:* 28 St Stephen's Hill, Canterbury, Kent. *Clubs:* United Service; Kent and Canterbury.

**GORDON, Sir John Charles,** 9th Bt, *cr* 1706; *b* 4 Jan. 1901; *s* of 8th Bt and Elizabeth, *d* of Rev. John Maitland Ware; *S* father, 1939; *m* 1928, Marion, 3rd *d* of James Wright, Springfield, Sydney; one *s* one *d*. *Heir: s* Robert James Gordon, *b* 1932. *Address:* Earlstoun, Guyra, New South Wales, Australia.

**GORDON, Brig. John Evison,** CIE 1947; OBE 1943; psc †; retired; *b* 21 June 1901; *s* of Webster Boyle Gordon, CIE, Monkstown, Co. Cork, Eire; *m* 1936, Frances Elizabeth, *d* of Lt-Gen. Sir Joseph Talbot Hobbs, KCB, KCMG; one *d*. *Educ:* Wellington Coll.; RMC, Sandhurst. Commissioned 1920; joined Probyn's Horse (5th King Edward VII's Own Lancers), 1922. Staff Coll., 1935-36. Served NWF of India, 1930-31 and 1937-39; War of 1939-45: DAQMG, 4 Ind. Div., 1940; GSO 1, Staff Coll., Quetta, 1942; AQMG 4 Corps, 1943; temp. Col 1944; temp. Brig. 1945; retired, 1948. *Address:* Manor Farm, Wootton, Boars Hill, Oxford. *T:* Oxford 35186. *Club:* Army and Navy.

**GORDON, Brig. John Keily,** DSO 1919; *b* 31 March 1883; *m* 1921, Beatrice Mary Grove, *d* of Comdr Hans Fell White and *widow* of Capt. G. E. S. Cotter; one *s*. *Educ:* Wellington; RMA, Woolwich. Served Mesopotamia, 1917-18 (despatches, DSO). Comdr, RA 50th (Northumbrian) Div., TA, 1935-39; retired 1939; re-employed as Comdr Catterick Area, 1939-41. *Address:* Fir Holt, Crowthorne, Berks. *Club:* Cavalry.

**GORDON, John Rutherford;** Editor-in-Chief, Sunday Express; Trustee of Beaverbrook Foundation; *b* 8 Dec. 1890; *Educ:* Morgan Academy, Dundee. Chief Sub-Editor, London Evening News, 1922; Chief Sub-Editor, Daily Express, 1924; Editor, Sunday Express, 1928; Dir Beaverbrook Newspapers Ltd, 1931-69; Dir, Sunday Express, 1946. Life Vice-President: Institute of Journalists, (Pres., 1948-49); Newspaper Press Fund; Press Club. Hon. LLD University of New Brunswick, 1966; *Address:* 78 Addiscombe Road, Croydon, Surrey. *Clubs:* Garrick, Press.

**GORDON, Kathleen Olivia,** CBE 1966; Director, The Royal Academy of Dancing, 1948-68; *b* 15 Jan. 1898; *d* of George R. Gordon, OBE, MD and Alice Maude Gordon. *Educ:* Manchester High Sch. for Girls; King's Coll., London Univ. With Royal Academy of Dancing, 1924-68. *Recreations:* reading, theatre, and ballet. *Address:* 23 Addisland Court, W14. *T:* 01-602 0430.

**GORDON, Keith Lyndell; Hon. Mr Justice Gordon;** Justice of Appeal, West Indies Associated States Supreme Court, since 1967; *b* 8 April 1906; 3rd *s* of late George S. E. Gordon, Journalist, and Nancy Gordon; *m* 1947, Ethel King; one *d*. *Educ:* St Mary's Coll., St Lucia, WI; Middle Temple, London. Magistrate, Grenada, 1938; Crown Attorney, Dominica, 1942; Trinidad and Tobago: Magistrate, 1943-46 and 1949-53; Exec. Off., Black Market Board, 1946-48; Puisne Judge, Windward Islands and Leeward Islands, 1954-59; Puisne Judge, British Guiana, 1959-62; Chief Justice, West Cameroon, 1963-67. *Recreations:* tennis, gardening. *Address:* Court of Appeal, St George's, Grenada.

**GORDON, Sir Lionel E. P. S.;** *see* Smith-Gordon.

**GORDON, Capt. Oliver Loudon,** CB 1946; MVO 1934; *b* 26 Jan. 1896; *s* of late W. M. Gordon, Brechin, Angus, Scotland; *m* 1923, Aileen Mabel Marguerite Baker (*d* 1969); two *s*. *Educ:* Aldenham; RN Colls Osborne and Dartmouth. Entered Navy as Cadet, 1909; Comdr 1931; Capt. 1939. Served in HM Yacht Victoria and Albert, 1932-34 (MVO). In Command of HMS Exeter from March, 1941, till sunk by Japanese Forces in the Java Sea on 1st March 1942. POW in Japan till Sept. 1945; HMS Cleopatra, in command, 1946-48; Retired List, 1948. *Publication:* Fight It Out (autobiography), 1958. *Recreation:* fishing. *Address:* 22 Marshal's Drive, St Albans, Herts. *T:* St Albans 53261.

**GORDON, Patrick W.;** *see* Wolrige-Gordon.

**GORDON, Percival Hector,** CBE 1943; retired as Judge of Court of Appeal for Saskatchewan, Canada, 1935-61, now associate counsel in firm of Embury, Molisky, Gritzfeld & Embury, Regina; *b* 27 Jan. 1884; *s* of Leslie Gordon, Craigmyle, Scotland, and Clara Elizabeth Hector, Toronto; *m* Harriet S. (*d* 1959), *d* of John and Mary Kennedy, Dixie, Ont.; one *d*. *Educ:* Trinity Coll. Sch., Port Hope, Ont.; Trinity Coll., Toronto Univ. (BA 1905, MA 1906, BCL 1909). Athletic champion of sch. and coll.; admitted Saskatchewan Bar 1908, Ont. Bar 1933; KC 1928; practised in

Saskatchewan, 1908-33, Ont. 1933-35; represented Saskatchewan in Natural Resources Royal Commission, 1933-34; Life Mem., Law Soc. of Sask., 1965. Chancellor Anglican Diocese of Qu'Appelle, 1921-42; Chm. of Executive Cttee Canadian Red Cross Soc. 1941-44 (Hon. Counsellor, Canadian Red Cross, 1934). lld (hon.) Manitoba Univ. 1943. Jubilee Medal, 1935; Coronation medal, 1937; Order of Polonia Restituta, 1946; Greek Red Cross Medal, 1949; Service Medal, Order of Canada, 1968. *Publication:* Fifty Years in the Canadian Red Cross, 1969. *Recreations:* shooting, gardening. *Address:* 2424 College Avenue, Regina, Sask., Canada. *Club:* Assiniboia (Regina).

**GORDON, Peter Macie,** CMG 1964; Assistant Secretary, University of Exeter, 1964-70; *b* 4 June 1919; *o s* of late Herbert and Gladys Gordon (*née* Simpson); *m* 1945, Marianne, *er d* of Dr Paul Meerwein, Basle; two *d. Educ:* Cotham Sch., Bristol; University Coll., Exeter; Merton Coll., Oxford. Served War, 1940-46; commissioned Argyll and Sutherland Highlanders, 1941; Campaign in North-West Europe, 1944-45 (despatches). Entered Colonial Administrative Service as District Officer, 1946; Senior District Commissioner, 1957; Asst Sec., Ministry of Agriculture, 1958; Under-Sec., 1960; Permanent Sec., Ministry of Agriculture Animal Husbandry, Kenya, 1961; retired, 1964. *Address:* The Old Rectory, Huxham, near Exeter. *Club:* Royal Over-Seas League.

**GORDON, Richard, (Dr Gordon Ostlere);** MA, MB, BChir Cambridge, FFARCS, DA; Author; *b* 15 Sept. 1921; *m* 1951, Mary Patten, MRCPE, FFARCS; two *s* two *d. Educ:* privately; Selwyn Coll., Cambridge; St Bartholomew's Hosp. Senior Resident Anaesthetist, St Bartholomew's (Hill End) Hosp., 1945-48; Asst Ed., BMJ, 1949-50; Ship Surg., 1950-51; Research Asst and Dep. First Asst, Nuffield Dept of Anaesthetics, Oxford Univ., 1951-52; left medical practice, 1952. *Publications:* Doctor in the House, 1952 (film, 1954, play 1956, radio series 1968, TV series 1969, 1970); Doctor at Sea, 1953 (film 1955, play 1961); The Captain's Table, 1954 (film 1959); Doctor at Large, 1955 (film 1957, radio series 1969); Doctor in Love, 1957 (film 1960, play 1966); Doctor and Son, 1959 (film: Doctor in Distress, 1963); Doctor in Clover, 1960 (film 1966); Doctor on Toast, 1961 (filmed as Doctor in Trouble, 1970); Doctor in the Swim, 1962; Nuts in May, 1964; The Summer of Sir Lancelot, 1965; Love and Sir Lancelot, 1966; The Facemaker, 1967; Surgeon at Arms, 1968; The Facts of Life, 1969; Doctor on the Boil, 1970; (with wife) A Baby in the House: A Guide to Practical Parenthood, 1966; text books and papers on anaesthesia. Contributions to Punch. *Recreations:* watching cricket, fishing, walking, gardening. *Address:* c/o 78 S Audley Street, W1. *Clubs:* Garrick, MCC.

**GORDON, Robert Wilson,** MC 1944; Deputy Chairman of the Stock Exchange, London, 1965-68; Senior Partner, Maguire, Roy Marshall & Co. (Stockbrokers); *b* 3 March 1915; *s* of late Malcolm Gordon and late Blanche Fayerweather Gordon; *m* 1st, 1946, Joan Alison (*d* 1965), *d* of late Brig. A. G. Kenchington, CBE, MC; one *d*; 2nd, 1967, Mrs Dianna E. V. Ansell (*née* Tyrwhitt-Drake). *Educ:* Harrow. Served War of 1939-45 (despatches); Royal Ulster Rifles, and Parachute Regt; Instructor, Staff Coll., 1943-44. Elected to the Council, Stock Exchange, London, 1956. *Recreation:* golf. *Address:* 41 Cadogan Square, SW1. *T:* 01-235 4496. *Club:* City of London.

**GORDON, Capt. Roderick Cosmo,** DSO 1941; RN, retired; *b* 17 Feb. 1902; *s* of Alexander S. Gordon; *m* 1932, Estelle Boulton; one *d. Educ:* RN Colls, Osborne and Dartmouth. Midshipman from 1918 in HMS New Zealand till end of European War, 1914-18; commanded destroyers HMS Verity, 1934-36, HMS Hereward, 1936-38; Comdr, 1938; commanded destroyers, HMS Intrepid, 1939-41, HMS Savage, 1943; Actg Capt., 1944-48; reverted to Comdr, 1948; Admiralty, 1948-51; retired, with rank of Capt., 1952. *Address:* Stream Cottage, Wrecclesham, Farnham, Surrey. *T:* Farnham 5715.

**GORDON, Seton,** CBE 1939; BA Oxon; FZS, Author and Nature Photographer; *b* 11 April 1886; *o s* of late William Gordon, LLD, OBE, Advocate, and late Mrs Ella Mary Gordon, FRSL; *m* 1st, 1915, Evelyn Audrey (*d* 1959), *d* of late Howard Pease of Otterburn, Northumberland; one *s* two *d*; 2nd, 1960, Betty, *d* of Mr and the Hon. Mrs G. Murray Smith, and *widow* of Col R. Badger, Biddlesden Park, Brackley. *Educ:* privately; Oxford Univ.; BA (hons) in Natural Science and Diploma in Rural Economy. Studied Forestry in Russia, Germany, and France; Admiralty Patrol Officer in Argyllshire and Inner Hebrides, 1914-16; afterwards served as Naval Centre Officer (Lieut RNVR); has lectured on Bird Life before the Royal Institution, Royal Scottish Geographical Society, Eton, Winchester, Harrow, etc.; Photographer with the Oxford Univ. Spitsbergen Expedition, 1921. JP Inverness-shire. *Publications:* Birds of the Loch and Mountain; The Charm of the Hills; Hill Birds of Scotland; The Land of the Hills and Glens; Wanderings of a Naturalist; Amid Snowy Wastes; Hebridean Memories; The Cairngorn Hills of Scotland; The Immortal Isles; Days with the Golden Eagle; The Charm of Skye; In the Highlands; Islands of the West; Highways and Byways in the Western Highlands; Thirty Years of Nature Photography; Afoot in Wild Places; Edward Grey of Fallodon and his Birds; Wild Birds in Britain; In Search of Northern Birds; A Highland Year; Highways and Byways in the Central Highlands (illustrated by Sir D. Y. Cameron, RA); Afoot in the Hebrides, 1950; The Highlands of Scotland, 1952; The Golden Eagle, 1955; Highland Days, 1963; and many contributions to periodicals and the Press. *Recreations:* golf, represented Oxford, 1911; mountain climbing; fishing; Highland pipe-playing (member of the Scottish Pipers' Soc.). *Address:* Upper Duntulm, Isle of Skye. *TA:* Portree. *T:* Duntulm 206. *Clubs:* Bath; Vincent's (Oxford).

**GORDON, Strathearn,** CBE 1967 (OBE 1953); Librarian of the House of Commons, 1950-67; *b* 3 Sept., 1902; 2nd *s* of Hon. Huntly D. Gordon, Sheriff-Substitute of Ross and Cromarty, and Violet, *d* of John Gaspard Fanshawe, Parsloes; *m* 1934, Elizabeth, *d* of Lovelace Serjeantson; two *s* one *d. Educ:* Edinburgh Academy; RMC Sandhurst. Joined 2nd Bn Highland Light Infantry, 1923; invalided 1927. Clerk in the House of Commons, 1930. *Publications:* Our Parliament, 1945; (with T. G. B. Cocks) A People's Conscience, 1952. *Address:* Quilter's Farm, East Hanningfield, Chelmsford, Essex. *T:* Woodham Ferrers 214. *Club:* Army and Navy.

**GORDON CUMMING, Sir William Gordon,** 6th Bt, *cr* 1804; Royal Scots Greys; *b* 19 June 1928; *s* of Major Sir Alexander Penrose Gordon-Cumming, 5th Bt, and Elizabeth Topham, *d* of J. Topham Richardson, Harps Oak, Merstham; *S* father, 1939; *m* 1953, Elisabeth, *d* of Maj.-Gen. Sir William Hinde, *qv*; one *s* three *d*. *Educ:* Eton; RMC, Sandhurst. Late Royal Scots Greys; retired 1952. *Heir:* *s* Alexander Penrose Gordon Cumming, *b* 15 April 1954. *Address:* Altyre, Forres, Morayshire.

**GORDON DAVIES, Rev. John;** *see* Davies, Rev. John G.

**GORDON-DUFF, Col Thomas Robert,** MC 1945; JP; Lord-Lieutenant of Banffshire since 1964; Convener of County Council, 1962-70; *b* 1911; *er s* of Lachlan Gordon-Duff (killed in action, 1914); *m* 1946, Jean, *d* of late Leslie G. Moir, Bicester; one *s*. *Educ:* Eton; RMC, Sandhurst. Entered Army, 2nd Lieut, Rifle Brigade, 1932; served War of 1939-45 (MC); retired, 1947. Lt-Col 5/6 Bn Gordon Highlanders (TA), 1947, retiring as Col. DL 1948, JP 1959. Vice-Lieut 1961, Banffshire. *Address:* Drummuir, Keith, Banffshire. *T:* Drummuir 224. *Clubs:* Army and Navy; Royal Northern (Aberdeen).

**GORDON-FINLAYSON, Air Vice-Marshal James Richmond,** DSO 1941; DFC 1940; *b* 19 Aug. 1914; *s* of late Gen. Sir Robert Gordon-Finlayson, KCB, CMG, DSO, and late Lady (Mary) Gordon-Finlayson, OBE; *m* 1953, Margaret Ann (*d* 1965), *d* of Col G. C. Richardson, DSO, MC; one *s* one *d* by a former marriage. *Educ:* Winchester; Pembroke Coll., Cambridge (MA). Mem. Inner Temple, 1935; joined RAF, 1936; ADC to Gov. of Kenya, 1938-39; served in Libya, 1940 and 1941-42, Greece, 1940-41 (despatches), Syria, 1941; Sqdn Ldr 1940; OC 211 Sqdn, 1940-41; RAF Staff Coll., 1942; Air Staff, Air Min., 1942-45; RAF Liaison Offr to HQ, US Army Strategic Air Force, Guam, 1945; Air Staff, Air Comd, SEA, 1945-46; SASO, AHQ, Burma, 1946; OC 48 Sqdn, 1946-47; on directing staff, JSSC, Group Capt. 1951; Air Staff, Air Min., 1951-54, OC, RAF Deversoir, 1954; OC, RAF Khormaksar, 1954-56; on staff of HQ Bomber Command, 1956, Asst Comdt, RAF Staff Coll., Bracknell; Air Cdre, 1958; Air Vice-Marshal, 1961; Dir-Gen. of Personal Services, Air Ministry, 1960-63; retired, June 1963. Greek DFC, 1941; Sheikh el Bilharith. *Publications:* articles on strategic and air and military affairs in various jls; verse. *Recreations:* fishing, sailing, travel and literary interests. *Clubs:* United Service, Marylebone Cricket.

*See also Maj.-Gen. R. Gordon-Finlayson.*

**GORDON-FINLAYSON, Maj.-Gen. Robert,** OBE 1957 (MBE 1945); *b* 28 Oct. 1916; *yr s* of late Gen. Sir Robert Gordon-Finlayson, KCB, CMG, DSO, DL; *m* 1945, Alexandra, *d* of late John Bartholomew, Rowde Court, Rowde, Wilts; two *s*. *Educ:* Winchester Coll.; RMA, Woolwich. 2 Lt RA, 1936; Major, BEF, 1940; Staff Coll., 1941; Middle East, 1942-43; NW Europe, 1944-45; India and Burma, 1945-47; GSO 1 1945; RHA, 1952-53; JSSC, 1953; Bt Lieut-Col, 1955; AA and QMG, 3 Inf. Div., 1955-57; Near East (Suez Ops), 1956; Middle East, 1958; Lieut-Col 1958; Comdr, 26 Field Regt RA, 1958-59; Col 1959; GSO 1, Staff Coll., 1960-62; Brig. CRA, 49 Div. TA, 1962-64; Brig. DQMG, HQ, BAOR, 1964-66. GOC 49 Inf. Div., TA/N Midland Dist, 1966-67; GOC E Midland District, 1967-70; retd, 1970. *Recreations:* shooting, fishing, ski-ing, gardening, walking. *Address:* South Collingham Manor, near Newark, Notts. *T:* Collingham 204; c/o Lloyds Bank Ltd, Cox's & King's Branch, 6 Pall Mall, SW1. *Clubs:* MCC, United Service.

*See also Air Vice-Marshal J. R. Gordon-Finlayson.*

**GORDON-HALL, Maj.-Gen. Frederick William,** CB 1958; CBE 1945; *b* 28 Dec. 1902; *s* of Col Frederick William George Gordon-Hall and Clare Frances (*née* Taylor); *m* 1930, Phyllis Dorothy Miller; one *s* one *d*. *Educ:* Winchester Coll.; RMC Sandhurst. Gazetted Royal Tank Corps, 1923; Staff Capt., War Office, 1935-39; Ministry of Supply, 1939-43; HQ Allied Armies in Italy, 1943-45; Military Dir of Studies, Mil. Coll. of Science, 1946-49; Dir of Technical Services (Land), British Joint Staff Mission, Washington, 1950-52; Dir of Inspection of Fighting Vehicles, Ministry of Supply, Dec. 1952-June 1955. Dir-Gen. of Fighting Vehicles, Min. of Supply, 1955-58, retd. *Recreations:* model engineering, foreign travel, cabinet making. *Address:* Whitegates, Salisbury Road, Horsham, Sussex. *T:* Horsham 3304.

**GORDON JONES, Air Marshal Sir Edward,** KCB 1967 (CB 1960); CBE 1956 (OBE 1945); DSO 1941; DFC 1941; idc; jssc; *qs*; Air Officer Commanding-in-Chief, Near East Air Force, and Administrator, Sovereign Base Areas, 1966-69; Commander, British Forces Near East, 1967-69; retired 1969; *b* 31 Aug. 1914; *s* of Lt-Col Dr A. Jones, DSO, MC, MD, DPh; *m* 1938, Margery Thurston Hatfield, BSc, DipEd; two *s*. Served War of 1939-45 (despatches, DFC, DSO, OBE, Greek DFC). ACOS (Intelligence), Allied Air Forces Central Europe, 1960-61; Air Officer Commanding RAF Germany, 1961-63; Senior RAF Directing Staff, Imperial Defence Coll., 1963-65; AOC, RAF, Malta, and Dep. C-in-C (Air), Allied Forces, Mediterranean, 1965-66. MBIM. Comdr Order of Orange Nassau. *Recreations:* sport, photography, travel, music. *Address:* 14 Chaucer Road, Cambridge. *Club:* *Royal Air Force.*

**GORDON-LENNOX,** family name of **Duke of Richmond.**

**GORDON LENNOX, Rear-Adm. Alexander Henry Charles,** CB 1962; DSO 1942; Serjeant at Arms, House of Commons, since 1962; President, Royal Naval College, Greenwich, 1961-62; *b* 9 April 1911; *s* of Lord Bernard Charles Gordon Lennox and Evelyn (*née* Loch); *m* 1936, Barbara, *d* of Maj.-Gen. Julian Steele; two *s*. *Educ:* Hetherdown, Ascot; RNC Dartmouth. Served as Young officer in small ships in Far East and Home Fleet; communication specialist. Served War of 1939-45 (despatches 1943); in ME, East Coast Convoys, Russian Convoys; subsequently commanded HMS Surprise, HMS Mermaid and 2nd Frigate Sqdn, HMS Mercury and HMS Newcastle. Dep. Chief of Supplies and Transport, 1959-62. Liberty Medal (Norway). *Recreations:* shooting, fishing and gardening. *Address:* Fishers Hill, Iping, Midhurst, Sussex. *T:* Midhurst 3623. *Club:* Naval (Portsmouth).

**GORDON LENNOX, Lieut-Gen. Sir George (Charles),** KBE 1964; CB 1959; CVO 1952; DSO 1943; General Officer Commanding-in-Chief (Scottish Command) and Governor of Edinburgh Castle, 1964-66; King of Arms, Order of British Empire, since 1968; *b* 29 May 1908; *s* of late Lord Bernard Charles Gordon Lennox, 3rd *s* of 7th Duke of Richmond and Gordon and late Evelyn Loch, *d* of 1st Baron Loch; *m* 1931, Nancy Brenda Darell; two *s*. *Educ:* Eton; Sandhurst. Served Grenadier Guards, 1928-52; Lieut-Col Commanding Grenadier Guards, Jan. 1951-July 1952; Comdr 1st Guards Brigade, 1952-54; Imperial Defence Coll., 1955; BGS (SD and Trg), HQ, BAOR, 1956-57; Gen. Officer Commanding 3rd Div., 1957-59; Commandant Royal Military Acad. Sandhurst, 1960-63; Dir-Gen. of Military Training, 1963-64. Served with Regt and on staff throughout War of 1939-45, in Europe, Africa and Far East. Col, Gordon

Highlanders, 1965. *Recreations:* field sports. *Address:* Gordon Castle, Fochabers, Morayshire. *T:* Fochabers 275. *Club:* Guards.

**GORDON-SMITH, David Gerard;** Legal Counsellor, Foreign and Commonwealth Office, since 1968 (Commonwealth Office, 1966-68); *b* 6 Oct. 1925; *s* of late Frederic Gordon-Smith, QC, and of Elsie Gordon-Smith (*née* Foster); *m* 1952, Angela Kirkpatrick Pile; one *s* one *d*. *Educ:* Rugby Sch.; Trinity Coll., Oxford. Served in RNVR, 1944-46. BA (Oxford) 1948; called to Bar, Inner Temple, 1949; Legal Asst, Colonial Office, 1950; Sen. Legal Asst, 1954; CRO, 1963-65; Asst Legal Adviser, CO, 1965-66. *Recreations:* tennis, sailing, bird-watching. *Address:* Kingscote, Westcott, Surrey. *T:* Dorking 5702.

**GORDON-SMITH, Ralph;** Chairman, Smiths Industries Ltd, since 1951 (formerly Smith and Sons (England) Ltd); *b* 22 May 1905; *s* of late Sir Allan Gordon-Smith, KBE, DL and Hilda Beatrice Cave; *m* 1932, Beryl Mavis Cundy; no *c*. *Educ:* Bradfield Coll. Joined Smiths Industries, 1927; trained in all deaprtments; Dir, 1933. Dir of EMI Ltd, 1951. FBHI 1961. *Recreations:* yachting, shooting, fishing. *Address:* The Old Ship, Bosham, Sussex. *T:* Bosham 2372; 23 Kingston House East, Princes Gate, SW7. *T:* 01-584 9428. *Clubs:* Royal Thames Yacht, Bosham Sailing.

**GORDON WALKER, Rt. Hon. Patrick Chrestien,** PC 1950; CH 1968; MP (Lab) Leyton, since 1966; *b* 7 April 1907; *s* of Alan Lachlan Gordon Walker and Dora Marguerite Chrestien; *m* 1934, Audrey Muriel Rudolf; twin *s* three *d*. *Educ:* Wellington Coll; Christ Church, Oxford, MA, BLitt. Student and History Tutor, Christ Church, 1931-40; BBC European Service (German workers), 1940-44; Chief Editor, Radio Luxemburg, 1944; Asst German Service Dir, BBC, 1945. Chm. British Film Institute, 1946; Vice-Chm. British Council, 1947. MP (Lab) Smethwick, 1945-64; contested (Lab) Leyton, Jan. 1965. PPS to Mr Herbert Morrison, MP, 1946; Parliamentary Under-Sec. of State, Commonwealth Relations Office, 1947-50; Sec. of State for Commonwealth Relations, 1950-51; Sec. of State for Foreign Affairs, Oct. 1964-Jan. 1965; Leader, UK Delegn to Council of Europe, 1966; Chm., Book Development Council, 1965-67; Minister without Portfolio during 1967; Sec. of State for Educn and Science, 1967-68. *Publications:* The Sixteenth and Seventeenth Centuries, 1935; Outline of Man's History, 1939; The Lid Lifts, 1945; Restatement of Liberty, 1951; The Commonwealth, 1962; The Cabinet, 1970. *Recreations:* reading and writing. *Address:* 22 South Square, NW11.

**GORDON WATSON, Hugh;** *see* Watson.

**GORE,** family name of **Earl of Arran.**

**GORE;** *see* Ormsby Gore.

**GORE, Frederick John Pym,** ARA 1964; Painter; Head of Painting Department, St Martin's School of Art, WC2, since 1951 and Vice-Principal since 1961; *b* 8 Nov. 1913; *s* of Spencer Frederick Gore and Mary Johanna Kerr. *Educ:* Lancing Coll.; Trinity Coll., Oxford; studied art at Ruskin, Westminster and Slade Schs. Taught at: Westminster Sch. of Art, 1937; Chelsea and Epsom, 1947; St Martin's, 1946-. *One-man exhibitions:* Gall. Borghèse, Paris, 1938; Redfern Gall., 1937, 1949, 1950, 1953, 1956, 1962; Mayor Gall., 1958, 1960; Juster Gall., NY, 1963. *Paintings in public collections include:* Contemporary Art Soc., Leicester County Council, GLC, Southampton, Plymouth, Rutherston Collection and New Brunswick. Served War of 1939-45: Mx Regt and RA (SO Camouflage). *Publications:* Abstract Art, 1956; Painting, Some Principles, 1965. *Recreation:* Russian folk dancing. *Address:* Flat 3, 35 Elm Park Gardens, SW10. *T:* 01-352 4940. *Club:* Garrick.

**GORE, John Francis,** CVO 1941; TD; journalist and author; *b* 15 May 1885; *y s* of late Sir Francis Gore, KCB; *m* 1926, Lady Janet Helena Campbell, *er d* of 4th Earl Cawdor; one *s* two *d*. *Educ:* Radley Coll.; Trinity Coll., Oxford (MA). Barrister-at-Law, Inner Temple, 1909; served European War, 1914-19 (despatches); Captain Bedfordshire Yeomanry; Sec. Training Grants Cttee, Ministry of Labour, 1920; took up journalism, 1923; pen-name The Old Stager, of the Sphere's Newsletter, 1928-64. Chm. Midhurst Bench, 1944-58. JP Sussex, 1932-59. *Publications:* The Trial Stone, 1919; A Londoner's Calendar, 1925; The Way In, 1927; The Ghosts of Fleet Street, 1929; Charles Gore, father and son, 1932; Creevey's life and times, 1934; Nelson's Hardy and his wife, 1935; Sydney Holland, Lord Knutsford, 1936; Geoffrey Colman; Mary, Duchess of Bedford (privately printed), 1938; King George V, 1941 (awarded J. T. Black Memorial Prize, 1941); Creevey, 1948; Edwardian Scrapbook, 1951; Three Howard Sisters (with another), 1955. *Address:* Littlehay, Burley, Ringwood, Hants. *T:* Burley 3306. *Clubs:* MCC, I Zingari. *See also Sir Charles Cave.*

**GORE, Paul Annesley,** CMG 1964; CVO 1961; Secretary, Oxford University Physical Chemistry Laboratory; *b* 28 Feb. 1921; *o s* of late Charles Henry Gore, OBE and late Hon. Violet Kathleen (*née* Annesley); *m* 1946, Gillian Mary, *d* of T. E. Allen-Stevens; three *s*. *Educ:* Winchester Coll.; Christ Church, Oxford MA (war degree). Military Service, 1941-46: 16/5 Lancers (despatches). Colonial Service, 1948-65; Dep. Governor, The Gambia, 1962-65. County Comr, Scouts, Oxfordshire. *Publication:* (with B. E. R. Kirwan) Elementary Luganda, 1952. *Recreations:* sailing, bird-watching. *Address:* The Old Manor House, Beckley, Oxford. *T:* Stanton St John 251.

**GORE, Lieut-Col Sir Ralph St George Brian,** 11th Bt, *cr* 1621; *b* 31 May 1908; *s* of Sir Ralph St George Claude Gore, 10th Bt, and Elsie Vaughan Grigg; *S* father, 1961; *m* 1947, Phyllis Gabrielle Brooke-Hitching (marr. diss., 1965), *d* of M. Von der Porten, New York; one *d*. *Educ:* Eton; RMC. Formerly Royal Dragoons. *Recreation:* yachting. *Address:* c/o Royal Bank of Scotland, Burlington Gardens, W1. *Club:* Royal Yacht Squadron.

**GORE-BOOTH,** family name of **Baron Gore-Booth.**

**GORE-BOOTH,** Baron *cr* 1969 (Life Peer), of Maltby; **Paul Henry Gore-Booth,** GCMG 1965 (KCMG 1957; CMG 1949); KCVO 1961; Director: National and Grindlays Bank, since 1969; United Kingdom Provident Institution, since 1969; Head of HM Diplomatic Service, 1968-69; Registrar, Order of St Michael and St George, since 1966; *b* 3 Feb. 1909; *m* 1940, Patricia Mary Ellerton; twin *s* two *d*. *Educ:* Eton; Balliol Coll., Oxford. Joined Foreign Service, 1933; FO 1933-36; Vienna, 1936-37; Tokyo, 1938-42; Washington, 1942-45; FO, 1945-49; Head of UN (Economic and Social) and Refugees Depts, 1947-48; Head of European Recovery Dept, Foreign Office, 1948-49; Dir British Information Services in United States, 1949-53; Ambassador to

Burma, 1953-56; Dep. Under-Sec. (Economic Affairs), Foreign Office, 1956-60; British High Commissioner in India, 1960-65; Permanent Under-Sec. of State, FO, 1965-69. Hot Springs Food Conference, 1943; UNRRA Conference, 1943; Chicago Civil Aviation Conference, 1944; San Francisco Conf., 1945; UN Assembly, 1946 (Sec. of UK Deleg.) Jan. and Oct. and 1947. Pres. Sherlock Holmes Soc. of London, 1967; Dir, Windsor Festival Soc. *Address:* 29 The Vale, Chelsea, SW3. *Club:* Athenæum, Royal Automobile, Baker Street Irregulars.

**GORE-BOOTH, Sir Michael;** *see* Booth.

**GORE-LANGTON;** *see* Temple-Gore-Langton.

**GORELL,** 4th Baron *cr* 1909; **Timothy John Radcliffe Barnes;** *b* 2 Aug. 1927; *e s* of 3rd Baron Gorell and Elizabeth Gorell, *d* of Alexander Nelson Radcliffe; *S* father, 1963; *m* 1954, Joan Marion, *y d* of John Collins, Moseley, Birmingham; two adopted *d. Educ:* Eton Coll.; New Coll., Oxford. Lieut, Rifle Brigade, 1946-48. Barrister, Inner Temple, 1951. Joined Royal Dutch/Shell Group, 1959. *Heir: b* Hon. Ronald Alexander Henry Barnes [*b* 28 June 1931; *m* 1957, Gillian Picton Hughes-Jones; one *s* one *d*]. *Address:* 4 Roehampton Gate, SW15. *T:* 01-876 6042. *Club:* Roehampton Golf.

**GORELL BARNES, Sir William (Lethbridge),** KCMG 1961 (CMG 1949); CB 1956; Director: Royal Group of insurance companies; Limmer Holdings Ltd (Deputy Chairman); Doulton & Co. Ltd (Deputy Chairman); Minister Assets Ltd; Thames Aeroport Group Ltd (Chairman); Trinidad Canadian Oils Ltd; *b* 23 Aug. 1909; *y s* of late Sir Frederic Gorell Barnes and Caroline Anne Roper Lethbridge; *m* 1935, Barbara Mary Louise, *e d* of late Brig. A. F. B. Cottrell, DSO, OBE; one *s* three *d*. *Educ:* Marlborough Coll.; Pembroke Coll., Cambridge, 1st Cl. Classical Tripos Pt 1, 1st Cl. Mod. Langs Tripos Pt 2. Served in HM Diplomatic Service, 1932-39; Offices of War Cabinet, 1939-45, and HM Treasury, 1945-46; Personal Asst to Prime Minister, Oct. 1946-Feb. 1948; Seconded to Colonial Office, 1948; Asst Under-Sec. of State, 1948-59; Dep. Under-Sec. of State, 1959-63. Mem. UK delegn for negotiations with European Economic Community, 1962, retired 1963. *Recreations:* gardening, lawn tennis. *Address:* Mulberry House, Church Row, Hampstead, NW3. *T:* 01-435 7526. *Club:* Reform.

**GORHAM, Maurice Anthony Coneys;** Author and Journalist; *b* London 1902; *o s* of late J. J. Gorham, MD, Clifden, Connemara. *Educ:* Stonyhurst; Balliol Coll., Oxford. Entered journalism, 1923; on editorial staffs of Weekly Westminster, Westminster Gazette; joined Radio Times, 1926; Art Ed., 1928; Ed., 1933-41; North American Service Dir, BBC, 1941-44; Dir of Allied Expeditionary Forces Programme, 1944-45; Head of Light Programme, 1945; Head of Television Service, 1946-47; Dir of Radio Eireann (Irish broadcasting service), 1953-60. Pres., Irish UN Association, 1967-. *Publications:* The Local, 1939; Sound and Fury (Twenty-One Years in the BBC), 1948; Back to the Local; Television, Medium of the Future, 1949; Professional Training for Radio (enquiry for Unesco); Inside the Pub, 1950; Showmen and Suckers; Londoners, 1951: Broadcasting and Television since 1900, 1952; Forty Years of Irish Broadcasting, 1967. *Address:* 33 Sydney Parade Avenue, Dublin. *T:* Dublin 692587. *Club:* University (Dublin).

**GORING, Marius;** Actor; *b* Newport, IOW, 23 May 1912; *s* of Dr Charles Buckman Goring, MD, BSc, and Katie Winifred Macdonald; *m* 1931, Mary Westwood Steel (marriage dissolved); one *d*; *m* 1941, Lucie Mannheim, *qv*. *Educ:* Perse Sch., Cambridge; Universities of Frankfurt, Munich, Vienna, and Paris. Studied for stage under Harcourt Williams and at Old Vic dramatic school. First stage appearance in London in one of Jean Sterling Mackinlay's matinées, 1927; toured in France and Germany with English Classical Players, 1931; played two seasons at Old Vic and Sadler's Wells, 1932-34. First West End appearance as Hugh Voysey in The Voysey Inheritance, Shaftesbury, 1934; toured France, Belgium, and Holland with Compagnie des Quinze (acting in French), 1934-35; appeared London, 1935-39, in: Hamlet, Noah, The Hangman, Sowers of the Hills, Mary Tudor, The Happy Hypocrite, Girl Unknown, The Wild Duck, The Witch of Edmonton, Twelfth Night, Henry V, Hamlet, The Last Straw, Surprise Item, The White Guard; Satyr. In management at Duke of York's, 1939; produced Nora (A Doll's House); played Ariel in, and partly produced, The Tempest, Old Vic, 1940. Served War of 1939-45, Army, 1940-41; Foreign Office, 1941-45; supervisor of productions of BBC broadcasting to Germany, 1941. Toured British zone of Germany, 1947 (playing in German), 1948; Rosmersholm, Too True to be Good, Cherry Orchard, Marriage, The Third Man, at Arts Theatre; Daphne Laureola, Berlin (playing in German), 1949; The Madwoman of Chaillot, St James's, 1951; Richard III, Antony and Cleopatra, Taming of the Shrew, King Lear, Sratford-upon-Avon, 1953; Antony and Cleopatra, Princes, 1953; Marriage, Wuppertal, 1954; has toured France, Holland, Finland, 1957, and India, 1958, with own company of English comedians; Tonight at 8.30 (in German), Berlin Fest., 1960; Measure for Measure, Stratford-upon-Avon, 1962; A Penny for a Song, Aldwych, 1962; Ménage à Trois, Lyric, 1963; The Poker Session, Globe, 1964; The Apple Cart, Cambridge, 1965; The Bells, Vaudeville, 1968; The Demonstration, Nottingham, 1969. Was one of founders of London Theatre Studio. Has appeared in a number of films since 1936, including: The Case of the Frightened Lady, A Matter of Life and Death, Take my Life, The Red Shoes, Mr Perrin and Mr Traill, Odette, Circle of Danger, Highly Dangerous, So Little Time, Nachts auf den Strassen (Germany), The Man Who Watched the Trains Go By, Rough Shoot, The Barefoot Contessa, Family Doctor, Ill Met by Moonlight, The Inspector, The Crooked Road, Up from the Beach, 25th Hour. Has broadcast over a number of years and written several radio scripts. Co-prod. and played lead in television series, The Scarlet Pimpernel, 1955; The Expert, 1968-70. has appeared on TV in England, Germany and France. Vice-Pres. British Actors' Equity Assoc., 1963-65. *Recreations:* skating and riding. *Address:* Middle Court, The Green, Hampton Court, Surrey. *T:* 01-977 4030. *Club:* Garrick.

**GORING, Sir William (Burton Nigel),** 13th Bt, *cr* 1627; Member of London Stock Exchange since 1963; *b* 21 June 1933; *s* of Major Frederick Yelverton Goring (*d* 1938) (6th *s* of 11th Bt) and Freda Margaret, *o d* of N. V. Ainsworth, Woolbeding Glebe, Midhurst; *S* uncle, Sir Forster Gurney Goring, 12th Bt, 1956; *m* 1960, Hon. Caroline Thellusson, *d* of 8th Baron Rendlesham, *qv*, and of Elizabeth Lady Rendlesham. *Educ:* Wellington; RMA Sandhurst, 2nd Lieut, The Royal Sussex Regt, 1953, Lieut 1st Bn, 1955. *Recreation:* lawn tennis. *Heir: b* Edward Yelverton Combe Goring, *b* 20 June 1936. *Address:* 89 Cornwall Gardens, SW7. *T:* 01-584 3421.

**GORLEY PUTT, Samuel;** *see* Putt, S. G.

**GORMAN, Sir Eugene,** KBE 1966 (CBE 1960); MC 1917; QC (Melbourne); Chairman, Australian Dried Fruit Export Board, retired, 1968; *b* Goornong, Victoria, 10 April 1891; *s* of Patrick and Mary Gorman; *m* 1920, Marthe Vallée (*d* 1966); one *s*. *Educ:* St Joseph's Coll. (Sydney, NSW). Barrister, 1914; KC 1929; AIF, 1914-19 and 1940-44 (despatches 1942); Capt., 1st AIF; Brig. 1944. Consul for Greece, 1955, retd. Consul-Gen., NEI, 1942 until Japanese occupation. Chief Comr, Aust. Comforts Fund, 1941-42; Chief Inspector, Australian Army Admin, 1942. President: Opportunity Youth Clubs, 1953-; Australian Branch, Internat. Social Services, retd 1969. Gold Cross of Greek Red Cross; Kt Comr, Royal Order of Phoenix (Greece), 1953. *Publication:* With the 22nd Battalion, 1919. *Recreation:* racing. *Address:* Equity Chambers, 472 Bourke Street, Melbourne, Victoria 3000, Australia. *T:* 67-3164. *Clubs:* Portland (London); Athenæum (Melbourne); Victoria Racing (Committeeman 27 years).

**GORMAN, William Moore;** Professor of Economics, University of London, since 1967; *b* 17 June 1923; *s* of late Richard Gorman, Lusaka, Northern Rhodesia, and Sarah Crawford Moore, Kesh, Northern Ireland; *m* 1950, Dorinda Scott. *Educ:* Foyle Coll., Derry; Trinity Coll., Dublin. Asst Lectr, 1949, Lectr, 1951, and Sen. Lectr, 1957, in Econometrics and Social Statistics, University of Birmingham; Prof. of Economics, University of Oxford, and Fellow of Nuffield Coll., Oxford, 1962-67. Visiting Professor: Iowa State Coll. of Agriculture and the Mechanic Arts, 1956-57; Stanford Univ., 1967. *Publications:* articles in various economic journals. *Address:* London School of Economics, Houghton Street, WC2. *T:* 01-405 7686.

**GORMANSTON,** 17th Viscount *cr* 1478; **Jenico Nicholas Dudley Preston;** Baron Gormanston (UK), 1868; Premier Viscount of Ireland; *b* 19 Nov. 1939; *s* of 16th Viscount and Pamela (who *m* 2nd, 1943, M. B. O'Connor, Irish Guards; he *d* 1961), *o d* of late Capt. Dudley Hanly, and of Lady Marjorie Heath (by her 1st marriage); *S* father, who was officially presumed killed in action, France, 9 June 1940. *Educ:* Downside. *Heir: u* Hon. Robert Francis Hubert Preston, formerly Capt. 11th Hussars [*b* 7 Dec. 1915; *m* 1941, Jean Helen (marriage dissolved, 1955), *o c* of late Capt. Charles Shaw, 15th Hussars; one *d* (and one *d* decd).] *Address:* c/o 33 Tite Street, SW3.

**GORST, Elliot Marcet,** QC 1953; *b* 18 Nov. 1885; *o s* of Herbert Charles Gorst, Liverpool, and Jessie Elliot-Blake; *m* 1914, Hester Gaskell, 3rd *d* of Walter Holland, Carnatic Hall, Mossley Hill, Liverpool; one *d*. *Educ:* Temple Grove; Harrow; Jena; Sorbonne; Florence. Barrister, Inner Temple, 1912. Served European War, 1915-19. Contested (MR) Bow and Bromley, 1926, S Poplar, 1928; contested (C) Poplar (South), 1929. Mem. of Bar Coun., 1932 and 1948-52; Deputy Judge, Bloomsbury County Court, 1940-42. Mem. of Legal Deleg. to USSR, 1954. Chm., Kent and Sussex Poetry Soc., 1953-; Chm. Bournemouth Swanage Motor Road and Ferry Co., 1925-61; Dir Carbon Electric Holdings Ltd (Chm. 1962-64). Farms in Kent (Pedigree herd of Sussex cattle and flock of Hampshire Down Sheep). *Publications:* Guide to Railway Rates Tribunal and Title on Railways and Canals in Halsbury's Statutes. *Recreations:* fishing, riding. *Address:* 6 Pump Court, Temple, EC4. *T:* 01-353 7242; 16 Abingdon Villas, W8. *T:* 01-937 7494; Catt's Place, Paddock Wood, Kent. *T:* Paddock Wood 2232. *Club:* United Hunts.

**GORST, John Michael;** MP (C) Hendon North since 1970; *b* 28 June 1928; *s* of Derek Charles Gorst and Tatiana (*née* Kolotinsky); *m* 1954, Noël Harington Walker; four *s*. *Educ:* Ardingly Coll.; Corpus Christi Coll., Cambridge (MA). Advertising and Public Relations Manager, Pye Ltd, 1953-63; and Public Relations Consultant, John Gorst & Associates, 1964-70. Public relations adviser to: British Lion Films, 1964-65; Fedn of British Film Makers, 1964-67; Film Production Assoc. of GB, 1967-68; BALPA, 1967-69; Guy's Hosp., 1968-70. Dir, Cassius Film Productions Ltd, 1969-. Founder, Telephone Users' Assoc., 1964- (Sec. 1964-70); Founder, Local Radio Assoc. 1964- (Sec., 1964-70). Contested (C) Chester-le-Street, 1964; Bodmin, 1966. *Recreations:* chess, book collecting, squash, organising campaigns. *Address:* 35 Connaught Square, W2. *T:* 01-723 4836. *Club:* Garrick.

**GORT,** 7th Viscount (Ireland) *cr* 1816; **Standish Robert Gage Prendergast Vereker;** MC; Baron Kiltarton, 1810; *b* 12 Feb. 1888; *s* of 5th Viscount and Eleanor (*d* 1933), *d* and *co-heiress* of R. S. Surtees of Hamsterley Hall, Co. Durham [she *m* 2nd, 1908, Col S. M. Benson]; *S* brother 1946; *m* 1921, Bessy, CStJ 1969, *d* of late Aubone Surtees, Dinsdale Manor, Co. Durham. *Educ:* Harrow; Trinity Coll., Cambridge. Served European War, 1914-19 (MC, despatches, thrice wounded); Sheriff of Durham, 1934. KStJ. *Heir: kinsman,* Colin Leopold Prendergast Vereker, Lt-Comdr RNVR [*b* 21 June 1916; *s* of late Comdr Leopold George Prendergast Vereker, RD, RNR; *m* 1946, Bettine Green; two *s* one *d*]. *Address:* Hamsterley Hall, Rowlands Gill, Newcastle upon Tyne; Bunratty Castle, Co. Clare. *Clubs:* Carlton; Manitoba (Winnipeg); Kildare Street (Dublin).

**GORTON, Rt. Hon. John Grey,** PC 1968; MA; MP; Prime Minister of Australia since Jan. 1968; Member of House of Representatives since Feb. 1968; *b* 1911; *m* 1935, Bettina, *d* of G. Brown, Bangor, Me, USA; two *s* one *d*. *Educ:* Geelong Gram. Sch.; Brasenose Coll., Oxford (MA, Hon. Fellow, 1968). Orchardist. Enlisted RAAF, Nov. 1940; served in UK, Singapore, Darwin, Milne Bay; severely wounded in air ops; discharged with rank of Flt-Lt, Dec. 1944. Councillor, Kerang Shire, 1947-52 (Pres. of Shire); Mem., Lodden Valley Regional Cttee. Senator for State of Victoria, Parlt of Commonwealth of Australia, 1949-68 (Govt Leader in Senate, 1967-68); Minister for Navy, 1958-63; Minister Assisting the Minister for External Affairs, 1960-63 (Actg Minister during periods of absence overseas of Minister); Minister in Charge of CSIRO, 1962-68; Minister for Works and, under Prime Minister, Minister in Charge of Commonwealth Activities in Educn and Research, 1963-66; Minister for Interior, 1963-64; Minister for Works, 1966-67; Minister for Educn and Science, 1966-68. Mem., Liberal Party. *Address:* Parliament House, Canberra, ACT 2600, Australia.

**GOSCHEN,** family name of **Viscount Goschen.**

**GOSCHEN,** 3rd Viscount *cr* 1900; **John Alexander Goschen,** of Hawkhurst; OBE 1944; Colonel, Grenadier Guards; *b* 7 July 1906; *e surv. s* of late Hon. Sir William Henry Goschen, KBE (2nd *s* of 1st Viscount) and late Geraldine Elizabeth, *d* of Rt Hon. J. W. Mellor, PC, KC; *S* uncle, 1952; *m* 1st, 1934, Hilda Violet Ursula (from whom he obtained a divorce, 1950), *d* of late Lieut-Col Hon. St Leger Henry Jervis, DSO; no *c*; 2nd, 1955, Alvin, *yr d* of late H. England, Durban S Africa; one *s* one *d*. *Educ:* Eton; RMC Sandhurst. 2nd Lieut Grenadier Guards, 1926; served War of 1939-45, in Grenadier Guards (appointments on the staff), N Africa, Italy, France and Greece (OBE); Lt-Col 1941. Captain of the Yeomen of the Guard (Asst Govt Chief Whip in the Lords), 1962-64, 1970-. *Recreations:* hunting, shooting and fishing. *Heir: s* Hon. Giles John Harry Goschen, *b* 16 Nov. 1965. *Address:* Hilton House, Crowthorne, Berks. *Club:* Guards.

**GOSCHEN, Maj.-Gen. Arthur Alec,** CB 1935; DSO 1900; DL Glos 1953; *b* 6 Jan. 1880; 3rd *s* of H. Goschen, Heathfield, Surrey; *m* 1908, Marjorie Mary, *d* of late Major W. Blacker, Castle Martin, Newbridge, Co. Kildare; one *s* three *d*. *Educ:* Eton. Entered RA 1899; served S Africa, 1899-1901 (despatches, Queen's medal, 2 clasps, DSO); European War, 1914-18 (wounded, Bt Lieut-Col, 2 bars, DSO, Croix de Guerre); Instructor, Staff Coll., Quetta, 1925-29; Garrison Commander and Commandant, RA Depot, Woolwich, 1929-31; Brigadier, RA, Aldershot Command, 1931-34; ADC to the King, 1932-34; Comdt, Royal Military Academy, Woolwich, 1934-38; retired pay, 1938; Area Commander, 1939-41; Col Comdt RHA, 1942-48; Col-Comdt RA 1941-48. *Address:* King's Hay, Eastleach, Cirencester, Glos.

**GOSCHEN, Sir Edward (Christian),** 3rd Bt, *cr* 1916; DSO 1944; Rifle Brigade; *b* 2 Sept. 1913; *er s* of Sir Edward Henry Goschen, 2nd Bt, and Countess Mary, 7th *d* of Count Danneskiold, Samsoe, Denmark; *S* father, 1933; *m* 1946, Cynthia, *d* of late Rt Hon. Sir Alexander Cadogan, PC, OM, GCMG, KCB; one *s* one *d*. *Educ:* Eton; Trinity Coll., Oxford. Deputy Chairman, Stock Exchange, 1968-. *Heir: s* Edward Alexander Goschen, *b* 13 March 1949. *Address:* Jesmond Hill, Pangbourne, Berks.

**GOSFORD,** 7th Earl of, *cr* 1806; **Charles David Nicholas Alexander John Sparrow Acheson;** Bt (NS) 1628; Baron Gosford 1776; Viscount Gosford 1785; Baron Worlingham (UK) 1835; Baron Acheson (UK) 1847; *b* 13 July 1942; *o s* of 6th Earl of Gosford, OBE, and Francisca Augusta, *er d* of Francesco Cagiati, New York; *S* father, 1966. *Educ:* Harrow; Byam Shaw Sch. of drawing and painting; Royal Academy Schs. *Heir: u* Hon. Patrick Bernard Victor Montagu Acheson [*b* 1915; *m* 1946, Judith, *d* of Mrs F. B. Bate, Virginia, USA; three *s* two *d*].

**GOSLING, Sir Arthur Hulin,** KBE, *cr* 1955; CB 1950; BSc; FRSE; FRICS; Director-General, Forestry Commission, 1948-62, retired; *b* 26 July 1901; 5th *s* of late C. F. Gosling; *m* 1931, Jane Alexander (*d* 1969), *o d* of late Dr M. Bryson. *Educ:* Bell's Gram. Sch., Coleford, Glos; Edinburgh Univ. District Officer, Forestry Commission, 1928; Divisional Officer, Glasgow, 1938; Asst Comr, Scotland, 1940; Dep. Dir Gen., 1947. Chm. Commonwealth Forestry Assoc., 1963-. *Address:* The Old Manse, Cerne Abbas, Dorset.

**GOSS, Brig. Leonard George,** CB 1946; *b* 30 May 1895; *s* of Alfred Herbert Goss, Wellington, NZ; *m* 1920, Ella May, *d* of John Airth Mace, New Plymouth, NZ; one *d*. *Educ:* New Plymouth Boys' High Sch. (NZ); RMC of Australia. Commissioned in NZ Staff Corps, Lieut 1916; Captain 1919; Major, 1935; Lt-Col 1939; Temp. Brig. 1942. *Recreations:* Rugby, cricket, swimming, boxing. *Address:* 17 Waitui Crescent, Lower Hutt, NZ. *Club:* United Service (Wellington, NZ).

**GOSTLING, Maj.-Gen. Philip le M. S. S.;** *see* Stonhouse-Gostling.

**GOTHARD, Sir Clifford (Frederic),** Kt 1959; OBE 1956; JP; Chartered Accountant in practice, Coxon, Bannister & Gothard, Burton-on-Trent, since 1925; Chairman: Marston, Thompson & Evershed, Ltd; Burton Daily Mail Ltd; Director, The Portland Motor Group Ltd and Subsidiaries, etc; has estate at Drakelowe, Derbyshire; *b* 9 June 1893; *s* of Frederic Gothard and Mary Gothard (*née* Startin); *m* 1961, Margaret Vera Hall. *Educ:* Burton-on-Trent Grammar Sch.; Birmingham Univ. BScEng 1915. Served European War, 1914-18, Royal Artillery (Captain). Institute of Chartered Accountants: Associate, 1924; Fellow 1929. His interests include religious, educational, agricultural bodies. District Staff Officer, Midland Command, with rank of Squadron-Leader; supervised Air Training Corps Units, 1939/45. Mem. of certain special cttees of Assoc. of British Chambers of Commerce, etc; Chm. Burton Div. Conservative Assoc., 1945-; Mem. Council West Midlands Union of Conservative and Unionist Assocs and of Conservative Commonwealth and Overseas Council. JP for County Borough, Burton-on-Trent, 1940-. Life Member: Royal Agricultural Society of England, 1921-; Canadian Chamber of Commerce in Great Britain (Inc.). Court of Governors: Birmingham Univ. (Life Gov.); Keele Univ. *Recreations:* travel, shooting, fishing, sailing, gardening, reading. *Address:* Bearwood House, Burton-on-Trent, Staffs. *T:* 4866. *Club:* Abbey (Burton-on-Trent).

**GOTLEY;** *see* Henniker-Gotley.

**GOTTLIEB, Bernard,** CB 1970; Director, Telecommunications Department, Ministry of Posts and Telecommunications, since 1969; *b* 1913; *s* of late James Gottlieb and late Pauline Littaur; *m* 1955, Sybil N. Epstein; one *s* one *d*. *Educ:* Haberdashers' Hampstead Sch.; Queen Mary Coll., London Univ. BSc First Class Maths, 1932. Entered Civil Service as an Executive Officer in Customs and Excise, 1932. Air Ministry, 1938; Asst Private Sec., 1941, and Private Sec., 1944, to Permanent Under-Sec. of State (late Sir Arthur Street), Control Office for Germany and Austria, 1945; Asst Sec., 1946. Seconded to National Coal Board, 1946; Min. of Power, 1950; Under-Sec., 1961, Dir of Establishments, 1965-69. Gwilym Gibbon Research Fellow, Nuffield Coll., Oxford, 1952-53. *Address:* 113 The Vale, NW11. *T:* 01-455 5482. *Club:* Reform.

**GOTTMANN, Prof. Jean,** FRGS; Professor of Geography, University of Oxford, since 1968; Fellow of Hertford College, Oxford, 1968; *b* 10 Oct. 1915; *s* of Elie Gottmann and Sonia-Fanny Ettinger Gottmann; *m* 1957, Bernice Adelson. *Educ:* Lycée Montaigne; Lycée St Louis; Sorbonne. Research Asst Human Geography, Sorbonne, 1937-40; Mem., Inst. for Advanced Study, Princeton, NJ, several times, 1942-65; Lectr, then Associate Prof. in Geography, Johns Hopkins Univ., Baltimore, 1943-48; Dir of Studies and Research, UN Secretariat, NY, 1946-47; Chargé de Recherches, CNRS, Paris, 1948-51; Lectr, then Prof., Institut d'Etudes Politiques, University of Paris, 1948-56; Research Dir, Twentieth Century Fund, NY, 1956-61; Prof. Ecole des Hautes Etudes, Sorbonne, 1960-. Hon. Mem., Royal Netherlands Geog. Soc., 1963. Hon. LLD: Wisconsin, 1968; S Illinois, 1969. charles Daly Medal of Amer. Geograph.

Soc., 1964; Prix Bonaparte-Wyse, 1962; Palmes Académiques, 1968, etc. *Publications:* Relations Commerciales de la France, 1942; L'Amérique, 1949 (3rd edn 1960); A Geography of Europe, 1950 (4th edn 1969); La politique des Etats et leur géographie, 1952; Virginia at Mid-century, 1955; Megalopolis, 1961; Essais sur l'Aménagement de l'Espace habité, 1966, etc. *Recreations:* travelling, chess. *Address:* 19 Belsyre Court, Woodstock Road, Oxford. *T:* Oxford 57076.

**GÖTZ, Hon. Sir Frank Leon Aroha,** KCVO 1963; New Zealand High Commissioner, Ottawa, since 1965; *b* Auckland, NZ, 12 Sept. 1892; *s* of Henry F. Götz and Violet Frances (Pavitt); *m*; one *s* two *d*; *m* 1962, Mary Spencer Ranson. *Educ:* Ecole de Prangins, Nyon; Ecole de l'Ile de France, Liancourt; King's Coll., Auckland; Wanganui Collegiate Sch.; Otago Univ. Planter in Malaya, 12 years; teacher of Languages in NZ; General Manager, NZ Reparation Estates, W Samoa; commercial life in NZ. Entered Parliament, 1949; Minister of Crown, 1960; Minister for Internal Affairs, Island Territories and Civil Defence, 1961-63. *Recreations:* now reduced to shooting and fishing. *Address:* 337 Fenton Street, Rotorua, New Zealand.

**GOUDGE, Elizabeth de Beauchamp;** *b* 24 April 1900; *d* of late Henry Leighton Goudge, Regius Professor of Divinity in the University of Oxford, and late Ida de Beauchamp Collenette; unmarried. *Educ:* Grassendale, Southbourne; Reading Univ. Writer of novels, children's books, short stories and plays. *Publications: novels:* Island Magic, 1932; The Middle Window. 1933; A City of Bells, 1934; Towers in the Mist, 1936; The Bird in the Tree, 1939; The Castle on the Hill, 1942; Green Dolphin Country, 1944; The Herb of Grace, 1948; Gentian Hill, 1950; The Heart of the Family, 1953; The Rosemary Tree, 1956; The White Witch, 1958; The Dean's Watch, 1960; The Scent of Water, 1963; The Child from the Sea, 1970; *collections of short stories:* Make-Believe; The Reward of Faith; White Wings; *plays:* Three Plays, 1937; *Children's books:* Smokey House, 1938; Henrietta's House (in America: The Blue Hills), 1942; The Little White Horse, 1946 (awarded Carnegie Medal for 1947); The Valley of Song, 1951; Linnets and Valerians, 1964; *biography:* God so Loved the World (Life of Christ), 1951; St Francis of Assisi, 1959. Anthology of Verse and Prose: A Book of Comfort, 1964; 2nd Anthology of Verse and Prose: A Book of Peace, 1967. *Recreations:* reading and gardening. *Address:* Rose Cottage, Peppard Common, Henley-on-Thames, Oxon.

**GOUGH,** family name of **Viscount Gough.**

**GOUGH,** 5th Viscount (of Goojerat, of the Punjaub, and Limerick), *cr* 1849; **Shane Hugh Maryon Gough;** Irish Guards, 1961-67; *b* 26 Aug. 1941; *o s* of 4th Viscount Gough and Margaretta Elizabeth, *o d* of Sir Spencer Maryon-Wilson, 11th Bt; *S* father 1951. *Educ:* Abberley Hall, Worcs; Winchester Coll. *Heir:* none. *Address:* Keppoch Estate Office, Strathpeffer, Ross-shire, Scotland. *T:* Strathpeffer 224; 26 Markham Street, SW3. *T:* 01-584 4136. *Clubs:* Guards, White's.

**GOUGH, Sir Arthur (Ernest),** Kt 1966; JP; *b* 7 Jan. 1878; *s* of Richard and Elizabeth Gough; *m* 1913, Florence Tomkins; one *s* (decd). Railway Official. Mem., Cardiff City Council, 1919-32; Lord Mayor of Cardiff, 1933-34. Mem., S Wales Electricity Board, 1948-52. JP Cardiff, 1932-. *Address:* 2 Tydraw Road, Cardiff. *T:* 36959.

**GOUGH, Cecil Ernest Freeman,** CMG 1956; Managing Director, Airwork (Overseas) Ltd; Director, Airwork Services Ltd; *b* 29 Oct. 1911; *s* of Ernest John Gough; *m* 1938, Gwendolen Lily Miriam Longman; one *s* one *d*. *Educ:* Southend High Sch.; London Sch. of Economics (evening student) (School of Economics Scholar in Law, 1932). LLB 1934. Asst Examiner Estate Duty Office, Board of Inland Revenue, 1930; Air Ministry, 1938; Principal, 1944; Ministry of Defence, 1947; Asst Sec., 1949; on loan to Foreign Office, as Counsellor, United Kingdom Delegation to NATO, Paris, 1952-56; Chairman: NATO Infrastructure Cttee, 1952-53; Standing Armaments Cttee Western European Union, 1956; returned Ministry of Defence, 1956; Under-Sec., 1958; Under-Sec. at the Admiralty, 1962-64; Asst Under-Sec. of State, Min. of Defence, 1964-68. Medal of Freedom (USA), 1947; Coronation Medal, 1953. *Recreations:* cookery, gardening, reading, travel. *Address:* 13 Canonbury Park South, N1. *T:* 01-226 6378. *Club:* Naval and Military.

**GOUGH, Col (Charles) Frederick (Howard),** MC 1943; TD 1948; *b* 16 Sept. 1901; *yr s* of late Lt-Col Charles Hugh Henry Gough, IA; *m* 1929, Barbara May Pegler; one *s* one *d*. *Educ:* RN Colls., Osborne and Dartmouth. Midshipman in HMS Ramillies and HMS Witherington, 1917-20; left Navy, 1920. Took up farming and horse-breeding in India; returned to UK, 1922, and joined a firm of Lloyd's insurance brokers; Dir of a number of companies. Joined London Rifle Bde (TA), 1924, served until 1929 when he went on to TARO; rejoined London Rifle Bde, 1939, and served War of 1939-45; comd 1st Airborne Reconnaissance Squadron, Italy; qualified parachutist (Holder, Royal Aero Club Parachutist Certificate no 1); demobilised 1945 (despatches 1940; MC 1943; prisoner at Arnhem, 1944, escaped 1945); commanded 11th Bn Parachute Regt TA 1946-48. Hon. Col, Sussex Yeomanry, 1959-63. MP (C) Horsham Division of West Sussex, 1951-64. Vice-Pres. of Lloyd's Branch of British Legion, and Trustee of Airborne Forces Security Fund; Pres. South Lewisham Conservative Assoc.; Chm. Horsham Div. Cons. Assoc., 1964-70 (Pres., 1970); Pres. City of London Young Conservatives, 1964-70; Governor Cutty Sark Soc. *Address:* Weavers, Lodsworth, Sussex. *Clubs:* Buck's, Royal Aero (Chm. 1958-68).

**GOUGH, Frederick;** *see* Gough, Charles F. H.

**GOUGH, Brig. Guy Francis,** DSO MC; late Royal Irish Fusiliers; *b* 9 Aug. 1893; *e s* of late Hugh George Gough, Hyderabad, Deccan; *m* 1st, 1914, Dorothy (*d* 1953), *d* of late Edwin Paget Palmer, Patcham House, Sussex; one *s* one *d*; *m* 2nd, 1954, Elizabeth Treharn, *d* of Lewis David Thomas, Newton, near Porthcawl. *Educ:* The Oratory Sch.; RMC Sandhurst. 2nd Lieut, Royal Irish Fusiliers, Aug. 1914; European War, 1914-18. France and Belgium with 1st Royal Irish Fusiliers, and on the Staff (wounded, despatches, MC, 1915 Star); Staff Course, 1916. Commanded 1st Bn Nigeria Regt, 1936-37; War of 1939-45: Commanded ITC Royal Irish Fusiliers, 1st Battalion Royal Irish Fusiliers (in France and Belgium, May 1940), 202nd and 11th Infantry Brigades, Advanced Base I Army (N Africa), North Aldershot Sub-District. DSO, 1939-45 Star, Africa Star (with 1st Army clasp); retd pay, 1946. Control Commission, Germany as a Senior Control Officer, 1947-48. Coronation Medal, 1937. *Recreation:* fly-fishing. *Address:* The Malt House, Talybont-on-Usk, near Brecon. *Club:* Army and Navy.

**GOUGH, Harold Robert;** President British-American Tobacco Co. Ltd, SW1. 1950-60, retired; *b* 15 Dec. 1889; *s* of late Robert and late Annie Gough, Bower Ashton, Som; *m* 1st, 1921, Elizabeth Gilchrist McIntyre (*decd*); 2nd, 1941, Barbara Hall Watson; no *c*. *Educ:* Merchant Venturers Sch. Joined British-American Tobacco Co. Ltd 1905; Dir 1926; Dep. Chm. 1932; Chm. 1947. *Recreations:* shooting, fishing. *Address:* Pilcot Farm, Dogmersfield, Basingstoke, Hants. *Club:* Oriental.

**GOUGH, Rt. Rev. Hugh Rowlands;** CMG 1965; OBE 1945; TD 1950; DD Lambeth; Rector of Freshford, diocese of Bath and Wells, since 1967; Chaplain and Sub-Prelate. Order of St John of Jerusalem, from 1959; *b* 19 Sept. 1905; *o s* of late Rev. Charles Massey Gough, Rector of St Ebbe's, Oxford; *m* 1929, Hon. Madeline Elizabeth, *d* of 12th Baron Kinnaird, *qv*; one *d*. *Educ:* Weymouth Coll.; Trinity Coll., Cambridge; London Coll. Divinity. BA 1927, MA Cantab 1931. Deacon, 1928; Priest, 1929; Curate of St Mary, Islington, 1928-31; Perpetual Curate of St Paul, Walcot, Bath, 1931-34; Vicar of St James, Carlisle, 1934-39; Chaplain to High Sheriff of Cumberland, 1937; CF (TA), 1937-45; Chaplain to 4th Bn The Border Regt, 1937-39; Vicar of St Matthew, Bayswater 1939-46; Chaplain to 1st Bn London Rifle Bde, 1939-43; served Western Desert and Tunisia (wounded); Senior Chap. to 1st Armd Div., Tunisia, 1943; DACG 10 Corps, Italy, 1943-45 (despatches); DACG, North Midland Dist, 1945. Hon. Chaplain to the Forces (2nd cl.) 1945. Vicar of Islington, Rural Dean of Islington, 1946-48. Preb. St Paul's Cathedral, 1948; Suffragan Bishop of Barking, 1948-59; Archdeacon of West Ham, 1948-58; Archbishop of Sydney and Primate of Australia, also Metropolitan of New South Wales, 1959-66, retired, 1966. Formerly Member Council: London Coll. of Divinity, Clifton Theol. Coll. (Chm.), Haileybury Coll., Monkton Combe Sch., St Lawrence Coll. (Ramsgate), Chigwell Sch., Stowe Sch., Kingham Hill Trust. Golden Lectr Haberdashers' Co., 1953 and 1955. Pres. Conference, Educational Assoc., 1956. Mem., Essex County Education Cttee, 1949-59; DL Essex, 1952-59. Hon. DD Wycliffe Coll., Toronto; Hon. ThD, Aust. *Recreations:* shooting, tennis. *Address:* Freshford Rectory, Bath, Som. *T:* Limpley Stoke 3135. *Club:* National (London).

**GOUGH, Prof. Jethro;** Professor of Pathology, Welsh National School of Medicine, Cardiff, 1948-69, retired; *b* 29 Dec. 1903; *s* of Jabez and Ellen Gough; *m* 1933, Anne (*née* Thomas); two *s*. *Educ:* Mountain Ash County Sch.: Welsh National Sch. of Medicine, Cardiff. BSc, 1924; MRCS, LRCP, 1926; MB, BCh, 1927; MD, 1930; FRCP 1967. Demonstrator in Pathology, Cardiff, 1927, Manchester Univ., 1928; Lecturer in Pathology, Cardiff, 1929; Senior Lecturer, Cardiff, 1933. *Publications:* on several subjects relating to Pathology, but especially silicosis and allied conditions. *Address:* 22 Park Road, Whitchurch, Cardiff. *T:* Cardiff 65011.

**GOUGH-CALTHORPE,** family name of **Baron Calthorpe.**

**GOULBURN;** *see* Canberra-Goulburn.

**GOULBURN, Maj.-Gen. Edward Henry,** DSO and Bar 1944; DL; *b* 27 May 1903; *s* of late Brig.-Gen. C. E. Goulburn, DSO, and of Grace Ethel, *d* of late W. H. Foster, Apley Park, Bridgnorth, Salop. *Educ:* Eton and Sandhurst. Grenadier Guards, 1924; Adjutant, 1st Bn, 1931-34; Adjutant, RMC, SAndhurst, 1938-40; OC 1st Bn Gren. Guards in France, Belgium and Holland, 1942-44; Brigadier Cmdg 8th British Infantry Bde Holland and Germany, 1944-45; 1st Guards Bde, Palestine, 1945-46; Maj.-Gen. Cmdg Allied Military Mission to Italian Army, 1946-47; Lt-Col Comdg Gren. Guards, 1948-50. DL Surrey, 1962. Comdr Order of Orange Nassau. *Recreations:* farming, sport, travel. *Address:* Betchworth House, Betchworth, Surrey. *T:* Betchworth 3315. *Clubs:* Guards, Turf, Pratt's.

**GOULD, Cecil Hilton Monk;** Deputy Keeper of the National Gallery since 1962 (Assistant Keeper, 1946); *b* 24 May 1918; *s* of late Lieut Commander R. T. Gould and of Muriel Hilda Estall. *Educ:* Westminster Sch. Served in Royal Air Force: France, 1940; Middle East, 1941-43; Italy, 1943-44; Normandy, Belgium and Germany, 1944-46. FRSA, 1968. *Publications:* An Introduction to Italian Renaissance Painting, 1957; National Gallery catalogues: the 16th-century Venetian School, 1959; the 16th-century Italian Schools (excluding the Venetian), 1962; catalogue of art section of exhibition of Leonardo da Vinci, Royal Academy, 1952; the Leonardo Cartoon (with Sir Kenneth Clark), 1962; Michelangelo's Battle of Cascina (Charlton lecture, 1964), 1966; Trophy of Conquest, 1965; Catalogues of Corot Exhibn, Edinburgh Fest., 1965, Sebastiano del Piombo's Raising of Lazarus, 1967; Titian's Bacchus and Ariadne, 1969; Raphael's Julius II, 1970; articles in Encyclopædia Britannica, Chambers's Encyclopedia, Dizionario Biografico degli Italiani, Burlington Magazine, Journal of the Warburg and Courtauld Institutes, Art Bulletin (USA), Art Quarterly (USA), etc. *Recreations:* music, ski-ing. *Address:* 6 Palace Gate, W8. *T:* 01-584 9151. *Club:* Reform.

**GOULD, Donald (William),** BSc (Physiol.), MRCS, DTM&H; writer and broadcaster on medical and scientific affairs; Medical Correspondent, New Statesman, since 1966; *b* 26 Jan. 1919; *s* of late Rev. Frank J. Gould; *m* 1940, Edna Forsyth (marr. diss., 1969); three *s* four *d*. *Educ:* Mill Hill Sch.; St Thomas's Hosp. Med. Sch., London. Orthopædic House Surg., Botley's Park Hosp., 1942; Surg. Lieut, RNVR, 1942-46; Med. Off., Hong Kong Govt Med. Dept, 1946-48; Lectr in Physiol., University of Hong Kong, 1948-51, Sen. Lectr, 1951-57; King Edward VII Prof. of Physiol., University of Malaya (Singapore), 1957-60; Lectr in Physiol., St Bartholomew's Hosp. Med. Coll., London, 1960-61, Sen. Lectr, 1961-63; External Examr in Physiol., University of Durham (Newcastle), 1961-63; Dep. Ed., Medical News, 1963-65; Editor: World Medicine, 1965-66; New Scientist, 1966-69. Mem., Physiol. Soc., 1958; Chm., Med. Journalists' Assoc., 1967; Mem. Cttee, Assoc. of British Science Writers, 1967. *Publications:* scientific papers in physiological jls; numerous articles on medical politics, ethics and science in lay and professional press. *Recreations:* writing poems nobody will publish, listening, talking, and occasionally walking. *Address:* 73 Burntwood Grange Road, SW18. *T:* 01-870 3113. *Club:* Savage.

**GOULD, Frederick,** OBE 1941; JP, Alderman CC Som., retired; *b* 28 June 1879; *s* of Joshua and Eliza Gould; *m* 1903; two *s* one *d*. *Educ:* Church of England Elementary Sch. Kitchen and stable boy, 3 years; boot operative, 24 years; political agent, 3 years; MP (Lab.) Frome Division Som, 1923-24, and 1929-31; Contested East Leicester 1935. *Recreations:* fishing, bowls. *Address:* Midsomer Norton, near Bath, Som. *T:* Midsomer Norton 2362. *See also Sir Ronald Gould.*

**GOULD, R(alph) Blair,** MB, ChB Sheffield; DA (England); FFARCS; physician, anæsthetist; Fellow Royal Society of Medicine (Member Section of Anæsthetists); Fellow, Internat. College of Anæsthetists, USA; Fellow, Association of Anæsthetists of Great Britain; Hon. Consultant Anæsthetist: St George's Hospital; Royal Throat Nose and Ear Hospital; *b* Manchester, 15 May 1914; *o s* of late Maurice Gould, Bournemouth. *Educ:* King Edward VII Sch., Sheffield; Sheffield Univ. Held Senior Resident appointments at Jessop Hospital for Women, Sheffield; Sheffield Royal Hosp., and West London Hosp., Hammersmith; Surg., Canadian Pacific Steamship Co.; lately: Hon. Asst in the Out-patient Dept., Central London Throat, Nose and Ear Hosp.; Clinical Asst, Central London Ophthalmic Hosp.; Clinical Asst, Aural and Children's Depts, West London Hosp.; Specialist in Anæsthetics: Metropolitan Reg. Hosp. Bds, etc; EMS for London; Senior Consultant Anæsthetist: German Hosp.; Brentwood Dist Hosp.; Royal Nat. Throat Hosp.; Sch. of Dental Surgery, Royal Dental Hosp. (also Lectr); Anæsthetist to LCC and Royal Eye Hosp.; Hon. Anæsthetist: St John's Hosp., Lewisham; Romford Victoria Hosp.; Queen Mary's Hosp., Sidcup; Editor, Anæsthesia; *Publications:* various communications to the medical journals. *Recreations:* music, photography. *Address:* 55 Harley Street, W1. *T:* 01-580 5070; 25 Briardale Gardens, NW3. *T:* 01-435 2646.

**GOULD, Sir Robert Macdonald,** KBE 1953; Kt 1948; CB 1946; War of 1914-18: Artists Rifles, 1914; Middlesex Regt, 1916, severely wounded; invalided 1919. Late Chief Industrial Commissioner, Ministry of Labour and National Service. Retired, 1952. Dir of cos, 1952-62. *Address:* Littleden, Tilford, near Farnham, Surrey. *Club:* United Service.

**GOULD, Sir Ronald,** Kt 1955; General Secretary, National Union of Teachers, 1947-70; (First) President of World Confederation of Organizations of the Teaching Profession, 1952-70; Deputy Chairman, Independent Television Authority, since 1967; Member, Community Relations Commission, since 1968; *b* 9 Oct. 1904; *s* of Fred Gould, *qv*; *m* 1928, Nellie Denning Fish; two *s*. *Educ:* Shepton Mallet Grammar Sch.; Westminster Training Coll. Asst Master Radstock Council Sch., 1924-41; Headmaster Welton County Sch., 1941-46; Chm. Norton Radstock UDC, 1936-46; Pres. NUT, 1943-44; Hon. Fellow; Educational Inst. of Scotland; College of Preceptors, 1965; a Governor of the Commonwealth Institute. Hon. MA Bristol, 1943; Hon. LLD: British Columbia, 1963; McGill, 1964; St Francis Xavier, NS, 1969. Officier, Ordre des Palmes Académiques, 1969. *Address:* Grasmere, 21 Lakenheath, Southgate, N14.

**GOULD, Thomas William,** VC 1942; late Lieutenant RNVR; *b* 28 Dec. 1914; *s* of late Mrs C. E. Cheeseman and late Reuben Gould (killed in action, 1916); *m* 1941, Phyllis Eileen Eldridge; one *s*. *Educ:* St James, Dover, Kent. Royal Navy, 1933-37; Submarines, 1937-45 (despatches); invalided Oct. 1945. Business Consultant, 1965-; company director.

**GOULD, Sir Trevor (Jack),** Kt 1961; *b* 24 June 1906; *s* of Percy Clendon and Elizabeth Margaret Gould; *m* 1934, May Milne; one *s* two *d*. *Educ:* Auckland Gram. Sch.; Auckland Univ. Coll., NZ. Barrister and Solicitor, Supreme Court of New Zealand, 1928; Supreme Court of Fiji, 1934; Crown Counsel, Hong Kong, 1938; served War, 1941-45 (prisoner of war). Actg Puisne Judge, Hong Kong, 1946, Puisne Judge, 1948; Acting Chief Justice, Hong Kong, 1953-55; Senior Puisne Judge, Hong Kong, 1953-58; Justice of Appeal, Court of Appeal for Eastern Africa, 1958-63; Vice-Pres. Court of Appeal for Eastern Africa, 1963-65. *Recreation:* sports. *Address:* 21 Mount St John Avenue, Auckland SE3, New Zealand.

**GOULDEN, Gontran Iceton,** OBE 1963; FRIBA; TD, 1946 (and 3 Clasps); Director-General, the London Group of Building Centres, since 1968; *b* 5 April 1912; *s* of late H. G. R. Goulden, Canterbury, and Alice Mildred Iceton; *m* 1937, Phyllis Nancye, *d* of J. W. F. Crawfurd, Dublin; two *s* one *d*. *Educ:* St Edmund's Sch., Canterbury; Paris; London Univ. (Dipl.). Commissioned RA (TA) 1931, Capt. 1936, Major 1939; served UK, Ceylon (GSO2 to C-in-C), India and SEAC (CO 6 Indian HAA Regt I Artillery; Comd 13 AA Bde), 1939-45; T/Lieut-Col 1943; A/Brig. 1945 (despatches twice); Lieut-Col 1947, Bt Col 1953. Col 1954; Deputy Commander, an AA Brigade, 1954-58; TARO 1960; Hon. Col 452 HAA Rgt RA (TA), 1960-61; Hon. Col 254 Fd Regt RA (TA) 1964-65; Mem. Middx TA & AFA, 1947-53. Surveyor to Wellcome Archæol. Exped. to Near East, 1934-35; Asst to Graham Dawbarn, 1935-39. Teaching staff of Architectural Association Sch. of Architecture, 1945-46. Chief Tech. Officer and Dep. Dir, the Building Centre, 1947-61, Dir, 1962-. Mem. of Council AA, 1949-58 (Pres., 1956-57). Hon. Sec. Modern Architectural Research (MARS) group, 1950-53. Member: Architects Registration Council of the UK, 1954-56, 1963-64; RIBA Council, 1956-57, 1962-65; Dir, VIth Congress Intern Union of Architects, 1961; Chm. UIA and Foreign Relations Cttee, RIBA, 1962-65. Treasurer UIA, 1965-; Mem., Franco-British Union of Architects; Honarary Corresponding Mem. Danish Architectural Assoc., 1965; Pres. International Union of Building Centres, 1962-63, Sec.-Gen. 1969-; Mem. Council, Modular Soc., 1955-59. Sec., The Architecture Club, 1958-64; Member: Min. of Transport Advisory Cttee on landscaping of trunk roads, 1963-64; Ministry of Public Building and Works Cttee on the Agrément System, 1964-65; General Council of BSI, 1964-67. Governor: St Edmund's Sch., Canterbury; St Margaret's Sch., Bushey, 1949-59. Lecturer and broadcaster on architectural subjects. Hereditary Freeman of City of Canterbury. *Publications:* Bathrooms, 1966; regular contrib. to architectural papers. *Recreations:* travel, sailing. *Address:* 28 St Peter's Square, Hammersmith, W6. *T:* 01-748 6621.

**GOULDEN, Mark;** Chairman, W. H. Allen & Co. Ltd, Publishers; *b* Clifton, Bristol; 2nd *s* of late Morris and Eve Goulden; *m*; two *s* one *d*. Began journalism with Cambridge Daily News; served Royal Engineers, Managing Editor and Dir, Eastern Morning News and Hull Evening News, 1923-30; Managing Editor, Yorkshire Evening News, Leeds, 1930-32; Managing Editor Sunday Referee, 1932-36; Editor-in-Chief, Argus Press Ltd; Managing Editor, Cavalcade and other publications: Director: Illustrated Publications Ltd, Bicycle Publishing Co. Ltd; Macfadden's Magazines Ltd, 1937-41; written and lectured extensively on newspapers, advertising and publishing. British Delegate World Advertising Convention, Philadelphia, 1927; former member Nat. Council Advertising Clubs: Council Newspaper Proprietors Assoc., etc.; inventor, Gouldris Matrix Machine; a pioneer of civil aviation in England. *Recreations:* flying, motoring, golf. *Address:* (Home) St James's Chambers, Ryder Street, SW1; 37 East 64th Street, New York, NY 10022, USA; (Office) 43 Essex Street, WC2; 444 Madison Avenue, New York. *Clubs:* Press, Paternosters, Savage; Players' (New York).

**GOULDING, Sir Basil;** *see* Goulding, Sir W. B.

**GOULDING, Ernest Irvine,** QC 1961; *b* 1 May 1910; *s* of late Dr Ernest Goulding; *m* 1935, Gladys, *d* of late Engineer Rear-Adm. Marrack Sennett; one *s* one *d*. *Educ:* Merchant Taylors' Sch., London; St Catharine's Coll., Cambridge. Served as Instructor Officer, Royal Navy, 1931-36 and 1939-45. Called to Bar, Inner Temple, 1936. Bencher, Lincoln's Inn, 1966. *Address:* 9 Constitution Hill, Woking, Surrey. *T:* Woking 61012. *Clubs:* Travellers', National Liberal.

**GOULDING, Lt-Col Terence Leslie Crawford P.;** *see* Pierce-Goulding.

**GOULDING, Sir (William) Basil,** 3rd Bt *cr* 1904; Director: W. & H. M. Goulding Ltd; National Bank of Ireland Ltd; Hibernian Insurance Co. Ltd; Rio-Tinto Zinc Corp. Ltd; Irish Pensions Trust; *b* 4 Nov. 1909; *s* of Sir Lingard Goulding, 2nd Bt, and Nesta Violet (*d* 1968) (she *m* 2nd, 1938, Stanley Adams, who *d* 1965), *d* of late Hon. Mr Justice Wright, and *g d* of Sir Croker Barrington, 4th Bt; *S* father, 1935; *m* 1939, Valerie Hamilton, LLD, *o d* of 1st Viscount Monckton of Brenchley, PC, GCVO, KCMG, MC, QC, and *g d* of Sir Thomas Colyer-Fergusson, 3rd Bt; three *s*. *Educ:* Winchester Coll.; Christ Church, Oxford. War of 1939-45, Wing Comdr RAFVR. *Heir:* *s* William Lingard Walter Goulding, *b* 11 July 1940. *Address:* Dargle Cottage, Enniskerry, Co. Wicklow, Eire.

**GOURLAY, Maj.-Gen. Basil Ian Spencer,** OBE 1956 (MBE 1948); MC 1944; Major-General Royal Marines, Porstmouth, since 1968; *b* 13 Nov. 1920; *er s* of late Brig. K. I. Gourlay, DSO, OBE, MC; *m* 1948, Natasha Zinovieff; one *s* one *d*. *Educ:* Eastbourne Coll. Commissioned, RM, 1940; HMS Formidable, 1941-44; 43 Commando, 1944-45; 45 Commando, 1946-48; Instructor, RNC Greenwich, 1948-50; Adjt RMFVR, City of London, 1950-52; Instructor, RM Officers' Sch., 1952-54; psc 1954; Bde Major, 3rd Commando Bde, 1955-57 (despatches); OC RM Officers' Trng Wing, Infantry Training Centre RM, 1957-59; 2nd in Comd, 42 Commando, 1959-61; GSO1, HQ Plymouth Gp, 1961-63; CO 42 Commando, 1963-65; Col GS, Dept of CGRM, Min. of Defence, 1965-66; Col 1965; Comdr, 3rd Commando Bde, 1966-68; Maj.-Gen. 1968. *Recreations:* cricket, squash, golf. *Address:* c/o Dept of CGRM, Ministry of Defence (Navy), SW1. *Club:* United Hunts.

**GOURLAY, Harry Philp Heggie,** JP; MP (Lab) Kirkcaldy Burghs since Oct. 1959; *b* 10 July 1916; *s* of William Gourlay; *m* 1942, Margaret McFarlane Ingram; no *c*. *Educ:* Kirkcaldy High Sch. Coachbuilder, 1932; Vehicle Examiner, 1947. Mem. Kirkcaldy Town Council, 1946, Hon. Treasurer, 1953-57; Magistrate, 1957-59; Vice-Chm. Fife Education Cttee, 1958; Mem. Hospital Management Cttee; Sec. Kirkcaldy Burghs Constituency Labour Party, 1945-59; Mem. Estimates Cttee, 1959-64; Chm. Scottish Parly Labour Group, 1963-64; Government Whip, 1964-66; a Lord Comr of the Treasury, 1966-68; Dep. Chm. of Ways and Means, 1968-70. *Recreations:* chess, golf. *Address:* 34 Rosemount Avenue, Kirkcaldy, Fife. *T:* Kirkcaldy 61919.

**GOURLAY, Dame Janet;** *see* Vaughan, Dame Janet.

**GOUSEV, Feodor Tarasovich;** Order of Lenin, 1944; Soviet Diplomatist; *b* Leningrad region, 29 April 1905; *m*; one *d*. *Educ:* Leningrad Univ. (graduated from the Law Faculty, 1931). Worked in Leningrad State Offices, 1931-36; held various responsible posts at the People's Commissariat for Foreign Affairs, 1937-39; Chief of the Second European Dept of the People's Commissariat for Foreign Affairs, 1939-42; Soviet Envoy Extraordinary and Minister Plenipotentiary in Canada, 1942-43; Ambassador of the USSR in Great Britain, 1943-46; Dep. Foreign Minister, USSR, 1946-52; Counsellor, Min. of For. Affairs, 1953-56, 1962-; Ambassador to Sweden, 1957-62. *Address:* Foreign Office, Moscow.

**GOW, Andrew Sydenham Farrar,** MA; FBA 1943; Hon. DLitt (Durham); Hon LLD (Edinburgh); Fellow of Trinity College, Cambridge; on committee of National Art-Collections Fund; *b* 27 Aug. 1886; *e s* of Rev. James Gow, LittD, sometime Headmaster of Westminster, and Gertrude Sydenham, *d* of G. P. Everett-Green. *Educ:* Rugby Sch.; Trinity Coll., Cambridge. Porson Prizeman, 1906, 1907; Browne Medallist, 1907, 1908; Charles Oldham Scholar, 1909, 1910; Fellow of Trinity Coll., 1911; Asst Master at Eton Coll., 1914-25; Trinity Coll., Cambridge: Lectr, 1925-46; Tutor, 1929-42; Praelector, 1946-51; University Lectr, 1925-51; Brereton Reader in Classics, 1947-51; a Trustee of the National Gallery, 1947-53. *Publications:* A. E. Housman: A Sketch and List of his Writings, 1936; Letters from Cambridge (1939-1944), 1945; Theocritus (text, translation, and commentary), 2 vols, 1950, 2nd edn 1953, rep. 1965; Bucolici Graeci (Oxford Classical Texts), 1952, 2nd impression 1958; The Greek Bucolic Poets (introd. and trans.), 1953; The Greek Anthology: sources and ascriptions, 1958; Machon (introd., text, and commentary), 1965; (with A. F. Scholfield) Nicander (text, trans., and notes), 1953; (with Prof. D. L. Page) The Greek Anthology: Hellenistic Epigrams (text and commentary), 2 vols, 1965; The *Garland* of Philip (text, translation and commentary) 2 vols, 1968; contribs to Jl of Hellenic Studies, Jl of Philology, Classical Quarterly, Classical Review, etc; editor of A. E. Housman's Manilius (edn 2), 1937, and with Prof. D. S. Robertson, of W. Ridgeway's The Early Age of Greece, vol. II, 1931. *Address:* Trinity College, Cambridge. *T:* Cambridge 58201. *Club:* United University.

**GOW, Brig. John Wesley Harper,** CBE 1958 (OBE 1945); DL; JP; retired Shipowner; *b* 8 April 1898; *s* of late Leonard Gow, DL, LLD, Glasgow, and Mabel A. Harper, *d* of John W. Harper, publisher, Cedar Knoll, Long Island, NY; *m* 1925, Frances Jean, JP, *d* of James Begg, Westlands, Paisley; three *s*. *Educ:* Cargilfield; Sedbergh; RMC Sandhurst; Trinity Coll., Oxford. Entered Scots Guards, 1917; severely wounded, France. Late partner, Gow Harrison & Co. Mem. Queen's Body Guard for Scotland (Royal Company of Archers), 1941. MFH, Lanarkshire and Renfrewshire, 1949-54; Pres. Royal Caledonian Curling Club, 1958-60; Chm. West Renfrewshire Unionist Assoc., 1947-60, Pres. 1960-68; Vice-Pres. of RNLI and Chm. Glasgow Branch; Mem. Council and Pres. Glasgow Branch, SS & AFA; Mem. Cttee Erskine Hosp., Earl Haig Fund Officers Assoc. (Scotland); Mem. Glasgow TA & AFA, 1947-56. Served War of 1939-45: Scots Guards, RARO; Lt-Col attached RA (LAA), NW Europe; commanded 77 AA Bde, RA (TA),

1947-48; Brig. 1948. Hon. Col 483 HAA (Blythswood) Regt RA, TA, 1951-56; Hon. Col 445 LAA Regt RA (Cameronians) TA, 1959-67, later 445 (Lowland) Regt RA (TA). DL City of Glasgow, 1948; JP Renfrewshire, 1952, Lord Dean of Guild, Glasgow, 1965-67. OStJ 1969. Chevalier Order of Crown of Belgium and Croix de Guerre (Belgian), 1945. *Recreations:* curling, hunting, shooting. *Address:* Hallhill, Howwood, Renfrewshire. *T:* Kilbarchan 2503. *Clubs:* Army and Navy; New (Edinburgh); Western (Glasgow); Prestwick Golf.

**GOW, Mrs Ronald;** *see* Hiller, Wendy.

**GOW, Very Rev. William Connell;** Dean of Moray, Ross and Caithness, since 1960; Canon of St Andrew's Cathedral, Inverness, since 1953; Rector of St James', Dingwall, since 1940; *b* 6 Jan. 1909; *s* of Alexander Gow, Errol, Perthshire; *m* 1938, Edith Mary, *d* of John William Jarvis, Scarborough; two *s*. *Educ:* Edinburgh Theological Coll.; Durham Univ. (LTh). Deacon, 1936; Priest, 1937; Curate St Mary Magdalene's, Dundee, 1936-39. Awarded Frihetsmedalje (by King Haakon), Norway, 1947. *Recreations:* fishing, bridge. *Address:* The Parsonage, Dingwall, Ross-shire. *T:* Dingwall 2204.

**GOWANS, Prof. James Learmonth,** FRS 1963; Henry Dale Research Professor of the Royal Society since 1962; Director, Medical Research Council, Cellular Immunology Research Unit, since 1963; *b* 7 May 1924; *s* of John Gowans and Selma Josefina Ljung; *m* 1956, Moyra Leatham; one *s* two *d*. *Educ:* Trinity Sch., Croydon; King's Coll. Hosp.; Lincoln Coll., Oxford. MB, BS (London) 1947; MA, DPhil (Oxford) 1953. Medical Research Council Exchange Scholar, Pasteur Institute, Paris, 1953; Staines Medical Research Fellow, Exeter Coll., Oxford, 1955-60. Fellow, St Catherine's Coll., Oxford, 1961-. Mem. MRC, 1965-69; Chm. Biological Research Bd, 1967-69. Hon. ScD Yale, 1966; Gairdner Foundn Award, 1968. *Publications:* articles in scientific journals. *Address:* Sir William Dunn School of Pathology, Oxford University, Oxford. *T:* Oxford 57321.

**GOWER;** *see* Leveson Gower.

**GOWER, Most Rev. Godfrey Philip;** *see* New Westminster, Archbishop of.

**GOWER, (Herbert) Raymond;** MP (C) Barry Division of Glamorganshire since 1951; solicitor, Cardiff, since 1948; Political Columnist for Western Mail for Cardiff, 1951-64; Chairman of Penray Press Ltd and Barry Herald Newspaper since 1955; Director: Nicholson Construction Ltd, since 1957; Welsh Dragon Securities Ltd, since 1961; Broughton & Co. (Bristol) Ltd since 1961; Assoc. of Conservative Clubs Ltd, 1962-65; Welsh Dragon Unit Trust (Management Co.), since 1962 (Jt Founder); Deane-Spence Ltd, Cranleigh and London, SW1 (Merchant Bankers) since 1963; Building and Construction Co. Ltd, Cardiff, 1962-64; Welsh Industrial Investment Trust Ltd; Welsh Industrial Securities Ltd, since 1965; Treasurer, Welsh Parliamentary Party, since 1966; journalist and broadcaster; *b* 15 Aug. 1916; *s* of Lawford R. Gower, FRIBA, County Architect for Glamorgan, and late Mrs Gower; unmarried. *Educ:* Cardiff High Sch.; Univ. of Wales; Cardiff Sch. of Law. Solicitor, admitted 1944; own practice at Cardiff, 1948-. Contested (C) Ogmore Division of Glamorgan, general election, 1950. Parliamentary Private Secretary: to Mr Gurney Braithwaite, 1951-54, to Mr R. Maudling, 1951-52, to Mr J. Profumo, 1952-57, to Mr Hugh Molson, 1954-57, Min. of Transport and Civil Aviation, and to Minister of Works, 1957-60. Governor, University Coll., Cardiff, 1951-; Member Court of Governors: National Museum of Wales, 1952-; National Library of Wales, 1951-; University Coll., Aberystwyth, 1953-; Vice-President: National Chamber of Trade, 1956-; Young Conservatives of Wales, 1952-; Cardiff Business Club, 1952; South Wales Ramblers, 1958-; Sec., Friends of Wales Soc. (Cultural); Mem., Welsh Advisory Council for Civil Aviation, 1959-62; President: Wales Area Conservative Teachers' Assoc., 1962-; Glamorgan (London) Soc., 1967-. FInstD 1958. *Recreations:* cricket, tennis, squash rackets, and travelling in Italy. *Address:* House of Commons, SW1; 1 Dorchester Avenue, Cardiff. *T:* Cardiff 44280. *Clubs:* Carlton, Royal Over-Seas League; St Mellons County (Mon); various (Cardiff).

**GOWER, John Hugh,** QC 1967; Deputy Chairman, Kent Quarter Sessions, since 1968; *b* 6 Nov. 1925; *s* of Henry John Gower, JP and Edith (*née* Brooks); *m* 1960, Shirley Mameena Darbourne; one *s* one *d*. *Educ:* Skinners' Sch., Tunbridge Wells. RASC, 1945-48 (Staff Sgt). Called to Bar, Inner Temple, 1948. SE Circuit, Central Criminal Court Bar Messes. Mem., Pembury (Kent) Parish Council, 1955-61; Pres., Kent Assoc. of Parish Councils, 1963-. Governor, Skinners' Sch., Tunbridge Wells, 1957-. Freeman, City of London (by purchase), 1960. *Recreations:* fishing, foxhunting, gardening. *Address:* The Coppice, Lye Green, Crowborough, Sussex. *T:* Crowborough 4395. *Clubs:* United and Cecil; Kent and Sussex (Tunbridge Wells).

**GOWER, Laurence Cecil Bartlett,** FBA 1965; Solicitor; Law Commissioner, since 1965; *b* 29 Dec. 1913; *s* of Henry Lawrence Gower; *m* 1939, Helen Margaret Shepperson, *d* of George Francis Birch; two *s* one *d*. *Educ:* Lindisfarne Coll.; University Coll., London. LLB 1933; LLM 1934. Admitted Solicitor, 1937. Served War of 1939-45, with RA and RAOC. Sir Ernest Cassel Prof. of Commercial Law in University of London, 1948-62, Visiting Prof., Law Sch. of Harvard Univ., 1954-55; Adviser on Legal Educn in Africa to Brit. Inst. of Internat. and Comparative Law and Adviser to Nigerian Council of Legal Educn, 1962-65; Prof. and Dean of Faculty of Law of Univ. of Lagos, 1962-65; Holmes Lectr, Harvard Univ., 1966. Fellow of University Coll., London; Comr on Company Law Amendment in Ghana, 1958; Member: Jenkins Cttee on Company Law Amendment; Denning Cttee on Legal Education for Students from Africa, 1960; Ormrod Cttee on Legal Education, 1967-. Trustee, British Museum, 1968-. Hon. LLD: York Univ., Ont; Edinburgh Univ. *Publications:* 15th edn Pollock's Law of Partnership; Principles of Modern Company Law, 1954, 3rd edn 1969; Independent Africa: The Challenge to the Legal Profession, 1967; numerous articles in legal periodicals. *Recreation:* travel. *Address:* Ladywell Lodge, East Heath Road, NW3. *T:* 01-435 8890. *Club:* Athenæum.

**GOWER, Raymond;** *see* Gower, Herbert R.

**GOWER-JONES, Ven. Geoffrey;** Archdeacon of Lancaster since 1966; Vicar of St Stephen-on-the-Cliffs, Blackpool, since 1960; *b* 30 April 1910; *s* of late Rev. William Gower-Jones; *m* 1938, Margaret, *d* of late John Alexander; one *s* one *d*. *Educ:* Brasenose Coll., Oxford; Wells Theological Coll. Ordained 1935; Curate: St Paul, Royton, 1934-39; Prestwich, 1939-43; Vicar, Belfield, 1943-50. Canon of Blackburn,

1962-66; Rural Dean of Fylde, 1962; Rural Dean of Blackpool, 1963-66. *Address:* St Stephen's Vicarage, Blackpool, Lancs. *T:* Blackpool 51484.

**GOWING, Rt. Rev. Eric Austin;** *see* Auckland, (NZ), Bishop of.

**GOWING, Lawrence Burnett,** CBE 1952; MA Dunelm 1952; painter and writer on painting; Professor of Fine Art, University of Leeds, since 1967; *b* 21 April 1918; *s* of late Horace Burnett and Louise Gowing; *m* Jennifer Akam Wallis; one *d. Educ:* Leighton Park Sch., and as a pupil of William Coldstream. Exhibitions: 1942, 1946, 1948, 1955, 1965; works in collections of Contemp. Art Soc., Tate Gallery, National Gallery of Canada, National Gallery of South Australia, British Council, Arts Council, Ashmolean Museum and galleries of Brighton, Bristol, Manchester, Middlesborough, Newcastle, Nottingham, etc. Prof. of Fine Art, Univ. of Durham, and Principal of King Edward VII Sch. of Art, Newcastle upon Tyne, 1948-58; Principal, Chelsea Sch. of Art, 1958-65; Keeper of the British Collection, and Dep. Dir of the Tate Gallery, 1965-67. Mem. Arts Council Art Panel, 1953-58, 1959-65, 1969-, Dep. Chm., 1970-; a Trustee of Tate Gallery, 1953-60 and 1961-64; a Trustee of National Portrait Gallery, 1960-; a Mem. of National Council for Diplomas in Art and Design, 1961-65; Chairman: Adv. Cttee on Painting, Gulbenkian Foundation, 1958-64; Art Films Cttee, 1970-. *Publications:* Renoir, 1947; Vermeer, 1952; Cézanne (catalogue of Edinburgh and London exhibns), 1954; Constable, 1960; Vermeer, 1961; Goya, 1965; Turner: Imagination and Reality, 1966; Matisse (Museum of Modern Art, New York), 1966, (London), 1968; many exhibition catalogues and writings in periodicals. *Address:* 50 Victoria Road, Leeds 6. *T:* 55316; 49 Walham Grove, SW6. *T:* 01-385 5941.

**GOWING, Dr Noel Frank Collett;** Consultant Pathologist and Director of the Department of Histopathology, The Royal Marsden Hospital, SW3, since 1957; Hon. Senior Lecturer, Institute of Cancer Research: The Royal Cancer Hospital; *b* 3 Jan. 1917; *s* of Edward Charles Gowing and Annie Elizabeth Gowing; *m* 1942, Rela Griffel; one *d. Educ:* Ardingly Coll., Sussex; London Univ. MRCS, LRCP 1941; MB, BS, London, 1947; MD London, 1948. Served RAMC (Capt.), 1942-46, 52nd (Lowland) Div. Lectr in Pathology, St George's Hosp. Med. Sch., 1947-52; Sen. Lectr in Pathology and Hon. Cons. Pathologist, St George's Hosp., 1952-57. Founder Fellow, Coll. of Pathologists, 1964. *Publications:* articles on pathology in medical journals. *Recreations:* gardening, astronomy. *Address:* 9 Top Park, Beckenham, Kent. *T:* 01-650 8556.

**GOWRIE,** 2nd Earl of, *cr* 1945; **Alexander Patric Greysteil Ruthven;** Baron Ruthven of Gowrie, 1919; Baron Gowrie, 1935; Viscount Ruthven of Canberra and Dirleton, 1945; *b* 26 Nov. 1939; *er s* of late Capt. Hon. Alexander Hardinge Patrick Hore-Ruthven, Rifle Bde, and Pamela Margaret (as Viscountess Ruthven of Canberra, she *m* 1952, Major Derek Cooper, MC, The Life Guards), 2nd *d* of late Rev. A. H. Fletcher; *S* grandfather, 1955; *m* 1962, Xandra, *yr d* of Col R. A. G. Bingley, *qv*; one *s. Educ:* Eton; Balliol Coll., Oxford. Visiting Lectr, State Univ. of New York at Buffalo, 1963-64; Tutor, Harvard Univ., 1965-68; Lecturer, University College, London, 1969-. *Recreation:* politics. *Heir: s* Viscount Ruthven of Canberra and Dirleton, *qv. Address:* Castlemartin, Kilcullen, Co. Kildare, Ireland. *T:* Curragh 81221; 34 King Street, Covent Garden, WC2. *T:* 01-240 2371.

**GOYDER, George Armin;** Chairman and Managing Director, British International Paper Ltd since 1935; Chairman, International Paper Co. Ltd, since 1969; *b* 22 June 1908; *s* of William Goyder and Lili Julia Kellersberger, Baden, Switzerland; *m* 1937, Rosemary, 4th *d* of Prof. R. C. Bosanquet, Rock, Northumberland; five *s* three *d. Educ:* Mill Hill Sch.; London Sch. of Economics; abroad. UK Rep., Internat. Paper Co., 1932. Gen. Man., Newsprint Supply Co., 1940-47 (responsible for supply and rationing of newsprint to British Press); The Geographical Magazine, 1935-58. Mem., Church Assembly, 1948; Chm., Liberal Party Standing Cttee on Industrial Partnership, 1966. Founder Trustee, William Blake Trust; Governor: Oversea Service Coll. (Chm. 1970); Mill Hill Sch., 1943-69; Monkton Combe Sch.; Trustee and Hon. Fellow, St Peter's Coll., Oxford; Mem. Council, Wycliffe Hall; Founder Mem., British-North American Cttee, 1969. *Publications:* The Future of Private Enterprise, 1951, 1954; The Responsible Company, 1961; The People's Church, 1966. *Recreations:* music, old books, theology. *Address:* 4-5 Grosvenor Place, SW1. *T:* 01-235 1672; Pindars, Rotherfield Greys, Henley-on-Thames, Oxon. *Club:* Reform.

**GRAAFF, Sir de Villiers,** 2nd Bt *cr* 1911; MBE 1946; BA Cape, MA, BCL Oxon; Barrister-at-Law, Inner Temple; Advocate of the Supreme Court of S Africa; MP for Hottentots Holland in Union Parliament 1948-58, for Rondebosch, Cape Town, since 1958; Leader of the United Party since 1956; *b* 8 Dec. 1913; *s* of 1st Bt and Eileen (*d* 1950), *d* of Rev. Dr J. P. Van Heerden, Cape Town; *S* father, 1931; *m* 1939, Helena Le Roux, *d* of F. C. M. Voigt, Provincial Sec. of Cape Province; two *s* one *d.* Served War of 1939-45 (prisoner, MBE). Hon. LLD, Rhodes. *Heir: s* David de Villiers Graaff, *b* 3 May 1940. *Address:* De Grendel, Tijgerberg, Cape, South Africa. *Club:* Civil Service (Cape Town).

**GRACE, Sir John (Te Herekiekie),** KBE 1968; MVO 1953; AEA (RNZAF) 1950; sheep and cattle station owner since 1958; *b* 28 July 1905; *s* of John Edward Grace, JP and Rangiamohia Herekiekie; *m* 1st, 1940, Marion Linton McGregor (*d* 1962); No *c*; 2nd, 1968, Dorothy Kirkcaldie. *Educ:* Wanganui Coll.; Te Aute Coll., Hawkes Bay. Served War of 1939-45, Royal NZ Air Force (Sqdn-Ldr). NZ Public Service, 1926-58: Private Sec. to Ministers of the Crown incl. three Prime Ministers, 1947-58; Member: NZ Historic Places Trust, 1952-68; NZ Geographic Bd, 1952-68; Maori Purposes Fund Bd, 1961-68; Maori Educn Foundn, 1962-68; Nature Conservation Coun., 1963-68; Nat. Coun. of Adult Educn, 1964-68; Vice-Pres. and Dominion Councillor, NZ Nat. Party, 1959-67. JP 1947. *Publication:* Tuwharetoa, a History of the Maori People of the Taupo District, NZ. *Recreations:* golf, trout fishing, gardening. *Address:* Te Waka Station, Parapara Road, RD3 Wanganui, New Zealand. *T:* Wanganui 49-133. *Clubs:* Wellesley (Wellington); Wanganui (Wanganui).

**GRACE, Dr Michael Anthony,** FRS 1967; Senior Research Officer, Department of Nuclear Physics, Oxford, since 1955; Student and Tutor in Physics, Christ Church, since 1959; *b* 13 May 1920; *er s* of Claude Saville Grace, Haslemere, Surrey, and late Evelyn Doris (*née* Adams); *m* 1948, Philippa Agnes Lois, *o d* of Sir (Vincent) Zachary Cope, *qv*; one *s* three *d. Educ:* St Paul's; Christ Church, Oxford. MA 1948; DPhil 1950. Mine Design Dept, HMS

Vernon, 1940-45. ICI Research Fellowship, Clarendon Laboratory, Oxford, 1951; University Sen. Res. Officer, 1955; Lectr in Physics, Christ Church, 1958, Censor, 1964-69. Governor: St Paul's Schools, 1959; Harrow School, 1969. *Publications:* papers in various jls including Phil. Mag., Proc. Royal Soc., Proc. Phys. Soc., Nuclear Physics. *Recreations:* lawn tennis, swimming. *Address:* 13 Blandford Avenue, Oxford, *T:* Oxford 58464. *Club:* Athenæum.

**GRACE, Sir Raymond Eustace,** 6th Bt *cr* 1795; Major Royal Inniskilling Fusiliers; *b* 6 Jan. 1903; *s* of Sir Valentine Raymond Grace, 5th Bt; *S* father, 1945. *Educ:* Downside Sch.; Trinity Coll., Dublin Univ. *Recreations:* golf, tennis. *Heir:* none. *Address.* 13 Leeson Park, Dublin, Eire.

**GRACIAS, His Eminence Cardinal;** *see* Bombay, Cardinal-Archbishop of.

**GRACIE, Alan James,** CMG 1957; *b* 23 March 1904; *s* of late David Smart Gracie and late Margaret MacArthur (*née* Campbell), Duddingston, Edinburgh; *m* 1933, Isobel, *d* of late James Dick Gracie, Lanark; two *s* one *d*. *Educ:* Royal High Sch., Edinburgh; Edinburgh Univ. Entered Malayan Civil Service, 1928; Asst Adviser, Trengganu, 1929-32; Sec. to Resident, Pahang, 1933-34; Asst Sec., Federal Secretariat, 1935-37; Asst Adviser, Segamat, Johore, 1937-39. Prisoner of War, Singapore, 1942-45. Malayan Establishment Officer, 1949-53; Federation Establishment Officer, 1954-57; retired, 1958. *Address:* 24 Regent Terrace, Edinburgh EH7 5BS. *T:* 031-556 7463.

**GRACIE, George H. H.;** *see* Heath-Gracie.

**GRACIE, Instructor Capt. Henry Stewart,** CB 1956; MA; FSA; RN retired; *b* 6 Aug. 1901; *s* of late Capt. G. S. Gracie, Leonard Stanley, Glos; *m* 1932, Dorothy Constance (*d* 1960), *d* of Rev. Edward Senior, Sheffield. *Educ:* Pocklington Sch.; St John's Coll., Cambridge (BA). Joined Rn as Instr Lt, 1923; Instr Comdr 1937; Instr Capt. 1949. Command Instructor Officer Portsmouth (actg Capt.), 1946-49; Fleet Instructor Officer, Mediterranean, 1949-52; Dir of Studies, RN Coll., Greenwich, 1953-56. Naval ADC to the Queen, 1955-56. Retired 1956. Hon. Editor, Trans Bristol and Glos Archæological Soc., 1956. *Publications:* papers in various archæological jls. *Recreations:* prehistoric archæology. *Address:* Thrupp House, Stroud, Glos GL5 2DD. *T:* Stroud 4572. *Club:* United Service.

**GRADE, Sir Lew,** Kt 1969; Chief Executive, Associated Television Corporation Ltd (Deputy Chairman); Deputy Chairman and Managing Director, ATV Network Ltd; Managing Director, Incorporated Television Company Ltd; *b* 25 Dec. 1906; *s* of late Isaac Winogradsky and of Olga Winogradsky; *m* 1942, Kathleen Sheila Moody; one *s*. *Educ:* Rochelle Street Sch. Joint Managing Dir of Lew and Leslie Grade Ltd, until Sept. 1955 when Dep. Managing Dir of Associated Television Ltd and Managing Dir of Incorporated Television Company Ltd. Director: Bermans (Holdings) Ltd; Bentray Investments Ltd; Associated Television Corp. (International) Ltd (Switzerland); Ambassador Bowling Ltd; Independent Television Corp. (USA); Planned Holdings Ltd; Pye Records Ltd; Century 21 Organisation Ltd. *Address:* ATV House, Great Cumberland Place, W1.

*See also Bernard Delfont.*

**GRADY, John William;** Executive Director, Samuel Montagu & Co. Ltd, since 1969; Director, Pearl Montagu Trust Managers Ltd, since 1970; Chairman, Optimation Services Ltd, since 1970; *b* London, 6 April 1915; *s* of late John William Grady and late Teresa (*née* Moore); *m* 1939, Edith Mary Green; one *s* one *d*. *Educ:* St Olave's Sch. Entered Post Office as Exec. Off., 1935; Higher Exec. Off., 1946; Sen. Exec. Off. in Organisation and Methods Br., 1950; Asst Accountant Gen., 1955; Financial Adviser, External Telecommunications, 1962; Dep. Dir of Finance, 1964; Dir of Giro and Remittance Services, PO, 1965-69. *Recreations:* music, walking. *Address:* 1 Richmond Terrace, Shernfold Park, Frant, Sussex. *T:* Frant 471.

**GRAEME, Bruce,** (Pseudonym of **Graham Montague Jeffries**); Novelist; *s* of late William Henry Jeffries; *m* 1925, Lorna Hélène, *d* of Capt. Hay T. Louch; one *s* one *d*. *Educ:* Privately. Finish of education interrupted by Great War; volunteered for Queen's Westminster Rifles; after demobilization became free-lance journalist; travelled several times to USA and France on various commissions, published short stories, 1921-25; interested in film work; financed, produced and sold one reel comedy, 1919-20; resumed this lifelong interest in films as script writer, and producer, 1942; entered Gray's Inn, 1930. *Publications:* The Story of Buckingham Palace, 1928; The Story of St James's Palace, 1929; A Century of Buckingham Palace, 1937; The Story of Windsor Castle, 1937; Blackshirt, 1925; The Trail of the White Knight, 1926; The Return of Blackshirt, 1927; Hate Ship, 1928; Trouble, 1929; Blackshirt Again, 1929; Through the Eyes of the Judge, 1930; The Penance of Brother Alaric, 1930; A Murder of Some Importance, 1931; Unsolved, 1931; Gigins Court, 1932; Alias Blackshirt, 1932; The Imperfect Crime, 1932; Impeached, 1933; Epilogue, 1933; An International Affair, 1934; Public Enemy No. 1, 1934; Satan's Mistress, 1935; Blackshirt the Audacious, 1936; Not Proven, 1935; Cardyce for the Defence, 1936; Blackshirt the Adventurer, 1936; Mystery on the Queen Mary, 1937; Blackshirt takes a Hand, 1937; Disappearance of Roger Tremayne, 1937; Racing Yacht Mystery, 1938; Blackshirt; Counter-Spy, 1938; The Man from Michigan, 1938; Body Unknown, 1939; Blackshirt Interferes, 1939; Poisoned Sleep, 1939; 13 in a Fog, 1940; Blackshirt Strikes Back, 1940; The Corporal Died in Bed, 1940; Seven Clues in Search of a Crime, 1941; Son of Blackshirt, 1941; Encore Allain, 1941; House with Crooked Walls, 1942; Lord Blackshirt, 1942; News Travels by Night, 1943; A Case for Solomon, 1943; Calling Lord Blackshirt, 1944; Work for the Hangman, 1944; Ten Trails to Tyburn, 1944; The Coming of Carew, 1945; A Case of Books, 1946; Without Malice, 1946; A Brief for O'Leary, 1947; No Clues for Dexter, 1948; And a Bottle of Rum, 1948; Tigers Have Claws, 1949; Cherchez la Femme; Dead Pigs at Hungry Farm, 1951; Lady in Black, 1952; Mr Whimset Buys a Gun, 1953; Suspense, 1953; The Way Out, 1954; So Sharp the Razor, 1955; Just an Ordinary Case, 1956; The Accidental Clue, 1957; The Long Night, 1958; Boomerang, 1959; Fog for a Killer, 1960; The Undetective, 1962; Almost Without Murder, 1963; Holiday for a Spy, 1964; Always Expect the Unexpected, 1965; The Devil was a Woman, 1966; Much Ado About Something, 1967; Never Mix Business With Pleasure, 1968; Some Geese Lay Golden Eggs, 1968; Blind Date for a Private Eye, 1969; The Quiet Ones, 1970; The Lady doth Protest, 1971. *Recreations:* travel, historical research. *Address:* Gorse Field Cottage, Aldington

Frith, nr Ashford, Kent. *T:* Aldington 383. *Club:* Paternosters.

**GRÆME, Maj.-Gen. Ian Rollo,** CB 1967; OBE 1955; Secretary, National Ski Federation of Great Britain, since 1967; *b* 23 May 1913; *s* of Col J. A. Græme, DSO, late RE; *m* 1941, Elizabeth Jean Dyas; two *d*. *Educ:* Boxgrove; Stowe; RMA Woolwich. King's Medal and Benson Memorial Prize, RMA, 1933. 2nd Lt RA 1933; pre-war service at regimental duty UK; War Service in Singapore, Java, India, Burma, Siam; psc 1942; Instructor Staff Coll., Quetta, 1944; CO 1st Burma Field Regt, 1945-46; OC, K Battery, RHA, 1949; jssc 1952; GSO1, HQ Northern Army Group, 1953-54; CO 27 Regt RA, 1955-57; Col GS Staff Coll., Camberley, 1957-59; idc 1960; Dep. Mil. Sec., WO, 1961-63; Dep. Dir Personnel Admin, WO, 1963-64; Dir Army Recruiting, 1964-67; Retd 1967. Mem. Royal Yachting Assoc., 1950-; Life Governor, Royal Life Saving Soc., 1956-; Life Mem., British Olympic Assoc., 1958-; Chm., Army Holiday Cttee for ski-ing, 1963-67; Council, Army Ski Assoc., 1958-; Mem. Council, Nat. Ski Fedn of GB, 1964-67 (Life Mem. Fedn). Mem. BIM, 1967. *Recreations:* ski-ing, sailing, mountains. *Clubs:* United Service, English-Speaking Union (Life Mem.); Ski Club of Great Britain, Army Ski Association, Alpbach Visitors Ski; Ranelagh Sailing, Royal Artillery Yacht.

**GRAFFTEY-SMITH, Sir Laurence Barton,** KCMG 1951 (CMG 1944); KBE 1947 (OBE 1932); *b* 16 April 1892; *s* of late Rev. Arthur Grafftey-Smith and late Mabel, *d* of Rev. Charles Barton, Cheselbourne, Dorset; *m* 1930, Vivien (marr. diss., 1937), *d* of G. Alexander Alderson; two *s*; *m* 1946, Evgenia Owen, *d* of late P. H. Coolidge, New York. *Educ:* Repton; Pembroke Coll., Cambridge. Student Interpreter, Levant Consular Service, 1914. HM Vice Consul, 1920; served at Alexandria, Cairo (Residency), Jeddah, Constantinople; Asst Oriental Sec. at the Residency, Cairo, 1925-35; HM Consul, Mosul, 1935-37; Baghdad, 1937-39; HM Consul-Gen. in Albania, 1939-40; attached British Embassy, Cairo, 1940; Chief Political Adviser, Diego Suarez, May 1942; Chief Political Officer, Madagascar, July 1942; Consul-Gen., Antananarivo, 1943; Minister to Saudi Arabia, 1945-47; High Comr for UK in Pakistan, 1947-51; retired from Govt service on 31 Dec. 1951; UK Rep. on Gov.-Gen.'s Commn, Khartoum, 1953-56. *Publications:* (with Godfrey Haggard) Visa Verses, 1915 (privately printed). *Address:* Broom Hill House, Coddenham, Suffolk. *Clubs:* Travellers', Royal Automobile.

**GRAFTON,** 10th Duke of *cr* 1675; **Captain Charles Alfred Euston FitzRoy;** Earl of Euston, Viscount Ipswich; JP West Suffolk; DL Suffolk; late Royal Welch Fusiliers; *b* 4 June 1892; *s* of late Rev. Lord Charles Edward FitzRoy, 4th *s* of 7th Duke, and late Hon. Ismay Mary Helen Augusta FitzRoy, *d* of 3rd Baron Southampton; *S* cousin, 1936; *m* 1st, 1918, Lady Doreen Maria Josepha Sydney Buxton (*d* 1923), *d* of 1st Earl Buxton; one *s* (and one killed in action, 1944) one *d*; 2nd, 1924, Lucy Eleanor (*d* 1943), *d* of late Sir George Stapylton Barnes, KCB, KCSI; one *s* (and one *s* decd); 3rd, 1944, Mrs Rita Currie (*d* 1970), *d* of late J. S. Carr-Ellison. *Educ:* Wellington Coll.; RMC Sandhurst. Joined RWF in Quetta, 1911; France, 1914; ADC and Comptroller to Lord Buxton, Governor Gen. South Africa, 1917-20; retired from Army, 1921; farmed at Coney Weston, Suffolk, 1921-27; Agent to Owen Hugh Smith, Langham, Oakham, Rutland, 1927-36. *Heir:* *s* Earl of Euston, *qv*. *Address:* Euston Hall, Thetford, Norfolk. *TA:* Euston Suffolk. *T:* Thetford 3282.

*See also Charles Robertson.*

**GRAFTON, NSW, Bishop of,** since 1961; **Rt. Rev. Robert Gordon Arthur;** *b* 17 Aug. 1909; *s* of George Thomas Arthur and Mary Arthur; *m* Marie Olive Cavell Wheen; two *s* two *d*. *Educ:* Launceston and Devonport High Schs, Tasmania; Queen's Coll., Univ. of Melbourne. MA (Hons) 1932. Rector of: Berridale, NSW, 1950-53; St John's, Canberra, aCT, 1953-60; Wagga Wagga, NSW, 1960-61; Archdeacon of Canberra, 1953-60; Asst Bp of Canberra and Goulburn, 1956-61. *Address:* Bishopsholme, Grafton, NSW, Australia. *T:* Grafton 70.

**GRAHAM,** family name of **Duke of Montrose.**

**GRAHAM, Marquis of; James Graham;** *b* 6 April 1935; *s* of 7th Duke of Montrose, *qv*; *m* 1970, Catherine Elizabeth MacDonell, *d* of late Captain N. A. T. Young, and of Mrs Young, Ottawa. *Educ:* Loretto. *Address:* Auchmar, Drymen, Glasgow. *T:* 221.

**GRAHAM, Captain Lord Alastair Mungo;** late Royal Navy; *b* 1886; *y s* of 5th Duke of Montrose; *m* 1st, 1916, Lady Meriel Olivia Bathurst (*d* 1936), *d* of 7th Earl Bathurst; two *s* two *d*; 2nd, 1944, Sheelah Violet Edgeworth, *d* of late Essex Edgeworth Reade and of Sheelah, Lady Ruggles-Brise. Served Dardanelles, 1915 and War of 1939-45. *Address:* Chantry Farm, Campsea Ashe, Woodbridge, Suffolk.

*See also I. J. A. Graham.*

**GRAHAM, Rev. Andrew Alexander Kenny;** Warden of Lincoln Theological College since 1970; *b* 7 Aug. 1929; *o s* of late Andrew Harrison and Magdalene Graham; unmarried. *Educ:* Tonbridge Sch.; St John's Coll., Oxford; Ely Theological College. Curate of Hove Parish Church, 1955-58; Chaplain and Lectr in Theology, Worcester Coll., Oxford, 1958-70; Fellow and Tutor, 1960-70. Examining Chaplain to Bishop of Carlisle, 1967-. *Recreation:* hill walking. *Address:* The Theological College, Lincoln. *T:* Lincoln 25879. *Club:* United University.

**GRAHAM, Angus,** MA, FSA; Member of Royal Commission on Ancient Monuments (Scotland) since 1960; *b* 1892; *yr s* of late R. C. Graham, Skipness, Argyll. *Educ:* Winchester Coll.; New Coll., Oxford. Served European War, 4th Highland LI, 1914-19. British Forestry Commission, 1920-22 (district officer); Price Bros and Co. Ltd, Quebec, 1922-25 (forester); Quebec Forest Industries Association, Ltd, 1925-33 (sec.-treasurer); Royal Commission on Ancient Monuments (Scotland), 1935-57 (sec.). *Publications:* Forests in the National Development, 1923; Quebec Limit-Holders' Manual, 1932; The Golden Grindstone, 1935; Napoleon Tremblay, 1939; papers in Proc. Society of Antiquaries of Scotland, Jl Royal Society Antiquaries of Ireland, Jl of Forestry. *Address:* 1 Nelson Street, Edinburgh EH3 6LF. *T:* 031-556 1534. *Club:* New (Edinburgh).

**GRAHAM, Admiral Sir Angus E. M. B. C.;** *see* Cunninghame Graham.

**GRAHAM, Billy;** *see* Graham, William F.

**GRAHAM, Maj.-Gen. Douglas Alexander Henry,** CB 1944; CBE 1942; DSO 1943; MC; *b* 26 March 1893. Capt. 1916; Major, 1930; Lt-Col 1937; Col 1940; Maj.-Gen. 1944. Served European War, 1914-18 (wounded, despatches, MC, French Croix de Guerre); Palestine, 1936-39; War of 1939-45 (despatches, CBE, DSO and Bar, CB; Legion of Merit, Comdr; French Legion of Honour, Officier; Croix de Guerre, Order of St Olaf). Retired pay, 1947. *Address:* 43 Airlie Street, Brechin, Angus. *T:* Brechin 2629. *Club:* Army and Navy.

**GRAHAM, Rev. Douglas Leslie,** MA (Dublin); Assistant Master and Chaplain, Williston Academy, since 1968; *b* 4 Oct. 1909; *s* of late Very Rev. G. F. Graham; *m* 1935, Gladys Winifred Ann, *y d* of J. W. Brittain, JP, Kilronan, Donnybrook, Co. Dublin; three *s*. *Educ:* Portora Royal Sch.; Dublin Univ. (BA); Munich Univ. Lectr in Classics, Dublin Univ., 1932-34; MA and Madden Prizeman, 1934; Asst Master, Eton Coll., 1934-41. Ordained, 1937. Served War as Temp. Chaplain, RNVR, 1941-45; HMS Trinidad, 1941; HMS King Alfred, 1942; HMS Daedalus, 1944; HMS Ferret, 1944; Headmaster, Portora Royal School, 1945-53; Headmaster, Dean Close Sch., 1954-68. Select Preacher to the Univs of Dublin, 1945, 1961 and 1965, and Oxford, 1956-57. FRSA. *Publications:* occasional articles on classical subjects. *Recreations:* books, birds and boxing. *Address:* Williston Academy, Easthampton, Mass 01027, USA; Treanoughtragh, Glenbeigh, Co. Kerry, Ireland. *Club:* University (Dublin).

**GRAHAM, Brig. Lord (Douglas) Malise,** CB 1936; DSO 1917; MC; RA; *b* 14 Oct 1883; 2nd *s* of 5th Duke of Montrose; *m* 1919, Hon. Rachael Mary Holland, *y d* of 2nd Viscount Knutsford; two *s*. *Educ:* Cheltenham; Woolwich. ADC to Gen. Sir Charles Fergusson, 1914; Brigade-Major, 1916; served European War, 1914-18 (despatches, MC, DSO); Asst Dir of Artillery, War Office, 1931-34; Comdt, Sch. of Artillery, Larkhill, 1934-36; retired, 1936; Military Attaché, Paris, 1940; reverted to retired pay, 1945. *Address:* Kingfisher Lodge, Brambridge, Eastleigh, Hants. *T:* Twyford 2136. *Club:* Cavalry.

**GRAHAM, Maj.-Gen. Frederick Clarence Campbell,** CB 1960; DSO 1945; DL; *b* Ardencaple Castle, Helensburgh, Scotland, 14 Dec. 1908; *s* of Sir Frederick Graham, 2nd Bt, and Lady Irene Graham (*née* Campbell); *m* 1936, Phyllis Mary, *d* of late Maj.-Gen. H. F. E. MacMahon, CB, CSI, CBE, MC; three *s*. *Educ:* Eton Coll.; RMC Sandhurst. Commissioned Argyll and Sutherland Highlanders, 1929; served 1st and 2nd Bn Argyll and Sutherland Highlanders in China, India, UK and Palestine, 1929-39; Adjutant 1st Bn, 1937; War of 1939-45, served Palestine, N Africa, Crete, Syria, India, Italy; commanded 1st Bn Argyll and Sutherland Highlanders, 1944-end of war in Europe. Since 1945: GSO1, Home Counties District and Home Counties Div.; Joint Services Staff Coll.; Staff Coll., Camberley (Col); Comdr 61 Lorried Infantry Brigade (Brigadier); Asst Commandant, RMA Sandhurst; Dep. Comdr, Land Forces, Hong Kong; Adviser in recruiting, MoD; Comdr Highland District and 51st (Highland) Div., TA, 1959-62; retd from HM Forces, 1962. Col, The Argyll and Sutherlanders, 1958-. Col Comdt, The Scottish Div., 1968-69. Mem. of Royal Company of Archers, The Queen's Body Guard for Scotland, 1958-. DL Perthshire, 1966. *Address:* Mackeanston House, Doune, Perthshire. *Clubs:* Caledonian, Army and Navy.

**GRAHAM, Sir (Frederick) Fergus,** 5th Bt *cr* 1783; KBE 1956; HM Lieutenant, Cumberland, 1958-68; formerly Captain Irish Guards; *b* 10 March 1893; *er s* of Sir Richard Graham, 4th Bt, and Lady Cynthia Duncombe (*d* 1926), 3rd *d* of 1st Earl of Feversham; *S* father, 1932; *m* 1918, Mary Spencer Revell, CBE, *o c* of late Maj.-Gen. Raymond Reade, CB, CMG; one *s*. *Educ:* Eton; Christ Church, Oxford. BA 1914; MA 1920; is Lieut-Col late 6th Bn Border Regt (TA); formerly Hon. Col 4th Battalion Border Regt TA; TD; JP for Cumberland; Patron of 2 Livings. Served European War, 1914-19 (wounded, despatches); MP (U) North Cumberland, 1926-35, (C) Darlington, 1951-Sept. 1959. *Heir: s* Major Charles Spencer Richard Graham, Scots Guards [*b* 16 July 1919; *m* 1944, Susan, *o d* of Major R. L. Surtees, Redworth Cottage, Littlestone-on-Sea, Kent; two *s* one *d*. Served War of 1939-45 (despatches)]. *Recreation:* shooting. *Address:* Netherby, Longtown, Cumberland. *T:* Longtown 206. *Club:* Farmers'.

**GRAHAM, George,** MD Cambridge, FRCP; Retired Consultant Physician St Bartholomew's Hospital; *b* 27 Feb. 1882; *s* of late William Edgar Graham and late Jane, *d* of Thomas Newton. *Educ:* St Paul's Sch.; Trinity Coll., Cambridge (Exhibitioner); Natural Science Tripos, Class I, 1903, Part II, Class II, 1904; Senior Entrance Scholarship, St Bartholomew's Hosp.; München; Otto Beit memorial Fellow, 1912-14; late Physician Royal Northern Hosp., and East London Hosp. for Children; late Mem. of North-East Regional Metropolitan Hospital Board, 1948-57; late chm. Hosp. Management Cttee (Central Group), 1949-59; Governor St Bartholomew's Hospital. Senior Censor, 1947-48, Goulstonian Lecturer, 1921, Croonian Lecturer, 1940 Harveian Orator, 1953, of Royal Coll. of Physicians. Lettsomian Lectures, Medical Soc. of London, 1938; Harben Lectr, Royal Inst. of Public Health and Hygiene, 1949. Master, Worshipful Company of Barbers, 1963-64. Temp. Capt., RAMC, 1916-19 (despatches). *Publications:* various contributions to scientific and medical publications. *Recreations:* golf and walking. *Address:* 49a Acacia Road, NW8. *T:* 01-722 8930. *Clubs:* Savile, Athenæum; Denham Golf (Denham); St Enodoc Golf (Wadebridge).

**GRAHAM, George Boughen,** QC 1964; *b* 17 July 1920; *s* of Sydney Boughen and Hannah Graham, Keswick, Cumberland; unmarried. *Educ:* Keswick Sch. Royal Signals, 1940-46. Barrister, Lincoln's Inn, 1950. Chancellor, Diocese of Wakefield, 1959. Common Councilman, City of London, 1960-66. Member of Lloyd's, 1968. Alderman, City of London (Ward of Queenhithe), 1966. Liveryman: Worshipful Co. of Merchant Taylors, 1954; Worshipful Co. of Painter Stainers (Mem. Court), 1967. *Publications:* Covenants, Settlements and Taxation, 1953; Estate Duty Handbook, 1954. *Recreations:* walking and dining. *Address:* 5 Paper Buildings, Temple, EC4. *T:* 01-353 4763; Brocklehurst, Keswick, Cumberland. *T:* Keswick 70042. *Clubs:* Athenæum, United Service.

**GRAHAM, Sir George (Goldie),** Kt 1952; OBE 1947; DL; JP; retired as Secretary of The Scottish Football Association (1928-57); Director (Scottish Board) Legal and General Assurance Society; *b* 10 Feb. 1892; *s* of William John Graham, contractor, Glasgow; *m* 1916, Mary France Watson, Glasgow; two *s*. *Educ:* Allan Glen's Sch., Glasgow. DL 1955, Glasgow. CStJ 1964. *Address:* Norden, Largs, Ayrshire. *T:* Largs 2767.

**GRAHAM, Gerald Sandford,** MA, PhD, FRHists; Rhodes Professor of Imperial History, London University, 1949-70; *b* Sudbury, Ontario, 27 April 1903; *s* of Rev. H. S. Graham and Florence Marian Chambers; *m* 1929, Winifred Emily Ware (marr. diss. 1950); one *s*; *m* 1950, Constance Mary Greey,

Toronto; one *s* two *d. Educ:* Queen's Univ., Canada. Queen's Univ. Travelling Fellowship to Harvard, 1926-27; Sir George Parkin Scholarship at Trinity Coll., Cambridge, 1927-29; Rockefeller Fellowship to Germany, 1929-30; Instructor in History, and Tutor, Harvard Univ., 1930-36; successively Asst Assoc. and Prof. of History, Queen's Univ., 1936-46; Guggenheim Fellowship to US, 1941; RCNVR, 1942-45; Historical Section, Canadian Army Overseas, 1945-46; Reader in History, Birkbeck Coll., Univ. of London, 1946-48. Mem., Inst. for Advanced Study, Princeton, 1952. *Publications:* British Policy and Canada, 1774-1791, 1930; Sea Power and British North America, 1783-1820, 1941; Contributor to Newfoundland, Economic, Diplomatic and Strategic Studies, 1946; Empire of the North Atlantic, 1950 (2nd edn 1958); Canada, A Short History, 1950; The Walker Expedition to Quebec, 1711 (Navy Records Soc., and Champlain Soc.), 1953; The Politics of Naval Supremacy, 1965; contributor to Cambridge History of the British Empire, Vol. III, 1959; (with R. A. Humphreys) The Navy and South America, 1807-1823 (Navy Records Soc.), 1962; Britain in the Indian Ocean, 1810-1850, 1967; A Concise History of Canada, 1968; A Concise History of the British Empire, 1970; Canadian Historical Review, Mariner's Mirror, Economic History Review, Times Literary Supplement. *Address:* Hobbs Cottage, Beckley, Rye, Sussex. *Clubs:* Athenæum, Royal Commonwealth Society.

**GRAHAM, (Godfrey) Michael,** CMG 1954; OBE 1946; Director of Fishery Research, 1948-58; Lecturer in Biology Department, University of Salford, since 1966; *b* 22 Feb. 1898; *s* of J. W. Graham, Principal of Dalton Hall, Manchester; *m* 1925, Edith Mary, *d* of Prof. Alex. Meek Durham; two *s* one *d. Educ:* Bootham, York; King's Coll., Cambridge. Served European War: Telegraphist, RNVR, 1917; Sub-Lt, 1918; Naturalist, Fisheries Dept, from 1920; served War, 1942-45 (despatches), Hon. Wing Comdr (Op. Res.), RAFVR. *Publications:* The Victoria Nyanza and its Fisheries, 1929; Soil and Sense, 1941; The Fish Gate, 1943; Rational Fishing of the North Sea Cod, 1948; Human Needs, 1951, illustr. 1955; Sea Fisheries, 1956; articles on crowds in Human Relations, 1964. *Recreation:* farming. *Address:* Rivington, near Bolton, Lancs.

**GRAHAM, Air Vice-Marshal Henry Rudolph,** CB 1958; CBE 1955; DSO 1941; DFC 1942; *b* 28 March 1910; *s* of Major Campbell Frederick Graham, late Cape Mounted Rifles and South African Mounted Rifles, and Frances Elizabeth Cheeseman; *m* 1949, Maisie Frances Butler; two *s. Educ:* Rondebosch; SA Trng Ship General Botha, S Africa. Union Castle Line, 1926-31; RAF, 1931-62. National Trust, 1966-69. Hon. Treas., Council of Social Service, Reading; Pres., St John Ambulance Bde, Reading; Gov., Feathers Clubs Assoc. Military Cross (Czechoslovakia), 1940. *Recreations:* cricket, golf, Rugby football. *Address:* The Cedar, 60a Bath Road, Reading, Berks. *Club:* Royal Air Force.

**GRAHAM, Lieut-Col H(oward) Boyd,** DSO 1918; MC; MD; FRACP; AAMC (Retired); RAMC (Retired); *b* 30 Aug. 1891; *s* of late John Duncan Graham and late Jeanne Austin; *m* 1925, Adele Norman Metzner; one *s. Educ:* Scotch Coll., Melbourne; Melbourne Univ. RAMC on active service with 64th Field Ambulance, BEF, 1915-19; Cons. Physician, Royal Children's Hosp. Hon. Life Member: Australian Pædiatric Assoc.; Pædiatric Soc. of Victoria; Eltham Community Youth Club. Private Med. Practitioner. MO, Judge Book Memorial Village, Eltham; Pres., BMA (Victoria Br.), 1941-42; Pres., Book Collectors of Australia Vic. Br. *Publications:* technical contributions to medical journals, and Australian historical items. *Address:* Yarramalong, Luck Street, Eltham, Vic., Australia. *T:* 439-9321. *Club:* Melbourne (Melbourne).

**GRAHAM, Lt-Gen. Howard Douglas,** SM 1967; CBE 1946; DSO 1943 and Bar 1944; ED; CD; QC (Canada); retired as Lieut-Gen. Canadian Army; *b* 1898. Served War of 1914-18: Canadian Infantry in France, Germany and Belgium; served War of 1939-45 (DSO and Bar, CBE), UK, Sicily and Italy; Senior Canadian Army Liaison Officer, London, and Army Adviser to the Canadian High Commissioner in London, 1946-48; Vice-Chief of Canadian General Staff, 1948-50; Gen. Officer Commanding Central Command, Canada, 1951-55; Chief of Canadian Gen. Staff, 1955-58; undertook, on behalf of Canadian Govt, during 1958, a comprehensive survey of all aspects of Canada's civil def. policy and programme. Acted as Canadian Sec. to the Queen, 1959 and 1967. Pres. (retd), Toronto Stock Exchange. Officer, US Legion of Merit; Chevalier Legion of Honour (France); Croix de Guerre with palm (France). *Address:* 33 Colonial Crescent, Oakville, Ont., Canada.

**GRAHAM, Hugh,** DSc; 2nd *s* of late John Graham, Belfast, N Ireland; *m* 1933, Patricia Millar. *Educ:* Queen's Univ., Belfast (Research Scholar of HM Commissioners of the Exhibition of 1851); Durham Univ. Sometime Lecturer in Chemistry, University of London (King's Coll.); and Reader in Organic Chemistry, Queen's Univ., Belfast. Formerly Chief Alkali Inspector for Northern Ireland. Mem. of Soc. of Chemical Industry; ARIC. *Publications:* (with A. W. Stewart) Recent Advances in Organic Chemistry (7th edn), 1948-49; numerous publications in scientific jls. *Address:* Fairway Cottage, Castlerock, Co. Derry, N Ireland.

**GRAHAM, Ian James Alastair;** Research Fellow, Peabody Museum of Archaeology, Harvard University; *b* 12 Nov. 1923; *s* of Captain Lord Alastair Graham, *qv*; unmarried. *Educ:* Winchester Coll.; Trinity Coll., Dublin. RNVR (A), 1942-47; TCD 1947-51; Nuffield Foundn Research Scholar at The National Gallery, 1951-54; independent archaeological explorer in Central America from 1959. Occasional photographer of architecture. *Publications:* Splendours of the East; Great Houses of the Western World; Archaeological Explorations in El Peten, Guatemala, 1967; other reports in learned jls. *Address:* Chantry Farm, Campsey Ash, Suffolk. *T:* Wickham Market 217; c/o Peabody Museum, Harvard University, Cambridge, Mass, USA.

**GRAHAM, John;** Fisheries Secretary, Ministry of Agriculture, Fisheries and Food, since 1967; *b* 17 March 1918; *s* of late John Graham; *m* 1940, Betty Ramage Jarvie; two *s* three *d. Educ:* Fettes Coll., Edinburgh; Trinity Coll., Cambridge (Schol.). Classical Tripos, MA Cantab. Entered Post Office as Asst Principal, 1939; Min. of Food, 1940. *Address:* 24 Vanbrugh Hill, SE3. *T:* 01-858 1665. *Club:* United University.

**GRAHAM, John Alexander Noble;** Principal Private Secretary to the Foreign and Commonwealth Secretary; *b* 15 July 1926; *s* and *heir* of Sir John Reginald Noble Graham, Bt, *qv*; *m* 1956, Marygold Ellinor Gabrielle Austin; two *s* one *d. Educ:* Eton Coll.; Trinity Coll., Cambridge. Army, 1944-47; Cambridge,

1948-50; HM Foreign (now Diplomatic) Service, 1950-. *Address:* c/o Foreign and Commonwealth Office, SW1; Caerlaverock House, Glencaple, Dumfries. *Club:* Army and Navy.

**GRAHAM, Prof. John Macdonald,** CBE 1955; JP; Professor of Systematic Theology, University of Aberdeen, since 1937; *b* 17 March 1908; *s* of Thomas Graham and Elizabeth Macdonald; *m* 1933, Jessie Huntley Carmichael; two *s* twin *d. Educ:* Allan Glen's Sch., Glasgow; University of Glasgow. MA. First Cl. Hons in Mental Philosophy, 1930; Ferguson Scholar in Philosophy, 1931. Minister of Radnor Park, Clydebank, 1933-37. Mem. of Aberdeen Town Council, 1947-64; Lord Provost of the City of Aberdeen, 1952-55 and 1961-64; DL 1956; Hon. DD Glasgow, 1959; Hon. LLD Aberdeen, 1964. FEIS 1964. *Publication:* Christianity, Democracy and Communism, 1958. *Address:* 3 The Chanonry, Aberdeen. *T:* 44347; Ruchil House, Comrie, Perthshire. *T:* Comrie 307.

**GRAHAM, Sir John (Moodie),** 2nd Bt *cr* 1964; Director: John Graham (Dromore) Ltd, since 1966 (Chairman); Electrical Supplies Ltd, since 1967; Concrete (NI) Ltd, since 1967; Irish Terrazzo Ltd; Kwik-Mix Ltd; Ulster Quarries Ltd; *b* 3 April 1938; *s* of Sir Clarence Graham, 1st Bt, MICE, and Margaret Christina Moodie (*d* 1954); *S* father, 1966; *m* 1970, Valerie Rosemary, *d* of Frank Gill, Belfast. *Educ:* Trinity Coll., Glenalmond; Queen's Univ., Belfast. BSc, Civil Engineering, 1961. Joined family firm of John Graham (Dromore) Ltd, Building and Civil Engineering Contractors, on graduating from University. Pres., Northern Ireland Leukaemia Research Fund, 1967; Iveagh Unionist Assoc., 1968. Patron, N Ireland Foreign Bird and Zebra Finch Assoc., 1967. *Recreations:* sailing, squash, water ski-ing, photography. *Address:* Lisroyan, 154 Malone Road, Belfast BT9 5LJ. *T:* Belfast 666037. *Clubs:* Royal County Down Golf (Newcastle, Co. Down); Malone Golf (Belfast); Kongelig Dansk Yachtclub (Copenhagen).

**GRAHAM, Hon. Sir (John) Patrick,** Kt 1969; **Hon. Mr Justice Graham;** Judge of the High Court of Justice, Chancery Division, since 1969; *b* 26 Nov. 1906; *s* of Alexander Graham and Mary Adeline Cock; *m* 1931, Annie Elizabeth Newport Willson; four *s. Educ:* Shrewsbury; Caius Coll., Cambridge. Called to Bar, Middle Temple, 1930; read with Sir Lionel Heald, QC, MP; QC 1953. Served War of 1939-45: RAF (VR), demobilised, 1945, with rank of Group Capt. Director, Shrewsbury Club Co. Ltd. Dep.-Chm., Salop Quarter Sessions, 1961-69. *Publication:* Awards to Inventors, 1946. *Recreations:* golf, tennis, sailing. *Address:* Tall Elms, Radlett, Herts. *T:* Radlett 6307.

**GRAHAM, Sir (John) Reginald (Noble),** 3rd Bt *cr* 1906; VC 1917; OBE 1946; Major, Argyll and Sutherland Highlanders, TF and MGC; *b* 17 Sept. 1892; *e s* of Sir J. F. N. Graham, 2nd Bt; *S* father, 1936; *m* 1920, Rachel Septima, *d* of Col Sir Alexander Sprot, 1st and last Bt; one *s* one *d. Educ:* Cheam; Eton; Cambridge. Served European War (Mesopotamia and Palestine), 1914-18 (VC); Emergency Commission Sept. 1939 (Staff Capt.); Served on Staff at War Office, Essex Div. and Scottish Comd, temp. Lt-Col 1942-46 (OBE). Gentleman Usher of the Green Rod to the Most Noble Order of the Thistle, 1959-. *Heir: s* John Alexander Noble Graham, *qv. Address:* The Mailens, Gullane, East Lothian. *Club:* New (Edinburgh).

**GRAHAM, Kathleen Mary,** CBE 1958 (MBE 1945); Executive Director of the English-Speaking Union, since 1970; *d* of late Col R. B. Graham, CBE, and of Mrs M. G. Graham, London; unmarried. *Educ:* Cheltenham Ladies' Coll.; Univ. of London (Courtauld Inst. of Art). Courtauld Inst., Dept of Technology War-time Laboratory, 1940-41; Political Warfare Executive, 1942-45; entered HM Foreign Service, 1945; served in FO, 1946-49; Consul (Information) at San Francisco, Calif, 1949-53; served in FO, 1953-55; made Counsellor in HM Foreign Service in 1955 and appointed Dep. Consul-Gen. in New York, 1955-59; HM Consul-Gen. at Amsterdam, 1960-63; in FO, 1964-69, retired. *Recreations:* music, history of art. *Address:* 20a Montpelier Street, SW7. *T:* 01-584 5998.

**GRAHAM, Lord Malise;** *see* Graham, Brig. Lord Douglas Malise.

**GRAHAM, Martha;** dancer; choreographer; director and teacher of dancing at the Martha Graham School of Contemporary Dance in New York; *b* Pittsburgh, Pa; *d* of Dr and Mrs George Graham. *Educ:* privately, and with Ruth St Denis and Ted Shawn. First appeared in Xochitl, New York, 1920; first recital by pupils, 1926; danced lead in Stravinsky's La Sacre du Printemps, 1930; founded Dance Repertory Theatre, 1930; choreographer of 144 solo and ensemble productions inc. three films (A Dancer's World, 1957; Appalachian Spring, 1958; Night Journey, 1960). Foreign tours, 1954, 1955-56, 1958, 1962, 1963, 1967; performed and lectured in major cities of Europe, Middle East, Iron Curtain countries, and throughout the Orient; has given solo performances with leading orchestras of United States. Three by Martha Graham, TV, 1969. Teacher: Neighbourhood Sch. of Music; Juilliard Sch. of Music. In the last five years her sch. has taken students from over forty foreign countries. Guggenheim Fellow, 1932, 1939; holds many doctorates and awards, including the Capezio Award, 1959, and the Aspen Award in the Humanities, 1965. *Relevant publication:* Martha Graham: Portrait of a Lady as an Artist, by LeRoy Leatherman, 1966. *Address:* Martha Graham School of Contemporary Dance, 316 East 63rd Street, New York, NY 10021, USA. *Club:* Cosmopolitan (New York).

**GRAHAM, Michael;** *see* Graham, Godfrey Michael.

**GRAHAM, Maj.-Gen. Sir Miles (William Arthur Peel),** KBE 1945 (CBE 1943; OBE 1942); CB 1944; MC; Hon. President: GRA Trust Ltd and subsidiaries; GRA and White City (Manchester) Associated and subsidiaries; Chairman: A. C. Cossor Ltd, 1947-68; Totalisators Ltd and subsidiaries; Deputy Chairman, Franco Signs Ltd and subsidiaries; Director, Times Publishing Co., 1946-62; *b* 11 Aug. 1895; *s* of late Major Henry Graham and late Ellen, CBE (*née* Peel; she *m* 2nd, 1908, the first and last Baron Askwith); *m* 1st, 1918, Lady Evelyn King, *e d* of 3rd Earl of Lovelace; (one *s* killed in action, 1944) one *d*; 2nd, 1943, Irene Lavender, *widow* of Lieut-Col William Seely and *d* of Richard Francklin. *Educ:* Eton (scholar); Trinity Coll., Cambridge. Joined 2nd Life Guards, 1914; served European War, 1914-18 (twice wounded, despatches twice, MC); Capt. and Adjutant, 1916; rejoined Life Guards from Reserve, Sept. 1939, as Capt.; Maj.-Gen. 1944; served War of 1939-45, Chief Administrative Officer to FM The Viscount Montgomery, 1942-46 (OBE, CBE, CB, KBE, despatches, Comdr of Legion of Merit, US, Officier Légion d'Honneur, Croix de Guerre avec Palmes, Knight Grand Officer of Orange-

Nassau). CC Notts. Has travelled extensively. *Recreations:* shooting and fishing. *Address:* Wiverton Hall, Bingham, Notts. *T:* Bingham 2372; 3 West Eaton Place, SW1. *T:* 01-235 3646. *Club:* Turf.

**GRAHAM, Sir Montrose Stuart,** 12th Bt *cr* 1629; *b* 4 Aug. 1904; *s* of Sir Montrose Stuart Graham, 11th Bt and Helen Ursula, *d* of John Henderson, Lerwick; *S* father, 1939; *m* 1932, Elizabeth Ann, *d* of John Gerken; two *d*. *Heir: cousin* Ralph Wolfe Graham [*b* 14 July 1908; *m* 1949, Geraldine, *d* of Austin Velour, Brooklyn, New York; two *s*]. *Address:* 45 Aster Avenue, North Merrick, Long Island, New York 11566, USA.

**GRAHAM, Norman William,** CB 1961; Secretary, Scottish Education Department, since 1964; *b* 11 Oct. 1913; *s* of William and Margaret Graham; *m* 1949, Catherine Mary Strathie; two *s* one *d*. *Educ:* High Sch. of Glasgow; Glasgow Univ. Dept of Health for Scotland, 1936; Private Sec. to Permanent Under-Sec. of State, 1939-40; Ministry of Aircraft Production, 1940; Principal Private Sec. to Minister, 1944-45; Asst Sec., Dept of Health for Scotland, 1945; Under-Sec., Scottish Home and Health Dept, 1956-63. *Recreations:* golf, gardening. *Address:* Suilven, Longniddry, East Lothian. *T:* Longniddry 2130. *Club:* New (Edinburgh).

**GRAHAM, Hon. Sir Patrick;** *see* Graham, Hon. Sir J. P.

**GRAHAM, Sir Reginald;** *see* Graham, Sir J. R. N.

**GRAHAM, Sir Richard Bellingham,** 10th Bt of Norton Conyers, *cr* 1662; OBE 1946; DL, JP; Wing Commander, RAFVR; Chairman, Yorkshire Television, since 1968; *b* 17 May 1912; *e s* of Sir Guy Graham, 9th Bt, and Katharine Noel (*d* 1966), *d* of Frank Stobart, Selaby, Darlington; *S* father, 1940; *m* 1939, Beatrice Mary, *o d* of late Michael Seymour Spencer-Smith, DSO; three *s*. *Educ:* Eton Coll.; Magdalene Coll., Cambridge. JP 1952, DL 1961, N Riding of Yorks; High Sheriff of Yorkshire, 1961. *Heir: s* James Bellingham Graham, *b* 8 Oct. 1940. *Address:* Norton Conyers, Melmerby, Ripon, Yorks.

**GRAHAM, Colonel Robert M.;** *see* Mould-Graham.

**GRAHAM, Samuel Horatio,** CMG 1965; OBE 1962; Puisne Judge, British Honduras, since 1966; *b* 3 May 1912; *o s* of late Rev. Benjamin Graham, Trinidad; *m* 1943, Oris Gloria (*née* Teka); two *s* four *d*. *Educ:* Barbados; External Student, London Univ. BA (London) 1945; LLB (London) 1949. Teacher and journalist until called to Bar, Gray's Inn, 1949. Private practice as Barrister in Grenada, 1949-53; Magistrate, St Lucia, 1953-57; Crown Attorney, St Kitts, 1957-59; Attorney-General, St Kitts, 1960-62; Administrator of St Vincent, 1962-66. Chairman Inquiries into: Income Tax Reliefs; Coconut Industry, St Lucia, 1955; Legislators' Salaries, St Kitts, 1962. Acted Administrator of St Lucia, St Kitts and Dominica on various occasions. Acted Chief Justice, British HOnduras, Feb.-May 1968. CStJ 1964. *Recreations:* cricket, bridge, swimming. *Address:* Courts of Justice, Belize, British Honduras, Central America. *Clubs:* West Indian, St John's House; St Vincent Aquatic.

**GRAHAM, Stanley Galbraith,** MD, LLD (Hon.), FRCPGlas, FRCPE; retired; *b* 2 Oct. 1895; *s* of Dr Peter Graham and Mary Reid; *m* 1925, Grace Anderson; two *s*. *Educ:* Toronto, Vienna, Glasgow. MB 1916, MD (Hons) 1924, Toronto. Served European War, 1914-18, Mesopotamia (RAMC). Fellow in Pathological Chemistry, 1919-20, University of Toronto; Assistant to Professor of Medical Paediatrics, University of Glasgow, 1924-30; Leonard Gow Lecturer, University of Glasgow, 1930-47; Professor of Child Health, University of Glasgow, 1947-61. Hon. Member American Acad. of Pediatrics and of Canadian Paediatric Society; Member: Association of Physicians of Great Britain and Ireland; British Paediatric Association (Pres. 1954-55). President Royal Faculty of Physicians and Surgeons, Glasgow, 1954-56. Hon. LLD, Toronto, 1955. *Publications:* (co-author) Acidosis and Alkalosis; Notes on Infant Feeding; numerous papers in medical journals. *Address:* Westerton, Callander, Perthshire. *T:* Callander 6. *Club:* Royal Scottish Automobile.

**GRAHAM, Stephen;** author; *b* 1884; *s* of P. Anderson Graham; *m* 1909, Rosa Savory (*d* 1956); *m* 1956, Vera Mitrinovic. Attracted to Russia by the spirit in Russian literature, gave up life in London and took his chances with Russian peasants and students, with whom he lived in Little Russia and Moscow; has tramped in the Caucasus and the Crimea, in the Ural Mountains, in the Far North of Russia, has accompanied the Russian peasant pilgrims to Jerusalem, and has also followed up the tide of emigration to America, tramping to the farms of the West; travelled in Central Asia, 1914, Egypt, Bulgaria, and Roumania, 1915, Northern Norway and Murmansk, 1916; served European War in 2nd Bt Scots Guards as private, 1917-18; walked across Georgia, 1919; tramping with Vachel Lindsay In Far West, 1921; Tour in Mexico with friend Wilfrid Ewart, in which the latter was accidentally shot on Old Year's Night, 1922-23; explored Soviet frontier from Lake Ladoga to the Black Sea, 1924; Dalmatia and the Balkans, 1925; Carpathian Russia, 1926; Bosnia, 1929-30; Macedonia, 1935; Swaziland and Transvaal, 1936; FRSL 1950; BBC Foreign Service, 1941-65; Tour of Southern States of America, 1967-68; Councillor of The Poetry Society, 1949; contributed series of signed articles to The Times, 1914-15, 1916, 1924, 1926; Order of St Sava, Jugoslavia, 1936. *Publications:* A Vagabond in the Caucasus; Undiscovered Russia; A Tramp's Sketches; Changing Russia; With the Russian Pilgrims to Jerusalem, 1913; With Poor Emigrants to America, 1914; Russia and the World, 1915; The Way of Martha and the Way of Mary, 1915; Through Russian Central Asia, 1916; Russia in 1916, 1917; Priest of the Ideal, 1917; Quest of the Face, 1918; Private in the Guards, 1919; Children of the Slaves, 1920; The Challenge of the Dead, 1921; Europe–whither bound?, 1921; Tramping with a Poet in the Rockies, 1922; Under-London, 1923; In Quest of El Dorado, 1924; Life and Last Words of Wilfrid Ewart, 1924; Russia in Division, 1925; London Nights, 1925; Midsummer Music, 1926; Gentle Art of Tramping, 1927; New York Nights, 1928; The Lay Confessor, 1928; (editor) The Tramp's Anthology, 1928; Life of Peter the Great, 1929; The Death of Yesterday, 1930; St Vitus' Day, 1930; A Modern Vanity Fair, 1931; (editor) Great Russian Short Stories, 1929; Great American Short Stories, 1931; Stalin: an Imperial Study, 1931; Life of Ivan the Terrible, 1932; One of the Ten Thousand, 1933; Twice Round the London Clock, 1933; Boris Godunof, 1933; The Padre of St Jacobs, 1934; Lost Battle, 1934; Balkan Monastery, 1935; A Life of Alexander II, Tsar of Russia, 1935; African Tragedy, 1937; Alexander of Yugoslavia, 1938; The Moving Tent, 1939; From War to War, 1940; Thinking of Living,

1949; Summing-Up on Russia, 1951; 100 Best Poems in the Language, 1953; Pay as You Run, 1955; Part of the Wonderful Scene–an Autobiography, 1964. *Address:* 60 Frith Street, Soho, W1. *T:* 01-437 3771.

**GRAHAM, Walter Gerald Cloete,** CBE 1952; Research Adviser in Joint Foreign Office/Commonwealth Office Research Department, since 1967; *b* 13 May 1906; *s* of late Lance Graham Cloete Graham, of HBM Consular Service in China; *m* 1937, Nellor Alice Lee Swan; one *s*; *m* 1949, Cynthia Anne, *d* of late Sir George Clayton East, Bt; one *s* one *d*. *Educ:* Malvern Coll.; The Queen's Coll., Oxford. Laming Travelling Fellow of Queen's, 1927-29. Entered Consular Service in China, 1928; served in Peking, Nanking, Shanghai, Mukden Chefoo and Tientsin; Consul: Port Said, 1942-44, Chengtu, 1944-45, Urumchi (Chinese Turkestan), 1945-47; Consul-General, Mukden, 1947-49, Peking, 1949-50; Counsellor, Foreign Office, 1951-52; Minister to Republic of Korea, 1952-54; Ambassador to Libya, 1955-59; Asia Adviser to Defence Intelligence Staff (formerly Jt Intell. Bureau), Min. of Defence, 1959-67. *Recreations:* cricket, golf, gardening. *Address:* Milland, Herstmonceux, Sussex. *T:* Herstmonceux 2156. *Club:* MCC.

**GRAHAM, William,** CB 1950; MBE 1920; Acting Secretary-General of the Intergovernmental Maritime Consultative Organisation (IMCO), 1961-63, Deputy Secretary-General, 1959-61; *b* 14 Dec. 1894; *s* of late A. Graham, Bradford, Yorks; *m* 1917, Elizabeth Young Warnock; one *s* one *d*. *Educ:* Bradford. Entered CS, 1911; served in Board of Trade until formation of Ministry of Shipping, 1939; Asst Secretary, Commercial Services Division, Ministry of Transport, 1940-46; Head of British Merchant Shipping Mission in Washington, DC, 1946; Under-Secretary, Ministry of Transport, 1946-59; Vice-Chairman, Maritime Transport Cttee, OEEC, 1948-59. *Address:* 115 Downs Court Road, Purley, Surrey. *T:* 01-660 1263.

**GRAHAM, William Franklin, (Billy Graham);** Evangelist; *b* Charlotte, NC, 7 Nov. 1918; *s* of William Franklin Graham and Morrow (*née* Coffey); *m* 1943, Ruth McCue Bell; two *s* three *d*. *Educ:* Florida Bible Institute, Tampa (ThB); Wheaton Coll., Ill (AB). Ordained to Baptist ministry, 1940; first Vice-Pres., Youth for Christ Internat., 1946-; Pres., Northwestern Coll., Minneapolis, 1947-52; Evangelistic campaigns, 1946-; world-wide weekly broadcast, 1950-; many evangelistic tours of Great Britain, Europe, the Far East, South America and Australia. Chairman, Board of World Wide Pictures Inc. Editor-in-Chief, Decision Magazine. FRGS. Holds numerous honorary degrees in Divinity, Laws, Literature and the Humanities, from American universities and colleges; also varied awards from organisations, 1954-. *Publications:* Calling Youth to Christ, 1947; Revival in Our Time, 1950; Hour of Decision, 1952; I Saw Your Sons at War, 1953; Peace with God, 1954; Secret of Happiness, 1955; My Answer, 1961; World Aflame, 1965. *Recreation:* golf. *Address:* (office) 1300 Harmon Place, Minneapolis, Minnesota 54403, USA. *T:* 332-8081.

**GRAHAM, Col William James,** MC 1917; Vice-Lieutenant of Kincardineshire, 1959-64; *b* 14 March 1890; *e s* of D. W. Graham, Hilston Park, Monmouth, and late Emmilene, *d* of late Major Carnegy, Royal Scots Fusiliers; *m* 1st, 1915, Yvette (marr. diss., 1930), *d* of late Baron Jules d'Anethan, Brussels; one *s*; 2nd, 1933, Alexandra Mary, 3rd *d* of late James Finlayson, Johnstone, Renfrewshire. *Educ:* Cheltenham Coll.; Pembroke Coll., Cambridge. 2nd Lt, 3rd (SR) Bn Gordon Highlanders, 1910-12; 2nd Lt Gordon Highlanders, 1912; served in European War, 1914-18, France and Belgium (wounded, despatches); commanded 3rd King's African Rifles, Kenya, 1929-33; Lieut-Colonel, 1938; served War of 1939-45, Malaya; Colonel, 1941; retired, 1946. Colonel The Gordon Highlanders, 1948-58. Member of Royal Company of Archers, Queen's Body Guard for Scotland, 1940. DL Kincardineshire, 1953. Chevalier, Order of the Crown of Belgium. *Address:* Hill House, Donhead St Andrew, Shaftesbury, Dorset. *T:* Donhead 388. *Clubs:* Army and Navy, MCC.

**GRAHAM, Winston Mawdsley,** FRSL; *b* Victoria Park, Manchester; *m* 1939, Jean Mary Williamson; one *s* one *d*. *Publications:* some early novels (designedly) out of print, and: Night Journey, 1941; The Forgotten Story, 1945; Ross Poldark, 1945; Demelza, 1946; Take My Life, 1947; Cordelia, 1949; Night Without Stars, 1950; Jeremy Poldark, 1950; Fortune is a Woman, 1953; Warleggan, 1953; The Little Walls, 1955; The Sleeping Partner, 1956; Greek Fire, 1957; The Tumbled House, 1959; Marnie, 1961; The Grove of Eagles, 1963; After the Act, 1965; The Walking Stick, 1967; Angell, Pearl and Little God, 1970; The Japanese Girl, 1971. *Recreations:* golf, gardening, swimming. *Address:* Abbotswood House, Buxted, Sussex. *T:* Buxted 3233. *Club:* Savile.

**GRAHAM BRYCE, Dame Isabel,** DBE 1968; Chairman: Oxford Regional Hospital Board, since 1963; National Nursing Staff Committee, since 1967; National Staff Committee, since 1969; Member, Maternity and Midwifery Standing Committee, since 1957; Member Board: British Transport Hotels, since 1962; ATV Network Ltd, since 1968; Vice-President, Princess Christian College, Manchester, since 1953; *b* 30 April 1902; *d* of late Prof. James Lorrain Smith, FRS; *m* 1934, Alexander Graham Bryce, FRCS (*d* 1968); two *s*. *Educ:* St Leonards Sch., St Andrews; Edinburgh Univ. (MA). Investigator, Industrial Fatigue Research Board, 1926-27; HM Inspector of Factories, 1928-34; Centre Organiser, WVS, Manchester, 1938-39; Dir of Organization, Ontario Div., Canadian WVS, 1941-42; Tech. Adviser, American WVS, 1942-43; Res. Fellow Fatigue Lab. Harvard Univ., 1943-44; Nat. Council of Women: Chm., Manchester Br., 1947-50; Vice-Chm., Education Cttee, 1950-51. JP and Mem. Juvenile Court Panel, Manchester City, 1949-55; Vice-Chairman: Assoc. of HMC's, 1953-55; Bd of Visitors, Grendon Prison, 1962-67. Member: Nurses and Midwives Whitley Council, 1953-57; General Nursing Council, 1956-61; Bd of Governors, Eastman Dental Hosp., 1957-63; Public Health Insp., Education Bd, 1958-64; Independent Television Authority, 1960-65 (Chm., General Advisory Council, 1964-65); Ancillary Dental Workers Cttee, 1956-68; Experimental Scheme for Dental Auxiliaries, 1958-69. *Publications:* (joint) reports on research into industrial psychological problems. *Recreations:* home decorating, gardening. *Address:* 20 Penny Piece, Goring, Reading RG8 9BY. *T:* Goring 2064. *Club:* Cowdray.

**GRAHAM-CAMPBELL, Rt. Rev. Archibald Rollo,** CBE, 1965; Assistant Bishop of Peterborough, since 1965; *b* 18 Feb. 1903; *s* of late Sir Rollo Frederick Graham-Campbell. *Educ:* Eton; King's Coll., Cambridge; Cuddesdon Theological Coll., 1st class Classical Tripos, Pt I, 1923; 1st class Classical

Tripos Pt II, 1924; 2nd class Theological Tripos, Pt II, 1925; BA 1924; MA 1929; Deacon, 1926; Priest, 1927; Curate of St John, Middlesbrough, 1926-30; Assistant Master, Eton Coll., 1930-37; Vicar of St Paul, King Cross, 1937-42; Fellow, Dean and Chaplain of King's Coll., Cambridge, 1942-48; Examining Chaplain to Bishop of St Albans and to Bishop of Lincoln, 1946-48; Bishop of Colombo, 1948-64; Rector of Kislingbury with Rothersthorpe, 1965-68. Hon. Canon of Peterborough, 1967-. *Address:* 4 Penfold Drive, Great Billing, Northampton. *T:* Cogenhoe 498. *Clubs:* MCC, Oxford and Cambridge University.

*See also D. J. Graham-Campbell.*

**GRAHAM-CAMPBELL, David John,** MA Cantab; Warden, Trinity College, Glenalmond, since Sept. 1964; *b* 18 Feb. 1912; *s* of late Sir R. F. Graham-Campbell; *m* 1940, Joan Sybil, *d* of late Major H. F. Maclean; three *s. Educ:* Eton Coll.; Trinity Coll., Cambridge (Exhibitioner). Assistant Master, Eton Coll., 1935-64. Served with 2nd Bn KRRC and on the staff, 1939-45 (Lt-Col). *Publication:* Writing English, 1953. *Recreations:* fishing, gardening, walking. *Address:* Trinity College, Glenalmond, Perthshire.

*See also Rt Rev. A. R. Graham-Campbell, Major Sir Charles Maclean, Bt.*

**GRAHAM-DIXON, Leslie Charles,** QC 1950; retired 1956; *b* 17 June 1901; *m* 1926, Dorothy Rivett; two *s. Educ:* Merchant Taylors' Sch.; St John's Coll., Oxford. Called to the Bar, 1925, Inner Temple. Western Circuit. *Address:* Chapelwood Manor, Nutley, Sussex. *T:* Nutley 2877.

**GRAHAM DOW, R.;** *see* Dow, R. G.

**GRAHAM-GREEN, Graham John,** TD 1945; Master of the Supreme Court, since 1953; *b* 16 Dec. 1906; *m* 1933, Eirene Mary Baston; one *d. Educ:* Dulwich. Admitted solicitor, 1929; Partner Kingsford, Dorman & Co., 1935-52; and Director of Companies. Served HAC, 1924-33; RA (TA), 1935-45. Freeman of City of London, 1945; Member of Solicitors Company, 1945; Co-Founder of Catholic Marriage Advisory Council, 1946. *Publications:* Cordery's Law Relating to Solicitors (5th edn), 1961, Supplements 1962, 1963, 1965 and 1966; (6th edn), 1968, Supplement 1970; Criminal Costs and Legal Aid, 1965, 2nd edn 1969, etc. *Recreations:* riding, travelling. *Address:* Marysmead, Hungershall Park, Tunbridge Wells, Kent. *T:* Tunbridge Wells 30800. *Clubs:* Army and Navy, City Livery, Challoner.

**GRAHAM-HARRISON, Francis Laurence Theodore,** CB 1962; Deputy Under-Secretary of State, Home Office, since 1963; *b* 30 Oct. 1914; *s* of late Sir William Montagu Graham-Harrison, KCB, KC, and Lady Graham-Harrison, *d* of Sir Cyril Graham, 5th and last Bt, CMG; *m* 1941, Carol Mary St John, 3rd *d* of late Sir Francis Stewart, CIE; one *s* three *d. Educ:* Eton; Magdalen Coll., Oxford. Entered Home Office, 1938. Private Secretary to Parliamentary Under-Secretary of State, 1941-43; Asst Private Secretary to Prime Minister, 1946-49; Secretary, Royal Commission on Capital Punishment, 1949-53; Asst Secretary, Home Office, 1953-57; Asst Under-Secretary of State, Home Office, 1957-63. *Address:* 14 Hill Road, NW8. *T:* 01-286 0621.

**GRAHAM-MOON, Sir P. W. G.;** *see* Moon.

**GRAHAM SMITH, Stanley,** CBE 1949; *b* 18 Jan. 1896; *s* of late George Graham Smith and Minnie Elizabeth Graham Smith; *m* 1929, Mrs Blanche Violet Horne, *widow* (née Venning); one *s. Educ:* Strand Sch. and King's Coll., London. Entered Civil Service, 1914 (Admiralty). Served European War as pilot in Royal Naval Air Service, Dec. 1916-Jan. 1919. Rejoined Admiralty, 1919. Private Secretary to Accountant-General of the Navy, 1922-32; Private Secretary to Civil Lord of Admiralty, 1932-35; Head of Air Branch, Admiralty, 1941-49; Under Secretary (Naval Staff), Admiralty, 1950-56, retired from Civil Service, 1956.

**GRAHAM-TOLER,** family name of the **Earl of Norbury.**

**GRAHAM-VIVIAN, (Richard) Preston,** MVO 1961; MC; Norroy and Ulster King of Arms, since 1966; *b* 10 Aug. 1896; 2nd *s* of late Sir Richard James Graham, Bt, and Lady Cynthia Duncombe; assumed additional surname of Vivian by Royal Licence, 1929; *m* 1921, Audrey Emily, *o c* of late Major Henry Wyndham Vivian and late Lady Maude Clements (who *m* 2nd, Christopher Foulis Roundell, CBE; he *d* 1958); one *s* one *d. Educ:* Eton; Trinity Coll., Cambridge (BA). Served European War, 1915-19, as Lieut in 21st and 7th Bns KRRC (twice wounded, prisoner, MC). Bluemantle Pursuivant of Arms, 1933-47; Windsor Herald of Arms, 1947-66; Earl Marshal's Secretary, 1954-61. FZS (Life). Hon. FSG; Vice-Pres., Irish Genealogical Res. Soc., 1968-. OStJ, 1949. *Address:* College of Arms, Queen Victoria Street, EC4. *T:* 01-248 6140; Wealden House, Warninglid, Haywards Heath, Sussex. *T:* Warninglid 272. *Club:* Travellers'.

**GRAHAME-THOMSON, Leslie;** *see* MacDougall, Leslie Grahame.

**GRAHAMSTOWN, Bishop of,** since 1969; **Rt. Rev. Bill Bendyshe Burnett,** MA; *b* 31 May 1917; *s* of Richard Evelyn Burnett and Louisa Dobinson; *m* 1945, Sheila Fulton Trollip; two *s* one *d. Educ:* Bishop's College (Rondebosch); Michaelhouse (Natal); Rhodes University College; St Paul's Theological College and Queen's College, Birmingham. Schoolmaster, St John's College, Umtata, 1940; Army, 1940-45; Deacon, S Thomas', Durban, 1947; Priest, 1948; Assistant priest, St Thomas', Durban, 1947, 1949; Chaplain, Michaelhouse, 1950-54; Vicar of Ladysmith, 1954-57; Bishop of Bloemfontein, 1957-67; Gen. Secretary, Christian Council of S Africa, 1967-69; Asst Bishop of Johannesburg, 1967-69. *Publications:* Anglicans in Natal, 1953. *Recreations:* tennis; painting. *Address:* Bishopsbourne, Grahamstown, Cape Province, S Africa.

**GRAHAMSTOWN, Assistant Bishop of;** *see* Cowdry, Rt Rev. R. W. F.

**GRAINGER, Leslie,** BSc, FIM; MInstF; Member for Science, National Coal Board, since June 1966; *b* 8 Aug. 1917. *Address:* National Coal Board, Hobart House, SW1. *T:* 01-235 2020.

**GRAINGER-STEWART, Brig. Thomas,** CB 1952; MC 1917; TD 1934 (3 bars); DL; retired as Deputy Secretary, Scottish Education Department; *b* 12 Jan. 1896; *s* of late Alexander Arthur Grainger-Stewart and of late Emily Francis Adam; *m* 1931, Pansy Gertrude Kemp, *d* of late J. T. Salvesen, shipowner, Leith; no *c. Educ:* Edinburgh Academy; Edinburgh Univ. Called to Scottish Bar, 1921; Secretary, Educational Endowments (Scotland) Commn, 1929-36; Asst Sec., Scottish Education Dept, 1937-46; Under-Secretary, 1947-48; Deputy Secretary, 1949-59. Served European War, 1914-18, with 16th and 17th (Service)

Battalions, The Royal Scots, 1914-19; France and Flanders, 1916-19, 2 Lt to Captain. Joined 7th/9th (Highlanders) Bn, The Royal Scots, TA, 1920; comd the Bn, 1932-38; Colonel 1936; Brigadier 1939; War of 1939-45, comd 155th (East Scottish) Infantry Bde, TA, 1939-42 (France, 1940); ADC to King George VI, 1943, and to Queen Elizabeth II, 1952-53. Hon. Colonel, 7th/9th (Highlanders) Bn, The Royal Scots, TA, 1955-60. Joined HM's Body Guard for Scotland, the Royal Company of Archers, 1931; Brigadier, 1940; Ensign, 1950; Lieutenant, 1953; Captain, 1965. DL County of City of Edinburgh, 1960. Member Scottish Cttee of Arts Council of Great Britain, 1961-66; Member Restrictive Practices Court, 1961-64. *Recreations:* archery, swimming, gardening. *Address:* Easter Belmont, 1 Easter Belmont Road, Edinburgh 12. *T:* 031-337 6920. *Clubs:* Royal Automobile; New (Edinburgh); Royal Scottish Automobile (Glasgow).

**GRANADO, Donald Casimir;** High Commissioner for Trinidad and Tobago, in London, since 1969; concurrently Ambassador to France, Federal Republic of Germany, Switzerland, Holland, Luxembourg, European Common Market; *b* 4 March 1915; *m* 1959, Anne-Marie Faustin Lombard; one *s* two *d*. *Educ:* Trinidad. Gen. Sec., Union of Commercial and Industrial Workers, 1951-53; Sec./Treas., Fedn of Trade Unions, 1952-53; Elected MP for Laventille, Trinidad, 1956 and 1961; Minister of: Labour and Social Services, 1956-61; Health and Housing, and Dep. Leader House of Representatives, 1961-63. Ambassador to Venezuela, 1963-64; High Comr to Canada, 1964-69; Ambassador to Argentina and to Brazil, 1965-69. Led Trinidad and Tobago delegn to UN, 1965; led govt delegn and went on govt business to various parts of the World. First Gen. Sec., People's National Movement; reads and writes French and Spanish. *Recreations:* played cricket, soccer, chess, table-tennis, checkers, bridge and golf; music (tape-recording), photography, writing. *Address:* 42 Belgrave Square, SW1. *T:* 01-245 9351.

**GRANARD,** 9th Earl of, *cr* 1684; **Arthur Patrick Hastings Forbes,** AFC, 1941; Bt 1628; Viscount Granard and Baron Clanehugh, 1675; Baron Granard (UK), 1806; Air Commodore late RAFVR; *b* 10 April 1915; *e s* of 8th Earl of Granard, KP, PC, GCVO, and Beatrice, OBE, *d* of Ogden Mills, Staatsburg, Dutchess County, USA; *S* father, 1948; *m* 1949, Marie-Madeleine Eugènie, *y d* of Jean Maurel, Millau, Aveyron, formerly wife of late Prince Humbert de Faucigny Lucinge; two *d*. *Educ:* Eton; Trinity Coll., Cambridge. Served War of 1939-45 (despatches, AFC). Commandeur Légion d'Honneur; Croix de Guerre with Palm; Officer Legion of Merit, USA; Croix des Vaillants of Poland. *Heir:* *b* Flt-Lt Hon. John Forbes, RAF [*b* 8 Oct. 1920; *m* 1947, Joan, *d* of A. Edward Smith, Algoa, Westminster Road, Foxrock, Co. Dublin; one *s* three *d*]. *Address:* Castle Forbes, Newtown Forbes, Co. Longford; 73 Rue de Varenne, Paris 7. *Club:* White's.
*See also Marquess of Bute.*

**GRANBY, Marquis of; David Charles Robert Manners;** *b* 8 May 1959; *s* and *heir* of 10th Duke of Rutland, *qv*.

**GRAND, Keith Walter Chamberlain;** MInstT; Chairman: Coast Lines Ltd; Penarth Engineering Co.; Director, Advance Laundries Ltd; *b* 3 July 1900; *m* 1925, Alice M. (*d* 1969), *d* of late Henry Gates, Brockville, Ont., Canada; one *d* (one *s* decd). *Educ:* Rugby. Joined GWR 1919; USA 1926-29; General Manager, British Railways, Western Region, 1948-59. Member (full-time) British Transport Commn, 1959-62; Member Coastal Shipping Advisory Cttee, 1959-62. *Recreation:* golf. *Address:* Porchester Lodge, 101 Bayswater Road, W2. *T:* 01-262 7400. *Clubs:* Carlton, Royal Thames Yacht.

**GRAND, Maj.-Gen. Laurence Douglas,** CB 1950; CIE 1946; CBE 1943 (MBE 1923); FICE; Director of Fortifications and Works, War Office, 1949-52; *b* 10 Aug. 1898; *s* of late D. H. Grand; *m* 1930, Irene Lola Hilda Mathew; one *s* one *d*. *Educ:* Rugby; Woolwich; Cambridge. *Recreation:* sailing. *Address:* Delaford Manor, Iver, Bucks. *Club:* United Service.
*See also Earl of Bessborough.*

**GRANDI,** Count (di Mordano) *cr* 1937, **Dino;** retired; President Chamber of Fasci and Corporazioni, Italy, 1939-43; late Member of the Chamber of Deputies and of the Fascist Grand Council; *b* Mordano (Bologna), 4 June 1895; *m* 1924, Antonietta Brizzi; one *s* one *d*. Graduated in Law at the University of Bologna, 1919; volunteered for the war and was promoted to Captain for merit and decorated with silver medal, bronze medal, and three military crosses for valour; journalist and political organiser, after the war led the Fascist movement in the North of Italy and took part in the March on Rome as Chief of the General Staff of the Quadrunvirato; elected member of the Chamber of Deputies, 1921, 1924, 1929, 1934, and 1939; member of the General Direction of the Fascist Party Organisation, 1921-23-24; Deputy President of the Chamber of Deputies, 1924; Italian Delegate to the IV, V, International Labour Conference, 1922, 1923; Under-Secretary of State for the Interior, 1924; Under Secretary of State for Foreign Affairs, 1925-29; Italian Delegate, Locarno Conference, 1925; to Conferences for Settlement of War Debt, Washington, 1925 and London, 1926; and Hague Conference on War Debts, 1929; Head of Italian Delegation, London Naval Conference, 1930; Italian Delegate, Danubian Conference, London, 1932; Head of Italian Delegation, Geneva Disarmament Conference, 1932; Minister of Foreign Affairs, 1929-32; Permanent Italian Delegate to the Council of the League of Nations, 1925-32; Italian Ambassador in London, 1932-39; Keeper of the Seal and Minister of Justice, Italy, 1939-43; Head of Italian Delegation to London Naval Conference, 1936; Italian Representative to London Session of Council of League of Nations, 1936; at London Meeting of Locarno Powers, 1936; and on the London International Cttee for Non-Intervention in Spain, 1936, 1937, 1938, 1939. *Publications:* Origins of Fascism, 1929; Italian Foreign Policy, 1931; The Spanish War in the London Committee, 1939; The Frontiers of the Law, 1941, etc. *Recreations:* book collecting, riding, gardening, mountaineering. *Address:* Albareto Di Modena, Italy.

**GRANDY, Air Chief Marshal Sir John,** GCB 1967 (KCB 1964; CB 1956); KBE 1961; DSO 1945; RAF; Chief of the Air Staff, since 1967; *b* Northwood, Mddx, 8 Feb. 1913; *s* of late Francis Grandy and Nellie Lines Grandy; *m* 1937, Cecile Elizabeth Florence, *yr d* of Sir Robert Rankin, 1st and last Bt; two *s*. *Educ:* University College Sch., London. Joined RAF 1931. No 54 (Fighter) Sqdn, 1932-35; 604 (Middx) Sqdn., RAuxAF, 1935-36; Adjt and Flying Instructor, London Univ. Air Sqdn, 1937-39; Comd No 249 (Fighter) Sqdn during Battle of Britain; Staff Duties, HQ Fighter Comd, and Wing Comdr Flying RAF Coltishall, 1941; commanded: RAF Duxford, 1942 (First Typhoon Wing); HQ No 210 Group, No 73 Op Training Unit, and Fighter

Conversion Unit at Abu Sueir, 1943-44; No 341 Wing (Dakotas), SE Asia Comd, 1944-55; DSO 1945, despatches 1943 and 1945. SASO No 232 Gp, 1945; *psc* 1946; Dep. Dir operational Training, Air Min., 1946; Air Attaché, Brussels, 1949; Comd Northern Sector, Fighter Comd, 1950; Air Staff HQ Fighter Comd, 1952-54; Comdt, Central Fighter Estab., 1954-57; *idc* 1957; Comdr, Task Force Grapple (British Nuclear Weapon Test Force), Christmas Is., 1957-58; Assistant CAS (Ops), 1958-61; Commander-in-Chief, RAF, Germany and Comdr, Second Allied TAF, 1961-63; AOC-in-C, Bomber Command, 1963-65; C-in-C, Far East Command, 1965-67. Air Cdre 1956; Air Vice-Marshal 1958; Air Marshal 1962; Air Chief Marshal 1965. Hon. PMN 1967. Hon. Liveryman, Haberdashers' Co., 1968. *Recreations:* sailing, golf, shooting. *Address:* c/o Ministry of Defence (Air), Whitehall, SW1. *Clubs:* White's, Pratt's, Royal Air Force; Royal Thames Yacht, Royal Yacht Squadron (Cowes).

**GRANER, Most Rev. Lawrence L.,** CSC, DD, BA; *b* Franklin, Pa, USA, 3 April 1901; *s* of W. D. Graner. *Educ:* Holy Cross Seminary, Notre Dame, Indiana, USA; Notre Dame Univ.; Holy Cross Coll., Washington, DC, USA. BA (Notre Dame), 1924; member of congregation of Holy Cross, 1921; priest, 1928; missionary, diocese of Dacca, 1928-45; delegate to Gen.-Chapter of the Congregation of Holy Cross, 1945; Vicar-General of Dacca, 1937-45; member of Provincial Council of Congregation of Holy Cross; War of 1939-45, Chaplain to US Air Forces; Bishop of Dacca, 1947-50; Archbishop of Dacca, 1950-67. *Address:* c/o Archbishop's House, Dacca, Pakistan.

**GRANGE, Kenneth Henry,** RDI, FSIA; self-employed Consultant Designer since 1958; *b* 17 July 1929; *s* of Harry Alfred Grange and Hilda Gladys (*née* Long); *Educ:* various London schs; Willesden Sch. of Art. Technical Illustrator, Royal Engineers, 1948-50; Design Asst, Arcon Chartered Architects, 1948; Bronek Katz & Vaughn, 1950-51; Gordon Bowyer & Partners, 1951-54; Jack Howe & Partners, 1954-58. RDI 1969; FSIA 1959. *Recreations:* tennis, ski-ing, photography. *Address:* 7a Hampstead High Street, NW3. *T:* 01-435 7624. *Club:* Arethusa.

**GRANGE-BENNETT, Rev. Canon Ronald du Pre,** TD; LTh; HCF; Licensed Preacher, Diocese of Oxford; *b* Bolton, Lancashire, 18 Feb. 1901; *s* of Rev. John Grange-Bennett, of Bewsey Old Hall, Warrington, Lancs., and Matilda Agnes du Pré, of Cape House, Samarés, Jersey; *m* 1925, Violet Edith Bryant, Clifton; two *s*. *Educ:* Kingswood Sch.; RMC Sandhurst; Lichfield Theological Coll.; LTh Serampore Univ., India. Commission East Lancashire Regt on Passing out of Sandhurst, 1920; retired 1922 and studied for Holy Orders; Priest, 1925; Curate Holy Trinity, Birchfield, Birmingham; Royal Army Chaplain's Dept, 1925-27; Principal, S Paul's Theological Coll., Mauritius, 1927-31. Bishop's Domestic Chaplain, Mauritius, 1928-31. Short service Commn in RAF Chaplain's Dept, 1931-34; Vicar of S Augustine-the-Less, Bristol, 1934-38; Campaign Director, Bishop of Lichfield's Campaign Appeal, 1938-39. Rejoined Royal Army Chaplains Dept (TA), 1939; served in UK, France, and Middle East (8th Army); demobilised, 1945. Religious Editor of English Service of French Radio, Paris, and Hon. Assistant Chaplain, St George's Paris, 1945-46; Vicar of Minehead, 1946-52; Vicar of Ruislip, Middlesex, 1952-62; Rector of Ascot, Berks., Oct. 1962-67; Hon. Canon of Mauritius, 1961. Golden Lecturer to the Haberdashers' Company, 1951-52. *Recreations:* photography, oil painting, ballet. *Address:* The Beam House, Winkfield Road, Windsor, Berks. *T:* Windsor 63872.

**GRANGER, Stewart; (James Lablache Stewart);** Actor (Stage and Film); *b* London, 6 May 1913; *s* of late Major James Stewart, RE, and Frederica Lablache; *m* 1st, Elspeth March (marr. diss., 1948); two *c*; 2nd, 1950, Jean Simmons, *qv* (marr. diss., at Nogales, Arizona, 1960); one *d*; 3rd, 1964, Viviane Lecerf. *Educ:* Epsom Coll. Began training as doctor but decided to become an actor. Studied at Webber-Douglas School of Dramatic Art; played at Little Theatre, Hull, and with Birmingham Repertory Company; appeared at Malvern Festivals, 1936-37; first London appearance as Captain Hamilton in The Sun Never Sets, Drury Lane, 1938; appeared on London stage, 1938-39; joined Old Vic Company, 1939; Dr Fleming in Tony Draws a Horse, Criterion, 1940; George Winthrop in A House in the Square, St Martin's, 1940; toured, 1940; served War of 1939-45, Army, 1940-42 (invalided). Toured, 1942; succeeded Owen Nares as Max de Winter in Rebecca, Lyric, 1942. Began film career in 1938, and has appeared in many films, including: The Man in Grey, The Lamp Still Burns, Fanny by Gaslight, Blue for Waterloo, The Love Story, The Madonna of the Seven Moons, Cæsar and Cleopatra, The Magic Bow, Captain Boycott, Blanche Fury, Saraband for Dead Lovers, Woman Hater, Adam and Evelyne, King Solomon's Mines, Soldiers Three, Light Touch, Wild North, Scaramouche, Young Bess, Salome, Beau Brummell, Footsteps in the Fog, Green Fire, Bhowani Junction, The Little Hut, North to Alaska, Swordsman of Siena, The Secret Invasion. *Address:* 141 El Camino Drive, Beverly Hills, California, USA.

**GRANIT, Prof. Ragnar Arthur,** Commander, Order of Nordstjernan, Sweden, 1964; Professor Emeritus, since 1967, Karolinska Institutet, Stockholm; *b* 30 Oct. 1900; *s* of Arthur W. Granit and Albertina Helena Granit (*née* Malmberg); *m* 1929, Baroness Marguerite (Daisy) Bruun; one *s*. *Educ:* Swedish Normallyceum; Helsingfors University. MagPhil 1923, MD 1927. Prof. of Physiology, Helsingfors, 1937; Prof. of Neurophysiology, Stockholm, 1940; Dir of Dept of Neurophysiology, Medical Nobel Inst., 1945; retired, 1967. President, Royal Swedish Acad. Science, 1963-65. Silliman Lecturer, Yale Univ., 1954; Visiting Prof., Rockefeller Univ., NY, 1956-66; Visiting Prof., St Catherine's Coll., Oxford, 1967. Hon. MD, Oslo, 1951; Hon. DSc: Oxford, 1956; Hong Kong, 1961; Catedr. Hon., Lima, Santiago, Bogotá, 1958. Retzius Gold Medal, 1957; Donders Medal, 1957; Jahre Prize (Oslo), 1961; III Internat. St Vincent Prize, 1961; Nobel Prize for Medicine (jointly), 1967; Sherrington Medal, 1967; Purkinje Gold Medal. For. Mem., Royal Soc., 1960; Nat. Acad. Sci., Washington, 1968; Mem. and Hon. Mem. of several learned societies. Cross of Freedom (Finland), 1918. *Publications:* Sensory Mechanisms of the Retina, (UK) 1947 (US 1963); Receptors and Sensory Perception, (US) 1955; Charles Scott Sherrington: An Appraisal, (UK) 1966; Basis of Motor Control, (UK) 1970; Ung Mans Väg till Minerva, 1941. *Recreations:* sailing, island life, gardening. *Address:* The Medical Nobel Institute, Karolinska Institutet, Stockholm 60, Sweden.

**GRANSDEN, Sir Robert,** Kt 1946; CBE 1942; *b* 10 Dec. 1893; *m* 1925, Dorothy Irene McCord; three *s*. *Educ:* Foyle Coll., Londonderry. British Civil Service, 1914; 2nd Lieut Royal Air Force, 1919; HM Treasury, 1920-22; transferred to NI Civil Service, 1922; Private

Secretary to Minister of Finance, 1923-25; Principal Officer, Ministry of Home Affairs, 1925-33; Cabinet Secretariat, Deputy Clerk Privy Council, 1933; Asst Secretary to Cabinet, 1937; Secretary to Cabinet, Clerk of Privy Council and Private Secretary to Prime Minister, 1939-57; Agent for the Government of N Ireland in Great Britain, 1957-62. Past Pres., Foyle Coll. Old Boys' Assoc., Londonderry. American Medal of Freedom (Bronze Palm). *Address:* Flat 3, 44 Wilbury Road, Hove, Sussex. *Clubs:* Constitutional (Hon.); London and Hove (Hove).

**GRANT,** family name of **Baron Strathspey.**

**GRANT, Rt. Hon. Lord; Rt. Hon. Lord Justice-Clerk; William Grant,** PC 1958; TD; Lord Justice-Clerk of Scotland, since 1962; *b* 19 June 1909; *s* of late Edward Grant and Margaret Jane Kennedy; *m* 1936, Margaret Katharine, *d* of J. W. Milne, CA, London; two *s* one *d*. *Educ:* Fettes Coll.; Oriel Coll., Oxford (BA); Edinburgh Univ. (LLB). Admitted to Faculty of Advocates, 1934. Served War of 1939-45, 2nd Lieut RA (TA), 1939, DAAG, War Office, 1944. Resumed practice as Advocate, 1945; QC (Scot.) 1951; Chairman, National Health Service (Scotland) Tribunal, 1949-54; Solicitor-General for Scotland, 1955-60; MP (C) Woodside Division of Glasgow, 1955-62; Lord Advocate, 1960-62. Governor, Fettes, 1952 (Chairman 1965); Director, Scottish Opera Ltd, 1965. Member Royal Company of Archers (Queen's Body Guard for Scotland); Hon. LLD Manitoba, 1961; Hon. Mem. Canadian Bar Assoc., 1961. Hon. Fellow, Oriel Coll., Oxford, 1963. Hon. Colonel 357 (Lowland) Light Regt RA (TA), 1956-61. *Recreations:* golf, shooting. *Address:* 30 Moray Place, Edinburgh. *T:* 031-225 4406. *Clubs:* Caledonian, United Service; Scottish Arts, New (Edinburgh).

**GRANT, Alexander Ludovic,** TD 1940; DL; JP; Director, Barclays Bank Ltd, since 1945 (Chairman, Manchester, and Deputy Chairman, Liverpool, Local Boards; Local Director, Liverpool, 1930, Manchester, 1940); Director, Barclays Bank (DCO), since 1948; *b* 26 March 1901; *s* of late John Peter Grant, of Rothiemurchus, Aviemore, Inverness-shire, and late Lady Mary Grant, *d* of 3rd Earl Manvers; *m* 1946, Elizabeth Langley, *widow* of Capt. J. G. F. Buxton, Grenadier Guards, and *d* of late Major Robert Barbour, Bolesworth Castle, Tattenhall, Cheshire; two *d*. *Educ:* Winchester; New Coll., Oxford (MA). Entered Barclays Bank Ltd, 1925; General Manager, Union Bank of Manchester, 1938-39 (Union Bank of Manchester was absorbed by Barclays Bank, 1940). Served Lovat Scouts, 1920-40 (Major 1935), and with Cheshire Home Guard, 1940-45. High Sheriff of Cheshire, 1956; DL Cheshire, 1963. *Recreations:* hunting, shooting, and fishing. *Address:* Marbury Hall, Whitchurch, Salop. *T:* Marbury 231; 7 Sloane Terrace Mansions, SW1. *T:* 01-730 1151. *Clubs:* Turf, Pratt's, MCC.

**GRANT, Alexander (Marshall),** CBE 1965; Principal Dancer, Royal Ballet Company; *b* Wellington, New Zealand, 22 Feb. 1928; *s* of Alexander and Eleather Grant. *Educ:* Wellington Coll., NZ. Arrived in London, Feb. 1946, to study with Sadler's Wells School on Scholarship given in New Zealand by Royal Academy of Dancing, London; joined Sadler's Wells Ballet (now Royal Ballet Company), Aug. 1946. Danced leading rôles in following: Mam'zelle Angot, Clock Symphony, Boutique Fantasque, Donald of the Burthens, Rake's Progress, Job, Three Cornered Hat, Ballabile, Cinderella, Sylvia, Madame Chrysanthème, Façade, Daphnis and Chloé, Coppélia, Petrushka, Ondine, La Fille Mal Gardée, Jabez and the Devil; Persèphone; The Dream. *Recreations:* gardening, cinephotography. *Address:* Royal Opera House, Covent Garden, WC2.

**GRANT, Alexander Thomas Kingdom,** CB 1965; CMG 1949; MA; Secretary of the Faculty of Economics, Cambridge, and Fellow of Pembroke College, since 1966; *b* 29 March 1906; *s* of late Harold Allan Grant and of Marie F. C. Grant; *m* 1930, Helen Frances, *d* of late Dr and Mrs H. Newsome, Clifton, Bristol. *Educ:* St Olave's Sch.; University College, Oxford (Scholar in Modern History). Research on International financial problems at RIIA, 1932-35. Leverhulme Research Fellow, 1935-37. Lecturer in Dept of Political Econ., UCL, 1938-39. Joined HM Treasury, 1939; Under-Secretary, 1956; Under Secretary, ECGD, 1958-66. UK member on Managing Board of European Payments Union, 1952-53. *Publications:* Society and Enterprise, 1934; A Study of the Capital Market in Post-War Britain, 1937; The Machinery of Finance and the Management of Sterling, 1967; miscellaneous articles. *Address:* 66 Gough Way, Cambridge. *T:* Cambridge 63119. *Club:* United University.

**GRANT, Andrew Francis Joseph,** BSc, MICE; Director, Home Regional Services, Ministry of Public Building and Works, since 1968; *b* 25 Feb. 1911; *er s* of Francis Herbert and Clare Grant; *m* 1934, Mary Harrison; two *s* two *d*. *Educ:* St Joseph's Coll., Beulah Hill; King's Coll., London. Asst Civil Engr with Contractors on London Underground Rlys, 1931; Port of London Authority, 1935; entered Civil Engineer-in-Chief's Dept, Admiralty, and posted to Singapore, 1937; Suptg Civil Engr, Durban, 1942; Civil Engr. Adviser, RN Home Air Comd, 1947; Suptg Civil Engr, Malta, 1951; Asst Dir, Navy Works, 1959; Fleet Navy Works Officer, Mediterranean, 1960; Director for Wales, MPBW, 1963; Regional Director, Far East, 1966. *Recreations:* painting, golf, travel. *Address:* Whitefriars, 9 Dormer Wells Lane, Southall, Middx. *T:* 01-574 0156; Ministry of Public Building and Works, Lambeth Bridge House, SE1. *T:* 01-735 7611. *Club:* Civil Service.

**GRANT, Anthony;** *see* Grant, J. A.

**GRANT, Sir Archibald,** 13th Bt, *cr* 1705; *b* 2 Sept. 1954; *e s* of Captain Sir Francis Cullen Grant, 12th Bt, and of Lady Grant (Jean Margherita, *d* of Captain Humphrey Douglas Tollemache, RN); *S* father, 1966. *Heir: b* Francis Tollemache Grant, *b* 18 Dec. 1955. *Address:* House of Monymusk, Aberdeenshire. *T:* Monymusk 220.

**GRANT, Brian;** *see* Grant, H. B.

**GRANT, Cary;** actor; *b* Bristol, 18 Jan. 1904; *s* of Elias Leach and Elsie Kingdom; became US citizen, 1942; *m* 1st 1934, Virginia Cherill (marr. diss., 1934); 2nd, 1942, Barbara Hutton (marr. diss., 1945); 3rd, 1949, Betsy Drake; 4th, 1965, Diane Cannon (marr. diss., 1968); one *d*. *Educ:* Fairfield Academy, Somerset. Started acting, New York, 1921; appeared in: Golden Dawn; Polly; Boom Boom; Wonderful Night; Street Singer; Nikki. *Films include:* Arsenic and Old Lace; None but the Lonely Heart; The Bishop's Wife; The Bachelor and the Bobby Soxer; Mr Blandings Builds His Dream House; To Catch a Thief; The Pride and the Passion; An Affair to Remember; Indiscreet; North by North-West; Operation Petticoat; A Touch of Mink; Charade; Father Goose; Walk, Don't Run. *Recreation:* riding.

*Address:* Universal-International Pictures, Universal City, California, USA; West Pico Boulevard, Los Angeles 64.

**GRANT, Rt. Rev. Charles Alexander;** *see* Northampton, Bishop of, (RC).

**GRANT, Prof. Colin King,** MA, DPhil; Professor of Philosophy in the University of Durham, since Oct. 1959; *b* 22 March 1924; *s* of Edward Harold Stewart Grant and Leila Ellen Grant (*née* King); *m* Alison Stoddart Wallace, MB, MRCS, DMRT, DCH; two *s*. *Educ:* Clayesmore Sch.; Wadham Coll., Oxford. First Class Philosophy, Politics and Economics, 1944; Pollard Student of Wadham Coll., 1944-46; DPhil 1950. Assistant in Moral Philosophy Dept, University of Glasgow, 1946-49; Lecturer in Philosophy, University of Nottingham, 1949-59. Visiting Lecturer, University of Chicago, 1950-51; Visiting Professor: University of Maryland, 1964; University of Bergen, 1967. *Publications:* articles in Mind, Philosophy, Proc. of Aristotelian Society, etc. *Recreations:* travel, reading. *Address:* 202 Gilesgate, Durham.

**GRANT, Derek Aldwin,** DSO 1944; QC 1962; **His Honour Judge Derek Grant;** an Additional Judge of the Central Criminal Court, since 1969; *b* 22 Jan. 1915; *s* of late Charles Frederick Grant; *m* 1954, Phoebe Louise Wavell-Paxton; one *s* three *d*. *Educ:* Winchester Coll.,; Oriel Coll., Oxford. Called to Bar 1938. Served in RAF, 1940-46 (King's Commendation, DSO). Master of the Bench, Inner Temple, 1969. Deputy Chairman, East Sussex County Sessions, 1962-; Recorder of Salisbury, 1962-67, of Portsmouth, 1967-69; *Address:* Carters Lodge, Handcross, Sussex. *Club:* Travellers'.

**GRANT, Douglas Marr Kelso;** Sheriff-Substitute of the Sheriffdom of Ayr and Bute, at Ayr, since 1966; *b* 5 April 1917; *s* of John Marr Grant, JP, and Helen (*née* Kelso), Glasgow; *m* 1952, Audrey Stevenson Law; two *s* two *d*. *Educ:* Rugby; Peterhouse, Cambridge. Entered Colonial Admin. Service, Uganda Protectorate, 1939. Army Service, 1940-46; Kenya Regt, 7 Bn King's African Rifles; Military Admins. of Ethiopia, Madagascar, Tripolitania, Malaya; GSO2, Civil Affairs, Cairo, Delhi, London. Called to Bar, Gray's Inn, 1945; transferred Colonial Legal Service, 1946; Judicial and Legal Dept, Malaya, 1946-57 (Legal Adviser, Government of Johore, 1953-55); retired from Colonial Service, 1957. Admitted to Faculty of Advocates and Scottish Bar, 1959; Junior Counsel to Secretary of State under Private Legislation Procedure (Scotland) Act, 1936, 1961-66. Hon. Sheriff-Substitute: of Lothians and Peebles, 1962; of Lanarkshire, 1963. *Recreation:* shooting. *Address:* Drumellan, Maybole, Ayrshire. *T:* Maybole 2279. *Clubs:* Public Schools; Royal Over-Seas League (Edinburgh).

**GRANT, Duncan James Corrowr,** RDI; Painter; *b* Rothiemurchus, Inverness, 1885; *s* of Major Bartle Grant and Ethel Grant; unmarried. *Educ:* St Paul's Sch. Studied at Westminster School of Art, Slade School, in Italy and in Paris, under Jacques Emile Blanche. Original Member London Artists' Association, Member of Camden Town Group and of London Group. *Address:* Charleston, Firle, Sussex.

**GRANT, Brig. Eneas Henry George,** CBE 1951; DSO 1944 and Bar, 1945; MC 1936; JP; DL; retired; *b* 14 Aug. 1901; *s* of late Col H. G. Grant, CB, late Seaforth Highlanders and late Mrs Grant, Balnespick, Inverness-shire; *m* 1926, Lilian Marion, *d* of late S. O'Neill, Cumberstown House, Co. Westmeath; one *s* (and *er s*, Lieut Seaforth Highlanders, killed in action, Korea, 1951). *Educ:* Wellington Coll., Berks; RMC, Sandhurst. 2nd Lieut Seaforth Highlanders, 1920; Adjt Lovat Scouts, 1928-33; served in Palestine, 1936; War of 1939-45; France 1940; France and Germany, 1944-45. Lieut-Colonel 1942 (Subs. 1947); Colonel 1944 (Subs. 1948); Brigadier 1944 (Subs. 1952); Bde Commander, 1944-49; Comdr Gold Coast District, 1949-52. Col Comdt Gold Coast Regt, 1949-52; Deputy Commander, Northumbrian District, 1952-55; retired 1955. JP Inverness-shire, 1957. DL Inverness-shire, 1958. Chairman Inverness-shire TA and Air Force Association, 1961-65. *Recreations:* country pursuits. *Address:* Inverbrough Lodge, Tomatin, Inverness-shire. *Club:* Highland (Inverness).

**GRANT, Maj.-Gen. Ferris Nelson,** CB 1967; Commander, Plymouth Group, Royal Marines, 1965-68; retired, 1968; *b* 25 Dec. 1916; *s* of late Lieut-Gen. H. G. Grant and of Mrs N. L. B. Grant (*née* Barker); *m* 1940, Patricia Anne (*née* Jameson); one *s* one *d*. *Educ:* Cheltenham Coll. Joined Royal Marines, 1935. Capt., HMS Suffolk, 1940-42; US Marine Corps Staff Coll., Major, 1943; Staff of SACSEA, Lieut-Col 1943; 45 Commando 1947; Army Staff Coll., Camberley, 1946; Chief Instructor, Commando Sch., 1949; CO 41 Commando, Korea, 1950; Joint Services Staff Coll., 1951; Bde Major, Commando Bde, 1952; Instructor, USMC Staff Coll., 1958; CO Amphibious Training Unit, 1960; CO Depot RM, 1961; CO Infantry Training Centre, 1963. Mem. Council, Sail Training Assoc. Legion of Merit (US). *Recreations:* sailing, riding, gardening, painting; Past Pres. RN Boxing Assoc. *Address:* c/o Lloyds Bank, Chatham, Kent. *Clubs:* Army and Navy; Royal Naval Sailing Association.

**GRANT, Frank,** CB 1953; OBE 1939; former Under-Secretary, Ministry of Agriculture and Fisheries; *b* 1890; *s* of late J. F. Grant, Evesham; *m* 1926, Eileen, *d* of late T. H. Carey; one *s* one *d*. *Address:* 9 Harefield Gardens, Middleton-on-Sea, Sussex. *T:* Middleton-on-Sea 3511.

**GRANT, George;** MP (Lab) Morpeth, since 1970; *b* 11 Oct. 1924; *m* 1948, Adeline (*née* Conroy), Morpeth; one *s* four *d*. *Educ:* Netherton Council Sch. and WEA. Member Bedlingtonshire UDC, 1959-70 (Chm. for two years). Member: Labour Party, 1947-; NUM (Chm., 1963-70). *Recreations:* sport, gardening. *Address:* House of Commons, SW1; 30 Sheepwash Bank, Choppington, Northumberland. *Clubs:* Working Men's, in the Bedlington and Ashington area.

**GRANT, Gordon,** CB 1956; Secretary, Trade Marks, Patents and Designs Federation, since 1970; *b* 13 Oct. 1907; *o s* of Harry Wykeham and Blanche Grant; *m* 1932, Lilian, *d* of William Gunner, two *d*. *Educ:* Christ's Hosp. Asst Traffic Supt, GPO, 1926; Principal Min. of Supply, 1939; Min. of Labour, 1940; Prin. Private Sec. to Rt Hon. Ernest Bevin, 1942-44; Asst Sec., 1944; Sec. Catering Wages Commission, 1944-45; idc 1949; Under Sec., Min. of Materials, 1951-54; Under Sec., Board of Trade, 1954-58; Comptroller-Gen., Patents, Designs and Trade Marks, 1958-69. *Address:* 4 Camborne House, Camborne Road, Sutton, Surrey. *T:* 01-643 2582. *Club:* National Liberal.

**GRANT, (Hubert) Brian; His Honour Judge Grant;** Judge of County Courts since 1965; *b* 5 Aug. 1917; *m* 1946, Jeanette Mary Carroll; one *s* three *d*. *Educ:* privately; Trinity Coll., Cambridge (Sen. Schol.). 1st cl. hons, Law

Tripos, 1939; MA. war service, 1940-44: Commandos, 1942-44. Called to Bar, Gray's Inn, 1945 (Lord Justice Holker Senior Scholar). Vice-Chm., Nat. Marriage Guidance Council, 1970-. *Publications:* Marriage, Separation and Divorce, 1946; Family Law, 1970. *Recreations:* travel and reading. *Address:* 56 The Pryors, East Heath Road, NW3; 15 High Wickham, Hastings, Sussex.

**GRANT, Maj.-Gen. Ian Hallam L.;** *see* Lyall Grant.

**GRANT, Isabel Frances,** MBE 1959; LLD (Edinburgh); *d* of late Colonel H. G. Grant, CB, late the Seaforth Highlanders; *g d* of late Field Marshal Sir Patrick Grant, KCB, GCMG; unmarried. *Educ:* privately. Founder of the Highland Folk Museum at Kingussie. *Publications:* Everyday Life on an Old Highland Farm, 1922; Social and Economic Development of Scotland before 1603, 1929; In the Tracks of Montrose, 1931; Everyday Life in Old Scotland, 1933; Social and Economic History of Scotland, 1934; Lordship of the Isles, 1935; Highland Folk Ways, 1961; Angus Og of the Isles, 1969. *Recreations:* reading, gardening, needlework. *Address:* 35 Heriot Row, Edinburgh.

**GRANT, James Currie;** Editor, The Press and Journal, Aberdeen, since 1960; *b* 5 May 1914; *s* of Alexander Grant, Elgin; *m* 1940, Lillias Isabella Gordon; one *d*. *Educ:* Elgin Academy. With the Northern Scot, Elgin, 1930-36; joined The Press and Journal, as reporter, 1936; Sub-editor, 1946, Dep. Editor, 1955. Served with Royal Artillery, 1940-46. *Recreations:* golf, gardening. *Address:* 42 Fonthill Road, Aberdeen. *T:* 22090.

**GRANT, Sir James Monteith,** KCVO 1969; Lord Lyon King of Arms since 1969; Writer to the Signet; *b* 19 Oct. 1903; *m* 1st, 1935, Agnes Winifried Comrie Lorimer (*d* 1955); 2nd, 1958, Yvonne Margaret Wilkinson; one *d*. *Educ:* The Edinburgh Academy; Univ. of Edinburgh. MA, LLB Edinburgh; WS 1927. Carrick Pursuivant, 1946; Marchmont Herald, 1957. FSA (Scot). KStJ 1970 (OStJ 1967). *Address:* 40 Corstorphine Road, Edinburgh 12. *T:* 031-337 1209. *Clubs:* New, Scottish Arts (Edinburgh).

**GRANT, James Shaw,** CBE 1968 (OBE 1956); Chairman, Crofters' Commission, since 1963; *b* 22 May 1910; *s* of William Grant and Johanna Morison Grant, Stornoway; *m* 1951, Catherine Mary Stewart; no *c*. *Educ:* Nicolson Inst.; Glasgow Univ. Editor, Stornoway Gazette, 1932-63; Mem., Crofters' Commn, 1955-63; Dir, Grampian Television, 1969-. Governor, Pitlochry Festival Theatre, 1954-. Has written several plays. *Recreations:* golf, photography. *Address:* Ardgrianach, Inshes, Inverness. *T:* Inverness 31476. *Clubs:* Royal Over-Seas League; Highland (Inverness).

**GRANT, Joan, (Mrs Denys Kelsey);** *b* 12 April 1907; *d* of John Frederick Marshall, CBE; *m* 1st, 1927, Arthur Leslie Grant; one *d*; 2nd, 1940, Charles Robert Longfield Beatty; 3rd, 1960, Denys Edward Reginald Kelsey, MB, MRCP. Is engaged in psychotherapy as well as in writing. *Publications:* Winged Pharaoh, 1937; Life as Carola, 1939; Eyes of Horus, 1942; The Scarlet Fish and other Stories, 1942; Lord of the Horizon, 1943; Redskin Morning, 1944; Scarlet Feather, 1945; Vague Vacation, 1947; Return to Elysium, 1947; The Laird and the Lady, 1949; So Moses Was Born, 1952; Time out of Mind (autobiography), 1956; A Lot to Remember, 1962; (with Dr Kelsey) Many Lifetimes, 1969. *Address:* Les Lucarnes, Collonges, Corrèze, France. *T:* Brive-la-Gaillarde 25.32.11.

**GRANT, Rear-Adm. John,** CB 1960; DSO 1942; Director and Secretary, Conference of the Electronics Industry, since 1965; *b* 13 Oct. 1908; *s* of late Maj.-Gen. Sir Philip Grant, KCB, CMG, and of late Annette, Lady Grant, Park Lodge, East Lulworth, Dorset; *m* 1935, Ruth Hayward Slade; two *s* two *d*. *Educ:* St Anthony's, Eastbourne; RN Colls, Dartmouth and Greenwich. Midshipman, HMS Queen Elizabeth, 1926; Sub-Lieut, HMS Revenge, 1930; Lieut, HMS Kent, China Station, 1932; specialised in anti-submarine warfare, 1933-39; Staff Officer Convoys, Rosyth, 1940; in comd HMS Beverley, 1941-42 (DSO); Trng Comdr, HMS Osprey, 1942, and subseq. in HMS Western Isles; in comd HMS Philante, 1943; Trng Comdr, HMS Osprey, 1944; in comd HMS Opportune, Fame and Crispin, 1945-47; Joint Staff Coll., 1947; Executive Officer, HMS Vernon; Capt. 1949; Dep. Dir Torpedo Anti-Submarine and Mine Warfare Div., Naval Staff, Admiralty, 1949-51; in comd HMS Cleopatra, 1952-53; Imperial Defence Coll., 1954; in comd HMS Vernon, 1955-57; on staff of Chief of Defence Staff, Min. of Defence, 1957-59; Rear-Adm., 1959; Flag Officer Commanding Reserve Fleet, 1959-60; retired list, 1961. Rank Organisation, 1961-65. CompIERE, 1963. *Address:* 14 Rivermead Court, Ranelagh Gardens, SW6. *Club:* United Service.

**GRANT, (John) Anthony;** MP (C) Harrow Central since 1964; Parliamentary Under-Secretary of State, Department of Trade and Industry, since Oct. 1970; Solicitor; *b* May 1925; *s* of late Arthur Ernest Grant, MA; *m* 1953, Sonia Isobel, *d* of late George Henry Landen; one *s* one *d*. *Educ:* St Paul's Sch.; Brasenose Coll., Oxford. Admitted a Solicitor, 1952; Past Chm., Young Conservatives; Liveryman, Worshipful Company of Solicitors; Freeman, City of London; Mem., Court of Guild of Freemen. Served in the Far East, 1943-48, with Third Dragoon Guards (Capt.). Opposition Whip, 1966-70; Parly Sec., Board of Trade, June-Oct. 1970. *Recreations:* Rugby, cricket, swimming; very amateur rose-growing. *Address:* 34 Nicholas Lane, Lombard Street, EC4. *T:* 01-623 8881. *Clubs:* Gresham, United and Cecil.

**GRANT, John Douglas;** MP (Lab) Islington East since 1970; *b* 16 Oct. 1932; *m* 1955, Patricia Julia Ann; two *s* one *d*. *Educ:* Stationers' Company's Sch., Hornsey. Reporter on various provincial newspapers until 1955; Daily Express, 1955-70 (Chief Industrial Correspondent, 1967-70). Contested (Lab) Beckenham, 1966; Chm., Bromley Constituency Labour Party, 1966-70. Chm., Labour and Industrial Correspondents' Group, 1967. *Recreations:* tennis, swimming, watching soccer. *Address:* 16 Magpie Hall Lane, Bromley, Kent. *T:* 01-467 0227.

**GRANT, John Leslie,** CIE 1942; *b* 12 Oct. 1890; *m* 1927, Joy Edith Horn; one *s* one *d*. *Educ:* Felsted Sch. Entered Indian Service of Engineers in 1913 and served in Sind and Iraq on Irrigation work and also on roads and building works, 1918-20; Chief Engineer in Sind and Sec. to Govt Public Works Dept, Sind, 1941-46; retired, 1948. Officer in RE in European War, 1914-18. *Recreations:* collection of antiques, archæology, travel. *Address:* The House on the Bend, Sea Lane, East Preston, Sussex. *T:* Rustington 3408.

**GRANT, Captain John Moreau,** CBE 1944; Royal Canadian Navy, retired; *b* 22 July 1895; *s* of late Hon. MacCallum Grant and Laura

MacNeil Parker; *m* 1923, Jocelyn Clare Weaver-Bridgman; one *d*. *Educ:* Heidelberg Coll., Germany; RCN Coll., Halifax, NS. *Address:* 601 Transit Road, Victoria, British Colombia, Canada. *T:* 384-3837.

**GRANT, John Sharp,** MD, FRCSE, MRCPE; Chief Medical Officer, British Railways Board, since 1965; Medical Consultant, National Freight Corporation; *b* 2 April 1909; *s* of late Andrew MacKenzie Grant, JP, and Elsie Ann Sharp; *m* 1938, Sheena Marjory, *d* of late Rev. D. M. Cameron; one *d*. *Educ:* Kingussie Sch., Inverness-shire; Edinburgh Univ. MB, ChB 1934; FRCSE 1937; MD 1949; MRCPE 1969. Cons. MO, L & NER, London, 1946-47; Regional MO, Eastern Region, British Railways, London, 1947-63; Med. Adviser, British Railways Bd, 1963-65. Lectr, Royal College of Nursing, England, 1957; Visiting Lectr in Industrial Medicine: Westminster Hosp. Med. Sch., 1962-64; Queen's Coll., Dundee (now Dundee Univ.), 1962-; St George's Hosp. Med. Sch., 1964-; Examr in Industrial Med., St Andrews Univ., 1963-66; Examr for DIH Exam. Bd in England, 1966-; Chm. of Commn of Enquiry: to Examine and Report on Transport Med. Services in Fedn of Central Africa, 1960; into Railway Med. Services in Rhodesia and Zambia, 1965; Vice-Pres., Union Internat. des Services Médicaux des Chemins de Fer, 1954-; Mem. Council, Royal Inst. Public Health and Hygiene, 1961-; Mem., Soc. of Occupational Med., 1965-; Pres.-elect (Pres. from Oct. 1971), Occupational Health Sect., RSM (Vice-Pres., 1966); Member: Industrial Injuries Adv. Council, 1966-; Med. Adv. Council, Migraine Trust, 1970. KStJ. *Publications:* contrib. Occupational Health, Medical Annual, 1963-67; (Jt Editor) Medical Services in Transport, 1966; various papers in med. jls. *Recreations:* golf, fishing. *Address:* 84 Chiltern Court, Baker Street, W1M 1DL. *T:* 01-935 8801. *Club:* Caledonian.

**GRANT, Sir (Kenneth) Lindsay,** Kt 1963; OBE 1956; ED 1944; Director, T. Geddes Grant Ltd (Chairman, 1946-64); Chairman, Vice-Chairman, or Director of numerous other companies; *b* Trinidad, 10 Feb. 1899; *s* of T. Geddes Grant (Canadian); *m* 1923, (Edith) Grace Norman; no *c*. *Educ:* Queen's Royal College, Trinidad; Maritime Business Coll., Halifax, NS. Served European War: (3rd Trinidad Contingent, 1916-17, 5th BWI Regt, 1917, RFC, 1917) 2nd Lieut; (RAF 1917-19) Flying Officer; War of 1939-45: (Trinidad Volunteers) Major, 2nd in Comd, 1944-45. Joined T. Geddes Grant Ltd, 1919; Manager, Office Appliances Dept, 1921; Director, 1927; Chm. and Man. Dir, 1946 (retd as Man. Dir, Sept. 1962; Chm. until 1964). Past and present activities; Church (Elder, Greyfriars); Boy Scouts; Cadets; Social Service. Chaconia Gold Medal, Trinidad, 1969. *Recreations:* none now; played cricket, Association football, tennis, golf. *Address:* (office) T. Geddes Grant Ltd, Box 171, Port of Spain, Trinidad. *T:* 54441; (home) 50 Ellerslie Park, Maraval, Trinidad. *T:* 25202, Port of Spain. *Clubs:* West Indian, Royal Commonwealth Society, Royal Over-Seas League, (Hon. Life) MCC (all London); Union, Country, Queen's Park Cricket, etc (Trinidad).

**GRANT, Leonard Bishopp,** CIE 1936; TD 1923; ED 1943; Secretary United Service Club, Simla, 1922-47; Colonel Commanding The Simla Rifles Auxiliary Force, India, 1923-47; *b* 16 Nov. 1882; *s* of W. Leonard Grant, Sittingbourne, Kent; *m* 1922, Eileen Staveley, *d* of late E. Neild Shackle, Botwell House, Hayes, Middlesex; three *d*. *Educ:* Felsted Sch. 4th Bn The Buffs, 1909-23; served European War, active service, 1915-16-18-19 (Brevet Major, despatches twice); General Staff Officer, Aden, 1919-20; DAAG Army HQ, India, 1920-22. *Address:* Burnt House, Benenden, Kent.

**GRANT, Sir Lindsay;** *see* Grant, Sir K. L.

**GRANT, Michael,** CBE 1958 (OBE 1946); MA, LittD (Cambridge); *b* 21 Nov. 1914; *s* of late Col Maurice Harold Grant and of Muriel, *d* of C. Jörgensen; *m* 1944, Anne Sophie Beskow, Norrköping, Sweden; two *s*. *Educ:* Harrow Sch.; Trinity Coll., Cambridge. Porson Prizeman, First Chancellor's Classical Medallist, Craven Student; Fellow Trinity Coll., Cambridge, 1938-49. Served War of 1939-45, Army, War Office, 1939-40, Actg Capt.; first British Council Rep. in Turkey, 1940-45; Prof. of Humanity at Edinburgh Univ., 1948-59; first Vice-Chancellor, Univ. of Khartoum, 1956-58; Pres. and Vice-Chancellor of the Queen's Univ. of Belfast, 1959-66; Pres., 1953-56, and Medallist, 1962, Royal Numismatic Soc.; Huntington Medallist, American Numismatic Soc., 1965. J. H. Gray Lectr, Cambridge, 1955; Donnellan Lectr, Trinity Coll., Dublin, 1962; FSA. Chairman: National Council for the Supply of Teachers Overseas, 1963-66; Advisory Council for Education, N Ireland, 1959-66. Pres. Virgil Soc., 1963-66. Mem., Milan Acad. of Sciences and Letters; Chm., Commonwealth Conf. on Teaching of English as 2nd Language at Makerere, Uganda, 1961. Hon. LittD (Dublin); Hon. LLD Queen's, Belfast. *Publications:* From Imperium to Auctoritas, 1946; Aspects of the Principate of Tiberius, 1950; Roman Anniversary Issues, 1950; Ancient History, 1952; The Six Main Aes Coinages of Augustus, 1953; Roman Imperial Money, 1954; Roman Literature, 1954; translation of the Annals of Tacitus, 1956; Roman Readings (ed), 1958; Roman History from Coins, 1958; Greeks, 1958, Romans, 1960 (with Don Pottinger); translations of selected works of Cicero, 1960, 1969; The World of Rome, 1960; Myths of the Greeks and Romans, 1962; Birth of Western Civilization (ed), 1964; The Civilizations of Europe, 1965; Cambridge, 1966; The Gladiators, 1967; The Climax of Rome, 1968; The Ancient Mediterranean, 1969; Julius Caesar, 1969; The Ancient Historians, 1970; The Roman Forum, 1970; Nero, 1970. *Address:* Le Pitturacce, Gattaiola, Lucca, Italy. *Club:* Athenæum.

**GRANT, Neil Forbes,** CBE 1918; MA; late London Editor of Cape Times, Natal Mercury, Rand Daily Mail, and Sunday Times of Johannesburg; *b* Forres, Morayshire, 1882; *s* of James Grant; *m* Nancy Elizabeth Puckett (*d* 1954). *Educ:* Edinburgh Univ.; Brasenose Coll., Oxford (scholar). Joined Staff of Morning Post, 1907; Foreign Editor, 1918-25; Editor, Wireless and Cable Section, Ministry of Information; officer of the Order of Crown of Belgium, Comdr of Order of Dannebrog. *Publications:* Possessions, Getting Mother Married, A Valuable Rival, Thy Name is Woman, Petticoat Influence, The Nelson Touch, Dusty Ermine, and other plays; ed Willy Nicky Letters. *Recreation:* music. *Address:* Flat 2, 6 Third Avenue, Hove, Sussex. *Club:* Royal Commonwealth Society (Sussex Branch).

**GRANT, Sir Patrick Alexander Benedict,** 14th Bt *cr* 1688; *b* 5 Feb. 1953; *e s* of Sir Duncan Alexander Grant, 13th Bt, and Joan Penelope, *o d* of Capt. Sir Denzil Cope, 14th Bt; *S* father, 1961. *Educ:* St Conleth's Coll., Dublin; The Abbey Sch., Fort Augustus. *Heir: b* Denzil Mohun Bede Grant, *b* 19 April 1955. *Address:*

34 Morehampton Road, Donnybrook, Dublin. *T:* Dublin 680536.

**GRANT, Prof. Peter John,** MA, PhD, MIMechE, FInstP; Professor of Nuclear Power, Imperial College of Science and Technology, London, since 1966; *b* London, 2 July 1926; *s* of Herbert James Grant; *m* Audrey, *d* of Joseph Whitham; one *s*. *Educ:* Merchant Taylors' Sch.; Sidney Sussex Coll., Cambridge. BA 1947, MA, PhD 1951, Cantab. Research in Nuclear Physics at Cavendish Laboratory, 1947-50; Lectr in Natural Philosophy, Univ. of Glasgow, 1950-55; Chief Physicist, Atomic Energy Div., GEC Ltd, 1956-59; Reader in Engineering Science, Imperial Coll. of Science and Technology, 1959-66. *Publications:* Elementary Reactor Physics, 1966; papers on radioactivity, nuclear reactions, physics of nuclear reactors. *Address:* 49 Manor Road South, Esher, Surrey. *T:* 01-398 2001.

**GRANT, Ronald Thomson,** OBE; FRS 1934; MD, FRCP, DPH; formerly physician on staff of Medical Research Council; *b* 5 Nov. 1892. *Educ:* Glasgow Univ. *Publications:* articles to scientific journals. *Address:* Guy's Hospital, SE1; Farley Green Cottage, Albury, Guildford, Surrey. *T:* Shere 2164.

**GRANT, Air Vice-Marshal Stanley Bernard,** CB 1969; DFC 1942; bar to DFC 1943; RAF; *b* 31 May 1919; *s* of late Harry Alexander Gwatkin Grant and Marjorie Gladys Hoyle; *m* 1948, Barbara Jean Watts (*d* 1963); one *s* one *d*; *m* 1965, Christiane Marie Py; one step *s* two step *d*. *Educ:* Charterhouse; RAF Coll., Cranwell. Joined RAF, 1937; War of 1939-45; service in UK, Malta, Egypt and Italy. Air Ministry, 1946-47; Flying Training Command, 1948-54; Fighter Command, 1955-56; SEATO, Bangkok, 1957-59; Fighter Command, 1960-61; idc course, 1962; NATO, Fontainebleau, 1963-64; Directing Staff, IDC, 1965-68; Comdr, British Forces, Gulf, 1968-69; retired 1970. *Address:* 8/69 Courtfield Gardens, SW5. *Club:* Royal Air Force.

**GRANT, Rt. Hon. William;** *see* Grant, Rt Hon. Lord.

**GRANT, Prof. Willis,** DMus, Hon. RAM, FRCO, ARCM; Stanley Hugh Badock Professor of Music, since 1958, Dean of Faculty of Arts, 1968-70, Bristol University; *b* Bolton, 1 May 1907; *o s* of Herbert Grant; *m* Grace Winifred, *d* of C. A. Baker, Moseley, Birmingham. *Educ:* Astley Bridge Sch.; privately. Studied music with several teachers including Sir Edward C. Bairstow, York Minster; Organist and Choirmaster, All Souls' Parish Church, Bolton, 1929-31; Asst Organist, Lincoln Minster, 1931-36; Music Master, South Park High Sch., 1931-36; conducted Gate Burton Choral Soc., 1932-35; Extra-mural lectr for the University Coll. of Nottingham, 1936-37; Organist and Master of the Choristers, Birmingham Cathedral, 1936-58; Tutor in Special Music Course for Teachers at Sheffield City Training Coll., 1938-39; Conductor, Birmingham Bach Soc., 1938-58 (now Hon. Life Mem.); Lecturer in Music, Sheffield Univ., 1934-47; Extra-mural lecturer for WEA and Sheffield Univ., 1938-47; Dir of Music, King Edward's Sch., Birmingham, 1948-58; Extra-mural lectr for Birmingham Univ., 1956-58. Rep. of Royal School of Church Music for Birmingham Dio., 1936-58. Pres. Birmingham Organists Assoc., 1950-55 (now Hon. Life Mem.); Mem., Management and Music Advisory Cttees of City of Birmingham Symphony Orchestra, 1950-58; Special Comr, Royal School of Church Music, 1953-; Mem. Musical Adv. Board, 1952-55; Mem. Council: RCO; Incorporated Soc. of Musicians, 1956-59, 1960- (Mem. Exec. Cttee, 1958-); President: Music Masters' Assoc., 1958; Incorporated Assoc. of Organists, 1964. Mem. Management Cttee, Western Orchestral Soc.; Gov. Newton Park Coll., Bath. Served with HM Forces, RASC, 1941-42; AEC Major, lecturing on music in India Comd, 1942-46. *Publications:* An Album of Songs; Music in Education. *Recreations:* photography, gardening. *Address:* The Old Rectory, Compton Martin, Somerset BS18 6JP. *T:* West Harptree 350. *Club:* Athenæum.

**GRANT-FERRIS, Wing Comdr Sir Robert (Grant),** Kt 1969; MP (C) Nantwich Division of Cheshire since 1955; Chairman of Ways and Means and Deputy Speaker of the House of Commons, since 1970; Chairman Board of Management, Hospital of St John and St Elizabeth (now integrated with St Andrew's, Dollis Hill), since 1963; Privy Chamberlain of the Sword and Cape to Popes Pius XII, John XXIII and Paul VI; *b* 1907; *s* of late Robert Francis Ferris, MB, ChB; *m* 1930, Florence, *d* of Major W. Brennan De Vine, MC; one *s* one *d*. *Educ:* Douai Sch. Called to Bar, Inner Temple, 1937; joined RAuxAF, 1933, 605 (County of Warwick) Fighter Sqdn; Flight Comdr 1939-40; Wing Comdr, 1941; Air Efficiency Award, 1942; MP (C) North St Pancras, 1937-45; Parly. Private Sec. to Minister of Town and Country Planning (Rt Hon. W. S. Morrison, KC, MP), 1944-45; Temp. Chm. House of Commons and Chairman of Cttees 1962-; contested Wigan, 1935, North St Pancras, 1945, Central Wandsworth, 1950, 1951. Pres. Southdown Sheep Soc. of England, 1950-52 and 1959-60; Pres. Nat. Sheep Breeders' Assoc., 1956-58; a Vice-Pres. Smithfield Club, 1964. Knight Grand Cross of Magistral Grace, the Sovereign and Military Order of Malta; holds Grand Cross of Merit with Star of same Order; Comdr, Order of Leopold II (Belgium), 1964. *Recreations:* hunting, golf, yachting. *Address:* 16 Stafford Place, SW1; 8 Dysart Buildings, Nantwich, Cheshire. *Clubs:* Carlton, Royal Thames Yacht, House of Commons Yacht (Hon. Admiral).

**GRANT LAWSON, Sir P.;** *see* Lawson.

**GRANT-SUTTIE;** *see* Suttie.

**GRANT WATSON, Herbert Adolphus,** CMG 1933; *b* 4 Jan. 1881; *s* of Robert Grant Watson, Diplomatic Service; *m* 1st, 1905, Anna (*d* 1953), *d* of William G. Low, New York; one *s* (and one *s* killed on active service); 2nd, 1953, Katherine, *d* of John J. Whelan, Frant, Sussex. *Educ:* Eton; Trinity Coll., Cambridge. Attaché in Diplomatic Service, 1905; attaché at HM Embassy, Washington, 1906; 3rd Sec., 1907! transferred to Rio, 1908; to Brussels, 1910; 2nd Sec., 1912; transferred to Foreign Office, Feb. 1915; to Copenhagen, Aug. 1915; 1st Sec., 1919; employed on special service in the Baltic Provinces, 1919; transferred to Lisbon, 1920; Counsellor of Embassy, 1925; Envoy Extraordinary and Minister Plenipotentiary to Central American Republics, 1928-33; to Cuba, 1933-35; to Finland, 1935-37; to Cuba, 1937-40. *Publication:* Mission to the Baltic in 1919. *Address:* Woodberry, West Overcliff Drive, Bournemouth. *Clubs:* St James', Vikings.

**GRANTCHESTER,** 1st Baron, *cr* 1953, of Knightsbridge in the City of Westminster; **Alfred Jesse Suenson-Taylor,** Kt, *cr* 1935; OBE, MA Cantab; FRGS; FCII; FRSA; Barrister-at-Law; *b* 14 Aug. 1893; *s* of late Alfred George and Mary Taylor; *m* 1920, Mara Henriette (Mamie), *d* of late Albert Suenson,

Copenhagen; one *s* one *d*. *Educ:* Epsom Coll.; King's Coll., Cambridge. Served Gallipoli and France 1914-18 (despatches twice, OBE, two French decorations, rank of Major); Contested Isle of Thanet Div. of Kent, 1922 and 1929; Member: Royal Institute of International Affairs; Mont Pelerin Soc. (international economic); Gov. Brit. Soc. for Internat. Understanding; Delegate to Assemblies Council of Europe and WEU, 1957-66; Mem. Delegns to Washington, Iran, Turkey, and Greece; visits to SE Asia, 1966, 1968; originator of unofficial meetings at Strasbourg of delegates from EFTA countries; Pres. Emeritus, London Liberal Party; Pres. Insurance Inst. of Kent, 1933-34; Pres. Free Trade League; Vice-Pres. Insurance Institute of London; Vice-Pres. United Nations Assoc.; Director: County Fire Office Ltd, 1934-68; London and Manchester Assurance Co. Ltd, 1934-67 (Chm. 1953-61); Canal Randolph Corp. (USA); United Stockyards Corporation (USA); Chm., Brightstone Estates Ltd. Dato Seri Laila Jasa, Brunei; DHBS, Brunei. *Publications:* Industrial Assurance Law; Editor, the Owl, a quarterly jl of internat. thought. *Heir:* *s* Hon. Kenneth Suenson-Taylor, LLM [*b* 18 Aug. 1921; *m* 1947, Betty Moores; three *s* three *d*]. *Address:* 49 Grosvenor Square, W1. *T:* 01-629 3883; 52 Westminster Mansions, 1 Little Smith Street, SW1. *T:* 01-799 3782. *Clubs:* National Liberal, English-Speaking Union.

**GRANTHAM, Bishop Suffragan of,** since 1965; **Rt. Rev. Ross Sydney Hook,** MC 1945; *b* 19 Feb. 1917; *o s* of late Sydney Frank and Laura Harriet Hook; *m* 1948, Ruth Leslie, *d* of late Rev. Herman Masterman Biddell and Violet Marjorie Biddell; one *s* one *d*. *Educ:* Christ's Hosp.; Peterhouse, Cambridge (MA); Ridley Hall, Cambridge, Asst Curate, Milton, Hants, 1941-43. Chaplain, RNVR (Royal Marine Commandos), 1943-46. Chaplain, Ridley Hall, Cambridge, 1946-48. Select Preacher, University of Cambridge, 1948; Rector, Chorlton-cum-Hardy, Manchester, 1948-52; Rector and Rural Dean, Chelsea, 1952-61; Chaplain: Chelsea Hosp. for Women, 1954-61; St Luke's Hosp., Chelsea, 1957-61; Residentiary Canon of Rochester and Precentor, 1961-65; Treasurer, 1965; Diocesan Dir of Post Ordination Training, 1961-65; Examining Chaplain to Bishop of Rochester, 1961-65, to Bishop of Lincoln, 1966-; Prebendary of Brampton (Lincoln Cathedral), 1966-. Chm., Inspections Cttee, Central Advisory Council for the Ministry, 1966- (Sec., 1960-66). *Recreation:* cricket. *Address:* Stoke Rochford, Grantham, Lincs. *T:* Great Ponton 214.

**GRANTHAM, Sir Alexander (William George Herder),** GCMG 1951 (KCMG 1945; CMG 1941); *b* 15 March 1899; *s* of F. W. Grantham and A. von Herder; *m* 1925, Maurine Samson (*d* 1970), San Francisco; no *c*. *Educ:* Wellington; RMC, Sandhurst; Pembroke Coll., Cambridge, MA. Gazetted 18th Hussars, 1917; Colonial Administrative Service, Hong Kong, 1922; called to Bar, Inner Temple, 1934; attended Imperial Defence Coll., 1934; Colonial Sec., Bermuda, 1935-38; Colonial Sec., Jamaica, 1938-41; Chief Sec., Nigeria, 1941-44; Governor, Fiji, and High Commissioner for Western Pacific, 1945-47; Governor Hong Kong, 1947-57. Hon. Fellow, Pembroke Coll., Cambridge. Hon. LLD Hong Kong Univ. *Address:* 90 Piccadilly, W1. *Club:* Cavalry.

**GRANTHAM, Adm. Sir Guy,** GCB, 1956 (KCB 1952; CB 1942); CBE 1946; DSO 1941; retired; Governor and Commander-in-Chief of Malta, 1959-62; *b* 9 Jan. 1900; *s* of late C. F. Grantham, The Hall, Skegness, Lincs; *m* 1934, Beryl Marjorie, *d* of late T. C. B. Mackintosh-Walker, Geddes, Nairn; two *d*. Served War of 1939-45 (despatches, twice, DSO, CB, CBE); Chief of Staff to C-in-C, Mediterranean, 1946-48; Naval ADC to the King, 1947-48; Flag Officer (Submarines), 1948-50; Flag Officer, Second-in-Command, Mediterranean Fleet, 1950-51; Vice-Chief of Naval Staff, 1951-54; Comdr-in-Chief, Mediterranean Station, and Allied Forces, Mediterranean, 1954-57; Comdr-in-Chief, Portsmouth, Allied Comdr-in-Chief, Channel and Southern North Sea, 1957-59; First and Principal Naval ADC to the Queen, 1958-59. Retired list, 1959. Hon. Freeman of Haberdashers' Company. Mem., Commonwealth War Graves Commn 1962- (Vice-Chm. 1963-70). Governor and Mem. Administrative Board, Corps of Commissionaires, 1964-. *Address:* Stanleys, Hatch Lane, Liss, Hants. *T:* Liss 2135.

**GRANTHAM, Alderman Mrs Violet Hardisty;** member of Newcastle upon Tyne City Council since 1937; Alderman of City, 1951-58; *o d* of Thomas Taylor, BSc, and Sarah Taylor; *m* John Grantham (*d* 1945), formerly Sheriff of Newcastle upon Tyne, and Lord Mayor, 1936-37. *Educ:* privately. Dir of Private Companies. Lady Mayoress of Newcastle upon Tyne, 1936-37 and 1949-50; Sheriff of Newcastle upon Tyne, 1950-51 (first woman to hold this office); Lord Mayor, 1952-53 (first woman to hold this office); mem. Newcastle upon Tyne Hosp. Management Cttee; Mem. of Cttee, Percy Hedley Home for Spastic Children. Northern Area Chm. of Women's Junior Air Corps; formerly Pres. Newcastle upon Tyne Branch of Royal College of Nursing; active in Townswomen's Guilds and other women's organisations. *Address:* 4 Grange Road, Fenham, Newcastle upon Tyne 4. *T:* 33816.

**GRANTLEY,** 7th Baron, *cr* 1782; **John Richard Brinsley Norton,** MC 1944; Baron of Markenfield, 1782; a Member of Lloyd's; Director, Leslie & Godwin Ltd; *b* 30 July 1923; *o s* of 6th Baron and Jean Mary (*d* 1945), *d* of Sir David Alexander Kinloch, CB, MVO, 11th Bt; *S* father 1954; *m* 1955, Deirdre Mary Freda, *o d* of 5th Earl of Listowel, *qv*; two *s*. *Educ:* Eton; New Coll., Oxford. Served War of 1939-45, 1942-45, in Italy as Capt. Grenadier Guards (MC). *Heir:* *s* Hon. Richard William Brinsley Norton, *b* 30 Jan. 1956. *Address:* 53 Lower Belgrave Street, SW1; Markenfield Hall, Ripon, Yorks. *Clubs:* White's, Pratt's.

**GRANVILLE,** family name of **Baron Granville of Eye.**

**GRANVILLE,** 5th Earl, *cr* 1833; **Granville James Leveson Gower,** MC 1945; Viscount Granville, 1815; Baron Leveson, 1833; Major Coldstream Guards (Supplementary Reserve); *b* 6 Dec. 1918; *s* of 4th Earl Granville, KG, KCVO, CB, DSO, and Countess Granville, GCVO; *S* father, 1953; *m* 1958, Doon Aileen, *d* of late Hon. Brinsley Plunket and of Mrs V. Stux-Rybar, Luttrellstown Castle, Co. Dublin; two *s* one *d*. *Educ:* Eton. Served throughout War, 1939-45, Tunisia and Italy (twice wounded, despatches, MC). *Heir:* *s* Lord Leveson, *qv*. *Address:* 49 Lyall Mews, SW1. *T:* 01-235 1026; Callernish, Sollas, North Uist, Outer Hebrides, Inverness-shire. *T:* Bayhead 213.

**GRANVILLE OF EYE,** Baron *cr* 1967, of Eye (Life Peer); **Edgar Louis Granville;** *s* of Reginald and Margaret Granville; *b* Reading, 12 Feb. 1899; *m* 1943, Elizabeth *d* of late Rev. W. C. Hunter; one *d*. *Educ:* High Wycombe, London and Australia. Served as officer in AIF, Gallipoli, Egypt and France. Capt. RA, 1939-40. MP (L) Eye Div. of Suffolk, 1929-51;

Hon. Sec., Liberal Agricultural Group, House of Commons, 1929-31; Hon. Sec. Foreign Affairs Group, Vice-Pres. National League of Young Liberals; Chm., Young Liberals Manifesto Group; Parliamentary Private Sec. to Sir Herbert Samuel, first National Government, 1931; Parliamentary Private Sec. to Sir John Simon, National Government, 1931-36; Mem. of Inter-Departmental Cttee for the World Economic Conference, 1933. *Recreations:* cricket, football, ski-ing. *Address:* Charlton Lane, Cheltenham.

**GRANVILLE, Keith,** CBE 1958; MInstT: Deputy Chairman, since 1964, Managing Director, since 1969, BOAC; Member Board: British Travel Association since 1954; BOAC, since 1959; Chairman: International Aeradio Ltd, 1965 (Deputy-Chairman, 1962-65); BOAC Engine Overhaul Ltd; *b* 1 Nov. 1910; *m* 1st, 1933, Patricia Capstick; one *s* one *d*; 2nd, 1946, Truda Belliss; one *s* four *d*. *Educ:* Tonbridge Sch. Joined Imperial Airways as Trainee, 1929 and served Italy, Tanganyika, Southern and Northern Rhodesia, Egypt, India. BOAC: Manager African and Middle East Div., 1947; Commercial Dir, 1954; Dep. Managing Dir, 1958-60; Chm., BOAC Associated Companies Ltd, 1960-64. Pres., Inst. of Transport, 1963-64. *Address:* Hurstbourne, Portnall Drive, Virginia Water, Surrey. *T:* Wentworth 2371; Exbury, Sea Road, Westgate-on-Sea. *T:* Thanet 31415. *Clubs:* Royal Aero; Wentworth (Virginia Water).

**GRANVILLE SLACK, George;** *see* Slack, G. G.

**GRANVILLE-SMITH, Stuart Hayne,** OBE 1946; **His Honour Judge Granville-Smith;** Judge of No. 38 County Court Circuit; *b* 7 May 1901; *s* of Granville Smith, Master of the Supreme Court of Justice, 1900-25, and Nellie Claire Mead; *m* 1935, Elisabeth Mary Woodcock; one *s* one *d*. *Educ:* Marlborough Coll.; Oriel Coll., Oxford. Called to Bar, Inner Temple, 1925; Midland Circuit; North London Sessions. Prosecuting Counsel for Post Office, Midland Circuit, 1932. Served War of 1939-45, on active service with RAF 1940-46 (Wing Comdr); Control Office and Control Commission for Germany, 1946-47. *Recreations:* tennis, walking, climbing. *Address:* 379 Woodstock Road, Oxford. *Club:* United University.

**GRANVILLE-WEST;** *see* West (family name).

**GRANVILLE-WEST,** Baron, *cr* 1958 (Life Peer), of Pontypool, in the County of Monmouthshire, **Daniel Granville West;** Senior Partner in the firm of D. Granville West, Chivers and Dunford, Newbridge and Pontypool; *b* 17 March 1904; *s* of John West, Newbridge, Monmouthshire, and Elizabeth West (*née* Bridges); *m* 1937, Vera (JP Monmouthshire, 1956), *d* of J. Hopkins, Pontypool; one *s* one *d*. Admitted a Solicitor, 1929. Served War of 1939-45: Royal Air Force Volunteer Reserve, Flight Lt. MP (Lab) Pontypool Div. of Monmouthshire, July 1946-58. PPS to Home Sec., 1950-51. Mem. of Abercarn Urban District Council, 1934-38 and of Monmouthshire County Council, 1938-47. *Address:* Brynderwen, Abersychan, Pontypool, Monmouthshire. *T:* Talywain 236.

**GRASAR, Rt. Rev. William Eric;** *see* Shrewsbury, Bishop of, (RC).

**GRASETT, Lt-Gen. Sir (Arthur) Edward,** KBE 1945; CB 1940; DSO 1919; MC 1915; Colonel Commandant Royal Engineers, 1945-55; *b* 1888, *e s* of late A. W. Grasett, Toronto; *m* 1935, Joan Mary, 2nd *d* of late J. K. Foster, Egton Manor, Yorks; one *d*. *Educ:* Upper Canada Coll., Toronto; Royal military Coll., Kingston. Entered RE 1909; served European War (despatches five times, DSO, MC); Operations on NW Frontier of India, 1921-23; Staff Coll., Camberley, 1920; Imperial Defence Coll., 1931; GSO1 Staff Coll., Camberley, 1935-37; Brig., Gen. Staff, Northern Command, 1937-38; GOC China, 1938-41; Divisional Comdr, 1941; Corps Comdr, 1941-43; War Office, 1944; SHAEF 1944-45; Lt-Governor and C-in-C OF Jersey, 1945-53; retired pay, 1947. KStJ. Chief Comdr Legion of Merit (USA); Grand Cross of the Crown (Belgium); Comdr of the Legion of Honour, Croix de Guerre (France); Order of the Red Banner (USSR). *Address:* St Amands, Adderbury, Oxon. *Clubs:* Army and Navy, Leander.

**GRASS, Günter Wilhelm;** German writer and artist; *b* Danzig, 16 Oct. 1927; *m* 1954, Anna Schwarz; three *s* (inc. twin *s*) one *d*. *Educ:* Volksschule and Gymnasium, Danzig; Düsseldorf Kunstakademie; Hochschule für Bildende Künste. Lecture Tour of US, 1964, and many other foreign tours. Member: Akademie der Künste, Berlin; Deutscher PEN, Zentrum der Bundesrepublik; Verband Deutscher Schriftsteller; Amer. Academy of Arts and Sciences. Prizes: Lyric, Süddeutscher Rundfunk, 1955; Gruppe 47, 1959; Bremen Literary, 1959 (zurückgezogen); Literary, Assoc. of German Critics, 1960; Meilleur livre étranger, 1962; George-Büchner, 1965; Theodor-Heuss, 1969. *Publications: novels:* Die Blechtrommel, 1959 (The Tin Drum, 1962); Katz und Maus, 1961 (Cat and Mouse, 1963); Hundejahre, 1963 (Dog Years, 1965); Örtlich Betäubt, 1969 (Local Anaesthetic, 1970); *poetry:* Die Vorzüge der Windhühner, 1956; Gleisdreieck, 1960; Ausgefragt, 1967; *poetry in translation:* Selected Poems, 1966; Poems of Günter Grass, 1969; *drama:* Hochwasser, 1957 (Flood, 1968); Noch zehn Minuten bis Buffalo, 1958 (Only Ten Minutes to Buffalo, 1968); Onkel, Onkel, 1958 (Onkel, Onkel, 1968); Die bösen Köche, 1961 (The Wicked Cooks, 1968); Die Plebejer proben den Aufstand, 1966 (The Plebeians rehearse the Uprising, 1967); Davor, 1969; *prose:* Uber das Selbsverständlische, 1968; (Speak Out!, 1969). *Address:* Niedstrasse 13, Berlin 41, Germany.

**GRATIAEN, Edward Frederick Noel,** CMG 1952; QC 1962; *b* 30 Dec. 1904; *s* of late W. E. Gratiaen, Ceylon; *m* 1936, Zillah Weinman; one *d*. *Educ:* St Thomas' Coll., Ceylon; Exeter Coll., Oxford; QC (Ceylon) 1946; formerly Attorney Gen. and Puisne Justice, Ceylon. Past Pres., Blackheath Football Club. *Address:* 1 Radnor House, Manor Way, Blackheath, SE3. *Clubs:* Athenæum; Army and Navy.

**GRATTAN-BELLEW, Sir Arthur (John),** Kt 1959; CMG 1956; QC (Tanganyika), 1952; *b* 23 May 1903; *s* of Sir Henry (Christopher) Grattan-Bellew, 3rd Bt, and Lady Sophia Forbes, *d* of 7th Earl of Granard, KP; *m* 1931, Freda Mary Mahony; one *s* one *d*. *Educ:* Downside Sch.; Christ's Coll., Cambridge (BA). Called to Bar, Lincoln's Inn, 1925; practised in London until 1935, Legal Service, Egyptian Govt, 1936-38; Colonial Legal Service, Malaya, 1938-41. Military Service, 1941-45 (POW 1942-45). Colonial Legal Service; Malaya, 1946-48; Attorney-General: Sarawak, 1948-52; Tanganyika, 1952-56; Chief Sec., Tanganyika, 1956-59, retired. Legal Adviser's Dept, Foreign and Commonwealth Office. *Address:* Pledgdon Green, Henham, near Bishop's Stortford, Herts.

**GRATTAN-BELLEW, Sir Henry Charles,** 5th Bt, *cr* 1838; *b* 12 May 1933; *s* of Lt-Col Sir Charles

Christopher Grattan-Bellew, 4th Bt, MC, KRRC and Maureen Peyton, *niece* and adopted *d* of late Sir Thomas Segrave, Shenfield, Essex; *S* father, 1948; *m* 1956, Naomi Ellis, *yr d* of late Dr Charles Cyril Morgan, Chester. *Educ:* St Gerard's, Bray, Co. Wicklow; Ampleforth Coll., York. *Heir: c* Patrick Edward Grattan-Bellew, *b* 26 Sept. 1934.

**GRATTAN-COOPER, Rear Admiral Sidney,** CB 1966; OBE 1946; *b* 3 Dec. 1911; *s* of Sidney Cooper; *m* 1940, Felicity Joan Pitt; two *s*. *Educ:* privately. Entered RN 1936; served in war of 1939-45; Chief of Staff Flag Officer (Air) Home, 1957-59; Staff of Supreme Allied Cdr Atlantic (NATO), 1961-63; Dep. Controller (Aircraft) RN, Min. of Aviation, 1964-66; retired 1966. *Recreations:* golf, swimming. *Address:* Hursley, St James, Cape, S Africa. *Club:* Army and Navy.

**GRATTIDGE, Capt. Harry,** OBE 1940; retired 31 Dec. 1953, as Commodore, Cunard Line; *b* 30 Dec. 1890; *s* of George Grattidge and Nellie Tildesley; *m* 1917, Dorothy K. Sale (marriage dissolved), Plymouth; one *s*. *Educ:* Stafford Grammar Sch. Joined Cunard Line as Junior Officer, 1914; in command SS Ascania, 1943-44. After comdg various other ships became Capt. of Queen Mary, 1949-52; Queen Elizabeth, 1952-53. Lecture tour in USA, 1957. *Publication:* Captain of the Queens. *Address:* 41 Dudley Court, Upper Berkeley Street, W1. *Club:* County Conservative (Stafford).

**GRATWICK, John;** Managing Director, Urwick, Orr & Partners Ltd, since 1968; Member (part-time), Monopolies Commission, since 1969; *b* 23 April 1918; *s* of Percival John and Kathleen Mary Gratwick; *m* 1944, Ellen Violet Wright; two *s* two *d*. *Educ:* Cranbrook Sch., Kent; Imperial Coll., Univ. of London. Asst Production Manager, Armstrong Siddeley, 1941-45; Director, Urwick, Orr & Partners Ltd, 1959. Member: Economic Develt Cttee for the Clothing Industry, 1967-; Senate of Univ. of London, 1967-; Univ. of London Appts Bd, 1962-. *Recreations:* golf, sailing, photography, philately. *Address:* Silver Howe, Nuns Walk, Virginia Water, Surrey. *T:* Wentworth 3121. *Clubs:* Reform, National Liberal; Wentworth (Surrey).

*See also Stephen Gratwick.*

**GRATWICK, Stephen,** QC 1968; *b* 19 Aug. 1924; *s* of late Percival John Gratwick, Fawkham, Kent; *m* 1954, Jocelyn Chaplin, Horton Kirby, Kent; four *d*. *Educ:* Charterhouse, Balliol Coll., Oxford. Oxford 1942-44; Signals Research and Develt Estab., 1944-47. BA (Physics) 1946; MA 1950. Called to Bar, Lincoln's Inn, 1949. *Recreations:* sailing, ski-ing, tennis, swimming, making and mending things. *Address:* Queen Elizabeth Building, Temple EC4. T: 01-353 1234. *Clubs:* Ski Club of Great Britain; Catamaran Yacht.

*See also John Gratwick.*

**GRAVE, Walter Wyatt,** CMG 1958: MA (Cambridge); Hon. LLD (Cambridge and McMaster); Master of Fitzwilliam College, Cambridge, since 1966; *b* 16 Oct. 1901; *o s* of late Walter and Annie Grave; *m* 1932, Kathleen Margaret, *d* of late Stewart Macpherson; two *d*. *Educ:* King Edward VII Sch., King's Lynn; Emmanuel Coll., Cambridge (Scholar); Fellow of Emmanuel Coll., 1926-66; Tutor, 1936-40; University Lecturer in Spanish, 1936-40; Registrary of Cambridge Univ., 1943-52; Principal of the University Coll., of the West Indies, Jamaica, 1953-58; Censor of Fitzwilliam House, Cambridge, 1959-66. Temporary Administrative Officer, Ministry of Labour and National Service, 1940-43. *Address:* 18 Luard Road, Cambridge. *T:* 47415.

**GRAVELY, Sir Walter B.;** *see* Booth-Gravely.

**GRAVES,** family name of **Baron Graves.**

**GRAVES,** 8th Baron, *cr* 1794; **Peter George Wellesley Graves;** Actor; *b* 21 Oct. 1911; *o s* of 7th Baron Graves; *S* father, 1963; *m* 1960, Vanessa Lee. *Educ:* Harrow. First appeared on London stage in 1934, and has subsequently played many leading parts. Mem. Windsor repertory co., 1941. Has appeared in films since 1940. *Recreation:* lawn tennis. *Heir: kinsman,* Evelyn Paget Graves [*b* 17 May 1926; *m* 1957, Marjorie Ann, *d* of late Dr Sidney Ernest Holder; two *s* two *d*]. *Address:* c/o Messrs Coutts & Co., 440 Strand, WC2. *Club:* All England Lawn Tennis.

**GRAVES, Charles Patrick Ranke,** MA; Writer; *b* 1 Dec. 1899; *s* of late Alfred Perceval Graves and late Amalie von Ranke; *m* Margaret Ethel (Peggy) (*d* 1962), *o d* of late Hon. Rowland Leigh; *m* 1966, Vivien Winch (*née* St George). *Educ:* Charterhouse; St John's Coll., Oxford. Edited Isis; later columnist, Sunday Express, Daily Express, Sunday Chronicle, Sunday Graphic, Bystander, Sunday Dispatch, Daily Mail, News of the World. *Publications:* And the Greeks; Gone abroad; Panorama; Gone abroad again; The Price of Pleasure; Triptyque to Spain; Deauville Taxi; Other People's Money; Swiss Summer; You're Welcome; War over Peace; The Pope Speaks; The Thin Blue Line; Life Line; Off the Record; The Avengers; Londoner's Life; Seven Pilots; The Home Guard of Britain; The Black Beret; Great Days; Five Survive; Pride of the Morning; Dusk to Dawn; Atlantic Queens at War; Switzerland Revisited; The Riviera Revisited; Women in Green; the Story of St Thomas's; Ireland Revisited; Italy Revisited; The Big Gamble; The 3rd vol. of Regimental history of The Royal Ulster Rifles; The Cochran Story; The Bad Old Days; Royal Riviera; Champagne and Chandeliers; The Art of Egmontese; None But the Rich; Palace Extraordinary; Leather Armchairs; Fourteen Islands in the Sun; The Rich Man's Guide to Europe; The Legend of Linda Martel; Invasion by Virus; Enjoy Life Longer. *Recreations:* golf, and gin rummy. *Address:* Les Rocques Barrées, Guernsey, CI. *Clubs:* Curzon House; Cercle des Capucines (Paris), Royal Channel Islands Yacht, Royal Guernsey Golf.

**GRAVES, Sir Hubert (Ashton),** KCMG, *cr* 1953 (CMG 1947); MC; *b* 10 Aug. 1894; *m* 1st, 1921, Madeleine Constance Marie Michelle Bourdillon (*deceased*); one *s*; 2nd, 1929, Albertine Louise Macon; one *d*. European War, 1914-18, Served with Leics Regt and Machine Gun Corps; entered Consular Service, 1926; served in various posts in Japan and Far East until 1941; seconded to Naval Board and Dept of External Affairs, Australia, for special duties, 1942-45; Controller, Far Eastern Div., Political Intelligence Dept, 1945; Counsellor British Embassy, Washington, DC, USA, 1946-51; Minister to Associate States of Vietnam, Cambodia and Laos, 1951-Oct. 1954, when became Ambassador to Vietnam (on the raising of status of the post to an Embassy); retired, 1955. *Address:* East Dean, St Mary's Road, Leatherhead, Surrey. *T:* Leatherhead 2541.

**GRAVES, Robert Ranke;** writer; Professor of Poetry, University of Oxford, 1961-66; *b* London, 1895; *s* of late Alfred Perceval and Amy Graves; *m* 1st, Nancy, *d* of late Sir Wm Nicholson; one *s* two *d* (and one *s* killed in

Burma); 2nd, Beryl, *d* of late Sir Harry Pritchard; three *s* one *d. Educ:* Charterhouse; St John's Coll., Oxford. Served in France with Royal Welch Fusiliers; Prof. of English Literature, Egyptian Univ., 1926. Clarke Lecturer at Trinity Coll., Cambridge, 1954. Arthur Dehon Little Memorial Lecturer, Massachusetts Institute of Technology, 1963. Books (over 100) and manuscripts, on permanent exhibition, at Lockwood Memorial Library, Buffalo, NY. Bronze Medal for Poetry, Olympic Games, Paris, 1924; Gold Medal for Poetry, Cultural Olympics, Mexico, 1968; Gold Medal of Nat. Poetry Soc. of America, 1960; Queen's Gold Medal for Poetry, 1968. Adoptive son of Deyá village, Mallorca, 1968, where resident since 1929. *Publications:* Goodbye to All That, An Autobiography, 1929 (revised 1957); But it Still Goes on, 1930; The Real David Copperfield, 1933; I, Claudius, 1934 (awarded Hawthornden and James Tait Black Memorial Prizes for 1934); Claudius the God, 1934; Antigua Penny Puce, 1936; T. E. Lawrence to his Biographer, 1938; Count Belisarius, 1938 (awarded Stock Prize, 1939); Sergeant Lamb of the Ninth, 1940; The Long Week End: A Social History (with Alan Hodge), 1940; Proceed, Sergeant Lamb, 1941; Wife to Mr Milton, 1943; The Reader Over Your Shoulder (with Alan Hodge), 1943; The Golden Fleece, 1944; King Jesus, 1946; The White Goddess, 1947; Collected Poems, 1948; Seven Days in New Crete, 1949; The Common Asphodel (Collected Essays on Poetry), 1949; The Isles of Unwisdom, 1949; Occupation: Writer, 1950; Poems and Satires, 1951; The Nazarene Gospel Restored (with Joshua Podro), 1953; The Greek Myths, 1955 (new edn, Greek Myths and Legends, 1968); Homer's Daughter, 1955; The Crowning Privilege, 1955; Adam's Rib, 1955; Catacrok (stories), 1956; Jesus in Rome (with Joshua Podro), 1957; They hanged my saintly Billy, 1957; (ed) English and Scottish Ballads, 1957; Steps, 1958; Collected Poems, 1959; The Penny Fiddle, 1960; More Poems, 1961; Oxford Addresses, 1962; New Poems, 1962; (with Raphael Patai) Hebrew Myths; Genesis, 1964; Collected Short Stories, 1964; Man Does, Woman Is (poems), 1964; Mammon and the Black Goddess, 1964; Hebrew Myths: Genesis (with Rafael Patai), 1965; Ann at High Wood Hall, 1965; Collected Short Stories, 1965; Love Respelt, 1965; Majorca Observed, 1965; Collected Poems, 1965; Seventeen Poems Missing from Love Respelt, 1966; Two Wise Children, 1967; Colophon, 1967; Poetic Craft and Principle, 1967; The Poor Boy who followed his Star, 1968; Poems 1965-68, 1968; The Crane Bag and other disputed subjects, 1968; Beyond Giving, 1969; Poems 1968-1970, 1970; The Song of Songs (with lithographs by Hans Erni), 1970; *translations:* The Golden Ass, 1949; Alarcón's Infant with the Globe, 1956; Galvan's The Cross and the Sword, 1956; George Sand's Winter in Majorca, 1957; Suetonius's Twelve Cæsars; Lucan's Pharsalia; Homer's Anger of Achilles, 1959; Terence's Comedies, 1962; Rubaiyyat of Omar Khayaam (with Omar Ali-Shah), 1967. *Address:* c/o A. P. Watt & Son, 26/28 Bedford Row, WC1.

**GRAVESON, Prof. Ronald Harry,** QC 1966; Barrister-at-Law; Professor of Law since 1947 and Head of the Department of Laws, King's College, University of London; Visiting Professor: Harvard Law School, 1958-59; New York University Law School, 1959; *b* 2 Oct. 1911; *o s* of Harry Graveson, Sheffield; *m* 1937, Muriel, *o d* of John Saunders, Sheffield; one *s* two *d. Educ:* King Edward VII Sch., Sheffield; Universities of Sheffield, Harvard and London. LLB (Hons) 1932, LLM 1933, LLD 1955 Sheffield, SJD Harvard 1936; PhD London 1941; LLD London 1951; Scholar of Sheffield Univ.; Gregory Scholar in International Law of Harvard Univ. 1934; Solicitor (Hons). In private practice, 1935-40; Asst Lecturer in Law, King's Coll., University of London, 1938-40. Army, 1940-46 (Driver, RE; Lieut-Col RASC). Called to Bar, Gray's Inn, 1945; Bencher, 1965; Reader in English Law, University Coll., University of London, 1946-47; Dean of the Faculty of Laws, University of London, 1951-54, and King's Coll., London, 1951-58, 1959-63, 1966-70. Chm., UK, National Cttee of Comparative Law, 1955-57; Hon. Mem. Louisiana State Law Inst.; Deputy Chm. of Convocation of Univ. of London, 1955-59 and Mem. of the Senate, 1958-69; Mem. of the Senate of the Inns of Court, 1967-69; President: Council of Legal Educn, 1965-70; Harvard Law Sch. Assoc. of the UK, 1959-61; Dir Commonwealth-American Legal Studies. Consultant Editor of the Law Reports and the Weekly Law Reports, 1970-. Pres. International Association of Legal Science (UNESCO), 1960-62. Mem. Exec. Cttee, Internat. Social Science Council; Assoc. Mem. Inst. of International Law; Corr. Member: Rome Inst. for the Unification of Private Law; Internat. Acad. of Comparative Law. FKC 1962. LLD (*hc*) Ghent, 1964; Dr Juris (*hc*) Freiburg, 1969. JP St Alban's City, 1961-66. Rep. HM Govt at Cttee of Council of Europe and at 8th, 9th, 10th and 11th Sessions of Hague Conf. of Private Internat. Law, leading UK Delegn at 10th and 11th Sessions. Commandeur de l'Ordre de la Couronne de Chêne, 1964; Comdr, Order of Oranje Nassau, 1970. *Publications:* English Legal System, 1939; Conflict of Laws, 1948 (6th edition 1969); Cases on the Conflict of Laws, 1949; The Comparative Evolution of Principles of the Conflict of Laws in England and the USA 1960; General Principles of Private International Law, 1964; (jtly) The Conflict of Laws and International Contracts, 1951; Status in the Common Law, 1953; (jtly) A Century of Family Law, 1957; Law: An Introduction, 1967; (jtly) Unification of the International Law of Sale, 1968; Jt Editor, International and Comparative Law Quarterly, 1955-61; various articles, notes or reviews since 1936 in English and foreign law reviews. Contributor to: Current Legal Problems; Bentham and the Law; Chambers's Encyclopædia; Bibliography of UK Law; British Year Book of International Law; The teaching of the Social Sciences in the UK (UNESCO, 1953); Legal Institutions, Today and Tomorrow, 1959; The Jubilee Lectures, 1960; XXth Century Comparative and Conflicts Law, 1961; *De Conflictu Legum*, 1962; Vom Deutschen zum Europäischen Recht, 1963; Essays in Honour of Austin W. Scott, 1964 and G. W. Keeton, 1967; Apollo; Connoisseur. *Recreations:* tennis, works of art. *Address:* 2 Raymond Buildings, Gray's Inn, WC1. *T:* 01-242 8492. *Clubs:* Athenæum, Royal Commonwealth Society.

**GRAY,** 22nd Baron, *cr* 1445; **Angus Diarmid Ian Campbell-Gray;** *b* 3 July 1931; *s* of Major Hon. Lindsay Stuart Campbell-Gray, Master of Gray, MC (**d** 1945), and Doreen (*d* 1948), *d* of late Cyril Tubbs, Thedden Grange, Alton, Hants; *S* grandmother 1946; *m* 1959, Patricia Margaret, *o d* of late Capt. Philip Alexander and of Mrs Alexander, Kilmorna, Lismore, Co. Waterford; one *s* three *d. Heir: s* Master of Gray, *qv. Address:* The Malt House, Bran End, Stebbing, Dunmow, Essex CM6 3RX. *Club:* Carlton.

**GRAY,** Master of; **Hon. Andrew Godfrey Diarmid Stuart Campbell-Gray;** *b* 3 Sept. 1964; *s* of 22nd Baron Gray, *qv.*

**GRAY, Air Vice-Marshal Alexander,** CB 1944; MC; RAF retired; Deputy Air Commander, RAF Component, Eastern Air Command, South-East Asia Command, 1944; Dir of Flying Training, Air Ministry, 1945; Air Officer Commanding, Air Headquarters, Iraq, 1947; retired, 1949. *Address:* Gatcombe, Greenwood Avenue, Ferndown, Dorset.

**GRAY, Alexander Stuart,** FRIBA; Consultant to Watkins, Gray, Woodgate International, since 1968; *b* 15 July 1905; *s* of Alexander and Mary Gray; *m* 1932, Avis, *d* of John Radmore, Truro; one *s* two *d*. *Educ:* Mill Hill Sch. Articled to R. S. Balgarnie Wyld, ARIBA; studied at Central Sch. of Arts and Crafts; Royal Academy Schools (Bronze Medal, 1928; Silver Medal and Travelling Studentship, 1932; Gold Medal and Edward Stott Trav. Studentship (Italy), 1933); Brit. Instn Schol., 1929. Lectr on Arch. subjects at Central Sch. of Arts and Crafts, Brixton Sch. of Bldg, and Hammersmith Sch. of Bldg, 1936-39; Lectr on Hosp. Planning at King Edward VII Hosp. Fund Colleges, 1950-. In partnership with W. H. Watkins won architectural comp. for new St George's Hosp., Hyde Park Corner, London (partnership 1939-68); before retirement Architect with partners to: Radcliffe Infirmary, Oxford, United Bristol Hospitals, Royal Free Hospital, Guy's Hospital, London Hospital, Eastman Dental Hospital, St Mary's, Manchester, and other hosps in London and the provinces; also in West Indies, where they were responsible for banks, and commercial buildings as well; hospitals for Comptroller of Development and Welfare in BWI, 1941-46; rebuilding of centre of Georgetown, British Guiana, after the fire of 1945, including new GPO, Telecommunications Building, etc. In Nigeria, University Coll. Hosp., Ibadan, and other works, also in Qatar (Persian Gulf), etc. *Publications:* various papers read at confs on Hosp. Planning with special ref. to designing for the tropics, and contrib. Tech. Jls. *Address:* 76 Jermyn Street, SW1. *T:* 01-930 0981; 19 Middleway, NW11. *T:* 01-455 3998. *Clubs:* Arts, West Indian.

**GRAY, Andrew Aitken,** MC 1945; Chairman, Wellcome Foundation Ltd, since 1970; *b* 11 Jan. 1912; *s* of John Gray and Margaret Eckford Gray (*née* Crozier); *m* 1939, Eileen Mary Haines; three *s*. *Educ:* Wyggeston School, Leicester; Christ Church, Oxford. Served Royal Engineers, 1939-46 (MC, despatches). Unilever Ltd, 1935-52. Dir, Wellcome Foundation Ltd, 1954, Dep. Chm., 1967; Chm. and Man. Dir, Cooper, McDougall & Robertson, 1963-70. Comdr, Orden del Mérito Agricola. *Recreations:* fishing, gardening, theatre. *Address:* Rainhill Spring, Bovingdon, Herts. *T:* Bovingdon 3277. *Clubs:* East India and Sports, Farmers'.

**GRAY, Basil,** CB 1969; CBE 1957; MA; FBA 1966; Keeper of Oriental Antiquities, British Museum, 1946-69, Acting Director and Principal Librarian, 1968; *b* 21 July 1904; *s* of late Surgeon-Major Charles Gray and Florence Elworthy, *d* of Rev. H. v. H. Cowell; *m* 1933, Nicolete, *d* of late Laurence Binyon, CH; two *s* three *d*. *Educ:* Bradfield; New Coll., Oxford. British Academy excavations in Constantinople, 1928; entered British Museum (Printed Books), 1928; transferred to sub-Dept of Oriental Prints and Drawings, 1930; in charge of Oriental Antiquities (including Oriental Prints and Drawings) from 1938; Dep. Keeper, 1940; Mem. of Art Panel of the Arts Council, 1952-57, and 1959-68; President: Oriental Ceramic Soc., 1962-65. 6th Internat. Congress of Iranian Art and Archaeology, Oxford, 1972. A Visitor of Ashmolean Museum, Oxford, 1969-. *Publications:* Persian Painting, 1930; Persian Miniature Painting (part author), 1933; Chinese Art (with Leigh Ashton), 1935; The English Print, 1937; Persian Painting, New York, 1940; Rajput Painting, 1948; (joint) Commemorative Catalogue of the Exhibition of the Art of India and Pakistan, 1947-48, 1950; Treasures of Indian Miniatures in the Bikanir Palace Collection, 1951; Early Chinese Pottery and Porcelain, 1953; Japanese Screen-paintings, 1955; Buddhist Cave paintings at Tun-huang, 1959; Treasures of Asia; Persian Painting, 1961; (with D. E. Barrett) Painting of India, 1963; (Ed) Faber Gallery of Oriental Art. *Address:* Dawber's House, Long Withenham, Berks. *Club:* Savile.

**GRAY, Charles Herbert,** FRCS; Consultant Orthopædic Surgeon, Royal Free Hospital and British Postgraduate Medical School, Hammersmith Hospital; Consulting Orthopædic Surgeon, Connaught Hospital, Walthamstow. *Educ:* Victoria University, Manchester. BSc; MB, ChB (hons) 1932; MRCS, LRCP, 1932; FRCS, 1935. Temp. Lt-Col, Royal Army Medical Corps. Hunterian Prof., Royal College of Surgeons, 1946, 1949. Formerly, Fracture and Orthopædic Registrar, Middlesex Hosp.; Surg. Registrar, Royal Nat. Orthopaedic Hospital. Fellow: British Orthopaedic Assoc.; Hunterian Soc.; Membre Societé Internationale de Chirurgie, Orthopédie et Traumatologie. *Publications:* various articles in medical jls. *Address:* 27 Harley Street, W1. *T:* 01-580 5307.

**GRAY, Charles Horace,** MD (London). DSc, FRCP, FRIC, FCPath; Professor of Chemical Pathology in the University of London at King's College Hospital Medical School since 1948, and Consultant Chemical Pathologist, King's College Hospital Group, Denmark Hill, London, SE5, since 1938; *b* 30 June 1911; *s* of Charles H. Gray and Ethel Hider, Erith, Kent; *m* 1938, Florence Jessie Widdup, ARCA, *d* of Frank Widdup, JP, Barnoldswick, Yorks; two *s*. *Educ:* Imperial Coll. and University Coll., London; University Coll. Hospital Medical Sch. Demonstrator in Biochemistry, University Coll., London, 1931-36; Bayliss-Starling Scholar in Physiology and Biochemistry, 1932-33; Visiting Teacher in Biochemistry, Chelsea Polytechnic, 1933-36; Demonstrator and Lecturer in Physiology, University Coll., 1935-36; Graham Scholar in Pathology, UCH Medical Sch., 1936-38; Pathologist in Charge Sector Biochemical Laboratory, Sector 9, Emergency Health Service. 1939-44. Member: Clinical Res. Bd of Med. Res. Council, 1964-68; Cttee of Management, Inst. of Psychiatry, 1966; Assoc. of Biochemists (Pres. 1969-71). *Publications:* The Bile Pigments, 1953; Clinical Chemical Pathology, 1953, 1959, 1963, 1965, 1968; The Bile Pigments in Health and Disease, 1961; (Editor) Laboratory Handbook of Toxic Agents; (Joint Editor) Hormones in Blood, 1961, 1967; contributions to medical and scientific journals. *Recreations:* music and travel. *Address:* Barn Cottage, Linden Road, Leatherhead, Surrey. *T:* 2415; 34 Cleaver Square, SE11. *T:* 01-735 9652; Owls Mount, Portland, Dorset. *T:* Portland 3374. *Club:* Athenæum.

**GRAY, David;** *b* 2 April 1906; *er s* of W. S. Gray; *m* 1938, Betty R. Humphry, Southsea; one *s*. *Educ:* The Grammar School, Carlisle; Merton Coll., Oxford; London Sch. of Economics. Cadet, Malayan Civil Service, 1930; Chinese Secretariat, Singapore, 1934; interned, Singapore, 1942-45; Dept of Labour, Federation of Malaya, 1947; Sec. for Chinese Affairs, Fedn of Malaya, 1951; Actg Chief

Sec., Fedn of Malaya, 1952; Resident Councillor, Penang, 1954; Actg Chief Sec., Fedn of Malaya, and Officer Administering the govt of Fedn, 1955-56. Secretary-General, Engineering Industries Assoc., 1956; Sec., The Industrial Soc., 1958-68. *Recreation:* golf. *Address:* 48 Bryanston Square, W1. *T:* 01-262 2401. *Club:* Royal Over-Seas League.

**GRAY, Dulcie;** *see* Denison, D. W. C.

**GRAY, Geoffrey Leicester,** CMG 1958; OBE 1953; Secretary for Local Government, N Borneo, 1956-61, retired; *b* 26 Aug. 1905; *s* of late Leonard Swainson Gray, Resident Magistrate of Kingston, Jamaica, and of late Marion Scotland, Vale Royal, Kingston, Jamaica; *m* 1932, Penelope Milnes, MBE, 1962, *o c* of late Philip Henry Townsend, OBE and late Gwenyth Gwendoline Roberts. *Educ:* Latymer Upper Sch. Cadet, North Borneo Civil Service, under British North Borneo (Chartered) Co., 1925; served in various admin. posts, 1925-30; studied Chinese in Canton, 1931; attached Secretariat for Chinese Affairs and Educ. Dept, Hong Kong, 1931; Dist Officer, Jesselton, Supt, Govt Printing Office, and Editor, British North Borneo Herald and Official Gazette, 1932-35; Dist Officer, Kudat, 1935; Under-Sec., 1935-38; Govt Sec. Class 1b and *ex-officio* MLC, 1938-46; Additional Sessions and High Court Judge, 1938-46; interned by Japanese, 1941-45; Class 1a, 1946; accredited to HQ Brit. Mil. Admin (Brit. Borneo) at Labuan, 1946; assimilated into HM Colonial Admin. Service (later HM Overseas Service) on cession of North Borneo to the Crown, 1946; Actg Dep. Chief Sec., 1946; Protector of Labour and Sec. for Chinese Affairs, 1947; Resident, E Coast, in addition, 1947; Mem. Advisory Council, 1947-50; Comr of Immigration and Labour, 1948-51: Official MLC and MEC, 1950-61; Actg Fin. Sec., 1951-52; Dep. Chief Sec., Staff Class, 1952-56; represented North Borneo at Coronation, 1953; Chm. Board of Education, 1956-61; Actg Chief Sec. (intermittently), 1952-60; administered Govt twice, 1958, 1959; acted as High Comr, Brunei, 1959; retd, 1961. Life Associate, N Borneo and UK Branches, CPA, 1961. Chm., Borneo Mission Assoc., 1961; Commissary for Bp of Jesselton (later Sabah), 1961. Elected Incorporated Mem. of SPG (Mem., Standing Cttee, 1964-66; Mem., East Asia and Pacific Sub-Cttees, 1964-69; Mem. USPG Council, 1965, Mem. Gen. Cttee, 1966; Mem. Overseas Cttee, Grants and Budget Groups, 1969. *Address:* 4 Trafalgar Road, Twickenham, Middx. *T:* 01-894 4142. *Club:* Royal Commonwealth.

**GRAY, George Charles,** DMus (Cantuar) 1968; FRCO 1920; FRSCM 1967; Organist and Master of the Music, Leicester Cathedral, 1931-69; Conductor of Leicester Bach Choir, 1931-69; Senior Lecturer in Music, Leicester College of Education, since 1946; Lay Canon of Leicester Cathedral, 1942; Examiner, Trinity College of Music, since 1958; *b* 1897; *s* of late Charles Wilson Gray and Alice Gray; *m* 1925, Gladys Gofton, York; two *s* one *d* (and one *d* decd). *Educ:* Rotherham Grammar Sch. MusB (Dunelm) 1927. Articled pupil of late Sir Edward Bairstow at York Minster, 1919-22; Lafontaine Prize winner, Royal Coll. of Organists, 1920, also winner, Worshipful Company of Musicians Silver Medal, 1922; Organist and Choirmaster successively of S Michael-le-Belfry, York, S Martin's, Leeds, and Alnwick Parish Church; Conductor of Alnwick Choral Union, and Wooler Choral Union Organist and Choirmaster, St Mary le Tower, Ipswich, 1926; Founder and Conductor of Ipswich Bach Choir 1927-30; Conductor of Ipswich Choral Society, 1928-30; Extra-mural Lecturer in Musical Appreciation at Vaughan Coll., Leicester, 1931-51; Lecturer in Singing, University Coll., 1931-58. Pres. Cathedral Organists' Assoc., 1968-70. Hon. MusM Leicester, 1965. *Recreation:* cricket. *Address:* 8 Knighton Court, Knighton Park Road, Leicester LE2 1ZB. *T:* 705167. *Club:* Rotary.

**GRAY, His Eminence Cardinal Gordon;** *see* St Andrews and Edinburgh, Archbishop of, (RC).

**GRAY, Gordon;** Chairman, National Trust for Historic Preservation; Chairman of the Board, Triangle Broadcasting Corporation; Member, President's Foreign Intelligence Advisory Board, since 1961; *b* 30 May 1909; *s* of Bowman and Nathalie Lyons Gray; *m* 1938, Jane Boyden Craige (*d* 1953); four *s*; *m* 1956, Nancy Maguire Beebe; three step *d*. *Educ:* Woodberry Forest Sch., Woodberry Forest, Va; University of N Carolina, Chapel Hill, NC; Yale Law Sch., New Haven, Conn. Admitted to NY Bar, 1934, and associated with Carter, Ledyard & Milburn, 1933-35; with Manly, Hendren & Womble, Winston-Salem, NC, 1935-37; admitted to North Carolina Bar, 1936; Pres., Piedmont Publishing Company, 1937-47. N Carolina Senate, 1939, 1941, 1945. Enlisted in US Army as private, 1942; Capt., 1945. Asst Sec. of Army, 1947; Under-Sec. of Army, 1949; Sec. of Army, 1949; Special Asst to the President, USA, April-Nov. 1950; Dir, Psychological Strategy Board, July-Dec. 1951. Pres. of Univ. of N Carolina, Feb. 1950-Nov. 1955; Asst Sec. of Defense, International Sec. Affairs, US, 1955-57; Dir, Office of Defense Mobilization, 1957-58; Special Asst to President, USA, for National Security Affairs, 1958-61. Chm. Nat. Trust for Historic Preservation; Mem. Civil Defense Adv. Council; Director: R. J. Reynolds Tobacco Co.; American Security & Trust Co.; Media General, Inc.; Trustee: Corcoran Art Gallery; Brookings Instn; Federal City Council. Pres., Kensington Orchids Inc. Holds several Hon. degrees. *Address:* 1224 30th Street NW, Washington, DC 20007, USA; (Office) 800 17th Street NW, Washington, DC 20006, USA. *Clubs:* Alibi, Chevy Chase, Burning Tree, Metropolitan (all Washington); The Brook (New York).

**GRAY, Rear-Adm. Gordon Thomas Seccombe,** CB 1964; DSC 1939; *b* 20 Dec. 1911; *s* of late Rev. Thomas Seccombe Gray and Edith Gray; *m* 1939, Sonia Moore-Gwyn; one *s* one *d*. *Educ:* Nautical Coll., Pangbourne. Entered RN, 1929; Sub-Lieut and Lieut, Mediterranean Fleet, 1934-36, ashore Arab revolt in Palestine (despatches); 1st Lieut, HMS Stork, 1939, Norwegian campaign (despatches, DSC); Comd HMS Badsworth, 1942-43 (despatches); Comd HMS Lamerton, 1943-45 (despatches). After the War comd destroyers Consort, Contest and St Kitts; JSSC, 1948; Comdr 1949; Directing Staff, RN Staff Coll., Greenwich, 1950; Exec. Officer, cruiser HMS Glasgow, 1951-53; Capt. 1953; Naval Deputy to UK Nat. Military Representative, at SHAPE; Capt. of 5th Frigate Sqdn, and Comd HMS Wakeful and HMS Torquay, 1956-59; Asst Chief of Staff to C-in-C Eastern Atlantic Command, 1959-61; in comd of Naval Air Anti-Submarine Sch. at Portland and Chief Staff Officer to Flag Officer Sea Trng, 1961-62; Senior Naval Instructor, Imperial Defence Coll., 1963-65, retd. *Recreation:* yachting. *Address:* Hollies, Wispers, Midhurst, West Sussex. *Club:* East India and Sports.

**GRAY, Hamish;** *see* Gray, J. H. N.

**GRAY, Harold James,** CMG 1956; Director of Legal Affairs, Confederation of British Industry, since 1965; *b* 17 Oct. 1907; 2nd *s* of late John William Gray and of Amelia Frances (*née* Miller); *m* 1928, Katherine Gray (*née* Starling); one *d. Educ:* Alleyn's Sch.; Dover County Sch.; Queen Mary Coll., London Univ. (MSc, LLB); Gray's Inn; Harvard University, USA (Master of Public Administration). Customs and Excise Dept, 1927; Asst Examiner, Patent Office, 1930, Examiner, 1935; Industries and Manufactures Dept, Board of Trade, 1938; Ministry of Supply, 1939; Asst Sec., Min. of Supply, 1942. transf. to Bd of Trade, 1946; Commercial Relations and Exports Dept, Board of Trade, 1950; Under-Sec., 1954; UK Senior Trade Comr and Economic and Commercial Adviser to High Commissioner in Australia, 1954-58; United Kingdon Senior Trade Commissioner and Economic Adviser to the High Commissioner in the Union of South Africa, 1958-60; Dir, National Association of British Manufacturers, 1961-65. Associate Mem. Inst. of Physics; Commonwealth Fund Fellowship, 1949-50. Dir NUMAS Ltd. *Publications:* Electricity in the Service of Man, 1949; Economic Survey of Australia, 1955; Dictionary of Physics, 1958. *Recreations:* golf, swimming, riding. *Address:* (office) 21 Tothill Street, SW1; Four Oaks, Marlings Park Avenue, Chislehurst, Kent. *Clubs:* Devonshire, Hurlingham.

**GRAY, Harriet;** *see* Robins, Mrs Denise.

**GRAY, Hugh,** BSc(Soc), PhD; *b* 19 April 1916; *s* of William Marshall Kemp Gray; *m* 1954, Edith Esther (*née* Rudinger); no *c. Educ:* Battersea Gram. Sch.; London Sch. of Economics. Army Service (Intelligence Corps), 1940-45. UNRRA, 1945-48; Internat. Refugee Organisation, 1948-52; Social Worker, 1952-57; Student on Leverhulme Adult Schol. at LSE, 1957-60; Fellow in S Asian Studies, SOAS, 1960-62; Lectr in Sociology with ref. to S Asia, SOAS, University of London, 1962-66; MP (Lab) Yarmouth, 1966-70. *Publications:* various articles on Indian politics in Jl of Commonwealth Studies, Asian Survey, etc. *Recreations:* ski-ing, skating, theatre, ballet. *Address:* 22 Bridstow Place, W2.

**GRAY, Sir James,** Kt 1954; CBE 1946; MC; FRS; ScD; Fellow of King's College Cambridge, since 1914; Professor of Zoology, Cambridge Univ., 1937-59; Development Commission, 1951-59; Chairman of the Fishery Advisory Committee of Development Commission; Trustee of British Museum, 1948-60; *b* 14 Oct. 1891; *s* of James Gray; *m* 1921, Norah C. King; one *s* one *d. Educ:* Merchant Taylors' Sch., London; King's Coll., Cambridge (Scholar). Capt. The Queen's Royal West Surrey Regt, 1914-18; Balfour Student, 1919-23; Reader in Experimental Zoology, Cambridge Univ. Fullerian Prof. of Physiology, Royal Institution, 1943-47; Mem. Agricultural Research Council, 1942-47; President: Marine Biological Assoc., 1945-55; Brit. Assoc. for the Advancement of Science, 1959; Eugenics Soc., 1962-. Hon. LLD (Edinburgh, Aberdeen); Hon. DSc (Durham, Manchester, Wales). *Publications:* Scientific papers; Ciliary Movement; Experimental Cytology; How Animals Move; Animal Locomotion. *Recreations:* golf, angling. *Address:* King's Field, West Road, Cambridge. *T:* 50439.

**GRAY, James Hector Northey, (Hamish Gray);** MP (C) Ross and Cromarty since 1970; Director in Family and other Cos; *b* 28 June 1927; *s* of J. Northey Gray, Inverness, and Mrs. E. M. Gray; *m* 1953, Judith Waite Brydon, BSc, Helensburgh; two *s* one *d. Educ:* Inverness Royal Academy. Served in Queen's Own Cameron Hldrs, 1945-48. Member, Inverness Town Council, 1965-70. *Recreations:* golf, walking, family life. *Address:* The Cedars, Drummond Road, Inverness. *Club:* Highland (Inverness).

**GRAY, John;** *see* Gray, R. J.

**GRAY, Rev. Prof. John;** Professor of Hebrew, University of Aberdeen; *b* 9 June 1913; *s* of James Telfer Gray; *m* Janet J. Gibson; five *c. Educ:* Kelso High Sch.; Edinburgh Univ. (MA, BD, PhD). Colonial Chaplain and Chaplain to Palestine Police, 1939-41; Minister of the Church of Scotland, Kilmory, Isle of Arran, 1942-46; Lectr in Semitic Languages and Literatures, Manchester Univ., 1946-53; Lectr in Hebrew and Biblical Criticism, University of Aberdeen, 1953-61. Mem., Soc. for Old Testament Study. *Publications:* The Kt Text in the Literature of Ras Shamra, 1955 (2nd edn 1964); The Legacy of Canaan, 1957 (2nd edn 1965); Archæology and the Old Testament World, 1962; The Canaanites, 1964; Kings I and II: a Commentary, 1964; Joshua, Judges and Ruth, 1967; A History of Jerusalem, 1969; Near Eastern Mythology, 1969; contribs to various Bible Dictionaries, memorial volumes and learned journals. *Recreations:* beekeeping, gardening, trout-fishing. *Address:* Inverawe, Persley, Aberdeen. *T:* Bucksburn 2729.

**GRAY, John Archibald Browne,** MA, MB, ScD; Secretary, Medical Research Council, since 1968; *b* 30 March 1918; *s* of late Sir Archibald Gray, KCVO, CBE; *m* 1946, Vera Kathleen Mares; one *s* one *d. Educ:* Cheltenham Coll.; Clare Coll., Cambridge; University Coll. Hospital. BA 1939; MA 1942; MB, BChir 1942; ScD 1962. Service Research for MRC, 1943-45; Surg. Lieut, RNVR, 1945-46; Scientific Staff of MRC at Nat. Inst. for Med. Research, 1946-52; Reader in Physiology, University Coll., London, 1952-58; Prof. of Physiology, University Coll., London, 1959-66; Second Sec., Medical Research Council, 1966-68. QHP 1968-. FIBiol. *Publications:* papers, mostly on sensory receptors and sensory nervous system, in Jl of Physiology, etc. *Recreations:* painting, sailing, tennis. *Address:* Medical Research Council, 20 Park Crescent, W1. *Club:* Athenæum.

**GRAY, Air Vice-Marshal John Astley,** CB 1945; CBE 1943; DFC; GM; retired; *b* 1899. *Educ:* Framlingham Coll. Served European War, 1917-19; War of 1939-45. Air Officer Commanding, RAF, Greece, 1946; Air Officer Administrating Middle East, 1949-54; retired, 1954. *Club:* Royal Air Force.

**GRAY, Vice-Adm. Sir John (Michael Dudgeon),** KBE 1967 (OBE 1950); CB 1964; General Secretary, Victoria League, since 1968; *b* Dublin, 13 June 1913; British; *m* 1939, Margaret Helen Purvis; one *s* one *d. Educ:* RNC, Dartmouth. HMS Nelson, 1931; Midshipman, HMS Enterprise, 1932-33; Sub-Lieut, HMS Devonshire, 1934; specialised in Gunnery, 1938. Served War of 1939-45; HMS Hermes; HMS Spartan; with US in Anzio; 8th Army in Italy; French Army in France (despatches). HMS Duke of York, 1945, Comdr 1947; Naval Adviser, UK Mission, Japan, 1947-50 (OBE Korean War); HMS Swiftsure, 1950, Capt. 1952; HMS Lynx, 1956; HMS Victorious, 1961; Rear-Adm. 1962; Dir-Gen. of Naval Trng, Min. of Def., 1964-65 (Admiralty, 1962-64); Vice-Adm. 1965; C-in-C, S Atlantic and S America, 1965-67. *Recreations:* squash, tennis, athletics (represented RN in 220 and 440 yds). *Address:*

55 Elm Park Gardens, SW10. *T:* 01-352 1757. *Club:* Naval and Military.

**GRAY, Rt. Rev. Joseph;** Titular Bishop of Mercia and Auxiliary Bishop of Liverpool, (RC), since 1969; *b* 20 Oct. 1919; *s* of Terence Gray and Mary Gray (*née* Alwill). *Educ:* St Patrick's Coll., Cavan, Eire; St Mary's Seminary, Oscott, Birmingham; Dunboyne House, St Patrick's Coll., Maynooth, Eire; Pontifical Univ. of St Thomas Aquinas, Rome. Priest, 1943; Asst Priest, Sacred Heart, Aston, Birmingham, 1943-48; Dunboyne House, 1948-50 (Licentiate in Canon Law, 1950); Sec. to Archbp of Birmingham, 1950-55. Diocesan Chancellor, Birmingham, 1951-69; Pontifical Univ., 1959-60 (Doctorate in Canon Law, 1960); Vicar-Gen., Birmingham, 1960-69; Parish Priest, St Michael's, Birmingham, 1955-69. Papal Chamberlain, 1960; Domestic Prelate, 1966. *Recreations:* music, reading, travel. *Address:* Martland House, Spencer Road, Wigan, Lancashire. *T:* Wigan 42740.

**GRAY, Margaret Caroline,** MA Cantab; Headmistress, Godolphin and Latymer School, since 1963; *b* 25 June 1913; *d* of Rev. A. Herbert Gray, DD, and Mrs Gray (Mary C. Dods, *d* of Principal Marcus Dods of New Coll., Edinburgh). *Educ:* St Mary's Hall, Brighton; Newnham Coll., Cambridge. Post graduate fellowship to Smith Coll., Mass, USA, 1935-36. Asst History mistress, Westcliff High Sch. for Girls, 1937-38; Head of History dept, Mary Datchelor Girls' Sch., Camberwell, 1939-52; Headmistress, Skinners' Company's Sch., Stamford Hill, 1952-63. *Recreations:* gardening, motoring, walking. *Address:* 28 Bishop's Close, Ham Common, Richmond, Surrey. *T:* 01-940 8010.

**GRAY, Mary Elizabeth,** CBE 1946 (OBE 1942); WVS Administrator, Midland Region, since 1949; resigned as County Commssioner, Gloucestershire Girl Guides (1949-61); *b* 19 May 1903; *d* of late Edward Wilmot Butler and Ethel Margaret Gray. *Educ:* Lanherne House, Dawlish; Switzerland. Joined WVS 1938; WVS Administrator, Eastern Counties Region 4, 1938-44; Deputy Vice-Chm., WVS, 1944; WVS Administrator SEAC and FE, 1944-48. *Recreation:* dog breeding. *Address:* Woodgate, Albert Road North, Great Malvern, Worcs.

**GRAY, Milner Connorton,** CBE 1963; RDI 1938; FSIA; AGI; MInstPack; Designer, Senior Partner, Design Research Unit, since 1946: Past Master, Faculty of Royal Designers for Industry; Past President, Society of Industrial Artists and Designers; Past Master Art Workers' Guild; British President, Alliance Graphique Internationale; *b* 8 Oct. 1899; *s* of late Archibald Campbell Gray and Katherine May Hart, Eynsford, Kent; *m* 1934, Gnade Osborne-Pratt; no *c*. *Educ:* studied painting and design, London Univ., Goldsmiths' Coll. Sch. of Art. Head of Exhibitions Branch, Ministry of Information, 1940-41, and Adviser on Exhibitions, 1941-44; Senior Partner in Industrial Design Partnership, 1934-40; Principal, Sir John Cass Sch., 1937-40; on Visiting Staff: Goldsmiths' Coll. Sch. of Art, London Univ., 1930-40; Chelsea Sch. of Art, 1934-37; Royal Coll. of Art, 1940; Founder Mem., Soc. of Industrial Artists, 1930, Hon. Sec., 1932-40, Pres., 1943-48 and 1968; Member of Council: Design and Industries Assoc., 1935-38; RSA, 1959-65; Artists Gen. Benevolent Instn; Adviser to BBC "Looking at Things" Schs Broadcasts, 1949-55. Member: Min. of Education Nat. Adv. Cttee on Art Examinations, 1949-52; Nat. Adv. Council on Art Education, 1959-69; Royal Mint Adv. Cttee, 1956-. Mem. Council, RCA, 1963-67, Mem. Court 1967-. Consultant Designer: BR Bd for BR Corporate Identity Prog., 1963-67; (jointly) to Orient Line, SS Oriana, 1957-61; Ilford Ltd, 1946-66; Internat. Distillers and Vintners, 1954-; Watney Mann Group, 1956-; British Aluminium Co., 1965-; ICI, 1966-; Min. of Technology, 1970-. Governor: Central Sch. of Art and Design, 1944-46; Hornsey Coll. of Art and Design, 1959-65. Hon. Des. RCA; Hon. DA Manchester. Served in 19th London Regt, and Royal Engineers, attached Camouflage Sch., 1917-19. Gold Medal, Soc. of Ind. Artists and Designers, 1955. *Publications:* The Practice of Design (jointly), 1946; Package Design, 1955; Lettering for Architects and Designers, 1962; articles, lectures and broadcasts on various aspects of design. *Address:* 8 Holly Mount, Hampstead, NW3. *T:* 01-435 4238; Felix Hall, Kelvedon, Essex. *Clubs:* Arts, Garrick.

**GRAY, Prof. Peter,** MA, PhD, ScD (Cantab); FRIC; Professor and Head of Department of Physical Chemistry, University of Leeds, since 1965; *b* 25 Aug. 1926; *er s* of late Ivor Hicks Gray and Rose Ethel Gray; *m* 1952, Barbara Joan Hume, PhD, 2nd *d* of J. B. Hume, London; two *s* two *d*. *Educ:* Newport, High Sch.; Gonville and Caius Coll., Cambrdige. Major Schol., 1943; Prizeman, 1944, 1945 and 1946, Gonville and Caius Coll.; BA 1st cl hons Nat. Sci. Tripos, 1946; Dunlop Res. Student, 1946; Ramsay Mem. Fellow, 1949-51; PhD 1949; Fellow, Gonville and Caius Coll., 1949-53; ICI Fellow, 1951; ScD 1963. University Demonstrator in Chem. Engrg, University of Cambridge, 1951-55; Physical Chemistry Dept, University of Leeds: Lectr, 1955; Reader, 1959; Prof., 1962. Vis. Prof., Univ. of BC, 1958-59. Mem. Council: Faraday Soc., 1965; Chemical Soc., 1969. Meldola Medal, Royal Inst. Chem., 1956; Marlow Medal, Faraday Soc., 1959. *Publications:* papers on phys. chem. subjects in scientific jls. *Recreation:* walking. *Address:* 4 Ancaster Road, Leeds LS16 5HH. *T:* Leeds 52826.

**GRAY, Maj.-Gen. (Reginald) John;** Deputy Director-General of Army Medical Services, since 1969; QHS 1970; *b* 26 Nov. 1916; *s* of late Dr Cyril Gray and Frances Anne Higgins, Higginsbrook, Co. Meath; *m* 1943, Esme, *d* of late G. R. G. Shipp; one *s* one *d*. *Educ:* Rossall Sch.; Coll. of Medicine, Univ. of Durham. MB, BS. Commissioned into RAMC, 1939; served War of 1939-45 in India; later Burma, NW Europe, Egypt, Malta, BAOR. Comd of 9 (Br.) CCS, 1945; Asst Dir-Gen., AMS, WO, AMD3, 1954-57; comd of David Bruce Mil. Hosp., Mtarfa, 1957-60; 14 Field Amb., 4 Guards Bde, 1960-63; Brit. Mil. Hosp., Rinteln, 1963-64; The Queen Alexandra Mil. Hosp., Millbank, 1964-67; Asst Dir-Gen., AMS, Min. of Defence AMD1, 1967-69. FRSM; FMedSoc. Lond. OStJ 1957. *Recreations:* horticulture, philately. *Address:* 11 Hampton Close, Wimbledon, SW20. *T:* 01-946 7429. *Club:* Army and Navy.

**GRAY, Roger Ibbotson,** QC 1967; *b* 16 June 1921; *o s* of late Arthur Gray and of Mary Gray (*née* Ibbotson), Seaford, Sussex; *m* 1952, Anne Valerie, 2nd *d* of late Capt. G. G. P. Hewett, CBE, RN; one *s*. *Educ:* Wycliffe Coll.; Queen's Coll., Oxford. 1st cl. hons Jurisprudence, Oxon, 1941. Commissioned RA, 1942; served with Ayrshire Yeomanry, 1942-45; Normandy and NW Europe, 1944-45; GSO3 (Mil. Ops), GHQ, India, 1946. Pres. of Oxford Union, 1947. Called to Bar, Gray's Inn, 1947; South-Eastern Circuit. Contested (C) Dagenham, 1955. *Publication:* (with Major I. A. Graham Young) A Short History of the Ayrshire Yeomanry (Earl of Carrick's Own) 151st Field Regiment, RA, 1939-46, 1947. *Recreations:* cricket, reading, talk. *Address:* 34 Halsey

Street, SW3. *T:* 01-589 0221. *Clubs:* Carlton, MCC.

**GRAY, Stephen Alexander Reith;** Managing Director of Strip Mills Division, British Steel Corporation, since 1970; *b* 18 June 1926; *er s* of Alexander Reith Gray and Catherine Mary Thompson. *Educ:* Winchester Coll.; Trinity Coll., Cambridge. Stewarts & Lloyds Ltd, 1950-53; John Summers & Sons Ltd, 1953-68; Member for Engineering, BSC, 1968-70. *Address:* Lower Soughton, Northop, Mold, Flints. *T:* Northop 203. *Club:* Leander.

**GRAY, Prof. Thomas Cecil,** MD, FRCS, FFARCS; FFARACS (Hon.); FFARCSI (Hon.); Professor of Anæsthesia, The University of Liverpool, since 1959; Dean of Postgraduate Medical Studies, 1966-70, of Faculty of Medicine, since 1970; *b* 11 March 1913; *s* of Thomas and Ethel Gray; *m* 1937, Marjorie Kathleen (*née* Hely); one *s* one *d*. *Educ:* Ampleforth Coll.; University of Liverpool. General Practice, 1937-39. Hon. Anaesthetist to various hospitals, 1940-47. Active Service, Royal Army Medical Corps, 1942-44. Demonstrator in Anæsthesia, University of Liverpool, 1942, 1944-46; Reader in Anæsthesia, University of Liverpool, 1947-59; Hon. Cons Anæsthetist: United Liverpool Hosps, Royal Infirmary Branch; Liverpool Thoracic Surgical Centre, Broadgreen Hosp.; Mem. Bd, Faculty of Anæsthetists, RCSEng, 1948-69 (Vice-Dean, 1952-54; Dean, 1964-67). Member Council: RCS, 1964-67; Assoc. of Anæsthetists of Great Brit. and Ire., 1948-67 (Hon. Treas. 1950-56; Pres. 1957-59); FRSocMed (Mem. Council, 1958-61; Pres. Anæsthetic Section, 1955-56; Mem. Council, Sect. of Med. Educn, 1969-); Chm. BMA Anæsthetic Group, 1957-62; Mem., Liverpool Regional Hosp. Board, 1968- (Chm., Anæsthetic Adv. Cttee, 1948-70; Chm., Med. Adv. Council); Mem., Bd of Governors, United Liverpool Hosp., 1969-; Mem. Clinical Res. Bd, Med. Res. Council, 1965-69; Hon. Civilian Consultant in Anæsthetics to the Army at Home. Hon. Consultant to St John's Ambulance; Member Council: Order of St John, County Palatine of Lancaster; Med. Defence Union. Examiner in FFARCS, 1953-70; FFARCSI 1967-70: Dip. Vet. Anæsth., RCVS, 1968-70. Hon. Member: Sheffield and East Midlands Soc. of Anæsthetists; Yorks Soc. of Anæsthetists; Soc. Belge d'Anesthesie et de Reanimation; Brazilian Soc. of Anesthesiologists; Argentinian Soc. of Anesthesiologists; Australian Soc. of Anæsthetists; Assoc. of Veterinary Anæsthetists. Hon. Corresp. Member: Sociedade das Ciencias Medical di Lisboa; W African Assoc. of Surgeons. Clover Lecturer and Medallist, RCS of England, 1953; Simpson-Smith Memorial Lecturer, W London Sch. of Med., 1956; Jenny Hartmann Memorial Lectr, University of Basle, 1958; Eastman Lectr, University of Rochester, NY, 1958; Sims Commonwealth Travelling Prof., 1961; Sir James Young Simpson Memorial Lectr, RCS Edinburgh, 1967. Medallist, University of Liège. *Publications:* Consultant Ed. British Journal of Anæsthesia; Jt Ed., Modern Trends in Anæsthesia, Jt Ed., General Anæsthesia. Many contrib. gen. med. press and specialist jls. *Recreations:* music and amateur dramatics. *Address:* Dalkey, Burbo Bank Road North, Liverpool L23 8TA. *T:* 051-924 5805. *Clubs:* National Liberal; Liverpool University.

**GRAY, Vernon Foxwell,** CIE 1936; *b* Singapore, 1 Sept. 1882; *s* of Alfred Thomas Gray and Jane Ann Foxwell; *m* 1st, 1919, Bertha Marie (*d* 1928), *d* of late James Walter Champion Stevens; one *d*; 2nd, 1929, Marian Agnes Conley (*d* 1931), *d* of late Col Peter Burke; 3rd, 1937, Frances Buckland (*d* 1957), *d* of late Arthur Newman. *Educ:* Solihull Sch. Chm. and Pres., Punjab Chamber of Commerce, 1920-27 and 1938-39; Mem. of Punjab Legislative Council, 1923-29; Sole Representative Associated Chambers of Commerce of India-Ceylon at 10th Congress Assoc. Chambers of Commerce of Empire, in London, 1924; late Dir R. J. Wood and Co., Ltd, India; late Dir of John Bolton and Co., Ltd, Manchester; Jubilee Medal, 1935; Coronation Medal, 1937. *Recreations:* riding, fishing, tennis, golf. *Address:* Whittam, Hartley Road, Altrincham, Cheshire, *T:* 061-928 4374.

**GRAY, Sir William,** 2nd Bt, *cr* 1917; DL; Director, Hartlepools Water Company; Local Director, Royal Insurance Group; late Yorkshire Regiment; *b* 18 Aug. 1895; *o s* of 1st Bt and Kate, *d* of late C. T. Casebourne, CE; *S* father, 1924; *m* 1st, 1929, Josephine (*d* 1943), *d* of William Henry Eveleigh; two *s*; 2nd, 1947, Mrs Beryl Henshaw, *d* of Alfred Stott, Liverpool. *Educ:* Loretto Sch., Edinburgh. Served European War, 1914-18, as Capt. Yorks Regt (despatches; wounded, prisoner); High Sheriff of Co. Durham, 1938-39. *Recreations:* shooting, fishing. *Heir: s* William Talbot Gray [*b* 4 July 1931; *m* 1954, Rosemarie Elliott-Smith; one *s* two *d*]. *Address:* Egglestone Hall, Egglestone, Barnard Castle, Durham. *T:* Cotherstone 228.

**GRAY, William Macfarlane,** OBE 1961; JP; FACCA; Senior Partner Macfarlane Gray & Co., Stirling, since 1934; Hon. Sheriff Substitute for Stirling and Clackmannan since 1964; *b* 28 March 1910; *s* of Peter M. Gray and Isabella Bain Macfarlane; *m* 1938, Muriel Agnes Elizabeth Lindsay, *d* of James R. Lindsay, Glasgow; two *d*. *Educ:* The High Sch. of Stirling. Provost of Royal Burgh of Stirling, 1958-64; Nat. Pres., Assoc. of Certified and Corporate Accountants, 1954-56; Chm. Stirling Festival of the Arts Cttee, 1958-67; Chm. Stirlingshire Savings Cttee, 1959-; Member: Court, Univ. of Stirling, 1968-; Executive Cttee, Scottish Council (Development and Industry), 1961-; Scottish Tourist Board, 1963-64; Council, National Trust for Scotland, 1962; Chairman: PO Advisory Cttee for Stirlingshire and Clackmannan; of Trustees, Smith Art Gallery and Museum, Stirling, 1958-64; Sponsoring Cttee for University of Stirling, 1963-65. Member: South of Scotland Electricity Board, 1961-66; Independent Television Authority (Chm. Scottish Adv. Cttee), 1964-70; Nat. Savings Cttee for Scotland, 1969-; Exec. Cttee, British Council (Chm. Scottish Adv. Cttee), 1970-. Hon. Freeman of Royal Burgh of Stirling, 1964. Hon. DUniv. Stirling, 1968. OStJ. *Recreation:* golf. *Address:* 27 Snowdon Place, Stirling. *T:* Stirling 4776. *Club:* Stirling and County.

**GRAY, (William) Nicol,** CMG 1948; DSO 1944, Bar, 1945; Administrator, MacRobert Trusts, Douneside, Tarland; *b* 1 May 1908; *e s* of late Dr W. Gray, Westfield, West Hartlepool; *m* 1st, 1953, Jean Marie Frances Backhouse (marr. diss. 1966), *o c* of Lieut-Col G. R. V. Hume-Gore, MC and Mrs W. Lyne-Stephens, and *widow* of Major Sir John Backhouse, Bt, MC; two *d*; 2nd, 1967, Margaret Clare Galpin, *widow* of Commander Walter Galpin, RN. *Educ:* Trinity Coll., Glenalmond. Royal Marines, 1939-46; Inspector-Gen., Palestine Police, 1946-48; Commissioner of Police, Federation of Malaya, 1948-52. Agent to the Jockey Club, Newmarket, 1953-64. *Address:* The Lodge, Tarland, Aberdeenshire. *Clubs:* Boodle's; Royal Northern.

**GRAY DEBROS, Mrs E.;** *see* Fox, W. M.

**GRAY HORTON, Lieut-Col W.**; *see* Horton, W. G.

**GRAYSON, Prof. Cecil,** MA; Serena Professor of Italian Studies in the University of Oxford, and Fellow of Magdalen College, since 1958; *b* 5 Feb. 1920; *s* of John M. Grayson and Dora Hartley; *m* 1947, Margaret Jordan; one *s* three *d*. *Educ:* Batley Grammar Sch.; St Edmund Hall, Oxford. Army service (UK and India), 1940-46 (Major); First Class Hons (Mod. Langs), 1947; Univ. Lectr in Italian, Oxford, 1948; Lectr at St Edmund Hall, 1948; Lectr at New Coll., 1954. Corresp. Fellow, Commissione per i Testi di Lingua, Bologna, 1957; Mem., Accademia Letteraria Ital. dell' Arcadia, 1958; Corresp. Mem., Accademia della Crusca, 1960; Accademia delle Scienze, Bologna, 1964; Accademia dei Lincei, 1967; Barlow Lecturer, University Coll., London, 1963; Resident Fellow, Newberry Library, Chicago, 1965; Visiting Professor: Yale Univ., 1966; Berkeley, Calif, 1969. An editor of Italian Studies. *Publications:* Early Italian Texts (with Prof. C. Dionisotti), 1949; Opuscoli inediti di L. B. Alberti, 1954; Alberti and the Tempio Malatestiano, 1957; Vincenzo Calmeta, Prose e Lettere edite e inedite, 1959; A Renaissance Controversy: Latin or Italian?, 1960; L. B. Alberti, Opere volgari, I, 1960, II, 1966; L. B. Alberti e la prima grammatica volgare, 1964; (trans.) The Lives of Savonarola, Machiavelli and Guicciardini by Roberto Ridolfi, 1959, 1963, 1967; (ed) selected works of Guicciardini, 1964. Articles in Bibliofilia, Burlingon Mag., English Misc., Giorn. Stor. d. Lett. Ital., Ital. Studies, Lettere Italiane, Lingua Nostra, Rassegna d. Lett. Ital., Rinascimento, The Year's Work in Mod. Languages. *Recreation:* music. *Address:* 11 Norham Road, Oxford. *T:* 57045.

**GRAYSON, Sir Ronald Henry Rudyard,** 3rd Bt of Ravens Point, *cr* 1922; *b* 15 Nov. 1916; *s* of Sir Denys Henry Harrington Grayson, 2nd Bt, and Elsie May, *d* of Richard Davies Jones; *S* father 1955; *m* 1st, 1936, Babette Vivienne (marriage dissolved, 1944), *d* of Count Vivien Hollender; 2nd, 1946, Dorothy Vera Hoare, *d* of Charles Serrel. *Educ:* Harrow Sch. Engineering apprenticeship Grayson, Rollo & Clover Docks Ltd, 1934. Dir, 1940-49; Emigrated to Australia, 1953. Served War of 1939-45, RAF. *Heir: uncle* Rupert Stanley Harrington Grayson [*b* 22 July 1897; *m* 1st, 1919, Ruby Victoria, *d* of Walter Henry Banks; 2nd, 1950, Vari Colette, *d* of Major Henry O'Shea]. *Recreations:* books, travel. *Address:* 22 Kimberly Street, Vaucluse, Sydney, New South Wales, Australia.

**GRAYSTON, Rev. Prof. Kenneth,** MA; Professor of Theology, Bristol University, since 1965; *b* Sheffield, 8 July 1914; *s* of Ernest Edward and Jessie Grayston; *m* 1942, Elizabeth Alison, *d* of Rev. Walter Mayo and Beatrice Aste, Elsfield, Oxon.; no *c*. *Educ:* Colfe's Grammar Sch., Lewisham; Universities of Oxford and Cambridge. Ordained Methodist Minister, 1942; Ordnance Factory Chaplain, 1942-44; Asst Head of Religious Broadcasting, BBC, 1944-49; Tutor in New Testament Language and Literature, Didsbury Coll., 1949-64; Special Lecturer in Hellenistic Greek, Bristol University, 1950-64; Select Preacher to University of Cambridge, 1952, 1962; Sec. Studiorum Novi Testamenti Societas, 1955-65. *Publications:* The Epistles to the Galatians and to the Philippians, 1957; The Letters of Paul to the Philippians and the Thessalonians, 1967; (contrib. in): A Theological Word Book of the Bible, 1950; The Teacher's Commentary, 1955; The Interpreter's Dictionary of the Bible, 1962, etc. (Contrib. to): Expository Times, New Testament Studies, Theology, London Quarterly and Holborn Review, etc. *Recreations:* tennis, travel. *Address:* 11 Rockleaze Avenue, Bristol BS9 1NG. *T:* Bristol 683872.

**GREATBATCH, Sir Bruce,** Kt 1969; CMG 1961; CVO 1956; MBE 1954; Governor and Commander-in-Chief, Seychelles, and Commissioner for the British Indian Ocean Territory, since 1969; *b* 10 June 1917; *s* of W. T. Greatbatch; unmarried. *Educ:* Malvern Coll.; Brasenose Coll., Oxford. Appointed Colonial Service, 1940, Northern Nigeria. War Service with Royal W African Frontier Force, 1940-45, rank of Major, Burma Campaign (despatches). Resumed Colonial Service, Northern Nigeria, 1945; Resident, 1956; Sec. to Governor and Executive Council, 1957; Senior Resident, Kano, 1958; Sec. to the Premier of Northern Nigeria and Head of Regional Civil Service, 1959; Dep. High Comr, Nairobi, Kenya, 1963. KStJ 1969. *Recreations:* shooting, gardening, *Address:* Government House, Seychelles; c/o National Provincial Bank, Ltd, Cornmarket Street, Oxford. *Club:* Public Schools.

**GREAVES, Maj.-Gen. Charles Granville Barry,** CB 1947; CBE 1945 (OBE 1941); late Royal Engineers; *b* 1900; *s* of late Charles Gregory Heritage Greaves, Inverness; *m* 1926, Maud Frances Mary, *d* of late Frank Euting, Durban, S Africa; three *s*. *Educ:* Inverness Royal Academy; RMA Woolwich. Commissioned RE 1920. Dir of Movements, War Office, 1949-53; retired 1953; American Bronze Star, 1945. *Address:* Devon Lodge, 15 Kimbolton Avenue, Bedford. *T:* 53368.

**GREAVES, Prof. Harold Richard Goring;** Professor of Political Science in the University of London since 1960; *s* of Harold Frederick Greaves, Derbyshire, and Beatrice Violet (*née* Heather); unmarried. *Educ:* London Sch. of Economics, University of London; Graduate Institute, Geneva. Has taught at the London Sch. of Economics and Political Science since 1931; previously worked in business, a bank, and free lance journalism. Visiting Professor, Columbia Univ., New York, 1959-60; Literary Editor, Political Quarterly; English Editor, International Political Science Abstracts. Contested (Lab) Camborne, Cornwall, 1935. War-time service BBC and RIIA. *Publications:* The League Committees and World Order, 1931; The Spanish Constitution, 1933; Reactionary England, 1936; Raw Materials and International Control, 1936; The British Constitution, 1938; Federal Union, 1940; The Civil Service and the Changing State, 1947; The Foundations of Political Theory, 1958; Democratic Participation and Public Enterprise (Hobhouse Memorial Lecture), 1964; contrib. to Political Quarterly, Political Science Quarterly, Modern Law Review, The Civil Service in Britain and France, etc. *Address:* The Forge, Stoke by Clare, Suffolk. *Club:* Reform.

**GREAVES, Sir John (Bewley),** Kt, *cr* 1953; CMG 1948; OBE 1944; *b* 6 June 1890; 2nd *s* of late John and Mary Greaves; *m* 1918, Grace Anne, *d* of late W. T. Lock. *Educ:* Cardiff High Sch.; University Coll., Cardiff. Served European War, 1914-19, 21st Royal Fusiliers and 12th South Wales Borderers. Joined Dept of Overseas Trade, 1919; Asst Trade Commissioner, Vancouver, 1931; Trade Commissioner, Winnipeg, 1937-39; Trade Commissioner, Toronto, 1939-45. Acting Senior Trade Commissioner in Canada for periods during 1938, 1943 and 1944; Commercial Counsellor, British Embassy, Washington, 1945-47; United Kingdom Senior Trade Commissioner in Australia and

Economic Adviser to United Kingdom High Commissioner, 1948-54, retired 1954. *Address:* 1 Sandgate, Portsmouth Road, Esher, Surrey.

**GREAVES, Prof. Robert William;** Professor of History, University of Kansas, since 1968; *b* 27 May 1909; *s* of William Atkins Greaves and Olive Greaves (*née* Whatnall), Leicester; *m* 1955, Rose Louise Coughlin, Kansas City, Kansas, USA. *Educ:* Alderman Newton's Sch., Leicester; Merton Coll., Oxford (Exhibr, Harmsworth Schol.). BA, 1st cl. Mod. History, 1930; 2nd cl. PPE, 1931; MA 1934; DPhil 1936. Temp. Lectr, Queen's University of Belfast, 1935; Asst in History, Bedford Coll., London, 1935-39. Temp. Admin Officer, HM Treasury, 1940-42, Min. of Production, 1942-45; Asst Private Sec. to Chancellor of Exchequer, 1942, to Minister of Production, 1942-43. Bedford Coll., University of London: Lectr in History, 1945-50; Reader in History, 1950-62; Prof. of Modern History, 1962-68; Head of Dept of History, 1962-68; Vice-Princ., 1964-65. Birkbeck Lectr in Eccles. History, Trinity Coll., Cambridge, 1963-64. Vis. Professor: University of Kansas, 1965-66; University of Toronto, 1967-68. Hon. Sec., Royal Historical Society, 1955-58. *Publications:* The Corporation of Leicester 1689-1836, 1939; The First Ledger Book of High Wycombe, 1957; Autobiography and Court Papers of Archbishop Secker;contrib. to Victoria County History of Leicestershire and to New Cambridge Modern History; articles and reviews in English Historical Review, Jl Eccles. History, History, etc. *Address:* 1920 Hillview Road, Lawrence, Kansas 66044, USA. *T:* 913-842-9161. *Clubs:* Reform, Royal Commonwealth Society.

**GREBENIK, Eugene,** MSc (Economics); Principal of the Civil Service College since 1970; Joint Editor, Population Studies; Secretary-Treasurer, International Union for the Scientific Study of Population; *b* 20 July 1919; *s* of S. Grebenik; *m* 1946, Virginia, *d* of James D. Barker; two *s* one *d*. *Educ:* abroad; London Sch. of Economics. Statistician, Dept of Economics, Univ. of Bristol, 1939-40; London Sch. of Economics: Asst. 1940-44 and Lecturer, 1944-49, in Statistics (on leave, 1944-46; served in RN, 1944; Temp. Statistical Officer, Admiralty, 1944-45; Secretariat, Royal Commn on Population, 1945-46); Reader in Demography, Univ. of London, 1949-54; Research Sec., Population Investigation Cttee, 1947-54; Prof. of Social Studies, Univ. of Leeds, 1954-69. Mem., Impact of Rates Cttee, Ministry of Housing, 1963-64. Social Science Research Council: Statistics Cttee, 1966-69; Cttee on Social Science and Government, 1968-. Hon. Fellow, LSE, 1969. *Publications:* (with H. A. Shannon) The Population of Bristol, 1943; (with D. V. Glass) The Trend and Pattern of Fertility in Great Britain; A Report on the Family Census of 1946, 1954; various articles in statistical and economic journals. *Address:* Civil Service College, Sunningdale Park, Ascot, Berks. *T:* Ascot 23178.

**GRECH, Herbert F.,** CVO 1954; *b* 18 May 1899; *m* 1923, Alice Machell (*d* 1969); two *d* (one *s* decd). *Educ:* St Aloysius' Coll., Malta. Served in Army, 1917-20, Lieut King's Own Malta Regt of Militia. Malta Police Force, 1920-54; Commissioner of Police, Malta, 1951-54; retired 1954. *Address:* Flat 1, 27 Creche Street, Sliema, Malta. *T:* Sliema 30086. *Club:* Union (Malta).

**GREEN, Alan;** MP (C) Preston South, 1955-64 and since 1970; Director: Walmsley (Bury) Group (Chairman since 1970); Scapa Group Ltd; Wolstenholme Bronze Powders Ltd (Vice-Chairman); Porritts & Spencer (Asia) Ltd, since 1969; Local Director, Barclays Bank, Manchester District, since 1969; *b* 29 Sept. 1911; *s* of Edward and Emily Green; *m* 1935, Hilda Mary Wolstenholme; three *d*. *Educ:* Brighton Coll. Schoolmaster, 1931-35; joined Scapa Dryers Ltd, Blackburn, 1935. Army Service, 1940-45. Formerly: Dir of Scapa Dryers Ltd, 1945; Vice-Chm. of Scapa Dryers Ltd, 1956; Dir of Scapa Dryers Inc., 1955; Dir of companies associated with Walmsley (Bury) Group, 1950; Chm. of Walmsley Operating Companies, 1954. Contested (C) Nelson and Colne, 1950-51; Parly. Sec., Min. of Labour. 1961-62; Minister of State, Board of Trade, 1962-63; Financial Sec. to the Treasury, 1963-64. Mem., Australia Cttee, BNEC, 1968-; frequent business visits to Northern and Western Europe and North America. *Recreations:* cricket, golf, tennis, gardening, history. *Address:* The Stables, Sabden, near Blackburn, Lancs. *T:* Padiham 71528; Flat 125, 4 Whitehall Court, SW1. *T:* 01-930 3160. *Clubs:* Carlton, Royal Automobile.
*See also D. C. Waddington.*

**GREEN, Prof. Albert Edward,** FRS 1958; MA, PhD, ScD (Cambridge); Sedleian Professor of Natural Philosophy, University of Oxford, since 1968; *m* 1939, Gwendoline May Rudston. *Educ:* Jesus Coll., Cambridge Univ. (Scholar). PhD 1937; MA 1938; ScD 1943. Formerly: Lecturer in Mathematics, Durham Colls, University of Durham; Fellow of Jesus Coll., Cambridge, 1936; Prof. of Applied Mathematics, University of Newcastle upon Tyne, 1948-68. *Address:* Mathematical Institute, 24-29 St Giles, Oxford.

**GREEN, Arthur Eatough,** CIE 1946; OBE 1937; MC 1917; MSc (Leeds); FICE; JP; Chief Engineer, Public Works Department, Bihar, India, retired; *b* 16 Dec. 1892; *s* of late William Green; *m* 1929, Frances Margaret, *d* of late Col William Henry Savage, CMG; two *s* one *d*. *Educ:* King's Sch., Pontefract; Leeds Univ. Served European War, 1914-18, in 5th Bn West Yorks Regt and RE. Appointed to PWD, India, 1919; served province of Bihar and Orissa, 1919-47; Chief Engineer and Sec. to Govt of Orissa, in PWD, 1942-44, to Govt of Bihar, 1944-47. JP 1964. *Recreation:* fishing. *Address:* Drumawillin House, Ballycastle, Co. Antrim, N Ireland. *T:* Ballycastle 349.

**GREEN, Rev. Canon Bryan Stuart Westmacott,** BD; DD (*hc*); Canon Emeritus of Birmingham Cathedral since 1970 (Hon. Canon, 1950-70); *b* 14 Jan. 1901; *s* of late Hubert Westmacott Green and late Sarah Kathleen Green (*née* Brockwell); *m* 1926, Winifred Annie Bevan; one *s* one *d*. *Educ:* Merchant Taylors' Sch.; London Univ. BD 1922; Curate, New Malden, 1924-28; Staff of Children's Special Service Mission, 1928-31; Chap., Oxford Pastorate, 1931-34; Vicar of Christ Church, Crouch End, 1934-38; Vicar of Holy Trinity, Brompton, 1938-48; Rector of Birmingham, 1948-70. Conducted evangelistic campaigns: Canada and America, 1936, 1944, and 1947-70; Australia and New Zealand, 1951, 1953, 1958; West Africa, 1953; S Africa, 1953, 1955, 1956, 1957, 1959 and 1960; Ceylon, 1954, 1959. DD Hon. St John's Coll. Winnipeg, 1961. *Publications:* The Practice of Evangelism, 1951; Being and Believing, 1956; Saints Alive, 1959. *Recreation:* golf. *Address:* West Field, Southern Road, Thame, Oxon. *T:* Thame 2026. *Club:* National.

**GREEN, Prof. Cecil Alfred,** MD, PhD, DPH Edinburgh; FCPath; FInstBiol; Professor of Bacteriology, University of Newcastle upon Tyne, since 1963; Director of Department of Microbiology, Royal Victoria Infirmary,

Newcastle upon Tyne, since 1947; *b* 5 Nov. 1908; *s* of George Alfred Green and Anne Bell; *m* 1940, Jemina Stewart Scott; one *s* one *d*. *Educ:* Dunfermline High Sch.; Edinburgh Univ. MB, ChB Edinburgh, 1932, and Vans Dunlop Scholar; Crichton Research Fellow, Edinburgh Univ., 1933-35; Lecturer in Bacteriology, Dept of Bacteriology, Edinburgh Univ., 1935-38; Bacteriologist to Edinburgh Royal Infirmary; Empire Rheumatism Council Research Scholar, 1938-39. Professor of Bacteriology, University of Durham, 1960-63; MD Gold Medal (Edinburgh) 1941. Surg. Comdr, RNVR, 1939-45. *Publications:* articles in med. jls on researches into and control of infectious diseases. *Address:* Department of Microbiology, Medical School, Newcastle upon Tyne.

**GREEN, Prof. Dennis Howard;** Professor of Modern Languages, University of Cambridge, since 1966; Fellow of Trinity College, Cambridge, since 1949; Head of the Department of Other Languages since 1956; *b* 26 June 1922; *s* of Herbert Maurice Green and Agnes Edith Green (*née* Fleming). *Educ:* Latymer Upper Sch., London; Trinity Coll., Cambridge; Univ. of Basle. Univ. of Cambridge, 1940-41 and 1945-47; Univ. of Basle (Dr Phil.), 1947-49; Military service (RAC), 1941-45; Univ. Lecturer in German, St Andrews, 1949-50; Research Fellowship, Trinity Coll., Cambridge (first year held *in absentia*), 1949-52; Univ. Asst Lectr in German, Cambridge, 1950-54; Teaching Fellowship, Trinity Coll., Cambridge, 1952-66; Visiting Professor: Cornell Univ., 1965-66; Auckland Univ., 1966; Yale Univ., 1969. *Publications:* The Carolingian Lord, 1965; The Millstätter Exodus: a crusading epic, 1966. Reviews and articles in learned journals. *Recreations:* walking and foreign travel. *Address:* Trinity College, Cambridge. *T:* Cambridge 58201.

**GREEN, Rev. Edward Michael Bankes;** Principal, St John's College, Nottingham (until July 1970 The London College of Divinity), since 1969; *b* 20 Aug. 1930; British; *m* 1957, Rosemary Wake (*née* Storr); two *s* two *d*. *Educ:* Clifton Coll.; Oxford and Cambridge Univs. BD Cantab 1966. Exeter Coll., Oxford, 1949-53 (1st cl. Lit. Hum.); Royal Artillery (Lieut, A/Adjt), 1953-55; Queens' Coll., Cambridge, 1955-57 (1st cl. Theol. Tripos Pt III; Carus Greek Testament Prize; Fencing Blue), and Ridley Hall Theol Coll., 1955-57; Curate, Holy Trinity, Eastbourne, 1957-60; Lectr, London Coll. of Divinity, 1960-69, Principal, 1969. *Publications:* Called to Serve, 1964; Choose Freedom, 1965; The Meaning of Salvation, 1965; Man Alive, 1967; Runaway World, 1968; Commentary on 2 Peter and Jude, 1968; Evangelism in the Early Church, 1970; contribs to various jls. *Recreations:* family, countryside pursuits, cricket, squash. *Address:* St John's College, Bramcote, Nottingham. *T:* Nottingham 251114.

**GREEN, Sir (Edward) Stephen (Lycett),** 4th Bt, *cr* 1886; CBE 1964; DL, JP; Chairman, East Anglian Regional Hospital Board, since 1959; *b* 18 April 1910; *s* of Sir E. A. Lycett Green, 3rd Bt, and Elizabeth Williams; *S* father, 1941; *m* 1935, Constance Mary, *d* of late Ven H. S. Radcliffe; one *d*. *Educ:* Eton; Magdalene Coll., Cambridge. Called to Bar, Lincoln's Inn, 1933. Served War of 1939-45 (Major, RA). CC 1946-49, JP 1946, DL 1961, Norfolk; Dep. Chairman Norfolk Quarter Sessions, 1948; Chairman: King's Lynn Hospital Management Cttee, 1948-59; Assoc. of Hosp. Management Cttees, 1956-58; Cttee of Inquiry into Recruitment, Training and Promotion of Administrative and Clerical Staff in Hospital Service, 1962-63; Docking RDC, 1950-57. *Recreations:* shooting, racing. *Heir:* *b* Lt-Col Simon Green, TD, Yorks Dragoons Yeomanry [*b* 1912; *m* 1935, Gladys, *d* of late Arthur Ranicar, JP, Springfield, Wigan; one *d*]. *Address:* Ken Hill, Snettisham, King's Lynn. *TA:* Snettisham, Norfolk. *T:* Snettisham 202; 60 Pont Street, SW1. *T:* 01-589 5958. *Clubs:* White's; Norfolk (Norwich).

**GREEN, Ernest,** CBE 1950; JP; LLD, MA; *b* 28 Jan. 1885; *s* of Horatio E. Green, Engineer; *m* 1911, Emma, 3rd *d* of John T. Wilde, cutlery manufacturer, Sheffield; no *c*. *Educ:* elementary sch. Organising Sec. (Yorks) Clerical Workers Union, 1916-23; Yorks District Sec., Workers' Educational Association, 1923-29; National Organising Sec., 1929-34; General Sec., 1934-50; Hon. Treasurer, 1951-62. Member: Civil Service Arbitration Tribunal, 1949-63; Management Cttee of Workers' Travel Assoc., 1934-64. JP for Surrey, 1933; Hon. MA, Manchester, 1937; Hon. LLD Leeds, 1952. *Publications:* Education for a New Society; Adult Education–why this apathy?, 1954; contributor to Year Book of Education, and leading educational journals. *Recreation:* gardening. *Address:* 15 Nidd Rise, Birstwith, near Harrogate, Yorks.

**GREEN, Francis Henry Knethell,** CBE 1949; MD, FRCP; Retired; *b* 27 August 1900; *e s* of late Knethell Wade Green; *m* 1933, Elsie Joyce, *o d* of late Karl Hinde; no *c*. *Educ:* Highgate Sch.; St Bartholomew's Hosp., London. Joined administrative staff of Medical Research Council, 1929; asst Sec., 1946-49, formerly Publications Officer; Principal Medical Officer on headquarters staff, 1949-55; Sec., War Wounds Cttee, 1940-45. Member of: Grand Council, British Empire Cancer Campaign, 1951-55; National Radium Commission, 1941-46; Sec., Scientific Advisory Cttee, Lady Tata Memorial Trust, 1934-55; Scientific Sec., Wellcome Trust, 1955-63; Scientific Adviser, British Heart Foundation, 1963-67. Bradshaw Lecturer, Royal College of Physicians, 1954. *Publications:* various papers in scientific jls, dealing chiefly with the organisation of medical research and clinical trials in Great Britain; jt editor, Medical Research volume of Official Medical History of the Second World War. *Address:* 129 Nether Street, N12. *T:* 01-445 4195. *Club:* Athenæum.

**GREEN, Geoffrey; His Honour Judge Green;** Judge of County Courts since 1969; Deputy Chairman, Herefordshire County Quarter Sessions, since 1966; *b* 10 Sept. 1918; *s* of Arthur Green, Ombersley, Worcs; *m* 1955, Olive Mary Elizabeth Batchelor; two *s* one *d*. *Educ:* Worcester Royal Grammar Sch.; Hertford Coll., Oxford. Served in RA and Indian Mountain Artillery, 1939-46 (despatches); Major. Barrister, Lincoln's Inn, 1947. Chm., Agricultural Land Tribunal, Midlands Area, 1965-69; Chm., Industrial Tribunals, 1965-68. *Recreation:* golf. *Address:* 239 Wells Road, Malvern Wells, Worcs WR14 4HR. *T:* Malvern 4020.

**GREEN, Geoffrey Hugh;** Assistant Under-Secretary of State (Research and Development) Ministry of Defence, since 1969; *b* 24 Sept. 1920; *o s* of late Duncan M. Green, Bristol, and of Mrs Kate Green; *m* 1948, Ruth Hazel Mercy; two *d*. *Educ:* Bristol Grammar Sch.; Worcester Coll., Oxford (Exhibr). Oxford, 1939-41, 1945-47 (MA). Served with Royal Artillery (Ayrshire Yeomanry): N Africa and Italy, 1942-45 (Captain). Entered Min. of Defence, Oct. 1947; Principal, 1949; Asst Sec., 1960; Under-

Sec., 1969. *Recreations:* travel, music. *Address:* 47 Kent Avenue, Ealing W13.

**GREEN, George Conrad,** CMG 1948; MBE 1926; *b* 5 April 1897; 3rd *s* of late J. F. Green, Lancs and British Guiana; *m* 1932, Dorothy Elizabeth, *d* of late Mrs E. Hill, Enfield, Middx; one *s* one *d*. *Educ:* British Guiana. Entered Colonial Service, British Guiana (Colonial Sec.'s Office), 1912; Principal Asst Colonial Sec., 1932; Administrator of Grenada, 1942; retired from Colonial Service, 1951; attached to Colonial Office, 1951-59. Sec., Br Guiana section, Wembley Exhib., 1924; Sec., Br. Guiana delegn, West Indies Conf., London, 1926; Sec. to various Cttees and Commissions, including Br. Guiana Constitution Commission, 1927. Organised Civil Defence in Br. Guiana, 1941-42; Actg Governor, Windward Islands, various periods, 1947 and 1949; Governor's Deputy on many occasions. *Address:* Lamaha, Marina Park, Brixham, Devon.

**GREEN, Sir George (Ernest),** Kt 1963; Chairman of Eagers Holdings Ltd; *b* 1892; *s* of Jabez Green, Brisbane, and Catherine Genevieve, *d* of T. Crouin; *m* Ailsa Beatrice, *d* of Charles George Rools Crane. *Educ:* Maryborough Grammar Sch. Pres., Royal National Agricultural and Industrial Assoc. of Qld, 1955-61. *Address:* 35 Markwell Street, Hamilton, Brisbane, Qld, Australia.

**GREEN, Henry;** Managing Director of Engineering Co., Birmingham; *b* 1905; *m* 1929; one *s*. *Educ:* Public Sch.; Oxford Univ. Engineer in Food and Drink Trade; War of 1939-45, full time NFS (in the ranks), 1939-43. *Publications:* Blindness, 1926; Living, 1929; Party Going, 1939; Pack My Bag, 1940; Caught, 1943; Loving, 1945; Back, 1946; Concluding, 1948; Nothing, 1950; Doting, 1952. *Relevant publication:* The Novels of Henry Green by Edward Stokes, 1959. *Recreation:* romancing over the bottle, to a good band. *Address:* c/o The Hogarth Press, 40-42 King William IV Street, WC2.

**GREEN, Henry Rupert,** CBE 1960; MA; Legal Senior Commissioner of Board of Control, 1953-60, later Ministry of Health; *b* 29 Dec. 1900; *o s* of late Henry Green, JP, solicitor, and Margaret Helen Green, Stockport, Cheshire; *m* 1937, Marie Elizabeth Patricia Bailey; three *s* one *d*. *Educ:* Charterhouse; Hertford Coll., Oxford (Exhibitioner). Barrister, Lincoln's Inn, 1926; practised on Northern Circuit, 1926-36; Commissioner of Board of Control, 1936. War of 1939-45: commissioned RAF, 1940; served as Operations Staff Officer, Malta, 1941-43; released, 1944. Governor, St Mary's Sch. for Girls, Gerrards Cross. *Publications:* title: Persons Mentally Disordered (Pts 2 and 3), Halsbury's Laws of England, 3rd Edn, 1960; title: Persons of Unsound Mind, Halsbury's Statutes (Burrows Edn), 1950 and similar title: Encyclopædia of Court Forms, 1949. *Recreation:* carpentry. *Address:* The Square House, Latchmoor Grove, Gerrards Cross, Bucks. *T:* Gerrards Cross 82316.

**GREEN, Hon. Howard Charles,** PC (Canada); QC (Canada); LLD (University of British Columbia); *b* Kaslo, BC, 5 Nov. 1895; *s* of Samuel Howard and Flora Isabel Green; *m* 1st, 1923, Marion Jean (decd), *d* of Lewis Mounce, Vancouver; two *s*; 2nd, 1956, Donna Enid, *d* of Dr D. E. Kerr, Duncan, BC. *Educ:* High Sch., Kaslo; University of Toronto (BA); Osgoode Hall Law Sch. Served European War, 1915-19. Called to Bar of British Columbia, 1922; elected to Federal Parliament, 1935; Minister of Public Works and Acting Minister of Defence Production, 1957-59; Canadian Sec. of State for External Affairs, 1959-63. Is a Progressive Conservative. *Address:* 4160 W 8th Avenue, Vancouver, British Columbia, Canada. *Club:* Terminal City (Vancouver, BC).

**GREEN, (James) Maurice (Spurgeon),** MBE, TD, MA; Editor, The Daily Telegraph, since 1964 (Deputy Editor, 1961-64); *b* 8 Dec. 1906; *s* of Lieut-Col James Edward Green, DSO; *m* 1st 1929, Pearl (*d* 1934), *d* of A. S. Oko, Cincinnati, USA; 2nd, 1936, Janet Grace, *d* of Maj.-Gen. C. E. M. Norie, CB, CMG, DSO; two *s*. *Educ:* Rugby Sch. (scholar); University Coll., Oxford (scholar, 1st Class, Honour Mods and Lit. Hum.). Editor of The Financial News, 1934-38; Financial and Industrial Editor of The Times, 1938-39 and 1944-53; Asst Editor, 1953-61. Served in Royal Artillery, 1939-44. *Recreations:* books, music, fishing. *Address:* 15 Sloane Avenue, SW3. *T:* 01-584 1649; Billing Cottage, Colden Common, near Winchester, Hants. *T:* Twyford 3040. *Club:* Reform.

**GREEN, Sir John,** Kt, *cr* 1949; JP; President, Thos Firth & John Brown Ltd since 1966 (Chairman, 1955-66); Deputy Chairman, Firth Brown Ltd, 1962-66; Chairman: William Beardmore & Co. Ltd, 1957-66; Past Director: Mitchell Engineering Ltd; Richard Thomas & Baldwins Ltd; John M. Henderson & Co. Ltd; GKN Steel Company Ltd; *b* 1892; *s* of late William Henry Green, Ecclesfield; *m* 1930, Hannah Isabella, *d* of late Edward Smith, Clonsilla, Co. Dublin. Chm., Iron and Steel Corporation of Great Britain, 1952-53 (Dep. Chm. 1950-52); Mem. Iron and Steel Holding and Realisation Agency, 1953-55. Hon. LLD, Sheffield, 1966. *Address:* Loughlinstown House, Mulhuddart, Co. Dublin, Eire. *T:* 256171.

**GREEN, John Dennis Fowler;** Member: Executive Committee, Council for the Protection of Rural England (Chairman Gloucestershire Branch); Executive Committee, Land Settlement Association; *b* 9 May 1909; *s* of late Capt. Henry and Amy Gertrude Green, Chedworth, Glos; *m* 1946, Diana Judith, JP, *y d* of late Lt-Col H. C. Elwes, DSO, MVO, Colesbourne, Glos. *Educ:* Cheltenham Coll.; Peterhouse, Cambridge. President of the Union. Called to the Bar, Inner Temple, 1933; BBC, 1934-62; established agricultural broadcasting, 1935; Special Agric. Mission to Aust. and NZ, 1945-47; Controller, Talks Div., 1956-61. Pres. National Pig Breeders Assoc., 1955-56; Chm., Agricultural Adv. Council, 1963-68. Chm., Cirencester and Tewkesbury Conservative Assoc. *Publications:* Mr Baldwin: A Study in Post War Conservatism, 1933. Articles and broadcasts on historical and agricultural subjects. *Recreations:* forestry, field sports. *Address:* The Manor, Chedworth, Cheltenham. *T:* Fossbridge 233. *Clubs:* Bath, Buck's, Farmers'.

**GREEN, Julian Hartridge;** Writer; *b* Paris, France, 6 Sept. 1900. *Educ:* Lycée Janson, Paris; Univ. of Virginia. Grand Prix, Académie Française, 1970. *Publications:* Mont-Cinere, 1925; Le Voyageur sur la Terre, 1926; Adrienne Mesurat, 1927; Leviathan, 1929; Epaves, 1932; Le Visionnaire, 1934; Minuit, 1936; Journal, 1928-35, 2 vols 1938-39 (published in England as Personal Record, 1928-1939, 1940); Varouna, 1940; Memories of Happy Days, 1942; Journal, 1940-43, 1946; Si j'étais vous. . ., 1947; Journal, 1943-45, 1949; Moira, 1950; Sud, 1953; L'Ennemi, 1954; Journal, 1949-1954, 1955; Le Malfaiteur, 1956; L'Ombre, 1956; Le Bel Aujourd'hui, 1958; Chaque Homme dans sa Nuit, 1960; Partir avant le jour, 1963; Mille Chemins ouverts, 1964; Terre lontaine, 1966; Vers l'invisible, 1967. *Address:* c/o Plon, 8 rue Garancière, Paris 5e, France.

**GREEN, Dame Mary Georgina,** DBE 1968; BA; Head Mistress, Kidbrooke School, SE3, since 1954; a Governor of the BBC since 1968; *b* 27 July 1913; *er d* of late Edwin George Green and Rose Margaret Green (*née* Gibbs). *Educ:* Wellingborough High Sch.; Westfield Coll., University of London. Assistant Mistress: Clapham High Sch., 1936-38; Streatham Hill and Clapham High Sch., 1938-40; William Hulme's Sch., Manchester, 1940-45; Head Mistress, Colston's Girls' Sch., Bristol, 1946-53. Member: Central Advisory Council for Education (Eng.), 1956-63; Church of England Board of Education, 1958-65; Council King George's Jubilee Trust, 1963-68; Court of Governors, London Sch. of Economics and Political Science, 1964-; Royal Commission on Trade Unions and Employers' Assocs, 1965-68; Council, City University, 1969-. Governor: Royal Ballet Sch., 1969-; Centre for Educnl Develt Overseas, 1970-. *Address:* 45 Winn Road, SE12. *T:* 01-857 1514.

**GREEN, Maurice;** *see* Green, J. M. S.

**GREEN, Brig. Michael Arthur,** CBE 1945 (OBE 1939); MC 1918; *b* 3 Oct. 1891; *s* of William Wheeler Green and Georgina (*née* Day). *Educ:* Wimbledon Coll., Surrey. Commissioned Glos Regt, 1914; served European War, 1914-18, France, Belgium; Adjt 1st Bn Glos Regt; GSO3 IV Army; Bde Major 14th Inf. Bde, 30th Inf. Bde; GSO2 EEF; Bde Major Cairo, 1919-22; accelerated, Northampton Regt, 1922; served India. Instructor, RMC Sandhurst, 1924-28. GSO2 PT Eastern Command, 1934-36; Gold Coast Regt, Comdg Sierra Leone Bn, 1930-32; Bt Major 1932; Sec., Army Boxing, 1934-36; Comdg Gold Coast Regt, 1936-39; Comdt, Army Physical Training Sch., 1939-40; Officer Commanding Brigade, France, 1940; Commanding Sierra Leone, 1940-41; East Africa, 1942; Commanding RAF Regt 2nd TAF, 1943-46 (France and Germany); retired, 1946. Sec. Worcs County Cricket Club, 1946-51; Sec., Royal Selangor Golf Club, Kuala Lumpur, Malaya, 1953-63. Chm. Army Cricket and Army Association Football; Manager, MCC Touring Team, South Africa, 1948-49. MCC Touring Team Australia, 1950-51. OStJ 1935. *Recreations:* formerly: cricket (Glos CCC, Army, MCC); Rugby football (Army, Surrey, Harlequins); Association football (Army, Corinthians, Casuals, Surrey). *Publication:* Sporting Campaigner, 1956. *Clubs:* Naval and Military, MCC (Hon. Life Mem.).

**GREEN, Paul Eliot,** LittD; Writer; *b* 17 March 1894; *s* of William Archibald Green and Betty Lorine Byrd; *m* 1922, Elizabeth Atkinson Lay; one *s* three *d. Educ:* Buie's Creek Academy; University of North Carolina; Cornell Univ. Editor of The Reviewer, a literary quarterly, 1925; winner of Pulitzer Prize for best American Play, 1927, In Abraham's Bosom; Guggenheim Fellow for study abroad, 1928, 1929; Member, National Institute of Arts and Letters. *Publications: plays:* The Lord's Will and other Plays, 1925; Lonesome Road (one-act plays), 1926; The Field God and In Abraham's Bosom, 1927; In the Valley and other Plays, 1928; The House of Connelly and other Plays, 1931; Roll Sweet Chariot, 1934; Shroud my Body Down, 1935; Hymn to the Rising Sun, 1936; Johnny Johnson, 1937; The Lost Colony (with music), 1937; Out of the South (The Life of a People in Dramatic Form), 1939; The Enchanted Maze, 1939; Native Son (co-author), 1941; The Highland Call (with music), 1941; The Common Glory (with music), 1947; Peer Gynt (modern adaptation of Ibsen's play), 1951; Wings for to Fly (three Negro plays), 1959; Five Plays of the South, 1963; The Sheltering Plaid, 1965; Sing All a Green Willow (play with music), 1969; numerous screen plays and outdoor dramas. *novels:* The Laughing Pioneer, 1932; This Body the Earth, 1935. *miscellaneous:* Wide Fields (short stories), 1928; The Lost Colony Songbook, 1938; Salvation on a String (stories), 1946; Dog on the Sun (stories), 1949; The Hawthorn Tree (essays), 1943; Forever Growing (essay), 1945; The Common Glory Song-book, 1951; Dramatic Heritage (essays), 1953; Wilderness Road (symphonic drama), 1955; The Founders (symphonic drama), 1957; Drama and the Weather (essays), 1958; The Confederacy (symphonic drama), 1959; Stephen Foster (musical drama), 1959; Plough and Furrow (essays), 1963; Cross and Sword (symphonic drama), 1964; Texas (symphonic drama), 1966; Texas Songbook, 1967; Words and Ways (stories), 1968; Home to My Valley (stories), 1970. *Recreation:* farming. *Address:* Old Lystra Road, Chapel Hill, North Carolina 27514, USA. *T:* 942-3858.

**GREEN, Brig. Percy William Powlett,** CBE 1960 (OBE 1956); DSO 1946; *b* 10 Sept. 1912; *er s* of late Brig.-Gen. W. G. K. Green, CB, CMG, DSO, Indian Army; *m* 1943, Phyllis Margery Fitz Gerald May, *d* of late Lieut-Col A. H. May, OBE; one *s* one *d. Educ:* Wellington Coll.; RMC. Commnd Northamptonshire Regt, 1932; Op. NW Frontier, India, 1936-37; BEF 1939-40; Lt-Col Comdg 2nd W Yorks Regt, 1945-46; Burma, 1944-45; Lt-Col Comdg 1 Malay Regt, 1946-47; Comd 4th King's African Rifles, 1954-56; Op. against Mau Mau; Col, Gen. Staff, War Office, 1956-57; Chief of Staff (Brig.) E Africa Comd, 1957-60; DDMI, War Office, 1961-63; Chief of Staff, N Ireland Command, 1963-65; Dep. Comdr, Aldershot District, 1965-67; retired, 1967. ADC to the Queen, 1965-67. Dep. Colonel, Royal Anglian Regt, 1966-. *Recreations:* field sports. *Address:* Grudds, South Warnborough, Basingstoke, Hants. *Club:* United Service.

**GREEN, Peter Morris;** author and translator since 1953; *b* 22 Dec. 1924; *o c* of Arthur Green, CBE, MC, LLB, and Olive Slaughter; *m* 1951, Lalage Isobel Pulvertaft; two *s* one *d. Educ:* Charterhouse; Trinity Coll., Cambridge. Served in RAFVR, 1943-47: overseas tour in Burma Comd, 1944-46. 1st Cl. Hons, Pts I and II, Classical Tripos, 1949-50; MA and PhD Cantab 1954; Craven Schol. and Student, 1950; Dir of Studies in Classics, 1951-52; Fiction Critic, London Daily Telegraph, 1953-63; Literary Adviser, The Bodley Head, 1957-58; Cons. Editor, Hodder and Stoughton, 1960-63; Television Critic, The Listener, 1961-63; Film Critic, John o'London's, 1961-62; Mem. Book Soc. Cttee, 1959-62. Former Mem. of selection cttees for literary prizes: Heinemann Award, John Llewellyn Rhys, W. H. Smith £1000 Award for Literature. Translator of numerous works from French and Italian, including books by Simone de Beauvoir, Fosco Maraini, Joseph Kessel. FRSL 1956; Mem. Council, Royal Society of Literature, 1958-63 (resigned on emigration). In 1963 resigned all positions and emigrated to Greece as full-time writer. *Publications:* The Expanding Eye, 1953; Achilles His Armour, 1955; Cat in Gloves (Pseud. Denis Delaney), 1956; The Sword of Pleasure (W. H. Heinemann Award for Literature), 1957; Kenneth Grahame, 1859-1932: A Study of his Life, Work and Times, 1959; Essays in Antiquity, 1960; Habeas Corpus and other stories, 1962; Look at the Romans, 1963; The Laughter of Aphrodite, 1965; Juvenal: The Sixteen Satires (trans.),

1967; Armada from Athens: The Failure of the Sicilian Expedition, 415-413 BC, 1970; Alexander the Great: a biography, 1970; The Year of Salamis, 480-479 BC, 1970. *Recreations:* travel, swimming, spear-fishing, table-tennis, historical research, amateur archæology, avoiding urban life. *Address:* 20 Efkalypton Road, Amaroussi, near Athens, Greece. *T:* Athens 8-020-392. *Club:* Savile.

**GREEN, Roger James N.**; *see* Northcote-Green.

**GREEN, Roland,** FZS; MBOU; *b* Rainham, Kent, 9 Jan. 1895; *s* of Roland Green, Naturalist; unmarried. *Educ:* Sir Joseph Williamson's Sch., Rochester. Artist; Specialises in Bird and Animal life; Annual one man show of paintings and etchings in Nov. at Ackermann Galleries; painted large frescoes in oil of Bird Life for Lord Desborough KG, at White Slea Lodge, Hickling Bird Sanctuary; Lecturer on Bird Watching and How to draw Birds: Hon. Fellow, Royal Society Protection of Birds; Associate Mem. of American Ornithologists' Union. *Publications:* Birds in Flight (Pycraft); Birds and their Young (Coward); Illustrations to Avicultural Magazine; Etchings published, Snipe, Canada Geese, Mallard, Over the Sand Hills, Kingfishers, How I Draw Birds, etc. *Recreations:* music, golf, nature study. *Address:* The Studio, Hickling Broad, Norfolk.

**GREEN, Prof. Ronald Bramble,** CBE 1961; MA Dunelm; MB, BS London; FRCS; Hon. DCL Dunelm; late Dean of Medicine and Professor of Anatomy, King's College, University of Durham, now Professor Emeritus; *b* 1 Aug. 1895; *s* of Frank E. Green and Christina Swanson; *m* 1925, Doris Kathleen Conway; one *s*. *Educ:* University Coll. and University Coll. Hospital, London. Demonstrator of Anatomy, University Coll.; Demonstrator and Lecturer in Anatomy, University of Durham; late Lieut-Col RAMC, TA (Durham Univ. Senior Training Corps). *Recreation:* fishing. *Address:* 30 Brandling Park, Newcastle upon Tyne NE2 4RR.

**GREEN, Ronald Frank,** CB 1958; Permanent Secretary, Ministry of Health and Social Services, Northern Ireland, since 1964 (Ministry of Health and Local Government, Northern Ireland, 1958); *b* 20 Sept. 1905; *s* of Ernest and Ethel Cranstone Green; *m* 1932, Margaret Mitchell McBride; two *s*. *Educ:* Friends Sch., Lisburn; Bootham Sch., York. Civil Service, NI 1923; Private Sec. to Minister of Labour, NI, 1934; Asst Sec., Ministry of Public Security, 1940; Asst Sec., Ministry of Health and Local Govt, 1944; Second Sec., Ministry of Finance, 1955. *Recreation:* yachting. *Address:* Plymouth Hoe, Stoney Road, Dundonald, Belfast. *T:* Belfast 63175. *Clubs:* Irish Cruising (Dublin); Strangford Lough Yacht (Co. Down).

**GREEN, Sam,** CBE 1960; Chairman: Industrial Advisers to the Blind, since 1970 (Director since 1964); Dula (ISMA) Ltd, since 1969; Green & Associates Ltd, since 1970; Spear Bros Ltd, since 1970; Chairman and Managing Director, Ralli Brothers (Industries) Ltd, 1964-69; Director: J. E. Lesser Group Ltd, since 1969; British Legion Poppy Factory, Richmond, since 1964; British Legion Industries, since 1967; *b* Oldham, Lancs, 6 Feb. 1907; *s* of Fred Green; *m* 1942, Dr Lilly (*née* Pollak); one *d*. *Educ:* Manchester Coll. of Technology. Apprentice, Platt Bros, Oldham, 1920-34; Designer and Development Engr, British Northrop Automatic Loom Co., Blackburn, 1934-39 (invented 4-colour loom); Chief Engr, Betts & Co., London, 1939-42; Works Manager, Morphy-Richards Ltd, St Mary Cray, Kent, 1942-44; General Works Manager, Holoplast Ltd, New Hythe, near Maidstone, 1944-47; Industrial Adviser, Industrial and Commercial Finance Corp., London, 1947-52; Managing Dir of Remploy Ltd, 1952-64. Vice-Chm., Inst. of Patentees and Inventors, 1961; FRSA 1962. CEng; FIEE; FIProdE. *Recreations:* reading, gardening, cycling, walking, golf. *Address:* Holly Lodge, 39 Westmoreland Road, Bromley, Kent. *T:* 01-460 3306. *Clubs:* Reform, Directors', Pickwick (oldest Bicycle Club).

**GREEN, Sir Stephen;** *see* Green, Sir E. S. L.

**GREEN, Thomas Charles;** Chief Charity Commissioner since 1966; *b* 13 Oct. 1915; *s* of late Charles Harold Green and late Hilda Emma Green (*née* Thomas); *m* 1945, Beryl Eva Barber, *widow* of Lieut N. Barber; one *d* (and one step *d*). *Educ:* Eltham Coll.; Oriel Coll., Oxford. Entered Home Office, 1938. Served with RAF, 1940-45. Asst Secretary: Home Office, 1950-64; Charity Commn, 1964-65. UK representative on UN Commn on Narcotic Drugs, 1957-64. Nuffield Travelling Fellowship, 1959-60. *Recreations:* gardening, photography. *Address:* Silver Birch Cottage, Burntwood Road, Sevenoaks, Kent. *T:* Sevenoaks 52933. *Club:* Oxford and Cambridge University.

**GREEN, Rev. Vivian Hubert Howard,** DD, FRHistS; Fellow and Tutor in History, Lincoln College, Oxford, since 1951 (Senior Tutor 1953-62; Chaplain, 1951-69); *b* 18 Nov. 1915; *s* of Hubert James and Edith Eleanor Playle Green; unmarried. *Educ:* Bradfield Coll., Berks; Trinity Hall, Cambridge (Scholar). Goldsmiths' Exhibnr; 1st Cl. Hist. Tripos, Parts I and II; Lightfoot Schol. in Ecclesiastical Hist.; Thirlwall Medal and Prize, 1941; MA 1941; MA Oxon by incorp., 1951; DD Cambridge, 1958; DD Oxon by incorp., 1958. Gladstone Research Studentship, St Deiniol's Library, Hawarden, 1937-38; Fellow of St Augustine's Coll., Canterbury, 1939-48; Chaplain, Exeter Sch. and St Luke's Training Coll., Exeter, 1940-42; Chaplain and Asst Master, Sherborne Sch., Dorset, 1942-51. Deacon, 1939; Priest, 1940. Select Preacher, Oxford, 1959-60. *Publications:* Bishop Reginald Pecock, 1945; The Hanoverians, 1948; From St Augustine to William Temple, 1948; Renaissance and Reformation, 1952; The Later Plantagenets, 1955; Oxford Common Room, 1957; The Young Mr Wesley, 1961; The Swiss Alps, 1961; Martin Luther and the Reformation, 1964; John Wesley, 1964; Religion at Oxford and Cambridge (historical survey), 1964; The Universities, 1969. Contributor to: Dictionary of English Church History (ed Ollard, Crosse and Bond); The Oxford Dictionary of the Christian Church (ed Cross). *Address:* Lincoln College, Oxford. *T:* Oxford 43658; Calendars, Burford, Oxford. *T:* Burford 3214.

**GREEN, William Allan McInnes,** CMG 1964; Consultant; retired as Town Clerk and Chief Executive Officer, City of Perth, WA, (1944-66); *b* 27 Jan. 1896; *s* of Thompson and Margaret Green, Adelaide, South Australia; *m* 1932, Edyth Irene, *d* of E. J. Thomas, Adelaide; two *d*. *Educ:* Adelaide High Sch.; South Australian Sch. of Mines; University of Adelaide (BE). Served European War, 1914-18, with AIF, Second Tunnelling Company. Design Engineer, Adelaide City Council, 1928-34; Asst Engineer and Architect, Launceston, 1934-37; City Building Surveyor and City Architect, Perth City, 1937-44. FSASM 1928; FRAIA 1944 (ARAIA 1932); AMIEA 1932. *Recreations:* golf, bowls. *Address:* 30 Mountjoy

Road, Nedlands, Western Australia 6009, Australia. *T:* 86 3435. *Club:* Weld (Perth, WA).

**GREEN, Lt-Gen. Sir (William) Wyndham,** KBE 1945; CB 1942; DSO 1918; MC 1916 and bar 1917; *b* 1887; *s* of Captain Percy Green, The Buffs; *m* 1st, 1916, Madge Bellairs; one *d*; 2nd, 1924, Primrose, *d* of A. Townshend Cobbold, OBE; one *d* (one *s* decd). Served European War, 1914-18 (despatches, MC with bar, DSO, Croix de Guerre); NW Frontier, 1930 (despatches); Bt Lieut-Col, 1929; Lieut-Col 1935; Col 1937; Maj.-Gen. 1941; Acting Lieut-Gen. 1945. Chief Instructor (Equipments), School of Artillery, 1937-38; Commandant, Military Coll. of Science, Woolwich, 1938; 2nd in Comd Gibraltar, 1941-42; GOC AA Div. and Gps, 1942-45; GOC-in-C, AA Command, 1945-46; retired, 1946, as Lt-Gen. Vice-Chm., Kent T & AFA, 1948-52, Chm., 1952-54; Vice-Pres., 1954-56; Hon. Col 410 Coast Regt RA (Kent) TA, 1949-56; Chm. Canterbury Diocesan Bd of Finance, 1953-61. Col Commandant RA, 1947-52, DL Kent, 1949. A Governor Dover Coll., 1959-. Polonia Restituta 3rd Class, 1943. *Address:* Little Gables, New Romney, Kent. *T:* New Romney 2137. *Clubs:* Army and Navy, MCC, Band of Brothers.

**GREEN, Lieut-Gen. Sir Wyndham;** *see* Green, Lieut-Gen. Sir William Wyndham.

**GREEN-PRICE, Sir Robert (John),** 5th Bt, *cr* 1874; ADC to the Governor of Bermuda; *b* 22 Oct. 1940; *o s* of Sir John Green-Price, 4th Bt, and Irene Marion (*d* 1954), *d* of Major Sir (Ernest) Guy Lloyd, 1st Bt, *qv*; *S* father, 1964. *Educ:* Shrewsbury. Army Officer, 1961-69; Captain, RCT, retd. *Heir: kinsman* Lieut-Col Francis Chase Green-Price [*b* 12 Aug. 1896; *m* 1934, Joan Atcherley Dobell; one *s* one *d*]. *Address:* Gwernaffel, Knighton, Radnorshire. *T:* Knighton 80.

**GREENACRE, Brigadier Walter Douglas Campbell,** CB 1952; DSO 1945; MVO 1927; late Welsh Guards; Extra Equerry to the Queen since 1952 (to King George VI, 1936-52); *b* Durban, S Africa, 20 March 1900; *er s* of late Walter Greenacre, OBE, Durban; *m* 1928, Gwendolen Edith, *d* of late Lieut-Col L. R. Fisher-Rowe; three *s* two *d*. *Educ:* Leys Sch., Cambridge. Equerry to Prince of Wales, 1924-26; Extra Equerry to Prince of Wales, 1926-36; Welsh Guards, 1918-47; raised 3rd Bn Welsh Guards, 1941; commanded: 2nd Armoured Bn Welsh Guards, 1941-43; Col 5th Guards Armoured Bde, 1943-44; Brig. (temp.), 1944; 6th Guards Armoured Bde, NW Europe, 1944-45; 6th Guards Brigade, 1945-47, BAOR; Schleswig-Holstein Sub Area, 1947-48; 128 Inf. Bde TA, 1948-49; 17th Infantry Bde & Dist, MELF, 1950-52; Col, Gen. Staff, 1947; Brigadier, 1951; retired pay, 1952. *Recreations:* shooting, golf. *Address:* Rendham Barnes, Saxmundham, Suffolk. *T:* Rendham 467. *Clubs:* Guards, White's Pratt's.

**GREENALL,** family name of **Baron Daresbury.**

**GREENAWAY, Alan Pearce,** JP; Vice-Chairman and Joint Managing Director, Daniel Greenaway & Sons Ltd; *b* 25 Nov. 1913; *yr s* of Sir Percy Walter Greenaway, 1st Bt, and Lydie Amy (*d* 1962), *er d* of James Burdick; *m* 1948, Patricia Frances, *yr d* of Ald. Sir Frederick Wells, 1st Bt; one *s* one *d*. *Educ:* Canford. Served in King's Liverpool Regt during War of 1939-45, reaching rank of Captain. Liveryman, Worshipful Co. of Merchant Taylors and Worshipful Co. of Stationers and Newspaper Makers. Mem. Court of Common Council for Ward of Bishopsgate, 1952-; Sheriff for the City of London, 1962-63; JP, Co. London, 1964; Alderman, Lime Street Ward, City of London, 1965-. Officer, l'Ordre de la Valeur Camerounaise, 1963; Commandeur, l'Ordre de Leopold Class III, 1963; Commander, Royal Order of the Phoenix, 1964. *Recreations:* golf, fishing, swimming. *Address:* The Doone, Byfleet Road, Cobham, Surrey; Dashwood House, 69 Old Broad Street, EC2. *T:* 01-588 7525. *Clubs:* Carlton, City Livery, Royal Automobile, United Wards, St George's Hill Golf.

**GREENAWAY, Sir Derek (Burdick),** 2nd Bt *cr* 1933; TD; JP; Chairman and Managing Director of Daniel Greenaway & Sons Ltd, 69 Old Broad Street, EC2 and its subsidiary and associated companies; *b* 27 May 1910; *er s* of Sir Percy Walter Greenaway, 1st Bt and Lydie Amy (*d* 1962), *er d* of James Burdick; *S* father 1956; *m* 1937, Sheila Beatrice, *d* of late Richard Cyril Lockett, 58 Cadogan Place, SW1; one *s* one *d*. *Educ:* Marlborough. Served in Field Artillery during War of 1939-45, reaching rank of Major. Hon. Col: 44 (HC) Signal Regt (Cinque Ports) TA, 1966; 36th (Eastern) Signal Regt (V), 1967. Joint Master, Old Surrey and Burstow Foxhounds, 1958-66. Chm. Sevenoaks Constituency C & U Assoc., 1960-63; Pres. 1963-66. Asst Area Treasurer, SE Area Nat. Union of Cons. Assocs, 1966, Treasurer, 1969. JP County of Kent, 1962. *Recreations:* hunting, shooting. *Heir: s* John Michael Burdick Greenaway, The Life Guards, *b* 9 Aug. 1944. *Address:* Dunmore, Four Elms, Edenbridge, Kent. *T:* Four Elms 275. *Clubs:* Carlton, City of London, MCC.
*See also A. P. Greenaway, H. F. R. Sturge.*

**GREENAWAY, Frank,** FRIC, FMA; Keeper, Department of Chemistry, The Science Museum, since 1967; Reader in the History of Science, Davy-Faraday Research Laboratory of the Royal Institution, since 1970; *b* 9 July 1917; 3rd *s* of late Henry James Greenaway; *m* 1942, Margaret (Miranda), 2nd *d* of late R. G. Heegaard Warner and *widow* of John Raymond Brumfit; two *s* three *d*. *Educ:* Cardiff High Sch.; Jesus Coll., Oxford (Meyricke Exhibitioner); University Coll. London. MA Oxon, MSc London. Served War of 1939-45, RAOC, as Inspecting Ordnance Officer, 1940-41 (invalided). Science Master: Bournemouth Sch., 1941-42; Epsom Gram. Sch., 1942-43; Research Labs, Kodak Ltd, 1944-49; Asst Keeper, Science Museum, 1949; Dep. Keeper, 1959; Keeper, 1967. Mem. Council: Brit. Soc. for the Hist. of Science, 1958-68 (Vice-Pres. 1962-65); Museums Assoc., 1961- (Hon. Editor, 1965-70). Chm., Cttee of Visitors, Royal Instn, 1964-65; Mem. Brit. Nat. Cttee of Internat. Council of Museums, 1956-58 and 1962-; Membre Correspondant de l'Académie Internationale d'Histoire des Sciences, 1963. Sec., Soc. for Study of Alchemy and Early Chemistry, 1967-; Mem., History of Medicine Adv. Panel, The Wellcome Trust 1968-. Boerhaave Medal, Leyden Univ., 1968. *Publications:* Science Museums in Developing Countries, 1962; John Dalton and the Atom, 1966; Official Publications of the Science Museum; Papers on history of chemistry and on museology. *Recreations:* music, travel. *Address:* 135 London Road, Ewell, Epsom, Surrey. *T:* 01-393 1330. *Club:* Athenæum.

**GREENAWAY, Sir Thomas Moore,** Kt 1968; Hon. Consulting Physician, Royal Prince Alfred Hospital, since 1930; *b* 1 June 1902; *s* of T. C. Greenaway, Grafton, NSW; *m* 1927, Lavinia, *d* of late G. H. Figtree, Wollongong, NSW; one *s* two *d*. *Educ:* N Sydney High Sch.; University of Sydney. MB, ChM, 1927; MRCP 1934; FRCP 1950. Foundn Fellow, RACP, 1938; Censor-in-Chief, 1952-56; Pres., RACP, 1960-62. Councillor, BMA (NSW Br.), 1944-

48; Mem., NSW Med. Bd; Mem. Bd of Dirs, RPA Hospital. Lectr in Clinical Med., University of Sydney, 1940-62. Hon. Fellow, RACGP, 1968. *Publications:* contribs to various med. jls. *Recreation:* golf. *Address:* 143 Macquarie Street, Sydney, NSW, Australia. *T:* 27-3325. *Clubs:* Australian (Sydney); Elanora Country.

**GREENE, Edward Reginald,** CMG 1953; *b* Santos, Brazil, 26 Nov. 1904; *s* of late Edward Greene and of Eva Greene; *m* Irmingard Fischges. *Educ:* Bedales Sch.; St John's Coll., Cambridge (BA 1926). After Continental banking experience joined coffee merchant firm E. Johnston & Co. Ltd, 1927; has since travelled and traded in coffee, Brazil, USA, East Africa, Continent, Dir of Coffee, Ministry of Food, 1943, subsequently Dir of Raw Cocoa; resigned 1952. *Recreations:* painting, antiques. *Address:* Orbell House, Castle Hedingham, Essex. *T:* Hedingham 298. *Clubs:* Royal Societies, City of London, Garrick.

**GREENE, Graham,** CH 1966; Chevalier de la Légion d'Honneur, 1969. Hon. LittD, Cambridge, 1962; Hon. Fellow of Balliol, 1963; Hon. DLitt, Edinburgh, 1967; *b* 2 Oct. 1904; *s* of late Charles Henry Greene; *m* 1927, Vivien Dayrell-Browning; one *s* one *d*. *Educ:* Berkhamsted; Balliol Coll., Oxford. On staff of The Times, 1926-30; Literary Editor, The Spectator, 1940-41; department of Foreign Office, 1941-44. Director: Eyre & Spottiswoode Ltd, 1944-48; Bodley Head, 1958-68. Shakespeare Prize, Hamburg, 1968. *Publications:* Babbling April, 1925; The Man Within, 1929; The Name of Action, 1930; Rumour at Nightfall, 1931; Stamboul Train, 1932; It's a Battlefield, 1934; The Old School (Editor), 1934; The Bear Fell Free (limited edn), 1935; England Made Me, 1935; The Basement Room (short stories), 1935; Journey without Maps (account of a journey through Liberia), 1936; A Gun for Sale, 1936; Brighton Rock, 1938; The Lawless Roads, 1939; The Confidential Agent, 1939; The Power and the Glory, 1940 (Hawthornden Prize for 1940); British Dramatists, 1942; The Ministry of Fear, 1943; Nineteen Stories, 1947; The Heart of the Matter, 1948; The Third Man, 1950; The End of the Affair, 1951; The Lost Childhood and other essays, 1951; Essais Catholiques, 1953; Twenty one Stories, 1954; Loser Takes All, 1955; The Quiet American, 1955; Our Man in Havana, 1958; A Burnt-Out Case, 1961; In Search of a Character, Two African Journals, 1961; A Sense of Reality, 1963; The Comedians, 1966; May we borrow your Husband? And other Comedies of the Sexual Life (short stories), 1967; Collected Essays, 1969; Travels with my Aunt, 1969; *plays:* The Living Room, 1953; The Potting Shed, 1957; The Complaisant Lover, 1959; Carving a Statue, 1964; *for children* (with Dorothy Craigie): The Little Train, 1947; The Little Fire Engine, 1950; The Little Horse Bus, 1952; The Little Steamroller, 1953; *film plays:* Brighton Rock, 1948; The Fallen Idol, 1948; The Third Man, 1949; Our Man in Havana, 1960; The Comedians, 1967. *Address:* c/o The Bodley Head, 9 Bow Street, WC2.

*See also R. O. Dennys, Sir Hugh and Raymond Greene.*

**GREENE, Sir Hugh (Carleton),** KCMG 1964; OBE 1950; Chairman, The Bodley Head, since 1969; a Governor of the BBC, since 1969; Director, Greene, King & Sons Ltd, Westgate Brewery, Bury St Edmunds; Member, Observer Editorial Trust, since 1969; *b* Nov. 1910; *s* of late Charles Henry Greene; *m* 1934, Helga Guinness (marr. diss.); two *s*; *m* 1951, Elaine Shaplen (marr. diss.); two *s*; *m* 1970, Tatjana Sais. *Educ:* Berkhamsted; Merton Coll., Oxford (MA). Daily Telegraph Berlin staff, 1934; Chief Correspondent, 1938; expelled from Germany as reprisal, May 1939; Warsaw correspondent, 1939; after the outbreak of war reported events in Poland, Rumania, Bulgaria, Turkey, Holland, Belgium, and France. Joined BBC as head of German Service, 1940, after service in RAF; Controller of Broadcasting in British Zone of Germany, 1946-48; Head of BBC East European Service, 1949-50; Head of Emergency Information Services, Federation of Malaya, 1950-51; Asst Controller, BBC Overseas Services, 1952-55; Controller, Overseas Services, 1955-56; Chm. Federal Commn of Inquiry into Organisation of Broadcasting in Fed. of Rhodesia and Nyasaland, 1955; Dir of Administration, BBC, 1956-58; Dir, News and Current Affairs, BBC, 1958-59; Director-General, 1960-69. Vice-Pres., European Broadcasting Union, 1963-69. FBIM, 1966. Hon. DCL E Anglia, 1969. *Publications:* The Spy's Bedside Book (with Graham Greene), 1957; The Third Floor Front, 1969; The Rivals of Sherlock Holmes, 1970. *Address:* Earl's Hall, Cockfield, Suffolk.

*See also R. O. Dennys, Graham and Raymond Greene.*

**GREENE, Ian Rawdon;** retired as Chief Justice, Somaliland Protectorate; *b* 3 March 1909; *o s* of Rawdon Greene and Marie Louise, Rahan, Bray, County Wicklow, Ireland; *m* 1937, Eileen Theodora Stack; one *d*. *Educ:* Cheltenham Coll.; Trinity Coll., Dublin (BA, LLB). Crown Counsel, Tanganyika, 1935; Resident Magistrate, Zanzibar, 1937. Military Service, Kenya, 1940-41. Sen. Resident Magistrate, Zanzibar, 1955; Actg Asst Judge, Zanzibar, on numerous occasions; Actg Chief Justice, Zanzibar, June 1954, and May-Oct. 1955; Judge-in-charge, Somaliland Protectorate, 1955; Chief Justice, Somaliland Protectorate, 1958-60; Stipendiary Magistrate, North Borneo, 1961-64. Order of Brilliant Star of Zanzibar (4th Cl.), 1953. *Publications:* Jt Ed., Vols VI and VII, Zanzibar Law Reports. *Recreations:* cricket, golf, bridge, chess. *Address:* Malindi, Kilmacanogue, Co. Wicklow, Ireland. *Clubs:* Royal Over-Seas League; English (Zanzibar); Hargeisa (Somaliland); Friendly Brothers (Dublin).

**GREENE, Mrs Luther;** *see* Anderson, Dame Judith.

**GREENE, Raymond;** Chevalier of the Legion of Honour; Hon. Consultant Physician, Royal Northern Hospital, and New End Hospital; Chairman, Heinemann Medical Books Ltd; *b* 17 April 1901; *s* of late Charles Henry Greene, MA, FRHistSoc; *m* 1934, Eleanor Craven, *d* of late Hamilton Gamble, St Louis, USA; one *s* one *d*. *Educ:* Berkhamsted; Pembroke Coll., Oxford (Theodore Williams Scholar in Medicine and Senior Open Scholar); Westminster Hospital (Scholar in Anatomy and Physiology), BA (Hons) Oxon. 1924, MA 1927, DM 1935; MRCP, 1943; FRCP 1954; held various appointments at Westminster Hospital, Queen Charlotte's Hospital, and Radcliffe Infirmary, Oxford. Mem. Kamet Expedition, 1931; Mem. Everest Expedition, 1933. Schorstein Research Fellow in Medical Science, University of Oxford, 1932-34; Senior Clinical Asst in charge of the Endocrine Clinic, Westminster Hosp., 1938-45; Physician: Metropolitan Hosp., 1945-54; Whittington Hosp., 1948-66. Hunterian Professor, RCS of England, 1943 and 1956; Mem. British Pharmacopœia Commission, 1948-53; Vice-Pres., Royal Society of Medicine and Pres. Section of Endocrinology, 1953; Chm. Fourth

Internat. Goitre Conf., 1960; Vice-Pres., Fifth Internat. Thyroid Conf., 1965; Vice-Pres., European Thyroid Assoc., 1966; Corresp. Mem., Amer. Thyroid Assoc.; Ex-Pres., Thyroid Club; Vice-Pres., Alpine Club, 1948-49; Hon. Mem., Oxford Univ. Exploration Club and Oxford Univ. Mountaineering Club. Chm., Cttee, Nuffield Inst. of Comparative Medicine; FZS (Vice-Pres.). *Publications:* The Practice of Endocrinology; Myasthenia Gravis; Human Hormones; many scientific and medical papers on the effects of great altitude and exposure to cold, and on endocrinology. *Recreations:* mountain climbing and travel. *Address:* 106 Harley Street, W1. *T:* 01-935 3889; 10 Cheltenham Terrace, Chelsea, SW3. *T:* 01-730 1434. *Clubs:* Athenæum, Alpine, Savile.

*See also R. O. Dennys, Graham and Sir Hugh Greene.*

**GREENE, Sir Sidney (Francis),** Kt 1970; CBE 1966; General Secretary, National Union of Railwaymen, since 1957; *b* 12 Feb. 1910; *s* of Frank James Greene and Alice (*née* Kerrod); *m* 1936, Masel Elizabeth Carter; three *d. Educ:* elementary. Joined Railway Service, 1924; appointed Union Organiser, 1944; Asst Gen. Sec., 1954. Mem., TUC Gen. Council, 1957- (Chm., 1969-70); Chm., TUC Economic Cttee, 1968. Member: National Economic Development Council, 1962-; Advisory Council, ECGD, 1967-; part-time Mem. Southern Electricity Board, 1964-; a Dir, Bank of England, 1970-. JP London, 1941-65. *Recreations:* cricket, reading, gardening, foreign travel. *Address:* 10 Hillview Avenue, Kenton, Middx.

**GREENEWALT, Crawford Hallock;** Chairman of the Board, E. I. du Pont de Nemours & Co., Inc., since 1962, Chairman of the Finance Committee since 1967; Member, Board of Directors: Christiana Securities Co.; Morgan Guaranty Trust Co.; The Boeing Co.; *b* Cummington Mass, 16 Aug. 1902; *s* of Frank Lindsay and Mary Hallock Greenewalt; *m* 1926, Margaretta Lammot du Pont; two *s* one *d. Educ:* William Penn Charter Sch.; Mass. Institute of Technology (BS). With E. I. du Pont de Nemours & Co., Inc. from 1922; Asst Dir Exptl Station, Central Research Dept, 1939; Dir Chem. Div., Industrial and Biochemicals Dept, 1942; Technical Dir, Explosives Department, 1943; Asst Dir, Development Dept, 1945; Asst Gen. Man. Pigments Dept, 1945-46; Vice-Pres., 1946; Vice-Pres. and Vice-Chm. Exec. Cttee, 1947; Pres., Chm. Exec. Cttee and Mem. Finance Cttee, 1948-; Chm. Board, 1962-, Chm. Finance Cttee, 1967-; Member Board of Directors of various other organisations. Member: Amer. Acad. of Arts and Sciences, National Academy of Sciences, Amer. Philos. Soc.; Board of Trustees, Nat. Geographic Soc.; Carnegie Inst. of Washington, etc; A regent, Smithsonian Instn. Holds hon. degrees in Science, Engineering and Laws, and has various scientific awards and medals. *Publications:* The Uncommon Man, 1959; Hummingbirds, 1960; Bird Song: acoustics and physiology, 1969. *Recreation:* photography. *Address:* Greenville, Delaware 19807, USA; (office) Du Pont Building, Wilmington, Delaware 19898, USA. *Clubs:* Wilmington, Wilmington Country, Du Pont Country (USA); Royal Bermuda Yacht.

**GREENFIELD, Prof. Archibald David Mant;** Dean of the Medical School and Professor of Physiology in the University of Nottingham, since 1966; *b* 31 May 1917; *s* of late A. W. M. Greenfield, MA, Parkstone, Dorset; *m* 1943, Margaret (*née* Duane); one *s* one *d. Educ:* Poole Grammar Sch.; St Mary's Hospital Medical Sch. BSc London, 1st class hons Physiology, 1937; MB, BS, 1940; MSc, DSc; MRCP; Kitchener Scholar; St Mary's Hosp. Med. Sch. Entrance Scholar. Dunville Prof. of Physiology in the Queen's Univ. of Belfast, 1948-64; Prof of Physiology in the Univ. of London, at St Mary's Hosp. Med. Sch., 1964-67. WHO Visiting Prof., India, 1960; Visiting Prof., Univ. of California, San Francisco Medical Center, 1962-63. Member: Sheffield Regional Hospitals Bd; Nottingham Univ. Hosp. Management Cttee. Mem., Physiological, Biochemical and Medical Research Societies. Sometime examiner in Universities of London, Edinburgh, Oxford, Cambridge, Liverpool, Belfast, Adelaide, Sydney, Bristol, Birmingham, Malaya, Ibadan, Ghana, NUI and Royal Colls of Surgeons of England and in Ireland. *Publications:* Papers in Lancet, Journal of Physiology, Clinical Science, and Journal of Applied Physiology. *Recreations:* sketching, travel. *Address:* 25 Sutton Passeys Crescent, Nottingham NG8 1BX. *T:* Nottingham 72424. *Club:* Athenæum.

**GREENFIELD, Sir Cornelius (Ewen MacLean),** KBE 1965 (MBE 1944); CMG 1956; Director: Netherlands Bank of Rhodesia Ltd; Rio Tinto (Rhodesia) Ltd; Member, Agricultural Marketing Authority, etc., Rhodesia; *b* 2 May 1906; *s* of Rev. C. E. Greenfield; *m* 1934, Brenda, *d* of E. M. Diaper; one *s* two *d.* Formerly Sec. to the Treasury, Rhodesia. Trustee, Automobile Assoc. of Rhodesia. *Recreation:* bowls. *Address:* Windsmoor, Hazeldean Road, Borrowdale, Salisbury, Rhodesia. *Club:* Salisbury (Salisbury).

**GREENFIELD, Sir Harry,** Kt 1948; CSI 1946; CIE 1938; Director, The Chartered Bank, and of various companies; Adviser, British-Amercian Tobacco Co.; *b* 2 Oct. 1898; *m* 1931, Hilda Adeline Wilkinson; one *s.* Served European War, Berks Yeomanry and TAnk Corps in UK, France and Germany, 1916-19. In Civil Service in India, from 1919, retiring, 1947, as Chairman Central Board of Revenue, Govt of India. Delegate of India to Narcotics Commn of UN, 1946; Pres., Internat. Narcotics Control Board, Geneva, 1968-; Pres., Permanent Central Narcotics Board, 1953-68 (Vice-Pres., 1948-52); Chm., Inst. for the Study of Drug Dependence, 1968-; Mem. Cttee appointed to review Customs and Excise Organisation, 1951-53. Governor, Polytechnic of Central London, 1970- (Regent Street Polytechnic, 1956-70); Chm. Council, The Leprosy Mission, 1962-; Chm., Royal Society for India, Pakistan and Ceylon; Vice-Chm., Westminster Chamber of Commerce, 1963-65; Mem. Advisory Cttee Chelsea Sch. of Art, 1958-64. *Recreations:* gardening and fly-fishing. *Club:* Oriental.

**GREENFIELD, Brigadier Hector Robert Hume,** CBE 1945; retired; *b* 21 June 1893; *o s* of late Col Hume Greenfield, JP, Fascadale, Ardrishaig, Argyll, and Edna Constance, *d* of Robert Leake, MP; *m* 1st, 1918, Ivy Maud (*d* 1947), *e d* of Sir Henry Dering, 10th Bt, of Surrenden Dering, Kent, and *widow* of Capt. R. A. C. Murray, Seaforth Highlanders; one *d*; 2nd, 1948, Mary Patricia, *d* of Major H. E. O'B. Traill, DSO, Dundooan, Coleraine, Co. Londonderry; one *s. Educ:* Eton; RMC, Sandhurst. Served for a year in Merchant Navy, going as an apprentice in a sailing ship to Australia and round Cape Horn. 2nd Lieut Argyll and Sutherland Highlanders, 1912; European War, 1914-19 (severely wounded, Serbian Order of the White Eagle). Specially employed War Office; Asst to Military Attaché, Paris, 1918-19; Asst Military Sec., Gibraltar, 1921-22; psc †, 1926-27; Staff Capt., DAAG and GSO2; Sec., War Block

Cttee, AHQ, India, 1934-35; commanded 2nd Bn Argyll and Sutherland Highlanders, 1938-40. War of 1939-45: Col (AA and QMG) 1940; Brig. 1940; Commander 15th Infantry Brigade, 1940-43; Commandant, Middle East Staff Coll., Haifa, 1943-44; Commander, Eritrea District, MEF, 1944-46 (despatches, CBE). Retired 1946. Dep., Sec., Govt Hospitality Fund, 1946-49; Ceremonial Officer. Festival of Britain, 1950-51. Chm., Lochgilphead Hospitals Board. Mem. Queen's Body Guard for Scotland (Royal Company of Archers). Commander Order of Dannebrog (Denmark), 1951. *Address:* Fascadale, Ardrishaig, Argyll. *Club:* Naval and Military.

**GREENFIELD, Hon. Julius MacDonald,** CMG 1954; Judge of the High Court of Rhodesia, since 1968; *b* Boksburg, Transvaal, 13 July 1907; *s* of late Rev. C. E. Greenfield; *m* 1935, Florence Margaret Couper; two *s* one *d*. *Educ:* Milton Sch., Bulawayo; Universities of Capetown and Oxford. BA, LLB Cape; Rhodes Scholar, 1929; BA, BCL Oxon. Called to the Bar at Gray's Inn, 1933. QC 1948; practised at Bar in S Rhodesia, 1933-50; elected MP for Hillside, S Rhodesia, 1948, and appointed Minister of Internal Affairs and Justice, 1950; participated in London Conferences on Federation in Central Africa. MP Federal Parliament, in Umguza Constituency, 1953-63; Minister of Law, Federation of Rhodesia and Nyasaland, 1954-63; Minister for Home Affairs, 1962-63. *Address:* 34 Weir Avenue, Hillside, Bulawayo, Rhodesia. *Clubs:* Bulawayo, Salisbury (Rhodesia).

**GREENHAM, Peter George,** RA 1960 (ARA, 1951); RP; RBA; NEAC; Keeper of the Royal Academy Schools, since 1964; *b* 1909; *s* of George Frederick Greenham, MBE, civil servant; *m* 1964, Jane, *d* of Dr G. B. Dowling, *qv*; one *s* one *d*. *Educ:* Dulwich Coll.; Magdalen Coll., Oxford (Hist. Demy, BA); Byam Shaw Sch. of Art. *Recreation:* music. *Address:* c/o Royal Academy, Piccadilly, W1.

*See also R. D. Greenham.*

**GREENHAM, Robert Duckworth,** RBA; ROI; Professional Artist and Author; *b* Streatham, 6 Sept. 1906; *s* of George F. Greenham, MBE, MIEE, and Isobel Greenham; *m* 1937, Kay Gilbert Fahey (divorced, 1942); *m* 1943, Joan Anne Benbow (*d* 1962); two *d*; *m* 1964, Janet Phyllis Williams. *Educ:* Dulwich Coll. Studied art at Byam Shaw, and later at the Royal Academy Schs; silver medals, Landseer Scholarship, and British Institute Scholarship. Exhibits at Royal Academy, Royal Portrait Society, etc., and the New English Art Club, Provincial exhibitions, and Internat. Exhibitions at Carnegie Institute, Pittsburgh, USA; paints many portraits of film stars, including Anna Sten, exhibited at RA 1935, Elisabeth Bergner, exhibited RA 1936, Greta Garbo, exhibited RA 1937, and Ann Todd, exhibited RBA 1943; one-man show in New York, 1937; Poster work for London and N Eastern Railway, 1938-39. Conscripted into Inns of Court Regt, 1941; 2nd Lieut 1941, Corps Camouflage Officer; Lieut 1942; invalided from Army, 1943; exhibited again Royal Academy and other shows. Picture bought by Australian Govt from Royal Academy, 1945; Council of Imperial Arts League, 1946-48; Council of Royal Society of British Artists, 1946-49. Did a series of figure paintings for Lintas International Advertising Ltd. RBA Bronze Medal for painting, 1946. Since 1949 has turned almost entirely to landscapes and seashore paintings; temporary Art Critic for The Scotsman, 1959 and 1960. Teacher (part-time) of Advanced Art, Camberley Adult Further Educn Centre, 1968-; Teacher (part-time) of Art Therapy, Coldingley Prison, Bisley, 1969. *Publications:* many technical articles on Art. *Recreations:* cine-photography, gardening and Modern English Competitive-style Ballroom Dancing (International Award and Gold Medals). *Address:* Collingwood Hall, Camberley, Surrey. *T:* Camberley 21881; 14B Langham Mansions, SW5. *T:* 01-373 0814. *Club:* Chelsea Arts.

*See also P. G. Greenham.*

**GREENHILL,** family name of **Baron Greenhill.**

**GREENHILL,** 2nd Baron, *cr* 1950, of Townhead; **Stanley E. Greenhill,** MD, DPH; Professor and Head, Department of Community Medicine, University of Alberta, Edmonton, Alberta, since 1959; *b* 17 July 1917; *s* of 1st Baron Greenhill and Ida Goodman; *S* father, 1967; *m* 1946, Margaret Jean, *d* of Thomas Newlands Hamilton, Ontario, Canada; two *d*. *Educ:* Kelvinside Academy, Glasgow; California and Toronto Univs. MD Toronto, DPH Toronto, CRCP Canada, FACP US, FRSH, FRSM. British Information Services, 1941; RAF, 1944. Lecturer, Dept of Medicine, University of Alberta, 1952. *Publications:* many articles in medical journals; Editor, Alberta Medical Bulletin. *Recreations:* photography, fishing, travel and the outdoors. *Heir:* *b* Hon. Malcolm Greenhill, *b* 1924. *Address:* 10223, 137th Street, Edmonton, Alta, Canada. *T:* Edmonton 488-8677; c/o 68 Glencairn Drive, Glasgow, S1, Scotland. *T:* 041-423 0129. *Club:* Faculty (Edmonton, Alta).

**GREENHILL, Basil Jack,** CMG 1967; FRHistS; Director, National Maritime Museum, Greenwich, since 1967; *b* 26 Feb. 1920; *o c* of B. J. and Edith Greenhill; *m* 1st, 1950, Gillian (*d* 1959), *e d* of Capt. Ralph Tyacke Stratton, MC; one *s*; 2nd, 1961, Ann, *d* of Walter Ernest Giffard; one *s*. *Educ:* Bristol Grammar Sch.; Bristol Univ. (T. H. Green Scholar). Served War of 1939-45: RNVR (Air Br.). Joined Commonwealth (subseq. Diplomatic) Service, 1946; served: Dacca, 1950-52; Peshawar, 1952-53; Karachi, 1953-54; UK Delegation, New York, 1954; Tokyo, 1955-58; UK Delegate to Conference on Law of the Sea, Geneva, 1958; British Deputy High Comr in E Pakistan, 1958-59; Ottawa, 1961-64; Commonwealth Office, 1965-66. *Publications:* The Merchant Schooners, Vol. I, 1951, Vol. II, 1957, rev. edn, 1968; The Boats of East Pakistan, 1957; (ed and prefaced) W. J. Slade's Out of Appledore, 1959; Sailing For A Living, 1962; Westcountrymen in Prince Edward's Isle (with Ann Giffard), 1967 (Amer. Assoc. Award); The Great Migration, 1968; The Nonsuch, 1969; The Merchant Sailing Ship: A Photographic History (with Ann Giffard), 1970; Women under Sail (with Ann Giffard), 1970; Captain Cook, 1970. Numerous articles and reviews on maritime history subjects. *Recreations:* writing, travel. *Address:* c/o National Maritime Museum, Greenwich, SE10. *Clubs:* Travellers'; North Devon Yacht (Instow); Karachi Yacht (Karachi).

**GREENHILL, Sir Denis (Arthur),** KCMG 1967 (CMG 1960); OBE 1941; Permanent Under-Secretary of State, Foreign and Commonwealth Office, and Head of the Diplomatic Service, since 1969; *b* 7 Nov. 1913; *s* of James and Susie Greenhill, Loughton; *m* 1941, Angela McCulloch; two *s*. *Educ:* Bishop's Stortford Coll.; Christ Church, Oxford. Served War of 1939-45 (despatches thrice): Royal Engineers; in Egypt, N Africa, Italy, India and SE Asia; demobilised with rank of Col. Entered Foreign Service, 1946; served: Sofia, 1947-49; Washington, 1949-52; Foreign

Office, 1952-54. Imperial Defence Coll., 1954; UK Delegation to NATO, Paris, 1955-57; Singapore, 1957-59; Counsellor, 1959-62; Minister, 1962-64, Washington DC; Asst Under-Sec. of State, FO, 1964-66; Dep. Under-Sec. of State, FO, 1966-69. *Address:* 25 Hamilton House, Vicarage Gate, W8. *T:* 01-937 8362. *Club:* Travellers'.

**GREENIDGE, Charles Wilton Wood;** Vice-President, Anti-Slavery Society, 1968 (Secretary 1941-56, Director 1957-68); *b* 1889; *y s* of late Charles Joseph Greenidge, member of the Colonial Parliament of Barbados West Indies; unmarried. *Educ:* Harrison Coll., Barbados; Downing Coll., Cambridge. Magistrate, St Kitts, LI 1919; Magistrate Barbados, 1923; Judge of Court of Appeal, Barbados, 1925; Magistrate, Port of Spain, Trinidad, 1927; acted Solicitor-Gen. and Attorney-Gen. of Trinidad; mem. of the Legislative Council of Trinidad; Chief Justice of British Honduras, 1932-36; Solicitor-Gen., Nigeria, 1936-41; Member: Commission on Development of British Guiana and British Honduras, 1947; UN's Cttee of Experts on Slavery, 1950-51. MLC Barbados, 1958-62. *Publication:* Slavery, 1958. *Recreations:* music and walking. *Address:* Fontabelle, New Street, Santa Venera, Malta. *Club:* National Liberal.

**GREENING, Wilfrid Peter,** FRCS; Consultant Surgeon to: Royal Marsden Hospital since 1952; Charing Cross Hospital since 1955; Lecturer in Surgery to Charing Cross Hospital Medical School; *b* 16 May 1914; *s* of Rev. W. Greening and M. M. Waller, Saxlingham, Norfolk; *m* 1st, 1939, Hilary Berryman (marr. diss., 1961); one *d*; 2nd, 1962, Susan Ann Clair Huber. *Educ:* St Edmund's Sch., Canterbury; King's Coll.; Charing Cross Hospital Medical Sch. MRCS 1937; LRCP 1937; FRCS 1939. Houseman and Surgical Registrar, Charing Cross Hosp., 1938. Served War of 1939-45 (despatches); Wing Comdr i/c Surgical Div., RAFVR, 1943. Surgical Registrar, Gordon Hospital, 1946; Consultant Surgeon: Woolwich Hospital, 1948; Bromley and District Hospital, 1947-66. *Publications:* contributions to medical literature. *Recreations:* fishing, golf. *Address:* 49 Harley House, Regent's Park, NW1. *T:* 01-935 2567. *Club:* Garrick.

**GREENLEAVES, Herbert Leslie,** CBE 1958; retired, Foreign Service, 1960; *b* 10 May 1897; *s* of late Herbert Greenleaves and Jane Elizabeth Ford; *m* 1938, Cecilia Joyce, *d* of late Commander F. W. Parker; one *d* (one *s* decd). *Educ:* Liverpool Coll. 2nd Lieut (Territorials), 1915; active service Egypt, France, Belgium, 1916-19. British Vice-Consul, Florence, 1939; Acting Consul there, 1939-40; British Vice-Consul, Tangier, 1940-43, and Casablanca, 1943. Hon. Commission Lieut-Comdr RNVR (Special Branch), 1943. Service French North Africa and Italy. Consul, Florence, 1945-52; Consul, Lille, 1952-55; Consul-Gen., Lyons, 1955-60. *Recreations:* chess, bridge. *Address:* Peel House, North Perrott, Crewkerne, Somerset.

**GREENLEES, Ian Gordon,** OBE 1963; MA; Director of the British Institute of Florence, since 1958; *b* 10 July 1913; *s* of Samuel Greenlees and Rosalie Stewart. *Educ:* Ampleforth Coll.; Magdalen Coll., Oxford. Reader in English Literature at University of Rome, 1934-36; supervisor of cultural centres of English for the British Council and Acting British Council Representative in Italy, 1939-40; Dir, British Institute, Rome, 1940; commissioned in Army, 1940; served in North African and Italian Campaigns, 1942-45, with rank of Major (despatches). Second Sec. (Asst Press Attaché) at British Embassy, Rome, Jan.-Dec. 1946; Asst British Council Representative, Italy, May 1947-Sept. 1948; Deputy British Council Representative, Italy, 1948-54. Medagilia d'Argento ai Benemeriti della Cultura (Italy), 1959; Cavaliere Ufficiale dell' Ordine del Merito della Repubblica Italiana, 1963. *Publication:* Norman Douglas, 1957. *Recreations:* swimming, walking, and talking. *Address:* Via Santo Spirito 15, Florence, Italy. *T:* Florence 291978; Villa Fraita, Anacapri, Prov. di Napoli, Italy. *T:* Capri 778031. *Clubs:* Athenæum; Leonardo da Vinci (Florence).

**GREENOCK, Lord; Charles Alan Andrew Cathcart;** *b* 30 Nov. 1952; *s* and *heir* of 6th Earl Cathcart, *qv*.

**GREENSLADE, Brigadier Cyrus,** CBE 1940; psc; *b* 13 May 1892; *s* of late William Francis Greenslade and R. B. Greenslade, St Mary Church, Torquay; *m* 1917, Edith Margaret Johnson; one *d*. *Educ:* Blundell's Sch., Tiverton. 2nd Lieut Devonshire Regt 1914; Capt. South Staffordshire Regt; Major York and Lancaster Regt; Lieut-Col North Staffordshire Regt; Brevets of Major and Lieut-Col; Instructor at Staff Coll., Camberley, 1932-35; GSO2 Army HQ, India, 1936-37; Col. 1936; Brigadier 1940; served European War, 1914-18, France, Salonica; 1919, The Baltic States (despatches, OBE); War of 1939-45, War Office as AQMG and Dir of Quartering; France, as Dep. QMG (CBE); 2 Corps HQ as DA&QMG. Combined Ops Training Centre as 2nd i/c to Vice-Adm. and Chief Instructor; Middle East, Comdr Eritrea Area and Comdr 2nd Bde Sudan Defence Force, 1942-44 (despatches); Palestine, as Comdr Southern Palestine Area, 1944-46; retd pay, 1946. Dep. Chief, Displaced Persons Operation, UNRRA, Germany and Paris, 1946-47; International Refugee Organisation, Geneva HQ, 1947-48; Chief UK Officer, IRO, 1948-51. Exec. Officer, Royal Commonwealth Society for the Blind, 1953-59. Legion of Merit, USA (Commander). *Recreation:* fishing. *Address:* 11 Eresby House, Rutland Gate, SW7. *T:* 01-589 3684. *Clubs:* Athenæum, United Service.

**GREENSLADE, Rev. Canon Stanley Lawrence,** DD; FBA 1960; Canon of Christ Church and Regius Professor of Ecclesiastical History, Oxford University, 1960; *b* 14 May 1905; *s* of late William Greenslade and Alice Sear; *m* 1929, Phyllis Dora Towell; one *s* one *d*. *Educ:* Christ's Hosp.; Hertford Coll., Oxford (Open Classical Scholar, Class I, Hon. Classical Mods, Lit. Hum. II, Theology I); Wycliffe Hall, Oxford. Curate of St Mary's, Beeston, Leeds, 1929-30; Fellow, Chaplain, and Tutor in Theology, St John's Coll., Oxford, 1930-43; Lightfoot Prof. of Divinity, Univ. of Durham, 1943-50; Van Mildert Prof. of Divinity, Univ. of Durham, 1950-58; Ely Prof. of Divinity, Cambridge Univ., 1958-59; Fellow of Selwyn Coll., Cambridge, 1958-59. Senior Denyer-Johnson Scholar (Oxford Univ.), 1933. Canon of Durham, 1943-58; Examining Chaplain to Bishop of Durham, 1943-58; to Bishop of Bradford, 1956-61; to Bishop of Chelmsford, 1933-43; to Bishop of Leicester, 1932-47. Hon. DD Edinburgh. *Publications:* The Work of William Tindale, 1938; The Christian Church and the Social Order, 1948; Schism in the Early Church, 1953; Church and State from Constantine to Theodosius, 1954; Early Latin Theology, 1956. ed The Cambridge History of the Bible: The West from the Reformation to the Present Day, 1963; Shepherding the Flock, 1967. *Recreations:* music, bibliography. *Address:* Christ Church, Oxford.

**GREENSMITH, Edwin Lloydd,** CMG 1962; Chairman, New Zealand Wool Commission, since 1965; *b* 23 Jan. 1900; *s* of Edwin Greensmith; *m* 1932, Winifred Bryce; two *s* two *d*. *Educ:* Victoria Univ., Wellington, NZ. MCom (Hons), 1930. Chartered Accountant; Solicitor. Chief Accountant, Ministry of Works, New Zealand, to 1935; then Treasury (Secretary, 1955-64). Dir, Tasman Pulp & Paper Co. *Recreations:* tennis, gardening. *Address:* Lowry Bay, Wellington, NZ. *T:* 60-623. *Clubs:* Wellington (Wellington NZ); Northern (Auckland, NZ).

**GREENWAY,** family name of **Baron Greenway.**

**GREENWAY,** 3rd Baron *cr* 1927; **(Charles) Paul Greenway;** Bt 1919; Insurance Broker and Underwriter, Lloyd's, London; *b* 31 Jan. 1917; *s* of 2nd Baron Greenway and Eileen (*d* 1963), *d* of late Maj.-Gen. Sir Harry Triscott Brooking, KCB, KCSI, KCMG; *S* father, 1963; *m* 1939, Cordelia Mary, *d* of late Major H. C. Stephen, late Northumberland Fusiliers; three *s*. *Educ:* Winchester; Cambridge (MA). Private, Royal Hampshire Regt; Commissioned The Buffs, 1940; Major, 6 Airborne Div., 3rd Parachute Bde, 1942-46, France, India, Palestine. Citizen and Vintner Freeman of the City of London, 1938. *Recreations:* sailing, ocean cruising. *heir:* *s* Hon. Ambrose Charles Drexel Greenway, *b* 21 May 1941. *Address:* 52 Chester Row, SW1. *Clubs:* City Livery; Royal London Yacht, Royal Fowey Yacht, Island Sailing, House of Lords Yacht, Lloyd's Yacht, Mylor Sailing.

**GREENWELL, Captain Sir Peter (McClintock),** 3rd Bt, *cr* 1906; TD; formerly 98th (Surrey and Sussex Yeomanry) Field Brigade (TA); *b* 23 May 1914; *s* of 2nd Bt and Anna Elizabeth (*d* 1957), *e d* of late Adm. Sir Francis Leopold McClintock, KCB; *S* father, 1939; *m* 1940, Henrietta, 2nd *d* of late Peter and of Lady Alexandra Haig-Thomas, Harbridge House, Ringwood; two *s* one *d*. *Educ:* Winchester; Trinity Coll., Cambridge (BA). Served War of 1939-45 (despatches, 1946, prisoner). JP Suffolk, resigned, 1958. Chm., Ransomes, Sims and Jefferies Ltd, 1969-. High Sheriff of Suffolk, 1966. *Heir:* *s* Edward Bernard Greenwell, *b* 10 June 1948. *Address:* Butley Abbey Farm, Woodbridge, Suffolk. *T:* Orford 233.

**GREENWOOD,** family name of **Viscount Greenwood and of Baron Greenwood of Rossendale.**

**GREENWOOD,** 2nd Viscount, *cr* 1937 of Holbourne; **David Henry Hamar Greenwood,** Baron, *cr* 1929; Bt, *cr* 1915; *b* 30 Oct. 1914; *e s* of 1st Viscount Greenwood, PC, KC, LLD, and Margery (*d* 1968), 2nd *d* of late Rev. Walter Spencer; *S* father 1948; unmarried. *Educ:* privately and at Bowers Gifford. Agriculture and Farming. *Heir:* *b* Hon. Michael George Hamar Greenwood, *b* 5 May 1923. *Recreations:* shooting and reading. *Address:* 13 Kingston House East, Princes Gate, SW7.

**GREENWOOD OF ROSSENDALE,** Baron *cr* 1970 (Life Peer), of East Mersea, Essex; **Arthur William James Greenwood, (Anthony Greenwood),** PC 1964; Member, Commonwealth Development Corporation, since 1970; *b* Leeds, 14 Sept. 1911; *s* of late Rt Hon. Arthur Greenwood, PC, CH; *m* 1940, Gillian Crawshay Williams; two *d*. *Educ:* Merchant Taylors' Sch.; Balliol Coll., Oxford (MA). President Oxford Union, 1933. National Fitness Council, 1938-39; Ministry of Information in UK, Russia and Middle East, 1939-42; Intelligence Officer in RAF (Flight Lieut), 1942-46; Allied Reparation Commission, Moscow, Potsdam Conference, Allied Reparation Conference, Paris, 1945; Organising Cttee, Inter-Allied Reparation Agency, 1945-46. Mem. Hampstead Borough Council, 1945-49. MP (Lab), Heywood and Radcliffe, 1946-50, Rossendale, 1950-70. Vice-Chairman: Parly Labour Party, 1950, 1951; Parly Cttee of Labour Party, 1951-52 and 1955-60; Vice-Chm., Nat. Exec. Cttee of Labour Party, 1962-63, Chm., 1963-64 (Mem., 1954-70); Sec. of State for Colonial Affairs, Oct. 1964-Dec. 1965; Minister of Overseas Development, Dec. 1965-Aug. 1966; Minister of Housing and Local Government, 1966-70. Member: Council, British Council for Rehabilitation; Cttee of Inquiry on Rehabilitation of Disabled Persons, 1953; Vice-President: Central Council for Care of Cripples; Brit. Rheumatic Assoc.; RSPCA; President: National Soc. for Abolition of Cruel Sports; Socialist Educational Assoc.; Vice-Pres., Nat. Marriage Guidance Council; Chm., Labour Parly Assoc., 1960-; JP London, 1950. *Address:* 38 Downshire Hill, Hampstead, NW3. *Clubs:* Savile, Royal Automobile.

**GREENWOOD, Brig. Harold Gustave Francis,** CBE 1942; MC; retired; *b* 15 Nov. 1894; *s* of late Lieut-Col H. S. Greenwood, VD, Kingston, Canada, and Matilda, *d* of Sir Henri Joly de Lotbinière, KCMG; *m* 1928, Gwyneth Francis, *d* of late E. B. Lemon, Winnipeg and late Mrs Ogilvie, Victoria, Canada; one *d*. *Educ:* Bishops Coll. Sch., Lennoxville, Canada; RMC, Canada. Served European War, 1914-18 (despatches twice, MC); NW Frontier Province, India, 1923-24 (despatches twice, Bt Major); lately Brigadier Engineer Staff, GHQ, India; and Chief Engineer 11th Army Group, SE Asia Command; retired pay, 1947. *Address:* c/o Lloyds Bank Ltd, Pall Mall, SW1; 3 Highlands Road, Buckingham, Bucks.

**GREENWOOD, James Russell;** Counsellor (Information), British Embassy, Tokyo, since 1968; *b* 30 April 1924; *s* of J. and L. Greenwood, Padiham; *m* 1957, Mary Veronica, *d* of late Dr D. W. Griffith and Dr Grace Griffith, Bures; one *s*. *Educ:* RGS, Clitheroe; Queen's Coll., Oxford. Army Service, 1943-47. BA, MA (Oxon) 1949; Foreign Office, 1949; subseq. service in Bangkok, 1950-52; Tokyo and Osaka, 1952-54; London, 1955-58; Rangoon, 1958-61; Rome, 1961-63; Bangkok, 1964-68. *Recreations:* travel, golf, cricket. *Address:* c/o Foreign and Commonwealth Office, SW1. *Clubs:* Oxford and Cambridge, MCC.

**GREENWOOD, Joan;** Actress; Theatre, Films, Radio, Television; *b* 4 March 1921; *d* of late Earnshaw Greenwood, Artist; *m* 1960, André Morell; one *s*. *Educ:* St Catherine's Sch., Bramley, Surrey. First professional stage appearance in Le Malade Imaginaire, 1938; since then has appeared in: Little Ladyship; The Women; Striplings; Damaged Goods; Heartbreak House; Hamlet; Volpone; A Doll's House; Frenzy; Young Wives' Tale; The Confidential Clerk (New York); Peter Pan 1951; The Moon and the Chimney, 1955; Bell, Book and Candle, 1955; Cards of Identity, 1956; Lysistrata, 1957-58; The Grass is Greener, 1959; Hedda Gabler, 1960, 1964; The Irregular Verb to Love, 1961; Oblomov (later Son of Oblomov), 1964; Fallen Angels, 1967; The Au Pair Man, 1969. Acted at Chichester Festival, 1962. *Films include:* They Knew Mr Knight, Latin Quarter, Girl in a Million, Bad Sister, The October Man, Tight Little Island, Bad Lord Byron, Train of Events, Flesh and Blood, Kind Hearts and Coronets, The Man in the White Suit, Young Wives Tale, Mr Peek-a-Boo, The Importance of Being Earnest, Monsieur Ripois, Father Brown, Moonfleet,

Stage Struck, Tom Jones, The Moonspinners. *Recreations:* reading, ballet, music, painting. *Address:* c/o Westminster Bank, 1 Brompton Square, SW3.

**GREENWOOD, John Eric;** Director Boots Pure Drug Co. Ltd, 1920-53 (Joint Vice-Chairman, 1951); *b* 23 July 1891; 4th *s* of late Thomas Greenwood; *m* 1921, Doris Mary Radford; one *s* two *d*. *Educ:* Dulwich; King's Coll., Cambridge. Served European War 1914-18, E Surrey Regt and Grenadier Guards (wounded, despatches); retd with rank of Capt. MA, LLB Cantab; FCA 1960; JP Nottingham 1947-53. Civil Service Arbitration Tribunal, Chancellor of Exchequer's Panel, 1936-49. Member of: Board of Trade Retail Trade Cttee, 1941; Catering Wages Commn, 1943-46; Royal Commn on Taxation of Profits and Income, 1950-55; Court of Inquiry into Omnibus Industry Dispute, 1946; Court of Inquiry into Road Haulage Dispute, 1947. President Rugby Football Union, 1935-6-7. *Recreations:* fishing, gardening; played Rugby football for Cambridge Univ. 1910-11-12-13-19 (Capt. 1912-19), for England 13 times (Capt. 1920). *Address:* The Priory of Lady St Mary, Wareham, Dorset. *T:* Wareham 2772. *Club:* White's.

**GREENWOOD, Prof. John Neill,** DSc, MMetE; Emeritus Professor, University of Melbourne, since 1965; *b* St Helens, 12 Dec. 1894; *s* of late Ellen and Walter Greenwood; *m* 1934, Winifred, *d* of Katherine and James Borrie; two *s* one *d*. *Educ:* St Helen's Technical Sch. Victoria University, Manchester, 1st class hons metallurgy, 1913-16; Chief Research Asst, Sir W. G. Armstrong Whitworth & Co. (Openshaw), 1916-19; MSc, by thesis, 1917; Chief of Research Dept, Sam. Fox & Co., Ltd, 1919-24; Prof. of Metallurgy, Melbourne Univ., 1924-46. DSc 1922; MMetE (Melbourne), 1931; designing pilot plant for wrought tungsten for Australian Ministry of Munitions, 1942-44; Research Prof. of Metallurgy, 1946-59 (Sen. Prof. of Univ. from 1956), retd; Prof. (personal chair) and Dean of Faculty of Applied Sciences, 1960-64, retd. Past-Pres. and Mem. of Council, 1933-44, Australian Inst. Mining and Metallurgy. Royal Commissioner, King's Bridge Failure, 1962-63. Hon. Life Mem. Victorian Coll. of Optometry, 1964. Hon. DAppSc Melbourne, 1968. Silver Medal, Aust. Inst. Metals, 1958; Bronze Medal, Aust. Inst. Mining and Metallurgy, 1961. *Publications:* Glossary of metallographic terms; various original researches in metallurgy and pyrometry, in Journal Iron and Steel Inst., and Journal Institute of Metals, Faraday Soc., Birmingham Met. Soc., Staffs Iron and Steel Institute, Australasian Institute of Mining and Metallurgy. *Address:* c/o 55 St George's Road, Toorak, Victoria 3142, Australia. *See also Prof. Norman N. Greenwood.*

**GREENWOOD, Prof. Norman Neill,** MSc, DSc Melbourne; PhD; ScD Cambridge; FRIC; Professor and Head of Department of Inorganic and Structural Chemistry, University of Leeds, since 1970; *b* Melbourne, Vic., 19 Jan. 1925; *er s* of Prof. J. Neill Greenwood, *qv*; *m* 1951, Kirsten Marie Rydland, Bergen, Norway; three *d*. *Educ:* University High School, Melbourne; University of Melbourne; Sidney Sussex Coll., Cambridge. Laboratory Cadet, CSIRO Div. of Tribophysics, Melbourne, 1942-44; BSc Melbourne 1945, MSc Melbourne 1948; DSc Melbourne 1966. Masson Memorial Medal, Royal Australian Chem. Institute, 1945. Resident Tutor and Lecturer in Chemistry, Trinity Coll., Melbourne, 1946-48. Exhibnr of 1851, Overseas Student, 1948-51; PhD Cambridge 1951; ScD Cambridge 1961. Senior Harwell Research Fellow, 1951-53; Lectr, 1953-60 Senior Lectr, 1960-61, in Inorganic Chemistry, Univ. of Nottingham; Prof. of Inorganic Chemistry, Univ. of Newcastle upon Tyne, 1961-70. Vis. Professor: Univ. of Melbourne 1966; Univ. of Western Australia, 1969; Tilden Lectr (Chem. Soc.), 1966-67; National Science Foundation Distinguished Vis. Prof., Michigan State Univ., USA, 1967. Mem., 1963-69, and Chm. 1969-, Internat. Commn on Atomic Weights of Internat. Union of Pure and Applied Chemistry. *Publications:* Principles of Atomic Orbitals, 1964 (rev. edn 1968); Ionic Crystals, Lattice Defects, and Nonstoichiometry, 1968; (jointly) Spectroscopic Properties of Inorganic and Organometallic Compounds, vols I-III, 1968-70; (with W. A. Campbell) Contemporary British Chemists, 1970; numerous original papers and reviews in chemical jls and chapters in scientific monographs. *Recreations:* ski-ing, Squash, tennis. *Address:* Department of Inorganic and Structural Chemistry, The University, Leeds.

**GREENWOOD, Ranolf Nelson,** MC 1917; JP; *b* 10 May 1889; *m* 1st, 1916, Beatrice Marion (*d* 1947), *d* of late Rev. Llewellyn L. Montford Bebb, DD, Principal of Lampeter Coll., S Wales; four *s* two *d*; 2nd, 1953, Kathleen Winifred Whiteside. *Educ:* Uppingham. Admitted a Solicitor, 1913; partner, firm Travers, Smith Braithwaite & Co., 1919-67. Served European War, 1914-19; 3rd Bn (Res.), Cheshire Regt, Adjt, 1st Bn, 1916; Major, DAAG 16th Div. 1918 (despatches twice); returned to City, 1919. Comdg Home Guard Bn, 1942-45. JP Herts 1932. *Address:* Croft Corner, 26 Harmer Green Lane, Digswell, Welwyn, Herts.

**GREENWOOD, Robert;** novelist and short-story writer; *b* Crosshills, Yorks, 8 March 1897; *m* 1932, Alice Ross; no *c*. *Publications:* novels: Mr Bunting, 1940; Mr Bunting at War, 1941; The Squad Goes Out, 1943; Wagstaff's England, 1947; Mr Bunting in the Promised Land, 1949; Good Angel Slept, 1953; O Mistress Mine, 1955; A Breeze in Dinglesea, 1957; A Stone from the Brook, 1960; Spring at the Limes, 1963; Summer in Bishop Street, 1965. Books published in England and/or USA and translated into Swedish, Spanish, German, French, Hebrew and Russian. Short stories published in England and USA. Adapted Bunting novels for the British film, Salute John Citizen. *Address:* 111 St Andrews Road, Felixstowe, Suffolk.

**GREENWOOD, Rt. Rev. Tom,** DD; *b* 1 Jan. 1903; *s* of Mitchell and Ellen Greenwood; *m* 1934, Isabel Dunham Gilbert; one *s* three *d* (and one *s* decd). *Educ:* Trinity Coll., Toronto (LTh). DD (*Jure Dignitatis*) Trinity Coll., 1952. Deacon, 1933; Priest, 1934. Arctic Mission at Fort McPherson, 1934-36; in American Ch., 1936-37; Diocese of London: Permission to Officiate (Colonial Clergy Act) at St John the Baptist, Greenhill, 1937-38; Curate, 1938-40; Vicar of St Peter's, Hale, 1940-46; Curate-in-charge of St Elizabeth's, Ashley, 1944-46; Proctor in Convocation, Chester, 1945-46; Rector of Fort McMurray, 1946-49; Rector of Yellowknife, 1949-52; Bishop of Yukon, 1952-61; Vicar of Whitegate, Asst Bishop, Dio. Chester and Hon. Canon of Chester Cathedral, 1962-65, Canon Emeritus, 1965; Asst Bishop of Cariboo, 1965-69, retired. *Address:* 2 Farnham Crescent, Ottawa 7, Ontario, Canada.

**GREENWOOD, Walter;** novelist and dramatist; *b* Salford, Lancs, 17 Dec. 1903; *e s* of late Tom and Elizabeth M. Greenwood. *Educ:*

Langworthy Road Council Sch., Salford; by self. Began part-time work as milk-roundsman's boy and pawnbroker's clerk at twelve years of age; left school at thirteen; worked as office boy, and as stable boy at millionaire's private stable, then at racing stable; clerk, packing-case maker, sign-writer, car-driver, warehouseman, salesman; never earned more than 35/- a week until employed for few months in automobile factory; on "dole" three or four times. *Publications:* Lancashire (County Books), 1949; *novels:* Love on the Dole, 1933 (play (jointly), 1934; film, 1941); His Worship the Mayor, 1934; Standing Room Only, 1936; The Cleft Stick (short stories), 1937; The Secret Kingdom, 1938; Only Mugs Work, 1938 (play, 1938); How the Other Man Lives, 1939; Something in My Heart, 1944; So Brief the Spring, 1950; What Everybody Wants, 1953; Down by the Sea, 1956; *plays:* My Son's My Son (jointly), 1935; Give Us This Day, 1936; The Practised Hand (one act play), 1936; The Cure for Love, 1945 (film, 1949); So Brief the Spring, 1945; Too Clever for Love, 1951; Saturday Night at the Crown, 1953 (novel, 1959); Happy Birthday (one act play), 1954; Happy Days, 1959; Fun and Games, 1961; This is your Wife, 1964; *autobiography:* There Was a Time, 1967 (play, 1968); *films:* No Limit (George Formby film), 1935; Sidney Howard Film, 1936; Merchant Navy Film, 1942; Six Men of Dorset, 1944; Eureka Stockade, 1947; Chance of a Lifetime, 1949. The Secret Kingdom (BBC TV serial), 1960. *Recreations:* riding, rowing, fishing. *Address:* Whitegates, Cannan Avenue, Kirk Michael, Isle of Man. *Club:* Royal Automobile.

**GREENWOOD WILSON, J.**; *see* Wilson, John G.

**GREER, Rt. Rev. William Derrick Lindsay;** *b* 28 Feb. 1902; *s* of Rev. Richard Ussher Greer and Elizabeth Lindsay Greer; *m* 1946, Marigold, *d* of late Rev. E. Stogdon; one *s* two *d. Educ:* St Columba's Coll., Co. Dublin; Trinity Coll., Dublin. Assistant Principal, Ministry of Home Affairs, N Ireland, 1925-29; Curate, 1929-32, and Vicar, 1932-35, of St Luke's Church, Newcastle upon Tyne; General Sec. Student Christian Movement of Gt Britain and Ireland, 1935-44; Principal of Westcott House, Cambridge, 1944-47; Bishop of Manchester, 1947-70, retired. DD (jure dig.), TCD, 1947; Hon. DD Univ. of Edinburgh, 1951. *Recreations:* walking, gardening. *Address:* The Old Rectory, Woodland, Broughton in Furness, N Lancs. *T:* Broughton in Furness 442.

**GREESON, Surgeon Vice-Adm. Sir (Clarence) Edward,** KBE, *cr* 1950; CB 1945; retired; *b* 29 Nov. 1888; *s* of Rev. John Greeson; *m* 1st, 1911, Katharine Whyte (*d* 1959); one *d*; 2nd, 1959, Mrs Marion Meredith Edgecombe (*d* 1968); 3rd, 1969, Hon. Mrs Michael Scott. *Educ:* Aberdeen Univ. (MB, ChB 1910; MD 1913). Surgeon, Royal Navy, 1914; Surgeon Capt., 1939; Surgeon Rear-Adm., 1945; Surgeon Vice-Adm., 1948. Served European War, 1914-19; War of 1939-45 (CB); Medical Dir-Gen. of the Navy, 1949-52; KHP 1946-52; QHP 1952; retd list, 1952. CStJ, 1948. *Address:* 2 Oakwood Court, Bolsover Road, Eastbourne, Sussex.

**GREEVES, Rev. Derrick Amphlet;** Superintendent Minister, Worcester Methodist Circuit; *b* 29 June 1913; *s* of Edward Greeves, Methodist Minister; *m* 1942, Nancy (*née* Morgans); one *s* three *d. Educ:* Bolton Sch.; Preston Gram. Sch.; Manchester and Cambridge Univs. Manchester Univ. 1931-34 (BA); Cambridge Univ. (Wesley Hse), 1934-37 (MA). Entered Methodist Ministry, 1935; Barnet, 1937-39; Bristol, 1939-43. RAF Chaplain, 1943-47. S Norwood, 1947-52; Bowes Park, 1952-55; Westminster Central Hall, 1955-64; Guildford, 1964-69. *Publication:* Christ in Me, a study of the Mind of Christ in Paul. *Address:* 29 Battenhall Road, Worcester. *T:* Worcester 23670.

*See also Rev. F. Greeves.*

**GREEVES, Rev. Frederic,** MA; LLD; Principal, 1949-67, and Randles Chair of Systematic Theology and Philosophy of Religion, 1946-67, Didsbury College; President, Methodist Conference, 1963-64; *b* 1 June 1903; *s* of Rev. Edward Greeves and Mabel Barnsley Greeves; *m* 1929, Frances Marion Barratt; one *s* one *d. Educ:* Merchant Taylors' Sch., Crosby; Manchester Univ. (BA); Didsbury Coll., Manchester; Cambridge Univ. Asst Tutor, Didsbury Coll., Manchester, 1924-28; Methodist Minister, Cheltenham, 1928-30; BA Cambridge, 1932 (MA 1936); Burney Prize, 1933; Minister, Cambridge, 1930-33; Epsom, 1933-39; Oxford, Chaplain to Methodists in Univ., 1939-46. Chm. West Regional Religious Adv. Council, BBC, 1952-57; Fernley-Hartley Lecture, 1956; Cato Lectr, 1960; Select Preacher, Cambridge, 1964. Hon. LLD (Bristol), 1963. *Publications:* Jesus the Son of God, 1939; Talking about God, 1949; The Meaning of Sin, 1956; Theology and the Cure of Souls, 1960; The Christian Way, 1963. *Address:* 13 Eastmead Lane, Bristol 9. *T:* Bristol 684251.

*See also Rev. D. A. Greeves.*

**GREEVES, John Ernest,** CB 1966; Permanent Secretary, Ministry of Home Affairs for N Ireland; *b* 9 Oct. 1910; *s* of late R. D. Greeves, Grange, Dungannon, Co. Tyrone; *m* 1942, Hilde Alexandra, *d* of E. Hülbig, Coburg, Bavaria; one *s* one *d. Educ:* Royal School, Dungannon. Entered Min. of Labour, NI, 1928; Asst Sec., 1956-62; Permanent Sec., 1962-64; subseq. Min. of Home Affairs. *Address:* 22 Downshire Road, Belfast 6. *T:* 648380.

**GREEVES, Maj.-Gen. Sir Stuart,** KBE, *cr* 1955 (CBE 1945; OBE 1940); CB 1948; DSO 1944; MC 1917; (ex-Indian Army) Deputy Adjutant General, India, until 1957, retired; *b* 2 April 1897; *s* of late J. S. Greeves; unmarried. *Educ:* Northampton Sch. Served European War, 1914-18 (MC and Bar); War of 1939-45 (DSO and Bar, CBE). *Recreation:* golf. *Address:* c/o Lloyds Bank, 6 Pall Mall SW1. *Club:* United Service.

**GREG, Barbara,** RE 1946; *b* 30 April 1900; *d* of H. P. and J. E. Greg; *m* 1925, Norman Janes, *qv*; one *s* two *d. Educ:* Bedales. Studied at Slade Sch. of Fine Art. Has exhibited wood engravings in London, provincial and foreign exhibitions since 1926. ARE 1940. Books illustrated include A Fisherman's Log by Major Ashley Dodd, Enigmas of Natural History and More Enigmas of Natural History by E. L. Grant Watson, The Poacher's Handbook by Ian Niall, Fresh Woods, Pastures New, by Ian Niall. *Address:* 70 Canonbury Park South, Canonbury, N1. *T:* 01-226 1925.

**GREGG, Humphrey P.**; *see* Procter-Gregg.

**GREGG, James Reali;** *b* 16 Nov. 1899; *e s* of late James Gregg, OBE, JP, Carnmoney, Co. Antrim, N Ireland; *m* 1930, Nina Hamilton Smith, *d* of late William H. Smith, Upton Park, Templepatrick, N Ireland; no *c. Educ:* Royal Belfast Academical Institution; Lathrop Sch., Mo; Hampden-Sidney Coll., Va, USA; Harvard Coll., Harvard Univ.; St

Catharine's Coll, Cambridge Univ. (MA). Called to Bar, King's Inn, Dublin, 1923; Gray's Inn, London, 1939; KC (Uganda) 1944. Chm., Court of Referees, NI, 1928; Nyasaland: Acting Attorney General, 1937-38; Uganda: Solicitor General, 1939, Attorney General, 1943; Puisne Judge, Nigeria, 1948; Judge of the Supreme Court, Hong Kong, 1953; Sen. Judge of Supreme Court of Hong Kong, 1959-61 (Acting Chief Justice, Hong Kong, Feb.-Nov. 1960); retired. *Recreation:* golf. *Address:* Hermanus, Cape Province, South Africa. *Club:* Hong Kong (Hong Kong).

**GREGG, Milton Fowler,** VC 1918; SM 1967; CBE 1946; MC 1917, and Bar 1918; Canadian Commissioner to Guyana, 1964-67, retired; *b* Mountain Dale, NB, Canada, 10 April 1892; *m* 1919, Amy Dorothy Alward, of Havelock, NB; one *d*; *m* 1964, Erica, *widow* of Kjeld Deichmann, Sussex, NB. *Educ:* Public Sch., New Brunswick; Provincial Normal Sch., Fredericton NB; Acadia Univ., Wolfville, NS (hon. MA). As a boy lived on a farm; enlisted as a private while at coll., 1914; went to France with 13th Batt. Royal Highlanders of Canada 1915 (wounded, Festubert); later obtained Commission in KORLR; transferred to Royal Canadian Regt; in France, 1917 (wounded, MC) (bar to MC, wounded, Cambrai, 1918, VC); Adjt; returned Canada, 1919; Major in Governor-General's Foot Guards; Dominion Treasurer Canadian Legion, BESL 1934-39; On outbreak of war, 1939 was posted 2nd in command Royal Canadian Regt and proceeded to England with it 1939; Lieut-Col commanding West Nova Scotia Regt 1940; Commandant, Canadian OCTU, England, 1941; Col Commandant Officers' Training Centre, Canada, 1942; Brig. Commandant Canadian Sch. of Infantry, 1943. Minister of Fisheries, Canada, 1947-48; Minister of Veterans' Affairs, 1948-50; Minister of Labour, 1950, till defeated in General Election, 10 June 1957. United Nations Technical Assistance in Iraq, 1958-59; United Nations Children's Fund in Indonesia, 1960-63. *Recreations:* Rugby football, hunting, motoring, and fishing. *Address:* Fredericton, New Brunswick, Canada.

**GREGOIRE, Most Rev. Paul;** see Montreal, Archbishop of, (RC).

**GREGOR, James Wyllie,** CBE 1961; PhD, DSc, FRSE; Director, Scottish Plant Breeding Station, 1950-65; *b* 14 Jan. 1900; *s* of C. E. Gregor, Innerwick, East Lothian; *m* 1929, Mary Joanne Farquharson, *d* of A. Robertson Wilson, MD. *Educ:* St Mary's Sch., Melrose; Edinburgh Univ. *Publications:* scientific papers in various international journals. *Recreations:* various. *Address:* Old Mill House, Balerno, Midlothian. *T:* 031-449 3273.

**GREGORY, Arnold;** industrial consultant; *b* Salford, Lancs, 14 Nov. 1924; *s* of Samuel Gregory and Ethel (*née* Aspinall-Stockwell); *m* 1945, Elizabeth Spooner; one *d*. *Educ:* Manchester and Salford Municipal Schs; Manchester Coll. of Technology. Parly Agent, Manchester (Wythenshawe), 1955; contested (Lab) Stafford and Stone, 1959. Lectr and Tutor, Nat. Council of Labour Colls, 1956-64. MP (Lab) Stockport North, 1964-70. Contracts Manager and Consultant (Textiles), 1958-. Mem., Parly Select Cttee on Science and Technology, 1968-70. *Publications:* contribs to Labour periodicals and newspapers. *Recreations:* reading, gardening, theatre. *Address:* 6 Avalon Road, Orpington, Kent. *T:* Orpington 36816.

**GREGORY, Vice-Adm. Sir David;** *see* Gregory, Vice-Adm. Sir G. D. A.

**GREGORY, Vice-Adm. Sir (George) David (Archibald),** KBE 1964; CB 1962; DSO 1939; retired, 1966; *b* 8 Oct. 1909; *s* of late Lt-Col G. M. A. Gregory, RA (retired), Tayfletts House, Perth; *m* 1933, Florence Eve Patricia, *yr d* of late James Hill, Lambourne House, Bagshot; two *s*. *Educ:* RN Coll., Dartmouth. Joined Submarine Service, 1931, and served in it at home and in China; served War of 1939-45, in comd of HM Submarines and on Staff of C-in-C Home Fleet (DSO and Bar, despatches); Capt. (S/M) 2nd and 5th Submarine Squadrons, 1954-57; Commodore, Hong Kong, 1957-60; Admiral Superintendent HM Dockyard, Devonport, 1960-64; Flag Officer, Scotland and Northern Ireland, 1964-66. Mem., Queen's Body Guard for Scotland (Royal Company of Archers). *Recreations:* shooting, fishing. *Address:* Guthrie Castle, By Forfar, Angus. *T:* Friockheim 209. *Club:* United Service.

**GREGORY, Philip Herries,** PhD, DSc London, DIC; FRS 1962; Head of Plant Pathology Department, Rothamsted Experimental Station, Harpenden, Hertfordshire, 1958-67; *b* Exmouth, Devon, 24 July 1907; *s* of late Rev. Herries Smith Gregory, MA and late Muriel Edith Gregory (*née* Eldridge), Hove, Sussex; *m* 1932, Margaret Fearn Culverhouse; one *s* one *d*. *Educ:* Brighton Technical Coll.; Imperial Coll. of Science and Technology, London. Research in medical mycology, Manitoba Med. Coll., 1931-34; Research plant pathologist, Seale-Hayne Agric. Coll., Newton Abbot, Devon, 1935-40; Rothamsted Experimental Station, Hardenden: Agric. Research Council Research Officer, 1940-47 (seconded for penicillin research to ICI, Manchester, 1945-46); Mycologist, Rothamsted Experimental Station, 1948-54; Prof. of Botany, University of London, Imperial Coll. of Science and Technology, 1954-68. Pres. British Mycological Soc., 1951. *Publications:* The Microbiology of the Atmosphere, 1961; papers on mycology, plant pathology, and virology. *Address:* 11 Topstreet Way, Harpenden, Herts.

**GREGORY, Roderic Alfred,** FRS 1965; George Holt Professor of Physiology, University of Liverpool, since 1948; *b* 29 Dec. 1913; *o c* of Alfred and Alice Gregory, West Ham, London; *m* 1939, Alice, *o c* of J. D. Watts, London; one *d*. *Educ:* George Green's Sch., London; University Coll. and Hospital, London. BSc Hons Physiology, 1934; MSc Biochemistry, 1938; MRCS, LRCP, 1939; PhD Physiology, 1942; DSc Physiology, 1949; Paul Philip Reitlinger Prize, 1938; Schafer Prize, 1939; Bayliss-Starling Scholar, 1935; Sharpey Scholar, 1936-39 and 1941-42; Rockefeller Fellow, 1939-41; Lecturer in Physiology, University Coll., London (Leatherhead), 1942-45; Senior Lecturer in Experimental Physiology, University of Liverpool, 1945-48; Mem. Biolog. Res. Bd, MRC, 1965, Chm. 1969; Mem., MRC, 1967; Hon. Mem., Amer. Gastroenterological Soc., 1967. Inaugural Bengt Ihre Lecture and Anniversary Medal, Swedish Med. Soc., 1963; Lectures: Purser, TCD, 1964; Waller, Univ. of London, 1966; Memorial Lecture, Amer. Gastroenterolog. Assoc., 1966; Ravdin, Amer. Coll. of Surgeons, 1967; Harvey, 1968; William Mitchell Banks, Liverpool Univ., 1970; Finlayson, RCPGlas, 1970. Baly Medal, RCP, 1965; John Hunter Medal, RCS, 1969. Fellow, University Coll., London, 1965; Feldberg Foundn Prize, 1966. Hon. DSc, Univ. of Chicago, 1966. *Publications:* Secretory Mechanisms of the Gastro-intestinal Tract, 1962; various papers in Jl Physiol., Quart. Jl exp. Physiol. and elsewhere since 1935. *Recreation:* music. *Address:* University of Liverpool, PO Box 147, Liverpool L69 3BX.

**GREGORY, Sir Theodore,** Kt, *cr* 1942; DSc (Econ.) London; sometime British member of the Currency Committee, Bank of Greece, and Financial Adviser to British Economic Mission to Greece; *b* London, 10 Sept. 1890; *m* 1st, 1917 (marriage dissolved, 1951); no *c*; 2nd, 1952, Mme Iphigenia Toumba (*d* 1969), *widow* of Admiral Nikola Toumba, RHN. *Educ:* Owen's School, Islington; Stuttgart; London Sch. of Economics; Asst and Lecturer, London Sch. of Economics, 1913-19; Cassel Reader in International Trade, 1920; Acting Professor of Economics at University Coll., Nottingham, 1915-16; some-time Mem. of Council, REconS; Dean of the Faculty of Economics, University of London, 1927-30; Pres., Section F of British Assoc., 1930; Senator of the Univ., 1928-30; Newmarch Lecturer, University Coll., 1929; Mem., Macmillan Cttee on Industry and Finance, 1929-31; Economic Adviser, Niemeyer Mission to Australia and New Zealand, 1930; Sir E. Cassel Prof. of Economics in the University of London, 1927-37; Economic Adviser to Govt of India, 1938-46; Mem., Irish Free State Banking Commission, 1934-37; Chm., Foodgrains Policy Cttee (India), 1943; Prof. of Social Economics in the University of Manchester, 1930-32; Examiner in the Universities of London, Cambridge, Oxford, Edinburgh, etc. Hon. Fellow, London Sch. of Economics, 1958. Comdr, Order of George 1st (Greece); Comdr Austrian Order of Merit. *Publications:* Tariffs, a Study in Method; Foreign Exchange, before, during, and after the War; Present Position of Banking in America; The Return to Gold; First Year of the Gold Standard; The Practical Working of the Federal Reserve System in the US; Introduction to Tooke and Newmarch's History of Prices; Select Statutes, Documents and Reports relating to British Banking; The Gold Standard and its Future, 1932; Gold, Unemployment, and Capitalism, 1933; The Westminster Bank Through a Century, 1936; India on the Eve of the Third Five-Year Plan, 1960; Ernst Oppenheimer and the Economic Development of Southern Africa, 1962; joint editor, Ricardo's Notes on Malthus and various official publications. *Club:* Reform.

**GREGORY, Theophilus Stephen;** Author and Journalist; *b* 23 Nov. 1897; *s* of Stephen Herbert and Mabel Gregory; *m* 1925, Hilda Harper Road; one *d. Educ:* Kingswood Sch.; New Coll., Oxford. Served European War, 1914-18, HAC and 13th KRR (MC), 1916-18. Methodist Minister, 1921-35; received into Catholic Church, 1935. Editor of The Dublin Review, 1945-47. Pres. Aquinas Soc., 1945. *Publication:* The Unfinished Universe, 1935. *Address:* The Cottage, Badby House, Daventry, Northants NN11 4NH. *T:* Daventry 2035.

**GREGORY, William King,** PhD, DSc; Da Costa Professor emeritus of Vertebrate Palæontology, Columbia University, since 1945; Curator emeritus of Comparative Anatomy, American Museum of Natural History, and Curator emeritus of Ichthyology, 1944; *b* New York, 19 May 1876; *s* of George Gregory and Jane King; *m* 1st, 1899, Laura Grace (decd), *d* of Daniel Foote, Mystic, Conn., no *c*; 2nd, 1938, Angela, *d* of Charles E. Du Bois, Kingston, NY. *Educ:* Trinity Sch., New York City; School of Mines, School of Arts, Graduate Sch., Columbia Univ. Mem. of the National Academy of Sciences, American Philosophical Soc., New York Academy of Sciences (Pres., 1932-33), New York Zoological Soc., AAAS; Geological Soc. of America, American Association of Physical Anthropologists (Pres., 1941-43), American Soc. of Herpetologists and Ichthyologists (Pres., 1936-38), Internat. Assoc. of Dental Research, etc.; foreign FZS; foreign FGS; foreign mem., Linnean Soc., London, etc.; mem. Royal Society of Sciences of Upsala, State Russian Palæontological Soc., etc.; Explorers Club; Phi Beta Kappa; Sigma Xi; Delta Upsilon. Research Associate, Lerner Marine Zoolog. Laboratory, Bimini, Bahamas, 1949. *Publications:* The Orders of Mammals, 1910; Studies on the Evolution of the Primates, 1916; On the Structure and Relations of Notharctus, an American Eocene Primate, 1920; The Origin and Evolution of the Human Dentition, 1922; The Dentition of Dryopithecus and the Origin of Man (with Milo Hellman), 1926; Our Face from Fish to Man, 1929; Fish Skulls; A Study of the Evolution of Natural Mechanisms, 1933; Man's Place among the Anthropoids, 1934; A Half Century of Trituberculy, 1934; In Quest of Gorillas, 1937; Studies on the Origin and Early Evolution of Paired Fins and Limbs (with H. C. Raven), 1941; Pareiasaurs versus Placodonts as Near-ancestors to the Turtles, 1946; The Roles of Motile Larvae and Fixed Adults in the Origin of the Vertebrates, 1946; The Monotremes and the Palimpsest Theory, 1947; Evolution Emerging: A Survey of Changing Patterns from Primeval Life to Man, 2 vols, 1951; Essays presented to D. M. S. Watson, 1958 (London); Cone Shells and their Color Patterns–an Approach to Evolution and Natural Philosophy, 1959-61. *Address:* Box 35, Woodstock (NY), New York 12489, USA.

**GREGSON, Maj.-Gen. Guy Patrick,** CB 1958; CBE 1953; DSO 1943 and Bar 1944; MC 1942; retired as General Officer Commanding 1st Division, Salisbury Plain District (1956-59); *b* 8 April 1906; *m*; one *s* one *d. Educ:* Gresham's Sch., Holt; RMA. 2nd Lieut RA, 1925. Served War of 1939-45 (despatches twice, MC, DSO and Bar, Croix de Guerre); Lt-Col 1942; Brig. 1950. Korea, 1953 (CBE). Regional Dir of Civil Defence, Eastern Region, 1960-68. *Address:* Bear's Farm, Hundon, Sudbury, Suffolk. *T:* Hundon 205. *Club:* Army and Navy.

**GREIG, Prof. James,** MSc (London), PhD (Birmingham); William Siemens Professor of Electrical Engineering, University of London, King's College, since 1945; *b* 24 April 1903; *s* of James Alexander Greig and Helen Bruce Meldrum, Edinburgh; *m* 1931, Ethel May, *d* of William Archibald, Edinburgh; one *d. Educ:* George Watson's Coll. and Heriot-Watt Coll., Edinburgh; University Coll., University of London. Experience in telephone engineering with Bell Telephone Company, Montreal, 1924-26; Mem. research staff, General Electric Company, London, 1928-33; Asst lectr, University Coll., London, 1933-36; Lectr, Univ. of Birmingham, 1936-39; Head of Dept of Electrical Engineering, Northampton Polytechnic, 1939-45. MIEE (Chm. Measurement Section, 1949-50; Mem. Council, 1955-58); Dean of the Faculty of Engineering, Univ. of London, 1958-62, and Mem. Senate, 1958-70; Mem. Court, Univ. of London, 1967-70. MRI; FIEEE; Fellow Heriot-Watt Coll., 1951; FRSE 1956; FKC 1963. Member Council: Electrical Research Assoc.; British Assoc. for the Advancement of Science (Mem. General Cttee); Regional Advisory Council for Technological Educn., London and Home Counties; Nat. Advisory Council on Educn for Industry and Commerce; Member: Educn Cttee, Herts CC; Governing Body, University of Surrey. *Publications:* papers (dealing mainly with subject of electrical and magnetic measurements) to: Jl Inst. Electrical Engineers, The Wireless Engineer, and Engineering. *Address:* Flat 15, Selwyn House,

Lansdowne Terrace, WC1. *T:* 01-278 1388. *Club:* Athenæum.

**GREIG, James Dennis,** CMG 1967; Africa Region Liaison Officer, International Planned Parenthood Federation, since 1968; *b* 1926; *o s* of Dennis George Greig and late Florence Aileen Marjoribanks; *m* 1st, 1952, Pamela Marguerite Stock (marr. diss., 1960); one *s* one *d*; *m* 2nd, 1960 (marr. diss., 1967); one *s*; *m* 3rd, 1968, Paula Mary Sterling. *Educ:* Winchester Coll.; Clare Coll., Cambridge; London Sch. of Economics. Military Service (Lieut, The Black Watch, seconded to Nigeria Regt), 1944-47. HMOCS: Administrative Officer, Northern Nigeria, 1949-55; Fedn of Nigeria, 1955-59; Dep. Financial Sec. (Economics), Mauritius, 1960-64; Financial Secretary, Mauritius, 1964-67; retired voluntarily on Mauritius achieving internal self-government, 1967. With Booker Bros. (Liverpool) Ltd, 1967-68. *Recreations:* rough shooting, golf, cricket, bridge. *Address:* 6 Beverley Close, Barnes, SW13. *T:* 01-876 5354. *Clubs:* East India and Sports; Hurlingham.

**GREIG, Maysie, (Mrs Jan Sopoushek);** author; pen-names: Maysie Greig and Jennifer Ames; *d* of Dr Robert Greig-Smith, bacteriologist, NSW; *m* 1937, Maxwell Murray (*d* 1956), author; one *s*; *m* 1959, Jan Sopoushek. *Educ:* Presbyterian Ladies' Coll., Pymble, NSW. Started as journalist on Sydney Sun and came to London to write a London column. Started writing short stories for Westminster Gazette and serials for Daily Sketch and Mirror. Went to New York and Boston where her first novel was published and later filmed; has had several novels filmed in Hollywood. Most novels serialised in leading women's jls in Eng. and Amer. Life Mem. Romantic Novelists' Assoc., London. *Publications:* 200 novels in England and America. *Address:* 15 Craven Hill, W2. *Clubs:* (Vice-Pres. NSW, Sydney European Rep.) PEN; Women Writers (Sydney).

**GREIG, Rear-Adm. Morice Gordon,** CB 1963; DSC 1944; Chairman, Public Service Commission, Bermuda, since 1968; *b* 20 March 1914; *s* of late Gordon Eastley Greig, Malayan Civil Service, and late Elsie Challoner Greig (*née* Lake); *m* 1st; two *s* three *d*; 2nd, 1960, Stephanie Margaret; one step *d*. *Educ:* RNC, Dartmouth. Joined Royal Navy as Cadet, 1927. War of 1939-45: Western Approaches, Mediterranean (HMS Orion) and Combined Ops. Comdr, 1947-52, Admiralty, Staff Course, HMS Vigo, in command; Captain, 1952-61, Admiralty, course at IDC and HMS Girdle Ness, in command; Rear-Adm 1962-65, Chief of Staff and Dep. to Chm., Brit. Defence Staffs, Washington. Dir-Gen., Winston Churchill Memorial Trust, 1965-67. *Recreations:* painting, music, sailing, outdoor life, with my wife. *Address:* Flying Bridge, Ely's Harbour, Bermuda. *Club:* United Service.

**GREIG DUNBAR, Sir John;** *see* Dunbar, Sir J. G.

**GRENFELL,** family name of **Barons Grenfell** and **St Just.**

**GRENFELL,** 2nd Baron *cr* 1902, of Kilvey; **Pascoe Christian Victor Francis Grenfell;** late Colonel KRRC; *b* 12 Dec. 1905; *s* of 1st Baron and Hon. Aline (*d* 1911), *o d* of late Lewis A. Majendie of Hedingham Castle, Essex; *S* father, 1925; *m* 1st, 1932, Elizabeth Sarah Polk (Betty) (whom he divorced, 1946; she *m* 1946, Berkeley Stafford), *o d* of late Capt. Hon. Alfred Shaughnessy and of Hon. Lady Legh; one *s* one *d*; 2nd, 1946, Irene Lilian, *er d* of H. A. G. Cartwright, Buenos Aires; one *d*. Deputy Chairman of Committees, House of Lords. Chairman: Finance Cttee, ICAA; Exec. Cttee, Grenfell Assoc. of GB and Ireland; Fountain and Carshalton Group Hosps; Hon. Treasurer, Nat. Soc. for Mentally Handicapped Children. *Heir: s* Hon. Julian Pascoe Francis St Leger Grenfell, [*b* 23 May 1935; *m* 1961, Loretta, *e d* of Alfredo Reali, Florence, Italy; one *d*]. *Address:* 13 Liphook Crescent, Forest Hill, SE23. *T:* 01-699 8528.

**GRENFELL, Joyce Irene,** OBE 1946; Actress and Writer (all own material, talks, articles, etc.); *b* 10 Feb. 1910; *d* of late Paul Phipps; *m* 1929, Reginald Pascoe Grenfell. *Educ:* Claremont, Esher, Surrey. Radio critic on the Observer 1936-39; Farjeon's Little Revue, 1939-40; Farjeon's Diversion, 1940-41; Farjeon's Light and Shade, 1942. Entertained troops, N Ireland, 1942; Welfare Officer, Can. Red Cross, 1941-43; entertained troops in hosps, Algiers, Malta, Sicily, Italy, Egypt, Trans-Jordania, Palestine, Syria, the Lebanon, Irak, Iran, India in 2 tours 1944 and 1945. Noel Coward's Sigh No More, 1945-46; Tuppence Coloured, 1947-48; Penny Plain, revue, 1951-52. Films from 1949: Poets Pub, Stage Fright, Run for Your Money, The Happiest Days of Your Life, The Galloping Major. Laughter in Paradise, Pickwick Papers, Genevieve, The Million Pound Note, Forbidden Cargo, Belles of St Trinian's, The Good Companions, Here Comes the Bride, Blue Murder at St Trinian's, The Pure Hell of St Trinian's, The Americanization of Emily, Radio: We Beg to Differ, from Sept. 1949. Toured Canal Zone, entertaining troops, 1953. Joyce Grenfell Requests the Pleasure, Fortune Theatre, 1954, also Bijou Theatre, New York, 1955. Appeared on TV, New York, 1955. during 1956: concert tour, N Rhodesia; TV Series, BBC; TV and 20 concerts, USA; during 1957: tour of solo show; 4-week season, London; during 1958: Recital tour, Canada and USA; 3-week season, New York; during 1959: played 13 weeks solo engagement, Sydney, Australia; during 1960: toured USA, Canada, etc.; Seven Good Reasons, Scala Theatre, London; 6-week concert tour Great Britain; during 1962: solo show, Theatre Royal, Haymarket; 4-week concert tour, Great Britain; during 1963: Festival Performing Arts, TV, New York; concert tour (July-Oct.), Hong Kong, Singapore, Australia, New Zealand; during 1964: Two "Joyce Grenfell" (45 min.) shows for BBC2; concert tours of Switzerland and Canada; played in film The Yellow Rolls-Royce; during 1965: four-week season, Queen's Theatre, London; concert tour, England; two more (50 min.) solo programmes for BBC; during 1966: concert tour of Great Britain (7 weeks); tour of Australia New Zealand; during 1967: concert tour of Great Britain (7 weeks); tour of Colls and Univs, USA; during 1968: concert tour GB; Solo BBC TV show; during 1969: Concert tour Hong Kong, Australia; solo BBC TV show; during 1970: Spring tour of England (8 weeks). Pres. of the Soc. of Women Writers and Journalists, 1957-; Mem. Pilkington Cttee on Broadcasting, 1960-62. *Publications:* contributions of light verse to Punch, of poetry to Observer, etc.; further contributions, light articles for various women's magazines. *Recreations:* listening to music; writing letters; going to the theatre; radio. *Address:* Flat 8, 34 Elm Park Gardens, SW10.

**GRENFELL PRICE, Sir Archibald;** *see* Price, Sir A. G.

**GRENVILLE;** *see* Freeman-Grenville.

**GRESFORD JONES, Rt. Rev. Edward Michael,** KCVO 1968; DD (Lambeth), 1950; Hon. Assistant Bishop of Monmouth, since 1970; *b* 21 Oct. 1901; *s* of Rt. Rev. Herbert Gresford Jones; *m* 1933, Lucy, *d* of R. Carr Bosanquet, Rock, Northumberland; three *d*. *Educ:* Rugby; Trinity Coll., Camb. Curate of St Chrysostom's, Victoria Park, Manchester, 1926-28; Chaplain of Trinity College, Cambridge, 1928-33; Vicar of Holy Trinity, South Shore, Blackpool, 1933-39; Rural Dean of the Fylde, 1938-39; Vicar of Hunslet, Leeds, 1939-42; Rector of St Botolph-without-Bishopsgate, 1942-50; Bishop Suffragan of Willesden, 1942-50; Bishop of St Albans, 1950-69; Lord High Almoner, 1953-70. Chairman of C of E Youth Council, 1942-50; Chm. of C of E Moral Welfare Council, 1951-61; Member of Council of Boy Scouts' Assoc. *Recreations:* riding, bird watching and fishing. *Address:* Braeside, St Arvans, Chepstow, Mon. *T:* Chepstow 2482. *Club:* United University.

**GRESLEY, Sir Nigel,** 12th Bt, *cr* 1611; *b* 22 April 1894; *s* of Sir Robert Gresley, 11th Bt, and Lady Frances Louisa Spencer Churchill (*d* 1954), *e d* of 8th Duke of Marlborough; *S* father, 1936. *Heir: b* Laurence Gresley [*b* 1896; *m* 1936, Mrs Kathleen Agnes Chater (*d* 1969), *o d* of late Lt-Col W. E. Bradish-Ellames, Manor House, Little Marlow, Bucks].

**GRESSON, Rt. Hon. Sir Kenneth (Macfarlane),** PC 1963; KBE 1958; Judge of Supreme Court of New Zealand 1947-57; President of New Zealand Court of Appeal, 1957-63; Member Judicial Committee of the Privy Council, since 1963; President, Indecent Publications Tribunal (NZ); *b* 18 July 1891; *s* of John Beatty Gresson; *m* 1917, Athole Bruce; one *s* one *d*. *Educ:* Wanganui Coll. Sch.; Univ. of NZ. LLB 1914. Served European War, 1914-18, with 1st NZ Expeditionary Force (Major). In practice as Barrister and Solicitor, Christchurch, NZ, 1918-47. Chancellor, Diocese of Christchurch (C of E); Dean of Faculty of Law, Canterbury Univ. Coll., 1936-47. *Address:* 54 Aurora Terrace, Wellington, NZ.

**GRESWELL, Air Cdre Jeaffreson Herbert,** CB 1967; CBE 1962 (OBE 1946); DSO 1944; DFC 1942; RAF, retired; *b* 28 July 1916; *s* of William Territt Greswell; *m* 1939, Gwyneth Alice Hayes; one *s* three *d*. *Educ:* Repton. Joined RAF, 1935, Pilot. Served War of 1939-45, in Coastal Command, Anti-Submarine No. 217 Sqdn, 1937-41; No. 172 Sqdn, 1942; OC No. 179 Sqdn, Gibraltar, 1943-44. Air Liaison Officer, Pacific Fleet, 1946-47; Staff of Joint Anti-Submarine Sch., 1949-52; Staff of Flying Coll., Manby, 1952-54; Planning Staff, Min. of Defence, 1954-57; OC, RAF Station Kinloss, 1957-59; Plans HQ, Coastal Comd, 1959-61; Standing Group Rep. to NATO Council, Paris, 1961-64; Commandant, Royal Observer Corps, 1964-68. Sqdn Ldr 1941; Wing Comdr 1942; Gp Capt. 1955; Air Cdre 1961. *Recreations:* none special. *Address:* Picket Lodge, Ringwood, Hants.

**GRESWELL, Richard Egerton,** CMG 1963; MBE 1946; with Ministry of Transport, Taunton, Somerset; *b* 6 May 1916; *s* of late Ernest Arthur Greswell, Wayvile House, Bicknoller, Taunton, Som., and Grace Lillian (*née* Egerton); *m* 1948, Jean Patricia, *d* of Lieut-Col J. R. Hutchison, DSO; two *s* one *d*. *Educ:* Repton Sch.; Hertford Coll., Oxford (MA). HM's Overseas Civil Service in Northern Nigeria, 1938-63. War Service Royal West African Frontier Force (Artillery), East Africa and Burma Campaigns. Lt-Col, 1939-46. Sir John Hodsoll Award, 1966-67. *Publication:* Civil Defence and the County Council, 1967. *Recreations:* shooting, golf. *Address:* Wayvile House, Bicknoller, Taunton, Somerset. *T:* Stogumber 335. *Club:* Royal Commonwealth Society.

**GRETTON,** family name of **Baron Gretton.**

**GRETTON,** 2nd Baron, *cr* 1944, of Stapleford; **John Frederic Gretton,** OBE 1950; *b* 15 Aug. 1902; *o s* of 1st Baron Gretton, PC, CBE, and Hon. Maud Helen de Moleyns, *y d* of 4th Baron Ventry; *S* father, 1947; *m* 1930, Margaret, *s d* of Capt. H. Loeffler; two *s* two *d*. *Educ:* Eton. MP (C) Burton Div. of Staffs, 1943-45. *Recreations:* yachting, shooting, travelling. *Heir: s* Hon. John Henrik Gretton [*b* 9 Feb. 1941; *m* 1970, Jennifer, *o d* of Edmund Moore, York]. *Address:* Stapleford Park, Melton Mowbray. *T:* Wymondham (Leicestershire) 229; 77 Sussex Square, W2. *Club:* Carlton.

**GRETTON, Vice-Adm. Sir Peter (William),** KCB 1963 (CB 1960); DSO 1942; OBE 1941; DSC 1936; MA; Domestic Bursar of University College, Oxford, since 1965; *b* 27 Aug. 1912; *s* of Major G. F. Gretton; *m* 1943, D. N. G. Du Vivier; three *s* one *d*. *Educ:* Roper's Preparatory Sch.; RNC, Dartmouth. Prize for Five First Class Certificates as Sub.-Lieut; Comdr 1942; Capt. 1948; Rear-Adm. 1958; Vice-Adm. 1961. Served War of 1939-45 (despatches, OBE, DSO and two Bars). Senior Naval Mem. of Directing Staff of Imperial Defence Coll., April 1958-60; Flag Officer, Sea Training, 1960-61; a Lord Commissioner of the Admiralty, Dep. Chief of Naval Staff and Fifth Sea Lord, 1962-63, retd. Vice-Pres., Royal Humane Soc.; Testimonial of Royal Humane Society, 1940. Member Cttee, Automobile Assoc. *Publications:* Convoy Escort Commander, 1964; Maritime Strategy: A Study of British Defence Problems, 1965; Former Naval Person: Churchill and the Navy, 1968. *Recreations:* shooting, golf, real tennis. *Address:* University College, Oxford. *Club:* United Service.

**GREVILLE,** family name of **Baron Greville,** and of **Earl of Warwick.**

**GREVILLE,** 4th Baron, *cr* 1869; **Ronald Charles Fulke Greville;** *b* 11 April 1912; *s* of 3rd Baron and Olive Grace (*d* 1959), *d* of J. W. Grace, Leybourne Grange, Kent, and *widow* of Henry Kerr; *S* father 1952. *Educ:* Eton; Magdalen Coll., Oxford Univ. *Recreations:* music, travel, sport. *Heir:* none. *Address:* 4 Paulton's Square, SW3. *T:* 01-352 7207; Cubberley, Ross-on-Wye, Herefordshire. *T:* Ross-on-Wye 2323. *Clubs:* Bath; Hurlingham.
*See also Sir Hamilton Kerr, Bt.*

**GREW, Major Benjamin Dixon,** OBE 1954; Governor HM Prison, Wormwood Scrubs, 1945-56; *b* 25 June 1892; *s* of Benjamin Grew and Minnie Jane Moore; *m* 1921, Eleanor Flora Enid, *d* of Burton Swift, JP, High Sheriff, Montgomeryshire, 1913; one *d*. *Educ:* Wordsworth Sch. Joined Scots Guards, 1910; Northumberland Fusiliers, 1915-23; Egyptian Army, 1917, 1919; Palestine Administration, 1919-22; Dep. Mil. Governor, Nazareth, and Senior Inspector, Nablus, Palestine, 1919-22; Governor HM Prisons: Maidstone, 1930-37; Durham 1937-40; Wandsworth, 1940-45. Bar Student, Mem. Gray's Inn, 1932. New Forest RDC, 1958-64. Chm. of Governors, Priestlands Sch., Lymington, 1963-67. *Publication:* Prison Governor, 1958. *Address:* Latchmoor Farm, Tile Barn Lane, Brockenhurst, Hants.

**GREY,** family name of **Earl Grey,** and of **Baron Grey of Naunton** and **Earl of Stamford.**

**GREY;** *see* De Grey.

**GREY**, 6th Earl, *cr* 1806; **Richard Fleming George Charles Grey;** Bt 1746; Baron Grey, 1801; Viscount Howick, 1806; *b* 5 March 1939; *s* of late Albert Harry George Campbell Grey (Trooper, Canadian Army Tanks, who *d* on active service, 1942) and Vera Helen Louise Harding; *S* cousin, 1963; *m* 1966, Margaret Ann, *e d* of Henry Bradford, Ashburton. *Educ:* Hounslow Coll.; Hammersmith Coll. of Bldg (Quantity Surveying). Mem. Young Conservatives. *Recreations:* golf, sailing. *Heir: b* Philip Kent Grey, *b* 11 May 1940; *m* 1968, Ann Catherine, *y d* of Cecil Applegate, Kingsbridge, Devon.

**GREY OF NAUNTON,** Baron, *cr* 1968 (Life Peer); **Ralph Francis Alnwick Grey,** GCMG 1964 (KCMG 1959, CMG 1955); KCVO 1956; OBE 1951; Governor of Northern Ireland since Dec. 1968; *b* 15 April 1910; *o s* of late Francis Arthur Grey and Mary Wilkie Grey (*née* Spence); *m* 1944, Esmé, CStJ, *widow* of Pilot Officer Kenneth Kirkcaldie, RAFVR, and *d* of late A. V. Burcher and of Florence Burcher, Remuera, Auckland, New Zealand; two *s* one *d*. *Educ:* Wellington Coll., NZ; Auckland Univ. Coll.; Pembroke Coll., Cambridge. LLB (NZ). Barrister and Solicitor of Supreme Court of New Zealand, 1932; Associate to Hon. Mr Justice Smith, 1932-36; Probationer, Colonial Administrative Service, 1936; Administrative Service, Nigeria: Cadet, 1937; Asst Financial Sec., 1949; Administrative Officer, Class I, 1951; Development Sec., 1952; Sec. to Governor-Gen. and Council of Ministers, 1954; Chief Sec. of the Federation, 1955-57; Dep. Gov.-Gen., 1957-59; Gov. and C-in-C, British Guiana, 1959-64; Governor and C-in-C of The Bahamas, 1964-68, and of the Turks and Caicos Islands, 1965-68. KStJ; Kt Comdr, Commandery of Ards. *Recreation:* golf. *Address:* Government House, Hillsborough, Northern Ireland; Overbrook, Naunton, near Cheltenham, Glos. *T:* Guiting Power 263. *Clubs:* Travellers'; New (Cheltenham).

**GREY, Beryl, (Mrs S. G. Svenson);** Prima Ballerina, Sadler's Wells Ballet, now Royal Ballet, 1942-57; Artistic Director, London's Festival Ballet, since 1968; *b* London, 11 June 1927; *d* of Arthur Ernest Groom; *m* 1950, Dr Sven Gustav Svenson; one *s*. *Educ:* Dame Alice Owens Girls' Sch., London. Professional training: Madeline Sharp Sch., Sadler's Wells Sch. (Schol.), de Vos Sch. Début Sadler's Wells Co., 1941, with Ballerina rôles following same year in Les Sylphides, The Gods Go A'Begging, Le Lac des Cygnes, Act II, Comus. First full-length ballet, Le Lac des Cygnes on 15th birthday, 1942. Has appeared since in leading rôles of many ballets including: Sleeping Beauty, Giselle, Sylvia, Checkmate, Ballet Imperial, Donald of the Burthens, Homage, Birthday Offering, The Lady and the Fool. Film: first 3 Dimensional Ballet Film ever made, The Black Swan, 1952. Left Royal Ballet, Covent Garden (as permanent Mem.) Spring 1957, to become free-lance ballerina. Regular guest appearances with Royal Ballet at Covent Garden and on Continental, African, American and Far Eastern Tours. Guest Artist, London's Festival Ballet in London and abroad, 1958-64. First Western ballerina to appear with Bolshoi Ballet: Moscow, Leningrad, Kiev, Tiflis, 1957-58; First Western ballerina to dance with Chinese Ballet Co. in Peking and Shanghai, 1964. Engagements and tours abroad include: Central and S America, Mexico, Rhodesia and S Africa, Canada, NZ, Lebanon, Germany, Norway, Sweden, Denmark, Finland, Belgium, Holland, France, Switzerland, Italy, Portugal, Austria, Czechoslovakia, Poland, Rumania. Regular television and broadcasts in England and abroad. Dir-Gen., Arts Educational Trust, 1966-68; Gov. of Dame Alice Owens Girls' Sch., London. Hon. DMus Leicester, 1970. *Publications:* Red Curtain Up, 1958; Through the Bamboo Curtain, 1965. *Relevant publications:* biographical studies (by Gordon Anthony), 1952, (by Pigeon Crowle), 1952; Beryl Grey, Dancers of Today (by Hugh Fisher), 1955; *Recreations:* music, painting, books and swimming. *Address:* 78 Park Street, W1. *T:* 01-629 0477.

**GREY, Charles Frederick,** CBE 1966; miner; Independent Methodist Minister; *b* 25 March 1903; *m* 1925, Margaret, *d* of James Aspey. Mem. of Divisional Labour Exec. MP (Lab) Durham, 1945-70; Opposition Whip (Northern), 1962-64; Comptroller of HM Household, 1964-66, Treasurer, 1966-69. *Address:* 1a, Moor House Gardens, Four Lane Ends, Hetton-le-Hole, Co. Durham. *T:* Hetton-le-Hole 2292.

**GREY, Sir Paul (Francis),** KCMG 1963 (CMG 1951); *b* 2 Dec. 1908; *s* of Lt-Col Arthur Grey, CIE, and Teresa (*née* Alleyne); *m* 1936, Agnes Mary, *d* of late Richard Weld-Blundell, Ince-Blundell Hall, Lancs; three *s*. *Educ:* Charterhouse; Christ Church, Oxford. Entered Diplomatic Service, 1933; served in Rome, 1935; Foreign Office, 1939; Rio de Janeiro, 1944; The Hague, 1945; Counsellor, Lisbon, 1949; Minister, British Embassy, Moscow, 1951-54; Assistant Under Sec., Foreign Office, Sept. 1954-57; HM Ambassador to Czechoslovakia, 1957-60; HM Ambassador to Switzerland, 1960-64. *Recreations:* shooting and fishing. *Address:* Pounds Bridge Manor, Penshurst, Kent. *T:* Langton 3117. *Club:* Brooks's.

**GREY, Rex Burton;** Director, Standard Telephones & Cables Ltd (Chairman, 1965-68); *b* El Paso, Texas, 27 Oct. 1920; *s* of Rex Grey and Georgie Mary (*née* Ferris); *m* 1942, Natalie C. Tandy; one *s*. *Educ:* Texas A and M Univ.; University of Houston; Harvard Univ. Gen. Electric, 1945-55; Texas Apparatus Co. (Pres. and owner), 1955-58; Manager, Controls and Automation Div., Dresser Industries, 1958-61; Man. Dir, Standard Telephones & Cables Ltd, 1961-65. Chairman: STC (South Africa); Supersonic (South Africa); Supersonic (Rhodesia); Supersonic (Zambia); ITT (Zambia); ITT (Maroc); Standard Elec. (Iran); Standard Elec. (Turkey); SACT (Algeria); ITT (Nigeria); Creed & Co. Ltd; Pres., ITT Africa and Middle East; Vice-President: Internat. Telephone and Telegraph Corp.; ITT Europe; ITT Industries Europe; Director: Standard Telecommunication Labs; Commercial Cable Co. Ltd; Internat. Marine Radio Co. Ltd; Kolster-Brandes Ltd; Stanelco Industrial Services Ltd; Abbey Life Assurance Co. Ltd. *Recreations:* collecting antique guns, golf, hunting. *Address:* 10 Park Crescent, W1. *T:* 01-580 8266; 190 Strand, WC2.

**GREY, Sir Robin (Edward Dysart),** 6th Bt, *cr* 1814; retired banking executive; *b* 12 Nov. 1886; *s* of Edward George Grey; *S* Kinsman, Sir (Harry) Martin Grey, 5th Bt, 1960; *m* 1918, Maude Wilson; one *s*. *Educ:* Rockhampton Grammar Sch., Qld, Australia. Joined The Union Bank of Australia Ltd, as a junior, and retired as Inspector for Queensland. *Heir: g s* Anthony Dysart Grey, *b* 19 Oct. 1949. *Address:* 35 Abbott Street, Ascot, Queensland, Australia. *Club:* Brisbane (Brisbane).

**GREY EGERTON, Sir (Philip) John (Caledon),** 15th Bt *cr* 1617; *b* 19 Oct. 1920; *er s* of Sir Philip Grey Egerton, 14th Bt; *S* father, 1962; *m* 1952, Margaret (Voase) (who *m* 1941, Sqdn Ldr

Robert A. Ullman, *d* 1943), *er d* of late Rowland Rank. *Educ:* Eton. Served Welsh Guards, 1939-45. *Recreation:* fishing. *Heir: b* Brian Balguy Le Belward Egerton, *b* 5 Feb. 1925. *Address:* Thornes, Mill Lane, Sidlesham, West Sussex. *T:* Sidlesham 307. *Clubs:* Pratt's, Marylebone Cricket (MCC).

**GREY-SMITH, Sir Ross,** Kt 1966; *b* 22 July 1901; *s* of Francis Grey-Smith and Sybella Anne (*née* Ross); *m* 1932, Betty, *d* of Charles Fairbairn; no *c*. *Educ:* Melbourne C of E Grammar Sch.; Univ. of Melbourne. Admitted to Victorian Bar, 1926; commenced practice as Solicitor, 1926. Served with RAAF in New Guinea, NEI, and commanded advance Echelon at Labuan landing (Borneo), 1945. Pres., Old Colonists' Assoc., 1948-49. Member Committee: Royal Victorian Aero Club, 1931-32; Oaklands Hunt Club, 1932-38 (Vice-Pres., 1955-); Victoria Racing Club, 1938- (Chm., 1962-); Moonee Valley Racing Club, 1935-38. Notary Public (Pres. Soc. of Notaries, 1962-63). Chm., Wm Drummond Ltd (Jewellers). *Recreations:* racing, shooting. *Address:* 7 Fairlie Court, South Yarra, Victoria, Australia. *T:* 26-2718; Collins House, Melbourne. *T:* 67-8481. *Clubs:* Melbourne, VRC, VATC, MVRC, MCC, RACV (all in Melbourne).

**GREY WALTER, William;** *see* Walter, W. G.

**GRIBBLE, Rev. Canon Arthur Stanley,** MA; Canon Residentiary and Chancellor of Peterborough Cathedral since 1967; *b* 18 Aug. 1904; *er s* of J. B. Gribble; *m* 1938, Edith Anne, *er d* of late Laurence Bailey; one *s*. *Educ:* Queen's Coll. and Westcott House, Cambridge (Burney Student); University of Heidelberg. Curate: St Mary, Windermere, 1930-33, Almondbury, 1933-36; Chaplain Sarum Theological Coll., 1936-38; Rector of Shepton Mallet, 1938-54. Examining Chaplain to Bp of Bath and Wells, 1947-54; Proctor in Convocation, diocese Bath and Wells, 1947-54; Rural Dean of Shepton Mallet, 1949-54; Prebendary of Wiveliscombe in Wells Cathedral, 1949-54; Principal, Queen's Coll., Birmingham, 1954-67; Recognised Lectr, Univ. of Birmingham, 1954-67. Hon. Canon, Birmingham Cathedral, 1954-67. Commissary for the Bishop of Kimberley and Kuruman, 1964-66. Examng Chaplain to Bishop of Peterborough, 1968-. *Recreation:* mountaineering. *Address:* Prebendal House, Minster Precincts, Peterborough. *T:* Peterborough 69441.

**GRIBBLE, Leonard Reginald;** Author; *b* 1 Feb. 1908; *s* of late Wilfred Browning Gribble and late Ada Mary Sterry; *m* 1932, Nancy Mason; one *d*. In 1928 wrote first detective story; literary adviser various London publishers: inaugurated The Empire Bookshelf series for the BBC; judge in two international novel competitions; has devised and written commercial radio programmes and commercial films; founder mem. Paternosters Club; in Press and Censorship Div. of Ministry of Information, 1940-45; co-founder Crime Writers Assoc., 1953. *Publications:* The Gillespie Suicide Mystery, A Christmas Treasury, 1929; The Jesus of the Poets, The Grand Modena Murder, 1930; Is This Revenge?, 1931; The Stolen Home Secretary, Queens of Crime, 1932; Famous Feats of Detection and Deduction, The Secret of Tangles, 1933; The Riddle of the Ravens, The Death Chime, 1934; Mystery at Tudor Arches; All The Year Round Stories (with Nancy Gribble), 1935; Riley of the Special Branch; The Case of the Malverne Diamonds, 1936; The Case-book of Anthony Slade, 1937; Tragedy in E flat, 1938; The Arsenal Stadium Mystery (filmed), 1939 and 1950; Heroes of the Fighting RAF, 1941; Death by Design (a film), 1942; Epics of the Fighting RAF, 1943; Heroes of the Merchant Navy, 1944; Toy Folk and Nursery People (verse), 1945; Best Children's Stories of the Year (editor), 1946-50; Profiles from notable Modern Biographies (editor); Atomic Murder, 1947; Hangman's Moon, 1949; They Kidnapped Stanley Matthews, 1950; The Frightened Chameleon, 1951; Murder Out of Season, 1952; Famous Manhunts, 1953; Adventures in Murder, 1954; Triumphs of Scotland Yard, 1955; Death Pays the Piper, 1956; Famous Judges and their Trials, 1957; Great Detective Exploits, 1958; Don't Argue with Death, 1959; Hands of Terror, 1960; Clues that Spelled Guilty, 1961; When Killers Err, 1962; They Challenged the Yard, 1963; Heads You Die, 1964; Such Women are Deadly, 1965; Great Manhunters of the Yard, 1966; Strip Tease Macabre, 1967; Stories of Famous Conspirators, 1968; Famous Stories of Scientific Detection, 1969; Strange Crimes of Passion, 1970; The Element of Horror, 1971; also writes fiction (some filmed) under several pseudonyms; translations in fourteen languages; contribs on sociology to Chambers's Encyclopædia, Encyclopedia Americana; book-reviews, feature articles, short stories and serials to various publications. *Recreations:* motoring abroad, watching things grow. *Address:* Chandons, Firsdown Close, High Salvington, Worthing, Sussex. *T:* Worthing 61976.

**GRIBBON, Maj.-Gen. Nigel St George,** OBE 1960; Assistant Chief of Staff (Intelligence), SHAPE, since 1970; *b* 6 Feb. 1917; *s* of late Brig. W. H. Gribbon, CMG, CBE; *m* 1943, Rowan Mary MacLeish; two *s* one *d*. *Educ:* Rugby Sch.; Sandhurst. King's Own, 1937-42; GSO3 10th Indian Div., 1942; Staff Coll. Quetta, 1943; GSO3 55th Div., 1944; Bde Major, 1st Parachute Bde, 1946; RAF Staff Coll., 1947; GSO2 GHQ FARELF, 1948-50; DAQMG WO, 1953-55; DAAG WO, 1957-58; OC 5 King's Own, 1958-60; AMS WO, 1960-62; Comdr 161 Bde, 1963-65; ndc 1965-66; DMC MoD, 1966-67; ACOS NORTHAG, 1967-69. *Recreations:* ski-ing, sailing. *Address:* c/o National and Grindlay's Bank, 13 St James's Square, SW1. *Club:* Army and Navy.

**GRIDLEY,** family name of **Baron Gridley.**

**GRIDLEY,** 2nd Baron, *cr* 1955; **Arnold Hudson Gridley;** *b* 26 May 1906; *er surv s* of 1st Baron Gridley, KBE, Culwood, Lye Green, Chesham, Bucks; *S* father, 1965; *m* 1948, Edna Lesley, *d* of late Lesley Richard Wheen of Shanghai, China and Penselwood, Somerset; one *s* three *d*. *Educ:* Oundle. Appointed to the Colonial Service in 1928. Served in various Government appointments in the Federated Malay States of Perak, Selangor and Pahang; Mem. of Penang Port Advisory Cttee; Dep.-Comptroller of Customs and Excise, Malaya, 1956; retired 1957. Entered the House of Lords, 1965. Mem. Council, HM Overseas Service Pensioners Assoc., 1966-; Mem., Somerset CC Rating Appeals Tribunal; a Dir, New Homes Building Soc. *Recreations:* photography, sea-fishing in Cornwall. *Heir: s* Hon. Richard David Arnold Gridley, *b* 22 Aug. 1956. *Address:* Coneygore, Stoke Trister, Wincanton, Somerset. *T:* Wincanton 2209. *Clubs:* Carlton; Bath and County (Bath).

**GRIER, Anthony MacGregor,** CMG 1963; General Manager, Redditch Development Corporation, since 1964; *b* 12 April 1911; *e s* of late Very Rev. R. M. Grier, St Ninian's House, Perth, Scotland, and late Mrs E. M. Grier; *m* 1946, Hon. Patricia Mary Spens, *er d* of 1st Baron Spens, *qv*; two *s* one *d*. *Educ:* St

Edward's Sch.; Exeter Coll., Oxford. Colonial Administrative Service, Sierra Leone, 1935; attached to Colonial Office in London and Delhi, 1943-47; appointed to North Borneo, 1947; Development Sec., 1953; Under-Sec., 1956; Resident, Sandakan, 1963; retired, 1964. Chm., Sabah Electricity Board, 1956-64. *Recreations:* tennis, golf, shooting. *Address:* Callow Hill House, Redditch, Worcs. *T:* Redditch 64303. *Club:* East India and Sports.

**GRIERSON, John,** CBE 1961; British Film Producer; *b* Kilmadock, Scotland, 26 April 1898; *s* of Robert Morrison and Jane (Anthony) Grierson; *m* 1930, Margaret Taylor. *Educ:* Glasgow and Chicago Univs. MA, LLD, Glasgow. RNVR, 1915-19. Associated in formation of Empire Marketing Board and GPO Film Units, Central Film Library, Film Centre, Films of Scotland Cttee, National Film Board of Canada and Group 3. Gen. Man. Canadian Wartime Information Board, 1942-43; Dir Mass Communications, Unesco, 1946-48; Controller Films Central Office of Information, 1948-50. Productions include: Drifters, 1929; Song of Ceylon, 1934; Night Mail, 1936; World in Action Series, 1942-43; The Brave Don't Cry, 1952; Man of Africa, 1953; This Wonderful World, TV, 1961. Hon. DLitt, Heriot-Watt, 1969. Golden Thistle Award, 1968. *Publications:* articles collected in Grierson on Documentary, 1946. *Address:* Tog Hill, Calstone, Calne, Wilts.

**GRIERSON, Philip,** MA; FBA; FSA; Fellow, since 1935, Librarian, 1944-69, and President, since 1966, Gonville and Caius College, Cambridge; Reader in Medieval Numismatics, University of Cambridge, since 1959; Professor of Numismatics and the History of Coinage, University of Brussels, since 1948; Hon. Keeper of the Coins, Fitzwilliam Museum, Cambridge, since 1949; Adviser in Byzantine Numismatics to the Dumbarton Oaks Library and Collections, Harvard University, at Washington, USA, since 1955; *b* 15 Nov. 1910; *s* of Philip Henry Grierson and Roberta Ellen Jane Pope. *Educ:* Marlborough Coll.; Gonville and Caius Coll., Cambridge. University Lectr in History, Cambridge, 1945-59; Literary Dir of Royal Historical Society, 1945-55; Ford's Lectr in History, University of Oxford, 1956-57. Pres. Royal Numismatic Society, 1961-66. Corresp. Mem., Koninklijke Vlaamse Acad., 1955; Assoc. Mem., Acad. royale de Belgique, 1968. Hon. LittD (University of Ghent), 1958. *Publications:* Les Annales de Saint-Pierre de Gand, 1937; Books on Soviet Russia, 1917-42, 1943; Sylloge of Coins of the British Isles, Vol. I (Fitzwilliam Museum: Early British and Anglo-Saxon Coins), 1958; Bibliographie numismatique, 1966. Editor: C. W. Previté-Orton, The Shorter Cambridge Medieval History, 1952; H. E. Ives, The Venetian Gold Ducat and its Imitations, 1954; Studies in Italian History presented to Miss E. M. Jamison, 1956; (with A. R. Bellinger) Catalogue of the Byzantine Coins in the Dumbarton Oaks Collection and in the Whittemore Collection, Vols 1, 2, 1966-68. Trans. F. L. Ganshof, Feudalism, 1952. *Recreations:* squash racquets, science fiction. *Address:* Gonville and Caius College, Cambridge. *T:* Cambridge 53275.

**GRIERSON, Sir Richard Douglas,** 11th Bt *cr* 1685; *b* 25 June 1912; *o s* of Sir Robert Gilbert White Grierson, 10th Bt, and Hilda (*d* 1962), *d* of James Stewart, Surbiton, Surrey; *S* father 1957; unmarried. *Educ:* Imperial Service Coll., Windsor. Journalist. *Heir: cousin* Michael John Bewes Grierson, *b* 24 July 1921. *Address:* 4 Modena Road, Hove 3, Sussex. *T:* Brighton 30398.

**GRIERSON, Ronald Hugh;** Vice-Chairman, General Electric Co., since 1968; Chairman: R. H. Grierson & Co. Ltd, since 1969; Scientific Enterprise Associates, Geneva, since 1969; *b* Nürnberg, Bavaria, 1921; *s* of E. J. Griessmann (name changed by Deed Poll in 1943 from Griessmann); *m* 1966, Elizabeth Heather, Viscountess Bearsted, *er d* of Mrs G. Firmston-Williams; one *s. Educ:* Lycée Pasteur, Paris; Highgate Sch., London; Balliol Coll., Oxford. Served in HM Forces, 1940-46. Economist Newspaper, 1947-48; entered S. G. Warburg & Co., 1948. Dep. Chm. and Man. Dir, IRC, 1966-67; Executive Dir, S. G. Warburg & Co. 1958-68. Member of Council: Atlantic Coll.; RIIA; Mem. Bd of Governors, Weizmann Inst. of Science. *Address:* 27 Grosvenor Crescent Mews, SW1; Ascott Lodge, Wing, near Leighton Buzzard, Beds.

**GRIEVE, Christopher Murray,** JP, Angus; (writes under pseudonym of Hugh McDiarmid); author and journalist; *b* Langholm, Dumfriesshire, 11 Aug. 1892; *m* 1st, Margaret Skinner; one *s* one *d*; 2nd, Valda Trevlyn; one *s. Educ:* Langholm Academy; Edinburgh Univ. One of the Founders of the Scottish Nationalist Party; Founder of Scottish Centre of PEN Club; regular contributor on literary, political, and general matters to many British and foreign newspapers and periodicals. Hon. Fellow, Modern Language Assoc. of America. Hon. LLD Edinburgh, 1957; *Publications:* Prose: Annals of the Five Senses; Contemporary Scottish Studies; Albyn, or the Future of Scotland; The Present Condition of Scottish Arts and Affairs; Scottish Scene; At the Sign of the Thistle; Scottish Eccentrics; The Handmaid of the Lord (a novel, from the Spanish of Ramon Maria de Tenreiro); The Scottish Islands; Lucky Poet (autobiography), etc. Poetry: Sangschaw; Penny Wheep; A Drunk Man looks at the Thistle; To Circumjack Cencrastus; Stony Limits and other poems; First Hymn to Lenin and other Poems; Second Hymn to Lenin and other Poems; Cornish Heroic Song for Valda Trevlyn; The Birlinn of Clanranald (from the Scots Gaelic of Alexander MacDonald); Direadh; Golden Treasury of Scottish Poetry; Speaking for Scotland (pub. USA only); A Kist of Whistles; R. B. Cunninghame Graham, a Centenary Study; The Golden Treasury of Scottish Poetry; In Memoriam James Joyce; The Battle Continues; Three Hymns to Lenin; Burns today and tomorrow; Collected Poems (1920-61); The Kind of Poetry I Want; The Company I've Kept; A Lap of Honour; Celtic Nationalism; The Uncanny Scot; A Clyack Sheaf; More Collected Poems, etc. *Recreation:* Anglophobia. *Address:* The Cottage, Brownsbank, by Biggar, Lanarkshire.

**GRIEVE, Sir (Herbert) Ronald (Robinson),** Kt 1958; Medical Practitioner; *b* 6 June 1896; 2nd *s* of Lieut Gideon James Grieve (killed in action, 1900) and Julia Australia Grieve (*née* Robinson), Sydney, Australia; *m* 1945, Florence Ross Timpson, formerly of Cheadle Heath, Cheshire; one *s* two *d. Educ:* Sydney Gram. Sch.; University of Sydney. Grad. in Medicine and Surgery. Resident Medical Officer, Newcastle Gen. Hosp., NSW, 1920-21; House Physician, Manchester Royal Infirmary, 1922-23; Hon. Clinical Asst in Medicine, Royal Prince Alfred Hospital, Sydney, 1941-47. Pres. BMA (NSW Branch), 1947; Mem. NSW Medical Board, 1938-63; Chm. Medical Benefits Fund of Australia, from inception, 1947-; Pres. Internat. Fedn of Voluntary Health Service Funds, 1968; Mem. Commonwealth of Australia Advisory Cttee on National Health Act, 1953-. MLC, NSW, 1933-34. *Recreations:* angling, the turf;

formerly rowing and cricket (rep. Sydney Univ.). *Address:* Earlwood, Sydney, NSW 2206, *T:* LL 1514. *Clubs:* University, Old Sydneians, Australian Jockey (Sydney).

**GRIEVE, Percy;** *see* Grieve, W. P.

**GRIEVE, Prof. Sir Robert,** Kt 1969; MA, MTPI, AMICE, AMIME; Professor of Town and Regional Planning, University of Glasgow, since 1964 (seconded as Chairman, Highlands and Islands Development Board, 1965-70); *b* 11 Dec. 1910; *s* of Peter Grieve and Catherine Boyle; *m* 1933, Mary Lavinia Broughton Blackburn; two *s* two *d*. *Educ:* N. Kelvinside Sch., Glasgow; Royal College of Science and Technology (now University of Strathclyde), Glasgow. Trng and qual. as Civil Engr with Corp. of Glasgow, 1927-32; Civil Engr and finally Chief Planning Asst, Renfrew CC, 1933-39; Town Planning Engr, and Civil Defence Construction, 1939-44; Sen. Techn Off. on preparation of Clyde Valley Regional Plan, 1944-46; Regional Planning Off., Dept of Health for Scotland: Highlands and Islands, 1946-49; W Scotland, 1949-60; Chief Planner, Scottish Office, 1960-64. *Publications:* part-author and collaborator in several major professional reports and books; many papers and articles in professional and technical jls. *Recreations:* mountaineering, ski-ing, canoeing. *Address:* Braids, 2a Green Drive, Inverness. *T:* Inverness 34400; 12 Nelson Street, Edinburgh 3. *Clubs:* Scottish Arts (Edinburgh); Highland (Inverness).

**GRIEVE, Sir Ronald;** *see* Grieve, Sir H. R. R.

**GRIEVE, Thomas Robert,** CBE 1968; MC 1944; Vice-Chairman and Managing Director Shell-Mex and BP Ltd, since 1965; Chairman, United Kingdom Oil Pipelines Ltd, since 1965; *b* 11 Sept. 1909; *s* of Robert Grieve and Annie Craig (*née* Stark); *m* 1946, Doreen Bramley Whitehead; two *d*. *Educ:* Cargilfield and Fettes Coll., Edinburgh. Joined Anglo-Saxon Petroleum Co. Ltd, 1930; served in London, 1930-40. Commissioned 9th Highland Lt Inf. (TA), 1928, seconded Movement Control, Royal Engineers, 1943-45; served NW Europe, rank of Major. Vice-Pres. in charge of Operations, Shell Oil Co. of Canada, 1945; Exec. Asst to Regional Vice-Pres. of Shell Oil Co., Houston, Texas, 1949; Manager of Distribution and Supply Dept, Shell Petroleum Co. Ltd, London, 1951; Director: Shell-Mex and BP Ltd, Shell Refining Co. Ltd, Shell Co. UK Ltd, 1959-65; Shell International Petroleum Co. Ltd, 1963-65. *Recreations:* golf, travel. *Address:* 6 Laverton Place, SW5. *T:* 01-373 6793. *Club:* Caledonian.

**GRIEVE, William Percival, (W. Percy Grieve),** QC 1962; MP (C) Solihull Division of Warwickshire since 1964; Recorder of Northampton since 1965; Deputy-Chairman of Quarter Sessions, County of Lincoln (parts of Holland) since 1962; *b* 25 March 1915; *o s* of 2nd Lieut W. P. Grieve, the Middlesex Regt (killed in action, Ypres, Feb. 1915), Rockcliffe, Dalbeattie; *m* 1949, Evelyn Raymonde Louise, *y d* of late Comdt Hubert Mijouain, Paris, and of Liliane, *e d* of late Sir George Roberts, 1st and last Bt; one *s* one *d* (and one *s* decd). *Educ:* privately; Trinity Hall, Cambridge. Exhibitioner, Trinity Hall, 1933; Lord Kitchener Nat. Memorial Schol., 1934; BA 1937, MA 1940. Harmsworth Law Schol., 1937, called to Bar, 1938, Middle Temple; Bencher, 1969. Joined Midland Circuit, 1939. Commissioned the Middlesex Regt, 1939; Liaison Officer, French Mil. Censorship, Paris, 1939-40; Min. of Information, 1940-41; HQ Fighting France, 1941-43; Staff Capt. and Exec. Officer, SHAEF Mission to Luxembourg, 1944; Major and GSO2 Brit. Mil. Mission to Luxembourg, 1945; DAAG, BAOR, 1946. Asst Recorder of Leicester, 1956-65. Mem. Mental Health Review Tribunal, Sheffield Region, 1960-64. Has served on Gen. Council of the Bar. Contested (C) Lincoln, Parly. by-election, 1962. Member: House of Commons Select Cttee on Race Relations and Immigration, 1968-; UK Delegn, Council of Europe and WEU, 1969-. Mem. Council, Officers' Assoc., 1969-. Officier avec Couronne, Order of Adolphe of Nassau; Chevalier, Order of Couronne de Chêne and Croix de Guerre avec Palmes (Luxembourg), 1945-46; Bronze Star (USA), 1945. *Recreations:* swimming, travel, the theatre. *Address:* 1 King's Bench Walk, Temple, EC4. *T:* 01-353 8436; 6 Fitz James Avenue, W14. *T:* 01-603 0376. *Clubs:* Carlton, Hurlingham.

**GRIEVE, William Robertson,** VRD 1958; QC (Scotland) 1957; Sheriff of Renfrew and Argyll since 1964; Procurator of the Church of Scotland, since 1969; *b* 21 Oct. 1917; *o s* of late William Robertson Grieve (killed in action, 1917) and of Mrs Grieve, Edinburgh; *m* 1947, Lorna St John, *y d* of late Engineer Rear-Adm. E. P. St J. Benn, CB; one *s* one *d*. *Educ:* Glasgow Academy; Sedbergh; Glasgow Univ. MA 1939, LLB 1946 (Glasgow); Pres. Glasgow Univ. Union, 1938-39. John Clark (Mile-end) Scholar, 1939. RNVR: Sub-Lt 1939; Lieut 1942; Lt-Comdr 1950; served with RN, 1939-46. Admitted Mem. of Faculty of Advocates, 1947. Junior Counsel in Scotland to Bd of Inland Revenue, 1952-57. Advocate-Depute (Home), 1962-64. *Recreations:* golf, painting. *Address:* 20 Belgrave Crescent, Edinburgh 4. *T:* 031-332 7500. *Clubs:* New (Edinburgh); Hon. Company of Edinburgh Golfers.

**GRIEVES, Joseph Arthur,** QC 1958; **His Honour Judge Grieves;** Chairman of SE Area, Greater London Quarter Sessions, since 1967 (Deputy Chairman: Middlesex 1965-67; Peterborough, 1960-64; Co. London, 1964-65); *b* 15 July 1907; *s* of Arthur Grieves, Leicester; *m* 1935, Anna Lloyd Amphlett; two *s* two *d*. *Educ:* Wyggeston Sch., Leicester; Exeter Coll., Oxford. Called to Bar, Inner Temple, 1933; joined Midland Circuit, 1933. Recorder: of Lincoln, Jan.-Aug. 1960; of Birmingham, 1960-64. RAFVR, 1941-45. *Address:* 5 Pump Court, Temple, EC4. *T:* 01-353 2628; 53 Central Hill, Upper Norwood, SE19. *T:* 01-670 0455. *Club:* Reform.

**GRIFFIN, Vice-Adm. Anthony Templer Frederick Griffith,** CB 1967; Controller of the Navy, since 1971; *b* Peshawar, 24 Nov. 1920; *s* of late Col F. M. G. Griffin, MC, and B. A. B. Griffin (*née* Down); *m* 1943, Rosemary Ann Hickling; two *s* one *d*. *Educ:* RN Coll., Dartmouth. Joined RN, 1934; to sea as Midshipman, 1939; War Service in E Indies, Mediterranean, Atlantic, N Russia and Far East; specialised in navigation, 1944; Staff Coll., 1952; Imp. Defence Coll., 1963; comd HMS Ark Royal, 1964-65; Asst Chief of Naval Staff (Warfare), 1966-68; Flag Officer, Second-in-Command, Far East Fleet, 1968-69; Flag Officer, Plymouth, Comdr Central Sub Area, Eastern Atlantic, and Comdr Plymouth Sub Area, Channel, 1969-71. Comdr 1951; Capt. 1956; Rear-Adm. 1966; Vice-Adm. 1968. *Recreations:* sailing, ski-ing, riding, golf. *Address:* Shedfield Cottage, Shedfield, near Southampton, Hants. *T:* Wickham (Hants) 2239. *Clubs:* United Service, Royal Navy.

**GRIFFIN, Col Edgar Allen,** CMG 1965; OBE 1943; ED 1945; Regional Director, Northern Region, Commonwealth War Graves Commission, since 1969; *b* 18 Jan. 1907; 3rd *s* of Gerald Francis and Isabella Margaret Griffin; *m* 1936, Alethea Mary Byrne; two *s* two *d.* Retired from AMF, 1947; Australian Govt Nominee to Staff of War Graves Commn, 1947; Chief Admin. Officer, Eastern Dist (Cairo), 1947-54; UK Dist (London), 1954-58; Regional Dir, Southern Region (Rome), 1958-69. *Address:* 100 rue Emile Zola, Arras, Pas-de-Calais, France.

**GRIFFIN, Sir Elton Reginald,** Kt 1970; CBE 1967; General Manager of Boral Ltd, Sydney, Australia, since 1947; *b* 1906; *s* of late Frank Carlton Griffin, Gordon, New South Wales; *m* Betty Maud, *d* of late Arthur Vickery, Bellevue Hill, NSW. *Educ:* Sydney Grammar Sch. Served War of 1939-45: Capt. AIF. FCA (Aust.). *Address:* c/o Boral Ltd, 221 Miller Street, North Sydney, NSW, Australia; (private) 81 Kambala Road, Bellevue Hill, NSW. *Club:* Royal Yacht Squadron.

**GRIFFIN, Mrs Francis D.;** *see* Dunne, Irene.

**GRIFFIN, Maj.-Gen. John Arnold Atkinson,** DSO 1918; *b* 1891; *s* of late Comdr John Griffin, RN; *m* 1915, Marjorie Annie (*d* 1968), *d* of Rev. Alan Williams; one *s* one *d. Educ:* Sherborne; RMC Sandhurst. Served European War, 1914-18 (despatches thrice, DSO); commanded 1st Bn, Lincs Regt, 1935-39; retired pay, 1945; Col Royal Lincs Regt, 1948-58. *Recreations:* yacht racing, shooting. *Address:* Harepath, East Boldre, Brockenhurst, Hants. *T:* East End 267. *Club:* Royal Lymington Yacht.

**GRIFFIN, Sir John Bowes,** Kt 1955; QC 1938; *b* 19 April 1903; *o s* of late Sir Charles Griffin; *m* Eva Orrell, 2nd *d* of late John Mellifont Walsh, Wexford; two *d. Educ:* Clongowes; Dublin Univ. (MA, LLD, First Cl. Moderatorship, Gold Medallist); Cambridge. Barrister-at-Law, Inner Temple, 1926. Administrative Officer, Uganda, 1927; Asst District Officer, 1929; Registrar, High Court, 1929; Crown Counsel, 1933; Actg Solicitor-Gen. and Attorney-Gen., various periods; Attorney-Gen., Bahamas, 1936 (Acting Governor and Acting Chief Justice, various periods); Solicitor-Gen., Palestine, 1939, Acting Attorney-Gen., various periods; Attorney-Gen., Hong Kong, 1946; Chief Justice of Uganda, 1952-56. Secretary: East Africa Law Officers Conference, 1933; Commission of Enquiry Admin. of Justice, East Africa, 1933; Chm. Prisons Enquiry, Bahamas, 1936; miscellaneous Bds and Cttees; Chairman: Tel Aviv Municipal Commn of Enquiry, Palestine, 1942; Review Cttees, Detainees (Defence and Emergency Regulations), Palestine, 1940-46. Retired, Dec. 1956; Actg Chief Justice, N Rhodesia, 1957; Chm. Commn of Enquiry Gwenbe Valley Disturbances, N Rhodesia, 1958; Speaker, Legislative Council, Uganda, 1958-62; Speaker, Uganda National Assembly, 1962-63, retd. Chairman: Public Service Commissions, 1963 and Constitutional Council, 1964, N Rhodesia; retd 1965. CStJ 1960. *Publications:* Revised Edn of Laws (Uganda), 1935; (joint) Hong Kong, 1950. *Recreation:* golf. *Clubs:* East India and Sports; Kampala (Uganda); Union (Malta). *Address:* c/o National Bank Ltd, 15 Whitehall, SW1. *See also A. J. Boase.*

**GRIFFIN, Paul,** MBE 1961; MA Cantab; Headmaster of Aldenham School since 1962; *b* 2 March 1922; *s* of late John Edwin Herman Griffin; *m* 1946, Felicity Grace, *d* of Canon Howard Dobson; one *s* one *d. Educ:* Framlingham Coll.; St Catharine's Coll., Cambridge. Served War in Gurkhas, India, Burma, Malaya, 1940-46; North-West Frontier, 1941-43; Chindits, 1943-44. Asst Master and Senior English Master, Uppingham Sch., 1949-55; Principal, English Sch. in Cyprus, 1956-60. *Publications:* various poems, articles and broadcast talks. *Recreation:* sea fishing. *Address:* Headmaster's House, Aldenham School, Elstree, Herts. *T:* Radlett 6131. *Club:* Public Schools.

**GRIFFIN, Mrs R. L.;** *see* Chapman, Mrs H. W.

**GRIFFIN, Very Rev. Victor Gilbert Benjamin;** Dean of St Patrick's Cathedral, Dublin, since 1969; *b* 24 May 1924; *s* of Gilbert B. and Violet M. Griffin, Carnew, Co. Wicklow; *m* 1958, Daphne E. Mitchell; two *s. Educ:* Kilkenny Coll.; Mountjoy Sch., and Trinity Coll., Dublin. MA, 1st class Hons in Philosophy. Ordained, 1947; Curacy, St Augustine's, Londonderry, 1947-51; Curacy, Christ Church, Londonderry, 1951-57; Rector of Christ Church, Londonderry, 1957-69. Lecturer in Philosophy, Magee Univ. Coll., Londonderry, 1950-69. *Recreations:* music, golf. *Address:* The Deanery, St Patrick's Cathedral, Dublin 8. *T:* Dublin 752451. *Club:* Friendly Brothers of St Patrick (Dublin).

**GRIFFITH, Rev. Arthur Leonard;** Minister, Deer Park United Church, Toronto, since 1966; *b* 20 March 1920; *s* of Thomas Griffiths and Sarah Jane Taylor; *m* 1947, Anne Merelie Cayford; two *d. Educ:* Public and High Schs, Brockville, Ont; McGill Univ., Montreal (BA, McGill, 1942); United Theological Coll., Montreal (BD 1945; Hon. DD 1962); Mansfield Coll., Oxford, England, 1957-58. Ordained in The United Church of Canada, 1945; Minister: United Church, Arden, Ont, 1945-47; Trinity United Church, Grimsby, Ont, 1947-50; Chalmers United Church, Ottawa, Ont, 1950-60; The City Temple, London, 1960-66. *Publications:* The Roman Letter Today, 1959; God and His People, 1960; Beneath The Cross of Jesus; What is a Christian?; Barriers to Christian Belief; The Eternal Legacy, 1963; Pathways to Happiness, 1964; God's Time and Ours, 1964; The Crucial Encounter, 1965; This is Living!, 1966; God in Man's Experience, 1968; Illusions of our Culture, 1969. *Recreations:* music, drama, golf. *Address:* Deer Park United Church, 129 St Clair Avenue West Toronto 7, Canada.

**GRIFFITH, Cyril Cobham,** OBE 1962; MC 1917; President, Engineering Components Ltd, since 1968 (Chairman, 1948-68); *b* 2 Jan. 1891; *s* of Patrick Gill and Josephine Ellen Griffith; *m* 1920, Louisa Ellen Mathews; two *s* (and two *s* decd). *Educ:* Highgate Sch., Highgate, London. Joined Edwin Cooper & Co., 1909. Served European War, 1914-18, with Royal Hants Regt, in Gallipoli and Macedonia (MC, despatches). Rejoined Edwin Cooper, 1919, and subsequently Coopers Mechanical Joints Ltd, 1920. Mem. of Council of Soc. of Motor Manufacturers and Traders Ltd, 1935-39; Dep. Regional Controller, Eastern Region, MAP, 1940-42; Pres., Slough Social Fund, 1951; Chm., Southern Regional Board for Industry, 1949-52. Mem. of the Livery of the Worshipful Co. of Coachmakers and Coach Harness Makers, London. High Sheriff of Bucks, 1959. Greek Military Cross, 1918. *Recreations:* golf, fishing. *Address:* Stoke Lodge, Stoke Poges, Bucks. *T:* Fulmer 67. *Club:* Royal Automobile.

**GRIFFITH, Grosvenor Talbot;** retired; Warden of Missenden Abbey, 1958-66; *b* 27 Jan. 1899; *s* of late Thomas Wardrop Griffith, CMG, and Louisa, *d* of late Grosvenor Talbot, JP, Leeds; *m* 1934, Hilda Mary, *d* of late Eric Nisbet, JP Ryton-on-Tyne; one *s* one *d. Educ:* Charterhouse; Trinity Coll., Cambridge. 1st Class Historical Tripos Pt 1 1921, 2nd Class Pt 2, 1922: RFA 1917-19; BEF France, 1918 (wounded Nov. 1918); Trinity Coll., Cambridge, 1919-23; Asst Master and Tutor Wellington Coll., 1923-34; called to Bar, Inner Temple, 1934; Headmaster, Oakham Sch., Rutland, 1935-57. Dep. Chm., Rutland Quarter Sessions, 1946-57; Chm. Rutland Magistrates, 1954-57. Mem. Governing Body English-Speaking Union, 1962. JP Bucks, 1962-66. *Publication:* Population Problems of Age of Malthus, 1926 (repr. 1967). *Recreations:* walking, painting. *Address:* Old Swindon House, Swindon Village, Cheltenham. *T:* Cheltenham 25565. *Club:* English-Speaking Union.

**GRIFFITH, Guy Thompson,** FBA 1952; MA; Laurence Reader in Classics, Cambridge University, since 1951; Fellow of Gonville and Caius College since 1931, Lecturer in Classics since 1937; *b* 7 Jan. 1908; *m* 1940, Josephine Marjorie Rainey; three *s* one *d*. *Educ:* The Leys Sch., and Gonville and Caius Coll., Cambridge. Served in RAFVR, 1941-45. Joint Editor Classical Quarterly, 1947-51. *Publications:* The Mercenaries of the Hellenistic World, 1935; (with Michael Oakeshott) A Guide to the Classics, 1936; The Greek Historians, in Fifty Years of Classical Studies (ed M. Platnauer), 1954. Articles mostly on Greek History in periodicals. *Recreation:* racing. *Address:* 1 Springfield Road, Cambridge. *T:* Cambridge 54040.

**GRIFFITH, Hugh Emrys;** Actor since 1938; *b* 30 May 1912; *s* of William and Mary Griffith, Marian Glas, Anglesey; *m* 1947, Adelgunde Margaret Beatrice von Dechend; no *c*. *Educ:* Llangefni Gram. Sch., Anglesey. Banking, 1929-37; Leverhulme Schol., RADA, 1938-39; Bancroft Gold Medallist, RADA, 1939; various West End Productions, 1939-40; 1st Bn Royal Welch Fusiliers, with service in the Far East, 1940-46. Stratford-upon-Avon Festival Season, 1946; Trinculo, Touchstone, Holofernes, First Witch, King of France, and Mephistophiles in Dr Faustus, Cardinal Montichelso in The White Devil, Duchess, 1947; The Playboy of the Western World and Machiavelli's Mandragola, Mercury, 1947 and 1948. The Comedy of Good and Evil, Arts, 1948; Swansea Festival, 1949, King Lear; also King Lear in Welsh, BBC 1949; Lyric and Duke of York's, 1950-51: Point of Departure (Anouilh's Eurydice), The Father, also the same part in New York. Stratford-upon-Avon Festival of Britain, 1951: John of Gaunt, Glendower, and Caliban. Andrew Deeson in Escapade, St James's and Strand, 1952-53; Bellman, in The Dark is Light Enough, Aldwych, 1954; General St Pé, in The Waltz of the Toreadors, Arts and Criterion, 1956-57; W. O. Gant in Look Homeward, Angel, Barrymore Theatre, New York, 1957-58; Count Cenci, in The Cenci, Old Vic, 1959; Azdak, in The Caucasian Chalk Circle, Aldwych, 1962; the Teacher in Andorra, Biltimore Theatre, New York, 1963; Falstaff, in Henry IV, Parts I and II, Stratford-upon-Avon Festival Season, 1964. *Films include:* A Run for Your Money, The Galloping Major, The Titfield Thunderbolt, The Beggar's Opera, The Sleeping Tiger, Gone to Earth, Passage Home, The Good Companions, Lucky Jim, Ben Hur (American Oscar, 1959), Exodus, The Counterfeit Traitor, Mutiny on the Bounty, The Inspector, Term of Trial, Tom Jones, The Bargee, Hide and Seek, Oh Dad! Poor Dad! Mama's hung you in the Closet, and we're all feeling so sad, How to steal a Million, Danger Grows Wild, A Sailor from Gibraltar, Brown Eye-Evil Eye, Dare I Weep, Dare I Mourn, The Chastity Belt, The Fixer, Oliver!. Various broadcasts and TV incl. series Walrus and the Carpenter, 1965, etc. Hon. DLitt, Univ. of Wales, 1965. *Recreations:* golf, repairing old property, breeding Welsh corgis, writing, small farming. *Address:* Old Red Lion, Cherington, Shipston on Stour, Warwicks. *Club:* Garrick.

**GRIFFITH, Prof. John Aneurin Grey,** LLB London, LLM London; Barrister-at-law; Professor of Public Law, London School of Economics and Political Science, University of London, since 1970; *b* 14 Oct. 1918; *s* of Rev. B. Grey Griffith and Bertha Griffith; *m* 1941, Barbara Eirene Garnet, *d* of W. Garnet Williams; two *s* one *d*. *Educ:* Taunton Sch.; LSE. British and Indian armies, 1940-46. Lectr in Law, UCW, Aberystwyth, 1946-48; Lectr in Law and Reader, LSE, 1948-59, Prof. of English Law, 1959-70. Mem., Marlow UDC, 1950-55, and Bucks CC, 1955-61. Vis. Prof. of Law, Univ. of California at Berkeley, 1966. Editor Public Law, 1956-. *Publications:* (with H. Street) A Casebook of Administrative Law, 1964; Central Departments and Local Authorities, 1966; (with H. Street) Principles of Administrative Law, 4th edn, 1967; articles in English, Commonwealth and American jls of law, public administration and politics. *Recreations:* drinking beer and writing bad verse. *Address:* London School of Economics and Political Science, Houghton Street, WC2. *Clubs:* Tatty Bogle; Le Petit Club Français.

**GRIFFITH, John Eaton,** CMG 1949; OBE 1941; *b* 1894; *s* of L. J. Griffith, Brondesbury; *m* 1921, Violet Godson (*d* 1958); two *d*. *Educ:* University Coll. RA., 1914-19, Egypt and France; retd disabled, 1919. 1920-45, UK Civil Service; Air Ministry; Ministry of Aircraft Production; Ministry of Production and Ministry of Fuel and Power; Principal Private Sec. to successive Ministers of Aircraft Production, Lord Beaverbrook and Lord Brabazon; Under-Sec., Ministry of Supply, 1949-50; retired, 1950. Chm. European Coal Organisation, 1946-47; Organising Cttee XIV Olympiad, 1948; Pres. International Lawn Tennis Federation; Vice-Pres. The Lawn Tennis Assoc.; Pres. Bucks Lawn Tennis Assoc.; Chm. National Recreation Centre, Bisham. *Address:* St Martins, Grimm's Hill, Great Missenden, Bucks. *T:* Gt Missenden 2244. *Clubs:* Junior Carlton; All England (Wimbledon).

**GRIFFITH, (Llewelyn) Wyn,** CBE 1961 (OBE 1918); Hon. DLitt University of Wales; Chairman of Council of Honourable Society of Cymmrodorion; Vice-Chairman, Arts Council, 1952-61; *b* 30 Aug. 1890; *e s* of John Griffith, BSc, Dolgelley; *m* 1915, Winifred Elizabeth Frimston; one *s* (and one *s* killed in action, 1942). *Educ:* Grammar Sch., Dolgellau. Asst Surveyor of Taxes, 1909; Asst Sec., Inland Revenue, 1945-52. Served European War, Capt. RWF and General Staff, 1914-19. Chm. Welsh Cttee of Arts Council, 1949-56; Chm., National Book League, 1957-58; Vice-Pres. of London Centre of PEN; Mem., Departmental Cttee on Foot and Mouth Disease, 1952-54. Cymmrodorion Medal, 1970. Croix de Guerre (French), 1918. *Publications:* Up to Mametz, 1931; Branwen, 1934; Spring of Youth, 1935; The Wooden Spoon, 1937; Can Wales Unite?, 1940; Word from Wales, 1941; The Barren Tree and other Poems, 1945; The Way Lies West, 1945; The Voice of Wales, 1946; The Welsh and Their Country, 1947; The Welsh, 1950; Thomas Edwards (Twm o'r Nant), 1953; The British Civil Service, 1854-1954, 1954; Libretto of Menna, opera, by Arwel Hughes, 1954; Wales in Colour, 1958; T. E. Ellis, MP, 1959; The Saga of Pryderi, 1962; (trans.) Tea in the Heather, 1968; short stories in Welsh. *Recreations:* broadcasting in Welsh and English. *Address:* 4 Park View Road,

Berkhamsted, Herts. *T:* Berkhamsted 5042. *Clubs:* Athenæum, PEN.

**GRIFFITH, Stewart Cathie,** DFC 1944; TD 1954; Secretary, MCC, since 1962; *b* 16 June 1914; *yr s* of H. L. A. Griffith, Middleton, Sussex; *m* 1939, Barbara Reynolds; one *s* one *d*. *Educ:* Dulwich Coll.; Pembroke Coll., Cambridge (MA). Asst Master, Dulwich Coll., 1937-39. Army, 1939-46. Glider Pilot Regt, Lieut-Col. Sec., Sussex County Cricket Club, 1946-50; Cricket Correspondent, Sunday Times, 1950-52; Asst Sec., MCC, 1952-62. *Recreations:* cricket, golf, real tennis, walking. *Address:* 20 Elm Tree Road, NW8. *T:* 01-286 6246. *Clubs:* East India and Sports, MCC; Hawks (Cambridge), etc.

**GRIFFITH, Wyn;** *see* Griffith, (L.) W.

**GRIFFITH-JONES, Sir Eric (Newton),** KBE 1962; CMG 1957; QC (Kenya) 1954; Chairman: The Guthrie Corporation Ltd and associated companies; Property Holdings (Pennine) Ltd; Director: Provident Mutual Life Assurance Association; Provident Clerks' Benevolent Fund; Sutcliffe Mitchell (Insurances) Ltd; *b* 1 Nov. 1913; *s* of late Oswald Phillips Griffith-Jones and Edith Sydney (*née* Newton); *m* 1946, Mary Patricia, *widow* of F. E. Rowland, and *d* of late Capt. W. T. Heagerty and of Mrs T. H. Holyoak; one *s* two *d* (and one *s* decd). *Educ:* Cheltenham Coll. Barrister-at-law, Gray's Inn, 1934; Advocate and Solicitor, Straits Settlements, and Johore, 1935; Crown Counsel, SS (Singapore), 1939; Mil. service, 1941-46. Capt., SS Volunteer Force (Efficiency Medal; POW 1942-45). Crown Counsel, Malayan Union, 1946; Federation of Malaya: Sen. Federal Counsel, 1948; Legal Adviser: Selangor, 1948-49, Perak, 1949-51. Actg Sol.-Gen. and Actg Attorney-Gen., 1951. Solicitor-Gen., Kenya, 1952-55. Dep. Speaker, Kenya Legislative Council, 1954-55; Attorney-Gen. and Minister for Legal Affairs, Kenya, 1955-61; Acting Chief Sec. Kenya, 1955-61 (occasions); Dep. Governor, 1961-63; Actg Governor (on occasions), 1959, 1961, 1962, 1963. *Recreations:* tennis, shooting and water ski-ing. *Address:* 52-54 Gracechurch Street, EC3. *T:* 01-626 1301; The Combe, Rogate, near Petersfield, Hants. *T:* Rogate 566. *Club:* MCC.

**GRIFFITH-JONES, (John) Mervyn (Guthrie),** MC 1943; **His Honour Judge Griffith-Jones;** Common Serjeant in the City of London, since Oct. 1964; Chairman, Norfolk Quarter Sessions, since 1965; a Deputy Chairman, City of London Quarter Sessions, since 1969; *b* 1 July 1909; *e s* of late John Stanley Griffith-Jones, JP; *m* 1947, Joan Clare Baker; two *s* one *d*. *Educ:* Eton; Trinity Hall, Cambridge. Called to the Bar, Middle Temple, 1932; Master of the Bench of the Middle Temple, 1958. Served War of 1939-45. Coldstream Guards in Western Desert, North Africa and Italy (despatches). One of the British Prosecuting Council at the trial of Major War criminals at Nuremberg, 1945-46; Counsel to the Crown at North London Sessions, 1946-50; one of the Counsel to the Crown at the Central Criminal Court, 1950-59, and First Senior, 1959-64. Recorder of Grantham, 1957; Recorder of Coventry, 1959. Mem. Standing Cttee on Criminal Law Revision, 1958; Councillor, Westminster City Council, 1948-54. Liveryman, Glazier's Company; Lieutenancy, City of London. Mem. of the Pilgrims of Great Britain. First one-man show of paintings, John Whibley Gallery, 1969. *Recreations:* painting, shooting, sailing. *Address:* 5 Blithfield Street, W8. *T:* 01-937 1105; Creake Abbey, North Creake, Fakenham, Norfolk. *T:* Burnham Market 228. *Clubs:* MCC, White's, Pratt's; Royal West Norfolk Golf.

**GRIFFITH-WILLIAMS, Brig. Eric Llewellyn Griffith,** CBE 1945; DSO 1919; MC and Bar; psc; late RA; 5th *s* of late A. L. G. Griffith-Williams, Highfields, Marlow, Bucks; *b* 2 May 1894; *m* 1938, Delia (*d* 1964), *o c* of late Lt-Col H. S. Follett, CBE, Rockbeare Manor, Devon; one *d*. *Educ:* Tonbridge Sch.; RMA, Woolwich. Served European War, 1914-19; Bt. Lt-Col, 1937; War of 1939-45; Col 1940; Brig. 1940; retired pay, 1946. High Sheriff of Devonshire, 1966; DL Devon 1966. *Address:* Rockbeare Manor, Devon. *Club:* Army and Navy.

**GRIFFITHS, Bruce (Fletcher),** QC 1970; *b* 28 April 1924; *s* of Edward Griffiths and Nancy Olga (*née* Fuell); *m* 1952, Mary Kirkhouse Jenkins, *y d* of late Judge George Kirkhouse Jenkins, QC and Mrs A. D. Kirkhouse Jenkins; two *s* one *d*. *Educ:* Whitchurch Grammar Sch., Cardiff; King's Coll., London. RAF, 1942-47. LLB (Hons) London, 1951 (Jelf Medallist). Chm., Local Appeals Tribunal (Cardiff), Min. of Social Security, 1964-70; Vice-Chm., Mental Health Review Tribunal for Wales, 1968. Mem., Arts Cttee of Welsh Arts Council. *Address:* Lamb Building, Temple, EC4. *T:* 01-353 4843; 34 Park Place, Cardiff. *T:* 22454. *Clubs:* Bath; Cardiff and County (Cardiff).

**GRIFFITHS, David;** Miner; member of the Dearne UDC, 1924-46 (Chairman three times); MP (Lab) Rother Valley Div., West Riding of Yorkshire, 1945-70. Member, Commonwealth War Graves Commission, 1961-. Formerly Member Don Valley Board of Guardians, and of Swinton and District Isolation Hospital Committee. *Address:* 6 Lincoln Gardens, Goldthorpe, Rotherham, Yorks.

**GRIFFITHS, Edward;** MP (Lab) Brightside Division of Sheffield since June 1968; *b* 7 March 1929; Welsh; *m* 1954, Ella Constance Griffiths; one *s* one *d*. *Educ:* University Coll. of N Wales, Bangor. Industrial Chemist, 1951. Mem., Flintshire CC, 1964. *Recreation:* sport. *Address:* Treuddyn House, 14 Mill View Road, Shotton, Deeside, Flintshire.

**GRIFFITHS, Eldon Wylie,** MA Cantab, MA Yale; MP (C) Bury St Edmunds, since May 1964; Parliamentary Under-Secretary of State, Department of the Environment, since Oct. 1970; *b* 25 May 1925; *s* of Thomas H. W. Griffiths and Edith May; *m* 1949, Sigrid Griffiths; one *s* one *d*. *Educ:* Ashton Grammar Sch.; Emmanuel Coll., Cambridge. Fellow, Saybrook Coll., Yale, 1948-49; Correspondent, Time and Life magazines, 1949-55; Foreign Editor, Newsweek, 1956-63; Columnist, Washington Post, 1962-63; Conservative Research Department, 1963-64. Parly Sec., Min. of Housing and Local Govt, June-Oct. 1970. Consultant/Adviser, Nat. Police Federation, 1966-70; Pres., Eastern Centre Public Health Inspectors, 1966-. *Recreations:* reading, swimming, cricket. *Address:* The Little Mill House, Great Ashfield, Bury St Edmunds, Suffolk. *T:* Elmswell 585; 44 Carlisle Mansions, SW1. *Clubs:* Carlton, Lord's Taverners'; Dutch treat (New York); Farmers' (Bury St Edmunds).

**GRIFFITHS, Gilbert,** BA, LLB; Barrister-at-Law; Recorder of Dudley since 1944; Assistant Recorder of Birmingham, since 1968; *b* 21 July 1901; *s* of Harry Griffiths, Bilston, Staffs; *m* 1927, Bertha Verena, *yr d* of late Dan Gill, JP, Old Hill, Staffs; no *c*. *Educ:* King Edward's Sch., Birmingham; Trinity Hall, Cambridge. BA and LLB 1924; called to Bar, Inner

Temple, 1925; joined Oxford Circuit. Arbitrator under Conciliation Agreement between NCB and Association of Colliery Management. *Recreation:* gardening. *Address:* 2 Fountain Court, Birmingham 4. *T:* 021-236 3882. *Club:* Sutton Coldfield.

**GRIFFITHS, Harold Morris;** Head of Information Division, HM Treasury, since 1968; *b* 17 March 1926; *s* of Rt Hon. James Griffiths, *qv*; *m* 1st, 1951, Gwyneth Lethby (*d* 1966); three *s* one *d*; 2nd, 1966, Elaine Burge (*née* Walsh); one *s*. *Educ:* Llanelly Grammar Sch.; London Sch. of Economics. Editorial Staff: Glasgow Herald, 1949-55; Guardian, 1955-67; Deputy Head of Information Div., HM Treasury, 1967-68. *Address:* 32 Teddington Park, Teddington, Middlesex. *T:* 01-977 2464.

**GRIFFITHS, Capt. Hubert Penry,** OBE 1953; Assistant Commissioner, City of London Police, 1940-60; *b* 24 April 1894; *yr s* of late Henry Griffiths; *m* 1926, Beryl Rees, *o c* of late I. Newton Rees; one *s* (and one *s* one *d* decd). *Educ:* St Paul's Sch. Gazetted to 5th Special Res. Bn, Middlesex Regt, Oct. 1914; seconded to Nigeria Regt, Royal W African Frontier Force, 1915-20; served German W and E African Campaigns, 1915-18; Second in Command, 2nd Bn, 1918; served Egba Rising, 1918; Asst Comr, Nigeria Police, 1920, Commissioner, 1927; Actg Asst Inspector Gen., Northern Provinces, 1935-36; Police Div., Home Office, 1937; Actg Comr, City of London Police, 1952-53 and again for one year in 1954. Liveryman of Gold and Silver Wyre Drawers Company. OStJ 1952. Commander, Order of North Star (Sweden); Commander Star of Ethiopia. *Address:* 33 Seacliffe Avenue, Takapuna, Auckland 9, NZ. *Club:* City Livery.

**GRIFFITHS, Hugh;** *see* Griffiths, W. H.

**GRIFFITHS, Rt. Hon. James,** PC 1945; CH 1966; JP; *b* Ammanford, Sept. 1890; *m* 1918, Winnie Rutley, Overton, Hants; two *s* two *d*. *Educ:* Bettws Council Sch., Ammanford; Labour Coll., London. Hon. LLD University of Wales, 1946. Sec. Ammanford Trade Council, 1916-19; Agent Llanelly Labour Party, 1922-25; Miners' Agent Anthracite Mines Association, 1925-36; Pres., South Wales Miners' Federation, 1934-36; Mem. Executive Cttee of Miners' Federation of Great Britain, 1934-36. MP (Lab) Llanelly, 1936-70; Minister of National Insurance, 1945-50; Sec. of State for the Colonies, 1950-51. Mem. National Executive Labour Party, 1939-59 (Chm., 1948-49); Deputy Leader and Vice-Chm., Parliamentary Labour Party, 1956-59; Sec. of State for Wales, 1964-66. Mem. BBC Gen. Advisory Council, 1952. *Publication:* Pages from Memory, 1969. *Address:* 32 Combemartin Road, SW18.

*See also H. M. Griffiths.*

**GRIFFITHS, Dr James Howard Eagle,** OBE 1946; President, Magdalen College, Oxford, since 1968; *b* 6 Dec. 1908; *s* of Rev. James David Griffiths and Olive Arnold (*née* Chataway). *Educ:* Denstone Coll.; Magdalen Coll., Oxford (Demy). 1st cl. National Science (Physics), 1930; DPhil 1933; MA 1934. Sec., CVD (Admty), 1943-45. Magdalen Coll., Oxford: Fellow, 1934-68; Sen. Dean of Arts, 1947-50, 1956-60, 1965-66; Vice-Pres., 1951-52; University Demonstrator and Lectr in Physics, 1945-66; Reader in Physics, 1966-68; Vice-Chancellor, University of Malaya, Kuala Lumpur, 1967-68. C. V. Boys Prize, Physical Soc., London, 1951. Mem., Hebdomadal Council, Oxford, 1951-63, 1968-; Mem., Hale Cttee on Univ. Teaching Methods. Hon. DEd, Univ. of Mindanao, Philippines, 1968. *Publications:* papers in Proc. Royal Soc., Proc. Phys. Soc. London and other physics jls. *Recreations:* music, wine. *Address:* Magdalen College, Oxford. *T:* Oxford 41781. *Club:* Leander (Henley-on-Thames).

**GRIFFITHS, John Edward Seaton,** CMG 1959; MBE 1934; Administrative Training Officer, Government of Botswana, 1967-70; *b* 27 Sept. 1908; *s* of A. E. Griffiths, MA, Cape Town; *m* 1937, Helen Parker, *d* of C. C. Wiles, MA, Grahamstown, SA; two *s* one *d*. *Educ:* South African Coll. Sch.; Cape Town Univ.; Selwyn Coll., Cambridge. Apptd Cadet Administrative Officer, Colonial Service (later HM Oversea Civil Service), Tanganyika, 1931; District Officer, 1943; Provincial Comr, 1954; Senior Provincial Comr, 1958; retd 1959; Asst Comr, East African Office, 1960-63; Director of Studies, Royal Inst. Public Administration, 1963-67. Actg Sec., Trade and Economics, Tanganyika, 1954, and Adviser, Local Government, Tanganyika, 1954-55. *Publications:* articles in Tanganyika Notes and Records and in Journal of African Administration. *Recreations:* mountaineering, golf, photography. *Address:* Hathersage, Glebe Lane, Sevenoaks, Kent. *Clubs:* Royal Commonwealth Society; Mountain Club of South Africa (Cape Town).

**GRIFFITHS, Sir Percival Joseph,** KBE 1963; Kt 1947; CIE 1943; ICS (retired); President, India, Pakistan and Burma Association; Director of various companies; *b* 15 Jan. 1899; *s* of late J. T. Griffiths, Ashford, Middx; *m* Kathleen Mary, *d* of late T. R. Wilkes, Kettering; three *s*. *Educ:* Peterhouse, Cambridge (MA). BSc London; entered Indian Civil Service, 1922; retired, 1937. Leader, European Group, Indian Central Legislature, 1946; Central Organiser, National War Front, India, and Publicity Adviser to Government of India; Mem. Indian Legislative Assembly, 1937. *Publications:* The British in India, 1947; The British Impact on India, 1952; Modern India, 1957; The Changing Face of Communism, 1961; The Road to Freedom, 1964; History of the Indian Tea Industry, 1967; Empire to Commonwealth, 1969. *Address:* St Christopher, Abbotts Drive, Wentworth, Virginia Water, Surrey. *Clubs:* Oriental, City of London.

**GRIFFITHS, Peter Harry Steve;** Senior Lecturer in Economic History, The Polytechnic, Portsmouth (formerly Portsmouth College of Technology), since 1967; *b* 24 May 1928; *s* of W. L. Griffiths, West Bromwich; *m* 1962, Jeannette Christine (*née* Rubery); no *c*. *Educ:* City of Leeds Training Coll. BSc (Econ.) Hons London, 1956; MEd Birmingham, 1963. Headmaster, Hall Green Road Sch., West Bromwich, 1962-64. Fulbright Exchange Prof. of Economics, Pierce Coll., Los Angeles, Calif, 1968-69. Chm., Smethwick Education Cttee; Leader, Conservative Group of Councillors in Smethwick, 1960-64. MP (C) Smethwick, 1964-66. *Publication:* A Question of Colour?, 1966. *Recreations:* motoring, writing. *Address:* 1 Gloucester Mews, Southsea, Hants. *Club:* Conservative (Smethwick).

**GRIFFITHS, Sir Peter N.;** *see* Norton-Griffiths.

**GRIFFITHS, Richard Cerdin;** Director, Inter-University Council for Higher Education Overseas, since 1970; *b* 21 Oct. 1915; *s* of James Griffiths, MBE, and Gwendolen Griffiths, Swansea; *m* 1944, Pamela de Grave Hetherington; three *s* one *d*. *Educ:* Swansea Grammar Sch.; Jesus Coll., Oxford (Exhibnr, Hon. Schol.). 1st Cl. Hons Maths Mods, 2nd Cl. Finals; MA. Entered Admiralty as Asst

Principal, 1939; served Royal Navy (Ord. Seamen), 1940-41; British Admiralty Delegn, Washington, DC, 1941-43. Private Sec. to Sec. to Admiralty (Sir Henry Markham), 1943-44; transf. to Treasury, 1946; Private Sec. to Sec. of Treasury (Sir Edward Bridges), 1948-49; Asst Sec., 1949; Treasury Representative in Australia and New Zealand, 1952-53; Imperial Defence Coll., 1957; Sec., UK Delegn to Commonwealth Trade and Economic Conf., Montreal, 1958; Head of Arts and Science Div., 1958-63; Under-Sec., Treasury, 1963; Dep. Sec., UGC, 1963-70. Mem., University Grants Cttee, Hong Kong; Hon. Sec., Civil Service Sports Council; Vice Chm., Civil Service Lifeboat Fund; Hon. Treasurer, Highgate Literary and Scientific Instn. Mem. Council, Hon. Soc. of Cymmrodorion. *Recreations:* cricket, sailing. *Address:* 2 St Albans Villas, NW5. *T:* 01-485 1862. *Clubs:* Athenæum; MCC.

**GRIFFITHS, Roger Noel Price,** MA Cantab; Headmaster of Hurstpierpoint College since Sept. 1964; *b* 25 Dec. 1931; *er s* of William Thomas and Annie Evelyn Griffiths; *m* 1966, Diana, *y d* of Capt. J. F. B. Brown, RN; three *d. Educ:* Lancing Coll.; King's Coll., Cambridge. Asst Master at Charterhouse, 1956-64. MA Oxon, by incorporation, 1960. *Recreations:* music, theatre, bowls. *Address:* Hurstpierpoint College, Hassocks, Sussex. *T:* Hurstpierpoint 3178. *Club:* Athenæum.

**GRIFFITHS, Trevor,** BScEng, CEng, FIMechE, FIEE; Chief Inspector of Nuclear Installations since 1964; *b* 17 April 1913; *m* 1939, Evelyn Mary Colborn; one *d. Educ:* Bishop Gore Gram. Sch., Swansea; University Coll., London. Metropolitan Vickers Electrical Co. Ltd, 1934; Air Min., 1938; UKAEA, 1955; Min. of Power, 1960; Min. of Technology, 1969. *Address:* Flat 8, 24 Hyde Park Square, W2. *T:* 01-262 6829.

**GRIFFITHS, William;** MP (Lab) Moss Side Division of Manchester, 1945-50, Exchange Division of Manchester since 1950; *b* Moss Side, Manchester, 7 April 1912; *m* 1949, Decia, *o d* of Noel and Jean Robinson, Blackpool, Lancs; one *s* one *d. Educ:* Manchester Elementary Sch.; private tutor. Profession, consulting ophthalmic optician; Fellow of British Optical Assoc. Joined Labour Party, 1932. Adopted as prospective Parliamentary Candidate, 1937; Parly Private Sec. to Min. of Health, 1950-51, to Min. of Labour, Jan.-April 1951. Served War of 1939-45, in Army, 1940-46; was with 8th Army at Alamein; commissioned in Middle East, 1944. *Recreation:* walking. *Address:* 11 Park Avenue, Wythenshawe, Manchester. *T:* 061-998 3165; 24 Onslow Avenue, Richmond, Surrey. *T:* 01-940 4887.

**GRIFFITHS, (William) Hugh,** MC 1944; QC 1964; Recorder of Cambridge, since 1964; *b* 26 Sept. 1923; *s* of late Sir Hugh Griffiths, CBE, MS, FRCS; *m* 1949, Evelyn, *d* of Col K. A. Krefting; one *s* three *d. Educ:* Charterhouse; St John's Coll., Cambridge. Commissioned in Welsh Guards, 1942; demobilised after war service, 1946. Cambridge, 1946-48. BA 1948. Called to the Bar, Inner Temple, 1949; Recorder of Margate, 1962-64. Mem., Bar Council, 1968-69. *Recreations:* golf, fishing. *Address:* 31 Chelsea Park Gardens, SW3. *T:* 01-352 2738. *Clubs:* Garrick; MCC; Hawks (Cambridge); Woking Golf.

**GRIGG, John (Edward Poynder);** political journalist; *b* 15 April 1924; *s* of 1st Baron Altrincham and Joan, *d* of 1st Baron Islington; *S* to father's barony, 1955, but did not apply for Writ of Summons to the House of Lords; disclaimed title, 31 July 1963; *m* 1958, Patricia, *d* of H. E. Campbell, Belfast; two *s* (adopted). *Educ:* Eton (Capt. of the Oppidans); New Coll., Oxford (Exhibitioner). MA, Modern History; Gladstone Memorial Prize. Served Grenadier Guards, 1943-45. Editor, National and English Review, 1954-60 (formerly Associate Editor). Contested (C) Oldham West, 1951 and 1955. *Publication:* Two Anglican Essays. *Heir; (to disclaimed barony): b* Hon. Anthony Ulick David Dundas Grigg [*b* 12 Jan. 1934; *m* 1965, Eliane de Miramon; two *s* one *d*]. *Address:* 32 Dartmouth Row, SE10. *T:* 01-692 4973. *Club:* Beefsteak.

**GRIGG-SMITH, Rev. Canon Thomas,** MA; Canon Emeritus, 1955; Perpetual Curate of Yelverton, 1954-58. *Educ:* Gonville and Caius Coll., Cambridge (Choral Exhib.); Egerton Hall, Manchester, BA 1912; MA 1916; deacon, 1913; priest, 1914; Curate, Burnley Parish Church, 1913-15; Christ Church, Harwood, 1916; Dir of Religious Educ., Diocese of Manchester, 1916-29; Lecturer in Voice Production and Elocution (1913-29) and Education (1921-29) at Egerton Hall; Vicar of Warley, Yorks, 1929-37; Rector of Chipstead, Surrey, 1939-45; Churches' Cttee Representative, S-E Command, 1942-45; Dir of Education, Diocese of Portsmouth, 1945-52; Canon Residentiary, 1945-55, and Canon-Chancellor, 1949-55, Portsmouth Cathedral. OCF. *Publications:* The Use of the Voice, 1917; The Child's Knowledge of God, 1929; Macmillan Syllabuses of Religious Instruction, 1921-22; For Youth and the Years, 1935; Intinction and the Administration of the Chalice, 1950; Church Teaching for Confirmation and After, 1954; Editor: Prayers for Day and Sunday School, 1921; Training in Faith, Worship and Service, 1922-24; Hosanna, 1930; revised Handbook of Christian Teaching, 1938; Prayers for School, Church and Home, 1951. *Recreations:* tennis, walking, fishing, riding, music. *Address:* 2 Place House Close, Catisfield, near Fareham, Hants. *T:* Titchfield 3003.

**GRIGOROV, Mitko;** Order of G. Dimitrov, 1964; Ambassador of the People's Republic of Bulgaria since 1969; *b* 9 Sept. 1920; *m* 1956, Stanka Stanoeva; one *d. Educ:* Sofia University. Mem. of Parliament from 1953, Minister without Portfolio, 1962-66. Mem., Editorial Board of magazine Problems of Peace and Socialism, 1966-69. *Recreation:* mountaineering. *Address:* 24 Queen's Gate Gardens, SW7. *T:* 01-584 9400.

**GRIGSON, Geoffrey;** poet; *b* 2 March 1905; 7th *s* of late Canon W. S. Grigson, Pelynt, Cornwall and of Mary Beatrice Boldero. Editor of New Verse, 1933-39; *Publications:* Several Observations, 1939; Under the Cliff and other poems, 1943; Henry Moore, 1943; The Isles of Scilly and other poems, 1946; Samuel Palmer, 1947; The Harp of Aeolus, 1947; Places of the Mind, 1949; The Crest on the Silver, 1950; William Barnes (Muses Library), 1950; John Clare (Muses Library), 1950; Essays from the Air, 1951; A Master of Our Time (Wyndham Lewis), 1951; Gardenage, 1952; Legenda Suecana (poems), 1953; Freedom of the Parish, 1954; The Englishman's Flora, 1955; Gerard Manley Hopkins, 1955; English Drawings, 1955; The Painted Caves, 1957; Art Treasures of the British Museum, 1958; The Three Kings, 1958; A Herbal of All Sorts, 1959; The Cherry Tree, 1959; English Excursions, 1960; Christopher Smart, 1961; The Shell Country Book, 1962; Collected Poems, 1963; Poems of Walter Savage Landor, 1964; (with Jane Grigson) Shapes and Stories, 1964; The Shell Country Alphabet, 1966; A Skull in Salop and Other Poems, 1967; Poems and Poets,

1968; A Choice of William Morris's Verse, 1968; Ingestion of Ice-Cream and Other Poems, 1969; Notes from a Queer Country, 1970; Faber Book of Popular Verse, 1971. *Address:* Broad Town Farm, Broad Town, Swindon. *T:* Broad Hinton 259.

**GRILLER, Sidney Aaron,** CBE 1951; Leader of Griller String Quartet since 1928; *b* London, 10 Jan. 1911; *s* of Salter Griller and Hannah (*née* Green); *m* 1932, Elizabeth Honor, *y d* of James Linton, JP, Co. Down, N Ireland; one *s* one *d*. *Educ:* Royal Academy of Music. Toured British Isles, Holland, Germany, Switzerland, France, Italy, 1928-38; first concert tour in USA, 1939. Served RAF, 1940-45. Lecturer in Music, University of California, 1949; world tours, 1951, 1953. Prof. of Music: Royal Irish Acad. of Music, 1963; Royal Academy of Music, 1964. Worshipful Company of Musicians Medal for Chamber Music, 1944; FRAM, 1945; Mem. Royal Society of St George, 1955. *Address:* 63 Marloes Road, W8. *T:* 01-937 7067.

**GRILLET, Alain R.;** *see* Robbe-Grillet.

**GRIME, Sir Harold (Riley),** Kt 1959; DL; JP; Chairman and Editor-in-Chief of the West Lancashire Evening Gazette and associated newspapers; Editor of the Blackpool Gazette, 1926-62; *b* 12 May 1896; *s* of late Frederick Alexander Grime, JP, and late Fannie Grime (*née* Riley); *m* 1925, Mary (Mollie) Bowman (*d* 1970), *d* of late W. Powell Bowman, Leeds; two *d*. *Educ:* Arnold Sch., Blackpool; Bonn, Germany. East Lancs Regt, 1915-17; Indian Army, 1917-20. Yorkshire Evening Post and London Evening News, 1920-23. Dir, Press Association, 1942-51 (Chm. 1946-47); Dir, Reuters, 1945-47; Chm., Guild of Editors (NW Region), 1957-58. Hon. Sec., Blackpool Victoria Hosp., 1938-48; Hon. Treas., Blackpool Conservative and Unionist Assoc., 1938-45; Dir, Blackpool Tower and Winter Gardens Cos., 1944-68 (Vice-Chm. 1953-68); Pres., Preston and District Chamber of Commerce, 1962-67. Mem., Gen. Advisory Council, BBC, 1960-64. Hon. Freeman of Blackpool, 1950. DL Lancs, 1968. JP for Blackpool, 1943-. *Publications:* The Silver Trumpet, 1942; Sand in My Shoes, 1950. *Address:* Corin Doone, Poulton-le-Fylde, Lancs.

**GRIMES, Ven. (Cecil) John;** Archdeacon of Northampton and Canon Residentiary of Peterborough, 1941-59; Treasurer, 1946-59; Examining Chaplain to Bishop of Peterborough, 1939-59; Archdeacon and Canon Emeritus, 1959; *b* Stratford-on-Avon, 1881; *y s* of Joseph Grimes, Stratford-on-Avon; *m* 1st, 1905, Sophie (*d* 1923), *y d* of late Charles Alfred Perkin, London; 2nd, 1925, Caroline Blanche, 3rd *d* of late Sir G. B. Bowen, KBE, DL; three *s*. *Educ:* Stratford-on-Avon; London Univ.; Cuddesdon Coll., Oxford. Trained as Civil Engineer; MIEE; DD 1945; FSA 1959; Resident Engineer at HM Dockyard, Devonport, 1903-7, Asst Engineer, Calcutta Port Comrs, 1907-10; Deacon, 1912; Priest, 1913; St Giles', Reading, 1912-15; Chap., Indian Ecclesiastical Establishment (Bengal), 1915-24; served with Mesopotamia Expeditionary Force in RE as Dep.-Asst and Asst Dir of Military Works, 1917-19; Vicar of St Matthew's, Westminster, 1924-25; Archdeacon of Calcutta and Examining Chaplain to the Bishop of Calcutta, 1926-33; Commissary to Bishop of Calcutta, 1934-51; Vicar of St John the Baptist, Peterborough, 1933-38; Proctor in Convocation for Diocese of Peterborough, 1937-41; Canon of Peterborough, (non. res.), 1937-41; Rector of Thorpe Malsor, Kettering, 1938-41; Rural Dean of Peterborough First Deanery, 1934-38; Surrogate, 1934; Rural Dean of Rothwell Second Deanery 1938-41; Mem. Canon Law Commission, 1939-47; Fellow of Woodard Corporation, 1943-52, 1969-; Select Preacher Cambridge, 1946; Oxford, 1947. Mem. Bd and Admin. Cttee of Church Comrs, 1948-63; Pro-Prolocutor Canterbury Convocation, 1950-59. *Publication:* Towards an Indian Church, 1946; (ed) Spencer Leeson, 1958. *Address:* The Vineyard, Minster Precincts, Peterborough PE1 1XU. *T:* Peterborough 62406. *Club:* United Service.

**GRIMES, Prof. William Francis,** CBE 1955; DLitt, FSA; FMA; Director of the Institute of Archæology, and Professor of Archæology, University of London, since Oct. 1956; *b* 31 Oct. 1905; *e s* of Thomas George Grimes, Pembroke; *m* 1st, 1928, Barbara Lilian Morgan (marr. diss., 1959); one *s* one *d*; 2nd, 1959, Audrey Williams (*née* Davies). *Educ:* University of Wales (MA); DLitt Wales, 1961. Asst Keeper of Archæology, National Museum of Wales, Cardiff, 1926-38; Asst Archæology Officer, Ordnance Survey, 1938-45; seconded to Min. of Works to record historic monuments on defence sites, 1939-45; Dir London Museum, 1945-56. Mem. Royal Commn on Ancient Monuments in Wales and Mon, 1948- (Chm., 1967-), and of Ancient Monuments Boards, England, 1954-, Wales, 1959-; Mem. Commn on Historical Monuments (England), 1964-. Sec. to Coun. for British Archæology, 1949-54, Pres. 1954-59, Vice-Pres., 1961-65, Treas, 1964-; Pres. London and Middlesex Archæological Soc., 1950-59; Pres. Royal Archæological Institute, 1957-60 (Vice-Pres. 1951-57); Vice-President: Soc. of Antiquaries, 1953-57; Soc. for Medieval Archæology; Prehistoric Soc., 1958-61; Hon. Dir of Excavations for the Roman and Mediæval London Excavation Council, 1946-; Chm., London Topographical Soc., 1961-. Pres., Cambrian Archæological Assoc., 1963-64 (G. T. Clark Prize, 1946); Chm., Faculty of Archæology, History and Letters, British Sch. at Rome, 1963-66; Chm., Field Studies Council, 1966-; Pres., Stanmore Archæological Soc., 1962-. *Publications:* Holt, Denbighshire, Legionary Works Depôt (Y Cymmrodor), 1930; Pre-history of Wales, 1951; (Ed.) Aspects of Archæology in Britain and Beyond, 1951; (with M. D. Knowles) Charterhouse, 1954; (with others) Brooke House, Hackney (London Survey, Vol. XXVIII), 1960; Excavations in Defence Sites, 1939-1945, I, 1960; The Excavation of Roman and Mediæval London, 1968; many papers in learned jls. *Address:* Institute of Archæology, 31-4 Gordon Square, WC1.

**GRIMOND, Rt. Hon. Joseph;** TD 1957; PC 1961; LLD Edinburgh; MP (L) Orkney and Shetland since 1950; Leader of the Parliamentary Liberal Party, 1956-67; Director, The Manchester Guardian and Evening News Ltd, since 1967; Rector of Aberdeen University since 1969; Chancellor of University of Kent at Canterbury, since 1970; *b* 29 July 1913; *s* of Joseph Bowman Grimond and Helen Lydia Richardson; *m* 1938, Hon. Laura Miranda, *d* of late Sir Maurice Bonham Carter, KCB, KCVO, and Baroness Asquith of Yarnbury, DBE; two *s* one *d* (and one *s* decd). *Educ:* Eton; Balliol Coll., Oxford (Brackenbury Scholar). 1st Class Hons (Politics, Philosophy, and Economics). Called to the Bar, Middle Temple (Harmsworth Scholar), 1937. Served War of 1939-45, Fife and Forfar Yeomanry and Staff 53 Div. (Major). Contested Orkney and Shetland (Liberal), 1945. Dir of Personnel, European Office, UNRRA, 1945-47; Sec. of the National Trust for Scotland, 1947-49. Rector of Edinburgh Univ., 1960-63. Senior

Trustee, Young Volunteer Force Foundation, 1968-, Jt Vice-Chm., 1970-. Hon. LLD Edinburgh. *Publications:* The Liberal Future, 1959; The Liberal Challenge, 1963. *Recreation:* golf. *Address:* Old Manse of Firth, Kirkwall, Orkney.

**GRIMSBY, Bishop Suffragan of,** since 1966; **Rt. Rev. Gerald Fitzmaurice Colin,** MA; *b* 13 July 1913; *s* of Frederick Constant Colin and Jemima Fitzmaurice; *m* 1941, Iris Susan Stuart Weir; three *s* two *d. Educ:* Mountjoy Sch.; Trinity Coll., Dublin. MA (TCD) 1946. Deacon, 1936; Priest, 1937. St George's, Dublin, 1938; Chancellor's Vicar, St Patrick's Cathedral, Dublin, 1938; RAFVR, 1939-47; Vicar of Frodingham, Dio. of Lincoln, 1947-66; Canon of Lincoln Cathedral, 1960; Rural Dean of Manlake, 1960; Proctor in Convocation, 1960-65, 1966-70. *Recreations:* family life, fishing. *Address:* 21 Westgate, Louth, Lincs.

**GRIMSDITCH, Herbert Borthwick;** Executive editor, The Book of Knowledge, 1951-63; a biographical correspondent of Dictionary of National Biography since 1934, and of The Times since 1938; *b* 28 Feb. 1898; *o s* of Frederick J. D. Grimsditch, Liverpool; *m* 1928, Marie Sophie Gibson; one *s. Educ:* private sch., Liverpool; University of Liverpool, BA 1st class hons English and University Schol., 1923; MA (by Thesis) 1925. Asst., University Library, Liverpool, 1914-20 (broken by 15 months in RAF Naval kite balloon section); undergraduate, 1920-23; Asst Editor, The Studio, 1923-29; Prof. of English, University of Neuchâtel, Switzerland, 1930-33; freelance writer, chiefly for Cambridge Bibliogr. of Eng. Lit., 1934-36; Asst Editor, The Artist, 1936-38; freelance, chiefly for The Times, 1938-41; Cipher Officer, War Office, 1942; BBC monitoring editorial, 1942-45; on Illustrated, 1945-47; Chambers's Encyclopædia (in charge of make-up), 1947-50; freelance, 1950-51. *Publications:* Character and Environment in the Novels of Thomas Hardy, 1925; William Hogarth, 1926; Wm Beckford's Vathek (a new trans.), 1929, 1953, 1958; Pitfalls in Everyday French, 1933; Kunitz and Haycraft, British Authors of the Nineteenth Century (part-author), 1937; This is England, 1941; Kunitz and Haycraft, Twentieth Century Authors (part-author), 1942; The Paintings of H. H. Newton, 1952; sundry translations. Contributions to Works of Reference: The Artist's Year-Book, 1937-38; Cambridge Bibliography of English Literature, 1940; Dictionary of National Biography, 3 decennial supplements, 1937, 1949, 1959 (and a 4th in press); Chambers's Encyclopædia, 1950, and rev. edn; Cassell's Encyclopædia of Literature, 1953; The Book of Knowledge, 1954, 1959 (London); The World of Music, 1954; New Universal Encyclopedia, 1959; Children's Encyclopedia, 1961, 1963; The Book of Knowledge, 1963 (New York); Junior Year Book, 1964. Contributions to: The Times; Current Biography (New York); London Mercury; Bookman; Studio; Architects' Journal; Artist; Art Review; Observer; Spectator; Illustrated; John Bull; Everybody's; Liverpool Daily Post, etc. *Recreations:* intelligent conversation, listening to classical music. *Address:* 84 West Heath Road, Hampstead, NW3. *T:* 01-455 9422.

**GRIMSHAW, Maj.-Gen. Ewing Henry Wrigley,** CB 1965; CBE 1957 (OBE 1954); DSO 1945; *b* 30 June 1911; *s* of Col E. W. Grimshaw; *m* 1943, Hilda Florence Agnes Allison; two *s* one *d. Educ:* Brighton Coll. Joined Indian Army, 1931. Served War of 1939-45, Western Desert and Burma (despatches twice). Transferred to Royal Inniskilling Fusiliers, 1947; Active Service in Malaya, Kenya and Suez, 1956 and Cyprus, 1958. GOC 44th Div. (TA) and Home Counties Dist, 1962-65. Col, The Royal Inniskilling Fusiliers, 1966-68; Dep. Col, The Royal Irish Rangers, 1968-. *Address:* The Trellis House, Copford Green, near Colchester, Essex.

**GRIMSTON,** family name of **Baron Grimston of Westbury** and of **Earl of Verulam.**

**GRIMSTON OF WESTBURY,** 1st Baron, *cr* 1964; **Robert Villiers Grimston,** Bt *cr* 1952; BSc, ACGI; *b* 8 June 1897; *e s* of late Hon. Robert Grimston, Canon of St Albans; *m* 1923, Sybil, *e d* of late Sir Sigismund Neumann, Bt; three *s* two *d. Educ:* Repton; City and Guilds Engineering Coll., London Univ. Commissioned RGA (6" Howitzers), 1916; served in Salonika and Palestine, 1916-19. MP (C) Westbury Div. Wilts, 1931-64; Junior Lord of the Treasury, 1937; Asst Whip (Unpaid), 1937; Vice-Chamberlain of HM's Household, 1938-39, Treasurer, 1939-42; Asst Postmaster-Gen., 1942-45; Parliamentary Sec., Ministry of Supply, 1945; Dep. Chm. of Ways and Means, 1962-64. Mem., UK Delegn to Gen. Assembly of UN, 1960. Pres. Urban District Councils Association, 1949-70. Comdr Parly. Home Guard, 1941-42. *Heir: s* Hon. Robert Walter Sigismund Grimston [*b* 14 June 1925; *m* 1949, Hon. June Mary Ponsonby, *d* of 5th Baron de Mauley; two *s* one *d*]. *Address:* 25 Westminster Gardens, SW1. *T:* 01-834 4315. *Clubs:* Carlton, MCC.

**GRIMSTON, Viscount; John Duncan Grimston;** *b* 21 April 1951; *s* and *heir* of 6th Earl of Verulam, *qv.*

**GRIMTHORPE,** 4th Baron, *cr* 1886; **Christopher John Beckett,** Bt 1813; OBE 1958; DL; Deputy Commander, Malta and Libya, 1964-67; *b* 16 Sept. 1915; *e s* of 3rd Baron Grimthorpe, TD, and Mary Lady Grimthorpe (*d* 1962); *S* father, 1963; *m* 1954, Elizabeth Lumley, 2nd *d* of 11th Earl of Scarbrough, KG, PC, GCSI, GCIE, GCVO; two *s* one *d. Educ:* Eton. 2nd Lieut, 9 Lancers, 1936; Lt-Col, 9 Lancers, 1955-58; AAG, War Office, 1958-61; Brigadier, Royal Armoured Corps, HQ, Western Command, 1961-64. ADC 1964-68. DL East Riding of Yorkshire, 1969. *Recreations:* travel, horse sports. *Heir: s* Hon. Edward John Beckett, *b* 20 Nov. 1954. *Address:* 87 Dorset House, Gloucester Place, NW1. *T:* 01-486 4374; Westow Hall, York. *T:* Whitwell-on-the-Hill 225. *Clubs:* Cavalry; York (York).

**GRIMWOOD, Frank Southgate,** DPhil; Warden and Director of Studies, Moor Park College, Farnham, Surrey, since 1961; *b* 14 July 1904; *s* of late Frank Grimwood, Ipswich and Newbury, and Rose Grimwood (*née* Lake), Bucklebury, Berks; *m* 1935, Mary Habberley Price, MA Oxon; one *s* one *d. Educ:* Isleworth County High Sch.; Reading Univ. (Wantage Hall); Queen's Coll., Oxford. DPhil Oxon; BA Hons University of Reading. Sub-Warden and Foreign Student Sec., SCM, 1929-30; Lecturer in Philosophy and Psychology, City Literary Institute, 1930-40; Welfare Officer (Oxon., Bucks, and Berks), Min. of Labour and Nat. Service, 1940-48. Advanced Student, The Queen's Coll., Oxford, 1948-56, including one year (1951) at Cuddesdon Theological Coll. (thesis on psycho-analysis, group-therapy and unbelief). Lecturer and Tutor, Oxford Univ. Extra-Mural Delegacy, 1956-61. Mem. of Brit. Psychological Soc. *Recreations:* painting, drawing, walking in the country, reading poetry and biography, conversation. *Address:* Moor Park College, Farnham, Surrey. *T:* Farnham 6401.

**GRINDLE, Capt. John Annesley,** CBE 1943; RN; JP; *b* 17 Sept. 1900; *s* of late George Annesley Grindle and late Eveleen Grindle; *m* 1925, Joyce Lilian Alton, *d* of J. W. A. Batchelor, Blackheath; two *s*. *Educ:* Pembroke Lodge, Southbourne; RN Colleges, Osborne and Dartmouth; Pembroke Coll., Cambridge; Midshipman, 1917; Comdr 1934; Captain 1941. Retired list, 1950. JP (Hants) 1952. *Recreation:* gardening. *Address:* Lark Hill, Portchester, Hants. *T:* Cosham 76067.

**GRINDON, John Evelyn,** CVO 1957; DSO 1945; AFC 1948; Group Captain, RAF retired; General Manager, Thomas Skinner & Co. (Publishers) Ltd, since 1966; *b* 30 Sept. 1917; *s* of Thomas Edward Grindon (killed in action, 1917), and Dora Eastlake. *Educ:* Dulwich Coll. Cadet at RAF Coll., Cranwell, 1935-37. Served in Bomber Command during War of 1939-45. Commanded The Queen's Flight, 1953-56; retired at own request 1959. *Address:* c/o Lloyds Bank Ltd, Cox's and King's Branch, 6 Pall Mall, SW1. *Club:* Royal Air Force.

**GRINDROD, Rt. Rev. John Basil Rowland;** *see* Riverina, NSW, Bishop of.

**GRINKE, Frederick,** FRAM; Solo Violinist; Professor of Violin, Royal Academy of Music, London; *b* Winnipeg, Canada, 8 Aug. 1911; *s* of Arthur Grinke, Winnipeg; *m* 1942, Dorothy Ethel Sirr Sheldon; one *s*. *Educ:* Winnipeg; Royal Academy of Music, London (all prizes for solo and chamber music playing. Studied with Adolf Busch in Switzerland, with Carl Flesch in London and Belgium. Was leader and soloist with the Boyd Neel Orchestra for 10 years. Appeared regularly as Soloist with leading orchestras; has played in many countries in Europe also in America, Australia and New Zealand. Has appeared at Festivals: Edinburgh, Bath, Cheltenham, Three Choirs, Salzburg. Has taken part in many Promenade Concerts. A sonata was dedicated to him by Vaughan Williams; his sonata partner is Joseph Weingarten. Has made numerous recordings, including many works with the composers as pianists (such as Rubbra, Ireland, Berkeley, Benjamin). Has acted as mem. of the Jury for several international violin competitions. *Recreations:* music, good food, wine, reading, the theatre. *Address:* 34 Castlebar Road, Ealing, W5. *T:* 01-997 3607; Frog's Hall, Braiseworth, near Eye, Suffolk. *T:* Eye 483.

**GRINT, Edmund Thomas Charles,** CBE 1960; *b* 14 Feb. 1904; *e s* of Edmund Albert Grint; *m* 1930, Olive Maria, *d* of Albert Cheyne Sherras; one *s* two *d*. *Educ:* London Univ. (Dip. Econs). Joined ICI 1929; Commercial Dir, Nobel Div., 1946; Director: Billingham Div., 1952-61; Alkali Div., 1961-63; Mond Div., 1964. Dep. Chief Labour Officer, 1951; Chief Labour Officer, 1952-63; Gen. Manager Personnel, 1963-65. Chm., Nat. Dock Labour Board, 1966-69. Has served on Tribunals and Cts of Inquiry in industrial relations problems. *Recreations:* golf, gardening. *Address:* Old Walls, Seal, Sevenoaks, Kent. *T:* Sevenoaks 61364.

**GRIPENBERG, Georg Achates,** MA, LLB; Finnish Diplomat; *b* 18 May 1890; *s* of Claes Alexis Constantin Gripenberg, Conseiller d'Etat Actuel and Finnish Minister to Stockholm, and Agnes Maria, *d* of Victor von Haartman, Conseiller Intime and Marshal of House of Nobles; *m* 1927, Margaret, *d* of Edward Moseley-Williams; one *d*. *Educ:* Helsingfors and Upsala Univs; London Sch. of Economics and Political Science. Entered Finnish Foreign Service, 1918; Chargé d'Affaires, Brussels, 1921, The Hague, 1922, Madrid, 1923; Minister, 1925; Minister in Rio de Janeiro, Buenos Aires, Santiago de Chile, 1929-32; to Court of St James, 1933-41; to the Holy See, 1942-43; Minister in Stockholm, 1943-54. Ambassador, 1954-56; Permanent Finnish Delegate to the United Nations, 1956-59. D *hc*, University of Helsinki, Finland. *Publications:* Life of Major-General Hans Henrik Gripenberg, 1937; Reminiscences of a Chief of Mission, 1959; London–the Vatican–Stockholm, 1960. *Recreations:* reading, tennis, riding, ski-ing. *Address:* 11 Ostra Brunnsparken, Helsingfors, Finland.

**GRISEWOOD, Frederick Henry,** OBE 1959; free-lance broadcaster and lecturer, since retirement, 1948; Outside Broadcasts Department, and headquarters staff, BBC, 1929-48; Announcer, BBC, 1929-37; *b* 11 April 1888; *e s* of A. G. Grisewood, Rector of Daylesford, Worcs; *m* 1st, 1915, Gladys Elizabeth (marriage dissolved), *e d* of W. T. Roffey, Writtle, Chelmsford, Essex; one *d*; 2nd, 1941, Aileen Croft, *er d* of E. C. Scriven, Leeds, Yorks. *Educ:* Radley; Magdalen Coll., Oxford. Studied singing; opera and concert work in London, Paris, and Munich under Victor Beigel, R. von zur Mühlen and George Henschel; sang bass solo part in first performance in England of Henschel's Requiem at Queen's Hall with Carrie Tubb, Muriel Foster, Gervase Elwes, 1913; served European War, 1914-18, 1/4th Oxon. and Bucks Light Infantry, France, 1915, Adjutant, 1915; invalided out of Army, 1918; Agent for Daylesford Estate, 1918-29. *Publications:* Our Bill, 1934; The World Goes By (Autobiography), 1952; My Story of the BBC, 1959; many articles in magazines and periodicals. *Recreations:* played cricket and tennis for Worcs, hockey for Oxon and Southern Trials; collecting antiques and old glass; fishing and gardening. *Address:* Hewshotts, Liphook, Hants. *T:* Liphook 3229.

**GRISEWOOD, Harman Joseph Gerard,** CBE 1960; Chief Assistant to the Director-General, BBC, 1955-64, retired; *b* 8 Feb. 1906; *e s* of late Lieut-Col Harman Grisewood and Lucille Cardozo; *m* 1940, Clotilde Margaret Bailey; one *d*. *Educ:* Ampleforth Coll., York; Worcester Coll., Oxford. BBC Repertory Co., 1929-33; Announcer, 1933-36; Asst to Programme Organiser, 1936-39; Asst Dir Programme Planning, 1939-41; Asst Controller, European Div., 1941-45; Actg Controller, European Div., 1945-46; Dir of Talks, 1946-47; Planner, Third Programme, 1947-48; Controller of the Third Programme, BBC, 1948-52; Dir of the Spoken Word, BBC, 1952-55. Vice-Pres., European Broadcasting Union, 1953-54. Chm., The Latin Mass Soc., 1969. King Christian X Freedom Medal, 1946. Mem. Hon. Soc. of Cymmrodorion, 1956. Knight of Magistral Grace, Sovereign and Military Order of Malta, 1960. *Publications:* Broadcasting and Society, 1949; The Recess, 1963 (novel); The Last Cab on the Rank, 1964 (novel); David Jones: Welsh National Lecture, 1966; One Thing at a Time (autobiography), 1968; The Painted Kipper, 1970. *Address:* Field House, Widford, near Ware, Herts. *T:* Much Hadham 2611. *Clubs:* Oriental, Beefsteak.

**GRIST, Prof. Norman Roy,** FRCPEd; Professor of Infectious Diseases, University of Glasgow, since 1965; *b* 9 March 1918; *s* of Walter Reginald Grist and Florence Goodwin Grist (*née* Nadin); *m* 1943, Mary Stewart McAlister. *Educ:* Shawlands Acad., Glasgow; University of Glasgow, Postgrad. studies at Dept of Bacteriology, University of Liverpool, 1948-49; Virus Reference Lab., Colindale, London, 1951-52; Dept of Epidemiology, University of Michigan, 1956-57. BSc 1939; MB, ChB (Commendation), 1942; Mem. 1950, Fellow

1958, RCP, Edinburgh. Founder Mem., 1963, FCPath., 1967. Ho. Phys. Gartloch Hosp., 1942-43; RAMC, GPO 223 Fd Amb. and RMO 2/KSLI, 1943-46; Ho. Surg. Victoria Inf., Glasgow, 1946-47; Res. Phys. Ruchill Hosp., Glasgow, 1947-48; Research Asst, Glasgow Univ. Dept of Infectious Diseases, 1948-52; Lectr in Virus Disease, Glasgow Univ., 1952-62, and Regional Adviser in Virology to Scottish Western Reg. Hosp. Bd from 1960; Reader in Viral Epidemiology, Glasgow Univ., 1962-65. Consultant for WHO. Interregional Virology Course, Singapore, 1962. *Publications:* Diagnostic Methods in Clinical Virology, 1965; numerous contribs. to British, US, French and international med. jls. *Recreations:* lazing, travelling, bird-watching. *Address:* 6 Sydenham Road, Glasgow W2. *T:* 041-339 5242. *Clubs:* Royal Automobile; Royal Scottish Automobile (Glasgow).

**GROHMAN, Vice-Adm. H. T. B.;** *see* Baillie-Grohman.

**GROMYKO, Andrei A.;** Order of Lenin (triple award); Minister of Foreign Affairs of the USSR, since 1957; *b* 6 July 1909; *m* Lydia D. Grinevich; one *s* one *d. Educ:* Agricultural Institute and Institute of Economics, Moscow. Scientific worker (senior), Acad. of Sciences USSR, 1936-39, also lecturing in Moscow Universities. Chief of American Division National Council of Foreign Affairs, 1939; Counsellor, USSR Washington Embassy, 1939-43; Ambassador to USA and Minister to Cuba, 1943-46; Soviet Representative on UN Security Council, 1946-48; Deputy Foreign Minister, 1946-49, 1953-54; 1st Deputy Minister of Foreign Affairs, 1949-52; Soviet Ambassador in London, 1952-53; First Deputy Foreign Minister in Moscow, 1954-57. Chm. of Delegates, Conference on Post-War Security, Dumbarton Oaks, USA. 1944. Hero of Socialist Labour, 1969. *Address:* Moscow.

**GRONCHI, Giovanni;** Member of Senate of the Italian Republic; President of Italy, 1955-62; *b* Pontedera, 10 Sept. 1887; *s* of Sperandio Gronchi and Maria (*née* Giacomelli); *m*; two *c*. *Educ:* Pisa Univ. Served European War of 1914-18 as a Volunteer. A founder of Italian Popular Party (Popolare), 1919; Head of Confederation of Christian Workers, 1919. Elected MP, 1919, and became Under-Sec. for Commerce and Industry, 1922; retired (parliamentary mandate), 1923-42; Minister for Industry, Commerce and Labour, 1944-45; Minister of Commerce, 1945. Elected to Constituent Assembly of Republic of Italy, 1946; Pres. Christian Democrat Parliamentary Group, 1946-48; Speaker, Chamber of Deputies, 1948-55. *Address:* Senato della Repubblica, Rome, Italy.

**GROOM, Sir (Thomas) Reginald,** Kt 1961; Chartered Accountant; Senior Partner, Groom, Sanderson & Co., Brisbane, Qld; Commissioner, Australian National Airlines Commission, since 1961; Director: Brolite Industries Ltd (Chairman); Consolidated Rutile Ltd (Chairman); Mount Isa Mines Ltd; P & O Australian Holdings Ltd; Fire Fighting Enterprises Ltd; Besser (Qld) Ltd; Elder Smith Goldsbrough Mort Ltd (Chairman Qld Board); Member, Commonwealth Banking Corporation Board, since 1964, and of several private companies; *b* 30 Dec. 1906; *s* of Roy Graeme Groom and May Augusta Groom; *m* 1932, Jessie Mary Grace Butcher; two *s* one *d*. *Educ:* Brisbane Grammar Sch.; University of Qld (BA, BCom). Admitted to Institute of Chartered Accountants in Australia, 1932; in public practice, 1932-. Alderman, Brisbane City Council, 1943-; Lord Mayor of Brisbane, 1955-61. Dir, Australian Elizabethan Theatre Trust. *Recreations:* farming, fishing, golf. *Address:* 61 The Esplanade, St Lucia, Brisbane, Qld 4067, Australia. *T:* 2-4982. *Clubs:* Queensland, Johnsonian (Brisbane); Athenæum (Melbourne); Union (Sydney); Royal Queensland Golf.

**GROOM, Air Marshal Sir Victor E.,** KCVO, *cr* 1953; KBE, *cr* 1952 (CBE 1945; OBE 1940); CB 1944; DFC 1918, and Bar, 1921; RAF retired; *b* 4 Aug. 1898; *e s* of late William E. Groom; *m* 1st, 1924, Maisie Monica Maule (*d* 1961); two *s*; 2nd, 1969, Mrs Muriel Constance Brown. *Educ:* Alleyns, Dulwich. Served European War, 1916-18 (DFC); Egypt, Iraq, 1919-22 (bar to DFC); RAF Staff Coll. (psa 1928); India, 1929-34; Bomber Command, 1936-41 (OBE); Directorate of Plans, Air Min., 1941-42; Head of RAF Staff planning the invasion under Chief of Staff to the Supreme Allied Commander, 1942-43; SASO 2nd Tactical Air Force, 1943-45; AOA Flying Trg Command, 1945-46; Dir-Gen. of Manning, Air Ministry, 1947-49; AOC 205 Group RAF, MEAF, 1949-51; C-in-C, MEAF, 1952; AOC-in-C, Technical Training Command, 1952-55, retired 1955. Officer Legion of Honour (France). *Address:* 8 Somerville House, Manor Fields, SW15. *T:* 01-788 1290. *Club:* Royal Air Force.

**GROPPER, William;** artist; *b* 3 Dec. 1897; *s* of Harry Gropper and Jenny Nidel; *m* 1924, Sophie Frankle; two *s. Educ:* Ferrer Sch. of Art; National Academy of Design; New York Sch. of Fine and Applied Art. Began as artist New York Tribune, 1919; later illustrator of many books; Murals: US Post Office, Freeport, LI; New Interior Bldg, Washington, DC; Northwestern PO, Detroit, Mich.; Schenley Corp., NY; five stain-glass windows for Temple Har-Zion, at River Forest, Ill, 1966. *Represented in:* Metropolitan Museum of Art, Museum of Modern Art, Whitney Museum of Am. Art (all New York); St Louis Museum, Mo.; Museum of Western Art, Moscow, USSR, Hartford Museum, Conn.; Art Institute of Chicago, Ill.; Gimbel Pa Art Coll.; Phillips Memorial Museum, Washington; Newark Museum, NJ; Pa Acad. of Art Museum, Philadelphia, Pa; Walker Museum of Minneapolis, Minn.; Fogg Art Museum, Cambridge, Mass; Los Angeles County Museum, Calif.; Encyclopædia Britannica Collection; National Gallery, Prague; City Museum, Sofia; Brooklyn Museum, New York; Museum of City of New York; Syracuse Univ.; Boston Museum of Fine Art; Brandeis Univ.; IBM Collection; Hirshhorn Collection. Collier prize for Illustration, 1920; Harmon prize, 1930; John Simon Guggenheim Fellowship, 1937; First prizes in lithography, John Herron Art Inst., Ind.; Artist for Victory, Metropolitan Museum of Art; Patron's purchase prize, Los Angeles County Museum, Calif., purchase award, first biennial exhibition drawings, USA (St Paul, Minnesota). Ford Foundation Award, 1965; Tamarind Fellowship Award, 1966-67. Mem., Nat. Inst. of Arts and Letters, 1968. *Publications:* The Golden Land (Political Cartoons), 1927; 56 Drawings of USSR (Paris), 1928; Alay-Oop (Story in Pictures), 1930; Gropper (Collection of Art), 1938; Lidice (Portfolio drawings), 1943; Your Brother's Blood Cries Out (War sketches), 1945; Never to Forget (Warsaw Ghetto), 1947; Portfolio Caucasian Studies, 1950; Portfolio American Folklore Lithographs, 1953; Hound Dog Moses and the Promised Land (with Walter D. Edmonds), 1954; The Little Tailor, 1955; Capricios (Portfolio of lithographs), 1957; Twelve Etchings (Portfolio), 1965; illustrated thirty books.

*Address:* Croton-on-Hudson, New York 10520, USA. *T:* Croton 3619. *Club:* Artists Equity.

**GROSS, Anthony Imre Alexander;** Painter, etcher; *b* 19 March 1905; *s* of Alexander Gross and Isabelle Crowley; *m* 1930, Marcelle Florenty; one *s* one *d*. *Educ:* Repton; Slade; Académie Julien. Exhibits London, Paris, New York, etc. Has also made films and illustrated books. Lives several months each year in France. Teaches etching, Slade Sch. *Address:* 115 King George Street, Greenwich, SE10.

**GROSS, Solomon Joseph,** CMG 1966; Minister, British Embassy, Pretoria, since 1969; *b* 3 Sept. 1920; *s* of late Abraham Gross; *m* 1948, Doris Evelyn (*née* Barker); two *d*. *Educ:* Hackney Downs Sch.; University Coll., London. RAF, 1941-46, Burma, India. Ministry of Supply, 1947; Attached OEEC, Paris, 1948-51; Raw Materials Dept, British Embassy, Washington, 1951-53; Board of Trade, 1954-57; British Trade Commr, Pretoria, SA, 1958-62; Principal British Trade Commr, Ghana, 1963-66; British Deputy High Commr, Ghana, 1966-67; Board of Trade, 1967-69. *Recreations:* squash, tennis, do-it-yourself. *Address:* British Embassy, 6 Hill Street, Pretoria, South Africa. *Club:* Royal Automobile.

**GROSVENOR,** family name of **Baron Ebury,** and of **Duke of Westminster.**

**GROSVENOR, Earl; Gerald Cavendish Grosvenor;** *b* 22 Dec. 1951; *s* and *heir* of 5th Duke of Westminster, *qv*. *Educ:* Harrow.

**GROSVENOR, Mrs Beatrice Elizabeth Katherine,** CBE 1952; United Kingdom Representative on the Executive Committee of the Programme of the United Nations High Commissioner for Refugees, 1959-60; *b* 6 Nov. 1915; *d* of late Lord Edward Grosvenor and late Lady Dorothy Charteris; *m* 1944 (marr. annulled, 1945), Major Richard Girouard. *Educ:* Holy Child Convent, Cavendish Square, W1. Served War of 1939-45 (despatches), with St John Ambulance Brigade; Asst Superintendent-in-Chief SJAB, 1946-52; Deputy Superintendent-in-Chief, 1952-59; County Pres. for Co. Cork, Eire, SJAB, 1960. DStJ 1958. *Address:* Kenmare House, Killarney, Co. Kerry. *T:* Killarney 41.

**GROTRIAN, Sir John (Appelbe) Brent,** 2nd Bt, *cr* 1934; *b* 16 Feb. 1904; 2nd and *o surv. s* of Sir Herbert Brent Grotrian, 1st Bt, KC, JP, and Mary Lilian, *d* of late Robert Adams, Barrister-at-law of Hamilton, Ont., Canada; *S* father 1951. *Educ:* Eton Coll.; Trinity Coll., Oxford. Served in War of 1939-45 (despatches). *Heir: nephew* Philip Christian Brent Grotrian [*b* 26 March 1935; *s* of Robert Philip Brent Grotrian (*d* on active servce, 1945; *y s* of 1st Bt) and Elizabeth Mary Hardy-Wrigley; *m* 1960, Anne Isabel, *d* of Robert Sieger Whyte, Toronto, Canada; one *s*]. *Address:* Raughmere House, Lavant, Chichester, Sussex.

**GROUES, Henri Antoine;** *see* Pierre, Abbé.

**GROUNDS, George Ambrose,** CBE 1958; DSO 1917 (Bar 1918); TD 1933; DL; Retired; *b* 19 Nov. 1886; *s* of Frederick and Elizabeth Grounds; *m* 1950, Kathleen Burton Sale (*d* 1968). *Educ:* St Ives (Hunts) Gram. Sch.; Lowestoft Coll. Banking, 1903-45. Served European War, 1914-18, Royal Tank Corps, France (wounded); served War of 1939-45, RA; Lieut-Col 1936. DL Lincs, 1951; Chm. Holland (Lincs) CC, 1963-67; Alderman HCC, 1961-. *Address:* 16 Witham Bank West, Boston, Lincs. *T:* Boston 2772.

**GROUNDS, Sir Roy (Burman),** Kt 1969; FRAIA; Governing Director, Roy Grounds & Co. Pty Ltd, Architects, since 1963; *b* Melbourne, 18 Dec. 1905; *s* of Herbert Algernon Haslett and Maude Hawksworth (*née* Hughes); *m* 1940, Alice Bettine James; one *s* one *d* (and one *d* decd). *Educ:* Melbourne Grammar Sch.; Univ. of Melbourne. BArch Melbourne, 1947. Partner, Mewton & Grounds, 1932-38; Two Centenary Gold Medal awards for completed bldgs, 1935; practice in Europe and Melbourne, 1938-41. Commissioned RAAF, SW Pacific, 1941-45; Sen. Lectr in Architecture, Univ. of Melbourne, 1945-52; Sen. partner, Grounds, Romberg & Boyd, Architects, Melbourne, 1953-62. RVIA Arch. Award, 1954; RAIA Arch. Award (for Aust. Acad. of Science Bldg, Canberra), 1957; Pan-Pacific Architectural Citation of AIA, 1960; Sulman Award for Arch., 1961; RAIA Gold Medal, 1968. *Address:* 24 Hill Street, Toorak, Victoria 3142, Australia. *T:* 24-3110. *Club:* Commonwealth (Canberra).

**GROUNDS, Stanley Paterson,** CBE 1968; Charity Commissioner, 1960-69; *b* 25 Oct. 1904; 2nd *s* of late Thomas Grounds and Olivia Henrietta (*née* Anear), Melbourne, Australia; *m* 1932, Freda Mary Gale Ransford; twin *s* and *d*. *Educ:* Melbourne High Sch.; Queen's Coll., Melbourne Univ. (1st Cl. hons, MA). With Melbourne Herald, 1926-28; British Empire Producers' Organisation, London, 1928-33. Called to Bar, Middle Temple, 1933; at Chancery Bar, 1934-40. Served Royal Air Force, 1940-45 (Squadron Leader). Asst Charity Commissioner, 1946-58; Sec., Charity Commission, 1958-60. *Publications:* contrib. Encyclopædia of Forms and Precedents, Encyclopædia of Court Forms (on Charities), Halsbury's Laws of England, 3rd ed. (on Charities). Articles in law jls. *Recreation:* other men's flowers. *Address:* 23 Boundary Road, St John's Wood, NW8. *T:* 01-624 9776. *Clubs:* Australia, United Service.

**GROVE, George Alexander,** QC 1969; Professor of Equity since 1952, Dean of Faculty of Law, 1968-70, University of Birmingham; *b* 14 Oct. 1908; *s* of Alexander Oliver George Mantle Grove; *m* 1934, Marion Jessie Greaves; one *s*. *Educ:* King Edward's Sch., Birmingham; University of Birmingham. Solicitor, 1930-46. RAF (Squadron Leader), 1940-46 (despatches). Barrister-at-Law, 1946-; Reader in Equity, University of Birmingham, 1946-52. *Address:* 1 Stone Buildings, Lincoln's Inn, WC2; *T:* 01-242 3118; The Mill House, Naunton, Glos. *T:* Guiting Power 215. *Club:* Garrick.

**GROVE, Sir Walter Felipe (Philip),** 4th Bt *cr* 1874, of Ferne, Wilts; *b* 18 March 1927; *s* of late Walter Peel Grove (3rd *s* of Sir Walter John Grove, 2nd Bt) and Elena Rebecca, *d* of late Felipe Crosthwaite, Santa Rosa, Lower Californa, Mexico; *S* uncle, Sir Gerald Grove, 3rd Bt, 1962. Resides abroad. *Heir: b* Charles Gerald Grove, *b* 10 Dec. 1929. [*But his name does not, at the time of going to press, appear on the Official Roll of Baronets.*

**GROVER, Anthony Charles;** Chairman: Lloyd's Register of Shipping, since July 1963; Lifeguard Assurance Ltd, since 1964; *b* 13 Oct. 1907; *s* of F. J. Grover, Harrow, Middx; *m* 1931, Marguerite Beatrice Davies; one *s* one *d*. *Educ:* Westminster Sch. War of 1939-45 (despatches): joined Coldstream Guards, 1940; served in Italy, 1942-44; rose to rank of Major. Underwriting Mem. of Lloyd's, 1936-

(Dep. Chm., 1958; Chm., 1959-60). Dep. Chm. and Treas, Lloyd's Register of Shipping, 1956-58, 1961-63. Mem. Export Council for Europe; Chm., N European Section, London Chamber of Commerce. Comdr, Order of Leopold II, 1967; Comdr, Order of Oranje Nassau, 1968. *Recreation:* golf. *Address:* Marella, Hook Heath, Woking, Surrey. *T:* Woking 3928. *Clubs:* White's, Pratt's, Guards; Woking Golf; Royal St George's Golf (Sandwich); Honourable Company of Edinburgh Golfers; Rye Golf; Royal Worlington; Newmarket.

**GROVER, Maj.-Gen. John Malcolm Lawrence,** CB 1945; MC; *b* 6 Feb. 1897; *s* of late General Sir M. H. S. Grover, KCB, KCIE; *m* 1930, Betty Chune, *d* of late Maj.-Gen. L. Humphry, CB, CMG, Army Medical Service; one *s*. *Educ:* Winchester; RMC, Sandhurst. Commissioned King's Shropshire LI, 1914; served European War, 1914-18, France and Belgium (wounded thrice, MC and Bar); Operations NW Frontier, India, 1930-31; War of 1939-45. France and Belgium, 1939-40 (despatches); India and Assam, (Kohima–Imphal operations), 1942-44. Commanded 1st KSLI, 1938-39; 11th Inf. Brigade, 1940; 29th Independent Brigade Gp, 1941; 2nd Division, 1941-44; Dir of Army Welfare Services, War Office, 1944-48; retired, 1948. General Sec., Officers' Association, 1948-61. Col. KSLI, 1947-55. Commissioner, Royal Hospital, Chelsea, 1957-66. *Address:* Bowmans, Crowborough, Sussex. *Club:* Army and Navy.

**GROVES, Charles Barnard,** CBE 1968 (OBE 1958); FRCM, Hon. RAM; conductor; Musical Director and Resident Conductor, Royal Liverpool Philharmonic Orchestra, since 1963; Associate Conductor, Royal Philharmonic Orchestra, since 1969; *b* 10 March 1915; *s* of Frederick Groves and Annie (*née* Whitehead); *m* 1948, Hilary Hermione Barchard; one *s* two *d*. *Educ:* St Paul's Cathedral Choir Sch.; Sutton Valence Sch.; Royal College of Music. Free lance accompanist and organist. Joined BBC, Chorus-Master Music Productions Unit, 1938; Asst Conductor BBC Theatre Orchestra, 1942; Conductor BBC Revue Orchestra, 1943; Conductor BBC Northern Orchestra, 1944-51; Dir of Music, Bournemouth Corporation, and Conductor, Bournemouth Municipal Orchestra, 1951-54; Conductor of Bournemouth Symphony Orchestra, 1954-61; Resident Musical Dir, Welsh National Opera Company, 1961-63. FRCM 1961; Hon. RAM 1967. Conductor of the Year Award, 1968. Has toured Australia, South Africa, America and Europe. Hon. DMus Liverpool, 1970. *Recreations:* gardening and English literature. *Address:* 23 Fulwood Park, Liverpool L17 5AD. *T:* 051-727 1121.

**GROVES, John Dudley,** OBE 1964; Chief of Public Relations, Ministry of Defence, since 1968; *b* 12 Aug. 1922; *y s* of late Walter Groves; *m* 1943; Pamela Joy Holliday; one *s* two *d*. *Educ:* St Paul's Sch. Reporter, Richmond Herald, 1940-41; Queen's Royal Regt, 1941-42; commnd in 43rd Reconnaissance Regt, 1942; served in NW Europe, 1944-45 (despatches); Observer Officer, Berlin, 1945; Press Association (Press Gallery), 1947-51; Times (Press Gallery and Lobby), 1951-58; Head of Press Sect., Treasury, 1958-62; Dep. Public Relations Adviser to Prime Minister, 1962-64 (Actg Adviser, 1964); Chief Information Officer, DEA, 1964-68. *Publication:* (with R. Gill) Club Route, 1945. *Recreation:* walking. *Address:* Mortimers, Manningford Bohune, Pewsey, Wilts.

**GROVES, Ronald,** MA, BSc Oxon; FRIC; Master, Dulwich College, 1954-66; Adviser, Joint Working Party of the Governing Bodies' Association and the Headmasters' Conference, since 1966; *b* 19 Aug. 1908; *s* of late John Ackroyd Groves and Annie Groves, Bradford, *m* 1939, Hilary Annot, *yr d* of late George Smith; two *s*. *Educ:* Bradford Grammar Sch.; Christ Church, Oxford. 1st Class Hons Nat. Sci. (Chemistry), 1931; Asst Master, Bradfield Coll., 1931-32; Worksop Coll., 1932-35; Senior Science Master and Housemaster, King's Sch., Canterbury, 1935-43; Bursar, 1937-43; Headmaster, Campbell Coll., Belfast, 1943-54. Governor of King's Coll. Hospital and Mem. King's Coll. Hospital Medical Sch. Council. Chm., Food Standards Cttee, 1959-62. *Address:* Great Wallis Oast, Mayfield, Sussex. *Clubs:* Athenæum, MCC.

**GRUBB, Sir Kenneth (George),** KCMG 1970 (CMG 1942); Kt 1953; Chairman, House of Laity, Church Assembly, since 1959; *b* 9 Sept. 1900; *s* of Rev. H. P. Grubb and M. A. Crichton-Stuart; *m* 1st, 1926, Eileen Sylvia Knight (*d* 1932); 2nd, 1935, Nancy Mary Arundel; three *s* one *d*. *Educ:* Marlborough Coll. Exec. Trustee, Survey Application Trust; President: CMS, 1944-69; Cheltenham Training Colls, 1948-; Grubb Inst. of Behavioural Studies; Chairman: Commission of Churches on Internat. Affairs, 1946-68; Missionary and Ecumenical Council, Church Assembly, 1964-67; Royal Foundation of St Katharine, 1957-; Vice-President: Inst. of Race Relations; British Council of Churches, 1965-68. Vice-Pres. or Trustee of many other institutions including Inst. of Strategic Studies; a Church Commissioner; Hon. Fellow, St Peter's Coll., Oxford. Missionary, 1923-28; Survey Application Trust, 1928-39, 1953-; Controller, in Ministry of Information, 1941-46; Sec.-Gen., Hispanic Council, 1946-53; Publicity Consultant, Rank Organisation, 1955-59. Director: Argentine Club Ltd; Ashmount Properties Ltd; Hooker Craigmyle & Co. Ltd, and subsidiaries. United Kingdom Delegate: Unesco, 1954; Atlantic Congress, 1959. Hon. LLD Muhlenberg, Pa, 1951. *Publications:* numerous works on Latin America; World Christian Handbook, 1949, 1953, 1957, 1962, 1968. *Recreations:* gardening, yachting. *Address:* The Moot Farm, Downton, Salisbury, Wilts. *T:* Downton 433. *Clubs:* Canning; Nikaean.

**GRUBB, Violet Margaret,** DSc London; FRGS; retired; *b* Oxton, Notts, 1898; *o d* of Rev. H. Percy Grubb and M. A. Crichton-Stuart. *Educ:* Bournemouth High Sch.; Westfield Coll., University of London. BSc Hons London, 1920; DSc London, 1925; Asst Lecturer in Botany, Westfield Coll., 1923-25; Science teacher in I Fang Sch., Changsha, Central China and Lecturer in Hunan Provincial Univ., 1925-30; Lecturer in Dept of Botany, Westfield Coll., University of London, 1931-37; Headmistress, Westonbirt Sch., Tetbury, Glos, 1937-55; Principal, The Training Coll., Salisbury, 1955-62. Pres., Assoc. Head Mistresses of Boarding Schs, 1943-45. Chm., Assoc. of Independent and Direct Grant Schs, 1950-53; Member: Central Advisory Council for Education (England), 1956-59; Science Museum Advisory Council, 1957-64. *Publications:* Articles on Ecology and Reproduction of Marine Algæ and on distribution of Far Eastern Algæ, in scientific journals in England and abroad. *Address:* Moot Farm, Downton, Salisbury, Wilts. *T:* Downton 461. *Clubs:* Cowdray, Royal Over-Seas League.

**GRUENTHER, Gen. Alfred (Maximilian);** (Hon.) CB (UK) 1943; DSM (US) (with 2 Oak Leaf Clusters) 1943, 1945, 1956; US Army, retired; Director: Pan American World

Airways; New York Life Insurance Co.; Dart Industries; Federated Department Stores; Member: The Business Council; Board of Trustees, Institute for Defense Analyses; President's Commission on an All-Volunteer Armed Force, since 1969; Editorial Board, Foreign Affairs Magazine, since 1969; *b* Nebraska, 3 March 1899; *s* of Christian M. Gruenther and Mary Shea; *m* 1922, Grace Elizabeth Crum; two *s*. *Educ:* Military Academy, West Point (BS). Commissioned, Field Artillery, 1918; routine peacetime assignments, including 8 years as instructor and asst professor chemistry and electricity at West Point; Deputy Chief of Staff, Allied Force Headquarters (London, North African Campaign, Algiers), 1942-43; Chief of Staff, Fifth Army (Italy), 1943-44; Chief of Staff, 15th Army Group (Italian Campaign), 1944-45; Dep. Comdr, US Forces in Austria, 1945; Dep. Comdt, Nat. War Coll. Washington, 1945-47; Dir Jt Staff, Jt Chiefs of Staff, 1947-49; Dep. Chief of Staff for Plans and Operations, Army Gen. Staff, 1949-51; Gen., US Army, 1951; Chief of Staff, SHAPE, 1951-53; Supreme Allied Commander, Europe, 1953-56; retd 1956. Member: Presidential Arms Control Gen. Adv. Cttee, 1966-69; Presidential Adv. Cttee on Foreign Assistance, 1965-69. Pres., American Red Cross, 1957-64. Chm., English-Speaking Union of US, 1966-68. Hon. Pres., World Bridge Federation. Several decorations, including Grand Cross of Légion d'Honneur, 1954, and Médaille Militaire, 1956. Hon. degrees from 37 universities including Harvard, Yale, Columbia, Dartmouth and Holy Cross. *Publications:* Famous Hands of the Culbertson-Lenz Match, 1932; Duplicate Contract Complete, 1933. *Address:* Cathedral Apartments, 4101 Cathedral Avenue, NW, Washington, DC 20016, USA.

**GRUMMITT, J. H.;** Principal, Royal Academical Institution, Belfast, 1940-59; *b* 29 Jan. 1901; *s* of Charles C. Grummitt and Annie E. Halliday; *m* 1931, Mary Christine Bennett; two *s* two *d*. *Educ:* Cheltenham; Caius Coll., Cambridge. Schs Sec., Student Christian Movement, 1923-28; Senior Classical Master, Ipswich Sch., 1929-30; Head of Classical Dept, Epsom Coll., 1930-33; Headmaster, Victoria Coll., Jersey, 1933-40. *Publication:* The Sacrament of Life, 1931. *Recreations:* music, bridge. *Address:* Clovelly, Holywood, Co. Down. *T:* H.2434.

**GRUNDY, Air Marshal Sir Edouard (Michael FitzFrederick),** KBE 1963 (OBE 1942); CB 1960; Chairman, Short Brothers and Harland, since 1968; *b* 29 Sept. 1908; *s* of late Frederick Grundy and Osca Marah Ewart; *m* 1945, Lucia le Sueur (*née* Corder); three *s* (and one *d* decd). *Educ:* St Paul's Sch.; RAF Coll., Cranwell. 56 (F) Sqdn 1928; 403 Flight FAA, 1929-31; Signals Specialist Course, 1932; RAF North Weald, 1933-36; RNZAF HQ, 1937-40; OC No. 80 (S) Wing, 1941-42; CSO, NW African AF, 1942-43; CSO Mediterranean Allied Tactical Air Forces, 1943-44; CSO, RAF, Middle East, 1944-45; Commandant, Empire Radio Sch., 1945-46; Dep. Dir Air Staff Policy, Air Ministry, 1947-49; Air Adviser, Royal Norwegian AF, 1949-51; Dep. CSO, Supreme HQ Allied Powers Europe, 1951-52; idc 1953; Senior Air Staff Officer, Brit. Jt Services Mission in USA, 1954-55; Chm. NATO Military Agency for Standardisation, 1955-58: Air Officer i/c Administration, FEAF, 1958-61; Commandant-Gen. RAF Regt, 1961-62; Controller, Guided Weapons and Electronics, Ministry of Aviation, 1962-66; retired, 1966. Chevalier, Royal Norwegian Order of St Olaf, 1953. *Recreations:* usual. *Address:* c/o Lloyds Bank Ltd, 6 Pall Mall, SW1. *Clubs:* United Service, Royal Air Force.

**GRUNDY, Fred,** MD; MRCP; DPH; Barrister-at-law; Assistant Director-General, World Health Organization, Geneva, 1961-66; retired; *b* 15 May 1905; *s* of Thomas Grundy, Manchester; *m* 1932, Ada Furnell Leppington, Hessle, Yorks; one *s* one *d*. *Educ:* Leeds and London Univs. MB, ChB (Hons), Leeds; MRCS, LRCP, 1927; DPH, RCPS, 1931; MD Leeds, 1933; MRCP, 1951. Called to the Bar, Inner Temple, 1934. Resident hospital appts and gen. practice, 1927-31; Asst County Medical Officer, E Suffolk, 1931-34; Asst MOH to Borough of Willesden, 1934-35; Deputy MOH to Borough of Luton, 1935-37; MOH to Borough of Luton, 1937-49; Mansel Talbot Prof. of Preventive Medicine, Welsh Nat. Sch. of Medicine, 1949-61. *Publications:* A Note on the Vital Statistics of Luton, 1944; (with R. M. Titmuss) Report on Luton, 1945; Handbook of Social Medicine, 1945; The New Public Health, 1949; Preventive Medicine and Public Health: An Introduction for Students and Practitioners, 1951; papers on public health and scientific subjects. *Recreations:* mountaineering, yachting, golf, etc. *Address:* Galmington, Radyr, near Cardiff. *Club:* Yacht (Penarth).

**GRUNDY, John Brownsdon Clowes,** TD 1953; Officier d'Académie, 1937; MA, PhD; *b* 21 April 1902; *m* 1939, Carol Dorothea, *d* of Enid Pennington; two *s* three *d*. *Educ:* Emanuel Sch.; Fitzwilliam Hall, Cambridge (Exhibitioner); University Coll., London (research). Asst Master, St Paul's Sch., 1923-27; English Lektor, University of Göttingen, 1928; "The Connoisseur", 1928-29; Sen. Mod. Langs Master, Shrewsbury Sch., 1929-39. Served War of 1939-45, The Rangers (KRRC); principally in Gen. Staff (Intell.); Normandy-Holland, 1944; rank at release, temp. Col. First Rep. of Brit. Council in Finland, 1945-49; Dir, Brit. Institute, Cairo, 1949-50; head of mod. langs, Harrow Sch., 1950-53; Headmaster of Emanuel Sch., 1953-63; Head of Dept of Modern Languages, University Coll. of Sierra Leone, 1964-66. *Publications:* Tieck and Runge, 1929; Brush Up Your German, series, 1931-61; French Style, 1937; Life's Five Windows, 1968; various edns and translations of foreign texts. *Recreations:* antiquities, hills, foreign parts. *Address:* 44 Abbey Foregate, Shrewsbury.

**GRUNDY, R(upert) F(rancis) Brooks;** General Manager, Corby Development Corporation, 1950-68, and Industrial Projects Consultant to the Corporation since 1968; *b* 6 Sept. 1903; *s* of J. F. E. Grundy, fine art publisher, London and Emily Grundy (*née* Brownsdon); *m* 1938, Heather Mary, *d* of William and Mabel Thomas, Swansea; one *s* one *d*. *Educ:* Emanuel Sch., London; University Coll., London. BSc (Eng.) London; FICE, FIMunE; Registered Architect. Municipal Engrg, 1922-44, at Croydon, Bournemouth, Swansea, Carlisle and Harrow; Borough Engr and Surveyor: Mansfield, 1944-45; Wallasey, 1945-49; Wandsworth, 1949-50. Mem., BBC Midlands Region Adv. Coun., 1966-68. *Publications:* Builders' Materials, 1930; Essentials of Reinforced Concrete, 1939, 1948; papers presented to ICE and IMunE. *Recreations:* golf, walking, reading. *Address:* The Mill House, Brigstock, Kettering, Northants. *T:* Brigstock 218. *Club:* Royal Automobile.

**GRÜNEBERG, Prof. Hans,** FRS 1956; PhD Berlin, MD Bonn, DSc London; Professor of Genetics, University College, London, since 1956; Hon. Director of the Medical Research Council Experimental Genetics Research

Unit, since 1955; *b* 26 May 1907; *o s* of late Dr Levi Grüneberg and late Mrs Else Grüneberg (*née* Steinberg), Wuppertal-Elberfeld, Germany; *m* 1st, 1933, Elsbeth (*d* 1944), *d* of late Hugo Capell; two *s*; 2nd, 1946, Hannah (*d* 1962), *d* of late Albrecht Blumenfeld. *Educ:* Städt. Gymnasium, Wuppertal-Elberfeld, Germany. Hon. Research Asst, University Coll., London, 1933-38; Moseley Research Student of Royal Society, 1938-42. Captain, RAMC, 1942-46. Reader in Genetics, University Coll., London, 1946-55. *Publications:* The Genetics of the Mouse, 1943, 1952; Animal Genetics and Medicine, 1947; The Pathology of Development, 1963. Numerous papers in scientific jls. *Recreation:* foreign travel. *Address:* University College, Wolfson House, 4 Stephenson Way, NW1. *T:* 01-387 7050.

**GRUNFELD, Henry;** Chairman: Mercury Securities Ltd, since 1964; S. G. Warburg & Co. Ltd; *b* 1 June 1904; *s* of Max Grunfeld and Rosa Grunfeld (*née* Haendler); *m* 1931, Berta Lotte Oliven; one *s* one *d*. *Educ:* Berlin. Studied law in Berlin and Breslau; Doctor of Law, 1926. Partner in family firm, 1927; Manager: New Trading Co. Ltd, 1938; S. G. Warburg & Co. Ltd, 1946; Director, S. G. Warburg & Co. Ltd, 1951-. *Address:* 34 Ennismore Gardens, SW7. *T:* 01-584 4047; Moxley, Holmbury St Mary, Surrey. *T:* Dorking 730461.

**GRUNSELL, Prof. Charles Stuart Grant,** PhD; Professor of Veterinary Medicine in the University of Bristol since 1957; *b* 6 Jan. 1915; *s* of Stuart and Edith Grunsell; *m* 1939, Marjorie Prunella Wright; one *s* two *d*. *Educ:* Shanghai Public Sch.; Bristol Grammar Sch. Qualified as MRCVS at The Royal (Dick) Veterinary Coll., Edinburgh, 1937. In general practice at Glastonbury, Som., 1939-48. PhD Edinburgh, 1952. Senior Lecturer in Veterinary Hygiene and Preventive Medicine, University of Edinburgh, 1952. Editor, Veterinary Annual. A Diocesan Reader. Defence Medal 1946. *Publications:* papers on the Erythron of Ruminants, on Vital Statistics in Veterinary Medicine, and on Preventive Medicine. *Recreations:* squash, tennis. *Address:* Towerhead House, Banwell, near Weston-super-Mare, Somerset. *T:* Banwell 2461.

**GRUTSCHNIG, Karl;** painter and sculptor; late Professor at Academy of Fine Arts, Vienna; Member of Board of Examiners for Teachers at Grammar Schools; *b* Gurk, Carinthia, 19 Nov. 1888; *s* of Johann and Marie Grutschnig; *m* 1921, Rosa Tauchen. *Educ:* Elem. Sch., Raab, Upper Austria; Gram. Sch.; Training Colls for Wood and Metal-work, Ebensee and Hallstatt, Upper Austria; Academy for Design, Vienna. Apprenticeship in wood and stone sculpture, modelling and theatre scenery painting, 1907-11; Academy of Fine Arts, studio of Prof. Rumpler, 1911-15. Mil. Service as Lieut of Reserve, 1915-18. Has been an active teacher of art and arts and crafts, 1919-. *Publications:* Der Handarbeitsunterricht an der Bundeserziehungasnstalt; Der Handarbeitsunterricht für Knaben an Mittelund Hauptschulen als Mitarbeiter; in verschiedenen österreichischen Tageszeitungen; in England in Teachers' World, Sept., 1935; Schöpferische Handarbeit 1937. *Address:* Kaiserstrasse 51, Wien VII, Austria.

**GRYLLS, Rear-Adm. Henry John Bedford,** CB 1956; *b* 24 Aug. 1903; *s* of late C. B. Grylls, CB, CBE, and late Mrs Grylls; *m* 1938, Ruth Ellison, *d* of S. E. Minnis, *qv*; one *s* one *d*. *Educ:* RN Colleges Osborne and Dartmouth. Midshipman, HMS Durban, 1921; Sub-Lieut 1924; Engineering Courses and Advanced Engineering Course, 1924-28; Lieut (E), HMS London, 1928-31; HM Dockyard, Chatham, 1931-34; Lieut-Comdr (E), HMS Rodney, 1934-37; Comdr (E) 1937; Engineer-in-Chief's Dept, Admiralty, 1938-41; Engineer Officer, HMS Duke of York, 1941-44; HM Dockyard, Devonport, 1944-45; Dockyard Dept, Admiralty, 1945-47; Capt. (E) 1946; Chief Engineer, HM Dockyard, Singapore, 1948-51; Asst Engineer-in-Chief, 1951-54; Rear-Adm. (E) 1954; Engineer Manager, HM Dockyard, Devonport, 1954-58, retired. *Address:* Penshurst, 6 Mornington Park, Wellington, Som. *T:* Wellington 2931.

**GRYLLS, Rosalie G.;** *see* Mander, Lady (Rosalie).

**GRYLLS, William Michael John;** MP (C) Chertsey Division of Surrey since 1970; *b* 21 Feb. 1934; *s* of Brig. W. E. H. Grylls, OBE; *m* 1965, Sarah Smiles Justice Ford; one *d*. *Educ:* RN College, Dartmouth; Univ. of Paris. Lieut, Royal Marines, 1952-55. Mem., St Pancras Borough Council, 1959-62; contested (C) Fulham, Gen. Elecs, 1964 and 1966; Mem. GLC, 1967-70; Dep. Leader, Inner London Educn Authority, 1969-70; Chm., Further and Higher Educn, 1968-70; Mem., Nat. Youth Employment Council, 1968-70; Governor, Polytechnic of Central London. *Recreations:* sailing, riding, gardening. *Address:* Walcot House, 139 Kennington Road, SE11. *Club:* Carlton.

**GUAZZELLI, Rt. Rev. Victor;** Auxiliary Bishop of Westminster (RC), and Titular Bishop of Lindisfarne since 1970; *b* 19 March 1920; *s* of Cesare Guazzelli and Maria (*née* Frepoli). *Educ:* Parochial Schools, Tower Hamlets; English Coll., Lisbon. Priest, 1945. Asst, St Patrick's, Soho Square, 1945-48; Bursar and Prof. at English Coll., Lisbon, 1948-58; Westminster Cathedral: Chaplain, 1958-64; Hon. Canon, 1964; Sub-Administrator, 1964-67; Parish Priest of St Thomas', Fulham, 1967-70; Vicar General of Westminster, 1970. *Address:* Archbishop's House, Westminster, SW1. *T:* 01-834 4717.

**GUBBINS, Sir Colin McVean, (Maj.-Gen., retired),** KCMG 1946 (CMG 1944); DSO 1940; MC; *b* 2 July 1896; *s* of late J. H. Gubbins, CMG, Diplomatic Service, and late Helen Brodie, *d* of late C. A. McVean, JP; *m* 1919, Norah Creina Somerville (marriage dissolved, 1944), *d* of late Surgeon-Comdr Philip Somerville Warren, RN; one *s* (*er s* killed in action, Italy, 1944); *m* 1950, Anna Elise, *widow* of Lieut R. T. Tradin, Royal Norwegian Air Force, Oslo. *Educ:* Cheltenham Coll.; Royal Military Academy. 2nd Lieut RFA 1914; served European War, 1914-19, France, Belgium, North Russia (wounded, MC, 1914 Star with clasp, Order of St Stanislas 3rd Class); Acting Capt., 1915; Acting Major, 1917; Brigade Major, RA, 1921-22, Ireland; GSO3, AHQ, India, 1925-28; Staff Coll., 1928-29; GSO3, War Office, 1931-32; Brigade Major, RA, 1933-34; Brevet Major, 1934; GSO2, War Office, 1935-39; Brevet Lieut-Col, 1939; Acting Col, 1940; Acting Brigadier, 1940; Lieut-Col 1941; Col 1942; temp. Maj.-Gen. 1943; served War of 1939-45 (DSO, CMG, KCMG, Polish Croix de Vaillance). in Poland. (Chief of Staff to Brit. Mil. Mission), France, Norway (raised and commanded Independent Companies, later Commandos), N Africa, Italy, Far East. Raised and commanded Auxiliary Units, June 1940, for special duties under GHQ, Home Forces; Special Operations Exec. (SOE), Nov. 1940-Jan. 1946). Retd pay, 1946. Officier Légion d'Honneur; Grand Officier Order of Leopold;

Belgian Croix de Guerre; Order of Dannebrog, 1st cl.; Royal Order of St Olaf; Grand Officer Order of Orange Nassau and Polonia Restituta; Commander Legion of Merit, USA. Comdr Order of White Lion. *Publication:* (jt author) The Fourth Dimension of Warfare, 1968. *Recreations:* shooting, fishing. *Address:* Obbe, Isle of Harris; White House Farm, Lacey Green, Bucks. *Clubs:* Army and Navy, Special Forces.

**GUBBINS, Major William John Mounsey,** TD 1946; DL; *b* 23 Aug. 1907; *s* of late Col R. R. Gubbins, DSO, JP, The Old Hall, Rockcliffe, Carlisle; *m* 1932, Marjorie Mary, *d* of late T. O. Carter, The Place, Armathwaite, Cumberland; two *s*. *Educ:* Sherborne Sch. High Sheriff of Cumberland, 1959-60; DL of Cumberland, 1961-. *Recreations:* shooting, fishing, gardening. *Address:* Eden Lacy, Lazonby, Cumberland. *T:* Lazonby 337. *Club:* County (Carlisle).

**GUÐMUNDSSON, Guðmundur I.,** Comdr with Star, Order of the Falcon, 1957; Ambassador of Iceland to the Court of St James's and to the Netherlands, Portugal and Spain, since 1965; *b* 17 July 1909; *m* 1942, Rósa Ingólfsdóttir; four *s*. *Educ:* Reykjavík Grammar Sch.; Univ. of Iceland. Grad. in Law 1934. Practised as Solicitor and Barrister from 1934; Barrister to Supreme Court, 1939; Sheriff and Magistrate, 1945-56. Mem. Central Cttee, Social Democratic Party, 1940-65, Vice-Chm. of Party, 1954-65; Member of Althing (Parlt), 1942-65; Minister of Foreign Affairs, 1956-65; Minister of Finance, 1958-59; Chm., Icelandic Delegn to UN Conf. on Law of the Sea, Geneva, 1958 and 1960; Mem. and Chm. of Board of Dirs, Fishery Bank in Reykjavík, 1957-65. Establishment of Republic Medal, 1944. Hon. KBE; Grand Cross, Order of: White Rose (Finland); North Star (Sweden); Orange-Nassau (Netherlands); Chêne (Luxembourg); Southern Cross (Brazil); St Olav (Norway); Phoenix (Greece). *Address:* 101 Park Street, W1. *T:* 01-629 8660.

**GUDMUNDSSON, Dr Kristinn;** Commander of the Icelandic Falcon (1st Class); Ambassador of Iceland to the USSR, 1961-68; concurrently Ambassador at Bucharest (1964-68), Sofia (1965-68) and Budapest (1966-68); *b* 14 Oct. 1897; *s* of Gudmundur Sigfredsson and Gudrún Einarsdóttir; *m* 1927, Elsa Alma Kalbow; one *d*. *Educ:* University of Reykjavik; Berlin and Kiel. Master, Akureyri Coll., 1929-44; Tax Dir, Akureyri, 1944-53; Minister for Foreign Affairs, Iceland, Sept. 1953-July 1956; Minister to the UK, 1956, subsequently Ambassador, until 1960; concurently both at The Hague. Grand Cross: Dannebrog (Denmark); Vasa (Sweden); White Rose (Finland); St Olav (Norway); Verdienstorden (Germany); Crown of Oak (Luxembourg). *Publication:* Die dänischenglischen Handelsbeziehungen, 1931. *Address:* Grettisgata 96, Reykjavik, Iceland.

**GUERISSE, Dr Albert Marie Edmond,** GC 1946; DSO 1942 (under name of Patrick Albert O'Leary); medical officer; Major-General in the Belgian Army; Director-General, Medical Service, Belgian Forces; *b* Brussels, 5 April 1911; *m* 1947, Sylvia Cooper Smith; one *s*. *Educ:* in Belgium; Louvain; Brussels University. Medical Officer, Lieut, 1940; after Belgian capitulation embarked at Dunkirk and became, in Sept. 1940, Lieut-Comdr, RN; first officer of "Q" ship, HMS Fidelity (under name of P. A. O'Leary). Engaged on secret work in France from April 1941 until arrest by Gestapo in March 1943 (chief of an escape organisation). After 2 years in Concentration Camps returned to England. After demobilisation from RN rejoined Belgian Army (1st Lancers); joined Belgian Volunteer Bn, 1951, as Chief of Medical Service in Korea; Officier Légion d'Honneur, 1947; Medal of Freedom with golden palm, 1947; Officier Ordre Léopold, 1946; French Croix de Guerre, 1945; Polish Croix de Guerre, 1944. *Address:* 100 avenue General Lartigue, Brussels 15, Belgium. *T:* 357555.

**GUERITZ, Rear-Adm. Edward Findlay,** OBE 1957; DSC 1942, and Bar, 1944; Commandant, Joint Warfare Establishment, since 1970; *b* 8 Sept. 1919; *s* of Elton and Valentine Gueritz; *m* 1947, Pamela Amanda Bernhardina Britton, *d* of Commander L. H. Jeans; one *s* one *d*. *Educ:* Cheltenham Coll. Entered Navy, 1937; Midshipman, 1938; served War of 1939-45 (wounded; DSC and Bar): HMS Jersey, 5th Flotilla, 1940-41; Combined Ops (Indian Ocean, Normandy), 1941-44; HMS Saumarez (Corfu Channel incident), 1946; Army Staff Coll., Camberley, 1948; Staff of C-in-C S Atlantic and Junior Naval Liaison Officer to UK High Comr, S Africa, 1954-56; Near East Operations, 1956 (OBE); Dep. Dir, RN Staff Coll., 1959-61; Naval Staff, Admty, 1961-63; idc 1964; Captain of Fleet, Far East Fleet, 1965-66; Dir of Defence Plans (Navy), 1967; Dir, Jt Warfare Staff, MoD, 1968; Admiral-President, Royal Naval Coll., 1968-70. Lt-Comdr 1949; Comdr 1953; Captain 1959; Rear-Adm. 1969. *Recreations:* history, reading. *Address:* Joint Warfare Establishment, Old Sarum, Salisbury, Wilts. *Clubs:* Army and Navy; Royal Naval (Portsmouth).

**GUERNSEY, Lord; Heneage Charles Finch-Knightley;** *b* 27 March 1947; *s* and *heir* of 11th Earl of Aylesford, *qv*. *Educ:* Oundle. *Address:* Packington Hall, Coventry.

**GUERNSEY, Dean of;** *see* Cogman, Very Rev. F. W.

**GUEST,** family name of **Viscount Wimborne.**

**GUEST,** *see* Haden-Guest.

**GUEST,** Baron (Life Peer), *cr* 1961; **Christopher William Graham Guest,** PC 1961; a Lord of Appeal in Ordinary since 1961; *b* 7 Nov. 1901; *s* of Edward Graham and Mary Catherine Guest; *m* 1941, Catharine Geraldine Hotham; four *s* one *d*. *Educ:* Merchiston Castle; Cambridge (MA, LLB); Edinburgh (LLB). Called to Scots Bar, 1925, Inner Temple, 1929; Bencher, Inner Temple, 1961. 2nd Lieut Royal Artillery, TA, 1939; Major, Judge Advocate General's Branch, War Office, 1942. QC, Scots Bar, 1945. Contested (U) Kirkcaldy Burghs, 1945; Advocate Depute, 1945; Pres. Transport Arbitration Tribunal, Scotland, 1947-55; Sheriff of Ayr and Bute, 1952-54; Trustee National Library of Scotland, 1952-57; Sheriff of Perth and Angus, 1954-55; Chm. Building Legislation Cttee, 1954-57; Chm. Scottish Agricultural Wages Board, 1955-61; Chm. Scottish Licensing Law Cttee, 1959-63. Dean of the Faculty of Advocates, 1955-57; a Senator of the College of Justice in Scotland, 1957-61. *Publication:* Law of Valuation in Scotland, 1930. *Address:* 3 Ainslie Place, Edinburgh. *T:* 031-225 5508; Woodend, Dirleton, E Lothian. *T:* Dirleton 276. *Clubs:* Buck's, Oriental.

**GUEST, Prof. Anthony Gordon;** Barrister-at-Law; Professor of English Law, King's College, University of London, since 1966; Reader in Common Law to the Council of Legal Education (Inns of Court), since 1967; *b* 8 Feb. 1930; *o s* of Gordon Walter Leslie Guest and Marjorie (*née* Hooper), Maidencombe, Devon; unmarried. *Educ:* Colston's Sch.,

Bristol; St John's Coll., Oxford (MA). Army service, 1948-50 (Lieut). Exhibr and Casberd Schol., Oxford, 1950-54; 2nd cl. Class. Hon. Mods 1952, 1st cl. Final Hon. Sch. of Jurisprudence, 1954. Bacon Schol., Gray's Inn, 1955; Barstow Law Schol., 1955; called to Bar, Gray's Inn, 1955. University Coll., Oxford: Lectr, 1954-55; Fellow and Prælector in Jurisprudence, 1955-65; Dean, 1963-64; Travelling Fellowship to S Africa, 1957; Mem., Lord Chancellor's Law Reform Cttee, 1963; Mem., Adv. Cttee on establishment of Law Faculty in University of Hong Kong, 1965; UK Deleg. to UN Commn on Internat. Trade Law, NY and Geneva, 1968-70; Mem., Board of Athlone Press, 1968. *Publications:* (ed) Anson's Principles of the Law of Contract, 21st to 23rd edns, 1959-69; Chitty on Contracts: (Asst Editor) 22nd edn, 1961; (Gen. Editor) 23rd edn, 1968; (ed) Oxford Essays in Jurisprudence, 1961; The Law of Hire-Purchase, 1966; articles in legal jls. *Address:* 6 Carrington House, Hertford Street, W1. *T:* 01-499 1322. *Club:* Garrick.

**GUEST, Air Marshal Sir Charles Edward Neville,** KBE 1954 (CBE 1945; OBE 1936); CB 1946; Advisor on Flight Safety, BOAC, since 1961; *b* 1900; *s* of Rev. H. J. Guest; *m* 1945, Moira, *d* of late K. Cameron, Motherwell; two *s. Educ:* King Edward's Sch., Birmingham. AOC No 229 Group, India, 1943-45; AOC Transport Command Group in India, 1945; Senior Air Staff Officer, HQ Air Command, Singapore, 1946-47; AOC No 1 Group, Bomber Command, 1947-48; Asst Chief of the Air Staff (Ops), 1948-52; AOC-in-C, Transport Command, 1952-54; Inspector-Gen. of the RAF, 1954-56, retired. *Recreations:* golf, tennis, philately. *Clubs:* Royal Air Force; Moor Park (Northwood).

**GUEST, Douglas Albert,** MA Cantab and Oxon; MusB Cantab; FRCM, Hon. RAM, Hon. FRCO; Organist and Master of the Choristers, Westminster Abbey, since 1963; Professor, Royal College of Music; Examiner to Associated Board of Royal Schools of Music; *b* 9 May 1916; 2nd *s* of late Harold Guest, Henley-on-Thames, Oxon.; *m* 1941, Peggie Florentia, *d* of late Thomas Falconer, FRIBA, Amberley, Gloucester; two *d. Educ:* Reading Sch.; Royal College of Music, London; King's Coll., Cambridge. Organ Scholar, King's Coll., Cambridge, 1935-39; John Stewart of Rannoch Scholar in Sacred Music, Cambridge Univ., 1936-39. Served War of 1939-45, Major, Royal Artillery (HAC) (despatches). Gazetted Hon. Major, April 1945. Dir of Music, Uppingham Sch., 1945-50; Organist and Master of the Choristers, Salisbury Cathedral, 1950-57. Conductor of Salisbury Musical Soc., 1950-57; Dir of Music St Mary's Sch., Calne, 1950-57; Master of the Choristers and Organist, Worcester Cathedral, 1957-63; Conductor Worcester Festival Chorus and Three Choirs Festival, 1957-63. Chm. Council of National Youth Orchestra of Great Britain, 1953-. *Recreations:* fly fishing, golf. *Address:* 8 Little Cloister, Westminster Abbey, SW1. *T:* 01-222 6222. *Club:* Athenæum.

**GUEST, Eric Ronald;** Metropolitan Magistrate (West London), 1946-68; Barrister-at-Law; *b* 7 June 1904; *s* of late William Guest; *m* 1932, Sybil Blakelock; one *d. Educ:* Berkhamsted Sch.; Oriel Coll., Oxford. BA 1925 (1st Class Hons Sch. of Jurisprudence); BCL 1926; called to Bar, 1927; practised in London and on Oxford Circuit. Recorder of Worcester, 1941-46; served as Sqdn Leader with RAFVR, 1940-45. *Recreations:* reading, fishing. *Address:* 71 Arthur Road, SW19. *Club:* Arts.

**GUEST, Col Hon. Sir Ernest Lucas,** KBE, *cr* 1944 (OBE 1938); CMG 1949; CVO 1947; JP; Hon. LLD; Minister of Air, 1939, of Internal Affairs, 1944, of Finance, Defence, and Air, 1946, Southern Rhodesia; *b* 20 Aug. 1882; *s* of H. M. Guest, JP, Kerksdorp, Transvaal; *m* 1911, Edith May Jones, Singapore; (two *s* killed in War) two *d. Educ:* St Andrew's Coll. Sch., Grahamstown; South African Coll., Cape Town. Solicitor; Mem. of firm of Coghlan, Welsh & Guest, Salisbury. Elected to Parliament, 1928 (Charter); Minister of Mines and Works, 1938. Served Anglo-Boer War (King's and Queen's Medal, 5 clasps); European War, German South-West Africa and Western Front (1915 Star, Gen. Service and Victory medals) Lecture tour, 1919, in USA on behalf Dept Public Information. Knight, Order of the Phœnix (Greece); Companion, Order of the White Eagle (Serbia). *Recreations:* shooting, golf. *Address:* PO Box 53, Salisbury, Rhodesia. *Clubs:* Salisbury (Salisbury, Rhodesia); Bulawayo (Bulawayo); Umtali (Umtali).

**GUEST, George Howell,** MA, MusB; FRCO; Organist of St John's College, Cambridge since 1951; Fellow, 1956; University Lecturer in Music, Cambridge University, since 1956; Special Commissioner, Royal School of Church Music; Examiner to Associated Board of Royal Schools of Music; Member of Council, Royal College of Organists; Director of Studies in Music at St John's, Emmanuel, Downing, Queens' and Christ's Colleges; *b* 9 Feb. 1924; *s* of late Ernest Joseph Guest and late Gwendolen (*née* Brown); *m* 1959, Nancy Mary, *o d* of W. P. Talbot; one *s* one *d. Educ:* Friars Sch., Bangor; King's Sch., Chester; St John's Coll., Cambridge. Chorister: Bangor Cath., 1933-35; Chester Cath., 1935-39. Served in RAF, 1942-46. Sub-Organist, Chester Cath., 1946-47; Organ Student, St John's Coll., Cambridge, 1947-51; John Stewart of Rannoch Scholar in Sacred Music, 1948; University Asst Lectr in Music, Cambridge, 1953-56; Prof. of Harmony and Counterpoint, RAM, London, 1960-61. Dir, Berkshire Boy Choir, USA, 1967, 1970. *Recreations:* watching Chester AFC; playing croquet. *Address:* 9 Gurney Way, Cambridge. *T:* Cambridge 54932. *Club:* Union Society (Cambridge).

**GUI, Vittorio;** Commander of the Crown of Italy, 1923; Gold Medal for Culture (Italy) 1957; orchestral conductor; Artistic Counsellor at Glyndebourne, Sussex, since 1960; *b* 14 Sept. 1885; *m* 1st, 1911, Mary Bourbon del Monte S Maria; three *s*; 2nd, 1936, Elda Salaroli-Enriques; two step *s. Educ:* Rome. Debut as conductor of orchestra, Dec. 1907; has conducted orchestras all over Europe. Founder of Teatro di Torino, Italy, 1925; Founder of Orch. Stabile, Florence, and of Maggio Musicale, 1933. Hon. citizen of Pesaro. Order of St Iago y Espada, Portugal, 1921; Comdr of Order of Gustavus Vasa, Sweden, 1941, etc. *Publications:* several musical compositions including songs and an opera for children (Fairy-tale), 1927; also a book of musical essays, articles in magazines, and a study of Boito's Nerone. *Address:* Villa San Maurizio, Fiesole (Florence), Italy. *T:* 59232.

**GUIDOTTI, Gastone,** FRSA; Italian Ambassador to the Court of St James's, 1964-68; *b* 29 Sept. 1901; *m* 1931, Raffaellina Betocchi; one *d. Educ:* St Carlo's Coll., Modena and University of Siena, Italy. Head of Dept at Ministry of Foreign Affairs, Rome, 1935; First Sec., Belgrade; First Sec., Stockholm; Italian Rep. to Allied Govts, London, 1945; in charge of Italian Legation,

Prague, 1945, Athens, 1946; Head of Liaison Office of Min. of Foreign Affairs with Allied Govt, Trieste, 1947; Gen. Dir of Polit. Affs, Italian Min. for For. Affs, Rome, and Mem. various Italian Delegns to Nato Confs, Coun. of Europe Meetings, etc., 1948; Head of Italian Representation to UNO, 1951; Italian Ambassador: Belgrade, 1955; Vienna, 1958; Bonn, 1961. Holds foreign decorations including 4 grand crosses. *Recreations:* shooting, art collecting. *Address:* c/o Ministero degli Affari Esteri, Rome, Italy. *Clubs:* Unione (Florence), Circolo della Caccia (Rome).

**GUILD, Surgeon Captain William John Forbes;** CBE 1952; FRCS, MD; RN retd; House Governor, King Edward VII Convalescent Home for Officers, Osborne House, IW, since 1965; *b* 30 Aug. 1908; *s* of late William Guild and Jessie Guild, Dundee; *m* 1st, 1942, Joan (*d* 1957), *d* of Charles Innes, Hornsey; one *s* one *d*; 2nd, 1958, Jessie, *d* of John MacLennan, Mallaig. *Educ:* Harris Academy, Dundee; St Andrews Univ. MB, ChB 1930; MD (StA) 1936, FRCS (Ed.) 1941. Post-grad. House appts, Royal Infirmary, Dundee. Served RN Med. Service, 1933-65: Ophthalmic Specialist and Surgical Specialist; final appt as Med. Officer i/c RN Hosp., Gibraltar; ret. with rank of Surgeon Captain. Sen. Fellow, Assoc. of Surgeons; Mem., Faculty of Ophthalmologists. *Publications:* various papers on naval medical matters. *Recreations:* tennis, gardening, hill-walking. *Address:* The Manse, The Mall, Brading, Isle of Wight. *T:* Brading 316. *Clubs:* Royal Over-Seas League; Royal Naval (Portsmouth).

**GUILDFORD, Bishop of,** since 1961; **Rt. Rev. George Edmund Reindorp,** DD; *b* 19 Dec. 1911; *s* of Rev. Hector William Reindorp and Dora Lucy (*née* George), Goodmayes, Essex; *m* 1943, Alix Violet Edington, MB, ChB, *d* of Alexander Edington, MD, and Helen Edington, Durban, Natal; three *s* one *d* (and one *d* decd). *Educ:* Felsted Sch.; Trinity Coll., Cambridge; Westcott House, Cambridge. MA Cantab, 1939. Deacon, 1937; priest, 1938; Curate, S Mary Abbots, Kensington, 1937-39; Chaplain RNVR, 1938-46; Vicar St Stephen with St John, Westminster, 1946-57. Commissary for: Bishop of Natal, 1948; Bishop of New Guinea, 1956; Provost of Southwark and Rector of St Saviour with All Hallows, Southwark, 1957-61. Chaplain, RCGP, 1965. DD Lambeth 1961. *Publications:* What about You?, 1956; No Common Task, 1957; Putting it Over: ten points for preachers, 1961; Over to You, 1964. *Recreations:* ski-ing; radio and television; avoiding committees. *Address:* Willow Grange, Stringer's Common, Guildford, Surrey. *T:* Guildford 73922. *Clubs:* Ski Club of Great Britain, Kandahar. *See also Sir Humphrey Mynors, Bt.*

**GUILDFORD, Assistant Bishops of;** *see* Pike, Rt Rev. St John S., Usher-Wilson, Rt Rev. Lucian C.

**GUILDFORD, Dean of;** *see* Bridge, Very Rev. A. C.

**GUILFORD,** 9th Earl of *cr* 1752; **Edward Francis North;** Baron Guilford, 1683; *b* 22 Sept. 1933; *s* of Major Lord North (*d* 1940) and Joan Louise (she *m* 2nd, 1947, Charles Harman Hunt, JP), *er d* of late Sir Merrik Burrell, 7th Bt, CBE; *S* grandfather, 1949; *m* 1956, Osyth Vere Napier, *d* of Cyril Napier Leeston Smith, Trottiscliffe, near West Malling, Kent. *Educ:* Eton. *Heir: uncle* Hon. John Montagu William North [*b* 28 Feb. 1905; *m* 1st, 1927, Muriel Norton (marr. diss., 1939), *d* of Sir William Norton Hicking, 1st Bt; one *s* (*see* Sir W. J. F. North, Bt) one *d*; 2nd, 1939, Marion Dyer, *d* of Frank Erving Chase, Boston, Mass]. *Address:* Waldershare Park, Dover, Kent. *T:* Kearsney 2244. *See also Major Hon. Sir Clive Bossom, Bt.*

**GUILLEBAUD, Claude William,** CBE 1948; Fellow in 1915, Tutor, 1926-52, Senior Tutor, 1952-56, St John's College, Cambridge; Emeritus University Reader in Economics, Cambridge; *b* 2 July 1890; *s* of Rev. Ernest Delabere Guillebaud and Mabel Louisa Marshall; *m* 1918, Marie-Thérèse Prunner; two *d*. *Educ:* Repton Sch.; Manchester Univ.; St John's Coll., Cambridge. Adam Smith Prize, 1914; with Supreme Economic Council in Paris, 1919-20; Sec. of Cttee on Prices under Profiteering Acts, 1920-21; Senior Proctor of Cambridge Univ., 1933-34; Chm. of Baking Wages Council, 1940; unlicensed Place of Refreshment Wages Board, 1945, Road Haulage Wages Council, 1947, National Joint Wages Council for the Biscuit Industry, 1942; Independent Mem. of Agricultural Wages Boards for England and Wales, and Scotland, 1956; Member: Council Royal Economic Society; Industrial Disputes Tribunal, 1952; Royal Commission on Scottish Affairs, 1952; East Anglian Regional Hosp. Board, 1958; Bd of Govs, United Cambridge Hosps, 1963; Chm. Cttee of Investigation into Cost of the Nat. Health Service, 1953; Chm. Railway Pay Cttee of Enquiry, 1959; Lay Mem., Gen. Medical Council, 1959. *Publications:* The Works Council: A German Experiment in Industrial Democracy, 1928; The Economic Recovery of Germany, 1933-38; Contributor to second vol. Cambridge History of the British Empire; The Wages Council System in Great Britain, 2nd edn 1962; Economic Survey of the Sisal Industry of Tanganyika, 1959 (3rd edn 1966); Wage Determination and Wages Policy, 2nd edn 1967; Variorum edn of Marshall's Principles of Economics, 1961. *Recreation:* golf. *Address:* St John's College, Cambridge; 36 Wilberforce Road, Cambridge. *T:* Cambridge 50829.

**GUILLEBAUD, Walter Henry,** CBE 1951; *b* 2 July 1890; *s* of Ernest Delabere Guillebaud and Mabel Louisa (*née* Marshall); *m* 1st, 1916, Alice Betty Stocks (*d* 1919); 2nd, 1921, Dorothy Joyce Young; two *d*. *Educ:* Monkton Combe Junior Sch.; Repton Sch.; Victoria Coll., Manchester Univ.; St John's Coll., Cambridge Univ. BA Nat. Sci. Tripos; Diploma of Agriculture and Diploma of Forestry, Cambridge. Asst Inspector in Forestry Branch of Board of Agriculture and Fisheries, 1914; Forestry Commission: Research Officer, 1919; Divisional Officer in charge of Div. 5, 1925; Chief Research Officer, 1928; Actg Dep. Surveyor, Forest of Dean, 1939; Dir of Research and Education, 1945; Dep. Dir-Gen., 1948-53; Mem. of Standing Cttee of International Union of Forest Research Organizations, 1949. Sec., Retired Men's Club, Gerrards Cross, 1962. *Publications:* numerous contributions to technical journals. *Recreations:* gardening, reading. *Address:* Yatesbury, Oval Way, Gerrards Cross, Bucks. *T:* Gerrards Cross 83608.

**GUILLUM SCOTT, Sir John (Arthur),** Kt 1964; TD 1945; Secretary-General, General Synod of the Church of England, since 1970 (Secretary, Church Assembly, 1948-70); *b* 27 Oct. 1910; *e s* of late Guy H. Guillam Scott; *m* 1939, Muriel Elizabeth, *d* of late James Ross; one *d*. *Educ:* King's Sch., Canterbury. Queen Anne's Bounty, 1929-46; Asst Sec., Church Assembly, 1946-48. Inns of Court Regt TA, 1929-53; war service, 1939-45 (despatches); Lieut-Col commanding Inns of Court Regt, 1950-53; Bt Col, 1953. DCL (Lambeth) 1961. *Recreations:*

gardening, field sports. *Address:* Lower Farm House, Drayton Beauchamp, Aylesbury, Bucks. *Club:* Royal Automobile.

**GUILLY, Rt. Rev. Richard Lester;** *see* Georgetown, Bishop of, (RC).

**GUINNESS,** family name of **Earl of Iveagh** and **Baron Moyne.**

**GUINNESS, Sir Alec,** Kt 1959; CBE 1955; actor; *b* Marylebone, 2 April 1914; *m* 1938, Merula Salaman; one *s. Educ:* Pembroke Lodge, Southbourne; Roborough, Eastbourne. On leaving school went into Arks Publicity, Advertising Agents, as copywriter. First professional appearance walking on in Libel at King's Theatre, Hammersmith, 1933; played Hamlet in modern dress, Old Vic, 1938; toured the Continent, 1939. Served War of 1939-45; joined Royal Navy as a rating, 1941; commissioned 1942. Rejoined Old Vic, 1946-47. Hon. D Fine Arts Boston Coll., 1962. Pres., Mermaid Theatre Trust, 1967-. *Films include:* Oliver Twist, Kind Hearts and Coronets, The Lavender Hill Mob, Captain's Paradise, The Bridge on the River Kwai (Oscar for best actor of the year, 1957); The Horse's Mouth; Tunes of Glory; Lawrence of Arabia; The Comedians; Cromwell. *Plays include:* The Cocktail Party (New York), The Prisoner, Hotel Paradiso, Ross, Dylan (New York); Wise Child. *Recreation:* fishing. *Address:* Kettlebrook Meadows, Steep Marsh, Petersfield, Hants. *Clubs:* Athenæum, Garrick.

**GUINNESS, Bryan;** *see* Moyne, 2nd Baron.

**GUINNESS, Henry Samuel Howard;** Director, Guinness & Mahon Ltd, Dublin; formerly Senior Partner in Guinness Mahon & Co., London; *b* 1888; *e s* of late Howard Guinness and Mary Alice (*née* Guinness), Dublin; *m* 1913, Alfhild Holter, Oslo; three *d. Educ:* Winchester; Balliol Coll., Oxford. Banking education in USA and Germany; Hon. Financial Adviser at Foreign Office, 1919-20; joined family banking firm of Guinness Mahon & Co. as a Partner, 1923, Senior Partner, 1937-65; created, simultaneously with his wife, Chevalier Order of St Olav, Norway, 1947. Has travelled extensively in USA, Canada and Scandinavia. *Recreations:* salmon fishing and travelling in Norway. *Address:* 17 College Green, Dublin; East View, Seapoint Avenue, Monkstown, Co. Dublin; 3 Gracechurch Street, EC3. *Clubs:* Kildare Street (Dublin); Royal St George Yacht (Co. Dublin).

**GUINNESS, Sir Kenelm (Ernest Lee),** 4th Bt, *cr* 1867; International Bank for Reconstruction and Development, at Washington, DC, since 1954; *b* 13 Dec. 1928; *s* of late Kenelm Edward Lee Guinness and of Mrs Josephine Lee Guinness; *S* uncle 1954; *m* 1961, Mrs Jane Nevin Dickson; two *s. Educ:* Eton Coll.; Massachusetts Institute of Technology, USA. Late Lieut, Royal Horse Guards. *Heir: s,* Kenelm Edward Lee Guinness, *b* 30 Jan. 1962. *Address:* (home) 2814 35th Street NW, Washington, DC 20007, USA. *T:* FE7-3933. *Club:* Buck's.

**GUINNESS, Loel;** *see* Guinness, T. L. E. B.

**GUINNESS, (Thomas) Loel Evelyn Bulkeley,** OBE 1942; late Irish Guards; *s* of late Benjamin S. Guinness; *m* 1st, 1927, Hon. Joan Yarde-Buller (from whom he obtained a divorce, 1936); one *s* decd; 2nd, 1936, Lady Isabel Manners (marr. diss., 1951), *yr d* of 9th Duke of Rutland; one *s* one *d*; 3rd, 1951, Gloria, *d* of Raphael Rubio, Mexico. *Educ:* Sandhurst. MP (U) City of Bath, 1931-45; Contested Whitechapel, 1929, and By-election, 1930; Group Captain Auxiliary Air Force Reserve. Served War of 1939-45: RAF (despatches five times). Comdr Order of Orange Nassau; Officer Legion of Honour, France; Croix de Guerre. *Address:* Villa Zanroc, Epalinges, Vaud, Switzerland. *Clubs:* White's, Buck's, Guards, Beefsteak; Royal Yacht Squadron (Cowes).

**GUISE, Sir John (Grant),** 7th Bt *cr* 1783; Jockey Club Official since 1968; *b* 15 Dec. 1927; *s* of Sir Anselm William Edward Guise, 6th Bt and of Lady Guise (Nina Margaret Sophie, *d* of Sir James Augustus Grant, 1st Bt); *S* father, 1970. *Educ:* Winchester; RMA, Sandhurst. Regular officer, 3rd The King's Own Hussars, 1948-61. *Recreations:* hunting, shooting. *Heir: b* Christopher James Guise [*b* 10 July 1930; *m* 1969, Mrs Carole Hoskins Benson, *e d* of Jack Master]. *Address:* Elmore Court, Gloucester. *T:* Hardwicke 293.

**GULBENKIAN, Nubar Sarkis;** Hon. Counsellor at the Turkish Embassy since 1966; *b* 2 June 1896; *o s* of C. S. Gulbenkian and Nevarte (*née* Essayan); *m* 1st, 1922, Herminia Elena Josefa Rodriguez Feijôo; 2nd, 1928, Dore Freeland; 3rd, 1948, Marie Berthe Edmée, *o d* of Louis de Ayala, Château d'Ay, Marne, France, and of Annette (*née* Gunning). *Educ:* Orley Farm; Harrow; Bonn Univ.; Trinity Coll., Cambridge (MA, LLB); Middle Temple. Attached French Ministry of Supply (Petroleum Section), 1917-21; with Royal Dutch Shell Group, 1922-25; worked with his father in oil and finance, 1925-55; engaged in Middle East Oil negotiations, 1926-28 and 1948-54; Dir, Iraq Petroleum Co., 1917-25 and 1928-38. Commercial Attaché to Iranian Embassy, 1926-51 and again 1956-65. Hon. Pres., Armenian Church Trustees, 1955-, and of Assoc. of Economic Representatives, 1956-. Vice-Pres. Royal Central Asian Soc., 1967-. FRGS Legion of Honour, Chevalier, 1919, Comdr 1928; Order of St Gregory the Illuminator (with diamonds), 1957; Order of Taj, 1962. *Publication:* (autobiography) Pantaraxia, 1965. *Recreations:* hunting and pantaraxia. *Address:* Domaine des Colles, 06 Valbonne, France. *T:* 93.67.63.56; The Old House, Hoggeston, near Bletchley, Bucks; 8/55 Park Lane, W1Y 3DH. *T:* 01-493 1316. *Clubs:* St James'; Travellers' (Paris).

**GULL, Sir Michael Swinnerton Cameron,** 4th Bt, *cr* 1872; *b* 24 Jan. 1919; *o s* of 3rd Bt and of Dona Eva Swinnerton, *e d* of late Sir Thomas Swinnerton Dyer, 11th Bt; *S* father 1960; *m* 1950, Mrs Yvonne Bawtree, *o d* of Dr Albert Oliver Macarius Heslop, Cape Town; one *s* one *d. Educ:* Eton. Late 2nd Lieut, Scots Guards (SRO). *Heir: s* Rupert William Cameron Gull, *b* 14 July 1954. *Address:* Phyllis Road, Claremont, Cape Town, S Africa.

**GULLIVER, James Gerald;** Chairman since 1967 and Managing Director since 1965, Fine Fare (Holdings) Ltd; *b* 17 Aug. 1930; *s* of William Frederick and Mary Gulliver; *m* 1958, Margaret Joan (*née* Cormack); three *s* two *d. Educ:* Campbeltown Grammar Sch.; Univs of Glasgow and Harvard. Royal Navy (Short Service Commn), 1956-59; Dir, Concrete (Scotland) Ltd, 1960-61; Management Consultant, Urwick, Orr & Partners Ltd, 1961-65. *Recreations:* golf, ski-ing, music, painting. *Address:* Ayres End House, Harpenden, Herts. *T:* Harpenden 2345. *Clubs:* Royal Automobile; Royal Scottish Automobile (Glasgow).

**GULLY,** family name of **Viscount Selby.**

**GUMBLEY, Douglas William,** CBE 1932; ISO; Rafidain, 1934; *b* 14 Aug. 1880; *s* of William Gumbley, AMICE; unmarried. Formerly

Indo-European Telegraph Department (Government of India). Served European War, 1914-18, Major Royal Engineers (despatches, OBE), Inspector-Gen. of Posts and Telegraphs, and Dir of Civil Aviation, Iraq, 1919-34; Dir of Civil Aviation, Palestine, 1934-47; Iraq Petroleum Co. Ltd, 1947-52. *Address:* Green Patch, Yew Tree Shute, Sandford, Wroxall, Isle of Wight. *Club:* East India and Sports.

**GUMMER, John Selwyn;** MP (C) Lewisham West since 1970; *b* 26 Nov. 1939; *s* of Canon Selwyn Gummer, Brighton, and Sybille (*née* Mason). *Educ:* King's Sch., Rochester; Selwyn Coll., Cambridge (Exhibr). BA Hons History 1961; Chm., Cambridge Univ. Conservative Assoc., 1961; Pres., Cambridge Union, 1962; Chm., Fedn of Conservative Students, 1962. Editor, Business Publications, 1962-64; Editor-in-Chief, Max Parrish & Oldbourne Press, 1964-66; BPC Publishing: Special Asst to Chm., 1967; Publisher, Special Projects, 1967-69; Editorial Coordinator, 1969-; Dir, Shandwick Publishing Co., 1966-. Mem., ILEA Educn Cttee, 1967-70; Mem., Southwark Diocese Pastoral Reorganisation Cttee, 1969-. Contested (C) Greenwich, 1964 and 1966. *Publications:* (jtly) When the Coloured People Come, 1966; (contrib.) To Church with Enthusiasm, 1969. *Address:* 7 Vauxhall Walk, SE11. *T:* 01-735 8500. *Club:* United Universities.

**GUNASEKERA, Percival Reginald;** Ceylonese diplomat and lawyer; Managing Director, Associated Cables Ltd; *b* 5 March 1897; *s* of late S. D. S. Gunasekera, Colombo; *m* 1924, Constance de Silva; two *s* one *d*. *Educ:* Royal Coll., Colombo; Clare Coll., Cambridge. MA (Cantab.) 1926. Barrister-at-Law, Middle Temple, 1923; Lectr, Ceylon Univ., 1923-24; Principal, Mahinda Coll., Galle, Ceylon, 1924-32; practised at Galle Bar, 1932-45; Crown Advocate, Galle, 1941; joined Judicial Service, Ceylon, 1946; High Commissioner for Ceylon in Australia and New Zealand, 1955-57; Ambassador for Ceylon in France, 1958-60, also High Commissioner for Ceylon in UK, Oct. 1958-Jan. 1960; Ambassador to France and Minister to Switzerland, 1960-61. *Address:* 171/3 Buller's Road, Colombo 3, Ceylon.

**GUNDRY, Rev. Canon Dudley William,** MTh; Canon Residentiary and Chancellor of Leicester since 1963; Rural Dean of Christianity (Leicester); Examining Chaplain to Bishop of Leicester; *b* 4 June 1916; *e s* of late Cecil Wood Gundry and of Lucy Gundry; unmarried. *Educ:* Sir Walter St John's Sch.; King's Coll., London. BD (1st cl. Hons) 1939, AKC (1st cl. Hons Theology) 1939, MTh 1941. Deacon, 1939; Priest 1940. Curate of St Matthew, Surbiton, 1939-44; Lectr in History of Religions, University Coll. of North Wales, Bangor, 1944-60; Mem. Senate and Warden of Neuadd Reichel, 1947-60; Dean of Faculty of Theology, 1956-60; Hon. Sec., British Section, Internat. Assoc. for History of Religions, 1954-60; Select Preacher, Trinity Coll., Dublin, 1957; Prof. Head of Dept of Religious Studies, and Mem. of Senate University Coll., Ibadan, 1960-63; Commissary to Bishop of Northern Nigeria, 1963-69. Sometime Examining Chaplain to Bishops of Bangor and St Davids; Examiner to Universities of Leeds, London, St David's Coll., Lampeter, Gen. Ordination Examination. *Publications:* Religions: An Historical and Theological Study, 1958; Israel's Neighbours (in Neil's Bible Companion), 1959; The Teacher and the World Religions, 1968; many articles and signed reviews in theological and kindred journals. *Recreations:* motoring, architecture. *Address:* 3 Morland Avenue, Leicester LE2 2PF. *T:* Leicester 704133. *Clubs:* National; Leicestershire (Leicester).

**GUNEWARDENE, Ratnakirti Senarat Serasinghe,** Kt 1956; High Commissioner for Ceylon in Canada, 1963-69, also Permanent Representative at the United Nations; *b* 1899; *m* 1927, Sumana Gunewardene; two *d*. *Educ:* Ceylon (BA); University of London. Advocate of Ceylon Supreme Court. Mem. Ceylon State Council, 1936-47; Mem. first Parliament of Ceylon, 1947-52; Minister without Portfolio for short period and Chief Govt Whip; Minister of Ceylon to Italy, 1952-54; Ambassador in Washington, 1954-61; concurrently accredited as Ceylon's High Commissioner in Canada, 1957-58 and as Ambassador to Cuba, 1958-61, and Ambassador to Mexico, 1958-61; Permanent Representative at UN, 1956-58; Vice-Pres. United National General Assembly, 1957; Chm. UN Human Rights Commn, 1958-59. Served on Advisory Cttee of UN Emergency Force and UN Commn on Problem of Hungary, 1956. Ceylon Ambassador in France, 1961, with concurrent accreditation as MInister in Switzerland, 1961, until March 1962; Ceylon High Comr in Britain, 1961-63. Head of Ceylon's Mission to the European Economic Community, with rank of Ambassador. *Recreations:* reading and travelling. *Address:* c/o Department of External Affairs, Colombo, Ceylon.

**GUNLAKE, John Henry,** CBE 1946; FIA; FSS; FIS; consulting actuary; *b* 23 May 1905; *s* of late John Gunlake, MRCS, LRCP, and late Alice Emma Gunlake; unmarried. *Educ:* Epsom Coll. Institute of Actuaries: Fellow, 1933; Hon. Sec., 1952-54; Vice-Pres., 1956-59; Pres., 1960-62. A Statistical Adviser, Min. of Shipping, 1940-47. Member: Cttee on Econ. and Financial Problems of Provision for Old Age, 1953-54; Royal Commn on Doctors' and Dentists' Remuneration, 1957-60; Permanent Advisory Cttee on Doctors' and Dentists' Remuneration, 1962-70. *Publications:* Premiums for Life Assurances and Annuities, 1939. Contrib. to Jl of Inst. of Actuaries. *Recreations:* reading, music, walking. *Address:* 20 Belgrave Mews West, SW1. *T:* 01-235 7452. *Club:* Reform.

**GUNN, Alistair Livingston,** VRD; MD Wales; FRCSE, FRCOG; Consulting Obstetrician, Lewisham and Bromley, Kent, Hospitals; Consulting Gynæcologist to numerous hospitals and public authorities; *b* 14 Feb. 1903; *s* of George H. Gunn and Mary Tait; *m* 1930, Sibyl Marian Thomas, *d* of late Lieut-Col G. C. Thomas, DSO, OBE; two *s* one *d*. *Educ:* Cardiff High Sch.; Universities of Wales and Edinburgh. Chm. Cardiff Medical Students Club; resident hospital appointments at Cardiff Royal Infirmary, Redhill Hosp., Edgeware and Mile End Hospital; Obstetrician and Gynæcologist, St Mary's, Mayday and Borough Hosps, Croydon, 1933-36. Served War of 1939-45, Surgeon Comdr RNVR; MO i/c RN hosp., Duncraig, Scotland, 1940-43; Surgical Specialist RN Hosp., Durban and HMS Westcliff. Lectr and Examr Central Midwives Bd; Examr in Obst. and Gynæc. for London Univ. MB, BS; to conjoint Examining Bd in England and for Membership of RCOG; Mem. Ct of Assts of Worshipful Soc. of Apothecaries of London; Hon. Librarian and Mem. Council of RCOG; James Young Simpson Orator, 1967; FRSocMed (Vice-Pres., Sect. of Obst. and Gynæc); Fellow and Mem. Council, Hunterian Soc.; Hunterian Orator, 1968. Rep. of Royal College on SE Reg. Cttee of Brit. Postgrad. Med. Fedn; Chm. Maternity Liaison Cttees for Lewisham and Bromley; Past Pres.; W Kent Medico-

Chirurgical Soc.; New Cross Med. Soc.; Sec. Gynæcolog. Sect, BMA Meeting, 1952. Freeman of City of London; Conservator of Chislehurst Common; Chairman Chislehurst Playing Fields Assoc. *Publications:* Treatment of Uterine Hæmorrhage, 1942; articles and clinical reports, mainly obstetrical. *Recreations:* travel, book-collecting. *Address:* 82 Harley Street, W1. *T:* 01-580 4357; 9 Holbrook House, Chislehurst, Kent. *T:* 01-467 1625. *Clubs:* Athenæum; Chislehurst Golf; Gynæcological Travellers'.

**GUNN, Air Marshal Sir George (Roy),** KBE 1967 (OBE 1946); CB 1965; QHP 1965; Director-General of Medical Services (Royal Air Force) 1967-71, retired; *b* 23 Dec. 1910; *s* of late Donald Gunn, Edinburgh; *m* 1937, Violet Eleanor Munro, Evanton, Ross-shire; one *s* one *d*. *Educ:* Royal High School and Edinburgh Univ. MB ChB (Edinburgh) 1934; MRCP (Edinburgh); DPHLondon 1952. Served War of 1939-45, RAF: Lossiemouth, 1939-43; India and Burma, 1943-45; OC RAF, Hosp., Changi, Singapore, 1952-54; Dep. Dir Med. Org. AM, 1958-61; PMO, RAF Germany, 1961-63; Dir Health and Research, Min. of Defence Air Dept, 1963-65; PMO, RAF Bomber Command, 1965-67. *Recreations:* golf, gardening, etc. *Address:* 27 Moor Lane, Rickmansworth, Herts. *T:* Rickmansworth 74897. *Clubs:* Royal Air Force; Royal and Ancient (St Andrews).

**GUNN, Prof. John Currie,** MA (Glasgow and Cambridge); FRSE, FIMA; Cargill Professor of Natural Philosophy, University of Glasgow, since 1949; *b* 13 Sept. 1916; *s* of Richard Robertson Gunn and Jane Blair Currie; *m* 1944, Betty Russum; one *s*. *Educ:* Glasgow Acad.; Glasgow Univ.; St John's Coll., Cambridge. Engaged in Admiralty scientific service, first at Admiralty Research Laboratory, later at Mine Design Dept, 1939-45; Research Fellow of St John's Coll., Cambridge, 1944; Lecturer in Applied Mathematics: Manchester Univ., 1945-46; University Coll., London, 1946-49. Mem., SRC, 1968-. *Publications:* papers on mathematical physics in various scientific journals. *Recreations:* golf, music, chess. *Address:* 13 The University, Glasgow W2. *T:* 041-334 3042.

**GUNN, Neil M.,** LLD; writer; *b* 8 Nov. 1891; *m* 1921, Jessie D. Frew. *Educ:* Highland Sch.; privately. Resigned from Civil Service, 1937. *Publications: novels:* Grey Coast, 1926; Morning Tide, 1931; The Lost Glen, 1932; Sun Circle, 1933; Butchers Broom, 1934; Highland River, 1937 (Tait Black Prize); Wild Geese Overhead, 1939; Second Sight, 1940; The Silver Darlings, 1941; Young Art and Old Hector, 1942; The Serpent, 1943; The Green Isle of the Great Deep, 1944; The Key of the Chest, 1946; The Drinking Well, 1947; The Shadow, 1948; The Silver Bough, 1948; The Lost Chart, 1949; The Well at the World's End, 1951; Bloodhunt, 1952; The Other Landscape, 1954; *short stories:* Hidden Doors, 1929; The White Hour, 1950; *essay:* Whisky and Scotland, 1935; *travel:* Off in a Boat, 1938; Highland Pack, 1950; *autobiography:* The Atom of Delight, 1956; various one-act plays. *Address:* Dalcraig, Kessock, Inverness.

**GUNN, Thomson William, (Thom Gunn);** *b* 29 Aug. 1929; *s* of Herbert Smith Gunn, and Ann Charlotte Gunn (*née* Thomson); unmarried. *Educ:* University Coll. Sch., Hampstead; Trinity Coll., Cambridge. British Army (National Service), 1948-50; lived in Paris six months, 1950; Cambridge, 1950-53; lived in Rome, 1953-54; has lived in California since 1954 except for a year in San Antonio, Texas (1955-56) and three months in Berlin (1960). Regular poetry reviewer for the Yale Review, 1958-64. Formerly Associate Prof., English Dept, University of Calif (Berkeley). Levinson Prize, 1955; Somerset Maugham Award, 1958; Arts Council Award, 1959. *Publications:* Poetry from Cambridge, 1953; Fighting Terms, 1954; The Sense of Movement, 1957; My Sad Captains, 1961; Selected Poems (with Ted Hughes), 1962; Five American Poets (ed. with Ted Hughes), 1962; Positives (with Ander Gunn), 1966; Touch (poems), 1967; Poems 1950-1966: a selection, 1969. *Recreations:* reading, drinking, going to films. *Address:* 975 Filbert Street, San Francisco, Calif, USA.

**GUNN, Sir William (Archer),** KBE 1961; CMG 1955; JP; Australian grazier and company director; Chairman: Australian Wool Board, since 1963; International Wool Secretariat, since 1961; *b* Goondiwindi, Qld, 1 Feb. 1914; *s* of late Walter and Doris Isabel Gunn, Goondiwindi; *m* 1939, Mary (Phillipa), *d* of F. B. Haydon, Murrurundi, NSW; one *s* two *d*. *Educ:* The King's Sch., Parramatta, NSW. Director: Rothmans of Pall Mall (Australia) Ltd; Grazcos Co-op. Ltd; Amagraze Ltd; Clausen Steamship Co. (Australia) Pty Ltd; Walter Reid and Co. Ltd; Douglas Pastoral Co. Pty Ltd; Lizard Island Pty Ltd; Ta Hing (Australia) Pty Ltd; Managing Director: Elsey Pastoral Pty Ltd; The Elsey Station Ltd; Hodgson Downs Ltd; Gunn Rural Management Pty Ltd; Gunn Development Pty Ltd; Gunn Resources & Exploration (Australia) Pty Ltd; Pres., Gunn Land & Exploration Partnership; Member: Commonwealth Bank Bd, 1952-59; Reserve Bank Bd, 1959-; Aust. Meat Bd, 1953-66; Aust. Wool Bureau, 1951-63 (Chm. 1958-63); Aust. Wool Growers Council, 1947-60 (Chm. 1956-57); Graziers Federal Council of Aust., 1951-60 (Pres. 1951-54); Aust. Wool Growers and Graziers Council, 1960-66; Export Develt Council, 1962-65; Faculty of Veterinary Science, University of Qld; Exec. Council, United Graziers Assoc. of Qld, 1944-69 (Pres., 1951-59; Vice-Pres., 1947-51); Aust. Wool Testing Authority, 1958-63; Exec., Internat. Wool Secretariat, 1958-63 (Chm. 1961-63); Council, NFU of Aust., 1951-54; CSIRO State Cttee, 1951-68; Chairman: The Wool Bureau Inc., New York, 1962-69; Qld Advisory Bd, Develt Finance Corp, 1962-; Trustee: Ian Clunies Ross Memorial Foundation; Qld Cancer Fund; Australian Pastoral Research Trust. Coronation Medal, 1953; Golden Fleece Achievement Award (Bd of Dirs of Nat. Assoc. of Wool Manufrs of America), 1962. Interest in properties: Goondiwindi District: Tarewinnabar; Eukabilla; Talinga; Rugby; Kington; Northern Territory: Gimbat; Elsey; Douglas; Dungowan; Noonamah Hotel & Store; Hayes Creek Inn; NT Stock Feeds. *Recreations:* formerly football, athletics, rowing and shot putting. *Address:* (home) 98 Windermere Road, Ascot, Qld 4007, Australia. *T:* Brisbane 68 2688; (office) Gunn Rural Management Pty Ltd, Wool Exchange, 69 Eagle Street, Brisbane, Qld 4000. *T:* Brisbane 21 4044. *Clubs:* Queensland, Tattersalls, Turf (Brisbane); Union (Sydney); Australian (Melbourne); Darwin (Darwin); McIntyre (Goondiwindi).

**GUNNARSSON, Gunnar;** StkF (Grand Cross, Order of Icelandic Falcon); RD (Kt of Dannebrog); FIAL; author; Hon. Professor; Dr hc; Hon. President, Bandalag Islenzkra Listamanna, Congress of Cultural Freedom, Icelandic Centre; Hon. Member Mark Twain International Society; *b* Valpjófsstad in Fljótsdal in Nordur-Múlasysla, Island (Iceland) 18 May 1889; *s* of Gunnar H. Gunnarsson and Katrin Dórarinsdóttir; *m*

1912, Franzisca Jörgensen; two *s*. *Publications:* Borgarættin, 1912-14 (Guest the One-Eyed, 1920); Ströndin, 1915; Vargur í véum, 1916; Drengurinn, 1917; Fostbræður, 1918 (The Sworn Brothers, 1920); Sælir eru einfaldir, 1920 (Seven Days' Darkness, 1930); Fjallkirkjan I-V, 1923-28 (Ships in the Sky, 1937; The Night and the Dream, 1938. Icelandic edition in 1 volume with illus by G. G. jr 1951); Svartfugi, 1929 (The Black Cliffs, 1967); Jón Arason, 1930; Vikivaki, 1932; Blindhús, 1933; Jörö, 1933; Hvitikristur, 1934; Grámann, 1936; Aöventa, 1937 (Eng. Advent, Amer. The Good Shepherd, 1940); Heiöaharmur, 1940; Sálumessa, 1952; Brimhenda, 1954; 6 vols short stories; 4 plays. *Address:* Dyngjuvegi 8, Reykjavik, Island (Iceland). *Club:* PEN (hon.).

**GUNNING, John Edward Maitland,** CBE 1960 (OBE 1945); Barrister-at-Law; *b* 22 Sept. 1904; *s* of late John Elgee Gunning, Manor House, Moneymore, Co. Derry, and late Edythe, *er d* of T. J. Reeves, London; *m* 1936, Enid Katherine, *o d* of George Menhinick; two *s*. *Educ:* Harrow; Magdalene Coll., Cambridge. Called to Bar, Gray's Inn, 1933. Practised South Eastern Circuit, Central Criminal Court, North London Sessions, Herts and Essex Sessions. Joined Judge Advocate General's office, Oct. 1939. War of 1939-45: served BEF, France, 1939-40; N Africa, 1942-43; Italy, 1943-45 (despatches, OBE). Middle East, 1945-50; Deputy Judge Advocate Gen. with rank of Col, CMF, 1945, Middle East, 1946; Deputy Judge Advocate Gen. (Army and RAF): Germany, 1951-53, 1960-63, 1968-70; Far East, 1957-59, 1965-67; Senior Asst Judge Advocate Gen., 1965-70. *Recreations:* bridge, watching cricket, reading. *Address:* c/o Midland Bank Ltd, 16a Curzon Street, W1. *Clubs:* United Service, MCC.

**GUNNING, Sir Robert Charles,** 8th Bt, *cr* 1778; gold-mine owner and farmer; *b* 2 Dec. 1901; *o s* of late Charles Archibald John Gunning and Beatrice Constance Purvis; *S* cousin 1950; *m* 1934, Helen Nancy, *d* of late Vice-Adm. Sir T. J. Hallet, KBE, CB; eight *s* two *d*. *Educ:* St Paul's Sch.; Leeds Univ. Business in the Sudan and Nigeria, 1924-33; prospecting and gold-mining in Nigeria, 1933-38; pegged first Nigerian lode gold-mine of the least importance, this in 1935 at Bin Yauri; served AA Command, 1939-46, temp. Capt. Emigrated to Alberta, 1948. *Recreations:* gardening, cricket, and almost any ball game. *Heir:* *s* Lieut Charles Theodore Gunning, RCN, *b* 19 June 1935. *Address:* c/o Postmaster, Peace River, Alberta, Canada.

**GUNSTON, Major Sir Derrick Wellesley,** 1st Bt, *cr* 1938; MC; *b* 1891; *s* of late Major Bernard Hamilton Gunston, late 5th Dragoon Guards; *m* 1917, Evelyn (Gardenia), OBE 1944, *d* of Howard St George, Cam House, Campden Hill, W8; one *s*. *Educ:* Harrow; Trinity Coll., Cambridge. Pres. of the New Carlton Club at Cambridge; joined army at outbreak of war; second in command 1st Battalion Irish Guards at Armistice; War of 1939-45, Major 7th Bn Glos Regt; MP (C) Thornbury Division Glos, 1924-45; Parliamentary Private Sec. to Rt Hon. Sir Kingsley Wood, Parliamentary Sec. to the Ministry of Health in Conservative Government, 1926-29; Parliamentary Private Sec. to Rt Hon. Neville Chamberlain, Chancellor of the Exchequer, 1931-36, to Sir Edward Grigg, Joint Under-Sec. for War 1940-42. *Heir:* *s* Richard Wellesley [*b* 1924; *m* 1st, 1947, Elizabeth Mary (from whom he obtained a divorce, 1956), *e d* of Arthur Colegate, Hillgrove, Bembridge, IOW; one *d*; 2nd, 1959, Mrs Joan Elizabeth Marie Coldicott, *o d* of Reginald Forde, Johannesburg]. *Address:* Fram Cottage, Bembridge, IoW; 14 Pelham Crescent, SW7. *Clubs:* Carlton, Pratt's; Royal Yacht Squadron (Cowes); Bembridge Sailing (Bembridge, IoW).

**GUNTER, Rt. Hon. Raymond Jones;** PC 1964; MP (Lab) Southwark since Oct. 1959; *b* 30 Aug. 1909; *s* of Miles Gunter, Llanhilleth, Mon; *m* 1934, Elsie, *d* of James Elkins, Nantyglo, Mon; one *s*. *Educ:* Abertillery and Newbridge Secondary Schs. Railway Clerks Assoc. branch officer, 1929-41; joined Royal Engineers, 1941, as Sapper; commissioned, 1943; Staff Capt. 1944-45. MP (Lab.) South Eastern Div. of Essex, 1945-50, Doncaster, 1950-51. Mem, National Executive of the Labour Party, 1955-; Minister of Labour, 1964-68; Minister of Power, April-June 1968. Pres. Transport Salaried Staff Association, 1956-64. Chm., Labour Party, 1965. Director: Securicor Ltd, 1969-; Industrial Communications Ltd, 1970-. *Address:* 12 Westminster Palace Gardens, SW1.

**GUNTER, Sir Ronald Vernon,** 3rd Bt, *cr* 1901; Temporary Lieutenant RNVR; *b* 8 March 1904; *s* of Sir Nevill Gunter, 2nd Bart, and Clara Lydia, *widow* of John Pritchard-Barrett of Sydenham; *S* father, 1917; *m* 1st, 1925, Anne (who obtained a divorce, 1932, and *m* 2nd, 1939, William Johnston Dyson), *d* of C. Lovell Simmonds, St John's Coll. Park; two *d*; 2nd, 1932, Dorothy Eleanor Johnston (marriage dissolved, 1950), *d* of H. E. Capes; 3rd, 1950, Mrs Vera Irene Wynn Parry (marriage dissolved, 1955), *d* of Sir Henry Philip Price, Bt; 4th, 1955, Phyllis Lesley Wallace, *d* of William St Clair Johnston. *Heir:* none. *Address:* Mill Hamlet Cottage, Sidlesham, Chichester, Sussex.

*See also Sir William R. Younger.*

**GUNTHER, John Thomson,** CMG, 1965; OBE, 1954; MB, DTM&H Sydney; Vice-Chancellor, University of Papua and New Guinea; Assistant Administrator, Papua and New Guinea, 1957-66; MEC and MLC, Papua and New Guinea; *b* 2 Oct. 1910; *s* of C. M. Gunther; *m* 1938; one *s* three *d*. *Educ:* King's Sch.; Sydney Univ. Dir of Public Health, Papua and New Guinea, 1949-56; Levers Pacific Plantations Pty Ltd, Brit. Solomon Is, 1935-37; Chm., Med. Bd (Mt Isa, Qld), investigating Plumbism, 1938-41; MO, RAAF, 1941-46; Malariologist, RAAF, 1943; CO 1 Trop. Research Fld Unit, 1944-45; Mem. S Pacific Commn Research Coun. (Chm. 1st meeting); Chm. Select Cttee on Polit. Devel t for Papua and NG; Mem. Commn on Higher Educn, Papua and NG. *Publications:* reports to govt of Qld on Plumbism, 1939-40; reports to RAAF on Malaria and Scrub Typhus. *Recreation:* gardening. *Address:* Port Moresby, Papua and New Guinea. *T:* 4223. *Club:* University (Sydney).

**GUPPY, Ronald James,** CB 1967; Secretary, Commission on the Constitution, since 1969; *b* 7 July 1916; *s* of late James Guppy; *m* 1943, Elsie Fuller; one *s* one *d*. *Educ:* Victoria Coll., Jersey; St John's Coll. Cambridge. Home Office, 1939-67. Served War of 1939-45, in RE and RA. Principal Private Sec. to Home Sec., 1953-55; Asst Sec., 1955; Asst Under-Sec. of State: Home Office, 1961-67; Dept of Educn and Science, 1967-69. *Address:* Rozel House, Broad Lane, Hampton-on-Thames, Mddx. *T:* 01-979 2409. *Club:* Oxford and Cambridge.

**GURD, Surg. Rear-Adm. Dudley Plunket,** CB 1968; Medical Officer-in-Charge, Royal Naval Hospital, Malta, 1966-69; now in private practice; *b* 18 June 1910; *s* of Frederick Plunket Gurd and Annie Jane Glenn; *m* 1939, Thérèse Marie, *d* of John and Frances Delenda,

Salonika, Greece; one *s* one *d. Educ:* Belfast Royal Academy; Queen's Univ., Belfast, MB, BCh, BAO (Hons) 1932; MD (High Commend) 1942; FRACS 1945; MCh 1959; FRCS (Eng.) 1964. Gilbert Blane Medal, 1943. Sen. Consultant and Adviser in Ophthalmology to the Navy, 1952; Warden, Ophthalmic Hosp. of St John, Jerusalem, Jordan, 1952-55. Joined RN as Surg. Lieut, 1934; Lieut-Comdr 1939; Comdr 1945; Capt. 1958; Rear-Adm. 1966; retired 1969; Served in Royal Naval Hosps at Malta, Barrow Gurney, Hong Kong, Plymouth and Haslar. QHS 1964. KStJ 1967. Hon. DSc QUB, 1969. Chevalier de l'Ordre Nationale du Viet-Nam, 1949; Gold Cross, Order of Holy Sepulchre, 1955. *Publications:* various contribs to ophthalmic literature. *Recreations:* interested in all kinds of sport and athletics, also in languages, religion and medical education. *Address:* Shanklin Lodge, Eastern Villas Road, Southsea, Hants. *Clubs:* Athenæum; Union (Malta).

**GURDEN, Harold Edward;** MP (C) Selly Oak Division of Birmingham, since 1955; *s* of late Arthur William and late Ada Gurden; *m* Lucy Isabella Izon; three *d.* Birmingham City Council, Selly Oak Ward, 1946-56; Pres. Birmingham and Dist Dairyman's Assoc., 1947-50; Chm. Soc. of Dairy Technology, Midland Div.; Pres.-Elect, Nat. Dairyman's Assoc., 1951; Chm., Northfield Div. Conservative Assoc., 1950-52. Mem. of Speaker's Panel, House of Commons, 1966. *Recreations:* bridge, golf, numismatics. *Address:* House of Commons, SW1.

**GURDON,** family name of **Baron Cranworth.**

**GURION, David B.;** *see* Ben-Gurion.

**GURNEY, Norman William,** CBE 1959; JP; retired land agent; *b* 4 May 1880; *s* of James and Elizabeth Gurney; *m* 1910, Millicent Surman (*d* 1960), two *s. Educ:* St George's Sch., Harpenden. County Council, 1922, CA 1934-70, JP 1938, Bucks; High Sheriff, Bucks, 1952. Member: Amersham RDC, 1922-49 (Chm., 1927-41); Beaconsfield UDC, 1922-47 (Chm. 1938); Chairman: Bucks Agricultural Wages Bd, 1948-69; Bucks Local Valuation Panel, 1952-67; Chalfont & District Permanent Building Soc., 1940-; Pres. Bucks Parish Councils Assoc., 1947-65; Chm. Bucks County Council, 1947-62. Horner and Freeman of City of London. Served City of London Rough Riders, S Africa, 1902; Worcs Regt European War, 1914-18, Capt. *Address:* Woodlands, Beaconsfield, Bucks. *T:* 3184.

**GURNEY, Oliver Robert,** MA DPhil Oxon; FBA 1959; Shillito Reader in Assyriology, Oxford University, since 1945; Professor, 1965; Fellow of Magdalen College, 1963; *b* 28 Jan. 1911; *s* of Robert Gurney, DSc, and Sarah Gamzu, *d* of Walter Garstang, MD, MRCP; *m* 1957, Mrs Diana Hope Grazebrook (*née* Esencourt); no *c. Educ:* Eton Coll.; New Coll., Oxford. Served War of 1939-45, in Royal Artillery and Sudan Defence Force. Freeman of City of Norwich. *Publications:* The Hittites (Penguin), 1952; (with J. J. Finkelstein and P. Hulin) The Sultantepe Tablets, 1957, 1964; (with John Garstang) The Geography of the Hittite Empire, 1959. Articles in Annals of Archæology and Anthropology (Liverpool), Anatolian Studies, etc. *Recreations:* lawn tennis, golf. *Address:* Bayworth Corner, Boar's Hill, Oxford. *T:* Oxford 35322.

**GUSEV, F. T.;** *see* Gousev.

**GUTCH, Sir John,** KCMG 1957 (CMG 1952); OBE 1947; *b* 12 July 1905; *s* of late Clement Gutch, MA, King's Coll., Cambridge, and late Isabella Margaret Newton; *m* 1938, Diana Mary Worsley; three *s. Educ:* Aldenham Sch.; Gonville amd Caius Coll., Cambridge. Classical scholar, 1924; 1st class Classical Tripos, Part I, 1926; 2nd class Classical Tripos, Part II, 1927; BA 1927; MA 1931. Cadet, Colonial Administrative Service, 1928; Asst District Commissioner, Gold Coast, 1928; Asst Colonial Secretary, Gold Coast, 1935; Asst Secretary, Palestine, 1936, Principal Asst Secretary, 1944, Under Sec., 1945; Asst Sec., Middle East Department, Colonial Office, 1947; Chief Secretary, British Administration, Cyrenaica, 1948; Adviser to the Prime Minister, Government of Cyrenaica, 1949; Chief Secretary, British Guiana, 1950-54; High Commissioner for Western Pacific, 1955-60. British Electric Traction Co. Ltd, 1961-69; Dir, Aldershot and District Traction Co. Ltd, 1970-. Member: Governing Body, Aldenham School; Cttee of Management, Institute of Opthalmology. *Address:* Littleworth Cross, Seale, near Farnham, Surrey. *T:* Runfold 2081.

**GUTHRIE, Douglas James,** MD, DLitt, FRCSE, FRCPE, FRSE; Formerly Lecturer on History of Medicine, Edinburgh University; Cons. Aural Surgeon, Edinburgh Royal Hospital for Sick Children; *b* 8 Sept. 1885; *s* of late Rev. William Guthrie, Dysart, Fife; *m* 1st, 1909, Helen (*d* 1950), *d* of James Stark, Glasgow and Rangoon; 2nd, 1953, Margaret Jean, *d* of James Guthrie, Dunblane. *Educ:* Edinburgh, Jena and Paris. MB, ChB (with Hons), 1907; DLitt Edinburgh, 1967. awarded McCosh Travelling Scholarship post graduate study in Hamburg, Jena, Berlin and Vienna; engaged in general practice for six years; MD, 1909; FRCS, 1913; FRCP, 1961; served RAMC for 2 years and later with RAF as Commandant, RAF Officers Hospitals; specialised in Otology and Laryngology, 1919-; retired from practice, 1946; Ear and Throat Surgeon, Royal Hospital for Sick Children and Surgeon to Ear and Throat Infirmary, 1919; Lecturer on Diseases of Ear, Nose and Throat, School of Medicine of Royal Colleges, Edinburgh, 1920; Lecturer on History of Medicine, University of Edinburgh, 1945-56; FRSM 1920, and since then Member of Council, Sections of Otology and Laryngology, 1956-57; President, Section of Otology, 1936-37, Section History of Medicine, 1956-57; Assistant Editor, Journal of Laryngology, 1921-29; President: Edinburgh Branch, BMA, 1935-36; Founder and Hon. President Scottish Society of History of Medicine, 1948; Royal Physical Society; FSA; Hon. FRSGS, 1958; Vice-President, Royal Society of Edinburgh, 1960; President, British Society for History of Medicine, 1965. Hon. FRSM 1967. *Publications:* A History of Medicine, 1945; Lord Lister, His Life and Doctrine, 1949; From Witchcraft to Antisepsis (Clendening Lectures, University Kansas), 1954; Janus in the Doorway, 1964; and many papers on otolaryngology and on the history of medicine. *Recreations:* travel, photography, writing. *Address:* 21 Clarendon Crescent, Edinburgh EH4 1PU. *T:* 031-332 1820. *Club:* New (Edinburgh).

**GUTHRIE, Sir Giles (Connop McEacharn),** 2nd Bt, *cr* 1936; OBE 1946; DSC 1941; JP; Merchant Banker; Chairman, Air Transport Insurance SA, Lausanne, Switzerland; *b* 21 March 1916; *s* of Sir Connop Guthrie, 1st Bt, KBE, and late Eila, *d* of Sir Malcolm McEacharn of Galloway House, Wigtownshire; *S* father, 1945; *m* 1939, Rhona, *d* of late Frederic Stileman and Mrs Stileman, Jersey, CI; two *s* (and one *s* decd). *Educ:* Eton; Magdalene Coll., Cambridge. Winner with late

C. W. A. Scott, of Portsmouth-Johannesburg Air Race, 1936; Served War of 1939-46 in Fleet Air Arm, Lieutenant Commander, 1943. Chairman and Chief Executive, BOAC, 1964-68; Mem. Bd, BEA, 1959-68; formerly: a Man. Dir, Brown Shipley & Co. Ltd; Dep. Chm., North Central Finance Ltd; Director: Prudential Assurance Co; Radio Rentals Ltd, and other cos. Governor, The London Hospital, 1965-68; a Vice-Chairman, 1968. JP West Sussex, 1955. *Heir: s* Malcolm Connop Guthrie [*b* 16 Dec. 1942; *m* 1967, Victoria, *o d* of late Brian Willcock and of Mrs Willcock, Belbroughton, Worcs; one *d*]. *Address:* Rozel, Jersey, Channel Islands. *Clubs:* MCC; Royal Yacht Squadron (Cowes).

**GUTHRIE, Air Vice-Marshal Kenneth MacGregor,** CB 1946; CBE 1944; CD 1948; retired; *b* 9 Aug. 1900; *s* of Rev. Donald and Jean Stirton Guthrie; *m* 1926, Kathleen Mary Fidler; one *d*. *Educ:* Baltimore, USA; Montreal and Ottawa, Canada. RFC and RAF, 1917-19; RCAMC 1919-20; Canadian Air Board and RCAF since 1920. Asst Director of Military and Air Force Intelligence, General Staff, Ottawa, 1935-38; CO, RCAF Station, Rockcliffe, 1938-39; Senior Air Staff Officer, Eastern Air Command, 1939-41; CO, RCAF Station, Gander, Nfld, 1941; Air Officer i/c Administration, Western Air Command, 1942; Deputy Air Member Air Staff (Plans) AFHQ, Dec. 1942-44; AOC Northwest Air Command, RCAF, 1944-49. Retired, 1949. Legion of Merit (USA), 1946. *Recreations:* hunting, fishing, gardening. *Address:* 12809 Stony Plain Road, Edmonton, Canada. *Clubs:* Garrison Officers' (Edmonton); Royal Vancouver Yacht (Vancouver).

**GUTHRIE, Prof. Malcolm,** PhD, BSc; FBA 1968; Professor of Bantu Languages, University of London, 1951-70, Professor Emeritus 1970; Head of Department of African Languages and Cultures, School of Oriental and African Studies, 1950-68; *b* 10 Feb. 1903; *s* of Malcolm Guthrie and Maude Louise Lindeboom; *m* 1931, Margaret Helen Near (*d* 1968). *Educ:* Northgate, Ipswich; University of London. Missionary, Belgian Congo, 1932-41; Lecturer in Bantu Languages, London, 1942-47; Reader in Bantu Languages, 1947-51. *Publications:* Grammaire et Dictionnaire de Lingala, 1939; The Classification of the Bantu Languages, 1948; Bantu Word Division, 1948; The Bantu Languages of Western Equatorial Africa, 1953; Comparative Bantu, Vol. 1, 1967, vols 3 and 4, 1970; Collected Papers in Bantu Linguistics, 1970; articles in Bulletin of School of Oriental and African Studies, Africa, African Language Studies. *Address:* Brambletye, Cowden, Kent.

**GUTHRIE, Robin Craig;** RP 1961; portrait, genre and landscape painter and draughtsman; Member of: Royal Society of Portrait Painters; Society of Mural Painters; Past Member of NEAC; *b* Harting, Hampshire, 15 June 1902; *s* of late James Joshua Guthrie and of Marion Stuart Craig; *m* Cathleen Maltby; one *s*; *m* Deborah Dering; one *d* (one *s* decd). *Educ:* Home; Slade Sch.; University College, London. Exhibited first at Goupil Gallery, also at New English Art Club, Royal Academy, etc., and abroad; One-man exhibitions: Goupil Gallery, 1926, Fine Art Society, 1939, Colnaghi's Gallery, 1946; paintings and drawings have been acquired by or presented to the Tate Gallery, Victoria and Albert Museum, National Portrait Gallery, British Museum, Contemporary Art Society, the Duveen Fund, Manchester Art Gallery, Manchester Whitworth Institute, Stoke-on-Trent Art Gallery, National Gallery of Canada, Fogg Art Museum, Cambridge, Mass., USA, and National Gallery of New South Wales; National War Records Collection; Director of Boston Museum School of Fine Art, USA, 1931-33; Instructor in drawing at the Royal College of Art, 1950-52; Instructor: St Martin's School of Art; City and Guilds of London Art School. Has painted Royal and commemorative occasions for Royal Marines, Royal Scots Greys and Royal Tank Regiments. *Publications:* illustrated editions from the Pear Tree Press, the Morland Press, etc. *Recreation:* fishing. *Address:* 1 Sydney Close, 76 Fulham Road, SW3. *T:* 01-584 1726. *Club:* Chelsea Arts.

**GUTHRIE, Hon. Sir Rutherford (Campbell),** Kt 1968; CMG 1960; *b* 28 Nov. 1899; *s* of late Thomas O. Guthrie, Rich Avon, Donald; *m* 1927, Rhona Mary McKellar, *d* of late T. McKellar; two *s*. *Educ:* Melbourne Church of England Grammar Sch;; Jesus Coll., Cambridge (BA). Farmer and grazier, Skipton, Victoria. Served European War of 1914-18 and War of 1939-45 (wounded, despatches): 9 Australian Div., Alamein. MP Ripon, Victoria, 1947-50; Minister for Lands and for Soldier Settlement, Australia, 1948-50. Director: Phosphate Co-op Co. Ltd; Perpetual Executors & Trustees Association. *Recreations:* fishing and golf. *Address:* Warrawidgee, Linton, Victoria, Australia. *Clubs:* Melbourne, Naval and Military; Royal Melbourne Golf; Hawks, Pitt (Cambridge); Leander.

**GUTHRIE, Sir Tyrone;** *see* Guthrie, Sir W. T.

**GUTHRIE, William Keith Chambers,** LittD; FBA; Master of Downing College, Cambridge, since 1957; Hon. Fellow of Peterhouse, Cambridge; Laurence Professor of Ancient Philosophy; Public Orator of the University, 1939-57; *b* 1 Aug. 1906; *s* of Charles Jameson Guthrie; *m* 1933, Adele Marion Ogilvy, MA; one *s* one *d*. *Educ:* Dulwich Coll.; Trinity Coll., Cambridge. Browne Scholar, 1927. Craven Student, 1928, Chancellor's Classical Medallist, 1929; Member of expeditions of American Society for Archaeological Research in Asia Minor, 1929, 1930 and 1932; Bye-Fellow of Peterhouse, 1930, Fellow, 1932-57; University Proctor, 1936-37; P. M. Laurence Reader in Classics, 1947-52; Intelligence Corps, 1941-45 (temp. Major 1945); Messenger Lecturer, Cornell Univ., 1957; James B. Duke Visiting Professor of Philosophy, Duke Univ., 1966. President, Classical Assoc., 1967-68. LittD Cambridge, 1959; Hon. DLitt: Melbourne, 1957; Sheffield, 1967. *Publications:* Monumenta Asiae Minoris Antiqua, IV (with W. M. Calder and W. H. Buckler), 1933; Orpheus and Greek Religion, 1935 (repr. 1952); Aristotle De Caelo, text, trans., introduction and notes (Loeb Classical Library), 1939; The Greek Philosophers, 1950; The Greeks and their Gods, 1950; F. M. Cornford, The Unwritten Philosophy (edited with a memoir by W. K. C. G.), 1950; Greek Philosophy: The Hub and the Spokes (Inaugural Lecture), 1953; In the Beginning: some Greek views of the origins of life and the early state of man, 1957; A History of Greek Philosophy, Vols 1-3, 1962-69. Contributions to various classical journals. *Address:* Downing College, Cambridge CB2 1DQ. *T:* Cambridge 56638.

**GUTHRIE, Sir (William) Tyrone,** Kt 1961; Chancellor, Queen's University, Belfast, 1963-70; *b* 2 July 1900; *s* of Thomas Clement Guthrie, surgeon; *m* 1931, Judith, *d* of E. G. Bretherton; no *c*. *Educ:* Wellington Coll.; St John's Coll., Oxford. Administrator Old Vic and Sadler's Wells, 1939-45; Director of the

Old Vic. 1951-52; founded Tyrone Guthrie Theatre, Minneapolis, 1963. Many productions in London, New York, also Australia, Finland, Israel; Repertory and Tour, including musical comedy, farce, opera, but mostly of classical nature. Hon. Fellow, St John's Coll., Oxford, 1964. Hon. DLitt: Trinity Coll., Dublin, 1964; Queen's Univ., Belfast; St Andrews Univ.; Franklyn and Marshall Univ., Penn., USA; University of Western Ontario; Ripon Coll., Wisconsin, USA; Citadel Military Coll., Charleston, SC. *Publications:* Squirrel's Cage, The Flowers Are Not For You To Pick, and Matrimonial News (microphone plays), 1931; Theatre Prospect, 1932; Top of the Ladder, 1950; A Life in the Theatre, 1960; A New Theatre, 1964; In Several Directions, 1965; (ed) Three Plays of Armand Salacrou, 1968. *Address:* Annagh-ma-Kerrig, Doohat, Newbliss, Co. Monaghan, Eire.

**GUTT, Camille;** Belgian Minister of State; became one of partners in Banque Lambert, 1951; *b* Brussels, 14 Nov. 1884; *s* of Max Gutt and Pauline Schweizer; *m* 1906, Claire Frick; one *s* (and two *s* killed on active service). *Educ:* Brussels University (graduated in Political and Social Sciences, 1904; Doctor of Law, 1906). Barrister and journalist, 1906; Volunteer in Belgian Army, 1914-18; Secretary-General of Belgian War Material Purchasing Commission, London, 1916; Secretary-General of Belgian Delegation to Reparations Commission, Aug. 1919; Chief Secretary (Chef de Cabinet) to Belgian Minister of Finance, 1920. Assistant Delegate for Belgium to Reparations Commission, 1924; Assistant to M. Francqui, Chancellor of the Exchequer, 1926; Belgian Member of the Young Cttee, Jan. 1929; Plenipotentiary for Belgium in discussions which led to an agreement with Germany about reimbursement of the Marks of Occupation in June 1929; Plenipotentiary for Belgium in negotiations connected with the Hoover Moratorium, 1931; sent on official mission to USA, May 1934; Minister of Finance in the Theunis Cabinet, Nov. 1934; Minister of Finance in the Pierlot Cabinet, Feb. 1939; arrived in London, Aug. 1940; Minister of Finance, 1939-45, National Defence, 1940-42, Communications, 1940-42, and Economic Affairs, 1940-45; Man. Dir International Monetary Fund, 1946-51; President International Chamber of Commerce, 1955. Grand Cordon de l'Ordre de Léopold; Grand Cross of the Order of the British Empire (GBE); Grand Cordon de l'Ordre d'Orange Nassau; Grand Cordon de l'Ordre de la Couronne de Chêne; Grand Cordon de l'Ordre pour le Mérite; Grand Officier de l'Ordre de la Légion d'Honneur; and various other distinctions including war medals, 1914-18. *Publications:* Pourquoi le franc belge est tombé, 1935; numerous articles in daily newspapers and magazines. *Recreation:* racing. *Address:* 70 avenue Bel Air, Brussels.

**GUTTERIDGE, Joyce Ada Cooke,** CBE 1962; retired; *b* 10 July 1906; *d* of late Harold Cooke Gutteridge, QC, and late Mary Louisa Gutteridge (*née* Jackson). *Educ:* Roedean Sch.; Somerville Coll., Oxford. Called to the Bar, Middle Temple, Nov. 1938. Served in HM Forces (ATS), War of 1939-45. Foriegn Office: Legal Assistant, 1947-50; Asst Legal Adviser, 1950-60; Legal Counsellor, 1960-61; Counsellor (Legal Adviser), UK Mission to the United Nations, 1961-64; Legal Counsellor, FO, 1964-66; re-employed on legal duties, FO, 1966-67. Hon. LLD, Western College for Women, Oxford, Ohio, 1963. *Publications:* articles in British Year Book of International Law and International and Comparative Law Quarterly. *Recreations:* reading, travel. *Address:* 8 Westberry Court, Grange Road, Cambridge. *Clubs:* (Associate Lady Member) Oxford and Cambridge, University Women's.

**GUTTMANN, Sir Ludwig,** Kt 1966; CBE 1960 (OBE 1950); MD, FRCP, FRCS; FRSA; Emeritus Consultant, Stoke Mandeville Hospital; Director: National Spinal Injuries Centre, Stoke Mandeville Hospital, Aylesbury, 1944-66; Stoke Mandeville Sports Stadium for the Paralysed and other Disabled, since 1969; Consultant to: Duchess of Gloucester House (Ministry of Labour) 1950; Star and Garter Home for Ex-Servicemen, Richmond; Chasely Home for Ex-Servicemen, Eastbourne; *b* 3 July 1899; *s* of Bernhard and Dorothea Guttmann; *m* 1927, Else (*née* Samuel); one *s* one *d*. *Educ:* Breslau and Freiburg Universities (Germany). MD Freiburg, 1924; MRCP, 1947. FRCS, 1961; Hon. DChir Durham, 1961; FRCP, 1962 Hon. LLD Dublin, 1969. Lecturer in Neurology, University of Breslau, 1930; Director, Dept of Neurology and Neuro-Surgery, Jewish Hospital, Breslau, 1933-39; Research Fellow, Dept of Surgery, Oxford Univ. (Senior Common Room, Balliol Coll.) 1939-43; Founder of Stoke Mandeville Games, 1948. First Albee Memorial Lecturer (Kessler Institute, New Jersey, USA), 1952; Ord. Professor (Emeritus), University Cologne, Germany, 1954. FRSocMed; Hon. Member of Medical Societies. President: Med. International Society of Paraplegia, 1961-69; British Sports Association for the Disabled, 1962; International Sports Association for the Disabled, 1966. OStJ 1957. Hon. Freeman, Borough of Aylesbury, Bucks., 1962. Commandeur de l'Ordre Oeuvre Humanitaire, France, 1952; First Recipient of Rehabilitation Prize, World Veterans Federation, 1954; Gold Medal for Verdiensten, Holland, 1958; Commendatore dell' ordine Al Merito, Italy, 1961; Officer, Order Oranje-Nassau, Holland, 1962; Grand Cross of Merit, Germany, 1962; Commandeur de l'Ordre de Léopold II, Belgium, 1963; Ordre du Mérite Combattant, France, 1963; Order of the Rising Sun, Japan, 1964. *Publications:* Vol. VII Handbuch der Neurologie (Germany), 1936; Surgical Practice Vols 2 and 6, 1948 and 1949; Vol. Surgery, Official British Medical History of Second World War, 1953; Modern Trends in Diseases of the Vertebral Column, 1959. Editor International Journal, Paraplegia, 1962. *Recreations:* sport, photography, travelling. *Address:* Menorah, Daws Hill Lane, High Wycombe, Bucks. *T:* High Wycombe 27678. *Club:* Athenæum.

**GUY, Rt. Rev. Basil Tudor;** *see* Gloucester, Bishop of.

**GUY, Geoffrey Colin,** CMG 1964; CVO 1966; OBE 1962 (MBE 1957); *b* 4 Nov. 1921; *s* of E. Guy, 14 Woodland Park Road, Headingley, Leeds, and Constance Reed Taylor; *m* 1946, Joan Elfreda Smith. *Educ:* Chatham House Sch., Ramsgate; Brasenose Coll., Oxford. Served as Pilot, RAF, 1941-46, Middle East and Burma (Flight Lieut). Colonial Administrative Service, Sierra Leone: Cadet, 1951; District Commissioner, 1955; seconded Administrator, Turks and Caicos Islands, 1958-65; Administrator, Dominica, 1965-67, Governor, March-Nov. 1967. *Recreations:* swimming, riding. *Address:* Tamarisk Cottage, Kirk Hammerton, York. *Club:* Royal Commonwealth Society.

**GUY, Hon. James Allan,** CBE 1968; JP; MEC; Senator, Australian Parliament, 1949 and 1951, retired 1956; *b* Launceston, Tas, 30 Nov. 1890; *s* of James Guy, Senator in

Commonwealth Parliament, and Margaret McElwee; *m* 1st, 1916, Amy Louisa Adams (*d* 1951); one *s*; 2nd, 1952, Madge Kernohan. *Educ:* Tasmanian State Education. Member for Bass in Tasmania State Parliament, 1916-29; Chief Secretary and Minister for Mines, 1923-24; Chief Secretary and Minister for Railways, 1924-28; Deputy Premier, 1925-28; acting Premier, July 1926-Dec. 1926; Deputy Leader of the Opposition, June 1928-Sept. 1929. Member for Bass in Commonwealth Parliament, 1929-34; Asst Minister of State for Trade and Customs, 1932-34; Member for Wilmot, 1940-46; Government Whip, 1941-42; Opposition Whip, 1942-46. Represented Tasmanian Government at the opening of the Commonwealth Parliament at Canberra, May 1927; Member: Commonwealth Parliamentary Joint Cttee of Public Accounts, 1929-31; Commonwealth Parliamentary Standing Cttee on Broadcasting; Senate Standing Cttee on Regulations and Ordinances, 1950-55; Empire Parliamentary Delegation visiting Great Britain, Canada, and America, 1943; Temp. Chairman of Committees. Life Title of "Honourable" conferred by King George VI, 1936. Alderman Launceston City Council, 1928-31. *Recreations:* motoring, bowling. *Address:* 166 George Street, Launceston, Tasmania 7250. *TA:* Launceston. *T:* Launceston 2-4555; (business) Box 109 B, GPO, Launceston, Tasmania 7250.

**GUY, Oswald Vernon,** CBE 1947; DSO 1918; MA; *b* 15 Dec. 1890; *s* of late Rev. Canon D. S. Guy; *m* 1920, Ethel Frances (*d* 1964), *d* of late Colonel R. K. Teversham, DSO, OBE. *Educ:* Marlborough; Jesus Coll., Cambridge. 9th PWO West Yorkshire Regt, Sept. 1914; Tank Corps, 1917-19 (Major, DSO, MC and bar, Legion of Honour). Secretary, Cambridge Univ. Appointments Board, 1932-52; Temp. Assistant Secretary Ministry of Labour, 1940-44. *Address:* Teversham, Orchard Close, Ferndown, Dorset.

**GUY, Sydney Slater,** FIMechE, MIEE, MSAE; Founder of Guy Motors Ltd (1913), Chairman and Managing Director of the Company, retired 1957 (organizations acquired by Jaguar Co. in 1961, subsequently by Leyland Motor Group); *b* 31 Oct. 1884; *m* Leila Brooks, Hale Barns; two *s* one *d*. Pupil, Bellis & Morcom; Repairs Manager, Humber Ltd, 1905-08; Works Manager, Sunbeam Motor Car Co. Ltd, 1908-13. Council Member, Society Motor Manufacturers, for 33 years; Vice-President 1928-29; Hon. Member, 1957. Responsible for first British V8 cylinder car in 1919 and first rear engined 4 wheel driven armoured car in 1937. Past President: Flatcoated Retriever Association; Leintwardine Fishing Club. Liveryman Worshipful Company of Carmen. FRSA. *Publications:* various. *Recreations:* fly fishing, shooting, photography. *Address:* Sauchieleigh, Albrighton, Salop. *T:* Albrighton 2288. *Clubs:* Royal Automobile; Royal Anglesey Yacht.

**GUYANA, Bishop of;** *see* West Indies, Archbishop of.

**GUYMER, Maurice Juniper,** DL; JP; Metropolitan Stipendiary Magistrate, since 1967; *b* 29 Aug. 1914; *s* of Frank and Florence Mary Guymer. *Educ:* Northcliffe House, Bognor Regis; Westminster School. Admitted Solicitor, 1936. Served with RAF, 1940-45. Royal Borough of Kingston upon Thames: Council, 1953; Mayor, 1959-60 and 1960-61; Alderman, 1960-65; JP 1956. DL, Co. Surrey, 1960. *Address:* Desborough Cottage, 132 Lower Ham Road, Kingston upon Thames, Surrey. *T:* 01-546 5529.

**GWANDU, Emir of; Alhaji Haruna, (Muhammadu Basharu),** CMG 1961; CBE 1955; 18th Emir of Gwandu, 1954; President, Northern Nigeria House of Chiefs, since 1957 (Dep. President 1956); *b* Batoranke, 1911; *m* 1933; fifteen *c*. *Educ:* Birnin Kebbi Primary Sch.; Katsina Training Coll. Teacher, Sokoto, 1933-37; Gusau Native Admin. Sub-Treasurer, 1937-43; Birnin Kebbi Native Admin. Treas., 1943-45; District Head, Kalgo, 1945-54. Member N. Reg. Marketing Board. *Recreations:* hunting, shooting. *Address:* c/o Central Office, No. 1 Block, Birnin Kebbi, Sokoto Province, N. Nigeria.

**GWATKIN, Frank T. A. A.;** *see* Ashton-Gwatkin.

**GWATKIN, Brig. Sir Norman (Wilmshurst),** GCVO 1963; KCMG 1964; DSO 1944; Comptroller, Lord Chamberlain's Office, 1960-64; Secretary and Registrar of the Order of Merit since 1963; Extra Equerry to King George VI, 1950-52, to the Queen since 1952; *b* 2 Aug. 1899; *m* 1957, June Wilson. *Educ:* Clifton; Royal Military Coll. Coldstream Guards, 1918; Adjt 1st Bn Coldstream Guards; Adjt RMC, Sandhurst, 1930; Bt Major, 1935; Lieut-Colonel, 1940; retired pay, 1946. *Recreations:* shooting, fishing. *Address:* Bedwells, Knodishall, Saxmundham, Suffolk. *T:* Leiston 647. *Club:* United Service.

**GWILLIAM, John Albert,** MA Cantab; Headmaster of Birkenhead School, since Sept. 1963; *b* 28 Feb. 1923; *s* of Thomas Albert and Adela Audrey Gwilliam; *m* 1949, Pegi Lloyd George; three *s* two *d*. *Educ:* Monmouth Sch.; Trinity Coll., Cambridge. Assistant Master: Trinity Coll., Glenalmond, 1949-52; Bromsgrove Sch., 1952-56; Head of Lower Sch., Dulwich Coll., 1956-63. *Address:* The Lodge, Beresford Road, Birkenhead, Cheshire.

**GWILLIM, Calvert Merton,** MD, FRCS, FRCP; Obstetric Surgeon, St George's Hospital; Consulting Physician, Lying-in Hospital, York Road; Surgeon, Samaritan Hospital for Women. *Educ:* St Bartholomew's Hospital; St George's Hospital. DPH 1923; MD London (Obst. and Gyn.), 1924; MD (Med.), 1924; MRCS, LRCP 1921; MRCP, 1925; FRCS, 1927; FRCP, 1940; FRCOG, 1942. Formerly: Gynæcological Registrar and Obst. Tutor and Asst Medical Registrar, St George's Hospital; Registrar-General, Lying-in Hospital, York Road. FRSocMed; Member BMA. *Address:* 26 Alexandra Road, Reading, Berks RG1 5PD.

**GWILT, Richard Lloyd,** CBE 1953; FFA, FIA, FRSE; formerly General Manager and Actuary, Scottish Widows Fund and Life Assurance Society (retired 1961); Director, Scottish Widows' Fund; *b* 25 July 1901; *m* 1926, Marjory, 2nd *d* of late David Beveridge Mair; three *s* one *d*. *Educ:* George Watson's Coll., Edinburgh. FFA 1922; FIA 1923; President: Insurance Society of Edinburgh, 1951-52; Faculty of Actuaries, 1952-54. Chairman: Associated Scottish Life Offices, 1956-58; Scottish Hospital Endowments Research Trust, 1954-66; Dir, Scottish-American Investment Co. Ltd, 1939-69. *Publications:* contributions to actuarial journals. *Recreation:* fishing. *Address:* 23a Dick Place, Edinburgh. *T:* 031-667 6263. *Clubs:* Scottish Mountaineering; New (Edinburgh).

**GWYER, Barbara Elizabeth,** MA; Hon. Fellow, St Hugh's College, Oxford, since 1946; *o d* of late John Edward Gwyer. *Educ:* The Grove Sch., Highgate; Lady Margaret Hall, Oxford. Educational Organiser, WRCC Educational Dept, 1906-08; Vice-Warden, Ashburne Hall,

Manchester Univ., 1910-13; Warden, University Hall, Leeds, 1917-24; Principal, St Hugh's Coll., Oxford, 1924-46. *Address:* New Patch, Stokenchurch, High Wycombe, Bucks. *T:* Radnage 3368.

**GWYNEDD, Viscount; David Richard Owen Lloyd George;** *b* 22 Jan. 1951; *s* and *heir* of 3rd Earl Lloyd George of Dwyfor, *qv. Educ:* Eton.

**GWYNN, Denis Rolleston,** DLitt, MRIA, FRHistS; Member of the Irish Academy of Letters; Research Professor of Modern Irish History, University College, Cork, 1946-63; Editor Cork University Press, 1954-63; *b* 1893; *s* of late Stephen Gwynn; *m* 1963, Alice, widow of John A. McEnery and *d* of late Dr Edward Trudeau and Lady Lavery. *Educ:* Clongowes Wood Coll.; London University; National University of Ireland. Served in France as Lieut, Royal Munster Fusiliers; attached Ministry of Information; Assistant Editor Everyman and Review of Reviews, and Editor National Press Agency, 1918-20; spent three years as a journalist in France; London Editor, The Freeman's Journal, 1924; editorial staff, Westminster Gazette, 1925; literary adviser and a Director of Burns, Oates and Washbourne and Editor of the Dublin Review, 1933-39; contributor to leading reviews and to Encyclopædia Britannica and other encyclopædias. *Publications:* The Catholic Reaction in France; The Action Française Condemnation; The Irish Free State, 1922-27; The Struggle for Catholic Emancipation; A Hundred Years of Catholic Emancipation; Daniel O'Connell; Cardinal Wiseman; Edward Martyn and the Irish Revival; The Life and Death of Roger Casement; The Life of John Redmond; Pius XI; De Valera; The O'Gorman Mahon; The Vatican and War in Europe; The Second Spring; Lord Shrewsbury, Pugin and the Catholic Revival; Father Dominic Barberi; Bishop Challoner; Young Ireland and 1848; O'Connell, Davis and the Colleges Bill; The History of Partition, 1950; Father Luigi Gentili, 1951; Thomas Francis Meagher, 1962; (ed) Dr Walter McDonald's Reminiscences of a Maynooth Professor, 1967. *Address:* Rosenallis, Seamount Road, Malahide, Co. Dublin.

**GWYNN, Edward Harold,** CB 1961; Deputy Under-Secretary of State, Ministry of Defence, since 1966; *b* 23 Aug. 1912; *y s* of late Dr E. J. Gwynn, Provost of Trinity Coll., Dublin, and of Olive Ponsonby; *m* 1937, Dorothy, *d* of late Geoffrey S. Phillpotts, Foxrock, Co. Dublin; one *s* four *d. Educ:* Sedbergh School; TCD. Entered Home Office, 1936; Assistant Secretary, 1947; Assistant Under Secretary of State, 1956; Principal Finance Officer (Under-Secretary), Ministry of Agriculture, 1961-62; Deputy Under-Secretary of State, Home Office, 1963-66. *Recreation:* gardening. *Address:* Tyrrelcote, Woodcote Green Road, Epsom, Surrey. *T:* 20130. *Club:* Athenæum.

**GWYNNE, Lieut-Colonel Sir Roland Vaughan,** Kt 1957; DSO 1917; DL; JP; *s* of late James Eglinton Gwynne and Mary Earle Gwynne of Folkington Manor, Polegate, Sussex, and 97 Harley Street, W1; unmarried. *Educ:* privately; Trinity Hall, Cambridge. Called to Bar, Inner Temple, 1910; practised Probate and Divorce Courts; served in the Sussex Yeomanry since 1904; European War, commanded the 10th Queen's Royal West Surrey Regt (twice wounded, despatches, DSO); High Sheriff of Sussex, 1926-27; Mayor of Eastbourne, 1928-29, 1929-30, and 1930-31; Chairman, Hailsham Rural District Council, 1924-47; Alderman and Chairman of the East Sussex Co. Council, 1937-40; JP Sussex and Eastbourne; Chairman Hailsham Justices, 1932-, and Chairman Eastbourne Justices. *Address:* Wootton Manor, Folkington, Polegate, Sussex. *TA:* Gwynne, Polegate. *T:* Polegate 2036.

**GWYNNE-EVANS, Sir Ian William,** 3rd Bt, *cr* 1913; Managing Director and Chairman, Real Estate Corporation of South Africa Ltd, since 1950; *b* 21 Feb. 1909; *er s* of Sir Evan Gwynne-Evans, 2nd Bt; *m* 1st, 1935, Elspeth Collins (marr. diss.); two *d*; 2nd, 1945, Monica Dalrymple. *Educ:* Royal Naval College, Dartmouth. Entered Royal Navy as Cadet, 1922; retired as Lieut, 1934. Served War, 1940-45, Lieut, Royal Navy. *Recreation:* bowls. *Heir: b* Francis Loring Gwynne-Evans [*b* 22 Feb. 1914; *m* 1st, 1937, Elisabeth Fforde (marr. diss., 1958), *d* of J. Fforde Tipping; two *s* one *d*; 2nd, 1958, Gloria Marie Reynolds; two *s* three *d*]. *Address:* 57 Eastwood Road, Dunkeld, Johannesburg, S Africa. *Club:* Rand (Johannesburg).

**GWYNNE JONES,** family name of **Baron Chalfont.**

**GWYNNE-JONES, Allan,** DSO 1916; RA 1965 (ARA 1955); painter, etcher; *b* 27 March 1892; *s* of Ll. Gwynne-Jones; *m* 1937, Rosemary Elizabeth, *d* of H. P. Allan; one *d. Educ:* Bedales Sch. Abandoned study of law for painting; student at Slade School for a short time before the first European War, returned as student after war, 1919-23. Served European War, 1914-18: Lieut HM Welsh Guards (DSO, wounded twice, despatches twice). Professor of Painting, Royal College of Art till 1930 when appointed Staff, Slade School, retired from Slade, 1959. Trustee of Tate Gallery, 1939-46. Represented by pictures in the collections of HM The Queen and HM The Queen Mother, and in the Tate Gallery and the public galleries of Birmingham, Newcastle, Leeds, Oldham, Carlisle, Manchester, Sheffield, and Merthyr Tydfil, and the National Galleries of Wales, South Africa and Australia, and in the collections of the Arts Council and Contemporary Art Society; and by drawings, etchings and engravings in the British Museum, Victoria and Albert Museum, and National Museum of Wales. *Publications:* A Way of Looking at Pictures; Portrait Painters; Notes for art students; Introduction to Still-Life. *Address:* Eastleach Turville, near Cirencester, Glos. *T:* Southrop 214. *Club:* Athenæum.

**GYEE, Sir Maung,** Kt 1942; Burmese Ambassador in India, since 1949; *b* 1886; *s* of U San U of Shwegyin; *m* Ma Aye Yee; two *s* three *d. Educ:* Rangoon, Calcutta, London and Oxford. MA Calcutta, 1909; called to English Bar (Middle Temple), 1911. Minister of Education, Burma Government, 1923-25; Delegate to Round Table Conference, 1931; to Coronation, 1937; President of the Senate, 1937-40; Counsellor to Governor of Burma, 1940-42; Judge of Supreme Court, 1943-44; Minister for Public Works and Rehabilitation, Executive Council, 1946-47; High Commissioner for Burma in the UK, 1947; Ambassador of Republic of Burma in UK, Jan.-Oct. 1948. President Burma branch Empire Parliamentary Association. *Address:* Embassy of the Union of Burma, New Delhi, India; 313 Prome Road, Rangoon, Burma.

**GYÖRGYI, Albert S.;** *see* Szent-Györgyi.

# H

**HAARHOFF, T. J.,** BA (Cape), BLitt (Oxon), LittD (Amsterdam); FRSA (London); FIAL (Switzerland); Hon. DLitt: Natal; Cape Town; Emeritus Professor of Classics, University of the Witwatersrand, Johannesburg, South Africa; formerly South African Representative on UNESCO; a Governor of SA Broadcasting Corporation; *b* 30 April 1892; *s* of Rev. Dr B. J. Haarhoff, Inspector of Schools, Cape Province, and Magdalena Johanna Marais, Paarl, CP; *m* Jessie Kilburn Davis, MA (Oxon); two *s*. *Educ:* S. A. College Sch. and College, Cape Town; Porter Scholarship (Hon.) and Rhodes Scholarship, 1913; Worcester Coll., Oxford. Lecturer in English Literature, University, Cape Town, 1916; Lecturer in Classics, University, Cape Town, 1919. *Publications:* Schools of Gaul, 1920; Primi Gradus, 1922; Studies in Roman Imperialism (with Jan H. Hofmeyr), 1921; Die Romeinse Boer, 1925; Die Klassieke in S. Afrika, 1930; Tria Corda (Afrikaans Verse), 1930; Vergil in the Experience of S. Africa, 1931; Coming of Age: Essays in S. African Citizenship and Politics (with J. H. Hofmeyr and others), 1930; The Holistic Attitude in Education, 1932; Die liefde van Catullus (narrative poem), 1933; The Achievement of Afrikaans (with C. M. van den Heever), 1934; The Short Story in the Classics (Afrikaans), 2 vols, 1934; Afrikaans, its origin and development, 1936; Briewe aan Reinhard (Travels in the Aegean); The Stranger at the Gate: a study in racial co-operation, 1938; Life and Thought in the Greek and Roman World (with M. Cary), 1940; SA and the Crisis of Civilisation, 1940; Spiritual Evolution in S. Africa, 1945; Vergil the Universal, 1949; Why not be Friends?, 1957; The ABC of Afrikaans; Die Antieke Drama, I; Smuts the Humanist, 1970. *Recreation:* walking. *Address:* Almondbury, Stanford Road, Rondebosch, CP, S Africa.

**HABAKKUK, Hrothgar John,** FBA 1965; Principal of Jesus College, Oxford, since 1967; *b* 13 May 1915; *s* of Evan Guest and Anne Habakkuk; *m* 1948, Mary Richards; one *s* three *d*. *Educ:* Barry County Sch.; St John's Coll., Cambridge (scholar and Strathcona student). Historical Tripos: Part I, First Class, 1935. Part II, First Class (with distinction), 1936; Fellow, Pembroke Coll., Cambridge, 1938-50; Director of Studies in History and Librarian, 1946-50. Temporary Civil Servant: Foreign Office, 1940-42, Board of Trade, 1942-46. University Lecturer in Faculty of Economics, Cambridge, 1946-50; Chichele Prof. of Economic History, Oxford, and Fellow of All Souls Coll., 1950-67. Visiting Lecturer, Harvard University, 1954-55; Ford Research Professor, University of California, Berkeley, 1962-63. Member: Grigg Cttee on Departmental Records, 1952-54; Advisory Council on Public Records, 1958-; Social Science Research Council, 1967-; Nat. Libraries Cttee, 1968-69; Civil Service Arbitration Tribunal. Foreign Member: Amer. Phil. Soc.; Amer. Acad of Arts and Sciences. *Publications:* American and British Technology in the Nineteenth Century, 1962; articles and reviews. *Address:* The Lodgings, Jesus College, Oxford. *T:* Oxford 48140.

**HABGOOD, Rev. John Stapylton,** MA, PhD; Principal of Queen's College, Birmingham, since 1967; *b* 23 June 1927; *s* of Arthur Henry Habgood, DSO, MB, BCh, and Vera (*née* Chetwynd-Stapylton); *m* 1961, Rosalie Mary Anne Boston; one *s* two *d*. *Educ:* Eton; King's Coll., Cambridge; Cuddesdon Coll., Oxford. Univ. Demonstrator in Pharmacology, Cambridge, 1950-53; Fellow of King's Coll., Cambridge, 1952-55; Curate of St Mary Abbots, Kensington, 1954-56; Vice-Principal of Westcott House, Cambridge, 1956-62; Rector of St John's Church, Jedburgh, 1962-67. *Publication:* Religion and Science, 1964. *Recreation:* making toys. *Address:* Queen's College, Somerset Road, Birmingham B15 2QH. *T:* 021-454 1527.

**HACKER, Prof. Louis M.,** MA (Columbia); Emeritus Professor of Economics, Columbia University, USA, 1967 (Economics Department, 1935; Dean of School of General Studies, 1952-58, Director, 1949-52; Professor of Economics, 1948-67); *b* 17 March 1899; *s* of Morris Hacker; *m* 1st, 1921, Lillian Lewis (*d* 1952); one *s* one *d*.; 2nd, 1953, Beatrice Larson Brennan. *Educ:* Columbia Coll.; Columbia University. Assistant and contributing Editor of New International Encyclopædia, Social Science Encyclopædia, Columbia Encyclopædia; taught economics and history at University of Wisconsin, Ohio State University, Utah State Agricultural College, University of Hawaii, Yeshiva University, Penn State University, Univ. of Puget Sound, Army War College, National War College. Executive sec. American Academic Freedom Study; Editor, American Century Series; Chairman, Academic Freedom Cttee, American Civil Liberties Union, resigned 1968; Guggenheim Fellow, 1948, 1959; Relm Foundation Fellow, 1967. Harmsworth Professor of American History, Oxford Univ., 1948-49; Lecturer, Fulbright Conference on American Studies, Cambridge, 1952. Visiting Distinguished Professor of Economics, Fairleigh Dickinson, 1967-68. Fellow, Queen's Coll., Oxford, and MA (Oxon); Benjamin Franklin Fellow of RSA; Hon. LLD Hawaii. Students Army Training Corps, 1918. *Publications:* (with B. B. Kendrick) United States since 1865, 1932, 4th edn 1949; The Farmer is Doomed, 1933; Short History of the New Deal, 1934; The US: a Graphic History, 1937; American Problems of Today, 1939; Triumph of American Capitalism, 1940; (with Allan Nevins) The US and Its Place in World Affairs, 1943; The Shaping of the American Tradition, 1947; New Industrial Relations (jointly), 1948; Government Assistance and the British Universities (jointly), 1952; (with H. S. Zahler) The United States in the 20th Century, 1952; Capitalism and the Historians (jointly), 1954; Alexander Hamilton in the American Tradition, 1957; American Capitalism, 1957; Larger View of the University, 1961; Major Documents in American Economic History, 2 vols, 1961; The World of Andrew Carnegie, Part 1, 1861-1901, 1968; The Course of American Economic Growth and Development, 1970; contributions to learned journals and reviews. *Recreations:* walking, bridge, travel. *Address:* 430 W 116th Street, New York, NY 10027, USA. *Clubs:* Athenæum (London); Faculty, Columbia University (New York); Pilgrims (USA).

**HACKETT, Prof. Cecil Arthur,** MA Cantab, Docteur de l'Université de Paris; Professor of French, University of Southampton, since 1952; *b* 19 Jan. 1908; *s* of Henry Hackett and Alice Setchell; *m* 1942, Mary Hazel Armstrong. *Educ:* King's Norton Grammar Sch., Birmingham; University of Birmingham; Emmanuel Coll., Cambridge (Scholar and Prizeman). Assistant d'Anglais, Lycée Louis-le-Grand, Paris, 1934-36; Lecturer in French and English, Borough Road Coll., Isleworth, 1936-39. Served War of 1939-45: enlisted 1/8th Bn Middlesex Regt, 1939; Intelligence Corps in France, N Ireland, N Africa, Italy, 1940-45. Education Representative, British Council,

Paris, 1945-46; Lecturer in French, University of Glasgow, 1947-52. Chevalier de la Légion d'Honneur. *Publications:* Le Lyrisme de Rimbaud, 1938; Rimbaud l'Enfant, 1948; An Anthology of Modern French Poetry, 1952 (revised and enlarged edn 1967); Rimbaud, 1957; Autour de Rimbaud, 1967; contributions to English and French Reviews. *Address:* Shawford Close, Shawford, Winchester, Hants. *T:* Twyford 3506.

**HACKETT, Dennis William;** Director of Publicity, IPC Newspapers Ltd, since 1969; Proprietor of Twentieth Century; *b* 5 Feb. 1929; *s* of James Joseph Hackett and Sarah Ellen Hackett (*née* Bedford); *m* 1953, Agnes Mary Collins; two *s* one *d*. *Educ:* De La Salle College, Sheffield. Served with RN, 1947-49. Sheffield Telegraph, 1945-47 and 1949-54; Daily Herald, 1954; Odhams Press, 1954; Deputy Editor, Illustrated, 1955-58; Daily Express, 1958-60; Daily Mail, 1960; Art Editor, Observer, 1961-62; Deputy Editor, 1962, Editor, 1964-65, Queen; Editor, Nova, 1965; Editorial Dir, George Newnes Ltd, 1966-69; Dir in charge Mirror Magazine, 1969-70. FInstD. *Recreations:* reading, squash, riding. *Address:* 44 The Pryors, East Heath Road, Hampstead, NW3. *T:* 01-435 1368. *Club:* Royal Automobile.

**HACKETT, Felix E. W.,** PhD; Professor of Physics and Electrical Engineering, University College, Dublin, 1926-52; *b* 15 Aug. 1882; *s* of Daniel Hackett, Omagh; *m* Mary, *e d* of George Murnaghan, Omagh. *Educ:* University College, Dublin; Johns Hopkins University, Baltimore. Junior Fellow Royal University of Ireland, 1905-09; Lecturer in Physics, Royal College of Science, Dublin, 1909-21; Professor of Physics, Royal College of Science, Dublin, 1921-26; Dean Royal College of Science for Ireland, 1922-24; Treasurer Royal Irish Academy, 1930-62; President, Royal Dublin Society, 1953-56 (Hon. Secretary 1933-53, Vice-President 1956-); Chairman Governing Board, School of Theoretical Physics, Dublin Institute for Advanced Studies, 1951-; Member: Senate, NUI, 1934-54; Industrial Research Cttee, 1946-58; Standards Cttee (Chairman 1958-62, consultant 1963-), Institute for Industrial Research and Standards (Dublin); Library Council (Ireland). President, Irish Youth Hostel Association, 1944-67; Chairman Dublin Branch, Institute of Physics and Physical Society, 1964-66. *Address:* 20 Zion Road, Rathgar, Dublin 6.

**HACKETT, Gen. Sir John Winthrop,** GCB 1967 (KCB 1962; CB 1958); CBE 1953 (MBE 1938); DSO 1942 and Bar 1945; MC 1941; BLitt, MA Oxon; Principal of King's College, London, since 1968; *b* 5 Nov. 1910; *s* of late Sir John Winthrop Hackett, KCMG, LLD, Perth, WA; *m* 1942 Margaret, *d* of Joseph Frena, Graz, Austria; one *d* (and two adopted *step d*). *Educ:* Geelong Grammar Sch., Australia; New Coll., Oxford. Regular Army, commissioned 8th KRI Hussars, 1931; Palestine, 1936 (despatches); seconded to Transjordan Frontier Force, 1937-39 (despatches twice); Syria, 1941 (wounded); Sec. Commn of Control Syria and Lebanon; GSO2 9th Army; Western Desert, 1942 (wounded); GSO1 Raiding Forces GHQ, MELF; Comdr 4th Parachute Brigade, 1943; Italy, 1943 (despatches); Arnhem, 1944 (wounded); Comdr Transjordan Frontier Force, 1947; idc 1951; DQMG, BAOR, 1952; Comdr 20th Armoured Bde, 1954; GOC 7th Armoured Div., 1956-58; Comdt, Royal Mil. Coll. of Science, 1958-61; GOC-in-C, Northern Ireland Command, 1961-63; Dep. Chief of Imperial Gen. Staff, 1963-64; Dep. Chief of the Gen. Staff, Ministry of Defence, 1964-66. Comdr-in-Chief, British Army of the Rhine, and Comdr Northern Army Gp, 1966-68. ADC (Gen.), 1967-68. Col. Commandant, REME, 1961-66; Hon. Col: 10th Bn The Parachute Regt, TA, 1965-67; 10th Volunteer Bn, The Parachute Regt, 1967-; Oxford Univ. Officers Training Corps, 1967-; Col, Queen's Royal Irish Hussars, 1969-. Hon. LLD: Queen's Univ. Belfast; Perth, WA, 1963. Fellow King's Coll., London, 1968; Hon. Fellow St George's Coll., University of Western Australia, 1965. *Address:* 48 Aubrey Walk, W8; Loughros, Lifford, Co. Donegal. *Clubs:* Cavalry, Carlton, United University, White's.

**HACKETT, Sir Maurice Frederick,** Kt 1970; OBE 1958; Chairman: SE Region Economic Planning Council, since 1966; NW Metropolitan Regional Hospital Board, since 1965 (Member since 1949); Member, Land Commission, since 1969; *b* Wood Green, N22, 11 Nov. 1905; British; *m* 1924, Deborah Levene (*d* 1969); one *s*. *Educ:* Glendale Secondary Sch., Wood Green. Press Dept, Labour Party Headquarters, 1935-40. With Min. of Information, then Central Office of Information, 1940-65 (Head of Speakers' Sect.; Chief Reg. Officer, London SE Region; Head of Tours Divn). 1st Nat. Chm., Labour Party League of Youth; Chm., Southgate, Sth Kensington, Barnet and Herts Federation Labour Parties. Mem., East Barnet UDC, 1942-46. Chairman: Barnet Group Hosp. Management Cttee, 1948-60; St Bernards Hosp. Management Cttee, 1960-62; SW Middx Hosp. Management Cttee, 1962-65; Mem., Gen. Nursing Council for England and Wales, 1969-. *Recreations:* cinema, travel. *Address:* 2 Chesterfield House, South Grove, Highgate, N6. *T:* 01-348 2667.

**HACKING,** family name of **Baron Hacking.**

**HACKING,** 2nd Baron, *cr* 1945, of Chorley; **Douglas Eric Hacking,** 2nd Bt, *cr* 1938; Major RA; BA (Cantab); *b* 7 Dec. 1910; *s* of 1st Baron, PC, OBE, DL, JP, and Margery Allen, OBE 1956, *e d* of late H. H. Bolton, JP, Newchurch-in-Rossendale; *S* father 1950; *m* 1936, Daphne Violet, *e d* of late Robert Leslie Finnis, Kensington, W; two *s* two *d*. *Educ:* Charterhouse; Clare Coll., Cambridge. Admitted Solicitor, 1935; Partner, Baileys, Shaw & Gillett, 1945-64. Mem. North West Metropolitan Regional Hospital Board, 1953-60; Pres., National Deaf Children's Soc.; Governor: Middlesex Hospital, 1953-56, St Mary's Hospital, 1956-59; University Coll. Hospital, 1959-65; Star and Garter Home for Disabled Sailors, Soldiers and Airmen, 1955-65; Member: Council British Travel and Holidays Association; Council of Trust Houses Group Ltd (Chm.); Nat. Council for Care of Old People; Chm. of Trustees of Whiteley Homes. Directorships include: Gen. Accident Fire & Life Assurance Corp. Ltd; Incledon & Lamberts Ltd; Stud Stock (Internat.) Ltd; Associated, Grievson Grant & Co., Stockbrokers, 1964-66. Consultant, Wedlake Letts & Birds. Court of Worshipful Co. of Makers of Playing Cards. Served War of 1939-45, Royal Artillery. *Recreations:* listening to music, and watching most sports. *Heir: s* Hon. Douglas David Hacking [*b* 17 April 1938; *m* 1965, Rosemary Anne, *e d* of F. P. Forrest; one *s* one *d*]. *Address:* c/o Messrs Wedlake Letts & Birds, 6 Store Buildings, Lincolns Inn, WC2; 46 Phillimore Gardens, W8. *T:* 01-937 6070. *Clubs:* MCC, Pilgrims.
*See also Col G. G. H. Bolton.*

**HACKNEY, Archdeacon of;** *see* Hodgins, Ven. M. M.

**HACKNEY, Arthur,** RE 1960; RWS 1957; ARCA 1949; Head of Department (Printmaking), West Surrey College of Art and Design (Farnham Centre) (formerly Farnham School of Art), since 1968; *b* 13 March 1925; *s* of late J. T. Hackney; *m* 1955, Mary Baker, ARCA; two *d*. *Educ:* Burslem Sch. of Art; Royal Coll. of Art, London. Served in Royal Navy, 1942-46. Travelling scholarship, Royal College of Art, 1949; part-time Painting Instructor, Farnham Sch. of Art, 1949, Lecturer, 1962; Head of Dept (Graphic), 1963-68. Work represented in Public Collections, including Bradford City Art Gallery, Victoria and Albert Museum, Ashmolean Museum, Wellington Art Gallery (NZ), Nottingham Art Gallery, Keighley Art Gallery (Yorks.), Wakefield City Art Gallery, Graves Art Gallery, Sheffield, GLC, Preston Art Gallery; Kent Educn Cttee; Staffordshire Educn Cttee. *Address:* Woodhatches, Spoil Lane, Tongham, Surrey. *T:* Aldershot 23919. *Club:* Chelsea Arts.

**HADDEN-PATON, Major Adrian Gerard Nigel,** DL, JP; *b* 3 Dec. 1918; *s* of late Nigel Fairholt Paton, Covehithe, Suffolk; *m* 1951, Mary-Rose, *d* of Col A. H. MacIlwaine, DSO, MC, Troutbeck, S Rhodesia; two *s* (and two step *s*). *Educ:* Rugby; Worcester Coll., Oxford. 2nd Lt, 1st The Royal Dragoons, 1940; Adjutant, 1943-44; served 1940-45: Western Desert, Tunisia, Italy, France, Belgium, Holland, Germany and Denmark; (despatches); Maj. 1945. Instructor, RMA, Sandhurst, 1947-50; retired 1950. Mem. Estates Cttee of Nat. Trust, 1956, and Properties Cttee, 1970; Mem. Exec. Cttee, 1959, and Finance Cttee, 1961 (Chm. 1962-68) of Country Landowners Association. Is an Underwriting Mem. of Lloyd's; Chm. Holland & Holland Ltd; Chm. Hertfordshire Agricultural Soc., 1961-69; Past Pres. Hertfordshire & Middlesex Trust for Nature Conservation. Vice-Chm. of Governors, Berkhamsted Sch. and Berkhamsted Sch. for Girls, 1963- (Governor 1950). JP 1951, DL 1962, Herts; High Sheriff, 1961. *Recreations:* shooting, forestry, gardening. *Address:* Rossway, Berkhamsted, Herts. *T:* Berkhamsted 3264. *Club:* Cavalry.

**HADDINGTON,** 12th Earl of, *cr* 1619; **George Baillie-Hamilton,** KT 1951; MC; TD; FRSE; FSAScot; LLD (Glasgow); Baron Binning, 1613; Scottish Representative Peer, 1922-63; HM Lieutenant County of Berwick, 1952-69; *b* 18 Sept. 1894; *s* of late Lord Binning; *e s* of 11th Earl, and Katharine Augusta Millicent (*d* 1952), *o c* of W. Severin Salting; *S* grandfather, 1917; *m* 1923, Sarah, *y d* of G. W. Cook, of Montreal; one *s* one *d*. *Educ:* Eton; Sandhurst. Served European War (Royal Scots Greys), 1915-18 (MC, wounded); late Major 19th (L and BH) Armoured Car Coy. Served European War of 1939-45; Wing Comdr RAFVR, 1941-45; Capt. Queen's Body Guard for Scotland, Royal Company of Archers, 1953-. Pres. Soc. of Antiquaries of Scotland; Pres. Scottish Georgian Soc.; Chm. of Trustees, National Museum of Antiquities, Scotland; Trustee, National Library of Scotland. *Heir:* *s* Lord Binning, *qv*. *Address:* Mellerstain, Gordon, Scotland. *Club:* New (Edinburgh).

*See also Lieut-Col H. B. O'Brien.*

**HADDO, Earl of; David George Ian Alexander Gordon,** CBE 1963; TD 1947; Vice-Lieutenant of Aberdeenshire since 1959, County Councillor since 1961, Chairman, Education Committee, since 1970; managing family estate since 1944; *b* 21 Jan. 1908; *e s* and *heir* of 3rd Marquis of Aberdeen and Temair, *qv*; *m* 1939, Beatrice Mary June, *d* of A. P. Boissier, sometime Headmaster of Harrow Sch.; two adopted *s* two adopted *d*. *Educ:* Harrow; Balliol, Oxford (MA). Chartered Land Agent, 1932; Fellow Chartered Land Agents Soc., 1946-69, FRICS 1969-. Land Agent: to Major W. R. D. Mackenzie, at Fawley Court, Henley-on-Thames and at Carradale, Argyll, 1932-38; to Earl of Derby, at Knowsley, 1938-39; to Lord Aberdeen (transferred Family Estate of Haddo House), Aberdeenshire, 1944. Landowner managing own property, 1944-. DL 1949, JP 1955, Aberdeenshire. Mem. Queen's Body Guard for Scotland (Royal Company of Archers), 1955. Chm. County of Aberdeen TAA, 1963-68; Convenor of Scottish Landowners Federation, 1962-66, Vice-Pres., 1967; Pres. East Aberdeenshire Unionist Association, 1959-63; Chm. of various Committees. President: British Assoc. of Experiment in Internat. Living, 1964-; Royal Scottish Agric. Benevolent Instn, 1965-70. Served War of 1939-45; 5th Gordons, BEF, 1940 (despatches); 9th Gordons and 2nd London Scottish, Bde Major, 1940-43 (Home Stations); Staff Officer to Provost Marshal, MEF, 1943-45. Knight Order of St John of Jerusalem, 1964; Prior, Order of St John in Scotland, 1970. *Recreations:* Rugby football (OU Greyhounds RFC, German tour 1930; London Scottish RFC, 1st XV, 1932-38, Capt. 1938; Kent RFC, 1933-38; Scottish Trials, 1934-35; Oxfordshire RFC, Capt. 1934-38), cricket, swimming, walking, music, model railways. *Address:* Haddo House, Aberdeenshire. *T:* Tarves 216 and 664. *Clubs:* Bath, MCC; New (Edinburgh); Royal Northern (Aberdeen).

**HADDOCK, Maurice Robert,** CBE 1963 (OBE 1945); ERD; General Manager and Secretary, National Dock Labour Board, 1955-70; *b* 26 July 1909; *s* of late Percy G. Haddock; *m* 1938, Rita Claridge; one *d*. *Educ:* St Paul's Sch.; Magdalene Coll., Cambridge. Served War, 1939-46, Royal Engineers (Transportation). Hon. Col 81 Port Regt, RE (AER) (incorporated in RCT, 1965), 1955-67; ADC to the Queen, 1959-64. Port Controller, Hamburg, 1945-49. Asst Sec., Docks & Inland Waterways Executive, 1949-52; Asst Gen. Manager and Sec., National Dock Labour Board, Sept. 1952-Oct. 1955. Officer Order of Leopold, 1945. *Address:* 14 Copse Edge Avenue, Epsom Surrey. *T:* Epsom 21479. *Club:* United University.

**HADDON, Eric Edwin,** CB 1965; BSc, FRIC; retired; Director, Chemical Defence Establishment, Ministry of Defence, 1961-68; *b* 16 March 1908; *s* of late William Edwin Haddon, York; *m* 1934, Barbara Fabian, York; no *c*. *Educ:* Archbishop Holgate's Grammar Sch., York; Queen Mary Coll., London Univ. BSc (Special) Chemistry, ARIC 1929; FRIC 1943. Joined Scientific Staff of Admiralty, 1929; Scientific Staff of War Dept, 1929; Sec., Scientific Advisory Council, Min. of Supply, 1945-52; Dir, Chemical Defence Research and Development, Min. of Supply, 1957-61. *Recreations:* gardening, bridge. *Address:* Knavesmire, St Leonards Road, Thames Ditton, Surrey. *T:* 01-398 5944.

**HADDOW, Prof. Sir Alexander,** Kt 1966; MD, DSc, PhD; FRS 1958; FRSE; Professor of Experimental Pathology, University of London, since 1946; Director, Chester Beatty Research Institute, Institute of Cancer Research, Royal Cancer Hospital, Fulham Road, SW3, 1946-69; *b* 18 Jan. 1907; *s* of William and Margaret Haddow, Broxburn, West Lothian, Scotland; *m* 1st, 1932, Lucia Lindsay Crosbie Black (*d* 1968); one *s*; 2nd, 1969, Feo Standing. *Educ:* Broxburn High Sch.; University of Edinburgh (MB, ChB 1929; PhD 1937; MD (Gold Medal) 1937; DSc 1938). Wellcome Gold Medal, History of Medicine.

Carnegie Research Student and House Physician, Royal Infirmary of Edinburgh; Davidson Research Fellow and Lecturer in Bacteriology, University of Edinburgh; Laura de Saliceto Student, University of London; Life Mem., Royal Medical Society of Edinburgh; Foreign Hon. Member, Amer. Acad. Arts and Sciences, 1961; Pres. Med. Assoc. for the Prevention of War; Pres., British Assoc. for Cancer Research, 1968; Vice-Pres., British Cancer Council. Fellow Inst. of Biology; Acad. royale de Méd. de Belgique; RSA; FRSocMed; Pres., Section of Oncology, RSM, 1970-71; late Mem., Press Council; Member: Executive Council, Ciba Foundation Executive Council, British Assoc. for World Govt and Parly Group for World Govt; Grand Council, British Empire Cancer Campaign; Pres. International Union Against Cancer, 1962-66; Member: Society for Study of Growth and Development (US); New York Acad. of Sciences; American Association for Cancer Research; Soviet Academy of Medical Sciences, 1961; Katherine Berkan Judd Award (Memorial Hosp., NY), 1948; Walker Prize (RCS of England), 1951; Officer, Order of Don Carlos Finlay, Cuba, 1957; Robert Roesler de Villiers Award (Leukemia Soc., NY), 1960; Claude Perchot Prize (Fac. de Méd., Paris, 1960); Gold Medal in Therapeutics (Soc. of Apothecaries of London, 1963); Harben Lecture, 1969; Karnofsky Meml Lecture, Houston, 1970; Sidney Farber Med. Res. Award, Boston, 1970; Internat. Union against Cancer Award, 1970. MD *hc* University Perugia, 1957. Officier de l'Ordre de la Santé Publique, (RF); Late Chm., BBC Science Consultative Gp. Hon. FRCP London, 1968; Hon. Member: Czechoslovak Med. Soc., 1966; Hungarian Acad. of Sciences, 1967. Hon. DSc Edinburgh, 1967; DUniv Liège, 1967; Doctor *hc* University of Helsinki, 1965. Croix de Chevalier de la Légion d'Honneur, 1965. *Publications:* papers in various scientific and medical journals. *Recreations:* bibliography, painting, music. *Address:* Chester Beatty Research Institute, Institute of Cancer Research, Royal Cancer Hospital, Fulham Road, SW3. *TA:* Cancer, London, SW3. *T:* 01-352 8133; The Lodge, Pollards Wood, Nightingales Lane, Chalfont St Giles, Bucks. *T:* Little Chalfont 2474. *Clubs:* Athenæum, Royal Automobile; Chelsea Arts.

**HADDOW, Alexander John,** CMG 1959; DSc, MD, FRCPGlas, DTM&H; FRSE; Associate Dean, Faculty of Medicine, and Titular Professor of Tropical Medicine, University of Glasgow, since 1970; *b* 27 Dec. 1912; *s* of Alexander and Margaret Blackburn Haddow; *m* 1946, Margaret Ronald Scott Orr; two *s*. *Educ:* Hillhead High Sch., Glasgow; Glasgow Univ. Strang-Steel Research Scholar (zoology), Glasgow Univ., 1934-35; Medical Research Council Junior Research Fellow in Tropical Medicine, 1938-41. Entomologist, Yellow Fever Research Institute, Entebbe, 1942-45; Staff Mem., International Health Div., Rockefeller Foundation, 1945-49; Overseas Research Service, 1950-65; Epidemiologist, East African Virus Research Institute, 1950-52; Acting Dir, 1952-53; Dir, 1953-65; Sen. Lectr in Epidemiology, Univ. of Glasgow, 1965-70, also Dir, Cancer Registration Bureau, W of Scotland Hosp. Region, 1966-70. Hon. Prof. of Medical Entomology, Makerere Coll., The University Coll. of East Africa, 1962-65. Mem. WHO expert panel on virus diseases, 1953. Trustee, Uganda National Parks, 1955-65; Life Honorary Park Warden, 1965-. Chalmers Gold Medal, Royal Soc. Tropical Medicine and Hygiene, 1957. Stewart Prize, BMA, 1962; Keith Prize, RSE, 1968. *Publications:* contributions to learned journals. *Address:* Faculty of Medicine, Glasgow University, Glasgow W2.

**HADDOW, Sir (Thomas) Douglas,** KCB 1966 (CB 1955); FRSE; Permanent Under-Secretary of State, Scottish Office, since 1965; *b* 9 Feb. 1913; *s* of George Haddow, Crawford, Lanarkshire; *m* 1942, Margaret R. S. Rowat (*d* 1969); two *s*. *Educ:* George Watson's Coll., Edinburgh; Edinburgh Univ.; Trinity Coll., Cambridge. MA (Edinburgh) 1932; BA (Cambridge) 1934. Department of Health for Scotland, 1935; Private Sec. to Sec. of State for Scotland, 1941-44. Commonwealth Fund Fellow, 1948. Secretary: Dept of Health for Scot., 1959-62; Scottish Develt Dept, 1962-64. Hon. LLD Strathclyde Univ., 1967. *Recreation:* golf. *Address:* 54 Northumberland Street, Edinburgh EH3 6JE. Castle View, Dirleton, East Lothian. *T:* Dirleton 266. *Clubs:* Caledonian, Royal Commonwealth Society.

**HADEN, William Demmery,** TD, MA; Headmaster, Royal Grammar School, Newcastle upon Tyne, since 1960; *b* 14 March 1909; *s* of Reverend William Henry and Gertrude Haden, Little Aston; *m* 1939, Elizabeth Marjorie, *d* of R. S. Tewson, Chorley Wood; one *s* two *d*. *Educ:* Nottingham High Sch.; Wadham Coll., Oxford, 2nd Class Lit. Hum.; MA 1934. English Master, Merchant Taylors' Sch., 1938-46; Headmaster, Mercers' Sch., 1946-59. War Service, 1940-45: served as Battery Comdr RA with Fourteenth Army throughout Burma Campaign (despatches twice); Administrative Commandant, Hmawbi Area, S Burma District, 1945. *Recreations:* games, gardening, listening to music. *Address:* 39 The Grove, Gosforth, Newcastle upon Tyne 3.

**HADEN-GUEST,** family name of **Baron Haden-Guest.**

**HADEN-GUEST,** 2nd Baron, *cr* 1950, of Saling, Essex; **Stephen Haden Haden-Guest;** translator and editor of scientific works; *b* 7 June 1902; *er s* of Leslie Haden Haden-Guest, 1st Baron, MC, and Edith (*d* 1944), *d* of Max Low, London; *S* father 1960; *m* 1948, Barbara Ann (marr. diss., 1954), *d* of late James Harvey Pinson, of West Virginia, USA; one *d*. *Educ:* St John's House Sch.; Institut St Cyr, Nevers, France; University Coll., London; London Sch. of Economics. BA (Hons), London, 1922. Served War of 1939-45: with British Information Services, New York, 1941-45 (Ed. and Translator). With United Nations Information Office, 1943-46; Editorial Adviser to the American Geographical Soc., 1948-54. *Heir:* *b* Hon. Richard Haden Haden-Guest [*b* 1904; *m* 1st, 1926, Hilda (marr. diss., 1934), *d* of late Thomas Russell-Cruise; one *d*; 2nd, 1934, Olive Maria, *d* of late Anders Gotfrid Nilsson; one *s* decd; 3rd, 1949, Marjorie, *d* of late Dr Douglas F. Kennard, of Clacton-on-Sea. *Educ:* Bembridge, IOW]. *Address:* 19 East 54th Street, New York City, USA. *Club:* English-Speaking Union (New York).

**HADFIELD, Ellis Charles Raymond,** CMG 1954; part-time Member, British Waterways Board, 1963-66; *b* 5 Aug. 1909; *s* of Alexander Charles Hadfield, South Africa Civil Service; *m* 1945, Alice Mary Miller, *d* of Lt-Col Henry Smyth, DSO; one *s* one *d* (and one *s* decd). *Educ:* Blundell's Sch.; St Edmund Hall, Oxford. Joined Oxford University Press, 1936; Dir of Publications, Central Office of Information, 1946-48; Controller (Overseas), 1948-62. Editor, Quaker Monthly, 1963-69. *Publications:* British Canals, 1950; The Canals of South Wales and the Border, 1960; The Canals of the East Midlands, 1966; The Canals of the West Midlands, 1966; The Canals of South West England, 1967; (with Michael Streat), Holiday Cruising on Inland Waterways, 1968; The Canal Age, 1968; The Canals of South and South East England, 1969. *Recreations:* writing; exploring canals. *Address:* Silver Street House, South Cerney, Glos. *T:* South Cerney 218. *Club:* Authors.

**HADFIELD, Esmé Havelock,** FRCS; Consultant Ear, Nose and Throat Surgeon, High Wycombe, Amersham and Chalfont Hospitals; Associate Surgeon (Hon.), Ear, Nose and Throat Department, Radcliffe Infirmary, Oxford; *b* 1921; *o d* of late Geoffrey Hadfield, MD. *Educ:* Clifton High Sch.; St Hugh's Coll., Oxford; Radcliffe Infirmary Oxford. BA (Oxon.) 1942; BM, BCh Oxon 1945; FRCS 1951; MA Oxon. 1952. House Officer appts, Radcliffe Infirmary, Oxford, 1945; Registrar to ENT Dept, Radcliffe Infirmary, Oxford, 1948; Asst Ohren, Nase, Hals Klinik, Kantonspital, University of Zurich, 1949. First Asst ENT Dept, Radcliffe Infirmary, Oxford, 1950. British Empire Cancer Campaign Travelling Fellow in Canada, 1953; Hunterian Prof., RCS, 1969-70. *Publications:* articles on ENT surgery in Medical Journals. *Recreation:* travel. *Address:* Linaver, Lane End, near High Wycombe, Bucks. *T:* Lane End 473.

**HADFIELD, John Charles Heywood;** author; Editor of The Saturday Book; Editorial Director, the Rainbird Publishing Group, Ltd; *b* 16 June 1907; 2nd *s* of H. G. Hadfield, Birmingham; *m* 1931, Phyllis Anna, *o d* of Captain Leonard McMullen; one *s*. *Educ:* Bradfield. Editor, J. M. Dent & Sons, Ltd, 1935-42; Books Officer for British Council in the Middle East, 1942-44; Dir of the National Book League, 1944-50; Organiser, Festival of Britain Exhibition of Books, 1951. *Publications:* The Christmas Companion, 1939; Georgian Love Songs, 1949; Restoration Love Songs, 1950; A Book of Beauty, 1952; A Book of Delights, 1954; Elizabethan Love Songs, 1955; A Book of Britain, 1956; A Book of Love, 1958; Love on a Branch Line, 1959; A Book of Pleasures, 1960; A Book of Joy, 1962; A Chamber of Horrors, 1965; (ed) The Shell Guide to England, 1970. (With Miles Hadfield): The Twelve Days of Christmas, 1961; Gardens of Delight, 1964. *Recreations:* books, pictures, gardens. *Address:* Barham Manor, near Ipswich, Suffolk. *T:* Claydon 236. *Club:* Savile.

**HADHAM, John;** *see* Parkes, Rev. J. W.

**HADLEY, Dr George Dickinson;** Physician, Middlesex Hospital, since 1946; *b* 30 June 1908; *s* of Laurence Percival Hadley and Norah Katherine Hadley (*née* Alabaster); *m* 1947, Jean Elinor Stewart; three *d*. *Educ:* King Edward VI Sch., Birmingham; Clare Coll., Cambridge. 1st Class Natural Sciences Tripos, Part I 1930, Part II 1931, Cambridge; MB, ChB Cantab 1934; MRCP 1937; MD Cantab 1939; Elmore Clinical Research Student, University of Cambridge, 1936-38; FRCP 1947. Major RAMC and Medical Specialist, 1939-45 (POW, Germany, 1940-45). Physician, Middlesex Hospital, 1946. Examiner in Medicine: Cambridge Univ., 1955-57; University of London, 1956-60. *Publications:* articles in various medical journals. *Recreations:* angling, 'cello playing. *Address:* 149 Harley Street, W1. *T:* 01-935 4444. *Club:* Athenæum.

**HADLEY, Patrick Arthur Sheldon,** MA, MusD Cantab; FRCM; composer; Emeritus Professor of Music in the University of Cambridge (Professor of Music and Precentor of Caius, 1946-62); *b* 5 March 1899; 2nd and *o surv. s* of late Dr W. S. Hadley, Master of Pembroke Coll., Cambridge, 1912-27, and of late Edith Jane, *d* of Rev. Robert Foster, one-time Vicar of St Peter's, Athlone; unmarried. *Educ:* Winchester Coll.; Pembroke Coll., Cambridge; Royal Coll. of Music (where studied composition under Vaughan Williams and conducting under Boult and Sargent). Served War of 1914-18 in RFA, 1917-18 (wounded in France). Mem. of Teaching Staff of RCM, 1925-62. Fellow of Gonville and Caius Coll., Cambridge, 1938, and Lecturer in University Faculty of Music; deputised during most of War of 1939-45 for Mr Boris Ord as conductor of Cambridge Univ. Musical Soc., introducing to Cambridge two major works by Delius, Appalachia and The Song of the High Hills. *Publications:* various songs and choral pieces; a few large-scale concert works for chorus and orchestra with soli, such as Fen and Flood (words by C. L. Cudworth), performed King's Lynn Festival, 1956; Norwich Festival, 1958. Music for the Greek Play, Antigone (Sophocles), at Cambridge, 1939; Agamemnon (Aeschylus), 1953; A Latin Coronation Ode for chorus and orchestra perf. at Cambridge, June 1953. Many compositions remain in manuscript, including a Cantata for Lent perf. at the St Bees Festival, 1963, and subsequently by the Cambridge Univ. Musical Soc. *Address:* Shallcross, Heacham, near King's Lynn, Norfolk. *T:* Heacham 220. *Club:* Oxford and Cambridge.

**HADOW, Sir Gordon,** Kt 1956; CMG 1953; OBE 1945; Deputy Governor of the Gold Coast (now Ghana), 1954-57; *b* 23 Sept. 1908; *e s* of late Rev. F. B. Hadow and Una Ethelwyn Durrant; *m* 1946, Marie, *er d* of late Dr L. H. Moiser; two *s*. *Educ:* Marlborough; Trinity Coll., Oxford. Administrative Service, Gold Coast, 1932; Dep. Financial Sec., Tanganyika, 1946; Under-Sec. Gold Coast, 1948; Sec. for the Civil Service, 1949; Sec. to Governor and to Exec. Council, 1950-54. *Address:* Garlands, Westerham, Kent. *Club:* Athenæum.

**HADOW, Reginald Michael,** CMG 1962; Ambassador to Argentina, since 1969; *b* 17 Aug. 1915; *s* of Malcolm McGregor Hadow and Constance Mary Lund; *m* 1955, Dolores Frances Main. *Educ:* Berkhamsted Sch.; King's Coll., Cambridge. Selected for ICS, 1937; Private Sec. to HM Ambassador, Moscow, 1942; Under-Sec., External Affairs Dept, Delhi, 1946-47; transferred to Foreign Office, 1948; FO, 1948-52; Private Sec. to Minister of State, 1949-52; Head of Chancery, Mexico City, 1952-54; FO, 1955; Head of Levant Dept and promoted Counsellor, 1958; Coun., Brit. Embassy, Paris, 1959-62; Head of News Dept, FO, 1962-65; Ambassador to Israel, 1965-69. *Recreations:* all field sports. *Address:* British Embassy, Buenos Aires, Argentina. *Club:* Travellers'.

**HADRILL, John Michael W.;** *see* Wallace-Hadrill.

**HAENDEL, Ida;** Violinist; *b* Poland, 15 Dec. 1924; Polish parentage. Began to play at age of 3½; amazing gift discovered when she picked up her sister's violin and started to play. Her father a great connoisseur of music, saw in her an unusual talent and decided to abandon his own career as an artist (painter) to devote himself to his daughter; studied at Warsaw Conservatorium and finished with a gold medal at age of ten; also studied with such great masters as Carl Flesch and Georges Enesco. Has played in Europe, US, and Middle East with great conductors like Sir Henry Wood, Sir Thomas Beecham, Sir Malcolm Sargent, Klemperer, Szell, Molinari. During

War of 1939-45 gave concerts for British and American troops, as well as concerts in factories. *Address:* 74 Upper Park Road, NW3. *T:* 01-722 2357.

**HAFFENDEN, Maj.-Gen. D. J. W.;** *see* Wilson-Haffenden.

**HAGART-ALEXANDER, Sir C.;** *see* Alexander.

**HAGEN, Dr John P(eter),** Presidential Certificate of Merit (US), 1947; DSM (US), 1959; Professor of Astronomy and Head of Department of Astronomy, Pennsylvania State University, since 1967; Director, Office of United Nations Conference, National Aeronautics and Space Administration, 1960-62 (Director, Vanguard Division, 1958-60); *b* 31 July 1908; *s* of John T. and Ella Bertha Hagen (*née* Fisher); *m* 1935, Edith W. Soderling; two *s*. *Educ:* Boston, Wesleyan, Yale and Georgetown Univs. Res. Associate, Wesleyan Univ., 1931-35; Supt Atmosphere and Astrophysics Div., US Naval Res. Lab., 1935-38; Dir, Project Vanguard, 1955-58. Lecturer, Georgetown Univ., 1949-. FRAS 1969. Hon. ScD: Boston Univ., 1958; Adelphi Univ., Loyola Univ., Fairfield Univ., 1959; Mt Allison Univ., 1960. Phi Beta Kappa. *Publications:* contrib. to Astrophysical Journal and to Proc. Inst. Radio Engrg; contributor to Encyclopædia Britannica. *Address:* 613 W Park Avenue, State College, PA 16801, USA. *T:* 237-3031. *Club:* Cosmos (Washington, DC).

**HAGEN, Victor W. V.;** *see* Von Hagen.

**HAGERTY, James C., (Jim Hagerty);** Vice-President, American Broadcasting Co., since 1961; *b* Plattsburg, 9 May 1909; *s* of James A. Hagerty; *m* 1937, Marjorie Lucas; two *s*. *Educ:* Blair Acad.; Columbia Univ. Joined staff of New York Times, 1934; Legislative Correspondent, 1938-42; Executive Asst to Governor Dewey, 1943-50; Sec. to Governor, 1950-52. Press Sec. to President Dwight D. Eisenhower, 1953-61. Mem. of Delta Kappa Epsilon. *Address:* (home) 7 Rittenhouse Road, Bronxville, NY 10708, USA.

**HAGESTADT, Leonard,** CMG 1966; OBE 1955; Counsellor (Labour), British Embassy, Paris, 1960-68, retired; *b* 12 June 1907; *s* of William Samuel Hagestadt and Emma (*née* Fish); *m* 1934, Constance Margaret Louise Valentine, Edinburgh; one *s* one *d*. *Educ:* Boulevard Sch., Kingston-upon-Hull, BCom (London). Various posts in Min. of Labour, 1930-60. *Address:* 58 Park Hall Road, SE21. *T:* 01-670 8011.

**HAGGART, Very Rev. Alastair Iain Macdonald;** Provost of St Paul's Cathedral, Dundee, since 1959; *b* 10 Oct. 1915; *s* of Alexander Macdonald Haggart and Jessie Mackay; *m* 1945, Margaret Agnes Trundle; two *d*. *Educ:* Hatfield Coll. (Exhibr); Durham Univ. (Exhibr); Edinburgh Theol College. LTh 1941; BA 1942; MA 1945. Deacon 1941; Priest 1942. Curate: St Mary's Cath., Glasgow, 1941-45; St Mary's, Hendon, 1945-48; Precentor, St Ninian's Cath., Perth, 1948-51; Rector, St Oswald's, King's Park, Glasgow, 1951, and Acting Priest-in-Charge, St Martin's, Glasgow, 1953-58; Synod Clerk of Glasgow Dio. and Canon of St Mary's Cath., Glasgow, 1958-59. Exam. Chap. to Bp of Brechin, 1964. Hon. LLD Dundee, 1970. *Recreations:* walking, reading, asking questions. *Address:* 4 Richmond Terrace, Dundee DD1 1BQ. *T:* 68548.

**HAGGERSTON of Haggerston, Captain Sir (Hugh) Carnaby de Marie,** 11th Bt, *cr* 1642; Captain late 5th Fusiliers; JP Northumberland; *b* March 1906; *s* of 10th Bt and Florence (*d* 1955), 3rd *d* of W. H. Perrin; *S* father, 1925; *m* 1933, Mary Ridgway, *e d* of late Mrs L. P. Macy, Beauly, Charlottesville, Va, USA; three *d* (and one *s* and one *d* decd). *Educ:* The Oratory Sch. Owns about 3,500 acres in Northumberland. *Heir:* *b* Ralph Stanley de Marie Haggerston [*b* 6 Aug. 1912; *m* 1956, Joan Adelene Blythe-Perrett]. *Address:* Harelaw House, Chathill, Northumberland. *T:* Chathill 24.

*See also P. D. Gadsden.*

**HÄGGLÖF, Gunnar,** GCVO (Hon.), 1954; Swedish Ambassador to France since 1967; *b* 15 Dec. 1904; *s* of Richard Hägglöf and Sigrid Ryding, Stockholm, Sweden; *m* Anna, *d* of Count Folchi-Vici, Rome. *Educ:* Upsala Univ., Sweden. Entered Swedish Diplomatic Service, 1926; served Legations in Paris, Madrid, Moscow (1930), and at Disarmament Conf. in Geneva, 1932-34; Head of Economic Dept; sec.–Gen., Industrial Commn; Minister without Portfolio, 1939. During War of 1939-45, led various Swedish delegns to Berlin, London, and Washington; Envoy to Belgian and Dutch Govts in London, 1944; Envoy in Moscow, 1946; permanent delegate to UN, 1947; Ambassador to Court of St James's, 1948-67. Delegate to Conf. for Constitution, European Council, 1949; delegate to Suez Confs, 1956; Mem. of Menzies Cttee to Cairo, 1956. Grand Cross of Swedish Order of North Star. Hon. DCL Birmingham, 1960. *Publications:* several books and essays in economics, politics and history. *Recreations:* ski-ing, swimming, reading and writing. *Address:* Ambassade de Suède, 11 Avenue d'Jena, Paris 16e.

**HAGUE, Sir (Charles) Kenneth (Felix),** Kt 1953; CEng, FIMechE, FIEE; *b* 17 Sept. 1901; *s* of late Albert Hague and Florence Muriel Flux; *m* 1926, Marjorie, *d* of Samuel Thornton; one *s* one *d*; *m* 1960, Mrs Helen Wallace Sutherland. *Educ:* New College Sch., Oxford; Leeds University. Joined Babcock & Wilcox Ltd, 1924; Chairman, 1960-68. Deputy Chairman, Royal Ordnance Factories Board, 1951-58; Member, Iron and Steel Board, 1959-64. Member UK Management/Labour Delegation to USA, 1941; British Representative on Public Utilities Cttee of Combined Production and Resources Board, Washington, 1944; Member Engineering Advisory Council, 1947-52; Past-President (1948-50), British Engineers' Association; Past President, Institute of Mech. Engineers, 1961-62, Hon. Fellow, 1967; Past President, Engineering Employers' Federation, 1958-60. Founder-Chairman, Council of Engineering Institutions, 1962-64. Hon. LLD Glasgow. *Recreation:* golf. *Address:* Poland Mill, Odiham, Hants. *T:* Odiham 2251. *Clubs:* Junior Carlton, Travellers'; Rand (Johannesburg).

**HAGUE, Prof. Douglas Chalmers;** Professor of Managerial Economics, University of Manchester, since 1965; *b* Leeds, 20 Oct. 1926; *s* of Laurence and Marion Hague; *m* 1947, Brenda Elizabeth Fereday; two *d*. *Educ:* Moseley Grammar Sch.; King Edward VI High Sch., Birmingham; University of Birmingham. Assistant Tutor, Faculty of Commerce, Birmingham Univ., 1946; Assistant Lecturer, University College, London, 1947, Lecturer, 1950; Reader in Political Economy in University of London, 1957; Newton Chambers Professor of Economics, University of Sheffield, 1957-63. Visiting Professor of Economics, Duke Univ., USA, 1960-61; Head of Department of Business Studies, University of Sheffield, 1962-63; Professor of Applied Economics, University of Manchester, 1963-65. Rapporteur to International Economic Association, 1953-; Member Working Party of

National Advisory Council on Education for Industry and Commerce, 1962-63; Consultant to Secretariat of NEDC, 1962-63; Member: Treasury Working Party on Management Training in the Civil Service, 1965-67; EDC for Paper and Board, 1967-; Part-time Member, N Western Gas Board, 1966-; Mem. Working Party, Local Govt Training Bd, 1969-; Director: Manchester School of Management and Administration, 1964-65; Centre for Business Research, Manchester, 1964-66. Member Council, Manchester Business School, 1964-; Chairman, Manchester Industrial Relations Society, 1964-66; President, NW Operational Research Group, 1967-; British Chm., Carnegie Project on Accountability, 1968-. Industrial Consultant. *Publications:* (with P. K. Newman) Costs in Alternative Locations: The Clothing Industry, 1952; (with A. W. Stonier) A Textbook of Economic Theory, 1953; (with A. W. Stonier) The Essentials of Economics, 1955; The Economics of Man-Made Fibres, 1957; Stability and Progress in the World Economy (ed), 1958; The Theory of Capital (ed), 1961; Inflation (ed), 1962; International Trade Theory in a Developing World (ed) (with Sir Roy Harrod), 1965; Price Formation in Various Economies (ed), 1967; Managerial Economics, 1969; The Dilemma of Accountability in Modern Government (ed) (with Bruce L. R. Smith), 1970; articles in economic and financial journals. *Recreation:* church organs. *Address:* 8 Knutsford Road, Wilmslow, Cheshire. *T:* Wilmslow 28898.

**HAGUE, Sir Kenneth;** *see* Hague, Sir C. K. F.

**HAHN, Prof. Frank Horace;** Professor of Economics, London School of Economics, since 1967; Fellow of Churchill College, Cambridge, since 1960; *b* 26 April 1925; *s* of Dr Arnold Hahn and Maria Hahn; *m* 1946, Dorothy Salter; no *c*. *Educ:* Bournemouth Grammar School; London School of Economics. PhD London, MA Cantab. Univ. of Birmingham, 1948-60, Reader in Mathematical Economics, 1958-60; Visiting Professor: Massachusetts Inst. of Technology, 1956-57; Univ. of California, Berkeley, 1959-60; Univ. Lecturer in Economics, Cambridge, 1960. Fellow, Inst. of Advanced Studies in Behavioural Sciences, Stanford, 1966-67. Fellow, Econometric Soc., 1962; Vice-Pres., 1967-68; Pres., 1968-69. Managing Editor, Review of Economic Studies, 1965-68. *Publications:* articles in learned journals. *Address:* 16 Adams Road, Cambridge. *T:* Cambridge 52560; 30 Tavistock Court, Tavistock Square, WC1. *T:* 01-387 4293. *Club:* Reform.

**HAHN, Kurt (Matthias Robert Martin),** CBE 1964; Hon. LLD; *b* Berlin, Germany, 5 June 1886; *s* of Oskar Hahn and Charlotte (*née* Landau); became British citizen, 1938. *Educ:* Wilhelmgymnasium, Berlin; Christ Church, Oxford; Universities of Berlin, Heidelberg, Freiburg, Göttingen. Returned to Germany, Aug. 1914; during war: Lector of English newspapers (first for German Foreign Office, then for Supreme Command); Private Secretary: to Prince Max von Baden, the last Imperial Chancellor, Jan. 1919; to Dr Melchior, a delegate in Versailles, April-June 1919; returned to Prince Max and helped him to found Salem Co-educational School at Salem Castle, 1920; arrested by Nazis, March 1933; released and protected through intervention of Ramsay MacDonald; emigrated to Britain, July 1933; founded Gordonstoun Sch., 1933-34; retired, 1953; Co-Founder with Lawrence Holt of Outward Bound Sea Sch., Aberdovey, 1941; announced at Bruges, Atlantic Colleges project, 1957; Co-Founder with Sir Lawrence Darvall of United World Coll. of the Atlantic, Wales, 1962. Hon. LLD, Edinburgh, 1953; Hon. Dr phil: Göttingen, 1956; Tübingen, 1961; Berlin, 1966. Grosses Verdienstkreuz des Verdienstordens der Bundesrepublik Deutschland, 1961; Freiherr-vom-Stein Prize, 1962; Foneme Prize, Milan, 1968. *Recreations:* lawn tennis, walking, applied history. *Address:* 7777 Salem, Baden, Federal Republic of Germany; Brown's Hotel, London, W1.

**HAIDER, Michael Lawrence;** Chairman, Chief Executive Officer, and Chairman of Executive Committee, Standard Oil Co. (NJ), 1965-69, retired; *b* 1 Oct. 1904; *s* of Michael Haider and Elizabeth (*née* Milner). *Educ:* Stanford Univ. BS 1927. Chemical Engineer, Richfield Oil Co., 1927-29; Carter Oil Co., Tulsa, Okla., 1929-38 (Chief Engineer, 1935-38); Manager, Research and Engineering Dept, Standard Oil Development Co., 1938-45; Standard Oil Co. (NJ): Executive, Producing Dept, 1945-46; Deputy Co-ordinator of Producing Activities, 1952-54; Vice-President, 1960-61; Executive Vice-President, 1961-63; President and Vice-Chairman, Executive Cttee, 1963-65. Was with: Imperial Oil Ltd, Toronto, 1946-52 (Vice-President and Director, 1948-52); International Petroleum Co. Ltd (President and Director), 1954-59. President, American Institute of Mining and Metallurgical Engineers, 1952. *Publications:* (Ed.) Petroleum Reservoir Efficiency and Well Spacing, 1943; articles in technical journals. *Address:* (office) 30 Rockefeller Plaza, New York, NY 10020, USA; (home) River Road, Essex, Conn 06426, USA.

**HAIG,** family name of **Earl Haig.**

**HAIG,** 2nd Earl, *cr* 1919; **George Alexander Eugene Douglas Haig,** OBE 1966; Viscount Dawick, *cr* 1919; Baron Haig and 30th Laird of Bemersyde; is a painter; Member, Queen's Body Guard for Scotland; Vice-Lieutenant of Berwickshire since 1967; *b* March 1918; *o s* of 1st Earl and Hon. Dorothy Vivian (*d* 1939) (Author of A Scottish Tour, 1935), *d* of 3rd Lord Vivian; *S* father, 1928; *m* 1956, Adrienne Thérèse, *d* of Derrick Morley, Quaives, Wickambreux, Kent, and Mrs Edmund Seyd, 9 Lyme Terrace, London; one *s* two *d*. *Educ:* Stowe; Christ Church, Oxford. MA Oxon. 2nd Lieut Royal Scots Greys, 1938; retired on account of disability, 1951, rank of Captain; Hon. Major on disbandment of HG 1958; studied painting Camberwell School of Art; paintings in collections of Arts Council and Scottish Modern Arts Association. War of 1939-45 (prisoner). Member: Society of Scottish Artists; Royal Fine Art Commission for Scotland, 1958-61; Council and Executive Cttee, Earl Haig Fund, Scotland, 1950-65 and 1966-; Scottish Arts Council, 1969-; President, Scottish Craft Centre. Member Council, British Commonwealth Ex-Services League; Chairman, NS&E Area, Officers' Association (Scottish Cttee); Vice-President: Scottish National Institution for War Blinded; Saltire Society; President Border Area British Legion, 1955-61; Chairman SE Scotland Disablement Advisory Cttee, 1960; Vice-Chairman, British Legion, Scotland, 1960, Chairman, 1962-65; Trustee, Scottish National War Memorial, 1961; Trustee, National Gallery of Scotland, 1962-. DL Berwickshire, 1953. FRSA 1951. *Heir: s* Viscount Dawick, *qv*. *Address:* Bemersyde, Melrose, Scotland. *T:* St Boswells 2762. *Clubs:* White's, Cavalry; New (Edinburgh). *See also Hon. Gavin Astor, H. R. Trevor-Roper.*

**HAIGH, Anthony;** *see* Haigh, A. A. F.

**HAIGH, (Austin) Anthony (Francis),** CMG 1954; retired as Director of Education and of Cultural and Scientific Affairs, Council of Europe, 1962-68; *b* 29 Aug. 1907; *s* of late P. B. Haigh, ICS, and Eliza (*d* 1963), *d* of George Moxon; *m* 1935, Gertrude, 2nd *d* of Frank Dodd, Rio de Janeiro; two *s* two *d*. *Educ:* Eton; King's Coll., Cambridge. Entered Diplomatic Service, 1932; served in Foreign Office and at HM Embassies at Rio de Janeiro, Tokyo, Lisbon, Ankara, Cairo and Brussels; Head of Cultural Relations Department, Foreign Office, 1952-62. Chairman Cttee of Cultural Experts, Council of Europe, 1960-61; Chairman, Admin. Board, Cultural Fund of Council of Europe, 1961-62. *Publication:* A Ministry of Education for Europe, 1970. *Address:* 17 Clarendon Road, W11. *Clubs:* Athenæum, Leander.

**HAIGH, Clifford;** Editor, The Friend, since 1966; *b* 5 Feb. 1906; *yr s* of Leonard and Isabel Haigh, Bradford, Yorks; *m* 1st, 1934, Dora Winifred Fowler (*d* 1959); one *s* one *d*; 2nd, 1970, Grace Elizabeth Cross. Editorial Staff: Yorkshire Observer, 1924-27; Birmingham Post, 1928-46; The Times, 1947-61; Assistant Editor, The Friend, 1961-65. *Recreation:* walking. *Address:* 15 Granville Square, WC1. *T:* 01-837 7361.

**HAIGHT, Gordon Sherman,** PhD; Professor of English, Yale University, 1950, Emily Sanford Professor, 1966, Emeritus 1969; *b* 6 Feb. 1901; *s* of Louis Pease Haight and Grace Carpenter; *m* 1937, Mary Treat Nettleton. *Educ:* Yale Univ. BA 1923, PhD 1933. Master in English: Kent Sch., 1924-25; Hotchkiss Sch., 1925-30; taught English at Yale, 1931-69; Master of Pierson Coll., Yale Univ., 1949-53. Visiting Prof. of English: Columbia Univ., 1946-47; Univ. of Oregon, 1949. Guggenheim Fellow, 1946, 1953, 1960. Fellow Royal Society of Literature, Corres. Fellow British Academy. Member: Berzelius; Zeta Psi. *Publications:* Mrs Sigourney, 1930; George Eliot and John Chapman, 1940, 1969; George Eliot, A Biography, 1968 (James Tait Black Award, Heinemann Award of Royal Society of Literature, Van Wyck Brooks Award, 1969; Amer. Acad. of Arts and Letters Award, 1970); Editor: Miss Ravenel's Conversion (J. W. De Forest), 1939, 1955; Adam Bede, 1948; The George Eliot Letters, 7 vols, 1954-55; Middlemarch, 1955; The Mill on the Floss, 1961; A Century of George Eliot Criticism, 1965; Portable Victorian Reader, 1971; contribs to various literary jls. *Recreations:* garden, water colours. *Address:* 145 Peck Hill Road, Woodbridge, Conn 06525, USA. *Clubs:* Yale, Century (New York); Elizabethan (New Haven).

**HAILE SELLASSIE, I, Emperor;** *see* Ethiopia, Emperor of.

**HAILES,** 1st Baron, *cr* 1957, of Prestonkirk; **Patrick George Thomas Buchan-Hepburn,** PC 1951; GBE 1957; CH 1962; *b* 2 April 1901; *y s* of late Sir Archibald Buchan-Hepburn, 4th Bt of Smeaton-Hepburn, East Lothian; *uncle* and *heir-pres.* to Sir Ninian Buchan-Hepburn, 6th Bt, *qv*; *m* 1945, Diana, *d* of late Brig.-Gen. Hon. Charles Lambton, DSO, and *widow* of Major W. Hedworth Williamson. *Educ:* Harrow; Trinity Coll., Cambridge. Hon. Attaché HM Embassy, Constantinople, 1926-27; contested (C) Wolverhampton East, 1929; Member of the LCC (North Kensington), 1930-31. MP (C) E Toxteth Division of Liverpool, Feb. 1931-Feb. 1950, Beckenham Division, 1950-57; Parliamentary Private Secretary to Rt Hon. Oliver Stanley, 1931; Junior Lord of the Treasury, 1939, and again 1944; Conservative Deputy Chief Whip, July 1945, and Chief Whip, 1948. Parliamentary Secretary to the Treasury and Government Chief Whip, 1951-55; Minister of Works, 1955-57; Governor-General and C-in-C of the West Indies, 1958-62. Served in the War, 1940-43, with RA and on staff. Chairman Historic Buildings Council for England, 1963-. KStJ. *Address:* 1 Pelham Place, SW7. *T:* 01-589 1870. *Clubs:* Carlton, Travellers'.

**HAILSHAM,** 2nd Viscount, *cr* 1929, of Hailsham; Baron, *cr* 1928 [disclaimed his peerages for life, 20 Nov. 1963]; *see under* Baron Hailsham of St Marylebone.

**HAILSHAM OF SAINT MARYLEBONE,** Baron *cr* 1970 (Life Peer), of Herstmonceux; **Quintin McGarel Hogg,** PC 1956; QC; Lord High Chancellor of Great Britain since 1970; *b* 9 Oct. 1907; *er s* of 1st Viscount Hailsham, PC, KC, and Elizabeth (*d* 1925), *d* of Judge Trimble Brown, Nashville, Tennessee, USA, and *widow* of Hon. A. J. Marjoribanks; *S* father, 1950, as 2nd Viscount Hailsham, but disclaimed his peerages for life, 20 Nov. 1963 (Baron *cr* 1928, Viscount *cr* 1929); *m* 1944, Mary Evelyn, *d* of Richard Martin (of Ross), London, SW; two *s* three *d*. *Educ:* Eton (Schol., Newcastle Schol.); Christ Church, Oxford ( (Scholar). First Class Hon. Mods, 1928; First Class Lit Hum, 1930; Pres., Oxford Union Soc., 1929. Served War of 1939-45: commissioned Rifle Bde Sept. 1939; served Middle East Forces, Western Desert, 1941 (wounded); Egypt, Palestine, Syria, 1942; Temp. Major, 1942. Fellow of All Souls Coll., Oxford, 1931-38, 1961-; Barrister, Lincoln's Inn, 1932; a Bencher of Lincoln's Inn, 1956; QC 1953. MP (C) Oxford City, 1938-50, St Marylebone, (Dec.) 1963-70; Jt Parly Under-Sec. of State for Air, 1945; First Lord of the Admiralty, 1956-57; Minister of Education, 1957; Dep. Leader of the House of Lords, 1957-60; Leader of the House of Lords, 1960-63; Lord Privy Seal, 1959-60; Lord Pres. of the Council, 1957-59 and 1960-64; Minister for Science and Technology, 1959-64; Minister with special responsibility for: Sport, 1962-64; dealing with unemployment in the North-East, 1963-64; higher education, Dec. 1963-Feb. 1964; Sec. of State for Education and Science, April-Oct. 1964. Chm. of the Conservative Party Organization, Sept. 1957-Oct. 1959. Rector of Glasgow Univ., 1959-62. Pres. Classical Assoc., 1960-61. John Findley Green Foundation Lecture, 1960. Hon. Student of Christ Church, Oxford, 1962; Hon. Mem. Inst. of Civil Engineers, 1963. Hon. DCL, Westminster Coll., Fulton, Missouri, USA, 1960, Newcastle, 1964; Hon. LLD Cambridge, 1963. *Publications:* The Law of Arbitration, 1935; One Year's Work, 1944; The Law and Employers' Liability, 1944; The Times We Live In, 1944; Making Peace, 1945; The Left was never Right, 1945; The Purpose of Parliament, 1946; Case for Conservatism, 1947; The Law of Monopolies, Restrictive Practices and Resale Price Maintenance, 1956; The Conservative Case, 1959; Interdependence, 1961; Science and Politics, 1963; The Devil's Own Song, 1968. *Heir:* (*to disclaimed viscountcy*): *s* Hon. Douglas Martin Hogg [*b* 5 Feb. 1945; *m* 1968, Sarah, *d* of Rt Hon. J. A. Boyd-Carpenter, *qv*; one *d*]. *Recreations:* walking, climbing, shooting, etc. *Address:* House of Lords, SW1; The Corner House, Heathview Gardens, SW15. *Clubs:* Carlton, Alpine, MCC.

**HAILSTONE, Bernard,** RP; painter; *b* 6 Oct. 1910; *s* of William Edward Hailstone; *m* 1934, Joan Mercia Kenet Hastings; one *s*. *Educ:* Sir Andrew Judd's Sch., Tonbridge. Trained at Goldsmiths' Coll. and Royal Academy Schs; Practising Artist, 1934-39; NFS, London (Fireman Artist), 1939-42; Official War Artist to Ministry of Transport, 1942-44; Official War Artist to SEAC, 1944-45. *Recreation:* tennis. *Address:* Hadlow Castle, near Tonbridge, Kent. *T:* Hadlow 322. *Club:* Chelsea Arts.

**HAIMENDORF, Christoph von F.;** *see* Fürer-Haimendorf.

**HAIN, Henry William Theodore,** CBE 1943; retired; *b* 17 Aug. 1899; *e s* of late H. M. Hain, Leamington Spa, Warwicks; *m* 1928, Dorothy Eileen, 2nd *d* of Mrs E. Wysard; one *s* one *d.* *Educ:* Warwick Sch.; Birmingham Univ. BSc (Hons) in Civil Engineering, 1923; commissioned Royal Artillery, 1918-19. Joined Braithwaite & Co., Engineers, Ltd of Westminster, 1923; Managing Dir, 1961-64, retired 1965. Chm., Indian Engineering Assoc., 1939-43; Managing Dir, Braithwaite & Co. (India), Ltd, 1935-50. Dir, Braithwaite & Co., Engineers Ltd. *Recreation:* gardening. *Address:* Heather Cottage, The Barton, Cobham, Surrey. *T:* Cobham 2727. *Clubs:* Oriental; Bengal (Calcutta).

**HAINE, Reginald Leonard,** VC, MC; Captain HAC; *s* of late H. J. Haine, Clipsham, Ringley Avenue, Horley; *b* 10 July 1896; *m* 1923, Dora Beatrice, *er d* of late E. Holder, Monticello, South Border, Purley; one *d.* Lieut-Col Home Guard. *Address:* Dawslea Cottage, Hollist Lane, Midhurst, Sussex.

**HAINES, Sir Cyril (Henry),** KBE 1962 (CBE 1953; MBE 1930); Chairman, South West London Rent Tribunal, 1962-66; *b* 2 March 1895; *s* of late Walter John Haines, OBE, formerly Deputy Chief Inspector of Customs and Excise; *m* 1934, Mary Theodora, *d* of late Rev. J. W. P. Silvester, BD, Hon. CF, Vicar of Wembley; two *d.* *Educ:* Hele's Sch., Exeter. Apptd to Scottish Education Dept, 1914. On active service with Army, 1915-19. Appt to Foreign Office, Dec. 1919. Called to Bar, Middle Temple, 1926. Asst Brit. Agent to Anglo-Mexican Revolutionary Claims Commn, 1928; Registrar, HM Supreme Court, for China, 1930 (acted as Asst Judge during absences from China of one of Judges); Asst Judge, HM Consular Court in Egypt, and, for Naval Courts, HM Consul at Alexandria, Egypt, 1943; Judge of HM Consular Court in Egypt, 1946. Indep. Referee for War Pension Appeals in Egypt, 1946; Asst Judge of HM Chief Court for the Persian Gulf, 1949-59, and Head of Claims Dept, Foreign Office, 1949-54; Judge of HM Chief Court for the Persian Gulf, 1959-61. *Address:* Wood Lea, The Glen, Farnborough Park, Kent. *T:* Farnborough, Kent, 54507.

**HAINES, Geoffrey Colton,** OBE 1965; FCA, FSA; Deputy Chairman, Royal Masonic Benevolent Institution; Member, Board of Management, Royal Masonic Hospital; Fellow, The Royal Numismatic Society, (Hon. Treasurer, 1930-61); *b* Barrow-in-Furness, 18 Sept. 1899; *e surv s* of late Harry Colton Haines, FCA, and Margaret Elizabeth Haines (*née* Barnes); *m* Olive (JP, Mayor of Wandsworth, 1956-57), *er d* of late Philip Scott Minor, Solicitor, Manchester; one *d.* *Educ:* St Paul's Sch. 2nd Lieut The East Surrey Regt, 1919; Dep. Dist Warden, Putney, 1939-45; Bomb Reconnaissance Officer, Civil Defence, 1943-45; Asst Chief Warden, Civil Defence Corps, Wandsworth, 1954-55. Chief Executive Officer, London Association for the Blind, 1932-64, Vice-Pres., 1965; former Mem. of Executive Cttee of Royal National Institute for the Blind and other Charities for Blind Welfare; Hon. Mem., Nat. Assoc. of Workshops for the Blind. *Publications:* Revised, The Roman Republican Coinage (by late Rev. E. A. Sydenham), 1952; various papers to Numismatic Chronicle, etc. *Recreations:* Archæology, Roman and Byzantine history and Numismatics, travel, motoring, walking. *Address:* 31 Larpent Avenue, Putney, SW15. *T:* 01-788 0132.

**HAINES, Maj.-Gen. James Laurence Piggott,** CB 1952; CBE 1950; *b* 27 Nov. 1896; *s* of W. J. Haines, Witney; *m* 1st, 1930, Edith Nancy Freeman (*d* 1956); no *c*; 2nd, 1957, Jane Elizabeth, *d* of G. Drury, PC, Cootehill, County Cavan. *Educ:* Brighton Coll., Royal Military Academy, Woolwich. Served European War, 1916-19; Iraq Levies, 1925-27; Military Coll. of Science, pac, 1927-30; Technical Staff Appointments, UK, Canada and USA, 1930-49; Vice-Pres. Ordnance Board, 1949; Pres. Ordnance Board, 1951-52; retired pay, 1952. Managing Dir, Aron Electricity Meter, Ltd, 1952-59. *Address:* 29 Park Gate, Somerhill Road, Hove BN3 1RL. *Club:* United Service.

**HAINES, Joseph Thomas William;** Press Secretary to the Prime Minister, 1969-70; *b* 29 Jan. 1928; *s* of Joseph and Elizabeth Haines; *m* 1955, Irene Betty Lambert; no *c.* *Educ:* Elementary Schools, Rotherhithe, SE16. Parly Correspondent, The Bulletin (Glasgow) 1954-58, Political Correspondent, 1958-60; Political Correspondent: Scottish Daily Mail, 1960-64; The Sun, 1964-68; Dep. Press Sec. to Prime Minister, Jan.-June 1969. Mem. Tonbridge UDC, 1963-69. *Recreations:* heresy and watching football. *Address:* 7 Hazel Shaw, Tonbridge, Kent. *T:* Tonbridge 3460.

**HAINSWORTH, Col John Raymond,** CMG 1953; CBE 1945; retired; *b* 14 March 1900; *s* of William Henry Hainsworth, Keighley, Yorks; *m* 1925, Dora Marguerite Skiller, Rochester, Kent; one *s* one *d.* *Educ:* Taunton Sch.; RMA, Woolwich. Commissioned in Royal Engineers, 1919; posted to India, 1922. Served War of 1939-45 (despatches twice, CBE): Burma Campaign, 1942-45; apptd Dir of Works, GHQ, India, March 1945; seconded to Civil Employment in PWD, NWFP, India, 1946; Chief Engineer and Secretary to Government, PWD, NWFP, Pakistan, 1948-52; retired with rank of Col, 1952. *Recreations:* shooting, fishing. *Address:* Painswick House, Cavendish, near Sudbury, Suffolk. *T:* Glemsford 352.

**HAINWORTH, Henry Charles,** CMG 1961; Ambassador to Indonesia, 1968-70; *b* 12 Sept. 1914; *o s* of late Charles S. and Emily G. I. Hainworth; *m* 1944, Mary, *yr d* of late Felix B. and Lilian Ady; two *d.* *Educ:* Blundell's Sch.; Sidney Sussex Coll., Cambridge. Entered HM Consular Service, 1939; HM Embassy, Tokyo, 1940-42; seconded to Ministry of Information (Far Eastern Bureau, New Delhi), 1942-46; HM Embassy, Tokyo, 1946-51; Foreign Office, 1951-53; HM Legation, Bucharest, 1953-55; NATO Defence Coll., Paris, 1956; Political Office, Middle East Forces (Nicosia), 1956; Foreign Office, 1957-61 (Head of Atomic Energy and Disarmament Dept, 1958-61); Counsellor, United Kingdom Delegation to the Brussels Conference, 1961-63; HM Minister and Consul-Gen. at British Embassy, Vienna, 1963-68. *Recreations:* tennis, fishing. *Address:* c/o Foreign and Commonwealth Office, SW1. *Club:* Hurlingham.

**HAITINK, Bernard;** Artistic Director and Permanent Conductor, Concertgebouw Orchestra, Amsterdam, since 1964; also Principal Conductor and Artistic Adviser, London Philharmonic Orchestra, since 1967; *b* Amsterdam, 1929. *Educ:* Amsterdam Conservatory. Studied conducting under Felix Hupka, but started his career as a violinist with the Radio Philharmonic; in 1954 and 1955 attended annual conductors' course (org. by Netherlands Radio Union) under Ferdinand Leitner; became 2nd Conductor with Radio Union at Hilversum with co-responsibility for 4 radio orchs and conducted the Radio Philharmonic in public during the Holland Fest., in The Hague, 1956; conducted that choir with the Concertgebouw Orch. (as a subst. for Guilini) Oct. 1956; then followed guest engagements with this and other orchs in the Netherlands and elsewhere. Debut in USA, with Los Angeles Symph. Orch., 1958; 5 week season with Concertgebouw Orch., 1958-59, and toured Britain with it, 1959; apptd (with Eugen Jochum) as the Orchestra's permanent conductor, Sept. 1961; 2nd US tour 1961; 4 week tour of Japan, 1962; Edinburgh Fest., 1963; became sole artistic dir and permanent conductor of the orch., 1967. Undertook to conduct the LPO as principal conductor for 4 periods per season (Nov., Jan., March, May), 1967-, and in 1970 assumed title of LPO's Artistic Director. Has been a guest conductor all over the world, and has been interested in conducting youth orchs. Bruckner Medal of Honour, 1970. *Address:* c/o London Philharmonic Orchestra Ltd, 53 Welbeck Street, W1M 7HE.

**HAJNAL, John,** FBA 1966; Reader in Statistics, London School of Economics, since 1966; *b* 26 Nov. 1924; *s* of Kálmán and Eva Hajnal-Kónyi; *m* 1950, Nina Lande; one *s* three *d. Educ:* University Coll. Sch., London; Balliol Coll., Oxford. Employed by: Royal Commission on Population, 1944-48; UN, New York, 1948-51; Office of Population Research, Princeton Univ., 1951-53; Manchester Univ., 1953-57; London Sch. of Economics, 1957-. Mem. Internat. Statistical Institute. *Publications:* papers on demography, statistics, etc. *Address:* London School of Economics and Political Science, Houghton Street, WC1. *T:* 01-405 7686.

**HAKE, Herbert Denys,** OBE 1961; MA; retired as Headmaster, The King's School, Parramatta, NSW, Australia (1939-64); *b* 8 Nov. 1894; *s* of late E. D. Hake; *m* 1938, Elizabeth Barton; three *d. Educ:* Haileybury Coll.; Queens' Coll., Cambridge. Served European War, Hants Regt, 1914-19, India and Mesopotamia (Capt., despatches); Asst Master, Haileybury Coll., 1921-38; Temporary Asst Master, St John's Coll., Johannesburg, 1927-28; Chm., Headmasters' Conference of Australia, 1951-54. FACE 1962. *Address:* Hailey, Mills Road, Glenhaven, NSW 2154, Australia. *Clubs:* MCC (London); Australian (Sydney).

**HAKEWILL SMITH, Maj.-Gen. Sir Edmund,** KCVO 1967; CB 1945; CBE 1944; MC; psc; JP; Deputy Constable and Lieutenant-Governor of Windsor Castle since 1964; Governor, Military Knights of Windsor since 1951; *b* Kimberley, S Africa, 17 March 1896; *s* of George Cecil Smith and Mildred, 2nd *d* of J. B. Currey; *m* 1928, Edith Constance, *e d* of Brigadier-Gen. H. Nelson, DSO, Shovel, Somerset; one *d. Educ:* Diocesan Coll., South Africa; RMC Sandhurst. Commissioned into Royal Scots Fusiliers as 2nd Lieut, 1915; ADC to Governor of Bengal, 1921-22; Adjutant, 2nd RSF, 1927-30; Staff Coll., Quetta, 1930-32; Staff Capt., War Office, 1934-36. Employed Air Staff Duties, RAF, 1936-37; DAAG War Office, 1938-40. Comdr 5 Devons, March-June 1940; Comdr 4/5 RSF, 1940-41; Comd 1957 Inf. Bde, 1941-42; Dir of Organisation, War Office (Maj.-Gen.), 1942-43; Comdr 155 Inf. Bde (Brig.), Feb.-Nov. 1943; Comdr 52nd Lowland Div. (Maj.-Gen.), 1943 till disbandment, 1946; Commander, Lowland District, 1946; retired pay, 1949. Served European War, 1915-18 (wounded twice, MC); War of 1939-45 (despatches, CBE, CB. Order of St Olaf, Order of Orange-Nassau). Col, The Royal Scots Fusiliers, 1946-57; Berks County Commandant, Army Cadet Force, 1952-57. Grand Officer of Order of Orange Nassau, 1947; Order of St Olaf, Second Class, 1947. *Address:* Mary Tudor Tower, Lower Ward, Windsor Castle, Berks.

**HALABY, Najeeb Elias;** Chairman of the Board, President and Chief Executive Officer, Pan American World Airways, since 1970 (Senior Vice-President, President, then President and Chief Executive Officer, 1965-70); Member Board, and Executive Committee of Board; Director: Whirlpool Corporation; Chrysler Corporation; Bank of America; *b* 19 Nov. 1915; *s* of late Najeeb Elias Halaby and of Laura Wilkins Halaby; *m* 1946, Doris Carlquist; one *s* two *d. Educ:* Stanford Univ. (AB); Yale Univ. (LLB); Bonar Law Coll., Ashridge, (Summer) 1939. Practised law in Los Angeles, Calif, 1940-42, 1958-61; Air Corps Flight Instructor, 1940; Test pilot for Lockheed Aircraft Corp., 1942-43; Naval aviator, established Navy Test Pilot Sch., 1943; formerly Chief of Intelligence Coordination Div., State Dept; Foreign Affairs Advisor to Sec. of Defense; Chm., NATO Military Production and Supply Board, 1950; Asst Administrator, Mutual Security Economic Cooperation Administration, 1950-51; Dep. Sec. of Defense for Internat. Security, 1952-54; Vice-Chm., White House Advisory Group whose report led to formation of Federal Aviation Agency, 1955-56, Administrator of the Agency, 1961-65. Associate of Laurance and Nelson Rockefeller, 1954-57; Past Exec. Vice-Pres. and Dir, Servomechanisms Inc.; Sec.-Treas., Aerospace Corp., 1959-61, Trustee, 1965-; Pres., American Technology Corp.; Monsanto Safety Award; FAA Exceptional Service Medal. Hon. LLB: Allegheney Coll., Pa, 1967; Loyola Coll., LA, 1968. *Recreation:* golf. *Address:* (office) Pan American World Airways, Pan Am Building, New York, NY 10017, USA; (home) 1120 Fifth Avenue, New York, NY 10028, USA. *Clubs:* Aviation, Metropolitan, Chevy Chase (Washington); California (Los Angeles); River (NYC); Burning Tree (Bethesda, Md).

**HALDANE, Archibald Richard Burdon,** CBE 1968; *b* 18 Nov. 1900; *s* of late Sir William Haldane; *m* 1941, Janet Macrae Simpson-Smith; one *s* one *d. Educ:* Edinburgh Academy; Winchester Coll.; Balliol Coll., Oxford; Edinburgh University. LLB Edinburgh, 1926; WS 1926; DLitt Edinburgh, 1950. Dep. Chm., Trustee Savings Banks Assoc., 1959-61; Chm., Trustee Savings Banks Inspection Cttee, 1960-67; Trustee, National Library of Scotland. *Publications:* By Many Waters, 1940; The Path by the Water, 1944; The Drove Roads of Scotland, 1950; New Ways through the Glens, 1962; Three Centuries of Scottish Posts, 1970. *Recreations:* fishing, walking. *Address:* Foswell, Auchterarder, Perthshire. *T:* Auchterarder 2610; 4 North Charlotte Street, Edinburgh. *T:* 031-225 4181. *Club:* New (Edinburgh).

**HALE, Arthur James,** BSc London; Chemist (retd); *b* 25 Jan. 1877; *m* 1st, 1907, Gertrude Ann (*d* 1945); 2nd, 1947, Winifred F. E. Clifford (*d* 1966). *Educ:* Manor House Sch., Clapham; S-Western Polytechnic. Demonstrator, Chemical Dept Borough Polytechnic, 1903-6; Lecturer in Chemistry and Physics, Waterford Technical Institute, 1906-10; Lecturer, Dept of Applied Chemistry, City and Guilds' Technical Coll., Finsbury, 1910-17; Chief Asst, 1918-21;

Professor of Applied Chemistry, City and Guilds' Technical Coll. Finsbury, 1921-26. *Publications:* Practical Chemistry for Engineering Students; The Synthetic Use of Metals in Organic Chemistry; The Applications of Electrolysis in Chemical Industry; The Manufacture of Chemicals by Electrolysis; Modern Chemistry, Pure and Applied. *Address:* c/o Lloyds Bank Ltd, Terminus Road, Eastbourne, Sussex.

**HALE, (Charles) Leslie;** *b* 13 July 1902; *s* of Benjamin George Hale, Managing Director of Stableford & Co. Ltd, Coalville, Leics; *m* 1926, Dorothy Ann Latham; one *s* one *d*. *Educ:* Ashby-de-la-Zouch Boys' Grammar Sch. Articled to Evan Barlow, Solicitor, Leicester; practised in Coalville, Nuneaton and London. Mem. Leics County Council, 1925-50. Contested (L) S Nottingham, 1929. MP (Lab) for Oldham, Lancs, 1945-50, West Division of Oldham, 1950-Jan. 1968, resigned. Freedom of Oldham, 1969. *Publications:* Thirty Who Were Tried, 1955; John Philpot Curran, 1958; Blood on the Scales, 1960; Hanged in Error, 1961; Hanging in the Balance, 1962; None So Blind, 1963. *Recreations:* chess, trying to paint. *Address:* 92 College Road, SE21.

**HALE, Sir Edward,** KBE 1952; CB 1942; Hon. LLD Leeds, 1959, Belfast, 1959, London, 1961; *b* 1895; *er s* of late Dr G. E. Hale, Eton; *m* 1930, Joan Latham, *er d* of late Sir Alexander (Hon. Mr Justice) Bateson; two *d*. *Educ:* Tonbridge Sch.; Corpus Christi Coll., Oxford. MA; entered Treasury, 1921; Secretary to University Grants Cttee, 1951-57; Administrative Head, Historical Branch, Cabinet Office, 1958-60. *Address:* Jordleys, Goring, Reading, Berks. *Club:* United University.

**HALE, Comdr John William,** DSO 1940; RN retired; *b* 30 March 1907; 4th *s* of late Warren Stormes Hale and late Cora Hale; *m* 1938, Ada Elizabeth Bowden; one *s* two *d*. *Educ:* Highgate Sch.; RN Coll., Dartmouth. Went to sea as midshipman in HMS Resolution, 1924; Lieut and joined Fleet Air Arm, 1929; Lieut Cdr 1937; at beginning of war of 1939-45, served in HMS Glorious and then HMS Illustrious; Commander, 1940; retired, 1957; Freeman of City of London; Past Master of Tallow Chandlers Company. *Recreations:* sailing, gardening. *Address:* Letheringham Mill, Woodbridge, Suffolk. *Clubs:* United Service, MCC.

**HALE, Joseph;** engineer; formerly Merchant Navy; *b* 28 Oct. 1913; *s* of J. Gordon Tyson Hale and M. Hale (*née* Johnston); *m* 1939, Annie Irene Clowes; one *s* one *d*. *Educ:* elementary and secondary technical schs. Mem. Bolton Town Council until 1950; Junior Whip to Labour Group; Chm. Bolton West Divisional Party, 1949; Mem. Amalgamated Engineering Union District Cttee, 1943-50. MP (Lab) Rochdale, 1950-51. *Recreations:* literature, music; Methodist lay preacher and church worker. *Address:* 30 Thorpe Street, Bolton, Lancs.

**HALE, Kathleen, (Mrs Douglas McClean);** artist; illustrator and author of books for children; *b* 24 May 1898; *d* of Charles Edward Hale and Ethel Alice Aylmer Hughes; *m* 1926, Dr Douglas McClean (*d* 1967); two *s*. *Educ:* Manchester High Sch. for Girls; Manchester Sch. of Art; Art Dept (scholar) of University Coll., Reading; Central Sch. of Art; East Anglian Sch. of Painting and Drawing. Has exhibited paintings at: New English Art Club, London Group, Grosvenor Galleries, Vermont Gallery, Warwick Public Library Gallery; metal groups and pictures at: Lefevre Galleries; Leicester Galleries. Mural for South Bank (Festival) Schs Section, 1951; Orlando Ballet for Festival Gardens, 1951. *Publications:* The Orlando The Marmalade Cat Series, since 1938: Camping Holiday; Trip Abroad; Buys a Farm; Becomes a Doctor; Silver Wedding; Keeps a Dog; A Seaside Holiday; The Frisky Housewife; Orlando's Evening Out; Orlando's Home Life; Orlando's Invisible Pyjamas; Orlando the Judge; Orlando's Zoo; Orlando's Magic Carpet; Henrietta, the Faithful Hen, 1946; Puss-in-Boots Peep-Show, 1950; Manda, 1952; Orlando's Country Peep-Show; Orlando Buys a Cottage; Orlando and The Three Graces; Orlando Goes to the Moon; TV and radio programmes. *Recreation:* painting. *Address:* Tod House, Forest Hill, near Oxford. *T:* Stanton St John 390.

**HALE, Leslie;** *see* Hale, Charles L.

**HALE, Lionel Ramsay;** journalist and dramatist; *b* 26 Oct. 1909; 2nd *s* of James and Lylie Hale; *m* 1939, Betty Tayler (*d* 1952); one *s* one *d*; *m* 1955, Crystal Pudney, *e d* of Sir Alan Herbert; one *d*. *Educ:* Charterhouse; Balliol Coll., Oxford. Asst Lit. Ed., News Chronicle, 1933-37; Dramatic Critic, News Chronicle, 1937-40; Govt service, 1940-46; Dramatic Critic, Daily Mail, 1946-48. General Editor, Evans Plays, 1949. Organiser, Nat. Library Week, 1969; Festival Organiser, Islington '70. Dramatic and literary criticism for various newspapers and magazines, including Observer, and frequent broadcasting for BBC Plays: Beargarden, 1931; She Passed Through Lorraine, 1931; These Two, 1933; The Mocking Bird, 1933; Festival Time, 1937; Gilt and Gingerbread, 1959. *Publications:* The Old Vic, 1949-50; A Fleece of Lambs, 1961. *Address:* 76 Noel Road, N1. *T:* 01-226 4597; Little Lodge, Great Bardfield, Essex. *T:* 450.

**HALEY, Sir William (John),** KCMG, 1946; Hon. LLD Cambridge 1951, Dartmouth, New Hampshire, 1957, London, 1963, St Andrews, 1965; Hon. Fellow Jesus College, Cambridge 1956; FRSL; Editor-in-Chief, Encyclopædia Britannica, 1968-69; *b* Jersey, CI, 24 May 1901; *s* of Frank Haley, Bramley, Leeds, and Marie Sangan; *m* 1921, Edith Susie Gibbons; two *s* two *d*. *Educ:* Victoria Coll., Jersey. Joined Manchester Evening News, 1922; Chief Sub-Editor, 1925; Managing Editor, 1930; Dir Manchester Guardian and Evening News, Ltd, 1930; Jt Managing Dir, 1939-43; Dir Press Association, 1939-43; Dir Reuters, 1939-43; Editor-in-Chief, BBC, 1943-44; Dir-Gen., BBC, 1944-52; Editor of the Times, 1952-66; Dir and Chief Executive, The Times Publishing Co. Ltd, 1965-66; Chm., Times Newspapers Ltd, 1967. Pres., Nat. Book League, 1955-62. Chevalier Legion of Honour, 1948; Grand Officer, Order of Orange Nassau, 1950. *Address:* Beau Site, Gorey, Jersey, Channel Islands. *T:* Jersey East 68.
*See also Prof. J. N. Hunt.*

**HALFORD, Maj.-Gen. Michael Charles Kirkpatrick,** DSO 1946; OBE 1957; *b* 28 Oct. 1914; *s* of Lieut-Col M. F. Halford, OBE, and Violet Halford (*née* Kirkpatrick); *m* 1945, Pamela Joy (*née* Wright); three *s*. *Educ:* Wellington Coll.; Trinity Coll., Cambridge. Commissioned Royal Guernsey Militia, 1932; 2nd Lieut York and Lancaster Regt, 1935; served Egypt and Palestine, 1936; France 1940; N Africa, Italy, France and Germany; comd Hallamshire Bn, York and Lancaster Regt, 1945, 1st Bn, 1954; Asst Army Instr, Imperial Defence Coll., 1957; comd 147 Inf. Bde (TA), 1960; GOC 43 (Wessex) Div./District, 1964-67; retd, 1967. Col The York and Lancaster Regt, 1966. *Recreations:* shooting, golf.

*Address:* c/o Lloyds Bank Ltd, Cox's & King's Branch, Pall Mall, SW1. *Club:* Army and Navy.

**HALFORD-MacLEOD, Aubrey Seymour,** CMG 1958; CVO 1965; HM Ambassador to Iceland, 1966-70; *b* 15 Dec. 1914; *o s* of late Joseph and Clara Halford; changed name by deed poll from Halford to Halford-MacLeod, 1964; *m* 1939, Giovanna Mary, *o d* of late W. H. Durst; three *s* one *d. Educ:* King Edward's Sch., Birmingham; Magdalen Coll., Oxford. Entered HM Diplomatic (subseq. Foreign, now again Diplomatic) Service as Third Sec., 1937; Bagdad, 1939; Second Sec., 1942; transferred to Office of Minister Resident in N Africa, 1943; First Sec., 1943; British mem. of Secretariat of Advisory Council for Italy, 1944; British High Commission in Italy, 1944; Asst Political Adviser to Allied Commission in Italy, Sept, 1944, Political Adviser, 1945; transferred to HM Foreign Office, 1946, Principal Private Sec. to Permanent Under-Sec.; Dep. Exec. Sec. to Preparatory Commission for Council of Europe, May 1949, and promoted Counsellor; Dep. Sec. Gen. of the Council of Europe, 1949-52; Counsellor, HM Embassy, Tokyo, 1953-55; in charge of HM Legation, Seoul, 1954; Counsellor at HM Embassy in Libya, 1955-57; HM Political Agent at Kuwait, 1957-59; HM Consul-Gen., Munich, 1959-65. *Publication:* (with G. M. Halford) The Kabuki Handbook, 1956. *Recreations:* fishing, shooting, ornithology. *Address:* Mulag House, Ardvourlie, N Harris. *Clubs:* Brooks's, Royal Central Asian Society.

**HALIFAX,** 2nd Earl of, *cr* 1944; **Charles Ingram Courtenay Wood,** Bt 1784; Baron Irwin, 1925; Viscount Halifax, 1866; Lord Lieutenant for East Riding of Yorks, since 1968; *b* 3 Oct. 1912; *e s* of 1st Earl of Halifax, KG, PC, OM, GCSI, GCMG, GCIE, TD, and Lady Dorothy Evelyn Augusta Onslow (*see* Dowager Countess of Halifax); *S* father 1959; *m* 1936, Ruth (JP 1956 ER Yorks), *d* of late Captain Rt Hon. Neil James Archibald Primrose, MC, sometime MP; one *s* two *d. Educ:* Eton; Christ Ch., Oxford. 2nd Lieut Royal Horse Guards, 1934-37; War of 1939-45, Middle East, Captain. MP (U) York, 1937-45. High Steward of York Minster, 1970-. Mem. of Jockey Club; Senior Steward, 1950, 1959. Mem. of National Hunt Cttee; Joint Master, Middleton Foxhounds, 1946-; DL, E Riding of Yorks and Kingston upon Hull, 1955-68; JP, E Riding of Yorks, 1963-68; Chm., E Riding of Yorks CC, 1968. KStJ 1970. *Recreations:* hunting, shooting. *Heir: s* Lord Irwin, *qv. Address:* Swynford Paddocks, Six Mile Bottom, Newmarket. *T:* Six Mile Bottom 211; Garrowby, York. *T:* Bishop-Wilton 236. *Clubs:* Turf, White's.

*See also Rt Hon. R. F. Wood.*

**HALIFAX, Dowager Countess of, (Dorothy Evelyn Augusta Wood),** CI 1926; DCVO 1953; JP; an Extra Lady of the Bedchamber to Queen Elizabeth the Queen Mother since 1946; *b* 7 Feb. 1885; *yr d* of 4th Earl of Onslow, PC, GCMG; *m* 1909, Hon. Edward Frederick Lindley Wood (later 1st Earl of Halifax, KG, PC, OM, GCSI, GCMG, GCIE; he died 1959); two *s* (and one *s* killed in action, 1942) one *d. Educ:* privately. Vicereine of India, 1926-31. A Lady of the Bedchamber to Queen Elizabeth the Queen Mother, when Queen, 1937-46. JP East and West Ridings of Yorks, 1935. Hon. LLD Leeds, 1939. DGStJ. *Recreations:* gardening, travel, reading. *Address:* 14 Eaton Place, SW1. *T:* 01-235 1892.

*See also Earl of Halifax.*

**HALIFAX (NS), Archbishop of, (RC),** since 1967; **Most Rev. James Martin Hayes;** *b* 27 May 1924; *s* of late L. J. Hayes. *Educ:* St Mary's Univ., Halifax; Holy Heart Seminary, Halifax; Angelicum Univ., Rome. Asst, St Mary's Basilica, 1947-54; Chancellor and Sec. of Archdiocese of Halifax, 1957-65; Rector, St Mary's Basilica, 1964-65; Auxil. Bp of Halifax, 1965-66; Apostolic Administrator of Archdiocese of Halifax, 1966-67. Hon. Dr of Letters, St Anne's Coll., Church Point, NS; Hon. Dr of Sacred Theology, King's Coll., Halifax, NS. *Address:* 6541 Coburg Road, PO Box 1527, Halifax, Nova Scotia, Canada. *T:* 902-429-9388.

**HALIFAX, Archdeacon of;** *see* Lister, Ven. John Field.

**HALL,** family name of **Viscount Hall.**

**HALL,** 2nd Viscount, *cr* 1946, of Cynon Valley; **(William George) Leonard Hall;** Chairman of the Post Office, since 1969; *b* 9 March 1913; *s* of 1st Viscount Hall, PC, and Margaret, *d* of William Jones, Ynysybwl; *S* father, 1965; *m* 1st, 1935, Joan Margaret (*d* 1962), *d* of William Griffiths, Glamorganshire; two *d*; 2nd, 1963, Constance Ann Gathorne, *d* of Rupert Gathorne Hardy, London. *Educ:* Christ Coll., Brecon; University Coll. Hospital. MRCS; LRCP. Asst MOH, Merthyr Tydfil, 1938-40. Surgeon Lt-Comdr, RNVR, 1940-46. Powell Duffryn Group, 1946-60; Dir of Investments, Africa, Asia and ME, Internat. Finance Corp. (affiliate of IBRD), 1962-64; Advisor for Special Projects, Internat. Finance Corp., 1963-64. Liveryman, Hon. Co. of Carmen. *Recreations:* country activities. *Address:* Belgrave Cottage, Upper Belgrave Street, SW1. *T:* 01-235 8918.

**HALL, Alfred Rupert,** MA, PhD; Professor of the History of Science and Technology, Imperial College of Science and Technology, University of London, since 1963; *b* 26 July 1920; *s* of Alfred Dawson Hall and Margaret Ritchie; *m* 1st, 1942, Annie Shore Hughes; two *d*; 2nd, 1959, Marie Boas. *Educ:* Alderman Newton's Boy's Sch., Leicester; Christ's Coll., Cambridge (scholar). Served in Royal Corps of Signals, 1940-45. 1st cl. Historical Tripos Part II, 1946; Allen Scholar, 1948; Fellow, Christ's Coll., 1949-59, Steward, 1955-59; University Lectr, 1950-59. Medical Research Historian, University of Calif, Los Angeles, 1959-60, Prof. of Philosophy, 1960-61; Prof. of History and Logic of Science, Indiana Univ., 1961-63. FRHistS. Pres., British Soc. for History of Science, 1966-68; Mem. Internat. Acad. of the History of Science. Co-editor, A History of Technology, 1951-58. Corresp. Mem., Soc. for the History of Technology, 1970. *Publications:* Ballistics in the Seventeenth Century, 1952; The Scientific Revolution, 1954; From Galileo to Newton, 1963; The Cambridge Philosophical Society: a history, 1819-1969, 1969. With Marie Boas Hall: Unpublished Scientific Papers of Isaac Newton, 1962; Correspondence of Henry Oldenburg, 1965-. Contributor to Isis, Annals of Science, etc. *Address:* Imperial College, Prince Consort Road, SW7. *T:* 01-589 5111; 23 Chiswick Staithe, W4. *T:* 01-994 3490.

**HALL, Sir Arnold (Alexander),** Kt 1954; FRS 1953; MA; Pro-Chancellor, University of Warwick, since 1964; Chairman and Managing Director, Hawker Siddeley Group Ltd, since 1967 (Director, Hawker Siddeley Group, Nov. 1955-, Vice-Chairman, 1963-67); Chairman: Hawker Siddeley Aviation Ltd; Hawker Siddeley Dynamics Ltd; Hawker Siddeley Diesels Ltd; Hawker Siddeley Electric Ltd; Hawker Siddeley Holdings Ltd; High Duty Alloys Ltd; Director: Lloyd's Bank; Phoenix Assurance; ICI; *b* 23 April 1915; married. *Educ:* Clare Coll., Cambridge (Rex Moir Prize in

Engineering, John Bernard Seely Prize in Aeronautics, Ricardo Prize in Thermodynamics). Res. Fellow in Aeronautics of the Company of Armourers and Brasiers (held at University of Cambridge), 1936-38; Principal Scientific Officer, Royal Aircraft Establishment, Farnborough, Hants, 1938-45; Zaharoff Prof. of Aviation, University of London, and Head of Dept of Aeronautics, Imperial Coll. of Science and Technology, 1945-51; Dir of the Royal Aircraft Establishment, Farnborough, 1951-55; Pres., Royal Aeronautical Society, 1958-59, Hon. Fellow, 1965; Dep. Pres., BEAMA, 1966-67, Pres., 1967-68; Vice-Pres., Engineering Employers' Fedn, 1968; Pres., Locomotive and Allied Manufacturers Assoc. of GB, 1968-69, 1969-70. Member: Advisory Council on Scientific Policy, 1962-64; Air Registration Board, 1963-; Electricity Supply Research Council, 1963-; Advisory Council on Technology (Min. of Technology), 1965-67; Nat. Defence Industries Council, 1969-. Fellow, Imperial Coll. of Science and Technology, 1963-; Hon. Fellow, Clare Coll., Cambridge, 1967; Hon. ACGI; Hon. FRAeS; Hon. FAIAA; Hon. MIMechE, 1968. Gold Medal, RAeS, 1962. *Address:* Hawker Siddeley Group Ltd, 18 St James's Square, SW1. *Club:* Athenæum.

**HALL, Arthur Henderson,** RWS 1970; RE 1961; MSIA; ARCA; painter, etcher, freelance illustrator; Head of School of Graphic Design, Kingston Polytechnic; *b* 25 June 1906; *s* of Charles and Mary Hall; *m* 1942, Frances Bruce; one *s* one *d*. *Educ:* Sedgefield; Royal College of Art; British Sch., Rome. Prix de Rome, Engraving, 1931; Glass Designer for Webb & Corbett, 1933-36; Part-time Teacher, Kingston Sch. of Art, 1933-41; Part-time Teacher, London Central Sch. of Art, 1936-39. RAF, 1942-46. Teacher, London Central Sch. of Art, 1946-52; exhibits paintings and etchings at: RA, RWS, RE. *Publications:* numerous illustrations for children's books and books on gardening. *Recreations:* gardening, travel. *Address:* 15 Church Road, East Molesey, Surrey. *T:* 01-979 5681. *Club:* Nash House.

**HALL, Arthur Herbert;** Librarian and Curator, Guildhall Library and Museum, 1956-66, retired; Director of Guildhall Art Gallery, 1956-66; *b* 30 Aug. 1901; *y s* of Henry and Eliza Jane Hall, Islington, London; *m* 1927, Dorothy Maud (*née* Barton); two *s* one *d*. *Educ:* Mercers' Sch., Holborn, London. Entered Guildhall Library as junior asst, 1918; Dep. Librarian, 1943-56. Hon. Librarian, Clockmakers' and Gardeners' Companies, 1956-66. Served with RAOC, 1942-46. Chm. Council, London and Middlesex Archæological Soc., 1957-64, Vice-Pres., 1962-; Member: Council of London Topographical Soc., 1960-67; Soc. of Archivists; Exec. Cttee, Friends of Nat. Libraries, 1965-69. Hon. Secretary: Middlesex Victoria County History Council; Enfield Archæological Soc.; Hon. Clerk, Civic Guild of Old Mercers. Liveryman of the Clockmakers Co.; FLA 1930; FSA 1963. *Address:* 23 Uvedale Road, Enfield, Mddx. *T:* 01-363 2526.

**HALL, Basil Brodribb,** MC 1945; TD 1952; Principal Assistant Solicitor, Treasury Solicitor's Department, since 1968; *b* 2 Jan. 1918; *s* of Alfred Brodribb Hall and Elsie Hilda Hall, Woking, Surrey; *m* 1955, Jean Stafford Gowland; two *s* one *d*. *Educ:* Merchant Taylors' Sch. Articled Clerk with Gibson & Weldon, Solicitors, 1935-39; admitted Solicitor, 1942. Served War of 1939-45: Trooper, Inns of Court Regt, 1939; 2nd Lieut, 12th Royal Lancers, 1940; Capt., 27th Lancers, 1941; Major, 27th Lancers, 1942. Legal Asst, Treasury Solicitor's Dept, 1946; Sen. Legal Asst, 1951; Asst Treasury Solicitor, 1958. *Recreations:* military history, travel. *Address:* Woodlands, Danes Way, Oxshott, Surrey. *T:* Oxshott 2032. *Club:* Cavalry.

**HALL, Catherine Mary,** CBE 1967; General Secretary, Royal College of Nursing and National Council of Nurses of the United Kingdom, since 1957 (designate, 1956-57); *b* 19 Dec. 1922; *d* of late Robert Hall, OBE and of Florence Irene Hall (*née* Turner). *Educ:* Hunmanby Hall Sch. for Girls, Filey, Yorks. Gen. Infirmary, Leeds: nursing trng, 1941-44 (SRN); Ward Sister, 1945-47; sen. nursing appts, 1949-53; midwifery trng, Leeds and Rotherham, 1948 (SCM); travelling fellowship, US and Canada, 1950-51; student in nursing administration, Royal College of Nursing, 1953-54; Asst Matron, Middlesex Hosp., London, 1954-56. *Address:* Peveril, Pilgrims' Way, Westhumble, Dorking, Surrey. *T:* Dorking 2229. *Club:* Cowdray.

**HALL, Dr Cecil Charles,** CB 1968; retired; formerly Director, Warren Spring Laboratory, Ministry of Technology, 1964-68; *b* 10 May 1907; *s* of Frederick Harrington and Alice Hall; *m* 1950, Margaret Rose Nicoll; no *c*. *Educ:* Beckenham Gram. Sch.; London Univ. Jun. Chemist, S Metropolitan Gas Co., 1925-30: BSc 1st Hons Chem. (London), 1929; MSc (London), 1931. Jun. Asst, Fuel Research Stn, DSIR, 1930: PhD (London), 1934. Research in high pressure hydrogenation of coal tar and synthesis of oils and chemicals from coal by catalytic processes. Special Merit Promotion to Sen. Princ. Scientific Off., 1952; Dep. Chief Chemist, Fuel Res. Stn, DSIR, 1953; Dep. Dir, Warren Spring Lab., 1959. FRIC 1944; FInstF 1954. *Publications:* (with T. P. Hilditch) Catalytic Processes in Industrial Chemistry, 1937; numerous research and review papers in scientific and techn. jls dealing with chemistry of high pressure hydrogenation processes and with Fischer Tropsch synthesis. *Recreation:* gardening, specialising in iris growing and hybridising (Pres., British Iris Soc., 1967-). *Address:* Tanglewood, Sollershott West, Letchworth, Herts. *T:* Letchworth 4339. *Clubs:* Civil Service; Rotary (Stevenage).

**HALL, Daniel George Edward,** MA, DLit, FRHistS, FRAS; Professor Emeritus in the University of London since 1959; *b* 1891; *e s* of Daniel Hall of Offley, Hitchin, Herts, and Elinor Ann Field; *m* 1919, Helen Eugenie (*d* 1962), *o d* of late John Banks, Wynberg, SA; two *s* (and *e s* killed in action Nov. 1943) two *d*. *Educ:* Hitchin Grammar Sch.; King's Coll., University of London. BA 1st Class Hons in History, University of London, 1916; Gladstone Memorial Prize and Inglis Studentship, King's Coll., 1915; Asst Lecturer in History, King's Coll., 1916-17; MA 1918; DLit 1930; with the Lena Ashwell Concert Parties on the Western Front in 1916 and early 1917; Inns of Court OTC at Berkhampstead, 1917-19; Senior History Master at Royal Grammar School, Worcester, Jan.-July 1919; Senior History Master at Bedales Sch., 1919-21; Professor of History, University of Rangoon, 1921-34; Headmaster of Caterham Sch., 1934-49; temp. Mem. Legislative Council of Burma, 1923-24; Corr. Mem. Indian Historical Records Commission, 1925; Mem. Panel of Additional Lecturers, Sch. of Oriental and African Studies, University of London, 1940-49; Prof. of the History of South-East Asia in the University of London, 1949-59. Visiting Lecturer, Johns Hopkins University Sch. of Advanced Internat. Studies Summer Sch., Washington, DC, 1955. Visiting Professor: Cornell Univ. Dept Far Eastern

Studies, 1959-60 and 1963; University of Syracuse Summer Sch., 1963; University of BC, 1964-65; Monash Univ., Vic, Aust., 1965; University of BC, 1965-66; Cornell Univ., 1966, 1967-69; University of Michigan, 1966; University of BC, 1967. Royal Society of Arts Silver Medal, 1944. Hon. Fellow Sch. of Oriental and African Studies, 1959. *Publications:* Imperialism in Modern History, 1923; A Brief Survey of English Constitutional History, 1925, revised and enlarged, 1939; Early English Intercourse with Burma, 1587-1743, 1927, 2nd edn 1968; The Dalhousie-Phayre Correspondence, 1852-56, 1929; The Tragedy of Negrais, 1752-59, 1931; Studies in Dutch Relations, with Arakan, 1936; Dutch Trade with Burma in the 17th Century, 1939; Europe and Burma, 1945; Burma, 1950, rev. and enlarged, 1956, 1960; A History of South-East Asia, 1955, rev. and enlarged, 1964, 3rd edn 1968; Michael Symes: Journal of his second mission to Ava in 1802, 1955. Joint-author: a Handbook to the League of Nations for India, Burma and Ceylon, 1926; A High School British History, 1714-1930, 1935, rev. and enlarged, 1946; A Handbook of Oriental History, 1951; (ed) Historians of South-East Asia, 1961; articles in historical journals. *Recreation:* music. *Address:* 4 Chiltern Road, Hitchin, Herts. *T:* Hitchin 51662.

**HALL, Rt. Rev. Denis Bartlett;** *b* 9 April 1899; *s* of Frank Marshall Hall and Caroline Beatrice Hall (*née* Bartlett), both of Bristol. *Educ:* Tudor House Sch., Henleaze, Bristol; Bristol Grammar Sch.; Bristol Univ. (BA). RNVR, 1917-19. University of Bristol, 1919-23; Ridley Hall, Cambridge, 1923-24. Curate, St Gabriel's Sunderland, 1924-28; Chaplain, HMS Conway Sch. Ship, 1928-30; Vicar of Bishopston, Bristol, 1930-47; Asst Bishop on The Niger, 1947-57; Vicar of St Paul's, Thornton Heath, Surrey, 1957-61; Asst Bishop of Canterbury, 1960-61; Rector of Tormarton with W Littleton, Glos, 1961-66. *Address:* c/o The Vicarage, Corsham, Wilts. *T:* Corsham 3232.

**HALL, Denis C.;** *see* Clarke Hall.

**HALL, Denis Whitfield,** CMG 1962; late Provincial Commissioner, Kenya; *b* 26 Aug. 1913; *s* of late H. R. Hall, Haslemere, Surrey; *m* 1940, Barbara Carman; two *s*. *Educ:* Dover College; Wadham Coll., Oxford. Dist Officer, Kenya, 1936; Personal Asst to Chief Native Comr, 1948; Senior Dist Comr, 1955; Provincial Comr, Coast Province, 1959. *Recreations:* sailing, tennis, walking, motoring. *Address:* Tillington Cottage, Petworth, Sussex. *Clubs:* Mombasa (Kenya); Oxford University Yacht.

**HALL, Sir Douglas (Basil),** KCMG 1959 (CMG 1958); *b* 1 Feb. 1909; *s* of late Capt. Lionel Erskine Hall and late Jane Augusta Hall (*née* Reynolds); *m* 1933, Rachel Marion Gartside-Tippinge; one *s* two *d* (and one *s* decd). *Educ:* Radley Coll.; Keble Coll., Oxford (MA). Joined Colonial Admin. Service, 1930; posted to N Rhodesia as Cadet; District Officer, 1932; Senior District Officer, 1950; Provincial Commr, 1953; Administrative Sec., 1954; Sec. for Native Affairs to Government of Northern Rhodesia, 1956-59, Acting Chief Sec. for a period during 1958; Governor and C-in-C, Somaliland Protectorate, 1959-60. JP Co. Devon, 1964. *Publications:* various technical articles. *Recreation:* vintage cars. *Address:* Barnford, Ringmore, near Kingsbridge, Devon. *T:* Bigbury-on-Sea 401. *Club:* Royal Commonwealth Society.

**HALL, Ven. Edgar Francis,** MA; Archdeacon of Totnes, 1948-62, Archdeacon Emeritus, 1962; Canon Residentiary of Exeter, 1934-62; Treasurer, Exeter Cathedral, 1951-62; *b* 14 Aug. 1888; *s* of Francis R. Hall, Oxford; *m* 1915, Anstice, *d* of Dr Louis Tosswill, Exeter; three *d*. *Educ:* Oxford High Sch.; Jesus Coll., Oxford (Scholar). Asst Master, Exeter Sch., 1911; Deacon 1914; Priest 1915; Curate of St James', Exeter, 1914; Chaplain of Exeter Sch., 1917; Vicar of Leusden, Devon, 1921; Diocesan Dir of Relig. Education, Exeter, 1934; Proctor in Convocation, 1944; Gen. Sec. Nat. Soc., 1943-47; Chm. Church of England Council for Education, 1949-58 (Sec. 1948-49). Retired, 1962. *Address:* Leusden Vicarage, Poundsgate, Newton Abbot, Devon.

**HALL, Lady (Edna);** *see* Clarke Hall.

**HALL, Edward,** RP 1958; *b* 5 Feb. 1922; *s* of James and Elizabeth Hall; *m* 1946, Daphne Cynthia, (*née* Grogan); two *s* one *d*. *Educ:* Wyggeston Sch., Leicester. Leicester Coll. of Art, 1939-41; Royal Air Force, 1941-46; Wimbledon Sch. of Art, 1946-48; Slade Sch. of Fine Art, 1949-52. Since 1952, portrait painting; part-time teaching and lecturing in various London and provincial art schools, including Sir John Cass Coll., Hammersmith Coll. of Art and Building, Heatherley Sch. of Fine Art, Canterbury Coll. of Art, Medway Coll. of Art. *Recreations:* music playing the piano. *Address:* 51 St George's Drive, SW1. *T:* 01-834 5366.

**HALL, Maj.-Gen. Edward Michael,** CB 1970; MBE 1943; *b* 16 July 1915; *s* of late Brig. E. G. Hall, CB, CIE; *m* 1948, Nina Diana (*née* McArthur); three *s*. *Educ:* Sherborne; RMA; Peterhouse, Cambridge. Commissioned RE, 1935; BA (Cantab) 1937. Served 1939-46, with Royal Bombay Sappers and Miners; Western Desert, India, Burma. CRE, 10th Armd and 3rd Inf. Div., 1957-59; Comd Training Bde, RE, 1962-63; Chief of Staff, Western Command, 1965-66; Military Deputy to Head of Defence Sales, 1966-70. *Recreation:* country pursuits. *Address:* Treworgey Manor, Liskeard, Cornwall. *Club:* United Service.

**HALL, Edwin G. S.;** *see* Sarsfield-Hall.

**HALL, Sir (Frederick) John (Frank),** 3rd Bt, *cr* 1923; *b* 14 Aug. 1931; *er s* of Sir Frederick Henry Hall, 2nd Bt, and Olwen Irene, *yr d* of late Alderman Frank Collis, Stokeville, Stoke-on-Trent, and Deganwy, Llandudno; *S* father, 1949; *m* 1st, 1956, Felicity Anne (marr. diss. 1960), *d* of late Edward Rivers-Fletcher, Norwich, and of Mrs L. R. Galloway; 2nd, 1961, Patricia Ann Atkinson (marr. diss., 1967); two *d*; re-married, 1967, 1st wife, Felicity Anne Hall. *Heir:* *b* David Christopher Hall [*b* 30 Dec. 1937; *m* 1962, Irene, *d* of William Duncan, Aberdeen; one *s*]. *Address:* Carradale, 29 Embercourt Road, Thames Ditton, Surrey. *T:* 01-398 2801.

**HALL, Maj.-Gen. Frederick William G.;** *see* Gordon-Hall.

**HALL, Geoffrey William,** CEng, FRAeS; retired as Director of The Fairey Co. Ltd and as Chairman of Roger Laurent SA Belgium and of Fairey SA Belgium (both subsidiaries of Fairey Co.); *b* 18 Oct. 1906; *s* of Henry Clayton Hall and Frances Rebecca Jackson; *m* 1946, Eileen Florence Tripp; two *s*. *Educ:* City and Guilds Engineering Coll.; Royal College of Science. Apprenticed to Fairey Aviation Co. Ltd; learned to fly, London Aeroplane Club, 1927; Experimental Engineer, Aero Engine Test and Development, Rolls-Royce Ltd, 1928-32. Re-joined Fairey Aviation Co. Ltd; engaged on Aircraft and Engine Development; appointed Asst Chief Engineer, Chief

Development Engineer and then Chief Research Engineer; Dir, 1949, becoming Engineering Dir, 1950, Asst Managing Dir, 1955 and Managing Dir, 1956; Chm. and Managing Dir, 1957-59; Chm., The Fairey Company Ltd, 1960-61. Mem., Radio Soc. of Gt Britain (RSGB). Licensed Radio Amateur with Call Sign G3UBQ. First Fairey Memorial Lecture, RAeS, 1959. Liveryman, Worshipful Co. of Coachmakers and Coach Harness Makers. *Recreations:* flying, sailing, radio. *Address:* Dellwood, 11 Pinewood Close, Iver Heath, Bucks. *T:* Iver 828. *Club:* Royal Aero.

**HALL, George Derek Gordon;** President of Corpus Christi College, Oxford, since 1969; *b* 8 Nov. 1924; *e s* of late Albert Avondale Hall and of Elizabeth Winifred Hall; *m* 1952, Susan Penelope, *d* of Vice-Adm. J. W. Carrington. *Educ:* South Shields High Sch.; Appleby Grammar Sch.; The Queen's Coll., Oxford (MA). Served in RAF, 1943-46. Lectr in Law, University Coll. of Wales, Aberystwyth, 1948-49; Fellow and Tutor in Law, Exeter Coll., Oxford, 1949-69; Junior Proctor, 1962-63; Hebdomadal Council, 1963-; Gen. Bd of the Faculties, 1963- (Vice-Chm., 1967-69); Asst Lit. Dir, Selden Soc. *Publications:* Glanvill (Nelson's Medieval Texts), 1965; articles in historical and legal periodicals. *Recreation:* fishing. *Address:* Corpus Christi College, Oxford. *T:* Oxford 49431. *Club:* Oxford and Cambridge University.

**HALL, Grahame;** *see* Muncaster, Claude.

**HALL, Harold Percival,** CMG 1963; MBE 1947; Assistant Under Secretary of State, Ministry of Defence, since 1968; *b* 9 Sept. 1913; *s* of late Major George Charles Hall; *m* 1939, Margery Hall, *d* of late Joseph Dickson; three *s* (including twin *s*). *Educ:* Portsmouth Grammar Sch.; Royal Military College, Sandhurst. Commissioned Indian Army, 1933. Indian Political Service, 1937-47. Private Sec. to Resident, Central India States, 1937; Magistrate and Collector, Meerut, 1938-39. Military Service, 1938-43 (Major). Staff Coll., Quetta, 1941. Asst Political Agent, Loralai, 1943, Nasirabad, 1944; Dir, Food and Civil Supplies, and Dep. Sec., Revenue, Baluchistan, 1945-46; Principal, Colonial Office, 1947; Asst Sec. (Head of Pacific and Indian Ocean Dept), Colonial Office, 1955-62; Seconded to Office of UK Comr-Gen. for SE Asia, 1962-63; British Dep. High Comr for Eastern Malaysia, Kuching, Sarawak, 1963-64; Asst Sec., Colonial Office, 1965-66; Asst Under-Sec. of State, Commonwealth Office, 1966-68. *Recreations:* cricket, tennis, squash, golf. *Address:* 77 Moss Lane, Pinner, Middlesex.

**HALL, Prof. Henry Edgar;** Professor of Physics, University of Manchester, since 1961; *b* 1928; *s* of John Ainger Hall; *m* 1962, Patricia Anne Broadbent; two *s* one *d*. *Educ:* Latymer Upper Sch., Hammersmith; Emmanuel Coll., Cambridge. BA 1952; PhD 1956. At Royal Society Mond Laboratory, Cambridge, 1952-58; Senior Student, Royal Commission for the Exhibition of 1851, 1955-57; Research Fellow of Emmanuel Coll., 1955-58; Lecturer in Physics, Univ. of Manchester, 1958-61. Simon Memorial Prize (with W. F. Vinen), 1963. Visiting Professor: Univ. of Western Australia, 1964; Univ. of Oregon, 1967-68. *Publications:* papers in scientific journals. *Recreations:* mountain walking, cinema-going. *Address:* The Physical Laboratories, The University, Manchester 13.

**HALL, Jean Graham,** LLM (London); Metropolitan Stipendiary Magistrate since Dec. 1965; *b* 26 March 1917; *d* of Robert Hall and Alison (*née* Graham). *Educ:* Inverkeithing Sch., Fife; St Anne's Coll., Sanderstead; London Sch. of Economics. Gold Medal (Elocution and Dramatic Art), Incorporated London Acad. of Music, 1935; Teacher's Dipl., Guildhall Sch. of Music, 1937; Social Science Cert., London Sch. of Economics, 1937; LLB (Hons), London, 1950. Club Leader and subseq. Sub-Warden, Birmingham Univ. Settlement, 1937-41; Sec., Eighteen Plus (an experiment in youth work), 1941-44; Probation Officer, Hants, subseq. Croydon, 1945-51. Called to Bar, Gray's Inn, 1951. Pres., Gray's Inn Debating Soc., 1953; Hon. Sec., Soc. of Labour Lawyers, 1954-64. Chm. Departmental Cttee on Statutory Maintenance Limits, 1966-68. Contested (Lab) East Surrey, 1955. *Recreations:* travel, theatre, congenial debate. *Address:* 45 West Hill, Sanderstead, Surrey. *T:* 01-657 3607. *Club:* University Women's.

**HALL, Joan Valerie;** MP (C) Keighley since 1970; *b* 31 Aug. 1935; *d* of Robert Percy Hall and Winifred Emily Umbers, Deffer House, High Hoyland, Barnsley. *Educ:* Queen Margaret's Sch., York; Ashridge House of Citizenship. Contested (C) Barnsley, 1964 and 1966. *Address:* House of Commons, SW1; Wheathead Cottage, Wheathead Lane, Keighley, Yorks. *T:* Keighley 4535.

**HALL, Sir John;** *see* Hall, Sir F. J. F.

**HALL, John,** OBE 1945; MP (C) Wycombe Division of Bucks, since Nov. 1952; chartered secretary; chairman and director of companies concerned with chemicals and brewing; *b* 21 Sept. 1911; *m* 1935, Nancy, *er d* of late W. Hearn Blake; one *s* one *d*. Served War of 1939-45, RA, TA; Commissioned RAOC, 1940; Staff Coll., Camberley, 1941-42; various Staff appts, 1942-45. Mem. Grimsby Borough Council, 1946-48; contested (C) Grimsby, 1950, (C) East Fulham, 1951; Parliamentary Private Sec. to Minister of Fuel and Power, 1956 and to Minister of Supply, 1957-59. Mem., Select Cttee on Public Accts, 1958-64; Vice-Chm., Cons. Parly Trade and Industry Cttee, 1964-65, and of Finance Cttee, 1965-68, 1969-. Treasurer, 1967, Vice-Chm., 1968-70, Chm., 1970-, Inter-Parly Union (British Br.), and Mem., Internat. Executive. *Address:* 41 Carlisle Mansions, Carlisle Place, SW1; Marsh, Great Kimble, Bucks. *Club:* United Service.

**HALL, John Anthony Sanderson,** DFC 1943; QC 1967; Barrister-at-Law; *b* 25 Dec. 1921; *s* of late Rt Hon. W. Glenvil Hall, PC, MP, and late Rachel Ida Hall (*née* Sanderson); *m* 1945, Nora Ella Hall (*née* Crowe); one *s* two *d*. *Educ:* Leighton Park Sch.; Trinity Hall, Cambridge (BA). Served RAF, 1940-46, 85 Squadron and 488 (NZ) Squadron (Squadron Leader; DFC and Bar). Called to Bar, Inner Temple, 1948; Western Circuit; Dep. Chm., Hants Quarter Sessions, 1967. Member: Gen. Council of the Bar, 1964; Senate of the Four Inns of Court, 1966. *Recreations:* walking, sailing, fishing. *Address:* 2 Dr Johnson's Buildings, Temple, EC4.

**HALL, Sir John (Bernard),** 3rd Bt; a Director: J. Henry Schroder Wagg & Co. Ltd (Merchant Bankers); The Antofagasta (Chile) and Bolivia Railway Co. Ltd, and associated cos; *b* 20 March 1932; *s* of Lieut-Col Sir Douglas Hall, DSO, 2nd Bt, and Ina Nancie Walton, *d* of late Col John Edward Mellor, CB (she *m* 2nd, 1962, Col Peter J. Bradford, DSO, OBE, TD); *S* father, 1962; *m* 1957, Delia Mary, *d* of late Lieut-Col J. A. Innes, DSO; one *s* two *d*. *Educ:* Eton; Trinity Coll., Oxford (MA). Lieut, Royal Fusiliers (RARO). *Recreations:* travel, fishing. *Heir:* *s* David Bernard Hall, *b* 12 May 1961. *Address:* Penrose House, Patmore Heath, Albury, Much Hadham, Herts. *T:* Albury 255. *Clubs:* Boodle's, Lansdowne, Overseas Bankers'.

**HALL, John Edward Beauchamp,** CMG 1959; Plunkett Foundation for Co-operative Studies, London, WC1, since 1964; *b* 9 Dec. 1905; *s* of Henry William Hall, MA, and Emily (*née* Odam); *m* 1936, Jane Gordon (*née* Forbes); two *d. Educ:* Bradfield Coll., Berks; Worcester Coll., Oxford. Foundation Scholar, Bradfield Coll., 1919-24; Exhibitioner, Worcester Coll., Oxford, 1924-28. Appointed to Colonial Administrative Service, Nigeria, 1930; Permanent Sec., Federal Government of Nigeria, 1958-60; retired, 1961. *Recreation:* gardening. *Address:* Meads, Stream Lane, Hawkhurst, Kent. *T:* Hawkhurst 2108.

**HALL, Sir John Hathorn,** GCMG 1950 (KCMG 1941; CMG 1935); DSO 1919; OBE 1931; MC; *b* 19 June 1894; *m* 1927, Torfrida Trevenen Mills; two *d. Educ:* St Paul's Sch.; Lincoln Coll., Oxford. Served European War, 1914-19 (despatches, MC, DSO, Croix de Guerre (Belgium)); Egyptian Civil Service, Ministry of Finance, 1919-21; Asst Principal, Colonial Office, 1921; Principal, 1927; seconded to Foreign Office, 1932; Chief Sec. to Govt of Palestine, 1933-37; British Resident, Zanzibar, 1937-40; Governor and C-in-C, Aden, 1940-44. Governor and C-in-C of Uganda, 1944-51; retd, 1951. Director: Midland Bank Ltd; Midland Bank Executor and Trustee Co. Ltd; Brixton Estate Ltd; Director: Clerical, Medical & General Life Assurance Soc. (Past Chm.); General Reversionary and Investment Co. (Past Chm.); Hon. Pres. Limmer & Trinidad Lake Asphalt Co. (Past Pres. and Chm.). 1st Cl. Order of the Brilliant Star of Zanzibar; KStJ. *Address:* 128 Rivermead Court, Hurlingham, SW6. *Clubs:* Athenæum, Hurlingham.

**HALL, Sir Julian Henry,** 11th Bt, *cr* 1687; *b* 22 Feb. 1907; *s* of Sir Martin Julian Hall, OBE, 10th Bt; *S* father 1958. *Educ:* Eton; Balliol Coll., Oxford (BA). Editor of Colour, 1931. Served with Intelligence Corps and in Special Forces, 1939-45. Home Talks Dept, BBC, 1948-51; contrib. articles on the contemporary theatre. *Publications:* Laura Seaborne, 1932; The Senior Commoner, 1934; Two Exiles, 1936. *Heir: cousin* Col Lionel Reid Hall, MC [*b* 1 Feb. 1898; *m* 1921, Mary Marjoribanks Moore, *d* of late Maj.-Gen. Sir Gerard Moore Heath, KCMG, CB, DSO, and *widow* of Capt. J. D. G. MacNeece, MC, RFA; three *d*]. *Address:* c/o Coutts & Co., 440 Strand, WC2. *Club:* Garrick.

**HALL, Kenneth Lambert,** CMG 1938; *b* 14 May 1887; *s* of late Thomas Lambert Hall, MRCS and *g g s* of William Hall of Arlington Manor, Bibury, Glos; *m* 1915, Mabel, *d* of Towry Piper of Barnard Castle, Durham; one *s* decd. *Educ:* Hereford Sch.; Brasenose Coll., Oxford (Somerset Scholar). Entered Northern Nigerian Political Service as Asst Resident, 1912; Principal Asst Sec., Nigerian Secretariat, 1927; acting Dep. Chief Sec., 1927-30; Mem., Legislative Council, Nigeria; acting Sec., Southern Provinces, Nigeria, 1930; Chief Sec., Nyasaland, 1931-41; acting Governor and Comdr-in-Chief, Nyasaland on various occasions; Sec. Nyasaland Northern and Southern Rhodesia Inter-territorial Conference, 1941; retired, 1945. *Address:* 74 Linkside Avenue, Oxford. *T:* Oxford 56092.

**HALL, Magdalen K.;** *see* King-Hall.

**HALL, Sir Noel (Frederick),** Kt 1957; Principal, Brasenose College, Oxford, since Nov. 1960; Chairman, Academic Advisory Committee for University of Lancaster, since 1964; Director: Babcock & Wilcox Ltd, since 1961; City Centre Properties (College Developments), since 1962; *b* 23 Dec. 1902; *s* of late Cecil Gallopine Hall and late Constance Gertrude Upcher; *m* 1st, 1927, Edith Evelyn Pearl Haward (marr. diss. 1944); no *c*; 2nd, 1946, Elinor Hirschborn Marks; one *s* one *d. Educ:* Royal Grammar Sch., Newcastle on Tyne; Bromsgrove Sch.; Brasenose Coll., Oxford. 1st Class hons Modern History, 1924; Senior Hulme Scholar, 1924-25; Certificate Social Anthropology, 1925; BA 1924; MA 1933. Commonwealth Fund Fellow in Economics, Princeton Univ., 1925-27, AM (Economics) Princeton, 1926; Lecturer in Political Economy, head of Dept of Political Economy, and Civil Service Tutor, University of London, University Coll., 1927-29; Senior Lecturer, 1929-35; Prof. of Political Economy in the University of London (University Coll.,) 1935-38; Sec. of Fellowship Advisory Cttee of Rockefeller Foundation for Social Sciences in Great Britain and Ireland, 1930-36; Dir, National Institute for Economic and Social Research, 1938-43; Mem. of International Commission for Relief of Child Refugees in Spain, 1939; Joint Dir, Ministry of Economic Warfare, 1940; Minister in charge of War Trade Department, British Embassy, Washington, 1941-43; Development Adviser West Africa, 1943-45; Principal of the Administrative Staff Coll., Greenlands, Henley-on-Thames, 1946-61. Ford Foundation Distinguished Visiting Prof., New York Univ., 1958 (University Medal, 1958). Hon. Associate, College of Advanced Technology, Birmingham, 1963. Hon. LLD Univ. of Lancaster, 1964. *Publications:* Measures of a National and International character for Raising Standards of Living (Report to Economic Committee of League of Nations, 1938); The Exchange Equalisation Account, 1935; Report on Grading Structure of Administrative and Clerical Staff in the Hospital Service, 1957; The Making of Higher Executives, 1958; (with Stephen King Hall) The Economist in the Witness Box, 1933, articles on economic subjects. *Recreations:* golf, bridge. *Address:* Brasenose College, Oxford; Homer End, Ipsden, Oxon. *T:* Checkendon 294. *Club:* English-Speaking Union.

**HALL, Percival Stanhope,** CMG 1952; CBE 1921 (OBE 1920; MBE 1919); late Chairman John Loudon & Co. Ltd, London Bridge, SE1; *b* 1879; *s* of William Henry Hall, JP, Aldeburgh; *m* 1926, Edith (*d* 1964), *widow* of T. P. Tebbutt, Northampton. *Educ:* Ipswich Sch. Dir of Meat Contracts, Min. of Food, in European War, 1914-18, Temp. Lieut RASC; Dir of Bacon Imports, Ministry of Food, War of 1939-45; also Dir of bacon and ham, 1946-52. Orders of Crown of Italy and Crown of Belgium, and Medal Agricole, France; Coronation Medal, 1953. *Address:* Kingsworthy, 26 Tangiers Road, Guildford, Surrey.

**HALL, Peter Reginald Frederick,** CBE 1963; director of plays, films and operas; Co-Director, Royal Shakespeare Company, since 1968 (Managing Director at Stratford-on-Avon and Aldwych Theatre, London, 1960-68); Member, Arts Council, since 1969; *b* Bury St Edmunds, Suffolk, 22 Nov. 1930; *s* of Reginald Edward Arthur Hall and Grace Pamment; *m* 1956, Leslie Caron (marr. diss., 1965); one *s* one *d*; *m* 1965, Jacqueline Taylor; one *s* one *d. Educ:* Perse Sch., Cambridge; St Catharine's Coll., Cambridge (MA Hons; Hon.

Fellow, 1964). Dir, Arts Theatre, London, 1955-56 (directed several plays incl. first productions of Waiting for Godot, South, Waltz of the Toreadors); formed own producing company, International Playwrights' Theatre, 1957, and directed their first production, Camino Real. At Sadler's Wells, directed his first opera, The Moon and Sixpence, 1957. First productions at Stratford: Love's Labour's Lost, 1956; Cymbeline, 1957; first prod. on Broadway, The Rope Dancers, Nov. 1957. Plays in London, 1956-58; Summertime; Gigi; Cat on a Hot Tin Roof; Brouhaha; Shadow of Heroes; Madame de . . .; Traveller Without Luggage; A Midsummer Night's Dream, Coriolanus (Stratford), The Wrong Side of the Park, 1959; apptd Dir of Royal Shakespeare Theatre, Jan. 1960; The Two Gentlemen of Verona, Twelfth Night, Troilus and Cressida, 1960; Ondine, Becket, Romeo and Juliet, 1961; The Collection, Troilus and Cressida, A Midsummer Night's Dream, 1962; The Wars of the Roses (adaptation of Henry VI Parts 1, 2, & 3, and Richard III), 1963; Sequence of Shakespeare's histories for Shakespeare's 400th anniversary at Stratford: Richard II, Henry IV Parts 1 & 2, Henry V, Henry VI, Edward IV, Richard III, 1964; The Wars of the Roses on BBC Television, 1965; The Homecoming, Moses and Aaron (Covent Garden), Hamlet, 1965; The Government Inspector, The Magic Flute (Covent Garden), Staircase, 1966; The Homecoming (New York), Macbeth (Stratford), 1967; Work is a Four Letter Word (film), 1968; A Midsummer Night's Dream (film), A Delicate Balance, Silence and Landscape, Three into Two Won't Go (film), 1969; Perfect Friday (film), The Battle of Shrivings, La Calisto (Glyndebourne), The Knot Garden (Covent Garden), 1970. Associate Prof. of Drama, Univ. of Warwick, 1966-. Hon. DUniv York, 1966. Tony Award (NY) for best director, 1966; Hamburg Univ. Shakespeare Prize, 1967. Chevalier de l'Ordre des Arts et des Lettres, 1965. *Recreation:* music. *Address:* The Wall House, Mongewell Park, Wallingford, Berks.

**HALL, Prof. Philip,** FRS 1942; MA; Sadleirian Professor of Pure Mathematics, Cambridge University, 1953-67, now Emeritus (University Lecturer in Mathematics, 1933-51; Reader in Algebra, 1951-53); Fellow of King's College, Cambridge, 1927; *b* 11 April 1904. *Educ:* Christ's Hosp. Hon. Sec. London Mathematical Soc., 1938-41, 1945-48, Pres., 1955-57. Sylvester Medal, Royal Society, 1961. de Morgan Medal and Larmor Prize of the London Mathematical Soc., 1965. Hon. DSc (Tübingen), 1963. *Address:* King's College, Cambridge; 50 Impington Lane, Histon, Cambs.

**HALL, Col (Hon.) Philip de Havilland,** DSO 1919; MC; TD; Consulting Engineer; *b* 28 Aug. 1885; *s* of late Dr F. de Havilland Hall; *m* 1925, Eleanor Louise Kirby; one *s* one *d. Educ:* Tonbridge Sch. (Foundation Scholar); Glasgow Univ.; BSc(Eng). MInstCE; Col RE, TA; OC 323rd Anti-Aircraft Co. RE, 1934; CRE Somerset 1941-42; Dep. Chief Engineer S Midlands Dist, 1942-43; retired, 1945, with Hon. rank of Col. Served European War, CRE 50th Div., 1914-19 (despatches thrice, MC, DSO). *Address:* 19 Hartington Mansions, Eastbourne, Sussex. *T:* Eastbourne 26934. *Clubs:* East India and Sports; Devonshire (Eastbourne).

**HALL, Sir Robert de Zouche,** KCMG 1953 (CMG 1952); MA; FSA; JP; *b* 27 April 1904; *s* of late Arthur William Hall, Liverpool; *m* 1932, Lorna Dorothy (*née* Markham); one *s* one *d. Educ:* Willaston Sch.; Gonville and Caius Coll., Cambridge. MA, 1932; Colonial Administrative Service, Tanganyika, 1926; Provincial Comr, 1947; Senior Provincial Comr, 1950; Mem. for Local Government, Tanganyika, 1950-53. Governor, Comdr-in-Chief, and Vice-Adm., Sierra Leone, 1953-56. Hon. Sec. Vernacular Architecture Group, 1959-; Chm. Governing Body, Somerset County Museum, 1961-. Member Hosp. Management Cttees: Sandhill Park, 1961-67 (Chm., 1965-67); South Somerset, 1962-. *Address:* 9 East Coker Road, Yeovil, Somerset. *T:* 21666.

**HALL, Robert King,** PhD; international consultant, educator and executive; *b* Kewanee, Ill, 13 March 1912; *s* of Dr Nelson Hall and Nellie Jean Hyer; *m* 1938, Margaret Wheeler, Belmont, Mass.; one *s* two *d. Educ:* Lake Forest Univ. (AB); Harvard Univ. (AM); Univ. of Chicago (AMEduc); Columbia Univ. (AM); Sch. of Asiatic Studies, NY (AM); Univ. of Michigan (PhD). Master: Cranbrook Sch. (Mich), 1936-40; Dir Research Milwaukee Country Day Schs, 1940-41; Asst Dir, Commn on Eng. Lang. Studies, Harvard Univ., 1941-43; Lt-Comdr, USNR, 1943-46; Assoc. Prof. Teachers Coll., Columbia Univ., 1947-50, Prof. of Comparative Education, 1950-55; Dir of Trng, Arabian Amer. Oil Co., Saudi Arabia, 1955-60. Hon. Lectr, Teachers Coll., Columbia Univ., 1955-57; Internat. Consultant, 1960-64; Sen. Advisor, Coll. of Petroleum and Minerals, Dhahran, 1964-. Vis. Prof. and Lectr, English, American and foreign Univs; special assignments in connection with education, in Japan, South America, Iran, Arabia; Jt Editor, Year Book of Education (London), 1952-57. Deleg. to numerous internat. educnl congresses. Holder of hon. degrees. *Publications:* Federal Control of Education in ABC Republics, 1942; The Teaching of English, 1942; Report of Latin-American Workshop, 1941; A Basic English for South America, 1943; Ingles Basico Para Brasil, 1943; Education for a New Japan, 1949; Kokutai no Hongi (with J. O. Gauntlett), 1949; Shūshin: The Ethics of a Defeated Nation, 1949; Educación en Crisis, 1950; Problemas de Educação Rural, 1950; Report of a Study of YMCA World Services Policy and Practices, 1962; A Strategy for the Inner City, 1963. Articles in English and foreign educnl jls; numerous monographs and consulting reports. *Recreations:* swimming, ski-ing, riding, shooting, tennis. *Address:* College of Petroleum and Minerals, Dhahran, Saudi Arabia.

**HALL, Roger Wilby,** MVO 1944; DL; JP; *b* 6 Oct. 1907; *s* of late A. W. Hall, London and Southwick, Sussex; *m* 1937, Audrey Mary Stuart, *d* of late Sir Henry Wheeler, KCSI, KCIE; two *s* two *d. Educ:* Charterhouse; Jesus Coll., Cambridge. Mem. of London Stock Exchange, 1932. Joined 72nd (Middx) S/L Regt, TA, May 1939; commissioned Dec. 1939; transferred to Life Guards, Jan. 1943; Temp. Major, 1943. Served 1939-45, with RA (TA) AA Home Service, and 2nd Household Cavalry Regt (BLA and BAOR). DL Sussex, 1956; High Sheriff of Sussex, 1957-58; JP W Sussex, 1961. *Recreation:* shooting. *Address:* Glebe House, West Grinstead, Horsham, Sussex. *T:* Partridge Green 341. *Clubs:* Buck's, Turf.

**HALL, Ronald;** Librarian, John Rylands Library, Manchester, retired 1970; *b* 8 Feb. 1900; *s* of Alfred and Elizabeth Hall; *m* 1925, Jessie Isobel Coggan (*d* 1966); two *s. Educ:* Manchester Grammar Sch.; London Univ. (Ext.). BA 1930; Hon. MA Manchester, 1966. Asst Librarian, John Rylands Library, 1915; Keeper of Printed Books, 1950; Acting Librarian, 1960. Served with RAF, 1938-45.

*Publications:* contributions to journals; co-editor, Bulletin of the John Rylands Library. *Recreations:* walking, gardening, amateur theatre. *Address:* Trafford House, 442 Bury Old Road, Prestwich, Manchester M25 5PQ. *T:* 061-773 4774.

**HALL, Rt. Rev. Ronald Owen,** CMG 1966; MC; *s* of Rev. Cecil Gallopine Hall, MA, and Constance Gertrude, *d* of Rev. Henry Berners Upcher; *m* 1923, Nora Kathleen Suckling-Baron; one *s* one *d* (and *er s* decd). *Educ:* Royal Grammar School, Newcastle upon Tyne; Bromsgrove Sch.; Brasenose Coll., Oxford (Schol.). MA Oxford, 1965. Served European War, 1914-19 (despatches, MC and Bar); Distinction in Literæ Humaniores and BA, 1920 (shortened course after war service); ordained to Newcastle Cathedral for work with Student Christian Movement; Missionary Sec., Student Christian Movement up to 1925; Sec. YMCA, China till 1926; Vicar, St Luke, Newcastle upon Tyne, 1926-32; Bishop of Victoria, Hong Kong, 1932; Bishop of Hong Kong and S China until 1951; then of smaller see of Hong Kong, 1951-66. Chm., Council of the Church of South-East Asia, 1955-62. Hon. DD: Hong Kong Univ., 1965; Church Divinity Sch. of Pacific, 1966. *Publications:* A Family in the Making, 1925; China and Britain, 1927; The Art of the Missionary, 1942. *Address:* The Home Farm, Lewknor, Oxford. *T:* Kingston Blount 275.

**HALL, Thomas Donald Horn,** CMG 1939; LLB (NZ); *b* 4 Oct. 1885 (of English parentage); *s* of J. H. Hall, Accountant, and Mary Brown; *m* 1922, Annie Catherine, *d* of late Prof. Hugh Mackenzie, CMG. *Educ:* Wanganui Collegiate Sch.; Wellington Coll.; Victoria Univ. Coll. Entered service of NZ Govt in Dept of Agriculture, attaining position of Senior Clerk and Legal Officer; Asst Law Draftsman, 1921; Clerk of the House of Representatives, 1930-45; retired 1945; Past Pres., NZ Library Assoc. and Hon. Life Mem.; Past Mem. of Cttee of Management, National Art Gallery; served European War with NZEF, 1915-19. *Publications:* Captain Joseph Nias and the Treaty of Waitangi, 1938; Contributor to NZ Affairs, 1929, to Legal Status of Aliens in Pacific Countries, 1937, and to Cyclopaedia of the Social Sciences. *Recreations:* reading, gardening. *Address:* 3 Braithwaite Street, Wellington, W3, NZ.

**HALL, Vernon F.,** CVO 1960; Anæsthetist, King's College Hospital, 1931-69, retired; *b* 25 Aug. 1904; *s* of Cecil S. and M. M. Hall; *m* 1935, C. Marcia Cavell; one *s* two *d. Educ:* Haberdashers' Sch.; King's Coll. Hosp., London. MRCS, LRCP, 1927; DA, 1938; FFARCS, 1948. Served War of 1939-45 in Army (Emergency Commission), 1942-46; Consultant Anæsthetist, India Command (Local Brig.), 1945; Dean, King's Coll. Hosp. Medical Sch., 1951-65. *Publications:* chapters on Anaesthesia–Rose & Carless, Surgery, etc. *Recreations:* riding, walking, reading and music. *Address:* Deercombe, Brendon, N Devon. *T:* Brendon 281.

**HALL, Lieut-Col Walter D'Arcy,** MC; *b* Australia, 10 Aug. 1891; *s* of late Thomas Skarratt Hall, of Weeting Hall, Brandon, Norfolk; *m* 1920, Ann Madelaine Brook (marr. diss.); two *s* one *d*; *m* 1957, Ruth Penelope Owen. *Educ:* Eton; Sandhurst. Joined 20th Hussars, 1911; served European War, 1914-19 (MC and Bar, Croix de Guerre avec Palme et Etoile); served War 1939-45. MP (U) Brecon and Radnor, 1924-29 and 1931-35. *Address:* Magnolia Cottage, Lower Woodford, Salisbury, Wilts. *Club:* Cavalry.

**HALL, Prof. William Bateman;** Professor of Nuclear Engineering, University of Manchester, since 1959; *b* 28 May 1923; *s* of Sidney Bateman Hall and Doris Hall; *m* 1950, Helen Mary Dennis; four *d. Educ:* Urmston Grammar Sch.; College of Technology, Manchester. Engineering apprenticeship, 1939-44; Royal Aircraft Establishment, 1944-46; United Kingdom Atomic Energy Authority (formerly Dept of Atomic Energy, Min. of Supply), 1946-59: Technical Engineer, 1946-52; Principal Scientific Officer, 1952-56; Senior Principal Scientific Officer, 1956-58; Dep. Chief Scientific Officer, 1958. *Publications:* Reactor Heat Transfer, 1958; papers to scientific and professional institutions. *Recreations:* music, fell walking. *Address:* Maple Bank, Macclesfield Road, Alderley Edge, Cheshire. *T:* Alderley Edge 3034.

**HALL, Brig. Sir William (Henry),** Kt 1968; CBE 1962; DSO 1942; ED; Comptroller of Stores, State Electricity Commission of Victoria, 1956-70; Colonel Commandant, RAA Southern Command, since 1967; *b* 5 Jan. 1906; *s* of William Henry Hall, Edinburgh, Scotland; *m* 1930, Irene Mary, *d* of William Hayes; one *s* four *d. Educ:* Morgan Acad., Dundee; Melbourne Univ. Joined Staff of State Electricity Commn of Vic, 1924. Enlisted AIF, 1939: Capt. Royal Aust. Artillery, Palestine, Egypt; Syria, Papua, New Guinea, 1941 (Major); Aust. Dir of Armaments at AHQ, 1942 (Lt-Col); Dir of Armament at AHQ, 1945 (Col); CRA 3 Div. Artillery CMF, 1955-59 (Brig.). Chm., Anzac Day Commemoration Coun.; Dir, Royal Humane Society of Vic.; Mem., Patriotic Funds Coun.; Chm., War Widows and Widowed Mothers' Trust; State Pres. Vic Br, Returned Services League, 1964; Mem., Discharged Servicemen's Employment Bd and Victorian Raffle Bd, 1969. Assoc. Fellow, Aust. Inst. Management; Mem., Inst. of Purchasing and Supply (London). *Recreation:* golf. *Address:* Rosemont, 112 Kooyong Road, Caulfield, Victoria 3162, Australia; The Moorings, Flinders, Victoria 3929. *Clubs:* Naval and Military (Melbourne); Melbourne Cricket, Peninsula Country Golf, Flinders Golf.

**HALL, William Telford,** CSI 1947; CIE 1942; *b* 4 June 1895; *s* of John Hall, Edinburgh; *m* 1922, E. winifred, *d* of late Col Sir George McCrae, DSO, DL; two *s* one *d. Educ:* George Heriot's Sch. Served European War, 1914-18, Capt. Royal Irish Fusiliers and Machine Gun Corps, Salonica and France. Joined Indian Forest Service, 1921; Chief Conservator of Forests, United Provinces, India. *Address:* 38 Cramond Terrace, Edinburgh 4.

**HALL, Willis;** writer; *b* 6 April 1929; *s* of Walter and Gladys Hall; *m* 1966, Dorothy Kingsmill-Lunn; three *s* (one by previous marr.). *Educ:* Cockburn High Sch., Leeds. *Publications: plays:* The Long and the Short and the Tall, 1959; A Glimpse of the Sea, 1959; (with Keith Waterhouse): Billy Liar, 1960; Celebration, 1961; All Things Bright and Beautiful, 1962; England Our England, 1962; Squat Betty and The Sponge Room, 1963; Say Who You Are, 1965; Whoops-a-Daisy, 1968; Children's Day, 1969. *Recreation:* greyhound racing. *Address:* Waterhall Productions, 32 Shaftesbury Avenue, W1. *T:* 01-437 3565. *Club:* Garrick.

**HALL-DAVIS, Alfred George Fletcher;** MP (C) Morecambe and Lonsdale Division of Lancs since 1964; *b* 21 June 1924; *s* of late George Hall-Davis, BA, MB, and of Mrs J. B. Cowan; *m* 1956, Margaret Carr, *d* of George Rushworth, JP, Colne, Lancs; one *d. Educ:* Clifton Coll., Bristol. Dir, Bass Charrington

Ltd. *Recreations:* racing, sailing, walking. *Address:* Low Graythwaite Hall, Ulverston, Lancs.

**HALL-PATCH, Sir Edmund Leo,** GCMG 1951 (KCMG 1947; CMG 1938); Director: Standard Bank (Chairman, 1957-62); Commercial Union Assurance Company and other public companies; *b* 1896; *s* of W. F. McD. Hall-Patch. Asst Sec., Treasury, 1935-44; HBM Financial Commissioner in the Far East, 1940; Asst Under-Sec. of State, Foreign Office, 1944; a Dep. Under-Sec. of State, Foreign Office, 1946-48; Chm. of Executive Cttee of Organization for European Economic Co-operation, with rank of Ambassador, 1948; late Permanent UK Representative on Organization for European Economic Co-operation, at Paris; UK Executive Dir of International Monetary Fund and of the International Bank for Reconstruction and Development, 1952-54, with the personal rank of Ambassador. Retired 1954. *Club:* Brooks's.

**HALLAM-HIPWELL, H.;** *see* Vivenot, Baroness Raoul de.

**HALLAND, Col Gordon Herbert Ramsay,** CIE 1931; OBE 1918; HM Inspector of Constabulary for England and Wales, 1938; retired, 1953; *b* 1888; *e s* of late Rev. J. T. Halland, MA, Rector of Blyburgh, Kirton-in-Lindsey, Lincs; *m* 1st, 1916, Helen Claudine Blanche (*d* 1946), *o d* of late Maj.-Gen. J. M. Walter, CB, CSI, DSO; two *d*; 2nd, 1947, Baroness Sigrid von der Recke (*née* von Lutzau), Windau, Latvia. *Educ:* private; Royal Latin Sch., Buckingham. Science Master at Kirton Grammar Sch., Lincs, 1906-08; Entered Indian Police, 1908 and posted to Punjab; served Ambala, Lahore, Rohtak, Hoshiarpur, Rawalpindi, Lyallpur, and Amritsar Districts; on police duty with the King at Delhi Durbar, 1911; Served European War, 1914-18 in Army in India Reserve of Officers (Major and Gen. Staff Officer, 2nd Grade, Army Headquarters, India) (despatches, OBE); Principal, Punjab Police Training Sch., Phillaur, 1921-26; on police duty with Duke of Connaught at Delhi, 1921; on police duty with Prince of Wales at Delhi, 1922; Lt-Col, Army in India Reserve of Officers, 1927; attached Gen. Staff, Headquarters of Shanghai Defence Force and subsequently North China Command, 1927-30; Senior Superintendent of Police, Delhi, 1930-31; Hon. ADC to the Viceroy, 1930, with hon. rank of Col; Chief Constable of Lincs, 1931-34; Dep. Asst Commissioner in charge of the Metropolitan Police Coll., 1934-38; Inspector-Gen. of Police, Ceylon, 1942-44; services lent to Foreign Office, Aug. 1944-Oct. 1947, as Inspector Gen. of Public Safety, CCG (British Element). Mem. County Council for Parts of Lindsey, Nov. 1953-March 1957. DL County of Lincoln, 1954-57. *Recreations:* gardening; (past) shooting, riding, polo, cricket, tennis. *Address:* Box Green House, Minchinhampton, Gloucestershire. *T:* Nailsworth 2508. *Club:* Lincolnshire County.

**HALLETT;** *see* Hughes-Hallett.

**HALLETT, Vice-Adm. Sir Cecil Charles;** *see* Hughes Hallett.

**HALLETT, Cecil Walter;** retired as General Secretary, Amalgamated Engineering Union, 1957-64; *b* 10 Dec. 1899; *m*; two *s* two *d*. *Educ:* New City Road Elementary Sch., London. Messenger, Commercial Cable Co., 1913-15; apprentice fitter and turner, Gas Light and Coke Co., Becton, N Woolwich, 1916-18. HM Forces, 10th London Regt, 1918-19; journeyman fitter and turner, various firms, 1923-48; Asst Gen. Sec. AEU, 1948-57. Former Editor, AEU Monthly Jl and The Way. *Address:* Ystad, Vines Cross Road, Horam, Sussex.

**HALLETT, Prof. George Edward Maurice,** MDS; Professor of Children's Dentistry in the University of Newcastle upon Tyne (formerly King's College, University of Durham), since 1951; Dean, Sutherland Dental School, since 1960, and Hospital since 1970; *b* 30 July 1912; *s* of Edward Henry and Berthe Hallett; *m* 1936, Annetta Eva Grant Napier; three *d*. *Educ:* Birkenhead Institute; Liverpool Univ. (LDS, Gilmour Medal and other prizes). HDD RCSE 1939; FDS RCS 1948; MDS Durham, 1952; DOrth RCS, 1954; FDS RCSE 1960; FFD RCSI 1964. House Surgeon, Liverpool Dental Hosp., 1934-35; School Dental Officer, Doncaster CB, 1935-36, Notts, 1936-40; served War, 1940-46: Army Dental Corps, Major, despatches. University of Durham: Lecturer in Children's Dentistry, 1946, Reader, 1948; Lectr in Orthodontics, 1946. Examiner in Dental subjects, Universities of Durham, Edinburgh and Glasgow; RCS of Eng., 1954-59; Consultant, United Teaching Hosps, Newcastle upon Tyne; Head of Children's Dept, Dental Hosp., Newcastle upon Tyne; Past President: Société Française d'Orthopedie Dento-Faciale; European Orthodontic Soc. (also former Editor); North of England Odontological Soc.; Brit. Soc. for the study of Orthodontics; former Mem., Newcastle RHB; Chm. Dental Advisory Cttee, RHB; Mem., Bd of Governors, Newcastle United Teaching Hosps; Mem. General Dental Council. *Publications:* contribs to scientific and dental jls. *Recreations:* dilettantism in the glyptic arts, club flying. *Address:* 63 Runnymede Road, Ponteland, Newcastle upon Tyne. *T:* Ponteland, 2646. *Club:* Newcastle Aero.

**HALLIDAY, Edward Irvine,** RP 1952; RBA 1942; ARCA (London) 1925; portrait painter; President: Royal Society of British Artists, since 1956; Royal Society of Portrait Painters, since 1970; Vice-President and Chairman, Artists General Benevolent Institution, since 1965; Chairman, Federation of British Artists, since 1970; *b* 7 Oct. 1902; *s* of James Halliday and Violet Irvine; *m* 1928, Dorothy Lucy Hatswell; one *s* one *d*. *Educ:* Liverpool; Paris; Royal College of Art, London; British Sch. at Rome. Rome Scholar 1925. War of 1939-45: service with RAF Bomber Command until seconded for special duties with Foreign Office. Mural paintings in: Athenæum Club, Liverpool; SS Hilary; several London restaurants. Posters of Western Highlands for British Railways. Principal Portraits include: The Queen, for various cities, regiments, etc.; The Queen and The Duke of Edinburgh, for SS Caronia; The Duke of Edinburgh, for Gordonstoun Sch., Baltic Exchange and the Press Club; Queen Elizabeth the Queen Mother; HRH Princess Alice, Countess of Athlone; Admiral of the Fleet the Earl Mountbatten of Burma; Countess Mountbatten of Burma; Pandit Nehru (painted in New Delhi, 1954); Sir Edmund Hillary; President Azikiwe (painted in Nigeria); Dr Kaunda (painted in Zambia); King Olaf of Norway. Conversation Pieces include: The Royal Family; The Marquess of Salisbury with his brother and sisters; Undergraduates at Worcester Coll., Oxford, 1937 and 1952. Broadcasts on many subjects, 1932-. Gold Medal, Paris Salon, 1953, 1965. FRSA 1970. *Address:* 62 Hamilton Terrace, NW8. *T:* 01-286 7030. *Clubs:* Athenæum, Arts, Chelsea Arts, Garrick, Savage; Artists' (Liverpool).

**HALLIDAY, Frank Ernest;** author; *b* 10 Feb. 1903; *s* of James Herbert Halliday, Bradford, and Anne Louise Anderson, Scarborough; *m* 1927, Nancibel Beth Gaunt; one *s*. *Educ:* Giggleswick Sch.; King's Coll., Cambridge. Asst Master, Cheltenham Coll., 1929-48. Resident in St Ives as a writer, 1948-. Shakespeare Lectr, Stratford, Ont., 1964, and for British Coun. in Portugal and Spain, 1965. *Publications:* Five Arts, 1946; Shakespeare and his Critics, 1949 (rev. edn 1958); A Shakespeare Companion, 1952 (rev. edn 1964); Richard Carew of Antony, 1953; The Poetry of Shakespeare's Plays, 1954; The Legend of the Rood, 1955; Shakespeare in his Age, 1956; Shakespeare, A Pictorial Biography, 1956; The Cult of Shakespeare, 1957; A History of Cornwall, 1959; Indifferent Honest, 1960; The Life of Shakespeare, 1961; Unfamiliar Shakespeare, 1962; Meditation at Bolerium (Poems), 1963; A Concise History of England, 1964; A Cultural History of England, 1967; A Cornish Chronicle, 1967; Dr Johnson and his World, 1968; Chaucer and his World, 1968; Wordsworth and his World, 1969. *Recreations:* walking, swimming, music, archæology, and, more than a recreation, the preservation of St Ives. *Address:* 12 Barnaloft, St Ives, Cornwall. *T:* St Ives 6650.

**HALLIDAY, Sir George Clifton,** Kt 1967; Consultant Otolaryngologist, Royal Prince Alfred and Prince Henry Hospitals; *b* 22 April 1901; *s* of late Edward James Halliday, NSW; *m* 1927, Hester Judith Macansh; two *s* one *d*. *Educ:* The King's Sch., Parramatta; St Paul's Coll., Univ. of Sydney. MB, ChM Sydney Univ., 1925; FRCSE 1934; FRACS 1954. Surg., St George Hosp., 1935; Surg., Royal Prince Alfred Hosp., 1936; Lectr in Otolaryngology, Sydney Univ., 1948-61. Served in AAMC, Middle East, 1940-43 (Lt-Col). *Recreations:* tennis, cricket, golf. *Address:* 67 Cranbrook Road, Rose Bay, NSW 2029, Australia. *T:* FM 2280. *Clubs:* Union, Royal Sydney Golf, Elanora Country (all Sydney).

**HALLIDAY, Prof. Michael Alexander Kirkwood;** Professor of General Linguistics in the University of London, at University College, since 1965; *b* 13 April 1925; *s* of Wilfrid J. Halliday and Winifred Halliday (*née* Kirkwood). *Educ:* Rugby School; University of London. BA London; MA, PhD, Cambridge. Served Army, 1944-47. Asst Lectr in Chinese, Cambridge Univ., 1954-58; Lectr in General Linguistics, Edinburgh Univ., 1958-60; Reader in General Linguistics, Edinburgh Univ., 1960-63. Linguistic Soc. of America Prof., Indiana Univ., 1964; Vis. Prof. of Linguistics, Yale, 1967. Dr *hc* Nancy. *Publications:* The Language of the Chinese 'Secret History of the Mongols', 1959; (with A. McIntosh and P. Strevens) The Linguistic Sciences and Language Teaching, 1964; (with A. McIntosh) Patterns of Language, 1966; Intonation and Grammar in British English, 1967; articles in Jl of Linguistics, Word, Trans of Philological Soc., etc. *Address:* 31 The Lawns, SE3. *T:* 01-852 2777.

**HALLIFAX, Mrs Joanne Mary,** JP; Central President of Mothers' Union, 1962-70; *b* 28 Nov. 1900; *d* of Sir Robert Hughes, 12th Bt (*d* 1951) and Edith Lady Hughes; *m* 1923, Vice-Adm. R. H. Hallifax, CB, CBE (killed on active service, 1943); one *s* two *d*. *Educ:* privately. JP, Hants, 1948. *Recreations:* travelling, gardening, music. *Address:* Longcroft, Shedfield, near Southampton. *T:* Wickham 3145.

**HALLINAN, (Adrian) Lincoln,** DL; Barrister-at-law; *b* 13 Nov. 1922; *e s* of Sir Charles Hallinan, *qv*; *m* 1955, Mary, *d* of Dr E. Parry-Evans; two *s* two *d*. *Educ:* Downside. Lieut, Rifle Bde, 1942-47; TA, 1950-52 (Captain), RAMC. Called to Bar, Lincoln's Inn, 1950; Wales and Chester Circuit. A Legal Pres., Mental Health Review Tribunal for Wales. Cardiff CC, 1949; Alderman, 1961, re-elected 1967; Lord Mayor of Cardiff, 1969-70. Contested (C), Aberdare, 1946, Cardiff West, 1951, 1959. Chm., Cardiff Educn Cttee, 1961-63 and 1965-70; Chm., Gov. Body, Cardiff Coll. of Art, and Cardiff Coll. of Music and Drama, 1961-; First Chm., Nat. Court of Govs, Welsh Coll. of Music and Drama, 1970; Vice-Chm., Court of Govs, Nat. Theatre for Wales, 1967-; Mem., Court of Govs: and Coun., UC of S Wales and Mon; and Coun., Nat. Musuem of Wales; Inst. of Science and Technology; Univs of Wales and Aberystwyth; Member: Bd of Govs, Welsh Theatre Co.; Assoc. of Educn Cttees; Educn Cttee of AMC; Welsh Jt Educn Cttee; Exec. Cttee of Llandaff Festival; Cttee, 20th Century Music Festival. Chm., Cardiff Arts Cttee, 1966-69; Pres., Cardiff Music Club, 1967-70; Founder and Chm., Cardiff 2000-Cardiff Civic Trust; Chm., Cardiff-Nantes Fellowship, 1961-68. Mem., Wales and Monmouth T&AVR; former Member: Cardiff East Glamorgan War Pensions Cttee; Cardiff and District Disablement Cttee. Chevalier, Ordre des Palmes Academiques, 1965. OStJ 1969. DL Glamorgan, 1969. *Recreations:* education and the arts. *Address:* (home) 63 Cathedral Road, Cardiff. *T:* Cardiff 20511; (chambers) 33 Park Place, Cardiff. *T:* Cardiff 33313. *Club:* Cardiff and County (Cardiff).

**HALLINAN, Sir Charles (Stuart),** Kt 1962; CBE 1954; solicitor; Alderman, Cardiff City Council; *b* 24 Nov. 1895; *o s* of John Hallinan and Jane Hallinan (*née* Rees); *m* 1921, Theresa Doris Hallinan, JP (*née* Holman) (decd); three *s* one *d*; *m* 1966, Mme Paule Reboul, *er d* of Count Nicholas Debane, and *widow* of M. Gabriel Reboul. *Educ:* Monkton House Sch., Cardiff; Ratcliffe Coll., near Leicester; also privately. Solicitor, admitted 1919. Served European War, 1914-18, with Inns of Court OTC (Cav.) RFA and RFC; War of 1939-45: Comd 21st Bn (Glam.) Home Guard, Lt-Col. Deputy Lord Mayor of Cardiff, 1945-46, 1960-61, and 1969-70; Chm., Cardiff Trading Services Cttee. Past Chm. and Life Vice-Pres., Wales and Monmouth Conservative Area Provincial Council; Patron, Wales and Monmouth Conservative Clubs' Council; Life Vice-Pres. Assoc. of Cons. Clubs (England and Wales); Mem. Executive Cttee, Nat. Union of Conservative and Unionist Associations, and Mem. various local Cons. organisations; Mem. Grand Council, Primrose League; Pres., Cardiff West Conservative and Unionist Association; Contested (C) Central Div. Cardiff July 1945 and Cardiff W Div. Feb. 1950. Former Nat. Vice-Pres. British Legion; now Patron, Wales. Past Pres., Cardiff and District Law Society. Trustee, S Wales East and Mon. Trustee Savings Bank. Member Court of Governors: Nat. Museum of Wales; Univ. of Wales; Governor, St Illtyd's Coll., Cardiff; Mem., Nat. Council for Inland Transport, etc. *Address:* Yscallog, Llandaff, Cardiff. *T:* Cardiff 563686. *Clubs:* County (Cardiff); Royal Porthcawl (Glam).
*See also A. L. Hallinan.*

**HALLINAN, Sir Eric,** Kt 1955; *b* 27 Oct. 1900; *s* of Edward Hallinan, Midleton, Co. Cork, and Elizabeth, *d* of Maj.-Gen. Sir Thomas Dennehy; *m* 1936, Monica, *d* of George Waters, Midleton, Co. Cork; one *s* one *d*. *Educ:* Downside; Trinity Coll., Dublin. BA, LLB Dublin, 1924; Barrister-at-Law (King's Inns, 1923; Gray's Inn, 1927). Practised at Irish Bar, 1924-29. Colonial Administrative

Service, Nigeria, 1930-36; Colonial Legal Service, Nigeria, 1936-40; Attorney-Gen., Bahamas, 1940-44; Puisne Judge: Trinidad, 1944-48; Nigeria, 1948-52; Chief Justice, Cyprus, 1952-57; Chief Justice of The West Indies, 1958-61; Justice of Appeal, Bahamas and Bermuda, 1966-68. LLD (*jure dig.*) Dublin, 1958. *Address:* Lakeview House, Midleton, Co. Cork. *T:* Midleton 62. *Club:* Royal Commonwealth Society.

**HALLINAN, Lincoln;** *see* Hallinan, A. L.

**HALLOWES, Basil John Knight,** CIE 1941; ICS (retired); *b* 27 Aug. 1884; *s* of Rev. J. F. T. Hallowes, MA Cantab; *m* 1st, Mary Catherine Lascelles Ward; 2nd, Joyce Mortimer. *Educ:* Mill Hill; Caius Coll., Cambridge. Entered Indian Civil Service, 1909; retired, 1944. *Recreations:* shooting; played hockey for Cambridge Univ., South of England and Mddx. *Address:* The Beauthorns, Hatherley Road, Cheltenham. *T:* Cheltenham 22508.

**HALLOWES, Odette Marie Celine,** GC 1946; MBE 1945; Légion d'Honneur, 1950; Vice-President, Women's Transport Services (FANY); Member Royal Society of St George; housewife; *b* 28 April 1912; *d* of Gaston Brailly, Croix-de-Guerre, Médaille Militaire; *m* 1931, Roy Sansom (decd); three *d*; *m* 1947, Capt. Peter Churchill, *qv*; *m* 1956, Geoffrey Macleod Hallowes. *Educ:* The Convent of Ste Therèse, Amiens (France) and privately. Entered Special Forces and landed in France, 1942; worked as British agent until capture by Gestapo, 1943; sentenced to death June 1943; endured imprisonment and torture until 28 April 1945, when left Ravensbrück Concentration Camp (MBE, GC). Member: Military Medallists League (Vice-Pres.) Cttee, Victoria Cross and George Cross Assoc. Pres., 282 (East Ham) Air Cadet Sqdn. *Recreations:* reading, travelling, cooking. *Address:* 25 St James's Place, SW1. *Clubs:* FANY, Special Forces; Royal Scottish Automobile.

**HALLPIKE, Charles Skinner,** CBE 1958; FRS 1956; FRCP, FRCS; *b* 19 July 1900; *s* of Frank Robert Hallpike and Rosamund Helen Skinner; *m* 1935, Barbara Lee Anderson; two *s* one *d*. *Educ:* St Paul's Sch., W14; Guy's Hospital, SE1 (Entrance Schol. in Arts and Beaney Prizeman in Pathology); MB, BS London 1926; FRCS 1931; FRCP 1945. William J. Mickle Fellow, London Univ., 1941; Dalby Prizeman, 1943, Gamble Prizeman, 1934 and 1947, Hughlings Jackson Memorial Lecturer and Medallist, 1967, Royal Society of Medicine; Bárány Medallist, Univ. of Uppsala, 1958; Guyot Medallist, Univ. of Groningen, 1959. House Surg., Aural Depts Guy's Hosp. and Cheltenham Gen. Hosp., 1924-27; Bernhard Baron Research Fellow, Ferens Inst. of Otology, Middx Hosp., 1929; Duveen Travelling Student, Univ. of London, 1930; Rockefeller Travelling Fellow, 1931; Foulerton Research Fellow, Royal Society, 1934; Mem. Scientific Staff, Med. Research Council, 1940; Aural Physician and Dir of Otological Research Unit, of Medical Research Council, National Hosp. for Nervous Diseases, Queen Square, WC1, 1944-65; Dir of Research, Ferens Inst. of Otolaryngology, Middlesex Hosp., 1965-68. Mem. Collegium Otorhinolaryngologicum Amicitiae Sacrum (Shambaugh Prizeman, 1955); Hon. Fellow Royal Academy of Medicine, Ireland; FRSocMed (Hon. Sec. 1938, and Editorial Rep., 1946-52, Pres., 1965, Hon. Mem., 1970, Sect. Otol.); Mem. Flying Personnel Research Cttee, 1938-55. *Publications:* papers on otology, physiology, and pathology of the ear in Proc. Royal Society, Jl Physiology, Jl Pathology, Jl Laryngology and Otology, etc. *Address:* Fern Lodge, Ashurst Road, West Moors, Dorset. *T:* Ferndown 4118.

**HALLSTEIN, Walter;** (Professor and Doctor); Grand Cross of Merit, Federal Republic of Germany; President, Commission of the European Economic Community, 1958-67; President, European Movement (international); *b* Mainz, Germany, 17 Nov. 1901; *s* of Jakob Hallstein and Anna Hallstein (*née* Geibel); unmarried. *Educ:* Humanistisches Gymnasium, Darmstadt and Mainz; Bonn, Munich and Berlin Univs. Doctorate of Law, University of Berlin. Prof, Rostock Univ., 1930-41; Prof., 1941-, Dir, 1941-44, Inst. for Comparative Law, Frankfort; Rector, Frankfort Univ., 1946-48; Visiting Prof., Georgetown Univ., Washington, DC, USA; Pres., German Unesco activities, 1949-50; Head, German Schumanplan delegn, Paris, 1950; Staatssekretär: Federal Chancellery, 1950; German Foreign Office, 1951-58. Adviser, Action Cttee for the United States of Europe, 1969-. Director: Farbwerke Hoechst, 1968-; Gebrüder Stumm GmbH, 1968-. Holds eighteen hon. doctorates. Grand Cross of thirty foreign orders, etc.; International Charlemagne Prize of City of Aix-le-Chapelle, 1961; Robert Schuman Prize, 1969. *Publications:* Die Aktienrechte der Gegenwart, 1931; Die Berichtigung des Gesellschaftskapitals, 1942; Wiederherstellung des Privatrechts, 1946; Wissenschaft und Politik, 1949; United Europe–Challenge and Opportunity, 1962; Der unvollendete Bundesstaat, 1969. *Recreation:* travelling. *Address:* 5439 Rennerod/Oberwesterwaldkreis, Germany; (office) Europa Büro, 53 Bonn, Oelbergstrasse 3, Germany.

**HALLSWORTH, Prof. Ernest Gordon,** DSc, ARIC; Chief of Division of Soils, Commonwealth Scientific and Industrial Research Organisation, Adelaide, since 1964; *b* 1913; *s* of Ernest and Beatrice Hallsworth, Ashton-under-Lyne, Lancs; *m* 1943, Elaine Gertrude Seddon, *d* of R. C. Weatherill, Waverley, NSW; two *s* one *d* (and one step *s*). *Educ:* Ashton Grammar Sch., Ashton-under-Lyne, Lancs; Univ. of Leeds. University of Leeds: First Cl. Hons in Agric. Chem., Sir Swire Smith Fellow, 1936; Asst Lectr in Agric. Chem., 1936; PhD 1939; DSc 1964. Lectr in Agric. Chem., Univ. of Sydney, 1939; Prof. of Soil Science, Univ. of West Australia, 1960-61; Prof. of Agric. Chem. and Head Dept Agric. Sci., Univ. Nottingham, 1951-64 (Dean, Faculty of Agric. and Hort., 1951-60). Pres. Lecturers' Assoc., 1946. Treas., Aust. Assoc. of Scientific Workers, 1943; Member: Science Advisory Panel, Australian Broadcasting Commn, 1949-51; Pasture Improvement Cttee, Australian Dairy Produce Bd (NSW), 1948-51; Chm. Insecticides and Fungicides Cttee, Australian Standards Inst., 1949-51. Pres. Internat. Soc. of Soil Science, 1964-68. Mem. Council, Flinders Univ. *Publications:* (Ed) Nutrition of the Legumes, 1958; (ed with D. V. Crawford) Experimental Pedology, 1964; Surface Chemistry, 1970; contributions to: Aust. Jl Science, Jl Soc. Chem. Indust., Empire Jl Experimental Agric, Jl Agric. Science, Aust. Medical Jl, Jl Soil Science. *Recreations:* talking, pedology. *Address:* 30 Fowlers Road, Glen Osmond, S Australia 5064. *T:* 796318. *Club:* Farmers'.

**HALLSWORTH, Sir Joseph,** Kt 1946; Hon. MA Manchester, 1942; Hon. LLD Manchester, 1954; *b* Audenshaw, near Manchester, 2 Dec. 1884; *s* of Samuel and Elizabeth Hallsworth; *m* 1908, Jessie Schofield (*d* 1946), Fairfield,

Manchester; one *d* (and one *s* decd). *Educ:* elementary, commercial, and tech. schools in Manchester district. Entered service of Co-operative Employees' Union, later the NUDAW, as confidential clerk to then Sec., 1902; Asst Sec.; contested (Lab) Stretford, Lancs, Parliamentary Division, 1918; Sec. of Trade Unions' Side of National Conciliation Boards for the Co-operative Service, 1927-47; Mem. of Trade Boards Administration Cttee, 1921; Mem. of General Council of TUC, 1926-47, Pres., 1938-39; visited India for the Congress in 1927-28; was mem. British representation International Labour Conference, Geneva, 1927-37; Workers' Delegate in 1938 and 1939 and again (at New York and Washington) 1941, (Philadelphia and Washington) 1944, (Paris) 1945, (Montreal) 1946, (Geneva) 1947. Pres. of Internat. Federation of Commercial, Clerical, and Technical Employees until 1947; travelled much in connection therewith since 1920; Mem. Governing Body of ILO, Geneva until 1948; Sec.-Gen., Nat. Union of Distributive and Allied Workers (now Union of Shop, Distributive and Allied Workers), 1916-49. Mem. Home Office Cttee on Hours of Work of Young Persons in Unregulated Occupations, 1936; Mem. Ministry of Labour Cost of Living Advisory Cttee, 1936 and 1946-47; Mem. Holidays with Pay Cttee, 1937; Mem. Central Price Regulation Cttee under Prices of Goods Act, 1939, and Goods and Services (Price Control) Act, 1941-47; also of Joint Consultative Cttee and Nat. Joint Advisory Council to Ministry of Labour until 1947; Mem. of Ministry of Labour Factory and Welfare Board until 1947 and of other Govt Cttees including the War Damage Commission; Mem. of National Coal Board and Chm. of Miners' Welfare Commission, 1947-49; Chm. North Western Electricity Board, 1949-55, retired. *Publications:* Protective Legislation for Shop and Office Employees; The Legal Minimum; Commercial Employees and Protective Legislation; Road Transport Workers' Wages; Co-operative Shop Managers' Wages; Trade Board Rates and Standard Rates of Wages; Union by Industry; Labour after the War, and others; (jointly) Working Life of Shop Assistants; Labour Conditions in India. *Address:* 9 Alan Road, Withington, Manchester M20 9NQ. *T:* 061-445 1764.

**HALLWARD, Bertrand Leslie,** MA; *b* 24 May 1901; *er s* of late N. L. Hallward, Indian Educational Service, and Evelyn A. Gordon; *m* 1926, Catherine Margaret, 2nd *d* of late Canon A. J. Tait; four *d*. *Educ:* Haileybury Coll. (Scholar); King's Coll., Cambridge (Scholar). Fellow of Peterhouse, 1923-39. Hon. Fellow 1956. Headmaster of Clifton Coll., 1939-48; Vice-Chancellor, Nottingham Univ., 1948-65; Governor of: Trent Coll., Loughborough Coll. of Technology. Hon. LLD: Sheffield, 1964; Nottingham, 1965. *Publications:* Chapters II, III, IV, and part of VII (the Second and Third Punic Wars) in Cambridge Ancient History, Vol. VIII, 1930; Editor of the Classical Quarterly, 1935-39. *Recreation:* cruising with Delphis in Mediterranean seas. *Address:* 52 Saxmundham Road, Aldeburgh, Suffolk. *T:* Aldeburgh 3395.

*See also W. O. Chadwick, DD.*

**HALPIN, Miss Kathleen Mary,** CBE 1953 (OBE 1941); Chief Administrator, Regions, WRVS (formerly WVS), since 1945; *b* 19 Nov. 1903; unmarried. *Educ:* Sydenham High Sch. (GPDST). Organising Sec., Women's Gas Council, 1935, and represented Gas Industry at International Management Congress, Washington, USA, 1936, Sweden, 1947. Appointed Chief of Metropolitan Dept, WVS, 1939; lent to Min. of Health and went to Washington as UK representative on Standing Technical Cttee on Welfare, UNRRA; Comr, Trainer, and Camp Adviser, Girl Guides Assoc., 1924-48; Comdt, BRCS, 1937-39; Mem. Council London Hostels Assoc., 1941-; Chm. Women's Gas Fedn, 1945-49, Pres., 1949-60. A Governor of St Bartholomew's Hospital, 1948-; President Fedn of Soroptomist Clubs of Gt Britain and Ireland, 1959-60. Trustee, Fawcett Library; Chm., Fawcett Soc., 1967-. OStJ. *Recreations:* motoring, reading, theatre. *Address:* 12 Ashley Court, SW1. *T:* 01-834 4281.

**HALSBURY,** 3rd Earl of, *cr* 1898; **John Anthony Hardinge Giffard,** FRS 1969; Baron Halsbury, 1885; Viscount Tiverton, 1898; Director: The Distillers Co. Ltd; Head, Wrightson & Co. Ltd; Joseph Lucas (industries) Ltd; Chairman Committee of Institute of Cancer Research, Royal Cancer Hospital, since 1962; President, National Institute of Industrial Psychology, since 1963; Member: Standing Commission on Museums and Galleries, since 1960; North Thames Gas Board; Decimal Currency Board, since 1966; Chancellor of Brunel University, London, since November 1966; Chairman, Meteorological Committee, since 1970; *b* 4 June 1908; *o s* of 2nd Earl and Esmé, *d* of late James Stewart Wallace; *S* father, 1943; *m* 1st, 1930, Ismay Catherine, *er d* of late Lord Ninian Crichton-Stuart and Hon. Mrs Archibald Maule Ramsay; one *s*; 2nd, 1936, Elizabeth Adeline Faith, *o d* of late Major Harry Crewe Godley, DSO, Northamptonshire Regt and of late Mrs Godley, of Claremont Lodge, Cheltenham; two *d*. *Educ:* Eton. Man. Dir, Nat. Research Development Corporation, 1949-59. Chairman: Science Museum Advisory Council, 1951-65; Cttee on Decimal Currency, 1961-63; Pres., Institution of Production Engineers, 1957-59; Member: Adv. Council to Cttee of Privy Council for Scientific Research, 1949-54; SRC, 1965-69; Computer Bd for Univs and Research Councils, 1966-69. Nationalised Transport Advisory Council, 1963-67. A Governor, BBC, 1960-62. Hon. DTech, Brunel Univ., 1966; Hon. DUniv, Essex, 1968. *Heir: s* Viscount Tiverton, *qv*. *Address:* (Correspondence) Flat 2, 17 Stanhope Terrace, W2. *T:* 01-723 3955; (home) 4 Campden House, 29 Sheffield Terrace, W8. *T:* 01-727 3035. *Clubs:* Athenæum, Savile, Beefsteak, Royal Automobile.

*See also Sir C. N. G. Blois, Bt.*

**HALSEY, Rt. Rev. Henry David;** *see* Tonbridge, Bishop Suffragan of.

**HALSEY, Rev. Sir John Walter Brooke,** 4th Bt *cr* 1920; *b* 26 Dec. 1933; *s* of Sir Thomas Edgar Halsey, 3rd Bt, DSO, and of Jean Margaret Palmer, *d* of late Bertram Willes Dayrell Brooke; *S* father, 1970. *Educ:* Eton; Magdalene College, Cambridge (BA 1957). Deacon, 1961, priest, 1962, Diocese of York; Curate of Stocksbridge, 1961-66. *Heir: uncle* William Edmund Halsey [*b* 8 Jan. 1903; *m* 1931, Barbara Dorothea, *d* of late Charles Lindsay Orr Ewing; one *d* (one *s* decd)]. *Address:* The Fraternity, 23 Manse Road, Roslin, Midlothian.

**HALSEY, Reginald John,** CMG 1957; BScEng; FCGI; DIC; CEng; FIEE; a Director of Cable and Wireless Ltd, since 1959; *b* 16 Dec. 1902; *s* of Edwin J. Halsey, Portsmouth; *m* 1930, Edna May Tonkin; one *d*. *Educ:* Secondary Sch. and HM Dockyard Sch., Portsmouth; Imperial Coll. of Science and Technology. Entered Post Office, 1927, and engaged on research in telecommunications; Asst Engineer-in-Chief, 1953-58; Dir of Research, 1958-64. Fellow of

Imperial Coll., 1965. *Publications:* many scientific and engineering. *Address:* 12 Oakridge Avenue, Radlett, Herts. *T:* Radlett 6488.

**HALSTED, Maj.-Gen. John Gregson,** CB 1940; OBE; MC; *b* 16 Aug. 1890; 2nd Lieut Loyal Regt, 1910; Capt., 1915; Bt Major, 1919; Major, 1928; Bt Lieut-Col, 1931; Lieut-Col, 1935; Col, 1937; Maj.-Gen., 1941; served European War, 1914-18 (wounded twice, despatches twice, Bt Major, MC); Palestine, 1936-39 (despatches, OBE); War of 1939-45 (CB), France 1939-40; MGA 1941; Vice-QMG, War Office, 1945; retired pay, 1946. *Address:* c/o Lloyds Bank, Cox's and King's Branch, 6 Pall Mall, SW1. *Club:* United Service.

**HAM, Rear-Adm. John Dudley Nelson,** CB 1955; RN retired; *b* 7 Sept. 1902; *s* of Eng. Rear-Adm. John William Ham and Lily Frances Nelson; *m* 1927, Margery Lyne Sandercock; no *c. Educ:* Edinburgh House, Lee-on-Solent; RN Colleges, Osborne and Dartmouth. Junior Service, 1920-37; HMS Ramillies, HMS Ceres; staff of RN Engineering College; Destroyers; Commander, 1937; Engineer Officer, Yangtse, China, 1938-40; served War of 1939-45: Chief Engineer, HMS Danae, 1940-41; Asst Dir Combined Operations Material, 1942; Chief Engineer, HMS Indomitable, 1945; Capt., 1946; Fleet Engineer Officer, Home Fleet, 1949; Staff Air Engineer Officer, 1951; Rear-Admiral, 1953; Dir of Aircraft Maintenance and Repair, 1953-55; Flag Officer Reserve Aircraft, 1955-57, retired. *Recreations:* golf, cabinet-making. *Address:* Green Lane Cottage, Lee-on-Solent, Hants. *T:* Lee-on-Solent 79660.

**HAMBIDGE, Rt. Rev. Douglas Walter;** *see* Caledonia, Bishop of.

**HAMBLEDEN,** 4th Viscount, *cr* 1891; **William Herbert Smith;** *b* 2 April 1930; *e s* of 3rd Viscount and Lady Patricia Herbert, DCVO 1953, *o d* of 15th Earl of Pembroke, MVO; *S* father 1948; *m* 1955, Donna Maria Carmela Attolico di Adelfia, *d* of late Count Bernardo Attolico and of Contessa Eleonora Attolico di Adelfia, Via Porta Latina, Rome; five *s. Educ:* Eton. *Heir: s* Hon. William Henry Bernard Smith, *b* 18 Nov. 1955. *Address:* The Manor House, Hambleden, Henley-on-Thames, Oxon. *TA:* Hambleden. *T:* Hambleden 335.
*See also Baron Margadale, Hon. D. J. Smith.*

**HAMBLING, Sir (Herbert) Hugh,** 3rd Bt, *cr* 1924; BOAC Representative at the Boeing Company, Seattle, Washington, USA, since 1957; *b* 3 Aug. 1919; *s* of Sir (Herbert) Guy (Musgrave) Hambling, 2nd Bt; *S* father 1966; *m* 1950, Anne Page Oswald, Spokane, Washington, USA; one *s. Educ:* Wixenford Preparatory Sch.; Eton Coll. British Airways Ltd, 1937-39. RAF Training and Atlantic Ferry Command, 1939-46. British Overseas Airways: Montreal, 1948; Seattle, 1950; Manager, Sir Guy Hambling & Son, 1956. *Heir: s* Herbert Peter Hugh Hambling, *b* 6 Sept. 1953. *Address:* 1219 Evergreen Point Road, Bellevue, Washington 98004, USA. *T:* GL4 0905 (USA); Rookery Park, Yoxford, Suffolk, England. *T:* Yoxford 310.

**HAMBRO, Jocelyn Olaf,** MC 1944; Managing Director, Hambros Bank Ltd, since 1947, and Chairman since 1965; Director: Phœnix Assurance Co. Ltd; Charter Consolidated Ltd; Diamond Development Co. Ltd; Chairman, Shipping Industrial Holdings; *b* 7 March 1919; *s* of late Ronald Olaf Hambro and late Winifred Martin-Smith; *m* 1942, Ann Silvia, *d* of R. H. Muir; three *s. Educ:* Eton; Trinity Coll., Cambridge. Coldstream Guards, 1939-45. Hambros Bank Ltd, 1945. *Recreations:* racing, shooting. *Address:* Coopersale House, Epping, Essex. *T:* Epping 2423; 43 Wilton Crescent, SW1. *T:* 01-235 6510. *Clubs:* Jockey, Pratt's, White's.

**HAMBURGER, Michael Peter Leopold,** MA (Oxon); *b* Berlin, 22 March 1924; *e s* of late Prof. Richard Hamburger and Mrs L. Hamburger (*née* Hamburg); *m* 1951, Anne Ellen File; one *s* two *d. Educ:* Westminster Sch.; Christ Church, Oxford. Army Service, 1943-47; Freelance Writer, 1948-52; Asst Lectr in German, UCL, 1952-55; Lectr, then Reader in German, Univ. of Reading, 1955-64. Florence Purington Lectr, Mount Holyoke Coll., Mass, 1966-67; Vis. Prof., State Univ. of NY at Buffalo, 1969; Vis. Fellow, Center for Humanities, Weslyan Univ., Conn, 1970. Bollingen Foundn Fellow, 1959-61, 1965-66. Translation Prizes: Deutsche Akademie für Sprache und Dichtung, Darmstadt, 1964; Arts Council, 1969. *Publications: poetry:* Flowering Cactus, 1950; Poems 1950-1951, 1952; The Dual Site, 1958; Weather and Season, 1963; Feeding the Chickadees, 1968; Penguin Modern Poets, (with A. Brownjohn and C. Tomlinson) 1969; Travelling, 1970. *translations:* Poems of Hölderlin, 1943, rev. edn as Hölderlin: Poems, 1952; C. Baudelaire, Twenty Prose Poems, 1946, repr. 1968; J. C. F. Hölderlin, Selected Verse, 1961; G. Trakl, Decline, 1952; A. Goes, The Burnt Offering, 1956; (with others) H. von Hofmannsthal, Poems and Verse Plays, 1961; (with C. Middleton) Modern German Poetry 1910-1960, 1962; (with others) H. von Hofmannsthal, Selected Plays and Libretti, 1964; B. Brecht, Tales from the Calendar, 1961; G. Büchner, Lenz, 1966; (with J. Rothenberg and the author) H. M. Enzensberger, The Poems of Hans Magnus Enzensberger, 1968; H. M. Enzensberger, Poems, 1966; H. M. Enzensberger, Poems For People Who Don't Read Poems, 1968; (with C. Middleton) G. Grass, Selected Poems, 1966; (with C. Middleton), G. Grass, The Poems of Gunter Grass, 1969; L. van Beethoven, Letters, Journals and Conversations, 1951, repr. 1967; J. C. F. Hölderlin, Poems and Fragments, 1967; P. Bichsel, And Really Frau Blum Would Very Much Like To Meet The Milkman, 1968; G. Eich, Journeys, 1968; N. Sachs, Selected Poems, 1968; *criticism:* Reason and Energy, 1957; From Prophecy to Exorcism, 1965; The Truth of Poetry, 1970. *Recreations:* gardening, tennis, walking. *Address:* c/o Glyn Mills & Co., Kirkland House, Whitehall, SW1. *Club:* PEN.
*See also P. B. Hamlyn.*

**HAMBURGER, Sidney Cyril,** CBE 1966; JP; Member, Supplementary Benefits Commission, since 1967; Member, Manchester Regional Hospital Board, since 1966; *b* 14 July 1914; *s* of Isidore and Hedwig Hamburger; *m* 1940; three *s. Educ:* Salford Grammar Sch. Served in Army, 1940-46, Capt. Salford City Council: Mem., 1946; Alderman, 1961; Mayor of Salford, 1968-69. Chairman: NE Manchester Hosp. Management Cttee, 1970; Finance Cttee, Manchester Regional Hosp. Bd. Pres. Council, Manchester-Salford Jews, 1962-65; Pres., Jewish Homes for the Aged, 1965-. JP, Salford, 1957. *Recreation:* football. *Address:* 26 New Hall Road, Salford 7, Lancs. *T:* 061-792 3939.

**HAMER, John,** MBE 1944; Secretary, Royal Horticultural Society, since 1962; *b* 14 June 1910; 2nd *s* of late John and Katherine Hamer; *m* 1940, Marjorie Agnes Martin (*d* 1970); one *s* one *d. Educ:* University of Leeds (BA). Asst Master, 1932-39. War Service, 1939-46 (despatches, MBE): The Loyal Regt, Royal

Tank Regt, Combined Operations, 1943-45; Lieut-Col; Controller of Supplies, Singapore, 1945. Joined Malayan Civil Service, 1946: District Officer, Jasin 1948, Klang 1952; British Adviser, Perlis, 1955; Deputy Chm., Rural Industrial Development Authority, Federation of Malaya, 1957; Ministry of Agriculture, 1958; State Sec., Penang, 1958-61. Joined Royal Horticultural Soc., 1961. *Recreation:* gardening. *Address:* Wildacres, Itchingfield, Sussex. *T:* Slinfold 467.

**HAMES, Sir George C. H.;** *see* Hayter Hames.

**HAMILTON,** family name of **Duke of Abercorn,** and of **Barons Belhaven, Hamilton of Dalzell,** and **Holm Patrick.**

**HAMILTON;** *see* Baillie-Hamilton.

**HAMILTON;** *see* Dalrymple-Hamilton.

**HAMILTON;** *see* Douglas-Hamilton.

**HAMILTON,** 14th Duke of, *cr* 1643, Scotland, and **BRANDON,** 11th Duke of, *cr* 1711, Great Britain; **Douglas Douglas-Hamilton;** PC 1940; KT 1951; GCVO 1946; AFC 1935; Royal Victorian Chain, 1964; LLD, Universities of St Andrews and Edinburgh; FRCSE; FRGS; DL; Hereditary Keeper of Palace of Holyroodhouse; Lord High Commissioner to the General Assembly of the Church of Scotland, 1953, 1954, 1955 and 1958; Lord Steward of HM Household, 1940-64; Chancellor St Andrews University since 1948; President, Air League of the British Empire; *b* 3 Feb. 1903; *e s* of 13th Duke; *S* father 1940; *m* 1937, Lady Elizabeth Percy, *er d* of 8th Duke of Northumberland, KG; five *s*. *Educ:* Eton; Balliol Coll., Oxford. Mem. of Royal Company of Archers. Hon. Pres. of Boys' Brigade, 1963 (Treas., 1938-62); Director: Scottish Aviation Ltd, Prestwick; Securicor (Scotland) (Pres.); Pres. Building Societies Assoc., 1961-65 (now Vice-Pres.). Served in 602 City of Glasgow RAAF Squadron which he commanded, 1927-36; served Royal Air Force, 1939-45 (despatches), Hon. Air Cdre. MP (U) East Renfrewshire, 1930-40; Chief Pilot Mount Everest Flight Expedition, 1933. Pres. British Air Line Pilots' Assoc., 1937-, and Chm. Cttee on Pilot Training. Liveryman, Guild of Air Pilots and Air Navigators, 1963. Pres. of Air League. *Publication:* (with Gp Capt. D. F. McIntyre) The Pilot's Book of Everest, 1936. *Recreations:* boxing, gliding, ski-ing, swimming. *Heir: s* Marquess of Clydesdale, *qv*. *Address:* Lennoxlove, East Lothian. *T:* Haddington 2156. *Clubs:* Royal Air Force, Royal Aero; Western (Glasgow); New (Edinburgh).

**HAMILTON, Marquess of; James Hamilton;** company director; *b* 4 July 1934; *er s* of 4th Duke of Abercorn, *qv*; *m* 1966, Alexandra, *e d* of Lt-Col Harold Phillips, Checkendon Court, Reading; one *s*. *Educ:* Eton Coll.; Royal Agricultural Coll., Cirencester, Glos. Joined HM Army, Oct. 1952; Lieut, Grenadier Guards. MP (UU) Fermanagh and South Tyrone, 1964-70. High Sheriff of Northern Ireland, 1970-. *Recreations:* shooting, water-ski-ing. *Heir: s* Viscount Strabane, *qv*. *Address:* Barons Court, Co. Tyrone, Northern Ireland. *T:* Newtown Stewart 215; 7 Upper Belgrave Street, SW1. *T:* 01-235 3161. *Club:* Turf.

**HAMILTON OF DALZELL,** 3rd Baron, *cr* 1886; **John d'Henin Hamilton,** MC 1945; DL; JP; Vice-Lieutenant of Surrey since 1957; Chairman: Surrey Council of Social Service since 1960; Guildford Borough Bench, since 1968; President, National Association of Probation Officers, since 1964; Member, Council on Tribunals, since 1964; a Lord-in-Waiting to the Queen, since 1968; *b* 1 May 1911; *s* of late Major Hon. Leslie d'Henin Hamilton, MVO, and Amy Cecile, *e d* of late Col Horace Ricardo, CVO; *S* uncle, 1952; *m* 1935, Rosemary Olive, *d* of late Major Hon. Sir John Coke, KCVO; two *s* one *d*. *Educ:* Eton; RMC, Sandhurst. Coldstream Guards, 1931-37 and 1939-45 (Major). Chm., Surrey Agricultural Exec. Cttee, 1958-68; Min. of Agriculture's Liaison Officer in South-East, 1960-64. Chm., Guildford Cathedral Council, 1958-69. DL Surrey, 1957; JP Guildford, 1957. *Heir: s* Hon. James Leslie Hamilton [*b* 11 Feb. 1938; *m* 1967, Corinna, *yr d* of late Sir Pierson Dixon, GCMG, CB and of Lady Dixon; one *s*]. *Address:* Snowdenham House, Bramley, Guildford, Surrey. *T:* Bramley 2002. *Club:* Guards.

**HAMILTON, Bishop of,** (RC), since 1937; **Rt. Rev. Joseph F. Ryan,** DD, JCD; *b* Dundas, Ontario, 1 March 1897; *s* of Wm Ryan and Ellen Manion. *Educ:* St Mary's Sch., Hamilton; St Jerome's Coll., Kitchener; St Augustine's Seminary, Toronto; Appolinaris Univ., Rome, Italy. Ordained 1921; Asst Priest, St Mary's CAthedral, Hamilton, 1921-25; Rector, 1925; First Rector of new Cathedral of Christ the King, Hamilton, 1933; Administrator of diocese after serving several years as Chancellor. *Address:* 722 King Street West, Hamilton, Ont, Canada. *T:* Jackson 2-6112.

**HAMILTON, Rt. Rev. Alexander Kenneth;** *see* Jarrow, Bishop Suffragan of.

**HAMILTON, His Honour Allister McNicoll;** Judge of County Courts Circuit No 23 (Coventry, Northampton), 1947-66; *b* 23 Jan. 1895; *s* of Donald Hamilton; *m* 1944, Mary Glen Rankin; one *s* one *d*. *Educ:* Liverpool Univ. (LLB Hons). Served throughout European War, 1914-18, as officer with Infantry and Trench Mortar Battery (wounded); called to Bar, Gray's Inn, 1919; in business, 1919-22; Northern Circuit, 1922-47. *Address:* Mayriggs, Brechin Road, Kirriemuir, Angus. *T:* Kirriemuir 2576.

**HAMILTON, Anthony Norris;** Headmaster, Hardye's School, Dorchester, since Sept. 1955; *b* 19 July 1913; 3rd *s* of Capt. Claude Hamilton, RD, RNR, and Kathleen Sophia Hamilton (*née* Mack); *m* 1942, Jean Philippa, 3rd *d* of Rev. David Railton, MC; one *s* three *d*. *Educ:* Kelly Coll.; Exeter Coll., Oxford. Asst Master Clifton Coll., 1935-40. Served War of 1939-45: commnd 6 Bn Argyll and Sutherland Highlanders, 1940; Gen. Staff, V Corps HQ, 1942, X Corps HQ 1943, VIII Army HQ, 1944. Ops Editor of VIII Army History of Italian Campaign, 1945. House Master, Clifton Coll., 1946-48; Headmaster, Strathallan Sch., 1948-51; Headmaster, Queen Mary's Grammar Sch., Walsall, 1951-55. Chm. Dorchester Branch, Save the Children Fund. *Recreations:* fishing, painting. *Address:* Hardye's School, Dorchester, Dorset.

**HAMILTON, Archibald;** Sheriff Substitute of Aberdeen, Kincardine and Banff, since 1952; *b* 28 June 1895; 2nd *s* of late Archibald Hamilton and Mrs Hannah Hamilton, Motherwell; *m* 1930, Janet Gibson McBride, MA, *d* of late John McBride, Motherwell; no *c*. *Educ:* Dalziel High Sch., Motherwell; Glasgow University. Graduated BL, and passed as Solicitor, 1920; partner Maclay Murray and Spens, Solicitors, Glasgow, 1929-44; Sheriff Substitute of Fife and Kinross, 1944-52. *Address:* 73 Fountainhall Road, Aberdeen. *T:* 23587.

**HAMILTON, (Arthur Douglas) Bruce,** CMG 1964; *b* 3 July 1900; *s* of Walter Bernard

Hamilton, Author and Barrister-at-Law, and Ellen Adèle Hamilton (*née* Hockley); *m* 1934, (Marie) Aileen (Lorna) Laurie. *Educ:* Westminster Sch.; University College, London. BA London 1926; PhD London 1947. Asst Master, Harrison Coll., Barbados, 1926-29. Senior History Master, 1938-50; Principal, Barbados Evening Institute and Technical Institute, 1950-55; Chm., Barbados Public Service Commission, 1957-64; Pres., Barbados Arts Council, 1959-60. *Publications: novels include:* To be Hanged, 1930; Middle Class Murder, 1935; Pro, 1946; Let Him have Judgment, 1947 (US and play title, Hanging Judge); So Sad, So Fresh, 1952; Too Much of Water, 1958, etc.; *play:* (with Diana Hamilton) The Home Front, 1930; *historical:* Barbados and the Confederation Question, 1957. *Recreations:* music, literary studies, cricket. *Address:* 26 West Hill Street, Brighton, Sussex.

**HAMILTON, Arthur Plumptre Faunce,** CIE 1947; OBE 1938; MC 1918; Inspector-General of Forests, Indian Forest Service, 1945-49; *b* 7 Oct. 1895; *s* of Francis Robert Abingdon Hamilton and Alice Emilia Plumptre; *m* 1925, Olivia Urmston Seth-Smith; one *s* one *d*. *Educ:* Trent Coll., Derbyshire; Lincoln Coll., Oxford. Served European War, 1914-19, in British Army, 8th Bn Sherwood Foresters and 2nd Bn Royal Tank Corps (temp. Major). Joined Indian Forest Service, 1921; served in Punjab. Forestry Commissioner, 1953-60. *Recreations:* shooting, fishing. *Address:* c/o Barclays Bank Ltd, Saxmundham, Suffolk.

**HAMILTON, Bruce;** *see* Hamilton, A. D. B.

**HAMILTON, (Charles) Denis,** DSO 1944; Editor-in-Chief and Chief Executive, Times Newspapers Ltd since 1967; *b* 6 Dec. 1918; *er s* of Charles and Helena Hamilton; *m* 1939, Olive, *yr d* of Thomas Hedley Wanless and Mary Anne Wanless; four *s*. *Educ:* Middlesbrough High Sch. Editorial Staff: Evening Gazette, Middlesbrough, 1937-38; Evening Chronicle, Newcastle, 1938-39; Editorial Asst to Viscount Kemsley, 1946-50; Editorial Dir, Kemsley (now Thomson) Newspapers, 1950-67; Editor of the Sunday Times, 1961-67. Director: Evening Gazette Ltd; Newcastle Chronicle and Journal Ltd; Times Newspapers Ltd (Chm. Exec. Bd); Thomson Organisation Ltd; Reuters, Ltd; Member: Council, Newspaper Publishers' Association; Press Council; National Council for the Training of Journalists (Chm., 1957); Executive Cttee, International Press Institute; National Council for Academic Awards; Trustee of British Museum, 1969-. Served War of 1939-45, TA, Durham Light Infantry; Lt-Col comdg 11th Bn Durham LI and 7th Bn Duke of Wellington's Regt. *Publication:* Jt Editor Kemsley Manual of Journalism, 1952. *Recreation:* sailing. *Address:* 25 Roebuck House, Palace Street, SW1. *T:* 01-828 0410; Weston House, Nutbourne, Chichester, Sussex. *T:* Emsworth 3351; (office) Printing House Square, EC4. *Clubs:* Garrick, Grillions.

**HAMILTON, Charles Keith Johnstone,** MC; BA, BM Oxford; FRCP; Consulting Physician, Children's Department, Charing Cross Hospital; *b* 1890; *s* of late C. W. Hamilton, MD; *m* Christine Mary (*d* 1959), *y d* of late Ernest Durrant. *Educ:* privately; Lincoln Coll., Oxford; St Thomas' Hospital. Served European War 1914 in King Edward's Horse and Royal Field Artillery (wounded, MC); late Hon. Medical Dir Violet Melchett Infant Welfare Centre; late Consulting Paediatrician to LCC, and to Taunton and Somerset Hospital. John Temple Research Fellow, St Thomas' Hosp.; Mem., British Pædiatric Assoc. *Publications:* The Principles of Infant Nutrition (with K. Tallerman); Heart Disease in Childhood (with H. B. Russell); contributions to medical journals. *Recreations:* hunting, fishing, gardening. *Address:* Castle Farm, Exford, Som. *Club:* United University.

**HAMILTON, Capt. Lord Claud (Nigel),** GCVO 1949 (KCVO 1937; CVO 1933; MVO 1916); CMG 1920; DSO 1914; late Grenadier Guards; *b* 10 Nov. 1889; 7th *s* of 2nd Duke of Abercorn; *m* 1933, Mrs Violet Newall. *Educ:* Wellington. Entered Army, 1911; served European War, 1914-19 (despatches twice, DSO); Equerry to Prince of Wales, 1919-22; Deputy-Master of HM's Household, 1922-24; Equerry to King George V, 1924-36; Comptroller and Treasurer in Queen Mary's Household, 1936-53; Extra Equerry to the Queen, 1953-. *Address:* Jannaways, Bagnor, Newbury, Berks. *T:* Newbury 553; 8 Russell Court, Cleveland Row, St James's, SW1. *T:* 01-930 1152.

**HAMILTON, Cyril Robert Parke;** Deputy Chairman: The Standard Bank Ltd, since 1963; Standard Bank of West Africa Ltd, since 1965; Vice-Chairman, Standard and Chartered Banking Group Ltd, since Dec. 1969; *b* 4 Aug. 1903; *s* of Alfred Parke and Annie Hamilton; *m* 1929, Cecily May Stearn (*d* 1966); one *s* one *d*. *Educ:* High Sch., Ilford; King's Coll., London Univ. Entered Bank of England, 1923, and retired as Deputy Chief Cashier, 1963, after career mainly concerned with internat. financial negotiations and Exchange Control. Director: Rank Organisation and subsidiary cos; A. Kershaw & Sons Ltd; Rank Xerox Ltd; The Standard Bank of South Africa Ltd; Midland and International Banks Ltd; Banque Belge d'Afrique; Chm., Malta Internat. Banking Corp. Ltd. *Recreations:* golf, gardening. *Address:* 67 Roebuck House, Palace Street, SW1. *T:* 01-834 0659; Peat Moor, Harborough Hill, Pulborough, Sussex. *T:* West Chiltington 2171. *Clubs:* Brooks's, Bath, MCC.

**HAMILTON, Denis;** *see* Hamilton, C. D.

**HAMILTON, Sir Edward (Sydney),** 7th and 5th Bt, *cr* 1776 and 1819; *b* 14 April 1925; *s* of Sir (Thomas) Sydney (Percival) Hamilton, 6th and 4th Bt, and Bertha Muriel, *d* of James Russell King, Singleton Park, Kendal; *S* father, 1966. *Educ:* Canford Sch. Served Royal Engineers, 1943-47; 1st Royal Sussex Home Guard, 1953-56. *Recreations:* spiritual matters, music. *Address:* The Cottage, East Lavant, near Chichester, Sussex. *T:* Chichester 7414.

**HAMILTON, Emily Moore,** MBE; *d* of late Rev. J. S. Hamilton, MA, Abbey Church, Dublin; *m* Prof. J. H. Richardson (*d* 1970); twin *d*. *Educ:* Victoria Coll., Belfast. Associate of the Royal College of Music, London. During European War, 1914-18, organised Girl Messenger System for West End Government Offices, 1915-18; Asst Commandant Women's Royal Air Force, 1918-19. First Staff officer, International Labour Office, League of Nations, Geneva, 1920-23; Save the Children Fund refugee work in Greece, 1923-24; War of 1939-45: supervision of women in explosives factory, Torontö, 1940. Red Cross work in Bermuda and Bahamas, 1941-43. *Address:* 2 Claremont Road, Mont Millais, Jersey, CI. *T:* Central 34717.

**HAMILTON, Maj.-Gen. Godfrey John,** CB 1966; CBE 1959 (OBE 1956); DSO 1935; *b* 31 March 1912; *s* of late Lieut-Col F. A. Hamilton, OBE, DL, JP, and of Mrs Hamilton, Osbaston, Monmouth; *m* 1st, 1937, Mary Penelope Colthurst; one *d*; 2nd, 1942, Mary Margaret Kaye (Novelist); two *d*. *Educ:* Radley Coll.;

RMC, Sandhurst. Commnd, 1932; served in Guides Infantry, IA, 1932-48 (despatches): India, Burma and Malaya; Royal Irish Fusiliers (despatches twice): Palestine, Egypt, Germany, Korea, Kenya, N Ireland, Berlin. Chief, Joint Services Liaison Organization, BAOR, 1963-66. Retired, 1967. *Recreations:* fishing, painting. *Address:* The Old House, Boreham Street, near Hailsham, Sussex. *Club:* Army and Navy.

**HAMILTON, Hamish;** Managing Director of Hamish Hamilton, Ltd, Publishers, since 1931; *b* 15 Nov. 1900; *o s* of James Neilson Hamilton, Glasgow, and Suzanne van Valkenberg, New York; *m* 1940, Countess Yvonne Pallavicino, of Rome; one *s*. *Educ:* Rugby; Caius Coll., Cambridge (Medical Student, 1919). MA (Hons Mod. Langs), LLB. Travelled in USA, 1922-23; called to Bar (Inner Temple), 1925; London Manager Harper and Brothers, Publishers, 1926; founded Hamish Hamilton Ltd, 1931; served in Army, 1939-41 (Holland and France, 1940); seconded to American Division, Ministry of Information, 1941-45; Hon. Sec. Kinsmen Trust, 1942-56; a Gov. of the Old Vic; Member Council, English-Speaking Union; a Gov., British Institute, Florence. Chevalier de la Légion d'Honneur. *Publications:* articles on publishing, Anglo-American relations and sport. Commemorative Anthologies: Decade, 1941, Majority, 1952. *Recreations:* music, the theatre, travel, tennis; formerly rowing (spare stroke Cambridge Eight, 1921; stroked Winning Crews Grand Challenge Cup, Henley, 1927 and 1928, and Olympic Eight, Amsterdam, 1928 (silver medal)), ski-ing, flying, squash. *Address:* 43 Hamilton Terrace, NW8. *T:* 01-286 2269. *Clubs:* Garrick, White's, Leander.

**HAMILTON, Rev. Herbert Alfred;** *b* 16 June 1897; *s* of Alfred and Ada Elizabeth Hamilton; *m* 1st, 1929, Winifred Alice Johnson (*d* 1936); two adopted *s*; 2nd, 1937, Phyllis Noella Pye (*d* 1944); one *d*; 3rd, 1944, Ellen Crossman Allen; one *s* one *d*. *Educ:* Merchant Taylors', Crosby; Manchester Univ.; Lancs Independent Coll. Ordained, 1924; Pastorates: Bolton, 1924-29; Birmingham, 1929-33; Sec. for Education and Youth Service, Congregational Union of England and Wales, 1933-45; Principal, Westhill Training Coll., Birmingham, 1945-54; Minister, Union Church, Brighton, 1954-63. Chm., Congregational Union of England and Wales, May 1961-62; Associate Gen. Sec., World Council of Christian Education, 1963-65; Asst Gen. Sec., World Council of Churches, 1965-66. Retired as consultant to the World Council of Christian Education, 1966. *Publications:* How to Say your Prayers, 1933; The Family Church, 1940; Church Youth Training, 1944; Conversation with God, 1955; contrib. to Expository Times, Times Educl Supplement, etc. *Recreations:* music, painting, conversation. *Address:* 22 Damian Way, Keymer, Hassocks, Sussex.

**HAMILTON, Sir Horace (Perkins),** GCB 1942 (KCB 1921; CB 1918); UK Member, Commonwealth Economic Committee, 1947-61 (Chairman, 1947-49); *b* 20 Nov. 1880; *o s* of Horace Hamilton, Ashford, Kent; *m* 1915, Amy (*d* 1970), *d* of Sydney Turner Klein; one *s* two *d*. *Educ:* Tonbridge Sch.; Hertford Coll., Oxford. Entered Inland Revenue Dept, 1904; transferred to Treasury, 1912; Private Sec. to Chancellor of the Exchequer, 1912-18; Dep. Chm. Board of Inland Revenue, 1918-19; Chm. Board of Customs and Excise, 1919-27; Permanent Sec., Board of Trade, 1927-37; Permanent Under-Sec. of State for Scotland, 1937-46. Advised Control Office for Germany and Austria on application of Whitley system to British civilian staffs in Control Service, 1946; advised Syrian Govt on taxation system of Syria, 1946-47; Mem., Interdepartmental Cttees on remuneration of specialists and of dentists, 1947-48; Vice-Chm. Advisory Cttee on Awards for Consultants and Specialists, 1948-60; Chm., OEEC Cttee on Internal Financial Stability, Paris, 1949; Mem., Deptl Cttee on Scottish Financial and Trade Statistics, 1950-52; Chm. Cttee on Regional Bds for Industry, 1953; Pres., Old Tonbridgian Soc., 1950-60; Pres., Tonbridge Sch. Clubs, St Pancras, 1934-64. *Address:* Leigham Grange, Leigham Court Road, SW16. *Club:* Athenæum.

*See also P. P. Henderson.*

**HAMILTON, Brig. Hugh Gray Wybrants,** CBE 1964 (MBE 1945); General Manager, Corby Development Corporation, since 1968; *b* 16 May 1918; *s* of Lt-Col H. W. Hamilton, late 5th Dragoon Guards; *m* 1944, Claire Buxton; two *d*. *Educ:* Wellington Coll., Berks; Peterhouse, Cambridge; Royal Mil. Academy. Commissioned with Royal Engineers, 1938. War Service in BEF, BNAF, BLA, 1939-45. Post War Service in Australia, BAOR, France and UK. Instructor, Army Staff Coll., Camberley, 1954-56; Student, IDC, 1965; retired, 1968. *Recreations:* riding, sailing, ski-ing. *Address:* Marston Trussell Hall, Market Harborough, Leics. *T:* Market Harborough 4209. *Club:* Army and Navy.

**HAMILTON, Iain (Bertram);** writer; Drama Critic, Times Educational Supplement; Fiction Reviewer, Daily Telegraph; Columnist, Illustrated London News; *b* 3 Feb. 1920; *s* of John Hamilton and Margaret Laird MacEachran; *m* 1944, Jean Campbell Fisher; one *s* one *d*. *Educ:* Paisley Grammar Sch. Editorial staff: Daily Record, 1944-45; The Guardian, 1945-52; The Spectator, 1952; Asst Editor, 1953, Associate Editor, 1954-56, The Spectator; Editor-in-Chief, 1957, Editorial Director, The Hutchinson group of publishing cos, 1958-62; Editor of The Spectator, 1962-63. Has contrib. prose and verse to radio, Encounter, Interplay, The Times Literary Supplement, Spectator, World Review, Twentieth Century, Scots Review, Student of Edinburgh Univ. Former Art Critic of Public Opinion. *Publications:* Scotland the Brave, 1957; The Foster Gang (with H. J. May), 1966. *Play:* The Snarling Beggar, 1951. *Recreations:* fishing, walking, travelling, talking, listening, arguing. *Address:* 31 Highgate West Hill, N6. *T:* 01-340 8270; Kames, Tighnabruaich, Argyll. *Club:* Garrick.

**HAMILTON, Iain Ellis,** BMus, FRAM; composer; pianist; Mary Duke Biddle Professor of Music (Chairman of the Department, 1966), Duke University, North Carolina, USA; *b* Glasgow, 6 June 1922; *s* of James and Catherine Hamilton. *Educ:* Mill Hill; Royal Academy of Music. Engineer (Handley Page Ltd), 1939-46; RAM (Scholar) 1947-51; BMus (London University), 1951. Lecturer at Morley Coll., 1952-58; Lecturer, London Univ., 1956-60. Prizes and awards include: Prize of Royal Philharmonic Society, 1951; Prize of Koussevitsky Foundation (America), 1951; Butterworth Award, 1954; Arnold Bax Gold Medal, 1956. FRAM, 1960. Chm. Composers' Guild, 1958; Chm. ICA Music Cttee, 1958-60. *Works:* 2 Symphonies; Sinfonia for Two Orchestras (Edinburgh Festival Commission); Concertos, for Piano, Clarinet, Organ and Violin; The Bermudas, for Baritone, Chorus and Orchestra (BBC Commission); Symphonic Variations for String Orchestra; Overture, Bartholomew Fair; Overture, 1912; Ecossaise for Orchestra; Concerto for Jazz Trumpet and Orchestra

(BBC Commn); Scottish Dances; Sonata for Chamber Orchestra; 5 Love Songs for Tenor and Orchestra; (BBC Commission) Cantos for Orchestra; Jubilee for Orchestra; Arias for Small Orchestra; Circus for Orchestra (BBC Commn); Epitaph for this World and Time: 3 choruses and 2 organs; Voyage for horn and orchestra; Clerk Saunders, a ballet; chamber works include: two String Quartets; String Octet; Sonatas for Piano, Viola, Clarinet and Flute; Flute Quartet; Clarinet Quintet; 3 Nocturnes for Clarinet and Piano; 5 Scenes for Trumpet and Piano; Sextet; Sonatas and Variants for 10 Winds; Dialogues for Soprano and 5 Instruments; Nocturnes with Cadenzas for Solo Piano; 4 Border Songs and the Fray of Suport for unaccompanied voices; Opera: Agamemnon; Royal Hunt of the Sun; Pharsalia; Threnos: 1966 for solo organ. Music for theatre and films. Hon. DMus Glasgow, 1970. *Publications:* articles for many journals. *Address:* 40 Park Avenue, New York, NY 10016, USA. *Club:* Williams (New York).

**HAMILTON, James;** MP (Lab) Bothwell since 1964; an Opposition Whip, since 1970; *b* 11 March 1918; *s* of George Hamilton and Margaret Carey; *m* 1945, Agnes McGhee; one *s* three *d* (and one *s* decd). *Educ:* St Bridget's, Baillieston; St Mary's, High Whifflet. District Councillor, 6th Lanarks, 1955-58; Lanarks County Council, 1958-64. National Executive Mem., Constructional Engrg Union, 1958-, Pres., 1968-; Chm., Trade Union Group, Parly Labour Party, 1969-. Asst Govt Whip, 1969-70. *Recreations:* tennis, badminton, golf. *Address:* 57 Cochrane Street, Bellshill, Lanarks. *T:* Bellshill 2071.

**HAMILTON, Prof. James;** Professor of Physics, Nordic Institute for Theoretical Atomic Physics, since 1964; *b* 29 Jan. 1918; *s* of Joseph Hamilton, Killybegs, Co. Donegal; *m* 1945, Glen, *d* of Charles Dobbs, Verwood, Dorset; two *s* one *d*. *Educ:* Royal Academical Institution, Belfast; Queen's Univ., Belfast; Institute for Advanced Study, Dublin; Manchester Univ. Scientific Officer, Admiralty, London, and South East Asia Command, 1943-45; ICI Fellow, Manchester Univ., 1945-48; Lectr in Theoretical Physics, Manchester Univ., 1948-49; University Lectr in Mathematics, Cambridge Univ., 1950-60. Fellow of Christ's Coll., Cambridge, 1953-60; Research Associate in Nuclear Physics, Cornell Univ., NY, 1957-58; Prof. of Physics, University Coll., London, 1960-64. Donegall Lectr, TCD, 1969. Foreign Mem., Royal Danish Acad. *Publications:* The Theory of Elementary Particles, 1959; papers and articles on elementary particle physics and related topics. *Address:* Nordita, Blegdamsvej 17, 2100 Copenhagen, ø, Denmark.

**HAMILTON, James Arnot,** MBE 1952; Director-General Concorde, Ministry of Technology, since 1966; *b* 2 May 1923; *m* 1947, Christine Mary McKean; three *s*. *Educ:* University of Edinburgh (BSc). Marine Aircraft Experimental Estab., 1943: Head of Flight Research, 1948; Royal Aircraft Estab., 1952; Head of Projects Div., 1964; Dir, Anglo-French Combat Aircraft, Min. of Aviation, 1965. *Publications:* papers in Reports and Memoranda series of Aeronautical Research Coun., Jl RAeS, and technical press. *Address:* Pentlands, 9 Cedar Road, Farnborough, Hants. *T:* Farnborough 43254. *Club:* Oxford and Cambridge University.

**HAMILTON, James Gilbert Murdoch,** FRCPEd; Consultant Physician, Royal Infirmary, Edinburgh, since 1939; Principal Medical Officer, Scottish Widows Fund and Life Assurance Society, since 1954; *b* 14 July 1907; *s* of William Henry Hamilton, SSC, and Margaret Paterson Mackenzie; *m* 1937, Elizabeth Frary King, Boston, Mass, USA; two *s* one *d* (and one *d* decd). *Educ:* George Watson's Coll., Edinburgh; Edinburgh Univ. MB, ChB, Edinburgh, 1931; MRCP, 1934, FRCPEd, 1939. Commonwealth Fund Fellow, Boston, Mass, 1935-37. Mem., Gen. Medical Council, 1958-. Vice-Pres., BMA, 1966-. *Publications:* contrib. to Brit. Medical Jl, Lancet, Brit. Heart Jl, Amer. Heart Jl; chapter on Life Assurance in Encyclopaedia of General practice. *Recreations:* formerly golf, now committee work. *Address:* 24 Mortonhall Road, Edinburgh 9. *T:* 031-667 5439. *Club:* University Staff (Edinburgh).

**HAMILTON, Brig. James Melvill,** DSO 1916; retired; *b* 4 Nov. 1886; *o s* of late Lewis Hamilton; *m* 1st, 1913, Violet Anne Colquhoun (*d* 1950); 2nd, 1950, Amelia Grenfell. *Educ:* Winchester; Sandhurst. Joined The Gordon Highlanders, 1907; Lt-Col 1934; Col 1938; Brig. 1938-41; Comd 144 Inf. Bde, Sub-Area Comd 1941-43; Col CA/Military Government, 1943-46; Served European War, 1914-19 (despatches five times, DSO, Legion of Honour); War of 1939-45 (despatches). *Address:* 6 Orchard Rise, Richmond, Surrey. *Club:* Royal Automobile.

**HAMILTON, John Almeric de Courcy,** CMG 1946; MC; Sudan Political Service (retired); *b* 7 Oct. 1896; *s* of late Henry de Courcy Hamilton; *m* 1960, Noreen, 2nd *d* of late Lieut-Col and Mrs H. K. Hamilton-Wedderburn. *Educ:* Cheltenham; King's Coll., Cambridge. BA 1920; MA 1933; served with 4th Bn Royal Hampshire Regiment, 1914-19 (wounded, MC); Sudan Political Service, 1920; District Commissioner, 1920-32; Sudan Agent, Cairo, 1932-34; seconded to Egyptian Govt, 1935-37 and to British Embassy, Cairo, 1937-41. Counsellor at the Legation, Beirut, 1941-42; Minister of State's Office, Bagdad and Cairo, 1942-46; Counsellor, British Embassy, Cairo, 1947-56; retired 1957. *Address:* 15 Collingham Road, SW5. *Club:* Athenæum.

**HAMILTON, John Cole;** *see* Cole-Hamilton.

**HAMILTON, Adm. Sir John (Graham),** GBE 1966 (KBE 1963; CBE 1958); CB 1960; Director-General, Institute of Marketing, since 1968; *b* 12 July 1910; *s* of late Col E. G. Hamilton, CMG, DSO, MC, and Ethel Marie (*née* Frith); *m* 1938, Dorothy Nina Turner, 2nd *d* of late Col J. E. Turner, CMG, DSO; no *c*. *Educ:* RN Coll., Dartmouth. Joined RN 1924; specialised in Gunnery, 1936. Served War of 1939-45: destroyers; on staff of Adm. Cunningham, Mediterranean; Gunnery Officer, HMS Warspite; Admiralty; SE Asia; Comdr, 1943 (despatches). In command, HMS Alacrity, Far East, 1946-48; Capt., 1949; Dep. Dir, Radio Equipment, 1950-51; in command, 5th Destroyer Squadron, 1952-53; Dir of Naval Ordnance, Admiralty, 1954-56; in command HMS Newfoundland, Far East, 1956-58; despatches, 1957; Rear-Adm., 1958; Naval Sec. to First Lord of the Admiralty, 1958-60; Vice-Adm., 1961; Flag Officer: Flotillas, Home Fleet, 1960-62; Naval Air Command, 1962-64; C-in-C Mediterranean, and C-in-C Allied Forces, Mediterranean, 1964-67; Adm. 1965. *Recreations:* walking, climbing, photography. *Address:* White Cottage, Church Oakley, Basingstoke, Hants. *T:* Oakley 279. *Club:* United Service.

**HAMILTON, Maj.-Gen. (Retired) John Robert Crosse,** CB 1957; CBE 1950; DSO 1944; late RE; *b* 1 April 1906; *s* of late Major, J. A. C. Hamilton, Fyne Court, Bridgwater, Somerset; *m* 1938, Rosamond Budd, *d* of late Richard

Hancock, Hong Kong; one *s* one *d*. *Educ:* Radley; Royal Military Academy; Caius Coll., Cambridge. 2nd Lieut RE, 1925. Served War of 1939-45 (DSO); France, Belgium, Germany; acting Brig., 1947; Lieut-Col 1948; Col, 1950; Maj.-Gen., 1956. Chief of Staff, HQ Malaya Command, 1955-56; Dir of Military Operations, War Office, 1956-59; retired, 1959. Bursar, Churchill Coll., Cambridge, 1959-. Col Comdt, RE, 1962-. *Address:* Orchard House, Comberton, Cambridge. *Club:* Naval and Military.

**HAMILTON, Michael Aubrey;** MP (C) Salisbury since Feb. 1965; Director: Army & Navy Stores Ltd; Royal Exchange Assurance; Hop Marketing Board; *b* 5 July 1918; *s* of late Rt Rev. E. K. C. Hamilton, KCVO; *m* 1947, Lavinia, 3rd *d* of Col Sir Charles Ponsonby, Bt, *qv*; one *s* three *d*. *Educ:* Radley; Oxford. Served War of 1939-45, with 1st Bn, Coldstream Guards. MP (C) Wellingborough Div. Northants, 1959-64; Asst Govt Whip (unpaid), 1961-62; a Lord Comr of the Treasury, 1962-64. *Address:* 45 Pont Street, SW1. *T:* 01-589 9993; Lordington House, Chichester, Sussex. *T:* Emsworth 2171.

**HAMILTON, Myer A. B. K.;** *see* King-Hamilton.

**HAMILTON, Sir Patrick George,** 2nd Bt, *cr* 1937; Chairman, Expanded Metal Co. Ltd; Director: Simon Engineering Ltd; Simon Carves Chemical Engineering Ltd; Simon Carves Ltd; Renold Chains Ltd; Lloyds Bank Ltd; *b* 17 Nov. 1908; *o s* of Sir George Clements Hamilton, 1st Bt, and Eleanor (*d* 1958), *d* of late Henry Simon and *sister* of 1st Baron Simon of Wythenshawe; *S* father, 1947; *m* 1941, Winifred Mary Stone (OBE 1957, MA), *o c* of Hammond Jenkins, Maddings, Hadstock, Cambs. *Educ:* Eton; Trinity Coll., Oxford (MA). First Managing Director and later Chairman of Tyresoles Ltd, 1934-53. Director of Propeller Production, Ministry of Aircraft Production, 1943-44. Chairman, Advisory Committee on Commercial Information Overseas, 1957-59. Dep. Chm., Export Publicity Council, 1960-63. Chm., Transport Users Consultative Cttee, NW Area, 1957-64; Mem., Central Transport Consultative Cttee, 1963-64. Treas., Fedn of Commonwealth Chambers of Commerce, 1962-64. Mem., ITA, 1964-69. Chm., Central Mddx Gp Hosp. Management Cttee, 1964-70. *Recreations:* gardening, travel. *Heir:* none. *Address:* 23 Cheyne Walk, SW3. *T:* 01-352 5577. *Club:* Carlton.

**HAMILTON, Sir Richard Caradoc;** *see* Hamilton, Sir Robert C. R. C.

**HAMILTON, Sir (Robert Charles) Richard (Caradoc),** 9th Bt, *cr* 1647; *b* 8 Sept. 1911; *s* of Sir Robert Caradoc Hamilton, 8th Bt, and Irene Lady Hamilton (*née* Mordaunt) (*d* 1969); *S* father, 1959; *m* 1952, Elizabeth Vidal Barton; one *s* three *d*. *Educ:* Charterhouse; St Peter's Coll., Oxford (MA). Served in the Intelligence Corps, 1940-45. Schoolmaster at Ardingly Coll., Sussex, 1946-60. *Recreation:* dramatist. *Heir:* *s* Andrew Caradoc Hamilton, *b* 23 Sept. 1953. *Address:* Walton, Warwick. *T:* Wellesbourne 460.

**HAMILTON, Robert William,** FBA 1960; Keeper of the Ashmolean Museum, Oxford, since 1962; Keeper of the Department of Antiquities, since 1956; *b* 26 Nov. 1905; *s* of William Stirling Hamilton and Kathleen Hamilton (*née* Elsmie); *m* 1935, Eileen Hetty Lowick; three *s* two *d*. *Educ:* Winchester Coll.; Magdalen Coll., Oxford. Chief Insp. of Antiquities, Palestine, 1931-38; Dir of Antiquities, Palestine, 1938-48; Sec.-Librarian, British Sch. of Archæology, Iraq, 1948-49; Senior Lecturer in Near Eastern Archæology, Oxford, 1949-56. FSA. fellow Magdalen Coll., Oxford. *Publications:* The Church of the Nativity, Bethlehem, 1947; Structural History of the Aqsa Mosque, 1949; Khirbat al Mafjar, 1959. *Address:* 20 Charlbury Road, Oxford.

**HAMILTON, Captain Sir Robert William Stirling-,** 12th Bt, *cr* 1673; JP, DL; RN, retired; *b* 5 April 1903; *s* of Sir William Stirling-Hamilton, 11th Bt, and late Mabel Mary, *d* of Maj.-Gen. Tyndall; *S* father 1946; *m* 1930, Eileen, *d* of late Rt Rev. H. K. Southwell, CMG; one *s* two *d*. *Educ:* RNC, Dartmouth. Commodore, RN Barracks, Portsmouth, 1952-54, retired 1954. DL, Sussex, 1970-. *Heir:* *s* Bruce Stirling-Hamilton [*b* 5 Aug. 1940; *m* 1968, Stephanie, *e d* of Dr William Campbell; one *d*]. *Address:* Puriton Lodge, Hambrook, Chichester, Sussex. *T:* West Ashling 363.

**HAMILTON, Walter,** MA; Hon. DLitt Durham; FRSL; Master of Magdalene College, Cambridge, since 1967; *b* 10 Feb. 1908; *s* of late Walter George Hamilton and Caroline Mary Stiff; *m* 1951, Jane Elizabeth, *o d* of Sir John Burrows, *qv*, Cronklands, Limpsfield Chart, Surrey; three *s* one *d*. *Educ:* St Dunstan's Coll.; Trinity Coll., Cambridge (Scholar). 1st Class Classical Tripos, Part I, 1927; Part II, 1929; Craven Scholar, 1927; Chancellor's Classical Medallist, 1928; Porson Prizeman and Craven Student, 1929. Fellow of Trinity Coll., 1931-35; Asst Lecturer, University of Manchester, 1931-32; Asst Master, Eton Coll., 1933-46, Master in Coll., 1937-46; Fellow and Classical Lecturer, Trinity Coll., 1946-50; Tutor, 1947-50; University Lectr in Classics, 1947-50; Head Master: of Westminster Sch., 1950-57; of Rugby Sch., 1957-66. Editor, Classical Quarterly, 1946-47. Chairman: Scholarship Cttee, Lord Kitchener Nat. Memor. Fund, 1953-59, Exec. Cttee, 1967-; Headmasters' Conference, 1955, 1956, 1965, 1966; Governing Body, Shrewsbury Sch., 1968-; Governing Bodies Assoc., 1969-. Member: Exec. Cttee, British Council, 1958-70; Council of Senate of Cambridge Univ., 1969-. *Publications:* A New translation of Plato's Symposium (Penguin Classics), 1951; Plato's Gorgias, (Penguin Classics) 1960; contributions to Classical Quarterly, Classical Review, etc. *Address:* Magdalene College, Cambridge; Ardbeg, Dervaig, Isle of Mull. *Club:* Athenæum.

**HAMILTON, William Aitken Brown,** CMG 1950; *b* 3 June 1909; *e s* of Brown Hamilton, Milltimber, Aberdeenshire; *m* 1936, Barbara, *e d* of S. T. Gano, Belmont, Massachusetts, USA; one *s* (and one *s* decd). *Educ:* Aberdeen Grammar Sch.; Aberdeen Univ. 1st Class Hons Classics. Administrative Civil Service, Board of Education, 1931; Principal, 1936; Joint Sec., Athlone Cttee on Nursing Services, 1937-39; Ministry of Food, 1939-44; Asst Sec., 1943; Ministry of Education, 1944-49; Dir of Establishments and Under-Sec., 1946; Dir of Establishments and Asst Under-Sec. of State, Commonwealth Relations Office, 1949; Dir of Personnel, United Nations, 1959-62; Asst Under-Sec. of State, Commonwealth Office, 1962-67, retired. *Address:* Bullingstone Lane, Speldhurst, Kent. *T:* Speldhurst 164.

**HAMILTON, Prof. William James,** MD, BCh (Belfast), DSc (Glasgow); FRCS; FRCOG; FRSE; Professor of Anatomy, University of London, at Charing Cross Hospital Medical School, 1947-70; Dean, Charing Cross Hospital Medical School, 1956-62; Professor of Anatomy at the Royal Academy of Arts; *b* 1903; *s* of late Andrew and late Emmeline G.

Hamilton, Roselle, Whitehead, Co. Antrim, N Ireland; *m* 1933, Maimie, *o d* of late Samuel Young, Ingleside, Myrtlefield Park, Belfast; four *s* one *d*. *Educ:* Queen's Univ. Belfast, BSc, 1926, First Class Hons; MB, BCh, BAO, 1929, First Class Hons and First Place; MSc 1931; MD 1936, High Commendation, Queen's Univ., Belfast; DSc, 1934, Glasgow Univ.; various Scholarships and Exhibitions at Queen's Univ. and Royal Victoria Hosp., Belfast, 1925-29; Struthers Anatomical Prize and Gold Medal, University of Glasgow, 1932; Neill Prize, Royal Society of Edinburgh, 1938; formerly Lecturer in Anatomy in University of Glasgow and Dep. Dir of Anatomy at St Thomas's Hosp. Medical Sch.; Prof. of Anatomy in Univ. of London at St Bartholomew's Hosp. Medical Coll.; Regius Prof. of Anatomy at Glasgow Univ., 1945-47. Pres. Anatomical Soc. of Great Britain and Ireland, 1953-55, Sec., 1964-67. Chm. Special Adv. Bd of Vet. Med. in Univ. of London. Member: Senate, University of London, 1962-64; Sch. Council, Royal Vet. Coll.; Bd of Governors, Queen Charlotte's and Chelsea Hosps, 1966-69; Bd of Govs, Charing Cross Hosp., 1953-64, 1967-70; SW Metropolitan Regional Hosp. Bd, 1959-68. Sometime External Examr in Univs of: Aberdeen, Belfast, Bristol, Cambridge, Cardiff, Liverpool and Manchester; also in Primary FRCS, RCS of England. FRCS 1968. Hon. DSc Queen's Univ., Belfast, 1968. *Publications:* Memoirs on Embryology and related subjects in Transactions of Royal Society of Edinburgh and Journal of Anatomy; Text Book on Surface and Radiological Anatomy (with Appleton and Tchaperoff), 1938, 5th edn 1970; Textbook on Human Embryology (with Boyd and Mossman), 1945, 4th edn 1971; Editor Textbook of Human Anatomy, 1956; The Human Placenta (with Boyd), 1970; contributions to: Vol. 2 of Marshall's Physiology of Reproduction (ed Parkes), 3rd edn, 1952; Queen Charlotte's Textbook of Obstetrics (ed Tomkinson), 11th edn, 1956, 12th edn, 1970; British Obstetric and Gynaecological Practice (ed Claye and Bourne), 2nd edn, 1953, 3rd edn, 1963; Modern Trends in Obstetrics (ed Bowes), 1st series, 1950, 2nd series, 1955; Diseases of the Ear, Nose and Throat (ed Scott-Brown, Ballantyne and Groves) 2nd edn, 1965, 3rd edn, 1970; Scientific Foundations of Obstetrics and Gynaecology (ed Philipp, Barnes and Newton), 1970. *Address:* Tara, 45 Wolsey Road, Moor Park, Northwood, Middlesex. *T:* Northwood 22258.

**HAMILTON, William Winter;** MP (Lab) West Fife since 1950; *b* 26 June 1917; *m* (wife died 1968); one *s* one *d*. *Educ:* Washington Grammar Sch., Co. Durham; Sheffield Univ. (BA, DipEd). Joined Lab. Party, 1936; contested W Fife, 1945; Chairman, H. of C. Estimates Cttee, 1964-; Vice-Chm., Parly Labour Party, 1966-. School teacher; Mem. National Union of Teachers. Served War of 1939-45, Middle East, Capt. *Address:* House of Commons, SW1; 35 Hitherwood Drive, College Road, Norwood, SE19.

**HAMILTON-DALRYMPLE, Sir Hew;** *see* Dalrymple.

**HAMILTON-KING, Mrs Grace M.;** Principal, Royal School of Needlework, 1950-66; *d* of late Canon Arthur West and of Mrs Louisa Oliver; *m* 1932, Edward Hamilton-King (decd). *Educ:* St Clair, Tunbridge Wells; Effingham House, Bexhill; Lytton House, London. London Academy of Music, 1922-23; Miss Kerr-Sander's Secretarial Coll., 1930-31; Temp. Administrative Officer, Home Office, 1941-45. Coronation Medal, 1953. *Address:* Flat Three, 2 Fortfield Terrace, Sidmouth, Devon. *T:* Sidmouth 3582.

**HAMILTON-RUSSELL,** family name of **Viscount Boyne.**

**HAMILTON-SPENCER-SMITH, Sir John;** *see* Spencer-Smith.

**HAMLING, William,** JP; MP (Lab) Woolwich West since 1964; an Opposition Whip, since 1970; *b* 10 Aug. 1912; *s* of William and Charlotte Hamling, Liverpool; *m* 1940, Olive Victoria, *d* of William and Henrietta Sophia Fraser, Liverpool; two *d*. *Educ:* Liverpool Inst. High Sch. for Boys; University of Liverpool. Schoolmaster and Lecturer. Commissioned in Royal Marines, 1941; served until 1946. An Asst Govt Whip, 1969-70. Trustee, Nat. Maritime Museum, 1967-; Governor, The Foudroyant Trust; Mem. Council, Navy League. JP Liverpool, 1948-51; JP Blackheath, 1963. *Address:* 4 Commonwealth Way, SE2. *T:* 01-854 6778.

**HAMLYN, Paul (Bertrand);** Joint Managing Director, News of the World, since 1970; *b* 12 Feb. 1926; 2nd *s* of late Prof. Richard Hamburger and Mrs L. Hamburger (*née* Hamburg); *m* 1952, Eileen Margaret (Bobbie) (marr. diss. 1969), *d* of Col Richard Watson; one *s* one *d*; *m* 1970, Mrs Helen Price Guest. *Educ:* St Christopher's Sch., Letchworth, Herts. Formed: Books for Pleasure, 1949; Prints for Pleasure, 1960; Records for Pleasure, Marketing long-playing classical records, and Golden Pleasure Books (jt co. with Golden Press Inc., NY), 1961; Music for Pleasure (with EMI), 1965. Paul Hamlyn Gp acquired by Internat. Publishing Corp, 1964; joined IPC Bd with special responsibility for all Corporation's book publishing activities; Butterworth & Co. acquired 1968; Director, IPC, 1965-70; Chm., IPC Books, controlling Hamlyn Publishing Gp, 1965-70 (formerly Chm., Paul Hamlyn Holdings Ltd, and associated Cos). *Address:* 8 Chelsea Embankment, SW3. *T:* 01-352 8369.

**HAMMARSKJÖLD, Knut (Olaf Hjalmar Åkesson);** Director-General, International Air Transport Association, since 1966; *b* Geneva, 16 Jan. 1922; Swedish; *m*; two *s*. *Educ:* Sigtunaskolan, Sigtuna, Sweden; Stockholm Univ. Swedish Foreign Service, 1946; served in: Stockholm; Paris; Vienna; Moscow; Bucharest; Sofia; Kabul; OEEC/OECD, Paris; seconded to EFTA as Dep. Sec.-Gen., 1960; Minister, Swedish Foreign Service, 1966. Order of Oranje Nassau (Netherlands), 1945; Order of Black Star (France), 1949; 1st cl. Order of Falcon (Iceland), 1958; Comdr, Order of Lion (Finland), 1966. *Publications:* contribs to Ekonomisk Revy (Swed. Bankers Assoc.), etc. *Recreations:* music, painting, ski-ing. *Address:* c/o IATA, 1155 Mansfield Street, Montreal 113, PQ, Canada. *T:* 866-1011; IATA, Cointrin Airport, Geneva, Switzerland. *Clubs:* Nya Sällskapet (Stockholm); University (Montreal).

**HAMMETT, Hon. Sir Clifford (James),** Kt 1969; Chief Justice, Fiji, since 1967; *b* 8 June 1917; *s* of late Frederick John and Louisa Maria Hammett; *m* 1946, Olive Beryl Applebee; four *s* one *d*. *Educ:* Woodbridge. Admitted Solicitor, 1939. Indian Army, 1st Punjab Regt, 1939, North Africa, 1940; captured at Singapore, 1942 (despatches); POW on Siam Railway, 1942-45. Magistrate, Nigeria, 1946-52. Called to the Bar, Middle Temple, 1948. Transferred to Fiji, 1952; Senior Magistrate, Fiji, 1954, Puisne Judge, 1955; conjointly Chief Justice, Tonga, 1956-68. *Recreation:* gardening. *Address:* Chief Justice's Chambers, Suva, Fiji.

*Clubs:* United Service, Royal Commonwealth Society; Fiji.

**HAMMETT, Harold George;** British Deputy High Commissioner, Peshawar, 1964-66; *b* 2 Aug. 1906; 2nd *s* of Arthur Henry Hammett; *m* 1st, 1936, Daphne Margaret Vowler; one *s*; 2nd, 1947, Natalie Moira Sherratt; one *s* one *d*. *Educ:* St Olave's; Clare Coll., Cambridge. Malayan Civil Service, 1928-57; Commonwealth Office (formerly CRO), 1958-66. *Recreations:* woodwork, gardening. *Address:* Hole Head, Holcombe, Dawlish, Devon. *T:* Dawlish 2114. *Clubs:* East India and Sports, Royal Commonwealth Society.

**HAMMICK, Sir Stephen (George),** 5th Bt, *cr* 1834; *b* 27 Dec. 1926; *s* of Sir George Hammick, 4th Bt; *S* father, 1964; *m* 1953, Gillian Elizabeth Inchbald; two *s* one *d*. *Educ:* Stowe. Royal Navy as Rating (hostilities only), 1944-48; RAC Coll., Cirencester, 1949-50; MFH Cattistock hunt, 1961 and 1962. County Councillor (Dorset), 1958. Farmer, with 450 acres. *Recreations:* hunting, fishing, sailing. *Heir:* *s* Paul St Vincent Hammick, *b* 1 Jan. 1955. *Address:* Badgers, Wraxall, Dorchester. *T:* Evershot 343.

**HAMMILL, Capt. Charles Ford,** CIE 1944; *b* 27 Nov. 1891; *s* of Capt. Tynte Ford Hammill, CB, RN; *m* 1933, Cynthia, *d* of late Adm. Sir Howard Kelly, GBE, KCB. Entered RNC, Osborne, 1904. Served in HMS Colossus, European War, 1914-18. Commanded HMS Enterprise, 1938, HMS Cornwall, 1939-41; Naval Attaché, Paris, 1934-37; Commodore, Senior Naval Officer Persian Gulf, 1942-44; Commodore in Charge Royal Naval Establishments, Durban, 1944-46; retired, 1943. *Address:* Bleak House, Slindon, Arundel, Sussex. *T:* Slindon 281. *Club:* United Service.

**HAMMOND, Maj.-Gen. Arthur Verney,** CB 1944; DSO 1943; Indian Army, retired; *b* 16 Oct. 1892; *s* of late Col Sir Arthur G. Hammond, VC, KCB, DSO; *m* 1919, Mary Ellen Eaton; two *d*; *m* 1947, E. Boyes Cooper. *Educ:* Streete Court; Wellington Coll.; Royal Military College, Sandhurst. 2nd Lieut 1911, attached R West Kent Regt; Joined QVO Corps of Guides (Cavalry), 1912; European War, 1914-18 (despatches); NW Persia, 1920-21; Staff Coll., Quetta, 1925-26; Brigade Major, 1928-32; commanded The Guides Cavalry, 1937-39; War Office, London, 1939-40 (Col on the Staff); Brigade Comd 1941-43; served in Burma, 1942-43 (DSO); Maj.-Gen. 1942; ADC to the King, 1942-43; Comdg Lucknow District, 1944-45; retired, 1947. *Address:* 2 Connaught Place, Dun Laoghaire, Eire.

**HAMMOND, Catherine Elizabeth,** CBE 1950; Colonel, WRAC (retired); *b* 22 Dec. 1909; *d* of late Frank Ernest Rauleigh Eddolls and Elsie Eddolls (*née* Cooper); *m*; one *s* one *d*. *Educ:* Lassington House, Highworth, Wilts; Chesterville Sch., Cirencester, Glos. Joined ATS (TA) (FANY), 1938; Private, 7th Wilts MT Co. 1939; 2nd Subaltern 1940; Capt., 1942; Major, Commanding Devon Bn, 1942; Lieut-Col, Asst Dir ATS Oxford, 1943; Col, Dep. Dir ATS (later WRAC), Eastern Command 1947-50; Hon. Col 54 (East Anglia) Div./Dist WRAC/TA, 1964-67. Chm., WRAC Assoc., 1966-. *Recreations:* Hockey–Army (women), 1947-48; all games; racing. *Address:* Red Down, Highworth, Wilts. *T:* Highworth 331.

**HAMMOND, Joan Hood,** CBE 1963 (OBE 1953); Australian operatic, concert, oratorio, and recital singer; *b* 24 May 1912; *d* of late Samuel Hood Hammond and Hilda Mary Blandford. *Educ:* Presbyterian Ladies Coll., Pymble, Sydney, Australia. Student of violin and singing at Sydney Conservatorium of Music; played with Sydney Philharmonic Orchestra for three years. Sports writer, Daily Telegraph, Sydney. Commenced public appearances (singing) in Sydney, 1929; studied in Europe from 1936; made operatic debut, Vienna, 1939; London debut in Messiah, 1938. World Tours: British Isles, USA, Canada, Australasia, Malaya, India, E and S Africa, Europe, Scandinavia, Russia, etc. Guest Artist: Royal Opera House, Covent Garden; Carl Rosa; Sadler's Wells; Vienna Staatsoper; Bolshoi, Moscow; Marinsky, Leningrad; Riga, Latvia; New York City Centre; Australian Elizabethan Theatre Trust; Netherlands Opera; Barcelona Liceo. Operatic roles: Aida, Madame Butterfly, Tosca, Salome, Otello, Thais, Faust, Don Carlos, Eugene Onegin, Invisible City of Kitej, La Traviata, Il Trovatore, La Bohème, Pique Dame, Manon, Manon Lescaut, La Forza del Destino, Fidelio, Simone Boccanegra, Turandot, Tannhauser, Lohengrin, Damnation of Faust, Martha, Pagliacci, Der Freischutz, Oberon, Magic Flute, Dido and Aeneas; World Premieres: Trojan Women, Wat Tyler, Yerma; British Premiere, Rusalka. Has made recordings. Volunteer Ambulance Driver, London, War of 1939-45. Sir Charles Santley Award, Worshipful Co. of Musicians, 1970. Coronation Medal 1953. *Publication:* A Voice, A Life, 1970. *Recreations:* golf (won first junior Golf Championship of NSW, 1930 and 1931; NSW. LGU State Title, 1932, 1934, 1935; runner-up Australian Open Championship, 1933; Mem. first LGU team of Australia to compete against Gt Brit., 1935) (runner-up NSW State Squash Championship, 1934), yachting, swimming, tennis, writing, reading. *Address:* c/o Bank of New South Wales, Sackville Street, London, W1; Private Bag 101, Geelong PO, Victoria 3220, Australia. *Clubs:* New Century (London); Royal Dornoch Golf (Scotland); Barwon Heads Golf (Victoria); Royal Sydney Golf (Sydney, Australia); Royal Motor Yacht (Dorset, England).

**HAMMOND, John Colman,** OBE 1959; MA; Retired as Headmaster, Harrison College, Barbados, WI (1949-65); *b* 24 Nov. 1906; *s* of late Ven. T. C. Hammond; *m* 1943, Majorie (*née* Cruse); one *s* one *d*. *Educ:* Rossall Sch.; Pembroke Coll., Cambridge (MA). Senior History Master, St John's Sch., Leatherhead, Surrey, 1929-46; House Master, 1934-46; Headmaster, Sompting Abbotts Sch., Sussex. 1947-49. Coronation Medal, 1953. *Recreation:* bridge. *Address:* 23 Riggindale Road, Streatham, SW16.

**HAMMOND, Kay, (Dorothy Katharine);** Actress; *b* 18 Feb.; *d* of late Sir Guy Standing, KBE, and late Dorothy Plaskitt (professionally known as Dorothy Hammond); *m* 1st, 1932, Sir Ronald George Leon, 3rd Bt (marriage dissolved); two *s*; 2nd, 1946, Sir John Selby Clements, *qv*. *Educ:* The Lodge, Banstead, Surrey. Studied at Royal Academy of Dramatic Art. Among London appearances are: Beatrice in Nine Till Six, Arts and Apollo, 1930; Evergreen, Adelphi, 1930; Daphne Hibberd in Can the Leopard . . .?, Haymarket, 1931; Emmie in My Hat, New, 1932; Elsa Frost in Woman Kind, Phoenix, 1933; Elizabeth Rimplegar in Three-Cornered Moon, Westminster, 1934; Dorothy Wilson in Youth at the Helm, Globe, 1935; Hon. Ursula Maddings in Bees on the Boatdeck, Lyric, 1936; Diana Lake in French Without Tears, Criterion, 1936-38; Adeline Rawlinson in Sugar Plum, Criterion, 1939; Elvira in Blithe Spirit, Piccadilly, St James's and Duchess, 1941-44; Amanda in Private Lives (revival),

Apollo, 1944-45; Lady Elizabeth Grey in The Kingmaker; Melantha in Marriage à la Mode, by John Dryden, St James's, 1946; Mrs Sullen in The Beaux' Stratagem, by George Farquhar, Phoenix and Lyric, 1949; Ann in Man and Superman, New, 1951; The Happy Marriage, Duke of York's, 1952; Eliza in Pygmalion, St James's, 1953-54; The Little Glass Clock, Aldwych, 1954-55; Lydia Languish in The Rivals, Saville, 1956; Millamant in The Way of the World, Saville, 1956; The Rape of the Belt, Piccadilly, 1957; Gilt and Gingerbread, Duke of York's, 1959; The Marriage-Go-Round, 1959. In numerous films, 1931-. *Address:* 7 Royal Crescent, Brighton, Sussex.
*See also Sir J. R. Leon, Bt.*

**HAMMOND, Prof. Nicholas Geoffrey Lemprière,** DSO 1944; FBA 1968; DL; Henry Overton Wills Professor of Greek, University of Bristol, since 1962; a Pro-Vice-Chancellor, 1964-66; *b* 15 Nov. 1907; *s* of late Rev. James Vavasour Hammond, Rector of St Just-in-Roseland, Cornwall, and Dorothy May; *m* 1938, Margaret Campbell, *d* of James W. J. Townley, CBE, MIEE; two *s* three *d*. *Educ:* Fettes Coll. (schol.); Caius Coll., Cambridge (schol.). 1st Cl. Classical Tripos Pts I and II, dist. in Hist., Pt II; Montagu Butler Prize; Sandys Student; Pres. CU Hockey Club; Treas. Union Soc. Fellow Clare Coll., Cambridge, 1930; University Lectr in Classics, 1936; Junior Proctor, 1939; Sen. Tutor, Clare Coll., 1947-54; Headmaster, Clifton Coll., 1954-62. Served War of 1939-45, as Lt-Col, campaigns in Greece, Crete, Syria, and Mem. Allied Mil. Mission, Greece, 1943-44 (despatches twice, DSO). Pres., Hellenic Soc., 1965-68. DL, Bristol, 1965. Officer, Order of the Phœnix, Greece, 1946. *Publications:* Memoir of Sir John Edwin Sandys, 1933; History of Greece, 1959; Epirus, 1967; articles and reviews in learned jls; editor: Clifton Coll Centenary Essays, 1962; Cambridge Ancient History, rev. edn, vols I and II. *Address:* 27 Woodstock Road, Bristol. *T:* Bristol 41064.

**HAMMOND, Stanley Alfred Andrew,** CMG 1943; Adviser on Establishment, Organization and Training, Barbados, 1959-64, retired; *b* 24 Oct. 1898; *s* of Alfred Gauntlett Hammond; *m* 1946, Adèle Alice Viola, *d* of William Wallace Cathcart Dunlop. *Educ:* Bancrofts Sch.; Trinity Coll. Oxford. 2nd Lieut RE 1917; Superintendent of Education, Nigeria, 1922; Dir of Education, Jamaica, 1928; Senior Education Commissioner, West Indies, 1936; Educn Adviser to Comptroller for Development and Welfare, West Indies, 1940; Chief Adviser Development and Welfare Organization, West Indies, 1948. Commissioner, Enquiry into Organization of the Civil Service, Leeward Islands, 1951. Adviser with special Duties, Development and Welfare Organisation, West Indies, 1950-53; retired, 1953. Dir of Training, Barbados, 1956. *Address:* c/o Midland Bank Ltd, 52 Oxford Street, W1; Little Edgehill, St Thomas, Barbados, West Indies.

**HAMMOND INNES, Ralph;** author and traveller; *b* 15 July 1913; *s* of late William Hammond and Dora Beatrice Innes; *m* 1937, Dorothy Mary Lang. Staff of Financial News, 1934-40. Served Artillery, 1940-46. Works regularly translated into numerous languages. *Publications include:* Wreckers Must Breathe, 1940; The Trojan Horse, 1940; Attack Alarm, 1941; Dead and Alive, 1946; The Lonely Skier, 1947; The Killer Mine, 1947; Maddon's Rock, 1948; The Blue Ice, 1948; The White South (Book Society Choice), 1949; The Angry Mountain, 1950; Air Bridge, 1951; Campbell's Kingdom (Book Society Choice), 1952; The Strange Land, 1954; The Mary Deare (chosen by Literary Guild of America), 1956; The Land God Gave to Cain, 1958; Harvest of Journeys, 1959; The Doomed Oasis (chosen by Literary Guild of America), 1960; Atlantic Fury (Book Society Choice), 1962; Scandinavia, 1963; The Strode Venturer, 1965; Sea and Islands (Book Society Choice), 1967; The Conquistadors (Book of the Month and Literary Guild), 1969; *films:* Snowbound, Hell Below Zero, Campbell's Kingdom, The Wreck of the Mary Deare. *Recreation:* cruising and ocean racing. *Address:* Kersey, Suffolk. *T:* Hadleigh (Suffolk) 3294. *Clubs:* Royal Ocean Racing, Royal Cruising.

**HAMNETT,** family name of **Baron Hamnett.**

**HAMNETT,** Baron *cr* 1970 (Life Peer), of Warrington; **Cyril Hamnett;** Chairman: Warrington New Town Development Corporation since 1969; Co-operative Press Ltd since 1953 (Director since 1947); Director, Nor-West Co-operative Society Ltd since 1946; *b* 20 May 1906; *e s* of James Henry Hamnett and Gertrude Hilton; *m* 1929, Elsie Cox (*d* 1970); one *d*. *Educ:* elementary and Manchester Technical School. Engineering Journalism, Editor and Publicity Officer to Union of Shop, Distributive & Allied Workers until 1952; Admin. Officer, 1953-66. Chm., Reynolds News and Sunday Citizen, 1953-67; Mem., Newspaper Proprietors' Assoc., 1953-67; Mem., British Press Council, 1956-65; Mem., Central Exec., Co-operative Union, 1953- (Chm. Parly Cttee, 1969-); Manchester City Magistrate, 1956- (Chm. of Licensing Bench, 1962-65, 1968-); Mem., Licensing Planning Cttee, 1960-; Mem. of Industrial Tribunals. *Publications:* pamphlets and articles to magazines, newspapers, on industrial, trade union and co-operative subjects. *Recreation:* the pursuit of the unattainable. *Address:* 11 Bolton Avenue, Manchester M19 1RP. *T:* 061-432 4801. *Clubs:* Didsbury Golf, Warrington Sports.

**HAMPDEN;** *see* Hobart-Hampden.

**HAMPDEN,** 5th Viscount, *cr* 1884; **David Francis Brand;** Chairman, English Scottish and Australian Bank Ltd, since 1948; *b* 14 June 1902; 2nd *s* of 3rd Viscount Hampden, GCVO, KCB, CMG; *S* brother, 4th Viscount, 1965; *m* 1936, Imogen Alice Rhys, *d* of 7th Baron Dynevor; one *s* two *d*. *Educ:* Eton; Trinity Coll., Cambridge. Herts Regt, 1938; served with 29th Independent Brigade Group; DAA&QMG, Madagascar, 1942; Bde Major, Burma, 1944 (despatches); Lt-Col 1944. *Heir: s* Hon. Anthony David Brand [*b* 7 May 1937; *m* 1969, Cara Fiona, *e d* of Claud Proby; one *s*]. *Address:* Trevor House, Glynde, Sussex. *T:* Glynde 295. *Club:* White's.

**HAMPDEN, John,** MA Oxon; author and publishers' editor; *b* 6 Feb. 1898; *e s* of Francis John Hampden; *m* 1st, Doreen Springall; one *s* one *d*; 2nd, Rosalind Vallance, author and playwright; one *d*. *Educ:* St Martin's, Dover; privately; Exeter Coll., Oxford. Skeat Prize, 1921. Served European War, Macedonia, 1915-19 (despatches). English Master, Royal Grammar Sch., Guildford, 1922-29; Lectr in and later Prof. of English Literature, Queen's Coll., London, 1929-32; Gen. Editor, Thomas Nelson & Sons Ltd, 1932-37; Nat. Book Council, 1938-39; Min. of Information, 1940-41. British Council, 1941-63: Books and Periodicals Adviser, 1959-63; Head of Literature Group of Depts, 1947-59; Dep. Controller, Arts and Science Div., 1950-59; etc. Editor, British Book News, 1942-46; Mem. Council and Exec., Nat. Book League, 1946-63; a Dir, British Nat. Bibliography,

1950-63; Hon. Life Mem., Soc. of Bookmen and PEN. *Publications:* Critical editions of many 16th, 17th and 18th century English plays; Havelok and Sir Orfeo; Drake's Raid on the Treasure Trains (with Janet Hampden); An Eighteenth Century Journal; edns of Lamb's Essays, Hazlitt's Essays, Johnson's Lives of the Poets (with Rosalind Vallance); The Book World Today; Books, from Papyrus to Paperback (with Esther S. Harley); A Picture History of India; New Worlds Ahead; The Yellow Dragon; The Black Monkey; The House of Cats; Drake's Early Voyages; The Spanish Armada; The Tudor Venturers, etc. Anthologies, textbooks, contribs to literary jls and BBC programmes. Much pseudonymous work. *Recreations:* walking, talking. *Address:* Robin House, 55 St Mary's Terrace, Hastings, Sussex. *T:* Hastings 29065.

**HAMPSHIRE, Sir (George) Peter,** KCMG 1967 (CMG 1963); HM Diplomatic Service, retired; *b* 1 Dec. 1912; *s* of late G. N. Hampshire and Marie Hampshire (*née* West); *m* 1956, Eve Buhler (*née* Rowell); no *c*. *Educ:* Repton; Oriel Coll., Oxford. Apptd to War Office, 1935; Control Office for Germany and Austria and Foreign Office (German Section), 1946-48; Office of UK High Commission, Ottawa, 1948-51; UK Dep. High Comr, Dacca, 1953-55; IDC, 1956; Counsellor, British Embassy, Buenos Aires, 1957-60; Asst Under-Sec. of State, CRO, 1961-64, DSAO, 1965-66; High Comr, Trinidad and Tobago, 1966-70. *Address:* Sorrels House, Dagworth, Stowmarket, Suffolk. *T:* Haughley 285. *Club:* Travellers'.

**HAMPSHIRE, Margaret Grace,** MA; Principal of Cheltenham Ladies' College, since 1964; *b* 7 Sept. 1918; *o d* of Dr C. H. Hampshire, CMG, MB, BS, BSc, sometime Sec. of British Pharmacopœia Commission, and Grace Mary Hampshire. *Educ:* Malvern Girls' Coll.; Girton Coll., Cambridge. BA 1941; MA 1945. Entered Civil Service, Board of Trade, 1941. Joined Staff of Courtaulds, 1951. Head of Government Relations Department, 1959-64. Member: Board of Governors, University Coll. Hosp., 1961-64; Marylebone Borough Council, 1962-64; SW Regional Hosp. Board, 1967-70. *Recreations:* music, reading, foreign travel. *Address:* The Ladies' College, Cheltenham, Glos. *Club:* Royal Over-Seas League.

**HAMPSHIRE, Sir Peter;** *see* Hampshire, Sir G. P.

**HAMPSHIRE, Prof. Stuart Newton,** FBA 1960; Warden of Wadham College, Oxford University, since 1970; *b* 1 Oct. 1914; *s* of G. N. Hampshire and Marie West; *m* 1961, Renee Ayer. *Educ:* Repton; Balliol Coll., Oxford. 1st Cl. Lit Hum, Oxford, 1936. Fellow of All Souls Coll., and Lecturer in Philosophy, Oxford, 1936-40. Service in Army, 1940-45. Personal Asst to Minister of State, Foreign Office, 1945; Lecturer in Philosophy, University Coll., London, 1947-50; Fellow of New Coll., Oxford, 1950-55; Domestic Bursar and Research Fellow, All Souls Coll., 1955-60; Grote Prof. of Philosophy of Mind and Logic, University of London, 1960-63; Prof. of Philosophy, Princeton Univ., 1963-70. Fellow, Amer. Acad. of Arts and Sciences, 1968. *Publications:* Spinoza, 1951; Thought and Action 1959; Freedom of the Individual, 1965; Modern Writers and other essays, 1969; articles in philosophical journals. *Address:* Wadham College, Oxford.

**HAMPSON, Arthur Cecil,** MC; MA, MD, FRCP; Consulting Physician to Guy's Hospital; Hon. Consulting Physician to Queen Mary's Hospital for the East End, and to Bromley, Beckenham and Purley Hospitals; *b* 1894; *s* of late Robert Hampson, Southport; *m* 1926, Anne Ramsbottom. *Educ:* Southport; Cambridge; Guy's Medical School. Served European War, 1915-19, Major, RA (SR). Hilda and Ronald Poulton Research Fellow, Guy's Hosp., 1926-30; Asst Physician Children's Dept, Guy's Hosp., 1930-35. Fellow Royal Society of Medicine; Mem. Assoc. of British Physicians and other societies. Hon. Visiting Physician to Johns Hopkins Hosp., USA, 1952. *Publications:* contributions to medical journals. *Recreations:* gardening, golf. *Address:* Little Hurnford, Snowshill, Broadway, Worcs. *T:* Broadway 3204. *Club:* Athenæum.

**HAMPSON, Prof. Elwyn Lloyd,** MDS, FDSRCS; HDD RCSE; Professor of Operative Dental Surgery, University of Sheffield, since 1960; Dean, Dental School, University of Sheffield, consultant Dental Surgeon to United Sheffield Hospitals; *b* 31 Jan. 1916; *s* of John and Mary Hampson; *m* 1940, Anne Cottrell; one *s* one *d*. *Educ:* Calday Grange Grammar Sch., W Kirby, Cheshire; Univ. of Liverpool. BDS with 1st Class Hons 1939; HDD RCSE 1944; FDSRCS 1949; MDS 1954; FDSE 1964. House surg., Liverpool Dental Hosp., 1939; Royal Army Dental Corps, 1941-45; Lecturer in Operative Dental Surgery, Edinburgh Dental Sch., 1945-47; Lecturer and later Senior Lecturer in Operative Dental Surgery, Univ. of Sheffield, 1947-60. Mem. Council, RCSE. *Publications:* Textbook of Operative Dental Surgery, 1961. Many papers in scientific jls. *Recreation:* water colour painting. *Address:* 6 Chorley Place, Fulwood, Sheffield 10. *T:* Sheffield 302104.

**HAMPSTEAD, Archdeacon of;** *see* Pink, Ven. H. A. S.

**HAMPTON,** 5th Baron, *cr* 1874; **Humphrey Arthur Pakington,** Bt 1846; OBE 1942; DL; *b* 8 Sept. 1888; 4th *s* of 3rd Baron (*d* 1906); *S* brother, 1962; *m* 1913, Grace Dykes (*d* 1959), 3rd *d* of Rt Hon. Sir A. Spicer, 1st Bt, PC; one *s* three *d*. Entered Navy, 1903; retired 1920 as Lieut-Comdr; Comdr, retired, 1928. Trained at Architectural Association; Holloway Scholarship, 1922; Architectural Association Diploma and FRIBA (retired); Pres. of Architectural Assoc., 1934-36; partner in Pakington & Enthoven, Architects, 10 Bayley Street, Bedford Square, WC1; rejoined Navy, 1939; Staff of C-in-C, Western Approaches, 1939-45. DL, Worcs, 1953. *Publications:* various novels including: Four in Family; Aston Kings; The Washbournes of Otterley; Catherine Chailey; John Brandon; How the World Builds, an Introduction to Architecture; English Villages and Hamlets; Bid Time Return, an autobiography. *Heir: s* Hon. Richard Humphrey Russell Pakington [*b* 25 May 1925; *m* 1958, Jane Elizabeth Farquharson, *d* of T. F. Arnott, OBE, TD, MB, ChB; one *s* two *d*]. *Address:* The Old Rectory, Holt, near Worcester. *T:* Ombersley 243. *Club:* Athenæum.

**HAMSON, Prof. Charles John;** Professor of Comparative Law, University of Cambridge, since 1953; Fellow of Trinity College, since 1934; Barrister-at-Law, Gray's Inn, Bencher, 1956; Editor, Cambridge Law Journal, since 1955; Corr. Mem. Institut de France (Acad. Sci. Mor. et Pol.); Doctor *hc* Universities of Grenoble, Nancy, Poitiers, Bordeaux, Brussels, Montpellier; Mem. International Acad. of comparative Law, 1956, Vice-Pres., 1965, Pres., 1966; Chevalier de la Légion d'Honneur; *b* 23 Nov. 1905; *er s* of Charles Edward Hamson (formerly of Constantinople), and of Thérèse Boudon; *m*

1933, Isabella Stewart Robertson Drummond, *y d* of Duncan Drummond and Grace Gardiner of Auchterarder; one *d*. *Educ:* Downside; Trinity Coll., Cambridge. Entrance and Sen. Scholar in Classics; Classical Tripos Part I 1925, Part II 1927 (distinction); Capt. CU Epée Team, 1928; Davison Scholar, Harvard Law Sch., 1928-29; Linthicum Foundation Prize (North-western Univ.) 1929; Yorke Prize, 1932; LLB 1934; LLM 1935. Asst Lecturer, 1932, Lecturer, 1934, Reader in Comparative Law, 1949; Chm. Faculty Board of Law, 1954-57. Served War of 1939-45; commissioned in Army, 1940; detached for service with SOE; Battle of Crete, 1941; POW Germany, 1941-45. Hamlyn Lectures on Conseil d'Etat, 1954; Visiting Prof., University of Michigan Law Sch. (Ann Arbor), 1957; Paris Faculty of Law, 1959; Sherrill Lecturer, Yale Law Sch., 1960, etc. *Address:* 7 Cranmer Road, Cambridge. *T:* 50638.

**HAMSON, Vincent Everard;** *b* 2 Nov. 1888; 2nd *s* of late John Hamson, Bedford; *m* 1912, Florence Reynolds, St Albans; one *s* one *d*. *Educ:* Bedford. Reporter Bedfordshire Times and various provincial papers; Exchange Telegraph Co., 1920; Official Report (Hansard), 1927, Asst Editor, 1947; Editor, Official Report of Debates, House of Commons (Hansard), 1951-54, retired Nov. 1954. Librarian and Archivist, Parliamentary Press Gallery, 1931-37. Pres., Incorporated Phonographic Soc., 1952. *Recreation:* alpine gardening. *Address:* Bedford, Pickhurst Rise, West Wickham, Kent. *T:* Springpark 1331.

**HAN SUYIN, (Mrs Elizabeth Comber);** doctor and author; (*née* Elizabeth K. Chow); *b* 12 Sept. 1917; *d* of Y. T. Chow (Chinese) and M. Denis (Belgian); *m* 1st, 1938, General P. H. Tang, (*d* 1947); one *d*; 2nd, 1952, L. F. Comber. *Educ:* Yenching Univ., Peking, China; Brussels Univ., Brussels, Belgium; London Univ., London, England. Graduated MB, BS, London (Hons) in 1948, since when has been a practising doctor. *Publications: as Han Suyin:* Destination Chungking, 1942; And the Rain My Drink, 1956; The Mountain Is Young, 1958; Cast but One Shadow and Winter Love, 1962; The Four Faces, 1963; China in the Year 2001, 1967; *autobiography:* A Many Splendoured Thing, 1952; The Crippled Tree, 1965; A Mortal Flower, 1966; Birdless Summer: China, Autobiography, History, 1968. *Recreations:* botany, riding, swimming, lecturing. *Address:* c/o Jonathan Cape Ltd, 30 Bedford Square, London, WC1.

**HANBURY, Lt-Col Hanmer Cecil,** MVO 1953; MC 1943; DL; JP; Vice-Lieutenant of Bedfordshire, since 1970; *b* 5 Jan. 1916; *yr s* of late Sir Cecil Hanbury, MP, FLS, and of Mrs Hanbury-Forbes, OBE, of Kingston Maurward, Dorchester, Dorset, and La Mortola, Ventimiglia, Italy; *m* 1939, Prunella Kathleen Charlotte, *d* of late Air Cdre T. C. R. Higgins, CB, CMG, DL, JP, Turvey House, Beds; one *s* one *d*. *Educ:* Eton; RMC, Sandhurst. 2nd Lieut Grenadier Guards, 1936; served 1939-45 with Grenadier Guards, France, Belgium, N Africa, Italy; Capt. 1943; Temp. Major, 1944; Major 1948; retired 1958. DL 1958, JP 1959, Beds; High Sheriff, Beds, 1965. Dir, British Red Cross Soc., Beds, 1959. *Recreations:* shooting, travelling. *Address:* Turvey House, Turvey, Beds. *T:* Turvey 227. *Clubs:* White's, Guards, Pratt's, Royal Automobile.

**HANBURY, Harold Greville,** QC 1960; DCL; Vinerian Professor Emeritus of English Law, Oxford; Hon. Fellow, Lincoln College, Oxford; Hon. Master of the Bench, Inner Temple; *b* 19 June 1898; *s* of late Lt-Col Basil Hanbury and late Hon. Patience Verney; *m* 1927, Anna Margaret, *d* of late Hannibal Dreyer, Copenhagen, Denmark. *Educ:* Charterhouse; Brasenose Coll., Oxford (Scholar). Vinerian Law Scholar, 1921; Fellow of Lincoln Coll., Oxford 1921-49; Fellow of All Souls Coll., 1949-64. Vinerian Prof. of English Law, Oxford, 1949-64. Visiting Prof., Univ. of Ife, 1962-63; Univ. of Nigeria, 1964-66. Barrister-at-Law, Inner Temple, 1922; Rhodes Travelling Fellow, 1931-32; Senior Proctor, Oxford Univ., 1933-34 and 1944-45. President: Bentham Club, UCL, 1954; Soc. of Public Teachers of Law, 1958-59. Chairman: Court of Inquiry into Provincial Omnibus Industry, 1954; Board of Inquiry into West Indian Airways, 1958; Tribunal for Industrials, Gibraltar, 1960; Independent Mem. Commns of Inquiry on Retail Distributive Trades, 1946; Minimum Wage Arbitrator in Nigeria, 1955. Sponsor, Britain/Biafra Assoc. *Publications:* Essays in Equity, 1934; Modern Equity, 1935 (9th edn by R. H. Maudsley, 1969); Traité Pratique des Divorces et des Successions en Droit Anglais (with R. Moureaux), 1939 (2nd edn 1952); English Courts of Law, 1944 (4th edn by D. C. M. Yardley, 1967); Principles of Agency, 1952 (2nd edn, 1960); The Vinerian Chair and Legal Education, 1958; Biafra: a challenge to the conscience of Britain, 1968; articles in legal periodicals. *Recreations:* travelling, aelurophily (Vice-Pres. Oxford and District Cat Club), formerly cricket. *Address:* Marlborough House, Falmouth, Cornwall.

**HANBURY, John Capel,** CBE 1969; Chairman, Allen and Hanburys Ltd, since 1954 (Director, 1944); *b* 26 May 1908; *e s* of late Frederick Capel Hanbury; *m* 1935, Joan Terry Fussell; two *s* one *d* (and one *s* decd). *Educ:* Downside; Trinity Coll., Cambridge. Apptd to Pharmacopoeia Commn, 1948; Member: Central Health Services Council; Standing Pharmaceutical Adv. Cttee, Dept of Health and Social Security; Pres. Assoc. of Brit. Pharmaceutical Industry, 1950-52; Chm., Assoc. of Brit. Chemical Manufacturers, 1961-63; Pres. Franco-British Pharmaceutical Commn, 1955; Chm., Harlow Group Hosp. Man. Cttee. FRIC 1947; FPS 1955. *Recreations:* horticulture, archæology. *Address:* Amwellbury House, Ware, Herts. *T:* Ware 2108. *Club:* United University.

**HANBURY, Brig. Richard Nigel,** CBE 1954; TD 1943; DL; JP; retired; *b* 7 Oct. 1911; *s* of Nigel Hanbury, Green End House, Ware, Herts; *m* 1936, Anne Mildred, *d* of E. Perceval Alers Hankey, Stourton, Wilts; two *d*. *Educ:* Eton; Magdalene Coll., Cambridge. Served War of 1939-45, with RA (France, N Africa, Italy and Austria); Lieut-Col 1943; Brig. 1950. Hon. Col: Herts Yeo. (479 HAA), 1954; Herts Yeo. (286 Fd), 1957; Hon. Brig. TA retired. ADC (TA) to the Queen, 1958-63, retd. Chm. and Managing Dir, Gripper and Wrightman Ltd, malsters, 1946-59. DL, 1951, JP 1962, Herts; High Sheriff of Herts, 1960. Hon. Colonel: 286 The Hertfordshire and Bedfordshire Yeomanry, 1963-67; The Bedfordshire and Hertfordshire (T), 1967-69. *Recreations:* hunting, sailing. *Address:* Hay Lodge, Braughing, Ware, Herts. *T:* Puckeridge 372. *Club:* Leander (Henley).

**HANBURY-TENISON, Richard;** Counsellor, HM Diplomatic Service; *b* 3 Jan. 1925; *e s* of late Major G. E. F. Tenison, Lough Bawn, Co. Monaghan, Ireland, and Ruth, *o surv. c* of late Col J. C. Hanbury, JP, DL, Pontypool Park, Monmouthshire; *m* 1955, Euphan Mary, *er d* of late Major A. B. Wardlaw-Ramsay, Whitehill, Midlothian; three *s* two *d*. *Educ:* Eton; Magdalen Coll., Oxford. Served Irish Guards, 1943-47 (Captain, wounded). Entered HM

Foreign Service, 1949: 1st Sec., Vienna, 1956-58; 1st Sec. (and sometime Chargé d'Affaires), Phnom Penh, 1961-63, and Bucharest, 1966-68; Counsellor, Bonn, 1968-70. Pres., Monmouthshire Rural Community Council, 1959-. *Recreations:* shooting, fishing, conservation. *Address:* 59 Egerton Crescent, SW3. *T:* 01-584 0578; Bryngwyn Manor, Raglan, Mon. *T:* Raglan 210. *Clubs:* Boodle's; Kildare Street (Dublin).

**HANBURY-TRACY,** family name of **Baron Sudeley.**

**HANCOCK, Lt-Col Sir Cyril (Percy),** KCIE 1946 (CIE 1941); OBE 1930; MC; *b* 18 Sept. 1896; *m* Joyce, *d* of F. R. Hemingway, ICS; three *s* one *d. Educ:* Wellington Coll.; RMC, Sandhurst. Indian Political Service: Resident 1st class. *Address:* Woodhayes, Yateley, near Camberley, Surrey. *T:* Yateley 3240. *Club:* MCC.

**HANCOCK, Dame Florence (May),** DBE *cr* 1951 (CBE 1947; OBE 1942); Chief Woman Officer, Transport and General Workers' Union, 1942-58; Director of Remploy Ltd, 1958-66; *b* 25 Feb. 1893; *d* of Jacob and Mary Hancock; *m* 1964, John Donovan, *qv. Educ:* Chippenham Elementary Sch. Full-time official of Workers' Union, 1917; Mem. of General Council of the TUC, 1935-58; Pres. of British TUC 1947-48; Dir Daily Herald, July 1955-March 1957. A Governor of the BBC, 1956-62. *Recreations:* reading and needlework. *Address:* 4 Melita Road, Bristol 6. *T:* Bristol 43880. *Club:* English-Speaking Union.

**HANCOCK, Prof. Sir Keith;** *see* Hancock, Prof. Sir W. K.

**HANCOCK, Maj.-Gen. Michael Stephen,** MBE 1953; Vice-Quarter-Master-General, Ministry of Defence, since 1970; *b* 19 July 1917; *s* of late Rev. W. H. M. Hancock and late Mrs C. C. Hancock (*née* Sherbrooke); *m* 1941, Constance Geraldine Margaret Ovens; one *s* one *d. Educ:* Marlborough Coll.; RMA, Woolwich. Commnd into Royal Signals, 1937; Comdr, Corps Royal Signals, 1st British Corps, 1963-66; Sec., Mil. Cttee, NATO, 1967-68; Chief of Staff, FARELF, 1968-70. Col Comdt, Royal Signals, 1970-. *Recreation:* sailing. *Address:* Brakey Hill, Godstone, Surrey. *T:* Godstone 273. *Club:* Army and Navy.

**HANCOCK, Sir Patrick (Francis),** KCMG 1969 (CMG 1956); HM Ambassador in Rome, since 1969; *b* 25 June 1914; *s* of late R. E. Hancock, DSO; *m* 1947, Beatrice Mangeot; one *s* one *d. Educ:* Winchester Coll.; Trinity Coll., Cambridge. Entered HM Foreign Service, 1937. Appointed Principal Private Sec, to Foreign Sec., 1955; Head of Western Dept, Foreign Office, 1956; Ambassador to Israel, 1959-62; Ambassador to Norway, 1963-65; Asst Under-Sec. of State, FO, 1965-68. Dep. Under-Sec. of State, FCO, 1968-69. Commander, Order of North Star, 1956. *Recreation:* salmon fishing. *Address:* HM Embassy, Villa Wolkonsky, via Conte Rosso 25, I-000185 Rome; The Old Vicarage, Affpuddle, Dorset. *T:* Puddletown 315.

**HANCOCK, P(ercy) E(llis) Thompson,** FRCP; Senior Physician and Director of the Department of Clinical Research, The Royal Marsden Hospital; Physician: The Royal Free Hospital; The Lister Hospital, Hitchin; Consultant Gastroscopist, Queen Mary's (Roehampton) Hospital; *b* 4 Feb. 1904; *s* of Frank Hancock; *m* 1932, Dorothy Barnes (*d* 1953); two *d*; *m* 1955, Laurie Newton Sharp. *Educ:* Wellington Coll., Berks; Caius Coll., Cambridge; St Bartholomew's Hospital. MB 1937, BCh, 1930, Cantab; FRCP 1944. Senior Examiner in Medicine, Univ. of London. Member: Cttee of Management of Inst. of Cancer Research; Grand Council, British Empire Cancer Campaign for Research; Exec. Cttee, British Cancer Council; Pres., Leukaemia Soc. Hosp. Visitor, King Edward's Hosp. Fund for London; Member: King Edward's Hosp. Fund for London Aux. Hosps Cttee, 1970-; London Medical Appeals Tribunals, 1970-. Hon. Member: American Gastroscopic Soc., 1958; Sociedad Chilena de Cancerología; Sociedad Chilana de Hematología; Sociedad Médica de Valparaíso. Dir, Steel Scaffolding Co. Ltd and Subsidiaries. *Publications:* (joint) Cancer in General Practice; The Use of Bone Marrow Transfusion with massive Chemotherapy, 1960; (joint) Treatment of Early Hodgkin's Disease, 1967. *Recreations:* dining and wining. *Address:* Welbeck House, Welbeck Street, W1. *T:* 01-935 6726.

**HANCOCK, Sheila;** actress; *d* of Enrico Hancock and Ivy Woodward; *m* 1955, Alexander Ross; one *d. Educ:* Dartford County Grammar Sch.; Royal Academy of Dramatic Art. Acted in Repertory, Theatre Workshop, Stratford East, for 8 years. West End starring roles in: Rattle of a Simple Man, The Anniversay and A Delicate Balance, etc, for Royal Shakespeare Co.; So What About Love?. Has starred in several successful revues; repeated stage role in film of The Anniversary. Appeared on Broadway in Entertaining Mr Sloane. Many Television successes, including her own colour spectacular for BBC2, and several comedy series. Awards: Variety Club, London Critics, Whitbread Trophy (for best Actress on Broadway). *Recreations:* reading, music, driving fast cars. *Address:* 60 Black Lion Lane, W6; Tarleton, Glos.

**HANCOCK, Air Marshal Sir Valston Eldridge,** KBE 1962 (CBE 1953); CB 1958; DFC 1945; retired; grazier; *b* 31 May 1907; *s* of R. J. Hancock, Perth, W Australia; *m* 1932, Joan E. G., *d* of Col A. G. Butler, DSO, VD; two *s* one *d. Educ:* Hale Sch., Perth; RMC, Duntroon; psa; idc. Joined Royal Military College, Duntroon, 1925; transferred RAAF, 1929; Dir of Plans, 1940-41; commanded 71 (Beaufort) Wing, New Guinea, 1945; Commandant RAAF Academy, 1947-49; Deputy Chief of Air Staff, 1951-53; Air Mem. for Personnel, Air Board, 1953-54; Head of Australian Joint Services Staff, UK, 1955-57; Extra Gentleman Usher to the Royal Household, 1955-57; AOC 224 Group, RAF, Malaya, 1957-59; Air Officer Commanding Operational Command, 1959-61; Chief of Air Staff, Royal Australian Air Force, 1961-65. Commissioner-Gen., Australian Exhibit Organization Expo, 1967. *Recreations:* literature and sport. *Address:* 108a Victoria Avenue, Dalkeith, Western Australia 6009, Australia.

**HANCOCK, Prof. Sir (William) Keith,** KBE 1965; Kt 1953; MA; FBA 1950; Emeritus Professor and Hon. Fellow; Professor of History, Australian National University, Canberra, 1957-65; first President, Australian Academy of the Humanities, since 1969; *b* Melbourne, 26 June 1898; *s* of Archdeacon William Hancock, MA; *m* 1st, 1925, Theaden Brocklebank (*d* 1960); 2nd, 1961, Marjorie Eyre. Fellow of All Souls Coll., Oxford, 1924-30; Prof. of Modern History in the University of Adelaide, 1924-33; Prof. of History, Birmingham Univ., 1934-44; Chichele Prof. of Economic History, University of Oxford 1944-49; Dir, Institute of Commonwealth Studies, and Prof. of British Commonwealth Affairs in the University of London, 1949-56; Dir of the Research Sch. of Social Sciences, Australian

National Univ., 1957-61; appointed to War Cabinet Offices as Supervisor of Civil Histories, 1941. Hon. Fellow, Balliol Coll.; Corresp. Mem., Sch. of Oriental and African Studies. Hon. DLitt (Rhodes, Cambridge, Birmingham, Oxford, Cape Town, Melbourne, ANU). Foreign Hon. Member: American Historical Association; American Academy of Arts and Sciences. Order of Merit of Republic of Italy. *Publications:* Ricasoli, 1926; Australia, 1930; Survey of British Commonwealth Affairs, 1937, 1940, and 1942; Argument of Empire, 1943; Politics in Pitcairn, 1947; (with M. M. Gowing) British War Economy, 1949; Wealth of Colonies, 1950; Country and Calling, 1954; War and Peace in this Century, 1961; Smuts: The Sanguine Years, 1870-1919, Vol. 1, 1962; The Fields of Force, 1919-1950, Vol. II, 1968; Attempting History, 1969. *Address:* The Australian National University, Box 4, GPO, Canberra, ACT 2601, Australia. *Club:* Athenæum.

**HANCOX, Leslie Pascoe,** CIE 1946; OBE 1939; *b* 18 May 1906; *s* of Thomas and Maria Pascoe Hancox; *m* 1936, Heather Alexandra Thomson; one *s* one *d. Educ:* St Olave's Sch.; Christ's Coll., Cambridge. Entered Indian Civil Service, 1929; Asst Magistrate, United Provinces, 1929-30; Joint Magistrate, United Provinces, 1931-35; District Magistrate, United Provinces, 1935-42; Sec. to Govt United Provinces, Civil Supplies Dept, 1942-44; Finance Sec., Government of the United Provinces, Lucknow, UP, India, 1945-47, retired from ICS, 1947. The British Oxygen Co. Ltd, 1949-. *Recreations:* cricket, tennis, squash rackets. *Address:* 1 Rutland Lodge, 1 Clifton Road, SW19.

**HAND, Rt. Rev. Geoffrey David;** *see* New Guinea, Bishop of.

**HANDCOCK,** family name of **Baron Castlemaine.**

**HANDFIELD-JONES, Ranald Montagu,** MC; Consulting Surgeon, St Mary's Hospital; Consulting General Surgeon, the Hospital for Women, Soho Square; Member Court of Examiners, RCS; Examiner in Surgery to Universities of London, Cambridge, Liverpool, Leeds and Manchester; *b* 12 May 1892; *s* of late C. R. Handfield-Jones, MD, and Alice Jervis; *m* 1920; three *s* one *d. Educ:* Epsom Coll.; St Mary's Hospital Medical Sch.; London Univ.; Epsom Scholarship to St Mary's Hosp.; Master of Surgery (University of London), MB, BS (Hons in Surgery and Midwifery, University Gold Medallist); FRCS; Hunterian Prof., RCS. Served European War in France, Oct. 1914-May 1918; prisoner of war, May-Nov. 1918. *Publications:* The Essentials of Modern Surgery (with A. E. Porritt), 5th edn, 1955; Surgery of the Hand, 2nd edn 1946; papers to medical journals. *Recreations:* entomology, cricket, golf, photography. *Address:* 9 Hurlingham Gardens, SW6. *T:* 01-736 5671.

**HANDFORD, Stanley Alexander,** MA Oxon; *b* Manchester 1898; *s* of late Thomas Edward Handford, Harrogate; *m* 1923, Doris, *d* of late James Henry Ollerhead, Oswestry. *Educ:* Bradford Grammar Sch.; Balliol Coll., Oxford (Classical Schol.); 1st class Hon. Classical Moderations and Craven Scholarship, 1920; Ireland Scholarship, 1921; 1st Class Literae Humaniores and Charles Oldham Prize, 1922; Asst Lecturer in Classics, University Coll. of Swansea, 1922-23; Asst Lectr and Lectr, King's Coll., London, 1923-46; Reader, 1946-66. *Publications:* Revision of L. W. Hunter's Aeneas on Siegecraft, 1927; Xenophon's Anabasis, Books III and IV, 1928; The Latin Subjunctive, 1947; Caesar's Conquest of Gaul (Penguin Classics), 1951; Caesar's Gallic War, Books II and III, 1952; Fables of Aesop (Penguin Classics), 1954; Pocket Latin-English Dictionary, 1955; Sallust's Jugurthine War and Conspiracy of Catiline (Penguin Classics), 1963; Tacitus's Agricola and Germania (Penguin Classics), 1970. *Recreation:* music. *Address:* Hurstleigh, Elm Park Road, Pinner, Mddx HA5 3LE.

**HANDLEY, Prof. Eric Walter;** FBA 1969; Professor of Greek, University College, London, since 1968, and Director of the Institute of Classical Studies, University of London, since 1967; *b* 12 Nov. 1926; *s* of Alfred W. Handley and late A. Doris Cox; *m* 1952, Carol Margaret, *d* of late Claude Hilary Taylor and Margaret E. Peebles. *Educ:* King Edward's Sch., Birmingham; Trinity Coll., Cambridge. Stewart of Rannoch Schol. and Browne Medal, 1945. Asst Lectr in Latin and Greek, University Coll. London, 1946; Lectr, 1949; Reader, 1961; Prof. of Latin and Greek, 1967-68. Cromer Greek Prize (jtly), 1958; Vis. Lectr on the Classics, Harvard, 1966. *Publications:* (with John Rea) The Telephus of Euripides, 1957; The Dyskolos of Menander 1965; papers in class. jls, etc. *Recreations:* boating, hill-walking, travel. *Address:* University College London, Gower Street, WC1E 6BT. *T:* 01-387 7050. *Club:* Oxford and Cambridge University.

**HANDLEY, Richard Sampson,** OBE 1946; Surgeon, The Middlesex Hospital, W1, since 1946 (Senior Surgeon, 1965); *b* 2 May 1909; *e s* of late W. Sampson Handley; *m* 1942, Joan, *d* of Dr Cyril Gray, Newcastle upon Tyne; one *s* one *d. Educ:* Uppingham Sch.; Gonville and Caius Coll., Cambridge; The Middlesex Hospital. Entrance Schol., Middx Hosp., 1930; BA Cantab 1930 (Pts 1 and 2, Nat. Sci. Tripos); MRCS, LRCP and MA, MB, BCh Cantab, 1933; University Demonstrator of Anatomy, Cambridge, 1936; Asst Pathologist, 1937, and Surgical Registrar, 1939, Middx Hosp. FRCS 1938; Mem. Council, RCS 1966; Hon. Sec. RSM, 1967. Served, 1939-46 (despatches, OBE); Temp. Major RAMC and Surgical Specialist, serving with BEF, 1939, and MEF, 1940; Temp. Lieut-Col, RAMC, 1944, serving BLA. Late Examiner in Surgery, Cambridge Univ.; late Mem. Court of Examiners, RCS; late Hon. Sec., Assoc. of Surgeons of GB and Ireland. *Publications:* papers and lectures on surgical subjects, especially with reference to malignant disease. *Recreations:* sailing, model-making. *Address:* 13 Holly Lodge Gardens, Highgate, N6. *T:* 01-340 1272; 107 Harley Street, W1.

**HANDY, Gen. Thomas Troy,** Hon. KBE 1945; DSC (US) 1918; DSM (US) 1945 (Oak Leaf Cluster, 1947); Legion of Merit, 1945; formerly Deputy to General Ridgway (Supreme Allied Commander in Europe and Commander-in-Chief US European Command, 1952-53); *b* Tennessee, 11 March 1892; *s* of Rev. T. R. Handy and Caroline (*née* Hall); *m* 1920, Alma Hudson, Va; one *d. Educ:* Va Mil. Inst. (BS). Served European War, 1917-18 (DSC, French Croix de Guerre); War of 1939-45; when US a belligerent, 1942, became Asst Chief of Staff, Ops Div,; Dep. Chief of Staff, US Army, 1944; Lieut-Gen. 1945. Comdg-Gen. 4th Army, Texas, 1947; C-in-C all Amer. Troops in Europe (except in Austria and Trieste), 1949-52. *Address:* 3325 Runnymede Place, NW, Washington, DC 20015, USA.

**HANES, Prof. Charles Samuel,** FRS 1942; FRSC 1956; Professor of Biochemistry, University of Toronto, 1951-68, now Emeritus; Hon.

Fellow of Downing College, Cambridge; *b* 1903. *Educ:* University of Toronto (BA 1925); University of Cambridge, PhD Cantab 1929; ScD Cantab 1952. Lately Reader in Plant Biochemistry, University of Cambridge, and Director, Agricultural Research Council Unit of Plant Biochemistry; previously Dir of Food Investigation, Dept of Scientific and Industrial Research. Flavelle Medal, Royal Society of Canada, 1958. *Address:* Department of Biochemistry, University of Toronto, Toronto 5, Canada.

**HANHAM, Sir Henry (Phelips),** 11th Bt, *cr* 1667; *b* 6 April 1901; *s* of Sir John Alexander Hanham, 9th Bt and Hon. Cordelia Lucy (*d* 1945), 2nd *d* of 1st Lord Ludlow; *S* brother 1955. *Educ:* Winchester; Magdalen Coll., Oxford. Served War of 1939-45, RA. *Heir: kinsman* Michael William Hanham, DFC [*b* 31 Oct. 1922; *m* 1954, Margaret Jane, *o d* of Wing-Comdr Harold Thomas, RAF; one *s* one *d*]. *Address:* Dean's Court, Wimborne, Dorset.

**HANKEY,** family name of **Baron Hankey.**

**HANKEY,** 2nd Baron *cr* 1939, of The Chart; **Robert Maurice Alers Hankey;** KCMG 1955 (CMG 1947); KCVO 1956; *b* 4 July 1905; *s* of 1st Baron Hankey, PC, GCB, GCMG, GCVO, FRS, and Adeline, *d* of A. de Smidt; *S* father, 1963; *m* 1st, 1930, Frances Bevyl Stuart-Menteth (*d* 1957); two *s* two *d*; 2nd, 1962, Joanna Riddall Wright, *d* of late Rev. James Johnstone Wright. *Educ:* Rugby Sch.; New Coll., Oxford. Diplomatic Service, 1927; served Berlin, Paris, London, Warsaw, Bucharest, Cairo, Teheran, Madrid, Budapest. HM Ambassador at Stockholm, 1954-60. Permanent UK Delegate to OEEC and OECD, and Chm., Economic Policy Cttee, 1960-65; Vice-Pres., European Inst. of Business Administration, Fontainebleau, Dir, Alliance Bldg Soc., 1970. Member: Internat. Council of United World Colleges, 1966-; Council, Internat. Baccalaureati Foundn, Geneva. Pres., Anglo-Swedish Soc., 1969-. Grand Cross of Order of the North Star (Sweden), 1954. *Recreations:* reading, tennis, ski-ing, music. *Heir: er s* Hon. Donald Robin Alers Hankey [*b* 12 June 1938; *m* 1963, Margaretha, *yr d* of H. Thorndahl, Copenhagen]. *Address:* Hethe House, Cowden, Edenbridge, Kent. *T:* Cowden 538. *Club:* Travellers'.
*See also Sir John Benn, Hon. H. A. A. Hankey.*

**HANKEY, Very Rev. Cyril Patrick;** Dean of Ely, 1951-69, Emeritus since 1969; *b* 1886; *s* of Rev. Claude Hankey; *m* 1925, Frances Mary Harris (*d* 1966); one *s* one *d*. *Educ:* Haileybury; Pembroke Coll., Cambridge; Ely Theological Coll. Principal, Dorchester Missionary Coll., 1916-22; Vicar of St Matthew's, Westminster, 1922-24; Vicar of St Mary's the Less, Cambridge, 1925-38; Chaplain of St John, Menton, France, 1938-41; Vicar of Aldenham and Rural Dean of Watford, 1941-46; Vicar of St Paul's, Bedford, and Rural Dean of Bedford, 1946-51. *Publications:* Lives of the Serbian Saints, 1921; The Young Priest, 1933; A Confession of My Faith, 1940; Signposts on the Christian Way, 1962 (USA). *Address:* Lychgate Cottage, Dorchester-on-Thames, Oxford. *T:* Warborough 476.

**HANKEY, Col George Trevor,** OBE 1945; TD; late RAMC (TA); Consulting Dental and Oral Surgeon; *b* London, 15 March 1900; *er s* of J. Trevor Hankey, Lingfield, Surrey; *m* 1933, Norah (*d* 1939), *y d* of late R. H. G. Coulson, Tynemouth; (one *s* decd); *m* 1945, Mary Isobel, *d* of late R. H. G. Coulson, Tynemouth. *Educ:* Oakham Sch; Guy's Hosp. LDSEng, 1922; LRCP, MRCS 1925; elected FDS, RCS, 1948; Consultant Dental Surgeon, St Bartholomew's Hospital, 1928-65, retd; Consultant, The London Hosp. Dental Sch., 1928-66; Lectr in Oral Surg., University of London. Fellow, Royal Society of Medicine; Examr in Dental Surgery, RCS England, 1948-54; Examiner in Dental and Oral Surgery, University of London, 1948-56; Pres. Odontological Section, RSM 1957-58; Charles Tomes Lecturer, RCS, 1953; Mem. Bd Dent. Faculty RCS, 1958-; Vice-Dean, 1966-67. John Tomes Prize, RCS, 1960, Mem. Bd Govs, London Hosp., 1954-63, and NE Metrop. Reg. Hosp. Bd, 1959-62; Fellow, Brit. Assoc. Oral Surgeons, Pres., 1963-64; Sprawson Lectr, 1967. Commissioned RAMC(TA), 1927; OC 141 Field Ambulance, 1939; OC 12 Gen. Hosp., 1952; Hon. Col 1957-62. Served War of 1939-45 (despatches, prisoner, OBE). Officer, Legion of Merit, USA, 1951. *Publications:* chapter on Mandibular Joint Disorders, in Surgical Progress, 1960; contrib. Brit. Dental Jl and British Jl of Oral Surgery; various communications on Oral Surgery and Pathology to Proc. Royal Society of Medicine. *Recreations:* golf, fishing. *Address:* 3 Harcourt House, 19a Cavendish Square, W1. *T:* 01-580 1141.

**HANKEY, Hon. Henry Arthur Alers,** CMG 1960; CVO 1959; HM Diplomatic Service; Assistant Under-Secretary of State, Foreign and Commonwealth Office, since 1969; *b* 1 Sept. 1914; *y s* of 1st Baron Hankey, PC, GCB, GCMG, GCVO, FRS; *m* 1941, Vronwy Mary Fisher; three *s* one *d*. *Educ:* Rugby Sch.; New Coll., Oxford. Entered HM Diplomatic Service, 1937; Third Sec., HM Embassy, Paris, 1939; Second Sec., Madrid, 1942; First Sec., Rome, 1946; Consul, San Francisco, 1950; First Sec., Santiago, 1953; promoted Counsellor and apptd Head of American Dept, Foreign Office, Sept. 1956; Counsellor, HM Embassy, Beirut, 1962-66; Ambassador, Panama, 1966-69. *Recreations:* tennis, music. *Address:* Hosey Croft, Hosey Hill, Westerham, Kent. *T:* Westerham 2309. *Club:* United University.

**HANKIN, Arthur Maxwell,** CMG 1955: Sudan Political Service, retired; Comptroller, Forces Help Society and Lord Roberts Workshops, since Oct. 1963; *b* 27 Nov. 1905; *e s* of Seymer and Ethel Hankin; *m* 1938, Helen Elizabeth English; one *s* two *d*. *Educ:* Bromsgrove Sch.; Worcester Coll., Oxford. Joined Sudan Political Service, 1928; Private Sec. to Governor General of Sudan, 1938; Dir of Establishments, Sudan Govt, 1953; retired from Sudan 1955. Order of the Nile (4th class), 1940. *Recreations:* tennis and gardening. *Address:* Ivor Lodge, Milton Lilbourne, Pewsey, Wilts. *T:* Pewsey 3207. *Club:* United University.

**HANKINSON, Cyril Francis James,** Editor of Debrett's Peerage, 1935-62; journalist and lecturer; *b* 4 Nov. 1895; *e s* of late Charles James Hankinson, MBE, JP (pen-name Clive Holland), of Ealing, W5, and formerly of Bournemouth, and late Violet, *d* of William Downs, CE; *m* 1942, Lillian Louise, *e surv d* of late Walter Herbert Read, FSI, 29 Castlebar Road, Ealing, W5; one *s*. *Educ:* Queen Elizabeth's Grammar Sch., Wimborne, Dorset. European War, 1915-19 with Kite Balloon Section RFC, France, Belgium and subsequently at Air Ministry; Asst Editor of National Roll of the Great War, 1919-21; Assist Editor of Debrett, 1921-35. *Publications:* My Forty Years with Debrett, 1963. Contributor to London, Commonwealth, and American Press of articles regarding Royal Family, Peerage, Heraldry, etc; also lectures and broadcasts on these subjects. *Recreations:* reading biographies, watching cricket. *Address:* 13 Welsby Court, Eaton Rise, Ealing, W5. *T:* 01-997 5018. *Club:* MCC.

**HANKINSON, Sir Walter Crossfield,** KCMG 1948 (CMG 1941); OBE 1936; MC; *b* 1894; *y s* of late A. W. Hankinson; *m* 1936, Sheila, *d* of Dr Frederick Watson, Sydney. *Educ:* Manchester Grammar Sch.; Jesus Coll., Oxford. MA. Served European War, 1914-18 (MC); Colonial Office, 1920; transferred to Dominions Office, 1925; Acting Representative in Australia of HM Govt in the United Kingdom, 1931-32 and 1935-36; Principal Private Sec. to successive Secretaries of State for Dominion Affairs, 1937-39; Principal Sec., Office of High Commissioner for the United Kingdom in Canada, 1939-41; Principal Sec. to United Kingdom Representative to Eire, 1942-43; Dep. High Comr in Australia, 1943-47; Acting High Comr June 1945-June 1946; UK High Commissioner in Ceylon, 1948-51; British Ambassador to Republic of Ireland, 1951-55, retired. *Recreations:* bowls, gardening. *Address:* 25 Beauchamp Street, Deakin, Canberra, ACT 2600, Australia. *Club:* United University.

**HANLEY, Denis Augustine;** *b* 1903; *s* of late Edmund Hanley, Kintbury, Berks; *m* 1935, Kathleen Mary, *d* of J. P. Eyre, 56 York Terrace, Regent's Park; three *d*. *Educ:* Downside; Trinity Coll., Cambridge. MP (C) Deptford, 1931-35. Royal Naval Scientific Service, 1938-54. *Address:* Woodcombe, Oxbridge, Bridport, Dorset. *T:* Netherbury 343.

**HANLEY, Gerald Anthony;** author; *b* 17 Feb. 1916; *s* of Edward Michael Hanly and Bridget Maria Roche. *Publications:* Monsoon Victory, 1946; The Consul at Sunset, 1951; The Year of the Lion, 1953; Drinkers of Darkness, 1955; Without Love (Book Society Choice), 1957; The Journey Homeward (Book Society Choice), 1961; Gilligan's Last Elephant, 1962; See You in Yasukuni, 1969. *Recreations:* music, languages. *Address:* c/o David Higham Associates, Authors' Agents, 76 Dean Street, Soho, W1.

**HANLEY, Howard Granville,** MD, FRCS; Urologist: St Peter's and St Paul's Hospitals; Royal Masonic Hospital London; Consulting Urologist, King Edward VII's Hospital for Officers, W1; Urological Consultant to the Army; Hon. Consulting Urologist, Royal Hospital, Chelsea; Dean of Institute of Urology, University of London; *b* 27 July 1909; *s* of F. T. Hanley; *m* 1939, Margaret Jeffrey; two *s*. *Educ:* St Bees Sch., Cumberland. MB 1932; MD 1934; FRCS 1937. Hunterian Prof., Royal College of Surgeons, 1955; Visiting Prof. of Urology: University of Calif, Los Angeles, 1958; Ohio State Univ., Columbus, 1961; University of Texas Southwestern Medical Sch., 1963; Tulane University, New Orleans, 1967. Pres., Urological Section Royal Society of Medicine, 1964-65; Dep. Chm., Central Consultative Cttee, BMA, Mem. Jt Consultants Cttee; Mem. Council, RCS, 1969. Fellow, Association of Surgeons of Great Britain and Ireland; Treasurer and Past Sec., British Assoc. Urological Surgeons; Sec., Hunterian Soc.; Hon. Librarian, Royal Society of Medicine. Member: Internat. Soc. Urology; German Urol. Soc.; Soc. Française d'Urologie; Med. Soc. London; Chelsea Clinical Soc. Corresp. Mem., Amer. Assoc. Genito-urinary Surgeons; Hon. Member: Mexican Urological Soc.; Western Sect. Amer. Urological Assoc. Liveryman, Worshipful Soc. of Apothecaries of London. Hon. FACS. *Publications:* Recent Advances in Urology, 1957; chapters in: British Surgical Practice, 1960; Modern Trends in Urology, 1960; A Text Book of Urology, 1960. *Recreation:* gardening. *Address:* 147 Harley Street, W1. *T:* 01-935 4444; Brandon House, North End Avenue, NW3. *T:* 01-458 2035. *Club:* Athenæum.

**HANLEY, James;** novelist, short story writer; *b* 1901. *Publications:* Men in Darkness (stories), 1931, New York, 1932; The Furys (novel), 1934; Stoker Bush (novel), 1935; The Maelstrom (novel), 1935; The Furys, New York, 1935; The Secret Journey, 1936; The Wall, 1936; Broken Water (an Autobiography), 1937; Grey Children (A Sociological Study), 1937; Half-an-Eye (stories), 1937; Hollow Sea (novel), 1938; Soldiers Wind (Essays), 1938; People Are Curious (stories), 1938; Between the Tides (Essays), 1939; Our Time is Gone (novel), 1940; The Ocean, 1941; No Directions (novel), 1943; At Bay (stories), 1943; Sailor's Song (novel), 1943; Crilley (stories); 1945; What Farrar Saw (novel), 1945; Winter Song (novel), 1950; A Walk in the Wilderness (stories), 1950; The Closed Harbour (novel), 1952; Don Quixote Drowned (essays), 1953; The Welsh Sonata (novel), 1954; Levine (novel), 1955; An end and a beginning, 1958; Say Nothing, 1962. *Recreations:* fishing, music. *Address:* c/o David Higham Associates, 76 Dean Street, Soho, W1.

**HANLON, John Austin Thomas,** JP; Chairman of Quarter Sessions, County of Northumberland, since 1965; Chairman of Traffic Commissioners, Northern Traffic Area, since 1953; *b* 18 Dec. 1905; *s* of late Thomas Peter Hanlon; *m* 1933, Marjorie Edith (Nesta), *d* of late John W. Waltham Taylor, Portsmouth. *Educ:* Portsmouth Grammar Sch. Joined Portsmouth Police, 1924; served through ranks CID, Det. Sgt, Det. Inspector; Dep. Chief Constable, Scarborough, 1934; Chief Constable, Leamington, 1938; Home Office Regional Comr's Staff, 1940; admitted student Gray's Inn, 1934; called to the Bar, 1944; practised NE Circuit. Deputy Chm. of Quarter Sessions: Co. Northumberland, 1955-65; Co. Durham, 1958-65. JP Northumberland, 1954-. *Recreations:* athletics (British Team, Olympic Games, 1928; AAA 220 yds and 440 yds Champion, 1929; many internat. teams and events); fishing, shooting, motoring, music. *Address:* Hartburn, Morpeth, Northumberland. *T:* Hartburn 269. *Club:* Northern Counties (Newcastle upon Tyne).

**HANLON, Air Vice-Marshal Thomas James,** CB 1969; CBE 1959; Air Officer i/c Administration, HQ Maintenance Command, RAF Andover, since 1968; *b* 15 July 1916; *s* of late James Francis Hanlon, Dublin; *m* 1965, Susan Janet Elizabeth (*née* Williams); one *s*. *Educ:* Belvedere Coll. Dublin; RAF Coll., Cranwell. Sqdn Service, Bomber Comd, 1937-39; No. 8 Sqdn, Aden, 1939-42; Air Min., 1943-46; Bomber Comd, 1946-47; OC, RAF White Waltham, 1948; HQ No. 65 (London) Gp, 1949; HQ Allied Forces Central Europe (NATO), 1950-53; Air Sec.'s Dept, Air Min., 1953-58; HQ Transport Comd, 1958-60; OC, RAF Stn Steamer Point, Aden, 1961-62; SASO, RAF Record Office, Glos, 1964-65; AOC, RAF Record and Pay Office, Glos, 1965-68; psc 1943; jssc 1947; idc 1963; MBIM 1967. *Address:* c/o Westminster Bank Ltd, 36 St James's Street, SW1. *Club:* Royal Air Force.

**HANMER, Lt-Col Sir (Griffin Wyndham) Edward,** 7th Bt, *cr* 1620, *re-cr* 1774; late Shropshire Yeomanry and Royal Air Force; JP Flintshire; High Sheriff, 1932; Master of Sir W. W. Wynn's Hounds, 1946-53; *b* 30 Aug.

1893; *s* of 6th Bt, and Essex (*d* 1952), *d* of W. Selby Lowndes, Whaddon Hall, Bucks; *S* father, 1922; *m* 1st, 1921, Aileen Mary (*d* 1967), *er d* of Capt. J. E. Rogerson; one *s* three *d*; 2nd, 1968, Mrs Angela Mary Bromley, *widow* of Richard Nightingale Bromley. *Educ:* Wellington Coll. Owns about 7000 acres; Mem. of Jockey Club (Sen. Steward, 1944) and National Hunt Cttee. *Recreations:* hunting, shooting, racing, stud farm, and farming (Red Polls). *Heir: s* John Wyndham Edward Hanmer, Capt. The Royal Dragoons [*b* 27 Sept. 1928; *m* 1954, Audrey Melissa, *d* of Major A. C. J. Congreve, Cockspur Hall, Tenbury Wells, Worcs; two *s*]. *Address:* Bettisfield Park, Whitchurch, Salop. *TA* and *T:* Bettisfield 280. *Clubs:* Cavalry, Jockey. *See also M. F. Hanmer, Sir T. D. Wilson, Bt.*

**HANMER, Marguerite Frances;** *b* 1895; 2nd *d* of late Sir Wyndham Hanmer, 6th Bart, and Essex, Lady Hanmer (*d* 1952). *Educ:* Private. High Sheriff, Montgomeryshire, 1946. *Address:* Bryn Conroy, Llanbrynmair, Mont. *T:* Llanbrynmair 219. *Club:* English-Speaking Union.

**HANNAFORD, Charles Arthur,** RBA; *b* Aug. 1887; *er s* of C. E. Hannaford; *m* 1920, Phyllis, *yr d* of late Frederick A. Allchin, JP, Fowey, Cornwall. *Publication:* The Charm of the Norfolk Broads, 1949. *Recreation:* yachting. *Address:* The Boat House, Wroxham, Norfolk. *T:* Wroxham 2716. *Club:* Norfolk Broad Yacht (Wroxham).

**HANNAFORD, Guy George,** CMG 1957; OBE 1951; Director, Marconi Italiana, Genoa, and Delegate of English Electric Company for Italy, since 1961; *b* 31 Aug. 1901; *s* of Charles Archibald Hannaford and Marguérite Fillhard. *Educ:* privately; Sorbonne, Paris. Served, 1939-47, with gen. staff (France, Gibraltar, N Africa, Italy) (despatches twice), Lieut-Col. Entered Foreign Office, 1947; Counsellor and Legal Adviser, Rome, from 1947; British Rep. on Anglo-Italian Conciliation Commn, 1949-60; resigned from Foreign Office, 1961. Cross, Order of Merit of Knights of Malta; Medal of Freedom with Silver Palm (USA); Hon. Comdr Order St Maurice and Lazarus, Italy. *Publications:* articles in legal and political reviews. *Recreations:* tennis; collecting early Italian maiolica. *Address:* via Porta Pinciana 6, Rome, Italy.

**HANNAM, John Gordon;** MP (C) City of Exeter, since 1970; *b* 2 Aug. 1929; *s* of Thomas William and Selina Hannam; *m* 1956, Wendy Macartney; one *d. Educ:* Yeovil Grammar Sch. Studied Agriculture, 1945-46. Served in: Royal Tank Regt (commissioned), 1947-48; Somerset LI (TA), 1949-51. Studied Hotel industry, 1950-52; Managing Dir, Hotels and Restaurant Co., 1952-61; Developed Motels, 1961-70; Chm., British Motels Fedn, 1967-; Mem. Council, BTA, 1968-69; Mem. Economic Research Council, 1967-. *Recreations:* music (opera), art (modern), sailing (anything), skiing (fast), Cresta tobogganing (foolish); formerly tennis (Somerset Co. tennis champion, 1953). *Address:* Crooked House, Chiselborough, near Stoke-under-Ham, Somerset. *Clubs:* Carlton, Institute of Directors.

**HANNAM, Michael Patrick Vivian;** Counsellor, British Embassy, Tripoli, since 1969; *b* 13 Feb. 1920; *s* of Rev. Wilfrid L. Hannam, BD, and Dorothy (*née* Parker); *m* 1947, Sybil Huggins; one *s* one *d. Educ:* Westminster Sch. LMS Railway, 1937-40. Served in Army, 1940-46 (Major, RE). LMS Railway, 1946-50; Malayan Railway, 1950-60. FO, 1960-62; First Sec., British Embassy, Cairo, 1962-65; Principal British Trade Comr, Hong Kong, 1965-69 (and Consul, Macao, 1968-69). *Recreations:* music, swimming, tennis, photography. *Address:* Little Oaklands, Langton Green, Kent. *T:* Langton 163. *Clubs:* Royal Commonwealth Society; Lake (Kuala Lumpur); Turf (Cairo); Hong Kong, Country (Hong Kong).

**HANNAN, William;** MP (Lab) Maryhill Division of Glasgow since 1945; insurance agent; Town Councillor, Glasgow; *b* 30 Aug. 1906; *m*; one *d*. *Educ:* North Kelvinside Secondary Sch. Lord Commissioner of HM Treasury, 1946-51; an Opposition Whip, Nov. 1951-53; PPS to Rt Hon. George Brown as First Sec. and Sec. of State for Economic Affairs, 1964-66, as Sec. of State for Foreign Affairs, 1966-68. Mem., British Delegation to Council of Europe. *Recreation:* music. *Address:* House of Commons, SW1.

**HANNAY, Lady Fergusson;** *see* Leslie, Doris.

**HANNEN, Mrs Nicholas;** *see* Seyler, Athene.

**HANNEN, Nicholas James,** OBE; Actor; *b* London, 1 May 1881; *s* of Sir Nicholas John Hannen and Jessie Maria Harriette Woodhouse; *m* 1st, 1907, Muriel Melbourne Victoria Morland (*d* 1960); two *d* (one *s* decd); 2nd, Athene Seyler, *qv*. *Educ:* Radley; Heidelberg; Rouen. Spent sixteen years of his early life in China and Japan; after leaving sch. studied for the Foreign Office before becoming apprenticed as an architect under Sir Edwin Lutyens; finally went on the Stage in 1910 under the management of late George Edwardes; remained in Musical Comedy for four years during which he studied under the late Rosina Filippi; joined the Glasgow Repertory Company early in 1914; at St James Theatre under George Alexander when war broke out, and made his first London success subsequently as Nelson in Thomas Hardy's The Dynasts under Harley Granville Barker; played in New York in Granville Barker's repertory season of Shakespeare and Shaw early in 1915; returned to England May 1915 and joined the RASC serving throughout in France in the 40th Div., SO 120th Brigade; SO Div'l Troops; SSO Div. (despatches, OBE); has played many parts from Greek Tragedy to Modern Comedy; his special successes in the latter being the Conquering Hero, Escape, The Fanatics, Many Waters, To see Ourselves, Sour Grapes, Accent on Youth, Winter Sunshine, and Waste; has toured with Athene Seyler (Mrs Athene Hannen) in South Africa, Egypt and Australia, and played in representative British Companies in Finland, France and USA; mem., Old Vic Company, 1944-47; has since appeared in Shakespeare, Shaw and Tchekov in Old Vic and John Clements's companies; film appearances include Who killed John Savage?, Fear, King Henry V, Quo Vadis, and Richard III; is uncompromisingly opposed to the opening of Theatres on Sundays. *Recreations:* trying to play games. *Address:* Lamb's Cottage, Ludham, Norfolk. *Clubs:* Leander, Garrick, Beefsteak, Green Room.

**HANNON, Ven. Arthur Gordon,** MA, TCD; retired, with General Licence from the Bishop of Down and Dromore, 1960; *b* 16 April 1891; *s* of John Alexander Hannon and Martha Matilda, *d* of Rev. James Rice, BD, TCD; *m* 1923, Hilda Catherine Stewart-Moore Denny, *g d* of late Provost Traill of TCD; five *s* one *d*. *Educ:* Corrig Sch., Kingstown; Trinity Coll., Dublin; Honoursman Literature, Logic and Ethics, and Modern History (1st Class), Exhibitioner. Auditor of Coll. Theological Soc. TCD, represented Dublin Univ. in Athletics. Flour Milling Industry, 1911-13;

Curate of Drumcondra and North Strand, Dublin, 1915-17; Head of Trinity Coll. Mission in Belfast, 1917-20; Rector of Ballymoney, 1920-24; Rector of Shankill Parish, Lurgan, 1924-40; Precentor of Dromore, 1924-32; Archdeacon of Dromore, 1933-40; Examining Chaplain to Bishop of Down, 1935-40; General Licence from Bishop of Down, 1940-54; Head of Industrial Relations Training Centre, 1940-54; Vicar of Kilbroney, Co. Down, 1954-60. Irish Representative, Congress of Europe, 1948. Chm., Churches' Industrial Council, 1959-61. *Publications:* The War and Foreign Missions, 1915; The Kingdom of God in Ireland, 1936. *Address:* Ramoan Lodge, Ballycastle, Co. Antrim, N Ireland. *T:* Ballycastle 605.

**HANSEN, Alvin H.,** PhD, LLD; Lucius N. Littauer Professor of Political Economy, Harvard University; *b* 23 Aug. 1887; *s* of Niels Hansen and Bergita Marie Nielnen; *m* 1916, Mabel Lewis; two *d. Educ:* Yankton Coll. (BA 1910, LLD 1936); University of Wisconsin (MA 1915, PhD 1918). John Simon Guggenheim Fellowship, 1928-29; Dir of Research and Sec. of Commission of Inquiry on National Policy in International Economic Relations, 1933-34; Chief Economic Analyst, State Dept, Washington, DC, 1934-35; Economic Adviser to Prairie Provinces on Canadian Dominion-Provincial Relations, 1937-38; Mem. Advisory Council on Social Security, 1937-38; Chm., US-Canadian Joint Economic Cttee, 1941-43; Special Economic Adviser, Federal Reserve Board, 1940-45; Pres., American Economic Assoc., 1938. *Publications:* Cycles of Prosperity and Depression, 1921; Business Cycle Theory, 1927; Principles of Economics (with F. B. Garver), 1928, revised edition 1937, 1947; Economic Stabilization in an Unbalanced World, 1932; Full Recovery or Stagnation, 1938; Fiscal Policy and Business Cycles, 1941; State and Local Finance in the National Economy (with H. S. Perloff), 1944; America's Role in the World Economy, 1945; Economic Policy and Full Employment, 1946. Monetary Theory and Fiscal Policy, 1949; Business Cycles and National Income, 1951; A Guide to Keynes, 1953; The American Economy, 1957; Economic Issues of the 1960's, 1960; The Dollar and the International Monetary System, 1965. *Address:* 56 Juniper Road, Belmont, Mass, USA. *T:* Belmont 484-4721.

**HANSEN, David Ernest,** CMG 1949; Principal, Christchurch Technical College, Christchurch, NZ, 1919-50, retired 1950; *b* Auckland, New Zealand, 9 May 1884; *s* of Lars and Mary Anne Hansen; *m* 1916, Margaret Emma Hampson; one *s* one *d* (and one *s* decd). *Educ:* Thames High Sch.; Auckland Grammar Sch.; Auckland Univ.; Canterbury Univ., NZ. Was a Post-graduate research student, Berlin Univ., Karlsruhe Technische Hochschule, 1909-11. MSc 1st Hons, MA, Dr Ingenieur. Science Master, Christchurch Technical Coll., 1908, 1909; Research Student Berlin and Karlsruhe (Electro-Chemistry), 1909, 1910, 1911; Principal Southland Technical Coll., 1912-19; Pres. Southland WEA, 1918-19; Christchurch District Cttee, WEA: Mem. 1952, Hon. Life Mem. 1961; Member: Canterbury Univ. Council, 1952-61; Regional Council of Adult Education, 1952-60; Risingholme Community Centre, Exec., 1944, Life Mem. and Patron, 1961; Life Mem., New Zealand Disabled Servicemen's Rehabilitation Board; Chm. Te Waipounamu Coll. (Maori Girls') Coun., 1956-64; Mem., Cttee of Crippled Children's Soc., 1950-61; Mem. Canterbury and Westland Auxil. Brit. and Foreign Bible Soc., 1950 (Chm. 1956-64, Mem. of Dominion Council, 1956-64). *Recreation:* gardening. *Address:* 30 Locarno Street, Christchurch, New Zealand. *T:* 101964.

**HANSEN, Harry;** Vice-President, Hastings House, Publishers, Inc., since 1965; *b* Davenport, Iowa, 26 Dec. 1884; *s* of Hans Hansen and Christine Jochims; *m* 1914, Ruth McLernon; two *d. Educ:* University of Chicago (PhB 1909). Ed. University of Chicago Magazine and Alumni Secretary, 1909-11; war corr. Chicago Daily News, 1914-16; corr. at Paris Peace Conference, 1919; literary ed. Chicago Daily News, 1920-26, New York World, 1926-31; New York World-Telegram, 1931-48; Editor, World Almanac, 1948-65; Chm., editorial board, East and West Association; mem. editorial board, Armed Services Editions; judge, Metro-Goldwyn-Mayer novel award; Lectr Columbia Univ., University of Colorado, Miami Univ., etc. *Publications:* The Adventures of the Fourteen Points, 1919; Midwest Portraits, 1923; Carl Sandburg the Man and his Poetry, 1924; Your Life Lies Before You (novel), 1935; The Chicago (Rivers of America), 1942; North of Manhattan, 1950; Scarsdale; Colonial Manor to Modern Community, 1954; Old Ironsides, 1955; The Story of Illinois, 1956; History of the American Civil War, 1961; The Boston Massacre, 1970. Co-author, Writing Up the News, 1940; Journalism in Wartime, 1943; The Aspirin Age, 1949; contr. Encyc. Britann., Universal Jewish Encyc. Editor O. Henry Prize Stories, 1933-40; American Guide Series, 1966; New England Legends and Folklore, 1967. Translations from German, inc. Wasserman. *Address:* 10 E 40th Street, New York, NY 10016, USA. *Clubs:* Coffee House, Overseas Press (New York); Tavern (Chicago).

**HANSFORD, S(idney) Howard,** MA, DLit; Professor Emeritus of Chinese Art and Archæology in the University of London and Hon. Fellow, School of Oriental and African Studies, 1966; *b* London, 22 June 1899; *s* of late Sidney Robert Hansford; *m* 1929, Doris Irene, *er d* of late Capt. Herbert Mansfield Pinkham; two *s* one *d. Educ:* Mill Hill Sch.; University of London. Served in France, 1918, 2nd Lieut, RFA. Partner in firm of Wright & Hansford, China and Japan Merchants, 1923-35; Universities' China Cttee. Student in China, 1938-39; Special Intelligence Officer, Foreign Office, 1940-45; Chinese Government Scholar, University of London, 1945-47; Lectr in Chinese Art and Archæology, Courtauld Inst. of Art, 1947-55; Prof. of Chinese Art and Archæol. in University of London (Sch. of Oriental and African Studies) and Head of the Percival David Foundation of Chinese Art, 1955-66. Vis. Lectr in the Fine Arts, Harvard Univ., 1960. Vice-Chm., China Soc.; Member: Univs' China Cttee in London; Exec. Coun. of Oriental Ceramic Soc.; MRAS. *Publications:* Chinese Jade Carving, 1950; A Glossary of Chinese Art and Archæology, 1954; The Seligman Collection of Chinese and Central Asian Bronzes and Chinese Jades and Sculptures, 1957; Great Buildings of China, 1965; Chinese Carved Jades, 1968; Jade, Essence of Hills and Streams, the von Oertzen Collection, 1969; articles in Jl of Royal Asiatic Soc., Trans of Oriental Ceramic Soc., Oriental Art, etc. *Address:* Cherrywood, Granville Road, Limpsfield, Oxted, Surrey. *T:* Oxted 2714.

**HANSFORD JOHNSON, Pamela;** *see* Johnson, P. H.

**HANSON, Prof. Albert Henry;** Professor of Politics, University of Leeds, since 1963; *b* 20 April 1913; *s* of Henry Herbert Hanson and Rosa Anne Hanson (*née* Duck); *m* 1937, Joan Madge Cansick; one *s* one *d. Educ:* Jesus Coll.,

Oxford; London Univ. Inst. of Education. Served as Major, RA, 1941-46. History Master: Grammar Sch. for Boys, Preston, 1935-39; City Boys' Sch., Leicester, 1939-41; Sen. Lectr in History, Cooper's Hill (Emergency) Trng Coll., 1946-48; Lectr in Public Administration, University of Leeds, 1948-56; Dir of Research, Public Administration Inst., Ankara, 1953-54; Reader in Public Admin., University of Leeds, 1956-63; Res. Fellow, Nuffield Coll., Oxford, 1960-61. *Publications:* Public Enterprise and Economic Development, 1959 (2nd edn, 1965); Parliament and Public Ownership, 1961; Nationalisation, 1963; (with Prof. H. V. Wiseman) Parliament at Work, 1963; The Process of Planning: A Study of India's Five Year Plans, 1966; Planning and the Politicians, 1969; (with Dr Malcolm Wallis) Governing Britain, 1970; articles and reviews for Times Lit. Supp., Public Administration, Parly Affairs, etc. *Recreations:* music, travel. *Address:* 15 Park View Crescent, Roundhay, Leeds 8. *T:* Leeds 662092.

**HANSON, Sir Anthony (Leslie Oswald),** 4th Bt, *cr* 1887; *b* 27 Nov. 1934; *s* of Sir Gerald Stanhope Hanson, 2nd Bt, and Flora Liebe (*d* 1956), *e d* of late Lieut-Col W. A. R. Blennerhassett; *S* half-brother, 1951; *m* 1964, Denise Jane (Tuppence), *e d* of R. S. Rolph. *Educ:* Hawtrey's, Savernake, Wilts; Gordonstoun, Elgin, Morayshire. Career in Royal Navy until 1955; farming, 1956-. *Recreation:* hunting.

**HANSON, Dr Bertram Speakman,** CMG 1963; DSO 1942; OBE 1941; ED; *b* 6 Jan. 1905; *s* of William Speakman Hanson and Maggie Aitken Hanson; *m* 1932, Mayne, *d* of T. J. Gilpin; three *s* one *d*. *Educ:* St Peter's Coll., Adelaide; University of Adelaide (MB, BS). War Service: Comd 2/8 Aust. Field Amb., 1940-43; ADMS, 9 Aust. Div., 1943-44. Pres., SA Branch of BMA, 1952-53; Pres. College of Radiologists of Australasia, 1961-62; Member: Radiation Health Cttee of Nat. Health and Med. Research Coun., 1963-67; Radiological Advisory Cttee, S Aust., 1957-; Hon. Radiotherapist, Royal Adelaide Hospital, 1952-64; Pres., The Australian Cancer Soc., 1964-67; Chm., Exec. Board, Anti-Cancer Foundation, University of Adelaide, 1955-; Mem. Council, International Union Against Cancer, 1962-. FFR (Hon.) 1964; FAMA 1967. *Publications:* sundry addresses and papers in Med. Jl of Australia. *Recreation:* gardening. *Address:* 7 Glenroy Avenue, Beaumont, South Australia 5066. *T:* 79-3016. *Clubs:* Adelaide, Naval, Military and Air Force (Adelaide).

**HANSON, Sir (Charles) John,** 3rd Bt *cr* 1918; Member of the London Stock Exchange; *b* 28 Feb. 1919; *o s* of Major Sir Charles Edwin Bourne Hanson, 2nd Bt, and Violet Sybil (*d* 1966), 3rd *d* of late John B. Johnstone, Coombe Cottage, Kingston Hill, Surrey; *S* father 1958; *m* 1st, 1944, Patricia Helen (marr. diss. 1968), *o c* of late Adm. Sir (Eric James) Patrick Brind, GBE, KCB; one *s* one *d*; 2nd, 1968, Mrs Helen Yorke. *Educ:* Eton; Clare Coll., Cambridge. Late Captain, The Duke of Cornwall's Light Infantry; served War of 1939-45. *Heir:* *s* Charles Rupert Patrick Hanson, *b* 25 June 1945. *Address:* 7 Abingdon Gardens, Abingdon Villas, W8. *T:* 01-937 1297. *Clubs:* MCC, United University; Royal Fowey Yacht (Fowey).

**HANSON, Prof. (Emmeline) Jean,** FRS 1967; Member of Staff of Medical Research Council since 1948; Professor of Biology, School of Biological Sciences, King's College, University of London, since 1966; *b* Newhall, Derbyshire, 1919; *d* of late Thomas Hanson and of Emma Jane Badger. *Educ:* High Sch. for Girls, Burton-on-Trent; Bedford Coll., University of London. BSc (Zoology) 1941, PhD 1951, London. Cancer Research, Strangeways Research Lab., Cambridge, 1942-44; Demonstrator in Zoology, Bedford Coll., London, 1944-48; Mem. Scientific staff of MRC Biophysics Research Unit, King's Coll., London, 1948-. Rockefeller Foundn Res. Fell., Dept of Biol, MIT, 1953-54; Hon. Lectr in Biophysics, King's Coll., London, 1964. *Publications:* articles in scientific periodicals. *Recreations:* music, reading, fell-walking, travel, cooking. *Address:* 3 Eliot Lodge, Kirkdale, SE26. *T:* 01-699 8719.

**HANSON, Frederick Horowhenua Melrose,** CMG 1961; DSO 1943, and Bar 1945; OBE 1942; MM 1918; ED 1954; New Zealand Commissioner of Works, 1955-62, retired; Member of NZ Council for Technical Education; Chairman, NZ Defence Survey Committee, 1962; *b* Levin, New Zealand, 9 July 1896; *s* of Frederick Hanson; *m* 1924, Constance M., *d* of Edward Grindley. *Educ:* Wellington Coll.; Victoria Univ. Coll. Served European War, 1914-18 (MM), 1st NZEF, Wellington Regt. Educated and trained as civil engineer. With Public Works Dept, 1921-39. Served War of 1939-45 (despatches, DSO, bar, wounded thrice): 2 NZEF, CRE 2 NZ Div., CE 2 NZEF; Brig. NZ Chief Highways Engineer, 1946-49; Dep. Commissioner of Works, 1949-55. Territorial Mem. Army Bd, 1948-55. First Chm., NZ Nat. Roads Bd, 1954-55; Past Pres., NZ Instn of Engineers. FICE; FNZIE; MSINZ. *Publications:* on soil mechanics, foundations and road engineering. *Recreations:* shooting and fishing. *Address:* 17 Portland Crescent, Wellington, N1, NZ. *Club:* United Services Officers' (Wellington, NZ).

**HANSON, Prof. Jean;** *see* Hanson, Prof. E. J.

**HANSON, Sir John;** *see* Hanson, Sir Charles John.

**HANSON, Rt. Rev. Richard Patrick Crosland;** *see* Clogher, Bishop of.

**HANWORTH,** 2nd Viscount, *cr* 1936, of Hanworth; **David Bertram Pollock,** CEng, MIMechE, FRPS, FIEE; Baron, *cr* 1926; Bt, *cr* 1922; Lt-Col Royal Engineers, retired; Barrister-at-Law (Inner Temple), 1958; Assistant Director, The Consumer Council; *b* 1 Aug. 1916; *s* of Charles Thomas Anderson Pollock and Alice Joyce Becher; *S* grandfather, 1936; *m* 1940, Isolda Rosamond, *yr d* of Geoffrey Parker, of Cairo; two *s* one *d*. *Educ:* Wellington Coll.; Trinity Coll., Cambridge. (Mechanical Science Tripos, 1939). *Publications:* Amateur Carbro Colour Prints, 1950; Amateur Dye Transfer Colour Prints, 1956. *Recreations:* ski-ing, photography, gardening. *Heir:* *s* Hon. David Stephen Geoffrey Pollock [*b* 16 Feb. 1946; *m* 1968, Elizabeth Liberty, *e d* of Lawrence Vambe]. *Address:* Folly Hill, Ewhurst, Surrey. *Club:* Athenæum.

*See also Sir W. L. Farrer.*

**HAPPELL, Sir Arthur Comyn,** Kt, *cr* 1947; ICS (retired); *b* 20 Oct. 1891; *s* of late W. A. Happell, Indian Civil Service, and Mrs Happell, Tunbridge Wells, Kent; unmarried. *Educ:* Tonbridge; King's Coll., Cambridge. Served in Suffolk Regt during European War, 1914-18; demobilised with rank of Capt. 1919; Indian Civil Service, 1921; served in Madras Presidency, Asst and Sub-Collector and Joint Magistrate, 1921-25; Under and Dep. Sec. to Govt, 1925-26; Registrar, High Court, 1926-29; District and Sessions Judge, 1930-41; Judge, High Court, Madras, 1941-48.

*Recreations:* golf and reading. *Clubs:* East India and Sports, Roehampton.

**HAPPELL, Brig. william Horatio,** CIE 1943; Indian Army, retired; *b* 15 April 1890; *s* of W. A. Happell, ICS; *m* 1925, Ivy Ellen Grimley. *Educ:* Tonbridge; RMC, Sandhurst. Commissioned, 1909; despatches, 1918; Judge Advocate-Gen. in India, 1938-44; retired, 1944. *Address:* Pond Mead, 37 Village Way, Dulwich, SE21.

**HAPPOLD, Prof. Frank Charles,** PhD, DSc (Manchester); Professor of Biochemistry, University of Leeds, 1946-67; *b* Barrow-in-Furness, 23 Sept. 1902; *s* of Henry Happold and Emma Happold (*née* Ley); *m* 1926, A. Margaret M. Smith, MA, Brighton; one *s* one *d*. *Educ:* privately; Barrow Gram. Sch.; University of Manchester. PhD (Manchester) 1927; DSc (Manchester) 1934. University of Leeds: Department of Bacteriology, 1926-36; Dept of Physiology, 1936-46; Dept of Biochemistry, 1946-67; Research Prof., University of Florida, 1958-59. First Chm., Fedn of European Biochem. Socs, 1964. Leverhulme Fellowship to Harvard Univ. Post Graduate Medical Sch., 1939; Visiting Prof., University of Ghana, 1967-70. Co-founder with wife of International Tramping Tours, 1929. *Publications:* numerous scientific publications, mainly in Microbiological Chemistry and Enzymology. *Recreations:* gardening and travel. *Address:* Three Roods, Arnside, Westmorland. *Club:* Athenæum.

**HAPPOLD, Frederick Crossfield,** DSO 1916; *b* 15 Feb. 1893; *s* of A. C. Happold, Lancaster; *m* 1933, Dorothy Vectis Halbach; one *s*. *Educ:* Rydal Sch.; Peterhouse, Cambridge, MA; Hon. LLD Melbourne. Served European War, 1914-18 (despatches, DSO); Asst Master, The Perse Sch., Cambridge, 1920-28; Lecturer in History at Cambridge Univ., 1922-28; Headmaster, Bishop Wordsworth's Sch., Salisbury, Wilts, 1928-60. *Publications:* The Adventure of Man; The Finding of the King; The Approach to History; Citizens in the Making; This Modern Age; Towards a New Aristocracy; Everyone's Book about the English Church; Adventure in Search of a Creed; Mysticism; Religious Faith and Twentieth Century Man; The Journey Inwards; Prayer, its Nature and Practice, and other books and articles on religious, educational and historical subjects. *Address:* High Elms, Sandy Lane, Redlynch, Salisbury, Wiltshire. *T:* Downton 280.

**HARBERTON,** 9th Viscount, *cr* 1791; **Henry Ralph Martyn Pomeroy;** Baron Haberton, 1783; *b* 12 Oct. 1908; *s* of 8th Viscount and Mary Katherine, *o d* of A. W. Leatham, JP; *S* father 1956. *Educ:* Eton. *Heir:* *b* Lieut-Col Hon. Thomas de Vautort Pomeroy [*b* 19 Oct. 1910; *m* 1st, 1939, Nancy Ellen (marriage dissolved, 1946), *d* of late C. A. Penoyer; 2nd, 1950, Pauline Stafford, *d* of late Wilfred Sidney Baker, Stoke, Plymouth]. *Address:* 5 Thurloe Street, SW7. *T:* 01-589 6767.

**HARBISON, Air Cdre William,** CBE 1965; AFC 1956; Director of Control (Operations), National Air Traffic Control Services, since Dec. 1968; *b* 11 April 1922; *s* of W. Harbison; *m* 1950, Helen, *d* of late William B. Geneva, Bloomington, Illinois; two *s*. *Educ:* Ballymena Academy, N Ireland. Joined RAF, 1941; 118 Sqdn Fighter Comd, 1943-46; 263, 257 and 64 Sqdns, 1946-48; Exchange Officer with 1st Fighter Group USAF, 1948-50; Central Fighter Estabt, 1950-51; 4th Fighter Group USAF, Korea, 1952; 2nd ATAF Germany: comd No 67 Sqdn, 1952-55; HQ No 2 Group, 1955; psc 1956; Air Min. and All Weather OCU, 1957; comd No 29 All Weather Sqdn Fighter Comd, Acklington and Leuchars, 1958-59; British Defence Staffs, Washington, 1959-62; jssc 1962; comd RAF Leuchars Fighter Comd, 1963-65; ndc 1965-66; Gp Capt. Ops: HQ Fighter Comd, 1967-68; No 11 Group Strike Comd, 1968. *Recreations:* flying, motoring. *Address:* c/o Lloyds Bank, Cox's & King's Branch, 6 Pall Mall, SW1. *Club:* Royal Air Force.

**HARBORD, Rev. Derek** (formerly **Hon. Mr Justice Harbord**); Rector of St Botolph-without-Aldgate *with* Holy Trinity, Minories, since 1962; *b* 25 July 1902; *yr s* of F. W. Harbord, Birkenhead, and Isabella (*née* Gardner), Sale; *m* Grace Rosalind (*d* 1969); *o d* of A. S. Fowles, Birmingham; two *s* one *d*. *Educ:* Mount Radford Sch., Exeter; Gray's Inn; St Michael's Theol Coll., Llandaff. Barrister-at-Law, 1925; Deacon, 1925; Priest, 1926; Curate, W. Norwood, 1925-27; Streatham, 1927-29; Vicar, Stoke Lyne, 1929; Royal Army Chaplains Dept, 1929; Chaplain i/c Depot RAMC, Crookham, and V Lt Bde RA, Ewshott, 1929-30; Vicar, Hindolveston, 1930-33; Vicar, Good Shepherd, W Bromwich, 1933-35; resigned to become a Roman Catholic, 1935; reconciled with Anglican Communion and licensed to offic. Accra dioc., 1959-61. Practised at English Bar, 1935-40: Central Criminal Court, SE Circuit, Mddx and N London Sess; Sec., Bentham Cttee for Poor Litigants, 1937-40; AOER, 1938; HM Colonial Legal Service, 1940; Dist Magistrate and Coroner, Gold Coast, 1940-44; Registrar of High Court of N Rhodesia and High Sheriff of the Territory, 1944-46; Resident Magistrate and Coroner, N Rhodesia, 1946-53; Chm., Reinstatement in Civil Employment (Mining Industry) Cttee; Chm., Liquor Licensing Appeal Tribunal for N Rhodesia; a Judge of High Court of Tanganyika, and Mem. Ct of Appeal for E Africa, 1953-59; ret. 1959; admitted to Ghana Bar, 1959; Senior Lecturer, Ghana Sch. of Law, and Editor of Ghana Law Reports, 1959-61. Granted armorial bearings, 1967. *Publications:* Manual for Magistrates (N Rhodesia), 1951; Law Reports (N Rhodesia), 1952; Law Reports (Ghana), 1960. *Recreations:* 15 grandchildren. *Address:* Aldgate Rectory, 1 Woodcote Valley Road, Purley, Surrey. *T:* 01-660 8168; St Botolph's Vestry, Aldgate, EC3. *T:* 01-283 1670. *Club:* Athenæum.

**HARBORD-HAMOND,** family name of **Baron Suffield.**

**HARBOUR, Brian Hugo,** CBE 1964; Director, Transport Holding Company, since 1963; *b* 5 Oct. 1899; *s* of late Samuel and Georgina Harbour; *m* 1928, Joan Kirsten, *er d* of Rev. Charles and Mrs Emily Sykes, Halifax; two *s*. *Educ:* elementary sch.; Brockley County Sch., London, SE; London Sch. of Economics. Joined Underground group of companies as a junior clerk, 1913; transferred to London Passenger Transport Bd, 1933; Personal Asst to Chm. of Bd and Sec. of Standing Jt Cttee of LPTB and main line railway companies, 1937-43; Commercial Manager, 1943-46; Operating Manager (country buses and coaches), 1946-54; Member: London Transport Executive, 1954-62; London Transport Board, Nov. 1962-Nov. 1963; London and Home Counties Traffic Advisory Cttee, 1956-62; London Travel Cttee, 1958-62. MInstT. *Recreations:* reading, walking. *Address:* 7 Selwyn House, Selwyn Road, Eastbourne, Sussex. *T:* Eastbourne 27284.

**HARCOURT,** family name of **Viscount Harcourt.**

**HARCOURT,** 2nd Viscount, *cr* 1917; **William Edward Harcourt,** KCMG 1957; OBE 1945 (MBE 1943); Baron Nuneham, *cr* 1917; Chairman: Morgan Grenfell & Co. Limited; Legal and General Assurance Society Limited; Gresham Life Assurance Society Ltd; Gresham Fire and Accident Insurance Society Ltd; British Commonwealth Insurance Co. Ltd; Trustee: London Museum (Chairman); Rhodes Trust; Oxford Preservation Trust (Chairman); Board of Governors of Museum of London (Chairman); Vice-Lieutenant of Oxfordshire since 1963; Hon. Fellow, St Antony's College, Oxford; *b* 1908; *o s* of 1st Viscount and Mary Ethel (*d* 1960), GBE, *o d* of late Walter H. Burns of New York and North Mymms Park, Hatfield; *S* father, 1922; *heir-pres.* to 10th Baron Vernon, *qv*; *m* 1st, 1931, Hon. Maud Elizabeth Grosvenor (marr. diss., 1942), *o d* of 4th Baron Ebury, DSO, MC; three *d*; 2nd, 1946, Elizabeth Sonia (*d* 1959), *widow* of Capt. Lionel Gibbs, and *d* of late Sir Harold Snagge, KBE. *Educ:* Eton; Christ Church, Oxford, MA. Served War of 1939-45, with 63rd (Oxford Yeomanry) AT Regt RA and on staff. Minister (Economic) HM Embassy, Washington, and Head of UK Treasury Delegation in USA, 1954-57; UK Exec. Dir of International Bank for Reconstruction and Development and of International Monetary Fund, 1954-57; Mem., Departmental (Radcliffe) Cttee on Working of Monetary and Credit Policy of United Kingdom, 1957-59 and of Departmental (Plowden) Cttee on Overseas Representational Services, 1962-64. *Address:* 23 Culross Street, W1. *T:* 01-629 6061; Staunton Harcourt, Oxon. *T:* Standlake 296.

*See also Baron Ashburton, Hon. Mrs John Mulholland.*

**HARDEN, Donald Benjamin,** CBE 1969 (OBE 1956); MA Cantab, MA Oxon, PhD Mich; FSA, FMA; Director of the London Museum, 1956-70; Acting Director of the Museum of London, 1965-70; *b* Dublin, 8 July 1901; *er s* of late John Mason Harden and Constance Caroline Sparrow; *m* 1st, 1934, Cecil Ursula (*d* 1963), *e d* of late James Adolphus Harriss; one *d*; 2nd, 1965, Dorothy May, *er d* of late Daniel Herbert McDonald. *Educ:* Kilkenny Coll.; Westminster Sch.; Trinity Coll., Cambridge; University of Michigan. Travelled in Italy and Tunisia, 1923-24; Senior Asst, Dept of Humanity, University of Aberdeen, 1924-26; Commonwealth Fund Fellow, University of Michigan, 1926-28; Asst University of Michigan Archæol Exped. to Egypt, 1928-29; Asst Keeper, Dept of Antiquities, Ashmolean Museum, Oxford, 1929-45; Keeper, Dept of Antiquities, and Sec., Griffith Institute, 1945-56. Temp. Civil Servant Ministries of Supply and Production, 1940-45: Vice-Pres. Soc. of Antiquaries of London, 1949-53, 1964-67; President: Council for British Archæology, 1950-54; Oxford Architectural and Historical Soc., 1952-55; Section H, British Assoc., 1955; London and Middlesex Archæol. Soc., 1959-65; Royal Archæol Inst., 1966-69; Internat. Assoc. for History of Glass, 1968-; Chm., Directors' Conf. (Nat. Museums), 1968-70; Hon. Sec. Museums Assoc., 1949-54, Chm. Educ. Cttee 1954-59, Pres. 1960. Hon. Editor, Soc. for Medieval Archæology, 1957-; Mem. of Council: British Schools of Archæology in Iraq and Jerusalem; Member: Ancient Monuments Board for England; Royal Commission on Historical Monuments (England); Trustee, RAEC Museum. Leverhulme Fellowship for research on ancient glass, 1953. *Publications:* Roman Glass from Karanis, 1936; (with E. T. Leeds) The Anglo-Saxon Cemetery at Abingdon, Berks, 1936; The Phoenicians, 1962; (jointly) Masterpieces of Glass, British Museum, 1968; (ed) Dark-Age Britain, 1956. Numerous articles on archæology and museums. *Address:* 12 St Andrew's Mansions, Dorset Street, W1H 3FD. *T:* 01-935 5121. *Club:* Athenæum.

**HARDEN, Major James Richard Edwards,** DSO, MC, DL, JP; farmer; *b* 12 Dec. 1916; *s* of late Major J. E. Harden, DL, JP, Royal Irish Fusiliers, and L. G. C. Harden; *m* 1948, Ursula Joyce, *y d* of G. M. Strutt, Newhouse, Terling, Chelmsford, Essex; one *s* two *d*. *Educ:* Oriel House, St Asaph; Bedford Sch.; Sandhurst. Commissioned into Royal Tank Regt 1937; retired on agricultural release, 1947; MP (UU) for County Armagh, 1948-54. JP County Armagh, 1956. DL Caernarvonshire, 1968. *Recreations:* shooting, fishing. *Address:* Nanhoran, Pwllheli, Cærnarvonshire, North Wales. *T:* Botwnnog 610.

**HARDIE, Sir Charles (Edgar Mathewes),** Kt 1970; CBE 1963 (OBE 1943); chartered accountant; Partner in Dixon, Wilson, Tubbs & Gillett, since 1934; *b* 10 March 1910; *s* of Dr C. F. and Mrs R. F. Hardie (*née* Moore), Barnet, Herts; *m* 1st, 1937, Dorothy Jean (*née* Hobson) (*d* 1965); one *s* three *d*; 2nd, 1966, Mrs Angela Richli, *widow* of Raymond Paul Richli. *Educ:* Aldenham Sch. Qualified as Chartered Accountant, 1932; practised in London, 1934-. War Service, 1939-44 (Col). Chairman: BOAC; White Fish Authority; The British Printing Corporation Ltd; Metropolitan Estate and Property Corp. Ltd; Vokes Group Ltd; Director: British American and General Trust Ltd; NAAFI (Dep. Chm.); Melbray Group Ltd (Dep. Chm.); Hill Samuel Group Ltd; Royal Bank of Canada; Fitch Lovell (Dep. Chm.); Mann Egerton & Co. Ltd; Member: BEA Board; Council, Inst. of Directors. Legion of Merit, 1944. *Address:* Framfield Grange, Framfield, Sussex. *T:* Framfield 264. *Clubs:* Boodle's, Gresham; Royal Thames Yacht.

**HARDIE, Colin Graham;** Official Fellow and Tutor in Classics, Magdalen College, Oxford, since 1936; Public Orator of Oxford University, since Oct. 1967; *b* 16 Feb. 1906; 3rd *s* of William Ross Hardie, Fellow of Balliol Coll. and Prof. of Humanity in Edinburgh Univ., and Isabella Watt Stevenson; *m* 1940, Christian Viola Mary Lucas; two *s*. *Educ:* Edinburgh Acad.; Balliol Coll., Oxford (Warner Exhibitioner and Hon. Scholar); 1st class Classical Moderations, 1926, and Lit Hum BA, 1928; MA, 1931; Craven Scholar, 1925; Ireland Scholar, 1925; Hertford Scholar, 1926; Gaisford Prize for Greek Prose, 1927; Junior Research Fellow of Balliol, 1928-29; Fellow and Classical Tutor, 1930-33; Dir of the British Sch. at Rome, 1933-36. *Publications:* Vitae Vergilianae antiquae, 1954; papers on Dante. *Recreation:* gardening. *Address:* 63 High Street, Oxford. *T:* Oxford 47364.

**HARDIE, John William Somerville,** MA Cantab; Principal, Loughborough College of Education, since 1963; *b* 21 Aug. 1912; 2nd *s* of late Most Rev. W. G. Hardie, CBE, DD; *m* 1938, Evelyn Chrystal, 5th *d* of J. C. Adkins, Uppingham, Rutland; one *s* two *d*. *Educ:* St Lawrence Coll., Ramsgate; Trinity Coll., Cambridge. Second Cl. Hon. (Div. I) Modern and Medieval Lang. Tripos. Asst Master St Lawrence Coll., 1933-35; Asst Master Uppingham Sch., 1935-40; Headmaster Cornwall Coll., Montego Bay, Jamaica 1940-42; Headmaster Jamaica Coll., Kingston, Jamaica, 1943-46; Asst Master Blundell's Sch., 1946-47; Headmaster, Canford Sch., 1947-60; Headmaster-Elect, Hesarack Sch., Iran, 1960-61; consultant Voluntary Service Overseas, 1961; Managing Dir, The Broadcasting Company of Northern Nigeria Ltd (seconded by Granada TV Ltd), 1961-62; Head of Information and Research, The Centre for Educational Television Overseas, Nuffield Lodge, 1962-63. *Recreation:* hockey (Cambridge Univ. Hockey XI, 1931, 1932, Capt. 1933; Welsh Hockey XI, 1931, 1932, Capt. 1933-39). *Address:* Loughborough College of Education, Loughborough, Leics; Blue Seas, Trelawney Road, St Mawes, Truro, Cornwall.

**HARDIE, Captain Maurice Linton,** CBE 1961; DSC 1944; RN retired; *b* 29 July 1909; *s* of late Martin Hardie and Agnes Madeline Pattisson; *m* 1942, Patricia Josephine, *d* of G. St Noble, Barcelona; one *s* one *d*. *Educ:* RN Coll., Dartmouth. Specialised in navigation, 1933. War Service included Inglefield, 1939-42; Minelaying Sqdn, 1942-43; invasion of Normandy, 1944; Fleet Navigating Officer, Mediterranean, 1944-47. Comd Starling, 1947-48; Staff of C-in-C, East Indies, 1948-50; Capt. (D) Portsmouth, in Boxer, 1951-52; Naval Officer-in-Charge, Auckland, NZ, 1952-54; comd Defender, 1955-56; Dir of Naval Equipment, Admlty, 1957-59; Capt. of Coll., at Greenwich, 1959-60; retired, 1961. Bursar and Clerk to the Governors, Portsmouth Grammar Sch., 1962-70. *Address:* Kentons, 16 Havant Road, Emsworth, Hants PO10 7JE. *T:* Emsworth 2586. *Clubs:* United Service, MCC, Royal Naval (Portsmouth).

**HARDIE, Rt. Rev. William Auchterlonie;** *see* Ballarat, Bishop of.

**HARDIE, William Francis Ross;** President, Corpus Christi College, Oxford, 1950-69; Hon. Fellow, 1969; *b* 25 April 1902; *s* of late W. R. Hardie, Professor of Humanity, University of Edinburgh; *m* 1938, Isobel St Maur Macaulay; two *s*. *Educ:* Edinburgh Academy; Balliol Coll., Oxford. Fellow by Examination, Magdalen Coll., 1925; Fellow and Tutor in Philosophy, Corpus Christi Coll., Oxford, 1926-50. *Publications:* A Study in Plato, 1936; Aristotle's Ethical Theory, 1968; articles in philosophical journals. *Address:* Hogan, Frilford Heath, Abingdon, Berks. *T:* Frilford Heath 201.

**HARDING,** family name of **Baron Harding of Petherton.**

**HARDING OF PETHERTON,** 1st Baron *cr* 1958, of Nether Compton; **Field-Marshal John Harding,** GCB 1951 (KCB 1944); CBE 1940; DSO 1941; MC; *b* 1896; *s* of late Francis E. Harding, Compton Way, S Petherton, Somerset; changed his Christian names from Allan Francis to John, 1944; *m* 1927, Mary G. M., *d* of late Wilson Rooke, JP, Knutsford, Cheshire; one *s*. *Educ:* Ilminster Grammar Sch. Served European War, 1914-19, with TA and Machine Gun Corps (MC); Lieut Somerset Light Infantry 1920; Capt. 1923; psc 1928; Brigade Major British Force, Saar Plebiscite; Bt Major, 1935; Bt Lieut-Col 1938; Lieut-Col 1939; Brig. 1942; Maj.-Gen. 1942; Lieut-Gen. 1943; General, 1949; Field-Marshal, 1953. Served War of 1939-45 (despatches, CBE, DSO and two Bars, KCB). GOC CMF, 1946-47; GOC-in-C Southern Command, 1947-49; C-in-C, Far East Land Forces, 1949-51; Comdr-in-Chief, British Army of the Rhine, 1951-52; Chief of the Imperial Gen. Staff, 1952-55. Governor and Comdr-in-Chief, Cyprus, 1955-Nov. 1957. Director: Nat. Provincial Bank, 1957-69; Standard Bank, 1965-; Chairman: Williams (Hounslow) Ltd, 1962-; Plessey Co. Ltd, 1967-70 (Dir, 1962-; Dep. Chm., 1964-67). ADC Gen. to King George VI, 1950-52, to the Queen, 1952-53. Col 6th Gurkha Rifles, 1951-61; Col Somerset and Cornwall LI (Somerset LI, 1953-60); Col, The Life Guards, and Gold Stick to the Queen, 1957-64. KStJ. Hon. DCL (Durham). *Recreation:* gardening. *Heir:* *s* Major Hon. John Charles Harding [*b* 12 Feb. 1928; *m* 1966, Harriet, *yr d* of late Maj.-Gen. J. F. Hare, and Mrs D. E. Hare; one *s* one *d*]. *Address:* Lower Farm, Nether Compton, Sherborne, Dorset. *Clubs:* Cavalry, Naval and Military.

**HARDING, Ann;** Actress; *b* Fort Sam Houston, San Antonio, Texas, USA, 7 Aug. 1902; *d* of General George Grant Gatley; *m* 1937, Werner Janssen, Symphony Conductor (marr. diss. 1963; Court restored Ann Harding as her legal name); one *d* from a former marriage. *Educ:* American public schs; Baldwin Sch., Bryn Mawr, Penna. First appearance as Madeline in Inheritors, with The Provincetown Players, New York; Tarnish, Trial of Mary Dugan, New York; Candida, London, 1937; Glass Menagerie, California, 1948; Garden District, New York, 1958. *Films include:* Holiday, East Lynn, Life of Vergie Winters, When Ladies Meet, The Fountain, Peter Ibbetson, Gallant Lady, Love From A Stranger (British picture), Mission to Moscow, Janie (Warners), Christmas Eve, It Happened on Fifth Avenue, The Man in the Grey Flannel Suit. *Recreations:* tennis, motoring, knitting. *Club:* Cosmopolitan (New York).

**HARDING, Denys Wyatt,** MA; Emeritus Professor of Psychology, University of London, since 1968; *b* 13 July 1906; *s* of Clement and Harriet Harding; *m* 1930, Jessie Muriel Ward; no *c*. *Educ:* Lowestoft Secondary Sch.; Emmanuel Coll., Cambridge. Investigator and Mem. of research staff, National Institute of Industrial Psychology, 1928-33; Asst (later Lecturer) in Social Psychology, London Sch. of Economics, 1933-38; Senior Lecturer in Psychology, University of Liverpool, 1938-45 (leave of absence for national service, 1941-44); part-time Lecturer in Psychology, University of Manchester, 1940-41 and 1944-45; Prof. of Psychology, Univ. of London, at Bedford Coll., 1945-68. Hon. Gen. Sec., British Psychological Soc., 1944-48. Mem. of editorial board of Scrutiny, a Quarterly Review, 1933-47. Editor, British Journal of Psychology (Gen. Section) 1948-54. *Publications:* The Impulse to Dominate, 1941; Social Psychology and Individual Values, 1953; Experience into Words: Essays on Poetry, 1963. Edited (with Gordon Bottomley) The Complete Works of Isaac Rosenberg, 1937. Translated (with Erik Mesterton) Guest of Reality, by Pār Lagerkvist, 1936; various papers on psychology and literary criticism. *Address:* Ashbocking Old Vicarage, near Ipswich, Suffolk. *T:* Helmingham 347.

**HARDING, George Richardson,** DSO 1918; MBE 1944; Member: Board of Referees since 1953; Post Office Advisory Council, since 1946; *b* 15 Sept. 1884; *s* of George S. and Margaret Harding; *m* 1921, Grace Henley, *d* of late Thomas H. Darby; two *s*. *Educ:* Brighton. Civil Engineer, Railway and gen. construction work, England and Canada, 1901-14; Royal Engineers, 1914-19 (despatches 4 times, DSO); Home Guard, Hampstead Rocket AA Battery, 1942-45 (MBE). Vice-Chm. Aplin & Barrett, Ltd, 1949-56; Chm., 1956-60; Chm. Maconochie Bros, Ltd, 1926-42; Mem. of Exec. Cttee The Canners' (War Time) Assoc., 1942-43; Member: National Advisory Council for Fire Prevention, 1941-45; Food Prices Control Cttee, 1940-; Chm. of Council London Chamber of Commerce, 1941-44, Vice-Pres. 1944-; Pres., Food Manufacturers Federation Inc., 1937-44; Chairman: Council, British Food Manufacturers Research Assoc., 1942-50, Vice-Pres., 1950-; Food Manufacturers Export Group, 1940-; Vice-

Pres. Assoc. of British Chambers of Commerce, 1948-55; Member Council of Foreign Bondholders, 1944-56. *Recreation:* gardening. *Address:* Wildwood, Abbots Drive, Virginia Water, Surrey. *T:* Wentworth 2137. *Club:* Wentworth.

**HARDING, Gerald William Lankester,** CBE 1957; FSA; Fellow of University College, London; Director, Department of Antiquities, Hashemite Kingdom of Jordan, 1936-56; *b* 8 Dec. 1901; *s* of William Arthur Harding and Florence Maud Lankester. Excavating with Sir Flinders Petrie near Gaza, Palestine, 1926-32; Asst Dir, Wellcome Archæological Research Expedition to Near East at Tell Duweir (Lachish), Palestine, 1932-36. Star of Jordan, Second Class, 1952. *Publications:* (with E. Mackay) Bahrein and Hamamieh, 1928; (with E. Macdonald and J. L. Starkey) Beth Pelet II, 1930; (with others) Lachish I; (with O. Tufnell and C. H. Inge) Lachish II; Some Thamudic Inscriptions from Jordan, 1952; Four Tomb Groups from Jordan, 1953; The Antiquities of Jordan, 1959; Archæology in the Aden Protectorate, 1964. Articles in Quarterly of the Dept of Antiquities of Palestine Annual of the Jordan Dept of Antiquities, Palestine Exploration Quarterly, etc. *Address:* PO Box 54, Jounieh, Lebanon. *Club:* Lansdowne.

**HARDING, Sir Harold (John Boyer),** Kt 1968; BSc, FCGI, DIC, FICE; Consulting Civil Engineer; individual practice since 1956; Consultant to Channel Tunnel Study Group since 1958; *b* 6 Jan. 1900; *s* of late Arthur Boyer Harding, Elvetham, Hants, and Helen Clinton (*née* Lowe); *m* 1927, Sophie Helen Blair, *d* of E. Blair Leighton, RI; two *s* one *d*. *Educ:* Christ's Hosp.; City and Guilds (Engrg) Coll.; Imperial Coll. of Science and Technology. Joined John Mowlem & Co. Ltd, Civil Engrg Contractors, 1922; Dir, John Mowlem & Co., 1950-56; Dir, Soil Mechanics Ltd, 1949-56. Governor: Westminster Techn Coll., 1948-53; Northampton Engrg Coll., 1950-53; Imperial Coll., 1955-. Mem., Building Res. Bd, 1952-55; Pres., ICE, 1963-64; Mem., Aberfan Disaster Tribunal, 1966-67; Vice-Pres., Parly and Scientific Cttee, 1968. James Forrest Lectr, ICE, 1952. AMICE 1927; MICE 1939; FCGI 1952; Fellow, Imperial Coll. of Science and Technology, 1968. Prix Coiseau, Soc. des Ingénieurs Civils de France, 1964. *Publications:* numerous papers to ICE. *Recreations:* varied. *Address:* 79 Mount Ephraim, Tunbridge Wells, Kent. *T:* Tunbridge Wells 32592. *Club:* United Service.

**HARDING, Hugh Alastair,** CMG 1958; Under-Secretary, Department of Education and Science, since 1967; *b* 4 May 1917; 2nd *s* of Roland Charles Harding, Norton-le-Moors, Staffordshire; *m* 1943, Florence Esnouf; one *s* one *d*. *Educ:* Rugby; Trinity Coll., Cambridge. Colonial Office, 1939; Asst Sec., 1950; Asst Sec., Treasury, 1961; Under-Sec., Treasury, 1962-64; Minister, UK Delegation to OECD, 1964-67. Served War of 1939-45, Army (Captain RA). *Address:* Department of Education and Science, Elizabeth House, York Road, SE1.

**HARDING, Mrs J. P.;** *see* Manton, Sidnie M.

**HARDING, John Philip,** PhD; Keeper of Zoology, British Museum (Natural History), since 1964; *b* 12 Nov. 1911; *s* of Philip William and Eleanor Harding, Rondebosch, Cape Town; *m* 1936, Sidnie Manton, *qv*; one *s* one *d*. *Educ:* Torquay; University Coll., Exeter; University of Cincinnati; King's Coll., Cambridge. Ministry of Agriculture and Fisheries, 1936-37; British Museum (Natural History), 1937-. *Publications:* scientific papers on Crustacea. *Recreations:* bee-keeping, mechanical devices, photography. *Address:* 88 Ennerdale Road, Richmond, Surrey. *T:* 01-940 2908. *Club:* Athenæum.

**HARDING, Maj.-Gen. Reginald Peregrine,** CB 1953; DSO 1940; DL; late 5th Royal Inniskilling Dragoon Guards; *b* 3 July 1905; *s* of late John Reginald Harding, JP, and Elizabeth Margaret Harding; *m* 1941, Elizabeth Mary Baker (marr. diss. 1970); one *s* one *d*. *Educ:* Wellington Coll. Joined 5th Royal Inniskilling Dragoon Guards, 1925; served Palestine, 1938-39 (despatches); France and Flanders, 1940 (DSO); NW Europe, 1944 (Bar to DSO); Comdr N Midland District and 49 Armoured Div., Dec. 1951-55; Comdr, East Anglian District, 1955-58; retired, 1958. DL Essex, 1958. *Recreations:* steeplechasing, hunting, polo, fishing, shooting, racquets. *Address:* Abbots Croft, Chappel, Essex. *T:* Fordham 232.

**HARDING, Rosamond Evelyn Mary,** PhD, LittD; *b* 1898; *d* of late W. A. Harding and Ethel Adela Harding, Madingley Hall, Cambs. *Educ:* Newnham Coll., Cambridge. PhD (Cambridge), 1931, LittD, 1941 (for research on subjects connected with music). Held Airplane Pilot's "A" Licence, 1936-39. *Publications:* A History of the Piano-Forte, 1933; Origins of Musical Time and Expression, 1938; edition of the Twelve Piano-Forte Sonatas of L. Guistini di Pistoia, 1732, 1933; edition of Il Primo Libro d'Intavolaura di Balli d'Arpicordo di Gio, Maria Radino, 1592, 1961 (in MS Thematic Cataloque of the works of Matthew Locke). Towards a Law of Creative Thought, 1936; An Anatomy of Inspiration, 3rd edn 1948 (corrected repr. of 2nd edn with new preface, 1967); Matthew Locke: thematic catalogue, with calendar of the main events of his life, 1970. *Address:* 49 Whitecroft Road, Meldreth, near Royston, Herts.

**HARDING, Rowe; His Honour Judge Rowe Harding,** DL; County Court Judge, Circuit No 31, since 1965 (Circuit No 28, 1953-56; Circuit No 30, 1956-64); *b* 10 Sept. 1901; *s* of late Albert Harding, Swansea, and of Elizabeth Harding; *m* 1933, Elizabeth Adeline, *d* of John Owen George, Hirwaun, S Wales; one *s* one *d* (and one *s* decd). *Educ:* Gowerton County Sch.; Pembroke Coll., Cambridge. Qualified as solicitor, 1924; called to Bar, Inner Temple, 1928. Capt. Wales, Cambridge and Swansea, Rugby football, 1924-28. Home Guard, 1940-44. Contested (Lib. Nat. and C) Swansea East, 1945; Gower, 1950 and 1951. Mem. Swansea Town Council, 1945-48; Dep. Chm. Haverfordwest Quarter Sessions, 1945; Chm., 1948-49; Chancellor Diocese of St David's, 1949-; Member Governing and Rep. Bodies of Church in Wales; Mem. Council of Lampeter Coll.; Mem. Court of Governors, Univ. Coll. of Swansea, 1956-; Council, 1957. Past Chm. Radnorshire Quarter Sessions; Chm. Breconshire Quarter Sessions; Dep. Chm., Pembrokeshire Quarter Sessions; Past Dep. Chm. Carmarthenshire Quarter Sessions; Dep. Chm. Glamorganshire Quarter Sessions; Dep. Chm. Local Tribunal for Conscientious Objectors in Wales. Vice-Pres. Welsh Rugby Union, 1953-56; Chm., Glamorgan County Cricket Club, 1959-; Pres. Royal Institution of S Wales, 1960-61. Chm. Welsh Regional Cttee, Cheshire Homes, 1961-63; Cheshire Foundation Trustee, 1962-70. Mem., Nat. Advisory Coun. on the Training of Magistrates, 1964. Judge of Provincial Court of Church in Wales, 1966-. DL Glamorgan, 1970. *Publication:* Rugby Reminiscences and Opinions, 1929; Rugby in Wales, 1970. *Recreations:* walking, gardening, watching Rugby football and cricket. *Address:* The Old

Rectory, Ilston, Gower, near Swansea, Glamorgan. *T:* Penmaen 243.

**HARDINGE,** family name of **Viscount Hardinge** and **Baron Hardinge of Penshurst.**

**HARDINGE,** 4th Viscount *cr* 1846, of Lahore, and of King's Newton, Derbyshire; **Caryl Nicholas Charles Hardinge,** MBE 1946; Chairman: Greenshields Incorporated (investment dealers) and Greenshields Ltd; Ritz-Carlton Hotel Co. of Montreal Ltd; Member: Montreal Stock Exchange; Canadian Stock Exchange; Toronto Stock Exchange; Director: The Jockey Club Ltd; Jamaica Public Service Co., Ltd; Mt Royal Jockey Club Inc.; Electra Investments (Canada), Ltd; Holt, Renfrew & Co. Ltd; Phœnix Assurance Company; Markborough Properties Ltd; Trizec Corporation Ltd; *b* London, England, 25 Dec. 1905; *s* of 3rd Viscount Hardinge of Lahore, and Mary, Marchioness of Abergavenny (*d* 1954); *S* father 1924; *m* 1928, Margaret Elizabeth Arnott, *d* of Hugh Fleming, Ottawa; one *s* two *d. Educ:* Harrow. Served with 7th Queen's Own Hussars as Lieut and as ADC to Governor-Gen. of Canada, 1926-28. Partner, Kitcat & Aitken, London, 1931-51, and mem., London Stock Exchange. Served as Military Asst, with rank of Major, to Adjt-Gen. to the Forces, 1941-45. *Heir: s* Hon. (Henry) Nicholas (Paul) Hardinge [*b* 15 Aug. 1929; *m* 1955, Zoë Molson, Canada; three *s*]. *Address:* 1523 Summerhill Avenue, Montreal, Canada. *Clubs:* Turf; Toronto, York (Toronto); Mount Royal, Mount Bruno Country, Montreal Racket, St James's (Montreal); Links (NY); Lyford Cay (Nassau).
*See also Maj.-Gen. F. G. Beaumont-Nesbitt, Earl Fortescue.*

**HARDINGE OF PENSHURST,** 3rd Baron *cr* 1910; **George Edward Charles Hardinge;** *b* 31 Oct. 1921; *o s* of 2nd Baron Hardinge of Penshurst, PC, GCB, GCVO, MC, and Helen Mary Cecil; *S* father, 1960; *m* 1st, 1944, Janet Christine Goschen (marr. diss. 1962, she *d* 1970), *d* of late Lt-Col F. C. C. Balfour, CIE, CVO, CBE, MC; three *s*; 2nd, 1966, Margaret Trezise; one *s*. *Educ:* Eton; Royal Naval College, Dartmouth. RN 1940-47; subsequently in publishing. *Recreations:* reading, fishing, gardening. *Heir: s* Hon. Julian Alexander Hardinge, *b* 23 Aug. 1945. *Address:* Hunts Barn, Mayfield, Sussex. *T:* Mayfield 2151. *Clubs:* Brooks's, Savile.
*See also Lieut-Col J. F. D. Johnston.*

**HARDINGE, Sir Robert,** 6th Bt *cr* 1801; *b* 3 Dec. 1887; *s* of Edmond Cecil Hardinge (*d* 1890) (*g s* of 2nd Bt) and Harriet, *d* of James Fontaine; *S* kinsman, Sir Charles Edmund Hardinge, 5th Bt, 1968; *m* 1st, 1911, Emma Vera (marr. diss., 1938), *d* of Charles Arnold; one *s* one *d*; 2nd 1947, Mrs. Nellie May Houser. *Heir: s* Robert Arnold Hardinge, *b* 19 Dec. 1914. *Address:* The Rockland Hotel, Denver, Colorado, USA.

**HARDINGHAM, Sir Robert (Ernest),** Kt 1969; CMG 1953; OBE 1947; Chief Executive, Air Registration Board, 1947-68; *b* 16 Dec. 1903; *s* of late Robert Henry Hardingham and Florence Elizabeth Hardingham; *m* 1929, I. Everett; one *s* one *d. Educ:* Farnborough; de Havilland Technical Coll. RAE Farnborough, 1918-21; de Havilland Aircraft Co., 1921-34; Air Min., 1934-37; Air Registration Board, 1937-. CEng; FRAeS 1949 (Empire and Commonwealth Lecturer, 1952). Wakefield Gold Medal, RAeS, 1965; Silver Medal, Royal Aero Club, 1965. Cavaliere Ordino Merito della Repubblica Italiana. *Publications:* many technical papers. *Recreation:* golf. *Address:* Brackenwood, Dukes Kiln Drive, Gerrard's Cross, Bucks. *T:* Gerrard's Cross 84490. *Clubs:* Royal Aero, Airways Flying.

**HARDISTY, Charles William,** CB 1950; *b* 18 Jan. 1893; *s* of late Charles Henry Hardisty, Manchester; *m* 1922, Dorothy Mayhew Girling. *Educ:* Manchester Grammar Sch.; St John's Coll., Cambridge. Served in Army, 1916-18, and Naval Intelligence Service, 1918-19. Joined HM Customs and Excise, 1919; Commissioner of Customs and Excise, and Dir of Establishments and Organisation, 1946-54, retired. *Address:* Fjaerland, Pine Trees Close, Worlingham, Beccles, Suffolk.

**HARDMAN, Amy Elizabeth;** Matron, The Royal Free Hospital, London, 1953-70; *b* 23 Dec. 1909; *d* of late Charlton James Hardman and Elizabeth Clark. *Educ:* Godolphin and Latymer Sch., Hammersmith; Rosebery Sch. for Girls, Epsom. General Training, St Bartholomew's Hosp., London, 1930-34 (SRN); Midwifery Training, Kingston County Hosp., 1937 (SCM); Asst Matron, Sister Tutor, Metropolitan Hosp., E8, 1937-42; Matron, The Guest Hospital, Dudley, Worcs, 1942-49; Matron, St Margaret's Hospital, Epping, 1949-53. *Publication:* An Introduction to Ward Management, 1970. *Address:* Apple Tree Cottage, Main Street, Northiam, Rye, Sussex. *T:* Northiam 2319.

**HARDMAN, David Rennie,** MA, LLB; JP; Secretary, Cassel Educational Trust; Secretary, Stafford Cripps Memorial Appeal and Trustees; *b* 1901; *s* of David Hardman, MSc, and Isobel Rennie, Mansfield House University Settlement; *m* 1928, Freda Mary Riley; one *d*; *m* 1946, Barbara, *er d* of late Herbert Lambert, Bath; *one s* one *d. Educ:* Coleraine Academical Instn; Christ's Coll., Cambridge. Mem. Railway Clerks' Assoc., 1919-21; Pres. Cambridge Union Soc., 1925; Contested (Lab) Cambridge Borough, 1929. Cambridge Borough Councillor and Cambridge County Councillor, 1937-46; late Chm. Cambs Education Cttee; JP Cambridge, 1941-47; MP (Lab) Darlington, 1945-51; Parl. Sec., Min. of Education, 1945-51; contested (Lab) Rushcliffe Div. of Notts, 1955; leader UK delegns UNESCO, Paris 1946, Mexico 1947, Beirut 1948, Paris 1949, Florence 1950, Paris 1951; Vice-Pres. Shaw Soc.; Pres., Holiday Fellowship, 1962-69. Visiting Prof. of English Literature, Elmira, New York, 1964-66. Barclay Acheson Prof. Internat. Studies, Macalester Coll., Minn, 1967. *Publications:* What about Shakespeare?, 1939; Poems of Love and Affairs, 1949; Telscombe: A Sussex Village, 1964. *Recreation:* gardening. *Address:* Bankyfield, Hurstpierpoint, Sussex. *T:* Hurstpierpoint 3194. *Club:* Savile.

**HARDMAN, Air Chief Marshal Sir Donald;** *see* Hardman, Sir J. D. I.

**HARDMAN, Sir Henry,** KCB 1962 (CB 1956); Chairman: Covent Garden Market Authority, since 1967; Home-Grown Cereals Authority, since 1968; Governor and Trustee, Reserve Bank of Rhodesia, since 1967; *b* 15 Dec. 1905; *s* of late Harry and late Bertha Hardman; *m* 1937, Helen Diana, *d* of late Robert Carr Bosanquet; one *s* two *d. Educ:* Manchester Central High Sch.; University of Manchester. Lecturer for Workers' Educational Association, 1929-34; Economics Tutor, University of Leeds, 1934-45; joined Ministry of Food, 1940; Deputy Head, British Food Mission to N America, 1946-48; Under-Sec., Ministry of Food, 1948-53; Minister, UK Permanent Delegation, Paris, 1953-54; Dep. Sec., Ministry of Agriculture, Fisheries and Food, 1955-60; Dep. Sec., Ministry of Aviation, 1960; Permanent Sec., 1961-63:

Permanent Sec., Ministry of Defence, 1963-64; Permanent Under Sec. of State, Min. of Defence, 1964-66; Mem., Monopolies Commn, 1967-70 (Dep. Chm., 1967-68). Hon. LLD Manchester, 1965. *Address:* 31 Cholmeley Park, N6. *T:* 01-340 7559. *Clubs:* Reform, Farmers'.

**HARDMAN, Air Chief Marshal Sir (James) Donald Innes,** GBE 1958 (OBE 1940); KCB 1952 (CB 1945); DFC; Royal Air Force retired; *b* 1899; *s* of James Hardman, MA, Delph, Yorks; *m* 1930, Dorothy, *d* of William Ashcroft Thompson, JP, Larkenshaw, Chobham; two *s* one *d*. *Educ:* Malvern; Hertford Coll., Oxford. Served European War, 1916-19; joined RAF 1918; Wing Comdr, 1939; Air Commodore, 1941; Air Vice-Marshal, 1945; Air Officer i/c Administration, Air Comd, SE Asia, 1946-47; Asst Chief of Air Staff (Ops), 1947-49; Comdt RAF Air Staff Coll., 1949-51; AOC-in-C, Home Comd, 1951-52; Air Marshal 1952; Chief of Air Staff, RAAF, 1952-54; Air Chief Marshal, 1955; Air Mem. Supply and Organisation, 1954-57; retired, 1958. *Address:* Lower Baybridge, Owslebury, Hants. *Clubs:* Oxford and Cambridge University, Royal Air Force.
*See also Sir W. J. F. North, Bt.*

**HARDWICK, Christopher,** MD, FRCP; Physician, Guy's Hospital, since 1946; *b* 13 Jan. 1911; *s* of Thomas Mold Hardwick and Harriet Taylor; *m* 1938, Joan Dorothy Plummer; two *s*. *Educ:* Berkhamsted Sch.; Trinity Hall, Cambridge; Middlesex Hospital. MRCS, LRCP 1935; MA (Cambridge) 1937; MD (Cambridge) 1940; FRCP 1947. House Physician, House Surgeon and Med. Registrar, Middlesex Hosp., 1935 and 1938-41; House physician and Registrar, Hosp. for Sick Children, Gt Ormond Street, 1936-38. Wing Comdr, Medical Specialist, RAF Med. Service, 1941-46. Cons. Phys., Dorking Hosp., 1946-; Hon. Vis. Phys., Johns Hopkins Hosp., Baltimore, 1954. Mem. Council, RCP, 1965-68; Member: Assoc. of Physicians of Great Britain and Ireland; British Gastro-Enterological Soc.; Board of Governors, Guy's Hospital, 1967-. *Publications:* contribs to medical literature. *Recreations:* gardening, reading. *Address:* 107 Harley Street, W1. *T:* 01-935 2255. *Club:* United University.

**HARDWICK, Donald Ross,** CIE 1947; *b* 26 Feb. 1895; *s* of Arthur Hardwick, MD; *m* 1st, 1918, Lilian Rosa (*d* 1956), *d* of George Thomas Rees; (one *s* decd); 2nd, 1957, Madeleine Bosworth (*d* 1964); 3rd, 1965, Doris Maud Noakes. *Educ:* Blundells Sch., Tiverton, Devon. Joined Indian Police, 1914; Deputy Inspector-General, Intelligence Branch, Bengal, 1943; Commissioner of Police, Calcutta, 1946-47. King's Police Medal, 1944, Indian Police Medal, 1939; Jubilee Medal, 1935, Coronation Medal, 1937. *Recreations:* golf, bridge. *Address:* 1 Wykeham Lodge, Woodend Road, Torquay, Devon. *T:* Torquay 23353. *Clubs:* Royal Torbay Yacht (Torquay); Torquay Golf.

**HARDWICK, Prof. James Leslie,** MDS, MSc, PhD; FDSRCS; Professor of Preventive Dentistry, University of Manchester, since 1960; President, European Organisation for Caries Research; *b* 27 March 1913; *o s* of George Hardwicke and Mary Ann Hardwick; *m* 1954, Eileen Margaret Isobel Gibson; two *s* two *d*. *Educ:* Rugby Sch.; Birmingham Univ. MDS 1948, PhD 1950, Birmingham; FDSRCS 1954; MSc 1964. Private and hospital dental practice, 1935-39. Served War of 1939-45, Army Dental Corps. University of Birmingham: Lecturer, 1945-48, Sen. Lecturer, 1948-52, in Operative Dental Surgery; Reader in Dental Surgery, 1952-60. *Publications:* editor of and contributor to dental and other scientific journals and textbooks. *Address:* 167 Stanley Road, Cheadle Hulme, Cheshire SK8 6RF. *T:* 061-437 3555.

**HARDWICKE,** 9th Earl of *cr* 1754; **Philip Grantham Yorke;** Baron Hardwicke, 1733; Viscount Royston, 1754; Major SAS; company director; *b* 9 April 1906; *s* of late Hon. Alfred Yorke, 2nd *s* of 7th Earl and Gladys Dunlop (*d* 1933), *d* of Andrew Vans Dunlop Best (she *m* 2nd, Hon. Percy Thellusson); *S* uncle, 1936; *m* 1st, 1934, Sarah (*d* 1965), *d* of late Rt Hon. Sir Francis Lindlay, PC, GCMG; one *s* three *d*; 2nd, 1970, Mrs Enid Boulting. *Educ:* Eton; RMC. *Recreations:* yachting, shooting, fishing, hunting. *Heir: s* Viscount Royston, *qv*. *T:* 01-589 1716. *Clubs:* Travellers' (Paris); White's; Royal Yacht Squadron (Cowes); Household Brigade Yacht; Brook, Racquet and Tennis (New York).
*See also Earl of Leicester.*

**HARDY;** *see* Cozens-Hardy and Gathorne-Hardy.

**HARDY, Sir Alister (Clavering),** Kt 1957; FRS 1940; MA, DSc Oxon; FLS, FZS; Hon. Fellow of Exeter College, Oxford; Hon. Fellow of Merton College, Oxford (Fellow, 1946-63); Professor Emeritus, University of Oxford; Director, Religious Experience Research Unit, Manchester College, Oxford; *b* Nottingham, 10 Feb. 1896; *y s* of late Richard Hardy; *m* 1927, Sylvia Lucy, 2nd *d* of late Prof. Walter Garstang; one *s* one *d*. *Educ:* Oundle Sch.; Exeter Coll., Oxford. Lieut and Capt. 2/1 Northern Cyclist Bn, 1915-19; attached RE, Asst Camouflage Officer, Staff of XIII Army Corps, 1918; Christopher Welch Biological Research Scholar, 1920; Oxford Biological Scholar at the Stazione Zoologica, Naples, 1920; Asst Naturalist in Fisheries Dept, Min. of Agriculture and Fisheries, 1921-24; Chief Zoologist to the Discovery Expedition, 1924-28; Prof. of Zoology and Oceanography, University Coll., Hull, 1928-42; Regius Prof. of Natural History, University of Aberdeen, 1942-45; Linacre Prof. of Zoology, University of Oxford, 1946-61; Prof. of Zoological Field Studies, Oxford, 1961-63; Gifford Lectr, Univ. of Aberdeen, for 1963-65. Scientific Medal of Zoological Soc., 1939. Hon. LLD Aberdeen; Hon. DSc: Southampton; Hull. *Publications:* The Open Sea, Part I, The World of Plankton, 1956; The Open Sea, Part II, Fish and Fisheries, 1958; The Living Stream, 1965; The Divine Flame, 1966; Great Waters, 1967; Memoirs on Biological Oceanography; joint editor of Bulletins of Marine Ecology. *Recreation:* water-colour sketching. *Address:* 7 Capel Close, Oxford. *Club:* Athenæum.

**HARDY, Rev. Basil Augustus;** Canon Residentiary of Chester Cathedral since 1946 and Precentor since 1943; *b* 1901; *s* of Rev. Henry Hardy, MA; *m* 1935, Helena Edgar English. *Educ:* Trinity Coll., Glenalmond; Keble Coll., Oxford; Westcott House, Cambridge. Asst Curate St Matthew's, Thorpe Hamlet, Norwich, 1924-27; Chaplain and Asst Master, Elstree Sch., 1927-38; Headmaster of the Choir Sch. and Chaplain Choral, Chester Cathedral, 1938-46. MA 1927, MRST 1944, FTCL 1954; Hon. Sec. Choir Schools Assoc., 1946-57; Chaplain to High Sheriff of Cheshire, 1947; Proctor in Convocation and Mem. of Church Assembly, 1955-64; Chaplain to Mayor of Chester, 1956; Headmaster of the Choir Sch., Chester Cathedral, 1955-63. *Recreations:* woodwork and clocks. *Address:* 13 Abbey Street, Chester. *T:* Chester 20157.

**HARDY, Gen. Sir Campbell Richard,** KCB 1957 (CB 1954); CBE 1951; DSO 1944 (and 2 Bars); RM retired; Director of the Coal Utilisation Council, 1960-70; *b* 24 May 1906; *s* of Major Frank Buckland Hardy, OBE; *m* 1931, Phyllis Cole Sutton; one *s* one *d*. *Educ:* Felsted Sch. 2nd Lieut RM, 1924; HMS Renown, 1927-29; courses, 1929-30; HMS Rodney, 1930-31; Physical Training Officer, Portsmouth Div., RM, 1932-37; RNC Dartmouth, 1937-38; HMS Vindictive, 1938-39; served War of 1939-45; Adjt Ports Div., RM, 1939-40; RM Div., 1940-43; 46 Commando, RM, 1943-44; Comd 3 Commando Bde, 1944-45; Staff, RM Office, 1946-47; Chief Instructor, Sch. of Combined Ops, 1947-48; Comd 3 Commando Bde, 1948-51; CO Depot, RM, Deal, 1951; Chief of Staff Royal Marines, 1952-55; Commandant General of the Royal Marines, 1955-59; retired, 1959; Col Comdt, Royal Marines, 1961-66. *Address:* Bunch Lane House, Haslemere, Surrey. *T:* Haselmere 3177. *Club:* United Service.

**HARDY, Sir Edward,** Kt 1945; *b* 1 Aug. 1887; *s* of Col Charles Stewart Hardy, Chilham Castle, Canterbury, and Fanny Alice, *d* of Matthew Bell, Bourne Park, Canterbury. *Educ:* Eastbourne Coll.; Wye Coll. Positions held at various times and now relinquished: Member of Kent County Council for 33 years (Alderman, 1935-58, Chm., 1936-49); Governor of Wye Coll. for 26 years (Chm. 16 years; Chm. Finance and General Purposes Cttee 25 years); Chm. and/or President Ashford Division of Kent Conservative Assoc. for 30 years; Deputy Chm. Kent War Agricultural Executive Cttee, 1939-46. Formerly: JP for Kent; Mem. LPTB; Mem. London Transport Executive; Vice-Chm. Kent Standing Joint Cttee; Supervisor of Special Constables, Ashford Div.; responsible for organising the first Royal Observer Corps Posts in Kent; Canterbury Diocesan Conf.; Canterbury Diocesan Board of Finance; Pres. Kent or Romney Marsh Sheepbreeders' Assoc.; Kent River Authority; Vice-Pres., County Councils Assoc.; Chm., Kent Br. of CLA; Chm., Kent Jt Adv. Water Cttee; Vice-Pres., Nat. Fedn of Young Farmers' Clubs; Dep. Chm., Sponsors of the University of Kent at Canterbury. Is a Life Vice-Pres. (Past Pres.), Kent Fedn of Young Farmers' Clubs. Hon. Fellow, Wye Coll., University of London. Hon. DCL University of Kent at Canterbury. Farms 1497 acres in Kent. *Recreations:* shooting, fishing, producing dramatic performances. *Address:* Boughton Court, Ashford, Kent. *T:* Wye 413. *Club:* Junior Carlton.

**HARDY, Francis,** MA, LLD; *b* 26 March 1879. *Educ:* Trinity Coll., Dublin. Headmaster, Elizabeth Coll., Guernsey, 1924-39; called to Bar, Gray's Inn, 1945. *Publication:* A Headmaster Remembers, 1969. *Address:* Etrenne, Grandes Rocques, Guernsey, CI.

**HARDY, Alderman Sir Harry,** Kt 1956; JP; ATI; chartered textile technologist; Director, Harry Hardy Ltd, W. E. Tetley Group; *b* 10 Sept. 1896; *e s* of Friend and Elizabeth Ann Hardy, Rods Mills, Morley; *m* 1922, Remie (*d* 1955), *d* of Benjamin Siddle, Morley; *m* 1957, Mollie, *d* of Henry Dixon, Morley. *Educ:* Univ. of Leeds. Chemical and fibre manufacturer. Lectr in Textiles, Dewsbury Technical Coll., 1920-35, Head of Textile Industries Dept, 1925-35; Lecturer in Textiles, Huddersfield Technical Coll., 1922-25; Examiner to City and Guilds of London Institute, 1941-44. Pres. Morley and District Textile Soc., 1936-; Founder Pres. Morley Musical Soc., 1943-58; Chm. Youth Employment Cttee, 1943-; Chm. Local Employment Cttee, 1950-68; Founder Pres., Rotary Club of Morley, 1949-; Vice-Pres. Textile Inst., 1956-59; Liveryman, Cordwainers' Co., 1946-. Hon. Life Pres., Batley and Morley Conservative Assoc. (55 years active service). County Councillor, West Riding of Yorks, 1945-49, County Alderman, 1949-; JP Borough of Morley, 1948-. *Recreations:* education for textiles, science and technology of textiles; youth employment, music and the arts; Parish Church Men's Fellowship. *Address:* 45 The Roundway, Dartmouth Park, Morley, near Leeds. *T:* Morley 5150.

**HARDY, Sir James (Douglas),** Kt 1962; CBE 1955 (OBE 1953); Project Manager and Chief United Nations Adviser, UN Special Fund Public Service Reform and Training Project, Tehran, since 1968; *b* 8 June 1915; *s* of James Percy Hardy; *m* 1937, Robina, *d* of Robert Bookless; two *s*. *Educ:* Gonville and Caius Coll., Cambridge. ICS, 1937-47; Pakistan Civil Service, 1947-61. Dist and Sessions Judge and Dep. Comr, Punjab, up to 1952; Jt Sec. to Govt of Pakistan, 1953; served in: Min. of Communications, as Jt Sec. in charge, 1953-56; Cabinet Secretariat; Min. of Law. Apptd Jt Sec. in charge Estabt Div., President's Secretariat, 1959; promoted Sec., Govt of Pakistan President's Secretariat, 1960; retired, 1961. Ford Foundation representative, in N Africa, 1961-67. Star of Pakistan (SPk), 1961; Comdr Order of Tunisia, 1967. *Recreations:* riding, golf and motoring. *Address:* PO Box 1555, 10 Kh. Namdar, Elahieh, Shemiran, Tehran, Iran. *T:* Tehran 830744. *Club:* Oxford and Cambridge University.

**HARDY, Peter;** MP (Lab) Rother Valley since 1970; *b* 17 July 1931; *s* of Lawrence Hardy and of Mrs I. Hardy, Wath upon Dearne; *m* 1954, Margaret Anne Brookes; one *s* (decd). *Educ:* Wath upon Dearne Grammar Sch.; Westminster Coll., London; Sheffield Univ. Schoolmaster in S Yorkshire, 1953-70. Member: Wath upon Dearne UDC, 1960-70 (Chm. Council, 1968-69); Governing Body of Wath Grammar Sch. (Chm. of Governors, 1969-70); Pres., Wath upon Dearne Labour Party, 1960-68; contested (Lab): Scarborough and Whitby, 1964; Sheffield, Hallam, 1966. *Publications:* various articles on educational and other subjects. *Recreations:* watching wild life, notably badgers; exhibiting a Samoyed dog. *Address:* 4 Buckleigh Road, Wath upon Dearne, Rotherham, Yorkshire. *T:* Wath upon Dearne 3375. *Club:* Rawmarsh Trades and Labour.

**HARDY, Sir Rupert (John),** 4th Bt, *cr* 1876; Lieutenant-Colonel Life Guards, retired; *b* 24 Oct. 1902; *s* of 3rd Bt and Violet Agnes Evelyn, *d* of Hon. Sir Edward Chandos Leigh, KCB, KC; *S* father 1953; *m* 1930, Hon. Diana Joan Allsopp, *er d* of 3rd Baron Hindlip; one *s* one *d*. *Educ:* Eton; Trinity Hall, Cambridge. BA 1925. Joined The Life Guards, 1925; Major, 1940; retired, 1948, and rejoined as RARO, 1952; Lieut-Col comdg Household Cavalry Regt, 1952-56; ceased to belong to R of O, Dec. 1956; granted hon. rank of Lieut-Col. *Recreations:* hunting and shooting. *Heir: s* Richard Charles Hardy, *b* 6 Feb. 1945. *Address:* Spratton House, Spratton, Northampton, *T:* Creaton 259. *Club:* Turf.

*See also Sir Robert Black, Bt.*

**HARDY-ROBERTS, Brig. (temp.) Geoffrey Paul,** CB 1945; CBE 1944 (OBE 1941); JP; DL; Master of HM's Household since 1967; Extra Equerry to the Queen since 1967; Secretary-Superintendent of Middlesex Hospital, 1946-67; *b* 1907; *s* of A. W. Roberts; *m* 1945, Eldred, *widow* of Col J. R. Macdonell, DSO. *Educ:*

Eton; RMC Sandhurst. Regular Commission, 9th Lancers, 1926-37. Served War of 1939-45 (OBE, CBE, CB). JP 1960, DL 1964, High Sheriff, 1965, Sussex. Officer, Legion of Merit, 1945. *Address:* The Mill House, Fittleworth, Sussex; St James's Palace, SW1. *Clubs:* Turf, Beefsteak.

**HARE,** family name of **Viscount Blakenham** and **Earl of Listowel.**

**HARE, Frederick Kenneth,** PhD; FRSC; Professor of Geography and Physics, University of Toronto, since 1969; *b* Wylye, Wilts, 5 Feb. 1919; *s* of Frederick Eli Hare and Irene Smith; *m* 1st, 1941, Suzanne Alice Bates (marr. diss. 1952); one *s*; 2nd, 1953, Helen Neilson Morrill; one *s* one *d*. *Educ:* Windsor Grammar Sch.; King's Coll., University of London (BSc); Univ. of Montreal (PhD). Lectr in Geography, Univ. of Manchester, 1940-41; War service in Air Min., Meteorological Office, 1941-45; Asst and Assoc. Prof. of Geography, McGill Univ., Montreal, 1945-52; Prof. of Geography and Meteorology, McGill Univ., 1952-64, Chm. of Dept, 1962-64; Dean of Faculty of Arts and Science, 1962-64; Prof. of Geography, Univ. of London (King's Coll.), 1964-66; Master of Birkbeck Coll., Univ. of London, 1966-68; Pres., Univ. of British Columbia, 1968-69. fellow, King's Coll., London, 1967-. Mem. Nat. Research Coun. of Canada, 1962-64; Chm. of Bd, Arctic Inst. of N America, 1963; Mem., NERC, 1965-68; Dir, Resources for the Future, 1969-. Pres., Canadian Assoc. of Geographers, 1964; FRSC 1968; Fellow, Amer. Meteorological Soc., 1969; Hon. Fellow, American Geographical Soc., 1963; Hon. Pres., Assoc. of Amer. Geographers, 1964. Hon. LLD: Queen's (Canada) Univ., 1964; Univ. of W Ontario, 1968; Hon. DSc McGill, 1969. *Publications:* The Restless Atmosphere, 1953; On University Freedom, 1968; numerous articles in Quarterly Jl Royal Meteorological Soc., Geography, and other learned jls. *Recreation:* music. *Address:* University Toronto, Toronto 5, Ont, Canada. *Clubs:* Athenæum; McGill Faculty (Montreal) (Hon. Life Mem.).

**HARE, Rt. Rev. John Tyrrell Holmes;** *see* Bedford, Bishop Suffragan of.

**HARE, Prof. Patrick James;** Grant Professor of Dermatology, University of Edinburgh, since 1968; *b* 18 Jan. 1920; *yr s* of John Henry Hare and Isabella McIntyre; *m* 1945, Mary, *yr d* of late Col A. H. Bridges, CB, CIE, DSO, and Dorothea Seth-Smith; two *s*. *Educ:* Westminster City Sch.; University Coll., London (Andrews Scholar); University Coll. Hosp. Med. Sch.; Johns Hopkins Univ. (Rockefeller Student). MB, BS, 1944; MD Johns Hopkins, 1944; RAMC 1945-48 (Burma, Singapore); Registrar, Dept of Dermatology, 1948; MRCP 1949; FRCP 1964; MRCPE 1968. Travelling Fellow, Univ. of London, 1951 (Paris, Zürich); Consultant Dermatologist, UCH, 1951-68; Research worker and Senior Lecturer in Dermatology, UCH Med. Sch., 1952-59; MD London 1954; Cons. Dermatologist, Whittington Hosp., London, 1959-68. Editor, British Journal of Dermatology, 1959-67. Sec. Sect. of Dermatology, Royal Society of Medicine, 1961-62. *Publications:* The Skin, 1966; Basic Dermatology, 1966; scientific and med. articles in various jls. *Recreations:* gardening, music. *Address:* Department of Dermatology, Royal Infirmary, Edinburgh. *T:* 031-229 2477, Ext. 112; 7 East Castle Road, Edinburgh 10. *T:* 031-229 3054.

**HARE, Kenneth;** *see* Hare, F. K.

**HARE, Major Sir Ralph Leigh,** 4th Bt *cr* 1818; late Coldstream Guards; *b* 19 Jan. 1903; *s* of 3rd Bt and Lady Florence Mary Constance Marsham, *d* of 4th Earl of Romney; *S* father, 1933; *m* 1st, 1928, Doreen (marr. diss. 1944), *e d* of late Sir Richard Bagge, DSO; one *s* one *d*; 2nd, 1945, Natalie (marr. diss. 1958), *o c* of Mrs E. Vincent Irwin and of late Capt. Baron de Langué; two *d*; 3rd, 1960, Barbara, *y d* of late Joseph Walton; one *d*. *Educ:* Eton. *Heir: s* Thomas Hare [*b* 27 July 1930; *m* 1961, Lady Rose Amanda Bligh, *d* of late Earl of Darnley, and of Mrs Nancy Cotterell; two *d*]. *Address:* Stow Bardolph, King's Lynn, Norfolk. *Club:* Guards.

**HARE, Hon. Mrs Richard;** *see* Gordine, Dora.

**HARE, Ven. Richard;** *see* Hare, Ven. (Thomas) Richard.

**HARE, Richard Mervyn,** FBA 1964; White's Professor of Moral Philosophy and Fellow of Corpus Christi College, Oxford, since 1966; *b* 21 March 1919; *s* of late Charles Francis Aubone Hare and late Louise Kathleen (*née* Simonds); *m* 1947, Catherine, *d* of Sir Harry Verney, 4th Bt, *qv*; one *s* three *d*. *Educ:* Rugby (Schol.); Balliol Coll., Oxford (Schol.). Commissioned Royal Artillery, 1940; Lieut, Indian Mountain Artillery, 1941; Prisoner of War, Singapore and Siam, 1942-45. 1st Lit. Hum. 1947. Fellow and Tutor in Philosophy, Balliol Coll., Oxford, 1947-66; Vis. Fellow, Princeton, 1957; Wilde Lecturer in Natural Religion, Oxford, 1963-66; Vis. Fellow, Australian Nat. Univ., Canberra, 1966; Vis. Prof., University of Michigan, 1968. Mem. Nat. Road Safety Advisory Council, 1966-68. *Publications:* Oxford's Traffic, 1948; The Language of Morals, 1952; Freedom and Reason, 1963; papers in Mind, Proc. Aristotelian Soc., Traffic Engrg and Control, etc. *Recreations:* music, gardening, the study of architecture, town planning and transport problems. *Address:* Saffron House, Ewelme, Oxford.

**HARE, Robertson;** actor; *b* 17 Dec. 1891; *s* of Frank Homer Hare and Louisa Mary Robertson; *m* 1915, Irene Mewton (*d* 1969); one *d*. *Educ:* Margate Coll. Trained under Cairns James; first walked on as torch bearer in Sir John Martin Harvey's production of Oedipus Rex, Covent Garden, 1912; first big part Grumpy in the play of that name, 1914-16; joined the Army and served in France, 1917-18; opened with Tom Walls Leslie Henson management at Shaftesbury Theatre, 1922, in farce Tons of Money; continued association with this management when they transferred to Aldwych Theatre and remained there with the Ben Travers farces for eleven years; film work in parts created in the farces: teamed up with Alfred Drayton, 1936, in Vernon Sylvaine's Aren't Men Beasts, Strand Theatre, followed by Spot of Bother by same author, Ben Travers' two farces Banana Ridge and Spotted Dick, Sylvaine's Women Aren't Angels, Ben Travers' play She Follows Me About; with Alfred Drayton in Sylvaine's farce, Madame Louise, Garrick; with Ralph Lynn in Ben Travers' Outrageous Fortune, Winter Garden; with Alfred Drayton, then Arthur Riscoe, in Sylvaine's farce, One Wild Oat, Garrick, 1948 (filmed, 1951); with Arthur Riscoe in Sylvaine's farce, Will Any Gentleman?, Strand, 1950; with Ralph Lynn in Ben Travers' Wild Horses, Aldwych, 1952; The Party Spirit, 1954; Man Alive, Aldwych, 1956; The Bride and the Bachelor, Duchess, 1956; Fine Fettle, Palace, 1959; The Bride Comes Back, Vaudeville, 1960-61; A funny thing happened on the way to the Forum, Strand, 1963; Oh Clarence!, Lyric, 1968. Has appeared in many films, from 1929. BBC TV Series, All Gas and Gaiters, 1968-70. *Publication:* Yours Indubitably, 1957. *Recreations:* writing, swimming, golf. *Address:* 105 St Mary Abbots' Court, W14. *Club:* Savage.

**HARE, Ronald,** MD (London); Emeritus Professor of Bacteriology in University of London since 1964 and Hon. Consulting Bacteriologist to St Thomas's Hospital since 1951; *b* 30 Aug. 1899; *s* of late Frederick Hare, MD, and Elizabeth Roxby Hare, Esh Winning, Co. Durham; *m* 1932, Barbara Thurgarland Wintle (*d* 1966); one *s*. *Educ:* Royal Masonic Sch.; Birkbeck Coll.; St Mary's Hosp., London. Scholar, Institute of Pathology and Research, 1925, and asst in Inoculation Dept, St Mary's Hospital, London, 1926-30; first asst in Research Laboratories, Queen Charlotte's Hospital, London, 1931-36; Research Associate in Connaught Laboratories, Univ. of Toronto, and Lectr in Dept of Hygiene and Preventive Medicine, 1936; has carried out extensive researches on the streptococci (Catherine Bishop Harman Prize of BMA and Nicholls Prize of Royal Society of Medicine); largely responsible for the planning and building of the penicillin plant set up in the University of Toronto by the Govt of Canada. Professor of Bacteriology, University of London, 1946-64. Mem. Council: Wright-Fleming Inst., 1952-60; Nuffield Inst. of Comparative Med., 1960-68; Fountains and Carshalton Gp Hospital Management Cttee, 1966. Pres., Pathology Sect., 1963-64, and Mem. Council, Royal Society of Medicine, 1965-68; Examr in Universities of: London, Malaya, Birmingham, West Indies, East Africa, Ibadan. *Publications:* Pomp and Pestilence, 1954; An Outline of Bacteriology and Immunity, 1956; Bacteriology and Immunity for Nurses, 1961; The Birth of Penicillin, 1970; many papers in scientific and medical jls. *Recreations:* water-colour painting, the history of pestilence. *Address:* 13 Warwick Square, SW1. *T:* 01-834 6038.

**HARE, Ven. Thomas Richard;** Archdeacon of Westmorland and Furness, since 1965, and Vicar of Winster, since 1969; *b* 1922; *m* 1963, Sara, *d* of Lt-Col J. E. Spedding, OBE; one *s* one *d*. *Educ:* Marlborough; Trinity Coll., Oxford; Wescott House, Cambridge. RAF, 1942-45. Curate of Haltwhistle, 1950-52; Domestic Chaplain to Bishop of Manchester, 1952-59; Canon Residentiary of Carlisle Cathedral, 1959-65; Vicar of St George with St Luke, Barrow-in-Furness, 1965-69. *Address:* Winster Vicarage, Windermere, Westmorland. *T:* Windermere 3639.

**HARE DUKE, Rt. Rev. Michael Geoffrey;** *see* St Andrews, Dunkeld and Dunblane, Bishop of.

**HAREWOOD,** 7th Earl of, *cr* 1812; **George Henry Hubert Lascelles;** Baron Harewood, 1796; Viscount Lascelles, 1812; Artistic Director, Leeds Festival, since 1958; Artistic Adviser, New Philharmonia Orchestra, London, since 1966; *b* 7 Feb. 1923; *er s* of 6th Earl of Harewood, KG, GCVO, DSO, and HRH Princess Mary (Princess Royal; who *d* 28 March 1965); *S* father, 1947; *m* 1st, 1949, Maria Donata (marr. diss. 1967), *d* of late Erwin Stein; three *s*; 2nd, 1967, Patricia (Elizabeth), *d* of Charles Tuckwell, Australia; one *s* and one step *s*. *Educ:* Eton; King's Coll., Cambridge (MA). Served War of 1939-45, Capt. Grenadier Guards (wounded and prisoner, 1944, released May 1945); ADC to Earl of Athlone, 1945-46, Canada. Editor of magazine "Opera" 1950-53; Royal Opera House, Covent Garden: a Dir, 1951-53; on staff, 1953-60; a Dir, 1969-; Artistic Dir, Edinburgh Internat. Festival, 1961-65. Chm., Music Advisory Cttee of British Council, 1956-66; Chancellor of the Univ. of York, 1963-67; Member: Arts Council, 1966-; Gen. Adv. Council of BBC, 1969-. President: English Football Assoc.; Leeds United Football Club; English Opera Group; Rural Music Schools Assoc.; Royal Manchester College of Music; British-Italian Soc.; Dir, English Stage Company; Overseas Dir, Australian Opera. Hon. LLD: Leeds, 1959; Aberdeen, 1966; Hon. DMus Hull, 1962. *Heir:* *s* Viscount Lascelles, *qv*. *Address:* Harewood House, Leeds; 121 Hamilton Terrace, NW8.

**HARFORD, Sir James (Dundas),** KBE 1956; CMG 1943; *b* Great Yarmouth, 7 Jan. 1899; *s* of late Rev. Dundas Harford, MA; *m* 1st, 1932, Countess Thelma, *d* of Count Albert Metaxa; one *s*; 2nd, 1937, Lilias Madeline, *d* of Major Archibald Campbell; two *d*. *Educ:* Repton; Balliol Coll., Oxford (Hon. Scholar, MA). Served European War, France and Belgium, 1917-19; Asst Master, Eton Coll., 1922-25; Administrative Service, Nigeria, 1926; District administration, Bornu Province, 1926-29; Asst Sec., Nigerian Secretariat, 1930-34 and Clerk to Exec. and Legislative Councils; seconded to Colonial Office, 1934-36; Administrator of Antigua and Federal Sec. of the Leeward Islands, 1936-40; Administrator, St Kitts-Nevis, 1940-47; administered Government of Leeward Islands, on various occasions; seconded to Colonial Office, 1947-48; administered Government of Mauritius, on various occasions; Colonial Sec., Mauritius, 1948-53; Governor and Commander-in-Chief of St Helena, 1954-58. Conference Organiser, Commonwealth Institute, 1959-64. *Address:* Links Cottage, Rother Road, Seaford, Sussex.

**HARFORD, Sir (John) Timothy,** 3rd Bt *cr* 1934; Director of Singer & Friedlander Ltd, since 1970 (Local Director, 1967-69); *b* 6 July 1932; *s* of Sir George Arthur Harford, 2nd Bt and Anstice Marion, *d* of Sir Alfred Tritton, 2nd Bt; *S* father, 1967; *m* 1962, Carolyn Jane Mullens; two *s* one *d*. *Educ:* Harrow Sch.; Oxford Univ.; Harvard Business Sch. Philip Hill Higginson Erlangers Ltd, 1960-63; Dir, Birmingham Industrial Trust Ltd, 1963-67. *Recreations:* wine and food, viticulture. *Heir:* *s* Mark John Harford, *b* 6 Aug. 1964. *Address:* South House, South Littleton, Evesham, Worcs. *T:* Evesham 830478. *Clubs:* Cavalry; Union (Birmingham).

**HARGRAVE, John Gordon,** FRSA; artist and writer; *b* 1894; *s* of Gordon Hargrave, landscape painter; *m* 1919, Ruth Clark (marr. diss. 1952); one *s*. *Educ:* Wordsworth's Sch., Hawkshead. Illustrated Gulliver's Travels, and the Rose and the Ring at the age of fifteen; chief cartoonist, London Evening Times, at the age of seventeen; joined the staff of C. Arthur Pearson Ltd, 1914; enlisted in RAMC, and served with 10th (Irish) Division in Gallipoli campaign (Suvla Bay Landing), and later in Salonika; invalided out, end of 1916; Art Manager, C. Arthur Pearson Ltd, 1917-20; founded the Kibbo Kift, 1920 (later Social Credit Party, The Green Shirts); Hon. Adviser to the Alberta Govt Planning Cttee, 1936-37; issued the Alberta Report, July 1937; invented the Hargrave Automatic Navigator for Aircraft, 1937; created animal character, "Bushy", for The Sketch, 1952. *Publications:* Lonecraft, 1913, and five other handbooks on camping and the outdoor life; At Suvla Bay, 1916; Harbottle, 1924; Young Winkle, 1925; And Then Came Spring, 1926; The Pfenniger Failing, 1927; The Confession of the Kibbo Kift, 1927; The Imitation Man, 1931; Summer Time Ends, 1935; Professor Skinner alias Montagu Norman, 1939; Words Win Wars,

1940; Social Credit Clearly Explained, 1945; The Life and Soul of Paracelsus, 1951; The Paragon Dictionary, 1953; The Suvla Bay Landing, 1964; The Facts of the Case concerning the Hargrave Automatic Navigator for Aircraft (privately pr.), 1969. *Recreation;* work. *Club:* Royal Societies.

**HARGREAVES, Alfred;** *b* 15 Feb. 1899. Hon. Secretary West Derby (Liverpool) Labour Party, 1926; President Liverpool Trades Council and Labour Party, 1945. Mem., Liverpool City Council, 1928-. MP (Lab) Carlisle, 1950-55. Min. of Transport's nominee on Mersey Docks and Harbour Board. Mem., Transport Salaried Staffs Assoc.; Chm., Liverpool, North Wales and Cheshire Divisional Council. *Address:* 52 Warmington Road, Liverpool 14. *T:* Stoneycroft 3049.

**HARGREAVES, Eric Lyde;** Emeritus Fellow since 1963 (Fellow, 1925, Tutor, 1930, Senior Tutor, 1937-56), Oriel College, Oxford; *b* 13 Oct. 1898; *s* of George Harrison and Emily Frances Hargreaves. *Educ:* St Paul's Sch.; Corpus Christi Coll., Oxford (Scholar). Wounded and taken prisoner, April 1918; 1st Class Lit. Hum., 1921; PhD London, 1924; University Lecturer in Economics, 1929-35, and 1954-59; Historian, Official History of Second World War (Civil Series), 1942-52; Fellow of Royal Economic and Royal Statistical Societies. *Publications:* Restoring Currency Standards, 1926; National Debt, 1930; (with M. M. Gowing) Civil Industry and Trade, 1952; essays and articles on economic subjects. *Recreation:* walking. *Address:* Oriel College, Oxford.

**HARGREAVES, His Honour Sir Gerald de la Pryme,** Kt 1944; County Court Judge Circuit No 18, 1922-23; Circuit No 46, 1923-28; Circuit No 48, 1928; Circuit No 37, 1928-55; *s* of Thomas and Constance Hargreaves, Oakhurst, Birkdale, Lancs; *m* 1955, Mrs Winifred Elsie Johnson. *Educ:* Eton; Magdalen Coll., Oxford. Called to Bar, 1905; Mem. of Northern Circuit; Unionist candidate for Osgoldcross Div. of Yorks, Jan. 1910; Monmouth Boroughs, Dec. 1910; prospective Unionist candidate for Bedford, 1911-18; served with Bedfordshire Yeomanry, 1914-17; attached as Court-Martial Officer Xth Army Corps, 1917-19 (despatches, Belgian Croix de Guerre). Served with Home Guard, 1942-45. Chm. of London Tribunal for Conscientious Objectors, from 1939. *Publications:* Deeds of Arrangement; Operettas. *Recreations:* lawn tennis, golf, music, painting. *Address:* Mount Rise, Gorey, Jersey, CI. *T:* East 71. *Clubs:* 1900, United and Cecil, Queen's, All England Lawn Tennis and Croquet, International Lawn Tennis, Bar Lawn Tennis Society.

**HARGREAVES, Prof. John Desmond;** Professor of History, University of Aberdeen, since 1962; *b* 25 Jan. 1924; *s* of Arthur Swire Hargreaves and Margaret Hilda (*née* Duckworth); *m* 1950, Sheila Elizabeth (*née* Wilks); one *s* two *d*. *Educ:* Skipton Grammar Sch.; Bootham; Manchester Univ. War service, 1943-46. Asst Princ., War Office, 1948; Lectr in History: Manchester Univ., 1948-52; Fourah Bay Coll., Sierra Leone, 1952-54; Aberdeen Univ., 1954-62. Vis. Prof., Union Coll. Schenectady, New York, 1960-61. Mem., Kidd Cttee on Sheriff Court Records, 1966; Mem., Scottish Records Adv. Council. *Publications:* A Life of Sir Samuel Lewis, 1958; Prelude to the Partition of West Africa, 1963; West Africa: the Former French States, 1967; France and West Africa, 1969; many articles and chapters in jls and collaborative volumes. Jt Editor, Oxford Studies in African Affairs. *Recreations:* inhabiting dilapidated shooting-lodge; hill-walking; occasional lawn tennis. *Address:* 146 Hamilton Place, Aberdeen 26852. *Club:* Royal Commonwealth Society.

**HARGREAVES, Brig. Kenneth,** CBE 1956 (MBE 1939); TD 1942; Chairman, Hargreaves Group Ltd, 1964 (Managing Director, 1938-64); Director: Lloyds Bank Ltd, 1965 (Chairman, Yorkshire Regional Board, 1967); Yorkshire Bank, 1969; Richards Longstaff (Insurance) Ltd, 1948; Member: Eastern Railway Board, British Rail, 1964 (Chairman since 1970); Sadler's Wells Trust Ltd, 1969; Lord Lieutenant, West Riding of Yorkshire, since 1970; *b* 23 Feb. 1903; *s* of late Henry Hargreaves, Leeds, and late Hope Hargreaves; *m* 1st, 1958, Else Margareta Allen (*d* 1968); one step *s* one step *d* (both adopted); 2nd, 1969, Hon. Mrs Margaret Packe; two step *d*. *Educ:* Haileybury Coll. Commissioned 8th (Leeds Rifles) Battalion W Yorks Regt TA, 1922; Lieut-Col comdg 96th HAA Regt RA, 1939-41; Brig. comdg 3rd Ind. AA Bde, 1942-45; Hon. Col, 496 (M) HAA Regt TA, 1947-55; 466 (Leeds Rifles) LAA Regt RA TA, 1958-61 and Leeds Rifles TA, 1963-66. Chairman: Coal Industry Society, 1933-34; Coal Trade Benevolent Assoc., 1958. President: Chartered Inst. of Secretaries, 1956, (FCIS 1930); W Yorks Branch, BRCS, 1965; Yorks Agricultural Soc., 1971-; Vice-President: Yorks Council of Social Service, 1970; Leeds Chamber of Commerce, 1946-47; Dep. Chm., Leeds Musical Festival, 1961; Mem. Court, University of Leeds, 1950-; Parly Candidate: Pontefract, 1945; Keighley, 1950 and 1951; Hon. Treasurer, Yorks Provincial Area Conservative and Unionist Assoc., 1946-54; Governor, Swinton Conservative Coll., 1952-70; Lay Reader, Ripon Diocese, 1954-. Liveryman, Clothworkers' Co., 1938, First Warden, 1965, Master, 1969-70. DL for WR of Co. of York and City and Co. of York, 1956-70; High Sheriff of Yorks, 1962-63. LLD, Leeds Univ., 1970. KStJ 1970. *Recreations:* sailing, beagling. *Address:* Castle Garth, Wetherby, Yorks. *T:* Wetherby 2413. *Clubs:* Army and Navy; Carlton; Royal Yorks Yacht (Bridlington).

**HARGREAVES, Maj.-Gen. William Herbert,** CB 1965; OBE 1945; FRCP; Chief Medical Adviser, Shell International Petroleum Company Ltd, since 1965; *b* 5 Aug. 1908; *s* of Arthur William Hargreaves; *m* 1946, Pamela Mary Westray; one *s* one *d*. *Educ:* Merchant Taylors' Sch.; St Bartholomew's Hospital. FRCP 1950; FRCPE 1965. Served War of 1939-45. Medical Liaison Officer to Surgeon-Gen., US Army, Washington, DC, 1946-48; Prof. of Medicine, Univ. of Baghdad, 1951-59; Physician to late King Faisal II of Iraq, 1951-58; Hon. Consulting Physician, Iraqi Army, 1953-59; Consulting Physician to the Army, 1960-65; retd 1965. Lectr in Tropical Medicine, Middlesex Hosp. Med. Sch., 1960-65, and London Hosp. Med. Sch., 1963-65; Hon. Consulting Physician, Royal Hosp., Chelsea, 1961-65. Examiner: RCP, 1964-66; Soc. Apothecaries, 1966-. Mem. of Council, Royal Society of Medicine, 1966-69, Vice-Pres., Library (Scientific Research) Section, 1967-69. Counsellor, Royal Soc. of Tropical Med. and Hygiene, 1961-65; Member: Hosp. Cttee, St John's Ophthalmic Hosp., Jerusalem, 1965-; Finance Cttee, RCP. OStJ 1965. Iraq Coronation Medal, 1953. *Publications:* The Practice of Tropical Medicine (with R. J. G. Morrison), 1965; chapters in: Textbook of Medicine (Conybeare), 1964; Modern Trends in Gastro-Enterology (Avery Jones), 1951; numerous articles in med. jls. *Recreations:* art and music. *Address:* 12 Vicarage Gardens, W8. *T:* 01-229 3871.

**HARINGTON, Gen. Sir Charles,** GCB 1969 (KCB 1964; CB 1961); CBE 1957 (OBE 1953); DSO 1944; MC 1940; ADC (General) to the Queen, since 1969; *b* 5 May 1910; *s* of Lt-Col H. H. Harington and Dorothy Pepys; *m* 1942, Victoire Marion Williams-Freeman; one *s* two *d*. *Educ:* Malvern; Sandhurst. Commissioned into 22nd (Cheshire) Regt, 1930. Served War of 1939-45: France and Belgium, 2nd Bn Cheshire Regt, 1939-40; CO, 1st Bn Manchester Regt and GSO1, 53 (W) Div., NW Europe, 1944-45. DS Staff Coll., 1946; GSO1 Mil. Mission Greece, 1948; CO 1st Bn The Parachute Regt, 1949; Mil. Asst to CIGS, 1951; SHAPE, 1953; Comdr 49 Inf. Bde in Kenya, 1955; idc 1957; Comdt Sch. of Infantry, 1958; GOC 3rd Div., 1959; Comdt, Staff Coll., Camberley, 1961; C-in-C Middle East, 1963; DCGS, 1966; Chief of Personnel and Logistics, to Secretary of State for Defence, 1968-71; Col The Cheshire Regt, 1962-68. Col Comdt, Small Arms Sch. Corps, 1964-70; Col Comdt, The Prince of Wales Div., 1968-71. Pres., milocarian Athletic Club; Knight Officer with swords, Order of Orange Nassau (Netherlands), 1945. *Club:* Army and Navy.

**HARINGTON, Sir Charles (Robert),** KBE 1962; Kt 1948; FRS 1931; MA, PhD; Hon. ScD Cambridge; Dr (*hc*), Paris; Hon. DSc London; Consultant Adviser to Medical Research Council, 1966-67; *b* 1 Aug. 1897; *er s* of Rev. Charles Harington; *m* 1923, Jessie, 2nd *d* of Rev. James Craig; one *s* two *d*. *Educ:* Malvern Coll.; Magdalene Coll., Cambridge; University of Edinburgh. Research Asst in Department of Therapeutics, University of Edinburgh, 1920; Lecturer in Pathological Chemistry, University Coll. Hospital Medical Sch., London, 1922; Reader in Pathological Chemistry, Univ. of London, 1928; Prof. of Chemical Pathology in the Univ. of London, 1931-42; Dir of Graham Medical Research Laboritories, UCH Medical Sch., 1937-42; Dir of National Institute for Medical Research, 1942-62; Consultant Adviser to the Secretary, Medical Research Council, 1962-64; Second Sec. (Acting), Medical Research Council, 1965-66. Editor of the Biochemical Journal, 1930-42; Mem. of Med. Research Council, 1938-42; Mem. of Agricultural Research Council, 1941-45; Croonian Lectr of Royal Society, 1944; Hon. Fellow of Magdalene Coll., Cambridge, 1944; Hon. Freeman, Soc. of Apothecaries, 1949; Hon. FRSM 1959; Hon. FRCP 1963. Royal Medal, Royal Society, 1944; Gold Medal, Soc. of Apothecaries, 1953; Nuffield Lectr and Medallist, RSM, 1963. *Publications:* The Thyroid Gland: its Chemistry and Physiology, 1933; papers on chemical and biochemical subjects, mainly in the Biochemical Journal. *Recreation:* fishing. *Address:* 33 Sylvan Avenue, Mill Hill, NW7. *T:* 01-959 4278. *Club:* Athenæum.

**HARINGTON, Maj.-Gen. John,** CB 1967; OBE 1958; Secretary, Army Ski Association; *b* 7 Nov. 1912; *s* of late Col Henry Harington, Kelston, Folkestone, Kent; *m* 1943, Nancy, *d* of Stanley Allen, Denne Hill, Canterbury; one *s*. *Educ:* Lambrook, Bracknell; Aldenham Sch.; RMA Woolwich. Commnd RA, 1933. Served War of 1939-45: BEF, 1939-40; Capt., RHA, France and Germany; Major 1943; 1st Airborne Corps; Lt-Col 1945. GSO1, British and Indian Div., Japan, 1946-47; CO 18th Regt RA, 1954-55; College Comdr, RMA, Sandhurst, 1956-57; Head of Defence Secretariat, Middle East, 1958-59; commanded 1st Artillery Brigade, 1960-61; BRA, Far East Land Forces, 1962; DMS (2), War Office, 1962-64 (Min. of Defence, 1964); Chief of Staff to C-in-C, Far East Comd, 1964-67, retired. *Recreations:* polo, ski-ing, shooting, golf, tennis. *Address:* Harkaway, Goodworth Clatford, Andover, Hants. *Clubs:* Army and Navy, Ski Club of Great Britain.

**HARINGTON, John Charles Dundas,** QC 1957; **His Honour Judge Harington;** Judge of County Courts (Staffordshire Circuit) since 1961; Chairman, Herefordshire Quarter Sessions, since 1957; *b* 27 June 1903; *yr s* of Sir Richard Harington, 12th Bt, and *heir-pres.* to Sir Richard Harington, 13th Bt, *qv*; *m* 1941, Lavender Cecilia, *d* of late Major E. W. Denny, Garboldisham Manor, Diss, Norfolk; two *s* one *d*. *Educ:* RN Colleges, Osborne and Dartmouth; Christ Church, Oxford. Called to Bar, 1928. Served War of 1939-45, RNVR, 1939-44. Recorder of Banbury, 1951-55; Recorder of New Windsor, 1955-58; Judge of County Courts (Hants Circuit), 1958-61. Dep. Chm., Herefordshire QS, 1953-57. *Recreations:* various. *Address:* Whitbourne Court, Worcester.

**HARINGTON, Kenneth Douglas Evelyn Herbert;** Metropolitan Magistrate since 1967; *b* 30 Sept. 1911; *yr s* of late His Honour Edward Harington; *m* 1st, 1939, Lady Cecilia Bowes-Lyon (*d* 1947), *er d* of 15th Earl of Strathmore; 2nd, 1950, Maureen Helen McCalmont, *d* of Brig.-Gen. Sir Robert McCalmont, KCVO, CBE, DSO; two *s*. *Educ:* Stowe. War of 1939-45: Served NW Europe (Major, Coldstream Guards). Hon. Attaché, British Legation, Stockholm, 1930-32; Barrister, Inner Temple, 1952; Acting Deputy Chm., Inner London and NE London Quarter Sessions, 1966-67. *Recreations:* shooting, fishing and breeding donkeys. *Address:* 21 Milner Street, SW3. *T:* 01-589 8951; Sotchers, Bury Gate, Pulborough, Sussex. *T:* Fittleworth 227. *Club:* Guards.

**HARINGTON, Sir Richard Dundas,** 13th Bt *cr* 1611; *b* 16 Oct. 1900; *s* of 12th Bt and Selina Louisa Grace (*d* 1945), *d* of 6th Viscount Melville; *S* father, 1931. *Educ:* Eton. *Heir: b* John Charles Dundas Harington, *qv*. *Address:* c/o Coutts & Co., Bankers, 440 Strand, WC2.

**HARINGTON HAWES, Derrick Gordon;** Director General, International Hospital Federation since 1962; *b* 22 May 1907; *s* of late Col Charles Howard Hawes, DSO, MVO, Indian Army; *m* 1932, Drusilla Way; one *s* two *d*. *Educ:* Wellington Coll; RMC Sandhurst. Regimental Officer, 14th Punjab Regt, IA, 1927-34; Officer of Indian Political Service, 1934-47; King Edward's Hospital Fund for London, 1949-62 (Dep. Sec., 1960). *Address:* c/o National Westminster Bank Ltd, Warwick Gardens, W14. *Club:* Oriental.

**HARKNESS, Sir Douglas (Alexander Earsman),** KBE 1956 (CBE 1946); retired Civil Servant; Councillor, Clifton Ward, Belfast Corporation, 1967; *b* 12 Sept. 1902; *o c* of late George Wightman Harkness and Jane Earsman Harkness; *m* 1936, Annie, *o d* of late J. C. M. Blow and of Jane Sibbald Blow; one *s* one *d*. *Educ:* Newport (Mon.) High Sch.; University of Glasgow. 2nd Class Hons in History, 1922; 1st Class Hons in Economic Science, 1923; Reid Stewart Fellow, 1923-24. Min. of Agriculture, Northern Ireland, 1924; Lecturer in Agricultural Economics, Queen's Univ., Belfast, 1926; Asst Sec., Min. of Agriculture, 1936; Perm. Sec., 1948; Second Sec., Min. of Finance, 1952; Perm. Sec. to Min. of Finance, Northern Ireland, and Head of Northern Ireland Civil Service, 1953-61; Economic Adviser to the Government of Northern Ireland, 1961-63. LLD (*hc*) Queen's Univ. of Belfast, 1962. *Publications:* War and British Agriculture, 1941; A Tract on Agricultural Policy, 1945; Bolingbroke, 1957; various articles on economic and agricultural subjects. *Recreations:* golf, fishing. *Address:* 33 Knockdene Park, Belfast 5. *T:* 654051.

**HARKNESS, Lt-Col Hon. Douglas Scott,** PC (Canada) 1957; GM 1943; ED 1944; MP (Canada) for Calgary Centre since 1968; Minister of National Defence, Canada, 1960-63; *b* 29 March 1903; *s* of William Keefer and Janet Douglas Harkness (*née* Scott); *m* 1932, Frances Elisabeth, *d* of James Blair McMillan, Charlottetown and Calgary; one *s*. *Educ:* Central Collegiate, Calgary; University of Alberta (BA). Served overseas in War (Italy and NW Europe), 1940-45; Major and Lt-Col, Royal Canadian Artillery; with Reserve Army, CO 41st Anti-Tank Regt (SP), Royal Canadian Artillery. MP (Calgary E) gen. elecs, 1945, 1949; re-elected (Calgary N) gen. elecs, 1953, 1957, 1958, 1962, 1963, 1965, 1968; Min. for Northern Affairs and Nat. Resources and Actg Minister of Agric., June 1957; Minister of Agric., Aug. 1957; relinquished portfolios of Northern Affairs and Nat. Resources, Aug. 1957, of Agriculture, Oct. 1960. Mem. Alta Military Institute. *Address:* 4232 Elbow Drive, Calgary, Alta, Canada. *Clubs:* Ranchmen's, Calgary Petroleum (Calgary); Rideau (Ottawa).

**HARKNESS, Rear-Adm. James Percy Knowles;** Director-General of Naval Manpower since 1970; *b* 28 Nov. 1916; *s* of Captain P. Y. Harkness, West Yorkshire Regt, and Gladys Dundas Harkness (*née* Knowles); *m* 1949, Joan, *d* of late Vice-Adm. N. A. Sullivan, CVO; two *d*. *Educ:* RN Coll., Dartmouth. Entered Royal Navy, 1930; transferred to Supply Branch, 1934; Comdr, 1951; Staff course, 1955; Captain 1961; Asst Dir of Plans, 1962; IDC, 1965; Cdre Naval Drafting, 1966. *Recreations:* sailing, working with hands. *Address:* c/o Midland Bank, High Street, Gosport, Hants. *Clubs:* Royal Naval Sailing Association; Island Sailing (Cowes).

**HARKNESS, Captain Kenneth Lanyon,** CBE 1963; DSC 1940; Royal Navy; *b* 24 Aug. 1900; *s* of late Major T. R. Harkness, RA, and late Mrs G. A. de Burgh; *m* 1932, Joan Phyllis Lovell; one *d*. *Educ:* RN Colls, Osborne and Dartmouth; Cambridge Univ. Midshipman, HMS Bellerophon, 1917; Cambridge Univ., 1922; Qual. Gunnery, 1926; Comdr Admty, 1935; Sqdn Gunnery Off., 2nd Battle Sqdn, 1937; Comd HMS Winchelsea, 1938; Comd HMS Fearless, 1939-40; Capt. 1940; Chief of Intell. Service, Far East, 1940-42; Dep. Dir of Naval Ordnance, Admty, 1943-44; Comd HMS Ceylon, 1945; Comd HMS Sheffield, 1946; Chief of Staff to C-in-C Portsmouth, 1947; retired from RN, 1949. Civil Defence Officer, Portsmouth, 1949; Home Office, Asst Chief Trg Off. (CD), 1952; Prin. Off., later Reg. Dir of CD, London Reg., 1954; Temp. seconded as CD Adviser, Cyprus, 1956; later Regional Dir of Civil Defence, London Region, 1954-65. *Recreation:* gardening. *Address:* Far Rockaway, Durford Wood, Petersfield, Hants. *T:* Liss 3173. *Clubs:* United Service; Nuffield United Service Officers' (Portsmouth).

**HARLAN, John M.;** US Legion of Merit; Associate Justice, Supreme Court of the United States since 1955; *b* Chicago, Ill., 20 May 1899; *s* of John Maynard Harlan and Elizabeth Palmer (*née* Flagg); *m* 1928, Ethel Andrews, New Haven, Conn.; one *d*. *Educ:* Chicago Latin Sch.; Appleby Sch.; Lake Placid Sch.; Princeton Univ.; Balliol Coll., Oxford; New York Law Sch. AB Princeton, 1920; Rhodes Scholar, Oxford Univ., 1921-23; BA Jurisprudence, MA; Hon. Fellow, Balliol Coll., 1955; LLB New York Law Sch., 1924. Admitted to New York Bar, 1925; joined firm of Root, Clark, Buckner & Howland (subsequently Root, Ballantine, Harlan, Bushby & Palmer), 31 Nassau Street, New York City, as an associate, 1923; mem. of firm, 1931-54; specialised in litigation throughout. Asst US Attorney, Southern District of New York, 1925-27; Chief Counsel to NY State Crime Commission, 1951. US Court of Appeals, Second Circuit, 1954. Member: American Bar Assoc.; NY State Bar Assoc.; Assoc. of the Bar of City of NY; NY County Lawyers Assoc. (Dir 1938-42); American Law Institute; Dir of National Legal Aid Assoc. Hon. Master of the Bench, Inner Temple, 1969. Hon. LLD: Brandeis Univ., Evansville Coll., New York Law Sch., Princeton Univ., 1955; Columbia Univ., Oberlin Coll., 1956. Served War as Col, US Army Air Force; stationed in England, 1943-45 as Chief of Operations Analysis Section Eighth Air Force, and subsequently mem. of Planning Section for Occupation of Germany, US Strategic Air Forces in Europe. Croix de Guerre (France); Croix de Guerre (Belgium). *Address:* 1677 31st Street, NW, Washington, DC, USA; Weston, Conn. *Clubs:* Century Association, University (NYC); Country (Fairfield, Conn.); Ivy (Princeton, NJ).

**HARLAND, Ven. Lawrence Winston,** MBE 1952; Archdeacon of Rochester and Residentiary Canon of Rochester Cathedral, 1951-69, now Emeritus; *b* 19 Nov. 1905; *s* of Harry Harland, Bradford, Yorks; *m* 1933, Rita Doreen Harrison; two *s* one *d*. *Educ:* Sidney Sussex Coll., Cambridge; Chichester Theological Coll. BA (Cantab) 1931; MA 1934. Curate of: Holy Trinity, Bingley, 1933; Christ Church, Skipton, 1936; Priest in Charge, St Martin's, Bradford, 1937; Vicar of Menston in Wharfedale, 1939. War of 1939-45: CF, RARO, 1939; Dunkirk, 1940; HCF 1942. Priest-Vicar of Lichfield Cathedral, 1946; Vicar of St Nicholas, Rochester, 1965-69; Gen. Sec., Christian Reconstruction of Europe, 1947; Gen. Sec. Advisory Cttee of Christian Churches for the Festival of Britain, 1951. Chaplain to the Queen, 1966-. *Address:* Innisfree, 153 Pear Tree Lane, Little Common, Bexhill-on-Sea, Sussex. *T:* Cooden 2027.

**HARLAND, Rt. Rev. Maurice Henry,** MA, DD; *b* 17 April 1896; *s* of late Rev. William George Harland and late Clara Elizabeth Harland; *m* 1923, Agnes Hildyard Winckley, MBE 1967; two *d*. *Educ:* St Peter's Sch., York; Exeter Coll., Oxford (MA); Leeds Clergy Sch. DD (Lambeth) 1948. 2nd Lieut West Yorks Regt, 1914-15; 2nd Lieut R Field Artillery, 1915-16; Lieut Royal Flying Corps and afterwards RAF, 1916-19; Curate St Peter's, Leicester, 1922-27; Priest in Charge St Anne's Conventional District, 1927-33; Perpetual Curate of St Matthew's Holbeck, Leeds, 1933-38; Vicar of St Mary's, Windermere, 1938-42; Rural Dean of Ambleside; Vicar of Croydon, 1942-47; Archdeacon of Croydon, 1946-47; Hon. Canon of Canterbury, 1942-47; Bishop Suffragan of Croydon, 1942-47; Bishop of Lincoln, 1947-56; Bishop of Durham, 1956-66. Select Preacher, Oxford Univ., 1949-50. Pres., Edinburgh Sir Walter Scott Soc., 1940-50; Hon. Fellow, Exeter Coll., Oxford, 1950; Hon. DD Durham Univ., 1956. Introduced to House of Lords, 1954 and again in 1956 on becoming Bishop of Durham. *Recreations:* fishing, riding. *Address:* White Chimneys, Rookwood Road, West Wittering, near Chichester, Sussex. *T:* West Wittering 2351.

**HARLAND, Air Vice-Marshal Reginald Edward Wynyard;** AOC No 24 Group, RAF Rudloe Manor, since 1970; *b* 30 May 1920; *s* of Charles

Cecil Harland and Ida Maud (*née* Bellhouse); *m* 1942, Doreen Rosalind, *d* of W. H. C. Romanis, *qv*; three *s* two *d*. *Educ:* Summer Fields, Oxford; Stowe; Trinity Coll., Cambridge (MA). Served War of 1939-45: RAE Farnborough, 1941-42; N Africa, Italy and S France, 1942-45. Techn. trng, techn. plans and manning depts, Air Min., 1946-49; pilot trng, 1949-50; Chief Engrg Instructor, RAF Coll., Cranwell, 1950-52; Guided Weapon trng, RMCS Shrivenham, 1952-53; Thunderbird Project Officer: RAE Farnborough, 1953-55; Min. of Supply, 1955-56; psa 1957; Ballistic Missile Liaison Officer, (BJSM) Los Angeles, 1958-60; CO, Central Servicing Develt Estab., Swanton Morley, 1960-62; STSO, HQ No 3 (Bomber) Gp, Mildenhall, 1962-64; AO i/c Engrg, HQ Far East Air Force, Singapore, 1964-66; Harrier Project Dir, HQ Min. of Technology, 1967-68; idc 1969. CEng 1966; FIMechE 1967; FIEE 1964; FRAeS 1967; MBIM 1968; FIE (Singapore) 1967; MIE (Malaysia) 1966. *Publications:* occasional articles in Jl RAeS and other engrg jls. *Recreations:* sailing, bridge, reading. *Address:* Heleigh House, Middle Hill, Box, Chippenham, Wilts. *T:* Box 389. *Club:* Royal Air Force.

**HARLAND, Sydney Cross,** FRS 1943; DSc (London); FRSE 1951; FTI (Hon.) 1954; George Harrison Professor of Botany, Manchester University, 1950-58, retired, Emeritus Professor, 1958; Member, Agricultural Research Council, 1950-55; *b* 19 June 1891; *s* of Erasmus and Eliza Harland, Cliff Grange, Snainton, Yorks; *m* 1st, 1915, Emily Wilson Cameron; two *d*; 2nd, 1934, Olive Sylvia Atteck; one *s*. *Educ:* High Sch., Scarborough; King's Coll., London. Asst Supt Agric., St Vincent, BWI, 1915; Asst for Cotton Research, Imp. Dept Agric. for West Indies, 1918; Head Botanical Dept, British Cotton Industry Res. Assoc., Manchester, 1920; Prof. Botany and Genetics, Imperial Coll. Trop. Agric., Trinidad, 1923; Chief Geneticist, Empire Cotton Growing Corp., Cotton Research Station, Trinidad, and Cotton Adviser to Comr of Agric., 1926; Gen. Adviser to State Cotton Industry of Sao Paulo, Brazil, 1935; Dir, Institute of Cotton Genetics, National Agricultural Soc., Peru, 1939-50. Fellow, New England Inst. of Medical Res., 1963. *Publications:* The Genetics of Cotton, 1939; also papers on cotton, cocoa, other tropical crops, and applied genetics. *Recreations:* travel, gardening, human genetics. *Address:* Cliff Grange, Snainton, Scarborough, Yorks. *T:* Snainton 549; Correo Naña, Carretera Central, Peru. *Club:* Athenæum.

**HARLECH,** 5th Baron *cr* 1876; **William David Ormsby Gore,** PC 1957; KCMG 1961; *b* 20 May 1918; *e surv. s* of 4th Baron Harlech, KG, PC, GCMG, and Lady Beatrice Cecil (*see* Dowager Lady Harlech); *S* father, 1964; *m* 1st, 1940, Sylvia (*d* 1967), 2nd *d* of late Hugh Lloyd Thomas, CMG, CVO; two *s* three *d*; 2nd, 1969, Pamela, *o d* of Ralph F. Colin, New York. *Educ:* Eton; New Coll., Oxford. Joined Berks Yeomanry, 1939, Adjutant, 1942; Major (GS), 1945. MP (C) Oswestry Div. of Salop, 1950-61; Parliamentary Private Sec. to Minister of State for Foreign Affairs, 1951; Parliamentary Under-Sec. of State for Foreign Affairs, Nov. 1956-Jan. 1957; Minister of State for Foreign Affairs, 1957-61; British Ambassador in Washington, 1961-65. Dep.-Leader of the Opposition, House of Lords, 1966-67. President: British Bd of Film Censors, 1965-; The Pilgrims (Soc. of UK); Trustee, The Pilgrim Trust, 1965-; Chairman: Harlech Television; Kennedy Mem. Trust; Papworth and Enham Village Settlements. Member: Adv. Cttee, Kennedy Inst., Harvard; Exec. Cttee, Nat. Trust. Governor, Yehudi Menuhin Sch. Hon. Chm., Shelter, 1969-. Hon. Fellow, New Coll., Oxford, 1964. Hon. DCL, Univ. of Pittsburgh, 1962; Hon. LLD: Brown Univ., 1963; New York Univ., 1964; William and Mary Coll., 1965; Manchester, 1966. DL Salop, 1961. KStJ. *Publication:* Must the West Decline?, 1966. *Heir: s* Hon. Julian Hugh Ormsby Gore [*b* 23 Dec. 1940. *Educ:* Eton; McGill Univ., Canada]. *Address:* 14a Ladbroke Road, W11. *T:* 01-229 6701; House of Lords, Westminster, SW1; Woodhill, Oswestry, Salop. *T:* Oswestry 3134. *Club:* Pratt's.

*See also M. V. Macmillan, A. L. Mayall, Baron Wardington.*

**HARLECH, Dowager Lady,** DCVO 1947; **Beatrice Mildred Edith;** Extra Lady of the Bedchamber to the Queen Mother; *b* 10 Aug. 1891; *d* of 4th Marquess of Salisbury, KG, GCVO; *m* 1913, 4th Baron Harlech, KG, PC, GCMG (*d* 1964); one *s* three *d* (and one *s* decd). *Address:* 14 Ladbroke Road, W11. *T:* 01-229 6679.

*See also Baron Harlech.*

**HARLEY, John Laker,** FRS 1964; MA, DPhil Oxon; Professor of Forest Science, Oxford University, since 1969; *b* 17 Nov. 1911; *s* of Charles Laker Harley and Edith Sarah (*née* Smith); *m* 1938, Elizabeth Lindsay Fitt; one *s* one *d*. *Educ:* Leeds Grammar Sch.; Wadham Coll., Oxford. Open Exhibition, Wadham Coll., 1930, Hon. Scholar 1933, Christopher Welch Scholar, Oxford, 1933-37; Senior Student 1851 Exhibition, 1937-38. Departmental Demonstrator, Oxford, 1938-44. Served in Royal Signals, 1940-45: attached Operation Research Group No. 1, India, Lieut-Col GSO1. University Demonstrator, Oxford, 1945-62; Browne Research Fellow, Queen's Coll., Oxford, 1946-52; Official Fellow, Queen's Coll., Oxford, 1952-65; Reader in Plant Nutrition, Oxford Univ., 1962-65; Prof. of Botany, Sheffield Univ., 1965-69. Editor, New Phytologist, 1961-. President: British Mycological Soc., 1967; British Ecological Soc., 1970-72. *Publications:* Biology of Mycorrhiza, 1969; scientific papers in New Phytologist, Annals of Applied Mycology, Annals of Botany, Biochemical Jl, Plant Physiology, Proc. Royal Soc., Jl of Ecology. *Recreation:* gardening. *Address:* The Orchard, Old Marston, Oxford.

**HARLEY, Sir Stanley (Jaffa),** Kt 1958; DL; Chairman and Managing Director, Coventry Gauge Ltd, since 1963; Director, Tube Investments Ltd, since 1969; *b* 12 Nov. 1905; *s* of late Sir Harry Harley, CBE and Mrs Lydia Harley; *m* 1931, Rhona Townsend; two *s* one *d*. *Educ:* Wrekin Coll., Wellington, Salop; Birmingham Univ. Apprenticed to Coventry Gauge & Tool Co. Ltd, 1926; completed training at Coventry, on Continent, and in USA; Joint Man. Dir, Coventry Gauge & Tool Co. Ltd, 1935; Man. Dir, 1946, 1951; Dep. Chm. 1946; Chm. 1951. DL, Co. Warwick, 1967. Hon. Controller of Jigs, Tools and Gauges, Machine Tool Control, Min. of Supply and Min. of Production, 1940-46. *Recreations:* golf, travel. *Address:* Walsh Hall, Meriden, Warwicks. *T:* Meriden 262. *Clubs:* Carlton, Royal Automobile; Coventry and County (Coventry).

**HARLEY, Sir Thomas (Winlack),** Kt 1960; MBE 1944; MC 1918; DL; Senior Partner, Simpson North Harley & Co., solicitors, Liverpool and London, admitted 1922; *b* 27 June 1895; *o s* of George Harley and Annie Thomson (*née* Macwatty); *m* 1924, Margaret Hilda, 2nd *d* of late Canon J. U. N. Bardsley; three *s*. *Educ:* Birkenhead Sch.; Eton. Served European War,

1914-19, France and Balkans, Major The King's Own Regt (despatches, MC); War of 1939-45, Major RA (TA); comd (HG) AA Battery (MBE), 1942-45. Chm. Liverpool Regional Hosp. Bd, 1959-68; Mem. Board of Governors, United Liverpool Hosps, 1955-; Mem., Liverpool Cathedral Cttee; a Vice-Pres., Liverpool Conservative Assoc.; Pres., Bebington Conservative Constituency, etc. DL County of Chester, 1962. *Recreations:* shooting, golf and gardening. *Address:* Hesketh Hey, Thornton Hough, Wirral, Cheshire. *T:* 051-336 3439. *Clubs:* Brooks's, Royal Over-Seas League; Royal Liverpool Golf.

**HARLOCK, Maj.-Gen. Hugh George Frederick,** CBE 1953; *b* 20 Aug. 1900; *s* of James Harlock, Camperdown, Victoria; *m* 1935, Florence Madge, *d* of W. C. Ewing, Sydney, NSW; one *s* one *d*. *Educ:* Wesley Coll., Melbourne; RMC Duntroon. Commnd Aust. Staff Corps, 1921; Regimental and Staff appts in Royal Australian Artillery, 1922-39; Aust. Imperial Force, 1940-47; Staff appts, AHQ, 1947-49; Aust. Army Rep., UK, 1950-52; Brig. i/c Admin., E Comd, 1953; Maj.-Gen. 1954; Gen. Officer Commanding, Northern Command, Australian Military Forces, 1954-57. *Address:* 12 Patrick Lane, Toowong, Queensland 4066, Australia. *Club:* United Services (Brisbane).

**HARLOW, Christopher Millward,** CIE 1942; BSc; *b* 5 Jan. 1889; *s* of late John Starcke Harlow; *m* 1921, Doris Gertrude Chittenden; two *s* one *d*. Joined Indian Forest Service, 1911; Chief Conservator of Forests, Central Provinces and Berar; retired, 1946. *Address:* The Glebe House, Occold, near Eye, Suffolk. *T:* Occold 239.

**HARMAN, Sir Cecil W. F. S. K.;** *see* Stafford-King-Harman.

**HARMAN, Rt. Hon. Sir Charles Eustace,** PC 1959; Kt 1947; a Lord Justice of Appeal, 1959-70; *b* 22 Nov. 1894; *e surv. s* of John E. Harman and Ethel Frances Birch; *m* 1924, Helen Sarah Le Roy Lewis; two *s*. *Educ:* Eton (scholar); King's Coll., Cambridge (scholar). Served in war with Middlesex Regt (Prisoner); called to Bar, Lincoln's Inn, 1921. KC 1935; Judge of the High Court of Justice, Chancery Div., 1947-59. Treas., Lincoln's Inn, 1959-. *Recreations:* fishing, shooting. *Address:* Tully, Louisburgh, Co. Mayo; 6 Stone Buildings, Lincoln's Inn, WC2. *Club:* United University.
*See also J. L. Harman.*

**HARMAN, Sir (Clement) James,** GBE 1964; JP; one of HM Lieutenants for City of London, 1952-69; Chairman: Provincial Flats Ltd; Harman Properties Ltd; Managing Director, Bryanston Property Co. Ltd, and other companies; *b* 15 May 1894; *e s* of late Clement Valentine Harman, Frinton Hall, Essex; *m* 1917, Mary Abigail (*d* 1967), *d* of Arthur John Childe-Freeman, Gaines, Worcs; one *s* (one *d* decd). *Educ:* London Univ.; Zürich and Paris. Freeman, City of London, 1936; Liveryman, Worshipful Cos of Painter-Stainers, Clockmakers (Mem. Court of Assts; Master, 1961, 1963), Plumbers (Mem. Court of Assts; Master, 1958); Mem. Court of Common Council for Ward of Bread Street, 1949; Governor: Christ's Hosp., 1952-69; Royal Bridewell Hosp. (King Edward Sch., Witley); Chm., City of London Licensing Planning Cttee, 1955-63; Life Gov., Sheriffs' Fund Soc.; Sheriff of City of London, 1951-52; Alderman, City of London, 1952-69 (Ward of Candlewick); Lord Mayor of London, 1963-64. A Church Comr for England, 1966-69. Served European War, 1914-18: Royal Welch Fusiliers; subseq. Gen. Staff (Intelligence) 31st Divl HQ, 7th Corps HQ, 2nd Army HQ; BEF France and Flanders; MEF campaigns, Gallipoli and Salonika. Capt., 7th Surrey Home Guard, 1940-45. Hon. Col, TA, 1963. KStJ; Order of the Falcon with Star (Iceland), 1963; Order of Two Niles (Sudan), 2nd Class, 1964. *Address:* 12 South Audley Street, W1. *T:* 01-499 1601, 01-499 2180; Croft House, Buxton Road, Eastbourne, Sussex. *T:* Eastbourne 34256. *Clubs:* Athenæum, Garrick, City Livery (Pres. 1961-62), United Wards; Walton Heath Golf; Royal Eastbourne Golf.

**HARMAN, Ernest Henry,** OBE 1961; Chairman, South Western Gas Board, since 1964; *b* 1908; *m* 2nd, 1958, Dorothy Anne Parsons; (two *d* by 1st *m*). *Educ:* London Univ. BSc (Hons). Sec., 1936, Gen. Manager, 1944, Commercial Gas Co.; Gen. Manager, Sheffield and Rotherham Div., East Midlands Gas Board, 1949; Dep. Chm., East Midlands Gas Board, 1952. *Recreations:* tennis, motoring, music. *Address:* c/o SW Gas Board, 9a Quiet Street, Bath, Somerset.

**HARMAN, Maj.-Gen. Jack Wentworth,** OBE 1962; MC 1943; General Officer Commanding 1st Division, since 1970; *b* 20 July 1920; *s* of late Lt-Gen. Sir Wentworth Harman, KCB, DSO, and late Dorothy Harman; *m* 1947, Gwladys May Murphy (*widow* of Lt-Col R. J. Murphy) (decd), *d* of Sir Idwal Lloyd; one *d* and two step *d*. *Educ:* Wellington Coll.; RMC Sandhurst. Commissioned into The Queen's Bays, 1940, Bt Lt-Col, 1958; Commanding Officer, 1st The Queen's Dragoon Guards, 1960-62; commanded 11 Infantry Bde, 1965-66; attended IDC, 1967; BGS, HQ Army Strategic Command, 1968-69. *Address:* Bathurst Cottage, Teffont Magna, near Salisbury, Wilts. *T:* Teffont 288. *Club:* Cavalry.

**HARMAN, Sir James;** *see* Harman, Sir C. J.

**HARMAN, Jeremiah LeRoy,** QC 1968; *b* 13 April 1930; *er s* of Rt Hon. Sir Charles Eustace Harman, *qv*; *m* 1960, Erica Jane, *e d* of Hon. Sir Maurice Richard Bridgeman, *qv*; two *s* one *d*. *Educ:* Horris Hill Sch.; Eton Coll. Served Coldstream Guards and Parachute Regt, 1948-51; Parachute Regt (TA), 1951-55. Called to the Bar, Lincoln's Inn, 1954; Mem., Bar Council, 1963-67. *Recreations:* fishing, shooting, stalking, watching birds. *Address:* 22 Stafford Terrace, W8. *T:* 01-937 8995; Sra-na-Cloya, near Louisburgh, Co. Mayo; 9 Old Square, Lincoln's Inn, WC2. *T:* 01-405 3806. *Club:* Garrick.

**HARMAN, John Bishop,** FRCS, FRCP; Physician, St Thomas' Hospital since 1938, Royal Marsden Hospital since 1947; *b* 10 Aug. 1907; *s* of late Nathaniel Bishop Harman and of Katharine (*née* Chamberlain); *m* 1946, Anna Charlotte Malcolm Spicer; four *d*. *Educ:* Oundle; St John's Coll., Cambridge (Scholar); St Thomas's Hospital (Scholar). Fearnsides Scholar, Cantab, 1932; 1st Cl. Nat. Sci. Tripos Pt I, 2nd Cl. Pt II, Cantab; MA 1933; MD 1937; FRCS 1932; FRCP 1942. Late Lt-Col RAMC (despatches). *Publications:* contribs to medical literature. *Recreation:* horticulture. *Address:* 108 Harley Street, W1. *T:* 01-935 7822; 32 Carlton Hill, NW8. *T:* 01-624 9505.

**HARMAN, R. D. K.;** *see* King-Harman.

**HARMER, Cyril Henry Carrington;** Chairman and Managing Director, H. R. Harmer Ltd, since 1967; Director, H. R. Harmer (Pty) Ltd, Sydney; *b* 17 Aug. 1903; *s* of Henry Revell Harmer and Edith Annie Harmer; *m* 1935, Elizabeth Boyd Baird; two *d*. *Educ:* Brighton Grammar Sch. Joined H. R. Harmer, 1921;

Partner, 1927; Dir, 1946. Lieut RA, 1939-45; POW, 1941-45. FInstD; FRSoc.; Roll of Distinguished Philatelists, 1969. *Publications:* (with R. E. R. Dalwick) Newfoundland Air Mails, 1953; contribs to philatelic jls. *Recreations:* rowing, cricket. *Address:* 20 Wildcroft Manor, SW15. *T:* 01-788 0710. *Clubs:* Hurlingham; Collectors (New York).

**HARMER, Sir Frederic (Evelyn),** Kt 1968; CMG 1945; Deputy Chairman P & OSN Company; Chairman, International Chamber of Shipping, since 1968; *b* 3 Nov. 1905; *yr s* of late Sir Sidney Frederic Harmer, KBE, FRS; *m* 1931, Barbara Susan, *er d* of late Major J. A. C. Hamilton, JP, Fyne Court, Bridgwater, Som.; one *s* three *d. Educ:* Eton; King's Coll., Cambridge. Wrangler, Maths Tripos Part II, 1926; Class 1, Div. 1, Econs Tripos Part II 1927; BA 1927; MA 1934. Entered Treasury, Oct. 1939; Temp. Asst Sec., 1943-45; served in Washington, March-June 1944 and again in Sept.-Dec. 1945 for Anglo-American economic and financial negotiations; resigned Dec. 1945. Chm., Cttee of European Shipowners, 1965-68; HM Govt Dir, British Petroleum Co. Ltd, 1953-70; Director: BP Tanker Co. Ltd; National Westminster Bank Ltd, and other cos. Vice-Chm. of Governors, London Sch. of Economics, 1952-69. *Recreations:* sailing, golf. *Address:* Stanny, Aldeburgh, Suffolk. *T:* Aldeburgh 2774. *Club:* Royal Yacht Squadron.

**HARMER, Lewis Charles,** MA, PhD Cantab; Licencié ès Lettres Bordeaux; Drapers' Professor of French, University of Cambridge, since 1951; Fellow of Trinity College, Cambridge, since 1944; *b* 22 June 1902; *s* of Charles Collins Harmer and Kate Lewis; *m* 1940, Nina, *o d* of Eugène Le Prévost; two *s* two *d. Educ:* Universities of London, Bordeaux and Cambridge. Modern and Medieval Languages Tripos, Cambridge, 1930-33; Lecturer in French, University of Cambridge, 1936-51. *Publications:* The French Language Today, 1954; Vocabulary in French and English, A Facsimile of Caxton's edition *c* 1480 (Textual Introduction), 1964; (with F. J. Norton) A Manual of Modern Spanish; contribs to Encyclopædias and learned jls. *Address:* Trinity College, Cambridge.

**HARMER, Michael Hedley,** MA, MB Cantab, FRCS; Surgeon: Paddington Green Children's Hospital, since 1948; Royal Marsden Hospital and Institute of Cancer Research since 1949; St Andrew's Hospital, Dollis Hill, since 1950; *b* 6 July 1912; *y s* of late Douglas Harmer, MC, FRCS, and May (*née* Hedley); *m* 1939, Bridget Jean, *d* of James Higgs-Walker, *qv*; one *s* one *d. Educ:* Marlborough; King's Coll., Cambridge; St Bartholomew's Hosp., London. St Bart's Hosp.: Pres. Abernethian Soc., 1938; jun. surgical appts, 1938-43; Westminster Hosp., 1946-47; Royal Cancer Hospital, 1947-48. Surgical Specialist, RAFVR, 1943-46. Chairman, Cttee on TNM Classification, of Internat. Union against Cancer; Sec. to Clin. Section, 8th Internat. Cancer Congress, London, 1958; FRSM. Bellman Snark Club, Cambridge, 1934-; Pres., King's Coll. Assoc., 1961. Freeman of Norwich by Patrimony, 1935. *Publications:* (jt): A Handbook of Surgery, 1951; Aids to Surgery, 1962; (Jt Editor) Rose and Carless's Manual of Surgery, 19th edn, 1959; paper on cancer of the mouth, and other papers, mostly on malignant disease. *Recreations:* mountaineering, music. *Address:* 6 Hale House, 34 De Vere Gardens, W8. *T:* 01-937 7974.

**HARMOOD-BANNER, Sir George Knowles,** 3rd Bt, *cr* 1924; *b* 9 Nov. 1918; *s* of Sir Harmood Harmood-Banner, 2nd Bt, and Frances Cordelia, *d* of late George Duberly, JP, Plansworth, Co. Durham; *S* father 1950; *m* 1947, Rosemary Jane, *d* of Col M. L. Treston, CBE, FRCS, FRCOG, late IMS, and late Mrs Sheila Treston; two *d. Educ:* Eton; University of Cambridge. Served War of 1939-45; 2nd Lieut Royal Welch Fusiliers, 1942, attached to East African Engineers (SEAC); transferred RASC, 1945. *Recreations:* tennis, ski-ing and swimming. *Heir:* none. *Address:* c/o The Bank of Nova Scotia, 11 Waterloo Place, SW1.

**HARMSWORTH,** family name of **Viscount Rothermere** and **Baron Harmsworth.**

**HARMSWORTH,** 2nd Baron, *cr* 1939, of Egham; **Cecil Desmond Bernard Harmsworth;** painter; *b* 1903; *e s* of 1st Baron Harmsworth and Emilie Alberta (*d* 1942), *d* of William Hamilton Maffett, Finglas, Co. Dublin; *S* father, 1948; *m* 1926, Dorothy Alexander, *d* of late Hon. J. C. Heinlein, Bridgeport, Ohio, USA; one *d. Educ:* Eton Coll.; Christ Church, Oxford (MA); (in drawing) Académie Julian, Paris; (in painting) public galleries. Was successively newspaperman and book publisher before becoming a painter. Exhibitions: Galerie des Quatre-Chemins, Paris, 1933; Wildenstein Gall., London, 1938; Bonestell Gall., New York, 1944; Swedish Modern, Dallas, Texas, 1950; Messrs Roland, Browse & Delbanco, London, 1954. Has been regular contributor to Salon d'Automne and group exhibitions in Paris; has exhibited in many London and New York galleries, and at the Phillips Memorial Gallery, Washington, DC. Portraits of Norman Douglas, Havelock Ellis, Lord Inverchapel, James Joyce, Consuelo de Saint-Exupéry, Sir Osbert Sitwell, Swami Nikhilananda, etc. Chairman, Dr Johnson's House Trust. Served in British Information Services, New York, 1940-46. *Publications:* occasional prose and verse contributions to English, Irish, and US periodicals; drawings and paintings reproduced in US magazines. *Heir:* *b* Hon. Eric Beauchamp Northcliffe Harmsworth [*b* 1905; *m* 1935, Hélène (*d* 1962), *d* of Col Jules-Raymond Dehove, Paris; one *s* one *d*; *m* 1964, Mrs Helen Hudson, London. *Educ:* Eton Coll.; Christ Church, Oxford (MA)]. *Address:* Lime Lodge, Egham, Surrey. *T:* Egham 379.

**HARMSWORTH, Sir (Arthur) Geoffrey (Annesley),** 3rd Bt *cr* 1918; FSA; Chairman: Harmsworth Press Ltd; West Country Holdings Ltd; West Country Publications Ltd; Western Morning News Co. Ltd; Western Times Co. Ltd; Director: Daily Mail & General Trust Ltd; F. Hewitt & Son (1927) Ltd; News Holdings Ltd; *b* 29 March 1904; *y s* of Sir Leicester Harmsworth, 1st Bt and late Annie Louisa Scott; *S* brother, 1962. *Educ:* Harrow. War Correspondent, 1939-40. Sqdn Leader RAFVR. *Publications:* The Maid of the Mountains, Her Story (with Miss José Collins), 1932; Abyssinian Adventure, 1935; I Like America, 1939; Northcliffe (with Reginald Pound), 1959. *Address:* 8 Stratton Street, W1.

**HARMSWORTH, Sir Geoffrey;** *see* Harmsworth, Sir A. G. A.

**HARMSWORTH, Sir Hildebrand Alfred Beresford,** 2nd Bt, *cr* 1922; *b* 27 May 1901; *s* of 1st Bt and Kathleen Mary (*d* 1966), *d* of E. D. Berton, MB; *S* father, 1929; *m*; one *s* one *d. Educ:* Harrow. *Heir:* *s* Hildebrand Harold Harmsworth, *b* 5 June 1931. *Address:* Deepdene, Haslemere, Surrey. *T:* Haslemere 2092.

**HARMSWORTH, St John Bernard Vyvyan;** Metropolitan Magistrate since 1961; *b* 28 Nov. 1912; *e s* of Vyvyan George Harmsworth and

Constance Gwendolen Mary Catt; *m* 1937, Jane Penelope, *er d* of Basil Tandridge Berry Boothby; three *d*. *Educ:* Harrow; New Coll., Oxford. Called to the Bar, Middle Temple, 1937. Served in RNVR, Lieut-Comdr, Oct. 1939-Feb. 1946. *Recreations:* fly fishing, shooting, tennis. *Address:* Horsted Keynes, Sussex. *T:* Danehill 332. *Clubs:* Boodle's, Pratt's.

**HARNDEN, Arthur Baker,** CB 1969; BSc, CEng, FIEE, MBIM; *b* 6 Jan. 1909; *s* of Cecil Henry Harnden and Susan (*née* Baker); *m* 1935, Maisie Elizabeth Annie (*d* 1970), *d* of A. H. Winterburn, LRIBA; one *s*. *Educ:* various state schools. Exec. Engr, GPO, 1933; Royal Corps of Signals, 1939-45; Dir, London Telecommunications Region, GPO, 1962; Senior Dir, Operations, PO (Telecommunications), 1967-69. *Recreation:* painting. *Address:* 108 Friern Park, N Finchley, N12. *T:* 01-445 3296; Comrie, Dipley, Hartley Wintney, Hants.

**HAROLD, Eileen,** MA Oxon; FRSA; Headmistress, Haberdashers' Aske's School for Girls, West Acton, 1944-68; *b* 7 Dec. 1909; *d* of Charles and Margaret Harold. *Educ:* Herts and Essex High Sch., Bishop's Stortford; Lady Margaret Hall, Oxford. On Classical Staff of Sherborne Sch. for Girls, Dorset, 1931-34; on Classical Staff of Haberdashers' Aske's Sch. for Girls, West Acton, 1934-40; Headmistress of North London Collegiate Sch., 1940-44. *Address:* c/o Midland Bank, Sherborne, Dorset.

**HARPER, Prof. Alfred Alexander,** MA, MD; Professor of Physiology, University of Newcastle upon Tyne, since 1963; *b* 19 June 1907; *er s* of James and Elizabeth Harper. *Educ:* Aberdeen Gram. Sch.; Aberdeen Univ. Lecturer in Physiology, University of Leeds, 1935-36; Demonstrator in Physiology, St Thomas's Hosp., London, 1936-39; Lectr, later Reader, in Human Physiology, Univ. of Manchester, 1939-49; Prof. of Physiology, Univ. of Durham, 1949-63. *Publications:* papers in Jl of Physiology mostly on physiology of digestion. *Address:* Department of Physiology, Medical School, University of Newcastle upon Tyne, Newcastle upon Tyne, NE1 7RU. *T:* Newcastle 28511.

**HARPER, Sir Arthur (Grant),** KCVO 1959 (CVO 1954); CBE 1954; now retired; Director: Electronic Development and Applications Co. Ltd (Chm.); Williams Development Holdings Ltd (Chm.); Wareham Associates Ltd (Chm.); a Consultant to Philips Electrical Industries of New Zealand; Trustee, Wellington District Savings Bank; *b* 16 July 1898; *s* of William John and Robina Harper; *m* 1925, Hilda Mary Evans; two *s* one *d*. *Educ:* Hastings High Sch. Entered NZ Civil Service, 1914; held various positions; Sec. for Internal Affairs, also Clerk of the Writs, NZ, 1948-58. Chief Electoral Officer, 1945-50; Dir of Royal Tours of NZ, 1953-54, 1956, 1958. Patron, Pres., Vice-Pres., Chm., Trustee or Mem. of numerous national and local voluntary organizations. JP. *Recreations:* cricket and hockey (past), bowls; interested in most sports; keen walker. *Address:* 23 Ashleigh Crescent, Miramar, Wellington, NZ. *T:* 886-425. *Club:* United Services Officers' (Wellington).

**HARPER, Prof. Denis Rawnsley,** BArch, PhD, MSc Tech, FRIBA, AMTPI, AILA, FIOB, MIA (SA); Professor of Building at the University of Manchester Institute of Science and Technology, since 1957; Warden, Wright Robinson Hall; *b* 27 May 1907; *s* of James William Harper, Harrogate; *m* 1934, Joan Mary Coggin (*d* 1968); one *s* one *d*. *Educ:* Harrogate Grammar Sch.; Univ. of Liverpool Sch. of Architecture. Asst Architect in Hosp. practice in London, 1930-38; RIBA Saxon Snell Prizeman, 1939; Lectr in Sch. of Architecture, University of Cape Town, 1939-49. In private practice (with Prof. Thornton White), in Cape Town, as architect and town planner, 1940-50; Associate Architect in BBC TV Centre, 1950-52; Chief Architect to Corby New Town, Northants, 1952-57. Chm., CNAA Architectural Board; Vice-Chm., Univ. of Lancaster Building Cttee; Vice-President: Inst. of Building; Manchester Soc. of Architects. Mem. the Architectural Assoc. *Publications:* various contribs to technical jls. *Recreations:* walking, cricket and boating. *Address:* Wright Robinson Hall, Manchester. *T:* 061-236 6627; Rose Cottage, Frith Lane, Wrenbury, Cheshire. *T:* Aston 320.

**HARPER, George Clifford;** *b* 8 Aug. 1900; *s* of Charles George and Emily Harper, Newcastle upon Tyne; *m* 1925, Georgette Marie Aimée Guéry; one *s* two *d*. *Educ:* Shrewsbury Sch.; Christ Church, Oxford. Traffic Apprentice LNER; Asst Master at Stowe and Bedford; Headmaster of King Edward VI Sch., Southampton, until 1946; HM Inspector of Schools, 1947-60 (Metropolitan Divisional Inspector, 1952-60); Mem., Anglo-French Mixed Cultural Commn, 1954-60; Chm. and Dir, British Cttee for Interchange of Teachers with USA, 1960-65. Officier d'Académie. Governor: Shrewsbury Sch.; Dartford Coll. of Education. *Address:* 172 Coleherne Court, SW5. *T:* 01-373 4426.

**HARPER, George MacGowan;** *b* 18 March 1899; 3rd *s* of James Harper, MD; *m* 1930, Ruth Musgrave, 2nd *d* of Sir Ernest Musgrave Harvey, KBE (marriage dissolved, 1947); one *d* (one *s* decd). *Educ:* Tonbridge; Royal Military Academy, Woolwich. Served with RHA, France, 1918. Entered Lloyd's, 1921; first served on Cttee of Lloyd's, 1945; Dep. Chm. of Lloyd's, 1953. *Recreation:* golf. *Address:* 12 Arundel Court, Jubilee Place, SW3. *T:* 01-352 2711. *Clubs:* Brooks's, United Service; Honourable Company of Edinburgh Golfers.

**HARPER, Heather (Mary), (Mrs Buck),** CBE 1965; soprano; *b* 8 May 1930; *d* of late Hugh Harper, Belfast; *m* 1952, Leonard Buck. *Educ:* Trinity Coll. of Music, London. Has sung many principal roles at Covent Garden, Glyndebourne and Sadler's Wells; has also sung at many Festivals and at every Promenade Concert season since 1957; she sang the soprano role in Benjamin Britten's War Requiem at the World Première in Coventry Cathedral in 1962, and since then in Europe and Australia; she has also sung in the US, Middle East and Far East. FTCL. Hon. DMus, Queen's Univ., Belfast, 1966. *Recreations:* gardening, cooking. *Address:* 15 Lancaster Grove, Hampstead, NW3.

**HARPER, Joseph,** JP; MP (Lab) Pontefract since March 1962; an Opposition Whip, since 1970; *b* 17 March 1914; *m* 1939, Gwendoline Hughes; two *s* two *d*. *Educ:* Featherstone Elementary Sch. Started work at Snydale Colliery, Yorks, 1928. Deleg. for Local Branch of NUM, 1943-62; served on Yorks area NUM Exec. Cttee, 1947-48 and 1950-52. Mem. Featherstone UDC, 1949-63 (Chm., 1955-56 and 1961-62); Chm. Featherstone Managers of Primary Schs and Governors of Secondary Sch., 1955-62; Vice-Chm. Divl Educn Executive, 1955-62; Mem. Osgoldcross Cremation Board, 1957-62; Mem. Pontefract and Castleford Hospital Management Cttee, 1958-; an Asst Government Whip, 1964-66; a Lord Comr of the Treasury, 1966-70. JP, WR Yorks, 1959. *Recreations:* music, first aid.

*Address:* 11 Bedford Close, Purston, Featherstone, near Pontefract, Yorks.

**HARPER, Norman Adamson;** Chairman, Gemmological Association of Great Britain, since 1965; Founder-Director, Perry Greaves Ltd, 1964; Director: W. A. Perry & Co. Ltd, 1953; Gemmological Instruments Ltd, 1965; *b* 15 Oct. 1913; *s* of Andrew Adamson Harper, Newcastle-upon-Tyne; *m* 1st, 1935, Priscilla (*d* 1956), *d* of William George Hoverd; three *s* one *d*; 2nd, 1957, Brenda, *d* of Robert Watts; one *s*. *Educ:* Rutherford Coll.; Durham Univ. Dip. Nat. Assoc. Goldsmiths, 1946. FGA 1934; FRGS 1946; Fellow, Nat. Jewellers' Assoc., 1947; FInstD 1953. Chm., Nat. Assoc. of Goldsmiths, 1961-63; Guardian of Standard of Wrought Plate in Birmingham, 1963-; Sen. Lectr on Gemstones and Jewellery, City of Birmingham Sch. of Jewellery and Silversmithing, 1946-66; Founder, Course on Gem Diamonds for Jewellers, 1962. Freedom of Goldsmiths' Co. (Special Award), 1947; Freedom of City of London, 1947. Winner of Greenough Trophy, 1946. *Publications:* Introduction to Gemstones, 1955; Handbook on Gem Diamonds, 1965; articles in Jl of Gemmology, British Jeweller, Watchmaker and Jeweller, etc. *Recreations:* keyboard music, historical studies. *Address:* 61 Chester Road, Streetly, Sutton Coldfield, Warwicks. *T:* 021-353 2230. *Clubs:* Royal Aero; Conservative (Birmingham); Sutton Coldfield (Sutton Coldfield).

**HARPER, Alderman Sir Richard Stephenson,** Kt 1958; JP; *b* 30 Dec. 1902; *o s* of late Alderman Richard S. Harper, JP and Mrs Edith C. Harper, JP, Harnham House, Slade Lane, Manchester 19; *m* 1942, Lily, *o d* of late Nathaniel and Elizabeth Walker, Manchester; one *s*. *Educ:* Manchester Gram. Sch.; Chorlton-cum-Hardy Gram. Sch.; Bonar Law Coll., Ashridge, Herts. Electrical and Gen. Engineering, 1920-25; Priv. Sec. to Ald. R. S. Harper Sen., 1925-32; City Councillor, Manchester, 1932-51; Alderman, City of Manchester, 1951-; Lord Mayor of Manchester, 1954-55. Chm. of several Corporation Cttees at various times; Dir (apptd by Manchester Corp.) of Manchester Ship Canal Co. Ltd, 1945-; contested (C) Exchange Div. Gen. Election, 1950. Religion: Church of England; special interest housing. Divl Warden Civil Defence, Manchester, 1937-46 (CD Medal, 1946). *Publications:* political pamphlets. *Address:* Harnham House, Slade Lane, Manchester 19. *T:* 061-224 4419. *Clubs:* local political.

**HARPHAM, Sir William,** KBE 1966 (OBE 1948); CMG 1953; Director, Great Britain-East Europe Centre, 1967; *b* 3 Dec. 1906; *o s* of W. Harpham and N. Harpham (*née* Stout); *m* 1943, Isabelle Marie Sophie Droz; one *s* one *d*. *Educ:* Wintringham Secondary Sch., Grimsby; Christ's Coll., Cambridge. Entered Dept of Overseas Trade, 1929; transferred to Embassy, Brussels, 1931, Rome, 1934; Private Sec. to Parliamentary Sec. for Overseas Trade, 1936; seconded to League of Nations, 1937; reverted to Dept of Overseas Trade, 1939; served: Cairo, 1940-44; Beirut, 1944-47; appointed Counsellor (Commercial) at Berne, 1947; Head of Gen. Dept, Foreign Office, 1950-53; Dep. to UK Delegate to OEEC, 1953-56; Minister, British Embassy, Tokyo, 1956-59; Minister (Economic), Paris, 1959-63; Ambassador to Bulgaria, 1964-66; retd 1967. Order of Madara Horseman, Bulgaria, 1969. *Address:* 9 Kings Keep, Putney Hill, SW15. *T:* 01-788 1383. *Clubs:* Travellers', Royal Automobile.

**HARRER, Prof. Heinrich;** author and explorer; (awarded title of Professor by President of Austrian Republic, 1964); *b* 6 July 1912; *m*; one *s*; *m* 1953, Margaretha Truxa (marriage dissolved 1958); *m* 1962, Katharina Haarhaus. *Educ:* University of Graz, Austria (graduated in Geography, 1938). First ascent, Eiger North Wall, 1938; Himalayan Expedition, 1939; interned in India, 1939-44; Tibet, 1944-51; Himalayan Expedition, 1951; expedition to the Andes, 1953; to Alaska, 1954; to Ruwenzori (Mountains of the Moon), Africa, 1957; to West New Guinea, 1961-62; to Nepal, 1965; to Xingu Red Indians in Mato Grosso, Brazil; to Bush Negroes of Surinam (Surinam Expedn with King Leopold of Belgium), 1966. Austrian National Amateur Golf Champion, 1958; Pres., Austrian Golf Association, 1964. *Publications:* Seven Years in Tibet, 1953 (Great Britain, and numerous other countries); Meine Tibet-Bilder, 1953 (Germany); The White Spider, History of the North Face of the Eiger, 1958; Tibet is My Country: Biography of Thubten Jigme Norbu, *e b* of Dalai Lama, 1960 (Eng.); I Come from the Stone Age, 1964 (London). *Address:* c/o Liechtenstein Verlag, Vaduz, Liechtenstein.

**HARREY, C. O. W.;** *see* Wakefield-Harrey.

**HARRIES, Rear-Adm. David Hugh,** CB 1961; CBE 1952; RAN (Retired); *b* 27 June 1903; *s* of David Henry Harries, Melbourne, Australia; *m* 1933, Margaret, *d* of Edric H. Street, Camden, New South Wales; two *s*. *Educ:* Melbourne Church of England Gram. Sch.; Royal Australian Naval College, Jervis Bay, NSW; 2nd Naval Mem., Aust. Naval Bd, 1952-53; Rear-Adm. 1954; Head of Australian Joint Service Staff, Washington, DC, USA, 1953-55; Flag Officer comdg HM Australian Fleet, 1956-58; retired 1960. US Legion of Merit, 1955. *Recreations:* golf, foreign languages. *Address:* 3 Graylind Place, Vaucluse, NSW, Australia. *Clubs:* Union, Royal Sydney Golf (Sydney); Naval and Military (Melbourne).

**HARRIES, Air Vice-Marshal Sir Douglas,** KCB, *cr* 1947 (CB 1943); AFC 1918; retired; *b* 31 March 1893; 2nd *s* of W. J. Harries, Sidcup, Kent; *m* 1924. *Educ:* Royal Naval Colleges, Osborne and Dartmouth. Retired list, 1946. *Address:* Mill Lane Cottage, Crondall, near Farnham, Surrey.

**HARRIES, Victor Percy,** CB 1953; Secretary and Solicitor, British Airports Authority, since 1965; *b* 27 Oct. 1907; *s* of late Henry Percy Harries; *m* 1932, Etheldreda (Audrey), *d* of late Joseph Lorkin; one *s* two *d*. *Educ:* Ealing Priory Sch.; St Benedict's; University of London (LLB Hons). Admitted Solicitor (Hons), 1930; Partner in firm of Reynolds, Sons & Gorst, London, until 1939; Principal, Min. of Supply (later Aviation), 1939; Asst Sec. Lands and Legal Branch, 1940; Principal Asst Sec., 1944; Under Sec., 1949, in charge successively of Metals, Electronics and Guided Weapons, Contracts, and Airports Divisions. Mem. Catholic Union of GB; Mem., Hon. Soc. of Cymmrodorian. *Address:* 89 Exeter House, Putney Heath, SW15.

**HARRIMAN, Averell;** *see* Harriman, William A.

**HARRIMAN, Sir George,** Kt 1965; CBE 1951 (OBE 1943); President, British Leyland Motor Corporation, since 1968 (Chairman, 1968). Joined Austin Motor Company, 1940; appointed to Board, 1945; Works Director; Deputy Chairman, Austin Motor Co., 1952-61; appointed to Board of British Motor Corporation on its formation, 1952; Deputy Managing Director, 1952-56; Deputy Chairman and Joint Managing Director, 1956-58; Deputy Chairman and Sole Managing Director, 1958-61; Chairman and Managing

Director, 1961; Executive Chairman, 1967-68. Chairman, British Motor Holdings, 1967-68; Chairman and Managing Director, Austin Motor Co., 1961-68. President Society of Motor Manufacturers and Traders, 1967, 1968. *Recreations:* golf, fishing. *Address:* British Leyland Motor Corporation Ltd, Longbridge Works, Birmingham. *T:* 021-475 2101.

**HARRIMAN, (William) Averell;** US Ambassador-at-Large, 1965-69; *b* 15 Nov. 1891; *s* of late Edward Henry Harriman and Mary Williamson Averell; *m* 1st, 1915, Kitty Lanier Lawrence (decd); two *d*; 2nd, 1930, Mrs Marie Norton Whitney. *Educ:* Groton Sch., Yale Univ., BA 1913. Partner Brown Brothers Harriman & Co. since 1931, Limited partner since 1946; Chairman of the Board, Union Pacific Railroad Co. 1932-46; Mem. Business Advisory Council for the Dept of Commerce since 1933 (Chm., 1937-40). Vice-Pres. in Charge of Purchases and Supplies of Union Pacific Railroad Co., 1914-18; Chm. Board of Merchant Ship-building Corp., 1917-25; Chm. Board of W. A. Harriman & Co., Inc. (merged with Brown Brothers, 1931), 1920-30; Chm. Exec. Cttee Ill. Central Railroad Co., 1931-42; National Recovery Administration: Division Administrator of Div. II, Jan.-March 1934, Special Asst Administrator, March-May, 1934, Administrative Officer, Nov. 1934-June 1935; Associated with Industrial Materials Div., National Defense Advisory Commission, 1940; Chief, Materials Branch, Production Div., Office of Production Management, Jan.-March 1941; Pres. Roosevelt's Special Representative in Great Britain with rank of Minister, March 1941; Special Rep. of the Pres. and Chm. of the President's Special Mission to USSR with rank of Ambassador, 1941; US Representative in London of Combined Shipping Adjustment Board, 1942; Mem. London Combined Production and Resources Board, 1942; US Ambassador to USSR, 1943-46; to Britain, 1946; US Sec. of Commerce, 1946-48; US Special Representative in Europe under Economic Co-operation Act of 1948 (with rank of Ambassador) until 1950; US Rep. on N Atlantic Defence, Financial and Economic Cttee, 1949; Special Asst to Pres. Truman, 1950-51; Chm. NATO Commission on Defense Plans, 1951; Dir of Foreign Aid under Mutual Security Act, 1951-53; Governor, State of New York, Jan. 1955-Nov. 1958; US Ambassador-at-Large, Feb.-Dec. 1961 and 1965-69; Asst Sec. of State for Far Eastern Affairs, 1961-63; Under-Sec. for Political Affairs, 1963-65. US Representative, Vietnam Peace Talks, Paris, 1968-69. Democrat. *Publication:* Peace with Russia?, 1960. *Address:* (residence) 16 E 81st Street, New York City, NY 10028, USA.

**HARRINGTON,** 11th Earl of, *cr* 1742; **William Henry Leicester Stanhope;** Viscount Stanhope of Mahon and Baron Stanhope of Elvaston, Co. Derby, 1717; Baron Harrington, 1729; Viscount Petersham, 1742; late Captain RAC; *b* 24 Aug. 1922; *o s* of 10th Earl and Margaret Trelawney (Susan), (*d* 1952), *d* of Major H. H. D. Seaton; *S* father, 1929; *m* 1st, 1942, Eileen (from whom he obtained a divorce, 1946), *o d* of late Sir John Grey, Enville Hall, Stourbridge; one *s* two *d*; 2nd, 1947, Anne Theodora (from whom he obtained a divorce, 1962), *o d* of late Major Richard Arenbourg Blennerhassett Chute; one *s* two *d*; 3rd, 1964, Priscilla Margaret, *d* of Hon. A. E. Cubitt and Mrs Ronald Dawnay; one *s* one *d*. *Educ:* Eton; RMC, Sandhurst. Served War of 1939-45, demobilised 1946. Owns about 700 acres. Became Irish Citizen, 1965. *Heir: s* Viscount Petersham, *qv*. *Address:* Greenmount Stud, Patrickswell, Co. Limerick, Eire.
*See also Baron Ashcombe.*

**HARRIS,** family name of **Baron Harris** and of **Earl of Malmesbury.**

**HARRIS,** 5th Baron (of Seringapatam and Mysore, and of Belmont, Kent, *cr* 1815); **George St Vincent Harris,** MC; JP; Vice-Lieutenant of Kent; *b* 3 Sept. 1889; *e s* of 4th Baron and Hon. Lucy Ada Jervis, CI (*d* 1930), *d* of 3rd Viscount St Vincent; *S* father, 1932; *m* 1918, Dorothy Mary, *d* of Rev. W. J. Crookes, late Vicar of Borden; one *s*. *Educ:* Eton; Christ Church, Oxford (MA). Capt. late Royal East Kent Imperial Yeomanry; served European War, 1914-18 (MC, wounded, despatches). Grand Master, Mark Master Masons of England, etc; Grand Master, Masonic Knights Templar of England, etc. Commissioner St John Amb. Brigade for Kent, 1940-45; Chm. Kent Police Authority, 1945-64; KStJ 1949-. JP, Kent, 1919. *Heir: s* Hon. George Robert John Harris, *b* 17 April 1920. *Address:* Belmont Park, Faversham, Kent. *Clubs:* Carlton, Beefsteak.

**HARRIS, Sir Archibald,** Kt, *cr* 1944; *b* 10 Dec. 1883; *s* of Rev. Isidore Harris, MA, London; *m* 1919, Phoebe (*d* 1962), *d* of Ernest Meyer, Ladbroke Grove, London, and West Street House, Eastry, Kent. *Educ:* University Coll. Sch. Entered firm of Louis Bamberger & Sons, London (Timber Importers), in 1901, Partner, 1919; Dir Bambergers Ltd until 1963 (a former Vice-Chm.). Temporary 2nd Lieut RASC (T) Aug. 1914 and Temporary Capt. Oct. 1914; served France and Macedonia, 1915-18 (despatches twice, Bt Major). Pres. Timber Trade Federation of UK 1937-39; Mem. Timber Trade Federation's delegation to Imperial Conference, Ottawa, 1932; Timber Controller, Ministry of Supply, 1939-47. Officier de l'ordre de la Mérite Agricole, 1937; American Medal of Freedom, 1947. *Recreations:* travel, bridge. *Address:* 32 London House, Avenue Road, NW8. *T:* 01-586 0995. *Clubs:* Bath, Hardingham, East India and Sports; Royal Thames Yacht.

**HARRIS, Marshal of the Royal Air Force Sir Arthur Travers,** 1st Bt, *cr* 1953; GCB 1945 (KCB 1942; CB 1940); OBE 1927; AFC 1918; *b* 13 April 1892; *m* 1st, 1916; one *s* two *d*; 2nd, 1938, Thérèse Hearne; one *d*. Served European War, 1914-19, 1st Rhodesian Regt, RFC, and RAF; Group Capt. 1933; Air Commodore, 1937; Air Vice-Marshal, 1939; Air Marshal, 1941; Air Chief Marshal, 1943; AOC, RAF Palestine and Transjordan, 1938-39; AOC, 5 Bomber Group, 1939-41; Deputy Chief of Air Staff, 1940-41; Head of Royal Air Force Delegation to USA, 1941; Commander-in-Chief Bomber Command 1942-45. Marshal of the RAF 1945. Managing Director South African Marine Corporation, 1946-53. Order of Suvorov (1st class) (Russia), 1944, Grand Cross Polonia Restituta (Poland), 1945, Chief Commander Legion of Merit (US), 1944; Grand Cross Order of the Southern Cross (Brazil), 1945; Grand Officier Légion d'Honneur, Croix de guerre avec palme (France), 1945; DSM (US), 1945. Freeman of Honiton and of Chepping Wycombe; Hon. LLD Liverpool, 1946. *Heir: s* Anthony Kyrle Travers Harris, *b* 18 March 1918. *Address:* The Ferry House, Goring-on-Thames, Oxon. *Clubs:* Royal and Ancient (St Andrews); Bankers (New York); Nederlandsche (Cape Town).

**HARRIS, Rt. Rev. Augustine;** Titular Bishop of Socia and Auxiliary Bishop of Liverpool, (RC), since 1965; *b* 27 Oct. 1917; *s* of Augustine Harris and Louisa Beatrice (*née*

Rycroft). *Educ:* St Francis Xavier's Coll., Liverpool; Upholland Coll., Lancs. Ordained, 1942; Curate at: St Oswald's, Liverpool, 1942-43; St Elizabeth's, Litherland, Lancs, 1943-52; Prison Chaplain, HM Prison, Liverpool, 1952-65; Sen. RC Priest, Prison Dept, 1957-66; English Rep. to Internat. Coun. of Sen. Prison Chaplains (RC), 1957-66. Mem. Vatican Delegn to UN Quinquennial Congress on Crime, London, 1960 and Stockholm, 1965; Liaison between English and Welsh Hierarchy (RC) and Home Office, 1966-. *Publications:* articles for criminological works. *Recreations:* golf, walking. *Address:* Archbishop's House, Liverpool. *T:* 051-428 1233.

**HARRIS, Sir Charles (Felix),** Kt 1968; MD, FRCP; Hon. FRCS; Officier Orde van Oranje-Nassau; Consulting Physician for Diseases of Children, late Physician i/c the Children's Department St Bartholomew's Hospital; Physician, The Westminster Children's Hospital, Vincent Square; Consultant Pædiatrist to London County Council; Chairman of Convocation, University of London, since Oct. 1961; Member of Senate since 1950, of Court since 1951 (Vice-Chancellor of the University, 1958-61); *b* 30 March 1900; *s* of G. Felix Harris and Ellen Charles; *m* 1929, Edith Nadejda Goldsmith; no *c.* *Educ:* Epsom Coll.; St Bart.'s Hosp. Medical Coll. House Physician, and Chief Asst St Bartholomew's Hospital (Kirkes Scholarship, 1922, Lawrence Research Scholarship, 1925), House Physician Hospital for Sick Children, Great Ormond Street; Asst, with Rockefeller Fellowship, Pediatrics Dept Johns Hopkins Hospital, Baltimore, USA; Med. Off. i/c (EMS) St Bartholomew's Hospital, London, 1939-46; sometime Examiner in Children's Diseases, Leeds, Birmingham and Aberdeen; Dean, Faculty of Medicine, University of London, 1952-56; Dean, St Bartholomew's Hosp. Med. Coll., 1945-52, Warden, 1936-45, Vice-Pres., 1960-65. Hon. Sec., Royal Society Medicine, 1941-46; Pres. British Pædiatric Assoc., 1962-63. Editor Archives of Disease in Childhood, 1934-38. *Publications:* various in medical and scientific journals. *Recreations:* shooting, gardening. *Address:* Combe Wood Cottage, Ewshott, Hants. *T:* Crondall 203. *Clubs:* Oriental; North Hampshire Golf.

**HARRIS, Sir Charles Herbert S.;** *see* Stuart-Harris.

**HARRIS, Sir Charles Joseph William,** KBE 1961 (CBE 1927); Kt 1952; Private Secretary to successive Parliamentary Secretaries to Treasury, 1919-24, 1924-29 and 1931-61; retired as Assistant Secretary, HM Treasury, 1961; *b* 1901; *m* 1924, Emily Kyle Thompson; one *s* two *d.* *Educ:* Christ Church Sch., Ramsgate; privately. Private Sec. to Conservative Chief Whip, 1924 and 1929-31. Freeman, City of London; Mem., Court of Assistants, Guild of Freemen of City of London; Liveryman, Scriveners' Company; Is a dir of public companies. *Address:* 3 Burcote Road, SW18. *T:* 01-874 8226. *Club:* City Livery.

**HARRIS, Charles Reginald Schiller,** MA, DPhil Oxon, PhD Princeton and Adelaide; MInstT; *b* 10 April 1896; *e s* of late Sir Charles Harris, GBE, KCB; *m* 1931, Lucia Marie Ghislaine, *o d* of late Dom José de Figueiredo de Pitinga and of late Mrs C. T. Terry; one *d.* *Educ:* Clifton Coll.; Corpus Christi Coll., Oxford (Scholar). 1st Class Lit. Hum., 1920; Senior Demy, Magdalen Coll., Oxon, 1920-21; Jane Eliza Procter Visiting Fellow, Princeton Univ., New Jersey, 1922-23; Fellow of All Souls Coll., Oxford, 1921-36; Editor of The Nineteenth Century and After, 1930-35; Leader Writer on the Staff of the Times, 1925-35, and the Economist, 1932-35; Dir-Gen., Buenos Aires Gt Southern and Western Railways, 1935-59; Dir, Entre Rios, Argentine North Eastern and Central Uruguay Railways, 1939-47. Commercial Counsellor HM Legation, Reykjavik, Iceland, 1940-42; Lieut-Col General List; Dir Property Control, AMGOT, Sicily, 1943, Allied Control Commission, Italy, 1944; Reader in Studies in the Humanities for Medical Students and Tutor of St Mark's Coll., Adelaide Univ., 1958-65. Hon. Fellow, St Mark's Coll., Adelaide. *Publications:* Duns Scotus, 1927; Germany's Foreign Indebtedness, published under the auspices of the Royal Institute of International Affairs, 1935; vol. on Allied Administration of Italy, 1943-45, in the Official History of the Second World War, 1958. *Recreation:* fishing. *Address:* Rock House, Wheatley, Oxon. *Club:* Athenæum.

**HARRIS, Colin Grendon,** CMG 1964; HM Diplomatic Service, retired; *b* 25 Oct. 1912; *m* 1941, Adelaide Zamoiska (decd); *m* 1947, Monique Jacqueline Marcuse-Baudoux; four *s* two *d.* *Educ:* Rossall Sch.; Pembroke Coll., Cambridge. Entered Foreign (subseq. Diplomatic) Service, 1935; served Antwerp, Elisabethville, Leopoldville, Lisbon, Montevideo, Rio de Janeiro, Vienna, Tokyo, Oslo, retired 1969. *Recreations:* tennis, swimming. *Address:* c/o Foreign and Commonwealth Office, SW1.

**HARRIS, Diana R.;** *see* Reader Harris.

**HARRIS, Rev. Donald Bertram;** Vicar of St Paul's, Knightsbridge, since 1955; *b* 4 Aug. 1904; unmarried. *Educ:* King's Coll. Choir Sch., Cambridge; Haileybury Coll.; King's Coll., Cambridge; Cuddesdon Coll., Oxford. Chorister, King's Coll. Choir, 1915-19; Choral Scholar, King's Coll., Cambridge, 1923-26; BA 1925; MA 1929; Ordained Deacon, 1927; Priest, 1928; Curate of Chesterfield Parish Church, 1927-31; St Mary the Less, Cambridge, 1931-36. Chaplain of King's Coll., Cambridge, 1932-33; Examg Chaplain to Bishop of Wakefield, 1932-36; Rector of Great Greenford, Middx, 1936-45; Archdeacon of Bedford 1946-55, and Rector of St Mary's Bedford, 1945-55, Life Governor, Haileybury and Imperial Service Coll., 1946-. Pres. Association for Promoting Retreats, 1968. *Address:* St Paul's Vicarage, Wilton Place, SW1. *T:* 01-235 1810. *Club:* Royal Thames Yacht.

**HARRIS, (Emanuel) Vincent,** OBE; Hon. DLitt, Exeter; RA 1942 (ARA 1936); FRIBA; Treasurer of the Royal Academy, retired, 1954; *s* of Major Emanuel Harris and Mary Vincent; *m* Edith (*d* 1965), *d* of William Maule, MD. *Educ:* Kingsbridge Gram. Sch. Architect for Manchester Central Library and Town Hall Extension, Sheffield City Hall, Leeds Civic Hall, University Coll. of SW, Exeter, Glamorgan County Hall, Surrey County Hall, Somerset County Hall, Bristol Council House; Science Buildings taunton Sch.; Nottinghamshire County Hall; selected Architect in competition for HM New Government Buildings, Whitehall, and many other public buildings. Royal Gold Medal for Architecture, 1951. *Address:* Chard School, Chard, Somerset. *Clubs:* Savage, Reform; Nottinghamshire (Nottingham).

**HARRIS, Euan Cadogan;** Principal Assistant Solicitor, Ministry of Agriculture, Fisheries and Food, since 1964; *b* 6 June 1906; *s* of late Charles Poulett Harris, MD and Violet Harris; *m* 1931, Brenda, *er d* of late William Turnbull Bowman, OBE and Jessie Bowman; two *d.*

*Educ:* Epsom Coll.; Clare Coll., Cambridge. BA 1927; LLB 1928. Admitted Solicitor (Edmund Thomas Child Prize), 1930. Entered Legal Dept of Min. of Agric. and Fisheries, 1935. *Recreations:* walking, swimming; reading, especially history. *Address:* 6 Newlands Road, Rottingdean, Sussex. *T:* Brighton 32019.

*See also A. K. Rothie.*

**HARRIS, Frank;** *see* Harris, W. F.

**HARRIS, Frederic Walter;** Chairman and Managing Director, Marshall's Universal Ltd; Chairman: Marshall's (East Africa) Ltd; Marshall's Investments Ltd; Kenya Orchards Ltd; Maryland Estates Ltd; Marshall's Proprietaries Ltd; Marshall House Ltd; Distributors Peugeot Ltd; Tanganyka Motors Ltd; Delta Ltd; Martint Universal Sales Ltd; *b* 6 March 1915; *s* of Alice and Walter Harris; *m* 1st, 1939, Betty Eileen Benson (*d* 1955); one *s* two *d*; 2nd, 1957, Joan Hope, *d* of David N. K. Bagnall, Overmist, Tadworth, Surrey. *Educ:* Belmont Coll. Streatham. Founded food-producing company as Dir, 1934; Joint Man. Dir of same company known as Marshall's Universal Ltd, 1939, Man. Dir, 1945-63, Chm and Man. Dir, 1964- (company's capital now £ 386,368); Owner of Maryland Estates Ltd, a large farming estate in Kenya. MP (C), North Croydon, 1948-55, North West Croydon, 1955-70. Freeman of City of London; Freedom of Croydon, 1970; Liveryman of Basketmakers. *Address:* Wood Rising, The Ridge, Woldingham, Surrey. *T:* Woldingham 2365. *Clubs:* Surrey Conservatives and Unionists, Constitutional (Croydon).

**HARRIS, Lieut-Gen. Sir Frederick,** KBE, *cr* 1953 (CBE 1944); CB 1949; *b* 21 June 1891; *s* of J. Porter Harris; *m* 1918, Sheila Isabel (*d* 1967), *d* of W. Boyd; one *s* one *d*. *Educ:* Coleraine Sch.; Trinity Coll., Dublin. Lieut RAMC 1915; Capt. 1916; Major 1927; Lieut-Col 1940; Temp. Col 1941; Temp. Brig. 1944; Col 1945; Actg Maj.-Gen. 1947; Temp. Maj.-Gen. 1947; Maj.-Gen. 1948. European War, 1914-19, Gallipoli Egypt, France, Italy (MC, 1915 star, Allied and Victory medals, despatches, twice wounded); NW Frontier of India, 1936 37 (medal and clasp); War of 1939-45 on staff of Northern Command, India, 1939-41; on staff of GHQ India Command, 1941-45; Deputy Dir Medical Services 12 Army, Sept.-Dec. 1945 (Burma Star, Defence Medal, 1939-45 War medal); DDMS, Burma Command, Jan.-July 1946; Asst Dir Med. Services, Aldershot and Hants District, 1946-47; DMS, MELF, 1947-48; Dep. Dir.-Gen., Army Med. Services, Dec. 1948-Apr. 1952; Dir-Gen., Army Medical Services, WO, April 1952-56; QHS, 1946-56; retired May 1956. *Address:* 609 Nelson House, Dolphin Square, SW1.

**HARRIS, Prof. Geoffrey Wingfield,** CBE 1965; FRS 1953; MA, MD, ScD Cantab; DM Oxford, 1962; Dr Lee's Professor of Anatomy, University of Oxford, since Oct. 1962; Hon. Director of MRC Neuroendocrinology Research Unit, since 1962; Hon. Consultant in Psychiatry, Oxford United Hospitals and Oxford Regional Hospital Board; *b* 4 June 1913; *s* of late Tom Harris, Ballistics Research Dept, Woolwich Arsenal; *m* 1st, 1936 (marr. diss. 1951); one *s*; 2nd, 1951, Margaret, *d* of late Dr M. J. O'Kane, Cushendall; two *d*. *Educ:* Dulwich Coll.; University Coll., London Univ.; Emmanuel Coll., Cambridge; St Mary's Hospital, London. Scholar (Emmanuel); Colin Mackenzie Prize, 1935; Marmaduke Shield Student in Anatomy, Cambridge, 1935; Harmsworth Scholar, St Mary's Hosp., 1936; Agnes Cope Prize and Wallace Memorial Prize, 1939. Res. MO, Hillingdon County Hosp., 1939-40. Univ. of Cambridge: Demr in Anat., 1940-47; Lectr in Anat. 1947-48; Lectr in Physiology, 1948-52. Senior Lecturer in Physiology, Univ. of London, 1952; Fitzmary Prof. of Physiology, Institute of Psychiatry, London Univ., 1952-62. Claude Bernard Visiting Prof. Univ. of Montreal, 1950; Visiting Prof.: Univ. of Calif., Los Angeles, 1953; Univ. of Calif., San Francisco, 1954-55; Rockefeller Univ., NY, 1967. Lectures: Herter, Johns Hopkins Hosp., 1955; Sharpey-Schafer, Edinburgh Univ., 1957; Richardson, Massachusetts Gen. Hospital, 1958; Upjohn, San Francisco, 1964; Feldberg, Cologne, 1964; Keith Harrison Memorial, Melbourne, 1965; Charnock Bradley, Edinburgh, 1966; Rehfuss, Philadelphia, 1967; Harry Burr Ferris, Yale, 1967; Member: Society for Endocrinology; Society for Study of Fertility; Anatomical Soc.; Physiol. Soc. Hon. Member: Swiss Soc. for Endocrinology; Amer. Acad. of Arts and Sciences; Royal Acad. of Denmark; Amer. Assoc. Anatomy, 1970; Corresp. Mem., Sociedad Argentina de Biologia, 1970. Fred Lyman Adair Award, Amer. Gynaec. Soc., 1969; Baly Medal, RCP, 1969; Amory Prize, Amer. Acad. Arts and Sciences, 1970. DSc (Detroit), 1965; Hon. DUniv, Strasbourg, 1969. *Publications:* Neural Control of the Pituitary Gland, 1955; scientific papers dealing with Neuroendocrinology, Jl Physiol, etc. *Recreations:* reading, forestry, and travel. *Address:* Department of Human Anatomy, South Parks Road, Oxford. *T:* 58686; Campsfield Wood, Woodstock, Oxon.

**HARRIS, Professor Harry,** FRS 1966; Galton Professor of Human Genetics, University of London at University College, since 1965; Hon. Director, Medical Research Council Human Biochemical Genetics Research Unit, since 1962; Hon. Consulting Geneticist, University College Hospital, since 1966; *b* 30 Sept. 1919; *m* 1948, Muriel Hargest; one *s*. *Educ:* Manchester Gram. Sch.; Trinity Coll., Cambridge. (MA, MD). Research Asst, Galton Laboratory, Dept of Eugenics, Biometry, and Genetics UC, London, 1947-50; Leverhulme Scholar, RCP, 1947-48; Lund Research Fellow, Diabetic Assoc., 1949; Lectr, Dept of Biochem., UC, London, 1950-53; Sen. Lectr, 1953-58, Reader in Biochem. Genetics, 1958-60, Dept of Biochem., The London Hosp. Med. Coll.; Prof. of Biochem., University of London, at King's Coll., 1960-65. Hon. Lectr, 1950-55, Hon. Research Associate, 1955-60, Dept of Eugenics, Biometry, and Genetics, UC, London. Nat. Research Coun. of Canada and Nuffield Foundation Vis. Lectr, British Columbia and McGill, 1967. Lectures: Thomas Young, St George's Hosp. Med. Sch., 1966; De Frees, University Penna, 1966; Walter R. Bloor, Univ. Rochester, 1967; Langdon Brown, RCP, 1968; Sir William Jackson Pope, RSA, 1968; Darwin, Inst. Biol., 1969; Leonard Parsons, Birmingham Univ., 1969; Sidney Ringer, UCH Med. Sch., 1970. William Allan Meml Award, Amer. Soc. of Human Genetics, 1968. *Publications:* An Introduction to Human Biochemical Genetics (Eugenics Laboratory Memoir Series), 1953; Human Biochemical Genetics, 1959; The Principles of Human Biochemical Genetics, 1970. *Address:* 25 Southwood Avenue, Highgate, N6. *T:* 01-340 2416.

**HARRIS, Prof. Henry,** FRS 1968; Professor of Pathology, University of Oxford, since 1963; Hon. Director, Cancer Research Campaign, Cell Biology Unit, since 1963; Fellow of Lincoln College; *b* 28 Jan. 1925; *s* of Sam and Ann Harris; *m* 1950, Alexandra Fanny Brodsky; one *s* two *d*. *Educ:* Sydney Boys' High Sch. and University of Sydney, Australia;

Lincoln Coll., Oxford. Public Exhibnr, University of Sydney, 1942; BA Mod. Langs, 1944; MBBS 1950; Travelling Schol. of Austr. Nat. Univ. at Univ. of Oxford, 1952; MA; DPhil (Oxon.), 1954. Dir of Research, Brit. Empire Cancer Campaign, at Sir William Dunn Sch. of Pathology, Oxford, 1954-59; Visiting Scientist, Nat. Institutes of Health, USA, 1959-60; Head of Dept of Cell Biology, John Innes Inst., 1960-63; Vis. Prof., Vanderbilt Univ., 1968; Walker-Ames Prof., University of Washington, 1968; Mem. ARC, 1968-. Lectures: Sigma Xi, Yale, 1967; Almroth Wright, 1968; Hoffman La Roche, Rutgers, 1969; Harvey, Harvey Soc. NY, 1969; Dunham, Harvard, 1969; Jenner Meml, 1970. Foreign Hon. Mem., Amer. Acad. Arts and Sciences. *Publications:* Nucleus and Cytoplasm, 1968; Cell Fusion, 1970; numerous papers on cellular physiology and biochemistry, in scientific books and jls. *Recreation:* history. *Address:* Sir William Dunn School of Pathology, South Parks Road, Oxford. *T:* Oxford 57321.

**HARRIS, Rev. Preb. Herbert,** MVO 1962; MA; retired; *b* 2 Sept. 1884; *s* of Alfred and Mary Harris; unmarried. *Educ:* Merchant Taylors' Sch., London; St Catharine's Coll. and Westcott House, Cambridge. BA 1906, MA 1911, Cambridge. Ordained, 1907; Curate of Gt Torrington, 1907-11; of S. Saviour, Alexandra Park, N22, 1911-24; Vicar of S Saviour, Alexandra Park, N22, 1924-47; Rural Dean of Tottenham, 1934-46; Chaplain at Hampton Court Palace, 1947-61; Rural Dean of Hampton, 1948-56. Prebendary of St Paul's Cathedral, 1944-61, Emeritus, 1961. *Recreation:* cricket. *Address:* 38 St Cross Road, Winchester, Hants. *T:* Winchester 2923.

**HARRIS, Lt-Gen. Sir Ian (Cecil),** KBE 1967 (CBE 1958); CB 1962; DSO 1945; farming, Ballykisteen Stud, Tipperary; *b* 7 July 1910; *y s* of late J. W. A. Harris, Victor Stud, Golden, Tipperary; *m* 1945, Anne-Marie Desmotreux; two *s*. *Educ:* Portora Royal Sch., Enniskillen, Northern Ireland; RMC, Sandhurst. 2nd Lt Royal Ulster Rifles, 1930; served War of 1939-45, NW Frontier of India, 1939 (despatches); comd 2nd Bn Royal Ulster Rifles, 1943-45; GSO1, 25 Ind. Div. and 7 Div. in Burma and Malaya, 1945-46 (despatches), India and Pakistan, 1946-47; AQMG Scottish Comd, 1949-51; comd 6th Bn Royal Ulster Rifles (TA), 1951-52; Chief of Staff, Northern Ireland, 1952-54; Comdr 1 Federal Infantry Bde, Malaya, 1954-57 (despatches); Dep. Dir of Staff Duties (A), WO, 1957-60; GOC Singapore Base District, 1960-62; Chief of Staff, Contingencies Planning, Supreme HQ, Allied Powers, Europe, 1963-66; GOC-in-C, then GOC, N Ireland, 1966-69. Colonel: Royal Ulster Rifles, 1962-68; Royal Irish Rangers, 1968-. *Recreations:* riding and tennis. *Address:* Acraboy House, Monard, Co. Tipperary. *T:* Tipperary 51564. *Club:* Army and Navy.

**HARRIS, Sir Jack A. S.;** *see* Sutherland-Harris.

**HARRIS, Sir Jack Wolfred Ashford,** 2nd Bt, *cr* 1932; Governing Director, Bing Harris & Co. Ltd, Wellington, NZ, since 1942; *b* 23 July 1906; *er s* of Rt Hon. Sir Percy Harris, 1st Bt, PC, and Frieda Bloxam (*d* 1962); *S* father 1952; *m* 1933, Patricia, *o d* of A. P. Penman, Wahroonga, Sydney, NSW; two *s* one *d*. *Educ:* Shrewsbury Sch.; Trinity Hall, Cambridge. BA (Cantab.) History; then one year's study in Europe. Joined family business in New Zealand, 1929, and became director shortly afterwards; Chm., 1935. President NZ Wholesale Softgoods Federation; Past Pres. Wellington Chamber of Commerce. Served during War of 1939-45, for three years in NZ Home Forces. *Recreations:* gardening, fishing, swimming. *Heir: s* Christopher John Ashford Harris [*b* 26 Aug. 1934; *m* 1957, Anna, *d* of F. de Malmanche, Auckland, NZ; one *s* one *d*]. *Address:* Te Rama, Waikanae, near Wellington, NZ. *Clubs:* Royal Automobile; Wellington (Wellington).

**HARRIS, Kenneth Edwin,** MA, MD Cantab; FRCP; Senior Physician and Cardiologist, University College Hospital; Consulting Physician to the Republic of the Sudan in London; Consulting Physician Royal Chest Hospital; Senior Censor, Royal College of Physicians; Examiner in Medicine Universities of Cambridge, London and Bristol, and Conjoint Examining Board of England; *s* of late Dr Thomas Harris, MD, FRCP, Physician, Manchester Royal Infirmary, and late I. M. Harris (*née* Brockbank); *m* 1932, Edith I. L. Abbott, MB, BS (London), DPH(Eng.); no *c*. *Educ:* Shrewsbury Sch.; Gonville and Caius Coll. Cambridge; University Coll. Hospital. BA (Hons); Fellowes Silver Medal for Clinical Medicine; Liston Gold Medal for Surgery; Erichsen Prize for Practical Surgery. Liveryman, Apothecaries Soc.; Vice-Pres. of Cambridge Graduates Medical Club. Freeman of City of London. Mem., English-Speaking Union. *Publications:* Minor Medical operations (with E. I. L. Harris), 1938. Contributions to: Heart, Lancet, BMJ, 1929-. *Recreations:* philately, gardening, colour photography, foreign travel and architecture. *Address:* The White House, 4 Grand Avenue, Worthing, Sussex. *T:* Worthing 48056.

**HARRIS, Dr Leslie J.,** ScD Cantab, DSc Manchester, PhD Cantab; FRIC; Fellow Royal Society of Medicine; first Director of Dunn Nutritional Laboratory (Medical Research Council and University of Cambridge), 1927-63, retired; *b* Liverpool, 1898; *s* of late John and Edith Harris; *m* 1927, Rose, *d* of late Dr and Mrs J. Snowman; two *s*. *Educ:* Liverpool Coll.; Dalton Hall, University of Manchester; Emmanuel Coll., Cambridge. Leblanc Medal, 1921; Meldola Medallist of Royal Institute of Chemistry, 1925; Coronation Medal, 1953; Emeritus Mem. Biochem. Soc.; Hon. Member: Physiolog. Soc.; Chem. Soc., Royal Institute of Chemistry, etc; Mem. Regent House, University of Cambridge; ex-Assessor, Food Investigation Board; joint founder, first Hon. Sec. (1941-47) and Pres. (1953-56), The Nutrition Soc.; Founder, and Sec.-Gen. (1946-60), Internat. Union of Nutritional Sciences; ex-Mem. Accessory-Food-Factors Cttee (Med. Res. Council); Past-Pres. Biological Methods Gp, Soc. for Analytical Chemistry; Past member: Cttee of Biochemical Soc.; Survey Gp on Animal Nutrition (Agric. Res. Council); various Govt Cttees (on Welfare Foods; Chemical Additives; Scientific Promotions, etc.); Biological Council; Joint Editor: Internationale Zeitschrift für Vitaminforschung; World Review of Nutrition and Dietetics, and formerly of Br. Journ. of Nutrition, of Proceedings of the Nutrition Soc. and of Br. Journ. of Social Medicine; past Trustee, Assoc. of Scientific Workers; ex-Mem. of Cambridge Univ. Educational Film Council; a Vice-Pres., Annual Meeting, BMA, 1948; Hon. Sec. Section I, 1st International Congress of Biochemistry, 1949; Vice-Pres., Ann. Congress of Royal Sanitary Institute, 1951; an Hon. Chm., 12th Internat. Congress of Pure and Applied Chemistry, NY, 1951; Pres. of Honour, Internat. Vitamin Congress, Milan, 1953; Contrib. of articles, on Vitamins in British Encylopædia of Medical Practice, in Annual Reviews of Biochemistry, 1932-35, in Chemical Society's Annual Reports, 1939-42, in Thorpe's Dictionary of Pure and Applied Chemistry, in Chambers's Encyclopædia, 1950, etc.; Royal Instn. Lectr on Vitamins, 1934; Boyle Lectr, Univ. of Oxford, 1942; De Lamar Lecturer, Johns Hopkins University, 1951; Visiting Lecturer: Harvard, Yale, Berkeley, Cornell, and Columbia Univs, 1951; India, Israel, 1958; Prague, 1959, etc. *Publications:* Vitamins in Theory and Practice (1st edn, 1935; 4th edn, 1955; Dutch, Polish, American and Italian edns, 1936, etc); Vitamins and Vitamin Deficiencies, Vol. I, 1939; (with J. Needham and others) Hopkins and Biochemistry, 1949; Vitamins, a Digest of Current Knowledge, 1951; (with A. S. MacNalty and others) The British Medical Dictionary, 1961; (with J. Needham and others) The Chemistry of Life, 1970; papers in Proc. Royal Society, Biochem. J., Lancet, Brit. Jl of Nutrit, etc. *Recreations:* painting (Past Hon. Treas., Cambridge Drawing Soc.), sculpture, etc. *Address:* 40 Highsett, Hills Road, Cambridge. *T:* Cambridge 54058.

**HARRIS, Brigadier Lewis John,** CBE 1961 (OBE 1949; MBE 1943); Consultant to Federal Surveys and Mapping, Canada, since 1967; *b* 19 Dec. 1910; *e s* of late David Rees and of Cecilia Harris. *Educ:* Christ Coll., Brecon; Royal Military Academy, Woolwich; Pembroke Coll., Cambridge (Exhibitioner) (MA). Commissioned RE 1930; Triangulation of Jamaica, 1937-39; served War of 1939-45: British Expeditionary Force, 1939-40 (despatches); First Army in North Africa, 1942-43, AFHQ and American Seventh Army, Italy, 1944; Land Forces SE Asia, India, Burma and Malaya, 1944-46; Chief Instructor, Sch. of Mil. Survey, 1946-49; War Office, Geog. Section GS, 1949-52; Ordnance Survey, 1952-53; Survey Dir GHQ, Middle East, and GHQ, E Africa, 1953-55; Land Survey Adviser, Allied Forces, Mediterranean, 1954-55; Ordnance Survey of Great Britain, 1955-61; Dir, Map Production and Publication, 1956-59; Dir, Field Surveys, 1959-61; Dir of Military Survey, Ministry of Defence and Chief of Geographical Section Gen. Staff, 1961-65. Brig. 1956. Hon. Col 135 Survey Engineer Regt, TA, 1965-67 Chm., Nat. Cttee for Cartography, Royal Society, 1961-67. Hon. Foreign Sec., Royal Geographical Soc., 1964-67. *Publications:* various papers on cartography in learned jls. *Recreations:* outdoor sports. *Address:* 315 Holmwood Avenue, Apt 1102, Ottawa 1, Ontario, Canada. *Club:* United Service.

**HARRIS, Brigadier (Hon.) Sir Lionel Herbert,** KBE 1957 (CBE 1945; OBE 1943); TD 1942; Engineer-in-Chief, GPO, 1954-60, retired; *b* 15 April 1897; *s* of Thomas Harris, London; *m* 1920, Daisy Edith Barkel, London; one *s*. *Educ:* Sir Walter St John's, London; Imperial Coll. of Science. FCGI, BScEng, MScEng, MIEE. Served European War, 1914-18, Australian Signals, 1915-19; Engineering Dept, GPO, 1922-39; 44th Home Counties Division Signals, TA, 1926, Hon. Col, 1950-55; War of 1939-45, commanded GHQ, Signals, 1941-42; CSO, Lines of Communication, 1942-43; Chief, Telecommunications, SHAEF, 1943-45; Regional Dir, GPO Scotland, 1945-49; Controller of Research, GPO. 1949-54. Legion of Merit, US, 1945; Legion of Honour, Croix de Guerre, France, 1945. *Publication:* Signal Venture, 1951. *Address:* 21 Dove Park, Hatch End, Middx. *T:* 01-428 5013.

**HARRIS, Lyndon Goodwin,** RI 1958; RSW 1952; RWA 1947; Artist in oil, water-colour, stained glass, and etching; *b* 25 July 1928; *s* of S. E. Harris, ACIS and Mary Elsie Harris. *Educ:* Halesowen Grammar Sch. Studied Art at: Birmingham Coll. of Art; Slade Sch. of Fine Art, 1946-50; University of London Inst. of Education, 1950-51; Courtauld Inst.; Central Sch. of Art and Crafts, London. Leverhulme Schol., Pilkington Schol., Slade Schol., and Slade Anatomy Prizeman; Dip. Fine Art (London) 1949; Courtauld Certificate, 1950; ATD 1951. *Works exhibited:* Paris Salon (Gold Medal, Oil Painting; Honourable Mention, Etching); RA (first exhibited at age of 13), RSA, RI, RSW, NEAC, RBA, RGI, RWA, and principal provincial galleries. *Works in permanent collections:* Ministry of Works; University Coll., London; Birmingham and Midland Inst.; City of Worcester; (stained glass) Gorsty Hill Methodist Church, Halesowen. *Recreation:* music (organ and pianoforte). *Address:* The Uplands, Waxland Road, Halesowen, Worcs.

**HARRIS, Margaret Frances;** Resident Designer, Sadler's Wells Theatre, since 1962; Director, Sadler's Wells Design Course, since 1966; *b* 28 May 1904; *d* of William Birkbeck Harris and Kathleen Marion Carey. *Educ:* Downe House. In partnership with Elizabeth Montgomery and late Sophie Devine as firm of Motley, 1931-. Has designed many productions in London and New York of drama, opera and ballet: first notable production, Richard of Bordeaux, for John Gielgud, 1932; recently, sets for The Mastersingers, at Sadler's Wells, 1968. *Publication:* Designing and Making Costume, by Motley, 1965. *Address:* 40 Smith Square, SW1. *T:* 01-222 5431.

**HARRIS, Noël H. V.;** *see* Vicars-Harris.

**HARRIS, Sir Percy W.;** *see* Wyn-Harris.

**HARRIS, Philip;** Principal Assistant Registrar, Office of the Registrar of Restrictive Trading Agreements, since 1966; *b* Manchester, 15 Dec. 1915; *er s* of S. D. Harris and Sarah Chazan; *m* 1939, Sarah Henriques Valentine; three *d*. *Educ:* Manchester Grammar Sch.; Trinity Hall, Cambridge (Open Scholarship, BA 1st Cl (with dist.), Historical Tripos). Asst Principal, Board of Trade, 1938-40. Served War, 1940-45; Anti-Aircraft Command and Western Europe; 2nd Lieut RA, 1941; Lieut, 2/8th Lancs Fusiliers, 1944; Capt., 6th Royal Welch Fusiliers, 1945. Principal, Board of Trade, 1946; Asst Sec., Board of Trade, 1948-64; Asst Registrar, Office of the Registrar of Restrictive Trading Agreements, 1964-66. Nuffield Travelling Fellowship, 1956-57 (study of Indian Industrial Development). Leader, UK Delgn to Internat. Cotton Advisory Cttee, 1960, 1963. *Recreation:* history. *Address:* 23 Courthouse Gardens, Finchley, N3. *T:* 01-346 3138. *Club:* Arts Theatre.

**HARRIS, Richard Reader;** *b* 4 June 1913; *s* of Richard Reader Harris; *m* 1940, Pamela Rosemary Merrick Stephens; three *d*. *Educ:* St Lawrence Coll., Ramsgate. Called to the Bar, 1941. Fire Service, 1939-45. MP (C) Heston and Isleworth, 1950-70. *Recreations:* squash, tennis. *Address:* 2 Carlyle Mansions, Cheyne Walk, SW3.

**HARRIS, Robert;** actor since 1922; *b* 28 March 1900; *s* of Alfred H. Harris and Suzanne Amelie (*née* Anstie). *Educ:* Sherborne; New Coll., Oxford. Has appeared in Shakespearean rôles with the Old Vic-Sadler's Wells Company at Stratford-on-Avon, and in the West End (Hamlet, Oberon, Prospero, Angelo, Henry IV, King John, Shylock, Dr Faustus, J. Robert Oppenheimer). Other parts include: St Bernard, in The Marvellous History of St Bernard; Charles Tritton, in The Wind and The Rain; Eugene Marchbanks, in Candida; Orin Mannon, in Mourning Becomes Electra;

Thomas More, in A Man for all Seasons (USA); Pope Pius XII in The Deputy (NY); 40 Years on (Canada); Prendergast, in Decline and Fall (film). Television and radio plays and verse reading, 1923-. *Recreation:* travel. *Address:* 18 Pitt Street, W8. *T:* 01-937 8825. *Club:* Garrick.

**HARRIS, Sir Ronald (Montague Joseph),** KCVO 1960 (MVO 1943); CB 1956; First Church Estates Commissioner, since 1969; *b* 6 May 1913; *o s* of late Rev. J. Montague Harris; *m* 1st, 1939, Margaret Julia Wharton (*d* 1955); one *s* three *d*; 2nd, 1957, Marjorie, *widow* of Julian Tryon, and *e d* of Sir Harry Verney, *qv*; one step *d* (one step *s* decd). *Educ:* Harrow; Trinity Coll., Oxford. India Office and Burma Office, 1936-38; Private Sec. to Sec. of Cabinet, 1939-43; India Office and Burma Office, 1944-47; Imperial Defence Coll., 1948; HM Treasury, 1949-52; Cabinet Office, 1952-55; Second Crown Estate Commissioner, 1955-60; Third Sec., HM Treasury, 1960-64; Sec. to Church Commissioners, 1964-68. Director: Yorks Insurance Co., 1966-69; Yorkshire General Life Assurance Co., 1969-; St Martins Property Corp. *Address:* Slyfield Farm House, Stoke D'Abernon, Cobham, Surrey. *Club:* Boodle's.

**HARRIS, Sidney;** Member, British Steel Corporation, 1968-70 (Member Organising Committee, 1967); Director, Iron & Steel Corporation, 1967; *b* 28 July 1903; *m* 1929, Elsie May South; one *s* one *d*. *Educ:* Harden, Yorks. Started work in textile industry as a half-timer, 1915; started work in iron and steel industry at Rotherham, with Steel Peech & Tozer (now United Steel Cos), 1922. Mem., Rotherham Co. Borough Coun., 1943-67 (Mayor and Alderman, 1958). Nat. Pres., British Iron & Steel Workers' Union, 1956; Exec. Mem., BISAKTA, 1948-66 (a Founder, 1930, and Sec., 1935-66, Temple 2 Br.). *Recreations:* (now watching) football; fishing. *Address:* 242 Badsley Moor Lane, Rotherham, Yorks. *T:* Rotherham 78096.

**HARRIS, (Theodore) Wilson;** *b* 24 March 1921; of mixed parentage (Amerindian, European, African); *m* 1st, 1945, Cecily Carew; 2nd, 1959, Margaret Whitaker (*née* Burns). *Educ:* Queen's Coll., Georgetown, British Guiana. Studied land surveying, British Guiana, 1939, and subseq. qualified to practise; led many survey parties (mapping and geomorphological research) in the interior; Senior Surveyor, Projects, for Govt of British Guiana, 1955-58. Came to live in London, 1959. Writer in Residence, Univ. of West Indies and Univ. of Toronto, 1970; Vis. Lectr, State Univ. of NY, Buffalo, 1970. *Publications:* Eternity to Season (poems, privately printed), 1954; Palace of the Peacock, 1960; The Far Journey of Oudin, 1961; The Whole Armour, 1962; The Secret Ladder, 1963; Heartland, 1964; The Eye of the Scarecrow, 1965; The Waiting Room, 1967; Tradition, the Writer and Society: Critical Essays, 1967; Tumatumari, 1968; Ascent to Omai, 1970; The Sleepers of Roraima (a Carib Trilogy), 1970; The Age of the Rainmakers, 1971. *Address:* c/o Faber and Faber, 24 Russell Square, WC1.

**HARRIS, Thomas Maxwell,** FRS 1948; Professor of Botany, University of Reading, 1935-68, Professor Emeritus 1968; *b* 8 Jan. 1903; *s* of Alexander Charles Harris and Lucy Frances Evans; *m* 1928, Katharine Massey; one *s* three *d*. *Educ:* Bootham, York; Wyggeston Sch., Leicester; University Coll., Nottingham; Christ's Coll., Cambridge (scholar). Natural Science Tripos, Parts I and II, 1st Class Hons; London BSc, 1st Class Hons; ScD Cambridge; Mem. of Danish Expedition to E Greenland, 1926-27; Demonstrator in Botany, 1928; Fellow of Christ's Coll., 1928. Vice-Pres., Royal Society, 1960-61; President, Linnæan Soc., 1961-64; Vice-Pres., 1964. Trustee, Natural History Museum, 1963-. *Publications:* communications to scientific journals on Palæobotany. *Recreation:* gardening. *Address:* Department of Geology, The University, Reading, Berks.

**HARRIS, Vincent;** *see* Harris, E. V.

**HARRIS, Hon. Walter Edward,** PC (Canada), QC (Canada); DCL; Director, Homewood Sanitarium Ltd; President of Victoria and Grey Trust Co.; *b* 14 Jan. 1904; *s* of Melvin Harris and Helen (*née* Carruthers); *m* 1933, Grace Elma Morrison; one *s* two *d*. *Educ:* Osgoode Hall, Toronto. Served War of 1939-45. First elected to House of Commons, Canada, 1940 (re-elected 1945, 1949, 1953), MP (Canada) until 1957. Parliamentary Asst to Sec of State for External Affairs, 1947; Parly Asst to Prime Minister, 1948; Minister of Citizenship and Immigration, 1950; of Finance, 1954-57. Mem. of the firm of Harris & Dunlop, Barristers, Markdale. *Address:* Markdale, Ontario, Canada.

**HARRIS, (Walter) Frank;** Director and Comptroller, Massey-Ferguson (United Kingdom), since 1969; *b* 19 May 1920; *m* Esther Blanche Hill; two *s* two *d*. *Educ:* King Edward's Sch., Birmingham; University of Nottingham. Served Royal Air Force, 1939-46. University, 1946-49. Ford Motor Company, 1950-65; Principal City Officer and Town Clerk, Newcastle upon Tyne, 1965-69. *Recreations:* fell walking, gardening. *Address:* Massey-Ferguson Manufacturing Co., PO Box 62, Banner Lane, Coventry.

**HARRIS, William Barclay,** QC 1961; *b* 25 Nov. 1911; *s* of W. Cecil Harris, Moatlands, E Grinstead, Sussex; *m* 1937, Elizabeth, 2nd *d* of Capt. Sir Clive Milnes-Coates, 2nd Bt, *qv*; one *s* two *d*. *Educ:* Harrow; Trinity Coll., Cambridge (MA). Served 1940-45: with Coldstream Guards, N Africa, Italy, Germany (despatches), Major. Barrister, Inner Temple, 1937. Chm., Rowton Hotels, 1965-. A Church Commissioner, 1966. *Address:* Moatlands, East Grinstead, Sussex. *T:* Sharpthorne 228; 29 Barkston Gardens, SW5. *T:* 01-373 8793. *Clubs:* Athenæum, MCC.

**HARRIS, Sir William (Gordon),** KBE 1969; CB 1963; MA (Cantab); CEng; FICE; Director-General, Highways (previously Director of Highway Engineering), Ministry of Transport, since 1965; *b* 10 June 1912; *s* of Capt. James Whyte Harris, Royal Naval Reserve, and Margaret Roberta Buchanan Forsyth; *m* 1938, Margaret Emily Harvie; three *s* one *d*. *Educ:* Liverpool Coll.; Sidney Sussex Coll., Cambridge. Mechanical Sciences Tripos and BA 1932, MA 1937. London Midland & Scottish Railway, 1932-35; Sudan Irrigation Dept, 1935-37; Joined Civil Engineer in Chief's Dept, Admiralty, 1937; Asst Civil Engineer in Chief, 1950; Deputy Civil Engineer in Chief, 1955; Civil Engineer in Chief, 1959; Dir-Gen., Navy Works, 1960-63; Dir-Gen. of Works, Ministry of Public Building and Works, 1963-65. Commonwealth Fund (of New York) Fellowship, 1950-51. Mem., Smeatonian Soc. of Civil Engineers. *Address:* 5 Moor Park Road, Northwood, Mddx. *T:* Northwood 25899. *Club:* Royal Automobile.

**HARRIS, Sir William (Henry),** KCVO, *cr* 1954 (CVO 1942); MA, DMus Oxon; FRCO, FRCM, Hon. RAM; Organist of St George's Chapel, Windsor, 1933-61; Professor of Organ and Harmony, Royal College of Music, 1921-

53; *b* 1883; *m* Kathleen Doris (*d* 1968), *y d* of late J. P. Carter, Redland, Bristol; two *d.* Organ Scholar RCM 1899; Organist of New Coll., Oxford, 1919-28; of Christ Church Cathedral, Oxford, 1928-33; Conductor of Oxford Bach Choir, 1926-33; President Oxford University Musical Soc., 1921; Dir Balliol Concerts, 1925-33; Conductor St George's Chapel Special Choir, 1933; Conductor Slough Philharmonic Soc., 1941-44. Windsor and Eton Choral Soc., 1944-49. Pres. Royal Coll. of Organists, 1946-48; Dir, Musical Studies, Royal School of Church Music, 1956-61. *Publications:* including a Carnegie award, a setting of The Hound of Heaven for Baritone Solo, Chorus, and Orchestra; Michael Angelo's Confession of Faith, for Solo, Chorus, and Orchestra; Psalm 103 for double Choir, etc. *Address:* 64a Heath Road, Petersfield, Hants. *T:* 2168.

**HARRIS, Wilson;** *see* Harris, T. W.

**HARRISON, Alastair Brian Clarke,** MP (C) Maldon Division of Essex, since 1955; *b* 3 Oct. 1921; *s* of late Brig. E. F. Harrison, Melbourne; *m* 1952, Elizabeth Hood Hardie, Oaklands, NSW, Aust.; one *s* one *d. Educ:* Geelong Grammar Sch.; Trinity Coll., Cambridge. Capt. AIF. Parliamentary Private Secretary to: Min. of State, Colonial Office, 1955-56; Sec. of State for War, 1956-58; Min. of Agriculture, Fisheries and Food, 1958-60. Mem. Victoria Promotion Cttee (London); Mem. One Nation Gp which published The Responsible Society, and One Europe; toured USA on E-SU Ford Foundation Fellowship, 1959; Commonwealth Parliamentary Assoc. Delegation, Kenya and Horn of Africa, 1960. *Recreations:* photography, gardening. *Address:* Copford Hall, Colchester, Essex. *Clubs:* Carlton; Melbourne (Australia).

**HARRISON, Albert Norman,** CB 1966; CVO 1955; OBE 1946; RCNC; MRINA; *b* 12 July 1901; *s* of William Arthur and Sarah Jane Harrison, Portsmouth, Hants; *m* 1941, Queenie Perpetua Parker, Luton, Beds; one *d. Educ:* Portsmouth; Royal Naval Coll., Greenwich. Asst Constructor, Royal Corps of Naval Constructors, 1926; Constructor, 1937; Principal Ship Overseer. Vickers-Armstrong, Barrow-in-Furness, 1936-39; Staff of RA (D), Home Fleet, 1940-41; Naval Constructor-in-Chief, Royal Canadian Navy, 1942-48; Chief Constructor, Admiralty, 1948-51; Asst Dir of Naval Construction, Admiralty, 1951-61; Dir of Naval Construction, Min. of Defence (N) (formerly Admiralty), 1961-66. *Address:* Whiteoaks, 126 Bloomfield Road, Bath, Som. *T:* Bath 61866. *Clubs:* Royal Automobile; Bath and County (Bath).

**HARRISON, Alexander,** CBE 1955; CA; Vice-President, Trustee Savings Bank Association (Deputy-Chairman, 1947-59); *b* 26 Feb. 1890; *s* of John Harrison, CBE, LLD, FRSE, DL, and Helen Georgina Roberts; *m* 1931, Jean Muriel Small; one *s* three *d. Educ:* Merchiston Castle Sch. Chartered Accountant, 1914 (Distinction). Chm. Edinburgh Savings Bank, 1945-54. Mem. Edinburgh Town Council, 1946-48. Served European War, 1914-18; temp. Major, Royal Scots, attached Machine Gun Corps in France and Italy, FRSGS. Hon. Pres., Scottish Mountaineering Club. *Recreation:* mountaineering. *Address:* 4 Whitehouse Terrace, Edinburgh 9. *T:* 031-447 2898. *Clubs:* Alpine; New (Edinburgh).

**HARRISON, Sir Archibald Frederick,** Kt 1955; CBE 1947; Secretary, Trade Marks, Patents and Designs Federation, 1959-69, retired; Solicitor to the Ministry of Labour and National Service, 1949-59; Government Delegate to the ILO Conferences, 1956-58; *s* of F. W. Harrison, journalist; *m* 1923, Mabel Glendinning (*d* 1970); two *d. Educ:* Appleby, Westmorland; Queen's Coll., Oxford. Called to Bar, 1919, Inner Temple. *Address:* 58 Nightingale Road, Rickmansworth, Herts. *T:* Rickmansworth 73849.

**HARRISON, Arthur Neville John,** CIE 1936; *b* 15 Sept. 1881; *s* of late John Henry Harrison, ICS; *m* 1st, 1914, Helen Zoë Foote (*d* 1934); 2nd, 1934, Frances Mary De Havilland (*d* 1962); no *c. Educ:* Cheltenham Coll.; Lincoln Coll., Oxford (scholar). Government of India PWD, Accounts, 1904; Madras, 1905-9; Eastern Bengal Railway (Calcutta), 1909-14; Auditor Jodhpur-Bikanir Railway (Rajputana), 1914-24; Chief Auditor Bombay, Baroda and Central India Railway (Bombay), 1924-36; officiated Agent BB & CI Railway, Bombay, 1933, 1934, and 1935; retired, 1936; Treasurer of the International Zone of Tangier (Morocco), 1940; Petrol Rationing Authority, Delhi, 1941-42; Deputy Military Accountant Gen. Administration, Delhi, India, 1942-43; Admiralty Courier, 1945; Finances Officer, East Asia, Rice Commn, Bangkok, 1945-47. *Recreation:* bridge. *Address:* c/o National Westminster Bank, High Street, St Peter's Port, Guernsey, CI.

**HARRISON, Sir (Bernard) Guy,** Kt, *cr* 1951; late Chairman, Harrison & Sons, Ltd; *b* 2 July 1885; *s* of Bernard Bowles Harrison; *m* 1st, 1907, Cicely Ann (*d* 1957), *d* of late H. N. Vicat; one *s* one *d*; 2nd, 1958, Iris, *y d* of late E. R. C. Hall. *Educ:* Sevenoaks Sch. Chm., Harrison Properties Ltd; Pres. London Master Printers' Assoc., 1931-32; Pres. British Federation of Master Printers, 1933-34; Pres. Printing & Allied Trades Research Assoc., 1952-56; Chm., Joint Industrial Council (Printing & Allied Trades), 1939-45; Master of Stationers' Company, 1948-49. Governor, North Western Polytechnic, 1947-57. Pres., Printers' Pension Corporation, 1959-60. *Publications:* occasional contribs to Astronomical and Ornithological Jls. *Recreations:* astronomy, ornithology, botany and entomology. *Address:* Beenleigh Manor, Habertonford, Totnes, Devon. *T:* Habertonford 234. *Club:* Athenæum.

**HARRISON, Rev. Cecil Marriott;** Vicar of Aislaby, Diocese of York, since 1969; *b* 16 March 1911; *s* of late Tom Marriott Harrison, Davidson's Mains, Midlothian; *m* 1944, Phyllis Edith McKenzie. *Educ:* Westminster Sch.; Trinity Coll., Cambridge. 1st Class Classical Tripos Pt I, 1930; Pt II, 1932; BA 1932, MA 1936; Classical Sixth Form Master, Nottingham High Sch., 1932; Dulwich Coll., 1934; Charterhouse, 1936-47. Served War of 1939-45; Royal Signals, 1940-46; Headmaster of Felsted Sch., 1947-51; Headmaster, King's School, Peterborough, 1951-69. Deacon, 1966, Priest, 1967. *Address:* Aislaby Vicarage, Whitby, Yorks. *T:* Sleights 350. *Club:* Leander.

**HARRISON, Prof. Charles Victor;** Professor of Morbid Anatomy, Royal Postgraduate Medical School, University of London, since 1955; *b* Newport, Mon, 1907; *s* of Charles Henry Harrison, LDS, and Violet Harrison (*née* Witchell); *m* 1937, Olga Beatrice Cochrane; one *s* one *d. Educ:* Dean Close Sch., Cheltenham; University Coll., Cardiff; University Coll. Hosp., London. MB, BCh, BSc (Wales), 1929; MB, BS (London), 1929; MD (London), 1937; FCPath 1965; FRCP 1967. Demonstrator in Pathology, Welsh National School of Medicine, 1930; Asst Morbid Anatomist, British Postgraduate Medical Sch., 1935; Senior Lecturer, Liverpool Univ., 1939; Reader in Morbid

Anatomy, Postgraduate Medical Sch. of London, 1946. Willie Seager Gold Medal in Pathology, 1927. *Publications:* (ed) Recent Advances in Pathology, 1967; various scientific papers in Jl of Pathology and Bacteriology, British Heart Journal, Jl Clin. Pathology, etc. *Recreations:* carpentry and gardening. *Address:* 23 Woodville Gardens, Ealing, W5. *T:* 01-997 5156.

**HARRISON, Claude William,** RP 1961; Artist; portrait painter and painter of conversation pieces, imaginative landscapes and murals, etc; *b* Leyland, Lancs, 31 March 1922; *s* of Harold Harrison and Florence Mildred Ireton; *m* 1947, Audrey Johnson; one *s. Educ:* Hutton Grammar Sch., Lancs. Served in RAF, 1942-46. Royal Coll. of Art, 1947-49; Studio in Ambleside, 1949-52. Exhibited since 1950 at: RA; RSA; Royal Society Portrait Painters; New English Art Club, etc. *Publication:* The Portrait Painter's handbook, 1968. *Recreation:* painting. *Address:* Easedale House, Grasmere, Westmorland. *T:* Grasmere 231.

**HARRISON, Sir Colin;** *see* Harrison, Sir R. C.

**HARRISON, Sir Cyril (Ernest),** Kt 1963; Chairman, English Sewing Cotton Co. Ltd, 1963-68 (Director 1942; Managing Director, 1948; Vice-Chairman 1952); Joint Deputy Chairman, Williams Deacon's bank Ltd, since 1961; a Deputy Chairman, Williams and Glyn's Bank, since 1969; former Director, The Royal Bank of Scotland; *b* 14 Dec. 1901; *s* of Alfred John Harrison, MIGasE, and Edith Harrison, Great Harwood, Lancs; *m* 1927, Ethel, *d* of Edward Wood, FCA, JP, Burnley; two *s. Educ:* Burnley Grammar Sch. President: Manchester Chamber of Commerce, 1958-60; Cotton, Silk and Man-made Fibres Res. Assoc. Member: NW Electricity Bd; S Manchester Hosp. Management Cttee; Council, Manchester Business Sch.; Grand Council, CBI; Court of Govs, University of Manchester. Chm., Christie Hospital and Holt Radium Inst., 1959-61; Chm., NW Regional Council of FBI, 1957-59; Pres., FBI, 1961-63. Mem. National Economic Development Council, 1962-64. Chm., Bd of Governors, United Manchester Hospitals, 1967-. Hon. MA, Victoria Univ. of Manchester, 1960. Comp. Textile Inst.; FBIM. *Recreation:* golf. *Address:* 4 Harefield Drive, Holly Road South, Wilmslow, Cheshire. *T:* Wilmslow 22186.

**HARRISON, Denis Byrne;** Town Clerk and Chief Executive Officer, City of Sheffield, since 1966; *b* 11 July 1917; *y s* of late Arthur Harrison and of Priscilla Harrison; *m* 1956, Alice Marion Vickers. *Educ:* Birkenhead Sch.; Liverpool Univ. (LLM). Articled to late E. W. Tame, OBE (Town Clerk of Birkenhead). Admitted Solicitor, 1939; Asst Solicitor to Birkenhead Corp., 1939. Served War, 1939-46: 75th Shropshire Yeo. (Medium Regt) RA, Combined Ops Bombardment Unit; Staff Captain at HQ of OC, Cyprus. First Asst Solicitor, Wolverhampton Co. Borough, 1946-49; Dep. Town Clerk of Co. Boroughs: Warrington, 1949-57; Bolton, 1957-63; Sheffield, 1963-66. Mem., Advisory Council on Noise, 1970. *Recreations:* foreign travel, music, ski-ing, golf. *Address:* Town Hall, Sheffield S1 2HH. *T:* 26444 (Ext. 202); Norfolk Lodge, Hollow Meadows, near Sheffield S6 6GH. *T:* Sheffield 303229. *Clubs:* Sheffield (Sheffield); Lindrick Golf.

**HARRISON, Maj.-Gen. Desmond,** CB 1946; DSO 1940; MICE; Civil Engineer; *b* 11 Nov. 1896; *s* of R. J. Harrison, JP; *m* 1920; one *s* two *d. Educ:* Kilkenny Coll.; Mountjoy Sch., Dublin; RMA, Woolwich; Cambridge Univ. Temp. Maj.-Gen. 1944; Maj.-Gen. 1947; Comdt SME 1942; Engineer-in-Chief, SEAC, 1943; Director of Fortifications and Works, War Office, 1946; retired 1947. Mem. Overseas Food Corp., 1947; resigned 1949. Comdr Legion of Merit, USA. *Recreations:* golf, shooting, fishing. *Address:* 55 Hans Road, SW3. *T:* 01-584 4867. *Club:* Army and Navy.

**HARRISON, Prof. Donald Frederick Norris,** MD, MS, FRCS; Professor of Laryngology and Otology (University of London), at the Institute of Laryngology, Gray's Inn Road, WC1, since 1963; Surgeon, Royal National Throat, Nose and Ear Hospital; *b* 9 March 1925; *s* of Frederick William Rees Harrison, OBE, JP, and Florence, *d* of Robert Norris, Portsmouth, Hants; *m* 1949, Audrey, *o d* of Percival Clubb, Penarth, Glam.; two *d. Educ:* Newport High Sch., Mon.; Guy's Hosp. MD (London) 1960; MS (London) 1959; FRCS 1955. Ho. Surg., Guy's Hosp. and Royal Gwent Hospital, Newport; Surg. Registrar, Shrewsbury Eye and Ear Hosp.; Senior Registrar, Throat and Ear Dept, Guy's Hosp.; University Reader in Laryngology, Inst. of Laryngol. and Otol. Hunterian Prof., Royal College of Surgeons, Eng., 1962; Chevalier Jackson Lectr, 1964. Mem. of Court of Examiners, RCS; Examr, National Univ. of Ireland; External Examr, Univs of Melbourne and Sydney; Fellow Medical Soc. London; Scientific Fellow, Royal Zoological Soc. of London; FRSM (Mem. Council, Sect. of Laryngology and Otology); Mem. BMA; Mem. Council, Brit. Assoc. of Otolaryngologists on Brit. Standards Instn; Member: Collegium Oto-Rhino-Laryngologium; Anatomical Soc. of Great Britain; Res. Cttee, Nat. Deaf Children's Soc.; Cttee of Management, Institute of Cancer Research; Internat. Cttee for Cancer of Larynx. Editorial Board: Clinical Trials Journal; Acta Otolaryngologica; Practica Oto-Rhino-Laryngologica; Annals of Oto-Rhino-Laryngology. Hon. Mem., Otolaryngological Soc., Australia; For. Mem., Internat. Broncho-œsophagological Soc.; Corresp. Member: Amer. Head and Neck Soc.; Soc. Française d'Otorhinolaryngologie; Otolaryngological Soc., Denmark; Amer. Acad. of Facial Plastic Reconstr. Surgery; Pacific Coast Oto-Opthalmological Soc. *Publications:* articles on familial hæmorrhagic telangiectases, meatal oseomata, cancer chemotherapy, head and neck surgery in learned jls; chapters in Text Books on Ent. and Gen. Surgery. *Recreation:* work. *Address:* Institute of Laryngology and Otology, Gray's Inn Road, WC1. *T:* 01-837 8855; Springfield, Fisher's Farm, Horley, Surrey. *T:* Horley 4307.

**HARRISON, Douglas Creese,** DSc London, PhD Cantab, ARIC; Professor of Biochemistry, Queen's University, Belfast, 1935-67; *b* 29 April, 1901; *s* of Lovell and Lillian E. Harrison, MBE, JP; *m* 1926, Sylva Thurlow, MA, PhD, Philadelphia, USA; one *s. Educ:* Highgate Sch.; King's Coll., London; Emmanuel Coll., Cambridge. Keddey Fletcher-Warr Research Studentship, 1925-28; Lecturer at Sheffield Univ., 1926-35. *Publications:* various papers in the Biochemical Journal, Proc. Royal Society, Lancet, etc. *Address:* 4 Broomhill Park Central, Belfast. *T:* Belfast 665685.

**HARRISON, Very Rev. Douglas Ernest William;** Dean of Bristol since 1957; *b* 30 March 1903; *s* of late Ernest and Beatrice Harrison, Downend, Bristol; *m* 1933, Monica Aileen, *d* of Rev. A. L. F. Baker; one *s* two *d. Educ:* Bristol Grammar Sch.; St John's Coll., Oxford (Scholar); Wycliffe Hall, Oxford. 1st class Hons, Sch. of Nat. Sci. 1925; MA 1928! Curate St John, Waterloo, Liverpool, 1926-30; Chaplain St Peter's Hall, Oxford, and Curate of St Peter-le-Bailey, 1930-31; Chaplain Wycliffe Hall, Oxford, 1931-33, Vice-Principal, 1933-42; Acting Chaplain, Wadham Coll., Oxford, 1939-42, Examining Chaplain to the Bishop of Rochester, 1940-45; Canon Residentiary of Sheffield Cathedral, Examining Chaplain to Bishop of Sheffield and Director of Ordinands, 1942-57; Archdeacon of Sheffield, 1943-57; Examining Chaplain to the Bishop of Blackburn, 1966-. Select Preacher at Oxford, 1947-48, Cambridge, 1960. Mem. of C of E Bd of Educn; Vice-Chm., Council of Church Colls of Education; Vice-Chm. Liturgical Commission; Chm., The Churches' Joint Liturgical Group; Mem. Council of Religious Communities. OStJ. Hon. DLitt Bristol, 1969. *Publication:* Common Prayer in the Church of England, 1946. *Recreations:* carpentry, church architecture. *Address:* The Deanery, Charlotte Street, Bristol 1. *T:* Bristol 22443.

**HARRISON, Maj.-Gen. Eric George William Warde,** CB 1945; CBE 1943; MC 1915; MA (hon.) Oxford; DL; JP; *b* 23 March 1893; *s* of Major W. C. Warde Harrison, Indian Army; *m* 1961, Mrs Roza M. Stevenson, *widow* of J. B. Stevenson (she *d* 1967). *Educ:* Royal Military Academy, Woolwich. Commissioned Royal Artillery, 1913; European War, France and Belgium, 1914-19, GSOII 58 Div. and III Corps (despatches four times, MC, Crown of Italy, Bt Major); Staff Coll. Camberley, 1925-26; GSOII Lahore District, India, 1928-32; Major, 1932; Bt Lieut-Col 1934; Commanding Oxford Univ. OTC 1934-38; Lieut-Col 1939; Col 1939. War of 1939-45, CRA 12 Div., BRA Northern Ireland, CCRA 9 Corps, MGRA AFHQ, Comdr Surrey and Sussex District. War Service North Africa and Italy, 1943-45 (despatches, CBE, CB); Temp. Maj.-Gen. 1944; ADC to the King, 1945-46; retired pay, 1946. JP Cornwall, 1951; DL 1955; High Sheriff of Cornwall, 1958. Chm. St Lawrence's Hospital Management Cttee, 1952-66. *Publications:* Riding, 1949; To Own a Dog, 1951. *Recreations:* shooting, fishing, gardening, painting; Rugby football Mother Country XV 1919, Army 1920; Athletics, represented England in 120 yds Hurdles, 1914 and 1920, Olympic Games, 1924; Master RA Harriers, 1920-24, Staff Coll. Drag 1925-26, Lahore Hounds 1928-31, South Oxon Foxhounds, 1935-38, North Cornwall Foxhounds, 1940-48. *Address:* Tremeer, St Tudy, Bodmin, Cornwall. *T:* St Tudy 313. *Club:* Army and Navy.

**HARRISON, Rt. Hon. Sir Eric John,** PC 1952; KCMG 1962; KCVO 1954; Freeman of City of London, 1957; Company Director; *b* 7 Sept. 1892; *s* of Arthur Harrison, Birmingham, England, and Sydney, Australia; *m* 1st, 1920, Mary McCall (decd); three *d*; 2nd, 1944, Linda R., *d* of John Fullerton, Sydney. *Educ:* Crown Street Sch., Sydney. Served European War, 1914-18, with AIF (France) and 1939-45 as Capt. and Liaison Officer to US Forces; MHR, Australia, (L) Wentworth, NSW, 1931-56; Minister for Interior, 1934; Mem. Jt Cttee, Public Works, 1937 and 1943-46; Minister without portfolio, 1938-39; PMG and Repatriation Minister, 1939-40; Minister for Trade and Customs, 1940-41; Mem. Economic Cabinet, 1939-41; Dep. Leader, Liberal Party, 1944; Dep. Leader, Opposition, 1944-49 (actg Leader Oppn, latter half 1948); Minister for Defence, 1949-50; Resident Minister for Commonwealth of Australia in London and Minister for Interior, Australia, 1950-51. Vice-Pres. of Executive Council, Leader of the House of Representatives, and Minister for Defence Production, Australia, 1951-56. Minister in charge of Royal Visit, 1952 (cancelled); Minister in charge, Royal Tour, 1954; Acting Prime Minister, June 1954; Acting Treasurer, June 1954; Minister for the Army and Minister for the Navy, 1955-56; High Commissioner for the Commonwealth of Australia in London, 1956-64. *Recreations:* rowing (Mem. Australian team, Henley-on-Thames, 1919), sailing, golf, reading. *Address:* Stoke Lodge, 95 Neerim Road, Castle Cove, Sydney, NSW, Australia. *Clubs:* Union; Elanora Country (Sydney).

**HARRISON, Ernest,** CMG 1935; BSc; *b* 30 July 1886; *s* of Thomas Harrison and Louise Goodwin; *m* 1st, 1911, Annie Gladys Anyan (*d* 1920); 2nd, 1925, Josephine ffolliott Highett (*d* 1957); two *s* (and two killed on active service); 3rd, Helen Day Price. *Educ:* Holmes Chapel; Edinburgh Univ.; Ames, Iowa, USA. Lecturer Grootfontein Sch. of Agriculture, Cape Colony, 1910-12; Principal, Sch. of Agriculture, Cedara, Natal, 1913-17; Dep. Dir of Agriculture, Kenya Colony, 1921-30; Dir of Agriculture, Tanganyika, 1930-37; Prof. of Agriculture, Imperial Coll. of Tropical Agriculture, Trinidad, BWI, 1938-43, 1943-47. Agricultural Consultant, Lima, Peru. *Address:* 876 Somenos Street, Victoria, BC, Canada.

**HARRISON, Francis Anthony Kitchener;** Assistant Director, Civil Service Selection Board, since 1967; *b* 28 Aug. 1914; *s* of late Fred Harrison, JP, and Mrs M. M. Harrison (*née* Mitchell); *m* 1955, Sheila Noëlle, *d* of late Lt-Col N. D. Stevenson and of Lady Nye; three *s* one *d*. *Educ:* Winchester; New Coll., Oxford. Asst Principal, India Office, Nov. 1937; 1st Sec., UK High Commn, New Delhi, 1949-51; Commonwealth Relations Office, 1951-56; Asst Sec., 1954; Dep. High Comr for the UK at Peshawar, 1956-59; Asst Sec., CRO, 1959-61; British Dep. High Comr, New Zealand, 1961-64; Asst Secretary: Cabinet Office, 1965-67. *Recreations:* golf, fishing. *Address:* Four Winds, Snowdenham Links Road, Bramley, Surrey. *T:* Bramley 2312. *Club:* United University.

**HARRISON, Francis Laurence Theodore G.;** *see* Graham-Harrison.

**HARRISON, Dr Francis Llewelyn,** FBA 1965; Professor of Ethnomusicology, University of Amsterdam, since 1970; *b* Dublin, 29 Sept. 1905; *s* of Alfred Francis and Florence May Harrison; *m* 1966, Joan Rimmer; (two *d* of a former marriage). *Educ:* St Patrick's Cathedral Gram. Sch., Dublin; Mountjoy Sch., Dublin; Trinity Coll., Dublin; Oxford Univ. MusB Dublin, 1926; MusD Dublin, 1929; MA, DMus Oxon, 1952. Organist, St Canice's Cath., Kilkenny, 1927; Prof. of Music; Queen's Univ., Kingston, Ontario, 1935; Colgate Univ. 1946; Washington Univ., St Louis, 1947; Lectr in Music, 1952, Sen. Lectr, 1956, Reader in History of Music, 1962-70, University of Oxford; Senior Research Fellow, Jesus Coll., 1965-70. Vis. Prof. of Musicology, Yale Univ., 1958-59; Vis. Prof. of Music, Princeton Univ., 1961, 1968-69; Vis. Mem., Inst. for Advanced Study, Princeton, 1957; Fellow of Center for Advanced Study in the Behavioral Sciences, Stanford, Calif., 1965-66; Gen. Editor; Early English Church Music, 1961; Polyphonic Music of the Fourteenth Century, 1963. *Publications:* The Eton Choirbook (3 vols), 1956-61; Music in Medieval Britain, 1958; Collins Music Encyclopaedia (with J. A. Westrup), 1956; Musicology (with M. Hood and C. V. Palisca), 1963; European Musical Instruments (with J. Rimmer), 1964; Polyphonic Music of the Fourteenth Century, vol. V (Motets of French Provenance), 1969; (with E. J. Dobson) Medieval English Songs, 1971; edns of music by William Mundy, John Sheppard and others; contribs to New Oxford History of Music, and to musical jls, etc. *Recreations:* travel, eating. *Address:* 2 Chapel Lane, Littlemore, Oxford OX4 4QB. *T:* Oxford 78838.

**HARRISON, Sir Geoffrey (Wedgwood),** GCMG 1968 (KCMG 1955; CMG 1949); KCVO 1961; *b* Southsea, 18 July 1908; *s* of late Lieut-Comdr Thomas Edmund Harrison, Royal Navy, and Maud, *d* of Percy Godman; *m* 1936, Amy Katharine, *d* of late Rt Hon. Sir R. H. Clive, PC, GCMG; three *s* one *d*. *Educ:* Winchester; King's Coll., Cambridge. Entered FO, 1932; served HM Embassy, Tokyo, 1935-37; HM Embassy, Berlin, 1937-39; Private Sec. to Parly Under-Sec., FO, 1939-41; First Sec., FO, 1941-45; Counsellor, HM Embassy, Brussels, 1945-47; Brit. Minister in Moscow, 1947-49; Head of Northern Dept, FO, 1949-51; Asst Under-Sec., FO, 1951-56; Ambassador: to Brazil, 1956-58; to Persia, 1958-63; Dep. Under-Sec. of State, FO, 1963-65; Ambassador to the USSR, 1965-68. Order of Homayoun (1st Class), 1959. *Recreations:* fishing, golf, gardening. *Address:* Timbers, Plummersplain, near Horsham, Sussex. *T:* Handcross 266; 6 Ormonde Gate, SW3.

**HARRISON, George Bagshawe,** MA Cantab; PhD London; Emeritus Professor of English, University of Michigan, 1964 (Professor, 1949-64); *b* 14 July 1894; *s* of late Walter Harrison, Brighton; *m* 1919, Dorothy Agnes, *o d* of late Rev. Thomas Barker; one *d* (three *s* decd). *Educ:* Brighton Coll.; Queens' Coll., Cambridge (Classical Exhibitioner; 1st Class English Tripos, 1920. Commnd to 5th Bn The Queen's Royal Regt, and served in India and Mesopotamia, 1914-19; Staff Capt. 42nd Indian Infantry Brigade (despatches); War of 1939-45, RASC and Intelligence Corps, 1940-43. Asst Master, Felsted Sch., 1920-22; Senior Lecturer in English, St Paul's Training Coll., Cheltenham, 1922-24; Asst Lecturer in English Literature, King's Coll., University of London, 1924-27; Lecturer, 1927-29; Frederic Ives Carpenter Visiting Prof. of English, University of Chicago, 1929; Reader in English Literature, University of London, 1929-43; Head of English Dept and Prof. of English, Queen's Univ., Kingston, Ont., Canada, 1943-49; lectured at Sorbonne, 1933, in Holland, 1940; Alexander Lecturer, University of Toronto, Canada, 1947. Mem., Internat. Cttee on English in the Liturgy. Hon. LittD Villanova, 1960, Holy Cross, 1961; Marquette, 1963; Hon. LLD Assumption, 1962. Campion Award for long and eminent service in cause of Christian literature. *Publications:* Shakespeare: the Man and his Stage (with E. A. G. Lamborn); Shakespeare's Fellows; John Bunyan: a Study in Personality; England in Shakespeare's Day; An Elizabethan Journal, 1591-94; A Second Elizabethan Journal 1595-98; A Last Elizabethan Journal, 1599-1603; A Jacobean Journal, 1603-1606; A Second Jacobean Journal, 1607-1610; Shakespeare at Work; The Life and Death of Robert Devereux, Earl of Essex, 1937; The Day before Yesterday (a Journal of 1936); Elizabethan Plays and Players, 1940; Shakespeare's Tragedies, 1951; Profession of English, 1962; The Fires of Arcadia, 1965, etc.; Editor: The Bodley Head Quartos; The New Readers' Shakespeare (with F. H. Pritchard); The Pilgrim's Progress and Mr Badman; The Church Book of Bunyan Meeting; Breton's Melancholike Humours; The Lancaster Witches, 1612; The Earl of Northumberland's Advice to his son; translated and edited The Journal of De Maisse (with R. A. Jones); A Companion to Shakespeare Studies (with Harley Granville-Barker); The Letters of Queen Elizabeth; The Penguin Shakespeares; Contributor to The Road to Damascus, 1949; etc. *Address:* 113 West Lupita Road, Santa Fe, New Mexico 87501, USA.

**HARRISON, Sir Guy;** *see* Harrison, Sir B. G.

**HARRISON, Sir Harwood;** *see* Harrison, Sir James Harwood.

**HARRISON, Rear-Adm. Hubert Southwood,** CBE 1951; DSC 1941; *b* Glasgow, 7 Aug. 1898; *s* of T. S. Harrison; *m* 1935, Beth Rowson Saynor (*d* 1962). *Educ:* Trinity Coll., Glenalmond. Cadet, RN, 1916; Midshipman, 1917; Sub-Lieut, 1918; Lieut (E), 1920; Lieut-Comdr (E), 1927; Comdr (E), 1930; Capt. (E), 1941; Rear-Adm. (E), 1948; Asst Dir of Dockyards, Admiralty, 1946-52; retired, 1952. *Recreations:* golf, sailing, fishing. *Address:* House in the Wood, Budock Vean, Falmouth. *T:* Mawnan Smith 337.

**HARRISON, Maj.-Gen. Ian Stewart,** CB 1970; Director-General, British Food Export Council, since 1970; *b* 25 May 1919; *s* of Leslie George Harrison and Evelyn Simpson Christie; *m* 1942, Winifred Raikes Stavert; one *s* one *d*. *Educ:* St Albans Sch. Commissioned, Royal Marines, 1937; service at sea, in Norway, Middle East, Sicily, BAOR, 1939-45; Staff Coll., Camberley (student), 1948; HQ 3rd Commando Bde, 1949-51 (despatches); Staff of Comdt-Gen., RM, 1951-52; Staff Coll., Camberley (Directing Staff), 1953-55; Commandant, RM Signal Sch., 1956-58; Joint Services Staff Coll. (Student), 1958; CO 40 Commando, RM, 1959-61; Dir, Royal Marines Reserves, 1962; Staff of Comdt-Gen., RM, 1963-64; Joint Warfare Estabt, 1965-67; British Defence Staff, Washington, DC, 1967-68; Chief of Staff to Comdt-Gen., RM, 1968-70, retired. MBIM. *Recreations:* sailing, real tennis, lawn tennis, golf, painting. *Address:* Apuldram Cottage, Dell Quay, Chichester, W Sussex. *T:* Chichester 85480. *Clubs:* United Service; Royal Yacht Squadron, Royal Naval Sailing Association, Royal Thames Yacht, Itchenor Sailing.

**HARRISON, His Honour James Fraser;** Judge of County Courts, 1940-62; retired; Commissioner of Divorce; JP Lancs, 1938, Cheshire, 1942; *b* 7 May 1890; *s* of late James Fraser Harrison, Caerwys, Flintshire; *m* 1915, Betty (*d* 1960), *er d* of late Alfred Broadhurst, Bramhall, Cheshire; one *s*. *Educ:* Liverpool Coll.; Sedbergh; Liverpool Univ. LLM (Hon.) Liverpool Univ., 1942. Called to Bar, Inner Temple, 1912; practised Liverpool and Northern Circuit; Army, 1914-18; Asst Recorder of Liverpool, 1929-40; Dep. Chm. Preston, Manchester and Liverpool County Quarter Sessions, 1938-40; Aliens Tribunal, 1939; a Dep. Chm. of Appeal Cttees for County of Lancaster, 1943-60 and Chester, 1943-46; Hon. Independent Referee Lancs and Cheshire Coal Mining Conciliation Board, 1945-62; HM Commissioner of Assize, Northern Circuit, 1946. *Address:* Alexandra Court Hotel, Liverpool 17. *T:* 051-727 2551. *Club:* Lyceum (Liverpool).

**HARRISON, Sir (James) Harwood,** 1st Bt *cr* 1961, of Bugbrooke; TD (2 bars) 1947; MA; MP (C) Eye Division of Suffolk since 1951; *b* 6 June 1907; *e s* of late Rev. E. W. Harrison, MA, Bugbrooke, Northampton; *m* 1932, Peggy Alberta Mary, *d* of late Lieut-Col V. D. Stenhouse, TD, JP, Minehead; one *s* one *d*. *Educ:* Northampton Grammar Sch.; Trinity Coll., Oxford. Hons degree (jurisprudence), 1928; MA 1946. Mem. Ipswich County Borough Council, 1935-46; Chm. Mental Hosp., 1938. Commissioned 4th Bn The Suffolk Regt, TA, 1935; Capt. 1939; Major

1940; captured (Singapore), 1942; on Burma Railway, 1943; Lieut-Col comdg 4th Suffolks, 1947; Bt-Col 1951; TARO 1951-65. Mil. Mem. Suffolk T and AFA, 1951-. Contested Eye Div. of Suffolk, 1950. Presented and sponsored Private Member's Bills: The Road Transport Lighting (Rear Lights) Act, 1953; The Road Traffic Act, 1964. PPS to Mr Harold Macmillan, Minister of Housing and Local Govt, 1953-54; Asst Whip, 1954-56; a Lord Commissioner of the Treasury, 1956-59; Comptroller of HM Household, 1959-61. Pres., Nat. Union of Conservative and Unionist Assocs Eastern Area, 1963-66 (Chm. 1956-59, Vice-Chm. 1953-56); Chm., Unionist Club, 1966-. Pres. Ipswich and District Far East POW Fellowship, 1953. Chm., Cap Estate (St Lucia) Ltd; Dir of Chalwyns Ltd and other companies. Has lectured extensively in America, Europe and Africa. Patron, Lord of Manor and Land-Owner at Bugbrooke. *Recreations:* sailing, ski-ing. *Heir:* *s* Michael James Harwood Harrison [*b* 28 March, 1936; *m* 1967, Rosamund Louise, *d* of Edward Clive, Bishops Waltham; one *d*]. *Address:* Little Manor, Hasketon, Woodbridge, Suffolk. *T:* Woodbridge 242; 17 Tufton Court, Tufton Street, SW1. *T:* 01-799 6619. *Clubs:* Carlton, Crockford's, Pratt's; House of Commons Yacht (Commodore).

**HARRISON, Maj.-Gen. Sir James (William),** KCMG 1968; CB 1968; CBE 1958; idc; Governor of South Australia, since 1968; *b* 25 May 1912; *s* of James Samuel Harrison, Camperdown, Vic.; *m* 1940, Patricia Hellen, *d* of Col. F. W. Lennox; two *s*. *Educ:* Geelong Coll.; RMC Duntroon. Commnd RAA, 1932; regimental appts until 1939; served 1939-45 in Middle East (despatches), SW Pacific Area, NW Europe. Aust. Staff UK, 1954-56; GOC, W Comd, 1957-59; Chm., Jt Planning Cttee, Dept of Defence, 1960-61; QMG Australian Army, 1962-63; Adjt Gen., 1963-66. GOC Eastern Comd, Australia, 1966-68. KStJ 1969. *Recreations:* golf, books. *Address:* Government House, Adelaide, South Australia. *Club:* Naval and Military (Melbourne).

**HARRISON, John H.;** *see* Heslop-Harrison.

**HARRISON, Maj.-Gen. John Martin Donald W.;** *see* Ward-Harrison.

**HARRISON, John Vernon,** MA, DSc; FRSE; Geologist; formerly Reader in Structural Geology, Oxford University; *b* 16 March 1892; *s* of late J. Frederick Harrison, MInstCE; *m* 1939, Janet Mitchell, *d* of D. M. Dingwall, Flisk, Newburgh, Fife. *Educ:* George Watson's Coll., Edinburgh; Allan Glen's Sch., Glasgow; Glasgow Univ. Explored in Persia, Central and South America, West Indies, and Borneo. Grand Officer, Order for Distinguished Services to Peru. *Publications:* Papers on Geology and Geography. *Recreation:* hill-climbing. *Address:* 59 Bagley Wood Road, Kennington, Oxford. *Club:* Athenæum.

**HARRISON, Kathleen, (Mrs J. H. Back);** leading character actress, stage and films; *d* of Arthur Harrison, MICE, Civil Engineer, and Alice Harrison; *m* 1916, John Henry Back; two *s* one *d*. *Educ:* Clapham High Sch. Trained at RADA. *Notable plays include:* Badger's Green, Prince of Wales Theatre, 1930; Night Must Fall, Duchess, 1935; The Corn is Green, Duchess, 1938; Flare Path, Apollo, 1942; The Winslow Boy, Lyric, 1946; All for Mary, Duke of York's, 1955; Nude with Violin, Globe, 1956; How Say You? Aldwych, 1959; Watch it, Sailor!, Aldwych, 1960; The Chances, Chichester Festival, 1962. Norman, Duchess, 1963; title role in Goodnight Mrs Puffin, New Theatre, Bromley. *Films include:* In Which We Serve; The Huggett films; Alive and Kicking; The Winslow Boy; Bank Holiday; Holiday Camp; Barabbas; West 11; Scrooge. *TV includes:* Martin Chuzzlewit serial (Betsy Prig); title role in Mrs Thursday series; Waters of the Moon. *Address:* c/o International Famous Agency, 11/12 Hanover Street, W1. *T:* 01-629 8080.

**HARRISON, Kenneth Cecil,** MBE 1945; FLA; City Librarian, Westminster, since 1961; *b* 29 April 1915; *s* of Thomas and Annie Harrison; *m* 1941, Doris Taylor; two *s*. *Educ:* Grammar Sch., Hyde. Asst, Hyde Public Library, 1931-36; Branch Librarian, Coulsdon and Purley Public Libraries, 1936-39; Borough Librarian: Hyde, 1939-47; Hove (also Curator), 1947-50; Eastbourne, 1950-58; Hendon, 1958-61. HM Forces, 1940-46; Commnd RMC Sandhurst, 1942; served with E Yorks Regt in Middle East, Sicily and NW Europe (wounded, 1944; Major 1944-46). Member: Council Library Assoc.; Exec. Bd, Internat. Assoc. Metropolitan Libraries; Exec. Cttee, National Central Library; Central Music Library Council; National Book League Council; Chm. Jt Organising Cttee for Nat. Library Week, 1966, 1967, 1969. Hon. Sec., Westminster Arts Council. Has lectured on librarianship at European, US, and Brit. Univs and Library schools. Governor, Westminster Technical Coll. Editor, The Library World, 1961-. *Publications:* First Steps in Librarianship, 1950; Libraries in Scandinavia, 1961; The Library and the Community, 1963; Public Libraries Today, 1963; Facts at your Fingertips, 1964; British Public Library Buildings (with S. G. Berriman), 1966; Libraries in Britain, 1968. Contributions to many international and foreign jls. *Recreations:* reading, writing, travel, cricket. *Address:* 50 West Hill Way, N20. *T:* 01-445 1298. *Clubs:* Authors', MCC; Surrey County Cricket.

**HARRISON, Laurence,** CMG 1952, retired; *b* 3 Oct. 1897; *s* of late George Henry Harrison; *m* 1st, 1923, Nellie Florence (Serving Sister of Order of St John; *d* 1963); one *d*; 2nd, 1969, Jenny Margaret Wallace Pritchard (*née* Duncan), Sandown, Johannesburg. *Educ:* St Dunstan's Coll.; Strand Sch. Served BEF France (RE), 1916-19. Entered Min. of Pensions, 1919; transf. to Dept of Overseas Trade, 1930; Asst Trade Commissioner (Grade II), Johannesburg, 1945, Trade Commissioner (Grade I), New Delhi, 1947, Johannesburg, 1953-57. *Recreations:* horticulture, field natural history. *Address:* 6 Berg Street, Barberton, East Transvaal, S Africa.

**HARRISON, Mrs Molly,** MBE 1967; Curator, Geffrye Museum, 1941-69; *b* Stevenage, 1909; *d* of late Ethel and late Ernest Charles Hodgett; *m* 1940, Gordon Frederick Harrison; three *d*. *Educ:* Friends Sch., Saffron Walden; Convent in Belgium; Sorbonne. Teaching in various Schs, 1934-39; Asst to Curator, Geffrye Museum, 1939-41. FMA 1952; Member: Council Museums Assoc., 1953-56; Council of Industrial Design, 1958-61; Cttee of Management, Society of Authors, 1967-. Lectr on varied educational topics. FRSA 1968. Editor, Local Search Series, 1969-. *Publications:* Museum Adventure, 1950; Picture Source Books for Social History, 1951, 1953, 1955, 1957, 1958, 1960 and 1966; Furniture 1953; Learning out of School, 1954; Food, 1954; Homes, 1960; Children in History, 1958, 1959, 1960, 1961; Your Book of Furniture, 1960; Shops and Shopping, 1963; How They Lived, 1963; Changing Museums, 1967; Hairstyles and Hairdressing, 1968; The English Home, 1969; numerous articles and reviews. *Recreations:* writing, children, gardening. *Address:* The Coach House, Horse Leas, Bradfield, Berks. *T:* Bradfield 437.

**HARRISON, Patrick Kennard;** Secretary, Royal Institute of British Architects, since 1968; *b* 8 July 1928, *e s* of late Richard Harrison and Sheila Griffin; *m* 1955, Mary Wilson, *y d* of late Captain G. C. C. Damant, CBE, RN; one *d*. *Educ:* Lord Williams's Sch., Thame; Downing Coll., Cambridge. Asst Principal, Dept of Health for Scotland, 1953; Private Sec. to Deptl Sec. and to Parly Secs, Scottish Office, 1958-60; Principal, Scottish Develt Dept and Regional Develt Div., Scottish Office, 1960-68. *Address:* 11 Forres Street, Edinburgh 3. *T:* 031-225 6271. *Club:* New (Edinburgh).

**HARRISON, Rex Carey;** actor; *b* 5 March 1908; *s* of William Reginald and Edith Carey Harrison; *m* 1st, 1934, Marjorie Noel Collette Thomas; one *s*; 2nd, 1943, Lilli Palmer (marriage dissolved 1957); one *s*; 3rd, 1957, Kay Kendall (*d* 1959); 4th, 1962, Rachel Roberts. *Educ:* Birkdale Preparatory Sch.; Liverpool Coll. Made first appearance on the stage at Liverpool Repertory Theatre, 1924; remained until 1927. Toured with Charley's Aunt playing Jack, 1927; also toured at intervals during subsequent years until 1935, and appeared with Cardiff Repertory, and in the West End. First appearance on London stage as Rankin in The Ninth Man, Prince of Wales Theatre, 1931; First appearance on New York stage at Booth Theatre, 1936, as Tubbs Barrow in Sweet Aloes. Played in French Without Tears at Criterion, 1936-37-38, and at Haymarket Theatre, 1939-41, in Design for Living (Leo) and No Time for Comedy (Gaylord Esterbrook). Volunteered RAFVR, 1941, and served till 1944. Released from Forces to make Blithe Spirit (film), and, 1945, Rake's Progress (film). Filmed in Hollywood, 1945-46-47. (Maxwell Anderson's) Anne of the Thousand Days, Schubert Theatre, NY, 1948-49; in The Cocktail Party, New Theatre, London, 1950; acted in and produced Bell, Book and Candle, Ethel Barrymore Theatre, NY, 1951, and Phœnix Theatre, London, 1954; in Venus Observed, Century Theatre, NY, 1952; directed and played in Love of Four Colonels, Schubert Theatre, NY, 1953; produced Nina, Haymarket Theatre, London, 1955; acted in: My Fair Lady (Henry Higgins), Mark Hellinger Theatre, NY, 1956-57, and Drury Lane, London, 1958-59; The Fighting Cock, Anta Theatre, NY, 1959; Platonov, Royal Court, 1960; August for the People, Edinburgh Festival, 1961, and Royal Court Theatre; The Lionel Touch, Lyric, 1969, etc. Began acting in films in 1929. Best known films: Storm in a Teacup, 1936; St Martin's Lane, 1937; Over the Moon, 1938; Night Train to Munich, Major Barbara, 1940-41; Blithe Spirit, 1944; I Live in Grosvenor Square, 1944; The Rake's Progress, 1945; (Hollywood, 1945) Anna and the King of Siam, 1946; The Ghost and Mrs Muir, 1947; The Foxes of Harrow, 1947; (Galsworthy's) Escape (in England), 1948; Unfaithfully Yours (in America), 1948; The Long Dark Hall, 1951; King Richard and the Crusaders, 1954; The Constant Husband, 1955; The Reluctant Debutante, 1958; Midnight Lace, 1960; The Happy Thieves, 1961; Cleopatra (Julius Caesar), 1962; My Fair Lady, 1964; The Yellow Rolls Royce, 1965; The Agony and the Ecstacy, 1965; The Honey Pot, 1967; Doctor Dolittle, 1967; A Flea in her Ear, 1967; *Recreations:* golf, tennis, fishing. *Address:* c/o International Famous Agency, 11/12 Hanover Street, W1. *Clubs:* Beefsteak, Green Room, Garrick; Players' (New York); Travellers' (Paris).

**HARRISON, Air Vice-Marshal Richard,** CB 1944; CBE 1943; DFC; AFC; late RAF; *b* 29 June 1893; *s* of late Mansfield Harrison, Pocklington, Yorks; unmarried. *Educ:* Highgate; Scarborough Coll.; Sheffield Univ. European War, 1914-19 (despatches); Palestine; Iraq (despatches twice); Egypt; War of 1939-45 (despatches thrice); retired, 1946. Officier Légion d'Honneur; Croix de Guerre (France). *Club:* Royal Air Force.

**HARRISON, Prof. Richard John,** MD, DSc; Professor of Anatomy, Cambridge University, since 1968; Fellow of Downing College, Cambridge; *b* 8 Oct. 1920; *er s* of Geoffrey Arthur Harrison, MD, and late Theodora Beatrice Mary West; *m* 1st, 1943, Joanna Gillies; two *s* one *d*; 2nd, 1967, Barbara, *o d* of James and Florence Fuller, Neston, Cheshire. *Educ:* Oundle; Gonville and Caius Coll., Cambridge (Scholar); St Bartholomew's Hosp. Medical Coll. LRCP, MRCS, 1944. House Surgeon, St Bartholomew's Hosp., 1944. MB, BChir, 1944; MA 1946. Demonstrator in Anatomy, St Bartholomew's Hosp. Medical Coll., 1944; Lectr in Anatomy, Glasgow Univ., 1946, DSc Glasgow 1948; Sen. Lectr, 1947, and Reader in Anatomy, 1950, Charing Cross Hosp. Medical Sch. (Symington Prize for research in Anatomy); Reader in charge of Anatomy Dept, London Hosp. Medical Coll., 1951-54; Prof. of Anatomy, University of London, at London Hosp. Medical Coll., 1954-68; Fullerian Prof. of Physiology, Royal Institution, 1961-67. Editor, Jl Anatomy, 1964-68. MD, Cambridge, 1954; FZS, FLS. *Publications:* Anatomical Terms, 3rd edn, 1967; Man the Peculiar Animal, 1958; (with F. Goldby) Recent Advances in Anatomy, 1961; (with J. E. King) Marine Mammals, 1965; Reproduction and Man, 1967; numerous papers on embryology, comparative and human anatomy in Jl of Anatomy, Nature, Proc. and Trans. Zoolog. Soc., etc. *Recreations:* marine biology, painting, golf. *Address:* The Beeches, 8 Woodlands Road, Great Shelford, Cambs. *T:* Shelford 3287. *Club:* Garrick.

**HARRISON, Sir (Robert) Colin,** 4th Bt, *cr* 1922; *b* 25 May 1938; *s* of Sir John Fowler Harrison, 2nd Bt, and Kathleen, *yr d* of late Robert Livingston, The Gables, Eaglescliffe, Co. Durham; *S* brother, 1955; *m* 1963, Maureen, *er d* of E. Leonard Chiverton, Fairfield, Evenwood, West Auckland, Co. Durham; one *d*. *Educ:* St Peter's Coll., Radley; St John's Coll., Cambridge. Commissioned with Fifth Royal Northumberland Fusiliers (National Service), 1957-59. *Address:* Keld Close, Hutton-le-Hole, York. *T:* Lastingham 329.

**HARRISON, Prof. Ronald George;** Derby Professor of Anatomy, University of Liverpool, since 1950; *b* 5 April 1921; *s* of James Harrison and Alice Hannah Harrison (*née* Edmondson); *m* 1945; two *s* one *d*; *m* 1966, Dr M. J. Hoey, Southport, Lancs; one *d*. *Educ:* Ulverston Grammar Sch.; Oxford Univ. BA Oxon, 1942; BM, BCh, Oxon 1944; MA Oxon, 1946; DM Oxon, 1949. Demy, Magdalen Coll., Oxford, 1939-42; Pres., OU Scientific Club, 1942. Junior Gynæcological House Surg., Nuffield Dept of Obstetrics and Gynæcology, Oxford, 1943; Gynæc. and Obst. House Surgeonships, Radcliffe Infirmary, Oxford, 1944-45; Demonstrator and Lecturer, Dept of Human Anatomy, Univ. of Oxford, 1945-49. Lectr in Anatomy, Ruskin Sch. of Drawing and Fine Art, 1946-50; Univ. Demonstrator, Dept of Human Anatomy, Univ. of Oxford, 1949-50; Lectr in Anatomy, Pembroke Coll., Oxford, 1950. BBC TV film, Tutankhamen Post-mortem, 1969. Fellow Eugenics Soc. Chm., Bd of Governors, Liverpool Coll. of

Occupational Therapy, 1968; Pres., Liverpool Univ. Med. Sciences Club, 1954-55. For. Corr. Mem., Royal Belgian Soc. of Obstetrics and Gynæcology, 1964-. Vice-Pres., Rotary Club of Liverpool, 1970. *Publications:* A Textbook of Human Embryology, 1959, 1963; The Adrenal Circulation, 1960; Chapters in Cunningham's Textbook of Anatomy, 1964; contrib. to various medical and scientific journals. Editor, Studies on Fertility, 1954-58. *Recreations:* riding, music. *Address:* The Stables, Fernhill, Upper Brighton, Wallasey, Cheshire. *T:* 051-639 6327.

**HARRISON, Ven. Talbot D.;** *see* Dilworth-Harrison.

**HARRISON, Walter,** JP; MP (Lab) Wakefield, since 1964; Deputy Chief Opposition Whip, since 1970; *b* 2 Jan. 1921; *s* of Henry and Ada Harrison; *m* 1948, Enid Mary (*née* Coleman); one *s* one *d*. *Educ:* Dewsbury Technical and Art Coll. Electrical Inspector and Electrical Foreman, Electricity Supply Industry, 1937-64. Asst Govt Whip, 1966-68; a Lord Comr of the Treasury, 1968-70. West Riding CC, 1958; Alderman, Castleford Borough Council, 1959 (Councillor, 1952); JP West Riding, Yorks, 1962. *Address:* 1 Milnthorpe Drive, Sandal, Wakefield, Yorks. *T:* Wakefield 55550.

**HARRISON, Prof. Wilfrid;** Professor of Politics and Pro-Vice-Chancellor, University of Warwick, since 1964; *b* 30 May 1909; *s* of W. T. and Amy Harrison, Glasgow; *m* 1943, Elizabeth Sara, *d* of Rev. P. J. and Linda Sweeny, Ardagh, Co. Limerick; two *d*. *Educ:* Hyndland Sch., Glasgow; University of Glasgow; Queen's Coll., Oxford. MA 1931, University of Glasgow; BA 1933, MA 1937, University of Oxford. Senior Demy of Magdalen Coll., Oxford, 1933; Lecturer in Politics, Queen's Coll., Oxford, 1935; Fellow of Queen's Coll., 1939-57, Dean, 1940; Prof. of Political Theory and Institutions, University of Liverpool, 1957-64. Temporary Civil Servant, Ministry of Supply, 1940-45. Editor of Political Studies, 1952-63. *Publications:* The Government of Britain, 1948; Conflict and Compromise, 1965; (ed) Bentham's Fragment on Government and Introduction to the Principles of Morals and Legislation, 1948; articles in Chambers's Encyclopædia and various journals. *Recreations:* piano; cooking. *Address:* 73 Coten End, Warwick.

**HARRISON, William Herbert;** Chairman of Power Plant Gears Limited; Director: Parkwood Engineering Co. Ltd; Amalgamated Anthracite Holdings Ltd; Amalgamated Anthracite Subsidiaries Ltd; Amalgamated Anthracite Partners Ltd; British Anthracite Sales Ltd; Weevsown Ltd; Garner Motors Ltd; Hawson Ltd; New Blaenhirwaun Anthracite Collieries Ltd; *b* 1909; *s* of late Lt-Col William Edward Harrison, OBE, Wychnor Park; *m* 1934, Elcha Cecelia (marr. diss.), *d* of late Charles Hore-Ruthven, Norwich; four *d*. *Educ:* Harrow. High Sheriff of Staffordshire, 1964. *Recreations:* racing, shooting and fishing. *Address:* Wychnor Park, near Burton-on-Trent, Staffs. *T:* Alrewas 209. *Club:* Boodle's.

**HARRISON-CHURCH, Prof. Ronald James;** Professor of Geography, University of London, at London School of Economics, since 1964; *b* 26 July 1915; *s* of late James Walter Church and late Jessie May Church; *m* 1944, Dorothy Violet, *d* of late Robert Colchester Harrison and late Rose Harrison; one *s* one *d*. *Educ:* Westminster City Sch.; Universities of London and Paris. BSc (Econ) 1936, PhD 1943, London. LSE: Asst Lectr, 1944-47; Lectr, 1947-58; Reader, 1958-64. Consultant to UN Economic Commn for Africa on large scale irrigation schemes, 1962. Vis. Prof., University of Wisconsin, 1956; Vis. Prof., Indiana Univ., 1965. Has lectured in many other univs in US, Belgium, France, Germany and Brazil. Back Award, RGS, 1957. *Publications:* Modern Colonization, 1951; West Africa, 1957 (6th edn, 1968); Environment and Policies in West Africa, 1963; (jtly) Africa and the Islands, 1964 (3rd edn, 1971); (jtly) An Advanced Geography of Northern and Western Europe, 1967; contribs to Geograph. Jl, W Africa, etc. *Recreations:* travel, good food and wine. *Address:* 8 Mannicotts, Welwyn Garden City, Herts. *T:* Welwyn Garden City 23293.

**HARRISSON, Tom,** DSO 1946; OBE 1959; Senior Research Associate in Anthropology and South-east Asia Program, Cornell University; Emeritus Curator, Sarawak Museum; Research Fellow and Director of Mass-Observation Archive, University of Sussex; *b* 26 Sept. 1911; *s* of late Gen. G. H. Harrisson, DSO, and D. Cole; *m* 1st, 1941, Mrs Betha Clayton (marr. diss., 1954; she *d* 1961), *d* of late T. Pellatt, Durnford Sch., Dorset; one *s*; 2nd, 1956, Barbara, *d* of Dr Gerhart Güttler, Berlin, Nikolassee and Bad Tolz, Germany. *Educ:* Harrow; Pembroke Coll., Cambridge. Biological upbringing and training; left Harrow (where wrote standard book on the birds of the district) to go on Oxford Univ. Expedn to Arctic Lapland; spent time on uninhabited British islands; in Central Borneo where led large Oxford Expedition, and then for two years in New Hebrides, Western Pacific; one year living among cannibal mountain tribes of Malekula–Cuthbert Peak award of Royal Geographical Society. On return to England, 1938, determined, instead of studying primitive people, to study the cannibals of Britain, so started with Charles Madge new type of social research organisation, called Mass-Observation. Radio critic Sunday Observer, 1941-44; served in KRRC, Green Howards and Reconnaissance Corps, 1942-44; Paratroop Major with Special Operations Executive, 1944-45 (DSO); first white man to be dropped in Borneo, to organise guerillas in Sarawak and Dutch Borneo prior to Allied landings; Officer Administrating Interior Borneo for Mil. Admin., 1946; Govt Ethnologist and Curator of Museum, Sarawak, 1947-66; Vis. Prof., Cornell, 1967-69. Editor, Sarawak Museum Jl; Ethnological Expedns for Sarawak Govt to Kelabit Plateau Central Borneo, 1947-64. Speleological Soc. Award, USA, 1960; José Rizal Centennial Medal, Philippines, 1961; Founder's Medal of Royal Geographical Soc., 1962; RSA Medallist, 1964. *Publications:* Birds of NW Middlesex, 1930; The Great Crested Grebe Census, 1931; Letter to Oxford, 1933; numerous papers in scientific journals on biological studies and exploratory work, 1932-36; Savage Civilisation, 1937; Borneo Jungle, 1938; Living Among Cannibals, 1942. Mass-Observation, 1937; Britain, by Mass-Observation, 1939; War begins at Home, 1940; Home Propaganda, 1941; People in Production, 1942; The Pub and the People, 1943; People's Homes, 1943; World Within: a Borneo Story, 1959; Britain Re-visited, 1961; The Peoples of Sarawak, 1961; Brunei: Background to a Revolt, 1963; The Malays of Sarawak, 1969; papers on ethnology of South East Asia in Jls of Asiatic Soc. Polynesian Soc., South Seas Soc., Man, etc., 1948-69; (with Prof. S. J. O'Connor) The Prehistoric Iron Age Workings of Sarawak, 1969; Gold and the Megalithic in Borneo, 1970. *Recreations:* living among strange people and listening to them talk about themselves; collecting strange objects; television (with Hugh Gibb, won Eurovision Grand Prix, Cannes Film Festival for TV film, Birds' Nest Soup, one of a series of 6, in The Borneo Story). *Address:* c/o South-east Asia Program, Cornell University, Ithaca, NY 14850, USA; c/o Vice-Chancellor's Office, University of Sussex, Brighton, Sussex. *Clubs:* Reform, Travellers', Special Forces; Brunei Yacht; International House of Japan.

**HARROD, Sir Roy (Forbes),** Kt 1959; FBA; Hon. Dr (Law), Poitiers; Hon. LLD Aberdeen; Hon. Dr (Laws) University of Pennsylvania; Hon. DLitt: Glasgow; Warwick; Hon. Student of Christ Church, since 1967; Hon. Fellow of Nuffield College; *b* 13 Feb. 1900; *s* of Henry Dawes Harrod and Frances Marie Desiree Harrod; *m* 1938, Wilhelmine, *e d* of late Capt. F. J. Cresswell, The Norfolk Regt, and of Lady Strickland, *qv*; two *s*. *Educ:* Westminster Sch. (Scholar); New Coll., Oxford (Scholar); 1st class in Lit. Hum., 1921; 1st class in Modern History, 1922. Enlisted, Sept. 1918; Lecturer at Christ Church, 1922-24; Student, 1924-67; Junior Censor, 1927-29; Senior Censor, 1930-31; Mem. of the Hebdomadal Council of Oxford University, 1929-35; Bodleian Library Commission, 1930-31; University Lecturer in Economics, 1929-37 and 1946-52; Nuffield Reader in Economics, 1952-67. Pres. of Sect. F of Brit. Assoc., 1938; served under Lord Cherwell on Mr Churchill's private statistical staff in Admiralty, 1940, and in Prime Minister's office, at full time, 1940-42, and subsequently in advisory capacity; also statistical adviser to Admiralty, 1943-45; Vice-Pres., the Royal Economic Society (Mem., Council since 1933); Jt Editor, Economic Journal, 1945-61; Mem. of UN Sub-Commission on Employment and Economic Stability, 1947-50; Fellow of Nuffield Coll., 1938-47, and 1954-58; Hon. Fellow, 1958. Economic Adviser, International Monetary Fund, 1952-53; Sir George Watson Lecturer in American History, 1953; Bernard Harms Prize (Keil), 1966. Mem. Migration Board, Commonwealth Relations Office, 1953-66. Curator of Christ Church Pictures, 1956-64. Exec. Cttee of sponsors of East Anglia Univ., 1959-64; Pres. Royal Economic Soc., 1962-64. *Publications:* International Economics, 1933 (revised edn, 1957); The Trade Cycle, an Essay, 1936; Britain's Future Population, 1943; A Page of British Folly, 1946; Are These Hardships Necesary?, 1947; Towards a Dynamic Economics, 1948; The Life of John Maynard Keynes, 1951; And So It Goes On, 1951; Economic Essays, 1952; The Dollar, 1953; The Foundations of Inductive Logic, 1956; Policy Against Inflation, 1958; The Prof. (A Personal Memoir of Lord Cherwell), 1959; Topical Comment, 1961; The British Economy, 1963; Reforming the World's Money, 1965; Towards a New Economic Policy, 1967; Dollar-Sterling Collaboration, 1968; Money, 1969. Papers in the Economic Journal, the Quarterly Journal of Economics, Economica, Mind, etc. *Address:* The Old Rectory, Holt, Norfolk. *T:* Holt 2204; 51 Campden Hill Square, W8. *T:* 01-727 8485.

**HARROP, Maj.-Gen. William Harrington H.;** *see* Hulton-Harrop.

**HARROWBY,** 6th Earl of, *cr* 1809; **Dudley Ryder;** Baron Harrowby, 1776; Viscount Sandon, 1809; Major, late RFA (TAR); *b* 11 Oct. 1892; *e s* of 5th Earl of Harrowby and Hon. Mabel Danvers Smith, DBE (*d* 1956), *y d* of late Rt Hon. W. H. Smith, MP, and 1st Viscountess Hambleden; *S* father 1956; *m* 1922, Lady Helena Blanche Coventry, *e d* of late Viscount Deerhurst; two *s* one *d*. *Educ:* Eton; Christ Church, Oxford (BA). Asst Private Sec. to Viscount Milner, Sec. of State for the Colonies, Jan. 1919-Aug. 1920; MP (U) Shrewsbury Division of Salop, Nov. 1922-Nov. 1923, and Oct. 1924-May 1929; Parliamentary Private Sec. to Sir S. Hoare, Sec. of State for Air, Dec. 1922-Nov. 1923; Alderman LCC, 1932-37, Mem. for Dulwich, 1937-40; served European War, Major RA, 1914-19 (wounded); served War of 1939-45. Col Commandant Staffs Army Cadet Force, 1946-50. DL Staffs, 1925; JP Staffs, 1929; Mem. of Royal Commission on Historical Manuscripts, 1935-66. Hon. DLitt Oxon, 1964. *Publications:* England at Worship; (joint) Geography of Everyday Things. *Heir:* *s* Viscount Sandon, *qv*. *Address:* Sandon Hall, Stafford; Burnt Norton, Campden, Gloucestershire. *Club:* Travellers'.

**HARSANT, Maj.-Gen. Arnold Guy,** CB 1952; OBE 1935; FRCS; MD; MS; Limb-fitting Surgeon, Queen Mary's Hospital, Roehampton; *b* 16 Nov. 1893; *s* of F. A. Harsant, LDS, and Rosetta Harsant; *m* 1934, Mabel Sarah Bailey; one *d*. *Educ:* St Paul's Sch., West Kensington; The London Hosp. MRCS, LRCP, 1916; DTM and H 1922; MB, BS 1930; FRCS 1930; MD 1931; MS London 1933. Commissioned in Regular Army RAMC; served in Salonica Campaign, 1916-18 (despatches); subsequently served in Mesopotamia, India, China, Egypt; Maj.-Gen., 1951; Cons. Surgeon, Egypt and Palestine Forces, Sept.-Dec. 1936; Prof. of Surgery, Egyptian University, 1937-45; Cons. Surgeon, BAOR, 1945-49; Dir of Surgery and Consulting Surgeon to the Army, 1949-53. KHS 1949. Order of St Sava, 1916; Order of the Nile, 1937. *Address:* 16 Roehampton Gate, SW15. *T:* 01-876 8924.

**HARSCH, Joseph Close,** CBE (Hon.) 1965; writer and broadcaster; Commentator, American Broadcasting Company since 1967; Columnist Christian Science Monitor; *b* Toledo, Ohio, 25 May 1905; *s* of Paul Arthur Harsch and Leila Katherine Close; *m* 1932, Anne Elizabeth Wood; three *s*. *Educ:* Williams Coll., Williamstown, Mass, (MA); Corpus Christi Coll., Cambridge (MA). Joined staff Christian Science Monitor, 1929; Washington corresp., then foreign corresp.; Asst Dir, Intergovt Cttee, London, 1939; Monitor Corresp. in Berlin, 1940, SW Pacific area, 1941 and 1942. Began radio broadcasting, 1943; Senior European Correspondent, NBC, 1957-65; Diplomatic Correspondent, NBC, 1965-67. *Publications:* Pattern of Conquest, 1941; The Curtain Isn't Iron, 1950. *Address:* 2806, 29th Street, NW Washington, DC 20008, USA; Highland Drive, Jamestown, Rhode Island 02835, USA. *Clubs:* Garrick, St James'; Metropolitan (Washington, DC); Century (New York).

**HARSTON, Major Sir Ernest (Sirdefield),** Kt 1958; CBE 1953 (OBE 1947); Hon. Recorder, British Commonwealth Ex-Services League, since 1962 (Hon. Secretary, 1942-62. Executive Chairman 1961-62); Solicitor, New Zealand, since 1918, England since 1935; *b* 21 Aug. 1891; *s* of Harry Loversedge Harston; *m* 1919, Ruth Barbara, *d* of Sir George Shirtcliffe, Wellington, NZ; one *d* (one *s* killed in action). *Educ:* Napier High Sch.; St John's Coll., New Zealand Univ. Served European War, 1914-18 (despatches), with New Zealand Forces; Egypt, Dardanelles, France; Defence Headquarters, Wellington; Major, 1917. Secretariat, League of Nations, 1926-30; Mem. Marylebone Borough Council, 1944-50. War of 1939-45, Home Guard and Admiralty Ferry Crews. Mem., Arts Educational Trust Ltd, 1966-. OStJ 1960. *Recreation:* sailing. *Address:* The Hard, Swanwick Shore, near Southampton. *T:* Locksheath 2107. *Clubs:* Carlton, Royal Thames Yacht (Rear Cdre, 1954, 1955); Royal Cruising; Law Society Yacht (Cdre, 1960-62).

**HART, Edward Watson,** MBE 1945; MD; FRCP; Physician, Children's Department, Middlesex Hospital; Pædiatrician, Hampstead General Hospital; Consulting Pædiatrician, Finchley Memorial Hospital. *Educ:* St John's Coll., Cambridge; Middlesex Hosp. MB, BChir, Cambridge, 1937, MD 1942; MRCS, LRCP, 1936; MRCP, 1938; FRCP, 1949; DCH England, 1946. Formerly: Pædiatric Registrar, Middlesex Hosp.; House Physician, Brompton Hosp. and Hosp. for Sick Children, Gt Ormond Street. Mem. Brit. Pædiatric Assoc. *Address:* 90 Harley Street, W1.

**HART, F(rancis) Dudley,** FRCP; Physician since 1946 and Physician-in-charge Rheumatism Unit, Westminster Hospital, SW1; Physician, St Stephen's Hospital, Fulham; Consulting Physician: Chelsea Hospital for Women; Hospital of St John and St Elizabeth, London; Queen Alexandra's Military Hospital, Millbank; *b* 4 Oct. 1909; *s* of Canon C. Dudley Hart and Kate Evelyn Bowden; *m* 1944, Mary Josephine, *d* of late Luke Tully, Carrigaline, Co. Cork; one *s* two *d*. *Educ:* Grosvenor Sch., Nottingham; Edinburgh Univ. MB, ChB Edinburgh 1933, MD 1939; MRCP 1937, FRCP 1949. House physician and clinical asst, Brompton Hosp., 1937; Med. Registrar, Royal Northern Hosp., 1935-37; Med. Registrar, Westminster Hosp., 1939-42; Med. Specialist and Officer i/c Med. Div., RAMC, 1942-46. Ex-Pres. Heberden Soc.; Member: BMA; RSM, Assoc. of Physicians; Med. Soc. of London; Hunterian Soc. Arris and Gale Lecturer, RCS, 1955. Executive Member: Arthritis and Rheumatism Council; Kennedy Inst. for Research into Rheumatism; Actions and Uses Sub-Cttee, British Pharmaceutical Codex; Hon. Member: Ligue Française contre le Rheumatisme; American Rheumatism Association; Australian Rheumatism Association. *Publications:* (co-author) Drugs: Actions, Uses and Dosage, 1963; contributions to: Pye's Surgical Handicraft, 1939-62; Copeman's Textbook of the Rheumatic Diseases, 1964; Cortisone and ACTH, 1953; Miller's Modern Medical Treatment, 1962; Encyclopedia of General Practice, 1964; Chambers's Encyclopædia, 1964. Articles on General Medicine and Rheumatism. *Recreations:* music, travelling. *Address:* 8 Devonshire Place, W1. *T:* 01-935 4252; (private) 19 Ranulf Road, Hampstead, NW2. *T:* 01-794 2525. *Club:* Athenæum.

**HART, Sir Francis Edmund T.;** *see* Turton-Hart.

**HART, Frank Thomas,** JP; House Governor and Secretary to the Board, Charing Cross Hospital, since 1952; *b* London, 9 Nov. 1911; *s* of late Samuel Black and Ada Frances Laura Hart; *m* 1938, Eveline Brenda Deakin, Leek, Staffs; three *s*. *Educ:* Gravesend and Sheerness Junior Technical Schs. Asst Sec., Buchanan Hospital, St Leonards-on-Sea, 1931-34; Sec., 1934-42; Sec., Central London Eye Hospital, 1942-44; Sec.-Superintendent, Princess Louise Hospital, 1944-48; Superintendent, Royal Infirmary, Sheffield, 1948-52. Chm., League of Friends, Charing Cross Hosp.; Pres., Assoc. of Hosp. Secretaries; Past Pres. of the Hospital Officers' Club; Lectr on Hospital Administration, Royal Coll. of Nursing; Examiner, Medical Records Officers' Association. FHA; DPA (London); Diploma of Economics (London). JP Co. Mddx, 1955-65, Co. Surrey, 1965-. Mem., Worshipful Soc. of Apothecaries. *Publications:* (jointly) A Study of Hospital Administration, 1948; articles in The Hospital, Hospital and Social Service Journal, etc. *Recreations:* all games, especially cricket, Rugby football, tennis, walking, reading. *Address:* Five Ways, Chapel Lane, Westhumble, near Dorking, Surrey. *T:* Dorking 2097.

**HART, George Vaughan;** Principal Assistant Legal Adviser, Home Office, since 1967; *b* 9 Sept. 1911; *e s* of George Vaughan Hart and Maude (*née* Curran); *m* 1949, Norah Marie, *d* of Major D. L. J. Babington; one *s* one *d*. *Educ:* Rossall; Corpus Christi Coll., Oxford. Called to Bar, Middle Temple, 1937. Served Royal Irish Fusiliers, 1940-45. Entered Home Office as Legal Asst, 1946. Sec., Criminal Law Revision Cttee, 1959-. *Recreations:* walking, bird-watching. *Address:* Egham's Farm, Knotty Green, Beaconsfield, Bucks. *T:* Beaconsfield 4120. *Clubs:* Athenæum; University (Dublin).

**HART, Prof. Herbert Lionel Adolphus;** FBA 1962; Research Fellow of University College, Oxford, since 1969 (Fellow 1952-68); Senior Research Fellow, Nuffield Foundation, since 1969; Delegate of the Oxford University Press since 1960; Member, Monopolies Commission, 1967; *b* 18 July 1907; 3rd *s* of Simeon Hart and Rose (*née* Samson); *m* 1941, Jenifer, 3rd *d* of Sir John Fischer Williams, CBE, KC; three *s* one *d*. *Educ:* Cheltenham Coll.; Bradford Grammar Sch.; New Coll., Oxford (Hon. Fellow 1968). Open Classical Scholar, New Coll., Oxford, 1926; First Class Lit. Hum., 1929. Practised at the Chancery Bar, 1932-40. Served War of 1939-45, in War Office, 1940-45. Fellow and Tutor in Philosophy, New Coll., Oxford, 1945; University Lecturer in Philosophy, Oxford, 1948; Prof. of Jurisprudence, Oxford, 1952-68. Visiting Professor: Harvard Univ., 1956-57; Univ. of California, LA, 1961-62. pres., Aristotelian Soc., 1959-60. Hon. Master of the Bench, Middle Temple, 1963. Hon. Dr of Law, Univ. of Stockholm, 1960; Hon. LLD: Univ. of Glasgow, 1966; Univ. of Chicago, 1966; Hon. DLitt, Univ. of Kent, 1969. Fellow, Accademia delle Scienze, Turin, 1964; For. Mem. Amer. Acad. of Arts and Sciences, 1966. *Publications:* (with A. M. Honoré) Causation in the Law, 1959; The Concept of Law, 1961; Law Liberty and Morality, 1963; The Morality of the Criminal Law, 1965; Punishment and Responsibility, 1968; articles in philosophical and legal journals. *Address:* 11 Manor Place, Oxford. *T:* 42402.

**HART, Rt. Hon. Mrs Judith (Constance Mary),** PC 1967; MP (Lab) Lanark Division of Lanarkshire since 1959; *d* of Harry Ridehalgh and late Lily Ridehalgh; *m* 1946, Anthony Bernard Hart, PhD, BSc, FRIC; two *s*. *Educ:* Clitheroe Royal Grammar Sch.; London School of Economics, London University (BA Hons 1945). Contested (Lab) Bournemouth West, 1951, and South Aberdeen, 1955. Jt Parly. Under-Sec. of State for Scotland, 1964-66; Minister of State, Commonwealth Office, 1966-67; Minister of Social Security, 1967-68; Paymaster-General, 1968-69; Minister of Overseas Development, 1969-70. Mem., Nat. Executive of Labour Party, 1969-. Govt Co.-Chm., Women's Nat. Commn, 1969-. *Recreations:* theatre; gardening; spending time with her family. *Address:* 3 Ennerdale Road, Kew Gardens, Richmond-upon-Thames. *T:* 01-948 1989.

**HART, Michael,** MA; FRSA; Headmaster of Mill Hill School since 1967; *b* 1 May 1928; *yr s* of late Dr F. C. Hardt; *m* 1956, Lida Dabney Adams, PhD (Wisconsin Univ.). *Educ:* Collège Français, Berlin; Landerziehungsheim Schondorf; Keble Coll., Oxford (Exhib.). 1st Cl. Hons History, 1951. Administrative Asst, UNRRA, 1945-47; Asst Master and Head of History, Sherborne Sch., 1951-56; Head of History, 1956-61, and Housemaster of School

House, 1961-67, Shrewsbury Sch. *Publications:* contrib. to Reader's Digest World Atlas and Atlas of British Isles. *Recreations:* tennis, climbing. *Address:* Headmaster's House, Mill Hill School, NW7. *T:* 01-959 1006.

**HART, P(hilip) M(ontagu) D'Arcy,** CBE 1956; MA, MD (Cambridge), FRCP; Director, Tuberculosis Research Unit, Medical Research Council, 1948-65; *b* 25 June 1900; *s* of late Henry D'Arcy Hart and late Hon. Ethel Montagu; *m* 1941, Ruth, *d* of late Herbert Meyer and of Grete Meyer-Larsen; one *s*. *Educ:* Clifton Coll.; Gonville and Caius Coll., Cambridge; University Coll. Hospital. Dorothy Temple Cross Fellowship to USA, 1934-35; Asst Physician, UCH, 1934-37; Mem. Scientific Staff, MRC, 1937-65; Mem. Expert Cttee on Tuberculosis, WHO, 1947-64. Goldsmith Entrance Exhibnr, Filliter Exhibnr, Magrath Scholarship, Tuke Medals, UCH Medical Sch., 1922-25; Horton Smith MD Prize, Cambridge, 1930; Royal College of Physicians: Milroy Lecture, 1937; Mitchell Lecture, 1946; Weber-Parkes Prize, 1951; Marc Daniels Lecture, 1967; Stewart Prize, BMA, 1964. *Publications:* scientific papers on respiratory disease, and on epidemiological and microbiological subjects. *Address:* National Institute for Medical Research, Mill Hill, NW7. *T:* 01-959 3666; 37 Belsize Court, NW3.

**HART, Capt. Raymond,** CBE 1963; DSO 1945; DSC 1941, Bar 1943; Royal Navy; Nautical Adviser and Director of British and Commonwealth Shipping Company Ltd; Director: Cayzer Irvine & Co. Ltd; Union-Castle Mail Steamship Co. Ltd; Clan Line Steamers Ltd; *b* 24 June 1913; *o s* of late H. H. Hart, Bassett, Southampton; *m* 1945, Margaret Evanson, *o d* of Capt. S. B. Duffin, Danesfort, Belfast; two *s* one *d*. *Educ:* Oakmount Preparatory Sch.; King Edward VII Sch. Joined Royal Navy, 1937; HMS Hasty, 2nd Destroyer Flotilla, 1939-42; in command: HMS Vidette, 1942-44 (despatches); HMS Havelock, 1944; Sen. Officer, 21st Escort Gp, 1944-45; served in HMS Vanguard during Royal Tour of S Africa, 1947. RN Staff Course, 1949-52; in command, HMS Relentless, 1952-53; Joint Services Staff Course, 1953-54. Staff C-in-C Allied Forces Mediterranean, as Liaison Officer to C-in-C. Allied Forces Southern Europe, HQ Naples, Italy, 1954-56; in command, HMS Undine, and Capt. 6th Frigate Sqdn, 1957-58; Cdre Naval Drafting, 1960-62; retd from RN, 1963. Mem. Coun., Missions to Seamen; Mem. Cttee of Management of: Seamen's Hosp. Soc.; Royal Alfred Merchant Seamen's Soc.; Marine Soc.; School of Navigation, Warsash; Mem., Inst. of Navigation. Officer, Order of Merit of Republic of Italy, 1958. *Recreations:* swimming, shooting, golf, tennis, gardening, painting. *Address:* Three Firs, Bramshott Chase, Hindhead, Surrey. *T:* Hindhead 489. *Club:* United Service.

**HART, Thomas Mure,** CMG 1957; *b* 1 March 1909; *s* of late Maxwell M. Hart and of Elizabeth Watson, Aiknut, West Kilbride; *m* 1936, Eileen Stewart Lawson; one *s* one *d*. *Educ:* Strathallan; Glasgow Univ.; Brasenose Coll., Oxford. Colonial Administrative Service, 1933; seconded Colonial Office, 1933-36; Malayan Civil Service, 1936; Dir of Commerce and Industry, Singapore, 1953; Financial Sec., Singapore, 1954; retired, 1959. Bursar, Loretto Sch., Musselburgh, 1959-69. *Recreation:* golf. *Address:* 44 Frogstone Road West, Edinburgh EH10 7AJ. *T:* 031-445 2152. *Club:* Royal and Ancient (St Andrews).

**HART, Rt. Rev. Mgr W. A.;** *see* Dunkeld, Bishop of (RC).

**HART, Sir William (Ogden),** Kt 1961; CMG 1946; Chairman, Northampton New Town Development Corporation, since 1968; *b* 25 May 1903; *s* of late Sir William Edward Hart, OBE; *m* 1927, Dorothy Eileen, *d* of late Col D. W. Churcher, Royal Irish Fusiliers; three *s* one *d*. *Educ:* Rugby Sch.; New Coll., Oxford. Called to Bar (Lincoln's Inn), 1928; Fellow of Wadham Coll., Oxford, 1926-47; Tutor, 1934-47; Bursar, 1928-40; Hon. Fellow, 1962; Min. of Shipping, 1940-41; joined British Merchant Shipping Mission, Washington, 1941, and Head of the Mission, 1944-46. Gen. Man., Hemel Hempstead Development Corp., 1947-55; Dir-Gen. and Clerk to the Greater London Council, 1964-68 (Clerk of London County Council from 1956). Member: Social Science Research Council, 1965-; Bd, Nat. Bus Company, 1968-. *Publication:* (with Sir William E. Hart) Introduction to the Law of Local Government and Administration, 1934. *Address:* Turweston Lodge, near Brackley, Northants. *Club:* United University.

**HART-DAVIS, Sir Rupert (Charles),** Kt 1967; author, editor and former publisher; Director of Rupert Hart-Davis, Ltd, Publishers, 1946-68; Chairman, Committee of the London Library, 1957-69; *b* 28 Aug. 1907; *o s* of Richard Vaughan Hart-Davis and Sybil Mary Cooper, *er sister* of 1st Viscount Norwich; *m* 1st, 1929, Peggy Ashcroft (now Dame Peggy Ashcroft) (marr. diss.); 2nd, 1933, Catherine Comfort Borden-Turner (marr. diss.), *d* of Mary Borden and George Douglas Turner; two *s* one *d*; 3rd, 1964, Winifred Ruth (*d* 1967), *d* of C. H. Ware, Bromyard, and *widow* of Oliver Simon; 4th, 1968, June (*née* Clifford), *widow* of David Williams. *Educ:* Eton; Balliol Coll., Oxford. Student at Old Vic, 1927-28; Actor at Lyric Theatre, Hammersmith, 1928-29; office boy at William Heinemann Ltd, 1929-31; Manager of Book Soc., 1932; Dir of Jonathan Cape Ltd, 1933-40. Served in Coldstream Guards, 1940-45. Founded Rupert Hart-Davis Ltd, 1946. Hon. DLitt, Reading, 1964. *Publications:* Hugh Walpole: a biography, 1952; *edited:* George Moore: Letters to Lady Cunard, 1957; The Letters of Oscar Wilde, 1962; Max Beerbohm: Letters to Reggie Turner, 1964. *Recreations:* reading, book-collecting, watching cricket. *Address:* The Old Rectory, Marske-in-Swaledale, Richmond, Yorks. *Clubs:* Garrick, MCC.
*See also Hon. D. M. Trustram Eve.*

**HART-SYNNOT, Ronald Victor Okes,** DSO 1900; OBE 1919; late Lieutenant East Surrey Regiment; Emeritus Fellow of St John's College, Oxford, 1949; *b* 24 July 1879; *s* of late Maj.-Gen. FitzRoy Hart-Synnot, CB, CMG; *m* 1912, Violet, *e d* of late Rev. Lord Theobald Butler; one *s*. *Educ:* King William's Coll.; Sandhurst; South-East Agricultural Coll., Wye; MA Oxon, BSc London. Joined Regiment, 1899; served South Africa, 1899-1902, including Colenso, and as ADC to Maj.-Gen. FitzRoy Hart, including Spion Kop, Potgieter's Drift, Pieters Relief of Ladysmith, etc. (despatches twice); in Orange River and Cape Colonies, 1901-02 (Queen's Medal with 5 clasps, King's medal with 2 clasps); resigned commission, 1904; Private Sec. to Sir Horace Plunkett, 1909; Dean, Faculty of Agriculture and Horticulture, University Coll., Reading, 1909-14 and 1919-20; ADC to HE Gen. Sir Reginald Hart in Guernsey, 1915; Headquarters Staff, Southern Command, Salisbury, Feb. 1916; Dep. Asst Dir of Labour, 1918; temp. Capt., 1915; temp. Major, 1918. Bursar, 1920-49, Fellow, 1922-49, of St John's Coll., Oxford. *Publications:* articles on agricultural subjects in Quarterly Review, XIX Century, Banker, and other periodicals. *Address:* 21 Belsyre Court, Oxford.

**HARTE, Wilma Pansy;** Assistant Under-Secretary of State, Department of Education and Science; *b* 19 Nov. 1916; *d* of late William and Mary Harte. *Educ:* St Christopher Sch., Letchworth, Herts; University Coll., London. Min. of Labour, Third Class Officer, later Asst Principal, 1939-47; Asst Sec., Royal Commn on Equal Pay, 1944-46; Min. of Education: Asst Principal, 1947-48; Principal, 1948-60; Asst Sec., 1960-68; Dept of Educn and Science, Asst Under-Sec. of State and Head of Schools Branch, 1968-. *Recreation:* listening. *Address:* 9 Kent Terrace, Park Road, NW1. *T:* 01-723 4961. *Club:* Ladies' Oxford and Cambridge.

**HARTFALL, Prof. Stanley Jack,** TD 1942; BSc, MD; FRCP; Professor of Clinical Medicine, University of Leeds, 1948-64, now Emeritus; *b* 27 Feb. 1899; *m* 1931, Muriel Ann Hunter; two *s* (one *d* decd). *Educ:* University of Leeds; Guy's Hosp. House Surg. and House Physician. Resident Medical Officer, Leeds Gen. Infirmary, 1926-30; Medical Asst to Sir A. Hurst, Guy's Hosp., 1930-32; Leverhulme Research Scholar, Royal College of Physicians, London, 1932-33; Hon. Physician and Consulting Physician, Leeds Gen. Infirmary and Leeds Regional Hosp. Board, Harrogate Royal Bath Hosp., Dewsbury and District Gen. Hosp., Prof. of Therapeutics, University of Leeds, 1937. Lieut-Col RAMC (TA). *Publications:* numerous papers on pathological and clinical subjects, gastro-intestinal diseases, anaemias and blood diseases, arthritis and rheumatism. *Recreations:* cricket and tennis. *Address:* West Garth, Creskeld Lane, Bramhope, Leeds. *T:* Leeds 67-3959.

**HARTHAN, John Plant,** MA, FLA; Keeper of the Library, Victoria and Albert Museum, since 1962; *b* 15 April 1916; *y s* of late Dr George Ezra Harthan, Evesham, Worcs, and Winifred May Slater. *Educ:* Bryanston; Jesus Coll., Cambridge; University Coll., London. Asst-Librarian, Southampton Univ., 1940-43; Royal Society of Medicine Library, 1943-44; Asst Under-Librarian, Cambridge Univ. Library, 1944-48; Asst-Keeper of the Library, Victoria and Albert Museum, 1948. *Publications:* Bookbindings in the Victoria and Albert Museum, 1950 and 1961; co-editor, F.D. Klingender, Animals in Art and Thought, 1970. *Recreations:* music, architecture. *Address:* 20 Pelham Street, SW7. *Club:* Travellers'.

**HARTINGTON, Marquess of; Peregrine Andrew Morny Cavendish;** *b* 27 April 1944; *s* of 11th Duke of Devonshire, *qv*; *m* 1967, Amanda Carmen, *d* of late Comdr E. G. Heywood-Lonsdale, RN, and of Mrs Heywood-Lonsdale; one *s*. *Educ:* Eton; Exter Coll., Oxford. *Heir:* *s* Earl of Burlington, *qv*. *Address:* 15 Christ Church Road, SW14. *T:* 01-878 2272. *Clubs:* Turf; Jockey Club Rooms (Newmarket).

**HARTLAND, Alderman William John,** CBE 1965; JP; Executive Officer and Council Member, Tenovus Cancer Information Centre; *b* 19 Feb. 1909; *s* of William Edward Hartland and Minnie Evelyn (*nēe* Herbert); *m* 1934, Phyllis, *y d* of Annie and Late John Lewis Morris, Cardiff; one *s*. *Educ:* Llandovery Coll. Partner in Meat Manufacturing Firm, 1930-59. Member: Cardiff CC, 1946- (Whip to Conservative Gp, 1948-57; Leader, Conservative Gp, 1957-70); Bd of Govs, Cardiff Royal Infirmary, 1939-48; Bd of Govs, Nat. Library of Wales, 1949-56; Govs, Nat. Museum of Wales, 1949-56; Cardiff North HMC, 1948-; Health Educn Council, 1968-; Chairman: Cardiff SE Conservative Assoc.; Health Cttee, AMC; Vice-Pres., Internat. Union of Local Authorities; Lord Mayor of Cardiff, 1964-65; Deputy Lord Mayor, 1967-68. JP Cardiff, 1950. OStJ 1966. MRSH 1965. *Recreations:* football, cricket, reading. *Address:* 27 Princes' Avenue, Roath Court, Cardiff. *T:* Cardiff 42851 (business), 25333 (private). *Clubs:* (Pres.) Roath Conservative, (Hon. Life Mem.) Splott Conservative (Cardiff).

**HARTLEY, Arthur Coulton,** CIE 1946; OBE 1943; ICS (retired); *b* 24 March 1906; *s* of late John Aspinall Hartley and Jennie Hartley, Stream Mill, Chiddingly, Sussex; *m* 1943, Mrs Cecilie Leslie; one *s*. *Educ:* Cowley Grammar Sch.; Manchester Univ.; Balliol Coll., Oxford. Entered Indian Civil Service, 1929; Asst Magistrate, Comilla, Bengal, 1929-30; Subdivisional Magistrate, Sirajganj, Bengal, 1930-32; Asst Settlement Officer, Rangpur, Bengal, 1932-34; Settlement Officer, Rangpur, Bengal, 1934-37; Asst Sec. to Governor of Bengal, 1938-40; District Magistrate, Howrah, Bengal, 1940-43; Controller of Rationing, Calcutta, Bengal, 1943-45; Dir-Gen. of Food, Bengal, India, 1945-47. *Publication:* Report on Survey and Settlement Operations of Rangpur, 1938. *Recreations:* hill walking, painting.

**HARTLEY, Brian Joseph,** CMG 1950; OBE 1945 (MBE 1934); Project Manager, UNSF Survey of Northern Rangelands Project, Somalia, since 1970; *b* 1907; *s* of late John Joseph Hartley, Tring, Herts; *m* 1951, Doreen Mary, *d* of Col R. G. Sanders; three *s* one *d*. *Educ:* Loughborough; Midland Agricultural Coll.; Wadham Coll., Oxford; Imperial Coll. of Tropical Agriculture, Trinidad. Entered Colonial Service; Agricultural Officer, Tanganyika, 1929; Aden Protectorate: Agricultural Officer, 1938; Agricultural Adviser, 1944; Dir of Agriculture, 1946-54; retd 1954; Chief, FAO(UN), mission in Iraq, 1955; Mem., Tanganyika Agricultural Corporation, 1956-62; Trustee, Tanganyika Nat. Parks, 1957-64; Mem., Ngorongoro Conservation Authority Advisory Board, 1963-64. UN (Special Fund) Consultant Team Leader: Kafue Basin Survey, N Rhodesia, 1960; Livestock Develt Survey, Somalia, 1966; Chief Livestock Adviser, FAO, Somalia, 1967-70. *Address:* c/o UNDP, PO Box 24, Mogadishu, Somalia; Hill Farm, Winkleigh, Devon.

**HARTLEY, Air Marshal Sir Christopher (Harold),** KCB 1963 (CB 1961); CBE 1957 (OBE 1949); DFC 1945; AFC 1944; BA Oxon; Deputy Chairman, British Hovercraft Corporation, since 1970; *b* 31 Jan. 1913; *s* of Brig.-Gen. Sir Harold Hartley, *qv*; *m* 1st, 1937, Anne Sitwell (marr. diss., 1943); 2nd, 1944, Margaret, *d* of Harold Watson; two *s*. *Educ:* Eton; Balliol Coll., Oxford (Williams Exhibnr); King's Coll., Cambridge. Zoologist on Oxford Univ. expeditions: to Sarawak, 1932; Spitsbergen, 1933; Greenland, 1937. Asst Master at Eton Coll., 1937-39. Joined RAFVR, 1938. Served War of 1939-45: 604 Sqdn, 256 Sqdn, Fighter Interception Unit, Central Fighter Establishment. Permanent Commission, 1945; AOC 12 Group, Fighter Command, 1959; ACAS (Operational Requirements), Air Min., 1961; DCAS, 1963-66; Controller of Aircraft, Min. of Aviation and Min. of Technology, 1966-70, retired. *Recreations:* shooting, fishing, sailing. *Address:* Froghole Farm House, Petworth, Sussex. *Club:* Travellers'.

**HARTLEY, Frank,** CBE 1970; PhD London, FPS, FRIC; Dean of the School of Pharmacy, University of London, since 1962; *b* 5 Jan. 1911; *s* of late Robinson King Hartley and Mary Hartley (*née* Holt); *m* 1937, Lydia May England; two *s. Educ:* Municipal Secondary (later Grammar) Sch., Nelson, Lancs; Sch. of Pharmacy, University Coll., and Birkbeck Coll., University of London. Jacob Bell Schol., 1930, Silver Medallist in Pharmaceutics, Pharmaceut. Chem. and Pharmacognosy, 1932. Pharmaceutical Chemist, 1932, Demonstrator and Lectr, 1932-40, at Sch. of Pharmacy; 1st cl. hons BSc (Chem.), University of London, 1936, and PhD, 1941; Chief Chemist, Organon Laboratories Ltd, 1940-43; Sec., Therapeutic Research Corp., 1943-46; Sec., Gen. Penicillin Cttee (Min. of Supply), 1943-46; Dir of Research and Sci. Services, The British Drug Houses, Ltd, 1946-62; Chm. Brit. Pharmaceut. Conf, 1957, and of Sci. Adv. Cttee of Pharmaceut. Soc. of Great Britain, 1964-66; Mem. Council, 1955-58, 1961-64, Vice-Pres., 1958-60, 1964-65, 1967-69, Pres., 1965-67, of Royal Institute of Chemistry; Hon. Treasurer, 1956-61, Chm. 1964-68 of Chem. Council; Mem. 1953-, Vice-Chm. 1963-68, Chm. 1970, of British Pharmacopoeia Commn, and a UK deleg., 1964-, to European Pharmacopoeia Commn; Member: Poisons Bd (Home Office), 1958-66; Cttee on Safety of Drugs (Min. of Health), 1963-70; Medicines Commn, 1970-; Chairman: Bd of Studies in Pharmacy, Univ. of London, 1964-68; Pharmacy Bd, Council for Nat. Academic Awards, 1965-; Collegiate Council, 1969-. Co-opted Mem. Senate, 1968, Senate Mem. of Court, 1970, University of London; Member Council: St Thomas's Hosp. Medical Sch., University of London, 1968-; Royal Free Hosp. Med. Sch., 1970-; Mem. Bd of Governors, Kingston Polytechnic, 1970-. Sir William Pope Memorial Lectr, RSA, 1962. Liveryman, Worshipful Soc. of Apothecaries of London. *Publications:* papers on chem. and pharmaceut. research in Quarterly Jl of Pharmacy, Jl of Pharmacy and Pharmacology and Jl of Chem. Soc. Reviews and articles in sci. and tech. jls. *Recreations:* reading, motoring. *Address:* 146 Dorset Road, SW19. *T:* 01-542 7198. *Club:* Athenæum.

**HARTLEY, Gilbert Hillard; His Honour Judge Hartley;** Judge of County Courts, since 1967; Deputy Chairman, West Riding of Yorkshire Sessions, since 1965; *b* 11 Aug. 1917; *s* of late Percy Neave Hartley and late Nellie Bond (*née* Hillard); *m* 1948, Jeanne, *d* of late C. W. Gall, Leeds; one *s* two *d*. *Educ:* Ashville, Harrogate; Exeter Coll. Oxford. Called to Bar, 1939. Served with Army, 1940-46. Recorder of Rotherham, 1965-67. *Address:* South Lawn, East Keswick, Leeds, Yorks.

**HARTLEY, Brig.-Gen. Sir Harold,** GCVO 1957 (KCVO 1944); CH 1967; Kt 1928; CBE 1919; FRS 1926; MC; MA, Oxford; Hon. DCL Oxford; Hon. LLD Edinburgh; Hon. DSc Sheffield, Birmingham, Princeton, Southampton; Hon. Associate, Manchester College of Technology; Hon. Fellow Balliol College, Oxford, 1941; Director, Readex Microprint Corporation (UK), Ltd; *b* London, 3 Sept. 1878; *o s* of late Harold T. Hartley; *M e d* of late A. L. Smith, Master of Balliol; one *s* one *d*. *Educ:* Dulwich Coll.; Balliol Coll., Oxford (1st Class Nat. Science). Natural Science Tutor and Bedford Lectr in Physical Chemistry, Balliol Coll., Oxford, 1901-31; Jowett Fellow, 1928-31; Research Fellow, 1931-41. Capt. 7th Leics Regt, 1914-15; Chemical Adviser to the 3rd Army, 1915-17; Asst Dir Gas Services, GHQ, France, 1917-18; Controller Chemical Warfare Dept, Ministry of Munitions, 1918-19 (MC, despatches thrice). A Dir, Gas Light and Coke Co., 1922-45 (a Dep. Governor, 1942-45). Chm. of Fuel Research Board, 1932-47; Dir of Times Publishing Co., 1936-60; Hon. Adviser on development of home-produced fuels, Ministry of Fuel and Power, 1939-47; Vice-Pres, and Dir of Research, LMS Railway, 1930-45; Chm., Railway Air Services, 1934-45; Prime Warden of Goldsmiths' Company, 1941-42; Chairman: British European Airways Corporation, 1946-47; British Overseas Airways Corporation, 1947-49; Electricity Supply Research Council of British Electricity Authority, 1949-52; Pres. Institute of Chemical Engineers, 1951-52, and 1954-55. Pres. British Assoc. for the Advancement of Science for 1950; Chairman: British National Cttee and International Executive Council, World Power Conference, 1935-50; Fourth World Power Conference, 1950; Pres. World Power Conference, 1950-56; Chairman: Energy Commission, OEEC, 1955-56; Council, Duke of Edinburgh's Study Conference on Human Problems of Industrial Communities, 1954-56; Pres., Soc. of Instrument Technology, 1957-61; Scientific Adviser to Constructors John Brown Ltd, 1954-61. Lubbock, Citrine and Romanes Lectureships, 1964. Rly Engrg Medal Inst. of Transport, 1932; Wilhelm Exner Medal, 1937; Osborne-Reynolds Medal of Instn of Chem. Engrs, 1954; Birmingham Medal of Instn of Gas Engrs, 1958; Kelvin Gold Medal, 1965; Herbert Hoover Medal, 1968. *Publications:* Balliol Men, 1963; ed, The Royal Society: Its Origins and Founders, 1960; Man and Nature (Romanes Lecture), 1964; Humphry Davy, 1966. *Address:* c/o 20 Fitzjames Avenue, W14. *Clubs:* Athenæum, Travellers'.

*See also Air Marshal Sir Christopher Hartley.*

**HARTLEY, Leslie Poles,** CBE 1956; author and critic; *b* 30 Dec. 1895; *s* of H. B. Hartley, JP, Fletton Tower, Peterborough; unmarried. *Educ:* Harrow; Balliol Coll., Oxford. Has written literary criticism for the weekly reviews (Spectator, Week-end Review, Sketch, Time and Tide, etc.) since 1923. Clark Lecturer, Trinity Coll., Cambridge, 1964. *Publications:* Night Fears (short stories), 1924; Simonetta Perkins (novel), 1925; The Killing Bottle (short stories), 1932; The Shrimp and the Anemone (novel), 1944; The Sixth Heaven (novel), 1946; Eustace and Hilda (novel, James Tait Black Memorial Prize), 1947; The Boat (novel), 1950; The Travelling Grave and other Stories, 1951; My Fellow Devils (novel), 1951; The Go-Between, 1953 (W. H. Heinemann Foundation award); The White Wand (short stories), 1954; A Perfect Woman (novel), 1955; The Hireling (novel), 1957; Facial Justice (novel), 1960; Two for the River (short stories), 1961; The Brickfield (novel), 1964; The Betrayal, 1966; The Novelists' Responsibility (lectures and essays), 1967; Poor Clare, 1968; The Collected Stories of L. P. Hartley, 1968; The Love-Adept (novel), 1969; My Sisters' Keeper, 1970. *Recreations:* rowing, swimming, walking. *Address:* Avondale, Bathford, Somerset. *T:* Bath 88117; Flat 10, 53 Rutland Gate, SW7. *Clubs:* Athenæum, Beefsteak; Bath and County (Bath).

**HARTLEY, Percival Hubert Graham Horton-Smith,** OBE 1945; on the staff of O. Gross & Sons Ltd, Managers for the Power Steamship Co., since 1957; *b* 27 Sept. 1896; *s* of late Sir Percival Horton-Smith Hartley, CVO, MD; *m* 1923, Mary Grizel, *d* of late Sir George Seaton Buchanan, CB, MD. *Educ:* Eton; St John's Coll., Cambridge (Entrance Scholar). Asst Master at Eton Coll., 1922-56 (House Master, 1933-51). Served European War 1915-18 Coldstream Guards (Special Reserve) and again 1940-45 in Staff appointments, and in Allied Military Government, Italy (Freedom of City of Bologna, 1945); released with rank of Col, 1946. Master of the Worshipful Company of Ironmongers, 1953-54. *Recreations:* rowing (Eton VIII 1915, Cambridge crew 1920-21-22), climbing, sailing. *Address:* Dorney House, Dorney, near Windsor, Berks. *T:* Burnham 4983. *Clubs:* Athenæum, Leander.

**HARTLINE, Prof. Haldan Keffer;** Professor of Biophysics, Rockefeller University, New York, since 1953; *b* Bloomsburg, Pa, 22 Dec. 1903; *s* of Daniel S. Hartline and Harriet F. Keffer; *m* 1936, Elizabeth Kraus; three *s. Educ:* Lafayette Coll. (BS); Johns Hopkins Univ. (MD), Nat. Res. Fellow, Medicine, Johns Hopkins Univ., 1927-29; Reeves Johnson Trav. Res. Schol., Universities of Leipzig and Munich, 1929-31; University of Pa; Fellow, Med. Physics, 1931-36; Asst Prof. Biophysics, Eldridge Reeves Johnson Foundn for Med. Physics, 1936-40; Assoc. Prof. Physiology, Cornell Univ. Med. Coll., NY, 1940-41; Asst Prof. Biophysics, Johnson Foundn, University of Pa, 1941-42; Assoc. Prof. Biophysics, University of Pa, 1943-48; Prof. Biophysics and Chm. of Dept, Johns Hopkins Univ., 1949-53. Mem., Nat. Acad. of Sciences; For. Mem., Royal Soc. (London). Hon. ScD, Lafayette Coll., 1959; Hon. Dr of Laws, Johns Hopkins Univ., 1969. William H. Howell Award (Physiol.), 1927; Howard Crosby Warren Medal, 1948; A. A. Michelson Award, 1964; Nobel Prize in Physiology or Medicine (jointly), 1967; Lighthouse Award, NY Assoc. for the Blind, 1969. *Publications:* articles in: Amer. Jl Physiol; Jl Gen. Physiol.; Jl Cell. Comp. Physiol.; Cold Spring Harbor Symposia on Quant. Biol.; Jl Opt. Soc. Amer.; Harvey Lectures; Science; Rev. Mod. Physics, etc. *Recreations:* ski-ing, sailing, mountain climbing. *Address:* 447 East 65 Street, New York, NY 10021, USA; Patterson Road, Hydes, Maryland 21082. *T:* 301 592 8162.

**HARTNELL, Air Vice-Marshal Geoffrey Clark,** CBE 1955; RAAF, retired; *b* Melbourne, 15 April 1916; *s* of late F. B. Hartnell, Melbourne; *m* 1941, Joyce M., *d* of late J. T. Webster; two *s* one *d. Educ:* Wesley Coll. Cadet RAAF Pt Cook, 1936; service Aust., SW Pacific, UK, 1939-45; Air Staff RAAF HQ, 1946-50; CO RAAF Amberley, Qld, 1951-53; Dir of Air Staff Plans and Policy, RAAF HQ Melbourne, 1953-56; Senior Air Staff Officer, HQ Home Command, 1956-58; idc 1959; Officer Commanding RAAF Butterworth, 1960-62; Dir Gen. of Plans and Policy, Dept of Air, Canberra, 1960-63; Head, Australian Joint Services Staff and RAAF Representative, 1964-66; Extra Gentleman Usher to the Royal Household, 1964-66; Dir, Joint Service Plans, Dept of Defence, Canberra, 1966-68. Trustee, Australian War Memorial, Canberra. *Recreation:* woodwork. *Address:* 48 Endeavour Street, Red Hill, ACT 2603, Australia. *Clubs:* Legacy, Commonwealth (Canberra).

**HARTNELL, Norman,** MVO 1953; Dressmaker by appointment to HM the Queen, and to HM Queen Elizabeth the Queen Mother; Member Incorporated Society of London Fashion Designers (Chairman 1947-56); Ex-Vice-President Clothing Institute; *b* 12 June 1901. *Educ:* Magdalene Coll., Cambridge. Awarded Officier d'Académie by French Government, 1939; Royal Warrant, 1940; Neiman-Marcus Award, USA, for world influence on fashion, 1947. *Publication:* Silver and Gold (autobiography), 1955. *Recreations:* painting, riding, swimming. *Address:* 26 Bruton Street, Mayfair, W1.

**HARTNETT, Sir Laurence (John),** Kt 1967; CBE 1945; FRSA; MIE (Australia); industrial consultant, chairman and director of a number of companies; *b* Woking, Surrey, 26 May 1898; *s* of John Joseph Hartnett, MD and Katherine Jane Hartnett; *m* 1925, Gladys Winifred, *d* of Charles Walter Tyler, Bexleyheath, Kent; three *d. Educ:* Kingston Grammar Sch.; Epsom Coll., England. Cadet, Vickers Ltd, England. Served European War, 1914-18, as Flt-Lieut and Flt Sub-Lieut, RNAS; War of 1939-45: Dir of Ordnance Production, Min. of Munitions, and Chm. Army Inventions Bd, Australia. Started own engrg and motor business; Man. Motor Dept, Guthrie & Co. Ltd, Singapore; Zone Man., General Motors, USA; Vice-Pres., General Motors Export Co., NY; Sales Man., General Motors, Nordeska, Sweden; Dir, Vauxhall Motors Ltd, England; Man. Dir, General Motors Holdens, Australia; Regional Dir of the overseas operations. Mem. Exec. and Past Pres., Aust. Industries Develt Assoc.; Trustee, Inst. of Applied Sciences, Vic.; Mem. Gov. Bd, Corps of Commissionaires. FAIM. *Publication:* Big Wheels and Little Wheels, 1964. *Recreations:* yachting, tennis. *Address:* Rubra, Mt Eliza, Victoria 3930, Australia. *T:* Melbourne 78-71271; Flat 4, 24 Hill Street, Toorak, Victoria 3142, Australia. *T:* Melbourne 245381. *Clubs:* Royal Aero; Athenæum (Melbourne); Canadian Bay (Mt Eliza).

**HARTOG, Harold Samuel Arnold;** Knight, Order of the Netherlands Lion; KBE (Hon.) 1970; Chairman, Unilever, NV, 1966-May 1971; *b* Nijmegen, Holland, 21 Dec. 1910; *m* 1963, Ingeborg Luise Krahn. *Educ:* Wiedemann Coll., Geneva. Joined Unilever, 1931. After service with Dutch forces during War of 1939-45 he joined management of Unilever interests in France, and subseq. took charge of Unilever cos in the Netherlands; elected to Bds of Unilever, 1948; Mem. Rotterdam Group Management and responsible for Unilever activities in Germany, Austria and Belgium, 1952-60; subseq. Mem. Cttee for Unilever's overseas interests, in London; became, there, one of the two world co-ordinators of Unilever's foods interests, 1962. *Recreations:* history of art; collecting Chinese pottery and porcelain. *Address:* 21 St James's Place, SW1. *T:* 01-493 5558. *Club:* Dutch.

**HARTOPP, Sir John Edmund Cradock-,** 9th Bt, *cr* 1796; TD; Director, Firth Brown Tools Ltd; *b* 8 April 1912; *s* of late Francis Gerald Cradock-Hartopp, Barbrook, Chatsworth, Bakewell, Derbyshire (kinsman of 8th Bt) and Elizabeth Ada Mary (*née* Stuart); *S* kinsman, Sir George Francis Fleetwood Cradock-Hartopp, 1949; *m* 1953, Prudence, 2nd *d* of Sir Frederick Leith-Ross, *qv*; three *d. Educ:* Summer Fields, Oxford; Uppingham Sch. Travelled in United States of America before joining at age of 18, Staff of Research Laboratories, Messrs Thos Firth & John Brown Ltd, Steel Makers, Sheffield, 1930; has since served in the Works and on the Commercial Staff; travelled in India and the Far East, 1948-49. War of 1939-45 (despatches twice); joined TA and served with Royal Engineers in UK; Norway, 1940; North Africa (1st Army), 1943; Italy, 1943-45; released, 1945, with rank of Major. Mem. Council, Machine Tool Research Assoc., 1965. *Recreations:* golf (semi-finalist English Golf Champ., 1935; first reserve, Eng. *v* France, 1935); cricket, tennis, motoring. *Heir: cousin* Lt-Comdr Kenneth Alston Cradock-Hartopp, MBE, DSC, RN [*b* 26 Feb. 1918; *m* 1942, Gwendolyn Amy Lilian Upton; one *d*]. *Address:* c/o John Brown and Co. Ltd, 8 The Sanctuary, Westminster, SW1; The Cottage,

27 Wool Road, Wimbledon Common, SW20. *Clubs:* East India and Sports, MCC; Sheffield (Sheffield); Royal and Ancient (St Andrews); Royal Colombo Yacht.

**HARTRIDGE, Hamilton,** FRS 1926; MA, MD, ScD (Cambridge); MRCP; Emeritus Professor of Physiology, University of London, since 1949; *b* 7 May 1886; *e s* of Henry Hill Hartridge, Oakwood Hill, Surrey; *m* 1916, Kathleen, *d* of Hugo Wilson, Kegworth, Leicestershire; one *s* three *d. Educ:* St Vincent's, Eastbourne; Harrow Sch.; King's Coll., Cambridge (Exhibitioner 1907, Fellow 1912-26). Horton-Smith Prize, 1918; Experimental Officer, Kingsnorth Airship Station (RAF), 1915-19; Lecturer in Special Senses and Senior Demonstrator in Physiology at Cambridge Univ., 1919-27; Prof. of Physiology at St Bartholomew's Hosp. Med. Coll., 1927-47; Dir, Vision Research Unit, MRC, 1947-51. Many inventions, from intrinsic electric light and scale for mirror galvanometer, 1904, to a projection microscope for large audiences, 1932. Hon. Fellow of Royal Photographic Society, 1957; FInstP 1962; Hon. Mem., Physiol Soc., 1968. *Publications:* Colours and how we see them, 1949; Recent advances in the Physiology of Vision, 1950; Editor (with Prof. J. d'Silva) of Bainbridge and Menzies Essentials of Physiology, 1929; papers and research on the optics of the eye, on the visual perception of fine detail, on the optics of the microscope, on the resonance theory of hearing, on carbon monoxide gas in tobacco smoke and in the blood of a cigarette smoker, and on bats' radar. *Recreations:* motoring, metal working, and sketching. *Address:* Benridge, Frithwood Avenue, Northwood, Middx. *T:* Northwood 21844.

**HARTUNG, Ernst Johannes,** DSc; Professor of Chemistry, University of Melbourne, 1928-53; Emeritus Professor since 1953; *b* Victoria, 23 April 1893; 2nd *s* of Carl August Ernst Hartung, Leipzig, and Ida Emilie, *d* of F. A. Hagenauer, Vic.; *m* 1922, Gladys, *d* of F. W. Gray, Glos; two *d. Educ:* Wesley Coll., Melbourne; University of Melbourne. BSc, 1913; DSc, 1919; Tutor in Chemistry, Trinity Coll., Melbourne, 1914; Lecturer and Demonstrator in Chemistry, University of Melbourne, 1919; Associate Prof., 1924; Winner of David Syme Scientific Research Prize, Australia, 1926; President of the Australian Chemical Institute, 1928. *Publications:* The Screen Projection of Chemical Experiments, 1953; Astronomical Objects for Southern Telescopes, 1968. Various scientific papers, including a series on Studies with the Micro-balance, and Studies in Membrane Permeability in Journal of Chemical Society, London, Transactions of Faraday Society, London. *Recreation:* astronomy. *Address:* Lavender Farm, Woodend, Victoria 3442, Australia.

**HARTWELL,** Baron, *cr* 1968 (Life Peer), of Peterborough Court in the City of London; **(William) Michael Berry,** MBE 1944; TD; Chairman and Editor-in-Chief of The Daily Telegraph and Sunday Telegraph; *b* 18 May 1911; 2nd *s* of 1st Viscount Camrose and Mary Agnes, *e d* of late Thomas Corns, London; *m* 1936, Lady Pamela Margaret Elizabeth Smith (*see* Lady Hartwell), *yr d* of 1st Earl of Birkenhead, PC, GCSI, KC; two *s* two *d. Educ:* Eton; Christ Church, Oxford (MA). 2nd Lieut 11th (City of London Yeo.) Light AA Bde, RA (TA), 1938; served War of 1939-45; Capt. and Major, 1940; Lieut-Col 1944 (despatches twice, MBE). Chm. Amalgamated Press Ltd, 1954-59. *Publication:* Party Choice, 1948. *Address:* 18 Cowley Street, Westminster, SW1. *T:* 01-930 3673; Oving House, Whitchurch, near Aylesbury, Bucks. *T:* Whitchurch 307. *Clubs:* White's, Beefsteak; Royal Yacht Squadron.

*See also Viscount Camrose.*

**HARTWELL, Lady; Pamela Margaret Elizabeth Berry;** President, Incorporated Society of London Fashion Designers, since 1954; 2nd *d* of 1st Earl of Birkenhead, PC, GCSI, KC, and of Margaret, Countess of Birkenhead; *m* 1936, Hon. (William) Michael Berry (now Baron Hartwell, *qv*); two *s* two *d. Address:* Oving House, Aylesbury, Bucks; 18 Cowley Street, Westminster, SW1.

**HARTWELL, Benjamin James,** OBE 1959; Clerk to Southport Borough Justices since 1943; *b* Southport, 24 June 1908; *s* of late Joseph Hartwell, Bucks, and late Margaret Ann Hartwell; *m* 1937, Mary (*née* Binns), Southport: one *s* one *d. Educ:* King George V Sch., Southport; London Univ. (LLM). Admitted a Solicitor of the Supreme Court, 1936; Hon. Sec. Justices' Clerks' Soc., 1947-59; Pres. Lancs and Cheshire Dist of Boys' Brigade, 1950-63; Chm. Council, Congregational Union of England and Wales, 1952-58; Chm. Congregational Union of England and Wales 1959-60. Mem. Home Secretary's Advisory Council on the Treatment of Offenders, 1955-63. *Address:* 3 Dunbar Road, Southport, Lancs. *T:* Southport 67178.

**HARTWELL, Sir Brodrick William Charles Elwin,** 5th Bt, *cr* 1805; *b* 7 Aug. 1909; *s* of Sir Brodrick Cecil Denham Arkwright Hartwell, 4th Bt, and Joan Amy (*d* 1962), *o d* of Robert Milne Jeffrey, Esquimault, Vancouver; *S* father, 1948; *m* 1st, 1937, Marie Josephine, *d* of late S. P. Mullins (marriage dissolved 1950); one *s*; 2nd, 1951, Mary Maude, MBE, *d* of J. W. Church, Bedford; one *d* decd. *Educ:* Bedford Sch. Sometime Pilot Officer RAF. Served War of 1939-45; Capt. Leics Regt, 1943. *Heir: s* Francis Antony Charles Peter Hartwell, *b* 1 June 1940. *Address:* Little Dale, 50 High Street, Lavendon, Olney, Bucks.

**HARTWELL, Sir Charles (Herbert),** Kt 1960; CMG 1954; Chairman, Public Services Commission, Hong Kong, since 1967; *b* 1904. *Educ:* St John's Coll., Cambridge. Ceylon CS, 1927; Administrative Sec., Palestine, 1940; reverted to Ceylon Civil Service, 1942, and became Sec. to the Governor of Ceylon. Dir of Establishments, Kenya, 1947; Deputy Chief Sec. and Mem. for Education and Labour of Legislative Council of Kenya, 1952; Minister for Education, Labour and Lands, Kenya, 1955; Chief Sec., Uganda, 1955-60; retired from Colonial Service, July 1960; assumed duties as Chm. of Public Service Commission and Police Service Commission in Northern Rhodesia, Oct. 1960; retired, 1963; Ministry of Overseas Development, 1963-66; Adviser to the Government of Mauritius, 1966-67. *Address:* Public Services Commission, Room 573a, Central Government Offices, Lower Albert Road, Hong Kong.

**HARTY, Maj.-Gen. Arthur Henry,** CIE 1942; KHP 1945; MB, BS, MRCS, LRCP, 1914; IMS, retired; *b* 13 Aug. 1890; *s* of T. Harty and M. E. Fowles; *m* 1919, Gladys Maud Davies; one *s* one *d* (and one *s* decd). *Educ:* Jamaica Coll., Jamaica; Queen's Univ., Kingston, Canada (MB, BS 1912). Joined Royal Navy as Surgeon, Aug. 1914; served in Grand Fleet and Mediterranean Fleet in European War; joined Indian Medical Service, 1919; Burma, 1920-23; Bombay Presidency and Sind 1923-42; Inspector-Gen., Civil Hospitals, Central Provinces, 1942-45; Surgeon-Gen., Bombay, 1945. *Address:* c/o National and Grindlay's

Bank Ltd, 13 St James's Square, SW1; 80 East Street, Kingston, Jamaica, West Indies.

**HARTY, Most Rev. Michael;** *see* Killaloe, Bishop of, (RC).

**HARUNA, Alhaji;** *see* Gwandu, Emir of.

**HARVATT, Thomas,** CMG 1960; Secretary and Deputy Director, Council of Legal Education, 1934-68; *b* 5 Nov. 1901; *s* of Thomas Joseph Harvatt, Sheffield; *m* 1931, Nellie Adelaide, *d* of James Stephen Blythe, Sydenham; two *d. Educ:* King Edward VII Sch., Sheffield; University Coll., London; Inner Temple. Personal Asst to Dir of Educn, Sheffield, 1923-27; first Sec. for Educn, NALGO, 1927-34; Sec. to Council of Legal Education, 1934-68, and Dep. Dir of Inns of Court Sch. of Law, 1958-68; Mem. Cttee on Legal Education for Students from Africa, 1960. *Address:* 72 Old Lodge Lane, Purley, Surrey.

**HARVEY,** family name of **Baron Harvey of Tasburgh.**

**HARVEY OF TASBURGH,** 2nd Baron, *cr* 1954, of Tasburgh, Norfolk; **Peter Charles Oliver Harvey;** Bt 1868; Chartered Accountant; Investment Manager, Bank of London & South America Limited, since 1968; *b* 28 Jan. 1921; *er s* of 1st Baron Harvey of Tasburgh, GCMG, GCVO, CB, and Maud Annora (*d* 1970), *d* of late Arthur Watkin Williams-Wynn; *S* father, 1968; *m* 1957, Penelope Anne, *d* of Lt-Col Sir William Makins, 3rd Bt; two *d. Educ:* Eton; Trinity College, Cambridge. Served 1941-46 with Royal Artillery, Tunisia, Italy. Bank of England, 1948-56; Binder Hamlyn & Co., 1956-61; Bank of London & South America, 1961-. *Recreations:* sailing, music. *Heir: b* Hon. John Wynn Harvey [*b* 4 Nov. 1923; *m* 1950, Elena Maria-Teresa, *d* of late Marchese Giambattista Curtopassi, Rome; two *s* one *d*]. *Address:* 2 Halsey Street, SW3; Mill House, Mylor Bridge, near Falmouth, Cornwall. *Clubs:* Brooks's, Royal Cornwall Yacht, Royal Fowey Yacht.

**HARVEY, Alexander,** PhD, BSc, FInstP; Principal, University of Wales Institute of Science and Technology, 1946-68 (formerly Cardiff Technical College, later Welsh College of Advanced Technology); Pro-Vice-Chancellor, University of Wales, 1967-68; *b* 21 Sept. 1904; *s* of Andrew Harvey, Bangor, Co. Down; *m* 1933, Mona Anderson, Newcastle upon Tyne; one *s* two *d. Educ:* Gateshead Grammar Sch.; Armstrong (King's) Coll., Univ. of Durham. Commonwealth Fund Fellowship, Univ. of California, 1929-31; Scientific Asst, Adam Hilger Ltd, London, 1931-33; Asst Lecturer, Physics Dept, University of Manchester, 1933-34; Head of Physics Dept, Wigan and District Mining and Tech. Coll., 1934-42; Principal, Scunthorpe Tech. Sch., 1942-46. President: Assoc. of Principals of Technical Instns, 1957-58; South Wales Instn of Engineers, 1970-71; Chm. Council of Assoc. of Technical Instns, 1961-62. Hon. LLD Wales, 1970. *Publications:* Science for Miners, 1938; One Hundred Years of Technical Education, 1966; various papers on optical, spectroscopic and educational subjects. *Address:* 110 Pencisely Road, Llandaff, Cardiff. *T:* Cardiff 563795.

**HARVEY, Arthur Douglas;** Assistant Under-Secretary of State, Ministry of Defence, since 1969; *b* 16 July 1916; *o s* of William Arthur Harvey and late Edith Alice; *m* 1940, Doris Irene Lodge; two *s. Educ:* Westcliff High Sch.; St Catharine's Coll., Cambridge. Wrangler, Maths Tripos, 1938. Entered War Office, 1938; served in Army, 1940-45; Princ. 1945; Registrar, Royal Military College of Science, 1951-54; Asst Sec. 1954; Under-Sec. 1969. *Address:* 36b Lovelace Road, Long Ditton, Surrey. *T:* 01-399 0587.

**HARVEY, Air Cdre Sir Arthur Vere,** Kt 1957; CBE 1942; MP (C) Macclesfield Division of Cheshire since 1945; *b* 31 Jan. 1906; *e s* of A. W. Harvey, Kessingland, Suffolk; *m* 1st, 1940, Jacqueline Anne (marr. diss., 1954), *o d* of W. H. Dunnett; two *s*; 2nd, 1955, Mrs Hilary Charmian Williams. *Educ:* Framlingham Coll. Royal Air Force 1925-30, qualified as flying instructor; Dir of Far East Aviation Co. Ltd and Far East Flying Training Sch. Ltd, Hong-Kong, 1930-35; Adviser to Southern Chinese Air Forces with hon. rank of Maj.-Gen., 1932-35; Sqdn Leader AAF, 1937, and founded 615 County of Surrey Squadron and commanded the Squadron in France, 1939-40 (despatches twice); Group Capt. 1942. Director: CIBA Limited, Basle; CIBA United Kingdom Ltd; CIBA Cos in Gt Britain (Chm.); Mullard Ltd; Mullard Overseas Ltd; Philips Electrical Industries Ltd; Ilford Ltd (Chm., 1969-). Chairman Conservative Members' 1922 Cttee, 1966-70. vice-Pres. British Air Line Pilots' Assoc., 1965. Hon. Freeman: Macclesfield, 1969; Congleton, 1970. Comdr, Order of Oranje Nassau, 1969. *Recreations:* private flying (4th King's Cup Race, 1937), sailing. *Address:* 96 Piccadilly, W1. *Clubs:* Carlton, Buck's; Royal Yacht Squadron (Cowes).

**HARVEY, Benjamin Hyde,** OBE 1968; FIMTA, FSAA, DPA; General Manager, Harlow Development Corporation, since 1955; *b* 29 Sept. 1908; *s* of Benjamin Harvey and Elizabeth (*née* Hyde); *m* 1938, Heather Frances Broome; one *d. Educ:* Stationers' Company's Sch. Local Govt, 1924-40; Treas., Borough of Leyton, 1940-47; Comptroller, Harlow Develt Corp., 1947-55. *Recreations:* books, sport. *Address:* 188 Hugh's Tower, Harlow, Essex. *T:* Harlow 24031; Brick House, Broxted, Essex. *Club:* Royal Automobile.

**HARVEY, Hildebrand Wolfe,** CBE 1958; FRS 1945; ScD; formerly on scientific staff of Marine Biological Assoc. of the UK, 1921-58; *b* 31 Dec. 1887; *m* 1923, Elsie Marguerite, *d* of late H. Sanders; *m* 1933, Marjorie Joan, *d* of late J. Sargeant; one *s. Educ:* Gresham's Sch., Holt; Downing Coll., Cambridge. Alexander Agassiz Medal, Nat. Acad. of Science, New York, 1952. *Publications:* Biological Chemistry and Physics of Sea Water, 1927 (Moscow 1933); The Chemistry and Biology of Sea Water, 1945 (Paris, 1949); Chemistry and Fertility of Sea Waters, 1956; scientific papers relating to the fertility of the sea. *Address:* Southern House, 123 Furzehatt Road, Plymstock, Plymouth, South Devon.

**HARVEY, Ian Douglas,** TD 1950; psc 1944; author; public relations consultant; *b* 25 Jan. 1914; *s* of late Major Douglas Harvey, DSO, and of late Mrs Bertram Bisgood (*née* Dorothy Cundall); *m* 1949, Clare, *y d* of late Sir Basil E. Mayhew, KBE; two *d. Educ:* Fettes Coll.; Christ Church, Oxford. Pres., Oxford Union Soc., 1936; BA, 1937; MA, 1941. Served War of 1939-45, Adjutant, 123 LAA Regt, RA, 1940; Bde Major, 38 AA Bde, RA, 1943; GSO2 (ops), HQ AA command, 1944; Bde Major 100 AA Bde, NW Europe, 1945; Lieut-Col Comdg 566 LAA Regt, RA (City of London Rifles) TA, 1947-50. Contested Spelthorne Div. of Mddx, 1945; MP (C) Harrow East, 1950-58. Mem. of Council, Royal Borough of Kensington, 1947-52; Mem. of LCC for S Kensington, 1949-52; Rep. of LCC on County of London TA Assoc. 1949-52; Governor Birkbeck Coll., 1949-52; Deleg. Advertising Assoc. to Advertising Federation of America Convention (Detroit),

1950; Chm. Press Relations Cttee of International Advertising Conference (Great Britain), 1951; Member: Advertising Association; Inst. of Public Relations; Parliamentary Select Cttee for reform of the Army and Air Force Acts, 1952-54; Advisory Cttee on Publicity and Recruitment for Civil Defence, 1952-56; Soc. of Authors; London Soc. of Rugby Union Football Referees; Writers' Guild of GB, 1969; Rep. of Church Assembly on Standing Cttee of Nat. Soc., 1951-55; Dir of W. S. Crawford Ltd, 1949-56; Dir, Colman, Prentis and Varley Ltd, 1962-63; Advertising Controller, Yardley of London Ltd, 1963-64 (Advertising Dir, 1964-66). Parly Sec., Min. of Supply, Nov. 1956-Jan. 1957; Jt Parliamentary Under-Sec. of State, Foreign Office, 1957-58. *Publications:* Talk of Propaganda, 1947; The Technique of Persuasion, 1951; Arms and To-morrow, 1954. *Recreations:* squash, swimming, tennis. *Address:* Pitwell House, Edington, Bridgwater, Somerset. *T:* Chilton Polden 282. *Club:* Royal Automobile.

**HARVEY, John Edgar;** European Divisional Director, and Director, subsidiary companies in Burmah Oil Group; *b* Londonderry, 24 April 1920; *s* of John Watt Harvey and Charlotte Elizabeth Harvey; *m* 1945, Mary Joyce Lane, BA, JP; one *s*. *Educ:* Xaverian Coll., Bruges, Belgium; Lyme Regis Grammar Sch. Radio Officer, in the Merchant Navy, 1939-45. Contested (C): St Pancras North, 1950; Walthamstow East, 1951; Mem. Nat. Exec. Cttee., Conservative Party, 1950-55; Chm., Woodford Conservative Assoc., 1954-56. MP (C) Walthamstow East, 1955-66. Mem., NSPCC Central Executive Cttee, 1963-68. Governor, Forest Sch., 1966-. *Recreations:* various in moderation. *Address:* Colway, 87 Woodford Road, South Woodford, E18. *T:* 01-989 8466. *Club:* Carlton.

**HARVEY, Laurence,** (born **Larushka Mischa Skikne**); actor; *b* Yonishkis, Lithuania, 1 Oct. 1929; *s* of Ber and Ella Skikne; *m* 1957, Margaret Leighton (marr. diss., 1961), *qv*; *m* 1968, Joan Cohn. *Educ:* Meyerton Coll., Meyerton; Earl of Athlone High Sch., Johannesburg, South Africa. Johannesburg Repertory, 1943. Served South African Army, 1943-46; arrived England, 1946; studied at RADA for 3 months. Manchester Library Theatre, 1946-47. Appeared in Hassan, London, 1951. Stratford-on-Avon: 1952: Tullus Aufidius in Coriolanus; Orlando in As You Like It; Malcolm in Macbeth; also appeared in Volpone; 1954: Romeo in Romeo and Juliet; Troilus in Troilus and Cressida. Further parts, taken in London, New York, etc.: Angelo in Island of Goats, New York, 1955; Captain Absolute in The Rivals, and Horner in The Country Wife, London, 1955-56; The Country Wife, London and New York, 1957-58. Directed Simply Heavenly (Coloured Musical), London, 1958. Played title role in Henry V, Old Vic tour of America, 1958-59, and at Old Vic, London, 1959-60; Time of the Barracudas, USA, 1963; The Outrage, USA, 1963; Arthur, in Camelot, Drury Lane, 1964; The Winter's Tale: (Edinburgh, Cambridge), 1966; subseq. (Edinburgh, London); Arms and the Man and The Alchemist, Chichester, 1970. First film, House of Darkness, 1947. *Films include:* Man From Yesterday; Man on the Run; Cairo Road; Black Rose; The Scarlet Thread; The Wall of Death; Gathering Storm; I Believe in You; Women of Twilight; Innocents in Paris; Romeo and Juliet; The Good Die Young; King Richard and the Crusaders (in Hollywood); I Am A Camera; Storm Over The Nile; Three Men In A Boat; After the Ball; Truth About Women; The Silent Enemy; Room At The Top; Expresso Bongo; The Alamo (Texas) USA; Butterfield 8 (New York); The Long and the Short and the Tall; Summer and Smoke; The Manchurian Candidate; Two Loves, Walk on the Wild Side, Brothers Grimm, Tamiko (all in Hollywood); The Running Man; The Ceremony (prod, dir and acted); Of Human Bondage; Darling; Life at the Top; The Spy with the Cold Nose; The Winter's Tale; Dial M for Murder (film TV); Dandy in Aspic; Cherry with Creme de Cacao; Struggle for Rome; The Magic Christian; He and She; Hall of Mirrors. TV appearances in London and in America. *Recreations:* swimming, tennis, Rugby football, physical culture. *Address:* c/o Romulus Films Ltd, Brook House, Park Lane, W1. *T:* 01-493 7741. *Club:* Royal Automobile.

**HARVEY, Prof. Leslie Arthur;** Professor, 1946-69, and Head of Department of Zoology, University of Exeter, 1930-69; *b* 23 Dec. 1903; *s* of Arthur Harvey; *m* 1925, Christina Clare Brockway; one *s* one *d*. *Educ:* Bancroft's Sch.; Imperial Coll., London. ARCS 1923; BSc 1923; Beit Mem. Research Student, Imperial Coll., 1923-25; MSc 1925. Asst Lecturer, subsequently Lecturer in Zoology, University of Edinburgh, 1925-30. *Publications:* (with D. St Leger Gordon) Dartmoor, 1952; contributions to various learned journals, 1925-. *Recreations:* alpine gardening, bridge. *Address:* Benhams, The Garrison, St Mary's, Isles of Scilly. *T:* Scillonia 686.

**HARVEY, Air Marshal Sir Leslie Gordon,** KBE 1955; CB 1946; retired; *b* 11 April 1896; *s* of Thomas Gordon Harvey, Cowden, Kent; *m* 1926, Mary Sophia Clowser; one *d*. *Educ:* Commercial Sch., Maidstone, Kent. Served in Royal Warwicks Regt, 1914-17; Active Service with 7th Bn 48th Div. in France; seconded as 2nd Lieut Royal Warwick Regt to RFC, 1917; with 20 Squadron in India on North-West Frontier, 1919-24; specialised in Aeronautical Engineering at RAF Engineering Coll., 1925-27; Wing Commander in Dept of Dir of Research and Development, 1938-39; Group Capt. Commanding Airborne Forces Experimental Establishment, Ringway, Manchester, and later at Sherbourn-on-Ilmet, 1939-42; Group Capt. Commanding No. 8 Sch. of Technical Training, Weeton, Technical Training Command, 1942-43; Chief Engineer No. 45 (Atlantic) Group, Transport Command, Dorval, 1943-44; Temp. Air Commodore, HQ Transport Command as Chief Maintenance Officer and latterly as Senior Technical Staff Officer; Air Commodore, 1946; Air Officer Commanding No. 47 Group Transport Command, Milton Ernest, Bedford, 1946-48; Air Vice-Marshal, 1948; Air Officer Commanding No. 24 Group, Technical Training Command, 1948-50; SASO Technical Trg Comd, 1950-52; AOC-in-C Maintenance Comd, 1952-55 (Actg Air Marshal). Retired, 1955. *Recreations:* cricket, Adastrian and RAF. *Address:* Stanfield, Begbroke, Oxford.

**HARVEY, Mary Frances Clare,** MA; Headmistress, Badminton School, Westbury on Trym, Bristol, since Sept. 1969; *b* 24 Aug. 1927; *d* of Rev. Oliver Douglas Harvey, Highfield, Southampton. *Educ:* St Mary's Sch., Colchester; St Hugh's Coll., Oxford. BA Oxon, Final Honour Sch. of Mod. Hist., 1950; Diploma in Educn, 1951; MA 1954. History Mistress, St Albans High Sch., 1951; Head of History Dept, Portsmouth High Sch., GPDST, 1956; Headmistress, Sch. of St Clare, Penzance, 1962-69. *Recreations:* music, travel, reading, needlework. *Address:* 1 Great Brockeridge, Westbury on Trym, Bristol BS9 3TY. *T:* Bristol 628983.

**HARVEY, Sir Richard Musgrave,** 2nd Bt, *cr* 1933; Lieutenant-Commander, RN retired; Director, Price, Forbes (Agencies) Ltd; *b* 1 Dec. 1898; *s* of Sir Ernest Musgrave Harvey, 1st Bt, KBE and Sophia (*d* 1952), *y d* of late Capt. Catesby Paget; *S* father 1955; *m* 1930, Frances Estelle, *er d* of late Lindsay Crompton Lawford, Montreal; one *s* one *d*. *Educ:* Royal Naval Colls, Osborne and Dartmouth. *Heir: s* Charles Richard Musgrave Harvey [*b* 7 April 1937; *m* 1967, Celia Vivien, *d* of G. H. Hodson]. *Address:* Chisenbury Priory, Pewsey, Wilts.

**HARVEY, Major Thomas Cockayne,** CVO 1951; DSO 1945; Extra Gentleman Usher to the Queen, since 1952 (to King George VI, 1951-52); *b* 22 Aug. 1918; *s* of late Col John Harvey, DSO; *m* 1940, Lady Katharine Mary Coke, (Woman of the Bedchamber to Queen Elizabeth the Queen Mother, 1961-63), *yr d* of 3rd Earl of Leicester; one *s* two *d*. *Educ:* Radley; Balliol Coll., Oxford. Joined Scots Guards SRO, 1938. Served Norway, 1940, Italy, 1944; Private Sec. to the Queen, 1946-51. *Recreations:* golf, shooting. *Address:* 93 Eaton Place, SW1. *T:* 01-235 8725; Warham House, Warham, Wells, Norfolk. *T:* Wells 457. *Clubs:* White's, Beefsteak.

**HARVEY, Wilfred John;** Governor, HM Prison, Pentonville, 1954-57, retired; *b* 21 June 1895; *m* 1921, Susan Sansom; one *s* one *d*. *Educ:* Temple Cowley Sch., Cowley, Oxford. Served European War, 1914-18, regular soldier, RA. Prison Officer, Wandsworth Prison, 1926; Housemaster, Feltham Borstal Instn, 1933; Dep.-Governor, 1942; Governor i/c: Boys' Prison, Wormwood Scrubs Prison, 1942; Borstal at Sherwood, Nottingham, 1945; Borstal Instn, Feltham, 1948. *Recreations:* cricket, soccer, boxing. *Address:* Pasadena, 38 Preston Road, Weymouth, Dorset.

**HARVEY EVERS, H.;** *see* Evers, H. H.

**HARVEY-JAMIESON, H. M.;** *see* Jamieson, H. M. H.

**HARVIE ANDERSON, (Margaret) Betty, (Mrs J. F. P. Skrimshire),** OBE 1955; TD 1959; MP (C) East Renfrewshire since Oct. 1959; Deputy Chairman of Ways and Means, House of Commons, since 1970; *d* of late T. A. Harvie Anderson, CB, Quarter and Shirgarton, and Mrs Harvie Anderson; *m* 1960, John Francis Penrose Skrimshire, MD, FRCP. *Educ:* St Leonard's Sch., St Andrews. CC, Stirlingshire, 1945-59; Leader, moderate group, Stirling CC, 1953-59; Member: Sec. of State for Scotland's Advisory Council on Education, 1955-59; Council St Leonard's Sch.; Bd of Management Royal Scottish Nat. Instn; City of Glasgow T & AFA, 1949-51; Stirlingshire T & AFA, 1953-59; Exec. Cttee Princess Louise Scottish Hosp.; W Stirlingshire Unionist Assoc., 1938-54; Western Div. Council Scottish Unionist Assoc., 1939-59; convener Western Div. Council Women's Cttee, 1955-58; Pres. Scottish Young Unionists, 1955-58; Chm. Scottish Assoc. of Mixed and Girls' Clubs, 1952-55. Company Comdr, ATS, 1938; Adj. Reception Depot, 1940; Sen. Comdr, Mixed Heavy Anti-Aircraft Regt, RA, 1942-43; Chief Comdr Mixed Heavy Anti-Aircraft Bde, 1943-46. Contested (C) W Stirlingshire, 1950 and 1951, Sowerby (Yorks), 1955; Member: Chairman's Panel, House of Commons, 1966-; Historic Buildings Council for Scotland, 1966; Royal Commission on Local Government in Scotland, 1966-69; Mr Speaker's Conf., 1966-68. *Address:* Quarter by Denny, Stirlingshire. *T:* Denny 271.

**HARVIE-WATT, Sir George Steven,** 1st Bt, *cr* 1945; QC 1945; TD 1942 (with three Bars); DL; *b* 23 Aug. 1903; *s* of late James McDougal Watt of Armadale; *m* 1932, Bettie, *o d* of late Paymaster-Capt. Archibald Taylor, OBE, RN; two *s* one *d*. *Educ:* George Watson's Coll., Edinburgh; Glasgow Univ.; Edinburgh Univ. Called to Bar, Inner Temple, 1930; practised in London and on North Eastern Circuit. Commissioned RE TA 1924, 52nd (Lowland) Scottish Div., 1924-29; 56th (1st London) Div., 1929-38; Bt Major, 1935; Lt-Col Commanding 31st Bn RE TA, 1938-41; promoted Brig. to command 6th AA Bde, 1941; Brig. Commanding 63rd AA Bde TA, 1948-50; Hon. Col 566 LAA Regt, 1949-62. ADC to King George VI, 1948-52; ADC to the Queen, 1952-58; MP (U) Keighley Div. of Yorks, 1931-35; (U) Richmond, Surrey, Feb. 1937-Sept. 1959; PPS to late Rt Hon. Euan Wallace when Parly Sec. to Board of Trade, 1937-38; Asst Government Whip, 1938-40; PPS TO Rt Hon. Winston S. Churchill when Prime Minister, July 1941-July 1945; Hon. Treas. UK Branch of Commonwealth Parly Assoc., 1945-51; Mem. UK Deleg. to CPA Confs, Ottawa and Washington, 1949, Australia and New Zealand, 1950; Mem. of Borough Council, Royal Borough of Kensington, 1934-45. Formerly Mem. of City of London TA Association; TA Rep. Council of RUSI, 1948-57; DL: Surrey, 1942; Greater London, 1966; JP County of London, 1944-56. Pres. Printers' Pension Corporation, 1956-57. Chm., monotype Corporation Ltd; Director: Gold Fields Mining & Industrial Ltd; Clydesdale Bank Ltd; Consolidated Gold Fields Ltd (Chief Executive, 1954-69, Dep. Chm., 1954-60, Chm. 1960-69); Midland Bank, Standard Bank Ltd, Eagle Star Insurance Company, and other Companies. Formerly Dir, Great Western Railway Co. Member of Queen's Body Guard for Scotland, Royal Company of Archers. Gold Medal, Inst. Mining and Metallurgy, 1969. *Heir: s* James Harvie-Watt [*b* 25 Aug. 1940; *m* 1966, Roseline, *d* of Baron Louis de Chollet; one *s* one *d*]. *Recreation:* Territorial Army. *Address:* 1 Belgrave Place, SW1. *T:* 01-235 8197; Earlsneuk, Elie, Fife. *T:* Elie 506. *Clubs:* Pratt's, Caledonian (Chm. 1953-61, Vice-Pres. 1961); New (Edinburgh).

**HARWOOD, Basil Antony,** MA Oxon; Barrister-at-Law; a Master of the Supreme Court (Queen's Bench Division), 1950-70; Senior Master and Queen's Remembrancer, 1966-70; *b* 25 June 1903; 2nd *s* of late Basil Harwood, DMus, Woodhouse, Olveston, Glos; *m* 1929, Enid Arundel, *d* of late Philip Grove, Quorn House, Leamington; two *s*. *Educ:* Charterhouse; Christ Church, Oxford. Called to the Bar, Inner Temple, 1927. Served War of 1939-45 in Italy. Prosecuting Counsel to Post Office, Western Circuit, 1948-50. Pres. Medico-Legal Soc., 1967-69. *Address:* West Hill, Great Rissington, Glos.

**HASELDEN, Edward Christopher,** CMG 1952; *b* 14 Aug. 1903; *s* of E. N. Haselden, Minieh, Upper Egypt; *m* 1929, Lily Jewett Foote; two *d*. *Educ:* Cheltenham Coll.; Pembroke Coll., Cambridge. Joined Sudan Political Service, 1925; Sudan Agent in Cairo, 1945-53; retired, 1953. Chm. of Anglo-Egyptian Aid Soc. Cttee, 1960. Order of the Nile (4th Class), 1936. *Address:* 14 Gilston Road, SW10. *Club:* Athenæum.

**HASELDEN, Prof. Geoffrey Gordon;** Brotherton Professor of Chemical Engineering, University of Leeds, since 1960; *b* 4 Aug. 1924; *s* of George A. Haselden and Rose E. (*née* Pleasants); *m* 1945, Eileen Doris Francis; three *d*. *Educ:* Sir Walter St John's Sch.; Imperial

Coll. of Science and Technology. BScChemEng London 1944; ACGI; PhD (Eng) Chem Eng London, 1947; DScEng London, 1962; DIC; CEng; FIMechE; MIChemE; AMInstR. Mem. Gas Research Bd, 1946-48; Lectr in Low Temperature Technology, Chemical Engrg Dept, 1948-57, Senior Lectr in Chemical Engrg, 1957-60, Imperial Coll. Chm., British Cryogenics Council, 1967. Dir, Hall Thermotank International Ltd, 1968. *Publications:* research papers in Trans. Inst. Chem. Eng., etc. *Recreation:* Methodist lay preacher. *Address:* 12 High Ash Drive, Wigton Lane, Leeds 17. *T:* Leeds 687047; The University, Leeds. *T:* Leeds 31751.

**HASELDINE (Charles) Norman;** Public Relations Officer, Sheffield & Ecclesall Co-operative Society, since 1957; *b* 25 March 1922; *s* of Charles Edward Haseldine and Lily White; *m* 1946, Georgette Elise Michelle Bernard; four *s*. *Educ:* Nether Edge Grammar Sch., Sheffield. Education Officer, Doncaster Co-operative Soc., 1947-57. MP (Lab and Co-op) Bradford West, 1966-70; PPS to Minister of Power, 1968-69; PPS to Pres. Bd of Trade, 1969-70; Mem. Select Cttee on Nationalised Inds; Sec., Public and Cooperative Enterprise. *Recreation:* classical music. *Address:* 31 Roland Gardens, SW7; 115 Psalter Lane, Sheffield S11 8YR. *T:* Sheffield 55974.

**HASELDINE, Norman;** *see* Haseldine, C. N.

**HASELGROVE, Dennis Cliff,** CB 1963; MA; Under Secretary, Ministry of Transport, since 1957; *b* 18 Aug. 1914; *s* of late H. Cliff Haselgrove, LLB, Chingford; *m* 1941, Evelyn Hope Johnston, MA, *d* of late R. Johnston, Edinburgh; one *s*. *Educ:* Uppingham Sch.; King's Coll., Cambridge. 1st Class, Classical Tripos, Parts I and II. Entered Ministry of Transport, Oct. 1937; Private Sec. to Permanent Sec., and Asst Priv. Sec. to Minister, 1941. Served in Intelligence Corps and 10th Baluch Regt, IA, 1941-45. Asst Sec., 1948. Govt Delegate to: ILO Asian Maritime Conf., 1953; Internat. Conf. on Oil Pollution of the Sea, 1954, 1962; Internat. Lab. Conf. (Maritime Session), 1958; Internat. Conf. on Safety of Life at Sea, 1960. Imperial Defence Coll., 1955. Chairman of: Management Cttee for Slough Road Safety Experiment, 1956; Working Party on Child Cyclists, 1956. *Recreations:* archæology, travel, philately. *Address:* 10 Church Gate, SW6. *T:* 01-736 5213.

**HASELHURST, Alan Gordon Barraclough;** MP (C) Middleton and Prestwich since 1970; *b* 23 June 1937; *s* of John Haselhurst and Alyse (*née* Barraclough); unmarried. *Educ:* King Edward VI Sch., Birmingham; Cheltenham Coll.; Oriel Coll., Oxford. Pres., Oxford Univ. Conservative Assoc., 1958; Sec., Treas. and Librarian, Oxford Union Soc., 1959-60; Nat. Chm., Young Conservatives, 1966-68. *Recreations:* squash, theatre, music. *Address:* Spring Bank, Broad Oak Park, Worsley, Manchester, M28 4NS. *T:* 061-794 2494. *Clubs:* Carlton; St James's (Manchester).

**HASELL, Edward William;** *b* 16 Jan. 1888; *m* 1920, Gertrude, OBE 1958, *d* of John Stroyan, Lanrick Castle, Perthshire and Kirkchrist, Wigtownshire; two *d*. *Educ:* Rossall; Queen's Coll., Oxford. Served European War, 1914-18, with Westmorland and Cumberland Yeomanry, Major 1919. JP 1922, DL, 1927, and High Sheriff, 1927, Westmorland; Vice-Lieut of Westmorland, 1958-65. *Recreations:* shooting, farming, forestry. *Address:* Dalemain, Penrith, Cumberland. *T:* Pooley Bridge 223.

**HASKARD, Sir Cosmo (Dugal Patrick Thomas),** KCMG 1965 (CMG 1960); MBE 1945; Governor and Commander-in-Chief, Falkland Islands, and High Commissioner for the British Antarctic Territory, 1964-70; *b* 25 Nov. 1916; *o c* of late Brig.-Gen. J. McD. Haskard, CMG, DSO; *m* 1957, Phillada, *o c* of Sir Robert Stanley, *qv*; one *s*. *Educ:* Cheltenham; RMC Sandhurst; Pembroke Coll., Cambridge (MA). Served War of 1939-45 (MBE); 2nd Lieut, TA (Gen. List), 1938; Emergency Commn, RIF, 1939; seconded KAR, 1941; served 2nd Bn, E Africa, Ceylon, Burma; Major 1944. Cadet, Tanganyika, 1940; transf. Nyasaland, 1946; Dist Comr, 1948; Provincial Commissioner, 1955; acting Secretary for African Affairs, 1957-58; Sec. for Labour and Social Development, 1961; Sec. for Local Government, 1962; Sec. for Natural Resources, 1963. Served on Nyasaland-Mozambique Boundary Commission, 1951-52. *Address:* Tragariff, Bantry, Co. Cork, Ireland. *T:* Bantry 74.

**HASKELL, Arnold Lionel,** CBE 1954; Chevalier de la Légion d'Honneur, 1950; writer, lecturer, and journalist; Hon. Director, Royal Ballet School, 1946-65, Governor, since 1966; a Governor, The Royal Ballet since 1957; *b* 1903; *s* of late J. S. Haskell and Emmy Mesritz; *m* 1st, 1927, Vera Saitzoff (*d* 1968); two *s* one *d*; 2nd, 1970, Vivienne Marks. *Educ:* Westminster; Trinity Hall, Cambridge (MA). Mem., editorial staff, William Heinemann Ltd, 1927-32; joint founder of Camargo Soc., 1930; visited America with Russian Ballet, 1933-34; dance critic, Daily Telegraph, 1935-38; Founder the Vic-Wells Ballet Benevolent Fund, 1936; visited Australia, guest critic for Melbourne Herald and Sydney Daily Telegraph, 1936-37; Australia, 1938-39; toured Spain, Portugal and Germany for British Council, 1950-51, Italy, Yugoslavia and Greece, 1953, Germany and Italy, 1954, Italy 1955; visited USSR to study ballet and to lecture, 1960 and 1962, and as guest of Youth Organisation, 1967. Visited Cuba as guest of National Council of Culture, 1967, and lectured there for three months, 1968. Advised Dutch Government Commission on formation of a National ballet, 1954; Vice-Pres. jury, Varna dance competition, 1964, 1965, 1966 and 1970; Mem. jury, Internat. Ballet contest, Moscow, 1969; Vice-Pres. Royal Academy of Dancing; Vice-Pres., Catholic Stage Guild; Governor, Trent Park Training Coll., 1953-58 and 1961; Council, Royal West of England Academy, 1961. *Publications:* Some Studies in Ballet, 1928; The Sculptor Speaks, 1932; Black on White, 1933; Balletomania, 1934; Diaghileff, 1935; Prelude to Ballet, Balletomane's Scrapbook, 1936; Dancing Round the World, 1937; Ballet Panorama, 1938; Ballet, a complete guide to appreciation, 1938; Balletomane's Album, 1939; Waltzing Matilda: a background to Australia, 1940; Australia, 1941; The Australians, 1943; The National Ballet, 1943; The Dominions–Partnership or Rift?, 1943; British Ballet, 1939-45; The Making of a Dancer, 1946; Ballet Vignettes, 1949; In His True Centre (autobiography), 1951; edited Ballet–to Poland in aid of Polish Relief Funds, 1940, and Ballet Annual, 1947-; Saints Alive, 1953; co-edited Gala Performance, 1956; The Russian Genius in Ballet, 1962; Ballet Retrospect, 1964; What is Ballet, 1965; Heroes and Roses, 1966; Ballet Russe: the Age of Diaghilev, 1968; (ed) Infantilia, 1971. Contrib. Encyclopædia Britannica, British Journal of Aesthetics, Chambers's Encyclopædia and Annual Register. *Recreations:* travelling, opera-going, collecting sculpture, photography and juvenilia. *Address:* Beechwood House, Bath,

Somerset. *Club:* Garrick.
*See also F. J. H. Haskell.*

**HASKELL, Francis James Herbert;** Professor of Art History, Oxford University and Fellow of Trinity College, Oxford, since October 1967; *b* 7 April 1928; *s* of Arnold Haskell, *qv*; *m* 1965, Larissa Salmina. *Educ:* Eton Coll.; King's Coll., Cambridge. Junior Library Clerk, House of Commons, 1953-54; Fellow of King's Coll., Cambridge, 1954-67; Librarian of Fine Arts Faculty, Cambridge Univ., 1962-67. *Publications:* Patrons and Painters: a study of the relations between Art and Society in the Age of the Baroque, 1963; Géricault (The Masters), 1966; articles in Burlington Mag., Jl Warburg Inst, etc.; reviews in New Statesman, NY Review of Books, etc. *Recreation:* foreign travel. *Address:* 7 Walton Street, Oxford and Trinity College, Oxford.

**HASLEGRAVE, Herbert Leslie,** WhSch (Sen.), MA Cantab, PhD London, MSc (Eng), CEng, FIMechE, FIEE, FIProdE; educational consultant; formerly Vice-Chancellor, Loughborough University of Technology; *b* 16 May 1902; *s* of late George Herbert Haslegrave and Annie (*née* Totty), Wakefield; *m* 1938, Agnes Mary, *er d* of Leo Sweeney, Bradford; one *d*. *Educ:* Wakefield Gram. Sch.; Bradford Technical Coll.; Trinity Hall Cambridge (Scholar). Rex Moir Prizeman, John Bernard Seeley Prizeman, Ricardo Prizeman, 1928; 1st Cl. Mechanical Sciences Tripos, 1928. English Electric Co. Ltd: Engineering Apprentice, 1918-23, Asst Designer, Stafford, 1928-30; Lecturer: Wolverhampton and Staffs, Technical Coll., 1931; Bradford Technical Coll., 1931-35; Head of Continuative Education Dept, Loughborough Coll., 1935-38; Principal: St Helens Municipal Technical Coll., 1938-43; Barnsley Mining and Technical Coll., 1943-46; Leicester Coll. of Technology, 1947-53; Loughborough Coll. of Technology, 1953-66. Member of: Productivity Team on Training of Supervisors, visiting USA, 1951; Delegation on Education and Training of Engineers visiting USSR, 1956; Council, IMechE, 1965-66; Council, IEE, 1956-58. Chairman: Council, Assoc. of Technical Institutions, 1963-64; Cttee on Technician Courses and Examinations, 1967-69. Hon. Dr of Technology, Loughborough Univ. of Technology. *Publications:* various on engineering, education and management in Proceedings of professional engineering bodies and educational press; chapter in Management, Labour and Community. *Recreations:* motoring, swimming, music. *Address:* 7 Heath Rise, Brixham, Devon; 14c Kennington Oval, SE11. *Club:* Challoner.

**HASLEGRAVE, Neville Crompton;** Town Clerk of Leeds since 1965; Solicitor; *b* 2 Aug. 1914; *o s* of late Joe Haslegrave, Clerk of Council, and late Olive May Haslegrave; *m* 1943, Vera May, *o d* of Waldemar Julius Pedersen, MBE, and late Eva Pedersen; two *d*. *Educ:* Exeter Cathedral Choristers School; Leeds Univ. Asst Examr, Estate Duty Office, Bd of Inland Revenue, 1940-44; Asst Solicitor, Co. Borough of Leeds, 1944-46. Chief Prosecuting Solicitor, Leeds, 1946-51; Principal Asst Solicitor, Leeds, 1951-60; Dep. Town Clerk, Leeds, 1960-65. *Recreations:* cricket, golf, tennis, music, walking. *Address:* 23 Grove Court, Leeds, 6. *T:* Leeds 59531; Low House, Halton Gill, Arncliffe, Skipton, Yorks. *Club:* National Liberal.

**HASLEWOOD, Geoffrey Arthur Dering;** Professor of Biochemistry at Guy's Hospital Medical School, University of London, since 1949; *b* 9 July 1910; *s* of N. A. F. Haslewood, Architect, and Florence (*née* Hughes); *m* 1943, B. W. Leeburn (*d* 1949); two *d*; *m* 1953, E. S. Blakiston, Geelong, Vic, Australia. *Educ:* St Marylebone Grammar Sch.; University Coll., London. Research on polycyclic aromatic hydrocarbons, etc, at Royal Cancer Hosp. (Free), 1933-35; Asst in Pathological Chemistry at British Postgraduate Med. Sch., 1935-39; Reader in Biochemistry at Guy's Hosp. Med. Sch., 1939-49. MSc 1932, PhD 1935, DSc 1946, London. FRIC 1946. *Publications:* various articles and original memoirs in scientific literature, mainly on steroids. *Recreation:* fishing. *Address:* 28 Old Fort Road, Shoreham-by-Sea, Sussex.

**HASLIP, Joan;** author; *b* 27 Feb. 1912; *yr d* of late George Ernest Haslip, MD, original planner of the Health Service. *Educ:* privately in London and on the continent. Grew up in Florence. Sub-editor, London Mercury, 1929-39, contributed verse, reviews, etc; travelled extensively Europe, USA, Middle East; Editor, European Service, BBC, 1941-45 (Italian Section); lectured for British Council, Italy and Middle East; broadcast and contributed articles to BBC and various publications and newspapers. FRSL 1958. *Publications:* (several translated); Out of Focus (novel), 1931; Grandfather Steps (novel), 1932 (USA 1933); Lady Hester Stanhope, 1934; Parnell, 1936 (USA 1937); Portrait of Pamela, 1940; Lucrezia Borgia, 1953 (USA 1954); The Sultan, Life of Abdul Hamid, 1958; The Lonely Empress, a life of Elizabeth of Austria, 1965 (trans. into nine languages). *Recreations:* travelling and conversation. *Address:* 208 Carrington House, Hertford Street, W1. *T:* 01-629 6232.

**HASLUCK, Rt. Hon. Sir Paul,** PC 1966; GCMG 1969; GCVO 1970; Governor-General of Australia, since 1969; *b* 1 April 1905; *s* of E. M. C. Hasluck and Patience (*née* Wooler); *m* 1932, Alexandra Margaret Martin Darker; two *s*. *Educ:* University of Western Australia (MA). Journalist until 1938. Lectr in History, University of Western Australia, 1939-40; Australian Diplomatic Service, 1941-47; Head of Australian Mission to United Nations, 1946-47; Representative on Security Council, Atomic Energy Commn, General Assembly, etc. Research Reader in History, University of Western Australia, 1948. Official War Historian. Mem. (L) House of Representatives, 1949; Minister for Territories in successive Menzies Governments, 1951-63; Minister for Defence, 1963-64; Minister for External Affairs, 1964-69. KStJ 1969. *Publications:* Black Australians, 1942; Workshop of Security, 1946; The Government and the People (Australian Official War History, vol. 1, 1951, vol. 2, 1970; Collected Poems, 1970. *Recreations:* horse riding, book collecting (Australiana). *Address:* Government House, Canberra, ACT 2600, Australia. *Club:* Weld (Perth).

**HASSALL, Joan,** RE 1948; FSIA 1958; painter and wood engraver; *b* 3 March 1906; *d* of late John Hassall, RI, RWA, and late Constance Brooke-Webb. *Educ:* Parsons Mead, Ashtead; Froebel Educational Institute, Roehampton. Sec. to London Sch. of Art, 1925-27; studied Royal Academy Schs, 1928-33; studied Wood Engraving, LCC Sch. of Photo-engraving and Lithography. Teacher of Book Production (deputy), Edinburgh Coll. of Art, 1940; resumed her own work in London, chiefly wood engraving, 1945. Work represented in: British Museum, Victoria and Albert Museum and collections abroad. Designed the Queen's Invitation Card to her guests for Coronation, 1953. *Publications:* first published engraving in Devil's Dyke, by Christopher Hassall, 1935; The Wood Engravings of Joan Hassall, 1960.

Her engraved and drawn work appears in many classic and contemporary books of prose and poetry, and in advertising. *Recreations:* music, literature and printing. *Address:* 88 Kensington Park Road, W11. *T:* 01-727 5826.

**HASSAN, Sir Joshua (Abraham),** Kt 1963; CBE 1957; MVO 1954; QC (Gibraltar) 1961; JP; Leader of the Opposition, Gibraltar House of Assembly, since 1969; *b* 1915; *s* of late Abraham M. Hassan, Gibraltar; *m* 1945, Daniela (marr. diss. 1969), *d* of late José Salazar; two *d*; *m* 1969, Marcelle Bensimon. *Educ:* Line Wall Coll., Gibraltar. Called to Bar, Middle Temple, 1939. HM Deputy Coroner, Gibraltar, 1941-64; Mayor of Gibraltar, 1945-50 and 1953-69; Mem. Executive Council, Chief Mem. Legislative Council, Gibraltar, 1950-64; Chief Minister of Gibraltar, 1964-69. Chairman: Cttee of Management, Gibraltar Museum, 1952-65; Gibraltar Govt Lottery Cttee, 1955-70; Central Planning Commn, 1947-70. *Address:* 11/18 Europa Road, Gibraltar. *T:* A2295. *Clubs:* Oxford and Cambridge University; Royal Gibraltar Yacht.

**HASSEL, Prof. Odd;** Knight of the Order of St Olav; Guldber-Waage and Gunnerus Medals; Emeritus Professor of the University, Oslo; *b* 17 May 1897; *s* of Ernst August Hassel and Mathilde Klaveness. *Educ:* Oslo, Munich and Berlin Universities. Lectr, Oslo Univ., 1925, docent 1926, full Professor, 1934; Director, Department of Physical Chemistry of Univ. of Oslo, 1934-64. Hon. Fellow: Chemical Soc., London; Norwegian Chemical Soc., Oslo; Fellow of Academies in Oslo, Trondheim, Stockholm, Copenhagen, etc. Nobel Prize for Chemistry, 1969. Hon. Dr phil, Univ. of Copenhagen, 1950; Hon. Fil dr, Univ. of Stockholm, 1960. *Publications:* Kristallchemie, 1934, trans. English and Russian; about 250 scientific papers, chiefly on molecular structure problems. *Address:* Chemistry Department, University of Oslo, Blindern, Oslo 3, Norway; (home) Holsteinveien 10, Oslo 8. *T:* 232062.

**HASSETT, Maj.-Gen. Francis George,** CB 1970; CBE 1966 (OBE 1945); DSO 1951; MVO 1954; Chairman, Army Review Committee, since 1970; *b* 11 April 1918; *s* of John Francis Hassett, Sydney, Australia; *m* 1946, Margaret Hallie Roberts, *d* of Dr Edwin Spencer Roberts, Toowoomba, Qld; two *s* two *d*. *Educ:* RMC, Duntroon, Australia. Graduated RMC, 1938. Served War of 1939-45, Middle East and South West Pacific Area (Lt-Col; despatches twice); CO 3 Bn Royal Australian Regt, Korea, 1951-52; Marshal for ACT Royal Tour, 1954; Comd 28 Commonwealth Bde, 1961-62; DCGS, 1964-65; Head of Aust. Jt Services Staff, Australia House, 1966-67; GOC Northern Comd, Australia, 1968-70; Extra Gentleman Usher to the Queen, 1966-68. *Recreations:* golf, tennis, boating. *Address:* 42 Mugga Way, Red Hill, Canberra, ACT 2603, Australia. *Clubs:* Commonwealth, Queensland.

**HASTED, Maj.-Gen. William Freke,** CB 1946; CIE 1943; CBE 1941; DSO 1937; MC; late Royal Engineers; *b* 28 Sept. 1897; *s* of late W. A. Hasted, Lindfield, Sussex; *m* 1920, Hella Elizabeth Mary (*d* 1961), *d* of Lieut-Col A. E. Cuming, Doneraile, Co. Cork; no *c*. *Educ:* Cheltenham Coll.; Cambridge Univ.; Royal Military Academy, Woolwich. First Commission, 1915; European war (2nd Division) 1916-18 (despatches, MC); Instructor RM Academy Woolwich, 1924-26; Instructor RMC of Canada, Kingston, Ont. 1926-30; OCRE South Irish Coast Defence, 1932-36; Bengal Sappers-Miners (Peshawar), 1936-37; Headquarters Northern Command, India, 1937; Waziristan Operations, 1937 (despatches twice, DSO); CRE Waziristan District, 1938-41; Waziristan Admadzai Operations, 1940 (despatches CBE); Deputy Chief Engineer, HQ Xth Army, 1941-42; Deputy Engineer-in-Chief (Air), GHQ, New Delhi, 1942-43; Chief Engineer 14 Army, 1944-45 (CB); Chief Engineer, Allied Land Forces SEAC, 1945-46; Engineer-in-Chief in India, 1946-47; late Controller of Aerodromes; retired pay, 1948. Pres., Loughborough Coll., Leics, 1951. Controller of Development, Kuwait, Persian Gulf, 1952; retired from Persian Gulf, 1954. *Recreations:* shooting, fishing, tennis; International Hockey, England, 1923; Hockey, Army and Combined Services, 1922-25. *Address:* c/o Lloyds Bank, Pall Mall, SW1.

**HASTILOW, Cyril Alexander Frederick,** CBE 1955 (OBE 1947); Chairman, Smith & Nephew Associated Companies Ltd, 1962-68 (Director, 1958); *b* Birmingham, 31 May 1895; *s* of Frederick Hastilow; *m* 1922, Doreen Madge, MA, *d* of J. H. Hateley; two *s* one *d*. *Educ:* Central Gram. Sch., Birmingham; Birmingham Univ. MSc 1919; BCom. 1920; FRIC 1926. Chief Chemist, Docker Bros., 1920-32; Sales Manager, 1932-39; General Manager, 1939-46; Chairman, 1946-60. Asst Controller, Miscellaneous Chemicals Control, Ministry of Supply, 1942-44; Dir, Paint Materials, Min. of Supply, 1944-45. Pres. Paint Materials Trade Association, 1945-47; Dir Pinchin Johnson & Associates Ltd, 1946-62; Mem. Industrial Estates Management Corporation for England, 1960-65. Pres. Birmingham Chamber of Commerce, 1953-54; Vice-Pres. Soc. of Brit. Paint Manufacturers, 1958-60. Mem. Court of Governors, Birmingham Univ., 1946-; Mem. Bd of Governors, United Birmingham Hosps, 1949-57; Mem. House Cttee, Queen Elizabeth Hosp., 1947-60. Chm. and Hon. Sec. Warwicks County Cricket Club, 1948-62, Vice-Pres., 1966-; Pres. Warwicks Youth Cricket Council, 1961- (Chm. 1951-61); Member: MCC Cttee, 1964-67; MCC Youth Cricket Assoc., 1952-. *Recreations:* interested in all outdoor sports, particularly cricket. *Address:* 43 Moor Green Lane, Moseley, Birmingham 13. *T:* 021-449 0883. *Club:* Royal Aero.

**HASTINGS,** family name of **Earl of Huntingdon.**

**HASTINGS;** *see* Abney-Hastings, family name of Countess of Loudoun.

**HASTINGS,** 22nd Baron, *cr* 1290; **Edward Delaval Henry Astley,** Bt 1660; *b* 14 April 1912; *s* of 21st Baron and Lady Marguerite Nevill, *d* of 3rd Marquess of Abergavenny; *S* father 1956; *m* 1954, Catherine Rosaline Ratcliffe Coats, 2nd *d* of late Capt. H. V. Hinton; two *s* one *d*. *Educ:* Eton and abroad. Supplementary Reserve, Coldstream Guards, 1934; served War of 1939-45, Major 1945; farming in Southern Rhodesia, 1951-57. Mem. of Parliamentary delegation to the West Indies, 1958; a Lord in Waiting, 1961-62; Jt Parly Sec., Min. of Housing and Local Govt, 1962-64. Chm. British-Italian Soc., 1957-62. Grand Officer, Order of Merit (Italy), 1968. *Heir: s* Hon. Delaval Thomas Harold Astley, *b* 25 April 1960. *Address:* Fulmodeston Hall, Fakenham, Norfolk. *T:* Thursford 231; Seaton Delaval Hall, Northumberland. *Clubs:* St James'; Northern Counties (Newcastle); Norfolk County (Norwich).

**HASTINGS, Archdeacon of;** *see* Mayfield, Ven. G.

**HASTINGS, Anne Wilson;** formerly HM Superintending Inspector of Factories; *b* Kinneff, Kincardineshire; *d* of Rev. James Hastings, DD, Editor of the Dictionary of the Bible, etc, and Wilson Hastings; *m* Leonard J. Page, CEng, MRINA. *Educ:* Leeds Girls' High Sch.; Aberdeen Univ. MA (1st class Hons Mental Philosophy); Bain Gold Medallist, 1916; Fullerton Scholar, 1916-17. Joint-Editor of Expository Times, 1922-65. *Address:* 105 Argyle Road, W13. *T:* 01-997 1959.
*See also Rev. E. Hastings.*

**HASTINGS, Rev. Edward,** MA, DD; *b* Kinneff, Kincardineshire; *s* of late Rev. James Hastings, DD. *Educ:* Aberdeen Univ.; New Coll., Edinburgh. Ordained minister at Errol, Perthshire in 1921; resigned charge 1923 to undertake editorial work. *Publications:* The Speaker's Bible; The Local Colour of the Bible (with Rev. Dr Charles W. Budden); Joint-Editor of The Expository Times, 1922-65. *Address:* King's Gate, Aberdeen AB2 6BL. *T:* Aberdeen 26048.
*See also A. W. Hastings.*

**HASTINGS, Hubert De Cronin;** Chairman, Architectural Press; Editor, Architectural Review since 1927; Editor, Architects' Journal since 1932; *b* 18 July 1902; *s* of Percy Hastings and Lilian Bass; *m* 1927, Hazel Rickman Garrard; one *s* one *d*. *Address:* 9/13 Queen Anne's Gate, Westminster, SW1. *Club:* Arts.

**HASTINGS, Stephen Lewis Edmonstone,** MC 1944; MP (C) Mid-Bedfordshire since Nov. 1960; *b* 4 May 1921; *s* of late Lewis Aloysius MacDonald Hastings, MC, and of Edith Meriel Edmonstone; *m* 1948, Harriet Mary Elisabeth, *d* of Col Julian Latham Tomlin, CBE, DSO; one *s* one *d*. *Educ:* Eton; RMC, Sandhurst. Gazetted Ensign, Scots Guards, 1939; served 2nd Bn, Western Desert, 1941-43 (despatches); SAS Regt, 1943. Joined Foreign Office, 1948. British Legation, Helsinki, 1950-52; British Embassy, Paris, 1953-58; First Sec., Political Office, Middle East Forces, 1959-60. Director: Oxley Developments; Roger Tomlin Ltd. *Publication:* The Murder of TSR 2, 1966. *Recreations:* painting, ski-ing, shooting. *Address:* c/o House of Commons, SW1. *Clubs:* Buck's, Guards; Kandahar.

**HASZELDINE, Robert Neville,** FRS 1968; MA Cantab, PhD Birmingham, PhD Cantab, DSc Birmingham, ScD Cantab; FRIC; Professor of Chemistry and Head of Department of Chemistry, University of Manchester Institute of Science and Technology (Faculty of Technology, The University of Manchester), since 1957; *b* Manchester, 3 May 1925; *s* of late Walter Haszeldine and Hilda Haszeldine (*née* Webster); *m* 1954, Pauline Elvina Goodwin; two *s* two *d*. *Educ:* Stockport Grammar Sch.; University of Birmingham; University of Cambridge. John Watt Memorial Scholarship, 1942. University of Cambridge: Asst in Research in Organic Chemistry, 1949; University Demonstrator in Organic and Inorganic Chemistry, 1951; Asst Dir of Research, 1956; Fellow and Dir of Studies, Queens' Coll., until 1957; Mem. of Sidney Sussex Coll. Tilden Lectr, 1968; Vis. Lectr at Universities and laboratories in the USA, Russia, Switzerland, Austria, Germany and France. Meldola Medal, 1953; Corday-Morgan Medal and Prize, 1960. *Publications:* numerous scientific publications in chemical jls. *Recreations:* mountaineering, gardening, good food, wine. *Address:* Windyridge, Lyme Road, Disley, Cheshire. *T:* Disley 2223; Department of Chemistry, University of Manchester Institute of Science and Technology, Manchester 1. *T:* 051-236 3311.

**HATHAWAY, Dame Sibyl Mary,** DBE 1965 (OBE 1949); Dame de Serk; *d* of late W. F. Collings, Seigneur of Serk; *widow* of Dudley Beaumont, *s* of Capt. Spencer Beaumont; two *s* (and *e s* killed in 1941) one *d* (and two *d* decd); *m* 1929, Robert Woodward Hathaway (*d* 1954), *s* of Charles Hathaway, New York. *Publications:* Maid of Sark, 1939; Dame of Sark, 1961. *Heir to title: g s* Michael Beaumont. *Address:* La Seigneurie, Island of Sark.

**HATHERTON,** 6th Baron, *cr* 1835; **John Walter Stuart Littleton;** *b* 9 Aug. 1906; *s* of 4th Baron Hatherton and Hester Edithe (*d* 1947), *d* of Thomas Tarrant Hoskins, MD, Tasmania; *S* brother, 1969; *m* 1932, Nora Evelyn (*d* 1955), *d* of R. C. Smith, Edgbaston; one *d*. *Educ:* Cranleigh. *Heir: b* Hon. Thomas Charles Tasman Littleton, TD [*b* 6 Oct. 1907; *m* 1933, Ann Scott, *o d* of late Lt-Comdr Thomas McLeod, RN; one *d*]. *Address:* Madeira House, Church Stretton, Salop.

**HATTERSLEY, Alan Frederick,** MA, DLitt; Professor Emeritus of History, University of Natal; Member Union Archives Commission, 1948-64; *b* 6 April 1893; *o s* of F. Kilvington Hattersley, Fairlawn, Harrogate. *Educ:* Leeds Grammar Sch.; Downing Coll., Cambridge. Professor of History and Political Science, University of Natal, 1923-53. Hon. DLitt (Natal), 1957. *Publications:* A Short History of Western Civilisation 1927; A History of Democracy, 1930; South Africa (Home University Library), 1933; History Teaching in Schools, 1935; More Annals of Natal, 1936; Pietermaritzburg Panorama, 1938; Later Annals of Natal, 1938; Portrait of a Colony, 1940; The Natalians, 1940; Hilton Portrait, 1945; Journal of J. S. Dobie, 1945; The British Settlement of Natal, 1950; Carbineer, 1950; A Victorian Lady At the Cape, 1951; A Hospital Century, 1955; Oliver the Spy and Others, 1959; The First South African Detectives, 1960; The Convict Crisis and Growth of Unity, 1965; An Illustrated Social History of S Africa, 1969. *Recreation:* Emeritus Commissioner, Boy Scouts Association, South Africa. *Address:* Inglemoor House, 1 Sanders Road, Pietermaritzburg, S Africa. *TA:* Univcoll. *Club:* Authors'.

**HATTERSLEY, Roy Sydney George,** BSc (Econ.); MP (Lab) Sparkbrook Division of Birmingham since 1964; *b* 28 Dec. 1932; *s* of Frederick Roy Hattersley, Sheffield; *m* 1956, Molly, *d* of Michael Loughran, Consett, Co. Durham. *Educ:* Sheffield City Grammar Sch.; Univ. of Hull. Journalist and Health Service Executive, 1956-64; Mem. Sheffield City Council, 1957-65 (Chm. Housing Cttee and Public Works Cttee). PPS to Minister of Pensions and National Insurance, 1964-67; Jt Parly Sec., DEP (formerly Min. of Labour), 1967-69; Minister of Defence for Administration, 1969-70. Dir, Campaign for a European Political Community, 1966-67. *Address:* House of Commons, SW1. *Club:* Reform.

**HATTO, Professor Arthur Thomas,** MA; Head of the Department of German, Queen Mary College, University of London, since 1938; *b* 11 Feb. 1910; *s* of Thomas Hatto, LLB and Alice Walters; *m* 1935, Margot Feibelmann; one *d*. *Educ:* Dulwich Coll.; King's Coll., London; University Coll., London. BA (London) 1931; MA (with Distinction), 1934. Lektor für Englisch, University of Berne, 1932-34; Asst Lectr in German, KCL, 1934-38; Queen Mary Coll., University of London, 1938 (Head of Dept of German). Temp. Sen. Asst, Foreign Office, 1939-45; Part-time Lectr in German, University Coll., London, 1944-45; returned to Queen Mary Coll., 1945; Reader in

German Language and Literature, University of London, 1946; Prof. of German Language and Literature, University of London, 1953. Governor, School Of Oriental and African Studies, Univ. of London, 1960; Governor and Mem. Standing Cttee, Queen Mary Coll., Univ. of London, 1968-70. Chairman: London Seminar on Epic; Cttee 'A' (Theol. and Arts), Central Research Fund, Univ. of London, 1969. Fellow: Royal Anthropological Institute; Royal Asiatic Society. *Publications:* (with R. J. Taylor) The Songs of Neidhart von Reuental, 1958; Gottfried von Strassburg, Tristan (trans. entire for first time) with Tristran of Thomas (newly trans.) with an Introduction, 1960; The Niblungenlied: a new translation, with Introduction and Notes, 1964; editor of Eos, an enquiry by fifty scholars into the theme of the alba in world literature, 1965; articles in learned periodicals. *Recreations:* reading, gardening, walking. *Address:* 11 Gills Hill, Radlett, Herts. *T:* Radlett 6490. *Club:* The Confrères.

**HATTON;** *see* Finch Hatton, family name of Earl of Winchilsea.

**HATTON, Maj.-Gen. George Seton,** CB 1950; DSO 1942; OBE 1941; psc 1935; *b* 13 Feb. 1899; *s* of late Edwin Fullarton Hatton and late Marion Isobella (*née* Seton-Browne); *m* 1949, Hilda Mary Arthur (*widow*), OBE 1955; no *c*. *Educ:* Upper Canada Coll.; Royal Military Coll. of Canada; Cambridge Univ. Commnd as 2nd Lieut, Royal Engineers, 1917; served European War, 1914-18, with RE in France and Belgium, and on Staff in Turkey, 1920-23; regimental duty with RE in Egypt and at home, 1924-34; on Staff India, 1936-39 and accompanied 11th Ind. Inf. Bde to Middle East as Brigade Major, 1939; served War of 1939-45; Staff services in Middle East, 1939-44, including appointments in Western Desert as AA and QMG 7th Armoured Div., and BGS 30 Corps; also senior administrative appointments with Ninth Army and GHQ (despatches). Served in North West Europe, 1945, on Staff SHAEF and 21 Army Group and in comd as Brig. (despatches). Dep. Comdr L of C, 1946, and later Comdr of Br troops Low Countries. Returned to UK, 1947, as Brig. A/Q; Chief of Staff HQ Southern Command, Salisbury, 1949-51; Maj.-Gen., Administration, BAOR, 1951-54; Maj.-Gen. 1950; retired 1955. Deputy Federal Civil Defence Co-ordinator for Canada, 1955-59. *Recreation:* photography. *Address:* 4 Beechwood Drive, Marlow, Bucks. *Club:* United Service.

**HATTY, Hon. Sir Cyril (James),** Kt 1963; director of companies; *b* 22 Dec. 1908; *o s* of James Hatty and Edith (*née* Russen); *m* 1937, Doris Evelyn, *o d* of James Lane Stewart and Mable Grace Stewart; two *s*. *Educ:* Westminster City Sch. Deputy Dir, O and M Division, UK Treasury, until Jan. 1947; emigrated to S Africa, in industry, Feb. 1947; moved to Bulawayo, in industry, Jan. 1948. MP for Bulawayo North, Sept. 1950-Dec. 1963; Minister of Treasury, Jan. 1954-Sept. 1962, also Minister of Mines, Feb. 1956-Dec. 1962. FCIS; Fellow Inst. of Cost and Works Accountants; Fellow Brit. Inst. of Management. *Publication:* Digest of SR Company Law, 1952. *Recreations:* painting, music. *Address:* Merton Park, Norton, Rhodesia. *T:* 74520. *Clubs:* Polytechnic, Salisbury, New (Salisbury).

**HAUFF, Mrs Janet Alderson;** Assistant Under-Secretary of State, Department of Health and Social Security (formerly Ministry of Health), since 1966; *b* 24 Sept. 1913; *d* of William Fitzjohn Crisp and Ethel May Crisp; *m* 1940, Charles Kenneth Hauff (*d* 1967). *Educ:* Mexborough Grammar Sch.; Girton Coll., Cambridge (BA). Entered Civil Service, 1941. FRGS. *Recreations:* Antarctic travel, photography. *Address:* 31 Campden Grove, Kensington, W8. *T:* 01-937 3852.

**HAUGHTON, Dr Sidney Henry,** FRS 1961; FGS 1914; DSc; *b* 7 May 1888; *s* of Henry Charles Haughton and Alice Haughton (*née* Aves), London; *m* 1914, Edith Hoal, Cape Town; one *s* one *d*. *Educ:* Walthamstow Technical Institute; Trinity Hall, Cambridge. BA Cantab 1909; DSc Cape Town, 1921. Palæontologist, S African Museum, Cape Town, 1911, Asst Dir, 1914; Sen. Geologist, S African Geological Survey, 1920, Dir, 1934; Chief Geologist, S African Atomic Energy Board, 1948-54. Mem., at various times of Governmental Bds and Commns on Industrial Requirements, Fuel Research, Scientific and Industrial Research, Museums, University Finances. Hon. LLD (Cape Town) 1948; Hon. DSc (Witwatersrand) 1964; Hon. DSc (Natal) 1967; Corresponding Mem., Geological Soc. Amer., 1948, etc. *Publications:* Stratigraphical Geology of Africa South of the Sahara, 1962; Geological History of Southern Africa, 1969; numerous, on geol., palæontolog. and geograph. subjects, in learned jls; rev. and ed Geology of South Africa, by A. L. Du Toit (3rd edn), 1954. *Recreations:* music, reading, walking; formerly: cricket, hockey, tennis. *Address:* Private Bag 112, Pretoria, South Africa. *Club:* Country (Pretoria).

**HAUSER, Frank Ivor,** CBE 1968; Director of Productions, Meadow Players, Oxford Playhouse, since 1956; *b* 1 Aug. 1922; *s* of late Abraham and of Sarah Hauser; unmarried. *Educ:* Cardiff High Sch.; Christ Church, Oxford. Oxford, 1941-42; RA, 1942-45; Oxford, 1946-48. BBC Drama Producer, 1948-51; Director: Salisbury Arts Theatre, 1952-53; Midland Theatre Co., 1945-55. Formed Meadow Players Ltd, which re-opened the Oxford Playhouse, 1956; took Oxford Playhouse Co. on tour of India, Pakistan and Ceylon, 1959-60. Produced at Sadler's Wells Opera: La Traviata, 1961; Iolanthe, 1962; Orfeo, 1965; produced: at Oxford Playhouse: Antony and Cleopatra, 1965; Phèdre, 1966; The Promise, 1966; The Silent Woman, 1968; Pippa Passes, 1968; Uncle Vanya, 1969; Curtain Up, 1969; also: Il Matrimonio Segreto, Glyndebourne, 1965; A Heritage and its History, Phoenix, 1965; The Promise, Fortune, 1967; Volpone, Garrick, 1967; The Magic Flute, Sadler's Wells, 1967. *Recreation:* piano. *Address:* 5 Stirling Mansions, Canfield Gardens, NW6. *T:* 01-624 4690.

**HAVELOCK, Eric Henry Edwardes,** CB 1950; CBE 1943 (OBE 1936); Secretary, Development Commission, 1934-55; *b* 9 July 1891; *s* of late George Eric Havelock and Elizabeth Maria Caroline, *d* of late Lewis Nanney, Horne Hall, Co. Durham; *m* 1st, 1919, Christina Ramsay Scott (*d* 1958), *d* of late Alexander Moodie, Edinburgh; one *d*; 2nd, 1962. Eileen, *widow* of Maj.-Gen. W. R. Paul, CBE. *Educ:* Norfolk House Sch., Beaconsfield, Bucks; Highgate Sch.; Merton Coll., Oxford. BA 1918. War Refugees Cttee, 1914-15; Underground Rlys, 1915-16; Cabinet Reconstruction Cttee and Min. of Reconstruction, 1916-19 (private sec. to Sec.); Asst Sec., Develt Commn, 1919-34; Asst Sec., Agric. Research Council, 1931-34, Admin. Sec., 1934-50. Hon. Mem. Marine Biological Assoc.; Freshwater Biological Assoc.; Challenger Soc. for Promotion of Oceanography. Trustee, Rural Industries Bureau, retired 1968. FRSE 1945. Gold Palms of Order of Crown of Belgium, 1916. *Address:*

c/o Barclays Bank Ltd, 27 Regent Street, SW1.

**HAVELOCK, Sir Wilfrid (Bowen),** Kt 1963; *b* 14 April 1912; *s* of late Rev. E. W. Havelock and Helen (*née* Bowen); *m* 1938, Mrs M. E. Pershouse (*née* Vincent) (marriage dissolved, 1967); one *s*. *Educ:* Imperial Service Coll., Windsor, Berks. Elected to Kenya Legislative Council, 1948; Chairman, European Elected Members, 1952; Mem., Kenya Executive Council, 1952; Minister for Local Government, Kenya 1954; Minister for Agriculture, Kenya, 1962-63. *Address:* PO Box 154, Malindi, Kenya. *Clubs:* Lansdowne (London); Mombasa, Muthaiga Country (Kenya).

**HAVELOCK-ALLAN, Anthony James Allan;** film producer; *b* 28 Feb. 1905; *s* of Allan (2nd *s* of Sir Henry Havelock-Allan, 1st Bt, VC, GCB, MP), and Annie Julia, *d* of Sir William Chaytor, 3rd Bt; *m* 1939, Valerie Louis Hobson, *qv* (marr. diss. 1952), *d* of late Comdr Robert Gordon Hobson, RN; two *s*. *Educ:* Charterhouse; Switzerland. Entered films 1933. Produced: A Spot of Bother; This Man is News; Lightning Conductor; The Lambeth Walk, 1938; This Man in Paris; Silent Battle, 1939; Unpublished Story, 1941; Produced and directed, From the Four Corners; Associate Producer, In Which We Serve, 1943; Produced or co-produced: This Happy Breed; Blithe Spirit; Brief Encounter; Great Expectations; Take My Life; Blanche Fury; The Small Voice; The Interrupted Journey; Shadow of The Eagle; Never Take No for an Answer; Meet me Tonight; The Young Lovers; Orders to Kill, 1963; Produced and co-directed: An Evening with The Royal Ballet, 1965; Olivier's Othello, 1967; Zeffirelli's Romeo and Juliet, 1968. Director: British Home Entertainment Ltd; Constellation Films Ltd; Liger Films Ltd. Member: National Film Production Council, 1947-48; Cinematograph Films Council, 1948-51; Governor, British Film Institute, 1961-67; Twice Chairman, British Film Academy and Society of Film and Television Arts. *Recreations:* fishing, golf, travelling. *Address:* c/o Messrs Gorrie Whitson & Sons, 9 Cavendish Square, W1. *Club:* Royal Automobile Club.

*See also Sir Henry Havelock-Allan, Bt, Baron Gainford.*

**HAVELOCK-ALLAN, Sir Henry Ralph Moreton,** 3rd Bt, *cr* 1858; *b* 31 Aug. 1899; *s* of Allan Havelock-Allan (*d* 1949), (2nd *s* of 1st Bt) and of late Annie Julia, *d* of Sir William Chaytor, 3rd Bt; *S* uncle 1953. *Educ:* Sandroyd Sch.; Charterhouse. Formerly Lieut Scots Guards. *Heir:* *b* Anthony James Allan Havelock-Allan, *qv*. *Address:* c/o Lloyds Bank Ltd, Berkeley Square House, Berkeley Square, W1.

**HAVERGAL, Henry MacLeod,** OBE 1965; MA Oxon, BMus Edinburgh; Hon. DMus Edinburgh; FRCM; Hon. RAM; *b* 21 Feb. 1902; *er s* of Rev. Ernest Havergal; *m* 1st, 1926, Hyacinth (*d* 1962), *er d* of Arthur Chitty; two *s*; 2nd, 1964, Nina Davidson, Aberdeen. *Educ:* Choristers Sch., Salisbury; St Edward's Sch. and St John's Coll., Oxford. Dir of Music, Fettes Coll., Edinburgh, 1924-33; Haileybury Coll., 1934-36; Harrow Sch., 1937-45; Master of Music, Winchester Coll., 1946-53; Principal, Royal Scottish Academy of Music (later Royal Scottish Academy of Music and Drama), 1953-69. Hon. LLD Glasgow, 1969. *Recreation:* fishing. *Address:* 2 Bellevue Terrace, Edinburgh 7. *Club:* Oxford and Cambridge University; New (Edinburgh).

**HAVERS, Sir Cecil (Robert),** Kt 1951; QC 1939; retired as Judge of the High Court of Justice, 1967 (Probate, Divorce and Admiralty Division, 1951-52; Queen's Bench Division, 1952-67); *b* 12 Nov. 1889; *s* of Daniel Havers and Agnes Buckingham; *m* 1916, Enid F. O. Snelling (*d* 1956); three *s* one *d*. *Educ:* Norwich Grammar Sch.; Corpus Christi Coll., Cambridge. Classical Scholar, Corpus Christi Coll., 1909, BA (Hons) Classics, 1912, LLB (Hons), 1913; MA; served European War, 1914-19, Capt. 5th Hants RTF and Tank Corps (despatches); Recorder of Chichester, 1939-51; Commissioner in Gold Coast, 1944-45; HM Commissioner of Assize, Oxford and Midland Circuits, 1949; called to Bar, Inner Temple, 1920, Certificate of Honour; Bencher, Inner Temple, 1946. *Publication:* Landlord and Tenant Act, 1927, 1928. *Recreations:* lawn tennis, golf. *Address:* 8 Lichfield Road, Kew Gardens, Surrey. *T:* 01-940 2658. *Clubs:* United University, Garrick.

*See also R. M. O. Havers.*

**HAVERS, Air Vice-Marshal Sir E. William,** KBE 1946 (CBE 1941); CB 1944; *b* 15 Oct. 1887; *m* 1920, Blanche Mary Somerville Macey (*d* 1968); one *s* one *d*; *m* 1970, Mary Elizabeth Ritchie. Served European War, RFC, 1915-19, France (despatches); Air Ministry, Industrial Whitley Council, 1921-23; Iraq, 1923-25; Coastal Command, 1926-28; RAF Staff Coll., 1929; Senior Equipment Staff Officer Air Defences, Great Britain, 1930-32; HQ Middle East, Egypt, 1932-34; Dir-Gen. of Equipment, Air Ministry, 1940-42; AOC No. 40 Group, RAF, 1943-46; retired 1946; Govt Missions in Middle East, HQ Cairo, 1946-48; Consultant to Ministry of Supply, 1952-53. District Comr S Wight Scouts, 1950-55. *Address:* Tenter Lodge, Waterside, Knaresborough, Yorks. *T:* Knaresborough 2312. *Club:* Royal Automobile.

**HAVERS, Michael;** *see* Havers, R. M. O.

**HAVERS, (Robert) Michael (Oldfield),** QC 1964; MP (C) Wimbledon, since 1970; Barrister-at-Law; Recorder of Norwich, since 1968; Chancellor of the Diocese of St Edmundsbury and Ipswich, since 1965; Chancellor of the Diocese of Ely, since 1969; *b* 10 March 1923; 2nd *s* of Sir Cecil Havers, *qv*; *m* 1949, Carol Elizabeth, *d* of Stuart Lay, London; two *s*. *Educ:* Westminster Sch.; Corpus Christi Coll., Cambridge. Lieut RNVR, 1941-46. Called to Bar, Inner Temple, 1948; Recorder of Dover, 1962-68. Chm., West Suffolk Quarter Sessions (Dep. Chairman 1961-65). Chm., Lakenheath Anglo-American Community Relations Cttee, 1966-. *Recreations:* golf, photography, reading. *Address:* 2 Dr Johnson's Buildings, Temple, EC4. *T:* 01-583 2583; White Shutters, Ousden, Newmarket. *T:* Ousden 267. *Clubs:* Garrick, Royal Automobile; Norfolk (Norwich).

**HAVILAND, Denis William Garstin Latimer,** CB 1957; Chairman and Managing Director, Staveley Industries Ltd, 1965-69 (Joint Managing Director and Deputy Chairman, 1964); *b* 15 Aug. 1910; *s* of late William Alexander Haviland and of Edyth Louise Latimer. *Educ:* Rugby Sch., St John's Coll., Cambridge (MA, exam. of AMInstT). LMS Rly, 1934-39. Army, RE (Col), 1940-46. Prin., Control Office for Germany and Austria, 1946; Asst Sec., 1947; transf. FO (GS), 1947; seconded to IDC, 1950; transf. Min. of Supply, 1951; Under Sec., 1953; Deputy Sec., 1959; trans. Min. of Aviation, 1959, deputy Sec., 1959-64. Director: Short Bros & Harland Ltd; Wheelabrator Corp. of Mishawaka, USA. Member Council: CBI, BIM. *Address:* 113 Hampstead Way, NW11. *T:* 01-455 2638. *Clubs:* Bath, St James'.

**HAVILLAND;** *see* de Havilland.

**HAVINDEN, Ashley Eldrid,** OBE 1951; RDI 1947; FSIA; Hon. DA Manchester, 1961; Designer, Typographer, Painter, signs work Ashley; Master of Faculty of Royal Designers for Industry, 1967-69; Director, W. S. Crawford Ltd, Advertising Agents, 1929-67 (joined 1922); Director, Design International Ltd, Industrial Research and Design, 1949-67; *b* 13 April 1903; *s* of G. E. Havinden and Nellie, *d* of J. Latter; *m* 1928, Margaret Kirk, *d* of John Sangster; one *s* one *d*. *Educ:* Christ's Hospital. Held retrospective exhibition of posters and advertisement designs at Lund, Humphries Gallery, 1937; work included in Exhibitions in Paris (Union des Artistes Moderne, 1933; French Pavillon de Publicité, Paris Exposition, 1937) and USA; Mem. Display Cttee for British Pavilion, Paris Exhibition, 1937; Fellow of Soc. of Industrial Artists, 1946 (Mem. of Council, 1946-47; Pres. 1953); NRD; Fellow of Central Institute of Art and Design, FRSA, Fellow of Institute of Practitioners in Advertising; President: Advertising Creative Circle, 1955 (Hon. Mem., 1966); The Double Crown Club, 1956; Président D'Honneur (Prés., 1957-59), Alliance Graphique Internationale; Gov. London Coll. of Printing, 1950-67 (Chm., 1955-56, 1958-59); Visitor Graphic Sch. of Royal College of Art, 1955-57. Gov. The Central Sch. of Arts and Crafts, 1959-67; Mem. Advisory Cttee, the new Sch. of Art at Chelsea, 1958-65. Governor, 1965-67. First one-man exhibition of paintings at The London Gallery, 1937; paintings also represented in Exhibitions at Reid and Lefevre Gallery, 1939, and Leicester Galleries, 1939, Marlborough Fine Arts, 1965; one-man exhibition of Rugs and Fabrics at Duncan Miller Gallery, 1937; Designer of Men's Wear Section for Council of Industrial Design Exhibition, Britain Can Make It, Victoria and Albert Museum, 1946. Textiles and Rugs represented in Exhibitions in London, Paris, and San Francisco. Exhibited posters and advertising designs in National Museum, Stockholm, 1952; AGI Exhibitions, Louvre, Paris, 1955; RBA Gallery, London, 1956; Lausanne, 1957; Milan, 1961; Amsterdam, 1962; Hamburg, 1964; New York 1966. Served in War of 1939-45 Capt., Staff Officer, Camouflage. *Publications:* Line Drawing for Reproduction, 1933, revised edn, 1941; Advertising and the Artist, 1956; numerous articles on Industrial Art and allied subjects. *Address:* Roxford, Hertingfordbury, Herts. *T:* Hertford 2151. *Clubs:* Arts, Garrick.

**HAWARDEN,** 8th Viscount, *cr* 1791; **Robert Leslie Eustace Maude;** farming his own estate since 1952; *b* 26 March 1926; *s* of 7th Viscount Hawarden and of Viscountess Hawarden (*née* Marion Wright); *S* father 1958; *m* 1957, Susannah Caroline Hyde Gardner; two *s* one *d*. *Educ:* Winchester; Christ Church, Oxford. Cirencester Agricultural Coll., 1948-50. Served for a short time in the Coldstream Guards and was invalided out, 1945-46. *Recreation:* shooting. *Heir:* *s* Hon. Robert Connan Wyndham Leslie Maude, *b* 23 May 1961. *Address:* Wingham Court, near Canterbury, Kent. *T:* Wingham 222. *Club:* Guards.

**HAWES, Derrick Gordon H.;** *see* Harington Hawes.

**HAWES, Maj.-Gen. Leonard Arthur,** CBE 1940; DSO 1918; MC; MA (Hon.) Oxon; Royal Artillery; *b* Throcking, Herts, 22 July 1892; *s* of C. A. Hawes, Uckfield, Sussex; *m* 1919, Gwendolen Mary (*d* 1970), *d* of D. H. Grimsdale, JP, Uxbridge, Middlesex; one *d* (one *s* decd). *Educ:* Bedford; RM Academy, Woolwich. Lieut Royal Garrison Artillery, 1911; Capt., 1916; Temp. Major, 1917; Major, 1929; Bt Lieut-Col 1932; Lieut-Col and Col 1938; served European War, 1914-18 (wounded, DSO, MC, despatches, Order of Crown of Italy); served War of 1939-45; retired pay, 1945. *Address:* Old Manor House, West Harting, Petersfield, Hants. *Club:* Army and Navy.

**HAWGOOD, John Arkas;** Professor of American History, University of Birmingham, since 1964 (of Modern History, 1945-64, and of Government, 1945-58); *b* Brighton, Sussex, 20 Nov. 1905; *m* 1927, Alison, *d* of late Rev. J. H. Bowker; four *s* one *d*. *Educ:* Leyton Sch.; University Coll., London (Andrews Scholar, Pollard Prize); Universities of Heidelberg, Vienna, Yale, Wisconsin, etc. BA (London) 1st class hons in history, 1926; MA 1928; DLit 1944; PhD (Heidelberg) in Political Science and Sociology, 1928; MCom (Birmingham) *ex officio*, 1946; Anglo-German Exchange Scholar, Heidelberg, 1926-27; Hon. Hilfslektor, Univ. of Vienna, 1927-28; Research Fellow in the Social Sciences of Rockefeller Foundation, in Austria and Germany, 1927-28, and in the USA, 1928-29 and 1934-35. Asst Lectr in History, University Coll., London, 1929-31; Reader in Modern History, University of Birmingham, 1931-45. Seconded for service under Foreign Office, 1939-45 (Head of German Section, Foreign Research and Press Service, 1939-40; with Political Intelligence Dept, 1940-43; with Political Warfare Executive, 1943-45); Dir, Europa Publications, Ltd, 1945-68. Research Associate, Hoover Inst., Stanford Univ., 1950; Consultant, Library of Congress, 1952 and 1960; Mem. Council European Assoc. for American Studies, 1954-, Council International Political Science Assoc., 1955-58; Resident Fellow, Newberry Library, Chicago, 1956; Vis. Prof., Univ. of Kansas, 1969. First Alfred A. Knopf Western History Prize, 1966; Western Heritage and Western Writers of America Non-Fiction Awards, 1967. *Publications:* Political and Economic Relations between the USA and the German Provisional Central Government at Frankfurt-am-Main in 1848-49, 1928; Modern Constitutions since 1787, 1939; The Tragedy of German-America, 1940, repr. 1970; The Citizen and Government, 1947; The Evolution of Germany, 1955; First and Last Consul (T. O. Larkin and the Americanization of California), 1962, 2nd edn 1970; The American West (US title America's Western Frontiers), 1967, etc.; contrib. to Chambers's, Collier's and other Encyclopædias. *Address:* The University of Birmingham, PO Box 363, Birmingham 15; Court Place, Old Marston, Oxford OX3 0PQ. *T:* Oxford 41198.

**HAWKE,** family name of **Baron Hawke.**

**HAWKE,** 9th Baron, *cr* 1776, of Towton; **Bladen Wilmer Hawke;** *b* 31 Dec. 1901; *s* of 8th Baron and late Frances Alice, *d* of Col J. R. Wilmer, Survey of India; *S* father 1939; *m* 1934, Ina Mary, *e d* of late Henry Faure Walker, Highley Manor, Balcombe, Sussex; seven *d*. *Educ:* Winchester; King's Coll., Cambridge (MA). Bombay Company, India, 1923-38; Temp. Civil Servant, Ministry of Economic Warfare, 1940-43, War Office, 1943-45. Lord-in-Waiting to the Queen and Government Whip, House of Lords, 1953-57. Chm. Conservative Back Bench Peers Assoc., 1949-53; Executive Cttee, National Union Conservatives, 1950-53; Mem., House of Laity, Church Assembly, 1955; Church Commissioner, 1958; Chm., Chichester Diocesan Board of Finance. Chm., Rhodesia Fairbridge Scholarship Fund. Director: Initial Services Ltd; Ecclesiastical Insurance Office, Ltd. *Recreations:* golf, gardening. *Heir:* b Squadron Leader Hon. (Julian Stanhope) Theodore Hawke, Auxiliary Air Force [*b* 1904; *m* 1st, 1933, Angela Margaret Griselda (marriage dissolved, 1946), *d* of late Capt. Edmund W. Bury; two *d*; 2nd, 1947, Georgette Margaret, *d* of George S. Davidson; one *s* three *d*]. *Address:* Faygate Place, Faygate, Sussex. *T:* Faygate 252. *Club:* Carlton.

**HAWKER, Albert Henry,** CMG 1964; OBE 1960; a Director, The Thomson Organisation, since 1969; *b* 31 Oct. 1911; *s* of late H. J. Hawker, Cheltenham and of Mrs G. A. Hawker, Exeter; *m* 1944, Margaret Janet Olivia, *d* of late T. J. C. Acton (ICS) and of Mrs M de C. Acton, BEM, Golden Furlong, Brackley, Northants; two *s*. *Educ:* Pate's Sch., Cheltenham. Served War of 1939-45: Bde Major 12th Bde, 1941-43; Staff Coll., Camberley, 1943-44; Lieut-Col Mil. Asst to CGS in India, 1944-46. RARO; Lieut-Col The Gordon Highlanders, 1946-61. Barclays Bank Ltd, Birmingham and Oxford Local Districts, 1929-39. Joined HM Overseas Civil Service, 1946; served in: Palestine, 1946-48; N Rhodesia, 1948-52; Zanzibar, 1952-64 (Development Sec., Admin. Sec., Perm. Sec. in Min. of Finance, Prime Minister's Office, Vice-President's Office and President's Office); retd, 1964. Director: Thomson Regional Newspapers Ltd, 1965-69; The Times Ltd and The Sunday Times Ltd, 1968-69. Gold Cross, Royal Order of George I of Greece, 1948; Brilliant Star of Zanzibar, 1957. *Recreations:* sailing, cricket, tennis, golf, photography (Cdre, Zanzibar Sailing Club, 1955 and 1961). *Address:* (business) 200 Gray's Inn Road, WC1. *T:* 01-837 1234; Bowling Green Farm, Cottered, near Buntingford, Herts. *T:* Cottered 234. *Clubs:* East India and Sports, Royal Commonwealth Society, Royal Yachting Association.

**HAWKER, Sir Cyril;** *see* Hawker, Sir F. C.

**HAWKER, Sir (Frank) Cyril,** Kt 1958; Chairman: The Standard Bank Ltd, 1962-69, Standard and Chartered Banking Group, since 1969; The Bank of West Africa, since 1965; Director, Head Wrightson & Co. Ltd, since 1962; Deputy-Chairman: Agricultural Mortgage Corporation, since 1964 (Director, since 1962); Midland and International Banks, since 1969; Chairman, Finance Committee, National Playing Fields Association; *b* 21 July 1900; *s* of late Frank Charley and Bertha Mary Hawker; *m* 1931, Marjorie Ann, *d* of late Thomas Henry and Amelia Harriett Pearce; three *d*. *Educ:* City of London Sch. Entered service Bank of England, 1920; Dep. Chief Cashier, 1944-48; Chief Accountant, 1948-53; Adviser to Governors, 1953-54; Executive Director, Bank of England, 1954-62. High Sheriff of County of London, 1963. President, MCC, 1970. *Recreation:* cricket. *Address:* The Standard Bank Ltd, 10 Clements Lane, EC4. *T:* 01-623 7500; Pounsley Lodge, Blackboys, near Uckfield, Sussex. *T:* Hadlow Down 250. *Clubs:* Athenæum, MCC.

**HAWKER, Sir Richard (George),** Kt 1965; MA Cantab; *b* 11 April 1907; *s* of late R. M. Hawker; *m* 1940, Frances C., *d* of late S. Rymill; two *s* two *d* (and one *s* decd). *Educ:* Geelong Grammar Sch.; Trinity Hall, Cambridge. Returned SA, 1929; took over management Bungaree Merino Stud, 1932. Mem. Blyth Dist Coun., 1936-42, 1946-. War service: 9/23 Light Horse Regt, 1939-41; 1st Armoured Div., AIF, 1941-44. Member: Cttee SA Stud Merino Breeders Assoc., 1939-40, 1959- (Pres. 1962-63, 1963-64); Council, Aust. Assoc. of Stud Merino Breeders, 1962- (Pres., 1968-); Australian Wool Industry Conf., 1963-65 (as nominee of Federal Graziers' Council). Chm., Roseworthy Agricultural Coll. Council, 1964-. Director: Adelaide Steamship Co. Ltd, 1949 (Chm. 1952-); Coast Steamship Co., 1949 (Chm. 1952-); SA Tug Co., 1949 (Chm. 1952-); Coal & Allied Industries, NSW, 1961-; Waratah Tug & Salvage Co., NSW, 1963-; Associated Steamships Pty Ltd, 1963-; (local bd in SA) Queensland Insurance Co. Ltd, 1955-. *Recreations:* shooting, fishing. *Address:* Bungaree, Brinkworth, S Australia 5464, Australia. *T:* Clare 2676. *Clubs:* Bath, Oriental; Australian (Sydney); Adelaide (SA).

**HAWKES, (Charles Francis) Christopher;** Professor of European Archaeology in the University of Oxford since 1946; Fellow of Keble College since 1946; Secretary, Committee of Research Laboratory for Archæology and History of Art, since 1955; *b* 5 June 1905; *o s* of late Charles Pascoe Hawkes; *m* 1st, 1933, Jacquetta (from whom he obtained a divorce 1953) (*see* Jacquetta Hawkes), *yr d* of late Sir Frederick Gowland Hopkins, OM; one *s*; 2nd, 1959, Sonia Elizabeth, *o d* of Albert Andrew Chadwick. *Educ:* Winchester Coll. (Scholar); New Coll. Oxford (Scholar). 1st in Classical Hon. Mods 1926, in Final Lit. Hum. 1928; BA 1928; MA 1931; entered British Museum, Dept. of British and Medieval Antiquities, 1928; Asst Keeper 1st Class, 1938; in charge of Prehistoric and Romano-British Antiquities, 1946. Principal in Ministry of Aircraft Production, 1940-45. Retired from British Museum, 1946. I/c Inst. of Archæology, 1961-67. FBA, 1948; FSA 1932; Fellow of Royal Archæological Institute, Hon. Sec. 1930-35, and Hon. Editor of Archæological Journal, 1944-50; Pres. Prehistoric Soc., 1950-54; a National Sec. for Great Britain, 1931-48, and Mem. of Permanent Council since 1948, International Congress (since 1958 Union) of Prehistoric and Protohistoric Sciences; Hon. Sec. of Colchester Excavation Cttee and in joint charge of its excavations, 1930-62; in charge of excavations elsewhere variously since 1926, on Romano-British and prehistoric sites, especially in Hants for the Hants Field Club; conducted archæological expedns in N Portugal, 1958-59. Dalrymple Lectures, University of Glasgow, 1948; George Grant McCurdy Lecturer, Harvard Univ., 1953; travelled in Europe as Leverhulme Research Fellow, 1955-58 a Visitor, Ashmolean Museum, 1961-67. President: Section H., Brit. Assoc., 1957; Hants Field Club, 1960-63; Member: Council for British Archæology 1944- (Pres., 1961-64; Group 9 Convener, 1964-67); Ancient Monuments Board for England, 1954-69. Editor of *Inventaria Archæologia* for Great Britain, 1954-. Various British Acad. awards, 1963-. *Publications:* St Catharine's Hill, Winchester (with J. N. L. Myres and C. G. Stevens), 1931; Archæology in England and Wales, 1914-31 (with T. D. Kendrick), 1932; Winchester College: An Essay in Description and Appreciation, 1933; The Prehistoric Foundations of Europe, 1940; Prehistoric Britain (with Jacquetta Hawkes), 1943, 1947, 1957; Camulodunum: The Excavations at Colchester, 1930-39 (with M. R. Hull), 1947; articles in encyclopædias, collaborative books, and many archæological journals. *Recreations:* archæology, travelling, music, the theatre. *Address:* Institute of Archæology, 35 Beaumont Street, Oxford; Keble College, Oxford; 19 Walton Street, Oxford. *Club:* Oxford and Cambridge.

**HAWKES, Christopher;** *see* Hawkes, C. F. C.

**HAWKES, Prof. David,** MA, DPhil; Professor of Chinese, Oxford University, since Oct. 1959; *b* 6 July 1923; *s* of Ewart Hawkes and Dorothy May Hawkes (*née* Davis); *m* 1950, Sylvia Jean

Perkins; one *s* three *d. Educ:* Bancroft's Sch. Open Scholarship in Classics, Christ Church, Oxford, 1941; Chinese Hons Sch., Oxford, 1945-47; Research Student, National Peking Univ., 1948-51. Formerly University Lecturer in Chinese, Oxford. Visiting Lecturer in Chinese Literature, Harvard Univ., 1958-59. *Publications:* Ch'u Tz'ŭ, Songs of the South, 1959; A Little Primer of Tu Fu, 1967.

**HAWKES, Frederic Clare,** CBE 1957; *b* 25 Sept. 1892; *er s* of late F. J. Hawkes, London; *m* 1st, 1921, Erica Heinrich (*d* 1932); no *c*; 2nd, 1938, Phyllis Elizabeth Watson; two *s* one *d. Educ:* St Paul's Sch.; Merton Coll., Oxford (MA); Clare Coll., Cambridge (MA by incorporation). Served European War, 1915-19. Min. of Agriculture and Fisheries, 1919-21. Sec., 1920-33, and Asst Dir, 1925-33, of National Inst. of Agricultural Botany, Cambridge. Sec. of Wheat Commission, 1933-37; Sec. of Chartered Auctioneers' and Estate Agents' Institute, 1938-57, Hon. Fellow, 1957-70. Pres. of the College of Estate Management, 1957-58. Master, Worshipful Company of Farmers, 1959-60. Hon. Mem. RICS, 1970-. *Address:* Martin Cottage, West Wittering, Chichester, Sussex. *T:* West Wittering 2057. *Club:* United University.

**HAWKES, Jacquetta,** OBE 1952; author and archaeologist; *b* 1910; *yr d* of Sir Frederick Gowland Hopkins, OM and Jessie Anne Stephens; *m* 1st, 1933, Christopher Hawkes (*see* Prof. C. F. C. Hawkes) (marr. diss., 1953); one *s*; 2nd, 1953, J. B. Priestley, *qv. Educ:* Perse Sch.; Newnham Coll., Cambridge. MA. Associate, Newnham Coll., 1951. Research and excavation in Great Britain, Eire, France and Palestine, 1931-40; FSA, 1940. Asst Principal, Post-War Reconstruction Secretariat, 1941-43; Ministry of Education, becoming established Principal and Sec. of UK National Commn for UNESCO, 1943-49; retired from Civil Service to write, 1949. Vice-Pres. Council for Brit. Archæology, 1949-52; Gov. Brit. Film Inst., 1950-55. Archæological adviser, Festival of Britain, 1949-51. Mem., UNESCO Culture Advisory Cttee, 1966. *Publications:* Archæology of Jersey, 1939; Prehistoric Britain (with Christopher Hawkes), 1944; Early Britain, 1945; Symbols and Speculations (poems), 1948; A Land, 1951 (£100 Kemsley Award); Guide to Prehistoric and Roman Monuments in England and Wales, 1951; Dragon's Mouth, (play) (with J. B. Priestley); Fables, 1953; Man on Earth, 1954; Journey Down a Rainbow (with J. B. Priestley), 1955; Providence Island, 1959; Man and the Sun, 1962; Unesco History of Mankind, Vol. I, Part 1, 1963; The World of the Past, 1963; King of the Two Lands, 1966; The Dawn of the Gods, 1968. Contrib. learned jls and national periodicals. *Recreation:* natural history. *Address:* Kissing Tree House, Alveston, Stratford-on-Avon, Warwicks; B3 Albany, W1.

**HAWKES, Prof. Leonard,** FRS 1952; Head of Department of Geology, Bedford College, 1921-56; Professor Emeritus since 1956; *b* 6 Aug. 1891; *s* of Rev. Philip Hawkes; *m* 1926, Hilda Kathleen, *d* of late L. V. Cargill; one *s*. *Educ:* Armstrong Coll.; Kristiania Univ. 1851 Exhibitioner, 1914. Served European War, 1914-18, Capt. RAMC, 1917-19 (despatches). Lecturer in Geology, Armstrong Coll., 1919-21. Sec., Geological Soc. of London, 1934-42 (Pres., 1956-58); Pres. Mineralogical Soc., 1954-57. Murchison Medallist, 1946. Wollaston Medallist, 1962. Geol. Soc. of London. *Publications:* papers dealing with geology of Iceland. *Address:* 26 Moor Lane, Rickmansworth, Herts. *T:* Rickmansworth 72955.

**HAWKEY, Rt. Rev. Ernest Eric;** *see* Carpentaria, Bishop of.

**HAWKEY, Sir Roger (Pryce),** 2nd Bt, *cr* 1945 of Woodford; Company Director; *b* 25 June 1905; *o s* of Sir James Hawkey, 1st Bt, and Vera Kathleen (*d* 1949), *d* of late F. E. Price; *S* father 1952; *m* 1st, 1931, Julia Elizabeth Austin; one *d*; 2nd, 1947, Mabel Dorothy, *d* of Sir Thomas McConnell, CBE, MP, of Belfast. *Educ:* Chigwell Sch. Served War of 1939-45, with RN; Lieut-Comdr, RNVR. *Heir:* none. *Address:* Great Coopers, Takeley, Essex. *T:* Takeley 362. *Club:* MCC.

**HAWKINS, Arthur (Ernest),** BSc (Eng), FIMechE, FIEE; Member, Central Electricity Generating Board, since 1970; Midlands Regional Director (CEGB) since 1964; *b* 10 June 1913; *s* of Rev. H. R. and Louisa Hawkins; *m* 1939, Laura Judith Tallent Draper; one *s* two *d. Educ:* The Grammar Sch., Gt Yarmouth; City of Norwich Technical Coll. Served (prior to nationalisation) with Gt Yarmouth Electricity Dept, Central Electricity Bd and Islington Electricity Dept (Dep. Engr and Gen. Manager); Croydon Dist Manager of SE Elec. Bd, 1948; joined Brit. Electricity Authority as Chief Asst Engr in System Operation Br., 1951; Personal Engrg Asst to Chief Engr, 1954. He has been with the CEGB since its formation in 1957, at first as System Planning Engr and then as Chief Ops Engr, 1959-64. *Publications:* contrib. Jl of Management Studies; various papers to technical instns. *Recreations:* fell walking, swimming, motoring. *Address:* 61 Rowan Road, W6. *T:* 01-603 2849. *Club:* Royal Automobile.

**HAWKINS, Clive David B.;** *see* Black-Hawkins.

**HAWKINS, Desmond,** OBE 1963; BBC Controller, South and West, 1967-69; *b* 1908; *m* Barbara Hawkins (*née* Skidmore); two *s* two *d*. Novelist, critic and broadcaster, 1935-39; Literary Editor of New English Weekly and Purpose Quarterly; Fiction Chronicler of The Criterion; Features Producer, BBC West Region, 1946; Head of Programmes, 1955; founded BBC Natural History Unit, 1959. Silver Medal, RSPB, 1959. *Publications:* Poetry and Prose of John Donne, 1938; Hawk among the Sparrows, 1939; Stories, Essays and Poems of D. H. Lawrence, 1939; Lighter than Day, 1940; War Report, 1946; Sedgmoor and Avalon, 1954; The BBC Naturalist, 1957; Hardy the Novelist, 1965. *Address:* Pinehurst, Verwood, Dorset. *T:* Verwood 2479. *Clubs:* BBC; Christchurch Sailing.

**HAWKINS, Air Vice-Marshal Desmond Ernest,** CBE 1967; DFC and Bar, 1942; Senior Air Staff Officer, Headquarters RAF Strike Command, RAF, since 1969; *b* 27 Dec. 1919; *s* of Ernest and Lilian Hawkins; *m* 1947, Joan Audrey (*née* Munro); one *s. Educ:* Bancroft Sch. Commissioned in RAF, 1938. Served War of 1939-45: Coastal Command and Far East, commanding 36, 230 and 240 Sqdns, 1940-46 (despatches). Commanded RAF Pembroke Dock, 1946-47 (despatches). Staff appts, 1947-50; RAF Staff Coll., 1950; Staff appts, 1951-55; commanded 38 Sqdn, OC Flg, RAF Luqa, 1955-57; jssc, 1957; Staff appts, 1958-61; SASO 19 Gp, 1961-63; commanded RAF Tengah, 1963-66; idc 1967; commanded RAF Lyneham, 1968. *Recreations:* sailing (Commodore RAFSA), fishing. *Address:* c/o Barclays Bank, Bridgwater, Somerset. *Clubs:* Royal Air Force, Royal Commonwealth Society, Cruising Association.

**HAWKINS, Frank Ernest;** Chairman and Managing Director, International Stores Ltd,

Mitre Square, EC3; *b* 12 Aug. 1904; 2nd *s* of late George William and late Sophie Hawkins; *m* 1933, Muriel, *d* of late Joseph and Isabella Sinclair; two *s* one *d*. *Educ:* Leyton County High Sch. Joined staff of International Stores Ltd as boy clerk, 1919; apptd: Asst Sec., 1934; Sec., 1935; Director, 1949; Managing Dir, 1956; Vice-Chm., 1958; Chairman, 1959. *Recreation:* golf. *Address:* Merton Court, Page's Croft, Wokingham, Berkshire. *Clubs:* City Livery; East Berkshire Golf.

**HAWKINS, Adm. Sir Geoffrey Alan Brooke,** KBE *cr* 1952; CB 1949; MVO 1925; DSC 1917; *b* 13 July 1895; *e s* of late Capt. Hawkins, St Fentons, Baldoyle, Co. Dublin; *m* 1926, Lady Margaret Scott, *d* of 7th Duke of Buccleuch; one *s* two *d*. *Educ:* Royal Naval Colls, Osborne and Dartmouth. Served European War, 1914-18 (DSC); War of 1939-45 (despatches). ADC to Governor-Gen. of South Africa, 1924-27; attached to staff of Prince of Wales, S African tour, 1925. Flag Officer, Malta, 1950-52; retired list, 1952. Attached to staff of Princess Royal, WI tour, 1960 and 1962. *Address:* Grafton Underwood, Kettering. *T:* Cranford 245. *Club:* White's.

**HAWKINS, Maj.-Gen. George Ledsam Seymour,** CB 1943; MC; Indian Army, retired; *b* 13 May 1898; *s* of G. L. S. Hawkins, Apton Hall, Rochford, Essex; *m* 1921, Katharine Marian (*d* 1957), *d* of George Hancock, Templecombe, Somerset; one *s* one *d*. Served European War, RFA (MC). Indian Army, 1923; Comdt IAOC Sch., India, 1928-33; ADOS India, 1936-37; Ordnance Consulting Officer, 1937-41; retired, 1945. Col Comdt, IAOC, 1945-56. *Address:* Apton, Upper Basildon, Berks.

**HAWKINS, Sir Humphry (Villiers) Caesar,** 7th Bt, *cr* 1778; MB, ChB; Medical Practitioner; *b* 10 Aug. 1923; *s* of Sir Villiers Geoffry Caesar Hawkins, 6th Bt and Blanche Hawkins, *d* of A. E. Hampden-Smithers; *S* father 1955; *m* 1952, Anita, *d* of C. H. Funkey, Johannesburg; two *s* three *d*. *Educ:* Hilton Coll.; University of Witwatersrand. Served War of 1939-45 with 6th SA Armoured Div. *Heir: s* Howard Cæsar Hawkins, *b* 17 Nov. 1956. *Address:* 41 Hume Road, Dunkeld, Johannesburg, S Africa. *Club:* Johannesburg Country.

**HAWKINS, Jack,** CBE 1958; actor and producer; *b* 14 Sept. 1910; *s* of Thomas George Hawkins and Phoebe Goodman; *m* 1st, 1932, Jessica Tandy; one *d*; 2nd, 1947, Doreen Lawrence; two *s* one *d*. *Educ:* Trinity County Sch., Mddx. Studied with Italia Conti; first appearance on stage, Dec. 1923; subsequently appeared regularly in the Theatre and Films in London and New York until War of 1939-45. Joined Royal Welch Fusiliers, 1940; served with 2nd Div. in India and Burma; demobilised, 1946, with Hon. rank of Col; reappeared in the Theatre and Films, 1947. Mem. Bd of Governors, London Independent Television Producers Ltd, 1963. *Films include:* The Cruel Sea, Man in the Sky, The Long Arm, Bridge on the River Kwai, Ben Hur, League of Gentlemen, Lawrence of Arabia, Lord Jim, Guns at Batasi, La Fayette, Masquerade, Great Catherine, Shalako, Battle of Waterloo. *Recreations:* music, riding and fishing. *Address:* Westmead Lodge, Westmead, Roehampton, SW15. *Clubs:* Garrick, Royal Automobile.

**HAWKINS, Leonard Cecil,** CBE 1962; *b* 23 April 1897; 2nd *s* of late Fred and Martha Hawkins, Churchill, Somerset; *m* 1926, Janet Grace Seager; one *s*. After service with BEF in France (31/10th Royal Fusiliers) joined staff of City firm of chartered accountants, 1918-29; admitted Incorporated Accountant (hons), 1925; Fellow, 1944; Mem. Coun., 1947; CA and Mem. Coun. Inst. of Chartered Accts in England and Wales, 1957-62; joined Underground Railways and London Gen. Omnibus Co., 1929; Asst Comptroller, London Passenger Transport Bd, 1933; Comptroller, 1940-47; concurrently Joint Gen. Man., London Aircraft Production, 1943-45; full time Mem., London Transport Exec., 1947-62; Mem., National Incomes Commn, 1962-65. Chm. Transport Commission of Inquiry, Singapore, 1955; Leader, UK Advisory Mission under Colombo Plan to advise Ceylon Govt on reorganisation of Ceylon's omnibus services, 1957; an Hon. Adviser, Admin. Staff Coll., 1949-59. OStJ 1962. *Publications:* Accountancy in a Large-Scale Industrial Undertaking, 1947; Financial Control in Industry, 1950; Measurements of Efficiency, 1950; Mass Transportation in the Future, 1961, etc. *Address:* 29 Clarence Road North, Weston-super-Mare, Somerset. *T:* 983. *Clubs:* Weston-super-Mare; Royal Mid-Surrey Golf.

**HAWKINS, Sir Michael Babington Charles,** KCVO 1968 (CVO 1960; MVO 1951); MBE 1944; Private Secretary to the Duke of Gloucester since 1958 (Asst Private Secretary and Equerry, 1948-57); *b* 27 July 1914; *s* of L. G. Hawkins, West Bilney Hall, Norfolk; *m* 1947, Virginia Anne, *d* of Gp Capt. Noel Heath, Sydney, Aust.; one *d*. *Educ:* Cheltenham Coll. Solicitor, Supreme Court, 1935. Served 10th Royal Hussars; Western Desert, 1940-42; Hqrs Allied Armies, Sicily and Italy, 1942-44. ADC to Gov.-Gen. of Australia, 1945-47. Director: Samuel Dobie of Chester Ltd; Carters Tested Seeds Ltd; Laxton and Bunyard Ltd. Dep. Chm., British Boys Movement for Australia. Mem. Council, Royal Over-Seas League. Governor, Royal Nat. Orthopaedic Hosp. Order of Dannebrog, 1948. *Recreations:* fishing, gardening. *Address:* Weston Patrick House, near Basingstoke, Hants. *T:* Long Sutton 396; Engine Court, St James's Palace, SW1. *T:* 01-930 0242. *Clubs:* Cavalry, Pratt's.

**HAWKINS, Paul Lancelot,** TD 1945; JP; MP (C) South West Norfolk since 1964; an Assistant Government Whip, since 1970; Principal in firm of Chartered Surveyors in Rural practice; *b* 7 Aug. 1912; *s* of L. G. Hawkins and of Mrs Hawkins (*née* Peile); *m* 1937, E. Joan Snow; two *s* one *d*. *Educ:* Cheltenham Coll. Joined Family Firm, 1930; Chartered Surveyor, 1933. Served in TA, Royal Norfolk Regt, 1933-45; POW Germany, 1940-45. CC Norfolk, 1949-, Alderman, 1968; JP Norfolk. *Recreations:* tennis, riding, gardening, travel. *Address:* Stables, Downham Market, Norfolk. *T:* Downham Market 2117. *Club:* Carlton.

**HAWKINS, Rt. Rev. Ralph Gordon;** *see* Bunbury, Bishop of.

**HAWKINS, Vice-Adm. Sir Raymond (Shayle),** KCB 1965 (CB 1963); Director of Engineering, English Electric Diesels Ltd, since 1968; *b* 21 Dec. 1909; *s* of late Thomas Hawkins and Dorothy Hawkins, Bedford; *m* 1936, Rosalind, *d* of late Roger and Ada Ingpen; three *s* one *d*. *Educ:* Bedford Sch.; RN Engineering Coll. Entered Royal Navy, 1927, as a Cadet; HMS Iron Duke 1932; HMS Resolution, 1933; served with Submarines, 1935-43; HMS Orion, 1943. Asst Naval Attaché, Paris, 1947; Exec. Officer, RN Engineering Coll., 1951; Naval Asst to Controller, 1954; Commanding Officer, HMS St Vincent, 1957; Rear-Adm., Nuclear Propulsion, 1959; Dir of Marine Engineering, 1961-63; Chief Naval Engineering Officer, 1962-63; Vice-Adm., 1964; a Lord Comr of the Admiralty, Fourth Sea Lord and Vice-Controller, 1963-64; Chief of Naval Supplies and Transport and Vice-Controller of the Navy, MoD, 1964-67; retd, 1967. CEng; FIMechE; MIMarE. *Recreations:* golf and motoring. *Address:* Hodshill, South Stoke, Bath, Somerset. *T:* Combe Down 3021. *Club:* Army and Navy.

**HAWKINS, Reginald Thomas,** CBE 1949; *b* 13 May 1888; *s* of Robert William Hawkins; *m* 1914, Margaret T., *e d* of James Rennie Addison; one *d* (one *s* killed in action, RAF, 1944). *Educ:* Owen's Sch., Islington; Edinburgh Univ. (MA). Entered Civil Service, 1904; Scottish Education Dept, 1910. Served European War, 1914-18, with London-Scottish Regt in France, Salonika and Egypt. Asst Sec., Scottish Education Dept, 1939; Under-Sec., Scottish Education Dept, 1949-52; retired, 1952. Sec. to Advisory Council on Education in Scotland, 1935-38. *Publications:* articles on educational finance. *Address:* The Laurels, Great Bromley, near Colchester, Essex. *T:* Great Bentley 389.

**HAWKINS, Rev. Canon Robert Henry;** Canon of St George's Windsor, 1958-70; *b* 3 March 1892; *s* of Rev. Francis Henry Albert Hawkins and Mary Anna Ridley Hawkins (*née* Morris); *m* 1917, Margaret, *e d* of Rev. T. A. Lacey, DD, Canon of Worcester; two *s* three *d*. *Educ:* Forest Sch., Essex; St Edmund Hall, Oxford. BA 1913, MA 1919. Served European War: commissioned 3rd S Staffs Regt, 1914; France and Salonika, 1915-17; RFC (Flight Comdr), 1917-19. Ordained Deacon, 1919, Priest, 1920; Vicar of: Maryport, Dio. Carlisle, 1923-27; St George, Barrow in Furness, 1927-34; Dalston, 1934-43; Vicar of St Mary, Nottingham, Rural Dean of Nottingham and Hon. Canon of Southwell, 1943-58. *Address:* 4a The Cloisters, Windsor Castle. *T:* Windsor 64736.

**HAWKINS, William Francis Spencer,** CB 1968; a Master of the Supreme Court (Chancery Division), 1933-Jan. 1969, Chief Master, 1959-Jan. 1969; *b* Richmond, Surrey, 13 Feb. 1896; *s* of Francis William Hawkins; *m* 1933, Eva Lilian, *d* of William Graham; one *s* one *d*. *Educ:* Rugby. Served European War, 1914-18: on active service, 1915-19, Salonika and British Army of the Black Sea, Signal Officer with 27th Div. Artillery and 80th Inf. Bde (despatches twice). Admitted a solicitor, 1921; Partner with Bird and Bird, Gray's Inn, 1928. Post Invasion Warden, War of 1939-45. Trustee United Law Clerks Soc. Pres. of Wimbledon Hockey Club, 1952-60, and of Old Rugbeian Soc., 1957-59. Sometime Mem. Coulsdon and Purley, UDC and Council of the Magistrates Assoc. JP Surrey, 1947; Chm. Wallington Petty Sessions Div. Bench, Oct. 1958-60. *Address:* Rossley, Copthorne, Sussex. *T:* Copthorne 2013.

**HAWKS, Ellison,** FRAS, FZS; Captain RFA, TF; Managing Director Poland's Packing Cases Ltd; Real Photographs Ltd; Direct Trading Organisation Ltd; Ellison Hawks Ltd; New Mornington Hotels Ltd; Broadstairs Photo. Works Ltd; *b* Hull, 13 March 1889; *o s* of Matthew H. Hawks, Derwenthaugh, Gateshead-on-Tyne, and Rowena Reynard Hull; *m* 1921, Edna, *e d* of J. Dawson Fawcett, Leeds and Harrogate; one *s* two *d*. *Educ:* Bebington Coll., Rock Ferry, Wirral; William Hulme Grammar Sch., Manchester. Chief Clerk, Accident Dept, Commercial Union Assurance Co. Ltd, Leeds, 1913-15. Active Service, 1915-19, Asst Provost Marshal, D Area, Northern Command, 1916-19; Advertising Manager, Meccano Ltd, Liverpool, 1921-35; Gen. Editor Amalgamated Press, Ltd, London, 1936-40; Lecturer in Astronomy (Lecture League, London). *Publications:* Scientific publications of general interest, covering Astronomy, Geology, Microscopy, Nature Wonders, Radio, etc. include: Stars Shown to the Children; The Starry Heavens; Engineering for Boys; Pioneers of Wireless; Pioneers of Plant Study; Remarkable Machinery; Electrical Wonders; Nature Wonders; Water Wonders; Marvels and Mysteries of Science; How it Works; The Triumph of Man in Science and Invention; How it is Made, etc; Scientific papers; articles in encyclopædias and in general science works, magazines, periodicals, and newspapers; Editor: Romance of Reality Series; Meccano Magazine, 1921-35; The Dog Owner. Author of most of the current volumes in Cassell's Motoring Series (popular cars). *Recreations:* dogs (English Setters), photography, philately. *Address:* 20 Delamere Road, Ainsdale, Southport, Lancs. *T:* Southport 77549. *Clubs:* Author's, Royal Aero.

**HAWKSLEY, John Callis,** CBE 1946; PhD, MD, FRCP; formerly Physician, University College Hospital and St Peter's, St Paul's and St Philip's Hospitals, London; *b* 30 Nov. 1903; *s* of late Joseph Hawksley, Great Yarmouth; *m* 1933, Margaret, *er d* of late Engineer Vice-Adm. Sir Reginald Skelton, KCB, CBE, DSO; two *s* two *d*. *Educ:* Dulwich Coll.; University Coll., London; University Coll. Hospital. Appts on resident staff, University Coll. Hosp., 1926-28; ship's surg., BISN Co., 1929; research appts, Birmingham Children's Hosp., 1930-32; Sebag-Montefiore Research Fellow, Hospital for Sick Children, Gt Ormond Street, 1933-34; Bilton Pollard Travelling Fellowship, University Coll. Hosp., 1935, devoted to work at Bispebjerg Hosp., Copenhagen; Asst Physician, University Coll. Hosp., 1936-39; Physician to University Coll. Hosp., 1940; retd, 1969. Temp. commission RAMC 1939; served with rank of Lieut-Col in MEF, 1941-44 (despatches); Consulting Physician, local Brig., with South East Asia Command, 1945. Fellow of University Coll., London, 1946; Dean of University Coll. Hosp. Med. Sch., 1949-54; Senior Vice-Pres., RCP, 1966-. *Publications:* contributions to various medical journals. *Recreations:* mountaineering, music. *Address:* The Old Vicarage, East Kennett, Wilts. *T:* Lockeridge 237. *Clubs:* Alpine; Savile.

**HAWKSLEY, Richard Walter Benson,** TD 1948; Executive Chairman, Mann Egerton & Co. Ltd (Chairman and Managing Director since 1957); *b* Birkenhead; *s* of late Dr Walter Linney Hawksley; *m* 1939, Jean, *d* of Harold Lilley; three *s* one *d*. *Educ:* Stamford Sch. Joined Mann Egerton as pupil, 1934; has remained throughout career, serving with the Company at Norwich, London, and Bury St Edmunds; Director, 1950. Joined TA, 9th Bn Royal Fusiliers, 1937. Served with Royal Fusiliers throughout War of 1939-45, in UK and Middle East. Attended Staff Coll., Camberley; demobilised, rank Major, 1946. Pres., Motor Agents Assoc., 1968-69, Dep. Pres., 1969-70. *Recreations:* cruising and sailing on Norfolk Broads; travel. *Address:* (private) 67 The Close, Norwich; (business) Mann Egerton & Co. Ltd, 5 Prince of Wales Road, Norwich. *T:* Norwich 28383. *Clubs:* Naval and Military; Norfolk (Norwich); Norfolk Broads Yacht (Wroxham).

**HAWKSWORTH, Frederick William,** JP; FIMechE; *b* 10 Feb. 1884; unmarried. *Educ:* Swindon. Apprenticeship GWR, Swindon; Chief Draughtsman, 1925-31; Asst to Chief Mechanical Engineer, 1932-41; Chief Mechanical Engineer, Great Western Railway, 1941-48; British Railways Western Region, 1948-49; retired Dec. 1949. Mem. of: Council of Institution of Mechanical Engineers, 1939-49; Education Cttee of Swindon Borough;

Chm. Swindon Borough Magistrates, 1951-59; Chm. Swindon Permanent Building Soc.; formerly Mem. Regional Council for Further Education (for the South West). Freeman of the Borough of Swindon, 1960. *Recreation:* music. *Address:* Kingswood, Westlecott Road, Swindon, Wilts. *T:* Swindon 22287.

**HAWLEY, Major Sir David Henry,** 7th Bt, *cr* 1795; MA; FRICS; DL; late KRRC; Member of firm of Jas Martin & Co., Chartered Surveyors, Land Agents and Valuers, 8 Bank Street, Lincoln; *b* 13 May 1913; *e s* of Capt. Cyril Francis Hawley and Ursula Mary, *d* of Henry Percy St John; *S* uncle, 1923; *m* 1938, Hermione, 2nd *d* of late Col L. Gregson; one *s* two *d*. *Educ:* Eton; Magdalene Coll., Cambridge. Served Palestine, 1936-39 (medal and clasp), War of 1939-45 (prisoner, 1939-45 Star, despatches). DL 1952, High Sheriff, 1962-63, Lincs. *Heir:* *s* Henry Nicholas Hawley, *b* 26 Nov. 1939. *Address:* Tumby Lawn, Mareham-le-Fen, Boston, Lincs. *T:* Coningsby 337.

**HAWLEY, Donald Frederick,** CMG 1970; MBE 1955; Counsellor (Commercial) British Embassy, Baghdad, since 1968; Barrister-at-law; *b* 22 May 1921; *s* of F. G. Hawley, Stag Wood, Ringshall, Berkhamsted, Herts and late Mrs Hawley; *m* 1964, Ruth Morwenna Graham Howes, *d* of late Rev. P. G. Howes and of Mrs Howes, Charmouth, Dorset; three *d*. *Educ:* Radley; New Coll., Oxford (MA). Served in HM Forces, 1941. Sudan Political Service, 1944; joined Sudan Judiciary, 1947. Called to Bar, Inner Temple, 1951. Chief Registrar, Sudan Judiciary, and Registrar-Gen. of Marriages, 1951; resigned from Sudan Service, 1955; joined HM Foreign Service, 1955; FO, 1956: Political Agent, Trucial States, in Dubai, 1958; Head of Chancery, British Embassy, Cairo, 1962; Counsellor and Head of Chancery, British High Commission, Lagos, 1965; Vis. Fellow, Dept of Geography, Durham Univ., 1967. Chargé d'Affaires in Iraq, 1969 and 1970. *Publications:* Handbook for Registrars of Marriage and Ministers of Religion, 1963 (Sudan Govt pubn); Courtesies in the Trucial States, 1965; The Trucial States, 1970. *Recreations:* tennis, squash, sailing, book collecting; Hon. Sec., Sudan Football Assoc., 1952-55. *Address:* West Pulridge, Little Gaddesden, near Berkhamsted, Hertfordshire. *T:* Little Gaddesden 3439. *Clubs:* Athenæum, Travellers'.

**HAWORTH, Sir (Arthur) Geoffrey,** 2nd Bt, *cr* 1911; MA; JP; farmer; *b* 5 April 1896; *s* of Sir Arthur Haworth, 1st Bt, and Lily (*d* 1952), *y d* of late John Rigby, Altrincham; *S* father, 1944; *m* 1926, Emily Dorothea, *er d* of H. E. Gaddum, The Priory, Bowdon; two *s* two *d*. *Educ:* Rugby Sch.; New Coll., Oxford. Served European War, 1914-19, Lieut Queen's Own Royal West Kent Regiment and Machine Gun Corps (despatches). Chm., Hallé Concert Soc., 1965-. FRSA 1969. JP 1937. *Recreation:* music. *Heir:* *s* Philip Haworth [*b* 17 Jan. 1927; *m* 1951, Joan Helen, *d* of late S. P. Clark, Ipswich; four *s* one *d*]. *Address:* The Red Brook, Lower Peover, Cheshire. *Club:* Farmers'.

**HAWORTH, Sir Geoffrey;** *see* Haworth, Sir Arthur Geoffrey.

**HAWORTH, James;** Member, London Midland Railway Board, 1956-67; *b* 10 Nov. 1896; *m* 1919, Cassie Pughe (*d* 1946), *d* of T. R. Thomas, Towyn. Councillor, Bootle, 1923-30, Alderman, JP, 1930-42. Contested (Lab) West Derby (Liverpool), 1935; MP (Lab) Walton Div. of Liverpool, 1945-50. Mem., National Executive, The Labour Party, 1953-55; Hon. Treasurer, National Federation of Professional Workers, 1949-56; Mem. Council, Industrial Soc.; Pres., Transport Salaried Staffs Assoc., 1953-56. *Recreation:* making socialists. *Address:* 34 Byculláh Road, Enfield, Middlesex. *T:* 01-363 8823.

**HAWORTH, Very Rev. Kenneth William;** Dean of Salisbury, 1960-71; *b* 21 Jan. 1903; *s* of William Bell and Helen Haworth; *m* 1937, Sybil Mavrojani; two *s* two *d*. *Educ:* Cheltenham Coll.; Clare Coll., Cambridge; Wells Theological Coll. Curate of St Giles, Willenhall, 1926; Domestic Chaplain 1931, Examining Chaplain, 1937, to Bp of Lichfield; Chaplain of Wells Theological Coll., 1938; CF (4th cl.), 1939; Rector of Stratton w. Baunton, Dio., Gloucester, 1943; Vice-Principal of Wells Theol. Coll., 1946, Principal, 1947-60; Prebendary of Combe II in Wells Cathedral, 1947-60; Exam. Chap. to Bishop of Bath and Wells, 1947; Proctor in Convocation, 1956-59; Exam. Chap. to Bishop of Salisbury, 1962. *Address:* The Common, Woodgreen, Fordingbridge, Hants.

**HAWORTH, Robert Downs,** FRS 1944; DSc, PhD Victoria, BSc Oxon, FRIC; Firth Professor of Chemistry, University of Sheffield, 1939-63, now Emeritus; *b* 1 March 1898; *s* of J. T. and Emily Haworth, Cheadle, Cheshire; *m* 1930, Dorothy, *d* of A. L. Stocks, Manchester; one *d*. *Educ:* Secondary Sch., Stockport; University of Manchester, Mercer Scholar, 1919; Beyer Fellow, 1920; 1851 Exhibition Scholar, 1921-23; 1851 Exhibition Sen. Student, 1923-25; Demonstrator in Organic Chemistry, Oxford, 1925-26; Lecturer in Chemistry, King's Coll., Newcastle upon Tyne, 1927-39. Visiting Prof. of Organic Chemistry, University of Madras, 1963-64. Davy Medal, Royal Society, 1956. *Publications:* papers on organic chemistry in Journal of Chemical Society. *Address:* The University, Sheffield; 67 Tom Lane, Sheffield S10 3PA. *T:* Sheffield 302595.

**HAWORTH, Hon. Sir William (Crawford),** Kt 1969; *b* 15 April 1905; *s* of Edward Haworth; *m* 1927, Winifred Senior. *Educ:* Essendon; Melbourne Univ.; Victorian Pharmacy Coll. PhC 1925; MPS. War of 1939-45: Captain, 2nd AIF, 9th Divn; served in Egypt, Tobruk, Palestine and Syria; R of O 1944. Municipal Councillor, S Melb., 1923-38; Mem. Bd of Management, Vic Infectious Diseases Hosp., 1936-38; Mem. Council, S Melb. Technical Sch., 1939-62 (Pres., 1947-48). MLA for Albert Park, Vic Parliament, 1937-45; Minister for Health and Housing, Vic Govt, Oct.-Nov. 1945. MHR for Isaacs, Aust. Commonwealth Parliament, 1949-69. Mem. Jt Parly Cttee for For. Affairs, 1959-66; Leader of Aust. Delegn to Inter-Parly Union Conf., Warsaw, 1959 (Mem. IPU Council, 1959-60); Dep. Chm. of Cttees, 1960-69. *Recreations:* golf. *Address:* 11 Findon Avenue, North Caulfield, Vic 3161, Australia. *T:* 50 6008. *Clubs:* Commonwealth (Canberra); Naval and Military, Royal Melb. Yacht Squadron, Amateur Sports, Victoria Racing, Royal Automobile Club of Victoria, Kingston Heath Golf (Vic).

**HAWSER, Cyril Lewis,** QC 1959; Recorder of Portsmouth since 1969; *b* 5 Oct. 1916; *s* of Abraham and Sarah Hawser; *m* 1940, Phyllis Greatrex; one *s* one *d*. *Educ:* Cardiff High Sch.; Balliol Coll., Oxford (MA). Called to the Bar, 1938. Recorder of Salisbury, 1967-69. *Recreations:* tennis, chess, conversation. *Address:* 57 Eaton Place, SW1. *T:* 01-235 6566.

**HAWTHORN, Maj.-Gen. Douglas Cyril,** CB 1946; DSO 1945; *b* 1897; *s* of late Edgar Hawthorn; *m* 1919, Maude Marie, *d* of late

John Henry Price. 2nd Lieut KOYLI, 1917; transferred to Indian Army 1918, 1st Punjab Regt; served European War, 1914-18; France, NW Frontier of India, Palestine; Mahsud and Waziristan operations, NW Frontier of India, 1920-23; passed Staff Coll., Quetta, 1930-31; asst Commandant and Chief Instructor Tactical Sch., India, 1941-42; served War of 1939-45; commanded 62 Indian Inf. Bde, Chief of Staff 15 Indian Corps, Arakan (DSO); commanded 23rd Indian Div., Malaya (CB), and Java (despatches), Comdr of Java in Netherland East Indies, 1945-46, took the surrender of the Japanese Comdr in Java; Dir of Military Trng, India, 1946-47; Dep. Chief of Gen. Staff to Supreme Comdr India and Pakistan, 1947; retired, 1948. Chm. Burma Star Assoc., 1949-55. *Address:* 29 Ramsden Road, SW12. *Club:* United Service.

**HAWTHORNE, Prof. Sir William (Rede),** Kt 1970; CBE 1959; FRS 1955; MA; ScD; FIMechE; FRAeS; Master of Churchill College, Cambridge, since 1968; Hopkinson and ICI Professor of Applied Thermodynamics, University of Cambridge, since 1951; Head of Department of Engineering since 1968; *b* 22 May 1913; *s* of William Hawthorne, MInstCE, and Elizabeth C. Hawthorne; *m* 1939, Barbara Runkle, Cambridge, Massachusetts, USA; one *s* two *d*. *Educ:* Westminster Sch.; Trinity Coll., Cambridge; Massachusetts Institute of Technology, USA. Development Engineer, Babcock & Wilcox Ltd, 1937-39; Scientific Officer, Royal Aircraft Establishment, 1940-44; British Air Commission, Washington, 1944; Dep. Dir Engine Research, Min. of Supply, 1945; Associate Prof. of Mechanical Engineering, 1946, George Westinghouse Prof. of Mechanical Engineering, 1948, Massachusetts Institute of Technology; Jerome C. Hunsaker Prof. of Aeronautical Engineering, MIT, 1955-56. Visiting Institute Prof., MIT, 1962-63. Mem. Council, Royal Soc., 1968-; a Vice-Pres., Royal Soc., 1970. Foreign Associate, US Nat. Acad. of Sciences, 1965. Chm. Advisory Council on Scientific Research and Technical Development, 1966-. Dir, Dracone Developments Ltd, 1958-. Governor, Westminster Sch., 1956-. Medal of Freedom (US), 1947. *Publications:* papers in mechanical and aeronautical journals. *Address:* The Master's Lodge, Churchill College, Cambridge; Engineering Laboratory, Cambridge. *Club:* Athenæum.

**HAWTON, Sir John (Malcolm Kenneth),** KCB 1952 (CB 1947); *b* 18 Sept. 1904; *s* of John Francis Hawton; *m* 1935, Hilda Cawley; one *d*. *Educ:* Emanuel Sch.; St John's Coll., Cambridge (1st Class Classical Tripos, Foundation Scholar, Graves Prizeman). Barrister (Middle Temple); entered Ministry of Health, 1927; various duties in that Ministry, concerning local government, housing, water supply, private bill legislation, public health, wartime emergency services, also inception and running of National Health Service; Permanent Sec., Ministry of Health, 1951-60. Chm., British Waterways Board, 1963-68, Vice-Chm., 1968-. Mem., Advertising Standards Authority, 1962-. *Recreations:* erstwhile. *Address:* Roundway Cottage, The Roundway, Rustington, Sussex. *Club:* Reform.

**HAWTREY, John Havilland Procter,** CBE 1958; FICE; Director, Associated Railway Consultants, London, SW1; *b* 16 Feb. 1905; *e s* of late Edmond Charles Hawtrey and late Helen Mary Hawtrey (*née* Durand); *m* 1947, Kathleen Mary, *d* of late Captain M. T. Daniel, RN, Henley-on-Thames; one *s* one *d*. *Educ:* Eton; City and Guilds Engineering Coll., London (BSc 1927). Asst Engineer, later Dist Engineer, Burma Railways, 1927-47. Served War of 1939-45: with RE, 1940-46; Major 1942, in India and Burma, 1942-46 (despatches). Entered office of Crown Agents for Oversea Govts and Administrations, 1948: Chief Civil Engineer, 1956; Crown Agent and Engineer-in-Chief, 1965; retired, 1969. *Address:* 11 Curzon Avenue, Beaconsfield, Bucks. *T:* Beaconsfield 4220; Associated Railway Consultants, North House, Great Peter Street, SW1. *Club:* East India and Sports.

*See also S. C. Hawtrey.*

**HAWTREY, Sir Ralph (George),** Kt 1956; CB 1941; FBA; Hon. DSc (Econ) London; *b* 1879; *s* of George Procter Hawtrey; *m* 1915, Hortense Emilia d'Aranyi (*d* 1953). *Educ:* Eton; Trinity Coll., Cambridge (19th Wrangler). Entered Admiralty, 1903; Treasury, 1904-45; Dir of Financial Enquiries, 1919-45; special leave from the Treasury to lecture on Economics at Harvard Univ., 1928-29; Pres. Royal Econ. Society, 1946-48; Price Prof. of International Economics, Chatham House (RIIA), 1947-52. Hon. Fellow Trinity Coll. Cambridge, 1959. *Publications:* Good and Bad Trade, 1913; Currency and Credit, 1919 (4th edn 1950); The Exchequer and the Control of Expenditure, 1921; Monetary Reconstruction, 1923, 2nd edn 1926; The Economic Problem, 1926; The Gold Standard in Theory and Practice, 1927, 5th edn 1947; Trade and Credit, 1929; Economic Aspects of Sovereignty, 1930 (2nd edn 1952); Trade Depression and the Way Out, 1931 (2nd edn 1933); The Art of Central Banking, 1932; Revision of G. Armitage Smith's Principles and Methods of Taxation, 1935; Capital and Employment, 1937 (2nd edn 1952); A Century of Bank Rate, 1938; Economic Destiny, 1944; Economic Rebirth, 1946; Bretton Woods for Better or Worse, 1946; Western European Union (for a Chatham House Study Group), 1949; The Balance of Payments and the Standard of Living, 1950; Towards the Rescue of Sterling, 1954; Cross Purposes in Wage Policy, 1955; The Pound at Home and Abroad, 1961; Incomes and Money, 1967. *Address:* 29 Argyll Road, W8. *T:* 01-937 3805. *Club:* United University.

**HAWTREY, Stephen Charles,** CB 1966; Clerk of the Journals, House of Commons, since 1958; *b* 8 July 1907; *s* of Edmond C. Hawtrey; *m* 1934, Leila Winifred, *e d* of late Lieut-Col Wilmot Blomefield; two *s* one *d*. *Educ:* Eton; Trinity Coll., Cambridge (MA). Asst Clerk, House of Commons, 1930; Senior Clerk, 1944. Temporarily attached: to Min. of Home Security, 1939; to Secretariat of Council of Europe, Strasbourg, France, at various sessions between 1950 and 1964. *Publication:* (With L. A. Abraham) A Parliamentary Dictionary, 1956 and 1964; 3rd edn (with H. M. Barclay), 1970. *Address:* 52 New Street, Henley-on-Thames, Oxon. *T:* Henley 4521. *Clubs:* Oxford and Cambridge University, Railway.

*See also J. H. P. Hawtrey.*

**HAY,** family name of **Countess of Erroll, Earl of Kinnoull,** and of **Marquis of Tweeddale.**

**HAY, Lord; Merlin Sereld Victor Gilbert Hay;** Master of Erroll; *b* 20 April 1948; *s* and *heir* of Countess of Erroll, *qv* and of Sir Iain Moncreiffe of that Ilk, 11th Bt, *qv*. *Educ:* Eton; Trinity College, Cambridge. Page to the Lord Lyon, 1956. The Queen's Royal Rifles (parachutist), 1966. *Address:* Easter Moncreiffe, Perthshire. *T:* Bridge of Earn 338; Old Slains, Collieston, Aberdeenshire. *T:* 248. *Clubs:* Turf; Puffin's (Edinburgh).

**HAY, Sir (Alan) Philip,** KCVO 1960 (CVO 1953); TD; Treasurer to the Duke of Kent and to Prince Michael of Kent; Private Secretary to Princess Marina, Duchess of Kent, 1948-68; *b* 27 Feb. 1918; *y s* of late E. Alan Hay and of Mrs Hay, 72 Albert Hall Mansions, SW7; *m* 1948, The Lady Margaret Katharine Seymour (*see* Lady Margaret Hay); three *s*. *Educ:* Harrow; Trinity Coll., Cambridge (BA). Commissioned Herts Yeomanry, TA (135 Field Regt RA). 1939; prisoner, Singapore, 1942-45. *Address:* 10 Kensington Palace, W8. *Club:* Boodle's.

**HAY, Sir Arthur Thomas Erroll;** 10th Bt of Park, *cr* 1663; DiplArch; ARIBA 1935; Principal Architect, Civil Service; *b* 13 April 1909; *o s* of 9th Bt and Lizabel Annie (*d* 1957), *o d* of late Lachlan Mackinnon Macdonald, Skeabost, Isle of Skye; *S* father, 1923; *m* 1st, 1935, Hertha Louise (who was granted a divorce, 1942), *d* of late Herr Ludwig Stölzle, Nagelberg, Austria, and of H. E. Frau Vaugoin, Vienna; one *s*; 2nd, 1942, Rosemarie Evelyn Anne, *d* of late Vice-Adm. Aubrey Lambert and of Mrs Lambert. *Educ:* Fettes Coll., Edinburgh. Student of architecture, University of Liverpool, 1927-31; Diploma in Architecture, Architectural Assoc., July 1934. Served War of 1939-45; 2nd Lieut RE 1943; Lieut 1944; service in Normandy, Belgium, Holland and Germany in 21 Army Group. *Heir: s* John Erroll Audley Hay, *b* 3 Dec. 1935. *Recreation:* golf. *Address:* c/o Lloyds Bank, 67/69 Old Brompton Road, SW7.

**HAY, David Osborne,** CBE 1962; DSO 1945; Secretary, Department of External Territories, Canberra, since 1970; *b* 29 Nov. 1916; 2nd *s* of late H. A. Hay, Barwon Heads, Victoria; *m* 1944, Alison Marion Parker Adams; two *s*. *Educ:* Geelong Grammar Sch.; Brasenose Coll., Oxford; Melbourne Univ. Joined Commonwealth Public Service, 1939. Australian Imperial Force, 1940-46: Major, 2nd Sixth Infantry Bn; served in Western Desert, Greece, New Guinea. Rejoined External Affairs Dept, 1947; Imp. Def. Coll., 1954; Minister (later Ambassador) to Thailand, 1955-57; High Comr in Canada, 1961-64; Ambassador to UN, New York, 1964-65; First Asst Secretary, External Affairs, 1966; Administrator of Papua and New Guinea, 1967-70. *Recreations:* reading, ski-ing, golf. *Address:* c/o Department of External Territories, Canberra, ACT, Australia. *Clubs:* Australian (Melbourne); Naval and Military (Melbourne); Commonwealth (Canberra).

**HAY, Prof. Denys,** MA; FBA 1970; Professor of Medieval History, University of Edinburgh, since Oct. 1954; *b* 29 Aug. 1915; *s* of Rev. W. K. Hay and Janet Waugh; *m* 1937, Sarah Gwyneth, *d* of S. E. Morley; one *s* two *d*. *Educ:* Royal Grammar Sch., Newcastle upon Tyne; Balliol Coll., Oxford. 1st Cl. hons, Modern History, 1937; senior demy, Magdalen Coll., 1937. Temporary Lecturer, Glasgow Univ., 1938; Bryce Studentship, Oxford Univ., 1939; Asst Lecturer, University Coll., Southampton, 1939; RASC 1940-42; War Historian (Civil Depts), 1942-45; Lecturer in Medieval History, Edinburgh Univ., 1945; Literary Dir, Royal Historical Soc., 1955-58; Italian Lecturer, British Acad., 1959; Wiles Lecturer, Queen's Univ., Belfast, 1960; Visiting Prof., Cornell Univ., 1963; Senior Fellow, Newberry Library, Chicago, 1966; Trustee, Nat. Library of Scotland, 1966-; Pres., Historical Association, 1967-70. Editor, English Historical Review, 1958-65. Hon. DLitt, Newcastle, 1970. *Publications:* Anglica Historia of P. Vergil, 1950; Polydore Vergil, 1952; From Roman Empire to Renaissance Europe, 1953 (The Medieval Centuries, 1964); ed. R. K. Hannay's Letters of James V, 1954; Europe: the emergence of an idea, 1957; Italian Renaissance in its Historical Background, 1961; Design and Development of Weapons (History of Second World War) (with M. M. Postan and J. D. Scott), 1964; Europe in the 14th and 15th Centuries, 1966; ed. (with W. K. Smith) Aeneas Sylvius Piccolomini, *De Gestis Concilii Basiliensis,* 1967; ed The Age of the Renaissance, 1967; articles in historical journals. *Address:* 31 Fountainhall Road, Edinburgh. *T:* 031-667 2886.

**HAY, Sir Frederick Baden-Powell,** 10th Bt of Alderston, *cr* 1703; *b* 24 June 1900; *s* of late Frederick Howard Hay; *S* uncle 1936; *m* 1935, Henrietta Margaret, *d* of Herbert William Reid; no *c*. *Recreations:* golf, turf, motoring. *Heir: b* Ronald Nelson Hay [*b* 9 July 1910; *m* 1940, Rita, *d* of John Munyard; one *s* one *d*]. *Address:* Haddington, 21 Stewart Street, Ormond, Melbourne, Australia. *T:* UL 8273. *Club:* Royal Caledonian (Melbourne).

**HAY, Sir James B. D.;** *see* Dalrymple-Hay.

**HAY, Col James Charles Edward,** CBE 1937; MC, TD, DL; Sheriff-Substitute of Lanarkshire at Glasgow, 1946-59, at Hamilton, 1959-61; Solicitor; *b* 6 June 1889; *s* of late William Thomas Hay, solicitor, Hamilton; *m* 1929, Mary Buchanan Thomson; two *s*. *Educ:* Academy, Hamilton; Glasgow Univ. Hon. Col (late CO) 6th Battalion The Cameronians; late Comdr 156 (West Scottish) Infantry Bde; late Hon. Col 3rd (Lanarkshire) Army Cadet Bn; served European War, 1914-18; War of 1939-45 (despatches). Late Vice-Chm., Secretary, and Military Mem., Lanarkshire T & AF Assoc. DL Co. of Lanark. *Recreations:* bowls, motoring, fishing. *Address:* Erroll, Bothwell, Lanarkshire. *T:* Bothwell 2180.

**HAY, Sir James (Lawrence),** Kt 1961; OBE 1918 (MBE 1918); President, Hay's-Wright Stephenson Ltd, Christchurch, New Zealand, since 1967 (Managing Director, 1929-61; Chairman, 1955-67); *b* 17 May 1888; *s* of William Hay, Lawrence, NZ; *m* 1st, 1918, Davidina Mertel (*d* 1969), *d* of William Gunn, Christchurch, NZ; two *s* two *d*; 2nd, 1970, Olive Musgrove, Christchurch. *Educ:* Lawrence District High Sch. Sen. YMCA Sec., 1st NZEF in France and Egypt, 1915-19 (MBE, OBE). Gen. Sec. New Zealand YMCA, Wellington, 1921-25. Founded Hay's Ltd, Department Store, 1929. Christchurch City Council, 1944-53. Chm. Canterbury Nat. Savings Cttee, 1939-45. Chm. Christchurch Civic Music Council, 1944-63; Chm. Canterbury Museum Trust Bd, 1946-53. President: NZ Retailers Fedn, 1940; NZ Council of YMCA; NZ Inst. of Management (Canterbury); Royal Christchurch Musical Society; Mem. NZ Savings Cttee, 1962-65. Hon. Fellow, NZ Institute of Management; Hon. FTCL 1968. Jubilee Medal, 1935; Coronation Medal, 1953; Canterbury Soc. of Arts Medal for services to the Arts. *Recreations:* bowls, music. *Address:* Braemore, 111 Puriri Street, Christchurch, NZ. *T:* 46-680.

**HAY, John Albert;** MP (C) Henley Division of Oxfordshire since 1950; *b* 24 Nov. 1919; *er s* of Alderman J. E. Hay; *m* 1947, Beryl Joan, *o d* of Comdr H. C. Found, RN (retired); one *s* one *d*. *Educ:* Brighton, Hove and Sussex Grammar Sch. Solicitor admitted May 1945. Chairman: Brighton and Hove Young Conservatives, 1945-47; Sussex Federation of Young Conservatives, 1945-47; Young Conservative and Unionist Central Cttee, 1947-49; Conservative Party Housing and Local

Government Cttee, 1956-59; formerly Dir London Municipal Soc.; Vice-Pres. Urban District Councils Assoc.; Hon. Sec. UK Council of the European Movement, 1965-66; Mem. of Executive Cttee, National Union of Conservative and Unionist Association, 1947-49 and 1950-51. Served War of 1939-45, in RNVR; temporary Sub-Lieut, RNVR, 1940-44; temporary Lieut, RNVR, 1944; invalided 1944. Company Dir. Member: British Delegation, Congress of Europe, 1948; UK Delegations, Council of Europe and Western European Union, 1956-59. Parliamentary Private Sec. to President of Board of Trade, 1951-56; Parliamentary Sec., Ministry of Transport, 1959-63; Civil Lord of the Admiralty, 1963-64; Parliamentary Under-Sec. of State for Defence for the Royal Navy, April-Oct. 1964. Mem. Court, Reading Univ., 1968-. *Recreations:* gardening, travel, historical study. *Address:* 14 Soho Square, W1. *T:* 01-437 3934.

**HAY, Prof. John Duncan,** MA, MD, FRCP; Professor of Child Health, University of Liverpool, since 1957; *b* 6 Feb. 1909; *s* of late Prof. John Hay; *m* 1936, Jannett Ceridwen Evans; one *s* two *d*. *Educ:* Liverpool Coll.; Sidney Sussex Coll., Cambridge; Liverpool Univ. MB, ChB, 1st Cl. Hons, Liverpool, 1933; MA 1934, MB 1935, Cambridge; MD Liverpool, 1936; DCH London, MRCP 1939; FRCP 1951. Holt Fellowship in Pathology, Liverpool, 1935; Cons. Pædiatrician to: Royal Liverpool Children's Hospital, 1939-; Royal Liverpool Babies' Hospital, 1939-61; Birkenhead Children's Hosp., 1937-54; Liverpool Maternity Hosp. 1946-; Lancashire County Hosp., Whiston, 1942-51; Liverpool Open-Air Hospital, Leasowe, and Mill Road Maternity Hosp., 1947-; Alder Hey Children's Hosp., 1957-; Liverpool Education Cttee, 1951-. Demonstrator in Pathology, University of Liverpool, 1935 and 1938; Asst Lectr in Clinical Pædiatrics, University of Liverpool, 1948-57. RAMC (Major and Lieut-Col), 1942-46. *Publications:* contribs to Archives of Disease in Childhood, British Heart Journal, BMJ, Lancet, Practitioner, Brit. Encyclopædia of Medical Practice, Medical Progress, 1957, Cardiovascular Diseases in Childhood. *Recreations:* music, fell walking. *Address:* Foenum Lodge, Oldfield Road, Heswall, Wirral, Cheshire. *T:* 051-342 2607.

**HAY, Lady Margaret Katharine,** CVO 1953; Woman of the Bedchamber to the Queen since 1953; *b* 9 May 1918; *o d* of late Brig.-Gen. Lord Henry Seymour, DSO, and of Lady Helen Seymour; *m* 1948, Sir Alan Philip Hay, *qv*; three *s*. Lady-in-Waiting to Princess Elizabeth, 1947-52, to the Queen, 1952. *Address:* 10 Kensington Palace, W8. *T:* 01-937 5514.

**HAY, Noel Grant,** QC (Nigeria) 1955; Attorney-General, Western Region, Nigeria, 1954-58, retired; *b* 21 Dec. 1910; *s* of William Grant Hay, Barrister, NZ, and Jessie Margaret Talboys; *m* 1937, Clare Morton. *Educ:* Otago Univ., Dunedin, New Zealand (BA; LLM Hons); Oxford Univ. Asst District Officer, Nigeria, 1937; Magistrate, Nigeria, 1939-42; Legal Dept, Nigeria, 1943-53; Senior Crown Counsel, 1949. Legal Sec., 1950. *Recreations:* golf, tennis, fishing. *Address:* 63a Weka Street, Christchurch, New Zealand. *Club:* South Canterbury (Timaru).

**HAY, Sir Philip;** *see* Hay, Sir Alan Philip.

**HAY, Lt-Gen. Sir Robert,** KCIE 1947 (CIE 1942); MB, ChB Edinburgh 1912; DPH Glasgow 1928; DTM&H Liverpool, 1927; *b* 8 March 1889; *s* of late Robert Erskine Hay, The Kilt, Castlecary; *m* 1928, Mary Carnegie McAusland; two *d* (one *s* decd). *Educ:* George Watson's; Edinburgh Univ., IMS 1917; late Dir-Gen. IMS; KHP, 1944-48; retired, 1948, KStJ 1948. Hon. FRCPE, 1969. *Address:* Little Rulwood, Denholm, Harwick, Roxburghshire. *T:* Denholm 302. *Club:* Royal Scots (Edinburgh).

**HAY, Maj.-Gen. Robert Arthur,** CB 1970; MBE 1946; Commander, First Australian Division, 1970; Chief, Military Planning Office, SEATO, 1971; *b* 9 April 1920; *s* of Eric Alexander Hay and Vera Eileen Hay (*née* Whitehead); *m* 1944, Endree Patricia Hay (*née* McGovern); two *s* one *d* (and one *s* decd). *Educ:* Brighton Grammar Sch., Melbourne, Victoria; RMC Duntroon, ACT (graduated Dec. 1939). Lt-Col, 1945; Col, 1955; Col GS HQ Eastern Comd; Military Attaché, Washington, DC, 1956; Dir Administrative Planning, AHQ, 1959; Defence Representative, Singapore and Malaya, 1962; Brig., 1964; IDC London, 1965; Dir Military Ops and Plans, AHQ, 1966; Maj.-Gen., 1967; Dep. Chief of the General Staff, AHQ; Comdr, Australian Forces, Vietnam, 1969. *Recreations:* tennis, golf. *Address:* 5 Borrowdale Street, Red Hill, ACT 2603, Australia. *T:* 95 9506. *Clubs:* Melbourne Cricket, Naval and Military (Melbourne); Commonwealth (Canberra); Tanglin (Singapore).

**HAY, Robert Edwin, (Roy Hay);** formerly Editor, Gardeners' Chronicle (1954-64); *b* 20 Aug. 1910; *o s* of late Thomas Hay, CVO, sometime Superintendent Central Royal Parks; *m* 1946, Elizabeth Jessie, *d* of late Rev. H. C. Charter; two *d*. *Educ:* Marylebone Grammar Sch. Horticultural seed trade, 1928; Asst Editor, Gardeners' Chronicle, 1936; Editor, Royal Horicultural Soc.'s publications, 1939; Min. of Agriculture, 1940; Horticultural Officer, Malta, 1942; Controller of Horticulture and Seed Divs, British zone of Germany, 1945. Officier du Mérite Agricole: Belgium, 1956; France, 1959. *Publications:* Annuals, 1937; In My Garden, 1955; Gardening the Modern Way, 1962; (with P. M. Synge) The Dictionary of Garden Plants, 1969. *Recreation:* philately. *Address:* Hurtmore Farm House, Hurtmore, Godalming, Surrey. *Club:* Farmers'.

**HAY, Rt. Rev. Robert Milton,** MA, BD; Suffragan Bishop of Buckingham, 1944-60; Hon. Canon of Christ Church, Oxford, since 1937; Hon. Assistant Bishop, Diocese of Oxford, 1960-70; *b* 30 Aug. 1884; *er s* of Robert Hay, Lauder, Scotland, and London; *m* 1909, Esmay Alice (*d* 1959), 2nd *d* of Joseph Foster, Hon. MA Oxon; one *s* one *d*; *m* 1960, Agnes Mary, *e d* of late Bishop and Mrs E. D. Shaw. *Educ:* Merchant Taylors' Sch., London; St John's Coll., Oxford (scholar); Wells Theological Coll. BA (2nd class Lit. Hum.) 1907; MA 1910; BD 1924; Curate of St Pancras, London, 1909-15; Vicar of Summertown, Oxford, 1915-23; of SS Philip and James, Oxford, 1923-39; Rector of Taplow, Bucks, 1939-53. Proctor in Convocation, 1929-57. Hon. Clerical Sec. Oxford Diocesan Conference, 1934-44; Rural Dean of Oxford, 1937-39; Archdeacon of Buckingham, 1944-57. *Address:* Greenhills, Wooburn Green, High Wycombe, Bucks. *T:* Bourne End 20944.

**HAYBALL, Frederick Ronald,** CMG 1969; with Longman Group Ltd, Publishers, since 1969; *b* 23 April 1914; *s* of Frederick Reuben Hayball and late Rebecca Hayball; *m* 1938, Lavinia Violet Palmer; one *s* one *d*. *Educ:* Alleyn's Sch., Dulwich. Accountant, Myers, Gondouin & Co. Ltd, 1932-39. Flying Officer, RAF, 1939-45. Foreign and Commonwealth Office, 1945-69 (Counsellor, retired). *Recreations:* cricket, angling, motoring. *Address:* 42 Theydon Park Road, Theydon Bois, Essex. *T:* Theydon Bois 2195. *Club:* RAF Reserves.

**HAYCOCKS, Prof. Norman,** CBE 1969; Professor of Education, University of Nottingham, since 1946; Deputy Vice-Chancellor, University of Nottingham, 1962-66, Pro-Vice-Chancellor, since 1969; *b* 17 Nov. 1907; unmarried. *Educ:* Salford Grammar Sch.; Univs of Manchester (open Schol.), Paris and Grenoble. BA First Cl. Hons in French, Manchester, 1928 (Research Schol.), MA 1929 (by research, Mediaeval French). Lecturer Univ. of Grenoble, 1928-29; Asst Master, North Manchester Sch. (branch of Manchester Gram. Sch.), 1929-33; Lecturer in Education, University of Manchester, 1933-46. Chairman, Standing Conference of National Voluntary Youth Organisations, 1952-70; Mem. Schools Broadcasting Council, 1958-68, and Chm., Secondary I Programme Cttee, 1958-64; Governor, National Coll. for Training of Youth Leaders, 1960-70; Mem., Youth Service Development Council, 1963-; Mem. Television Research Cttee, 1963-. Vice-Chm., Universities' Council for the Education of Teachers, 1967-69, Chm., 1969-. Squadron Leader in Intelligence Branch of Royal Air Force, 1941-45 (despatches). *Publications:* articles and papers in educational journals. *Recreations:* theatre and gardening. *Address:* 109 Derby Road, Bramcote, Nottingham NG9 3GZ. *T:* Nottingham 255024. *Clubs:* Athenæum, National Liberal.

**HAYDAY, Sir Frederick,** Kt 1969; CBE 1963; National Industrial Officer, National Union of General and Municipal Workers, since 1946; Chairman, International Committee, Trades Union Congress; Member: General Council of the Trades Union Congress (Chairman, 1962-63, Vice-Chairman, 1964-); ITA, since 1969; British Railways Board. *Address:* 42 West Drive, Cheam, Surrey. *T:* 01-642 8928.

**HAYDON, Maj.-Gen. Joseph Charles,** CB 1948; DSO 1940 and bar 1942; OBE; *b* 1899; *s* of late Frank Knowles Haydon; *m* 1926, Florence (*d* 1957), *d* of late John Stephen Keogh, Chicago, USA; one *d. Educ:* Downside; RMC Sandhurst. Served European War, 1914-19 (despatches); 2nd Lieut Irish Guards, 1917. Military Asst to Sec. of State for War, 1938. Lieut-Col Commanding 2nd battalion of the Irish Guards, 1939; Brigadier, 1941 (commanding Commandos, 1940-42); Col, 1942; Vice-Chief of Combined Operations Staff, 1942; Comd 1st Guard Bde, Italy, 1944; Brit. Jt Services Mission, Washington, DC, 1944-45; Brit. Army Rep., Jt Chiefs of Staff, Australia, 1946-47; Chief Intelligence Div., Control Commn, Germany, 1948-50; Major-Gen., 1944; retired pay, 1951. Served in Foreign Office, 1951-58. Served with F. G. Miles Ltd and Beagle Aircraft Ltd. Chevalier Legion of Honour (France); Officer Legion of Merit (USA). *Address:* College Cottage, Winson, near Cirencester, Glos. *Club:* Royal Aero.

**HAYDON, Walter Robert,** CMG 1970; HM Diplomatic Service; Head of News Department, Foreign and Commonwealth Office (formerly Foreign Office), since 1967; *b* 29 May 1920; *s* of Walter Haydon and Evelyn Louise Thom; *m* 1943, Joan Elizabeth Tewson; one *s* one *d* (and one *d* decd). *Educ:* Dover Grammar Sch. Served in Army in France, India and Burma, 1939-46. Entered Foreign Service, 1946; served at Berne, London, Turin, Sofia, Bangkok, London, Khartoum, UK Mission to UN (New York), Washington. *Recreations:* walking, tennis, swimming. *Address:* 7L Hyde Park Mansions, Cabbell Street, NW1.

**HAYDON-LEWIS, J;** *see* Lewis, Jack H.

**HAYEK, Friedrich August von,** FBA 1944; Dr Jur, DrScPol, Vienna; DSc (Econ.) London; Visiting Professor, University of Salzburg; *b* Vienna, 8 May 1899; *s* of late August von Hayek, Prof. of Botany at University of Vienna; certificate of naturalisation, 1938; *m* 1st, Hella von Fritsch (*d* 1960); one *s* one *d*; 2nd, Helene Bitterlich. *Educ:* University of Vienna. Austrian Civil Service, 1921-26; Dir, Austrian Institute for Economic Research, 1927-31; Lecturer in Economics, University of Vienna, 1929-31; Tooke Prof. of Economic Science and Statistics in University of London, 1931-50; Prof. of Social and Moral Science, University of Chicago, 1950-62; Prof. of Economics, Univ. of Freiburg i B, 1962-69. Dr jur *hc* Rikkyo Univ., Tokyo, 1964. *Publications:* Prices and Production, 1931; Monetary Theory and the Trade Cycle, 1933 (German edition, 1929); Monetary Nationalism and International Stability, 1937; Profits, Interest, and Investment, 1939; The Pure Theory of Capital, 1941; The Road to Serfdom, 1944; Individualism and Economic Order, 1948; John Stuart Mill and Harriet Taylor, 1950; The Counter-revolution of Science, 1952; The Sensory Order, 1952; The Political Ideal of the Rule of Law, 1955; The Constitution of Liberty, 1960; Studies in Philosophy, Politics and Economics, 1967; Freiburger Studien, 1969; edited: Beiträge zur Geldtheorie, 1933; Collectivist Economic Planning, 1935; Capitalism and the Historians, 1954; and the works of H. H. Gossen, 1927; F. Wieser, 1929; C. Menger, 1933-36; and H. Thornton, 1939; articles in Economic Journal, Economica, and other English and foreign journals. *Address:* 17a Firmianstrasse, A5020 Salzburg, Austria. *Clubs:* Reform, Alpine (London).

**HAYES, Claude James,** CMG 1969; MA, BLitt; Chairman, Crown Agents for Oversea Governments and Administrations, since 1968; Vice-Chairman, E. D. Sassoon Banking Co. Ltd; *b* 23 March 1912; *er s* of late J. B. F. Hayes, West Hoathly, Sussex; *m* 1940, Joan McCarthy, *yr d* of Edward McCarthy Fitt, Civil Engineer; two *s* one *d. Educ:* Ardingly Coll.; St Edmund Hall, Oxford (Scholar); Sorbonne; New Coll., Oxford (Sen. Scholar). Heath Harrison Travelling Scholarship; Zaharoff Travelling Fellowship; Paget Toynbee Prize; MA, BLitt. Asst Dir of Examinations, Civil Service Commn, 1938. Capt RASC 1st Inf. Div. BEF, 1939; Major 1940, Combined Ops; Lieut-Col, 1942-45 (N Africa, Sicily, Italy, NW Europe). Dep. Dir of Examinations, Civil Service Commn, 1945; Dir and Comr, 1949, also Sec., 1955; Nuffield Foundn Fellowship, 1953-54, toured Commonwealth studying public service recruitment and management. Asst Sec., HM Treasury, 1957; British Govt Mem., Cttee on Dissolution of Central African Fedn, 1963; Under-Sec., HM Treasury, 1964-65; Prin. Finance Officer, Min. of Overseas Development, 1965-68. *Recreations:* travel; music; unaided gardening; antique furniture; 18th century bourgeois silver; getting value for money from shops. *Address:* Prinkham, Chiddingstone Hoath, Kent. *T:* Cowden 335. *Club:* Oxford and Cambridge.

**HAYES, Colin Graham Frederick,** RA 1970 (ARA 1963); Tutor, Royal College of Art, since 1949; painter; *b* 17 Nov. 1919; *s* of Gerald Hayes and Winifred (*née* Yule); *m* 1949, Jean Westbrook Law; three *d. Educ:* Westminster Sch.; Christ Church, Oxford. Served Royal Engineers, 1940-45 (Middle East) (Capt.). Ruskin Sch. of Drawing, 1946-47. Work in Collections: Arts Council; British Council;

Carisle Museum; etc. Hon. ARCA and Fellow, Royal College of Art, 1960. *Publications include:* Renoir, 1961; Stanley Spencer, 1963; Rembrandt, 1969; many articles on painting in jls. *Address:* 26 Cleveland Avenue, W4. *T:* 01-994 8762.

**HAYES, Helen, (Mrs Charles MacArthur);** actress; *b* Washington, DC 10 Oct. 1900; *d* of Francis Van Arnum Brown and Catherine Estelle Hayes; *m* 1928, Charles MacArthur (*d* 1956); one *s* one *d*. *Educ:* Sacred Heart Academy, Washington, DC. As actress has appeared in USA in stage plays, among others;–Pollyana, Dear Brutus, Clarence, Bab, Coquette, The Good Fairy, To the Ladies, Young Blood, Mary of Scotland, Victoria Regina, Ladies and Gentlemen, Twelfth Night, Harriet, Happy Birthday; The Wisteria Trees, 1950; Mrs McThing, 1952. First appearance in England in The Glass Menagerie, 1948. Is also radio actress. Has appeared in films;–Farewell to Arms, The Sin of Madelon Claudet, Arrowsmith, The Son-Daughter, My Son John, Anastasia, Airport, etc. Awarded gold statuette by Motion Picture Academy of Arts and Sciences, 1932, as outstanding actress, based on performance in the Sin of Madelon Claudet; Hon. degrees: Smith Coll., Hamilton Coll., Columbia Univ., Princeton Univ., St Mary's Coll. *Publication:* A Gift of Joy, 1965. *Address:* Nyack, New York, USA. *Clubs:* Cosmopolitan, River, etc.

**HAYES, Most Rev. James Martin;** *see* Halifax (NS), Archbishop of, (RC).

**HAYES, Vice-Admiral Sir John (Osler Chattock),** KCB 1967 (CB 1964); OBE 1945; Flag Officer, Scotland and N Ireland, 1966-68; retired; *b* 9 May 1913; *er s* of late Major L. C. Hayes, RAMC and Mrs Hayes; *m* 1939, Hon. Rosalind Mary Finlay, *o d* of 2nd and last Viscount Finlay of Nairn; two *s* one *d*. *Educ:* RN Coll., Dartmouth. Entered RN, 1927. Served War of 1939-45; Atlantic, HMS Repulse, Singapore, Russian Convoys, Malta. The Naval Sec., 1962-64; Flag Officer, Flotillas, Home Fleet, 1964-66. Comdr 1948; Capt. 1953; Rear-Adm. 1962; Vice-Adm. 1965. Mem., Queen's Body Guard for Scotland (Royal Company of Archers), 1969. Pres., Scottish Council, King George's Fund for Sailors, 1968. CC Ross and Cromarty, 1969. King Gustav V of Sweden Jubilee Medal, 1948. *Address:* Arabella House, by Tain, Ross and Cromarty. *T:* Nigg Station 213. *Club:* United Service.

**HAYES, John Philip;** Deputy Director General of Economic Planning, Ministry of Overseas Development, since 1969; *b* 1924; *s* of late Harry Hayes and of Mrs G. E. de Garston (*née* Hallsworth); *m* 1956, Susan Elizabeth, *d* of Sir Percivale Liesching, *qv*; one *s* one *d*. *Educ:* Cranleigh Sch.; Corpus Christi Coll., Oxford. RAFVR, 1943-46. Barnett Memorial Fellowship, 1948-49; Political and Economic Planning, 1950-53; OEEC, 1953-58; Internat. Bank for Reconstruction and Develt, 1958-64; Head, Economic Develt Div., OECD, 1964-67; Dir, World Economy Div., Economic Planning Staff, ODM, 1967-69. *Recreations:* music, lawn tennis. *Address:* Stoke House, Pensford Avenue, Kew, Richmond, Surrey. *T:* 01-876 2964.

**HAYES, John Trevor,** MA Oxon, PhD London; Director of the London Museum since 1970; *b* 21 Jan. 1929; *er s* of Leslie Thomas Hayes and Gwendoline (*née* Griffiths), London. *Educ:* Ardingly; Keble Coll., Oxford (Open Exhibr); Courtauld Inst. of Art, London; Inst. of Fine Arts, New York. Asst Keeper, London Museum, 1954-70; Commonwealth Fund Fellow, 1958-59 (NY Univ.); Vis. Prof. in History of Art, Yale Univ., 1969. *Publications:* London: a pictorial history, 1969; The Drawings of Thomas Gainsborough, 1970; Catalogue of Oil Paintings in the London Museum, 1970; various London Museum pubns; numerous articles in The Burlington Magazine, Apollo and other jls. *Recreations:* music, walking, travel. *Address:* c/o The London Museum, Kensington Palace, W8. *T:* 01-937 9816.

**HAYES, Michael,** MA, BL; Professor of Modern Irish, University College, Dublin, retired Oct. 1960; *b* 1 Dec. 1889; *s* of John and Jane Hayes; *m* 1917, Margaret Kavanagh; one *s* one *d* (and *er s* decd). *Educ:* Christian Schs, Synge Street, and University Coll., Dublin. Asst Prof. of French in University Coll., Dublin, until 1922; Minister for Education, Dail Eireann, 1922; Speaker, Dail Eireann, and Chm. of the Civil Service Commission, Saorstat Eireann, 1922-32; Leader of Fine Gael Party in Senate, Republic of Ireland, 1938-65; retired 1965. *Recreation:* golf. *Address:* 143 Templeogue Road, Dublin.

**HAYES, Thomas William Henry;** Regional Director of Prisons, South West Region, since 1969; *b* 1 Aug. 1912; *s* of Henry Daniel and Joanna Hayes; *m* 1933, Alice Frances; one *s*. *Educ:* Central Foundation Sch., London; London Univ. After 3 years in teaching and 2 in industry joined Prison Service, 1937, as Borstal Housemaster. Served in RA, 1940-45. Dep. Gov. Rochester Borstal, 1945-48; Staff Officer, with Police and Prisons Mission to Greece, 1948-51; Governor, subseq. of Lewes Prison, Hatfield and Lowdham Grange Borstals, Ashford Remand Centre and Wormwood Scrubs Prison; Asst Dir of Borstals, Home Office, 1964-69. *Recreations:* golf, contract bridge. *Address:* 2 Cedar Row, Shirehampton, Bristol BS11 0UJ. *T:* Avonmouth 3827. *Clubs:* Broad Arrows CC, Shirehampton Golf.

**HAYES, Prof. William,** FRS 1964; FRSE 1968; Professor of Molecular Genetics, University of Edinburgh, since 1968, and Hon. Director, Medical Research Council, Molecular Genetics Unit (Director, 1957-68); Past Hon. Senior Lecturer in Bacteriology, Royal Postgraduate Medical School of London; *b* 18 Jan. 1913; *s* of William Hayes and Miriam (*née* Harris), Co. Dublin, Ireland; *m* 1941, Honora Lee; one *s*. *Educ:* College of St Columba, Rathfarnham, Co. Dublin; Dublin Univ. BA (1st Cl. Mods. Nat. Sci.) Dublin, 1936; MB, BCh, Dublin, 1937; FRCPI 1945; ScD, Dublin, 1949. Served in India as Major, RAMC, Specialist in Pathology, 1942-46. Lectr in Bacteriology, Trinity Coll., Dublin, 1947-50; Sen. Lectr in Bacteriology, Postgraduate Medical Sch. of London, 1950-57. Hon. DSc Leicester, 1966; Hon. LLD, Dublin, 1970. *Publication:* The Genetics of Bacteria and their Viruses, 1964. *Recreations:* painting, reading or doing nothing. *Address:* 15 Moray Place, Edinburgh 3. *T:* 031-225 3471.

**HAYGARTH JACKSON, Harold;** *see* Jackson, H. H.

**HAYHOE, Bernard John, (Barney),** CEng, MIMechE; MP (C) Heston and Isleworth, since 1970; *b* 8 Aug. 1925; *s* of Frank Stanley and Catherine Hayhoe; *m* 1962, Anne Gascoigne Thornton, *o d* of Bernard William and Hilda Thornton; two *s* one *d*. *Educ:* State schools; Borough Polytechnic. Tool Room Apprentice, 1941-44; Armaments Design Dept, Ministry of Supply, 1944-54; Inspectorate of Armaments, 1954-63; Conservative Research Dept, 1965-70.

*Address:* 20 Wool Road, SW20. *T:* 01-947 0037. *Clubs:* Carlton; Conservative (Hounslow).

**HAYHOE, Prof. Frank George James,** MD, FRCP; Leukaemia Research Fund Professor of Haematological Medicine, University of Cambridge, since 1968; Fellow and Vice-Master, Darwin College, Cambridge, since 1964; *b* 25 Oct. 1920; *s* of Frank Stanley and Catharine Hayhoe; *m* 1945, Jacqueline Marie Marguerite (*née* Dierkx); two *s. Educ:* Selhurst Grammar Sch.; Trinity Hall, Cambridge; St Thomas's Hospital Medical Sch. BA Cantab 1942; MRCS, LRCP 1944; MB, BChir Cantab 1945; MRCP 1949; MA Cantab 1949; MD Cantab 1951; FRCP 1965. Captain RAMC, 1945-47. Registrar, St Thomas' Hosp., 1947-49. Elmore Research Student, Cambridge Univ., 1949-51; Lectr in Medicine, Cambridge Univ., 1951-68. *Publications:* (ed) Lectures in Haematology, 1960; Leukaemia: Research and Clinical Practice, 1960; Cytology and Cytochemistry of Acute Leukaemia, 1964; (ed) Current Research in Leukaemia, 1965; An Atlas of Haematological Cytology, 1969; contribs to med. and scientific jls, on haematological topics, especially leukaemia. *Address:* Department of Medicine, University of Cambridge. *T:* Cambridge 45171.
*See also B. J. Hayhoe.*

**HAYMAN, Perceval Mills Cobham;** *b* 31 Oct. 1883; 2nd *s* of Canon Henry Telford Hayman, TD, MA, and Mrs Hayman, JP; *m* 1st, 1914, Susan Moon (*d* 1924), *d* of late W. H. Hartley, Hoarstones and Fence Gate, Lancs; one *s* (and one *s* killed in action, 1943); 2nd, 1928, Agnes Vera, *d* of late Gerald Hall Kennedy; one *d. Educ:* Eastbourne; abroad. Called to Bar, Inner Temple, 1913. Served European War, 1914-19, with E Lancs Regt (wounded, 1918), and as District Courts Martial Officer; retired from active list, 1919, with rank of Capt. Admitted Solicitor, 1919; Group Registrar of County Courts, 1932-56; District Registrar, High Court, 1939-56 and Hon. Mem. Registrars Assoc.; re-admitted to the Bar, Inner Temple; Hon. Mem. Oxford Circuit. Member: Glos Diocesan Board of Finance, 1942-67; Standing Joint Cttee, 1942-58; a Founder, Lilian Faithfull Homes for Old People (Chm. 1952-59); Chm. Council Friends of Tewkesbury Abbey, 1958-66. Home Guard, 1940-44; Corp. Mem. Cheltenham Ladies' Coll., 1944. Deputy Chm. Glos QS, 1947-58. JP Co. Glos, 1942. FRGS, Hon. FZS. District and Asst County Comr, NE Lancs Scouts, 1922-39; Scout Medal of Merit and Hon. Comr, 1939. Coronation Medal, 1953. Masonry: Deputy Provincial Grand Master, Glos, 1950. *Publications:* Some Elementary Notes on Military Law and Procedure (4 Editions, 1941). Numerous contributions on military law to legal publications, etc. *Recreations:* formerly cricket, hockey; now watching cricket. *Address:* Dolphin House, Charlton Park Gate, Cheltenham, Glos. *T:* Cheltenham 24725. *Clubs:* Junior Carlton, Marylebone Cricket, Farmers'; New (Cheltenham).

**HAYMAN, Peter Telford,** CMG 1963; CVO 1965; MBE 1945; British High Commissioner in Canada, since 1970; *b* 14 June 1914; *s* of C. H. T. Hayman, The Manor House, Brackley, Northants; *m* 1942, Rosemary Eardley Blomefield; one *s* one *d. Educ:* Stowe; Worcester Coll., Oxford. Asst Principal: Home Office, 1937-39; Min. of Home Security, 1939-41; Asst Priv. Sec. to Home Sec. (Rt Hon. Herbert Morrison, MP), 1941-42; Principal, Home Office, 1942. Served War, 1942-45, Rifle Bde, Major. Principal, Home Office, 1945-49; transf. to Min. of Defence as Personal Asst to Chief Staff Officer to the Minister, 1949-52; Asst Sec, Min. of Defence, 1950; UK Delegation to NATO, 1952-54; transf. to FO, 1954; Counsellor, Belgrade, 1955-58; seconded for temp. duty with Governor of Malta, 1958; Couns., Baghdad, 1959-61; Dir-Gen. of British Information Services, New York, 1961-64; Minister and Dep. Comdt, Brit. Milit. Govt in Berlin, 1964-66; Asst Under-Sec., FO, 1966-69; Dep. Under-Secretary of State, FCO, 1969-70. *Recreations:* fishing, travel. *Address:* c/o Foreign and Commonwealth Office, SW1; Uxmore House, Checkendon, Oxon. *T:* 658. *Club:* Travellers'.

**HAYMAN, Prof. Walter Kurt,** FRS 1956; MA; ScD (Cambridge); Hon. ARCS (Imperial College); Professor of Pure Mathematics at the Imperial College of Science and Technology, London; *b* 6 Jan. 1926; *s* of late Franz Samuel Haymann and Ruth Therese (*née* Hensel); *m* 1947, Margaret Riley Crann, MA Cantab, *d* of Thomas Crann, New Earswick, York; three *d. Educ:* Gordonstoun Sch.; St John's Coll., Cambridge. Lecturer at King's Coll., Newcastle upon Tyne, 1947, and Fellow of St John's Coll., Cambridge, 1947-50; Lecturer, 1947, and Reader, 1953-56, Exeter. 1st Smiths prize, 1948, shared Adams Prize, 1949, Junior Berwick Prize, 1955; Senior Berwick Prize, 1964. Visiting Lecturer at Brown Univ., USA, 1949-50, at Stanford Univ., USA (summer) 1950 and 1955, and to the American Mathematical Soc., 1961. Co-founder with Mrs Hayman of British Mathematical Olympiad. *Publications:* Multivalent Functions (Cambridge, 1958) Meromorphic Functions (Oxford, 1964); Research Problems in Function Theory (London, 1967); papers in various mathematical journals. *Recreations:* music, travel. *Address:* Imperial College, Exhibition Road, SW7. *T:* 01-589 5111.

**HAYMAN, Ven. William Samuel;** Archdeacon of Lewisham since 1960; Chaplain to The Queen's Household since 1961; *b* 3 June 1903; *s* of late Rev. William Henry Hayman, Rector of Leckford, and late Louise Charlotte Hayman; *m* 1930, Rosemary Prideaux Metcalfe; one *s* one *d. Educ:* Merchant Taylors' Sch.; St John's Coll., Oxford (MA). Deacon, 1926; Priest, 1927; Curate: St Matthew, Brixton, 1926-32; Wimbledon (in charge of St Mark), 1932-34; Vicar of Finstall, Worcs, 1934-38; Rector of Cheam, 1938-. Hon. Canon of Southwark 1952-60; Rural Dean of Beddington, 1955-60. *Recreations:* fly-fishing, photography, music, amateur operatics, scouting. *Address:* The Rectory, 15 Malden Road, Cheam, Surrey. *T:* 01-644 9110.

**HAYNES, Denys Eyre Lankester;** Keeper of Greek and Roman Antiquities, British Museum, since 1956; *b* 15 Feb. 1913; 2nd *s* of late Rev. Hugh Lankester Haynes and late Emmeline Marianne Chaldecott; *m* 1951, Sybille Edith Overhoff. *Educ:* Marlborough; Trinity Coll., Cambridge. Scholar, British School at Rome, 1936; Asst Keeper: Victoria and Albert Museum, 1937; British Museum, 1939-54 (released for war service, 1939-45); Dep. Keeper, British Museum, 1954. Corr. Mem., German Archæological Inst., 1953; Ordinary Mem., 1957. *Publications:* Porta Argentariorum, 1939; Ancient Tripolitania, 1946; Antiquities of Tripolitania, 1956; The Parthenon Frieze, 1958; The Portland Vase, 1964. *Address:* Flat 3, 24 Hereford Square, SW7. *Club:* Travellers'.

**HAYNES, Edwin William George;** Under-Secretary, Ministry of Technology; *b* 10 Dec. 1911; *s* of Frederick William George Haynes and Lilian May Haynes (*née* Armstrong); *m* 1942, Dorothy Kathleen Coombs; one *s* one *d.*

*Educ:* Regent Street Polytechnic Secondary Sch.; University of London (BA, LLM). Barrister-at-law, Lincoln's Inn, 1946. Estate Duty Office, Inland Revenue, 1930-39; Air Min., 1939; Min. of Aircraft Production, 1940; Min. of Supply, 1946; Min. of Aviation, 1959; Under-Sec., 1964. *Recreations:* gardening, tennis. *Address:* 92 Malmains Way, Beckenham, Kent. *T:* 01-650 0224.

**HAYNES, Ernest Harry,** FIA; Chairman: Royal London Mutual Insurance Society Ltd, since 1956; Span Developments Ltd; Director, Hammersons Property & Investment Trust Ltd; *b* 19 Sept. 1904; *m* 1931, Doris Shackleton; one *s* two *d*. *Educ:* Alleyn's Sch., Dulwich. Royal London Mutual Insurance Soc.; Asst Actuary, 1939; Actuary 1947; Dir, 1952; Joint Managing Dir, 1955-69. Vice-Chm., Hosp. Saving Assoc.; Trustee, Yvonne Arnaud Theatre Trust. Hon. Treasurer, Soldiers', Sailors' and Airmen's Families Association. *Recreation:* gardening. *Address:* Wishing Well Cottage, Wormley, Surrey. *T:* Wormley 3435.

**HAYNES, Sir George (Ernest),** Kt 1962; CBE 1945; Hon. President of International Conference of Social Work (President, 1948-56); *b* 24 Jan. 1902; *e s* of Albert Ernest and Sarah Anne Haynes, Middlewich, Ches; *m* 1930, Kathleen Norris Greenhaigh; two *d*. *Educ:* Sandbach Sch.; Liverpool Univ. BSc 1922; school master and educational and social research, 1923-28; Warden of University Settlement, Liverpool, 1928-33; Dir, Nat. Council of Social Service, 1940-67; Mem., Lord Chancellor's Cttee: on Procedure of County Courts, 1948; on Legal Aid, 1944 and 1950-; Chairman of Temp. Internat. Council for Educational Reconstruction of UNESCO, 1947-48; Mem. Colonial Office Advisory Cttee, on Social Development, 1947-63. Pres., National Birthday Trust; Chairman: National Bureau for Co-operation in Child Care, 1963-68; Invalid Children's Aid Association, 1964-69; Rural Industries Loan Fund Ltd, 1949-68; Social Services Cttee, National Association for Mental Health, 1955-58; Standing Conference of British Organisations for Aid to Refugees, 1953-60; Council of British Assoc. of Residential Settlement, 1963-68; Adv. Council, Rural Industries Bureau, 1962-68; Exec. Cttee, British National Conference on Social Welfare, 1950-67; Social Science Cttee, Nat. Fund for Research into Crippling Diseases. vice-Chm., Family Welfare Assoc., 1961-66. Mem. Council of Brit. Red Cross Soc.; Crown Trustee, City Parochial Foundation; UK Delegate to UN Social Commission, 1962-66, and to UN Commn for Social Develt 1967. René Sand Memorial Award, 1958. *Address:* 12 Celia Court, Holmesdale Road, Kew, Surrey. *T:* 01-940 6589. *Club:* Athenæum.

**HAYNES, Rear-Adm. William Allen,** CB 1968; OBE 1941; retired 1970; *b* 29 Sept. 1913; *s* of late Paymaster Capt. W. F. Haynes, Royal Navy and late Mrs M. W. Haynes (*née* Wilkinson); *m* 1964, Mary Theodosia Peploe; two *d*. *Educ:* Royal Naval Colleges, Dartmouth, Keyham and Greenwich. HMS Leander, 1935-36; HMS Glasgow, 1938-41; HM Dockyard, Chatham, 1941-44; HMS Gabbard, 1944-47; Admty i/c development of steam catapult, 1947-51; HMS Ceylon (Korean War), 1951-53; Apprentice Trng in HMS Fisgard, 1953-55; HM Dockyard, Chatham, 1955-60; Imp. Def. Coll., 1961; Dir of Naval Ship Production, 1962-67; Dir-Gen., Dockyards and Maintenance, 1967-69. Comdr 1947; Capt. 1958; Rear-Adm. 1966. *Recreations:* sailing, ski-ing, do-it-yourself. *Address:* Bowden House, Dartmouth, Devon. *T:* Stoke Fleming 234. *Clubs:* Army and Navy, Royal Ocean Racing.

**HAYNES DIXON, Margaret Rumer, (Rumer Godden);** writer, playwright, poet; *b* 10 Dec. 1907; *d* of late Arthur Leigh Godden, Lydd House, Aldington, Kent, and Katherine Norah Hingley; *m* 1934, Laurence Sinclair Foster, Calcutta; two *d*; *m* 1949, James Haynes Dixon, London. *Educ:* abroad and Moira House, Eastbourne. *Publications:* Chinese Puzzle, 1935; Lady and Unicorn, 1937; Black Narcissus (novel and play), 1938; Gypsy Gypsy, 1940; Breakfast with the Nikolides, 1941; Fugue in Time (novel and play), 1945; The River, 1946 (filmed, 1950); Rungli-Rungliot (biography), 1943; Candle for St Jude, 1948; In Noah's Ark (poetry), 1949; A Breath of Air, 1950; Kingfishers Catch Fire, 1953; Hans Christian Andersen (biography), 1955; An Episode of Sparrows, 1955 (filmed 1957); Mooltiki, 1957; The Greengage Summer, 1958 (filmed, 1961); China Court, 1961; The Battle of the Villa Florita, 1963 (filmed 1964); Two Under the Indian Sun (with Jon Godden), 1966; The Kitchen Madonna, 1967; Swans and Turtles, 1968; In This House of Brede, 1969. Contributor to periodicals, journals, children's books, etc; published internationally (11 languages). *Address:* Lamb House, Rye, East Sussex.

**HAYTER,** 3rd Baron *cr* 1927 of Chislehurst, Kent; **George Charles Hayter Chubb;** Bt 1900; Managing Director since 1941, Chairman since 1957 of Chubb & Son's Lock & Safe Co. Ltd; Director of Charles Early & Marriott (Witney) Ltd since 1952; *b* 25 April 1911; *e s* of 2nd Baron Hayter and Mary (*d* 1948), *d* of J. F. Haworth; *S* father, 1967; *m* 1940, Elizabeth Anne Rumbold; three *s* one *d*. *Educ:* Leys Sch., Cambridge; Trinity Coll., Cambridge (MA). Chairman: Royal Society of Arts, 1965-66; Management Cttee, King Edward's Hospital Fund for London, 1965-; Executives Assoc. of GB, 1960; Duke of Edinburgh's Countryside in 1970 Cttee. President: Canadian Chamber of Commerce in Great Britain, Inc., 1966-67; Royal Warrant Holders Association, 1967; Business Equipment Trades Association, 1954-55. Member: Council of Industrial Design, 1964-; BNEC, 1969-. Worshipful Company of Weavers': Liveryman, 1934-; Upper Bailiff, 1961-62. *Publication:* Security offered by Locks and Safes (Lecture, RSA), 1962. *Heir: s* Hon. George William Michael Chubb, *b* 9 Oct. 1943. *Address:* Ashtead House, Ashtead, Surrey. *T:* Ashtead 3476. *Club:* Carlton.

**HAYTER, Stanley William,** CBE 1967 (OBE 1959); artist; *b* 27 Dec. 1901; *s* of William Harry Hayter and Ellen Mercy Palmer; *m* 1st, 1926, Edith Fletcher (marriage dissolved at Reno, Nevada, 1929); one *s* decd; 2nd, 1940, Helen Phillips; two *s*. *Educ:* Whitgift Middle Sch.; King's Coll., London. Chemist, Anglo-Iranian Oil Co., Abadan, Iran, 1922-25. Founded Atelier 17, Paris, 1927. Has exhibited since 1927 in various cities of Europe, America and Japan (incl. London: 1928, 1938, 1957, 1962, 1967). Paintings and prints in principal museums in Gt Britain, France, Belgium, Switzerland, Sweden, Italy, Canada, USA, Japan. Legion of Honour, 1951; Chevalier des Arts et Lettres, 1967. *Publications:* New Ways of Gravure, 1949 (New York also) (revised edn, 1966); Nature and Art of Motion, New York, 1964; About Prints, 1962. *Address:* 63 rue Daguerre, Paris 14e. *T:* SEG 61-33.

**HAYTER, Sir William Goodenough,** KCMG 1953 (CMG 1948); Warden of New College, Oxford, since 1958; *b* 1 Aug. 1906; *s* of late Sir William Goodenough Hayter, KBE; *m* 1938,

Iris Marie, *d* of late Lieut-Col C. H. Grey (formerly Hoare), DSO; one *d*. *Educ:* Winchester; New Coll., Oxford. Entered HM Diplomatic Service, 1930; served Foreign Office, 1930; Vienna, 1931; Moscow, 1934; Foreign Office, 1937; China, 1938; Washington, 1941; Foreign Office, 1944 (Asst Under-Sec. of State, 1948); HM Minister, Paris, 1949; Ambassador to USSR, 1953-57; Deputy Under-Sec. of State, Foreign Office, 1957-58. Fellow of Winchester Coll. Pres. British Institute in Paris, and Anglo-Austrian Soc.; Trustee, British Museum, 1960-70. Grosses Goldenes Ehrenzeichen mit dem Stern für Verdienste (Austria), 1967. *Publications:* The Diplomacy of the Great Powers, 1961; The Kremlin and the Embassy, 1966; Russia and the World, 1970; William of Wykeham, Patron of the Arts, 1970. *Address:* The Warden's Lodgings, New College, Oxford. *Club:* Brooks's.

**HAYWARD, Sir Alfred,** KBE 1961 (CBE 1960); retired; *b* England, 14 Jan. 1896; *s* of Thomas and Minnie Hayward, Sudbourne, Suffolk; *m* 1923, Margaret Fromm; one *s* two *d*. Came to New Zealand, 1911. Served European War, 1914-18, in France, 1916-18. Took up farming in Waikato district. Dir, NZ Co-op. Dairy Co., 1933-61. Chm., 1947-61; Deputy Chm., NZ Dairy Board, 1958. JP 1957. *Address:* 36 Rita Street, Mount Maunganui, New Zealand.

**HAYWARD, Alfred Robert,** RP; ARWS 1960; NEAC; artist; portrait, water colours and landscape painter; mural decorator; *b* London, 1875; *m*; one *d*. *Educ:* privately; S Kensington; The Slade Sch. Freeman of City of London. Examples of his paintings are included in the following permanent collections: Brighton Museum; Municipal Gallery, Johannesburg; National Museum of Wales, Cardiff; Public Art Gallery, Christchurch, New Zealand; Imperial War Museum; International Gallery of Modern Art, Venice; Tate Gallery, Millbank; Whitworth Institute, Manchester; Municipal Gallery, Southampton; Emmanuel Coll., Cambridge; an Exhibition of Water Colours and Paintings of Venice held at the Leicester Galleries, Jan. 1924; Exhibition of Paintings held at Wildenstein Galleries, 1936; exhibited pictures in London since 1896, principally at The New English Art Club, The Royal Society of Portrait Painters, The Royal Academy, and at Paris, Rome, Venice, and Pittsburgh. Retrospective Exhibition: Federation of British Artists, 1964; FBA Gallery, 1967; Harvane Gallery, 1970. Joined Artists Rifles beginning of European War, 1914-18; 2nd Lieut RGA (SR) 1916 (Anti-Aircraft); Lieut 1917; Official War Artist during last few months of the War; awarded Mention Honorable Paris Salon, 1921; a Decoration representing the First Governor and presented by the Bank of England placed in Royal Exchange, 1923; the decoration of the Safety Curtain, De La Warr Pavilion, Bexhill-on-Sea, 1939; awarded a Civil List Pension, 1943; lately teaching painting and drawing from life, City and Guilds School of Art. *Address:* 14 Manor Gardens, Hampton-on-Thames, Middx. *T:* 01-979 4223. *Clubs:* Chelsea Arts, National Book League.

**HAYWARD, Charles William,** CBE 1970; Chairman and Joint Managing Director of Firth Cleveland Ltd and of constituent companies in Group at home and abroad at varying dates since 1936; *b* 3 Sept. 1892; *s* of John and Mary Hayward, Wolverhampton; *m* 1915, Hilda, *d* of late John and Alexandra Arnold; one *s*. *Educ:* St John's School, Wolverhampton. Director of Electric and General Industrial Trusts Ltd, 1928, Chairman and Managing Director, 1932; Vice-Chairman, The Grand Bahama Port Authority. Mem. of Post Office Advisory Council, 1952. Held Directorships since 1920 in various companies, public and private, including engineering, farming and horticulture. Trustee, The Hayward Foundn, 1961 (Chm.); Pres., Royal Wolverhampton Sch. Liveryman of Barbers' Company; Freeman of the City of London, 1938; Worshipful Company of Masons. Hon. FRCS, 1970; Hon. Fellow, Inst. of Ophthalmology, 1967. *Recreations:* yachting, collecting antiques and works of art. *Address:* Lydhurst, Warninglid, Haywards Heath, Sussex. *T:* Warninglid 247. *Clubs:* Royal Thames Yacht, Royal Automobile.

**HAYWARD, Rev. Edward,** MA; retired as Rector of Maresfield (1956-59); *b* 15 June 1884; *s* of Joseph and Annie Hayward, Stanbridge House, Holt, Wiltshire; *m* 1st, 1908, Constance Alethe Perry (*d* 1930); one *s* one *d*; 2nd, 1933, Eileen, *o d* of Charles A. Swan, Lisbon; two *s*. *Educ:* Monkton Combe School; Sidney Sussex College (Senior Classical Scholar, 1903, Stewart of Rannoch Scholarship, 1904), and Ridley Hall, Cambridge. 2nd Class Honours, Theo. Tripos, 1906; 3rd Class Honours, Theo. Trip., Part ii, 1907. Curate of S Silas Lozells, Birmingham, 1907-11; CMS Missionary at Panyam, N Nigeria, 1911-19; Organising Secretary, CMS, 1920-23; Secretary for Far East Missions, CMS, 1923-26; Headmaster, Monkton Combe School, 1926-46; Rector of Eastrop, Basingstoke, 1949-55. *Address:* 3 Rotherfield Road, Boscombe, Bournemouth, Hants. *T:* Bournemouth 44995.

**HAYWARD, Sir Edward (Waterfield),** Kt 1961; grazier and company director, Australia; Chairman and Managing Director, John Martin & Co. Ltd; Chairman of Directors: South Australian Insurance Co. Ltd since 1948; Coca Cola Bottlers Ltd since 1948; The Bank of Adelaide; Director: Finance Corporation of Australia since 1955; Bennett & Fisher Ltd since 1960; SA Telecasters Ltd; *b* 10 November 1903; *s* of Arthur Dudley Hayward and Mary Anne Hayward; *m* 1935, Ursula, *y d* of late Mr and Mrs T. E. Barr Smith. *Educ:* St Peter's Coll., Adelaide, S Australia. Lt-Col, 2nd AIF, Middle East, New Guinea and Borneo (despatches: 1944 in New Guinea, 1945 in Borneo). Chm., Council of St John in South Australia, 1946; Purchased (in conjunction with wife) Silverton Park, Delamere, SA 1942, and established Border Leicester Stud and later Hereford Stud. KStJ 1960; Bronze Star Medal, USA, 1945. *Recreations:* polo (represented S Australia, Interstate, 1936-57); golf, swimming. *Address:* 100 Rundle Street, Adelaide, SA 5001, Australia. *T:* 23-0200; Carrick Hill, Springfield, SA 5062, Australia. *T:* 79-3886. *Clubs:* Adelaide, Naval, Military & Air Force, Royal Adelaide Golf, Adelaide Polo (Adelaide SA); Australian, Royal Sydney Golf (Sydney, NSW).

**HAYWARD, Graham William,** MD London; FRCP; Physician, St Bartholomew's Hospital, London, since 1956; Senior physician, National Heart Hospital, London, since 1947; Adviser in Cardiology, Ministry of Health, since 1961; Cardiologist, King Edward VII Hospital for Officers, since 1964; *b* 7 June 1911; *s* of William George Hayward, OBE; *m* 1946, Mary Anna Harding, Philadelphia, USA; two *s* one *d* (and one *s* decd). *Educ:* Cardiff High School; St Bartholomew's Hosp. and University of London. MD London, 1937, MB, BS (Hons Med., Path., Surgery, Midwifery and Forensic Med. and Univ. Gold Medal), 1935; FRCP 1946. Kirkes Schol. and

Gold Medal, Clin. Med., 1933; Brackenbury Schol. in Med., 1933; Willett Medal, Op. Surg., 1934 (St Bartholomew's Hosp.). Fellowships: Rockefeller Foundation, USA, 1937-38; Research in Med., Penna. Hosp., Philadelphia, 1937-38; Mackenzie Mackinnon Research, Royal Coll. Physicians, 1939. Lieut-Col. NZ Med. Corps; served in Middle East and Italy as OC Med. Div., 3rd NZ Hosp., 1940-45. Asst Dir Med. Professorial Unit, St Bartholomew's, and Reader in Med., Univ. of London, 1945-47; Asst Physician, St Bartholomew's, 1944-55. Dean, Inst. of Cardiology, Univ. of London, 1948-61. Examiner in Medicine: Univ. of London, 1952-58; Univ. of Khartoum, 1956; Univ. of Cambridge, 1958; University Coll. of The West Indies, 1959-60. Member: Association Physicians Great Britain; Cardiac Soc. *Publications:* articles in medical and scientific journals on cardio-vascular subjects. *Recreation:* gardening. *Address:* 149 Harley Street, W1. *T:* 01-935 4444; Colyton, Totteridge Lane, N20. *T:* 01-445 1761.

**HAYWARD, Sir Isaac (James),** Kt 1959; LLD; JP; *b* Blaenavon, Monmouthshire, 17 Nov. 1884; *m* 1st, 1913, Alice Mayers (decd); three *s* (and one *s* killed 1944); 2nd, 1951, Violet Cleveland. *Educ:* non-provided elementary school. Trade Union Office for 28 years, National Union of Enginemen, Firemen, Mechanics, and Elec. Workers; from 1938, until retirement in 1946, Gen. Sec. to Union. London County Council: Member, 1928-65; Chairman of General Purposes Committee, 1937-38; Public Assistance Committee, 1934-37; Education Committee, 1945-47; Welfare of the Blind Committee, 1938-39; Chief Whip, 1932-47; Leader of the Council, 1947-65. Chairman, London Electricity Consultative Council, 1948-60. Member of London and Home Counties Jt Electricity Authority from inception, 1925, until nationalisation, 1949; late Member of No 9 and 10 Areas (London) of District Jt Industrial Council for Electrical Supply Industry; Member: BEA Board, 1946-48; London Electricity Bd, 1948-60; Court of University of London; South Bank Theatre and Opera House Board, 1962-. *Recreations:* bowls, chess. *Address:* 140 Chudleigh Road, SE4. *T:* 01-690 0323.

**HAYWARD, Sir Richard (Arthur),** Kt 1969; CBE 1966; Member for Industrial Relations, Post Office Board since 1969; *b* 14 March 1910; *m* 1936, Ethel Wheatcroft; one *s* one *d. Educ:* Catford Central Sch. Post Office: Boy Messenger; Counter Clerk; Union of Post Office Workers: Assistant Secretary, 1947; Deputy General Secretary, 1951. Secretary General, Civil Service National Whitley Council (Staff Side), 1955-66; Chm., Supplementary Benefits Commn, 1966-69. UK Rep., Meeting of Experts on Conditions of Work and Service of Public Servants, ILO, 1963; overseas visits, inc. Israel, Mauritius, Canada, to advise on Trade Unionism in Public Services. Chm., Civil Service Sports Council, 1968-; Pres., Civil Service Cricket Assoc., 1966-. Governor, Guy's Hosp., 1949-. *Recreations:* topography of Southwark; Kent cricket. *Address:* 49 Hayes Way, Beckenham, Kent BR2 3RR. *T:* 01-650 5210. *Clubs:* MCC, Royal Automobile.

**HAYWARD, Tom Christopher,** CBE 1946; DL; Clerk of the Peace and County Council for West Sussex, 1938-66 and Clerk to Lieutenancy for Sussex, 1938-68, retired; *b* 25 Nov. 1904; *s* of Major P. C. G. Hayward, Needham Market, Suffolk; *m* 1930, Sybil Lisette Grainger-Brunt; one *s* one *d. Educ:* Cheltenham Coll.; Corpus Christi Coll., Cambridge (BA). Solicitor, 1929; Assistant Solicitor, Bath City Council, 1929, Oxfordshire County Council, 1929; Senior Asst Solicitor, E Sussex County Council, 1930; Deputy Clerk of the Peace and of County Council for Staffs, 1934. Controller for Civil Defence for W Sussex. Lord of the Manor, Thorndon-cum-Hestley Hall, Suffolk. DL Sussex, 1968. *Recreations:* hunting, shooting, golf, cricket. *Address:* Threeways, Canon's Close, Aldwick, Sussex. *Clubs:* Royal Automobile, MCC; Sussex.

**HAYWOOD, Thomas Charles Stanley,** OBE 1962; JP; Lord Lieutenant of Rutland since 1963; *b* 10 March 1911; *s* of late Charles B. Haywood, Woodhatch, Reigate, Surrey; *m* 1937, Anne, *d* of J. B. A. Kessler, London; two *s* one *d. Educ:* Winchester; Magdalene Coll., Cambridge. Served 1939-42 with Leics Yeomanry, Capt. 1940. Chm. Trustees, Oakham Sch., 1964-. DL 1962, JP 1957, High Sheriff 1952, County of Rutland. *Address:* Gunthorpe, Oakham, Rutland. *T:* Manton 203. *Clubs:* Bath, MCC.

**HAZAN, John Boris Roderick,** QC 1969; JP; Barrister-at-law; *b* 3 Oct. 1926; *s* of Selik and Eugenie Hazan. *Educ:* King's Coll., Taunton; King's Coll., Univ. of London. Called to Bar, Lincoln's Inn, 1948. Prosecuting Counsel to Inland Revenue, South Eastern Circuit, 1967-69. Dep. Chm., Surrey QS, 1969-. JP Surrey, 1969. *Recreations:* music, opera, walking. *Address:* 4 Brick Court, Temple, EC4. *T:* 01-353 2725. *Club:* Savile.

**HAZELL, Bertie,** CBE 1962 (MBE 1946); District Organiser, National Union of Agricultural Workers, since 1937 and President, 1966; *b* 18 April 1907; *s* of John and Elizabeth Hazell; *m* 1936, Dora A. Barham; one *d. Educ:* various elementary schs in Norfolk. Agricultural worker, 1921; apptd Sec. and Agent to E Norfolk Divisional Labour Party, Sept. 1933; Mem. W Riding of Yorks, War Agricultural Executive Cttee, 1939 (Chm. several of its Cttees, throughout war period). Contested (Lab) Barkston Ash Parliamentary Division, 1945 and 1950 Gen. Elections; MP (Lab) North Norfolk, 1964-70. Chm., E and W Ridings Regional Bd for Industry, 1954-64; Member: E Riding Co. Agricultural Exec. Cttee, 1946-64; Agricultural Wages Board, 1946-; Leeds Regional Hosp. Board, 1948- (Chm. Works and Buildings Cttee); Magistrate, City of York, 1950-; Chm. York and District Employment Cttee, 1963; Vice-Chm., Leeds Regional Hosp. Bd, 1967-. *Recreation:* gardening. *Address:* 42 Fellbrook Avenue, Beckfield Lane, Acomb, York. *T:* York 78443.

**HAZI, Dr Vencel,** Golden Grade of Order of Merit for Labour, 1962, and of Medal of Merit of Hungarian People's Republic, 1953; Ambassador of Hungary to the Court of St James's since 1970; *b* 3 Sept. 1925; *m* 1952, Judit Zell; one *d. Educ:* Technical Univ. and Univ. of Economics, Budapest. Entered Diplomatic Service, 1950; served in Min. of Foreign Affairs, Budapest, 1950; Press Attaché, Hungarian Legation, London, 1951-53; Counsellor, Legation, Stockholm, 1957-58; Ambassador: to Iraq, and to Afghanistan, 1958-61; to Greece, and to Cyprus, 1962-64; Head of Western Dept, Min. of For. Affairs, Budapest, 1964-68; Dep. For. Minister, Budapest, 1968-70. Grand Cordon of Order of Omayoum, 1st Class, Iran. *Recreations:* reading, music, swimming, chess. *Address:* Hungarian Embassy, 35 Eaton Place, SW1. *T:* 01-235 4048/7191. *Club:* Opera Fans (Budapest).

**HAZLERIGG,** family name of **Baron Hazlerigg.**

**HAZLERIGG,** 2nd Baron, *cr* 1945, of Noseley; **Arthur Grey Hazlerigg,** Bt, *cr* 1622; MC 1945; DL, JP; *b* 24 Feb. 1910; *e s* of 1st Baron and Dorothy Rachel, *e d* of John Henry Buxton, Easneye, Ware, Herts; *S* father 1949; *m* 1945, Patricia, *e d* of late John Pullar, High Seat, Fields Hill, Kloof, Natal, SA; one *s* two *d*. *Educ:* Eton; Trinity Coll., Cambridge. BA 1932. Served War of 1939-45, Leics Yeomanry (MC); Major, 1941; served in Italy. DL 1946; JP 1946. *Recreations:* tennis, shooting. *Heir: s* Hon. Arthur Grey Hazlerigg, *b* 5 May 1951. *Clubs:* Army and Navy, MCC.

**HAZLEWOOD, Air Cdre Frederick Samuel,** CB 1970; CBE 1967 (OBE 1960); AFC 1951 (Bar to AFC, 1954); Air Officer Commanding and Commandant, Central Flying School, since 1970; *b* 13 May 1921; *s* of Samuel Henry and Lilian Hazlewood; *m* 1943, Isabelle Mary (*née* Hunt); one *s*. *Educ:* Kimbolton Sch. Served War of 1939-45: joined RAF, 1939; ops with Bomber Command, 1941; MEAF and UK Coastal Command, 1940-45. CFS, 1948; Lancaster Units, 1948-53 (Sqdn Ldr); Staff Coll. course, 1955; Comdg Officer, No 90 Valiant Sqdn, 1958-61 (Wing Comdr); HQ, Bomber Comd, 1961-63; HQ, RAF, Germany, 1963-64 (Gp Capt.); OC, RAF, Lyneham, 1965-67; HQ, RAF, Germany, 1968-69 (Air Cdre). *Recreations:* golf, tennis, squash. *Address:* Holly Ditch Farm, Calne, Wilts. *Club:* Royal Air Force.

**HEAD,** family name of **Viscount Head.**

**HEAD,** 1st Viscount *cr* 1960, of Throope; **Antony Henry Head;** PC 1951; GCMG 1963 (KCMG 1961); CBE 1946; MC 1940; *b* 1906; *s* of late Geoffrey Head; *m* 1935, Lady Dorothea Ashley-Cooper, *d* of 9th Earl of Shaftesbury, KP, PC, GCVO, CBE; two *s* one *d* (and one *d* decd). *Educ:* Eton; Royal Military Coll., Sandhurst, Adjt Life Guards, 1934-37; Staff Coll., 1939; Brigade Major 20th Gds Bde, 1940; Asst Sec. Cttee Imperial Defence, 1940-41; Guards Armd Div., 1941-42 (GSO2); representative with Directors of Plans for Amphibious Operations (Brigadier), 1943-45. MP (C) Carshalton Division of Surrey, 1945-60; Sec. of State for War, 1951-56; Minister of Defence, Oct. 1956-Jan. 1957. High Commissioner (first) of the United Kingdom in the Federation of Nigeria, 1960-63; High Commissioner to the new Federation of Malaysia, 1963-66. Trustee of the Thomson Foundation, 1967-. Chm., RNIB, 1968-. Col Comdt, SAS Regt, 1968-. *Recreations:* sailing, shooting. *Heir: s* Hon. Richard Antony Head [*b* 27 Feb. 1937. *Educ:* Eton; Royal Military Coll., Sandhurst. *Address:* Throope Manor, Bishopstone, near Salisbury, Wilts.

**HEAD, Alice Maud;** *b* London; *y d* of F. D. Head. *Educ:* privately; North London Collegiate Sch. for Girls. Editor of Woman at Home, 1909-17; Managing Director of the National Magazine Company, Ltd, and editor of Good Housekeeping, 1924-39; re-joined the firm of George Newnes Ltd, 1941-49; Director, Country Life Ltd, 1942-49. *Publications:* It Could Never Have Happened, 1939; contributions to various daily and weekly publications. *Recreations:* travelling, reading, theatre-going. *Address:* 22 Whitelands House, Chelsea, SW3. *T:* 01-730 1967. *Club:* PEN.

**HEAD, Major Sir Francis (David Somerville),** 5th Bt, *cr* 1838; late Queen's Own Cameron Highlanders; *b* 17 Oct. 1916; *s* of 4th Bt and Grace Margaret (*d* 1967), *d* of late David Robertson; *S* father, 1924; *m* 1st, 1950, Susan Patricia (marr. diss. 1965), *o d* of A. D. Ramsay, OBE; one *s* one *d*; 2nd, 1967, Penelope, *d* of late Wilfred Alexander. *Educ:* Eton; Peterhouse, Cambridge, BA 1937. Served War of 1939-45 (wounded and prisoner); retired 1951. *Heir: s* Richard Douglas Somerville Head [*b* 16 Jan. 1951. *Educ:* Eton]. *Address:* 10 Fairway, Merrow, Guildford, Surrey. *Club:* Naval and Military.

**HEADFORT,** 6th Marquis of, *cr* 1800; **Thomas Geoffrey Charles Michael Taylour;** Bt 1704; Baron Headfort, 1760; Viscount Headfort, 1762; Earl of Bective, 1766; Baron Kenlis (UK), 1831; *b* 20 Jan. 1932; *o s* of 5th Marquis and Elsie Florence, *d* of J. Partridge Tucker, Sydney, NSW, and *widow* of Sir Rupert Clarke, 2nd Bt of Rupertswood; *S* father, 1960; *m* 1958, Hon. Elizabeth Nall-Cain (from whom he obtained a divorce, 1969), *d* of 2nd Baron Brocket; one *s* two *d*. *Educ:* Stowe; Christ's Coll., Cambridge (MA). Chm., Bective Electrical Co. Ltd. 2nd Lieut Life Guards, 1950; acting Pilot Officer, RAFVR, 1952. Freeman, Guild of Air Pilots and Air Navigators, 1958. Piloted Prospector aircraft around Africa, 1960, etc. Associate, Chartered Land Agents' Soc., 1955; Council, Royal Agricultural Society of England, 1961. *Heir: s* Earl of Bective, *qv*. *Address:* Ellerslie, Crosby, Isle of Man. *T:* Marown 521. *Clubs:* Cavalry, Royal Aero; Kildare Street (Dublin); RAF Reserves.

**HEADING, Hon. Sir James Alfred,** Kt 1961; CMG 1955; DCM 1917; MM 1918; *b* Payneham, SA, 26 Jan. 1884; *s* of William Heading, Burn, Eng., and Rhoda Heading, Adelaide; *m* 1919, Ruby Jeanie, *d* of John Henry Thomas, Clarence Park, SA; one *s* three *d*. *Educ:* Netherby, Vic. Served European War, 1914-18 (DCM, MM), 47 and 45 Bns, AIF, 1915-19. Retired farmer. Chairman: Queensland Co-op Bacon Assoc. (now Queensland Bacon Pty Ltd), 1926-57; S Burnett Co-op. Dairy Assoc., 1930-57; Dir Producers Co-op. Distrib. Soc., Sydney, Brisb., Melb., 1938-57. MLA Wide Bay, Qld, 1947-50, Marodian, Qld, 1950-60; Minister for Public Works, Local Govt and Immigration, Qld, 1957-60. Pres. Royal National Agric. and Industrial Assoc. of Qld, 1951-55 (Vice-Pres., 1948-51). *Address:* Highfields, Murgon, Qld, Australia. *Club:* United Service (Brisbane).

**HEADLAM, Air Vice-Marshal Frank,** CB 1965; CBE 1958 (OBE 1954); Head, Australian Joint Services Staff, London, since 1968; *b* 15 July 1914; *s* of Malcolm Headlam, Oatlands, Tasmania; *m* 1940, Katherine Beatrice (marriage dissolved 1956), *d* of P. S. Bridge, Victoria; one *s* one *d*. *Educ:* Clemes Coll., Hobart. Pilot Officer RAAF 1934. Served War of 1939-45 (SE Asia, Northern Australia). Gp Capt. 1942; Air Cdre 1953; Dir-Gen. of Plans, 1958; Mem. for Personnel Dept of Air, 1957 and 1959; Air Vice-Marshal 1961; Air Officer Commanding Operational Command, RAAF Penrith, NSW, 1961-62; Air Officer Commanding 224 Gp, Far East Air Force, 1962-64; Dep. Chief of Air Staff, RAAF, 1965-66; AOC Support Comd, RAAF, Melbourne, 1966-67. ADC to the Queen, 1954. *Recreations:* tennis, golf, fishing, shooting. *Address:* Australia House, Strand, WC2; 7 Argyll Road, Kensington, W8. *Clubs:* Melbourne; Melbourne Cricket; Lawn Tennis Association of Victoria.

**HEADLAM-MORLEY, Prof. Agnes,** MA, BLit; Montague Burton Professor of International Relations, Oxford University, since 1948; *b* 10 Dec. 1902; *o d* of late Sir James Wycliffe Headlam-Morley, CBE, Historical Adviser to the Foreign Office. *Educ:* Wimbledon High Sch., GPDST; Somerville Coll., Oxford. Fellow and Tutor, St Hugh's Coll., Oxford, 1932. Adopted Prospective Conservative

Candidate, Barnard Castle Div. of Durham, 1936. Hon. Fellow Somerville Coll., Oxford, 1948; Mem., St Antony's Coll. Received into the Roman Catholic Church, 1948. *Publications:* The New Democratic Constitutions of Europe, 1929. Editor (with K. Headlam-Morley) of Studies in Diplomatic History by J. W. Headlam-Morley, 1930; Arthur Cayley Headlam (a memoir published in The Fourth Gospel as History by A. C. Headlam, 1948); Last Days, 1960. *Address:* 29 St Mary's Road, Wimbledon, SW19; St Hugh's College, Oxford. *T:* 01-946 6134.

**HEADLAM-MORLEY, Kenneth Arthur Sonntag,** OBE 1962; Secretary, The Iron and Steel Institute, 1933-67; *b* 24 June 1901; *o s* of late Sir James Headlam-Morley, CBE (who assumed additional surname of Morley by Royal Licence, 1917), Historical Adviser to the Foreign Office, and of Else, *y d* of late Dr August Sonntag, Lüneburg; *m* 1951, Lorna Dione, *d* of late Francis Kinchin Smith; three *s* two *d. Educ:* Eton; New Coll., Oxford (Schol.). Staff of Dorman, Long & Co Ltd, 1924; Secretary: Inst. of Metals, 1944-47; Instn of Metallurgists, 1945-48; Dep. Controller Chrome Ore, Magnesite and Wolfram Control, Foundry Bonding Materials Control and assoc. Controls of Min. of Supply, 1940-43. Hon. Life Member: Amer. Inst. of Mining and Metallurgical Engrs, 1955; Amer. Soc. for Metals, 1955. Hon. Member: l'Assoc. des Ingénieurs sortis de l'Ecole de Liège, 1955; Verein deutscher Eisenhüttenleute, 1955; Soc. Française de Métallurgie, 1956; The Indian Institute of Metals, 1963. Chevalier Order of Vasa (Sweden), 1954; Chevalier Order of the Crown (Belgium), 1955. *Recreation:* gardening. *Address:* Whorlton Hall, near Barnard Castle, Co. Durham. *T:* Whorlton 278; 01-730 0061. *Club:* Athenæum.

**HEADLEY,** 7th Baron *cr* 1797; **Charles Rowland Allanson-Winn;** Bt 1660 and 1776; retired; *b* 19 May 1902; *s* of 5th Baron Headley and Teresa (*d* 1919), *y d* of late W. H. Johnson; *S* brother, 1969; *m* 1927, Hilda May Wells-Thorpe; one *s* three *d. Educ:* Bedford School. *Recreations:* golf, fishing. *Heir:* *s* Hon. John Rowland Allanson-Winn, *b* 14 Oct. 1934. *Address:* Torton Top, Torton Hill Road, Arundel, Sussex. *T:* Arundel 3269. *Club:* Public Schools.

**HEADLY, Derek,** CMG 1957; lately Malayan Civil Service; *b* 1908; *s* of L. C. Headly, The House-on-the-Hill, Woodhouse Eaves, Leics; *m* 1946, Joyce Catherine, *d* of C. F. Freeman; one *s* one *d. Educ:* Repton Sch.; Corpus Christi Coll., Cambridge (BA). Military Service, 1944-46, Lieut-Col, Special Ops Exec., Force 136 (despatches). Cadet, Malaya, 1931; served Muar, Trengganu, etc; Palestine, 1938-44; Resident N Borneo, 1949; ret. as Brit. Adv., Kelantan, 1957. Mem. Melton and Belvoir RDC, 1958-67. Midlands Sec., Public Schs Appointments Bureau. Officer (Brother) Order of St John. *Recreations:* hunting, fishing, tennis, golf. *Address:* The Grange, Hoby, Melton Mowbray, Leics. *T:* Rotherby 214. *Club:* Special Forces.

**HEAF, Prof. Frederick Roland George,** CMG 1957; MA; MD 1923; FRCP 1946; MRCS 1918; Emeritus Professor University of Wales, since 1961; Consultant to Ministry of Health, 1947-63, to Scottish Health Department, and to Colonial Office, 1948-68; *b* 21 June 1894; *o s* of late Julius R. Heaf, Cambridge; *m* 1920, Madeleine (*d* 1966), *y d* of John Denison, Ilkley, Yorks; two *s* one *d. Educ:* Oundle; Sidney Sussex Coll., Cambridge; St Thomas' Hosp., London. Medical Superintendent: Warwick Sanatorium, 1922-30; Colindale Hosp., 1930-36; Sen. Medical Officer, LCC, 1936-49; David Davies Prof., University of Wales, 1949-60. Hon. Consulting Physician: Welsh Hosp. Board and SE Metrop. Hosp. Bd, 1949-; British Legion, 1944. Hon. Member: Brit. Tuberc. Assoc.; (Sen. Mem.) Thor. Soc., 1961; Med. Soc. of Sweden; Salonika Med. Assoc.; Tuberculosis Assoc. of Turkey. FRGS 1961. *Publications:* Rehabilitation of the Tuberculous (jointly), 1938; Recent Advances in Respiratory Tuberculosis (6th Edn) (jointly), 1968; Symposium of Tuberculosis (Ed.), 1957. *Recreations:* archæology, geology, photography. *Address:* Broadgate, Witney Road, Freeland, Oxon. *T:* Freeland 311. *Club:* National Liberal.

*See also P. J. D. Heaf.*

**HEAF, Peter Julius Denison,** MD, FRCP; Consultant Physician, University College Hospital, since 1958; *b* 1922; *s* of Prof. F. R. G. Heaf, *qv*; *m* 1947, Rosemary Cartledge; two *s* two *d. Educ:* Stamford Sch., Lincs; University Coll., London. MB, BS 1946; MD London 1952; MRCP 1954; FRCP 1965. House Physician and Surg., also RMO, University Coll. Hosp., and Capt. RAMC, 1946-51; Research Asst, Brompton Hosp., 1953-54; Sen. Registrar, St Thomas' Hosp., 1955-58. *Publications:* papers on chest disease and pulmonary physiology, in Lancet, etc. *Recreations:* painting, sailing. *Address:* 16 Gordon Mansions, Torrington Place, WC1E 7HE. *T:* 01-580 6981.

**HEAKES, Air Vice-Marshal Francis Vernon,** CB 1944; Commander, Legion of Merit (US); RCAF retired; *b* 27 Jan. 1894; *s* of Frank R. Heakes, Architect, and Susie Pemberton Heakes; *m* 1920, Edna Eulalie Watson, BA; one *s* three *d. Educ:* University of Toronto. Canadian Expeditionary Force, Lieut 1916-17; RFC (seconded), 1917-18; RAF 1918-19; CAF 1919; CAF and RCAF since 1923; Air Mem. Permanent Joint Board, Canada and US; Dir Air Personnel, RCAF; Dir Plans & Operations; AOC, RCAF, Newfoundland; AOC Western Air Command, Canada. *Recreations:* sports, all kinds, writing prose and verse, oil painting, musical composition. *Address:* 1876 West 63rd Avenue, Vancouver, BC, Canada.

**HEAL, Anthony Standerwick;** Chairman, Heal & Son Holdings Ltd (formerly Heal & Son Ltd), since 1952; *b* 23 Feb. 1907; *s* of Sir Ambrose Heal and Lady Edith Florence Digby Heal; *m* 1941, Theodora Caldwell (*née* Griffin); two *s. Educ:* Leighton Park Sch., Reading. Joined Heal & Son Ltd 1929; Dir 1936. Chm. Council, London and S Eastern Furniture Manufrs Assoc., 1947-48; Master, Furniture Makers Guild (now Worshipful Co. of Furniture Makers), 1959-60; Mem. Council of Industrial Design, 1959-67; Mem. Council, City and Guilds of London Inst., 1969, Vice-Chm., Licentiateship Cttee, 1963-; Pres., Design and Industries Assoc., 1965; Chm. Indep. Stores Assoc., 1970-. RSA Bi-Centenary Medal, 1964; Order of White Rose of Finland, 1970. *Recreations:* vintage cars and steam engines. *Address:* Baylins Farm, Knotty Green, Beaconsfield, Bucks. *Clubs:* Vintage Sports Car, National Traction Engine.

**HEALD, Charles Brehmer,** CBE 1919 MD Cantab; FRCP; Consulting Physician Royal Free Hospital; Consulting Physician for Rheumatic Diseases, Middlesex Hospital; late Medical Consultant, RAF; Medical Adviser, Department of Civil Aviation, Air Ministry; late Chairman and Medical Director, Rural Rheumatism Centre (Cotswolds); *b* 3 Dec. 1882; *s* of Walter Heald and Emily Krabbé; *m* Edith Hildegarde, *d* of Arthur Mason, Walton-on-Thames; three *d. Educ:* Tonbridge; Caius

Coll., Cambridge; St Bartholomew's Hosp. Temp. Surg., Royal Navy; Lieut-Col (temp.) RAMC; Principal Medical Officer, RAF, Middle East; FRSM. *Publications:* Injuries and Sport; The Genesis of Aviation Medicine (Historical Section, Cabinet Office) (restricted edn), 1966; on Rheumatism and Physical Health to medical journals. *Recreations:* woodwork, gardening. *Address:* Tally-Ho Cottage, Chipping Campden, Glos. *T:* Campden 401. *Club:* United University.
*See also V. C. Fairfax.*

**HEALD, Edith Shackleton;** journalist; *yr d* of late J. T. Heald and Mary Shackleton. Formerly dramatic critic and leader writer on the Evening Standard; book reviewer. *Address:* The Chantry House, Steyning, Sussex. *T:* Steyning 3163.

**HEALD, Henry Townley;** Chairman, Heald Hobson and Associates, Inc., since 1966; President of the Ford Foundation, 1956-65; Director: American Telephone & Telegraph Co.; Equitable Life Assurance Society of the US; Lever Brothers Co.; United States Steel Corporation; Crowell, Collier and Macmillan, Inc.; *b* 8 Nov. 1904; *s* of Frederick De Forest and Nellie Townley Heald; *m* 1928, Muriel Starcher; no *c*. *Educ:* State Coll. of Washington, Pullman, Washington; University of Ill, Urbana, Ill. BS (State Coll. of Washington), 1923; MS (University of Ill), 1925. Successively Asst Prof., Associate Prof., Prof. of Civil Engineering, Dean of Freshmen, Dean of Engineering, and Pres., Illinois Inst. of Technology, Chicago, Ill, 1927-52; Pres., New York Univ., Feb. 1952-Sept. 1956. Hon. degrees: DEng, Rose Polytechnic Inst, 1942, Clarkson Coll. of Technology, 1948; LLD, Northwestern Univ., 1942, Rutgers Univ., 1952, Hofstra Coll., 1955, Fairleigh Dickinson Coll., 1956, Princeton Univ., 1956, University of Pittsburgh, 1956, Columbia Univ., 1954, University of State of New York, 1962; University of Ill, 1963, Case Western Reserve Univ., 1968; LHD, Rollins Coll., 1953, Pacific Lutheran Univ., 1966, Northern Illinois Univ., since 1966, Brandeis Univ., 1966, College of Wooster, 1966; DSc, Newark Coll. of Engineering, 1954, Union Coll., 1956, Pratt Inst., 1954; DCL New York Univ., 1956; DH, Cornell Coll., 1967. *Publications:* articles and addresses. *Address:* 1 Mitchell Place, New York, NY 10017, USA. *Clubs:* Chicago (Chicago, Ill); University (Chicago and New York); Century Association (New York City).

**HEALD, Rt. Hon. Sir Lionel Frederick,** PC 1954; Kt 1951; QC 1937; JP; Governor, Middlesex Hospital, since 1946; Air Commodore RAF (VR); *b* 7 Aug. 1897; *yr s* of late James Heald, Parrs Wood, Lancs; *m* 1st, 1923, Flavia, *d* of Lieut-Col J. S. Forbes; one *s* one *d*; 2nd, 1929, Daphne Constance, OBE 1955, *d* of late Montague Price; two *s* one *d*. *Educ:* Charterhouse; Christ Church, Oxford (Holford Exhibitioner). BA Litt Hum 1920. Served RE (SR) 1915-19 (Italian Bronze Medal); RAF (VR), 1939-45. Borough Councillor (MR), St Pancras, 1934-37. Called to Bar, Middle Temple, 1923, Bencher, 1946; Junior Counsel to Board of Trade in technical matters, 1931-37; additional mem. of Bar Council, 1947. Contested (Nat C) SW St Pancras Div., 1945; MP (C) Chertsey, 1950-70. JP Surrey, 1946. Attorney-Gen., 1951-54. *Address:* Queen Elizabeth Building, Temple, EC4; *T:* 01-353 1234; Chilworth Manor, Guildford, Surrey. *Club:* Garrick.

**HEALD, Mervyn,** QC 1970; *b* 12 April 1930; *s* of Rt Hon. Sir Lionel Heald, *qv*; *m* 1954, Clarissa Bowen; three *d*. *Educ:* Eton College; Magdalene College, Cambridge. Called to the Bar, Middle Temple, 1954. *Recreations:* country pursuits. *Address:* Headfoldswood Farm, Loxwood, Sussex. *T:* Loxwood 248.

**HEALD, Thomas Routledge; His Honour Judge Heald;** County Court Judge, Circuit 18, since 1970; *b* 19 Aug. 1923; *s* of late John Arthur Heald and Nora Marion Heald; *m* 1950, Jean, *d* of James Campbell Henderson; two *s* two *d*. *Educ:* Merchant Taylors' Sch.; St John's Coll., Oxford. Fish Schol., St John's Coll., Oxford, 1941; Lieut, RAC, 1943-45; BA (Jurisprudence) 1947; MA 1949. Called to Bar, Middle Temple, 1948; Midland Circuit; Dep. Chm., Lindsey QS, 1965; Prosecuting Counsel to Inland Revenue (Midland Circuit), 1965-70; Dep. Chm., Notts QS, 1969. *Address:* Rebbur House, Nicker Hill, Keyworth, Nottingham. *T:* Plumtree 2676.

**HEALEY, Rt. Hon. Denis Winston,** PC 1964; MBE 1945; MP (Lab) South East Leeds, Feb. 1952-55, Leeds East since 1955; *b* 30 Aug. 1917; *s* of William Healey, Keighley, Yorks; *m* 1945, Edna May, *d* of Edward Edmunds, Coleford, Gloucestershire; one *s* two *d*. *Educ:* Bradford Grammar Sch.; Balliol Coll., Oxford. First Cl. Hons Mods 1938; Jenkyns Exhib. 1939; Harmsworth Sen. Schol., First Cl. Lit. Hum., BA 1940; MA 1945. War of 1939-45; entered Army, 1940; served N Africa, Italy. Major RE 1944 (despatches). Contested (Lab) Pudsey and Otley Div., 1945; Sec., International Dept, Labour Party, 1945-52. Mem. Parliamentary Cttee Labour Party, 1959-64. Secretary of State for Defence, 1964-70. Councillor, Royal Institute of International Affairs, 1948-60; Councillor, Institute of Strategic Studies, 1958-61; Mem. Brit. Delegn to Commonwealth Relations Conf., Canada, 1949; British Delegate to: Consultative Assembly, Council of Europe, 1952-54; Inter Parly Union Conf., Washington, 1953; Western European Union and Council of Europe, 1963-65. Mem. Exec. Fabian Soc., 1954-61. Mem., Labour Party Nat. Exec. Cttee, 1970-. *Publications:* The Curtain Falls, 1951; New Fabian Essays, 1952; Neutralism, 1955; Fabian International Essays, 1956; A Neutral Belt in Europe, 1958; NATO and American Security, 1959; The Race Against the H Bomb, 1960; Labour Britain and the World, 1963. *Recreations:* travel, photography, music, painting. *Address:* House of Commons, SW1. *T:* 01-930 6240.

**HEALEY, Sir Edward Randal C.;** *see* Chadwyck-Healey.

**HEALEY, Rt. Rev. Kenneth;** an Assistant Bishop, Diocese of Lincoln since 1966; *b* 7 Aug. 1899; *s* of late Harry Healey; *m* 1925, Marjorie, *d* of late Harry Wright Palmer, Friday Bridge, Cambs; two *d*. *Educ:* Moulton Grammar Sch. Deacon, 1931; Priest, 1932; Asst Curate, Grantham, 1931; Rector of Bloxholm with Digby, 1935; and Vicar of Ashby de la Launde (in plurality), 1939: Rural Dean of Lafford North, 1938; Vicar of Nocton, 1943; Rector of Algarkirk, 1950-58; Archdeacon of Lincoln, 1951-58; Bishop Suffragan of Grimsby, 1958-65. Proctor in Convocation, 1945-70; Church Commissioner, 1952-70. Chm. (formerly Vice-Chm.) Lindsey and Kesteven Agricultural Wages Cttee, 1945-69. MA Lambeth, 1958. *Address:* Gedney Dyke, Spalding, Lincs. *T:* Long Sutton 2030. *Club:* English-Speaking Union.

**HEALY, Rt. Rev. John F.;** *see* Gibraltar, Bishop of, (RC).

**HEANEY, Brig. George Frederick,** CBE 1943; late Royal Engineers (retd); fruit grower; *b* 1 June 1897; 2nd *s* of late George Robert

Heaney, Dublin; *m* 1929, Doreen Marguerite, *e d* of late Lieut-Col R. H. Hammersley-Smith, CBE; one *s* two *d* (and one *s* decd). *Educ:* St Lawrence; RMA Woolwich; Christ's Coll., Cambridge. 2nd Lieut RE 1916; European War in France, 1917-18 (wounded, despatches twice); apptd to Survey of India, 1921; in India and Burma, 1920-41; served in Persia-Iraq Forces, 1941-43 (CBE); D Survey, Allied Land Forces, SEAC, 1944-45; retired from Army, 1948; Surveyor-Gen. of India, 1946-51; Pres. Inst. of Surveyors (India), 1950-51; Managing Dir, North Essex Growers Ltd, 1963-64. *Address:* Crepping House, Wakes Colne, near Colchester, Essex. *T:* Fordham 236. *Club:* Army and Navy.

**HEANEY, Leonard Martin,** CMG 1959; Overseas Civil Service, retired; *b* 28 Nov. 1906; *s* of Alexander John and Lilian Heaney; *m* 1947, Kathleen Edith Mary Chapman; no *c*. *Educ:* Bristol Grammar Sch.; Oriel Coll., Oxford. Joined Colonial Service on leaving Oxford, 1929; served in Tanganyika, retiring as a Senior Provincial Commissioner, 1959. Military service with East African Forces in Abyssinia, Madagascar, Ceylon, Burma, 1940-45. *Recreations:* reading and golf. *Address:* Kindai, Philpot Lane, Chobham, Surrey. *T:* Chobham 8344.

**HEANLEY, Charles Laurence,** TD 1950; FRCS; Consulting Surgeon, Worthing Hospital; Member of Lloyd's; *b* 28 Feb. 1907; *e s* of Dr C. M. Heanley; *m* 1935; three *s*. *Educ:* Epsom Coll.; Downing Coll., Cambridge (Exhib., Schol.); London Hosp. BA Cambridge (Nat. Sci. Tripos) 1929, MA 1934; MRCS, LRCP 1932; MB, BCh Cambridge 1934; FRCS 1933; MRCP 1935. London Hosp., 1929; Surg. First Asst, 1936. Served War of 1939-45; France, Surgical Specialist, 17th Gen. Hosp., 1939-40; Surgeon Specialist, RAMC Park Prewitt Plastic Unit, 1941-42; India, OC No. 3 British Maxillo-Facial Surgical Unit and Lieut-Col OC Surgical Div., 1942-45; Surg. in charge of Dept of Plastic Surg., London Hosp., 1946-64. Cons. Surg. Worthing Hosp., Bethnal Green Hosp., and Plastic Unit Queen Victoria Hosp., East Grinstead, 1945; Plastic Surg. London Hosp.; Hon. Cons. Plastic Surg. Royal National and Golden Square Hosps, 1969. *Publications:* varied medical articles. *Recreations:* swimming, archæology. *Address:* Kymer House, Hassocks, Sussex. *T:* Hassocks 2828; 145 Heene Road, Worthing, Sussex. *T:* Worthing 35344.

**HEAP, Sir Desmond,** Kt 1970; LLM, PPTPI; Comptroller and City Solicitor to the Corporation of London, since 1947; *b* 17 Sept. 1907, *o s* of late William Heap, Architect, Burnley, Lancs, and of Minnie Heap; *m* 1945, Adelene Mai, *o d* of late Frederick Lacey, Harrogate, and of Mrs F. N. Hornby; one *s* two *d*. *Educ:* Burnley Grammar Sch.; Victoria University of Manchester. LLB Hons 1929; LLM 1936; admitted, 1933; Hons Final Law Examination; Mem. of Council Law Soc. since 1954, Chm. Law Reform Cttee, 1955-60, and Chm., Town Planning Cttee, 1964-. Past Master, Worshipful Company of Solicitors of City of London; Liveryman of Worshipful Company of Carpenters of City of London; Legal Mem. of Town Planning Institute, 1935-, Mem. of Council, 1947-, Pres., 1955-56; Assoc. Mem. Royal Institute of Chartered Surveyors, 1953-, Mem. of Council, 1957-; Mem. of Colonial Office Housing and Town Planning Adv. Panel, 1953-65; Prosecuting Solicitor, 1935-38 and Chief Asst Solicitor for City of Leeds, 1938-40; Dep. Town Clerk of Leeds, 1940-47; Lecturer in the Law of Town and Country Planning and Housing, Leeds Sch. of Architecture, 1935-47; mem. of Editorial Board of Journal of Planning Law since 1948; Dep. Pres., City of London Branch, British Red Cross Soc. *Publications:* Planning Law for Town and Country, 1938; Planning and the Law of Interim Development, 1944; The Town and Country Planning Act, 1944, 1945; An Outline of Planning Law, 1943 to 1945, 1945; The New Towns Act, 1946, 1947; Introducing the Town and Country Planning Act, 1947, 1947; Encyclopædia of Planning, Compulsory Purchase and Compensation, Vol. 1, 1949; Heap on the Town and Country Planning Act, 1954, 1955; Encyclopædia of Town Planning Law, 1960; Introducing the Land Commission Act 1967, 1967; Encyclopædia of Betterment Levy, 1967; The New Town Planning Procedures, 1969; An Outline of Planning Law, 5th edn 1969; articles in legal jls. *Recreations:* swimming, fell walking, the amateur theatre. *Address:* Quarry House, Oak Hill Road, Sevenoaks, Kent. *T:* Sevenoaks 53688; Guildhall, EC2. *T:* 01-606 3030.

**HEAPE, William Leslie,** CMG 1942; Colonial Service, retired; *b* 1896; 2nd *s* of late H. Heape, Forde, Ashford Carbonel, Ludlow; *m* Anice, *d* of Capt. Chandler, Army Medical Service; one *s* one *d*. *Educ:* Rugby; RMC, Sandhurst. Commissioned East Lancs Regt, 1914; BEF France, 1915 (severely wounded); served ground staff, RAF 1917; War Office, 1918-19; entered Colonial Civil Service, 1919, Asst Sec., Somaliland Protectorate; attached for duty, Colonial Office, 1926; Secretariat Tanganyika Territory, 1929; Private Sec. to Governor of Barbados, 1933-35; Colonial Sec., Grenada, 1935-40; Bahamas, 1940-43; Colonial Sec., British Guiana, 1944-50; Officer Administering the Government, 1944, 1946, 1947, 1948 and 1949; retired from Colonial Service 1949; re-employed, Colonial Office, 1950-58. *Address:* Colway Dene, Roman Road, Lyme Regis, Dorset.

**HEARD, Gerald;** *see* Heard, H. F. G.

**HEARD, Henry Fitz Gerald;** author; *b* 6 Oct. 1889; *y s* of late Prebendary H. J. Heard; unmarried. *Educ:* Sherbourne; Gonville and Caius Coll., Cambridge. Literary Editor of The Realist, 1929; Fortnightly Broadcast on This Surprising World, 1930-34; Broadcast Series; Science in the Making, 1934; Ayer Lecturer, Colgate Rochester Seminary, 1946; visiting consultant (dept of Philosophy), Washington Univ., St Louis, USA, 1951 and 1952, 1955-56; two-year Bollinger Foundation Grant, 1955-56; Haskell Foundation Lecturer at Oberlin Coll., Oberlin, Ohio, 1958. *Publications:* Narcissus (To-day and To-morrow Series); The Ascent of Humanity (awarded by British Academy grant from Henrietta Hertz Fund); The Social Substance of Religion; The Emergence of Man; This Surprising World; These Hurrying Years; Science in the Making; The Source of Civilisation; Exploring the Stratosphere: The Third Morality; Pain, Sex and Time; The Creed of Christ; The Code of Christ; Man the Master; Taste for Honey; Reply Paid; Desert Dialogue; Preface to Prayer; Gamaliel's Gospel; The Eternal Gospel; Dopplegangers; Is God Evident?; The Lost Cavern; The Black Fox; The Book of Wishes; The Riddle of the Flying Saucers (Is Another World Watching?), publ. GB (and US); The Human Venture; The Perennial Praxis; The Five Ages of Man; Five Cloven Men; The Four Classes of Men. *Address:* 322 East Rustic Road, Santa Monica, Calif 90402, USA.

**HEARD, Brig. Leonard Ferguson,** CBE 1943; JP; *b* 30 Oct. 1903; *er s* of late Lieut-Col Samuel Ferguson Heard, and late Florence Roberta

Heard (*née* Allan), Magilligan, Co. Londonderry; unmarried. *Educ:* Shrewsbury Sch.; RMA, Woolwich. Entered RE 1923; Capt. 1934; Major, 1940; Col 1947; Brig. 1949; ADC to the Queen, 1954-57; retired, 1957; French Croix de Guerre (with palm) 1945. High Sheriff, Co. Londonderry, 1964. *Address:* Magilligan, Co. Londonderry, N Ireland. *T:* Bellarena 208. *Clubs:* Naval and Military; Northern Counties (Londonderry).

**HEARD, His Eminence Cardinal William Theodore,** BA (Oxon.); DPh, DD DCL; Auditor of the Sacred Roman Rota since 1927 (Dean, 1958-); Prelate of the Sacred Congregation of the Rites, 1944; *b* Edinburgh, 24 Feb. 1884; *s* of Rev. W. A. Heard, LLD. *Educ:* Fettes Coll., Edinburgh; Balliol Coll., Oxford; English Coll., Rome. Rowed in Oxford Eight, 1907; admitted Solicitor, 1910; received into Catholic Church, 1910; ordained Priest, 1918; stationed at Dockhead, Bermondsey, 1921-27; Mem. Pontifical Commn for the interpretation of the Codex, 1959; Cardinal, Dec. 1959. Hon. LLD Edinburgh, 1968. *Address:* Via Monserrato 45, Roma, Italy.

**HEARN, Col George William Richard,** CBE 1959; DL; Chief Constable of Staffordshire, 1950-61; *b* 11 Aug. 1893; *e s* of Sir Walter Risley Hearn, KBE, Buckingham; *m* 1st, 1921, Mabel Jean Winifred (*d* 1963), *e d* of late John T. C. Eadie, JP, Aldershawe, Lichfield; (one *s* decd); 2nd, 1964, Pamela Frances Mary, *widow* of John Francis Phillips, Brocton Leys, near Stafford. *Educ:* Uppingham. Served European War, 1914-18, joined DLI, 1914. South Staffs Regt 1915; Dep. Asst Provost-Marshal, 59th Div. Capt. 1921; retd 1935; Bt Major 1940; Hon. Col 5th Bn The South Staffs Regt (TA), 1946-58. Asst Chief Constable of Staffs, 1935-50; actg Inspector of Constabulary, NE Civil Defence Region, 1940-43. DL Staffs, 1947. King's Police Medal, 1947; OStJ 1951. *Address:* Farley Hill Court, near Reading, Berks. *T:* Eversley 3386. *Club:* Army and Navy.

**HEARNSHAW, Prof. Leslie Spencer;** Professor of Psychology, University of Liverpool, since 1947; *b* Southampton, 9 Dec. 1907; *o s* of late Prof. F. J. C. Hearnshaw, Prof. of History, King's Coll., London; *m* 1937, Gwenneth R. Dickins, Perth, Western Australia; one *s* three *d*. *Educ:* King's Coll. Sch., Wimbledon; Christ Church, Oxford; King's coll., London. 1st Class Lit Hum, 1930; 1st Class Psychology Hons (London), 1932. Investigator, Nat. Institute of Industrial Psychology, London, 1933-38; Lecturer in Psychology, Victoria Univ., Coll., Wellington, NZ, 1939-47; Dir, Industrial Psychology Div., DSIR, Wellington, NZ, 1942-47; Mem. of Council, British Psychological Soc., 1949-57; Chm., Industrial Section, 1953-54; Pres., British Psychological Soc., 1955-56. Pres. Section J (Psychology), Brit. Assoc., 1954; Hon. Dir, Medical Research Council, Research Group into occupational aspects of ageing, 1955-59, 1963-70. Hobhouse Memorial Lecturer, 1966. Vice-Pres., International Assoc. of Applied Psychology, and Editor of its Journal. *Publications:* (with R. Winterbourn) Human Welfare and Industrial Efficiency, 1945; A Short History of British Psychology, 1840-1940, 1964; articles on industrial psychology and the psychology of thinking. *Address:* 18 Kirby Park, West Kirby, Cheshire. *T:* 051-625 5823.

*See also C. T. C. Wall.*

**HEARST, William Randolph, Jun.;** journalist; Editor-in-Chief, The Hearst Newspapers, and Chairman of the Board, The Hearst Corp.; *b* NYC, 27 Jan. 1908; *s* of William Randolph Hearst and Millicent Veronica (*née* Willson); *m* 1st, 1928, Alma Walker (marr. diss., 1932); 2nd, 1933, Lorelle McCarver (marr. diss., 1948); 3rd, 1948, Austine McDonnell; two *s*. *Educ:* Collegiate Sch.; St John's Manlius Mil. Acad., Syracuse; Berkeley High Sch., Berkeley, Calif.; Hitchcock Mil. Acad., San Rafael, Calif; University of Calif. Began career with New York American, NYC, as a reporter, 1928; publisher, 1936-37; publisher, NY Journal-American, 1937-56; The American Weekly, 1945-56; War Correspondent, 1943-45. Member Boards: 20th Century-Fox; United Press International; San Luis Mining. *Address:* (home) 810 Fifth Avenue, New York, NY 10021, USA; (office) 959 Eighth Avenue, New York, NY 10019, USA. *Clubs:* Overseas Press, Brook, Madison Square Garden (New York City); F Street, Sulgrave, National Press, Metropolitan, Burning Tree (Washington); Bohemian, Pacific Union (San Francisco).

**HEATH, Rt. Hon. Edward Richard George,** PC 1955; MBE 1946; MP (C) Bexley since 1950; Prime Minister and First Lord of the Treasury since 1970; *b* Broadstairs, Kent, 9 July 1916; *s* of William George and Edith Anne Heath. *Educ:* Chatham House Sch., Ramsgate; Balliol Coll., Oxford (Scholar; Hon. Fellow, 1969). Pres. Oxford Univ. Conservative Assoc., 1937; Chm. Federation of Univ. Conservative Assocs, 1938; Pres. Oxford Union, 1939; Oxford Union debating tour of American Univs, 1939-40; Smith-Mundt Fellowship, USA, 1953; Pres. Federation of University Conservative and Unionist Associations, 1959-. Served War of 1939-45 (despatches, MBE); in Army, 1940-46, in France, Belgium, Holland and Germany; gunner in RA, 1940; Lieut-Col 1945. Lieut-Col comdg 2nd Regt HAC, TA, April 1947-Aug. 1951; Master Gunner within the Tower of London, 1951-54. Administrative Civil Service, 1946-47 resigning to become prospective candidate for Bexley. Asst Conservative Whip, Feb. 1951; Lord Commissioner of the Treasury, Nov. 1951, and Joint Deputy Govt Chief Whip, 1952, and Dep. Govt Chief Whip, 1953-55; Parliamentary Sec. to the Treasury, and Government Chief Whip, Dec. 1955-Oct. 1959; Minister of Labour, Oct. 1959-July 1960; Lord Privy Seal, with Foreign Office responsibilities, 1960-63; Sec. of State for Industry, Trade, Regional Development and Pres. of the Board of Trade, Oct. 1963-Oct. 1964; Leader of the Opposition, 1965-70. Chm., Commonwealth Parly Assoc., 1970-. Mem. Council, Royal College of Music, 1961; Vice-Pres., Bach Choir, 1970-; Visiting Fellow, Nuffield Coll., Oxford, 1962; Chm. London Symphony Orchestra Trust, 1963. Charlemagne Prize, 1963. Winner, Sydney to Hobart Ocean Race, 1969. *Publication:* (joint) One Nation–a Tory approach to social problems, 1950; Old World, New Horizons, 1970. *Recreations:* sailing, travel, music. *Address:* 10 Downing Street, SW1. *Clubs:* Buck's, Carlton.

**HEATH, Maj.-Gen. Gerard William Egerton,** CB 1949; CBE 1945; DSO 1945; MC 1916; retired; *b* 17 March 1897; *s* of late Maj.-Gen. Sir G. M. Heath, KCMG, CB, and Mary (*née* Egerton); *m* 1923, Hilda Mary, (*née* Houldsworth) (from whom he obtained a divorce, 1931); two *d*; *m* 1933, Gwendda Curtis (*née* Evans). *Educ:* Wellington Coll.; RMA Woolwich. Commissioned RA, 1915; served European War, 1915-18 (wounded); War of 1939-45 (despatches, 1940); CRA 43rd Div., 1942-44; CCRA 12 Corps, 1944-45; CCRA 1st Airborne Corps, 1945; Commandant Sch. of Artillery, Larkhill, 1945-47; GOC 1st Anti-Aircraft Group, 1947-49; GOC Troops, Malta, 1949-51. Pres. Regular Commissions Board, 1951-

54, retired Nov. 1954. Col Comdt RA and Royal Malta Artillery, 1955, RHA 1957. *Recreations:* shooting and all forms of mounted sport. *Address:* Westbrook Farm, Avebury, Wilts. *T:* Avebury 248. *Club:* United Service.

**HEATH, Harry Cecil;** Managing Director, United Kingdom Temperance Alliance Ltd, since 1963; *b* 1898; *e s* of Harry Heath, Wellington, Shropshire; *m* 1st, 1924, Margaret (*d* 1928), *e d* of George Harvey, JP, Wellington; two *d*; 2nd, 1930, Muriel Grace, *e d* of Joseph B. Adams, Ambergate. *Educ:* Newport Grammar Sch.; Pembroke Coll., Oxford, BA (Hons English). Commissioned in the Cheshire Regt, 1917; Mem. Inner Temple; called to Bar, 1938; General Sec. of the United Kingdon Alliance, 1926-62; Editor of The Licensing Magistrate; Joint Hon. Sec. National Temperance Federation; Pres. Nat. Assoc. of Temperance Officials, 1935-37; Hon. Sec. British Section Internat. Temp·rance Union; Extension Lecturer, University of London, 1946; Vice-Chm., Churches' Council on Gambling; Chairman, Good Templar Children's Home; Chm., Friends' Temperance Union; Chm., Temperance Collegiate Assoc.; Chm. Internat. Cttee on Alcohol and Road Traffic, 1950-60; Pres., National United Temperance Council; Pres., National Brotherhood Movement, 1960-61; Pres., United Kingdom Alliance, 1963; Chm., Ansvar Insurance Co. Ltd. *Publications:* Drink and Sport; Temperance Exhibitions; The Case against the Public Ownership of the Drink Trade; Alcohol and Democracy; Drink and Motoring; a Survey of Magisterial Practice in relation to Occasional Licences; Alcohol and World Traffic Safety; The Drink Problem in War Time; A Citizen Addresses the Licensing Justices; A Post-War Plan for the Temperance Movement; It's Your Money They Want; End This Colossal Waste of Food; The Control of a Dangerous Trade; Social Economics in Relation to the Alcohol Problem; Some Fallacies concerning the Nationalisation of the Drink Trade; A Summary of the Licensing Act, 1949; Drink and the Press; The Citizen's Guide to Licensing Procedure; The Licensing Act, 1961; Academic Apathy, and other pamphlets; Contrib. to Everyman's Encyclopædia and Encyclopædia Britannica. *Recreations:* Member of the Magic Circle; motoring. *Address:* Alliance House, 12 Caxton Street, SW1. *T:* 01-222 5880; 62 Becmead Avenue, Streatham, SW16. *T:* 01-769 6649.

**HEATH, Henry Wylde Edwards,** CMG 1963; Commissioner of Police, Hong Kong, 1959-67, retd; *b* 18 March 1912; *s* of late Dr W. G. Heath and late Mrs L. B. Heath; *m* Joan Mildred Crichett; two *s* one *d*. *Educ:* Dean Close Sch.; HMS Conway. Probationer Sub-Inspector of Police, Leeward Islands, 1931; Asst Supt, Hong Kong, 1934; Superintendent, 1944; Asst Commissioner, 1950. Colonial Police Medal, 1953; QPM, 1957. *Recreations:* golf and sailing. *Address:* The Shepherd's Cottage, East Dean, near Eastbourne, Sussex. *Clubs:* Hong Kong, Royal Hong Kong Golf (Hong Kong).

**HEATH, John Baldwin;** Director, Economic Services Division, Board of Trade, since 1967; *b* 25 Sept. 1924; *s* of Thomas Arthur Heath and late Dorothy Meallin; *m* 1953, Wendy Julia Betts; two *s* one *d*. *Educ:* Merchant Taylors' Sch.; St Andrews Univ.; Cambridge Univ. RNVR, 1942-46. Spicers Ltd, 1946-50; Lecturer in Economics, Univ. of Manchester, 1956-64; Rockefeller Foundation Fellowship, 1961-62; Dir, Economic Research Unit, Bd of Trade, 1964-67. *Publications:* articles in many learned jls on competition and monopoly, productivity, cost-benefit analysis. *Recreations:* music, walking. *Address:* 20 Denmark Avenue, SW19. *T:* 01-946 5474. *Club:* Reform.

**HEATH, John Moore;** Counsellor (Commercial), British Embassy, Bonn, since 1969; *b* 9 May 1922; *s* of Philip George and Olga Heath; *m* 1952, Patricia Mary Bibby; one *s* one *d*. *Educ:* Shrewsbury Sch.; Merton Coll., Oxford (MA). Served War of 1939-45, France, Belgium and Germany: commnd Inns of Court Regt, 1942; Capt. GSO3 11th Armoured Div., 1944-45 (despatches). Merton Coll., 1940-42, 1946-47. Entered Foreign Service, 1950; 2nd Sec., Comr-Gen.'s Office, Singapore, 1950-52; 1st Sec. (Commercial), Jedda, 1952-56; 1st Sec., FO, 1956-58; Nat. Def. Coll., Kingston, Ont., 1958-59; Head of Chancery and HM Consul, Brit. Embassy, Mexico City, 1959-62; Head of Chancery, Brit. Embassy, Kabul, Afghanistan, 1963-65; Counsellor and Head of Establishment and Organisation Dept, FCO (formerly DSAO), 1966-69. *Recreations:* walking, travel. *Address:* British Embassy, Friedrich Ebert Allee 77, 53 Bonn, Germany. *Club:* United Service and Sports.

**HEATH, Air Marshal Sir Maurice (Lionel),** KBE 1962 (OBE 1946); CB 1957; Chief Hon. Steward, Westminster Abbey, since 1965; Gentleman Usher to the Queen, since 1966; *b* 12 Aug. 1909; *s* of Lionel Heath, Artist and Principal of the Mayo Sch. of Arts, Lahore, India; *m* 1938, Kathleen Mary *d* of Boaler Gibson, Bourne, Lincs; one *s* one *d*. *Educ:* Sutton Valence Sch.; Cranwell. Commissioned RAF, 1929; service with Nos 16 and 28 Squadrons; Specialist Armament duties, 1933-42; Chief Instructor, No 1 Air Armament Sch., 1942; Station Commander, Metheringham, No 5 Group, Bomber Comd, 1944 (despatches). Dep. to Dir-Gen. of Armament, Air Min., 1946-48; CO Central Gunnery Sch., 1948-49; Sen. Air Liaison Officer, Wellington, NZ, 1950-52; CO Bomber Comd Bombing Sch., 1952-53; idc, 1954; Dir of Plans, Air Min., 1955; Deputy Air Secretary, Air Ministry, 1955-57; Commander, British Forces, Arabian Peninsula, 1957-59; Commandant, RAF Staff Coll., 1959-61; Chief of Staff, HQ Allied Air Forces Central Europe, 1962-65, retd. *Recreations:* sailing, golf and travel. *Address:* Broom Cottage, Sunset Lane, West Chiltington, Pulborough, Sussex. *Clubs:* Royal Air Force; West Sussex Golf.

**HEATH, Oscar Victor Sayer,** FRS 1960; DSc (London); Professor of Horticulture, University of Reading, 1958-69, now Emeritus; Leverhulme Emeritus Research Fellow, since 1970; *b* 26 July 1903; *s* of late Sir (Henry) Frank Heath, GBE, KCB, and Frances Elaine (*née* Sayer); *m* 1930, Sarah Margery, *d* of Stephen Bumstead, Guestling, Hastings; two *s* one *d*. *Educ:* Imperial Coll., London (Forbes Medallist). Asst Demonstrator in Botany, Imperial Coll., 1925-26; Empire Cotton Growing Corp. Sen. Studentship, Imperial Coll. of Tropical Agriculture, Trinidad, 1926-27; Plant Physiologist, Empire Cotton Growing Corp., Cotton Experiment Station, Barberton, S Africa, 1927-36; Research Student, Imperial Coll., London, 1936-39; Leverhulme Research Fellow, 1937-39; Research Asst, 1939-40, and Mem. of Staff, Research Inst. of Plant Physiology of Imperial Coll., Rothamsted, 1940-46, London, 1946-58; Sen. Principal Scientific Officer, 1948-58; Special Lectr in Plant Physiology, Imperial Coll., 1945-58; Dir, ARC Research Council Unit of Flower Crop Physiology, 1962-70; Mem. ARC, 1965-70. *Publications:* chapters on physiology of leaf stomata in Encyclopædia of Plant Physiology (ed Ruhland) 1959, in Plant Physiology–a

Treatise (ed Steward), 1959, and (with T. A. Mansfield) in Physiology of Plant Growth (ed Wilkins), 1969; The Physiological Aspects of Photosynthesis, 1969; Investigation by Experiment, 1970; papers in scientific jls. *Address:* University of Reading Horticultural Research Laboratories, Shinfield Grange, Shinfield, Reading RG2 9AD; 4 Coley Avenue, Reading RG1 6LQ. *T:* Reading 50511.

**HEATH-GRACIE, George Handel,** MusB (Dunelm), 1932; FRCO 1915; Organist and Master of the Choristers, Derby Cathedral, 1933-57; Diocesan Choirmaster, 1936-57; Founder and Conductor, Derby Bach Choir, 1935; Member of panel of Examiners, Associated Board of the Royal Schools of Music; Special Commissioner, Royal School of Church Music; *m* 1922, Marjory Josephine Knight. *Educ:* Bristol Grammar Sch.; Bristol Cathedral. Organist of various Bristol Churches, 1909-14; of St John's, Frome, 1914-15; Service with HM forces, 1915-19; Organist of St Peter, Brockley, SE, 1918-33; Conductor South London Philharmonic Soc., 1919-21; Broadcast Church Music Series, 1936-38; Music Dir, Derby Sch., 1938-44; Sch. Music Adviser, Derbyshire Educn Cttee, 1944-57; Mem. Council, Incorporated Soc. of Musicians for SW England, 1964-67; Mem. Diocesan Adv. Cttee, to 1957; Extra-mural Lectr, University Coll., Nottingham; Festival Adjudicator and Lectr. Toured Canada and USA as adjudicator, lecturer and performer, 1949, return visit, 1953; travelled in Asia, and African Tour, 1959; Eastern Tour, Ceylon, Singapore, Malaya, 1960; Tour of W Indies, N and S America and New Zealand, 1966, and New Zealand, 1968. *Publications:* various Church Music and press articles. *Recreations:* gossip, grass-cutting, brewing, domestic repairs, and electrical engineering. *Address:* Shorms, near Stockland, Honiton, Devon. *T:* Stockland 403. *Clubs:* Savage; Exeter and County; (Hon.) Kiwanis (Peterborough, Ont).

**HEATH-STUBBS, John (Francis Alexander);** poet; Lecturer in English Literature, College of St Mark and St John, Chelsea, since 1963; *b* 1918; *s* of Francis Heath Stubbs and Edith Louise Sara (*née* Marr). *Educ:* Queen's Coll., Oxford. English Master, Hall Sch., Hampstead, 1944-45; Editorial Asst, Hutchinson's, 1945-46; Gregory Fellow in Poetry, Leeds Univ., 1952-55; Vis. Prof. of English: University of Alexandria, 1955-58; University of Michigan, 1960-61. FRSL 1953. *Publications: verse:* Wounded Thammuz; Beauty and the Beast; The Divided Ways; The Swarming of the Bees; A Charm against the Toothache; The Triumph of the Muse; The Blue Fly in his Head; Selected Poems; Satires and Epigrams; *drama:* Helen in Egypt; *Criticism:* The Darkling Plain; Charles Williams; The Pastoral; The Ode; The Verse Satire; *translations:* (with Peter Avery) Hafiz of Shiraz; (with Iris Origo) Leopardi, Selected Prose and Poetry; *edited:* Selected Poems of Jonathan Swift; Selected Poems of P. B. Shelley; Selected Poems of Tennyson; Selected Poems of Alexander Pope; (with David Wright) The Forsaken Garden; Images of Tomorrow; (with David Wright) Faber Book of Twentieth Century Verse. *Recreation:* taxonomy. *Address:* 35 Sutherland Place, W2. *T:* 01-229 6367.

**HEATHCOAT AMORY;** family name of **Viscount Amory.**

**HEATHCOAT-AMORY, Major Sir John,** Bt; *see* Amory.

**HEATHCOTE, Sir Michael Perryman,** 11th Bt, *cr* 1733; *b* 7 Aug. 1927; *s* of Leonard Vyvyan Heathcote, 10th Bt, and Joyce Kathleen Heathcote (*d* 1967); *S* father, 1963; *m* 1956, Victoria Wilford, *e d* of Comdr J. E. R. Wilford, RN, Retd; two *s* one *d*. *Educ:* Winchester Coll.; Clare Coll., Cambridge. Started farming in England, 1951, in Scotland, 1961. Is in remainder to Earldom of Macclesfield. *Recreations:* fishing, shooting and farming. *Heir:* *s* Timothy Gilbert Heathcote, *b* 25 May 1957. *Address:* Warborne Farm, Boldre, Lymington, Hants. *T:* Lymington 3478; Carie and Carwhin, Lawers, by Aberfeldy, Perthshire.

**HEATHCOTE-DRUMMOND-WILLOUGHBY;** family name of **Earl of Ancaster.**

**HEATHCOTE-SMITH, Clifford Bertram Bruce,** CBE 1963; HM Diplomatic Service; *b* 2 Sept. 1912; *s* of late Sir Clifford E. Heathcote-Smith, KBE, CMG; *m* 1940, Thelma Joyce Engström; two *s*. *Educ:* Malvern; Pembroke Coll., Cambridge. Entered Consular Service, 1936; served in China, 1937-44; Foreign Office, 1944-47; Political Adviser, Hong-Kong, 1947-50, Montevideo, 1951-56; Commercial Counsellor: Ankara, 1956-60; Copenhagen, 1960-64; Washington, 1964-65; Dep. High Comr, Madras, 1965-68. *Address:* c/o Foreign and Commonwealth Office, SW1.

**HEATON, Rev. Eric William;** Official Fellow and Tutor in Theology and Chaplain, St John's College, Oxford, since 1960, Senior Tutor since 1967; Chairman of Council, Headington School, Oxford, since 1968; *b* 15 Oct. 1920; *s* of Robert William Heaton and Ella Mabel Heaton (*née* Brear); *m* 1951, Rachel Mary, *d* of Charles Harold Dodd, *qv*; two *s* two *d*. *Educ:* Ermysted's, Skipton; (Exhibnr) Christ's Coll., Cambridge (MA). English Tripos, Part I; Theological Tripos, Part I (First Class). Deacon, 1944; Priest, 1945; Curate of St Oswald's, Durham, 1944-45; Staff Sec., Student Christian Movement in University of Durham, 1944-45; Chaplain, Gonville and Caius Coll., Cambridge, 1945-46; Dean and Fellow, 1946-53; Tutor, 1951-53; Bishop of Derby's Chaplain in University of Cambridge, 1946-53; Canon Residentiary, 1953-60, and Chancellor, 1956-60, Salisbury Cathedral. Examining Chaplain to: Archbishop of York, 1951-56; Bishop of Portsmouth, 1947-; Bishop of Salisbury, 1949-64; Bishop of Norwich, 1960-; Bishop of Wakefield, 1961-; Bishop of Rochester, 1962-; Select Preacher: Cambridge University, 1948, 1958; Oxford Univ., 1958-59, 1967. *Publications:* His Servants the Prophets, 1949 (revised and enlarged Pelican edn, The Old Testament Prophets, 1958); The Book of Daniel, 1956; Everyday Life in Old Testament Times, 1956; Commentary on the Sunday Lessons, 1959; The Hebrew Kingdoms, 1968. Articles in Jl of Theological Studies, Expository Times, etc. *Address:* St John's College, Oxford. *T:* Oxford 47671/2; 1 Wellington Place, Oxford. *T:* Oxford 57547.

**HEATON, Mrs Gwenllian Margaret,** CBE 1946; TD; *b* 12 March 1897; *o c* of late Lieut-Col B. E. Philips, DL, JP, Rhual, Mold, Flintshire; *m* 1921, Commander H. E. Heaton, DL, JP, RN (retd); two *s*. *Educ:* Privately. Local service as VAD European War, 1914-18. Enrolled in Auxiliary Territorial Service Sept. 1938; embodied Aug. 1939 with rank of Senior Commander. Served on Staff at HQ Western Command, 1940-44 and HQ Eastern Command, 1944-45; Chief Commander 1941; Controller, 1942, with appointment as DDATS. Released with Age and Service Group July 1945. *Address:* Garregwen, Pantymwyn, Mold, Flintshire. *T:* Pantymwyn 234.

**HEATON, Herbert,** MA (Leeds), MCom (Birmingham), DLitt (Leeds); Professor Emeritus Economic History, University of Minnesota (Professor 1927-58; Chairman History Department, 1954-58); *b* Silsden, Yorks, 6 June 1890; *s* of Fred and Eva Heaton; *m* 1914, Ellen Jane (*d* 1956), *d* of W. J. and A. Houghton, Cheltenham; one *s* two *d*; *m* 1959, Marjorie Edith Ronson, Cheltenham. *Educ:* Batley Gram. Sch. Morley Secondary Sch.; Leeds Univ.; London Sch. of Economics. 1st Class History Hons BA (Leeds 1911); Rutson Research Scholar, 1911; Fellow Leeds Univ., 1912; Asst Lecturer in Economics, Birmingham Univ., 1912-14; Lecturer in History and Economics, University of Tasmania, 1914-17; Lecturer in Economics and Dir of Tutorial Classes, University of Adelaide, 1917-25; Sir John A. Macdonald Prof. of Economic and Political Science, Queen's Univ., Kingston, Canada, 1925-27; Pres. WEA of Australia, 1919, 1922-25; Special lecturer on Australian problems in London, Cambridge, Toronto, Edmonton, 1924; Guggenheim Fellow, 1931-32; Visiting professor: Princeton Univ., 1939-40; Johns Hopkins Univ., 1961; University of Utah, 1962, 1969; University of British Colombia, 1962-63; University of Texas, 1964; University of California at Davis, 1965; University of California at Riverside, 1966; Michigan State University, 1968; Disting. Vis. Prof. Pennsylv. State Univ., 1958-60. Sec. of Social Science Research Council's Cttee on research in Econ. Hist., 1941-54; Pres. Econ. History Assoc., 1948-50. Corres. FBA 1967. *Publications:* History of Yorkshire Woollen and Worsted Industries, 1920, 1965; Mod. Econ. Hist., with Special Reference to Aust., 1920; Welfare Work, 1919; History of Trade and Commerce, with Special Reference to Canada, 1928 (rewritten 1953); The British Way of Recovery, 1934; An Economic History of Europe, 1936 (rewritten 1948); Edwin F. Gay: American Scholar in action, 1952; Articles in econ. jls, etc. *Recreations:* golf, motoring and music. *Address:* 5148 Luverne Avenue, Minneapolis, Minn 55419, USA. *Club:* Campus (Minn).

**HEATON, Sir (John Victor) Peregrine Henniker-,** 3rd Bt, *cr* 1912; RAF retired; *b* 15 Jan. 1903; *e s* of Sir John Henniker Heaton, 2nd Bt; *S* father, 1963; *m* 1st, 1927, Gladys (marr. diss., 1937), 2nd *d* of Peter E. Tyson, Alnwick, Northumberland; two *d*; 2nd, 1948, Margaret Patricia, *d* of late Lieut Percy Wright, Canadian Mounted Rifles (killed in action); one *s* one *d*. *Educ:* HMS Conway. Served War of 1939-45 (despatches), Pilot Officer RAF, 1940; Sqdn-Ldr, 1944; Asst Provost Marshal, Austria, 1945; Deputy Provost Marshal, Levant, 1945-48; Wing-Commander, 1948; retired, 1958; Mem. Council, Anglo-Arab Assoc. *Recreation:* yachting (Chm., Amateur Yacht Research Soc.). *Heir:* *s* Yvo Robert Henniker-Heaton, *b* 24 April 1954. *Address:* 14 Woodville Road, Ealing, W5. *T:* 01-997 2097. *Club:* Royal Thames Yacht.

**HEATON, Sir Peregrine;** *see* Heaton, Sir J. V. P. H.

**HEATON, Ralph Neville,** CB 1951; Deputy Secretary, Ministry of Housing and Local Government, since 1969; *b* 4 June 1912; *s* of late Ernest Heaton; *m* 1939, Cecily Margaret Alabaster; three *s* one *d*. *Educ:* Westminster; Christ Church, Oxford. Entered Board of Education 1934; Under-Sec., Ministry of Education, 1946-53; Deputy Sec., 1954-61; Deputy Sec., Ministry of Transport, 1961-68; Dep. Under-Sec. of State, DEA, 1968-69. Commonwealth Fund Fellow, 1951-52. *Address:* Rossmore, Manor Park Avenue, Princes Risborough, Bucks.

**HEATON, Rose Henniker (Mrs Adrian Porter);** *b* London, 1884; *d* of late Sir John Henniker-Heaton, Bt, Postal Reformer, and Rose Bennett; *m* 1914, Lieut-Col Adrian Porter (*d* 1954), King's Messenger; one *d*. *Publications:* The Perfect Hostess; The Perfect Schoolgirl; The Perfect Christmas; The Perfect Cruise; Mr Manners; Dinner with James; Chez James (with Sir Duncan Swann); Contract with James; Cruising with James; Life of Sir John Henniker-Heaton; Roseleaves (verses); The Perfect Address Book; Running a House without Help. *Recreations:* travelling and listening-in. *Address:* c/o Mrs L. Buckley, Sheepcote, Bartestree, Hereford.

**HEATON, Trevor Braby,** OBE 1919; DM, MA Oxon; MRCP; Student Emeritus of Christ Church, Oxford; *b* Oslo, Norway, 9 Aug. 1886; 2nd *s* of late Rev. A. F. Heaton, Rector of Covington, Hunts; *m* 1920 Constance Irene, *d* of late J. W. Wheeler-Bennett, JP; one *s* two *d*. *Educ:* Charterhouse; Christ Church, Oxford; Guy's Hospital. 1st class Natural Science, Oxford, 1909; Medical Registrar, Guy's Hospital, 1913; Capt. RAMC (SR), 1915-19. Dr Lee's Reader in Anatomy, Christ Church, Oxford, 1920-54. *Publication:* The Human Body, 1927. *Address:* 3 St Martin's Square, Chichester, Sussex. *T:* Chichester 83941.

**HEAUME, Sir Francis H. du;** *see* du Heaume.

**HEAWOOD, Geoffrey Leonard;** *s* of late Professor P. J. Heawood, OBE, DCL; *m* 1926, Norah Buchanan, 2nd *d* of late Rt Rev. J. T. Inskip, DD; one *s* one *d*. *Educ:* Blundell's; Wadham Coll., Oxford (Math. Mods and Lit. Hum.). Capt. 4th Bn Wilts Regt; attached 1st Oxford and Bucks LI; Major, Home Guard. Tutor Knutsford Test Sch., 1919-22; London Sec. Student Christian Movement, 1922-24; Resident Tutor, King's Coll. Hostel, London, 1924-26; Asst Master Alleyns Sch., 1925-29; Headmaster County Sch. for Boys, Bromley, 1929-37; Headmaster Cheltenham Grammar Sch., 1937-53; Sec. of the Central Advisory Council for the Ministry (CACTM), 1953-60, General Sec., 1960-62; retired, 1962. *Publications:* Religion in School; Vacant Possession; Westminster Abbey Trinity Lectures, 1961; The Humanist-Christian Frontier. *Address:* Vanbrugh Cottage, Selham Road, West Lavington, Midhurst, Sussex. *T:* Midhurst 2240.

**HEBB, Professor Donald Olding,** FRSC 1959; FRS 1966; Professor of Psychology, since 1947, and Chancellor, since 1970, McGill University (Chairman of Department, 1948-58; Vice-Dean of Biological Sciences, 1964-66); *b* 22 July 1904; *s* of Arthur Morrison Hebb and Mary Clara Olding; *m* 1st, 1931, Marion Isobel Clark (*d* 1933); 2nd, 1937, Elizabeth Nicholas Donovan (*d* 1962); two *d*; 3rd, 1966, Margaret Doreen Wright (*née* Williamson). *Educ:* Dalhousie Univ.; McGill Univ.; University of Chicago; Harvard Univ. PhD (Harvard), 1936. Taught in schools, Nova Scotia and Quebec, 1925-34; Instructor, Harvard Univ., 1936-37; Research Fellow, Montreal Neurological Inst., 1937-39; Lectr, Queen's Univ., 1939-42; Research Associate, Yerkes Labs of Primate Biology, 1942-47. Pres., Canadian Psychol Assoc., 1952; Pres., American Psychol. Assoc., 1960. Hon. DSc: Chicago, 1961; Waterloo, 1963; York, 1966; McMaster, 1967; Hon. DHL, Northeastern, 1963; Hon. LLD: Dalhousie, 1965; Queen's, 1967; Western Ontario, 1968. *Publications:* Organization of Behaviour, 1949; Textbook of Psychology, 1958, 1966; papers in technical psychological jls. *Address:* 21 Curzon Street, Montreal West 28, PQ, Canada. *T:* 481-8366.

**HEBBLETHWAITE, Sidney Horace,** CMG 1964; HM Diplomatic Service; Consul in Florence, since 1970; *b* 15 Nov. 1914; *s* of Sidney Horace Hebblethwaite and Margaret Bowler Cooke; *m* 1942, May Gladys Cook; two *d. Educ:* Reale Ginnasio-Liceo, Francesco Petrarca, Trieste, Italy; Pembroke Coll., Cambridge. Third Sec., FO, 1939; transferred to: Rome, 1939; FO, 1940; Lisbon, 1942; Second Sec. 1944; transferred to FO, 1945; Foreign Service Officer, 1948; 1st Sec. (Information), Athens, 1949; transferred to: Rome, 1951; FO, 1955; seconded to Treasury, 1957; transferred to Brussels, 1958; Counsellor: HM Embassy, Stockholm, 1958-62, Rangoon, 1962-65; Counsellor (Information), Washington, 1965-68; retired, in order to take up appt as HM Consul, Florence. *Recreations:* music, reading. *Address:* c/o Foreign and Commonwealth Office, SW1; 1 Paultons Street, SW3. *T:* 01-352 1541.

**HECKER, William Rundle,** CBE 1963; MA, BSc, FKC; Headmaster of St Dunstan's College, Catford, 1938-67; *b* 1899; *s* of late W. J. Hecker, Margate, and Elizabeth, *d* of Richard Rundle, Hazelbeech, Northants; *m* 1925, Ione Murray, *d* of late J. P. Topping, MD; one *s. Educ:* Chatham House, Ramsgate; King's Coll., London. Served European War, 1914-18, in France; London Regt, 1917-19; Senior Science Master, Boston Gram. Sch., 1924-25; Asst Master, Epsom Coll., 1925-28; Headmaster of Tavistock Gram. Sch., 1928-31, Wilson's Gram. Sch., Camberwell, 1931-38. Pres. Incorporated Assoc. of Headmasters, 1951. Chm. Jt Cttee of the Four Secondary Assoc., 1958-59. *Recreations:* walking, gardening, travel. *Address:* 8 Brokes Crescent, Reigate, Surrey. *Club:* Athenæum.

**HECKLE, Arnold,** CMG 1964; Chairman and President, Rubery Owen Canada Ltd; North American Director, The Owen Organisation; *b* 4 Dec. 1906; *s* of late James Allison Heckle; *m* 1954, Monique, *d* of late Alfred Choinière, Montreal. *Educ:* Padgate Sch., Lancs; Warrington Technical Coll. Entered Local Govt; subseq. Bd of Trade: Regional Controller, Midlands, 1941; Asst Sec., Bd of Trade; British Trade Comr, Johannesburg, 1957-60; Principal British Trade Comr, PQ, 1960-68. *Recreations:* fly-fishing, golf. *Address:* Apt 917, 21 Dale Avenue, Toronto 5, Ontario, Canada.

**HECKSTALL-SMITH, Hugh William,** MA; author; *b* 24 July 1896; *s* of late Malden and of Ada Victoria Heckstall-Smith; *m* Eileen Violet Mary, *d* of Surgn Rear-Adm. I. H. Anderson, Twyford, Hants; one *s. Educ:* Tonbridge Sch.; Sidney Sussex Coll., Cambridge. Served European War, 1915-19 (wounded). Stowe Sch. (Science Tutor), 1923-33; Headmaster, Grammar Sch., Ludlow, 1933-35; Headmaster, Chippenham Grammar Sch., Wilts, 1935-39; farming in Radnorshire, 1939-47; Chm., Knighton Branch NFU, 1946; Mem., Min. of Agric. Machinery Working Party, 1946-51; Mem. Management Cttee, Moorhaven (Mental) Hospital, Devon, 1951-69. Mem. Soc. of Friends (Quakers), 1935-. *Publications:* First Electrical Theory, 1930, revised 1950; Intermediate Electrical Theory, 1932, revised 1958; The Bases of Atomic Physics, 1956; Atomic Radiation Dangers, 1958; Doubtful Schoolmaster (an autobiography), 1962. *Recreation:* trying to understand, not only with the mind. *Address:* Brooking House, Tigley Cross, Totnes, Devon.

**HECTOR, Gordon Matthews,** CMG 1966; CBE 1961 (OBE 1955); Clerk to the University Court, Aberdeen; *b* 9 June 1918; *m* 1954, Mary Forrest, MB, ChB; *o d* of late Robert Gray, Fraserburgh, Aberdeenshire; one *s* two *d. Educ:* Edinburgh Academy; Lincoln Coll., Oxford. Military Service with East Africa Forces, 1940-45. Apptd Dist Officer, Kenya, 1946; Asst Sec., 1950; Sec. to Road Authority, 1951; Sec. to Govt of Seychelles, 1952; Acting Governor, 1953; Dep. Resident Comr and Govt Sec., Basutoland, 1956; Chief Sec., Basutoland, 1964; Deputy British Government Representative, Lesotho (lately Basutoland), 1965. Sec., Basutoland Constitutional Commn, 1957-58. Fellow of the Commonwealth Fund, 1939. Chm., Aberdeen Branch, Save the Children Fund; Member: Court of Directors, Edinburgh Acad.; Bd of Governors, Oakbank Sch.; Aberdeen Youth Council; Sec., Aberdeen Scouts Assoc. *Recreations:* various. *Address:* 9 Rubislaw Den North, Aberdeen AB2 4AL. *T:* Aberdeen 38064. *Clubs:* Royal Over-Seas League; Nairobi (Kenya); Vincent's (Oxford).

**HEDDY, Brian Huleatt;** HM Diplomatic Service; Head of Migration and Visa Department, Foreign and Commonwealth Office, since 1968; *b* 8 June 1916; *o s* of Dr William Reginald Huleatt Heddy, Barrister-at-Law, and Ruby Norton-Taylor; *m* 1st, 1940, Barbara Ellen Williams (*d* 1965); two *s* one *d*; 2nd, 1966, Ruth Mackarness (*née* Hogan) (*d* 1967); (one step *s* two step *d*); 3rd, 1969, Horatia Clare Kennedy. *Educ:* St Paul's Sch.; Pembroke Coll., Oxford. Commissioned in 75th (Highland) Field Regt, Royal Artillery, Nov. 1939; served in France 1940; WA, 1943; War Office and France, 1944-45; Mem. of Gray's Inn. Entered Foreign Service, 1945. Appointed to Brussels, 1946; Denver, 1948; Foreign Office, 1952; Tel Aviv, 1953; UK Delegation to ECSC, Luxembourg, 1955; Foreign Office, 1959; promoted Counsellor, 1963; ConsulGen. at Lourenço Marques, 1963-65; Head of Nationality and Consular Dept, Commonwealth Office, 1966-67. *Recreations:* tennis, golf. *Address:* c/o Foreign and Commonwealth Office, SW1; 16 Lexham House, Lexham Gardens, W8. *T:* 01-373 9107. *Clubs:* Public Schools, MCC.

**HEDGES, Sir John (Francis),** Kt 1962; CBE 1958; solicitor in private practice; *b* 1917; *o s* of Francis Reade Hedges and Nesta Violet (*née* Cavell); *m* 1957, Barbara Mary (*née* Ward), *widow* of Comdr Richard Scobell Palairet, RN; no *c. Educ:* St Andrew's, Eastbourne; Harrow. Commissioned Royal Signals, 1940; served India and SE Asia, TARO, 1950. Chm. Abingdon Conservative Assoc., 1948-60; Chm. Wessex Area, 1954-57 (Hon. Treas. 1960-67); Pres. Berks, Bucks and Oxon Justices' Clerks' Soc., 1955; Pres. Berks, Bucks and Oxon Inc. Law Soc., 1963; Chm. Turner's Court Sch. for Boys, 1955; Pres. League of Friends, Wallingford Hosps, 1953; Mem. Berks Exec. Council, Nat. Health Service, 1960 (Vice-Chm., 1969-). *Recreations:* shooting, gardening, music. *Address:* St Nicholas, High Street, Wallingford, Berks. *T:* 2217. *Club:* Berkshire (Reading).

**HEDGES, Sidney George;** author and journalist; *b* Bicester, Oxon, 25 March 1897; *s* of G. W. and M. A. Hedges; *m* 1930, Mary, *y d* of G. H. Dixon, Retford; one *s. Educ:* Oxford Wesleyan Sch. and evening classes. War service in Malta, 1915-19; tried carpentering, drapery trade, music teaching, orchestral playing, lecturing–freelance and for Empire Marketing Board, before settling as writer. Has been National Pres. of Methodist Assoc. of Youth Clubs; Mem. of Bd, Nat. Sunday Sch. Union; Chm., Nat. Harmonica League; Pres. of

British Temperance Youth; Founder-leader, Red Rhythmics pioneer harmonica band, 1935-56; European adjudicator, Fédération Internationale de l'Harmonica. *Publications:* more than one hundred books–a dozen novels; twenty works on swimming (originator of modern surface-diving and seal stroke); as many more on indoor and outdoor games, and on youth club and Sunday School work; others autobiographical and on music, skating, hobbies. (Some trans. into French, Dutch, Norwegian, Hindi). Editor of: Christian Youth Handbook; Things to Do books; Universal Book of Hobbies. Chief works: The Complete Swimmer, Indoor and Community Games, Youth Club Programmes, The Youth Sing Book, Pendlecliffe School stories; recent anthologies of prayers and scriptural excerpts from the world's Living Religions. Contributor to Chamber's Encyclopædia, to magazines on both sides of the Atlantic, and broadcaster on many subjects. *Recreations:* youth work, swimming, violin playing, travel, skating. *Address:* Banbury Road, Bicester, Oxon. *T:* Bicester 2239. *Club:* Royal Commonwealth Society.

**HEDLEY, Hilda Mabel;** Assistant Under-Secretary of State, Department of Health and Social Security (formerly Ministry of Health), since 1967; *b* 4 May 1918; *d* of late George Ward Hedley, Cheltenham, and late Winifred Mary Hedley (*née* Cockshott). *Educ:* Cheltenham Ladies' Coll.; Newnham Coll., Cambridge. Examiner, Uncommon Languages Dept., Postal Censorship, 1940-42; Temp. Asst Principal, Foreign Office, 1942-46; Asst Principal, Min. of Health (Private Sec. to Permanent Sec.), 1946-48; Principal, 1949; Asst Sec., 1956. Sec. to Royal Commn on Mental Health, 1954-57. Nuffield Foundation Travelling Fellowship, 1960-61. *Recreations:* house and garden, travel. *Address:* 28 Gilkes Crescent, SE21. *T:* 01-693 4321.

**HEDLEY, Maj.-Gen. Robert Cecil Osborne,** CB 1951; CBE 1947; DSO 1944; retired; *b* 31 Oct. 1900; *s* of late Major R. C. Hedley, Corbridge, Northumberland; *m* 1945, Lucy, *d* of late J. D. N. Strang and Mrs Strang, Oakwood, Hexham, Northumberland. *Educ:* St Bees Sch.; RMC, Sandhurst, 2nd Lieut IA, 1920; Lieut 5th Royal Gurkha Rifles (Frontier Force) 1923; Capt. 1928; Coy. Officer, RMC, Sandhurst, 1935-38; Major, 1938; Dep. Asst Military Sec., GHQ, MEF, 1941-42; Lieut-Col Comdt 2nd Bn 5th Royal Gurkha Rifles (Frontier Force), 1942-44; Brig. Comdg 48 Ind. Inf., Bde, 1944-45; HQ ALFSEA, 1945-46; Maj.-Gen. Comdg 26 Indian Division, 1946-47; Brig. Comdt School of Infantry, Mhow, 1947; Brig. Comdg Br. Gurkha Troops in India, 1948; Brig. Comdg Johore Sub-Dist, Malaya, 1948-49; Brig. Comdg 48th Gurkha Inf. Bde, 1949-50; Maj.-Gen. Bde of Gurkhas, and GOC South Malaya District, 1950-51; retired, 1952. Schools Liaison Officer, Western Command, 1952-61. IGS Medal with clasp, Waziristan, 1923-24; NW Frontier Clasp to IGS Medal, 1930. Served War of 1939-45, Middle East, 1941 (despatches): Burma, 1942-45 (despatches, DSO and 2 bars); Sumatra, 1946 (CBE, Gen. Service Medal and Clasp); Malaya (CB despatches twice and clasp), 1948-51. *Address:* The Dene, Haydon Bridge, Northumberland; c/o National and Grindlay's Bank, Ltd, 13 St James's Square, SW1.

**HEDLEY-WHYTE, Angus,** DSO 1940; TD; MB, MS, FRCS; FRCSE; LRCP; Honorary Consultant Surgeon: Royal Victoria Infirmary, Newcastle upon Tyne; Tynemouth Victoria Jubilee Infirmary and Preston Hospital, North Shields; lately Consulting Surgeon: Richard Murray Hospital; South Moor Hospital; *b* 23 Aug. 1897; *o s* of Dr John Whyte, JP, Gosforth, Newcastle upon Tyne; *m* 1930, Nancy Nettleton; two *s* one *d*. *Educ:* Ackworth Sch., Yorks; University of Durham, MB, MS (Hons) 1924; BS 1919, with 1st class Hons in Surgery; St Bartholomew's and London Hospitals. Successively House Surgeon in Special Depts, House Surgeon, House Physician, Hon. Registrar, Asst Hon. Surgeon, Royal Victoria Infirmary, Newcastle upon Tyne and Hon. Surgeon Hospital for Sick Children, Newcastle upon Tyne; lately Consulting Surgeon, AMS; Pres., Proctological Section, Royal Society of Medicine; Member: RCS, 1943-49; Court of Examiners Council, RCS, 1950-58; Medical Officer, Northumb Hussars Yeomanry, 1927-32; MO 149 (Northumbrian) Field Ambulance, 1932-40 (OC 1937-40); served War of 1939-45 (despatches, DSO). Hon. Col 50th (N) Div., RAMC units. *Publications:* various medical. *Address:* Ruthven, 10 Adderstone Crescent, Jesmond, Newcastle upon Tyne 2. *T:* 811660. *Clubs:* Thatched House, Junior Carlton.

**HEENAN, His Eminence Cardinal John Carmel;** *see* Westminster, Cardinal Archbishop of.

**HEENAN, Maurice,** CMG 1966; QC (Hong Kong) 1962; Deputy-Director, General Legal Division, Office of Legal Affairs, Offices of the Secretary-General, United Nations, New York; *b* NZ, 8 Oct. 1912; 2nd *s* of late David Heenan and of Anne Frame; *m* 1951, Claire, 2nd *d* of Emil Ciho, Trenčín, Bratislava, Czechoslovakia; two *d*. *Educ:* Canterbury Coll., University of New Zealand. Law Professional, LLB, Barrister and Solicitor of Supreme Court of New Zealand, Practised law in NZ, 1937-40. War of 1939-45; Major, 2nd NZEF; active service Western Desert, Libya, Cyrenica and Italy, 1940-45 (despatches). Crown Counsel, Palestine, 1946-48. Solicitor-Gen., Hong Kong, 1961; HM's Attorney-Gen., Hong Kong, and *ex officio* MEC and MLC, Hong Kong, 1961-66. *Recreations:* Rugby football, tennis, squash, ski-ing, golf. *Address:* Room 3450, Office of Legal Affairs, United Nations, New York, NY 10017, USA; Plane Trees, West Road, New Canaan, Conn 06840, USA. *Club:* Hong Kong.

**HEENEY, Arnold Danford Patrick,** CC (Canada) 1968; QC (Canada); MA, BCL, LLD; Chairman, Canadian Section, International Joint Commission (Canada and United States) since 1962; Canadian Chairman, Permanent Joint Board on Defence (Canada and United States), since 1967; *b* 5 April 1902; *s* of late Rev. Canon Bertal Heeney and late Eva Marjorie Holland; *m* 1931, Margaret Yuile, Montreal; one *s* one *d*. *Educ:* St John's Coll., Sch., Winnipeg; University of Manitoba; St John's Coll., Oxford (Rhodes Scholar, Mod. Hist.; Hon. Fellow, 1970); McGill Univ. (Law). MA (Manitoba and Oxford); BCL (McGill). Admitted to Bar of Quebec, 1929; practised law in Montreal, 1929-38; Sessional Lecturer, Faculty of Law, McGill Univ., 1934-38. Principal Sec. to Prime Minister, Oct. 1938; Clerk of Privy Council and Sec. to Cabinet, 1940; KC (Dominion), 1941; Under-Sec. of State for External Affairs, 1949. Ambassador and Permanent Representative of Canada to the North Atlantic Council and to the Organization for European Economic Co-operation, Paris, 1952; Canadian Ambassador to the US, 1953-57; Chm. of the CS Commission of Canada, 1957-59; Canadian Ambassador to the United States, 1959-62. Member, Board of Govs McGill Univ. Hon. Fellow, St John's Coll., Oxford, 1970. Hon. LLD: British Columbia, 1948; Manitoba, 1950; Franklin and Marshall Coll., 1954; Michigan State Univ., 1955; Kenyon Coll.,

1955; University of Rhode Island, 1960; McGill Univ., 1961; Alberta Univ., 1967; Hon. DCL: St John's Coll., Winnipeg, 1966; Bishop's Univ., Lennoxville, 1969; Royal Mil. Coll., Kingston, Ont, 1970. *Recreations:* golf and ski-ing. *Address:* (office) 850 Burnside Building, 151 Slater Street, Ottawa 4, Canada; (home) 428 Buena Vista Road, Rockcliffe, Ont, Canada. *Clubs:* Rideau, Royal Ottawa Golf (Ottawa); University (Montreal).

**HEES, Hon. George H.,** PC (Canada) 1957; MP (Canada) (Progressive C) Northumberland, Ontario, since Nov. 1965 (Broadview Riding, 1950); President, Montreal and Canadian Stock Exchanges, since 1964; *b* Toronto, 17 June 1910; *s* of Harris Lincoln Hees, Toronto, and Mabel Good, New York; *m* 1934, Mabel, *d* of late Hon. E. A. Dunlop; three *d. Educ:* Trinity Coll. Sch., Port Hope, Ont; RMC, Kingston, Ont; University of Toronto; Cambridge Univ. Formerly Dir, George H. Hees & Son & Co. Served War of 1939-45: Royal Canadian Artillery, 1941-44; 3rd Anti-Tank Regt, Royal Canadian Artillery; Bde Major, 5th Infantry Bde, Holland (wounded); retd as Major. Contested (Prog. C) Spadina Riding, 1945. Minister of Transport, Canada, 1957-60; Minister of Trade and Commerce, 1960-63. Executive with George H. Hees Son & Co., Toronto; Director: Expo 67; Wood Green Community Centre. Hon. Dr of Laws, 1961. *Recreations:* reading, ski-ing, swimming, golf, tennis, riding, bridge; formerly boxing. *Address:* 7 Coltrin Place, Ottawa, Ontario, Canada; Rathbunwood, Cobourg, Canada. *Clubs:* University, Toronto Golf, Toronto Badminton and Racquet, Osler Bluff Ski, Granite, Albany (Toronto); Rideau, Royal Ottawa Golf (Ottawa); Bonaventure (Montreal); Mid-Ocean (Bermuda).

**HEFFER, Eric Samuel;** MP (Lab) Walton Division of Liverpool since 1964; *b* 12 Jan. 1922; *s* of William George Heffer and Annie Heffer (*née* Nicholls); *m* 1945, Doris Murray. *Educ:* Bengeo Junior Sch. and Longmore Senior Sch., Hertford. Served RAF, 1942-45. Pres. Liverpool Trades Council and Labour Party, 1959-60, 1964-65, and Vice-Pres., 1960 and 1964. Liverpool City Councillor, 1960-66. Member: Council of Europe, 1965-68; WEU, 1969- (served on political, social and financial cttees). *Publications:* (part author) The Agreeable Autocracies, 1961, (USA); articles in Tribune, Liverpool Daily Post, Labour Voice, New Left Review, and in foreign jls. *Recreations:* hill-walking, mountaineering. *Address:* 54 Avondale Road, Liverpool 15, Lancs. *T:* 051-733 6009.

**HEGER, Prof. Robert;** President of State High School of Munich and First Conductor of State-Opera, Munich; *b* Strassbourgh, 19 Aug. 1886. *Educ:* Strassbourgh, Zurich, Lyon, Munich. Conductor at the Operas in Strassbourgh, Barmen; First Conductor at the Volks-opera in Vienna, 1911; Dir of the Opera in Nuremburg, 1912-19; First Conductor at the Munich Opera, 1919-25; First Conductor of the State Opera Vienna, 1925-33; Dir of the Concerts of the Soc. of Friends of Music, Vienna; Conductor at the State Opera, Berlin, 1933-45; Conductor at the Royal Opera in London, 1926-36. *Publications:* Trio for Piano; Ein Fest zu Haderslev, Opera; Concert for Violin, First Symphony; A Song of Peace, Chorus work; Second Symphony; Nine Songs; Verdi-Variations; Der Bettler Namenlos, Opera; Der Verlorene Sohn (the prodigal son), Opera: A Serious Prelude and a Gay Fugue for Orchestra, op. 26; Lady Hamilton, Opera; Dramatic Overture, op. 28; Henry the Lion, Opera; A serious Symphonie (the third one) op. 30; Variations and Fugue on a Baroque theme for Orchestra, op. 32a; Chaconne and Fugue on a twelve-tone series, op. 35; 4 alte Marienlieder for a high soprano and orchestra, op. 42; Concerto for Violoncello and Orchestra, op. 43; Don Carlos–Variations, op. 44; Te Deum for 2 soli, choir and orchestra, op. 45. *Address:* Widenmayerstrasse 46 I, Munich, Germany.

**HEGGS, G. B. M.;** *see* Mitchell-Heggs.

**HEGLAND, David Leroy,** DFC 1944; Chairman and Managing Director, Vauxhall Motors Ltd, Luton, 1966-70; Director: General Motors Ltd, London, since 1966; GMAC (UK) Ltd, Luton, since 1966; *b* 12 June 1919; *s* of Lee and Jennie Hegland; *m* 1944, Dagmar Cooke; two *s* one *d. Educ:* Whitman Coll., Washington, USA (BA). Managing Director: GM International, Copenhagen, 1956-58; GM South African, Port Elizabeth, 1958-61; GM Holden's Pty Ltd, Melbourne, 1962-65. Member: Nat. Adv. Coun. for Motor Manufacturing Industry; EDC for Motor Manufacturing Industry; Brit. Manufacturers' Exec. Cttee, SMMT; Delta Sigma Rho. FIMI. *Recreations:* tennis, golf, riding. *Clubs:* Royal Automobile; Harpenden Golf; Royal & Ancient Golf; Melbourne (Melbourne, Aust.).

**HEIDEGGER, Martin;** retired; *b* Messkirch, Baden, 26 Sept. 1889; *m* 1917, Elfride Petri; two *s* one *d. Educ:* Gymnasium and University, Freiburg i. Br., Privatdozent Freiburg i. Br., 1925; ordentlich Professor, University Marburg, 1923; Professor of Philosophy, University of Freiburg-i.-Br., 1928. *Publications:* Die Kategorienlehre des Duns Scotus, 1916; Sein und Zeit, 1927; Was ist Metaphysik?, 1929; Vom Wesen des Grundes, 1929; Kant und das Problem der Metaphysik, 1929; Brief über den Humanismus, 1947; Existence and Being (introd. Werner Brock), 1949; Holzwege, 1950; An Introduction to Metaphysics, 1960. *Address:* Freiburg i. Br., Rötebuckweg 47, Germany.

**HEIFETZ, Jascha;** Violinist, Soloist; Commander, Legion of Honour, 1957; 1st Vice-President of American Guild of Musical Artists, Inc., New York City; Hon. Member: Society of Concerts of Paris Conservatoire; Association des Anciens Elèves du Conservatoire; Cercle International de la Jeunesse Artistique; Hon. Vice-President of Mark Twain Society, USA; Hon. President, Musicians' Fund of America; *b* Vilna, Russia, 1901; father professional violinist and music teacher; *m* Florence Vidor; one *s* one *d*; *m* 1947, Mrs Frances Spiegelberg; one *s. Educ:* Music Sch. at Vilna; Petrograd Conservatory of Music under Professor Auer. Made his first public appearance at the age of 4½ when he played in Vilna Fantasie Pastorale; at 7 he played Mendelssohn Concerto before a full house in Kovno; entered Petrograd Conservatory when 10, and soon began to give concerts in Russia, Germany, Austro-Hungary, Scandinavia, and later met with a phenomenal success in the United States of America, 1917; from hence he proceeded to England; appeared as soloist with orchestras under Nikisch, Safonoff, Koussevitsky, Schneifoght, Stokowski, Toscanini, and others; toured Australia and New Zealand, 1921; Japan, China, Manchuria, Korea, 1923; tour of the World, 1925-27, including Europe, Northern Africa, South America, Mexico, India, Java, China, Australia, Philippines, etc; has made appearances in the Festival Hall, London, in recent years; his repertoire includes most of the classical and modern violin literature. *Recreations:* sailing, tennis, ping-pong (table tennis), motoring, aquatic sports, reading and dancing. *Address:* Beverly

Hills, Calif., USA. *Clubs:* Royal Automobile, Savage; Bohemian (New York); Newport Harbor Yacht (Newport); Beaux Arts, Inter-Allied (Paris).

**HEILBRON, Rose,** QC 1949; Recorder of Burnley since 1956; *b* 19 Aug. 1914; *d* of late Max and Nellie Heilbron; *m* 1945, Dr Nathaniel Burstein; one *d. Educ:* Belvedere Sch., GPDST; Liverpool University, LLB 1st Class Hons, 1935; Lord Justice Holker Scholar, Gray's Inn, 1936; LLM 1937. Called to Bar, Gray's Inn, 1939, Bencher, 1968; joined Northern Circuit. Hon. Col, WRAC(TA). *Address:* 1 Gray's Inn Square, WC1. *T:* 01-242 3815; 1 Verulam Buildings, Gray's Inn, WC1; Parklands, Allerton, Liverpool 18. *T:* 051-428 4059. *Clubs:* Federation of University Women, Soroptimist, Cowdray (Vice-Pres.).

**HEILBRONN, Hans Arnold,** FRS 1951; FRSC; PhD, MA; Professor of Mathematics, University of Toronto, since 1964; *b* 8 Oct. 1908; *m* 1964, Mrs Dorothy Greaves. Bevan Fellow of Trinity Coll., Cambridge, 1935-40; Henry Overton Wills Professor of Mathematics, University of Bristol, 1949-64. *Publications:* scientific papers in several periodicals. *Address:* 538 Kensington Towers, 21 Dale Avenue, Toronto 5, Canada.

**HEILPERN, Godfrey,** QC 1962; Recorder of Salford since 1964; *b* 29 Oct. 1911; *s* of Marcus and Rose Heilpern; *m* 1944, Anne Sheila Cohen; one *d. Educ:* Manchester Grammar Sch.; Hertford Coll., Oxford. Open classical exhibn to Hertford Coll., Oxford, 1930; First Class Hons in Final Sch. of Jurisprudence, 1934; Harmsworth Schol., Middle Temple, 1935, Bencher, 1968. Called to Bar, 1938; has practised on Northern Circuit, 1938. *Recreations:* golf, bridge, reading, travel. *Address:* 16 Ballbrook Avenue, Didsbury, Manchester 20. *T:* Didsbury 1326. *Clubs:* RAC; Dunham Forest Golf (Dunham).

**HEINZ, Henry John II;** Chairman, H. J. Heinz Company since 1959 (President, 1941-59); *b* Sewickley, Pa, USA, 10 July 1908; *s* of Howard and Elizabeth Rust Heinz; *m* 1st, 1935, Joan Diehl (divorced, 1942); one *s*; *m* 1953, Drue English Maher. *Educ:* Yale (BA 1931); Trinity Coll., Cambridge. Salesman, H. J. Heinz Co., Ltd, London, 1932; with H. J. Heinz Co., Pittsburgh, Pa, Pres., 1941-59; Chm., 1959-; Dir or Officer, various subsidiaries of H. J. Heinz Co. in England, Canada, Australia and elsewhere. Commander, Royal Order of the Phœnix, Greece, 1950; Chevalier de la Légion d'Honneur, France, 1950; Comdr of Order of Merit, Italian Republic. *Recreation:* ski-ing. *Address:* (residence) Goodwood, Sewickley, Pa 15143, USA. *Clubs:* Buck's, White's; The Brook, River, Stanwich (New York); Dunquesne, Rolling Rock, Fox Chapel Golf, Allegheny Country, Laurel Valley Golf (Pittsburgh).

**HEINZE, Prof. Sir Bernard (Thomas),** Kt, *cr* 1949; MA, LLD, MusDoc, FRCM; Degré Supérieur Schola Cantorum, Paris; Ormond Professor of Music, University of Melbourne, 1925-57; Director, State Conservatorium, NSW, 1957-66; Conductor Melbourne Philharmonic Society since 1928; Conductor under contract to ABC since 1947; Member, ABC Music Advisory Committee; *b* Shepparton, Vic., 1 July 1894; *m* 1932, Valerie Antonia, *d* of late Sir David Valentine Hennessy, of Melbourne; three *s. Educ:* St Patrick's Coll., Ballarat; Melbourne Univ. MA (Melbourne); LLD (Hon.) (Brit. Columbia); FRCM 1931; Won the Clarke Scholarship in 1912 and was sent to England to study at the Royal College of Music; studies interrupted by five years' service as an officer in the Royal Artillery; won the Gowland Harrison Scholarship, 1920; studied at the Schola Cantorum, Paris, under Vincent d'Indy and Nestor Lejeune; studied in Berlin under Willy Hess; returned to Australia, 1923; founded Melbourne String Quartette; Conductor: University Symphony Orchestra, 1924-32; Melbourne Symphony Orchestra, 1933-46. Officier de la Couronne, Belgium, 1938; Dir General for Music Australian Broadcasting Co. 1929-32. *Recreations:* golf and philately. *Address:* 101 Victoria Road, Bellevue Hill, Sydney, NSW, Australia. *Clubs:* Royal Automobile of Victoria, Savage, Canada (Melbourne); American (Sydney).

**HEISENBERG, Dr Werner;** Vice-President, Max-Planck Society; Director of the Max-Planck-Institute for Physics and Astrophysics, Munich, since 1958 and Professor at University of Munich; President, Alexander von Humboldt-foundation; *b* 5 Dec. 1901; *s* of August Heisenberg and Annie Wecklein; *m* 1937, Elisabeth Schumacher; three *s* four *d. Educ:* Universities Munich and Göttingen. Dr phil. Munich, 1923; Privatdozent, Göttingen, 1924; Lectr at Univ. of Copenhagen, 1926; Prof., University of Leipzig, 1927-41; Prof., University of Berlin and Dir of the Kaiser-Wilhelm-Institute for Physics in Berlin, 1941-45; Prof. University of Göttingen and Dir of the Max-Planck-Institute for Physics in Göttingen, 1946-58. Gifford Lecturer, St Andrews Univ., 1955-56. Foreign Member, Royal Society, 1955. Nobel Prize for Physics, 1932; Pour le mérite für Wissenschaften und Künste, 1957. *Publications:* papers about atomic physics, quantum theory etc., in different periodicals; Die physikalischen Prinzipien der Quantentheorie, Leipzig, 1930, 4th edn, 1944 (Engl. edn Chicago, 1930); Wandlungen in den Grundlagen der Naturwissenschaft, Leipzig, 1935, 9th edn, 1959; Vorträge über kosmische Strahlung, Berlin, 1943, 2nd edn, 1953; Die Physik der Atomkerne, Braunschweig, 1943; Das Naturbild der heutigen Physik, 1955; (trans. various langs); Physics and Philosophy, 1958 (New York) (trans. various langs); Introduction to the Unified Field Theory of Elementary Particles, 1966; Einführung in die einheitliche Feldtheorie der Elementarteilchen, 1967; Der Teil und das Ganze, 1969. *Address:* München 23, Rheinlandstrasse 1, West Germany. *T:* 327001.

**HEISER, Victor George,** MD; Consultant, Industrial Health; Consultant, Leonard Wood Memorial for Eradication of Leprosy, since 1970; *b* 5 Feb. 1873; *s* of George and Mathilde Lorentz; *m* 1940, Marion Phinny (*d* 1965). *Educ:* private tutors; Jefferson Medical Coll., Pennsylvania. Entered US Marine Hosp. Service, 1898; special detail to Europe to study plague, 1899; to Canada with regard to emigration, 1901; deleg. Internat. Congress on Medicine, Egypt, 1902; Chief Quarantine Officer, Philippine Islands, 1903-15, Dir of Health, 1905-15; Dir for East, Internat. Health Bd, Rockefeller Foundation, 1914-27; Assoc. Dir, Internat. Health Div., Rockefeller Foundation, 1927-34 (retd); Consultant to Cttee on Healthful Working Conditions, Nat. Assoc. of Manufacturers, 1938-; Pres. Internat. Leprosy Assoc., 1931-38; Chm., Advisory Cttee on Medicine and Public Health, NY World's Fair, 1939; Member: Amer. Red Cross Commission to Italy, 1917; Cttee on Health and Medical Relief, US Railroad Admin, 1918-20; Advisory Council, Nat. Health Admin., China; Director: Amer. Museum of Health 1940-; NY Post-Grad.

Hosp., 1932-49; connected with work of stamping out plague, cholera, smallpox, etc., in various countries, also with building of Philippine Gen. Hosp., Coll. of Medicine and Surgery (served as Prof. of Hygiene), and many hosps throughout the Philippines; Pres. NY Soc. of Tropical Medicine, 1948. *Publications:* Sanitary Code for the City of Manila; Manual for the Bureau of Health, Manila; An American Doctor's Odyssey, 1936; You're the Doctor, 1939; Toughen Up, America!, 1941; (co-author): Handbook of Medical Treatment, 1918; Oxford System of Medicine, 1921; Practice of Medicine in the Tropics, 1922; A System of Pediatrics, 1924; A Textbook of Medicine by American Authors, 1926; Cyclopedia of Medicine, 1932; articles in medical journals, magazines and Encyclopedia Americana. *Address:* Manhattan House, 200 East 66th Street, New York, NY 10021, USA. *Clubs:* Army and Navy (Manila, New York and Washington, DC); Century, New York Athletic (New York); The Sanctum (Litchfield).

**HEISKELL, Andrew;** Chairman of Directors, Time, Inc., since 1960; *b* Naples, 13 Sept. 1915; *s* of Morgan Heiskell and Ann Heiskell (*née* Hubbard); *m* 1937, Cornelia Scott (marriage dissolved); two *s*; *m* 1950, Madeleine Carroll (marriage dissolved); one *d*; *m* 1965, Marian, *d* of Arthur Hays Sulzberger, and *widow* of Orvil E. Dryfoos. *Educ:* Switzerland; France; University of Paris. Science teacher, Ecole du Montcel, Paris, 1935. Life Magazine: Science and Medicine Editor, 1937-39; Asst Gen. Manager, 1939-42; Gen. Manager, 1942-46; Publisher, 1946-60; Vice-Pres., Time, Inc., 1949-60. Co-Chm., Urban Coalition; Mem., Exec. Cttee, Inter-American Press Assoc.; Director: Council for Latin America; Center for Inter-American Relations; Actors Studio; Trustee: Bennington Coll.; Inst. of Internat. Educn; Internat. Exec. Service Corps. *Address:* Time, Inc., Time and Life Building, Rockefeller Center, New York, NY 10017; 870 United Nations Plaza, New York, NY 10028; Darien, Conn, USA.

**HEITLER, Walter Heinrich,** FRS 1948; PhD; Professor of Theoretical Physics, University of Zürich, since 1949; *b* 2 Jan. 1904; *m* 1942, Kathleen Winifred; one *s*. *Educ:* Universities of Berlin and Munich. Doctor's Degree, Munich, 1926; Privatdocent for Theoretical Physics, University of Göttingen, 1929-33; Research Fellow, University of Bristol, 1933-41; Professor of Theoretical Physics, 1941-45; Dir, School of Theoretical Physics, Dublin Institute for Advanced Studies, 1945-49. Hon. DSc, Dublin, 1954; Dr rer nat *hc*, Göttingen, 1969. Max Planck Medal, 1968. *Publications:* (with F. London) Theory of Chemical Bond, 1927; Quantum Theory of Radiation, 1936 (3rd edn 1954); Elementary Wave Mechanics, 1945 (2nd edn 1956); papers on Cosmic Rays, Meson theory, Quantum-electrodynamics; Der Mensch und die Naturwissenschaftliche Erkenntnis, 1961, 4th edn, 1966 (Eng. Trans. Man and Scientific Knowledge, 1963); Naturphilosophische Streifzüge, 1970. *Recreations:* mountaineering, ski-ing. *Address:* The University, Zürich.

**HELE, Desmond George K.;** *see* King-Hele.

**HELLER, Hans,** MD (Cambridge), PhD, FRCP; FIBiol; Professor of Pharmacology, University of Bristol, since 1949; Editor, Journal of Endocrinology, since 1963; Hon. Director, MRC Research Group on Neurosecretion; *b* Brno, Czechoslovakia, 25 Sept. 1905; *s* of Dr Joseph Heller, Brno; *m* 1933, Josephine Gertrude, *d* of Dr E. Libich; two *d*. *Educ:* Emmanuel Coll., Cambridge; University Coll. Hosp., London. University Lecturer in Pharmacology, Vienna, 1931-34; Research Grantee, University Coll. Hosp. London, 1935-39; Beit Memorial Fellow for Medical Research, 1939-41; Lecturer in Pharmacology, Bristol, 1942-44, Reader, 1944-49, Dean of Faculty of Medicine, 1966-69; Visiting Prof. NY University Medical Coll., 1949; Visiting Scientist, US Dept of Health, Washington, DC 1958. Pres. European Soc. for Comparative Endocrinology. *Publications:* papers on pharmacological subjects in Journal of Physiology, British Journal of Pharmacology, Jl of Endocrinology, etc.; Ed., The Neurohypophysis, 1957; Oxytocin, 1961; Neurosecretion, 1962; Comparative Endocrinology, 1963; Internat. Encyclopedia of Pharmacology and Therapeutics, Sect. 41, 1970. *Recreations:* travelling, numismatics. *Address:* 29 Druid Road, Bristol 9. *T:* 684152.

**HELLER, J. H. S.;** *see* Heller, Hans.

**HELLINGS, Lt-Gen. Sir Peter (William Cradock),** KCB 1970 (CB 1966); DSC 1940; MC 1943; Commandant-General, Royal Marines, since 1968; *b* 6 Sept. 1916; *s* of Stanley and Norah Hellings; *m* 1941, Zoya, *d* of Col Bassett; one *s* one *d*. *Educ:* Naut. Coll., Pangbourne. Joined Royal Marines, 1935; Company Cmdr, 40 Commando, 1942; GSO 2, Commando Group, 1944; Comdr 41 and 42 Commandos, 1945-46; Brigade Major, 3 Commando Bde in Malaya, 1949-51; joined Directing Staff of Marine Corps Schs, Quantico, USA, 1954; Comdr 40 Commando, 1958; Brigade Comdr, 3 Commando Bde, 1959; Comdr Infantry Training Centre, Royal Marines, 1960; idc 1962; Dep. Dir, Joint Warfare Staff, 1963; Maj.-Gen., 1964; Chief of Staff to Commandant-Gen., RM, 1964; Group Comdr, HQ Portsmouth Group RM, 1967-68; Lt-Gen., 1968. *Recreations:* shooting, fishing, sailing. *Address:* The Leys, Milton Combe, Devon. *T:* Yelverton 3355. *Clubs:* United Service, United Hunts.

**HELLMAN, Lillian;** Playwright; *b* New Orleans, Louisiana, USA, 20 June 1907; *d* of Max Bernard Hellman and Julia Newhouse; *m* 1925, Arthur Kober (divorced). *Educ:* New York Univ.; Columbia Univ. Worked for Horace Liveright, Publishers, 1925-26. Hon. LLD Wheaton Coll., MA Tufts Univ.; Hon. LLD: Rutgers Univ., 1963, Brandeis Univ., 1965; Creative Arts Award, Brandeis Univ.; Mem., National Academy of Arts and Letters (Gold Medal for Drama, 1964); Mem., American Academy of Arts and Sciences. Book reviews, Herald Tribune, wrote short stories. First produced play The Children's Hour, 1934. Wrote movie scenarios The Dark Angel, These Three (screen version of The Children's Hour), Dead End, The Little Foxes, North Star, The Searching Wind. *Publications:* plays produced: The Children's Hour, 1934; Days to Come, 1936; The Little Foxes, 1939; Watch on the Rhine, 1941; The Searching Wind, 1944; Another Part of the Forest, 1946; adapted from the French, Roblès' play, Montserrat, 1949; The Autumn Garden, 1951; adapted Anouilh's The Lark, 1955; adapted Voltaire's Candide as comic operetta, 1956; Toys in the Attic, 1960; adapted Blechman's novel How Much as play, My Mother, My Father and Me, 1963; edited: The Selected Letters of Anton Chekhov, 1955; (with introduction) Dashiell Hammett, The Big Knockover, 1966; (memoir) An Unfinished Woman, 1969. *Address:* 630 Park Avenue, New York, NY 10028, USA.

**HELLYER, Arthur George Lee,** MBE 1967; FLS; Gardening Correspondent to the Financial

Times; Editor of Amateur Gardening, 1946-67; Editor of Gardening Illustrated, 1947-56; *b* 16 Dec. 1902; *s* of Arthur Lee Hellyer and Maggie Parlett; *m* 1933, Grace Charlotte Bolt; two *s* one *d*. *Educ:* Dulwich Coll. Farming in Jersey, 1918-21; Nursery work in England, 1921-29; Asst Editor of Commercial Horticulture, 1929; Asst Editor of Amateur Gardening, 1929-46. Associate of Hon. of Royal Horticultural Society; Victoria Medal of Honour in Horticulture. *Publications:* The Amateur Gardener, 1948; Amateur Gardening Pocket Guide, 1941; Amateur Gardening Popular Encyclopædia of Flowering Plants, 1957; Encyclopædia of Garden Work and Terms, 1954; Encyclopædia of Plant Portraits, 1953; English Gardens Open to the Public, 1956; Flowers in Colour, 1955; Garden Pests and Diseases, 1966; Garden Plants in Colour, 1958; Practical Gardening for Amateurs, 1935; Shrubs in Colour, 1966; Your Garden Week by Week, 1938; Your New Garden, 1937; Starting with Roses, 1966; Find out about Gardening, 1967; Gardens to Visit in Britain, 1970. *Recreations:* gardening, photography, travelling. *Address:* Orchards, Rowfant, near Crawley, Sussex. *T:* Turners Hill 338.

**HELLYER, Hon. Paul Theodore,** PC (Canada) 1957; *b* Waterford, Ont, Canada, 6 Aug. 1923; *s* of A. S. Hellyer and Lulla M. Anderson; *m* 1945, Ellen Jean, *d* of Henry Ralph, Toronto, Ont; two *s* one *d*. *Educ:* Waterford High Sch., Ont; Curtiss-Wright Techn. Inst. of Aeronautics, Glendale, Calif; University of Toronto (BA). Fleet Aircraft Mfg Co., Fort Erie, Ont. Wartime service, RCAF and Cdn Army. Propr Mari-Jane Fashions, Toronto, 1945-56; Treas., Curran Hall Ltd, Toronto, 1950 (Pres., 1951-62). Elected to House of Commons, 1949; re-elected, 1953; Parly Asst to Hon. Ralph Campney, Minister of Nat. Defence, 1956; Associate Minister of Nat. Defence, 1957; defeated in gen. elections of June 1957 and March 1958; re-elected to House of Commons in by-election Dec. 1958 and again re-elected June 1962, April 1963, Nov. 1965, and June 1968; Minister of National Defence, 1963-67; Minister of Transport, 1967-69, and Minister i/c Housing, 1968-69; resigned 1969 on question of principle relating to housing. Chm., Federal Task Force on Housing and Urban Develt, 1968. Served as a Parly Rep. to NATO under both L and C administrations. *Recreations:* philately, music. *Address:* 1982 Rideau River Drive, Ottawa, Ont, Canada. *T:* 992-0047.

**HELMORE, Sir James (Reginald Carroll),** KCB 1954; KCMG 1948 (CMG 1946); *b* 1 July 1906; *s* of R. M. Helmore; *m* 1930, Margaret Eleanor, *er d* of Rev. H. J. Green; no *c*. *Educ:* St Paul's Sch. (Scholar); New Coll. (Scholar). Entered Bd of Trade, 1929; Private Sec. to the Pres., 1934-37; Under-Sec., 1946; Second Sec. Board of Trade, 1954-62; Mem. Economic Planning Board, 1952; Permanent Sec., Ministry of Materials, 1952; Permanent Sec., Ministry of Supply, 1953-56; retired July 1956. Chm. of UN Interim Co-ordinating Cttee, for Internat. Commodity Arrangements, 1947-53. *Club:* Travellers'.

**HELMSING, Most Rev. Charles H.;** Bishop (RC) of Kansas City-St Joseph, since 1962; *b* 23 March 1908; *s* of George Helmsing and Louise Helmsing (*née* Boschert). *Educ:* St Michael's Parochial Sch.; St Louis Preparatory Seminary; Kenrick Seminary. Sec. to Archbishop of St Louis, 1946-49; Auxiliary Bishop to Archbishop of St Louis, and Titular Bishop of Axum, 1949; first Bishop, Diocese of Springfield-CApe Girardeau, Mo, 1956-62. Member: Secretariat of Christian Unity, 1963; US Bishops Cttee for Ecumenical Affairs, 1964; Preparatory Cttee for Dialogue between Anglican Communion and Roman Catholic Church, 1966-67 (Chm., Roman Catholic Members); Chm., Special Cttee for Dialogue with Episcopal Church, US, 1964. Hon. Doctorates: Letters: Avila Coll. 1962; Humanities, Rockhurst Coll., 1963. Law: St Benedict's Coll. 1966. Order of Condor, Bolivia, 1966. *Address:* (Chancery Office) PO Box 1037, Kansas City, Missouri 64141, USA. *T:* (816), Jefferson 1-1475.

**HELPMANN, Sir Robert Murray,** Kt 1968; CBE 1964; dancer, actor (stage and films); choreographer; producer; director; *b* 9 April 1909; *s* of James Murray Helpman, Mount Gambia, South Australia, and Mary Gardiner, Mount Shank, SA. *Educ:* Prince Alfred's Coll., Adelaide. First appeared under J. C. Williamson's Management, Australia, 1926-30; Premier Danseur, Sadler's Wells Ballet, 1933-50; played in Stop Press, Adelphi Theatre, 1936; Oberon in A Midsummer Night's Dream, Old Vic. 1937-38; Gremio in Taming of the Shrew, 1939; title role in Old Vic production Hamlet, New Theatre, 1944; Flamineo in The White Devil and Prince in He Who Gets Slapped, Duchess Theatre, 1947; Stratford-on-Avon, 1948 Season; played Shylock, King John and Hamlet; produced Madame Butterfly, Royal Opera House, Covent Garden, 1950; appeared in Sir Laurence Olivier's Shaw-Shakespeare Festival Season, 1951, playing Apollodorus in Cæsar and Cleopatra, and Octavius Cæsar in Antony and Cleopatra; The Millionairess, New, 1952; Oberon in A Midsummer Night's Dream, Edinburgh Festival, in the USA and in Canada. 1954. Choreographer and Premier Danseur in Red Shoes; produced Murder in the Cathedral, Old Vic, 1953; Coq d'Or, Royal Opera House, 1954, 1956, 1962; After the Ball, Globe, 1954; appeared in Old Vic Australian tour as Petruchio in The Taming of the Shrew, Shylock in the Merchant of Venice, Angelo in Measure for Measure, 1955; Shylock in the Merchant of Venice, Old Vic, 1956; Launce in The Two Gentlemen of Verona, Old Vic, 1957; produced Antony and Cleopatra, Old Vic, 1957; Emperor in Titus Andronicus and Pinch in Comedy of Errors, Old Vic, 1957; King Richard in Richard III, Old Vic, 1957; Georges de Valera in Nekrassov, edinburgh Fest. and Royal Court Theatre, London, 1957; Sebastien in Nude with Violin, London, 1958, and Australian Tour, 1958; Guest dancer, Royal Opera House, London, for Spring Season, 1958; prod. The Marriage-Go-Round, Piccadilly, 1959; Duel of Angels: New York, 1960; Melbourne, 1961; Old Vic South American tour, 1962. Dir of Camelot, Drury Lane, 1964. Choreographer: Comus, Hamlet, The Birds, Miracle in the Gorbals, Adam Zero, The Soldier's Tale, Elektra, The Display (Australia, 1964); Yugen (Australia, 1964); Cinderella (Covent Garden, 1965); Elektra (Australia, 1966); Joint Artistic Dir, Australian Ballet, 1965-; Artistic Dir, Adelaide Festival, 1970-. *Films include:* One of our Aircraft is Missing, Wyecroft in Caravan, Henry V (Bishop of Ely), Tales of Hoffmann, The Iron Petticoat, Big Money, Red Shoes, 55 Days in Pekin, The Soldier's Tale, The Quiller Memorandum, Chitty Chitty Bang Bang. Has appeared on TV. Knight of the Northern Star (Sweden); Knight of the Cedar (Lebanon). *Address:* c/o Midland Bank Ltd, 70 St Martin's Lane, WC2.

**HELSBY,** family name of **Baron Helsby.**

**HELSBY,** Baron *cr* 1968 (Life Peer); **Laurence Norman Helsby,** GCB 1963 (CB 1950); KBE 1955; a Director: Rank Organisation, since 1968; Imperial Tobacco Group, since 1968;

Midland Bank, since 1968; Chairman, Midland Bank Executor and Trustee Co., since 1970; *b* 27 April 1908; *s* of late Wilfred Helsby; *m* 1938, Wilmett Mary, *yr d* of late W. G. Maddison, Durham; one *s* one *d*. *Educ:* Sedbergh; Keble Coll., Oxford. Lecturer in Economics, University Coll. of the South West, 1930-31; Lecturer in Economics, Durham Colls in the University of Durham, 1931-45; Asst Sec., HM Treasury, 1946; Principal Private Sec. to the Prime Minister, 1947-50; Dep. Sec., Min. of Food, 1950-54; First Civil Service Commissioner, 1954-59; Permanent Sec., Min. of Labour, 1959-62; Joint Permanent Sec. to the Treasury and Head of the Home Civil Service, 1963-68; Sec., Order of the British Empire, 1963-68. Hon. Fellow, Keble Coll., Oxford, 1959; Hon. LLD, University of Exeter, 1963; Hon. DCL, Univ. of Durham, 1963. *Address:* Logmore Farm, Dorking, Surrey. *Club:* Oxford and Cambridge.

**HELY, Brig. Alfred Francis,** CB 1951; CBE 1945; DSO 1943; TD 1944; DL; Chief Dental Officer, Cheshire County Council, 1957-68; *b* 3 Aug. 1902; *s* of Alfred Francis Hely; unmarried. *Educ:* St Edward's Coll., Liverpool; Liverpool Univ. Qualified as a Dental Surg., 1923; in private practice, 1923-26. Liverpool Univ. OTC, 1921-25; Cadet Corporal, Duke of Lancaster's Own Imperial Yeomanry, 1925-26; 106 (Lancs Hussars), RHA, 1926-41 (comd, 1937-41); served War of 1939-45 (despatches twice); 60th Field Regt, RA, 1941-42; CRA 7 Ind. Div., 1942-45; Comd 7 Ind. Div. 1945 until end of hostilities in Burma (3 months); war service in Palestine, Western Desert, Greece, Crete, Syria, 1940-42, North-West Frontier, India, 1942, Burma, 1943-45. CRA 42 (Lancs) Inf. Div. (TA), 1947-50. DL County Palatine of Lancaster, 1951. *Recreations:* outdoor country pursuits. *Address:* 37 Ashburton Road, Oxton, Birkenhead, Cheshire. *T:* 051-652 2132. *Club:* Army and Navy.

**HELY, Air Commodore Arthur Hubert McMath,** CB 1962; OBE 1945; Air Commodore Operations, HQ Maintenance Command, 1961-64, retired; *b* 16 Feb. 1909; *s* of Hamilton McMath Hely and Lubie Thrine Hely (*née* Jörgensen); *m* 1935, Laura Mary Sullivan, 6th *d* of Serjeant, A. M. Sullivan, QC; two *s* two *d*. *Educ:* Mt Albert, Auckland, NZ; Auckland University Coll. Joined Royal Air Force, 1934; Staff Coll., 1942; HQ SACSEA, 1944, 1945; Joint Chiefs of Staff, Australia, 1946-48; Joint Services Staff Coll., 1948; Group Capt. 1950; HQ Fighter Command, 1953-56; HQ Far East Air Force, 1956, 1958; Air Ministry (acting Air Commodore), 1958; Air Commodore, 1959. *Recreations:* sailing, golf, painting. *Address:* The Harrow Inn, Ightham Common, near Sevenoaks, Kent. *T:* Borough Green 3841. *Club:* RAF Changi Golf.

**HELY, Air Vice-Marshal William Lloyd,** CB 1964; CBE 1953; AFC 1938; psc, idc; retired as Air Member for Personnel, RAAF Headquarters, Canberra, ACT (1960-66); *b* Wellington, NSW, 24 Aug. 1909; *s* of late Prosper F. Hely, Sydney; *m* 1938, Jean A., *d* of F. McDonald; two *d*. *Educ:* Fort Street High Sch., Sydney; RMC, Duntroon. Pilot Officer, RAAF, 1930; grad. flying training, Pt Cook, 1931; comdg RAAF Detachment, N Aust. Aerial and Geological Survey, 1936; conducted air search and rescue operations in Northern Territory, 1937; RAF Staff Coll., Andover, 1939; HQ Coastal Command, 1939 (Sqdn Leader); Director: Air Staff Policy, HQ, RAAF, 1943-46; Personal Services, RAAF, 1946-50; Personnel Services, Dept of Air, Melbourne, 1947-48; AOC Western Area, 1951-53; Dep. Chief of the Air Staff, 1953; AOC Trng Comd, RAAF, 1956-57; Head of Australian Joint Services Staff, Washington, 1957-60. *Address:* 4 Hamelin Crescent, Narrabundah, ACT, Australia.

**HELY-HUTCHINSON,** family name of **Earl of Donoughmore.**

**HEMINGFORD,** 2nd Baron, *cr* 1943, of Watford; **Dennis George Ruddock Herbert,** MA; JP; Lord Lieutenant of Huntingford and Peterborough since 1968; Chairman, Huntingdon and Peterborough County Council, since 1967 (Vice-Chairman, 1965-67, County Alderman 1965); Vice-President, Africa Bureau (Chairman, 1952-63); *b* 25 March 1904; *s* of 1st Baron Hemingford, PC, KBE; *S* father 1947; *m* 1932, Elizabeth McClare, *d* of late Col J. M. Clark, Haltwhistle, Northumberland; one *s* two *d*. *Educ:* Oundle; Brasenose Coll., Oxford. Master, Achimota Coll., Gold Coast, 1926-39; Headmaster, King's Coll., Budo, Uganda (CMS), 1939-47; Rector Achimota Training Coll., Gold Coast, 1948-51. Mem., London Government Staff Commission, 1963-65. JP Huntingdon and Peterborough, 1965 (Hunts, 1960-65). CC 1952, CA 1959, Chm. CC, 1961-65, Hunts. *Heir:* *s* Hon. Dennis Nicholas Herbert [*b* 25 July 1934; *m* 1958, Jennifer Mary Toresen, *o d* of F. W. Bailey, 24 Kent Road, Harrogate; three *d*]. *Address:* The Old Rectory, Hemingford Abbots, Huntingdon. *T:* St Ives, Hunts, 2375. *Clubs:* Royal Commonwealth Society, National.

**HEMINGWAY, Albert,** MSc, MB, ChB; Emeritus Professor, University of Leeds (Professor of Physiology, 1936-67); *b* 1902; *s* of Herbert Hemingway, Leeds; *m* 1930, Margaret Alice Cooper; one *d*. *Educ:* University of Leeds. Demonstrator in Physiology, King's Coll., London, 1925; Senior Asst in Physiology, University Coll., London, 1926; Lecturer in Experimental Physiology, Welsh National Sch. of Medicine, 1927. Vis. Prof., Makerere University Coll., Uganda, 1968. Examiner in Physiology, Universities of St Andrews, Birmingham, Bristol, Cambridge, Durham, Glasgow, Liverpool, London, Manchester, Wales and RCS. Mem. various cttees of MRC on work and exercise physiology; Mem. Cttee, Physiological Soc. (Editor, Jl Physiology); Pres., Section I, British Assoc., 1959. *Publications:* original papers on the physiology of the circulation, exercise and the kidney in scientific and medical journals. *Recreations:* athletics, travel. *Address:* 4 Helmsley Drive, Leeds LS16 5HY. *T:* Leeds 53720.

**HEMLOW, Prof. Joyce;** Greenshields Professor of English Language and Literature, McGill University, Montreal, Canada, since 1955; author; *b* 30 July 1906; *d* of William Hemlow and Rosalinda Hemlow (*née* Redmond), Liscomb, NS. *Educ:* Queen's Univ., Kingston, Ont (MA) (LLD 1967): Harvard Univ., Cambridge, Mass (AM, PhD). Preceding a univ. career, period of teaching in Nova Scotia, Canada; lecturer in English Language and Literature at McGill Univ. FRSC 1960. Guggenheim Fellow, 1951-52, 1960-62 and 1966. Member: Phi Beta Kappa, The Johnsonians, and of other literary and professional organizations. James Tait Black Memorial Book Prize, 1958; Brit. Academy Award (Crawshay Prize), 1960. *Publications:* The History of Fanny Burney, 1958 (GB). Articles in learned jls on Fanny Burney's novels and unpublished plays. *Address:* (home) Liscomb, Nova Scotia, Canada; The Crestwood, 3555 Atwater Avenue, Montreal, Canada. *Club:* English-Speaking Union (Canadian Branch).

**HEMMING, Lt-Col Henry Harold,** OBE 1948; MC 1917; Chairman: Municipal Journal Group of Companies, since 1950; Glass Guide Service Ltd; Brintex Ltd; *b* Toronto, Canada, 5 April 1893; *o s* of late H. K. S. Hemming and late Louisa Hemming (*née* McFee); *m* 1931, Alice Louisa Weaver, one *s* one *d*. *Educ:* Aldenham Sch., England; McGill Univ., Montreal (BA); Ecole des Sciences Politique, Paris. Served European War, 1914-19, in France (Major; despatches 3 times). Banking in New York, 1920-24; Vice-Pres. Harris Forbes & Co. Ltd, London Investment Bankers, 1924-31; Mem. London Stock Exchange, 1933-50. War of 1939-45: Sch. of Artillery, Larkhill, Senior Instructor at Survey Wing, Lieut-Col. Vice-Pres. Frobisher Ltd, Canada, International Mining Finance, 1950-57. Chm. and Founder, Canadian-British Educational Cttee; Hon. Pres., Field Survey Assoc.; Member: Royal Institution; Royal Institute International Affairs; Royal Geographical Soc. Formerly: Pres., McGill Soc. of GB; Vice-Pres., Canadian Univ. Soc.; Dep.-Chm., Internat. Ballet. Liveryman of Worshipful Company of Stationers and Newspaper Makers. Freeman of City of London. *Publication:* translated the works of André Siegfried (the French economist), 1925-39. *Recreations:* sailing, motoring. *Address:* 35 Elsworthy Road, NW3. *T:* 01-722 6619. *Clubs:* Athenæum, Canada, Pilgrims.

**HEMMING, Air Commodore Idris George Selvin,** CB 1968; CBE 1959 (OBE 1954); retired; *b* 11 Dec. 1911; *s* of late George Hemming, Liverpool; *m* 1939, Phyllis, *d* of Francis Payne, Drogheda, Eire; two *s*. *Educ:* Chalford, Glos.; Wallasey, Cheshire. Joined RAF, 1928; served War of 1939-45, UK, India and Burma; Gp Capt. 1957; Air Cdre 1962; Dir of Equipment (Pol.) (RAF), MoD, 1962-66; Dir of Equipment (1) (RAF), MoD, Harrogate, 1966-68. *Recreations:* cricket, golf. *Address:* Ash House, St Chloe Green, Amberley, near Stroud, Glos. *T:* Amberley 3581. *Club:* Royal Air Force.

**HEMP, Prof. William Spooner,** MA, FRAeS; Stewarts and Lloyds Professor of Structural Engineering, Oxford University, since 1965; Professorial Fellow of Keble College, Oxford, since 1965; *b* 21 March 1916; *s* of late Rev. William James Hemp and Daisy Lilian Hemp; *m* 1938, Dilys Ruth Davies; one *s*. *Educ:* Paston Grammar Sch., North Walsham; Jesus Coll., Cambridge (Scholar, MA). Aeronautical Engineer, Bristol Aeroplane Co., 1938-46. Coll. of Aeronautics: Senior Lecturer, 1946-50; Prof. of Aircraft Structures and Aeroelasticity, 1950-65; Head of Dept of Aircraft Design, 1951-65; Dep. Principal, 1957-65. Mem. of various cttees of Aeronautical Research Council since 1948. Visiting Prof., Stanford Univ., Calif., 1960-61. *Publications:* research papers in the Theory of Structures, Solid Mechanics and Applied Mathematics. *Recreations:* mountain walking, music. *Address:* Department of Engineering Science, Park Road, Oxford. *T:* Oxford 59988.

**HEMPHILL,** 5th Baron *cr* 1906, of Rathkenny and Cashel; **Peter Patrick Fitzroy Martyn Martyn-Hemphill;** *b* 5 Sept. 1928; *o s* of 4th Baron Hemphill and Emily, *d* of F. Irving Sears, Webster, Mass.; *S* father 1957; *m* 1952, Olivia Anne, *er d* of Major Robert Francis Ruttledge, MC, Cloonee, Ballinrobe, County Mayo; one *s* two *d*; assumed surname of Martyn in addition to Hemphill, 1959. *Educ:* Downside; Brasenose Coll., Oxford (MA). *Heir: s* Hon. Charles Andrew Martyn Martyn-Hemphill, *b* 8 Oct. 1954. *Address:* Tulira, Ardrahan, Co. Galway, Eire. *T:* Ardrahan 4. *Clubs:* Royal Automobile, Turf, White's; Kildare Street (Dublin); County (Galway).

**HEMSLEY, Thomas Jeffrey;** free-lance opera and concert singer; *b* 12 April 1927; *s* of Sydney William Hemsley and Kathleen Annie Hemsley (*née* Deacon); *m* 1960, Hon. Gwenllian Ellen James, *d* of 4th Baron Northbourne, *qv*; three *s*. *Educ:* Ashby de la Zouch Grammar Sch.; Brasenose Coll., Oxford (MA). Vicar Choral, St Paul's Cathedral, 1950-51; Prin. Baritone, Stadttheater, Aachen, 1953-56; Deutsche Oper am Rhein, 1957-63; Opernhaus, Zurich, 1963-67; Glyndebourne, Bayreuth, Edinburgh Festivals, etc. *Address:* 10 Denewood Road, N6. *T:* 01-348 3397.

**HEMS, (Benjamin) Arthur,** FRS 1969; Managing Director, Glaxo Research Ltd, since 1965; *b* 29 June 1912; *er s* of late B. A. Hems and of L. D. Hems; *m* 1937, Jean Douglas Herd; one *s* one *d*. *Educ:* Glasgow and Edinburgh Univs. Joined Glaxo, 1937. *Recreations:* golf, avoiding gardening. *Address:* 18 Milton Court, Ickenham, Middx. *T:* Ruislip 39254.

**HENBEST, Prof. Harold Bernard;** Professor of Organic Chemistry at the Queen's University, Belfast, since 1958; *b* 10 March 1924; *s* of A. Bernard Henbest and Edith Winifred Herbert; *m* 1948, Rosalind Eve Skone James; two *s* one *d*. *Educ:* Barking Abbey Sch.; Imperial Coll. of Science, London. Beit Research Fellow, 1947-48; Lectr, University of Manchester, 1948-56; Research Fellow, Harvard Univ., 1953-54; Vis. Prof., Univ. of Calif. at Los Angeles, 1954; Reader, KCL, 1956-57. *Publications:* contrib. to Jl of Chemical Soc., etc. *Address:* Department of Chemistry, The Queen's University of Belfast. *T:* Belfast 30111; 8 Cleaver Gardens, Belfast 9. *T:* Belfast 660732.

**HENDEL, Prof. Charles William;** Professor Emeritus of Moral Philosophy and Metaphysics, Yale University; *b* 16 Dec. 1890; *s* of Charles William Hendel and Emma Stolz, American; *m* 1916, Elizabeth Phoebe Jones; two *s*. *Educ:* Princeton Univ. LittB 1913; PhD 1917. United States Army, 1917-18, 2nd Lieut Infantry. Instructor, Williams Coll., 1919-20; Asst and Associate Prof., Princeton Univ., 1920-29; MacDonald Prof. of Moral Philosophy, McGill Univ., 1929-40; Chm. of Philosophy, 1929-40; Dean of Faculty of Arts and Science, 1937-40; Clarke Prof. of Moral Philosophy and Metaphysics, Yale Univ., 1940-59; Chm. of Dept, 1940-45 and 1950-59; Prof. Emeritus, 1959-. Gifford Lecturer, University of Glasgow, 1962-63. Hon. MA Yale, 1940. President: American Philosophical Assoc. (Eastern Div.), 1940; American Soc. for Political and Legal Philosophy, 1959-61. *Publications:* Studies in the Philosophy of David Hume, 1925 (2nd edn enlarged with Supplement, 1963); (jointly) Contemporary Idealism in America, 1932; Jean Jacques Rousseau, Moralist, 2 vols 1934 (2nd edn with Preface, 1963); Citizen of Geneva, 1937; Civilization and Religion, 1948; The Philosophy of Kant and our Modern World; John Dewey: Philosophy and the Experimental Spirit, 1959; many translations, joint authorships, and edns of philosophical works. *Recreations:* music; out-of-doors, in woods, fields and mountains. *Address:* 245 East Rock Road, New Haven, Conn, USA. *T:* 203-624-9545; Yale University, New Haven, Conn, USA. *T:* State 203-432-4313.

**HENDERSON,** family name of **Barons Faringdon** and **Henderson.**

**HENDERSON,** 1st Baron, *cr* 1945, of Westgate in the City and County of Newcastle on Tyne; **William Watson Henderson,** PC 1950;

Chairman, Alliance Building Society, since 1966; journalist and political writer; *b* Newcastle upon Tyne, 8 Aug. 1891; *s* of late Rt Hon. Arthur Henderson, MP. *Educ:* Queen Elizabeth Grammar Sch., Darlington. Editorial Sec., Daily Citizen, 1912-14; Parliamentary Correspondent, Labour Press Dept, 1919-21; Lobby Correspondent, Daily Herald, 1919-21; Sec., Press and Publicity Dept, Labour Party, 1921-45; Private Sec. to Rt Hon. John Hodge, MP, Minister of Labour, 1917; Prospective Labour Candidate, Bridgwater Div. of Somerset, 1919-21; MP (Lab) Enfield, 1923-24 and 1929-31; Parliamentary Private Sec. to the Sec. of State for India, 1929-31; Personal Asst to Rt Hon. Arthur Greenwood, MP (Minister without Portfolio and Mem. of the War Cabinet), 1940-42; an additional mem. of the Air Council, 1945-47; a Lord in Waiting to the King, 1945-48; a Parly Under-Sec. of State, FO, 1948-51. A British Representative at Assembly of Council of Europe, 1954 and 1955; Labour Peers representative on Parliamentary Cttee of Parliamentary Labour Party, 1952-55. *Address:* 707 Collingwood House, Dolphin Square, SW1. *T:* 01-834 3800.

**HENDERSON, Sir Charles James,** KBE, *cr* 1946; Hon. President British Chamber of Commerce, France, and President, 1930-31, 1934-35, 1942-45; a former Trustee and Chairman of British Charitable Fund; Member and former Chairman, Cttee of Management of the Hertford British Hospital, Paris; President, Board of Governors, British American Hospital, Nice; Director of various companies operating in France; *b* London, 9 Nov. 1882; *s* of Henry Henderson and Marie Tharp; *m* 1st, 1909, Freda Marguerite Dorothy Seerancke Archer, MBE (*d* 1964); one *s* one *d*; 2nd, 1964, Emma Lilian Nikis (Chevalier, Légion d'Honneur; Médaille Militaire), *née* Tattersall, *widow* of Mario Nikis. *Educ:* privately; City of London Sch. Mem. of London Stock Exchange, 1904-19. Served European War, France, 1914-18; Chm. British Chamber of Commerce Delegation to France, Sept. 1944; former Chm., British Legion, Paris. Freeman, City of London, 1919. Chevalier, Légion d'Honneur. *Address:* Parc Springland, Avenue de Vallauris, Cannes, AM, France. *Clubs:* Junior Carlton; Union Interallié (Paris).

*See also Rear-Adm. G. A. Henderson, Air Cdre E. J. Morris.*

**HENDERSON, Rt. Rev. Edward Barry;** *see* Bath and Wells, Bishop of.

**HENDERSON, Ven. Edward Chance,** BD, ALCD; Archdeacon of Pontefract and Vicar of Darrington with Wentbridge since 1968; *b* 15 Oct. 1916; *s* of William Edward and Mary Anne Henderson; *m* 1942, Vera Massie Pattison; two *s* three *d Educ:* Heaton Gram. Sch.; London University. Asst Curate, St Stephen, Newcastle upon Tyne, 1939-42; Organising Sec., CPAS, 1942-45; Vicar of St Mary of Bethany, Leeds, 1945-51; Priest i/c: Annley Hall, Leeds, 1948-51; St John, New Wortley, Leeds, 1949-51; Vicar of: All Souls, Halifax, 1951-59; Dewsbury, 1959-68. *Address:* Darrington Vicarage, Pontefract, Yorks. *T:* Pontefract 4744.

**HENDERSON, Rear-Adm. Geoffrey Archer,** CB 1969; Chief Naval Supply and Secretariat Officer, 1968-70, and Director of Management and Support Intelligence, Ministry of Defence, 1969-70; *b* 14 Aug. 1913; *s* of Sir Charles James Henderson, *qv*; *m* 1959 Pamela (Rachel), *d* of late Sir Philip Petrides; one *s* one *d*. *Educ:* Christ's Hosp. Entered RN, 1931. Served War of 1939-45; HMS Onslow, 1941-42 (despatches); Sec. to Asst Chief of Naval Staff (F), 1943-44. HMS Newfoundland, 1952-55; HMS Victorious, 1957-58; Cabinet Office, 1959-61; idc 1962; Director of Naval Officer Appointments (S), 1963-65; Commodore, RN Barracks, Portsmouth, 1965-66; ADC 1966; Naval Mem. of Senior Directing Staff, Imperial Defence Coll., 1966-68. *Address:* Pigeon's Green, St Mary's Platt, Sevenoaks, Kent. *T:* Borough Green 2462. *Club:* Army and Navy.

**HENDERSON, Prof. George Patrick;** Professor of Philosophy in the University of Dundee (formerly Queen's College, Dundee), since 1959; *b* 22 April 1915; *e s* of Rev. George Aitchison Henderson, MA, and Violet Margaret Mackenzie; *m* 1939, Hester Lowry Douglas McWilliam, BSc, *d* of Rev. John Morell McWilliam, BA. *Educ:* Elgin Academy; St Andrews Univ. (Harkness Scholar); Balliol Coll., Oxford. 1st Class Hons in Philosophy, University of St Andrews, 1936; Miller Prize and Ramsay Scholarship; MA 1936; Ferguson Scholarship in Philosophy, 1936; 2nd Class Lit Hum, University of Oxford, 1938; BA 1938. Asst in Logic and Metaphysics, University of St Andrews, 1938; Shaw Fellow in Mental Philosophy, University of Edinburgh, 1938. MA Oxon, 1943. Army Service, 1940-46; Royal Artillery (commissioned 1940, Adjutant 1942-43) and Gen. Staff (GSO 3 1945); served in UK, Italy and Greece. Lecturer in Logic and Metaphysics, University of St Andrews, 1945; Senior Lecturer, 1953. Editor of the Philosophical Quarterly, 1962-. *Publications:* numerous articles and reviews in principal philosophical periodicals. *Recreations:* modern Greek studies, gardening. *Address:* Department of Philosophy, Dundee University, Dundee.

**HENDERSON, Sir Guy (Wilmot McLintock),** Kt 1956; BA, LLB Cantab; QC (Uganda) 1949; Chief Justice of the Bahamas, 1951-60, retired; *b* 13 July 1897; *e s* of late Arthur James and Charlotte West Henderson; *m* 1930, Ann, *d* of late George and Elizabeth Dring-Campion; two *s* one *d*. *Educ:* Blundell's, Tiverton; Collegiate Sch., Wanganui, NZ; Trinity Coll., Cambridge. Served European War, 1914-18, Lieut RFA (SR). Barrister-at-Law, Inner Temple, 1923; private practice, Rangoon, Burma, 1924-29; professional clerk, prosecuting staff GPO, London, 1930-32; stipendiary and circuit magistrate, Bahamas, 1932-37; Crown Counsel, Tanganyika Territory, 1937-40; legal draftsman, Nigeria, 1940-45; dep. Chief Legal Adviser, British Military Administration, Malaya, 1945-46; Solicitor-Gen., Colony of Singapore, 1946-48; Attorney-Gen., Uganda Protectorate, 1948-51. *Address:* PO Box 1241, Nassau, Bahamas.

**HENDERSON, Sir Ian (Leslie),** KBE 1958; CMG 1952; *b* 6 July 1901; *o s* of late Lieutenant-Colonel Hugh Leslie Henderson, 1st Bn (Princess Louise's) Argyll and Sutherland Highlanders) and of Martha Saumarez (*née* Grosvenor); *m* 1927, Phyllis Mary, *o d* of late James Thornton, JP. *Educ:* Rugby Sch. (Head of Sch.); Trinity Coll., Oxford (MA). Sen. Schol., Lit. Hum. Entered HM Consular Service, 1924; served at Genoa, 1926 and 1929, Zürich, 1928, Lourenço Marques, 1930, Antwerp, 1932, being Actg Consul-Gen. at all posts. Consul, Innsbruck, 1933; Civil Observer in Sudeten-German districts of Czechoslovakia, 1938, attached to Viscount Runciman's Mission to Prague, 1938; Consul, Rosario, 1939; Chargé d'Affaires, San Salvador, 1940; Foreign Office, 1942; Counsellor (Commercial), Prague, 1946; Ambassador at Asuncion, Paraguay, 1952-53 (Minister, 1949-52); Consul-Gen., Rotterdam,

1953-54; HM Ambassador to Panama, 1954-60, retired. Coronation Medal, 1953. *Recreations:* reading, gardening. *Address:* 2 Wellswood Park, Torquay, Devon. *T:* 23777. *Club:* Travellers'.

**HENDERSON, James Bell,** CBE 1942; retired; *b* 29 June 1883; *s* of David Henderson and Flora Falconer Bell; *m* 1917, D. N. Graham; two *s*. *Educ:* Dumbarton Academy; Royal Technical College, Glasgow. Joined British India Steam Navigation Co., 1904; Merchant Navy as Marine Engineer officer; joined BISN Co.'s engineers shore staff, Calcutta, 1916; Gen. Manager, 1939-42. *Recreations:* golf, billiards, fishing. *Address:* 6 Alexandra Avenue, Prestwick, Ayrshire, Scotland. *Club:* St Nicholas Golf (Prestwick).

**HENDERSON, James Ewart,** MA Chief Scientist (RAF) and Member of the Air Force Board, since Dec. 1969; *b* 29 May 1923; *s* of late Rev. James Ewart Henderson, MA, BD and Agnes Mary (*née* Crawford); *m* 1949, Alice Joan Hewlitt; one *d*. *Educ:* private sch.; Glasgow University. Research on air rockets and guns, MAP, 1943-44; hon. commn in RAFVR, 1944-46; operational assessment of air attacks in Belgium, Holland and Germany, 2TAF, 1944-45; exper. research on fighter and bomber capability, and on the use of radar and radio aids: RAF APC Germany, 1945-46, Fighter Comd, 1946-49 and CFE, 1949-52; research on weapons effects and capability: Air Min., 1952-54, AWRE 1955, Air Min., 1955-58; Asst Scientific Adviser (Ops), Air Min., 1958-63; Dep. Chief Scientist (RAF), MoD, 1963-69. *Recreations:* flying, sailing, golf, opera, photography. *Address:* Ministry of Defence, SW1. *T:* 01-930 7022, ext. 7430. *Clubs:* Royal Aero; Moor Park Golf.

**HENDERSON, Sir James Thyne,** KBE 1959; CMG 1952; *b* 18 Jan. 1901; *s* of late Sir Thomas Henderson; *m* 1930, Karen Margrethe Hansen; one *s* four *d*. *Educ:* Warriston, Moffat; Sedbergh Sch.; Queen's Coll., Oxford. Entered Diplomatic Service, 1925, apptd to FO; transf. to Tehran, 1927; Athens, 1929; Helsinki, 1932, where acted as Chargé d'Affaires in 1932, 1933, 1934 and 1935; Foreign Office, 1935. First Sec., 1936; attached to Representative of Finland at the Coronation of King George VI, 1937; Tokyo, 1938; Santiago, 1941; Foreign Office, 1944; Stockholm, 1946, Chargé d'Affaires there in 1946 and 1947; Counsellor, 1947; Consul-Gen., Houston, 1949; HM Minister to Iceland, 1953-56; HM Ambassador to Bolivia, 1956-60, retired. Chairman, Commonwealth Institute, Scotland. *Recreation:* gardening. *Address:* 10 Greenhill Park, Edinburgh 10. *T:* 031-447 6379. *Club:* Royal Automobile.

**HENDERSON, Dame Joan;** *see* Kelleher, Dame Joan.

**HENDERSON, Sir John,** Kt 1964; DL; JP Glasgow; former Chairman, J. Henderson, Ltd, Produce Importers, Glasgow; *b* 12 July 1888; *s* of John Henderson and Ellen Shiels; *m* 1918, Nessie Brander, Crosshill, Glasgow; one *s* one *d*. *Educ:* Martyrs Sch., Glasgow. Mem., Glasgow Corporation, 1926-46. Mem., Inter-Parliamentary Delegation to Finland, Israel, Austria, Western Germany, Belgium and Czechoslovakia. Magistrate and Police Judge, City of Glasgow; Chm. Scottish Unionist and Nat. Liberals' Cttee; Chm. Scottish Fact and Faith Films Soc.; House of Parliament Christian Fellowship; Pres. Internat. Council for Christian Leadership; Deacon, Incorporation of Bonnetmakers and Dyers. MP (C) Cathcart Div. of Glasgow, Feb. 1946-Sept. 1964. *Publications:* contribs to various religious periodicals. *Recreations:* President Glasgow Corporation Bowling Club; Hon. President Queen's Park Bowling and Tennis Club. *Address:* Dundrennan, 658 Clarkston Road, Netherlee, Glasgow. *T:* 041-637 4321; Strand Palace Hotel, WC2. *Club:* Conservative (Glasgow).

**HENDERSON, Sir John Craik,** Kt 1953; *b* 21 Dec. 1890; *s* of late Robert Jenkinson Henderson, JP, and Agnes Craik; *m* Ivie Hestor Mary, *d* of late Harry Lester Hertslet, MVO of Lord Chamberlain's Office; one *d*. *Educ:* George Watson's Coll., Edinburgh; University of Glasgow. Joined Royal Scots, 1914; commissioned, 1914, and served until 1919; Prof. of Mercantile Law at University of Glasgow, 1929-40; MP (C) for North-East Leeds, 1940-45; Mem. of Conscientous Objectors' Tribunal for South-West Scotland, 1939-40; formerly Pres. Scottish Unionist Assoc. Hon. President: Glasgow YMCA; Franco-Scottish Soc. (Glasgow and West of Scotland); Glasgow Old People's Welfare Cttee; Chm. Scottish Council, The People's Dispensary for Sick Animals; Chm. Group considering British Parly System (Gp responsible for "Parliament-A Survey"). Legion of Honour. *Recreations:* shooting, golf. *Address:* Bridge House, Loxwood, Sussex. *T:* Loxwood 328; 190 St Vincent Street, Glasgow. *T:* 041-221 9005.

**HENDERSON, Prof. John Louis,** MD, FRCPE; Professor of Child Health, University of Dundee, since 1967; *b* 25 March 1907; British; *m* 1938, Agnes Deneson McHarg, MB, ChB (*d* 1963); one *s* three *d*. *Educ:* Leighton Park Sch., Reading; University of Edinburgh. Sen. Pres., Royal Medical Society, Edinburgh 1934-35; Lecturer, Dept of Child Health, University of Edinburgh, 1939-45; Rockefeller Travelling Fellow at Yale and Harvard, USA, 1946; Senior Lecturer, Dept of Child Health, University of Edinburgh, 1947-51; Physician, Royal Edinburgh Hosp. for Sick Children, 1948-51; Prof. of Child Health, University of St Andrews, 1951-67. Member: Scottish Health Services Council, 1953-62; GMC, 1968-; Chm. Standing Med. Adv. Cttee, Dept of Health for Scotland, 1956-62. *Publications:* Cerebral Palsy in Childhood and Adolescence, 1961; articles in medical journals. *Recreations:* golf, ornithology. *Address:* Wayside, Longforgan, Perthshire. *T:* Longforgan 294.

**HENDERSON, John Nicholas,** CMG 1965; HM Ambassador to Poland, since 1969; *b* 1 April 1919; *s* of Prof. Sir Hubert Henderson; *m* 1951, Mary Barber (*née* Cawadias); one *d*. *Educ:* Stowe Sch.; Hertford Coll., Oxford. Mem. HM Diplomatic Service. Served Minister of State's Office, Cairo, 1942-43; Asst Private Sec. to the Foreign Sec., 1944-47; HM Embassy, Washington, 1947-49; Athens, 1949-50; Permanent Under Secretary's Dept, FO, 1950-53; HM Embassy, Vienna, 1953-56; Santiago, 1956-59; Northern Dept, FO, 1959-62; Permanent Under Secretary's Dept, 1962-63; Head of Northern Dept, Foreign Office, 1963; Private Sec. to the Sec. of State for Foreign Affairs, 1963-65; Minister in Madrid, 1965-69. *Publications:* Prince Eugen of Savoy (biography); various stories and articles in Penguin New Writing, Horizon and History Today. *Recreations:* tennis, gardening, dogs. *Address:* 6 Fairholt Street, SW7. *T:* 01-589 4291; School House, Combe, near Newbury, Berks. *T:* Inkpen 330; c/o Foreign and Commonwealth Office, King Charles Street, SW1. *Club:* Brooks's.

**HENDERSON, Keith,** OBE; RWS; RSW; ROI; *b* 1883; *er s* of George MacDonald Henderson and Constance Helen, *d* of James Keith; *m*

Helen, *d* of Charles Knox-Shaw. *Educ:* Marlborough; Paris. Served Aug. 1914 to end of war (despatches twice). Pictures in Public Galleries, Manchester, Preston, Birmingham, Worthing, Newport, Leamington, Dublin, Glasgow, Carlisle, Dundee. Author and illustrator of Letters to Helen; Palm-groves and Hummingbirds; Prehistoric Man; Burns by Himself; illustrator of The Romaunt of the Rose, The Conquest of Mexico, Green Mansions, No Second Spring, Buckaroo, Christina Strang, Highland Pack, Scotland before History, etc; War Artist to the Air Force, 1940. *Address:* Coirechoille, Spean Bridge, Inverness-shire. *T:* Spean Bridge 256.

**HENDERSON, Kenneth David Druitt,** CMG 1951; Secretary, Spalding Educational Trust and Union for the Study of Great Religions, since 1953; *b* 4 Sept. 1903; *s* of late George Gilfillan Henderson, MA, MB, CM (Edinburgh); *m* 1935, Margery Grant, *d* of John Atkinson, Sydney, NSW; one *s* two *d*. *Educ:* Glenalmond; University Coll., Oxford. Entered Sudan Political Service, 1926; Dept Asst Civil Sec., 1938-44; Sec. to Governor-General's Council, 1939-44, to N Sudan Advisory Council, 1944; Principal Sch. of Administration and Police, Omdurman, 1944; Deputy-Governor, Kassala Province, Sudan, 1945; Asst Civil Sec., 1946-49; Governor, Darfur Province, Sudan, 1949-53. Officer, Order of the Nile, 1937. *Publications:* History of the Hamar Tribe, 1935; Survey of the Anglo-Egyptian Sudan, 1898-1944, 1945; The Making of The Modern Sudan, 1952; Sudan Republic, 1965; contribs to Chambers's Encyclopædia, Encyclopædia Britannica, and Encyclopædia Americana. *Address:* Orchard House, Steeple Langford, Salisbury, Wilts. *T:* Stapleford 388. *Clubs:* Athenæum, Royal Commonwealth Society.

**HENDERSON, Air Vice-Marshal Malcolm,** CB 1942; CIE 1938; CBE 1953; DSO 1916; RAF, retired; Director General, Over-Seas League, 1946-56; 2nd *s* of late Lessels Henderson and *g s* of late George Malcolm, Dundee; *m* 1918, Elizabeth, *d* of late Frederick Craig, St Columb, North Cornwall; two *s* one *d* (one *s* killed in action, RAF, 1940). *Club:* East India and Sports.

**HENDERSON, Sir Malcolm (Siborne),** KCMG 1961 (CMG 1952); *b* 21 April 1905; *s* of late Lt-Col Kenneth Henderson; *m* 1933, Paula Elizabeth Wilms; two *d*. *Educ:* Winchester and privately. MA Edinburgh. Vice-Consul, Antwerp, 1927-30, Chicago, 1930-35, New York, 1935-42; Consul, Atlanta, 1942-44; Foreign Office, 1944-47; Counsellor (Commercial) and Consul-Gen., Lisbon, 1947-52; Land Commissioner, Hanover, 1952-55, and Consul-Gen., 1954-55; Ambassador: to Grand Duchy of Luxembourg, 1955-57; to Republic of Uruguay, 1957-61; to Austria, 1961-65, retd. *Address:* 32 Cadogan Place, SW1. *Club:* Travellers'.

**HENDERSON, Admiral Sir Nigel Stuart,** GBE 1968 (OBE 1944); KCB 1962 (CB 1959); Chairman, Military Committee, NATO, since 1968; *b* 1 Aug. 1909; *s* of late Lt-Col Selby Herriott Henderson, IMS; *m* 1939, Catherine Mary Maitland; one *s* two *d*. *Educ:* Cheltenham Coll. Entered RN, 1927; served War of 1939-45 in HM Ships and as Fleet Gunnery Officer, Mediterranean; Comdr 1942; Capt. 1948; Naval Attaché, Rome, 1949-51; in comd HMS Protector, 1951; in comd RN Air Station, Bramcote, 1952; Imperial Defence Coll., 1954; in command HMS Kenya, 1955; Rear-Admiral, 1957; Vice-Naval Dep. to Supreme Allied Comdr, Europe, 1957-Dec. 1959; Vice-Adm. 1960; Dir-Gen. of Training, Admiralty, 1960-62; C-in-C Plymouth, 1962-65; Adm. 1963; Head of British Defence Staffs, Washington, and UK Rep., Mil. Cttee, NATO, 1965-68. *Recreations:* golf, bird watching, shooting, fishing. *Address:* Hensol, Mossdale, Castle Douglas, Kirkcudbrightshire. *T:* Laurieston 207. *Clubs:* United Service, White's.

**HENDERSON, Peter,** CB 1965; MD; QHP 1962; Senior Principal Medical Officer, Ministry of Education, 1964-69; *b* 16 March 1904; *e s* of Peter and Margaret Henderson, Inverness; *m* 1933, Beatrice Chrissie Pashley, Bridlington, Yorks; no *c*. *Educ:* High Sch. and Royal Academy, Inverness; Aberdeen Univ. MB 1929; MD 1931; DPH London, 1932. Resident MO, Bradford City Sanatorium, 1929-30; House Physician, St Luke's Hospital, Bradford, 1930-31; Resident MO, Inst. of Ray Therapy, London, 1931-32; Asst MO, Somerset CC, 1933-35; Asst MO, St Helens, 1935-36; Dep. MOH, Leyton, 1936-39; MOH, Todmorden, 1939-40; MO, Min. of Educn, 1940-51, PMO, 1951-64. Consultant, WHO. Milroy Lectr, 1968. *Publications:* various papers on the health and disabilities of children in BMJ, Lancet and Practitioner; contribs to The Theory and Practice of Public Health (ed W. Hobson), 1961, 3rd edn 1968; chapter in The Humanist Outlook (ed A. J. Ayer), 1968. *Recreation:* gardening. *Address:* Lythe Ghyll, Merrowcroft, Guildford, Surrey. *T:* Guildford 5353.

**HENDERSON, Philip Prichard;** author; *b* 1906; *m* 1st, 1938, Millicent Rose (marr. diss. 1947); 2nd, 1948, Belinda, *e d* of Sir Horace Hamilton, *qv*; two *s*. *Educ:* Bradfield. Asst Editor, Everyman's Library, 1929-32; Fireman, National Fire Service, 1939-43; Co-Editor, British Book News, 1943-46; Editor, Feature Articles, British Council, 1958-63; Publications and Recorded Sound Dept, 1963-64. *Publications:* First Poems, 1930; A Wind in the Sand, 1932; Events in the Early Life of Anthony Price, a Novel, 1935; Literature and a Changing Civilization, 1935; The Novel Today, 1936; And Morning in His Eyes, A Book about Christopher Marlowe, 1937; The Poet and Society, 1939; Editor of: The Complete Poems of John Skelton, 1931 (4th edn 1964); Edmund Spenser's Shepherd's Calendar, and other poems, 1932; Shorter Novels: 16th-18th Century, 3 vols; George Crabbe: Poems, 1946; Emily Brontë: Poems, 1947; The Letters of William Morris, 1950; The Complete Poems of Emily Brontë, 1951; Christopher Marlowe, 1952; William Morris (Writers and Their Work: No. 32), 1952 (revised edn 1969); Samuel Butler, 1953 (new edn 1967); The Life of Laurence Oliphant, 1956; Christopher Marlowe (Writers and Their Work: No. 81), 1956 (revised edn 1966); Richard Cœur de Lion, 1958; William Morris, His Life, Work and Friends, 1967. *Address:* c/o A. M. Heath & Co. Ltd, 35 Dover Street, W1.

**HENDERSON, Ralph,** CB 1959; OBE 1946; Director of Stores, Admiralty, 1955-60, retired; *b* 15 Aug. 1897; *s* of James Ralph Henderson, Perth, Scotland (author, pen-name Sandy McNab); *m* 1923, Gladys Dunnett; two *s*. *Educ:* Perth Academy. Entered Civil Service, 1913. Served in Army, 1915-19, Lieut, Royal Field Artillery. Naval Store Officer, Naval Base, Singapore, 1939-42; Deputy Dir of Stores, Admiralty, 1944. French Croix de Guerre (with palm), 1918. *Recreation:* golf. *Address:* 18 Wykeham Court, Wykeham Road, Worthing, Sussex. *T:* Worthing 203187.

**HENDERSON, Richard McNeil,** CBE 1939; FInstCE; FIMechE; *b* Glasgow, 14 Jan. 1886; *s* of George Henderson and Margaret McNeil; *m*

1920, Mary Esme Woodcock, London; two *s* one *d*. *Educ:* Allan Glen's Institution; Royal Technical College, Glasgow. Entered Colonial Govt Service as Engineer, 1912; Dir of Public Works, Hong Kong, 1932; retired 1939. *Recreations:* golf, tennis, swimming, etc. *Address:* 1 Winton Drive, Edinburgh 10.

**HENDERSON, Robert Brumwell;** Managing Director, Ulster Television Ltd, since 1959; *b* 28 July 1929; *s* of late Comdr Oscar Henderson, CVO, CBE, DSO, RN, and of Mrs Henderson; *m* 1953, Joy Frances Duncan (marr. diss. 1970); two *d*; *m* 1970, Patricia Ann Davison. *Educ:* Brackenber House Sch., Belfast; Bradfield Coll., Berks; Trinity Coll., Dublin. BA (Hons) 1951, MA 1959. Journalism: London, Liverpool, Glasgow and Belfast, 1951-59. Chairman: British Regional Television Assoc.; Cinematograph and Television Benevolent Fund, N Ire.; Publicity Assoc. of N Ire., 1959-60; Director: Ulster Theatre Council; Independent Television News Ltd, 1964-68; Pres. (twice), Radio Industries Club of N Ire.; Member: Cttee to Review Higher Educn in N Ire.; Council of Belfast Chamber of Commerce, 1963-67; Appts Cttee of Trinity Coll., Dublin; Court of New University of Ulster; Network Planning Cttee (of ITV); Vice-Chm., Standing Consultative Cttee, and Programme Planning Cttee (of ITA); Independent Television Companies Assoc. *Publication:* Midnight Oil, 1962. *Recreations:* reading, theatre and cinema, golf. *Address:* Glenburn House, Dunmurry, Belfast. *T:* Dunmurry 3369.

**HENDERSON, Roy (Galbraith),** CBE 1970; FRAM; baritone; Teacher of Singing (private); Professor of Singing, RAM, London, since 1940; *b* Edinburgh, 4 July 1899; *er s* of late Rev. Dr Alex. Roy Henderson, formerly Principal of Paton Coll., Nottingham; *m* 1926, Bertha Collin Smyth; one *s* two *d*. *Educ:* Nottingham High Sch.; Royal Academy of Music, London (Worshipful Company of Musicians Medal). Debut as baritone singer, Queen's Hall, London, 1925; has sung at all leading Festivals in England, Internat. Festival for contemporary music, Amsterdam, 1933; recitals at first two Edinburgh Festivals, 1947 and 1948; principal parts in all Glyndebourne Opera festivals, 1934-40, associated chiefly with works of Delius, Elgar and Vaughan Williams, and sang many first performances of contemp. music. Retired from concert platform, 1951, to devote his whole time to teaching (among his pupils was late Kathleen Ferrier). Conductor, Huddersfield Glee and Madrigal Soc., 1932-39; Founder and Conductor, Nottingham Oriana Choir, 1937-52. Conductor of Bournemouth Municipal Choir, 1942-53. Adjudicator at International Concours, Geneva, 1952, and Triennially, 1956-65. Mem. of the Jury of the International Muziekstad s'Hertogenbosch, Holland, 1955-62, 1965, and Barcelona, 1965. Master classes in singing: Royal Conservatory of Music, Toronto, 1956; Toonkunst Conservatorium, Rotterdam, 1957, 1958; s'Hertogenbosch, 1967. Awarded the Sir Charles Santley memorial by Worshipful Company of Musicians for distinguished services to the art of singing, 1958. *Publications:* contributed to: Kathleen Ferrier, ed Neville Cardus, 1954; Opera Annual, 1958. *Recreations:* fishing, gardening and cricket. *Address:* 85 Belsize Park Gardens, Hampstead, NW3. *T:* 01-722 3144. *Club:* Royal Automobile.

**HENDERSON, Rupert Albert Geary;** Chairman: Australian Newsprint Mills Ltd, since 1960; Trustees of Reuters Ltd since 1961 (Trustee since 1952, Director, 1946-51); Amalgamated Television Services Pty Ltd, since 1958; *b* 26 Feb. 1896; *s* of late Robert Geary Henderson and Isabel Henderson; *m* 1st, 1914, Helene, *d* of Thomas Mason; one *s*; 2nd, 1939, Hazel, *d* of Herbert Harris; one *d*. *Educ:* Glebe Public Sch., Sydney. Literary staff, The Sydney Morning Herald, 1915; London rep., 1923-26; Advertising Manager, Sydney Mail, 1927; Circulation Manager, Sydney Morning Herald, 1928; Sec. to Gen. Manager, 1934; Gen. Manager, 1938; Chm., Australian Associated Press Pty Ltd, 1940-49; Managing Director: John Fairfax & Sons Pty Ltd, 1949-56; John Fairfax Ltd, 1956-64; Associated Newspapers Ltd, 1954-64; Pres. Australian Newspaper Proprietors' Association, 1942-47 and 1951-58; Director, Australian Assoc. Press Pty Ltd. *Recreation:* grazier. *Address:* John Fairfax Ltd, 23 Hamilton Street, Sydney, NSW 2000, Australia. *TA:* Herald, Sydney. *T:* BO 944.

**HENDERSON, William Crichton;** Advocate; Sheriff Substitute of Renfrew and Argyll, at Paisley, since 1968; *b* 10 June 1931; *s* of William Henderson, headmaster, and late Helen Philp Henderson (*née* Crichton); *m* 1962, Norma Sheila Hope Henderson (*née* Grant); two *d*. *Educ:* George Watson's Boys' Coll., Edinburgh; Edinburgh Univ. MA Edinburgh 1952, LLB Edinburgh 1954. Admitted Solicitor, 1954; Diploma in Administrative Law and Practice, Edinburgh, 1955; called to Scottish Bar, 1957; practised as Advocate, 1957-68. Chm., Supreme Court Legal Aid Cttee, 1967-68. *Recreations:* golf, photography, travel. *Address:* Erroldene, Kilmacolm, Renfrewshire; Old Station House, Lower Largo, Fife. *T:* Kilmacolm 2418. *Club:* The Club (Paisley).

**HENDERSON-STEWART, Sir David (James),** 2nd Bt *cr* 1957; *b* 3 July 1941; *s* of Sir James Henderson-Stewart, 1st Bt, MP, and of Anna Margaret (*née* Greenwell); *S* father, 1961. *Educ:* Eton Coll.; Trinity Coll., Oxford. *Address:* 25 Pembroke Place, W8. *T:* 01-937 1020. *Club:* Travellers'.

**HENDREY, Mrs Graeme;** *see* Lewis, Eiluned.

**HENDRY, (Alexander) Forbes,** OBE 1957; MC 1940; TD 1947; DL; *b* 24 Oct. 1908; *s* of late Alexander Hendry, Solicitor, Denny, and Catherine Ann Forbes; *m* 1939, Margaret Whitehead; one *s* two *d*. *Educ:* Stirling High Sch.; Univ. of Glasgow (MA, LLB). Admitted Solicitor, 1932; Town Clerk of Denny and Dunipace, 1934-59. Commissioned 7th Bn The Argyll and Sutherland Highlanders (TA), 1935. Joint Manager, National Commercial, now Royal, Bank of Scotland Ltd, Denny, 1938. Served War of 1939-45 in France, Middle East, North Africa, Sicily and North West Europe. Chairman and Managing Dir, Cannerton Brick Co. Ltd; Dir Craigend Refractories Ltd, and other companies. Lieut-Col, 1953; TARO 1956. Contested (C) Lanarkshire North, 1955. MP (C) West Aberdeenshire, 1959-66. Mem., Parliamentary Delegn to Tunisia, 1961; Vice-Chm., Anglo-Tunisian Parliamentary Group, 1965; Mem., Executive Cttee, British Branch, Inter-Parly Union, 1963-65; Chm., W Stirlingshire Cons. Assoc., 1968; Vice-Chm., Central and Southern Region, Scottish Cons. and Unionist Assoc., 1969. DL Stirlingshire, 1965; Town Councillor, Burgh of Denny and Dunipace, 1969. *Recreation:* gardening. *Address:* Braes, Dunipace, Denny, Stirlingshire. *T:* Denny 345. *Clubs:* Royal Automobile; Royal Northern (Aberdeen); Caledonian (Edinburgh).

**HENDRY, Prof. Arnold William;** Professor of Civil Engineering, University of Edinburgh, since 1964; *b* 10 Sept. 1921; *s* of late Dr George Hendry, MB, ChB, Buckie, Scotland; *m* 1st,

1946, Sheila Mary Cameron Roberts (*d* 1966), Glasgow; two *s* one *d*; 2nd, 1968, Elizabeth Lois Alice Inglis, Edinburgh. *Educ:* Buckie High Sch.; Aberdeen Univ. Civil engineer with Sir William Arrol & Co. Ltd, Bridge builders and Engineers, Glasgow, 1941-43; Asst in Engineering, University of Aberdeen, 1943-46; Lecturer in Civil Engineering, 1946-49; Reader in Civil Engineering, Univ. of London, King's Coll., 1949-51; Prof. of Civil Engrg and Dean of Fac. of Engrg, Univ. of Khartoum, 1951-57; Prof. of Building Science, University of Liverpool, 1957-63. *Publications:* An Introduction to Photo-Elastic Analysis, 1948; (with L. G. Jaeger) The Analysis of Grid Frameworks, 1958; The Elements of Experimental Stress Analysis, 1964; about 50 papers and articles in professional and technical jls. *Recrreation:* sailing. *Address:* Department of Civil Engineering, University of Edinburgh.

**HENDRY, Forbes;** *see* Hendry, A. F.

**HENDY, Sir Philip,** Kt 1950; Adviser to the Israel Museum, Jerusalem, since 1968; *b* 27 Sept. 1900; *s* of Frederick James Roberts Hendy and Caroline Isobel Potts. *Educ:* Westminster School; Christ Church, Oxford. Lecturer and Asst to the Keeper, The Wallace Collection, London, 1923-27; lived in Florence, Italy, 1927-30; Curator of Paintings, Museum of Fine Arts, Boston, Mass, USA, 1930-33; Dir, City Art Gallery and Temple Newsam, Leeds, 1934-45; Slade Prof. of Fine Art, Oxford Univ., 1936-46; Director, National Gallery, London, 1946-67. President: Internat. Council of Museums, 1959-65; ICOM Foundation, 1965-. *Publications:* Hours in the Wallace Collection, 1926; The Isabella Stewart Gardner Museum, Catalogue of Paintings and Drawings, Boston, 1931; Matthew Smith (Penguin Modern Painters), 1944; Giovanni Bellini, 1945; Spanish Painting, 1946; The National Gallery, London, 1955; Masaccio (Unesco), 1957; Piero della Francesca and the Early Renaissance, 1968. *Address:* The Israel Museum, Jerusalem, Israel. *Clubs:* Athenæum, Beefsteak.

**HENEAGE, Lt-Col Sir Arthur Pelham,** Kt 1945; DSO 1917; DL; Member, Central Advisory Water Committee, Ministry of Health; Alderman Lindsey CC; *b* 11 July 1881; *s* of late Capt F. W. Heneage, RE (*s* of late E. F. Heneage, MP for Grimsby), and Ann, *d* of late Maj.-Gen. E. C. A. Gordon, RE; *m* Anne, *d* of late Brig.-Gen. N. D. Findlay, CB, RA; two *s* two *d* (and one *s* decd). *Educ:* Eton; RM Academy, Woolwich. Joined the RFA 1900; served European War, 1914-18, on the French and Balkan Fronts as Staff Capt., Staff Officer, RA, and commanding a Field Artillery Brigade (despatches thrice); retired pay, 1924; JP parts of Lindsey; late a mem. of the Inter-allied Commission of Control in Berlin; Chm. Central and Associated Chambers of Agriculture, 1927; MP (C) Louth, 1924-45; Parliamentary Private Sec. to Minister of Transport, 1931-33, to Asst Postmaster-Gen., 1936-38; to Minister of Pensions, 1939-45; Mem. of Central Advisory Cttee to Min. of Pensions, 1939-45; Pres. Catchment and Rivers Boards Association; Chm. Cttee relating to Public Water Supply, 1939-; Gathering Grounds Sub-Cttee, 1948-; Land Drainage Sub-Cttee, 1951-; Mem. Lincolnshire River Board, 1951-. Mem. Central Advisory Water Cttee, Min. of Housing and Local Govt; late Hon. Col 529 Light AA Regt; late Hon. Col 53rd (City of London) AA Brigade (TA); late Mem. Central National Service Cttee for Great Britain; Vice-Pres. Urban District Council Association, 1925-45; Vice-Pres., Rural District Council Assoc., 1931-45; Chm. Lincs Branch Country Landowners' Assoc. DL Lincs 1936; High Sheriff of Lincs, 1947. *Recreation:* shooting. *Address:* Walesby Hall, Market Rasen, Lincs. *T:* Tealby 277. *Club:* Cavalry.

**HENIG, Sir Mark,** Kt 1965; Director, Henig & Sons Ltd, Leicester, since 1933; Chairman: East Midlands Economic Planning Council; East Midlands Gas Consultative Council; English Tourist Board; Member, Commission on the Constitution, since 1969; *b* 11 Feb. 1911; *e s* of Harry and Gertrude Henig; *m* 1937, Grace (*née* Cohen); one *s* one *d*. *Educ:* Wyggeston Grammar Sch., Leicester. Mem. Leicester City Council, 1945-70, Alderman, 1958-70; High Bailiff, City of Leicester, 1965, Lord Mayor, 1967-68. Chm., Assoc. of Municipal Corporations, 1966-67. *Address:* 35 Stanley Road, Leicester LE2 1RF. *T:* 708425. *Club:* Oxford and Cambridge University.
*See also S. Henig.*

**HENIG, Stanley;** *b* 7 July 1939; *s* of Sir Mark Henig, *qv*; *m* 1966, Ruth Beatrice Munzer; one *s*. *Educ:* Wyggeston Grammar Sch.; Corpus Christi Coll., Oxford. BA 1st Cl. Hons, 1961; MA 1965 Oxon. Teaching Asst, Dept of Politics, Univ. of Minnesota, 1961; Research Student, Nuffield Coll., 1962; Lecturer in Politics, Lancaster Univ., 1964-66. MP (Lab) Lancaster, 1966-70. Asst Editor, Jl of Common Market Studies, 1964-. *Publication:* (ed) European Political Parties, 1969. *Recreation:* collector of old gramophone records. *Address:* 22 Whinfell Drive, Lancaster. *T:* 66527. *Club:* Phœnix (Lancaster).

**HENLEY,** 7th Baron (Ire.), *cr* 1799; **Michael Francis Eden;** Baron Northington (UK) *cr* 1885; *b* 13 Aug. 1914; *er s* of 6th Baron Henley and Lady Dorothy Howard (*d* 1968), 3rd *d* of 9th Earl of Carlisle; *S* father, 1962; *m* 1st, 1943, Elizabeth, *d* of Sir A. L. Hobhouse (marriage dissolved by divorce, 1947); one *d*; 2nd, 1949, Nancy, *d* of Stanley Walton; two *s* three *d*. *Educ:* Eton; Balliol Coll., Oxford. Served War of 1939-45: Coldstream Guards, 1940-41; Household Cavalry, 1941-46. *Heir: s* Hon. Oliver Michael Robert Eden, *b* 22 Nov. 1953. *Address:* Scaleby Castle, Carlisle; (seat) Watford Court, Rugby, Warwicks. *Clubs:* Brooks's, Pratt's.

**HENLEY, Douglas Owen,** CB 1970; Third Secretary, HM Treasury, since 1969; *b* 5 April 1919; *s* of late Owen Henley and of Beatrice Mary Henley; *m* 1942, June Muriel Ibbetson; four *d*. *Educ:* Beckenham County Sch.; London Sch. of Economics. BSc (Econ.), 1939; Gerstenberg Studentship and Leverhulme Res. Studentship (not taken up). Served Army, 1939-46; Queen's Own Royal West Kent Regt and HQ 12th Inf. Bde (despatches twice, 1945). Treasury, 1946; Treas. rep. (Financial Counsellor) in Tokyo and Singapore, 1956-59; Asst Under-Sec. of State, DEA, 1964-69, Dep. Under-Sec. of State, 1969. *Address:* 1 The Ridge Way, Sanderstead, South Croydon, Surrey CR2 0LG. *T:* Sanderstead 4379.

**HENLEY, Rear-Adm. Sir Joseph (Charles Cameron),** KCVO 1963; CB 1962; *b* 24 April 1909; *e s* of Vice-Adm. J. C. W. Henley, CB; *m* 1934, Daphne Ruth (marr. diss. 1965), *d* of late A. A. H. Wykeham, of Pitt Place, Brighstone, IW; one *s* three *d*; *m* 1966, Patricia Sharp, MBE 1952, *d* of late Roy Eastman, Alberta, Canada. *Educ:* Sherborne. Joined Royal Navy, 1927. Served War of 1939-45, in HMS Birmingham and King George V. Capt., 1951, in command HMS Defender, 1954-55; Naval Attaché, Washington (as Commodore), 1956-57; Dir,

Royal Naval Staff Coll., 1958; Chief of Staff, Mediterranean Station, 1959-61, as Commodore; Rear-Adm. 1960; Flag Officer, Royal Yachts and Extra Naval Equerry to the Queen, 1962-65; retd 1965. *Address:* Wilkscliffe, Upton Estate, St Ann, Jamaica; 11a Hopewood Gardens, Darling Point, Edgecliff, NSW 2027, Australia. *Clubs:* United Service; Royal Yacht Squadron.

**HENMAN, Philip Sydney;** Founder of Transport Development Group Ltd; Director, Temperance Permanent Building Society. MInstT, 1943. Farmer. *Address:* 141 High Street, Dorking, Surrey. *T:* Dorking 4567.

**HENN, Thomas Rice,** CBE 1945; MA; Hon. DLitt (Dublin); Hon. LLD (Victoria); Emeritus fellow of St Catharine's College, Cambridge; Emeritus Reader in Anglo-Irish Literature; *b* 10 Nov. 1901; 2nd *s* of Francis Blackburn Henn, Barrister-at-Law, Paradise, Ennis, Co. Clare, Ireland; *m* 1926, May Enid, *d* of E. A. Roberts, MD; one *d* (one *s* decd). *Educ:* Aldenham Sch.; St Catharine's Coll., Cambridge. Mod. Lang. Scholar of St Catharine's Coll.; Class I English Tripos, 1922; Charles Oldham Shakespeare Scholar, Members' English Prizeman, 1923. Asst, Burmah Oil Co., 1923-25; Fellow of St Catharine's Coll., 1926-69; Prælector, 1927; Tutor, 1934; Special Pro-Proctor, 1934-39; Senior Tutor, 1945-57; Pres., 1957-61, 1968-69. Gov. of Aldenham Sch. Donnellian Lecturer, TCD, 1965; Warton Lecturer, British Academy, 1965. Served War of 1939-45, The Welch Regt; 2nd Lieut 1940; Brigadier, General Staff, 1945; France and Italian Campaigns (despatches twice); Staff Coll. (War Course); US Legion of Merit. Hon. Fellow of Trumbull Coll., Yale; FRSL. Seatonian Prizeman, 1957 and 1966. *Publications:* Longinus and English Criticism, 1934; The Lonely Tower, 1950; Practical Fly-Tying, 1950; The Apple and the Spectroscope, 1951; The Harvest of Tragedy, 1956; Prose for Science, 1960; Passages for Divine Reading, 1963; Synge's Plays and Poems, 1963; Poems, 1964; Rudyard Kipling, 1967; The Bible as Literature, 1970; articles and reviews. *Recreations:* shooting, fishing, sailing. *Address:* 32 Millington Road, Cambridge. *T:* Cambridge 50176; St Catharine's College, Cambridge. *T:* Cambridge 59445.

**HENNELL, Rev. Canon Michael Murray;** Residentiary Canon, Manchester Cathedral, since 1970; *b* 11 Sept. 1918; *s* of Charles Murray and Jessie Hennell; *m* 1951, Peggy Glendinning; four *s*. *Educ:* Bishops Stortford Coll. (Prep.); Royal Masonic Sch.; St Edmund Hall and Wycliffe Hall, Oxford. MA Oxon and, by incorporation, MA Cantab. Asst Curate: St Stephen's With St Bartholomew's, Islington, N1, 1942-44; All Saints, Queensbury, Middx, 1944-48; Tutor, Ridley Hall, Cambridge, 1948-51. St Aidan's Coll., Birkenhead: Sen. Tutor, 1951; Vice-Principal, 1952-59; Principal, 1959-63; Principal, Ridley Hall, Cambridge, 1964-70. Examining Chaplain to the Bishops of Chelmsford, Liverpool and Manchester. *Publications:* John Venn and the Clapham Sect, 1958; ed and contrib., Charles Simeon, 1759-1836, 1959; contrib., The Anglican Synthesis, 1964; articles in Theology. *Recreation:* golf. *Address:* 21 Morville Road, Chorlton-cum-Hardy, Manchester 21.

**HENNESSEY, Dennis;** Deputy Managing Director, National Research Development Corporation, since 1959 (Member since 1956); Chairman: Hovercraft Development Ltd, since 1959; Tracked Hovercraft Ltd, since 1967; *b* 24 July 1912; *s* of John Michael Hennessey and Rosina Marion Hennessey; *m* 1941, Gladys Rees Evans; one *d*. *Educ:* Haberdashers' Aske's Hampstead Sch. Practised as Patent Agent, 1930-39. War Service, Royal Signals, 1939-45 (Lieut-Col). Princ. Patents Officer, Min. of Supply, 1945-49; Patents Man., NRDC, 1949-56. *Publications:* contribs to learned jls. *Recreations:* golf, travel. *Address:* 12 Saxon Hall, Palace Court, W2. *T:* 01-727 0299.

**HENNESSEY, Robert Samuel Fleming,** CMG 1954; Assistant Research Director, Wellcome Foundation, 1967-70, retired; *b* 8 May 1905; *s* of late W. R. H. Hennessey and late Elizabeth Fleming; *m* 1930, Grace Alberta Coote; one *s* one *d*. *Educ:* St Andrew's Coll., Dublin; Dublin and London Universities. MD, FRCPI, DipBact, DTM&H. Pathologist, Uganda, 1929; Dep. Director (Laboratories), Palestine, 1944; Dep. Director, Medical Services, Palestine, 1946; Asst Medical Adviser, Colonial Office, 1947; Director of Medical Services, Uganda, 1949-55; Head of the Wellcome Laboratories of Tropical Medicine, London, 1956-58; Head of Therapeutic Research Division, Wellcome Foundation, 1958-66. *Publications:* papers on pathology in scientific jls. *Recreations:* golf, music, literature. *Address:* 51 Stone Park Avenue, Beckenham, Kent. *T:* 01-650 5336.

**HENNESSY,** family name of **Baron Windlesham.**

**HENNESSY;** *see* Pope-Hennessy.

**HENNESSY, Christopher;** journalist; Chairman, Associated Catholic Newspapers (1912) Ltd, since 1970 and Editor of The Universe since 1954; Director, The Catholic Association; *b* 29 Dec. 1909; *e s* of Daniel and Anne Hennessy; *m* 1942, Kathleen Margaret Cadley, Liverpool. *Educ:* St Edward's Coll., Liverpool. Served War of 1939-45 as Commissioned Officer in British and Indian Armies; commanded a Territorial Army Unit in the North-West, 1950-55. *Recreation:* travel. *Address:* Beech House, Montreal Road, Riverhead, Sevenoaks, Kent. *T:* Sevenoaks 54117. *Clubs:* Directors', Press.

**HENNESSY, Denis William,** OBE 1967; Counsellor, British Embassy, Bonn, since 1969; *b* 5 Dec. 1912; *s* of Daniel Hennessy and Rosina Gertrude Hennessy (*née* Griffiths); *m* 1937, Lorna McDonald Lappin; three *s* one *d*. *Educ:* private sch. Joined Foreign Office, 1930; served in the Foreign Office and in Prague, Washington, New York, Zürich, Bremen, Miami, Düsseldorf, Accra, and as Consul-Gen., Hanover. *Address:* c/o Foreign and Commonwealth Office, SW1. *Clubs:* Royal Commonweath Society, Civil Service.

**HENNESSY, Sir Patrick,** Kt, *cr* 1941; Chairman: Ford Motor Co. Ltd, 1956-68; Henry Ford & Son Ltd, Cork, Eire, since 1955; Director, Montego Freeport Ltd, Jamaica; *b* 18 April 1898; *s* of Patrick Hennessy, Ballyvodak House, Midleton, Co. Cork; *m* 1923, Dorothy Margaret (*d* 1949), *d* of Robert Davis, JP, Killaney Lodge, Boardmills, N Ireland; two *s* one *d*. Served European War, 1914-18, Royal Inniskilling Fus. Pres., Soc. of Motor Manufacturers & Traders, 1965 and 1966, Dep. Pres., 1967 and 1968. Mem. Council, Univ. of Essex, 1965-68; formerly Mem. Adv. Council, Min. of Aircraft Production. *Address:* 88 Regent Street, W1. *T:* 01-734 7272; Larkmead, Theydon Bois, Essex. *T:* Theydon Bois 2139. *Club:* Royal Automobile.

**HENNIKER,** 7th Baron, *cr* 1800; **John Ernest De Grey Henniker-Major;** Bt 1765; Baron Hartismere (UK) 1866; sits in House of Lords as Baron Hartismere; Land Agent for: Lord

Mostyn (N Wales); W. D. Mackenzie (Henley-on-Thames); Sir Percy Loraine, Bt and Lord Henniker (Suffolk); *b* 18 Jan. 1883; *y s* of 5th Baron Henniker and Alice Mary (*d* 1893), *o d* of 3rd Earl of Desart; *S* brother 1956; *m* 1914, Molly, *d* of late Sir Robert Burnet, KCVO; two *s*. *Educ:* Radley; Royal Agricultural College, Cirencester (Hons Diploma). Page of Honour to Queen Victoria, 1895-99; served in Army and RAF, 1914-19 (French Croix de Guerre). FLAS. *Heir: s* Hon. Sir John Patrick Edward Chandos Henniker-Major, *qv*. *Address:* Thornham Hall, Eye, Suffolk. *T:* Mellis 207 and 314.

**HENNIKER, Brig. Sir Mark Chandos Auberon,** 8th Bt, *cr* 1813; CBE 1953 (OBE 1944); DSO 1945; MC 1933; DL; retired, 1958; *b* 23 Jan. 1906; *s* of late F. C. Henniker, ICS, and of Ada Russell (*née* Howell); *S* cousin (Lieut-Col Sir Robert Henniker, 7th Bt, MC) 1958; *m* 1945, Kathleen Denys (*née* Anderson); one *s* one *d*. *Educ:* Marlborough Coll.; Royal Military Academy, Woolwich; King's Coll., Cambridge. Royal Engineers, 1926; served India, 1928-34 (MC); Aldershot, 1937-39; BEF, 1939-40; North Africa, 1943; Sicily, 1943 (wounded); Italy, 1943 (OBE); NW Europe, 1944-45 (DSO); India, 1946-47; Malaya, 1952-55 (CBE); Port Said, 1956 (despatches). Hon. Col, Parachute Engineer Regt (TA), 1959-68; Hon. Col, REME (TA), 1964-68. DL, County of Mon, 1963. *Publications:* Memoirs of a Junior Officer, 1951; Red Shadow over Malaya, 1955; Life in the Army Today, 1957; contributor to Blackwood's Magazine. *Recreations:* appropriate to age and rank. *Heir: s* Adrian Chandos Henniker, *b* 18 Oct. 1946. *Address:* c/o Lloyds Bank Ltd, Cox & King's Branch, 6 Pall Mall, SW1. *Club:* United Service.

**HENNIKER-GOTLEY, George Rainald,** CIE 1944; DSO 1918; *b* 5 Sept. 1893; *s* of Rev. George Henniker-Gotley; *m* Lorna Earle, *y d* of Stanley Dorling; one *s* one *d*. *Educ:* Sherborne Sch.; Brasenose Coll., Oxford. Served European War (DSO, despatches thrice). Indian Forest Service, 1921-47; Conservator of Forests, NW Frontier, 1939-45; Chief Conservator of Forests, Punjab, India, 1945-47. *Recreations:* fishing, gardening. *Address:* Twynax, Ford Lane, Farnham, Surrey. *T:* Farnham 3504. *Club:* Oxford and Cambridge.

**HENNIKER-GOTLEY, Roger Alwyn,** MA Oxon.; Headmaster of Sebright School, 1938-63, retired; *b* 8 Feb. 1898; 3rd *s* of late Rev. George Henniker-Gotley and late Louisa Sarah Lefroy; *m* 1931, Helen Hope Campbell, *d* of late Rev. Gerald Campbell Dicker; two *s*. *Educ:* Cheltenham Coll.; Brasenose Coll., Oxford. Served European War, 1914-18, Lancashire Fusiliers. Asst Master and Housemaster, Stamford School, 1924-25; Asst Master and Housemaster, Worksop Coll., 1925-27; Asst Master and Senior English Master, Cranleigh Sch., 1927-38. *Recreations:* cricket, ornithology, gardening. *Address:* 2 The Old Rectory, Codford St Mary, Warminster, Wiltshire. *T:* Codford St Mary 239. *Club:* Athenæum.

**HENNIKER HEATON;** *see* Heaton.

**HENNIKER-MAJOR,** family name of **Baron Henniker.**

**HENNIKER-MAJOR, Hon. Sir John (Patrick Edward Chandos),** KCMG 1965 (CMG 1956); CVO 1960; MC 1945; Director-General, British Council, since 1968; *b* 19 Feb. 1916; *s* and *heir* of 7th Baron Henniker, *qv; m* 1946, Margaret Osla Benning; two *s* one *d*. *Educ:* Stowe; Trinity Coll., Cambridge. HM Foreign Service, 1938; served 1940-45, Army (Major, The Rifle Brigade). HM Embassy Belgrade, 1945-46; Asst Private Secretary to Secretary of State for Foreign Affairs, 1946-48; Foreign Office, 1948-50; HM Embassy, Buenos Aires, 1950-52; Foreign Office, 1952-60 (Counsellor and Head of Personnel Dept, 1953); HM Ambassador to Jordan, 1960-62; to Denmark, 1962-66; Civil Service Commission, 1966-67; Asst Under-Secretary of State, FO, 1967-68. *Address:* 11 Campden Hill Road, W8. *Club:* Travellers'.

**HENNINGS, John Dunn,** CMG 1968; Counsellor and Head of Chancery, British High Commission, Delhi, since Dec. 1968; *b* 9 June 1922; *o c* of Stanley John and Grace Beatrice Hennings, Ipswich, Suffolk; *m* 1953, Joanna Anita, *er d* of J. Thompson Reed, Northampton; two *s*. *Educ:* Ipswich Sch.; University College, Oxford. Foreign Office and Berlin, 1947-49; Colonial Office, 1949-53; W. African Inter-Territorial Secretariat, Accra, 1953-55; Colonial Office, 1955-60; Attaché for Colonial Affairs, British Embassy, Washington, DC, 1960-63; Commonwealth Relations Office, 1963; Counsellor, HM Diplomatic Service, 1965; Head, British High Commission, Residual Staff, Salisbury, Rhodesia, 1966-68. Secretary, British Guiana Constitutional Commission, 1951. *Recreations:* reading, tennis, photography. *Address:* British High Commission, Chanakyapuri, New Delhi 11; c/o Foreign and Commonwealth Office, Downing Street, SW1

**HENNINGS, Richard Owen,** CMG 1957; retired as Deputy Chief Secretary, Kenya (1960-63); Hon. Editor Ski Notes and Queries, since 1964; *b* 8 Sept. 1911; *s* of W. G. Hennings; *m* 1939, Constance Patricia Milton Sexton; one *d*. *Educ:* Cheltenham; New Coll., Oxford. Newdigate Prize Poem, 1932. District Officer, Kenya, 1935; Political Officer, Ethiopia, 1941; Secretary for Agriculture, Kenya, 1953; Permanent Secretary, Ministry of Agriculture, Animal Husbandry and Water Resources, Kenya, 1956. Nominated Member of Kenya Legislative Council, 1960, and of East African Central Legislative Assembly, 1960. *Publications:* Arnold in Africa, 1941; African Morning, 1951; articles in The Geographical Magazine, Journal of African Administration, Corona, British Ski Year Book, Ski Notes and Queries. *Recreations:* ski-ing, tennis, gardening, reefing. *Address:* Wyngates, Pennymead Drive, East Horsley, Surrey. *T:* East Horsley 3703. *Clubs:* Ski Club of Great Britain; Nairobi (Nairobi).

**HENREY, Mrs Robert;** authoress; *b* Paris, 13 Aug. 1906; maiden name Madeleine Gal; *m* 1928, Robert Selby Henrey, *o s* of Rev. Thomas Selby Henrey, Vicar of Old Brentford, Middx, and Euphemia, *d* of Sir Coutts and Lady Lindsay of Balcarres; one *s*. *Educ:* Protestant Girls' Sch., Clichy; Convent of The Holy Family, Tooting, SW. *Publications:* The Little Madeleine (her girlhood), (Book Society Choice), 1951 (her own French version published Paris, under title La Petite Madeleine, 1954); An Exile in Soho (her adolescence), 1952; Madeleine Grown Up (her love story and marriage), 1952 (published Paris, under title Madeleine Jeune Fille, 1955); Madeleine Young Wife (incorporating A Farm in Normandy and The Return), 1960; Matilda and the Chickens (a winter on her farm), 1950; A Journey to Vienna, 1950; Paloma, 1951; Madeleine's Journal, 1953; A Month in Paris, 1954; Milou's Daughter (she visits the French Riviera), 1955; Bloomsbury Fair, 1955; This Feminine World, 1956; A Daughter for a Fortnight, 1957; The Virgin of Aldermanbury (rebirth of the City of London), 1958; Mistress of Myself, 1959; The Dream Makers, 1961; Spring in a Soho Street, 1962; Her April Days, 1963; Wednesday at Four, 1964; Winter Wild, 1966; She Who Pays, 1969; London under Fire 1940-45, 1969; Julia: a year as a London shopgirl, 1971. *Recreations:* sewing, ironing, knitting and cooking. *Address:* c/o J. M. Dent & Sons, Aldine House, Bedford Street, Strand, WC2; Ferme Robert Henrey, Villers-sur-Mer, Calvados 14, France. *T:* 8-703-88.

**HENRION, Frederick Henri Kay,** MBE 1951; RDI; PPSIA; General Consulting Designer for Industry and Commerce; Visiting Lecturer at Royal College of Art; *b* 18 April 1914; *m* 1947, Daphne Hardy, sculptress; two *s* one *d.* Textile design in Paris, 1932-33; worked in Paris and London, 1936-39; designed Smoke Abatement Exhibition, Charing Cross Station, and worked on Glasgow Empire Exhibition, 1939, and New York World Fair, 1940-45. Design of all exhibitions for ministry of Agriculture through Ministry of Information and exhibitions for Army Bureau of Current Affairs (WO), etc., 1943-45. Consultant Designer to US Embassy and US Office of War Information, 1945; Chief Cons. Designer to Sir William Crawford and Partners, 1946-47; Art Editor of Contact Publication, 1947-48; Art Director BOAC Publications, 1949-51, and of Future Magazine, 1951; Designer, Festival of britain pavilions (Agriculture and Natural History), 1950-51-54; Art Editor and Designer of the Bowater Papers, 1951-53; subseq. Cons. Designer for many firms. Posters for: GPO; BOAC; LPTB; Council of Industrial Design, and in exhibitions and permanent collections (both in Europe and America). One-man show, Designing Things and Symbols, at Institute of Contemporary Arts, 1960. Member Council and Vice-President, Society of Industrial Artists (President, 1961-63); Member, Council of Industrial Design, 1963-66; President: Alliance Graphique Internationale, 1962-67; ICOGRADA, 1968-70. member Advisory Council to Governors of London School of Printing; Past Governor, Central School of Art; Outside Assessor, Scottish Schools of Art; Outside Assessor and Examiner for NDD for Display and Exhibition at Ministry of Education. Consultant Designer to: BTC; KLM Royal Dutch Airlines; British Olivetti Ltd; Tate & Lyle Ltd; The Postmaster General; BEA; Blue Circle Group; Courage, Barclay & Simonds Ltd; Financial Times; Volkswagen, Audi, NSU, Porsche. Member: National Advisory Council on Art Education; National Council for Diplomas in Art and Design; Co-ordinating graphics designer for British Pavilion, Expo 67. Hon. Dip. Manchester, 1962. *Publications:* Design Co-ordination and Corporate Image, 1967 (USA). Contributor to: Graphis, Gebrauchgraphik, Design Magazine, Architectural Review, Art and Industry, Penrose Annual, etc. *Address:* 35 Pond Street, NW3. *T:* 01-435 7402. *Club:* Savile.

**HENRIQUES, Sir Cyril George Xavier,** Kt 1963; QC (Jamaica); LLB; President, Court of Appeal, Jamaica, since 1968; *b* Kingston, Jamaica, 5 July 1908; *m* Marjory Brunhilda (*née* Burrows); two *d. Educ:* St George's Coll., Jamaica; St Francis Xavier's Coll.; University College, London. Called to Bar, Inner Temple, 1936; Crown Counsel, Jamaica, 1939; Resident Magistrate, 1944; Attorney General, British Honduras, 1950; Puisne-Judge, Jamaica, 1955; appointment in British Honduras, 1956; Chief Justice of Supreme Court of Windward Islands and Leeward Islands, 1958; Judge of Appeal, Appeal Court of Jamaica, 1963-68. *Address:* Kingston, Jamaica.

**HENRIQUES, Prof. Louis Fernando,** MA, DPhil Oxon; Professorial Fellow and Director of Centre for Multi-Racial Studies (formerly Research Unit for Study of Multi-racial Societies), University of Sussex, since 1964; *b* Kingston, Jamaica, 1916; *y s* of Cyril Charles Henriques and of Mrs Edith Emily Henriques; *m* 1948, Rosamund Ann, *e d* of late Dr F. R. Seymour, Ministry of Health, London; three *s. Educ:* St Aloysius Coll., London, N6; London School of Economics; Brasenose Coll., Oxford. Senior History Scholar, Brasenose Coll., 1942-45; President, Oxford Union Society, Trin. Term, 1944; Carnegie Research Fellow, 1946-47. Grad. Asst, Institute of Social Anthropology, University of Oxford, 1947-48; Lecturer in Social Anthropology, University of Leeds, 1948-64; Director of sociological research projects, sponsored by Nuffield Foundation, 1952-54; Coal Industry Social Welfare Organisation, 1954-58; DSIR, 1955-56; Sociol. Member Un Tech. Assist. Admin. Rural Electrification Survey, Ghana, 1957; Dean, Faculty of Economics and Social Studies, University of Leeds, 1960-62; Wyndham Deedes Scholar, 1963; Member Council, Institute of Race Relations, London, 1965-; Member SE Economic Planning Council, 1966-68. National Fire Service, London, 1939-42. Broadcaster in Overseas Services of BBC, 1939-. *Publications:* Family and Colour in Jamaica, 1953, rev. edn, 1968; Jamaica, Land of Wood and Water, 1957; Coal is Our Life (with N. Dennis and C. Slaughter), 1956, rev. edn, 1969; Love in Action, 1959; Prostitution and Society, Vol. I, 1962, Vol. II, 1963, Vol. III, 1967. Contributions to: Handbook of Latin American Studies, 1966; Ciba Foundation Report on Immigration, 1966; Encyclopædia Britannica, 1966; English Language Editor, Library of Sexual Behaviour, 1970. Various papers in sociological journals. *Recreations:* bibliomania, camping sauvage, people. *Address:* The Coach House, Beechland, Newick, Sussex. *T:* Newick 2367. *Clubs:* Athenæum, Royal Commonwealth Society, West Indian, Centro Español de Londres.

**HENRY, Cyril Bowdler (C. Bowdler-Henry);** Knight (First Class) Royal Norwegian Order of St Olav; Chevalier de la Légion d'Honneur; Officer of Order of Orange Nassau; Czechoslovak Military Medal of Merit (First Class); LRCP, MRCS, FDSRCS (Eng.); Hunterian Professor, RCS, 1935-36; Vice-President Royal Society Medicine (President Sect. Odontology, 1954-55, Hon. Member, 1964); Menzies Campbell Lecturer (on Dental History), RCS 1962; Arris and Gale Lecturer, RCS, 1933-34; Life Governor, Hon. Consulting Surgeon Emeritus, late Senior Surgeon and Lecturer in Oral Surgery, Royal Dental Hospital and Chairman of Governing Body of The London School of Dental Surgery (University of London), in Centenary Year of School's foundation; Member Board of Studies in Dentistry, and Examiner in Oral Surgery for Mastership in Dental Surgery, University of London; Life Governor Westminster Hospital; a Governor of St George's Hospital, 1954-60; Oral Surgeon EMS, Sept. 1939; Hon. Oral Surgeon and Consulting Stomatologist to Royal Norwegian Armed Forces in UK, Royal Norwegian Ministry of Social Welfare, Polish Ministry of Labour and Social Welfare, Netherland Army, Czechoslovak Armed Forces, Fighting French Forces, Armed Forces of Yugoslavia; Czechoslovak and Polish Red Cross Societies; Hon. Fellow British Association of Oral Surgeons; Fellow

Harveian Society of London; Member European Orthodontic Society; Member British Society for Study of Orthodontics; Member BMA; Member British Dental Association; Hon. Member American Dental Society of London (President, 1960-61), etc; *b* Leire, Leics., 10 Oct. 1893; *s* of late Thomas Henry, Moorgate Park, Retford, and Rose Emily Bowdler, Shrewsbury; *m* 1920, Dorothy Mildred, 2nd *d* of late William Henry Bradley, Solicitor. *Educ:* King Edward VI's Grammar Sch., Retford; Sheffield Univ.; Royal Dental and Westminster Hospitals, and King's Coll., University of London. Lieut RAMC attached 22 CCS, BEF, 1915-16; House Physician, House Surgeon, Resident Obstetric Assistant, Westminster Hospital, 1917-20; Assistant Dental Surgeon, Metropolitan Hospital, 1919-22; Dental Surgeon, Westminster Hospital, 1922-29, Royal Dental Hospital, 1925-59; appointed to represent the Royal College of Surgeons at the IInd International Stomatological Congress (Bologna), 1935, and at the IXth International Dental Congress, Vienna, 1936. *Publications:* (with A. W. Marrett-Tims) Tomes' Dental Anatomy, 8th Edn; A Study of the Mandibular third molar tooth (with G. M. Morant), vol. 28, 1936; Chapters in a System of Dental Surgery by Sir Norman G. Bennett and in Post Graduate Surgery by Rodney Maingot; papers, lectures and reviews upon scientific subjects related to dental medicine, oral surgery, stomatology and dental history. *Address:* 62 Harley Street, W1. *T:* 01-580 1612, 2758.

**HENRY, Sir James Holmes,** 2nd Bt, *cr* 1922; CMG 1960; MC 1944; TD 1950; QC (Tanganyika) 1953, (Cyprus) 1957; *b* 22 Sept. 1911; *er s* of Rt Hon. Sir Denis Stanislaus Henry, 1st Baronet, Cahore, Co. Londonderry, 1st Lord Chief Justice of Northern Ireland, and Violet (*d* 1966), 3rd *d* of late Rt Hon. Hugh Holmes, Court of Appeal, Ireland; *S* father, 1925; *m* 1st, 1941, S. M. Blackwell (marriage terminated by divorce and rescript of Holy Office in Rome); 2nd, 1949, Christina Hilary, *widow* of Lieut-Commander Christopher H. Wells, RN, and *e d* of late Sir Hugh Holmes, KBE, CMG, MC, QC; three *d*. *Educ:* Mount St Mary's Coll., Chesterfield; Downside Sch.; University College, London. BA (Hons) Classics (1st Class), University Scholarships. Called to Bar, Inner Temple, 1934; practised, London, 1934-39. Served War of 1939-45, London Irish Rifles (wounded). Crown Counsel, Tanganyika, 1946; Legal Draftsman, 1949; jt comr, Revised Edn of Laws of Tanganyika (1947-49), 1950; Solicitor-General, 1952; Attorney-General, Cyprus, 1956-60. Member of Foreign Compensation Commission, 1960-. *Heir: b* Denis Valentine Henry [*b* 29 June 1917; *m* 1956, Elizabeth, *d* of Rowland Walker; one *s* two *d*]. *Address:* Kandy Lodge, 18 Ormond Avenue, Hampton-on-Thames, Middlesex. *Clubs:* Travellers', Royal Commonwealth Society.

**HENRY, Robert Llewellyn,** JD, DCL; retired Judge; *b* 4 Nov. 1882; *s* of Robert L. Henry, Chicago; *m* 1908, Elaine Goodale Read; two *s*. *Educ:* University of Chicago; Worcester Coll., Oxford. Member of bar of Illinois, Iowa, District of Columbia and Supreme Court of US; Prof. of Law, Louisiana State Univ., 1907-11; Asst Prof. of Law, University of Illinois, 1911-12; Prof. of Law and Dean of the College of Law, University of North Dakota, 1912-14; Prof of Law, State University of Iowa, 1914-16; Capt. Infantry and Instructor Officers' Training Corps in USA, 1917-18; Major on General Staff and Member of Construction Demobilisation Cttee, War Dept, Washington, DC, 1919; Mem. of Board of Contract Adjustment, War Dept, 1920; Lecturer, Oxford, 1921-22. Judge in Mixed Courts of Egypt, 1924-41; Justice on Mixed Court of Appeals, 1941-49. *Publication:* Contracts in the Local Courts of Mediæval England, 1926. *Address:* 3621 Brownsboro RD (C-2), Louisville 7, Ky, USA

**HENRY, Thomas Cradock,** FDS, RCS; MRCS; LRCP; Consultant Dental Surgeon, Hospital for Sick Children, Great Ormond Street; Consultant Maxillo-Facial Surgeon, Royal Surrey County Hospital; Consultant Oral Surgeon, Italian Hospital, London; *b* 30 Dec. 1910; *s* of late Thomas Henry and Rose Emily Bowdler, Moorgate, Park Retford; *m* 1939, Claire Mary, 7th *c* of late R. A. Caraman, The Grange, Elstree; two *s*. *Educ:* King Edward VI Grammar Sch., Retford; King's Coll., University of London; Middlesex and Royal Dental Hospital; Saunders Scholar; qualified as Doctor, 1935. Formerly: House Physician, House Surgeon and Resident Anæsthetist St James's Hosp., London; Dental House Surgeon, St Bartholomew's Hosp.; Squadron Leader and Surgical Specialist, RAFVR, 1939-46; Surgical Registrar, Plastic and Jaw Injuries Centre, East Grinstead, 1941-42; Surgeon in charge of Maxillo-Facial and Plastic Unit, RAF Hosp., Cosford, 1942-46; Hunterian Prof., RCS, 1944-45. Fellow Royal Society Med.; Fellow Hunterian Soc.; Member: European Orthodontic Soc.; British Assoc. of Plastic Surgeons; BMA. *Publications:* Fracture of the Facial Bones (chapter in Fractures and Dislocations in General Practice, 1949); Dental Sepsis (chapter in Medical Treatment, 1951); Irregularities of the Teeth and Jaws (chapter in Diseases of Children, Fifth Edn, 1953); numerous contrib. to leading medical and dental journals, including BMJ and Jl of Bone and Joint Surgery. *Recreations:* shooting and fishing. *Address:* 8 Upper Wimpole Street, W1. *T:* 01-935 1244; Fieldfares, Thursley, Surrey. *T:* Elstead 2279.

**HENRY, Hon. Sir Trevor (Ernest),** Kt 1970; Judge of the Supreme Court of New Zealand since 1955; *b* 9 May 1902; *s* of John Henry and Edith Anna (*née* Eaton); *m* 1930, Audrey Kate Sheriff; one *s* one *d*. *Educ:* Rotorua District High Sch.; Univ. of New Zealand (Auckland). LLB 1925, LLM Hons 1926, NZ. Solicitor of Supreme Court of NZ, 1923, Barrister, 1925. *Recreation:* fishing. *Address:* 123 St Heliers Bay Road, Auckland, New Zealand. *T:* 584-323. *Club:* Northern (Auckland).

**HENSLEY, John;** Member, Council, National Institute of Agricultural Botany, since 1970; *b* 28 Feb. 1910; *s* of late Edward Hutton and Marion Hensley; *m* 1940, Dorothy Betty (*d* 1969), *d* of Percy George and Dorothy Coppard; one *s*. *Educ:* Malvern; Trinity Coll., Cambridge (Chancellor's Classical Medal, MA). Entered Min. of Agriculture and Fisheries, 1933; Priv. Sec. to Chancellor of Duchy of Lancaster and Minister of Food, 1939; Priv. Sec. to Minister of Agriculture and Fisheries, 1945; Asst Sec., 1946; Under Sec., 1957; retired 1970. member Agricultural Research Council, 1957-59. *Recreations:* ice skating, genealogy. *Address:* 162 Addiscombe Road, Croydon CRO 7LA. *T:* 01-654-3964. *Club:* United University.

**HENSON, Ronald Alfred,** MD, FRCP; Physician and Neurologist, The London Hospital, since 1949; Physician, National Hospital for Nervous Diseases, Maida Vale Hospital, since 1952; Director, British Empire Cancer Campaign Neuropathological Research Unit, London Hospital Medical College, 1967; *b* 4 Oct. 1915; *s* of Alfred and Nellie Henson, Chippenham, Wilts; *m* 1941, Frances, *d* of A. Francis and Jessie Sims, Bath;

three *d. Educ:* King Edward VI Sch., Bath; London Hospital Medical Coll. Major, RAMC, 1940-46. Mem., Archbishops' Commission on Divine Healing, 1953-57. Dir of Studies, Institute of Neurology, University of London, 1955-64. Secretary: Neurological Section, Royal Society of Medicine, 1956-58; Association of British Neurologists, 1964-68. Commonwealth Fellow 1964. Member: Assoc. of Physicians of Great Britain and Ireland; British Neuropathological Soc.; Hon. Corresponding Mem. Amer. Neurological Assoc., 1966. *Publications:* various contributions to learned journals and books on neurological subjects. *Address:* 26 Stormont Road, Highgate, N6. *T:* 01-340 6092. *Clubs:* Athenæum, MCC.

**HENTSCHEL, Christopher Carl,** MSc; FLS, FZS, FIBiol; Principal, Chelsea College of Science and Technology, 1962-65, retired; *b* 4 July 1899; *s* of Carl and Bertha Hentschel; unmarried. *Educ:* St Paul's Sch. (Classical Scholar); King's Coll., London. Demonstrator, in Biology, St Bartholomew's Med. Coll., 1923-31; Chelsea Polytechnic, later Chelsea Coll. of Science and Technology; Lectr in Zoology, 1931-53; Head, Dept of Botany and Zoology, 1953-61; Vice-Principal, 1961-62. Mem. of Senate, University of London, 1956-64, 1966-70. Vice-Pres., Linnean Soc. of London, 1943-44, 1950-51, 1952-53; Formerly Governor: Sloane & Rutherford Schs, London; Paddington Technical Coll.; Governor, Morehall Sch., Folkestone. *Publications:* (with W. R. Ivimey Cook) Biology for Medical Students, 1932; papers on parasitic Protozoa. *Recreations:* motoring; continental travel. *Address:* Flat A, Dolphin House, 117 Sandgate High Street, Folkestone, Kent. *T:* Folkestone 3809. *Club:* Folkstone Racing.

*See also I. J. C. Brown.*

**HENTY, Hon. Sir (Norman Henry) Denham,** KBE 1968; Leader of the Government in the Senate, Australia, 1966-67; Minister for Supply, 1966-68; Senator for Tasmania 1950-68; Commissioner, Overseas Telecommunications, since 1968; *b* 13 Oct. 1903; *s* of Thomas Norman and Lily Henty; *m* 1930, Faith Gordon Spotswood; two *s* one *d. Educ:* Launceston Church Grammar Sch. Managing Director, T. Norman Henty Pty Ltd, 1937-50. Chm., Public Works Cttee, 1955-56; Minister for Custons and Excise, 1956-64; Minister for Civil Agiation, 1964-66. Alderman, Launceston City Coun., 1943-50; Mayor, City of Launceston, 1948-49. *Recreations:* golf, billiards. *Address:* 11 Beulah Gardens, Launceston, Tasmania 7250, Australia. *T:* Launceston 2-3031. *Clubs:* Tasmanian (Hobart); Launceston, Northern (Launceston); Commercial Travellers Association (Australia).

**HENZE, Hans Werner;** Professor of Composition at Academy Mozarteum, Salzburg, Austria, since 1961; *b* 1 July 1926; *s* of Franz Gebhard Henze and Margarete Geldmacher. *Educ:* Bünde i/W; Bielefeld i/W; Braunschweig. Studying music in Heidelberg, 1945; First Work performed (Chamber Concerto), at Darmstadt-Kranichstein, 1946; Musical Dir, Municipal Theatre, Constance, 1948; Artistic Dir of Ballet, Hessian States Theatre, Wiesbaden, 1950. Definite departure for Italy, living first in Forio d'Ischia, then Naples, then Castelgandolfo as a Composer. Frequent international conducting tours. Prix d'Italia, 1953; Robert Schumann Prize, 1952; Berlin Prize of Artists, 1958; Nordrhein-Westphalian Award, 1955; Great Prize for Artists, Hanover, 1962. *Publications:* a book of Essays; 5 symphonies; 7 full length operas, 3 one-act operas; 5 normal ballets and five chamber ballets; chamber music; choral works. *Address:* 18 Via dei Laghi, Castelgandolfo, Rome, Italy.

**HEPBURN;** *see* Buchan-Hepburn.

**HEPBURN, Audrey;** actress; *b* Brussels, 4 May 1929; *d* of J. A. Hepburn; *m* 1st, 1954, Mel Ferrer (marr. diss. 1968); one *s*; 2nd, 1969, Dr Andrea Dotti; one *s*. Studied ballet in Amsterdam and in Marie Rambert's ballet sch. First stage part in musical production, High Button Shoes; first film appearance in Laughter in Paradise. Played leading rôles in Gigi (play), New York, 1951 (tour of America, Oct. 1952-May 1953); Ondine (play by Jean Giraudoux), 1954. *Films:* One Wild Oat, The Lavender Hill Mob; The Young Wives' Tale; The Secret People; Nous Irons à Monte Carlo; Roman Holiday, 1952; Sabrina Fair, 1954; War and Peace, 1956; Funny Face, 1957; Love in the Afternoon, 1957; The Nun's Story, 1958, also Green Mansions; The Unforgiven, 1960; Breakfast at Tiffany's, 1961; Paris When it Sizzles, 1962; Charade, 1962; My Fair Lady, 1964, How to Make a Million, 1966; Two for the Road, 1967; Wait Until Dark, 1968. *Address:* c/o Paramount Pictures Corporation, Paramount Building, 1501 Broadway, New York, NY 10036, USA.

**HEPBURN, Bryan Audley St John,** CMG 1962; Financial Secretary, Sarawak, 1958-63; Member, Sarawak Legislative and Executive Councils, 1955-63; Member, Inter-Governmental Committee which led to establishment of Federation of Malaysia; *b* 24 Feb. 1911; *m* 1940, Sybil Isabel Myers; two *d. Educ:* Cornwall Coll., Jamaica. Jamaica Civil Service, 1930; Asst Sec., Colonial Service, 1944; Principal Asst Sec., Sarawak, 1947; Development Sec., 1951. chm., Sarawak Devel. Finance Corp., 1958-63; Chm., Sarawak Electricity Supply Co. Ltd, 1955-63; Dir, Malayan Airways Ltd, 1959-63; Dir, Borneo Airways Ltd, 1958-63; Dep. Chm., Malaysian Tariff Adv. Bd, 1963-65. Ministry of Overseas Development, 1966-. *Recreations:* golf, swimming, fishing. *Address:* 7 Weald Rise, Haywards Heath, Sussex. *Clubs:* Royal Over-Seas League; Royal Commonwealth Society; Sarawak (Sarawak).

**HEPBURN, Katharine;** actress; *b* 9 Nov. 1909; *d* of late Dr Thomas N. Hepburn and Katharine Houghton; *m* Ludlow Ogden Smith (marr. diss.). *Educ:* Hartford; Bryn Mawr College. First professional appearance on stage, Baltimore, 1928, in Czarina; first New York appearance, 1928, in Night Hostess (under name Katherine Burns), The Millionairess, New Theatre, London, 1952. Entered films, 1932; notable films: A Bill of Divorcement; Morning Glory; Little Women; The Little Minister; Mary of Scotland; Quality Street; Stage Door; The Philadelphia Story; Keeper of the Flame; Dragon Seed; Woman of the Year; Under-current; Without Love; Sea of Grass; Song of Love; State of the Union; Adam's Rib; The African Queen; Pat and Mike; Summer Madness; The Iron Petticoat; The Rainmaker; His Other Woman; Suddenly, Last Summer; Long Day's Journey into Night; Guess Who's Coming to Dinner; The Madwoman of Chaillot; The Lion in Winter. *Stage:* Warrior's Husband; The Philadelphia Story; Without Love; As You Like It; Taming of the Shrew; Merchant of Venice; Measure for Measure, Australia, 1955; Coco, 1970. Academy Awards for performances in Morning Glory, Guess Who's Coming to Dinner, The Lion in Winter. *Address:* 201 Bloomfield Avenue, West Hartford, Conn 06117, USA.

**HEPBURN, Surg. Rear-Adm. Nicol Sinclair,** CBE 1968; QHP 1966; Medical Officer-in-Charge, RN Hospital, Haslar, since 1969; *b* 2 Feb. 1913; *s* of late John Primrose and Susan Hepburn, Edinburgh; *m* 1939, Dorothy Blackwood; two *s*. *Educ:* Broughton; Edinburgh Univ. MB, ChB 1935; DPH London, 1948; DIH London, 1952. Barrister-at-law, Gray's Inn, 1956. Joined RN, 1935; served during war in Atlantic and Pacific Stations; SMO, HM Dockyard: Plymouth, 1952; Portsmouth, 1955; Naval Medical Officer of Health: Portsmouth, 1959; Malta, 1962; Surg. Cdre and Dep. Med. Dir-Gen., 1966; Surg. Rear-Adm. 1969. FRSM. *Address:* Royal Naval Hospital, Haslar, Gosport, Hants. *Club:* Royal Naval (Portsmouth).

**HEPBURN, Prof. Ronald William;** Professor of Philosophy, University of Edinburgh, since 1964; *b* 16 March 1927; *s* of late W. G. Hepburn, Aberdeen; *m* 1953, Agnes Forbes Anderson; two *s*. *Educ:* Aberdeen Grammar Sch.; University of Aberdeen. MA 1951, PhD 1955 (Aberdeen). National service in Army, 1944-48. Asst, 1952-55, Lecturer, 1955-60, Dept of Moral Philosophy, University of Aberdeen; Visiting Associate Prof., New York University, 1959-60; Prof. of Philosophy, University of Nottingham, 1960-64. Stanton Lecturer in the Philosophy of Religion, Cambridge, 1965-68. *Publications:* (jointly) Metaphysical beliefs, 1957; Christianity and Paradox, 1958; chapters in: Objections to Humanism, 1963; Collected Papers on Aesthetics, 1965; Christian Ethics and Contemporary Philosophy, 1966; British Analytical Philosophy, 1966; contrib. to learned journals; broadcasts. *Recreations:* music, hill-walking, photography. *Address:* Department of Philosophy, University of Edinburgh, David Hume Tower, George Square, Edinburgh EH8 9JX.

**HEPBURNE-SCOTT,** family name of **Baron Polwarth.**

**HEPPEL, Richard Purdon,** CMG 1959; *b* 27 Oct. 1913; 2nd *s* of late Engineer Rear-Admiral Walter George Heppel and Margaret, *d* of late Robert Stevens Fraser; *m* 1949, Ruth Theodora, *d* of Horatio Matthews, MD; two *s* one *d*. *Educ:* Rugby Sch.; Balliol Coll., Oxford. Laming Travelling Fellow, Queen's Coll., 1935. Entered Diplomatic Service, 1936; Third Sec., Rome, 1939; Second Sec., Tehran, 1942; First Sec., Athens, 1944; Private Sec. to Min. of State, 1946; seconded to Office of UK High Commissioner, Karachi, 1948; First Sec., Madrid, 1951; Counsellor, HM Legation, Saigon, 1953-54; Ambassador to Cambodia, 1954-56; Minister at Vienna, 1956-59; Head of South East Asia Dept, Foreign Office, 1959; Head of Consular Dept, Foreign Office, 1961-63; Imperial Defence Coll., 1960; Consul-Gen. at Stuttgart, 1963; retd, 1969. Freeman, Skinners' Company, 1961, Liveryman 1969. *Address:* The Manor House, Princes Risborough, Bucks; Lacona, Isola d'Elba, Italy. *Club:* Travellers'.

**HEPPELL, Ralph Gordon,** FCA, AHA; Administrator and Secretary, The Royal Free Hospital Group, 1947-70, retired; *b* 24 Nov. 1910; *s* of Ralph Nicol Heppell and Annie Gordon; *m* 1940, Yvonne Jean Grant; one *s* two *d*. *Educ:* Durham Sch. ACA 1937; FCA 1960; aHA 1941. Dep. Clerk to Governors, Guy's Hosp., SE1, 1940-44; Superintendent-Sec., Christie Hospital, Manchester, 1944-47; Mem. of Cttee of Management of the Institute of Dental Surgery, Eastman Dental Hospital. *Publications:* various articles in hospital journals. *Recreations:* gardening, reading. *Address:* 3 Canon Street, Islington, N1. *T:* 01-226 6067.

**HEPPENSTALL, (John) Rayner;** novelist, poet and literary critic; *b* 27 July 1911; *s* of Edgar and Lizzie Heppenstall, Huddersfield, Yorks; *m* 1937, Margaret Harwood Edwards, Newport, Mon; one *s* one *d*. *Educ:* in Yorks (variously); Calais; University of Leeds; University of Strasbourg. Graduated (Modern Languages), 1933; schoolmaster, 1934; freelance author, 1935-39. Served War of 1939-45 Army (RA, Field, RAPC), 1940-45. Feature-writer and producer, BBC, 1945-65, Drama producer, 1965-67. *Publications:* First Poems, 1935; Apology for Dancing, 1936; Sebastian, 1937; The Blaze of Noon, 1939 (Arts Council Prize, 1966); Blind Men's Flowers are Green, 1940; Saturnine, 1943 (revised as The Greater Infortune, 1960); The Double Image, 1946; Poems, 1933-1945, 1946; The Lesser Infortune, 1953; Léon Bloy, 1954; Four Absentees, 1960; The Fourfold Tradition, 1961; The Connecting Door, 1962; The Woodshed, 1962; The Intellectual Part, 1963; Raymond Roussel: a critical guide, 1966; Portrait of the Artist as a Professional Man, 1969; The Shearers, 1969; A Little Pattern of French Crime, 1969; French Crime in the Romantic Age, 1970; edited: Existentialism (G. de Ruggiero), 1946; Imaginary Conversations, 1948; Architecture of Truth, 1957; (with Michael Innes) Three Tales of Hamlet, 1950; translated: Atala and René (Chateaubriand), 1963; Impressions of Africa (Roussel) (with Lindy Foord), 1966; A Harlot High and Low (Balzac), 1970; Miscarriage of Justice (Floriot), 1971. *Recreations:* variable. *Address:* 14c Ladbroke Terrace, W11. *T:* 01-727 4458. *Club:* PEN.

**HEPPENSTALL, Rayner;** *see* Heppenstall, John R.

**HEPPER, Anthony Evelyn;** CEng; MIMechE; Chairman, Upper Clyde Shipbuilders Ltd, since 1968; *b* 16 Jan. 1923; *s* of Lieut-Col J. E. Hepper. *Educ:* Wellington Coll., Berks. Royal Engrs, 1942-47 (retd as Hon. Maj.); Courtaulds Ltd, 1947-53; Cape Asbestos Co. Ltd 1953-57; Thomas Tilling Ltd, 1957-68 (Dir from 1963 until secondment), seconded as Industrial Adviser, DEA, 1966-67, and Mem., SIB, 1967. *Recreation:* golf. *Address:* 95 (L) Eaton Square, SW1. *T:* 01-245 9108; *Club:* Western (Glasgow).

**HEPPLE, (Robert) Norman,** RA 1961 (ARA 1954); RP 1948; NEAC, 1950; *b* 18 May 1908; *s* of Robert Watkin Hepple and Ethel Louise Wardale; *m* 1948, Jillian Constance Marigold Pratt; one *s* one *d*. *Educ:* Goldsmiths' Coll.; Royal Acad. Schools. Figure subject and portrait painter. *Address:* (studio) 16 Cresswell Place, SW10; 24 Cathcart Road, S Kensington, SW10. *T:* 01-352 0366. *Club:* Chelsea Arts.

**HEPPLESTON, Prof. Alfred Gordon;** Professor of Pathology, University of Newcastle upon Tyne (formerly Durham), since 1960; *b* 29 Aug. 1915; *s* of Alfred Heppleston, Headmaster, and Edith (*née* Clough); *m* 1942, Eleanor Rix Tebbutt; two *s*. *Educ:* Manchester Grammar Sch. Chief Asst, Professorial Medical Unit, University of Manchester; Asst Lecturer in Pathology, Welsh Nat. Sch. of Medicine, Univ. of Wales, 1944-47; Dorothy Temple Cross Research Fellow, Univ. of Pennsylvania, 1947-48; Sen. Lectr in Pathology, Univ. of Wales, 1948-60. *Publications:* on pathological topics, largely in reference to pulmonary disorders. *Recreations:* ornithology, cricket and music. *Address:* Department of Pathology, University of Newcastle upon Tyne, Royal Victoria

Infirmary, Newcastle upon Tyne NE1 4LP. *T:* Newcastle 25131; 44 Oakfield Road, Gosforth, Newcastle upon Tyne NE3 4HS. *T:* Newcastle 851541.

**HEPTINSTALL, Leslie George;** Deputy Senior Trade Commissioner, Montreal, 1968-70; *b* 20 Aug. 1919; *s* of late Victor George Heptinstall and of Maud Maunder; *m* 1949, Marion Nicholls; one *d*. *Educ:* Thames Valley County Sch.; London Univ. (BSc Econ.). Served War of 1939-45: Capt., Royal Artillery; Middle East, Mediterranean, North-West Europe. Asst Principal, Colonial Office, 1948; Principal, 1951; seconded to West African Inter-Territorial Secretariat, Accra, 1955; Acting Chief Sec., 1958; Acting Administrator, W African Research Office, 1959; Principal, CRO, 1961; First Sec. on Staff of Brit. High Comr, Wellington, NZ, 1962-64; Brit. Dep. High Comr, Lahore, 1964-65; Head of South Asia Dept, ODM, 1966-68. *Recreations:* sailing, golf and tennis. *Address:* 141 Richmond Road, Twickenham, Mddx.

**HEPWORTH, Dame Barbara,** DBE 1965 (CBE 1958); Sculptor; a Trustee of the Tate Gallery since 1965; *b* Wakefield, Yorks, 10 Jan. 1903; *d* of late H. R. Hepworth, CBE, and Gertrude A. Johnson; *m* 1st, John Skeaping, *qv* (marr. diss., 1933); one *s* (killed in action, RAF, 1953); 2nd, Ben Nicholson, *qv* (marr. diss., 1951); triplets: one *s* two *d*. *Educ:* Wakefield High Sch.; Leeds Sch. of Art; Royal Coll. of Art; Florence; Rome. Grand Prix, 5th São Paulo Biennial, 1959. Foreign Minister's Award, Mainichi Exhibition 7th Biennial, Tokyo, 1963. Hon. ARCA 1964. Hon. Fellow, St Annes Coll., Oxford, 1968. Hon. DLitt: Birmingham, 1960; Leeds, 1961; Exeter, 1966; Oxford, 1968. Bard of Cornwall, 1968. Hon. Freeman, St Ives, 1968. *Works: one-man exhibition* at 25th Biennale in Venice, Brit. Pavilion, 1950; *retrospective exhibitions:* Whitechapel Art Gall., 1954 and 1962; also in Paris, Amsterdam, Brussels, New York, Philadelphia, Chicago, (touring) Scandinavia, 1964-65, Rijksmuseum, Kröller-Müller, Holland, 1965, etc; Battersea Park Sculpture Exhibns, 1949, 1951, 1960, 1963, 1966 and in Holland Park, 1954, 1957; (2 sculptures) Festival of Britain 1951; Tate Gallery, 1968; also *out-door* Sculpture exhibitions in Europe and USA. Permanent London Gallery: Gimpel Fils and Marlborough Fine Art Ltd. *Works in permanent collections:* in London: Tate Gallery; Arts Council of Gt Britain; British Council; LCC; Victoria and Albert Museum; in USA; United Nations, New York; Museums of Modern Art, New York, Albright Gallery, Buffalo; Smith Coll. Museum; Yale Univ., Museum, and Steinberg Hall at Washington Univ.; in Scottish National Gallery of Modern Art, Edinburgh; National Galleries of Canada, Australia and New Zealand; Museum of Modern Art, São Paulo, Brazil; Mus. of Fine Art, Valparaiso, Chile; Museo de Bellas Artes, Caracas; Middelheimpark, Antwerp, Belgium; Gemeentemuseum, the Hague, and Rijksmuseum, Kröller-Müller, Holland; Dag Hammarskjöld Museum, Backakra, Sweden; Carlsberg Foundation, Denmark; The Marie-Louise and Gunnar Didrichsen Art Foundation, Helsinki, Finland; The Israel Museum, Jerusalem; The Ulster Museum, Belfast; Ferens Art Gallery, Hull; Glynn Vivian Art Gall., Swansea; Leeds, Manchester, Wakefield, Bristol, Birmingham and Aberdeen City Art Galleries; also Herts CC and Harlow and St Ives (Cornwall) Borough Councils. *Films:* film on her sculpture produced by British Film Institute, 1953; (BBC TV) 'Barbara Hepworth' (commentary by Barbara Hepworth and Bernard Miles), 1961; Westward Television Colour Film, 1967. *Publications:* 'Barbara Hepworth' Ariel Series, foreword William Gibson, 1946; 'Barbara Hepworth' Carvings and Drawings, foreword Herbert Read, 1952; Monograph 'Barbara Hepworth' Europäische Bildhauer, Allert de Lange, Amsterdam, 1958; 'Barbara Hepworth', foreword J. P. Hodin, 1961 (Edn Griffon, Neuchâtel); 'Barbara Hepworth' (monograph) Art in Progress Series, text by Michael Shepherd, 1962; 'Barbara Hepworh–Drawings from a Sculptor's Landscape', by Alan Bowness, 1966; Barbara Hepworth (Monograph), World of Art Series, text by Prof. A. M. Hammacher, 1968; The Pictorial Autobiography of Barbara Hepworth, 1970. *Recreations:* music, reading, dancing, gardening. *Address:* Trewyn Studio, St Ives, Cornwall. *T:* St Ives 6226.

**HERBAGE, Julian Livingston-;** musicologist, writer, broadcaster; *b* Woking, 10 Sept. 1904; *yr s* of late Walter Herbage and late Ruth Ann Livingston; *m* 1944, Anna (OBE 1966), *d* of late Sir Samuel Instone. *Educ:* Royal Naval Coll., Osborne and Dartmouth; St John's Coll., Cambridge (Choral Student). Arranged and conducted Love in a Village, Everyman Theatre, 1923; Conductor and Composer of incidental music, Savoy Theatre, 1924; Liverpool Repertory Theatre, 1925; joined BBC 1927; edited and conducted revivals of Operas, Cantatas, and Masques by Purcell, Arne, Handel, etc; organised Foundations of Music programmes, including From Plainsong to Purcell with Sir Richard Terry, Bach Celebration with Dr Sanford Terry, Handel and Scarlatti Celebrations with Prof. E. J. Dent; edited Purcell's King Arthur for performance at Queen's Hall, 1935; Asst Dir of Music, British Broadcasting Corporation, 1940-44; resigned from BBC, 1946; edited Handel's Messiah for special bicentenary broadcast, 1942; Chm. Henry Wood Concert Society, 1959-61. *Publications:* Arne's "Comus" (Musica britannica); Perseus and Andromeda (Operatic Masque after Handel); Suite from Purcell's King Arthur; Arne's Overture in B flat; The Humours of Bath (Suite); songs and instrumental pieces. *Books:* Messiah; Arnold Bax (Penguin British Music of our Time); Sibelius (Penguin Symphony series); Handel's Oratorios (Handel Symposium); The Baroque Era; contributions on musical subjects to various journals. *Address:* 8 Treborough House, Nottingham Place, W1.

**HERBERT,** family name of **Earls of Carnarvon, Pembroke, Powis,** and **Barons Hemingford** and **Tangley.**

**HERBERT, Sir Alan Patrick,** CH 1970; Kt 1945; author and barrister-at-law; Staff of Punch (A.P.H.); *b* 24 Sept. 1890; *e s* of P. H. Herbert, India Office, and Beatrice Selwyn; *m* 1914, Gwendolen, 2nd *d* of late Harry Quilter; one *s* three *d*. *Educ:* Winchester (Exhibitioner); New Coll., Oxford (Exhibitioner); 1st Class, Jurisprudence, 1914. Served with Royal Naval Division (Hawke Batt.), 1914-17; Gallipoli Peninsula (despatches); France (wounded); called to Bar, Inner Temple, 1918, but never practised; for two years Private Sec. to Sir Leslie Scott, KC, MP; began writing for Punch, 1910, joined Staff, 1924; represented Punch at Third Imperial Press Conference, Melbourne, Australia, 1925; MP (Ind.) Oxford Univ., 1935-50, when Univ. seats abolished; introduced in House of Commons in 1937 a Marriage Bill, passed into law as the Matrimonial Causes Act, 1937. Served with River Emergency Service, Thames, London, from 3 Sept. 1939, and joined Naval Auxiliary Patrol, June 1940. Petty Officer–two good conduct badges; a Thames Conservator, 1940;

Trustee National Maritime Museum, 1947-53. President: London Corinthian Sailing Club; Black Lion Skittles Club; Inland Waterways Assoc.; Soc. of Authors; Chm., British Copyright Council. Freeman of Hammersmith, 1969. Hon. Doctor of Laws, Queen's Univ., Kingston, Ont, 1957; DCL Oxford, 1958. *Publications:* The Bomber Gipsy; The Secret Battle; The House-by-the-River, Light Articles Only; The Wherefore and the Why; Tinker, Tailor . . .; The Man About Town; The Old Flame; Laughing Ann; She Shanties; Riverside Nights; Plain Jane; Misleading Cases; The Trials of Topsy; Topsy, MP; Honeybubble & Co.; La Vie Parisienne (adaptation); The Water Gipsies; More Misleading Cases; Ballads for Broadbrows; No Boats on the River, 1932; Still More Misleading Cases, 1933; Holy Deadlock, 1934; What a Word, 1935; Uncommon Law, 1935; Mild and Bitter, 1936; The Ayes Have It, 1937; Sip!, Swallow!, 1937; General Cargo, 1939; Siren Song, 1940; Let us be Glum, 1941; Well, Anyhow . . ., 1942; Bring Back The Bells, 1943; A Better Sky, Less Nonsense, 1944; Light the Lights, The Battle of the Thames, 1945; The Point of Parliament, 1946; Topsy Turvy, 1947; Mr Gay's London, 1948; A Book of Ballads; Topsy Omnibus, 1949; Independent Member, 1950; Number Nine, Come to the Ball (with Reginald Arkell), 1951; Full Enjoyment, Codd's Last Case, Why Waterloo?, 1952; Pools Pilot, 1953; The Right to Marry, 1954; No Fine on Fun, 1957; Made for Man, 1958; Look Back and Laugh (selection), 1960; Silver Stream, 1962; Bardot MP? And Other Modern Misleading Cases, 1964; Watch This Space, 1964; The Thames, 1966; Wigs at Work, 1966; Sundials or Fun with the Sun, 1967; The Singing Swan, 1968; In the Dark, 1969; A.P.H.: his life and times, 1970. *stage:* Two Gentlemen of Soho; *musical plays:* King of the Castle (with William Armstrong), Fat King Melon (for children), Riverside Nights (with Nigel Playfair); Plain Jane, the Blue Peter, Perseverance, Policeman's Serenade (one act); La Vie Parisienne, Tantivy Towers, Helen, Derby Day, Mother of Pearl, Paganini (with Reginald Arkell), Big Ben, Bless The Bride, Tough at the Top, The Water Gipsies; Streamline (with Ronald Jeans), Home and Beauty (Cochran revues). *Recreations:* sailing, lawn tennis, the piano, skittles, etc. *Address:* 12 Hammersmith Terrace, Hammersmith, W6. *T:* 01-748 1627. *Clubs:* Savage, Beefsteak, Grillions.

**HERBERT, Desmond Andrew,** CMG 1966; DSc; Emeritus Professor of Botany, University of Queensland; *b* 17 June 1898; *s* of Andrew Herbert; *m* 1922, Vera McNeilance Prowse; two *s* two *d*. *Educ:* Melbourne C of E Grammar Sch.; University of Melbourne. BSc 1918; MSc 1920; DSc 1931. Govt Botanist, W Australia, 1919-21; Prof. of Plant Physiology, University of Philippines, 1921-24; University of Queensland: Lectr in Botany, 1924-40; Associate Prof. of Botany, 1941-50; Dean, Faculty of Science, 1950-63; Prof. of Botany, 1950-65; Emer. Prof., 1966. Pres. of various learned societies. *Publications:* Gardening in Warm Climates, 1952; numerous papers in scientific jls. *Recreation:* horticulture. *Address:* 47 Adamson Street, Wooloowin, Queensland, Australia. *T:* Brisbane 62-3975.

**HERBERT, Lieut-Gen. Sir (Edwin) Otway,** KBE 1955 (CBE 1944); CB 1946; DSO 1940; retired as General Officer Commanding-in-Chief, Western Command (1957-60); Colonel Commandant, Royal Artillery 1956-66; *b* 18 Nov. 1901; *s* of late Gustavus Otway Herbert; *m* 1925, Muriel Irlam Barlow; one *d*. *Educ:* Felsted Sch.; Royal Military Academy, Woolwich. Commissioned Royal Artillery, 1921: served war of 1939-45; BEF France and Belgium, 1939-40 (despatches, DSO); 1st Army, 78 Div., North Africa, 1942-43 (bar to DSO); 21 Army Group, 1943-45 (despatches, CBE, CB); GOC British Troops, Berlin, and British Commandant, Berlin, 1947-49; Dir Territorial Army and Cadets, War Office, 1949-52; GOC 44 (Home Counties) Div. and District, 1952-53; GOC-in-C, West Africa Command, 1953-56. High Sheriff of Anglesey, 1964-65. Officer of Legion of Merit (USA); Knight Commander Orange Nassau (Netherlands); Commander of Leopold II (Belgium). *Recreations:* most outdoor sports available. *Address:* Llanidan House, Brynsiencyn, Anglesey. *T:* Brynsiencyn 393. *Club:* Army and Navy.

**HERBERT, George,** MBE; *b* 1892; *s* of William Herbert, York; *m* 1916, Elsie (*d* 1952), *d* of late G. E. Barton, York; one *s*. Served European War, France, 1914-19 (despatches, MBE) Major; Active Service, 1939-44 (despatches), Food Controller Gibraltar. MP (C) Rotherham, 1931-33; dir of companies. *Publications:* Trade Abroad; British Empire Ltd; The Call of Empire; Can Land Settlement Solve Unemployment?. *Recreations:* golf, fishing, cricket. *Address:* 27 Swan Road, Harrogate.

**HERBERT, Jesse Basil,** MC 1918; QC 1949; **His Honour Judge Herbert;** a Judge of the County Courts, Circuit 44, Westminster, since 1959 (34, Brentford etc, 1958-59, 58 and 41, Southend etc., 1957-58); *b* 17 March 1899; *s* of late Sir Jesse Herbert; *m* 1922, Hon. Isabella Russell Rea, *er d* of 1st Baron Rea; two *d*. *Educ:* Westminster; Christ Church, Oxford. Served in Flanders, 1918; Private Sec. to Rt Hon. H. H. Asquith, 1923-25; called to Bar, 1924: Master of the Bench of the Inner Temple, 1957. *Address:* 2 Crown Office Row, Temple, EC4. *T:* 01-583 5144. *Club:* Garrick.
*See also Sir T. A. Beevor, Bt.*

**HERBERT, Lieut-Gen. Sir Otway;** *see* Herbert, Lieut-Gen. Sir E. O.

**HERBERT, Roscoe,** CB 1952; CMG 1944; Member, Agricultural Market Development Executive Committee, since 1962; *b* 1895; *s* of late James Herbert; *m* Lillie May, *er d* of late Elisha Steward, Wolverhampton; one *s* one *d*. *Educ:* Wolverhampton Sch. Called to Bar, Middle Temple, 1930; entered Civil Service, 1913; Chief British Economic Adviser, North African Economic Board, French North Africa, 1942-43; Asst Dep. Dir-Gen. UNRRA, 1944-46; Under-Sec., Ministry of Food, 1947-54; Dep. Sec., Ministry of Food, 1954-55; Gen. Manager, Potato Marketing Bd, 1955-60. *Address:* Downside, Tennyson's Lane, Haslemere. *T:* Haslemere 2663.

**HERBERT, Walter Elmes,** MRCS, LRCP 1928; LDS, RCS 1925; FDS, RCS 1948; FRSM; Professor of Dental Surgery, University of London, 1938-67, now Emeritus; Director of Department of Conservative Dental Surgery, Guy's Hospital Dental School, 1931-67; Lecturer in Operative Dental Surgery, 1933-67; *b* Sept. 1902; *s* of H. W. Herbert, Egham, Surrey; *m* 1933, Joyce Mary Griffith Clogg, MB, BS; one *s* one *d*. *Educ:* Queen' Coll., Taunton; Guy's Hospital Medical and Dental Schools (travelling Dental Scholar, 1928); North Western Univ., Chicago; Demonstrator in Operative Dental Surgery, Guy's Hospital, 1929-31; Univ. Reader in Conservative Dental Surgery, 1933-38. Vis. Prof. of Dentistry, Sch. of Dentistry, Nat. Univ. of Iran, Tehran, 1969-70. *Publications:* Operative Dental Surgery (with J. B. Parfitt), 4th edn 1939, 5th edn 1944, 6th edn, 1948, 7th edn 1955 (with W. A.

Vale), 8th edn, 1962; Cancer of Stomach, in London, in Stockholm and in Amsterdam (jointly) Guy's Hospital Reports, 1939; The Training of the Dental Surgeon, 1962; and various contributions to British Dental Journal. *Recreations:* mountaineering, gardening. *Address:* 28 Worcester Road, Sutton, Surrey. *T:* 01-642 6284. *Club:* Alpine.

**HERBERT, Walter William;** *b* 24 Oct. 1934; *s* of Captain W. W. J. Herbert and Helen (*née* Manton); *m* 1969, Marie, *d* of Prof. C. A. McGaughey. Trained as surveyor in RE; Egypt, 1953-54, demob. 1955; travelled in Middle East, 1955; Surveyor with Falkland Is Dependencies Survey; Hope Bay, Antarctica, 1955-58; travelled in S America, 1958-59; Mem. expedn to Lapland and Spitzbergen, 1960; travelled in Greenaland, 1960; Surveyor, NZ Antarctic Expedn, 1960-62; leader Southern Party; mapped 26,000 sq. miles of Queen Maud Range and descended Amundsen's route to Pole on 50th anniv.; led expedn to NW Greenland, 1966-67; dog-sledged 1,400 miles Greenland to Canada in trng for trans-Arctic crossing; led British Trans-Arctic Expedn, 1968-69, which made 3,800-mile first surface crossing of Arctic Ocean from Alaska via North Pole to Spitzbergen (longest sustained sledging journey in history of Polar exploration). Polar Medal 1962, and clasp 1969; Livingstone Gold Medal, RSGS, 1969; Founder's Gold Medal, RGS, 1970. *Publications:* A World of Men, 1968; Across the Top of the World, 1969; (contrib.) World Atlas of Mountaineering, 1969; The Long Cold Walk, 1970; The Polar Deserts, 1971. *Recreations:* writing, painting. *Address:* c/o Royal Geographical Society, SW7. *Club:* Lansdowne.

**HERBERTSON, James John William,** MVO 4th class 1943; OBE 1918; Officer of Order of Orange Nassau, 1949; MA Oxon; *b* 29 Dec. 1883; *s* of James Grozier Herbertson, Glasgow; *m* 1919, Lilian, *d* of A. Rawlinson Wood, Denstone Coll.; two *d*. *Educ:* St Albans Sch.; Jesus Coll., Oxford. European War, HAC 1st Bn, 1914; Capt. 1918, GSO3 IV Army; Political Officer Inter-allied Rhineland High Commission, 1919-29; Acting British High Commissioner, 1929-30. Air Ministry and Ministry of Civil Aviation, 1937-50; retired, 1950. *Address:* 7 Westbourne Mansions, Sandgate Road, Folkestone, Kent. *T:* 53054.
*See also Rev. Canon B. C. Pawley.*

**HERBISON, Rt. Hon. Margaret McCrorie,** PC 1964; Lord High Commissioner of the Church of Scotland, since 1970; *b* 11 March 1907. *Educ:* Dykehead Public Sch., Schotts; Bellshill Acad.; Glasgow Univ. Teacher of English and History in Glasgow Schs; MP (Lab) North Lanark, 1945-70; Jt Parly Under-Sec. of State, Scottish Office, 1950-51; Minister of Pensions and National Insurance, Oct. 1964-Aug. 1966, of Social Security, 1966-67. Chm., Select Cttee on Overseas Aid, 1969-. Member National Executive Cttee, Labour Party; Chm. Labour Party, 1957. *Recreations:* reading, gardening. *Address:* 61 Shotts Kirk Road, Shotts, Lanarkshire. *T:* Shotts 159.

**HERCHENRODER, Sir (Marie Joseph Barnabe) Francis,** Kt, *cr* 1953; QC; Assistant Legal Adviser, Commonwealth Office, retired, 1968; *b* 13 Feb. 1896; 3rd *s* of late Sir Alfred Herchenroder, KC and Lady Herchenroder (*née* Vinton); *m* 1923, Marie Charlotte Paule Geneve; two *d*. *Educ:* Royal College, Mauritius; Middle Temple, London. Called to the Bar, 1919; District Magistrate, Mauritius, 1923; Additional Substitute Procureur and Advocate General, Mauritius, 1934; Substitute Procureur and Advocate General, Mauritius, 1938; KC 1943; Puisne Judge, Supreme Court, Mauritius, 1944; Procureur and Advocate General, Mauritius, 1945; Chief Justice, Mauritius, 1949-60. Coronation Medals, 1937, 1953. *Address:* 11 Pelham Court, Chelsea, SW3. *T:* 01-584 3937.

**HERCUS, Sir Charles Ernest,** Kt 1947; DSO 1918; OBE 1919; FRCP; FRACP; fRACS; retired 1958, as Dean of the Medical Faculty, University of Otago, New Zealand; Professor of Bacteriology and Public Health, 1922-58, Emeritus Professor since 1959; *b* 13 June 1888; *s* of Peter and Jane Hercus; *m* 1923; two *s* one *d*. *Educ:* Christchurch Boys' High Sch.; Otago Univ. Qualified in Dentistry and Medicine. Served European War, 1914-18, in the Field throughout, and overseas, War of 1939-45, in NZ TA, as OC Otago Univ. Medical Corps. *Publications:* The Otago Medical School under the First three Deans, 1963; numerous in medical journals. *Recreation:* tennis. *Address:* 19 Wallace Street, Dunedin, NZ. *T:* 20451. *Clubs:* University, Otago (Dunedin).

**HERD, Frederick Charles;** Assistant Under-Secretary of State (Civilian Management, General), Ministry of Defence, since 1970; *b* 27 April 1915. *Educ:* Strode's Sch., Egham; Sidney Sussex Coll., Cambridge. Asst Principal, Admiralty, 1937; Principal, 1941; Asst. Sec., 1950; Asst Under-Sec. of State, 1964. *Recreations:* music, lawn tennis, bridge. *Address:* 21 Cleveland Square, W2. *T:* 01-262 9020. *Clubs:* United University; Cumberland Lawn Tennis.

**HERD, Harold;** author and journalist; *b* 1893; *m* 1923, Kate, *y d* of late John Lancaster, Skipton; one *d*. Began journalistic career as a reporter on the West Yorkshire Pioneer; was successively Editor of the Flintshire News, Editor and Manager of the Flintshire Observer. Asst Editor of Mayfair, Editor of the Magazine of To-day, and Editor of To-day and To-morrow. Founded The Regent Institute (Principal, 1919-67); edited the Fleet Street Annual, 1930-59; contributed extensively to daily and weekly Press. Served in the Cheshire Regt, etc., 1915-18. *Publications:* The Making of Modern Journalism, 1927; The Newspaper of Tomorrow, 1930; Press Days, 1936; Panorama 1900-1942, 1942; Roman Road (play), 1945; The March of Journalism (a history of the British Press), 1952; Seven Editors, 1955; A Press Gallery, 1958, etc. Edited, the English Collection, the Writer's Library, the Outline Series, and various anthologies. *Recreations:* travel, reading, walking. *Address:* 79 Westbourne Terrace, W2. *T:* 01-262 9375.

**HEREFORD,** 18th Viscount *cr* 1550; **Robert Milo Leicester Devereux;** Bt 1611; Premier Viscount of England; *b* 4 Nov. 1932; *o s* of Hon. Robert Godfrey de Bohun Devereux (*d* 1934) and Audrey Maureen Leslie, DStJ 1963 (she *m* 2nd, 1961, 7th Earl of Lisburne, who *d* 1965), *y d* of late James Meakin, Westwood Manor, Staffs and of late Countess Sondes; *S* grandfather, 1952; *m* 1969, Susan Mary, *o c* of Major Maurice Godley, Ide Hill, Sevenoaks, Kent, and Mrs Glen Godley, Kingham, Oxon. *Educ:* Eton. OStJ. *Heir: kinsman* Rupert Montague Devereux [*b* 1907; *m* 1940, Joan Ursula, *d* of D. W. Thomas; two *d*]. *Address:* Hampton Court, Leominster, Herefordshire. *T:* Bodenham 234/235. *Clubs:* Turf; House of Lords Yacht; Anglo-American Sporting.

**HEREFORD, Bishop of,** since 1961; **Rt. Rev. Mark Allin Hodson;** *b* 1907; *s* of Albert Edgar Hodson, Solicitor; *m* 1959, Susanna Grace, *e d* of late Arthur Hugh Lister, CMG. *Educ:* Enfield Grammar Sch.; University Coll.,

London (BA); Wells Theological Coll. Ordained 1931; Asst Curate St Dunstan, Stepney, 1931-35; Missioner St Nicholas, Perivale, 1935-40; Rector of Poplar, 1940-55. Officiating Curate-in-charge of All Hallows, E India Docks, 1942-52; St Stephen, Poplar, 1943-52; St Frideswide, Poplar, 1947-52; Prebendary of Newington in St Paul's Cathedral, London, 1951-55; Suffragan Bishop of Taunton, 1955-61, also Prebendary and Rector of St Michael and All Angels, Dinder, diocese of Bath and Wells, 1956-61. *Recreation:* travel. *Address'* Bishop's House, The Palace, Hereford. *T:* Hereford 2823. *Club:* Athenæum.

**HEREFORD, Assistant Bishop of;** *see* Partridge, Rt Rev. W. A.

**HEREFORD, Dean of;** *see* Rathbone, Very Rev. N. S.

**HEREFORD, Archdeacon of;** *see* Lewis, Ven. J. W.

**HEREN, Louis Philip;** American Editor and Chief Washington Correspondent of The Times; *b* 6 Feb. 1919; *s* of William Heren and Beatrice (*née* Keller); *m* 1948, Patricia Cecilia O'Regan; one *s* three *d. Educ:* St George's Sch., London. Army, 1939-46. Foreign Corresp. of The Times, 1947-; India, 1947-48; Israel and Middle East, 1948-50; Southeast Asian Corresp., 1951-53; Germany, 1955-60. War Correspondent: Kashmir, 1947; Israel-Arab war, 1948; Korean war, 1950. Hannan Swaffer Award for Internat. Reporting, 1967; John F. Kennedy Memorial Award, 1968. *Publications:* New American Commonwealth, 1968; No Hail, No Farewell, 1970. *Address:* 4016 48th Street NW, Washington, DC 20016, USA. *T:* 966-8284. *Club:* National Press (Washington, DC).

**HERFORD, Geoffrey Vernon Brooke,** CBE 1956 (OBE 1946); MSc; FIBiol; Director of Pest Infestation Research, Agricultural Research Council, 1946-68, retired; *b* 1905; *s* of late Henry J. R. Herford, Hampstead; *m* 1933, Evelyn Cicely, *d* of W. G. Lambert. *Educ:* Gresham's School, Holt; Magdalen College, Oxford (BA); Minnesota University (MSc). *Address:* 57 Langley Road, Slough, Bucks.

**HERIOT, Alexander John,** MS, FRCS; Surgeon, King's College Hospital; *b* 28 May 1914; *s* of Robert Heriot; *m* 1940, Dr Christine Stacey (*d* 1958); two *s*; *m* 1959, Dr Cynthia Heymeson; one *s* one *d.* Major RAMC. *Address:* 261 Trinity Road, SW18.

**HERITAGE, Rev. Canon Thomas Charles;** Canon Residentiary of Portsmouth Cathedral since 1964; *b* 3 March 1908; *s* of Thomas and Sarah Ellen Heritage; *m* 1934, Frances Warrington; twin *d. Educ:* The King's Sch., Chester; St Edmund Hall, Oxford. BA 1929; MA 1944; Diploma in Education (Oxford), 1930; ATCL 1931. Deacon, 1934; Priest, 1938. Curate of Christ Church, Chesterfield and Asst Master, Chesterfield Grammar Sch., 1934-38; Asst Master, Portsmouth Grammar Sch., 1938-64; Curate of St Mark, Portsmouth, 1938-40, St Christopher, Bournemouth, 1940-44; Chaplain of Portsmouth Cathedral, 1945-64. Hon. Canon, 1958-64. Examining Chaplain to the Bishop of Portsmouth, 1965-. Warden, Portsmouth Diocesan Readers' Assoc., 1966. *Publications:* A New Testament Lectionary for Schools, 1943; The Early Christians in Britain (with B. E. Dodd), 1966. *Recreations:* music, the theatre, reading, fell-walking. *Address:* 13 Pembroke Road, Old Portsmouth, Hants. *T:* Portsmouth 22673. *Club:* Royal Naval (Portsmouth).

**HERKLOTS, Geoffrey Alton Craig,** CBE 1961; MSc, PhD; FLS; *b* Naini Tal, India, 10 Aug. 1902; *er s* of late Rev. Bernard Herklots, MA; *m* 1932, Iris, *yr d* of late Capt. Philip Walter, RN; two *s* one *d. Educ:* Trent Coll., Derbyshire; University of Leeds; Trinity Hall, Cambridge. Reader in Biology, University of Hong Kong, 1928-45; interned at Stanley Camp, Hong Kong, Jan. 1942-Aug. 1945; Secretary for Development, Hong Kong, 1946-48; Secretary for Colonial Agricultural Research, Colonial Office, London, 1948-53. Principal and Director of Research, Imperial College of Tropical Agriculture, Trinidad, 1953-60, retired 1961. Colombo Plan Botanical Adviser to HM Government of Nepal, 1961-63. Corresp. Member Zoological Society. *Publications:* Common Marine Food Fishes of Hong Kong, 1936, 1940; The Birds of Hong Kong, Field Identification and Field Note Book, 1946, 1952; Vegetable Cultivation in Hong Kong, 1941, 1947; The Hong Kong Countryside, 1951; Hong Kong Birds, 1953; Birds of Trinidad and Tobago, 1961, etc. Editor: Hong Kong Naturalist, 1930-41; Journal of Hong Kong Fisheries Research Station, 1940. *Recreations:* drawing, gardening, walking. *Address:* Vanners, Chobham, Woking, Surrey. *T:* Chobham (Woking) 8109. *Club:* Athenæum.

**HERKLOTS, Rev. Hugh Gerard Gibson,** MA, DD; Moderator of the Church Colleges of Education, 1959-67; Residentiary Canon of Peterborough, since 1959; *b* Sikandra, India, 5 Sept. 1903; *s* of late Rev. Bernard Herklots, MA, and late Emily Frances Bazeley; *m* 1930, Helen Beveridge, *d* of late Professor Murgoci, Bucarest; two *s* two *d. Educ:* Trent Coll., Derbyshire; Ordination Test Sch., Knutsford; Trinity Hall and Ridley Hall, Cambridge. MA (Cantab) 1929. Editor of the Granta, 1925-26; President Cambridge Union Society, 1926; Curate of Holy Trinity, St Marylebone, 1927-30; Canon of St John's Cathedral, Winnipeg; Professor of Exegetical Theology in St John's Coll., 1930-36; Member of the Council of the University of Manitoba, 1933-36; Member of the General Synod of the Church of England in Canada, 1934; Rector of Flixton near Manchester, 1936-41; Commissary to Archbishop of Rupert's Land, 1936; Youth Secretary, British Council of Churches, 1942-45; Director of Religious Education, Diocese of Sheffield, 1945-51; Vicar of Doncaster, 1951-59; Hon. Canon of Sheffield, 1945-59; Examining Chaplain to the Bishop of Manchester, 1938-41; Select Preacher, Cambridge University, 1943, 1955; Member, Youth Advisory Council (Board of Education), 1942-45; Archbishops' Evangelistic Commission, 1944; Associate of the Sheffield Society of Artists, 1951; Delegate to Second Assembly of World Council of Churches, 1954; Member Commission for Revision of Catechism, 1958. Hon. DD, St John's Coll., Manitoba, 1967. *Publications:* Jack of All Trades, 1926; The New Universities, 1928; Hospital Sketches (edited), 1929; Paper Aeroplanes, 1931; Not as the Scribes, 1934; The First Winter, 1935; The Yoke of Christ, 1938; Hear our Prayer, 1940; For Such a Time as This, 1945; Philippians (Devotional Commentary), 1946; These Denominations, Grant us Thy Salvation, 1946; Pilgrimage to Amsterdam, 1947; Nathan Söderblom, 1948; Amsterdam 1948, 1948; A Fresh Approach to the New Testament, 1950; Magnificent Heritage, 1950; The Hope of our Calling, 1954; How Our Bible Came to Us, 1954; Publicans and Sinners, 1956; Operation Firm Faith, 1957; The Ten Commandments and Modern Man, 1958; The Gospel in a World of Conflict, 1960; Frontiers of the Church, 1961; The Call of God, 1962; Behind the New

Testament, 1962; The Church of England and the American Episcopal Church, 1966; The People of God, 1968; An Old Testament Dozen, 1970. *Recreations:* reading, writing, painting. *Address:* Canonry House, 14 Minster Precincts, Peterborough. *T:* 62125. *Club:* Athenæum.

**HERLIE, Eileen;** Actress; *b* 8 March 1920; *d* of Patrick Herlihy (Irish) and Isobel Cowden (Scottish); *m* 1st, 1942, Philip Barrett; 2nd, 1951, Witold Kuncewicz. *Educ:* Shawlands Academy, Glasgow. Varied repertoire with own company, 1942-44; Old Vic, Liverpool, 1944-45; Lyric Theatre, Hammersmith, 1945-46; Andromache in Trojan Women, Alcestis in Thracian Horses, Queen in Eagle has Two Heads, 1946-47; Gertrude in Hamlet (Film), 1948; Medea, 1949; Angel with the Trumpet (Film), 1949; Paula in The Second Mrs Tanqueray, Haymarket, 1950-51; Helen D'Oyly Carte in Gilbert and Sullivan (Film), 1952; Mother in Isn't Life Wonderful? (Film), 1952; John Gielgud Season, 1953: Mrs Marwood in The Way of the World; Belvidera in Venice Preserv'd; Irene in Sense of Guilt, 1953; Mrs Molloy in The Matchmaker, 1954; She Didn't Say No! (Film), 1958; acted in George Dillon (New York), 1958; Take Me Along (New York), 1959; All America (New York), 1963; The Queen in Hamlet (New York), 1964. *Recreations:* riding, reading, music. *Address:* c/o Witt Associates Inc., 34 West 57th Street, New York, USA.

**HERMAN, Josef;** painter; *b* 3 Jan. 1911; *m* 1955, Eleanor Ettlinger; one *s* (one *d* decd). *Educ:* Warsaw. First exhibition, Warsaw, 1932; left for Belgium, 1938; arrived in Britain, June 1940; lived in: Glasgow, 1940-43; Ystradgynlais (mining village, Wales), 1944-53. Exhibitions include: Glasgow, 1942; Edinburgh, 1942; London, 1943; Roland, Browse and Delbanco Gallery, 1946-; British Council; Arts Council; (retrospective) Whitechapel Art Gallery, 1962; New Grafton Gallery, 1970. Work in permanent collections: Arts Council; British Council; National Museum, Cardiff; Contemporary Art Society; National Museum Bezalel, Jerusalem; National Gallery, Johannesburg; Tate Gallery, London; Victoria and Albert Museum, London; National Gallery, Melbourne; National Gallery, Ottawa; National Gallery, Wellington, etc. Gold Medal, Royal National Eisteddfod, Llanelly, 1962; Contemporary Art Society prize, 1952 and 1953; prize, John Moore Exhibition, 1956; Trust House Award, 1962. *Address:* Holly Lodge, Little Cornard, near Sudbury, Suffolk. *T:* Sudbury 3187.

**HERMANN, Alexander Henry Baxter;** Counsellor of British Embassy, Washington, 1967; *b* 28 Dec. 1917; *m* 1944, Eudoksia Eugenia Domnina; one *d.* Joined Foreign Service, 1939; served 1942-55; Peking, Ahwaz, Chengtu, Chungking, Shanghai, Quito, Panama, Tamsui; Foreign Office, 1956; Commercial Counsellor and Consul-General, Rangoon, 1957-61; HM Consul-General at Marseilles, also to Monaco, 1961-65; Diplomatic Service Inspector, 1965-66. *Address:* c/o British Embassy, Washington, DC, USA. *Club:* Oriental.

**HERMES, Gertrude,** ARA 1963; RE; sculptor; wood engraver; Teacher of wood engraving, Royal Academy Schools, W1; *b* Bickley, Kent, 1901; *m*; one *s* one *d. Educ:* Belmont, Bickley, Kent; Leon Underwood's Sch., London. Portrait Sculpture and decorative carving for buildings; wood engraving decorations for books; fountain and door furniture, Shakespeare Memorial Theatre, Stratford-on-Avon; Britannia Window, British Pavilion, Paris, 1937; 3 glass panels, British Pavilion, World's Fair, NY, 1939; Engravings for books, for: Cressett Press, Swan Press, Golden Cockerel Press, Penguin Books Ltd, etc.; member of: London Group; Society of Wood-engravers. *Recreations:* swimming and fishing. *Address:* 31 Danvers Street, Chelsea, SW3. *T:* 01-352 4006.

**HERMON-HODGE,** family name of **Baron Wyfold.**

**HERNIMAN, Ven. Ronald George;** Archdeacon of Barnstaple, and Rector of Shirwell with Loxhore, since 1970; *b* 18 April 1923; *s* of George Egerton and Rose Herniman; *m* 1949, Grace Jordan-Jones; one *s* two *d. Educ:* Geneva; Bideford, Devon. Served RAF, 1941-46. Birkbeck Coll., London Univ., 1948-51 (BA); Oak Hill Theological Coll., 1951-53; Tutor, Oak Hill Coll., 1953-54; Asst Curate, Christ Church, Cockfosters, 1954-56; Dir of Philosophical Studies, Oak Hill, 1956-61; Rector of Exe Valley Group of Churches (Washfield, Stoodleigh, Withleigh, Calverleigh Oakford, Morebath, Rackenford, Loxbeare and Templeton), 1961-70. *Recreations:* sailing; making and mending things. *Address:* The Rectory, Shirwell, near Barnstaple, Devon. *T:* Shirwell 371.

**HERON, Conrad Frederick,** CB 1969; OBE 1953; Deputy Under Secretary of State, Department of Employment and Productivity, since 1968; *b* 21 Feb. 1916; *s* of Richard Foster Heron and Ida Fredrika Heron; *m* 1948, Envye Linnéa Gustafsson; two *d. Educ:* South Shields High Sch.; Trinity Hall. Entered Ministry of Labour, 1938; Principal Private Secretary to Minister of Labour, 1953-56; Under-Secretary, Industrial Relations Dept, 1965-68. (Industrial Relations Dept, 1963-64; Overseas Dept. 1964-65). *Address:* 80 Skeena Hill, SW18. *T:* 01-788 6881.

**HERON, (Cuthbert) George;** Recorder of Lichfield since 1968; *b* 8 April 1911; *s* of late Lieut-Commander George Heron, RN, and late Kate Heron; *m* 1937, Maud Mary Josephine Hogan; one *s* one *d. Educ:* St Bede's Coll., Manchester; Manchester Univ. (LLB). Solicitor, 1934; called to Bar, Middle Temple, 1944; Oxford Circuit. Served RAF, 1939-45 (Flt-Lieutenant). *Recreations:* reading, motoring, foreign travel. *Address:* 160 Wake Green Road, Moseley, Birmingham 13. *T:* 021-777 1960; 4 Fountain Court, Birmingham 4. *T:* 021-236 3476/7. *Clubs:* Union, Worcestershire (Worcester).

**HERON, George;** *see* Heron, C. G.

**HERON, Patrick;** painter; *b* 30 Jan. 1920; *e s* of T. M. and Eulalie Heron; *m* 1945, Delia Reiss; two *d. Educ:* St Ives, Cornwall; Welwyn Garden City; St Georges, Harpenden; Slade School. Art critic to: New English Weekly, 1945-47; New Statesman and Nation, 1947-50; London correspondent, Arts (NY), 1955-58. One-man exhibitions: Redfern Gallery, London, 1947, 1948, 1950, 1951, 1954, 1956 and 1958; Waddington Galleries, London, 1959, 1960, 1963, 1964, 1965, 1967, 1968, 1970; Bertha Schaefer Gallery, NY, 1960, 1962 and 1965; Galerie Charles Lienhard, Zürich, 1963; Traverse Theatre Gallery, Edinburgh, 1965, etc; Retrospective exhibitions: Wakefield City Art Gallery, Leeds, Hull, Nottingham, 1952; Richard Demarco Gallery, Edinburgh, 1967; Museum of Modern Art, Oxford, 1968; Kunstnernes Hus, Oslo, 1967. Twelve paintings shown at São Paulo Bienal II, Brazil, 1953-54. Carnegie International, Pittsburgh, 1961. One-man exhibition at São Paulo Bienal VIII, 1965 (awarded Silver Medal) (exhibition toured S America, 1966); exhibited in group and British Council exhibitions in many countries; works owned by: Tate Gallery; Arts Council; British Council; V&A Museum; British Museum; Gulbenkian Foundation; Leeds City Art Gallery; Stuyvesant Foundation; National Portrait Gallery; Broadcasting House; Warwick Univ.; Wakefield City Art Gallery; Manchester City Art Gallery; Contemporary Art Society; Cecil Higgins Art Gallery, Bedford; Oldham Art Gallery; CEMA, N Ireland; Abbot Hall Art Gallery, Kendal; The Art Gallery, Aberdeen; National Gallery of Wales, Cardiff; Toronto Art Gallery; Montreal Museum of Fine Art; Vancouver Art Gallery; Toledo Museum of Art, Ohio; Smith College Museum of Art, Mass; Brooklyn Museum, NY; Albright-Knox Art Gallery, Buffalo, NY; University of Michigan Museum of Art; Boymans Museum, Rotterdam; Musée d'Art Contemporain, Montreal; National Gallery of W Australia, Perth; Pembroke and Nuffield Colleges, Oxford; Stirling Univ.; Bristol City Art Gall., etc. Awarded Grand Prize by international jury, John Moores' 2nd Liverpool Exhibition, 1959. *Publications:* The Changing Forms of Art, 1955. *Address:* Eagle's Nest, Zennor, near St Ives, Cornwall. *T:* St Ives 6921.

**HERON-MAXWELL, Sir Patrick Ivor,** 9th Bt of Springkell, *cr* 1683; *b* 26 July 1916; *o s* of 8th Bt and Norah, *d* of late Hon. Francis Parker; *S* father, 1928; *m* 1942, D. Geraldine E., *y d* of late C. Paget Mellor, Letchworth, Herts, and Victoria, BC; three *s*. *Educ:* Stowe. *Heir: s* Nigel Mellor Heron-Maxwell, *b* 30 Jan. 1944. *Address:* 9 Cowslip Hill, Letchworth, Herts.

**HERRICK, Frederick Charles;** painter and designer; engaged on experimental research into the relationship between impression and design; Fellow British Institute of Industrial Art; Member Art Workers' Guild and Fellow Society of Industrial Artists; NRD; *b* Mountsorrel, Leicestershire, 20 Sept. 1887; *y s* of Thomas Herrick, Mountsorrel; *m* 1931, Lily, *y d* of William Ray, Basingstoke; one *s*. *Educ:* Alderman Newton's Sch., Leicester; Leicester College of Arts and Crafts (Mulready Prize); the Royal College of Art; gained Royal Exhibition tenable at the Royal College of Art, 1908; awarded Travelling Scholarship in painting, 1912; served with Grenadier Guards, 1914-19 (severely wounded at Hulluch, 1915); poster and commercial designer with the Baynard Press, 1919-26; awarded Diploma at the International Exhibition of Decorative Art, Italy, 1923; awarded Grand Prix at the International Exhibition of Modern Decorative and Industraial Art, Paris, 1925; formerly Instructor of Drawing at Royal College of Art; Instructor of Drawing and Illustrative Design at Sir John Cass Technical Institute; Instructor of drawing, painting, composition, and anatomy in action at Brighton College of Art; Examiner in Drawing and Painting for East Midlands Educational Union; Professional Inspector (Board of Education) in Illustrative Design; Professional Examiner (Board of Education) in Pictorial Design; Chief Professional Examiner (Board of Education) in Industrial Design; Assessor for Diploma (Scottish Education Department) in Industrial Design. *Principal Works:* Mural decorations at Plymouth, Southampton, Reading, and Brighton; many posters, chiefly for London Underground Railways, Royal Mail Steam Packet Co., LCC, and Empire Marketing Board; numerous commercial devices, including the Wembley Lion and the emblem Truth in Advertising, for the International Advertising Convention. *Recreations:* rowing and sailing. *Address:* 44 Selborne Road, Hove, Sussex BN3 3AH.

**HERRICK, Rev. Canon Richard William;** Canon Residentiary of Chelmsford Cathedral, since 1957; Vice-Provost of Chelmsford Cathedral since 1962; Director of Laity Training since 1967; *b* 3 Dec. 1913; *s* of W. Herrick, Retford, Notts; *m* 1943, Ann L. Sparshott; two *s* one *d*. *Educ:* King Edward VI Sch., Retford; Leeds University; College of the Resurrection, Mirfield. Civil Servant, 1930-34. BA Leeds, 1937; Deacon, 1939; Priest, 1940; Curate of Duston, 1939-41; Curate of St Mark's, Portsea, 1941-47; Vicar of St Michael's, Northampton, 1947-57; Director of Religious Education for the Diocese of Chelmsford, 1957-67. *Address:* 208 New London Road, Chelmsford, Essex. *T:* Chelmsford 54318.

**HERRIDGE, Geoffrey Howard,** CMG 1962; Chairman, Iraq Petroleum Co. Ltd and Associated Companies, 1965-70, retired (Managing Director, 1957-63; Deputy Chairman, 1963-65); *b* 22 Feb. 1904; 3rd *s* of late Edward Herridge, Eckington, Worcestershire; *m* 1935, Dorothy Elvira Tod; two *s* two *d*. *Educ:* Crypt Sch., Gloucester; St John's Coll., Cambridge. Joined Turkish Petroleum Co. Ltd (later Iraq Petroleum Co. Ltd), Iraq, 1926; served in Iraq, Jordan, Palestine, 1926-47; General Manager in the Middle East, Iraq Petroleum Co. and Associated Companies, 1947-51; Executive Director, 1953-57; Member of London Cttee, Ottoman Bank, 1964. Chairman, Petroleum Industry Training Board, 1967-70. *Address:* Flint, Sidlesham Common, Chichester, Sussex. *T:* Sidlesham 357. *Club:* Oriental.

**HERRIES, Michael Alexander Robert Young-,** OBE 1968; MC 1945; Chairman and Managing Director, Jardine Matheson & Co. Ltd, since 1963; *b* 28 Feb. 1923; *s* of Lieut-Colonel William Dobree Young-Herries and Ruth Mary (*née* Thrupp); *m* 1949, Elizabeth Hilary Russell (*née* Smith); two *s* one *d*. *Educ:* Eton; Trinity Coll., Cambridge (MA). Joined Jardine Matheson & Co. Ltd, 1948; served in Hong Kong, Japan and Singapore; Director, 1959; Managing Director, 1962. *Recreations:* shooting, walking, swimming, tennis. *Address:* Strawberry Hill, 36 Plantation Road, Hong Kong. *T:* Hong Kong 96148; Jardine Penthouse, Jardine House, Hong Kong. *T:* Hong Kong 228263; 9 Shek O, Hong Kong. *T:* Hong Kong 94489; Spottes, Castle Douglas, Kirkcudbrightshire. *T:* Haugh of Urr 202. *Clubs:* Caledonian, Farmers', City of London; Hong Kong Country, The Hong Kong, Royal Hong Kong Yacht, Hong Kong Cricket, Sheko Country (Hong Kong).

**HERRING, Lt-Gen. Hon. Sir Edmund Francis,** KCMG 1949; KBE 1943 (CBE 1941); DSO 1919; MC; ED; Lieutenant-Governor of Victoria since 1945; Chief Justice of Supreme Court of Victoria, 1944-64; Chancellor of Archdiocese of Melbourne since 1941; Hon. Fellow of New College, Oxford, 1949; Hon. Bencher Inner Temple, 1963; *b* 2 Sept. 1892; *s* of Edmund Selwyn Herring and Gertrude Stella Fetherstonhaugh; *m* 1922, Dr Mary Ranken Lyle (*see* Dame Mary Ranken Herring); three *d*. *Educ:* Melbourne Grammar Sch.; TRinity Coll., Melbourne; New Coll., Oxford. MA, BCL; Barrister, Inner Temple, 1920; called to Bar, Melbourne, 1921; KC 1936. King Edward's Horse, July-Dec. 1914; RFA, Dec. 1914-Feb. 1919; BEF France and Macedonia (DSO, MC, despatches); war of 1939-45 (CBE, KBE): CRA 6th Div., AIF, 1939-41; commanded 6th Div., AIF, 1941-42; General Officer Commanding: Northern Territory Force, 1942; New Guinea Force,

1942-43; 1 Australian corps, 1942-44; Director-General of Recruiting, Australia, 1950-51. GMC 1 (Greece) 1941; DSC (USA) 1943. Chairman Trustees, Shrine of Remembrance, Melbourne, 1945-; President: Toc H, Australia, 1947-; Australian Boy Scouts' Association, 1959-; Boy Scouts Assoc. of Victoria, 1945-68. Chairman Trustees, National War Memorial, Canberra, 1959-. Leader, Australian Coronation Contingent, 1953. Hon. DCL (Oxford) 1953. KStJ 1953. *Recreation:* golf. *Address:* 226 Walsh Street, South Yarra, Victoria 3141, Australia. *T:* 26 1000. *Clubs:* Melbourne, Naval and Military (Melbourne).

**HERRING, Dame Mary Ranken,** DBE 1960; *b* 31 March 1895; *d* of late Sir Thomas Lyle, DSc, FRS and Lady Lyle, CBE; *m* 1922, Edmund Francis Herring (*see* Lieut-General Hon. Sir Edmund Francis Herring); three *d. Educ:* Toorak College and Melbourne University. MB, BS, Melbourne, 1921. Medical Officer, Ante-Natal Clinics, Prahran and South Melbourne, 1926-45; Vice-President, Melbourne District Nursing Society; Vice-President and President, AIF Women's Association, 1939-47; President, Council of Toorak Coll., 1948-; Vice-Chairman, British Commonwealth Youth Sunday, 1947-59; Chairman of Trustees, V. S. Brown Memorial Fund; Dep. President, Victoria League in Victoria, 1945-; Dep. President, Red Cross in Victoria, 1945-; Member Advisory Council on Child Welfare, 1956-61. CStJ, 1953. *Recreations:* gardening, lawn Tennis and golf. *Address:* 226 Walsh Street, South Yarra, Victoria 3141, Australia. *T:* 26 1000. *Clubs:* Lyceum, Alexandra (Melbourne); Royal Melbourne Golf; Barwon Heads Golf.

**HERRING, Robert;** *b* London, 13 May 1903; *y s* of Arthur Herring and Clara Helena Williams. *Educ:* Clifton Coll.; King's Coll., Cambridge. MA (Cantab), 1928, History and 2nd Class Hons English; Asst Editor, The London Mercury, 1925-34; film critic on The Manchester Guardian, 1928-38; incorporated The London Mercury in Life and Letters, 1938; Editor, Life and Letters, 1935-50. *Publications:* The President's Hat (travel), 1926; Films of the Year, 1928; Adam and Evelyn at Kew (novel), 1930; Cactus Coast; The Impecunious Captain (play), 1944; Westward Look (poems), 1946; The Life and Death of St George; edited Plays of Sheridan and of Goldsmith in English Literature Series, 1927-34; (Jt) Leaves in the Storm, 1948; Happy Days and Holidays, 1949. *Recreation:* old age. *Address:* 7(W), Chelsea Embankment, SW3.

**HERRINGTON, Hugh Geoffrey,** CBE 1954; *b* 28 Sept. 1900; *s* of Hugh William Herrington; *m* 1926, Olive, *d* of James Procter. *Educ:* Bablake Sch., Coventry, Warwickshire. Director, High Duty Alloys Ltd. *Recreations:* cricket, tennis. *Address:* Clevehurst, Stoke Poges, Bucks.

**HERRON, Hon. Sir Leslie James,** KBE 1966; CMG 1964; Chief Justice of the Supreme Court of NSW since 1962; *b* 22 May 1902; *s* of Henry Herron; *m* 1930, Andree L., *d* of late F. Leverrier, KC; one *d. Educ:* Sydney Grammar Sch.; University of Sydney. Admitted Bar, 1925; KC 1939. Acting Judge, 1939; Judge of Supreme Court, 1941; Acting Chief Justice, March-Oct. 1962. Trustee: Australian Museum; Sydney Cricket Ground. President: NSW Div., St John Ambulance Assoc.; Australian Golf Club. KStJ 1964. *Recreation:* golf. *Address:* Mevagissey, 6 Mannerin Place, Castle Cove, NSW 2069, Australia. *T:* 403286. *Clubs:* Australian, Australian Jockey (Sydney); Royal Automobile of Australia.

**HERRON, Shaun;** Senior Leader Writer, Winnipeg Free Press, since 1964 (Correspondent in USA, 1960-64); *b* 23 Nov. 1912; *s* of late Thomas and Mary Herron, Carrickfergus, Co. Antrim, N. Ireland; *m*; two *s* two *d. Educ:* Belfast Royal Academy; Queen's Univ., Belfast; Edinburgh, and Princeton, New Jersey, USA. Ordained to Ministry of Scottish Congregational Churches, 1940; Editor, British Weekly, 1950-58; Minister, United Church of Canada, 1958; war service, 1941-44; Smith Lecturer, Union College, University of British Columbia, 1952; Cole Lecturer, Vanderbilt University, Nashville, Tenn., USA, 1956; Willson Lecturer, 1957, Oklahoma City University; Chancellor's Lecturer, Queen's Univ., Kingston, Ontario, 1959; service with Toc H in Yorkshire and Wales. Has travelled intermittently, writing, as correspondent; broadcaster, etc. *Publications:* (novel) Miro, 1968; (novel) To Make a Right Rose Tree, 1970. *Recreations:* travelling, writing. *Address:* FP Publications, 300 Carlton Street, Winnipeg, Manitoba, Canada.

**HERSCHELL,** family name of **Baron Herschell.**

**HERSCHELL,** 3rd Baron, *cr* 1886; **Rognvald Richard Farrer Herschell;** late Captain Coldstream Guards; *b* 13 Sept. 1923; *o s* of 2nd Baron and Vera (*d* 1961), *d* of Sir Arthur Nicolson, 10th Bt, of that Ilk and Lasswade; *S* father, 1929; *m* 1948, Heather, *d* of 8th Earl of Dartmouth, CVO, DSO; one *d. Educ:* Eton. Page of Honour to the King, 1935-40. *Heir:* none. *Address:* Westfield House, Ardington, Wantage, Berks. *T:* East Hendred 224.

**HERSEY, John;** writer; Master, Pierson College, Yale University, since 1965; *b* 17 June 1914; *s* of Roscoe M. and Grace B. Hersey; *m* 1st, 1940, Frances Ann Cannon (marr. diss. 1958); three *s* one *d*; 2nd, 1958, Barbara Day Kaufman; one *d. Educ:* Yale Univ.; Clare Coll., Cambridge. Secretary to Sinclair Lewis, 1937; Editor Time, 1937-42; War and Foreign Correspondent, Time, Life, New Yorker, 1942-46. Vice-President, Authors' League of America, 1948-55. Member American Academy of Arts and Letters, 1954; Pulitzer Prize for fiction, 1945. Hon. Fellow, Clare Coll., Cambridge, 1967. *Publications:* Men on Bataan, 1942; Into the Valley, 1943; A Bell for Adano, 1944; Hiroshima, 1946; The Wall, 1950; The Marmot Drive, 1953; A Single Pebble, 1956; The War Lover, 1959; The Child Buyer, 1960; Here to Stay, 1962; White Lotus, 1965; Too Far to Walk, 1966; Under the Eye of the Storm, 1967; The Algiers Motel Incident, 1968. *Address:* 231 Park Street, New Haven, Conn, USA.

**HERSHEY, Dr Alfred Day;** Director, Genetics Research Unit, Carnegie Institution of Washington, since 1962; *b* 4 Dec. 1908; *s* of Robert D. Hershey and Alma (*née* Wilbur); *m* 1946, Harriet Davidson; one *s. Educ:* Michigan State Coll. (now Univ.). BS 1930; PhD 1934. Asst Bacteriologist, Washington Univ. Sch. of Medicine, St Louis Missouri, 1934-36; Instructor, 1936-38; Asst Prof., 1938-42; Assoc. Prof., 1942-50; Staff Mem., Dept of Genetics (now Genetics Research Unit), Carnegie Instn of Washington, 1950-. Albert Lasker Award, Amer. Public Health Assoc., 1958; Kimber Genetics Award, Nat. Acad. Sci., US, 1965. Hon. DSc, Chicago, 1967; Hon. Dr Med. Science, Michigan State, 1970. Nobel Prize for Physiology or Medicine (jtly), 1969. *Publications:* numerous articles in scientific jls or books. *Address:* Post Office Box 200, Cold Spring Harbor, New York 11724, USA. *T:* 516 692 6660.

**HERTFORD,** 8th Marquess of, *cr* 1793; **Hugh Edward Conway Seymour;** Baron Conway of Ragley, 1703; Baron Conway of Killultagh, 1712; Earl of Hertford, Viscount Beauchamp, 1750; Earl of Yarmouth, 1793; DL Warwick, 1959; formerly Lieutenant Grenadier Guards; Chairman, Hertford Public Relations Ltd since 1962; *b* 29 March 1930; *s* of late Brig.-General Lord Henry Charles Seymour, DSO (2nd *s* of 6th Marquess) and Lady Helen Frances Grosvenor (*d* 1970), *d* of 1st Duke of Westminster; *S* uncle, 1940; *m* 1956, Comtesse Louise de Caraman Chimay, *o d* of Lieut-Colonel Prince Alphonse de Chimay, *qv*; one *s* three *d*. *Educ:* Eton. Chief interest is public relations; also is engaged in farming, estate management (Diploma, Royal Agricultural Coll., Cirencester, 1956) and opening Ragley to the public. *Heir: s* Earl of Yarmouth, *qv*. *Address:* Hertford Public Relations Ltd, 193 Fleet Street, EC4. *T:* 01-405 8141. Ragley Hall, Alcester, Warwickshire. *T:* Alcester 2455. *Club:* Turf.

**HERTFORD, Bishop Suffragan of,** since 1968; **Rt. Rev. Albert John Trillo,** MTh; *b* 4 July 1915; *s* of late Albert Chowns and late Margaret Trillo; *m* 1942, Patricia Eva Williams; two *s* one *d*. *Educ:* The Quintin Sch.; King's Coll., University of London. Business career, 1931-36; University, 1936-38, BD (1st Class Hons) and AKC (1st Class Hons), 1938; MTh 1943. Asst Curate, Christ Church, Fulham, 1938-41; Asst Curate, St Gabriel's, Cricklewood (in charge of St Michael's), 1941-45; Secretary, SCM in Schools, 1945-50; Rector of Friern Barnet and Lecturer in New Testament Greek, King's Coll., London, 1950-55; Principal, Bishops' Coll., Cheshunt, 1955-63; Bishop Suffragan of Bedford, 1963-68. Examining Chaplain to Bishop of St Edmundsbury and Ipswich, 1955-63, to Bishop of St Albans, 1963-. Hon. Canon, Cathedral and Abbey Church at St Albans, 1958-63; Canon Residentiary, 1963-65. Fellow of King's Coll., London, 1959. Proctor in Convocation for Dean and Chapter of St Albans, 1963-64; Proctor-in-Convocation for the Clergy, 1965. Governor: Aldenham Sch., 1963-; Harper Trust Schs, Bedford, 1963-68; Queenswood Sch., 1969. *Recreations:* reading and work. *Address:* Longcroft, 32 Crouch Hall Lane, Redbourn, Herts. *T:* Redbourn 2216.

**HERVEY,** family name of **Marquess of Bristol.**

**HERVEY-BATHURST, Sir F.;** *see* Bathurst.

**HERWARTH von BITTENFELD, Hans Heinrich;** Grand Cross (2nd Class), Order of Merit, Federal Republic of Germany, 1963; Hon. GCVO 1958; State Secretary, retired; President, Commission for the Reform of the German Diplomatic Service, since 1969; *b* Berlin, 14 July 1904; *s* of Hans Richard Herwarth von Bittenfeld and Ilse Herwarth von Bittenfeld (*née* von Tiedemann); *m* 1935, Elisabeth Frelin von Redwitz; one *d*. *Educ:* Universities of Berlin, Breslau and Munich (Law and Nat. Econ.). Entered Auswärtiges Amt, Berlin, 1927; Attaché, Paris, 1930; Second Secretary and Personal Secretary to Ambassador, Moscow, 1931-39. Military Service, 1939-45. Oberregierungsrat, Regierungs-direktor, Ministerialrat Bavarian State Chancellery, 1945-49; Ministerialdirigent and Chief of Protocol, Federal Government, 1950, Minister Plenipotentiary, 1952; German Ambassador to Court of St James's, 1955-61; State Secretary and Chief of German Federal Presidential Office, 1961-65; German Ambassador to Republic of Italy, 1965-69. *Recreations:* shooting, ski-ing, antiques. *Address:* 53 Bonn, Kaiser Friedrich Strasse 8, Germany.

**HERZBERG, Gerhard,** CC (Canada), 1968; FRS 1951; FRSC 1939; Director, Division of Pure Physics, National Research Council of Canada, 1949-69, now Distinguished Research Scientist, National Research Council of Canada; *b* Hamburg, Germany, 25 Dec. 1904; *s* of late Albin Herzberg and Ella Herzberg; *m* 1929, Luise Herzberg (*née* Oettinger); one *s* one *d*. *Educ:* Inst. of Technology, Darmstadt, Germany; University of Göttingen, Germany; University of bristol, England. Lecturer, Darmstadt Inst. of Technology, 1930; Research Professor, University of Saskatchewan, 1935; Professor of Spectroscopy, Yerkes Observatory, University of Chicago, 1945; Principal Research Officer, National Research Council of Canada, 1948. University Medal, University of Liège, Belgium, 1950; President, RSC, 1966 (Henry Marshall Tory Medal, 1953). Joy Kissen Mookerjee Gold Medal of Indian Association for Cultivation of Science, 1954 (awarded 1957). Gold Medal of Canadian Association Phys., 1957; Bakerian Lecture, Royal Society, 1960; Faraday Lecture and Medal, Chem. Soc., 1970. Hon. Fellow: Indian Academy of Science, 1954; Indian Physical Society, 1957; Chemical Society of London, 1968. Hon. Member: Hungarian Academy of Sciences, 1964; Optical Society of America, 1968; Royal Irish Acad., 1970; Hon. Foreign Member American Academy Arts and Sciences, 1965; Foreign Associate, National Academy of Sciences, US, 1968. President, Canadian Association of Physicists, 1956; Vice-President, International Union of Pure and Applied Physics, 1957-63. Holds numerous hon. degrees. *Publications:* Atomic Spectra and Atomic Structure, 1st edition (USA) 1937, 2nd edition (USA) 1944; Molecular Spectra and Molecular Structure: I, Spectra of Diatomic Molecules, 1st edition (USA), 1939, 2nd edition (USA), 1950; II, Infra-red and Raman Spectra of Polyatomic Molecules (USA), 1945; III, Electronic Spectra and Electronic Structure of Polyatomic Molecules (USA), 1966; original research on atomic and molecular spectra published in various scientific journals. *Address:* Division of Physics, National Research Council, Ottawa 7, Canada. *T:* 99-22350.

**HERZFELD, Gertrude,** MB, ChB, FRCSE; retired; Surgeon, Bruntsfield Hospital for Women and Children, 1920-55; Consulting Surgeon, Royal Edinburgh Hospital for Sick Children, 1920-45; Surgeon, Edinburgh Orthopedic Clinic; Vice-President, Trefoil School for Physically Handicapped Children, 1964; *b* 1890; *d* of late Michael Herzfeld. *Educ:* Private School; Edinburgh Univ. MB, ChB, Edinburgh, 1914; Dorothy Gilfillan Prize, 1914; FRCSE, 1920; Wm Gibson Scholarship, 1920-22; formerly House Surgeon, Royal Hospital for Sick Children and Chalmers Hospital, Edinburgh, 1914-17; Surgeon, attached RAMC Cambridge Hospital, Aldershot, 1917; senior House Surgeon, Bolton Infirmary, 1917-19; Hon. Assistant Surgeon, 1920-25, Hon. Surgeon, 1925-45, Royal Hospital for Sick Children, Edinburgh; President, Soroptimist Club, Edinburgh, 1930; President, Medical Women's Federation, 1947-49 (Vice-President, 1930); Vice-President, Edinburgh Cripple Aid Society, 1956-; President, Edinburgh Br. of Chartered Society of Physiotherapists, 1950-61. Vice-President Scottish Society of Women Artists, 1954; Chairman, City of Edinburgh Div., BMA, 1960-62. *Publications:* Section on Congenital Club Foot in Fraser's Surgery of Childhood; The Radical Cure of Hernia in Infants and Young Children, and various other papers in the Edinburgh Medical Journal, Lancet and British Medical Journal.

*Recreations:* motoring, gardening. *Address:* Ormelie, 20 Corstorphine Road, Edinburgh EH12 6HP. *T:* 031-337 7188. *Club:* Ladies Caledonian (Edinburgh).

**HERZOG, Frederick Joseph,** MC; Farmer; *b* 8 Dec. 1890; *s* of late F. C. Herzog, formerly of Mossley Hill, Liverpool; *m* 1918, Constance Cicely Broad; two *s* one *d. Educ:* Charterhouse; Trinity Coll., Cambridge. BA, Economics tripos, 1911. Served European War in Royal Artillery, 1914-19 (MC); retired with rank of Major. High Sheriff of Denbighshire, 1942; JP Denbighshire since 1946. *Recreations:* sketching, gardening. *Address:* The Grange, Ruthin, North Wales. *T:* Ruthin 2124.

**HESELTINE, Michael Ray Dibdin;** MP (C) Tavistock, since 1966; Parliamentary Under-Secretary of State, Department of the Environment, since Oct. 1970; *b* 21 March 1933; *s* of Colonel R. D. Heseltine, Swansea, Glamorgan; *m* 1962, Anne Harding Williams; one *s* two *d. Educ:* Shrewsbury Sch.; Pembroke Coll., Oxford. BA 2nd class in Politics, Philosophy and Economics; Pres. Oxford Union, 1954. National Service (commissioned), Welsh Guards, 1959. Contested (C): Gower, 1959; Coventry North, 1964. Director of Bow Publications, 1961-65; Chm., Haymarket Press, 1966-70. Television interviewer or chairman, 1960-64. Vice-Chm., Cons. Parly Transport Cttee, 1968; Opposition Spokesman on Transport, 1969; Parly Sec., Min. of Transport, June-Oct. 1970. *Address:* 24 Wilton Crescent, SW1. *T:* 01-235 1794. *Clubs:* Carlton, Coningsby.

**HESELTINE, William Frederick Payne,** CVO 1969 (MVO 1961); Press Secretary to the Queen since 1968; *b* E Fremantle, W Australia, 17 July 1930; *s* of H. W. Heseltine; *m* 1st, Ann Elizabeth (*d* 1957), *d* of late L. F. Turner, Melbourne; 2nd, Audrey Margaret, *d* of late S. Nolan, Sydney; one *s* one *d. Educ:* Christ Church Grammar Sch., Claremont, WA; University of Western Australia (1st class hons, History). Prime Minister's dept, Canberra, 1951-62; Private Secretary to Prime Minister, 1955-59; Asst Information Officer to The Queen, 1960-61; Acting Official Secretary to Governor-General of Australia, 1962; Asst Federal Director of Liberal Party of Australia, 1962-64; attached to Household of Princess Marina for visit to Australia, 1964; attached to Melbourne Age, 1964; Asst Press Secretary to The Queen, 1965-67. *Address:* 7 Trevor Street, SW7. *Club:* Press.

**HESKETH,** 3rd Baron, *cr* 1935, of Hesketh, **Thomas Alexander Fermor-Hesketh,** Bt 1761; *b* 28 Oct. 1950; *s* of 2nd Baron and Christian Mary, *o d* of Sir John McEwen, 1st Bt of Marchmont; *S* father 1955. *Educ:* Ampleforth. *Heir: b* Hon. Robert Fermor-Hesketh, *b* 1 Nov. 1951. *Address:* Easton Neston, Towcester, Northamptonshire. *T:* Towcester 445. *Club:* Turf.

**HESKETH, Air Vice-Marshal Allan,** CB 1946; CBE 1944; (OBE 1941); DFC; Royal Air Force, retired; AOC No 3 Group, Bomber Command, 1949; AOC No 23 Group, Flying Training Command, 1951-52; Air Vice-Marshal, 1949; AOA Flying Training Command, 1952-54; retired, 1954. *Address:* c/o Lloyds Bank Ltd, Cox's and King's Branch, 6 Pall Mall, SW1.

**HESKETH, (Charles) Peter Fleetwood Fleetwood-**, TD 1943; DL; *b* 5 Feb. 1905; 2nd *s* of late Charles Hesketh Fleetwood-Hesketh, and late Anne Dorothea, *e d* of Sir Thomas Brocklebank, 2nd Bt; *m* 1940, Mary Monica, 2nd *d* of Sir Ralph Cockayne Assheton, 1st Bt; one *d. Educ:* Eton. Studied architecture at London Univ. under Sir Albert Richardson, and at Architectural Association; Student RIBA and Registered Architect. Worked in office of late H. S. Goodhart-Rendel and later with Seely & Paget and other architects. Hon. district representative: for National Trust, 1947-68; for Georgian Group and other Societies; Founder Mem., Victorian Society, Secretary, 1961-63, Hon. Architectural Adviser, 1963-, Chm., Liverpool Gp, Victorian Soc., 1968-; Architectural Correspt, Daily Telegraph, 1964-67. Mem., Anglo-Rhodesian Soc., 1965-; Chm., Lancs and Cheshire Br., Anglo-Rhodesian Soc., 1969-. 2nd Lieut DLO Yeomanry (Cavalry) 1926, Captain 1938. Served, 1939-45, with DLO Yeomanry; WO, MI (Liaison); in occupied France with 2nd SAS and Maquis; Monuments, Fine Arts and Archives (Austria). High Sheriff, Lancs., 1960-61; DL Lancs, 1961. A Burgess of Preston. Governor of Rossall and other schools. *Publications:* Guide to the Palace of Schönbrunn, 1945; Murray's Lancashire Architectural Guide, 1955; Lancs section of Collins's Guide to English Parish Churches, 1958 (ed. John Betjeman); Life of Sir Charles Barry, in Peter Ferriday's Victorian Architecture, 1963; 1790-1840 section of Ian Grant's Great Interiors, 1967; chapters in: Shell Guide to England (ed John Hadfield), 1970; The Country Seat (ed Howard Colvin and John Harris), 1970. Illustrated John Betjeman's Ghastly Good Taste, 1933, new edn 1970. Contrib. articles to Country Life, etc. *Address:* The Manor House, Hale, Lancashire. *T:* Hale 3116; 57 Great Ormond Street, WC1. *T:* 01-242 3672. *Clubs:* Travellers', MCC.

**HESKETH, Roger Fleetwood,** OBE 1970; TD 1942; DL; *b* 28 July 1902; *e s* of Charles Hesketh Fleetwood-Hesketh; *m* 1952, Lady Mary Lumley, DStJ, *e d* of 11th Earl of Scarbrough, KG; one *s* two *d. Educ:* Eton; Christ Church, Oxford (MA). Called to the Bar, Inner Temple, 1928. MP (C) for Southport, 1952-59. High Sheriff, Lancs, 1947; DL 1948, JP 1950, Lancs; Mayor of Southport, 1950; Freeman of the Borough, 1966. Chairman, Lancashire Agricultural Executive Cttee, 1965-. Served War of 1939-45 (despatches, Bronze Star Medal, USA). Hon. Colonel, Duke of Lancaster's Own Yeomanry, 1956-67. *Address:* Meols Hall, Southport, Lancs. *T:* Southport 88171; H4 Albany, Piccadilly, W1. *T:* 01-734 5320. *Clubs:* White's, Travellers', Pratt's.

**HESLOP, Air Vice-Marshal Herbert William,** CB 1946; OBE; CEng; AFRAeS, MIEI; RAF, retired; *b* 29 Oct. 1898; *m* 1937, Phyllis Bletsoe, *d* of H. Brown, Sywell House, Sywell; two *s. Educ:* Durham School. Cadet RFC 1917; commissioned RFC 1917; 20 Squadron, France, 1918; 28 Squadron, India, 1919; instructor on engineering duties, Halton, 1923; Long engineering course, Henlow, 1924; chief engineer officer, Armament and Gunnery School, Eastchurch, 1925; Royal Canadian Air Force, Canada, on exchange engineering duties, 1927-29; 24 Communication Sqdn, Northolt, 1929; Squadron Leader 1933; chief engineer officer, Cranwell, 1933; chief RAF engineer officer, HMS Glorious, 1935; Wing Commander 1937; employed Directorate of Research and Development, 1937; head of RDA4 branch AMRD, Air Ministry; British Purchasing Commission, New York and Washington, 1940; Group Captain 1940; Flying Training Command HQ for engineer duties, 1943; Command Engineer Officer, 1943; Air Commodore 1943; Director Aeronautical Inspection Service, Air Ministry, 1947-51; Senior Technical Staff Officer,

Bomber Command, 1951-52; Senior Technical Staff Officer, Middle East Air Force, 1952-54; Air Vice-Marshal, 1953; retired 1955. *Address:* High Barn, Pound Lane, Sonning, Berks. *T:* 3150. *Club:* Royal Air Force.

**HESLOP-HARRISON, Prof. John,** FRS 1970; MSc, PhD, DSc, FRSE, MRIA, FLS; Professor of Botany in the Institute of Plant Development, University of Wisconsin, since 1967; Director designate, Royal Botanic Gardens, Kew; *b* 10 Feb. 1920; *s* of late Prof. J. W. Heslop-Harrison, FRS; *m* 1950, Yolande, *d* of late Captain J. H. Massey, Burnley, Lancashire; one *s. Educ:* Grammar School, Chester-le-Street, King's Coll. (University of Durham), Newcastle upon Tyne. MSc (Dunelm), PhD (Belfast), DSc (Dunelm). Radio Officer, Ministry of Supply, 1941-42; 2nd Lieut RAOC, 1942; Captain REME, 1942-45. Lecturer in Agricultural Botany, King's Coll., Univ. of Durham, 1945-46; Lecturer in Botany: Queen's Univ., Belfast, 1946-50, UCL, 1950-53; Reader in Taxonomy, UCL, 1953-54; Prof. of Botany, Queen's Univ., Belfast, 1954-60; Brittingham Vis. Prof., Univ. of Wisconsin, USA, 1965; Mason Prof. of Botany, Univ. of Birmingham, 1960-67; Vis. Prof., US Dept of Agriculture Institute of Forest Genetics, Rhinelander, Wis, 1968. Editor, Annals of Botany, 1961-67. Corresp. Mem., Royal Netherlands Botanical Soc., 1968. Trail-Crisp Award, Linnean Soc., 1967; Univ. of Liège Medal, 1967. *Publications:* New Concepts in Flowering-plant Taxonomy, 1953. Papers on botanical subjects in various British and foreign journals. *Recreations:* hill walking, photography and painting. *Address:* Institute of Plant Development, University of Wisconsin, Madison, Wis 53706, USA; (from June 1971) Royal Botanic Gardens, Surrey: Elm Cottage, Stretford Bridge, Herefordshire.

**HESS, Ellen Elizabeth,** NDH; Principal, Studley College, Warwickshire, 1956-69; *b* 28 Dec. 1908; *d* of Charles Michael Joseph Hess and Fanny Thompson Hess (*née* Alder). *Educ:* Grammar School for Girls, Dalston; Royal Botanic Society, Regents Park. Lecturer in Horticulture, Swanley Horticultural College for Women, 1934-39; Agricultural Secretary, National Federation of Women's Institutes, 1939-46; Ellen Eddy Shaw Fellowship, Brooklyn Botanic Gardens, New York, USA, 1946-47; School of Horticulture, Ambler, Pa., USA, 1947-48; HM Inspector of Schools (Agriculture and Further Education), 1948-56. Veitch Meml Medal, RHS, 1967. *Recreations:* travel, photography, walking. *Address:* The Croft, 54 Torton Hill Road, Arundel, Sussex.

**HESS, Prof. Walter R.;** Emeritus Professor (Professor of Physiology and Director of the Physiological Department, University of Zürich, 1917-51); *b* 17 March 1881; *s* of Prof. Dr Clemenz Hess, Switzerland, and Gertrud (*née* Fischer Saxon); *m* 1909, Luise Sandmeyer; one *s* one *d. Educ:* Gymnasium at Frauenfeld (Thurgau), Switzerland. Medical studies, 1900-05, at the Universities of Lausanne, Berne, Berlin, Kiel, Zürich. Postgraduate: Asst at Dept of Surgery and of Ophthalmology, 1905-08; MD Zürich 1906. Practitioner: oculist, 1908-12; Asst and lecturer in Physiol. at Zürich and Bonn, 1913-17. Retired, 1951. Dr hc: Philosophy, Berne, 1933; Medicine, Geneva, 1944; Science, McGill Univ., Montreal, 1953; Medicine, Freiburg (Br). Hon. member of different societies of Physiol., Ophthalm. and Neurol. Hon. and corresponding Member of different Academies. Ludwigmedaille der deutschen Gesellschaft für Kreislaufforschung, 1938; Marcel Benoist Prize, 1933; Nobel Prize, 1949. *Publications:* Monographs: Die Regulierung d. Blutkreislaufes, 1930; Die Regulierung d. Atmung, 1931; Die Methodik d. lokalisierten Reizung subkortikaler Hirnabschnitte, 1932; Das Zwischenhirn u. d. Regulation v. Kreislauf u. Atmung, 1938; Vegetative Funktionen u. Zwischenhirn, 1949; Die funktionelle Organisation d. vegetat. Nervensystems, 1948; Das Zwischenhirn, 1949; Diencephalon, 1954; Hypothalamus and Thalamus, 1956, 2nd edn 1968; The functional organisation of the Diencephalon, 1957; Psychologie in biologischer Sicht, 1962, 2nd edn, 1968. *Recreations:* taking care of the garden, fruit trees and vineyards. *Address:* Via Gabbio 6, 6612 Ascona, Switzerland. *T:* 093/25406.

**HETHERINGTON, Alastair;** *see* Hetherington, H. A.

**HETHERINGTON, Arthur Ford,** DSC 1944; Member and Deputy Chairman, Gas Council, since 1967; *b* 12 July 1911; *s* of late Sir Roger Hetherington and of Lady Hetherington; *m* 1937, Margaret Lacey; one *s* one *d. Educ:* Highgate Sch.; Trinity Coll., Cambridge (BA). Joined staff of Gas Light & Coke Company, 1935. Served War, RNVR, 1941-45. North Thames Gas Board, 1949-55; joined staff of Southern Gas Board, 1955; Deputy Chairman, 1956; Chairman 1961-64; Chairman, E Midlands Gas Board, 1964-66. *Address:* 32 Connaught Square, W2. *T:* 01-723 3128. *Clubs:* Athenæum; Royal Southampton Yacht.

**HETHERINGTON, Rear-Adm. Derick Henry Fellowes,** CB 1961; DSC 1941 (2 Bars 1944, 1945); MA (Oxon), 1963; Domestic Bursar and Fellow of Merton College, Oxford, since 1963; *b* 27 June 1911; *s* of Commander H. R. Hetherington, RD, Royal Naval Reserve, and Hilda Fellowes; *m* 1942, Josephine Mary, *d* of Captain Sir Leonard Vavasour, 4th Bt, RN (retired), *qv*; one *s* three *d* (and one *s* decd). *Educ:* St Neot's, Eversley, Hants; RNC Dartmouth. Cadet, HMS Barham, 1928-29; Midshipman-Comdr (HMS Effingham, Leander, Anthony, Wildfire, Kimberley, Windsor, Lookout, Royal Arthur, Cheviot), 1929-52; Captain 1950; Chief of Staff, Canal Zone, Egypt, 1950-52; Senior British Naval Officer, Ceylon, 1954-55; Captain (D) 4th Destroyer Squadron, 1956-57; Director of Naval Training, Admiralty, 1958-59; Flag Officer, Malta, 1959-61; retired 1961. Croix de Guerre (France) 1945. *Address:* Merton College, Oxford.

**HETHERINGTON, (Hector) Alastair;** Editor of the Guardian, since 1956; Director, Guardian Newspapers Ltd, since 1967; *b* Llanishen, Glamorganshire, 31 Oct. 1919; *yr s* of late Sir Hector Hetherington and Lady Hetherington; *m* 1957, Miranda, *d* of Professor R. A. C. Oliver, *qv*; two *s* two *d. Educ:* Gresham's Sch., Holt; Corpus Christi Coll., Oxford. Royal Armoured Corps, 1940-46. Editorial staff: The Glasgow Herald, 1946-50; the Manchester Guardian, 1950-; Asst Editor and Foreign Editor, 1953-56. Member, Royal Commission on the Police, 1960-62. *Recreation:* hill walking. *Address:* c/o The Guardian, 192 Gray's Inn Road, WC1. *T:* 01-837 7011. *Clubs:* Athenæum, National Liberal.

**HETHERINGTON, Thomas Chalmers, (Tony),** CBE 1970; TD; Legal Secretary, Law Officers' Department, since 1966; *b* 18 Sept. 1926; *er s* of William and Alice Hetherington; *m* 1953, June Margaret Ann Catliff; four *d. Educ:* Rugby Sch.; Christ Church, Oxford. Served in Royal Artillery, Middle East, 1945-48; Territorial Army, 1948-67. Called to Bar, Inner Temple, 1952; Legal Dept, Min. of Pensions and Nat. Insce, 1953; Law Officers' Dept, 1962.

*Address:* Rosemount, Lingfield, Surrey. *T:* Lingfield 2742.

**HEUSTON, Prof. Robert Francis Vere,** DCL Oxon 1970; Regius Professor of Laws, Trinity College, Dublin, since 1970; *b* Dublin, 17 Nov. 1923; *e s* of late Vere Douglas Heuston and of Dorothy Helen Coulter; *m* 1962, Bridget Nancy (*née* Bolland), *widow* of Neville Ward-Perkins; four step *c. Educ:* St Columba's Coll.; Trinity Coll., Dublin; St John's Coll., Cambridge. Barrister, King's Inns, 1947, Gray's Inn, 1951; Hon. Member, Western Circuit, 1966. Fellow, Pembroke Coll., Oxford, 1947-65 (Supernumary Fellow, 1965-), Dean, 1951-57, Pro-Proctor, 1953. Member, Law Reform Cttee, 1968-70. Visiting Professor: Univ. of Melbourne, 1956; Univ. of British Columbia, 1960; Gresham Professor in Law, 1964-70. *Publications:* (ed) Salmond on Torts, 11th edn 1953, 15th edn 1969; Essays in Constitutional Law, 2nd edn 1964; Lives of the Lord Chancellors, 1964; various in learned periodicals. *Address:* Kentstown Glebe, Brownstown, Navan, Ireland. *T:* Balroth 95. *Clubs:* Savile; University (Dublin).

**HEWAN, Gethyn Elliot;** Headmaster, Allhallows School, Rousdon, since Sept. 1965; *b* 23 Dec. 1916; *s* of late E. D. Hewan and of Mrs L. Hewan; *m* 1943, Peggy (*née* Allen); one *s* two *d. Educ:* Marlborough Coll., Wilts; Clare Coll., Cambridge (Exhibitioner); Yale Univ., USA (Mellon Schol). BA Hons 1938; MA 1943, Cambridge. Served War of 1939-45 (despatches): Middle East; Capt. 3rd Regt RHA 1943; Staff Coll., Camberley, psc 1944; BMRA 51st Highland Div., 1944-45. Asst Master, Wellington Coll., 1946-50; Headmaster, Cranbrook Sch., Bellevue Hill, NSW, 1951-63; Acting Bursar, Marlborough Coll., Wilts, 1963; Asst Master, Winchester Coll., 1963-64, Charterhouse Sch., 1964-65. Sec., NSW branch of HMC of Aust., 1956-63; Standing Cttee of HMC of Aust., 1958-63; Foundation Member, Aust. Coll. of Education, 1958; Exec. Cttee, Australian Outward Bound Foundation, 1958-63. *Recreations:* cricket (Cambridge blue, 1938), golf, fishing; formerly hockey (blue, 1936-37-38, Capt.) and billiards (½ blue, 1938). *Address:* Headmaster's House, Allhallows School, Rousdon, near Lyme Regis, Dorset. *T:* Seaton 8. *Clubs:* MCC; I Zingari; Free Foresters; Oxford and Cambridge Golfing Society; Royal Sydney Golf; Lyme Regis Golf.

**HEWARD, Air Marshal Anthony Wilkinson,** CB 1968; OBE 1952; DFC; AFC. Group Captain RAF, 1957; IDC, 1962; Dir of Operations (Bomber and Reconnaissance) Min. of Defence (RAF), 1963; Air Commodore, 1963; SASO, RAF Germany, 1966; Air Officer in charge of Administration, HQ, RAF Air Support Command, Upavon, Wilts, March 1968; Chief of Staff, HQ, RAF Strike Command, High Wycombe, Bucks, Jan. 1969. *Address:* HQ, RAF Strike Command, High Wycombe, Bucks.

**HEWARD, Edmund Rawlings;** Master of the Supreme Court (Chancery Division), since 1959; *b* 19 Aug. 1912; *s* of late Rev. Thomas Brown Heward and Kathleen Amy Rachel Rawlings; *m* 1945, Constance Mary Sandiford, *d* of George Bertram Crossley, OBE. *Educ:* Repton; Trinity Coll., Cambridge. Admitted a solicitor, 1937. Enlisted Royal Artillery as a Gunner, 1940; released as Major, DAAG, 1946. Partner in Rose, Johnson and Hicks, 9 Suffolk St, SW1, 1946. LLM 1960. *Publication:* Guide to Chancery Practice, 1962 (3rd edn 1966). *Address:* 36a Dartmouth Row, Greenwich, SE10. *T:* 01-692 3525. *Club:* United University.

**HEWAT, Aubrey Middleton,** MD, ChB (Edinburgh), DPH, RCP and SE; late Principal Medical Officer, Public Health Department, LCC; *b* 17 Sept. 1884; *er s* of late Richard G. Hewat, Edinburgh, and late Harriet Aitken Middleton; *m* 1912, Mary Victoria (*d* 1969), *e d* of late E. H. Claye, Derby; five *s. Educ:* Fettes Coll., Edinburgh; Edinburgh Univ. Research Scholar, Royal Victoria Hospital for Consumption, Edinburgh; Resident Medical Officer, Edinburgh Maternity Hospital; Asst Medical Officer of Health, Derby and East Suffolk; Tuberculosis Officer, Preston, Lancs; Medical Officer of Health, Borough of Nuneaton and Metropolitan Borough of Fulham; Fellow of Society of Medical Officers of Health and of Royal Institute of Public Health and Hygiene; Capt. RAMC (retired). *Publications:* Annual Reports on State of Health of Nuneaton (1919-21) and Fulham (1922-25); numerous papers on public health subjects. *Recreation:* gardening. *Address:* Borodale Hotel, Bexhill-on-Sea, Sussex. *T:* Cooden 2532. *Club:* Cooden Beach Golf.

**HEWER, Christopher Langton,** MB, BS (London); MRCP; Hon. FFARCS; Consulting Anæsthetist to St Bartholomew's Hospital and to Hospital for Tropical Diseases, London; Anæsthetist, Florence Nightingale Hospital; late Senior Anæsthetist, The Queen's Hospital for Children, Hackney Road; Seamen's Hospital, Royal Albert Dock; late Anæsthetist to Queen Mary's Hospital, Roehampton, Ministry of Pensions, Brompton Chest Hospital and Anæsthetic Specialist RAMC; Examiner in Anæsthesia to Royal College of Surgeons of England and Royal College of Physicians; late Consultant Anæsthetist to West Herts Hospital, Hemel Hempstead, to Luton and Dunstable Hospital, and to Harpenden Hospital; *s* of Joseph Langton Hewer, MD, FRCS; *m* 1925, Doris Phœbe, *d* of H. D'Arcy Champney, MA, Bristol; two *s* one *d. Educ:* University Coll. Sch; St Bartholomew's Hospital. Junior Scholarship in Anatomy and Physiology in St Bartholomew's Hospital Medical Coll.; MBBS London degree (distinction in Physiology), 1920; served as House Surgeon and Resident Anæsthetist at St Bartholomew's Hospital; FRSM; Sec. of the Anæsthetic Section of same, 1930 and 1931, Pres., 1936-37; late Vice-Pres. Assoc. of Anæsthetists of Great Britain and Ireland, and ed. of the Association's Journal, Anæsthesia; Member Anæsthetics Cttee of MRC and RSM; Pres., Section of Anæsthetics, BMA, 1953; Hon. Member Canadian Soc. of Anæsthetists; late Member Board of Faculty of Anæsthetists, RCS. Frederic Hewitt Lecturer, 1959. Henry Hill Hickman Medallist, 1966, John Snow Medallist, 1966. *Publications:* Anæsthesia in Children, 1922; Recent Advances in Anæsthesia and Analgesia, 1932, 10th edn 1957 (editor of); Practical Anæsthetics, 1923; (with H. E. G. Boyle) articles in medical journals and reports; Section on Anæsthesia in Post Graduate Surgery, edited by R. Maingot; Thoughts on Modern Anæsthesia, 1970; formerly editor Section on Anæsthesia in Medical Annual. *Address:* 33 Stormont Road, Highgate, N6. *T:* 01-340 1388.

**HEWER, Prof. Humphrey Robert,** OBE 1959; Professor of Zoology, Imperial College, University of London, since 1964; *b* 16 Aug. 1903; *s* of Basil Hewer and Annie Elizabeth (Hargroves); *m* 1927, Olive Mary La Trobe Stooke; two *d. Educ:* Fulneck Sch.; Imperial Coll. Lectr in Zoology, Imperial Coll., 1926-37; Asst Prof. and Reader in Zoology, Imperial Coll., 1937-64. Chief Rodent Officer, Min. of Food, 1941-45. Chairman: Adv. Cttee,

Infestation Control Laboratory, Min. of Agric. Fish. and Food, 1965-; Farm animal Welfare Adv. Cttee, Min. of Agric. Fish and Food, 1967-. *Publications:* various scientific publications in Proc. and Trans Royal Society London, J. Zool. Linn. Soc. London; Proc. Zool Soc. London, etc. *Recreations:* reading, natural history. *Address:* 6 Armstrong Close, Brockenhurst, Hants. *T:* Brockenhurst 2375.

**HEWER, Maj.-Gen. Reginald Kingscote,** CB 1945; CBE 1942 (OBE 1940); MC 1917; retired; *b* 24 Oct. 1892; *s* of late R. T. Hewer, Down Ampney, Cirencester, Glos; *m* 1925, Elizabeth Ivan Leslie, *d* of Col L. Findlay of Craigellachie, Banffshire; two *s* one *d. Educ:* Haileybury; Oxford (BA). Served European War in RA 1914-18 (despatches, MC); transferred to 7th Dragoon Guards, 1921, and to 7th Hussars, 1923; Major, 1935; Col 1942; Acting Brig. 1940; Acting Maj.-Gen. 1942; Temp. Maj.-Gen. 1943. Served War of 1939-45 (despatches four time, OBE, CBE, CB). Dep. Dir Gen., European Central Inland Transport Organisation, 1945-47. *Recreations:* hunting, shooting. *Address:* Bleeke House, Marston Mersey, Cricklade, Wilts. *T:* Kempsford 237. *Club:* United Hunts.

**HEWER, Thomas Frederick,** MD (Bristol); FRCP, FLS; Professor of Pathology, 1938-68, and Pro-Vice-Chancellor, 1966-68, University of Bristol; Professor Emeritus, 1968; *b* 12 April 1903; *s* of William Frederick Hewer and Kathleen Braddon Standerwick; *m* 1941, Anne Hiatt Baker; two *s* two *d. Educ:* Bristol Gram. Sch.; University of Bristol. Commonwealth Fund Fellow and Asst Pathologist, Johns Hopkins Univ., USA, 1927-29; Bacteriologist Sudan Government, 1930-35; Sen. Lectr in Pathology, University of Liverpool, 1935-38. Chm., Bristol Br., English-Speaking Union, 1942-67, Vice-Pres., 1967-. *Publications:* articles in medical and horticultural journals. *Recreations:* gardening and travel. *Address:* Vine House, Henbury, Bristol BS10 7AD. *T:* Bristol 628913. *Club:* English-Speaking Union.

**HEWETSON, Gen. Sir Reginald (Hackett),** GCB 1966 (KCB 1962; CB 1958); CBE 1945 (OBE 1943); DSO 1944; Adjutant-General, Ministry of Defence (Army), 1964-67; retired; *b* Shortlands, Kent, 4 Aug. 1908; *s* of late J. Hewetson, ICS, and E. M. M. Hackett-Wilkins; *m* 1935, Patricia Mable, *y d* of late F. H. Burkitt, CIE; one *s* one *d. Educ:* Repton; RMA, Woolwich. Regular Commission in RA, 1928; Service in India (including Active Service, 1930-32), 1929-35; RA depot and home stations, 1935-39; psc 1939; Staff Capt. RA 4 Div., 1938; Adjt 30 Fd Regt and Capt. 1939; France, Oct. 1939-Jan. 1940; 2nd war course at Staff Coll., Camberley, Jan.-April 1940; Brigade Major RA 43 (Wessex) Div. May-Sept. 1940. Temp. Major; various GSO2 jobs incl. instructor Senior Officers Sch., 1940-42; GSO1 (Lieut-Col) HQ. L of C North Africa, Sept.-Nov. 1942; 78 Div (in NOrth Africa) 1942-43 (OBE); Lieut-Col Comdg Fd Regt in 56 (London) Div in Italy, 1943-44 (DSO); BGS HQ 10 Corps, 1944-45; BGS, British Troops, Austria, 1945-47; Student, IDC, 1949; Dep. Dir Staff Duties, WO, 1950-52; CRA 2nd Infantry Div., BAOR, 1953-55; GOC 11th Armoured Div., March 1956; GOC, 4th Infantry Div. 1956-58; Commandant, Staff Coll., Camberley, 1958-61; Commander, British Forces, Hong Kong, Dec. 1961-March 1963; GOC-in-C, Far East Land Forces, 1963-64. Col Comdt, RA, 1962-; Col Comdt, Army PT Corps, 1966-; ADC (Gen.), 1966-67. Chm., Exec. Cttee, Army Benevolent Fund, 1968-. Gov. and Mem. Administrative Bd, Corps of Commissionaires, 1964. *Recreations:* cricket (Army and Kent 2nd XI MCC, IZ), hockey (Norfolk and RA), golf. *Address:* Cherry Orchard, Fairwarp, near Uckfield, Sussex. *Clubs:* MCC, Army and Navy.

**HEWETT, Sir John George,** 5th Bt, *cr* 1813; MC 1919; Captain KAR; *b* 23 Oct. 1895; *e surv s* of Sir Harold George Hewett, 4th Bt, and Eleanor (*d* 1946), *d* of Capt. Studdy, RN, and Mrs W. T. Summers; *S* father, 1949; *m* 1926, Yuilleen Maude, *o c* of Samuel F. Smithson, Lauriston, Camberley; two *s. Educ:* Cheltenham. Served European War, 1914-18, British East Africa, 1914-19. *Heir: er s* Peter John Smithson Hewett, MM [*b* 27 June 1931; *m* 1958, Jennifer Ann Cooper, *o c* of Emrys Thomas Jones, Limuru, Kenya; two *s* one *d. Educ:* Bradfield Coll.; Jesus Coll., Cambridge. Called to the Bar, Gray's Inn, 1954; now a practising Advocate in Kenya. Kenya Regt attached Special Branch, Kenya Police, 1957]. *Address:* Ol'Morogi, Naivasha, Kenya.

**HEWISH, Antony,** MA, PhD; FRS 1968; Reader in Radioastronomy, University of Cambridge, since 1969; Fellow of Churchill College since 1962; *b* 11 May 1924; *s* of Ernest William Hewish and late Frances Grace Lanyon Pinch; *m* 1950, Marjorie Elizabeth Catherine Richards; one *s* one *d. Educ:* King's Coll., Taunton; Gonville and Caius Coll., Cambridge. BA (Cantab.) 1948, MA 1950, PhD 1952; Hamilton Prize, Isaac Newton Student, 1952. RAE Farnborough, 1943-46; Research Fellow, Gonville and Caius Coll., 1952-54; Asst Dir of Research, 1954-62; Fellow, Gonville and Caius Coll., 1955-62; Lectr in Physics, Univ. of Cambridge, 1962-69. Visiting Prof. in Astronomy, Yale, 1963. Eddington Medal, Royal Astronomical Soc., 1969. *Publications:* Papers in Proc. Royal Society, Phys. Soc., Mon. Not. Royal Astr. Soc., etc. *Recreations:* music, gardening. *Address:* 4 Mailes Close, Barton, Cambridge. *T:* Comberton 2657. *Club:* Grafham Water Sailing.

**HEWITSON, Captain Mark;** retired as National Industrial Officer of General and Municipal Workers' Union, Oct. 1964; *b* 1897; *m* Gwynneth, *d* of James Wicks, Sunningwell. Served Northumberland Fus and West Yorks 1916-20, and in Pioneer Corps, 1940-42. Member Durham CC, 1930-40; Pres., Public and Civil Service International, 1937-40; Pres., General Factory Workers International, 1945-50. MP (Lab) Hull Central, 1945-55, Hull West, 1955-64. Past Member Nat. Exec. Cttee, Labour Party, *Address:* 57 Sunningwell Village, near Abingdon, Berks.

**HEWITT,** family name of **Viscount Lifford.**

**HEWITT, Cecil Rolph, (C. H. Rolph);** Member of the editorial staff, New Statesman; *b* London, 23 Aug. 1901; *s* of Frederick Thompson Hewitt and Edith Mary Speed; *m* 1st, 1926, Audrey Mary Buttery (marr. diss., 1946); one *d*; 2nd, 1947, Jenifer Wayne, author and scriptwriter; one *s* two *d. Educ:* State schools. City of London Police, 1921-46 (Chief Inspector); editorial staff, New Statesman, 1947; Dir, Statesman Publishing Co. Ltd, 1965-; editor The Author, 1956-60. Member, exec. cttee, Howard League for Penal Reform. frequently broadcasts topical talks and documentaries. *Publications:* A Licensing Handbook, 1947; Crime and Punishment, 1950; Towards My Neighbour, 1950; On Gambling, 1951; Personal Identity, 1956; (Ed.) The Human Sum, 1957; Mental Disorder, 1958; Commonsense About Crime and Punishment, 1961; The Trial of Lady Chatterley, 1961; (with Arthur Koestler) Hanged by the Neck, 1961; All Those in Favour? (The ETU Trial), 1962; The Police and The Public, 1962; Law and the Common Man, 1967; Books in the Dock, 1969; contributor to The Encyclopædia Britannica, Chambers's Encyclopædia, Punch, The Week-End Book, The Solicitor, The Law Guardian, The Author, The Nation (NY), daily and weekly press. *Recreations:* music, reading verse, odd jobbing. *Address:* Rushett Edge, Bramley, Surrey. *T:* Bramley 3227.

**HEWITT, Lieut-Col Dudley Riddiford,** CIE 1919; retired Indian Army; *b* 1877; 2nd *s* of late Capt. James Dudley Ryder Hewitt, RN; *m* 1913, Marjorie Middlemas (*d* 1954), 2nd *d* of late William Fleming Inglis, Shanghai; two *d*. *Educ:* Wanganui, New Zealand. Served with 4th New Zealand Regt, South African War, 1900; E Lanc. Regt 1900-02; Indian Army, 1902-28 (17th Cavalry, 1902-05; Remount Depart, 1905-28). *Address:* The Old Rectory, West Stow, Bury St Edmunds, Suffolk.

**HEWITT, Sir Edgar R. L.;** *see* Ludlow-Hewitt.

**HEWITT, Rev. Canon George Henry Gordon;** Residentiary Canon, Chelmsford Cathedral, since 1964; Chaplain to the Queen, since 1969; *b* 30 May 1912; *s* of Rev. G. H. Hewitt; *m* 1942, Joan Ellen Howden; two *s* one *d*. *Educ:* Trent Coll.; Brasenose, Oxford; Wycliffe Hall, Oxford. Asst Curate, St Clement, Leeds, 1936-39; Chaplain, Ridley Hall, Cambridge, 1939-41; Asst Curate, Leeds Parish Church, 1941-43; Religious Book Editor, Lutterworth Press, 1943-52; Diocesan Education Sec., Sheffield, 1952-58; Residentiary Canon, Sheffield Cathedral, 1953-58; Vicar of St Andrew, Oxford, 1958-64. *Publication:* Let the People Read, 1949. *Address:* 20 Rainsford Avenue, Chelmsford, Essex.

**HEWITT, Admiral H. Kent,** Hon. KCB; retired; *b* Hackensack, New Jersey, 11 Feb. 1887; *s* of Robert Anderson Hewitt and Mary Kent; *m* 1913, Floride Louise Hunt; two *d*. *Educ:* US Naval Academy (graduated 1906); Naval War Coll., 1928-29; Served European war, 1917-18; Capt. 1932; Rear-Adm. 1940; Vice-Adm. 1942; Adm. 1945. Commanded: Amphibious Force, Atlantic Fleet, 1942; landings in Morocco, 1942; US Naval Forces in North-West African Waters (US Eighth Fleet), Feb. 1943; American half of the invasion of Sicily, July 1943; Allied Forces which effected landing at Salerno, 1943; Allied Forces, which on 15 Aug. 1944, established the Seventh Army on shore in Southern France; US Twelfth Fleet (Naval Forces in Europe), 1945-46; US Naval Rep., UN Military Staff Cttee, 1946-49. Navy Cross with gold star, Navy DSM with gold star, Army DSM and Oak Leaf Cluster, Grand Officer Legion of Honour, France, Order of Leopold, Belgium, Order of Orange-Nassau, Holland, and many other decorations. *Recreations:* walking, riding. *Address:* Foretop, Orwell, Vermont 05760, USA. *Clubs:* Army Navy (Washington, DC); University, Century (NY City).

**HEWITT, John Francis,** CBE 1964; Secretary for Appointments to the Prime Minister, since Oct. 1961, and Ecclesiastical Secretary to the Lord Chancellor, since 1965; Trustee: Chevening Estate; Dorneywood Trust; *b* 12 Nov. 1910; *o s* of late Rev. John Francis Hewitt, MA and of late Frances Hilda Hewitt, BLitt; *m* 1938, Betty Mida Pantin Dale-Glossop, *o d* of late Lieut-Col H. Dale-Glossop and of Mrs T. E. Carew-Hunt; one *s* one *d*. *Educ:* St Lawrence Coll., Ramsgate and privately. London Stock Exchange, 1928; joined Board of Trade, 1941; Imperial Defence Coll., 1947; Asst Sec., Board of Trade, Tariff Div., 1947-55, CRE Div. (US Branch), 1955-57; HM Customs and Excise (International Div.), 1957-61. Chm., Ellison House (Probation Hostel) Camberwell, 1961. *Address:* Little Heath, Limpsfield, Surrey. *T:* Limpsfield Chart 2205. *Club:* Travellers'.

**HEWITT, Capt. John Graham,** DSO, 1940; RN (retired); *b* 15 Oct. 1902; *s* of J. G. L. Hewitt, SM, Marton, NZ; two *s*; *m* 1947, Mrs Rooney, *widow* of Col J. J. Rooney, IMS. *Educ:* RN Colls, Osborne and Dartmouth. Midshipman, 1919; Comdr, 1936; commanded HMS Winchelsea, 1937, HMS Auckland, 1940-41; HMS Dauntless, 1941-42; Capt. 1942; HMS Royalist, 1944; HMS Frobisher, 1945-46; Second Naval Member of NZ Navy Board, 1947; Director Tactical Sch., Woolwich, 1949-52; retired list, 1952. Norwegian War Cross, 1942. *Recreation:* fishing. *Address:* 16 Royston Court, Kew Gardens, Richmond, Surrey.

**HEWITT, Sir Joseph,** 2nd Bt, *cr* 1921; Major RA; *b* 8 Sept. 1907; *s* of 1st Bt and Margaret Eliza (*d* 1950), *d* of George Guest of Barnsley; *S* father, 1923; *m* 1940, Marguerite, *yr d* of Charles Burgess; two *s* one *d*. *Educ:* Uppingham Sch. *Recreation:* gardening. *Heir: s* Nicholas Charles Joseph Hewitt [*b* 12 Nov. 1947; *m* 1969, Pamela Margaret, *o d* of Geoffrey Hunt, Scalby]. *Address:* Lebberston Hall, near Scarborough, Yorks. *T:* Cayton 271.

**HEWITT, Air Vice-Marshal Joseph Eric,** CBE 1951 (OBE 1940); psa 1934; Royal Australian Air Force (retired); Member Panel of Military Experts, United Nations, since 1952; *b* 13 April 1901; *s* of late Rev. J. H. Hewitt, MA, BD and late Rose Alice Hewitt (*née* Harkness), Melbourne, Vic; *m* 1925, Lorna Pretoria, *d* of late Alfred Eugene Bishop and late Joanne Bishop (*née* Prismall), Melbourne, Vic; Three *d*. *Educ:* Scotch Coll., Melbourne; Royal Australian Naval Coll., Jervis Bay, NSW. Served in RAN, RN, RAAF and RAF, 1915-28; Cadet Midshipman, 1915; Midshipman, 1918; Sub-Lieut 1921; Lieut, 1922. Transferred to RAAF, 1928; Comdg Officer RAAF, HMAS Albatross, 1929-32; RAF Staff Coll., Andover, 1934; Asst Liaison Officer, Australia House, London, 1935; Comdg Officer, No 104 Sqdn, RAF, 1936-38; SASO, RAAF, Richmond, NSW, 1938-39; Sen. Admin. Staff Officer, Southern Area, HQ, 1939-40; DPS, HQ, RAAF, 1940-41; DCAS, RAAF, 1941; Director of Air Operations, Staff of C-in-C. Allied Command, NEI, Java, 1942; ACAS, 1942; Director of Allied Air Intelligence, SW Pacific Area, 1942 and 1944; AOC No 9 Op. Group, 1943 (Battle of Bismarck Sea, 1943); Air member for Personnel, RAAF, HQrs, 1945-48; Australian Defence Representative, London, 1949-51; Air Member for Supply and Equipment, Dept of Air, Melbourne, 1951-56, retired April 1956. Member, Council for Adult Education of Victoria, 1956-66. Manager, Education and Training, Internat. Harvester Co. (Aust.) Pty Ltd, 1956-66. FAIM 1956. *Recreations:* swimming, gardening, reading. *Address:* Langate, 3 Albany Road, Toorak, Melbourne, Victoria 3142, Australia. *T:* Melbourne 20 4116. *Club:* Naval and Military (Melbourne).

**HEWITT, Richard Thornton,** OBE 1945; Secretary of the Royal Society of Medicine since 1952; Executive Director, the Royal Society of Medicine Foundation, Inc., New York, since 1969; *b* 1917, *yr s* of Harold and Elsie Muriel Hewitt, Bramhall, Cheshire. *Educ:* King's Sch., Macclesfield; Magdalen Coll., Oxford (Exhibitioner). Served War, Lt-Col, infantry and special forces, 1939-46. Asst Registrar, Cambridge Univ., 1946. Incorporated MA, Magdalene Coll., Cambridge, 1946. Sec., Oxford Univ. Medical Sch., 1947-52. Hon. Fellow, Swedish Med.

Soc., 1968. Liveryman, Worshipful Society of Apothecaries of London, 1954. Freeman of the City of London, 1954. *Recreations:* most games, increasingly as a spectator; music. *Address:* 151 Dorset House, NW1. *T:* 01-935 4014; The White House, Iffley, Oxford. *T:* Oxford 79263. *Clubs:* Athenæum, MCC, Royal Automobile, Special Forces; Frewen (Oxford); Royal and Ancient (St Andrews).

**HEWLETT, Sir C.;** *see* Hewlett, Sir T. C.

**HEWLETT, Sir (Thomas) Clyde,** Kt 1964; CBE 1959; MA; MIEx; JP; Deputy Chairman since 1968, Managing Director since 1965, Anchor Chemical Co. Ltd (Export Director, 1950-61; Joint Managing Director, 1961-65), and Chairman of subsidiary Cos; Chairman, Marbon UK Ltd, since 1970; *b* 4 Aug. 1923; *s* of Thomas Henry Hewlett, JP (MP, Manchester Exchange, 1940-45); *m* 1949, Millicent, *d* of Sir John (William) Taylor, *qv*; two *s*. *Educ:* Clifton; Magdalene Coll., Cambridge. Served War of 1939-45, Royal Marines (Lieut). BA 1948 (2nd Cl. Hons, Econs and Polit. Tripos); MA 1952. Pres., Cambridge Union, 1948; Chm., Cambridge Univ. Conservatives, 1948; Sec. Cambridge Univ. Rifle Assoc., 1947. Chm., NW Br. of Inst. of Export, 1961-66 (Corporate MIEx, 1957). Mem. Manchester City Council, 1949-56; Mem. Manchester and Salford Street Children's (Wood Street) Mission Management Cttee, 1950-; President: 2/230th Boy Scouts, 1957-; 1st Wythenshawe Boy Scouts, 1958-67; Mem. Youth Cttee, Manchester City Council, 1959-65; Vice-Pres. Manchester Br. Cripples Aid Soc., 1963-; Mem. Manchester Cttee RNLI, 1964-. President: Altrincham and Sale Div. Young Conservs Assoc., 1961-; City of Manchester Young Conservs, 1967-68; Chairman: Altrincham and Sale Div. Cons. Assoc., 1954-61 (Vice-Pres. 1961-); NW Area Young Conservs, 1951-53 (Vice-Pres. 1963-); Dep. Chm., Wythenshawe Div. Cons. Assoc., 1953-54; Vice-Chm. Nat. Young Conservs, 1953; Mem. Nat. Union Exec. Cttee, Cons. Party, 1952-; Chm. Exec. Cttee, Nat. Union Cons. and Unionist Assocs, 1965- (Pres. NW Area, 1966-69, Chm. 1961-66, Vice-Chm. 1956); Mem. Gen. Cttee, Constitutional Club, 1967-. Member: Council, Theatre Sixty Nine; Court of Governors, Manchester Univ., 1966-. JP Manchester, 1965. FIRI 1966; FBIM 1969. *Recreations:* gardening, photography. *Address:* Dane Edge, Swettenham, Congleton, Cheshire. *T:* Lower Withington 363; Anchor Chemical Co. Ltd, Clayton, Manchester M11 4SR. *T:* 061-223 2461-6. *Clubs:* Carlton, Constitutional, Cambridge Union.

**HEWLINGS, David George,** DFC 1942; AFC 1945; Assistant Controller, Prison Department, Home Office, since 1969; *b* 23 April 1915; *s* of Ernest Patrick Hewlings and Hilda Louise Hewlings (*née* Fountain); *m* 1944, Diana Hippisley Packham (*widow, née* Meade); two *s* one step *d*. *Educ:* Cheltenham Coll.; Queen's Coll., Oxford. Entered RAFVR, trained as pilot; Coastal Command, 1940. Asst Man., Rugby Clubs, Notting Dale, 1935-38; joined Prison Service, 1938; Housemaster: Portland Borstal, 1938-40; Rochester Borstal, 1946; Hewell Grange Borstal, 1946-48; Dep. Governor, Portland Borstal, 1948-49; Governor, Hewell Grange Borstal, 1949-55; Chief Admin. Officer, Welwyn Garden City and Hatfield New Town Devt. Corps, 1955-58; Governor: Wetherby Borstal, 1958-61; Leyhill Prison, 1961-63; Principal, Prison Service Staff Coll., Wakefield, 1963-68; Governor, Wormwood Scrubs Prison, 1968-69. *Address:* 34a Eaton Rise, Ealing, W5.

**HEWSON, Sir Bushby;** *see* Hewson, Sir J. B.

**HEWSON, George Henry Phillips,** MA, MusD (Dublin); FRCO (hc); Professor of Music, Dublin University, 1937-62, now Emeritus; *b* 19 Nov. 1881; *s* of Edmund and Caroline Hewson; *m* 1929; three *d*. *Educ:* St Patrick's Cathedral Grammar Sch.; Trinity Coll., Dublin. Organist and Choirmaster. Chapel Royal, Dublin Castle; Armagh Cathedral. Hon. Fellow, Trinity Coll., Dublin, 1962. *Publications:* Anthems, Services, Part-songs. *Recreations:* motoring, tennis. *Address:* 18 Gilford Road, Sandymount, Dublin. *T:* Dublin 683614. *Clubs:* Hibernian Catch, University (Dublin).

**HEWSON, Sir (Joseph) Bushby,** Kt 1958; RD 1941; Judge of High Court of Justice, Probate, Divorce and Admiralty Division, 1958-66; *b* 1 June 1902; 2nd *s* of Wilfred Bushby Hewson; *m* 1933, Helen Mary Ropner; one *d*. *Educ:* HMS Conway, Rock Ferry, Ches. Midshipman, Royal Naval Reserve, 1920; Extra Master, 1928; called to Bar, Inner Temple, 1936; Bencher, 1958. Comdr Royal Naval Reserve, 1942. Served War of 1939-45, in Royal Navy. Junior Counsel to Admiralty (Admiralty Court), 1952-58; QC 1958. Fellow of Institute of Navigation, 1960. *Publications:* A History of the Practice of Navigation, 1951. *Address:* 77 Eyre Court, St John's Wood, NW8. *T:* 01-722 4041. *Club:* MCC.

**HEXHAM and NEWCASTLE, Bishop of, (RC),** since 1958; **Rt. Rev. James Cunningham;** *b* Manchester, 15 Aug. 1910; *s* of Patrick William Cunningham and Mary Elizabeth (*née* Meehan). *Educ:* Xaverian Coll., Manchester; St Joseph's Coll., Upholland, Lancs; Gregorian Univ., Rome. Ordained priest, Salford, 1937; Curate, Salford Cathedral, 1940-41; Bishop's Sec. and on staff of Salford Cathedral, 1941-53; Vicar Gen., Administrator and Canon of Salford Cathedral, 1953; Domestic Prelate, 1954-; Vicar Capitular, Salford Dio., 1955; Vicar Gen. of Salford Diocese, 1956-57; Auxiliary Bishop of Hexham and Newcastle, 1957-58, and Vicar Capitular, 1958-. *Address:* Bishop's House, East Denton Hall, 800 West Road, Newcastle upon Tyne, 5.

**HEXHAM and NEWCASTLE,** Auxiliary Bishop of (RC); *see* Lindsay, Rt Rev. H.

**HEXT, Maj.-Gen. Frederick Maurice,** CB 1954; OBE 1945; CEng; FIMechE; FIEE; *b* 5 May 1901; *s* of Frederick Robert Hext; *m* 1924, Kathleen Goulden; one *s*. *Educ:* Portsmouth Gram. Sch.; RMA, Woolwich. Commissioned RE 1921; served in India, 1925-28, and 1931-34; Instructor, Sch. of Military Engineering, 1939-42; served NW Europe Campaign (despatches) Comdr, REME, 53rd (Welsh) Div., and Dep. Dir of Mechanical Engineering, 12 Corps; DDME, 1 Corps, 1945-46; DDME, Burma Command, 1946-48; AAG, AG 21, War Office, 1949-51; DME, BAOR, 1951-53; Inspector of REME, 1953-56, retired 1956. Hon. Col 53 (Welsh) Inf. Div. REME, 1956-61. Maj.-Gen., 1953. Member Wessex RHB; Chm. Isle of Wight Group Hospital Management Cttee. *Address:* Orchard Dene, Undercliff, St Lawrence, Isle of Wight. *T:* Niton 387.

**HEY, Donald Holroyde,** FRS 1955, DSc (Manchester), PhD, BSc (London) MSc (Wales), FRIC; Daniell Professor of Chemistry, University of London, since 1950; President, Section B, British Association for the Advancement of Science, 1965; *b* Swansea, 1904; 2nd *s* of Arthur Hey, MusB, FRCO, LRAM, and Frances Jane Hey; *m* 1931, Jessie, MSc (Wales), *d* of Thomas and Katharine Jones; one *s* one *d*. *Educ:* Magdalen Coll. Sch., Oxford; University Coll., Swansea. Asst

Lecturer in Chemistry, University of Manchester, 1928-30; Lecturer in Chemistry, University of Manchester, 1930-38; Lecturer in Chemistry, Imperial Coll. of Science and Technology, London, 1939-41; Dir of British Schering Research Institute, 1941-45; University Prof. of Chemistry at King's Coll., London, 1945-50; Asst Principal, King's Coll., 1962-68. Vice-Pres. of Chemical Soc. 1951-54 (Tilden Lectr, 1951, Pedler Lectr, 1970, Hon. Secretary, 1946-51). Reilly Lectr, University of Notre Dame, Indiana, 1952; Visiting Prof. University of Florida, 1967. FKC; Fellow Imp. Coll. of Science and Technology, 1968. Hon. DSc, Wales, 1970. Intra-Science Res. Conf. Award and Medal, Santa Monica, Calif., 1968. *Publications:* The Radio Universe, 1971; articles in scientific journals, mainly in Journ. of Chem. Soc. *Recreations:* music, gardening. *Address:* King's College, Strand, WC2. *T:* 01-836 5454.

**HEY, Air Vice-Marshal Ernest,** CB 1967; CBE 1963 (OBE 1954); CEng; Air Member for Technical Services, Department of Air, Canberra, since 1960; *b* Plymouth, Devon, 29 Nov. 1912; *s* of Ernest Hey, Terrigal, NSW; *m* 1936, Lorna, *d* of Sqdn Ldr A. Bennett, Melbourne; one *s* one *d*. *Educ:* Sydney Technical High Sch.; Sydney University. RAAF cadet, 1934; served War of 1939-45; Dir Technical Services, 1947-54; AOC Maintenance Comd, 1956-57; Imp. Defence Coll., 1957; Liaison Air Material Comd, USAF, 1958-59. *Recreation:* sailing. *Address:* 36 Holmes Crescent, Campbell, Canberra, ACT 2601, Australia. *Club:* Canberra Yacht.

**HEY, James Stanley,** MBE 1945; DSc; retired; Research Scientist at Royal Radar Establishment, 1952-69; Chief Scientific Officer, 1966-69; *b* 3 May 1909; *s* of William Rennie Hey and Barbara Elizabeth Hey (*née* Matthews); *m* 1934, Edna Heywood. *Educ:* Rydal Sch.; Manchester Univ. BSc (Physics), 1930; MSc (X-ray Crystallography), 1931; DSc (Radio Astronomy and Radar Research), 1950. Army Operational Research Group, 1940-52 (Head of Estab., 1949-52). Eddington Medal, Royal Astron. Soc., 1959. *Publications:* research papers in scientific jls (RAS, Royal Society, Phys Soc., Philosophical Magazine, Nature, etc.) including pioneering papers in radio astronomy. *Address:* 4 Shortlands Close, Willingdon, Sussex.

**HEYCOCK,** Baron *cr* 1967 (Life Peer), of Taibach; **Llewellyn Heycock,** CBE 1959; DL, JP; Chairman, Glamorgan Education Committee since 1947; President, University of Wales Institute of Science and Technology; *b* 12 Aug. 1905; *s* of William Heycock and late Mary Heycock; *m* 1930, Olive Elizabeth (*née* Rees); one *s* (and one *s* decd). *Educ:* Eastern Sch., Port Talbot. Engine Driver, Dyffryn Yard Loco Sheds, Port Talbot. Glam CC, 1937- (Chm. 1962-63). Member: Council and Court, University of Wales; Council and Court, University Coll. of S Wales and Mon.; Gov. Body, Welsh Coll. of Adv. Tech.; Welsh Adv. Cttee for Civil Aviation; Chairman: Schools Museum Service for Wales; Port Talbot and Glyncorrwg Div. Exec. and Div. Health Cttee; Exec. Cttee, Royal National Eisteddfod of Wales, Port Talbot, 1966; Vice-Chm., Welsh Jt Educn Cttee; President: Coleg Harlech; Assoc. of Educn Cttees, 1964-65; Nat. Assoc. of Div. Execs for England and Wales, 1954-55, 1965-66; Exec. Mem., County Councils Assoc.; Hon. Druid, Nat. Eisteddfod of Wales, 1963; Vice-Pres., Nat. Theatre Co. for Wales. Hon. LLD, University of Wales, 1963. Hon. Freedom of Port Talbot, 1961. JP Glam; JP Port Talbot; DL Glam 1963. *Recreation:* Rugby football. *Address:* 1 Llewellyn Close, Taibach, Port Talbot, Glam. *T:* Port Talbot 2565.

**HEYCOCK, Air Commodore George Francis Wheaton,** CB 1963; DFC 1941; JP; Aviation Consultant; *b* 17 Sept. 1909; *s* of Rev. F. W. Heycock, MA, and Edith Rowlandson; *m* 1938, Betty Boyd; one *s*. *Educ:* Haileybury and Imperial Service Coll.; Cranwell Cadet Coll. Commnd in RAF, 1929; Flying Instructor at RAF Coll., Cranwell and Central Flying Sch., 111 Sqdn, Fleet Air Arm, 1935-37. Test Pilot, Farnborough, 1937-39. Command of 23 and 141 Sqdns, 1940-42. Dir of Ops, Indian Air Force, 1949; Command of RAF Syerston, 1950-52; Air Ministry, 1952-55; Chief of Staff, British Joint Services Mission (RAF Staff), Washington, and Air Attaché, Washington, 1955; Air Attaché, Paris, 1959-64. JP Northants, 1965. Comdr Légion d'Honneur. *Recreation:* golf. *Address:* 6 Carlton Tower Place, Sloane Street, SW1. *T:* 01-235 1726; The Manor House, Pytchley, Northants. *T:* Broughton 269. *Club:* Royal Air Force.

**HEYDON, Sir Peter (Richard),** Kt 1970; CBE 1959; Secretary, Department of Immigration, Australia, since 1961; *b* 9 Sept. 1913; *s* of Vigar and Emily Heydon; *m* 1942, Naomi Slater, Ottawa; one *s* two *d*. *Educ:* Fort Street High Sch., Sydney; Univ. of Sydney (BA, LLB). Admitted NSW Bar, 1936; Dept of External Affairs, 1936; Private Sec. to Minister, 1936-37 and to Attorney-General, 1938; 2nd Sec, Australian Legation, Washington, 1940-42 and Moscow, 1942-44; Counsellor, London, 1947-50 and the Hague, 1950; Minister to Brazil, 1951-53; High Comr to New Zealand, 1953-55 and to India, 1955-58; Asst Sec. 1959-60 and 1st Asst Sec. 1960-61, Dept of External Affairs. *Publications:* Quiet Decision (a study of G. F. Pearce), 1965; contrib. to Australian Dictionary of Biography. *Recreation:* golf. *Address:* 18 Tennyson Crescent, Forrest, ACT 2603, Australia. *T:* 73-2266. *Clubs:* Reform; University (Sydney); Commonwealth (Canberra).

**HEYER, Georgette;** novelist; *b* 16 Aug. 1902; *d* of George Heyer, MA, MBE; *m* 1925, George Ronald Rougier, *qv*; one *s*. *Educ:* various schools. *Publications:* The Black Moth, These Old Shades, Devil's Cub, The Conqueror, Regency Buck, An Infamous Army, Death in the Stocks, Behold, Here's Poison, A Blunt Instrument, Royal Escape, No Wind of Blame, The Spanish Bride, The Corinthian, Faro's Daughter, Penhallow, Friday's Child, The Reluctant Widow, The Foundling, Arabella, The Grand Sophy, Duplicate Death, The Quiet Gentleman, Cotillion, Detection Unlimited, The Toll-Gate, Bath Tangle, Sprig Muslin, April Lady, Sylvester, The Unknown Ajax, A Civil Contract, The Nonesuch, False Colours, Frederica, Black Sheep, Cousin Kate, Charity Girl. *Address:* 60 Jermyn Street, SW1.

**HEYERDAHL, Thor;** author and anthropologist, since 1938; *b* 6 Oct. 1914; *s* of Thor Heyerdahl and Alison Heyerdahl (*née* Lyng); *m* 1st, 1936, Liv Coucheron Torp (*d* 1969); two *s*; 2nd, 1949, Yvonne Dedekam-Simonsen; three *d*. *Educ:* University of Oslo, 1933-36. Researches in the Marquesas Islands (Pacific), 1937-38; Researches among Coast Indians of Brit. Columbia, 1939-40. Active service Free Norwegian Army-Air Force parachute unit, 1942-45. Organised and led Kon-Tiki expedition, 1947. Continued research in USA and Europe, with authorship, 1948-. Retzius Medal, Swedish Soc. for Anthropology and Geography, 1950; Mungo Park Medal, Royal Scottish Geographical Society, 1951; Prix Bonaparte-Wyse from Société de Géographie, Paris, 1951; Elish Kent

Kane Gold Medal, Geog. Soc. of Philadelphia, 1952; Vega Medal, Swedish Soc. of Anthropology and Geography, 1962; Lomonosov Medal, Moscow Univ., 1962; Royal Gold Medal, Royal Geog. Society, London, 1964. Oscar Prize for best documentary feature of 1951, Acad. of Motion Picture Arts and Sciences, 1952, etc; Comdr of Order of St Olav, Norway, 1951; Officer of El Order por Meritos Distinguidos, Peru, 1953; Gold Medal City of Lima; Gr.-Officer, Order Al Merito della Repubblica Italiana, Italy, 1965; Chm. Bd, Kon-Tiki Museum, Oslo; organised and led Norwegian Archæological Expedition to the Galapagos Islands, 1953; experiments revealing tacking principles of balsa raft in Ecuador, 1953; field research, Bolivia, Peru, Colombia, 1954. Produced Galapagos film, 1955. Organised and led Norwegian Archæological Expedition to Easter Island and the East Pacific, 1955-56. Continued research, 1957-59. Made crossing from Safi, Morocco, to W Indies in papyrus boat, Ra II, 1970. Participation in: Internat. Congress of Americanists, 1952-; Pacific Science Congresses, 1961-, all with lectures subseq. publ. in Proc. Congress. Vice-Pres., World Assoc. of World Federalists, 1966-. Mem., Royal Norwegian Acad. of Science, 1958; Fellow, New York Acad. of Sciences, 1960. Hon. Dr Oslo Univ., 1961. Hon. Mem. Geog. Soc.: Peru, 1953; Norway, 1953; Brazil, 1954; USSR, 1964. Chevalier, Grand Cross, Knights of Malta, 1970. *Publications:* Paa Jakt efter Paradiset, 1938 (Oslo, Copenhagen); The Kon-Tiki Expedition, 1948 (Oslo, etc. translated numerous languages); American Indians in the Pacific: the theory behind the Kon-Tiki expedition, 1952 (London, Stockholm, New York); Archæological Evidence of Pre-Spanish Visits to the Galapagos Islands, 1955 (New York); Aku-Aku: The Secrets of Easter Island, 1957 (Oslo, etc. trans. numerous languages); Reports of the Norwegian Achæological Expedition to Easter Island and the East Pacific, Vol. I: The Archæology of Easter Island, 1961, vol. II: Miscellaneous Papers, 1965, Vol. III, Art of Easter Island, 1969-70; Sea Routes to Polynesia, 1968. Co-editor (with E. N. Ferdon, Jr) Monograph of The School of American Research, Santa Fé, NM, USA; Navel of the World (Chapter XIV) in Vanished Civilizations, 1963. Indianer und Alt-Asiaten im Pazifik: Das Abenteuer einer Theorie, 1966 (Vienna). Contrib. National Geographical Magazine, Royal Geographical Journal, The Geographical Magazine, Archiv für Völkerkunde, Ymer, Swedish Geogr. Yearbook, South-western Journal of Anthropology, Russian Academy of Sciences Yearbook, American Antiquity, Antiquity (Cambridge). *Recreations:* outdoor life, travelling. *Address:* Laigueglia, Italy.

**HEYES, Sir Tasman (Hudson Eastwood),** Kt 1960; CBE 1953; Member, Immigration Planning Council; Director, P. Rowe (International) Pty Ltd; *b* 6 Nov. 1896; *s* of late Hudson Heyes and of Mary Heyes, Melbourne; *m* 1921, Ethel Brettell, *d* of late Archibald and Phoebe Causer, Melbourne; one *s* one *d*. *Educ:* Melbourne. Served European War, 1914-18, with 3rd Divisional Signal Co., AIF, France and Flanders, 1916-19. Attached to Historical Section, Cttee of Imperial Defence, London, and War Depts, Ottawa, Washington, and Wellington, 1924-28. Dir, Australian War Memorial, Canberra, 1939-42; Dept of Defence, Melbourne, 1942-46; Sec., Dept of Immigration, Australia, 1946-61. Mem., Australian Broadcasting Control Bd, 1963-68, retd. Nansen Medal, 1962. *Recreations:* gardening and golf. *Address:* 2 Myrnong Crescent, Toorak, Victoria 3142, Australia. *Clubs:* Melbourne; RACV (Vic.), Commonwealth Golf.

**HEYGATE, Sir John (Edward Nourse),** 4th Bt, *cr* 1831; writer (retd); *b* 19 April 1903; *s* of Arthur Connolly Gage and Frances Evelyn Rowley Heygate; *S* uncle, 1940. *Educ:* Eton; Balliol Coll., Oxford (BA). Served War of 1939-45 as Bombardier, RA. *Address:* Bellarena, Co. Londonderry, N Ireland.

**HEYMAN, Allan,** QC 1969; *b* 27 Feb. 1921; *e s* of late Erik Heyman and of Rita Heyman (*née* Meyer); *m* 1958, Anne Marie (*née* Castenschiold); one *d*. *Educ:* Stenhus Kostskole, Denmark; Univ. of Copenhagen. Master of Law (Univ. of Copenhagen), 1947. Called to Bar, Middle Temple, 1951. *Recreations:* shooting, stalking, reading, music. *Address:* 1 New Square, Lincoln's Inn, WC2; Marshland House, Iken, Woodbridge, Suffolk. *Clubs:* Bath, Shikar.

**HEYMAN, Dr Jacques,** MA, PhD; FICE; FSA; Reader in Engineering, University of Cambridge, and Fellow of Peterhouse; *b* 8 March 1925; *m* 1958, Eva Orlans; three *d*. *Educ:* Whitgift Sch.; Peterhouse, Cambridge. Fellow of Peterhouse, 1949, Senior Bursar, 1962-64; University Demonstrator, Engineering Dept, Cambridge Univ., 1951, University Lectr, 1954, Reader, 1968. Vis. Professor: Brown Univ., USA, 1957-58; Harvard Univ., 1966. mem. of Coun., Institution of Civil Engineers, 1960. *Publications:* The Steel Skeleton, vol. 2 (with Sir John Baker, M. R. Horne), 1956; Plastic Design of Portal Frames, 1957; Beams and Framed Structures, 1964; (with Sir John Baker) Plastic Design of Frames, vol. 1, 1969; articles on plastic design and general structural theory. *Address:* Engineering Laboratory, Trumpington Street, Cambridge. *T:* 55691.

**HEYTESBURY,** 5th Baron *cr* 1828; **William Leonard Frank Holmes à Court;** Bart 1795; *b* 17 April 1906; *o s* of 4th Baron and Sybil Mary (*d* 1937), *d* of late Capt. F. B. Morris; *S* father, 1949; *m* 1926, Beryl (*d* 1968), *y d* of A. E. B. Crawford, DCL, of Aston Clinton House, Bucks; one *s*. *Educ:* Pembroke Coll., Cambridge (BA). *Heir: s* Hon. Francis William Holmes à Court [*b* 8 Nov. 1931; *m* 1962, Alison, *e d* of Michael Graham Balfour; one *s* one *d*]. *Address:* Westover, Heytesbury, Wilts. *T:* Sutton Veny 324.

**HEYWOOD, Francis Melville,** MA; Warden of Lord Mayor Treloar College, 1952-69; *b* 1 Oct. 1908; 4th *s* of late Rt Rev. B. O. F. Heywood, DD; *m* 1937, Dorothea Kathleen, *e d* of late Sir Basil Mayhew, KBE; two *s* two *d*. *Educ:* Haileybury Coll. (Scholar); Gonville and Caius Coll. Cambridge (Scholar), 1st Class Hons, Classical Tripos, Part I, 1929; Part II, 1931; Rugby Football blue, 1928. Asst Master, Haileybury Coll., 1931-35; Fellow, Asst Tutor and Praelector, Trinity Hall, Cambridge, 1935-39; Master of Marlborough Coll., 1939-52. *Recreations:* gardening, shooting, walking. *Address:* The Old Bakery, Catcott, near Bridgwater, Somerset. *T:* Chilton Polden 627.

**HEYWOOD, Very Rev. Hugh Christopher Lempriere,** MA; Provost of Southwell and Rector of S Mary, Southwell, 1945-69; Priest-in-charge of Upton, Diocese of Southwell, since 1969; *b* 5 Nov. 1896; *s* of late Charles Christopher Heywood; *m* 1920, Margaret Marion, *d* of Herbert Vizard; one *s* one *d*. *Educ:* Haileybury; Trinity Coll., Cambridge (Scholar and Stanton Student). Manchester Regt 1914-17 (wounded, despatches); 74th Punjabis IA 1917-23 (Staff Capt., 1919-22); Ordained, 1926; Curate of St Andrew's the Great, Cambridge, 1926-27; of Holy Cross,

Greenford, 1927-28; Fellow and Dean, Gonville and Caius Coll., Cambridge, 1928-45; University Lecturer in Divinity, Cambridge, 1937-45; Examining Chaplain to Bishop of Southwark, 1932-41, and to Bishop of Southwell, 1941. Junior Proctor, Cambridge, 1934-35 and 1942-43. *Publications:* The Worshipping Community, 1938; On a Golden Thread, 1960. *Recreation:* walking. *Address:* Ashleigh, 31 Church Street, Southwell, Notts.

**HEYWOOD, Sir Oliver Kerr,** 5th Bt, *cr* 1888; *b* 30 June 1920; *s* of late Maj.-Gen. C. P. Heywood, CB, CMG, DSO (2nd *s* of 3rd Bt) and late Margaret Vere, *d* of late Arthur Herbert Kerr; *S* uncle 1946; *m* 1947, Denise Wymondham, 2nd *d* of late Jocelyn William Godefroi, MVO; three *s. Educ:* Eton; Trinity Coll. Cambridge (BA). Served in Coldstream Guards, 1940-46 (despatches). Profession: artist. *Heir: s* Peter Heywood [*b* 10 Dec. 1947; *m* 1970, Jacqueline Anne, *d* of R. F. Hunt, Greenacre, Charlton Park Gate, Cheltenham]. *Address:* Viner's Wood, Wickstreet, Stroud, Glos.

**HEYWOOD, Wilfred Lanceley,** CBE 1958 (OBE 1951); Member, Restrictive Practices Court, 1958-68, and since 1970; *b* 11 Sept. 1900; *s* of Edward James and Ellen Ann Heywood, Wooldale, Yorks; *m* Vera, *d* of Allen and Edith Boothroyd, Honley, Yorks; one *s. Educ:* Wooldale Council Sch.; evening classes, WEA. Formerly Gen. Sec., Nat. Union of Dyers, Bleachers and Textile Workers; Member: Gen. Council TUC, 1948-57; Brit. Wool Marketing Bd, 1950-57; Monopolies Commn, 1953-56; NCB, 1955-57; PIB, 1968-70; Royal Commission on the Working of the Tribunals of Inquiry (Evidence) Act, 1921, 1966-. *Address:* 41 Holland Avenue, SW20. *T:* 01-946 8176.

**HEYWOOD-LONSDALE, Lt-Col Arthur,** CBE 1968; MC 1943; JP; Lord Lieutenant of Shropshire, since 1970; *b* 13 May 1900; *m* 1931, Jean Katharine, *o d* of Hon. Claud Eustace Hamilton Russell; two *s. Educ:* Eton; Royal Military Coll. Sandhurst. Joined Grenadier Guards, 1919; retired 1931; re-employed 1940-45 (Major 1943). Capt. Shrops Yeomanry, 1931, Major 1938. Lieut-Col comdg Shrops Yeo., 1947-50. JP 1933, CC 1934, CA 1950, Chairman, CC, 1966-69, DL, 1951-70, High Sheriff, 1957-58, Salop. KStJ 1970. *Address:* Shavington Grange, Market Drayton, Salop. *T:* Calverhall 652. *Clubs:* Guards, Turf.

**HEYWORTH,** family name of **Baron Heyworth.**

**HEYWORTH,** 1st Baron, *cr* 1955, of Oxton; **Geoffrey Heyworth,** Kt 1948; Hon. LLD: St Andrews, 1950; Manchester, 1950; London, 1962; Bristol and Sussex, 1966, Southampton, 1970; Hon. DCL Oxon, 1957; Hon. DLitt Warwick, 1967; Hon. Fellow Nuffield College, Oxford; *b* 18 Oct. 1894; *s* of Thomas Blackwell Heyworth, Oxton, Birkenhead, and Florence Myers, Bradford, Yorks; *m* 1924, Lois Dunlop, Woodstock, Ontario, Canada; no *c. Educ:* Dollar Acad. Joined Lever Brothers Ltd at Liverpool, 1912; various positions in Canada and England until 1931; Canadian Army, 1915-18; Dir parent company, Lever Bros Ltd (now Unilever Ltd), from 1931; Chm. Unilever Ltd, 1942-60. Chm. Gas Industry Cttee, 1945; Mem. Company Law Amendment Cttee, Bd of Trade, 1943; formerly part-time mem., London Transport and NCB. Mem. Royal Commission on Taxation of Profits and Income, 1951. Chairman: Council on Productivity, Prices and Incomes, 1960-62; Cttee on Research in Social Sciences, 1963-65; Court of Governors, London Sch. of Hygiene and Tropical Medicine, 1964-70; Pres., Nat. Council of Social Service, 1961-70. Grand Officer, Order of Orange Nassau, 1947. *Address:* 29 Sussex Square, W2. *Club:* Athenæum.

**HEYWORTH, Peter Lawrence Frederick;** Music Critic of The Observer since 1955; *b* 3 June 1921; *er s* of Lawrence Ormerod Heyworth and Ella Stern. *Educ:* Charterhouse; Balliol Coll., Oxford. HM Forces, 1940-46; Balliol, 1947-50; University of Göttingen, 1950. Music critic of Times Educational Supplement, 1952-56; Record reviewer for New Statesman, 1956-58; Guest of the Ford Foundation in Berlin, 1964-65. *Recreations:* wine and escape. *Address:* 32 Bryanston Square, W1. *T:* 01-262 8906.

**HEZLET, Vice-Admiral Sir Arthur Richard,** KBE 1964; CB 1961; DSO 1944 (Bar 1945); DSC 1941; *b* 7 April 1914; *s* of late Maj.-Gen. R. K. Hezlet, CB, CBE, DSO; *m* 1948, Anne Joan Patricia, *e d* of late G. W. N. Clark, Carnabane, Upperlands, Co. Derry; two adopted *d. Educ:* RN College, Dartmouth. Comd HM Submarines: H44, Ursula, Trident, Thrasher and Trenchant, 1941-45; comd HMS Scorpion, 1949-50; Chief Staff Officer to Flag Officer (Submarines), 1953-54; Capt. (D), 6th Destroyer Squadron 1955-56; Dir, RN Staff Coll., Greenwich, 1956-57; comd HMS Newfoundland, 1958-59; Rear-Adm. 1959; Flag Officer (Submarines), 1959-61; Flag Officer, Scotland, 1961-62; Vice-Adm. 1962; Flag Officer, Scotland and Northern Ireland, 1963-64; retired 1964. Legion of Merit (Degree of Commander) (US), 1945. *Publication:* The Submarine and Sea Power, 1967; Aircraft and Sea Power, 1970. *Address:* Bovagh House, Aghadowey, Co. Derry, N Ireland. *Clubs:* Army and Navy, Royal Ocean Racing, Goat.

**HIBBERD, (Andrew) Stuart,** MBE; *b* 5 Sept. 1893; *y s* of late W. H. Hibberd, Canford Magna, Dorset; *m* 1923, Alice Mary, *e d* of late Lieut-Col Gerard Chichester, North Staffs Regt; no *c. Educ:* Weymouth Coll.; St John's Coll., Cambridge (MA). Served European War in 7th and 5th Batt. Dorset Regt; and 46th Punjabis IA; later 2/25th Punjabis IA; served in Gallipoli, Mesopotamia and Waziristan. Joined BBC, at Savoy Hill, 1924; on Headquarter Staff until retirement, 1951; for some years Chief Announcer. Fellow: Royal Society of Arts; Royal Society of St George. *Publication:* "This–is London", 1951. *Recreations:* gardening, music. *Address:* 2 West Field, Budleigh Salterton, Devon.

**HIBBERD, Prof. George,** PhD; ARTC, CEng, FIMinE; FRSE; Dixon Professor of Mining, University of Glasgow, and Professor of Mining, University of Strathclyde, Glasgow, 1947-67, now Emeritus; *b* Muirkirk, NB, 17 May 1901; *e s* of Charles Hibberd and Helen Brown; *m* 1931, Marion Dalziel Robb Adamson; two *s* two *d. Educ:* Muirkirk Public Sch.; Royal Tech. Coll., Glasgow. Walter Duncan Res. Scholar. Mining official, 1926-28; Coll. Lectr, 1928-46. Past Pres. Mining Inst. of Scotland. Mem. Council, Inst. Mining Engineers. *Publications:* A Survey of the Welsh Slate Industry; A Survey of The Caithness Flagstone Industry; numerous papers on mining and scientific subjects in technical press. (Jointly) A Survey of the Scottish Slate Industry and A Survey of the Scottish Free-Stone Quarrying Industry. *Recreations:* golf, gardening. *Address:* 120 Kings Park Avenue, Glasgow S4. *T:* 041-632 4608.

**HIBBERD, Stuart;** *see* Hibberd, A. S.

**HIBBERT, Christopher,** MC 1945; author; *b* 5 March 1924; *s* of Canon H. V. Hibbert; *m* 1948, Susan Piggford; two *s* one *d. Educ:* Radley;

Oriel Coll., Oxford (MA). Served in Italy, 1944-45; Capt., London Irish Rifles. Partner in firm of land agents, auctioneers and surveyors, 1948-59. Fellow, Chartered Auctioneers' and Estate Agents' Inst., 1948-59. Won Heinemann Award for Literature, 1962. FRSL. *Publications:* The Road to Tyburn, 1957; King Mob, 1958; Wolfe at Quebec, 1959; The Destruction of Lord Raglan, 1961; Corunna, 1961; Benito Mussolini, 1962; The Battle of Arnhem, 1962; The Roots of Evil, 1963; The Court at Windsor, 1964; Agincourt, 1964; (ed) The Wheatley Diary, 1964; Garibaldi and His Enemies, 1965; The Making of Charles Dickens, 1967; (ed) Waterloo: Napoleon's Last Campaign, 1967; (ed) An American in Regency England: The Journal of Louis Simond, 1968; Charles I, 1968; The Grand Tour, 1969; London: Biography of a City, 1969; The Search for King Arthur, 1970; (ed) The Recollections of Rifleman Harris, 1970; Anzio: the bid for Rome, 1970; The Dragon Wakes: China and the West, 1793-1911, 1970. *Recreation:* painting. *Address:* 64 St Andrew's Road, Henley-on-Thames, Oxon.

**HIBBERT, Denys Heseltine,** CBE 1954; Director of Education and Member of Legislative Council, British Solomon Islands Protectorate, 1966-70; *b* 17 Oct. 1905; *s* of late Rev. and Mrs E. H. Hibbert; *m* 1931, Siblie Langmuir Napier; three *d*. *Educ:* Radley Coll.; Worcester Coll., Oxford. Sudan Political Service, 1928; Warden, Gordon Coll., Khartoum, 1943-45; Asst Dir of Education, 1945-50; Dir of Education, Sudan, 1950-54. Headmaster, Portsmouth Grammar Sch., 1954-65. Adviser in Education, Abu Dhabi, Trucial States, Jan.-July, 1965. Life Governor, CMS, 1963. *Recreation:* bridge. *Address:* Little Acre, Godshill, Fordingbridge, Hants. *T:* Fordingbridge 3316.

**HIBBERT, Eleanor;** author; *b* London, 1906. *Educ:* privately. *Publications: as Jean Plaidy:* Together They Ride, 1945; Beyond The Blue Mountains, 1947; Murder Most Royal (and as The King's Pleasure, USA), 1949; The Goldsmith's Wife, 1950; Madame Serpent, 1951; Daughter of Satan, 1952; The Italian Woman, 1952; Sixth Wife, 1953, new edn 1969; Queen Jezebel, 1953; St Thomas's Eve, 1954; The Spanish Bridegroom, 1954; Gay Lord Robert, 1955; The Royal Road to Fotheringay, 1955, new edn 1968; The Wandering Prince, 1956; A Health Unto His Majesty, 1956; Here Lies Our Sovereign Lord, 1956; Flaunting Extravagant Queen, 1956, new edn 1960; Triptych of Poisoners, 1958, new edn 1970; Madonna of the Seven Hills, 1958; Light on Lucrezia, 1958; Louis the Wellbeloved, 1959; The Road to Compiegne, 1959; The Rise of the Spanish Inquisition, 1959; The Growth of the Spanish Inquisition, 1960; Castile For Isabella, 1960; Spain for the Sovereigns, 1960; The End of the Spanish Inquisition, 1961; Daughters of Spain, 1961; Katherine, The Virgin Widow, 1961; Meg Roper, Daughter of Sir Thomas More (for children), 1961; The Young Elizabeth (for children), 1961; The Shadow of the Pomegranate, 1962; The King's Secret Matter, 1962; The Young Mary, Queen of Scots, 1962; The Captive Queen of Scots, 1963; Mary, Queen of France, 1964; The Murder in the Tower, 1964; The Thistle and the Rose, 1965; The Three Crowns, 1965; Evergreen Gallant, 1965; The Haunted Sisters, 1966; The Queen's Favourites, 1966; The Princess of Celle, 1967; Queen in Waiting, 1967; The Spanish Inquisition, its Rise, Growth and End (3 vols in one), 1967; Caroline The Queen, 1968; Katharine of Aragon (3 vols in one), 1968; The Prince and the Quakeress, 1968; The Third George, 1969; Catherine de Medici (3 vols in one), 1969; Perdita's Prince, 1969; Sweet Lass of Richmond Hill, 1970; *as Eleanor Burford:* Daughter of Anna, 1941; Passionate Witness, 1941; Married Love, 1942; When All The World Was Young, 1943; So The Dreams Depart, 1944; Not In Our Stars, 1945; Dear Chance, 1947; Alexa, 1948; The House At Cupid's Cross, 1949; Behave The Heart, 1950; Love Child, 1950; Saint Or Sinner?, 1951; Dear Delusion, 1952; Bright Tomorrow, 1952; When We Are Married, 1953; Leave Me My Love, 1953; Castles in Spain, 1954; Hearts Afire, 1954; When Other Hearts, 1955; Two Loves In Her Life, 1955; Married in Haste, 1956; Begin To Live, 1956; To Meet A Stranger, 1957; Pride of the Morning, 1958; Blaze of Noon, 1958; Dawn Chorus, 1959; Red Sky At Night, 1959; Night of Stars, 1960; Now That April's Gone, 1961; Who's Calling?, 1962; *as Ellalice Tate:* Defenders of The Faith, 1956 (under name of Jean Plaidy, 1970); Scarlet Cloak, 1957 (2nd edn, under name of Jean Plaidy, 1969); Queen of Diamonds, 1958; Madame Du Barry, 1959; This Was A Man, 1961; *as Elbur Ford:* The Flesh and The Devil, 1950; Poison in Pimlico, 1950; Bed Disturbed, 1952; Such Bitter Business, 1953 (as Evil in the House, USA 1954); *as Kathleen Kellow:* Danse Macabre, 1952; Rooms At Mrs Oliver's, 1953; Lilith, 1954 (2nd edn, under name of Jean Plaidy, 1967); It Began in Vauxhall Gardens, 1955 (2nd edn under name of Jean Plaidy, 1968); Call of the Blood, 1956; Rochester–The Mad Earl, 1957; Milady Charlotte, 1959; The World's A Stage, 1960; *as Victoria Holt:* Mistress of Mellyn, 1961; Kirkland Revels, 1962; The Bride of Pendorric, 1963; The Legend of the Seventh Virgin, 1965; Menfreya, 1966; The King of the Castle, 1967; The Queen's Confession, 1968; The Shivering Sands, 1969. *Address:* c/o Robert Hale Ltd., 63 Old Brompton Road, SW7.

**HIBBERT, Francis Dennis,** CMG 1958; ED 1946; *b* 18 Aug. 1906; *s* of Preb. F. A. Hibbert, MA, Headmaster of Worksop Coll. and of Denstone Coll., and Prebendary of Lichfield Cathedral; *m* 1939, Annie Doreen Coomber; one *d*. *Educ:* Denstone Coll.; Bloxham Sch.; St John's Coll., Cambridge (MA). Joined Educ. Dept, Nigeria, as Supt of Education, 1929; served Bauchi, Katsina and Plateau Provinces, and Northern Provinces HQ Office, Kaduna, 1929-40. Commnd Supplementary Reserve, The Nigeria Regt, RWAFF, 1930; served 6th Bn The Nigeria Regt, HQ 3rd W African Infantry Bde, and The West African Trg and Reinforcement Camp, Nigeria and India, 1940-45 (Major). Rejoined Educ. Dept., Nigeria, 1946; served Bornu and Plateau Provinces, and HQ Offices, Lagos and Kaduna; Chief Educ. Officer, Northern Region, 1951; Dep. Dir of Education, Northern Region, 1952; Chm., Public Service Commn, Northern Region, Nov. 1954-Oct. 1958, retired. Min. of Overseas Develt, 1962-69. *Recreations:* watching cricket and gardening. *Address:* Hemphayes, Charlton Mackrell, Somerton, Somerset. *T:* Charlton Mackrell 386.

**HIBBERT, Maj.-Gen. Hugh Brownlow,** DSO 1940; *b* 10 Dec. 1893; *s* of late Adm. H. T. Hibbert, CBE, DSO; *m* 1926, Susan Louisa Mary Feilding; one *s* one *d*. *Educ:* Uppingham; RMC, Sandhurst. Retired pay, 1946. *Address:* Sunton House, Collingbourne Ducis, Wilts.

**HIBBERT, Hon. Julian Thurstan H.;** *see* Holland-Hibbert.

**HIBBERT, Reginald Alfred,** CMG 1966; HM Diplomatic Service; Political Adviser to Commander-in-Chief Far East, Singapore, since 1970; *b* 21 Feb. 1922; *s* of Alfred Hibbert, Barnet, Herts; *m* 1949, Ann Alun Pugh, *d* of Sir

Alun Pugh, Dunsfold, Surrey; two *s* one *d*. *Educ:* Queen Elizabeth's Sch., Barnet; Worcester Coll., Oxford. Served with SOE and 4th Hussars in Albania and Italy, 1943-45. Entered Foreign Service, 1946; served in Bucharest, Vienna, Guatemala, Ankara, Brussels; Chargé d'Affaires, Ulan Bator, 1964-66; Research Fellow, Leeds Univ., 1966-67; Political Adviser's Office, Singapore, 1967-70. *Address:* 79 Broad Lane, Hampton, Middx. *T:* 01-979 5714. *Club:* Reform.

**HICHENS, Mrs Mary Hermione,** CBE 1950; ARRC; JP Oxon; County Councillor Oxon since 1937, Alderman, 1951; *b* 15 Oct. 1894; 3rd *d* of Gen. Rt Hon. Sir N. G. Lyttelton, GCB, GCVO; *m* 1919, William Lionel Hichens (Chm. of Cammell Laird; killed by enemy action, 1940); two *s* three *d*. *Educ:* Alexander Coll., Dublin; in Paris. Saved as Military Probationer QAIMNS in England, 1915; in France, 1916-19 (despatches, ARRC); Mem. of Royal Commission on the Geographical Distribution of the Industrial Population, 1937-39, signed Minority Report; Mem. of Consultative Panel on Post-War Reconstruction to Minister of Works and Buildings; Mem. of Departmental Cttee on Land Utilisation, 1941; Mem. of Departmental Cttee on Training of Teachers, 1942; Chm. of Education Cttee, 1946-57; Commissioner under the Catering Act, 1943-58. *Recreation:* gardening. *Address:* North Aston Hall, Oxford. *T:* Steeple Aston 200.

**HICKIE, Brig. George William Clement,** CBE 1943 (OBE 1920); RIASC (retired); *b* 2 March 1897; *s* of late Major W. B. Hickie, IA; *m* 1924, Nora Margaret Peel Corbin; no *c*. *Educ:* Cheltenham; Imperial Services Coll.; RMC Sandhurst. Served European War, 1914-18; BEF France, EEF Egypt and Palestine (despatches twice); DADST, British Mil. Mission, South Russia, 1919-20 (despatches, OBE, 2nd class Order of St Stanislaus); Northern Command, India, ADS 1938-39. ADST Peshawar Dist 1939-40; Dep. Dir of Transport, Army HQ, India, 1940-41; DDS and T Tenth Army, British Forces in Iraq and Paiforce, 1941-43 (CBE); Brig. NW Army, India Command, 1943; DDST, GHQ, India, 1944-45; offg DST, GHQ, India, 1945 (Actg Maj.-Gen.); Brig. RIASC, Northern Command, India, 1945-47; retired, 1947. *Recreations:* tennis, cricket, golf. *Address:* c/o Lloyds Bank Ltd, 6 Pall Mall, SW1; 25 Southfields Road, Eastbourne, Sussex. *T:* Eastbourne 22602.

**HICKINBOTHAM, Rev. Canon James Peter;** Principal of Wycliffe Hall, Oxford, since 1970; *b* 16 May 1914; *s* of late F. J. L. Hickinbotham, JP and Mrs Hickinbotham; *m* 1948, Ingeborg Alice Lydia Manger; two *s* one *d*. *Educ:* Rugby Sch.; Magdalen Coll., Oxford; Wycliffe Hall, Oxford. Deacon, 1937; priest, 1938; curate: St John, Knighton, Leicester, 1937-39; St Paul, S Harrow, 1940-42; Chaplain, Wycliffe Hall, Oxford, 1942-45; Vice-Principal, 1945-50. Prof. of Theology, University Coll. of the Gold Coast, 1950-54. Principal, St John's Coll. and Cranmer Hall, Durham, 1954-70. Examining Chaplain: to Bishop of Manchester, 1947-50; to Bishop of Leicester, 1948-53; to Bishop of Durham, 1955-70. Proctor in Convocation, 1957-70. Hon. Canon, Durham Cathedral, 1959-70. *Address:* 2 Norham Gardens, Oxford OX2 6QB. *T:* Oxford 57539.

**HICKINBOTHAM, Sir Tom,** KCMG, 1953 (CMG 1951); KCVO 1954; CIE 1944; OBE 1939; Director, The Eastern Bank; Chairman, Board of Governors, The London Clinic, since 1968 (a Governor since 1959); *b* 27 April 1903; 2nd *s* of James Ryland Hickinbotham, MB, and Beatrice Elliot, *d* of Rev. Theophilus Sharp, MA. *Educ:* Royal Military Coll., Sandhurst. Entered Indian Army, 1923; served North West Frontier, 1924 (medal); posted to 5th Battalion Baluch Regiment, 1924; transferred to Indian Political Service, 1930; served in various appointments in Aden, 1931-32, 1933-35, and 1938-39; Political Agent, Bahrain, 1937, Muscat, 1939-41, Kuwait, 1941-43, Bahrain, 1943-45; Kalat, 1945-47; Chm. of the Aden Port Trust, 1948-51; Governor and Comdr-in-Chief of Colony and Protectorate of Aden, 1951-56, retired from Government Service. *Publication:* Aden, 1958. *Recreation:* fishing. *Address:* London Clinic, 20 Devonshire Place, W1. *Club:* Travellers'.

**HICKLING, Charles Frederick,** CMG 1951; MA, ScD Cantab; Fisheries Adviser, Department of Technical Co-operation, 1961, retired 1962; *b* 15 Aug. 1902; *s* of late R. A. Hickling, Chik Ballapura, S India; *m* 1930, Marjorie Ellerington, *d* of late Henry Blamey, Dovercourt; two *s*. *Educ:* Taunton Sch.; St Catherine's Coll., Cambridge (Scholar); Dept of Oceanography, Univ. of Liverpool, 1925-26; Ministry of Agriculture and Fisheries, 1927-45; Port Fishery Capt., Milford Haven, 1939-45; Buckland Prof., 1934; Acting Dir, Tropical Fish Culture Research Institute, Malacca, 1957-59; Fisheries Adviser to Sec. of State for the Colonies, 1945-61. *Publications:* Tropical Inland Fisheries, 1961; Fish Culture, 1962 (new edn, 1970); numerous publications and monographs on fisheries, fisheries biology and zoology. *Address:* 95 Greenway, Totteridge, N20.

**HICKLING, Reginald Hugh,** CMG 1968; Maritime Law Adviser, Ceylon, 1970; *b* 2 Aug. 1920; *er s* of late Frederick Hugh Hickling and Elsie May Hickling, Malvern, Worcs; *m* 1945, Beryl Iris (*née* Dennett); two *s* one *d* (and one *s* decd). *Educ:* Buxton Coll.; Nottingham Univ. RNVR, 1941-46. Dep. Solicitor, Evening Standard, London, 1946-50; Asst Attorney-Gen., Sarawak, 1950-55; Legal Adviser, Johore, 1956; Legal Draftsman, Malaya, 1957; Parly Draftsman, Malaya, 1959; Comr of Law Revision, Malaya, 1961; Commonwealth Office, 1964; Legal Adviser to High Comr, Aden and Protectorate of S Arabia, 1964-67; Maritime Law Adviser: Thailand, 1968-69; Malaysia, 1969. *Publications:* The Furious Evangelist, 1950; The English Flotilla, 1954 (US as Falconer's Voyage, 1956); Sarawak and Its Government, 1955; Festival of Hungry Ghosts, 1957; An Introduction to the Federal Constitution, 1960; Lieutenant Okino, 1968. *Recreation:* recorded music. *Address:* 1 Highfield Road, Malvern, Worcs. *T:* Malvern 3477.

**HICKMAN, Sir (Alfred) Howard (Whitby),** 3rd Bt, *cr* 1903; *b* 29 Jan. 1920; *s* of Major Sir Alfred Hickman, 2nd Bt, and Lilian Brenda, *o d* of late B. Howard Mander and Mrs Mander, of Trysull Manor, Wolverhampton; *S* father, 1947; *m* 1948, Mrs Margaret D. Thatcher, *o d* of Leonard Kempson; one *s*. *Educ:* Eton. *Heir: s* Richard Glenn Hickman, *b* 12 April 1949. *Address:* Shenley Cottage, Radlett, Herts. *T:* Radlett 6605.

**HICKMAN, Sir Howard;** *see* Hickman, Sir A. H. W.

**HICKMAN, John Kyrle;** Deputy High Commissioner, Singapore, since 1969; *b* 3 July 1927; *s* of late J. B. Hickman and Joan Hickman; *m* 1956, Jennifer Love; two *s* one *d*. *Educ:* Tonbridge; Trinity Hall, Cambridge. Served in RA, 1948-50. Asst Principal, WO, 1950; Principal, 1955; transf. to CRO, 1958; UK High Commn, Wellington, 1959-62; HM

Diplomatic Service, 1965; British Embassy, Madrid, 1966; Counsellor and HM Consul-General, Bilbao, 1967. *Recreations:* ski-ing, golf. *Address:* c/o Foreign and Commonwealth Office, King Charles Street, SW1. *Club:* Oxford and Cambridge University.

**HICKS;** *see* Joynson-Hicks.

**HICKS, Brig. Sir (Cedric) Stanton,** Kt 1936; CStJ; MSc (1st Class Hons), MB, ChB NZ; MD Adelaide; PhD Cantab; FRIC (London), FCS (London); FRSA; Emeritus Professor of Human Physiology and Pharmacology in University of Adelaide (Professor 1926-58); *b* Mosgiel, NZ, 2 June 1892; *s* of George Henry Hicks and Sarah, *d* of Stanton Evans; *m* 1st, Florence (marr. diss. 1948), *e d* of John Haggitt, Dunedin, NZ; two *s* (and one *s* decd); 2nd, 1948, Valerie, *d* of Lt-Col S. H. Hubbard, Peppermint Grove, WA. *Educ:* Otago Boys High Sch.; Otago Univ. (Selwyn Coll.); Trinity Coll., Cambridge; Universities of Zürich and Vienna. Junior National Scholar, 1906; erected and operated first wireless telegraph in NZ 1908; BSc 1913; MSc 1914; NZ National Research Scholar; produced report on Preservation of Structural Timber, 1915; Synthesis of Chloramine with J. K. H. Inglis for War Purposes and Enlistment, 1916 NZMC Expeditionary Force: AIF, 1939-45; Government Analyst, Otago and Southland, New Zealand, 1918-23; established Clinical Pathology Laboratory, Otago Medical Sch., 1922; Clinical Pathologist, Otago Hosp. and Medical Sch.; with A. M. Drennan initiated research into Endemic Goitre in New Zealand, 1920-23; Beit Memorial Research Fellow and Research Studentship, Trinity Coll., Cambridge, 1923; Mem. of Cttee on Endocrine Research, Medical Research Council, 1925-26; PhD Cantab 1925; Sheridan Research Fellow, Univ. of Adelaide, 1926-31; Mem. Commonwealth National Research Council, 1930; Commonwealth Nutrition Advisory Cttee, 1936-38; Nutrition Cttee Council National Health and Medical Research, 1939-59; Vice-Pres. Nat. Old People's Welfare Council. Dir Army Catering, Allied Land Forces, and AMF, 1942-52. Mem. Med. Advisory Cttee, Army, Navy and Air Force, 1940; Scientific Advisory Cttee, (Food Stuffs), 1941; Personnel Research Cttee, 1941. Founded Australian Army Catering Corps, 1942. Scientific Mission, US and UK, 1944; Pres. Council Social Services, SA, 1946-48; Chm. Defence Food Stuffs Res. Cttee, 1949-59. Scientific Food Consultant, Army, Australia, 1952-. *Publications:* scientific papers; Molecular Structure and Physiological Action; Physiological Observations on the Aboriginals of Central Australia on Expeditions in 1931-32-33, 1934, 1936 and 1937, and Chemistry and Pharmacology of Native Poisons; Sanderson Wells Lecturer, University of London, 1950; CIBA Lecturer, London, 1950. Managing Editor Australian Journal of Experimental Biology and Medical Science; Ed. Board, Excerpta Medica, Amsterdam; Ed. Board Internat. Jl of Vitamin Research, Bern; Food and Folly, 1952; Life from the Soil, 1953; Physiology of Nutrition, 1957; Terrestrial Animals in the Cold: Studies of Primitive Man, 1964; Land Reform in Southern Italy, 1969. *Recreations:* travel, gardening, mechanical tinkering. *Address:* Woodley, Glen Osmond, SA 5064, Australia. *Clubs:* Royal Societies; Naval and Military (Adelaide).

**HICKS, Col Sir Denys (Theodore),** Kt 1961; OBE 1950; TD 1943; DL; Member Council of The Law Society, 1948-69; *b* 2 May 1908; *s* of late Cuthbert Hicks, Bristol; *m* 1941, Irene Elizabeth Mansell Leach; four *d. Educ:* Clifton. Admitted a Solicitor of Supreme Court of Judicature, 1931. Served War of 1939-45; with RA in UK and on staff. Col 1953. Vice-President of The Law Society, 1959, Pres., 1960; Chairman: Internat. Bar Assoc., 1966-; Metropolitan and Country Racecourse Management and Holdings, 1969-. Member: Horserace Betting Levy Board, 1961; Royal Commission on Assizes and QS, 1967. Hon. Member: Amer. Bar Assoc., 1960; Il Ilustre y Nacional Collegio de Abagados de Mexico, 1964; Virginia State Bar Assoc., 1966. DL Glos, 1957. *Address:* 39 Durdham Park, Bristol 6. *T:* 33439; 12 Berkeley Square, Bristol 8. *T:* 294351. *Clubs:* Royal Automobile; Constitutional (Bristol).

**HICKS, Donald,** OBE 1968; MSc (London), MIChemE, FRIC; Director-General, British Coal Utilisation Research Association, 1962-67; *b* 26 June 1902; *e s* of late Benjamin and Matilda Hicks; *m* May, *y d* of late William and Margaret Sainsbury, Shirenewton, Chepstow; no *c. Educ:* Pontypridd Grammar Sch.; Glamorgan Coll. of Technology. Chief Coal Survey Officer, DSIR, S Wales, 1930-45; Supt of Coal Survey Organisation, DSIR, 1946; Dir of Scientific Control, Nat. Coal Bd, 1947-58; Carbonisation and Scientific Dir and Mem. East Midland Divisional Bd of NCB, 1959-62; Dir of Operational Research and Dir of Pneumoconiosis Field Research, Nat. Coal Bd, 1949-62. *Publications:* papers in various scientific and technical jls. *Recreations:* walking and reading. *Address:* 26 St Kingsmark Avenue, Chepstow, Mon NP6 5LY. *T:* Chepstow 3147.

**HICKS, Sir Edwin (William),** Kt 1965; CBE 1956; Australian High Commissioner, Wellington, New Zealand, since 1968; *b* 9 June 1910; *s* of late William Banks Hicks, Melbourne, Victoria; *m* 1st, 1937, Jean (*d* 1959), *yr d* of late Thomas MacPherson, Brighton, Victoria; four *s* one *d*; 2nd, 1961, Lois, *o d* of Norman S. Swindon, Canberra; one *s* one *d. Educ:* Haileybury; Melbourne Grammar Sch.; Canberra Univ. Coll. (BCom 1947). Commonwealth Public Service Bd, 1929-31; Commonwealth Statistician's Branch, 1931-38; Trade and Customs Dept, 1938-48; Senior Inspector, then Actg Asst Comr Commonwealth Public Service Bd, investigating organisation and methods of Commonwealth Govt Depts, 1948-51; Secretary: Dept of Air, Commonwealth of Australia, 1951-56; Dept of Defence, 1956-68. Served 1942-45 with Royal Australian Air Force in South West Pacific Area. *Recreations:* formerly: cricket, football, tennis; now golf. *Address:* c/o Australian High Commission, PO Box 12-145, Wellington, New Zealand.

**HICKS, Lt-Col James Hamilton,** OBE 1966; TD 1945; Vice-Lieutenant for the County of Bute since 1957; *b* 21 April 1909; *yr s* of late Major George Hicks, MC, TD, JP, and Elizabeth Young; *m* 1938, Roberta Kirk, *y d* of late Thomas Boag, Greenock; no *c. Educ:* Pannal Ash Coll., Harrogate. 2nd Lieut RA, Territorial Army, 1929; Capt., 1934; Major, 1939; served in War of 1939-45, OC Bute Battery RA; POW (Germany), 1940-45; despatches, 1945; Lieut-Col, 1950. Chm. Buteshire T&AFA, 1950-62; County Cadet Commandant, Bute, 1950-53; DL, JP, Bute, 1949. *Address:* 39 Crichton Road, Rothesay, Bute. *T:* Rothesay 12. *Club:* Royal Scottish Automobile (Glasgow).

**HICKS, John Donald;** A. F. and May T. Morrison Professor of History, University of California (Berkeley), 1942-57, Emeritus since 1957; *b* Pickering, Missouri, 25 Jan. 1890; *s* of Rev. John Kossuth Hicks and Harriett

Gertrude Wing; *m* 1921, Lucile Harriet Curtis, St James, Minn.; three *d. Educ:* Northwestern Univ.; Univ. of Wisconsin. BA, 1913, MA 1914, Northwestern University: PhD 1916, Wisconsin Univ. Asst Prof. and Prof. of History, Hamline Univ., 1916-22; Prof. of Hist., North Carolina Coll. for Women, 1922-23; Prof. of Amer. Hist., University of Nebraska, 1923-32; Prof. of Hist., University of Wisconsin, 1932-42. Teacher, summers, numerous Amer. Univs. Visiting Lecturer, Harvard Univ., 1st half year, 1931-32; Visiting Professor of American History and Institutions, Univ. of Cambridge. 1950-51 (Hon. MA). Professorial Fellow, Trinity Hall. Phi Beta Kappa Visiting Scholar, 1958-59. Hon. LLD: Northwestern Univ., 1956; Univ. of San Francisco, 1957; Univ. of California, 1960. *Publications:* The Populist Revolt, 1931; The Federal Union, 1937; The American Nation, 1941; A Short History of American Democracy, 1943; (co-author with Theodore Saloutos) Agricultural Discontent in the Middle West, 1900-39, 1950; The American Tradition, 1955; Republican Ascendency, 1921-1933, 1960; Rehearsal for Disaster: The Boom and Collapse of 1919-1920, 1961; My Life With History: an autobiography, 1968; numerous articles in historical publications and encyclopædias. *Address:* 66 Southampton Avenue, Berkeley, Calif 94707, USA.

**HICKS, Sir John (Richard),** Kt 1964; FBA 1942; Fellow of All Souls College, since 1952; *b* 1904; *s* of late Edward Hicks, Leamington Spa; *m* 1935, Ursula K. Webb (*see* U. K. Hicks). *Educ:* Clifton Coll.; Balliol Coll., Oxford. Lectr, London Sch. of Economics, 1926-35; Fellow of Gonville and Caius Coll., Cambridge, 1935-38; Prof. of Political Economy, University of Manchester, 1938-46; Official Fellow of Nuffield Coll., Oxford, 1946-52; Drummond Prof. of Political Economy, University of Oxford, 1952-65; Member: Revenue Allocation Commn, Nigeria, 1950; Royal Commn on the Taxation of Profits and Income, 1951. Hon. Fellow, LSE, 1969. *Publications:* The Theory of Wages, 1932 (revised edn, 1963); Value and Capital, 1939; The Taxation of War Wealth (with U. K. Hicks and L. Rostas), 1941; The Social Framework, 1942 (3rd edition, 1960); Standards of Local Expenditure (with U. K. Hicks), 1943; The Problem of Valuation for Rating (with U. K. Hicks and C. E. V. Leser), 1944; The Incidence of Local Rates in Great Britain (with U. K. Hicks), 1945; The Problem of Budgeting Reform, 1948; A Contribution to the Theory of the Trade Cycle, 1950; (with U. K. Hicks) Report on Finance and Taxation in Jamaica, 1955; A Revision of Demand Theory, 1956; Essays in World Economics, 1960; Capital and Growth, 1965; Critical Essays in Monetary Theory, 1967; A Theory of Economic History, 1969. *Address:* All Souls College, Oxford.

**HICKS, Lady (John Richard);** *see* Hicks, U. K.

**HICKS, Robert;** MP (C) Bodmin Division of Cornwall since 1970; *b* 18 Jan. 1938; *s* of W. H. Hicks; *m* 1962, Maria Elizabeth Ann Gwyther; two *d. Educ:* Queen Elizabeth Grammar Sch., Crediton; University Coll., London; Univ. of Exeter. Taught at St Austell Grammar Sch., 1961-64; Lecturer in Regional Geography, Weston-super-Mare Technical Coll., 1964-70. *Recreations:* cricket, gardening. *Address:* Little Court, Tarnock, Axbridge, Somerset. *T:* Edgingworth 214. *Club:* MCC.

**HICKS, Brig. Sir Stanton;** *see* Hicks, Brig. Sir C. S.

**HICKS, Thomas;** *see* Steele, Tommy.

**HICKS, Ursula Kathleen, (Lady Hicks);** University Lecturer in Public Finance, Oxford, 1947-65; Fellow of Linacre College, since 1965; *b* 17 Feb. 1896; *d* of W. F. and I. M. Webb, Dublin; *m* 1935 Sir John Hicks, *qv. Educ:* Roedean; Somerville College, Oxford; London Sch. of Economics. Asst Lecturer, London Sch. of Economics, Oct. 1935 (resigned on marriage); Lecturer in charge of Dept of Economics, Liverpool University, 1941-46; Fiscal Comr, Uganda, 1962, Eastern Caribbean, 1962-63. Hon. Fellow, Inst. of Social Studies, The Hague, 1967; Hon. DSc (Econ.), Belfast, 1966. *Publications:* Finance of British Government, 1920-36, 1938; Taxation of War Wealth, 1941, Standards of Local Expenditure, 1943, The Problem of Valuation for Rating, 1944, and The Incidence of Local Rates, 1945 (with J. R. Hicks); Indian Public Finance, 1952 (UN); Finance and Taxation in Jamaica (with J. R. Hicks), 1955; Public Finance, 1955; British Public Finances, their Structure and Development, 1880-1952, 1954; Development from Below (Local Government and Finance in Developing Countries of the Commonwealth), 1961; Federalism and Economic Growth (with others), 1961; Report of Fiscal Commission Eastern Caribbean (Command Paper No. 1991), 1963. Development Finance: Planning and Control, 1965. Articles in Economic Journal, Economica, Public Administration, etc. *Recreations:* painting, gardening. *Address:* Porch House, Blockley, Glos. *T:* Blockley 210.

**HICKS BEACH,** family name of **Earl St Aldwyn.**

**HICKS BEACH, Major William Whitehead,** TD; DL; solicitor; *b* 23 March 1907; *s* of late Ellis Hicks Beach, Witcombe Park, Glos; *m* 1939, Diana, *d* of C. G. Hoare, Yateley Hall, Elmham, Dereham, Norfolk; one *s* two *d. Educ:* Eton; Magdalene Coll., Cambridge. A solicitor since 1932 and a partner in Payne, Hicks Beach & Co., 10 New Square, Lincoln's Inn, WC2, since 1933. Served throughout War of 1939-45 with Royal Gloucestershire Hussars and retired as Major. Contested (C) Cheltenham, 1945; MP (C) Cheltenham, 1950-64. DL, Glos, 1963. *Recreations:* hunting, shooting and fishing. *Address:* Witcombe Park, near Gloucester. *Clubs:* Turf Bath; New (Cheltenham).

**HICKSON, Geoffrey Fletcher,** MA; Secretary of Board of Extra-Mural Studies, University of Cambridge, 1928-67; Fellow of Fitzwilliam College, 1963-67; *b* 4 July 1900; *s* of late Professor S. J. Hickson, FRS; *m* 1934, Jane Margaret Amy, *er d* of late Dr W. R. Cazenove; two *s* one *d. Educ:* Uppingham Sch. (Scholar); Clare Coll., Cambridge (Archdeacon Johnson Exhib.). Historical Tripos, 1921 and 1922; Gladstone Prize, 1924. Asst Master, Highgate Sch., 1924. Asst Sec., Board of Extra-Mural Studies, Univ. of Cambridge, 1925. Mem. Council of Senate, 1947-62; Mem. Cambridge City Council, 1943-; Chm. Cttee for Education, 1946-64; Mayor, 1947-49 and 1962-63; Alderman, 1952-; Mem. Gen. Purposes Cttee, Assoc. of Municipal Corporations, 1956- (Dep. Chm., 1969); Chm., Non-County Boroughs Cttee for England and Wales, 1969-. chm. Central Cttee for Adult Education in HM Forces 1957-60. Trustee of Uppingham Sch. *Recreations:* music and golf. *Address:* 16 Rathmore Road, Cambridge CB1 4AD. *T:* Cambridge 44472. *Club:* United University.

**HIDAYATULLAH, Hon. Mr Justice M.,** OBE 1946; Chief Justice, Supreme Court of India, since 1968; Acting President of India, 1969; *b* 17 Dec. 1905; *y s* of Khan Bahadur Hafiz M. Wilayatullah, ISO; *m* 1948, Pushpa Shah, *d* of A. N. Shah, ICS; one *s* (one *d* decd). *Educ:*

Govt High Sch., Raipur; Morris Coll., Nagpur (Phillips Schol.; BA); Trinity Coll., Cambridge (MA); Lincoln's Inn. Nagpur High Court: Advocate, 1930-46; Govt Pleader, 1942-43; Advocate General, CP & Berar, 1943-46; Puisne Judge, 1946-54; Chief Justice, 1954-56; Chief Justice, Madhya Pradesh High Court, 1956-58; Puisne Judge, Supreme Court of India, 1958-68. Dean, Faculty of Law, Nagpur Univ., 1950-54; Mem., Faculty of Law, Sagar, Vikram and Aligarh Univs; Pres., Indian Law Inst., 1968-; Pres., Internat. Law Assoc. (Indian Br.), 1968-; Pres., Indian Soc. of Internat. Law, 1968-; Internat. Inst. of Space Law, Paris; Internat. Coun. of Former Scouts and Guides (awarded Silver Elephant, bronze medal for gallantry); Exec. Coun., World Assembly of Judges; rep. India at Internat. Confs at Bangkok, Helsinki, Durham, Geneva and Port of Spain. Chancellor, Muslim Nat. Univ., New Delhi; Pro-Chancellor, Delhi Univ. Hon. Bencher, Lincoln's Inn, 1968. Hon. LLD: Univ. of Philippines; Ravishankar Univ. *Publications:* Democracy in India and the Judicial Process, 1966; The South-West Africa Case, 1967; (Ed.) Mulla's Mahomedan Law, 1968; A Judge's Miscellany, in preparation; numerous monographs and articles. *Recreations:* golf, bridge. *Address:* Chief Justice's Chambers, Supreme Court, New Delhi, India. *T:* New Delhi 45665; 5 Hastings Road, New Delhi 11. *T:* New Delhi 33317, 35439. *Club:* Delhi Gymkhana (New Delhi).

**HIEGER, Izrael,** DSc (London); Biochemist, Royal Marsden Hospital, 1924-66; *b* Siedletz, Russian-Poland, June 1901; *s* of F. E. Hieger. *Educ:* Birkbeck Coll. and University Coll., London. With colleagues, Anna Fuller Memorial Prize for Cancer Research, 1939. *Publications:* One in Six: An Outline of the Cancer Problem, 1955; Carcinogenesis, 1961; papers on the discovery of cancer producing chemical compounds. *Address:* Chester Beatty Research Institute, Royal Marsden Hospital, Fulham Road, SW3.

**HIGGIN, Walter Wynnefield;** DL County of Chester; Partner in Smith, Coney and Barrett, Liverpool, retired; *b* 18 Dec. 1889; *s* of W. S. Higgin and J., *d* of J. Saunders, Annan, Dumfries; *m* 1918, Olive, *d* of A. B. Earle, Old Hall, Puddington, Ches; three *s*. *Educ:* Gresham's Sch., Norfolk. Partner, W. S. Higgin and Co., Cotton Merchants, 1918; retired, 1924; joined Smith, Coney and Barrett, 1931; Pres. Liverpool Cotton Association Ltd, 1943-45; 2nd Lieut 6th Bn The King's Liverpool Regt 1910; joined RFC 1915; Capt., 1916; Major, 1918; High Sheriff of Ches., 1938. *Recreations:* shooting, fishing. *Address:* Puddington Hall, Wirral, Cheshire. *TA:* Neston, Wirral. *T:* 051-336 2120. *Club:* Travellers'.

**HIGGINS,** *see* Longuet-Higgins.

**HIGGINS, Rev. Canon John Denis P.;** *see* Pearce-Higgins.

**HIGGINS, Terence Langley;** MP (C) Worthing since 1964; Minister of State, Treasury, since 1970; *b* 18 Jan. 1928; *s* of Reginald Higgins, Dulwich; *m* 1961, Rosalyn, *d* of Lewis Cohen, London; one *s* one *d*. *Educ:* Alleyn's Sch., Dulwich; Gonville and Caius Coll., Cambridge. Brit. Olympic Team (athletics) 1948, 1952; BA (Hons) 1958. MA 1963; Pres. Cambridge Union Soc., 1958. NZ Shipping Co., 1948-55; Lectr in Economic Principles, Dept of Economics, Yale Univ., 1958-59; Economist with Unilever, 1959-64. Sec., Cons. Parly Finance Cttee, 1965-66; Opposition Spokesman on Treasury and Economic Affairs, 1966-70. Associate, Inst. of Chartered Shipbrokers. *Address:* 18 Hallgate, Blackheath Park, SE3. *T:* 01-852 3759. *Club:* Hawks (Cambridge).

**HIGGON, Col Laurence Hugh,** CBE 1958; MC 1916 and Bar 1917; *b* 3 Sept. 1884; 4th (and *o surv*) *s* of late Capt. J. D. G. Higgon, RA, DL, JP, Scolton, Pembrokeshire; *m* 1922, Neda Kathleen C., *er d* of late Lieut-Col F. Rennick; two *d*. *Educ:* Cheltenham; RMA, Woolwich. Entered RA 1903; retired, 1927; comd 102nd (Pembroke Yeo.) Bde RA, 1930-35 (Bt Col); Hon. Col 1948; Hon. Comr Toc H in Wales, 1931. Rejoined RA (Lieut-Col), 1939. Home Guard, Pembs (Lieut-Col), 1942-45. DL, JP, Pembrokeshire; JP Haverfordwest. Served European War, 1914-19, France and Flanders (despatches twice, MC and Bar). Chm. Pembroke County War Memorial Hospital 1934-53; Mem. West Wales Hosps Management Cttee, 1948-53; Chm. Standing Joint Cttee, 1949-54; Chm., Pembroke TA Assoc., 1944-47; Lord Lieutenant, Pembrokeshire, 1944-54. OStJ. *Address:* Castle Corner, Manorbier, Pembrokeshire. *T:* Manorbier 343. *Clubs:* Army and Navy; Pembroke County (Haverfordwest).

**HIGGS, Godfrey Walter,** CBE 1960; Vice-President, Bahamas Senate, 1964-68; *b* 28 Sept. 1907; *yr s* of late Charles Roger Higgs; *m* 1937, Marion Suzanne (marr. diss.), *y d* of Roscoe Hagen, Rochester, NY; three *s*; *m* Eleanor Claire, *y d* of Charles Frederick Beckmann, New York City, USA. *Educ:* Queen's Coll., Taunton. Called to Bahamas Bar, 1929; English Bar, Inner Temple, 1933 (Profumo Prize); Deputy Speaker, House of Assembly, Bahamas, 1937-42; Mem. Executive Council and Leader for the Govt, Bahamas House of Assembly, 1942-45 and 1946-49; Member: Legislative Council, Bahamas, 1950-64; Senate, 1964-68. *Recreations:* yachting, swimming, golf, shooting, fishing, etc. *Address:* Stanley, East Bay Street, Nassau, Bahamas. *Clubs:* Royal Nassau Sailing, Lyford Cay (Nassau).

**HIGGS, Rt. Rev. Hubert Laurence;** *see* Hull, Suffragan Bishop of.

**HIGGS, Sir (John) Michael (Clifford),** Kt 1969; solicitor; Partner, Higgs & Sons; *b* 30 May 1912; *s* of late Alderman A. W. Higgs, Cranford House, Stourton, Staffs; *m* 1st, 1936, Diana Louise Jerrams (*d* 1950); two *d*; 2nd, 1952, Rachel Mary Jones; one *s* one *d*. *Educ:* St Cuthberts, Malvern; Shrewsbury. LLB (Birmingham), 1932. Admitted solicitor, 1934. Served War of 1939-45 with 73 HAA Regt RA (TA), 1939-42; JAG Staff, 1942-46; demobilised, 1946, with rank of Lieut-Col. Mem. of Staffs County Council, 1946-49; MP (C) Bromsgrove Div. of Worcs, 1950-55; Mem. of Worcs CC, 1953- (Chm. 1959-); Alderman, 1963; Mem. West Midlands Economic Planning Council, 1965-; Chm., W Midlands Planning Authorities' Conf., 1969-. *Recreation:* tennis. *Address:* The Green, Sankyn's Green, Little Witley, Worcs. *T:* Great Witley 416. *Clubs:* 1900; Conservative (Birmingham); Worcestershire (Worcester).

**HIGGS, Sir Michael;** *see* Higgs, Sir J. M. C.

**HIGGS, Sydney Limbrey,** FRCS; Consulting Orthopædic Surgeon, St Bartholomew's Hospital; Hon. Consulting Surgeon, Royal National Orthopædic Hospital; Hon. Consulting Orthopædic Surgeon, North-East Metropolitan Regional Hospital Board; *b* 12 Sept. 1892; widower; one *d*. *Educ:* St John's Coll., Cambridge; St Bartholomew's Hospital. MB, BCh, MA, Cambridge, 1919; MRCS, LRCP 1917; FRCS 1922. Formerly: Regional

Orthopædic Consultant, EMS; Surgeon, Queen Mary's Hospital, Roehampton; Hon. Consulting Orthopædic Surgeon to the Army, Eastern Command. Fellow British Orthopædic Association; Fellow Royal Society of Medicine. *Publications:* contributions to medical journals. *Address:* Phœnix, West Wittering, near Chichester, Sussex. *Club:* Royal Yacht Squadron.

**HIGGS-WALKER, James Arthur,** MA Oxon; Headmaster of Sevenoaks School, 1925-54; *b* 31 July 1892; *s* of W. H. Higgs-Walker, Wychbury House, Hagley, Worcestershire; *m* 1917, Muriel Jessie, *e d* of Rev. Harold Earnshaw Smith, Himley Rectory, Staffs, and *g d* of Hon. Henley Eden; one *d. Educ:* Repton; St John's Coll., Oxford (Scholar). Served European War, Capt. in the Worcs Regt, in Egypt, Mesopotamia, Italy, 1914-19; House-Master and Chief History Master at Oundle Sch., 1919-25. *Publications:* European History, 1789-1815; Introduction to Eighteenth Century French Society; contributor to History and other periodicals. *Recreation:* member of Oxford University Authentics Cricket Club, and has played cricket for Worcs. *Address:* Long Barn, Chelwood Gate, Sussex.

*See also M. H. Harmer.*

**HIGHAM, Anthony Richard Charles,** TD 1945; Senior Surgeon, St Peter's Hospital Group, since 1968; Surgeon, St Paul's Hospital, since 1939; Surgeon i/c Genito-Urinary Department, Queen Mary's Hospital, Stratford, E15, since 1948; *b* 11 June 1907; *e s* of late Lieut-Col B. Higham, CIE; *m* 1931, Mary, *er d* of late J. W. W. Shepley, Highfield House, Glossop; two *s. Educ:* Epsom Coll.; St George's Hospital; FRCS 1932. Mem., Board of Governors St Peter's, St Paul's and St Philip's Hospitals, 1948-; Dean, St Paul's Hospital, 1948-51; Dean, Institute of Urology, University of London, 1951-67; Everidge Prize in Urology, 1952. FRSM 1930-; Mem. Urological Section, 1935- (Mem. of Council, 1952-56); Foundation Mem. British Assoc. of Urological Surgeons. Mem., International Society of Urology, 1951-. Commissioned RA (TA), 1927; transferred to RAMC (TA), 1930; served throughout War of 1939-45, in UK (with Commandos), Africa, Iraq, Sicily and Italy (Actg Col, OC 22 Gen. Hosp., 1945). Polish Golden Cross of Merit with Swords, 1948. *Publications:* occasional contrib. to medical literature. *Recreation:* motoring. *Address:* 27 Flood Street, SW3. *T:* 01-352 7891. *Club:* Royal Automobile.

**HIGHAM, John Drew,** CMG 1956; Assistant Secretary in the Ministry of Housing and Local Government; *b* 28 Nov. 1914; *s* of Richard and Margaret Higham, Pendleton, Lancs; *m* 1936, Mary Constance Bromage; three *d. Educ:* Manchester Grammar Sch.; Gonville and Caius Coll., Cambridge (Scholar). Asst Principal, Admiralty, 1936; Asst Private Sec. to First Lord, 1939; Private Sec. to Parliamentary Sec. and Parliamentary Clerk, 1940; Principal, Admiralty, 1941; transferred to Colonial Office, 1946; Asst Sec. Colonial Office, 1948; seconded to Singapore as Under Sec., 1953, and as Dir of Personnel, 1955-57 (acted on various occasions as Chief Sec.). Chevalier 1st Cl. Order of St Olaf (Norway), 1948. *Address:* 31 Morpeth Mansions, SW1. *T:* 01-828 7540.

**HIGHAM, Rear-Adm. Philip Roger Canning;** Assistant Chief of Naval Staff (Operational Requirements), since 1970; *b* 9 June 1920; *s* of Edward Higham, Stoke Bishop, Bristol; *m* 1942, Pamela Bracton Edwards, *er d* of Gerald Edwards, Southport, Lancs; two *s. Educ:* RNC Dartmouth. Cadet, 1937; Midshipman, 1938; Sub-Lt 1940; Lieut 1942; qual. Gunnery Officer, 1944; Second Gunnery Off., HMS Vanguard, Royal Tour of S Africa, 1947; psc 1948; Exper. Dept, HMS Excellent, 1951-52; Comdr, Devonport Gunnery Sch., 1953; Trials Comdr, RAE Aberporth, 1954-55; jssc 1956; Exper. Comdr, HMS Excellent, 1957-59; Admty (DTWP), 1960-61; Naval Attaché, Middle East, 1962-64; idc 1965; Dep. Chief Polaris Exec., 1966-68; Cdre i/c Hong Kong, 1968-70. Recreations: gardening, fishing. *Address:* Holmwood House, Emsworth, Hants. *T:* Emsworth 2195. *Club:* United Service.

**HIGHAM, Thomas Farrant;** Official Fellow, 1914-58, Dean, 1919-33, Senior Tutor, 1938-39 and 1945-48, and Emeritus Fellow, since 1958, Trinity College, Oxford; Public Orator, Oxford University, 1939-58 and sometime University Lecturer in Greek and Latin Literature; *b* 20 Sept. 1890; *y s* of late Sir Thomas Higham, KCIE; *m* 1915, Mary Elisabeth *e d* of late Dr B. M. H. Rogers; one *s* one *d. Educ:* Clifton Coll.; Trinity Coll., Oxford. 1st class, Class. Hon. Mods, 1911; Gaisford Prize, Greek Verse, 1912; 2nd Lieut 9th (Ser.) Bn OBLI, Dec. 1914; attached GSI, British Salonika Force and Constantinople, 1916-19; Capt., 1917 (despatches, Greek medal for Military Merit); Proproctor, Oxford Univ., 1921-22, 1927-28; Senior Proctor, 1932-33; Member: Oxford and Cambridge Schs Examination Board, 1927-41; Council St Hilda's Coll., Oxford, 1934-42; Governing Body, St Paul's Schs, 1934-64; Council, Clifton Coll., 1953-66; Council, The Oxford Soc., 1952-69. Vis. Prof. in Classics, Stanford Univ., Calif, 1962-63. Attached to Foreign Office, Jan. 1940-June 1945. *Publications:* Orationes Oxonienses Selectae, 1960; Dr Blakiston Recalled, 1968; co-editor: The Mind of Rome, 1926; The Oxford Book of Greek Verse, 1930, and the same in translation, 1938; From the Greek, 1943; Some Oxford Compositions, 1949; Ovidiana, Recherches sur Ovide, 1958; More Oxford Compositions, 1964. Articles in Greek Poetry and Life, 1936, Classical journals, etc. *Recreation:* conchology. *Address:* 2 William Orchard Close, Old Headington, Oxford OX3 9DR. *T:* Oxford 65113.

**HIGHET, Gilbert (Arthur);** Anthon Professor of the Latin Language and Literature, Columbia University, New York, since 1950 (Chairman, Department of Greek and Latin, 1965-68); *b* 22 June 1906; *o s* of Gilbert Highet, Superintendent, Postal Telegraphs, Glasgow, and Elizabeth Gertrude Boyle; *m* 1932, Helen Clark, *o d* of Donald McInnes, Glasgow (*see* Helen MacInnes); one *s. Educ:* Hillhead High Sch., Glasgow; Glasgow Univ.; Balliol Coll., Oxford. Snell Exhibitioner and Hon. Schol., Balliol. Fellow of St John's Coll., Oxford, 1932; Prof. of Greek and Latin, Columbia Univ., 1938-50; on leave for war service, 1941-46; with British mission in US and later in Mil. Govt, Germany (British Zone); commissioned, 1943; Lt-Col 1946. Became US citizen, 1951. DLitt Glasgow, 1951; Guggenheim Memorial Fellow, 1951; LHD, Case Inst. of Technology, 1952; DLitt Oxford, 1956; DLitt Syracuse, 1960; LHD Adelphi, 1964. FRSL 1959. Mem. Bd of Judges, Book-of-the-Month Club, 1954-; Chm. Adv. Bd, Horizon, 1958-. *Publications:* The Classical Tradition: Greek and Roman Influences on Western Literature, 1949; The Art of Teaching, 1950; People, Places and Books, 1953; Juvenal the Satirist, 1954; The Mind of Man, 1954; A Clerk of Oxenford, 1954; Poets in a Landscape, 1957; Talents and Geniuses, 1957; The Powers of Poetry, 1960; The Anatomy of Satire, 1962 (Award of Merit,

American Philological Association, 1963). Translator of Werner Jaeger's Paideia: the Ideals of Greek Culture, 1939-44. Contributor: The Classical Review, The American Journal of Philology, etc. *Recreations:* two-piano duets, photography. *Address:* 15 Jeffreys Lane, East Hampton, New York 11937, USA. *Clubs:* Century (New York); Maidstone (East Hampton).

**HIGHSMITH, Patricia;** writer since 1942; *b* 19 Jan. 1921; *o c* of Jay Bernard Plangman and Mary Coates (of German and English-Scots descent respectively); name changed to Highsmith by adoption; unmarried. *Educ:* Barnard Coll., Columbia Univ., New York. For a year after univ. had a mediocre writing job; after that she tried free-lance writing, with sufficient success (though modest) that she did not have to take another job; lived in Europe, 1951-53, and again in 1959; in Pennsylvania, 1960-63; subseq. four years in England, and now has been some years in France. *Publications:* Strangers on a Train, 1950; The Blunderer, 1955; The Talented Mr Ripley, 1956; Deep Water, 1957; A Game for the Living, 1958; This Sweet Sickness, 1960; The Cry of the Owl, 1962; The Two Faces of January, 1964; The Glass Cell, 1965; A Suspension of Mercy, 1965; Plotting and Writing Suspense Fiction, 1966; Those Who Walk Away, 1967; The Tremor of Forgery, 1969; Eleven Short Stories, 1970. *Recreations:* drawing, some painting, carpentering, snail-watching. *Address:* Montmachoux 77, France.

**HIGHTON, Rear-Adm. (Retd) Jack Kenneth,** CB 1959; CBE 1952; *b* 2 Sept. 1904; *s* of John Henry Highton and Kate (*née* Powers); *m* 1933, Eileen Metcalfe Flack; one *s* two *d. Educ:* Bedford Modern Sch. Joined Royal Navy, 1922; Captain 1951; Dir of Welfare and Service Conditions, 1955-57; Rear-Adm. 1957; Chief Staff Officer (Administration) to Commander-in-Chief, Plymouth, 1957-60; retired, 1960. *Recreations:* walking, sailing, gardening.

**HIGMAN, Prof. Graham,** FRS 1958; MA, DPhil; Waynflete Professor of Pure Mathematics, Oxford University, and Fellow of Magdalen College, Oxford, since Oct. 1960; *b* 1917; 2nd *s* of Rev. Joseph Higman; *m* 1941, Ivah May Treleaven; five *s* one *d. Educ:* Sutton Secondary Sch., Plymouth; Balliol Coll., Oxford. Meteorological Office, 1940-46; Lecturer, University of Manchester, 1946-55; Reader in Mathematics at Oxford Univ., 1955-60; Senior Research Fellow, Balliol Coll., Oxford, 1958-60. *Publications:* papers in Proc. London Math. Soc., and other technical jls. *Address:* 64 Sandfield Road, Headington, Oxford. *T:* 62974.

**HILALY, Agha,** SPk; Ambassador for Pakistan to the United States, since 1966; also accredited to Mexico, Venezuela and Jamaica; *b* 20 May 1911; *s* of late Agha Abdulla; *m* 1938, Malek Taj Begum, *d* of Mirza Kazim, Bangalore; three *s. Educ:* Presidency Coll., Madras (MA); King's Coll., Cambridge (MA). Entered former ICS (Bengal cadre), 1936; Under-Sec., Govt of Bengal, 1939-41; Govt of India, 1941-47; entered Pakistan Foreign Service at time of Partition; Jt Sec., Min. of Foreign Affairs, 1951; Imp. Def. Coll., 1955; Ambassador to Sweden, Norway, Denmark and Finland, 1956; Delegate to UN Gen. Assembly, 1958; Ambassador to USSR and Czechoslovakia, 1959; High Commissioner in India and Ambassador to Nepal, 1961; High Commissioner for Pakistan in the UK and Ambassador to Ireland, 1963-66. Star of Pakistan, Grand Cross, Order of the North Star, Sweden; Grand Cross, Prabol Gurkha Dakshana Bahu (Nepal). *Recreations:* colour photography, shooting. *Address:* Embassy of Pakistan, 2315 Massachusetts Avenue, NW, Washington, DC 20008, USA. *Clubs:* Travellers'; International (Washington); Sind (Karachi).

**HILBORNE, Rev. Frederick Wilfred,** CBE 1957; *b* 5 March 1901; *yr s* of Frank and Eleanor Hilborne; *m* 1929, Irene May Wheatland; one *s* one *d. Educ:* Eastbourne Coll.; Handsworth Theological Coll. Ordained into Ministry of Methodist Church, 1929. Commissioned in Royal Army Chaplains' Dept, 1929; served in Malta, 1932-35. War Service: BEF, 1939-40; MELF 1942; CMF, 1943-45. CF 3rd Class, 1939; CF 2nd Class, 1943; CF 1st Class, 1950. Appointed Dep. Chaplain-Gen. to the Forces and Hon. Chaplain to the Queen, 1953; relinquished both appointments and placed on retired pay, Dec. 1956. *Address:* 43 West Parade, Worthing, Sussex. *T:* Worthing 48204. *Club:* Army and Navy.

**HILDER, Ven. Geoffrey Frank;** Archdeacon of Taunton since 1951; Provost of Western Division of Woodard Corporation, 1960-70; *b* 17 July 1906; *s* of Albert Thomas and Lilian Ethel Hilder; *m* 1939, Enid, *d* of Rev. F. E. Coggin. *Educ:* Uppingham Sch.; Lincoln Coll., Oxford; Inner Temple; Ely Theological Coll. Called to the Bar, 1930. Deacon, 1931; Priest, 1932; Rector of Ruardean, Glos., 1937-41; Vicar of St Stephen's, Cheltenham, 1941-48; Vicar of Hambridge, 1948-59. Prolocutor of Lower House of Convocation of Canterbury, 1955-70; Dir of Ecclesiastical Insurance Office Ltd, 1957-61. *Recreations:* music, gardening. *Address:* Broom House, Stogumber, Taunton, Som. *T:* Stogumber 246. *Club:* Athenæum.

**HILDER, Rowland,** PRI (RI 1938); painter; *b* Greatneck, Long Island, USA, 28 June 1905, British parents; *m* 1929, Edith Blenkiron; one *s* one *d. Educ:* Morristown Sch., USA; Goldsmiths' Coll. Sch. of Art, London. *Publications:* Illustrated editions of: Moby Dick, 1926; Treasure Island, 1929; Precious Bane, 1930; The Bible for To-day, 1940; The Shell Guide to Flowers of the Countryside (with Edith Hilder), 1955; (jointly) Sketching and Painting Indoors, 1957; Starting with Watercolour, 1966. *Recreation:* sailing. *Address:* 5 Kidbrooke Grove, Blackheath, SE3. *T:* 01-858 3072.

**HILDRED, Sir William (Percival),** Kt 1945; CB 1942; OBE 1936; Grand Officer, Order of Orange-Nassau, 1946; Commander Order of Crown of Belgium; MA; Director-General Emeritus International Air Transport Association (Director-General, 1946-66); *b* 13 July 1893; *s* of late William Kirk Hildred; *m* 1920, Constance Mary Chappell, MB, ChB; two *s* one *d. Educ:* Boulevard Sch., Hull; University of Sheffield. Served European War, 1st York and Lancaster Regt, 1914-17; entered Treasury, 1919; Finance Officer, Empire Marketing Board, 1926-34; Head of Special Measures Branch, Ministry of Agriculture and Fisheries, 1934-35; Deputy General Manager, Export Credits Guarantee Dept, 1935-38; Deputy Dir-Gen. of Civil Aviation, Air Ministry, 1938; Principal Asst Sec., Ministry of Aircraft Production, 1940; assisted in formation of RAF Ferry Command, Montreal, 1941; Director-Gen. of Civil Aviation, Ministry of Civil Aviation, 1941-46. Edward Warner Award of ICAO, 1965. Hon. LLD: Sheffield; McGill Univ.; FRSA. Hon. Comp. RAeS. *Recreations:* cycling, music, carpentry. *Address:* Spreakley House, Frensham, Surrey. *Clubs:* Athenæum; Royal Yacht; Bermuda.

**HILDRETH, Maj.-Gen. Sir (Harold) John (Crossley),** KBE 1964 (CBE 1952; OBE 1945); Managing Director, Services Kinema Corporation; *b* 12 June 1908; *s* of late Lt-Col H. C. Hildreth, DSO, OBE, FRCS, and Mrs Hildreth, Camberley; *m* 1950, Mary, *d* of G. Wroe, Worthing; two *s* three *d*. *Educ:* Wellington Coll., Berks; RMA, Woolwich. 2nd Lieut, RA, 1928; transferred to RAOC, 1935, as Captain; Major 1944; Lieut-Col 1948; Col 1952; Brig. 1958; Maj.-Gen. 1961. War Office: Col 1942-44; Brig. 1944-47; Inspector of Establishments, 1947-50; Controller of Army Statistics, 1950-51; Comdr RAOC, Ammunition Org., 1951-53; Comdr, Bicester, 1953-57; DOS, BAOR, 1957-60; Inspector, RAOC, War Office, 1960-61; Dir of Ordnance Service, War Office, 1961-64; retired, Dec. 1964. Col Commandant, RAOC, 1963-. Legion of Merit (degree of Officer), USA. *Recreations:* shooting, sailing. *Address:* 59 Latymer Court, W6. *T:* 01-748 3107. *Club:* United Service.

**HILDRETH, (Henry) Jan (Hamilton Crossley);** Member, London Transport Board, since 1968; *b* 1 Dec. 1932; *s* of Maj.-Gen. Sir (Harold) John (Crossley) Hildreth, KBE, and Mrs Joan Elise Hallett (*née* Hamilton); *m* 1958, Wendy Moira Marjorie, *d* of late Arthur Harold Clough, CMG; two *s* one *d*. *Educ:* Wellington Coll.; The Queen's Coll., Oxford. National Service in RA, BAOR, 1952-53; 44 Parachute Bde (TA), 1953-58. Oxford, Hon. Mods (Nat. Sci.), BA (PPE) 1956, MA. Baltic Exchange, 1956; Royal Dutch Shell Group, 1957: served Philippines (marketing) and London (finance); Kleinwort, Benson Ltd, 1963; Nat. Economic Development Office, 1965. Member of Economic Development Cttees for the Clothing, the Hosiery and Knitwear, and the Wool Textile industries. *Recreations:* cross country running, photography; and others. *Address:* 50 Ridgway Place, Wimbledon, SW19. *T:* 01-946 0243. *Club:* Vincent's (Oxford).

**HILDYARD, Rev. Christopher,** MVO 1966; MA; Minor Canon and Sacrist of Westminster Abbey; *b* 28 April 1901; *s* of Lyonel D'Arcy and Dora Hildyard. *Educ:* St George's, Windsor Castle; Repton; Magdalene Coll., Cambridge; Cuddesdon Theological Coll. Curate at Glass Houghton, West Yorks, 1925-27; Curate at Gisborough, North Yorks, 1927-28; Asst Minor Canon, Westminster Abbey, 1928-32; Minor Canon, Westminster Abbey, 1932; Chaplain of Westminster Hospital, 1937-58; Custodian, Westminster Abbey, 1945-55; Sacrist, Westminster Abbey, 1958. *Recreation:* painting. *Address:* 2 The Cloisters, Westminster, SW1. *T:* 01-222 4982.

**HILDYARD, David Henry Thoroton,** CMG 1966; DFC 1943; Ambassador to Chile, since 1970; *b* 4 May 1916; *s* of late His Honour G. M. T. Hildyard, QC, and Sybil, *d* of H. W. Hamilton Hoare; *m* 1947, Millicent (*née* Baron), *widow* of Wing Commander R. M. Longmore, OBE; one *s* one *d*. *Educ:* Eton; Christ Church, Oxford. Served with RAF, 1940-46. Entered HM Foreign (subseq. Diplomatic) Service, 1948; Montevideo, 1950; Madrid, 1953; FO, 1957; Counsellor, Mexico City, 1960-65; Head of Economic Relations Dept, FO, 1965-68; Minister and Alternate UK Rep. to UN, 1968-70. *Recreations:* tennis, golf. *Address:* British Embassy, Santiago, Chile. *Clubs:* Turf, Hurlingham.

**HILEY, Joseph;** MP (C) Pudsey since Oct. 1959; *b* 18 Aug. 1902; *s* of Frank Hiley of Leeds; *m* 1932, Mary Morrison, *d* of Dr William Boyd; three *d*. *Educ:* West Leeds High Sch.; Leeds Univ., 1920-23. Formerly family business, Hiley Brothers, took over firm of J. B. Battye & Co. Ltd, 1924, Managing Dir 1927-59; Director: Readicut International Ltd (formerly Readicut Wool Co.), 1946-; J. B. Battye & Co., Ltd; Irish Spinners Ltd, 1952. Mem. of Lloyd's. Leeds City Councillor, 1930, Alderman, 1949, resigned, 1960; Lord Mayor of Leeds, 1957-58; Chm. West Leeds Area Board of Governors, 1947-; Pres., west Leeds Conservative Assoc.; Past President: Hand-Knitting Assoc.; Leeds Chamber of Commerce. *Recreations:* cricket, theatre. *Address:* Elmaran, Layton Road, Horsforth, Leeds. *T:* Horsforth 4787. *Clubs:* Constitutional; Stephen's Green (Dublin); Leeds and County Conservative, Leeds (Leeds); Pudsey (C) (Pudsey).

**HILEY, Sir Thomas (Alfred),** KBE 1966; Chartered Accountant, Australia, since 1932; *b* 25 Nov. 1905; *s* of William Hiley and Maria (*née* Savage); *m* 1929, Marjory Joyce (*née* Jarrott); two *s*. *Educ:* Brisbane Grammar Sch.; University of Qld. State Public Service, 1921; Public Accountancy, 1923; in practice (Public Accountant), 1925. Qld Parliament, 1944; Dep. Leader of Opposition, 1950; Treasurer of Qld and Minister for Housing, 1957; Treasurer, 1963; Deputy Premier, 1965; retired from Parliament, 1966. Pres., Inst. of Chartered Accts in Aust., 1946-47. Chm., State Award Cttee, Duke of Edinburgh Award. Hon. MCom, University of Qld, 1960. *Recreations:* shooting, fishing, cricket (Pres. Qld Cricket Assoc.). *Address:* Illawong, 39 The Esplanade, Tewantin, Qld 4565, Australia. *T:* 97-3754. *Clubs:* Number 10 (London); Queensland (Brisbane).

**HILL,** family name of **Marquess of Downshire, Baron Hill of Luton** and **Baron Sandys.**

**HILL;** *see* Clegg-Hill.

**HILL,** 7th Viscount, *cr* 1842; **Gerald Rowland Clegg-Hill;** Bt 1726-27; Baron Hill of Almarez and of Hawkstone, Salop, 1814; formerly Major, Royal Welch Fusiliers; *b* 31 March 1904; *s* of 6th Viscount Hill, DSO, and Mildred (*d* 1934), *d* of Thomas Bulteel, Radford, S Devon; *S* father 1957; *m* 1st, 1930, Betty (marriage dissolved, 1942), *yr d* of late Brig.-Gen. George Nowell Thomas Smyth-Osbourne, CB, CMG, DSO; one *s* (and one *s* decd); 2nd, 1942, Catherine Mary (Molly), *o d* of late Dr Rowland Venables Lloyd-Williams, Maiford, Denbigh. *Educ:* Shrewsbury; RMC, Sandhurst. *Heir:* *s* Hon. Antony Rowland Clegg-Hill, Lieut, Royal Artillery [*b* 19 March 1931; *m* 1963, Juanita Phyllis, *d* of John W. Pertwee, Salfords, Surrey]. *Address:* Coton Hall, Whitchurch, Salop. *T:* Whixall 353.

**HILL OF LUTON,** Baron, *cr* 1963 (Life Peer); **Charles Hill,** PC 1955; MA, MD, DPH, LLD; Chairman of Governors of the BBC, since 1967; Chairman, Laporte Industries Ltd, 1965-70; Chairman, National Joint Council for Local Authorities' Administrative, Professional, Technical and Clerical Services, since 1963; Director, Abbey National Building Society since 1964; *b* 15 Jan. 1904; *s* of late Charles Hill and Florence M. Cook; *m* 1931, Marion Spencer Wallace; two *s* three *d*. *Educ:* St Olave's Sch.; Trinity Coll., Cambridge; London Hosp. Formerly: House Physician and Receiving Room Officer, London Hospital; London University Extension Lecturer in Biology; Deputy Medical Supt, Coppice Mental Hospital, Nottingham; Deputy MOH, City of Oxford; President: World Medical Assoc.; Central Council for Health Educn; Hon. Sec., Commonwealth Medical Conf. sec., BMA, 1944-50. MP (L and C) Luton, 1950-63. Parly Sec., Min. of Food, 1951-April 1955;

Postmaster-Gen., April 1955-Jan. 1957; Chancellor of the Duchy of Lancaster Jan. 1957-Oct. 1961; Minister of Housing and Local Government and Minister for Welsh Affairs, Oct. 1961-July 1962. Chm., Independent Television Authority, 1963-67. Hon. Fellow Amer. Medical Assoc. *Publications:* What is Osteopathy? (jointly), 1937; Re-printed Broadcasts, 1941-50; Both Sides of the Hill, 1964, etc. *Recreations:* golf and walking. *Address:* Winch Hill House, Wandon End, near Luton, Beds. *Club:* Reform.

**HILL, Adrian Keith Graham,** PROI 1968 (ROI 1929); RBA 1926; RI 1928-36; Society of Graphic Arts, 1931; Painter in Water Colours and Oils; Life Master and Lecturer on Anatomy, Westminster School of Art, 1935-38; External Examiner for Teachers' Certificate, Durham Univ., 1938-39; Art Lecturer to HM Forces, 1943-44; Member Society for Education in Art, 1947; Governor: Chichester School of Art, 1951-62; Midhurst Grammar School, 1957-67; Federation of British Artists, 1968; President, Chichester Art Society, 1969; Vice-President: St James's Art Society, 1947; National League of Hospital Friends, 1950; Ancient Monuments Society, 1960; British Society of Aesthetics (founder member), 1960; British Association of Art Therapists, 1966; Broadcaster on Sound and TV; *b* Charlton, Kent, 24 March 1895; *s* of Graham Hill; *m* Dorothy Margaret Whitley; one *s*. *Educ:* Dulwich; St John's Wood Art Sch.; Royal College of Art; joined HAC 1914; overseas, 1916-19; Lieut 1917; Official War Artist, Collection of 190 War Pictures at Imperial War Museum, London. Work exhibited at Royal Acad. Salon, New English Art Club, London Gp, USA, Canada, S Africa, etc.; De Laszio Silver and Bronze Medals, Royal Society of British Artists; awarded Prix Catherine-Hadot, Académie Nationale de Médecine, Paris, 1947. Works represented in: Victoria and Albert Museum, Bradford Corp. Art Gall., Municipal Galls of Cork, Derby, Brighton, Northampton, Lane, Oldham, Hinckley, Letchworth, and Lever Art Galls; Collection of War Pictures at Headquarters of Hon. Artillery Company; One-man Exhibitions: 1938, 1940, 1961, 1964, 1966, 1968. Apptd under the Pilgrim Trust Grant to depict The Changing Face of Britain, 1940. Fellow, Soc. of Ancient Monuments, 1958. *Publications:* On Drawing and Painting Trees, 1936; On the Mastery of Water Colour Painting, 1938; Art versus Illness, 1945; Trees Have Names, 1949; Painting Out Illness, 1951; A Book of Trees, 1951; The Pleasures of Painting, 1952; Adventures in Line and Tone, 1954; What Shall We Draw?, 1956; Oil Painting for Beginners, 1957; Art as a Hobby, 1958; The Beginner's Book of Watercolour Painting, 1959; Knowing and Painting Trees, 1960; Sketching and Painting Out of Doors, 1961; Drawing the Countryside, 1961; Sketching and Painting Indoors, 1962; Basic Anatomy, 1962; Faces and Figures, 1962; Adventures in Painting, 1962; How to Draw, 1963; Seascapes and Landscapes, 1964; Flower Drawing and Painting, 1965; Architecture in Landscape, 1966; How to Paint in Water Colour, 1967; Further Steps in Oil Painting, 1969. *Address:* Old Laundry Cottage, Midhurst, Sussex. *T:* Midhurst 2018. *Clubs:* Alleyn, National Book League.

**HILL, Rev. Alexander Currie,** CB 1957; Minister Emeritus of Portknockie, Banffshire; Principal Finance Officer, Board of Trade, 1958-64; *b* 23 Jan. 1906; *o s* of late Alexander Hill and Jeanie Currie; unmarried. *Educ:* George Heriot's Sch., Edinburgh; University of Edinburgh; Christ's Coll., University of Aberdeen. Entered Administrative Class, Home Civil Service, 1928. Under-Sec., Board of Trade, 1950-58. *Address:* 62a Rubislaw Den North, Aberdeen AB2 4AN. *Clubs:* Reform; Royal Northern (Aberdeen).

**HILL, Archibald Vivian,** CH 1946; OBE 1918; FRS 1918; MA, ScD; Hon. LLD Edinburgh, Belfast; Hon. MD, Louvain, Brussels, Toulouse; Hon. DSc, Pennsylvania, Bristol, Manchester, Oxford, Algiers, Liège, Johns Hopkins, Brazil, Columbia, Rochester, Rockefeller, Exeter; Foulerton Research Professor, Royal Society, 1926-51; *b* 26 Sept. 1886; *m* 1913, Margaret Neville, *d* of late Dr J. N. Keynes; one *s* two *d* (and one *s* decd). *Educ:* Blundell's Sch., Tiverton; Trinity Coll., Cambridge (Scholar). 3rd Wrangler, 1907; Class I. Natural Sciences Tripos Part II. (Physiology), 1909; Fellow of Trinity Coll., Cambridge, 1910-16; Hon Fellow, 1941; Fellow of King's Coll., Cambridge, 1916-25; Hon. Fellow, 1927; Brackenbury Prof. of Physiology, Manchester Univ., 1920-23; Nobel Prize, Physiology and Medicine, 1922; Jodrell Prof. of Physiology, University Coll., London, 1923-25; Hon. Prof., 1926-51; Hon. Fellow, 1948; Mem. Cttee of Award, Commonwealth Fund Fellowships, 1934-39; Sec. of Royal Society, 1935-45, For. Sec., 1945-46, Royal Medal, 1926, Copley Medal, 1948; Mem. Univ. Grants Cttee, 1937-44; Chm. Executive Cttee National Physical Laboratory, 1939-45; Attaché, British Embassy, Washington, 1940; MP (Ind. C), Cambridge Univ., 1940-45; Member: War Cabinet Scientific Advisory Cttee, 1940-46, Inter-departmental Cttee on Medical Schs, 1942-44; Colonial Research Cttee, 1942; Science Cttee, British Council, 1946-56; Scientific Adviser, Govt of India, 1943-44; Trustee, British Museum, 1947-63; Trustee, Natural History Museum, 1963-65; Chairman: Research Defence Soc., 1940-51; Soc. for the Protection of Science and Learning, 1946-63 (Pres., 1963-); Pres., Society for Visiting Scientists, 1952-66; Pres. of the British Association for the Advancement of Science for 1952; Mem. Commission on Higher Education for Africans in Central Africa, 1952; Sec. General, Internat. Council of Scientific Unions, 1952-56; President: Marine Biological Asssociation, 1955-60. Foreign, Hon. or Assoc. Mem. of various foreign acads and socs. Served 1914-19, Captain and Brev. Major Cambs Regt and Dir of Anti-Aircraft Experimental Section, Munitions Inventions Dept; since then mem. of various cttees on air defence, etc (incl. Tizard Cttee, 1935-40). Medal of Freedom with Silver Palm, USA, 1947; Chevalier of the Legion of Honour, 1950. *Publications:* Living Machinery, 1927; The Ethical Dilemma of Science, 1960; Trails and Trials in Physiology, 1965; First and Last Experiments on Muscle Mechanics, 1969; monographs and papers in scientific jls, chiefly on physiological subjects. *Address:* 11a Chaucer Road, Cambridge CB2 2EB. *T:* Cambridge 54551.

*See also J. H. Humphrey.*

**HILL, (Arthur) Derek;** artist, writer, and organiser of exhibitions; *b* Bassett, Hampshire 6 Dec., 1916; *s* of A. J. L. Hill and Grace Lilian Mercer. *Educ:* Marlborough Coll. Has designed sets and dresses for Covent Garden and Sadler's Wells. *One-man exhibitions:* Nicholson Gall., London, 1943; Leicester Galls, London, 1947, 1950, 1953 and 1956. *Organised exhibitions:* 1934 onwards: Degas Exhibn for Edingburgh Fest. and Tate Gall., London, 1952; Landseer exhibn (with John Woodward) at Royal Academy, 1961, etc. Represented in exhibns, Europe and USA, 1957-; retrospective exhibn, Whitechapel Gall., London, 1961; exhibns in New York, 1966 and 1969. *Pictures owned by:* Tate Gall.;

Nat. Gall. of Canada; Arts Council; Fogg Museum, Harvard; City Art Galleries of: Southampton, Birmingham, Bradford, Coventry, Carlisle, etc. FRGS. *Publications:* Islamic Architecture and Its Decoration (with Prof. Oleg Grabar), 1965. Articles in Illustrated London News, Apollo, Burlington Magazine, etc. *Recreations:* gardening, travelling. *Address:* 18 Holly Hill, NW3. *Club:* Travellers'.

**HILL, Sir Austin Bradford,** Kt 1961; CBE 1951; FRS 1954; PhD (Econ.), 1926, DSc, 1929 (London); Emeritus Professor of Medical Statistics, London Sch. of Hygiene and Tropical Medicine, University of London, and Hon. Director, Statistical Research Unit of Medical Research Council, 1945-61; Dean of the London School of Hygiene and Tropical Medicine, 1955-57; *b* 8 July 1897; 3rd *s* of late Sir Leonard Erskine Hill, FRS; *m* 1923, Florence Maud, *d* of late Edward Salmon, OBE; two *s* one *d*. *Educ:* Chigwell Sch.; privately; University Coll., London. Flight Sub-Lieut in Royal Naval Air Service, 1916-18; on staff of Medical Research Council and its Industrial Health Research Board, 1923-33; Reader in Epidemiology and Vital Statistics, London Sch. of Hygiene and Tropical Medicine, 1933-45; seconded during the war to Research and Experiments Dept, Ministry of Home Security, 1940-42, and to Medical Directorate, Royal Air Force, 1943-45. Civil Consultant in Medical Statistics to RAF and mem. of Flying Personnel Research Cttee; Civil Consultant in Medical Statistics to RN; Pres. Royal Statistical Soc., 1950-52 (Hon. Sec. 1940-50); Gold Medallist, 1953; Pres. Section of Epidemiology, Royal Society of Medicine, 1953-55, Section of Occupational Medicine, 1964-65; Member: MRC, 1954-58; Cttee on Safety of Drugs; International Statistical Institute; Fellow of University Coll., London; Hon. Fellow: Royal College of Physicians; American Public Health Assoc.; Soc. of Medical Officers of Health; Institute of Actuaries; Soc. of Occupational Medicine; Faculty of Medicine, University of Chile; Royal Society of Medicine; Society for Social Medicine; Cutter Lecturer, Harvard, 1953; Harben Lecturer Royal Institute of Public Health and Hygiene, 1957; Alfred Watson Memorial Lectr Inst. of Actuaries, 1962; Marc Daniels Lectr RCP, 1963. Hon. DSc Oxford, 1963; Hon. MD Edinburgh, 1968. Galen Medallist, Soc. of Apothecaries, 1959; Harben Gold Medallist, 1961; Jenner Medallist, Royal Society of Medicine 1965; Heberden Medallist, Heberden Soc., 1965. *Publications:* Internal Migration and its Effects upon the Death Rates, 1925; The Inheritance of Resistance to Bacterial Infection in Animal Species, 1934; Principles of Medical Statistics, 1937, 8th edn 1966; Statistical Methods in Clinical and Preventive Medicine, 1962; reports to Industrial Health Research Board on industrial sickness and numerous papers in scientific journals, especially studies of cigarette smoking and cancer of the lung and of the clinical trial of new drugs. *Recreations:* travelling, gardening. *Address:* Green Acres, Little Kingshill, Great Missenden, Bucks. *T:* Gt Missenden 2380.

**HILL, Charles Loraine;** Chairman: Bristol City Line of Steamships Ltd; Charles Hill of Bristol Ltd; also Chairman or Director of several other companies; *b* 1891; *s* of late Chas Gathorne Hill, MA, JP; *m* 1st, 1916, Mary A. (marriage dissolved 1944). *d* of Major J. C. Harford; two *s* two *d* (and one *d* decd); 2nd, 1944, Mrs John Taylor (*née* Grant-Richards). *Educ:* Eton; Cambridge (BA). JP Som, 1923. *Address:* Grove House, Alveston, Glos. *T:* Thornbury 2273. *Club:* Brooks's.

**HILL, Christopher;** *see* Hill, J. E. C.

**HILL, Christopher Pascoe,** CB 1964; CBE 1956; Charity consultant; *b* 6 July 1903; *s* of late Charles Pascoe Grenfell Hill; *m* 1st, 1926, Elizabeth Ridding Oldfield (*d* 1931), *d* of late Lieut-Col H. Oldfield, RMA; one *d*; 2nd, 1934, Joan Elizabeth Smith, *d* of late R. W. Smith; two *s* one *d*. *Educ:* Merchant Taylors'; St John's Coll., Oxford, Galsford Prizeman, 1925. Entered Home Office, Asst Principal, 1925; Asst Sec., Ministry of Home Security, 1942; Home Office: Aliens Dept, 1943-47; Children's Dept, 1947-56; Asst Under-Sec. of State, 1957. Attached to Charity Commission, 1956, to prepare Charities Act, 1960; Chief Charity Commissioner, 1960-65; Sec. to Archbishops, Commission on Church and State, 1966. Member: Exec. Cttees National Council of Social Service, Herts Council of Social Service and Hertfordshire Soc.; Standing Conf. on Herts Countryside (Chm.); Gen. Adv. Council of BBC; BBC and ITA Central Appeals Adv. Cttees (Chm.). Legal Board, Church Assembly; Council, National Trust, 1969-. Director: WRVS Trustees Ltd; Internat. Standing Conf. on Philantrophy, Geneva. King Haakon VII Liberty Cross, Norway. *Publications:* A Guide for Charity Trustees, 1966; papers on delinquency and charity subjects in periodicals. *Recreations:* garden, painting, archæology, preserving Herts countryside. *Address:* The Grange, Therfield, Royston, Herts. *T:* Kelshall 358. *Club:* Athenæum.

**HILL, Colin de Neufville,** CMG 1961; OBE 1959; Deputy Bursar, University of Sussex, since 1964; *b* 2 Jan. 1917; *s* of Philip Rowland and Alice May Hill; *m* 1950, Mary Patricia Carson Wilson; two *s*. *Educ:* Cheltenham Coll.; St Edmund Hall, Oxford. BA. hons in Mod. Langs, Oxford, 1938. Selected for appt to Colonial Service, 1938; Administrative Officer, Colonial Admin. Service, Eastern Nigeria, 1939; served with Provincial and Regional Administration, Eastern Nigeria, 1939-53; transferred to Tanganyika and apptd Sec. for Finance, 1954; Permanent Sec. to the Treasury, Tanganyika Government, 1959-64. *Recreations:* photography, gardening, music. *Address:* Mount Pleasant Farm, Barcombe, near Lewes, Sussex.

**HILL, Sir Cyril Rowley;** *see* Hill, Sir (George) Cyril Rowley.

**HILL, Sir Denis;** *see* Hill, Sir John Denis Nelson.

**HILL, Derek;** *see* Hill, A. D.

**HILL, Prof. Dorothy,** FAA 1956; FRS 1965; Research Professor of Geology, University of Queensland, since 1959; *b* 10 Sept. 1907; *d* of R. S. Hill, Brisbane; unmarried. *Educ:* Brisbane Girls' Grammar Sch.; Univs of Queensland and Cambridge. BSc (Qld) 1928, 1st Cl. Hons in Geol. and Univ. Gold Medal. Foundn Trav. Fellowship of Univ. of Queensland held at Newnham Coll., Cambridge, 1930-32; PhD Cantab 1932; Old Students' Res. Fellowship, Newnham Coll., Cambridge, 1932-35; Sen. Studentship (Exhibn of 1851) held at Cambridge, 1935-37; Coun. for Sci. and Indust. Res. Fellowship, held at Univ. of Queensland, 1937-42; DSc (Qld) 1942. WRANS, Second Off., 1942-45 (RAN Ops Staff). Univ. of Queensland: Lectr in Geol., 1946-56, Reader, 1956-59. Hon. Editor, Geol. Soc. of Aust., 1958-64; Mem. Council, Australian Acad. of Science, 1968-70, Pres. 1970. lyell Medal, Geol. Soc. of London, 1964; Clarke Medal, Royal Society of NSW, 1966; Mueller Medal, ANZAAS, 1967; Foreign and Commonwealth Mem. Geol. Soc. London,

1967. *Publications:* numerous, in geol and palæontol jls on fossil corals, archæocyatha, brachiopods, reef sediments and Australian geology and stratigraphy. *Recreations:* travel, reading. *Address:* University of Queensland, St Lucia, Brisbane, Qld 4067, Australia.

**HILL, Rev. Canon Douglas George;** Hon. Canon of Ely and Rector of Leverington, since 1965; Examining Chaplain to the Bishop of Ely and Director of Studies in Ely Diocese, since 1965; *b* 1912; *s* of George and Edith Hill, Grimsby, Lincs; *m* 1944, Margaret Esther, *d* of late Judge Sir Gerald Hurst, QC; no *c. Educ:* St James' Choir Sch., Grimsby; Gonville and Caius Coll., Cambridge; Lincoln Theological Coll. Schol. Gonville and Caius Coll., 1931-35; John Stewart of Rannoch Schol. in Hebrew, 1932; 1st cl. Oriental Lang. Tripos pt 1, 1933, BA (1st cl. Oriental Lang. Tripos pt 2) 1934; 2nd cl. Theological Tripos pt 2 and Tyrwhitt Schol., 1935; MA 1938. Deacon, 1936, Priest 1937, Lincoln; Curate of: Louth with Welton-le-Wold, 1936-40; Crosby, Dio. of Lincoln, 1940-42; St Nicholas, Chislehurst, 1943-45; Vicar of Eynsford, Kent, Dio. of Rochester, 1945-56; Rector of Papworth Everard, Cambridge, Dio. of Ely, and Chaplain to Papworth Village Settlement and Hosp., 1956-60; Residentiary Canon of Ely Cathedral, 1960-65; Principal, Ely Theological Coll., 1960-64. *Recreations:* travel and walking. *Address:* The Rectory, Leverington, Wisbech, Cambs. *T:* Wisbech 4271.

**HILL, Douglas William,** CBE 1965; DSc; Chairman of Council and Pro-Chancellor, University of Salford, since 1967; *b* 3 March 1904; *o s* of Henry and Florence Mary Hill; *m* 1st, 1936, Margaret Eluned (*d* 1956), *y d* of Rev. O.M. Owen; one *s*; 2nd, 1958, Mabel Constance Prothero, *er d* of James Belford. *Educ:* St George's Sch., Bristol; Univs of Bristol, Liverpool and Illinois, PhD Liverpool, 1926; DSc Bristol, 1936. Research Chemist, Boots Pure Drug Co. Ltd, 1927-30; Commonwealth Fund Fellow, Univ. of Illinois and Rockerfeller Inst. for Med. Research, New York, 1930-33; Lectr in Organic Chemistry, UC Exeter and Special Lectr in Biochemistry, Bristol Univ., 1933-37; Asst to Dir, Shirley Inst., 1937-40; Min. of Supply, 1940-43; Combined Production and Rescources Board, Washington DC, 1943-44; Dep. Dir, Shirley Inst., 1944-56; Director, 1956-69. Mem. Council RIC, 1948-60 (Chm., Manchester and Dist Sect., 1953-54); Mem. Council, Chemical Soc., 1947-50; Vice-Pres., Parly and Sci. Cttee, 1962-65; Chairman: Cttee of Dirs of Research Assocs, 1960-63; Cttee of Dirs of Textile Research, Assocs, 1964-66; Cttee on Mule Spinners' Cancer; Chm. of Governors, Royal Coll. of Advanced Technology, Salford, 1962-67; Member: UGC Cttee on Libraries, 1962-68, Cttee of Management, Science of Science Foundn; Chm., Perkin Memorial Trust Dir, Shirley Developments Ltd, 1953-. Chm., Macclesfield Div. Liberal Assoc., 1948-56. Bernard Dyer Memorial Medallist and Lectr, 1962; Mather Lectr, 1970. Hon. DSc Salford, 1969. *Publications:* Insulin: Its Production, Purification and Properties, 1936; Impact and Value of Science, 1944, 2nd edn, 1946; Co-operative Research for Industry, 1946; papers and articles in scientific jls, press and reviews. *Recreations:* sketching, travel, writing and lecturing. *Address:* Flat 2, Underwood, Underwood Road, Alderley Edge, Cheshire. *T:* Alderley Edge 3411. *Club:* Athenæum.

**HILL, Captain Duncan C.,** DSO; Royal Navy retired; *b* 10 April 1900; 2nd *s* of late Alick S. Hill, Elmfield, Coventry; *m* 1944, Chief Officer Roseanne Maureen Uprichard, WRNS, Elmfield, Portadown, Northern Ireland; one *s* one *d. Educ:* Oundle; Royal Naval Colls, Osborne and Dartmouth. In various ships from 1917; at Royal Naval Staff Coll., 1936-37; Admiralty, 1937-39; HMS Vindictive, July-Aug. 1939; HMS Royal Arthur, 1939-40; HMS Nelson, 1940-42; HMS President, 1942-44; Naval Force Commander, Burma, 1944-45; Naval Attaché, Moscow, 1945-48; CO, HMS Sirius, 1948-49, HMS Cleopatra, 1949-50, HMS Ganges, Shotley, 1950-51; retd 1951. Gen. Manager, Massey Ferguson Training Centre (UK), 1951-69. *Recreations:* tennis, squash, golf, cricket; ex-football; RN and RM squash champion, 1935. *Address:* Park Farm House, Stareton, Kenilworth, Warwicks. *Clubs:* United Service, Incogniti; Jesters.

**HILL, Col (Edward) Roderick,** DSO 1944; JP; HM Lieutenant for Monmouthshire since 1965; Chairman, Chepstow Race Course Co. Ltd, since 1964; *b* 1904; *s* of late Capt. Roderick Tickell Hill; *m* 1934, Rachel, *e d* of Ellis Hicks Beach, Witcombe Park, Glos; one *s* one *d. Educ:* Winchester; Magdalen Coll., Oxford. Gazetted to Coldstream Guards, 1926; served War of 1939-45, with regt (despatches, DSO); commanded 5th Bn and 1st Bn Coldstream Guards and Guards Training Bn; comd Regt, 1949-52. JP Co. Monmouth; High Sheriff of Monmouthshire, 1956; DL Monmouthshire, 1957; Vice-Lieut, 1963-65. Chm. of the Curre Hunt, 1959-65. Chm. of Governors, Monmouth Sch. and Monmouth Sch. for Girls, 1961-66; Chm. Chepstow RDC, 1962-63. Hon. Col, 104 Light AD Regt RA(V), 1967-69. Freeman and Liveryman, Haberdashers Co., 1969. Officer, Order of Orange-Nassau (with swords), 1946. CStJ 1966. *Publications:* (with the Earl of Rosse) The Story of the Guards Armoured Division, 1941-1945, 1956. *Address:* St Arvan's Court, Chepstow, Mon. *T:* Chepstow 2091. *Clubs:* Guards; Monmouthshire County (Newport).

**HILL, Prof. Elizabeth;** Andrew Mellon Professor of Slavic Languages and Literatures, Pittsburgh University, USA, since 1968; *b* 24 Oct. 1900. *Educ:* University and King's Colls, London Univ. BA London 1924, PhD London 1928; MA Cantab 1937. War of 1939-45: Slavonic specialist, Min. of Information. University Lecturer in Slavonic, 1936-48; Prof. of Slavonic Studies, Univ. of Cambridge, 1948-68. Fellow of University Coll., London; Professorial Fellow, Girton Coll., Cambridge. *Address:* 10 Croft Gardens, Cambridge.

**HILL, Eveline, (Mrs J. S. Hill),** JP; *b* 16 April 1898; *d* of Richard and Mary A. Ridyard; *m* 1922, John Stanley Hill; one *s* two *d. Educ:* Manchester Education Cttee Schs. On leaving sch. entered parents' catering business and continued until marriage; assumed joint control, with brother, of the business on Father's death. Manchester City Council, Didsbury Ward, as Conservative rep., 1936-66; CA 1957; County Borough organizer, WVS, Manchester, 1943-50; MP (C) Wythenshawe Division of Manchester, 1950-64. JP Manchester, 1945; Hon. Alderman, 1966. *Address:* 115 Styal Road, Gatley, Cheadle, Cheshire SK8 3TG. *T:* 061-428 5087.

**HILL, Air Cdre Dame Felicity (Barbara),** DBE 1966 (OBE 1954); Director of the Women's Royal Air Force, 1966-69; *b* 12 Dec. 1915; *d* of late Edwin Frederick Hill and of Mrs Frances Ada Barbara Hill (*née* Cocke). *Educ:* St Margaret's Sch., Folkestone. Joined WAAF, 1939; commnd, 1940; served in: UK, 1939-46; Germany, 1946-47; Far East Air Force, 1949-51; other appts included Inspector of WRAF,

1956-59; OC, RAF Hawkinge, 1959-60; OC, RAF Spitalgate, 1960-62; Dep. Dir, 1962-65. Hon. ADC to the Queen, 1966-69. *Address:* Worcester Cottage, Mews Lane, Winchester, Hants. *Club:* Royal Air Force.

**HILL, Sir Francis;** *see* Hill, Sir J. W. F.

**HILL, Sir (George) Cyril Rowley,** 8th Bt, *cr* 1779 of Brook Hall, Londonderry; Journalist; *b* 18 Dec. 1890; *o s* of Sir George Rowley Hill, 7th Bt, and Alice Estelle Harley (*d* 1940), *d* of Edward Bacon, Eywood, Kington, Herefordshire; *S* father 1954; *m* 1919, Edith Muriel, *d* of W. O. Thomas, Oakhurst, Liverpool, and Bryn Glas, Mold, North Wales. *Educ:* St Cyprian's, Eastbourne; Wellington Coll., and abroad. *Heir: cousin* George Alfred Rowley Hill [*b* 11 Oct. 1899; *m* 1st, 1924 (marriage dissolved, 1938); one *s*; 2nd, 1938; one *s* one *d*]. *Address:* 100a Leighton Avenue, Leigh-on-Sea, Essex. *T:* Southend-on-Sea 78046.

**HILL, Gladys,** MA, MD; FRCS, FRCOG; retired as Obstetrician and Gynæcologist, Royal Free Hospital (1940-59); *b* 28 Sept. 1894; *d* of late Arthur Griffiths Hill and Caroline Sutton Hill. *Educ:* Cheltenham Ladies' Coll.; Somerville Coll., Oxford; Royal Free Hosp. Med. Sch. MA Oxon, MD, BS London, FRCS 1936; FRCOG 1943. *Publications:* contribs to medical journals. *Recreations:* mountain walking and reading. *Address:* The Captain's Cottage, Bishops Lydeard, near Taunton, Som. *T:* Bishops Lydeard 533. *Club:* English-Speaking Union.

**HILL, Graham,** OBE 1968; racing driver and company director; *b* 15 Feb. 1929; *s* of Norman H. D. Hill and Constance M. Hill; *m* 1955, Bette P. Hill; one *s* two *d. Educ:* Hendon Technical Coll. Served RN, 1950-52. Racing Driver: Team Lotus, 1958-59, 1967, 1968, 1969; BRM, 1960-66; Porsche, 1960; R. R. C. Walker, 1970. World Champion Racing Driver, 1962, 1968; Runner-up (or 2nd) World Champion Racing Driver, 1963, 1964, 1965; 1st, Dutch Grand Prix, May 1962; 1st, German Grand Prix, Aug. 1962; 1st, Italian Grand Prix, Sept. 1962; 1st, South African Grand Prix, Dec. 1962; 1st, Monaco Grand Prix, 1963, 1964, 1965, 1968, 1969; 1st, Tourist Trophy, Aug. 1963 and 1964; 1st, American Grand Prix, 1963, 1964, 1965; 1st, Spanish Grand Prix, 1968; 1st, Reims 12 hr, July 1964; 1st, Indianapolis, 1966. *Recreations:* rowing, squash, photography, flying, water ski-ing, shooting, golf. *Address:* 32 Parkside, Mill Hill, NW7. *T:* 01-959 2763. *Clubs:* London Rowing, British Racing Drivers, Leander.

**HILL, Harold G.;** *see* Gardiner-Hill.

**HILL, Sir Ian (George Wilson),** Kt 1966; CBE 1945; TD; FRSE; MB; FRCPE; FRCP; Hon. Physician to HM The Queen in Scotland; Professor of Medicine, University of Dundee (formerly University of St Andrews), 1950-69, now Professor Emeritus; *b* 7 Sept. 1904; *s* of late A. W. Hill, JP, and of Mrs J. M. Hill, Edinburgh; *m* 1st, 1933, Audrey (*d* 1966), 2nd *d* of late G. W. Lavender, Stoke-on-Trent; one *s* one *d*; 2nd, 1968, Anna, *o d* of late M. W. Hill. *Educ:* George Watson's Coll., Edinburgh; Universities of Edinburgh, Michigan and Vienna. MB, ChB (Hons), Edinburgh, 1928; FRCPE 1933; FRCP 1956; Ettles Scholar, Allan Fellow, Shaw-Macfie-Lang Fellow, etc, Univ. of Edinburgh; Rockefeller Travelling Fellow, 1932-33; Lecturer in Medicine, University of Aberdeen, 1933-37; Lectr in Therapeutics, University of Edinburgh, 1937-49; Asst Physician, Edinburgh Royal Infirmary, 1938-50; Physician, Deaconess Hosp., Edinburgh, 1946-50. Served War of 1939-45, Officer i/c Med. Div., Mil. Hosps in UK, MEF and India, 1939-44; Consulting Physician, XIVth Army, Burma and ALFSEA, 1944-45; Col, Royal Army Medical Corps (TARO) retd; Hon. Col 2nd Scottish Gen. Hosp., 1947-58; Examr in Med., Univs Edinburgh, Glasgow, Birmingham, E Africa, Leeds, Singapore, Hong Kong; Vis. Prof. of Medicine, McGill Univ., 1967; Vis. Consultant in Medicine, Hong Kong, Malaya, Borneo, etc, 1956 and 1961; Hon. Consulting Physician, Scottish Comd (Army), 1965-70. Gibson Lectr, RCPE, 1949; Patel Lectr, Bombay, 1961; Walker Lectr, RCP and S Glasgow, 1962; Centennial Lectr, Univ. of Illinois, 1967; Carey Coombs Lectr, Univ. of Bristol, 1968; Wilson Memorial Lectr, Univ. of Michigan, 1968. Former Senior Pres. Royal Medical Soc., Edinburgh; Pres., Royal Coll. of Physicians of Edinburgh, 1963-66; Member: British Cardiac Soc. (Chm. 1962); Assoc. of Physicians of Great Britain and Ireland (Pres. 1962); Scottish Soc. of Physicians (Pres., 1967). hon. Member: Cardiac and Endocrinological Socs of India; Cardiac Soc. of Hong Kong; Acad. Med., Singapore, 1966, etc. Hon. FRACP 1966; Hon. FACP 1967. *Publications:* various contribs to scientific and medical books and journals, principally on cardiology. *Address:* 21 Farington Street, Dundee, Angus. *Clubs:* Flyfishers', Royal Societies; Royal and Ancient (St Andrews); New (Edinburgh).

**HILL, Ian Macdonald,** MS, FRCS; Consultant Thoracic Surgeon, St Bartholomew's Hospital and SE Metropolitan Regional Hospital Board, since 1950; Sub Dean, St Bartholomews Hospital Medical College, since 1964; *b* 8 June 1919; British; *m* 1944, Agnes Mary Paice; three *s* one *d. Educ:* Stationers' Company's Sch.; St Bartholomew's Hosp. Medical Coll. Undergrad. schols and medals, 1937-41; MB, BS (Hons) London, 1942; MRCS, LRCP 1942; FRCS 1944; MS London 1945. Demonstrator of Anatomy, St Bartholomew's, 1943; Surgical Chief Asst St Bart.'s Hosp., 1944; RAF Medical Branch, 1946; Wing Comdr i/c Surg. Div. No 1 RAF Gen. Hosp., 1947; Senior Registrar, Thoracic Surg. Unit, Guy's Hosp., 1948; Surgical Chief Asst, Brompton Hosp. and Inst. of Diseases of the Chest, 1950. FRSocMed. Member: Soc. of Apothecaries; Soc. of Thoracic Surgeons; Thoracic and Cardiac Socs. Freeman of City of London. *Publications:* articles in professional jls, mainly relating to lung and cardiac surgery, 1942-61. *Recreations:* old cars, furniture, keyboard instruments; gardening and house care. *Address:* 98 Fox Lane, Palmers Green, N13. *T:* 01-886 7324; 152 Harley Street, W1. *T:* 01-935 8868.

**HILL, Ian Starforth,** QC 1969; Barrister; *b* 30 Sept. 1921; *s* of late Harold Victor John Hill; *m* 1950, Bridget Mary Footner; one *s* two *d. Educ:* Shrewsbury Sch.; Brasenose Coll., Oxford (MA). 11th Sikh Regt, Indian Army, 1940-45, India, Africa, Italy (despatches). Called to Bar, Gray's Inn, 1949; Dep. Chm., Isle of Wight QS, 1968; Western Circuit. *Address:* 1 Crown Office Row, Temple, EC4. *T:* 01-353 9272; The Dial House, Frensham, Surrey. *T:* Frensham 2774. *Club:* Hampshire (Winchester).

**HILL, Ivan Conrad,** CBE 1960; Deputy Chairman: Illingworth, Morris & Co. Ltd; Joshua Hoyle & Sons Ltd; Director: Kelsall & Kemp Ltd, since 1933; Winterbotham, Strachan & Payne Ltd; Chairman: Industrial Coal Consumers Council, since 1965; *b* 22 Jan. 1906; *s* of Wilfred Lawson Hill and Annie Jane England; *m* 1st, 1931, Alexandrina Ewart (marr. diss. 1962); four *d*; 2nd, 1963, Sheila

Houghton. *Educ:* Oakham Sch.; St John's Coll., Cambridge. Exhibitioner and Open Scholar of St John's Coll. 1st cl. Hons Law Tripos Cantab 1928. Apptd Jt Man. Dir. Kelsall & Kemp Ltd, 1933. Chm. Wool Industries Research Assoc., 1950-53; Mem. Monopolies and Restrictive Practices Commn, and Monopolies Commn, 1951-63; Chm. British Rayon Research Assoc., 1956-61; Chairman, Samuel Courtauld & Co. Ltd, 1962-66. Liveryman, Weavers' Company, 1938-. *Recreations:* tennis, ski-ing, riding. *Address:* Rookwoods, Sible Hedingham, Essex. *T:* Hedingham 266.

**HILL, Sir James,** 3rd Bt, *cr* 1917; Chairman of Directors of Sir James Hill & Sons, Ltd, Bradford; *b* 29 May 1905; *s* of Sir Albert Hill, 2nd Bt; *S* father 1946; *m* 1930, Marjory, *d* of late Frank Croft, Brocka, Lindale, Grange-over-Sands; one *s* four *d. Educ:* Wrekin Coll., Salop. *Heir: s* James Frederick Hill [*b* 5 Dec. 1943; *m* 1966, Sandra Elizabeth, *o d* of J. C. Ingram]. *Address:* Apperley Grange, Rawdon, near Leeds. *T:* Rawdon 2216. *Club:* Bradford.

**HILL, Brig. James;** *see* Hill, Brig. S. J. L.

**HILL, James;** *see* Hill, S. J. A.

**HILL, Sir (James William) Francis,** Kt 1958; CBE 1954; solicitor; company director; *b* 15 Sept. 1899; *s* of James Hill and Millicent (*née* Blinkhorn). *Educ:* City Sch., Lincoln; Trinity Coll., Cambridge. MA 1925, LLM 1926, LittD 1950 (Cambridge). 2nd Lieut KRRC, 1918. Admitted Solicitor, 1926. Senior partner Andrew and Co., Lincoln, Solicitors. Mem. Lincoln City Council, 1932- (Mayor, 1945-46); Hon. Freeman, Lincoln, 1961; Mem. Nottingham University Coll. Council, 1938-48; Pres. Nottingham Univ. Council, 1948-68; Pro-Chancellor, 1959-. Mem., Royal Commn on Local Govt in England, 1966-69. Chairman, Assoc. of Municipal Corporations, 1957-66; formerly Governor, Administrative Staff Coll.; President: European Conf. of Local Authorities, Strasbourg, 1966-68; International Union of Local Authorities, The Hague, 1967-; Member: Historic Buildings Council, 1968-; Archbishops' Commn on Redundant Churches, 1969-. chm. of Governors: Lincoln Christ's Hosp. Foundation, Girls' High Sch., and Lincoln Sch., 1935-66. Hon. LLD Nottingham and Birmingham. FSA, FRHistS. Contested (L) Peterborough, 1929, (C) Lincoln, 1950. *Publications:* Medieval Lincoln, 1948; Tudor and Stuart Lincoln, 1956; Georgian Lincoln, 1966; (ed) Banks Family Papers, 1952. *Recreation:* local history. *Address:* The Priory, Lincoln. *T:* Lincoln 25759. *Club:* United University.

**HILL, James William Thomas, (Jimmy);** Head of Sport, London Weekend Television, since Nov. 1967; *m* 1st, 1950, Gloria Mary (marr. diss. 1961) two *s* one *d*; 2nd, 1962, Heather Christine; one *s* one *d. Educ:* Henry Thornton School, Clapham. Player, Brentford FC, 1949-52, Fulham FC, 1952-61; Gen. Manager, Coventry City FC, 1961-67. Hon. Chm., The Professional Footballers Assoc., 1957-61. *Publications:* Striking for Soccer, 1961; Improve your Soccer, 1964. *Recreations:* golf, riding, tennis, soccer, bridge. *Address:* c/o London Weekend Television, Station House, Harrow Road, Wembley, Middx. *T:* 01-902 8846. *Clubs:* The Sportsman, Queen's.

**HILL, Jimmy;** *see* Hill, James William Thomas.

**HILL, Sir (John) Denis (Nelson),** Kt 1966; MB, BS; FRCP; DPM; Professor of Psychiatry, Institute of Psychiatry, since 1966; *b* 5 Oct. 1913; *s* of Lieut-Col John Arthur Hill, Orleton Manor, near Ludlow; *m* 1st, 1938, Phoebe Elizabeth Herschel, *d* of Lieut-Col H. H. Wade; one *s* one *d*; 2nd, 1962, Lorna, *d* of J. F. Wheelan; one *s* one *d. Educ:* Shrewsbury Sch.; St Thomas' Hosp., London. Chief Asst, Dept Psychol Medicine, St Thomas' Hosp., 1938-44; Psychiatric Specialist, Emergency Medical Service, 1939-46; Physician and Lecturer in Psychological Medicine, King's Coll. Hosp., London, 1947-60; Senior Lecturer, Institute of Psychiatry, Maudsley Hosp., London, 1948-60; Hon. Physician, Maudsley Hosp., 1948-60. Mem. Medical Research Council, 1956-60; Prof. of Psychiatry, Middlesex Hosp. Medical Sch., London, 1961-66. Mem. (Crown Representative), Gen. Medical Council, 1961-; Mem., Central Health Service Council, 1961-67. Rock Carling Fellow, 1969. *Publications:* Editor: Electro-encephalography: a symposium, 1950; contribs to textbooks on medical subjects and to scientific journals. *Recreations:* shooting, riding. *Address:* 71 Cottenham Park Road, Wimbledon, SW20.

**HILL, John Edward Bernard;** MP (C) South Norfolk since Jan. 1955; farming in Suffolk since 1946; *b* 13 Nov. 1912; *o s* of late Capt. Robert William Hill, Cambs Regt, and Marjorie Jane Lloyd-Jones, *d* of Edward Scott Miller; *m* 1944, Edith Luard, *widow* of Comdr R. A. E. Luard, RNVR, and 5th *d* of late John Maxwell, Cove, Dunbartonshire; one adopted *d. Educ:* Charterhouse; Merton Coll., Oxford (MA). Various journeys; Middle East, Far East, India, USA, 1935-37; Far East, 1956-57; USA, 1958. Called to Bar, Inner Temple (Certificate of Honour), 1938. RA (TA), 1939; Air Observation Post Pilot, 1942; War Office, 1942; 651 (Air OP) RAF, Tunisia, 1942; wounded, 1943; invalided out, 1945. Mem. Parliamentary delegns: W Germany and Berlin, 1959; Ghana, 1965; IPU Conf., Teheran, 1966; CPA Conf., Uganda, 1967; Bulgaria, 1970; Vice-Chm., Cons. Educn Cttee, 1968-69; Mem., Select Cttee on Agriculture, 1967-69; Asst Govt Whip, 1959-60; a Lord Comr of the Treasury, 1960-64. Mem. East Suffolk and Norfolk River Board, 1952-62. Member: Governing Body, Charterhouse Sch., 1958; Langley Sch., Norfolk, 1962; GBA Cttee, 1966-. *Recreations:* association football (Blue; Sec., OUAFC 1934); shooting, concerts, picture galleries. *Address:* Watermill Farm, Wenhaston, Halesworth, Suffolk. *T:* Blythburgh 207; 14 Cowley Street. SW1. *T:* 01-222 7149. *Clubs:* Garrick, MCC.

**HILL, (John Edward) Christopher,** FBA 1966; Master of Balliol College, Oxford, since 1965; *b* 6 Feb. 1912; *m* 1st, 1944, Inez Waugh; one *d*; 2nd, 1956, Bridget Irene Sutton; one *s* one *d* (and one *d* decd). *Educ:* St Peter's Sch., York; Balliol Coll., Oxford. Fellow of All Souls Coll., Oxford, 1934; Asst Lectr, University Coll., Cardiff, 1936; Fellow and Tutor in Modern History, Balliol Coll., Oxford, 1938. Private in Field Security Police, commissioned Oxford and Bucks Light Inf., 1940, Major; seconded to Foreign Office, 1943. Returned to Balliol, 1945; University Lectr in 16th- and 17th-century history, 1959; Ford's Lectr, 1962. DLitt Oxford, 1965; Hon. DLitt: Hull, 1966; E Anglia, 1968; Hon. LittD Sheffield, 1967. *Publications:* The English Revolution 1640, 1940; (under name K. E. Holme) Two Commonwealths, 1945; Lenin and the Russian Revolution, 1947; The Good Old Cause (ed. jointly with E. Dell), 1949; Economic Problems of the Church, 1956; Puritanism and Revolution, 1958; Oliver Cromwell, 1958; The Century of Revolution, 1961; Society and Puritanism in Pre-Revolutionary England, 1964; Intellectual Origins of the English

Revolution, 1965; Reformation to Industrial Revolution, 1967; God's Englishman, 1970; articles in learned journals, etc. *Address:* 21 Northmoor Road, Oxford. *T:* Oxford 58544.

**HILL, John Frederick Rowland,** CMG 1955; *b* 20 April 1905; *s* of Judge William Henry Hill; *m* 1930, Phyllys Esmé (*née* Fryer); one *s* two *d.* *Educ:* Pinewood Sch., Farnborough; Marlborough Coll.; Lincoln Coll., Oxford. BA Oxon, Hon. Sch. Jurisprudence, 1927; Cadet Colonial Civil Service, Tanganyika, 1928; Asst District Officer, 1930; District Officer, 1940; Dep. Provincial Comr, 1947; Provincial Comr, 1948; Sen. Provincial Comr, 1950; Mem. for Communications, Works and Development Planning, Tanganyika Govt, 1951-56; Chm., Tanganyika Broadcasting Corp. and Dir of Broadcasting, 1956-57; Govt Liaison Officer, Freeport, Bahamas, 1957-58; Supervisor of Elections, Zanzibar, 1959-60. *Recreations:* tennis, golf, cricket. *Address:* Box 1180, Zanzibar. *Club:* Royal Commonwealth Society.

**HILL, Sir John McGregor,** Kt 1969; BSc, PhD, FInstP; Chairman of the United Kingdom Atomic Energy Authority since 1967; *b* 21 Feb. 1921; *s* of John Campbell Hill and Margaret Elizabeth Park; *m* 1947, Nora Eileen Hellett; two *s* one *d.* *Educ:* King's Coll., London; St John's Coll., Cambridge. Flt Lieut, RAF, 1941. Cavendish Laboratory, Cambridge, 1946; Lecturer, London Univ., 1948. Joined UKAEA, 1950 (Mem. for Production, 1964-67). Mem., Advisory Council on Technology, 1968-. *Publications:* various papers on research physics. *Recreation:* golf. *Address:* Dominic House, Sudbrook Lane, Petersham, Surrey. *T:* 01-940 7221. *Clubs:* Athenæum, East India and Sports.

**HILL, John Maxwell,** CBE 1969; DFC 1945; Assistant Commissioner, Personnel and Training, New Scotland Yard, since 1968; *b* 25 March 1914; *s* of late L. S. M. Hill, Civil Servant, Plymouth; *m* 1939, Marjorie Louisa, *d* of late John Oliver Reynolds, Aylesbury, Bucks; one *s* one *d.* *Educ:* Plymouth Coll. Metropolitan Police Coll., Hendon, 1938-39; joined Metropolitan Police, 1933. Served with RAF, 1942-45. Dep. Comdr, New Scotland Yard, 1959; Metropolitan Police: Comdr, No 3 District, 1963, Comdr, No 1 District, 1964; HM Inspector of Constabulary, 1965. Asst Comr (Administration and Operations), 1966-68. *Recreations:* walking, golf. *Address:* 23 Beacon Way, Banstead, Surrey. *T:* Burgh Heath 52771.

**HILL, Mrs John Stanley;** *see* Hill, Eveline.

**HILL, Prof. Kenneth Robson;** Professor of Pathology, Royal Free Hospital School of Medicine, University of London; *b* 20 April 1911; *s* of Frederick and Lydia Hill; *m* 1938, Elsie Wade; one *s* one *d.* *Educ:* Washington Grammar Sch.; King's Coll. and Westminster Hosp., Univ. of London. BSc 1932; AKC 1932; MB, BS 1943; MD 1946; MRCP 1957; FRIC 1962; FRCPath 1964; FRCP 1970. Served RAMC, OC Med. Res. Unit, West Africa, 1939-45. Rockefeller Fellowship at Johns Hopkins Hosp., Baltimore, USA, 1947-48. Prof. of Pathology, University Coll. of the West Indies, 1949-56; WHO Consultant to Govt of Indonesia, 1950; WHO Consultant to India, Med. Educn, 1967; WHO Consultant for Treponematosis, 1950-70; Vis. Prof., Univ. of Alexandria, 1962; External Examr in Pathology; Univ. of Baghdad, 1961, 1962; Univ. of Khartoum, 1962; Malta, Singapore, 1963; Ibadan, 1966; Ghana, 1968-70. Chm., Group Adv. Med. Cttee, Royal Free Hosp. Chm., British Soc. of Clinical Cytology. Member: Overseas Cttee, BMA; Medical Advisory Cttee, Min. Overseas Development; British Voluntary Programme. Governor: Watford Tech. Coll.; Boreham Wood Grammar Sch. *Publication:* Atlas of Framboesia (WHO), 1951. *Recreations:* service overseas; medical education. *Address:* 12 Aldenham Avenue, Radlett, Herts. *T:* Radlett 6847. *Clubs:* Athenæum, MCC, Anglo-American Sporting.

**HILL, Maj.-Gen. Leslie Rowley,** OBE 1919; *b* Musselburgh, 28 Dec. 1884; 5th *s* of late Lieut-Col R. R. C. Hill; *m* 1916, Eileen Dorothy Hutchinson (*d* 1962); one *s* three *d.* *Educ:* Wellington Coll.; RMA Woolwich. Commissioned RA, 1904; Army student, Japan, 1910-14; served European War, 1914-16 (wounded), also War of 1939-45, 1939-40. Gen. Staff, 1917-21; Military Attaché, Tokyo, 1925-30; Lieut-Col, 1933; Col, 1933; Brig., 1936; Maj.-Gen., 1938; retired, 1940. *Recreations:* shooting and fishing. *Address:* Halketts, Kings Hill, Beech, Alton, Hants. *T:* Medstead 2258.

**HILL, Michael William;** Keeper, National Reference Library of Science and Invention, since 1968; *b* 1928; *o s* of late Geoffrey William Hill, Ross on Wye and Torquay; *m* 1st, 1957, Elma Jack Forrest; one *s* one *d*; 2nd, 1969, Barbara Joy Youngman. *Educ:* Nottingham High Sch.; Lincoln Coll., Oxford (BSc, MA). ARIC 1953. Research Chemist, Laporte Chemicals Ltd, 1953-56; Morgan Crucible Group: Laboratory Head, 1956; Asst Process Control Manager, 1958; Group Technical Editor, 1963. Asst Keeper, British Museum, 1964. Dep. Librarian, Patent Office Library, 1965. *Publications:* various articles on carbon and other ceramics in technological jls. *Address:* 9 Hillside Road, Cheam, Surrey. *T:* 01-642 2418. *Club:* Royal Torbay Yacht.

**HILL, Norman Hammond,** MD (London), MRCP; Consulting Physician: Belgrave Hospital for Children; Metropolitan and Wembley Hospitals; St Andrew's Hospital, Dollis Hill; *b* 10 March 1893; *s* of Lewis Gordon Hill and Amy Caroline Hammond; *m* 1938, Suzanne Mary, *y d* of Rev. H. S. Rees, Christchurch, Mon. *Educ:* Bradford Grammar Sch.; St Bartholomew's Hosp. MRCS, LRCP 1915. Served in Army, 1915-19, Capt. RAMC (TF); held appointment of House Surgeon, Chief Asst to a Medical Unit, and Casualty Physician St Bartholomew's Hosp. and House Physician and Senior Resident Medical Officer Metropolitan Hosp. *Publications:* articles on medical subjects to Lancet, British Medical Journal, Clinical Journal, and Medical Press and Circular. *Recreations:* golf, photography. *Address:* 22 Acacia Road, NW8. *T:* 01-722 7466.

**HILL, Osman;** *see* Hill, W. C. O.

**HILL, Reginald Dykers Richardson;** Judge of the Federal Court of Appeal, Malaysia, 1959-63; *b* 11 July 1902; *s* of Michael Dykers and Eliza Sophia Dasent, Brit. Guiana; *m* 1926, Gwendolen Emily Mary (*d* 1969), *e d* of Frank Sale, Birmingham; one *s.* *Educ:* Cranleigh Sch., Surrey. Called to the Bar, Gray's Inn, 1924. Private practice, Brit. Guiana, 1924; Stipendiary Magistrate, Brit. Guiana, 1930; Resident Magistrate, Jamaica, 1937; Chief Magistrate, Palestine, 1944; Puisne Judge, Malayan Union, 1947. Badlishah Decn of Loyalty, Kedah, 1958. *Recreations:* social. *Address:* 12 Wilbury Grange, Wilbury Road, Hove BN3 3GN. *Clubs:* West Indian; Hove (Hove).

**HILL, Reginald Harrison,** MA (Oxon); FLA 1928; Librarian and Secretary to the Trustees of the National Central Library, 1945-58, retired; *b* 24 Nov. 1894; *s* of William and Edith Margaret Hill, Oxford; *m* 1922, Winifred I. Langford (*d* 1956); two *s* decd. *Educ:* City of Oxford Sch.; St Catherine's Coll., Oxford. Bodleian Library, Oxford: Under-Asst, 1908-11; Senior Asst, 1911-33; Sec. to Bodley's Librarian, 1931-33; Sec. of the Library, 1933-44. Sec., Friends of the Bodleian, 1929-33. First Hon. Sec. of University and Research Section of Library Assoc., 1928-30. Rockefeller Research Fellow, visiting United States Libraries, 1934; Adviser (Libraries) to UK Delegn, UNESCO, Paris Conf., 1946; Chm., UK Libraries Advisory Cttee, UNESCO, 1948-66; Chm., Educn and Library Cttee of Polish Research Centre, 1958-67. Sec., British Academy Cttee on Provision for Research, 1958-61. Edited Bodleian Quarterly Record, 1914-17, 1919-31. Hon. Member: Osler Club; Polish Inst. *Publications:* The Shelley Correspondence in the Bodleian Library, 1926; Bibliotheca Osleriana, 1929 (with Dr W. W. Francis and Dr T. A. Malloch); reports and papers in Library Assoc. Record, etc. *Recreations:* bibliography, gardening. *Address:* Haydon House, 83 West Allington, Bridport, Dorset. *T:* Bridport 2539.

**HILL, Sir Reginald (Herbert),** KBE 1942; CB 1933; *b* 27 Nov. 1888; *s* of Herbert Charles Hill and Caroline Brown; *m* 1918, Mary Catherine (*d* 1964), *d* of T. H. McGinn; one *s* one *d*. *Educ:* Merchant Taylors' Sch.; St John's Coll., Oxford. Entered Board of Trade, 1912; Dep. Sec., Min. of Transport, 1940; Min. of War Transport, 1941-54; Dep. Dir-Gen. (Inland Transport), Min. of War Transport, 1941-47; Chm. Docks and Inland Waterways Board of Management, British Transport Commission, 1948-54. Medal of Freedom with silver palm, US, 1947; Ordre du Mérite Maritime, France, 1950. *Address:* Lammermoor Nursing Home, Shenfield Common, Brentwood, Essex.

**HILL, Reginald John James,** CIE 1947; MA; Principal, Ministry of Overseas Development, 1964; retired, 1965; *b* 1 July 1905; *s* of James Hill and Winifred Alexander; *m* 1932, Margaret St Barbe McNeil-Smith; one *s* one *d*. *Educ:* Dunfermline High Sch., Fife, Scotland; Universities of Edinburgh, Göttingen (Germany); Lyon (France); Emmanuel Coll., Cambridge. Joined ICS, 1928; Asst Comr, 1928; Dep. Comr, 1935; Financial Sec. to Govt, Central Provinces and Berar, 1944; entered HM Treasury, 1947; Colonial Office, 1949; Dept of Technical Co-operation, 1961. *Recreations:* fishing, gardening, cricket, field sports. *Address:* The Pound Cottage, Bisley, Surrey. *T:* Brookwood 3054.

**HILL, Robert,** ScD Cantab 1942; FRS 1946; biochemist; Member of Scientific Staff of Agricultural Research Council, 1943-66; *b* 2 April 1899; *s* of Joseph Alfred Hill and Clara Maud Jackson; *m* 1935, Amy Priscilla, *d* of Edgar Worthington; two *s* two *d*. *Educ:* Bedales Sch.; Emmanuel Coll., Cambridge (Scholar). Served European War, 1914-18: RE pioneer Anti-gas Dept, 1917-18. Emmanuel Coll., Cambridge, 1919-22; Senior Studentship (Exhibn of 1851), 1927; Beit Memorial Research Fellow, 1929; Senior Beit Memorial Research Fellow, 1935; Hon. Fellow of Emmanuel Coll., 1963. Royal Medal, Royal Society, 1963; 1st Award for photosynthesis, Soc. of American Plant Physiologists, 1963; Charles E. Kettering Research Award, 1963; Hon. Mem., Amer. Soc. of Biological Chemists, 1964. *Publication:* (with C. P. Whittingham) Photosynthesis, 1955. *Recreations:* growing plants and dyeing with traditional plant dyes, water-colour painting. *Address:* Department of Biochemistry, Tennis Court Road, Cambridge.

**HILL, Sir Robert E.;** *see* Erskine-Hill.

**HILL, Roderick;** *see* Hill, Colonel E. R.

**HILL, Dr Rodney,** FRS 1961; PhD; ScD; Reader in Mechanics of Solids, University of Cambridge, since 1969; *b* 11 June 1921; *o s* of Harold Harrison Hill, Leeds; *m* 1946, Jeanne Kathlyn, *yr d* of C. P. Wickens, Gidea Park; one *d*. *Educ:* Leeds Grammar Sch.; Pembroke Coll., Cambridge. MA, PhD, ScD Cambridge. Armament Research Dept, 1943-46; Cavendish Laboratory, Cambridge, 1946-48; British Iron and Steel Research Assoc., 1948-50; University of Bristol: Research Fellow, 1950-53, Reader, 1953; Univ. of Nottingham: Prof. of Applied Mathematics, 1953-62; Professorial Research Fellow, 1962-63; Berkeley Bye-Fellow, Gonville and Caius Coll., Cambridge, 1963-69. Editor, Jl of Mechanics and Physics of Solids, 1952-68. *Publications:* Mathematical Theory of Plasticity, 1950; Principles of Dynamics, 1964. *Address:* Dept of Applied Mathematics and Theoretical Physics, Cambridge.

**HILL, (Stanley) James (Allen);** MP (C) Southampton Test since 1970; company director; *b* 21 Dec. 1924; *s* of James and Florence Cynthia Hill; *m* 1958, Ruby Evelyn Ralph; two *s* three *d*. *Educ:* Regents Park Sch., Southampton; Southampton Univ.; North Wales Naval Training Coll. Former Pilot. Mem., Southampton City Council, 1966-70; Mem. Cttee, Southampton Conservative and Ratepayers Fedn. *Recreations:* private aviation, farming. *Address:* House of Commons, SW1; 24 John Islip Street, SW1; Gunsfield Lodge, Melchet Park, Plaitford, Hants. *Clubs:* Constitutional, St Stephen's, British Light Aviation; Royal Southampton Yacht.

**HILL, Brig. (Stanley) James (Ledger),** DSO 1942, and Bars, 1944, 1945; MC 1940; Director, Powell Duffryn Ltd, since 1961; Chairman, Cory Brothers & Co. Ltd, 1965-70; *b* 14 March 1911; *s* of late Maj.-Gen. Walter Pitts Hendy Hill, CB, CMG, DSO, West Amesbury House, Wilts; *m* 1937, Denys, *d* of late E. Hubert Gunter-Jones, MC, JP, Gloucester House, Ledbury; one *d*. *Educ:* Marlborough; RMC Sandhurst. 2nd Bn, Royal Fusiliers, 1931-35; 2nd Bn, RF, BEF, 1939; DAAG, GHQ, BEF, 1940; comd 1st Bn, Parachute Regt, N Africa landing, 1942; comd 3rd Parachute Bde, 1943-45; took part in Normandy and Rhine crossing (wounded thrice); comdr 4th Parachute Bde (TA), 1947-48. Apptd to Bd of Associated Coal & Wharf Cos Ltd, 1948; Pres., Powell Duffryn Group of Cos in Canada, 1952-58. Legion of Honour (France), 1942; Silver Star (USA), 1945; King Haakon VII Liberty Cross (Norway), 1945. *Recreations:* fishing, shooting and birdwatching. *Address:* 35 Thurloe Square, SW7. *T:* 01-589 0875. *Clubs:* Boodle's, Army and Navy, Hurlingham; Royal Solent Yacht; Island Sailing (IoW); University (Montreal and Toronto).

**HILL, Victor Archibald Lord,** MA; *b* 3 July 1905; *o s* of W. E. Hill; *m* 1938, Jean Melicent, *e d* of Dr D. N. Seth-Smith, Bournemouth; two *s*. *Educ:* Chigwell Sch.; Queen Mary Coll., London (Open Exhibr; Univ. Schol. in Classics; 1st cl. Hons BA); Hertford Coll., Oxford (Open Schol., 1st Cl. Hon. Mods, 3rd Cl. Lit. Hum.). MA (Oxon) 1934. Asst Master, Shrewsbury Sch., 1930-40, 1946-48; Headmaster, Allhallows Sch., 1948-65; Asst Master: Blundell's, 1965-66; Uppingham, 1966-67, 1968-69; Chigwell, 1969-70; Lectr in

Classics, Exeter Univ., 1967-68. Served 1940-45, with KSLI and RA (Major). *Recreations:* music, travel, golf. *Address:* Beggars' Roost, Morchard Bishop, near Crediton, Devon. *T:* Morchard Bishop 315. *Club:* National Liberal.

**HILL, William Charles Osman,** MD; *b* 13 July 1901; *s* of late James Osman Hill and of Fanny Martin; *m* 1947, Yvonne, *o d* of late Harold Stranger, KC, MP. *Educ:* King Edward VI Sch., Birmingham; Birmingham Univ. University of Birmingham: MB, ChB 1924, MD (Hons) 1925; Richards Memorial Prize; Junior Medical Prize; Ingleby Schol. in Midwifery; Asst Lecturer in Zoology, 1924-25; Lecturer in Anatomy, 1925-30; Prof. of Anatomy, Ceylon Medical Coll. (later University of Ceylon), 1930-44 (Registrar, 1938-40); Reader in Physical Anthropology, University of Edinburgh, 1945-50; Prosector to the Zoological Soc. of London, 1950-62; Associate Dir, Yerkes Primate Research Center, 1962-69. Editor-in-Chief, Ceylon Jl of Science, 1932-44; Gen. Editor, Zoo Penguins, 1957. Visiting Prof. of Anatomy, Emory Univ., Georgia, 1957-58. External Examiner in Univ. Coll., Colombo (Zoology), and in Universities of Cambridge, Edinburgh and Reading; Part-time Lecturer in Morphology, Charing Cross Hospital Medical Sch., 1954-62; Mem., Board of Studies in Anatomy, University of London; Hunterian Trustee, Royal College of Surgeons of England, 1962-. FRSE (Gold Medal, Makdougal-Brisbane Prize, 1955); FLS; FRAI; FZS; Anatomical Soc. of Great Britain and Ireland (Coun. Mem. and late Vice-Pres.). Asst Comr St John's Ambulance Assoc. (Ceylon Branch), 1938-43. *Publications:* Comparative Anatomy and Taxonomy of the Primates (7 vols), 1953, 1955, 1957, 1960, 1961, 1965, 1966, 1967; Man's Ancestry, 1954; Man as an Animal, 1957; numerous papers on primate morphology, anthropology and human anatomy. *Recreations:* field ornithology, botany, photography and travel. *Address:* c/o The Ulster Bank, College Green, Dublin, Ireland; Moonfleet, Frithsden Copse, Berkhamsted, Herts. *T:* Berkhamsted 4466.

**HILL, William Wills,** MA (Hon.) Birmingham. 1936; BSc London; Member of Standing Committee of Convocation, and former Member of the Senate, University of London; Editor of Schoolmaster and Woman Teacher's Chronicle, 1933-46; *b* 9 Sept. 1881; *m* 1905, May Frances (*d* 1960), *d* of William and Elizabeth Dixon, Kingston-upon-Thames; two *s*. *Educ:* Page Green Sch., Tottenham; East London Technical Coll.; Westminster Training Coll. Headmaster of Secondary Schs in Leics, 1907-33; Pres. of National Union of Teachers, 1928; Mem. of Executive, 1921-33; Pres. of Barwell Co-operative Soc., 1917-21. *Recreations:* swimming, dancing, bowls, gramophone, theatre. *Address:* 45 Queen's Avenue, Muswell Hill, N10. *T:* 01-883 2885. *Club:* Arts Theatre.

**HILL-NORTON, Adm. Sir Peter (John),** GCB 1970 (KCB 1967; CB 1964); Chief of the Defence Staff, since 1971; *b* 8 Feb. 1915; *s* of Capt. M. J. Norton and Mrs M. B. Norton; *m* 1936, Margaret Eileen Linstow; one *s* one *d*. *Educ:* RNC Dartmouth. Went to sea, 1932; commnd, 1936; specialised in Gunnery, 1939; War of 1939-45: Arctic Convoys; NW Approaches; Admiralty Naval Staff. Comdr 1948; Capt. 1952; Naval Attaché, Argentine, Uruguay, Paraguay, 1953-55; comd HMS Decoy, 1956-57; comd HMS Ark Royal, 1959-61; Asst Chief of Naval Staff, 1962-64; Flag Officer, Second-in-Command, Far East Fleet, 1964-66; Dep. Chief of the Defence Staff (Personnel and Logistics), 1966; Second Sea Lord and Chief of Naval Personnel, Jan.-Aug. 1967; Vice-Chief of Naval Staff, 1967-68; C-in-C Far East, 1969-70; Chief of the Naval Staff and First Sea Lord, 1970-71. *Recreations:* golf, shooting, water ski-ing. *Address:* King's Mill House, South Nutfield, Surrey. *T:* Nutfield Ridge 3309. *Club:* United Service.

**HILL-TREVOR,** family name of **Baron Trevor.**

**HILL-WOOD, Sir David (Basil),** 3rd Bt *cr* 1921; stockbroker since 1956; *b* 12 Nov. 1926; *s* of Sir Basil Samuel Hill Hill-Wood, 2nd Bt, and Hon. Joan Louisa Brand, *e d* of 3rd Viscount Hampden; *S* father, 1954. *Educ:* Eton. Served in Army (Grenadier Guards), 1945-48. Bank Clerk, 1948-55. *Recreations:* pig breeding, cricket and shooting. *Heir:* *u* Wilfred William Hill Hill-Wood, *qv*. *Address:* Dacre Farm, Farley Hill, Reading, Berks. *T:* Eversley 3185.

**HILL-WOOD, Wilfred William Hill,** CBE 1946; Member, Directors' Advisory Cttee, Morgan, Grenfell & Co. Ltd, since 1967 (Managing Director, 1939-67); *b* 8 Sept. 1901; 2nd *s* of Sir Samuel Hill Hill-Wood, 1st Bt; *m* 1947, Diana Marian, *widow* of Wing Comdr Harry Manners Mellor, MVO, RAF, and *d* of Major Hugh Wyld, Beverstone Old Rectory, Tetbury, Glos. *Educ:* Eton; Trinity Coll., Cambridge. Director: Anglo-American Debenture Corp. Ltd; North Atlantic Securities Corp. Ltd; R. A. Stephen & Co. Ltd. *Address:* Coldham, Sandwich Bay, Kent. *T:* Sandwich 3598; The House of Urrard, Killiecrankie, Perthshire; Flat 4, Cornwall Mansions, 33 Kensington Court, W8. *Club:* White's.

**HILLARD, Richard Arthur Loraine,** MBE 1946; **His Honour Judge Hillard;** County Court Judge (circuit 54, Bristol, etc) since 1956; *b* 1906; *e s* of Frederick Arthur Hillard, Puriton Manor, Bridgwater, Som; *m* 1st, 1936, Nancy Alford (*d* 1964), *d* of Dr Alford Andrews, Cambridge; one *s* one *d*; 2nd, 1969, Monica Constance, *er d* of John Healey Carus, Darwen, and *widow* of Paul Hillard; one step *s* one step *d*. *Educ:* Worcester Royal Grammar Sch.; Christ Church, Oxford. Barrister, Gray's Inn, 1931; South-Eastern circuit. Served, 1940-45: Military Dept, Judge Advocate General's Office, 1941-45, Lt-Col 1945. Asst Reader and Lecturer, Council of Legal Education, 1945-55. Chm. Agricultural Land Tribunal, South Eastern Province, 1955. *Recreation:* gardening. *Address:* West Wing, Lansdown, Bath. *T:* Bath 60124. *Club:* Oxford and Cambridge University.

**HILLARD, Ronald Johnstone,** CMG 1950; *b* 6 May 1903; *yr s* of late Rev. A. E. and late Mrs Hillard; *m* 1st, 1933 (marr. diss. 1950); one *s*; 2nd, 1950, Anne Josephine (*d* 1952), *yr d* of late B. J. F. Picton, Sherborne; one *d*; 3rd, 1954, Joan, *o c* of late Conyers Boldron Toller, Coldstream Guards. *Educ:* St Paul's Sch., London; Christ Church, Oxford. Scholar of Christ Church, Oxford, 1922-25; Rugby Blue, 1923-24, 1924-25; International (England) Rugby Cap, 1925. Sudan Political Service, Dec. 1925-46; Sec. to Governor-Gen.'s Council, 1932-34; Dir, Dept of Economics and Trade, Sudan Govt, 1946-49; Mem. of Governor-Gen.'s Council, 1946-48; Councillor without Portfolio on Executive Council and MLA, Sudan, 1949-52; Gen. Manager, Sudan Railways, 1949-52; Dir, Tunnel Portland Cement Co. Ltd, 1953-54; Chm. and Man. Dir, E African Portland Cement Co. Ltd, 1955-68. Pres., Nairobi Chamber of Commerce, 1961-62. Order of the Nile, 4th Class, 1936. *Recreations:* reading, writing. *Address:* 6 Egdon Glen, Crossways, near Dorchester, Dorset. *T:* Warmwell 342. *Club:* English-Speaking Union.

**HILLARY, Sir Edmund,** KBE 1953; Director, Field Educational Enterprises of Australasia Pty Ltd; Consultant to Sears Roebuck & Co., Chicago, on camping and outdoor equipment; author; lecturer; mountaineer; *b* 20 July 1919; *s* of Percival Augustus Hillary and Gertrude Hillary (*née* Clark); *m* 1953, Louise Rose; one *s* two *d. Educ:* Auckland Grammar Sch., Auckland, New Zealand. Apiarist, 1936-43. RNZAF, navigator on Catalina flying boats in Pacific Area, 1944-45. Apiarist (in partnership with brother W. F. Hillary), 1951-70. Himalayan Expeditions: NZ Gawhal Expedition, 1951; British Everest Reconnaissance, 1951; British Cho Oyu Expedition, 1952; Everest Expedition, 1953; with Sherpa Tenzing reached summit of Mount Everest, May 1953 (KBE). Leader of NZ Alpine Club Expedition to Barun Valley, East of Everest, 1954. Appointed, 1955, leader of New Zealand Transantarctic Expedition; completed overland journey to South Pole, Jan. 1958. Expeditions in Everest region, 1960-61, 1963, 1964, 1965; built first hosp. for Sherpas in Everest Area, with public subscription and NZ doctor, 1966; led expedition to Antarctic for geological and mountaineering purposes incl. first ascent of Mt Herschel, 1967; expedition to E Nepal (explored Himalayan rivers with two jet boats; first ascent of 180 miles of Sun Kosi river from Indian border to Katmandu), 1968. Pres., New Zealand Volunteer Service Abroad, 1963-. Hon. LLD: Univ. of Victoria, BC, Canada, 1969; Victoria Univ., Wellington, NZ, 1970. Hubbard Medal (US), 1954; Star of Nepal 1st Class; US Gold Cullum Geographical Medal, 1954; Founder's Gold Medal, Royal Geographical Society, 1958; Polar Medal, 1958. *Publications:* High Adventure; East of Everest, 1956 (with George Lowe); The Crossing of Antarctica, 1958 (with Sir Vivian Fuchs); No Latitude for Error, 1961; High in the Thin Cold Air, 1963 (with Desmond Doig); School House in the Clouds, 1965. *Recreations:* mountaineering, ski-ing, camping. *Address:* 278a Remuera Road, Auckland, SE2, New Zealand. *Clubs:* New Zealand Alpine (Hon. Mem.; Pres. 1965-67); Hon. Mem. of many other NZ and US clubs.

**HILLARY, Michael,** DSO 1917; OBE 1918; FASA; retired; *b* 20 Feb. 1886; *s* of Thomas Hillary, Adelaide, S Australia; *m* 1916, Edwyna Mary (*d* 1966), *d* of Dr J. W. Hope, Perth, WA; (one *s* killed on active service, 1943). *Educ:* private school; Adelaide Univ. Officer of the Commonwealth Treasury Dept, 1909-24; Sec., War Gratuities Board, 1920; War Pensions Branch, Repatriation Dept, 1921; Private Sec. to Prime Minister, 1922; Special Duty Australia House, London, including reporting to Royal Commission in Australia on Nat. Insurance in the UK, the Continent and USA, 1923-24; transferred to Sudan Govt, 1924: Asst Dir of Accounts, 1924-29; Dir of Accounts, 1929-33; Auditor-Gen., 1933-38. Served European War, 1914-18, in Mesopotamia (DSO, OBE, despatches twice). *Recreations:* sailing and golf. *Address:* 61 Clarewood Court, Seymour Place, W1. *T:* 01-723 0615. *Club:* United Service.

**HILLER, George François,** CMG 1962; DSO 1945; Commercial Counsellor, British Embassy, Brussels, since 1968; *b* 15 Dec. 1916; *s* of late George Spicer Hiller and Alice Prud'hon; *m* 1963, Judith, *e d* of John J. Buchanan, 67 Chester Square, SW1, and late Mrs Buchanan; one *s* two *d. Educ:* Lycée Janson de Sailly, Paris; Exeter Coll., Oxford. Served War of 1939-45 (DSO). Asst Principal, Dept of Overseas Trade, 1945; 2nd Sec. (Commercial), Madrid, 1946; 1st Sec. (Commercial), 1948, transferred to Lima, 1949; transferred to Foreign Office and attached to Joint Services Staff Coll., Nov. 1951-May 1952; 1st Sec. (Commercial), Tehran, 1954; Head of Chancery, Tehran, 1957; Counsellor, 1959; Head of Eastern Dept, Foreign Office, 1959-63; Counsellor: Political Advisers Office, Singapore, 1963-65; UK Delegation to NATO, 1965-68. *Recreations:* travelling, photography. *Address:* c/o Foreign and Commonwealth Office, SW1. *Club:* Travellers'.

**HILLER, Wendy;** actress; *b* 1912; *d* of Frank Watkin and Marie Hiller, Bramhall, Cheshire; *m* 1937, Ronald Gow; one *s* one *d. Educ:* Winceby House, Bexhill. Manchester Repertory Theatre; Sir Barry Jackson's tour of Evensong; Sally Hardcastle in Love on the Dole, London and New York; leading parts in Saint Joan and Pygmalion at Malvern Festival, 1936. *plays include:* Twelfth Night; Cradle Song (Apollo); The First Gentleman (Savoy); Tess of the d'Urbervilles (Piccadilly); The Heiress (Biltmore, NY, and Haymarket, London); Ann Veronica (Piccadilly); Waters of the Moon (Haymarket), 1951-53; The Night of the Ball (New), 1955; Old Vic Season, 1955-56; Moon for the Misbegotten (NY), 1957; Flowering Cherry (Haymarket), 1958; Toys in the Attic (Piccadilly), 1960; Aspern Papers (NY), 1962; The Wings of the Dove (Lyric), 1963; The Sacred Flame (Duke of York's), 1967; When We Dead Awaken (Edinburgh Festival), 1968; The Battle of Shrivings (Lyric), 1970. *Films:* Pygmalion; Major Barbara; I Know Where I'm Going; Outcast of the Islands; Separate Tables (Academy Award); Sons and Lovers; Toys in the Attic; A Man for All Seasons; David Copperfield, etc. *Address:* Spindles, Beaconsfield, Bucks.

**HILLGARTH, Capt. Alan Hugh,** CMG 1943; OBE 1937; RN, retired; *b* 7 June 1899; *s* of late Willmott Henderson Hillgarth Evans, MD, FRCS; assumed surname of Hillgarth by deed poll, 1928; *m* 1st, 1929, Hon. Mary Sidney Katherine Almina Hope-Morley (marriage dissolved, 1946), 3rd *d* of 1st Baron Burghclere; one *s*; 2nd, 1947, Jean Mary, *e d* of Frank Cobb; two *s* one *d. Educ:* Royal Naval Colls, Osborne and Dartmouth; King's Coll., Cambridge. Entered Royal Navy, 1912; Vice-Consul at Palma, 1932-37; Consul, 1937-39; Naval Attaché at Madrid, 1939-43; Chief of Intelligence Staff, Eastern Fleet, 1943-44; Chief of British Naval Intelligence, Eastern Theatre, 1944-46. *Publications:* various novels. *Recreation:* forestry. *Address:* Illannanagh House, Ballinderry, Co. Tipperary. *T:* Ballinderry 3. *Clubs:* Army and Navy, Garrick; Kildare Street (Dublin); Nuevo (Madrid).

**HILLIER, Arthur,** OBE 1947; retired as Chairman and Managing Director, Sperry Gyroscope Co. Ltd (1938-59); Chairman: Industrial Products (Speco) Ltd since 1949; New Holland Machine Co. Ltd since 1954; *b* 2 Dec. 1895; *s* of Thomas Hillier and Ann Hillier (*née* Holland); *m* 1st, 1919, Rita Mary (*d* 1955), *d* of John Wakeley; two *d*; 2nd, 1956, Margaret Howard. *Educ:* Judd Sch., Tonbridge, Kent. Joined Sperry Gyroscope Co. Ltd as Asst Sec., 1916; Sec., 1920; Dir, 1922; Dir and Gen. Manager, 1933; Man. Dir, 1934. Freeman of City of London, 1930; Freeman and Liveryman of: Needlemakers' Company, 1930; Shipwrights' Company, 1951. FCIS 1937; FIN 1953 (was Founder Mem.); JP Middlesex, 1951; High Sheriff County of Middlesex, 1956-57. Comdr, Order of Orange Nassau (Netherlands), 1950; Officer, Legion of Honour (France), 1952; Commendatore, Order of Merit (Italy), 1955. *Recreation:* ancient history. *Address:* Cranmore, Little Forest Road, Bournemouth, Hants. *T:*

Westbourne 65532. *Clubs:* Royal Automobile, City Livery.

**HILLIER, Tristram Paul,** RA 1967 (ARA 1957); painter and writer; *b* 11 April 1905; *s* of Edward Guy Hillier, CMG, and Ada Everett; *m* 1st, 1931, Irene Rose Hodgkins (marr. diss. 1935); two *s*; 2nd, 1937, Leda Millicent Hardcastle; two *d*. *Educ:* Downside; Christ's Coll., Cambridge. Studied at Slade Sch. and under André Lhôte, Paris. Has held eight one-man exhibitions in London at Lefevre Gall. (2) and Tooth's Gall. (6) and one exhibn in Paris at Galerie Barreiro. Rep. by official purchases of pictures in following public collections: Tate Gall.; National Galleries of Canada, NSW, and Victoria; Ferens Art Gall., Hull; Contemporary Art Soc.; City Art Galleries: Manchester, Aberdeen, Leeds, Southampton, Nottingham, Belfast; Art Galleries of Toronto, Brisbane, Rochdale, Oldham, Kettering; Min. of Works (for Brit. Embassies Fund); Harris Museum, Preston; Chantrey Bequest. Served as Lieut RNVR, 1940-45. *Publication:* Leda and the Goose (autobiography), 1954. *Recreations:* riding, walking, swimming. *Address:* c/o Arthur Tooth & Sons, 31 Bruton Street, W1; Yew Tree Cottage, East Pennard, Shepton Mallet, Somerset. *T:* Ditcheat 284. *Club:* Chelsea Arts.

**HILLIER-FRY, William Norman;** Counsellor, UK Disarmament Delegation, Geneva, since 1968; *b* 12 Aug. 1923; *o s* of William Henry and Emily Hillier Fry; *m* 1948, Elizabeth Adèle Misbah; two *s* two *d*. *Educ:* Colfe's Grammar School, Lewisham; St Edmund Hall, Oxford (BA 1946). Served Army, 1942-45; commissioned, Loyal Regt, 1942. HM Foreign Service, 1946; served: Iran, 1947-52; Strasbourg (Delegation to Council of Europe), 1955-56; Turkey, 1956-59; Czechoslovakia, 1961-63. *Recreations:* music, theatre. *Address:* UK Disarmament Delegation, 37-39 rue de Vermont, 1202 Geneva, Switzerland. *T:* 34-38-00.

**HILLINGDON,** 4th Baron *cr* 1886; **Charles Hedworth Mills;** Bt 1868; Captain, Life Guards; *b* 12 Jan. 1922; *er* and *o surv. s* of 3rd Baron and of Hon. Edith Mary Winifred, Cadogan (Edith, Lady Hillingdon, DBE), *e d* of Henry Arthur, Viscount Chelsea; *S* father 1952; *m* 1947, Lady Sarah Grey Stuart, 2nd *d* of 18th Earl of Moray; one *s* three *d*. *Educ:* Eton; Magdalen Coll., Oxford. 2nd Lieut Coldstream Guards, 1941; transferred Life Guards, 1942; Captain, 1943. *Heir: s* Hon. Charles James Mills, *b* 8 March 1951. *Address:* Messing Park, Kelvedon, Essex. *T:* Tiptree 364; 12 Markham Square, SW3. *T:* 01-584 0778. *Club:* White's.

**HILLIS, Arthur Henry Macnamara,** CMG 1961; Comptroller General, National Debt Office, 1961-68; *b* 29 Dec. 1905; *s* of late John David Hillis, FRCSI, Dublin; *m* 1936, Mary Francis; no *c*. *Educ:* Trinity Coll., Dublin. Called to Bar, Inner Temple, 1931. HM Treasury, 1941; Civil Service Commission, 1946-50; Harkness Fund Fellow, USA, 1950-51; Asst Sec., Treasury, 1951-58; Minister (Treasury Adviser), UK Permanent Mission to United Nations, 1958-61; Under-Sec., Treasury, 1961. *Address:* 2 Hare Court, Temple, EC4. *T:* 01-353 3443. *Clubs:* Athenæum, Garrick; University (Dublin).

**HILLS, Edwin Sherbon,** FRS 1954; FAA; Research Professor of Geology, University of Melbourne, since 1964, and Deputy Vice-Chancellor, since 1962; *b* Melbourne, 31 Aug. 1906; *s* of Edwin S. Hills, Melbourne; *m* 1932, Claire D. Fox; two *s* one *d*. *Educ:* Univs of Melbourne and London. DSc Melbourne; PhD London; DIC; DSc (Hon.) Dunelm; Foreign and Commonwealth FGS (Bigsby Medallist, 1951); David Syme Prize for Scientific Research (Melbourne), 1939; Trustee: National Museum of Victoria; Royal Soc. of Victoria. Fellow, Imperial Coll. of Science and Technology, London, 1966; Hon. Fellow Aust. Inst. of Geographers. *Publications:* Outlines of Structural Geology, 1940 (new edn 1953); Physiography of Victoria, 1941 (new edn 1967); Elements of Structural Geology, 1963 (new edn 1970); Arid Lands: a Geographical Appraisal (ed), 1966. *Address:* The University of Melbourne, Parkville, Victoria 3052, Australia; 25 Barry Street, Kew, Victoria 3101, Australia. *T:* 86-8572.

**HILLS, Lt-Col John David,** MC; MA; Head Master of Bradfield College, 1939-July 1955; *b* 1895; *s* of late Rev. Henry Gardner Hills and Isabel, *d* of Frederick Cattley, St Petersburg; *m* 1932, Lady Rosemary Baring, *er d* of 2nd Earl of Cromer, GCIE, GCVO; one *s* two *d*. *Educ:* Merchant Taylors' Sch.; Lincoln Coll., Oxford (Classical Exhibitioner). Served European War in 5th Bn Leics Regt (despatches twice, MC with bar, Croix de Guerre); Asst Master, Eton Coll., 1921, Housemaster, 1932, Sen. History Master, 1935-39; Comdg OTC, 1930-32; Lt-Col TA Reserve, 1932-50. Dir Schs Empire Tour, Canada, 1932; Lectr HM Forces, Middle East, 1945; Lectr for The Times. *Recreations:* genealogy and heraldry. *Address:* House by the Dyke, Chirk, Wrexham, N Wales. *T:* Chirk 3207.

**HILLYARD, Patrick Cyril Henry,** OBE 1956; Head of Sound Light Entertainment BBC, 1952-64, retd Nov. 1964; *s* of Rev. Dr H. J. Hillyard and Louie Charlotte Robinson; *m* 1932, Ena Violet, *d* of late Rev. C. Porter-Brickwell; one *s*. *Educ:* The High Sch., Dublin. Studied stage production under Donald Calthrop. Stage directed and produced plays and musical comedies in England and America, including: A Midsummer Night's Dream, Twelfth Night, The Fake, Jolly Roger, No More Ladies, The Desert Song, Gay Divorce, On Your Toes, Lilac Time. Joined BBC Television Service as Dep. Productions Manager, 1937; Asst Dir of Variety, BBC, 1941; Actg Dir of Variety, BBC, 1946; Dir of Television Presentation, BBC, 1947; Head of Television Light Entertainment, BBC, 1948. *Recreations:* going to the theatre, golf, tennis and swimming. *Address:* c/o Barclays Bank, 15 Langham Place, W1.

**HILTON OF UPTON,** Baron *cr* 1965 (Life Peer); **Albert Victor Hilton;** JP; CC; *b* 14 Feb. 1908; *s* of Thomas and Anne Hilton; *m* 1944, Nelly Simmons; (two *s* decd). *Educ:* Norfolk Elementary Schs. Labour Party Agent, E Norfolk, 1936-45. TU Officer, National Union of Agricultural Workers, 1946-59; MP (Lab) SW Norfolk, March 1959-Sept. 1964; a Lord in Waiting, 1966-70. vice-Pres., NUAW, 1963-; Member: Labour Party National Executive Cttee, 1963-; East Anglia Economic Planning Council, 1966-; Chm., National Brotherhood Movement, 1967. A Methodist Lay Preacher, 1932-. JP 1949, CC 1951, Norfolk. *Recreation:* Association football (County colours, Norfolk, 1932). *Address:* 9 Spinners Lane, Swaffham, Norfolk. *T:* Swaffham 341.

**HILTON, Conrad (Nicholson);** Chairman: Hilton Hotels Corporation, since (formation of company) 1946; Hilton International Company since 1968; *b* 25 Dec. 1887; *s* of August Holver Hilton and Mary Laufersweiler; *m* 1925, Mary Barron; two *s* (and one *s* decd). *Educ:* St Michael's Coll., Santa Fé; New Mexico Mil. Inst.; New Mexico

Sch. of Mines. MHR, New Mexico, 1912-13; Partner, A. H. Hilton & Sons, 1915. 2nd Lieut, US Army, 1917-19. Bought first hotel, Cisco, Texas, 1919; bought, sold and operated hotels, 1919-46; organized Hilton Hotels Corp., 1946; founded Hilton Internat. Co., 1948 (of which he is now Chm.); bought Waldorf-Astoria, 1949; bought Statler Hotel chain, 1954. Chm. of 2 companies, operating 125 hotels around the world. Holds several hon. doctorates; also knighthoods, etc in foreign Orders. *Publications:* Be My Guest, 1957; Inspirations of an Innkeeper, 1963. *Recreation:* golf. *Address:* 9990 Santa Monica Boulevard, Beverly Hills, Calif, USA. *T:* Crestview 1-6203. *Clubs:* Metropolitan (New York City); Chicago Athletic; Los Angeles Country; Bel Air Country.

**HILTON, Sir Derek (Percy),** Kt 1966; MBE 1945; *b* 11 April 1908; *o c* of Percy Hilton and Mary Beatrice Hilton (*née* Stott); *m* 1945, Joanna Stott, *er d* of late Sir Arnold Stott, KBE; three *d. Educ:* Rugby Sch.; Trinity Hall, Cambridge. Solicitor, 1932; subsequently private practice in Manchester. War of 1939-45, Manchester Regt; seconded to special operations executive, 1941. Mem. Council, Law Soc., 1951; Hon. Sec., Manchester Law Soc., 1950-59; Pres., Manchester Law Soc., 1957; Pres. of the Law Soc., 1965-66. Dir, Abbey National Building Soc., 1966-; Chm., Lancashire & Yorkshire Revisionary Interest Co. Ltd. Norwegian Liberty Cross, 1945. *Recreations:* gardening, walking, fishing. *Address:* Eaves, Chapel-en-le-Frith, Derbyshire. *T:* Chapel-en-le-Frith 2241. *Clubs:* Special Forces; St James's (Manchester).

**HILTON, Gwen,** CBE 1959; FRCS; Hon. Radiotherapist, University College Hospital, London; *b* 22 Sept. 1898; *d* of M. J. M. Hill, Professor of Pure Mathematics, University Coll., London; *m* 1925, Reginald Hilton (*d* 1969); one *d. Educ:* Roedean Sch.; University Coll. and Hosp. Hons BSc in Physiology, 1921; MB, BS London 1924; DMR&E 1932; FFR 1940; FRCS 1955. Fellow of University Coll. *Publications:* papers on radiotherapy treatment in cancer. *Recreations:* gardening, study of languages. *Address:* 8 Elm Tree Road, St John's Wood, NW8.

**HILTON, John Robert,** CMG 1965; HM Diplomatic Service (appointed to Foreign Service, 1943), retired 1969; *b* 5 Jan. 1908; *s* of Oscar Hilton, MD, and Louisa Holdsworth Hilton; *m* 1933, Margaret Frances Stephens; one *s* three *d. Educ:* Marlborough Coll.; Corpus Christi Coll., Oxford (MA); Bartlett Sch. of Architecture; University Coll., London (Diploma). ARIBA. Dir of Antiquities, Cyprus, 1934-36; Architect to E. S. & A. Robinson Ltd and private practice, 1936-41. Capt. RE, 1941-43. Foreign Service, 1943; transferred to Istanbul, 1944; 2nd Sec., Athens, 1945; Foreign Office, 1947; 1st Sec., Istanbul, 1956; Foreign Office, 1960. *Publications:* articles in Architectural Review and other jls, Mind and Analysis; Memoir on Louis MacNeice (as appendix to his autobiography, The Strings are False), 1965. *Recreations:* philosophy, walking. *Address:* Hope Cottage, Nash Hill, Lacock, Wilts. *T:* Lacock 369.

**HILTON, Peter John,** MA, DPhil Oxon, PhD Cantab; Professor of Mathematics, Cornell University, since 1962; *b* 7 April 1923; *s* of late Dr Mortimer Hilton and of Mrs Elizabeth Hilton; *m* 1949, Margaret (*née* Mostyn); two *s. Educ:* St Paul's Sch.; Queen's Coll., Oxford. Asst Lectr, Manchester Univ., 1948-51, Lectr, 1951-52; Lectr, Cambridge Univ., 1952-55; Senior Lecturer, Manchester Univ., 1956-58; Mason Prof. of Pure Mathematics, University of Birmingham, 1958-62. Visiting Professor: Cornell Univ., USA, 1958-59; Eidgenössische Techn. Hochschule, Zürich, 1966-67; Courant Inst., NY Univ., 1967-68. Mathematician-in-residence, Battelle Research Center, Seattle, 1970-71. Hon. Mem. Belgian Mathematical Soc., 1955. *Publications:* Introduction to Homotopy Theory, 1953; Differential Calculus, 1958; Homology Theory (with S. Wylie), 1960; Partial Derivatives, 1960; Homotopy Theory and Duality, 1965; (with H. B. Griffiths) Classical Mathematics, 1970; numerous research articles on algebraic topology in British and foreign mathematical journals. *Recreations:* travel, sport, reading, theatre, chess, bridge, broadcasting. *Address:* Department of Mathematics, Cornell University, Ithaca, NY 14850, USA.

**HILTON, Maj.-Gen. Richard,** DSO 1944; MC 1915; DFC and Bar, 1918; retired; *b* 18 Jan. 1894; 2nd *s* of John Edward Hilton, JP, Lambourn, Berks; *m* 1917, Phyllis Martha, *e d* of late Rev. S. H. Woodin, MA, Rector of Yarmouth, IoW; two *s. Educ:* Malvern; RMA Woolwich. Served European War, 1914-18, Western Front, in RA, RFC and RAF (wounded); commissioned 2nd Lieut, RGA, 1913; seconded to RFC, 1915; Lieut, 1915; Capt., 1917; Sqdn Comdr, 1918. Seconded to Tank Corps, 1922-23; Indian Mountain Artillery, 1924-30, 1934-38; Staff Capt., War Office, 1930-33; Major 1934; Bt Lt-Col 1937; Lt-Col 1939. War of 1939-45, BEF, 1939-40; Chief Instructor (Air), Sch. of Artillery, 1940; CRA 15th (Scottish) Div., 1941-44 (wounded); BGS to Allied Liberation Forces, Norway, 1945; Dep. Chief of British Mission to Soviet Zone of Germany, 1946-47; Military Attaché in Moscow, 1947-48; retd, 1948. Comdr, Order of St Olav, Norway, 1945. *Publications:* Military Attaché in Moscow, 1949; Nine Lives, 1955; The Indian Mutiny, 1957; The North-West Frontier, 1957; The Thirteenth Power, 1958; Imperial Obituary, 1968; contrib. to Blackwoods, Nineteenth Century and After, Service and other Journals. *Recreations:* yachting, mountain climbing, chess, world affairs, travel. *Address:* Little Tysoe, St John's Avenue, Leatherhead, Surrey. *T:* Leatherhead 3730.

**HILTON, Roger,** CBE 1968; Artist; *b* 23 March 1911; *s* of O. Hilton, MD, and Louisa Holdsworth (*née* Sampson); *m* 1st, 1957, Ruth Catherine David; one *s* one *d*; 2nd, 1965, Rosemary Julia Phipps; two *s. Educ:* Bishop's Stortford Coll.; Slade Sch., London. Served in HM Forces, 1939-45 (POW 1942-45). One Man Exhibitions: Gimpel Fils, 1952, 1954, 1956; Waddington Galls, 1960, 1962, 1964, 1966. 1st prize, John Moores Exhibition, Liverpool, 1963. Represented Great Britain at Venice Biennale, 1964 (UNESCO Prize). *Address:* c/o Waddington Galleries, 2 Cork Street, W1.

**HILTON, William (Samuel);** MP (Lab and Co-op) Bethnal Green since 1966; Director, Master Builders' Federation, since 1969; *b* 21 March 1926; *m* 1948, Agnes Aitken Orr; three *s. Educ:* Kyleshill, Saltcoats; Ardrossan Academy. Railway Fireman until 1949; Labour Party Agent to late Lord Kirkwood, 1949-52; Research and Education Officer for Building Trade Operatives, 1952-66. Mem. Agrément Bd for Building Industry, 1965-66; Mem. Economic Development Coun. for Building Industry, 1964-66. Editor, Builders Standard, 1954-66. *Publications:* Building by Direct Labour, 1954; Foes to Tyranny, 1964; Industrial Relations in Construction, 1968. *Address:* 95 Kingsmead Road, SW2.

**HILTON-SERGEANT, Maj.-Gen. Frederick Cavendish,** CB 1956; CBE 1955; retired 1957; Medical Adviser, British Red Cross, 1957-70; *b* 25 Feb. 1898; *s* of F. M. C. Sergeant, Liverpool; *m* 1929, Kathleen Margaret Howard, 2nd *d* of Howard J. Walker, Dalton Grange, Parbold; two *d. Educ:* Calday Sch.; Liverpool Univ. MB, ChB (Liverpool) 1921; DPH (Eng.) 1938; Leishman Prize, RAM Coll., 1932. 2nd Lieut, RFA, 1917-18; entered RAMC, 1923; served India, NW Frontier; China, Shanghai; and ME countries; Capt. 1926; Major 1934; Lieut-Col 1946; Brig. 1951; Maj.-Gen. 1953. Dep. Dir Hygiene, British Troops in Egypt and Ext. Examr in Preventive Medicine, Kasr-el-Aini Univ., Cairo, 1943-46; Dep. Dir Hygiene, W Comd, 1947-48; Prof. of Hygiene, RAM Coll., 1949; Comdt Army Sch. of Health, 1949-50; DDMS, Brit. troops in Egypt, 1951-52; DDMS, N Comd, 1953; Comdt and Dir of Medical Studies, Royal Army Medical Coll., 1953-57. QHP 1953-57. FRSM; FSocMOH. ostJ. *Publications:* contribs to Jl of RAMC. *Recreations:* ski-ing, sailing, tennis, golf. *Address:* Picket Wood, Merstham, Surrey. *T:* Merstham 3988.

**HIM, George,** PhD (Bonn); FSIA; FSTD; AGI; designer (freelance) and design consultant; Design Adviser of the Israeli Exhibition Authority and Design Consultant to El Al Israel Airlines; *b* 4 Aug. 1900; *m* Shirley Elizabeth (*née* Rhodes). *Educ:* Warsaw, Moscow, Bonn, Leipzig. In practice, first in Germany, then in Poland, from 1928; in London, since 1937. Field of work: book illustration, publicity design, exhibitions; designed Festival Clock in Battersea Park, 1951; The Observer Masada Exhibition, 1966; Masada Exhibition, New York, Chicago, Washington, etc, 1967-69, Paris, 1970; Chief Designer of Israel Pavilion, Expo 67, Montreal; designed covers for The New Middle East (monthly). Discoverer of the "County of Schweppshire" (with Stephen Potter) 1951-54. *Publications:* Israel, the Story of a Nation, 1957; children's books: Locomotive, 1937; The Little Red Engine, 1942 (with J. Lewitt); Squawky (with S. Potter), 1964; Folk Tales (with Leila Berg), 1966; Giant Alexander books (with F. Herrmann), 1964, 1966, 1967; The Day with the Duke (with Ann Thwaite), 1969; illustrations to Zuleika Dobson, 1960; Plays for Puritans, 1966. *Recreation:* work. *Address:* 37B Greville Road, NW6. *T:* 01-624 6663.

**HIMMELWEIT, Prof. Hilde T.;** Professor of Social Psychology, London School of Economics, University of London, since 1964; *b* Berlin; *d* of S. Litthauer and Feodore Litthauer (*née* Remak); *m* 1940, Prof. F. Himmelweit, MD, FRCPEd; one *d. Educ:* Berlin; Hayes Court, Kent; Newnham Coll., Cambridge. Degrees in Mod. Langs and Psych.; qual. Educational and Clinical Psychologist, 1943; PhD London 1945; Clin. Psychologist, Maudsley Hosp., 1945-48; joined LSE, 1949; Reader in Social Psychology, 1954. Dir Nuffield Television Enquiry, 1954-58; Vis. Prof., Univ. of Calif, Berkeley, 1959; Fellowship to Centre for Advanced Study of Behavioral Sciences, Stanford, Calif, 1967; Chm., Academic Adv. Cttee of Open Univ., 1969-; Fellow, Brit. Psycholog. Soc., 1952; Member: Council, Brit. Psycholog. Soc., 1961-64; Editorial Bd, Brit. Jl of Soc. and Clin. Psychology, 1962-; Council, Inst. of Race Relations, 1966-. *Publications:* Television and the Child, 1958; articles and chapters on: television, personality theory and measurement, attitude development and change, socialization, social mobility, school and higher education. *Address:* 154 Oakwood Court, Kensington, W14. *T:* 01-602 2152.

**HIMSWORTH, Eric,** CMG 1951; *b* 23 Nov. 1905; *s* of H. Himsworth and M. J. Macdonald; *m* 1941, Ethel Emily, *d* of Major Brook Pratt, DSO, Coldstream Guards; two *s. Educ:* Silcoates Sch., near Wakefield; Merton Coll., Oxford. MA, BCL Oxon; LLB, BSc (Econ.), DPA London. Colonial Administrative Service, 1928-55; Financial Sec., Malaya, 1952-55; UN Technical Assistance Administration, Nepal, 1956-64; IMF Financial Consultant, 1965-69. *Recreations:* travelling, swimming. *Address:* c/o Hongkong and Shanghai Banking Corporation, 9 Gracechurch Street, EC3.

**HIMSWORTH, Sir Harold (Percival),** KCB 1952; MD; FRS 1955; FRCP; Secretary, Medical Research Council, 1949-68, Member and Deputy Chairman, 1967-68; *b* 19 May 1905; *s* of late Arnold Himsworth, Huddersfield, Yorks; *m* 1932, Charlotte, *yr d* of William Gray, Walmer, Kent; two *s. Educ:* King James' Grammar Sch., Almondbury, Yorks; University Coll. and University Coll. Hosp., London. Asst, Medical Unit, University Coll. Hosp., 1930; Beit Memorial Research Fellow, 1932-35; William Julius Mickle Fellow, University of London, 1935; Fellow of University Coll., London, 1936; Deputy Dir, Medical Unit, University Coll. Hospital, 1936; Goulstonian Lecturer, 1939; Oliver-Sharpey Lectr, 1949, RCP; Prof. of Medicine, Univ. of London and Dir of the Medical Unit, University Coll. Hospital, London, 1939-49; Mem. of Medical Research Council, 1948-49; Sydney Ringer Lecturer, 1949; Lowell Lecturer, Boston, Mass, 1947; Harveian Orator, Royal College of Physicians, 1962. Pres., Sect. of Experimental Medicine, Royal Society of Medicine, 1946-47. Hon. Mem. Medical Soc. of Sweden, 1949; Docteur *hc* Toulouse, 1950; Hon. Mem., Amer. Assoc. of Physicians, 1950. Hon. LLD: Glasgow, 1953; London, 1956; Wales, 1959; Hon. DSc: Manchester, 1956; Leeds, 1968; Univ. of WI, 1968; Hon. ScD, cambridge, 1964. New York Univ. Medallist, 1958; Conway Evans Prize, RCP, 1968. Mem. of Norwegian Med. Soc., 1954; For. Hon. Mem., Amer. Acad. of Arts and Sciences, 1957; Mem., Royal Soc. of Arts and Sciences, Göteberg, Sweden, 1957; For. Corresp. Mem., Belgian Royal Acad. of Medicine, 1955; Hon. For. Mem., 1958. Hon. FFR 1958; Hon. FRCPE 1960; Hon. FRSM 1961; Hon. FRCS 1965. *Publications:* The Development and Organisation of Scientific Knowledge, 1970; medical and scientific papers. *Recreation:* fishing. *Address:* 13 Hamilton Terrace, NW8. *T:* 01-286 6996. *Club:* Athenæum.

**HINCHCLIFFE, Hon. Sir (George) Raymond,** Kt 1957; **Hon Mr Justice Hinchcliffe;** Judge of High Court of Justice, Queen's Bench Division, since 1957; *b* 2 March 1900; *s* of late A. E. T. Hinchcliffe, Woodside, Huddersfield; *m* 1st, Hilda Sydenham (*d* 1938); 2nd, Hannah Sophia Eadie. *Educ:* Leys Sch.; Trinity Hall, Cambridge. 2nd Lieut RAF, 1918; called to Bar, Middle Temple, 1924; KC 1947; Bencher Middle Temple, 1953; went North Eastern Circuit; Deputy Div. Food Officer, North Eastern Division, 1939-42; Dir of Services for North Eastern Region of Ministry of Fuel and Power, 1942-45; Recorder of Berwick-upon-Tweed, 1939-47, of Middlesbrough, 1947-50, of Leeds, 1950-57; Deputy Chm., Quarter Sessions, WR Yorks, 1947, Chm. 1954-57; Attorney-Gen., Co. Palatine of Durham, 1950-57 (Solicitor-Gen., 1947); Chancellor of Diocese of Bradford, 1950-57. Hon. Fellow, Trinity Hall, Cambridge, 1959. Hon. LLD Leeds, 1959. *Address:* Queen Elizabeth Building, Temple, EC4. *T:* 01-583 4040. *Club:* Bath.

**HINCHCLIFFE, Brig. John William,** DSO 1940; *b* 24 June 1893; *s* of late Rev. J. H. Hinchcliffe; *m* 1946, Millicent Damaris Reader Harris, *d* of late Sir Skinner Turner. *Educ:* Lancing Coll.; Caius Coll., Cambridge; RMC, Sandhurst. Joined Northamptonshire Regt, 1915; served European War, 1914-18; served India, 1919-25; China, 1927-29; Adjt, Shanghai Volunteer Corps, 1929-32; India, 1932-36; Northern Ireland, 1936-39; France, outbreak of war, 1939-40; Commanded 2nd Battalion The Northants Regt, 1940-42; Comdr Tehran Sub-Area, 1942-43; Commanded South Iraq Area, Paiforce, 1945; retired pay, 1946; Deputy Commissioner London (Prince of Wales's) District St John Ambulance Bde, 1952-66; KStJ 1964. *Address:* Grey Walls, Lymington Road, Milford-on-Sea, Hants SO4 0QN. *T:* Milford-on-Sea 2356. *Clubs:* Naval and Military, MCC.

**HINCHCLIFFE, Hon. Sir Raymond;** *see* Hinchcliffe, Hon. Sir G. R.

**HINCHEY, Herbert John,** CMG 1966; CBE 1955; Financial Adviser to Prime Minister of Mauritius, since 1967; *b* 13 Feb. 1908; *s* of late Edward and late Mary A. Hinchey, Sydney, NSW; *m* 1944, Amy E., *d* of late William and late Caroline Beddows, Vuni Vasa Estate, Taveuni, Fiji; no *c*. *Educ:* Sydney Gram. Sch.; University of Sydney; London Sch. of Economics. Bank of New South Wales, Sydney and Brisbane, 1932-40; Colonial Administrative Service, later HMOCS, 1940-65; Financial Secretary: Western Pacific High Commn, 1948-52; Govt of Mauritius, 1952-57; E Africa High Commn/Common Services Organization, 1957-65. Sometime Member: Mauritius Legislative Coun.; E African Central Legislative Assembly; Chairman: E African Industrial Coun.; E African Industrial Research Bd; E African Currency Bd, etc. *Recreations:* photography, swimming, walking. *Address:* Government House, Port Louis, Mauritius. *Clubs:* East India and Sports; Nairobi (Nairobi).

**HINCHINGBROOKE, Viscount;** *see* Montagu, J. E. H.

**HINCHLIFF, Rev. Canon Peter Bingham,** MA, DD Oxon, PhD Rhodes; Secretary, Missionary and Ecumenical Council of the Church Assembly, since 1969; *b* 25 Feb. 1929; *e s* of Rev. Canon Samuel Bingham Hinchliff and Brenda Hinchliff; *m* 1955, Constance, *d* of E. L. Whitehead, Uitenhage, S Africa; three *s* one *d*. *Educ:* St Andrew's Coll., Grahamstown, S Africa; Rhodes Univ., Grahamstown; Trinity Coll., Oxford. Deacon, 1952; Priest, 1953, in Anglican Church in S Africa; Asst in Parish of Uitenhage, 1952-55. Subwarden, St Paul's Theological Coll., Grahamstown, 1955-59; Lectr in Comparative Religion, Rhodes Univ., 1957-59; Prof. of Ecclesiastical History, Rhodes Univ., 1960-69; Canon and Chancellor, Grahamstown Cathedral, 1964-69. Public Orator, Rhodes Univ., 1965. Member: S African Jt Commn on Church Unity; Faith and Order Commn of World Council of Churches, etc. Provincial Hon. Canon, Cape Town Cathedral, 1959-; Hon. Canon, Grahamstown Cathedral, 1969-. *Publications:* The South African Liturgy, 1959; The Anglican Church in South Africa, 1963; John William Colenso, 1964; The One-Sided Reciprocity, 1966; A Calendar of Cape Missionary Correspondence, 1967; The Church in South Africa, 1968; The Journal of John Ayliff, 1970. Contributor to: Jl of Ecclesiastical History; Studia Liturgica, etc. *Recreations:* crossword puzzles, odd jobbery. *Address:* 19 Pollards Hill East, Norbury, SW16.

**HINCHLIFFE, Sir (Albert) Henry (Stanley),** Kt 1953; JP Manchester; DL Staffs; BA Oxon; Chairman Glazebrook Steel & Co. Ltd, Manchester; Director, Barclays Bank, 1952-69, also Local Director, Manchester Board; *b* 10 May 1893; *s* of Edward Stanley Hinchliffe, Mucklestone, Market Drayton; *m* 1921, Vera, JP, *d* of Frederick Liddell Steel, Ranton Abbey, Staffs; three *d*. *Educ:* Cheltenham; Keble Coll., Oxford. Enlisted North Staffs Regt 1914; commissioned, 1915 (wounded Loos); Finance Dept, India, 1916-19; India Office, 1919-20. County Councillor Staffs, 1942-55; High Sheriff of Staffs, 1944. Dir Manchester Chamber of Commerce, 1938-, Pres., 1944-45; Pres., Assoc. of British Chambers of Commerce, 1950-52; Chm. UK Cttee, Federation of Commonwealth Chambers of Commerce, 1961-63; Leader of British side in UK, Canada Trade Conference, 1949, 1951, 1954, 1955. Dir LNER, 1944 until nationalisation; Mem., Manchester Joint Research Council (Chm., 1944-48). Governor of Manchester Grammar Sch. Member: Central Transport Consultative Cttee, 1948-51; Advisory Council, DSIR, 1949-54; Dollar Exports Advisory Council, 1951-52; National Research Development Corp., 1955-58; Management Cttee, St Mary's Hospitals, Manchester, 1926-59; Chm., Min. of Health Cttee on Cost of Prescribing, 1957-59; Member: (original) ITA, 1954-59; Court of Governors, Manchester Univ.; Finance Cttee, Keele Univ. *Publications:* The Bar Sinister, 1935; contributor to Fortnightly Review and other periodicals. *Recreation:* ancient churches. *Address:* Mucklestone Old Rectory, Market Drayton, Staffs. *TA* and *T:* Norton-in-Hales 218. *Clubs:* Travellers', MCC; Union (Manchester).

**HINCHLIFFE, (Frank) Philip (Rideal),** QC 1968; *b* 13 Jan. 1923; *er s* of George Hinchliffe and Margaret Hinchliffe, JP, BSc; *m* 1954, Ann Rosamund Featherby; three *s*. *Educ:* Worksop Coll.; New Coll., Oxford. Pres., Oxford Union Soc., Trinity Term, 1942; 2nd cl. hons Jurisprudence Oxon, 1942; MA 1943. War Service, RA, 1942-46 (despatches, 1945); Capt. Called to Bar, Inner Temple, 1947 (Entrance Schol.). Dep. Chm., Westmorland QS, 1969-. *Recreations:* bridge, golf, caravanning. *Address:* Hunters Close, Dean Row, Wilmslow, Cheshire. *T:* Wilmslow 22131; 5 Essex Court, Temple, EC4. *T:* 01-353 4365. *Club:* Oxford and Cambridge University.

**HINCHLIFFE, Sir Henry;** *see* Hinchliffe, Sir (A.) H. (S.).

**HINCHLIFFE, Philip;** *see* Hinchliffe, F. P. R.

**HIND, Kenneth,** ERD 1955; Director, Central Services, GPO, since 1968; *b* 14 March 1920; *er s* of late Harry and Edith Hind; *m* 1942, Dorothy Walton; one *s*. *Educ:* Central Sec. Sch., Sheffield; Queens' Coll., Cambridge (Munro Schol.). Army, 1940-48: Major, REME. General Post Office: Asst Principal, 1948; Principal, 1950; Asst Sec., 1960; Dir, Radio and Broadcasting, 1967. *Recreations:* cricket, gardening. *Address:* 5 Brangwyn Crescent, Brighton BN1 8XJ. *T:* Brighton 504902.

**HIND, Maj.-Gen. Neville Godfray,** CSI 1943; MC; *b* 8 Jan. 1892; *s* of A. E. Hind, FRCS, Portland House, Jersey; *m* 1921, Marguerite Kay (*d* 1953), *d* of late Capt. A. R. K. Hall, Royal Irish Rifles; one *s* decd; *m* 1958, Mrs Noel Mansfield, *widow* of Humphrey Mansfield, and *d* of late Thomas Harvey Browne, Sydney, NSW. *Educ:* Winchester; Royal Military Academy, Woolwich. 2nd Lieut 1911; 2nd Gurkhas (The Sirmoor Rifles), 1912;

served in France, Egypt, and Baluchistan, 1914-18 (despatches); Waziristan, 1919-20 (despatches, MC); Staff Coll., 1923; Bde Major, Zhob, 1924; GSO2, Northern Command, India, 1926; Asst Sec. Cttee Imperial Defence, 1930; Comdt 2/2nd Gurkhas, 1935; Deputy Sec. Defence Dept, India, 1938; Comdr Jubblepur Area, 1940; Comdr Sind District, India, 1942; Maj.-Gen. 1943; retired, 1945. Order of Polonia Restituta, 1943. KStJ 1966. *Address:* Longueville Farm, Jersey. *T:* Central 20164. *Club:* United Service.

**HINDE, Lt-Col Reginald Graham;** Indian Political Service, retired; FLAS; *b* 19 May 1887; *o s* of late Arthur Percival Hinde, Beaumont Hall, Lancaster; *m* 1928, Eileen, *er d* of late Sir Henry Sutcliffe Smith, Ingerthorpe Grange, Markington, Yorks; two *s. Educ:* Eastbourne Coll.; Sandhurst. Commissioned in Indian Army, 1907; attached 89th (Princess Victoria's) Royal Irish Fusiliers; appointed to 124th (Duchess of Connaught's Own) Baluchistan Infantry, 1908; served in Baluchistan and China; proceeded to Persia with Sir Percy Sykes' Mission and DAA and QMG to Force, July 1916; recruiting duty in Kalat State, 1918; Comdt Sarhad Levy Corps, East Persia, 1919; transferred to Political Dept, 1920; Asst Political Agent, Makran, and Comdt Makran Levy Corps, 1920-21; Asst Commissioner Dera Ismail Khan and Sub-Divisional Officer, Tank, North-West Frontier Province, 1922; HBM's Vice-Consul Dizful Arabistan, Persia, 1923; HBM's Consul and Political Agent, Muscat, Oman, Arabia, 1923-24; Asst Resident in Kashmir and British Joint Commissioner, Ladakh, 1925-26; Sec. to the Agent to the Governor-Gen. Punjab States, 1927; Political Agent Southern States of Rajputana, 1929; Sec. to the Agent to the Governor-Gen. in Central India, 1929-30; Boundary Settlement Officer in Central India, 1930-31; Political Agent in Bundelkhand, 1931; in Bhopal, 1931-33; in Loraiai, 1933-36; in Raipur, 1936-38; Resident Agent, Castle Howard Estate, Yorks, 1940-51; Forestry Consultant, 1952-57. *Recreations:* fishing and racing. *Address:* Otterden Place, Eastling, Faversham, Kent. *T:* Eastling 342.

**HINDE, Prof. Robert Aubrey;** Royal Society Research Professor, University of Cambridge, since 1963; Fellow of St John's College, Cambridge, since 1968; *b* 26 Oct. 1923; *s* of late Dr and Mrs E. B. Hinde, Norwich; *m* 1948, Hester Cecily, *d* of late C. R. V. Coutts; two *s* two *d. Educ:* Oundle Sch.; St John's Coll., Cambridge; Balliol Coll., Oxford. Served Coastal Comd, RAF, Flt-Lt, 1941-45. Research Asst, Edward Grey Inst., Univ. of Oxford, 1948-50; Curator, Ornithological Field Station (now sub-Dept of Animal Behaviour), Madingley, Cambridge, 1950-65; St John's Coll., Cambridge: Research Fellow, 1951-54; Steward, 1956-58; Tutor, 1958-63. Zoological Society's Scientific Medal, 1961. *Publications:* Animal Behaviour: a synthesis of Ethology and Comparative Psychology, 1966; sundry papers in biological and psychological journals. *Address:* 108 Grantchester Meadows, Cambridge. *T:* 53376.

**HINDE, Thomas;** *see* Chitty, Sir Thomas Willes.

**HINDE, Maj.-Gen. (Hon.) Sir (William) Robert (Norris),** KBE 1956 (CBE 1948); CB 1955; DSO 1940 (and 2 Bars); *b* 25 June 1900; *s* of late Major H. Hinde, Fordlands, Northam, N Devon; *m* 1926, Evelyn Muriel Wright, *d* of late Capt. H. FitzHerbert Wright, Yeldersley Hall, Derby; one *s* three *d. Educ:* Wellington Coll.; RMC Sandhurst. 2nd Lieut 15th Hussars, 1919; served War of 1939-45: France, Belgium, 1939-40; Lt-Col 1940; Col 1944; comd 15/19th Hussars, 1940-42; comd 22nd Armd Bde, Libya, Italy, Normandy, 1943-44; Dep. Mil. Governor, Brit. Sector, Berlin, 1945-48; Dep. Comr, Land Niedersachsen, Hanover, 1949-51; Dist Comd, Cyrenaica, 1952-53; Maj.-Gen. 1957; Dep. Dir of Operations, Kenya, 1953-56; retd 1957. ADC 1950-56. Col 15th/19th Hussars, 1957-64. *Recreations:* shooting, fishing, ski-ing. *Address:* Shrewton House, Shrewton, Salisbury, Wilts. *T:* Shrewton 233. *Club:* Cavalry.

*See also Earl Cawdor, Sir William Gordon Cumming, Bt.*

**HINDERKS, Prof. Hermann Ernst,** MA, DrPhil; Professor of German in the Queen's University, Belfast, since 1954; *b* 19 Dec. 1907; *s* of Elrikus Hinderks and Alma Charlotte Jane (*née* Hildebrand); *m* 1935, Ingeborg (*née* Victor); three *d. Educ:* Lichtwark Schule, Hamburg; Univs of Hamburg, Freiburg i.Br and Basle (MA, DrPhil 1938). Teacher St George's Cathedral Grammar Sch., Capetown, 1935-37; Head of German Dept, Rhodes University Coll., Grahamstown, S Africa, 1938-39; Lecturer in German, University of Cape Town, 1939-53. *Publications:* Friedrich Nietzsche, ein Menschenleben und seine Philosophie (with H. A. Reyburn and J. G. Taylor), 1st edn 1946, 2nd edn 1947 (Eng. version, Nietzsche, The Story of a Human Philosopher, 1948); Uber die Gegenstandsbegriffe in der Kritik der reinen Vernunft, 1948. *Recreations:* music and walking. *Address:* c/o The University, Belfast.

**HINDLE, Edward,** FRS 1942; MA, ScD Cambridge, PhD California; Hon. FIBiol; Hon. Fellow of the Imperial College of Science and Technology, London University; Scientific Director of Zoological Society of London, 1944-51; *b* Sheffield, 21 March 1886; *s* of late Edward James Hindle and Sarah Elizabeth (*née* Dewar); *m* 1919, Irene Margaret (*d* 1933), *d* of late John Twist, Prescot, Lancs. *Educ:* Magdalene Coll., Cambridge; Royal Coll. of Science and King's Coll., London; institut Pasteur, Paris; California Univ., Berkeley; Rhodesian Gold Medallist, 1912; Charles Kingsley Lectr and Bye Fellow of Magdalene Coll., Cambridge, 1913; Prof. of Biology, Sch. of Medicine, Cairo, 1919-24; Milner Research Fellow, London Sch. of Hygiene and Tropical Medicine, 1924-27; Kala Azar Commission of the Royal Society to Northern China, 1925-27; Beit Memorial Research Fellow in Tropical Medicine, 1927-33; William Withering Lectr, Birmingham Univ., 1935; Regius Prof. of Zoology, Univ. of Glasgow, 1935-43; Joint Editor Parasitology and sectional Editor, Tropical Diseases Bulletin; Mem. Scientific Advisory Cttee, Laboratory Practice; Gen. Sec., British Assoc. for the Advancement of Science, 1946-51; Hon. Sec., RGS, 1951-61, Hon. Vice-Pres., 1962-; Founder-Pres., Inst. of Biology; Past Pres., Zoology Section of International Union of Biological Sciences; Pres., Universities Fedn of Animal Welfare; Founder Pres. and Hon. Vice-Pres., Zoological Soc. of Glasgow; Past Pres. Royal Phil. Soc. of Glasgow; Founder Dir Int. Wildfowl Research Bureau; Membre Correspondant: Soc. de Pathologie Exotique; Soc. Belge de Médecine Tropicale; Soc. Royale Entomologique d'Egypte. Médaille Geoffrey Saint-Hilaire (en or) de la Soc. d'Acclimatation de France, 1951; served European War, 1914-19, with Signal Service in France and Palestine, Lt-Col comdg Glasgow Univ. OTC, 1936-43; Belgian Croix Civique (1st class), 1931. *Publications:* Flies and Disease–Blood-sucking Flies, 1914; numerous papers relating chiefly to original work in protozoology and parasitology, especially insect-transmitted infections. *Recreations:* music, motoring, and travelling. *Address:* 51 Warwick Avenue, W9. *T:* 01-286 2603. *Club:* Athenæum.

**HINDLEY, Brig. Geoffrey Bernard Sylvester,** CBE 1955 (OBE 1943); *b* 25 Oct. 1902; 2nd *s* of late Sir Clement D. M. Hindley, KCIE, and of Lady Hindley; *m* 1934, Ruth, *d* of late T. H. and Mrs Corfield; one *s* one *d*. *Educ:* Oundle Sch.; RMA Woolwich. Commissioned, 1923; NW Frontier (Ind. Gen. Service Medal and clasp), 1930; Staff Coll., 1937-38; Temp. Lt-Col 1941, subst. 1947; Temp. Col 1943, subst. 1947; Temp. Brig. 1943, Brig. 1952. Served War of 1939-45, Middle East, Sicily, Italy. Dep. Dir Staff Duties, WO, 1945-47; Comdr Gold Coast District and Comdt Gold Coast Regt, RWAFF, 1947-49; Comdr 15th AA Bde, 1949-52; Dep. QMG, HQ Northern Army Group and BAOR, 1953-56; retd 1956. General Manager: Hemel Hempstead Development Corp., 1956-62; (Hemel Hempstead) Commission for the New Towns, April-Nov. 1962; Welwyn Garden City and Hatfield Development Corps, 1962-66; Welwyn Garden City and Hatfield, for the Commission for the New Towns, 1966-67. *Recreations:* travel, philately, gardening. *Address:* Allander Lodge, Upper Dicker, Hailsham, Sussex. *T:* Hellingly 337.

**HINDLEY, Henry Oliver Rait;** Member and Secretary, Canadian Telecommunications Commission; *b* 19 June 1906; 3rd *s* of late Sir Clement Hindley; unmarried. *Educ:* Oundle; Trinity Coll., Cambridge; Dundee School of Economics. Industrial Consultant, 1936-40; Treasury, 1940; Air Min., 1940-45; Dir-Gen., Brit. Air Commission, later British Supply Office, USA, 1945-46; Chairman: Northern Divisional Board of National Coal Board, Sept. 1946-47; Raw Cotton Commission, 1947-51. Canadian Civil Servant, 1961; Sec., Adv. Cttee on Broadcasting, 1965; Asst Under-Sec. of State, 1965-69. *Address:* 200 Rideau Terrace, Ottawa, Ontario, Canada.

**HINDLEY-SMITH, James Dury,** MA Cantab, MRCS, LRCP; Consultant Physician, retired; late Clinical Assistant Actino-therapy Department, St George's Hospital; Fellow of Royal Society of Medicine; Member of Senate, University of Cambridge; Member Royal Institution of Great Britain; *b* 6 Jan. 1894; *e s* of late W. Hindley-Smith, Wigan and Southport, Lancs and Mrs C. E. Hindley-Smith, JP; *m* 1st, Josephine (*d* 1953), *d* of E. McMaster, BA, LLB, Afton, Freshwater, Isle of Wight; two *s*; 2nd, 1956, Penelope King-King (*d* 1962), *d* of late H. D. Lynes; 3rd, Ruth, *d* of late A. J. Brough. *Educ:* Uppingham; Magdalene Coll., Cambridge; St George's Hosp. Served European War with Field Artillery and General Staff, 1914-19. *Publications:* Chronic Rheumatism and the Pre-Rheumatic State; Chronic Streptococcal Toxaemia; various contribs to contemporary medical literature. *Recreations:* golf and music. *Address:* Foxe's Bay, PO Box 31, Montserrat, West Indies. *Club:* Carlton.

**HINDLIP,** 5th Baron, *cr* 1886; **Henry Richard Allsopp;** Bt 1880; *b* 1 July 1912; 2nd *s* of 3rd Baron Hindlip and Agatha (*d* 1962), 2nd *d* of late John C. Thynne; *S* brother, 4th Baron, 1966; *m* 1939, Cecily Valentine Jane, *o d* of late Lieut-Col Malcolm Borwick, DSO, Hazelbech Hill, Northampton; two *s* one *d*. *Educ:* Eton; RMC, Sandhurst. 2nd Lieut, Coldstream Guards, 1932; Major, 1941; retired, 1948. Served War of 1939-45; NW Europe, 1944. JP 1957, DL 1956, Wilts. Bronze Star Medal, USA, 1945. *Recreations:* travel, shooting. *Heir:* *s* Hon. Charles Henry Allsopp [*b* 5 Aug. 1940; *m* 1968, Fiona Victoria, *d* of Hon. William McGowan]. *Address:* Vern Leaze, Calne, Wilts. *T:* Calne 3229. *Clubs:* White's, Pratt's, Turf.

*See also Sir R. J. Hardy, Bt.*

**HINDMARSH, Prof. W(illiam) Russell,** MA, DPhil; Professor of Atomic Physics, University of Newcastle upon Tyne, since 1961; *b* 7 Nov. 1929; *er s* of Clifford and Ruth Hindmarsh; *m* 1954, Margaret Mary Harrison; one *s* two *d*. *Educ:* Gosforth County Grammar Sch.; Wadham Coll. Oxford. Open minor schol., Wadham Coll., 1948, first class hons in Physics, 1951, MA and DPhil Oxford, 1954. Scientific Officer, 1954-55, and Sen. Scientific Officer, 1955-56, at AERE, Harwell; Demonstrator, 1956-59, and Sen. Research Officer, 1959-61, at University Observatory, Oxford. Vice-Pres., Methodist Conf. of Great Britain, 1970-71. *Publications:* Atomic Spectra, 1967; Science and Faith, 1968; papers in scientific journals. *Recreation:* music. *Address:* School of Physics, The University, Newcastle upon Tyne 1. *T:* 28511.

**HINDSON, William Stanley,** CMG 1962; BScEng, AIM, MIMechE; Managing Director, Wellman Engineering Corporation Ltd, since 1962 (Managing Director, Indian Steelworks Construction Co. Ltd, 1958-62); *b* 11 Jan. 1920; *s* of late W. A. L. Hindson, Darlington; *m* 1944, Mary Sturdy (*d* 1961); one *s* one *d*; *m* 1965, Catherine Leikine, Paris, France; one *s*. *Educ:* Darlington Grammar Sch.; Coatham Sch., Redcar. With Dorman Long (Steel) Ltd, Middlesbrough, 1937-55; Metallurgical Equipment Export Co. Ltd and Indian Steelworks Construction Co. Ltd, 1956-62. Mem., Inst. of Directors. *Recreations:* tennis, chess, philately. *Address:* Flat 12a, 51 South Street, W1. *T:* 01-499 1888.

**HINES, Gerald;** *see* Hines, V. G.

**HINES, (Vivian) Gerald,** QC 1964; JP; **His Honour Judge Hines;** Chairman, Greater London Quarter Sessions (Inner London), since Oct. 1969; *b* 24 Dec. 1912; 2nd *s* of late John Hines and Lizzie Emily (*née* Daniells), Essex; *m* 1st, 1950, Janet Graham, MA (*d* 1957), *e d* of late John Graham, Wigtownshire; 2nd, 1960, Barbara, *y d* of late Herbert Gunton, Colchester. *Educ:* Earls Colne Grammar Sch. Admitted Solicitor, 1935; private practice, 1935-42; Clerk to Colchester Borough Justices, 1942; called to Bar, Inner Temple, 1943; South-Eastern Circuit. Dep. Chairman: Essex QS, 1955-67; County of London QS, 1965; Chm., NE London QS, 1965-68; Judge of the Central Criminal Court, 1968-69; Chm., Greater London QS (Middlesex Area), 1969. Member: Council, Magistrates' Assoc., 1967-; Standing Joint Cttee, Essex, 1962-65; Essex CC, 1946-49; Coun. of Boy Scouts' Assoc., 1961-66; Gov., New Coll., London, 1963-65. JP Essex, 1955, Greater London, 1965. Mem., Court of Essex Univ., 1966-. *Address:* The Field House, Great Bentley, Colchester, Essex. *T:* Great Bentley 555; 3 Dr Johnson's Buildings, Temple, EC4. *T:* 01-583 0794; Sessions House, Newington Causeway, SE1.

**HINGESTON, Brig. William Henry,** CBE 1944; sugar cane planter; *b* 21 Nov. 1906; *s* of late Charles Sutherton and Elizabeth Leonore Hingeston, Transkei, South Africa; *m* 1936, Anne Emmett, *d* of late Mr Justice de Waal; one *s*. *Educ:* St Charles Coll., Pietermaritzburg. Cadet SA Military Coll., S Africa, 1929-30; (Lieut) Flying Instructor, SAAF, 1931-34; (Capt.) Adjt, SAAF, 1935; (Major and Lieut-Col) AAG, Defence Hqrs,

Pretoria, 1936-40; OC Waterkloof Air Station, Pretoria, 1941; (Col) Senior Administrative Officer (Air), SAAF, Middle East Forces, 1941; Dep. General Officer Adminis. (Air), SAAF, Mediterranean and Mid-East Theatre, 1943; Dep. Adjt-Gen., UDF, 1945; Adjt-Gen., UDF, 1946; OC Witwatersrand Comd, 1948; OC Natal Comd, 1953; retd 1955. *Recreations:* golf, bridge. *Address:* Stonehenge, Triangle, Pte Bag, Fort Victoria, Rhodesia. *Clubs:* Rand, Johannesburg Country.

**HINGLEY, Anthony Capper Moore,** CVO 1954; *b* 28 Nov. 1908; *e s* of late Lieut-Col S. H. Hingley and Dorothy, *d* of Thomas Capper; *m* 1947, Ruth, *d* of late C. P. Andrews; two *s* one *d. Educ:* Rugby Sch.; Trinity Coll., Oxford (MA). Ceylon Civil Service, 1931-47; Asst Establishment Officer, Kenya, 1947-49; Chief Establishment Officer, Nyasaland, 1949-50; Sec. to Governor-Gen., Ceylon, 1950-54; Chief Establishment Officer, Nyasaland, 1954-60; seconded as Mem., Interim Federal Public Service Commn, Fedn of Rhodesia and Nyasaland, 1955-59; Establishments Adviser, Seychelles, 1965. *Recreations:* golf, bridge. *Address:* Strangmans, Heale, Curry Rivel, Langport, Som. *Clubs:* East India and Sports, Crockford's; Colombo (Ceylon).

**HINGSTON, Lt-Col Walter George,** OBE 1964; psc; Member, Marlborough and Ramsbury Rural District Council; *b* Radcliffe on Trent, Notts, 15 Feb. 1905; *s* of late Charles Hingston and late Mildred (*née* Pleydell Bouverie), Cotgrave, Nottingham; *m* 1939, Elizabeth Margaret, *d* of Brig. Sir Clinton Lewis, *qv*; two *d. Educ:* Harrow; RMC Sandhurst; and Staff Coll. 2nd Lieut, KOYLI, 1925; Nigeria Regt, RWAFF, 1931-36; 1st Punjab Regt, Indian Army, 1936. Served War of 1939-45: 4th Indian Div., North Africa, Eritrea (despatches); Dep. Dir Public Relations, GHQ India, 1942; Chief Information Officer to C-in-C, Ceylon, 1943; retired (invalided), 1945. Chief Information Officer, DSIR, 1945-63; Editor, the Geographical Magazine, 1963-70. *Publications:* The Tiger Strikes, 1942; The Tiger Kills (with G. R. Stevens), 1944; Never Give Up, 1948. *Recreations:* shooting, fishing. *Address:* The Old Vicarage, Ramsbury, near Marlborough, Wilts. *Club:* United Service.

**HINKSON, Pamela;** novelist, journalist, writer of travel books and children's books; *o d* of late H. A. Hinkson, author, Resident Magistrate, Ireland, and late Katharine Tynan Hinkson, poet and prose writer. *Educ:* privately, and by living in France and Germany. During War, 1939-45: worked for Ministry of Information; mem. of Cttee of Shamrock (Irish Service) Club in London; lectured in USA for British Information Service, on India, 1944. Lecture Tours to HM Forces overseas, 1946 and 1947. Lecture Tour to German audiences, Germany, 1947. *Publications:* include: Wind from the West, 1930; The Ladies' Road, 1932; The Deeply Rooted, 1935; Seventy Years Young (collaboration with Elizabeth, Countess of Fingall), 1937; Irish Gold, 1940; Indian Harvest, 1941; Golden Rose, 1944; The Lonely Bride, 1951; contributor to The Fortnightly, Cornhill, Spectator, New Statesman, Time and Tide, Observer, Sunday Times, Guardian, Country Life, etc. *Recreations:* friendship, country life, animals. *Address:* c/o Lloyds Bank, 112 Kensington High Street, W8.

**HINSLEY, Prof. Francis Harry,** OBE 1946; Fellow of St John's College and Professor of the History of International Relations in the University of Cambridge, since 1969; *b* 26 Nov. 1918; *s* of late Thomas Henry Hinsley, and of Emma Hinsley; *m* 1946, Hilary Brett, *d* of late H. F. B. Brett-Smith and of Helena Brett-Smith, Oxford; two *s* one *d. Educ:* Queen Mary's Grammar Sch., Walsall; St John's Coll., Cambridge. HM Foreign Office, war service, 1939-46; Research Fellow, St John's Coll., Cambridge, 1944-50; Lectr in History, Univ. of Cambridge, 1949-65; Tutor, St John's Coll., Cambridge, 1956-63; Editor, The Historical Journal, 1960-; Reader in the History of International Relations, Univ. of Cambridge, 1965-69. *Publications:* Command of the Sea, 1950; Hitler's Strategy, 1951; (ed) New Cambridge Modern History, Vol. XI, 1962; Power and the Pursuit of Peace, 1963; Sovereignty, 1966. *Address:* St John's College, Cambridge. *T:* 61621; The Grove, Newnham, Cambridge. *T:* 50719.

**HINSLEY, Prof. Frederick Baden;** Professor of Mining and Head of Department of Mining Engineering, University of Nottingham, 1947-67, now Emeritus; *b* 20 May 1900; *m* 1932, Doris Lucy Spencer; three *s* two *d. Educ:* Coalville Technical Coll.; University of Birmingham. Lecturer and Vice-Principal, County Technical Coll., Worksop, 1932-39; Lecturer in Dept of Mining, University Coll., Cardiff, 1939-47. Pres. IMinE, 1968. Silver medal, Warwicks and S Staffs Inst. of Mining Engineers, 1940; Gold medal, South Wales Inst. of Engineers, 1946; Silver medal, Midland Counties Instn of Engineers, 1951; Douglas Hay medal, Instn of Mining Engineers, 1955; Van Waterschoot Van der Gracht medal, Royal Geol. and Mining Soc. of the Netherlands, 1962. *Publications:* contribs to: Proc. S Wales Inst. of Engineers; Proc. Nat. Assoc. of Colliery Managers; Trans Instn of Mining Engineers. *Recreations:* walking, gardening, reading. *Address:* 47 Ribblesdale Road, Sherwood, Nottingham. *T:* Nottingham 268981.

**HINTON,** family name of **Baron Hinton of Bankside.**

**HINTON OF BANKSIDE,** Baron *cr* 1965 (Life Peer); **Christopher Hinton,** KBE 1957; Kt 1951; FRS 1954; MA; FICE; FIMechE; FIChemE; FRSA; *b* 12 May 1901; *s* of late Frederick Henry Hinton, Lacock, Wilts; *m* 1931, Lillian, *d* of late Thomas Boyer; one *d. Educ:* Chippenham Grammar Sch.; Trinity Coll., Cambridge. Engineering apprenticeship, GWR Co., Swindon, 1917-23; Trinity Coll., Cambridge, 1923-26 (senior scholarship, 1st Class Hons Mech. Sciences Tripos, John Wimbolt Prize, Second Yeats Prize). ICI (Alkali), Northwich, 1926-40 (Chief Engineer, 1931-40); on loan from ICI to Ministry of Supply, 1940-46 (Dep. Dir-Gen. of Filling Factories, 1942-46); Mem. of Board for Engineering and Production, and Man. Dir (Industrial Gp), UKAEA, 1954-57; Chairman: Central Electricity Generating Board, 1957-64; Internat. Exec. Cttee of World Energy Conf., 1962-68; Dep. Chm., Electricity Supply Research Coun., 1965-; Special Adviser to the Internat. Bank for Reconstruction and Develt, 1965-70; Chancellor of The Bath Univ. of Technology, Nov., 1966-. Hon. Fellow of Trinity Coll., Cambridge, 1957; Hon. Associate, Manchester Coll. of Science and Technology. Hon. DEng, Liverpool, 1955; Hon. DSc (Eng), london, 1956; Hon. ScD, Cambridge, 1960; Hon. LLD, Edinburgh, 1958; Hon. DSc: Oxford, 1957; Southampton, 1962; Durham, 1966; Bath, 1966. Albert Medal (RSA), 1957. Glazebrook Medal and Prize, 1966. Pres., IMechE, 1966-67. Hon. Member: Inst. of Metals; Instn of Gas Engineers; Inst. of Welding. Imperial Order of The Rising Sun (Japan), 1966. *Address:* Tiverton Lodge, Dulwich Common, SE21. *T:* 01-693 6447.

**HINTON, Howard Everest,** FRS 1961; Professor of Entomology, University of Bristol, since 1964; *b* Mexico, 24 Aug. 1912; *s* of George Boole Hinton; *m* 1937, Margaret Rose Clark; two *s* two *d*. *Educ:* schools in Mexico and California; Univ. of California (BSc); King's Coll., Cambridge (PhD, ScD). Biological expeditions to Mexico, 1933, 1934, and to Peru, Bolivia, Brazil, 1937. Asst Keeper, British Museum (Natural History), 1939-49; Reader in Entomology, Univ. of Bristol, 1950-64. hon. Consulting Entomologist, Infestation Div., Min. of Agric., 1947-49. President: Soc. for British Entomology, 1954-55; Royal Entomological Soc. of London, 1969-70. Senior Fellowship, Australian Acad. of Sciences, 1963. Editor, Jl of Insect Physiology; Associate Editor, Royal Society. *Publications:* a monograph of the beetles associated with stored products, Vol. 1, 1945; (with A. M. S. Dunn) Mongooses; their natural history and behaviour, 1967; papers in learned journals. *Recreations:* entomology, shooting. *Address:* 16 Victoria Walk, Bristol 6. *T:* Bristol 41433; Department of Zoology, University of Bristol.

**HINTON-COOPER, Harold,** CIE 1945; ED 1943; retired; *b* 20 May 1891; *s* of Bernard Hinton-Cooper; *m* 1916, Winifred, *d* of late W. H. Lawson, JP, Swindon; one *s*. *Educ:* Deal Coll.; Swindon Technical Coll. Training on GWR, 1907-12; appointed Asst Loco. Supt, Indian State Rlys, 1914; Dep. Chief Mechanical Engr, India, 1936-39; Chief Mechanical Engr, 1939-46; retd 1946. Afghan Medal, 1919; Coronation Medal, 1937. *Recreations:* golf, photography. *Address:* The Coterie, Murray Road, Northwood, Middx. *T:* Northwood 25040. *Club:* Royal Over-Seas League.

**HINTZ, Orton Sutherland,** CMG 1968; former Editor, The New Zealand Herald, Auckland, New Zealand, 1958-70; *b* 15 Nov. 1907; *s* of late Alfred and late Cora Hintz; *m* 1st, 1931, Flora Margaret McIver (*d* 1943); 2nd, 1965, Caroline Jean Crawford (*née* Hutchinson). *Educ:* Mt Albert Grammar Sch., Auckland; Auckland Univ. Joined NZ Herald Staff, 1925; Parly Corresp., 1935-38; War service, Naval Intelligence, 1941-46; Night Ed., NZ Herald, 1946; Assoc. Ed., NZ Herald, 1952; Dir, Wilson & Horton Ltd, 1961; Dir, NZ Press Assoc., 1962 (Chm., 1965-66); Reuters Trustee, 1964-68. Mem. Coun., Outward Bound Trust of NZ, 1961; Delegate, Commonwealth Press Conf., India and Pakistan, 1961. *Publications:* The New Zealanders in England, 1931; HMNZS Philomel, 1944; Trout at Taupo, 1955. *Recreations:* trout fishing, cricket, Rugby football. *Address:* 36 Oregon Drive, Rainbow Point, Taupo, NZ. *T:* 1059M. *Clubs:* Flyfishers', Royal Naval Volunteer Reserve; Anglers' (New York); Northern, Auckland (Auckland).

**HIPWELL, Hermine H.;** *see* Vivenot, Baroness R. de.

**HIRSCH, Maj.-Gen. Charles Ernest Rickards,** CB 1956; CBE 1945; Chairman, Ex-Services Mental Welfare Society, since 1969; *b* 11 Jan. 1903; *s* of late Henry Hirsch, Armagh, N Ireland; *m* 1933, Margaret Agnes Mary, *d* of late Comdr L. E. Traherne, Coedarhydyglyn, near Cardiff; two *s*. *Educ:* Armagh Royal Sch.; Royal Military College, Sandhurst. Commissioned 2nd Lieut Welch Regt, 1923; served in Norway, 1940; Italy, as BGS (Intelligence), 15 Army Group, 1944-45. Dep. Dir, Military Intelligence, War Office, 1945-48; Senior Army Liaison Officer in S Africa, 1948-51; BGS to C-in-C (Designate), UK Land Forces, 1951-54; Dep. Chief of Staff, HQ, UN Command, Tokyo (Maj.-Gen.), 1954-56; Deputy Chief of Staff, HQ Allied Land Forces Central Europe, 1956-58, retd. Hon. Col, 5th Bn, The Welch Regt, 1959-65. Comdr Legion of Merit (USA), 1945. *Recreations:* golf, gardening. *Address:* Moorlands, Aldershot Road, Fleet, Hants. *T:* Fleet 6008.

**HIRSCH, Prof. Kurt August;** Professor of Pure Mathematics, University of London, Queen Mary College, since 1957; *b* Berlin, 12 Jan. 1906; *s* of Dr Robert Hirsch and Anna (*née* Lehmann); *m* 1928, Elsa Brühl; one *s* two *d*. *Educ:* University of Berlin; University of Cambridge. Dr phil (Berlin), 1930; PhD (Cambridge), 1937. Asst Lecturer, later Lecturer, University Coll., Leicester, 1938-47; Lecturer, later Sen. Lecturer, King's Coll., Newcastle upon Tyne, 1948-51; Reader, University of London, Queen Mary Coll., 1951-57. Editor, Russian Mathematical Surveys. *Publications:* (with A. G. Kurosh) Theory of Groups, 3 vols, 3rd English edn 1971; (with F. R. Gantmacher) Theory of Matrices, 2 vols, English edn 1960; (with A. G. Kurosh) Lectures on General Algebra, English edn 1964; contribs to learned jls. *Recreations:* chess, gardening. *Address:* 101 Shirehall Park, NW4. *T:* 01-202 7902.

**HIRSCH, Peter Bernhard,** MA, PhD; FRS 1963; Isaac Wolfson Professor of Metallurgy in the University of Oxford since 1966; Fellow, St Edmund Hall, Oxford, since 1966; *b* 16 Jan. 1925; *s* of Ismar Hirsch and Regina Hirsch (now Meyerson); *m* 1959, Mabel Anne Kellar (*née* Stephens), *widow* of James Noel Kellar; one step *s* one step *d*. *Educ:* Sloane Sch., Chelsea; St Catharine's Coll., Cambridge. BA 1946; MA 1950; PhD 1951. Reader in Physics in Univ. of Cambridge, 1964-66; Fellow, Christ's Coll., Cambridge, 1960-66. Has been engaged on researches with electron microscope on imperfections in crystalline structure of metals and on relation between structural defects and mechanical properties. *Publications:* Electron Microscopy of Thin Crystals (with others), 1965; numerous contribs learned jls. *Recreation:* bridge. *Address:* Department of Metallurgy, Parks Road, Oxford; 8 Lakeside, Oxford.

**HIRSHFIELD,** family name of **Baron Hirshfield.**

**HIRSHFIELD,** Baron *cr* 1967, of Holborn in Greater London (Life Peer); **Desmond Barel Hirshfield;** Senior Partner, Hesketh Hardy Hirshfield & Co., Chartered Accountants; Senior Partner, Horwath & Horwath (UK), Management Consultants; Founder and Chairman, Trades Union Unit Trust Managers Ltd, since 1961; Founder and Director, Foundation on Automation and Employment, since 1962; *b* 17 May 1913; *s* of late Leopold Hirshfield and Lily Hirshfield (*née* Blackford); *m* 1951, Bronia Eisen. *Educ:* City of London Sch. Chartered Accountant, 1939; Officer Refugee Organisations, 1937-40; Home Office Aliens Tribunal (Beds), 1940-42. Mem., Cttee on Consumer Credit, 1968-; Dep. Chm., Northampton New Town Develt Corp., 1968-; Mem., Central Adv. Water Cttee, 1969-; Admin. Trustee, Chevening Estate, 1970; Treasurer: UK Cttee of UNICEF, 1969-; Nat. Council for the Unmarried Mother and her Child, 1970-. Pres., Norwood Charitable Trust, 1960-; Treas., Norwood Homes for Jewish Children, 1968-; Mem., Bd of Deputies of British Jews, 1955-67. Capt., British Team, World Maccabi Games, Prague, 1934. *Publications:* pamphlets and reports on The Accounts of Charitable Institutions; Avoidance and Evasion of Income Tax; Scheme for Pay as You Earn; Investment of Trade Union Funds; Organisations and

Methods Reviews; articles in periodicals and newspapers. *Recreations:* travel, painting, caricaturing. *Address:* 53 Hanover Gate Mansions, Regent's Park, NW1. *T:* 01-262 9699. *Club:* Royal Automobile.

**HIRST, David Cozens-Hardy,** QC 1965; Barrister-at-Law; *b* 31 July 1925; *er s* of late Thomas William Hirst and of Margaret Joy Hirst, Aylsham, Norfolk; *m* 1951, Pamela Elizabeth Molesworth Bevan, *d* of Col T. P. M. Bevan, MC; three *s* two *d*. *Educ:* Eton; Trinity Coll., Cambridge. MA. Served 1943-47; RA and Intelligence Corps, Capt. 1946. Barrister, Inner Temple, 1951. Member: Lord Chancellor's Law Reform Cttee; Gen. Coun. of the Bar; Coun. on Tribunals. *Recreations:* shooting, lawn tennis, theatre and opera. *Address:* 1 Brick Court, Temple, EC4. *T:* 01-353 8845; Almond House, Hampton, Middx. *T:* 01-979 1666; Folly Cottage, Uploders, near Bridport, Dorset. *T:* Powerstock 284. *Clubs:* Boodles, MCC.

**HIRST, Sir Edmund (Langley),** Kt 1964; CBE 1957; FRS 1934; MA, PhD (St Andrews); DSc (Birmingham); MSc (Manchester); FRIC; FRSE; FH-WC (*hc*); Forbes Professor of Organic Chemistry, Edinburgh University, 1947-68, now Professor Emeritus; *b* 1898; *s* of Rev. Sim Hirst, BD; *m* 1st, 1925, Beda Winifred Phoebe Ramsay; 2nd, 1949, Kathleen Jennie Harrison, HMI. *Educ:* Northgate Sch., Ipswich; Madras Coll., St Andrews; St Andrews University. Asst in Chemistry, United Coll. of St Leonard and St Salvator, St Andrews Univ., 1920-23; Asst Lectr, Victoria University of Manchester, 1923-24; Lecturer in Chemistry, Armstrong Coll., University of Durham, 1924-26; Lecturer in Organic Chemistry, University of Birmingham, 1927-35; Reader in Chemistry, University of Birmingham, 1935-36; Alfred Capper Pass Prof. of Chemistry, Univ. of Bristol, 1936-44; Sir Samuel Hall Prof. of Chemistry and Dir of Chemical Lab., Univ. of Manchester, 1944-47. Davy Medal of Royal Soc., 1948; Longstaff Medal of Chem. Soc., 1957. Tilden lecture, Chem. Soc., 1939; Hugo Muller lecture, Chem. Soc., 1948; Bruce Preller lecture, RSE, 1951; Pedler lecture, Chem. Soc., 1955; Bakerian lecture, Royal Soc., 1959; Pres. Chem. Sect., British Association, 1950; Vice-Pres., Chem. Soc., 1952-55, Pres., 1956-58; Pres., RSE, 1959-64. Gunning Victoria Jubilee Prize, RSE, 1965. Hon. Mem., Polish Chemical Soc., 1959. Chm. Chemistry Research Bd, DSIR 1950-55; Vis. Lectr, Norwegian, Univs, 1953, and Univs in W Germany, 1955; Chm. Scientific Advisory Cttee, Inst. of Seaweed Research, 1952-63. Hon. Mem. RIA. Hon. LLD: St Andrews; Aberdeen; Birmingham; Strathclyde; Hon. ScD Trinity Coll., Dublin; Hon. DSc Heriot-Watt. *Publications:* in Jl Chem. Soc., Trans Faraday Soc., Biochemical Jl, mainly connected with chemistry of carbohydrates and Vitamin C. *Address:* 27 Mortonhall Road, Edinburgh EH9 2HS. *T:* 031-667 4701.

**HIRST, Sir (Frank) Wyndham,** KBE, *cr* 1953 (CBE 1947; OBE 1933); Public Trustee, 1949-56, retired. Formerly Assistant Public Trustee. Admitted Solicitor, 1912. *Address:* 61 Magdalen Road, Wandsworth Common, SW18; c/o Public Trustee Office, Kingsway, WC2.

**HIRST, Geoffrey A. N.,** TD 1945; *b* 14 Dec. 1904; *s* of late Col E. A. Hirst, CMG, TD, Wetherby, Yorks. *Educ:* Charterhouse; St John's Coll., Cambridge. Director: Samuel Webster & Sons Ltd; J. Hey & Co. Ltd; Hey & Humphries Ltd; Spinks (Caterers) Ltd; FBI: Mem. Grand Council and Executive Cttee, 1932-40, 1958-65; Mem. Economic Policy Cttee; Mem. Leeds Exec., 1930-46; East and West Riding Council and Exec., 1946-65, Vice-Chm., 1956, Chm., 1958-60. Mem. of Council, CBI: Mem., Economic Cttee, East and West Ridings and Humberside (Yorks) Regional Council, 1965-69. Leeds Chamber of Commerce: Mem. Council, 1932-; Junior Vice-Pres., 1948-49; Senior Vice-Pres., 1949-51; Pres., 1952-54; Mem., Bradford Chamber of Commerce, 1950-70; Vice-Pres., Urban Dist Councils' Assoc., 1951-; Mem., Nat. Advisory Council for Educn in Industry and Commerce, 1948-51; Chm., Yorks Regional Academic Bd, 1947-49; Mem., Leeds and Hull Academic Board, 1947-53 (Chm., 1949-50); Mem., Yorks Council for Further Educn, 1934-40 and 1949-51; Leeds Coll. of Technology: Mem. Bd of Governors, 1932-40; Vice-Chm., 1932-36 and 1938-40. Member: Leeds Nat. Service Cttee, 1938-40; UK Council of European Movement; Economic League, Central Council, 1934-67. Chm., W Yorks Regional Council and Exec., 1945-50; Mem., Nat. Council, Inst. of Marketing and Sales Management, 1932-35, 1960-62; Leeds Executive: Mem., 1930-; Chm., 1932-33; Pres., 1949-50; Vice-Pres. W Yorks Branch, English-Speaking Union. MP (C) Shipley Div., WR Yorks, 1950-70; Hon. Sec., Conservative Party's Parliamentary Trade and Industry Cttee, 1959-61, Vice-Chm., 1962, Chm., 1963-64. FCS, FSS, FREconS, FInstMSM. Territl Army, 1924-32, rejoined, 1939; served War of 1939-45; Battery Comdr, 1939-44; second in Comd 69th Fd Regt, RA, attached to Staff, 21 Army Gp, 1945. *Publications:* various contribs to the Press. *Recreations:* travel, music. *Address:* Fontaine St Donat, 06 Vence, France. *T:* 32.10.55. *Clubs:* Boodle's; Leeds (Leeds).

**HIRST, Dr John Malcolm,** DSC 1945; FRS 1970; Head of Plant Pathology Department, Rothamsted Experimental Station, Harpenden, since 1967; *b* 20 April 1921; *s* of Maurice Herbert Hirst and Olive Mary (*née* Pank); *m* 1957, Barbara Mary Stokes; two *d*. *Educ:* Solihull Sch.; Reading University. PhD London 1955. Royal Navy (Coastal Forces), 1941-46; Raading Univ. (BSc Hons Agric. Bot.), 1946-50; Rothamsted Exper. Stn., Harpenden, 1950-. Jakob Eriksson Gold Medal (Internat. Botanical Congress), 1959; Research Medal, RASE, 1970. *Publications:* papers in scientific jls mainly in Trans British Mycological Soc., Annals of Applied Biology, Jl of General Microbiology. *Address:* Rothamsted Experimental Station, Harpenden, Herts. *T:* Harpenden 4671.

**HIRST, Prof. Rodney Julian,** MA; Professor of Logic and Rhetoric, University of Glasgow, since Oct. 1961; *b* 28 July 1920; *s* of Rev. William Hirst and Elsie Hirst; *m* 1942, Jessica, *y d* of Charles Alfred Podmore; two *d*. *Educ:* Leeds Grammar Sch.; Magdalen Coll., Oxford. Demy, 1938-47; 1st Cl. Hons Classical Mods, 1940. War Service, 1940-45, mainly as REME Officer (Radar) at home and in Italy. First Class Hons Lit. Hum., Dec. 1947. Lectr in Logic and Metaphysics, St Andrews Univ., 1948; Lectr, 1949, and Sen. Lectr, 1959, in Logic, Glasgow Univ. *Publications:* Problems of Perception, 1959; (co-author) Human Senses and Perception, 1964; Perception and the External World, 1965; Philosophy: an outline for the intending student, 1968; contribs to Encyclopedia of Philosophy and philosophical journals. *Recreations:* music, mountains, meteorology. *Address:* 109 Maxwell Drive, Glasgow S1. *T:* 041-427 3554.

**HIRST, Sir Wyndham;** *see* Hirst, Sir F. W.

**HISCOCKS, Prof. Charles Richard,** MA, DPhil; Professor of International Relations,

University of Sussex, since Oct. 1964; *b* 1 June 1907; *y s* of F. W. Hiscocks; unmarried. *Educ:* Highgate Sch.; St Edmund Hall, Oxford; Berlin University. Asst Master, Trinity Coll. Sch., Port Hope, Ont, 1929-32; Bradfield Coll., 1936-39; Marlborough Coll., 1939-40. Served with Royal Marines, 1940-45, Lieut-Col; seconded to army for mil. govt duties in Germany, 1945; Brit. Council Rep. in Austria, 1946-49, S India, 1949-50; Prof. of Polit. Sci. and Internat. Relations, Univ. of Manitoba, 1950-64. UK Mem., UN Sub-Commn for Prevention of Discrimination and Protection of Minorities, 1953-62. Pres., Winnipeg Art Gall., 1959-60. *Publications:* The Rebirth of Austria, 1953; Democracy in Western Germany, 1957; Poland: Bridge for the Abyss?, 1963; Germany Revived, 1966. *Recreations:* music, art, riding. *Address:* 45 Wickham Hill, Hurstpierpoint, Sussex. *T:* Hassocks 2461. *Club:* Garrick.

**HISCOCKS, Edward Stanley,** CBE 1963; MSc; FRIC; *b* 2 Oct. 1903; *s* of late Edward and Annie Hiscocks, Bristol; *m* 1930, Joy M. L. Turner; one *s*. *Educ:* The Bishop Gore Sch., Swansea; University of Wales. Dept of Government Chemist, 1926-39; Head of Technical Branch, Raw Materials Dept, Ministry of Supply, 1939-44; Sec., National Physical Laboratory, DSIR, 1944-57; Dir, UK Scientific Mission (North America); Scientific Attaché, Washington, DC, 1957-60; Scientific Adviser to UK High Commissioner, Ottawa, 1957-60; Dir, Tropical Products Institute, 1960-66. *Publications:* Laboratory Administration, 1956; papers on physical chemistry and latterly articles and papers on organization and administration of scientific research. *Recreations:* travel, writing. *Address:* 1 Parsons Mead, East Molesey, Surrey. *T:* 01-979 8988. *Club:* Athenæum.

**HISLOP, Prof. Joseph,** FGSM 1953; Professor of Singing, Guildhall School of Music and Drama since 1952; Adviser on Singing to Royal Opera Covent Garden and Sadler's Wells Theatre, since 1949; formerly Principal Professor of Singing at Royal Academy of Music and of Royal School of Opera, Stockholm (title of Professor conferred by King of Sweden, 1949); *b* Edinburgh; *m* Karin Asklund, Gothenburg, Sweden; one *s* two *d*; *m* 1940, Agnes Fraser, *d* of Walter Passmore, London. *Educ:* Cathedral Sch. and Sch. of Arts, Edinburgh; Royal Sch. of Opera, Stockholm and Milan. Made debut Royal Opera House, Stockholm, 1914; has sung in most of the leading opera houses in Europe and of North and South America; has toured in Australia and South Africa. literis et Artibus, Sweden, 1922; Order of Dannebrog, Denmark, 1926; Order of the Vasa, Sweden, 1929. *Recreation:* painting. *Address:* Berryside Farm, By Leven, Fifeshire. *T:* Peat Inn 339.

**HISLOP, Margaret Ross,** RSA 1964 (ARSA 1950); *b* 27 June 1894; *d* of Thomas and Mary Grant; *m* 1921, Andrew Healey Hislop; one *d*. *Educ:* W. Calder (Midlothian) High Sch. Trained Edinburgh Coll. of Art (Diploma, Drawing and Painting, 1917). *Recreations:* gardening, etc. *Address:* 10 Inverleith Row, Edinburgh. *T:* 031-556 4291.

**HISS, Alger;** retailing since 1959 (manufacturing, 1957-59); *b* 11 Nov. 1904; *s* of Charles Alger Hiss and Mary L. Hughes; *m* 1929, Priscilla Fansler Hobson; one *s*. *Educ:* Johns Hopkins Univ. (AB 1926, Hon. LLD 1947); Harvard Univ. (LLB 1929). Sec. and law clerk to Supreme Court Justice Holmes, 1929-30; law practice, 1930-33; asst to gen. counsel and asst gen. counsel, Agricultural Adjustment Admin., 1933-35; legal asst, special Senate cttee investigating munitions industry, 1934-35; special attorney, US Dept of Justice, 1935-36; asst to Asst Sec. of State, 1936; asst to Adviser on Political Relations, 1939; special asst to Dir, Office of Far Eastern Affairs, 1944; special asst to Dir, Office of Special Political Affairs, May 1944; Dep. Dir, Nov. 1944, Dir, 1945; accompanied Pres. Roosevelt and Sec. of State Stettinius to Malta and Yalta Conferences, Feb. 1945; exec. sec., Dumbarton Oaks Conversations, Aug.-Oct. 1944; sec.-gen., United Nations Conference on International Organization, San Francisco, 1945; Principal Adviser to US Delegation, Gen. Assembly of United Nations, London, 1946; elected Pres. and Trustee of Carnegie Endowment for Internat. Peace, Dec. 1946 (Pres. until 1949); Mem., Alpha Delta Phi, Phi Beta Kappa. *Publication:* In the Court of Public Opinion, 1957. *Recreations:* tennis, swimming, ornithology. *Address:* c/o Davison-Bluth, 295 Lafayette Street, New York, NY 10012, USA. *T:* Worth 6-2492.

**HITCHCOCK, Alfred Joseph;** film producer-director; *b* 13 Aug. 1899; *s* of William and Emma Hitchcock; *m* 1926, Alma Reville; one *d*. *Educ:* St Ignatius Coll., London. Junior technician at Famous Players Lasky British Studios, 1920; Scenario writer, art dir, production manager, Gainsborough Pictures, 1923; Motion Picture Dir, 1925. Films include: The Lodger, Farmer's Wife, The Ring, Blackmail, Juno and the Paycock, Murder, Skin Game, Man Who Knew Too Much, Thirty-Nine Steps, Secret Agent, Sabotage, Young and Innocent, The Lady Vanishes, Jamaica Inn, Rebecca, Foreign Correspondent, Mr and Mrs Smith, Suspicion, Saboteur, Shadow of a Doubt, Lifeboat, Spellbound, Notorious, Paradine Case, Rope, Under Capricorn, Stage Fright, Strangers on a Train, I Confess, Dial M for Murder, Rear Window, To catch a Thief, The Trouble with Harry, The Wrong Man, Vertigo, North by Northwest, Psycho, The Birds, Marnie, Torn Curtain, Topaz. Television: Alfred Hitchcock Presents (1959-62), Alfred Hitchcock Hour (1963-65). *Address:* 10957 Bellagio Road, Bel Air, Los Angeles, California 90024, USA.

**HITCHCOCK, Henry-Russell;** Adjunct Professor, Institute of Fine Arts, University of New York, since 1969; *b* 3 June 1903; *s* of Henry R. Hitchcock and Alice Whitworth Davis. *Educ:* Middlesex Sch., Concord, Mass, USA; Harvard Univ. MA 1927. Asst Prof. of Art, Vassar Coll., 1927-28; Asst, Assoc., Full Prof., Wesleyan Univ., 1929-48; Lectr in Architecture, Massachusetts Institute of Technology, 1946-48; Prof. of Art, Smith Coll., Mass, 1948-68; Prof. of Art, Univ. of Massachusetts, 1968. Dir, Smith Coll. Museum of Art, 1949-55; Lectr, Inst. of Fine Arts, New York Univ., 1951-57; Lectr in Architecture, Yale Univ., 1951-52, 1959-60, Cambridge Univ., 1962, 1964, 1970. Fellow Amer. Acad. of Arts and Sciences. Hon. Corr. Mem. RIBA; Franklin Fellow, RSA; Pres., Soc. of Architectural Historians, 1952-54; Trustee, Pilgrim Soc.; Founder-Mem., Victorian Soc.; Pres., Victorian Soc. in America, 1969-. Hon. DFA New York Univ., 1969. *Publications:* Modern Architecture, 1929; J. J. P. Oud, 1931; The International Style (with Philip Johnson), 1932 (2nd edn 1966); The Architecture of H. H. Richardson, 1936 (3rd edn 1966); Modern Architecture in England (with others), 1937; Rhode Island Architecture, 1939 (2nd edn 1968); In the Nature of Materials, the Buildings of Frank Lloyd Wright, 1942 (2nd edn 1970); American Architectural Books, 1946 (2nd edn 1962); Painting towards Architecture, 1948; Early

Victorian Architecture in Britain, 1954; Latin American Architecture since 1945, 1955; Architecture: Nineteenth and Twentieth Centuries, 1958 (3rd edn 1969); German Rococo: The Brothers Zimmermann, 1968; Rococo Architecture in Southern Germany, 1968. *Address:* 152 E 62nd Street, New York, NY 10021, USA. *T:* PL8-6554. *Clubs:* Grolier, Century (NY).

**HITCHENS, Ivon;** *see* Hitchens, S. I.

**HITCHENS, (Sydney) Ivon,** CBE 1958; painter; *b* London, 3 March 1893; *o s* of Alfred Hitchens, painter and Ethel Margaret Seth-Smith; *m* 1935, Mary Cranford, *o d* of Rev. M. F. Coates, Hove; one *s. Educ:* Bedales; St John's Wood Art Schs; Royal Academy Schs. Member: 7 & 5 Soc.; London group. One-man Exhibitions: Mayor Gallery, 1925; Arthur Tooth & Son, 1928; London Artists Assoc., 1929; Mansard Gallery, 1930; Lefevre Galleries, 1932, 1935, 1937; Leicester Galleries, 1940, 1942, 1944, 1947, 1949, 1950, 1952, 1954, 1957, 1959; Waddington Galleries, 1960, 1962, 1964, 1966, 1968, 1969; Poindexter, New York, 1966. Works purchased by the Arts Council, and British Council; Stuyvesant Foundation; Ministry of Public Building and Works. Has also exhibited in New York World's Fair, 1939; UNESCO, Paris, 1946; British Painting since Whistler, National Gallery, 1940; Recent Tate Gallery Acquisitions, National Gallery, 1942; Tate Gallery Continental Exhibition, 1946-47. British Council Exhibitions. European Capitals, 1947, and Australia, 1949; Whitechapel Art Gallery, 1950; Contemporary Art Soc., The Private Collector, Tate Gallery, 1950, 1952. Purchase Prize, Arts Council Exhibition "50 painters for 1951"; British Council Hitchens and Nicholson Exhibition to Japan, 1953; Mural painting for Cecil Sharp House, London, 1954, Venezuela, 1955; twenty paintings in British Pavilion, XXVIII Biennale, Venice, 1956 (subseq. exhibited in Vienna and Munich, 1956, Paris and Amsterdam, 1957); Masters of British Painting, 1800-1950, Museum of Modern Art, New York, 1956; International Exhibition Brussels, 1958. Large landscape for Nuffield College, 1959; XI Premio, Lissone, Italy, 1959; 12th Exhibition International Assoc. art critics Exhibn, 1960; Exhibn British Paintings, 1720-1960, USSR, 1960. 3 Masters of Mod. Brit. Ptg; Arts Council, 1961; 20th Cent. Brit. Ptg: Brit. Council, Portugal, 1961; Kompas Sledelijk Museum, Eindhoven, Holland, 1962; Brit. Art Today, San Francisco, Dallas, Santa Barbara, 1962-63; Coll. E. LeBas, RA, 1963; Mural for Sussex Univ., 1963; Brit. Ptg in the "Sixties", Tate Gallery, 1963; Three British Painters, NZ, 1964; Ptg and Sculpture of a Decade, Gulbenkian Exhibn, 1964; The Bliss Travelling Collection. *Retrospective Exhibitions:* Temple Newsam, Leeds, 1945; Graves Art Gallery, Sheffield, 1948; Tate Gallery, London, 1963; Southampton, 1964; Worthing Art Gallery, 1966. *Represented in Public Collections of:* Leeds, Liverpool, Aberdeen, Wakefield, Shrewsbury, Salford, Hull, Manchester, Glasgow, Leicester, Bath, Birmingham, Bristol, Barnsley, Nottingham, Norwich, Southampton, Eastbourne, Newcastle upon Tyne, Huddersfield, Rochdale; also in Oxford and Cambridge Colls; Nat. Museum of Wales, Cardiff; Glynn Vivian Gall., Swansea; Victoria and Albert Museum, 1942; Cambridge, Fitzwilliam Museum; Tate Gall., 1938, 1941, 1942, 1959, 1965; Musée Nat. d'Art Moderne, Paris, 1957; Australian Nat. Galleries of Adelaide, Melbourne, Sydney; USA: Toledo Museum of Art and Albright Gall., Buffalo; Art Gall. of Seattle; Gothenberg Art Museum, Sweden; Nat. Gall., Oslo; Nat. Gall. of Canada, Ottawa; Art Gall. of Toronto; Nat. Gall. of New Zealand; Ashmolean Museum, Oxford; the Queen's private collection of pictures. *Relevant Publications:* Penguin Modern Painters, 1955; also represented in Tate Gallery colour catalogue, 1963, etc. *Recreation:* streams. *Address:* Greenleaves, Petworth, Sussex. *TA:* Hitchens Graffham. *T:* Graffham 200.

**HITCHIN, Aylwin Drakeford,** CBE 1970; Boyd Professor of Dental Surgery, Director of Dental Studies, University of Dundee (formerly University of St Andrews), Dean of Dundee Dental Hospital, and Dental Consultant, Dundee Royal Infirmary, and Maryfield Hospital, Dundee, since 1947; Consultant Dental Surgeon to Royal Navy since 1957; *b* 31 Dec. 1907; *s* of Alfred Leonard Hitchin, FRPS, and Ruth Drakeford; *m* 1942, Alice Stella Michie; one *s* one *d. Educ:* Rutherford College, Newcastle upon Tyne; Durham University Coll. of Medicine. LDS (Dunelm) 1931, BDS 1932, MDS 1935; DDSc 1957; FDSRCS Edinburgh 1951; FFDRCS Ire 1964; FDSRCPS Glasgow 1967. Asst Hon. Dental Surgeon and Demonstrator of Dental Surgery, Newcastle upon Tyne Dental Hosp., 1932-36; Private Dental Practice, Newcastle upon Tyne, 1932-46 (except for 6 yrs with AD Corps during War of 1939-45); Dental Surgical Specialist, Scottish Command, 1943-45, with rank of Major. Chairman: Dental Educn Advisory Council, 1951-52; Dental Hosp. Assoc., 1959-60; Dental Cttee, Scot. Post-Grad. Med. Assoc.; Member: Dental Cttee of MRC, Advisory Cttee on Medical Research (Scotland); Dental Adv. Cttee, Central Health Services Council (Scotland); Dental Council, RCSE; Jt Cttee on Higher Training in Dentistry; East Scotland Regional Hosp. Bd, 1948-52; Dental Sub Cttee, UGC; Nominated Mem., Gen. Dent. Council; External Examiner Dental Subjects, Universities, Durham, Edinburgh, Queen's, Belfast, Dublin, Manchester, Liverpool, Birmingham, Leeds, Bristol, Wales, RCS in Ireland; Examiner, FDSRCS Edinburgh, FFDRCS Ire, and FDSRCPS Glasgow. President: Oral Surgery Club, 1956-57; Christian Dental Fellowship, 1966-69; Brit. Soc. Dental Radiology, 1961-63; Royal Odonto-Chir. Soc. of Scotland, 1969-70; Vice-Pres., Inter-Varsity Fellowship (Pres., 1966-67); Foundation Fellow of the British Assoc. of Oral Surgeons; Hon. Mem., Swedish Dental Soc. Comr, Dundee Presbytery and Synod of Angus and Mearns. *Publications:* contribs to dental periodical literature. *Address:* Kyleakin, 8 Cedar Road, Broughty Ferry, Dundee, Angus. *TA* and *T:* Dundee 77320.

**HITCHINGS, Group Capt. John Phelp,** CBE 1944; Director, J. Cox & Co.'s Succrs Ltd, Bedminster, Bristol; *b* 2 Aug. 1899; *m* 1928, Gwendolyn Joyce Mary Newth; one *s* one *d. Educ:* Queen's Coll., Taunton. Served in RFC and RAF, 1917-18 and 1939-45; in business as Sole Leather Tanner, 1919-67. DL Glos and City and County of Bristol, 1953. *Recreation:* golf. *Address:* 19a The Avenue, Clifton, Bristol BS8 3HG. *T:* Bristol 36276.

**HITCHINS, Francis Eric,** CBE 1954; Member, Australian Wool Realization Commission, 1945-57; President Emeritus, Australian Wool and Meat Producers' Federation; sheep farming, Cranbrook, W Australia; *b* 15 Oct. 1891; *m* 1921, Bessie R. Paltridge; two *s* one *d.* Served European War, 1914-18, AIF, France. Inspector, Agric. Bank of W Australia, 1918-23; Land Valuer, Federal Taxation Dept, 1923-32; resumed sheep farming. Pres., Wool Sect., Primary Producers' Assoc. of WA; Pres., Australian Wool and Meat Producers' Fedn,

1941-52; Wool Grower Rep., Central Wool Cttee, War of 1939-45. Grower Rep., London Wool Confs, 1945 and 1950. *Publication:* Tangled Skeins: A Historic Survey of Australian Wool Marketing, 1956. *Address:* Pynup, Cranbrook, WA 6321, Australia. *T:* CB 12.

**HITCHMAN, Sir (Edwin) Alan,** KCB 1952 (CB 1948); Deputy Chairman, United Kingdom Atomic Energy Authority, 1964-66 (full-time Member, 1959); *b* 16 Nov. 1903; *s* of E. B. Hitchman, Newbury; *m* 1937, Katharine Mumford, *d* of Frank Hendrick, New York City; two *s. Educ:* St Bartholomew's Grammar Sch., Newbury; Downing Coll., Cambridge. Asst Principal, Ministry of Labour, 1926; Principal Private Sec. to Mr E. Brown, 1939, and to Mr E. Bevin, 1940, when Ministers of Labour; Principal Asst Sec., 1941; Under-Sec., 1946; transferred to HM Treasury, 1947; Dep. to Chief Planning Officer, 1948-49; Third Sec., HM Treasury, 1949-51; Perm. Sec. to Min. of Materials, 1951-52; Mem. Economic Planning Board, 1951-52; Chm. Agric. Improvement Council for England and Wales, 1952; Permanent Sec. to Min. of Agriculture and Fisheries, 1952-55, to Min. of Agriculture, Fisheries and Food, 1955-59. *Address:* 13 Wellington Square, Chelsea, SW3. *T:* 01-730 9359. *Club:* United University.

**HIVES,** family name of **Baron Hives.**

**HIVES,** 2nd Baron, *cr* 1950, of Duffield; **John Warwick Hives;** *b* 26 Nov. 1913; *s* of 1st Baron Hives and of Gertrude Ethel (*d* 1961), *d* of John Warwick; *S* father, 1965; *m* 1937, Olwen Protheroe Llewellin; no *c. Educ:* Manor School, Mickleover, Derby. *Recreation:* shooting. *Heir: b* Hon. Peter Anthony Hives [*b* 1921; *m* 1956, Dinah Wilson-North; three *d*]. *Address:* Bendalls, Milton, Derby. *T:* Repton 3319. *Club:* Farmers'.

**HIVES, Rt. Rev. Harry Ernest,** BA, DD; *b* 20 Sept. 1901; *s* of Richard Charles Hives and Rose Annie Watson; *m* 1927, Erla Ruth Wait; two *d. Educ:* Univ. of Saskatchewan (BA); Emmanuel Coll., Saskatoon (LTh Hons). Deacon, 1926; Priest, 1927. Curate-in-Charge, Cumberland House, 1926-27; Incumbent, 1927-29; Lac la Ronge, 1929-38; Paynton with Bresaylor, 1938-40; Lashburn, 1940-42; Rector of Battleford, 1943-50; Hon. Canon, St John's Cathedral, Saskatoon, 1943; Bishop's Commissary for Indian Affairs, 1945; Domestic Chaplain to Bishop of Saskatoon, 1949; Archdeacon of Indian Affairs, 1953; Bishop of Keewatin, 1953-69, retired 1969. DD (Emmanuel Coll., Saskatoon), 1954. *Publication:* Cree Grammar, 1948. *Address:* 4480 Shore Way, Victoria, BC, Canada.

**HOAD, Air Cdre Norman Edward,** CBE 1969; AFC 1951 and Bar, 1956; Defence and Air Attaché, British Embassy, Paris, since 1969; *b* 28 July 1923; *s* of Hubert Ronald Hoad and Florence Marie (*née* Johnson); two *s. Educ:* Brighton. Joined RAF, 1941, pilot trng, S Rhodesia; Lancaster pilot until shot down and taken prisoner in Germany, 1944; various flying and instructional duties, 1945-51; Sqdn Ldr 1951; OC No 192 Sqdn, 1953-55; psc 1956; Wing Comdr, HQ 2 ATAF, 1957-59; pfc 1960; OC No 216 Sqdn, 1960-62; jssc 1963; Gp Capt., MoD, 1963-65; idc 1966; Stn Comdr: RAF Lyneham, 1967, RAF Abingdon, 1968. *Recreation:* oil painting. *Address:* British Embassy, 35 rue du Faubourg St Honoré, Paris 16, France. *T:* Anjou 27-10. *Club:* Royal Air Force.

**HOAR, Arthur Stanley George,** CMG 1969; retired; *b* 17 July 1903; *s* of Arthur George Hoar and Emma Alice Hoar (*née* de Beaucamp); *m* 1930, Florence May Leigh; two *s* one *d. Educ:* Owen's Sch.; London Univ. Various positions, Bank of England, 1923-46; Dir-Gen. of Banking Branch, CCG (BE), 1945-46; Internat. Bank for Reconstruction and Development: Asst Loan Dir, 1946-51; Loan Dir, 1951-52; Dir of Operations for Europe, Africa and Australasia, 1952-55; Commonwealth Development Finance Co. Ltd: Gen. Manager, 1955-56; Managing Dir, 1956-68; Director: CDFC (Australia) Ltd, 1963-68; CDFC Holdings Ltd (Toronto), 1964-68; CDFC (Malaysia) Ltd, 1965-68. *Recreations:* archæology, history, gardening. *Address:* Chevy Chase, 26a Stratton Road, Beaconsfield, Bucks. *T:* Beaconsfield 3446.

**HOAR, Hon. Ernest Knight,** JP; *b* 20 Oct. 1898; *s* of Henry Knight Hoar and Sarah Ann Hoar, Luton, England; *m* 1924, Dorothy Helen Tomlin, Leicester, England; one *s. Educ:* Luton, England. Served European War, 1914-18, for 4½ years. Emigrated to Western Australia, 1922; entered Western Australian Parliament, 1943; Minister for Lands, Agriculture and Immigration, in the State Government, 1953-57; Agent-Gen. for Western Australia in London, 1957-65. Retired, 1965. *Recreation:* golf. *Address:* 61 Moreing Road, Attadale, WA 6156, Australia.

**HOARE, Sir Archer,** Kt 1955; CBE 1939; *b* 6 March 1876; *m* 1908, Agnes Falconer Harby (*d* 1969), *d* of Charles E. Harby, Southgate; one *s* one *d. Educ:* Richmond, Surrey. Entered Customs and Excise Dept, 1896; Dep. Chief Inspector, 1936; Collector, Port of London, 1938-40; Middlesex County Council: Councillor, 1940; Alderman, 1949; Chm. Establishment Cttee, 1949; Education Cttee, 1949-52, 1960-; Vice-Chm. of Council, 1951-52, Chm., 1953-54. Court of Univ. of London, 1952-67; Court of Mill Hill Sch., 1949-58; Hendon-Harrow War Pensions Cttee, 1940, Chm., 1941-63. LLD London, 1964. *Address:* 42 Love Lane, Pinner, Middlesex. *T:* 01-866 3449.

**HOARE, Cecil Arthur,** FRS 1950; DSc; FIBiol; *b* 6 March 1892; *m* Marie Leserson. *Educ:* XII St Petersburg Gymnasium; University of Petrograd (BSc 1917); University of London (DSc 1927). Fellow of Petrograd Univ., 1917-20; Lectr at Military Medical Academy, Petrograd, 1918-20; Researcher to Medical Research Council, 1920-23; Protozoologist to Wellcome Laboratories of Tropical Medicine, London, 1923-57; Wellcome Research Fellow, 1957-70; Trypanosomiasis Research Institute, Uganda Medical Service, 1927-29; in charge of Medical Protozoology at London Sch. of Hygiene and Tropical Medicine, 1941-45; Recorder of "Protozoa" in Zoological Record, 1926-57; Member: Editorial Panel of "Parasitology"; Expert Panel, WHO. Hon. Member: Soc. Protozool., USA; Brit. Soc. Parasitol.; Société de Pathologie Exotique, Paris; For. Member: Société Belge de Médecine Tropicale; Soc. Protistol. Franç. G. Vianna Medal, Brazil. Acad. Sci., 1962; Patrick Manson Prize, 1963. *Publications:* Handbook of Medical Protozoology, 1949; numerous papers dealing with the Protozoa. *Address:* 77 Sutton Court Road, W4. *T:* 01-994 4838.

**HOARE, Christopher Gurney,** MC 1918; Stockbroker in Hoare & Co.; *b* 29 June 1882; *s* of R. G. Hoare, Jesmond Park, Newcastle on Tyne; *m* 1907, Eveline Hamilton Lucas (*d* 1960); one *s* one *d. Educ:* Harrow; King's Coll., Cambridge (MA). At Cambridge Master of Trinity Foot Beagles; joined 2nd Line Essex Yeomanry, 1914; transferred to Royal Horse Guards. *Recreations:* hunting, shooting.

*Address:* Gateley Hall, Elmham, Dereham, Norfolk. *Clubs:* Buck's, Bath.

**HOARE, Rear-Adm. Dennis John,** CB 1945; FIMechE; *b* 16 April 1891; *s* of late Herbert K. Hoare, Portsmouth; *m* 1919, Madeline, *d* of T. Morris Prosser, JP, Newport, Mon.; two *s*. *Educ:* RNEC Keyham; RNC, Greenwich. HMS Collingwood, 1913-15, followed by service in HMS's Birkenhead, Goshawk and Glorious. Lecturer in Applied Mechanics at RNC Greenwich, 1919-24; then served in HM Ships Malaya and Shakespeare. Admiralty, 1926; HMS Exeter, 1930; later appointments included Fleet Engineer Officer, Mediterranean, Fleet Engineer Officer, Submarines, Asst Engineer-in-Chief, Superintendent Admiralty Engineering Laboratory; retired July 1945. Dir of Research, British Internal Combustion Engine Research Assoc., 1945-58. Chevalier Order of Aviz (Portugal), 1921; Grand Officer, Order of Orange-Nassau (Netherlands), 1947. *Address:* 11 Woodville Road, Newport, Mon NPT 4JB. *T:* Newport 59422.

**HOARE, Rear-Adm. Desmond John,** CB 1962; MIMechE; MRINA; Provost, United World Colleges, since 1969; *b* 25 June 1910; *s* of Capt. R. R. Hoare, OBE, Royal Navy; *m* 1941, Naomi Mary Gilbert Scott; one *s* two *d*. *Educ:* Wimbledon Coll.; King's Sch., Rochester. Joined RN, 1929; Engineering training, RNEC Keyham, 1930-33; Advanced engineering course, RNC Greenwich, 1934-36; HMS Exeter, 1936-39; Admiralty, 1939-41; HMS King George V, 1942-44; Admiralty, 1945-48; HMS Vanguard, 1949-51; HMS Condor (apprentice training), 1951-53; idc, 1955; Admiralty, 1956-59; Chief Staff Officer Technical to C-in-C Plymouth, 1960-62; retired, 1962. Headmaster, Atlantic Coll., 1962-69. Mem. Cttee, RNLI, 1969-. *Recreations:* sailing, power boats. *Address:* St Donat's Castle, Llantwit Major, Glamorgan. *T:* Llantwit Major 641. *Club:* Royal Automobile.

**HOARE, Sir Frederick (Alfred),** 1st Bt, *cr* 1962; Kt 1958: Managing Partner of C. Hoare & Co., Bankers, of 37 Fleet Street, since 1947; Deputy Chairman, National Mutual Life Assurance Society, since 1969; Director: Messrs Hoare Trustees; Mitre Court Securities Ltd; The Trust Union Ltd; Little New Street Development Ltd; City Arts Trust Ltd; St George Assurance Co. Ltd; Mitre Court Cranes Ltd; Grimersta Estate Ltd; Chairman: General Practice Finance Corporation; City of London Probation Committee; *b* 11 Feb. 1913; *s* of late Frederick Henry Hoare, 37 Fleet Street, EC4; *m* 1939, Norah Mary, *d* of A. J. Wheeler; two *d*. *Educ:* Wellington Coll. Clerk to C. Hoare & Co., 1931; Bankers' Agent, 1936, Managing Partner, 1947. Common Councilman City of London, 1948; Alderman for Ward of Farringdon Without, 1950; Sheriff, City of London, 1956; Lord Mayor of London, 1961-62. One of HM Lieutenants for City of London; Governor: Christ's Hosp.; Royal Bridewell Hosp.; Past Chm., St Bride's Institute; Mem., Court of Assistants and Prime Warden of Goldsmiths' Company, 1966-67. President: British Chess Federation, 1964-67; London Primary Schs Chess Assoc.; Cosmopolitan Banks Chess Assoc.; Upward Bound Young People's Gliding and Adventure Trust; Vice-Pres., Toc H. trustee: Lady Hoare Thalidomide Appeal; Historic Churches Preservation Trust; Member: Nat. Coun. of Social Service; Nat. Council, Noise Abatement Soc.; Adv. Panel, World Wildlife Fund. Chm., Family Welfare Assoc., 1961-68. Past Grand Deacon, United Grand Lodge of England. KStJ. Knight of Liberian Humane Order of African Redemption, 1962; Grand Officier de L'Ordre National de la République de Côte d'Ivoire, 1962. *Recreations:* chess, fishing, ornithology, photography, philately. *Heir:* none. *Address:* 78 Hamilton Terrace, St John's Wood, NW8. *T:* 01-286 8361. *Clubs:* Garrick, City Livery, Flyfishers'.

**HOARE, Maj.-Gen. Lionel Lennard,** DSO 1916; *b* Staplehurst, 24 July 1881; *s* of William Hoare of Staplehurst and Laura, 2nd *d* of Sir John Lennard, 1st Bt of Wickham Court, West Wickham, Kent; *m* 1912, Audrey (*d* 1963), *e d* of Lieut-Col G. H. Woodard; three *d*. *Educ:* Lambrook; Eton; RMA Woolwich. Joined Royal Field Artillery, 1899; served S Africa, 1901-02 (Queen's medal 5 clasps); transferred to Army Ordnance Dept, 1906; Capt. 1908; Major 1914; Temp. Lt-Col 1916-25; Lieut-Col 1925; Col 1932; Brig., 1935; Maj.-Gen. 1938; served European War, 1914-19 (despatches twice, DSO); Instructor RAOC Sch. of Instruction, 1926-31; Asst Dir of Ordnance Services, War Office, 1931-35; Dep. Dir of Ordnance Services, Royal Arsenal, Woolwich, 1935-38; Principal Ordnance Officer, War Office, 1938-39; retired pay, 1939; Dir of Progress and Inspection, and Military Adviser, Min. of Supply, 1939-45; Pres., Council of Big Ben Silent Minute Observance, 1941-62; Vice-Chm., Rochester Diocesan Board of Finance, 1949-67; Mem. of Church Assembly, 1950-65. *Recreations:* various. *Address:* South Lodge, Wrotham, Kent. *T:* Fairseat 382. *Club:* MCC.

**HOARE, Marcus Bertram,** CMG 1965; **Hon. Mr Justice Hoare;** Justice of Supreme Court of Queensland, since 1966; *b* 3 March 1910; *s* of John George and Emma Hoare; *m* 1936, Eileen Parker; four *s*. *Educ:* Brisbane Grammar Sch. Solicitor, 1933; Barrister-at-Law, 1944; QC (Australia) 1960. *Address:* 191 Laurel Avenue, Graceville, Brisbane, Qld 4075, Australia. *T:* 79-4181. *Clubs:* Queensland, Johnsonian, Anzac (Brisbane).

**HOARE, Sir Peter (William),** 7th Bt *cr* 1786, of Luscombe, Devon; Managing Partner of C. Hoare & Co., Bankers, of Fleet Street and Park Lane, London; Director: Messrs Hoare Trustees; Eagle Star Insurance Co. Ltd; *b* 22 July 1898; *o s* of late P. A. M. Hoare; *S* cousin 1947; *m* 1929, Laura Ray, *o d* of Sir John Esplen, 1st Bt, KBE; two *s*. *Educ:* Harrow. Served European War, 1917-19, France and Germany, Lieut RGA (TF). High Sheriff of Devon, 1955. *Recreations:* fishing and shooting. *Heir:* *s* Peter Richard Hoare, *b* 22 March 1932. *Address:* Luscombe Castle, Dawlish, Devon. *Clubs:* Travellers', Garrick, MCC; Royal Yacht Squadron.

**HOARE, Col Robert Rawdon,** DSO 1940; MC 1918; Director-General, Economic League, 1945-59; *b* 16 May 1897; *s* of late Gerald Eugene Hoare, Cromer, Norfolk, and Rosabelle Mary, *d* of late Rawdon Hunter-Muskett, DL, JP, Hingham Hall, Norfolk. *Educ:* Beaumont Coll., Windsor. Entered Army, Aug. 1914, RA; apptd Royal Horse Artillery, 1916 (wounded, MC); Regular Army Reserve of Officers, Major, 1922; recalled to command "K" (Hondeghem) Bty RHA, 1939; served War of 1939-45 (wounded twice, despatches twice, Africa Star, 8th Army Clasp, Italian Star); Temp. Lieut-Col RHA 1940; commanded 5 RHA, Aug. 1940-43; Head of RA Training Team, Free French and Polish Forces, 1943; Col 1943; Chief Artillery Adviser, Brit. Mil. Mission to the Egyptian Army, 1944. Croix de Guerre with gold star, 1947. Mem. Bd of Govs, Royal Nat. Orthopædic Hospital, 1947-59; Trustee of

Albany, 1955-67. *Publications:* two books on travel, 1936 and 1937; numerous articles on travel, 1928-37. *Recreations:* walking, reading, travel. *Address:* 2 Redbourne, Norwich Road, Cromer, Norfolk. *T:* Cromer 3101. *Club:* Turf.

**HOARE, Sir Samuel,** KBE 1970; Kt 1957; CB 1949; *b* 1896; *s* of Barnard George Hoare, Inverness. *Educ:* Inverness Royal Academy; Aberdeen Univ. Asst Under-Sec. of State, Home Office, 1946-61; Head of Internat. Div., 1950-61. Has represented UK on various international bodies, including Gen. Assembly and Economic and Social Council of UN; Member: Human Rights Commn of UN, 1952-69; Council of Europe Cttee on Human Rights, 1961-. *Address:* 11 Mulberry Close, Beaufort Street, SW3. *T:* 01-352 5697.

**HOARE, Sir Timothy Edward Charles,** 8th Bt *cr* 1784; *b* 11 Nov. 1934; *s* of Sir Edward O'Bryen Hoare, 7th Bt and of Nina Mary; *d* of late Charles Nugent Hope-Wallace, MBE; *S* father, 1969; *m* 1969, Felicity Anne, *o d* of Peter Boddington. *Educ:* Radley College; Worcester College, Oxford. *Heir: uncle* Terence O'Bryen Hoare [*b* 21 Jan. 1904; *m* 1939, Elizabeth, *d* of late William James Cambridge]. *Address:* 10 Prior Bolton Street, N1.

**HOBAN, Brian Michael Stanislaus;** JP; Head Master of Bradfield College, 1964-71; Head Master of Harrow, from Aug. 1971; *b* 7 Oct. 1921; 2nd *s* of late Capt. R. A. Hoban; *m* 1947, Jasmine, 2nd *d* of J. C. Holmes, MC, Charterhouse, Godalming; one *s* one *d* (and one *d* decd). *Educ:* Charterhouse (Scholar); University Coll., Oxford (Sch.). 2nd Cl. Hon. Mods, 1947; 2nd Cl. Lit. Hum., 1949; BA 1949, MA 1957. Served War of 1939-45: Capt., Westminster Dragoons; NW Europe, 1944-45 (despatches); demobilised, Nov. 1945. Capt. Northants Yeomanry, TA, 1950-56. Asst Master: Uppingham Sch., 1949-52; Shrewsbury Sch., 1952-59; Headmaster of St Edmund's Sch., Canterbury, 1960-64. JP Berks, 1967. *Recreations:* music, cricket, golf, walking. *Address:* Crossways, Bradfield, near Reading, Berks. *T:* Bradfield 203; (from Aug. 1971) The Head Master's, Harrow-on-the-Hill, Mddx. *Clubs:* Athenæum; Vincent's (Oxford).

**HOBART, Archbishop of, (RC),** since 1955; **Most Rev. Guilford Young,** DD (Rome); *b* Sandgate, Queensland, 10 Nov. 1916. Ordained, Rome, 1939; Auxiliary Bishop of Canberra and Goulburn, 1948; Co-Adjutor Archbishop of Hobart, 1954; succeeded to See of Hobart, Sept. 1955. *Address:* Archbishop's House, 31 Fisher Avenue, Sandy Bay, Hobart, Tasmania 7005, Australia.

**HOBART, Maj.-Gen. Patrick Robert Chamier,** CB 1970; DSO 1945; OBE 1944; MC 1943; Director, Royal Armoured Corps, since 1970; *b* 14 Nov. 1917; *s* of Robert Charles Arthur Stanley Hobart and Elsie Hinds. *Educ:* Charterhouse; Royal Military Academy Woolwich; 2nd Lieut, Royal Tank Corps, 1937; served in war of 1939-45: France, Western Desert, Tunisia, Italy and NW Europe (despatches 4 times), in 7th and Guards Armoured Divisions; Comdr, 20th Armoured Brigade, BAOR, 1961-63; Chief of Staff, 1 (British) Corps, BAOR, 1964-66; Dir Military Operations, MoD, 1966-68; Col Comdt Royal Tank Regt, 1968-; Chief of Staff Army Strategic Command, 1968-70. ADC to the Queen, 1961-66. *Address:* c/o Glyn Mills, Holts Branch, Kirkland House, Whitehall, SW1.

**HOBART, Lt-Comdr Sir Robert (Hampden),** 3rd Bt *cr* 1914; RN; JP, CC (Isle of Wight); *b* 7 May 1915; *o s* of Sir (Claud) Vere Cavendish Hobart, 2nd Bt, DSO, OBE and Violet Verve, MBE (*d* 1935), 2nd *d* of late John Wylie; *S* father 1949; *m* 1942, Sylvia (*d* 1965), *d* of H. Argo, Durban, Natal; three *s* one *d*. *Educ:* Wixenford; RN Coll., Dartmouth. Sub-Lieut, RN, 1935; Lieut-Comdr, 1945; served War of 1939-45 (wounded, two medals, four stars); retired, 1950. Contested (Nat Lib) Hillsborough Div. of Sheffield, 1945, (C and L) Itchen Div. of Southampton, 1950. *Heir: s* John Vere Hobart, *b* 9 April 1945. *Address:* Gatcombe Park, Newport, Isle of Wight. *Clubs:* Travellers', Royal London Yacht; Royal Yacht Squadron; Royal Southern Yacht, Royal Southampton Yacht, Bembridge Sailing.

**HOBART-HAMPDEN,** family name of **Earl of Buckinghamshire.**

**HOBBS, Harold William,** CB 1965; CBE 1955; Chartered Mechanical Engineer; Professional Adviser to the Royal Mint; *b* 1903; *s* of Thomas Harold Hobbs, London; *m* 1941, Greta Kathleen, *d* of Michael Boyne. *Educ:* Woolwich Polytechnic. Dep. Controller, Royal Ordnance Factories, MoD (Army), 1962-66. MIMechE. *Address:* 17 Riefield Road, Eltham, SE9. *T:* 01-850 5861; 41 Links Crescent, St Mary's Bay, Romney Marsh, Kent.

**HOBBS, Herbert Harry,** CB 1956; Under-Secretary, Ministry of Public Building and Works, since 1963; *b* 7 Nov. 1912; *s* of late Bertie Hobbs and Agnes Dora (*née* Clarke); *m* 1937, Joan Hazel Timmins; two *s* one *d*. *Educ:* Bedford Sch.; Corpus Christi Coll., Oxford. Entered War Office, 1935; Comptroller of Lands and Claims, 1956-60; Asst Under-Sec. of State (Works), War Office, 1960-63. Medal of Freedom with bronze palm (USA), 1946. *Recreation:* golf. *Address:* 57 Sunnybank, Epsom, Surrey. *T:* Epsom 22838. *Club:* Reform.

**HOBBS, Maj.-Gen. Reginald Geoffrey Stirling,** CB 1956; DSO 1942; OBE 1944; *b* 8 Aug. 1908; *e s* of late Brig.-Gen. Reginald Francis Arthur Hobbs, CB, CMG, DSO, Sutton Veny, Warminster, Wilts; *m* 1935, Mary Jameson, *d* of late Maj.-Gen. Hugo De Pree, CB, CMG, DSO, Beckley, Rye, Sussex; one *d*. *Educ:* Wellington; RMA Woolwich. 2nd Lieut RA, 1928; Staff Coll., 1940; BEF, 1940; RHA Eighth Army, Western Desert, 1942-43; Staff, 21 Army Group NW Europe, 1944-45; Lieut-Col 1942; temp. Brig. 1947; Chief of Staff, Combined Ops, 1948; idc, 1949; CRA 1st Inf. Div., 1950-51; Comd 2 Inf. Bde, 1952; Maj.-Gen. 1955; Comdt, RMA Sandhurst, 1954-56; Near East, 1956; Dir of Royal Artillery, War Office, 1957-59; GOC 1 Div., 1959-60; Col Comdt, Royal Regt Artillery, 1963-68; Hon. Col, Essex Yeomanry, 1961-66; Pres., Regular Commissions Bd, 1961-62; Lieut-Governor and Sec., Royal Hospital, Chelsea, 1962-67. Order of White Lion 3rd Class, and Military Cross (Czechoslovakia), 1945; Officer of Legion of Honour and Croix de Guerre with Palm (France), 1958. *Recreation:* English Rugby International, 1932; Pres. of the Rugby Football Union, 1961-62. *Address:* Lerags House, Oban, Argyll. *T:* Oban 2450. *Club:* Army and Navy.

**HOBBS, William Alfred,** CBE 1965; Deputy Chief Valuer, Inland Revenue Valuation Office; *b* 3 March 1912; *s* of A. V. Getland Hobbs; *m* 1937, Rose Winslade; one *s* one *d*. *Educ:* Brighton, Hove and Sussex Grammar Sch. Chartered Surveyor (FRICS). Private practice, 1928-38; joined Valuation Office, 1938; Dist Valuer (Maidstone), 1945;

Superintending Valuer, 1950 (London, Manchester and Birmingham); Asst Chief Valuer, 1958; Dep. Chief Valuer, 1966-. *Recreations:* fly-fishing, golf. *Address:* 7 Beech Grove, Epsom Downs, Surrey. *T:* Burgh Heath 56255. *Club:* Royal Automobile.

**HOBDEN, Dennis Harry;** *b* 21 Jan. 1920; *s* of Charles Hobden and Agnes Hobden (*née* Smith); *m* 1950, Kathleen Mary Hobden (*née* Holman) (marr. diss. 1970); two *s* two *d. Educ:* elementary sch. Entered GPO, 1934. Served as Air Crew, RAF, 1941-46 (Flt Lieut). MP (Lab) Kemptown Div. of Brighton, 1964-70. *Recreations:* politics, gardening, music, reading. *Address:* 3 Queens Park Terrace, Brighton 7, Sussex.

**HOBDEN, Reginald Herbert,** DFC 1944; Counsellor (Economic), British High Commission, Rawalpindi, since 1970; *b* 9 Nov. 1919; *s* of William Richard and Ada Emily Hobden; *m* 1945, Gwendoline Ilma Vowles; two *s* one *d. Educ:* Sir William Borlase's Sch., Marlow. Apptd Colonial Office, Dec. 1936. Served War of 1939-45 (despatches, DFC): RAFVR, Sept. 1940-Jan. 1946 (Sqdn Ldr). Returned to Colonial Office, 1946; seconded to Dept of Technical Co-operation, 1961; First Sec., UK Commn, Malta, 1962-64; HM Diplomatic Service, Nov. 1964: CRO until April 1968; Head of British Interests Section, Canadian High Commn, Dar es Salaam, April 1968; British Acting High Comr, Dar es Salaam, July-Oct. 1968, and Counsellor, Dar es Salaam, Oct. 1968-69. *Recreations:* cricket, tennis, chess, bridge. *Address:* 14 Belmont Close, Uxbridge, Mddx. *T:* Uxbridge 34754. *Club:* Royal Commonwealth Society.

**HOBHOUSE, Sir Charles Chisholm,** 6th Bt, *cr* 1812; TD; *b* 7 Dec. 1906; *s* of Sir Reginald A. Hobhouse, 5th Bt and Marjorie Chisholm Spencer (*d* 1967); *S* father, 1947; *m* 1st, 1946, Mary (*d* 1955), *widow* of Walter Horrocks, Salkeld Hall, Penrith; no *c*; 2nd, 1959, Elspeth Jean, *d* of T. G. Spinney, Mazagan, Morocco; one *s. Educ:* Eton. Commissioned North Somerset Yeomanry, 1927; Major 1940; Hon. Col 1966. *Recreations:* hunting, shooting. *Heir: s* Charles John Spinney Hobhouse, *b* 27 Oct. 1962. *Address:* The Manor, Monkton Farleigh, Bradford-on-Avon, Wilts. *T:* Bath 88558. *Clubs:* Brooks's, Cavalry, City of London.

**HOBHOUSE, Edmund W. Neill,** MA, MD Oxon, FRCP; Consulting Physician, Victoria Hospital for Children and West End Hospital for Nervous Diseases; Hon. Consulting Neurologist, Royal Free Hospital; *b* 1888; *e s* of late Rev. W. Hobhouse, DD, and Violet, *y d* of Edmund McNeill, DL, Craigdunn; *m* 1920, Phyllis, *d* of late Sir William J. Smyly; two *d. Educ:* Winchester; New Coll., Oxford. House Physician, etc, St Thomas's Hosp.; RMO City of London Hosp. for Diseases of Chest; served in RAMC; Physician to Out-patients, Hampstead Gen. Hosp.; Neurologist, Ministry of Pensions. *Publications:* Nervous Disorder in Infancy and Childhood, 1932; contributions to Lancet and other medical journals. *Address:* May Cottage, Mortimer Common, Berks.

**HOBKIRK, Col Elspeth Isabel Weatherley,** CBE 1951; TD 1952; WRAC (retired); Governor of HM Prison and of HM Borstal Institution, Greenock, 1955-69; also appointed Adviser to Scottish Home and Health Department on arrangements for Detention of Women and Girls in Scottish Penal Institutions, 1961, retired from Scottish Prison Service, Aug. 1969; *d* of late Brig.-Gen. C. J. Hobkirk, CMG, DSO, Cleddon Hall, Trellech, Mon. *Educ:* Sandecotes, Dorset; London Sch. of Art. JP Monmouthshire, 1938-49. Joined FANY, 1938; enrolled ATS, 1939; served War of 1939-45, Sen. Comdr, 1942; Chief Comdr, 1945; Controller and Dep. Dir ATS, HQ London District, 1946; Dep. Dir ATS, War Office, 1947-50; commissioned into Women's Royal Army Corps, 1949; Dep. Dir WRAC, War Office, 1949; Dep. Dir WRAC, HQ Eastern Command, 1950-52; Vice-Pres. Regular Commissions Bd, 1950-52; retired, 1952. Head Warden, Bristol Royal Hospital, 1952-54; Governor, HM Prison, Duke Street, Glasgow, 1954-55 (prison closed). Mem., Govt Adv. Cttee on Drug Dependence, 1967-70; Member: Parole Board for Scotland, 1970-; Civil Service Commn Panel of Interviewers, 1969-; Adv. Council on Social Work (Scotland), 1970-. *Recreations:* travel, painting, music, gardening; country pursuits generally. *Address:* 8 Moray Place, Edinburgh. *Clubs:* Army and Navy; Kelvin (Glasgow).

**HOBLER, Air Vice-Marshal John Forde,** CB 1958; CBE 1943; *b* Rockhampton, Qld, Australia, 26 Sept. 1907; *s* of late L. E. Hobler, Rockhampton; *m* 1939, Dorothy Evelyn Diana Halnes, Wilsford, Wilts; two *s* one *d. Educ:* Rockhampton, Qld. Served whole of War of 1939-45 in Bomber Command; commanded RAF Lossiemouth; Palestine, 1945; Staff Coll., 1946-48; Air Ministry, 1948-50; Comd Habbaniya, Iraq, 1950-52; HQ Flying Trg Comd, 1952-54; Air Ministry, 1954-56; AO i/c Administration, Middle East Air Force, 1956-58; Air Officer Commanding No. 25 GP, 1958-61; Air Officer i/c Administration, Far East Air Force, 1961-63, retd. *Address:* Bucknalla, Burnside Court, Southport, Qld 4215, Australia. *Club:* United Services (Brisbane).

**HOBSON, Alec,** CBE 1962 (OBE 1946); MVO 1955; *b* 29 Oct. 1899; *s* of Frederick Hobson, Esher, Surrey; *m* 1924, Elizabeth Josephine, *d* of Arthur Newman, Sudbury, Suffolk; one *s* (one *d* decd). Served Inns of Court and Royal West Surrey Regiments, 1918-19. Engaged in pedigree livestock improvement work, 1920-39; joint founder-partner Harry Hobson & Co. (pedigree livestock auctioneers), 1928. Domestic food production work for Min. of Agriculture, 1939-45. Sec., Royal Agricultural Soc. of England and of Nat. Agricultural Examinations Bds, 1946-61; Hon. Sec., Royal Agricultural Society of The Commonwealth, 1957-67. Founder Mem., Guild of Agricultural Journalists; Pres., Nat. Soc. of Master Thatchers; Liveryman, Past Master, and Court of Assts, Worshipful Co. of Farriers; Freeman, Worshipful Co. of Farmers. *Recreations:* golf, gardening. *Address:* Clare Cottage, Oulton, Norwich NOR 10Y. *T:* Saxthorpe 362. *Clubs:* Travellers', Farmers'.

**HOBSON, Alfred Dennis,** MA; FRSE; FZS; FIBiol; retired as Professor of Zoology, University of Newcastle upon Tyne (formerly King's College, University of Durham) and Hon. Director of Dove Marine Laboratory, Cullercoats (1932-66); now Emeritus Professor; *b* 25 July 1901; *o s* of late Alfred Edward Hobson and Anna Maria Magdalen Kershaw; *m* 1924, Mary Gladys Petra Paula, *o d* of late John Woods, Walton-le-Dale; no *c. Educ:* Highgate Sch.; Christ's Coll., Cambridge. Natural Sciences Tripos, Part I Class II and Part II Class II, Frank Smart Prizeman, 1923. Asst in Dept of Zoology, University Coll., London, 1923-25; Lecturer in Experimental Zoology, University of Edinburgh, 1925-32; Ray Lankester Investigator at the Marine Laboratory, Plymouth, 1928-29. A Vice-Pres. of Natural History Soc. of Northumberland, Durham and Newcastle upon Tyne. *Publications:* scientific papers, chiefly on experimental cytology and parasitology, in Proc. RSE, Jl of Experimental Biology, etc. *Recreations:* reading, philately. *Address:* 13 Kingsland, Newcastle upon Tyne 2. *T:* Newcastle 81.1689.

**HOBSON, Basil;** *see* Hobson, J. B.

**HOBSON, Harold;** consulting engineer; *b* 1 June 1891; *s* of John Atkinson and Florence Edgar Hobson; *m* 1914, Coralie Jeyes von Werner (*d* 1946); one *s* one *d*; *m* 1948, Margaret Hand (*née* Busvine). *Educ:* private schs in England and USA; King's Coll., London. Cons. Engineer with Merz and McLellan of 32 Victoria Street, 1914-25; Joint Manager, County of London Electric Supply Co. Ltd, 1925-28; Commercial Manager, Central Electricity Bd, 1928-35, Gen. Manager, 1935-44, Chm., 1944-47. *Recreation:* gardening. *Address:* 47 Montagu Square, W1. *T:* 01-262 5986; The Pastures, Hilton, Hunts. *T:* Papworth St Agnes 285. *Club:* Reform.

**HOBSON, Harold;** Dramatic Critic, The Sunday Times, since 1947; London Literary Editor, The Christian Science Monitor, since 1946; *b* Thorpe Hesley, near Rotherham, 4 Aug. 1904; *o s* of late J. and late Minnie Hobson; *m* 1935, Gladys Bessie (Elizabeth), *e d* of late James Johns; one *d*. *Educ:* privately; Oriel Coll., Oxford. Dramatic Critic, The Christian Science Monitor, 1932-; Asst Literary Editor, The Sunday Times, 1942-48; TV Critic, The Listener, 1947-51. Chevalier of the Legion of Honour (resigned 1968 in protest against dismissal of Jean-Louis Barrault from Théâtre de France). *Publications:* The First Three Years of the War, 1942; The Devil in Woodford Wells (novel), 1946; Theatre, 1948; Theatre II, 1950; Verdict at Midnight, 1952; The Theatre Now, 1953; The French Theatre of Today, 1953; (ed) The International Theatre Annual, 1956, 1957, 1958, 1959, 1960; Ralph Richardson, 1958. *Recreations:* Lord's, contemporary French literature; with his wife as partner plays a baffling game of bridge that is as mysterious in theory as it is startling in execution. *Address:* 905 Nelson House, Dolphin Square, SW1. *Clubs:* Athenæum, MCC.

**HOBSON, (John) Basil,** QC (Kenya, 1950; Nyasaland, 1953); **His Honour Judge Hobson;** a Deputy Chairman, Essex Quarter Sessions, 1964-68; Deputy Chairman, NE London Quarter Sessions, since 1968; *b* 1905; *s* of late J. D. Hobson, QC, Trinidad, British West Indies, and late Cecilia (*née* Johnstone); *m* 1932, Ursula, *y d* of late William Collie, Trinidad; no *c*. *Educ:* Sherborne. Solicitor, 1929; Dep. Registrar, Supreme Court, Trinidad, 1936; admitted Middle Temple and called to Bar, 1938; Crown Counsel, Uganda, 1939. Served War of 1939-45, King's African Rifles, 1939-41; Dep. Judge-Advocate, East Africa Command, 1941-44; Solicitor-Gen., Kenya, 1947; MLC, Kenya, 1947-51; Chm., Labour Advisory Board, Kenya, 1948-49; Attorney-Gen., MEC and MLC, Nyasaland, 1951-57; acted Chief Justice, April-Nov. 1954; Chm. Commn on Fishing Industry, 1956; Chm. Select Cttee on Non-African Agriculture, 1957. *Recreation:* watching cricket. *Address:* 5 Essex Court, Temple, EC4. *T:* 01-353 0366. *Clubs:* MCC, XL.

**HOBSON, Lawrence John,** CMG 1965; OBE 1960; with British Petroleum Co. Ltd since 1966; *b* 4 May 1921; *er s* of John Sinton Hobson and Marion Adelaide Crawford; *m* 1946, Patricia Fiona Rosemary Beggs (*née* Green); one step *s* (one *s* decd). *Educ:* Taunton Sch.; St Catharine's Coll., Cambridge. BA 1946, MA 1950. Served War, 1941-42. ADC and Private Sec. to Gov., Aden, 1942; Political Officer, 1944; Asst Chief Sec., 1956; Aden govt Student Liaison Officer, UK, 1960-62; Political Adviser to High Comr, Aden, 1963-66; retired from HMOCS, 1966. *Address:* Saffron House, Stanford Dingley, near Reading, Berks. *T:* Bradfield 536. *Club:* Bath.

**HOBSON, Neville,** MC; JP; Solicitor, Beverley; Director, Municipal Mutual Insurance Ltd; *b* 13 April 1886; *s* of Charles William Hobson, Solicitor, and Louisa Elizabeth Hobson; *m* 1919, Sarah Kathleen Darneley (*d* 1965); two *s* one *d*. *Educ:* Beverley Gram. Sch.; Bridlington Sch. Hons, Law Soc., 1908. Served European War, 1914-18, enlisted Yorks Regt, 1914; Lieut West Riding Regt, 1915; Capt. and Adjutant, 19th London Regt, 1916; HQ Staff, 60th Div., in France, Balkans and Palestine, 1917 (despatches, MC). Chm., Rural District Councils Assoc. of England and Wales, 1947-52; Rep. Rural District Councils before several Royal Commissions and Departmental Cttees; Mem. of Rly Assessment Authority, 1936-48. Founded CLB and Boys' Club, Beverley, 1908; original mem. of National Fitness Council; York Diocesan Lay Reader. Hon. Freedom, Borough of Beverley, 1958; Mayor of Beverley, 1966; Pres., Yorks Parish Councils Assoc., 1967. *Publications:* ABC of Rating and Valuation, 1925; The Bridge Players' Note Book, 1926; Bankruptcy and Deeds of Arrangement, 1931; A Treasury of Inspiration, 1934; Unity, Peace and Concord, 1940; The Borough, Urban and Rural Councillor, 1947; Law of Town and Country Planning, 1948; (Supervising Ed.), Hobson's Local Government, 1951; Reflections, 1964. *Recreations:* Youth Club activities, music. *Address:* North Bar Without, Beverley, E Yorks. *TA:* Beverley. *T:* Beverley 881618, 882278.

**HOBSON, Sidney;** business and company director; Lord Mayor of Nottingham, 1954-55; *b* 29 Sept. 1887; *s* of James and Mary A. Hobson; *m* 1919, Hilda Mary (*née* Scanlan) (*d* 1965); one *s* one *d*. *Educ:* Nottingham. President: Nottingham City Business Club, 1927-28; Nottingham Rotary Club, 1931-32; National Wood Box & Packing Makers Federation, 1943-44; Chm., Joint Industrial Council Wood Box & Packing Makers Federation, 1943-44. Councillor, Nottingham City, 1943; Alderman, 1957-58. Sheriff of Nottingham, 1951-52. *Recreation:* fishing. *Address:* 9a Villiers Road, Woodthorpe, Nottingham. *T:* 65437. *Club:* Nottingham Borough.

**HOBSON, Valerie Babette Louise, (Mrs Profumo);** film and stage actress; *b* Larne, Ireland; *d* of Comdr R. G. Hobson, RN, and Violette Hamilton-Willoughby; *m* 1st, 1939, Anthony James Allan Havelock-Allan (marr. diss. 1952), *qv*; two *s*; 2nd, 1954, John Dennis Profumo, *qv*; one *s*. *Educ:* St Augustine's Priory, London; Royal Academy of Dramatic Art. Was trained from early age to become ballet dancer; first stage appearance at Drury Lane in Ball at the Savoy, aged 15. The King and I, Drury Lane, 1953. First film, Badgers Green; went to Hollywood and appeared in Werewolf of London, Bride of Frankenstein, The Mystery of Edwin Drood, etc; at 18 returned to England. Films include: The Drum, This Man is News, This Man in Paris, The Spy in Black, Q Planes, Silent Battle, Contraband, Unpublished Story, Atlantic Ferry, The Adventures of Tartu, The Years Between, Great Expectations, Blanche Fury, The Small Voice, Kind Hearts and Coronets, Train of Events, Interrupted Journey, The Rocking Horse Winner, The Card, Who Goes There?, Meet Me Tonight, The Voice of Merrill, Background, Knave of Hearts.

*Recreations:* dancing, writing, reading, painting.

**HOBSON, Prof. William,** BSc (1st Cl. Hons), MD (Dist.), DPH (Dist.), Leeds; MRCS; LRCP; Chief, Staff Training, World Health Organization Headquarters, Geneva since 1968; *b* 5 Sept. 1911; *s* of William Hobson, The Langdales, Park Lane, Leeds; *m* 1937, Lucy Muriel Wilson; one *s* one *d*; *m* 1953, Heather McMahon Greer; one *d*. *Educ:* Fulneck; Bradford Grammar Sch.; Leeds Univ. Lecturer in Physiology and Hygiene, University of Leeds, 1936-38; Asst Sch. Medical Officer, Leeds, 1938-39; Asst County MO, Hants CC, 1939-40; Medical Officer of Health Borough of Lymington, Hants, 1940-42. Major, RAMC, 1942-46 (despatches). Senior Lecturer in Preventive Medicine, University of Bristol, 1946-48; Prof. of Social and Industrial Medicine, University of Sheffield, 1949-58; Chief, Educn and Training, WHO European Office, 1958-68. WHO visiting Prof. to India, 1957-58. *Publications:* The Health of the Elderly at Home (with J. Pemberton), 1955; (ed) Modern Trends in Geriatrics, 1956; (ed) Theory and Practice of Public Health, 1961, 1965, and 1969; World Health and History, 1963; contribs to Jl of Hygiene, BMJ. Jl of Phys. Med., Jl of Social Med., Bristol Med. Chir. Jl, Jl Med. Chir. Soc., The Naturalist, etc. *Recreation:* ornithology. *Address:* 23 Avenue de Budé, Genève, Suisse. *T:* Genève 33.54.19.

**HOCHHAUSER, Victor;** impresario; *b* 27 March 1923; *m* 1949, Lilian Hochhauser (*née* Shields); three *s* one *d*. *Educ:* City of London Coll. Impresario for: David Oistrakh; Sviatoslav Richter; Mstislav Rostropovich; Gilels, Kogan; Bolshoi Ballet season at Covent Garden, 1963, 1969; Leningrad State Kirov Ballet, Covent Garden, 1961, 1966, Royal Festival Hall, 1970; Moscow Philharmonic; Leningrad Philharmonic, and all other Soviet musicians, folk dance companies and classical dance companies; regular Sunday Evening Concerts, Royal Albert Hall. *Recreations:* reading, swimming, sleeping. *Address:* 4 Holland Park Avenue, W11. *T:* 01-727 0781.

**HOCHOY, Sir Solomon,** TC, GCMG 1962 (KCMG 1959; CMG 1957); GCVO 1966; OBE 1952; Governor-General and C-in-C of Trinidad and Tobago, since Aug. 1962 (Governor, 1960-62); *b* Jamaica, 20 April 1905; *m* 1935, Thelma Edna Huggins; one adopted *d*. *Educ:* St Mary's Coll., Port-of-Spain, Trinidad. Trinidad Government: Clerk, 1928-44; Labour Officer, 1944-46; Deputy Industrial Adviser, 1946-49; Commissioner of Labour, 1949-55; Deputy Colonial Sec., 1955-56; Chief Sec., Trinidad and Tobago, 1956-60. KStJ 1961. *Recreation:* fishing. *Address:* Governor-General's House, Port-of-Spain, Trinidad. *Clubs:* Royal Commonwealth Society, Corona; Clipper (International).

**HOCKADAY, Arthur Patrick,** CMG 1969; Assistant Under-Secretary of State, Ministry of Defence, since 1969; *b* 17 March 1926; *s* of William Ronald Hockaday and Marian Camilla Hockaday, *d* of Rev. A. C. Evans; *m* 1955, Peggy, *d* of H. W. Prince. *Educ:* Merchant Taylors' Sch.; St John's Coll., Oxford. BA (1st cl. Lit. Hum.) 1949, MA 1952. Apptd to Home Civil Service, 1949; Admty, 1949-62; Private Sec. to successive Ministers of Defence and Defence Secretaries, 1962-65; NATO Internat. Staff, 1965-69 (Asst Sec. Gen. for Defence Planning and Policy, 1967-69). *Address:* 2 Toll-Gate Drive, Dulwich, SE21. *T:* 01-693 1773.

**HOCKENHULL, Arthur James Weston,** OBE 1966; HBM Consul-General, Houston, Texas, since 1969; *b* 8 Aug. 1915; *s* of late Frederick Weston Hockenhull and late Jessie Gibson Kaye Hockenhull (*née* Mitchell); *m* 1955, Rachel Ann Kimber; two *d*. *Educ:* Clifton Coll.; Exeter Coll., Oxford. HM Overseas Civil Service; various appts in Far East, Cyprus and British Guiana, 1936-57. Interned by Japanese, in Singapore, 1942-45; First Sec., UK Commn, Singapore, 1958-63; Counsellor, British High Commn, Malaysia, 1964-68. *Recreations:* golf, gardening, swimming. *Address:* 930 Kirby Drive, Houston, Texas, USA. *T:* 713-522-6535. *Club:* Oxford and Cambridge University.

**HOCKING, Frederick Denison Maurice;** Cornwall County Pathologist; Consulting Biologist and Toxicologist, Devon River Board; late Consulting Pathologist, South-Western Regional Hospital Board; Acting Director Public Health Laboratory Service, Cornwall, and other hospitals in Cornwall; late Chemical Pathologist, Biochemist, and Assistant Pathologist, Westminster Hospital; Lecturer in General and Clinical Pathology, Westminster Hospital Medical School, University of London; *b* 28 Feb. 1899; *o s* of late Rev. Almund Trevosso Hocking and Gertrude Vernon Mary, *o d* of J. Parkinson; *m* 1st, 1927, Amy Gladys (*d* 1956), *y d* of A. T. Coucher; two *d*; 2nd, 1957, Kathleen, *e d* of Dr G. P. O'Donnell. *Educ:* High Sch., Leytonstone; City and Guilds of London Coll., Finsbury; Middlesex Hospital Medical Sch. RN Experimental and Ant-gas Station, 1917-18; Asst Laboratory Dir to the Clinical Research Assoc. mb, BS, BSc, MSc London, MRCS, LRCP, FRIC, FCS, FRMS; FRSA, MIBiol, FRSH. associate of the City and Guilds of London Tech. Coll., Finsbury; Member: Pathological Soc. of Great Britain and Ireland; Association of Clinical Pathologists (Councillor, 1944-46); Society of Public Analysts; Medico-Legal Society; Brit. Assoc. in Forensic Medicine; Court, Univ. of Exeter (representing Royal Institute of Chemistry); Pres. South-Western Branch, British Medical Association, 1946; Chm. South-Western Branch, RIC, 1955-57; Mem. Council, RIC, 1959-62, 1965-68. Consulting Biologist, Devon River Bd. Mem. Brit. Acad. of Forensic Sciences; Mem. Soc. for Forensic Science. *Publications:* The Employment of Uranium in the Treatment of Malignant New Growths, British Empire Cancer Campaign International Conference, London, 1928; Disseminated Sclerosis (with Sir James Purves-Stewart); Delayed Death due to Suicidal Hanging; Hanging and Manual Strangulation; Seaside Accidents; numerous scientific papers in medical journals, etc. *Recreations:* motoring, golf, sailing, hotels, good food. *Address:* Strathaven, Carlyon Bay, Cornwall.

**HOCKING, Philip Norman;** *b* 27 Oct. 1925; *s* of Fred Hocking, FIOB; *m* 1950, Joan Mable, *d* of Horace Ernest Jackson, CBE, Birmingham; three *d*. *Educ:* King Henry VIII Sch., Coventry; Birmingham Sch. of Architecture. Dir, F. Hocking & Sons Ltd. Mem. Coventry City Council, 1955-60. Prominent Mem. Young Con. Movement. MP (C) Coventry South, 1959-64; PPS to Minister of State, FO, 1963-64. Contested Coventry S, 1964 and 1966. Chm., Conservative Back Benchers' Housing and Local Govt Cttee, 1962-64. *Recreations:* gardening and sailing. *Address:* Tudor Grange, Warwick Road, Coventry. *T:* Coventry 27930. *Club:* Junior Carlton.

**HOCKLEY, Anthony Heritage F.;** *see* Farrar-Hockley.

**HOCKNEY, David;** artist; *b* 9 July 1937; *s* of Kenneth and Laura Hockney. *Educ:* Bradford

Grammar Sch.; Bradford Sch. of Art; Royal Coll. of Art. One-man shows: Kasmin Ltd, London, 1963, 1965, 1966, 1968, 1969; Alan Gallery, New York, 1964-67; Stedlijk Museum, Amsterdam, 1966; Whitworth Gallery, Manchester, 1969, etc; Retrospective Exhibn, Whitechapel Art Gall., 1970. 1st Prize, John Moores Exhibn, Liverpool, 1967. *Publication:* (ed and illustrated) 14 Poems of C. P. Cavafy, 1967. *Address:* c/o Kasmin Ltd, 118 New Bond Street, W1. *Club:* Le Duce.

**HODD, Ven. Henry Norman,** TD 1949; MA; Archdeacon of Blackburn since 1962; *b* 8 May 1905; *s* of Rev. Francis Arnold and Elizabeth Hodd; *m* 1930, Violet Murray Kennedy MacIntyre; two *s*. *Educ:* St Peter's Sch., York; Keble Coll., Oxford; Westcott House, Cantab. Curate, Leeds Parish Church, 1929-32; Senior Curate, Christ Church, Harrogate, 1932-35; Vicar, University Church, Leeds, 1935-42; Chaplain to the Forces, TA, 1937; Active Service, 1939-45; Staff Chaplain HQ Northern Command, 1942-45; Vicar and Rural Dean: Retford, 1945-51; Mansfield, 1951-59; Hon. Canon, Southwell, 1953; Adviser on Christian Stewardship to the Church of England, 1959-62. *Publications:* Prayers for Stewardship Campaigns, 1960; Before His Face, 1960. *Recreations:* occasional golf, and sea fishing. *Address:* Balderstone Vicarage, near Blackburn, Lancs. *T:* Mellor 2232. *Club:* District and Union (Blackburn).

**HODDER-WILLIAMS, Paul,** OBE 1945; TD; Publisher; Chairman: Matthew Hodder Ltd, 1961; Hodder & Stoughton Ltd; The Lancet Ltd; Brockhampton Press Ltd; Director: University of London Press Ltd; The English Universities Press Ltd; *b* 29 Jan. 1910; *s* of late Frank Garfield Hodder Williams, sometime Dean of Manchester, and Sarah Myfanwy (*née* Nicholson); *m* 1936, Felicity, 2nd *d* of late C. M. Blagden, DD, sometime Bishop of Peterborough; two *s* two *d*. *Educ:* Rugby; Gonville and Caius Coll., Cambridge (MA). Joined Hodder & Stoughton Ltd, 1931; Dir, 1936. Served with HAC (Major, 1942), 99th (London Welsh) HAA Regt RA (Lt-Col Comdg, 1942-45). *Recreations:* gardening, walking. *Address:* Court House, Exford, Minehead, Somerset. *T:* Exford 268.

**HODDINOTT, Alun,** DMus Wales; Professor of Music, University College of South Wales and Monmouthshire, since 1967; *b* 11 Aug. 1929; *s* of Thomas Ivor Hoddinott and Gertrude Jones; *m* 1953, Beti Rhiannon Huws; one *s*. *Educ:* University Coll. of S Wales and Mon. Lecturer: Cardiff Coll. of Music and Drama, 1951-59; University Coll. of S Wales and Mon, 1959-65; Reader, University of Wales, 1965-67. Mem., Welsh Arts Council, 1968-. Artistic Dir, Cardiff Music Festival. Governor: Welsh Nat. Theatre, 1968-; Cardiff Coll. of Music and Drama, 1968-. Walford Davies Prize, 1954; Arnold Bax Medal, 1957. *Publications: symphonies:* 1955, 1962, 1968, 1969; *concertos for:* clarinet, 1951; oboe, 1954; harp, 1958; viola, 1958; piano, 1940, 1960, 1967; violin, 1961; organ, 1967; horn, 1969; *sonatas for:* piano, 1959, 1962, 1965, 1966, 1968; harp, 1964; clarinet, 1967; violin, 1969, 1970; cellos, 1970; *other compositions:* Nocturne, 1951; Welsh Dances, 1958, 2nd suite 1969, Investiture Dances 1969; 2nd Nocturne, 1959; Two Welsh Nursery Tunes, 1959; Sextet, 1960; Rebecca, 1962; Septet, 1962; Folk Song Suite, 1962; Sonatina, 1963; Variations, 1963; Medieval Songs, 1963; Divertimento, 1963; Danegeld, 1964; 4 Welsh Songs, 1964; Dives and Lazarus, 1965; String Quartet, 1965; Concerto Grosso, 1965; Variants, 1966; Night music, 1966; Suite for harp, 1967; Aubade, 1967; Roman Dream, 1968; Nocturnes and Cadenzas, 1968; Divertimenti for 8 instruments, 1968; Sinfonietta, 1968, no 2, 1969, no 3, 1970; Fioriture, 1968; An apple tree and a pig, 1968; Black Bart, 1968; and numerous other shorter works. *Address:* Maesawelon, Mill Road, Lisvane, Cardiff. *Clubs:* East India and Sports; Cardiff and County (Cardiff).

**HODGE, Alan;** Joint Editor of History Today since 1951; *b* 16 Oct. 1915; *s* of late Capt. T. S. Hodge, RD, RNR; *m* 1948, Jane, *d* of Conrad Potter Aiken, *qv*; two *d*. *Educ:* Liverpool Collegiate Sch.; Oriel Coll., Oxford. Asst Private Sec. to Minister of Information, 1941-45. Editor of The Novel Library (Hamish Hamilton), 1946-52. *Publications:* (with Robert Graves) The Long Week-End, 1940; The Reader Over Your Shoulder, 1943; (with Peter Quennell) The Past We Share, 1960. *Address:* 6 Lancaster Road, SW19. *T:* 01-946 4101.

**HODGE, Alexander Mitchell,** GC 1940; VRD; Captain RNVR, retired; WS; Member of firm of Cowan & Stewart, WS, Edinburgh; *b* 23 June 1916; *y s* of James Mackenzie Hodge, Blairgowrie, Perthshire; *m* 1944, Pauline Hester Winsome, *o d* of William John Hill, Bristol; one *s* two *d*. *Educ:* Fettes Coll.; Edinburgh Univ. (MA 1936, LLB 1938). Joined RNVR, 1938; served with Royal Navy, 1939-45 (despatches, GC). Comdr RNVR, 1949, Capt. RNVR, 1953; CO of the Forth Div. RNVR, 1953-57. Chm., Edinburgh Dist Sea Cadet Cttee, 1959-63; Chm., Lady Haig's Poppy Factory, 1961-67; Mem. Council, Earl Haig Fund (Scotland), 1963-67; Chm., Edinburgh Western Gen. Hosp. Assoc. of Friends, 1962-68; Trustee and Mem. Cttee of Management: Royal Victoria Hosp. Tuberculosis Trust, 1964- (Pres., 1970-); Royal Edinburgh Inst. for Sailors, Soldiers and Airmen, 1964-; Chm. General Comrs of Income Tax, Edinburgh South Div., 1967-; Pres., Edinburgh Chamber of Commerce, 1968-70; Dir, The Cruden Foundn, 1969-; Governor, Fettes Coll., 1970-. dep. Chm., Standard Life Assurance Co. *Address:* Springbank, Barnton, Midlothian. *T:* 031-336 3054. *Clubs:* Royal Automobile; New (Edinburgh).

**HODGE, John Dennis;** Manager, Advanced Missions Program, National Aeronautics and Space Administration, Manned Spacecraft Center, USA, since 1968; *b* 10 Feb. 1929; *s* of John Charles Henry Hodge and Emily M. Corbett Hodge; *m* 1952, Audrey Cox; two *s* two *d*. *Educ:* Northampton Engineering Coll., University of London (now The City Univ.). Vickers-Armstrong Ltd, Weybridge, England (Aerodynamics Dept), 1950-52; Head, Air Loads Section, Avro Aircraft Ltd, Toronto, Canada, 1952-59; Tech. Asst to Chief, Ops Div., Space Task Group, NASA, Langley Field, Va, USA, 1959; Chief, Flight Control Br., Space Task Group, NASA, 1961; Asst Chief of Flight Control, 1962, Chief, Flight Control Div., Flight Ops Directorate, NASA, MSC, 1963-68. Hon. ScD, The City Univ., London, Eng., 1966; NASA Medal for Exceptional Service, 1966. *Publications:* contribs to NASA publications and various aerospace jls. *Recreation:* reading. *Address:* 501 Falling Leaf, Friendswood, Texas, USA. *T:* HU 2-7151.

**HODGE, John Douglass Vere,** CIE 1929; *b* 17 Oct. 1887; 4th *s* of late Rev. Edward Vere Hodge and Helen, *d* of late John Bacchus, JP; *m* 1920, Elspeth Stuart, 2nd *d* of late Robert Henderson; one *d*. *Educ:* Durham Sch.; Pembroke Coll., Cambridge. Entered Indian Civil Service, 1912; held various posts under

Government of Bengal and Government of India; Deputy Sec. to Government of India, 1926-29; Commissioner, Chittagong Division, Bengal, 1936-38; retired, 1939; Ministry of Home Security, 1939-45; Allied Commn for Austria, 1945-46. *Address:* Anchor Cottage, Portloe, near Truro, Cornwall. *T:* Veryan 359.

**HODGE, John Ernest,** CMG 1962; CVO 1956; QPM 1955; Inspector-General of Police, Republic of Nigeria, 1962-64; *b* 3 Nov. 1911; *s* of late Rev. J. Z. Hodge, DD; *m* 1950, Margaret Henrietta, *d* of late Rev. Hugh Brady Brew, Wicklow; one *s* one *d*. *Educ:* Taunton Sch., Taunton, Som. Jamaica Constabulary, 1931-35; The Nigeria Police, 1935-64. Colonial Police Medal, 1953. OStJ 1961. *Recreation:* golf. *Address:* Netherlea, Dirleton, East Lothian, Scotland. *T:* Dirleton 272. *Clubs:* Royal Over-Seas League; North Berwick.

**HODGE, Sir John Rowland,** 2nd Bt *cr* 1921; MBE 1940; FRHS; company director; *b* 1 May 1913; *s* of Sir Rowland Hodge, 1st Bt, and Mabel (*d* 1923), *d* of William Edward Thorpe; *S* father, 1950; *m* 1936, Peggy Ann (marr. diss. 1939), *o d* of Sydney Raymond Kent; *m* 1939, Joan (marr. diss. 1961), *o d* of late Sydney Foster Wilson; three *d*; *m* 1967, Vivien Jill, *d* of A. S. Knightley; one *s*. *Educ:* Wrekin Coll.; Switzerland. Served War of 1939-45, RNVR; Lt-Comdr, RNVR, 1938; formerly Oxford and Bucks Light Infantry. Mem. Inst. of Directors. *Heir: s* Andrew Rowland Hodge, *b* 3 Dec. 1968. *Address:* Casa Toro, St Andrews, Malta. *T:* 37583. *Clubs:* British Racing Drivers, Naval, Royal Motor Yacht, Royal Yachting Association, Cruising Association.
*See also Sir R. S. Isaacson.*

**HODGE, Sir Julian Stephen Alfred,** Kt 1970; Merchant banker; Chairman and Managing Director, Hodge Group Ltd; Chairman: Julian S. Hodge & Co. Ltd; Gwent & West of England Enterprises Ltd; Anglo Auto Finance Co. Ltd; Reliant Motor Group; Hodge Life Assurance Co. Ltd; Deputy Chairman and Managing Director, Hodge Unit Trust Managers Ltd; Financial Director: Avana Group Ltd; L. Ryan Holdings Ltd; *b* 15 Oct. 1904; *s* of late Alfred and Jane Hodge; *m* 1951, Moira (*née* Thomas); two *s* one *d*. *Educ:* Cardiff Technical Coll. Certified Accountant, 1930. Founded Hodge & Co., Accountants and Auditors. Founder and Trustee: The Jane Hodge Foundation, 1962-; The Julian S. Hodge Charitable Trust, 1964; Chm., Aberfan Disaster Fund Industrial Project Sub-Cttee; Member: Welsh Economic Council, 1965-68; Welsh Council, 1968; Council, Univ. of Wales Inst. of Science and Technology (Treasurer, 1968-); Foundation Fund Cttee, Univ. of Surrey; Management Cttee, Finance Houses Assoc. Pres., E Glamorgan Dist, St John Ambulance Bde. Governor, All Hallows (Cranmore Hall) Sch. Trust Ltd. Treasurer, Coleg Harlech. FTII 1941. OStJ. *Publication:* Paradox of Financial Preservation, 1959. *Recreations:* golf, walking, reading, gardening. *Address:* (business) 31 Windsor Place, Cardiff; (home) Ty Gwyn, Lisvane, Cardiff. *T:* Cardiff 752773. *Club:* Royal Automobile.

**HODGE, Stephen Oswald Vere,** CMG 1942; *b* 14 July 1891; *s* of late Rev. C. F. D. Hodge; *m* 1919; three *s*. *Educ:* Durham Sch.; Christ Church, Oxford. Served European War 1914-18, Lieut unattached list 1915-18 (despatches). Asst Dist Commissioner, Kenya, 1913; Sen. Dist Commissioner, 1935; MLC, Kenya, 1937-45; Provincial Comr, Kenya, 1939-46; retd, 1946. Provincial Comdt, Kenya Police Reserve, Rift Valley Prov., Kenya, 1952-53; Staff Officer to Prov. Comr, Rift Valley Prov., Kenya, 1953-54. *Address:* Sidai, PO Box 183, Nakuru, Kenya. *T:* Subukia 4Y10 (Kenya). *Clubs:* Royal Commonwealth Society; Muthaiga Country (Nairobi); Rift Valley Sports (Nakuru).

**HODGE, Sir William (Vallance Douglas),** Kt 1959; FRS 1938; MA, ScD; FRSE; Lowndean Professor of Astronomy and Geometry, Cambridge University, 1936-70; Master of Pembroke College, 1958-70 (Fellow, 1935-58, Hon. Fellow since 1970); *b* 17 June 1903; *s* of Archibald James Hodge and Janet Vallance; *m* 1929, Kathleen Anne Cameron; one *s* one *d*. *Educ:* George Watson's Coll. and University, Edinburgh; St John's Coll., Cambridge. Smith's Prizeman, 1927; Lecturer, Bristol Univ., 1926-31; Fellow of St John's Coll., 1930-33; 1851 Exhibtiion, Senior Studentship, 1931; University Lecturer, Cambridge, 1933-36; Visiting Lectr Harvard Univ., 1950; Pres. London Math. Soc., 1947-49; Pres. Cambridge Phil. Soc., 1947-49; Pres. Math. Assoc., 1955; Vice-Pres. Internat. Math. Union, 1954-58; Physical Sec. of Royal Society, 1957-65 (Vice-Pres. 1959-65); Pres. Internat. Congress of Mathematicians, 1958. Hon. Fellow, St John's Coll., Cambridge, 1964. For. Hon. Mem., Amer. Acad. of Arts and Sciences, 1958; For. Member: Amer. Phil. Soc.; Royal Danish Acad., 1966; For. Associate, Amer. Nat. Acad. Sci., 1959. Adams Prize, 1937; Berwick Prize, London Math. Soc. 1952; Royal Medal of Royal Society, 1957; De Morgan Medal, London Math. Soc., 1959; Grunning Victoria Jubilee Prize, Royal Society of Edinburgh, 1969. Hon. LLD Edinburgh, 1958; Hon. DSc: Bristol, 1958; Leicester, 1959; Sheffield, 1960; Exeter, 1961; Wales, 1961; Liverpool, 1961. *Publications:* Theory and Application of Harmonic Integrals, 1941 (2nd edn, 1952); (with D. Pedoe) Methods of Algebraic Geometry, vol. i, 1947, vol. ii, 1952, vol. iii, 1954; numerous papers in British and foreign mathematical jls. *Address:* 16 Amhurst Court, Grange Road, Cambridge. *Club:* Athenæum.

**HODGES, Rt. Rev. Evelyn Charles,** DD; *b* Towlerton House, Co. Carlow, 8 Aug. 1887; *s* of Rev. W. H. Hodges; *m* 1927, Violet Blanche, *d* of George Hill Crawford, Dublin; one *s* one *d*. *Educ:* Rathmines; Mountjoy; Trinity Coll., Dublin (BA, Moderator, Large Gold Medal, 1910, MA 1913, BD 1923, 2nd Class Divinity Testimonium 1911, Higher Diploma on Education 1920). Curate Asst of Drumcondra and North Strand, Dublin, 1911-14; of Rathmines, Dublin, 1914-17; Diocesan Inspector of Schs (Dublin, Glendalough and Kildare), 1917-24; Incumbent of Rathmines, 1924-28; Principal of Church of Ireland Training Coll (for Teachers), 1928-43; Canon of St Patrick's Cathedral, Dublin, 1934-43; Bishop of Limerick, Ardfert, and Aghadoe, 1943-60, retired. *Address:* 16 Stillorgan Park, Blackrock, Co. Dublin.

**HODGES, Herbert Arthur;** Professor of Philosophy in the University of Reading, 1934-69; Emeritus since 1969; *b* 4 Jan. 1905; *s* of Willis Hodges and Lily Malaingre Dyson; *m* 1939, Vera Joan, *y d* of late Rev. John Willis; two *s* one *d*. *Educ:* King Edward VII Sch., Sheffield; Balliol Coll., Oxford (Classical Scholar). Craven Scholar, 1923; First Class in Honour Moderations, 1924; First class in Literae Humaniores, and BA, 1926; John Locke Scholar, War Memorial Student of Balliol Coll., and Senior Demy of Magdalen Coll., 1926; Lecturer in Philosophy at New Coll., 1927; Lecturer in Philosophy in the University of Reading, 1928; MA, DPhil, 1932. Mem. of Royal Commission on Betting, Lotteries and Gaming, 1949-51; Master, Guild of St George, 1954-. *Publications:* Wilhelm Dilthey: an Introduction, 1944; Christianity and the Modern World View, 1949; The Philosophy of Wilhelm Dilthey, 1952; Languages, Standpoints and Attitudes, 1953; Anglicanism and Orthodoxy, 1955; The Pattern of Atonement, 1955; Death and Life have Contended, 1964; (with A. M. Allchin) A Rapture of Praise, 1966; articles in philosophical and theological journals. *Recreations:* listening to music, gardening. *Address:* 8 Mansfield Road, Reading RG1 6AJ. *T:* Reading 53560.

**HODGES, Air Marshal Sir Lewis (Macdonald),** KCB 1968 (CB 1963); CBE 1958; DSO 1944 and Bar 1945; DFC 1942 and Bar 1943; Air Member for Personnel, Ministry of Defence, since 1970; *b* 1 March 1918; *s* of late Arthur Macdonald Hodges and Gladys Mildred Hodges; *m* 1950, Elizabeth Mary, *e d* of G. H. Blackett, MC; two *s*. *Educ:* St Paul's Sch.; RAF Coll., Cranwell. Bomber Command, 1938-44; SE Asia (India, Burma, Ceylon), 1944-45; Palestine, 1945-47; Air Ministry and Min. of Defence, 1948-52; Bomber Command, 1952-59; Asst Comdt, RAF Coll., Cranwell, 1959-61; AO i/c Admin., Middle East Comd, Aden, 1961-63; Imperial Def. Coll., 1963; SHAPE, 1964-65; Ministry of Defence, 1965; Asst Chief of Air Staff (Ops) 1965-68; AOC-in-C, RAF Air Support Comd, 1968-70. Légion d'Honneur (French) 1950; Croix de Guerre (French) 1944. *Recreation:* sailing. *Address:* Allens House, Plaxtol, near Sevenoaks, Kent. *T:* Plaxtol 255. *Clubs:* Royal Air Force, United Service.

**HODGES, Captain Michael,** CB 1968; OBE 1946; Royal Navy (retired); Under-Secretary, Cabinet Office, 1964-68; *b* 8 Sept. 1904; *s* of Admiral Sir Michael Hodges, KCB, CMG, MVO, and Lady Hodges (*née* Tiarks); *m* 1946, Heather Hayes; one *s*. *Educ:* RN Colleges Osborne and Dartmouth. Entered Royal Navy, 1918; specialised in Signals, 1928; Fleet Signal Officer, Mediterranean, 1936-38; Chief Signal Officer, Combined Ops, 1942-44; Signal Officer-in-Chief, SE Asia, 1944-45. Dep. Dir of Signals, Admiralty, 1948-50. Invalided from RN and joined Civil Service, 1950; Under-Sec., Ministry of Defence, 1962-64. CEng; Fellow, Instn of Electronic and Radio Engineers. *Address:* 2 Elystan Mansions, SW3. *T:* 01-584 9391/2972. *Club:* Senior United Service.

**HODGES, Sir Reginald (John),** Kt 1951; JP; *b* 21 March 1889; *s* of late William Abraham Hodges, East Bridgford, Notts; *m* 1st, 1918, Doris Rhona Buchanan; one *d*; 2nd, 1930, Gwendoline Jeanie Buchanan (*d* 1961); 3rd, 1963, Mrs Claudia Roberts (*née* Lucas). *Educ:* Sedbergh Sch.; Trinity Coll., Oxford (MA); Grootfontein Sch. of Agriculture, Middelburg, Cape Province. Served European War in Egypt, Palestine, France, in Denbigh (Hussars) Yeomanry, 1914-18; Cunard Steam Ship Co., Ltd, 1919-30; Manager and, later, Dir of Anchor Line (Henderson Bros) Ltd, 1930-35; Asst General Manager, Mersey Docks and Harbour Board, 1935-39; Deputy General Manager, 1939-41; General Manager and Secretary, Mersey Docks and Harbour Board, 1941-54. Past Dir, British Insulated Callender's Cables Ltd; Dir, Humphreys Ltd. OStJ 1954. *Address:* Waverley House, Edgeworth, near Stroud, Glos. *T:* Miserden 340. *Club:* Royal Liverpool Golf (Hoylake).

**HODGINS, Ven. Michael Minden;** Archdeacon of Hackney since 1951; Secretary of London Diocesan Fund since 1946; *b* 26 Aug. 1912; *yr s* of late Major R. Hodgins, Indian Army, and Margaret Hodgins (*née* Wilson); unmarried. *Educ:* Wellington; Cuddesdon Theological Coll. Deacon, 1939; Priest, 1940; Asst Curate, S Barnabas, Northolt Park; Asst Secretary, London Diocesan Fund, 1943. MA Lambeth 1960. *Address:* 33 Bedford Square, WC1. *T:* 01-636 4155; St Mary's House, White Church Lane, Whitechapel, E1 7QR. *T:* 01-247 9683. *Club:* Reform.

**HODGKIN, Alan Lloyd,** FRS 1948; MA, ScD Cantab; Fellow of Trinity College, Cambridge, since 1936; John Humphrey Plummer Professor of Biophysics, University of Cambridge, since 1970; *b* 5 Feb. 1914; *s* of G. L. Hodgkin and M. F. Wilson; *m* 1944, Marion de Kay, *d* of late F. P. Rous; one *s* three *d*. *Educ:* Gresham's Sch., Holt; Trinity Coll., Cambridge. Scientific Officer working on Radar for Air Ministry and Min. of Aircraft Production, 1939-45. Lecturer and then Asst Dir of Research at Cambridge, 1945-52. Foulerton Research Prof., Royal Soc., 1952-69. Royal Medal of Royal Society, 1958; Nobel Prize for Medicine (jointly), 1963; Copley Medal of Royal Society, 1965. Mem. Royal Danish Acad. of Sciences, 1964. Pres., Marine Biological Assoc., 1966. For. Mem. Amer. Acad. of Arts and Sciences and Amer. Philosophical Soc.; Member: Leopoldina Acad.; Pontifical Acad. of Sciences, 1968. Hon. MD: Berne, Louvain; Hon. DSc: Sheffield, Newcastle and E Anglia. *Publications:* scientific papers dealing with the Nature of Nervous conduction, Journ. Physiology, etc. *Recreations:* travel and fishing. *Address:* Physiological Laboratory, Cambridge; 25 Newton Road, Cambridge. *T:* Cambridge 59284. *Club:* Athenæum.

**HODGKIN, Dorothy Crowfoot,** OM 1965; FRS 1947; Wolfson Research Professor, Royal Society, since 1960; Fellow of Somerville College, Oxford; *b* 1910; *d* of late J. W. Crowfoot, CBE; *m* 1937, Thomas Hodgkin, *qv*; two *s* one *d*. *Educ:* Sir John Leman Sch., Beccles; Somerville Coll., Oxford. Fellow: Australian Academy of Science, 1968; Akad. Leopoldina, 1968. Foreign Member: Royal Netherlands Academy of Science and Letters, 1956; Amer. Acad. of Arts and Sciences, Boston, 1958. Hon. DSc Leeds and Manchester; Hon. ScD Cambridge. Royal Medallist of the Royal Society, 1956; Nobel Prize for Chemistry, 1964. First Freedom of Beccles, 1965. *Publications:* various. *Recreations:* archæology, walking, children. *Address:* Somerville College, Oxford; 20c Bradmore Road, Oxford. *T:* Oxford 57125.

**HODGKIN, Eliot;** artist and writer; *b* 19 June 1905; *o s* of Charles Ernest Hodgkin and Alice Jane Brooke; *m* 1940, Maria Clara (Mimi) Henderson, (*née* Franceschi); one *s*. *Educ:* Harrow; Royal Academy Schs. Exhibited paintings, October, Royal Academy, 1936, and Undergrowth, Royal Academy, 1943 (both bought under Chantrey Bequest, for Tate Gallery); One Man Shows: London Leicester Galleries, 1956; New York, Durlacher, 1958; London, Arthur Jeffress Gallery, 1959; New York, Durlacher, 1962; London, Reid Gallery, 1963; Agnew's, 1966. *Publications:* She Closed the Door, 1931; Fashion Drawing, 1932; 55 London Views, 1948; A Pictorial Gospel, 1949. *Address:* Flat 12, Campden House Court, Church Street, W8.

**HODGKIN, Thomas Lionel;** Lecturer in the Government of New States, University of Oxford and Senior Research Fellow, Balliol College, Oxford, 1965-70; *b* 3 April 1910; *s* of late R. H. Hodgkin, Provost of Queen's Coll., Oxford, and D. F. Hodgkin, *d* of late A. L. Smith, Master of Balliol; *m* 1937, Dorothy Mary Crowfoot (*see* D. C. Hodgkin); two *s* one *d*. *Educ:* Winchester Coll. (Exhibitioner); Balliol Coll. (Schol.). Sen. Demy, Magdalen Coll., 1932-33; Asst Secretary, Palestine Civil

Service, 1934-36; Education Officer, Cumberland Friends' Unemployment Cttee, 1937-39; Staff Tutor in North Staffs, Oxford University Tutorial Classes Cttee, 1939-45; Sec. to the Oxford University Delegacy for Extra-Mural Studies, and Fellow of Balliol, 1945-52; Visiting Lecturer: Northwestern Univ., Illinois, 1957; University Coll. of Ghana, 1958; Research Associate, Institute of Islamic Studies, McGill Univ., Montreal, 1958-61; Dir, Institute of African Studies, University of Ghana, 1962-65. MA Oxon. *Publications:* Nationalism in Colonial Africa, 1956; Nigerian Perspectives, 1960; African Political Parties, 1961; articles on African affairs. *Recreations:* walking, conversation. *Address:* Crab Mill, Ilmington, Shipston-on-Stour. *T:* Ilmington 233; 20c Bradmore Road, Oxford. *T:* Oxford 57125.

**HODGKINSON, Very Rev. Arthur Edward;** Provost of St Andrew's Cathedral, Aberdeen, since 1965; *b* 29 Oct. 1913; *s* of Arthur and Rose Hodgkinson. *Educ:* Glasgow High School; Edinburgh Theol College. LTh Durham 1942. Deacon 1939; Priest 1940. Curate, St George's, Maryhill, Glasgow, 1939-43; Choir Chaplain, 1943, and Precentor of St Ninian's Cath., Perth, 1944-47; Curate-in-Charge, St Finnian's, Lochgelly, 1947-52, and Rector, 1952-54; Rector, Holy Trinity, Motherwell, 1954-65; Commissary to Bp of St John's, 1961; Canon of St Mary's Cath., Glasgow, 1963-65. Hon. Canon of Christ Church Cathedral, Connecticut, 1965. *Recreations:* motoring, travel. *Address:* Cathedral House, 10 Louisville Avenue, Aberdeen AB1 6TX. *T:* Aberdeen 39684.

**HODGKINSON, Commander Guy Beauchamp,** DSO 1940; RN retired; *b* 11 Jan. 1903; *s* of Commander George Hodgkinson, RN retired, and Helen Blanche Raggett; *m* 1930, Beryl Margaret, *d* of Harry Langley; two *d. Educ:* St Hugh's Sch., Chislehurst; RN Colleges Osborne and Dartmouth. War of 1939-45 (despatches twice, DSO). *Address:* Beech Hill, Frampton Cotterell, Glos.

**HODGKINSON, Terence William Ivan,** CBE 1958; Keeper of Department of Architecture and Sculpture, Victoria and Albert Museum, since 1967; *b* 7 Oct. 1913; *s* of late Ivan Tattersall Hodgkinson, Wells, Som, and of late Kathryn Van Vleck Townsend, New York (who *m* 2nd, 1929, Sir Gilbert Upcott, KCB; he *d* 1967); unmarried. *Educ:* Oundle Sch.; Magdalen Coll., Oxford. Served War of 1939-45 Major, Gen. Staff 1943. Joined staff of Victoria and Albert Museum (Dept of Architecture and Sculpture) 1946; Asst to the Dir, 1948-62; Secretary to the Advisory Council, 1951-67. *Publications:* (part author) Catalogue of Sculpture in the Frick Collection, New York, 1970; Catalogue of Sculpture at Waddesdon Manor, 1970; articles in Burlington Magazine, Bulletin and Yearbook of the Victoria and Albert Museum and for Walpole Society. *Recreation:* music. *Address:* 24 Southwood Lane, N6.

**HODGKINSON, Air Marshal William Derek,** CB 1969; CBE 1960; DFC; AFC; AOC-in-C, Near East Air Force, Commander British Forces Near East, and Administrator of the Soveriegn Base Area, Cyprus, since 1970; *b* 27 Dec. 1917; *s* of late E. N. Hodgkinson; *m* 1939, Nancy Heather Goodwin, Southampton; one *s* one *d. Educ:* Repton. Commnd, 1937; No. 220 Sqdn, 1938-40; POW Germany, 1942-45; OC No. 210 Sqdn, 1947-49; RAF Staff Coll., 1951; Chief Instructor, Jt Austr. Anti Submarine Sch., Nowra, Austr., 1952-54; Directing Staff, Jt Services Staff Coll., 1954-57; OC No. 240 Sqdn, 1957-58; OC RAF St Mawgan, 1960-61; ADC to the Queen, 1961-63; Staff of Chief of Defence Staff, 1961-63; Imp. Def. Coll., 1964; Comdt RAF Staff Coll., Andover, 1965; Assist Chief of the Air Staff, Operational Requirements, 1966-68; SASO, RAF Training Command, 1969-70. *Recreations:* cricket, fishing, painting. *Address:* The Old Rectory, Brampton, Hunts. *T:* Huntingdon 3782. *Clubs:* Royal Air Force, MCC.

**HODGSON, Arthur Brian,** CMG 1962; Director General, British Red Cross Society, Grosvenor Crescent, since 1970; *b* 24 Aug. 1916; *s* of late Major Arthur H. F. Hodgson, Westfields, Iffley, Oxford; *m* 1945, Anne Patricia Halse, *d* of late Lt-Col E. M. Ley, DSO, KRRC; two *s* two *d. Educ:* Edinburgh Academy; Eton Coll.; Oriel Coll., Oxford; Trinity Coll., Cambridge. Colonial Civil Service, Tanganyika Administration, 1939-62, retiring as Principal Sec. and Dir of Establishments. Dep. Dir-Gen., British Red Cross Society, 1966-70. *Recreations:* rowing, rifle shooting, tennis. *Address:* The Red House, West Hoathly, Sussex. *T:* Sharpthorne 416. *Clubs:* East India and Sports, MCC; Leander (Henley-on-Thames).

**HODGSON, His Honour Arthur John;** Judge of County Courts (Kingston and Wandsworth), 1950-60, retired; *b* 23 Aug. 1887; *y s* of Joseph and Emma Hodgson, Higher Bebington, Cheshire; *m* 1918, Ruth Irene Bateman, MB ChB, Kendal, Westmorland; one *d. Educ:* Birkenhead Sch.; Clare Coll., Cambridge (exhibitioner and scholar; Nat. Sci. Tripos; MA); Liverpool Univ. (LLB). Called to Bar, Inner Temple, 1913. Served European War in The King's (Liverpool) Regt and attached staff, 1914-19. Practised on Northern Circuit and in London, 1919-50. *Publications:* Shipping Documents, 1929; Carriage of Goods by Sea Act, 1932; (with G. R. Rudolf) Lowndes and Rudolf on General Average and the York-Antwerp Rules, 1948. *Recreations:* reading, crosswords and watching any sport. *Address:* The End House, 7 Stonehill Close, East Sheen, SW14.

**HODGSON, Derek;** *see* Hodgson, W. D. T.

**HODGSON, Ernest Atkinson,** PhD; *b* 15 Oct. 1886; *e s* of Henry Dent Hodgson, Penrith, and Ellen E. Young; *m* 1st, 1912, Elizabeth Humphrey; two *s*; 2nd, 1923, Gladys Prittie; 3rd, 1948, Eva Jarrett Astley. *Educ:* Hamilton Collegiate; University of Toronto; University of Chicago; Saint Louis Univ. Asst Seismologist, Dominion Observatory, Ottawa, 1914-17; Seismologist, 1917-19; Head Mathematical Master, Galt Collegiate, Galt, Ontario, 1919-20; Chief, Division of Seismology, Dominion Observatory, Ottawa, Canada, 1920-47; Asst Dir Dominion Observatory, Ottawa, Canada, and Chief, Division of Seismology, 1948-51; retired, 1951. Past Pres. Seis. Soc. Am. and Dir, 1920-50; Editor, Bibliography of Seismology, 1926-48; FRSC 1936; Soc. of the Sigma Xi, 1945. *Publications:* Technical papers on seismology and on rockbursts in mines, in scientific journals and in the Publications of the Dominion Observatory, Ottawa. *Recreation:* bowling. *Address:* Box 520, Port Perry, Ont., Canada. *T:* 985-2166.

**HODGSON, George Charles Day,** CMG 1961; MBE 1950; lately an Administrative Officer, Nyasaland; retired from HMOCS, Nov. 1964; Secretary, Old Diocesans' Union, Diocesan College, Rondebosch, Cape, South Africa, since 1965; *b* 21 Sept. 1913; *s* of late P. J. Hodgson and of A. E. Joubert; *m* 1940, Edna Orde, *d* of late G. H. Rushmere; one *s. Educ:* Diocesan Coll., Rondebosch, Capetown, S

Africa; Rhodes Univ., Grahamstown, S Africa; Cambridge Univ. Joined Colonial Administrative Service as Cadet, 1939. Military Service, 1940-42; Lieut, 1st Bn King's African Rifles. Returned to duty as Distr. Officer, Nyasaland, 1943; seconded for special famine relief duties in Nyasaland, 1949-50; Provincial Commissioner, 1952; Adviser on Race Affairs to Govt of Federation of Rhodesia and Nyasaland, 1958-59; Nyasaland Govt Liaison Officer to Monckton Commn, 1960; Permanent Sec., Ministry of Natural Resources and Surveys, Nyasaland, 1961-62; Permanent Sec., Ministry of Transport and Communications, Nyasaland, 1963-64. *Recreations:* Rugby football, cricket, golf. *Address:* Diocesan College, Rondebosch, Cape, South Africa. *Clubs:* Royal Cape Golf, Western Province Cricket (Cape Town).

**HODGSON, Sir Gerald Hassall,** Kt 1943; *b* Scawby, Lincs, 20 July 1891; *s* of Rev. F. D. Hodgson, late of St Peters, Broadstairs; *m* 1st, 1924, Margaret Emma Hogge (*d* 1925), Ferndown, Dorset; 2nd, 1929, Sylvia Joan Lawrence; one *s* one *d*. *Educ:* Westminster Sch. National Provincial Bank, 1908-11; Parry & Co. Ltd, Madras, 1911; Capt. 6th Bn Royal West Kent Regt (France), 1916-19; Director: Parry & Co. Ltd, Madras, 1928-44; The Royal Blackheath Golf Club. *Publication:* Thomas Parry, Freemerchant, Madras, 1788-1824, 1938. *Address:* 3 Darwin Court, North Park, Eltham, SE9. *T:* 01-850 7331.

**HODGSON, James;** Director of External Telecommunications, Post Office, since 1969; *b* 14 Oct. 1925; *s* of Frederick and Lucy Hodgson; *m* 1951, Patricia (*née* Reed); no *c*. *Educ:* Exeter Sch.; St John's Coll., Cambridge. Enetered GPO, 1950; Private Sec. to Asst PMG, 1952-55 and to Dir Gen. GPO, 1955-56; seconded to Cabinet Office, 1961-63; Head of Telephone Operating Div. of GPO Headquarters, 1965-67; Vice-Dir of External Telecommunications Executive, 1967-69. *Recreations:* travel, tennis, squash, archaeology. *T:* Rohan, Hatherley Road, Kew, Richmond, Surrey. *T:* 01-940 5986.

**HODGSON, Prof. Phyllis;** Professor of English Language and Mediæval Literature, Bedford College, University of London, since 1955; *b* 27 June 1909; *d* of late Herbert Henry Hodgson, MA, BSc, PhD FRIC. *Educ:* Bolling Grammar Sch. for Girls, Bradford; Bedford Coll., University of London (BA); (Sen. Schol.) Lady Margaret Hall, Oxford (BLitt, DPhil). Tutor of St Mary's Coll., Durham Univ., 1936-38; Jex-Blake Fellow, Girton Coll., Cambridge (MA), 1938-40; Lecturer in English Language (Part-time), Queen Mary Coll., University of London, and Lecturer in English, Homerton Coll., Cambridge, 1940-42; Lecturer in English Language and Mediæval Literature, Bedford Coll., University of London, 1942-49; Reader in English Language in the University of London, 1949-55; External examiner for Reading Univ., 1955-57, 1961-63. Mem. Council of Early English Text Soc., 1959; Chm. Bd of Studies in English, 1964-66. *Publications:* The Cloud of Unknowing (EETS), 1944, 1958; Deonise Hid Divinite (EETS), 1955, 1958; The Franklin's Tale, 1960; The Orcherd of Syon and the English Mystical Tradition (Proc. Brit. Acad. 1964), 1965; The Orcherd of Syon (EETS), 1966; Three 14th Century English Mystics, 1967; The General Prologue to the Canterbury Tales, 1969; articles in Review of English Studies, Modern Language Review, Contemporary Review, etc. *Recreations:* music, walking, travel. *Address:* 48 St Thomas Road, St Annes-on-Sea, Lancs. *T:* St Annes 21665; Bedford College, Regent's Park, NW1. *T:* 01-486 4400.

**HODGSON, Thomas Charles Birkett,** CVO 1970; OBE 1966; QPM 1969; Chief Constable, Thames Valley Constabulary, 1968-70; *b* 8 Dec. 1907; *s* of late Thomas Edward Birkett Hodgson, Preston, Lancs; *m* 1936, Gwyneth Cosslett Bowles, *d* of Ivor Willans Bowles, Llandaff, Cardiff; one *s* one *d*. *Educ:* St Peter's, York. Served with Lancashire Constabulary, 1927-55; Asst Chief Constable, Birmingham, 1955-59; Chief Constable, Berkshire, 1959-68. *Address:* Brackenhurst, Greenham Common South, Newbury, Berks. *T:* Newbury 510.

**HODGSON, Thomas Edward Highton,** CB 1958; Assistant Secretary, General Register Office, since 1968; *b* 22 Aug. 1907; *e s* of late Sir Edward Hodgson, KBE, CB; *m* 1935, E. Catherine, *d* of T. Robin Hodgson; four *s*. *Educ:* Felsted Sch.; St John's Coll., Oxford. Asst Master, Felsted Sch., 1931; Board of Trade: Principal, 1941; Asst Sec., 1945; Asst Sec., Ministry of Materials, 1951; Under Secretary: Ministry of Supply, 1954; Ministry of Aviation, 1959; Ministry of Health, 1960-68. *Address:* 8 Oakeshott Avenue, Highgate, N6. *T:* 01-340 2495.

**HODGSON, (Walter) Derek (Thornley),** QC 1961; Judge of the Salford Hundred Court of Record since 1965; Member, Lord Chancellor's Committee on Legal Education, since 1968; *b* 24 May 1917; *s* of late Walter Hodgson, Whitefield, Manchester; *m* 1951, Raymonde Valda (*née* de Villiers) (*d* 1965); no *c*. *Educ:* Malvern Coll.; Trinity Hall, Cambridge. Scholar, Trinity Hall; Harmsworth Scholar, Middle Temple; 1st Cl. Law Tripos, Part II, 1938; 1st Cl. LLB, 1939. Served throughout War 1939-46, Royal Artillery; Burma 1942-45; released with rank of Captain, 1946. Called to Bar, Middle Temple, 1946; Master of the Bench, Middle Temple, 1967-. Member: Senate of Inns of Court, 1966-69; Gen. Council of the Bar, 1965-69. *Recreations:* tennis, racquets, reading, music, travel. *Address:* 1 Parkfield Road, Didsbury, Manchester 20; 39 Clarence Terrace, Regent's Park, NW1; 2 Pump Court, Temple, EC4. *T:* 01-353 3106. *Clubs:* Oxford and Cambridge University; Manchester, Tennis and Racquets (Manchester).

**HODIN, Josef Paul,** LLD; author, art historian, art critic; *b* 17 Aug. 1905; *s* of Eduard D. Hodin and Rosa (*née* Klug); *m* 1945, Doris Pamela Simms; one *s* one *d*. *Educ:* Kleinseitner Realschule and Neustädter Realgymnasium, Prague; Charles Univ., Prague; London Univ.; Art Academies of Dresden and Berlin. Press Attaché to Norwegian Govt in London, 1944-45; Dir of Studies and Librarian, Inst. of Contemporary Arts, London, 1949-54; Hon. Mem. Editorial Council of The Journal of Aesthetics and Art Criticism, Cleveland, 1955-; Mem. Exec. Cttee British Soc. of Aesthetics; Editor: Prisme des Arts, Paris, 1956-59; Quadrum, Brussels, 1956-. 1st internat. prize for art criticism, Biennale, Venice, 1954. Hon. PhD Uppsala, 1969. DSM 1st cl. (Czechoslovakia), 1947; St Olav Medal (Norway), 1958; Comdr, Order of Merit (Italy) 1967; Grand Cross, Order of Merit, Austria, 1968. *Publications:* Monographs on Sven Erixson (Stockholm), 1940; Ernst Josephson (Stockholm), 1942, Edvard Munch (Stockholm), 1948, (Frankfurt a/M), 1951; Isaac Grünewald (Stockholm), 1949; Art and Criticism (Stockholm), 1944; J. A. Comenius and Our Time (Stockholm), 1944; The Dilemma of Being Modern (London), 1956, (New York), 1959; Henry Moore (Amsterdam,

Hamburg), 1956, (London, New York), 1958, (Buenos Aires), 1963; Ben Nicholson (London), 1957; Barbara Hepworth (Neuchatel, London, New York), 1961; Lynn Chadwick (Amsterdam, Hamburg, London, New York), 1961; Bekenntnis zu Kokoschka (Mainz), 1963; Edvard Munch (Mainz), 1963; Oskar Kokoschka: A Biography (London, New York), 1966; Walter Kern (Neuchatel, London), 1966; Ruszkowski (London), 1967; Bernard Leach (London), 1967; Oskar Kokoschka: Leben und Lebenswerk (Mainz), 1968; Kafka and Goethe (Hamburg), 1968; Emilio Greco, Life and Work (London, New York), 1970; Edvard Munch, A Norwegian Genius (London, New York, Oslo), 1970; The Four Pillars of Modern Art (London, Cleveland), 1970; Die Brühlsche Terrasse, Ein Künstlerroman (Hamburg), 1970; contribs on literary and art subjects to internat. periodicals. *Address:* 12 Eton Avenue, NW3. *T:* 01-794 3609.

**HODKIN, Rev. Canon Hedley;** Residentiary Canon, Manchester Cathedral, since 1957; Sub-Dean, since 1966; *b* 3 Jan. 1902; *s* of Walter and Elizabeth Hodkin; *m* 1932, Mary M., *d* of Dr J. A. Findlay; one *s* two *d*. *Educ:* University of Sheffield; Christ's Coll. and Westcott House, Cambridge. Curate of: Morpeth, 1935-38; St George's, Newcastle, 1938-40; Vicar of: St Luke's, Newcastle, 1940-47; Holy Trinity, Millhouses, Sheffield, 1947-57. Examining Chaplain: to Bishop of Newcastle, 1939-47; to Bishop of Sheffield, 1951-57; to Bishop of Manchester, 1957. Hon. Canon of Sheffield, 1955-57. Select Preacher, Cambridge, 1968. *Publication:* The Saving Name, 1954. *Recreation:* music. *Address:* 101 Slade Lane, Manchester 19. *T:* 061-224 5669. *Club:* The Old Rectory (Manchester).

**HODKINSON, William,** OBE 1952; Chairman, North Western Gas Board, since 1964; *b* 11 Aug. 1909; *s* of late William Hodkinson and late Ann Greenwood; *m* 1934, Ann, *d* of John Buxton; one *s*. *Educ:* St Anne's, Stretford; Salford Technical Coll. Stretford Gas Co.: Technical Asst, 1930-32; Asst Works Manager, 1932-35; UK Gas Corp. Ltd: Chief Technical Officer, 1935-39; Gen. Man., 1939-46; Tech. Dir and Gen. Man., 1946-49; North Western Gas Board: Chief Technical and Planning Officer, 1949-56; Dep. Chm., 1956-64. *Recreation:* golf. *Address:* 28 Moss Lane, Sale, Cheshire. *T:* 061-973 1730.

**HODSOLL, Wing Comdr Sir (Eric) John,** Kt 1944; CB 1934; *b* 1894; *s* of late Commander J. F. Hodsoll, RNR, and late Wilhelmina Ann White; *m* 1st, 1919, Winifred Joyce (*d* 1935), *d* of Col Morton Tomlin, OBE, TD, DL; one *d*; 2nd, 1937, Elisabeth Morton, *y d* of late Col Morton Tomlin; twin *d*. *Educ:* Christ's Hosp. Trained in engineering, Great Western Railway Works, Swindon, 1911-14; joined RNAS, 1914; served Calshot, 1915-17; Commanded Seaplane Base, Alexandria, 1918 (despatches thrice); Air Ministry, 1919-22; Staff Coll., Camberley, 1923-24; HQ RAF, India, 1925-29; Asst Sec., Cttee of Imperial Defence, 1929-35; retired list, RAF, 1935; Asst Under-Sec. of State, Home Office, in charge of Air Raid Precautions Department, 1935-37, Inspector-General, 1938-48; Dir-Gen., Civil Defence Training, 1948-54. Chief Civil Defence Adviser, and i/c Civil Emergency Planning Section, to North Atlantic Treaty Organization, 1954-61, retired. Pres., Nat. Voluntary Civil Aid Service, 1970-. Hon. Mem., Indian Inst. of Civil Defence. First Gold Medal of Inst. of Civil Defence, 1959. Gold Medal of Danish Civil Defence Assoc. Distinguished Service Award, Office of Civil and Defense Mobilization (US). OStJ. Hon. Chief of Scancee Tribe, Alberta, Canada. *Address:* Merlewood Cottage, Tarrant Rushton, Blandford Forum, Dorset. *T:* Blandford 2237.

**HODSON,** Baron (Life Peer), *cr* 1960, of Rotherfield Greys; **Francis Lord Charlton Hodson,** PC 1951; Kt 1937; MC; a Lord of Appeal in Ordinary since Oct. 1960; Mem. of Permanent Court of Arbitration at The Hague since 1949; Pres., Internat. Law Association, British Branch; *b* 1895; *s* of Rev. Thomas Hodson, MA, late Rector of Oddington, Glos, and Catherine Anne Maskew; *m* 1918, Susan Mary (*d* 1965), *d* of late Major W. G. Blake, DL; one *s* (and *er s* killed in Libya 23 Jan. 1942) one *d*. *Educ:* Cheltenham Coll.; Wadham Coll., Oxford (Hon. Fellow). 2nd Lieut 7th Bn Glos Regt, Sept. 1914; served in Gallipoli and Mesopotamia, 1915-17 (MC, Cavaliere of the Order of the Crown of Italy); retired as Captain, 1919; called to Bar, Inner Temple, 1921; Junior Counsel to Treasury (Probate), 1935; KC 1937; Judge of High Court of Justice (Probate Divorce and Admiralty Division), 1937-51; Bencher, Inner Temple, 1938; a Lord Justice of Appeal, 1951-60. *Address:* Rotherfield Greys, Oxon. *T:* Rotherfield Greys 303. *Clubs:* Bath, Brooks's; Huntercombe Golf (Henley-on-Thames).

**HODSON, Dr Cecil John,** MB, BS London; FRCP; FFR; DMRE; Director, X-Ray Diagnostic Department, University College Hospital, London, since 1960; Radiologist, Queen Elizabeth Hospital for Children, since 1948; Hon. Consultant Radiologist, Queen Alexandra Military Hospital, Millbank; *b* 20 Dec. 1915; *s* of Dr J. E. Hodson and Kate Bassnett; *m* 1960, Mary Selwyn-Clarke; one *s*. *Educ:* Eastbourne Coll.; St Mary's Hosp., Paddington. Junior medical posts: St Mary's Hosp. and St Giles Hosp., Camberwell; Brompton Hosp.; Harefield Emergency Hosp. RAMC, 1942-46 (despatches); served in N Africa, Sicily, Italy and Greece; Major, Specialist in Radiology. Dep. Dir, X-Ray Dept, University Coll. Hosp., 1949. Sec., Faculty of Radiologists, 1959-64, Vice-Pres., 1964-65. Baker Travelling Prof. of Royal Australasian College of Radiology, 1962. William Julius Mickie Fellow, University of London, 1966. *Publications:* numerous contributions to medical journals; (co-author) Renal Disease, 1962. *Recreations:* mountains, sailing, gardening. *Address:* 11 Perceval Avenue, NW3. *T:* 01-794 3661. *Clubs:* Alpine Ski; United Hospitals Sailing; Royal Sussex Yacht.

**HODSON, Donald Manly;** Director of Programmes, External Broadcasting, BBC, since 1970; *b* 10 Sept. 1913; 2nd *s* of late Prof. T. C. Hodson; *m* 1940, Margaret Beatson Bell, *er d* of late Sir Nicholas Beatson Bell, KCSI, KCIE; three *s* one *d*. *Educ:* Gresham's Sch.; Balliol Coll., Oxford. Editorial staff, the Economist, 1935; Leader writer, Financial Times, 1936; Asst Leader Page Editor, News Chronicle, 1937-38; Leader Page Editor, News Chronicle, 1939. BBC European Services: Sub-Editor, 1940; Chief Sub-Editor, 1942; Duty Editor, 1943; European Talks Editor, 1945; Asst Head of European News Dept, 1946; Head of European Talks and English Dept, 1948-51; Asst Controller, European Services, 1951-58; Controller, Overseas Services, 1958-68; Controller of Programmes, External Broadcasting, 1968-70. *Address:* 10 Wood Lane, Highgate, N6. *T:* 01-340 2007. *Club:* Five Farthings.

**HODSON, Major Sir Edmond Adair,** 5th Bt, *cr* 1789; DSO 1917; late Rifle Brigade; *b* 22 March 1893; *e s* of late R. E. Hodson and Margaret, *d* of Rev. Stanley Pemberton; *m* 1928, Anne

Elizabeth Adderley, *yr d* of Lt-Col H. Adderley Cradock, Hill House, Sherborne St John; *S* uncle, 1921; two *s*. *Educ:* Marlborough; Trinity Coll., Cambridge. Served European War, 1914-18 (DSO); retired pay, 1929. *Heir:* *s* Michael Robin Adderley Hodson [*b* 5 March 1932; *m* 1963, Katrin Alexa, *d* of Edwin Bernstiel, Dinas Powis, Glamorgan; two *d*]. *Address:* Hollybrooke, Bray, Co. Wicklow.

**HODSON, Prof. Frank,** BSc London 1949; PhD Reading 1951; FGS; Professor of Geology in the University of Southampton since 1958; *b* 23 Nov. 1921; *s* of late Matthew and Gertrude Hodson; *m* 1945, Ada Heyworth; three *d*. *Educ:* Burnley Grammar Sch.; Reading Univ. Demonstrator, Reading Univ., 1947-49; Lecturer, Reading Univ., 1949-58. Hon. Mem. Geol. Soc. de Belg. *Publications:* geological papers in publications of learned societies. *Recreations:* book collecting; geological field work. *Address:* Department of Geology, The University, Southampton.

**HODSON, Air Vice-Marshal George Stacey,** CB 1946; CBE 1942; AFC 1917; retired; *b* 2 May 1899; *s* of Percy George Hodson, London; *m* 1923, Eileen Marlon, *d* of Charles Sandell, Amesbury, Wilts; two *s*. *Educ:* Dulwich. Air Officer in charge of Training, Bomber Command, 1945; AOA Coastal Command, 1946; AOC No. 205 Group, RAF, Mediterranean and Middle East, 1947; SASO, Home Command, 1949-51; retired, 1951. *Address:* Woodham Place, Woking, Surrey. *T:* 2924.

**HODSON, Henry Vincent;** Provost of Ditchley since 1961; *b* 12 May 1906; *er s* of late Prof. T. C. Hodson; *m* 1933, Margaret Elizabeth Honey, Sydney; four *s*. *Educ:* Gresham's Sch.; Balliol Coll., Oxford. Fellow of All Souls Coll., Oxford, 1928-35; Staff of Economic Advisory Council, 1930-31; Asst Editor of the Round Table, 1931, Editor, 1934-39; Director, Empire Div., Ministry of Information, 1939-41; Reforms Commissioner, Govt of India, 1941-42; Principal Asst Sec., and later head of Non-Munitions Div., Min. of Production, 1942-45; Asst Editor, Sunday Times, 1946-50, Editor, 1950-61. *Publications:* Economics of a Changing World, 1933; (part) The Empire in the World, 1937; Slump and Recovery, 1929-37, 1938; The British Commonwealth and the Future, 1939; Twentieth Century Empire, 1948; Problems in Anglo-American Relations, 1963; The Great Divide: Britain-India-Pakistan, 1969; sections in annual Survey of International Affairs; many articles in reviews, etc. *Address:* Ditchley Park, Enstone, Oxford. *T:* Enstone 310; 52 Cadogan Lane, SW1. *T:* 07-235 4930. *Club:* Brooks's.

**HODSON, Prof. Joseph John,** BDS; PhD; FRCPath; Professor of Oral Pathology, University of Sheffield, since 1960; Hon. Consultant in Oral Pathology to the United Sheffield Hospitals, and to Sheffield Regional Hospital Board; *b* 7 March 1912; *e s* of late Rev. J. J. Hodson, MA, and late Mrs A. Hodson, Birmingham; *m* 1937, Mary Alice, *d* of late John and Florence Whitman, Hull; one *s* one *d*. *Educ:* Birmingham Univ.; Royal College of Surgeons, Edinburgh. Dental Surgeon to Warwicks CC, 1938-41. War Service, Capt., Royal Army Dental Corps, 1941-45. University of Sheffield: Research Asst, 1947-49, Lectr, 1949-53, Sen. Lectr, 1953-60, in Oral Pathology. Howard Mummery Research Prize, BDA, 1952-57. *Publications:* various papers in Medical and Dental Jls covering research in oral tumours, dental and other diseases of the mouth. *Recreations:* music, gardening. *Address:* 183 High Storrs Road, Sheffield 11. *T:* 61405; Dept of Oral Pathology, The University, Sheffield 10.

**HODSON, Leslie Manfred Noel,** CMG 1958; OBE 1953; QC 1943; retired as Advocate of the High Court of Southern Rhodesia (1929-63); now farming; *b* 2 Dec. 1902; *s* of late A. Hodson, JP, and Mrs Hodson; *m* 1927, Iona May Mackenzie; two *s* one *d*. *Educ:* Boys' High Sch., Salisbury, Rhodesia; University of the Witwatersrand. City Councillor, Salisbury, Rhodesia, 1932-36; contested by-election, Hartley, 1937; MP for Salisbury Central, 1946 and 1948. First Chm. Rhodesia Univ. Assoc., Inaugural Board and Council, of University Coll. of Rhodesia and Nyasaland, 1953-62. MP Federal Assembly of Rhodesia and Nyasaland, 1953-62. Dep. Speaker Legislative Assembly, 1951, 1953. *Recreation:* journalism. *Address:* Tor Fell, Private Bag 451G, Salisbury, Rhodesia. *T:* Salisbury 2066073. *Club:* Salisbury.

**HODSON, Rt. Rev. Mark Allin;** *see* Hereford, Bishop of.

**HOEHNE, Most Rev. John;** *see* Rabaul, Archbishop of, (RC).

**HOFF, H. S.;** *see* Cooper, William.

**HOFFMAN, Anna Rosenberg;** Senior Partner, Anna M. Rosenberg Associates, public and industrial relations consultants, New York; *b* Budapest, Hungary, 19 July 1902; *d* of Albert Lederer and Charlotte Bacskal; *m* 1919, Julius Rosenberg; one *s*; *m* 1962, Paul Gray Hoffman, *qv*; Member: President's Commn on Income Maintenance Programs, 1968-; States Urban Action Center, 1967-; NY Urban Coalition, Inc. of Nat. Urban Coalition, 1967-; Mayor Lindsay's Cttee on Rent Control, 1967-; National Citizens' Commn for Internat. Cooperation; Bd of Directors, United Nations Assoc. of the United States of America, Inc.; Population Crisis Cttee; Franklin Delano Roosevelt Memorial Commission; Board of Trustees, Eleanor Roosevelt Memorial Foundation; Board of Directors of World Rehabilitation Fund, Inc.; also Mem. of other Boards and Cttees, etc., in the United States. Formerly: Asst Sec. of Defense, USA, 1950-53; Regional Director of: War Manpower Commn, 1942-45; Social Security Admin., 1936-42; Office of Defense, Health and Welfare Services, 1941-42; Nat. Recovery Admin., 1934-35. Personal Representative of President Roosevelt, 1944, and of President Truman, 1945, to European Theatre of War; Sec. to President Roosevelt's Labor Victory Board, 1942-45; Member: US Nat. Commn for Unesco, 1946-50; Advisory Commn of the President on Universal Mil. Training, 1946-47; President Roosevelt's Industrial Relations Commn to Great Britain and Sweden etc.; Bd of Education, City of NY, 1961-63; Nat. Adv. Commn on Selective Service, 1966-67. Medal of Freedom, 1945 (first award by Gen. Eisenhower to a civilian); Medal for Merit, 1947; Dept of Defense Exceptional Civilian Service Award, 1953; Medallion of City of NY (for work on beautification of City), 1966. Holds Hon. Degrees in USA. *Publications:* chapter, Social Security and the National Purpose, in The Family in a World at War, 1942; article on history and status of American woman in business world, in The Great Ideas Today, 1966. *Recreations:* chiefly indoor gardening; collection of modern French art; antique china. *Address:* (office) 444 Madison Avenue, New York, NY 10022, USA; (home) 8 Sutton Square, New York, NY 10022, USA.

**HOFFMAN, Paul Gray;** Administrator, United Nations Development Programme since 1966;

Managing Director, United Nations Special Fund, 1959-65; *b* Chicago, Ill, 26 April 1891; *s* of George Delos Hoffman and Eleanor Lott; *m* 1915, Dorothy Brown (*d* 1961); five *s* two *d*. *m* 1962, Anna Rosenberg Hoffman, *qv*. *Educ:* La Grange (Ill) High Sch.; University of Chicago. Started in automobile business as porter for Chicago distributor of Halladay car; joined Studebaker, 1911; 1st Lieut, US Army, 1917-19. Vice-Pres. of Studebaker Corporation, 1925-33; Pres., 1935-48; Chm., 1953-56; Federal Reserve Bank (Chicago), 1942-49; Administrator of ECA (Marshall Plan), 1948-50; Pres. and Dir of the Ford Foundation, 1951-53. Mem. of US Delegation to United Nations, 1956-57. Director: NY Life Insurance Co.; Encyclopædia Britannica; Encyclopædia Britannica Films, Inc.; Adviser/Director, Time, Inc.; Director Emeritus, United Airlines. Chm., Public Policy Cttee, The Advertising Council, Inc.; Hon. Chm., UN Assoc. of USA; Member: American Soc. of French Legion of Honour; Automotive Safety Foundn (Pres., 1937-41, Pres. and Chm. 1941-42, Chm. 1942-48); Business Advisory Council, Dept of Commerce, 1941-61; Hon. Mem., The Business Council, 1962-. TRustee: Cttee for Economic Develt (Chm., 1942-48); Kenyon Coll., 1940-60; University of Chicago, 1937-50. Republican; Mason. Delta Tau Delta (Nat. Pres., 1940-42). Has numerous hon. degrees; many awards and medals. *Publications:* Seven Roads to Safety, 1939; Peace Can Be Won, 1951; World Without Want, 1962; various articles. *Address:* (office) United Nations, New York, NY 10017, USA; (home) 8 Sutton Square, New York, NY 10022. *Clubs:* Burning Tree, Metropolitan (Washington, DC); Century Association, Stanwich Country (New York); Thunderbird Country (California).

**HOFFMEISTER, Maj.-Gen. Bertram Meryl,** CB 1945; CBE 1944; DSO 1943; ED; President, Council of the Forest Industries of BC, Vancouver, since 1962; *b* 15 May 1907; *s* of Flora Elizabeth Rodway and Louis George Hoffmeister; *m* 1935, Donalda Strauss; one *s* one *d*. *Educ:* Public Schs, Vancouver. Previous to war of 1939-45 employed by H. R. MacMillan Export Co. Ltd, Vancouver, BC. 1st Lieut Seaforth Highlanders of Canada, 1927; Capt. 1934; Major 1939 and given command of a rifle Coy. Served with Seaforth Highlanders in England as Coy. Comdr, 1939-40; returned to Canada, 1942, to attend Canadian Junior War Staff Course; given Command of Seaforth Highlanders of Canada and commanded this Bn in assault on Sicily in July 1943 (DSO); Brig. Oct. 1943 and assumed command 2 Canadian Infantry Brigade (Bar to DSO battle of Ortona); Maj.-Gen. and commanded 5 Cdn Armoured Div. March 1944; operations on Hitler Line, May-June 1944 (2nd Bar to DSO, CBE); in NW Europe until conclusion of hostilities (CB). GOC Canadian Army Pacific Force, 1945. Gen. Manager, Canadian White Pine Co. Ltd, and MacMillan Industries Ltd (Plywood Div.), 1945-47; H. R. MacMillan Export Co. Ltd; Gen. Mgr Prod., 1947-49 and Vice-Pres. Prod., 1949; Pres., 1949-51; MacMillan & Bloedel Ltd; Pres. 1951-56; Chm. Bd, 1956-57. Agent-Gen. for British Columbia, 1958-61. *Recreations:* rugby, rowing, shooting and golf. *Address:* 5795 Newton Wynd, Vancouver 8, BC, Canada. *Clubs:* Vancouver, Capilano Golf and Country, Vancouver Rowing (Vancouver); Canadian.

**HOFSTADTER, Prof. Robert;** Professor of Physics, Stanford University, since 1954; Director, High Energy Physics Laboratory, Stanford University, since 1967; *b* Manhattan, New York, NY, 5 Feb. 1915; *s* of Louis and Henrietta Hofstadter; *m* 1942, Nancy Givan, Baltimore, Md; one *s* two *d*. *Educ:* City Coll. of New York (BS *magna cum laude*); Princeton Univ. (MA, PhD). Instructor in Physics: University of Pennsylvania, 1940-41; City Coll., New York, 1941-42; Associate Physicist and Physicist, Nat. Bureau of Standards, Washington DC, 1942-43; Asst Chief Physicist, Norden Laboratories Corp., New York, 1943-46; Asst Prof., physics, Princeton Univ., 1946-50; Associate Prof., physics, Stanford Univ., 1950-54. Associate Editor: Physical Review, 1951-53; Investigations in Physics, 1951-; Review of Scientific Instruments, 1954-56; Reviews of Modern Physics, 1958-61. Has held various fellowships, Nobel Prize in Physics, 1961. Fellow American Physical Soc.; FPS (London); Mem. Italian Phys. Soc.; Sigma Xi; Phi Beta Kappa. Hon. LLD, City Univ. of NY, 1962; Hon. DSc: Gustavus Adolphus Coll., Minn, 1963; Carleton Univ., Ottawa, 1967; Seoul Nat. Univ., 1967; *Laurea* (*hc*), Padua, 1965; Dr Univ. (*hc*), Univ. of Clermont, 1967. *Publications:* (with Robert Herman) High Energy Electron Scattering Tables, 1960 (US); (ed) Nuclear and Nucleon Structure, 1963 (US); (co-ed with L. I. Schiff) Nucleon Structure (Proc. Internat. Conf. at Stanford Univ., 1963), 1964; numerous scientific papers on various aspects of molecular structure, solid state physics, nuclear physics and review articles on crystal counters, electron scattering and nuclear and nucleon structure. *Recreations:* ski-ing, photography. *Address:* Department of Physics, Stanford University, Stanford, California, USA.

**HOG, Major Roger Thomas Alexander,** MC; DL; *b* 19 June 1893; *s* of late Steuart Bayley Hog, of Newliston and Kellie; *m* 1937, Marjorie St Clair, *d* of Charles F. Wood. *Educ:* Winchester Coll.; RMA Woolwich. Served European War, 1914-19; War of 1939-45, Royal Artillery, retired as Major. *Address:* Newliston, Kirkliston, West Lothian. *T:* Kirkliston 231. *Club:* New (Edinburgh).

**HOGAN, Air Vice-Marshal Henry Algernon Vickers,** CB 1955; DFC 1940; retired; *b* 25 Oct. 1909; *s* of Lieut-Col Edward M. A. Hogan, late IA; *m* 1939, Margaret Venetia, *d* of Vice-Adm. W. Tomkinson, *qv*; one *s* one *d*. *Educ:* Malvern Coll.; RAF Coll., Cranwell. Commissioned 1930. Served in Fighter Sqdns and Fleet Air Arm; Instructor CFS, 1936-37; Mem. RAF Long Distance Flight (Vickers Wellesleys) to Australia, 1938; Commanded No. 501 Sqdn throughout Battle of Britain; USA, 1941-43 (Arnold Scheme and RAF Delegation Washington); Asst Comdt, Empire CFS, 1944; Commanded No. 19 Flying Training Sch., RAF Coll., Cranwell, 1945; Staff Coll., 1946; Air Ministry, 1947-48; SPSO, MEAF, 1949-50; Commanded RAF, Wattisham 1951; Air Cdr 1953; Sector Comdr, Northern Sector, 1952-53; AOC No. 81 Group, 1954; Air Vice-Marshal, 1956; AOC No. 83 Group, 2nd ATAF, Germany, 1955-58; SASO, Flying Training Command, 1958-62. Led RAF Mission to Ghana, 1960, and Joint Services Mission to Ghana, 1961. Regional Dir, Civil Defence (Midland), 1964-68. USA Legion of Merit (Officer), 1945. *Recreations:* golf, shooting, fishing. *Address:* Arbour Hill House, Ross-on-Wye, Herefordshire. *T:* 3333. *Club:* Royal Air Force.

**HOGAN, Hon. Sir Michael (Joseph Patrick),** Kt 1958; CMG 1953; Chief Justice of Hong Kong, since 1955, of Brunei, since 1964; *b* 15 March 1908; *m* 1946, Patricia, *d* of late Thomas Galliford, no *c*. *Educ:* Belvedere Coll., Dublin; Stonyhurst Coll., Lancs; Trinity Coll., Dublin (BA, Gold Medal, 1st cl. hons; LLB).

Admitted Solicitor, Ireland, 1930; admitted to Kenya Bar, 1931; called to Irish Bar (Kings Inns), 1936; Chief Magistrate, Palestine, 1936; Crown Counsel, 1937; Attorney-Gen., Aden, 1945; called to English Bar (Inner Temple), 1946; KC (Aden) 1946; Solicitor-Gen., Palestine, 1947; attached Foreign Office, 1949; Malaya: Solicitor-Gen., 1950, QC (Malaya) 1952; Attorney-Gen., Federation of Malaya, 1950-55. British Mem., Anglo-Japanese Property Commission, 1960. Hon. LLD Dublin Univ., 1962. *Publications:* revised edition of the Laws of Aden, 1948. *Recreations:* tennis, ski-ing, polo, golf. *Address:* Chief Justice's House, Hong Kong. *Clubs:* Athenæum, Bath.

**HOGARTH, James;** Under-Secretary, Scottish Home and Health Department, since 1963; *b* 14 Aug. 1914; *s* of George Hogarth; *m* 1940, Katherine Mary Cameron; two *s* one *d*. *Educ:* George Watson's, Edinburgh; Edinburgh Univ.; Sorbonne, Paris. Joined Dept of Health for Scotland as Asst Principal, 1938; Principal, 1944; Asst Sec., 1948; Under-Sec., 1963. *Publications:* Payment of the General Practitioner, 1963; translations from French, Russian, etc. *Recreation:* travel. *Address:* 21 Crawfurd Road, Edinburgh EH16 5PQ. *T:* 031-667 3878.

**HOGARTH, Dr Margaret Cameron;** lately Chairman: Executive Committee, Central Council for District Nursing in London; Medical Advisory Committee Nursery School Association of Great Britain and Northern Ireland; Governor, Gipsy Hill Training College, Surrey County Council; Member Executive Committee, Children's Aid Society; a Vice-President of the Health Visitors Association; *b* 10 March 1885; *d* of Farquhar Macdonald, MA, Rector of Dingwall Academy, Ross-shire; *m* 1914, late Archibald Henry Hogarth, CBE, DCM, MA, MD Oxon, DPH; one *s*. *Educ:* Dingwall Acad.; Aberdeen Univ. Various Resident Hosp. appts, 1907-11, in London and Provinces, specialising in Obstetrics, Gynæcology, Eye and Ear and Child Diseases; Asst MOH and Dep. MOH, Bucks, 1911-12; Medical service under LCC, 1912-24; again with LCC, 1928-50 (Div. Med. Off., Principal Asst and Sen. MO); Ophthalmologist to two LCC eye clinics and, for a period, to LCC Schs for blind and blind and deaf children. Ext. Examr, Hygiene, to Goldsmiths' Trg Coll.; MO to certain Voluntary Maternity and Child Welfare centres and Ante-Natal Clinics. MO, Min. of Health, 1924-28; apptd Govt Rep. League of Nations Nutrition Cttee, 1936; Institute of Education, University of London: Ext. Examr Health Educ.; Mem. Health Educ. Panel, 1953-59; Lectr on Anatomy and Physiology to School of Dramatic Art and Speech Trg. *Publications:* various reports on specific subjects to LCC and Min. of Health; Public Health Reviews for Lancet; Survey of District Nursing in the Administrative County of London (publ. LCC); Medicine as a Career for Women (publ. Brit. Fedn University Women); Health in the Nursery School. *Recreations:* reading, picture galleries. *Address:* North Court Hotel, Hassocks, Sussex.

**HOGBEN, Herbert Edward;** Scientific Adviser to Commander, British Navy Staff, Washington, USA, 1968-70, retired; *b* 21 Dec. 1905; *s* of Herbert Edward Hogben; *m* 1929, Dorothy, *d* of Samuel Eastoe Pearson; three *d*. *Educ:* Borden Gram. Sch., Sittingbourne; King's Coll., London (BSc). Scientific Officer, Admiralty, 1927-; Princ. Scientific Officer, 1943; Sen. Princ. Sci. Off., 1952; Dep. Chief Sci. Off., 1961; Chief Sci. Off., Min. of Def. (Navy), 1965; Dep. Chief Scientist, Admiralty Surface Weapons Establishment, 1965-68. *Publications:* ASE monographs and technical notes, articles for Jl Inst. of Navigation. *Recreations:* gardening, travel. *Address:* 12 Portsdown Hill Road, Bedhampton, Havant PO9 3JX.

**HOGBEN, Lancelot,** FRS 1936; MA Cantab; DSc London; *b* Southsea, 9 Dec. 1895; *e s* of Thomas Hogben; *m* Enid (marr. diss., 1957), *d* of Rev. James Charles, Denbigh; two *s* two *d*; *m* Sarah Jane, *e d* of John Evans. *Educ:* Trinity Coll., Cambridge (Senr Scholar and Prizeman), Frank Smart Prizeman, Cambridge; Mackinnon Student of the Royal Society, 1923. Lecturer in Zoology, Imperial Coll. of Science, 1919-22; Asst Dir Animal Breeding Research Dept, 1923; Lecturer in Experimental Physiology, Edinburgh, 1923-25; Asst Prof. of Zoology, McGill, 1925-27; Prof. of Zoology, University of Cape Town, 1927-30; Prof. of Social Biology, University of London, 1930-37; Regius Prof. of Natural History, University of Aberdeen, 1937-41; Mason Prof. of Zoology, Birmingham Univ., 1941-47, Prof. of Medical Statistics, 1947-61; Vice-Chancellor, University of Guyana, 1963-65. Hon. Sen. Fellow in Linguistics, Birmingham Univ., 1961-64. Keith Prize and Gold Medal, Royal Society of Edinburgh, 1936; Croonian Lecture, 1942. Hon. LLD Birmingham; Hon. DSc Wales. *Publications:* The Comparative Physiology of Internal Secretion; The Nature of Living Matter; Nature and Nurture; Mathematics for the Million, 1936; Science for the Citizen, 1938; Dangerous Thoughts, 1939; Chance and Choice, Vol. I, 1950; Vol. II, 1955; Statistical Theory, 1957; Mathematics in the Making, 1960; Essential World English, 1963; The Mother Tongue, 1964; The Vocabulary of Science, 1970. Scientific memoirs on genetics, ductless glands, the physiology of colour change and medical statistics in Proc. Royal Society, B Journal Exper. Biology, Quarterly Journal Exper. Physiology, Biochem. Journal, Journal of Genetics, British Journal Soc. Medicine, etc; Articles in the Encyclopædia Britannica. *Address:* Tregeiriog, Denbighshire.

**HOGG,** family name of **Hailsham Viscountcy and of Baron Hailsham of Saint Marylebone.**

**HOGG, Alexander Hubert Arthur;** Secretary, Royal Commission on Ancient Monuments in Wales and Monmouthshire, since 1949; *b* 2 May 1908; *s* of A. F. Hogg; *m* 1943, Nellie, *d* of G. P. Henderson, MD; one *s* one *d*. *Educ:* Highgate Sch.; Sidney Sussex Coll., Cambridge (MA). Asst Engineer, Sir R. McAlpine & Sons, 1930-34; Junior Scientific Officer, Roads Research Laboratory, 1934-36; Lecturer, Engineering Dept, King's Coll., Newcastle upon Tyne, 1936-42; Temp. Experimental Officer, Admiralty Undex Works, Rosyth, 1942-45; ICI Fellowship, 1945-47; Lecturer Engineering Laboratory, University of Cambridge, 1947-49. FSA; FSAScot. *Publications:* papers in Philosophical Magazine and in Archæological periodicals. *Address:* Brynfield, Waun Fawr, Aberystwyth, Cards. *T:* Aberystwyth 3479.

**HOGG, Cecil;** *see* Hogg, J. C.

**HOGG, Cuthbert Stuart,** CMG 1965; Chartered Accountant since 1935; *b* 1 April 1911; *s* of J. S. Hogg; *m* 1939, Eileen Griffiths; three *s*. *Educ:* Whangarei High Sch. Mem. Cttee, Wellington Racing Club. Director: Alliance Textiles Ltd; Bryant & May Ltd, NZ; Kirkcaldie & Stains Ltd; Leopard Brewery Ltd; Lombard NZ Ltd, and others. *Address:* PO Box 230, Wellington, NZ. *T:* 71959. *Clubs:* Wellington, Wellesley, Commercial Travellers' (all in Wellington).

**HOGG, Edward Gascoigne,** CMG 1932; *b* 22 Jan. 1882; *s* of late Edward Hogg, Average Adjuster; *m* 1st, 1910, Beatrice, *d* of F. Filleul Hensley; two *s* one *d*; 2nd, 1928, Olivia Valentine, *d* of William Holmes; two *s* one *d*. *Educ:* Charterhouse; New Coll., Oxford. Egyptian Civil Service, 1906-31; Adviser to Ministry of Finance, Iraq, 1931. *Address:* Yattendon, Newbury, Berks.

**HOGG, George Robert Disraeli,** CB 1955; CBE 1946; *b* 23 June 1894; *s* of John Hogg; *m* 1919, Daisy Winifred Martin; two *d*. *Educ:* Westminster City Sch.; St John's Coll., Oxford. First Cl. Hons in Mathematics, 1916; BA 1919; Lecturer in Mathematics, Sir John Cass Technical Institute, 1919-20; entered Administrative Class, Home Civil Service and joined Dept of Scientific and Industrial Research, 1920; Under-Sec., 1950-57. Served European War, 1914-18, Army and Royal Air Force (meteorological officer, Lieut), 1916-19. *Recreations:* mathematical problems; chess. *Address:* 189 Sheen Lane, East Sheen, SW14. *T:* 01-876 3275.

**HOGG, Vice-Adm. Sir Ian (Leslie Trower),** KCB 1968 (CB 1964); DSC 1941, Bar to DSC 1944; Vice-Chief of the Defence Staff, 1967-70, retired; *b* 30 May 1911; 3rd *s* of Col John M. T. Hogg, IA, and Elma (*née* Brand); *m* 1945, Mary G. J., *e d* of Col and Mrs Marsden; two *s*. *Educ:* Cheltenham Coll. Entered Royal Navy, 1929; specialised in Navigation, 1937; HMS Cardiff, 1939; HMS Penelope, 1940; HMAS Napier, 1941-43; HMS Mauritius, 1944-45; Master of the Fleet, 1946-47; British Admiralty Delegation, Washington, DC, 1948-49; HMS Sluys, in comd, 1950-51; Staff of C-in-C Med., 1952-53; Captain RN, Dec. 1953; Brit. Joint Staff, Washington, DC, 1955-57; idc 1958; Staff of Chief of Defence Staff, 1959-60; Cdre, Cyprus, 1961-62; Dir, Chief of Defence Staff's Commonwealth Exercise, 1962-63; Flag Officer, Medway, and Admiral Superintendent, HM Dockyard, Chatham, 1963-66; Defence Services Sec., 1966-67. Rear-Adm. 1963; Vice-Adm. 1966. *Recreation:* golf. *Address:* Widcombe Hill House, Bath, Somerset. *T:* Bath 22638. *Club:* Army and Navy.

**HOGG, (James) Cecil,** CVO 1961; FRCS; Aurist to the Queen, since 1961; Dean of the Institute of Laryngology and Otology, University of London, 1961-65; late Examiner in Surgery, University of Bristol; Hon. Consulting Surgeon, Ear, Nose and Throat Department, St Bartholomew's Hospital, Royal National Throat, Nose and Ear Hospital; Consulting Laryngologist, King Edward VII Hospital, Midhurst, since 1960; *b* 25 Aug. 1900; *s* of late James Ewell Hogg; *m* 1936, Pollie Victoria Dalby; one *s* one *d*. *Educ:* Haileybury Coll.; Gonville & Caius Coll., Cambridge; St Bartholomew's Hosp. BA Cambridge 1922; MRCS, LRCP 1925; MA, BChir Cambridge 1926; FRCS 1930; House Surg. and House Surg., Ear, Nose and Throat Dept, St Bartholomew's Hosp., 1926-27; Chief Asst, Throat and Nose Dept, St Bartholomew's Hosp., 1931-35; Asst Surg., Throat and Ear Dept, Brompton Hosp. for Diseases of the Chest, London, 1936-46. FRSocMed (Pres., Section of Laryngology; Vice-Pres. Section of Otology; formerly Hon. Sec. Section of Laryngology and Section of Otology); Hon. Treasurer British Assoc. of Otolaryngology; Mem. BMA. *Publications:* various papers in medical jls and chapters in medical textbooks. *Recreations:* tennis, ski-ing. *Address:* 2 Upper Harley Street, NW1. *T:* 01-935 3884. *Clubs:* Bath, Ski Club of Great Britain.

**HOGG, Sir John (Nicholson),** Kt 1963; TD 1946; a Managing Director since 1950, and Chairman since 1968, Glyn, Mills & Co.; Deputy Chairman, Gallaher Ltd, since 1964; Director: National & Commercial Banking Group Ltd; The Prudential Assurance Co. Ltd; *b* 4 Oct. 1912; *o s* of late Sir Malcolm Hogg and of Lorna Beaman; *m* 1948, Barbara Mary Elisabeth, *yr d* of Capt. Arden Franklyn, Shedfield, Southampton and *widow* of Viscount Garmoyle (*d* of wounds, 1942); one *s* one *d*. *Educ:* Eton; Balliol Coll., Oxford. Joined Glyn, Mills and Co., 1934. Served War of 1939-45, with KRRC in Greece, Crete, Western Desert, Tunisia, NW Europe. Rejoined Glyn, Mills and Co. 1945, a Man. Dir., 1950-, Dep. Chm. 1963-68. Fellow of Eton Coll., 1951. Mem. of Commonwealth War Graves Commission, 1958-64; A Trustee Imperial War Graves Endowment Fund, 1965. Sheriff County of London, 1960; Chm., Export Credits Guarantee Department's Adv. Council, 1962-67. Chm., Abu Dhabi Investment Bd, 1967. *Recreations:* cricket, tennis. *Address:* The Red House, Shedfield, Southampton. *T:* Wickham 2121; 11 Melton Court, SW7. *T:* 01-589 9114. *Club:* Brooks's.

**HOGG, Sir Kenneth Weir,** 6th Bt, *cr* 1846; OBE 1946; Lieutenant-Colonel (retired); *b* 13 Sept. 1894; *s* of Guy Weir Hogg (*d* 1943); *S* to baronetcy of cousin, 4th Baron Magheramorne, 1957; *m* 1936, Hon. Aline Emily Partington, *o d* of 2nd Baron Doverdale. *Educ:* Haileybury; Christ Church, Oxford. Served in European War, 1914-18 and War of 1939-45; Irish Guards, 1915-33. *Recreations:* fishing, ski-ing. *Heir: cousin* Major Arthur Ramsay Hogg, MBE 1945 [*b* 24 Oct. 1896; *m* 1924, Mary Aileen Hester Lee, *d* of late P. H. Lee Evans; three *s* one *d*]. *Address:* 2 Curzon Place, Park Lane, W1. *Clubs:* St James', White's, Portland.

**HOGG, Margaret,** CBE 1917; SRN; Member, Trained Nurses Committee, and Regional Matron, Southern Area British Red Cross and Order of St John of Jerusalem, 1939-46; 3rd *d* of late Thomas T. Hogg, Gravesend, Kent. *Educ:* home and private sch. Was Civil Matron, Queen Alexandra's Imperial Army Nursing Board. Principal Matron, Mem. of Cttee and Acting Matron-in-Chief Territorial Army Nursing Service; Hosp. Visitor and Mem. of Gen. Nursing Council for England and Wales; Mem. Voluntary Advisory Nursing Board HM Prisons. Trained at Guys Hosp., SE; Night Superintendent, Ward Sister, Asst Matron and Matron of same Hosp.; retired, 1927. *Recreation:* music. *Address:* 9 Rosecroft Close, Lancing, Sussex. *Club:* Cowdray.

**HOGG, Norman,** CBE 1969; JP; Lord Provost of Aberdeen, 1964-67; Lord Lieutenant of the County of the City of Aberdeen, 1964-67; *b* 22 Nov. 1907; *s* of Hugh Hogg and Susan Gallow; *m* 1936, Mary Wilson; one *s*. *Educ:* Causewayend Sch., Aberdeen. Trade Union Officer, 1947-. Member: Aberdeen Town Council, 1943-48, 1951-; Guest Cttee on Scottish Licensing Law, 1959; Aberdeen Milk Marketing Board; Scottish After Care Council; Pt-time mem. of North of Scotland Hydro-Electric Board, 1961-; Chm., NE Consultative Group; Zone Comr, N Zone Scotland Civil Defence, 1970-. JP Aberdeen, 1948. Hon. LLD, Aberdeen, 1967. *Address:* 14 Sanday Road, Aberdeen. *T:* Aberdeen 34860.

**HOGG, Brig. Oliver Frederick Gillilan,** CBE 1943; pac; *b* 22 Dec. 1887; *s* of late Col Arthur Melvill Hogg, 6th Bombay Cavalry; *m* 1919, Ella Harold (*d* 1968), *d* of Arthur Harold Hallam, Shanghai; one *s*. *Educ:* Bedford Sch.; RMA, Woolwich. 2nd Lieut, RA 1907; Capt.

1914, Major, 1926; Lieut-Col 1934; Col 1935; Brig. 1939; retired, 1946; served European War (France) 1914-18 (1914 Star, British War and Victory Medals); Inspector of Danger Buildings, RGPF, 1915-16; Asst Supt RSAF, 1916-19; Asst Inspector Armaments Inspection Dept, 1921-25; Inspector AID, 1927-30; Mil. Asst to CSOF, 1933-36; War of 1939-45 (Defence and War Medals); Sec., Ordnance Board, 1936-39; Asst Master Gen. of the Ordnance, War Office, 1939; Dep. Dir of Military Administration, Ministry of Supply, 1939-41; Dir of Military Administration, Ministry of Supply, 1941-46; Leverhulme Research Fellow, 1950-51; FSA (Mem. Council, 1953-55); FRSA; FRGS; FRHistS; Fellow Soc. of Genealogists (Mem. Exec. Cttee, 1959-62); Soc. for Army Historical Research; Mem. Ancient Monuments Soc.; Vice-Pres. Greenwich Conservative Assoc., 1957- (Hon. Treasurer, 1956-57). Order of Polonia Restituta, 3rd class. *Publications:* The History of the 3rd Durham Volunteer Artillery, 1860-1960, 1960; English Artillery 1326-1716, 1963; The Royal Arsenal: Its Background, Origin and Subsequent History, 2 vols, 1963; Further Light on the Ancestry of William Penn, 1965; Clubs to Cannon, 1968; Artillery: its origin, heyday and decline, 1970; historical and technical articles dealing with artillery and small arm subjects in Army Jls, etc.; Contrib. on artillery, engines of war and The Board of Ordnance, to Chambers's Encycl. *Recreations:* walking and boating. *Address:* 1 Hardy Road, Blackheath, SE3. *T:* 01-858 3306. *Club:* United Service.

**HOGG, Percy Herbertson,** CBE 1965; retired; *b* 22 Dec. 1898; *s* of Andrew Herbertson Hogg, SCC, Edinburgh, and Mary Burrell Hogg; *m* 1925, Jean Kemp Selkirk; one *s* one *d*. *Educ:* Daniel Stewart's Coll., Edinburgh. Solicitor, Edinburgh, 1923-47; Dir, The Distillers Co. Ltd, 1952-65; Managing Dir, 1949-60, Chm., 1961-65, John Haig & Co. Ltd, Distillers. *Address:* 18 Queen's Road, Belmont, Surrey. *T:* 01-642 8339. *Club:* Royal Automobile.

**HOGG, Sir William Lindsay L.;** *see* Lindsay-Hogg.

**HOGGART, Richard;** an Assistant Director-General, UNESCO, since 1970; Professor of English, Birmingham University since 1962, and Director, Centre for Contemporary Cultural Studies, since 1964 (on leave of absence until 1973); *b* 24 Sept. 1918; 2nd *s* of Tom Longfellow Hoggart and Adeline Emma Hoggart; *m* 1942, Mary Holt France; two *s* one *d*. *Educ:* elementary and secondary schs, Leeds; Leeds Univ. (MA). Served 1940-46, RA; demobilised as Staff Capt. Staff Tutor and Sen. Staff Tutor, University Coll. of Hull and University of Hull, 1946-59; Sen. Lectr in English, University of Leicester, 1959-62. Visiting Prof., University of Rochester (NY), USA, 1956-57. Member: Albemarle Cttee on Youth Services, 1958-60; Brit. Council Brit. Books Overseas Cttee, 1959-64; BBC Gen. Advisory Council, 1959-60 and 1964-; Youth Service Development Council, 1960-62; (Pilkington) Cttee on Broadcasting, 1960-62; Culture Adv. Cttee of the UK Nat. Commn for UNESCO; Governor: Royal Shakespeare Theatre; Birmingham Repertory Theatre. FRSL, 1957-63. Mem. Editorial Board, Universities Quarterly. *Publications:* Auden, 1951; The Uses of Literacy, 1957; W. H. Auden, 1957; W. H. Auden–A Selection, 1961; chap. in Conviction, 1958; chapter in Pelican Guide to English Literature, 1961; Teaching Literature, 1963; chapter in Of Books and Humankind, 1964; The Critical Moment, 1964; How and Why Do We Learn, 1965; The World in 1984, 1965; Essays by Divers Hands XXXIII; Guide to the Social Sciences, 1966; Technology and Society, 1966; Essays on Reform, 1967; Your Sunday Paper (ed), 1967; Speaking to Each Other: vol. I, About Society; vol. II, About Literature, 1970. Numerous introductions, articles, pamphlets and reviews. *Recreation:* pottering about the house and garden. *Address:* UNESCO, 9 Place de Fontenoy, Paris 7, France.

**HOGGER, Rear-Adm. Henry Charles,** CB 1961; DSC 1942; Director, Production and Support Dockyards, since 1970; *b* 27 June 1907; *s* of Henry George and Maria Jane Hogger; *m* 1935, Ethel Mary Kreiner; two *s* one *d*. *Educ:* Portsmouth Grammar Sch. Entered Navy, Special Entry Cadet, 1925; specialised in Engineering at RNE Coll., Keyham and RN Coll., Greenwich. During War of 1939-45, served in HMS Kipling and Jervis, 1941-43. Chief Engineer, Hong Kong Dockyard, 1951-54; Asst Engineer-in-Chief, 1955-57; Manager, Engineering Dept, Portsmouth Dockyard, 1957; retired, 1961. Admiralty Regional Officer, Midlands, 1962; Dep. Head, Royal Naval Engineering Service, 1963-70. *Recreation:* golf. *Address:* Broome, Upper Lansdown Mews, Bath, Somerset. *T:* Bath 60108. *Clubs:* Royal Automobile, Army and Navy.

**HOGUE, Oliver Alfred John,** CVO 1954; Literary staff, Mirror Newspapers Ltd, Sydney, since 1962; *b* 16 Sept. 1910; *s* of Frank Arthur Hogue and Vida C. Hogue (*née* Robinson), Sydney; *m* 1st, 1936, Mary Barbour May (marr. diss., 1966); four *s*; 2nd, 1966, Mary Elizabeth Mofflin, *d* of Solomon Merkel, Lithuania. *Educ:* Newcastle (NSW) High Sch. Literary staff, Newcastle Herald, 1930; War Correspondent in Australia, 1940-43; Press Sec. to Hon. J. A. Beasley, Australian Minister for Supply, 1943-45; Political Corresp. for Sydney Sunday Sun, Canberra, 1945-53; literary staff, Sydney Sun, 1954-62. Pres., C'wealth Parly Press Gall., 1947-49. Aust. Govt PRO for Australian visit of the Queen and Prince Philip, 1954. *Address:* 5 Hill Street, Roseville, NSW, Australia. *T:* 41-6283. *Club:* Journalists' (Sydney).

**HOHLER, Henry Arthur Frederick,** CMG 1954; Ambassador to Switzerland 1967-70; *b* 4 Feb. 1911; *e s* of late Lt-Col Arthur Preston Hohler, DSO; *m* 1st, 1932, Mona Valentine (*d* 1944), *d* of late Lieut-Col Arthur Murray Pirie, DSO; two *s*; 2nd, 1945, Eveline Susan, *d* of late Lieut-Col Hon. Neville Albert Hood, CMG, DSO; two *d*. *Educ:* Eton; Sandhurst. 2nd Lieut Grenadier Guards, 1931. 3rd Sec. in Foreign Office, 1934; Budapest, 1936; 2nd Sec., 1939; Foreign Office, 1941; 1st Sec., 1945; Berne, 1945; Helsinki, 1948; Moscow, 1949; Counsellor, 1950; Head of Northern Dept, Foreign Office, 1951; Minister in Rome, 1956; Ambassador in Saigon, 1960-63; Minister in Paris, 1963-65; Asst Under-Sec., Foreign Office, 1966-67. Liveryman of the Grocers' Company. *Address:* Long Crendon Manor, Aylesbury, Bucks. *Club:* Boodle's.

**HOLBROOK, Col Sir Claude Vivian,** Kt, *cr* 1938; CBE 1919; JP; Officier Légion d'Honneur; Royal Army Service Corps (retired); *b* 1886; 3rd *s* of late Col Sir Arthur R. Holbrook, KBE; *m* 1st, 1913, Katharine (*d* 1966), *d* of late C. F. Elston; two *s*; 2nd, 1967, Joan, *d* of late Theodore Petersen and *widow* of Capt. J. L. Elston, The Northants Regt. Served European War, 1914-19; also 1939-43. DL, Warwicks, 1927-67. *Address:* Upper Durford, near Petersfield, Hants. *Club:* Royal Thames Yacht.

**HOLBROOK, Rear-Adm. Leonard Stanley,** MVO 1901; RN, retired; 2nd *s* of late Col Sir Arthur R. Holbrook, KBE; *b* 1882; *m* 1920, Gladys Nina (*d* 1968), *er d* of J. C. Grove of Stonehouse, Penn, Bucks, and *widow* of Major R. Spencer Britten; one *s*. *Educ:* privately. Entered HMS Britannia, 1896; Sub-Lt 1901; Lieut 1902; Lt-Comdr 1910; Comdr, 1914; Captain 1920; Rear-Adm. 1932; served with Naval Guard of Honour at Windsor at Queen Victoria's funeral; European War, 1914-17 (prom. Commander); lent to Australian Navy, 1929; commanded Australian Squadron, 1931-32; ADC to the King, 1932; retired list, 1932; War of 1939-45. *Address:* White Webbs, Bury, Pulborough, Sussex. *T:* Bury 412. *Club:* Savage.

**HOLBROOK, Cmdr Norman Douglas,** VC 1914; RN retired; *b* 9 July 1888; 4th *s* of late Col Sir Arthur R. Holbrook, KBE; *m* 1919, Viva (*d* 1952), *d* of late Frederick Woodin and *widow* of F. E. Dixon (one *s* killed in action, 1945); *m* 1953, Gundula, *d* of Dr A. Feldner, Innsbruck. When in command of submarine B11 in European War, 1914-17, dived under five rows of mines in the Dardanelles, 13 Dec. 1914, and torpedoed Turkish battleship Messudieh (VC, subsequently slightly wounded while on patrolling duties). *Address:* Stedham Mill, Stedham, near Midhurst, W Sussex. *T:* Midhurst 391. *Club:* Savage.

**HOLBURN, James;** *b* 1 Dec. 1900; *s* of late Rev. James Holburn, Alyth, Perthshire; *m* 1931, Elizabeth Margaret, *d* of late Rev. John McConnachie, DD, Dundee; three *s*. *Educ:* Harris Academy, Dundee; Univeristy of Glasgow (MA Hons). Editorial staff, the Glasgow Herald, 1921-34; joined The Times, 1934: asst correspondent and actg corresp. Berlin, 1935-39; correspondent Moscow, 1939-40; Ankara, 1940-41; War Correspondent, Middle East, 1941-42; Correspondent New Delhi, 1942-46; United Nations Headquarters, 1946-48; Diplomatic Corresp., 1948-51; Chief Corresp. Middle East, 1952-55; Editor, The Glasgow Herald, 1955-65. *Publications:* contributions to various periodicals. *Recreation:* golf. *Address:* Denford, Spring Elms Lane, Little Baddow, Chelmsford, Essex. *T:* Danbury 2581. *Club:* Western (Glasgow).

**HOLCROFT, Sir Reginald Culcheth,** 2nd Bt (2nd *cr*), *cr* 1921; TD; JP; *b* 6 April 1899; *s* of 1st Bt and Annie Gertrude (*d* 1929), *d* of late Rev. J. Coombes; *S* father, 1951; *m* 1st, 1928, Mary Frances (*d* 1963), *yr d* of late William Swire, CBE; two *s* two *d*; 2nd, 1965, Elizabeth, Countess of Bandon. *Educ:* Radley Coll.; RMC Sandhurst; Exeter Coll., Oxford. JP Shropshire since 1934, High Sheriff, 1950. *Heir: s* Peter George Culcheth Holcroft [*b* 29 April 1931; *m* 1956, Rosemary Rachel, *yr d* of G. N. Deas, Watery Gate, Weston-Sub-Edge, Campden, Glos; three *s* one *d*]. *Address:* Wrentnall House, Pulverbatch, Shrewsbury. *Club:* Cavalry.

**HOLDEN, Basil Munroe;** Rector, Glasgow Academy, since 1959; *b* 10 Nov. 1913; *m* 1951, Jean Watters; two *s* two *d*. *Educ:* Queen Elizabeth's Grammar Sch., Blackburn; King's Coll., Cambridge (Foundation Scholar). BA 1935, Maths Tripos (Wrangler), MA 1939. Mathematical Master, Highgate Sch., 1937. Instructor Lieut RN, 1940. Head of Mathematical Dept, Oundle Sch., 1947; Housemaster, Oundle Sch., 1956. *Recreations:* tennis, carpentry, dancing. *Address:* 98 Southbrae Drive, Glasgow W3. *T:* 041-959 1136.

**HOLDEN, David Charles Beresford,** CB 1963; ERD 1954; Secretary, Ministry of Finance, Northern Ireland, and Head of Northern Ireland Civil Defence, since 1970; *b* 26 July 1915; *s* of Oswald Addenbrooke Holden and Ella Mary Beresford; *m* 1948, Elizabeth Jean Odling; one *s* one *d*. *Educ:* Rosall Sch.; King's Coll., Cambridge. Northern Ireland Civil Service from 1937. Royal Artillery, 1939-46. Second Sec., Min. of Finance, N Ireland, 1958-70. *Address:* 7 Cross Avenue, Marlborough Park, Belfast 9, Northern Ireland. *T:* Belfast 667666. *Club:* Oriental.

**HOLDEN, Sir Edward,** 6th Bt *cr* 1893; Consultant Anæsthetist, Darlington & Northallerton Group Hospitals, since 1957; *b* 8 Oct. 1916; *s* of Sir Isaac Holden Holden, 5th Bt, and Alice Edna Byrom; *S* father, 1962; *m* 1942, Frances Joan, *e d* of John Spark, JP, Ludlow, Stockton-on-Tees; two adopted *s*. *Educ:* Leys Sch. and Christ's Coll., Cambridge (MA); St Thomas's Hosp. MRCS; LRCP 1942; DA Eng., 1946; FFA, RCS, 1958. Formerly Vis. Anæsth., Cumb. Infirm., Carlisle; Cons. Anæsth. W Cumb. Hospital Group. Managing Dir, Middleton-St-George Aero Club Ltd. *Recreations:* fishing and gardening. *Heir: b* Paul Holden [*b* 3 March 1923; *m* 1950, Vivien Mary Oldham; one *s* two *d*]. *Address:* Croft House, Croft, near Darlington, Co. Durham. *T:* Croft 225. *Club:* Farmers'.

**HOLDEN, Sir George,** 3rd Bt, *cr* 1919; London Area Manager for L. & G. Fire Appliance Co. Ltd, since 1967; *b* 6 Dec. 1914; *s* of Sir George Holden, 2nd Bt, and Margaret, *d* of Thomas Smith, JP, of Astley, near Manchester; *S* father, 1937; *m* 1937, Betty, *d* of late W. Shaw, 70 Portland Place, W1; two *s* two *d* (and one *s* decd). *Educ:* Oundle. *Heir: s* David George Holden [*b* 19 April 1938; *m* 1964, Nancy, *d* of H. W. D. Marwood; one *s*]. *Address:* Lynville, Portland Road, Dorking, Surrey. *T:* Dorking 3697.

**HOLDEN, Harold H.,** ARCA, AMC, RWS; *b* 1885. *Educ:* Settle; Skipton; Leeds School of Art; Royal College of Art, London. Head of the Art Dept, Leeds Modern Sch., 1910; Principal of the Sch. of Arts and Crafts, Cheltenham, 1914; Principal Leeds Coll. of Art, 1922; Dir of Art Education and Principal of The College of Arts and Crafts, Birmingham, 1928-46; retired, 1946. *Address:* 3 Southwood Drive, Westbury-on-Trym, Bristol.

**HOLDEN, Sir James (Robert),** Kt 1963; Resident Director, General Motors–Holden's Proprietary Ltd, Woodville, in the State of South Australia, since 1952; Director, Elder's Trustee & Executor Co. Ltd, Adelaide, since 1949; Director, Cellulose Australia Ltd, Adelaide, since 1954; *b* 1903; *s* of late Hubert William Holden, Turramurra, NSW, and Annie Maria, *d* of Robert Turner, Victoria; *m* 1934, Prudence Elsie Staughton; four *d*. *Educ:* Sydney C. of E. Grammar Sch., NSW. *Recreations:* golf, fishing. *Address:* General Motors–Holden's Pty Ltd, Woodville, S Australia; 27 Robe Terrace, Medindie, SA. *Club:* Adelaide.

**HOLDEN, Maj.-Gen. John Reid,** CB 1965; CBE 1960 (OBE 1953); DSO 1941; Director, RAC, 1965-68, retired 1968; *b* 8 Jan. 1913; 2nd *s* of late John Holden, MA, Edinburgh; *m* 1939, Rosemarie Florence, *d* of late William Henry de Vere Pennefather, Carlow; one *d*. *Educ:* Hamilton Academy; Glasgow Univ.; RMC, Sandhurst. 2nd Lieut Royal Tank Corps, 1937; Adjutant, 7th Royal Tank Regt, 1940-41 (despatches, DSO); Bde Major, 32nd Army Tank Bde, 1942; POW, 1942-45. GSO1, GHQ,

Far ELF, Singapore, 1951-52 (OBE); CO 3rd Royal Tank Regt, BAOR, 1954-57; AAG, War Office, 1958. Comdr, 7th Armoured Bde Group, BAOR, 1958-61 (CBE). Royal Naval War Coll., 1961. Chief of Mission, British Comdrs-in-Chief Mission to the Soviet Forces in Germany, 1961-63; GOC 43 (Wessex) Div. Dist, 1963-65. Col Comdt, RTR, 1965-68. *Recreations:* shooting, books, gardening. *Address:* Garden Cottage, Wareham, Dorset.

**HOLDEN, Kenneth Graham;** Chairman: Williams Deacon's Bank Ltd since 1964; Williams and Glyn's Bank Ltd, since 1969; Director: National Commercial Banking Group Ltd; Trustees Corporation Ltd; Geigy (UK) Ltd; G. N. Haden and Sons, Ltd; North Western Gas Board; The Manchester Ship Canal Co.; *b* 6 May 1910; *e s* of Norman Neill Holden; *m* 1937, Winifred Frances, *d* of Lt-Col T. F. S. Burridge; two *d. Educ:* Wellington Coll.; Pembroke Coll., Cambridge. Solicitor, 1935. Formerly Mem. Bd of Management (and sometime Jt Hon. Treasurer), Manchester Royal Infirmary. Governor, Manchester Grammar Sch. *Address:* Smithy Cottage, Birtles, Macclesfield, Cheshire. *T:* Chelford 521. *Clubs:* Bath, MCC, All England Lawn Tennis.

**HOLDEN, Philip Edward;** an Underwriting Member of Lloyd's since 1954; *b* 20 June 1905. *Educ:* King Edward VI Schs, Birmingham. Qualified, CA, 1929; Managing Dir Amalgamated Anthracite Colliers, from 1940. Past Chm., Amalgamated Anthracite Holdings Group of Cos. Has served on Exec. of Monmouthshire and S Wales Coal Owners Assoc., and as Chm. of its Commercial Cttee; also served on Exec. Bd of S Wales Coal Mines Scheme. Pres. Swansea Chamber of Commerce, 1952-53; Vice-Chm. Chamber of Coal Traders, 1953-65; Vice-Chm. Nat. Council of Coal Traders (Chm. 1953-65); Pres. Brit. Coal Exporters' Assoc., 1958-63; Mem. Industrial Coal Consumers' Council, 1958. A Dir of public and private cos (coal, shipping, manufactures, electronics, electro-chemical and general engineering, etc). *Recreations:* Pres. Swansea Town AFC Ltd; Vice-Pres. Clyne Golf Club, Ltd. *Address:* La Maison Blanche, Jerbourg Road, St Martin, Guernsey, CI. *T:* Guernsey 37985. *Clubs:* Carlton, Royal Automobile; Bristol Channel Yacht (Swansea).

**HOLDER, Prof. Douglas William,** MA, PhD, DSc; DIC; FRS 1962; FCGI; CEng; FICE; FRAeS; AFAIAA; Professor of Engineering Science and Head of Department of Engineering Science, Oxford University, since Oct. 1961; Fellow of Brasenose College, Oxford, since 1961; *b* 14 April 1923; *s* of late W. A. Holder and Ann Daniel; *m* 1946, Barbara Woods; two *d. Educ:* Imperial Coll. of Science and Technology. Aircraft and Armament Experimental Establishment, 1943; Nat. Physical Laboratory, 1944-61; Head of High Speed Laboratory, 1950-61 (dep. Chief SO (Personal Merit), 1957). Chairman: Enquiry into Precision Approach Radar, BoT, 1969; Royal Society ad hoc Cttee on Technology, 1963-65; Aerodynamic Cttee, RAeS, 1964-68. Mem. Aeronautical Research Coun., 1964-68 (Chm. Aerodynamics Cttee, Hypersonics Sub-Cttee; Mem. Fluid-motion Cttee, Guidance and Control Cttee); Mem., Advis. Coun. on Scientific Research and Tech. Development, MoD, 1964-68 (Mem., Maths and Physics Cttee, 1962-); Mem. or Chm., various cttees and working parties of MoD, 1964-; Member: Standing Adv. Cttee on Artificial Limbs, Dept Health and Social Security (formerly Min. of Health), 1966-; Hydraulic Research Bd, 1963-65; Vis. Bd, Nat. Physical Laboratory, 1967-69; Schools Council Science and Technology Cttee, 1964-; Academic Adv. Cttee, Coll. of Aeronautics, 1964-65; Adv. Council, RMCS, 1964-; RMA, 1969-; Council, Royal Society, 1969- (Mem. Educn Cttee, 1969-, Ind. Activities Cttee, 1969-); Court and Council, Cranfield Inst. Technology, 1970-. Visitor, Central Electricity Research Laboratory, 1962-; Chm. of Governors, Oxford Polytechnic, 1970-. Visiting Prof., University of Michigan, 1964. *Publications:* books, monographs and papers mainly on fluid mechanics and related topics. *Recreations:* tennis, golf. *Address:* Engineering Laboratory, Parks Road, Oxford. *T:* Oxford 56120; Grazely House, Iffley Turn, Oxford. *T:* Oxford 77040.

**HOLDER, Sir John Eric Duncan,** 3rd Bt, *cr* 1898; late Flight Lieutenant RAFVR; *b* 2 Aug. 1899; *s* of Sir Henry Holder, 2nd Bt, and Evelyn (*d* 1956), *d* of Sir Robert Ropner, 1st Bt; *S* father, 1945; *m* 1927, Evelyn Josephine (marriage dissolved, 1948), *er d* of late William Blain and Mrs Blain, The Old Manor House, Combe Florey; one *s* two *d. Educ:* Uppingham; Brasenose Coll., Oxford (MA). *Heir: s* John Henry Holder, Royal Armoured Corps [*b* 12 March 1928; *m* 1960, Catharine Harrison, *yr d* of Leonard Baker, Stone Lane, near Stourbridge, Worcs; two *s* (*twins*) one *d*]. *Address:* Staplegrove, 6 Church Street, Hampton, Middx.

**HOLDER, Air Marshal Sir Paul (Davie),** KBE 1965; CB 1964; DSO 1942; DFC 1941; Air Officer Commanding-in-Chief, RAF Coastal Command, and NATO Commander Maritime Air, Channel Command and Commander Maritime Air, Eastern Atlantic Area, 1965-68; retired 1968; *b* 2 Sept. 1911; *s* of Hugh John and Frances Rhoda Holder; *m* 1940, Mary Elizabeth Kidd; two *s. Educ:* Bristol Univ.; University of Illinois, USA. Graduated Bristol Univ., 1931; MSc 1933; Robert Blair Fellow, 1934; PhD 1935. Vice-Pres., RAF Selection Board, 1947-48; Student, Administrative Staff Coll., Henley on Thames, 1949; CO, RAF, Shallufa, Egypt, 1950-51; CO, RAF, Kabrit, Egypt, 1952; Dep. Dir, Air Staff Policy, Air Min., 1953-55; Student, Imperial Defence Coll., 1956; AOC, Singapore, 1957; AOC, Hong Kong, 1958-59; ACAS (Trng), Air Min., 1960-62; AOC No. 25 Gp, RAF Flying Trng Comd, 1963-64. FRAeS, 1966. *Recreations:* golf, sailing, bridge. *Address:* Ninford Cottage, Grayswood, Haslemere, Surrey. *T:* Haslemere 3227. *Club:* Royal Air Force.

**HOLDERNESS, Rt. Rev. George Edward,** ERD (with 2 clasps) 1955; Dean of Lichfield since 1970; *b* 5 March 1913; 2nd *s* of A. W. Holderness, Roundhay, Leeds; *m* 1940, Irene Mary, *er d* of H. G. Hird, Bedale, Yorkshire; one *s* two *d. Educ:* Leeds Grammar Sch.: Keble Coll., Oxford (MA); Westcott House, Cambridge. Assistant Curate of Bedale, 1936-39; Chaplain and Asst Master, Aysgarth School, Bedale, 1939-47. CF (RARO), 1940; SCF, 81st W African Div., 1943; DACG, India Command, 1945. Vicar of Darlington, 1947-55; Hon. Canon of Durham Cathedral, 1954; Suffragan Bishop of Burnley, 1955-70; Rector of Burnley, 1955-70; Canon of Blackburn Cathedral, 1955-70. DACG, TA, Northern Command, 1951-55. *Recreations:* cricket, shooting, fishing. *Address:* The Deanery, Lichfield, Staffs. *Clubs:* MCC, Forty, Lord's Taverners', Farmers'.

**HOLDERNESS, Sir Richard William,** 3rd Bt, *cr* 1920; *b* 30 Nov. 1927; *s* of Sir Ernest William Elsmie Holderness, 2nd Bt, CBE, and Emily Carlton (*d* 1950), *y d* of late Frederick McQuade, Sydney, NSW; *S* father, 1968; *m* 1953, Pamela, *d* of Eric Chapman, CBE; two *s* one *d. Educ:* Dauntsey's Sch.; Corpus Christi Coll., Oxford. *Heir: s* Martin William Holderness, *b* 24 May 1957. *Address:* Rosetree House, Boxgrove, Chichester.

**HOLDGATE, Martin Wyatt,** PhD; Head of Central Scientific Unit on Environmental Pollution, Department of the Environment (formerly in the Cabinet Office), since 1970; *b* 14 Jan. 1931; *s* of Francis Wyatt Holdgate, MA, JP, and Lois Marjorie Bebbington; *m* 1963, Elizabeth Mary (*née* Dickason), *widow* of Dr H. H. Weil; two *s. Educ:* Arnold Sch., Blackpool; Queens' Coll., Cambridge. BA Cantab 1952; MA 1956; PhD 1955; FInstBiol 1967. Senior Scientist, Gough Is. Scientific Survey, 1955-56; Lecturer in Zoology, Manchester Univ., 1956-57; Lecturer in Zoology, Durham Colleges, 1957-60; Leader, Royal Society Expedition to Southern Chile, 1958-59; Asst Director of Research, Scott Polar Research Institute, Cambridge, 1960-63; Senior Biologist, British Antarctic Survey, 1963-66; Dep. Dir (Research), The Nature Conservancy, 1966-70. Secretary, Working Group on Biology, Scientific Cttee on Antarctic Research, 1964-68. Chairman, British Schools Exploring Society, 1967-. *Publications:* Mountains in the Sea, The Story of the Gough Island Expedition, 1958; (Jt Ed) Antarctic Biology, 1964; (ed) Antarctic Ecology, 1969; numerous papers in biological journals and works on Antarctic. *Address:* 19 West Hill Road, Hoddesdon, Herts. *T:* Hoddesdon 63526.

**HOLDSWORTH, Albert Edward,** QC 1969; Barrister-at-law, Middle Temple; *b* 1909; *e s* of Albert Edward and Catherine Sarah Holdsworth; *m* 1st, 1941, Barbara Frances (*d* 1968), *e d* of Ernest Henry and Beatrice Maud Reeves; one *s*; 2nd, 1970, Brianne Evelyn Frances, *d* of Arthur James and Evelyn Lock. Educ: Sir George Monoux Sch., Walthamstow; Gonville and Caius Coll., Cambridge (Exhibitioner). Pres., Cambridge Union, 1932; Economics and Politics tripos; MA. Formerly journalist: Financial News, 1932-33; Special Correspondent, World Economic Conf., 1933; Yorkshire Post, 1933-46, Polit. Correspondent, later London Editor. Broadcasts for BBC on current affairs topics, 1935-56. Called to Bar, 1936. Conservative Candidate Ipswich, 1951; moved resolution in favour of UK entry into European Common Market, Conservative Conf., Llandudno, 1962. Dep.-Chm., SW Metropolitan Mental Health Tribunal, 1962-65. Pres., City Residents Conservative Council, 1966-. *Recreations:* cinema, theatre, reading. *Address:* 3 Temple Gardens, Temple, EC4. *T:* 01-353 1244; 2 Middle Temple Lane, Temple, EC4. *T:* 01-353 7926; 25 Norfolk Road, Brighton BN1 3AA. *T:* Brighton 70556. *Club:* Reform.

**HOLDSWORTH, Mrs Mary,** MA; Principal, St Mary's College, Durham University, since Oct. 1962; *b* Voronezh, Russia, 24 Oct. 1908; *d* of late Col A. Zvegintzov, Chev. Gardes, Member of Duma, and Catherine Sverbeev; *m* 1940, Richard William Gilbert Holdsworth, Fellow, University College, Oxford, Flt-Lieut RAFVR (killed on active service, 1942); one *d. Educ:* Cheltenham Ladies' Coll.; St Hugh's Coll., Oxford. Worked in banking and industry, 1931-37; College Sec., University College, Oxford, 1937-40; Air Ministry, 1942-43; Tutor for Education in the Forces, N. Ireland, 1943-45; WEA Tutor (part-time) in Oxon., 1945-48; Secretary and Senior Research Officer, OU Institute of Commonwealth Studies, 1948-62. Governor of two Oxon. schools, 1951-62. Member Royal Institute of International Affairs, 1961-. *Publications:* Turkestan in the 19th Century, 1959; Soviet African Studies, 1918-59 (annotated bibliography for RIIA), 1961. Articles, Reviews. *Recreations:* gardening, walking. *Address:* St Mary's College, Durham. *T:* Durham 3533.

**HOLDSWORTH, Max Ernest,** OBE; TD; DL; MA; LLB; Barrister-at-Law; Deputy-Chairman, Court of Quarter Sessions, Gloucestershire, 1954-68; Recorder of Lichfield, 1939-68; Colonel (TA); *b* 6 Nov. 1895; *o s* of late M. F. Holdsworth. *Educ:* King Edward's Sch., Birmingham; Christ's Coll., Cambridge. Served European War, 1915-19; also in War of 1939-45; called to the Bar, Gray's Inn, 1922. *Publication:* Law of Transport, 1932. *Address:* 5 Fountain Court, Steelhouse Lane, Birmingham 4. *T;* 021-236 5771. *Club:* Union (Worcester).

**HOLE, Edwyn Cecil,** CBE 1946; *s* of late George Walter Hole and Emma, *d* of George Jolly Grace; *m* 1919, Laura Hélène Marianne, *d* of late John Richard de Fonton; one *s* one *d. Educ:* St Olave's; Heidelberg; Paris; Pembroke Coll., Cambridge. Student Interpreter in the Levant, 1911; special service in Turkey, Bulgaria and Greece, 1914-16; served at Janina and Mitylene till 1919; on staff of British High Commissioner at Constantinople, 1919, Smyrna, 1919-22; acting Consul-Gen. Salonica, 1922-24; served with League of Nations Commission of Enquiry into the murder of Gen. Tellini, Janina, 1923; Corfu, 1925; Consul Damascus, 1926-32, Athens, 1932-36, Marrakesh, 1936; Dept of Overseas Trade, 1936; Consul-Gen. at Salonica, 1938-41; at Smyrna, 1941-45; at Nice 1945-50; retired 1950; Hon. Consul at Málaga, 1952-57. *Publications:* Syrian Harvest, 1955; Andalus: the Muslims in Spain, 1958; Also Ran, reminiscences, 1966. *Recreations:* historical research, music. *Address:* Running Tide, Smugglers Lane, Bosham, Sussex. *T:* Bosham 3115.

**HOLE, Francis George,** CBE 1963; FCA; *b* 29 Nov. 1904; *e s* of late Francis Hole; *m* 1934, Jean Mary, *d* of late Judge L. C. Thomas; one *s* one *d. Educ:* King's Coll. Sch. ACA 1929; senior asst, Thomson McLintock & Co., 1930; accountant, LMS Hotel Services, 1934; succeeded Arthur Towle, Controller, LMS Hotel Services, 1945; Mem. of Hotels Executive, British Transport, 1948-53; on discontinuance of Executive, Chief of British Transport Hotels and Catering Services, 1954-55; Gen. Manager, 1955-58; Chm. and Gen. Manager, 1959-62; Dir and Gen. Manager, British Transport Hotels Ltd, 1963-68, Man. Dir, 1969. Member: Council of Management, Executive Cttee and Scottish Cttee of British Hotels and Restaurants Assoc., 1944-; British Tourist and Holidays Board and Chm. of Hotels Cttee, 1947-48; Licensed Residential Establishment and Licensed Restaurant Wages Board, 1946-51; Board, BTA, 1964-70; Hotel and Catering Ind. Training Bd, 1969-. chm. of the Governing Body of King's Coll. Sch.; Mem. of Coun., Radley Coll. *Address:* Little Rex, St Andrews Square, Surbiton, Surrey. *T:* 01-399 1958.

**HOLE, George Vincer,** CBE 1969; Chief Executive, British Airports Authority, since 1966; *b* 26 Jan. 1910; *s* of George William Hole and Louisa Hole (*née* Vincer); *m* 1938, Gertraud Johanna Anna Koppe (Baroness von Broesigke); two *s. Educ:* Wilson's Grammar Sch., London; London Sch. of Economics. BSc (Econ.) 1933. Asst Auditor, Exchequer and Audit Dept, 1929; passed First Div. Exam., 1935; Asst Principal, Board of Trade, 1936; Principal, Ministry of Shipping, 1940; Asst

Sec. Min. of War Transport, 1946; Min. of Transport and Civil Aviation, 1953; Under-Sec., 1958; Min. of Aviation, 1959-66; student Imperial Defence Coll., 1948; Chm. First Div. Assoc., 1949-50; Chm. OEEC Productivity Group, on Traffic Engineering and Control, in the United States, 1954; Chm. W European Airports Assoc., 1970; Mem. Council, Internat. Bd of Airport Operators, 1970. MInstT. Hon. Treas., Caravan Club, 1960-66. Officer, Order of Orange Nassau, Netherlands, 1946; Officer, Order of the Crown, Belgium, 1946. *Recreation:* pottering. *Address:* 6 St Germans Place, Blackheath, SE3. *T:* 01-858 3917. *Clubs:* Reform, Royal Aero.

**HOLFORD,** Baron *cr* 1965, of Kemp Town (Life Peer); **William Graham Holford,** Kt 1953; RA 1968 (ARA 1961); FRIBA, MTPI; architect and planning consultant; Professor of Town Planning, University College, London, since 1948-70, now Emeritus Professor; *b* 22 March 1907; *s* of William George Holford and Katherine Palmer; *m* 1933, Marjorie, *d* of John and Caroline Brooks. *Educ:* Diocesan Coll., Capetown, S Africa; Liverpool Sch. of Architecture. American Scholar of the Soc. of Arts and Sciences, New York, USA, 1929; Degree of BArch (1st Class Hons), University of Liverpool; Rome Scholar in Architecture, 1930; Florence Bursar of RIBA, 1935; Pres., RIBA, 1960-62. Architect of houses, factories, university and public buildings; planning consultant to City of London, County of Cambridge, etc; Romanes Lectr, Oxford, 1969; Member: Royal Fine Art Commission, 1943-69; Historic Buildings Council for England, 1953-; (Pt-time) Central Electricity Generating Board; Hon. Mem., ICE, 1968. A Trustee, British Museum, 1969-; Governor: Wye Coll., Univ. of London, 1968-; Centre for Environmental Studies, 1967-. Prime Warden, Goldsmiths' Co., 1962-. Hon. DCL Dunelm 1960; Hon. LLD Liverpool, 1961; Hon. DLitt: Oxon, 1964; Exon, 1968. Gold Medal of Town Planning Institute, 1961; Royal Gold Medal for Architecture, 1963. *Publications:* The Great Baroque Masquerade, 1932; Town and City, 1942; Reconstruction in the City of London, 1947; Cambridge Planning Proposals, 1950; Corby New Town, 1952; Design in Town and Village, 1953; Report . . . on the Precincts of St Paul's, 1956; Durban 1985, a plan for central Durban in its regional setting, 1968. *Address:* 20 Eccleston Square, SW1; 133 Marine Parade, Brighton, Sussex. *Clubs:* Savile, Athenæum; University (Liverpool).

**HOLFORD, Rear-Adm. Frank Douglas,** CB 1969; DSC 1944; Director General of Naval Manpower, Ministry of Defence, 1967-69, retired 1970; *b* 28 June 1916; *y s* of late Capt. C. F. Holford, DSO, OBE, and Ursula Isobel Holford (*née* Corbett); *m* 1942, Sybil Priscilla, *d* of late Comdr Sir Robert Micklem and of Lady Micklem; two *s*. *Educ:* RN Coll., Dartmouth. Cadet, 1929, Midshipman, HMS Hood, 1933; Sub-Lieut, HMS Wolverine, 1937; Lieutenant: HMS Kent, 1938; HMS Anson, 1941; HMS Sheffield, 1943; Lieut-Comdr: HMS Excellent, 1945; HMS Triumph, 1948; Commander: Admlty, Naval Ordnance Dept, 1951; British Joint Services Mission, USA, 1953; HMS Excellent, 1955; Captain: Admlty, Dir Guided Weapons, 1957; Naval and Mil. Attaché, Buenos Aires, 1960; Staff C-in-C Portsmouth, 1962; Cdre-i-C Hong Kong, 1965. Rear-Adm. 1967. jssc 1947. *Address:* Great Down Cottage, Soberton, Hants. *T:* Droxford 448. *Club:* United Service.

**HOLFORD, Surgeon Rear-Adm. John Morley,** CB 1965; OBE 1954; Senior Medical Officer, Ministry of Health, since 1967; *b* 10 Jan. 1909; *o s* of late Rev. W. J. Holford and Amy Finnemore Lello; *m* 1935, Monica Peregrine, *d* of late Preb. P. S. G. Propert; two *s*. *Educ:* Kingswood, Bath; Trinity Hall, Cambridge. MA, MB, Cantab; FRCP; joined RN 1935. War service in HMS Nelson, 1940-42; RN Hosp. Plymouth, 1942-44. Surgeon Capt., 1957; Surgeon Rear-Adm. 1963; Medical Officer in Charge, RN Hosp. Haslar, 1963-66. Retired, 1966. MO, Min. of Health, 1966. CStJ 1964. *Publications:* Articles in medical journals. *Recreations:* chess (jt champion of South Africa, 1946), bridge. *Address:* c/o Lloyds Bank, 84 Park Lane, W1. *Clubs:* Army and Navy, Hurlingham.

**HOLGATE, Sidney;** Master of Grey College, University of Durham, since 1959; Chairman, Durham Local Radio Council, since 1968; *b* Hucknall, Notts, 9 Sept. 1918; *e s* of late Henry and Annie Elizabeth Holgate; *m* 1942, Isabel Armorey; no *c*. *Educ:* Henry Mellish Sch., Nottingham; Durham Univ. Open Scholar, Hatfield Coll., Durham, 1937; Univ. Mathematical Scholarship, 1940; BA (1st Cl. Hons Mathematics) 1940; MA 1943; PhD 1945. Asst Master, Nottingham High Sch., 1941-42; Lecturer in Mathematics, University of Durham, 1942-46; Sec. of the Durham Colls, 1946-59; Pro-Vice-Chancellor, Univ. of Durham, 1964-69. Member: Schools Council Gen. Studies Cttee, 1967-70; Academic Adv. Cttee, Open Univ., 1969-. *Publications:* mathematical papers in Proc. Camb. Phil. Soc. and Proc. Royal Soc. *Recreations:* cricket and other sports, railways, bridge. *Address:* Grey College, Durham. *T:* Durham 4778.

**HOLGATE, Surgeon Rear-Adm. (D) William,** CB 1962; OBE 1951; Chief Dental Officer, Ministry of Health, since 1961, and Ministry of Education and Science, since 1963; *b* 6 July 1906; *s* of Anthony and Jane Holgate; *m* 1933, Inga Ommanney Davis; one *s* one *d*. *Educ:* Scarborough Coll.; Guy's Hospital. LDS, RCS Eng., 1927; FDS, RCS Eng., 1963. Royal Navy, 1928-61. Director of Dental Services, 1960. *Address:* Winton, Woodham Road, Woking, Surrey. *Club:* Savage.

**HOLLAND, David Cuthbert Lyall;** Librarian of the House of Commons since 1967; *b* 23 March 1915; *yr s* of Michael Holland, MC, and Marion Holland (*née* Broadwood); *m* 1949, Rosemary Griffiths, *y d* of David Ll. Griffiths, OBE; two *s* one *d*. *Educ:* Eton; Trinity Coll., Cambridge (MA). War service, Army, 1939-46; PoW. Appointed House of Commons Library, 1946. *Publications:* book reviews, etc. *Recreation:* book collecting. *Address:* Trees, Sandridge Lane, Haywards Heath, Sussex. *T:* Lindfield 3345. *Club:* Athenæum.

**HOLLAND, David George;** Chief Economic Adviser, Foreign and Commonwealth Office (formerly Commonwealth Office), since 1967; *b* 31 May 1925; *s* of late Francis George Holland and Mabel Ellen Gulliver; *m* 1954, Marian Elizabeth Rowles; one *s* one *d*. *Educ:* Taunton Sch.; Wadham Coll., Oxford. Inst. of Economics and Statistics, Oxford, 1949-63; Internat. Bank for Reconstruction and Development, Washington, DC, 1963-65; Min. of Overseas Development, 1965-67. *Address:* 20 Woodside Avenue, Highgate, N6.

**HOLLAND, Edgar William,** CIE 1944; *b* 28 April 1899; *s* of Rev. Edgar Rogers Holland, MA, and Ellen Angela (*née* Jellicorse); *m* 1928, Doris Marjorie, 2nd *d* of George Waverling Schoneman, late Postmaster-Gen., Bengal and Assam, and Hilda Edith (*née* Hope Ross). *Educ:* Rossall Sch.; Brasenose Coll., Oxford. Served in European War, 1914-18, in Royal Artillery, France, 1918. Entered Indian Civil

Service, 1923, posted to Bengal Province; Commissioner of Commercial Taxes, 1941; Sec. to Government in Public Health Dept, 1943; Commissioner of Dacca Div., 1945; Chairman, Calcutta Improvement Trust, 1947; retired from ICS, 1948; Asst Governor HM Prison Service, 1951-56. *Recreations:* rowing, tennis, walking. *Address:* 44 Harlow Moor Drive, Harrogate.

**HOLLAND, Frank,** CBE 1964; retired as official of LCC, 1964; *b* 21 Sept. 1899; *s* of H. J. E. Holland; *m* 1931, Elsie Freda Smith; one *s*. *Educ:* King Edward VI Sch., Lichfield. Entered service of LCC, 1915; Dep. Comptroller, 1949, Comptroller, 1956-64. Incorporated Accountant, 1930. Mem. Coun., London Hostels Corp. and Chm. of Finance and Gen. Purposes Cttee. *Recreations:* walking, motoring, gardening, archaeology, geology. *Address:* Cherrywood, 6 Weedon Lane, Amersham, Bucks. *T:* Amersham 5577.

**HOLLAND, Sir Jim Sothern,** 2nd Bt, *cr* 1917; Major RA TARO, 1964-68; a Manager and Alternate Director, Charter Consolidated Ltd; *b* 31 March 1911; *er s* of Sir R. Sothern Holland, 1st Bt, and Stretta Aimée Holland (*née* Price) (*d* 1949); *S* father, 1948; *m* 1937, Elisabeth Hilda Margaret, *o d* of T. F. V. Prickard, *qv*; two *d*. *Educ:* Durnford; Marlborough; Trinity Coll., Oxon (MA). Central Mining and Investment, 1932-64; Dir, Price & Pierce (Finance) Ltd, 1959-66. Joined TA 1939. City of London Yeomanry; TD 1950. Served War of 1939-45; 1942-44, ADC to Field-Marshal Viscount Gort, when Governor of Malta. *Recreations:* botany, stalking, golf. *Heir: b* Guy Hope Holland, late Royal Scots Greys [*b* 19 July 1918; *m* 1945, Joan Marian, *o d* of late Capt. H. E. Street, 20th Hussars; two *d*. *Educ:* Christ Church, Oxford]. *Address:* Westwell Manor, Burford, Oxon. *T:* Burford 2123. *Club:* Bath.

**HOLLAND, Rt. Rev. John T.;** *see* Polynesia, Bishop in.

**HOLLAND, Capt. John Vincent,** VC 1916; Indian Army, retired; *b* Athy, Co. Kildare, July 1889; *e s* of John Holland, MRCVS, Model Farm, Athy, Co. Kildare; *m* Frances, *y d* of Joseph Grogan, JP, Manor House, Queenstown and Rossleague. *Educ:* Clongowes Wood Coll.; Liverpool Univ. Travelled extensively in South America (Brazil, Argentine, Chili and Bolivia), where engaged in ranching, railway engineering, and hunting; returned to England on Outbreak of war; enlisted in 2nd Life Guards, 2 Sept. 1914; gazetted to Leinster Regt Feb. 1915; attached to 2nd Royal Dublin Fusiliers in France (wounded in 2nd battle of Ypres); returned to France; attached to 7th Leinster Regt as Batt. Bombing Officer; saw service at Loos, Hulloch, and Somme, 1916 (despatches and awarded Parchment of 16th Irish Div.; VC for conspicuous bravery in leading an attack at the capture of Guillemont, 3 Sept. 1916); retired, 1922. *Recreations:* hunted a great deal with Kildare, Queen's County, and Co. Carlow foxhounds; big game abroad; tennis, cricket. *Address:* Model Farm, Athy, Co. Kildare. *TA:* Athy.

**HOLLAND, Philip Welsby;** MP (C) Carlton since 1966; *b* 14 March 1917; *s* of late John Holland, Middlewich, Cheshire; *m* 1943, Josephine Alma Hudson; one *s*. *Educ:* Sir John Deane's Grammar Sch. Northwich. Enlisted RAF 1936; commissioned 1943. Factory Manager, Jantzen Knitting Mills, 1946-47; Management Research, 1948-49; Manufacturers' Agent in Engineering and Refractories Products, 1949-60. Contested (C) Yardley Div. of Birmingham, Gen. Election, 1955; MP (C) Acton, 1959-64; PPS to Minister of Pensions and Nat. Insurance, 1961-62; PPS to Chief Sec. to Treasury and Paymaster-Gen., 1962-64. Personnel Manager, The Ultra Electronics Group of Companies, 1964-66; Personnel Consultant to Standard Telephones and Cables Ltd, 1969-. Councillor, Royal Borough of Kensington, 1955-59. *Recreation:* travel. *Address:* 2 Holland Park Mansions, Holland Park Gardens, W14. *T:* 01-603 5640; Orston, Notts. *Club:* Carlton.

**HOLLAND, Robert Henry Code,** CBE 1969; retired publisher; Chairman, Book Centre Ltd; formerly deputy Chairman, Sir Isaac Pitman & Sons Ltd; *b* Manchester, 22 Feb. 1904; *e s* of late Robert W. Holland, OBE, LLD, and Annie Glover Code; *m* 1st, 1927, Eveline Mary (*d* 1965), *d* of late W. J. Bonnett; one *s* two *d*; *m* 2nd, 1970, Dorothy, *d* of late Alfred Stockdale, Flixton. *Educ:* Newport (Mon.) High Sch.; University Coll., London. BA Hons Mod. Hist., 1924; Barrister-at-Law, Middle Temple, 1929. Editor, Butterworth & Co. (Publishers) Ltd, 1925-30; Legal Editor, Sir Isaac Pitman & Sons Ltd, 1931-37; Sales Manager, 1938-40; Publishing Director, 1940-65; Managing Director, 1966-68. President, Publishers' Association, 1949-51; Pres., Soc. of Commercial Teachers, 1959-62; Chairman: Legal Cttee of Publishers' Association. Liveryman, Stationers' Company; Freeman of City of London. *Publications:* (Joint Ed.) Slater's Mercantile Law, 7th-12th edns, 1931-50; Editor: Law and Practice of the Stock Exchange, 5th edn, 1932; Pitman's Commercial Law 12th edn, 1939; (Jt Ed) Law, Justice and Equity, 1967. *Recreation:* books. *Address:* Caunton House, 28 Watchbell Street, Rye, Sussex. *T:* Rye 2269. *Clubs:* Reform; Dawny (Rye).

**HOLLAND, Rt. Rev. Thomas;** *see* Salford, Bishop of, (RC).

**HOLLAND-HIBBERT,** family name of **Viscount Knutsford.**

**HOLLAND-HIBBERT, Hon. Julian Thurstan,** CBE 1957; JP; *b* 3 May 1920; *o s* and *heir* of 4th Viscount Knutsford, *qv*. *Educ:* Eton; Trinity Coll., Cambridge. Served War of 1939-45, Coldstream Guards. Mem. Ministry of Health Advisory Cttee on the Health and Welfare of Handicapped People. Mem. National Advisory Council on Employment of the Disabled. JP Herts, 1953. OStJ. *Address:* Munden, Watford, Herts. *T:* Garston 72002. *Club:* Guards.

**HOLLAND-MARTIN, Adm. Sir Deric (Douglas Eric),** GCB 1964 (KCB 1960; CB 1958); DSO 1943; DSC 1939, and Bar, 1943; DL; *b* 10 April 1906; 4th *s* of late R. M. Holland-Martin, CB, and late Mrs Holland-Martin, Overbury Court, Tewkesbury; *m* 1951, Rosamund Mary Hornby, OBE; one *s* one *d*. *Educ:* Royal Naval Coll., Osborne and Dartmouth. Midshipman HMS Iron Duke, 1924-27; Sub-Lieut HMY Victoria and Albert, 1928; HMS Effingham, 1929-31; Royal Naval Coll. Dartmouth, 1931-33; in comd of HM Ships, Tartar, Holderness, Nubian, Faulkner, during War of 1939-45; Comdr 1940; Capt. 1946; Naval Attaché to Argentine, Paraguay and Uruguay, 1947-49; in command of HMS Agincourt, 1949-50; idc 1951; Director of Plans, Admiralty, 1952-53; in command HMS Eagle, 1954; Flag Officer Flotillas, Mediterranean, 1955-57; Dep. Chief of Naval Personnel, 1957; Second Sea Lord and Chief of Naval Personnel, 1957-59; Flag Officer Air (Home), 1960-61; Comdr-in-Chief, Mediterranean, and C-in-C Allied Forces, Mediterranean, 1961-64; Commandant, Imperial Defence Coll., 1964-66. Rear-Adm.,

1955; Vice-Adm., 1958; Admiral, 1961. Retired, 1966. A Trustee, Imperial War Museum, 1966, Vice-Pres. and Chm. 1967-; Chairman: Cttee of Inquiry into Trawler Safety, 1968; Severn Region, Nat. Trust, 1967; White Ensign Association, 1966; Council, Malvern Coll., 1967. Dir, Barclays Bank, Bristol Local Bd, 1969. Mem., White Fish Authority and Herring Ind. Bd, 1969. DL Worcs, 1968. *Recreations:* shooting, fishing. *Address:* Bell's Castle, Kemerton, Tewkesbury, Glos. *T:* Overbury 333. *Clubs:* United Service, White's, MCC.
*See also Edward Holland-Martin.*

**HOLLAND-MARTIN, Edward;** Director: Agricultural Mortgage Corporation; Racecourse Holdings Trust Ltd; The Steeplechase Co. (Cheltenham) Ltd; *b* 8 March 1900; *s* of late R. M. Holland-Martin, CB; *m* 1955, Dagny Mary MacLean, *yr d* of late Major J. M. Grant and late Mrs Horace Webber; one *d. Educ:* Eton; Christ Church, Oxford. Dir Bank of England, 1933-48; Sheriff of County of London, 1941. Hon. Treasurer, Council for Preservation of Rural England; mem. Jockey Club. *Address:* Overbury Court, near Tewkesbury, Glos. *T:* Overbury 202; 28 St James's Place, SW1. *T:* 01-493 0937. *Club:* White's.
*See also Admiral Sir Deric Holland-Martin.*

**HOLLENDEN,** 2nd Baron, *cr* 1912; **Geoffrey Hope Hope-Morley;** Past President of the Wholesale Textile Association; High Sheriff County of London, 1917; JP Kent; *b* 28 Jan. 1885; *e s* of 1st Baron and Laura M. (*d* 1945), *d* of Rev. G. Royds Birch; *S* father, 1929; *m* 1st, 1914, Hon. Mary Gardner (from whom he obtained a divorce, 1928), 3rd *d* of late Lord Burghclere; two *d*; 2nd, 1929, Muriel Ivy (*d* 1962), 3rd *d* of Sir John E. Gladstone, 4th Bt; 3rd, 1963, Mrs Violet Norris Howitt, *widow* of Frank Howitt, Harley Street, W1. *Educ:* Eton; Trinity Coll., Cambridge. Pres., Salmon and Trout Association. *Heir; nephew* Gordon Hope Hope-Morley, *qv. Address:* Hall Place, Leigh, Tonbridge, Kent. *T:* Hildenborough 2255.
*See also D. F. Muirhead.*

**HOLLEY, Prof. Robert W.,** PhD; Resident Fellow, The Salk Institute, since 1968; *b* 28 Jan. 1922; *s* of Charles and Viola Holley, Urbana, Ill, USA; *m* 1945, Ann Dworkin; one *s. Educ:* Univ. of Illinois (AB); Cornell Univ. (PhD); Washington State Coll. Research Biochemist, Cornell Univ. Med. Coll., 1944-46; Instructor, State Coll. of Wash., 1947-48; Associate Prof. and Prof. of Biochem. (pt-time), Cornell Univ., 1948-57; Research Chemist, US Plant, Soil and Nut. Lab., ARS, USDA, 1957-64; Prof. of Biochem. and Molecular Biol., Biol. Div., Cornell Univ., 1964-. Various awards for research, 1965-. Hon. DSc Illinois, 1970. Nobel Prize in Physiology or Medicine, 1968. *Publications:* many contribs to: Jl Amer. Chem. Soc., Science, Jl Biol. Chem., Arch. Biochem., Nature, Proc. Nat. Acad. Sci., etc. *Recreations:* family enjoys walks along ocean and trips to mountains. *Address:* The Salk Institute, PO Box 1809, San Diego, California 92112, USA. *T:* 453-4100 (ext. 341).

**HOLLEY, William Stephen;** General Manager, Washington Development Corporation since 1965; *b* 26 March 1920; *m* 1947, Dinah Mary Harper; three *s. Educ:* King William's Coll. Student Accountant, 1937-39. War service, RA (TA), 1939-45 (Major). Colonial Service, and Overseas Civil Service, 1945-64; Mem. Legislature and State Sec., Head of Civil Service, Sabah, Malaysia, 1964. Hon. ADK (Malaysia). *Publications:* contribs to Sarawak Museum Jl and press articles on New Town Development. *Recreations:* tennis, shooting, sailing, theatre. *Address:* Ashfield House, 1 West Park Road, Cleadon, near Sunderland, Co. Durham. *T:* Boldon 2829. *Club:* Royal Commonwealth Society.

**HOLLIDAY, Gilbert Leonard Gibson,** CMG 1954; HM Ambassador to Morocco, 1965-69, retired; *b* 10 April 1910; *s* of late Rev. Andrew Barnes Holliday and late Violet Holliday (*née* White), Wigton, Cumberland; *m* 1934, Anita Lopez (*d* 1952); two *s*; *m* 1958, Jane Mary Wilkinson; one *s* two *d. Educ:* Rydal Sch.; Queen's Coll., Oxford. Laming Travelling Fellow, Queen's Coll., Oxford, 1931-32; entered HM Consular Service, 1932; served in Consular and Diplomatic Services at Buenos Aires, Valparaiso, Santiago, Katowice, Los Angeles, Foreign Office, New York; Warsaw; Paris; Berne and Stockholm; Ambassador to Laos, 1956-58; Foreign Office, 1958-60; Ambassador to Bolivia, 1960-64. *Recreations:* gardening, ski-ing, fishing, sketching. *Address:* (home) Notton Lodge, Lacock, Chippenham, Wilts; (business) Notton Nurseries, 4 Notton, Lacock, Chippenham, Wilts. *T:* Lacock 282.

**HOLLINGHURST, Air Chief Marshal Sir Leslie (Norman),** GBE 1952 (KBE 1945; CBE 1944; OBE 1932); KCB 1948 (CB 1942); DFC 1918; retired; *b* 2 Jan. 1895; *yr s* of late C. H. Hollinghurst, Brentwood, Essex. Served European War, 1914-19, Gallipoli, Salonika, France (DFC); transferred RFC from Middlesex Regt, 1916; Afghanistan and NW Frontier, 1919; graduated Royal Air Force Staff Coll., 1925; Shanghai Defence Force, 1927; NW Frontier, 1920-34 (despatches, OBE); commanded No. 20 Squadron, 1933-34; Instructor, RAF Staff Coll., 1935-37; graduated Imperial Defence Coll., 1928; Air Ministry, 1939; Group Catain 1939; Director of Organisation, 1940; Air Commodore, 1941; Air Vice-Marshal, 1942; Commendation, 1941; Director-General of Organisation, RAF, 1941-43; AOC No. 38 Group, 1943-44; Air Marshal Commanding Base Air Forces, South-East Asia, 1944-45; Temp. Air Marshal, 1946; Air Marshal, 1947; Air Member for Supply and Organisation on the Air Council, 1945-48; Inspector-General of the RAF, 1948-49; Air Council Member for Personnel, 1949-52. Retired 1952. *Address:* 12 Newnham House, Manor Fields, Putney Hill, SW15. *T:* 01-788 1065. *Clubs:* United Service, Royal Air Force, East India and Sports.

**HOLLINGS, (Alfred) Kenneth,** MC 1944; QC 1966; **His Honour Judge Hollings;** Judge of County Courts, Circuit 5 (E Lancs) since 1968; *b* 12 June 1918; *s* of Alfred Holdsworth Hollings and Rachel Elizabeth Hollings; *m* 1949, Harriet Evelyn Isabella (*née* Fishbourne); one *s* one *d. Educ:* Leys Sch., Cambridge; Clare Coll., Cambridge. Law Qualifying and Law Tripos, Cambridge, 1936-39; MA. Served RA (Shropshire Yeomanry), 1939-46. Called to Bar, Middle Temple, 1947, since when practised Northern Circuit. Recorder of Bolton, 1968. Standing Counsel for Inland Revenue, Northern Circuit, 1965-66. *Recreations:* walking, tennis, music. *Address:* Oakleigh, Dunham Road, Altrincham, Cheshire. *T:* 061-928 4596. *Clubs:* St James's, Tennis and Racquets (both Manchester).

**HOLLINGS, Rev. Michael Richard,** MC 1943; Parish Priest, St Anselm, Southall, Middlesex, since 1970; *b* 30 Dec. 1921; *s* of Lieut-Commander Richard Eustace Hollings, RN, and Agnes Mary (*née* Hamilton-Dalrymple). *Educ:* Beaumont Coll.; St Catherine's Society, Oxford (MA). St Catherine's, 1939; Sandhurst, 1941. Served War of 1939-45 (despatches): commnd Coldstream Guards, 1941; served N. Africa, Italy, Palestine, 1942-45; Major. Trained at Beda Coll., Rome, 1946-50. Ordained Rome, 1950; Asst Priest, St Patrick's, Soho Square, W1, 1950-54; Chaplain, Westminster Cathedral, 1954-58; Asst Chaplain, London Univ., 1958-59; Chaplain to Roman Catholics at Oxford Univ., 1959-70; Religious Adviser: ATV, 1958-59; Rediffusion, 1959-68; Thames Television, 1968. Mem., Nat. Catholic Radio and TV Commn, 1968; Lay Mem., Press Council, 1969-. Chaplain, Sovereign Military Order of Malta, 1957. *Publications:* Hey, You!, 1955; Purple Times, 1957; Chaplaincraft, 1963. Contributor Tablet, Clergy Review, Life of the Spirit. *Recreations:* reading, walking, people. *Address:* St Anselm's Rectory, The Green, Southall, Mddx. *T:* 01-574 0167.

**HOLLINGWORTH, John;** *b* 3 June 1885; *s* of Francis, *s* of Archdeacon Hollingworth, and Cecilia, *d* of Rev. W. Tomkins; unmarried. *Educ:* Bradfield Coll.; Peterhouse, Cambridge (Scholar). Wrangler, 1907; ACGI, 1909; BScEng London; 1st class hons, 1910; DSc London, 1928; MScTech Manchester, 1936; FIEE; FCGI 1937; Demonstrator, City and Guilds (Eng) Coll., 1911-13; Lecturer, College of Technology, Manchester, 1913-21; Lieut RNVR and later Captain RAF at Wireless Experimental Establishment, Biggin Hill, 1917-19; scientific assistant, National Physical Laboratory, 1921-26; Radio Research Station, Slough, 1926-31; Professor of Electrical Engineering in the University of Manchester and the College of Technology, 1932-52; retired 1952. *Publications:* various papers on Radio-Telegraphic subjects in Proceedings of Royal Society and Journal of Institution of Electrical Engineers. *Address:* The Manor House, Rowde, Devizes, Wilts.

**HOLLINGWORTH, John Harold;** *b* 11 July 1930; *s* of Harold Hollingworth, Harborne, Birmingham; *m* 1968, Susan Barbara, *d* of J. H. Walker, Gozo, Malta GC. *Educ:* Chigwell House Sch.; King Edward's Sch., Edgbaston. MP (C) All Saints Division of Birmingham, 1959-64. Chm., Edgbaston Div. Conservative Assoc., 1967; Vice-Chm., Birmingham Conservative Assoc., 1959-61 (Vice-Pres. 1960). *Publications:* contributions to political journals. *Recreations:* cricket, tennis. *Address:* 28 Viceroy Close, Edgbaston, Birmingham 5. *T:* 021-440 1678. *Club:* Constitutional.

**HOLLIS, Anthony Barnard,** QC 1969; *b* 11 May 1927; *er s* of late Henry Lewis Hollis and of Gladys Florence Hollis (*née* Barnard); *m* 1956, Pauline Mary (*née* Skuce); no *c*. *Educ:* Tonbridge Sch.; St Peter's Hall, Oxford. Called to Bar, Gray's Inn, 1951. *Recreation:* golf. *Address:* 1 King's Bench Walk, Temple, EC4. *T:* 01-353 4423. *Clubs:* Woking Golf; Royal St George's Golf (Sandwich).

**HOLLIS, Rt. Rev. (Arthur) Michael;** Assistant Bishop, Diocese of St Edmundsbury and Ipswich, since 1966; *b* 23 June 1899; *s* of late Right Rev. George Arthur Hollis, Bishop of Taunton; *m* 1935, Mary Cordelia, *d* of late Very Rev. Andrew Ewbank Burn, Dean of Salisbury. *Educ:* Leeds Grammar Sch.; Trinity Coll., Oxford (Scholar). Army, 1918-19; BA (2nd class Classical Hon. Mods) 1920; 1st class Litt. Hum., 1922; MA, 1924; BD, 1931; Leeds Clergy Sch., 1922; ordained deacon, 1923; priest, 1924; Curate S Andrew's, Huddersfield, 1923-24; Chaplain and Lecturer in Theology, Hertford Coll., Oxford, Fellow, 1926-31; Lecturer St Peter's Leeds, 1931; SPG Missionary, Bishop's Theological Seminary, Nazareth, diocese of Tinnevelly, India, 1931-37; Perpetual Curate of S Mary's Charlton Kings, diocese of Gloucester, 1937-42; CF 4th class (RARO), 1939-42; Bishop of Madras, 1942-47; Bishop in Madras, 1947-54; Moderator, Church of South India, 1948-54; Professor of Church History, United Theological Coll., Bangalore, 1955-60; Rector of Todwick, 1961-64; Second Assistant Bishop to the Bishop of Sheffield, 1963-66. Teaching, USA, 1960-61. *Publications:* Paternalism and the Church; The Significance of South India; Mission, Unity and Truth. *Address:* 72 Rembrandt Way, Bury St Edmunds, Suffolk.

*See also M. C. and Sir R. H. Hollis.*

**HOLLIS, Christopher;** *see* Hollis, M. C.

**HOLLIS, Daniel Ayrton,** VRD; QC 1968; Deputy Chairman of Kent Quarter Sessions, since 1970; *b* 30 April 1925; *s* of Norman Hollis; *m* 1st, 1950, Gillian Mary Turner (marr. diss., 1961), *d* of J. W. Cecil Turner, Cambridge; one *s* one *d*; 2nd, 1963, Stella Hydleman, *d* of Mark M. Gergel; one *s*. *Educ:* Geelong Grammar Sch., Australia; Brasenose Coll., Oxford. Served N Atlantic and Mediterranean, 1943-46. Lieut-Commander, RNVR. Called to Bar, Middle Temple, 1949. Standing Counsel to Inland Revenue at Central Criminal Court and London Sessions, 1965. *Recreation:* travel. *Address:* 3 Temple Gardens, EC4.

**HOLLIS, (Maurice) Christopher;** Chairman, Hollis and Carter; Member of Editorial Board of the Tablet; Member of Board of Punch; *b* 29 March 1902; 2nd *s* of late Rt Rev. George Arthur Hollis, Bishop of Taunton; *m* 1929, Margaret Madeline King; three *s* one *d*. *Educ:* Eton; Balliol Coll., Oxford. Toured USA, New Zealand, and Australia, as member of Oxford Union Debating Society, 1924-25; Asst Master Stonyhurst Coll., 1925-35; engaged in economic research at Notre Dame University, Indiana, USA, 1935-39; served War of 1939-45, with RAF. MP (C) Devizes Division of Wilts, 1945-55. *Publications:* American Heresy; Dr Johnson; Monstrous Regiment; Erasmus; Dryden; St Ignatius; Thomas More; Breakdown of Money; Two Nations; Foreigners Aren't Fools; We Aren't So Dumb; Lenin; Foreigners Aren't Knaves; Our Case; Italy in Africa, 1941; Noble Castle, 1941; Death of a Gentleman, 1943; Fossett's Memory, 1944; Rise and Fall of the ex-Socialist Government, Letters to a Sister, 1947; Can Parliament Survive?, 1949; A Study of George Orwell, 1956; The Ayes and the Noes, 1957; Along the Road to Frome, 1958; Eton, 1960; The Homicide Act, 1964; The Papacy, 1964; The Oxford Union, 1965; Newman and the Modern World, 1968; A History of the Jesuits, 1968; The Mind of Chesterton, 1969. general journalism. *Recreations:* tennis, watching cricket, squash rackets. *Address:* Little Claveys, Mells, near Frome. *T:* Mells 327.

*See also Rt Rev. A. M. and Sir R. H. Hollis.*

**HOLLIS, Rt. Rev. Michael;** *see* Hollis, Rt Rev. A. M.

**HOLLIS, Sir Roger (Henry),** KBE 1966 (OBE 1946); Kt 1960; CB 1956; Attached Ministry of Defence; retired; *b* 2 Dec. 1905; *s* of late Rt Rev. George Arthur Hollis, Bishop of Taunton; *m* 1st, 1937, Evelyn Esmé (*née* Swayne) (marr. diss., 1968); one *s*; 2nd, 1968, Edith Valentine (*née* Hammond). *Educ:* Clifton Coll.; Worcester Coll., Oxford. *Address:* Crossways Cottage, Catcott, near Bridgwater, Somerset.

*See also Rt Rev. A. M. and M. C. Hollis.*

**HOLLOM, Jasper Quintus;** Deputy Governor, Bank of England, since 1970; *b* 16 Dec. 1917; *s* of Arthur and Kate Louisa Hollom; *m* 1954,

Patricia Elizabeth Mary Ellis. *Educ:* King's Sch., Bruton. Entered Bank of England, 1936; appointed Deputy Chief Cashier, 1956; Chief Cashier, 1962-66; Director, 1966-70. *Address:* Tiryns, Forest Road, Wokingham, Berks. *T:* Wokingham 1527.

**HOLLOND, Prof. Henry Arthur,** DSO 1918; OBE 1919; Fellow of Trinity College, Cambridge, since 1909; Hon. Bencher Lincoln's Inn, since 1935; *b* 14 Oct. 1884; *o surv s* of late Arthur Edward Hollond of Great Ashfield House, Bury St Edmunds; *g s* of Rev. Edmund Hollond, Benhall Lodge, Saxmundham, Suffolk; *m* 1929, Marjorie, PhD Columbia Univ., Fellow of Girton Coll., Lecturer in Economics in the University of Cambridge, *er d* of Herman Tappan, Gloucester, Mass. *Educ:* Rugby Sch. (Classical Scholar, Head of the School); Trinity Coll., Cambridge (Classical Scholar); Classical Tripos Part I 1905, Law Tripos (both Parts) 1906, 1907; President of the Union Society, 1906; called to the Bar, Lincoln's Inn, 1911; attended the Law School of Harvard Univ., 1913-14; held a commission in Wessex (Hants) RGA (TF) 1914-20, retiring with rank of Major (DSO, OBE for services as DAAG on General Headquarters Staff, France); Reader in English Law, Cambridge Univ., 1919-43; Dean of Trinity Coll., 1922-50; Secretary, University of Cambridge Commissioners, 1923-27; Rouse Ball Professor of English Law, 1943-50; President Society of Public Teachers of Law, 1937-38; Chairman of Department of Criminal Science, Cambridge, 1949-55; Vice-Master of Trinity Coll., 1951-55; Reader in Legal History to the Inns of Court, 1945-68. *Address:* 3 Madingley Road, Cambridge. *T:* Cambridge 62811.

**HOLLOWAY, Gwendoline Elizabeth,** BA Hons; *b* 9 April 1893. *Educ:* University of Bristol (Hall of Residence, Clifton Hill House). Asst Mistress at Harrogate College for Girls, 1917-26; Vice-Principal, Queen's Coll., 1926-31; Acting Principal, 1931-32; Principal, 1932-40; First woman to be appointed Principal of Queen's Coll.; Lady Principal of Alexandra Coll., Dublin, 1940-61; Headmistress, Lowther Coll., North Wales, 1961-63. President: Federation of Soroptimist Clubs of Great Britain and Ireland, 1948-49; Alumni Assoc., Univ. of Bristol, 1968-69. *Recreations:* walking, motoring, golf. *Address:* 7 Gloucester Row, Clifton, Bristol BS8 4AW. *Clubs:* Cowdray; Soroptimist (Bristol).

**HOLLOWAY, John,** MA, DPhil, DLitt, LittD; University Reader in Modern English, Cambridge, since 1966; Fellow of Queens' College, 1955; *b* 1 Aug. 1920; *s* of George Holloway and Evelyn Astbury; *m* 1946, Audrey Gooding; one *s* one *d*. *Educ:* County Sch., Beckenham, Kent; New Coll., Oxford (Open History Scholar). 1st class Modern Greats, 1941; DPhil Oxon 1947; DLitt Aberdeen 1954; LittD Cambridge, 1969. Served War of 1939-45, commnd RA, 1942; subsequently seconded to Intelligence. Temporary Lecturer in Philosophy, New Coll., 1945; Fellow of All Souls Coll., 1946-60; John Locke Scholar, 1947; University Lecturer in English, Aberdeen, 1949-54; University Lecturer in English, Cambridge, 1954-66. FRSL 1956. Lecture Tour, Ceylon, India, Pakistan, 1958; Middle East, 1965; Byron Professor, University of Athens, 1961-63; Alexander White Professor, Chicago, 1965. *Publications:* Language and Intelligence, 1951; The Victorian Sage, 1953; The Charted Mirror (essays), 1960; (ed) Poems of the Mid-Century, 1957; (ed) Selections from Shelley, 1960; Shakespeare's Tragedies, 1961; The Colours of Clarity (essays), 1964; The Lion Hunt, 1964; Widening Horizons in English Verse, 1966; Blake, The Lyric Poetry, 1968; contributions to journals. *Verse:* The Minute, 1956; The Fugue, 1960; The Landfallers, 1962; Wood and Windfall, 1965; New Poems, 1970. *Recreation:* enjoyment. *Address:* Queens' College, Cambridge.

**HOLLOWAY, John Edward,** DSc; Hon. LLD, Hon. DCom; Director of Companies; *b* 4 July 1890; *s* of George John Holloway and Hester Maria Holloway (*née* Enslin); *m* 1913, Christina Maria Purchase (*d* 1967); one *s* three *d* (and one *d* decd). *Educ:* Stellenbosch Univ. (BA); London School of Economics. DSc (Econ) London, 1917, Hutchinson Research Medallist. Lecturer Grey University College, 1917-19; Lecturer and Professor Transvaal University College, 1919-25; Director Census and Statistics, 1925-33; Econ. Adviser to Treasury, 1934-37; Secretary for Finance, 1937-50; Chairman: Native Economic Commn, 1930-32; Customs Tariff Commn, 1934-35; Gold Mining Taxation Cttee, 1945; SW Africa Financial Commn, 1951; Univ. Finances Commn, 1951-53; Commn on Univ. Facilities for Non-Europeans, 1953; Member, SW Africa Commn, 1934-35; Transkeian Commn of Enquiry, 1962-63; Adviser Ottawa Conference, 1932, and Montreal Conference, 1958. World Economic Conference, 1933; Imperial Conference, 1937; Conferences of Finance Ministers, 1949, 1950, 1954; Delegate, Bretton Woods Conference, 1944; Leader S African Delegation: Conferences on Trade and Employment, Geneva, 1947, and Havana, 1948; formerly Alternate Governor IMF. Director: International Computers (SA) Ltd; Union Liquid Air Co.; Anglo-Alpha Cement; Consultant to Union Corp. and Barclays Bank DCO; formerly Director: South African Marine Corporation; South African Iron and Steel Corporation, and other cos; Member Atomic Energy Board. Resigned from these boards when appointed Ambassador in Washington, July 1954; High Commissioner for The Union of South Africa in London, 1956-58. Vice-President, S African Foundation; Member of Council, University of Pretoria. *Publications:* Apartheid: a challenge, 1964; various articles, chiefly about gold in the monetary system and race relations in South Africa. *Recreations:* golf, bowls, fly-fishing. *Address:* 1 Rockridge Road, Parktown, Johannesburg; Union Corporation Building, Johannesburg, South Africa. *Clubs:* Civil Service (Cape Town); Pretoria Country (Pretoria, SA); Bryanston Country, RSA (Johannesburg).

**HOLLOWAY, Stanley,** OBE 1960; Actor, Vocalist and Monologuist; *b* London; *m* 1st, 1913; 2nd, 1939, Violet Marion Lane. Formerly seaside concert artist; first West End appearance as Capt. Wentworth in Kissing Time, Winter Garden, 1919; René in A Night Out, Winter Garden, 1920; original member of the Co-Optimists, and remained as one until disbandment, 1927; Bill Smith in Hit the Deck, London Hippodrome, 1927; Lieut Richard Manners in Song of the Sea, His Majesty's, 1928; Cooee, Vaudeville, 1929; appeared with the revived Co-Optimists, 1929, The Co-Optimists of 1930, London Hippodrome; Savoy Follies, Savoy, 1932; Here We Are Again, Lyceum, 1932; Eustace Titherley in Three Sisters, 1934; first appearance in pantomime, Prince of Wales's, Birmingham, 1934, as Abanazar in Aladdin, and has played same part each succeeding Christmas at Leeds, Golders Green, Edinburgh and Manchester; All Wave, Duke of York's, 1936; London Rhapsody, London Palladium, 1938; All The Best, season at Blackpool, 1938; Saville: in Up and Doing,

1940 and 1941 in Fine and Dandy, 1942; Played First Gravedigger in Festival Production of Hamlet, New Theatre, 1951; Midsummer Night's Dream (with Old Vic at Edinburgh Festival, and subsequently Metropolitan Opera House, New York, followed by tour of USA and Canada); played Alfred Doolittle in New York production of My Fair Lady (musical version of Pygmalion), 1956-58 and in London production, Drury Lane, 1958-59; Burgess in Candida, Shaw Festival, Canada, 1970. *Films:* Hamlet (Gravedigger), This Happy Breed, The Way Ahead, The Way to the Stars, Cæsar and Cleopatra, Champagne Charlie, The Perfect Woman, Midnight Episode, One Wild Oat, The Lavender Hill Mob, The Magic Box (Festival Film), Lady Godiva Rides Again, Meet Me To-night, The Titfield Thunderbolt, The Beggar's Opera, Meet Mr Lucifer, A Day to Remember, Fast and Loose, An Alligator Named Daisy, Jumping for Joy, No Trees in the Street, Alive and Kicking, No Love For Johnnie, On The Fiddle, My Fair Lady (Alfred Doolittle), Ten Little Indians, Mrs Brown You Have A Lovely Daughter, Run a Crooked Mile, Private Life of Sherlock Holmes, What's in it for Harry. TV series: Our Man Higgins, Hollywood, 1962-; Thingamybob, London, 1968. *Publication:* Wiv a Little Bit o' Luck (autobiography), 1967. *Address:* Pyefleet, Tamarisk Way, East Preston, Sussex.

**HOLLOWOOD, A. Bernard,** MSc(Econ); FRSA; Editor of Punch, 1957-68; author, economist and cartoonist; contributor of articles and drawings to Punch since 1942; Member of Punch Table since 1945; *b* 3 June 1910; 2nd *s* of Albert and Sarah Elizabeth Hollowood, Burslem, Staffordshire; *m* 1938, Marjorie Duncan, *d* of Dr W. D. Lawrie, Hartshill, Stoke-on-Trent; one *s* two *d. Educ:* Hanley High School; St Paul's Coll., Cheltenham; London University. Lecturer in Economics, School of Commerce, Stoke-on-Trent, and Loughborough Coll., 1932-43; lecturer to HM Forces; on staff of The Economist, 1944-45; Research Officer, Council of Industrial Design, 1946-47; Editor of Pottery and Glass, 1944-50; Pocket cartoonist of Sunday Times, 1957-60; Sunday Telegraph, etc. Broadcaster since 1939. Visiting Prof. at American Univs. Member, Court of Governors, London School of Economics. Hon. MA Keele, 1968. *Publications:* Direct Economics, 1943; Money is No Expense, 1946; An Innocent at Large, 1947; Britain Inside-Out, 1948; Scowle and Other Papers, 1948; Pottery and Glass, 1949; Poor Little Rich World, 1948; The Hawksmoor Scandals, 1949; Cornish Engineers, 1951; The Story of Morro Velho, 1954; Tory Story, 1964; Pont, The Story of Graham Laidler, 1969; Cricket on the Brain, 1970; Tales of Tommy Barr, 1970; Pamphlets and Papers on Economics. *Recreation:* village cricket (formerly county cricket: Staffordshire 1930-46). *Address:* Blackmoor Paddock, Haldish Lane, Shamley Green, Surrey. *T:* Bramley 2118. *Clubs:* MCC, Lord's Taverners'.

**HOLM PATRICK,** 3rd Baron *cr* 1897; **James Hans Hamilton;** *b* 29 Nov. 1928; *s* of 2nd Baron and Lady Edina Alnsworth (*d* 1964), 4th *d* of 4th Marquess Conyngham; *S* father, 1942; *m* 1954, Anne Loys Roche, *o d* of Commander J. E. P. Brass, RN (retired); three *s. Heir: s* Hon. Hans James David Hamilton, *b* 15 March 1955. *Address:* Rye Bridge House, Leixlip, Co. Kildare, Ireland.

*See also Baron Swansea.*

**HOLMAN, Sir Adrian,** KBE, *cr* 1954; CMG 1936; MC; *b* 22 Dec. 1895; *s* of late Richard Haswell Holman; *m* 2nd, 1940, Betty, *o d* of Sir Gilbert Fox, 1st Bt. *Educ:* Copthorne Sch., Crawley, Sussex; Harrow; New Coll., Oxford. Served European War, 1915-18 (MC, despatches); entered Diplomatic Service as 3rd Secretary, 1920; HM Embassy, Brussels, 1921-24; 2nd Secretary, 1922; HM Embassy, Rome, 1924-26; Paris, 1926-31; First Secretary, 1931; First Secretary, HM Legation, Peking, 1931-35; Foreign Office, 1935-38; HM Embassy, Berlin, 1938-39; The Hague, 1939; Bagdad, 1940; Counsellor, 1940; Teheran, 1942; British Mission, Algiers; Minister at HM Embassy, Paris, 1944; British Political Representative in Rumania, 1946-47, Minister, 1947-49; Minister, Cuba, 1949-50, Ambassador to Cuba, 1950-54; retired from HM Foreign Service, May 1954. Coronation Medals, 1937, 1953; Chevalier of the Order of Leopold. *Recreations:* fishing and gardening. *Address:* Bohunt, Liphook, Hampshire. *T:* Liphook 2208. *Club:* Bath.

**HOLMAN, Norman Frederick;** Director of Postal Finance since 1967; *b* 22 Feb. 1914; *s* of late Walter John and Violet Holman, Taunton; *m* 1940, Louisa Young; one *s* two *d. Educ:* Huish's, Taunton. Entered Post Office as Exec. Officer, 1932; Higher Exec. Officer, 1942. Served in Royal Corps of Signals, 1942-46. Sen. Exec. Officer, 1950; Asst Accountant-Gen., 1953; Dep. Dir, 1956. *Recreations:* bridge, tennis, The Observer crossword; avoiding gardening. *Address:* 29 Melbourne Avenue, Pinner, Middlesex. *T:* 01-863 1669.

**HOLMAN, Percy,** BSc; Paper Merchant; *b* 5 April 1891; *s* of S. H. Holman; *m* 1918, Dorothy Anderson; one *s* two *d. Educ:* Mill Hill Sch.; London School of Economics (London Univ.). Entered business 1913. Service in France with BRCS, 1915-18. Member Middlesex CC, 1928-31; Member Teddington UDC, 1928-34. Contested (Lab) Twickenham, 1931, 1932, 1934 and 1935; MP (Lab.-Co-op) Bethnal Green, 1950-66, (Lab.-Co-op) Bethnal Green South-West, 1945-50). *Recreation:* walking. *Address:* 3 Arundel Court, Wimbledon, SW19. *T:* 01-946 3497.

**HOLMAN, Dr Portia Grenfell;** Senior Physician in Psychological Medicine, Elizabeth Garrett Anderson Hospital, since 1954; *b* 20 Nov. 1903; *d* of Hon. William Arthur Holman, KC, Premier of New South Wales, 1914-18, and Ada Augusta Kidgell. *Educ:* The Women's Coll., Sydney, NSW; Newnham Coll., Cambridge. Economics Tripos, 1923-26, BA Cantab, 1926. Research and lecturing at St Andrews Univ., 1927-33; MA Cantab 1923. Medical student, Cambridge and Royal Free Hospital, 1934-39. Consultant Psychiatrist to Twickenham Child Guidance Clinic, 1944, West Middlesex Hospital, 1945, Elizabeth Garrett Anderson Hospital, 1946. MD 1950; Burlingame Prize, 1952; FRCP 1961. Founder and first Chairman Association of Workers for Maladjusted Children, 1951. *Publications:* Bedwetting, 1954; Psychology and Psychological Medicine for Nurses, 1957; contributions to Journal of Mental Science. *Recreations:* mountain climbing, swimming. *Address:* 2 Prince Albert Road, NW1. *Club:* Royal Society of Medicine.

**HOLMBERG, Eric Robert Reginald;** Assistant Chief Scientist (Army) (formerly Director of Army Operational Science and Research), since Oct. 1961; *b* 24 Aug. 1917; *s* of Robert and May Holmberg; *m* 1940, Wanda Erna Reich; one *s* one *d. Educ:* Sandown (Isle of Wight) Grammar Sch.; St John's Coll., Cambridge (MA); Imperial Coll., London (PhD). Joined Mine Design Department, Admiralty, 1940; Admiralty Gunnery

Establishment, 1945; Operational Research Department, Admiralty, 1950; appointed Chief Supt. Army Operational Research Group, 1956. *Publications:* papers in Proc. Royal Astronomical Society. *Address:* 29 Westmoreland Road, Barnes, SW13. *T:* 01-748 2568.

**HOLME, Maj.-Gen. Michael Walter,** CBE 1966; MC 1945; GOC Near East Land Forces since 1969; *b* 9 May 1918; *s* of Thomas Walter Holme and Ruth Sangster Holme (*née* Rivington); *m* 1948, Sarah Christian Van Der Gucht; one *s* two *d*. *Educ:* Winchester College. Directing Staff, Staff Coll., Camberley, 1952-55; Comdr 1st Bn 3rd East Anglian Regt, 1960-62; Comdr Land Forces Persian Gulf, 1963-66; Chief of Staff, Western Comd, 1966-67; Divisional Brig., The Queen's Div., 1968-69; Dep. Col, The Royal Anglian Regiment, 1970-. *Recreations:* various. *Address:* c/o C. Hoare & Co., 37 Fleet Street, EC4. *Club:* Army and Navy.

**HOLMER, Paul Cecil Henry;** Counsellor in HM Diplomatic Service since 1966; *b* 19 Oct. 1923; *s* of Bernard Cecil and Mimi Claudine Holmer; *m* 1946, Irene Nora, *e d* of late Orlando Lenox Beater, DFC; two *s* two *d*. *Educ:* King's Sch., Canterbury; Balliol Coll., Oxford. Served in RA, 1942-46. Entered Civil Service, 1947; Colonial Office, 1947-49; transferred to HM Foreign Service, 1949; FO, 1949-51; Singapore, 1951-55; FO, 1955-56; served on Civil Service Selection Bd, 1956; FO, 1956-58; Moscow, 1958-59; Berlin, 1960-64; FO, 1964-66; Counsellor, 1966; Dep. High Comr, Singapore, 1966-69; Counsellor, Foreign and Commonwealth Office, 1969-. *Address:* Stoke Park Farm Cottage, Guildford, Surrey. *T:* Guildford 69639. *Club:* Oxford and Cambridge University.

**HOLMES, Hon. David Ronald,** CMG 1969; CBE 1962 (MBE 1943); MC 1943; ED 1956; Secretary for Home Affairs, Hong Kong, since 1969; also Member of Executive and Legislative Councils, Hong Kong; *b* 26 Dec. 1913; *s* of late Louis James Holmes and Emily Sutcliffe, Brighouse, W Yorks; *m* 1945, Marjorie Fisher, *d* of late Frank Hastings Fisher and Charlotte Fisher (*née* Gittins); two *s*. *Educ:* Bradford Grammar Sch.; Sidney Sussex Coll., Cambridge. Colonial Administrative Service, Hong Kong, 1938; various admin. posts. War service in Hong Kong and China, 1941-45, Major. Secretary for Chinese Affairs, Hong Kong, 1966 (title changed to Secretary for Home Affairs, 1969). *Recreations:* reading, travel, golf. *Address:* 19 Severn Road, Hong Kong. *T:* Hong Kong 96966. *Clubs:* Hong Kong, Royal Hong Kong Golf, etc.

**HOLMES, Eric Gordon,** MA, MD Cantab; MRCP London; retired; *b* 16 Aug. 1897; *s* of Rev. Richard Holmes and Catherine Emily Compton-Rickett; *m* 1st, 1924, Barbara Elizabeth (marr. diss., 1946), *d* of late Sir Frederick Gowland Hopkins, OM; one *s* one *d*; 2nd, 1946, Helen Merle, *d* of W. E. Stephen, Melbourne, Australia; three *s*. *Educ:* Rugby Sch.; Christ's Coll., Cambridge (Scholar); St Bartholomew's Hospital. 2nd Lieut RGA, 1917; served in France, 1917-18; Prisoner of War; Christ's Coll., Cambridge, 1919-21; 1st Class, Part II Nat. Science Tripos (Physiology), 1921; Demonstrator in Physiology, St Bartholomew's Hospital, 1923-24; Grocer's Company Research Scholar, 1924-26; Assistant to the Downing Professor of Medicine, Cambridge, 1926-31; University Lecturer in Pharmacology, 1931-33; Rockefeller Fellowship, held at University of Harvard, 1938; Fellow, 1930-46, and Tutor, 1931-46, of Downing College; University lecturer in Biochemistry, Cambridge, 1933-46; deputy for the professor of Biochemistry, 1940; Professor of Physiology and Director of Research Unit, Makerere Coll., Kampala, Uganda, 1946-55; Director, East African Institute for Medical Research, Mwanza, Tanganyika, 1955-60; Senior Research Fellow, CSIRO, University of Adelaide, 1960-66; Senior Research Officer, Inst. of Medical and Veterinary Science, Adelaide, 1966-69. Served War of 1939-45 in RAMC, Middle East and Burma, Lt-Col. *Publications:* The Metabolism of Living Tissues; Papers in The Biochemical Journal, British Journal of Experimental Pathology and elsewhere on the Metabolism of the Central Nervous System, the effects of Toxæmia upon Metabolism, Malnutrition and other subjects; contributor to the Annual Review of Biochemistry. *Recreations:* shooting, fencing, mountaineering. *Address:* 196 King William Road, Hyde Park, South Australia 5061, Australia. *Club:* Naval, Military and Air Force (Adelaide).

**HOLMES, Ven. George Hedley,** BA, LTh; Archdeacon of Prince Albert, 1933-41, now Hon. Archdeacon of British Columbia; *b* 24 May 1883; *s* of John Hedley Holmes, Liverpool, and Christina Shimmin; *m* 1915, Elsie Kathleen Lawley, Uttoxeter, Staffs; one *s* two *d*. *Educ:* Liverpool Coll.; Emmanuel Coll., Saskatoon; University of Saskatchewan. Deacon, 1913; Priest, 1914; Incumbent of Hardisty, Alta, 1914-19; Rector of St George's, Saskatoon, 1919-29; Rural Dean of Saskatoon, 1923-29; Canon Residentiary of St Alban's Cathedral, Prince Albert, 1929-33; Secretary-Treasurer and Registrar of Diocese of Saskatchewan, 1933-41; Rector of Salt Spring Island, BC, 1941-62, retired. Hon. DD, 1966. *Recreations:* gardening and motoring. *Address:* Box 17, Ganges, BC, Canada.

**HOLMES, Sir Horace (Edwin),** Kt 1966; NCLC Lecturer; *b* 30 March 1888; *s* of William and Martha Holmes; *m* 1912, Nellie Florence Marshall. *Educ:* elementary and technical schools; WEA classes. Miner and trade union official. Member of South Yorks Wages Board, Joint Board, Conciliation Board, advisory committees on mining, Recruitment, Safety, Welfare, etc. Member of Royston Urban District Council (Yorkshire) for 24 years; WR CC 12 years. Sergt, W. Yorks, 1915-18 (DCM). JP West Riding of Yorkshire, 1938-59. MP (Lab) Hemsworth Division of West Riding of Yorks, 1946-Sept. 1959. Parliamentary Private Secretary to Minister of Fuel and Power, 1947-51; one of the Opposition Whips, 1951-59. *Recreations:* music, books, gardening, walking. *Address:* 16 Park Avenue, Lakeside Estate, Hartsholme, Lincoln. *T:* Lincoln 21953.

**HOLMES, Brig. Kenneth Soar,** CB 1963; CBE 1954; Senior Director, Posts, Postal Headquarters, since 1970; *b* 1912; *s* of W. J. Holmes, Ellesmere, Chaddesden Park Road, Derby; *m* 1936, Anne, *d* of C. A. Chapman, Leicester; one *s*. *Educ:* Bemrose Sch., Derby, and at Derby Technical Coll. Entered Post Office as Asst Traffic Superintendent (Telephones), 1930; Asst Surveyor, 1936; Principal, 1947; Asst Secretary, 1950. Served War of 1939-45 as Officer Commanding 43rd Division Postal Unit, with 21st Army Group and 2nd Army Headquarters, and as Asst Director of Army Postal Services, British Army of the Rhine. Director of: Army Postal Services, War Office, 1950-59; Mechanisation and Buildings, GPO, 1956-60; Postal Services, GPO, 1960-65; London Postal Region, 1965-70. Chairman Executive Cttee of Universal Postal Union, 1960-64. *Address:* Beechcroft,

Gilhams Avenue, Banstead, Surrey. *T:* 01-393 4448.

**HOLMES, Brigadier Leonard Geoffrey,** CBE 1943; *b* 15 Jan. 1899; *s* of Lieut-Colonel L. Holmes, TD; *m* 1940, Gladys May Black; one *s*. *Educ:* Brighton Coll.; RMA, Woolwich. 2nd Lieut RA, Aug. 1916; European War, 1917-18; Staff Coll., Camberley, 1934-35; Middle East and North Africa, 1941-43; Brigadier 1949; retired 1953. *Address:* Headlams Well, Ipsden, Oxford.

**HOLMES, Sir Maurice (Andrew),** Kt 1969; South Eastern Circuit Administrator since 1970; *b* 28 July 1911; *o s* of Rev. A. T. Ellen Holmes; *m* 1935, Joyce Esther (*née* Hicks); no *c*. *Educ:* Felsted Sch., Essex. Served with RASC, 1941-45 (Major, despatches). Called to Bar, Gray's Inn, 1948; Practised at Bar, 1950-55. Director, 1955-60, Chairman, 1960-65, The Tilling Association Ltd; Chairman, London Transport Board, 1965-69. *Recreations:* golf, music. *Address:* The Limes, Felsted, near Dunmow, Essex. *T:* Felsted 352. *Clubs:* Forty, MCC.

**HOLMES, Maj.-Gen. Sir Noel Galway,** KBE 1946 (CBE 1940); CB 1943; MC; Chairman North Eastern Divisional Coal Board, 1946-57; *b* Galway, Ireland, 25 Dec. 1891; 4th *s* of late Capt. H. W. Holmes, Rockwood, Galway; *m* 1920, Mary, *er d* of late Sir Hugh Clifford, GCMG, GBE; one *s* one *d*. *Educ:* Bedford Sch. Joined Royal Irish Regt, 1912; India, 1912-14; served European War, France, 1914-18 (wounded, despatches four times, MC); Bt Major, 1919; Staff Coll., 1926-27; Bde Major, Dover, 1929-31; GSO Southern Command, India, 1933-37; Bt Lt-Col, 1935; Commanded 1 Bn East Yorkshire Regt, 1938-39; Maj.-Gen. 1943; Director of Movements, War Office, 1939-43; DQMG War Office, 1943-46; Commander Aldershot and Hampshire District, 1946; retired at own request, 1946. Croix d'Officier of the Legion d'Honneur and Croix de Guerre with Palme, 1945; American Legion of Merit (Commander), 1946. *Recreations:* Davis Cup Lawn Tennis (Ireland), 1930; golf, shooting, etc. *Address:* Rockwood, Branksome Wood Road, Fleet, Hants. *Club:* United Service.

**HOLMES, Air Vice-Marshal Peter Hamilton,** CB 1965; OBE 1945; CEng 1966; FRAeS 1965; *b* 4 Oct. 1912; *s* of late E. Hamilton Holmes, CMG, late Foreign Service; *m* 1940, Barbara Joan, *d* of late A. R. F. Bosman, Windlesham, Surrey; two *s*. *Educ:* Wellington Coll. Joined RAF on Short Service Commission, 1932; permanent commission, 1937; specialised in Signals, 1937; on Signals duties in UK and NW Europe, throughout War; Group Captain, 1945; Staff Coll., Bracknell, 1946; Directing Staff, JSSC, 1947-49; various Signals appointments at home and overseas as Group Capt., 1950-59; Air Commodore, Deputy Chief of Staff, HQ 2 ATAF Germany, 1959-61; Imperial Defence Coll., 1962; Air Vice-Marshal, 1963. Air Officer i/c Administration, Maintenance Command, 1963-65; retired 1965. *Recreations:* fishing, gardening. *Address:* Old Basing House, Basingstoke, Hants. *T:* Basingstoke 3555. *Clubs:* Royal Air Force, Royal Automobile.

**HOLMES, Stanley;** Chief Executive and Town Clerk of Liverpool since 1969; *b* 15 Dec. 1912; *s* of Stanley and Ethel Holmes, Liverpool; *m* 1939, Doris Elizabeth Burton; one *d*. *Educ:* Liverpool Collegiate School. Deputy Town Clerk, Liverpool, 1956, Town Clerk 1967. *Recreations:* people, places, paintings. *Address:* 38 Crompton Court, Cromptons Lane, Liverpool L18 3EZ. *T:* 051-722 5241.

**HOLMES, Sir Stephen (Lewis),** KCMG, *cr* 1950 (CMG 1942); MC 1918; MA; *b* 5 July 1896; *s* of late Basil Holmes and Isabella, *d* of Dr J. H. Gladstone, FRS; *m* 1922, Noreen, *o d* of late E. F. C. Trench, CBE, TD; two *s* one *d*. *Educ:* Westminster; Christ Church, Oxford. 2nd Lieut RGA (SR), 1915; served European War, France and Belgium, 1916-19 (MC, despatches twice, acting Major); entered Colonial Office, 1921; Principal, Dominions Office, 1928; Imperial Defence Coll., 1934; Senior Secretary, Office of High Commissioner for United Kingdom in Canada, 1936-39; Dominions Office representative, Washington, 1943-44; Deputy High Commissioner for the United Kingdom, Canada, 1944-46; Under Secretary, Board of Trade, 1946; Second Secretary, Board of Trade, 1947-51; Deputy Under-Secretary of State, Commonwealth Relations Office, 1951-52; High Commissioner for the UK in Australia, 1952-56. London Director, Bank of Adelaide. Master of the Leathersellers' Company, 1967-68. *Address:* Pinyons, Sandhurst, Hawkhurst, Kent. *Club:* Athenæum.

**HOLMES, Prof. William;** Professor of Agriculture, Wye College, University of London, since 1955; *b* Kilbarchan, Renfrewshire, 16 Aug. 1922; *s* of William John Holmes, Bank Manager; *m* 1949, Jean Ishbel Campbell, BSc; two *d*. *Educ:* John Neilson Institution, Paisley; Glasgow Univ.; West of Scotland Agricultural Coll. BSc (Agric), NDD, 1942; NDA (Hons), 1943; PhD Glasgow, 1947; DSc London, 1966. Asst Executive Officer, S Ayrshire AEC, 1943-44; Hannah Dairy Research Inst.: Asst in Animal Husbandry, 1944-45; Head of Department of Dairy and Grassland Husbandry, 1947-55. member, Cttee on Milk Composition in the UK, 1958-60; Governor, Grassland Research Inst., 1960-; Pres., British Grassland Soc., 1968-69; Pres., British Soc. of Animal Production, 1969-70; Member: Delegacy, Nat. Inst. for Research in Dairying, 1968-; Adv. Technical Cttee, Univ. of W Indies, 1969-; several technical cttees of ARC and Min. of Agriculture, 1960-. *Publications:* papers in technical agricultural journals. *Recreations:* gardening, beekeeping, travel. *Address:* Amage, Wye, Kent. *T:* Wye 372. *Club:* Farmers'.

**HOLMES à COURT,** family name of **Baron Heytesbury.**

**HOLMPATRICK;** *see* Holm Patrick.

**HOLROYD, Sir Ronald,** Kt 1963; FRS 1960; MSc; PhD; a Deputy Chairman of Imperial Chemical Industries Ltd, 1957-67; *b* 26 April 1904; *s* of Sykes Holroyd and Florence Holroyd (*née* Whitlam); *m* 1931, Kathleen Mary Addey (*d* 1966); one *s*. *Educ:* Holgate Grammar Sch., Barnsley; Sheffield Univ. Scientific Officer, Safety in Mines Research Board, 1926-28; Various appointments in ICI, 1928-52. Director: ICI, 1952-67; Canadian Industries Ltd, 1956-60; British Nylon Spinners, 1958-67 (Chm, 1964-67); African Explosives and Chemical Industries, 1960-67; Member: Board of Governors, Westminster Hospital, 1957-69; Trustees, Uppingham Sch., 1957-70; Academic Planning Cttee, University College of Sussex, 1958-67; Council, Sussex Univ., 1967-69; Ministry of Power Advisory Cttee on Research and Development, 1963-65; President, Soc. Chemical Industry, 1965; Chairman, Fire Service Inquiry, 1967; Hon. Fellow, Manchester Inst. of Science and Technology, 1968. DSc (*hc*): Oxford, 1958; Sheffield, 1959; Hull, 1960; TCD, 1966; Hon. DTech Bradford, 1967. Coal Science Medal (BCURA), 1953; Castner Medal of Society

Chemical Industry, 1958. FRSA 1963. *Recreations:* golf, motoring. *Address:* Rose Cottage, Buckden, near Skipton, Yorks. *T:* Kettlewell 218. *Club:* Athenæum.

**HOLT, Arthur Frederick;** Chief Executive, Holt Hosiery Co. Ltd, Bolton; *b* 8 Aug. 1914; *m* 1939, Kathleen Mary, *d* of A. C. Openshaw, Turton, nr Bolton; one *s* one *d*. *Educ:* Mill Hill Sch.; Manchester Univ. Army Territorial Officer (5th Loyals), 1939-45; taken prisoner, Singapore, 1942-45; despatches twice, 1946. MP (L) Bolton West, 1951-64; Liberal Chief Whip, 1962-63. *Recreation:* golf. *Address:* Harwood Lodge West, Harwood, near Bolton, Lancs. *T:* Bolton 21179. *Club:* Reform.

**HOLT, Ernest James Henry,** CMG 1957; CBE 1953; retired as Bank Manager, Lloyds Bank; Hon. Secretary Amateur Athletic Association, 1937-46; Hon. Secretary-Treasurer, International Amateur Athletic Federation, 1946-52; Director of Organisation, Olympic Games, 1948; Advisor, Olympic Games, 1956; *b* 2 Sept. 1883; *s* of Frank Ernest Holt and Florence Ann Holt (*née* Short); *m* 1914, Winifred Gladys, *d* of William D'Acier Baxter and Selina Baxter; two *s* one *d*. *Educ:* Rosemont House, Newport, Shropshire. Joined Lloyds Bank Ltd, 1900; Manager Belgravia Branch, London, 1927; retired, 1945. Director of Organisation, Olympic Games, London, 1946-48; Advisor and Technical Director, Olympic Games, Melbourne, 1953-56. *Recreations:* Athletics and Association Football. *Address:* Oakholme, 22 Fordbridge Road, Sunbury-on-Thames, Surrey. *T:* Sunbury 82309.

**HOLT, Herbert,** RP; portrait painter; *b* 7 Aug. 1894; *s* of Henry A. Holt, stained-glass artist, and Alice Seddon, schoolmistress; *m* Nora Norbury; one *s*. *Educ:* Cowley Sch., St Helens; St Helens, Liverpool and Slade Art Schools. *Publication:* Portrait Painting in Oils, 1958. *Address:* Broom Villa, Broomhouse Road, Hurlingham, SW6. *Clubs:* Chelsea Arts; Artists', Liverpool, Liver Sketching (Liverpool).

**HOLT, Major Herbert Paton,** MC; *b* Montreal, 10 Dec. 1890; *e s* of Sir Herbert Holt; *m* 1st, Aileen Elizabeth (*d* 1945), *d* of G. L. Cains, Montreal; (one *s* killed in action 1944); two *d*; *m* 2nd, 1946, Opal Eree M'Ilhenny, *d* of C. A. McCaulay, Meadville, USA. *Educ:* St Alban's Sch.; Royal Military Coll. of Canada. Joined 3rd Dragoon Guards, 1910; served European War, 1914-18 (wounded, MC); retired as Captain, 1920; MP (C) Upton Division of West Ham, 1924-29; High Sheriff of Wilts., 1935-36; served France Sept. 1939-Feb. 1940, Major attached Pioneer Corps; invalided out Sept. 1940. *Publication:* History of 3rd (P. of W.) Dragoon Guards, 1914-18. *Recreation:* racing. *Address:* Ballycrystal House, Nassau, Bahamas; Send Grove, Woking, Surrey. *Clubs:* Cavalry, Royal Automobile, Buck's, White's; Mount Royal (Montreal).

**HOLT, Sir James (Arthur),** Kt 1960; Co-ordinator General of Public Works, Queensland, 1954-68, retired; director of companies; *b* 30 April 1899; *s* of James and Delia Holt; *m* 1932, Audrey May Benson; three *s* one *d*. *Educ:* Sydney High Sch.; Sydney Univ. (BE). Engineering draftsman, Sydney Harbour Bridge, 1922-27; Supervising Engineer, Sydney Harbour Bridge, 1927-32; Engineer-in-Charge, District Office, Department of Main Roads, NSW, 1933; Supervising Engineer, for design and construction contract for Story Bridge, Brisbane, 1934-40; Chief Engineer, Bridge Board, Queensland, 1940-49 (Engineer-in-charge, Allied Works Council, Cairns, 1943-44); Chief Engineer, Co-ordinator General's Dept, Queensland, 1949-53. Peter Nicol Russell Memorial Medal, Institute of Engineers, Australia, 1961. DEng (*hc*), University of Queensland, 1965. *Publications:* contributions to Journal of Institution of Engineers, Australia; papers on: The Story Bridge, Brisbane; The Fitzroy Bridge, Rockhampton. *Recreations:* bowls and surfing. *Address:* 11 Hawken Drive, St Lucia, Brisbane, Queensland 4067, Australia. *T:* 70 7707. *Clubs:* University of Queensland; St Lucia Bowls.

**HOLT, Sir John Anthony L.;** *see* Langford-Holt.

**HOLT, Rear-Adm. John Bayley,** CB 1969; Director-General Aircraft (Naval), Ministry of Defence, 1967-70; *b* 1 June 1912; *s* of Arthur Ogden Holt and Gertrude (*née* Bayley); *m* 1940, Olga Esme Creake; three *d*. *Educ:* William Hulme Grammar Sch., Manchester; Manchester Univ. BScTech (hons) 1933. FIEE. Electrical Engineer with various cos and electric power undertakings, 1933-41. Joined RN; engaged on degaussing and minesweeping research and development, later on radar and electrical engineering, for Fleet Air Arm, 1941-48; served in HMS Cumberland on Gunnery Trials, Naval Air Stations, HQ and Staff appointments; comd HMS Ariel, 1961-63; subsequently Director of Naval Officer Appointments (Engineering Officers), Ministry of Defence. Former Naval ADC to HM The Queen. Commander 1948; Captain 1958; Rear-Admiral 1967. *Recreations:* sailing, poultry-keeping, gardening, sacred music. *Address:* Rowley Cottage, Thursley, Godalming, Surrey. *T:* Elstead 2140. *Club:* United Service.

**HOLT, Prof. John Riley,** FRS 1964; Professor of Experimental Physics, University of Liverpool, since 1966; *b* 15 Feb. 1918; *er s* of Frederick Holt and Annie (*née* Riley); *m* 1949, Joan Silvester Thomas; two *s*. *Educ:* Runcorn Secondary Sch.; University of Liverpool. PhD 1941. British Atomic Energy Project, Liverpool and Cambridge, 1940-45. University of Liverpool: Lecturer, 1945-53, Senior Lecturer, 1953-56, Reader, 1956-66. *Publications:* papers in scientific journals on nuclear physics and particle physics. *Recreations:* gardening, colour photography. *Address:* Rydalmere, Stanley Avenue, Higher Bebington, Cheshire. *T:* 051-608 2041.

**HOLT, Mary;** MP (C) Preston North since 1970; barrister-at-law; *d* of Henry James Holt, solicitor, and of Sarah Holt (*née* Chapman); unmarried. *Educ:* Park Sch., Preston; Girton Coll., Cambridge (MA, LLB). Called to the Bar, Gray's Inn, 1949. Practised on Northern circuit. Former Vice-Chm., Preston North Conservative Assoc.; Mem. Nat. Exec. Council and of Woman's Nat. Advisory Cttee, 1969-70; North-West representative, Central Council. *Publication:* 2nd edn, Benas and Essenhigh's Precedents of Pleadings, 1956. *Recreation:* walking. *Address:* House of Commons, SW1; 1a Chapel Street, Preston, Lancs. *T:* Preston 54462. *Clubs:* Constitutional, Royal Commonwealth Society; Preston Central Conservative.

**HOLT, Richard Anthony Appleby;** Chairman: Hutchinson Ltd since 1959; Hutchinson and Co. (Publishers) Ltd; Hutchinson Printing Trust; *b* 11 March 1920; *s* of Frederick Appleby Holt and Rae Vera Franz (*née* Hutchinson); *m* 1945, Daphne Vivien Pegram; three *s* two *d*. *Educ:* Harrow Sch.; King's Coll., Cambridge. Served War of 1939-45, commissioned in 60th Rifles, 1941; demobilised, 1946 (Major). Admitted solicitor, 1949. Governor Harrow Sch.

*Recreation:* lawn tennis. *Address:* 21 Pelham Crescent, SW7. *T:* 01-589 8469. *Clubs:* White's, Garrick, City of London, All England Lawn Tennis, MCC.

**HOLT, Sir Stanley (Silverwood),** Kt 1964; Hon. President: Stanley Holt & Son Ltd; Chairman, Victoria Buildings (Wigan) Ltd; *b* 5 June 1892; *s* of William Henry Holt, Manchester; *m* 1st, 1916, Dorothy Silverwood Clough (*d* 1943); one *s* three *d*; 2nd, 1955, Joan Freda Howarth Appleton. *Educ:* High Lane, Manchester. Formerly Director: Benmore Distilleries Ltd; Palace Theatre, Manchester; Severn & Co. Ltd; James Smith & Co. ltd; R. M. Bird & Co. President: Moss Side Conservative Association, 1945-; Wine and Spirit Trades Benevolent Society, 1957; Lancashire County Cricket Club, 1961-62; Chairman, City of Manchester Conservative Association, 1961-66, President, 1967. *Recreations:* political, charitable and cricket activities. *Address:* Mere Dene, Mere, Cheshire. *T:* Bucklow Hill 2106. *Clubs:* Constitutional, MCC.

**HOLT, Victoria;** *see* Hibbert, Eleanor.

**HOLT, Dame Zara (Kate),** DBE 1968; *b* 10 March; *d* of Sidney Herbert Dickens; *m* 1st, 1935, Captain James Fell; three *s*; 2nd, 1946, Rt Hon. Harold Edward Holt, PC, CH (*d* 1967), Prime Minister of Australia; 3rd, 1969, Henry Jefferson Percival Bate, MHR. *Educ:* Ruyton and Toorak Coll. Director: Trading and Agency; Berger & Fell; Magg; John Stafford & Co.; Colebrook Estates. Hon. Dr Lit and Hum, Ewha Women's Univ., Seoul, Korea, 1967. Coronation Medal, 1953. *Recreations:* tennis, reading, spear fishing. *Address:* 18 Millicent Avenue, Toorak, Victoria 3142, Australia. *T:* 24.1128.

**HOLT SMITH, Charles;** *see* Smith, Charles H.

**HOLTBY, Rev. Canon Robert Tinsley;** Secretary, Schools Council, Church of England Board of Education, and General Secretary, National Society, since 1967; *b* 25 Feb. 1921; *o s* of William and Elsie Holtby, Thornton-le-Dale, Yorkshire; *m* 1947, Mary, *er d* of late Rt Rev. Eric Graham; one *s* two *d*. *Educ:* York Minster Choir Sch.; Scarborough Coll. and High School. St Edmund Hall, Oxford, 1939; MA (2nd Class Mod. Hist.), 1946; BD 1957. Choral Scholar, King's Coll., Cambridge, 1944; MA (2nd Class Theol.), 1952. Cuddesdon Theological Coll. and Westcott House, Cambridge, 1943-46. Deacon, 1946; Priest, 1947. Curate of Pocklington, Yorks, 1946-48. Chaplain to the Forces, 1948-52: 14/20th King's Hussars, Catterick; Singapore. Acting Chaplain, King's Coll., Cambridge, 1952; Chaplain and Asst Master, Malvern Coll., 1952-54; Chaplain and Assistant Master, St Edward's Sch., Oxford, 1954-58; Canon Residentiary of Carlisle and Diocesan Director of Education, 1959-67, Canon Emeritus, 1967-; Chaplain to the High Sheriff of Cumberland, 1964, 1966. *Publications:* Daniel Waterland, A Study in 18th Century Orthodoxy, 1966; Carlisle Cathedral Library and Records, 1966; Eric Graham, 1888-1964, 1967; Carlisle Cathedral, 1969. *Recreations:* music, walking, history. *Address:* National Society, 69 Great Peter Street, SW1. *T:* 01-222 1672.

**HOLTTUM, Richard Eric,** MA; ScD; FLS; *b* Linton, Cambs, 20 July 1895; *s* of Richard Holttum; *m* 1927, Ursula, *d* of J. W. Massey, Saffron Walden; two *d*. *Educ:* Friends' Sch., Saffron Walden; Bootham Sch., York; St John's Coll., Cambridge (Foundation Scholar). Natural Sciences Tripos, Part 2 (Botany) Class 1, and Frank Smart Prize, 1920; Junior Demonstrator in Botany, Cambridge Univ., 1920-22; Assistant Director, Botanic Gardens, Singapore, 1922-25, Director, 1925-49. Professor of Botany, University of Malaya, 1949-54; President: Singapore Gardening Society, 1937-39, 1947-53; Singapore Rotary Club, 1939-41; British Pteridological Society, 1960-63; Section K (Botany) British Association for the Advancement of Science, 1961. Editor, Series II (Pteridophyta), Flora Malesiana, 1959-. Hon. DSc, University of Malaya, 1949. Linnean gold medal, 1964; has foreign gold medals, etc., for orchids. *Publications:* Orchids of Malaya, 1953; Gardening in the Lowlands of Malaya, 1953; Plant Life in Malaya, 1954; Ferns of Malaya, 1955; botanical and horticultural papers, especially on ferns and orchids. *Address:* 50 Gloucester Court, Kew Gardens, Richmond, Surrey. *T:* 01-940 6157.

**HOLYOAKE, Rt. Hon. Sir Keith Jacka,** PC 1954; GCMG 1970; CH 1963; MP (Nat) for Pahiatua, since 1943 (for Motueka, 1932-38); Prime Minister and Minister of External Affairs, New Zealand, since Dec. 1960; *b* 11 Feb. 1904; *s* of Henry Victor and Esther Holyoake; *m* 1935, Norma Janet Ingram; two *s* three *d*. *Educ:* Tauranga; Hastings; Motueka. President Golden Bay Rugby Union, 1930-33; Nelson Provincial Pres. Farmers' Union, 1930-41; Member Dominion Executive, Farmers' Union, 1940-50. Dominion Vice-Pres., 1940-50. President, NZ Hop Marketing Cttee, 1938-41; Member Exec.: NZ Tobacco Growers' Federation; NZ Fruit Exporters' Association. MP 1932 (Dep. Leader Opposition, NZ, 1947); Cabinet, 1949; Dep. Prime Minister and Minister of Agriculture, Marketing and Scientific Research, 1949-57; Prime Minister and Minister for Maori Affairs, Sept.-Dec. 1957; Leader of Opposition, 1957-60. Farmer; Represented New Zealand farmers at World Conference in London, 1946; Chairman FAO Conference, Rome, 1955; Member: SEATO meetings, 1962-; Conf. on Cambodia, Djakarta, 1970. Freeman, City of London, 1969. Hon. LLD: Victoria University of Wellington; Seoul Univ., Korea. *Recreations:* tennis, gardening. *Address:* 41 Pipitea Street, Wellington, NZ. *T:* 44-797. *Clubs:* Ruahine (Dannevirke); Pahiatua (Pahiatua); Wellington, National (Wellington).

**HOMAN, Philip John Lindsay;** Under Secretary, Ministry of Technology, since 1970; *b* 20 July 1916; *e s* of late Arthur Buckhurst Homan and Gertrude Homan; *m* 1940, Elisabeth Clemency Hobson; two *s* one *d*. *Educ:* Maidstone Grammar Sch.; London School of Economics. Estate Duty Office, Inland Revenue, 1935-49. Served in Royal Navy, 1941-46. Board of Trade, 1949-69: Asst Sec., Controller, Midland Region, 1960; Principal Controller, Scotland, 1966; Director, Min. of Technology Office for Scotland, 1970. *Address:* Skeldale, Kilmacolm, Renfrewshire.

**HOMANS, Prof. George Caspar;** Professor of Sociology, Harvard University, since 1953; Professor of Social Theory, University of Cambridge, 1955-56; *b* 11 Aug. 1910; *s* of Robert Homans and Abigail (*nee* Adams); *m* 1941, Nancy Parshall Cooper; one *s* two *d*. *Educ:* St Paul's Sch., Concord, New Hampshire; Harvard Univ. (AB). Harvard Univ.: Junior Fellow, 1934-39; Instructor in Sociology, 1939-41; Associate Professor of Sociology, 1946-53; Simon Visiting Professor, University of Manchester, 1953; Visiting Professor, University of Kent, 1967. President American Sociological Association, 1963-64. Officer, US Naval Reserve (Lieut-Commander), 1941-45. *Publications:* Massachusetts on the Sea, 1930; An Introduction to Pareto, 1934; Fatigue of

Workers, 1941; English Villagers of the 13th Century, 1941; The Human Group, 1950; Marriage, Authority and Final Causes, 1955; Social Behaviour, 1961; Sentiments and Activities, 1962; The Nature of Social Science, 1967. *Recreations:* forestry, sailing. *Address:* 11 Francis Avenue, Cambridge, Mass 02138, USA. *T:* 547-4737. *Club:* Tavern (Boston, USA).

**HOME,** 14th Earl of [Disclaimed his peerages for life, 23 Oct. 1963]; *see under* Douglas-Home, Rt Hon. Sir Alec.

**HOME, Rt. Hon. Sir Alec D.**; *see* Douglas-Home.

**HOME, Sir David George,** 13th Bt, *cr* 1671; late Temp. Major Argyll and Sutherland Highlanders; *b* 21 Jan. 1904; *o s* of Sir John Home, 12th Bt and Hon. Gwendolina H. R. Mostyn (*d* 1960), *sister* of 7th Baron Vaux of Harrowden; *S* father, 1938; *m* 1933, Sheila, *d* of late Mervyn Campbell Stephen; two *s* two *d*. *Educ:* Harrow; Jesus Coll., Cambridge (BA 1925). Member Royal Company of Archers (HM Body Guard for Scotland). FSA (Scotland). *Heir: s* John Home [*b* 1 June 1936; *m* 1966, Nancy Helen, *d* of H. G. Elliott, Perth, Western Australia, and *widow* of Commander Ian Macgregor, RAN; one *s* one *d*.] *Address:* Winterfield, North Berwick, East Lothian. *Clubs:* Brooks's; New (Edinburgh); Royal and Ancient (St Andrews).

*See also Sir Michael A. J. Malcolm.*

**HOME, Hon. William Douglas-;** dramatic author; *b* Edinburgh, 3 June 1912; *s* of 13th Earl of Home, KT; *m* 1951, Rachel Brand (*see* Baroness Dacre); one *s* three *d*. *Educ:* Eton; New Coll., Oxford (BA). Studied at Royal Academy of Dramatic Art, and has appeared on the West End stage. Formerly Captain RAC. Contested (Progressive Ind) Cathcart Division of Glasgow, April 1942, Windsor Division of Berks, June 1942, and Clay Cross Division of Derbyshire (Atlantic Charter), April 1944, (Liberal) South Edinburgh, 1957. Author of the following plays: Great Possessions, Passing By, Now Barabbas, The Chiltern Hundreds, Ambassador Extraordinary, Master of Arts, The Thistle and the Rose, Caro William, The Manor of Northstead, The Bad Samaritan, The Reluctant Debutante, The Iron Duchess, Aunt Edwina, The Bad Soldier Smith, The Cigarette Girl, The Reluctant Peer, Two Accounts Rendered, A Friend Indeed, Betzi, The Secretary Bird, The Queen's Highland Servant; The Jockey Club Stakes. *Address:* Drayton House, East Meon, Hants. *T:* East Meon 50. *Club:* Travellers'.

*See also Rt Hon. Sir Alec Douglas-Home.*

**HONDURAS, BRITISH, Bishop of,** since 1967; **Rt. Rev. Benjamin Noel Young Vaughan;** *b* 25 Dec. 1917; *s* of Alderman and Mrs J. O. Vaughan, Newport, Pembs; *m* 1945, Nesta Lewis. *Educ:* St David's Coll., Lampeter (BA); St Edmund Hall, Oxford (MA); Westcott House, Cambridge. Deacon, 1943; Priest, 1944. Curate of: Llannon, 1943-45; St David's, Carmarthen, 1945-48; Tutor, Codrington Coll., Barbados, 1948-52; Lecturer in Theology, St David's Coll., Lampeter, and Public Preacher, Diocese of St David's, 1952-55; Rector, Holy Trinity Cathedral, Port of Spain, and Dean of Trinidad, 1955-61; Bishop Suffragan of Mandeville, 1961-67. Examining Chaplain to Bishop of Barbados, 1951-52, to Bishop of Trinidad, 1955-61; Commissary for Barbados, 1952-55. Chairman: Nat. Council for Educn in British Honduras, 1968-; Govt Junior Secondary Sch.; Provincial Commn on Theological Educn in WI; Provincial Cttee on Reunion of Churches, Christian Social Council of British Honduras; Ecumenical Commn of British Honduras; Agric. Commn of Churches of British Honduras. *Publications:* Structures for Renewal, 1967; Wealth, Peace and Godliness, 1968. *Address:* Bishopthorpe, Belize City, British Honduras. *Club:* Rotary International.

**HONE, Sir Brian (William),** Kt 1970; OBE 1969; Headmaster, Melbourne Church of England Grammar School, 1950-70; *b* 1 July 1907; *s* of Dr F. S. Hone, CMG, Adelaide; *m* 1933, A. E. Boyce; three *s* one *d*. *Educ:* Prince Alfred Coll., Adelaide; Univs of Adelaide and Oxford. Asst Master, Marlborough Coll., Wilts, 1933-40; Headmaster, Cranbrook Sch., Sydney, 1940-50. Chm., HMC of Independent Schools of Australia, 1954-57; Mem. Council: Monash Univ., 1959-; Australian Nat. Univ., 1960-, etc. *Publications:* Cricket Practice and Tactics, 1937; (ed jtly) The Independent School, 1967. *Recreations:* tennis, walking. *Address:* 97 Sackville Street, Kew, Victoria 3101, Australia. *Club:* Melbourne (Melbourne).

**HONE, Sir Evelyn (Dennison),** GCMG 1965 (KCMG 1959; CMG 1953); CVO 1954; OBE 1946; Adviser to the West Africa Committee since 1967; *b* 13 Dec. 1911; 2nd *s* of late Arthur Rickman Hone, MBE, Salisbury, S Rhodesia, and late Olive Gertrude Fairbridge (*née* Scanlen); *m* 1946, Helen Joy Mellor; one *s* two *d*. *Educ:* Wellington Coll.; Rhodes Univ., S Africa; New College, Oxford Univ. Rhodes Scholar (Rhodesia), 1931; entered Colonial Service as Administrative Officer (cadet), Tanganyika Territory, 1935; Secretary to Government, Seychelles, 1944; Asst Secretary, Palestine, 1946; Colonial Secretary, British Honduras, 1948-53. Chief Secretary: Aden, 1953-57, N Rhodesia, 1957-59; Governor of Northern Rhodesia, 1959-64 (when the territory became the Republic of Zambia). Member: (part-time) Southern Gas Board, 1968-; Bd of Governors, Oversea Service Coll., 1969-; Central Council, Royal Over-Seas League, 1969-; Beit Trustee, 1970-. Hon. LLD, Rhodes Univ., 1964. *Address:* The Mill House, North Marston, Bucks.

**HONE, Maj.-Gen. Sir (Herbert) Ralph,** KCMG 1951; KBE 1946 (CBE 1943); MC; TD; QC Gibraltar 1934, QC Uganda 1938; barrister-at-law; *b* 3 May 1896; *s* of late Herbert Hone and Miriam Grace (*née* Dracott); *m* 1st, 1918 (marr. diss.); one *s* one *d*; 2nd, 1945, Sybil Mary, *widow* of Wing Commander G. Simond; one *s*. *Educ:* Varndean Grammar Sch., Brighton; London Univ. LLB (Hons). Barrister-at-law, Middle Temple. Inns of Court OTC. Gazetted London Irish Rifles, 1915; Lieut, 1916; Captain, 1918; served with BEF, France, 1916 and 1917-18 (wounded, MC), Staff Captain, Ministry of Munitions, 1918-20; Major R of O (TA); Asst Treas., Uganda, 1920; called to Bar; practised and went South Eastern Circuit, 1923-24; Registrar, High Court, Zanzibar, 1925; Resident Magistrate, Zanzibar, 1928; Crown Counsel, Tanganyika Territory, 1930; acted Asst Legal Adviser to the Colonial and Dominions Offices, jan.-Aug. 1933; Attorney-General, Gibraltar, 1933-36; Commissioner for the Revision of the laws of Gibraltar, 1934; King's Jubilee medal, 1935; Chm., Gibraltar Govt Commn on Slum Clearance and Rent Restriction, 1936; Coronation Medal, 1937; Acting Chief Justice, Gibraltar, on several occasions; Attorney-General, Uganda, 1937-43; Chairman, Uganda Government Cttee on Museum policy, 1938; Commandant, Uganda Defence Force, 1940; Chief Legal Adviser, Political Branch, GHQ, Middle East, 1941; Chief Political Officer, GHQ, Middle East, 1942-43; General Staff, War Office, 1943-45;

Chief Civil Affairs Officer, Malaya, 1945-46; Maj.-Gen., 1942-46 (despatches twice, CBE); Secretary-General to Governor-General of Malaya, 1946-48; Dep. Commissioner-General in SE Asia, 1948-49; Coronation Medal, 1953. Governor and C-in-C, North Borneo, 1949-54; Head of Legal Division, CRO, 1954-61. Resumed practice at the Bar, 1961. Retd TA with Hon. rank Maj.-Gen., 1956. KStJ 1949; Mem. Chapter Gen. Order of St John. Vice-Pres., Royal Commonwealth Society; Constitutional Adviser, Kenya Govt, Dec. 1961-Jan. 1962; Constitutional Adviser to Mr Butler's Advisers on Central Africa, July-Oct. 1962; Constitutional Adviser to South Arabian Government, Oct. 1965-Jan. 1966, and to Bermuda Government, July-Nov. 1966. Appeal Comr under Civil Aviation Licensing Act, 1961-. *Publications:* Index to Gibraltar Laws, 1933; revised edn of Laws of Gibraltar, 1935; revised edn of Laws of the Bahamas, 1965; Handbook on Native Courts, etc. *Recreations:* tennis, badminton and philately. *Address:* 1 Paper Buildings, Temple, EC4. *T:* 01-353 0165; 56 Kenilworth Court, Lower Richmond Road, SW15. *T:* 01-788 3367. *Clubs:* Athenæum, Royal Commonwealth Society.

**HONE, Sir Ralph;** *see* Hone, Sir H. R.

**HONE, Robert Monro,** MA; Headmaster, Exeter School, since 1966; *b* 2 March 1923; *s* of late Rt Rev. Campbell R. Hone; *m* 1958, Helen Isobel, *d* of late Col H. M. Cadell of Grange, OBE; three *d. Educ:* Winchester Coll. (Scholar); New Coll., Oxford (Scholar). Rifle Brigade, 1942-45. Asst Master, Clifton Coll., 1948-65 (Housemaster, 1958-65). *Address:* Exeter School, Exeter. *T:* Exeter 73679.

**HONEYCOMBE, Prof. Robert William Kerr;** Goldsmiths' Professor of Metallurgy, University of Cambridge, since 1966; *b* 2 May 1921; *s* of William and Rachel Honeycombe (*née* Kerr); *m* 1947, June Collins; two *d. Educ:* Geelong Coll.; Univ. of Melbourne. Research Student, Department of Metallurgy, University of Melbourne, 1941-42; Research Officer, Commonwealth Scientific and Industrial Research Organization, Australia, 1942-47; ICI Research Fellow, Cavendish Laboratory, Cambridge, 1948-49; Royal Society Armourers and Brasiers' Research Fellow, Cavendish Laboratory, Cambridge, 1949-51; Senior Lecturer in Physical Metallurgy, University of Sheffield, 1951-55; Professor, 1955-56. Rosenhain Medal of Inst. of Metals, 1959. Visiting Professor: University of Melbourne, 1962; Stanford Univ., 1965. Sir George Beilby Gold Medal, 1963. *Publications:* The Plastic Deformation of Metals, 1968; papers in Proc. Royal Soc., Jl Inst. of Metals, etc. *Recreations:* gardening, photography, tennis. *Address:* Barrabool, 46 Main Street, Hardwick, Cambridge. *T:* Madingley 501.

**HONEYMAN, Prof. Alexander Mackie,** MA, BLitt, PhD; Professor of Oriental Languages in University of St Andrews, 1936-67; Fellow of Royal Asiatic Society; *b* 25 Nov. 1907; *s* of late A. M. Honeyman, Cupar, Fife; *m* 1935, Cecilia Mary, 2nd *d* of late J. Leslie Milne, Edinburgh; one *s* two *d. Educ:* Universities of St Andrews, Edinburgh, London (School of Oriental Studies), Zürich and Chicago (Oriental Institute). 1st Class Hons Classics, 1929; BLitt in Ancient Languages, 1930; Guthrie Scholar, 1930, University of St Andrews; Commonwealth Fellow, New York and Chicago, 1932-34; PhD Chicago, 1934; Maclean Scholar of University of Glasgow, 1934-35, in Palestine, etc; Interim Lectr in Hebrew and Oriental Languages, Univ. of St Andrews, 1935-36. External Examiner to University of Glasgow, 1941-44, 1946, 1951-54, University of Edinburgh, 1946-48, Queen's Univ., Belfast, 1947-49; University of Leeds, 1954-56, 1959; University of London, 1959. Schweich Lecturer of British Academy, 1950; Leverhulme Fellowship, 1954. Travelled and excavated in S Arabia, 1950, 1954 and 1958. Trustee of National Library of Scotland, 1951-56; Mem. Council, Royal Asiatic Soc., 1952-56; Vice-Pres., British Branch, Hebrew Language Academy, 1954-. *Publications:* The Mission of Burzoe in the Arabic Kalilah wa-Dimnah, 1936; articles and reviews in archæological, philological and historical journals. *Address:* Cowan's Rigg, St Andrews, Fife, Scotland.

*See also Baron Bethell.*

**HONEYMAN, Sir George (Gordon),** Kt 1961; CBE 1953; QC 1955; JP; Chairman, Surrey QS, since 1969 (Deputy Chairman, 1962-69); *b* 10 March 1898; *y s* of Andrew Stark Honeyman, Glasgow, and Jemima Margaret, *d* of James Maclaren, Dundee; *m* 1933, Evelyn Goldsworth, Southport; two *d. Educ:* Glasgow High Sch.; Glasgow Univ. MA 1921, LLB 1923, LLD (Hon.), 1964. Served European War, 1914-18, Lieut Royal Sussex Regt, 1917-19. Called to Bar, Inner Temple, 1924; North East Circuit. Chairman: Retail Distributive Trades' Commissions of Inquiry, 1946; Unlicensed Places of Refreshment Wages Council; Hat, Cap and Millinery Wages Council; Commission of Inquiry, Copper Mining Industry, Nothern Rhodesia, 1957; Board of Inquiry, Sugar Milling Industry, Fiji, 1959; Commission of Inquiry, Sugar Industry, Trinidad, 1962-63; Civil Service Arbitration Tribunal, 1952-68; Agricultural Wages Board, 1953-68; a Chm., Industrial Court, 1949-67; Member: Nat. Arbitration Tribunal, 1951-59. Master of the Bench, Inner Temple, 1961. Chm., Approved Coal Merchants' Scheme, 1962. *Recreation:* gardening. *Address:* 5 Paper Buildings, Temple, EC4. *T:* 01-353 8494; Elm Bank, Godstone, Surrey. *T:* Godstone 295.

**HONEYMAN, Tom John,** JP; LLD; *b* 10 June 1891; 4th *s* of Tom Honeyman, Fife, and Elspeth Smith, Morayshire; *m* 1920, Victoria Catherine Burnett, Friockheim; two *s* one *d. Educ:* Queen's Park Sch. and University, Glasgow. Graduate in medicine, Glasgow, 1916. Served European War, 1914-18, Salonika and India, RAMC. FRCPGlas 1925; FMA 1951; FEIS 1955. Univ. Asst, Depts of Physiology and Medicine; practised until 1929. Dir, Lefevre Gallery, until 1939. Dir, Glasgow Art Gallery, 1939-54. Rector of Glasgow Univ., 1953-56. Awarded St Mungo Prize for Citizenship, 1943. Past Chairman: Scottish Tourist Cttee; Citizens' Theatre. Hon. Pres., The Provand's Lordship Soc.; Pres., Glasgow Tree Lovers' Soc. *Publications:* Monograph on Leslie Hunter, 1937; Three Scottish Colourists, 1950; The Clear Horizon, 1954; Patronage and Prejudice in Art, 1967; articles on art and tourism in various periodicals, weekly and daily newspapers, art catalogues, etc. *Recreations:* talking, travel, theatre. *Address:* 20 Queen's Gate, Glasgow. *T:* 041-339 2179. *Club:* Glasgow Art.

**HONG KONG, Bishop of, (RC),** since 1969; **Rt. Rev. Francis Hsu Chen-ping;** *b* 20 Feb. 1920. Ordained, 1959; consecrated Auxiliary Bishop of Hong Kong, 1967; nominated Apostolic Administrator of Hong Kong, 1968. *Address:* Bishop's House, 16 Caine Road, Hong Kong. *T:* H-232487/221009/220486.

**HONG KONG, Dean of;** *see* Foster, Very Rev. J. W.

**HONG KONG and MACAO, Bishop of,** since 1966; **Rt. Rev. John Gilbert Hindley Baker;** *b* 10 Oct. 1910; 3rd and *y s* of late Arthur Ernest

Baker, MRCS, LRCP, and Agnes Flora Baker (*née* Hindley), Bromley, Kent; *m* 1941, Martha Levering Sherman, *d* of late Rev. Arthur Sherman, STD and Mrs Martha Sherman, Wuchang, China and Ohio, USA; two *s* two *d*. *Educ:* Westminster Sch.; Christ Church, Oxford. Deacon, 1935; Priest, 1936. SCM Sec., London, 1932-34; Dio. of Hong Kong and S China, 1935-; taught at Lingnan Univ., Canton, 1936-38; in Kunming, Yunnan, 1939-45; St John's Univ., Shanghai, 1947-49; Union Theol. Coll., Lingnan, 1949-51; Rector of Christ Church, Guilford, Conn., 1952-55; Gen. Sec., Church Assembly Overseas Coun., London, 1955-63; Vicar, St Nicholas Cole Abbey, London, 1955-66; Actg Dir, Christian Study Centre, Hong Kong, 1966. *Publications:* The Changing Scene in China, 1946 (US 1948); The Church on Asian Frontiers, 1963; contrib., All One Body, 1969. *Recreations:* walking, swimming, listening to music. *Address:* Bishop's House, Hong Kong. *T:* Hong Kong 235851. *Club:* Royal Commonwealth Society.

**HONGLADAROM, Sunthorn;** Knight Grand Cordon, Order of Crown of Thailand, and Order of White Elephant; Ambassador of Thailand to the United States of America, since 1969; *b* 23 Aug. 1912; *m* 1937; five *s* one *d*. *Educ:* Trinity Coll., Cambridge. Asst Sec.-Gen. to Cabinet, 1946; Sec.-Gen., Nat. Economic Council, 1950; Ambassador to Fedn of Malaya (now Malaysia), 1957; Minister of Economic Affairs, 1959; Minister of Finance, 1960; Chairman of Boards of Governors; IBRD, IMF, IFC, and Internat. Development Assoc., 1961; Minister of Economic Affairs, 1966; Ambassador to UK, 1968. *Recreations:* golf, motoring. *Address:* Royal Thai Embassy, 2300 Kalorama Road, Washington, DC 20008, USA. *Club:* Roehampton.

**HONIG, Frederick; His Honour Judge Honig;** County Court Judge since 1968; *b* 22 March 1912; 2nd *s* of late Leopold Honig; *m* 1940, Joan, *o d* of late Arthur Burkart. *Educ:* Berlin and Heidelberg Univs. LLD (Hons) Heidelberg, 1934. Barrister, Middle Temple, 1937. War service, 1940-47: Capt., JAG's Dept; Judge Advocate in civilian capacity, 1947-48; subseq. practised at Bar. *Publications:* (jtly) Cartel Law of the European Economic Community, 1963; contribs to Internat. Law Reports (ed. Lauterpacht) and legal jls, incl. Amer. Jl of Internat. Law, Internat. and Comparative Law Quarterly, Law Jl, Propriété Industrielle, etc. *Recreations:* foreign languages, country walking. *Address:* Lamb Building, Temple, EC4. *T:* 01-353 1612; 23 Shilling Street, Lavenham, Suffolk. *T:* Lavenham 565.

**HONORÉ, Antony Maurice,** DCL Oxon; Professor of Comparative Law, University of Oxford, from Oct. 1971 (Rhodes Reader in Roman-Dutch Law, 1957-71); Fellow of Brasenose College, Oxford, from Oct. 1971 (Fellow of New College, 1964-71); *b* 30 March 1921; *o s* of Frédéric Maurice Honoré and Marjorie Erskine (*née* Gilbert); *m* 1948, Martine Marie-Odette, 2nd *d* of Pierre Genouville, Le Chesnay, France; one *s* one *d*. *Educ:* Diocesan Coll., Rondebosch; Univ. of Cape Town; New Coll., Oxford. Rhodes Scholar, 1940. Union Defence Forces, 1940-45; Lieut, Rand Light Infantry, 1942. BCL 1948. Advocate, South Africa, 1951; called to Bar, Lincoln's Inn, 1952. Lectr, Nottingham Univ., 1948; Fellow of Queen's Coll., Oxford, 1949-64. Visiting Professor: McGill, 1961; Berkeley, 1968. *Publications:* (with R. W. Lee) The South African Law of Obligations, 1950; (with R. W. Lee) The South African Law of Property etc, 1954; (with H. L. A. Hart) Causation in the Law, 1959; Gaius, 1962; The South African Law of Trusts, 1966. *Recreation:* cricket. *Address:* 97 Lonsdale Road, Oxford. *T:* Oxford 58718.

**HONYWOOD, Col Sir William Wynne,** 10th Bt *cr* 1660; MC; *b* 7 April 1891; 2nd *s* of Sir John William Honywood, 8th Bt of Evington; *S* brother, 1944; *m* 1923, Maud Naylor (*d* 1953) (who served in War of 1914-19 as special military probationer nurse), *d* of late William H. Wilson, Hexgreave Park, Southwell, Notts; one *s* two *d*. *Educ:* Downside. Joined 17th (DCO) Lancers, Aug. 1914; posted to RARO, 17th/21st Lancers, 1934; re-employed, Aug. 1939; Bt Major, Sept. 1939; Lieut-Col Pioneer Corps, 1940; Lieut-Col 8th Bn KSLI 1941; Chief Instructor, 210 Officer Cadet Training Unit, 1944; Col 1945; Deputy Dir Pioneers and Labour, Cyrenaica District, 1945-46; Comdt Royal Pioneer Corps Depôt, MEF, 1946-48. Served European War, 1914-19, in France, Belgium, and German East Africa (despatches thrice, MC); seconded to Air Ministry, Airship Pilot, 1918-19; Adjt Ceylon Mounted Rifles and Ceylon Planters Rifle Corps, 1928-31; War of 1939-45, served in France, 1939-40, and Middle East. *Heir: s* Filmer Courtenay William Honywood [*b* 20 May 1930; *m* 1956, Elizabeth Margaret Mary Cynthia Miller; two *s* two *d*]. *Address:* c/o Lloyds Bank Ltd, 6 Pall Mall, SW1.

**HOOD,** family name of **Viscounts Bridport** and **Hood.**

**HOOD;** *see* Fuller-Acland-Hood.

**HOOD,** 6th Viscount, *cr* 1796; **Samuel Hood,** GCMG 1969 (KCMG 1960; CMG 1953); Bt 1778; Baron 1782; Baron Hood (Great Britain), 1795; Deputy Under-Secretary of State, Foreign and Commonwealth Office (formerly Foreign Office), 1962-69; *b* 15 Oct. 1910; *s* of late Rear-Adm. Hon. Sir Horace Hood, KCB, DSO, MVO (3rd *s* of 4th Viscount), and late Ellen Touzalin; *S* uncle, 1933. *Educ:* Eton; Trinity Coll., Cambridge. Asst Private Sec. to Marquess of Zetland, Sec. of State for India, 1936-39; Private Sec. to Lord Macmillan, Sir John Reith and Mr A. Duff Cooper when Ministers of Information, 1939-41; served in the Foreign Office, 1942-47; mem. of the UK Delegns to meetings of Council of Foreign Ministers in London, Paris, New York and Moscow, 1945-47 and to the Peace Conf. in Paris, 1946; Dep. to Foreign Sec. for Austrian Peace Treaty, 1947; 1st Sec., HM Embassy, Madrid, 1947; Counsellor, HM Embassy, Paris, 1948; Asst Under-Sec. of State, Foreign Office, 1951; and British Representative, Council of Western European Union, 1956; HM Minister, Washington, 1957-62. *Heir: b* Hon. Alexander Lambert Hood, *qv*. *Address:* 80 Eaton Square, SW1. *Clubs:* Brooks's, Travellers', Turf; Swinley Forest Golf; Royal St George's Golf.
*See also Baron Ashburton.*

**HOOD, Lt-Gen. Sir Alexander,** GBE 1946 (CBE 1939); KCB 1943 (CB 1942); KCVO 1953; *b* 25 Sept. 1888; *s* of Alexander Hood, Trinity, Edinburgh; *m* 1st, 1918, Evelyn Dulcia, CStJ (from whom he obtained a divorce, in Reno, Nevada, USA, 1955), *d* of George Ellwood, Kensington, W; 2nd, 1955 (at Carson City, Nevada, USA), Mrs Helen Winifred Wilkinson, Hamilton, Bermuda. *Educ:* George Watson's Coll.; Edinburgh Univ. MB, ChB, 1910; MD 1931. House Surgeon Royal Infirmary, Edinburgh, 1910-11; Lieut RAMC, 1912. Served European War, 1914-18, in France and Belgium. Capt. 1915; Major 1924; Lieut-Col 1934; Col (Brevet) 1938, (Subst.) 1939; (despatches Palestine, 1939); Brig. 1940;

Maj.-Gen. 1941; Lt-Gen. 1941. Sometime DDMS, British Forces in Palestine and Trans-Jordan; Dir-Gen., Army Medical Services, 1941-48; Chm. of Governors of Star and Garter Home for Disabled Sailors, Soldiers and Airmen, 1948; Governor and C-in-C, Bermuda, 1949-55. KHP 1941. Hon. degrees: FRCSE, 1942; FRCP, 1944; LLD Edinburgh, 1945; DCL Durham, 1946; FRFPSG, 1946. Hon. Freeman of Barbers' Company. Knight of Order of White Lion of Czechoslovakia, 1944; Knight of Order of Orange Nassau, 1945; Commander of Order of Crown of Belgium, 1945; Commander of American Legion of Merit, 1945. *Address:* Montalto, Baileys Bay, Bermuda.

**HOOD, Hon. Alexander Lambert;** Director: J. Henry Schroder Wagg & Co. since 1957; George Wimpey & Co. Ltd since 1957; Inveresk Paper Co. Ltd since 1966 (Chairman 1967), etc; Part-time Member, British Waterways Board, since 1963; *b* 11 March 1914; *s* of late Rear-Adm. Hon. Sir H. L. A. Hood, KCB, DSO, MVO, and late Ellen Floyd Touzalin; *b* and *heir-pres.* to 6th Viscount Hood, *qv*; *m* 1957, Diana Maud, CVO 1957, *d* of late Hon. G. W. Lyttelton; three *s*. *Educ:* RN Coll., Dartmouth; Trinity Coll., Cambridge; Harvard Business Sch. RNVR, 1939-45. *Address:* 67 Chelsea Square, SW3. *T:* 01-352 4952; Loders Court, Bridport, Dorset. *T:* Bridport 2983. *Clubs:* Brooks's; Knickerbocker (New York).

**HOOD, Rev. Canon (Archibald) Frederic,** CBE 1967; Canon Residentiary, Chancellor and Chapter Treasurer of St Paul's Cathedral, 1961-Jan. 1970; Canon of Monmouth, 1940-69; Freeman of City of London, 1957; *b* 12 Dec. 1895; *s* of late Archibald Hood, MB, and Mrs Stanley Clay, *d* of late Ven. F. W. Edmondes, sometime Archdeacon of Llandaff; unmarried. *Educ:* St Andrew's, Eastbourne; privately; University Coll., Oxford. BA (1st Class Theology), 1916; Liddon Student, 1916; MA 1920; DD Nashotah, 1949; Senior Denyer and Johnson Scholar, 1921; FRGS 1920. Served in Volunteer Force, 1914-16; Asst Master at Lockers Park, Hemel Hempstead, 1916-18; Bishops Coll., Cheshunt, 1918-19; travelled round the world, 1919-20; Deacon, 1920; Priest, 1921; Vice-Principal of St Stephen's House, Oxford, 1920-22; studied at Bonn, 1922; Asst Chaplain, Exeter Coll., Oxford, 1922-23; Librarian, Pusey House, Oxford, 1922-34; Principal, 1934-52; Governor, 1957; Guild Church Vicar of St Mary Aldermary, EC4, 1954-61. Exam. Chaplain to Bishop of Monmouth, 1921-45; Mem. Governing Body of Church in Wales, 1933-; Ecclesiastical Judge of Provincial Court of Church in Wales, 1967; Chm. of Exec. Cttee of Church Union, 1935-36 (Vice-Pres.). Select Preacher, Oxford, 1946-48; August Preacher, 1946, Lent Preacher, 1949, New York Cathedral; University Preacher, Chicago, 1949, Yale, 1951, Harvard, 1951, Columbia, 1955 and 1957; Gore Lectr, Westminster Abbey, 1959; a Governor of St Stephen's House, Oxford, and St Michael's Coll., Llandaff, Liddon House; Member: Church of England Council on Foreign Relations; Central Cttee for Training og Ordinands in Province of Wales; Commissary to Bishop of St John's, CP, 1951; Chm., Church Moral Aid Assoc., 1952-58; Pres., Assoc. for Promoting Retreats, 1955-58; Past Pres., Sion Coll.; Pres., St Paul's Cathedral Lecture Soc., 1961-Jan. 1970; Sub Dean of Order of British Empire, 1962-. Chaplain and Mem. of the Chapter-General, Order of St John. Hon. Canon, St John's Cathedral, Umtata, S Africa, 1970-. *Publications:* The Christ of St Mark, 1928; God's Plan, 1955 (new edn 1961); The Chapel of the Most Excellent Order of the British Empire, 1967; contributor to Church Times; former contributor to: Catholic Sermons, 1932; Union of Christendom, 1938; Darwell Stone, 1943; Cowley Sermons, 1947; Chambers's Encyclopedia, 1950; Oxford Dictionary of the Christian Church, 1957; DNB, 1941-50; Anglo-Catholic Congress Report, 1930, 1948; The Church Quarterly Review, Time and Tide, Expository Times, etc. *Recreations:* travelling, swimming. *Address:* 66 Viceroy Court, Prince Albert Road, NW8. *T:* 01-722 1685. *Clubs:* Athenæum, Brooks's.

**HOOD, Clifford Firoved;** Director Emeritus, Trans World Airlines; Member Advisory Board, Liberty Mutual Insurance Co.; *b* Monmouth, Ill., 8 Feb. 1894; *s* of Edward Everett Hood; *m* 1917, Emilie R. Tener (decd); two *s*; *m* 1943, Mary Ellen Tolerton. *Educ:* Univ. of Illinois (BS). Technical apprentice Packard Electric Co., Ohio, 1915, Sales Engineer, 1915-17; with American Steel and Wire Co., 1917-49; operating clerk, 1917; war service, 1st Lieut, US Army, 1917-19; foreman, Amer. Steel and Wire Co., 1919-25; asst superintendent, South Works, Worcester, Mass, 1925-27; superintendent, 1927-28; asst manager, subseq. manager, Worcester district, 1928-35; Vice-Pres. in charge of operations, 1935-37; Exec. Vice-Pres., 1937; Pres., 1938-49; Pres., Carnegie-Illinois Steel Corp., 1950; Exec. Vice-Pres. in charge operations, US Steel Co., 1951-52; Pres. US Steel Corporation, 1953; retired May 1959. Mem. Amer. Iron and Steel Inst. Baptist. Holds several hon. degrees in law and engineering, from 1952. *Address:* Royal Palm Way Apartments, 100 Royal Palm Way, Palm Beach, Florida 33480, USA.

**HOOD, Douglas;** *see* Hood, J. D.

**HOOD, Prof. Francis Campbell,** MA (Edinburgh, Oxon and Dunelm); Professor Emeritus since 1955; Professor of Political Theory and Institutions, University of Durham, 1946-55; *b* 30 March 1895; *y s* of late Alexander Hood, Edinburgh; *m* 1st, 1921, Mary (marr. diss. 1939), *d* of Matthew Horsley, Hartlepool; one *s* killed on active service, 1945; 2nd, 1940, Muriel, *o d* of late Joseph Dodds, Kyleglas, Limerick; one *d*. *Educ:* Melville Coll.; University of Edinburgh (1st Cl. Hons in History, and Kirkpatrick Scholar, 1916); Balliol Coll., Oxford (Hon. Exhibitioner 1916, 1st Cl. Hons in Modern History, 1918). Board of Trade (temp.), 1918; Min. of Labour (temp.), 1919; Lectr in History, Univ. of Birmingham, 1919-20; National Federation of Iron and Steel Manufacturers, 1920-22; Lecturer in Economics and History, 1922-31; Lecturer in History, 1931-40; Reader in History, 1940-45, Univ. of Durham. *Publication:* The Divine Politics of Thomas Hobbes, 1964. *Address:* Kingsgate, Bow Lane, Durham. *T:* Durham 3651.

**HOOD, Rev. Canon Frederic;** *see* Hood, Rev. Canon (A.) F.

**HOOD, Sir Harold (Joseph),** 2nd Bt *cr* 1922, of Wimbledon, Co. Surrey; TD; Circulation Director Catholic Herald; Circulation Director, Universe, 1953-60; *b* 23 Jan. 1916; *e s* of Sir Joseph Hood, 1st Bt, and Marie Josephine (*d* 1956), *e d* of Archibald Robinson, JP, Dublin; *S* father, 1931; *m* 1946, Hon. Ferelith Rosemary Florence Kenworthy, *o d* of 10th Baron Strabolgi and of Doris, Lady Strabolgi, 137 Gloucester Road, SW7; two *s* two *d* (and one *s* decd). *Educ:* Downside Sch. Mem. Editorial Staff, The Universe, 1936-39; Asst Editor, The Catholic Directory, 1950,

Managing Ed., 1959-60; Editor, The Catholic Who's Who, 1952 Edition. 2nd Lieutenant 58th Middx Battalion RE (AA) (TA) 1939; Lieut RA, 1941. Kt of St Gregory (Holy See), 1964. *Heir:* s John Joseph Harold Hood, *b* 27 Aug. 1952. *Address:* 31 Avenue Road, NW8. *T:* 01-722 9088. *Clubs:* Carlton, Junior Carlton, MCC, Challoner.

**HOOD, (James) Douglas,** CBE 1956; Chairman: Scottish Worsteds & Woollens Ltd, Hawick (The Clan Royal Group); Wilson & Glenny Ltd (also Managing Director), Hawick; Simpson & Fairbairn Ltd, Earlston; National Wool Textile Export Corporation, Bradford; Director: William McGeoch & Co. Ltd, Glasgow; William McGeoch & Co. (Northern) Ltd, Glasgow; *b* 24 May 1905; *s* of late George B. W. Hood; *m* 1931, Evelyn Mary, 2nd *d* of late Lachlan A. McGeoch, Glasgow; one *d*. *Educ:* Sedbergh Sch., Yorks. Attended Scottish Woollen Technical Coll., Galashiels; entered Scottish tweed trade, joining Wilson & Glenny Ltd, Hawick, 1923; Chm. and Man. Dir, Wilson & Glenny Ltd, 1950. Pres., Nat. Assoc. of Scottish Woollen Manufrs, 1948-51; Chm., Scottish Woollen Publicity Council (on its formation), 1957-64; Chm. Nat. Wool Textile Export Corp., 1958-; Mem. Council, Royal Coll. of Art, 1961-; Advisory Council of Export Credits Guarantee Dept, 1963-; Chm. Textile Promotion Consultative Cttee, 1963-; Mem., British Nat. Export Council Australian Cttee, 1965-. *Recreations:* photography, music, gardening. *Address:* The Old Manse, Midlem, Selkirk. *T:* Lilliesleaf 294. *Clubs:* Caledonian; Conservative (Edinburgh).

**HOOD, (Martin) Sinclair (Frankland);** Archaeologist; *b* 31 Jan. 1917; *s* of late Lt-Comdr Martin Hood, RN, and late Mrs Martin Hood, New York; *m* 1957, Rachel Simmons; one *s* two *d*. *Educ:* Harrow; Magdalen Coll., Oxford. British Sch. at Athens: student, 1947-48 and 1951-53; Asst Dir, 1949-51; Dir, 1954-62. Student, British Inst. Archaeology, Ankara, 1948-49. Geddes-Harrower Vis. Prof. of Greek Art and Archaeology, Univ. of Aberdeen, 1968. Took part in excavations at: Dorchester, Oxon, 1937; Compton, Berks, 1946-47; Southwark, 1946; Smyrna, 1948-49; Atchana, 1949-50; Sakca-Gozu, 1950; Mycenae, 1950-52; Knossos, 1950-51, 1953-55, 1957-61; Jericho, 1952; Chios, 1952-55. *Publications:* The Home of the Heroes: The Aegean before the Greeks, 1967; various excavation reports and articles. *Address:* The Old Vicarage, Great Milton, Oxford. *T:* Great Milton 202. *Club:* Athenæum.

**HOOD, Sinclair;** *see* Hood, M. S. F.

**HOOD, Col Sir Tom (Fielden),** KBE 1967 (OBE 1944); CB 1959; TD 1944; DL; Chairman: Portman Building Society; National Employers' Life Assurance Co. Ltd; Director: National Employers' Mutual General Insurance Association Ltd (Deputy Chairman since 1967); Lennards Ltd, and other companies; Member: Bristol Regional Board, Lloyds Bank Ltd; Western Regional Board, Hill, Samuel & Co. Ltd; *s* of late Tom Hood, AMICE, AMIMechE, and Emmeline Clayton Hood (*née* Fielden); *m* 1931, Joan, *d* of Richmond P. Hellyar; two *s*. *Educ:* Clifton Coll. ACA 1930, FCA 1938. Partner, Lawrence, Gardner & Co., Chartered Accountants, Bristol, 1931-57. 2nd Lieut RE (TA), 1923; CRE 61 Div., 1939-42; DCE Scottish Command, 1942-44; DCE Second Army, 1944-45; Col 1945. Chm., Commn of Enquiry into Port of Aden, 1963. Governor of Clifton Coll., 1954-; Mem. of Court of Univ. of Bristol, 1956-. DL Co. Gloucester, 1950-. *Recreation:* shooting. *Address:* Sion Cottage, Sion Hill, Bath BA1 2UL. *T:* Bath 25123. *Clubs:* Army and Navy; Bath and County (Bath).

**HOOD, William Francis,** LLB London; Master of the Supreme Court (Taxing Office), 1946-70; *b* 27 Sept. 1902; *s* of Wm Charles Reginald Hood, solicitor, and Margaret Frances, *d* of John McKissock, Glaick, Leswalt, Stranraer; *m* 1928, Gwendolen Lloyd, *d* of Rex Lloyd Turner, Croydon; two *d*. *Educ:* Haileybury (Schol.). Asiatic Petroleum Co. Ltd, 1921-23; solicitor (Hons), 1929; Partner Barnett Tuson Hood & Co., 117 Old Broad Street, EC2, 1936-46; RNVR 1941-45; Lieut-Comdr, 1945; Board of Management, Metropolitan Ear, Nose and Throat Hospital, 1945-47. Editor Haileybury Register, 1962. *Recreations:* travel, music, drama. *Address:* Poyningshurst, Slaugham, Sussex. *T:* Handcross 336.

**HOOD PHILLIPS;** *see* Phillips.

**HOOFT, Willem Adolf Visser 't;** *see* Visser 't Hooft.

**HOOK, Very Rev. Norman;** Dean of Norwich, 1953-69, Dean Emeritus since 1969; *b* 1898; *e s* of late S. A. Hook and late Mrs Hook, Brough, Westmorland; *m* 1927, M. I. Sugden, *d* of Rev. E. H. Sugden; one *d* (and one *d* decd). *Educ:* Appleby Sch.; Univ. of Durham. Rector of Enborne, Berks, 1927-31; Vicar of West Norwood, SE27, 1931-37; Vicar of Knutsford, 1937-45; Vicar of Wimbledon, Rural Dean and Canon of Southwark, 1945-53. *Publications:* Holy is His Name: Studies in the Problem of Evil, 1957; The Eucharist in the New Testament, 1965; Christ in the Twentieth Century, 1968. *Recreations:* motoring and gardening. *Address:* 2 East Pallant, Chichester, Sussex.

**HOOK, Rt. Rev. Ross Sydney;** *see* Grantham, Bishop Suffragan of.

**HOOK, Prof. Sidney;** Professor, Department of Philosophy, Washington Square College, New York University, since 1939; Founder of The New York University Institute of Philosophy; *b* 20 Dec. 1902; *s* of Isaac Hook and Jennie Halpern; *m* 1924; one *s*; *m* 1935, Ann Zinken; one *s* one *d*. *Educ:* College of the City of New York; columbia Univ. BS (Coll. of City of New York), 1923; MA (Columbia Univ.), 1926; PhD, 1927; Columbia Univ. Fellowship in Philosophy, 1926-27; Guggenheim Research Fellowship in Philosophy for Study Abroad, 1928-29, 1953-; Ford Fellowship for the Study of Asian philosophy and culture, 1958. Teacher, New York City Public Schs, 1923-28; Lectr, Columbia Univ. Summer Session, 1927, 1930; Instr in Philosophy, Washington Square Coll., New York Univ., 1927-32; Asst Prof., 1932-34; Assoc. Prof. and Chm. of Dept of Philosophy, 1934-39; Lectr, New Sch. for Social Research, NYC, 1931-. Vis. Prof., Univ. of California, 1950, Harvard Univ., 1961; Thomas Jefferson Memorial Lectr, Univ. of California at Berkeley, 1961; Regents Prof., Univ. of California at Santa Barbara, 1966. Fellow at Center for Advanced Study in the Behavioral Sciences, Stanford Univ., 1961-62. Butler Silver Medal for distinction in Philosophy, Columbia Univ., 1945. Organiser: conf. on Methods in Philosophy and Sci., conf. on Sci. Spirit and Dem. Faith, and Cttee for Cultural Freedom; Organiser and Co-Chm., Americans for Intellectual Freedom; Member: American Philosophical Assoc. Vice-Pres., Eastern Div., 1958, Pres., 1959-60, Am. Assoc. Univ. Profs (past council Mem.), Internat. Cttees for Academic Freedom. Hon. degrees: Dr of Humane Letters, Univ. of Maine, 1960;

LLD, Univ. of California, 1966. Fellow, American Academy of Arts and Sciences, 1965. *Publications:* The Metaphysics of Pragmatism, 1927; Towards the Understanding of Karl Marx, 1933; American Philosophy–To-day and To-morrow, 1935; From Hegel to Marx, 1936; Planned Society–Yesterday, To-day, To-morrow, 1937; John Dewey: An Intellectual Portrait, 1939; Reason, Social Myths and Democracy, 1940; The Hero in History, 1943; Education for Modern Man, 1946; Heresy, Yes–Conspiracy No, 1953; The Ambiguous Legacy; Marx and the Marxists, 1955; Common Sense and the Fifth Amendment, 1957; Political Power and Personal Freedom, 1959; The Quest for Being, 1961; The Paradoxes of Freedom, 1962; The Fail-Safe Fallacy, 1963; Religion in a Free Society, 1967; Editor of various works; contrib. numerous articles to philosophical journals. *Recreation:* gardening. *Address:* New York University, New York, NY 10003, USA. *T:* 212-598-3262.

**HOOK, Sheriff William Thomson;** a Sheriff Substitute of the Lothians at Linlithgow, since 1968 (of Renfrew and Argyll at Greenock, 1956-68); *b* 6 Dec. 1918; *s* of Peter Dewar Hook, JP and Marianne Elizabeth Thomson; *m* 1947, Margaret, *d* of Robert Barr, Shadwell House, Leeds; one *s*. *Educ:* Edinburgh Acad.; Old Coll., Edinburgh (MA, LLB). Royal Northumberland Fusiliers, 1939-46 (despatches). Faculty of Advocates, 1948; Mem., College of Justice; Standing Jun. Counsel, Min. of Labour; a Chairman, Lothians Nat. Insce Tribunal; Mem. Cttee, Deaconess Hosp.; Mem., Probation and After Care Councils. Elder, West Kirk, Edinburgh. *Publication:* Gaelic Place Names of Bute. *Recreation:* Classical Association. *Address:* 10 Moray Place, Edinburgh. *Clubs:* New (Edinburgh); Royal Gourock Yacht.

**HOOKE, Sir Lionel (George Alfred),** Kt 1957; Chairman since 1962 and Managing Director, 1945-68, Amalgamated Wireless (Australasia) Ltd; *b* 31 Dec. 1895; *s* of Frank William and Ethel Margaret Hooke; *m* 1930, Eilleen Clarice Sparks; one *s*. *Educ:* Brighton Grammar Sch., Vic., Australia. Joined Amalgamated Wireless (A/asia) Ltd, 1913; Shackleton Polar Expedition, 1913-14; Pilot, Royal Naval Air Service, War of 1914-18. Executive, Amalgamated Wireless (A/asia) Ltd, 1919-. Mem., Senate, Univ. of Sydney, 1961-69. Chm., Electronics & Telecommunications Industry Adv. Cttee, 1965-. *Address:* Sidmouth, 26 Buckingham Road, Killara, NSW 2071, Australia. *T:* 49.3093. *Clubs:* Antarctic; Australian, Union (Sydney); Naval and Military (Melbourne).

**HOOKER, Stanley George,** CBE 1964 (OBE 1946); FRS 1962; DSc; DPhil; Technical Director, Rolls-Royce Ltd, Bristol Engine Division, since 1966; *b* 30 Sept. 1907; 5th *s* of William Harry and Ellen Mary Hooker; *m* 1st, 1936, Hon. Margaret Bradbury; one *d*; 2nd, 1950, Kate Maria Garth; one *d*. *Educ:* Borden Grammar Sch.; Imperial Coll., London; Brasenose Coll., Oxford. Scientific and Research Dept, Admiralty, 1935-38; Rolls Royce Ltd, 1938-48; Bristol Aero Engines, 1948-59. Apptd Chief Engr, Engine Div., Bristol Aeroplane Co. Ltd, 1951 and a Dir, 1952; Technical Dir (Aero), Bristol Siddeley Engines Ltd, 1959. MIMechE (Mem. Council, 1958-); FRAeS; Fellow, Imperial Coll. British Silver Medal for Aeronautics, awarded by RAeS, 1955; Diplôme Paul Tissandier, by Féd. Aero Internationale, 1955; Thulin Bronze Medal by Swedish Aero. Soc., 1960; Brit. Gold Medal for Aeronautics, by RAeS, 1961; James Clayton Prize (jointly), 1966; Churchill Gold Medal, Soc. of Engineers, 1968; Goddard Medal, Amer. Inst. of Aeronautics and Astronautics, 1969. *Address:* PO Box 3, Filton, Bristol; Orchard Hill, Milbury Heath, Wotton-under-Edge, Glos. *Club:* Athenæum.

*See also Sir John Barran, Bt.*

**HOOKWAY, Harry Thurston;** Assistant Under-Secretary of State, Department of Education and Science, since 1969; *b* 23 July 1921; *s* of William and Bertha Hookway; *m* 1956, Barbara Olive, *o d* of late Oliver and Olive Butler; one *s* one *d*. *Educ:* Trinity Sch. of John Whitgift; London Univ. (BSc, PhD); FRIC. Various posts in industry, 1941-49; DSIR, 1949-65; Asst Dir, National Chemical Laboratory, 1959; Dir, UK Scientific Mission (North America), Scientific Attaché, Washington, DC, and Scientific Adviser to UK High Comr, Ottawa, 1960-64; Head of Information Div., DSIR, 1964-65; CSO, Dept of Educn and Science, 1966-69. *Publications:* various contribs to jls of learned societies. *Recreations:* music, travel. *Address:* 35 Goldstone Crescent, Hove, Sussex.

**HOOLEY, Frank Oswald;** Senior Administrative Assistant, Manchester Polytechnic; *b* 30 Nov. 1923; *m* 1945, Doris Irene Snook; two *d*. *Educ:* King Edward's High Sch., Birmingham; Birmingham Univ. Admin. Asst, Birmingham Univ., 1948-52; Sheffield Univ.: Asst Registrar, 1952-65; Sen. Asst Registrar, 1965-66; Registrar, Fourah Bay Coll., Sierra Leone, 1960-62 (secondment from Sheffield). MP (Lab) Heeley Div. of Sheffield, 1966-70. *Address:* 41 Buckingham Mews, Sutton Coldfield, Warwicks.

**HOOLEY, Maj.-Gen. St John Cutler,** CB 1958; CBE 1954; *b* 30 Sept. 1902; *s* of late S. P. Hooley, Tharston, Norfolk; *m* 1931, Molly Isobel, *d* of late Dr A. Scott-Turner, MRCS, LRCP, JP, London; one *d*. *Educ:* RMA, Woolwich. Royal Artillery, 2nd Lieut 1923; Captain RAOC, 1934; Dep. Dir Ordnance Services: AA Comd, 1945-46; British Mil. Mission, Greece, 1947-50; HQ Eastern Comd, 1950-52; Dir, Ordnance Services, HQ BAOR and Northern Army Gp, 1952-57; Brig. 1954, Maj.-Gen. 1957; Inspector RAOC, 1957-58; Comdt, Mechanical Transport Organisation, Chilwell, 1958-60, retired. Served War of 1939-45 in Norway, Middle East and India (despatches). *Recreations:* golf, travel, photography. *Address:* Storrington Cottage, Sea Avenue, Rustington, Sussex.

**HOOPER, Sir Anthony (Robin Maurice),** 2nd Bt *cr* 1962; Director: Couper Gallery; Assistant Manager, Schweppes Ltd, since 1952; *b* 26 Oct. 1918; *o s* of Sir Frederic Collins Hooper, 1st Bt, and Eglantine Irene (Bland); *S* father, 1963; *m* 1970, Cynthia, *yr d* of Col W. J. H. Howard, DSO. *Educ:* Radley; New Coll., Oxford. Royal Artillery, 1939-41; Asst to Hubert Philips, News Chronicle, 1941-42; Political Research Centre, 1942-44; Actor (Liverpool, Windsor, Birmingham, Oxford, London, BBC), 1944-50; temp. Civil Servant, Cabinet Office, 1950-52. *Recreations:* music, conversation and people. *Address:* 3 St George's Court, Gloucester Road, SW7. *T:* 01-589 1771. *Club:* Savile.

**HOOPER, Ven. Charles German,** MA; Archdeacon of Ipswich, since 1963; Rector of St Lawrence's and St Stephen's, since 1967; *b* 16 April 1911; 2nd *s* of A. C. Hooper, Solicitor; *m* 1963, Lilian Mary, *d* of late Sir Harold Brakspear, KCVO; one *s* one *d*. *Educ:* Lincoln Coll., Oxford (MA 2nd cl. English). Curacies: Corsham, Wilts, 1934-36; Claremont, CP, South Africa, 1936-39; Rector, Castle Combe, Wilts, 1940; Chaplain, RAFVR, 1942-46 (despatches); Rector, Sandy, Beds, 1946-53;

Vicar and Rural Dean, Bishop's Stortford, Herts, 1953-63; Rector of Bildeston, Suffolk, 1963-67. *Recreations:* painting in water colours, sailing. *Address:* 63 Anglesea Road, Ipswich, Suffolk. *T:* Ipswich 51736.

**HOOPER, Howard Owen,** CB 1964; CMG 1952; Assistant Under Secretary of State, Ministry of Defence, since 1964 (War Office, 1960-64); *b* 1911; *s* of late R. H. Hooper and Mrs E. A. Hooper; *m* 1937, Margaret Oliff, *d* of late S. H. and C. L. Marshall, Newbury. *Educ:* St Austell Gram. Sch.; Merton Coll., Oxford (Exhibitioner). Served in Inland Revenue, Board of Trade, Cabinet Office, Ministry of Supply. *Address:* Englefield, Bridge Road, Cranleigh, Surrey. *Club:* Reform.

**HOOPER, John Robert Thomas,** TD, JP; Metropolitan Magistrate since 1961; Deputy Chairman, Buckinghamshire Quarter Sessions, since 1961; *b* 7 Nov. 1914; *s* of late F. C. Hooper, Eastington, Glos, and Liverpool, and H. L. Hooper (*née* Beale), Hyde, Glos; *m* 1948, Dorinda Marian, *d* of Lieut-Col G. B. de Courcy Ireland, *qv*; three *d. Educ:* Repton; Sidney Sussex Coll., Cambridge. BA (Hons) Cantab 1936, MA 1961. Served War of 1939-45: Middlesex Yeomanry, 2nd Lieut 1939, Major 1942; Greek, Iraq and Syrian Campaigns, 1941; Western Desert and N Africa, 1942-43 (wounded, despatches); passed Parachute Course, 1944; OC Beach Bde Signals, 1945. Barrister, Inner Temple, 1939 (Yarborough Anderson Scholar, 1950); London and Midland Circuit; an Asst Recorder of Birmingham, 1960-61. JP Bucks, 1961. *Recreations:* riding, reading. *Address:* Beech Lawn, Chalfont Heights, Chalfont St Peter, Bucks. *T:* Gerrards Cross 82283. *Club:* Cavalry.

**HOOPER, Sir Leonard (James),** KCMG 1967 (CMG 1962); CBE 1951; idc; Director, Government Communications Headquarters, since 1965; *b* 23 July 1914; *s* of James Edmond and Grace Hooper; *m* 1951, Ena Mary Osborn. *Educ:* Alleyn's, Dulwich; Worcester Coll., Oxford. 1st class hons Modern History, 1936. London Sch. of Economics, 1938. Joined Air Ministry, 1938, transferred Foreign Office (GCHQ), 1942. Imperial Defence Coll., 1953. *Recreations:* sport, motoring. *Address:* 3c Carlisle Place, SW1. *T:* 01-834 5172; The Meadows, Battledown, Cheltenham, Glos. *T:* Cheltenham 59172. *Club:* Royal Automobile.

**HOOPER, Mrs Mia Lilly Kellmer;** *see* Pringle, Dr M. L. K.

**HOOPER, Sir Robin (William John),** KCMG 1968 (CMG 1954); DSO 1943; DFC 1943; Deputy Secretary, Cabinet Office, since 1968; *b* 26 July 1914; *s* of late Col John Charles Hooper, DSO, and late Irene Annie Palmer Hooper (*née* Anderson), Harewell, Faversham, Kent; *m* 1941, Constance Mildred Ayshford, *d* of late Lieut-Col Gilbert Ayshford Sanford, DSO, DL, Triley Court, Abergavenny, Mon; three *s. Educ:* Charterhouse; The Queen's Coll., Oxford. 3rd Sec., Foreign Office, 1938-40. Served War of 1939-45; on active service with RAF, 1940-44 (Wing-Comdr). Second Sec., HM Embassy, Paris, 1944-47; First Sec., HM Embassy, Lisbon, 1947-49; transferred to FO, 1949; Counsellor, 1950; Head of Personnel Dept, 1950-53; Counsellor, HM Embassy, Bagdad, 1953-56; Head of Perm. Under-Sec.'s Dept, FO, 1956-60; Asst Sec.-Gen. (Political), NATO, 1960-66; Ambassador to Tunisia, 1966-67; Ambassador to Southern Yemen, 1967-68. Chevalier, Legion of Honour, 1945. Croix de Guerre, 1939-45 (2 Palms), 1945. *Address:* F3, Albany, Piccadilly, W1; Brook House, Egerton, near Ashford, Kent. *Club:* Travellers'.

**HOOSON, (Hugh) Emlyn,** QC 1960; MP (L) Montgomeryshire, since 1962; Chairman, Merioneth Quarter Sessions, since 1967; Deputy Chairman, Flint Quarter Sessions, since 1960; *b* 26 March 1925; *s* of late Hugh and Elsie Hooson, Colomendy, Denbigh; *m* 1950, Shirley Margaret Wynne, *d* of late Sir George Hamer, CBE; two *d. Educ:* Denbigh Gram. Sch.; University Coll. of Wales; Gray's Inn (Bencher, 1968). Called to Bar, 1949; Wales and Chester Circuit. *Recreation:* farming. *Address:* 1 Dr Johnson's Buildings, Temple, EC4. *T:* 01-353 7972.

**HOOTON, John Charles,** CMG 1963; MBE 1945; QC (Bermuda) 1959; *b* 1912; *m* 1938, Jessica Patricia, *d* of R. J. Manning; two *s.* Served War of 1939-45; Lt-Col General List (despatches, Croix de Guerre, MBE). Palestine Police, 1932; Police, Gold Coast, 1937-49. Called to the Bar, Gray's Inn, 1949. Crown Counsel, Gold Coast, 1951-53 (Senior Asst Legal Sec., East African Common Services Organisation, 1953); Attorney-Gen., Bermuda, 1958-61; Legal Sec. to East African Common Services Organisation, 1961, retd from Org., 1962, re-apptd on contract, 1962-63; temp. Senior Asst, CO, 1963-64. *Address:* Dingleden House, Benenden, Kent. *Club:* Oriental.

**HOOVER, Calvin Bryce,** PhD; Professor of Economics since 1927, and Dean of the Graduate School, 1938-48, Duke University; *b* Berwick, Illinois, 14 April 1897; *s* of John Calvin and Margaret Roadcap Hoover; *m* 1919, Faith Miriam Sprole; two *d. Educ:* Monmouth Coll. (AB); Univ. of Wisconsin (PhD). Phi Beta Kappa. 123rd Field Artillery, US Army, 1917-19, AEF, battles of St Mihiel and Meuse-Argonne. Instructor, Univ. of Minnesota, 1923-25; Asst Prof., Duke Univ., 1925-27; Social Science Research Fellow in Russia, 1929-30; Associate Editor, South Atlantic Quarterly; Economic Adviser, Dept of Agriculture, 1934; Consumers' Counsel, Agricultural Adjustment Administration, 1935; Consultant: National Resources Planning Board, 1937; Advisory Commn to Council of National Defense, 1940; Office of Price Administration and Civilian Supply, 1941; Pres., Southern Economic Assoc., 1936-37; Vice-Pres., Amer. Econ. Assoc., 1940; Pres., 1953; Econ. Adviser US Group Control Commn in Germany, 1945; President's Cttee on Foreign Aid, 1947; Economic Adviser US Special Representative in Europe, 1948. Distinguished Fellow, Amer. Econ. Assoc., 1966. Hon. Litt D: Columbia, 1934; Monmouth Coll., 1935; Hon. LLD, Case Western Reserve, 1968. Medal of Freedom, US, 1946. *Publications:* Economic Life of Soviet Russia, 1931; Germany Enters the Third Reich, 1933; Dictators and Democracies, 1937; International Trade and Domestic Employment, 1945; The Impact of Federal Policies on the Economy of The South, 1949; (jointly) Economic Resources and Policies of the South, 1951; The Economy, Liberty and The State, 1959; Economic Systems of the Commonwealth, 1962; Memoirs of Capitalism, Communism and Nazism, 1965. *Address:* Duke University, Durham, N Carolina 27701, USA. *Clubs:* Cosmos (Washington, DC); Century (New York).

**HOOVER, Herbert William, Jr;** President, 1954-66, and Chairman of the Board, 1959-66, The Hoover Company, North Canton, Ohio; *b* 23 April 1918; *s* of late Herbert William Hoover and Grace Hoover (*née* Steele); *m* 1941, Carl

Maitland Good; one *s* one *d. Educ:* Choate Sch., Wallingford, Conn.; Rollins Coll. (AB). Served in US Army as 2nd Lieut, 1943-45. Offices held with Hoover Co.: Exec. Sales, 1941; Dir Public Relations, 1945; Asst Vice-Pres., 1948; Vice-Pres. Field Sales, 1952; Exec. Vice-Pres., 1953. The Hoover Co. Ltd, Canada: Pres., 1954; Dir, 1952; Hoover Ltd, England: Dir 1954, Chm. 1956. Hoover Inc., Panama: Dir and Pres., 1955; Hoover (America Latina) SA, Panama: Dir and Pres., 1955; Hoover Mexicana, Mexico: Dir and Pres., 1955; Hoover Industrial y Comercial SA, Colombia: Dir and Pres., 1960; Hoover Worldwide Corp., NY City: Pres. and Chm., 1960; Dir, S. A. Hoover, France, 1965. Dir, Harter Bank & Trust Co., Canton, Ohio. Past Regional Vice-Chm., US Cttee for the UN. Hon. LLD, Mount Union Coll., 1959. Bd of Trustees. Univ. of Miami. Chevalier Légion d'Honneur, France, 1965. *Address:* 70 Park Drive, Bal Harbour, Fla 33154, USA.

**HOOVER, John Edgar,** Hon. KBE, *cr* 1947; Director, Federal Bureau of Investigation, United States Department of Justice, since 1924; *b* 1 Jan. 1895; *s* of Dickerson Naylor Hoover and Annie Marie Scheitlin; unmarried. *Educ:* George Washington Univ. Law Sch. (LLB 1916, LLM 1917). Started Government service with Library of Congress, Washington, DC, as clerk while attending law sch. at night. Upon obtaining legal degree and admission to the Bar in Washington, DC, entered US Dept of Justice in 1917; Special Asst to the Attorney Gen., 1919; Asst Dir of the then Bureau of Investigation, 1921. Trustee, George Washington Univ.; Mem. Bd of Dirs of Boys' Clubs of America. Holds numerous hon. degrees. Is a Mason, 33°; Grand Cross of Honour, Supreme Council, Scottish Rite, 33°, 1965. Medal of Merit (US), 1946; etc. *Publications:* Persons in Hiding, 1938; Masters of Deceit, 1958; A Study of Communism, 1962; J. Edgar Hoover on Communism, 1969; numerous articles on scientific crime detection, causation and prevention of crime. *Recreations:* baseball, tennis, football. *Address:* Federal Bureau of Investigation, 9th Street and Pennsylvania Avenue, Washington, DC 20535, USA. *Clubs:* Columbia Country (Washington, DC); Chevy Chase (Md).

**HOPE,** family name of **Baron Glendevon, Marquess of Linlithgow** and **Baron Rankeillour.**

**HOPE, Maj.-Gen. Adrian Price Webley,** CB 1961; CBE 1952; *b* 21 Jan. 1911; *s* of late Adm. H. W. W. Hope, CB, CVO, DSO; *m* 1958, Mary Elizabeth, *e d* of Grahame Partridge, Cotham Lodge, Newport, Pembrokeshire; no *c. Educ:* Winchester Coll.; RMC, Sandhurst. 2/Lt KOSB, 1931; Adjt, 1/KOSB, 1937-38; Staff Capt. A, Palestine, Egypt, 1938-40; DAQMG (Plans) Egypt, 1940-41; Instructor, Staff Coll., 1941; AQMG, Egypt, Sicily, Italy, 1941-44; Col Asst Quartermaster, Plans, India, 1945; Brig., Quartermaster, SE Asia, 1946; Comdt Sch. of Military Admin., 1947-48; Instructor, jssc, 1948-50; DQMG, GHQ, MELF, 1951-53; Student, idc, 1954; Brig. Quartermaster (ops), War Office, 1955-57; BGS, HQ, BAOR, 1958-59; MGA, GHQ, FARELF, 1959-61; Dir of Equipment Policy, War Office, 1961-64; Dep. Master-Gen. of the Ordnance, Ministry of Defence, 1964-66; retd 1966. *Recreations:* tennis, golf. *Address:* Monks Place, Charlton Horethorne, Sherborne, Dorset. *Club:* United Service.

**HOPE, Sir Archibald (Philip),** 17th Bt of Craighall, *cr* 1628; OBE 1945; DFC 1940; Group Treasurer, General Electric and English Electric Cos Ltd, since 1970; *b* 27 March 1912; *s* of 16th Bt and Hon. Mary Bruce, OBE, JP Midlothian, *e d* of 10th Lord Balfour of Burleigh; *S* father, 1924; *m* 1938, Ruth, *y d* of Carl Davis, Fryern, Storrington, Sussex; two *s. Educ:* Eton; Balliol Coll., Oxford. BA 1934; ACA 1939; FCA 1960; Mem. of Queen's Body Guard for Scotland (Royal Company of Archers). Served, RAFO, 1930-35; 601 (County of London) Sqdn AAF, 1935-39. Served War of 1939-45 (despatches twice, DFC, OBE). Wing Comdr (acting Group Capt.), AAF. Joined Airwork, 1945; Dir, 1951; resigned, June 1956; Dir, D. Napier & Son Ltd, 1956-61; Dir, Napier Aero Engines Ltd, 1961-68; Chief Exec., Napier Aero Engines Ltd, 1962-68. Chm., The Air League, 1966-69. FRAeS 1968. *Heir: s* John Carl Alexander Hope, *b* 10 June 1939. *Address:* Upton Grey Lodge, near Basingstoke, Hants. *T:* Long Sutton 374. *Clubs:* Bath, Royal Air Force; New (Edinburgh); Nairobi (Nairobi).

**HOPE, Bob, (Leslie Townes Hope);** Congressional Gold Medal, US, 1963; film, stage, radio, TV actor; *b* England, 1904; family migrated to US, 1907; *m* 1933, Dolores Reade. *Educ:* Fairmont Gram. Sch. and High Sch., Cleveland, O. Started career with Chandler Motor Co., but shortly went on stage. After Mid-West tours formed own Company in Chicago, finally going to New York and the RKO Vaudeville Circuit; first important stage part in Ballyhoo, 1932; first radio part, 1935. Entered films, 1938. *Films include:* The Cat and the Canary; Road to Singapore; The Ghost Breakers; Road to Zanzibar; Caught in the Draft; Nothing but the Truth; Louisiana Purchase; My Favorite Blonde; Road to Morocco; Let's Face It; Road to Utopia; Monsieur Beaucaire; They Got Me Covered; The Princess and the Pirate; Road to Rio; Where There's Life; The Great Lover; My Favorite Spy; Son of Paleface; Here Come the Girls; Casanova's Big Night; The Seven Little Foys; The Iron Petticoat; That Certain Feeling; Beau James; The Facts of Life; Bachelor in Paradise; The Road to Hong Kong; Call Me Bwana; A Global Affair; Boy, Did I Get a Wrong Number!; Eight on the Run; How to Commit Marriage. *TV Series:* The Bob Hope Show. *Publications:* I Never Left Home, 1944; This is on Me, 1954; I Owe Russia$1200, 1963. *Address:* c/o Paramount Pictures, 5451 Marathon Street, Hollywood, Calif, USA.

**HOPE, (Charles) Peter,** CMG 1956; TD 1945; Ambassador to Mexico since 1968; *b* 29 May 1912; *s* of G. L. N. Hope and H. M. V. Riddell, Weetwood, Mayfield, Sussex; *m* 1936, H. M. Turner, *d* of late G. L. Turner, company director; three *s. Educ:* Oratory Sch., Reading; London and Cambridge Univs. BSc (Hons), ACGI. Asst War Office, 1938; RA, TA, 1939; served until 1946 (TD). Transferred to Foreign Office and posted HM Embassy, Paris, as Temp. First Sec., 1946; transferred to United Nations Dept, Foreign Office, 1950; to HM Embassy, Bonn, as Counsellor, 1953; Foreign Office Spokesman (Head of News Dept Foreign Office), 1956-59; Minister, HM Embassy, Madrid, 1959-62; Consul-General, Houston, USA, 1963-64; Minister and Alternate UK Rep. to UN, 1965-68. *Recreations:* shooting and fishing. *Address:* c/o Foreign and Commonwealth Office, SW1. *Club:* White's.

**HOPE, Sir James,** 2nd Bt *cr* 1932; MM 1918; JP; farmer; *b* 2 May 1898; *s* of Sir Harry Hope, 1st Bt and Margaret Binnie Holmes Kerr; *S* father 1959. *Educ:* Fettes Coll. Served European War, 1916-19, with Black Watch (MM). District Chm., East Lothian Agricultural Executive Cttee, 1938-45. JP for East Lothian. *Heir: b* Robert Holmes Kerr Hope [*b* 12 April 1900; *m* 1928, Eleanor (*d* 1967), *d* of late Very

Rev. Marshall Lang, DD, Whittingehame, East Lothian]. *Address:* Eastbarns, Dunbar, East Lothian. *T:* Innerwick 212. *Club:* New (Edinburgh).

**HOPE, James Kenneth,** CBE 1946; DL; MA (Hon.); Recorder of City of Durham since 1942; Clerk of the Peace of County of Durham, Clerk of Durham County Council, and County Registration Officer, 1937-61; County Controller of Civil Defence, 1942-61; Clerk of Durham County Magistrates' Courts Cttee, 1952-61; *b* 12 July 1896; *s* of late J. Basil Hope, OBE, JP, and of Amy L. Hope, Bedford; *m* 1928, Mary Joyce, *yr d* of late Lieut-Col Rouse Orlebar, JP, DL, Hinwick, Beds; three *d. Educ:* Bedford Sch. Served European War, 1915-19: Commissioned Officer, 1st Bn Beds Regt. Solicitor, 1922; Asst Solicitor, Beds County Council, 1922-27; Dep. Clerk of the Peace and of County Council, Durham, 1927-37; T & AFA, County of Durham, 1937-61. Pres., Durham County Assoc. of Parish Councils, 1963-69. DL, Co. Durham, 1944; High Sheriff of Durham, 1966. *Address:* West Park, Lanchester, Co. Durham. *T:* Lanchester 339. *Club:* Durham County (Durham). *See also Baron Vivian.*

**HOPE, Capt. Laurence Nugent,** DL; JP; Landowner; Welsh Guards (SR); *b* 14 Oct. 1890; *s* of James L. A. Hope and Eliza, *d* of Sir Peter Coats, Auchendrane, Ayr; *m* 1st, Hilda Mary (*d* 1938) *d* of late M. J. Hunter, JP, Stoke Hall, Derbs; one *s* one *d*; 2nd, 1941, Constance Elizabeth, *d* of late E. A. Shell. *Educ:* Clifton Coll.; Trinity Hall, Cambridge (BA). Commission Royal North Devon Hussars (Yeo.), 1913-19, (Substantive Capt.), Gallipoli, Egypt, and Palestine; transferred as Capt. (SR) to the Welsh Guards, 1920. DL 1953, JP 1920, High Sheriff, 1923, Herefordshire. *Recreations:* hunting, shooting, fishing, photography. *Address:* Whitney Court, Whitney, Hereford. *T:* Clifford 213 (via Hereford and Hay). *Clubs:* Guards, Army and Navy.

**HOPE, Lt-Col Sir Percy (Mirehouse),** Kt 1954; OBE 1918; JP; DL; Chairman and Managing Director, Lake District Hotels and Pape's Garages, Coaches and Motors, and other cos; *b* Keswick, 17 July 1886; *s* of Joseph Fearon Hope; *m* 1919, Constance Maud Mark (*d* 1970); no *c. Educ:* Keswick Sch.; King's Coll., London. Articled J. J. Bell, MICE, County Surveyor and Bridge Master, Cumberland; Lieut The Border Regt, 1911; attached GS, Burma Div., 1916; Staff Coll., Mhow, India, 1917; RE Officer i/c Water Supplies, Mesopotamia, 1917; Deputy Dir of Works, Baghdad, 1917; Asst Dir of Works, GHQ, MEF, 1918-19 (OBE, Bt Major, despatches twice); LRIBA; CEng; Mem. Inst. Municipal and County Engineers; Chairman of Governors: Keswick Sch.; Lairthwaite School; Trustee Fitz Park; Trustee Hewitson Cottage Hosp.; Alderman, Cumberland County Council; Mem., Lake District Planning Board; Chm., National Council of British Hotels and Restaurants Association. Master Blencathra Foxhounds. DL Cumberland, 1961. *Recreations:* cricket, Rugby football (county cap), tennis, golf. *Address:* 39 Brundholme Terrace, Keswick, Cumberland. *T:* 162. *Clubs:* Royal Automobile; Border County (Carlisle).

**HOPE, Peter;** *see* Hope, C. P.

**HOPE-DUNBAR, Sir David,** 8th Bt *cr* 1664; *b* 13 July 1941; *o s* of Sir Basil Douglas Hope-Dunbar, 7th Bt, and of his 2nd wife, Edith Maude Maclaren, *d* of late Malcolm Cross; *S* father, 1961. *Educ:* Eton; Royal Agricultural College, Cirencester. Qualified: Associate Chartered Land Agents' Society, 1966; Mem. RICS, 1967. *Recreations:* fishing, shooting. *Heir: kinsman* John Alan Burns, Lieut-Col late Scots Guards [*b* 4 Oct. 1905; *m* 1944, Joyce Margaret August; two *d*]. *Address:* Banks Farm, Kirkcudbright. *T:* Kirkcudbright 424.

**HOPE GILL, Cecil Gervase,** MA; *b* 14 Dec. 1894; *s* of late Rt Rev. Charles Hope Gill and late Mary Hope Gill (*née* Thorp); *m* 1937, Kiti Colin, *e d* of Dr Alexander Campbell-Smith, Nelson, NZ. *Educ:* Windlesham House, Brighton; King William's Coll., IoM; Brighton Coll.; St John's Coll., Cambridge. Served in Royal Monmouthshire RE (Special Reserve), 1914-19 (wounded, despatches); Major 1919 (CRE Tournai); entered Levant Consular Service, 1920; served at Tangier (Vice-Consul), 1921; Casablanca, 1922; Saffi, 1923; Tetuan, 1923-25; Tangier (Asst Oriental Sec.), 1925-30; Jedda (Head of Chancery and Chargé d'Affaires), 1930-33; Alexandria (Consul), 1933-36; Addis Ababa, 1936; Imperial Defence Coll., 1937; Seattle, 1938-40; Baghdad (Asst Oriental Sec.), 1941; Léopoldville (Actg Consul-Gen.), 1941-42; Addis Ababa (First Sec.), 1942-44; Foreign Office, 1944-45; Tetuan (Consul-Gen.), 1945-52; retired from HM Foreign Service with rank of Consul-Gen., 1952. *Recreations:* travel, fruit growing, wine making, bee keeping, cinematography. *Address:* The High Threshing Floor, La Era Alta de Cotobros, Almuñecar (Granada), Spain. *Cables:* Hopegill Almunecarspain. *Club:* Royal Automobile.

**HOPE-JONES, Sir Arthur,** KBE 1964; CMG 1956; Chairman or Director of companies in UK and East Africa; Adviser or Consultant to companies in these and other countries since 1960; *b* 26 May 1911; *s* of William and Dinah Elizabeth Hope-Jones; *m* 1938, Lucile Owens, New York; one *s* one *d. Educ:* Kirkby Lonsdale; Christ's Coll., Cambridge (1st cl. hons Hist. Tripos); Columbia Univ., New York (Commonwealth Fund Fellow). Fellow of Christ's Coll., Cambridge, 1937-46. Served War, 1939-45 (TA Gen. List); seconded for duties at home and abroad; Economic Adviser in Persia to Anglo-Iranian Oil Co. Ltd (now BP), 1944-46; Economic Adviser Govt of Kenya, 1946-48; Mem., later Minister, for Commerce and Industry, Govt of Kenya, 1948-60; Member: Kenya Legislature, 1947-60; East African Legislative Assembly, 1956-60. *Publications:* Income Tax in the Napoleonic Wars, 1939; contribs to learned society jls, periodicals and the financial press, etc. *Recreations:* walking, fishing, reading. *Address:* 1 Buckland Court, Buckland, Betchworth, Surrey. *T:* Betchworth 2179; PO Box 30099, Nairobi, Kenya, East Africa. *Clubs:* East India and Sports; Muthaiga Country, Nairobi (Nairobi).

**HOPE-JONES, Ronald Christopher,** CMG 1969; Foreign and Commonwealth Office (formerly Foreign Office), since 1967; *b* 5 July 1920; *s* of William Hope-Jones and Winifred Coggin; *m* 1944, Pamela Hawker; two *s* one *d. Educ:* Eton; King's Coll., Cambridge. Served with HM Forces, 1940-45. 3rd Sec., Foreign Office, 1946, Paris, 1947; 2nd Sec., Beirut, 1949; 1st Sec., FO, 1952; Head of Chancery and Consul, Quito, 1955; Commercial Sec., Budapest, 1959; Head of Chancery, 1960; FO, 1961, Counsellor, 1963; UK Rep. to Internat. Atomic Energy Agency, Vienna, 1964. *Address:* c/o Foreign and Commonwealth Office, SW1; Kingsmead, Prey Heath Road, Mayford, Woking, Surrey. *T:* Woking 62759.

**HOPE-MORLEY,** family name of **Baron Hollenden.**

**HOPE-MORLEY, Gordon Hope;** I. & R. Morley Ltd, 1933-67, retired as Chairman; *b* 8 Jan. 1914; *s* of late Hon. Claude Hope-Morley and of Lady Dorothy Hope-Morley; *heir-pres.* to 2nd Baron Hollenden, *qv*; *m* 1945, Sonja Sundt, Norway; three *s. Educ:* Eton. War medals of 1939-45; King Haakon of Norway Liberation medal. *Address:* 19 Chelsea Square, SW3. *T:* 01-352 5389. *Club:* Brooks's.

**HOPE-WALLACE, (Dorothy) Jaqueline,** CBE 1958; Under-Secretary, retired; *b* 1909; 2nd *d* of Charles Nugent Hope-Wallace and Mabel Chaplin. *Educ:* Lady Margaret Hall, Oxford. Entered Ministry of Labour, 1932; transferred to National Assistance Board, 1934; Asst Sec., 1946-58; Under-Sec., 1958-65; Under-Sec., Min. of Housing and Local Govt, 1965-69. Commonwealth Fellow, 1952-53. Member Board: Corby Develt Corp., 1969-; Governors, UCH, 1970-. *Recreations:* Shakespeare, opera, paintings, travel. *Address:* 22 St Ann's Terrace, NW8. *Clubs:* Oxford and Cambridge University, Arts Theatre.

*See also P. A. Hope-Wallace.*

**HOPE-WALLACE, Philip Adrian;** dramatic critic, The Guardian; *b* 6 Nov. 1911; *o s* of Charles Nugent Hope-Wallace and Mabel Chaplin. *Educ:* Charterhouse; Balliol Coll., Oxford; abroad. International Broadcasting Co., France, 1934; Public Relations, Gas Light & Coke Co., 1935-36; Correspondent, The Times, 1935-39; Press Officer, Air Ministry, 1939-45. Critic of music and drama to various journals; Time and Tide, 1945-49; The Listener; The Manchester Guardian (now The Guardian), 1946-. Broadcasting, journalism. Lectured at home and abroad. *Publications:* A Key to Opera, 1939; pamphlets on the drama, music, etc.

*See also D. J. Hope-Wallace.*

**HOPETOUN, Earl of; Adrian John Charles Hope;** Stockbroker; *b* 1 July 1946; *s* and *heir* of Marquess of Linlithgow, *qv*; *m* 1968, Anne, *e d* of A. Leveson, Sunninghill, Berks; one *s. Educ:* Eton. Joined HM Navy, 1965. *Heir: s* Viscount Aithrie, *qv. Address:* Hopetoun House, South Queensferry; 31 Woodsford Square, W14. *Club:* Turf.

**HOPEWELL, John Prince;** Consultant Surgeon, Royal Free Hospital and Putney Hospital, Surrey, since 1957; *b* 1 Dec. 1920; *s* of Samuel Prince and Wilhelmina Hopewell; *m* 1959; one *s* one *d. Educ:* Bradfield Coll., Berks; King's Coll. Hosp., London. RAMC, 1945-48. Postgrad. education at King's Coll. Hosp. and Brighton, Sussex, and Hosp. for Sick Children, Gt Ormond Street. Hunterian Prof., RCS, 1958. *Publications:* contribs to Surgical Aspects of Medicine, Modern Treatment Year Book, and various medical journals. *Recreations:* photography, travel. *Address:* 90 Harley Street, W1. *T:* 01-935 7637; 3 Victoria Drive, SW19. *T:* 01-789 1666.

**HOPKIN, David Armand;** Metropolitan Stipendiary Magistrate, since Aug. 1970; *b* 10 Jan. 1922; *s* of Daniel and Edmée Hopkin; *m* 1948, Doris Evelyn (*née* Whitaker); one *s* three *d. Educ:* St Paul's Sch., W Kensington; University Coll., Aberystwyth; Corpus Christi Coll., Cambridge (BA). Served in Army, 1942-47, Hon. Major, 1947. Member of Staff of Director of Public Prosecutions, 1950-70. *Recreations:* fencing, tennis; administrative steward, British Boxing Board of Control. *Address:* 8 Crane Grove, N7. *T:* 01-607 0349.

**HOPKIN, William Aylsham Bryan,** CBE 1961; Deputy Chief Economic Adviser, Treasury, since 1970; *b* 7 Dec. 1914; *s* of late William Hopkin and Lilian Hopkin (*née* Cottelle); *m* 1938, Renée Ricour; two *s. Educ:* Barry (Glam.) County Sch.; St John's Coll., Cambridge; Manchester Univ. Ministry of Health, 1938-41; Prime Minister's Statistical Branch, 1941-45; Royal Commn on Population, 1945-48; Econ. Sect., Cabinet Office, 1948-50; Central Statistical Office, 1950-52; Dir, Nat. Inst. of Econ. and Soc. Research, 1952-57; Sec., Council on Prices, Productivity, and Incomes, 1957-58; Dep. Dir, Econ. Sect., HM Treasury, 1958-65; Econ. Planning Unit, Mauritius, 1965; Min. of Overseas Devlt, 1966-67; Dir-Gen. of Economic Planning, ODM, 1967-69; Dir-Gen., DEA, 1969. *Address:* 30 Laurier Road, NW5. *T:* 01-485 3779.

**HOPKINS, Alan Cripps Nind,** MA Cantab, LLB Yale; *b* 27 Oct. 1926; *s* of late Rt Hon. Sir Richard V. N. Hopkins, GCB and Lady Hopkins; *m* 1st, 1954, Margaret Cameron (from whom divorced, 1962), *d* of E. C. Bolton, Waco, Texas, USA; one *s*; 2nd, 1962, Venetia, *d* of Sir Edward Wills, Bt, *qv*; twin *s. Educ:* Winchester Coll.; King's Coll., Cambridge; Yale Univ. Law Sch., USA. BA Cantab 1947, MA 1950; LLB Yale 1952. Barrister, Inner Temple, 1948. PPS to Financial Sec. to Treasury, 1960-62. MP (C and Nat L) Bristol North-East, 1959-66. *Recreations:* travelling, ski-ing. *Address:* Great Shefford House, near Newbury, Berks. *T:* Great Shefford 212. *Club:* Brooks's.

**HOPKINS, Antony;** Gresham Professor of Music at the City University; composer and conductor; *b* 21 March 1921; *s* of late Hugh and of Marjorie Reynolds; adopted *c* of Major and Mrs T. H. C. Hopkins since 1925; *m* 1947, Alison Purves. *Educ:* Berkhamsted Sch.; Royal Coll. of Music. Won Chappell Gold Medal and Cobbett Prize at RCM, 1942; shortly became known as composer of incidental music for radio; numerous scores composed for BBC (2 for programmes winning Italia prize for best European programme of the year, 1952 and 1957). Composed music for many productions at Stratford and in West End. Dir, Intimate Opera Co., 1952-, and has written a number of chamber operas for this group; *ballets:* Etude and Café des Sports, for Sadler's Wells; *films (music) include:* Pickwick Papers, Decameron Nights, Cast a Dark Shadow, Billy Budd. Regular broadcaster with a series of programmes entitled Talking about Music. Hon. FRCM 1964. *Publications:* Talking about Symphonies, 1961; Talking about Concertos, 1964; Music All Around Me, 1968; Lucy and Peterkin, 1968. *Recreations:* motoring and motor sport. *Address:* Woodyard Cottage, Ashridge, Berkhamsted, Herts. *T:* Little Gaddesden 2257; 3 Elsham Road, W14.

**HOPKINS, Douglas Edward,** DMus (London); FRAM, FRCO, FGSM; Professor, Royal Academy of Music; Organist and Choirmaster, St Marylebone Parish Church; Conductor, Stock Exchange Male Voice Choir; Founder and Director, Holiday Course for Organists; *b* 23 Dec. 1902; *s* of Edward and Alice Hopkins; unmarried. *Educ:* St Paul's Cathedral Choir Sch.; Dulwich Coll.; Guildhall Sch. of Music (Ernest Palmer and Corporation Scholarships); Royal Academy of Music. Organist, Christ Church, Greyfriars, EC, 1921; Sub-Organist, St Paul's Cathedral, 1927; Master of the Music, Peterborough Cathedral, 1946; Organist, Canterbury Cathedral, 1953-55; Musical Dir, St Felix Sch., Southwold, 1956-65. Conductor of Handel Soc., 1928-33, and, since that, of various other musical societies. Mem. Court, Worshipful Co. of Musicians. *Address:* 244 Mytchett Road, Mytchett, Camberley, Surrey. *Club:* Savage.

**HOPKINS, Admiral Sir Frank (Henry Edward),** KCB 1964 (CB 1961); DSO 1942; DSC 1941; Commander-in-Chief, Portsmouth, 1966-67; retired, 1967; *b* 23 June 1910; *s* of late E. F. L. Hopkins and Sybil Mary Walrond; *m* 1939, Lois Barbara, *d* of J. R. Cook, Cheam, Surrey. *Educ:* Stubbington House; Nautical Coll., Pangbourne. Joined Navy as Cadet, 1927; served in HM Ships: London, Tiger, Whitehall, Vortigern, Winchester, Courageous, Furious, 1928-38; War of 1939-45 (despatches, 1941), in No 826 Fleet Air Arm Squadron (Formidable), 1940-41, and comd No 830 Sqdn, 1941-42, based on Malta; USS Hancock and USS Intrepid, American Pacific Fleet, 1944-45; took part in following operations: Dunkirk, air operations over Europe, Battle of Matapan, evacuation of Crete, bombardment of Tripoli, Malta, Battle of Leyte Gulf; Korean War, Theseus, 1950 (despatches); Capt., 1950; Dir of Air Warfare, Admiralty, comd Myngs, Tyrian, Grenville, and Ark Royal, 1954-58; comd RNC Dartmouth, 1958-60; Rear-Adm. 1960; Flag Officer: Flying Training, 1960-62; Aircraft Carriers, 1962-63; Vice-Adm. 1962; a Lord Comr of the Admiralty, Deputy Chief of Naval Staff and Fifth Sea Lord, 1963-64; Dep. Chief of Naval Staff, MoD, 1964-66; Adm. 1966. American Legion of Merit, 1948; Comdr, Order of Sword, Sweden, 1954. *Recreations:* sailing, golf. *Address:* Kingswear Court Lodge, Kingwear, S Devon. *Clubs:* Naval and Military, Royal Yacht Squadron; Royal Naval Sailing Assoc.; Britannia Yacht.

**HOPKINS, Col Harold Leslie,** CIE 1946; OBE 1942; *b* 1897; *s* of Walter Hopkins, York; *m* 1927, Louise; one *s*. *Educ:* York. Served European War, 1914-18; War of 1939-45, in Europe, Middle East and India; Colonel, 1943. General Manager, Bombay Port Trust, 1944-45. Chief Docks Manager, Hull, 1956-59, retd. *Address:* 3 Westbourne Grove, Scarborough, Yorks. *T:* Scarborough 2993.

**HOPKINS, Prof. Harry Geoffrey,** MSc, DSc London; MSc Manchester; Professor of Mathematics, University of Manchester Institute of Science and Technology, since 1966; *b* 14 April 1918; *s* of late Charles Thomas and late Violet Florence (*née* Johnson) Hopkins. *Educ:* Enfield Grammar Sch.; Harrow County Sch.; University Coll., London. Scientific Officer, Structural and Mechanical Engrg Dept, RAE, Farnborough, 1940-45; Asst in Mathematics, Queen's Univ., Belfast, 1946; Lectr in Mathematics, Manchester Univ., 1946-52; Fulbright Scholar, 1951, and Vis. Prof. of Applied Mathematics, Brown Univ., Providence, RI, 1951 and 1952-54; Senior Principal Scientific Officer, Basic Research Div., Royal Armament R&D Estabt, Fort Halstead, 1954-59; Dep. Chief Scientific Officer (Appleton, Individual Merit Award), 1959-66; Senior Foreign Scientist Fellow (Nat. Science Foundn), Dept of Physics, Washington State Univ., Pullman, Washington, 1965-66. Editor, Jl of Mechanics and Physics of Solids, 1969-; Mem., Court and Council, Univ. of Manchester Inst. of Science and Technology, 1968-70. FIMA 1964; FRAS 1964; Mem. Acoustical Soc. of America, 1967; Mem. ASME 1967. *Publications:* theoretical research on the mechanics and physics of solids; contributed to: Deformation and Flow of Solids, 1956; Progress in Solid Mechanics, 1960; Progress in Applied Mechanics, 1963; Stress Waves in Anelastic Solids, 1964; Applied Mechanics Surveys, 1966; Engineering Plasticity, 1968; papers in Proc. and Phil. Trans Royal Soc., Jl Mech. and Phys. Solids, Rep. and Memo. Aero. Res. Council, and other mathemat. and sci. jls. *Recreations:* music, alpine walking and photography, American history. *Address:* Department of Mathematics, University of Manchester Institute of Science and Technology, PO Box No 88, Sackville Street, Manchester M60 1QD. *T:* 061-236 3311.

**HOPKINS, James S. R. S.;** *see* Scott-Hopkins.

**HOPKINS, John Collier Frederick,** CMG 1962; DSc; AICTA; FIBiol; *b* 12 May 1898; *s* of late William and Edith Hopkins; *m* 1945, Elizabeth Callister, *d* of George and Helen Rothnie, Salisbury, Rhodesia; two *d*. *Educ:* Emanuel Sch.; King's Coll. and Imperial Coll., London; Imperial Coll. Trop. Agric., Trinidad. DSc (London) 1933; AICTA 1926. Hon. Artillery Co., 1916; RFC, 1916-18; RAF, 1918-19; Royal Rhodesia Regiment, 1940-45. Agricultural Officer, Uganda, 1924. Mycologist 1926, Senior Plant Pathologist 1933, Chief Botanist and Plant Pathologist, 1946, S Rhodesia. Asst Editor, Commonwealth Mycological Institute, 1954, Dir and Editor, 1956-64. Pres., Rhodesia Scientific Assoc., 1930, 1940-42; Pres., Section C, S African Assoc. for the Advancement of Science, 1940; Chm., London Branch, Inst. Biology, 1961-64. *Publications:* Diseases of Tobacco in Southern Rhodesia, 1931; Common Veld Flowers, 1940; Tobacco Diseases, 1956; numerous papers in scientific journals. *Address:* 26 St Helen's Park Road, Hastings, Sussex. *T:* Hastings 4170. *Club:* Salisbury (Rhodesia).

**HOPKINS, Rev. Canon Leslie Freeman;** Canon Residentiary and Treasurer, Liverpool Cathedral, since 1964; *b* 1914; *o s* of Joseph Freeman and Mabel Hopkins, London; *m* 1940, Violet, *d* of Edgar Crick, Crayford; three *s* one *d*. *Educ:* City of London Sch. (Abbott Schol.); Exeter Coll., Oxford (Squire Schol. and Exhib.); Wells Theological Coll. BA 1937, 2nd Cl. Hon. Mods, 2nd Cl. Hons Theology; MA 1940; BD Oxon 1953. Deacon 1938, priest 1939; Curate of Crayford 1938, Nympsfield 1942; Priest-in-Charge, Holy Trinity, Charlton, 1942-45; Vicar of St Chrysostom's, Peckham, 1945-56; Surrogate, 1946-62; Vicar of All Saints, Battersea Park, 1956-62; Chief Inspector of Schools, Dio. of Southwark, 1954-62; Dir of Religious Education, Dio. of Liverpool, 1962-; Chaplain of Josephine Butler Coll., 1962-; Governor of Chester Coll., St Elphin's, Darley Dale and of Grammar Schs; Mem. of Liverpool City Education Cttee and C of E Schs Council; Chm., Liverpool Council for Educn in Personal Relationships; Visiting Lectr in Religious Education; Mem. of Council, Guild of St Raphael, 1944-. *Publications:* contribs to press and Syllabuses of Religious Education. *Recreations:* architecture and music. *Address:* (office) Church House, 1 Hanover Street, Liverpool 1; (home) 17 Sandringham Drive, Liverpool L17 4JN. *Club:* Royal Commonwealth Society.

**HOPKINS, Maj.-Gen. Ronald Nicholas Lamond,** CBE 1943; Legion of Merit (US) 1944; psc; Australian Regular Army, retired; *b* 24 May 1897; *s* of Dr Wm F. Hopkins and Rosa M. B. Lamond; *m* 1926, Nora Frances Riceman; one *s*. *Educ:* Melbourne Grammar Sch.; RMC, Duntroon. Lieut Aust. Permt Forces, 1 Jan. 1918 and seconded 1st AIF; served with 6th Australian Light Horse Regt, Palestine, 1918; Staff Capt. 3rd Australian Light Horse Bde, 1919; Staff Coll., Quetta, 1927-28; attached Royal Tank Corps, England, 1937-38; 2nd AIF 1940; service in Middle East and New Guinea; Hon. ADC to Governor-Gen., 1943-45; late Dep. Chief of Gen. Staff (Australia). Chief Exec. Officer, Adelaide Festival of Arts, 1959-60. *Club:* Adelaide (Adelaide).

**HOPKINSON,** family name of **Baron Colyton.**

**HOPKINSON, Albert Cyril,** CBE 1970; FRIBA; Director of Works and Chief Architect, Home Office, since 1964; *b* 2 Aug. 1911; *s* of Albert Hopkinson and Isaline Pollard (*née* Cox); *m* 1943, Lesley Evelyn Hill; one *s* one *d*. *Educ:* Univs of Sheffield and London. BA 1933; MA 1934. FRIBA 1949 (ARIBA 1934); AMTPI 1938; Dipl. Town Planning and Civic Architecture, London, 1938. Min. of Public Building and Works, 1937-64. *Recreations:* reading, walking. *Address:* 110b High Street, Berkhamsted, Herts. *T:* Berkhamsted 5256.

**HOPKINSON, David Hugh;** Editor of The Birmingham Post since 1964; Director, Birmingham Post & Mail Ltd, since 1967; *b* 9 June 1930; *er s* of late C. G. Hopkinson; *m* 1952, Barbara Mary Lumb; three *s* one *d*. *Educ:* Sowerby Bridge Grammar Sch. Entered journalism on Huddersfield Examiner, 1950; Yorkshire Observer, 1954; Yorkshire Evening News, 1954; Evening Chronicle, Manchester, 1956; Chief Sub-Editor, Sunday Graphic, London, 1957; Asst Editor, Evening Chronicle, Newcastle upon Tyne, 1959; Chief Asst Editor, Sunday Graphic, 1960; Dep. Editor, Sheffield Telegraph, 1961, Editor, 1962-64. Member: National Training Council for Journalists; Midland Regional Advisory Cttee of National Training Council for Journalists (Vice-Chm.); International Press Institute; Associate Mem., Justice (British br. of Internat. Commn of Jurists). National Press Award, Journalist of the Year, 1963. *Address:* 63 Hampton Lane, Solihull, Warwicks. *T:* 021-705 1776. *Club:* Union (Birmingham).

**HOPKINSON, Maj.-Gen. Gerald Charles,** CB 1960; DSO 1945; OBE 1953; MC 1938; retired; *b* Wellington, Som, 27 May 1910; *s* of Capt. Charles Reginald Hopkinson; *m* 1938, Rhona Marion, *d* of Henry Turner, Farnham, Surrey; one *d*. *Educ:* Imperial Service Coll.; RMC Sandhurst. Second Lieut, Royal Tank Corps, 1930; served War of 1939-45 (India, Middle East, Italy and Europe); comd 1st RTR, Korea, 1952-53; 33rd Armoured Bde, BAOR, 1953-57; GOC 4th Div., BAOR, 1958-59; Dir, RAC, War Office, Oct. 1959-62. Lieut-Col 1952; Col 1953; Maj.-Gen. 1958. Order of the Crown and Croix de Guerre (Belgium). *Address:* Rosemount, Wrantage, Taunton, Somerset. *Club:* Army and Navy.

**HOPKINSON, Col Henry Somerset Parnell,** OBE 1944; JP; DL; *b* 16 Oct. 1899; *s* of Col H. C. B. Hopkinson, CMG, CBE, and Hon. M. F. L. Parnell, *d* of 3rd Baron Congleton; *m* 1928, Josephine Marie de Gilibert Addison, *d* of Lieut-Col A. J. R. Addison, Royal Irish Rifles; one *d* (and one *d* decd). *Educ:* Winchester and RMC. 2nd Lt Rifle Brigade, 1919; Major, 1938; Staff Coll., 1933-34; Brig. 1945; served War of 1939-45, Palestine, Burma, India; retd 1948. County Councillor Monmouthshire, 1958-64; JP 1950, DL 1951, High Sheriff 1964, Monmouthshire. FSA, FSG. *Recreations:* shooting, foreign travel. *Address:* Llanfihangel Court, Abergavenny, Monmouthshire. *T:* Crucorney 217. *Club:* Army and Navy.

**HOPKINSON, (Henry) Thomas,** CBE 1967; author, journalist; Director, Centre for Postgraduate Studies and Courses in Journalism, University College, Cardiff, since 1970; *b* 19 April 1905; 2nd *s* of late Archdeacon J. H. Hopkinson; *m* 1953, Dorothy, *widow* of late Hugh Kingsmill; (three *d* by previous marriages). *Educ:* St Edward's Sch., Oxford; Pembroke Coll., Oxford (Scholar). BA, 1927; MA, 1932. After working as a freelance journalist and in advertising and publicity, was appointed Asst Editor of the Clarion, 1934; Asst Editor, Weekly Illustrated, 1934-38; helped in preparation and launching of Picture Post; Editor, 1940-50; also edited Lilliput, 1941-46; Features Editor, News Chronicle, 1954-56; Editor, Drum Magazine, 1958-61. Dir for Africa of Internat. Press Inst., 1963-66. Senior Fellow in Press Studies, Univ. of Sussex, 1967-69. Vis. Prof. of Journalism and Mass Communication, University of Minnesota, 1968-69. *Publications:* A Wise Man Foolish, 1930; A Strong Hand at the Helm, 1933; The Man Below, 1939; Mist in the Tagus, 1946; The Transitory Venus (short stories), 1948; Down the Long Slide, 1949; Love's Apprentice, 1953; short life of George Orwell, 1953, in British Council series Writers and Their Work; The Lady and the Cut-Throat (short stories), 1958; In the Fiery Continent, 1962; South Africa, 1964 (New York); (ed) Picture Post, 1938-1950, 1970; Stories in English and American magazines, and for radio. *Address:* 6 Marine Parade, Penarth, Cardiff. *Club:* Savile.

**HOPKINSON, Thomas;** *see* Hopkinson, H. T.

**HOPLEY, Ven. Arthur;** Archdeacon of Bath since 1962; Prebendary of Yatton in Wells Cathedral since 1960; *b* 17 Oct. 1906; *o s* of Ernest Charles Hopley; *m* 1934, Marjorie Carswell Niven, *d* of John Niven; two *s*. *Educ:* Sir George Monoux Sch.; Wells Theological Coll. Asst Curate, St Mark's, Bath, 1941-44; Rector of Claverton, 1944-50; Vicar of Chard, 1950-62. *Address:* The Rectory, Shoscombe, Bath BA2 8NB. *T:* Radstock 2178. *Club:* English-Speaking Union.

**HOPPÉ, E. O.,** FRPS; author and photographer; *b* Munich, 1878. *Educ:* Paris and Vienna. Has devoted much of his time in theory and practice to the recognition of Photography as an Art Medium; is represented with works in National and Municipal Art Galleries and Museums; Japan, in 1924, acquired a collection of 400 of his prints for a permanent exhibition; travelled extensively throughout the world. Editor, Pictorial Geography. *Publications:* The Russian Ballet; Lovable London; In Gipsy Camp and Royal Palace; Picturesque Great Britain; This Romantic America; Cities Time has Passed By; Man and His Work; Achievement; In Passing; Bali; The Fifth Continent; London, 1932; Round the World with a Camera, 1935; A Camera on Unknown London; The Image of London; The London of George VI, 1937; Taken from Life (with J. D. Beresford); The Book of Fair Women (with Richard King); Gods of Modern Grub Street (with A. St John Adcock); More Gods (with A. St John Adcock); London Types (with Pett Ridge); Career with Camera; Hundred Thousand Exposures; Rural London; Jamaica - Island of many Waters; Pirates, Privateers and Gentlemen Adventurers; and numerous articles on art and travel. *Recreations:* fly-fishing, motoring, travelling off the beaten track, philately. *Address:* Wildhern, near Andover, Hants. *Clubs:* Savage, Authors'.

**HOPPER, Prof. Frederick Ernest,** MDS, FDSRCS; FFDRCSIre; Professor of Dental Surgery and Head of the Dental School, University of Leeds, since 1959; Consultant United Leeds Hospitals; Consultant Leeds Regional Hospital Board; *b* 22 Nov. 1919; *s* of Frederick Ernest Hopper, MPS and Margaret Ann Carlyle; *m* 1949, Gudrun Eik-Nes, LDSRCS, *d* of Prost Knut Eik-Nes and Nina Eik-Nes, Trondheim, Norway; three *s*. *Educ:* Dame Allan's Sch., Newcastle upon Tyne; King's Coll., University of Durham. BDS (with dist.) 1943; FDSRCS 1948; MDS 1958.

House Surg., Newcastle upon Tyne Dental Hosp. and Royal Dental Hospital, 1943-44; served in EMS in Maxillo-Facial Centres at E Grinstead and Shotley Bridge, 1944-46; successively Lecturer, 1946, and Sen. Lecturer, 1956, in Periodontal Diseases, King's Coll., University of Durham; Lecturer in Dental Pharmacology and Therapeutics, 1947-59; Examiner in Dental subjects, Univs of Durham, Edinburgh, St Andrews, etc; Dental Surgeon in charge Parodontal Dept, Newcastle upon Tyne Dental Hosp., and Sen. Dental Surg., Plastic and Jaw Unit, Shotley Bridge, 1946-59; Cons. Dent. Surg., United Newcastle Hosps, 1955-59. Hon. Treas., Brit. Soc. of Periodontology, 1949-53, Pres. 1954. Member: General Dental Council; Standing Dental Adv. Cttee; Brit. Dental Assoc.; Internat. Dental Fedn. *Publications:* contribs to med. and dental jls. *Recreations:* photography (still and cine); golf. *Address:* School of Dentistry, Leeds 1. *T:* 32006.

**HOPPER, Robert John;** Professor of Ancient History, University of Sheffield since 1955; *b* 13 Aug. 1910; *s* of Robert and Alice Hopper, Cardiff, Glamorgan; *m* 1939, Henriette, *d* of Edward and Ella Kiernan, Timperley, Cheshire; no *c.* *Educ:* Mount Radford Sch., Exeter; University of Wales; Gonville and Caius Coll., Cambridge. Served Royal Welch Fusiliers and Intelligence Corps, 1941-45. Macmillan Student of British Sch. at Athens, 1935-37; Fellow of Univ. of Wales (in Athens and Rome), 1936-38; Lectr in Classics, UCW Aberystwyth, 1938-41 and 1945-47; Senior Lecturer in Ancient History, Univ. of Sheffield, 1947-55, Dean of Faculty of Arts, 1967-70. FRNS 1949; FSA 1951; Trustee of British Sch. of Archæology, Athens. *Publications:* articles in classical and archæological periodicals. *Recreations:* numismatics; foreign travel. *Address:* 41 Barholm Road, Sheffield 10. *T:* Sheffield 302587. *Club:* National Liberal.

**HOPPS, Air Vice-Marshal Frank Linden,** CB 1945; CBE 1943; AFC; CIAgrE; retired, 1950. Directing Staff, RAF Staff Coll., 1938-39; AOC No. 16 Gp, Chatham, 1943-45 (despatches); Air Officer i/c Administration British Air Forces of Occupation (Germany), 1945-47; AOC No. 19 Group, Coastal Command, 1947. Chief Executive, Agricultural Engineers Assoc. Ltd, 1953-68. Order of Kutusov (USSR). *Address:* 77 Wick Hall, Hove, Sussex. *Clubs:* United Hunts, Farmers'.

**HOPSON, Sir Donald (Charles),** KCMG 1968 (CMG 1961); DSO 1945; MC 1944; TD 1948; HM Diplomatic Service; Ambassador to Venezuela, since 1969; *b* 31 Aug. 1915; *s* of late Charles Edward Hopson and of Ida Snowdown; *m* 1945, Denise, Croix de Guerre, *d* of late Roger Dreux, Bordeaux, France; one *d.* *Educ:* Christ's Hospital, Horsham; University Coll., Oxford (MA). Kelsall & Kemp Ltd, Rochdale, 1938-39. 2nd Lieut 5th (Territorial) Bn Lancs Fusiliers, April 1939; served France and Belgium, 1940; Capt. and Adjt 5 Lancs Fus., 1940; No 3 Commando, 1943, Sicily and Italy (despatches); Normandy, 1944, Major 2 i/c 3 Commando; Bde Major First Commando Bde, 1945, Belgium, Holland, Germany. HM Foreign (subseq. Diplomatic) Service, 1945; 2nd Sec., Copenhagen, 1946-48; Consul, Saigon, 1948-50; 1st Sec., Budapest, 1950-52; FO, 1952-55; Counsellor, Head of Chancery, Buenos Aires, 1955-57; Head of Information Research Dept, FO, 1958-62; Ambassador to Laos, 1962-65; Ambassador to Mongolia, 1965-66, and Chargé d'Affaires, Peking, 1965-68. *Address:* British Embassy, Caracas, Venezuela; 16 Chelsea Embankment, SW3. *T:* 01-352 4262. *Club:* Oxford and Cambridge University.

**HOPTHROW, Brig. Harry Ewart,** CBE 1946 (OBE 1940); UK Representative to Council of European Industrial Federations, since 1965; *b* 13 Nov. 1896; *s* of Frederick Hopthrow; *m* 1925, Audrey Kassel, *d* of J. Lewer; one *s* one *d.* *Educ:* Queen Elizabeth's Grammar Sch., Gainsborough; City Sch., Lincoln; Loughborough Coll. Civil and Mechanical Engineer, ICI Ltd, 1925-39; Asst Sec., ICI Ltd, 1945-58; Secretary and a Vice-Pres., Royal Institution, 1960-68. AMIMechE 1924, FIMechE 1933. Mem. Central Advisory Water Cttee (Min. of Housing and Local Govt), 1946-70; Mem. Cttee of Inquiry into Inland Waterways (Bowes Cttee), 1956-58; Vice-Chm. IoW River and Water Authority. Served European War, 1915-18, RE, France and Flanders; commanded 107 Company RE, 1931-35, Major; Asst Dir of Works, GHQ, BEF, 1939-40, Lieut-Col; Dep. Chief Engineer: Home Forces, 1940-41, and Western Command, 1941; Dep. Controller Mil. Works Service, War Office, 1941-43; Col; Dir of Fortifications and Works, War Office, 1943-45, Brig. Served France and Flanders, 1939-40 and 1944. Officer of American Legion of Merit, 1946. *Recreation:* yachting. *Address:* Surrey House, Cowes, Isle of Wight. *T:* Cowes 2430. *Clubs:* Army and Navy; Royal Engineer Yacht; Royal London Yacht, Island Sailing (Cowes).

**HOPWOOD,** family name of **Baron Southborough.**

**HOPWOOD, Brig. John Adam,** CBE 1958; DSO 1943 (and Bar 1944); *b* 26 Jan. 1910; *s* of Ernest Hopwood and Constance Marion Adam; *m* Cressida Mona Browning, *d* of R. Campbell Browning, Armsworth, Alresford, Hants; no *c.* *Educ:* St David's, Reigate; Eton; RMC Sandhurst. Commissioned Black Watch, 1930; served with 1st Bn in India, 1931-35; ADC to Governor of Bengal, 1935-37; with 1st Bn Black Watch, and BEF in France, 1939-40; Staff Coll., 1940; Bde Major, 154 Inf. Bde, 1941; Second in Comd, 7th Bn Black Watch, N Africa and Sicily, 1942; comd 1st Bn Black Watch, Sicily and NW Europe, 1943-45; comd 154 and 156 Inf. Bdes, Germany, 1946; Mem. Training Mission to Iraq Army, Baghdad, 1946-48; attended jssc, Latimer, 1948; Liaison Appt, RAF Fighter Comd, 1949; comd 44 Parachute Bde (TA) London, 1950-53; Col i/c Admin., Hong Kong, 1953-55; comd 3 Inf. Bde, Canal Zone, UK, Cyprus, 1955-58; Vice-Pres., Regular Commissions Board, 1958-60, retd. Awarded Bronze Lion of Netherlands. *Recreations:* ornithology (MBOU), field sports, travel. *Address:* Gilletts Farm, Yarcombe, Honiton, Devon. *T:* Chard 3121. *Club:* United Service.

**HORAM, John Rhodes;** MP (Lab) Gateshead West since 1970; Founder-Director, Commodities Research Unit Ltd, since 1968; *b* 7 March 1939; *s* of Sydney Horam, Preston; unmarried. *Educ:* Silcoates Sch., Wakefield; Univ. of Cambridge. Market Research Officer, Rowntrees & Co., 1960-62; leader and feature writer: Financial Times, 1962-65; The Economist, 1965-68. Contested (Lab) Folkestone and Hythe, 1966. Chm., Circle Thirty Three Housing Trust Ltd. *Recreations:* painting, playing tennis and squash. *Address:* Flat 4, 214 Piccadilly, W1. *T:* 01-734 2748. *Clubs:* Royal Automobile; Saltwell Social (Gateshead).

**HORAN, Rt. Rev. Forbes Trevor;** *see* Tewkesbury, Suffragan Bishop of.

**HORDER,** family name of **Baron Horder.**

**HORDER,** 2nd Baron *cr* 1933, of Ashford in the County of Southampton; **Thomas Mervyn Horder;** Bt, of Shaston, 1923; Chairman of Gerald Duckworth and Co. Ltd; *b* 8 Dec. 1910; *s* of 1st Baron Horder, GCVO, MD, FRCP, and Geraldine Rose (*d* 1954), *o d* of Arthur Doggett, Newnham Manor, Herts; *S* father, 1955. *Educ:* Winchester; Trinity Coll., Cambridge. BA 1932; MA 1937. Served War of 1939-45: HQ, RAF Fighter Comd, 1940-42 (despatches); Air HQ, India, 1942-44; Headquarters, South-EAst Asia Command, 1944-45; United Kingdom Liaison Mission, Tokyo, 1945-46. *Publications:* various simple works for piano, clarinet, oboe, etc, 1960-62; The Orange Carol Book (ed), 1962; Norfolk Dances for string orchestra, 1965; The Little Genius, 1966; Six Betjeman Songs, 1967; A Book of Love Songs (ed), 1969. *Recreations:* music, idling. *Address:* 3 Henrietta Street, WC2.

**HORDERN, Anthony,** CBE 1918; pastoralist; *b* Sydney, NSW, 21 Feb. 1889; *s* of late Samuel and Janie M. Hordern, Sydney; *m* 1st, 1911, Viola Sydney (*d* 1929), *d* of Col Bingham; one *s* two *d*; 2nd, 1932, Ursula Mary (*d* 1961), *d* of Dr H. H. Bullmore; two *d*. *Educ:* St Mark's Grammar Sch., Sydney; Oxford Univ. During European War service as Dep. Comr, with rank of Hon. Major, Australian Red Cross Soc.; Vice-Pres., Royal Agricultural Soc. of NSW; Patron Shorthorn Soc. of Australia; Pres., NSW Sheepbreeders' Assoc., 1954; Pres., NSW Romney Marsh Breeders Assoc.; owner of Mungadal Station, Hay, NSW, Milton Park, Bowral, NSW, and Wingadal, Albury, NSW; Anglican. *Recreation:* golf. *Address:* Milton Park, Bowral, NSW, Australia. *Clubs:* Union, Australian, NSW (Sydney).

**HORDERN, Michael Murray;** actor; *b* 3 Oct. 1911; *s* of Capt. Edward Joseph Calverly Hordern, CIE, RIN, and Margaret Emily (*née* Murray); *m* 1943, Grace Eveline Mortimer; one *d*. *Educ:* Brighton Coll. Formerly in business with The Educational Supply Assoc., playing meanwhile as an amateur at St Pancras People's Theatre. First professional appearance as Lodovico in Othello, People's Palace, 1937. Two seasons of repertory at Little Theatre, Bristol, 1937-39; War service in Navy, 1940-46; demobilised as Lieut-Comdr, RNVR. Parts include: Mr Toad in Toad of Toad Hall, at Stratford, 1948 and 1949; Ivanov in Ivanov, Arts Theatre, 1950. Stratford Season, 1952: Jacques, Menenius, Caliban. Old Vic Season, 1953-54: Polonius, King John, Malvolio, Prospero. "BB" in The Doctor's Dilemma, Saville, 1956; Old Vic Season, 1958-59: Cassius, Macbeth. Ulysses (Troilus and Cressida), Edinburgh Fest., 1962; Herbert Georg Beutler in The Physicists, Aldwych, 1963; Southman in Saint's Day, St Martin's, 1965; Relatively Speaking, Duke of York's, 1967; A Delicate Balance, Aldwych, 1969; King Lear, Nottingham Playhouse, 1969, National Theatre, 1970; Flint, Criterion, 1970. Also many leading parts in films, radio and television. *Recreation:* fishing. *Address:* 24 Kelso Place, W8; Bagnor, Newbury, Berks. *Club:* Garrick.

**HORDERN, Peter Maudslay;** MP (C) Horsham since 1964; *b* 18 April 1929; British; *m* 1964, Susan Chataway; two *s*. *Educ:* Geelong Grammar Sch., Australia; Christ Church, Oxford (MA). Commissioned 60th Rifles, 1947-49; Christ Church, Oxford, 1949-52. Mem. of Stock Exchange, London, 1957-. *Recreations:* cricket, golf, reading and travel. *Address:* 55 Cadogan Street, SW3.

**HORENSTEIN, Jascha;** Conductor; *b* Kiev, 6 May 1899; American citizen; *s* of Abraham Horenstein and Marie (*née* Jekels); *m* Ernestina Diaz; one *s*. *Educ:* Vienna Univ.; Vienna Academy. Conductor: Vienna Symphony Orchestra, 1923; Berlin Symphony Orchestra, 1925-28; Musical Dir, Düsseldorf Opera, 1929-33. Has conducted with the principal orchestras throughout the world, including the Berlin Philharmonic, Royal Philharmonic, New York Philharmonic, Amsterdam Concertgebauw, BBC Symphony, London Symphony, Brussels Philharmonic, Warsaw Philharmonic, Moscow Philharmonic, Leningrad Philharmonic, French National, and Israel Philharmonic Orchestras; also at La Scala and The Royal Opera House, Covent Garden. He has appeared at the Festivals of Vienna and Edinburgh, and the Maggio Fiorentino of Florence, among other festivals. Grand Prix du Disque (three times). *Recreations:* reading, collecting collages and abstract paintings. *Address:* 12 Chemin du Coteau, Lausanne-Pully, Switzerland. *T:* 28.62.05.

**HORLICK, Lt-Col Sir James Nockells,** 4th Bt *cr* 1914; OBE 1919; MC; 2nd *s* of Sir James Horlick, 1st Bt; *S* nephew (Sir Peter Horlick, 3rd Bt), 1958; *m* 1911, Flora Macdonald Martin (*d* 1955); one *s* one *d* (and one *d* decd); *m* 1956, Joan MacGill. *Educ:* Eton; Christ Church, Oxford. Coldstream Guards; served European War, 1914-18 (OBE, MC); MP (U) Gloucester, 1923-29; retired, 1929; Sheriff of Berks, 1938; late Hon. Col 1st Surrey Rifles. Victorian Medal of Honour and Gold Medal, Royal Horticultural Society, 1964. *Recreation:* gardening. *Heir:* *s* John James Macdonald Horlick [*b* 9 April 1922; *m* 1948, June, *d* of Douglas Cory-Wright; one *s* two *d*]. *Address:* Timbers, Nuffield, near Henley-on-Thames, Oxon; Isle of Gigha, Argyll, Scotland. *Clubs:* Bath, Beefsteak, Buck's.

**HORLOCK, Prof. John Harold;** Professor of Engineering, Cambridge University, since 1967, Deputy Head of Engineering Department, since 1969; *b* 19 April 1928; *s* of Harold Edgar and Olive Margaret Horlock; *m* 1953, Sheila Joy Stutely; one *s* two *d*. *Educ:* Edmonton Latymer Sch.; (Scholar) St John's Coll., Cambridge. 1st Class Hons Mech. Sci. Tripos, Pt I, 1948, Rex Moir Prize; Pt II, 1949; MA 1952; PhD 1955. Design and Development Engineer, Rolls Royce Ltd, Derby, 1949-51; Research Fellow, St John's Coll., Cambridge, 1954-57; Univ. Demonstrator, 1952-56; University Lecturer, 1956-58, at Cambridge Univ. Engineering Lab.; Harrison Prof. of Mechanical Engineering, Liverpool Univ., 1958-66. Professorial Fellow of St John's Coll., Cambridge, 1967-. Visiting Asst Prof. in Mech. Engineering, Massachusetts Inst. of Technology, USA, 1956-57; Vis. Prof. of Aero-Space Engineering, Pennsylvania State Univ., USA, 1966. CEng, FIMechE, FRAeS. Mem. ASME. *Publications:* The Fluid Mechanics and Thermodynamics of Axial Flow Compressors, 1958; The Fluid Mechanics and Thermodynamics of Axial Flow Turbines, 1966; contribs to mech. and aero. engineering jls and to Proc. Royal Society. *Recreations:* music, cricket, golf. *Address:* St John's College, Cambridge.

**HORN, Alan Bowes;** Consul-General, Istanbul, since 1970; *b* 6 June 1917; *m* 1946, Peggy Boocock; one *s* one *d*. *Educ:* London Sch. of Economics. Served in Army, 1940-46. Joined Foreign Service, 1946; Vice-Consul, Marseilles, 1948-49; 2nd Sec., HM Embassy, Tel Aviv, 1949; promoted 1st Sec. and later apptd: London, 1951-53; New York, 1953-56; Helsinki, 1957-60; FO, 1960-63; Ambassador to the Malagasy Republic, 1963-67; Counsellor, Warsaw, 1967-70. *Address:* c/o Foreign and Commonwealth Office, SW1.

**HORNBY, Sir Antony;** *see* Hornby, Sir R. A.

**HORNBY, Frank Robert,** MBE 1944; Chief Officer and Vice-Chairman, Council for National Academic Awards; *b* 20 Aug. 1911; *yr s* of late Robert Wilson Hornby and Jane Hornby; *m* 1939, Kathleen Margaret, *yr d* of late Dr Sidney Berry and Helen Berry. *Educ:* Heversham Sch., Westmorland; Magdalene Coll., Cambridge. 1st Class Natural Sciences Tripos Pts 1 and 2. Schoolmaster, 1933-41. RAOC, 1941-46 (Lieut-Col). Asst Educn Officer, Nottingham Co. Borough, 1946-56; Sec., Nat. Coun. for Technological Awards, 1956-64. *Address:* 15 Williams Way, Radlett, Herts. *T:* Radlett 5083. *Club:* Athenæum.

**HORNBY, Sir (Henry) Russell,** 2nd Bt, *cr* 1899; *b* 12 Sept. 1888; *s* of 1st Bt and Letitia (*d* 1937), *d* of Capt. W. R. Browne; *S* father 1928; *m* 1913, Dorothy Elma, *o d* of late Maj.-Gen. Sir W. Fry, KCVO, CB; one *d.* Was on active service in France. *Heir:* none. *Address:* Barraclough, Clitheroe, Lancs. *Club:* Junior Carlton.

**HORNBY, Prof. James Angus;** Professor of Law in the University of Bristol since 1961; *b* 15 Aug. 1922; twin *s* of James Hornby and Evelyn Gladys (*née* Grant). *Educ:* Bolton County Grammar Sch.; Christ's Coll., Cambridge. BA 1944, LLB 1945, MA 1948 Cantab. Called to Bar, Lincoln's Inn, 1947. Lecturer, Manchester Univ., 1947-61. *Publications:* An Introduction to Company Law, 3rd edn, 1969; contribs to legal journals. *Recreations:* hill walking, squash racquets. *Address:* The Faculty of Law, The University, Bristol. *Club:* Oxford and Cambridge University.

**HORNBY, Michael Charles St John;** retired as Vice-Chairman, W. H. Smith & Son Ltd (1944-65); *b* 2 Jan. 1899; *e s* of C. H. St J. Hornby and Cicely Hornby; *m* 1928, Nicolette Joan, *d* of Hon. Cyril Ward, MVO; two *s* one *d.* *Educ:* Winchester; RMC Sandhurst; New Coll., Oxford. Joined Grenadier Guards, 1918; served in France and Germany. New Coll., Oxford, 1919-21. Entered W. H. Smith & Son, 1921. Prime Warden, Goldsmiths' Company, 1954-55. Chm., National Book League, 1959. *Recreations:* fox-hunting, shooting, cricket, gardening. *Address:* Pusey House, Faringdon, Berks. *T:* Buckland 222. *Clubs:* White's, MCC.
*See also Sir R. A. Hornby.*

**HORNBY, Richard Phipps,** MA; MP (C) Tonbridge Division of Kent since June 1956; *b* 20 June 1922; *e s.* of late Rt Rev. Hugh Leycester Hornby, MC; *m* 1951, Stella Hichens; three *s* one *d.* *Educ:* Winchester Coll.; Trinity Coll., Oxford (Scholar). Served in King's Royal Rifle Corps, 1941-45. 2nd Cl. Hons in Modern History, Oxford, 1948 (Soccer Blue). History Master, Eton Coll., 1948-50; with Unilever, 1951-52; with J. Walter Thompson Co., 1952-63, 1964-. Contested (C) West Walthamstow: May 1955 (gen. election) and March 1956 (by-election). PPS, to Rt Hon. Duncan Sandys, MP, 1959-63; Parly Under-Sec. of State, CRO and CO, Oct. 1963-Oct. 1964. Member: BBC Gen. Adv. Council, 1969-; Cttee of Inquiry into Intrusions into Privacy, 1970-. *Recreations:* shooting, walking, riding and tennis. *Address:* 10 Hereford Square, SW7.

**HORNBY, Sir (Roger) Antony,** Kt 1960; Director of Savoy, Claridge's and Berkeley Hotel Cos; Director of Witan and other Investment Trusts; *b* 5 Feb. 1904; *s* of late C. H. St J. Hornby, Shelley House, Chelsea; *m* 1st, 1931, Lady Veronica Blackwood (marr. diss. 1940); one *d*; 2nd, 1949, Lily Ernst. *Educ:* Winchester Coll.; New Coll., Oxford. MA Oxon. Mem. of London Stock Exchange, 1928; Vice-Chm. King's Coll. Hosp., 1959; Chm. King's Coll. Hosp. Med. Sch. Council. Served War of 1939-45, Grenadier Guards. A Trustee of the Wallace Collection, 1963-; Mem., Exec. Cttee, Nat. Art Collections Fund. *Recreations:* travel, collecting pictures. *Address:* Claridge's Hotel, W1. *Clubs:* Buck's, Garrick, MCC, Hurlingham.
*See also M. C. St J. Hornby.*

**HORNBY, Sir Russell;** *see* Hornby, Sir H. R.

**HORNE, Sir Alan Edgar,** 2nd Bt *cr* 1929; MC; *b* 19 Sept. 1889; *s* of Sir Edgar Horne, 1st Bt, and Margery (*d* 1939), *d* of George Anderson May, Elford, Staffs; *S* father, 1941; *m* 1st, 1915, Henriette Kelly (*d* 1918); one *d*; 2nd, 1923, Roslyn (*d* 1961), *d* of John Brian Robinson; (one *s* decd). *Educ:* Eton; University Coll., Oxford. Served European War, 1914-19, in France and Balkans as Capt. Surrey Yeomanry and on Staff (despatches 4 times, MC, French Croix de Guerre); War of 1939-45, Basutoland and MELF, 1940-48, as Lt-Col Royal Pioneer Corps (African and Native Troops). *Heir:* *g s* Alan Gray Antony Horne, *b* 11 July 1948. *Address:* 1 The Paragon (Flat 4), Blackheath, SE3. *Clubs:* Cavalry, MCC.
*See also Major W. G. Horne.*

**HORNE, Alistair Allan;** author (formerly journalist); lecturer; *b* 9 Nov. 1925; *s* of late Sir (James) Allan Horne and Lady (Auriol Camilla) Horne (*née* Hay); *m* 1953, Renira Margaret Hawkins; three *d.* *Educ:* Le Rosey, Switzerland; Millbrook, USA; Jesus Coll., Cambridge (MA). Served War of 1939-45: RAF, 1943-44; Coldstream Gds, 1944-47; Captain, attached Intelligence Service (ME). Dir, Ropley Trust Ltd, 1948; Foreign Correspondent, Daily Telegraph, 1952-55. Founded Alistair Horne Res. Fellowship in Mod. History, St Antony's Coll., Oxford, 1969. FRSL. *Publications:* Back into Power, 1955; The Land is Bright, 1958; Canada and the Canadians, 1961; The Price of Glory: Verdun 1916, 1962 (Hawthornden Prize, 1963); The Fall of Paris: The Siege and The Commune 1870-71, 1965; To Lose a Battle: France 1940, 1969; Death of a Generation, 1970; contribs various periodicals. *Recreations:* skiing, shooting, painting. *Address:* 7 The Boltons, SW10; Membury House, Ramsbury, Wilts. *Clubs:* Garrick, Beefsteak.

**HORNE, Frank Robert,** CBE 1958; MA, NDA, NDD (Hons); FIBiol; Director of National Institute of Agricultural Botany, 1945-70; Scientific Adviser to Home Grown Cereals Authority, since 1970; *b* 9 June 1904; *m* 1929, Marjorie Bannister; one *s* three *d.* *Educ:* Hele's Sch., Exeter; Seale-Hayne Coll.; Christ's Coll., Cambridge; West of Scotland Agric. Coll. (Steven Memorial Prizeman); Gresham's Sch., Holt. Head of Botanical Dept, Seale-Hayne Agric. Coll., 1928-44 (Research Grant for Plant Breeding, 1931-44); Chief Tech. Officer and Dep. Exec. Officer, Devon War Agricultural Exec. Cttee, 1940-44; Chm. Min. of Agric. Cttee on Seeds (Horne Report), 1950; Chm. Pest Infestation Research Board, DSIR, 1952-57; Pres., British Grassland Soc., 1957-58. Chm., European Productivity Agency (OECD) Cttees on Herbage Varieties and Internat. Seed Certification, 1954-59; Chm. World Seed Year Meeting, FAO (UNO), Rome, 1962. Mem. Council, British Assoc., 1967- (Pres. Section M); Member: Internat. Commn, Nomenclature Cultivated Plants, 1956-; European Barley Cttee, 1950-. Foreign Mem. (Academician), swedish Acad. of

Forestry and Agriculture, 1968-; Hon. Life Mem., Swedish Seed Research Assoc., 1961. Commodore, Cambridge Univ. Cruising Club, 1961-63. *Address:* Angle Cottage, Longmeadow Lane, Lode, Cambridge. *T:* Bottisham 503. *Club:* Farmers'.

**HORNE, Frederic Thomas;** Master of the Supreme Court (Taxing Office) since 1967; *b* 21 March 1917; *y s* of Lionel Edward Horne, JP, Moreton-in-Marsh, Glos; *m* 1944, Madeline Hatton; two *s* two *d*. *Educ:* Chipping Campden Grammar Sch. Admitted a Solicitor (Hons), 1938. Served with RAFVR in General Duties Branch (Pilot), 1939-56. Partner in Iliffe Sweet & Co., 1956-67. *Recreations:* cricket, music. *Address:* Russetings, Shire Lane, Chorleywood, Herts. *Club:* MCC.

**HORNE, Maj.-Gen. Gerald Tom Warlters,** CB 1949; CBE 1945 (OBE 1944); *b* 4 March 1898; *s* of late Thomas Warlters Horne and late Cornelia Horne (*née* Ellis); *m* 1921, Janetta Marie Graham; one *d* (and one *s* killed in action, 1944). *Educ:* Repton; RMA Woolwich. Commissioned 2nd Lieut Royal Regt of Artillery, 1917; served European War, 1914-18, transferred to Royal Army Ordnance Corps, 1925; Capt., 1925; Major, 1936; Staff Coll., 1938-39; War of 1939-45, BEF France, 1939-40; War Office, 1940-44; Italy, 1944-45; War Office, Dep. Dir Ordnance Services (Brig.), 1945-48; Maj.-Gen., 1948; Dir of Ordnance Services (War Office), 1948-51; retired, 1951. Bronze Medal for Valour (Italian), 1918. *Recreations:* golf and gardening. *Address:* 28 Smarts Heath Road, Mayford, Woking, Surrey.

**HORNE, Prof. Michael Rex,** MA, PhD, ScD Cantab; MSc (Manchester); FICE; FIStructE; Professor of Civil Engineering, University of Manchester, since 1960; *b* 29 Dec. 1921; *s* of late Rev. Ernest Horne and of Mrs Katie Horne, Leicester; *m* 1947, Molly, *d* of late Mark Hewett, Royston, Herts; two *s* two *d*. *Educ:* Boston (Lincs) Grammar Sch.; Leeds Grammar Sch.; St John's Coll., Cambridge. MA Cantab 1945; PhD Cantab 1950, ScD Cantab 1956. John Winbolt Prize for Research, Cambridge Univ., 1944. Asst Engineer, River Great Ouse Catchment Bd, 1941-45; Scientific Officer, British Welding Research Assoc., 1945-51; Asst Dir of Research in Engineering, 1951-56, Lectr in Engineering, 1957-60, Univ. of Cambridge. Instn of Civil Engineers, Telford Premiums, 1956, 1966. Chm., NW Branch, IStructE, 1969-70. Fellow, St John's College, Cambridge, 1957. *Publications:* (with J. F. Baker and J. Heyman) The Steel Skeleton, 1956; (with W. F. Merchant) The Stability of Frames, 1965; contribs on structures, strength of materials and statistical theory of loads to learned journals. *Recreations:* photography, gardening, music. *Address:* Ganavan, 16 Temple Road, Buxton, Derbs.

**HORNE, Major William Guy;** *b* 19 Sept. 1889; *yr s* of Sir W. Edgar Horne, 1st Bt; *m* 1921, Louisa Carey (*d* 1962), *y d* of Herbert Carey Hardy, JP, Chilworth Manor, Surrey. *Educ:* Eton. Joined 19th Royal Hussars, 1912. Served European War in France, 1914-18; Cavalry Liaison Officer to Gen. Denikine in South Russia, 1919-20; transferred to 10th Royal Hussars, 1922; served in Europe, Egypt and Sudan; retired with rank of Major, 1931. AAF, 1938-43, retired with rank of Group Capt. Dir, Prudential Assurance Co. Ltd, 1931-42. Master, Clothworkers' Co., 1957-58. *Recreation:* golf. *Clubs:* Cavalry, MCC.

**HORNER, Arthur William,** CMG 1964; TD and clasp 1946; First Secretary, British High Commission, Kampala; *b* 22 June 1909; *s* of Francis Moore and Edith Horner; *m* 1938, Patricia Denise (*née* Campbell); two *s* one *d*. *Educ:* Hardenwick; Felsted. Marine Insurance, 1926-39. Served War, 1939-46, Rifle Brigade; Lieut-Col; psc. Farming in Kenya, 1948-50. Colonial Administrative Service (later HM Overseas Civil Service), Kenya, 1950-64; Commissioner of Lands, 1955-61; Permanent Sec., 1961-64; Dir of Independence Celebrations, 1963; Principal, ODM, 1964. *Recreation:* music. *Address:* Phoenix Cottage, New Road, Ham Common, Surrey.

**HORNER, John;** *b* 11 Nov. 1911; *s* of Ernest Charles and Emily Horner; *m* 1936, Patricia, *d* of Geoffrey and Alice Palmer; two *d*. *Educ:* elementary sch. and Sir George Monoux Grammar Sch., Walthamstow. Apprenticed Merchant Navy, 1927; Second Mate's Certificate, 1932. Joined London Fire Brigade, 1933; Gen. Sec. Fire Brigades Union, 1939-64; MP (Lab) Oldbury and Halesowen, 1964-70. Mem. Select Cttee on Nationalised Industries. *Recreations:* walking, gardening, talking, listening to music, studying history and art. *Address:* Yew Tree, Howle Hill, Ross on Wye, Herefordshire. *T:* Ross on Wye 2932. *Clubs:* Halesowen Labour (Halesowen, Worcs); Cradley Labour (Cradley, Staffs).

**HORNER, Lawrence John Hallam,** OBE 1959; Director, Chamber of Shipping of UK, since 1966; *b* 14 June 1907; *o s* of late David Aitken Horner and Louise Stuart Black; *m* 1935, Kathleen Joan, *o d* of late Charles D. Taite, Bowdon, Cheshire; two *d*. *Educ:* Malvern Coll.; Corpus Christi Coll., Oxford (MA). Served War of 1939-45, RSF and RAC (despatches). Admitted Solicitor (hons), 1931; Asst Solicitor, Cheshire CC, 1932-34; Rees & Freres, parly agents, 1934-51 (Partner, 1936); Sec., Canal Assoc., 1945-48; Parly Solicitor (later also Sec.), Dock and Harbour Authorities' Assoc., 1946-51; Asst Gen. Man. and Solicitor and Parly Agent, Chamber of Shipping of UK, 1951, Gen. Man., 1959; Sec., Adv. Cttee on New Lighthouse Works, etc, 1951-66; Mem., Adv. Cttee on Oil Pollution of the Sea, 1952-66; Mem., City of London Coll. Shipping Adv. Cttee, 1966-; Mem., Cttee of Management, British Ship Adoption Soc., 1968-; MInstT, 1970. Netherlands Bronze Cross, 1945. *Recreations:* stud farm, watching birds. *Address:* Salters Green Farm, Mayfield, Sussex. *T:* Rotherfield 472. *Club:* Reform.
*See also Sir T. C. Spenser-Wilkinson.*

**HORNER, Mrs Sibyl Gertrude,** CBE 1957; MB, BS; DPH Oxon; DIH; HM Senior Medical Inspector of Factories, 1957-61; *b* 18 Oct. 1895; 5th *d* of late Arthur Overton and Mary Overton, Forest Row, Sussex; *m* 1931, Bernard Stuart Horner, OBE; no *c*. *Educ:* London Sch. of Medicine and St Mary's Hosp., Paddington. MB, BS London 1919. HM Medical Inspector of Factories (Home Office), 1924; HM Dep. Senior Medical Inspector of Factories (Min. of Labour), 1948. Mem. Order of St John of Jerusalem. *Recreations:* horticulture, travel, walking. *Address:* Eaton Cottage, Esher, Surrey. *T:* Esher 63574.

**HORNIBROOK, Sir Manuel (Richard),** Kt 1960; OBE 1957; *b* 7 Aug. 1893; 2nd *s* of John and Katherine Hornibrook; *m* 1922, Daphne Winifred Brunckhorst; two *s* one *d* (and one *s* decd). *Educ:* S Brisbane Sch. Founded own business as building contractor, 1912; formed private Civil Engineering and Building Contracting Co. with position of Man. Dir, 1926; floated Hornibrook Ltd holding company for number of subsidiary civil engineering and building contracting companies throughout Australia. *Recreations:*

golf and bowls. *Address:* 175 Lancaster Road, Ascot, Brisbane, Qld, Australia. *T:* 68-4161. *Clubs:* Rotary, Brisbane, Royal Queensland Golf (Brisbane).

**HORNSBY, Harry Reginald,** MBE 1944; Headmaster, St Andrews School, Nukualofa, Tonga, since 1970; *b* 19 Dec. 1907; *s* of Rev. E. F. Hornsby, Hon. CF; *m* 1946, Mary Elizabeth Whitley; no *c*. *Educ:* Bromsgrove Sch.; Brasenose Coll., Oxford. Asst Master, Christ's Hosp., Horsham, 1929-39; Headmaster, The King's Sch., Peterborough, 1939-51; Headmaster: Christ's Coll., Christchurch, NZ, 1951-63; St Paul's Sch., Hamilton, NZ, 1963-69. Lay Canon of Christchurch Cathedral, 1962-63; Mem. of Council, Univ. of Canterbury, NZ, 1962-63. War Service, 1940-45 (despatches): Gunner RA, 1940; commissioned Worcs Regt, 1941; served 3rd Queen Alexandra's Own Gurkha Rifles, 1941-45. Chm. Independent Schools Assoc. of New Zealand, 1960-63; Member: Outward Bound Trust of New Zealand, 1961-64; Council, Univ. of Waikato, 1965-68. Lay Canon of Waikato Cathedral, 1967, 1968, 1969. *Recreations:* all games, mountaineering, gardening. *Address:* St Andrews School, Box 118, Nukualofa, Tonga.

**HORNSBY, Capt. James Arthur;** *b* 14 May 1891; *s* of James William Hornsby, late of Laxton Park, Stamford; *m* 1917, Cecily Mary Elizabeth, *d* of late Col S. W. Lane, CBE; one *s* two *d*. *Educ:* Eton; Magdalene Coll., Cambridge. Capt. late 5th Lancers; Sheriff of Rutland, 1940; Joint Master Meath Hounds, 1928-32; Master Duhallow Hounds, 1932-33; Joint Master Woodland Pytchley, 1933-35; Master Duhallow Hounds, 1946-62. *Address:* Rathkenny House, Drogheda, Co. Meath.

**HORNSBY-SMITH, Rt. Hon. Dame (Margaret) Patricia,** PC 1959; DBE 1961; MP (C) Chislehurst Division of Kent, 1950-66 and since 1970; *b* 17 March 1914; *o d* of F. C. Hornsby-Smith. *Educ:* Richmond. Ministry of Economic Warfare, 1941-45; Barnes Borough Council, 1945-49. Parliamentary Sec., Ministry of Health, 1951-57; UK delegate to Assembly of UN, 1958; Jt Parly Under-Sec. of State, Home Office, 1957-59; Jt Parly Sec., Min. of Pensions and Nat. Insurance, 1959-61. Led UK Parliamentary Delegation to Australasia, 1961. *Address:* 31 Stafford Mansions, Stafford Place, SW1. *Clubs:* Special Forces, Cowdray, Constitutional.

**HORNYOLD-STRICKLAND, Henry,** JP; FSA; Lord Lieutenant of Westmorland, 1957-65; *b* 1890; *s* of Alfred Hornyold, Blackmore Park, Worcs and Alice, *d* of Julien de La Chere and *niece* of 1st and last Viscount Llandaff; assumed by Royal Licence, 1932, additional name and arms of Strickland; *m* 1920, Mary Christina (*d* 1970), *d* of 1st and last Baron Strickland; one *s* one *d*. *Educ:* Beaumont; Magdalen Coll., Oxford. Elec. Engineer (retd); High Sheriff Co. Westmorland, 1937. *Publications:* Stricklands of Sizergh; Lancashire MPs, 1290-1550. *Address:* Sizergh Castle, near Kendal, Westmorland. *T:* Sedgwick 203. *Clubs:* Lansdowne; Union (Malta).

**HOROBIN, Sir Ian (Macdonald),** Kt, *cr* 1955; *b* 1899; *e s* of late Principal J. C. Horobin, Homerton Coll., Cambs, and of late Mrs M. A. Cloudesley Brereton. *Educ:* Highgate; Sidney Sussex Coll., Cambridge (MA). RAF, 1918-19 and 1939-46. Warden of Mansfield House Univ. Settlement, refounded and endowed, 1923-61. MP (Nat) Central Div. of Southwark, 1931-35; contested (C) Oldham (West), 1950; MP (C) Oldham East, 1951-Sept. 1959; Parl. Sec., Min. of Power, 1958-59. Gazetted a Life Peer, March 1962, but withdrew acceptance, April 1962. *Publications:* Pleasures of Planning, 1935; Poems, 1935; More Poems, 1939. *Address:* c/o The Chartered Bank, 38 Bishopsgate, EC2.

**HOROBIN, Norah Maud,** BSc (London); Head Mistress Roedean School, Brighton, 1947-61, retired; *b* 7 Feb. 1898; *d* of late J. C. Horobin, MA Cantab; Principal of Homerton Coll., Cambridge, and late Mrs M. A. Cloudesley Brereton. *Educ:* North London Collegiate Sch.; King's Coll., London. Head Mistress: Dulwich High Sch., 1935-38; Sunderland High Sch., 1938-47. *Address:* 1 Evelyn Terrace, Brighton BN2 2EP.

**HOROWITZ, Vladimir;** Pianist; *b* Kieff, Russia, 1 Oct. 1904; *s* of Samuel Horowitz and Sophie Bodik; *m* 1933, Wanda Toscanini. *Educ:* Kieff Conservatory; studied under Sergi Tarnowsky and Felix Blumenfeld. European Dêbut, 1925; dêbut with New York Philharmonic Orchestra, 1928. Soloist, New York Symphony Orchestra and other American orchestras. *Address:* c/o Columbia Records, 51 West 52nd Street, New York, NY 10019, USA.

**HORRIDGE, Prof. (George) Adrian,** FRS 1969; Professor of Behavioural Biology, Research School of Biological Sciences, Australian National University, ACT 2600, since 1969; *b* Sheffield, England, 12 Dec. 1927; *s* of George William Horridge and Olive Stray; *m* 1954, Audrey Anne Lightburne; one *s* three *d*. *Educ:* King Edward VII Sch., Sheffield. Fellow, St John's Coll., Cambridge, 1953-56; on staff, St Andrews Univ., 1956-60; Dir, Gatty Marine Laboratory, St Andrews, 1960-69. ScD Cantab 1968. *Publications:* Structure and Function of the Nervous Systems of Invertebrates (with T. H. Bullock), 1965; Interneurons, 1968; contribs numerous scientific papers on behaviour and nervous systems of lower animals, to jls, etc. *Recreations:* any outdoor. *Address:* PO Box 475, Canberra, ACT 2600, Australia. *T:* Canberra 494280.

**HORROBIN, Walter,** CMG 1959; engaged in sheep farming and primary production organisations in New Zealand; Past Chairman of New Zealand Wool Board; *b* 15 March 1894; *m* 1922, Lorna Pascoe; one *s* one *d*. *Educ:* Wellington, New Zealand. *Address:* Awatea, Waikanai, New Zealand; New Zealand House, Strand, London, WC2; 113 S Otaki, New Zealand. *Clubs:* Wellesley, Civil Service (New Zealand).

**HORROCKS, Lt-Gen. Sir Brian Gwynne,** KCB 1949 (CB 1943); KBE 1945; DSO 1943; MC; a Director of Bovis Holdings since 1963; President, National Television Rental Association; Director, Inter-Nation Television Trust Ltd; Gentleman Usher of the Black Rod, House of Lords, 1949-63; *b* 7 Sept. 1895; *o s* of late Col Sir William Heaton Horrocks, KCMG, CB; *m* 1928, Nancy, *d* of Brook and Hon. Mrs Brook Kitchin; one *d*. *Educ:* Uppingham; RMC Sandhurst. 2nd Lieut Middlesex Regt, 1914; served European War, France and Belgium, 1914, Russia, 1919 (wounded, MC); War of 1939-45 (wounded, DSO, CB, KBE); Comd 44 (HC Div.), 9 Armd Div., 13 Corps, 10 Corps in Egypt and Africa, 9 Corps Tunis, 30 Corps in BLA. GOC-in-C Western Comd, 1946; GOC-in-C British Army of the Rhine, 1948; retired, 1949. Hon. LLD (Belfast). *Publication:* A Full Life, 1960. *Address:* Manor Farm, East Compton, Shepton Mallet, Somerset. *Club:* United Service.

**HORROX, Lewis;** Professor of English Language and Literature, University of Exeter, 1924-61; *b* 27 April 1898; *s* of William Horrox, architect, and Annie Lewis; *m* 1920, Gladys Maud Cawston; one *d. Educ:* Caius Coll., Cambridge (scholar); Christopher James Research Studentship, 1920-23. Supervisor in English Studies at Caius Coll., and Lecturer for the English Tripos at Cambridge, 1920-24. *Publication:* Edition of Milton's Comus, etc, 1927. *Recreation:* walking. *Address:* 5 St James' Terrace, Winchester, Hants.

**HORSBRUGH-PORTER, Sir Andrew (Marshall),** 3rd Bt, *cr* 1902; DSO 1940; Col retired, 1953; *b* 1 June 1907; *s* of Sir John Horsbrugh-Porter, 2nd Bt, and Elaine Maud, *y d* of Thomas Jefferies; *S* father, 1953; *m* 1933, Annette Mary, *d* of late Brig.-Gen. R. C. Browne-Clayton, DSO, Browne's Hill, Carlow; one *s* two *d. Educ:* Winchester; RMC, Sandhurst. Subaltern 12th Royal Lancers, 1927; Capt., 1937; Acting Major, Sept. 1939; Temp. Major, Dec. 1939; Major, 1944; Lieut-Col, 1949. Served War of 1939-45 (DSO and Bar); commanded 27th Lancers, 1941-45; GSO1, Liaison attached to US Army, 1947; commanded 12th Royal Lancers, 1948-52; Military Adviser to UK High Commissioner, New Delhi, 1952. *Recreations:* polo and hunting. *Heir: s* John Simon Horsbrugh-Porter [*b* 18 Dec. 1938; *m* 1964, Lavinia Rose, *d* of Ralph Turton, Kildale Hall, Whitby, Yorks; two *d*]. *Address:* Manor Farm House, Salford, Chipping Norton, Oxon. *Club:* Cavalry.
*See also Sir J. D. Barlow, Bt.*

**HORSEFIELD, John Keith,** CB 1957; Historian, International Monetary Fund, 1966-69; *b* 14 Oct. 1901; *s* of Rev. Canon F. J. Horsefield, Bristol; *m* 1934, Lucy G. G. Florance. *Educ:* Monkton Combe Sch.; University of Bristol (MA 1948); London Sch. of Economics. Lecturer, LSE, 1939; Min. of Aircraft Production, 1940; International Monetary Fund, 1947; Under-Sec., Min. of Supply, 1951; Dep. Asst Sec.-Gen. for Economics and Finance, NATO, 1952; Supply and Development Officer, Iron and Steel Bd, 1954; Dir of Finance and Accounts, Gen. Post Office, 1955-60; Chief Editor, International Monetary Fund, 1960-66. *Publications:* The Real Cost of the War, 1940; British Monetary Experiments, 1650-1710, 1960; articles in Economica, etc. *Address:* 37 Clatterford Road, Carisbrooke, Newport, Isle of Wight.

**HORSFALL, Geoffrey Jonas,** CBE 1967; Judge of the Grand Court of the Cayman Islands, West Indies; *b* 22 Jan. 1905; *s* of late Major A. H. Horsfall, DSO, TD, Newcastle, NSW, Australia; *m* 1947, Robin, *y d* of late Curwin Maclure, Albury, NSW; one *s* two *d. Educ:* The King's Sch., Parramatta, NSW; Cheltenham Coll.; Keble Coll., Oxford. BA 1927; Barrister-at-Law, 1928, Gray's Inn; South-Eastern Circuit. Entered Colonial Legal Service, 1936, as Crown Counsel, Nigeria; Crown Counsel, Sierra Leone, 1943; Senior Magistrate, Fiji, 1947; Judicial Commissioner, British Solomon Islands Protectorate, 1953; Judge of the High Court, Zanzibar, 1958; Chief Justice of Zanzibar, retd 1964. *Recreations:* golf and gardening. *Address:* c/o Australia and New Zealand Bank Ltd, 71 Cornhill, EC3; Cayman Islands, West Indies.

**HORSFALL, Sir (John) Donald,** 2nd Bt, *cr* 1909; JP West Riding of Yorks; *b* 1 June 1891; *s* of Sir John Cousin Horsfall, 1st Bt of Hayfield, Crosshills, near Keighley; *S* father, 1920; *m* 1914, Henrietta (*d* 1936), *d* of W. Musgrave of Otley; three *s*; *m* 1953, Gladys, *widow* of Percy Taylor, Knowle Spring House, Keighley. *Educ:* Uppingham. Chairman: John C. Horsfall & Sons Ltd, Worsted Spinners, Glusburn, near Keighley; Underwriter at Lloyd's; Director: Halifax Building Soc., and others; Chm. Skipton Conservative Assoc., 1924-37; High Sheriff, Yorks, 1927-28. *Recreations:* shooting, golf, racing. *Heir: s* Major John Musgrave Horsfall, MC, TD, JP, 6th Bn Duke of Wellington's Regt [*b* 26 Aug. 1915; *m* 1940, Cassandra Nora Bernardine, *d* of late George Wright, Brinkworth Hall, Elvington, York; two *s* one *d*]. *Address:* Craiglands Hotel, Ilkley, Yorks. *Club:* Portland.

**HORSFALL TURNER, Harold;** Secretary-General, The Law Society, since 1969; *b* 1 June 1909; *s* of Stanley Horsfall Turner, Reader in Economics, Aberdeen University; *m* 1937, Eileen Mary Jenkins; two *s. Educ:* Rossall; The Queen's Coll., Oxford; Birmingham Univ. BA Oxford 1932, BCL Oxford 1934, LLB Birmingham 1935. Admitted Solicitor (with 1st Class Hons) 1936. Asst Solicitor, Dudley Corporation, 1936; Legal Asst, Inland Revenue, 1937; Sen. Legal Asst, Min. of National Insurance, 1945; Under-Sec., The Law Society, 1947; Second Secretary-Gen., The Law Society, 1964. *Recreations:* boating, opera, photography. *Address:* 42 Deansway, East Finchley, N2. *T:* 01-883 5605. *Club:* Garrick.

**HORSFIELD, Maj.-Gen. David Ralph,** OBE 1962; Chief Signal Officer, HQ British Army of the Rhine; Director, Rollalong Ltd; *b* 17 Dec. 1916; *s* of late Major Ralph B. Horsfield and Morah Horsfield (*née* Baynes); *m* 1948, Sheelah Patricia Royal Eagan; two *s* two *d. Educ:* Oundle Sch.; RMA Woolwich; Cambridge Univ. (MA). Commnd in Royal Signals, 1936; comd Burma Corps Signals, 1942; Instr, Staff Coll., 1944-45; comd 2 Indian Airborne Signals, 1946-47; Instr, RMA Sandhurst, 1950-53; comd 2 Signal Regt, 1956-59; Principal Army Staff Officer, MoD, Malaya, 1959-61; Dir of Telecommunications (Army), 1966-68; ADC to the Queen, 1968-69; Deputy Communications and Electronics, Supreme HQ Allied Powers, Europe, 1968-69. *Recreations:* ski-ing, the visual arts. *Address:* HQ British Army of the Rhine, BFPO 40; Southill House, Cranmore, Shepton Mallet, Somerset. *T:* Cranmore 395. *Club:* Ski Club of Great Britain.

**HORSFIELD, Brig. Herbert Eric,** CBE 1943; MC (2 Bars); *b* 23 Aug. 1895; *s* of H. Horsfield; *m* 1924, Harriet Beatrice Mills; one *s* one *d. Educ:* Bradfield Coll., Berks; Royal Military Academy, Woolwich. Commissioned RE 1914; France and Flanders, 1915-19; India, Royal Bombay Sappers and Miners, 1920-30; Military Engineer Services, 1930-36; Aldershot, DCRE 1936-37; India, RB Sappers and Miners, 1937-38; Commandant RB Sappers and Miners, 1938-42; Chief Engineer, Eastern Army, 1942-43; Chief Engineer, 14th Army, 1943-44; Chief Engineer, Southern Army, 1945-46; Commandant RE Depot, 1946; Comdr Engineer Stores Group, Long Marston; retired, 1948. John Mowlem & Co. Ltd, 1948-70. Councillor, Bognor Regis UDC, 1960-67 (Chm., 1964-65 and 1965-66). FRSA 1948-70. *Address:* St Julians, 34 Cross Bush Road, Felpham, Sussex. *T:* Middleton 2057. *Club:* Naval and Military.

**HORSFORD, Maj.-Gen. Derek Gordon Thomond,** CBE 1962 (MBE 1953); DSO 1944 and Bar 1945; Major-General, Brigade of Gurkhas, since 1969; Deputy Commander Land Forces, Hong Kong, since 1970; *b* 7 Feb. 1917; *s* of late Captain H. T. Horsford, The Gloucestershire Regt, and Mrs V. E. Horsford, Bexhill-on-Sea; *m* 1948, Sheila Louise Russell Crawford; one *s* (and one step *s* two step *d*). *Educ:* Clifton Coll.; RMC, Sandhurst. Commissioned into 8th Gurkha Rifles, 1937; comd 4/1 Gurkha Rifles, Burma, 1944-45; transf. to RA, 1948; Instructor Staff Coll., 1950-52; transf. to King's Regt, 1950; GSO1, 2nd Infantry Div., 1955-56; comd 1st Bn, The King's Regt, 1957-59; AAG, AG2, War Office, 1959-60; Comdr 24th Infantry Brigade Group, Dec. 1960-Dec. 1962; Imperial Defence Coll., 1963; Brig., Gen. Staff, HQ, BAOR, 1964-66. Maj.-Gen. 1966; GOC: 50 (Northumbrian) Div./Dist, 1966-67; Yorks Dist, 1967-68; 17 Div./Malaya District, 1969-70. Col, The King's Regt, 1965-70. *Recreations:* golf, tennis, sailing. *Address:* c/o Lloyds Bank Ltd, Cox's & King's Branch, 6 Pall Mall, SW1. *Club:* Army and Navy.

**HORSHAM, Suffragan Bishop of,** since 1968; **Rt. Rev. Simon Wilton Phipps,** MC 1945; *b* 6 July 1921; *s* of late Captain William Duncan Phipps, CVO, RN, and Pamela May Ross; single. *Educ:* Eton; Trinity Coll., Cambridge; Westcott House, Cambridge. Joined Coldstream Guards, 1940; commnd, 1941; Capt., 1944; ADC to GOC-in-C Northern Comd India, Nov. 1945; Mil. Asst to Adjt Gen. to the Forces, War Office, 1946; Major, 1946. BA (History) Cantab., 1948; Pres., Cambridge Univ. Footlights Club, 1949. Ordained, 1950. Asst Curate, Huddersfield Parish Church, 1950; Chaplain, Trinity Coll., Cambridge, 1953; Industrial Chaplain, Coventry Dio., 1958; Hon. Canon, Coventry Cath., 1965. *Publication:* God on Monday, 1966. *Recreations:* walking, cooking. *Address:* The Old Rectory, Worth, Crawley, Sussex.

**HORSLEY, Air Vice-Marshal (Beresford) Peter (Torrington),** CBE 1964; MVO 1956; AFC 1945; psa; pfc; Assistant Chief of the Air Staff (Operations), since 1968; *b* 26 March 1921; *s* of late Capt. Arthur Beresford Horsley, CBE; *m* 1943, Phyllis Conrad Phinney; one *s*. one *d*. *Educ:* Wellington Coll. Joined Royal Air Force, 1940; served in 2nd TAF and Fighter Command. Adjt Oxford Univ. Air Sqdn, 1948; Commands: No 9 and No 29 Sqdns, RAF Wattisham, RAF Akrotiri. Equerry to Princess Elizabeth and to the Duke of Edinburgh, 1949-52; Equerry to the Queen, 1952-53; Equerry to the Duke of Edinburgh, 1953-56. Dep. Comdt, Jt Warfare Establishment, RAF Old Sarum, 1966-68. Croix de Guerre, 1944. Holds Orders of Christ (Portugal), North Star (Sweden), and Menelik (Ethiopia). *Recreations:* ski-ing, philately. *Address:* c/o Barclays Bank Ltd, High Street, Newmarket.

**HORSLEY, Colin,** OBE 1963; Hon. ARCM; Pianist; Professor, Royal College of Music, London, and Royal Manchester College of Music; *b* Wanganui, New Zealand, 23 April 1920. *Educ:* Royal College of Music. Debut at invitation of Sir John Barbirolli at Hallé Concerts, Manchester, 1943. Soloist with all leading orchestras of Great Britain, the Royal Philharmonic Soc. (1953, 1959), Promenade Concerts, etc. Toured Belgium, Holland, Spain, France, Scandinavia, Malta, Ceylon, Malaya, Australia and New Zealand. Festival appearances include Aix-en-Provence, International Contemporary Music Festival, Palermo, British Music Festivals in Belgium, Holland and Finland. Broadcasts frequently, and records for His Master's Voice. *Recreation:* gardening. *Address:* Tawsden Manor, Brenchley, Kent. *T:* Brenchley 2323.

**HORSLEY, Air Commodore Peter;** *see* Horsley, B. P. T.

**HORSTEAD, Rt. Rev. James Lawrence Cecil,** CMG 1962; CBE 1956; DD (Hon.) 1956; Assistant Bishop in Diocese of Leicester and Hon. Canon of Leicester Cathedral since 1962; *b* 16 Feb. 1898; *s* of James William and Mary Leah Horstead; *m* 1926, Olive Davidson; no *c*. *Educ:* Christ's Hosp.; University and St John's Coll., Durham (Mathematical Scholar, Lightfoot Scholar). BA 2nd Cl. Maths Hons 1921; Theol. Hons 1923; MA 1924; Deacon, 1923; Priest, 1924; Curate St Margaret's Church, Durham, 1923-26; Sec. for Durham Student Christian Movement, 1923-26; Principal Fourah Bay Coll., 1926-36; Canon Missioner Diocese of Sierra Leone, 1928-36; Sec. Church Missionary Soc., Sierra Leone, 1926-36; Bishop of Sierra Leone, 1936-61; Archbishop of West Africa, 1955-61; Rector of Appleby Magna, 1962-68. *Publication:* Co-operation with Africans, International Review of Missions, April 1935. *Address:* 44 Ribble Drive, Barrow-upon-Soar, Loughborough, Leics.

**HORT, Sir James Fenton,** 8th Bt *cr* 1767; *b* 6 Sept. 1926; *s* of Sir Fenton George Hort, 7th Bt, and Gwendolene, *d* of late Sir Walter Alcock, MVO; *S* father 1960; *m* 1951, Joan, *d* of late Edward Peat, Swallownest, Sheffield; two *s* two *d*. *Educ:* Marlborough; Trinity Coll., Cambridge. MA, MB, BCh, Cambridge, 1950. *Recreation:* fishing. *Heir:* *s* Andrew Edwin Fenton Hort, *b* 15 Nov. 1954. *Address:* 40 Walter Street, Takapuna, Auckland 9, NZ.

**HORTON, Maj.-Gen. Frank Cyril,** CB 1957; OBE 1953; RM; *b* 31 May 1907; *s* of late Lieut-Comdr F. Horton, Royal Navy, and late Emma M. Hopper; *m* 1934, Jennie Ellaline Hammond: one *d*. *Educ:* Sir Roger Manwood's Sch. 2nd Lieut RM 1925; Lieut RM 1928; HMS Cumberland, China Station, 1928-29; HMS Royal Oak, Mediterranean Station, 1929-31; Captain RM, 1936; HMS Ajax, America and West Indies Station, 1936-37; psc 1941; Actg Lieut-Col 1942; GSO1, Staff of Chief of Combined Operations, 1942-43; Comdg Officer, 44 (RM) Commando, SE Asia, 1943-44; Directing Staff, Army Staff Coll., 1945-46; Plans Div., Admiralty, 1946-48; Directing Staff, Jt Services Staff Coll., 1948-51; Comdt, Amphibious Sch., RM, 1951-52; idc 1953; Col GS, Staff of Comdt Gen., RM, 1954; Chief of Staff to Commandant Gen. Royal Marines, 1955-58; Maj. 1946; Lieut-Col 1949, Col 1953; Maj.-Gen. 1955; retired, 1958. County Civil Defence Officer, Essex, 1959; Regional Dir of Civil Defence, S Eastern Region, 1961-68. *Address:* Southland, Florance Lane, Groombridge, Sussex. *T:* Groombridge 355. *Clubs:* United Service; Royal Naval (Portsmouth).

**HORTON, Lt-Col W(illiam) Gray,** MC 1917; Scots Guards, retired; Director, Rust Engineering Ltd; Senior Partner, Gray Horton Products; *b* 24 Aug. 1897; *s* of William S. and Lottie Gray Horton, New York; *m* 1st, 1930, Gwendolen Anna Le Bas (*d* 1944); one *s* one *d*; 2nd, 1949, Baroness Tornaco, Brussels. *Educ:* Harrow; RMC, Sandhurst (joined, 1916, when still an American citizen). Served European War, 1st Bn Scots Guards, 1917 (wounded, MC). Adjutant 1st Bn, 1926. Joined Le Bas Group of businesses, 1932; re-joined regt, July 1939. Served War of 1939-45: Eastern Comd, 1939; special service, France, 1940; comdg 70th Bn E Surrey Regt, 1941; formed and commanded Fighter Comd Battle Sch., 1943; commanded RAF Regt 85 gp, 1944, in England, Normandy, Belgium and Germany; GSO1, Berlin Air Comd, 1945 (despatches, 1946). One of Comdrs of Gold Staff Officers at Coronation; Coronation Medal, 1953. Inventor of Graphdex and Project Activating Signal Systems which are initiating a new science of Business Control; Co-inventor of lever type of tubular scaffold coupler. Mem. of Lloyd's; Mem., Worshipful Co. of Ironmongers. *Publication:* Data Display Systems, 1969. *Recreations:* hunting, winter sports (rep. Gt Britain, bobsleigh driver, Olympic games, Chamonix, 1924), cricket. *Address:* 22 Bruton Street, W1. *T:* 01-629 3716; 16 Roebuck House, SW1. *T:* 01-828 9216. *Clubs:* White's, Guards, MCC, All England Lawn Tennis.

**HORTON-SMITH-HARTLEY, P. H. G.;** *see* Hartley, P. H. G. H. S.

**HORWILL, Sir Lionel Clifford,** Kt, *cr* 1947; *b* 19 Sept. 1890; *s* of Frank James Horwill, Stoke, Devonport; *m* 1934, Dr Vera Merrick Walker, Edinburgh; one *s* one *d. Educ:* Royal Dockyard Sch., Devonport; Plymouth Technical Sch., Plymouth; Royal College of Science, London; Wadham Coll., Oxford. Entered Indian Civil Service, 1914; Indian Army Reserve of Officers, 1916-19, serving in India and Mesopotamia. Administrative posts of ICS, 1920-25; District and Sessions Judge in various parts of Southern India, 1925-36; Acting Judge, High Court, Madras, 1936; Judge, High Court, Madras, 1940-50, retired, 1950. *Recreation:* walking. *Address:* 220 Middleborough Road, Blackburn South, Victoria 3130, Australia. *T:* 890381. *Club:* Madras.

**HORWOOD, Prof. Owen Pieter Faure;** Member of South African Senate, since 1970; Principal and Vice-Chancellor, University of Natal, 1966-70 (William Hudson Prof. of Economics, 1957-65, and Director of University's Natal Regional Survey); *b* 6 Dec. 1916; *e s* of late Stanley Ebden Horwood and of Anna Johanna Horwood (*née* Faure); *m* 1946, Helen Mary Watt; one *s* one *d. Educ:* Boys' High Sch., Paarl, CP; University of Cape Town (BCom). South African Air Force, 1940-42. Associate Prof. of Commerce, University of Cape Town, 1954-55; Prof. of Economics, University Coll. of Rhodesia and Nyasaland, 1956-57. Director: Netherlands Bank of South Africa Ltd; Rembrandt Tobacco Corp. SA Ltd; Nat. Building Soc.; Trans-Natal Coal Corp.; Bonus Investment Corp. of S Africa; Netherlands INsurance Co. of SA Ltd. Financial Adviser to Govt of Lesotho, 1966-. *Publications:* (jtly) Economic Systems of the Commonwealth, 1962; contribs to SA Jl of Economics, SA Bankers' Jl, Economica (London), Optima, etc. *Recreations:* cricket, gardening, sailing. *Address:* Chartwell, 37 Ridge Road, Durban, South Africa. *T:* Durban 886976. *Clubs:* Durban (Durban); Kloof Country (Natal); Ruwa Country (Rhodesia); Western Province Cricket; Cape Town Cricket (Captain 1943-48).

**HOSFORD, John Percival,** MS, FRCS; retired; Surgeon, Lecturer on Surgery, St Bartholomew's Hospital (1936-60); Surgeon, King Edward VII Hospital for Officers and Florence Nightingale Hospital; Consulting Surgeon to Hospitals at Watford, Leatherhead, Hitchin, St Albans and to the Foundling Hospital and Reedham Orphanage; *b* 24 July 1900; 2nd *s* of Dr B. Hosford, Highgate; *m* 1932, Millicent Sacheverell Violet Sybil Claud, *d* of late Brig.-Gen. C. Vaughan Edwards, CMG, DSO; one *s* one *d. Educ:* Highgate Sch.; St Bartholomew's Hosp. MB, BS (London) 1922; FRCS Eng. 1925; MS (London); University Gold Medal, 1925. Formerly Registrar St Bartholomew's Hosp. and of Royal National Orthopædic Hosp. Hunterian Prof., Royal College of Surgeons, 1932. Retired, Oct. 1960. Formerly: Mem. of Court of Examiners of Royal College of Surgeons; Examiner in Surgery at Universities of Oxford, London, Sheffield, Belfast; Fellow Assoc. of Surgeons (on Council) and Royal Society Med. *Publications:* numerous articles in medical and surgical journals and encyclopædias. *Recreations:* viniculture and gardening. *Address:* Carril, Reguengo, Portalegre, Portugal.

**HOSIE, James Findlay,** OBE 1955; a Director, Science Research Council, since 1965; *b* 22 Aug. 1913; *m* 1951, Barbara Mary Mansell. *Educ:* Glasgow Univ. (MA Hons); St John's Coll., Cambridge (BA). Indian Civil Service, 1938-47; Principal, 1947-56, Asst Sec., 1956-58, Min. of Defence, London; Asst Sec. QMGF, War Office, 1958-61; Office of Minister for Science, later Dept of Educn. and Science, 1961-65. *Recreations:* bird-watching, gardening. *Address:* Beeches, Broomfield Park, Westcott, Surrey. *T:* Dorking 5535.

**HOSKING, Eric;** photographer, ornithologist, broadcaster; *b* 2 Oct. 1909; 3rd *s* of late Albert Hosking and Margaret Helen, *d* of William Steggall; *m* 1939, Dorothy, *d* of late Harry Sleigh; two *s* one *d. Educ:* Stationers' Company's Sch. London, N8. Hon. Fellow, Royal Photographic Society; a Vice-Pres., Royal Society for the Protection of Birds; Hon. Vice-Pres., London Natural History Soc.; a Vice-Pres., British Naturalists' Assoc.; Vice-President: Nature Photographic Society; British Ornithologists' Union; Chm., Photographic Advisory Cttee to Nature Conservancy. Scientific Fellow of Zoological Society. Exhibited at Royal Photographic Society, 1932- (Council, 1950-56; Fellowship & Associateship Admissions Cttee, 1951-56 and 1960-65); Member: BOU, 1935-; Brit. Trust for Ornithology, 1938-; Cornell Laboratory of Ornithology, America, 1961-. Dir of Photography to Coto Doñana Expedn, Spain, 1956 and 1957; Leader of Cazoria Valley Expedition, Spain, 1959; Dir of Photography, British Ornithologists' Expedition to Bulgaria, 1960, to Hungary, 1961, Mountfort-Jordan Expedition, 1963; British-Jordan Expedition, 1965; Pakistan Expedition, 1966; World Wildlife Fund Pakistan Expedition, 1967; Lindglad Galapagos Is Expedn, 1970. Photographic Editor: of New Naturalist, 1942-; of British Birds, 1960-. RGS Cherry Kearton Award, 1968. *Publications:* Intimate Sketches from Bird Life, 1940; The Art of Bird Photography, 1944; Birds of the Day, 1944; Birds of the Night, 1945; More Birds of the Day, 1946; The Swallow, 1946; Masterpieces of Bird Photography, 1947; Birds in Action, 1949; Birds Fighting, 1955; Bird Photography as a Hobby, 1961; Nesting Birds, Eggs and Fledglings, 1967; An Eye for a Bird, 1970. Illustrator of many books on natural history, by photographs. *Address:* 20 Crouch Hall Road, N8. *T:* 01-340 7703.

**HOSKINS, Sir Cecil (Harold),** Kt 1960; retired; *b* 11 Nov. 1899; *m* 1913, Dorothy Gwynn Loveridge; four *s* two *d. Educ:* Newington Coll., Sydney. Formerly: Ironmaster; Chm. Australian Mutual Provident Soc., Sydney. *Recreations:* motoring, gardening. *Address:* Cardrona, Moss Vale, NSW, Australia. *T:* Moss Vale 42. *Clubs:* Union, Elanora, Kensington (Sydney); Australian (Melbourne).

**HOSKINS, William George,** FBA 1969; MA, PhD; *b* Exeter, 22 May 1908; *e s* of late William George Hoskins and Alice Beatrice Dymond; *m* 1933, Frances Jackson; one *s* one *d. Educ:* Hele's Sch., Exeter; University Coll., Exeter. Lectr in Economics, University Coll., Leicester, 1931-41; 1946-48; Central Price Regulation Cttee, 1941-45; Reader in English Local History, University Coll. (now Univ.) of

Leicester, 1948-51; Reader in Econ. Hist., University of Oxford, 1951-65; Hatton Prof. of English History, University of Leicester, 1965-68, retired in despair, 1968; Emeritus Professor, 1968. Mem. Royal Commission on Common Land, 1955-58; Adv. Cttee on Bldgs of Special Architectural and Historical Interest (Min. of Housing and Local Govt), 1955-64; Vice-Pres. Leicestershire Archæol and Hist. Soc., 1952; Pres. Dartmoor Preserv. Assoc., 1962; Leverhulme Res. Fellow, 1961-63; Leverhulme Emeritus Fellowship, 1970-71. *Publications:* Industry, Trade and People in Exeter, 1935; Heritage of Leicestershire, 1946; Midland England, 1949; Essays in Leicestershire History, 1950; Chilterns to Black Country, 1951; East Midlands and the Peak, 1951; Devonshire Studies, (with H. P. R. Finberg), 1952; Devon (New Survey of England), 1954; The Making of the English Landscape, 1955; The Midland Peasant, 1957; The Leicestershire Landscape, 1957; Exeter in the Seventeeth Century, 1957; Local History in England, 1959; Devon and its People, 1959; Two Thousand Years in Exeter, 1960; The Westward Expansion of Wessex, 1960; Shell Guide to Rutland, 1963; The Common Lands of England and Wales (with L. Dudley Stamp), 1963; Provincial England, 1963; Old Devon, 1966; Fieldwork in Local History, 1967; Shell Guide to Leicestershire, 1970; History from the Farm, 1970. Numerous essays and papers in Quarterly Review, Past and Present, Agric. Hist. Review, The Listener, etc. *Recreation:* parochial explorations. *Address:* 2 Lyndhurst Road, Exeter. *T:* 56604.

**HOSKYNS, Sir Benedict (Leigh),** 16th Bt, *cr* 1676; *b* 27 May 1928; *s* of Rev. Sir Edwyn Clement Hoskyns, 13th Bt, MC, DD and Mary Trym, *d* of Edwin Budden, Macclesfield; *S* brother 1956; *m* 1953, Ann Wilkinson; two *s* two *d*. *Educ:* Haileybury; Corpus Christi Coll., Cambridge; London Hospital. BA Cantab 1949; MB, BChir Cantab 1952. House Officer at the London Hospital, 1953. RAMC, 1953-56. House Officer at Royal Surrey County Hospital and General Lying-In Hospital, York Road, SE1, 1957-58; DObstRCOG 1958; in general practice, 1958-. *Heir: s* Edwyn Wren Hoskyns, *b* 4 Feb. 1956. *Address:* Harewood, Great Oakley, Essex. *T:* Ramsey 341.

**HOSKYNS-ABRAHALL, Rt. Rev. A. L. E.;** *see* Lancaster, Suffragan Bishop of.

**HOSKYNS-ABRAHALL, Sir (Theo) Chandos,** Kt, *cr* 1950; CMG 1942; *b* 17 Dec. 1896; *o s* of Chandos William Hoskyns-Abrahall, MRCS, LRCP; *m* 1925, Clare Constance Drury; two *s* one *d*; *m* 1944, Lois Jennet Ogle. *Educ:* Epsom Coll. Served European War, 1915-20, Capt., London Regt in France, Salonika, and Palestine; Administrative Officer, Nigeria, 1921; Senior District Officer, 1936; Resident, 1937; Deputy Chief Sec., 1939; Acting Chief Sec., Nigeria, and Governor's deputy, various occasions, 1939 onwards; Chief Commissioner, Western Provinces, Nigeria, 1946-51; Lieut Governor, Western Region, 1951-52. Officer Legion of Honour, 1950. *Recreation:* painting (various one-man exhibitions London and elsewhere). *Address:* 6 The Green, Colne Engaine, Colchester, Essex. *T:* Earls Colne 770.

**HOTBLACK, Maj.-Gen. Frederick Elliot,** DSO 1917, MC; late Royal Tank Corps; *b* 1887; *s* of F. M. Hotblack, Norwich. Served European War, 1914-18 (DSO and bar, MC and bar, Legion of Honour, Order of St Anne, five times wounded); Brigade Major, 1st Rhine Brigade, 1921; General Staff Officer, War Office, 1927; Instructor Staff Coll., Camberley, 1932-35; Military Attaché, British Embassy, Berlin, 1935-37; General Staff, War Office, 1937-39; General Staff BEF Sept. 1939; Commander Division, 1939-40; ADC to the King, 1939; retired pay, 1941. Mem. Royal Tank Regimental Assoc. *Club:* Royal Automobile.

**HOTCHIN, Sir Claude,** Kt 1967; OBE 1952; JP; Company Director and Grazier, Western Australia; Art Patron and Philanthropist since 1916; *b* 7 March 1898; *s* of John Robert Hotchin and Bertha Mary Hotchin (*née* Brown); *m* 1925, Doris May Clarkson; one *d*. *Educ:* Quorn and Broken Hill Public Schs; Hayward's Coll., Adelaide. District Comr, Boy Scouts, 1931-35; Foundation Mem., WA Soc. for Crippled Children, 1938 (Hon. Mem., 1954-); Member: Bd of Trustees, Public Library, Museum and Art, Gallery, of WA, 1948-60; Board of Western Australian Art Gallery, 1960-65 (also first Chm.); Senate, University of WA, 1951-69. Chm., Commonwealth Australia Jubilee Art Cttee for Western Australia, 1951. Chm., Friends of Royal Perth Hosp., 1969-. *Recreations:* golf, swimming, motoring, gardening. *Address:* Chartwell, Great Eastern Highway, Mundaring, Western Australia 6073. *T:* 95-1076. *Clubs:* Western Australian, Perth Rotary (Hon. Sec., 1931-34; Pres., 1935-36) (Perth, WA); Albany, Albany Racing (WA).

**HOTHAM,** family name of **Baron Hotham.**

**HOTHAM,** 8th Baron, *cr* 1797; **Henry Durand Hotham;** Bt 1621; *b* 3 May 1940; *s* of 7th Baron Hotham, CBE, and Lady Letitia Sibell Winifred Cecil, *er d* of 5th Marquess of Exeter, KG; *S* father, 1967. *Educ:* Eton; Cirencester Agricultural Coll. Late Lieut, Grenadier Guards; ADC to Governor of Tasmania, 1963-66. *Heir: b* Hon. Peter William Hotham, *b* 10 March 1944. *Address:* Dalton Hall, Dalton Holme, Beverley, Yorks; Scorborough Hall, Driffield, Yorks.

**HOTHFIELD,** 4th Baron, *cr* 1881; **Thomas Sackville Tufton;** Bt 1851; *b* 20 July 1916; *s* of Hon. Sackville Philip Tufton (*d* 1936; 2nd *s* of 1st Baron), and Winifred Mary Ripley Dalton (*d* 1970); *S* cousin, 1961. *Educ:* Eton; Cambridge Univ. *Heir: cousin* Lieut-Col George William Anthony Tufton, TD [*b* 28 Oct. 1904; *m* 1936, Evelyn Margarette Mordaunt; two *s* one *d*]. *Address:* 4 St Augustine's Road, Canterbury, Kent.

**HOTSON, Leslie,** LittD (Cambridge); FRSL; Shakespearean scholar and writer; *b* Delhi, Ont, Canada, 16 Aug. 1897; *s* of John H. and Lillie S. Hotson; *m* 1919, Mary May, *d* of Frederick W. Peabody. *Educ:* Harvard Univ. Sheldon Travelling Fellow, Harvard, 1923-24; Sterling Research Fellow, Yale, 1926-27; Associate Prof. of English, New York Univ., 1927-29; Guggenheim Memorial Fellow, 1929-31; Prof. of English, Haverford Coll., Pa, 1931-41; served War of 1939-45, 1st Lieut and Capt. Signal Corps, US Army, 1943-46; Fulbright Exchange Scholar, Bedford Coll., London, 1949-50; Research Associate, Yale, 1953; Fellow, King's Coll., Cambridge, 1954-60. *Publications:* The Death of Christopher Marlowe, 1925; The Commonwealth and Restoration Stage, 1928; Shelley's Lost Letters to Harriet, 1930; Shakespeare versus Shallow, 1931; I, William Shakespeare, 1937; Shakespeare's Sonnets Dated, 1949; Shakespeare's Motley, 1952; Queen Elizabeth's Entertainment at Mitcham, 1953; The First Night of Twelfth Night, 1954; Shakespeare's Wooden O, 1959; Mr W. H., 1964. *Recreation:* boating. *Address:* Northford, Conn 06472, USA.

**HOTTER, Hans;** opera and concert singer; producer; *b* Offenbach, Germany; *m* 1936, Helga Fischer; one *s* one *d*. *Educ:* Munich. Concert career began in 1929 and opera career in 1930. Mem. of Munich, Vienna and Hamburg State Operas; guest singer in opera and concerts in all major cities of Europe and USA; concert tours in Australia; for the past 10 years, connected with Columbia Gramophone Co., England; guest singer, Covent Garden Opera, London, 1947-. Festivals: Salzburg, Edinburgh and Bayreuth. *Address:* Emil Dittlerstrasse 26, München-Solin, West Germany.

**HOUBLON, Mrs Doreen A.;** *see* Archer Houblon.

**HOUCHEN, Harry Owen,** FIMechE; Member of Board, Transportation Systems & Market Research Ltd; *b* 24 Sept. 1907; *s* of late Henry Houchen and Eliza Katherine, *d* of Burgoyne Owen; *m* 1935, Beatrix Elizabeth (*née* Ellett); one *s* one *d*. *Educ:* Canterbury Coll.; University of New Zealand. BE (Civil) 1932. From 1933 concerned with Transport and Civil Aviation, holding overseas appointments. Dir of Current Ops, BOAC, 1956; Man. Dir, Brookhirst Igranic Ltd, 1958; joined BTC as Gen. Man., BR Workshops, 1962; Member BR Bd for Mech. and Electr. Engrg and Workshops, 1964-69; Industrial Consultant, 1969-70. Order of Merit (1st cl.), Syria, 1956; Gold Medal of Merit, Lebanon, 1956. AFRAeS 1936; MIMechE 1964. *Recreations:* travelling, yachting. *Address:* 19 Laxford House, Cundy Street, SW1. *T:* 01-730 4415. *Club:* United Service.

**HOUGH, Prof. Graham Goulder;** Praelector and Fellow of Darwin College, Cambridge, since 1964; Professor of English since 1966 (University Reader in English, 1965-66); *b* 14 Feb. 1908; *s* of Joseph and Clara Hough; *m* 1st, 1942, Rosamund Oswell; one *s* one *d*; 2nd, 1952, Ingeborg Neumann. *Educ:* Prescot Grammar Sch.; University of Liverpool; Queens' Coll., Cambridge. Lecturer in English, Raffles Coll., Singapore, 1930. Served War of 1939-45, with Singapore Royal Artillery (Volunteer), 1942-45. Professor of English, University of Malaya, 1946; Visiting Lecturer, Johns Hopkins Univ., 1950; Fellow of Christ's Coll., Cambridge, 1950 (Tutor, 1955-60); Visiting Prof. Cornell University, 1958. Hon. DLitt, Malaya, 1955; LittD, Cambridge, 1961. *Publications:* The Last Romantics, 1949; The Romantic Poets, 1953; The Dark Sun, 1957; Image and Experience, 1960; Legends and Pastorals, 1961; A Preface to the Faerie Queene, 1962; The Dream and the Task, 1963; An Essay on Criticism, 1966; Style and Stylistics, 1969. *Recreation:* travel. *Address:* The White Cottage, Grantchester, Cambridge. *T:* Trumpington 2227. *Club:* Oxford and Cambridge.

**HOUGH, Rev. Lynn Harold,** AB, BD, DD; LHD Vermont, 1932; ThD; LittD; LLD Pittsburgh; JUD, Boston; Dean of Drew Theological Seminary, 1934-47, and Professor of Homiletics and the Christian Criticism of Life, 1930-47; *b* 10 Sept. 1877; *s* of Franklin M. Hough and Eunice R. Giles; *m* 1936, Blanche, *widow* of Stephen Van R. Trowbridge, *d* of late Byron Horton. *Educ:* Scio Coll.; Drew Theological Seminary. For 16 years was the Pastor of Methodist Churches in New Jersey, New York, and Maryland; Prof. of Historical Theology in Garrett Biblical Institute, 1914-19; sent to Great Britain by Lindgren Foundation of Northwestern Univ. to interpret America and the moral and spiritual aims of the War, 1918; preaching and speaking in Gt Britain at invitation of Ministry of Information, 1942; Merrick Lecturer, Ohio Wesleyan Univ., 1923; Cole Lecturer at Vanderbilt Univ., 1919-20; Pres. Northwestern Univ., USA, 1919-20; Pastor, Central Methodist Episcopal Church, Detroit, 1920-28; Pres., Detroit Council of Churches, 1926-28; Minister, American Presbyterian Church, United Church of Canada, 1928-30; Pres. of the Religious Education Council of Canada, 1929-30; Samuel Harris Lecturer, Bangor Theological Seminary, 1930; Ayer Lecturer, Colgate-Rochester Divinity Sch., 1930; Sam P. Jones Lecturer at Emory Univ., 1935; Fred J. Cato Lecturer, General Conference of Methodist Church of Australasia, Brisbane, 1941; Easter Lecturer, Bexley Hall, Kenyon Coll., 1945; Southwestern Lecturer, Southwestern Univ., 1945; Chancellor's Lecturer at Queen's Univ., Kingston, Ont., Christian Humanism and the Modern World; Pres. of the Assoc. of Methodist Theological Schs, USA, 1942; Mem. Exec. Cttee Federal Council of Churches of Christ in America, 1936-48. *Publications:* Athanasius the Hero; The Lure of Books; The Theology of a Preacher; The Men of the Gospels; The Quest for Wonder; The Man of Power; The Clean Sword; The Productive Beliefs; Flying over London; The Eyes of Faith; The Opinions of John Clearfield, 1921; Life and History; A Little Book of Sermons, 1922; Synthetic Christianity (Merrick Lectures); The Imperial Voice, 1924; The Lion in his Den; Evangelical Humanism (Fernley Lecture), 1925; Adventures in the Minds of Men, 1927; Imperishable Dreams, 1929; (ed and contrib.) Whither Christianity, 1929; The Artist and the Critic (Samuel Harris Lectures), 1930; Personality and Science (Ayer Lectures), 1930; The University of Experience, 1932; Vital Control (Forest Essays, First Series), 1934; The Church and Civilization, 1934; The Great Evangel, 1936; The Civilized Mind (Forest Essays, Second Series), 1937; Free Men (Forest Essays, Third Series), 1939; The Christian Criticism of Life, 1941; Adventures in Understanding, 1941; Patterns of the Mind, 1942; Living Democracy, 1943; The Meaning of Human Experience, 1945; Christian Humanism and the Modern World (Chancellor Lectures), 1948; The Dignity of Man, 1950; Great Humanists, 1952; The Great Argument, 1953; The Living Church, 1959. *Address:* 1165 Fifth Avenue, New York, NY 10029, USA. *Clubs:* National Liberal, Authors'; University, Century, The Pilgrims (New York).

**HOUGHTON, Albert Morley;** Under-Secretary, Ministry of Technology (Head of Electronics and Telecommunications Division), since 1965; *b* 26 June 1914; *s* of late George Albert Houghton and late Alice Lucy Houghton; *m* 1939, Lallie Whittington Hughes; no *c*. *Educ:* Hamond's Grammar Sch., Swaffham, Norfolk; King's Coll., London Univ. BSc (Special) Hons in Maths, and College Prizeman, 1935; MSc (Maths) 1937. Schoolmaster, 1937-39. Royal Navy, 1939-46 (Instructor Lieut Comdr RN). Lecturer (Maths), College of St Mark and St John, 1946; Sec. of Training Coll. Delegacy, University of London, 1946. Entered Civil Service, Administrative class, 1946; Civil Service Selection Board, 1946-49; Ministry of Transport, 1949-65; UK Delegn to NATO 1954-56; Shipping Attaché to Comr Gen. for SE Asia, 1956-60; Head of Gen. Shipping Policy Div., 1961-62 and Head of Road Safety Div., 1962-65, Min. of Transport. *Recreations:* trying to understand people; reading (history, literature, theology); music (and playing the piano); one-time campanologist; gardening, because he has to. *Address:* 21 Sugden Road, Thames Ditton, Surrey. *T:* 01-398 4808.

**HOUGHTON, Rev. Alfred Thomas,** MA, LTh; General Secretary Bible Churchmen's Missionary Society, 1945-66, Vice-President 1968; Hon. Canon, Diocese of Morogoro, Central Tanganyika, 1965; *b* Stafford, 11 April 1896; *s* of Rev. Thomas Houghton (Editor of the Gospel Magazine and Vicar of Whitington, Stoke Ferry, Norfolk) and Elizabeth Anne Houghton; *m* 1924, Coralie Mary, *d* of H. W. Green, and *g d* of Maj.-Gen. Green, Indian Army; two *s* four *d*. *Educ:* Clarence Sch. (now Canford Sch.); Durham Univ. (University Coll.); London Coll. of Divinity. BA Durham, 1923; MA Durham, 1929. Commissioned 2/5th PA Som LI, Burma, 1917; Staff Officer to Inspector of Infantry, South, AHQ India, 1918; Staff Capt., QMG's Br, AHQ India, 1919; demobilised, 1919; Deacon, 1921; Priest, 1922; Missionary Sch. of Medicine, 1923-24; Supt of BCMS Mission in Burma, 1924-40; Asst Bishop-Designate of Rangoon, 1940-44 (cancelled owing to Japanese occupation of Burma); Travelling Sec., Inter-Varsity Fellowship of Evangelical Unions, 1941-44, and Asst Sec., 1944-45. Pres. Missionary Sch. of Medicine, 1948-; Trustee Keswick Convention Council, 1948, and Chm., 1951-69; Chairman: Conference of British Missionary Socs, 1960; Church of England Evangelical Council, 1960-66; Pres. Mt Hermon Missionary Training Coll., 1960-; Vice-President: Evangelical Alliance; Young Life Campaign; Lord's Day Observance Soc. *Publications:* Tailum Jan, 1930; Dense Jungle Green, 1937; Preparing to be a Missionary, 1956. *Address:* 2 Queen Elizabeth Court, Park Road, Barnet, Herts. *T:* 01-449 1741.

**HOUGHTON, Arthur A., Jr;** President, Steuben Glass, since 1933; *b* Corning, New York, USA, 12 Dec. 1906; *s* of Arthur Amory and Mabel Hollister Houghton; *m* Elizabeth Douglas McCall; one *s* three *d*. *Educ:* St Paul's Sch.; Harvard Univ. Entered employment of Corning Glass Works, 1929; successively in manufacturing dept, in treasury dept, Asst to Pres., and Vice-Pres. Served War of 1942-45; Chairman: Academic Planning Bd, US Army Air Forces Intelligence Sch. (Lieut-Col); Wye Institute (Maryland). Director: Corning Glass Works; US Steel Corporation; New York Life Insurance Company; Trustee: United States Trust Company; New York Public Library; Chm., Metropolitan Museum of Art; Vice-Pres. Pierpont Morgan Library; Mem., Bibliographical Socs of London, Oxford and Cambridge; Past President: Keats-Shelley Assoc. of America; Shakespeare Assoc. of America; a Senior Fellow: Royal College of Art, London; RSA, London. Holds numerous hon. doctorates in Law, Letters and Science. Michael Friedsam Medal in Industrial Art. Officer Legion of Honour (France); Commandeur de l'Ordre des Arts et des Lettres. Assoc. CStJ. *Publication:* Design Policy Within Industry as a Responsibility of High-Level Management, 1951. *Address:* 715 Fifth Avenue, New York, NY 10022, USA. *T:* PL2-1441. *Clubs:* Century, Union, Harvard, Knickerbocker, Fifth Avenue (New York); Club of Odd Volumes (Boston); Philobiblon (Philadelphia).

**HOUGHTON, Rt. Hon. (Arthur Leslie Noel) Douglas,** PC 1964; CH 1967; MP (Lab) Sowerby Division, West Riding of Yorks, since March 1949; Member, Commission on the Constitution, since 1969; Chairman, Parliamentary Labour Party, 1967-70 and since Nov. 1970; *b* 11 Aug. 1898; *s* of John and Martha Houghton, Long Eaton, Derbyshire; *m* 1939, Vera Travis; no *c*. Sec., Inland Revenue Staff Fedn, 1922-60. Broadcaster in "Can I Help You?" Programme, BBC, 1941-64. Alderman LCC, 1947-49; Mem. Gen. Council, TUC, 1952-60. Chm., Staff Side, Civil Service National Whitley Council, 1956-58. Chm. Public Accounts Cttee, 1963-64. Chancellor of the Duchy of Lancaster, 1964-66; Minister Without Portfolio, 1966-67. Chairman: Commonwealth Scholarships Commn, 1967-68; Jt Vice-Chm., Young Volunteer Force Foundation, 1970- (Chm. 1967-70). *Publication:* Paying for the Social Services, 2nd edn, 1968. *Address:* 110 Marsham Court, SW1. *T:* 01-834 0602; Becks Cottage, Whitehill Lane, Bletchingley, Surrey. *T:* Bletchingley 340.

**HOUGHTON, Charles Thomas,** CB 1951; CBE 1941; Under-Secretary Ministry of Agriculture and Fisheries, 1946-56; *b* 12 Aug. 1892; *m* 1921, Anne, *d* of Thos Hunt, Ince, Lancs; one *s* one *d*. *Educ:* Hindley and Abram Grammar Sch.; London Sch. of Economics. Entered Board of Agriculture and Fisheries, 1912; Private Sec. to Permanent Sec., Ministry of Agriculture and Fisheries, 1920-21; Private Sec. to five successive Ministers of Agriculture 1921-29; an Asst Sec. to United Kingdom Delegation to Imperial Economic Conference, Ottawa, 1932; Asst Sec., Ministry of Agriculture and Fisheries, 1934; First Sec. to Cattle Cttee (under Cattle Subsidy Scheme), 1934-35; Agricultural Representative on UK Delegation to Conference of British Commonwealth Statisticians, Ottawa, 1935; Principal Finance Officer, Ministry of Agriculture, 1937-39; Asst Sec., Ministry of Food, 1939-42; Principal Asst Sec., Ministry of Agriculture, 1944; Under-Sec., 1946; Principal Establishment Officer, 1944-55. *Publication:* Paper on A New Index Number of Agricultural Prices, before Royal Statistical Society, Jan. 1938. *Address:* 2 The Bower Garden, London Road, Maldon, Essex. *T:* 01-942 3963. *Club:* Royal Commonwealth Society.

**HOUGHTON, Rt. Hon. Douglas;** *see* Houghton, Rt Hon. A. L. N. D.

**HOUGHTON, Rt. Rev. Frank;** *b* Stafford; *s* of Thomas and Elizabeth Houghton; *m* Dorothy Cassels, *d* of first Bishop in Western China. *Educ:* Clarence Sch., Weston-super-Mare; St John's Hall, Highbury; BA London Univ., 1913. Ordained 1917 to Curacy of St Benedict, Everton; Curate of All Saints, Preston, 1919-20; Missionary in China, China Inland Mission, 1920-26; Editorial Sec., China Inland Mission, London, 1928-36; Bishop of Eastern Szechwan, 1937-40; Gen. Dir, China Inland Mission, 1940-51; Vicar of St Marks, New Milverton, Leamington, 1953-60; Rector of St Peter's, Drayton, Banbury, 1960-63; retired, 1963. *Publications:* The Two Hundred, 1932; China Calling, 1936; If We Believe 1952; Amy Carmichael of Dohnavur, 1953; The Fire Burns on, 1964; Living your Life, 1966. *Address:* 4 Wellington Road, Parkstone, Poole, Dorset.

**HOUGHTON, Maj.-Gen. Robert Dyer,** CB 1963; OBE 1947; MC 1942; General Secretary, The Royal United Kingdom Beneficent Association; *b* 7 March 1912; *s* of J. M. Houghton, Dawlish, Devon; *m* 1940, Dorothy Uladh Lyons; two *s* one *d*. *Educ:* Haileybury Coll. Royal Marines Officer, 1930-64, retired, 1964. *Recreations:* gardening, sailing, model engineering. *Address:* Vert House, Whitesmith, near Lewes, Sussex. *Club:* United Service.

**HOUGHTON, Sir William (Frederick),** Kt 1967; Education Officer of the Inner London Education Authority, since 1965 (of LCC, 1956-65); *b* 30 Nov. 1909; *m* 1936, Mary Newton; one *s* (and one *s* decd). *Educ:* Christ's Coll., Cambridge Univ. BA 1931; MA 1936.

Teaching, Methodist Coll., Belfast, and Wirral Grammar Sch., Cheshire, 1932-36; Asst to Sec., E Suffolk Educ. Cttee, 1936-38; Dep. Dir of Education, W Sussex, 1938-41; Chief Education Officer, Darlington, 1941-47; Dep. Education Officer, Birmingham, 1947-52; Dep. Education Officer, London, 1952-56. Hon. FCP 1965. Hon. DUniv Surrey, 1968. *Publication:* Greeks and Romans, 1935. *Recreations:* reading, theatre, sport, travel. *Address:* 42 Brookfield, Highgate West Hill, N6.

**HOUGHTON, Rev. Canon William Reginald;** Canon Residentiary of Gloucester Cathedral, since 1969; *b* 28 Sept. 1910; *s* of late William Houghton and Elizabeth Houghton; unmarried. *Educ:* St John's Coll., Durham; Westcott House, Cambridge. BA (Durham) 1940; Dipl. in Th. (Durham) 1941; MA (Durham) 1943. Curate, St Clement, Leeds, 1941-43, Leeds Parish Church, 1943-47 (Senior Curate, 1945-47); Vicar of Beeston, Leeds, 1947-54. Surrogate, 1949-54. Public Preacher, Dio. Southwark, 1954-62; Asst Sec. South London Church Fund and Southwark Diocesan Board of Finance, 1954-56, Dep. Sec., 1956-60, Sec., 1960-61; Sec. Southwark Dio. Bd of Dilapidations, 1956-60; Canon Residentiary (Treas.) of Southwark Cathedral, 1959-62. Rector of St Mary de Crypt with St John the Baptist, Gloucester, 1962-69. *Recreations:* travel and reading. *Address:* 8 College Green, Gloucester. *T:* Gloucester 23987.

**HOULDEN, George Houldsworth,** CBE 1955 (MBE 1942); CEng; MRINA; Chairman of Vickers Ltd Shipbuilding Group, 1965-67; *b* 10 Sept. 1902; *s* of late George Houldsworth Houlden, Knutsford, Cheshire; *m* 1924, Winifred Crawford, *d* of David Lindsay Largie of Montrose; three *s* one *d. Educ:* Robert Gordon's Technical Coll., Aberdeen. Apprenticed with Hall, Russell & Co. Ltd, Aberdeen. Joined Vickers Ltd, Barrow-in-Furness, 1924; joined Management Staff at Barrow, 1933; transferred to Walker Yard as Personal Asst to Gen. Manager, 1943; Dep. Gen. Manager of Walker Yard and a Special Dir, Vickers-Armstrongs Ltd, 1946; Gen. Manager of Walker Yard, 1950; Dir, 1953, Managing Dir, 1954, Chm. and Man. Dir, 1962-64, Chm., 1964-65, of Vickers-Armstrongs (Shipbuilders) Ltd. Member: Board of Cockatoo Docks and Engineering Co. (Pty) Ltd, Sydney, 1954-65; Board of Vickers Ltd, 1957-67. *Recreation:* fishing. *Address:* Beda Lodge, Hookergate, Rowlands Gill, Co. Durham. *T:* Rowlands Gill 2236.

**HOULDEN, Rev. James Leslie;** Principal, Cuddesdon Theological College, since 1970; *b* 1 March 1929; *s* of James and Lily Alice Houlden. *Educ:* Altrincham Grammar Sch.; Queen's Coll., Oxford. Asst Curate, St Mary's, Hunslet, Leeds, 1955-58; Chaplain, Chichester Theological Coll., 1958-60; Chaplain Fellow, Trinity Coll., Oxford, 1960-70. *Publications:* Paul's Letters from Prison, 1970; (ed) A Celebration of Faith, 1970; reviews and articles in learned jls. *Address:* Cuddesdon College, Oxford OX9 9EX. *T:* Garsington 227.

**HOULDSWORTH, Sir Basil;** *see* Houldsworth, Sir H. B.

**HOULDSWORTH, Sir (Harold) Basil,** 2nd Bt, *cr* 1956; Consultant Anæsthetist, Barnsley and District Hospitals, since 1954; *b* 21 July 1922; *s* of Sir Hubert Stanley Houldsworth, 1st Bt, QC and (Hilda Frances) Lady Houldsworth (*née* Clegg); *S* father 1956; *m* 1946, Norah Clifford Halmshaw; one *d. Educ:* Heckmondwike Grammar Sch.; Leeds Sch. of Medicine, MRCS, LRCP 1946; FFA RCS 1954; DA Eng. 1951. Junior Registrar Anæsthetist, Leeds Gen. Infirmary, 1946-48; Graded Specialist Anæsthetist, RAMC, 1948-50; Registrar Anæsthetist, Leeds General Infirmary and St James Hospital, Leeds, 1950-53; Senior Registrar, Sheffield City General Hospital, 1953-54. *Recreations:* theatre, ballet and gardening. *Heir:* none. *Address:* Shadwell House, Lundhill Road, Wombwell, near Barnsley, Yorks. *T:* Wombwell 3191.

**HOULDSWORTH, Sir Reginald (Douglas Henry),** 4th Bt, *cr* 1887, OBE 1945; TD 1944; DL; landowner; *b* 9 July 1903; *s* of Sir Thomas Houldsworth, 3rd Bt, CBE; *S* father 1961; *m* 1934, Margaret May, *d* of late Cecil Emilius Laurie; one *s* two *d. Educ:* Shrewsbury Sch.; Cambridge Univ. Hon. Col Ayrshire ECO Yeomanry, 1960-67; Commanded: Ayrshire Yeomanry, 1940-42; 4 Pack Mule Group, 1943-45. DL Ayrshire, 1970-. *Heir: s* Richard Thomas Reginald Houldsworth, [*b* 2 Aug. 1947; *m* 1970, Jane, *o d* of Alistair Orr, Sydehead, Beith]. *Address:* Kirkbride, Maybole, Ayrshire. *T:* Crosshill 202. *Clubs:* Cavalry; Western Meeting (Ayr); Prestwick (Prestwick).

**HOULT, Norah;** novelist and journalist; *b* Dublin; *d* of Powis Hoult and Margaret O'Shaughnessy. *Educ:* Various boarding schools. *Publications:* Poor Women, 1928; Time, Gentlemen! Time!, 1929; Apartments to Let, 1931; Youth Can't be Served, 1933; Holy Ireland, 1935; Coming From the Fair, 1937; Nine Years is a Long Time, 1938; Four Women Grow Up, 1940; Smilin' on The Vine, 1941; Augusta Steps Out, 1942; Scene for Death, 1943; There Were No Windows, 1944; House Under Mars, 1946; Farewell, Happy Fields, 1948; Cocktail Bar, 1950; Frozen Ground, 1952; Sister Mavis, 1953; Journey into Print, 1954; A Death Occurred, 1954; Father Hone and the Television Set, 1956; Father and Daughter, 1957; Husband and Wife, 1959; Last Days of Miss Jenkinson, 1962; Poet's Pilgrimage, 1966; Only Fools and Horses Work, 1969. *Address:* Jonquil Cottage, Greystones, Co. Wicklow, Ireland. *Club:* United Arts (Dublin).

**HOULTON, Sir John (Wardle),** Kt 1947; CSI 1945; CIE 1939; President of the Senate of Swaziland, since 1968; *b* 28 Jan. 1892; *m* 1927, Gwynneth Clause, *d* of Dr Muspratt Comley (marr. diss. 1958); one *d*; *m* 1960, Lily, *widow* of Frederic Kingsley. *Educ:* Perse Sch.; Christ's Coll., Cambridge. 2nd Lieut Suffolk Regt, Spec. Res. of Officers, Sept. 1914. Served European War (wounded); acting Lieut-Col 1918. Entered ICS, Bihar Prov., 1920; Dist Magistrate, 1924; Dir of Land Records, 1928; Revenue and Commerce Sec., 1933; Chief Sec., 1943; Adviser to the Governor, 1944; retd, 1948. *Publication:* Bihar, the Heart of India, 1950. *Recreations:* writing, golf, shooting. *Address:* South Wind, Malkerns, Swaziland.

**HOURIGAN, Thomas,** JP; Chairman, Manchester Regional Hospital Board, since 1966; *b* 1 Dec. 1904; *m* 1929, Agnes Cassidy; one *s* two *d. Educ:* St Joseph's Primary Sch., Leigh. NUPE Trade Union Organising Officer, 1938-57; Sec. Manager, Leigh Rugby League Football Club, 1957-69; Member: Leigh Borough Council, 1934-; Lancs CC, 1946-; Manchester Regional Hosp. Bd, 1948-; Past Member: Lancs Exec. Coun.; United Manchester Hosps; Mayor of Leigh Borough, 1949-50; Former Chairman: Lancs County Fire Bde Cttee; Lancs Co. Health Cttee; Vice-Chairman: former Mersey River Bd; Mersey and Weaver River Authority (since inception).

Contested (Lab) Preston North, 1951. JP Leigh Borough, 1949-; Lancs County Alderman, Lancs, 1957-; Borough Alderman, Leigh, 1953-. Hon. MA (Manchester), 1963. *Recreations:* sports, gardening, reading. *Address:* 10 Wenlock Road, Leigh, Lancs. *T:* Leigh 73858.

**HOUSDEN, Rt. Rev. J. A. G.;** *see* Newcastle (NSW), Bishop of.

**HOUSE, Donald Victor;** Lay Member, Restrictive Practices Court, since 1962; *b* 31 Jan. 1900; *s* of Dr S. H. House, Liverpool; *m* 1925, Cicely May Cox-Moore; one *s* two *d*. *Educ:* Liverpool Coll. Lieut, Royal Garrison Artillery, 1918. Mem. (Fellow) Inst. of Chartered Accountants in England and Wales, 1922- (Mem. Council, 1942-62; Pres. 1954-55). Senior Partner, Harmood Banner & Co., 1946-62. Mem. Board of Governors, Guy's Hosp. and Chm. of Finance Cttee; Director: National Film Finance Corporation; Finance Cttee, Friends of the Poor and Gentlefolks Help; Mem., London Rent Assessment Panel. Hon. Sec., Herts Golf Union; Mem. Council, English Golf Union. Dir of several public and other companies (to 1962); Chm., House Cttee enquiring into Northern Ireland shipping facilities. Special Constabulary Long Service Medal, 1943. *Recreations:* golf, amateur dramatics. *Address:* 155 Stanmore Hill, Stanmore, Mddx HA7 3EF. *T:* 01-954 0525. *Clubs:* East India and Sports, Royal Commonwealth Society; Sandy Lodge Golf.

**HOUSE, Ven. Francis Harry,** OBE 1955; MA; Officer Royal (Hellenic) Order of Phoenix, 1947; Archdeacon of Macclesfield since 1967; Rector of St James, Gawsworth, since 1967; *b* 9 Aug. 1908; *s* of late Canon William Joseph House, DD; *m* 1938, Margaret Neave; two *d*. *Educ:* St George's Sch., Harpenden; Wadham Coll., Oxford; Cuddesdon Theological Coll. Sec. of Student Christian Movement of Gt Britain and Ireland, 1931-34; Deacon, 1936; Priest, 1937. Asst Missioner, Pembroke Coll. (Cambridge) Mission, Walworth, 1936-37; Travelling sec. of World's Student Christian Federation, Geneva, 1938-40; Curate of Leeds Parish Church, 1940-42; Overseas Asst, Religious Broadcasting Dept, BBC, London, 1942-44; representative of World Student Relief in Greece, 1944-46; Sec. Youth Dept World Council of Churches, Geneva, and World Conference of Christian Youth, Oslo, 1946-47; Head of Religious Broadcasting BBC, London, 1947-55; Associate Gen. Sec. of the World Council of Churches, Geneva, 1955-62; Vicar of St Giles, Pontefract, 1962-67. Select Preacher, Cambridge Univ., 1949. Examining Chaplain to Bishop of Chester, 1969-. *Publications:* articles contributed to: The Student Movement, The Student World, East and West, the Ecumenical Review, etc. *Address:* Gawsworth Rectory, Macclesfield, Cheshire. *T:* North Rode 201. *Club:* Travellers'.

**HOUSE, Harry Wilfred,** DSO 1918; MC; MA; Master of Wellington College, 1941-Aug. 1956; *b* Malvern, 26 Sept. 1895; 2nd *s* of late H. H. House, Acre End, Eynsham, Oxon.; *m* 1926, Marjorie Stracey, *yr d* of late Arthur Gibbs, of Bramley, Surrey; two *s* one *d*. *Educ:* Lockers Park, Hemel Hempstead; Rugby Sch.; Queen's Coll., Oxford. Served in HM Forces on leaving Rugby in 1914; temp. 2nd Lieut 7th East Lancs Regt, Sept. 1914; served in France from July 1915 (wounded July 1916; MC; DSO); relinquished commission with rank of Temp. Major, March, 1919; total service in France 3 years 5 months; temp. appointment Colonial Office, March to Dec. 1919; matriculated Oxford Univ., Jan. 1920; 2nd Class Hon. Mods, March 1921; studied at the University of Paris, 1921-23; Fellow and Lecturer Queen's Coll., Oxford, 1923-41; Laming Resident Fellow, Queen's Coll., Oxford, 1924-41; Junior Proctor, Oxford Univ., 1931-32; Major, Oxford and Bucks Light Infantry, 1939-41; Military Asst to Quarter Master Gen., 1940-41. Supernumerary Fellow, Queen's Coll., Oxford, 1953. Governor of Highgate, Ipswich, Holbrook, and Woolverstone Hall Schs. *Address:* The Old Rectory, Stutton, near Ipswich, Suffolk. *T:* Holbrook 205.

**HOUSEHOLD, Geoffrey Edward West,** TD; Author; *b* 30 Nov. 1900; *s* of H. W. Household, MA, Barrister-at-Law; *m* 1942, Ilona M. J. Zsoldos-Gutmán; one *s* two *d*. *Educ:* Clifton Coll.; Magdalen Coll., Oxford. Mostly commerce in foreign capitals. *Publications: novels:* The Third Hour, Rogue Male, Arabesque, The High Place, A Rough Shoot, A Time to Kill, Fellow Passenger, Watcher in the Shadows, Thing to Love, Olura, The Courtesy of Death, Dance of the Dwarfs; *autobiography:* Against the Wind; *short stories:* The Salvation of Pisco Gabar, Tales of Adventurers, The Brides of Solomon, Sabres on the Sand; *for children:* The Spanish Cave, Xenophon's Adventure, Prisoner of the Indies. *Recreation:* Atlantic Spain. *Address:* Church Headland, Whitchurch, Aylesbury, Bucks.

**HOUSSAY, Prof. Doctor Bernardo Alberto;** President, National Scientific Research Council, Buenos Aires; Director, Instituto de Biologia y Medicina Experimental, Obligado 2490, Buenos Aires; *b* Buenos Aires, 10 April 1887; *s* of Alberto Houssay and Clara Laffont; *m* 1920, Maria Angélica Catán; three *s*. *Educ:* Buenos Aires. Pharmacist, 1904; Med. Doctor, Buenos Aires, 1911. Prof. of Physiology: Veterinary Sch., Buenos Aires, 1910-19; Medical Sch., Buenos Aires, 1919-43, 1945-46, 1955-57; Research Prof. of the University of Buenos Aires, 1957-69. Hitchcock Prof., University of California, 1948. Mem. Advisory Cttee of Medical Research: WHO; Pan-American Health Organization. Mem. numerous societies and academies, both Argentinian and Foreign; Foreign Mem. Royal Society. Former President: Nat. Acad. of Medicine (Buenos Aires); Argentine Assoc. for Advancement of Sciences (Hon Pres.); Internat. Union of Physiological Sciences; President: Argentine Soc. of Biology; Argentine Soc. of Physiology. Holds numerous hon. presidencies, hon. professorships, and hon. doctorates (including Dr *hc* Oxford, Cambridge and Glasgow), etc. Winner of: National Prize Sciences, Buenos Aires, 1923; Charles Mickle Fellowship, Toronto, Canada, 1945; Banting Medal, American Diabetes Assoc., 1946; Research Award, American Pharmaceutical Manufacturers' Assoc., 1947; Baly Medal, Royal Coll. of Physicians, London, 1947; Nobel Prize for Physiology and Medicine, 1947; James Cook Medal, Sydney, 1948; Dale Medal, Soc. for Endocrinology, London, 1960; Weizmann Prize in Sciences and Humanities, 1967. Has several foreign orders. *Publications:* Textbook on Human Physiology (Spanish, English, French, Portuguese, Italian, Greek edns); many scientific papers on Hypophysis, Diabetes, Hypertension of Renal Origin, Pancreas, Adrenals, Thyroid, Endocrinology, Alloxan, Thymus, Venoms, Pharmacodynamics, Medical Education, etc. *Address:* (private) Viamonte 2790, Buenos Aires, Argentina. *T:* 87-8748.

**HOUSSEMAYNE du BOULAY, Roger William;** HM Diplomatic Service; Counsellor, since 1967; *b* 30 March 1922; *s* of Charles John Houssemayne du Boulay, Captain, RN, and

Mary Alice Veronica, *née* Morgan; *m* 1957, Elizabeth Home; one *d. Educ:* Winchester; Oxford. Served RAFVR, 1941-46 (Pilot). HM Colonial Service, Nigeria, 1949-58; HM Foreign, later Diplomatic, Service, 1959-. *Recreations:* riding, hunting, skiing. *Address:* Anstey House, near Buntingford, Herts. *T:* Barkway 241. *Clubs:* Hunts; Manila Polo (Manila).

**HOUSTON, Aubrey Claud D.;** *See* Davidson-Houston.

**HOUSTON, James Caldwell,** MD, FRCP; Physician to Guy's Hospital, since 1953; Dean of the Medical and Dental Schools, Guy's Hospital, since 1965; *b* 18 Feb. 1917; *yr s* of late David Houston and of Minnie Walker Houston; *m* 1946, Thelma Cromarty Cruickshank, MB, ChB, 2nd *d* of late John Cruickshank, CBE; four *s. Educ:* Mill Hill Sch.; Guy's Hosp. Medical Sch. MRCS, LRCP 1939; MB, BS (London) 1940; MRCP 1944; MD 1946; FRCP 1956. Late Major RAMC; Medical Registrar, Guy's Hospital, 1946; Asst Ed., 1954, Jt Ed., 1958-67, Guy's Hosp. Reports; Member: Bd of Governors, Guy's Hosp., 1965-; SE Metropolitan Regional Hosp. Bd, 1966-; Court of Governors, London Sch. of Hygiene and Tropical Med., 1969-; Senate, Univ. of London, 1970. Dir, Clerical, Medical & Gen. Life Assurance Soc., 1965; Vice-Pres., Medical Defence Union, 1970-. *Publications:* Principles of Medicine and Medical Nursing (jtly), 1956, 2nd edn 1966; A Short Text-book of Medicine (jtly), 1962, 3rd edn rev. 1970; articles in Quart. Jl Med., Brit. Med. Bull., Lancet, etc. *Recreations:* golf, gardening. *Address:* 108 Harley Street, W1. *T:* 01-935 9338; 16 Hocroft Road, NW2. *T:* 01-435 3434; Cockhill Farm, Detling, Maidstone, Kent. *T:* Medway 31395.

**HOUSTOUN, Robert Alexander,** MA, PhD, DSc, FRSE, FInstP; Hon. Research Fellow, University of Glasgow; *b* 1883; unmarried. *Educ:* Hillhead High Sch.; Universities of Glasgow (was Metcalfe Fellow and 1851 Research Fellow), Göttingen, and Cambridge (Scholar of Emmanuel Coll.). On the Staff of the Natural Philosophy Dept of the University of Glasgow, 1906-48. *Publications:* Studies in Light Production, 1912; An Introduction to Mathematical Physics, 1912; A Treatise on Light, 1915; Elements of Physics, 1919; Light and Colour, 1922; Intermediate Light, 1925; Intermediate Electricity and Magnetism, 1928; Intermediate Heat, 1929; Intermediate Physics, 1930; Vision and Colour Vision, 1932; Physical Optics, 1957; numerous scientific papers in the Proceedings of the Royal Society, The Proceedings of the Royal Society of Edinburgh, the Philosophical Magazine, etc. *Address:* The University, Glasgow.

**HOUSTOUN-BOSWALL, Sir Thomas,** 7th Bt, *cr* 1836; Chairman: Sir Thomas HB Properties Ltd; Continental Sales Agency Co. Ltd; Director: TC Motors Ltd; Sun Chinese Restaurants Ltd; Philip Developments Ltd; Southern Television (Pty) Ltd; *b* 13 Feb. 1919; *s* of Major Sir Gordon Houstoun-Boswall, 6th Bt; *S* father 1961; *m* 1945, Margaret, *d* of George Bullen-Smith; one *s* one *d. Educ:* Windlesham House Sch.; Nautical Coll., Pangbourne. Fighter Pilot, RAFVR, 1939-45 (Middle East and UK). *Heir: s* Thomas Alford Houstoun-Boswall, *b* 23 May 1947. *Address:* 240 Brompton Road, SW3. *T:* 01-589 2433; Heath Grange, Lingfield, Surrey. *T:* Lingfield 3291. *Club:* English-Speaking Union.

**HOVDE, Frederick Lawson;** President's Medal for Merit (USA), 1948; President, Purdue University, since 1946; *b* 7 Feb. 1908; *s* of Martin Rudolph Hovde and Julia Essidora Hovde (*née* Lawson); *m* 1933, Priscilla Louise Boyd; one *s* two *d. Educ:* University of Minnesota; Oxford Univ. Asst Dir Gen. Coll., University of Minnesota, 1932-36; Asst to Pres. and Exec. Sec. of Rochester Prize Scholarships, University of Rochester, 1936-41; Head, London Mission, Office of Scientific Research and Development, 1941-42; Exec. Asst to Chm., Nat. Defense Research Cttee, 1942-43; Chief, Rocket Ordnance Research Div., Nat. Defense Research Cttee, 1943-46. Hon. degrees: DSc: Hanover Coll., 1946; Case Inst. of Technology, 1948; Tri-State College, 1967; DEng Rose Polytechnic Inst., 1948; LLD: Wabash Coll., 1946; North Dakota Agricultural Coll., 1949; New York Univ., 1951; Michigan State Univ., 1955; Minnesota, 1956; Northwestern Univ., 1960; Notre Dame, 1964; Ball State Univ., 1965; Indiana State Univ., 1966; Indiana Univ., 1969; DHL Cincinnati, 1956; DCL Oxford, 1957; Dr *hc* University Rural do Estado de Minas Gerais, Brazil, 1965; DEd Valparaiso Univ., 1967; PhD Findlay Coll., 1961; DHum Northwood Inst., 1969. King's Medal for Service in the Cause of Freedom (Britain), 1948; Washington Award, Western Soc. of Engineers, 1967; Gold Medal, Nat. Football Foundn and Hall of Fame, 1967; Theodore Roosevelt Award, Nat. Collegiate Athl. Assoc., 1970; Dist. Public Service Medal, Dept of Defense, 1970. comdr, Order of the Southern Cross, Brazil, 1968. *Recreation:* golf. *Address:* 515 South Seventh Street, Lafayette, Indiana 47901, USA. *T:* (office) 317-749-2108; (home) 317-742-5485. *Clubs:* University (Chicago); Vincent's (Oxford, England).

**HOVELL-THURLOW-CUMMING-BRUCE,** family name of **Baron Thurlow,** and *see* Cumming-Bruce.

**HOVING, Thomas (Pearsall Field);** Director, The Metropolitan Museum of Art, since 1967; *b* 15 Jan. 1931; *s* of Walter Hoving and Mary Osgood (*née* Field); *m* 1953, Nancy Melissa Bell; one *d. Educ:* Princeton Univ. BA Highest Hons, 1953; Nat. Council of the Humanities Fellowship, 1955; Kienbusch and Haring Fellowship, 1957; MA 1958; PhD 1959. Dept of Medieval Art and The Cloisters, Metropolitan Museum of Art: Curatorial Asst, 1959; Asst Curator, 1960; Associate Curator, 1963; Curator, 1965; Commissioner of Parks, New York City, 1966; Administrator of Recreation and Cultural Affairs, New York City, 1967. Distinguished Citizen's Award, Citizen's Budget Cttee, 1967. Hon. Mem. AIA, 1967. Hon. LLD, Pratt Inst., 1967. *Publications:* The Sources of the Ada Group Ivories (PhD thesis), 1959; Guide to The Cloisters, 1962; Metropolitan Museum of Art Calendar, 1966; articles in Apollo magazine and Metropolitan Museum of Art Bulletin. *Recreations:* sailing, ski-ing, skating, tennis, bicycling. *Address:* 150 East 73rd Street, New York, NY 10021, USA.

**HOW, Sir Friston (Charles),** Kt 1958; CB 1948; Member, Air Transport Licensing Board, since 1960; *b* 17 Sept. 1897; *o c* of Charles Friston and Jane Ethel How, Leytonstone; *m* 1932, Ann Stewart, *e d* of late Alexander Chisholm Hunter, Aberdeen; no *c. Educ:* County High Sch. for Boys, Leyton; London Univ. Joined HAC, 1916; commissioned RM, 1917; served in France, 1917-18; demobilised 1919. Exchequer and Audit Dept, 1920; HM Inspector of Taxes, 1920-37; Air Ministry, 1937-40; MAP, 1940-45; Ministry of Supply, 1946-53; Sec., Atomic Energy Office, 1954-59; retired, 1959; Mem. Air Transport Advisory Council, 1960-61; BSc (War) (London), 1917. Called to Bar (Middle Temple), 1927. *Address:* Desswood, Dess, Aboyne, Aberdeenshire. *T:*

Kincardine O'Neil 246. *Club:* Royal Automobile.

**HOWARD;** *see* Fitzalan-Howard.

**HOWARD,** family name of **Earls of Carlisle, Effingham, Suffolk,** and **Wicklow,** of **Barons Howard of Glossop, Howard of Penrith,** and **Strathcona.**

**HOWARD DE WALDEN,** 9th Baron *cr* 1597; **John Osmael Scott-Ellis,** TD; Baron Seaford, 1826; *b* 27 Nov. 1912; *s* of 8th Baron and Margherita, CBE 1920, *d* of late Charles van Raalte of Brownsea Island, Dorset; *S* father, 1946; *m* 1934, Countess Irene Harrach, *y d* of Count Hans Albrecht Harrach; four *d. Educ:* Eton; Magdalene Coll., Cambridge. (BA 1934, MA). Director: Alliance Assurance Co. Ltd; Howard de Walden Estates Ltd (Chm.); Sun Alliance & London Insurance Ltd. Member of the Jockey Club (Senior Steward, 1957, 1964). *Heir:* four co-heiresses. *Address:* Ormeley Lodge, Ham Common, Surrey; Avington Manor, Hungerford, Berks. *Clubs:* Royal Yacht Squadron, Turf.
*See also Capt. D. W. S. Buchan of Auchmacoy.*

**HOWARD OF GLOSSOP,** 3rd Baron *cr* 1869; **Bernard Edward Fitzalan-Howard,** MBE 1920; *b* 10 May 1885; *s* of 2nd Baron and Clara, *d* of J. Greenwood of Swarcliffe, Ripley, Yorks; *c* and *heir-pres.* of 16th Duke of Norfolk, *qv*; *S* father, 1924; *m* 1914, 11th Baroness Beaumont, *qv*; four *s* four *d. Educ:* Oratory Sch., Edgbaston; Trinity Coll., Cambridge. *Heir: s* Maj.-Gen. Hon. Miles Francis Fitzalan-Howard, *qv. Address:* 23 Lennox Gardens, SW1. *T:* 01-589 2824.
*See also Maj.-Gen. Hon. Michael Fitzalan-Howard.*

**HOWARD OF PENRITH,** 2nd Baron, *cr* 1930; **Francis Philip Howard,** DL; Captain late RA; *b* 5 Oct. 1905; *s* of 1st Baron and Lady Isabella Giustiniani-Bandini (*d* 1963) (*d* of Prince Giustiniani-Bandini, 8th Earl of Newburgh); *S* father, 1939; *m* 1944, Anne, *widow* of Anthony Bazley; four *s. Educ:* Downside; Trinity Coll., Cambridge (BA); Harvard Univ. Called to Bar, Middle Temple, 1931; served in War, 1939-42 (wounded). DL County of Glos, 1960. *Heir: s* Hon. Philip Esme Howard [*b* 1 May 1945; *m* 1969, Sarah, *d* of late Barclay Walker and of Mrs Walker, Perthshire]. *Address:* Dean Farm, Hatherop, Glos.
*See also Hon. Edmund B. C. Howard, Lieut-Col Hon. Henry A. C. Howard.*

**HOWARD, Capt. Alan Frederic William,** DSO 1940; RN, retired; *b* 11 April 1883; *s* of late William Howard *m* 1921, Kathleen Jocelyn, *d* of Charles Campbell Riley; two *s. Educ:* late Mr C. Luton, Farnborough Park, Hants; HMS Britannia. Served European War and War of 1939-45 (despatches twice, Croix de Guerre with palm, DSO). *Address:* Hazelgrove, Slindon, Sussex. *T:* Slindon 255.

**HOWARD, Alexander Edward;** Headmaster, Wandsworth School, London, since 1963; *b* 2 Aug. 1909; *o s* of Alexander Watson Howard and Gertrude Nellie Howard; *m* 1937, Phyllis Ada Adams; no *c. Educ:* Swindon Coll.; University Coll. and Westminster Coll., London Univ. BSc (London) 1930; Pt I, BSc (Econ.) 1934. Flt-Lieut, RAF, 1940-46. Asst Master, Sanford Boys' Sch., Swindon, 1931-34; Lectr in Maths, Wandsworth Techn. Coll., 1935-40; Maths Master, Wilson's Grammar Sch., 1946-48; Headmaster: Northfleet Sch. for Boys, Kent, 1948-51; Borough-Beaufoy Sch., London, 1951-54; Forest Hill Sch., London, 1955-63. Member: Naval Educn Adv. Cttee, 1966-; Army Educational Adv. Bd, 1957-. FRSA 1970. *Publications:* The Secondary Technical School in England, 1955; Longman Mathematics Stages 1-5, 1962-67; Teaching Mathematics, 1968; articles in Times Educational Supplement, The Teacher, Technology, Inside the Comprehensive Sch. *Recreations:* amateur theatre, old-time dancing, music, cricket, travel, rotary. *Address:* 19 Downsway, Sanderstead, Surrey CR2 OJB. *T:* 01-657 3399. *Club:* Surrey County Cricket.

**HOWARD, Hon. Sir Arthur Jared Palmer,** KBE 1953; CVO 1937; Treasurer, St Thomas' Hospital, 1943-64; Chairman of Delegacy, King's College, University of London since 1951; Chairman City Parochial Foundation; late Captain Scots Guards; *b* 1896; *b* of 3rd Baron Strathcona; *m* 1922, Lorna Stanley, *d* of 1st Earl Baldwin, KG, PC, FRS; two *s* two *d.* Served European War, 1914-17 (wounded, Croix de Guerre); Principal Warden London Civil Defence Region, 1939-42. MP (C) S George's Division of Westminster, 1945-50. Mem. (part-time), S Eastern Electricity Bd, 1953-64. JP West Sussex, 1939. *Address:* Wappingthorn, Steyning, Sussex; 6 Chesterfield Street, W1. *Club:* Guards.
*See also Baron Russell of Liverpool.*

**HOWARD, Sir Douglas Frederick,** KCMG, *cr* 1953 (CMG 1944); MC; *b* 15 Feb. 1897; *s* of late John Howard Howard and of late Mrs Howard, Biddenham House, Bedford. *Educ:* Harrow. Served European War, 1915-18, France 1916 and 1918. Entered Diplomatic Service as 3rd Sec. Christiania, 1922; Bucharest, 1924; 2nd Sec., 1925; Rome, 1926; FO 1929. BA 1932. 1st Sec., 1934; Sofia, 1935; FO 1936; Madrid, 1939; Counsellor, FO, 1941; Madrid, 1945, where he was Chargé d'Affaires, Dec. 1946-Nov. 1949; Ambassador to Uruguay, 1949-53; HM Minister to the Holy See, 1953-57, retired. *Address:* Clophill House, Clophill, Bedford. *T:* Silsoe 285. *Club:* Travellers'.

**HOWARD, Hon. Edmund Bernard Carlo,** CMG 1969; MVO 1961; retired from HM Diplomatic Service, 1969; HM Consul-General, Genoa, 1965-69; *b* 8 Sept. 1909; *s* of 1st Baron Howard of Penrith, PC, GCB, GCMG, CVO, and Lady Isabella Giustiniani-Bandini (*d* of Prince Giustiniani-Bandini, 8th Earl of Newburgh); *m* 1936, Cécile Geoffroy-Dechaume; three *s* one *d* (and one *d* decd). *Educ:* Downside Sch.; Newman Sch., Lakewood, NJ; New Coll., Oxford. Called to the Bar, 1932; Sec., Trustees and Managers, Stock Exchange, 1937. Served in HM Forces, KRRC, 1939-45. Joined HM Diplomatic Service, 1947; served in: Rome, 1947-51; Foreign Office, 1951-53; Madrid, 1953-57; Bogotá, 1957-59; Florence, 1960-61; Rome, 1961-65. *Recreations:* travel, mountain climbing and walking, ski-ing. *Address:* Jerome Cottage, Marlow Common, Bucks. *T:* Marlow 2129. *Club:* English-Speaking Union.
*See also Lieut-Col Hon. H. A. C. Howard.*

**HOWARD, Sir Edward;** *see* Howard, Sir H. E. de C.

**HOWARD, Edwin Johnston,** MA, PhD; Professor of English, Miami University, Oxford, Ohio, 1942-68; *b* 10 July 1901; *s* of William Bakewell Howard and Elizabeth Johnston; *m* 1934, Miriam Elizabeth White; one *d. Educ:* Cornell Univ. Instructor of English at the University of Rochester, 1925-26; Asst Prof. of English at Beloit Coll., 1929-30; Associate Prof. of English, Miami Univ., 1930-42; Exchange Prof., 1941 summer term, University of Washington (Seattle). Editor, The Fisherman magazine, 1957-58. *Publications:* articles on Old English,

Elizabethan literature, angling and fishing tackle, and photography in journals; (ed) Ten Elizabethan Plays, 1931; (ed) Sir Thomas Elyot's The Defence of Good Women, 1940; (ed) Pleasant Quippes for Upstart Newfangled Gentle-women, 1942; (co-editor) The Canterbury Tales, 1946; (ed) Of the Knowledge Which Maketh a Wise Man, 1946; Geoffrey Chaucer, 1964; English Around the World, 1969. *Recreations:* photography and fishing. *Address:* 5035 Bonham Road, Oxford, Ohio 45056, USA. *T:* Oxford 35044. *Club:* Torch.

**HOWARD, Elizabeth Jane;** novelist; *b* 26 March 1923; *d* of David Liddon and Katherine M. Howard; *m* 1st, 1942, Peter M. Scott; one *d*; 2nd, 1959, James Douglas-Henry; 3rd, 1965, Kingsley Amis, *qv*. *Educ:* home. Trained at London Mask Theatre Sch. Played at Stratford-on-Avon, and in repertory theatre in Devon; BBC, Television, modelling, 1939-46; Sec. to Inland Waterways Assoc., 1947; subsequently writing, editing and reviewing. John Llewellyn Rhys Memorial Prize for The Beautiful Visit, 1950; Book Critic, Queen Magazine, 1959-61. Hon. Artistic Dir, Cheltenham Literary Festival, 1962. *Publications:* The Beautiful Visit, 1950; The Long View, 1956; The Sea Change, 1959; After Julius, 1965; Something in Disguise, 1969. *Recreations:* music, gardening, enjoying all the arts, travelling, natural history. *Address:* Lemmons, Hadley Common, Barnet, Herts.

**HOWARD, Francis Alex; (Frankie Howerd);** *b* 6 March 1922. *Educ:* Shooters Hill Sch., Woolwich, London. *Revues:* Out of this World, 1950; Pardon my French, 1953; Way Out in Piccadilly, 1966. *Plays:* Charlie's Aunt, 1955; Hotel Paradiso, 1957; A Midsummer Night's Dream (playing Bottom), 1958; Alice in Wonderland, 1960; A Funny Thing Happened on the Way to the Forum, 1963 (Critics' Award for Best Musical Actor, 1964); The Wind in the Sassafras Trees, Broadway, 1968. *Films:* The Ladykillers, 1956; Runaway Bus, 1956; Touch of the Sun, 1956; Jumping for Joy, 1956; Further up the Creek, 1958; Carry On, Doctor, 1968; Carry on Jungle Boy, 1970. *TV Series:* Fine Goings On, 1959; series for BBC, 1965, 1966, 1970. Royal Variety Performances, 1950, 1954, 1961, 1966. Variety Club of GB Award (Show Business Personality of the Year), 1966, 1969. *Recreations:* tennis, swimming, music, reading. *Address:* c/o ALS Management Ltd, 67 Brook Street, W1.

**HOWARD, Frederick Richard,** CB 1956; CMG 1950; lately Assistant Secretary, Air Ministry; *b* 7 June 1894; *m* 1920, Nellie Lewis. *Educ:* Strand Sch.; King's Coll., London; privately. Entered HM Civil Service, 1913, National Insurance Audit Dept. Served European War, 1914-18, in Civil Service Rifles, Aug. 1914-Jan. 1919; transferred to Air Ministry on release from Army, 1919; Private Sec. to successive Parliamentary Under-Secs of State for Air, 1937-39; Sec. to Riverdale Mission to Canada to plan Empire Air Training Scheme for Aircrew, 1939-40. *Recreations:* motoring, gardening, photography. *Address:* 22 Hadley Road, Enfield, Mddx.

**HOWARD, His Honour Geoffrey;** former Judge of County Courts (1952-63); Master of the Bench, Inner Temple, 1951-68; *b* Nov. 1889; *y s* of late E. Howard; widower; one *d*; *m* 1969, Mrs Ingwelde von Heitmann-Gorke. *Educ:* Haileybury Coll.; Christ Church, Oxford (BA 1912; MA 1967). "Temporary Gentleman", Royal Fusiliers, 1914-18. Called to Bar, 1919; practised London and Western Circuit. *Publications:* (as Marmaduke Dixey) Hell's Bells (novel), 1936; Words, Beasts and Fishes (verse), 1937; Tight Little Island (novel), 1938; The Beauties of Bridge (verse), 1939. *Address:* 1 King's Bench Walk, Temple, EC4. *T:* 01-236 8436; Belvedere, Mellieha Heights, Malta. *T:* Mellieha 73-815.

**HOWARD, Hon. Sir Gerald;** *see* Howard, Hon. Sir Stephen Gerald.

**HOWARD, Maj.-Gen. Gordon Byron,** CBE 1945; Consultant, Canadian Industrial Preparedness Association; *b* 8 May 1895; *s* of Samuel William and Maud Margaret Howard; *m* 1919, Ada Becket Woods, Montreal; one *d*. *Educ:* Toronto Public Schs; Upper Canada Coll.; Royal Military College, Kingston. Joined Royal Canadian Ordnance Corps, 1914; Ordnance Coll., Woolwich, 1919; Military Coll. of Science, 1928-31; Chief Inspector Armaments, Canada, 1934-40; Deputy Inspector-Gen., Inspection Board, 1940-43; Controller-Gen. and Chairman Inspection Board of UK and Canada, 1943-47; retired, 1947. *Recreation:* badminton. *Address:* Room 744, Dominion Square Building, Montreal, Canada.

**HOWARD, Hon. Greville (Reginald);** *b* 7 Sept. 1909; 3rd *s* of 19th Earl of Suffolk and Berks; *m* 1945, Mary Ridehalgh; one *d*. *Educ:* Eton; RMC Sandhurst. Commissioned in King's Shropshire LI, 1930-35. London Manager of G. W. Joynson, Cotton Merchants and Brokers, 1935-39. Councillor Westminster City Council, 1937; Naval Service, War of 1939-45; destroyers commanded: HMS Viscount (temp.), 1943; HMS Sabre, 1943-44; HMS Nith, 1944. Rejoined Westminster City Council, 1945; Mayor of Westminster, 1946-47; Chm. Public Cleansing, Transport, Baths and Contracts Cttee, 1945 and 1947-49; Vice-Chm. Establishments Cttee, 1949; Vice-Chm. Refuse Sub-Cttee, Metropolitan Boroughs Standing Joint Cttee, 1947-49. MP (Nat L and C) St Ives Division of Cornwall 1950-66; retired, 1966. Dir, Colour Processing Laboratories Ltd. Mem. Cttee of Management and Vice-Pres., Royal National Life-Boat Institution; Joint Pres., Nat. Assoc. of Inshore Fishermen. *Recreations:* photography, sailing, bicycling, riding, fishing. *Address:* Brouch, near Mersch, Grand Duché de Luxembourg. *T:* 63560. *Clubs:* White's, Pratt's, RNVR; Royal Cornwall Yacht.

**HOWARD, Sir (Hamilton) Edward (de Coucey),** 2nd Bt *cr* 1955; Partner of Stockbroking Firm of Charles Stanley and Company; Chairman, Advance Electronics Ltd; Director: LRC International Ltd; Toye & Co. Ltd; *b* 29 Oct. 1915; *s* of Sir (Harold Walter) Seymour Howard, 1st Bt, and Edith M. (*d* 1962), *d* of Edward Turner; *S* father 1967; *m* 1943, Elizabeth Howarth Ludlow; two *s*. *Educ:* Le Rosey, Rolle, Switzerland; Radley Coll., Abingdon; Worcester Coll., Oxford. Mem. of the Stock Exchange, London, 1946. Sheriff of the City of London, 1966 (Common Councillor, 1951; Alderman, 1963). Master of the Gardeners' Company, 1961. *Recreation:* gardening. *Heir: s* David Howarth Seymour Howard [*b* 29 Dec. 1945; *m* 1968, Valerie Picton, *o d* of Derek W. Crosse]. *Address:* Hithe House, Bridle Way, Addington Hills, Surrey. *T:* 01-777 3520. *Clubs:* City of London, City Livery, United Wards.

**HOWARD, Lieut-Col Hon. Henry Anthony Camillo,** CMG 1960; *b* 3 March 1913; *s* of 1st Baron Howard of Penrith, PC, GCB, GCMG, CVO, and Lady Isabella Giustiniani-Bandini (*d* of Prince Giustiniani-Bandini, 8th Earl of Newburgh); *m* 1937, Adele Le Bourgeois, *d* of late Reese Denny Alsop, New York City, USA; four *d* (and one *d* decd). *Educ:* Newman

Sch., NJ, USA; Downside; RMC Sandhurst. Commissioned, Coldstream Guards, 1932; seconded Somaliland Camel Corps, 1935-36; resigned commission, 1937; Asst Sec., Council of Foreign Bondholders, 1937-39. Served War of 1939-45 (despatches). Entered Colonial Service, 1946; Administrative Officer, Kenya, 1947; Private Sec. to Governor, 1952-53; seconded as Commissioner, Virgin Islands, 1954; Administrator, 1956; Administrator of St Kitts, Nevis and Anguilla, 1956-65. *Recreation:* shooting. *Address:* Bushby House, Greystoke, Penrith, Cumberland.

*See also Hon. Edmund B. C. Howard.*

**HOWARD, Sir Henry Rudolph;** *see* Howard, Sir Harry.

**HOWARD, James Boag;** Assistant Under-Secretary of State, Home Office, since 1963; *b* 10 Jan. 1915; *yr s* of William and Jean Howard, Greenock; *m* 1943, Dorothy Jean Crawshaw; two *d. Educ:* Greenock High Sch.; Glasgow Univ. (MA, BSc; 1st cl. Hons Mathematics and Natural Philosophy). Asst Principal, Home Office, 1937; Private Sec. to Permanent Sec., Ministry of Home Security, 1940-41; Principal, 1941; Asst Sec., 1948. *Address:* 12 Windhill, Bishop's Stortford, Herts. *T:* Bishop's Stortford 51728. *Club:* Reform.

**HOWARD, Sir John,** Kt 1954; FICE; Chairman and Managing Director, John Howard and Co. Ltd, Civil Engineering Contractors; Managing Director, Thames Estuary Development Co. Ltd; Chairman: Nuclear Industrial Structures; John Howard & Co. (Africa) Ltd; John Howard (Holdings) Ltd; John Howard & Co. (Northern) Ltd; Director: Parkinson Howard (Ghana) Ltd; Steel Structures Ltd; *b* 17 Nov. 1901; *s* of John Golding Howard, Biddenham, Bedford; *m* 1931, Margaret Mary, *d* of Herbert Edward Kemp; three *s* one *d. Educ:* Bedford Sch. Chm., National Union of Conservative and Unionist Assocs, 1962. *Recreations:* shooting, golf. *Address:* Crossland Fosse, Box End, Bedford. *T:* Kempston 2125; John Howard & Co. Ltd, 13 Buckingham Gate, SW1. *T:* 01-834 8951. *Clubs:* Carlton, City Livery, Royal Automobile.

**HOWARD, Sir John Curtois,** Kt 1942; Chairman, Police Council for Great Britain, 1953-57, retired; *b* Spalding, 15 Jan. 1887; *s* of late Fitzalan Howard, Holyrood House, Spalding; *m* 1912, Norah Carey, *d* of late Capt. John Lakes; one *s* three *d. Educ:* Uppingham; Clare Coll., Cambridge (Exhibitioner). BA 1909; Barrister-at-Law, Inner Temple, 1913; served European War, 1915-20; Brigade Trench Mortar, Officer, 177th Brigade, 59th Div.; Staff Capt. British Troops France and Flanders, 1919-20; Pres. District Court, Cyprus, 1920-24; Attorney-Gen., Cyprus, 1924-26; Solicitor-Gen., Nigeria, 1926-33; KC, Gold Coast, 1934; Attorney-Gen. of the Gold Coast, 1933-36; Attorney-Gen., Ceylon, 1936; KC, Ceylon, 1936; Legal Sec., Ceylon, 1936-39; Acting Governor, Ceylon, July 1946-Feb. 1947 and July 1947-Aug. 1947; Chief Justice of Ceylon, 1939-49. *Publication:* Joint Edition, Laws of Cyprus, 1924. *Recreation:* golf. *Address:* 19 Denton Road, Meads, Eastbourne, Sussex. *Club:* East India and Sports.

**HOWARD, Mrs John E.;** *see* Laski, Marghanita.

**HOWARD, John Melbourne;** Chartered Accountant; Director: Lonsdale and Bartholomew, Ltd; H. Sichel & Sons Ltd; Epsom Glass Industries Ltd; a Partner in John Howard & Co. and A. J. Pickard & Co., both firms of Chartered Accountants; *b* 10 Aug. 1913; *er s* of Harry Howard, Warlingham, Surrey; *m* 1948, Maisie Alexandra, *d* of Alexander Bartlett Gilbert. *Educ:* Whitgift Sch. ACA 1935; FCA 1945. Served in Royal Navy, 1941-45; commissioned in RNVR. MP (C) Test Division of Southampton, 1955-64; Parliamentary Private Secretary: to Financial Sec. to the Treasury, 1957-58; to Financial and Parliamentary Sec. to Admiralty and to Civil Lord, 1958-59; to Rt Hon. Edward Heath, MP, as Minister of Labour, 1959-60 and as Lord Privy Seal at the Foreign Office, 1960-63. *Recreation:* sailing. *Address:* Capel Manor House, Horsmonden, Kent. *Clubs:* Royal Automobile, Junior Carlton, Royal Naval Volunteer Reserve.

**HOWARD, Leon Alexander L.;** *see* Lee Howard.

**HOWARD, Leonard Henry,** RD 1941; retired; *b* 5 Aug. 1904; *m* 1st, 1938, Betty Scourse; one *s* one *d*; 2nd, 1960, Barbara Davies-Colley. *Educ:* Stubbington House Sch.; Nautical Coll., Pangbourne. Sea career in Royal Navy and P. & O.–Orient Lines (Merchant Navy), 1922-64; Commodore, P. & O.–Orient Lines, 1963-64 (now P. & O. Steam Navigation Co.), retired. Mem., Honourable Company of Master Mariners, HMS Wellington, Temple Stairs, London. *Recreations:* golf, gardening. *Address:* Port, Heyshott, Midhurst, W Sussex. *T:* Midhurst 2560. *Club:* Cowdray Park Golf.

**HOWARD, Hon. Mabel Bowden;** Member for Sydenham, Labour Party, Parliament of New Zealand, since 1943; *b* Adelaide, S Australia; 2nd *d* of Edwin John Howard, Deputy Speaker in first Labour Government in New Zealand; came to NZ on death of mother, Harriet Howard, in 1903. *Educ:* New Brighton Sch. and Technical Coll. Was sec. for many years of one of largest industrial unions in NZ, only woman ever to hold such a position; mem. City Council, Drainage Board, Hosp. Bd, Tramway Bd, for many years. Elected to Parliament (NZ) in 1943; in 1946 elections secured highest individual vote and majority ever recorded in NZ; first woman to be elected to Cabinet in NZ; Minister for Health in the Government of New Zealand, 1947-49; Ministry of Social Security, Minister for Welfare of Women and Children, and Minister in Charge of Child Welfare Dept, NZ, 1957-60. During war years was Chm. of Women's War Service Auxiliary in home town of Christchurch. Pres. Soc. Prevention Cruelty to Animals (SPCA); responsible for Act for protection of animals, passed in NZ, 1960. *Recreations:* reading, needlework, gardening; caring for old folk. *Address:* 147 Pages Road, Christchurch, New Zealand; Parliament House, Wellington, New Zealand.

**HOWARD, Michael Eliot,** MC 1943; FBA 1970; FRHistS; Fellow of All Souls, Oxford, since 1968; *b* 29 Nov. 1922; *y s* of Geoffrey Eliot Howard, Ashmore, near Salisbury, and of Edith Julia Emma, *o d* of Otto Edinger. *Educ:* Wellington; Christ Church, Oxford. BA 1946, MA 1948. Served War, Coldstream Guards, 1942-45. Asst Lecturer in History, University of London, King's Coll., 1947; Lecturer, 1950; Lecturer in War Studies, 1953-61; Prof. of War Studies, 1963-68; Dean of Faculty of Arts, 1964-68. Ford's Lectr in English History, Oxford, 1971. Member: Senate, University of London, 1966-68; Council, Institute for Strategic Studies; RIIA (Vice-Chm.); RUSI; RMA Academic Adv. Council; Chm., Army Educational Adv. Bd; Trustee, Imp. War Museum. Governor: Haileybury Coll.; Wellington Coll. *Publications:* The Coldstream Guards, 1920-46 (with John Sparrow), 1951; Disengagement in Europe, 1958; Wellingtonian Studies, 1959; The Franco-Prussian War, 1961 (Duff Cooper Memorial Prize, 1962); The Theory and Practice of War,

1965; The Mediterranean Strategy in the Second World War, 1967; Studies in War and Peace, 1970; contributions to The New Cambridge Modern History. *Address:* Eastbury, Newbury, Berks. *T:* Lambourn 387. *Clubs:* Brooks's, Garrick.

**HOWARD, Very Rev. Richard Thomas,** MA; Provost of Coventry Cathedral, 1933-58; Provost Emeritus since 1958; *b* 1884; *m* Ethel Marjorie Corfield; two *s* three *d*. *Educ:* Weymouth Coll.; Jesus Coll., Cambridge (Rustat Scholar; 23rd Wrangler, First-Class in the Theological Tripos); Ridley Hall. Ordained, 1908; Chaplain of Jesus Coll., Cambridge, 1908-12; went out to St John's Coll., Agra, under the Church Missionary Soc., 1912; Vice-Principal, St Paul's Divinity Sch., Allahabab, 1913-18; Principal of St Aidan's Coll., Birkenhead, 1919-29; Vicar of Luton, 1929-33; Archdeacon of Coventry, 1941-46; Proctor in Convocation for Diocese of St Albans, 1931, and Coventry Cathedral Chapter, 1933. *Address:* Ufton Rectory, Leamington, Warwicks. *T:* Harbury 268.

**HOWARD, Rev. Ronald Claude;** Headmaster, Hurstpierpoint College, 1945-64; *b* 15 Feb. 1902; 2nd *s* of Henry H. and Florence Howard, The Durrant, Sevenoaks. *Educ:* Sidney Sussex Coll., Cambridge; Westcott House, Cambridge. Ordained, 1926; Curate of Eastbourne, 1926-28; Chaplain, Bradfield Coll., 1928-30; Asst Master, Tonbridge Sch., 1930-37; Asst Master, Marlborough Coll., 1937, Chaplain there, 1938-43; Chaplain and Asst Master, Radley Coll., 1943-45. Canon of Chichester, 1957; Communar of Chichester Cathedral, 1964-67. *Recreations:* painting, collecting water-colours. *Address:* 11 Mount Harry Road, Sevenoaks, Kent. *Club:* Travellers'.

**HOWARD, Hon. Sir (Stephen) Gerald,** Kt 1961; JP; **Hon. Mr Justice Howard;** Judge of the High Court of Justice (Queen's Bench Division) since 1961; Barrister-at-law; *b* 7 June 1896; *o s* of late Major S. G. Howard, CBE, DL, and Mary M. Howard, The Moat, Upend, Newmarket; *m* 1934, Claudia Primrose, *d* of late Graves Stoker, MD, FRCS, Dublin and London, and Mrs Stoker, Gaddesden Hall, Gaddesden, Herts; two *s*. *Educ:* Harrow; Balliol Coll., Oxford. Flight Lieut RFC and RAF, 1916-18; Balliol Coll., Oxford, 1918-21; called to Bar, Lincoln's Inn, 1924; Bencher, 1942; QC 1950. Recorder of Bury St Edmunds, 1943-45; a senior Prosecuting Counsel, 1945-50; Recorder of Ipswich, 1947-58; Recorder of Southend, 1958-61. Chm. of Quarter Sessions: for Cambridgeshire, 1947-52; for East and West Suffolk, 1952-61. MP (C) Cambridgeshire, 1950-61. JP Cambridgeshire, 1942; High Sheriff of Cambs and Hunts, 1945-46. *Recreation:* shooting. *Address:* The Moat, Upend, Newmarket, Cambs. *T:* Cheveley 234. *Clubs:* Oxford and Cambridge; Norfolk County (Norwich).

**HOWARD, Trevor Wallace;** actor; *b* 29 Sept. 1916; father English, mother Canadian; *m* 1944, Helen Mary Cherry. *Educ:* Clifton Coll. Shakespeare Festival, Stratford-on-Avon, 1936 and 1939. Served War in Army, 1940-43, 1st Airborne Division. Played in the Recruiting Officer and Anna Christie, 1944; Old Vic Season, 1947-48, Petruchio in the Taming of the Shrew. *Films include:* Brief Encounter, 1945; The Third Man, 1949; An Outcast of the Islands, 1951; The Heart of the Matter, 1953; Lovers of Lisbon (French); Cockleshell Heroes, 1955; The Key, Roots of Heaven, 1958; Sons and Lovers, 1960; Mutiny on the Bounty, 1962; Von Ryan's Express, 1965; The Liquidator, 1966; The Charge of the Light Brigade, 1968; Ryan's Daughter, 1970. *Plays include:* The Devil's General, 1953; Lopahin in The Cherry Orchard, Lyric, 1954; Two Stars for Comfort, Garrick, 1962; The Father, Piccadilly, 1964. TV: The Invincible Mr Disraeli, 1963 (Acad. Award); Napoleon at St Helena, 1966 (Acad. nom.). *Recreations:* cricket, travel. *Address:* Rowley Green, Arkley, Herts. *Club:* MCC.

**HOWARD, Sir Walter Stewart,** Kt 1963; MBE 1944; DL; *b* 1888; *y s* of late Henry Blunt Howard; *m* 1917, Alison Mary Wall, *e d* of late Herbert F. Waring, Farningham Hill, Kent. *Educ:* Wellington; Trinity Coll., Cambridge. Vice-Chm., Warwicks CC, 1955 (Chm., 1956-60); Chm. Whiteley Village Trust, 1952-62; Governor: King Edward VI Sch., Birmingham; Warwick Sch.; Pres., Association of Education Cttees, 1962-63. Trustee of Shakespeare's birthplace. JP 1931, CC 1939, CA 1948, DL 1952, Warwicks. *Recreation:* foreign travel. *Address:* Barford, Warwick. *T:* Barford 208. *Club:* United University.

**HOWARD, William McLaren,** QC 1964; Deputy Chairman of Norfolk Quarter Sessions since 1967; Recorder of Ipswich, since 1968; *b* 27 Jan. 1921; 3rd *s* of William George Howard and Frances Jane (*née* McLaren). *Educ:* Merchant Taylors' Sch. Entered RN as Cadet, 1938. Served at sea throughout War of 1939-45; Lieut 1942; resigned commission, 1946. Called to the Bar, Lincoln's Inn, 1947; joined Inner Temple (*ad eundem*), 1960. *Address:* 3 King's Bench Walk, Temple, EC4. *T:* 01-353 0431. *Club:* Garrick.

**HOWARD-DOBSON, Maj.-Gen. Patrick John;** Chief of Staff, Far East Command, since 1969; *b* 12 Aug. 1921; *s* of Canon Howard Dobson, MA; *m* 1946, Barbara Mary Mills; two *s* one *d*. *Educ:* King's Coll. Choir Sch., Cambridge; Framlingham College. Joined 7th Queen's Own Hussars, Egypt, Dec. 1941; served in: Burma, 1942; Middle East, 1943; Italy, 1944-45; Germany, 1946; psc 1950; jssc 1958; comd The Queen's Own Hussars, 1963-65 and 20 Armoured Bde, 1965-67; idc 1968. Virtuti Militari (Poland), 1945; Silver Star (US), 1945. *Recreations:* cricket, golf, ski-ing. *Address:* c/o Barclays Bank, Halesworth, Suffolk. *Club:* Cavalry.

**HOWARD-JOHNSTON, Rear-Admiral Clarence Dinsmore,** CB 1955; DSO 1942; DSC 1940; *b* 13 Oct. 1903; *m* 1955, Paulette, *d* of late Paul Helleu. *Educ:* Royal Naval Colls Osborne and Dartmouth. Midshipman, 1921; Commander, 1937; Capt., 1943; Rear-Adm., 1953; Dir of Studies, Greek Naval War Coll., Athens, 1938-40; Dir Anti-U-Boat Div., Admiralty, 1943-45; Naval Attaché, Paris, 1947-50; apptd Naval ADC to the Queen, 1952; Chief of Staff to Flag Officer Central Europe, 1953-55; retired RN 1955. Order of Phœnix (Greece), 1940; Legion of Merit (USA), 1945. *Address:* 45 Rue Emile Menier, Paris 16e. *Clubs:* White's, Naval and Military, (Naval Member) Royal Yacht Squadron; Jockey (Paris).

**HOWARD-JONES, Maj.-Gen. Leonard Hamilton,** CB 1959; CBE 1945 (OBE 1942); *b* 4 April 1905; *s* of late Hubert Stanley Howard-Jones, Maindee Park, Newport, Mon; *m* 1st, 1934, Irene Lucy Gillespie (*d* 1944); 2nd, 1945, Violet, *d* of Sidney Alfred Butler, and *widow* of Lieut-Col Francis John Leland; one *s* one *d*. *Educ:* Imperial Service Coll.; Cardiff Univ. (BSc Eng). Served War of 1939-45 (despatches; OBE; CBE). Commandant REME Training Centre, 1953-57; Inspector, Royal Electrical and Mechanical Engineers, War Office, 1957-60. MIMechE; AMIEE. *Address:* Rifle Range

Farm, Hartley Wintney, Hants. *T:* Hartley Wintney 2358. *Club:* United Service.

**HOWARD-VYSE, Lt-Gen. Sir Edward (Dacre),** KBE 1962 (CBE 1955); CB 1958; MC 1941; Vice-Lieutenant of the East Riding of Yorkshire since 1968; *b* 27 Nov. 1905; *s* of late Lieut-Col Cecil Howard-Vyse, JP, Langton Hall, Malton, Yorks; *m* 1940, Mary Bridget, *er d* of late Col Hon. Claude Henry Comaraich Willoughby, CVO; two *s* one *d. Educ:* Wellington Coll., Berks; RMA. 2nd Lieut, Royal Artillery, 1925; served War of 1939-45: British Expeditionary Force, France, 1939-40; Lieut-Col, 1941; Mediterranean Expeditionary Force, 1941-44; In command 1st Royal Horse Artillery, Central Mediterranean Force, 1944-45. Brigadier, 1949; CRA 7th Armoured Division, BAOR, 1951-53; Commandant, Sch. of Artillery, 1953; Maj.-Gen., 1957; Maj.-Gen., Artillery, Northern Army Group, 1956-59; Dir, Royal Artillery, War Office, 1959-61; GOC-in-C, Western Command, 1961-64; retired, 1964. Lieut-Gen., 1961. Col Comdt: RA 1962; RHA 1968. Chm. Army Cadet Force Assoc., 1964-; Vice-Pres., Nat. Artillery Assoc., 1965-. DL E Riding of Yorks and Kingston upon Hull, 1964, Vice-Lieut, 1968. *Recreations:* foxhunting and fishing; British Olympic Equestrian Team, 1936. *Address:* Langton House, Malton, Yorks. *Club:* Army and Navy.

**HOWARTH, David Armine;** author; *b* 18 July 1912; *s* of Dr O. J. R. Howarth and Mrs E. K. Howarth; *m* 1944, Nanette Russell Smith; one *s* three *d. Educ:* Tonbridge Sch.; Trinity Coll., Cambridge. BBC Talks Asst etc, 1934-39. War Correspondent, 1939-40; RNVR, 1940-45. Knight 1st class, Order of St Olav (Norway), 1955; Cross of Freedom (Norway) 1945. *Publications:* The Shetland Bus, 1951; We Die Alone (also under title Escape Alone), 1955; The Sledge Patrol, 1957; Dawn of D-Day, 1959; The Shadow of the Dam, 1961; The Desert King, A Biography of Ibn Saud, 1964; The Golden Isthmus, 1966; A Near Run Thing: the Day of Waterloo, 1968; Trafalgar: The Nelson Touch, 1969; *fiction:* Group Flashing Two, 1952; One Night in Styria, 1953; *for children:* Heroes of Nowadays, 1957; Great Escapes, 1969. As Editor: My Land and My People (by HH The Dalai Lama), 1962. *Address:* Vines Gate, Brasted Chart, Westerham, Kent. *T:* Westerham 3608.

**HOWARTH, Herbert Lomax;** *b* 3 March 1900; *er s* of Herbert and Emma Margaret Howarth; *m* 1926, Mildred, *e d* of James and Janet Dodd; no *c. Educ:* Darlington Gram. Sch.; Preston Gram. Sch.; Magdalen Coll., Oxford. Joined Westminster Gazette, 1922. Council of the Newspaper Soc., 1939-64 (Chm. Labour Cttee, 1948-50; Chm. Technical Cttee, 1952-55). Dir Press Association Ltd, 1954-61 (Chm. 1958-59); Dir Birmingham Post & Mail Ltd, 1957-66; Dir Reuters Ltd, 1958-61, Trustee, 1963-. Managing Dir, Westminster Press Provincial Newspapers Limited, 1953-64, retired. *Address:* Top End, Storth, Milnthorpe, Westmorland. *T:* Milnthorpe 3195. *Club:* Oxford and Cambridge University.

**HOWARTH, Prof. Leslie,** OBE 1955; FRS 1950; FRAeS; BSc, MA, PhD; Henry Overton Wills Professor of Mathematics, University of Bristol, since 1964; *b* 23 May 1911; *s* of Fred and Elizabeth Ellen Howarth; *m* 1934, Eva Priestley; two *s. Educ:* Accrington Grammar Sch.; Manchester Univ.; Gonville and Caius Coll., Cambridge. Mathematical tripos, 1933; Smith's Prize, 1935; PhD, 1936. Berry-Ramsey Research Fellow, King's Coll., Cambridge, 1936-45; Lecturer in Mathematics in the University of Cambridge, 1936-49; Fellow of St John's Coll., Cambridge, 1945-49; Prof. of Applied Mathematics, University of Bristol, 1949-64; Adams Prize, 1951. Worked at External Ballistics Dept, Ordnance Board, 1939-42, and at Armament Research Dept, 1942-45. *Publications:* (ed) Modern Developments in Fluid Dynamics: High Speed Flow; papers on aerodynamics. *Address:* 10 The Crescent, Henleaze, Bristol BS9 4RW. *T:* Bristol 62-6346; School of Mathematics, University of Bristol, University Walk, Bristol BS8 1TW. *T:* Bristol 24161.

**HOWARTH, Robert Lever;** *b* 31 July 1927; *s* of James Howarth and Bessie (*née* Pearson); *m* 1952, Josephine Mary Doyle; one *s* one *d. Educ:* Bolton County Grammar Sch.; Bolton Technical Coll. Draughtsman with Hawker Siddeley Dynamics. MP (Lab) Bolton East, 1964-70. *Recreations:* gardening, reading, walking, films. *Address:* 11 Kinloch Drive, Bolton, Lancs. *T:* Bolton 44121.

**HOWARTH, Thomas Edward Brodie,** MC 1945; TD; High Master, St Paul's School since 1962; *b* 21 Oct. 1914; *e s* of Frank Fielding Howarth; *m* 1943, Margaret Teakle; three *s* one *d. Educ:* Rugby Sch.; Clare Coll., Cambridge (Scholar, MA, 1st cl. Hons Parts I and II, History Tripos). Asst Master, Winchester Coll., 1938-39, 1946-48; Headmaster King Edward's Sch., Birmingham, 1948-52; Second Master, Winchester Coll., 1952-62. Served War of 1939-45, King's (Liverpool) Regt; Brigade Major, HQ Mersey Garrison; Brigade Major 207 Infantry Bde; NW Europe, June 1944; Personal Liaison Officer to C-in-C 21st Army Group. Trustee, Imperial War Museum, 1964-. Mem., Public Schs Commission, 1966-. Chm., Headmasters' Conference, 1969. *Publications:* Citizen-King, 1961; Culture, Anarchy and the Public Schools, 1969. *Recreations:* lawn tennis, golf. *Address:* St Paul's School, Lonsdale Road, Barnes, SW13. *T:* 01-748 6420. *Clubs:* Savile, Queen's.

**HOWE,** 6th Earl, *cr* 1821; **Edward Richard Assheton Penn Curzon,** CBE 1961; DL; JP; Baron Howe, 1788; Baron Curzon, 1794; Viscount Curzon, 1802; Lieutenant-Commander RNVR; President of South Bucks Conservative and Unionist Association since 1965; Alderman CC Bucks, since 1958; *b* 7 Aug. 1908; a godson of King Edward VII; *o s* of 5th Earl Howe, PC, CBE, VD; *S* father, 1964; *m* 1st, 1935, Priscilla (whom he divorced, 1942), *o c* of Lieut-Col Sir Archibald Weigall, 1st Bt, KCMG; 2nd, 1946, Gay, *e d* of late Stephen Frederick Wakeling, Durban, South Africa; two *d. Educ:* Eton; Corpus Christi Coll., Cambridge. RNVR, 1928-46; Mem. (MR) LCC for South Battersea, 1937-46. Commissioner of Bucks St John Ambulance Bde, 1953-55; Pres., St John Ambulance, Bucks. Trustee, King William IV Naval Asylum. JP 1946, DL 1960, Bucks. Pres., Brit. Automobile Racing Club; Member: RAC Cttee; Nat. Motor Rallies Adv. Cttee; RAC Competitions Cttee. Mem. Management Cttee, Arethusa Training Ship. CStJ. *Recreations:* motoring, cricket, shooting, golf. *Heir: cousin* (Chambré) George (William Penn) Curzon (George Curzon, actor) [*b* 19 Oct. 1898; *m* 1st, 1927, Louise Merrill Rowe (*d* 1942); 2nd, 1950, Jane Victoria (marr. diss., 1965), *d* of late M. M. Fergusson, Toronto; one *s* one *d.* Comdr RN retd]. *Address:* Penn House, Amersham, Bucks. *T:* Holmer Green 3366; 20 Pitts Head Mews, W1. *T:* 01-499 4706. *Clubs:* 1900, Royal Naval Volunteer Reserve.

**HOWE, Sir Geoffrey;** *see* Howe, Sir R. E. G.

**HOWE, Prof. Geoffrey Leslie,** TD 1962 (Bar 1969); Professor of Oral Surgery, Royal Dental

Hospital, London School of Dental Surgery, since 1967; *b* 22 April 1924; *e s* of late Leo Leslie John Howe, Maidenhead, Berks; *m* 1947, Heather Patricia Joan Hambly; one *s*. *Educ:* Royal Dental and Middlesex Hospitals. LDS RCS 1946; LRCP, MRCS 1954; FDS RCS 1955; MDS Dunelm, 1961; FFD RCSI 1964. Dental and Medical Sch. Prizeman; Begley Prize, RCS, 1951; Cartwright Prize, RCS, 1961. Dental Officer, Royal Army Dental Corps, 1946-49. House appointments, etc., Royal Dental and Middlesex Hospitals, 1949-55. Registrar in Oral Surgery, Eastman Dental Hosp. (Institute of Dental Surgery), 1955-56; Senior Registrar in Oral Surgery, Plastic and Oral Surgery Centre, Chepstow, Mon, 1956; Senior Registrar in Oral Surgery, Eastman Dental Hospital, 1956-59; Professor of Oral Surgery, University of Newcastle upon Tyne (formerly King's Coll., University of Durham), 1959-67; Cons. Oral Surgeon, United Newcastle upon Tyne Hosps, 1959-67. FRSM. *Publications:* The Extraction of Teeth, 1961, 2nd edn 1970; Minor Oral Surgery, 1966; contribs to: Medical Treatment Yearbook, 1959; Modern Trends in Dental Surgery, 1962, and to numerous medical and dental journals. *Recreations:* sailing; Territorial Army Volunteer Reserve (Lieut-Col, graded Cons. Dental Surgeon RADC, TAVR). *Address:* c/o Royal Dental Hospital, Leicester Square, WC2. *T:* 01-930 8831; 1 Langton Way, Croydon, Surrey CRO 5JS. *T:* 01-686 4201. *Clubs:* Savage, Oral Surgery.

**HOWE, Jack,** RDI 1962; FRIBA 1953; Senior Partner Jack Howe & Partners, Architects and Industrial Designers; *b* 24 Feb. 1911; *s* of Charles Henry and Florence Eleanor Howe; *m* 1960, Margaret Crosbie Corrie; one *s* one *d* (by former marriage). *Educ:* Enfield Grammar Sch.; Polytechnic Sch. of Architecture. Asst to E. Maxwell Fry, 1933-37; Chief Asst to Walter Gropius and Maxwell Fry, 1937-39; Drawing Office Manager to Holland, Hannan & Cubitts Ltd for Royal Ordnance Factories at Wrexham and Ruskill, 1939-43; Associate Partner, Arcon, 1944-48; private practice, 1949; Partnership with Andrew Bain, 1959. Architectural work includes: Highbury Quadrant Primary School, (LCC); Windmill House, Lambeth (LCC Housing Scheme); Television Research Lab. for AEI Ltd; Kodak Pavilion, Brussels Exhibn, 1958; Official Architects for British Trade Fair, Moscow, 1961; Industrial Designs include: Diesel Electric Locomotives and Express Pullman Trains; also Rly equipment. Industrial Design Consultant to various large firms and to BR Board. Mem. Design Index Cttee and Street Furniture Cttee, Council of Industrial Design, 1956-; Mem. Cttee on Traffic Signs, Min. of Transport, 1962, 1963. FSIA (Pres. 1963-64). Duke of Edinburgh's design prize, 1969. *Publications:* articles for various architectural and design jls. *Recreations:* music, tennis. *Address:* 4 Leopold Avenue, Wimbledon, SW19. *T:* 01-946 7116.

**HOWE, Rt. Rev. John William Alexander;** Executive Officer of the Anglican Communion, since 1969; *b* 1920. *Educ:* Westcliff High Sch.; St Chad's Coll., Durham Univ. BA 1943; MA, BD 1948. Ordained, 1943; Curate, All Saints, Scarborough, 1943-46; Chaplain, Adisadel Coll., Gold Coast, 1946-50; Vice-Principal, Edinburgh Theological Coll., 1950-55; Hon. Chaplain, St Mary's Cathedral, Edinburgh, 1951-55; Bishop of St Andrews, Dunkeld and Dunblane, 1955-69. Hon. Canon, St Mary's Cath., Glasgow, 1969. *Address:* 21 Chester Street, SW1. *T:* 01-235 7461.

**HOWE, Sir (Richard Edward) Geoffrey,** Kt 1970; QC 1965; MP (C) Reigate since 1970; Solicitor-General since 1970; Deputy Chairman, Glamorgan Quarter Sessions since 1966; *b* 20 Dec. 1926; *er s* of late B. E. Howe and Mrs E. F. Howe, JP (*née* Thomson), Port Talbot, Glamorgan; *m* 1953, Elspeth Rosamund Morton Shand; one *s* two *d*. *Educ:* Winchester Coll. (Exhibitioner); Trinity Hall, Cambridge (Scholar, MA, LLB). Lieut Royal Signals 1945-48. Chm. Cambridge Univ. Conservative Assoc., 1951; Chm. Bow Group, 1955; Managing Dir, Crossbow, 1957-60, Editor 1960-62. Called to the Bar, Middle Temple, 1952; Bencher, 1969-; Mem. General Council of the Bar, 1957-61; Mem. Council of Justice, 1963-. Contested (C) Aberavon, 1955, 1959; MP (C) Bebington, 1964-66. Sec. Conservative Parliamentary Health and Social Security Cttee, 1964-65; an Opposition Front Bench spokesman on labour and social services, 1965-66. Mem., (Latey) Interdeptl Cttee on Age of Majority, 1965-67; Chm. Ely Hospital, Cardiff, Inquiry, 1969. Mem. Council of Management, Private Patients' Plan, 1969-. *Publications:* various political pamphlets for Bow Group and Conservative Political Centre. *Address:* c/o Barclays Bank, Cavendish Square Branch, 4 Vere Street, W1. *Club:* Carlton.

**HOWE, Sir Robert George,** GBE 1949; KCMG 1947 (CMG 1937); *b* Derby, 19 Sept. 1893; *s* of H. Howe; *m* 1919, Loveday Mary Hext (*d* 1970); one *s*. *Educ:* Derby Sch.; St Catharine's Coll., Cambridge. Third Sec. at Copenhagen, 1920; Second Sec., 1920; Belgrade, 1922; Rio de Janeiro, 1924; First Sec., 1926; Bucharest, 1926; Foreign Office, 1930; Acting Counsellor at Peking, 1934; Counsellor, 1936; Minister in Riga, 1940; Minister in Abyssinia, 1942-45; Asst Under-Sec. of State, Foreign Office, 1945; Governor-Gen. of the Sudan, 1947-55; retired 1955. *Recreation:* riding. *Address:* Cowbridge, Lostwithiel, Cornwall.

**HOWE, Sir Ronald (Martin),** Kt 1955; CVO 1950; MC 1916; Chairman, Group 4 Total Security; Director: Louis Dreyfus & Co. Ltd; City Wall Properties Ltd and many other cos; *b* 5 Sept. 1896; *s* of Frank Gull Howe, journalist, and Clara Harriet Mackenzie; bachelor. *Educ:* Westminster Sch. (King's scholar); Christ Church, Oxford (scholar). Served Royal Sussex Regt, 1915-19 (MC, wounded), Capt., 1917. Called to Bar, Inner Temple, 1924; Legal Officer, Dir of Public Prosecutions Dept, 1924-31; Chief Constable CID, New Scotland Yard, 1932; Asst Commissioner in charge of CID, 1945-53; Dep. Commissioner, 1953-57. Studied police methods in USA, Canada and all principal European countries; British Representative on Internat. Criminal Police Commission, 1945-57. Officer French Legion of Honour; Commander Royal Danish Order of Dannebrog; Officer Royal Netherlands Order of Orange-Nassau. *Publications:* The Pursuit of Crime, 1961; The Story of Scotland Yard, 1965. *Address:* White Walls, Roehampton, SW15. *T:* 01-788 9562. *Clubs:* United Service, Buck's.

**HOWELL, Charles Alfred,** OBE 1965; Clerical Officer, National Carriers Ltd (formerly British Railways); *b* 22 Oct. 1905; *s* of Charles and May Louise Howell; *m* 1927, Ivy Jeanette Silvester; one *d*. *Educ:* Winshill Secondary Sch., Burton-on-Trent. A railway guard; Branch Sec., Derby No 1 Branch, NUR, 1939-55; Mem. of LM Region Sectional Council No 3 (Traffic Grades), 1943-55; Mem. of National Executive Cttee, NUR, 1951-53; Voluntary Tutor, National Council of Labour Colls; Mem. of Derby County Borough Council, 1943-53; Sec. of Derby Trades Council, 1945-56; Chm. of Derby Borough Labour Party,

1950-51; Mem. Derby and S Derbyshire Assessment Tribunal, 1948-59; Member: Derby No 2 Hosp. Management Cttee 1948-66; Derby No 1 Hosp. Management Cttee, 1966-; Chairman: Derwent Hosp. (Derby), 1948-; Draycot Hosp., 1967-. MP (Lab) Perry Barr Div. of Birmingham, 1955-64; an Opposition Whip, 1959-64. Sec., Derby Area Trades Union Council, 1966-. *Address:* 36 Cardigan Street, Cowsley Estate, Derby DE2 6DW. *T:* Derby 43878.

**HOWELL, David Arthur Russell;** MP (C) Guildford since 1966; Lord Commissioner of the Treasury and Parliamentary Secretary, Civil Service Department, since 1970; *b* 18 Jan. 1936; *s* of Colonel A. H. E. Howell, DSO, TD, DL and Beryl Howell, 5 Headfort Place, SW1; *m* 1967, Davina Wallace; two *d. Educ:* Eton; King's Coll., Cambridge. Lieut Coldstream Guards, 1954-56; 1st class hons Cantab, 1959. Joined Economic Section of Treasury, 1959; resigned, 1960. Leader-Writer and Special Correspondent, The Daily Telegraph, 1960; Chm. of Bow Gp, 1961-62; Editor of Crossbow, 1962-64; Dir of Conservative Political Centre, 1964-66. Trustee, Federal Trust for Educn and Research. Jt Hon. Sec., UK Council of European Movement. Contested (C) Dudley, 1964. *Publications:* (co-author) Principles in Practice, 1960; Report of the Chatham House Conference on International Trade, 1964; The Conservative Opportunity, 1965; various pamphlets and articles. *Recreations:* travel, books. *Address:* 22 Ponsonby Terrace, SW1. *T:* 01-828 6166; Wintershall, Dunsfold, Surrey. *T:* Dunsfold 478. *Clubs:* Carlton; County (Guildford).

**HOWELL, Denis Herbert;** MP (Lab) Small Heath since 1961; Member, Birmingham City Council since 1946; *b* 4 Sept. 1923; *s* of Herbert and Bertha A. Howell; *m* 1955, Brenda Marjorie, *d* of Stephen and Ruth Wilson, Birmingham; three *s* one *d. Educ:* Gower Street Sch.; Handsworth Grammar Sch., Birmingham. Hon. Sec. Birmingham City Council Labour Group, 1950-55 (served Catering Establishment, General Purposes, Health and Watch Cttees); Chm. Catering Cttee, 1952-55; Health (Gen. Purposes) Sub-Cttee for setting up of first smokeless zones. MP (Lab) All Saints Div., Birmingham, 1955-Sept. 1959; Jt Parly Under-Sec. of State, Dept of Educn and Science (with responsibility for sport), 1964-69; Minister of State, Min. of Housing and Local Govt (with responsibility for sport), 1969-70. Member: Dudley Road Hosp. Group Management Cttee; the Albemarle Cttee on the Youth Service; Management Cttee, City of Birmingham Symphony Orchestra, 1950-55. Governor, Handsworth Grammar Sch. Chairman: Birmingham Assoc. of Youth Clubs, 1963-64; Birmingham Settlement, 1963-64; Sports Council, 1965-; Youth Service Develt Council, 1964-. *Publication:* Soccer Refereeing, 1968. *Recreations:* sport, theatre, music; active football referee. *Address:* 33 Moor Green Lane, Moseley, Birmingham 13. *T:* 021-449 0885. *Clubs:* Reform; Warwickshire County Cricket (Birmingham); Birmingham Press.

**HOWELL, Dorothy,** FRAM; Professor of Harmony and Composition, Royal Academy of Music, 1924-70; *b* Handsworth, Birmingham, 1898. *Educ:* Royal Academy of Music. *Publications:* Symphonic Poem, Lamia; various works for Piano, Violin, etc. *Address:* Studley, Malvern Wells, Worcs.

**HOWELL, Sir Evelyn Berkeley,** KCIE 1932 (CIE 1916); CSI 1919; *b* Calcutta, 1877; *s* of A. P. Howell, ICS; *m* 1912, Laetitia Cecilia, *d* of Brig.-Gen. G. P. Campbell, RE; two *s* one *d. Educ:* Charterhouse; Emmanuel Coll., Cambridge. Entered ICS 1900; Political Asst, NWF Province, 1906; Dep. Commissioner, 1907; District Judge, 1907; served Zakha Khel Expedition, 1908 (medal and clasp); Dep. Commissioner, Kohat, 1910; Censor of Indian Mails, Indian Expeditionary Force, France, 1914-16 (CIE); HM's Consul, Muscat, 1916; Dep. Civil Commissioner, Basrah Wilayat, Mesopotamia, 1917-18 (CSI); Military Governor, Baghdad, 1918; Revenue Sec., Mesopotamia, 1918-20; Dep. Foreign Sec., India, 1922; Officiating Foreign Sec., 1923-24 and 1926-27; Resident in Waziristan, 1924-26, in Kashmir, 1927-29; Foreign Sec. to Government of India 1930-32; retired 1933; Pres. of the Frontier Defence Cttee under the Government of India, 1931. *Publications:* Poems of Khushhal Khan (with Sir Olaf Caroe), 1963; contrib. NWFP Gazetteer and various articles. *Address:* 18 Manor Court, Pinehurst, Cambridge. *T:* 50702.

*See also Air Vice-Marshal E. M. T. Howell.*

**HOWELL, Air Vice-Marshal Evelyn Michael Thomas,** CBE 1961; CEng, FRAeS; General Manager, Van Dusen Aircraft Supplies Co., Oxford, since 1967; *b* 11 Sept. 1913; *s* of Sir Evelyn Berkeley Howell, *qv*; *m* 1937, Helen Joan, *o d* of late Brig. W. M. Hayes, CBE, FRICS; one *s* three *d. Educ:* Downside Sch.; RAF Coll., Cranwell. Commissioned, 1934; Dir of Air Armament Research and Devt, Min. of Aviation, 1960-62; Comdt, RAF Techn. Coll., 1963-65; SASO, HQ Technical Training Command RAF, 1966-67; retired, 1967. Mem. Livery of Clothworkers' Co., 1938. *Recreations:* swimming, rifle shooting, tennis, boating. *Address:* c/o Lloyds Bank Ltd, 6 Pall Mall, SW1. *Club:* Royal Air Force.

**HOWELL, Rt. Rev. Kenneth Walter;** *see* Chile, Bolivia and Peru, Bishop in.

**HOWELL, Paul Philip,** CMG 1964; OBE 1955; Fellow of and Director of Development Studies at University College, Cambridge; Director of Cambridge University Course on Development; *b* 13 Feb. 1917; *s* of Brig.-Gen. Philip Howell, CMG (killed in action, 1916) and Mrs Rosalind Upcher Howell (*née* Buxton); *m* 1949, Bridgit Mary Radclyffe Luard; two *s* two *d. Educ:* Westminster Sch.; Trinity Coll., Cambridge (Sen. Schol., MA); Christ Church, Oxford (MA, DPhil). Asst District Comr, Sudan Polit. Service, 1938; commnd in Sudan Defence Force, ADC to Gov.-Gen., 1940; Overseas Enemy Territory Administration, Eritrea, 1941; Asst District Comr, Zeraf Valley, 1942; District Comr, Central Nuer, 1944; District Comr, Baggara, Western Kordofan, 1946; Chm., Jonglei Investigation Team, 1948; Chm. (Dep. Gov.), Southern Development Investigation, 1953; Asst Chief Sec., Uganda Protectorate, 1955; Sen. Asst Sec., Min. of Natural Resources, 1955; Perm. Sec., Min. of Corporations and Regional Communications, 1957; Perm. Sec. Min. of Commerce and Industry, 1959; Chm., E African Nile Waters Co-ordinating Cttee, 1956-61; seconded to FO and Min. of Overseas Development; Head of Middle East Develt Div., Beirut, 1961-69. *Publications:* A Manual of Nuer Law, 1954; (ed) The Equatorial Nile Project and its Effects in the Anglo-Egyptian Sudan, 1954; (ed) Natural Resources and Development Potential in the Southern Sudan, 1955. *Recreation:* fishing. *Address:* University College, Cambridge. *T:* Cambridge 53951; 4 Marlborough Court, Grange Road, Cambridge. *T:* Cambridge 62601; Burfield Hall, Wymondham, Norfolk. *T:* Wymondham 3389. *Club:* Travellers'.

**HOWELL, Ralph Frederic;** MP (C) North Norfolk since 1970; *b* 25 May 1923; *m* 1950, Margaret (*née* Bone); two *s* one *d*. *Educ:* Diss Grammar Sch., Norfolk. Navigator/Bomb-aimer, RAF, 1941-46; farming near Dereham, Norfolk, 1946-; Dir, Mid-Norfolk Farmers Trading Co., 1963-. *Address:* Wendling Grange, Dereham, Norfolk. *T:* Wendling 247. *Clubs:* Carlton, Farmers'; Norfolk (Norwich).

**HOWELLS, Gilbert Haywood,** FRCS; *b* 23 Aug. 1897; *s* of Henry Haywood and Hannah Elizabeth Howells; *m* 1926, Dorothy Mary Jones; no *c*. *Educ:* Newport High Sch.; University Coll., Cardiff; St Thomas' Hosp. MB, BS London 1923; FRCS 1928. Consulting Surgeon: Royal National Ear Nose and Throat Hospital; (ENT), St George's Hosp.; (ENT), Moorfields Eye Hosp.; King Edward VII Hosp., Windsor; Upton Hosp., Slough; Fellow Royal Society of Medicine and British Association of Otolaryngologists; Mem. BMA; Corresp. Mem. Societé Française d'Otorhin. *Publications:* sundry articles in medical journals. *Address:* 46 Wimpole Street, W1. *T:* 01-935 5678; Breydon, South Park Drive, Gerrards Cross, Bucks. *T:* Gerrards Cross 3368.

**HOWELLS, Herbert Norman,** CBE 1953; DMus Oxon; FRCO; FRCM; Hon. RAM; composer; King Edward Professor of Music, University of London, Emeritus 1962; Professor of Composition at Royal College of Music; Director of Music, St Paul's Girls' School, Brook Green, 1936-62; sometime Editor RCM Magazine; Master, Worshipful Company of Musicians, 1959 (first John Collard Fellow; elected to John Collard Life Fellowship, 1959); *b* 17 Oct. 1892; *y s* of late Oliver Howells and Elizabeth Burgham; *m* 1920, Dorothy, *y d* of late William Goozee; one *d* (one *s* decd). *Educ:* Lydney Grammar Sch.; Gloucester Cathedral; RCM. Became pupil of Sir Herbert Brewer, Gloucester Cathedral, 1905; Open Schol. in Composition at RCM, 1912; studied there under Stanford, Parratt, Parry, Charles Wood, and Walford Davies till 1917; succeeded to the Grove Scholarship, 1915, and became Bruce Scholar, 1916; first work heard in London was the Mass produced by Sir Richard Terry at Westminster Cathedral, 1912; was for short time sub-organist at Salisbury Cathedral. President: RCO, 1958-59; Incorporated Soc. of Musicians, 1952; Plainsong and Mediæval Soc. Hon. MusD Cambridge, 1961; Hon. Fellow RSCM, 1963; Hon. Fellow, St John's Coll., Cambridge, 1962. *Publications:* Sir Patrick Spens; Sine Nomine (Chorus and Orchestra) Procession; Puck's Minuet; Piano Concerto; Elegy for Strings; Concerto for Strings; Lady Audrey's Suite; Phantasy Quartet; Piano Quartet; Rhapsodic Quintet (Clar. and Str.); First and Third Sonatas for violin and pianoforte; Lambert's Clavichord; In Green Ways, five songs for Soprano and Orchestra; Peacock Pie song-cycle; Sonata for Organ; Hymnus Paradisi for Sopr., Ten., Chor. and Orchestra; Missa Sabrinensis for 4 solo voices, Chorus and Orchestra; Pageantry (Suite for Brass Band); A Kent Yeoman's Wooing Song for 2 Soli, Choir and Orchestra; Four Organ Rhapsodies; Six Psalm Preludes; Music for a Prince (for HRH Prince Charles); Introit (composed for Coronation Service, 1953); Inheritance (commissioned by The Arts Council of Great Britain for A Garland for the Queen, 1953); An English Mass, 1955 (for Chorus and Orch.); Howell's Clavichord (20 pieces); Missa Aedis Christi (for Christ Church, Oxford); Missa, Collegium Regale (for King's Coll., Cambridge); Three Figures (suite for Brass Band); Sequence for St Michael (commnd by St John's Coll., Cambridge); Coventry Antiphon (commnd for Coventry Cath.); Stabat Mater for Tenor, Chorus and Orchestra (commnd by the London Bach Choir); The Coventry Mass. *Recreations:* seeking quiet; English literature. *Address:* 3 Beverley Close, Barnes, SW13. *T:* 01-876 5119. *Club:* Savile.

**HOWERD, Frankie;** *see* Howard, F. A.

**HOWES, Bobby;** actor; *b* Chelsea; *s* of Robert William Howes and Rose Marie Butler; *m* Patricia Malone; one *s* one *d*. *Educ:* privately. Started on stage with Sable Fern, stayed 1 year; then with dancing team for 1 year; Royal Gotham Quartette followed for 3 years; served European War, 1914-18: in 12th London Rangers for 3 years; took part in most big battles, but was unharmed; joined Jack Hulbert's Pot Luck, after war, then Little Revue, Six-Cylinder Love, We, Blue Kitten, Vaudeville Varieties, Blue Train, The Yellow Mask, Mr Cinders, Sons O'Guns; signed contract for Drury Lane Song of The Drum. *Films include:* Guns of Loos, Third Time Lucky, Lord Babs, For the Love of Mike, Over the Garden Wall, Please Teacher, Sweet Devil, Yes, Madam, Happy Go Lovely, Good Companions, Watch it Sailor. *Theatre:* as Dir Saville Theatre, appeared in For the Love of Mike, followed by Tell her The Truth and He Wanted Adventure, based on Ambrose Applejohn's Adventure; left Saville Theatre to play at London Hippodrome in Yes, Madam; followed by Please Teacher, Big Business and Hide and Seek; Bobby, Get Your Gun, Adelphi; All Clear, Queen's; Shephard's Pie, Princes; Lady Behave, His Majesty's; Let's Face It, Hippodrome; Halfway to Heaven, Princes; Cinderella, Winter Garden; Here Come the Boys, Saville; Roundabout, Saville; Paint Your Wagon, Her Majesty's, The Geese are Getting Fat, Phœnix, etc. Went to New York, to play Finian in Finian's Rainbow, 1960 (also name-part in Liverpool prod., 1958; Melbourne, 1963-64). Tours: Harvey, The Entertainer, Finian's Rainbow, Gazelle in Park Lane. Has appeared on television both in Britain and in USA. *Recreations:* golf, motoring, swimming, cricket. *Address:* 62 Holland Park, W11. *T:* 01-727 6201.
*See also Sally Ann Howes.*

**HOWES, Ernest James;** *b* 27 Aug. 1895; 2nd *s* of William Quinton Howes and Eleanor Brett; *m* 1922 (marriage dissolved); one *d*; *m* 1944, Sheila Burke; one *s*. *Educ:* privately. Served European War, 1914-18. Comdt of Police, Jerusalem. 1920; Comdt, Arab Legion Training Sch., 1921; ADC to HH Amir (later King) Abdulla, 1921-25; Air Liaison Officer, RAF, in Iraq, 1926-35; Asst Political Sec., Aden, 1936-42. In charge of British Information Services, Middle East, 1945. First Sec. (Information) British Legation, Beirut, 1946; Political Adviser to British Resident, Benghazi, 1951; Consul, Kermanshah, 1951-52; Consul, Aleppo, 1952. HM Consul-Gen., Asmara 1954. Retired from the Foreign Service, 1957. *Recreations:* gardening, cooking. *Address:* 11 Cedar Grove, Blendon, Bexley, Kent.

**HOWES, Frank Stewart,** CBE 1954; MA; FRCM; Hon. RAM; Lecturer at the Royal College of Music since 1938; *b* 2 April 1891; *s* of George Howes, Oxford; *m* 1929, Barbara Tidd Pratt; one *s* three *d*. *Educ:* Oxford High Sch.; St John's Coll., Oxford; Royal College of Music. Joined staff of The Times, 1925, and of the Royal College of Music, 1938; Editor, Folk Song Journal (later Journal of the English Folk Dance and Song Society), 1927-46; Chm. Musicians' Benevolent Fund, 1938-56; Music Critic of The Times, 1943-60: Pres. Royal

Musical Association, 1948-58; Chm. BBC Central Music Advisory Council, 1950-55. *Publications:* Borderland of Music and Psychology, 1926; Byrd, 1928; Key to the Art of Music, 1935; (with Philip Hope-Wallace) Key to Opera, 1939; Full Orchestra, 1942; Man, Mind and Music, 1948; The Music of Vaughan Williams, 1954; Music and its Meanings, 1958; The Music of William Walton, 1965; The English Musical Renaissance, 1966; Folk Music of Britain and Beyond, 1970. *Recreations:* aquatics and motoring. *Address:* Newbridge Mill, near Witney, Oxon. *T:* Standlake 245. *Club:* Athenæum.

**HOWES, Henry William,** CMG 1951; OBE 1948; MA, MSc, PhD London; lecturer, reviewer, author; *b* 1896; *e s* of late William and Laura Howes, Norwich; *m* 1923, Clarisse Vera, *y d* of late James Charles Bond, Rattlesden, Suffolk; one *d. Educ:* Bracondale and Grammar Schs, Norwich; Univs of London and Wales. Served European War, 1914-18, Royal Marines, 1915-17. Teaching in Essex and Middlesex, 1921-30, and in Polytechnics and Institutes, 1927-36; Principal, Norwich City Coll. and Sch. of Art, 1936-44; Mem. of Exec. of Eastern Counties Cttee for Adult Educn. In HM Forces, 1940-44; first Dir of Educn, Gibraltar, 1944-49, City Councillor, 1945-49; Dir of Education, Ceylon, 1949-54; Hon. Educn Adviser, Ceylon Army, 1951-; Mem. Court and Council, University of Ceylon, 1949-54. Educational Survey of the Caribbean Region for Unesco, 1954; Educational Adviser, Odhams, 1956-57; Dir of Education, British Honduras, 1958-60; Mem. Council, University Coll. of West Indies, 1958-60; Adviser on Secondary Education, British Honduras, 1960; Unesco Adviser on Adult and Youth Education, Dominica, West Indies, 1962. Overseas Educational Adviser, Harrap's, 1963-67; Hon. Historical Adviser to Govt of Gibraltar, 1964-. Hon. Life Mem., Ceylon Nat. Assoc. for Prevention of Tuberculosis. Chevalier of Order of Crown (Belgium), 1937; Officer of Order of Leopold II (Belgium), 1970; Officier d'Académie (France) 1936; Kt Comdr, Order of Alfonso X, el Sabio (Spain), 1966; Kt of Order of St Gregory the Great, 1957. *Publications:* Bruges, 1935; Santiago de Compostela and its Prehistoric Origin, 1936; The Story of Gibraltar, 1948; The Gibraltarian:–The Origin and Development of Population in Gibraltar since 1704, 1951; Presenting Modern Britain, 1965; We Go to Spain, 1967. *Recreation:* Spanish studies. *Address:* 11 Franklins Road, Stevenage, Herts. *T:* Stevenage 2512.

**HOWES, Rear-Adm. Peter Norris,** CB 1966; DSC 1941; Private Secretary to Lord Mayor of London, since 1968; *b* 1 July 1916; *s* of Percy Groom Howes; *m* 1952, Priscilla Hamilton, *d* of Maj.-Gen. G. W. E. Heath, *qv*; three *s* one *d*. *Educ:* St Peter's Court, Broadstairs; Royal Naval College, Dartmouth. Served in HM Ships Hood, Furious, Fortune, Albury, Aberdeen, Westminster, Adamant, Newcastle, Liverpool; commanded 6th Motor Gunboat Flotilla; HMS Chaplet; HMS Mercury; Dartmouth Training Sqdn; HMS Devonshire; specialised as Communications Officer, 1942; Senior Aide-de-Camp to Viceroy of India, 1947; Naval Asst to First Sea Lord, 1955-58; Flag Officer, Middle East Station, 1964-66. *Publication:* The Viceregal Establishments in India, 1948. *Recreations:* riding, shooting, fishing, photography. *Address:* Sutton Parva House, Heytesbury, Wilts. *T:* Sutton Veny 333. *Club:* White's.

**HOWES, Sally Ann;** actress (stage, film and television); *b* 20 July 1930; *d* of Bobby Howes, *qv*; *m* 1958, Richard Adler; *m* 1969, Morgan Maree. *Educ:* Glendower, London; Queenswood, Herts; privately. First appeared in films, 1942. *Films include:* Thursday's Child; Halfway House; Dead of Night; Nicholas Nickleby; Anna Karenina; My Sister and I; Fools Rush In; History of Mr Polly; Stop Press Girl; Honeymoon Deferred; The Admirable Crichton. First appeared West End stage in (revue) Fancy Free, at Prince of Wales's, and at Royal Variety Performance, 1950. *Stage Shows include:* Bet Your Life; Paint Your Wagon; Babes in the Wood; Romance by Candlelight; Summer Song; Hatful of Rain; My Fair Lady (NY); Kwamina (musical), NY City Center, 1961; Brigadoon (revival), NY City Center, 1962. Has appeared on television: in England from 1949 (Short and Sweet Series, Sally Ann Howes Show, etc); in USA from 1958 (Perry Como Show, Ed Sullivan Show, Patti Page Show, (6 times) Jack Parr Show). TV: Play of the Week; Panel Shows: To Tell the Truth; Password; Bell Telephone Hour; US Steel Hour, etc. *Recreations:* reading, riding, theatre. *Address:* 130 East 67th Street, New York, USA.

**HOWGILL, Richard John Frederick,** CBE 1949; Music Controller, BBC, 1952-59; *b* 21 April 1895; *s* of late Richard Frederick Howgill by first wife; *m* 1925, Hilda Mary, *d* of late Edwin Alexander; one *s* one *d*. *Educ:* Emanuel Sch.; studied piano, violin and composition, privately. He has made many arrangements and transcriptions of musical works. Served European War, 1914-18, in France and Mesopotamia; Mesopotamian Railways, 1919-21; Performing Right Soc., 1922-23; joined BBC, 1923, to take charge of its copyright dept; was subsequently Asst Dir of Programme Administration; Dir of Programme Administration; Asst Controller, Administration; Asst Controller, Programmes; Controller, Entertainment. *Address:* Branscombe, Sullington Warren, Storrington, Sussex. *T:* Storrington 2471. *Club:* Savile.

*See also Sir H. M. R. Newton, Bt.*

**HOWICK OF GLENDALE,** 1st Baron, *cr* 1960; **Evelyn Baring,** GCMG 1955 (KCMG, 1942); KCVO 1947; DL; late Indian Civil Service; a Director of the Swan Hunter Group Limited; Chairman of the Commonwealth Development Corporation since 1963 (Deputy Chairman, 1960, Chairman 1960-63, Colonial Development Corporation); Chairman, Nature Conservancy, since 1962 (Member, 1961-); *b* 29 Sept. 1903; *s* of 1st Earl of Cromer and (*o c* by 2nd wife) Lady Katharine Thynne (*d* 1933), 2nd *d* of 4th Marquess of Bath; *m* 1935, Lady Mary Cecil Grey, *er d* of 5th Earl Grey; one *s* two *d*. *Educ:* Winchester; New Coll., Oxford. First Cl. Hons History, 1924. Entered ICS, 1926; Sec. to Agent of Govt of India in S Africa, 1929; retired, 1934; Governor of S Rhodesia, 1942-44; High Commr for UK in Union of SA, and High Commr for Basutoland, the Bechuanaland Protectorate and Swaziland, 1944-51; Governor and C-in-C, Kenya, also Chm. of the East Africa High Commn, 1952-59. Mem., The Times Trust, 1967-; Vice-Pres., Liverpool Sch. of Tropical Medicine, 1967-. Hon. Fellow, New Coll., Oxford, 1960. DL Northumberland, 1968. Queen's Commendation for Brave Conduct, 1959. KStJ. *Heir: s* Hon. Charles Evelyn Baring [*b* 30 Dec. 1937; *m* 1964, Clare, *d* of Col Cyril Darby; two *d*. *Educ:* Eton; New Coll., Oxford]. *Address:* Howick, Alnwick, Northumberland. *Club:* Brooks's.

**HOWIE, Sir James (William),** Kt 1969; MD (Aberdeen); FRCP, FRCPGlas; FRCPath;

Director of the Public Health Laboratory Service, since 1963; *b* 31 Dec. 1907; *s* of late James Milne Howie and late Jessie Mowat Robertson; *m* 1935, Isabella Winifred Mitchell, BSc; two *s* one *d*. *Educ:* Robert Gordon's Coll., Aberdeen; University of Aberdeen. University lectureships in Aberdeen and Glasgow, 1932-40; Pathologist, RAMC, 1941-45 (served Nigeria and War Office); Head of Dept of Pathology and Bacteriology, Rowett Research Institute, Aberdeen, 1946-51; Prof. of Bacteriology, University of Glasgow, 1951-63. Mem. Agricultural Research Council, 1957-63. Convener, Medical Research Council Working Party on Sterilisers, 1957-64; Pres., Royal College of Pathologists, 1966-69 (Vice-Pres., 1962-66); Pres. BMA, 1969-70. QHP, 1965-68. Hon. LLD Aberdeen, 1969. *Publications:* various publications in medical and scientific periodicals, particularly on bacteriology and nutrition. *Recreations:* golf, music. *Address:* Knockmalloch, Newtonmore, Inverness-shire. *T:* Newtonmore 348; Public Health Laboratory Service, 24 Park Crescent, W1. *T:* 01-636 2223. *Club:* Athenæum.

**HOWIE, William;** civil engineer; *b* Troon, Ayrshire, 2 March 1924; *er s* of Peter and Annie Howie, Troon; *m* 1951, Mairi Margaret, *o d* of Martha and late John Sanderson, Troon; two *s* two *d*. *Educ:* Marr Coll., Troon; Royal Technical Coll., Glasgow (BSc, Diploma). MP (Lab) Luton, Nov. 1963-70; Asst Whip, 1964-66; Lord Comr of the Treasury, 1966-67; Comptroller, HM Household, 1967-68. A Vice-Chm., Parly Labour Party, 1968-. Mem., Instn of Civil Engineers, 1951; Member: Council, Instn of Civil Engineers, 1964-67; Governing Body, Imperial Coll. of Science and Technology, 1965-67; Council, City Univ., 1968-. *Recreations:* opera, watching football, trying to find time to play golf. *Address:* 34 Temple Fortune Lane, NW11. *T:* 01-455 0492. *Clubs:* Luton Trades Unionists, Luton Labour; Seretse.

**HOWITT, W(illiam) Fowler,** DA (Dundee), FRIBA; Partner in Firm of Cusdin Burden and Howitt, Architects; *b* Perth, Scotland, May 1924; *s* of Frederick Howitt, Head Postmaster, Forfar; *m* 1951, Ann Elizabeth, *o d* of late A. J. Hedges, Radipole, Dorset; three *s* one *d*. *Educ:* Perth Academy. Royal Marines, 1943-46. Sch. of Architecture, Dundee, 1948; RIBA Victory Scholar, 1949. Asst Louis de Soissons, London (housing and flats), 1949-52; Prin. Asst to Vincent Kelly, Dublin (hosps & offices), 1952-55; Architect to St Thomas' Hosp. (Hosp. rebuilding schemes, flats, offices), 1955-64. Present projects include: Grosvenor Road Site Develt and New Royal Victoria Hosp., Belfast; New Site Develt for Addenbrooke's Hosp. Cambridge. Prepared report for Health and Med. Sciences Centre, Univ. of Riyad, S Arabia. *Recreations:* reading, golf, childish pursuits. *Address:* 1-4 Yarmouth Place, Piccadilly, W1Y 8JQ. *T:* 01-493 8913; (home) 32 Gloucester Road, Teddington, Mddx. *T:* 01-977 5772.

**HOWKINS, John,** MD, FRCS; Gynæcological Surgeon to St Bartholomew's Hospital, 1946-69 (Hon. Consultant Gynæcologist since 1969), to Hampstead General Hospital 1946-67 (Hon. Consultant Gynæcologist, since 1968), and to Royal Masonic Hospital, since 1948; *b* 17 Dec. 1907; *m* 1940, Lena Brown; one *s* two *d*. *Educ:* Shrewsbury Sch.; London Univ. Arts Scholar, Middlesex Hospital, 1926; MRCS, LRCP, 1932; MB, BS, London, 1933; FRCS, 1936; MS London, 1936; MD (Gold Medal) London, 1937; MRCOG 1937, FRCOG 1947. House Surgeon and Casualty Surgeon, Middlesex Hosp., 1932-34; RMO Chelsea Hosp. for Women, 1936; Gynæcological Registrar, Middlesex Hosp., 1937-38; Resident Obstetric Surg., St Bartholomew's Hosp., 1938 and 1945; Temp. Wing-Comdr, RAFVR Med. Br., 1939-45. Hunterian Prof., RCS 1947. Sometime Examiner in Midwifery to Univs of Cambridge and London, RCOG, Conjoint Bd of England. Chm., Council Ski Club of Great Britain, 1964-67 (Hon. Life Member, 1968, Trustee, 1969-). *Publications:* Shaw's Textbook of Gynæcology, 1956 (8th edn 1962); Shaw's Textbook of Gynæcological Surgery, 3rd edn, 1967; (jointly) Bonney's Textbook of Gynæcological Surgery, 1963. *Recreations:* ski-ing, salmon fishing and sheep farming. *Address:* Caen Hen, Abercegir, Machynlleth, Montgomeryshire, Wales. *Club:* Ski Club of Great Britain.

**HOWLAND, Lord; Andrew Ian Henry Russell;** *b* 30 March 1962; *s* and *heir* of Marquess of Tavistock, *qv*.

**HOWLAND, Robert Leslie,** MA; Fellow of St John's College, Cambridge; University Lecturer in Classics; Warden of Madingley Hall; *b* 25 March 1905; *s* of Robert and Mary Howland; *m* 1930, Eileen, *d* of Robert Reid Tait; two *s* one *d*. *Educ:* Shrewsbury Sch.; St John's Coll., Cambridge. Mem. of Cambridge Univ. Athletic Team, 1925-28; Mem. of British National Athletic Team, 1927-39 (Capt. 1934-35), and British Olympic Team, 1928. Holder of English native record for putting the weight, 1930-48. *Publications:* papers in classical journals. *Address:* St John's College, Cambridge; Madingley Hall, Cambridge. *Clubs:* United University, Achilles; Hawks (Cambridge).

**HOWLETT, Jack,** CBE 1969; MA Oxon, PhD Manchester; MIEE, FRSS, FIMA; Atlas Computer Laboratory, Chilton, Didcot, Berks, since 1961 (under Science Research Council since April 1965); *b* 30 Aug. 1912; *s* of William Howlett and Lydia Ellen Howlett; *m* 1939, Joan Marjorie Simmons; four *s* one *d*. *Educ:* Stand Grammar Sch., Manchester; Manchester Univ. Mathematician, LMS Railway, 1935-40 and 1946-48; mathematical work in various wartime research estabts, 1940-46; Head of Computer Group, Atomic Energy Research Estabt, Harwell, 1948-61. Fellow by special election, St Cross Coll., Oxford, 1966. *Publications:* reviews and gen. papers on numerical mathematics and computation. *Recreations:* hill walking, music. *Address:* The Old Farm House, Tubney, Abingdon, Berks. *T:* Frilford Heath 298. *Clubs:* New Arts, Savile.

**HOWMAN, Brig. Ross Cosens,** CIE 1945; OBE 1939; retired; *b* 11 July 1899; *s* of late Martin Langston Howman, OBE; *m* 1930, Cecil, *d* of late Edmond Hardie Elles, OBE; two *s*. *Educ:* Edinburgh Academy; Cadet Coll., Wellington, S India; Commissioned IA, 1918; served European War, 1914-18; Third Afghan War, 1919 (7th Gurkha Rifles); OC Escort Naga Hills Expedn, 1926-27; psc 1933; Wa Operations, Burma Frontier, 1933 (Burma Rifles); GSOIII, 1934; DAAG, 1935, Waziristan District; DAAG, Waziristan Div.; DAA and QMG, Waziristan Force, 1936-39 (despatches thrice); GSO II, GHQ (India), 1940. Raised 1st Assam Regt, 1941. GSO I, 1942; DDMI, 1943; Dir of Security, India Comd, 1944-45; Gen. Staff, War Office, 1946-47; retired, 1948. *Publications:* contributor to journals and magazines. *Recreations:* shooting, fishing, writing. *Address:* Balmacneil, Strathtay, Perthshire. *T:* Ballinluig 254. *Club:* Naval and Military.

**HOWSAM, Air Vice-Marshal George Roberts,** CB 1945; MC 1918; RCAF, retired: also retired from Federal Emergency Measures Organization (Coordinator, Alberta Civil Defence, 1950-57) and from business; *b* 29 Jan. 1895; *s* of Mary Ida and George Roberts Howsam, Port Perry, Ont; *m* 1918, Lillian Isobel, *d* of Mary and William Somerville, Toronto; one *s*. *Educ:* Port Perry and Toronto. Joined Canadian Expeditionary Force, March 1916 and RFC 70 Sqdn and 43 Sqdn, 1917-18; served as fighter pilot France and Belgium, 1917-18 (wounded twice, MC); with Army of Occupation in Germany; returned to Canada, 1921; RCAF photographic survey, NW Canada; RAF Staff Coll., England, 1930 (psa); Senior Mem., RCAF 1st Aerobatic Team (Siskin) Display, Cleveland, USA, 1929; Staff Mem. CGAO Operations at AFHQ, 1931-32; SASO MD2 Toronto, 1933-36; OC 2 Army Co-operation Sqdn, Ottawa, 1937; Dir of Training for RCAF, Ottawa, 1938-40; England and France, 1940; later in 1940, SASO, No 4 Training Command, Regina; commanded No. 11 Service Flying Training Sch., Yorkton, 1941; AOC No 4 Training Command, Calgary, 1942-44, also AOC Air Staging Route to Alaska, 1942-43; Chm. Organisation Cttee, Air Force HQ, Ottawa, 1945; retired 1946. Dominion Dir The Air Cadet League of Canada, 1946-47; Alberta Chm. RCAF Assoc., 1958-59. Legion of Merit in Degree of Comdr (US), 1945; Order of White Lion (Czecho-Slovakia), 1946; Commandeur de l'ordre de la Couronne (Belgium), 1948. *Publications:* Rocky Mountain Foothills Offer Great Chance to Gliders (Calgary Daily Herald), 1923; Industrial and Mechanical Development: War (Canadian Defence Qtly Prize Essay), 1931. *Recreations:* gardening, writing, shooting. *Address:* 2040 Pauls Terrace, Victoria, BC, Canada; c/o Bank of Montreal, Government Street, Victoria, BC. *Clubs:* Union, Canadian (Victoria, BC); Empire (Toronto); Ranchmen's (Calgary).

**HOWSON, Rear-Adm. John,** CB 1963; DSC 1944; Regional Officer, North Midlands, British Productivity Council, since 1964; *b* 30 Aug. 1908; *s* of late George Howson and Mary Howson, Glasgow; *m* 1937, Evangeline Collins; one *s* one *d*. *Educ:* Kelvinside Academy, Glasgow; Royal Naval College, Dartmouth, 1922-25; Lieut, 1930; specialised in gunnery, 1934; Gunnery Officer, HMS Furious, 1936-38; served War of 1939-45 (despatches, DSC); HMS Newcastle, 1939-41; HMS Nelson, 1943-44; Comdr 1945; Fleet Gunnery Officer, British Pacific Fleet, 1947-48; Staff of C-in-C, Far East Stn, 1948-49; Exec. Officer, HMS Superb, 1949-50; Capt. 1951; served on Ordnance Bd, 1950-52; Comdg Officer, HMS Tamar, 1952-54; at SHAPE, 1955-57; Chief of Staff to C-in-C, Plymouth, 1958-61; Rear-Adm. 1961; Comdr, Allied Naval Forces, Northern Europe, 1961-62; Naval Dep. to C-in-C Allied Forces, Northern Europe, 1963-64. *Recreations:* walking, golf. *Address:* The Vinery, 14 Main Street, Burton Joyce, Notts NG14 5DZ. *T:* Burton Joyce 3355. *Club:* Naval and Military.

**HOY,** family name of **Baron Hoy.**

**HOY,** Baron *cr* 1970 (Life Peer), of Leith, Edinburgh; **James Hutchison Hoy,** PC 1969; *b* 21 Jan. 1909; 3rd *s* of William and Sarah Hoy, Edinburgh; *m* 1942, Nancy Hamlyn Rae McArthur; one *s*. *Educ:* Causewayside and Sciennes Public Schs, Edinburgh. Interior Decorator. MP (Lab) Leith, 1945-50, Leith Div. of Edinburgh, 1950-70; PPS to Sec. of State for Scotland, 1947-50; Joint Parly Sec., Min. of Agriculture, Fisheries and Food, 1964-70. Vice-Pres. Trustee Savings Bank Assoc., 1957; joint Pres., Nat. Assoc. of Inshore Fishermen, 1963. DL Edinburgh, 1958. *Address:* 77 Orchard Road, Edinburgh 4.

**HOY, Rev. David,** SJ; Rector of Stonyhurst College since 1964; *b* 1 March 1913; *s* of Augustine Hilary Hoy and Caroline Lovelace. *Educ:* Mount St Mary's Coll. Entered Society of Jesus, 1931. Senior English Master, Wimbledon Coll., 1947, Asst Head Master, 1957-59. Rector of St Robert Bellarmine, Heythrop, Chipping Norton, 1959-64. *Recreation:* walking. *Address:* Stonyhurst College, Whalley, Blackburn, Lancs.

**HOYER-MILLAR, Dame Elizabeth,** DBE 1960 (OBE 1952); JP; Director, Women's Royal Naval Service, 1958-61; Hon. ADC to the Queen, 1958-61; *b* 17 Dec. 1910; *o d* of late Robert Christian Hoyer Millar, Craig, Angus, Scotland, and Muriel (*née* Foster). *Educ:* privately. VAD 1939-41; joined WRNS, 1942. JP Angus, 1968. *Recreations:* needlework, gardening, country pursuits. *Address:* The Croft, Hillside, Angus. *T:* Hillside 304. *Club:* Service Women's.

**HOYLE, Prof. Fred,** FRS 1957; MA Cantab; Plumian Professor of Astronomy and Experimental Philosophy, Cambridge University, since 1958; Director Institute of Theoretical Astronomy, Cambridge; Fellow of St John's College, Cambridge; Professor of Astronomy, Royal Institution of Great Britain, since 1969; *b* 24 June 1915; *s* of Ben Hoyle, Bingley, Yorks; *m* 1939, Barbara Clark; one *s* one *d*. *Educ:* Bingley Grammar Sch.; Emmanuel Coll., Cambridge. Mayhew Prizeman, Mathematical Tripos, 1936; Smith's Prizeman, 1938. Senior Exhibitioner of Royal Commission for Exhibition of 1851. University Lecturer in Mathematics, 1945-58. Staff Mem., Mount Wilson and Palomar Observatories, 1956-. Mem. SRC, 1968-. Kalinga Prize, 1968. Vice-Pres., Royal Society, 1970. Foreign Associate, Amer. Nat. Acad. of Sciences, 1969. *Publications: astronomy:* Some Recent Researches in Solar Physics, 1949; The Nature of the Universe, 1950; A Decade of Decision, 1953; Frontiers of Astronomy, 1955; Of Men and Galaxies, 1965; Galaxies, Nuclei and Quasars, 1966; Man in the Universe, 1966; *novels:* The Black Cloud, 1957; Ossian's Ride, 1959; Fifth Planet, 1963 (with G. Hoyle); October the First is Too Late, 1966; (with G. Hoyle) Seven Steps to the Sun, 1970; *play:* Rockets in Ursa Major, 1962; scientific papers. *Address:* Institute of Theoretical Astronomy, Madingley Road, Cambridge.

**HOYLE, George,** CMG 1954; HM Deputy Chief Inspector of Mines and Quarries, 1958-66; *b* 8 May 1900; 3rd *s* of George Harry and Mary Elizabeth Hoyle, Leeds; *m* 1936, Margaret Stewart, *d* of Ernest and Beatrice Reed, Bridlington; two adopted *s*. *Educ:* Leeds Grammar Sch.; The Queen's Coll., Oxford. Colliery Undermanager, 1930-33; Junior Inspector of Mines, 1933-41; Senior Inspector, 1941-50; Divisional Inspector, 1950-58. *Recreations:* collecting old glass, gardening. *Address:* Mackery End, Greenway, Hutton, Brentwood, Essex. *T:* Brentwood 653.

**HOYLE, John Clifford;** retired; lately Physician and Director, Department of Medicine, King's College Hospital; Consulting Physician, King Edward VII and Brompton Hospitals; *b* 4 July 1901; *s* of John and Esther Hoyle; *m* 1931, Mary Irene Rosewarne; two *s*. *Educ:* Rydal; Manchester Univ. MB, BS (London), 1925; MD (London) 1929 (Gold Medal in Medicine); MRCP 1931; FRCP 1938; Ernest Hart Scholar, British Medical Assoc., 1928-30; Gillson Scholar, Society of Apothecaries,

1932-34; Medical First Asst London Hosp., 1930-33; Paterson Research Scholar, Cardiac Dept, London Hosp., 1933-35; Mem., Assoc. Physicians; Hon. Mem., Thoracic Soc.; FRSM. *Publications:* various contributions to medical journals on physiology and diseases of lungs and cardiovascular system. *Recreations:* idling, literature. *Address:* Tremethick, Budock Vean, Falmouth, Cornwall. *T:* Mawnan Smith 555.

**HSIUNG, Shih I;** Author; President, Tsing Hua College, Hong Kong (Founder, and Director, since 1963); Hon. Secretary of China Society, London, since 1936 (Secretary 1934-36); Member of Universities China Committee, London, since 1935; *b* Nanchang, China, 14 Oct. 1902; *s* of Hsiung, Yuen-Yui and Chou, Ti-Ping; *m* 1923, Tsai, Dymia, (author of Flowering Exile, 1952); three *s* three *d*. *Educ:* Teachers' Coll., National Univ., Peking. Associate Manager of Chen Kwang Theatre, Peking, 1923; Managing Director of Pantheon Theatre, Shanghai, 1927; Special Editor of Commercial Press, Shanghai; Prof. at Agriculture Coll., Nanchang; Prof. at Min-Kuo Univ., Peking, till 1932. Chinese Delegate to International PEN Congress at Edinburgh, 1934; at Barcelona, 1935; at Prague, 1938; at London, 1941; at Zürich, 1947; Chinese Delegate to First Congress of International Theatre Institute at Prague, 1948; lectured on Modern Chinese and Classical Chinese Drama, University of Cambridge, 1950-53; Visiting Prof., University of Hawaii, Honolulu. Dean, College of Arts, Nanyang Univ., 1954-55; Man.-Dir, Pacific Films Co. Ltd, Hong Kong, 1955-; Dir, Konin Co. Ltd, Hong Kong, 1956-; Dir, Success Co. Ltd, Hong Kong, 1956; Chm., Bd of Dirs Standard Publishers, Ltd, Hong Kong, 1961-. *Publications:* various Chinese books including Translations of Bernard Shaw, James Barrie, Thomas Hardy, Benjamin Franklin, etc.; English Publications: The Money-God, 1934; Lady Precious Stream, 1934; The Western Chamber, 1935; Mencius Was A Bad Boy, 1936; The Professor From Peking, 1939; The Bridge of Heaven, 1941; The Life of Chiang Kai-Shek, 1943; The Gate of Peace, 1945; Changing China: History of China from 1840 to 1911, 1946; The Story of Lady Precious Stream, 1949; Chinese Proverbs, 1952; Lady on the Roof, 1959. *Recreation:* theatre-going. *Address:* 41 Buckland Crescent, NW3. *T:* 01-586 1979; 1620-21-23 Central Building, Hong Kong; Tsing Hua College, Kowloon, Hong Kong. *T:* Hong Kong 820305. *TA:* Dr Hsiung, Hong Kong.

**HSU CHEN-PING, Rt. Rev. Francis;** *see* Hong Kong, Bishop of (RC).

**HUBBACK, David Francis,** CB 1970; Under Secretary, Board of Trade, Civil Aviation Division 1, since 1969; *b* 2 March 1916; *s* of late Francis William and Eva Hubback; *m* 1939, Elais Judith, *d* of late Sir John Fischer Williams; one *s* two *d*. *Educ:* Westminster Sch.; King's Coll., Cambridge. Mines Dept, Bd of Trade, 1939. War of 1939-45: Army, 1940-44; Capt., Royal Signals; Western Desert, Sicily, Normandy; Cabinet Office, 1944. UK Delegn to OEEC, 1948; Treasury, 1950; Principal Private Sec. to Chancellor of the Exchequer, 1960-62; Under-Sec., Treasury, 1962-68. *Recreations:* mountain walking, reading. *Address:* 5 Mount Vernon, Hampstead, NW3. *T:* 01-435 4512. *Club:* Reform.

**HUBBARD,** family name of **Baron Addington.**

**HUBBARD, Charles Edward,** CBE 1965 (OBE 1954); *b* 23 May 1900; *s* of Charles Edward Hubbard and Catherine Billing; *m* 1st, 1927, Madeleine Grace Witham (*d* 1961); one *s*; 2nd, 1963, Florence Kate Hubbard. *Educ:* King Edward VII Grammar Sch., King's Lynn. Royal Gardens, Sandringham, Norfolk, 1916-20; Royal Gardens, Oslo, Norway, 1919. RAF, 1918-19. Royal Botanic Gardens, Kew, 1920-65: Student Gardener, 1920-22; Tech. Asst, 1922-27; Asst Botanist, 1927-30; Botanist, 1930-46; Prin. Sci. Officer, 1946-56; Sen. Prin. Sci. Officer 1956-69; Dep. CSO, 1959-65; Dep. Dir of Royal Botanic Gardens, Kew, 1959-65, and Keeper of Herbarium and Library there, 1957-65. Linnean Gold Medal, 1967. Hon. DSc, Reading. *Publications:* Grasses, 1954, 1968. Numerous pubns on the Gramineae (Grasses) in various botanical books and jls. *Recreations:* walking; natural history. *Address:* 51 Ormond Crescent, Hampton, Middlesex. *T:* 01-979 6923.

**HUBBARD, Cdre Lancelot F.;** *see* Hubbard, Cdre R. L. F.

**HUBBARD, Commodore (Robert) Lancelot F(ortescue),** CBE 1957; RD, RNR retired; Elder Brother, Trinity House; *b* 16 March 1887; *s* of Commander R. R. F. Hubbard, RNR, and Lizzie Hubbard (*née* Sydenham); *m* 1st, 1914, Jessie Baldwin (*d* 1952), *d* of late Harry Staniland; three *s* two *d*; 2nd, Patience Eva, *d* of late Arthur Shipton. *Educ:* Dulwich Coll. Merchant Navy; served Loch Garry, 1902-9, leaving as First Mate; Orient Steam Navigation Co., 1909, and later commanded several of their liners till elected an Elder Brother in 1937, retired as active Elder Brother, 1957. Passed Extra Master, 1910; Royal Navy: Midshipman, RNR, 1908; served in many of HM Ships; attached HMS Fox, during Persian Gulf operations, 1910; served European War, 1914-18 (despatches thrice) on Belgian coast and against Königsberg in E Africa; commanded Destroyers 1916-18; served War of 1939-45, Commodore of convoys. Rep. Trinity House on Internat. Conference, Safety of Life at Sea, 1946. Reserve Decoration, 1920; Bronze Medal, Royal Humane Society, 1910. *Recreations:* golf, gardening. *Address:* Orontes, Shute Road, Kilmington, near Axminster, Devon; Trinity House, Tower Hill, EC3. *T:* 01-480 6601. *Club:* National Liberal.

**HUBBLE, Prof. Douglas Vernon,** CBE 1966; MD (London); FRCP; Dean of the Faculty of Medicine at Haile Selassie I University, Addis Ababa, since 1969; *b* 25 Dec. 1900; *s* of Harry Edward Hubble and Agnes Kate (*née* Field); *m* 1928, Marie Arnott Bryce; three *d*. *Educ:* St Bartholomew's Hospital, London. Physician, Derbyshire Children's Hospital, 1932; Physician, Derbyshire Royal Infirmary, 1942; Prof. of Pædiatrics and Child Health, and Dir, Inst. of Child Health, Univ. of Birmingham, 1958-68; Dean, Faculty of Medicine, Univ. of Birmingham, 1963-68. Pres., Paediatric Section, Royal Society of Medicine, 1956; Mem., British Pharmocopoeia Commission 1958-68; Burns Lectr, RFPS(G), 1957; Honeyman Gillespie Lectr, University of Edinburgh, 1958; Langdon Brown Lectr, RCP, 1960; Felton Bequest Travelling Lectr, Royal Children's Hosp., Melbourne, Australia, 1961; Lawson Wilkins Memorial Lectr, Johns Hopkins Univ., 1965; Lloyd Roberts Memorial Lectr, Univ. of Manchester, 1966. Tisdall Lectr, Canadian Med. Assoc., 1967; Osler Lectr, Soc. of Apothecaries of London, 1968. Council Mem., RCP, 1960-62; Public Orator, University of Birmingham, 1962-66; Mem., Clinical Research Board, MRC, 1962-66; Pædiatric Consultant, Josiah Macy, Jr, Foundation, 1968-; Chm. Council for Investigation of Fertility Control, 1963-68. Corr. Mem. Amer. Pediatric Soc., 1963. Pres. Lichfield Johnson Soc., 1956. Member: Tropical Med. Research

Bd, MRC, 1965-; GMC, 1965-. *Publications:* contrib. to medical and literary journals. *Recreation:* eighteenth-century literature. *Address:* Haile Selassi I University, PO Box 1176, Addis Ababa, Ethiopia. *Club:* Savile.

**HUBRECHT, J. B.,** PhD Ultraj; MA Cantab; FRAS; *b* 13 April 1883; 2nd *s* of late Professor A. A. W. Hubrecht, Utrecht, Holland; *m* 1907, Jonkvrouwe Leonore van Alphen; two *s* three *d. Educ:* High Sch., Utrecht; University, Utrecht; Christ's Coll., Cambridge. Isaac Newton student, 1907; did research in Astrophysics at Solar Physics Observatory, Cambridge, 1907-12; lectured on Astrophysics, University of Manchester, 1913; entered Dutch Diplomatic Service, 1915; Attaché, London, 1915; Tokio, 1917; Foreign Office, the Hague, 1919; Second Sec., 1919; Washington, 1919; First Sec., 1923; Madrid, 1924; Counsellor, 1926; London 1927; Netherland Minister: Rio de Janeiro, 1930; Bucharest, 1934; Rome, 1937; handed his passports by Italian Govt upon Italy's entry into War, 1940; proceeded to Indonesia and was interned there for over two years by Japanese, 1941. *Publication:* The Solar Rotation by Spectroscopic Observations, 1915. *Recreations:* books, travelling. *Address:* Witte Huis, Doorn, Holland.

**HUCKFIELD, Leslie (John);** MP (Lab) Nuneaton since March 1967; *b* 7 April 1942; *s* of Ernest Leslie and Suvla Huckfield; single. *Educ:* Prince Henry's Grammar Sch., Evesham; Keble Coll., Oxford; Univ. of Birmingham. Lectr in Economics, City of Birmingham Coll. of Commerce, 1963-67. Contested (Lab) Warwick and Leamington, 1966. PPS to Minister of Public Building and Works, 1969-70. Air Safety Adviser, British Safety Council, 1970-. *Publications:* various newspaper and periodical articles. *Recreations:* piano-playing, rowing, long-distance lorry driving. *Address:* 145 Windermere Avenue, Nuneaton, Warwicks. *T:* Nuneaton 5588.

**HUCKLE, Henry George,** OBE 1969; Chairman of Agricultural, Horticultural and Forestry Industry Training Board since 1970; Consultant to Shellstar Ltd and Shell International Chemical Co. since 1970; *b* 9 Jan. 1914; *s* of George Henry and Lucy Huckle; *m* 1st, 1935, L. Steel (*d* 1947); one *s*; 2nd, 1949, Mrs Millicent Mary Hunter; one *d* and one step *d. Educ:* Latymer Sch.; Oxford Univ. (by courtesy of BRCS via Stalag Luft III, Germany). Accountant trng, 1929-33; sales management, 1933-39; RAF bomber pilot, 1940-41; POW, Germany, 1941-45; Shell Group, 1945-70: Man. Dir, Shellstar Ltd, 1965-70, retd. *Recreations:* golf, gardening, following daughter's interest in horse eventing. *Address:* One Acre, Whiteleaf, Princes Risborough, Bucks. *T:* Princes Risborough 3357. *Clubs:* Farmers', Directors, Hanstown.

**HUDDIE, Sir David (Patrick),** Kt 1968; Managing Director, Aero Engine Division, Rolls-Royce Ltd, since 1965; Chairman, Rolls Royce Aero Inc., since 1969; *b* 12 March 1916; *s* of James and Catherine Huddie; *m* 1941, Wilhelmina Betty Booth; three *s. Educ:* Mountjoy Sch., Dublin; Trinity Coll., Dublin. Aero Engine Division, Rolls-Royce Ltd: Asst Chief Designer, 1947; Chief Development Engineer, 1953; Commercial Dir, 1959; General Manager, 1962; Dir, Rolls-Royce Ltd, 1961. Member Council: Air Registration Bd; Soc. of British Aerospace Cos. Hon. DSc Dublin, 1968. *Recreations:* gardening, shooting, fishing. *Address:* Pendle House, Milford, Derby DE5 1RD. *T:* Belper 2562.

**HUDDLESTON, Rt. Rev. (Ernest Urban) Trevor;** *see* Stepney, Suffragan Bishop of.

**HUDLESTON, Air Chief Marshal Sir Edmund C.,** GCB 1963 (KCB 1958; CB 1945); CBE 1943; Commander Allied Air Forces, Central Europe, 1963-67; Air ADC to the Queen, 1962-67, retired 1967; *b* 30 Dec. 1908; *s* of late Ven. C. Hudleston; *m* 1936, Nancye Davis; one *s* one *d. Educ:* Guildford Sch., W Australia; Royal Air Force Coll., Cranwell. Entered Royal Air Force 1927; served in UK until 1933; India, NWFP, 1933-37 (despatches); RAF Staff Coll., 1938; lent to Turkish Govt 1939-40; served Middle East and N Africa, Sicily, Italy, 1941-43 (despatches thrice); AOC 2nd TAF Group, Western Front, 1944; Imperial Defence Coll., 1946; Head of UK's military delegation to the Western Union Military Staff Cttee, 1948-50; AOC No. 1 Group, Bomber Command, 1950-51; Deputy Chief of Staff, Supreme Headquarters, Allied Command, Europe, 1951-53; AOC No. 3 Group, Bomber Command, 1953-56; RAF Instructor, Imperial Defence Coll., 1956-57; Vice-Chief of the Air Staff, 1957-62; Air Officer Commanding-in-Chief, Transport Command, 1962-63. Comdr Legion of Merit (USA), 1944; Knight Commander Order of Orange-Nassau (Netherlands), 1945; Commander Order of Couronne, Croix de Guerre (Belgium), 1945; Officer, Legion of Honour, 1956, Croix de Guerre (France), 1957. *Recreations:* cricket, squash, tennis, shooting, etc. *Address:* The King's House, 2 Ingram Avenue, NW11. *Clubs:* Royal Air Force, United Hunts.

**HUDSON, Rt. Rev. A(rthur) W(illiam) Goodwin,** ThD; Vicar of St Paul's, Portman Square, W1, since 1965; *s* of Alfred and Anne Goodwin Hudson; *m* Dr Elena E. de Wirtz; one *s. Educ:* London Univ.; London Coll. of Divinity. Ordained Deacon, 1940; Priest, 1941. Curate of St Paul, Chatham, 1940-42; Vicar of Good Easter, Essex, 1942-45; Diocesan Missioner, Chelmsford Diocese, 1943-45; Head Master, Windsor Sch., Santiago, 1945-48; Chaplain, Santiago, Chile, 1945-48; Vicar of St Mary Magdalene, Holloway, 1948-55 (with St James, 1953-55); Vicar of All Saints, Woodford Wells, 1955-60; Coadjutor Bishop and Dean of Sydney, 1960-65. Hon. Gen. Sec., S Amer. Missionary Soc., 1949-60; Hon. Sec., Spanish and Portuguese Church Aid Soc., 1950-55. *Recreations:* yachting, tennis; and profession! *Address:* St Paul's, Portman Square, W1. *Club:* National.

**HUDSON, Sir Edmund (Peder),** Kt 1963; FRSE 1948; FBIM 1960; Chairman: Scottish Technical Education Consultative Council, since 1959; Academic Advisory Committee, Heriot-Watt University, since 1966; Director: Scottish Investment Trust Co. Ltd; Second Scottish Investment Trust Co. Ltd; Scottish Widows' Fund & Life Assurance Society (Chairman, 1967-69); Vice-President, Association of Agriculture; Member Council, Outward Bound Trust; *b* 1 May 1903; *e s* of late Harold Hudson and Helen Ingeborg Olsen; *m* 1934, Bodil Catharina Böschen, Bergen, Norway; three *s. Educ:* Marlborough Coll.; King's Coll., Cambridge. Open Schol., 1922; Harold Fry Research Student, 1925; MA; Imperial Chemical Industries Ltd, Billingham, 1929-34; Scottish Agricultural Industries Ltd: Dir 1934, Asst Man. Dir, 1947, Managing Dir, 1957-62. Pres. Fertiliser Manufacturers' Assoc., 1948-49; Chm. Assoc. of Chemical & Allied Employers, 1953-55. Member: Pilkington Cttee on Broadcasting, 1960-62; Chancellor of Exchequer's Panel, Civil Service Arbitration Tribunal, 1963-68. Rector's Assessor, University Court, University of

Edinburgh, 1961-63. Chm., Napier Coll. of Science and Technology, Edinburgh, 1965-68. Hon. DSc Heriot-Watt Univ., 1966. *Recreation:* yachting. *Address:* 35 Ravelston Dykes, Edinburgh EH12 6HG. *T:* 031-337 3457. *Clubs:* New, Royal Forth Yacht (Edinburgh).

**HUDSON, Eleanor Erlund,** RE 1946 (ARE 1938); RWS 1949 (ARWS 1939); ARCA (London); Artist; *b* 18 Feb. 1912; *d* of Helen Ingeborg Olsen, Brookline, Boston, USA, and Harold Hudson. *Educ:* Torquay; Dorking; Royal College of Art (Diploma 1937, Travelling Scholarship 1938). Mem. Chicago Print Soc. and Soc. of Artist Print-Makers. Studied and travelled in Italy summer 1939. Interrupted by war. Exhibited in London, Provinces, Scandinavia, Canada, USA, etc.; works purchased by War Artists Advisory Council, 1942-43. *Recreations:* music, country life. *Address:* 6 Hammersmith Terrace, W6. *T:* 01-748 3778.

**HUDSON, Eric Hamilton,** FRCP; Hon. Consulting Physician: West London Hospital; London Chest Hospital; King Edward VII Hospital, Midhurst; Papworth Village Settlement; Consultant Physician, Manor House Hospital; Senior Medical Officer, Prudential Assurance Co.; *b* 11 July 1902; *s* of James Arthur and Edith Hudson; *m* 1940, Jessie Marian MacKenzie (*d* 1968); two *s* one *d*. *Educ:* Radley Coll.; Emmanuel Coll., Cambridge; Guy's Hosp., London. MRCS, LRCP, 1927; MA, MB, BCh Cantab, 1931; MRCP 1933, FRCP 1941. Late Wing Commander RAF, Officer in charge Medical Div., 1941-45. Late Examr in Medicine, RCP; Past Pres., W London Medico-Chirurgical Soc., 1959. *Publications:* Section on diagnosis and treatment of respiratory Tuberculosis, Heaf's Symposium of Tuberculosis, 1957; contrib. to Perry and Holmes Sellors Diseases of the Chest, 1964; contrib. to medical jls on diseases of the lungs. *Recreation:* fishing. *Address:* 135 Harley Street, W1. *T:* 01-935 4343.

**HUDSON, Havelock Henry Trevor;** Lloyd's Underwriter since 1952; Deputy Chairman of Lloyd's, 1968; *b* 4 Jan. 1919; *er s* of Savile E. Hudson and Dorothy Hudson (*née* Cheetham); *m* 1st, 1944, Elizabeth (marr. diss., 1956), *d* of Brig. W. Home; two *s*; 2nd, 1957, Cathleen Blanche Lily, *d* of 6th Earl of St Germans; one *s* one *d*. *Educ:* Rugby. Merchant Service, 1937-38. Served War of 1939-45: Royal Hampshire Regt (Major), 1939-42; 9 Parachute Bn, 1942-44. Member: Cttee Lloyd's Underwriters Assoc., 1963; Cttee of Lloyd's, 1965-68, 1970-; Gen. Cttee of Lloyd's Register of Shipping, 1967-. *Recreation:* shooting. *Address:* The Old Rectory, Stanford Dingley, Berkshire. *T:* Bradfield 346.

**HUDSON, Ian Francis;** Assistant Under-Secretary of State, Department of Employment and Productivity, since 1968; *b* 29 May 1925; *s* of Francis Reginald Hudson and Dorothy Mary Hudson (*née* Crabbe); *m* 1952, Gisela Elisabeth Grettka; one *s* one *d*. *Educ:* City of London Sch.; New Coll., Oxford. Royal Navy, 1943-47. Customs and Excise, 1947-53; Min. of Labour, 1953-56, 1959-61, 1963-64; Treasury, 1957-58; Dept of Labour, Australia, 1961-63; DEA, 1964-68. *Recreation:* philately. *Address:* 29 Westwood Avenue, South Harrow, Mddx. *T:* 01-422 0927.

**HUDSON, James Ralph,** FRCS; Surgeon, Moorfields Eye Hospital, since 1956; Ophthalmic Surgeon, Guy's Hospital, since 1963; Hon. Ophthalmic Surgeon, Hospital of St John and St Elizabeth, since 1953; Teacher of Ophthalmology, Guy's Hospital since 1964, Institute of Ophthalmology, University of London, since 1961; Consultant Adviser in Ophthalmology, Department of Health and Social Security; *b* 15 Feb. 1916; *o s* of late William Shand Hudson and Ethel Summerskill; *m*; two *s* two *d*. *Educ:* The King's Sch., Canterbury; Middlesex Hosp. (Edmund Davis Exhibnr), Univ. of London. MRCS, LRCP 1939; MB, BS London 1940; DOMS (England) 1948; FRCS 1949. RAFVR Med. Service, 1942-46; FO, Flt Lt, Sqdn Ldr; Res. Med. Appts, Tindal House Emergency Hosp. (Mddx Hosp. Sector), 1939-42. Moorfields Eye Hosp., Clin. Asst, 1947, Ho. Surg., 1947-49; Sen. Resident Officer, 1949, Chief Clin. Asst, 1950-56; Middlesex Hosp., Clin. Asst Ophth. Outpatients, 1950-51; Ophth. Surg., W Middlesex Hosp., 1950-56, Mount Vernon Hosp., 1953-59. Civilian Consultant in Ophthalmology to RAF, 1970-. Examr in Ophthalmology (Dipl. Ophth. of Examg Bd of Eng., RCP and RCS, 1960-65; Mem. Court of Examrs, RCS, 1966-). FRSocMed 1947 (Vice-Pres. Sect. of Ophthalmology, 1965); Member: Ophthal. Soc. UK, 1948 (Hon. Sec. 1956-58, Vice-Pres., 1969-); Faculty of Ophthalmologists, 1950 (Mem. Council, 1960-; Hon. Sec. 1960-70; Vice-Pres., 1970-; Rep. on Council of RCS, 1968-); Soc. Française d'Ophtal., 1950- (membre délégue étranger, 1970-); Scientific Cttee Les Entretions Annuels d'Ophtalmologie, 1970-; Hon. Mem. Aust. Coll. Ophthalmologists; Pilgrims of Gt Britain. Liveryman, Soc. of Apothecaries, and Freeman of City of London. *Publications:* (with T. Keith Lyle) chapters in Matthews's Recent Advances in the Surgery of Trauma; contrib. to chapters in Rob and Rodney Smith's Operative Surgery, 1969; articles in: Brit. Jl of Ophthalmology; Trans Ophth. Soc. UK; Proc. Royal Soc. Med. *Recreations:* motoring, golf. *Address:* 36 Wimpole Steet, W1M 7EE. *T:* 01-935 5038, 01-486 3236. *Club:* Garrick.

**HUDSON, John Arthur,** CB 1970; Deputy Under-Secretary of State, Department of Education and Science, since 1969; *b* 24 Aug. 1920; *s* of Francis Reginald Hudson and Dorothy Mary (*née* Crabbe); *m* 1960, Dwynwen Davies; one *s* one *d*. *Educ:* City of London Sch.; Jesus Coll., Oxford. Served Royal Corps of Signals, 1941-45 (despatches). Entered Board of Education, 1946. Mem., South Bank Theatre Bd, 1967-. *Recreations:* gardening, microscopy. *Address:* 30 Syke Cluan, Iver, Bucks. *T:* Iver 690.

**HUDSON, Prof. John Pilkington,** MBE 1943; GM 1944 and Bar 1945; BSc, MSc, PhD; NDH; FIBiol; Director, Long Ashton Research Station, and Professor of Horticultural Science, University of Bristol, since 1967; *b* 24 July 1910; *o s* of W. A. Hudson and Bertha (*née* Pilkington); *m* 1936, Mary Gretta, *d* of late W. N. and Mary Heath, Westfields, Market Bosworth, Leics; two *s*. *Educ:* New Mills Grammar Sch.; Midland Agricultural Coll.; University Coll., Nottingham. Hort. Adviser, E Sussex CC, 1935-39. Served War of 1939-45, Royal Engineers (Major). Horticulturist, Dept of Agric., Wellington, NZ, 1945-48; Lecturer in Horticulture, University of Nottingham Sch. of Agric., 1948-50; Head of Dept of Horticulture, University of Nottingham, 1950-67 (as Prof. of Horticulture, 1958-67, Dean, Faculty of Agriculture and Horticulture, 1965-67); seconded part-time to Univ. of Khartoum, Sudan, to found Dept of Horticulture, 1961-63. Associate of Honour, Royal New Zealand Institute of Horticulture, 1948. Member: Horticultural Advisory Council; Advisory Cttee on Agricultural Education; ARC Standing Cttee on

Agricultural Engineering Research; Adv. Technical Cttee, Caribbean Regional Research Centre; Meteorological Cttee, MoD. Governor: East Malling Research Station; Nat. Vegetable Research Station. Editor, Experimental Agriculture, 1965-. *Publications:* (ed) Control of the Plant Environment, 1957; contributions on effects of environment on plant behaviour to scientific jls. *Recreations:* travel, theatre, music, gardening. *Address:* The Spinney, Wrington, Bristol. *Club:* Farmers'.

**HUDSON, Prof. Liam,** MA, PhD; Professor of Educational Sciences, University of Edinburgh, since 1968; Director, Research Unit on Intellectual Development, since 1964; *b* 20 July 1933; *er s* of Cyril and Kathleen Hudson; *m* 1st, 1955, Elizabeth Ward; 2nd 1965, Bernadine Jacot de Boinod; three *s* one *d*. *Educ:* Whitgift Sch.; Exeter Coll., Oxford. Post-graduate and post-doctoral research, Psychological Laboratory, Cambridge, 1957-65, and King's Coll., Cambridge, 1965-68. Fellow, King's Coll., Cambridge, 1966-68. *Publications:* Contrary Imaginations, 1966; Frames of Mind, 1968; papers on various psychological and educational topics. *Recreations:* painting, sculpture, otherwise largely domestic. *Address:* 30 Dick Place, Edinburgh 9.

**HUDSON, Maurice William Petre;** Hon. Consulting Anæsthetist: National Dental Hospital; University College Hospital; Westminster Hospital; Western Ophthalmic Hospital; Samaritan Hospital for Women; Roehampton; Emeritus Consultant Anæsthetist, Princess Beatrice Hospital; *b* 8 Nov. 1901; *s* of late Henry Hudson, ARCA, and Anna Martha Rosa (*née* Petre); *m* 1922, Fredrica Helen de Pont; two *s* one *d* (and one *s* decd). *Educ:* Sherborne Sch.; St Thomas' Hosp. MB, BS London, 1925; MRCS, LRCP, 1924; DA England, 1936; FFARCS, 1948. Formerly; Resident House Surg., Resident Anæsthetist, and Clin. Asst, Nose and Throat Dept, St Thomas' Hosp. Fellow Assoc. Anæsthetists of Gt Brit. Mem. Royal Soc. Med. *Publications:* contrib. to med. jls. *Recreations:* swimming, photography. *Address:* 15 Harley Street, W1. *T:* 01-580 1850, 01-580 3977.

**HUDSON, Brig. Peter,** CBE 1970 (MBE 1965); Imperial Defence College, 1971; *b* 14 Sept. 1923; *s* of Captain William Hudson, late The Rifle Bde, and Ivy (*née* Brown); *m* 1949, Susan Anne Knollys; one adopted *s* one *d* and one adopted *d*. *Educ:* Wellingborough; Jesus Coll., Cambridge. Commnd into The Rifle Bde, 1944; psc 1954; comd company in Mau Mau and Malayan campaigns, 1955-57; jssc 1963; comd 3rd Bn The Royal Green Jackets, 1966-67; Regimental Col The Royal Green Jackets, 1968; Comdr 39 Infantry Bde, 1968-70. *Recreations:* travel, fishing, most games. *Address:* Little Orchard, Frilsham, Newbury, Berks. *T:* Yattendon 266. *Clubs:* Naval and Military, MCC; Green Jackets; Free Foresters.

**HUDSON, Peter John;** Under-Secretary, Cabinet Office, since 1969; *b* 29 Sept. 1919; *o s* of late A. J. Hudson; *m* 1954, Joan Howard FitzGerald; one *s* one *d*. *Educ:* Tollington Sch.; Birkbeck Coll., London. Exchequer and Audit Dept, 1938; Lieut, RNVR, 1940-46; Asst Principal, Air Min., 1947; Private Sec. to Perm. Under Sec. of State for Air, 1948-51; Asst Sec., 1958; Head of Air Staff Secretariat, 1958-61; Imperial Defence Coll., 1962; Head of Programme and Budget Div., Min. of Defence, 1966-69. *Address:* 20 The Ridings, W5. *T:* 01-997 5521.

**HUDSON, Rowland Skeffington,** CMG 1946; *b* 1 April 1900; *s* of late Commander William Joseph Villiers Hudson, Royal Navy; *m* 1928, Jean Mallagh Fegan; two *s*. *Educ:* St Edward's Sch., Oxford. 2nd Lieut Royal Air Force, April 1918; Probationer, BSA Co., N Rhodesia, 1919; Asst Native Commissioner, N Rhodesia, 1922; Native Commissioner, 1925; Asst Chief Sec., 1936; Labour Commissioner, 1940; Provincial Commissioner, 1944; Sec. for Native Affairs, 1945; Mem. Royal Commission on land and population in East Africa, 1953; Commissioner, Provincial Devolution, N Region, Nigeria, 1956; Head of African Studies Branch, Colonial Office, 1949-61; Special Administrative Adviser, Barotseland, 1963-64; Head of Administrative Services Branch, Ministry of Overseas Development, 1964-65; retired, 1966. *Recreation:* gardening. *Address:* Brook House, Ardingly, Sussex. *T:* Ardingly 408. *Club:* Royal Societies.

**HUDSON, Rt. Rev. Wilfrid John,** AKC; Bishop Coadjutor of Brisbane and Head of Brotherhood of S Paul since 1961; *b* 12 June 1904; *s* of late John William and late Bertha Mildred Hudson, Worthing, Sussex; unmarried. *Educ:* Brighton Coll.; King's Coll., London. AKC, first Cl. and Jelf Prize, 1931. Deacon 1931, Priest 1932, London. Curate of St Barnabas, Pimlico, 1931-36; Principal of Brotherhood of Good Shepherd, Dubbo, Diocese of Bathurst, and Examining Chaplain to Bishop of Bathurst, 1937-42; Curate of All Saints, Woodham, Surrey, 1942-43; Acting Curate of St Barnabas, Ealing, 1944; Rector of Letchworth, Diocese of St Albans, 1944-50; Bishop of Carpentaria, 1950-60. Associate of Inst. of Chartered Accountants, 1928. *Address:* 12 Gregory Street, Brisbane, Qld 4011, Australia.

**HUDSON, Sir William,** KBE 1955; FRS 1964; MICE; Chairman, Hawker-Siddeley Australia, since 1967; Commissioner, Snowy Mountains Hydro-Electric Authority, Australia, 1949-67; *b* 27 April 1896; *s* of Dr James Hudson, Nelson, NZ; *m* 1927, Eileen, OBE 1959, *d* of John Trotter, Fairlie, NZ; two *d*. *Educ:* Nelson Coll., NZ; University of London; Post-graduate course in Hydro-Electric Engineering, Grenoble, France. BSc (1st Cl. Hons), Univ. of London; Diploma (with distinction) in Civil Engineering, University Coll., London; Head Medal for Civil Engineering, University Coll., London. Served European War, France, 1916-17. Civil Engineering and Contracting Dept, Armstrong-Whitworth & Co. Ltd, London, 1920-21; Public Works Dept, New Zealand, 1923-24; Armstrong-Whitworth & Co. Ltd, Arapuni Hydro-Electric Scheme, NZ, 1924-27; Public Works Dept, NSW, 1928; First Asst to Resident Engineer, Metropolitan Water, Sewerage and Drainage Board, Sydney, NSW, 1928-30; Sir Alexander Gibb & Partners, London, Engineer-in-charge of construction work, Galloway (Scotland) Hydro-Electric Scheme, 1931-36; Metropolitan Water, Sewerage and Drainage Board, Sydney: Resident Engineer in charge of construction, Woronora Dam, 1937; Inspecting Engineer and Chief Construction Engineer, 1938-43; Engineer-in-Chief, 1948-49. Coronation Medal, 1953. Australasian Engineer Award for 1957 and Kernot Memorial Medal for Distinguished Engineering Achievement in Australia, 1959. Fellow University Coll., London, 1961-. Hon. Mem. Australasian Inst. of Mining and Metallurgy, 1961; Hon. Mem. Instn of Engrs, Australia, 1962; Dr of Laws (*hc*) Australian National University, 1962; Hon. Dr of Engineering, Monash Univ., Melbourne, 1968. James Cook Medal (Royal Society NSW), 1966. *Recreation:* yachting.

*Address:* 39 Flanagan Street, Garran, ACT 2605, Australia.

**HUDSON, William Meredith Fisher,** QC 1967; Barrister-at-law; *b* 17 Nov. 1916; *o s* of late Lt-Comdr William Henry Fisher Hudson, RN (killed in action, Jutland, 1916); *m* 1st, 1938, Elizabeth Sophie (marr. diss., 1948), *d* of late Reginald Pritchard, Bloemfontein, SA; one *s* one *d*; 2nd, 1949, Pamela Helen, *d* of late William Cecil Edwards, Indian Police; two *d*. *Educ:* Imperial Service Coll.; Trinity Hall, Cambridge. BA 1938; Harmsworth Law Scholar, 1939; MA 1940. Called to the Bar, Middle Temple, 1943; South Eastern Circuit, 1945; Mem. of Central Criminal Court Bar Mess. Commissioned Royal Artillery (TA), 1939; served War of 1939-45, Eritrea and Sudan. Chm., Blackfriars Settlement, 1970-. *Recreations:* trains, travel, theatre; formerly athletics (Cambridge Blue, Cross Country half Blue; rep. England and Wales, European Student Games, 1938). *Address:* 5 King's Bench Walk, Temple, EC4. *T:* 01-353 4713; (home) 62 Erpingham Road, SW15. *T:* 01-788 6524. *Clubs:* Hurlingham; Achilles; Hawks (Cambridge).

**HUDSON DAVIES, (Gwilym) Ednyfed;** *see* Davies, G. E. H.

**HUDSON-WILLIAMS, Prof. Harri Llwyd,** MA; Professor of Greek in the University of Newcastle upon Tyne (formerly King's College, Newcastle upon Tyne, University of Durham), since 1952 and Head of Department of Classics, since 1969; *b* 16 Feb. 1911; *yr s* of late Prof. T. Hudson-Williams; *m* 1946, Joan, *er d* of late Lieut-Col H. F. T. Fisher; two adopted *d*. *Educ:* University College of North Wales; King's Coll., Cambridge (Browne Medallist; Charles Oldham Scholar); Munich University. Asst Lectr in Greek, Liverpool Univ., 1937-40; Intelligence Corps, 1940-41; Foreign Office, 1941-45; Lectr in Greek, Liverpool Univ., 1945-50; Reader in Greek, King's Coll., Newcastle upon Tyne, 1950-52; Dean of the Faculty of Arts, 1963-66. *Publications:* contribs to various classical jls, etc. *Recreation:* gardening. *Address:* Toft Hill Cottage, Apperley Road, Stocksfield, Northumberland. *T:* Stocksfield 2341.

**HUDSPETH, Major Henry Moore,** DSO 1918; MC; MSc; FInstD; *b* 10 May 1886; *s* of J. W. Hudspeth, Willington, Durham; *m* 1919, *o d* of T. S. Gill, Doncaster; one *s* two *d*. *Educ:* King James Grammar Sch., Bishop Auckland; Armstrong Coll., Newcastle. Mining Apprenticeship with R. L. Weeks, Durham; County Council Senior Exhibitioner at Armstrong Coll.; Daglish Fellow abroad in France and Germany; Colliery Under-manager; Asst Agent; HM Inspector of Mines, Leeds and Doncaster; Officer RE, 3½ years in Belgium (despatches); HM Senior Inspector of Mines in West Scotland; HM Divisional Inspector of Mines, Yorks; Witness before Subsidence Commission; Assessor, Royal Commission Coal Industry, 1925; Chief Mining Engineer and Mem. of the Safety in Mines Research Board; HM Deputy Chief Inspector of Mines; Joint Managing Dir Airedale Collieries Ltd; T. & R. W. Bower Limited; Dir Glass Houghton and Castleford Collieries, Ltd; Pontefract Collieries Ltd; Yorkshire Coking and Chemical Co. Ltd; Deputy Dir of Production, North Eastern Division, National Coal Board; Deputy Chm. South Wales District Valuation Board; Past Pres. Midland Institute of Mining Engineers. Retired Mining Engineer. *Publications:* Electricity at Shamrock Colliery, Germany; Electric Winding; joint author Magnitude and Variation of Haulage Loads; Forces induced by the Extraction of Coal, and some of their effects on Coal Measure Strata, The Léon-Montluçon Firedamp Detector, Trans. Inst. Min. E. *Recreation:* golf. *Address:* Meads Way, Chesterfield Road, Eastbourne.

**HUFTON, Philip Arthur,** CB 1969; Deputy Director, Royal Aircraft Establishment, since 1966; *b* 13 Oct. 1911; *s* of Mr and Mrs J. W. Hufton, Widnes, Lancs. *Educ:* Wade Deacon Grammar Sch., Widnes; Manchester Univ. MSc 1934. Joined Royal Aircraft Establishment, 1934; Superintendent of Performance, Aircraft and Armament Establishment, Boscombe Down, 1947; Head of Aerodynamics Dept, RAE, 1959-66. *Publications:* Reports and Memoranda of the Aeronautical Research Council. *Address:* The Old Coach House, The Old Manor, Hartley Wintney, Hants. *T:* Hartley Wintney 2120.

**HUGESSEN;** *see* Knatchbull-Hugessen.

**HUGGETT, Mrs Helen K.;** *see* Porter, Prof. H. K.

**HUGGINS,** family name of **Viscount Malvern.**

**HUGGINS, Alan Armstrong; Hon. Mr Justice Huggins;** Judge of the Supreme Court of Hong Kong since 1965; *b* 15 May 1921; *yr s* of late William Armstrong Huggins and Dare (*née* Copping); *m* 1950, Catherine Davidson, *d* of late David Dick; two *s* one *d*. *Educ:* Radley Coll.; Sidney Sussex Coll., Cambridge (MA). TARO (Special List), 1940-48 (Actg Major); Admiralty, 1941-46. Called to Bar, Lincoln's Inn, 1947. Legal Associate Mem., TPI, 1949. Resident Magistrate, Uganda, 1951-53; Stipendiary Magistrate, Hong Kong, 1953-58; Diocesan Reader, Dio. of Hong Kong and Macao, 1954; District Judge, Hong Kong, 1958-65. Chm., Justice (Hong Kong Br.), 1965-68; Judicial Comr, State of Brunei, 1966-. Hon. Life Governor, Brit. and For. Bible Soc. Liveryman, Leathersellers' Company. *Recreations:* boating, archery. *Address:* Courts of Justice, Hong Kong; Maple Cottage, 64 Staines Road, Laleham, Staines, Middx.

**HUGGINS, Prof. Charles B.;** Professor of Surgery, University of Chicago; *b* Halifax, Canada, 22 Sept. 1901; *s* of Charles Edward Huggins and Bessie Huggins (*née* Spencer); citizen of USA by naturalization, 1933; *m* 1927, Margaret Wellman; one *s* one *d*. *Educ:* Acadia Univ.; Harvard. BA Acadia, 1920; MD Harvard, 1924; DSc Acadia, 1946. University of Michigan: Interne in Surgery, 1924-26; Instructor in Surgery, 1926-27; Univ. of Chicago, 1927-; Instructor in Surgery, 1927-29; Asst Prof., 1929-33; Assoc. Prof., 1933-36; Prof. of Surgery, 1936-; Dir, Ben May Laboratory for Cancer Research, 1951-; William B. Ogden Distinguished Service Prof., 1962-. Alpha Omega Alpha, 1942; Mem. Nat. Acad. of Sciences, 1949; Mem. Amer. Philosophical Soc., 1962. Sigillum Magnum, Bologna Univ., 1964; Hon. Prof., Madrid Univ., 1956; Hon. FRSocMed (London), 1956; Hon. FRCSE 1958; Hon. FRCS 1959; Hon. FACS 1963. Hon. MSc, Yale, 1947; Hon. DSc: Washington Univ., St Louis, 1950; Leeds Univ., 1953; Turin Univ., 1957; Trinity Coll., Hartford, Conn., 1965; Wales, 1967; Univ. of California, Berkeley, 1968; Univ. of Michigan, 1968; Hon. LLD: Aberdeen Univ., 1966; York Univ., Toronto, 1968; Hon. DPS, George Washington Univ., 1967. Has given many memorial lectures and has won numerous gold medals, prizes and awards for his work on urology and cancer research, including Nobel Prize for Medicine (jtly), 1966. Holds foreign orders. *Address:* Ben May Laboratory for

Cancer Research, University of Chicago, 950 East 59th Street, Chicago, Ill 60637, USA.

**HUGGINS, Sir John,** GCMG, *cr* 1949 (KCMG, *cr* 1943; CMG 1939); MC; *b* 17 Sept. 1891; *s* of late William Huggins; *m* 1st, 1929, Molly (marriage dissolved, 1958), *d* of Charles Francis Joseph Green; three *d*; 2nd, 1958, Mrs Margaret Hitchcock. *Educ:* Bridlington Sch.; Leeds Univ. Served European War, 1914-19; Capt., Yorks Regt; active service, Gallipoli, Egypt, France (despatches, MC); Malayan CS, 1920-38; held various appointments in that Service, including Private Sec. to Governor of Straits Settlements and High Commissioner for Malay States, 1926-27; Acting Malayan Establishment Officer, 1934-38; Colonial Sec., Trinidad, 1938-42; Governor's Deputy, Sept.-Nov. 1938; Acting Governor, 1938-39, 1941, and 1942; Head of British Colonies Supply Mission, Washington, 1942-43; Captain-General and Governor-in-Chief of Jamaica, 1943-51. KStJ 1945. *Recreations:* cricket, tennis, golf. *Address:* Fieldway, West Strand, West Wittering, Sussex.

**HUGGINS, Kenneth Herbert,** CMG 1960; *b* 4 Dec. 1908; *s* of late Herbert John Huggins and Nelly Bailey; *m* 1934, Gladys E. Walker; one *s* one *d*. *Educ:* Hitchin Grammar Sch.; Tollington Sch.; University Coll., London. BSc London 1930; PhD Glasgow, 1940. Asst and Lecturer in Geography, Glasgow Univ., 1930-41; Principal, Ministry of Supply, 1941; Staff of Combined Raw Materials Board, Washington, 1942-46; Board of Trade, 1947, Asst Sec., 1949; Staff of Administrative Staff Coll., Henley, Jan. 1954-March 1955; Commercial Counsellor, British Embassy, Washington, 1957-60; UK Trade Commissioner, subsequently Consul-General, Johannesburg, 1960-62. Dir, British Industrial Develt Office, NY, 1962-68. *Publications:* atlases and articles in geographical journals. *Recreation:* travelling. *Address:* Finnart House, Melton Drive, Storrington, Sussex. *T:* Storrington 2838. *Club:* Reform.

**HUGH-JONES, Evan Bonnor,** CB 1953; MC 1915; *b* 1890; 2nd *s* of Ll. Hugh-Jones, CBE, Wrexham; *m* 1st, 1918, Elsie M. Iggulden (*d* 1950); one *s* one *d*; 2nd, 1952, Mrs Maud Lundon (*née* O'Gorman), Co. Cork. *Educ:* Oundle; McGill Univ., Montreal. Major in Royal Engineers, European War (despatches twice, MC); Chief Engineer (Roads), Ministry of Transport 1949-54, retired. *Address:* 1 Clavering Walk, Cooden, Sussex. *T:* Cooden 4210.

**HUGH-JONES, Wynn Normington,** MVO 1961; Counsellor and Head of Chancery, British High Commission, Ottawa, since 1968; *b* 1 Nov. 1923; *s* of late Hugh Hugh-Jones and of May Hugh-Jones; *m* 1958, Ann Muriel, *d* of S. L. Purkiss; one *s* two *d*. *Educ:* Ludlow; Selwyn Coll., Cambridge. Served in RAF, 1943-46. Entered Foreign Service (now Diplomatic Service), 1947; Foreign Office, 1947-49; served in: Jedda, 1949-52; Paris, 1952-56; FO, 1956-59; Chargé d'Affaires, Conakry, 1959-60; Head of Chancery, Rome, 1960-64; FO, 1964-66. Counsellor, 1964. Consul, Elizabethville (later Lubumbashi), 1966-68. *Recreations:* golf, tennis, etc. *Address:* 1 Poyle Road, Guildford, Surrey. *Clubs:* Anglo-Belgian; Rideau (Ottawa); Hindhead Golf.

**HUGHES,** family name of **Baron Hughes.**

**HUGHES,** Baron, *cr* 1961, of Hawkhill (Life Peer); **William Hughes,** PC 1970; CBE 1956 (OBE 1942); DL, JP; President, Save the Children Fund, Dundee; Vice-Chairman: Advisory Committee King George VI Memorial Club for Old People, Dundee; Hon. Vice-President: Dundee Old People's Welfare Committee; Boy Scouts' Assoc., County of City of Dundee; Dundee Union of Boys' Clubs; Dundee Repertory Theatre Club; *b* 22 Jan. 1911; *e s* of late Joseph and of Margaret Hughes; *m* 1951, Christian Clacher, *o c* of late James and Sophia Gordon; two *d*. *Educ:* Balfour Street Public Sch., Dundee; Dundee Technical Coll. ARP Controller Dundee, 1939-43; Armed Forces, 1943-46; Commissioned RAOC, 1944; demobilised as Capt., 1946. Hon. City Treasurer, Dundee, 1946-47; Chairman, Eastern Regional Hospital Board, Scotland, 1948-60; Lord Provost of Dundee and HM Lieut of County of City of Dundee, 1954-60; Member: Dundee Town Council, 1933-36 and 1937-61; Court of St Andrews Univ., 1954-63; Council of Queen's Coll., Dundee, 1954-63; Cttee on Civil Juries, 1958-59; Cttee to Enquire into Registration of Title to Land in Scotland, 1960-62; Chm. Glenrothes Dev. Corp., 1960-64; Mem., North of Scotland Hydro-Electric Bd, 1957-64; Scottish Transport Council, 1960-64. Jt Parly Under-Sec. of State for Scotland, 1964-69; Joint Minister of State for Scotland, 1969-70. Contested (Lab) E Perthshire, 1945 and 1950. Hon. LLD St Andrews, 1960. Chevalier, Légion d'Honneur, 1958. *Recreation:* gardening. *Address:* East Claverhouse, Dundee, Angus. *T:* Dundee 42121.

**HUGHES, Albert Henry,** OBE 1961; Head of Finance Department, Foreign and Commonwealth Office, and Finance Officer of the Diplomatic Service, since 1968; *b* 20 Sept. 1917; *s* of George Albert Hughes; *m* 1939, Nancy Russell; two *s* one *d*. *Educ:* The Judd Sch., Tonbridge, Kent. Appointed to the Foreign Office, 1935. War of 1939-45: Served in HM Forces, 1940-45, HM Vice-Consul, Rouen, France, 1949; HM Consul, Tehran, Iran, 1949-52; HM Consul, Philadelphia, USA, 1953-55; HM Consul, Bilbao, Spain, 1962-64; Counsellor (Administration) and HM Consul-General, Washington, 1964-68. *Address:* The Cottage, Matfield Green, near Tonbridge, Kent.

**HUGHES, Andrew Anderson;** Managing Director, Crudens Ltd, since 1969; *b* 27 Dec. 1915; *s* of Alexander and Euphemia Hughes; *m* 1946, Margaret Dorothy Aikman; no *c*. *Educ:* Waid Academy; St Andrews Univ.; Marburg Univ.; Emmanuel Coll., Cambridge. Colonial Administrative Service, 1939; Private Sec. to Governor, Gold Coast, 1940-42; Staff Minister Resident West Africa, 1943; Colonial Office, 1946; Dept of Health for Scotland, 1947; Asst Sec., 1956; Under-Sec., 1964; Under-Sec., Scottish Development Dept, 1967-69. Mem. Scottish Tourist Bd, 1969-. *Recreations:* gardening, golf. *Address:* West Colinton House, Colinton, Edinburgh. *T:* 031-441 4296. *Clubs:* Royal Commonwealth Society; New (Edinburgh).

**HUGHES, Arthur Montague D'Urban,** MA; Emeritus Professor, University of Birmingham, since 1940; *b* Worthing, Sussex, 3 Nov. 1873; *s* of Rev. Edwin M. M. Hughes, Curate of St Thomas, Exeter, and Margaret Ann Richmond; *m* 1906, Wilhelmina Langenheim, Kiel, Germany; one *d*. *Educ:* St Edmund's Sch., Canterbury; St John's Coll., Oxford (Classical Scholar, Second Class Moderations, First Class Lit. Hum.). Lecturer for Oxford Univ. Extension Delegacy; English Lektor, Univ. of Kiel, 1905-14; Mem. of Staff, Oxford Univ. Press, 1915-21; Lecturer in English Literature, Birmingham Univ., 1921-31; Lectr St John's Coll., Oxford, 1923-29; Reader in English, Birmingham Univ., 1931-35; Prof. of English Language and Literature,

University of Birmingham, 1935-39. *Publications:* The Nascent Mind of Shelley, 1947; Editions: Carlyle's Past and Present, Shelley's Poems, 1820, Tennyson's Poems, 1842, and several volumes in Clarendon English Series. *Recreation:* walking. *Address:* 42 Weoley Hill, Selly Oak, Birmingham. *T:* 021-472 0371.

**HUGHES, Maj.-Gen. Basil Perronet,** CB 1955; CBE 1944; Chairman, Royal Artillery Institution; *b* 13 Jan. 1903; *s* of late Rev. E. B. A. Hughes; *m* 1932, Joan Marion Worthington; two *s*. *Educ:* Eton Coll.; RMA, Woolwich. Commissioned RFA 1923; Staff Coll., 1935-36; Directing Staff, Staff Coll., 1940. Served NW Frontier of India, 1930-31 (medal and clasp); Mohmand, 1933 (clasp); War of 1939-45 (star and despatches). Formerly: Hon. Col 2nd (London) Bn, Mobile Defence Corps; Hon. Colonel 571 LAA Regt (9th Battalion The Middx Regt DCO) RA, TA. ADC to the Queen, 1952-54; GOC 4 Anti-Aircraft Group, 1954; Maj.-Gen. RA (AA), War Office, 1955-58; retired, 1958. Col Comdt RA 1961-63; Hon. Colonel: 5th Bn, The Middx Regt (DCO), TA, 1964-69; 10th Bn, The Queen's Regt (Mddx), T&AVR, 1970-. *Clubs:* United Service, Leander.

**HUGHES, Brodie;** *see* Hughes, E. B. C.

**HUGHES, Rt. Hon. Cledwyn;** PC 1966; MP (Lab) Anglesey since 1951; *b* 14 Sept. 1916; *er s* of Rev. Henry David and Emily Hughes; *m* 1949, Jean Beatrice Hughes; one *s* one *d*. *Educ:* Holyhead Grammar Sch.; University Coll. of Wales, Aberystwyth (LLB). Solicitor, 1940. Served RAFVR, 1940-45. Mem. Anglesey County Council, 1946-52. Contested (Lab) Anglesey, 1945 and 1950. Chm. Welsh Parliamentary Party, 1953-54; Chm. Welsh Labour Group, 1955-56. Mem. Cttee of Public Accounts, 1957-64. Minister of State for Commonwealth Relations, 1964-66; Sec. of State for Wales, 1966-68; Min. of Agriculture, Fisheries and Food, 1968-70. Mem. Parly. Delegn to Lebanon, 1957; Represented British Govt at Kenya Republic Celebrations, 1964; led UK Delegn to The Gambia Independence celebrations, 1965. Mission to Rhodesia, July 1965; Led UK Mission on Contingency Planning to Zambia, 1966. Mem. County Councils' Assoc. *Publication:* Report on Conditions in St Helena, 1958. *Address:* Ty Gwyn, Holyhead, Anglesey. *T:* Holyhead 2452. *Club:* Travellers'.

**HUGHES, Sir David (Collingwood),** 14th Bt *cr* 1773; East European Operations Manager, Pye Unicam Ltd; *b* 29 Dec. 1936; *s* of Sir Richard Edgar Hughes, 13th Bt and Angela Lilian Adelaide Pell (*d* 1967); *S* father, 1970; *m* 1964, Rosemary Ann Pain, MA, LLB (Cantab), *d* of Rev. John Pain; three *s*. *Educ:* Oundle and Magdalene College, Cambridge (MA). National Service, RN, 1955-57. United Steel Cos Ltd, 1960-65; Unicam Instruments Ltd (subsequently Pye Unicam Ltd), export executive, 1965-70. *Recreations:* carpentry, music, shooting, fishing. *Heir:* *s* Thomas Collingwood Hughes, *b* 16 Feb. 1966. *Address:* The Old Fox, Balsham, Cambs. *T:* West Wratting 488.

**HUGHES, Mrs David (John);** *see* Zetterling, Mai.

**HUGHES, Prof. David Leslie,** PhD, FRCVS, DipBact; Professor of Veterinary Pathology, University of Liverpool, since 1955; Warden of Roscoe Hall, University of Liverpool; *b* 26 Oct. 1912; *s* of John and Eva Hughes; *m* 1938, Ann Marjorie Sparks. *Educ:* Wycliffe Coll., Stonehouse; Royal Veterinary Coll., London (MRCVS). Agricultural Research Council Studentship in Animal Health, 1934-37 (DipBact London, 1936); Research Officer, Veterinary Laboratory, Min. of Agriculture, 1937-38; Lecturer in Bacteriology, Royal Veterinary College, 1938-40; Second Scientific Asst, Agricultural Research Council's Field Station, Compton, 1940-46; Head of Veterinary Science Div., Research Dept, Boots Pure Drug Co. Ltd, 1948-55; PhD Nottingham, 1959; Dean of Faculty of Veterinary Science, University of Liverpool, 1965-68. FRCVS 1952; Mem. Council, RCVS, 1964-. Pres., British Veterinary Assoc., 1963-64. Scientific Editor, Research in Veterinary Science. *Publications:* scientific articles in Veterinary Record, British Veterinary Journal, Journal of Comparative Pathology, Journal of Hygiene, etc. *Recreations:* gardening, painting and travel. *Address:* Warden's House, Roscoe Hall, Greenbank Lane, Liverpool 17. *T:* 051-733 1847. *Club:* Farmers'.

**HUGHES, Desmond;** *see* Hughes, F. D.

**HUGHES, Rev. Edward Marshall,** MTh, PhD (London); Vicar of St Augustine's, South Croydon, since 1965; *b* London, 11 Nov. 1913; *o s* of late Edward William Hughes, Newhouse, Mersham, Ashford, Kent, and Mabel Frances (*née* Faggetter); descendant of Edward Hughes, *b* 1719, of Little Swanton, Mersham; unmarried. *Educ:* City of London Sch.; King's Coll., London; Cuddesdon Coll., Oxford. Deacon, 1936, Priest, 1937, Canterbury; Curate, St Martin's, Canterbury, 1936-41; Chaplain RAFVR 1941 (invalided Oct. 1941); Curate Bearsted, Kent, 1941-46; Vicar of Woodnesborough, Kent, 1946-52; Chap. St Bartholomew's Hosp., Sandwich, 1947-52; Off. Chap. RAF Station, Sandwich, 1948-52; Warden of St Peter's Theological Coll., Jamaica, 1952-61; Canon Missioner of Jamaica, 1955-61; Examining Chap. to the Bp of Jamaica, 1953-61; Hon. Chap. Jamaica, RAFA, 1954-61; Mem. Board of Governors Nuttall Memorial Hospital, Kingston, 1956-61, and St Jago High Sch., Spanish Town, 1957-61; Visiting Lecturer, McGill Univ., Canada, 1957; Hon. Lecturer, Union Theological Seminary, Jamaica, 1957-58; Visiting Lecturer, Séminaire de Théologie, Haiti, 1959; Acting Rector, St Matthew's Church, Kingston, and Chap. Kingston Public Hospital, 1959-60; JP (St Andrew, Jamaica), 1959-63; Commissary to Bishop of Jamaica, 1968-. Fellow (Librarian, 1962-65), St Augustine's Coll., Canterbury (Central Coll. of the Anglican Communion), 1961-65; Hon. helper for Kent, RAF Benevolent Fund, 1961-65, for London (Croydon), 1965-; Divinity Master, VI Forms, The King's Sch., Canterbury, 1962-63; Officiating Chap., Canterbury Garrison, 1963-64. Proctor in Convocation, Dio. Canterbury, 1966-. Examining Chap. to Archbishop of Canterbury, 1967-. *Publications:* various papers on theological education overseas. *Recreations:* television-viewing and bibliophagy. *Address:* Vicarage, 23a St Augustine's Avenue, South Croydon, Surrey CR2 6JN. *T:* 01-688 2663. *Club:* West Indian.

**HUGHES, Emmet John;** Newsweek columnist and editorial consultant to the Washington Post Co. since 1963; *b* 26 Dec. 1920; *s* of Judge John L. Hughes, Summit, NJ; *m* (div.); one *s* two *d*. *Educ:* Princeton Univ. (AB *summa cum laude*); Columbia Univ. (Graduate Sch.). Press Attaché, American Embassy, Madrid, 1942-46. Chief of Bureau for Time and Life Magazines: Rome, 1947-48, Berlin, 1948, 1949; Articles Editor, for Life Magazine, New York, 1949-53. Administrative Asst to the President of the United States, 1953, Special European Correspondent, Life Magazine, 1953-57; Chief of Foreign Correspondents, Time and Life, 1957-60; Senior Advisor on Public Affairs to the Rockefeller Brothers, 1960-63. *Publications:* The Church and the Liberal Society, 1944; Report from Spain, 1947; America the Vincible, 1959; The Ordeal of Power, 1963. *Address:* 444 Madison Avenue, New York, NY, USA. *T:* HA 1-1234.

**HUGHES, (Ernest) Brodie (Cobbett),** FRCS; Professor of Neurosurgery, University of Birmingham, since 1948; *b* 21 Sept. 1913; *o s* of E. T. C. Hughes, surgeon, and D. K. Cobbett, Richmond, Surrey; unmarried. *Educ:* Eastbourne Coll.; University Coll. and Hospital, London. MB, BS London 1937, FRCS 1939, ChM Birmingham 1949; resident appointments, UC Hospital, and at National Hospital for Nervous Diseases, Queen Square, London. After various appointments in neurosurgery was appointed Neurosurgeon, Birmingham United Hospitals, 1947. *Publications:* The Visual Fields, 1955; various publications in medical journals on neurosurgery and on perimetry and visual fields in particular. *Recreations:* playing the oboe, fly-fishing for trout; unsuccessful attempts to paint and draw in oils, water-colour, pen-and-ink and other media. *Address:* 68 Wellington Road, Edgbaston, Birmingham 15. *T:* 021-440 3427. *Clubs:* Athenæum; Union (Birmingham).

**HUGHES, Air Vice-Marshal (Frederick) Desmond,** CBE 1961; DSO 1945; DFC and 2 bars, 1941-43; AFC 1954; Commandant, RAF College, Cranwell, since 1970; *b* Belfast, 6 June 1919; *s* of late Fred C. Hughes, company dir, Donaghadee, Co. Down, and Hilda (*née* Hunter), Portballintrae, Co. Antrim; *m* 1941, Pamela, *d* of late Julius Harrison, composer and conductor; two *s. Educ:* Campbell Coll., Belfast; Pembroke Coll., Cambridge (MA). Joined RAF from Cambridge Univ. Air Sqdn, 1939; Battle of Britain, No. 264 Sqdn, 1940; night fighting ops in Britain and Mediterranean theatre, 1941-43; comd No. 604 Sqdn in Britain and France, 1944-45; granted perm. commn, 1946; served in Fighter Comd, 1946-53; Directing Staff, RAF Staff Coll., 1954-56; Personal Staff Off. to Chief of Air Staff, 1956-58; comd. RAF Stn Geilenkirchen, 1959-61; Dir of Air Staff Plans, Min. of Def., 1962-64; ADC to the Queen, 1963; Air Officer i/c Administration, HQ Flying Training Command, RAF, 1966-68; AOC, No 18 Group, RAF Coastal Command, and Air Officer, Scotland and N Ireland, 1968-70. *Recreations:* fishing, ski-ing, lawn tennis, sailing, music. *Address:* c/o Northern Bank Ltd, 14 Donegall Square West, Belfast 1, N Ireland; The Lodge, Cranwell, Sleaford, Lincs. *Club:* Royal Air Force.

**HUGHES, G. Bernard,** FRSA; author; formerly Editor-in-Chief of The Queen; *o s* of late Charles Bernard Hughes, Heath Town, and Lydia, *o d* of William Shepherd, Lane Head, Staffs; *m* Therle Marguerite Conway, *o d* of C. Conway Plumbe, BSc; two *s. Educ:* Wolverhampton Sch. Volunteered for active service; served with 1st Royal Marine Batt. at Arras, Paschendaele and Cambrai, 1916-19; HM Inspector of Factories, 1940-45. *Publications:* The Story of the Locomotive; The Circus; Dry Batteries, 1940; Modern Industrial Lighting, 1941; Collecting Antiques, 1949; More About Collecting Antiques, 1952; Living Crafts, 1953; Old English, Scottish and Irish Table Glass, 1956; Horse Brasses and Other Curios, 1956; Small Antique Silverware, 1957; English Glass for the Collector, 1958; Victorian Pottery and Porcelain, 1959; English and Scottish Earthenware, 1960; English Pottery and Porcelain Figures, 1964; Country Life Collector's Pocket Book of China, 1965; Old Sheffield Plate, 1970; Old English Snuff-Boxes, 1971. (With Therle Hughes): English Painted Enamels, 1950; Three Centuries of English Domestic Silver, 1952 and After the Regency, 1952; Old English Porcelain and Bone China, 1955; The Collector's Encyclopædia of English Ceramics, 1956; Small Antique Furniture, 1958; Country Life Collector's Pocket Book, 1963. Contributions to: Encyclopædia Britannica; The Connoisseur Concise Encyclopædia of Antiques, vols 1 to 5; The Connoisseur Period Guides, 1956, 1957; Country Life; The Connoisseur; Apollo. *Address:* Fairlight House, Hythe, Kent. *T:* Hythe 67512.

**HUGHES, George Ravensworth,** CVO 1943; *b* 16 June 1888; *s* of Thomas McKenny Hughes, formerly Professor of Geology at Cambridge Univ.; *m* 1917, Margaret (*d* 1967), *d* of His Honour Judge Graham; one *s* one *d. Educ:* Eton; Trinity Coll., Cambridge. Clerk of the Worshipful Company of Goldsmiths, 1938-53. *Publications:* The Plate of the Goldsmiths' Co. (with J. B. Carrington), 1926; The Goldsmiths' Company as Patrons of their craft, 1919 to 1953; Articles on Antique and Modern Silverwork. *Recreations:* music, gardening, and golf. *Address:* Plummers, Bishopstone, Seaford, Sussex. *T:* Seaford 2958. *Club:* Athenæum.

**HUGHES, Brig. Gerald Birdwood V.;** *see* Vaughan-Hughes.

**HUGHES, Guy Erskine,** CMG 1949; *b* 7 March 1904; *s* of late Major C. G. E. Hughes, the Cheshire Regt, and Florence, *d* of late S. A. Waters, sometime of Royal Irish Constabulary; *m* 1930, June, *d* of Donald Spicer, Ghent; three *s* one *d. Educ:* Harrow Sch.; Trinity Coll., Cambridge. Messrs Mather & Platt, Ltd; apprentice engineer, 1925-28; ICI Ltd, 1928-35; Messrs Ed. Sharp & Sons, Ltd; Dir, 1935-39. Served War of 1939-45, in RNVR; demobilised as Temp. Comdr RNVR (Sp.), 1945. Chief, Food, Agriculture and Forestry, CCG, 1946; Overseas Food Corp., Urambo, 1950. Managing Dir, Imperial Chemical Industries (South Africa) Ltd, 1952-58; Managing Dir, African Explosives and Chemical Industries Ltd, 1958-66. *Recreation:* fly-fishing. *Address:* Waterbank, Norham, Berwick upon Tweed. *Clubs:* Boodle's, Naval and Military; Rand, Country (Johannesburg).

**HUGHES, Rear-Adm. Henry Hugh,** CB 1966; Director of Naval Electrical Engineering, 1964; Chief Naval Engineer Officer, 1967-68; retired, 1968; *b* 9 March 1911; British; *m* 1939, Margaret (*née* Lycett); two *d. Educ:* Clydebank High Sch.; Glasgow Univ. (BSc Hons). English Electric Co. Ltd, Stafford, 1932-42; Electrical Officer, RNVR, 1942-45; transf. to RN as Lieut-Comdr, 1945; Comdr 1947; Capt. 1956; Rear-Adm. 1964. HMS Vanguard, 1947-49; subsequently: various appts in Admty and Dockyards; in comd, HMS Collingwood; Dep. Dir of Electrical Engrg. *Recreation:* tennis. *Address:* Little Morgrove, Perrymead, Bath, Somerset; Tigh Failté, Argyll Terrace, Tobermory, Isle of Mull, Scotland. *T:* Tobermory 2132.

**HUGHES, Rev. Henry Trevor,** MA; Minister, Attleborough Methodist Church, since 1969; *b* 27 Feb. 1910; *s* of late Rev. Dr H. Maldwyn Hughes; *m* 1946, Elizabeth Catherine Williams; one *s* one *d. Educ:* Perse Sch., Cambridge. National Provincial Bank, 1926-31; Wesley House, Cambridge, 1932-35 (2nd

Class Hons Theol Tripos, 1935); Chaplain, Culford Sch., Bury St Edmunds, 1935-41; Chaplain, Royal Air Force, 1941-45 (despatches). Asst Minister, Central Hall, Westminster, 1945-46; Vice-Principal and Chaplain, Westminster College of Education, 1946-53, Principal, 1953-69. Incorporated MA, Oxford Univ. through Lincoln Coll., 1959. Governor, East Anglian Sch., Bury St Edmunds. Select Preacher, University of Oxford, 1965; Methodist representative, British Council of Churches Preachers' Exchange with the USA, 1964. *Publications:* Prophetic Prayer, 1947; Teaching the Bible to Seniors, 1948; Teaching the Bible to Juniors, 1949; Why We Believe, 1950; The Piety of Jeremy Taylor, 1960; Faith and Life, 1962; Life Worth Living, 1965; pamphlets: Letters to a Christian, 1947; Teaching the Bible Today, 1957; contributor to London Quarterly Review. *Recreation:* painting. *Address:* The Manse, Station Road, Attleborough, Norfolk. *T:* Attleborough 2110.

**HUGHES, Herbert Delauney,** MA; Principal of Ruskin College, Oxford, since 1950; *b* 7 Sept. 1914; *s* of late Arthur Percy Hughes, BSc, and late Maggie Ellen Hughes; *m* 1937, Beryl Parker. *Educ:* Cheadle Hulme Sch.; Balliol Coll., Oxford (State and County Major Scholar). BA (Hons) in Modern History, 1936; Asst Sec., New Fabian Research Bureau, 1937-39; Organising Sec., Fabian Soc., 1939-46; Mem. Exec. Fabian Soc., 1946- (Vice-Chm. 1950-52, 1958-59, Chm. 1959-60); MP (Lab) Wolverhampton (West), 1945-50; Parliamentary Private Sec. to Minister of Education, 1945-47; to Financial Sec. to War Office, 1948-50; Mem. Lambeth Borough Council, 1937-42. Governor of Educational Foundation for Visual Aids, 1948-56. Member: Civil Service Arbitration Tribunal, 1955-; Commonwealth Scholarship Commn, 1968-; Cttee on Adult Educn, 1969-. Vice-Pres., Workers' Educational Assoc., 1958-67, Dep. Pres., 1968-. Trustee, Oxford Preservation Trust, 1959-. Served War of 1939-45, with 6 Field Regt Royal Artillery. *Publications:* (part author) Democratic Sweden, 1937, Anderson's Prisoners, 1940, Six Studies in Czechoslovakia, 1947. Advance in Education, 1947; Towards a Classless Society, 1947; A Socialist Education Policy, 1955; The Settlement of Disputes in The Public Service, 1968; (jt author) Planning for Education in 1980, 1970. *Recreations:* walking and foreign travel. *Address:* Ruskin College, Oxford; The Old Rectory, Noke, near Islip, Oxon. *T:* Kidlington 2832.

**HUGHES, H(ugh) L(lewelyn) Glyn,** CBE 1945; DSO 1916; MC; QHP; MRCS, LRCP; FRCGP; Director, South East London General Practitioner Centre, 1958-68; Senior Administrative Medical Officer, South-East Metropolitan Regional Hospital Board, 1947-57; President Harveian Society, 1947; President, Casualties Union, since 1953; Secretary and Secretary, Research Committee, Medical Council on Alcoholism, since 1969; Foundation Member, Hon. Treasurer, 1952-65, and Hon. Fellow, Royal College of General Practitioners; Vice-President (Hon. Secretary 1940-41) Medical Society of London; *b* 25 July 1892; *s* of Dr H. G. Hughes, formerly of Ventersburg, ORC; *m* 1920, Armorel Anselma Swynford-, *o d* of late T. Rought Jones, East Grinstead; one *s* two *d*; *m* 1949, Thelma Marion, *d* of Edward Pembroke, Eltham, Kent. *Educ:* Epsom Coll.; University Coll. Hosp., London (Scholar); Carr Exhibition, matric. 1st Class; Fellowes Medal for Clinical Medicine, 1914. Asst Physician Child Welfare Dept, University Coll. Hosp.; House Physician and House Surg. University Coll. Hosp., Asst Surg. Cheltenham Eye, Ear and Throat Hosp.; Obstetric Asst University Coll. Hosp. Served European War, 1914-18 (DSO and bar, MC, despatches, Croix de Guerre avec palme). Attached 1st Wilts, 1915-18; Grenadier Guards, 1918-19; War of 1939-45 (despatches, CBE, 2nd bar to DSO), Comdr Legion of Merit, US, OStJ. ADMS Guards Armoured Div.; Brig. DDMS VIII Corps; Brig. DDMS 2nd Army; Vice-Dir Medical Services BAOR, 1945; Comdt Depot RAMC, 1945-47; Inspector of Training, 1946-47; Hon. Col RAMC. Pres. The Bridge in Britain, 1967. Pres. Barbarian Football Club; Pres. Blackheath Football Club, 1930-55. *Publications:* Peace at the Last, 1960; Death (contrib. to Encyclopedia of General Practice), 1964. *Recreations:* Rugby Football, golf, rifle-shooting. *Address:* 17 Cadogan Square, SW1. *T:* 01-235 5161. *Clubs:* Army and Navy, Pratt's; Royal and Ancient (St Andrews); Royal St George's; Pine Valley (USA).

**HUGHES, Very Rev. John Chester;** Provost of Leicester since Sept. 1963; *b* 20 Feb. 1924; *m* 1950, Sybil Lewis McClelland; three *s* two *d* (and one *s* decd). *Educ:* Dulwich Coll.; St John's Coll., Durham. Curate of Westcliffe-on-Sea, Essex, 1950-53; Succentor of Chelmsford Cathedral, 1953-55; Vicar of St Barnabas, Leicester, 1955-61; Vicar of Croxton Kerrial with Branston-by-Belvoir, 1961-63. *Recreation:* golf. *Address:* Provost's House, 1 St Martin's East, Leicester, LE1 5FX. *T:* Leicester 25294/5.

**HUGHES, Rt. Rev. John Richard Worthington Poole;** *see* South-West Tanganyika, Bishop of.

**HUGHES, Rt. Rev. John Taylor;** *see* Croydon, Suffragan Bishop of.

**HUGHES, John Turnbull,** OBE 1959; Chief Information Officer, Civil Service Commission; Commonwealth Office, 1947-67; *b* 8 June 1919; *s* of Maurice and Helen Hughes. *Educ:* City Grammar Sch., Chester; Liverpool Univ., Officer, 2nd King Edward VII's Own Gurkha Rifles, 1940-46. Private Sec. to Governor of Bengal, 1945-46. FRSA. *Recreations:* theatre, walking, painting. *Address:* 15 Sackville Gardens, Hove, Sussex, BN3 4GJ. *T:* Brighton 777800. *Clubs:* Garrick, Le Petit Club Français.

**HUGHES, Richard (Arthur Warren),** OBE 1946; DLitt (*honoris causa*) University of Wales, 1956; FRSL; Hon. Member, American Academy of Arts and Letters and National Institute of Arts and Letters (Blashfield Foundation Address, 1969); author; *b* 1900; *s* of Arthur Hughes and Louisa Warren; *m* 1932, Frances, 2nd *d* of late Gardner S. Bazley and of Mrs Francis Cadogan, Hatherop Castle, Fairford, Glos.; two *s* three *d*. *Educ.* Charterhouse; Oriel Coll., Oxford. First play, The Sisters' Tragedy, produced London, 1922; contributor to London and American literary journals; co-founder of the Portmadoc Players; A Comedy of Good and Evil, produced London, 1925; also first author in the world of wireless plays; Vice-Chm. (till 1936) of the Welsh National Theatre; Petty-Constable of Laugharne, 1936. Served in Admiralty, 1940-45 (OBE). *Publications:* Gipsy-Night, and other Poems, 1922; The Sisters' Tragedy, 1922; The Sisters' Tragedy, and other Plays (The Sisters' Tragedy, The Man Born to be Hanged, A Comedy of Good and Evil, Danger), 1924; Poems by John Skelton (edited), 1924; A Moment of Time (Collected Stories), 1926; Confessio Juvenis

(Collected Poems), 1926; Plays, 1928; A High Wind in Jamaica (The Innocent Voyage), 1929 (filmed 1965); The Spider's Palace (children's stories), 1931; In Hazard, 1938; Don't Blame Me (children's stories), 1940. Volume in Official History of the War (Civil Series); The Administration of War Production (with J. D. Scott), 1956; The Fox in the Attic (Vol. I of the Human Predicament), 1961; Gertrude's Child (children's story) 1966. *Recreations:* sailing, travel. *Address:* c/o Chatto & Windus, 40-42 William IV Street, WC2. *Clubs:* Pratt's, United University, Garrick, Beefsteak; Royal Welsh Yacht (Caernarvon).

**HUGHES, Robert;** MP (Lab) Aberdeen North since 1970; *b* Pittenweem, Fife, 3 Jan. 1932; *m* 1957, Ina Margaret Miller; two *s* three *d*. *Educ:* Robert Gordon's Coll., Aberdeen; Benoni High Sch., Transvaal; Pietermaritzburg Techn. Coll., Natal. Emigrated S Africa, 1947, returned UK, 1954. Engrg apprentice, S African Rubber Co., Natal; Chief Draughtsman, C. F. Wilson & Co. (1932) Ltd, Aberdeen, until 1970. Mem., Aberdeen Town Council, 1962-70; Convener: Health and Welfare Cttee, 1963-68; Social Work Cttee, 1969-70. Mem., AEU, 1952-. Contested (Lab) North Angus and Mearns, 1959. Chm., Aberdeen City Labour Party, 1961-69. Founder Mem. and Aberdeen Chm., Campaign for Nuclear Disarmament; Member: Movement for Colonial Freedom, 1955- (Chm. Southern Africa Cttee); Scottish Poverty Action Group; Aberdeen Trades Council and Exec. Cttee, 1957-69; Labour Party League of Youth, 1954-57. *Recreation:* golf. *Address:* House of Commons, SW1; 23 Lisburne Road, Hampstead, NW3.

**HUGHES, Air Marshal Sir Rochford;** *see* Hughes, Air Marshal Sir S. W. R.

**HUGHES, Royston John;** MP (Lab) Newport, Mon, since 1966; *b* 9 June 1925; *s* of John Hughes, Coal Miner; *m* 1957, Florence Marion Appleyard; three *d*. *Educ:* Ruskin Coll., Oxford. Miner, Nine Mile Point Colliery, Mon., until 1944; served with HM Forces, 1944-47. Administrative Officer, Standard Motor Co. Ltd, Coventry, 1958-66. Mem. Coventry City Council, 1962-66; various offices in Transport and General Workers' Union, 1959-66. *Recreation:* follows Rugby football, Newport and Wales. *Address:* 34 St Kingsmark Avenue, Chepstow Mon. *T:* 3266. *Club:* Pontllanfraith Workingmen's Social.

**HUGHES, Air Marshal Sir (Sidney Weetman) Rochford,** KCB 1967 (CB 1964); CBE 1955 (OBE 1942); AFC 1947; Air Adviser, Civil and Military, to Government of Singapore, since 1969; *b* 25 Oct. 1914; *s* of late Capt. H. R. Hughes, Master Mariner, and late Mrs Hughes (*née* Brigham), Auckland, NZ; *m* 1942, Elizabeth, *d* of A. Duncum, Colombo, Ceylon; one *d*. *Educ:* Waitaki; Oamaru, NZ. Editorial Staff, NZ Herald, 1933-36; RNZ Air Force, 1937-38; RAF, Far East and Middle East, 1939-44 (despatches; Greek DFC); CO, No 511 Sqdn, 1945-47; Chief Ops, USAF All Weather Centre, 1948-49; Air Min., Operational Requirements, 1950-52; CO Farnborough, 1952-54; Imperial Defence Coll., 1955; CO RAF Jever, Germany, 1956-59; Min. of Defence, 1959-61; Air Officer Commanding No 19 Group, RAF Mt Batten, Plymouth, 1962-64; Dep. Controller Aircraft (RAF), Ministry of Aviation, 1964-66; Air Comdr, Far East Air Force, 1966-69, retd 1969. Livery Guild of Air Pilots and Air Navigators; FRAeS. *Recreations:* yachting, motoring, photography. *Address:* Cliff House, Bukit Chermin, Singapore 4; c/o Bank of New Zealand, 1 Queen Victoria Street, EC4. *Clubs:* Royal Air Force, Royal Commonwealth Society.

**HUGHES, Ted;** author; *b* 1930; *s* of William Henry Hughes and Edith Farrar Hughes; *m* 1956, Sylvia Plath (*d* 1963); one *s* one *d*. *Educ:* Pembroke Coll., Cambridge Univ. Awards: first prize, Guinness Poetry Awards, 1958; John Simon Guggenheim Fellow, 1959-60; Somerset Maugham Award, 1960; Hawthornden Prize, 1961. *Publications:* The Hawk in the Rain, 1957; Lupercal, 1960; Meet My Folks! (children's verse), 1961; The Earth-Owl and Other Moon People (children's verse), 1963; How the Whale Became (children's stories), 1963; (ed, jtly) Five American Poets, 1963; Selected Poems of Keith Douglas (ed, with Introduction), 1964; Nessie, The Mannerless Monster (children's verse story), 1964; Wodwo, 1967 (City of Florence Internat. Poetry Prize, 1969); Poetry in the Making, 1968; The Iron Man (children's story); (Ed) A Choice of Emily Dickinson's Verse, 1968; The Coming of the Kings (4 plays), 1970; *poems and stories in:* The London Magazine, Encounter, The Observer, The New Statesman, The Spectator, Vogue, Harper's Bazaar, The Times Literary Supplement, The Atlantic Monthly, Harper's, The New Yorker, Partisan Review, Sewanee Review, The Nation, etc. *Address:* c/o Faber and Faber Ltd, 24 Russell Square, WC1.

**HUGHES, Thomas Lewis,** CBE 1943; Chairman, Eton Rural District Council; *b* 27 July 1897; *s* of late R. D. Hughes; *m* 1927, Helen Mary Beynon; three *s*. *Educ:* Birkenhead Sch. Served European War, 1915-18 (France); Indian Army, 1918-22; Indian Civil Service, Burma, 1923-39; Political Sec. to Burma Chamber of Commerce, 1939-42; despatches; Sec. to Governor of Burma, 1942-46; Treasury, 1948-50. Hon. Sec. Stoke Poges Golf Club, 1955-62. *Address:* Redwood Cottage, Stoke Poges, Bucks. *T:* Farnham Common 2383. *Club:* East India and Sports.

**HUGHES, Thomas Lowe;** Minister and Deputy Chief of Mission, American Embassy, London, 1969-70; *b* 11 Dec. 1925; *s* of Evan Raymond Hughes and Alice (*née* Lowe); *m* 1955, Jean Hurlburt Reiman; two *s*. *Educ:* Carleton Coll., Minn (BA); Balliol Coll., Oxford (Rhodes Schol., BPhil); Yale Law Sch. (LLB). USAF, 1952-54 (Major). Member of Bar: Supreme Court of Minnesota; US District Court of DC; Supreme Court of US. Professional Staff Mem., US Senate Sub-cttee on Labour-Management Relations, 1951; part-time Prof. of Polit. Sci. and Internat. Relations, Univ. of Southern California, Los Angeles, 1953-54, and George Washington Univ., DC, 1957-58; Exec. Sec. to Governor of Connecticut, 1954-55; Legislative Counsel to Senator Hubert H. Humphrey, 1955-58; Admin. Asst to US Rep. Chester Bowles, 1959-60; Staff Dir of Platform Cttee, Democratic Nat. Convention, 1960; Special Asst to Under-Sec. of State, Dept of State, 1961; Dep. Dir of Intelligence and Research, Dept of State, 1961-63; Dir of Intell. and Res. (Asst Sec. of State), 1963-69. Arthur S. Flemming Award, 1965. *Publications:* occasional contribs to professional jls, etc. *Recreations:* swimming, tennis, music, 18th century engravings. *Address:* 5636 Western Avenue, Chevy Chase, Md 20015, USA. *Clubs:* Yale, Council on Foreign Relations (New York).

**HUGHES, Rt. Rev. Thomas Maurice;** Assistant Bishop of Llandaff since 1961; Archdeacon of Llandaff, 1965-69; *b* 17 April 1895; *s* of David and Jane Hughes, Conwil, Carmarthen; *m* 1926, Margaret, *d* of Rev. D. C. Morris, Vicar of Port Talbot; one *s* one *d*. *Educ:* St John's Coll., Ystradmeurig; St David's Coll., Lampeter; Keble Coll., Oxford (Hons Theol). Served European War, 1915-17: 29th and 9th RF (wounded). Asst Curate, Port Talbot, 1922; Minor Canon, Llandaff Cathedral, 1928; Vicar of Cadoxton Neath, 1931; Vicar of St Catherine, Cardiff, 1937; Rector and Rural Dean, Merthyr Tydfil, 1942. Canon of Llandaff Cathedral, 1943; Vicar of St John Baptist, Cardiff, 1946-61; Canon and Precentor of Llandaff Cathedral, 1946-61; Rural Dean of Cardiff, 1954-61; Archdeacon of Margam, 1961-65. *Recreation:* gardening. *Address:* St Andrew, High Street, Llandaff. *T:* Cardiff 73212.

**HUGHES, Sir Trevor Denby L.;** *see* Lloyd-Hughes.

**HUGHES, William,** CB 1953; Second Secretary, Board of Trade, since 1963; *b* 21 Aug. 1910; *o s* of William Hughes, Bishop's Stortford, Herts, and Daisy Constance, *y d* of Charles Henry Davis; *m* 1941, Ilse Erna, *o d* of late E. F. Plohs; one *s* one *d*. *Educ:* Bishop's Stortford Coll.; Magdalen Coll., Oxford (demy). Board of Trade, 1933; Asst Sec., 1942; Under-Sec., 1948-63 (Sec., Monopolies and Restrictive Practices Commission, 1952-55). *Recreation:* music. *Address:* 250 Trinity Road, SW18. *T:* 01-870 3652. *Clubs:* Leander, Reform.

**HUGHES, Maj.-Gen. (Retd) William Dillon,** CB 1960; CBE 1953; QHP 1957; MD; FRCP(I); DTM & H; Commandant, Royal Army Medical College, 1957-60; *b* 23 Dec. 1900; *s* of R. Hughes, JP; *m* 1929, Kathleen Linda Thomas; one *s*. *Educ:* Campbell Coll., Belfast; Queen's Univ., Belfast. MB, BCh, BAO, 1923; Lieut, RAMC, 1928; Officer i/c Medical Div. 64 and 42 Gen. Hosps, MEF, 1940-42; Officer i/c Medical Div. 105 Gen. Hosp., BAOR, 1944-46; Sen. MO, Belsen, 1945; consulting Physician, Far East Land Forces, 1950-53; ADMS, Aldershot Dist, 1954. Prof. in Tropical Medicine and Consulting Physician, RAM Coll., 1955-56; Vice-Pres., Royal Society of Tropical Medicine and Hygiene, 1959-60. Mitchiner Medal, RCS 1960. Col Comdt RAMC, 1961-65. *Address:* 11 Morley Road, Farnham, Surrey.

**HUGHES, William Henry;** a Metropolitan Magistrate, North London, since 1967; *b* 6 Jan. 1916; *s* of late William Howard Hamilton Hughes; *m* 1961, Jenny, *d* of Theodore Francis Turner, *qv*; one *d*. *Educ:* privately; Keble Coll., Oxford. Served War of 1939-45; AA & QMG, BEF, France and Belgium, N Africa, Italy (despatches, Croix de Guerre and palm); Staff Coll.; Lieut-Col 1944. Called to the Bar, Inner Temple, 1949. Dep. Chm., Isle of Ely QS, 1959-63; Dep. Chm., Essex QS, 1961-63. Formerly a mem., General Council of the Bar. *Address:* Old Wardour House, Tisbury, Wilts. *T:* Tisbury 431; 19 John Spencer Square, N1. *T:* 01-359 1623. *Clubs:* Brooks's, Garrick.

**HUGHES, Rt. Rev. William James,** DD; Rector of Port Burwell, Ontario, Canada, since 1970; *m* 1958, Ada Maud Baker. *Educ:* College of Resurrection, Mirfield, University of Leeds (BA 1919). Hon. DD Leeds, 1947; DD Lambeth 1958. Deacon, 1921; Priest, 1922; Vicar of St Benedict, Bordesley, 1927-30; Rector of St George's Cathedral, Georgetown, Guiana, 1930-44; Sub-Dean, 1930-37; Dean, 1937-44; Bishop of British Honduras, 1944-45; Bishop of Barbados, 1945-51; resigned, 1951; Vicar of St George, Edgbaston, and Assistant Bishop of Birmingham, 1951-53; Hon. Canon, Birmingham Cathedral, 1952-53; Bishop of Matabeleland, 1953-61; Archbishop of Central Africa, 1957-61; Bishop of Trinidad and Tobago, 1961-70. Formerly MLC Barbados. Sub-Prelate, Order of St John of Jerusalem, 1958. *Publication:* Think Again, 1947. *Address:* PO Box 179, Port Burwell, Ontario, Canada.

**HUGHES, William Mark;** MP (Lab) Durham since 1970; *b* 18 Dec. 1932; *s* of late Edward Hughes, sometime Prof. of History at Durham, and Sarah (*née* Hughes), Shincliffe, Durham; *m* 1958, Jennifer Mary, *d* of Dr G. H. Boobyer; one *s* two *d*. *Educ:* Durham Sch.; Balliol Coll., Oxford (MA). BA Oxon 1956; PhD Newcastle 1963. Sir James Knott Research Fellow, Newcastle-upon-Tyne, 1958-60; Staff Tutor, Manchester Univ. Extra-Mural Dept, 1960-64; Lectr, Durham Univ., 1964-70. *Recreations:* varied and private. *Address:* Oaklea, The Avenue, Durham City.

**HUGHES, William Reginald Noel,** FRINA, RCNC; General Manager, HM Dockyard, Chatham, since 1970; *b* 14 Dec. 1913; *s* of Frank George Hughes and Annie May Hughes (*née* Lock); *m* 1936, Doris Margaret (*née* Attwool); two *s* two *d*. *Educ:* Prince Edward Sch., Salisbury, Rhodesia; Esplanade House Sch., Southsea, Hants; Royal Dockyard Sch., Portsmouth; RN Coll., Greenwich. Constr Sub Lieut, Chatham, 1933; Constr Sub Lieut and Lieut, RN Coll., Greenwich, 1934; Admty, London, 1937; HM Dockyard, Chatham, 1938; Admty, Bath, 1940; Constr Comdr, Staff of C-in-C Home Fleet, 1944; HM Dockyard, Hong Kong, 1947; Admty, Bath, 1951; Chief Constr, HM Dockyard, Devonport, 1954; Admty, Bath, 1958; Admty Repair Manager, Malta, 1961; Manager, Constructive Dept, Portsmouth, 1964; Dep. Dir of Dockyards, Bath, 1967-70. *Recreations:* sailing, foreign travel, photography. *Address:* 6 The Terrace, HM Dockyard, Chatham. *Clubs:* Little Ship; Royal Naval Sailing Association.

**HUGHES HALLETT, Vice-Adm. (retd) Sir (Cecil) Charles,** KCB 1954 (CB 1950); CBE 1942; Chairman: Gas Purification and Chemical Co. Ltd, 1958-60; Edwards High Vacuum International Ltd, 1964-68; Mount Row Holdings Ltd, 1962-68; Director: John Tysack & Partners Ltd; Avdel Ltd; *b* 6 April 1898; *s* of Col W. Hughes Hallett and Clementina Mary Loch; *m* 1920, Eileen Louise Richardson; two *d*. (one *s* one *d* decd); *m* 1944, Joyce Plumer Cobbold; one *s* one *d*. *Educ:* Bedford; RN Colls, Osborne and Dartmouth; Emmanuel Coll., Cambridge. Went to sea as Midshipman in Aug. 1914; present at Dardanelles and Battle of Jutland: specialised in gunnery, 1921, in staff duties, 1933; Comdr 1932; Capt. 1939; Rear-Adm. 1949; Vice-Adm. 1952; retd Feb. 1955. Comdg destroyer 1934-35, anti-aircraft ship, 1940-42, aircraft carrier, 1944-46, during War of 1939-45 (despatches twice, CBE); present at operations against Japanese mainland, 1945. Dir of Administrative Plans and Joint Planning Staff, 1942-44; Dep. Chief of Naval Air Equipment, 1946-48; Admiralty for Special Duty, 1948-50; Chief of Staff to C-in-C Home Fleet, 1950-51; Admiral, British Joint Services Mission, Washington, 1952-54; Personal Asst to Chm., Charterhouse Group, 1955-59. Younger Brother of Trinity House, 1938; Renter Warden, Co. of Glovers, 1967, Master, 1968. Fellow, British Inst. of Management. Legion of Merit, Degree of Officer (USA), 1945. *Address:* The Dairy Cottage, Corton, Warminster, Wilts. *T:* Codford St Mary 313.

**HUGHES-HALLETT, Vice-Adm. John,** CB 1945; DSO 1942; Royal Navy, retired; *b* 1 Dec. 1901; *s* of late Col Wyndham Hughes-Hallett; unmarried. *Educ:* Bedford Sch.; Osborne and Dartmouth; Gonville and Caius Coll.,

Cambridge. Midshipman in HMS Lion, May 1918; Norwegian campaign, 1940, in HMS Devonshire (despatches); Naval Comdr at Dieppe Raid (DSO); Commodore Commanding Channel Assault Force and Naval Chief of Staff (X), 1942 and 1943; Capt. of HMS Jamaica, Dec. 1943; in command of HMS Vernon, 1946-48 and of HMS Illustrious, 1948-49; Vice-Controller of the Navy, 1950-52; Flag Officer, Heavy Sqdn, Home Fleet, 1952-53; retired in Sept. 1954 on adoption as Conservative candidate. MP (C) East Croydon, 1954-55, North-East (constituency altered), 1955-64; British Representative at the Council of Europe, 1958-60; Parliamentary Sec. to the Ministry of Transport for Shipping and Shipbuilding, 1961-64. Gov. Westminster Hosp., 1957-60. Consultant Dir, British Shippers' Council, 1964-69. W Sussex CC, 1969-70. *Recreation:* cycling. *Address:* New House, Slindon, Arundel, Sussex. *T:* Slindon 274. *Club:* Travellers'.

**HUGHES-MORGAN, Lt-Col Sir David (John),** 3rd Bt *cr* 1925; MBE 1959; *b* 11 Oct. 1925; *s* of Sir John Hughes-Morgan, 2nd Bt and of Lucie Margaret, *d* of late Thomas Parry Jones-Parry; *S* father, 1969; *m* 1959, Isabel Jean, *d* of J. M. Lindsay; three *s*. *Educ:* RNC, Dartmouth. Royal Navy, 1943-46. Admitted solicitor, 1950. Commissioned, Army Legal Services, 1955. *Recreation:* gliding. *Heir: s* Ian Parry David Hughes-Morgan, *b* 22 Feb. 1960. *Address:* c/o National Westminster Bank Ltd, Brecon; DALS, HQ BAOR, BFPO 40.

**HUGHES-ONSLOW, Sir Geoffrey Henry,** KBE 1959; DSC 1918; Lord Lieutenant of Ayrshire, 1950-69; *b* 28 Oct. 1893; *s* of Major Arthur Hughes-Onslow, 10th Hussars, and Anne Kathleen Whitehead; *m* 1918, Hon. Eileen Mabel Lowther Crofton, *d* of 4th Baron Crofton; four *d*. *Educ:* Cheam; RN Colls, Osborne and Dartmouth. Served in RN until 1920, retiring with rank of Lieut; War of 1939-45, in RN, as Lieut-Comdr and Comdr. Mem. Ayrshire CC 1922-55; Convener, 1949-55. Succeeded to estate of Alton Albany on death of father in 1914, now farms a large part of the estate. *Recreations:* shooting, fishing, ornithology. *Address:* Alton Albany, Barr, Ayrshire. *T:* Barr 228. *Clubs:* Naval and Military; New (Edinburgh).

**HUGHES-STANTON, Blair Rowlands;** Painter and Engraver; Member of The London Group; Member of Society of Wood Engravers; *b* 22 Feb. 1902. *Educ:* Colet Court, London; HMS Conway. Studied at Byam Shaw Sch., 1919-21, Royal Academy Schools and Leon Underwood Sch., 1921-24. Hon. Academician, Accademia Delle Arti Del Disegno, Florence, 1963. Made Decorations at Wembley, 1925, and Paris Exhibition, 1926. Produced numerous Books at Gregynog Press, Wales, 1930-33, and Illustrated Books for Golden Cockerel, Cresset Presses; also Allen Press, California. International Prize for Engraving at Venice Biennale, 1938. Represented with Engravings in British Museum, Victoria and Albert Museum, Whitworth Gall. (Manchester), etc. and Galls and Museums in Australia, Canada, New Zealand. *Recreation:* travel. *Address:* North House, Manningtree, Essex. *T:* Manningtree 2717.

**HUGHES-YOUNG,** family name of **Baron St Helens.**

**HUGILL, Michael James,** JP; Headmaster, Whitgift School, Croydon, 1961-70; *b* 13 July 1918; 2nd *s* of late Rear-Adm. R. C. Hugill, CB, MVO. *Educ:* Oundle; King's Coll., Cambridge, Exhibitioner, King's Coll., 1936-39; MA 1943. War Service in the RN; Mediterranean, Home and Pacific Fleets, 1939-46; rank on demobilisation, Lieut-Comdr. Mathematics Master, Stratford Grammar Sch., 1947-51; Senior Mathematics Master, Bedford Modern Sch., 1951-57; Headmaster, Preston Grammar Sch., 1957-61. JP 1966. *Address:* The Stables, The River House, Ashton Keynes, Wilts. *Club:* Army and Navy.

**HUGO, Lt-Col Sir John (Mandeville),** KCVO 1969 (CVO 1959); OBE 1947; Gentleman Usher to the Queen, 1952-69, an Extra Gentleman Usher since 1969; *b* 1 July 1899; *s* of R. M. Hugo; *m* 1952, Joan Winifred, *d* of late D. W. Hill; two *d*. *Educ:* Marlborough Coll.; RMA, Woolwich, Commissioned RA, 1917; transf. to Indian Cavalry, 1925; Military Sec. to Governor of Bengal, 1938-40; rejoined 7th Light Cavalry, 1940; Military Sec. to Governor of Bengal 1946-47; Asst Ceremonial Sec., Commonwealth Relations Office, 1948-52; Ceremonial and Protocol Secretary, 1952-69. *Address:* The Cottages, Nizels, Hildenborough, Kent. *T:* Hildenborough 2359. *Club:* United Service.

**HULBERT, Jack;** actor, dramatic author, manager, producer; *b* Ely, 24 April 1892; *s* of Dr H. H. Hulbert; *m* Cicely Courtneidge, *qv*; one *d*. *Educ:* Westminster; Gonville and Caius Coll., Cambridge. First appearance on professional stage, in The Pearl Girl, Shaftesbury Theatre, 1913; played in: Bubbly and Hullo Paris in Paris, 1919; Bran Pie; Little Dutch Girl; Pot Luck. Produced: The Blue Train; prod. and played in: By the Way, London and New York; Lido Lady; Clowns in Clover; The House that Jack Built; Follow a Star; prod. Folly to be Wise. Spent 10 years in *films:* Ghost Train; Sunshine Susie; Jack's the Boy; Jack Ahoy; Bulldog Jack; Jack of all Trades; Falling for You, etc.; Produced and played in: Under your Hat; Something in the Air; Full Swing (Palace Theatre); prod. Under the Counter; prod. and played in Here come the Boys; prod. and played for TV: Here come the Boys; Cinderella; Dick Whittington; The Golden Year; played in Hulbert Follies; Housemaster; Smith; The Squeaker; The White Sheep of the Family; prod. Gay's the Word; played in: The Reluctant Debutante; The Bride Comes Back; The Spider's Web; Let's Be Frank; Dear Octopus, etc. Served European War, 1917-19. Commandant in Special Constabulary, 1940-57. *Address:* 18a Charles Street, W1.

**HULBERT, Wing Comdr Sir Norman (John),** Kt 1955; DL; *b* 1903; *s* of late Norman Hulbert; *m* 1938, Eileen Pearl, MB, BChir, JP (marr. diss., 1960), *d* of late Dr Gretton-Watson, London; two *d*; *m* 1966, Eliette, *d* of Baron F. G. von Tschirschky und Boegendorff, CVO, Salzburg. *Educ:* Cranbrook; Tonbridge. Served RN Transport, 1918; served in an operational cmd of RAF, 1939-43; British Liaison officer with Polish Forces in Gt Britain, 1943-45. Mem. LCC, East Islington, 1934-37; MP (C) Stockport, 1935-50, North Div. of Stockport, 1950-64; PPS to Pres. of Board of Trade and Minister of Production, 1944-45; Mem. of House of Commons Select Cttee on Estimates, 1945-50; Temp. Chm. of House of Commons and Chm. of Standing Cttees, 1950-64; Freeman of City of London; Liveryman: Shipwright's Co.; Guild of Air Pilots and Navigators. Hon. Col 461 HAA Regt RA (TA), 1952-55; DL Middlesex, 1952-65; DL London, 1965. Order of Polonia Restituta, 1945. *Address:* The Priory, Dorchester-on-Thames, Oxon. *T:* Warborough 249. *Clubs:* Carlton, Press, Royal Automobile.

**HULL, Suffragan Bishop of,** since 1965; **Rt. Rev. Hubert Laurence Higgs,** MA Cantab; *b* 23 Nov. 1911; *s* of Frank William and Mary Ann Higgs; *m* 1936, Elizabeth Clare (*née* Rogers); one *s* one *d*. *Educ:* University Coll. Sch.; Christ's Coll., Cambridge; Ridley Hall, Cambridge. Curate: Holy Trinity, Richmond, 1935; St Luke's, Redcliffe Square, London, 1936-38; St John's, Boscombe (and Jt Sec. Winchester Youth Council), 1938-39. Vicar, Holy Trinity, Aldershot, 1939-45; Editorial Sec., Church Missionary Soc., 1945-52; Vicar, St John's, Woking, 1952-57 (Rural Dean, 1957); Archdeacon of Bradford and Canon Residentiary of Bradford Cathedral, 1957-65. *Recreations:* numismatics, gardening. *Address:* Hullen House, Woodfield Lane, Hessle, Yorks. *T:* Hull 642244.

**HULL, Sir Hubert,** Kt 1959; CBE 1945; *b* 10 Sept. 1887; 2nd *s* of Robert Hull, Preston, Lancs; *m* 1915, Judith, *e d* of P. F. S. Stokes, Barrister-at-Law; two *s* four *d*. *Educ:* Stonyhurst. Called to Bar, Inner Temple, 1910; Bencher 1945. Temp. Civil Servant, 1914-19, Junior Counsel to Ministry of Agriculture and Fisheries and Commissioners of Crown Lands; temp. Civil Servant, 1939-48, Asst Procurator-Gen.; an Official Referee of Supreme Court, 1949-50; Mem. Royal Commission on Press, 1947. Pres. of Transport Tribunal, 1951-62. Officer Order of Oranje Nassau, 1949. *Publications:* Legal only. *Recreations:* walking and housework. *Address:* 59 Campden Hill Road, Kensington, W8. *T:* 01-937 5503. *Club:* Reform.

**HULL, Field Marshal Sir Richard (Amyatt),** GCB 1961 (KCB 1956; CB 1945); DSO 1943; Constable of the Tower of London, since 1970; *b* 7 May 1907; *m* 1934, Antoinette Mary Labouchère de Rougemont; one *s* two *d*. *Educ:* Charterhouse; Trinity Coll., Cambridge (MA). Joined 17th/21st Lancers, 1928; Commanded 17/21st Lancers, 1941; Commanded 12th Infantry Bde, 1943; Commanded 26 Armd Bde, 1943; Comd 1st Armd Div., 1944; Cmd 5th Infantry Div., 1945; Commandant Staff Coll. Camberley, 1946-48; Dir of Staff Duties, War Office, 1948-50; Chief Army Instructor, Imperial Defence Coll., 1950-52; Chief of Staff, GHQ, MELF, 1953-54; General Officer Commanding, British Troops in Egypt, 1954-56; Dep. Chief of the Imperial Gen. Staff, 1956-58; Comdr-in-Chief, Far East Land Forces, 1958-61; Chief of the Imperial Gen. Staff, 1961-64; ADC Gen. to the Queen, 1961-64; Chief of the Gen. Staff, Ministry of Defence, 1964-65; Chief of the Defence Staff, 1965-67. Pres., Army Benevolent Fund (to 1971); Dir, Whitbread & Co. Ltd (Chm., Western Region Bd, 1969-). Col Comdt, RAC, 1968-71. Hon. LLD, Exeter, 1965. *Address:* Beacon Downe, Pinhoe, Exeter. *Clubs:* Cavalry, Flyfishers'.

*See also Maj.-Gen. H. R. Swinburn.*

**HULLAH-BROWN, J.,** MusBac (Dunelm), LRAM, ARCM, ARCO, AMusTCL; Professor of Music; *b* 8 Oct. 1875; *s* of James Conway Brown; *m* 1923, Hilda May Chatfield; one *d*. *Educ:* Farnham; privately; self-taught in music and art. Organist and choir-master, Cobham (Surrey) Parish Church, 1899-1906; Music and Art Master, Sandroyd Preparatory Sch., Cobham; Active Service, 1914-19; private teacher, lecturer (Music and Art). *Publications:* Water-Colour Guidance; Sketching Without a Master, and other works on Art; Technique of the Fiddle Bow; Children's Violin Books; Violin Glissando; Peter Pan Class Violin Tutor; Bow-craft Series, Concertinos, and other musical works. Author of the Violinda method and books. *Address:* c/o Post Office, Opotiki, New Zealand.

**HULME, Suffragan Bishop of,** since 1953; **Rt. Rev. Kenneth Venner Ramsey;** *b* 26 Jan. 1909; *s* of James Ernest and Laura Rebecca Ramsey, Southsea, Hants; unmarried. *Educ:* Portsmouth Grammar Sch.; University Coll., Oxford; Manchester Univ. Curate of St Matthew, Stretford, 1933-35; Vice-Prin., Egerton Hall, Manchester, and Lectr in Christian Ethics, Manchester Univ., 1935-38; Vice-Prin., Bishop Wilson Coll., Isle of Man, 1938-39; Prin. Egerton Hall, Manchester, 1939-41; Vicar of St Paul, Peel, Little Hulton, Lancs, 1941-48; Rector of Emmanuel Church, Didsbury, Manchester, 1948-55; Hon. Canon, Manchester Cathedral, 1950-53. Proctor in Convocation and mem. Church Assembly, 1950-55; Rural Dean of Heaton, 1950-53. *Address:* 22 Pine Road, Didsbury, Manchester M20 0UZ. *T:* 061-445 6748. *Club:* Old Rectory (Manchester).

**HULME, Sgt Alfred Clive,** VC 1941; Transport Contractor, New Zealand, since 1945; *b* 24 Jan. 1911; *s* of Harold Clive Hulme, Civil Servant, and Florence Sarah Hulme; *m* 1934, Rona Marjorie Murcott; one *s* one *d*. *Educ:* Dunedin High Sch. New Zealand Military Forces, War of 1939-45 (VC). Formerly tobacco farming; water and metal divining successfully in New Zealand, Australia, South Africa, and England. *Recreations:* tennis, boating, landscape gardening. *Address:* Te Puke, Bay of Plenty, New Zealand. *Club:* Returned Services Association.

**HULME, Dr Henry Rainsford;** Chief of Nuclear Research, Atomic Weapons Research Establishment; *b* 9 Aug. 1908; *s* of James Rainsford Hulme and Alice Jane Smith; *m* 1955, Margery Alice Ducker, *d* of late Sir James A. Cooper, KBE, and of Lady Cooper. *Educ:* Manchester Grammar Sch.; Gonville and Caius Coll., Cambridge; University of Leipzig. BA (Math. Tripos) 1929; Smiths' Prizeman, 1931; PhD (Cambridge) 1932; ScD (Cambridge) 1948. Fellow of Gonville and Caius Coll., Cambridge, 1933-38; Chief Asst Royal Observatory, Greenwich, 1938-45; on loan to Admiralty during war. Scientific Adviser Air Ministry, 1946-48. *Publications:* on Mathematical Physics and Astronomy in learned jls. *Recreations:* various. *Address:* Heathrow, Baughurst, Hants.

**HULME-MOIR, Rt. Rev. Francis Oag,** ED 1949; Senior Coadjutor Bishop of Sydney, since 1967; *b* 30 Jan. 1910; 2nd *s* of Alexander Hugh and Violet Beryl Hulme-Moir; *m* 1937, Ena Dorothy Smee; two *s* one *d*. *Educ:* Moore Theological Coll.; Sydney Univ. ThL, ACT, 1935. Deacon, 1936; Priest, 1937. Chaplain to Forces, 1936; Chaplain, AIF, 1939-45 (despatches, 1944); Dep. Asst Chaplain-Gen., 1942; Asst Chaplain-Gen., 1945; Senior Chaplain, NSW, 1946; Archdeacon of Ryde, 1947; Archdeacon of Cumberland, 1950; Bishop of Nelson, New Zealand, 1954-65; Coadjutor Bishop and Dean of Sydney, 1965-67; Coadjutor Bishop, Northern Region, 1968. senior Anglican Chaplain to all NZ Services, 1959-64; Bishop to the Australian Armed Forces, 1965. *Recreations:* golf, gardening, fishing. *Address:* Diocesan Church House, George Street, Sydney, NSW 2000, Australia. *T:* 262371. *Clubs:* Union (Sydney); Royal Sydney Motor Yacht.

**HULSE, Sir (Hamilton) Westrow,** 9th Bt, *cr* 1739; Barrister-at-Law, Inner Temple; *b* 20 June 1909; *o s* of Sir Hamilton Hulse, 8th Bt, and Estelle (*d* 1933) *d* of late William Lorillard Campbell, of New York, USA; *S* father, 1931;

*m* 1st, 1932, Philippa Mabel (marr. diss., 1937), *y d* of late A. J. Taylor, Strensham Court, Worcs; two *s*; 2nd, 1938, Amber (*d* 1940), *o d* of late Captain Herbert Stanley Orr Wilson, RHA, Rockfield Park, Mon; 3rd, 1945 (marr. diss.); 4th, 1954, Elizabeth, *d* of late Col George Redesdale Brooker Spain, CMG, TD, FSA. *Educ:* Eton; Christ Church, Oxford. Wing Comdr RAFVR, served 1940-45 (despatches). *Heir: s* Edward Jeremy Westrow Hulse [*b* 22 Nov. 1932; *m* 1957, Verity Ann, *d* of William Pilkington, Wardington House, Banbury, Oxon.; one *s*. one *d*]. *Address:* Breamore, Hants. *TA:* Breamore. *T:* Breamore 233. *Clubs:* Carlton, Bath.

**HULSE, Sir Westrow;** *see* Hulse, Sir H. W.

**HULTON, Sir Edward (George Warris),** Kt 1957; Magazine publisher; writer; *b* 29 Nov. 1906; *s* of late Sir Edward Hulton, former proprietor of Evening Standard; *m* 1st, Kira Pavlovna (from whom he obtained a divorce), *d* of General Paul Goudime-Levkovitsch, Imperial Russian Army; no *c*; 2nd, 1941, Princess Nika Yourivietch (marr. diss., 1966), 2nd *d* of Prince Serge Yourievitch, Russian Councillor of State, Chamberlain to His Imperial Majesty, Officier de la Légion d'Honneur (France), sculptor, and Helene de Lipovatz, *d* of Gen. de Lipovatz. Cetinje, Montenegro; two *s* one *d*. *Educ:* Harrow; Brasenose Coll., Oxford (open scholarship. Contested Leek Div. Staffs, as Unionist, 1929; Harwich Div., 1931. Called to Bar, Inner Temple; practised on South-Eastern Circuit; Chm. and Managing Dir of Hulton Publications Ltd, Periodical Publishers. Pres., European Atlantic Group; a Vice-President: British Atlantic Cttee; European League for Economic Co-operation; Mem. Exec. Cttee, British Council of the European Movement. editor-in-Chief, European Review. Liveryman and Freeman of Company of Stationers; Freeman of City of London. *Publications:* The New Age, 1943; When I Was a Child, 1952; Conflicts, 1966; contrib. various newspapers and books. *Recreation:* reading. *Address:* 59 Old Mint Street, Valletta, Malta GC. *Clubs:* Athenæum, Beefsteak, Carlton, Garrick, St James', Travellers'.

**HULTON, Sir Geoffrey (Alan),** 4th Bt, *cr* 1905; JP; *b* 21 Jan. 1920; *s* of Sir Roger Braddyll Hulton, 3rd Bt and Hon. Marjorie Evelyn Louise (*d* 1970), *o c* of 6th Viscount Mountmorres; *S* father 1956; *m* 1945, Mary Patricia Reynolds. *Educ:* Marlborough. Entered Royal Marines, Sept. 1938; Lieut, 1940; sunk in HMS Repulse, Dec. 1941; prisoner-of-war, Far East, Feb. 1942-Aug. 1945; Captain, 1948; retired (ill-health), 1949. Owner of Hulton Park estate. Chief Scout's Commissioner. Pres., Westhoughton Divisional Conservative Association; Vice-Pres., Country Landowners' Assoc. (Lancashire). Chm., SSAFA (E Lancs). JP Lancs, 1955. KCSG 1966. *Recreations:* country pursuits. *Heir:* none. *Address:* The Cottage, Hulton Park, Over Hulton, near Bolton, Lancs. *T:* Bolton 63224. *Clubs:* Lansdowne, Victory, Milverton Lodge (Manchester), Constitutional (Bolton).

**HULTON-HARROP, Maj.-Gen. (Retd) William Harrington,** CB 1959; DSO 1944; General Officer Commanding Catterick Area, 1959, retired; *b* 7 May 1906; *s* of Hugh de Lacy Hulton-Harrop and Delitia Mary (*née* Hulton); *m* 1937, Pamela Scholefield; one *d*. *Educ:* Charterhouse; RMA Sandhurst. 2nd Lieut KSLI, 1926; served War of 1939-45, N Africa, Sicily, Italy and Palestine. Lieut-Col 1942; Brig. 1949; Maj.-Gen. 1957; Commander 50th Division (TA) and Northumbrian District, 1956. *Address:* c/o Lloyds Bank, 6 Pall Mall, SW1.

**HUMBLE, Joseph Graeme,** CVO 1955; Reader in Haematology, Westminster Medical School, London University, since 1965; Hon. Consultant Haematologist, Westminster Hospital, since 1949; *b* 10 July 1913; 2nd *s* of late Wensley Taylor Humble and late Louisa Ann (*née* Witham), Mansfield, Notts; *m* 1942, Elsie May (Anne), *d* of late A. Hunt, Mendlesham, Suffolk; three *s* (and two *s* decd). *Educ:* Bedford Modern Sch.; Westminster Hosp. Med. Sch., University of London. MRCS, LRCP 1937, MRCP 1959, FCPath 1955, FRCP 1970. Westminster Hospital: House Physician Children's Dept, 1937-38; Junior Asst Pathologist, 1938-39; Acting Asst Pathologist and Temp. Lecturer in Pathology and Bacteriology, 1939-46; Haematologist, 1946-49. Member: Royal Society of Medicine; London Med. Soc. *Publications:* Westminster Hospital 1716-1966: a history; various articles in Med. Jls. *Recreations:* cricket, golf, history. *Address:* 199 Barnettwood Lane, Ashtead, Surrey. *T:* Ashtead 72603.

**HUME, Alan Blyth,** CB 1963; Secretary, Scottish Development Department since 1965; *b* 5 Jan. 1913; *s* of late W. Alan Hume; *m* 1943, Marion Morton Garrett; one *s* one *d*. *Educ:* George Heriot's Sch.; Edinburgh Univ. Entered Scottish Office, 1936. On staff of Regional Commissioner for Civil Defence (Scotland), 1939-45. Scottish Home Department, 1945-59; Under-Sec., 1957; Asst Under-Sec. of State, Scottish Office, 1959-62; Under-Sec., Min. of Public Bldg and Works, 1963-64. *Recreations:* golf, fishing. *Address:* 12 Oswald Road, Edinburgh 9. *T:* 031-667 2440. *Clubs:* New (Edinburgh); English-Speaking Union.

**HUME, Basil;** *see* Hume, John Basil.

**HUME, Major Charles Westley,** OBE 1962; MC; BSc; late Senior Examiner, Patent Office; Founder and Vice-President, Universities Federation for Animal Welfare; Scientific Intelligence Officer (CD), Finchley 1950-61; Fellow of Physical and Zoological Societies; Member: Institute of Biology; Mammal Society of the British Isles; Association for Study of Animal Behaviour; Hon. Life Member, British Deer Society; *b* 13 Jan. 1886; *s* of Charles William Hume (formerly a Pampas rancher), and Louisa, *d* of Captain Waldron Kelly, 26th Cameronians; *m* 1966, Margaret Pattison. *Educ:* Christ's Coll., Finchley; Strand Sch.; Birkbeck Coll. (University of London). Served in France (Royal Engineers Signals) in European War of 1914-18, and afterwards in 47th Divisional signals, TA; 3rd Signal Training Centre, 1939-41; qualified as Instructor, Fire Control (radar), 1941; Signals Experimental Establishment, 1942; HQ staff for Army Operational Research Group under Controller of Physical Research and Signals Development, 1942-45. Editor to the Physical Society, 1919-40; as Hon. Sec. of the British Science Guild, organised the campaign which issued in the Patents Act, 1932; founded (1926) the University of London Animal Welfare Soc. and (1939) Universities Federation for Animal Welfare; campaigned successfully for prohibition (1956) of gin traps. Citoyen d'Honneur de Meurchin, Pas-de-Calais, 1953-; medal 'en témoignage de reconnaissance, la Ville de Meurchin', 1970; Prés. d'Honneur of Meurchin Sect., Union Nat. des Anciens Combatants; Sòci dóu Felibrige, e de l'Escolo de la Targo, 1958-; Sòci d'Ounour di Cardelin de Maiano. *Publications:* The Status of Animals in the Christian Religion, 1956; Man and Beast, 1962. Articles on religion, animal welfare, statistical analysis, patent law, Provence and rabbit-control. *Address:* 2 Cyprus Gardens, Finchley, N3. *Club:* Athenæum.

**HUME, Rt. Rev. George Basil;** Abbot of Ampleforth since 1963; *b* 2 March 1923; *s* of Sir William Hume, CMG, FRCP. *Educ:* Ampleforth Coll.; St Benet's Hall, Oxford; Fribourg Univ., Switzerland. Ordained priest 1950. Ampleforth College: Senior Modern Language Master, 1952-63; Housemaster, 1955-63; Prof. of Dogmatic Theology, 1955-63; Magister Scholarum of the English Benedictine Congregation, 1957-63. *Address:* Ampleforth Abbey, York YO6 4EN. *T:* Ampleforth 421.

**HUME, John Basil,** MS, FRCS; Consulting Surgeon, St Bartholomew's Hospital; Surgeon St Andrew's Hospital, Dollis Hill; Member of Senate, University of London, Deputy Vice-Chancellor, 1965; Member of Board of Governors of St Bartholomew's Hospital; *b* 1893 *s* of David Hume, Whitby, Yorks; *m* 1925, Marjorie Poole; four *d. Educ:* Bootham Sch., York; St Bartholomew's Hospital (Brackenbury Scholar, Kirkes Gold Medal and Luther Holden Scholar). Captain RAMC (SR) during European War, served in German East Africa; subsequently Hunterian Professor: Examiner for Royal College of Surgeons; Lecturer in Anatomy and Surgery at St Bartholomew's Hospital. *Publications:* many articles in medical journals. *Recreation:* fly-fishing. *Address:* 73 Southway, NW11. *T:* 01-455 5041.

**HUME-WILLIAMS, Sir Roy Ellis,** 2nd Bt, *cr* 1922; schoolmaster; *b* 31 July 1887; *s* of Rt Hon. Sir Ellis Hume-Williams, 1st Bt, PC, KBE, KC; *S* father, 1947; *m* 1st, 1915, Norah (marr. diss., 1949, she *d* 1964), *y d* of late David Anderson, Sydney, NSW; 2nd, 1949, Frances Mary (Molly), *er d* of Major Arthur Groom, OBE, Warham Wells, Norfolk. *Educ:* Eton; Trinity Hall, Cambridge. Cons. Engineer, 1910-14. Served in European War, 1914-19; retired with rank of Captain, RASC. Schoolmaster, 1920-. *Recreations:* cricket, hockey, tennis, golf, skating. *Heir:* none. *Address:* Ardlui, The Highlands, East Horsley, Surrey. *Clubs:* Royal Automobile, MCC; County (Guildford).

**HUMMEL, Frederick Cornelius,** MA, DPhil, BSc; Commissioner for Harvesting and Marketing, Forestry Commission, since 1968; *b* 28 April 1915; *s* of Cornelius Hummel, OBE, and Caroline Hummel (*née* Riefler); *m* 1st, 1941, Agnes Kathleen Rushforth (marr. diss., 1961); one *s* (and one *s* decd); 2nd, 1961, Floriana Rosemary Hollyer; three *d. Educ:* St Stephan, Augsburg, Germany; Wadham Coll., Oxford. District Forest Officer, Uganda Forest Service, 1938-46; Forestry Commn, 1946-; Mensuration Officer, 1946; Chief, Management Sect., 1956; released for service with FAO as Co-Dir, Mexican Nat. Forest Inventory, 1961-66; Controller, Management Services, Forestry Commn, 1966-68. *Publications:* several for Forestry Commn; papers in British, foreign and internat. forestry jls. *Recreations:* walking, ski-ing. *Address:* Sunset Ridge, Copper Beech Close, Hook Hill Lane, Woking, Surrey. *T:* Woking 63314.

**HUMPHREY, Air Marshal Sir Andrew (Henry),** KCB 1968 (CB 1959); OBE 1951; DFC 1941; AFC 1943 (and two bars, 1945, 1955); Air Officer Commanding-in-Chief, RAF Strike Command, since 1971; Commander United Kingdom Air Defence Region (NATO), since 1971; *b* 10 Jan. 1921; *m* 1952, Agnes Stevenson, *yr d* of late James Wright and of Mrs Marjorie Wright. *Educ:* Bradfield Coll.; RAF Coll. Cranwell. RAF service since 1940, both at home and overseas. Station Commander, Royal Air Force, Akrotiri, Cyprus, 1959-61; Imperial Defence Coll., 1962; Dir of Defence Plans, Air, at Ministry of Defence, 1962-65; AOC Air Forces Middle East, 1965-68 (despatches); Air Member for Personnel, 1968-70. *Address:* Springfields, Great Kingshill, Bucks. *Club:* Royal Air Force.

**HUMPHREY, Arthur Hugh Peters,** CMG 1959; OBE 1952; Hon. PMN (Malaya), 1958; Controller of Special Projects, Ministry of Overseas Development, since 1961; Malayan Civil Service, 1934-60, retired; *b* 18 June 1911; *s* of late Arthur George Humphrey, Bank Manager; *m* 1948, Mary Valentine, *d* of late Lieut-Col J. E. Macpherson; three *d. Educ:* Eastbourne Coll.; Merton Coll., Oxford. Appointed Malayan Civil Service, 1934; Private Sec. to Governor of Straits Settlements and High Comr for Malay States, 1936-38; Resident, Labuan, 1940-42; interned by Japanese in Borneo, 1942-45; idc 1948; Sec. for Defence and Internal Security, Fedn of Malaya, 1953-57; Mem. of Federal Legislative and Executive Councils, 1953-56; Sec. to the Treasury, Federation of Malaya, 1957-59; Director of Technical Assistance, Commonwealth Relations Office, 1960-61. Official Leader, United Kingdom delegations at Colombo Plan conferences: Tokyo, 1960, and Kuala Lumpur, 1961. Coronation Medal, 1953. *Recreations:* music, tennis. *Address:* Falham House, Worth, Sussex. *T:* Pound Hill 2197. *Club:* East India and Sports.

**HUMPHREY, Frank Basil;** Parliamentary Counsel since 1967; *b* 21 Sept. 1918; *s* of late John Hartley Humphrey and of Alice Maud Humphrey (*née* Broadbent); *m* 1947, Ol'ga Černa, *y d* of late František Černý, Trenčín, Czechoslovakia; two *s. Educ:* Brentwood Sch.; St Catharine's Coll., Cambirdge (Schol.). 2nd cl. hons Pt I. Mod. Langs Tripos, 1st cl. hons Pt II Law Tripos. Served RA, 1939-45: Adjt 23rd Mountain Regt and DAAG 4 Corps, India and Burma. Called to Bar, Middle Temple, 1946 (Harmsworth Schol.). Seconded as First Parly. Counsel, Fedn of Nigeria, 1961-64. *Recreations:* gardening, mountain walking, music. *Address:* The Yews, Rookery Close, Fetcham, Surrey. *T:* Leatherhead 2619.

**HUMPHREY, Senator Hubert Horatio, Jr;** United States Senator from Minnesota (Democrat), 1949-64 and since 1970; Member Board, Encyclopædia Britannica, Inc., since 1969; *b* Wallace, South Dakota, USA, 27 May 1911; *s* of Hubert Horatio Humphrey; *m* 1936, Muriel Fay Buck; three *s* one *d. Educ:* Denver Coll. of Pharmacy; University of Minnesota (AB) and Louisiana State Univ. (AM). State Dir, War Production Training and Re-employment Div., 1941-42; Asst Regional Dir, War Manpower Commn, 1943; Professor of Political Science, Macalester Coll., Minnesota, 1943-44; Radio News Commentator, 1944-45; Mayor, City of Minneapolis, 1945-48; US Senate Asst Majority Leader, 1961-64; Vice-President of the US, 1965-69. Jt Prof., Macalester Coll. at St Paul and Univ. of Minnesota at Minneapolis, 1969-70. American delegate to UN, 1956-57. Member: Phi Beta Kappa; Delta Sigma Rho; Amer. Polit. Sci. Assoc. Holds many honorary degrees. Democrat. *Publications:* The Cause is Mankind, 1964; The War On Poverty, 1964; School Desegregation: Documents and Commentaries, 1964. *Address:* Waverley, Minnesota 55390, USA; Washington, DC, USA.

**HUMPHREY, John Herbert,** CBE 1970; FRS 1963; BA; MD; Head of Division of Immunology, 1957, and Deputy Director, 1961, National Institute for Medical Research; *b* 16 Dec. 1915; *s* of Herbert Alfred Humphrey and Mary Elizabeth Humphrey (*née* Horniblow); *m* 1939, Janet Rumney, *d* of Archibald Vivian Hill, *qv*; two *s* three *d*. *Educ:* Winchester Coll.; Trinity Coll., Cambridge; UCH Med. Sch. Jenner Research Student, Lister Inst., 1941-42; Asst Pathologist, Central Middx Hosp., 1942-46; External Staff, Med. Research Council, 1946-49; Member: Scientific Staff, Nat. Inst. for Med. Research, 1949-; Expert Cttee on Biological Standardization, WHO, 1955-70; Expert Cttee on Immunology, WHO, 1962-. Editor, Advances in Immunology, 1960-67; Asst Editor, Immunology, 1958-68. Mem. Council, Royal Society, 1967-69. Fellow, Winchester Coll., 1967; Hon. Prof., Middlesex Hosp. Med. Sch., 1970. *Publications:* Immunology for Students of Medicine (with Prof. R. G. White), 1963. Contrib. to Jls of immunology, biochemistry, physiology, etc. *Recreations:* walking; politics (*sensu stricto*). *Address:* Lawn House, 12 Hampstead Square, NW3. *T:* 01-435 0646.

**HUMPHREY, William Gerald,** MA Oxon and Cantab, DPhil Oxon; Assistant Secretary, University of Cambridge Appointments Board, 1962-68; Headmaster of The Leys School, Cambridge, 1934-58; Group personnel officer, Fisons Ltd, 1958-62; *b* 2 Aug. 1904; *e s* of late Rev. William Humphrey and Helen Lusher; *m* 1936, Margaret, *er d* of late William E. Swift, Cornwall, Conn., USA; one *s*. *Educ:* King Edward VII Sch., Sheffield; Queen's Coll., Oxford (Hastings Scholar, Taberdar, University Sen. Research Student); 1st Class Final Honour Sch. of Natural Science, 1926; DPhil, 1928; Commonwealth Fund Fellow, Harvard Univ., 1929-31; Senior Science Master, Uppingham Sch., 1932-34. Trustee, Uppingham Sch.; Governor, Queenswood Sch. Mem. Ministry of Agriculture Cttee on demand for Agricultural Graduates. *Publications:* The Christian and Education, 1940; Papers in Journal of the Chemical Soc. *Recreation:* mountain walking. *Address:* 14 Wingate Way, Trumpington, Cambridge. *T:* Trumpington 2296.

**HUMPHREYS, Professor Arthur Raleigh;** Professor of English, University of Leicester, since 1947; *b* 28 March 1911; *s* of William Ernest Humphreys and Lois (*née* Rainforth); *m* 1947, Kathryn Jane, *d* of James and Jessie Currie, Drumadoon, Isle of Arran. *Educ:* Grammar Sch., Wallasey, Ches; St Catharine's Coll., Cambridge; Harvard Univ., USA. Charles Oldham Shakespeare Schol., Cambridge, 1932; BA (Cambridge), 1933, MA 1936; Commonwealth Fund Fellow, Harvard, 1933-35; AM (Harvard), 1935. Supervisor in English, Cambridge Univ., 1935-37; Lectr in English, Liverpool Univ., 1937-46. Served War of 1939-45, RAF Intelligence, 1940-42 (Flying Officer); British Council Lecturer in English, Istanbul Univ., 1942-45. Fellow Folger Shakespeare Library, Washington, DC, 1960, 1961, 1964. *Publications:* William Shenstone 1937; The Augustan World, 1954; Steele, Addison, and their Periodical Essays, 1959; (ed) Henry IV, Part I, 1960, Part II, 1966; Melville, 1962; (ed) Joseph Andrews, 1962; (ed) Tom Jones, 1962; (ed) Amelia, 1963; (ed) Jonathan Wild, 1964; (ed) Melville's White-Jacket, 1966; Shakespeare, Richard II, 1967; (ed) Henry V, 1968; (ed) Henry VIII, 1971; contrib. to From Dryden to Johnson (ed B. Ford), 1957, and to learned journals. *Address:* 144 Victoria Park Road, Leicester. *T:* Leicester 705118.

**HUMPHREYS, Christmas;** *see* Humphreys, T. C.

**HUMPHREYS, Emyr Owen;** Author; *b* 15 April 1919; *s* of William and Sarah Rosina Humphreys, Prestatyn, Flints; *m* 1946, Elinor Myfanwy, *d* of Rev. Griffith Jones, Bontnewydd, Caerns; three *s* one *d*. *Educ:* University Coll., Aberystwyth; University Coll., Bangor. *Publications:* The Little Kingdom, 1946; The Voice of a Stranger, 1949; A Change of Heart, 1951; Hear and Forgive, 1952 (Somerset Maugham Award, 1953); A Man's Estate, 1955; The Italian Wife, 1957; Y Tri Llais, 1958; A Toy Epic, 1958 (Hawthornden Prize, 1959); The Gift, 1963; Outside the House of Baal, 1965; Natives, 1968; Ancestor Worship, 1970. *Recreations:* rural pursuits. *Address:* Ysgubor Fawr, Marianglas, Anglesey. *T:* Tynygongi 286.

**HUMPHREYS, Maj.-Gen. George Charles,** CB 1952; CBE 1948 (OBE 1945); *b* 5 Oct. 1899; *s* of late George Humphreys, formerly of Croft House, Croft-on-Tees, Co. Durham, and of Caroline Huddart; *m* 1931, Doris Isabelle, *d* of late A. B. Baines, Shanghai; no *c*. *Educ:* Giggleswick Sch., Yorks; RMC Sandhurst. 2nd Lieut Royal Northumberland Fusiliers, 1918; Lieut 1920; Capt. 1930; Bt-Major, Major 1938; Lieut-Col 1946; Col 1947; Brig. 1951; Maj.-Gen, 1952. Served with 2nd Bn Royal Northumberland Fusiliers, Iraq, India and China, 1919-31, Adjt 1925-28 (Iraq medal and clasp, 1920); War of 1939-45, in UK and Italy; GSO1 War Office, 1939-40; successively (Jan. 1941-May 1946), AA and QMG 55th Inf. Div., 1st and 3rd Armd Gps, 79th Armd Div., Col (Q) ops War Office, Col A/Q (BUCO) 21 Army Gp, Col A/Q, 1944-46; Dep. Chief Mil. Div. (Brig.), 1946, Allied Commn for Austria; Brig. i/c Admin Burma Comd, 1946-48; BGS, HQ Scottish Comd, 1948-51; Maj.-Gen. Adminstration, GHQ Middle East Land Forces, 1951-54; Military Adviser to Contractors for Canal Base (War Office, July 1954-31 May 1955); retired from Army, June 1955, and appointed General Manager, Suez Contractors Management Co. Ltd; appointed Chief Executive to Governing Body of Suez Contractors (Services) Ltd, Jan. 1956 until Liquidation of Suez enterprise, July 1957; Chief Organizer, Dollar Exports Council Conference, 1958. *Recreations:* reading, travel and shooting. *Address:* Lauriston Cottage, Old Green Lane, Camberley, Surrey. *T:* Camberley 21078.

**HUMPHREYS, Humphrey Francis,** CBE 1957 (OBE 1928); MC; TD; LLD (Birmingham and Glasgow), MB, ChB; MDS; FDS England; Hon. FDS RCS, Edinburgh; FSA; Hon. Colonel RAMC (TA); DL, Co. Warwickshire; *b* 19 June 1885; *s* of John Humphreys, MA, PhD, FSA, and Frances Lisseter; *m* 1920, Constance Evelyn Hudson; two *s*. *Educ:* Bromsgrove School; Birmingham University (Scholar); Harvard University, USA. In RAMC, TA, 1914-49; served European War, 1914-18, staff (despatches 3 times, MC); raised 1939 and commanded 1939-45, 14th General Hospital RAMC TA, UK, France, India, SE Asia; Hon. Phys. to the King, 1934-49; Professor of Dental Surgery, 1935-52; Vice-Principal, University of Birmingham, 1949-52; Vice-Chancellor, Univ. of Birmingham, 1952-53; President: Birmingham Archæological Society, 1953-58; Midland Medical Soc., 1954-55; Birmingham Nat. Hist. Soc., 1953-55; Section of Odontology RSM 1947-48; late Examiner to RCS and Univs Bristol and Sheffield; late member: Birmingham Regional Hospital Board; advisory committees to University Grants Committee, Medical Research Council, Nuffield Hospitals Trust,

Ministry of Health. *Publications:* Text Book of Surgery for Dental Students; numerous articles in medical, dental, and archæological periodicals. *Recreations:* gardening, archæology. *Address:* Church Farm, Hampton in Arden, Warwickshire. *T:* Hampton in Arden 2607. *Club:* Union (Birmingham).

**HUMPHREYS, Kenneth William,** BLitt, MA, PhD; FLA; Librarian, University of Birmingham, since 1952; *b* 4 Dec. 1916; *s* of Joseph Maxmillian Humphreys and Bessie Benfield; *m* 1939, Margaret, *d* of Reginald F. Hill and Dorothy Lucas; two *s*. *Educ:* Southfield Sch., Oxford; St Catherine's Coll., Oxford. Library Asst, All Souls Coll., Oxford, 1933-36; Asst, Bodleian Library, 1936-50; Dep. Librarian, Brotherton Library, University of Leeds, 1950-52. Hon. Lectr in Palaeography, University of Leeds, 1950-52; Hon. Lectr in Palaeography, University of Birmingham, 1952-; Hon. Sec., Standing Conf. of Nat. and University Libraries, 1954-69, Vice-Chm., 1969-; Mem. Library Adv. Council for England, 1966-; Mem. Council, Library Assoc., 1964-; Chm. Exec. Cttee, West Midlands Regional Library Bureau, 1963-; Chairman: Jt Standing Conf. and Cttee on Library Cooperation, 1965-; Nat. Cttee on Regional Cooperation, 1970-; Mem. Comité International de Paléographie, and Colloque International de Paléographie, 1955-; Pres., Nat. and University Libraries Section, Internat. Fedn of Library Assocs, 1968-69, Pres., University Libraries Sub-Section, 1967-. Editor, Studies in the History of Libraries and Librarianship; Associate Editor, Libri; Jt Editor, Series of Reproductions of Medieval and Renaissance Texts. Hon. LittD Dublin (Trinity Coll.), 1967. *Publications:* The Book Provisions of the Medieval Friars, 1964; The Medieval Library of the Carmelites at Florence, 1964; The Library of the Franciscans of the Convent of St Antony, Padua at the Beginning of the fifteenth century, 1966. Articles in library periodicals. *Recreation:* collection of manuscripts. *Address:* The Elms, Edgbaston Park Road, Edgbaston, Birmingham 15. *T:* 021-454 2980.

**HUMPHREYS, Sir Olliver (William),** Kt 1968; CBE 1957; BSc, FInstP, CEng, FIEE, FRAeS; Director, General Electric Co. Ltd, since 1953; *b* 4 Sept. 1902; *s* of late Rev. J. Willis Humphreys, Bath; *m* 1933, Muriel Mary Hawkins. *Educ:* Caterham Sch.; University Coll., London. Joined staff GEC Research Labs, 1925, Dir, 1949-61; Vice-Chm., GEC, 1963-67; Chm. all GEC Electronics and Telecommunications subsidiaries, 1961-66 and GEC (Research) Ltd, 1961-67. Mem. Bd, Inst. Physics, 1951-60 (Pres., 1956-58); Mem. Coun., IEE, 1952-55 (Vice-Pres., 1959-63; Pres., 1964-65); Faraday Lectr, 1953-54. Mem., BoT Cttee on Organisation and Constitution of BSI, 1949-50; Chm., BSI Telecommunications Industry Standards Cttee, 1951-63 (Mem. Gen. Coun., 1953-56; Mem. Exec. Cttee, 1953-60); Chm., Internat. Special Cttee on Radio Interference (CISPR), 1953-61; Chm., Electrical Res. Assoc., 1958-61; Chm., DSIR Radio Res. Bd, 1954-62; Pres., Electronic Engrg Assoc., 1962-64; Founder Chm., Conf. of Electronics Industry, 1963-67; Mem., Nat. ERC, 1963-67. Fellow UCL, 1963. Liveryman, Worshipful Co. of Makers of Playing Cards. *Publications:* various technical and scientific papers in proceedings of learned societies. *Recreations:* travel, walking, reading. *Address:* Branksome Cliff, Branksome Park, Poole, Dorset. *T:* Westbourne 66195.

**HUMPHREYS, Prof. Robert Arthur,** OBE 1946; MA, PhD Cantab; Director, Institute of Latin-American Studies, University of London, since 1965; Professor of Latin-American History in University of London, 1948-70; *b* 6 June 1907; *s* of late Robert and of Helen Marion Humphreys, Lincoln; *m* 1946, Elisabeth, *er d* of late Sir Bernard Pares, KBE, DCL. *Educ:* Lincoln Sch.; Peterhouse, Cambridge (Scholar). Commonwealth Fund Fellow, University of Michigan, 1930-32. Asst Lecturer in American History, University Coll., London, 1932; Lecturer, 1935; Reader in American History in University of London, 1942-48. Research Dept, Foreign Office, 1939-45. Mem., University Grants Cttee on Latin American Studies, 1962-64; Pres., Royal Historical Society, 1964-68. Hon. Vice-Pres., 1968; Enid Muir Memorial Lectr, University of Newcastle upon Tyne, 1962; Creighton Lectr, University of London, 1964; Raleigh Lectr, Brit. Acad., 1965. Corresp. Member: Argentine Acad. of History; Instituto Histórico e Geográfico Brasileiro; Sociedad Chilena de Historia y Geografia; Sociedad Peruana de Historia; Instituto Histórico y Geográfico del Uruguay; Academia Nacional de la Historia, Venezuela. Hon. DLitt (Newcastle) 1966. *Publications:* British Consular Reports on the Trade and Politics of Latin America, 1940; The Evolution of Modern Latin America, 1946; Liberation in South America, 1806-1827; 1952; Latin American History: A Guide to the Literature in English, 1958; The Diplomatic History of British Honduras, 1638-1901, 1961; (with G. S. Graham), The Navy and South America, 1807-1823 (Navy Records Soc.), 1962; (with J. Lynch) The Origins of the Latin American Revolutions, 1808-1826, 1965; Tradition and Revolt in Latin America and other Essays, 1969; The Detached Recollections of General D. F. O'Leary, 1969; The Royal Historical Society, 1868-1968, 1969; contrib. to The New Cambridge Modern History, vols VIII, IX and X. *Address:* 13 St Paul's Place, Canonbury, N1. *T:* 01-226 8930; Institute of Latin American Studies, 31 Tavistock Square, WC1. *T:* 01-387 5671/2. *Club:* United University.

**HUMPHREYS, (Travers) Christmas,** QC 1959; **His Honour Judge Humphreys;** Additional Judge, Central Criminal Court, since 1968; Deputy Chairman: East Kent Quarter Sessions, 1947; County of Kent Quarter Sessions, 1962; Barrister-at-Law, Inner Temple, 1924; Bencher, Inner Temple, 1955; *b* London, 1901; *o surv s* of late Rt Hon. Sir Travers Humphreys, PC; *m* 1927, Aileen Maude, *d* of Dr Charles Irvine and Alice Faulkner of Escrick, Yorks and Tunbridge Wells. *Educ:* Malvern Coll.; Trinity Hall, Cambridge (MA, LLB). Junior Counsel to Treasury for certain Appeals, 1932; Junior Counsel to Treasury at Central Criminal Court, 1934; Recorder of: Deal, 1942-56; Guildford, 1956-68. Senior Prosecuting Counsel to the Crown at the Central Criminal Court, 1950-59; a Commissioner, 1962-68. Founding Pres. of Buddhist Lodge, London, 1924 (now Buddhist Society); Pres. The Shakespearean Authorship Soc., 1955; Joint Vice-Chm. Royal India, Pakistan and Ceylon Society; a Vice-Pres. Tibet Soc., 1962. *Publications:* The Great Pearl Robbery of 1913, 1928; What is Buddhism?, 1928, and Concentration and Meditation, 1935; The Development of Buddhism in England, 1937; Studies in the Middle Way, 1940; Poems of Peace and War, 1941; Seagulls, and other Poems, 1942; Karma and Rebirth, 1943; Shadows and other Poems, 1945; Walk On, 1947; Via Tokyo, 1948; Zen Buddhism, 1949; Buddhism (Pelican books); The Way of Action, 1960; Zen Comes West, 1960; The Wisdom of Buddhism, 1960; Poems I Remember, 1960; A Popular Dictionary of

Buddhism, 1962; Zen, A Way of Life, 1962; Sixty Years of Buddhism in England, 1968; The Buddhist Way of Life, 1969; pamphlets, articles, etc. *Recreations:* music, ballet, entertaining; Eastern philosophy and Chinese Art. *Address:* 58 Marlborough Place, NW8. *T:* 01-624 4987.

**HUMPHREYS-DAVIES, Brian,** CB 1964; Assistant Under-Secretary of State, Ministry of Defence, since 1964 (Air Ministry, 1956-64); *b* 18 Feb. 1917; *y s* of late J. W. S. Humphreys-Davies, Southfields, Eastbourne; *m* 1948, Gillian *d* of late Major Colin Cooper, Barnwell Castle, Northants; one *s* one *d*. *Educ:* Sherborne; Balliol Coll., Oxford. Asst Principal, Air Ministry, 1938; served War of 1939-45, RA: BEF, 1939-40; British North Africa Force, 1943; Haifa Staff Coll., 1943; 40th Indian Inf. Bde, 1944; Control Commission for Germany, 1944-45, Lieut-Col 1945. Rejoined Air Ministry, 1945; Private Sec. to Chief of Air Staff, 1946-48; Imperial Defence Coll., 1955. Trustee, Imperial War Museum, 1968-. *Address:* c/o National Westminster Bank, Eastbourne, Sussex. *Club:* Reform.

**HUMPHREYS-DAVIES, (George) Peter,** CB 1953; Deputy Secretary, Ministry of Agriculture, Fisheries and Food, 1960-67; *b* 23 June 1909; *e s* of late J. W. S. Humphreys-Davies, Southfields, Eastbourne; *m* 1935, Barbara, *d* of late Lieut-Col F. G. Crompton, White Court, Alfriston, Sussex; two *s* one *d*. *Educ:* Sherborne; New Coll., Oxford. Craven Scholar, 1931. Asst Principal, Admiralty, 1932; HM Treasury, 1934; Private Sec. to Prime Ministers, 1936-38; Under-Sec., HM Treasury, 1949-56; Deputy Sec., Ministry of Supply, 1956-60; Directing Staff, Imperial Defence Coll., 1954. *Address:* Weyhurst Farm, Rudgwick, Sussex. *T:* Rudgwick 221.

**HUMPHRIES, George James,** CMG 1965; OBE 1954; *b* 23 April 1900. *Educ:* St James Sch., Tyresham; Magdalen Coll. Sch., Brackley; Reading Univ. Served War, 1939-46, Lieut-Col. Surveyor, Nigeria, 1928; Sen., 1945; Deputy Dir, Overseas Surveys, 1946; Dir and Surveys Adviser, Dept of Technical Co-operation, 1963; Dir and Surveys Adviser to Min. of Overseas Development, 1964. *Address:* Greenacre, Worplesdon Hill, Woking, Surrey.

**HUMPHRYS, Lt-Col Sir Francis Henry,** GCMG, 1932 (KCMG, 1929); GCVO, 1928; KBE, 1924; CIE, 1920; formerly of Charlton Park, Canterbury; *b* 24 April 1879; *e s* of late Rev. Walter Humphrys, MA, Oxford, and Helen Agnes, *d* of Rev. A. F. Boucher; *m* 1907, Gertrude Mary, DBE 1929, *e d* of Col Sir Harold Arthur Deane, KCSI, First Chief Commissioner, North-West Frontier Province, India; one *s* two *d*. *Educ:* Shrewsbury; Christ Church, Oxford. Gazetted 2nd Lieut, 2nd Worcestershire Regt 1900; served S African War, 1900-01 (Queen's medal, 3 clasps); held various political appointments on NW Frontier, India, 1904-17; Political Officer with troops, 1917 (despatches); served European War in Europe as pilot, RAF, 1918; Political Agent, Khyber, 1919; Deputy Foreign Sec. to the Government of India, 1921; HBM Envoy Extraordinary and Minister Plenipotentiary at Kabul, 1922-29; High Commissioner and Commander-in-Chief in Iraq, 1929-32; British Ambassador in Baghdad, 1932-35; Chm. British Sugar Corp., 1939-45; Chm. Iraq Petroleum Co., 1941-50; Vice-Chm. Associated Portland Cement Manufacturers, 1936-53; Chairman: Clerical Medical and General Life Assurance Society, 1948-59; Brixton Estates Ltd, 1950-63; Air Training Corps, Central Council of Welfare, 1940-57. Jubilee medal, 1935; Coronation medal, 1937; Order of Sardar-i-ala of Afghanistan, 1928; Grand Cordon Order of Two Rivers, Iraq, 1933. *Recreations:* cricket, shooting, fishing, aviation. *Address:* 4 Whitehall Court, SW1. *Clubs:* MCC, Royal Aero; Grillions.

**HUMPIDGE, Kenneth Palmer,** CMG 1957; Ministry of Transport, Cheltenham, 1965-69 (Nottingham, 1958-65); *b* 18 Nov. 1902; *s* of James Dickerson Humpidge, Stroud; *m* 1938, Jill Mary Russell, *d* of Russell Pountney, Bristol; two *d*. *Educ:* Wycliffe Coll.; Univ. of Bristol. BSc (Engineering). Public Works Dept, Nigeria, 1926; Director of Public Works, Northern Region, Nigeria, 1948-54; Director of Federal Public Works, 1954-57. FICE. *Address:* Pinfarthings, Amberley, Stroud, Glos. *T:* Nailsworth 198.

**HUNKIN, Leslie Claude,** CMG 1945; sometime Chairman Forestry Board, and Deputy Director Manpower, South Australia; *b* Lefroy, 1884; *s* of Joseph Hunkin, Mine Manager, and Elma Hunkin; *m* Florence M. Evans; two *s* one *d*. Business Career. Member of South Australian Parliament and later Public Service. Fellow of Instiiute of Public Administration. *Address:* Chatsworth Grove, Toorak Gardens, South Australia.

**HUNLOKE, Henry,** TD 1946; Lt-Col, Royal Wiltshire Yeomanry; *b* 1906; *o s* of late Major Sir Philip Hunloke, GCVO; *m* 1929, Lady Anne Cavendish (who obtained a divorce, 1945), *d* of 9th Duke of Devonshire, KG; two *s* one *d*; *m* 1945, Virginia Clive; one *d* (and one *d* decd). MP (U) Western Div. of Derbyshire, 1938-44. Served War of 1939-45 in Middle East (despatches). *Address:* St Catherine's Lodge, Bearwood, Wokingham, Berks. *T:* Wokingham 438. *Clubs:* Turf, Buck's, Pratt's, MCC.

*See also Viscount Astor.*

**HUNN, Jack Kent,** CMG 1964; LLM; Retired as Secretary of Defence, New Zealand. 1963-66; *b* 24 Aug. 1906; *m* 1932, Dorothy Murray; two *s*. *Educ:* Wairarapa Coll.; Auckland Univ. Public Trust Office, 1924-46; Actg Sec. of Justice, 1950; Public Service Comr, 1954-61; Actg Sec. of Internal Affairs and Dir of Civil Defence, 1959; Sec. for Maori Affairs and Maori Trustee, 1960-63. Reviewed Cook Islands Public Service, 1949 and 1954; Mem. NZ delegn to Duke of Edinburgh's Conf, 1956; Mem. UN Salary Review Cttee, 1956; reviewed organisation of South Pacific Commn, Noumea and Sydney, 1957, and of SEATO, Bangkok, 1959. Chairman: Wildlife Commission of Inquiry, 1968; Fire Safety Inquiry, 1969. *Publication:* Hunn Report on Maori Affairs, 1960. *Address:* 17 Kereru Street, Waikanae, Wellington, New Zealand. *T:* 177D.

**HUNSDON,** Baron; *see* Aldenham, Baron.

**HUNT,** family name of **Baron Hunt.**

**HUNT,** Baron, *cr* 1966, of Llanvair Waterdine (Life Peer); **(Henry Cecil) John Hunt;** Kt 1953; CBE 1945; DSO 1944; Chairman, Parole Board for England and Wales, since 1967; President, Council for Volunteers Overseas, since 1968; *b* 22 June 1910; *s* of late Capt. C. E. Hunt, MC, IA, and E. H. Hunt (*née* Crookshank); *m* 1936, Joy Mowbray-Green; four *d*. *Educ:* Marlborough Coll.; RMC, Sandhurst. Commissioned King's Royal Rifle Corps, 1930; seconded to Indian Police, 1934-35 and 1938-40 (Indian Police Medal, 1940). War of 1939-45: Comd 11th Bn KRRC, 1944; Comd 11th Indian Inf. Bde, 1944-46. Staff Coll., 1946; Joint Services Staff Coll., 1949; GSO 1,

Jt Planning Staffs, MELF, 1946-48; Western Europe C's-in-C Cttee, 1950-51; Allied Land Forces, Central Europe, 1951-52; Col, Gen. Staff, HQ I (British) Corps, 1952; Asst Comdt, The Staff Coll., 1953-56; retired, 1956; Hon. Brigadier. Dir, Duke of Edinburgh's Award Scheme, 1956-66. Rector, Aberdeen Univ., 1963-66. Leader, British Expedition to Mount Everest, 1952-53. President: The Alpine Club, 1956-58; Climbers' Club, 1963-66; British Mountaineering Council, 1965-68; The National Ski Fedn, 1968-. Hon. FRGS. Order 1st Class Gurkha Right Hand, 1953; Indian Everest Medal, 1953; Hubbard Medal (US), 1954; Founder's Medal, RGS, 1954; Lawrence Memorial Medal, RCAS, 1954; Hon. DCL (Durham) 1954; Hon. LLD (Aberdeen, London) 1954. *Publications:* The Ascent of Everest, 1953; Our Everest Adventure, 1954; (with C. Brasher) The Red Snows, 1959. *Recreations:* mountaineering, ski-ing. *Address:* Highway Cottage, Aston, Henley-on-Thames; Lloyds Bank Ltd, 6 Pall Mall, SW1. *Clubs:* Athenæum, Alpine.
*See also Hugh Hunt.*

**HUNT, Sir David (Wathen Stather),** KCMG 1963 (CMG 1959); OBE 1943; Ambassador to Brazil, since 1969; *b* 25 Sept. 1913; *s* of late Canon B. P. W. Stather Hunt, DD, and late Elizabeth Milner; *m* 1st, 1948, Pamela Muriel Medawar (marr. diss. 1967); two *s*; 2nd, 1968, Iro Myrianthousi. *Educ:* St Lawrence Coll.; Wadham Coll., Oxford. 1st Class Hon. Mods. 1934; 1st Class Lit. Hum. 1936; Thomas Whitcombe Greene Prize, 1936; Diploma in Classical Archæology, 1937; Fellow of Magdalen Coll., 1937. Served 1st Bn Welch Regt and General Staff in Middle East, Balkans, North Africa, Sicily, Italy, 1940-46 (despatches 3 times, OBE, US Bronze Star); GSO1 18th Army Group, 1943; 15th Army Group, 1943-45; Col General Staff, Allied Force HQ, 1945-46; attached staff Governor-General Canada, 1946-47; released and granted hon. rank of Colonel, 1947. Principal, Dominions Office, 1947; 1st Secretary, Pretoria, 1948-49; Private Secretary to Prime Minister (Mr Atlee), 1950-51, (Mr Churchill) 1951-52; Asst Secretary, 1952; Deputy High Commissioner for UK, Lahore, 1954-56; Head of Central African Dept, Commonwealth Relations Office, 1956-59; Asst Under Secretary of State, Commonwealth Relations Office, 1959-60; accompanied the Prime Minister as an Adviser, on African tour, Jan.-Feb. 1960; Dep. High Comr for the UK in Lagos, Fedn of Nigeria, oct. 1960-62; High Comr in Uganda, 1962-65; in Cyprus, 1965-67; in Nigeria, 1967-69. US Bronze Star 1945. *Publications:* A Don at War, 1966; articles in Annual of British School of Archæology at Athens and Journal of Hellenic Studies. *Recreations:* golf, history and sailing. *Address:* c/o Foreign and Commonwealth Office, SW1. *Clubs:* Athenæum, Travellers'.

**HUNT, Surgeon Rear-Adm. Frederick George,** CB 1952; CBE 1948; OStJ 1947; Royal Navy; *b* July 1894; *s* of Dr A. M. Hunt, Coolaney, Co. Sligo, Ireland; *m* 1926, Christina Leonard (*d* 1961); no *c*. *Educ:* Mount St Joseph's, Roscrea, Ireland; National Univ. of Ireland. Qualified MB, BCh, 1917; joined Royal Naval Medical Service: Surgeon Rear-Adm., 1949; KHP 1949; QHP 1952; retired list, 1952. *Recreations:* fishing, bridge. *Address:* The Old Cottage, Burgwallis, near Doncaster, Yorkshire. *Club:* Royal Automobile.

**HUNT, Rear-Adm. Geoffrey Harry C.;** *see* Carew Hunt.

**HUNT, Col (George) Vivian,** OBE 1943; TD 1943; MA 1926; LLB 1928; Senior Partner in Wake Smith and Company, solicitors, Sheffield; *b* 30 July 1905; *er s* of John Edwin Hunt, Crabtree Meadow House, Hope, Derbyshire; *m* 1935, Sylvia Anne, *d* of John Stanley Tyzack, Oakholme House, Sheffield; three *s*. *Educ:* Malvern Coll.; King's Coll., Cambridge (MA, LLB Hons). Commissioned RA (TA) 1926. Lt-Col 1940; invented Hunt Trainer, 1940; took part in North African, Sicilian and Italian campaigns with 78th Infantry Diviision, 1942-44; reconnoitred and laid out original defences North-East of Beja, Tunisia, which subseq. became known as 'Hunt's Gap'; Col 1944; Hon Col 513 LAA Regt RA (TA), 1947-55; retired from TA, 1956. JP for City of Sheffield, 1956-70. *Publication:* (Treatise) Finance of Voluntary Organizations, 1950. *Recreations:* golf, gardening. *Address:* The Lodge, Woodvale Road, Sheffield 10. *T:* Sheffield 60177. *Club:* Sheffield (Sheffield).

**HUNT, Gilbert Adams,** CBE 1967; Managing Director and Chief Executive Officer, Chrysler United Kingdom Ltd (formerly Rootes Motors Ltd), since 1967; *b* Wolverhampton, 29 Dec. 1914; *s* of Harold William Hunt, The Orchards, Alveley, Bridgnorth, Shropshire; *m* 1938, Sarah (marr. diss. 1946), *d* of Captain Wadman-Taylor; *m* 1946, Olive Doreen, *d* of late Maurice Martin O'Brien; no *c*. *Educ:* Old Hall, Wellington; Malvern Coll., Worcester. Director, High Duty Alloys, Slough, 1950-54; Dir and Gen. Man., High Duty Alloys (Dir, HDA, Canada, Northern Steel Scaffold & Engrg Co., all subsids. Hawker Siddeley Gp), 1954-60; Man. Dir, Massey-Ferguson (UK) Ltd; Jt Man. Dir, Massey-Ferguson-Perkins; Dir, Massey-Ferguson Holdings Ltd; Chm. and Man. Dir, Massey-Ferguson (Eire) Ltd; Chm., Massey-Ferguson (Farm Services) Ltd, 1960-67. Pres., Coventry Chamber of Commerce, 1962-64; Pres., Agricultural Engrs Association Ltd, 1965. CEng, CIMechE, FIProdE. *Recreations:* tennis, golfing, riding, sailing. *Address:* The Dial House, Alveston, Stratford-upon-Avon, Warwicks; 6 Lowndes Square, SW1. *Clubs:* Bath, Royal Thames Yacht; Royal Irish Yacht (Dublin).

**HUNT, Herbert James;** Senior Fellow in French, University of Warwick, since 1966; Professor of French Language and Literature, Royal Holloway College, University of London, 1944-66; *b* 2 Aug. 1899; *s* of James Henry and Mary Anne Hunt, Lichfield; *m* 1925, Sheila Jessamine Spielman (*d* 1961); two *s* three *d*. *Educ:* King Edward VI Grammar Sch., Lichfield; Magdalen Coll., Oxford. Asst Master: Imperial Service Coll., Windsor, 1923-25; Durham School, 1925-27. Lectr, Fellow, Tutor, St Edmund Hall, 1927-44; Fellow Emeritus 1953. Lecturer: Exeter Coll., Oxford, 1927-44; Jesus Coll., Oxford, 1930-44. *Publications:* Le Socialisme et le romantisme en France, 1935; The Epic in Nineteenth Century France, 1941; Victor Hugo: Légende des siècles (Selection and Annotations), 1944; Honoré de Balzac, a Biography, 1957; Balzac's Comédie Humaine, 1964; (ed) Eugénie Grandet, 1967; (trans.) Cousin Pons, 1968; articles in Mercure de France, Revue d'Histoire Littéraire de la France, Modern Language Review, French Studies, etc. *Address:* Mill Close, Tredington, Shipston-on-Stour, Warwicks. *T:* Shipston 581.

**HUNT, Hugh,** MA; Professor of Drama, University of Manchester, since 1961; Artistic Director, Abbey Theatre, Dublin, since 1969; *b* 25 Sept. 1911; *s* of Captain C. E. Hunt, MC, and Ethel Helen (née Crookshank); *m* 1940, Janet Mary (née Gordon); one *s* one *d*. *Educ:* Marlborough Coll.; Magdalen Coll., Oxford.

BA Oxon 1934, MA Oxon 1961. Hon. MA Manchester 1965. Pres. of OUDS, 1933-34; Producer: Maddermarket Theatre, Norwich, 1934; Croydon Repertory and Westminster Theatres, 1934-35; Producer, Abbey Theatre, Dublin, 1935-38; produced The White Steed, Cort Theatre, NY. Entered HM Forces, 1939; served War of 1939-45, with Scots Guards, King's Royal Rifle Corps, and Intelligence Service; demobilised, 1945. Director of Bristol Old Vic Company, 1945-49; Director Old Vic Company, London, 1949-53; Adjudicator Canadian Drama Festival Finals, 1954; Executive Officer, Elizabethan Theatre Trust, Australia, 1955-60. Produced: The Cherry Orchard, 1948, Love's Labour's Lost, 1949, Hamlet, 1950, New Theatre; Old Vic Seasons, 1951-53: Twelfth Night, Merry Wives of Windsor, Romeo and Juliet, Merchant of Venice, Julius Caesar. Produced The Living Room, New York, 1954; in Australia, Medea, 1955, Twelfth Night, 1956, Hamlet, 1957, Julius Caesar, 1959; The Shaughaun, World Theatre Season, Dublin, 1968; The Well of the Saints, 1969; The Hostage, 1970. *Publications:* Old Vic Prefaces; The Director in the Theatre; The Making of Australian Theatre; The Live Theatre; author or co-author of several Irish plays including The Invincibles and In The Train. *Address:* Department of Drama, University of Manchester, Manchester 13; Brant Wood, Red Lane, Disley, Cheshire. *Club:* Garrick.
*See also Baron Hunt.*

**HUNT, Prof. (Jack) Naylor,** DSc, MD; MRCP; Professor of Physiology at Guy's Hospital Medical School since Oct. 1962; *b* 29 April 1917; *s* of Charles Frank Hunt and Mary Anne Moss; *m* 1948, Claire, *d* of Sir William Haley, *qv*; no *c*. *Educ:* Royal Masonic School, Bushey; Guy's Hospital Medical School. Resident MO, Hertford British Hosp., Paris, 1940. Temp. Surgeon Lieutenant, RNVR, 1940-45. Dept of Physiology, Guy's Hospital Medical School, 1945-. Rockefeller Fellow, 1951; Arris and Gale Lecturer, 1951; Gillson Scholar, 1952. *Publications:* various papers on the alimentary tract. *Address:* 10 Noel Road, N1. *Club:* Athenæum.

**HUNT, John Francis,** CBE 1964; Under-Secretary and Controller of Supply, Ministry of Health, 1965-68, retired, 1968; *b* 10 Sept. 1906; *s* of late John William Hunt and late Beatrice (*née* Cass); *m* 1933, Vera Mary (*née* Jenkins); three *s*. *Educ:* Sir John Talbot Grammar Sch., Whitchurch, Shropshire; Liverpool Univ.; London Univ. (External). BSc Liverpool, 1st cl. hons Mathematics, 1928; Derby Scholar, 1928-29; LLB London, 2nd cl. hons (External), 1946. Entered Civil Service (District Audit), 1929; Asst District Auditor, 1929; Sen. Asst 1938; Deputy, 1947; transf. to Accountant-General's Dept, Min. of Health, 1947; Asst Acct-Gen., 1947; Deputy, 1951; Asst Secretary, 1958; Transf. to Supply Div., 1960. Mem. Surrey CC, Dorking North, 1970-. *Recreations:* reading, walking. *Address:* Fourways, Reigate Road, Dorking, Surrey. *T:* Dorking 4493. *Club:* Royal Automobile.

**HUNT, John Henderson,** CBE 1970; MA, DM Oxon, FRCP, FRCS; President, Royal College of General Practitioners; Cons. Physician, St Dunstan's, 1948-66; PMO, Provident Mutual Life Assurance Association, since 1947; Governor: Charterhouse School; Sutton's Hospital, Old Charterhouse; National Hospital, Queen Sq.; *b* 3 July 1905; *s* of late Edmund Henderson Hunt, MCh, FRCS, and Laura Mary Buckingham; *m* 1941, Elisabeth Ernestine, *d* of Norman Evill, FRIBA; two *s* two *d* (and one *s* decd). *Educ:* Charterhouse School; Balliol College, Oxford; St Batholomew's Hospital. Theodore Williams Scholar in Physiology, Oxford Univ., 1926; Radcliffe Scholar in Pharmacology, 1928. RAF Medical Service, 1940-45 (Wing Comdr). Hon. Cons in Gen. Practice, RAF; Pres. Gen. Practice Section, Royal Soc. Med., 1956; Vice-Pres. Brit. Med. Students' Assoc., 1956-69; Hon. Sec. Council, Coll. of Gen. Practitioners, 1952-67; Med. Soc. of London, 1964-65; Mem. Council: RCS (co-opted), 1957-61; Med. Protection Soc., 1948-69; St Dunstan's, 1966-69; Member: General Advisory Council, BBC, 1958-66; Med. Services Review Cttee, 1958-61; Med. Commn on Accident Prevention, 1967-69. Hon. Fellow: Aust. Coll. Gen. Practitioners; Amer. Acad. of Gen Practice; Hon. Mem. Coll. of Gen. Practice of Canada. Lloyd Roberts Lecturer (Manchester), 1956; Albert Wauden Lectr (RSM), 1968; Paul Hopkins Memorial Orator (Brisbane), 1969. Late House Surgeon, and Chief Assistant Medical Professorial Unit, St Bart's Hosp. and House Physician National Hosp. Queen Square. *Publications:* (ed) Accident Prevention and Life Saving, 1965; various papers in medical journals; chapter on Raynaud's Phenomenon, in British Encyclopaedia of Medical Practice, 1938 and 1948; chapter on Peripheral Vascular Disease, in Early Diagnosis, by Henry Miller, 1959. *Recreations:* tennis, golf, gardening. *Address:* 82 Sloane Street, SW1. *T:* 01-730 1811; 18 Wilton Place, SW1. *T:* 01-235 5566. *Clubs:* Royal Air Force, Caledonian, MCC.

**HUNT, John Joseph Benedict,** CB 1968; First Civil Service Commissioner, and Deputy Secretary, Civil Service Department, since 1968; *b* 23 Oct. 1919; *er s* of Major Arthur L. Hunt and Daphne Hunt; *m* 1941, Hon. Magdalen Mary Lister Robinson, *yr d* of 1st Baron Robinson; two *s* one *d*. *Educ:* Downside; Magdalene College, Cambridge. Served Royal Naval Volunteer Reserve, 1940-46, Lieut; Convoy escort, Western Approaches and in Far East. Home Civil Service, Admin. Class, 1946; Dominions Office, 1946; Priv. Sec. to Parly. Under-Sec., 1947; 2nd Sec., Office of UK High Comr in Ceylon, 1948-50; Principal, 1949; Directing Staff, IDC, 1951-52; 1st Sec., Office of UK High Comr in Canada, 1953-56; Private Secretary to: Sec. of Cabinet and Perm. Sec. to Treasury and Head of Civil Service, 1956-58; Asst Secretary: CRO 1958; Cabinet Office, 1960; HM Treasury, 1962-67; Under-Sec., 1965. Dep. Sec., 1968. *Recreations:* gardening, ski-ing. *Address:* 24 Parkside, SW19. *T:* 01-947 1046. *Clubs:* Oxford and Cambridge University, Hurlingham.

**HUNT, John Leonard;** MP (C) Bromley since 1964; *b* 27 Oct. 1929; *s* of late William John Hunt and of Dora Maud Hunt, Keston, Kent; unmarried. *Educ:* Dulwich Coll. Councillor, Bromley Borough Coun., 1953; Alderman, Bromley Borough Coun., 1961; Mayor of Bromley, 1963-64. Contested (C) S Lewisham, Gen. Election, 1959. Chm., All-Party Cttee on UK Citizenship, 1968-; Jt-Chm., British-Caribbean Assoc., 1968-. Mem. of London Stock Exchange. *Recreations:* foreign travel and good food. *Address:* 94 Park West, Marble Arch, W2. *T:* 01-262 7733.

**HUNT, John Maitland,** MA, BLitt; Headmaster of Roedean since Jan. 1971; *b* 4 March 1932; *s* of Richard Herbert Alexander Hunt and Eileen Mary Isabelle Hunt (*née* Witt); *m* 1969, Sarah, *d* of Lt-Gen. Sir Derek Lang, *qv*. *Educ:* Radley College; Wadham College, Oxford. BA 1956; BLitt 1959; MA 1960. Assistant master, Stowe School, 1958-70 (Sixth Form tutor in Geography). *Publications:* various articles on fine arts and architecture. *Recreations:* estate management, fine arts, writing, travel.

*Address:* Roedean School, Brighton, Sussex. *T:* Brighton 680791. *Club:* English-Speaking Union.

**HUNT, Sir Joseph (Anthony),** Kt 1966; MBE 1951; FBIM; Director, The Chloride Electrical Storage Co. Ltd, since 1965 (Deputy Managing Director since 1969); Director-in-charge, Overseas Operations, Chloride Group, since 1966; *b* 1 April 1905; *s* of Patrick and Florence Anne Hunt; *m* 2nd, 1960, Esme Jeanne, *d* of Albert Edward Langston; two *s* one *d*. *Educ:* St Gregory's Sch., Farnworth, Lancs; Salford Royal Tech. Coll.; Manchester Coll. of Technology. Gen. Man., Hymatic Engrg Co. Ltd, 1938-65. Chm., Hydrovane Compressor Co. Ltd, 1968- (Dir, 1960-68); Director: Hymatic Engrg Co. Ltd, 1960-; Ferrostatics Ltd, 1963-. Chairman: Economic Planning Council, West Midlands, 1965-67; Hunt Cttee on Intermediate Areas, 1967-69; Pro-Chancellor, Univ. of Aston in Birmingham, 1965-70; Member, Redditch Devel. Corp., 1964-; Central Training Council, 1964-; National Advisory Council on Education for Industry and Commerce, 1961-, Chm., 1967-; W Midlands Adv. Council for Further Education, 1960-; Vice-Pres., British Assoc. for Commercial and Industrial Educn, 1961- (Chm. Exec. Council, 1960-61); Mem. Council, Birmingham Chamber of Commerce, 1956-. Hon. ACT (Birmingham) 1950. Hon. DSc Aston; Hon. LLD Birmingham. *Publications:* contrib. to Technical Press: on Organisation, Management, Education and Training. *Recreations:* reading, architecture, theatre. *Address:* 216 Birchfield Road, Redditch, Worcs. *T:* Redditch 63562. *Club:* Royal Automobile.

**HUNT, Prof. Naylor;** *see* Hunt, J. N.

**HUNT, Prof. Norman Charles;** Professor of Business Studies, University of Edinburgh, since 1967 (Prof. of Organisation of Industry and Commerce, 1953-66); Chairman: R. and R. Clark Ltd, since 1967; William Thyne Ltd, since 1967; Director: William Thyne (Holdings) Ltd, since 1963; William Thyne (Plastics) Ltd, since 1967; *b* 6 April 1918; *s* of Charles Hunt and Charlotte (*née* Jackson), Swindon, Wilts; *m* 1942, Lorna Mary, 2nd *d* of Mary and William Arthur Mann, Swindon, Wilts; two *s*. *Educ:* Commonweal Sch.; Swindon Coll.; University of London (Sir Edward Stern Schol., BCom 1st cl. hons); PhD (Edinburgh). On Staff (Research Dept and Personal Staff of Chief Mechanical Engineers); former GWR Co., 1934-45. Lectr in Organisation of Industry and Commerce, University of Edinburgh, 1946-53; Dir of Studies in Commerce, 1948-53; Dean of Faculty of Social Sciences, 1962-64. Member: Departmental Cttee on Fire Service, 1967-70; Rubber Industry NEDC, 1968-; UGC, 1969-; ODM Working Party on Management Educn and Training in Developing Countries, 1968-69. *Publications:* Methods of Wage Payment in British Industry, 1951; articles in economic and management jls on industrial organisation, industrial relations, and management problems. *Recreations:* photography, motoring, foreign travel. *Address:* 65 Ravelston Dykes Road, Edinburgh 4.

**HUNT, Norman Crowther,** PhD; Fellow and Lecturer in Politics since 1952, Domestic Bursar since 1954, Exeter College, Oxford; Member, Commission on the Constitution, since 1969; *b* 13 March 1920; *s* of late Ernest Angus Hunt, and of Florence Hunt, Bradford, Yorks; *m* 1944, Joyce, *d* of late Rev. Joseph Stackhouse, Walsall Wood, Staffs; three *d*. *Educ:* Wellington Road Council Sch.; Belle Vue High Sch., Bradford; Sidney Sussex Coll., Cambridge. Exhibitioner, 1939-40, Open Scholar, 1945-47, Sidney Sussex Coll.; MA 1949; PhD 1951. Served RA, 1940-45; War Office (GSO3), 1944-45. First Cl. Hist. Tripos, 1946 and 1947; Res. Fellow, Sidney Sussex Coll., 1949-51; Commonwealth Fund Fellow, Princeton Univ., USA, 1951-52. Deleg., Oxford Univ. Extra-Mural Delegacy, 1956-; Vis. Prof., Michigan State Univ., 1961., Member: Council, Headington Sch., Oxford, 1966-; Cttee on the Civil Service (Fulton Cttee), 1966-68 (Leader of Management Consultancy Group); Civil Service Coll. Adv. Council, 1970-. *Publications:* Two Early Political Associations, 1961. (Ed.) Whitehall and Beyond, 1964. *Recreations:* playing tennis, squash and the piano; broadcasting. Cambridge Univ. Assoc. Football XI, 1939-40. *Address:* 14 Apsley Road, Oxford. *T:* Oxford 58342; Exeter College, Oxford. *T:* Oxford 44681.

**HUNT, Gen. Sir Peter (Mervyn),** KCB 1969 (CB 1965); DSO 1945; OBE 1947; Commander Northern Army Group and Commander-in-Chief, BAOR, since 1970; *b* 11 March 1916; *s* of H. V. Hunt, Barrister-at-law; *m* 1940, Anne Stopford (*d* 1966), *d* of Vice-Adm. Hon. Arthur Stopford, CMG; one *s* one *d*. *Educ:* Wellington Coll.; RMC Sandhurst. Commissioned QO Cameron Highlanders, 1936; commanded 7 Seaforth Highlanders, 1944-45; graduated Command and Gen. Staff Coll., Ft Leavenworth, USA. 1948; Instructor, Staff Coll., Camberley, 1952-55; Instructor, Imperial Defence Coll., 1956-57; commanded 1 Camerons, 1957-60; Comdr 152 (H) Infantry Brigade, TA, 1960-62; Chief of Staff, Scottish Command, 1962-64; GOC, 17 Div., also Comdr, Land Forces, Borneo, and Major-Gen., Bde of Gurkhas, 1964-65; Comdt, Royal Military Academy, Sandhurst, 1966-68; Comdr, FARELF, 1968-70. Col Queen's Own Highlanders (Seaforth and Camerons), 1966-; Col 10th Princess Mary's Own Gurkha Rifles, 1966-. Chevalier of the Order of Leopold II and Croix de Guerre (Belgium), 1940 (awarded 1945). *Recreations:* golf, philately and travel. *Address:* c/o Glyn, Mills and Co., Holt's Branch, Whitehall, SW1. *Club:* Naval and Military.

**HUNT, Reginald Heber,** DMus; FRCO; FLCM; Chairman of Corporation, London College of Music (Director, 1954-64); *b* 16 June 1891; *m* 1917, Lilian Blanche Shinton (*d* 1956); one *s* one *d*; *m* 1959, Mary Elizabeth Abbott. *Educ:* Wolverhampton; St John's Coll., Battersea; privately; Guildhall Sch. of Music. FRCO 1915; DMus London, 1925. Served European War, including France, 1915-19; Dir of Music, Sir Walter St John's Sch., Battersea, 1927-45; Lectr in Music, Coll. of St Mark and St John, Chelsea, 1933-39; Organist various London churches, 1919-39; Organist Godalming Parish Church, 1940-50, and Dir Music, County Gram. Sch., 1945-52; composer and arranger, BBC Military Band, 1929-40. Mem. Performing Rights Soc., 1929-. Sec. Union of Graduates in Music, 1948-50; Prof. and Examr, London Coll. of Music, 1947-; Mem. Senate, Univ. of London, 1951-64; Moderator in Music, General Certificate of Education, University of London, 1950-63. FLCM (Hon.) 1949; Editor, Boosey's Sch. Orchestra Series, 1928-40. Liveryman, Worshipful Co. of Musicians, 1961. *Publications* include: The Wondrous Cross (Passion setting), 1955; This Blessed Christmastide (Carol Fantasy), 1964; various church and organ works, incl. Communion Service in G, 1966, and Fantasy on *O Quanta Qualia*; Piano Sonatina in G, 1961; much Educational Music for Piano, Clarinet, Trumpet, Recorder, Sch. Orch., and many children's songs, incl. Fun with Tunes,

1969; *text-books* include: The Musical Touchstone I and II, 1947; School Music Method, 1957; Elements of Music, 1959; First Harmony Book, 1962; Second Harmony Book, 1966; Elements of Organ Playing, 1966; Extemporization for Music Students, 1968; Transposition for Music Students, 1969; Harmony at the Keyboard, 1969. *Address:* 2 Oyster Bend, Three Beaches, Paignton, Devon. *T:* 57475. *Club:* Royal Automobile.

**HUNT, Richard Henry;** Registrar of the High Court of Justice in Bankruptcy, since 1966; *b* 19 Jan. 1912; *s* of Francis John and Lucy Edwyna Louise Hunt; *m* 1947, Peggy Ashworth Richardson; two *s*. *Educ:* Marlborough Coll.; Queen's Coll., Oxford. Called to Bar, 1936. Served with RA, 1939-45: Western Desert, Greece and Crete campaigns (PoW, Crete, 1941). Elected Bencher, Middle Temple, 1964. *Recreations:* foreign travel, languages. *Address:* Handley Edge, Mill Green, Ingatestone, Essex. *Club:* Royal Ocean Racing.

**HUNT, Richard William,** FBA 1961; Keeper of Western Manuscripts, Bodleian Library, and Fellow of Balliol Coll., Oxford, since 1945; *b* 11 April 1908; *m* 1942, Katharine Eva Rowland; three *s*. *Educ:* Haileybury Coll.; Balliol Coll., Oxford. Lecturer in palaeography, University of Liverpool, 1934. *Publications:* articles in learned journals. *Address:* 44 Walton Street, Oxford. *T:* Oxford 57632.

**HUNT, Robert Frederick;** Deputy Chairman, Dowty Group Ltd, since 1959; *b* 11 May 1918; *s* of late Arthur Hunt, Cheltenham and Kathleen Alice Cotton; *m* 1947, Joy Patricia Molly, *d* of late Charles Leslie Harding, Cheltenham; four *d*. *Educ:* Pates Grammar Sch., Cheltenham; N Glos Techn. Coll. Apprenticed Dowty Equipment Ltd, 1935; Chief Instructor to Co.'s Sch. of Hydraulics, 1940; RAF Trng Comd, 1940; Export Man., Dowty Equipment Ltd, 1946; Vice-Pres. and Gen. Man., 1949, Pres., 1954, Dowty Equipment of Canada Ltd; Dir, Dowty Gp Ltd, 1956. Chm., Bd of Trustees, Improvement District of Ajax, Ont., 1954; Dir, Ajax and Pickering Gen. Hosp., 1954; Chm., Cheltenham Hosp. Gp Man. Cttee, 1959; Pres., Soc. of British Aerospace Cos Ltd, 1967-68. CEng; AFCAI 1954; FRAeS 1968. *Recreations:* family interests, gardening. *Address:* Dowty Group Ltd, Arle Court, Cheltenham, Glos. *T:* Cheltenham 21411. *Club:* New (Cheltenham).

**HUNT, Roland Charles Colin,** CMG 1965; British High Commissioner, Trinidad and Tobago, since 1970; *b* 19 March 1916; *s* of Colin and Dorothea Hunt, Oxford; *m* 1939, Pauline, 2nd *d* of late Dr J. C. Maxwell Garnett, CBE; three *s* two *d*. *Educ:* Rugby Sch. (scholar); The Queen's Coll., Oxford (scholar). Entered Indian Civil Service, 1938. Served in various districts in Madras as Sub-Collector, 1941-45; Joint Sec. and Sec., Board of Revenue (Civil Supplies), Madras, 1946-47; joined Commonwealth Relations Office, 1948; served on staff of United Kingdom High Commissioner in Pakistan (Karachi), 1948-50; Mem. UK Delegation to African Defence Facilities Conference, Nairobi, 1951; served in Office of UK High Comr in S Africa, 1952-55; Asst Sec., 1955; attached to Office of High Comr for Fedn of Malaya, Kuala Lumpur, 1956; Dep. High Commisioner for the UK in the Federation of Malaya, Kuala Lumpur, 1957-59; Imperial Defence Coll., 1960; Asst Sec., Commonwealth Relations Office, 1961; British Dep. High Comr in Pakistan, 1962-65; British High Commissioner in Uganda, 1965-67; Asst Under-Sec. of State, CO and FCO, 1967-70. *Recreations:* ball-games, piano-playing. *Address:* Charlton Lodge, near Banbury, Oxon. *T:* King's Sutton 437. *Clubs:* Oxford and Cambridge University; Selangor Golf (Kuala Lumpur).

**HUNT, Thomas Cecil,** CBE 1964; DM Oxford, FRCP, MRCS; Consulting Physician, St Mary's Hospital, Paddington; Physician: Royal Masonic Hospital; King Edward VII Hospital for Officers; Examiner Medicine, Royal College of Physicians and London University; late President: British Society Gastro-enterology; London Medical Society; World Organization Gastro-Enterology; President Oxford Graduate Medical Club; Hon. Member Societies of Gastro-enterology, France, Belgium, Mexico, Nigeria, Switzerland and Sweden; *b* 5 June 1901; *s* of Rev. A. T. G. Hunt; *m* 1930, Barbara, *d* of Egerton Todd, London; one *s* two *d*. *Educ:* St Paul's Sch.; Magdalen Coll., Oxford (Demy); 1st class hons final Physiology; Theodore Williams Scholarships Anatomy, 1922; Pathology, 1924; Demonstrator and Tutor Physiology, Oxford, 1924-25; Radcliffe Prize Pharmacology, 1924; University Scholar St Mary's Hosp., 1924; BM, BCh Oxford, 1926; Radcliffe Travellihg Fellowship, 1927; Asst Medical Unit Mary's, 1927-28; MRCP, 1928; Medical Registrar St Mary's Hosp., 1928-30; Mackenzie Mackinnon Res. Fellow, 1930-31; Mem. Assoc. of Physicians, Great Britain and Ireland, 1931; Fellow, Royal Soc. Medicine (Past Pres. Clinical Sect.); Senior Censor, RCP, 1956; 2nd Vice-Pres., RCP, 1967. Lt-Col 1940-44, Service West Africa, North Africa; Brig. RAMC, 1944-45; Consultant Persia Iraq Command. *Publications:* Peptic Ulcer, Brit. Ency. Med. Pract., 1938; various contribs to medical jls on digestive diseases. *Recreations:* books, gardening. *Address:* 4 Upper Harley Street, NW1. *T:* 01-935 4766; 53 Townshend Road, NW8. *T:* 01-722 5324. *Clubs:* Athenæum, MCC; Vincent's (Oxford).

**HUNT, Vernon Arthur Moore,** CBE 1958; Chief Inspector of Accidents, Board of Trade, since 1968; *b* 27 Dec. 1912; *s* of late Cecil Arthur Hunt, RWS, MA, LLB and late Phyllis Clara Hunt (*née* Lucas); *m* 1949, Betty Yvonne Macduff; two *s* one *d*. *Educ:* Sherborne; Trinity Coll., Cambridge (BA); Coll. of Aeronautical Engrg (Pilot's Licence). Airline Pilot, 1938; Capt., BOAC, 1939-46; Min. of Civil Aviation: Dep. Dir of Ops, 1947; Dir of Control and Navigation, 1949; Dir of Control (Plans), Nat. Air Traffic Control Service, 1962-68. Mollison Trophy, 1939; George Taylor Gold Medal, RAeS, 1954. CEng; FRAeS 1956; FIN 1956. *Publications:* contribs to RAeS and Inst. Navigation Jls. *Recreations:* sailing, gardening. *Address:* Foxworthy, Manaton, near Newton Abbot, South Devon. *T:* Manaton 310. *Clubs:* Athenæum, Royal Aero; Hayling Island Sailing.

**HUNT, Col Vivian;** *see* Hunt, Col G. V.

**HUNT, William Field,** JP; MA; Recorder of Newcastle under Lyme since 1945 (of Bridgnorth, 1941-45); Deputy Chairman Worcester County Quarter Sessions since 1956; Assistant Chairman: Ministry of National Insurance Tribunals for Birmingham District, since 1930; Industrial Tribunal, Birmingham Area, since 1968; A Deputy Chairman, Agricultural Land Tribunal, West Midlands Area; *b* 24 Oct. 1900; *s* of late Edwin James Hunt, JP, The Grange, Bescot, Walsall, and Charlotte Sheldon Field; *m* 1939, Helen Margaret (*d* 1961), *d* of late Dr Henry Malet, Wolverhampton; no *c*. *Educ:* Edgbaston Preparatory Sch., Birmingham; Rydal, Colwyn Bay; Exeter Coll., Oxford. On leaving school, 1919, went into an accountant's office,

1921 became a Bar Student of Inner Temple, to Oxford, called to Bar 1925, and joined Oxford Circuit; Chm. Court of Referees 1930. JP Worcestershire. *Recreations:* music, travel. *Address:* 1 Fountain Court, Steelhouse Lane, Birmingham 4. *T:* 02-236 5721; 30 Cotton Lane, Moseley, Birmingham 13; Windmill Cottage, Holberrow Green, Redditch, Worcs. *T:* Inkberrow 275. *Club:* Union (Birmingham).

**HUNT, Rt. Rev. William Warren;** *see* Repton, Suffragan Bishop of.

**HUNTER, Hon. Lord; John Oswald Mair Hunter,** BA, LLB; a Senator of the College of Justice in Scotland since Oct. 1961; Member of the English Bar since 1937. Member of the Faculty of Advocates, Scotland, 1937-61; QC (Scotland), 1961; Sheriff of Ayr and Bute, 1957-61. *Address:* Little Ruchlaw, Stenton, Dunbar, East Lothian.

**HUNTER, Adam;** MP (Lab) Dunfermline Burghs since 1964; Miner; *b* 11 Nov. 1908; *m*; one *s* one *d*. *Educ:* Kelty Public Elem. Sch. Joined Labour Party, 1933; Member: Exec. Cttee NUM (Scot. Area); Lochgelly Dist Council, 1948-52; Sec., Fife Co-op. Assoc. and Dist Coun., 1947-64. Mem. Fife CC, 1961-64. Voluntary Tutor, Nat. Coun. of Labour Colls. *Recreation:* reading. *Address:* Whitegates Terrace, Kelty, Fife, Scotland.

**HUNTER, Adam Kenneth Fisher;** Sheriff-substitute of Renfrew and Argyll at Paisley since 1953; *b* 1920; *o s* of late Thomas C. Hunter, MBE, AMIEE, and Elizabeth Hunter; *m* 1949, Joan Stella Hiscock, MB, ChB; one *s* two *d*. *Educ:* Dunfermline High Sch.; St Andrews Univ. (MA Hons); Edinburgh Univ. (LLB). Called to Bar, 1946; Chm. of the Supreme Court Legal Aid Cttee of the Law Society of Scotland, 1949-53; Standing Junior Counsel to HM Commissioners of Customs and Excise, 1950-53. *Recreations:* photography, music, motor boating. *Address:* Ravenswood, Bridge of Weir, Renfrewshire. *T:* 2017. *Club:* The Club (Paisley).

**HUNTER, Alastair;** *see* Hunter, M. I. A.

**HUNTER, Rt. Rev. Anthony George Weaver;** *see* Swaziland, Bishop of.

**HUNTER, Prof. Archibald Macbride,** MA, BD, PhD Glasgow, DD Glasgow, DPhil Oxon; Professor of New Testament Exegesis (formerly Biblical Criticism) in Aberdeen University since 1945; Master of Christ's College, Aberdeen, since 1957; *b* 16 Jan. 1906; *s* of late Rev. Archibald Hunter, Kilwinning, and Crissie Swan MacNeish; *m* 1934, Margaret Wylie Swanson; one *s* one *d*. *Educ:* Hutchesons' Grammar Sch., Glasgow; Universities of Glasgow, Marburg and Oxford. Minister in Comrie, Perthshire, 1934-37; Prof. of New Testament, in Mansfield Coll., Oxford, 1937-42; Minister in Kinnoull, Perth, 1942-45. Hastie Lecturer, Glasgow Univ., 1938; Lee Lecturer, 1950; Sprunt Lecturer (Richmond, Va), 1954. *Publications:* Paul and His Predecessors, 1940; The Unity of the New Testament, 1943; Introducing the New Testament, 1945; The Gospel according to St Mark, 1949; The Work and Words of Jesus, 1950; Interpreting the New Testament, 1951; Design for Life, 1953; Interpreting Paul's Gospel, 1954; The Epistle to the Romans, 1955; Introducing New Testament Theology, 1957; The Layman's Bible Commentary, Vol. 22, 1959; Interpreting The Parables, 1960; Teaching and Preaching the New Testament, 1963; The Gospel according to John, 1965; The Gospel according to St Paul, 1966; According to John, 1968; Bible and Gospel, 1969; articles and reviews in theological journals. *Recreation:* fishing. *Address:* 12 Westfield Terrace, Aberdeen. *T:* Aberdeen 25883.

**HUNTER, Dr Colin Graeme,** DSC 1939; FRCP; Director, Tunstall Laboratory of Toxicology, Shell Research Ltd, Sittingbourne, Kent, since 1958; *b* 31 Jan. 1913; *s* of Robert Hunter and Evelyn Harrison; *m* 1944, Betty Louise Riley; one *s* one *d*. *Educ:* Scots Coll., Univ. of Otago, New Zealand. MD 1958, DSc 1970. Christchurch Hosp. NZ, 1937-38; Royal Naval Medical Service, 1938-55; Univ. of Toronto, Canada, 1955-58; Shell Research Ltd, 1958-. Fellow: RCP (Lond.); Roy. Coll. of Pathologists; etc; also Mem. many societies; Freeman of City of London. *Publications:* scientific papers in many jls devoted to chemical and radiation toxicology. *Recreations:* sailing, squash. *Address:* 193 The Gateway, Dover, Kent. *T:* Dover 2172. *Clubs:* Army and Navy; Royal Cinque Ports Yacht, Royal Naval Sailing Association.

**HUNTER, Donald,** CBE 1957; MD, FRCP; Research Fellow in Occupational Health, Guy's Hospital, SE1; Consulting Physician to the London Hospital; Director, Department for Research in Industrial Medicine, MRC, London HOspital, 1943-63; Member World Health Organisation Expert Advisory Panel on Social and Occupational Health, Geneva; Member, Commission Permanente et Association Internationale pour la Médecine du Travail, Geneva; Member Editorial Board (formerly Editor), British Journal of Industrial Medicine; *b* 11 Feb. 1898; *s* of late George Hunter; *m* Mathilde, *d* of late Rev. Gustave Bugnion, Lausanne; two *s* two *d*. *Educ:* London Hospital. Medical Registrar, London Hosp., 1923-25; Res. Fellow, Harvard Medical Sch. and Massachusetts General Hospital, Boston, 1926; Goulstonian Lecturer, RCP, 1930; Arris and Gale Lecturer, RCS, 1931; Croonian Lecturer, RCP, 1942; Cutter Lecturer, Harvard, 1945; Frederick Price Lecturer, QUB, 1949, and Trinity Coll., Dublin, 1956; Ernestine Henry Lecturer, RCP, 1950; Maitland Oration, Sydney Hosp., 1950; McIlrath Guest Prof. in Medicine, Royal Prince Alfred Hospital, Sydney, Australia, 1950; visiting lecturer in Medicine, University of Cape Town, 1953; Sir Arthur Sims Commonwealth Travelling Prof., 1955; Prosser White Orator, 1956; Schorstein Lectr, 1956; Harveian Orator, RCP, 1957; Sir Charles Hastings lectr, 1958. Hon. DSc Durham; Hon. DIH Soc. Apoth., London; Hon. FRCPI; Hon. Foreign Mem. American Acad. of Arts and Sciences. Lately Cons. in Occupational and Environmental Medicine, The Middlesex Hosp., W1. Ex-member: Pharmacopœia Commission; Industrial Health Research Board; Poisons Board; ex-Senior Censor, Royal College of Physicians; ex-President, Association Physicians Great Britain and Ireland. *Publications:* (with Dr R. R. Bomford) Hutchison's Clinical Methods, 15th edn, 1968; The Diseases of Occupations, 4th edn, 1969; Health in Industry, 1959; various contributions to medical and scientific journals. *Address:* 13 Hitherwood Drive, Dulwich, SE19.

**HUNTER, Sir (Ernest) John,** Kt 1964; CBE 1960; DL; Chairman and Managing Director of Swan Hunter Group Ltd; Chairman: Swan Hunter Shipbuilders Ltd; Swan Hunter Shiprepairers Tyne ltd; M. W. Swinburne and Sons Ltd; Barclay Curle and Co.; Wallsend Slipway and Engineering Co.; Brims and Co. Ltd; *b* 3 Nov. 1912; 2nd *s* of George Ernest Hunter and Elsie Hunter (*née* Edwards); *m* 1st, 1937, Joanne Winifred Wilkinson; one *s*; 2nd, 1949, Sybil Malfroy (*née* Gordon); one *s* one *step d*. *Educ:*

Oundle Sch.; Cambridge Univ.; Durham Univ. (BSc). Apprentice, Swan, Hunter and Wigham Richardson Ltd, 1930-31; St John's Coll., Cambridge Univ., 1931-32; Durham Univ. (BSc) 1932-35; Draughtsman, SH and WR Ltd, 1935-37; Asst Manager: Barclay, Curle & Co. 1937-39; SH and WR Dry Docks, 1939-41; Asst Gen. Manager, SH and WR Dry Docks, 1941-43, Gen. Manager, 1943-45, Dir, 1945; Dir, Swan Hunter and Wigham Richardson Ltd, 1945, Chm., 1957-66. Director: Dorman Long Swan Hunter (Pty) Ltd; Shipbuilding Corporation Ltd; British Ship Research Association; Newcastle & Gateshead Water Co.; Common Bros Ltd; Midland Bank. Chairman: N-E Coast Ship-repairers' Association, 1957-58; Tyne Shipbuilders' Association, 1956-57. Dry Dock Owners' and Repairers' Central Council, 1961-62; President: NEC Institution, 1958-60; Shipbuilding Employers' Fedn, 1956-57; British Employers' Confedn, 1962-64; Shipbuilders' and Repairers' Nat. Assoc., 1968-. mem. NEDC, 1962-64. First Chm., Central Training Council, 1964-68. Part-time Mem., BR Bd, 1968-. Mem. of Cttees connected with shipping and with youth. Liveryman, Company of Shipwrights; Freeman of City of London. DL Northumberland, 1968. Hon. DSc Newcastle, 1968. *Publications:* contrib. to Trans NEC Instn. *Recreations:* golf and gardening. *Address:* The Dene, Stocksfield, Northumberland. *T:* Stocksfield 3124. *Clubs:* Garrick; Northern Counties (Newcastle upon Tyne).

**HUNTER, Ian Basil;** stage and screen actor; *b* Cape Town, S Africa, 13 June 1900; *s* of Robert and Isabella Hunter; *m* 1926, Casha (*née* Pringle); two *s. Educ:* St Andrew's Coll., Grahamstown, South Africa; Aldenham, Radlett, Herts; Bradfield Coll., Berks. Served European War, 1917-18, King Edward's Horse. First appearance New Theatre, 1919; subsequently London and New York; Hollywood, 1934-42. Served RNVR, 1942-45. Latterly stage screen and television, Hollywood, New York and London. *Recreations:* sailing, golf, ornithology. *Club:* Garrick.

**HUNTER, Ian Bruce Hope,** MBE 1945; Impresario; Chairman and Managing Director, Harold Holt Ltd; *b* 2 April 1919; *s* of late W. O. Hunter; *m* 1949, Susan, *d* of late Brig. A. G. Russell; four *d. Educ:* Fettes Coll., Edinburgh; abroad as pupil of Dr Fritz Busch and at Glyndebourne. Served War of 1939-45, Lieut-Col. Asst to Artistic Dir, Edinburgh Festival, 1946-48; Artistic Administrator, Edinburgh Festival, 1949-50; Artistic Dir, Edinburgh Festival, 1951-55. Director: Bath Festivals, 1948, 1955, 1958-68; Adviser, Adelaide Festivals, 1960-64; Artistic Director: Festivals of the City of London, 1962-; Brighton Festivals, 1967-; (with Yehudi Menuhin) Windsor Festival, 1969-; Dir-General, Commonwealth Arts Festival, 1965. Dir, British Nat. Day Entertainment, Expo' 67. Mem., Opera/Ballet Enquiry for Arts Council, 1967-69. Trustee, Chichester Festival Theatre Trust; Governor, Yehudi Menuhin Sch. R. B. Bennett Commonwealth Prize for 1966. FRSA (Mem. Council, 1968-). *Recreations:* gardening, sailing. *Address:* 122 Wigmore Street, W1. *T:* 01-935 2331. *Clubs:* Garrick; Seaview Yacht.

**HUNTER, Brig. Ian Murray,** CVO 1954; MBE 1943; psc 1943; fsc (US) 1955; FAIM 1964; Australian Regular Army; *b* Sydney, Aust., 10 July 1917; *s* of late Dr James Hunter, Stranraer, Scotland; *m* 1947, Rosemary Jane Batchelor; two *s* two *d. Educ:* Cranbrook Sch., Sydney; RMC, Duntroon. Lieut Aust. Staff Corps, and AIF 1939; 2/1 MG Bn, 1939-40; T/Capt. 1940; Staff Capt., 25 Inf. Bde, 1940-41; Middle East Staff Coll., Haifa, 1941; DA QMG (1), HQ 6 Div., 1941-42; T/Major 1942; AQMG, NT Force (MBE), 1942-43; Staff Sch. (Aust.), 1943; Gen. Staff 3 Corps and Advanced HQ Allied Land Forces, 1943-44; Lieut-Col 1945; Instructor, Staff Sch., 1945; AQMG, and Col BCOF, 1946-47; AQMG, AHQ and JCOSA, 1947; AA & QMG, HQ, 3 Div., 1948-50; Royal Visit, 1949; Exec. Commonwealth Jubilee Celebrations, 1950-51; CO 2 Recruit Trg Bn, 1952; CO 4 RAR, 1953; Executive and Commonwealth Marshal, Royal Visit, 1952, and 1954; Command and Gen. Staff Coll., Fort Leavenworth, USA, 1954-55; Military Mission, Washington, 1955-56; Officer i/c Admin., N Comd, 1956-59; Comd 11 Inf. Bde, 1959-60; Command 2nd RQR 1960-62; Chief of Staff 1st Div., 1963; Commandant, Australian Staff Coll., 1963-65; Comdr, Papua New Guinea Comd, 1966-69; DQMG, Army HQ, 1969. *Recreations:* golf, squash, swimming, riding. *Address:* Garthland, 42 Charlton Street, Ascot, Brisbane, Queensland 4007, Australia; Finchley, Hargreaves Street, Blackheath, NSW 2785, Australia. *Clubs:* Imperial Service (Sydney); Queensland (Brisbane); Royal Sydney Golf.

**HUNTER, Sir John;** *see* Hunter, Sir E. J.

**HUNTER, John Murray,** MC 1943; Counsellor and Consul-General, HM Embassy, Buenos Aires, since Dec. 1969; *b* 10 Nov. 1920; *s* of Rev. Dr J. M. Hunter; *m* 1948, Margaret, *d* of Stanley Cursiter, *qv*; two *s* three *d. Educ:* Fettes Coll.; Clare Coll., Cambridge. Served Army, 1941-45: Captain, The Rifle Bde. 3rd Sec., FO, 1947; UK High Comr's Office, Canberra, 1948; 2nd Sec., FO, 1951; 1st Sec., HM Embassy, Bogotá, 1953; HM Embassy, Baghdad, 1958; Imp. Def. Coll., 1961; HM Embassy, Prague, 1962; Counsellor, 1963; RNC, 1965; Head of Consular Dept, FO, 1966; Sen. Directing Staff, Jt Services Staff Coll., Latimer, 1967. *Recreations:* music, tennis, golf; formerly Rugby football. *Address:* c/o Foreign and Commonwealth Office, SW1.

**HUNTER, John Oswald Mair;** *see* Hunter, Hon. Lord.

**HUNTER, Major Joseph Charles,** CBE 1959; MC 1918; DL; Chairman Leeds Regional Hospital Board, 1955-63; *b* 1 Sept. 1894; *s* of W. S. Hunter, Gillingcastle, Yorks; *m* 1st, 1920, Cicely Longueville Heywood-Jones (marriage dissolved, 1930); one *s* two *d*; 2nd, 1934, Prudence Josephine Whetstone; two *s. Educ:* Harrow. Commissioned Yorkshire Hussars Yeo., 1912. Served European War, 1914-18, Europe; Regular Commission RA 1916; retired, 1920 (Major, R of O); War of 1939-45, in RA. alderman W Riding of Yorks County Council, 1955-61 (Mem. 1947-55); DL W Riding of Yorks and York, 1959. *Address:* Havikil Lodge, Scotton, Knaresborough, Yorks. *T:* Knaresborough 3400. *Club:* Boodle's.

**HUNTER, Rt. Rev. Leslie Stannard,** MA; DD Lambeth; Hon. LLD Sheffield; Hon. DCL Dunelm; Hon. DD Toronto, 1954; *b* 1890; *yr s* of late Rev. John Hunter, DD, Minister of the King's Weigh House Church, London, and Trinity Church, Glasgow, and Marion Martin; *m* 1919, Grace Marion, *yr d* of late Samuel McAulay, JP, of Aylesby, Lincs. *Educ:* Kelvinside Academy; New Coll., Oxford. Pres. of the Oxford University Lawn Tennis Club, 1911-12; Asst Sec. of the Student Christian Movement of Great Britain and Ireland, 1913-20; Curate of St Peter's, Brockley, SE, 1915-

18; served with YMCA, BEF, 1916, and the Army of Occupation, 1919; Mem. of the Army and Religion Inquiry Commission, 1917-19; Asst Curate of St Martin-in-the-Fields and Chaplain of Charing Cross Hospital, London, 1921-22; Residentiary Canon of Newcastle on Tyne, 1922-26 and 1931-39; Vicar of Barking, Essex, 1926-30; Archdeacon of Northumberland, 1931-39; Chm., Tyneside Council of Social Service, 1933-39; Chaplain to the King, 1936-39; Bishop of Sheffield, 1939-62; Chm. of Sheffield Hospitals Council, 1940-49. House of Lords, 1944-62. Foundation Mem., British Council of Churches; Select Preacher, Universities of: Oxford, Cambridge, Glasgow, Aberdeen, St Andrews and Edinburgh, various years; Birks Memorial Lecturer, McGill Univ., Montreal, 1951. Hon. Freeman of City of Sheffield, 1962. Comdr Order of the Dannebrog, 1952. *Publications:* John Hunter, DD: A Life, 1921; A Parson's Job: Aspects of Work in the English Church, 1931; Let Us Go Forward, 1944; Church Strategy in a Changing World, 1950; The Seed and the Fruit, 1953; A Mission of the People of God, 1961; (Editor and part author) A Diocesan Service Book, 1965; Scandinavian Churches, 1965; The English Church: a New Look, 1966. *Address:* Moorholme, Ashford Road, Bakewell, Derbyshire. *T:* Bakewell 2891.

**HUNTER, Prof. Louis,** PhD, DSc (London); FRIC; retired as Professor of Chemistry and Head of Department of Chemistry, University of Leicester (previously University College) (1946-65); Professor Emeritus, 1966; *b* 4 Dec. 1899; *s* of late George Hunter and Mary Edwards; *m* 1926, Laura Thorpe. *Educ:* East London College (subsequently Queen Mary College), University of London. Assistant Lecturer, University Coll. of North Wales, Bangor, 1920-25; Lecturer and Head of Dept of Chemistry, University Coll., Leicester, 1925, Prof. of Chemistry, 1946, and Vice-Principal, 1952-57, Pro-Vice-Chancellor, University of Leicester, 1957-60. Visiting Professor: Univ. of Ibadan, Nigeria, 1963, and Ahmadu Bello Univ., 1966. Mem. of Council: Chemical Soc., 1944-47, 1950-53, 1956-59; Royal Institute of Chemistry, 1947-50, 1961-64 (Vice-Pres., 1964-66; Chm. E Midlands Section, 1938-40); Sec. Section B (Chemistry), British Assoc. for the Advancement of Science, 1939-51, Recorder, 1951-56, mem. of Council, 1956-60. Hon. Fire Observer, Home Office, 1942-54; Scientific Adviser for Civil Defence, N Midlands, 1951-; Dep. Chm., 1939, Chm., 1952, Leicester Jt Recruiting Bd. *Publications:* mainly in Jl Chem. Soc. *Address:* Orchard Close, Gaulby, Leics. *T:* Billesdon 449. *Clubs:* Savage; Rotary (Leicester).

**HUNTER, (Mark Ian) Alastair,** MD, FRCP; Physician, St George's Hospital, SW1, since 1946; Dean of Medical School, St George's Hospital, since 1956; *b* 18 June 1909; *s* of Mark Oliver Hunter and Diana Rachel (*née* Jones); unmarried. *Educ:* Winchester Coll. (Entrance Exhibition); Trinity Coll., Cambridge. Qualified as Doctor, 1933. MD Cambridge, 1945; FRCP (London), 1947. Asst Registrar, Royal College of Physicians, 1950-57. *Publications:* medical subjects. *Recreations:* various. *Address:* St George's Hospital, 11 Knightsbridge, SW1; (home) 22 St Mark's Crescent, NW1. *Club:* Athenæum.

**HUNTER, Muir Vane Skerrett,** QC 1965; Lieutenant-Colonel (Hon.); MA Oxon; MRI; Barrister-at-Law; *b* 19 Aug. 1913; *s* of late Hugh Stewart Hunter, Home Civil Service; *m* 1939, Dorothea Eason (JP), *e d* of Philip Eason Verstone, *qv*; one *d*. *Educ:* Westminster Sch.; Christ Church, Oxford (Scholar). Called, Gray's Inn, 1938 (*ad eundem* Inner Temple, 1965); Holker Senior Scholar. Served 1940-46: RTR, Royal Glos Hussars, Royal Armoured Corps, 50 Ind. Tank Bde; General Staff Intelligence, GHQ (India), GSO 1 attd War and Legislative Depts, Govt of India; returned to the Bar, 1946; LCC rep. on Chelsea Borough Assessment Cttee, 1946-50; standing counsel (bankruptcy) to Bd of Trade, 1949-65; Dep. Chm., Advisory Cttee on Service Candidates, HO; Chairman: Grosvenor Square Housing Soc. Ltd; N Kensington Neighbourhood Law Centre; Mem. Exec. Cttee and Council of "Justice". *Publications:* editor of Williams on Bankruptcy, 1958-68; Emergent Africa and the Rule of Law, 1963. *Recreations:* theatre, travel (especially E and C Africa), gardening. *Address:* 19 Hillsleigh Road, Campden Hill, W8. *T:* 01-727 8946; (chambers) 3 Paper Buildings, Temple, EC4. *T:* 01-353 3721. *Clubs:* Oxford and Cambridge University; Little Ship.

**HUNTER, Norman Charles;** playwright and novelist; *b* 18 Sept. 1908; *s* of late Lieut-Col C. F. Hunter, DSO, late of 4th Dragoon Guards, and of Mrs N. W. Hunter (*née* Cobbett); *m* 1933, Germaine Dachsbeck, Brussels; no *c*. *Educ:* Repton; Royal Military College, Sandhurst. Commissioned 4/7 Dragoon Guards, 1930; relinquished commission, 1933; Mem. BBC staff, 1938-39; served War of 1939-45, in RA England and Italy. *Publications:* novels include: The Ascension of Mr Judson, 1949; The Losing Hazard, 1950; plays include: All Rights Reserved, 1935; Ladies and Gentlemen, 1937; Grouse in June, 1939; Waters of the Moon, 1951; A Day by the Sea, 1953; A Touch of the Sun, 1958; A Piece of Silver, 1960; The Tulip Tree, 1962; The Excursion, 1964; The Adventures of Tom Random, 1967. *Recreations:* fishing, travelling. *Address:* Pantlludw, Machynlleth, Montgomeryshire. *T:* Machynlleth 2218. *Clubs:* PEN, Dramatists.

**HUNTER, Philip Brown,** TD; Chairman, john Holt & Co. (Liverpool) Ltd, since 1967; *b* 30 May 1909; *s* of Charles Edward Hunter and Marion (*née* Harper); *m* 1937, Joyce Mary (*née* Holt); two *s* two *d*. *Educ:* Birkenhead Sch.; London University. Practised as Solicitor, 1933-. Director: Cammell Laird & Co. Ltd, 1949-70 (Chm. 1966-70); John Holt & Co. (Liverpool) Ltd, 1951- (Exec. Div., 1960); Lonrho Ltd; Guardian Royal Exchange; Guardian Assurance Co. Ltd, 1967. *Recreations:* sailing, gardening. *Address:* John Holt & Co. (Liverpool) Ltd, 380 India Buildings, Liverpool L20 QF; Highfield, Northop, Mold, Flintshire. *T:* Northop 221. *Club:* Caledonian.

**HUNTER, Robert Brockie,** MBE 1945; FRCP; Vice-Chancellor and Principal, University of Birmingham, since 1968; *b* 14 July 1915; *s* of Robert Marshall Hunter and Margaret Thorburn Brockie; *m* 1940, Kathleen Margaret Douglas; three *s* one *d*. *Educ:* George Watson's Coll. MB, ChB Edinburgh, 1938; FRCPE 1950; FACP 1963; FRSEd 1964; FInstBiol 1968. Asst Dir, Edinburgh Post-Graduate Bd for Medicine, 1947; Lectr in Therapeutics, University of Edinburgh, 1947; Commonwealth Fellow in Medicine, 1948; Lectr in Clinical Medicine, University of St Andrews, 1948; Dean of the Faculty of Medicine, 1958-62; Prof. of Materia Medica, Pharmacology and Therapeutics, University of St Andrews, 1948-67, and in University of Dundee, 1967-68; late Consultant Physician to Dundee General Hosps and dir, Post-graduate Medical Education. Hon. Lectr in Physiology, Boston Univ. Sch. of Medicine, USA, 1950. Member: GMC; Ministry of Health Cttee on

Safety of Drugs, 1963-68; Chm., Clinical Trials Sub-Cttee; Mem., UGC, 1964-68 (Chm., Medical Sub-Cttee, 1966-68). Malthe Foundation Lecturer, Oslo, 1958. Editor, Quarterly Journal of Medicine, 1957-67. Fellow (ex-President) Royal Medical Society. Major, Royal Army Medical Corps. Gained Purdue Frederick Medical Achievement Award, 1958. Senior Commonwealth Travelling Fellowship, 1960; Vis. Professor of Medicine: Post-Graduate school, University of Adelaide, 1965; McGill Univ., 1968. Hon. LLD Dundee, 1969. *Publications:* Clinical Science; contrib. to Br. Med. Journ., Lancet, Edinburgh Med. Journ., Quarterly Journ. of Medicine. *Recreation:* fishing. *Address:* 43 Edgbaston Park Road, Birmingham 15. *T:* 021-454 0925. *Club:* Athenæum.

**HUNTER BLAIR, Sir James,** 7th Bt, *cr* 1786; *b* 7 May 1889; *s* of Capt. Sir E. Hunter Blair, 6th Bt, and Cecilia (*d* 1951), *d* of late Sir W. Farrer; *S* father 1945; *m* 1st, 1917, Jean (*d* 1953), *d* of late T. W. McIntyre, Sorn Castle, Ayrshire; two *s*; 2nd, 1954, Mrs Ethel Norah Collins (*d* 1966). *Educ:* Wellington; Balliol Coll., Oxford (1st Hon. Mod., 2nd Greats); Christ's Coll., Cambridge (Forestry Diploma). Articled to solicitor, 1911-14; served with Seaforth Highlanders, 1915-19; District Officer with Forestry Commission, 1920-28. Forestry and Farming at Blairquhan, 1928-. *Publications:* articles on Forestry and cognate subjects in various journals. *Recreation:* collecting pictures. *Heir: s* Edward Thomas Hunter Blair [*b* 1920; *m* 1956, Norma, *d* of W. S. Harris; one adopted *s* one adopted *d*. *Educ:* Eton; Balliol Coll., Oxford]. *Address:* Blairquhan, Maybole, Ayrshire. *Clubs:* Oxford and Cambridge; New (Edinburgh).

**HUNTER JOHNSTON, David Alan;** Member, Monopolies Commission, since 1969; a Managing Director, J. Henry Schroder Wagg & Co. Ltd, since 1965; Chairman, Schroder Executor and Trustee Co. Ltd; a Director of six investment trust cos; Director: Clerical, Medical & General Life Assurance Society; Lindustries Ltd; *b* 16 Jan. 1915; *s* of James Ernest Johnston and Florence Edith Johnston (*née* Hunter); *m* 1949, Philippa Frances Ray; three *s* one *d*. *Educ:* Christ's Hospital; King's Coll., London. Royal Ordnance Factories, Woolwich, 1936-39; S Metropolitan Gas Co., 1939-44; Min. of Economic Warfare (Economic and Industrial Planning Staff), 1944-45; Control Office for Germany and Austria, 1945-47; Sec. to Scientific Cttee for Germany, 1946; FO (German Section), Asst Head, German Gen. Economic Dept, 1947-49; HM Treasury, Supply, Estabt and Home Finance Divs, 1949-53. Central Bd of Finance of Church of England: Sec. (and Fin. Sec. to Church Assembly), 1953-59, and Investment Manager, 1959-65; concurrently, Dir, Local Authorities Mutual Investment Trust, 1961-65, and Investment Man. to Charities Official Investment Fund, 1963-65. Fellow of King's Coll., London, and Hon. Treas. of the Corporation. *Publication:* Money in Christian Life, 1960. *Recreations:* (chief interests) family, theology, country life, music, architecture; a lay reader. *Address:* Sharpes Farm, Little Hadham, Herts. *T:* Much Hadham 2687; J. Henry Schroder Wagg & Co. Ltd, 120 Cheapside, EC2. *Clubs:* Farmers', City of London.

**HUNTER-TOD, Air Marshal John Hunter,** CB 1969; OBE 1957; Head of Engineer Branch and Director-General of Engineering (RAF), since 1970; *b* 21 April 1917; *s* of late Hunter Finlay Tod, FRCS; *m* 1959, Anne, *d* of late Thomas Chaffer Howard; one *s*. *Educ:* Marlborough; Trinity Coll., Cambridge (MA). DCAe 1948. Commissioned, 1940; Fighter Command and Middle East, 1939-45. Group Capt. 1958; Air Cdre 1963. Dir, Guided Weapons (Air), Min. of Aviation, 1962-65; AOEng, RAF Germany, 1965-67; AOC No 24 Group, RAF, 1967-70; Air Vice-Marshal, 1968; Air Marshal, 1970. CEng; FRAeS; FIEE. *Recreation:* gardening. *Address:* Whitetop, Larch Avenue, Sunninghill, Berks. *T:* Ascot 22264. *Clubs:* Army and Navy, Royal Air Force.

**HUNTING, Charles Patrick Maule,** TD 1952; FCA; Chairman of Hunting Group of Companies since 1962; *b* 16 Dec. 1910; *s* of Sir Percy Hunting, *qv*; *m* 1941, Diana, *d* of Brig. A. B. P. Pereira, DSO, of Tavistock, Devon; two *s* two *d*. *Educ:* Rugby Sch.; Trinity Coll., Cambridge. BA (Hons) Mod. and Mediaeval Langs; ACA 1936, FCA 1960. Served Royal Sussex Regt, 1939-45: France and Belgium, 1940; 8th Army, Western Desert, 1942; also in Palestine and Persia; Staff Coll., Camberley (psc), 1945. Entered Hunting Group, 1936, Dir 1946; Chm. Hunting Surveys Ltd, 1956; Pres. Hunting Associates Ltd (Canada), 1956; Vice-Chm. of Group, 1961 (Group includes: Hunting & Son Ltd; Northern Petroleum and Bulk Freighters Ltd; Hunting Associated Industries Ltd; Hunting Surveys and Consultants Ltd; E. A. Gibson & Co. Ltd; Hunting Engineering Ltd; Gibson Petroleum Co. Ltd, Canada; Brazos Young Corp., USA; Aircraft Operating Co., SA; Field Industries Africa Ltd). Director: Berry Wiggins & Co. Ltd; Cttee of London Steamship Owners Mutual Insurance Association Ltd. Mem. Council, Chamber of Shipping of UK 1960 (Chm. Tramp Tanker Section, 1962). *Recreations:* golf, fishing, model railways. *Address:* Merrifields, Lewes Road, Haywards Heath, Sussex. *T:* Scaynes Hill 370. *Clubs:* Bath, Royal Aero, MCC.

**HUNTING, Sir Percy (Llewellyn),** Kt 1960; Director, Hunting Group of Companies (Chairman, 1927-60); *b* 6 March 1885; *e s* of late Charles S. and Agnes Mona Hunting; *m* 1910, Dorothy Edith (*d* 1958), *e d* of late Daniel Maule Birkett, JP; one *s* (and one *s* lost on active service, HMS Repulse, 1941); *m* 1960, Evelyn Marion Birkett, Cranleigh. *Educ:* Loretto; Paris; Armstrong Coll., Newcastle on Tyne (marine engineering); North Eastern Marine Engineering Co. Served European War: 4th (Terr.) Bn Northumberland Fusiliers, 1914-16; seconded 30 Sqdn RFC and 3rd Wing, GHQ Mesopotamia, 1916-18 (despatches twice). International Tanker Owners' Assoc. Ltd (Dep. Chm.) 1934-50; British Chamber of Shipping Oil Tanker Cttee (Vice-Chm.), 1933-35, (Chm.), 1935-40; Tramp Tanker Cttee (Chm.), 1940-43. FICS; MInst Petroleum Technologists; Companion Royal Aeronautical Society; Mem. Photogrammetric Soc. of Gt Brit.; Mem. Soc. of Naval Architects and Marine Engineers (USA); Assoc. Mem. Indep. Petroleum Assoc. of America. *Publication:* The Group and I (private circulation). *Recreations:* arboriculture, travel. *Address:* Old Whyly, East Hoathly, near Lewes, Sussex. *T:* Halland 216. *Clubs:* Travellers', Royal Air Force.

*See also C. P. M. Hunting.*

**HUNTINGDON,** 15th Earl of, *cr* 1529; **Francis John Clarence Westenra Plantagenet Hastings,** MA; artist; *b* 30 Jan. 1901; *s* of 14th Earl and Margaret (*d* 1953), 2nd *d* of Sir Samuel Wilson, sometime MP for Portsmouth; *S* father, 1939; *m* 1st, 1925, Cristina (who obtained a divorce, 1943 and *m* 2nd, 1944, Hon. Wogan Philipps, who *S*, 1962, as 2nd Baron Milford, *qv*; she died 1953), *d* of the Marchese Casati, Rome; one *d*; 2nd, 1944, Margaret Lane, *qv*; two *d*. *Educ:* Eton; Christ Church, Oxford. MA Hons,

History. Played Oxford Univ. Polo team. ARP Officer and Dep. Controller Andover Rural district, 1941-45. Jt Parly Sec., Min. of Agriculture and Fisheries, 1945-50. A pupil of Diego Rivera; *Exhibitions:* Paris, London, Chicago, San Francisco; *murals:* Hall of Science, World's Fair, Chicago, 1933; Marx House, Buscot Park, Faringdon; Birmingham Univ.; Women's Press Club, London; Vineyards, Beaulieu, etc. Chm. of Cttee Soc. of Mural Painters, 1953-57. Pres., Solent Protection Soc., 1958-68. *Publications:* Commonsense about India; The Golden Octopus. *Heir: cousin* David Fox Godolphin Hastings [*b* 13 Dec. 1909; *m* 1945, Mary, *d* of late E. C. Jones, Llandovery, and *widow* of E. H. Power]. *Address:* A15 Albany, Piccadilly, W1; Blackbridge House, Beaulieu, Hants. *Clubs:* Garrick; House of Lords Yacht.
*See also W. L. Wyatt.*

**HUNTINGDON, Bishop Suffragan of,** since 1966; **Rt. Rev. Robert Arnold Schürhoff Martineau,** MA; Residentiary Canon of Ely Cathedral since 1966; *b* 22 Aug. 1913; *s* of late Prof. C. E. Martineau, MA, MCom, FCA, and Mrs Martineau, Birmingham; *m* 1941, Elinor Gertrude Ap-Thomas; one *s* two *d. Educ:* King Edward's Sch., Birmingham; Trinity Hall, Cambridge; Westcott House, Cambridge. Tyson Medal for Astronomy, 1935. Deacon 1938, priest 1939; Curate, Melksham, 1938-41. Chaplain, RAFVR, 1941-46. Vicar: Ovenden, Halifax, 1946-52; Allerton, Liverpool, 1952-65; St Christopher, San Lorenzo, Calif., 1961-62. Hon. Canon of Liverpool, 1961; Rural Dean of Childwall, 1964. Proctor in Convocation, 1964. *Publications:* The Church in Germany in Prayer (ed jtly), 1937; Rhodesian Wild Flowers, 1953; The Office and Work of a Reader, 1970. *Recreations:* gardening, swimming. *Address:* Whitgift House, Ely, Cambs. *T:* Ely 2137.

**HUNTINGDON, Archdeacon of;** *see* Page, Ven. Dennis Fountain.

**HUNTINGFIELD,** 6th Baron *cr* 1796; **Gerard Charles Arcedeckne Vanneck;** Bt 1751; international civil servant with United Nations Secretariat, since 1946; *b* 29 May 1915; *er s* of 5th Baron Huntingfield, KCMG, and Margaret Eleanor (*d* 1943) *o d* of late Judge Ernest Crosby, Grasmere, Rhinebeck, NY; *S* father, 1969; *m* 1941, Janetta Lois, *er d* of Capt. R. H. Errington, RN, Tostock Old Hall, Bury St Edmunds, Suffolk; one *s* three *d. Educ:* Stowe; Trinity College, Cambridge. *Heir: s* Hon. Joshua Charles Vanneck, *b* 10 Aug. 1954. *Address:* 147-47 Charter Road, Jamaica, NY 11435, USA. *T:* JA3-7898; Borley Green, Woolpit, Suffolk. *T:* Rattlesden 414.

**HUNTINGTON-WHITELEY, Sir H. M.;** *see* Whiteley.

**HUNTLEY, Arthur Geoffrey;** President, May Acoustics, Ltd, acoustical engineers; *b* 1897; *s* of Rev. A. H. Huntley, Hull; *m*; two *s. Educ:* Hereford Cathedral Sch. Commenced training as chemical engineer, 1913; commissioned to the Royal Engineers (TA), 1914; served in the Royal Engineers in France, Belgium, and India, 1914-19 (1914-15 Star, GS and allied ribbons, despatches, TD); Lieut-Col RA, retd; secured post with large contracting firm and studied sound, 1920; founded the May Construction Co. Ltd, to undertake the work of acoustical engineers and contractors, 1922; AMIStructE, 1921; Mem. of the Acoustical Soc. of America, 1931. *Publications:* Acoustics, Cantor Lectures, Royal Society of Arts, 1928, and other articles to the technical press; The Acoustics of Structures, paper before the Institute of Structural Engineers, 1925. *Recreation:* bridge. *Address:* Woodpeckers, Burchetts, North Chailey, Sussex.

**HUNTLY,** 12th Marquess of, *cr* 1599, Earl of, *cr* 1450; **Douglas Charles Lindsey Gordon;** Lord of Gordon before 1408; Earl of Enzie, Lord of Badenoch, 1599; Bt 1625; Baron Aboyne, 1627; Viscount Aboyne, 1632; Earl of Aboyne, Viscount Strathavon and Glenlivet, 1660; Baron Meldrum, 1815; sits under creation of 1815; Premier Marquess of Scotland; Gordon Highlanders; *b* 3 Feb. 1908; *s* of late Lieut-Col Douglas Gordon, CVO, DSO, and Violet Ida, *d* of Gerard Streatfeild; *S* great-uncle, 1937; *m* 1941, Hon. Mary Pamela Berry (marriage dissolved, 1965), *o d* of 1st Viscount Kemsley; one *s* one *d. Heir: s* Earl of Aboyne, *qv. Address:* Aboyne Castle, Aberdeenshire. *T:* Aboyne 136; 10 Duchess Street, W1. *T:* 01-580 1234. *Club:* Royal Northern (Aberdeen).
*See also Lord Adam Gordon.*

**HURCOMB,** family name of **Baron Hurcomb.**

**HURCOMB,** 1st Baron, *cr* 1950, of Campden Hill; **Cyril William Hurcomb,** GCB, 1946 (KCB 1938; CB 1922); KBE 1929 (CBE 1918); President, Society for the Promotion of Nature Reserves, 1951-61; Member, Nature Conservancy, 1953-62 (Chairman, 1961-62) and now Member of its Committee for England; Vice-President, International Union for the Protection of Nature, 1954-60; President, Royal Society for Protection of Birds, 1962-66; Chairman, Advisory Committee on Meteorological Office, 1958-70; Founder-President, Council for Nature, 1958; Trustee, British Museum, 1960-63; *b* 1883; *m* 1911, Dorothy Brooke (*d* 1947); two *d. Educ:* Oxford High Sch.; St John's Coll., Oxford (Hon. Fellow, 1938). Entered Secretary's Office, the Post Office, 1906; Private Sec. to Post-master General, 1911; Dep. Dir, and later, Dir of Commercial Services, Ministry of Shipping, 1915-18; Permanent Sec., Ministry of Transport, 1927-37; President, Institute of Transport, 1935-36; Chm., Electricity Commission, 1938-47; Dir-Gen., Ministry of Shipping, 1939-41; Dir-Gen., Ministry of War Transport, 1941-47; Chm. of British Transport Commission, 1947-53. Silver Medal, Zoological Soc. of London, 1965. Chevalier of the Legion of Honour; Grand Officer Order of Orange-Nassau; Knight Grand Cross Order of St Olav; Grand Officer Order of the Crown of Belgium; Grand Cross of Order of George I, King of the Hellenes. *Recreations:* fishing and birds. *Address:* 47 Campden Hill Court, W8. *Club:* Athenæum.

**HURLEY, Ven. Alfred Vincent,** CBE 1945 (OBE 1944); TD 1944; Archdeacon of Dudley, 1951-68; Rector of Old Swinford, 1948-64; *b* 12 Jan. 1896; *s* of Alfred Walter and Phoebe Hurley, Reading; *m* 1929, Jenny Drummond, 2nd *d* of Henry John Sansom, Pennsylvania Castle, Portland, Dorset; one *s* three *d. Educ:* Queen's Sch., Basingstoke; Keble Coll., Oxford (MA); Cuddesdon Coll. Artists' Rifles, 1915; Royal Flying Corps, 1916-19. Curate, Armley, Leeds, 1922; Chaplain: Leeds Prison, 1923-24; Portland Borstal Instn, 1924; Dep. Gov. Portland Borstal Instn, 1928; Rector of Portland, 1931; Rural Dean of Weymouth, 1937; Canon and Preb. of Salisbury, 1939. Chaplain to Forces, 4th Dorsets, 1939; SCF, 42 East Lancs Div. 1940; Asst Chaplain General, 8th Army, 1944 (despatches); Dep. Chaplain General, South East Asia Allied Land Forces, 1945-46; Hon. Canon of Worcester, 1951-; Exam. Chap. to Bishop of Worcester, 1951-68. *Address:* Old House, 1st Marine Avenue, Barton-on-Sea, Hants. *T:* New Milton 952.

**HURLEY, Sir Hugh;** *see* Hurley, Sir W. H.

**HURLEY, Sir John Garling,** Kt 1967; CBE 1959; Managing Director, Berlei United Ltd, Sydney, 1948-69; *b* 2 Oct. 1906; *s* of late John Hurley and late Annie Elizabeth (*née* Garling); *m* 1929, Alice Edith (*née* Saunders); three *d. Educ:* Sydney Techn. High Sch. With Berlei group of cos, 1922-69, incl. Berlei (UK) Ltd, London, 1931-36; Chm., William Adams & Co. Pty Ltd, Sydney; Director: Manufacturers' Mutual Insurance Ltd, Sydney; Develt Finance Corporation Ltd. Member: Associated Chambers of Manufactures of Austr. (Pres., 1955-57); Chamber of Manufactures of NSW (Pres., 1955-57); Manufacturing Industries Adv. Council, 1958-; Techn. Educn Adv. Coun. of NSW, 1958-; Industrial Design Coun. of Austr., 1958-; Institute of Directors; Australian-American Association; Council, Abbotsleigh Sch., 1960-66; Royal Agricultural Society, Sydney; Sydney Cricket Ground Trust. Chm., Standing Cttee on Productivity, Ministry of Labour Adv. Coun., 1957-58; Leader of Austr. Trade Mission to India and Ceylon, 1957; Dir on Hon. Bd, Austr. Nat. Travel Assoc., 1956-; Director: Med. Foundn of University of NSW; Royal North Shore Hosp. of Sydney, 1969-. Trustee, Museum of Applied Arts and Sciences, NSW, 1958-. FAIM 1949. *Recreations:* tennis, bowls, photography. *Address:* The Steps, 16 King Edward Street, Pymble, NSW 2073, Australia. *T:* 44-2762. *Clubs:* Australian, Royal Sydney Yacht Squadron, Australasian Pioneers' (Sydney); Warrawee Bowling.

**HURLEY, Sir (Wilfred) Hugh,** Kt 1963; Chief Justice, High Courts of Northern States of Nigeria, 1967-69; retired, 1969; *b* 16 Oct. 1910; *s* of Henry Hutchings Hurley and Elizabeth Louise (*née* Maguire); *m* 1940, Una Kathleen (*née* Wyllie); one *s* two *d. Educ:* St Stephen's Green Sch., Dublin; Trinity Coll., Dublin. Barrister-at-Law (King's Inns, Dublin), 1935; Magistrate, Nigeria, 1940; Chief Registrar, Supreme Court, Nigeria, 1949; Puisne Judge, Supreme Court, Nigeria, 1953-55, Judge, 1955-57, Senior Puisne Judge, 1957-60 and Chief Justice, 1960-67, High Court, Northern Nigeria. Chm., Judicial Service Commn, Northern Nigeria, and Mem., Judicial Service Commission, Federation of Nigeria, 1960-63. Hon. LLD Ahmadu Bello Univ., Nigeria, 1968. *Address:* Long Hill, Broadway, Worcs.

**HURLL, Alfred William,** CVO 1970; CBE 1955; Chief Executive Commissioner and Member of Council, The Scout Association, 1948-70; *b* 10 Sept. 1905; *s* of Charles Alfred Hurll; *m* 1933, Elsie Margaret, *d* of Frederick Sullivan; one *s* one *d. Educ:* Grammar Sch., Acton. Joined staff, The Scouts assoc. HQ, 1921; Sec., Home Dept, 1935; Asst Gen. Sec., 1938; Gen. Sec., 1941. *Publication:* (co-author) BP's Scouts, 1961. *Recreations:* cricket, theatre. *Address:* 106 Montrose Avenue, Whitton, Twickenham. *T:* 01-894 1957. *Club:* MCC.

**HUROK, Sol,** US Impresario; *b* Pogar, Russia, 9 April 1888; *s* of Israel and Naomi Hurok; *m*; one *d*; *m* 1939, Emma Runitch. *Educ:* Russia. Became US citizen, 1914. Manager of weekly concerts at Hippodrome, NYC, 1915. Since then has been impresario for many famous dancers and musicians, including: Anna Pavlova, Isadora Duncan, Feodor Chaliapin, and numerous living artistes of various countries. Has presented many ballet companies in America, including: Sadler's Wells (now the Royal Ballet), and famous continental ballet companies. Has also presented in America: Emlyn Williams as Charles Dickens, Jean Louis-Barrault in French plays, French theatre companies and the Old Vic Company; also Bands of British Regiments. Holds: Hon. doctorates; Legion of Honour (France); Hon. CBE 1960. *Address:* 730 Fifth Avenue, New York, NY 10019, USA.

**HURRELL, Col Geoffrey Taylor,** OBE 1944; Lord Lieutenant of Cambridgeshire and Isle of Ely since 1965; *b* 12 March 1900; *s* of Arthur Hurrell and Emily Taylor; *m* 1934, Mary Crossman; one *s* one *d. Educ:* Rugby; Sandhurst. Gazetted 17th Lancers, 1918; Lieut-Col comdg 17th/21st Lancers, 1940; Col 1944. High Sheriff, Cambridgeshire and Huntingdonshire, 1963; JP Cambs 1952. *Recreations:* hunting, shooting. *Address:* Park House, Harston, near Cambridge. *Clubs:* Cavalry, United Hunts.

**HURRELL, Ian Murray,** MVO 1961; HM Ambassador to Costa Rica since 1968; *b* 14 June 1914; *s* of Capt. L. H. M. Hurrell and Mrs Eva Hurrell; *m* 1939, Helen Marjorie Darwin; no *c. Educ:* Dover Coll. Anglo-Iranian Oil Co., 1932-34; Indian Police (United Provinces), 1935-47; entered HM Foreign (subseq. Diplomatic) Service, 1948; Vice-Consul, Shiraz, 1949-51; Consul, Benghazi, 1952; FO, 1952-53; 1st Sec., Quito, 1954 (Chargé d'Affaires, 1955); Bangkok, 1956-60; Tehran, 1960-64; Ankara (UK Delegn to CENTO), 1964-67. Imperial Order of the Crown (Iran). *Recreations:* rambling, photography, ski-ing, skin-diving, tennis, horses, gardening, chess, etc. *Address:* Embajada Británica, Apartado U, San José, Costa Rica; The Thatched Cottage, Brook Avenue, New Milton, Hants. *T:* New Milton 1163. *Clubs:* Royal Over-Seas League; Country (San José).

**HURRY, Leslie;** artist; *b* 10 Feb. 1909; *s* of Alfred George Hurry and Edith Louise Perry Butcher. *Educ:* St John's Wood Art Schs; Royal Academy Schools. Theatrical productions, settings and costumes: Hamlet Ballet, Sadler's Wells Co., 1942; Le Lac des Cygnes, Sadler's Wells Co., 1943 and 1952; La Scherzi della Sortie, Mercury Ballet, 1951; Hamlet, Old Vic, 1944; Turandot, Covent Garden Opera, 1947; Medea, Edinburgh Festival, 1948; Cymbeline, 1949, King Lear, 1950, Stratford Memorial Theatre; La Forza del Destino, Edinburgh Festival (Glyndebourne Opera), 1951; Tamburlaine, Old Vic, 1951; Living Room, Wyndhams, 1953; Venice Preserv'd, Lyric, Hammersmith; Der Ring des Nibelungen, Covent Garden Opera; The Tempest, Old Vic; Richard II, Old Vic; Measure for Measure, Old Vic (Australian Tour); Tamburlaine (Toronto and New York); Timon of Athens (Old Vic Theatre); The Gates of Summer (Provinces); The Moon and Sixpence, Sadler's Wells Opera Co.; Richard II, Old Vic Co. (Amer. and Canadian Tour); Richard III, Old Vic; The Hidden King, Edinburgh Festival; Henry VI, Parts I, II, III, Old Vic; Cat on a Hot Tin Roof, Comedy Theatre; King Lear, Old Vic; Hamlet Ballet (revival); Tristan and Isolde, Covent Garden Opera; costumes and setting for Mary Stuart (Edinburgh Fest., Old Vic), 1958; The Cenci, Old Vic; Andrea Chénier, Sadler's Wells Opera; St Joan, Old Vic; Troilus and Cressida, Royal Stratford Theatre; The Duchess of Malfi, Aldwych; Hamlet, Stratford upon Avon; Becket, Aldwych; Mourning Becomes Electra, Old Vic; St Joan, American Tour and Old Vic; A Village Romeo and Juliet (Delius Festival) Sadler's Wells Opera Co.; The Tempest, Old Vic; Beggar's Opera, Royal Shakespeare Co., Aldwych; (costumes) Maggie May, King Lear, Julius Cæsar, Stratford, Ont.; Swan Lake, Royal Ballet Touring Co.; Nicholas Romanov, Manitoba Theatre

Centre, Canada; Stratford Festival, Canada: Last of the Tsars; The Government Inspector; Albert Herring; A Midsummer Night's Dream; La Cenerentola; School for Scandal; Sadler's Wells Opera Co.: Fidelio; Queen of Spades; Hamlet, (opera, Humphrey Searle), Royal Opera, Covent Garden, 1969, etc. Exhibitions: Wertheim, 1937; Redfern, 1941, 1942, 1945; Rowland Browse Delblanco, 1946-50; Paintings and Theatre Designs (auspices Nat. Gall., Canada); Theatre Designs, Arts Council, 1964; paintings, Mercury Gall. *Works in galleries:* Victoria and Albert Museum; Birmingham City Art Gallery; Whitworth Art Gallery, Manchester; Brighton Art Gallery; Melbourne Art Gallery, Australia. *Publications:* (Theatre Design) Leslie Hurry, 1946; (Paintings and Drawings) Leslie Hurry, 1952. *Address:* The Bunting's, Hundon, near Clare, Suffolk. *T:* Hundon 269.

**HURST, Sir Alfred (William),** KBE 1929; CB 1926; *b* 1 Aug. 1884; *s* of G. E. Hurst; *m* 1909, Gertrude Alice, *e d* of W. H. Hurst; one *s* one *d*. *Educ:* Market Bosworth; Emmanuel Coll., Cambridge (Senior Scholar and Dixie Scholar); First Class Natural Sciences Tripos, 1905; Senior Optime Mathematical Tripos, 1906. Entered HM Treasury (first place in Civil Service (Class I) Exam.), 1907; Under-Sec. Treasury, 1932; seconded for Service with Import Duties Advisory Cttee as Adviser and Personal Asst to Chm., 1932; Under-Sec. for Mines, 1940-42; in charge of Reconstruction. Secretariat of the War Cabinet, 1942-44. Independent Chm. of London Builders' Conference, 1936-40 and 1944-57. *Address:* Burke's Grove, Burke's Road, Beaconsfield, Bucks.

**HURST, Sir Donald;** *see* Hurst, Sir J. H. D.

**HURST, Edward Weston,** MD, DSc (Birmingham); FRCP; retired 1969; formerly Consultant Pathologist to Industrial Hygiene Research Laboratories, Imperial Chemical Industries Ltd, Macclesfield; *b* Birmingham, 1900; *s* of Edward William Hurst and Clarinda, *d* of Thomas Wem; *m* 1926, Phyllis Edith, *d* of J. G. Picknett, MA, Leicester; three *d*; *m* 1942, Barbara Ternent, *d* of W. T. Cooke, DSc, Adelaide; one *s* one *d*. *Educ:* King Edward's Sch., Birmingham; Birmingham Univ. BSc 1920; MB, ChB, 1922; Hons in Obstetrics and Gynæcology, Queen's and Ingleby Scholarships; Walter Myers Travelling Student, Univ. of Birmingham, 1923-24; MD, 1924; Postgraduate study and research work at National Hospital, Queen Square, London, 1923-25; Pathologist to Miller General Hospital for South-East London, 1926-28; Pathologist to Milbank Fund for Research on Poliomyelitis, 1928-32; DSc, 1932; MRCP, 1932; FRCP, 1940; Associate at Rockefeller Institute, Princeton, NJ, 1932-34; Mem. of Research Staff, Lister Institute of Preventive Medicine, London, 1932-36; Reader in Experimental Pathology, University of London, 1932-36; Dir of the Institute of Medical and Veterinary Science, Adelaide, 1936-43; Keith Sheridan Professor of Experimental Medicine, University of Adelaide, 1938-43; William Withering Lecturer, University of Birmingham, 1935; Sir Joseph Bancroft Orator, Qld Branch BMA, 1940; G. E. Rennie Memorial Lecturer, RACP, 1941. *Publications:* Numerous contributions to pathology and allied subjects in English and foreign journals. *Recreation:* photography. *Address:* 9 Planet Court, Tigne Sea Front, Sliema, Malta, GC.

**HURST, George;** Artistic Advisor, Bournemouth Symphony Orchestra, since 1969; *b* 20 May 1926; Rumanian father and Russian mother. *Educ:* various preparatory and public schs. in the UK and Canada; Royal Conservatory, Toronto, Canada. First prize for Composition, Canadian Assoc. of Publishers, Authors and Composers, 1945. Asst Conductor, Opera Dept, Royal Conservatory of Music, of Toronto, 1946; Lectr in Harmony, Counterpoint, Composition etc, Peabody Conservatory of Music, Baltimore, Md, 1947; Conductor of York, Pa, Symph. Orch., 1950-55, and concurrently of Peabody Conservatory Orch., 1952-55; Asst Conductor, LPO, 1955-57, with which toured USSR 1956; Associate conductor, BBC Northern Symphony Orchestra, 1957; Principal Conductor, BBC Northern Symphony Orchestra (previously BBC Northern Orchestra), 1958-68. Since 1956 frequent guest conductor in Europe, Israel, Canada, South Africa. *Publications:* piano and vocal music (Canada). *Recreations:* ornithology, horse-riding, chess. *Address:* 21 Oslo Court, NW8. *T:* 01-722 3088.

**HURST, Harold Edwin,** CMG 1932; MA, DSc Oxon; FInstP; Professional Associate, Institution of Water Engineers; Hydrological Adviser, Ministry of Irrigation, Egypt; *b* 1 Jan. 1880; *s* of Charles Hurst, Wigston Magna, Leics; *m* 1st, Winifred, *d* of late Capt. A. B. Hawes; 2nd, Marguerite, *d* of late Dr G. C. B. Hawes, Pangbourne; two *s*. *Educ:* Alderman Newton's Sch., Leicester; Hertford Coll., Oxford. Lectr and demonstrator Oxford Univ. Electrical Laboratory, 1903-6; Joined Survey of Egypt, 1906; Dir-Gen., Physical Dept, Min. of Public Works, Egypt, 1919-46. Thrice awarded Telford Premium, and Telford Gold Medal, 1957, by Instn of Civil Engrs for work on the utilization of Nile waters; Order of the Nile 2nd Class; Order of Ismail 3rd Class; travelled extensively in the Nile Basin for purposes of hydrological reconnaissance. *Publications:* papers on physics, the measurement of water, the magnetic survey of Egypt, and the Nile Basin, 1931 onwards; The Nile, 1952, 1957; (with Black and Simaika) Long Term Storage, 1965. *Recreations:* mechanical work, fishing, shooting. *Address:* Sandford-on-Thames, Oxford OX4 4XZ. *T:* Oxford 77293. *Clubs:* Royal Societies; Gezira Sporting (Cairo).

**HURST, His Honour Sir (James Henry) Donald,** Kt 1954; retired as Judge of County Courts; *b* 1895; *er s* of late J. G. Hurst, KC, Recorder of Birmingham; *m* 1924, Laura Olive, *d* of late James Bannister, Leicester; two *d*. *Educ:* King Edward VI Sch., Birmingham; Wadham Coll., Oxford. Served European War, 1914-18, Argyll and Sutherland Highlanders (wounded). Judge of County Courts Circuit 23 (Coventry, Northampton, etc), 1937-41; Circuit 36 (Oxford, Reading, etc), 1941-62, and of Circuit 53 (Cheltenham, Tewkesbury, Northleach, etc), 1943-62; retd Oct. 1962. Chm. Oxfordshire QS, 1947-62, Dep. Chm., 1962-67. *Address:* Croft Northway, Godalming, Surrey. *T:* Godalming 5261. *Club:* National Liberal.

**HURST, Leonard Henry,** CBE 1949; *b* Shanghai, 22 April 1889; *y s* of late Richard Willett Hurst, HM Consular Service (China); *m* 1st, 1920, Annie (*d* 1922), *d* of Arthur Liley; 2nd, 1928, Olive Rose Madeline (*d* 1967), *widow* of Major R. M. F. Patrick. *Educ:* Tonbridge; Pembroke Coll., Cambridge. Entered Levant Consular Service, 1908; Vice-Consul at Sofia, 1914; Consul at Bengasi, 1924, at Port Said, 1926, and at Basra, 1932; Consul-Gen. at Rabat, 1936-40, at Istanbul, 1942-47, at Tunis, 1947-49; retired from HM Foreign Service, Nov. 1949; British Consul, Rhodes, 1953-1957; British Consul, Crete, 1957-58.

*Recreations:* mountaineering, numismatics. *Address:* Brynglas, Llechryd, Cards. *T:* Llechryd 393. *Club:* Alpine.

**HURST, Margery;** Joint Chairman and Managing Director, Brook Street Bureau of Mayfair Ltd; *b* 23 May 1913; *d* of late Samuel and Deborah Berney; *m* 1948, Eric Hurst, Barrister-at-law; two *d. Educ:* Brondesbury and Kilburn High Sch.; Minerva Coll. RADA. Joined ATS on Direct Commission, 1943 (1939-45 war medal); invalided out of the service, 1944. Commenced business of Brook St Bureau of Mayfair Ltd, 1946; founded Margery Hurst Schs and Colls for administrative and secretarial Studies. Co-opted Mem. of LCC Children's Cttee, 1956. Started non-profit making social clubs for secretaries, called Society for International Secretaries, in London, 1960; now in New York, San Francisco, Boston and Sydney; awarded Pimm's Cup for Anglo-American friendship in the business world, 1962. Member: American Cttee, BNEC, 1967-70; Exec. Cttee, Mental Health Research Fund, 1967-. *Publication:* No Glass Slipper (autobiography), 1967. *Recreations:* tennis, swimming, drama, opera. *Address:* Flutters Hill, Long Cross, near Chertsey, Surrey. *Club:* Wentworth Country.

**HURST, Dr Robert,** GM 1944; Director of Research, British Ship Research Association, since 1963; *b* Nelson, NZ, 3 Jan. 1915; *s* of late Percy Cecil Hurst and late Margery Hurst; *m* 1946, Rachael Jeanette (*née* Marsh); three *s. Educ:* Nelson Coll.; Canterbury Coll., NZ (MSc); Cambridge Univ. (PhD). Experimental Officer, Min. of Supply, engaged in research in bomb disposal and mine detection, 1940-45. Group Leader Transuranic Elements Group, AERE, Harwell, 1948-55; Project Leader, Homogeneous Aqueous Reactor Project, AERE, Harwell, 1956-57; Chief Chemist, Research and Development Branch, Industrial Group UKAEA, 1957-58; Director, Dounreay Experimental Reactor Establishment, UKAEA, 1958-63. *Publication:* Editor, Progress in Nuclear Engineering, Series IV (Technology and Engineering), 1957. *Recreations:* gardening, sailing. *Address:* 112 Moorside North, Newcastle upon Tyne NE4 9DX. *T:* Newcastle upon Tyne 39187. *Club:* Athenæum.

**HURSTFIELD, Joel,** DLit (London); Astor Professor of English History, University College, London, since 1962; *b* 4 Nov. 1911; *m* 1938, Elizabeth Valmai Walters, Hirwaun, Glam; one *s* one *d. Educ:* Owen's Sch.; University Coll., London. BA 1st Class Hons, 1934; Pollard and Gladstone Prizeman. Mem. Brit. Univs Debating Team (USA Tour), 1934. University of London Postgrad. Studentship, 1935-36; Asst Lectr (later Lectr) University Coll., Southampton, 1937-40; Asst Comr, Nat. Savings Cttee, 1940-42; Official Historian, Offices of War Cabinet, 1942-46. Lecturer: QMC, London, 1946-51; UC London, 1951-53; Reader in Mod. Hist., UC London, 1953-59; Prof. of Mod. Hist., UC London, 1959-62; Fellow of University Coll., London, 1963-. Visiting Prof., USA, 1967; Public Orator, University of London, 1967-; Shakespeare Birthday Lectr, Washington, 1969. *Publications:* Control of Raw Materials, 1953; The Queen's Wards, 1958; Elizabeth I and the Unity of England, 1960; The Elizabethan Nation, 1964; Jt Ed. Elizabethan Government and Society, 1961; Ed. Tudor Times (English History in Pictures), 1964; Jt Ed. Shakespeare's World, 1964; Ed. The Reformation Crisis, 1965. Articles and Reviews in History, Eng. Hist. Rev., Econ. Hist. Rev., Guardian, Daily Telegraph, etc. *Recreation:* walking. *Address:* 7 Glenilla Road, Hampstead, NW3. *T:* 01-794 2891; Northwood Cottage, 98 Northwood Road, Tankerton, Kent. *Club:* Athenæum.

**HUSAIN, Mohammad Arshad,** Sitara-i-Pakistan; *b* 9 Jan. 1910; *o s* of M. Afzal Husain; *m* Husanara, 3rd *d* of late Sir Fazl-e-Husain, KCSI, KCIE; one *s* one *d. Educ:* Govt Coll., Lahore; St Catharine's Coll., Cambridge; Middle Temple, London. Advertising Cons., Govt of India, 1943; Dir Publicity Govt of Pakistan, 1947; joined Pakistan Foreign Service, 1950; Dep. Sec., 1950-53; Chargé d'Affaires, Brussels, 1954-56, Jt Sec., 1957-59; Ambassador to Sweden, Denmark, Norway and Finland, 1959-61; Ambassador to USSR and Czechoslovakia, 1961-63; High Comr, New Delhi, 1963-68; Foreign Minister, Pakistan, 1968-69. *Address:* 18 Old F.C.C., Ferozpur Road, Lahore, Pakistan. *Club:* Karachi (Karachi).

**HUSBAND, Henry Charles,** CBE 1964; BEng, DSc, FICE, PPIStructE, FIMechE, FAmSCE; Senior Partner, Husband & Co., Consulting Engineers, Sheffield, London and Colombo, since 1937; *b* 30 Oct. 1908; *s* of Prof. Joseph Husband, DEng, MICE and Ellen Walton Husband; *m* 1932, Eileen Margaret, *d* of late Henry Nowill, Sheffield; two *s* two *d. Educ:* King Edward VII Sch., Sheffield; Sheffield Univ. Asst to Sir E. Owen Williams, MICE, 1931-33; Engr and Surveyor to First Nat. Housing Trust Ltd, 1933-36; planning and construction of large housing schemes in England and Scotland; from 1936, designed public works at home and overseas incl. major road, bridge, drainage and water supply schemes; Princ. Techn. Officer, Central Register, Min. of Labour and Nat. Service, 1939-40; Asst Dir, Directorate of Aircraft Prodn Factories, Min. of Works, 1943-45; designed first high altitude testing plant for continuous running of complete jet engines, 1946, also research estabs for Brit. Iron and Steel Res. Assoc., Prodn Engrg Res. Assoc. and other industrial organisations; designed and supervised construction of 250 ft diameter radio telescope, Jodrell Bank, and other large radio telescopes at home and abroad incl. steerable aerials for GPO satellite stn, Goonhilly Downs, Cornwall. Chm., Yorks Assoc. ICE, 1949; Pres., Instn Struct. Engrs, 1964-65; Chm., Adv. Cttee on Engrg and Metallurgy, University of Sheffield, 1962-65; Mem. Ct, University of Sheffield; Mem. Cons. Panel in Civil Engrg, Bradford Inst. of Technology, 1962-; Mem., Coun. of Engrg Instns, 1965-66; Chm., Assoc. of Consulting Engineers, 1967. Hon. DSc, Manchester Univ., 1964; Hon. DEng Sheffield Univ., 1967. Sir Benjamin Baker Gold Medal, ICE, 1959; (first) Queen's Gold Medal for Applied Science, Royal Society, 1965; Wilhelm Exner Medal for Science and Technology, University of Vienna, 1966. *Publications:* contributions to British and foreign engrg jls. *Recreations:* sailing, walking. *Address:* Jowitt House, School Green Lane, Sheffield 10. *T:* 303395. *Clubs:* Royal Thames Yacht, St Stephen's, Royal Automobile; Sheffield (Sheffield).

**HUSKISSON, Alfred,** OBE 1951; MC 1917, and Bar 1918; a Director of S. Simpson and of Simpson (Piccadilly) (Dep. Chm. 1959-64; Managing Director Simpson (Piccadilly), 1940-59, S. Simpson Ltd, 1942-59); *b* 27 June 1892; *s* of Joseph Cliffe and Martha Huskisson; *m* 1922, Constance, *d* of late Arthur Frederick Houfton, Nottingham; one *s* one *d. Educ:* privately. Served European War, 1914-18 (despatches); granted rank of Major, 1920. Managing Dir William Hollins & Co., Nottingham, 1929-38. Mem. Allies Welcome

Cttee, 1943-50. Life Member: Overseas League, 1943; National Playing Fields Assoc. 1952. Hon. Treas. Abbey Div., Westminster Conservative Assoc., 1945-54; No 1 Assoc. Mem. Variety Club of Gt Brit., 1950-; Chm. Wholesale Clothing Manufacturers Assoc., 1952; Pres. Appeal Cottage Homes, Linen and Woollen Drapers, 1953; Master of the Worshipful Co. of Woolmen, 1952-53, 1964-65; Past Pres. The Piccadilly and St James's Assoc. (Chm. 1950-53); Vice-Pres. Westminster Philanthropic Soc. (Chm. 1956); Vice-Chm. Machine Gun Corps Officers' Club, 1960; Member: Grand Council of FBI, 1953-65; British Olympic Assoc. Appeals Cttee, 1955-56; British Empire & Commonwealth Games Appeal Cttee, 1958; British Olympic Assoc. Appeals Cttee, 1959-60; Export Council for Europe, 1960-66; Empire & Commonwealth Games UK Industrial Appeal Cttee, 1961; Chm. various Westminster and other appeals in the past. *Recreation:* golf. *Address:* Rothwell Dene, Milner Road, Bournemouth, Hants. *Clubs:* Simpson Services, Lord's Taverners (Pres. 1954, 1955), MCC; British Sportsman's, Ferndown Golf, Isle of Purbeck Golf.

**HUSKISSON, Robert Andrews;** Director and General Manager, Shaw Savill & Albion Co. Ltd, since 1966; *b* 2 April 1923; *y s* of Edward Huskisson and Mary Huskisson (*née* Downing); *m* 1969, Alice Marian Swaffin. *Educ:* Merchant Taylors' Sch.; St Edmund Hall, Oxford. Served Royal Corps of Signals, 1941-47 (Major). Joined Shaw Savill, 1947. Director: Overseas Containers Ltd, 1967; Container Fleets Ltd, 1967; Cairn Line of Steamships Ltd, 1969. Chairman, British Shipping Fedn, 1968; President, International Shipping Fedn, 1969. *Recreations:* golf, music. *Address:* Merle Cottage, The Retreat, Shenfield, Essex. *Club:* Vincent's (Oxford).

**HUSSEIN, Amin Ahmed,** GCVO (Hon.) 1964; OBE (Hon.) 1952; Sudanese Ambassador: to USA, 1965-67; to the Court of St James's, 1961-65; *b* 1913; *m* 1940; no *c. Educ:* Gordon Memorial Coll., Khartoum. Joined the Ministry of the Interior as Sub Mamur (Police) and promoted to Commissioner of Police, Dec. 1954; Dep. Under-Sec. for Security in the Min. of Interior, 1957; Dep. Permanent Under-Sec. (personal rank of Ambassador), Min. of Foreign Affairs, 1957-61. Grand Officer of Ethiopian Star, 1960; Long Distinguished Service Decoration, 1962. *Address:* c/o Ministry of Foreign Affairs, Khartoum, Sudan.

**HUSSEY, Dyneley,** MA (Oxon); Music Critic to The Listener, 1946-60; *b* 27 Feb. 1893; *s* of Col Charles Edward Hussey, Salisbury; *m* 1st, 1926, Irene Letitia Melville Duncan (*d* 1941); one *s* two *d*; 2nd, 1946, Dr Florence Kathleen Costello. *Educ:* King's Sch., Canterbury; CCC, Oxford. Served European War, 1914-18, Lieut, Lancs Fusiliers, 1914-17; Asst to Asst Sec., Finance, Admiralty, 1917-22. Music Critic: on the Times, 1923-46; Saturday Review, Week-End Review, Spectator, successively, 1924-46. War of 1939-45: Administrative post at Admiralty. *Publications:* Wolfgang Amadeus Mozart, 1928; Verdi, 1940 (revised, 1968); Some Composers of Opera, 1952. *Recreations:* gardening, photography and foreign travel. *Address:* Hawksworth, Cheltenham. *Club:* United University.

**HUSSEY, Very Rev. John Walter Atherton;** Dean of Chichester, since 1955; *b* 15 May 1909; *yr s* of Rev. Canon John Rowden and Lilian Mary Hussey. *Educ:* Marlborough Coll.; Keble Coll., Oxford (MA); Cuddesdon Coll., Oxford. Asst Curate, S Mary Abbots, Kensington, 1932-37; Vicar of S Matthew, Northampton, 1937-55; Canon of Peterborough Cathedral, 1949-55; Master of S John's Hosp., Weston Favell, 1948-55; Rural Dean of Northampton, 1950-55. Chm. Diocesan Art Council. Mem., Redundant Churches Fund, 1969-. *Recreations:* enjoying the arts, gardening. *Address:* The Deanery, Chichester, Sussex. *T:* Chichester 83286.

**HUSTON, John;** film director and writer; *b* Nevada, Missouri, 5 Aug. 1906; *s* of Walter Huston and Rhea Gore; *m* 1st, 1946, Evelyn Keyes; 2nd, 1949, Enrica Soma (*d* 1969); one *s* one *d*; became an Irish Citizen, 1964. At beginning of career was reporter, artist, writer and actor at various times. Formerly: Writer for Warner Bros Studios, 1938; Director for Warner Bros 1941; Writer and Dir, Metro-Goldwyn-Mayer, 1949. Dir of several Broadway plays. Films directed or produced include: The Maltese Falcon; Key Largo; The Treasure of Sierra Madre; The Asphalt Jungle; The African Queen; Moulin Rouge; Beat the Devil; Moby Dick; Heaven Knows, Mr Allison; The Barbarian and the Geisha; The Roots of Heaven; The Unforgiven; The Misfits; Freud; The Night of the Iguana; The Bible . . . In the Beginning; Reflections in a Golden Eye; Sinful Davey; A Walk with Love and Death; The Kremlin Letter. Served US Army 1942-45, Major; filmed documentaries of the War. Hon. LittD, Trinity Coll., Dublin, 1970. *Recreation:* foxhunting. *Address:* St Clerans, Craughwell, Co. Galway, Ireland.

**HUTCHINGS, Arthur James Bramwell;** Professor of Music, University of Exeter, since 1968; *b* Sunbury on Thames, 14 July 1906; *s* of William Thomas Hutchings, Bideford, N Devon, and Annie Bramwell, Freckleton, Lytham, Lancs; *m* 1940, Marie Constance Haverson; one *d*. Formerly schoolmaster and organist; contributor to musical periodicals, critic and reviewer; served with RAF in SEAC; Prof. of Music, University of Durham, 1947-68. Mem. Bd of Governors of Trinity Coll. of Music, 1947-. Hon. FTCL, FRSCM, Hon. RAM. Compositions include: works for strings, comic operas and church music. *Publications:* Schubert (Master Musicians Series), 1941; Edmund Rubbra (contribution to Penguin Special, Music of Our Time), 1941; Delius (in French, Paris), 1946; A Companion to Mozart's Concertos, 1947; Delius, 1947; The Invention and Composition of Music, 1954; The Baroque Concerto, 1960; Pelican History of Music, Vol 3 (The 19th Century), 1962; Church Music in the Nineteenth Century, 1967. Contributions to: Die Musik in Geschichte und Gegenwart, 1956; The Mozart Companion, 1956; New Oxford History of Music, 1962. *Address:* Old Larkshayes, Dalwood, near Axminster, Devon. *T:* Wilmington 497.

**HUTCHINGS, Geoffrey Balfour,** CMG 1946; Formerly Senior Partner in Lovell, White & King, Solicitors, 1 Serjeants' Inn, EC4; *b* 24 Feb. 1904; 2nd *s* of late Charles Graham Hutchings, Seaford, Sussex; *m* 1st, 1928, Dorothy Guest (*d* 1967), *o d* of late Rev. J. Guest Gilbert; one *s* one *d*; 2nd, 1969, Mrs Stella Graham. Educ: Giggleswick Sch., Yorks. Served with 1/4 Bn South Lancs Regt, Sept. 1939-41; Principal Dir of Salvage and Recovery, Ministry of Supply, 1941-44; Dir-Gen. of British Ministry of Supply Commission, North West Europe, 1944-45; resumed professional practice, 1945. *Recreation:* golf. *Address:* 30 Marine Parade, Seaford, Sussex. *T:* Seaford 3482.

**HUTCHINGS, Sir Robert Howell,** KCIE 1946 (CIE 1935); CMG 1943; *b* 11 March 1897; *s* of late Charles Robert Hutchings, MA; *m* 1st, 1925, Irene Millicent (*d* 1953), *d* of Rev. A. Willifer Young; three *s*; 2nd, Lydia Gladys, *d* of J. H. Lightburn. *Educ:* St Paul's Sch., London; Trinity Coll., Oxford. Served European War, France, 1916-18; joined ICS 1920; Sec. to Government of India Food Dept, 1943; Mem. for Food and Agriculture, Governor General's Executive Council, India, July-Aug. 1946. Dir, Glaxo Laboratories Ltd, later Glaxo Group Ltd, 1947-67. Chairman: Joint UK Australian Mission on Rice Production in Ceylon, 1954; Cttee on National Security, Ghana, 1958; British and Foreign Bible Society, 1962-64. *Address:* Labadi, Pennington Cross, Lymington, Hants. *Club:* Oriental.

**HUTCHINS, Ven. George Francis;** Archdeacon of Cheltenham since 1965; *b* 8 Oct. 1909; *s* of late Frank and Lucy Hutchins; *m* 1935, Margaret Annie Powell; two *s* one *d*. *Educ:* Plymouth Coll.; University of Bristol (MA). Curate, St Matthew Moorfields, Bristol, 1934-35; Vicar: St Clement and St Swithin, Barbados, BWI, 1935-38; Holy Innocents, Barbados, 1938-43; St Matthias and St Lawrence, Barbados, 1943-48; All Saints, Gloucester, 1948-55; Rector, Dursley, Glos, 1955-61; Canon Missioner, Dio. Gloucester, 1961-65. Hon. Canon, Gloucester Cathedral, 1968. *Recreations:* walking, reading, railways. *Address:* 21 Eldorado Road, Cheltenham, Glos. *T:* 23488.

**HUTCHINS, Robert Maynard;** Chairman, The Fund for the Republic, USA, and Center for Study of Democratic Institutions; President University of Chicago, 1929; Chancellor University of Chicago, 1945-51; *b* 17 Jan. 1899; *s* of William James Hutchins and Anna Laura Murch; *m* 1921, Maude Phelps McVeigh (marriage dissolved, 1948); three *d*; *m* 1949, Vesta Sutton Orlick. *Educ:* Oberlin Coll.; Yale Univ. AB, Yale, 1921, Hon. AM 1922; LLB, 1925; LLD, WVaU, Lafayette Coll., and Oberlin Coll., 1929, Williams Coll., 1930, Berea Coll., 1931, Harvard Univ. 1936; Tulane Univ. 1938; Universities of Copenhagen, 1946; of Illinois (LittD), 1947; of Frankfurt, 1948; of Stockholm, 1949; Rollins Coll., 1950; Chicago, 1951; of Rochester, 1958. Master in English and Hist., Lake Placid Sch., 1921-23; Sec., Yale Univ., 1923-27; admitted to practice, Connecticut Bar, 1927; Lecturer, Yale Law Sch., 1925-27; acting Dean, 1927-28; Dean, 1928-29; Prof. of Law, 1927-29; Dir of Encyc. Britannica, Inc., Encyc. Brit., Ltd, and Encyc. Brit. Educnl Corp. (formerly EB Films Inc), since 1943; in ambulance service, USA, 1917-19; with Italian Army, 1918-19. Chairman: Commn on Internat. Economic Relations, 1933-34; Commn on Freedom of Press, 1945-47; Pres. Cttee to Frame a World Constitution, 1945-46; Chairman: Goethe Bicentennial Foundation, 1949; The Great Books Foundation, 1947-51; Bd of Editors, Measure, 1949-51; Bd of Editors, Encyc. Brit., 1946-. Associate Dir, Ford Foundation, 1951-54; Sir George Watson Prof. of American History, 1954; lectures given at Universities of Manchester, Birmingham, Edinburgh, Oxford, and University Coll. of North Staffs. Order of the Coif; Hon. Mem. Chicago Bar Assoc.; Officer of Legion of Honor; Croce di Guerra; Goethe plaque, City of Frankfurt, 1949; Grand Cross of Order of Merit (Germany), 1954. Aspen Founders Award, 1969. *Publications:* No Friendly Voice, 1936; The Higher Learning in America, 1936; Education for Freedom, 1943; St Thomas and the World State, 1949; Morals, Religion, and Higher Education, 1950; The Conflict in Education, 1953; The University of Utopia, 1953; Freedom, Education, and the Fund, 1956; Some Observations on American Education, 1956; The Learning Society, 1968. *Address:* c/o The Fund for the Republic, Inc., PO Box 4068, Santa Barbara, Calif 93103, USA. *Clubs:* Century (New York); (Hon.) Tavern, (Hon.) Law.

**HUTCHINS, Captain Ronald Edward,** CBE 1961; DSC 1943; International Computers Ltd, since 1961; Director: Data Recording Instrument Co., since 1964; RCA Magnetic Products Ltd since 1969; Dataset since 1969; *b* 7 Jan. 1912; *s* of Edward Albert Hutchins and Florence Ada (*née* Sharman); *m* 1937, Irene (*née* Wood); two *s*. *Educ:* St John's (elem. sch.), Hammersmith; TS Mercury, Hamble, Hants (C. B. Fry); RN Coll., Greenwich. Royal Navy, 1928-61. *Recreations:* walking, gardening. *Address:* Silvergarth, Badgers Hill, Wentworth, Virginia Water, Surrey. *T:* Wentworth 2622.

**HUTCHINSON;** *see* Hely-Hutchinson.

**HUTCHINSON,** family name of **Baron Ilford.**

**HUTCHINSON, Rev. Canon Archibald Campbell,** MA; Chaplain at Cossham Hospital, Bristol, 1950-63, and at Glenside Hospital, 1950-62; retired; now assisting at St Peter's Church, Henleaze, Bristol; *b* 9 Feb. 1883; *s* of Ven. Archdeacon Arthur Blockey Hutchinson; *m* 1912, Constance Clara Auden Stratton (*d* 1950), Newport, Isle of Wight; no *c*; *m* 1951, Dorothy May White, Sherborne, Dorset. *Educ:* St Lawrence Coll., Ramsgate; Corpus Christi Coll., Cambridge. Ordained, 1906; Curate of S John's, Carisbrooke, IoW; joined the Japan Mission of the CMS, 1909; formerly Lecturer at the Fukuoka Divinity Sch.; Lecturer for one year at The Central Theological Coll., Tokyo; Mem. of the Standing Cttee Diocese of Kyushu; Sec. of the CMS, Japan Mission; Hon. Canon of the Cathedral at Fukuoka in the diocese of Kyushu; left Japan, Dec. 1940; Asst Priest, St Andrew's Church, Halfway Tree, Jamaica, 1941-45; Asst Priest, St James' Church, Bristol, 1945-50. *Address:* 120 Howard Road, Westbury Park, Bristol BS6 7XA. *T:* Bristol 45740.

**HUTCHINSON, Arthur Stuart Menteth;** novelist; *b* 2 June 1879; *s* of late Lieut-Gen. H. D. Hutchinson, CSI; *m* 1926, Una Rosamond, *d* of late John Henry Bristow-Gapper; two *s*. Editor Daily Graphic, 1912-16. *Publications:* Once Aboard the Lugger, 1908; The Happy Warrior, 1912; The Clean Heart, 1914; If Winter Comes, 1921; This Freedom, 1922; The Eighth Wonder, 1923; One Increasing Purpose, 1925; The Uncertain Trumpet, 1929; The Golden Pound, 1930; The Book of Simon, 1930; Big Business, 1932; The Soft Spot, 1933; A Year That The Locust, 1935; As Once You Were, 1938; He Looked for a City, 1940; It Happened Like This, 1942; Bring Back The Days, 1958. *Address:* c/o Society of Authors, 84 Drayton Gardens, SW10.

**HUTCHINSON, Sir Arthur (Sydney),** KBE 1953; CB 1946; CVO 1937; *idc*; *b* 21 March 1896; 2nd and *o surv s* of late Sir Sydney Hutchinson, formerly Dir General of Telegraphs in India; *m* 1933, Charis Lyle, *d* of late Christopher Bathgate, Liverpool; no *c*. *Educ:* St Paul's Sch.; New Coll., Oxford. Army, 1916-18 (wounded); entered Home Office, 1919; Deputy Under-Sec. of State, 1948-57; retired, 1957. *Address:* 15a Pennington Road, Southborough, Tunbridge Wells. *T:* Tunbridge Wells 29782. *Club:* United University.

**HUTCHINSON, Rear-Adm. Christopher Haynes,** CB 1961; DSO 1940; OBE 1946; RN retired; *b* 13 March 1906; 2nd *s* of late Rev. Canon Frederick William Hutchinson; *m* 1941, Nancy Marguerite Coppinger. *Educ:* Lydgate House Prep. Sch., Hunstanton; Royal Naval Colleges, Osborne and Dartmouth. Naval Cadet RNC Osborne, Sept. 1919; served largely in submarines; served War of 1939-45, commanding submarine Truant which sank German cruiser Karlsruhe, 9 April 1940 (despatches, DSO); Staff Officer, British Pacific Fleet 1945 (OBE); Qualified RN Staff Coll. (1946) and Joint Services Staff Coll. (Directing Staff); Commanding 3rd Submarine Flotilla, 1950-52; Senior Naval Adviser to UK High Commissioner, Australia, 1952-54; Captain, RN Coll., Greenwich, 1954-56; Commodore, 1st Class, Chief of Staff Far East Station, 1956-59; Director-General of Personal Services and Officer Appointments, 1959-61; retired, 1962. *Recreation:* shooting. *Address:* Gillhurst, Warninglid, near Haywards Heath, Sussex. *T:* Warninglid 259.

**HUTCHINSON, Rev. Canon Deryck Reeves;** Canon Residentiary and Precentor of Chichester Cathedral since 1961; *b* 26 Aug. 1911; *s* of Charles Reeves Hutchinson and Alice Elizabeth (*née* Oldman); *m* 1942, Beatrice Maud Hammond. *Educ:* Merchant Taylors' Sch.; Oriel Coll., Oxford. BA (2nd cl. Mod. Hist.) 1933 (2nd cl. Theol., 1934), MA 1937; Deacon, 1935; Priest, 1936; Curate of Cranbrook, 1935-38; Chaplain, Salisbury Theological Coll., 1938-41, Vice-Principal, 1941-43; Lectr, St Boniface Coll., Warminster, 1939-41; Curate of Ripon, 1943-44; Vicar of Holy Trinity, Yeovil, 1944-49; Vice-Principal, Wells Theological Coll., 1949-58; Exam. Chaplain: to Bp of St Edmundsbury and Ipswich, 1941-54; to Bp of Bath and Wells, 1951-58; Editor, Bath and Wells Diocesan Gazette, 1952-56; Prebendary of Wells Cathedral, 1957-58; Lectr, Brasted Training Centre for Theological Students, 1958-61; Anglican Chaplain to Students, University of Reading, 1961. *Recreations:* motoring, gardening. *Address:* The Residentiary, Chichester, Sussex. *T:* Chichester 82961.

**HUTCHINSON, Frederick Heap,** CIE 1947; *b* 16 Oct. 1892; *s* of late William Henry Heap Hutchinson, Hull; *m* 1st, 1924, Dorothea Mary (*d* 1967), *d* of late Rev. G. F. Feild, Hampstead; three *s* one *d*; 2nd, 1968, Violet Mary, *d* of Major L. H. Robertson, RA, Romford, and *widow* of Major H. E. P. Yorke, MC, RAMC, Jersey. *Educ:* Rugby; Oundle; City and Guilds Coll., London. Served as Capt. i/c 120th Labour Corps, Persia, 1918-19. Indian Service of Engineers, 1914, posted to United Provinces; on deputation to Govt of Mauritius, 1938 and 1939; Chief Engineer, UP India, 1943-47; retired from ISE, 1947. Mem. of West Africa Rice Mission, 1948; Consulting Engineer for Drainage and Irrigation to the Government of British Guiana, 1949-52. *Recreations:* shooting, golf, yachting, reading. *Address:* 4 Victoria Crescent, Dover, Kent. *T:* Dover 1946.

**HUTCHINSON, Prof. George William,** MA, PhD, Cantab; Professor of Physics, Southampton University, since 1960; *b* Feb. 1921; *s* of George Hutchinson, farmer, and Louisa Ethel (*née* Saul), Farnsfield, Notts; *m* 1943, Christine Anne, *d* of Matthew Rymer and Mary (*née* Proctor), York; two *s*. *Educ:* Abergele Grammar Sch.; Cambridge. MA 1946, PhD 1952, Cantab. State Schol. and Schol. of St John's Coll., Cambridge, 1939-42. Research worker and factory manager in cotton textile industry, 1942-47; Cavendish Lab., Cambridge, 1947-52; Clerk-Maxwell Schol. of Cambridge Univ., 1949-52; Nuffield Fellow, 1952-53, and Lecturer, 1953-55, in Natural Philosophy, University of Glasgow; Research Assoc. of Stanford Univ., Calif, 1954. Lecturer, 1955, Sen. Lectr, 1957, in Physics, University of Birmingham. Duddell Medal, Physical Soc., 1959. FPhysS; FRAS. *Publications:* papers on nuclear and elementary particle physics, nuclear instrumentation and cosmic rays. *Recreations:* music, tennis, sailing. *Address:* Physical Laboratory, University of Southampton. *T:* Southampton 56331.

**HUTCHINSON, Sir Herbert John,** KBE, *cr* 1948 (CBE 1939); CB 1943; BSc (Econ.); *b* 22 Oct. 1889; *s* of late George Hutchinson, Lee; *m* 1926, Kathleen Eleanor (*d* 1969), *d* of late J. J. Byrne. *Educ:* St Dunstan's Coll.; University Coll. Sch.; London Univ. Entered Board of Trade, 1908; Asst Sec., Import Duties Advisory Cttee, 1932; Sec., 1939; Under-Sec., Ministry of Supply, 1941-46; Second Sec. Board of Trade, 1946-47; Sec. of NCB, 1947-51; Director-General, British Paper & Board Makers' Association, 1951-60. *Address:* Dean Cottage, Withdean Road, Brighton. *T:* Brighton 505444. *Club:* United Service.

**HUTCHINSON, Jeremy Nicolas,** QC 1961; Recorder of Bath since 1962; *b* 28 March 1915; *o s* of late St John Hutchinson, KC; *m* 1st, 1940, Dame Peggy Ashcroft (marriage dissolved, 1966); one *s* one *d*; 2nd, 1966, June Osborn. *Educ:* Stowe Sch.; Magdalen Coll., Oxford. Called to Bar, Middle Temple, 1939. RNVR, 1939-46. Practised on Western Circuit, N London Sessions and Central Criminal Court; formerly counsel to Post Office, Western Circuit. Mem. Cttee on Immigration Appeals, 1966-. *Address:* Queen Elizabeth Building, Temple, EC4. *T:* 01-353 7520 and 2576.

**HUTCHINSON, John,** FRS 1947; LLD (St Andrews); VMH, FLS; Corresponding Member of Philadelphia Academy of Science and the Botanical Society of America; Hon. Fellow and Herbert Medallist, American Amaryllis Society; Loder Cup for work on Rhododendrons, 1941; Hon. Fellow Botanical Society, Edinburgh, 1945; *b* 7 April 1884; *s* of Michael Hutchinson, Blindburn, Wark-on-Tyne, Northumberland; *m* 1910, Lilian Florence Cook, Richmond; two *s* three *d*. *Educ:* Wark; Rutherford Coll., Newcastle; privately. Asst for India, Royal Botanic Gardens, Kew, 1907-9, 1916-19; Asst for Africa, 1909-16; Asst in charge of African Section, 1919-36; Keeper of Museums of Botany, 1936-48; Botanical Tour in S Africa, 1928-29; in Rhodesia, 1930; Cameroons Mtn, 1937. Veitch Memorial Gold Medal, 1946; Darwin-Wallace Centenary Medal, 1958; Linnean Gold Medal, 1965. *Publications:* The Families of Flowering Plants, 1926 and 1934 (vol. ii), 2nd edn 1959; contributions towards a Phylogenetic Classification of Flowering Plants (Kew Bulletin); Floras of Tropical and South Africa (in part); Flora of West Africa; Common Wild Flowers, More Common Wild Floers, and Uncommon Wild Flowers I (Penguin Books); British Wild Flowers, 2 vols (Penguin Books); A Botanist in Southern Africa; Evolution and Classification of British Flowering Plants; (with R. Melville) The Story of Plants; (with H. Hahnewald) Wild Flowers in Colour (Penguin Books); (with C. Abbott) Bouquet of Wild Flowers; The Genera of Flowering Plants; Evolution and Phylogeny of Flowering Plants, 1969; numerous papers on the botany of Africa, Canary Islands, etc. *Recreations:* black and white drawing, botanical exploration. *Address:* 12 Kenmore

Close, Kent Road, Kew, Richmond, Surrey. *T:* 01-940 6811.

**HUTCHINSON, Sir Joseph (Burtt),** Kt 1956; CMG 1944; ScD Cantab; FRS 1951; Drapers' Professor of Agriculture, Cambridge, 1957-69, now Emeritus; Professorial Fellow, St John's College; *b* 21 March 1902; *s* of L. M. and Edmund Hutchinson; *m* 1930, Martha Leonora Johnson; one *s* one *d*. *Educ:* Ackworth and Bootham Schs; St John's Coll., Cambridge. Asst Geneticist, Empire Cotton Growing Corporation's Cotton Research Station, Trinidad, 1926-33; Geneticist and Botanist, Institute of Plant Industry, Indore, Central India, 1933-37; Geneticist, Empire Growing Corporation's Cotton Research Station, Trinidad, and Cotton Adviser to the Inspector-General of Agriculture, BWI, 1937-44. Chief Geneticist, Empire Cotton Growing Corp., 1944-49; Dir of its Cotton Research Station, Namulonge, Uganda, 1949-57. Chm. of Council of Makerere Coll., University Coll. of East Africa, 1953-57; Hon. Fellow, Makerere Coll., 1957. Pres., British Assoc., 1965-66. Royal Medal, Royal Society, 1967. DSc (*hc*), Nottingham, 1966. *Publications:* The Genetics of Gossypium; Genetics and the Improvement of Tropical Crops, 1958; Application of Genetics to Cotton Improvement, 1959; numerous papers on the Genetics, Taxonomy, and Economic Botany of cotton in the Journal of Genetics and other journals. *Address:* Huntingfield, Huntingdon Road, Cambridge. *T:* Cambridge 76272. *Club:* Farmers'.

**HUTCHINSON, Sir Lewis (Bede),** KBE 1952; CB 1947; Deputy Secretary, Ministry of Supply, 1949-59, retired; *b* 3 Jan. 1899; *o s* of late Lewis John Hutchinson, Leytonstone, Essex; *m* 1926, Eileen, *d* of late Arthur Eaton, Norwood, SE; one *d*. *Educ:* Leyton County High Sch. Barrister-at-law, Middle Temple, Cert. of Honour, 1928; served European War, 1914-18, with London Regt, 1917-19; served overseas (wounded); Inland Revenue Dept, 1916; Air Ministry, 1937; Ministry of Aircraft Production, 1940; Ministry of Supply, 1941. Chm. Woolwich Review Cttee, 1959-60. Dir, Projectile & Engineering Co. Ltd, 1959-65. *Address:* 16 Woodland Way, West Wickham, Kent. *T:* 01-777 1034. *Clubs:* United Service, Royal Automobile.

**HUTCHINSON, Ray Coryton,** FRSL; novelist; *b* London, 23 Jan. 1907; *yr s* of late Harry Hutchinson, Watford; *m* 1929, Margaret, *er d* of late Capt. Owen Jones, CBE; two *s* two *d*. *Educ:* Monkton Combe; Oriel Coll., Oxford. In the Army, 1940-45. *Publications:* Thou Hast A Devil, 1930; The Answering Glory, 1932; The Unforgotten Prisoner, 1933; One Light Burning, 1935; Shining Scabbard, 1936; Testament, 1938 (Sunday Times Gold Medal for Fiction, 1938); Last Train South, play, 1938; The Fire and the Wood, 1940; Interim, 1945; Elephant and Castle, 1949; Recollection of a Journey, 1952; The Stepmother, 1955; March the Ninth, 1957; Image of my Father, 1961; A Child Possessed, 1964 (W. H. Smith and Son Literary Award, 1966); Johanna at Daybreak, 1969. *Address:* Dysart, Bletchingley, Redhill, Surrey. *T:* Caterham 45041.

**HUTCHINSON, William James,** TD; Town Clerk and Chief Executive Officer, Bristol County Borough, since 1969; *b* 12 Dec. 1919; *s* of William James Hutchinson and Martha Allan Hutchinson (*née* Downie); *m* 1944, Barbara Olive Benaton; one *s* one *d*. *Educ:* Brighton Hove and Sussex Grammar School. Admitted Solicitor, 1947. Bury County Borough Council, 1947-49; Bristol CBC, 1949-. *Recreations:* gardening, walking, theatre. *Address:* 32 Woodland Grove, Coombe Dingle, Bristol, BS9 2BB. *T:* 683415.

**HUTCHISON, A(lan) Michael Clark;** MP (C) Edinburgh South since May 1957; *b* 26 Feb. 1914; *y s* of late Sir George A. Clark Hutchison, KC, MP, of Eriska, Argyll; *m* 1937, Anne, *yr d* of Rev. A. R. Taylor, DD, of Aberdeen; one *s* one *d*. *Educ:* Eton; Trinity Coll., Cambridge. Called to Bar, Gray's Inn, 1937. War of 1939-45 (despatches); served AIF, Middle East and Pacific theatres, psc. Mem. Australian Mil. Mission, Washington, USA, 1945-46. Entered Colonial Admin. Service, 1946, and served as Asst Dist Comr in Palestine till 1948; thereafter as Political Officer and Asst Sec. in Protectorate and Colony of Aden; resigned, 1955. Contested (C) Motherwell Div. of Lanarks, 1955. Parliamentary Private Secretary to: Parliamentary and Financial Sec. to the Admiralty, and to the Civil Lord, 1959; the Lord Advocate, 1959-60; Sec. of State for Scotland, 1960-62. Vice-Chm., Scottish Conservative Members' Cttee, 1965-66, 1967-68. *Recreations:* reading, Disraeliana. *Address:* 19 Newington Road, Edinburgh 9. *T:* 031-667 5783; 16 Maunsel Street, SW1. *T:* 01-828 1108. *Clubs:* Carlton; New, Conservative (Edinburgh).

*See also Lieut-Comdr Sir G. I. C. Hutchison.*

**HUTCHISON, Bruce;** *see* Hutchison, W. B.

**HUTCHISON, Hon. Sir Douglas;** *see* Hutchison, Hon. Sir J. D.

**HUTCHISON, Brig. Sir Eric Alexander Ogilvy,** 2nd Bt, *cr* 1923; RA; MB, ChB Edinburgh; *s* of 1st Bt and Jane Moir Ogilvy (*d* 1935), *d* of late Alexander Ogilvy Spence, banker; *b* 28 Feb. 1897; *S* father, 1925; *m* 1st, 1924, Bethia Maud (from whom he obtained a decree of divorce, 1943), *d* of Lieut-Col F. D. S. Fayrer, IMS; three *d*; 2nd, 1944, Olive, *d* of late Frederick Kerss, Newcastle; one *d*. *Educ:* Edinburgh Acad.; Royal Military Academy, Woolwich; Edinburgh Univ. Served in RA 1915-25 and RA (TA), 1925-47. Mem. of Royal Company of Archers (Queen's Body Guard for Scotland). *Heir:* none. *Recreations:* golf, motoring, metal working. *Address:* 9a, Palmerston Road, Edinburgh 9. *T:* 031-667 1341. *Clubs:* Caledonian United Service, Royal Forth Yacht (Edinburgh).

**HUTCHISON, Lt-Comdr Sir (George) Ian Clark,** Kt 1954; Royal Navy, retired; Member of the Queen's Body Guard for Scotland, Royal Company of Archers; *b* 4 Jan. 1903; *e s* of late Sir George Clark Hutchison, KC, MP, Eriska, Argyllshire; *m* 1926, Sheena (*d* 1966), *o d* of late A. B. Campbell, WS; one *d*. *Educ:* Edinburgh Academy; RN Colleges, Osborne and Dartmouth. Joined Navy as Cadet, 1916; Lieut, 1926; Lieut-Comdr 1934; specialised in torpedoes, 1929; emergency list, 1931; Mem., Edinburgh Town Council, 1935-41; Chm., Public Assistance Cttee, 1937-39; contested Maryhill Div. of Glasgow, 1935; rejoined Navy Sept. 1939; served in Naval Ordnance Inspection Dept, 1939-43; MP (U) for West Div. of Edinburgh, 1941-59. Mem. National Executive Council of British Legion (Scotland), 1943-51; Life Governor of Donaldson's Sch. for the Deaf, Edinburgh; Mem. Cttee on Electoral Registration, 1945-46; Mem. Scottish Leases Cttee, 1951-52. DL County of City of Edinburgh, 1958. *Recreations:* golf, fishing, walking, philately. *Address:* 16 Wester Coates Gardens, Edinburgh 12. *T:* 031-337 4888. *Clubs:* Carlton; New (Edinburgh).

*See also A. M. C. Hutchison.*

**HUTCHISON, Lt-Comdr Sir Ian Clark;** *see* Hutchison, Sir G. I. C.

**HUTCHISON, Isobel Wylie,** LLD; FRSGS; JP; *d* of Thomas Hutchison, Carlowrie, West Lothian, and Jeanie Wylie; unmarried. *Educ:* Rothesay House Sch., Edinburgh; Studley Horticultural Coll. for Women. Plant-collecting in Arctic regions, Greenland, Alaska, and Aleutian Islands for the Royal Horticultural Society, Royal Herbarium of Kew, and the British Museum. *Publications: verse:* Lyrics from West Lothian, The Northern Gate, How Joy was Found, The Calling of Bride; *novel:* Original Companions; *travel:* On Greenland's Closed Shore; North to the Rime-Ringed Sun; Arctic Nights Entertainments; Stepping Stones from Alaska to Asia, 1937, republished 1943 under title The Aleutian Islands. *Recreations:* sketching, walking, botany, etc. *Address:* Carlowrie, Kirkliston, West Lothian. *T:* Kirkliston 209.

**HUTCHISON, Hon. Sir (James) Douglas,** Kt 1959; Judge of Supreme Court of New Zealand, 1948-66, retired; *b* 29 Sept. 1894; *s* of Sir James Hutchison; *m* 1st, 1924, Mary Bethea Johnston (*d* 1943); two *s* two *d*; 2nd, 1954, Mary Elizabeth Averill. *Educ:* Otago Boys' High Sch.; Otago Univ.; Victoria University Coll. (now Victoria Univ. of Wellington). Served European War, 1914-18, with 1st NZEF in Gallipoli and France; War of 1939-45, DAAG, Southern Military District, NZ. Practised Carterton, 1920-24, Christchurch, 1924-48. *Recreations:* golf, tramping. *Address:* Main Road North, Paraparaumu, NZ. *Clubs:* Wellington, Canterbury (NZ).

**HUTCHISON, Prof. James Holmes,** OBE 1945; FRCP 1947; FRCPE 1960; FRCPGlas 1962; MD (Hons) 1939 (Glasgow); FRSE 1965; Samson Gemmell Professor of Child Health, University of Glasgow, since Oct. 1961; *b* 16 April 1912; *s* of Alexander Hutchison and Catherine Holmes; *m* 1940, Agnes T. A. Goodall; one *s* one *d*. *Educ:* High Sch. of Glasgow; University of Glasgow. Qualified MB, ChB (Glasgow) 1934; Resident Hosp. Posts, 1934-36; Royal Hosp. for Sick Children, Glasgow: McCunn Research Schol., 1936-38; Asst Vis. Phys., 1938-39; Physician in charge of Wards, 1947-61; also Consulting Pædiatrician, Queen Mother's Hospital, Glasgow; Leonard Gow Lectr on Med. Diseases of Infancy and Childhood, Univ. of Glasgow, 1947-61. President: Royal College of Physicians and Surgeons of Glasgow, Nov. 1966-Nov. 1968. British Paediatric Assoc., 1969-70. Hon. FACP 1968. RAMC, Major and Lieut-Col, 1939-45. *Publications:* Practical Pædiatric Problems, 1964 (2nd edn 1967); Rickets, in British Encyclopædia of Medical Practice, 2nd Edn, 1952; Disorders of Storage, Obesity and Endocrine Diseases; chapters 50-57, in Pædiatrics for the Practitioner, 1953 (ed Gaisford and Lightwood); Hypothyroidism, in Recent Advances in Pædiatrics, 1958 (ed Gairdner); chapter in Emergencies in Medical Practice (ed C. Allan Birch); chapter in Textbook of Medical Treatment (ed Davidson, Dunlop and Alstead); chapter in Endocrine and Genetic Diseases of Childhood (ed L. I. Gardner), 1969; Thyroid section in Paediatric Endrocrinology (ed D.Hubble), 1969; many contributions to Medical Journals. *Recreations:* golf, country dancing (Scottish), motoring. *Address:* 21 Victoria Park Gardens North, Glasgow, W1. *T:* 041-339 1791. *Clubs:* College (University of Glasgow); Royal Scottish Automobile.

**HUTCHISON, Sir James Riley Holt,** 1st Bt, *cr* 1956; DSO 1945; TD; JP; *s* of late Thomas Holt Hutchison, Shipowner, and Florence Riley; *m* 1928, Winefryde Eleanor Mary, *d* of late Rev. R. H. Craft; one *s* one *d*. *Educ:* Harrow; France. Shipowner, 1912. Served with Lanark Yeomanry and 17th Cavalry, Indian Army, throughout war, 1914-18; Hon. Col Lanarkshire Yeomanry, 1948-58. Dir of companies (Ailsa Shipbuilding Co. Ltd and others); President: Westminster Chamber of Commerce, 1963; Associated British Chambers of Commerce, 1960-62 (Dep.-Pres. 1958); UK Council of European Movement, 1955; Mem. Export Council for Europe, 1960; Nat. Pres. Incorporated Sales Managers' Assoc., 1949-51; Parl. Chm. Dock and Harbour Authorities Assoc. Served France, N Africa and on Staff, 1939-45. MP (U) Glasgow Central, 1945-50, Scotstoun Div. of Glasgow, Oct. 1950-Sept. 1959. Pres. Assembly of WEU, 1957-59. Parl. Under-Sec. of State and Financial Sec., War Office, 1951-54, and Vice-Chm. HM Army Council. JP Perthshire. Chevalier Legion of Honour, 1945; Croix de Guerre. *Recreations:* writing, music, shooting, games. *Heir: s* Peter Craft Hutchison [*b* 5 June 1935; *m* 1966, Virginia, *er d* of John M. Colville, Gribloch, Kippen, Stirlingshire]. *Address:* Rossie, Forgandenny, Perthshire. *T:* Bridge of Earn 265; 32 Moore Street, SW3. *Clubs:* Cavalry, Beefsteak; Western, Conservative (Glasgow).

**HUTCHISON, James Seller;** Chairman, The British Oxygen Co. Ltd and Associated Companies, since 1950; *b* 15 Oct. 1904; *s* of late R. F. Hutchison, Glasgow; *m* Kathleen, *d* of late William Maude, Leeds; two *d*. *Educ:* Greenock Academy; Glasgow Univ. Chartered Accountant, 1928. *Recreations:* golf, gardening. *Address:* Shenfield House, Orchard Way, Esher, Surrey. *Club:* Caledonian.

**HUTCHISON, Sir Kenneth;** *see* Hutchison, Sir W. K.

**HUTCHISON, Sir Peter,** 2nd Bt, *cr* 1939; Deputy-Clerk of the Peace and of the County Council for East Suffolk, since 1947; *b* 27 Sept. 1907; *er s* of Sir Robert Hutchison, 1st Bt, MD, CM, and Lady Hutchison (then Dr and Mrs Robert Hutchison); *S* father 1960; *m* 1949, Mary-Grace (*née* Seymour); two *s* two *d*. *Educ:* Marlborough; Lincoln Coll., Oxford. Admitted as a Solicitor, 1933. *Recreations:* walking, gardening, reading. *Heir: s* Robert Hutchison, *b* 25 April 1954. *Address:* Melton Mead, near Woodbridge, Suffolk. *T:* Woodbridge 2746. *Club:* Ipswich and Suffolk (Ipswich).

**HUTCHISON, Robert Edward;** Keeper, Scottish National Portrait Gallery, since 1953; *b* 4 Aug. 1922; *y s* of late Sir William Hutchison; *m* 1946, Heather, *d* of late Major A. G. Bird; one *s* one *d*. *Educ:* Gresham's Sch., Holt. Served War, 1940-46, Infantry and RA; Asst Keeper, Scottish National Portrait Gallery, 1949. *Publication:* (with Stuart Maxwell) Scottish Costume 1550-1850, 1958. *Address:* Edgelaw, Gorebridge, Midlothian. *T:* Temple 206. *Club:* Scottish Arts (Edinburgh).

**HUTCHISON, Sidney Charles,** MVO 1967; Secretary, Royal Academy of Arts, since 1968; *b* 26 March 1912; *s* of Henry Hutchison; *m* 1937, Nancy Arnold Brindley; no *c*. *Educ:* Holloway Sch., London; London Univ. (Dip. in Hist. of Art, with Dist.). Joined staff of Royal Academy, 1929. Served War of 1939-45: Royal Navy, rising to Lieut-Comdr (S), RNVR. Librarian of Royal Academy, 1949-68, also Sec. of Loan Exhibitions, 1955-68. Secretary: E. A. Abbey Memorial Trust Fund for Mural Painting, 1960-; Incorporated E. A. Abbey Scholarships Fund, 1965-; British

Institution Fund, 1968-; Chantrey Trustees, 1968-. Lectr in the History of Art, for Extra-Mural Dept of Univ. of London, 1957-. Governor, Holloway Sch., 1969-. Organist and Choirmaster of St Matthew's, Westminster, 1933-37. FRSA 1950; FSA 1955; FMA 1962. *Publications:* The Homes of the Royal Academy, 1956; The History of the Royal Academy, 1768-1968, 1968; articles for Walpole Society, Museums Jl, Encyclopædia Britannica, Apollo, etc. *Recreations:* music, travel, golf. *Address:* 60 Belmont Close, Mount Pleasant, Cockfosters, Herts. *T:* 01-449 9821. *Club:* Arts.

**HUTCHISON, Professor Terence Wilmot;** Professor of Economics, University of Birmingham since 1956; Dean of the Faculty of Commerce and Social Science, 1959-61; *b* 13 Aug. 1912; *m* 1935, Loretta Hack; one *s* two *d.* *Educ:* Tonbridge Sch.; Peterhouse, Cambridge. Lector, University of Bonn, 1935-38; Prof., Teachers' Training Coll., Bagdad, 1938-41. Served Indian Army, in intelligence, in Middle East and India, 1941-46; attached to Govt of India, 1945-46. Lecturer, University Coll., Hull, 1946-47; Lecturer, 1947-51 and Reader, 1951-56, London Sch. of Economics. Visiting Professor: Columbia Univ., 1954-55; University of Saarbrücken, 1962; Yale Univ., 1963-65; Dalhousie Univ., 1970; Visiting Fellow: University of Virginia, 1960; Aust. Nat. Univ., Canberra, 1967. Mem. Council, Royal Economic Soc., 1967-70. *Publications:* The Significance and Basic Postulates of Economic Theory, 1938 (2nd edn 1960); A Review of Economic Doctrines 1870-1929, 1953; Positive Economics and Policy Objectives, 1964; Economics and Economic Policy 1946-66, 1968; articles, reviews in jls. *Address:* 116 Oakfield Road, Birmingham 29. *T:* 021-472 2369.

**HUTCHISON, (William) Bruce,** SM 1967; Editorial Director, Vancouver Sun; *b* 5 June 1901; *s* of John and Constance Hutchison; *m* 1925, Dorothy Kidd McDiarmid; one *s* one *d.* *Educ:* Public and high schs, Victoria, BC. Political writer: Victoria Times, 1918; Vancouver Province, 1925; Vancouver Sun, 1938; editor, Victoria Times, 1950-63; associate editor, Winnipeg Free Press, 1944. Hon. LLD University of British Columbia, 1951. *Publications:* The Unknown Country, 1943; The Hollow Men, 1944; The Fraser, 1950; The Incredible Canadian, 1952; The Struggle for the Border, 1955; Canada: Tomorrow's Giant, 1957; Mr Prime Minister, 1964. *Recreations:* fishing, gardening. *Address:* 810 Rogers Avenue, Victoria, BC, Canada. *T:* Granite 9-2269. *Club:* Union (Victoria).

**HUTCHISON, William Gordon Douglas;** *b* London, 26 Sept. 1904; *y s* of late Col K. D. Hutchison, RGA, and late Mrs Rivers-Moore, Remenham House, near Henley-on-Thames. *Educ:* King William's Coll., Isle of Man. Old Vic, 1921; toured in several plays, 1924; Liverpool Repertory Theatre, 1925; The Right Age to Marry, Playhouse; toured with Arthur Bourchier in The Halo; The Old Adam, Kingsway, 1926; toured in The Street Singer, 1927; toured with Violet Vanbrugh in The Duchess Decides and Robert Atkins' Shakespearian Company to Egypt, 1928; The Trial of Mary Dugan, Queen's Theatre; Passing Brompton Road, with Dame Marie Tempest, Criterion, 1929; The Autocrat, Kingsway; toured in Magic Slippers; These Pretty Things, with Marie Löhr, Garrick; left the stage to study politics; MP (C) Romford Division of Essex, 1931-35; returned to the stage, 1936, to act in Lady Precious Stream, USA, 1937; The Dictator in Judgement Day, Embassy Theatre; a Kiss for Cinderella, Phœnix Theatre, 1938; Road to Gandahar, Garrick; The First Television Serial, Ann and Harold, 1939; Judgement Day, Phœnix, 1940; In Good King Charles Golden Days, Tour and New Theatre; Their Finest Hour, Comedy; Nineteen Naughty One, Prince of Wales, 1941; joined Royal Navy as ordinary seaman, Aug. 1941; Asst Instructor, Nov.; Able Seaman, May 1942; Sub-Lieut RNVR Sept. 1942; Acting Lieut Feb. 1943; Lieut March 1943; Liaison Officer with French Navy, 1942-43-44. Started firm, Sloane Decoration, Sept. 1946. Returned to Theatre, June 1947; Lady Precious Stream, Midsummer Night's Dream, Open Air Theatre, Regent's Park.

**HUTCHISON, Sir (William) Kenneth,** Kt 1962; CBE 1954; FRS 1966; MInstChemE; Hon. FInstGasE; Consultant; *b* 30 Oct. 1903; *m* 1929, Dorothea Marion Eva, *d* of late Commander Bertie W. Bluett, Royal Navy; one *d.* *Educ:* Edinburgh Academy; Corpus Christi Coll., Oxford. Joined staff of Gas, Light and Coke Co. as Research Chemist, 1926; seconded to Air Ministry as Asst Dir of Hydrogen Production, 1940, Dir, 1942; Dir of Compressed Gases, 1943; Controller of By-Products, Gas, Light and Coke Co., 1945, and a Managing Dir of the Company from 1947; Chm., South Eastern Gas Board, 1948-59; Deputy Chm., Gas Council, 1960-66; Chm., International Management and Engineering Group, 1967-69; Dir, Newton Chambers & Co. Ltd, 1967-; President: Institution of Gas Engineers, 1955-56; British Road Tar Assoc., 1953-55; Inst. of Chem. Engineers, 1959-61; Soc. of British Gas Industries, 1967-68; Nat. Soc. for Clean Air, 1969-. *Publications:* papers in Proc. Royal Society and other jls, 1926-. *Recreations:* sailing, golf. *Address:* 2 Arlington Road, Twickenham Park, Mddx. *T:* 01-892 1685; (office) 46/47 Pall Mall, SW1. *T:* 01-930 3921. *Clubs:* Athenæum, royal Thames Yacht; Royal Cruising.

**HUTSON, Hon. Sir Francis (Challenor),** Kt 1963; CBE 1960; Senior Partner, D. M. Simpson & Co., Consulting Engineers, Barbados, 1943-70, retired; *b* 13 Sept. 1895; *s* of Francis and Alice Sarah Hutson; *m* 1st, 1925, Muriel Allen Simpkin (*d* 1945); two *s* one *d*; 2nd, 1947, Edith Doris Howell. *Educ:* Harrison Coll., Barbados; Derby Technical Coll., Derby. Resident Engineer, Booker Bros, McConnell & Co. Ltd, British Guiana, 1920-30; Consulting Engineer, Barbados, 1930-35; D. M. Simpson & Co., 1935-. MLC, 1947-62, MEC, 1958-61, Barbados; PC (Barbados), 1961-. FIMechE. *Recreation:* bridge. *Address:* Fleetwood, Erdison Hill, St Michael, Barbados. *T:* 93905. *Clubs:* Bridgetown, Royal Barbados Yacht, Savannah, (all in Barbados).

**HUTSON, Maj.-Gen. Henry Porter Wolseley,** CB 1945; DSO 1917; OBE 1919; MC; *b* 22 March 1893; *s* of late Henry Wolseley Hutson, Wimbledon, SW19; *m* 1922, Rowena, *d* of Surg.-Gen. Percy Hugh Benson, IA; two *s* one *d.* *Educ:* King's Coll. Sch.; RMA; 2nd Lieut RE, 1913; Capt. 1917; Major, 1929; Lieut-Col 1937; Col 1939; Temp. Brig. 1940; Maj.-Gen. 1944. Employed with Egyptian Army, 1920-24; under Colonial Office (Road Engineer Nigeria), 1926-28; Chief Instructor, Field Works and Bridging, Sch. of Military Engineering, 1934-36; Chief Engineer, Forestry Commn, 1947-58. MICE; MBOU; Chm., British Trust for Ornithology. Served European War, 1914-18, France, Belgium, Egypt and Mesopotamia (wounded, despatches thrice, DSO, OBE, MC); War of 1939-45 (despatches); retired pay, 1947. *Address:* The Koppies, 23 Hoskins Road, Oxted, Surrey. *T:* Oxted 2354.

**HUTT, Sir (Alexander McDonald) Bruce,** KBE, *cr* 1956 (OBE 1943); CMG 1949; Administrator, East Africa High Commission, 1954-59; *b* 9 Feb. 1904; *s* of late John Hutt; *m* 1929, Margaret Helen, *er d* of late George Murray, Hill Crest, Natal, SA; two *s*. *Educ:* St Andrew's Coll., Grahamstown, S Africa; University Coll., Oxford (BA). Entered Tanganyika Administrative Service as Cadet, 1926; Asst Dist Officer, 1928; Private Sec. and ADC, 1933; Asst Sec., Secretariat, 1935-37; Dist Officer, 1938; Dep. Provincial Commissioner, 1944; Provincial Commissioner, 1946; Dep. Chm., Development Commission, 1946; Acting Chief Sec. and Governor's Deputy, 1948-49; Mem. for Development and Works, Tanganyika, 1949-50; Deputy Chief Sec., 1950-51; Chief Sec., Tanganyika, 1951-54. Acting Governor, Tanganyika, 1953. *Publications:* (jointly) Anthropology in Action, 1935; first editor, Tanganyika Notes and Records. *Recreations:* golf, swimming, fishing, and shooting. *Address:* PO Box 33, Hill Crest, Natal, South Africa. *Clubs:* Royal Commonwealth Society; Vincent's (Oxford); Royal and Ancient Golf (St Andrews); Durban.

**HUTT, Prof. William Harold;** Professor of Commerce and Dean of the Faculty of Commerce, University of Cape Town, 1931-64; Professor Emeritus since 1965; *b* 3 Aug. 1899; *s* of William Hutt and Louisa (*née* Fricker); *m* 1946, Margarethe Louise Schonken. *Educ:* LCC Schs; Hackney Downs Sch.; London Sch. of Economics, University of London. Personal Asst to Chm., Benn Bros Ltd, and Manager, Individualist Bookshop Ltd, 1924-28; Senior Lecturer, University of Cape Town, 1928-30. Visiting Professor of Economics at various Univs and Colls in USA, 1966-69; Vis. Research Fellow, Hoover Instn, Stanford Univ., Calif., 1969-71; Distinguished Vis. Prof. of Economics, Calif. State Coll., 1970-71. *Publications:* The Theory of Collective Bargaining, 1930; Economists and the Public, 1936; The Theory of Idle Resources, 1939; Plan for Reconstruction, 1943; Keynesianism–Retrospect and Prospect, 1963; The Economics of the Colour Bar, 1964; numerous articles in economic jls and symposia. *Recreations:* mountaineering, watching football and cricket. *Address:* De Witte Raaf, River Drive, Milnerton, Cape, South Africa. *T:* Cape Town 51-1714. *Club:* Civil Service (Cape Town).

**HUTTON, Air Vice-Marshal Arthur Francis,** CB 1955; CBE 1948; DFC 1935; FRAeS; FIMechE; *b* 9 Dec. 1900; *s* of Rev. A. W. Hutton; *m* 1927, Florence Strickland Oxley; one *s* two *d*. *Educ:* Queen Elizabeth's Gram. Sch., Darlington; Armstrong Coll., Newcastle; St Catharine's Coll., Cambridge (BA). Commissioned RAF 1924; DIC 1931; Officer Comdg No 28 Squadron, 1936; Officer Comdg No 52 Wing, 1939; Sen. Tech. Staff Officer, Far East, 1946; Dir of Engineering, Air Ministry, 1949; Sen. Tech. Staff Officer, Coastal Command, 1951; AOC No 43 Group, 1952; SASO Technical Training Command, 1953; Dir-Gen. of Engineering, Air Ministry, 1955-58, retd. Technical Consultant, Negretti & Zambra Ltd, 1959-61. MIMechE 1952. *Recreations:* shooting, golf. *Address:* Lower Berrick Farm, Berrick Salome, Oxford. *T:* Warborough 465. *Club:* Royal Air Force.

**HUTTON, (David) Graham,** OBE 1945; economist, author, consultant; Director of companies; *b* 13 April 1904; *er s* of David James and Lavinia Hutton; *m* 1st, Magdalene Ruth Rudolph, Zürich (marriage dissolved, 1934); 2nd, Joyce Muriel Green (marriage dissolved, 1958); three *d*; 3rd, Marjorie, *d* of late Dr and Mrs David Bremner, Chicago. *Educ:* Christ's Hospital; London Sch. of Economics; French and German Univs. Gladstone Memorial Prizeman, London Univ., 1929; Barrister-at-Law, Gray's Inn, 1932; Research Fellowship and teaching staff, London Sch. of Economics, 1929-33; Asst Editor, The Economist, 1933-38; Foreign Office and Min. of Information in England and USA, 1939-45. *Publications:* Nations and the Economic Crisis, 1932; The Burden of Plenty (as ed. and contributor, 1935); Is it Peace?, 1936; Danubian Destiny, 1939; Midwest at Noon, 1946; English Parish Churches, 1952; We Too Can Prosper, 1953; All Capitalists Now, 1960; Inflation and Society, 1960; Mexican Images, 1963; Planning and Enterprise, 1964; Politics and Economic Growth, 1968; essays in various collections, learned periodicals, etc. *Recreations:* ecclesiology, music, travel. *Address:* 38 Connaught Square, W2. *T:* 01-723 4067. *Cables:* Hutec, London, W2. *Clubs:* Reform, English-Speaking Union.

**HUTTON, Rear-Adm. FitzRoy Evelyn Patrick,** CB 1945; *b* 16 Jan. 1894; *s* of William Coats Hutton and Ethel FitzRoy Merriman; unmarried. *Educ:* RN Colleges, Osborne and Dartmouth. Lieut RN 1915; qualified as Gunnery Officer, 1917; Comdr 1927; Captain 1933. Commanded HM Ships Penelope (1936-39), Hermes (1939-40), Warspite (1942-43); Chief of Staff to C-in-C China, 1940-41; Commodore, Algeria, 1943-44; Commodore and Flag Officer, Belgium, 1944-45; Flag Officer, Western Germany, 1945-46; retired list, 1946; Grand Cross of Leopold II (Belgian), Commander Legion of Merit (American), Officier Légion d'Honneur (French). *Recreation:* shooting. *Address:* Talcotts, Colchester. *T:* Colchester 74693. *Club:* United Service.

**HUTTON, Graham;** *see* Hutton, D. G.

**HUTTON, John Campbell;** artist; *b* New Zealand, 8 Aug. 1906; *s* of Colin Campbell Hutton and Penrhyn Florence Olive Hutton (*née* Fleming). *Educ:* Wanganui Collegiate School, NZ. Studied law until age of 25 and then abandoned it for art, in which he is self-taught; came to England as an artist in 1935 and worked extensively as a mural painter. Mural paintings for Festival of Britain, 1951, orient liners Orcades and Orsova, Buckingham Palace, Southampton liner terminal, etc. In engraved glass, Dunkirk War Memorial window in France; Guildford Cathedral. Has developed a special technique for large-scale engraving of his designs on glass which has been used for the Great Glass Screen which forms the West Front of new Coventry Cathedral; large screen in engraved glass, Plymouth Civic Centre; engraved glass panels; Shakespeare Centre, Stratford upon Avon; new Nat. Lib. and Archives, Ottawa; Civic Centre, Newcastle upon Tyne; glass engraving represented in: Victoria and Albert Museum, London; National Museum of Scotland, Edinburgh; Corning Museum of Glass, New York. One man exhibn, Commonwealth Inst. Art Gallery, 1969. Designs also in stained glass and mosaic. *Recreation:* playing the Spanish guitar. *Address:* 3A Greville Place, NW6. *T:* 01-624 0525.

**HUTTON, Sir Leonard,** Kt, *cr* 1956; professional cricketer, retired 1956; *b* Fulneck, near Pudsey, Yorks, 23 June 1916; *s* of Henry Hutton; *m* 1939, Dorothy Mary Dennis, Scarborough; two *s*. First played for Yorks, 1934. First played for England *v* New Zealand, 1937; *v* Australia, 1938 (century on first appearance). *v* South Africa, 1938; *v* West Indies, 1939; *v* India, 1946. Captained England *v* India, 1952; *v* Australia, 1953; *v* Pakistan, 1954; *v* Australia, 1954. Captained MCC *v* West Indies, 1953-54. Made record Test score, 364, *v* Australia at the Oval, 1938; record total in a single month, 1294, in June 1949; has made over 100 centuries in first-class cricket. Hon. Mem. of MCC, 1955 (first Professional to be elected). Served War of 1939-45: in RA and APTC. *Publications:* Cricket is my Life, 1950; Just my Story, 1956. *Recreation:* golf. *Address:* 1 Coombe Nevile, Warren Road, Kingston-on-Thames, Surrey. *T:* 01-942 0604.

**HUTTON, Sir Noël (Kilpatrick),** GCB 1966 (KCB 1957; CB 1950); QC; First Parliamentary Counsel to Treasury, 1956-68, retired; *b* 27 Dec. 1907; *s* of late William Hutton and of late Mrs D. M. Hutton, Whiteacre, Kippington, Sevenoaks; *m* 1936, Virginia Jacomyn, *d* of Sir George Young, 4th Bt, MVO; two *s* two *d*. *Educ:* Fettes Coll. (Scholar); University Coll., Oxford (scholar). 1st class Hon. Mods; Craven Scholar; Gaisford Prize Greek Verse; 2nd cl. Litt. Hum.; OUBC crew 1930. Called to the Bar, Lincoln's Inn, 1932; QC 1962; Bencher, 1967; entered Parly Counsel Office, 1938; First Parly Counsel, 1956-68. Governor, Alleyn's College; Chm., Trusteeship Bd, Nat. Soc. for Mentally Handicapped Children. *Recreations:* music, golf, motoring. *Address:* 48 College Road, Dulwich, SE21. *Clubs:* Athenæum, Leander.

**HUTTON, Maj.-Gen. Reginald Antony,** CIE 1947; DSO 1944, and Bar 1945; OBE 1942; DL; *b* 18 April 1899; *s* of Charles Antony and Laura Beatrice Hutton, Earls Colne, Essex; *m* 1934, Margaret Isabel, *d* of Mark Feetham; two *d*. *Educ:* Haileybury and RMC, Sandhurst. Commissioned 1917, 2nd KEO Gurkha Rifles; Staff Coll., Camberley, 1934-35; Bde Major, 1938; GSO1 1940; Deputy Dir Military Intelligence, 1941; Bde Commander, 1944; Chief of Staff, 1 Corps, 1946. Served European War, 1914-18, General Service, 1917-18; 3rd Afghan War, 1919; Mahsud and NWF, 1919-20; Mohmand-Bajaur, 1933; Waziristan and NWF, 1938-40; War of 1939-45: (despatches 1940); Western Desert, Crete, Somaliland, Abyssinia, and Eritrea, 1940-42; Burma and Malaya, 1944-46; Chief of the General Staff, Pakistan Army, 1947-51; retired list, 1951. DL, Devon, 1962. *Address:* The Haven, Newton Ferrers, Devon. *T:* Newton Ferrers 325. *Club:* Naval and Military.

**HUTTON, Rear-Adm. Reginald Maurice James,** CB 1951; CBE 1945; DSO 1942 (Bars, 1942, 1943); Clerk to the Governors, Christ's Hospital, Sherburn, 1953-64; *b* 28 Sept. 1899; *s* of Reginald Hutton, Wootton Bridge, I of W; *m* 1930, Lois, *d* of M. P. Griffith-Jones, CBE; four *s*. *Educ:* Osborne and Dartmouth. Went to sea, 1915; served in battle cruisers and destroyers. Staff Coll., 1930. Commander, 1932; Captain, 1941; Rear-Admiral, 1950. Commanded HMS Laforey, 1941-43, in Mediterranean, as Captain D 19 Flotilla; commanded HMS Tyne, 1943-44; Commodore "D", Home Fleet, 1944-45; Chief of Staff to Naval C-in-C, Germany, 1945-46; Dir, Royal Naval Staff Coll., 1947-48; commanded HMS Triumph, 1949; Senior Naval Member on Staff of Imperial Defence Coll., 1950-52; retired list, 1953. *Recreation:* fishing. *Address:* Oaklawn, Wootton Bridge, Isle of Wight.

**HUTTON, Robert Crompton;** Recorder of Reading 1951-70 (of Oswestry, 1937-51); Chairman of Gloucestershire Quarter Sessions, 1943-70 (deputy Chairman, 1941-43); Chairman, Agricultural Land Tribunal, South Eastern Area, 1959-70; *b* 8 Aug. 1897; *s* of late Stamford Hutton, OBE; *m* 1927, Elfreda Bruce; three *s* one *d*. *Educ:* Winchester; Trinity Coll., Cambridge. Served European War, 1914-19, with 2/1 Royal Gloucestershire Hussars and Signals. Called to Bar, Inner Temple, 1923. TA, Royal Corps of Signals, 56th (1st London) Divl Signals, 1926-30. *Address:* 2 Harcourt Buildings, Temple, EC4; Harescombe Grange, Glos. *T:* Painswick 3260.

**HUTTON, Lt-Gen. Sir Thomas,** KCIE 1944; CB 1941; MC; idc; psc; *b* 27 March 1890; *e s* of W. H. Hutton, JP, Clevedon, Som; *m* 1921, Isabel (CBE 1948; she died 1960), *d* of James Emslie, Edinburgh. *Educ:* Rossall; Royal Military Academy, Woolwich. 2nd Lieut Royal Artillery, 1909; Capt. 1915; Bt Major 1918; Major 1927; Bt Lt-Col 1927; Col 1930; Maj.-Gen. 1938; Lieut-Gen. 1941; served European War, 1914-18 (wounded thrice, despatches four times, Bt Major, Legion of Honour, French and Italian War Crosses, MC and Bar); Palestine, 1936; GSO3, 1918; Bde-Major, 1918-19; Asst Military Sec., 1919-20; DAAG, War Office, 1923-24; GSO2 E Command, 1924-26; Military Asst to CIGS 1927-30; GSO1, Military Operations, 1933-36; GSO1, 1st Division, 1936-38; GOC Western Independent District, India, 1938-40; Deputy Chief of General Staff, Army Headquarters, India, 1940-41; Chief of the General Staff, India, 1941; GOC Burma, 1942; Sec. War Resources and Reconstruction Cttees of Council (India), 1942-44; retired pay, 1944; Officiating Sec., Viceroy's Executive Council; Sec., Planning and Development Dept, 1944-46; Regional Officer, Ministry of Health, 1947-49; General Manager, Anglo-American Council on Productivity, 1949-53; Dir, British Productivity Council, 1953-57. Chm. Organisation and Methods Training Council, 1957-64. Colonel Commandant RA, 1942-52. *Address:* 5 Spanish Place, W1. *T:* 01-935 8831. *Club:* Army and Navy.

**HUTTON, Thomas Winter;** *b* Kiukiang, China, 14 Oct. 1887; *s* of Thomas Hutton; *m* 1913, Katie Marguerite Thornbery; one *s* one *d*. *Educ:* King Edward's Sch., Birmingham; Merton Coll., Oxford (Postmaster). Asst Editor, Birmingham Gazette, 1910; Leader writer, Daily Dispatch, Manchester, 1911; Asst Editor, Liverpool Courier, 1911-13; Asst Editor, Birmingham Post, 1913; Editor, The Birmingham Post, 1945-49; retired, 1949. Served with Royal Warwickshire Regt, 1915-19. Chm. Sch. Cttee, King Edward's Sch., Birmingham; Bailiff of the Governors, 1953-54. Mem. Cttee Assoc. of Governing Bodies of Public Schs, 1954-67, Dep.-Chm. 1960-66; Mem. Council, Public Schs Appointments Bureau, 1953-66. *Publication:* King Edward's School, Birmingham, 1552-1952, 1952. *Address:* 27 Woodbourne, Augustus Road, Edgbaston, Birmingham. *T:* 021-454 2713.

**HUTTON, Maj.-Gen. Walter Morland,** CB 1964; CBE 1960; DSO 1943; MC 1936 and bar, 1942; MA (by decree, 1967); FIL (Arabic); Fellow since 1967 and Home Bursar since 1966, Jesus College, Oxford; *b* 5 May 1912; *s* of Walter Charles Stritch Hutton and Amy Mary Newton; *m* 1945, Peronelle Marie Stella Luxmoore-Ball; two *s* one *d*. *Educ:* Parkstone Sch.; Allhallows Sch.; RMC Sandhurst. Commissioned into Royal Tank Corps, 1932; served in Palestine, 1936 (MC); 1st Class Army Interpreter in Arabic, 1937; War of 1939-45: Western Desert, Alamein and N Africa (comdg 5 RTR); Italy (comdg 40 RTR); Comdt, Sandhurst, 1944-45; Instructor, Staff Coll., Camberley, 1949-51; BGS, Arab Legion, 1953-56; Imperial Defence Coll., 1957; Deputy Comd (Land), BFAP (Aden), 1957-59; Dir of Administrative Plans, War Office, 1959-60, Dir-Gen. of Fighting Vehicles, 1961-64; Chief Army Instructor, Imperial Defence Coll.,

1964-66. Mem., Bd of Governors, United Oxford Hosps, 1969-. *Address:* Jesus College, Oxford; Gate Burton, Combe, Oxon.

**HUTTON, William**, CBE 1962; FRSE; Solicitor and Notary Public; Member Council, Law Society of Scotland, 1962-67; Director of Mitchell-Camus Ltd; *b* 2 Feb. 1902; *e s* of late John Hutton, MPS, Brechin; *m* 1932, Marjorie Elizabeth, *d* of late John Philip Gibb, Director of Raimes, Clark & Co. Ltd, Leith; one *s* one *d*. *Educ:* Brechin High Sch.; Edinburgh Univ., MA 1925, LLB (dist.) 1927, Thow Schol. 1927. Legal experience with Tait & Crichton, WS and Davidson & Syme, WS; admitted Solicitor, 1928; Legal Asst to Dept of Health for Scotland and Asst Draftsman to Scottish Office, 1929-32; Town Clerk of Kirkcaldy, 1932-39; Sen. Depute Town Clerk of Edinburgh, 1939-48; Dep. Chm. former SW Scotland Electricity Bd, 1948-55; Deputy Chm. South of Scotland Electricity Board, 1955-63. Comp. IEE, 1949-63. Notary Public, 1958; FRSE 1960; JP (Glasgow), 1960-64. *Address:* 21 Craiglockhart Loan, Edinburgh. *T:* 031-443 3530. *Club:* Royal Scottish Automobile (Glasgow).

**HUWS JONES, Robin;** *see* Jones, R. H.

**HUXHAM, Henry William Walter**, CB 1967; CBE 1960; Legal Staff of Law Commission, since Oct. 1967; *b* 10 Feb. 1908; *s* of late William Henry Huxham; *m* 1st, 1934, Mabel Marion (*d* 1949), *d* of W. T. Swain; 2nd, 1950, Winifred Annie, *d* of G. W. Rogers; one *d*. LLB London, 1930; admitted Solicitor, 1933; joined Solicitor's Dept, Min. of Labour, 1934; Solicitor to Min. of Labour, Aug. 1962-Oct. 1967. Chm., Civil Service Legal Soc., 1952, 1953. Corresp. and Treasurer to Managers of Holy Trinity C of E Primary Sch., E Finchley. *Recreation:* ballroom dancing. *Address:* 21 Holyoake Walk, East Finchley, N2. *T:* 01-883 3196.

**HUXLEY, Andrew Fielding**, FRS 1955; MA Cantab; Royal Society Research Professor, in Department of Physiology, University College, London, since 1969 (Jodrell Professor 1960-69); *b* 22 Nov. 1917; *s* of late Leonard Huxley and Rosalind Bruce; *m* 1947, Jocelyn Richenda Gammell Pease; one *s* five *d*. *Educ:* University College Sch.; Westminster Sch.; Trinity Coll., Cambridge (MA). Operational research for Anti-Aircraft Command, 1940-42, for Admiralty, 1942-45. Fellow, 1941-60, and Dir of Studies, 1952-60, Trinity Coll., Cambridge; Hon. Fellow, Trinity Coll., 1967; Demonstrator, 1946-50, Asst Dir of Research, 1951-59, and Reader in Experimental Biophysics, 1959-60, in Dept of Physiology, Cambridge Univ.; Herter Lectr, Johns Hopkins Univ., 1959; Jesup Lectr, Columbia Univ., 1964; Alexander Forbes Lectr (Grass Foundation), 1966; Croonian Lectr, Royal Society, 1967. Fullerian Prof. of Physiology and Comparative Anatomy, Royal Institution, 1967. Foreign Hon. Mem., American Academy of Arts and Sciences, 1961; Mem., Leopoldina Academy, 1964; For. Mem. Danish Acad. of Sciences, 1964-. Nobel Prize for Medicine (jointly), 1963. Hon. MD University of the Saar, 1964; Hon. DSc: Sheffield, 1964; Leicester, 1967. *Publications:* papers in the Journal of Physiology, etc. *Recreations:* walking, shooting. *Address:* Manor Field, Grantchester, Cambridge. *T:* Trumpington 2207.

*See also Sir Julian Huxley.*

**HUXLEY, Anthony Julian;** Editor of Amateur Gardening since 1967; *b* 2 Dec. 1920; *s* of Sir Julian Huxley, *qv*; *m* 1943, Priscilla Ann Taylor; three *d*. *Educ:* Dauntsey's Sch.; Trinity Coll., Cambridge (MA). Operational Research in RAF and Min. of Aircraft Production, 1941-47; Economic Research in BOAC, 1947-48; with Amateur Gardening, 1949-. *Publications:* Cacti and Succulents, 1953; House Plants, 1954; (trans.) Exotic Plants of the World, 1955; (trans. and adapted) Orchids of Europe, 1961; (Gen. Ed.) Standard Encyclopedia of the World's Mountains, 1962; (Gen. Ed.) Standard Encyclopedia of Oceans and Islands, 1962; Garden Terms Simplified, 1962; Flowers in Greece: an outline of the Flora, 1964; (with O. Polunin) Flowers of the Mediterranean, 1965; (Gen. Ed.) Standard Encyclopedia of Rivers and Lakes, 1965; Mountain Flowers, 1967. *Recreations:* photography, wild flowers, travel. *Address:* 32 Beckley House, Eagle Street, WC1. *T:* 01-242 1974.

**HUXLEY, Elspeth Josceline, (Mrs Gervas Huxley)**, CBE 1962; JP; *b* 23 July 1907; *d* of Major Josceline Grant, Njoro, Kenya; *m* 1931, Gervas Huxley, *qv*; one *s*. *Educ:* European Sch., Nairobi, Kenya; Reading Univ. (Diploma in Agriculture); Cornell Univ., USA. Asst Press Officer to Empire Marketing Board, London, 1929-32; subsequently travelled in America, Africa and elsewhere; Mem. BBC Gen. Advisory Council, 1952-59; UK Independent Mem., Monckton Advisory Commission on Central Africa, 1959. *Publications:* White Man's Country; Lord Delamere and the Making of Kenya, 2 vols, 1935; Red Strangers (novel), 1939; Three detective stories; Atlantic Ordeal, 1943; Race and Politics in Kenya (with Margery Perham), 1944; The Walled City (novel), 1948; The Sorcerer's Apprentice (travel), 1948; I Don't Mind If I Do (light novel), 1951; Four Guineas (travel), A Thing to Love, 1954; The Red Rock Wilderness, 1957; The Flame Trees of Thika, 1959; A New Earth, 1960; The Mottled Lizard, 1962; The Merry Hippo, 1963; Forks and Hope, 1964; A Man from Nowhere, 1964; Back Street New Worlds, 1965; Brave New Victuals, 1965; Their Shining Eldorado: A Journey through Australia, 1967; Love Among the Daughters, 1968; press articles and broadcasts mainly on African affairs. *Recreation:* resting. *Address:* Woodfolds, Oaksey, near Malmesbury, Wilts. *TA:* Oaksey, Malmesbury. *T:* Crudwell 252.

**HUXLEY, Prof. George Leonard;** Professor of Greek, Queen's University of Belfast, since 1962; *b* Leicester, 23 Sept. 1932; *s* of Sir Leonard Huxley, *qv*; *m* 1957, Davina Best; three *d*. *Educ:* Blundell's Sch.; Magdalen Coll., Oxford. 2nd Mods, 1st Greats, Derby Scholar 1955, Cromer Greek Prize 1963. Commnd in RE, 1951. Asst Dir, British School at Athens, 1956-58. Fellow of All Souls Coll., 1955-61; Vis. Lectr, Harvard Univ., 1958 and 1961. FSA. *Publications:* Achaeans and Hittites, 1960; Early Sparta, 1962; Greek Epic Poetry from Eumelos to Panyassis, 1969; The Early Ionians, 1966; articles on Hellenic subjects. *Recreation:* studying railways. *Address:* 48 Marlborough Park North, Belfast BT9 6HJ, N Ireland. *Club:* Athenæum.

**HUXLEY, Gervas**, CMG 1954; MC; *b* 6 April 1894; *e s* of Henry Huxley and Sophy Wylde Stobart; *gs* of Rt Hon. Thomas Henry Huxley, PC, etc; *m* 1931, Elspeth Josceline Grant (*see* E. J. Huxley); one *s*. *Educ:* Rugby; Balliol Coll., Oxford. European War, 1914-18 (MC, despatches twice); Sec. Publicity Cttee Empire Marketing Board, 1926-32; Adviser to Minister of Information on publicity to and about the Empire and on relations with American Forces in UK until 1945; Organizing Dir and Vice-Chm., International Tea Market Expansion Board, 1935-67; Hon. Adviser on public relations matters to Sec. of State for the Colonies, 1947-63; Exec. Cttee, British

Council, 1953-64; Commissioner, Nat. Parks Commn, 1954-66. *Publications:* Talking of Tea, 1956; Endymion Porter, 1959; Lady Denman, 1961; Lady Elizabeth and the Grosvenors, 1965; Victorian Duke, 1967; Both Hands, 1970. *Recreation:* gardening. *Address:* Woodfolds, Oaksey, Malmesbury, Wilts. *T:* Crudwell 252. *Clubs:* Athenæum, Oriental.
*See also M. H. Huxley.*

**HUXLEY, Mrs Gervas;** *see* Huxley, Elspeth J.

**HUXLEY, Hugh Esmor,** MBE 1948; FRS 1960; MA, PhD; ScD; Member of Scientific Staff of Medical Research Council Laboratory of Molecular Biology, Cambridge, since 1962; *b* 25 Feb. 1924; *s* of late Thomas Hugh Huxley and Olwen Roberts, Birkenhead, Cheshire; *m* 1966, Frances Fripp, *d* of G. Maxon, Milwaukee. *Educ:* Park High Sch., Birkenhead; Christ's Coll., Cambridge (Exhibitioner and Scholar). Natural Science Tripos, Cambbridge, 1941-43 and 1947-48 (Pt II Physics); BA 1948, MA 1950, PhD 1952. Served War of 1939-45, Radar Officer, RAF Bomber Command and Telecommunications Research Establishment, Malvern, 1943-47; Mem. Empire Air Armaments Sch. Mission to Australia and NZ, 1946. Research Student, Med. Research Council Unit for Molecular Biology, Cavendish Lab., Cambridge, 1948-52; Commonwealth Fund Fellow, Biology Dept, Massachusetts Inst. of Technology, 1952-54; Research Fellow, Christ's Coll., Cambridge, 1953-56; Mem. of External Staff of Med. Res. Council, and Hon. Res. Associate, Biophysics Dept, University Coll., London, 1956-61. Harvey Soc. Lectr, New York, 1964-65; Hooke Lectr, Univ. of Texas, 1968; Dunham Lectr, Harvard Med. Sch., 1969. Fellow: King's Coll., Cambridge, 1961-67; Churchill Coll., Cambridge, 1967. Feldberg Foundation Award for Experimental Medical Research, 1963. William Bate Hardy Prize (Camb. Phil. Soc.) 1965. Mem., German Acad. of Science, Leopoldina, 1964; Foreign Hon. Mem., Amer. Acad. of Arts and Sciences, 1965. Hon. Dr of Science, Harvard Univ., 1969. *Publications:* contrib. to learned jls. *Recreations:* reading, ski-ing, sailing, tennis, travel. *Address:* Churchill College, Cambridge. *T:* Cambridge 61200; Binsted, Herschel Road, Cambridge. *T:* Cambridge 56117; 2 Chesterford Gardens, NW3. *T:* 01-435 9338.

**HUXLEY, Sir Julian (Sorell),** Kt 1958; FRS 1938; MA; DSc; biologist and writer; *b* 22 June 1887; *e s* of late Leonard Huxley; *m* 1919, Marie Juliette Baillot of Neuchâtel, Switzerland; two *s. Educ:* Eton (King's Scholar); Balliol Coll., Oxford (Brackenbury Scholar). Newdigate Prizeman, 1908; 1st in Nat. Sci. (Zoology), 1909; Naples Scholar, 1909-10; Lecturer in Zoology, Balliol Coll., 1910-12; Research Associate, 1912-13, and Asst Professor, 1913-16, The Rice Institute, Houston, Texas, USA; Staff Lieut GHQ, Italy, 1918; Fellow of New Coll. and Senior Demonstrator in Zoology, Oxford Univ., 1919-25; Oxford Univ. Expedition to Spitsbergen, 1921; Professor of Zoology, King's Coll., London, 1925-27; Hon. Lecturer, King's Coll., London, 1927-35; Pres. National Union of Scientific Workers, 1926-29; Fullerian Professor of Physiology in the Royal Institution, 1926-29; Sec., Zoological Soc. of London, 1935-42; Biological Editor, Ency. Brit., 14th edn; general supervisor of biological films for GB Instructional Ltd, 1933-36, and for Zoological Film Productions, Ltd, 1937; visited East Africa to advise on Native Education, 1929; Mem. of General Cttee for Lord Hailey's African Survey, 1933-38; Romanes Lectr, Oxford, 1943; mem. of Commission Higher Educn in W Africa, 1944; member: Editorial Board, New Naturalist, 1944-; Cttee on National Parks, 1946; Dir-Gen. of Unesco, 1946-48. Galton Lecturer, 1937 and 1962; William Alanson White Lecturer, Washington, DC, 1951; first Alfred P. Sloan Lecturer, Sloan-Kettering Inst. for Cancer Research, 1955; Vis. Prof., Chichago Univ., 1959. Coto Doñana Expedition, 1957; Adviser to Unesco on Wild Life Conservation in eastern Africa, 1960; Leader, Unesco Mission on Wild Life Conservation to Ethiopia, 1963; Jordan Expedition, 1963; Organizer, Royal Society Symposium on Ritualization in Animals and Man, 1965; Past Pres. Inst. of Animal Behaviour; Pres., Eugenics Soc.; Past Chm. Assoc. for the Study of Systematics. Dr *hc* Universities of: Caracas, 1947, San Carlos de Guatemala, 1947, San Marcos de Lima, 1947, Athens, 1949, Columbia, 1954, Birmingham, 1958; Hon. Mem. Fac. of Biology and Medicine, University of Santiago de Chile, 1947; Hon. Mem. Soc. of Biology, University of Montevideo, 1947; Corr. Mem. Acad. des Sciences (Paris), 1948; For. Mem. Hungarian Acad. of Science, 1948. Darwin Medal, Royal Society, 1957; Darwin-Wallace Commemorative Medal, Linnean Soc., 1958; Kalinga Prize, UNESCO, 1953. *Publications:* The Individual in the Animal Kingdom, 1911; Essays of a Biologist, 1923; The Stream of Life, 1926; Essays in Popular Science, 1926; Religion without Revelation, 1927; Animal Biology (with J. B. S. Haldane), 1927, revised edn 1957; The Science of Life (with H. G. and G. P. Wells), 1929; Ants, 1929; Bird-watching and Bird Behaviour, 1930; Africa View, 1931; What Dare I Think?, 1931; An Introduction to Science (with E. N. Da C. Andrade), vols 1-4 (Simple Science), 1931-35; Problems of Relative Growth, 1932; The Captive Shrew and other poems, 1932; The Elements of Experimental Embryology (with G. R. de Beer), 1934; Scientific Research and Social Needs, 1934; If I were Dictator, 1934; The Private Life of the Gannets (a film, with R. M. Lockley; Oscar Award), 1934; T. H. Huxley's Diary on the Rattlesnake (Ed.), 1935; We Europeans (with A. C. Haddon), 1935; At the Zoo, 1936; The Living Thoughts of Darwin, 1939; The New Systematics (Ed.), 1940; The Uniqueness of Man, 1941; Democracy Marches, 1941; Evolution, The Modern Synthesis, 1942, 2nd revised edition, 1963; TVA: Adventure in Planning, 1943; Evolutionary Ethics, 1943; On Living in a Revolution, 1944; Evolution and Ethics: 1893-1943 (part author), 1947; Man in the Modern World, 1947; Soviet Genetics and World Science, 1949; Evolution in action, 1952; Evolution as a Process (Ed.), 1953; From an Antique Land, 1954 (rev. edn 1966); Kingdom of the Beasts (with W. Suschitzky), 1956; Biological Aspects of Cancer, 1957; New Bottles for New Wine, 1957; (ed.) The Humanist Frame, 1961; Conservation of Wild Life in Central and East Africa, 1961; Essays of a Humanist, 1963; The Human Crisis, 1964; Darwin and his World (with H. B. D. Kettlewell), 1965; The Wonderful World of Evolution, 1969; Memories, 1970. Scientific papers, wireless talks and discussions, lectures, film commentaries, television programmes, miscellaneous articles. *Recreations:* travel, bird-watching, swimming, etc. *Address:* 31 Pond Street, Hampstead, NW3. *Club:* Athenæum.
*See also A. F. Huxley, A. J. Huxley.*

**HUXLEY, Sir Leonard (George Holden),** KBE 1964; MA, DPhil Oxon; PhD Adelaide; FAA; Emeritus Professor, University of Adelaide; Vice-Chancellor, The Australian National University, 1960-Dec. 1967; *b* London, UK, 29 May 1902; *s* of George H. and Lilian S. Huxley; *m* 1929, Elia M. C., *d* of F. G. and E. Copeland;

one *s* one *d*. *Educ:* The Hutchins Sch., Hobart; University of Tasmania; New Coll., Oxford. Rhodes Scholar, Tas., 1923; Jessie Theresa Rowden Scholar, New Coll., 1927; Scott Scholar, University of Oxford, 1929. Scientific staff, CSIR, Sydney, 1929-31; Head of Dept of Physics, University Coll. Leicester, 1932-40; Principal Scientific Officer, Telecommunications Research Estabt, MAP, 1940-46; Reader in Electromagnetism, University of Birmingham, 1946-49; Elder Prof. of Physics, University Adelaide, 1949-60; Mem. Executive, CSIRO, 1960; Mem. Council, University of Adelaide, 1953-60; Mem. Council, Aust. Nat. Univ., 1956-59; Foundation FAA, 1954 (Sec., Physical Sciences, 1959-62); Chm. Australian Radio Research Board, 1958-64; Chm. National Standards Commission, 1953-65; Chm. Radio Frequency Allocation Cttee, 1960-64; Mem. Nat. Library Council, 1961-; Mem. Bd, US Educl Foundn in Austr., 1960-65; Australian Deleg. on Cttee on Space Research, (COSPAR), 1959-60. First President Aust. Inst. of Physics, 1962-65. Mem., Queen Elizabeth II Fellowships Cttee, 1963-66; Chm., Gen. Coun. Encyclopædia Britannica Australia Awards, 1964-; Chm. Bd, Aust./Amer. Educl Foundn, 1965-; Trustee, Aust. Humanities Res. Council, 1968-. DSc (*hc*), Tas. *Publications:* Wave Guides, 1949. Numerous scientific papers on gaseous Electronics, the ionosphere, upper atmosphere and related subjects. *Address:* 19 Glasgow Place, Hughes, Canberra, ACT, Australia. *Club:* Commonwealth (Canberra).
*See also Prof. G. L. Huxley.*

**HUXLEY, Michael Heathorn;** *b* 9 Aug. 1899; *s* of Henry Huxley and Sophy Stobart; *m* 1926, Ottilie de Lotbinière Mills; one *s* one *d* (and one *s* decd). *Educ:* Rugby. Entered Diplomatic Service, 1922; served in Tehran and Washington and in the Foreign Office; Second Secretary, 1925; First Sec., 1934; resigned in order to launch and edit The Geographical Magazine, 1934; recalled for war service by Foreign Office, Sept, 1939; resumed editorial work, 1945; resigned editorship, 1959. *Address:* Buckhold, Lodsworth, near Petworth, Sussex. *Club:* National Liberal.
*See also Gervas Huxley.*

**HUXSTEP, Emily Mary,** CBE 1964; BA London: Headmistress of Chislehurst and Sidcup Girls' Grammar School, Kent, 1944-66; *b* 15 Sept. 1906; *d* of George T. and Nellie M. Huxstep (*née* Wood). *Educ:* Chatham Girls' Grammar Sch.; Queen Mary Coll. Headmistress, Hanson Girls' Grammar Sch., Bradford, Yorks, 1938-44. *Address:* 23 Homewood Crescent, Chislehurst, Kent. *T:* 01-467 3690.

**HUXTABLE, Rev. (William) John (Fairchild);** Minister Secretary, Congregational Church in England and Wales, since 1966; *b* 25 July 1912; *s* of Rev. John Huxtable and Florence Huxtable (*née* Watts); *m* 1939, Joan Lorimer Snow; one *s* two *d*. *Educ:* Barnstaple Gram. Sch.; Western Coll., Bristol; Mansfield and St Catherine's Colls, Oxford. BA Bristol 1933; BA Oxon 1937, MA 1940. Minister: Newton Abbot Congreg. Church, 1937-42; Palmers Green Congreg. Church, 1942-54; Princ., New Coll., University of London, 1953-64. Chm., 1962-63, Sec., 1964-66, Congregational Union of England and Wales. Vice-Pres., British Coun. of Churches, 1967-. Member: Central Cttee, World Council of Churches, 1968-; Jt Cttee of Translation of New English Bible, 1948-. *Publications:* The Ministry, 1943; (Ed.) John Owen's True Nature of a Gospel Church, 1947; (Jt Ed.) A Book of Public Worship, 1948; The Faith that is in Us, 1953; The Promise of the Father 1959; Like a Strange People, 1961; Church and State in Education (C. J. Cadoux Mem. Lect.), 1962; The Bible Says (Maynard Chapman Lects), 1962; Preaching the Law, (Joseph Smith Mem. Lect.), 1964; The Preacher's Integrity (A. S. Peake Mem. Lect), 1966; Christian Unity: some of the Issues (Congreg. Lects), 1966; contribs to symposia: The Churches and Christian Unity, 1962; A Companion to the Bible, 1963; From Uniformity to Unity, 1962; Renewal of Worship, 1965; Outlook for Christianity, 1967; also contribs to Congreg. Quarterly, Theology, London Quarterly and Holborn Review, and Proc. Internat. Congreg. Council. *Recreations:* reading, walking. *Address:* 10 Gerard Road, Harrow, Middlesex. *T:* 01-907 1420. *Club:* National Liberal.

**HUYGHE, René;** Commandeur de la Légion d'Honneur; Member of the Académie Française since 1960; Professor of Psychology of Plastic Arts, Collège de France, since 1950; Hon. Head Keeper, Musée de Louvre; *b* Arras, Pas-de-Calais, France, 3 May 1906; *s* of Louis Huyghe and Marie (*née* Delvoye); *m* 1950, Lydie Bouthet; one *s* one *d*. *Educ:* Sorbonne; École du Louvre, Paris. Attached to Musée du Louvre, 1927; Asst Keeper, 1930; Head Keeper, Département des Peintures. Dessins, Chalcographie, 1937. Mem. of Council, Musées Nationaux, 1952 (Vice-Pres. 1964); Pres. Assoc. internationale du Film d'Art, 1958. Holds foreign decorations. Praemium Erasmianum, The Hague, 1966. *Publications:* Histoire de l'Art contemporain: La Peinture, 1935; Cézanne 1936 and 1961; Les Contemporains, 1939 (2nd edn, 1949); Vermeer, 1948; Watteau, 1950; various works on Gauguin, 1951, 1952, 1959; Dialogue avec le visible, 1955 (trans. Eng.); L'Art et l'homme, Vol. I, 1957, Vol. II, 1958, Vol. III, 1961 (trans. Eng.); Van Gogh, 1959; Merveilles de la France, 1960; L'Art et l'Ame, 1960 (trans. Eng.); La peinture française aux XVIIe et XVIIIe Siècles, 1962; Delacroix ou le combat solitaire, 1963 (trans. Eng.); Puissances de l'Image, 1965; Sens et Destin de l'Art, 1967; L'Art et le monde moderne, 1969. *Address:* 3 rue Corneille, Paris VIe, France. *Club:* Union interalliée (Paris).

**HYAMSON, Derek Joseph;** Master of the Supreme Court, Queen's Bench Division, since 1969; *b* 12 Feb. 1914; *o s* of Lionel and Jane Hyamson; *m* 1952, Cynthia Mary O'Shea; one *d*. *Educ:* Brighton Coll.; St Catharine's Coll., Cambridge. Served War in R Artillery, 1939-46 (Lt-Col, 1944). Admitted as a Solicitor, 1939; called to the bar, Middle Temple, 1946; practised London and South Eastern Circuit, 1946-69. *Address:* 9 Ashmere Avenue, Beckenham, Kent BR3 2PQ. *T:* 01-650 3512.

**HYDE, Lady; (Marion Feoderovna Louise),** DCVO 1961 (CVO 1945); Woman of the Bedchamber to Queen Elizabeth the Queen Mother, 1937-61, Extra Woman of the Bedchamber since 1961; *b* 23 Aug. 1900; *er d* of 4th Baron Wolverton; *m* 1932, Lord Hyde (*d* 1935), *e s* and *heir* of 6th Earl of Clarendon, KG, PC, GCMG, GCVO; one *s* (*see* 7th Earl of Clarendon) one *d*. *Address:* Freckenham House, Bury St Edmunds, Suffolk. *TA:* Freckenham, Suffolk. *T:* Isleham 281.

**HYDE, Francis Edwin;** Chaddock Professor of Economics, University of Liverpool, since 1948; Dean of Faculty of Arts, 1949-53; Pro-Vice-Chancellor, 1960-64; *b* 18 July 1908; *s* of Walter Henry Hassall Hyde and Charlotte Ann Sharp; *m* 1935, Marian Rosa (*d* 1967), *d* of Thomas Abercromby Welton and Rosa Sheppard; one *d*; *m* 1970, Mrs Anne Evans.

*Educ:* Wolverton Grammar Sch.; University of Liverpool; University of London; Harvard Coll., USA. BA, First Cl. Hons in History (Liverpool), 1929; MA (Liverpool), 1931; PhD (Econ.) London Sch. of Economics, 1931. Commonwealth Fund Fellow, 1931-33; Gladstone Memorial Fellow and University Fellow, 1929-31; Houblon-Norman Fellow, 1948; FRHistS. Lecturer in Economics and Economic History, 1934-48; Board of Trade, 1941-45; Pres., Liverpool Economic and Statistical Soc.; Chm., University Press of Liverpool; Hon. Treasurer Joint Matriculation Board, 1955-66; Mem. University Council, 1957-. Editor of Business History. *Publications:* Mr Gladstone at the Board of Trade, 1934; The Import Trade of the Port of Liverpool, 1946; Economic History of Buckinghamshire, 1948; Stony Stratford, 1948; Blue Funnel: A History of Alfred Holt & Co., 1956; (with others) A New Prospect of Economics, 1958; Harrisons of Liverpool, 1830-1939, 1966; Shipping Enterprise and Management, 1967; (with Dr Sheila Marriner) The Senior: John Samuel Swire 1825-98, 1967. Reviews and articles in Economic Journals. *Recreations:* walking and rock climbing. *Address:* Savanna, Caldy Road, West Kirby, Cheshire. *T:* 051-625 8529. *Club:* University (Liverpool).

**HYDE, H(arford) Montgomery,** MA Oxon, DLit Belfast, FRHistS; FRSL; MRIA; author and barrister; *b* Belfast, 14 Aug. 1907; *o s* of late James J. Hyde, JP, Belfast, and Isobel Greenfield Montgomery; *m* 1st, 1939, Dorothy Mabel Brayshaw (from whom he obtained a divorce, 1952), *e d* of Dr J. Murray Crofts, CBE, Disley, Cheshire; 2nd, 1955, Mary Eleanor (marr. diss., 1966), *d* of Col L. G. Fischer, IMS; 3rd, 1966, Rosalind Roberts, *y d* of Comdr J. F. W. Dimond, RN. *Educ:* Sedbergh (Scholar); Queen's Univ. Belfast (Emily Lady Pakenham Scholar); 1st Class Hons Modern History, 1928; Magdalen Coll., Oxford (Open History Exhibitioner); 2nd Class Hons Jurisprudence, 1930; Harmsworth Law Scholar, Middle Temple, 1932. Called to Bar, Middle Temple, 1934; joined NE Circuit; Extension Lecturer in History, Oxford Univ., 1934; Private Sec. to Marquess of Londonderry, 1935-39; Asst Censor, Gibraltar, 1940; commissioned in Intelligence Corps, 1940; Military Liaison and Censorship Security Officer, Bermuda, 1940-41; Asst Passport Control Officer, New York, 1941-42; with British Army Staff, USA, 1942-44; Major, 1942; attached Supreme HQ Allied Expeditionary Force, 1944; Allied Commission for Austria, 1944-45; Lt-Col 1945; Asst Editor, Law Reports, 1946-47; Legal Adviser, British Lion Film Corp. Ltd, 1947-49; MP (U) North Belfast, 1950-59; UK Delegate to Council of Europe Consultative Assembly, Strasbourg, 1952-55; Hon. Col Intelligence Corps (TA), NI, 1958-61; Professor of Hist. and Polit. Sci., University of the Punjab, Lahore, 1959-61. Active in campaign for abolition of capital punishment; has travelled extensively in Russia, The Far East, West Indies, Mexico, and South America. *Publications:* The Rise of Castlereagh, 1933; The Russian Journals of Martha and Catherine Wilmot (with the Marchioness of Londonderry), 1934; More Letters from Martha Wilmot, Impressions of Vienna (with the Marchioness of Londonderry), 1935; The Empress Catherine and Princess Dashkhov, 1935; Air Defence and the Civil Population (with G. R. Falkiner Nuttall), 1937; Londonderry House and Its Pictures, 1937; Princess Lieven, 1938; Judge Jeffreys, 1940, new edn, 1948; Mexican Empire, 1946; A Victorian Historian, 1947; Privacy and the Press, 1947; John Law, 1948, new edn 1969; The Trials of Oscar Wilde, 1948, 1962; Mr and Mrs Beeton, 1951; Cases that changed the Law, 1951; Carson, 1953; The Trial of Craig and Bentley, 1954; United in Crime, 1955; Mr and Mrs Daventry, a play by Frank Harris, 1957; The Strange Death of Lord Castlereagh, 1959; The Trial of Roger Casement, 1960, 1964; The Life and Cases of Sir Patrick Hastings, 1960; Recent Developments in Historical Method and Interpretation, 1960; Simla and the Simla Hill States under British Protection, 1961; An International Crime Case Book, 1962; The Quiet Canadian, 1962; Oscar Wilde: the Aftermath, 1963; Room 3603, 1964; A History of Pornography, 1964; Norman Birkett, 1964; Cynthia, 1965; The Story of Lamb House, 1966; Lord Reading, 1967; Strong for Service: The Life of Lord Nathan of Churt, 1968; Henry James At Home, 1969; The Other Love, 1970; Their Good Names, 1970; Stalin, 1971; chapter 12 (The Congress of Vienna) in the Cambridge History of Poland, etc. *Recreations:* criminology, music. *Address:* Westwell House, Tenterden, Kent. *T:* Tenterden 3189. *Clubs:* Garrick; Dormy House (Rye); Ulster (Belfast); Grolier (New York).

**HYDE, Henry Armroid,** CIE 1936; MC; retired; *b* 17 Jan. 1885; *s* of Henry Thomas Hyde, late Administrator General of Bengal, and Amy Dougal; *m* 1921, G. H. A. Thompson; one *s*. *Educ:* Rugby; Coopers Hill. Joined Public Works Dept, India, 1906; commission in the Reserve of Officers, 1915; went to France, RFA, 1916 (MC); demobilised, 1919; rejoined PWD; Major AIRO, 1927-32; Chief Engineer and Sec. to Govt of Central Provinces, India, 1932-37; retired 1940; joined RAF as Pilot Officer, 1940, for station defence; discharged on medical grounds, 1943. *Recreations:* all forms of sport. *Address:* c/o National Provincial Bank Ltd, Trafalgar Square, WC2.

**HYDE, James Hazen;** *b* New York City, 6 June 1876; *s* of Henry Baldwin Hyde (founder and late President Equitable Life Assurance Society of the United States) and Annie Fitch Hyde; one *s*. *Educ:* Cutler's Sch., New York; AB Harvard Univ., 1898; Hon. MA Princeton University, 1903; Dr *hc* Rennes Univ., France, 1920; Hon. LLD Skidmore Coll., 1956; Vice-Pres. Equitable Life Assurance Soc., US, 1899-1905; founder (1902) and First Pres. of the Fédération des Alliances Françaises aux Etats-Unis (now Hon. Pres. and Mem. Exec. Cttee); founded Alliance Française in NY, in 1898 (now Hon. Pres.); Fellow RSL and RSA, London; Grand Croix of the Légion d'Honneur; Mem. of Académie des Sciences Morales et Politiques (Institut de France) since 1938. Chm. of Board, French Institute (New York); Vice-Pres. New York France-America Soc.; Hon. mem. Com. Amer. Field Service Fellowships, NY; Fellow, Metropolitan Museum of Art, NY City; Member: American Geographical Soc., NY; NY Historical Soc.; Exec. Cttee, American Soc. of French Legion of Honor; Life Fellow Cleveland Museum of Art (Ohio). Captain and Aide to High Comr, Amer. Red Cross in Paris during European War, 1914-18; organized Conreid Metropolitan Opera Co. NY, 1903; one of sponsors of New Theatre, NY, 1909. *Publications:* articles and lectures. *Recreations:* reading, collecting art objects on the allegorical representations of the Four Parts of the World. *Address:* Savoy Hilton Hotel, New York, NY, USA. *TA:* Hazenhyde, New York. *Clubs:* Century Association, Meadow Brook (hon. mem.), Harvard, Knickerbocker, University, union (New York); University (Albany).

**HYDE-CLARKE, (Ernest) Meredyth,** CBE 1962 (MBE 1942); Director of Organisation of Employers' Federations, etc (formerly Overseas Employers' Federation), since 1957 (Secretary, 1953-57); *b* London, 3 May 1905; *ys* of Percy Clarke, LLB and Alice Mary Young; *m* 1st, 1930, Edith Margaret, *e d* of late Albert and Florence Stevenson, Alderley Edge; two *d*; 2nd, 1970, Barbara Joan, *y d* of late Clare and of Florence Gilmour, London, Ont. Educ: St George's Sch., Harpenden; University of London; Wadham Coll., Oxford. Administrative Service, Kenya, 1927-50; Resident Magistrate, 1934; Dir of Manpower and Labour Commissioner, MLC Kenya, 1945-50; Permanent Sec., Ministry of Local Govt, Ghana, 1950-52; Establishment Sec., Ghana, 1952-53. Member: Honeyman Commn of Enquiry, N Rhodesia, 1957; Kenya Constitutional Commn (Boundaries), 1962; Council for Technical Education and Training for Overseas Countries (Management Gp), 1962-; Assoc. Mem. Commonwealth Parliamentary Assoc., 1953-. British Employers Technical Adviser/Delegate to various ILO conferences, 1953-60. *Publications:* various reports on industrial relations. *Address:* Cromer Hyde, Lemsford, Welwyn, Herts. *T:* Welwyn Garden 27114; Progress House, 10 Snow Hill, EC1. *T:* 01-248 5454. *Clubs:* Royal Commonwealth Society; Nairobi (Kenya).

**HYDE-PARKER, Sir R. W.;** *see* Parker.

**HYDE WHITE, Wilfrid;** *b* 12 May 1903; *s* of Edward William White, Canon of Gloucester and Ethel Adelaide White; *m* 1927, Blanche Hope Aitken; one *s*; *m* 1957, Ethel Korenman (stage name Ethel Drew); one *s* one *d*. *Educ:* Marlborough. First appeared in London in Beggar on Horseback, Queen's Theatre, 1925; successful appearances include: Rise Above It, Comedy; It Depends What You Mean, Westminster; Britannus in Cæsar and Cleopatra, St James's, London, and Ziegfield, New York; Affairs of State, Cambridge; Hippo Dancing, Lyric; The Reluctant Debutante, Cambridge, and Henry Miller's Theatre, New York; Not in the Book, Criterion; Miss Pell is Missing, Criterion; The Doctor's Dilemma, Haymarket; Lady Windermere's Fan, Phoenix. *Films include:* The 3rd Man, The Browning Version, Golden Salamander, The Million Pound Note, Libel, North West Frontier, Let's Make Love, His and Hers, On the Double, Ada, The Castaways, Crooks Anonymous, On the Fiddle, Aliki, My Fair Lady. *Address:* 67157 Santa Barbara Drive, Palm Springs, California, USA. *Clubs:* Green Room, Buck's.

**HYLTON,** 5th Baron, *cr* 1866; **Raymond Hervey Jolliffe,** ALAS; *b* 13 June 1932; *er s* of 4th Baron Hylton and of the Dowager Lady Hylton, *d* of late Raymond Asquith and *sister* of 2nd Earl of Oxford and Asquith, *qv*; *S* father, 1967; *m* 1966, Joanna Ida Elizabeth, *d* of late Andrew de Bertodano; two *s*. *Educ:* Eton (King's Scholar); Trinity Coll., Oxford (MA). Lieut R of O, Coldstream Guards. Asst Private Sec. to Governor-General of Canada, 1960-62; Trustee, Housing the Homeless Central Fund; Hon. Gen. Sec., Catholic Housing Aid Soc. Mem., Frome RDC, 1968. *Heir: s* Hon. William Henry Martin Jolliffe, *b* 1 April 1967. *Address:* Ammerdown, Radstock, Bath, Som.

**HYLTON-FOSTER,** family name of Baroness Hylton-Foster.

**HYLTON-FOSTER, Baroness,** *cr* 1965, of the City of Westminster (Life Peer); **Audrey Pellew Hylton-Foster;** President, County of London Branch, British Red Cross Society, since 1960; *b* 19 May 1908; *d* of 1st Viscount Ruffside, PC, DL (*d* 1958), and Viscountess Ruffside (*d* 1969); *m* 1931, Rt Hon. Sir Harry Hylton-Foster, QC (*d* 1965); no *c*. *Educ:* St George's, Ascot; Ivy House, Wimbledon. *Recreations:* gardening, trout fishing. *Address:* The Coach House, Tanhurst, Leith Hill, Dorking, Surrey. *T:* Dorking 6575.

**HYMAN, Joe;** Chairman, Viyella International, 1962-69; Underwriting member of Lloyd's; Governor, Bedales School; *b* 14 Oct. 1921; *yr s* of late Solomon Hyman and of Hannah Hyman; *m* 1st, 1950, Corinne I. Abrahams (marriage dissolved); one *s* one *d*; 2nd, 1963, Simone Duke; one *s* one *d*. *Educ:* North Manchester Gram. Sch. Has been in Textiles, 1939-. Trustee, Pestalozzi Children's Village Trust, 1967-; Governor, LSE. FRSA 1968; FBIM. Comp. TI. *Recreations:* music and golf. *Address:* Lukyns, Ewhurst, Surrey; Arlington House, Arlington Street, SW1. *Club:* Royal Automobile.

**HYND, Henry;** JP Middlesex; *b* Perth, Scotland, 4 July 1900; *s* of Henry Hynd; *m* 1925, Phyllis Jarman; one *d*. *Educ:* Perth Academy. Railway Clerk, 1915-20; Trade Union Official, 1920-45; Member Hornsey Borough Council, 1939-52; MP (Lab) for Central Hackney, 1945-50, for Accrington, 1950-66; Parliamentary Private Sec. to First Lord of the Admiralty, Dec. 1945-46 and to Min. of Defence, 1946-50. Vice-President: B-P Scout Guild; Hornsey Labour Party. Commander of Belgian Order of the Crown and Officer of Luxembourg Order of the Oak Crown. *Recreations:* travelling, bowls. *Address:* 31 Alford House, Stanhope Road, N6. *T:* 01-340 3308.

**HYND, John Burns;** *b* 4 April 1902; *s* of Henry Hynd, Perth, Scotland, and Ann Hynd, JP, Perth; *m* 1927, Elsie Margaret Doran; one *d*. *Educ:* St Ninian's Episcopal Sch., Perth; Caledonian Road Sch., Perth. Railway Clerk, District Office, LMSR, Perth, 1916-25; Trade Union Clerk (NUR), 1925-44; MP (Lab) Attercliffe Div. of Sheffield, 1944-70; Chancellor of the Duchy of Lancaster, and Minister for Germany and Austria, 1945-47; Minister of Pensions during 1947; Mem. of General Medical Council, 1950-55. Chm., Anglo-German and Anglo-Latin American Parly Groups. Grand Cross of Merit with Star (West German Republic), 1958; Chevalier of the Legion of Honour; Great Golden Cross of Honour with Star (Austria). *Publication:* Willy Brandt: A Pictorial Biography, 1966. *Recreations:* chess, golf, photography, etc. *Address:* 18 Lakeside, Enfield, Middx. *T:* 01-363 2920.

**HYND, Mrs Ronald;** *see* Page, Annette.

**HYSLOP, Robert John M.;** *see* Maxwell-Hyslop.

**HYTNER, Benet Alan,** QC 1970; *b* 29 Dec. 1927; *s* of Maurice and Sarah Hytner, Manchester; *m* 1954, Joyce, *er d* of Bernard and Vera Myers, Manchester; three *s* one *d*. *Educ:* Manchester Grammar Sch.; Trinity Hall, Cambridge (Exhibr). BA Hons Law, 1949. National Service, RASC, 1949-51 (commnd). Called to Bar, Middle Temple, 1952. *Recreations:* fell walking, music, theatre, reading. *Address:* 6 Linden Road, Didsbury, Manchester 20. *T:* 061-445 5722.

**HYTTEN, Torleiv,** CMG 1953; Vice-Chancellor, University of Tasmania, 1949-57, retired; *b* Drammen, Norway, 17 Feb. 1890; *s* of late E. O. Hytten, Tönsberg, Norway; *m* 1922, Margaret Frances (*née* Compton); one *s* (and one *s* decd). *Educ:* Tönsberg; University of

Tasmania. MA, 1st Cl. Hons Economics. Went to Australia, 1910; Journalist, 1920-26; University of Tasmania: Lecturer in Economics, 1926; Professor of Economics, 1929-35; Dir of Tutorial Classes, 1928-32. Economic Adviser: Tasmanian Govt 1929-35; Bank of NSW, 1935-49. Conducted case for Tasmanian Govt before Commonwealth Public Accts Cttee, 1930-31 before Commonwealth Grants Commn, 1933-34. Chm. Tasmanian State Employment Council, 1932; Delegate 16th Assembly, League of Nations, 1935; Chm. Aust. Nat. Cttee, Internat. Chamber of Commerce, 1949; Mem., Commonwealth Bank Bd, 1954-59. Conducted enquiry into Transport Problems in Qld, 1958. Knight 1st Class, Order of St Olav (Norway), 1951; Chevalier, Order of the Crown (Belgium), 1957. *Publications:* articles to Economic Record and similar periodicals, principally on economics of transport, and banking. *Address:* Forestgait, 22 King's Gate, Aberdeen AB9 2Y1. *T:* Aberdeen 28473. *Club:* Royal Northern (Aberdeen).

# I

**IBBOTSON, Lancelot William Cripps,** MBE 1948; General Manager of Southern Region, British Railways, and Chairman, Southern Railway Board, since 1968; *b* 10 Feb. 1909; *s* of William Ibbotson, FRCS and Mrs Dora Ibbotson (*née* Chapman), London; *m* 1931, Joan Marguerite Jeffcock; one *s* one *d*. *Educ:* Radley Coll. Traffic Apprentice, LNER, 1927; Chief Clerk to Dist. Supt, Newcastle, 1939; Asst Dist Supt, York, 1942; Dist Supt, Darlington, 1945; Asst to Operating Supt, Western Region, 1950; Asst Gen. Man., Western Region, 1959; Chief Operating Officer, British Railways, 1963; Gen. Man., Western Region, BR, and Chm., Western Railway Board, 1966-68. *Recreations:* foreign travel, photography. *Address:* Monk's Well, Waverley, Farnham, Surrey. *T:* Runfold 2328. *Club:* United Service.

**IBIAM, Sir Francis (Akanu),** GCON 1963; KCMG 1962; KBE 1951 (OBE 1949); LLD, DLit; Adviser to Military Governor of Eastern Provinces, Nigeria, from 1966; Chairman, Governing Council of the University of Nigeria, Nsukka, Nigeria, from 1966; Principal, Hope Waddell Training Institution, Calabar, 1957-60; *b* Unwana, Afikpo Division, Nigeria, 29 Nov. 1906; *s* of late Ibiam Aka Ibiam and late Alu Owora; *m* 1939, Eudora Olayinka Sasegbon; one *s* two *d*. *Educ:* Hope Waddell Training Instn Calabar; King's Coll., Lagos; University of St Andrews, Scotland. Medical Missionary with the Church of Scotland Mission, Calabar, Nigeria, 1936; started and built up new Hosp. in Abiriba, Bende Div., under Calabar Mission, 1936-45; Medical Supt, CSM Hosp., Itu, 1945-48; CSM Hosp., Uburu, 1952-57. MLC, Nigeria, 1947-52; MEC, 1949-52; retd from Politics, 1953; (on leave) Governor, Eastern Nigeria, 1960-66. Trustee: Presbyterian Church of Nigeria, 1945-; Queen Elizabeth Hosp., Umuahia-Ibeku, 1953-; Scout Movement of Eastern Nigeria, 1957-; Mem. Bd of Governors: Hope Waddell Trg Instn, Calabar, 1945-60; Queen Elizabeth Hosp., 1950-60; Mem. Provl Council of University Coll., Ibadan, 1948-54; Mem. Privy Council, Eastern Nigeria, 1954-60; Pres., Christian Council of Nigeria, 1955-58; Mem. Calabar Mission Council, 1940-60 (now integrated with Church); Mem. Admin. Cttee of Internat. Missionary Council, 1957-61; Chm. Provisional Cttee of All Africa Churches Conf., 1958-62; Chm., Council of University Coll., Ibadan, Nigeria, 1958-60; a Pres. of World Council of Churches, 1961-; a Pres. of All Africa Church Conf., 1962-; Pres., World Council of Christian Educn and Sunday Sch. Assoc.; Vice-Pres., Assoc. United Bible Societies. Presbyterian Church of Nigeria: Mem. Educ. Authority, 1940-; Mem. Missionaries' Cttee, Med. Bd, and Standing Cttee of Synod; Advanced Training Fund Management Cttee of Synod; Elder, 1940-. *Recreation:* reading. *Address:* 1 Mount Street, Enugu, Nigeria.

**IBRAHIM, Sir Kashim,** GCON 1963; KCMG 1962; CBE 1960 (MBE 1952); Governor of Northern Nigeria, 1962-66; Adviser to Military Governor, since 1966; *b* 1910; *s* of Mallam Ibrahim Lakkani; *m* 1st, 1943, Halima; 2nd, 1944, Khadija; 3rd, 1957, Zainaba; four *s* three *d* (and two *d* decd). *Educ:* Bornu Provincial Sch.; Katsina Teachers' Trng Coll. Teacher, 1929-32; Visiting Teacher, 1933-49; Educ. Officer, 1949-52. Federal Minister of Social Services, 1952-55; Northern Regional Minister of Social Develt and Surveys, 1955-56; Waziri of Bornu, 1956-62. Chm. Nigerian Coll. of Arts, Science and Technology, 1958-62; Chm. Provisional Council of Ahmadu Bello Univ. Hon. LLD: Ahmadu Bello, 1963; Univ. of Ibadan; Univ. of Nigeria (Nsukka); University of Lagos. *Publications:* Kanuri Reader Elementary, I-IV; Kanuri Arithmetic Books, I-IV, for Elementary Schs and Teachers' Guide for above. *Recreations:* walking, riding, polo playing. *Address:* Government Lodge, Kaduna, Northern Nigeria, West Africa. *T:* Kaduna 3167.

**ICELAND, Apostolic Administrator of;** *see* Theunissen, Most Rev. J. B. H.

**IDALOVICI, Mme Heinric;** *see* Oldenbourg-Idalovici, Zoé.

**IDDESLEIGH,** 4th Earl of, *cr* 1885; **Stafford Henry Northcote;** Bt 1641; Viscount St Cyres, 1885; *b* 14 July 1932; *e s* of 3rd Earl of Iddesleigh and of Elizabeth, *er d* of late F. S. A. Lowndes and late Marie Belloc; *S* father, 1970; *m* 1955, Maria Luisa Alvarez-Builla y Urquijo (Condesa del Real Agrado in Spain), *d* of late Don Gonzalo Alvarez-Builla y Alvera and Viscountess Exmouth, *step-d* of 9th Viscount Exmouth, *qv*; one *s* one *d*. *Educ:* Downside. 2nd Lieut, Irish Guards, 1951-52. *Heir: s* Viscount St Cyres, *qv*. *Address:* Shillands House, Upton Pyne Hill, Exeter, Devon EX5 5EB. *T:* Exeter 58916.

**IEVERS, Frank George Eyre,** CMG 1964; Postmaster-General, East Africa, 1962-65, retired; *b* 8 May 1910; *s* of Eyre Francis and Catherine Ievers; *m* 1936, Phyllis Robinson; two *s*. *Educ:* Dover Coll. Asst Traffic Supt, Post Office, 1933; Traffic Supt, East Africa, 1946; Telecommunications Controller, 1951; Regional Dir, 1959. *Recreations:* golf, photography. *Address:* Elgon, The Glade, Ashley Heath, Ringwood, Hants. *Clubs:* Nairobi (Kenya); Sudan (Khartoum).

**IEVERS, Rear-Adm. John Augustine,** CB 1962; OBE 1944; *b* 2 Dec. 1912; *s* of Eyre Francis Ievers, Tonbridge, Kent; *m* 1937, Peggy G. Marshall; one *s* two *d*. *Educ:* RN Coll., Dartmouth. CO Naval Test Squadron, Boscombe Down, 1945-47; RN Staff Coll., 1948-49; HMS Ocean, 1949; HMS Glory, 1949-50; HMS Burghead Bay, 1951-52; CO, RN Air Station, Lossiemouth, 1952-54; Dep. Dir Naval Air Warfare Div., 1954-57; Captain Air, Mediterranean, 1957-60; Deputy Controller

Aircraft, Min. of Aviation, 1960-63; retd, 1964. *Recreations:* golf, tennis. *Address:* Seven Firs, Swanland, East Yorks. *T:* Hull 631424.

**IFE, HH Aderemi I, The Oni of Ife** since 1930; **Sir Titus Martins Adesoji Tadeniawo Aderemi;** PC (Western Nigeria) 1954; KCMG 1962 (CMG 1943); KBE 1950; Governor, Western Region, Nigeria, 1960-63; President House of Chiefs, Western Nigeria, 1954-60; Chairman, Council of Obas and Chiefs, Western Nigeria, since 1966; Member, Western House of Chiefs, since 1951; *b* Ife, 1889; Akui House of Ife Royal family; *m* 1910 (polygamous marriage); several *c. Educ:* CMS Sch., Ife. Joined staff of govt railway construction, 1909; Civil Service, 1910; resigned, and started trading and motor transport business, 1921. Founded Oduduwa Coll. (first secondary sch. for boys in Ife Division), 1932. Mem. House of Assembly, Western Nigeria, 1946-. MLC, Nigeria, 1947-; Mem., Nigerian House of Representatives, 1951-54; Central Minister without Portfolio, 1951-55. Mem. Nigeria Cocoa Marketing Board, 1947-; Dir Nigerian Produce Marketing Company Ltd, 1947-. Visited England, July-Oct. 1948; attended meetings connected with cocoa industry; delegate to African Conference, London, 1948; led Nigerian Delegation to Coronation, 1953; delegate to Conference for revision of Nigerian Constitution, in London, July-Aug. 1953, and at Lagos, Jan. 1954; delegate to Nigerian Constitutional Confs, London, May-June 1957, Sept.-Oct. 1958. Hon. LLD University of Ife, 1967. *Recreations:* cricket and tennis; hunting game (before accession to the throne). *Address:* The Afin (Palace), Ife, Nigeria, West Africa.

**IGGULDEN, Sir Douglas (Percy),** Kt 1969; CBE 1954; DSO 1945; TD 1942; Chief Valuer, Valuation Office, Board of Inland Revenue since 1966 (Deputy Chief Valuer, 1950-66); *b* 4 May 1907; *s* of late Percy Edwin Iggulden, JP, and Agnes Iggulden, Herne Bay; *m* 1932, Mollie Gertrude Margaret, *d* of late Sydney Root, Herne Bay; one *d. Educ:* Kent Coll., Canterbury. FRICS; FAI. Articles and private practice as a surveyor, 1924-37; joined Valuation Office, Board of Inland Revenue, 1937. TA service: commissioned in 4th Bn The Buffs, 1924; mobilized, 1939; France (despatches), 1939-40; Malta, 1940-43, comd 4th Buffs, 1942; POW Leros, 1943; demobilized, 1945 (Major; Hon. Lt-Col). Commander Royal Order of the Dannebrog, Denmark. *Address:* 28 Anne Boleyn's Walk, Cheam, Surrey. *T:* 01-642 5048. *Club:* Royal Automobile.

**IGNATIEFF, George;** Canadian Ambassador and Permanent Representative to United Nations and other International Organisations at Geneva, since 1970; *b* 16 Dec. 1913; *s* of Count Paul N. Ignatieff and Princess Natalie Mestchersky; *m* 1945, Alison Grant; two *s. Educ:* St Paul's, London; Lower Canada Coll., Montreal; Jarvis Coll., Toronto; Univs of Toronto and Oxford. Rhodes Schol., Ont, 1935; BA Toronto 1936; MA Oxon 1938. Dept of External Affairs, Ottawa, 1940; 3rd Sec., London, 1940-44; Ottawa, 1944-45; Adviser, Canadian Delegn, UN Atomic Energy Commn, 1946; UN Assembly, 1946-47; Alt Rep., UN Security Council, 1946-48; Councillor, Canadian Embassy, Washington, DC, 1948-53; Imp. Def. Coll., London, 1953-54; Head of Defence Liaison Div., External Affairs, Ottawa, 1954-55; Canadian Ambassador to Yugoslavia, 1956-58; Dep. High Comr, London, 1959-60; Asst Under-Sec. of State for External Affairs, Ottawa, 1960-62; Perm. Rep. and Canadian Ambassador to NATO, 1962-66; Canadian Perm. Rep. and Ambassador to UN, NY, 1966-69, to Cttee on Disarmament, Geneva, 1969-70. Hon. LLD: Toronto, 1969; Brock, 1969; Guelph 1970. *Address:* 10a Avenue de Budé, Geneva, Switzerland. *Club:* Brooks's.

**IKERRIN, Viscount; David James Theobald Somerset Butler;** *b* 9 Jan. 1953; *s* and *heir* of 9th Earl of Carrick, *qv*.

**IKIN, Rutherford Graham;** Headmaster of Trent College, 1936-68; *b* 22 Jan. 1903; *s* of late Dr A. E. Ikin, formerly Dir of Education, Blackpool; *m* 1936, Elizabeth Mary Mason; two *d. Educ:* King Edward VI Sch., Norwich; King's Coll., Cambridge (Choral Scholar). BA 1925; MA 1928; Asst Master at King's Sch., Ely, 1926-29; History Master and House Master, St Bees Sch., 1929-36. *Publications:* A Pageant of World History; The Modern Age; The History of the King's School, Ely. *Address:* Eden Bank, Top Lane, Whatstandwell, Matlock, Derbyshire. *T:* Ambergate 2582. *Club:* Public Schools.

**ILCHESTER,** 9th Earl of, *cr* 1756; **Maurice Vivian de Touffreville Fox-Strangways;** Baron Ilchester and Strangways, 1741; Baron Ilchester and Stavordale, Baron of Redlynch, 1747; Wing Commander, Royal Air Force; *b* 1 April 1920; *s* of 8th Earl of Ilchester and of Laure Georgine Emilie, *d* of late Evanghelos Georgios Mazaraki, sometime Treasurer of Suez Canal Company, at Suez; *S* father, 1970; *m* 1941, Diana Mary Elizabeth, *e d* of late George Frederick Simpson, Cassington, Oxfordshire. *Educ:* Kingsbridge Sch. CEng; AFRAeS; FINucE; Mem., Soc. of Engineers; AMBIM; FRSA. *Recreations:* shooting, cricket, tennis. *Heir: b* Hon. Raymond George Fox-Strangways [*b* 11 Nov. 1921; *m* 1941, Margaret Vera, *d* of late James Force, North Surrey, BC; two *s*]. *Address:* 155 Babington Place, Biggin Hill 2987. *Clubs:* Brooks's, Royal Air Force.

**ILERSIC, Prof. Alfred Roman;** Professor of Social Studies, Bedford College, University of London, since 1965; *b* 14 Jan. 1920; *s* of late Roman Ilersic and Mary (*née* Moss); *m* 1944, Patricia Florence Bertram Liddle; one *s* one *d. Educ:* Polytechnic Sec. Sch., London; London Sch. of Economics. Lectr in Econs, University Coll. of S West, Exeter, 1947-53; Lectr in Social Statistics, Beford Coll., 1953; Reader in Economic and Social Statistics, Bedford Coll., London, 1963. Chm., Inst. of Statisticians, 1968-70. Hon. Mem., Rating and Valuation Assoc., 1968. *Publications:* Statistics, 1953; Government Finance and Fiscal Policy in Post-War Britain, 1956; (with P. F. B. Liddle) Parliament of Commerce 1860-1960, 1960; Taxation of Capital Gains, 1962; Rate Equalisation in London, 1968; Local Government Finance in Northern Ireland, 1969. *Recreations:* listening to music, walking. *Address:* 1 Park Road, Lewes, Sussex. *T:* Lewes 3913. *Clubs:* Reform, English-Speaking Union.

**ILES, Air Vice-Marshal Leslie Millington,** CBE 1942; AFC 1918; *b* 4 Oct. 1894; *s* of Henry and Mary Elizabeth Iles, The Orchard, Fairford, Glos; *m* 1st, 1924, Beatrice May Till (*decd*); one *s*; 2nd, 1936, Thelma Celia Newman; one *s. Educ:* Bancroft's Sch., Woodford Green, Essex; St Catharine's Coll., Cambridge (BA Hons, Mech. Sci. Tripos); Imperial Coll. Science and Technology (DIC). Territorial Gunners, Hants RHA, 1913; transferred to RFC 1917, continuous service with RFC and RAF since then; served European War, 1914-18 (despatches, AFC); War of 1939-45 (despatches, CBE). Commanded RAF Officers' Sch. of Aeronautical Engineering;

102 Sqn; 226 Gp, India; Controller of Technical Services, British Air Commn at Washington, 1945; Dep. Dir Military Aircraft R and D, 1947; retired from RAF, 1948. DIC; AFRAeS. *Recreations:* golf, shooting. *Address:* 6 Heathside, Hanger Hill, Weybridge, Surrey. *T:* 48350. *Club:* Burhill Golf (Walton-on-Thames).

**ILFORD,** Baron *cr* 1962, of Bury (Life Peer); **Geoffrey Clegg Hutchinson,** Kt 1952; MC 1916; TD; QC 1939; Hon. Freeman of Borough of Ilford, 1954, and of London Borough of Camden; Governor and Almoner of Christ's Hospital; Chairman, Commission appointed by Church Assembly on pastoral legislation, 1955; *b* 14 Oct. 1893; *y s* of late Henry Ormerod Hutchinson, VD, JP; *m* Janet Bidlake, *y d* of late Henry Frederick Keep. *Educ:* Cheltenham Coll.; Clare Coll., Cambridge (Scholar). MA, 1919; joined The Lancs Fusiliers, 1914; served Brit. Exped. Force, 1915-16, 1918-19 (wounded, MC); Brit. Exped. Force, France, 1940; Deputy-Asst Military Sec., War Office, 1941-42; Hon. Col 5th Bn The Lancs Fusiliers, 1948-54; called to Bar, Inner Temple, 1920; Bencher, 1946; Northern Circuit; MP (C) Ilford, 1937-45; Ilford North, 1950-54. Mem. of Select Cttee on National Expenditure, 1942-45, of Speaker's Conf., 1944, of Consolidation Cttee, 1951-53. Pres., British Waterworks Assoc., 1947; Pres., Water Companies Assoc., 1951-54; Chm., E Surrey Water Co., 1952-54; Dir, Colne Valley Water Co., 1944-54; Pres., Non-County Boroughs Assoc., 1937-44; Hon. Mem., National and Local Govt Officers' Assoc.; Mem. Hampstead Borough Council, 1931-37 (Chm., Finance Cttee, 1936-37); Alderman, LCC, 1944-49; represented Hampstead on Council, 1949-52. Chm. Home Counties North Provincial Area Council, Conservative Party, 1946. Chm., National Assistance Board, 1954-64; Pres., Assoc. of Municipal Corporations, 1964-68; Life Vice-Pres., Assoc. of Municipal Corporations, 1968; Comr (Appeals) London Govt Staff Commn, 1964; Gov. Nat. Corp. for Care of Old People, 1965-69; Master, Needlemakers' Company, 1967. *Address:* 2 Paper Buildings, Temple, EC4. *TA:* 57 Temple. *T:* 01-353 5835, 12 Church Row, NW3. *Clubs:* Athenæum, Carlton.

**ILIFF, Neil Atkinson,** CBE 1970; Managing Director, Shell Chemicals UK Ltd (previously Shell Chemical Co. Ltd), since 1960, Deputy Chairman since 1968; also Chairman, Petrochemicals Ltd and subsidiaries; Member, Royal Commission on Environmental Pollution, since 1970; *b* 23 May 1916; *s* of late Charles Wilkinson Iliff and Dorothy Atkinson; *m* 1950, Ann, *d* of Rt Hon. Sir Kenneth Pickthorn, Bt, *qv*; one *s* four *d*. *Educ:* Oundle; King's Coll., Cambridge (Major Scholar). Served with HM Forces, 1940-46 (despatches); Lt-Col, Royal Engineers. Fellow and Lectr, King's Coll., Cambridge, 1946-47. Joined Shell, 1948; USA, 1950-51; Germany, 1955-58. President: British Plastics Federation, 1965-67; Soc. of Chemical Industry, 1967-69 (Chm. Council, 1969-); Chemical Industries Assoc., 1968-. Chm., Economic Development Cttee for the Newspaper, Printing, and Publishing Industry, 1968-; Member: Adv. Council of Technology; Economic Development Cttee for the Chemical Industry; Governing Body, Imperial Coll., 1968; Governor, Sedbergh Sch., 1969. Hon. Fellow, Univ. of Manchester Inst. of Science and Technology, 1969. FRSA 1968. Hon. DSc Heriot-Watt, 1968. *Publications:* papers in Chemistry and Industry. *Recreation:* sailing. *Address:* 47 St George's Drive, SW1. *T:* 01-828 0907; Rosehill, Orford, Suffolk; *T:* Orford 344; Shell Centre, SE1. *T:* 01-934 3700. *Clubs:* Carlton; Aldeburgh Yacht.

**ILIFF, Sir William (Angus Boyd),** Kt 1961; CMG 1944; MBE 1924; Director: The De La Rue Company; Thomas De La Rue International; Pakistan Security Printing Corporation; *b* 2 Oct. 1898; *s* of late John Boyd Iliff, Kircubbin, Co. Down; *m*; two *d*; *m* 1947, Jacqueline Lois Christine Reepmaker-d'Orville; one *s*. *Educ:* Mountjoy School, Dublin; Cadet Coll., Wellington, India. Commissioned to IA, 1916. Served on NW Frontier, Mesopotamia, N Persia and S Russia. Entered N Ireland Civil Service, 1922. Private Sec. to Rt Hon. J. M. Andrews, DL, MP; Assist Sec., Ministry of Labour, 1935; Major Supp. Res. RA 1938; served in France, Dunkirk, 1940; Permanent Sec., Ministry of Public Security (Northern Ireland), 1940-41; Financial Counsellor at British Legation, Tehran, 1941-44; Financial Adviser to Governor of Burma, 1944; Representative of HM Treasury in Middle East, 1944-48; Loan Dir, International Bank, 1948, Asst to Pres., 1951, Vice-Pres., 1956-62. *Address:* Gasper, near Stourton, Wilts. *T:* Bourton 370. *Club:* Travellers'.

**ILIFFE,** family name of **Baron Iliffe.**

**ILIFFE,** 2nd Baron, *cr* 1933, of Yattendon; **Edward Langton Iliffe;** Vice-Chairman of the Birmingham Post and Mail Ltd; Chairman of the Coventry Evening Telegraph and of the Cambridge News; *b* 25 Jan. 1908; *er s* of 1st Baron Iliffe, GBE, and Charlotte Gilding; *S* father 1960; *m* 1938, Renée, *er d* of René Merandon du Plessis, Mauritius. *Educ:* Sherborne; France; Clare Coll., Cambridge. Served, 1940-46, with RAFVR (despatches). Governor, Royal Shakespeare Theatre, Stratford-on-Avon; Trustee, Shakespeare's Birthplace; Mem. Council, Univ. of Warwick, 1965-; Pres., Internat. Lawn Tennis Club of Gt Britain, 1965. High Sheriff of Berks, 1957. Hon. Freeman, City of Coventry. *Heir: n* Robert Peter Richard Iliffe [*b* 22 Nov. 1944; *m* 1966, Anne, twin *d* of Comdr Arthur Skipwith; two *s*]. *Address:* 26 St James's Place, SW1. *T:* 01-493 2717; Basildon Park, near Goring, Berks. *T:* Pangbourne 2447. *Clubs:* Carlton, White's; Royal Yacht Squadron.

**ILLINGWORTH, Sir Charles (Frederick William),** Kt 1961; CBE 1946; Regius Professor of Surgery, University of Glasgow, 1939, Emeritus, 1964; Hon. Surgeon to the Queen, in Scotland, 1961-65; Extra Surgeon since 1965; *b* 8 May 1899; *s* of John and Edith Illingworth; *m* 1928, Eleanor Mary Bennett; four *s*. *Educ:* Heath Grammar Sch., Halifax; Univ. of Edinburgh. Graduated Medicine, 1922. 2nd Lieut, RFC 1917. FRCSE 1925; FRCSGlas, 1963. Hon. FACS, 1954; Hon. FRCS, 1958; Hon. FRCSI, 1964; Hon. FRCS (Canada), 1965; Hon. Fellow, Coll. Surg. S Africa, 1965. DSc (Hon.): University of Sheffield, 1962; University of Belfast, 1963; Hon. LLD (Glasgow, Leeds) 1965. *Publications:* (jtly) Text Book of Surgical Pathology, 1932; Short Text Book of Surgery, 1938; Text Book of Surgical Treatment, 1942; Monograph on Peptic Ulcer, 1953; The Story of William Hunter, 1967; various contributions to surgical literature, mainly on digestive disorders. *Address:* 7 Winton Drive, Glasgow, W2. *T:* 041-339 5005.

**ILLINGWORTH, David Gordon,** MD, FRCPE; Surgeon Apothecary to HM Household at Holyrood Palace, Edinburgh, since 1970; Lecturer in General Practice Teaching Unit, Edinburgh University, since 1965; *b* 22 Dec. 1921; *yr s* of Sir Gordon Illingworth; *m* 1946, Lesley Beagrie, Peterhead; two *s* one *d*. *Educ:*

George Watson's Coll.; Edinburgh University. MB, ChB Edinburgh, 1943; MRCPE 1949; MD (with commendation) 1963; FRCPE 1965. Nuffield Foundn Travelling Fellow, 1966. RN Medical Service, 1944-46; medical appts, Edinburgh Northern Hosps Group, 1946-. *Publications:* contribs to BMJ, Jl of Clinical Pathology, Gut, etc. *Recreations:* golf, gardening. *Address:* 19 Napier Road, Edinburgh EH10 5AZ. *T:* 031-229 2392. *Club:* University (Edinburgh).

**ILLINGWORTH, Leslie Gilbert;** Political Cartoonist, Punch and Daily Mail; *b* Barry, Glam., 2 Sept. 1902; 2nd *s* of Richard Frederick Illingworth and Helen, *d* of Alexander MacGregor; unmarried. *Educ:* Barry County School; Royal College of Art; Slade School, London Univ. Political Cartoonist, Western Mail, Cardiff, 1921; first contributed to Punch, 1927; Free-lance Artist, 1926-39; joined Daily Mail, 1939; joined Punch as Junior Cartoonist, 1945. *Recreation:* gardening. *Address:* Silverdale, Robertsbridge, Sussex. *T:* Robertsbridge 154. *Clubs:* Chelsea Arts, Royal Automobile.

**ILLINGWORTH, Rear-Adm. Philip Holden Crothers,** CB 1969; Deputy Controller of Aircraft, Ministry of Technology, since 1969; *b* 29 Nov. 1916; *s* of late Norman Holden Illingworth, Woking; *m* 1944, Dorothy Jean, *d* of George Wells, Southbourne; three *s* three *d*. *Educ:* RN Coll., Dartmouth, RNEC. Joined RN 1930, Rear-Adm. 1967. *Address:* Manor House, Marston Magna, Somerset. *T:* Marston Magna 294. *Club:* Naval and Military.

**ILLINGWORTH, Ronald Stanley;** Professor of Child Health, University of Sheffield, since 1947; *b* 7 Oct. 1909; *s* of late H. E. Illingworth, ARIBA, ARPS, Fairleigh, Skipton Road, Ilkley; *m* Dr Cynthia Illingworth, MB, BS, MRCP, formerly Tutor in Child Health, Univ. of Sheffield; one *s* two *d*. *Educ:* Clifton House Sch., Harrogate; Bradford Grammar Sch. MB, ChB Leeds, 1934; MRCS, LRCP, 1934; MD Leeds, 1937; MRCP, 1937; DPH Leeds (distinction), 1938; DCH (RCP and S), 1938; FRCP 1947; FRPS, Fellow, Royal Society Medicine; Mem. British Paediatric Assoc.; Mem. BMA; Hon. Member: Swedish Pædiatric Assoc.; Academy of Pædiatricians of the USSR. West Riding County Major Scholar, 1928; Nuffield Research Studentship, Oxford, 1939-41; Rockefeller Research Fellowship, 1939 and 1946. Formerly Resident Asst, Hospital for Sick Children, Great Ormond Street, London, 1938-39; Medical Specialist and officer in charge of Medical Division (Lt-Col), RAMC, 1941-46. Asst to Prof. of Child Health, Univ. of London, 1946. *Publications:* The Normal Child: some problems of his first five years, 1953 (4th edn, 1968); (with C. M. Illingworth) Babies and Young Children: Feeding, Management and Care, 1954 (4th edn, 1968); ed, Recent Advances in Cerebral Palsy, 1958; Development of Infants and Children, Normal and Abnormal, 1960 (4th edn 1969); The Normal Schoolchild: His Problems, Physical and Emotional, 1964; (with C. M. Illingworth) Lessons from Childhood: some aspects of the early life of unusual men and women, 1966; Common Symptoms of Disease in Children, 1967, 2nd edn 1969; various medical and photographic papers. *Recreations:* climbing, photography, travel. *Address:* 8 Harley Road, Sheffield 11. *T:* 362774.

**ILOTT, Sir John (Moody Albert),** Kt 1954; JP; Chairman, J. Ilott Ltd; President, Golden Bay Cement Co. Ltd; Director of other companies; *b* 12 Aug. 1884; *s* of John and Elizabeth Ilott (*née* Baldwin); *m* 1912, Hazel E. M. Hall; one *s* one *d* (and one *d* decd). *Educ:* Terrace Sch., Wellington Coll.; Victoria Univ. Employed J. Ilott Ltd, 1903-. now Chm. President Emeritus, NZ Crippled Children Soc. (Inc); Member: Nuffield Trust; Trustees NZ National Library; J. R. McKenzie Trust; Vice-Pres., Wellington After-Care Assoc.; past Vice-President: Workers' Educational Assoc.; Rotary Internat.; Mem. Royal Econ. Soc., London. Trustee, National Art Gallery, NZ. Jubilee Medal, 1935; Coronation Medal, 1953. LLD (*hc*). *Recreation:* bowls. *Address:* Apartment 5, Broadwater, 214 Oriental Parade, Wellington, New Zealand. *Clubs:* Wellesley (Wellington); Wellington Golf (Life Mem.), Miramar Golf (Life Mem.), both Wellington.

**ILYUSHIN, Sergei Vladimirovich;** Order of Lenin (5 times); Soviet aircraft designer; Professor, N. E. Zhukovsky Air Force Engineering Academy; Lieutenant-General, Engineering Technical Service; *b* 1894. *Educ:* Air Force Engineering Academy. *Principal designs:* TsKB-30 twin-engine plane, 1936; IL-2 armoured attacker, 1939; IL-12 twin-engine passenger plane, 1946; IL-18 (Moscow) turbo-prop passenger plane, 1957; IL-62 passenger airliner, 1962. *Address:* Ministry of Defence, 34 Sophia Embankment, Moscow, USSR.

**IMBERT-TERRY, Major Sir Edward (Henry Bouhier),** 3rd Bt, *cr* 1917; MC 1944; *b* 28 Jan. 1920; *s* of Col Sir Henry B. Imbert-Terry, 2nd Bt, DSO, MC, DL, and of Dorothy Lady Imbert-Terry; *S* father, 1962; *m* 1944, Jean, 2nd *d* of late A. Stanley Garton; two *s* two *d*. *Educ:* Eton Coll.; New Coll., Oxford. Coldstream Guards, 1940-51; retired as Major, 1951. *Recreation:* golf. *Heir: er s* Andrew Henry Bouhier Imbert-Terry, *b* 5 Oct. 1945. *Address:* Brimshott Farm, near Chobham, Surrey. *T:* Chobham 8500; Strete Ralegh Estate, near Exeter, Devon. *T:* Whimple 243. *Clubs:* Guards, MCC.

**IMESON, Kenneth Robert,** MA; Headmaster, Nottingham High School, 1954-70; *b* 8 July 1908; *s* of R. W. Imeson; *m* 1st, 1934, Peggy (*d* 1967), *d* of late A. H. Mann, Dulwich; two *d*; 2nd, Peggy, *widow* of Duncan MacArthur, *d* of late Harold Pow. *Educ:* St Olave's; Sidney Sussex Coll., Cambridge (Schol.). Mathematical Tripos, Part 1 1928; Part II 1930. Asst Master, Llandovery Coll., 1930-33; Sen. Mathematical Master, Watford Grammar Sch., 1933-44; Headmaster, Sir Joseph Williamson's Mathematical Sch., 1944-53; Mem. Council SCM in Schools, 1948-58; Council of Friends of Rochester Cathedral, 1947-53; Board of Visitors, Nottingham Prison, 1956-57; Teaching Cttee, Mathematical Association, 1950-58; Trustee, Nottingham Mechanics Institution, 1955-70; Court of Nottingham Univ., 1955-64, 1968-70; Member: Oxford and Cambridge Examinations Board, 1957-61, 1962-70; Council Christian Education Movement, 1965-69; Cttee, Notts CCC, 1969-. *Publications:* articles in Journal of Education. *Recreations:* cricket and other games; music. *Address:* 16 Montagu Street, W1. *Club:* Public Schools.

**IMMS, George,** CB 1964; Commissioner and Director of Establishments and Organisation, HM Customs and Excise, since 1965; *b* 10 April 1911; *o s* of late George Imms; *m* 1938, Joan Sylvia Lance; two *s*. *Educ:* Grange High Sch., Bradford; Emmanuel Coll., Cambridge (Scholar). Joined HM Customs and Excise, 1933; Asst Sec., 1946; Commissioner, 1957-65. *Address:* Kings Beam House, Mark Lane, EC3.

**IMRIE, Sir John Dunlop,** Kt 1950; CBE 1942; JP; Chartered Accountant; *b* 16 Oct. 1891; *s* of late Alexander Imrie, Kinross; *m* 1953, Mary Isobel Rae Rowan. *Educ:* Dollar Academy; Edinburgh Univ. MA Edinburgh 1925; BCom Edinburgh 1923; FRSE 1943; City Chamberlain of Edinburgh, 1926-51; Hon. Financial Officer, Edinburgh Festival Society, 1945-51; Local Government Comr, Trinidad, BWI, 1951-53; Dir, Caledonian Insurance Co. Ltd, until 1965; Chairman: Wm Brown (Booksellers) Ltd; Edinburgh Bookshop Ltd; Scottish Bookshops Ltd; Past-Pres., Inst. Municipal Treasurers and Accountants; Hon. Governor Dollar Acad. Member: Scottish War Savings Cttee, 1940-64; Scottish Housing Advisory Cttee, 1942; Scottish Rating and Valuation Cttee, 1943; Cttee on Water Rating in Scotland, 1944; Cttee on Houses of National Importance, 1949; Hospital Endowments Commission, 1949; Cttee on Scottish Financial and Trade Statistics, 1950; Cttee on Economic and Financial Problems of Provision for Old Age, 1954; Historic Buildings Council for Scotland, 1954-58; South of Scotland Electricity Board, 1955-59; Public Works Loans Commission, 1956-65. *Publications:* Contributions to Local Government Finance, Public Administration, etc. *Recreations:* fishing and motoring. *Address:* Invervar Lodge, Glenlyon, Aberfeldy, Perthshire, Scotland. *T:* Glenlyon 203.

**INAYAT MASIH, Rt. Rev.;** *see* Lahore, Bishop of.

**INCE, Brigadier Cecil Edward Ronald,** CB 1950; CBE 1946 (OBE 1941); *b* 5 March 1897; 3rd *s* of late C. H. B. Ince, Barrister-at-Law; *m* 1924, Leslie, *o d* of late Robert Badham, Secretary of Midland & GW Rly, Ireland; two *d. Educ:* Sevenoaks. Regular Army; RA 1915, RASC 1919-49. Deputy Dir (Supplies), Middle East, 1940-42; War Office, 1943-47; Commandant RASC Trng Centre, 1947-49. Dir of Enforcement, subseq. Dir of Warehousing, Min. of Food and Agric., 1949-55. *Publications:* various military pamphlets and articles in Service publications. *Recreations:* mild golf, with progressive gardening. *Address:* Half-Acre, West Grove, Walton-on-Thames, Surrey. *T:* Walton-on-Thames 25035.

**INCE, Captain Edward Watkins W.;** *see* Whittington-Ince.

**INCE, Wesley Armstrong,** CMG 1968; Solicitor and Company Director; *b* 27 Nov. 1893; *s* of John and Christina Ince, Melbourne; *m* 1919, Elsie Maud Ince, *d* of Wm H. Smith, Melbourne; two *d. Educ:* Wesley Coll., Melbourne; Melbourne Univ. Admitted practice Barrister and Solicitor, 1917; Partner, Arthur Robinson & Co., 1919-67. Chm., Claude Neon Industries Ltd, 1932-; Chm., Rheem Australia Ltd, 1937-67; Foundn Mem. Coun., Inst. of Public Affairs, 1942-; Foundn Mem., Australian-American Assoc., 1941- (Federal Pres., 1962-63, 1965-67); Chm., Standard-Vacuum Refining Co. Ltd, 1952-61; Director: International Harvester Co. of Australia Pty Ltd, 1947-; W. R. Carpenter Holdings Ltd, 1961-; Hoyts Theatres Ltd, 1934-; Balm Paints Ltd, 1945-. *Recreations:* golf, bowls, swimming. *Address:* 372 Glenferrie Road, Malvern, Vic. 3144, Australia. *T:* 20-9516. *Clubs:* Athenæum, Victoria Racing (Melbourne); Royal Melbourne Golf, Melbourne Cricket.

**INCH, John Ritchie,** CVO 1969; CBE 1958 QPM 1961; Chief Constable, Edinburgh City Police, since 1955; *b* 14 May 1911; *s* of James Inch, Lesmahagow, Lanarkshire; *m* 1941, Anne Ferguson Shaw; one *s* two *d. Educ:* Hamilton Academy; Glasgow Univ. (MA, LLB). Joined Lanarkshire Constabulary, 1931; apptd Chief Constable, Dunfermline City Police, 1943, and of combined Fife Constabulary, 1949. OStJ 1964. Comdr, Royal Order of St Olav (Norway), 1962; Comdr, Order of Al-Kawkal Al Urdini (Jordan), 1966; Cavaliere Ufficiale, Order of Merit (Italy), 1969. *Recreations:* shooting, fishing, golf. *Address:* Fairways, Whitehouse Road, Barnton, Edinburgh. *T:* 031-336 3558. *Club:* Royal Scots (Edinburgh).

**INCHCAPE,** 3rd Earl of, *cr* 1929; **Kenneth James William Mackay;** Viscount Glenapp of Strathnaver, *cr* 1929; Viscount Inchcape, *cr* 1924; Baron Inchcape, *cr* 1911; Chairman, Inchcape & Co. Ltd; Director: P & O Steam Navigation Co.; The Chartered Bank; Royal Exchange Assurance; Burmah Oil Co. Ltd; British Petroleum Co. Ltd; Commonwealth Development Finance Co.; Bain Dawes Group; Deputy President: Royal Society for India, Pakistan and Ceylon; Commonwealth Society for the Deaf; *b* 27 Dec. 1917; *e s* of 2nd Earl and Joan (*d* 1933), *d* of late Lord Justice Moriarty; *S* father 1939; *m* 1st, 1941, Mrs Aline Thorn Hannay (from whom he obtained a divorce, 1954), *widow* of Flying Officer P. C. Hannay, AAF, and *d* of Sir Richard Pease, 2nd *Bt, qv*; two *s* one *d*; 2nd, 1965, Caroline Cholmeley, *e d* of Cholmeley Dering Harrison, 8 Bryanston Square, W1, and Woodstown House, County Waterford, Eire; one adopted *s. Educ:* Eton; Trinity Coll., Cambridge (MA). Served War of 1939-45: 12th Lancers BEF France; Major 27th Lancers MEF and Italy. Chm., Council for Middle East Trade, 1963-65. Prime Warden, Shipwrights' Co., 1967. Freeman, City of London. *Recreations:* shooting, fishing, golf. *Heir: s* Viscount Glenapp, *qv. Address:* Glenapp Castle, Ballantrae, Ayrshire. *T:* Ballantrae 212; Tulchan Lodge, Alyth, Perthshire; Quendon Park, Saffron Walden, Essex. *Clubs:* Brooks's, Buck's, Turf, City, Oriental.

*See also Baron Craigmyle, Sir Eugen Millington-Drake.*

**INCHIQUIN,** 17th Baron of, *cr* 1543; **Phaedrig Lucius Ambrose O'Brien;** Bt 1686; *b* 4 April 1900; 2nd *s* of 15th Baron of Inchiquin and Ethel Jane (*d* 1940), *d* of late Johnstone J. Foster, Moor Park, Ludlow; *S* brother, 1968; *m* 1945, Vera Maud, *d* of late Rev. C. S. Winter. *Educ:* Eton; Magdalen Coll., Oxford (MA); Imperial Coll., London Univ. Major (retd) Rifle Brigade; served War, 1940-45, attached E African Intelligence Corps, Somalia, Abyssinia, Madagascar (wounded, despatches). Farming and coffee planting, Kenya, 1922-36; Geologist, Anglo-American Corp., 1936-39 and 1946-54; Colonial Service, Overseas Geological Survey (retd), 1954-56. Consulting Geologist, 1960-67. *Heir: b* Hon. Fionn Myles Maryons O'Brien [*b* 28 Oct. 1903; *m* 1939, Josephine Reine, *d* of late J. E. Bembaron; one *s* one *d*]. *Address:* Hanway Lodge, Richard's Castle, Ludlow, Shropshire. *T:* Richard's Castle 210; Thomond House, Co. Clare, Ireland. *Club:* Royal Automobile.

**INCHYRA,** 1st Baron *cr* 1961; **Frederick Robert Hoyer Millar,** GCMG 1956 (KCMG 1949; CMG 1939); CVO 1938; *b* 6 June 1900; *s* of late R. Hoyer Millar; *m* 1931, Elizabeth de Marees van Swinderen; two *s* two *d. Educ:* Wellington Coll.; New Coll., Oxford. Hon. Attaché, HM Embassy, Brussels, 1922; entered HM Diplomatic Service, 1923; served as Third Sec. at Berlin and Paris, and as Second Sec. at Cairo; Asst Private Sec. to Sec. of State for Foreign Affairs, 1934-38; First Sec. at Washington, 1939; Counsellor, 1941-42; Sec., British Civil Secretariat, Washington, 1943;

Counsellor, FO, 1944; Asst Under-Sec. 1947; Minister, British Embassy, Washington, 1948; UK Deputy, North Atlantic Treaty Organisation, 1950; UK Permanent Representative on NATO Council, 1952; UK High Commissioner in Germany, 1953-55; British Ambassador to Bonn, 1955-57; Permanent Under-Sec. of State, Foreign Office, 1957-61. King of Arms, Order of St Michael and St George, 1961-. Director: General Accident, Fire and Life Assurance Corporation, 1962-; Stockholders Investment Trust, 1962-; Shell Transport and Trading Co., 1962; Grampian Holdings Ltd, 1962; Rootes Motors, 1963; British Linen Bank, 1963-. Chm., Executive Cttee, BRCS, 1963-70. *Recreation:* shooting. *Heir: s* Hon. Robert Charles Reneke Hoyer Millar [*b* 4 April 1935; *m* 1961, Fiona Sheffield; one *s* two *d*]. *Address:* 57 Eaton Place, SW1; *T:* 01-235 7675; Inchyra House, Glencarse, Perthshire. *Clubs:* Boodle's, Turf; Metropolitan (Washington).

**INCLEDON-WEBBER, Lt-Col Godfrey Sturdy, MA;** TD 1943; JP; DL; Managing Director, British Trusts Association Ltd, since 1953; *b* 1 July 1904; *er s* of William Beare Incledon-Webber, DL, JP, Braunton, Devon; *m* 1931, Angela Florence, *d* of Sir Pierce Lacy, 1st Bt; three *d*. *Educ:* Eton; Magdalen Coll., Oxford (BA 1926, MA 1947). Joined Royal Devon Yeomanry Artillery, 1925; served in War of 1939-45 (Lieut-Col Comdg 136 Lt AA Regt RA, 1942-45). Partner, Cutler Lacy, Stockbrokers, Birmingham, 1933-53; Director: United Dominions Trust Ltd, 1959; English Insurance Co. Ltd, 1955; Chairman: Osborn & Wallis Ltd Bristol, 1954; M. Hyam Ltd, 1956; Incledon Estate Co. Ltd, 1949. Alderman and JP, City of London, 1963-; one of HM's Lieutenants of City of London; Sheriff, City of London, 1968-69; Mem. Court of Assistants, Worshipful Co. of Clothworkers, 1965; Past Master (1961-62), Worshipful Co. of Saddlers. Hereditary Freeman of Barnstaple (1925); Lord of the Manor of Croyde and Putsborough, Devon. DL Devon, 1969; High Sheriff, Devon, 1970-71. *Recreations:* shooting, and interested in most kinds of sport and games; represented Eton at rackets and cricket, 1922-23, Oxford Univ. at tennis and squash rackets, 1925-26; mem. British Squash Rackets Team which toured USA and Canada, 1927. *Address:* 39 King Street, EC2. *T:* 01-606 4791; 1a Ennismore Gardens, SW7. *T:* 01-589 0908; St Brannocks, Braunton, N Devon. *T:* Braunton 270. *Clubs:* White's, Carlton, City of London, City Livery.

**INDORE, Ex-Maharaja of,** GCIE, *cr* 1918; **HH Tukoji Rao Holkar;** *b* 26 Nov. 1890; *S* as Maharaja of Indore, 1903, and as Premier Ruling Prince of Central India; *m* 1928, Nancy Miller (Maharanee Sharmishthabai Holkar); one *d*; abdicated in favour of his son (by a former marriage), 1926 (*s* Maharaja Sir Yeshwant Rao Holkar, GCIE, *d* 1961). *Educ:* Mayo Chiefs' Coll., Ajmere; Imperial Cadet Corps. Visited Europe, 1910; attended Coronation, 1911; again visited Europe, 1913 and 1921. *Recreations:* riding, shooting, lawn tennis. *Address:* The Darya Mahal, Barwaha, India.

**ING, Harry Raymond,** FRS 1951; *b* 31 July 1899; *s* of Arthur Frank William Ing and Anne (*née* Garrard); *m* 1941, Catherine Mills Francis, *d* of Bertie Mills and Sarah Francis. *Educ:* Oxford High Sch.; New Coll., Oxford. Sen. Scholar. New Coll., Oxford, 1921-23. Univ. Demonstrator in Chemistry, Oxford, 1921-26; Ramsay Memorial Fellow, 1926-27; Lecr, 1929, and Reader, 1935, in Pharmacological Chemistry, Univ. of London, University Coll.; Rockefeller Fellow, 1938-38; Univ. Reader in Chemical Pharmacology, Oxford, 1945-66. *Publications:* Chapters in Heterocyclic Compounds (ed Elderfield, New York); and in Advanced Organic Chemistry, Vol. III (Ed Gilman, New York); numerous papers in chemical, pharmacological and physiological journals, etc. *Recreation:* walking. *Address:* 6 Linton Road, Oxford OX2 6UG. *T:* Oxford 56968. *Club:* Athenæum.

**INGERSOLL, Ralph McAllister;** Editor and Publisher, USA; *b* 8 Dec. 1900; *s* of Colin Macrae and Theresa (McAllister) Ingersoll; *m* 1st, 1925, Mary Elizabeth Carden (marr. diss., 1935; she *d* 1965); 2nd, 1945, Elaine Brown Keiffer (*d* 1948); two *s*; 3rd, 1948, Mary Hill Doolittle (marr. diss., 1962); 4th, 1964, Thelma Bradford. *Educ:* Hotchkiss Sch., Lakeville, Connecticut; Yale and Columbia Univs. BS Yale, 1921; student, Columbia, 1922. Mining Engineer; Reporter for The New Yorker (mag.), 1925-30; Assoc. Editor, Fortune Magazine, 1930, Managing Editor, 1930-35; Vice-Pres. and General Manager, Time, Inc., publishing Time, Life, Fortune, etc. Publisher of Time Magazine, 1937-39; resigned to organise and finance company subsequently to publish PM (NY daily newspaper); Editor, PM, 1940-46. Enlisted as Private, Engr. Amphibian Command, US Army, 1942; advanced to Lt-Col, Gen. Staff Corps; served overseas, 1943-45; in Africa, England, Italy, France, Belgium, Luxembourg and Germany, on staffs of Gen. Jacob Devers, Field-Marshal Montgomery, and Gen. Omar Bradley. Legion of Merit, Bronze Arrowhead for assault landing in Normandy, and 7 campaign stars; Officer of Order of Crown (Belgium); returned to Editorship of PM; resigned, 1946; Pres., The RJ Company, Inc., 1948-59, investments, principally newspapers, including Middletown (NY) Times Herald, Union Gazette, Port Jervis, NY; President and Director of numerous newspapers and publishing concerns, in RI, NJ, Pa, Conn., NY and Mass; Pres., General Publications, Inc. (newspaper management), 1959-; Director: Central Home Trust Co., Eliz., NJ, 1963-67; Public Welfare Foundn, Washington DC, 1970-. *Publications:* Report on England, 1940; America is Worth Fighting For, 1941; Action on All Fronts, 1941; The Battle is the Pay-Off, 1944; Top Secret, 1946; The Great Ones, 1948; Wine of Violence, 1951; Point of Departure, 1961. *Address:* (home) Cornwall Bridge, Conn 06754, USA. *Clubs:* Racquet and Tennis, The Brook (NYC).

**INGESTRE, Viscount; Charles Henry John Benedict Crofton Chetwynd Chetwynd-Talbot;** *b* 18 Dec. 1952; *s* and *heir* of 21st Earl of Shrewsbury and Waterford, *qv*.

**INGHAM, John Henry,** CMG 1956; MBE 1947; *b* 1910. *Educ:* Plumtree School, S Rhodesia; Rhodes University College, S Africa; Brasenose College, Oxford. Administrative Officer, Nyasaland, 1936; Secretary for Agricultural and Natural Resources, Kenya, 1947; Administrative Secretary, 1952; Senior Secretary, East African Royal Commission, 1953-55; Secretary for African Affairs, Nyasaland, 1956-60; MEC, Nyasaland, 1961. Minister of Urban Development, Malawi, 1961. Representative of Beit Trust and Dulverton Trust in Central Africa, 1962-70. *Address:* 18 Jameson Avenue, Salisbury, Rhodesia.

**INGHAM, Prof. Kenneth,** OBE 1961; MC 1946; Professor of History, University of Bristol, since 1967; *b* 9 Aug. 1921; *s* of Gladson and Frances Lily Ingham; *m* 1949, Elizabeth Mary Southall; one *s* one *d*. *Educ:* Bingley Grammar

Sch.; Keble Coll., Oxford (Exhibitioner). Served with West Yorks Regt, 1941-46 (despatches, 1945). Frere Exhibitioner in Indian Studies, University of Oxford, 1947; DPhil 1950. Lecturer in Modern History, Makerere Coll., Uganda, 1950-56, Prof., 1956-62; Dir of Studies, RMA, Sandhurst, 1962-67. MLC, Uganda, 1954-61. *Publications:* Reformers in India, 1956; The Making of Modern Uganda, 1958; A History of East Africa, 1962; contrib. to Encyclopædia Britannica, Britannica Book of the Year. *Address:* The Woodlands, 94 West Town Lane, Bristol 4. *Club:* United University.

**INGILBY, Sir Joslan William Vivian,** 5th Bt, *cr* 1866; late Scots Guards; DL; JP; *b* 1 Sept. 1907; *o s* of Sir William Henry Ingilby, 4th Bt, and Hon. Alberta Diana Vivian (*d* 1968), 3rd *d* of 1st Baron Swansea; *S* father 1950; *m* 1948, Diana *o d* of late Sir George Colvin, CB, CMG, DSO; one *s* two *d*. *Educ:* Eton. Served War of 1939-45; Major, Scots Guards, retired. DL 1952, JP 1952, West Riding, Co. of York. *Heir: s* Thomas Colvin William Ingilby, *b* 17 July 1955. *Address:* Ripley Castle, Harrogate, West Riding, Yorks. *T:* Ripley 286. *Club:* Guards.

**INGLE, Charles Fiennes;** Barrister-at-Law; Recorder of Penzance since Dec. 1964; Deputy Chairman, Devon Quarter Sessions, since 1963; *b* 30 April 1908; *s* of F. S. Ingle and M. A. Ingle, Bath; *m* 1933, Mary (*née* Linaker); one *s* one *d*. *Educ:* Oundle; Jesus Coll., Cambridge (MA). Called to Bar, Inner Temple, 1931; Western Circuit. Sqdn Ldr, RAFVR, 1940-44. *Recreations:* yachting, shooting. *Address:* West Soar, Malborough, Devon. *T:* Galmpton 334.

**INGLE-FINCH, Peter;** *see* Finch, Peter.

**INGLEBY,** 2nd Viscount, *cr* 1955, of Snilesworth; **Martin Raymond Peake;** Landowner; Director, Hargreaves Group Ltd, since 1960; *b* 31 May 1926; *s* of 1st Viscount Ingleby, and of Joan, Viscountess Ingleby; *S* father, 1966; *m* 1952, Susan, *d* of late Henderson Russell Landale; one *s* four *d*. *Educ:* Eton; Trinity Coll., Oxford (MA). Called to the Bar, Inner Temple, 1956. Sec., Hargreaves Group Ltd, 1958-61. Administrative Staff Coll., 1961. CC Yorks (North Riding), 1964-67. Mem., Yorks Moors Nat. Park Planning Cttee, 1968-. *Heir: s* Hon. Richard Martin Herbert Peake, *b* 7 Aug. 1953. *Address:* Snilesworth, Osmotherley, Northallerton, Yorks. *T:* Osmotherley 214.

**INGLEFIELD, Sir Gilbert (Samuel),** GBE 1968; Kt 1965; TD; MA, ARIBA, AADip; Director, Inglefield Group of Companies; *b* 13 March 1909; 2nd *s* of late Adm. Sir F. S. Inglefield, KCB; *m* 1933, Laura Barbara Frances, *e d* of late Captain Gilbert Thompson, Connaught Rangers; two *s* one *d*. *Educ:* Eton; Trinity Coll., Cambridge. Architect; served War of 1939-45 with Sherwood Foresters, France, Far East. British Council Asst Rep. in Egypt, 1946-49 and in London, 1949-56. Alderman, City of London (Aldersgate Ward), 1959; Sheriff, 1963-64; Lord Mayor of London, 1967-68; one of HM Lieutenants for City of London; Church Commissioner for England, 1962; Governor: Thomas Coram Foundation; Royal Shakespeare Theatre; Chairman: Prisoners Welfare Centre; Appeal Cttee, Church Music Trust; Mem., Royal Fine Art Commission, 1968-. Chancellor of the Order of St John of Jerusalem, 1969-; GCStJ. FRSA; Hon. RBA; Hon. GSM. Hon. DSc, City Univ., 1967. Comdr Order of the Falcon (Iceland), 1963; Order of the Two Niles, Class III (Sudan), 1964. *Recreations:* music, travel. *Address:* Egginton House, Leighton Buzzard, Beds. *T:* Hockliffe 215. *Clubs:* Athenæum, Arts, City Livery.

**INGLEFIELD, Col Sir John (Frederick) C.;** *see* Crompton-Inglefield.

**INGLEFIELD-WATSON, Captain Sir Derrick W. I.;** *see* Watson.

**INGLESON, Philip,** CMG 1945; MBE 1926; MC 1917; Chairman, Revel Industrial Products Ltd; Chairman, Chair Centre Ltd; *b* 14 June 1892; *s* of William Frederick and Phoebe H. Ingleson; *m* 1921, Gwendoline, *o d* of Col R. Fulton, 1st KGVO Gurkha Rifles, IA; one *d*. *Educ:* Rossall Sch.; Queen's Coll., Cambridge (Senior Classical Scholar). Served European War (France), 1914-19, Royal Fusiliers and Staff Captain 198th Infantry Brigade 66 Div. (MC, despatches); joined Sudan Political Service, 1919; Governor Halfa Province 1931; Governor Berber Province, 1932; Governor Bahr-el-Ghazal Province, 1934; Governor Darfur Province, 1935-44; Ministry of Production, 1944; Board of Trade, 1945; UK Trade Commissioner in Queensland, 1949-53, and in Western Australia, 1954-56; Order of the Nile, 4th Class, 1929; Order of the Nile, 3rd Class 1935. *Recreation:* travel. *Address:* 36 Campden Hill Court, W8. *T:* 01-937 8993. *Clubs:* Bath; Weld (Perth).

**INGLEWOOD,** 1st Baron, *cr* 1964, of Hutton in the Forest; **William Morgan Fletcher-Vane,** TD; *b* 12 April 1909; *s* of late Col Hon. W. L. Vane and Lady Katharine Vane; assumed name of Fletcher-Vane by deed poll, 1931; *m* 1949, Mary (late Sen. Comdr ATS (despatches), JP, Mem. LCC, 1949-52, Cumberland CC, 1961-), *e d s* of Major Sir Richard G. Proby, Bt, *qv*; two *s*. *Educ:* Charterhouse; Trinity Coll., Cambridge (MA). 2nd Lt 6 Bn Durham Light Infantry, 1928; served Overseas: 1940, France, with 50 (N) Div. (despatches); 1941-44, Middle East with Durham LI and on the Staff, Lt-Col, 1943. MP (C) for Westmorland, 1945-64; Parliamentary Private Sec. to Minister of Agriculture, 1951-54, to Joint Under-Sec. of State, Foreign Office, 1954-55, and to Minister of Health, Dec. 1955-July 1956; Joint Parliamentary Secretary: Min. of Pensions and National Insurance, 1958-60; Min. of Agriculture, Oct. 1960-July 1962. DL Westmorland 1946; Landowner; Mem. Chartered Surveyors Institution and Chartered Land Agents Soc.; formerly Mem. of Historic Buildings Council for England; Leader of UK Delegation to World Food Congress (FAO) Washington, June 1963. Vice-Chm., Anglo-German Assoc., 1966-. Order of the Phoenix, Greece, 4th Class; Order of the Cedar, Lebanon. *Heir: s* Hon. William Richard Fletcher-Vane, *b* 31 July 1951. *Address:* Hutton-in-the-Forest, Penrith, Cumberland. *T:* Skelton 207; 19 Stack House, Ebury Street, SW1. *T:* 01-730 1559. *Club:* Travellers'.

**INGLIS, Allan,** CMG, 1962; Director of Public Works, Hong Kong, retired; *b* 25 Feb. 1906; *m* 1936, Constance M. Maclachlan; two *d*. *Educ:* Royal High Sch., Edinburgh; Heriot-Watt Coll., Edinburgh. Chartered Civil Engineer (MICE). Joined Colonial Service, 1930; Engrg Surveyor, Singapore, SS, 1930; Asst Engr, 1935, Exec. Engr, 1939, Malaya. Served War of 1939-45, Major Royal Engineers. Sen. Exec. Engr, 1946, State Engr, 1953, Malaya. *Address:* 26 Cramond Road South, Edinburgh 4. *T:* 031-336 1695. *Clubs:* Overseas; Royal Scots (Edinburgh).

**INGLIS, Brian (St John),** PhD; Journalist; *b* 31 July 1916; *s* of Sir Claude Inglis, *qv*; *m* 1958, Ruth Langdon; one *s* one *d*. *Educ:* Shrewsbury Sch.; Magdalen Coll., Oxford. BA 1939. Served in RAF (Coastal Command), 1940-46; Flight Comdr 202 Squadron, 1944-45; Squadron Ldr, 1944-46 (despatches). Irish Times Columnist, 1946-48; Parliamentary Corr., 1950-53. Trinity Coll., Dublin; PhD 1950; Asst to Prof. of Modern History, 1949-53; Lectr in Economics, 1951-53; Spectator: Asst Editor, 1954-59; Editor, 1959-62; Dir, 1962-63. TV Commentator: What the Papers Say, All Our Yesterdays, etc., 1957-. *Publications:* The Freedom of the Press in Ireland, 1954; The Story of Ireland 1956; Revolution in Medicine, 1958; West Briton, 1962; Fringe Medicine, 1964; Private Conscience: Public Morality, 1964; Drugs, Doctors and Disease, 1965; A History of Medicine, 1965; Abdication, 1966. *Address:* 20 Albion Street, W2. *T:* 01-262 8274.

**INGLIS, Sir Claude Cavendish,** Kt 1945; CIE 1936; FRS 1953; BA, BAI, MAI (*hc*); FICE; FAMSocCE; Chartered Civil Engineer; Consultant; *b* 3 March 1883; *s* of Sir Malcolm Inglis, DL, and Caroline Johnston; *m* 1912, Vera St John Blood; one *s*. *Educ:* Shrewsbury; Trinity Coll., Dublin. Irrigation branch Bombay PWD, 1906-38; Initiated and directed Irrigation Research and Development, Bombay Presidency and Sind, 1916-38; Dir Indian Waterways Experiment Stn, Poona, 1938-45; Initiated and directed Hydraulics Research Stn, Dept of Scientific and Industrial Research, Howbery Park, Wallingford., Berks, 1947-58. Ewing Medal, Inst. of Civil Engineers. *Publications:* The Behaviour and Control of Rivers and Canals; various Technical Papers dealing with training and control of rivers and estuaries, coast protection, irrigation and model investigation. *Address:* 7 Holmgarth, Furners Mead, Henfield, Sussex. *Club:* English-Speaking Union.

*See also B St J Inglis.*

**INGLIS, Maj.-Gen. Sir Drummond,** KBE 1945 (OBE 1939); CB 1944; MC 1916; Company Director; *b* 4 May 1895; *s* of late Major Thomas Drummond Inglis, RA, Colchester; *m* 1919, Monica, *d* of late Philip Percival Whitcombe, MB, London; one *s* (one *d* decd). *Educ:* Wellington Coll.; RMA, Woolwich. 2nd Lt RE 1914; served European War, 1914-19 (4th Class Order of White Eagle of Serbia with swords, Bt Major); Palestine, 1937-39 (despatches, OBE); War of 1939-45, France, Belgium, Holland, Germany; Chief Engineer, 21st Army Group, 1943-45 (Officer of the Legion of Honour, Croix de Guerre with palms, Knight Grand Officer of the Order of Orange Nassau with swords); retired pay, 1945; Col Comdt RE, 1955-60. *Address:* The Old Manor, Chelsworth, near Ipswich. *T:* Bildeston 257. *Club:* Army and Navy.

**INGLIS, Maj.-Gen. George Henry,** CB 1952; CBE 1950; JP; Vice-Lieutenant of Cumberland since 1969; *b* 22 Aug. 1902; *s* of late Col Henry Alves Inglis, CMG, Dalston, Cumberland; *m* 1940, Margaret Edith, *d* of C. H. Shaw, Ullswater. *Educ:* Ardvreck, Crieff; Wellington Coll.; RMA Woolwich. 2nd Lt RA 1922. Served War of 1939-45, France, SEAC, MELF (despatches Burma, 1946, Palestine, 1949), temp. Brig., 1944. Comdg 18 Trng Bde, Oswestry, 1948; Comdr 52 Lowland Div. TA and Lowland Dist, 1950-52; Maj.-Gen. 1951; Gen. Officer Commanding Nigeria District, 1953-56; retired, 1956. Chairman: Carlisle Diocesan Board of Finance, 1961-70; Carlisle & NW Counties Trustee Savings Bank, 1967-. JP Cumberland, 1958; High Sheriff of Cumberland, 1961; DL Cumberland, 1962. Col Comdt RA, 1960-67. *Address:* Crosby House, Crosby-on-Eden, Carlisle. *T:* Crosby-on-Eden 239. *Club:* Army and Navy.

**INGLIS, Maj.-Gen. Sir (John) Drummond;** *see* Inglis, Maj.-Gen. Sir Drummond.

**INGLIS, Vice-Adm. (retd) Sir John Gilchrist Thesiger,** KBE 1959 (OBE 1943); CB 1957; Director of Naval Intelligence, 1954-60; *b* 8 June 1906; *s* of Rupert Edward Inglis and Helen Mary Inglis, *d* of W. O. Gilchrist; *m* 1945, Maud Dorrien Frankland; one *d*. *Educ:* RNC, Osborne and Dartmouth, Lt RN, 1929; qualified as Signal Officer, 1932; Comdr 1940; Captain, 1944; Rear-Adm., 1954; Vice-Adm., 1958. *Recreations:* shooting and farming. *Address:* Wield Manor, Alresford, Hants. *T:* Medstead 3188. *Club:* Naval and Military.

**INGLIS of Glencorse, Sir Maxwell (Ian Hector),** 9th Bt (formerly Mackenzie of Gairloch, *cr* 1703); Lord-Lieutenant of Midlothian, since 1964; JP; *b* 18 Oct. 1903; *o s* of Hector Ian Maxwell Mackenzie-Inglis of Glencorse, and Dora, *d* of Robert Mole, Beoley Hall, Worcs; *S* kinsman (Sir Hector David Mackenzie, of Gairloch, Bt), 1958; *m* 1932, Dorothy Evelyn, MD, JP, *d* of Dr John Stewart, Tasmania; one *s*. *Educ:* Winchester; Trinity Coll., Cambridge. Gold Coast Political Service, 1928-37: Midlothian County Council, 1938-67; Convener of Co. 1946-47; Wing Comdr, RAFVR(T), retired. Mem. of Queen's Body Guard for Scotland, Royal Company of Archers. DL 1957, JP 1946, Midlothian. *Recreations:* shooting, travel. *Heir:* *s* Roderick John Inglis of Glencorse, Yr, MB, ChB [*b* 25 Jan. 1936; *m* 1960, Rachel, *d* of Lt-Col N. M. Morris, Dowdstown, Ardee, Co. Louth; three *s* (incl. twin *s*) one *d*]. *Address:* Loganbank, Milton Bridge, Penicuik, Midlothian. *T:* Penicuik 2686. *Club:* New (Edinburgh).

**INGLIS, Sheriff Robert Alexander;** Sheriff-Substitute of Inverness, Moray, Nairn and Ross and Cromarty at Fort William and Portree, since 1968; *b* 29 June 1918; *m* 1950, Shelagh Constance St Clair Boyd (marriage dissolved, 1956); one *s* one *d*. *Educ:* Malsis Hall, Daniel Stewart's Coll.; Rugby Sch.; Christ Church, Oxford (MA); Glasgow Univ. (LLB). Army, 1940-46; Glasgow Univ., 1946-48; called to Bar, 1948. Interim Sheriff-Sub., Dundee, 1955; perm. appt, 1956. *Recreations:* golf, fishing. *Address:* Inchree House, Onich, Inverness-shire.

**INGOLD, Cecil Terrence,** CMG 1970; DSc 1940; FLS; Professor of Botany in University of London, Birkbeck College, since 1944; Vice-Master, Birkbeck College, since 1965; *b* 3 July 1905; *s* of late E. G. Ingold; *m* 1933, Leonora Mary Kemp; one *s* three *d*. *Educ:* Bangor (Co. Down) Grammar Sch.; Queen's Univ., Belfast. Graduated BSc, QUB, 1925; Asst in Botany, QUB, 1929; Lectr in Botany, University of Reading, 1930-37; Lecturer-in-charge of Dept of Botany, University Coll., Leicester, 1937-44; Dean of Faculty of Science, London Univ., 1956-60. Dep. Vice-Chancellor, London Univ., 1966-67, Chm. Academic Council, 1969-. Chm., University Entrance and School Examinations Council, 1958-64. Chm., Council Freshwater Biolog. Assoc. Hon. DLitt, Ibadan, 1969. *Publications:* Spore Discharge in Land Plants, 1939; Dispersal in Fungi, 1953; The Biology of Fungi, 1961; Spore Liberation, 1965; papers in Annals of Botany, New Phytologist, and Transactions of British Mycological Soc. *Address:* Birkbeck College, Malet Street, WC1; Hinton, Sandy Lane, Platt, Sevenoaks, Kent. *T:* Borough Green 4131.

**INGOLD, Sir Christopher (Kelk),** Kt 1958; FRS 1924; DSc London; Hon. DSc Hull, Leeds, Sheffield, Southampton, Oxford, McMaster Univs and NUI; Hon. ScD Dublin; Hon. PhD

Oslo; Hon. Dr Faculty of Science Bologna, Paris, and Montpellier; ARCS, FIC; Professor of Chemistry, University of London, University College, 1930-61; Director of Chemistry Laboratories, 1937-61, since when Emeritus Professor and Special Lecturer; *b* 1893; *s* of William Kelk Ingold and Harriet Walker Newcomb, Forest Gate, London; *m* Edith Hilda, *d* of T. S. Usherwood, Finchley; one *s* two *d*. *Educ:* University Coll., Southampton; Imperial Coll. of Science and Technology, London. Research Chemist Cassel Cyanide Company, Ltd, 1918-20; Lecturer in Chemistry, Imperial Coll. of Science and Technology, 1920-24; Prof. of Organic Chemistry, University of Leeds, 1924-30. Visiting Lecturer, Stanford Univ., USA, 1932; Reilly, Glidden, Davis, American Cyanamide, and 3 M Lectr respectively at Univs of Notre Dame, Illinois, Kansas, Connecticut, and Minnesota, USA; Baker Lectr, Cornell Univ., USA, 1950; Redman Lecturer, McMaster Univ., Canada, 1957. Corresp. mem. of Royal Academy of Sciences of Spain, 1948; Hon. Counsellor for Higher Scientific Investigations in Spain; Hon. Foreign Member of: Weizmann Inst., Israel; New York Acad. of Science; Amer. Acad. of Arts and Sciences, 1958; Hon. Fellow, University Coll., London, 1964; Fellow, Imperial Coll. of Science and Technology, London; Foreign Academician, Bologna Academy of Science, 1965. pres. of the Chemical Soc., 1952-54. Meldola Medal, Royal Inst. Chem., 1922; Davy Medal of Royal Society, 1946; Longstaff Medal of Chemical Soc., 1951; Royal Medal of Royal Society, 1952; Faraday Medal of Chemical Soc., 1962; James Flack Norris Award for Physical Organic Chemistry, 1965. *Publications:* Structure and Mechanism in Organic Chemistry, 1953 (2nd edn 1969) (US); Introduction to Structure in Organic Chemistry, 1956. Scientific papers published mainly in the Journal of the Chemical Soc., since 1915. *Address:* 12 Handel Close, Edgware, Mddx; University College, Gower Street, WC1. *Club:* Athenæum.

**INGOLDBY, Eric,** CIE 1943; *b* 7 Jan. 1892; *m* 1925, Zyvee Elizabeth Taylor (*d* 1954); two *s*. Served European War of 1914-18, RGA. Joined Indian State Railways, 1921; Chief Mechanical Engineer, GIP Railway, 1934; Dir Railway Board, India, 1935-40; Chief Controller of Standardisation, Railway Board, Govt of India, 1941-47; retired 1949; mem. firm of Rendel, Palmer and Tritton, consulting engineers, 1947-55. *Address:* 5 Lynne Court, Chesham Road, Guildford, Surrey. *T:* Guildford 70878.

**INGRAM, Prof. David John Edward,** MA, DPhil; DSc Oxon 1960; Professor of Physics and Head of Physics Department, University of Keele, since 1959; Deputy Vice-Chancellor, since 1968; *b* 6 April 1927; *s* of late J. E. Ingram and late Marie Florence (*née* Weller); *m* 1952, Ruth Geraldine Grace McNair; two *s* one *d*. *Educ:* King's Coll. Sch., Wimbledon; New Coll., Oxford. Postgraduate research at Oxford Univ., 1948-52; Research Fellow and Lectr, University of Southampton, 1952-57; Reader in Electronics, University of Southampton, 1957-59; Dep. Vice-Chancellor, University of Keele, 1964-65. Hon. DSc (Clermont-Ferrand). *Publications:* Spectroscopy at Radio and Microwave Frequencies, 1955, 2nd edn, 1967; Free Radicals as Studied by Electron Spin Resonance, 1958; Biological and Biochemical Applications of Electron Spin Resonance, 1969. Various papers in Proc. Royal Soc., Proc. Phys. Soc., etc. *Recreations:* boating and debating. *Address:* 11 The University, Keele, Staffs. *T:* Keele Park 220.

**INGRAM, Sir Herbert,** 3rd Bt *cr* 1893; Partner, Cazenove & Co., 1947-70, retired; *b* 18 April 1912; *s* of Sir Herbert Ingram, 2nd Bt and Hilda Vivian Lake (*d* 1968); *S* father, 1958; *m* 1935, Jane Lindsay, *d* of J. E. Palmer Tomkinson; one *s* three *d*. *Educ:* Winchester; Balliol Coll., Oxford. Served War of 1939-45 (despatches): Grenadier Guards and REME, Major. *Recreations:* golf, ski-ing. *Heir:* *s* Herbert Robin Ingram [*b* 13 Jan. 1939; *m* 1963, Shiela, *o d* of Charles Peczenik and Mrs Edward Remington-Hobbs; one *s* one *d*]. *Address:* Hurst Lodge, near Reading, Berks. *T:* Hurst 88. *Club:* White's.

**INGRAM, Prof. John Thornton;** Professor of Dermatology, University of Newcastle upon Tyne, 1963-64, retired, now Emeritus; *b* 4 March 1899; *s* of Albert James and Florence Annie Ingram; *m* 1st, 1927, Lucy Graham; one *d*; 2nd, 1959, Kathleen Annie Raven (*see* Dame Kathleen Annie Raven). *Educ:* Hele's Sch.; University Coll., Exeter; London Univ., MB, BS London 1923; MD 1926; MRCS, LRCP 1923; MRCP 1926; FRCP 1936. Lectr in Dermatology, Univ. of Leeds, 1927-59; Prof. of Dermatology, Univ. of Durham, 1959-63; Physician i/c Dermatological Dept., Gen. Infirmary, Leeds, 1927-59; Physician, Royal Victoria Infirmary, Newcastle upon Tyne, 1959. Councillor Royal Coll. of Physicians, 1952-54; Lectures: Watson Smith, RCP, 1954; Paul O'Leary, Chicago, 1956; Litchfield, Oxford, 1960; Scott-Heron, Belfast, 1963; Pres. British Assoc. of Dermatology, 1947; Pres. Dermatology Section, RSM, 1957-59. Hon. Mem. Dermatological Socs of New York, America, France, Scandinavia, Denmark, Germany, Austria, Australia. *Publications:* (with R. T. Brain) Sequeira's Diseases of the Skin; Industrial Dermatoses and the Industrial Injuries Act, 1968; Clinical Dermatology: an individual Appraoch, 1969; Nursing Care of the Patient with Skin Diseases, 1970; contribs to numerous medical text books and numerous articles in British, American, Scandinavian, Pakistan and Australian medical journals. *Recreations:* painting and literature. *Address:* Jesmond, Burcott, Wing, near Leighton Buzzard, Beds LU7 0JU. *T:* Wing 244. *Club:* Athenæum.

**INGRAM, Prof. R. P. W.;** *see* Winnington-Ingram.

**INGRAM, Prof. Vernon M.,** FRS 1970; Professor of Biochemistry, Massachusetts Institute of Technology, since 1961; *b* Breslau, 19 May 1924; *s* of Kurt and Johanna Immerwahr; *m* 1950, Margaret Young; one *s* one *d*. *Educ:* Birkbeck Coll., Univ. of London. BSc (Gen.) 1943; BSc (Special) Chemistry, 1st cl., 1945; PhD Organic Chemistry, 1949; DSc Biochemistry, 1961. Analytical and Res. Chemist, Thos Morson & Son, Mddx, 1941-45; Lecture Demonstrator in Chem., Birkbeck Coll., 1945-47; Asst Lectr in Chem., Birkbeck Coll., 1947-50; Rockefeller Foundn Fellow, Rockefeller Inst., NY, 1950-51; Coxe Fellow, Yale, 1951-52; Mem. Sci. Staff, MRC Unit for Molecular Biology, Cavendish Lab., Cambridge, 1952-58; Vis. Assoc. Prof. 1958-59, Assoc. Prof. 1959-61, MIT; Lectr (part-time) in Medicine, Columbia, 1961-; Guggenheim Fellow, UCL, 1967-68. Jesup Lectr, Columbia, 1962; Harvey Soc. Lectr, 1965. Member: Amer. Acad. of Arts and Sciences, 1964; Amer. Chem. Soc.; Chemical Soc.; Biochemical Soc.; Genetical Society. William Allen Award, Amer. Soc. for Human Genetics, 1967. *Publications:* Haemoglobin and Its Abnormalities, 1961; The Hemoglobins in Genetics and Evolution, 1963; The Biosynthesis of Macromolecules, 1965; articles on human genetics, nucleic acids and differentiation in Nature, Jl Mol. Biol., Biochim., Biophys. Acta, Science, etc. *Recreation:* music. *Address:* Massachusetts Institute of Technology, Massachusetts Avenue, Cambridge, Mass 02139, USA. *T:* 617-864-6900, ext. 3706.

**INGRAMS,** family name of **Baroness Darcy de Knayth.**

**INGRAMS, William Harold,** CMG 1939; OBE 1933; *b* 3 Feb. 1897; *s* of Rev. W. S. Ingrams, The Schools, Shrewsbury; *m* 1930, Doreen, *y d* of Rt Hon. Edward Shortt, KC; two *d. Educ:* Shrewsbury. Served European War, KSLI, 1914-18 (wounded); 2nd Lieut Sept. 1914; Lt, Nov. 1914; Asst District Commissioner, Zanzibar, 1919; 2nd Asst Sec., 1925; Asst Col Sec. Mauritius 1927; Acting Colonial Sec., Jan.-May, and Aug. 1932-April 1933; Political Officer, Aden, 1934; British Resident Adviser at Mukalla, S Arabia, 1937-40; Acting Governor of Aden, 1940; Chief Sec. to Govt, Aden, 1940-42; Resident Adviser Hadhramaut States and British Agent Eastern Aden Protectorate, 1942-45; seconded as Asst Sec. Allied Control Commission for Germany (British Element) 1945-47; Chief Comr, Northern Territories, Gold Coast, 1947-48; Mission to Gibraltar, 1949, to Hong Kong, 1950, to Uganda, 1956; Adviser on Overseas Information, CO, 1950-54; Editor, Commonwealth Challenge, and If you ask me, 1952-66; Joint Research Dept, Foreign and Commonwealth Offices, 1966, retd 1968. Class IV Order of Brilliant Star, Zanzibar, 1927; awarded conjointly with wife, Lawrence Memorial Medal, 1939, and founder's Medal of RGS, 1940; Burton Memorial Medal, 1943. *Publications:* Dialects of Zanzibar Sultanate, 1924; Chronology and Genealogies of Zanzibar Rulers, 1926; Guide to Swahili Examinations, 1927; Zanzibar, Its History and People, 1931; School History of Mauritius, 1931; School Geography of Mauritius, 1932; Report on Social, Economic and Political Condition of the Hadhramaut, 1935; Arabia and the Isles, 1942 (3rd Edn, 1966); Seven Across the Sahara, 1949; Hong Kong, 1953; Uganda: a crisis of Nationhood, 1960; The Yemen: Imams, Rulers and Revolutions, 1963; numerous pamphlets, articles and broadcasts. *Address:* Uphousden, near Ash-next-Sandwich, Canterbury, Kent.

**INGRESS BELL, P.;** *see* Bell, Philip I.

**INIGO-JONES, Captain Henry Richmund,** CIE 1947; *b* 26 Aug. 1899; *s* of Rev. Ralph William Inigo-Jones, Kelston Park, Bath. Somerset; *m* 1st, 1925, Hester Rhoda (*d* 1948), *d* of late Herbert Smith, Great Ryburgh, Norfolk; one *s* one *d*; 2nd, 1951, Maidie Cubitt (from whom he obtained a divorce, 1961), London, SW. *Educ:* Elstow Sch., Bedford; Thames Nautical Training Coll.; HMS Worcester. Joined Royal Indian Marine (which later became Royal Indian Navy), 1920; transferred to Royal Navy on Indian Independence, and loaned to Indian Navy; Commodore-in-charge, Bombay, until 1951, when retired. *Address:* Ripton, Wodehouse Road, Hunstanton, Norfolk. *T:* Hunstanton 2849. *Club:* Naval.

**INMAN,** family name of **Baron Inman.**

**INMAN,** 1st Baron, *cr* 1946, of Knaresborough; **Philip Albert Inman,** PC 1947; JP County of London; President, former Chairman, Charing Cross Hospital; President, Charing Cross Hospital Medical School; Member of Council, King Edward's Hospital Fund; Patron, Independent Hospitals Association; director of publishing, hotel and industrial companies; an underwriting member of Lloyd's; *b* 12 June 1892; *s* of Philip Inman; *m* 1919, May Amélie, *o d* of Edward Dew, Harrow; one *d* (and one *s* decd). *Educ:* Harrogate; Leeds Univ. Former Chm. of BBC and of Central Bd of Finance of Church Assembly; Lord Privy Seal during 1947; Chm. Hotels Executive, British Transport, 1948-51; a Church Commissioner, 1946-57. Mem. of Court, Worshipful Co. of Needlemakers; Hon. FRSH. *Publications:* The Human Touch; The Silent Loom; The Golden Cup; Oil and Wine; Straight Runs Harley Street (Novel); No Going Back (Autobiography). *Recreations:* walking, reading, golf. *Address:* Knaresborough House, Warninglid, Haywards Heath, Sussex. *T:* Warninglid 225. *Club:* Athenæum.

**INMAN, Rt. Rev. Thomas George Vernon;** *see* Natal, Bishop of.

**INNES, Fergus Munro,** CIE 1946; CBE 1951; Director: Assam Trading (Holdings) Ltd; Rivers Steam Navigation Co. (Holdings) Ltd; Attock Oil Co. Ltd; *b* 12 May 1903; *s* of late Sir Charles Innes; *m* 1st, Evangeline, *d* of A. H. Chaworth-Musters (marriage dissolved); two *d*; 2nd, Vera, *d* of T. Mahoney; one *s* one *d*. *Educ:* Charterhouse; Brasenose Coll., Oxford. Joined Indian Civil Service, 1926; various posts in Punjab up to 1937; Joint Sec., Commerce Dept, Govt of India, 1944; Mem., Central Board of Revenue, 1947; retired, 1947; Adviser in Pakistan to Central Commercial Cttee, 1947-53; Sec., The West Africa Cttee, 1956-61. *Address:* Trilliums, Knowl Hill, The Hockering, Woking, Surrey. *T:* Woking 4626. *Club:* Oriental.

**INNES, Hammond;** *see* Hammond Innes, Ralph.

**INNES, Michael;** *see* Stewart, John I. M.

**INNES of Learney, Sir Thomas,** GCVO 1967 (KCVO 1946); Lord Lyon King of Arms, and Secretary to the Order of the Thistle, 1945-69; Marchmont Herald, since 1969; Heraldic and Peerage Lawyer; Hon. LLD St Andrews, 1956; FSA Scotland; Member of the Royal Company of Archers (Queen's Body Guard for Scotland); Baron of Aberkerder, Kinnairdy and Yeuchrie; Genealogist to Priory of Scotland in the Order of St John, 1947-70, Preceptor of Torphichen since 1970, KJStJ, 1947; Chairman of Postmaster General's Stamps Committee (Scotland), 1956-57; Commissioner of Supply for Aberdeenshire, 1926-29; Member of National Building Records Scottish Council since 1941; Member of Council of Scottish History Society, Scottish Record Society, Scottish Ecclesiological Society (President 1957-60), Scottish Ancestry Research Society; Vice-President Scottish Genealogy Society; Vice-President Society of Genealogists; Trustee of Sir William Fraser's Foundation; *b* 26 Aug. 1893; *o s* of late Lt-Col Francis N. Innes of Learney, DL, and Margaret Anne, *d* of Archer Irvine-Fortescue of Kingcausie, Kincardineshire, and *gs* of late Col Thomas Innes of Learney, CVO, LLD, DL; *m* 1928, Lady Lucy Buchan, 3rd *d* of 18th Earl of Caithness, CBE; three *s* one *d*. *Educ:* Neuchatel; Edinburgh Academy and Univ. Carrick Pursuivant of Arms, 1926-35; Advocate, Scots Bar, 1922; Albany Herald, 1935-45; was interim Lyon Clerk and Keeper of the Records in Court of Lord Lyon, May-Sept. 1929 and 1939-40. Herald-en-liaison with Armed Forces (Scotland), 1940-45. Hon. Sec. Scot. (Literary) Text Soc., 1932-54. *Publications:* many articles on Scots Heraldry, History, and Peerage Law; contributor to Green's Encyclopædia of the Laws of Scotland, Encyclopædia of Scot. Legal Styles and Encyclopædia Britannica; (ed) 4th and 5th edn Clans, Septs and Regiments of Scottish Highlands, 1952, 1955; Scots Heraldry, 1934, 1956; (ed) 25th edn Scottish Clans and Their Tartans, 1939; The Scottish Parliament, its Symbolism and its Ceremonial, 1933 (in Jur. Rev.) The Old Mansion House of Edingight, 1937; Observations on Armorial Conveyancing, 1940; Law of Succession in Ensigns Armorial, 1941; Tartans of the Clans and Families of Scotland, 1948; Robes of the Scots Feudal Baronage (in Soc. of Antiquaries of Scotland); Margaret Fair Tercentenary Book, 1950. *Recreations:* art, architecture, and literature (Scots and mediæval), visiting places of historic interest. *Heir: e s* Thomas [*b* 22 Jan. 1930 (Baron of Learney, Superior of Torphins); *m* 1958, Rosemary Elizabeth, *yr d* of late Brig. C. V. S. Jackson, CIE, CBE; one *d*]. *Address:* Laigh Riggs, Torphins, Aberdeenshire; Kinnairdy Castle, Bridge of Marnoch, Banffshire; 35 Inverleith Row, Edinburgh. *T:* 031-552 4924. *Club:* New (Edinburgh).

**INNES, Sir Walter James,** 15th Bt, *cr* 1628; *b* 8 Aug. 1903; *s* of late Hector Innes (6th *s* of 11th Bt) and Annie Jane, *d* of W. Fraser; *S* cousin 1950. *Heir: kinsman* Ronald Gordon Berowald Innes, OBE 1943 [*b* 24 July 1907; *m* 1st, 1933, Elizabeth Haughton (*d* 1958), *e d* of late A. Fayle, Merlin, Clonmel, Co. Tipperary; two *s* one *d*; 2nd, 1961, Elizabeth Christian, *e d* of late Lt-Col C. H. Watson, DSO. *Educ:* Harrow]. *Address:* Carlos Pellegrini 485, 4 piso, Dep. B., Buenos Aires, Argentina.

**INNES, William Arnold;** Commercial Consultant; Hon. President and Consultant to Cerebos Ltd and Associated Companies, 1962-69 (Chairman 1951-62); *b* 13 Nov. 1902; 3rd *s* of late Charles Robertson Innes, Edinburgh and Kingston upon Hull, and late Ann Florence Innes (*née* Buckley); *m* 1927, Dorothea Lois, *o d* of late William Douglas, WS, Edinburgh, and Jane Mary (*née* MacDonald); two *d* (and one *d* decd). *Educ:* Hymers Coll. Founder and Chm., The Alliance of Produce Importers and National Wholesale Distributors, and Chm. of Produce Importers (Alliance) Ltd, 1932-38; Dir Cerebos Ltd, 1939; formed and managed cttee set up in 1940 by agreement with Min. of Food to organise and maintain national distribution of salt; acted in advisory capacity to various sections of Bd of Trade and Min. of Supply, 1939-45; Formerly Chairman (retd 1962): Brand & Co. Ltd, Saxa Salt Co. Ltd, Bisto Ltd, The Middlewich Salt Co. Ltd, Henry Seddon & Sons Ltd, Scott (Midlothian) Ltd, John Crampton & Co. Ltd, Stamina Foods Ltd, Cerebos (Ireland) Ltd, Cerebos (Australia) Pty Ltd, Cerebos (Canada) Ltd, Cerebos (South Africa) Ltd. Mem., Court of Patrons RCS. Life Governor: Imperial Cancer Research Fund (Vice-Pres.); Royal Caledonian Schools; Heart Foundation. *Recreations:* travelling, gardening, golf, fishing. *Address:* Chapel Green House, Earlsferry, Elie, Fife. *T:* Elie 422. *Clubs:* Caledonian; Elie Golf House (Elie); Denham Golf (Denham).

**INNES-KER,** family name of **Duke of Roxburghe.**

**INNES-WILSON, Col Campbell Aubrey Kenneth,** CBE 1954 (OBE 1946, MBE 1943); *b* 20 June 1905; *s* of late Captain R. A. K. Wilson, KSLI; *m* 1939, Lorna Isabel, *d* of late Major G. G. P. Humphreys, Donaghmore House, Castlefinn, Co. Donegal; one *s*. *Educ:* Fettes; Royal Military Academy, Woolwich; St John's Coll., Cambridge. 2nd Lt, RE 1925. Joined Survey of India, 1929; Dir, Eastern Circle, Survey of India, 1946; Dep. Surveyor-Gen. of India, 1947; Surveyor Gen. of Pakistan, 1950-54. Served War of 1939-45; Iraq and Persia, 1941-43 (MBE); Burma, 1943-45 (OBE, despatches twice). FRICS; FRGS. *Address:* 27 Tufton Court, Tufton Street, SW1. *Club:* United Service.

**INNESS, Air Cdre William Innes Cosmo,** CB 1962; OBE 1954; Commandant, Air Cadets, London and South East, since 1968; *b* 25 March 1916; *y s* of Henry Atkinson Inness; *m* 1942, Margaret Rose Nolan, *er d* of Lt-Col P. E. Nolan, MBE, Royal Signals; two *s*. *Educ:* Richmond Sch., Yorkshire. Commissioned, RAF Coll., 1936; India, 1936-39; Iraq, 1939-41; Bomber Command, Flt, Sqdn and Station Comdr and GP Capt., Plans, 1941-45. Air Ministry Directorate-Gen. of Personnel, Brit. Bombing Survey Unit, and Directorate of Staff Duties, 1946-48; Air Attaché, Teheran, 1948-51; Sen. Personnel Staff Officer, No. 23 Gp, 1951-54; RAF Flying Coll., 1954-55; Station Comdr, St Eval, 1955-57; Dep. Asst Chief of Staff (Plans), HQ Allied Forces, Mediterranean, 1957-59; Air Officer i/c Administration, Coastal Command, 1959-62; AOC Gibraltar, 1962-65; Dir Personal Services (Provost Marshal), RAF, 1965-68, retired 1968. ADC 1966-68. Chevalier of the Military Order of Aviz (Portugal), 1956. *Recreations:* sailing, field sports. *Address:* c/o National Westminster Bank Ltd, Market Place, Sutton-in-Ashfield, Nottingham. *Club:* Royal Air Force.

**INNISS, Hon. Sir Clifford (de Lisle),** Kt 1961; Chief Justice of British Honduras since 1957; *b* Barbados, 26 Oct. 1910; *e s* of late Archibald de Lisle Inniss and Lelia Emmaline, *e d* of Elverton Richard Springer. *Educ:* Harrison Coll., Barbados; Queen's Coll., Oxford. BA (hons jurisprudence), BCL. Called to bar, Middle Temple, 1935. QC (Tanganyika) 1950, (Trinidad and Tobago) 1953; Practised at bar, Barbados; subseq. Legal Draughtsman and Clerk to Attorney-Gen., Barbados, 1938; Asst to Attorney General and Legal Draughtsman, 1941; Judge of Bridgetown Petty Debt Court, 1946; Legal Draughtsman, Tanganyika, 1947; Solicitor Gen., Tanganyika, 1949; Attorney-Gen., Trinidad and Tobago, 1953. *Recreations:* cricket, tennis, swimming. *Address:* Chief Justice's Residence, Belize City, British Honduras. *Clubs:* Royal Over-Seas League; Barbados Yacht; Kenya Kongonis (hon. mem.); Belize (British Honduras).

**INONU, Gen. Ismet;** Leader of the Republican People's Party, Turkey, since 1950; *b* Izmir, Asia Minor, 24 Sept. 1884; *s* of Reshid, judge and legal adviser to Governmental Depts, and Djevriye; *m* 1916, Mevhibe; two *s* one *d*. *Educ:* Military Artillery Coll. and Military Academy, Istanbul. Capt. Gen. Staff, 2nd Army, Edirne, 1906; Major, chief Gen. Staff, Army of Yemen, 1912; Lt-Col 1914; Col 1915; Comdr 4th Army Corps, 1916; Comdr 20th Army Corps, later 3rd Army Corps, 1917; Under-Sec., Ministry of War, Istanbul, 1918; left Istanbul, joined Mustafa Kemal (Atatürk) and National Struggle movement in Ankara; became dep. of Edirne and Chief of Great Gen. Staff, 1920; Comdr Western Front; victorious, 1st and 2nd Battles of Inönü, Brig.-Gen. 1921; Lt-Gen. 1922; appointed Minister of Foreign Affairs, while he kept his rank in army in accordance Constitution, 1922; signed Treaty of Lausanne, 1923; Prime Minister, Oct. 1923-Nov. 1924 and March 1925-Oct. 1937; Pres. of the Republic of Turkey, 1938-50; Leader of the Opposition, Turkish Parliament, 1950-60; Prime Minister of Turkey, 1961-65; again Leader of the Opposition, 1965-. Gen., 1926; retired from army, 1927. *Recreations:* fond of books; equitation, chess, bridge, billiards. *Address:* Office of the Republican People's Party, Ankara, Turkey.

**INSALL, Group Captain Gilbert Stuart Martin,** VC 1915; MC; RAF retired; *b* 1894; *e s* of G. J. Insall, Sevington, Kent; *m* 1926, Olwen Scott, *o d* of J. A. Yates; two *s*. *Educ:* Anglo-Saxon Sch., Paris. Was studying as a dentist in Paris on outbreak of war; enlisted as private in UPS Royal Fusiliers (18th Service Batt.); went to Brooklands on transfer to RFC 1915; flew to France in summer as pilot; on 7 Nov. he forced to earth an Aviatik and descended to less than 500 feet under heavy fire to allow his gunner to destroy the enemy machine within the German lines, was shot down in trenches on the way back at 200 feet, repaired machine during night under concentrated shell-fire, and flew back to his aerodrome at dawn (despatches, VC); pursued German machine on 14 Dec. across the lines; when well inside lines engaged the hostile machine and got hit by machine-gun bullet in petrol tank; while trying to plane back an anti-aircraft shell burst under the machine wounding him and his observer, Corpl Donald; unable to reach lines, he landed, and was taken prisoner, after trying to destroy his machine; underwent two operations whilst in captivity, one of which was the extraction of a large piece of anti-aircraft shell from his back; escaped from Heidelberg Camp, 1916; recaptured after five days; escaped from Crefeld, recaptured same day; sent to Ströhen, near Hanover; managed finally to reach Dutch Frontier, Aug. 1917 (MC); permanent Commission RAF Aug. 1919; retired from RAF, 1945. *Recreations:* hockey, shooting, fishing, archæology. *Address:* Monks Mill, Scrooby, near Doncaster, Yorks.

**INSKIP,** family name of **Viscount Caldecote.**

**INSKIP, John Hampden,** QC 1966; Deputy Chairman, Hampshire Quarter Sessions, since 1967; Recorder of Bournemouth, since 1970; *b* 1 Feb. 1924; *s* of Sir John Hampden Inskip, KBE, and Hon. Janet, *d* of 1st Baron Maclay, PC; *m* 1947; Ann Howell Davies. *Educ:* Clifton Coll.; King's Coll., Cambridge. BA 1948. Called to the Bar, Inner Temple, 1949. Mem. of Western Circuit. *Address:* 3 Pump Court, Temple, EC4. *T:* 01-353 7731; Clerks, Bramshott, Liphook, Hants.

**INSKIP, Maj.-Gen. Roland Debenham,** CB 1939; CIE 1938; DSO 1916; MC; IA; retired; *b* 1885; *s* of late Rev. O. D. Inskip, Rector of Harleston, Norfolk; *m* 1918, Evelyn (marriage dissolved, 1928), *d* of John Rickard, Tudor House, Fairford, Glos.; one *s* (and one killed in France Jan. 1944); *m* 1929, Mabel Louisa, *d* of Mackay John Scobie, Bournemouth. *Educ:* Framlingham Coll.; RMC, Sandhurst. Served NW Frontier of India, 1908 (medal and clasp); European War (France, Mesopotamia, Palestine), 1914-18 (despatches five times, DSO, MC); Bt Major, 1918; Bt Lt-Col, 1928, NW Frontier of India, 1930 (clasp); Waziristan, 1937-38-39 (CIE, despatches twice, medal and 2 clasps); Commandant 6th Royal Batt. 13th Frontier Force Rifles, 1932-34; Gen. Staff Officer First Grade, AHQ, India, 1934-35; Col 1935; Imperial Defence Coll., 1936; Comdr, 1st (Abbottabad) Infantry Brigade, India, 1937-39; Maj.-Gen. 1939; a District Comdr, India, 1941; GOC Ceylon, 1941-42; retired, Sept. 1942; re-employed Oct. 1942-Feb. 1946; Chief of Staff Bhopal State Forces, Feb. 1946-April 1947; Col 6th Royal Bn (Scinde) The FF Rifles, 1943-56; Hon. Col 1st Bn (Scinde) The FF Rifles, 1963- (Pakistan Army). *Address:* c/o Lloyd's Bank, 6 Pall Mall, SW1.

**INVERFORTH,** 2nd Baron, *cr* 1919, of Southgate; **Andrew Alexander Morton Weir;** Chairman and Governing Director of Andrew Weir & Company Ltd; *b* 12 Sept. 1897; *o s* of 1st Baron Inverforth, PC, and Anne (*d* 1941), *y d* of Thomas Kay Dowie; *S* father 1955; *m* 1929, Iris Beryl, *d* of late Charles Vincent, 4th Bn The Buffs; two *s*. *Educ:* St Paul's Sch. Comdr, Order of Dannebrog (Danish), 1947. *Recreation:* yachting. *Heir:* *s* Hon. (Andrew Charles) Roy Weir [*b* 6 June 1932; *m* 1966, Elizabeth, *o d* of John W. Thornycroft, Steyne, Bembridge, IW; one *s* one *d*]. *Address:* 24 Clarence Terrace, NW1. *Clubs:* Royal Automobile; Royal Yacht Squadron.

**INVERNESS, Provost of** (St Andrew's Cathedral); *see* Laming, Very Rev. F. F.

**IONESCO, Eugène;** Chevalier de la Legion d'Honneur, 1970; Chevalier des Arts et lettres, 1961; homme de lettres; Membre de l'Académie française, since 1970; *b* 13 Nov. 1912; *m* 1936, Rodica; one *d*. *Educ:* Bucharest and Paris. French citizen living in Paris. *Publications:* (most of which appear in English and American editions) Théâtre I; La Cantatrice chauve, La Leçon, Jacques ou La Soumission, Les Chaises, Victimes du devoir, Amédée ou Comment s'en débarrasser, Paris, 1956; Théâtre II: L'Impromptu de l'Alma, Tueur sans gages, Le Nouveau Locataire, L'Avenir est dans les œufs, Le Maître, La Jeune Fille à marier, Paris, 1958. Rhinocéros (play) in Collection Manteau d'Arlequin, Paris, 1959, Le Piéton de l'air, 1962, Chemises de Nuit, 1962; Le Roi se meurt, 1962; Notes et Contre-Notes, 1962; Journal en Miettes, 1967; Présent passé passé présent, 1968; Jeux de Massacre (play), 1970. Contrib. to: Avant-Garde (The experimental theatre in France) by L. C. Pronko, 1962; Modern French Theatre, from J. Giraudoux to Beckett, by Jean Guicharnaud, 1962; author essays and tales. *Relevant publication:* Ionesco, by Richard N. Coe, 1961. *Address:* c/o Editions Gallimard, 5 rue Sébastien Bottin, Paris 7e, France.

**IPSWICH, Viscount; James Oliver Charles FitzRoy;** *b* 13 Dec. 1947; *s* and *heir* of Earl of Euston, *qv*. *Educ:* Eton. *Address:* North Leys, Much Hadham, Herts.

**IPSWICH, Bishop of;** *see* St Edmundsbury.

**IPSWICH, Archdeacon of;** *see* Hooper, Ven. C. G.

**IQBAL AHMAD, Sir,** Kt 1941; BA, LLB; *b* 16 Sept. 1886; *s* of Ali Ahmad; *m* 1906, Abida Begum (*d* 1938); one *s*. *Educ:* Allahabad. Practised profession of law, 1908-26, and again since Chief Justiceship. Additional judge, Allahabad High Court, 1926-28; reverted to bar, 1928; acting judge, May-July 1929 and April-Aug. 1932; additional judge, 1932-33; permanent puisne judge, 1933-41; Chief Justice of High Court, Allahabad, 1941-46; acting Chief Justice, Feb.-July 1941. *Recreation:* shooting. *Address:* Butler Road, Lucknow, UP, India. *T:* Lucknow 23503.

**IRBY,** family name of **Baron Boston.**

**IRELAND, Frank;** Principal City Officer and Town Clerk, Newcastle upon Tyne, since 1969; *b* 2 May 1909; *s* of C. A. Ireland, Clitheroe, Lancs; *m* 1935, Elsie Mary (*née* Ashworth); one *s* two *d*. *Educ:* Clitheroe Royal Grammar Sch.; Victoria Univ., Manchester. Chartered Accountant, 1931; Hons, IMTA, 1936. Derby County Borough, 1933-37; Newcastle upon Tyne, 1937-: City Treasurer, 1962-69. *Recreations:* music, photography. *Address:* 61 Kenton Road, Newcastle upon Tyne NE3 4NJ. *T:* Gosforth 856930.

**IRELAND, Lt-Col G. B. de C.;** *see* De Courcy-Ireland.

**IRELAND, Ronald David,** QC (Scotland) 1964; Professor of Scots Law, University of Aberdeen, since 1958; *b* 13 March 1925; *o s* of William Alexander Ireland and Agnes Victoria Brown. *Educ:* George Watson's Coll., Edinburgh; Balliol Coll., Oxford (Scholar); Edinburgh Univ. Served Royal Signals, 1943-46. BA Oxford, 1950, MA 1958; LLB Edinburgh, 1952. Passed Advocate, 1952; Clerk of the Faculty of Advocates, 1957-58. Governor, Aberdeen Coll. of Education, 1959-64; Vice-Chm., 1962-64. Dean of the Faculty of Law, University of Aberdeen, 1964-67. Mem. Bd of Management, Aberdeen Gen. Hosps, 1961-. Chm., 1964-; Mem. Departmental Cttee on Children and Young Persons, 1961-64; Hon. Sheriff-Substitute for Aberdeenshire, 1963-. Member: North Eastern Regional Hosp. Bd, 1964- (Vice-Chm. 1966-); After Care Council, 1962-65; Nat. Staff Advisory Cttee for the Scottish Hosp. Service, 1964-65; Chm., Scottish Hosps Administrative Staffs Cttee, 1965-. *Recreations:* music, bird-watching. *Address:* 23 Don Street, Old Aberdeen AB2 1UH. *Clubs:* New (Edinburgh); University, Royal Northern (Aberdeen).

**IREMONGER, Thomas Lascelles;** MP (C) Ilford North, since Feb. 1954; *o s* of Lt-Col H. E. W. Iremonger, DSO, Royal Marine Artillery, and Julia St Mary Shandon, *d* of Col John Quarry, Royal Berks Regiment; *m* Lucille Iremonger, author and broadcaster; one *d. Educ:* Oriel Coll., Oxford. HM Overseas Service (Western Pacific), 1938-46. RNVR (Lt), 1942-46. PPS to Sir Fitzroy Maclean, Bt, CBE, MP, when Under-Sec. of State for War, 1954-57. Member: Royal Commn on the Penal System, 1964-66; Home Sec.'s Advis. Council on the Employment of Prisoners; Gen. Council, Institute for Study and Treatment of Delinquency. Underwriting Mem. of Lloyd's. *Publications:* Disturbers of the Peace, 1961; Money, Politics and You, 1963. *Recreations:* sailing, riding, shooting. *Address:* 34 Cheyne Row, SW3; The Giant's Cottage, Newbourn, near Woodbridge, Suffolk.

**IRENS, Alfred Norman,** CBE 1969; Chairman, South Western Electricity Board since 1956; *b* 28 Feb. 1911; *s* of Max Henry and Guinevere Emily Irens; *m* 1934, Joan Elizabeth, *d* of John Knight, FRIBA, Worsley, Manchester; two *s*. *Educ:* Blundell's Sch., Tiverton; Faraday House, London. College apprentice, Metropolitan Vickers, Ltd, Manchester. Subsequently with General Electric Co., Ltd, until joining Bristol Aeroplane Co., Ltd, 1939, becoming Chief Electrical Engineer, 1943; Consulting Engineer to Govt and other organisations, 1945-56. Part-time mem., SW Electricity Bd, 1948-56. Past Chm. IEE Utilization Section and IEE Western Sub-Centre; Chairman: British Electrical Development Assoc., 1962-63; SW Economic Planning Council, 1968-. Mem. Bd, Bristol Waterworks Co., 1967-. MSc, Univ. of Bristol, 1957. *Recreations:* general outdoor activities. *Address:* Crete Hill House, Cote House Lane, Bristol 9. *T:* Bristol 627471. *Club:* Junior Carlton.

**IRESON, Rev. Canon Gordon Worley;** Canon-Missioner of St Albans since September 1958; *b* 16 April 1906; *s* of Francis Robert and Julia Letitia Ireson; *m* 1939, Dorothy Elizabeth Walker; two *s* one *d. Educ:* Edinburgh Theological Coll.; Hatfield Coll., Durham. Asst Curate of Sheringham, 1933-36; Senior Chaplain of St Mary's Cathedral, Edinburgh, with charge of Holy Trinity, Dean Bridge, 1936-37; Priest-Lecturer to National Soc., 1937-39; Diocesan Missioner of Exeter Diocese, 1939-46; Hon. Chaplain to Bishop of Exeter, 1941-46; Canon Residentiary of Newcastle Cathedral, 1946-58; Examining Chaplain to Bishop of Newcastle, 1949-. *Publications:* Church Worship and the Non-Churchgoer, 1945; Think Again, 1949; How Shall They Hear?, 1957; Strange Victory, 1970. *Recreation:* making and mending in the workshop. *Address:* 10 Fishpool Street, St Albans. *T:* 57973.

**IRISH, Sir Ronald (Arthur),** Kt 1970; OBE 1963; Partner, Irish Young & Outhwaite, Chartered Accountants; Chairman, Rothmans of Pall Mall (Australia) Ltd; Director of other companies; *b* 26 March 1913; *s* of late Arthur Edward Irish; *m* 1960, Noella Jean Austin Fraser; three *s. Educ:* Fort Street High School. Pres., Inst. of Chartered Accountants in Australia, 1956-58; Pres., Tenth Internat. Congress of Accountants, 1972; Chm., Manufacturing Industries Adv. Council, 1966-. *Publications:* Practical Auditing, 1935; Auditing, 1947. *Recreations:* golf, swimming. *Address:* Cootharinga, Castle Hill, NSW 2154, Australia. *Clubs:* Australian, Union, Killara Golf (Sydney).

**IRON, Air Cdre Douglas,** CBE 1944; *b* 1 Aug. 1893; *s* of Captain John Iron, OBE, and Anne Iron; *m* 1917, Dorothy Bentham (from whom he obtained a divorce); one *d*; *m* 1930, Mrs P. V. Sankey (from whom he obtained a divorce). *Educ:* Tudor Hall Sch., Hawkhurst. Prob. Flight Sub.-Lt RNAS Sept. 1914; Flight Lt May 1915; Acting Lt-Col GSO1 (Air) April 1918; permanent commission, RAF, as Flight Lt 1919. Sqdn Leader, 1924; Wing Comdr 1930; attended Royal Naval Staff Coll., 1935; Group Capt. 1937; Air Officer i/c Administration, 4 Training Command, RCAF, Canada, with rank of Air Commodore, Dec. 1943; Air Officer Commanding 51 Group RAF, 1944-45; retired, 1945. *Recreation:* fishing. *Club:* Army and Navy.

**IRONMONGER, Sir (Charles) Ronald,** Kt 1970; Assistant Personnel Officer, AEI Attercliffe, since 1966; *b* 20 Jan. 1914; *s* of late Charles and Emily Ironmonger; *m* 1938 Jessie (*née* Green); one *s* one *d. Educ:* Huntsmans Gardens Elementary Sch., Firth Park Secondary Sch., Sheffield. Elected Sheffield City Council, Nov. 1945; Chairman, Water Cttee, 1951-66; Leader of City Council and Chairman, Policy Cttee, 1960-68, 1969-. *Recreations:* reading, sport. *Address:* 70 Chestnut Avenue, Sheffield S9 4AP. *T:* Sheffield 42329.

**IRONSIDE,** family name of **Baron Ironside.**

**IRONSIDE,** 2nd Baron, *cr* 1941, of Archangel and of Ironside; **Edmund Oslac Ironside;** Cryosystems Ltd, since 1963; International Research and Development Co., since 1969; *b* 21 Sept. 1924; *o s* of 1st Baron Ironside, GCB, CMG, DSO (Field Marshal Lord Ironside), and Mariot Ysobel Cheyne; *m* 1950, Audrey Marigold, *y d* of late Lt-Col Hon. Thomas Morgan-Grenville, DSO, OBE, MC; one *s* one *d. Educ:* Tonbridge Sch. Joined Royal Navy, 1943; retd as Lt, 1952. Marconi's Wireless Telegraph Co., 1952-60; English Electric Ltd, 1960. *Heir: s* Hon. Charles Edmund Grenville Ironside, *b* 1 July 1956. *Address:* Broomwood Manor, Chignal St James, Chelmsford, Essex. *T:* Broomfield 231. *Club:* Royal Ocean Racing.

**IRONSIDE, Christopher;** Artist and Designer; *b* 11 July 1913; *s* of Dr R. W. Ironside and Mrs P. L. Williamson (2nd *m*; *née* Cunliffe); *m* 1st, 1939, Janey (*née* Acheson) (marriage dissolved, 1961); one *d*; 2nd, 1961, Jean (*née* Marsden); one *s* two *d. Educ:* Central Sch. of Arts and Crafts. Served War of 1939-45, Dep. Sen. Design Off., Directorate of Camouflage, Min. of Home Security. In charge of Educn

Sect., Coun. of Industrial Design, 1946-48; part-time Teacher, Royal College of Art, 1953-63. Paintings in public and private collections. *One-man shows:* Redfern Gall., 1941; Arthur Jeffries Gall., 1960. *Design work includes:* Royal Coat of Arms, Whitehall and decorations in Pall Mall, Coronation, 1953; coinages for Tanzania, Brunei, Qatar and Dubai; reverses for Decimal Coinage, UK and Jamaican; many medals, coins and awards; theatrical work (with brother, late R. C. Ironside); various clocks; coat of arms and tapestry for Leather Sellers' Hall; firegrate for Goldsmiths' Co. FSIA 1970. *Recreation:* trying to keep abreast of modern scientific development. *Address:* 22 Abingdon Villas, W8. *T:* 01-937 9418.

**IRVINE, Rt. Hon. Sir Arthur (James),** PC 1970; Kt 1967; QC 1958; MP (Lab) Edge Hill Division of Liverpool, since 1947; *b* 14 July 1909; *s* of late J. M. Irvine, KC, Sheriff of Renfrew and Bute; *m* 1937, Eleanor, *d* of late E. E. T. Morris, Petersfield, Hants; four *s*. *Educ:* Angusfield Sch., Aberdeen; Edinburgh Academy; Edinburgh Univ. (MA 1929); Oriel Coll., Oxford (BA 1931, MA 1957). Pres., Oxford Union, 1932; called to Bar, Middle Temple, 1935; also Mem. of Inner Temple; Sec. to Lord Chief Justice of England, 1935-40; UK delegate to Council of Europe, 1961-62; Master of the Bench, Middle Temple, 1965; Chm. House of Commons Select Cttee on Procedure, 1965; Solicitor-General, 1967-70. Recorder of Colchester, 1965-67. Hon. Fellow, Oriel Coll., 1969. Contested Kincardine and West Aberdeenshire (L), 1935 and 1939 (by-election); DAAG HQ Eastern Command, 1944; DAMS HQ Land Forces, Greece, 1944-45 (despatches). Contested (Lab) Twickenham, 1945 and South Aberdeen (by-election), 1946. *Address:* 20 Wellington Square, SW3. *T:* 01-730 3117.

**IRVINE, B(ryant) Godman;** MP (C) Rye Division of East Sussex since 1955; Barrister-at-law; Farmer; *b* Toronto, 25 July 1909; *s* of late W. Henry Irvine and late Ada Mary Bryant Irvine, formerly of St Agnes, Cornwall; *m* 1945, Valborg Cecilie, *d* of late P. F. Carslund; two *d*. *Educ:* Upper Canada Coll.; St Paul's Sch.; Magdalen Coll., Oxford (MA). Sec. Oxford Union Soc., 1931. Called to Bar. Inner Temple, 1932. Chm. Agricultural Land Tribunal, SE Province, 1954-56. Mem. Executive Cttee, East Sussex NFU, 1947-; Branch Chm., 1956-58. Chm. Young Conservative Union, 1946-47; Prospective Candidate, Bewdley Div. of Worcs, 1947-49; contested Wood Green and Lower Tottenham, 1951. PPS to Minister of Education and to Parly Sec., Ministry of Education, 1957-59, to the Financial Sec. to the Treasury, 1959-60. Mem., Chm.'s Panel, House of Commons, 1965-; Jt Sec., 1922 Cttee, 1965-68; Vice-Chm., Cons. Agric. Cttee, 1964-; An Opposition spokesman on Agriculture; Mem., House of Commons Select Cttee on Agriculture, 1967-69; Mem., Exec. Cttee, UK Branch, Commonwealth Parly Assoc., 1964-; Jt Sec. and Vice-Chm., Cons. Commonwealth Affairs Cttee, 1957-66, 1967-68; Chm., Cons. Horticulture Sub-Cttee, 1960-62; All Party Tourist and Resort Cttee, 1964-66; Pres., Assoc. British Resorts, 1962-. Served War of 1939-45, Lt-Comdr RNVR, afloat and on staff of C-in-C Western Approaches and Commander US Naval Forces in Europe. Comp. InstCE. *Recreations:* skiing, travel by sea. *Address:* Great Ote Hall, Burgess Hill, Sussex. *T:* Burgess Hill 2179; Flat 51, 24 John Islip Street, SW1. *T:* 01-834 9221; 2 Dr Johnson's Buildings, Temple, EC4. 01-353 5371. *Clubs:* Carlton, Pratt's, Farmers', RNVR; Dormy House (Rye).

**IRVINE, Surg. Captain Gerard Sutherland,** CBE 1970; RN retired; *b* 19 June 1913; *s* of Major Gerard Byrom Corrie Irvine and Maud Andrée (*née* Wylde); *m* 1939, Phyllis Lucy Lawrie; one *s*. *Educ:* Imperial Service Coll., Windsor; Epsom Coll.; University Coll. and Hosp., London. MRCS, LRCP, MB, BS 1937; DLO 1940; FRCS 1967. Jenks Meml Schol. 1932; Liston Gold Medal for Surgery 1936. Surg. Sub-Lt RNVR 1935, Surg. Lt RNVR 1937; Surg Lt RN 1939; Surg. Lt-Comdr 1944; Surg. Comdr 1953; Surg. Capt. 1963. Served War of 1939-45 (1939-45 Star, Atlantic Star with Bar for France and Germany, Burma Star, Defence Medal, Victory Medal); subseq. service: Ceylon, 1946; Haslar, 1947-49 and 1957-60; Malta, 1953-56; HMS: Maidstone (Submarine Depot Ship), 1949-51; Osprey (T&A/S Trng Sch.), 1951-53; Collingwood, 1956-57; Lion, 1960-62; Vernon (Torpedo Sch.), 1962-63; Sen. Cons. in ENT, 1953-70; Adviser in ENT to Med. Dir-Gen. (Navy), 1966-70; Sen. MO i/c Surgical Div., RN Hosp. Haslar, 1966-70; QHS 1969-70; retd 1970. Member: BMA 1938; Sections of Otology and Laryngology, RSM, 1948- (FRSM 1948); British Assoc. of Otolaryngologists, 1945- (Council, 1958-70); S Western Laryngological Assoc., 1951-; Hearing Sub-Cttee of RN Personnel Res. Cttee, 1947-70; Otological Sub-Cttee of RAF Flying Personnel Res. Cttee, 1963-70. OStJ 1969. *Publications:* numerous articles in various medical jls. *Recreations:* gardening, philately, do-it-yourself. *Address:* 9 Alvara Road, Alverstoke, Gosport PO12 2HY. *T:* Gosport 80342. *Clubs:* Naval and Military; Royal Naval (Portsmouth).

**IRVINE, Rev. Canon John Murray;** Canon Residentiary, Prebendary of Hunderton, Chancellor and Librarian of Hereford Cathedral, and Director of Ordination Training in the Diocese of Hereford, since 1965; *b* 19 Aug. 1924; *s* of Andrew Leicester Irvine and Eleanor Mildred (*née* Lloyd); *m* 1961, Pamela Shirley Brain; one *s* two *d*. *Educ:* Charterhouse; Magdalene Coll., Cambridge; Ely Theological Coll. BA 1946, MA 1949. Deacon, 1948; Priest, 1949; Curate of All Saints, Poplar, 1948-53; Chaplain of Sidney Sussex Coll., Cambridge, 1953-60; Selection Sec. of CACTM, 1960-65. *Address:* The Close, Hereford. *T:* Hereford 66193.

**IRVINE, Very Rev. Thomas Thurstan;** Dean of the United Diocese of St Andrew's, Dunkeld and Dunblane, since 1959; Rector of St John's, Perth, since 1966; *b* 19 June 1913; 5th *s* of late William Fergusson Irvine; *m* 1943, Elizabeth Marian, *er d* of late Francis More, CA, Edinburgh; five *d*. *Educ:* Shrewsbury; Magdalen Coll., Oxford. BA 2nd Class History, 1934; Diploma in Theology, 1935; MA 1938. Cuddesdon Coll., 1937; deacon, 1938, priest, 1939, St Albans; Curate, All Saints, Hertford, 1938-40; Precentor, St Ninian's Cathedral, Perth, 1940-43; Priest in charge, Lochgelly, 1943-45; Rector of Bridge of Allan, 1945-47; Rector of Callander, 1947-66. Examining Chaplain to Bishop of St Andrews, 1950. *Recreations:* fishing, walking. *Address:* St John's Rectory, Dupplin Terrace, Perth.

**IRVINE, Prof. William Tait;** Professor of Surgery, University of London, at St Mary's Hospital, since Oct. 1960; *b* 19 March 1925; *s* of George Irvine; *m* 1950, May Warburton; two *d*. *Educ:* by his father and at Univs of Glasgow, McGill and Minnesota, USA. BSc 1944, MB, ChB, 1947, FRCSE 1950, FRCS 1952, ChM (Hons) 1956, MD (Hons) 1957. Archibald Fellow in Surgery, McGill Univ., 1954; Mayo Foundation Fellow, Mayo Clinic, USA, 1955; Lectr in Surgery, Univ. of Glasgow, 1956; Asst Surg., The London Hospital, E1, 1957-60.

*Publications:* various papers on surgical subjects. Editor: Modern Trends in Surgery; Scientific Basis of Surgery. *Recreations:* walking, reading. *Address:* St Mary's Hospital, W2. *T:* 01-262 1280.

**IRVINE-JONES, Douglas Vivian;** Sheriff-Substitute of Inverness, Moray, Nairn and Ross and Cromarty, since 1952; *b* 20 March 1904; *s* of late Henry Irvine-Jones, MD, and of Mrs Irvine-Jones, Edinburgh; *m* 1937, Angela Mary, *d* of late Sir John Couper MVO, OBE, and Lady Couper, North Berwick; no *c. Educ:* Daniel Stewart's Coll., Edinburgh; Edinburgh Univ. (MA, LLB). Solicitor, 1930; Advocate of the High Court of Judicature at Rangoon, 1930; Mem., Faculty of Advocates, 1945; Sheriff-Substitute of Dumfries, 1950-52. *Recreations:* fishing, shooting. *Address:* The Sheriff Court, Dingwall, Rossshire.

**IRVING, David Blair;** Chairman, London Electricity Board, 1956-68; *b* 9 Nov. 1903; *s* of late Mitchell B. Irving, Sorn, Ayrshire, and Mary Ross, Broadford, Isle of Skye; *m* 1933, Isabel Gibson; one *s. Educ:* Ayr Academy. BSc Hons (London), 1923. British Thomson-Houston Co. Ltd; trained Rugby; subseq. positions in London, Sheffield, Bombay and Calcutta. Joined Central Electricity Bd, 1932, and London Electricity Bd at Vesting Day, 1 April 1948: Chief Engineer, 1949-53; Dep. Chm., 1953-56. MIEE, 1945; FIEE, 1966; Mem. Société des Ingénieurs Civils de France, 1949-70; Mem. Royal Institution, 1957-69. Chm., British Electrical Development Assoc., 1960-61; Chm., Power Division IEE, 1962-63. Governor, Ashbridge Management Coll., 1965-68. *Publications:* papers to British and internat. engineering and scientific bodies. *Recreation:* golf. *Address:* Kinross, Ashridge Park, Berkhamsted, Herts. *T:* Little Gaddesden 2405. *Club:* Caledonian.

**IRVING, David J. M.;** *see* Mill Irving.

**IRVING, Rear-Adm. Sir Edmund (George),** KBE 1966 (OBE 1944); CB 1962; Hydrographer of the Navy, 1960-66, retired; *b* 5 April 1910; *s* of George Clerk Irving, British North Bornea, and Ethel Mary Frances (*née* Poole), Kimberley, SA; *m* 1936, Margaret Scudamore Edwards; one *s* one *d. Educ:* St Anthony's, Eastbourne; RN College, Dartmouth. Joined HMS Royal Oak, as Cadet and Midshipman, 1927; Sub-Lieut's Courses, 1930-31; HMS Kellett Surveying Service, Dec. 1931 (various surveying ships); HMS Franklin, in command, 1944; Hydrographic Dept, 1946; HMS Sharpshooter, in command, 1948; Hydrographic Dept, 1949; HMS Dalrymple, in command, 1950; HMS Vidal, in command, 1953; Hydrographic Dept, Asst Hydrographer, 1954; HMS Vidal, in command, Oct. 1956; Hydrographic Dept, Asst Hydrographer, 1959. ADC, 1960, Mem. Natural Environment Research Council, 1967. FRGS (Pres., 1969); FRICS; FRSA. *Recreation:* golf. *Address:* Camer Green, Meopham, Kent. *T:* Meopham 3253. *Club:* Army and Navy.

**IRVING, Prof. Harry Munroe Napier Hetherington;** Professor of Inorganic and Structural Chemistry, University of Leeds, since 1961; *b* 19 Nov. 1905; *s* of John and Clara Irving; *m* 1934, Monica Mary Wildsmith; no *c. Educ:* St Bees Sch., Cumberland; The Queen's Coll., Oxford. BA 1927; First Class in Final Honour Sch. (Chemistry), 1928; MA, DPhil 1930; DSc 1958 (all Oxon); LRAM 1930. Univ. Demonstrator in Chemistry, Oxford, 1934-61; Lectr in Organic Chemistry, The Queen's Coll., 1930-34; Fellow and Tutor, St Edmund Hall, 1938-51; Vice-Principal, 1951-61; Emeritus-Fellow, 1961-. Mem. Chem. Soc. 1935- (Council, 1954); Mem. Soc. for Analytical Chemists, 1950- (Council, 1952-57, 1965-67; Vice-Pres. 1955-57); Fellow Royal Inst. of Chemistry, 1948- (Council, 1950-52, 1962-65; Vice-Pres. 1965-67). Has lectured extensively in America, Africa and Europe; broadcasts on scientific subjects. Hon. DTech Brunel Univ., 1970. *Publications:* (trans.) Schwarzenbach and Flaschka's Complexometric Titrations; numerous papers in various learned jls. *Recreations:* music, foreign travel, mountain climbing, ice-skating. *Address:* 1 North Grange Mount, Leeds 6.

**IRVING, James Tutin,** MA Oxon and Cantab, MD, PhD Cantab; Professor of Physiology in the School of Dental Medicine at Harvard University and the Forsyth Dentral Center, 1961-68, Professor Emeritus, 1968; *b* Christchurch, New Zealand, 3 May 1902; *m* 1937, Janet, *d* of Hon. Nicholas O'Connor, New York. *Educ:* Christ's Coll., New Zealand; Caius Coll., Cambridge; Trinity Coll., Oxford; Guy's Hospital. Double First Class Hons, Nat. Sci. Tripos, Cambridge, 1923-24; Scholar and Prizeman, Caius Coll., 1923; Benn. W. Levy and Frank Smart Student, 1924-26; Beit Memorial Fellow, 1926-28; Lecturer in Physiology, Bristol Univ., 1931, and Leeds Univ., 1934; Head of Physiology Dept, Rowett Research Inst., and part-time lecturer, Aberdeen Univ., 1936; Prof. of Physiology, Cape Town Univ., 1939-53, Fellow 1948; Professor of Experimental Odontology, and Dir of the Joint CSIR and Univ. of Witwatersrand Dental Research Unit, 1953-59; Prof. of Anatomy, Harvard Sch. of Dental Med., 1959-61. Visiting Professor: Univ. of Illinois Dental Sch. 1947 and 1956; Univ. of Pennsylvania, 1951; Univ. of California, 1956. AM (Hon.) Harvard. Mem., National Nutrition Council, 1954-57; Hon. Life Mem., Nutrition Society of Southern Africa; late Hon. Physiologist to Groote Schuur Hosp.; Fellow Odont. Soc. S Africa. Hon. Life Mem. of New York Academy of Sciences. Mem. of Soc. of Sigma Xi. Hon. Mem. of Soc. of Omicron Kappa Upsilon. S African Medal for war services (non-military), 1948. *Publications:* Calcium Metabolism, 1957; Editor, Archives of Oral Biology; many papers in physiological and medical journals, chiefly on nutrition, and bone and tooth formation; also publications on nautical history. *Recreations:* music, gardening, nautical research. *Address:* Forsyth Dental Center, 140 The Fenway, Boston, Mass 02115, USA; Rockmarge, Prides Crossing, Mass 01965, USA. *Clubs:* Athenæum (London); Inanda (Johannesburg); Somerset (Boston).

**IRVING, Prof. John;** Freeland Professor of Natural Philosophy, University of Strathclyde, Glasgow, since 1961; *b* 22 Dec. 1920; *s* of John Irving and Margaret Kent Aird; *m* 1948, Monica Cecilia Clarke; two *s. Educ:* St John's Grammar Sch.; Hamilton Academy; Glasgow Univ. MA (1st Class Hons in Maths and Nat. Phil.), Glasgow Univ., 1940; PhD (Mathematical Physics), Birmingham Univ., 1951. Lectr, Stow Coll., Glasgow, 1944-45; Lectr in Maths, Univ. of St Andrews 1945-46; Lectr in Mathematical Physics, University of Birmingham, 1946-49; Nuffield Research Fellow (Nat. Phil.), University of Glasgow, 1949-51; Sen. Lectr in Applied Maths, University of Southampton, 1951-59; Prof. of Theoretical Physics and Head of Dept of Applied Mathematics and Theor. Physics University of Cape Town, 1959-61. Dean of Sch. of Mathematics and Physics, Glasgow Univ., 1964-69. *Publications:* Mathematics in Physics and Engineering, 1959 (New York); contrib. to: Proc. Physical Soc.; Philosophical Magazine, Physical Review. *Recreations:*

climbing, motoring. *Address:* Department of Natural Philosophy, University of Strathclyde, Glasgow, C1, Scotland. *T:* 041-552 4400 (Ext. 315).

**IRVING, Laurence Henry Forster,** OBE; RDI 1939; *b* 11 April 1897; *s* of late H. B. Irving, actor and author; *m* 1920, Rosalind Woolner; one *s* one *d. Educ:* Wellington Coll.; Royal Academy Schools. Served in RNAS and RAF, 1914-19 (Croix de Guerre, France); rejoined RAF Oct. 1939; served on Staff of British Air Forces in France, 1940 (despatches), and in 2nd Tactical Air Force, France, Belgium, 1943-44. Dir of the Times Publishing Co., 1946-62. Exhibited pictures at Royal Academy; held four exhibitions at the Fine Art Soc., 1925, 1928, 1936, 1950, and at Agnew and Sons, 1957; Art Dir to Douglas Fairbanks, 1928 and 1929, for film productions of The Iron Mask and The Taming of the Shrew; has designed a number of stage and film productions, including Pygmalion, Lean Harvest, The Good Companions, Punchinello, The First Gentleman, Marriage à la Mode, Hamlet (Old Vic), 1950, Man and Superman, 1951; The Happy Marriage, 1952; Pygmalion, 1953; The Wild Duck, 1955; produced and designed film production of Lefanu's Uncle Silas. *Publications:* Henry Irving; The Actor and his World, 1951; The Successors, 1967; Windmills and Waterways; edited and illustrated: The Maid of Athens; Bligh's narrative of The Mutiny of the Bounty; A Selection of Hakluyt's Voyages; illustrated: Masefield's Philip the King; Conrad's The Mirror of the Sea; St Exupery's Flight to Arras. *Address:* The Lea, Wittersham, Kent. *Club:* Garrick.

*See also Sir Felix Brunner.*

**IRVING, Robert Augustine,** DFC and Bar, 1943; Principal Conductor, New York City Ballet, New York, 1958; *b* 28 Aug. 1913; *s* of late R. L. G. Irving; unmarried. *Educ:* Winchester; New Coll., Oxford; Royal College of Music. Répétiteur, Royal Opera House, 1936; Music master, Winchester Coll., 1936-40. RA, 1940-41; RAF (Coastal Command), 1941-45. Associate Conductor, BBC Scottish Orchestra, 1945-48; Conductor, Royal Opera House (The Royal Ballet), 1949-58. Many recordings for HMV and Decca, with Philharmonia and Royal Philharmonic Orchestras, also public concerts with these orchestras and London Philharmonic Orchestra. Wrote music for film, Floodtide, 1948; for New York production of As You Like It, 1949. *Recreations:* racing, bridge, mountaineering. *Address:* c/o New York City Ballet, New York State Theatre, Columbus Avenue and 62nd Street, New York, NY 10023, USA. *Clubs:* Portland, Alpine.

**IRVING, Rt. Hon. Sydney,** PC 1969; *b* 1 July 1918; *s* of Sydney Irving, Newcastle upon Tyne; *m* 1942, Mildred, *d* of Chariton Weedy, Morpeth, Northumberland; two *s* one *d. Educ:* Pendower Sch., Newcastle upon Tyne; London School of Economics, University of London. BSc (Econ.); DipEd. War Service, 1939-46: West Yorks Regt, Major. Chairman Southern Regional Council of Labour Party, 1965-67. Alderman, Dartford Borough Council; Mem. North-West Kent Divisional Executive, Kent Education Cttee, 1952-; MP (Lab and Co-op) Dartford, 1955-70; Opposition Whip (S and S Western), 1959-64; Treasurer of the Household and Deputy Chief Government Whip, 1964-66; Dep. Chm. of Ways and Means, 1966-68; Chm. of Ways and Means, and Deputy Speaker, 1968-70. Mem. CPA delegations: to Hong Kong and Ceylon, 1958; to Council of Europe and WEU, 1963-64; Leader All Party Delegn to Malta, 1965. Pres., Thames-side Assoc. of Teachers, NUT, 1955; Mem. Min. of Education's Adv. Cttee on Handicapped Children, 1957-67; a dep. Pro-Chancellor, Univ. of Kent. *Address:* 10 Tynedale Close, Dartford, Kent. *T:* 25105.

**IRWIN, Lord; Charles Edward Peter Neil Wood;** *b* 14 March 1944; *s* and *heir* of 2nd Earl of Halifax, *qv. Educ:* Eton; Christ Church, Oxford. *Address:* Garrowby, York; 1 Eaton Place, SW1. *Club:* Turf.

**IRWIN, Maj.-Gen. Brian St George;** Director General, Ordnance Survey, since 1969; *b* 16 Sept. 1917; *s* of Lt-Col Alfred Percy Bulteel Irwin, DSO, and Eileen (*née* Holberton), Maumfin, Moyard, Co. Galway; *m* 1939, Audrey Lilla, *d* of Lt-Col H. B. Steen, IMS retd, Dunboe, Shepperton, Mddx; two *s. Educ:* Rugby Sch.; RMA Woolwich; Trinity Hall, Cambridge (MA). Commnd in RE, 1937; war service in Western Desert, 1941-43 (despatches); Sicily and Italy, 1943-44 (despatches); Greece, 1944-45; subseq. in Cyprus, 1956-59 (despatches) and 1961-63; Dir of Military Survey, MoD, 1965-69. FRICS (Council 1969-70); FRGS (Council 1966-70). *Recreations:* sailing, gardening. *Address:* Halterworth Lodge, Halterworth Lane, Romsey, Hants. *T:* Romsey 2402. *Club:* Army and Navy.

**IRWIN, John Conran;** Keeper, Indian Section, Victoria and Albert Museum, since 1959; *b* 5 Aug. 1917; *s* of late John Williamson Irwin; *m* 1947, Helen Hermione Scott (*née* Fletcher), *d* of late Herbert Bristowe Fletcher; three *s. Educ:* Canford Sch., Wimborne, Dorset. Temp. commission, Gordon Highlanders, 1939. Private Sec. to Gov. of Bengal, 1942-45; Asst Keeper, Victoria and Albert Museum, 1946; Exec. Sec., Royal Academy Winter Exhibition of Indian Art, 1947-48; UNESCO Expert on museum planning: on mission to Indonesia, 1956; to Malaya, 1962. Fellow Royal Asiatic Society. *Publications:* Jamini Roy, 1944; Indian art (section on sculpture), 1947; The Art of India and Pakistan (sections on bronzes and textiles), 1951, Shawls, 1955; Origins of Chintz, 1970. Articles in Encyclopædia Britannica, Chambers's Encyclopædia, Jl of Royal Asiatic Soc., Burlington Magazine, etc. *Recreations:* music, historical topography, gardening. *Address:* Bellmans Green, Edenbridge, Kent. *T:* Four Elms 272.

**IRWIN, Lt-Gen. Noel Mackintosh Stuart,** CB 1940; DSO 1918 and two bars 1918, 1919; MC; Croix de Guerre (France); *b* India, 24 Dec. 1892; *e s* of William Stuart Irwin of Motihari, Bihar and Orissa, India; *m* 1918, Margaret Maud (*d* 1963), *d* of late B. Bavin; one *s*; *m* 1966, Mrs Elizabeth Collier (*née* Fröhlich). *Educ:* Marlborough Coll.; RMC, Sandhurst; joined The Essex Regt, 1912; promoted Major, The Border Regt, 1927; Brevet Lt-Col 1931; Colonel, 1934; Major-Gen. 1940; temp. Lt-Gen. 1942; Lt-Gen. 1944; served France with Battalion Aug. 1914-17; commanded 2nd Batt. Lincs Regt 1917-18; 8th Batt. Leicester Regt 1918; 1st Batt. Lincs Regt 1918-19; Temp. Colonel, France 1919; (DSO and 2 bars; MC and Croix de Guerre; 1914 star; despatches 5 times); Staff Coll., 1924-25; General Staff, Rhine, 1926-27; India, 1929-33; Chief Instructor RMC, Sandhurst, 1933-35; Imperial Defence Coll., 1936; GSO 1st Grade, the British troops in China, 1937-38; Commander 6th Infantry Brigade, 1939; France, India and Burma, 1939-43; Commanded 2 Inf. Div., 38 (Welsh) Div., 11th Corps, 4th Indian Corps, Eastern Army, India, West Africa Command, 1946-48; retired, 1948. *Recreations:* Captain

Marlborough College Shooting VIII; hockey, Regt and Army. *Address:* Alfoxton Cottage, Holford, Somerset. *Club:* Army and Navy.

**IRWIN, Prof. Raymond,** MA Oxon; FLA; Professor of Library Studies, University of London, 1957-69, now Emeritus Professor; Director of the School of Librarianship and Archives, University College, London, 1944-69; *b* 14 March 1902; *s* of late John T. Irwin, Maryport, Cumberland, and Elizabeth (*née* Pollard), Eccles, Manchester; *m* 1929, Ivy Summerville Viggers. *Educ:* King's Coll., Taunton; St John's Coll., Oxford. County Librarian, Northamptonshire, 1924; County Librarian, Lancs, 1934. Hon. Treas. of Library Assoc., 1947-54, Vice-Pres., 1954, President, 1958, Hon. Fellow, 1963. *Publications:* The National Library Service, 1947; Librarianship: Essays on Applied Bibliography, 1949; (ed) The Libraries of London, 1949 (rev. edn 1961); British Bird Books: an Index to British Ornithology, 1951; British Birds and their Books: catalogue of exhibn for Nat. Book League, 1952; The Origins of the English Library, 1958; The Heritage of the English Library, 1964; The English Library: sources and history, 1966; many articles in periodicals. *Recreations:* wild flowers, birds, gardening, reading, music. *Address:* 13 Furzefield Crescent, Reigate, Surrey. *T:* Reigate 42508.

**IRWIN, William Henry;** Resident Judge, HM's Court of Sovereign Base Areas of Akrotiri and Dhekelia, Cyprus, 1961-65, retired; *b* 13 Sept. 1907; *o s* of William Irwin, JP, Aughnacloy, Co. Tyrone, and of Florence, *d* of Rev. J. A. Allison; *m* 1935, Olive, *d* of C. Jones Henry, Ardtarmon, Sligo; one *s* one *d*. *Educ:* Royal Belfast Academical Institution; Trinity Coll., Dublin (BA 1930). Called to Bar, Inn of Court of Northern Ireland, 1932; Northern Ireland Circuit; District Magistrate, Gold Coast, 1936; Acting Solicitor-Gen., Gold Coast, 1941-42 and 1947; Judge of the Supreme Court of Trinidad and Tobago, 1947; Mem. of West Indian Court of Appeal, 1951; Senior Puisne Judge, Trinidad and Tobago, 1952-54; Puisne Judge, Nigeria, 1954; Judge of High Court, Western Region, Nigeria, 1955-61; Acting Chief Justice, Western Region, Nigeria, 1958 and 1960. Mem. of HBM's Full Court for the Persian Gulf, 1962. *Address:* c/o Lloyds Bank Ltd, 6 Pall Mall, SW1.

**IRWIN, William Knox,** MD; FRCSE; Consulting Surgeon, St Peter's and St Paul's Hospitals for Genito-Urinary Diseases, London; *b* 1883; *s* of late William Irwin, Drumquin, Co. Tyrone; *m* 1930, Edith Isabel Mary, *d* of late Rev. J. T. Collins, MA; one *s*. *Educ:* Royal School, Dungannon; Aberdeen Univ.; Edinburgh; Berlin. MB, ChB 1908; MD (Hons), 1913; late Senior Resident Surgical Officer, W London Hospital; Hon. Consulting Genito-Urinary Surgeon, Eltham and Mottingham Hospital; Senior Surgeon, Hendon Emergency Hosp.; Lecturer, Post-Graduate Institute of Urology, University of London; etc. Hon. Corres. Mem. Italian Society of Urology; Membre de la Société Internationale d'Urologie; Fellow Royal Society of Medicine. *Publications:* Urinary Surgery, 2nd edn 1927; contributions to Surgery of Urinary Organs in British Journal of Surgery, Lancet, British Journal of Urology, British Medical Journal, Medical Press and Circular, Urologic and Cutaneous Review, etc. *Recreations:* riding, gardening, reading. *Address:* c/o National Westminster Bank Ltd, 1 Cavendish Square, W1. *Club:* Athenæum.

**ISAACS,** family name of **Marquess of Reading** and of **Stella, Marchioness of Reading** (*cr* Baroness Swanborough, Life Peeress, 1958).

**ISAACS, Rt. Hon. George Alfred,** PC 1945; DL, JP, Surrey; Past Chairman Kingston County Bench; *b* London, 1883. Past Alderman, Borough of Southwark; Mayor of Southwark, 1919-21; contested North Southwark, 1918; Gravesend, 1922; MP (Lab) Gravesend, 1923-24, North Southwark, 1929-31 and 1939-50, Southwark, 1950-Sept. 1959. Parl. Priv. Sec. to Sec. of State for Colonies, 1924, to Sec. of State for Dominions, 1929-31, to First Lord of the Admiralty, 1942-45; Minister of Labour and Nat. Service, 1945-Jan. 1951; Minister of Pensions, Jan.-Oct. 1951. Served on Govt's Departmental Cttee on Coroners and Departmental Cttee on Workmen's Compensation; also Mem. of Royal Commission on Workmen's Compensation. Sec. of Nat. Soc. of Operative Printers and Assistants, 1909-49; Past Pres., Printing and Kindred Trades Federation; Chm., Trades Union Congress General Council, 1945; Pres., World Trade Union Conference, London, 1945; Liveryman of the Worshipful Company of Stationers. Hon. Freeman of Borough of Southwark, 1957. *Publication:* The Story of the Newspaper Printing Press. *Address:* Mole Cottage, 166 Portsmouth Road, Cobham, Surrey.

**ISAACS, Jacob,** MA Oxon; Professor Emeritus, University of London, since 1964; Professor of English Language and Literature at Queen Mary College, University of London, 1952-64; *b* 1896; *s* of Rev. M. D. Isaacs and Jessie, *d* of Rev. Moses Bregman; *m* 1933, Enid Austin Dickie; two *d*. *Educ:* Exeter Coll., Oxford (1st Cl. Hons English). Civil Service, 1912-16; Lieut Royal Garrison Artillery (T), served in France; Asst Lecturer, University Coll. of N Wales, Bangor, 1921-24; Asst Lecturer, King's Coll., London, 1924-28; Lecturer, 1928-42; Professor of English Language and Literature, Univ. of Jerusalem, 1942-45; Mem. of Council, Stage Society and Film Society. *Publications:* Shakespeare as Man of the Theatre, 1927; Production and Stage Management at the Blackfriars Theatre, 1933; Shakespeare Scholarship, and Later Shakespeare Criticism, in Companion to Shakespeare Studies, 1933; Coleridge's Critical Terminology, 1936; Sixteenth Century Bible Versions, and The Authorised Version and after, 1940; An assessment of Twentieth Century Literature, 1951; The Background of Modern Poetry, 1951; Shakespeare's Earliest Years in the Theatre, 1953; William Poel's Prompt Book of Fratricide Punished, 1956; general editor, English Library Reprints; joint editor (with Dr W. Rose) of Contemporary Movements in European Literature; article on Dramatic Criticism, Encyclopædia Britannica (14th Edition); contributed to Times, Times Literary Supp., Art News and Review, Observer, Listener, Spectator, etc. *Recreations:* art history, theatrical history, book collecting, travelling, and reading dictionaries. *Address:* Little Court, Court Yard, Eltham, SE9. *T:* 01-850 7866.

**ISAACS, Mrs Nathan;** *see* Lawrence, E. M.

**ISAACSON, Sir Robert (Spencer),** KBE 1966; CMG 1955; *b* 11 Nov. 1907; *s* of late Arthur Spencer Isaacson and Dorothy Isaacson (*née* Lance); *m* 1938, Margaret Viola Lage, *e d* of Sir Rowland F. W. Hodge, 1st Bt. *Educ:* Radley. British Embassy, Rio de Janeiro, 1940-47; British Legation, Bucharest, 1948; British Embassy: Athens, 1948-52; Washington, 1952-55; Paris, 1955-59; Rio de Janeiro, 1959-63; Ambassador to Guatemala, 1963-64; Ambassador to Switzerland, 1964-67.

*Recreations:* fishing, shooting, bridge. *Address:* Flat 4, 3 Sloane Court East, SW3. *Club:* St James'.

**ISHAM, Sir Gyles,** 12th Bt, *cr* 1627; MA; FSA; DL; *b* 31 Oct. 1903; *o surv s* of Sir Vere Isham, 11th Bt, and Millicent (*d* 1961), *d* of late Henry Halford Vaughan; *S* father 1941. *Educ:* Rugby; Magdalen Coll., Oxford (Demy). MA 1930; Pres. of the OUDS, 1925; Pres. of the Oxford Union, 1926; adopted stage as a profession on coming down from Oxford, 1926, making his first appearance professionally under the management of the late J. B. Fagan; toured the English Provinces and the USA; appeared in New York and London, and later in films in both England and America; has played leading Shakespearean parts at the Old Vic, Memorial Theatre, Stratford-on-Avon, in the USA, and at the Open-Air Theatre, Regent's Park; has toured Canada and South Africa. Joined London Irish Rifles (TA) April 1939, Sergeant Aug. 1939; 2nd Lieut King's Royal Rifle Corps, Feb. 1940; served with 1st Bn Western Desert Campaign, Egypt, from 1 May 1940; on staff of Eighth Army when formed Sept. 1941; left for staff appt at GHQ ME (Major), July 1942; GSO1 (Intelligence) HQ Ninth Army, April 1943-Dec. 1944; on return to England, filled GSO1 appt War Office, March-Aug. 1945; Defence Security Officer HQ Palestine, Sept. 1945-Sept. 1946; demobilised (deferred) Lieut-Col, Dec. 1946. Contested (C) Kettering (Northants), 1950. Farms 700 acres of his own land. DL 1952, CC 1955-64, Northants; High Sheriff of Northants, 1958-59. A Trustee of the Nat. Portrait Gall., 1964-. Pres., Assoc. of Independent Hosps. 1969-. *Publications:* All Saints, Lamport, 1950; The Duppa-Isham Correspondence, 1650-60 (Northants Record Soc. Vol. XVII), 1955; The Story of Clipston Grammar School, 1956; Easton Mauduit, 1968. Editor, Northamptonshire Past and Present, 1960-. *Heir: cousin,* Ian Vere Gyles Isham, *b* 1923. *Address:* Lamport Hall, Northampton. *Club:* Beefsteak.

**ISHERWOOD, Christopher;** Author; *b* High Lane, Cheshire, 26 Aug. 1904; *s* of Lt-Col Francis B. Isherwood and Kathleen Machell-Smith. *Educ:* Repton Sch.; Corpus Christi, Cambridge. Private Tutor in London, 1926-27; Medical Student, Kings, London, 1928-29; Teacher of English, Berlin, 1930-33; Journalism, etc. in London, 1934-36; Film-Script work for Gaumont-British; went to China with W. H. Auden, 1938; worked for Metro-Goldwyn-Mayer, 1940, American Friends Service Cttee, 1941-42; editor of Vedanta and the West, 1943. Became a US citizen, 1946; travelled in South America, 1947-48. Elected Mem. US Nat. Inst. of Arts and Letters, 1949. Guest Prof., Los Angeles State Coll., and at University of California, Santa Barbara, 1959-62; Regents' Prof., University of California, 1965-66. *Publications: fiction:* All the Conspirators, 1928; The Memorial, 1932; Mr Norris Changes Trains, 1935; Goodbye to Berlin, 1939; Prater Violet, 1945; The World in The Evening, 1954; Down There on a Visit, 1962; A Single Man, 1964; A Meeting by the River, 1967; *biography:* Ramakrishna and his Disciples, 1965; *autobiography:* Lions and Shadows, 1938; *plays:* The Dog Beneath the Skin (with W. H. Auden), 1935; Ascent of F6 (with W. H. Auden), 1937; On the Frontier (with W. H. Auden), 1938; *travel:* Journey to a War (with W. H. Auden), 1939; The Condor and the Cows, 1949; *miscellaneous:* Exhumations, 1966; *translation:* (with Swami Prabhavananda) The Bhagavad-Gita, 1944; (with Swami Prabhavananda) Shankara's Crest-Jewel of Discrimination, 1947; Baudelaire's Intimate Journals, 1947; (with Swami Prabhavananda) How to Know God: the Yoga Aphorisms of Patanjali, 1953. *Recreations:* usual. *Address:* 145 Adelaide Drive, Santa Monica, Calif 90402, USA.

**ISITT, Air Vice-Marshal Sir Leonard (Monk),** KBE, *cr* 1946 (CBE 1939); retired as Chairman, Standard-Triumph (NZ) Ltd, and Chairman of Directors, NZ National Airways Corporation, and Tasman Empire Airways, Ltd; *b* 27 July 1891; *m* 1920; two *d*. *Educ:* Mostyn House, Parkgate, Cheshire, England; Christchurch Boys' High School, Christchurch, New Zealand. Farming early years; NZ Rifle Brigade, 1915-16; Royal Flying Corps/Royal Air Force, 1917-19; transferred Royal New Zealand Air Force, 1919; Air Force Mem. for Personnel, 1937; RNZAF Representative, Ottawa and Washington, 1940-41; Air Officer Commanding RNZAF, United Kingdom, 1942-43; Chief of the Air Staff, RNZAF, 1943-45. *Recreation:* fishing. *Address:* Golf Road, Paraparau Beach, NZ. *TA:* Wellington, New Zealand.

**ISLE, William Herbert Mosley,** CBE 1969; Chairman, Economic Development Committee for Wool Textile Industry, 1964-70; director of various companies; *b* 11 Oct. 1896; *s* of late William Mawson Isle and late Ellen Isle (*née* Ingham); *m* 1925, Victoria Constance Irene Feather (*d* 1963); one *s*. *Educ:* privately; Pembroke Coll., Cambridge. Qualified ACA, 1924; Partner in: Thoseby, Son & Co., Bradford, 1930; Peat, Marwick, Mitchell & Co., 1953; retired, 1964. *Recreation:* golf. *Address:* Badgergate, Burley Woodhead, near Ilkley, Yorkshire. *T:* Burley-in-Wharfedale 3044. *Clubs:* United University; Union (Bradford), Bradford (Bradford).

**ISLE OF WIGHT, Archdeacon of;** *see* Scruby, Ven. R. V.

**ISLES, Prof. Keith Sydney,** CMG 1967; Visiting Professor of Economics, New University of Ulster, 1968-69; *b* 4 Aug. 1902; 2nd, *s* of Sydney Henry Isles and Margaret Ellen Knight, Tasmania; *m* 1926, Irene Frances Clayton; one *s* two *d*. *Educ:* Universities of Tasmania, Adelaide and Cambridge. BCom, Tasmania; MA, MSc, Cambridge. Fellow of Laura Spelman Rockefeller Memorial at Univ. of Cambridge, 1929-31; Wrenbury Schol. and Adam Smith Prize of Univ. of Cambridge; Lecturer in Political Economy, University of Edinburgh, 1931-37; Prof. of Economics: University College of Swansea, 1937-39; University of Adelaide, 1939-45; Queen's Univ. of Belfast, 1945-57. Vice-Chancellor of the University of Tasmania, 1957-67. Economic Adviser to Commonwealth Rationing Commn, 1942. Served Commonwealth Mil. Forces (rank of temporary Lieut-Col) 1944-45. Jt Local Sec., meeting of British Assoc. for the Advancement of Science, in Belfast, 1952. Hon. LLD: St Andrews, 1963; Queen's Univ., Belfast, 1969; Hon. DLitt Tasmania, 1968. *Publications:* Wages Policy and the Price Level, 1934; Money and Trade, 1935; with N. Cuthbert: chapters in Ulster Home Rule (ed Wilson), 1955, and An Economic Survey of Northern Ireland (HMSO), 1957; articles in various journals. *Recreations:* golf and motoring. *Address:* 91 Esplanade, Rose Bay, Hobart, Tasmania 7015, Australia. *Club:* Tasmanian.

**ISMAY, Sir George,** KBE 1947; CB 1939; *b* 1891; *s* of late George Ismay, Carlisle; *m* 1919, Jeanette May, *d* of John Lloyd, Tredegar, Mon; two *d*. *Educ:* Private Schools, Carlisle. Entered Treasury, 1911; Asst Sec., 1934; Sec.

Macmillan Cttee on Finance and Industry, 1929-31; Comptroller and Accountant General, GPO, 1937; Asst Dir-General, 1942; Deputy Dir-Gen., General Post Office, 1947-52; Dir, Woolwich Equitable Building Society, 1952-; served European War, 1915-19, in Queen's Westminster Rifles. *Address:* Newstead, Golden Avenue, Angmering-on-Sea, Sussex. *T:* Rustington 2855.

**ISMAY, Walter Nicholas;** Deputy Chairman and Managing Director, Milton Keynes Development Corporation, since 1967; *b* 20 June 1921; *s* of John Ismay, Maryport, Cumberland. *Educ:* Taunton's Sch., Southampton; King's Coll., University of London (BSc). Royal Aircraft Establishment, 1939-40; Ministry of Supply, 1940-43; Served Army (Capt., General List), 1943-46; Imperial Chemical Industries, Metals Division, 1948-58 (Technical Dir, 1957-58); Dir, Yorkshire Imperial Medals, 1958-67; Dep. Chm. Yorkshire Imperial Plastics, 1966-67. FIMechE. *Recreation:* sailing. *Address:* Wavendon Tower, Wavendon, near Bletchley, Bucks. *T:* Bletchley 4000.

**ISPAHANI, Mirza Abol Hassan;** *b* 23 Jan. 1902; *s* of late Mirza Mohamed Ispahani and late Sakina Sultan; *m* 1st, 1930, Ameneh Sultan Shushtary; two *s* one *d*; 2nd, 1954, Ghamar Azimi. *Educ:* St John's Coll., Cambridge. Joined family business of M. M. Ispahani, 1925; was Dir of M. M. Ispahani Ltd, and other business undertakings; Pres., Muslim Chamber of Commerce, Calcutta; Leader, Indian Trade Delegation to Middle East, 1947. Elected to Calcutta Corporation, 1933; resigned to work for introduction of separate electorates in Calcutta Corp., 1935, re-elected, 1940, Dep. Mayor, 1941-42; Mem. Bengal Legislative Assembly, 1937-47; Mem. of All India Muslim League Working Cttee until end of 1947; Pakistan Constituent Assembly; represented Muslim League at New York Herald Tribune Forum, 1946; toured US as Personal Representative of Quaid-i-Azam, M. A. Jinnah; Ambassador of Pakistan to USA, 1947-52; Dep. Leader, Pakistan Delegn to UN, 1947; Leader Pakistan Delegn to Havana Conf. on Trade and Employment, 1947; Mem., Pakistan Delegn to UN (Jammu and Kashmir). High Comr for Pakistan in the UK, 1952-54; Minister of Industries and Commerce, 1954-55; Minister of Industries, Jan.-Aug. 1955; resigned and reverted to business; mem., Supreme Council, National Reconstruction Movement of Pakistan. Interested in sports, journalism and welfare work. *Publications:* 27 Days in China: Leningrad to Samarkand; Qaid-e-Azam Jinnah as I knew him (2nd end rev.). *Recreations:* travel, photography, golf. *Address:* 2 Reay Road, Karachi, Pakistan. *T:* 510665.

**ISSERLIS, Alexander Reginald;** Assistant Under-Secretary of State, Home Office, since 1970; *b* 18 May 1922; *y s* of late Isaak Isserlis, Ilford, Essex; *m* 1949, Eleanor Mary Ord, *d* of late Prof. R. D. Laurie, Aberystwyth; two *d*. *Educ:* Ilford High Sch.; Keble Coll., Oxford. British and Indian Army, 1942-46. Entered Civil Service, 1947. Principal, Min. of Health, 1950; Principal Private Secretary: to Lord President of the Council and Minister for Science, 1960-61; to Minister of Housing and Local Govt, 1962; Asst Sec., Min. of Housing and Local Govt, 1963; Under-Secretary: Cabinet Office, 1969; Min. of Housing and Local Government, 1969-70; Principal Private Secretary to the Prime Minister, 1970. *Recreations:* walking and Wales. *Address:* 5 Hartland Road, Epping, Essex. *T:* Epping 3299. *Club:* Farmers'.

**ISSERSTEDT, Hans S.;** *see* Schmidt-Isserstedt.

**ISSIGONIS, Sir Alec (Arnold Constantine),** Kt 1969; CBE 1964; RDI 1964; FRS 1967; Director of Research and Development, British Leyland (Austin-Morris) Ltd (formerly British Motor Corporation), since 1961; *b* Smyrna, 1906; British citizen. *Educ:* Battersea Polytechnic, London (Engrg Dip.). Draughtsman, Rootes Motors Ltd, 1933-36; Suspension Engineer, Morris Motors Ltd, 1936, subsequently Chief Engineer; Deputy Engineering Co-ordinator and Chief Engineer, British Motor Corporation, 1957-61; Technical Director, 1961; designs include: Morris Minor, 1948; Mini-Minor and Austin Seven, 1959; Morris 1100, 1962. Leverhulme Medal, Royal Society, 1966. *Address:* British Leyland (Austin-Morris) Ltd, Longbridge, Birmingham.

**ITHEL JONES, Rev. John;** *see* Jones, Rev. J. I.

**ITURBI, Jose;** Cross of Alphonso the Wise; Officier Légion d'Honneur; Companion Order of St Michael of Greece; Concert Pianist, Conductor, Composer, Film Actor; *b* Valencia, Spain, 28 Nov. 1895; *s* of Ricardo and Theresa Iturbi; *m* 1915, Maria Giner (*d* 1927); (one *d* decd). *Educ:* College and Academies at Valencia. Began to play piano at age of three; at seven, recognised as a child prodigy, was studying with and teaching pupils three and four times his age; attended local Conservatory in Valencia and later was sent to Barcelona to study. After graduating from Paris Conservatoire at age of 17½ with the Grand Prix, he became head of Piano Faculty at Geneva Conservatoire, a post once held by Liszt; American début, 1929. Regular conductor of Rochester Philharmonic, 1936-44; Guest Conductor New York Philharmonic, Philadelphia Orchestra, Detroit Symphony, and all leading symphony orchestras of United States; also all leading symphony orchestras of England, France, Spain, Mexico, S America, S Africa, etc. He averages 200 concerts a year. In several films. *Recreation:* flying. *Address:* Beverley Hills, Calif, USA.

**IVAMY, Prof. Edward Richard Hardy;** Professor of Law, University of London, since 1960; *b* 1 Dec. 1920; *o s* of late Edward Wadham Ivamy and Florence Ivamy; *m* 1965, Christine Ann Frances, *o d* of William and Frances Culver. *Educ:* Malvern Coll.; University Coll., London. Served War of 1939-45, RA: 67 Field Regt, N Africa, Italy and Middle East; 2nd Lieut 1942; Temp. Capt. 1945; Staff Capt., GHQ, Cairo, 1946. LLB (1st cl. hons) 1947; PhD 1953; LLD 1967. Barrister-at-law, Middle Temple, 1949. University Coll., London: Asst Lectr in Laws, 1947-50; Lectr, 1950-56; Reader in Law, 1956-60; Dean of Faculty of Laws, 1964 and 1965; Fellow, 1969. Hon. Sec., Soc. of Public Teachers of Law, 1960-63; Hon. Sec., Bentham Club, 1953-58; Mem. Editorial Bd, Jl of Business Law. *Publications:* Show Business and the Law, 1955; (ed) Payne's Carriage of Goods by Sea (7th edn 1963, 8th edn 1968); Hire-Purchase Legislation in England and Wales, 1965; Casebook on Carriage of Goods by Sea, 1965; Casebook on Sale of Goods, 1966, 2nd edn 1969; (ed) Chalmers's Marine Insurance Act 1906 (6th edn 1966); General Principles of Insurance Law, 1966, 2nd edn 1970; (ed) Topham and Ivamy's Company Law (14th edn 1970); Casebook on Mercantile Law, 1967; Fire and Motor Insurance, 1968; Casebook on Insurance Law, 1969; Marine Insurance, 1969; Casebook on Shipping Law, 1970; Casebook on Partnership Law, 1970; contrib. to Encyclopædia Britannica, Chambers's

Encyclopædia, Current Legal Problems, Jl of Business Law; Annual Survey of Commonwealth Law, 1967, 1968, 1969. *Recreations:* railways, cricket, tennis. *Address:* 143 Bishop's Mansions, SW6. *T:* 01-736 4736.

**IVATT, Henry George,** CEng, FIMechE, MILocoE; Retired; Director of Brush Traction Ltd as Consultant, 1957; Director and General Manager, Brush Traction Ltd, 1955; Director of Brush Bagnall Traction Ltd, as Consultant for diesel electric locomotives, 1951; Director, Remploy Ltd, 25 Buckingham Gate, SW1, 1952; *b* 4 May 1886; *s* of late H. A. Ivatt, Locomotive Engineer of former Great Northern Rly; *m* 1913, Dorothy Sarah Harrison (*d* 1962); no *c*. *Educ:* Uppingham. Mechanical and technical training at Locomotive Works, Crewe, of former London and North-Western Railway. Served European War, 1914-18, in France on staff of QMG, Mechanical Transport, with rank of Major. Dep. Locomotive Supt of former North Stafford Rly, 1919; Works Supt, Derby Locomotive Works, LMS Rly Co., 1928; Divisional Mechanical Engineer, Scottish Div., LMS Rly Co., 1932; Principal Asst for Locomotives to Chief Mechanical Engineer, LMS Rly Co., 1937; Chief Mechanical and Electrical Engineer, London Midland Region, British Railways, 1948-51; LMS Rly, 1946-48, retd 1951. Consultant for diesel traction, Brush Electrical Engineering Co. Ltd, 1958-64. *Address:* Chantry House, Melbourne, Derbyshire. *T:* Melbourne 2615.

**IVEAGH,** 3rd Earl of, *cr* 1919; **Arthur Francis Benjamin Guinness;** Bt 1885; Baron Iveagh 1891; Viscount Iveagh 1905; Viscount Elveden 1919; Chairman, Arthur Guinness Son & Co., Ltd; *b* 20 May 1937; *o s* of Viscount Elveden (killed in action, 1945) and Lady Elizabeth Hare, *yr d* of 4th Earl of Listowel; *S* grandfather, 1967; *m* 1963, Miranda Daphne Jane, *d* of Major Michael Smiley, Castle Fraser, Aberdeenshire; one *s* two *d*. *Educ:* Eton; Trinity Coll., Cambridge. *Heir:* *s* Viscount Elveden, *qv*. *Address:* Elveden Hall, Thetford, Norfolk; Farmleigh, Castleknock, Co. Dublin; 28 Upper Cheyne Row, SW3. *Clubs:* Carlton, White's; Royal Yacht Squadron (Cowes); Kildare Street (Dublin).

**IVELAW-CHAPMAN, Air Chief Marshal (Retd), Sir Ronald,** GCB 1957 (KCB 1953; CB 1949); KBE 1951 (CBE 1943); DFC 1918; AFC 1930; *b* 17 Jan. 1899; *s* of late Joseph Ivelaw-Chapman, Cheltenham; *m* 1930, Margaret, *d* of late C. W. Shortt, Beckenham; one *s* one *d*. *Educ:* Cheltenham Coll. 2nd Lieut Royal Flying Corps, 1917; European War, 1917-18; at home, India, and Iraq, 1919-20; Kabul evacuations (awarded AFC); served War of 1939-45: in various executive and staff appointments, 1939-43; prisoner of war, 1944-45. AOC No. 38 Group, 1945-46; Directing Staff, Imperial Defence Coll., 1947-49; C-in-C Indian Air Force, 1950-51; AOC-in-C Home Command, 1952; Deputy Chief of the Air Staff, 1952-53; Vice Chief of the Air Staff, 1953-57; retired, 1957. Pres. Cheltonian Society, 1956-57; Dir of Resettlement, Ministry of Labour, 1957-61. Mem. of Observer Trust, 1957-66. Pres. of Council, Cheltenham Coll.; Vice-Pres., RAF Escaping Society; Governor, Old Malthouse Sch. Trust. *Recreation:* fishing. *Address:* Knockwood, Nether Wallop, Hants. *Clubs:* Royal Air Force, United Service.

**IVERSEN, Johannes,** DrPhil; Senior Geologist at the Geological survey of Denmark since 1942; Lecturer at the University of Copenhagen, 1955-69; *b* 1904; *s* of Hans Iversen and Anna Iversen (*née* Asmussen); *m* 1939, Aase Thorlacius-Ussing; one *d*. *Educ:* Copenhagen. DrPhil 1936. FilDr *hc* Uppsala 1957; DSc *hc* Cambridge 1966. *Publications:* Land Occupation in Denmark's Stone Age, 1941 (2nd edn 1964); Textbook of Pollen Analysis (with Knut Faegri) 1950 (2nd rev. edn 1964). *Address:* Rörskaersvej 10, 2820 Gentofte, Denmark.

**IVES, Arthur Glendinning Loveless,** CVO 1954 (MVO 1945); *b* 19 Aug. 1904; *s* of late Rev. E. J. Ives, Wesleyan Minister; *m* 1929, Doris Marion, *d* of Thomas Coke Boden; three *s* one *d*. *Educ:* Kingswood Sch.; Queen's Coll., Oxford (classical scholar); MA. George Webb Medley Junior Scholarship for Economics, Oxford Univ., 1926. London Chamber of Commerce, 1928-29; joined staff of King Edward's Hosp. Fund for London, 1929; Sec., 1938-60; retired 1960. Seriously injured in railway accident at Lewisham, Dec. 1957. A Governor of Kingswood Sch., 1954-. *Publications:* British Hospitals (Britain in Pictures), 1948; Kingswood School in Wesley's Day and Since, 1970; contrib. to The Times, Lancet, etc, on hospital administration and allied topics. *Address:* The Cedars, Bordyke, Tonbridge, Kent. *Club:* Athenæum.

**IVES, Robert;** Recorder of Bury St Edmunds since 1963; Judge of Norwich Guildhall Court of Record, since 1952; Deputy Chairman of Norfolk Quarter Sessions since 1967; *b* 25 Aug. 1906; *o s* of Robert Ives; *m* 1931, Evelyn Harriet Hairby Alston (*d* 1965), *er d* of Rev. F. S. Alston; two *d*; *m* 1966, Vera Bowack, *widow* of Pilot Officer N. H. Bowack. *Educ:* privately; Gonville and Caius Coll., Cambridge (MA). Called to Bar, Gray's Inn, 1928. War Service, 1940-45: RASC and Judge Advocate General's Dept. Chairman: Mental Health Review Tribunal (E Anglia Region), 1960-63; Agricultural Land Tribunal (Eastern Area), 1961-; Mem. panel of Chairmen of Medical Appeal Tribunals, 1969-. *Recreations:* farm, garden, photography. *Address:* Erpingham House, Erpingham, Norwich, NOR 46 Y. *T:* Hanworth 208. *Club:* Norfolk (Norwich).

**IVINS, Prof. John Derek;** Professor of Agriculture, University of Nottingham, since Sept. 1958; *b* Eccleshall, Staffs, 11 March 1923; *s* of Alfred Ivins and Ann Ivins (*née* Holland); *m* 1952, Janet Alice Whitehead, BSc; one *s* one *d*. *Educ:* Wolstanton County Grammar Sch., Newcastle, Staffs. BSc Reading 1944, MSc 1951; PhD Nottingham 1954. Technical Officer, Seed Production Cttee of Nat. Inst. of Agricultural Botany, 1944-46; Regional Trials Officer, Nat. Inst. of Agricultural Botany, 1946-48; Lectr in Agriculture, 1948-58, Dean of Faculty of Agriculture and Horticulture, 1962-65, Deputy Vice-Chancellor, 1969-72, Univ. of Nottingham. *Publications:* papers in technical and agricultural journals. *Recreations:* shooting, gardening. *Address:* University of Nottingham School of Agriculture, Sutton Bonington, near Loughborough. *T:* Kegworth 2386.

# J

**JACK, Sir Alieu (Sulayman),** Kt 1970; Speaker, House of Representatives of the Republic of The Gambia, since 1962; *b* 14 July 1922; *m* 1946, Yai Marie Cham; four *s* four *d* (and one *d* decd). *Educ:* St Augustine's Elementary School. Entered Gambia Civil Service, 1939; resigned and took up local appt with NAAFI,

1940-44; Civil Service, 1945-48; entered commerce, 1948; Man. Dir, Gambia National Trading Co. Ltd. Mem., Bathurst City Council, 1949-62. Represented The Gambia Parlt at various internat. gatherings; Pres., CPA Gambia Branch. Comdr, National Order of Senegal, 1967; Comdr, Order of Merit of Mauritania, 1967. *Recreation:* golf. *Address:* House of Representatives, The Republic of The Gambia. *T:* (home) 93.639, (office) 241. *Club:* Bathurst (Bathurst).

**JACK, Sir Daniel (Thomson),** Kt 1966; CBE 1951; Hon. LLD Glasgow; MA; Chairman, Air Transport Licensing Board, 1961-70; David Dale Professor of Economics, University of Durham, King's College, Newcastle upon Tyne, 1935-61; Sub-Rector, King's College, 1950-55; *b* 18 Aug. 1901; *m* 1st, 1945, Nan (*d* 1949), *widow* of Prof. John Dall, Queen's Univ., Canada; 2nd, 1954, Elizabeth Witter Stewart (*d* 1970), Kingston, Ont. *Educ:* Bellahouston Academy, Glasgow; University of Glasgow. Asst to the Adam Smith Prof. of Political Economy, University of Glasgow, 1923-28; Lecturer in Political Economy, University of St Andrews, 1928-35. Asst Regional Controller, Northern Region, Ministry of Labour and National Service, 1941; Industrial Commissioner, Ministry of Labour, 1942; Labour Adviser to Govt of India, 1943; Chm. of Bd of Inquiry into proposed 40-hour week in Copper Mining Industry of N Rhodesia, 1950; Mem. Royal Commn on E Africa, 1953; Pres. Economics Sect., Brit. Assoc., 1952; Chm. Bd of Inquiry into sugar dispute in Trinidad, 1955; Special Investigator into wages dispute, Gibraltar, 1955; Visiting lecturer, University of the Witwatersrand, 1956; Chm. Courts of Inquiry into Shipbuilding and Engineering Wages Disputes, 1956; Economic Adviser, Urban African Affairs Commn, Southern Rhodesia, 1957; Chm. Court of Inquiry into London Airport dispute, 1958; Chm. Rural Transport Inquiry, 1959; UK Independent Mem., Monckton Advisory Commission on Central Africa, 1959; Chm. Court of Inquiry into Ford dispute, 1963. *Publications:* The Economics of the Gold standard, 1925; The Restoration of European Currencies, 1927; International Trade, 1931; The Crises of 1931, 1931; Currency and Banking, 1932; Studies in Economic Warfare, 1940; Economic Survey of Sierra Leone, 1958; Report on Industrial Relations in the Sisal Industry, 1959; Report on Wage Fixing Machinery in Tanganyika, 1959; (with others) Economic Survey of Nyasaland, 1959. Articles in various journals. *Address:* Gorselands, Nightingales Lane, Chalfont St Giles, Bucks. *T:* Chalfont St Giles 2309. *Clubs:* Reform, National Liberal.

**JACK, James,** CBE 1967; JP; General Secretary, Scottish Trades Union Congress, since 1963; Member, Scottish Gas Board, since 1970; *b* 6 Dec. 1910; *s* of late Andrew M. Jack and Margaret Reid; *m* 1936; one *s*. *Educ:* Auchinraith Primary Sch., Blantyre; St John's Gram. Sch., Hamilton. *Address:* 7 Stonefield Place, Blantyre, Glasgow. *T:* Blantyre 3304.

**JACK, Hon. Sir Roy (Emile),** Kt 1970; MP (Nat) for Waimarino, New Zealand, since 1963; Speaker of the House of Representatives, NZ, since 1967; barrister and solicitor, Jack, Riddet, Wallis & Tripe; *b* New Plymouth, 12 Jan. 1914; *s* of John Bain Jack; *m* 1946, Frances Anne, *d* of Dr G. W. Harty; one *d*. *Educ:* Wanganui Collegiate Sch.; Victoria University Coll., Wellington, NZ (LLB). Served War of 1939-45, RNZAF. Judge's Associate 1935-38; entered practice as solicitor and barrister, Wanganui, 1946. Mem., Wanganui City Council, 1946-55; Dep. Mayor, 1947-55. MP for Patea, 1954-63; Chm. of Cttees, House of Representatives, 1961-66. *Recreations:* music (especially violin), reading, skiing, flying, gliding. *Address:* Parliament House, Wellington, New Zealand; (private) 49 College Street, Wanganui, New Zealand. *T:* Wanganui 7640. *Club:* Wanganui.

**JACKLIN, Anthony,** OBE 1970; professional golfer; *b* 7 July 1944; *s* of Arthur David Jacklin; *m* 1966, Vivien; one *s*. Successes include: British Assistant Pro Championship, 1965; Pringle Tournament, 1967; Dunlop Masters, 1967; Greater Jacksonville Open, USA, 1968; British Open Championship, 1969; US Open Championship, 1970. *Publication:* Golf with Tony Jacklin, 1969. *Recreation:* shooting. *Address:* East Lodge, Elsham, Brigg, Lincs. *Clubs:* Potters Bar Golf; Hon. Mem. of others.

**JACKLING, Sir Roger William,** KCMG 1965 (CMG 1955); British Ambassador to the Federal Republic of Germany since 1968; *b* 10 May 1913; *s* of P. Jackling, OBE, and Lucy Jackling; *m* 1938, Joan Tustin; two *s* (and one *s* decd). *Educ:* Felsted. DPA, London Univ., 1932; Solicitor, Supreme Court, 1935; Actg Vice-Consul, New York, 1940; Commercial Sec., Quito, 1942; 2nd Sec., Washington, 1943; 1st Sec., 1945; HM Foreign Service, 1946; transf. Foreign Office, 1947; seconded to Cabinet Office, 1950 (Asst Sec.); Counsellor (commercial), The Hague, 1951; Economic and Financial Adviser to UK High Commr, Bonn; and UK commercial rep. in Germany, 1953; Minister (Economic), British Embassy, Bonn, 1955; Counsellor, British Embassy, Washington, 1957-59; Asst Under-Sec. of State, FO, 1959-63; Dep. Permanent UK Rep. to United Nations, 1963-67 (with personal rank of Ambassador from 1965); Dep. Under-Sec. of State, FO, 1967-68. *Recreation:* golf. *Address:* British Embassy, Bonn, Germany. *Club:* Travellers'.

**JACKMAN, Air Marshal Sir Douglas,** KBE 1959 (CBE 1943); CB 1946; RAF; idc 1948; Air Officer Commanding-in-Chief, Royal Air Force Maintenance Command, 1958-61, retired; *b* 26 Oct. 1902; twin *s* of late A. J. Jackman; *m* 1931, Marjorie Leonore, *d* of late A. Hyland, Kingsdown, Kent. *Educ:* HMS Worcester. Officer Royal Mail Line until 1926; joined RAF, 1926; served in Iraq, 1928-30, in No 55 Squadron; in UK with Wessex Bombing Area and at Cranwell until 1934; to Middle East Command in 1934 and served at Aboukir until 1938, when posted to HQ Middle East until 1943; with Mediterranean Air Command and Mediterranean Allied Air Forces HQ until 1944; HQ Balkan Air Force, 1944-45 (despatches five times, CB, CBE, Comdr Order George 1st of Greece with Swords, AFC [Greek]); Dir of Movements Air Ministry, 1946-47; Dir of Organization (forecasting and planning), Air Ministry, 1949-52; AOC N0 40 Group, 1952-55; Dir-Gen. of Equipment, Air Ministry, 1955-58; Co-ordinator, Anglo-American Relations, Air Ministry, 1961-64. *Publication:* technical, on planning, 1942. *Recreations:* golf (Member: RAF Golfing Soc.; Senior's Golfing Soc., Natal; Umkomass Golf Club); woodworking. *Address:* 136A Marriott Road, Durban, South Africa. *Clubs:* Royal Over-Seas League; Durban Country.

**JACKMAN, Frank Downer,** CMG 1964; Chairman, Bitumax Pty Ltd, since 1968; Commissioner of Highways and Director of Local Government for South Australia, 1958-66; *b* 14 May 1901; *s* of Arthur Joseph and Adela Mary Jackman; *m* 1930, Elaine Jean Nairn; two *d*. *Educ:* Prince Alfred Coll.; University of Adelaide. BE (Civil Engrg) 1923; FSASM 1923. Joined Engineer-in-Chief's

Dept, SA Govt, 1923; transferred to Highways and Local Govt Dept, 1929; Asst Engr, 1929-37; District Engr, 1937-49; Chief Engr, 1949-58. AMIE Aust., 1940; MInstT, 1963. *Recreations:* fishing, racing. *Address:* 7 Crompton Drive, Wattle Park, S Australia.

**JACKS, Graham Vernon,** MA, BSc; Director, Commonwealth Bureau of Soils, 1946-66; *b* 30 March 1901; *s* of late Dr L. P. Jacks; *m* 1933, Violet Elizabeth, *d* of late Henry Tompkins; one *s* one *d*. *Educ:* Dragon Sch., Oxford; Magdalen Coll. Sch., Oxford; Christ Church, Oxford (scholar). Min. of Agriculture Research Scholar, 1926-29; Lectr in Soil Science, Imperial Forestry Institute, 1929-31; Dep. Dir, Imperial Bureau of Soil Science, 1931-46; Editor, Journal of Soil Science, 1949-61; Mem. of Nature Conservancy, 1959-65. *Publications:* Soil, Vegetation and Climate, 1933; Tropical Soils in Relation to Tropical Crops, 1936; (with R. O. Whyte) Erosion and Soil Conservation, 1937; (with R. O. Whyte) The Rape of the Earth, 1938; (with H. Scherbatoff) The Minor Elements of the Soil, 1940; Land Classification, 1946; Soil, 1954. *Address:* 5 Kirkdale Road, Harpenden, Herts. *T:* Harpenden 3353.

**JACKS, Hector Beaumont,** MA; Headmaster of Bedales School, 1946-July 1962; *b* 25 June 1903; *s* of late Dr L. P. Jacks; *m* 1st, Mary (*d* 1959), *d* of Rev. G. N. Nuttall Smith; one *s* one *d*; 2nd, Nancy, *d* of F. E. Strudwick. *Educ:* Magdalen Coll. Sch. and Wadham Coll., Oxford. Asst master, Wellington Coll., Berks, 1925-32; Headmaster of Willaston Sch., Nantwich, 1932-37; Second Master, Cheltenham Coll. Junior Sch., 1940-46. *Recreation:* gardening. *Address:* Applegarth, Spotted Cow Lane, Buxted, Sussex. *T:* Buxted 2296.

**JACKSON,** family name of **Baron Allerton.**

**JACKSON, Brig. Alexander Cosby Fishburn,** CVO 1957; CBE 1954 (OBE 1943); Travel Films, Jersey; *b* 4 Dec. 1903; *s* of late Col S. C. F. Jackson, CMG, DSO, and Lucy B. Jackson (*née* Drake); *m* 1934, Margaret Hastings Hervey, Montclair, NJ, USA; one *s* (and one *s* decd). *Educ:* Yardley Court, Tonbridge; Haileybury Coll.; RMC Sandhurst. 2nd Lt, R Hants Regt, 1923; Brig. 1952; employed RWAFF, 1927-33; served in Middle East, 1940-45 (despatches twice, OBE); Dep. Dir of Quartering, War Office, 1945-48; Comdr Northern Area, Kenya, 1948-51; Comdr Caribbean Area, 1951-54; HBM Military Attaché, Paris, 1954-58. ADC to the Queen, 1955-58. Order of Kutuzov 2nd Class, USSR, 1944; Comdr Legion of Honour, France, 1957. *Recreation:* fishing. *Address:* Glenwhern, Grouville, Jersey. *Clubs:* Army and Navy; Kloof Country (Natal).

**JACKSON, Alexander Young,** CC (Canada) 1967; CMG 1946; RCA 1919; Landscape Painter; *b* Montreal, 3 Oct. 1882; *s* of Henry Jackson and Georgina Young; unmarried. *Educ:* Public Schools, Montreal. Worked in the lithographic business; studied art in Montreal, Chicago, and at the Académie Julian, Paris; has painted landscape all over Canada, as far north as Ellesmere Island; during European War served in France with the Canadian infantry; represented by paintings in the National Gallery of British Art, National Gallery of Canada, Art Galleries of Montreal, Toronto, Vancouver, etc. Hon. degrees from: Queen's Univ., Kingston, Ont (LLD); McMaster Univ., 1953; Carleton Univ., 1957; Univ. of British Columbia, 1964; McGill Univ., 1967. *Recreations:* canoeing, fishing. *Address:* c/o R. McMichael Esq, Kleinburg, Ont, Canada. *Club:* Arts and Letters (Toronto).

**JACKSON, Col Arnold N. S. S.-;** *see* Strode-Jackson.

**JACKSON, Mrs (Audrey) Muriel W.;** *see* Ward-Jackson.

**JACKSON, Lady (Barbara);** *see* Jackson, Lady (Robert); (Barbara Ward).

**JACKSON, Charles d'Orville Pilkington,** ARSA, FRBS, FRSA; sculptor; *b* Garlenick, Cornwall, 1887; *s* of late Louis Pilkington Jackson, MRCS, LRCP; *m* 1st, 1916, Eve Cornish Dening (*d* 1951); one *s* one *d*; 2nd, 1958, Audrey Ethelwyn O'Brien, *yr d* of late E. W. Clark, Oxford. *Educ:* Loretto Sch. Diploma of Sculpture and Travelling Scholarship, Edinburgh, 1910; British Sch. at Rome, 1910-11; served European War, 1914-19, RFA (despatches); War of 1939-45, AA, RA; Pres. Society of Scottish Artists, 1942-45; Mem. Royal Fine Art Commission for Scotland, 1944-63; Principal Works: Sculpture on Scottish National War Memorial, Stowe Sch. Chapel, Paisley Abbey, David Livingstone Memorial, Blantyre, Lanarks, and Royal Scots Monument, Edinburgh, Regimental Monument Royal Scots Fusiliers, Ayr. Portraiture: including David Livingstone at Newstead Abbey; James Clark Maxwell, Univ. of Aberdeen; and Lord Lugard, University of Hong Kong; works in Nat. Portrait Gallery. John Bruce Award of Merit (gold medal) for RCSE. Military Statuettes, 1633-1918, Scottish United Services Museum, and Imperial War Museum; Equestrian Statuette of Robert the Bruce, Prince Charles Stuart and Calgary Highlanders, at Calgary, Alberta; Equestrian Statue of King Robert the Bruce at Bannockburn, replica at Calgary. Maces of: Sch. of Medicine, University of St Andrews; City of Singapore; Coll. of Physicians, Surgeons and Gynæcologists of South Africa; Gillan Trophy ATC; (with David Linton, DSc) the Orographical Globe in Geological Survey and Museum, South Kensington, Eton Coll., etc. *Address:* 4 Polwarth Terrace, Edinburgh EH11 1NE. *T:* 031-229 4805. *Club:* Caledonian (London).

**JACKSON, Sir Christopher M. M.;** *see* Mather-Jackson, Sir G. C. M.

**JACKSON, Colin;** *see* Jackson, G. C.

**JACKSON, Derek Ainslie,** OBE; DFC; AFC; MA Cantab and Oxon; DSc Oxon; FRS 1947; *b* 23 June 1906; *s* of late Sir Charles James Jackson; *m* 1936, Hon. Pamela Freeman-Mitford (marr. diss., 1951), 2nd *d* of 2nd Baron Redesdale; *m* 1951, Janetta (marr. diss. 1956), *d* of Rev. G. H. Woolley, VC, OBE, MC; one *d*; *m* 1957, Consuelo Regina Maria (marr. diss., 1959), *d* of late William S. Eyre and *widow* of Prince Ernst Ratibor zu Hohenlohe Schillingsfürst; *m* 1968, Marie-Christine, *d* of Baron Georges Reille. *Educ:* Rugby; Trinity Coll., Cambridge. Formerly Prof. of Spectroscopy in the University of Oxford. Served War of 1939-45, Observer in RAFVR, 1940-45. Wing Comdr 1943. Officer Legion of Merit (USA); Chevalier, Légion d'Honneur, France. *Publications:* numerous papers in Proc. Royal Soc., Jl de Physique, Phys. Review, Zeitschrift für Physik. *Address:* 20 Avenue des Figuiers, Ouchy, Lausanne, Switzerland; 19 rue Auguste Vacquerie, Paris 16e.

**JACKSON, Sir Donald (Edward),** Kt 1953; *b* 1892; *e s* of late Joseph Waterton Jackson, OBE, JP, MLC; *m* 1937, Amy Beatrice, *e d* of late Walter Augustus Reynolds, British

Guiana; one *d*. *Educ:* The Middle Sch., British Guiana. LLB University of London, 1926. Called to Bar, Middle Temple, 1927; practised at Bar, British Guiana; Acting Asst Attorney-Gen., 1933, 1936, and Senior Magistrate, 1936; Registrar of Deeds, of Supreme Court and of West Indian Court of Appeal, British Guiana, 1944; Actg Puisne Judge, various periods, 1945-49; Puisne Judge, Windward and Leeward Islands, 1949; Chief Justice of Windward and Leeward Islands, and Judge of West Indian Court of Appeal, 1950-57, retired. Speaker, Legislative Council, British Guiana, 1959-61; Justice of Appeal, Federal Supreme Court of the West Indies, 1961-62; Justice of Appeal, British Caribbean Court of Appeal, 1962-66. Mem. of Commission on the Unification of the Public Services in the British Caribbean Area, 1948-49; Chm., Labour Commn of Enquiry, St Lucia, 1950; Chm., Commission of Inquiry into the Nutmeg Industry of Grenada, 1951; Mem. Brit. Guiana Constitutional Commn, 1954; Chm. of Commn of Inquiry into causes of Cessation of Work in Sugar Industry, St Lucia, 1957; Chm. Constitutional Cttee for British Guiana, 1958-59; Chm., Commn to review Salaries and Structure of W Indies Federal Civil Service, and also to enquire into remuneration of Ministers and other members of W Indies Fed. Legislature, 1960; Mem., Mixed Commn on Venezuela-Guyana Border Dispute, 1966-; Chm. Elections Commn, Guyana, 1966-; Mem. Boundaries Commn, Bermuda, 1967. OStJ, 1960. Cacique's Crown of Honour, Guyana, 1970. *Address:* Georgetown, Guyana. *Clubs:* West Indian; The Georgetown.

**JACKSON, Edward Francis,** MA; Director, Oxford University Institute of Economics and Statistics, and Professorial Fellow of St Antony's College, Oxford, since 1959; *b* 11 July 1915; *o s* of F. E. Jackson, schoolmaster, and Miriam Eveline (*née* Jevon); *m* 1st, 1942, Anne Katherine Cloake (marr. diss.); 2nd, 1954, Mrs Marion Marianne Marris, *o c* of late Arthur Ellinger; two *s*. *Educ:* West Bromwich Grammar Sch.; Univ. of Birmingham; Magdalen Coll., Oxford. BCom Birmingham with 1st cl. hons, 1934; Magdalen Coll., Oxford (Demy): 1st in PPE, 1937; Jun. G. W. Medley Schol., 1935-36; Sen. Demy, 1937; Lecturer in Economics: New Coll., 1938; Magdalen Coll., 1939. Temp. Civil Servant in War Cabinet Offices, 1941-45; established Civil Servant (Central Statistical Office), 1945; Dep. Dir, Res. and Planning Div., UN Econ. Commn for Europe, 1951-56. University Lectr in Economic Statistics, Oxford, and Research Fellow of St Antony's Coll., Oxford, 1956; Mem. Transport Adv. Coun., 1965. *Publications:* The Nigerian National Accounts, 1950-57 (with P. N. C. Obigbo), 1960; articles in economic journals. *Address:* The Manor House, Brill, Aylesbury, Bucks. *T:* Brill 205. *Club:* Reform.

**JACKSON, Egbert Joseph William,** CB 1950; MC 1918. *Educ:* Sheffield University (MA, Gladstone Memorial Prizeman, 1912). Assistant Lecturer, Sheffield University, 1913-14; Lecturer in Economics, Birmingham University, 1914-19. Served European War, 1916-18. Entered Ministry of Education, 1919; Staff Inspector of Commerce, 1936; Asst Secretary, Ministry of War Transport, 1940-45; Chief Inspector, Ministry of Education, 1945-51; retired, 1951. *Address:* Monkton, Elgood Avenue, Northwood, Middlesex. *T:* Northwood 25751.

**JACKSON, Eric Stead,** CB 1954; Under-Secretary, Ministry of Technology, since 1967; *b* 22 Aug. 1909; *yr s* of Stead Jackson, Shipley Glen, Yorks; *m* 1938, Yvonne Renée, *o d* of Devereux Doria De Brétigny, Victoria, BC; one *s* one *d*. *Educ:* Bradford Grammar Sch.; Corpus Christi Coll., Oxford (Scholar). 1st Class Hons Math. Mods, Math. Finals and Nat. Sci. Finals, Jun. Math. schol., 1930; MA. Asst Principal, Air Ministry, 1932; Sec., British Air Mission to Australia and NZ, 1939; Private Sec. to Minister of Aircraft Production, 1942, and to Resident Minister in Washington, 1943; Sec., British Supply Council in N America, 1944; Dir-Gen. Aircraft Branch, Control Commission, Berlin, 1945; Dep. Pres. Economic Sub-Commission, 1947; British Head of Bizonal Delegation to OEEC, Paris, 1948; Under Sec., Ministry of Supply, 1950-56; Dir-Gen., Atomic Weapons, Ministry of Supply, 1956-59; Under Sec., Min. of Aviation, 1959-67. *Address:* 48 Canonbury Park North, N1. *T:* 01-226 5752.

**JACKSON, Rt. Rev. Fabian Menteath Elliot;** Assistant Bishop of Bath and Wells since 1950; Prebendary of Wells Cathedral since 1954; *b* 22 Nov. 1902; *s* of William Henry Congreve and Maud Helen Jackson; unmarried. *Educ:* Westminster Sch.; University of London; Ely Theological Coll. BA Hons Classics, London, 1925; Deacon, 1926; Priest, 1927; S Augustine's, Kilburn, 1926-38; Priest-in-Charge of S Barnabas, Northolt Park, 1938-43; Vicar of All Saints, Clifton, 1943-46; Bishop of Trinidad, 1946-49, resigned, 1949; Rector of Batcombe with Upton Noble, Somerset, 1950-67. *Address:* Ullenwood, Lustleigh, Newton Abbot, Devon.

**JACKSON, Francis Alan;** Organist and Master of the Music, York Minster, since 1946; *b* 2 Oct. 1917; *s* of W. A. Jackson; *m* 1950, Priscilla, *d* of Tyndale Procter; two *s* one *d*. *Educ:* York Minster Choir Sch.; Sir Edward Bairstow. Chorister, York Minster, 1929-33; ARCO, 1936; BMus Dunelm 1937; FRCO (Limpus Prize), 1937; FRSCM, 1963; DMus Dunelm 1957. Organist Malton Parish Church, 1933-40. Served War of 1939-45, with 9th Lancers in Egypt, N Africa and Italy, 1940-46. Asst Organist, York Minster, 1946; Conductor York Musical Soc., 1947; Conductor York Symphony Orchestra, 1947. Pres. Incorp. Assoc of Organists, 1960-62. Hon. Fellow, Westminster Choir Coll., Princeton, NJ, 1970. *Publications:* Organ and Church Music, Songs, Monodramas. *Recreation:* gardening. *Address:* 1 Minster Court, York. *T:* York 53873.

**JACKSON, Col Sir Francis (James) Gidlow,** Kt, *cr* 1955; MC 1917; TD 1930; *b* 16 Sept. 1889; 2nd *s* of late Charles Gidlow Jackson, JP, CA; unmarried. *Educ:* Bilton Grange; Rugby. Admitted Solicitor, 1912; Served European War, 1914-19; Egypt, Gallipoli, France and Belgium. Served France, 1940. *Recreations:* hunting, shooting, fishing. *Address:* Domus, Enville Road, Bowdon, Cheshire. *Clubs:* St James's, The Manchester (Manchester).

**JACKSON, Col Frank Lawson John,** OBE 1959; TD; *b* 12 June 1919; *s* of S. V. Jackson. *Educ:* Oundle. Commissioned 6th Bn North Staffs Regt, TA, 1938. Served War of 1939-45 in Ireland, and as Chief Instructor. Commanded Bn, 1954-58; Lt-Col, 1954; Hon. Col, 1959; Col 1963. Mem. Burton-on-Trent Borough Council, 1950-54. MP (C) South-Eastern Div. of Derbyshire, Oct. 1959-Sept. 1964. Barley merchant; Mem. Inst. of Brewing. *Address:* 1 Hamilton Road, Burton-on-Trent, Staffs. *T:* 4615. *Clubs:* Public Schools, 1900; Burton.

**JACKSON, Frederick Hume,** OBE 1966; UK Resident Representative to the International Atomic Energy Agency, since 1969; *b* 8 Sept. 1918; *o s* of late Maj.-Gen. G. H. N. Jackson,

CB, CMG, DSO, Rathmore, Winchcombe, Glos and Eileen, *d* of J. Hume Dudgeon, Merville, Booterstown, Co. Dublin; *m* 1950, Anne Gibson; three *s* one *d*. *Educ:* Winchester; Clare Coll., Cambridge (MA) Military service, 1939-46: GSO3 (Intelligence), HQ 1 Corps District; Colonial Service (Tanganyika), 1946-57; FO, 1957-60; Head of Chancery, Saigon, 1960-62; 1st Sec., Washington, 1962-67; Counsellor and Dep. Head, UK Delegn to European Communities, Brussels, 1967-69. *Recreations:* fishing, sailing, shooting, riding. *Address:* c/o Barclays Bank Ltd, St Nicholas Street, Scarborough, Yorks; British Embassy, Vienna, Austria. *T:* Vienna 323574. *Club:* Flyfishers'.

**JACKSON, Geoffrey Holt Seymour,** CMG 1963; HM Diplomatic Service; HM Ambassador to Uruguay, since 1969; *b* 4 March 1915; *s* of Samuel Seymour Jackson and Marie Cecile Dudley Ryder; *m* 1939, Patricia Mary Evelyn Delany; one *s*. *Educ:* Bolton Sch.; Emmanuel Coll., Cambridge. Entered Foreign Service, 1937; Vice-Consul, Beirut, Cairo, Bagdad; Acting Consul-Gen., Basra, 1946; 1st Sec., Bogotá, 1946-50; Berne, 1954-56; Minister, Honduras, 1956, HM Ambassador to Honduras, 1957-60; Consul-Gen., Seattle, 1960-64; Senior British Trade Commissioner in Ontario, Canada, 1964; Minister (Commercial), Toronto, 1965-69. *Recreations:* ski-ing, golf, Latin-Americana. *Address:* British Embassy, Montevideo, Uruguay; 63B Cadogan Square, SW1. *Clubs:* Lansdowne, Canning.

**JACKSON, (George) Colin;** *b* 6 Dec. 1921; *s* of George Hutton and Agnes Scott Jackson. *Educ:* Tewkesbury Grammar Sch.; St John's Coll., Oxford. Called to the Bar, Gray's Inn, 1950. Lecturer, writer and broadcaster in Britain, America, throughout Africa and Asia, 1951-64. MP (Lab) Brighouse and Spenborough, 1964-70. *Publication:* The New India (Fabian Soc.). *Recreation:* travel. *Address:* 23 Ennismore Gardens, SW7. *T:* 01-584 0340. *Club:* Savile.

**JACKSON, Most Rev. George Frederick Clarence;** *see* Qu'Appelle, Archbishop of.

**JACKSON, Gerald Breck;** Senior Executive, Thomas Tilling Ltd, and Director, subsidiary cos, since 1969; *b* 28 June 1916; *o s* of Gerald Breck Jackson and Mary Jackson, Paterson, NJ; *m* 1940, Brenda Mary, *o d* of William and Mary Titshall; one *s*. *Educ:* various schs in USA; Canford Sch., Dorset; Faraday House Engrg Coll. Graduate Trainee, Central Electricity Bd, 1938. HM Forces, RE, 1939-43. Various appts in HV transmission with CEB and BEA, 1943-55; Overhead Line Design Engr, BEA, 1955-61; Asst Regional Dir, CEGB, 1961-64; Chief Ops Engr, CEGB, 1964-66; Regional Dir, NW Region, CEGB, 1966-68; Dir Engineering, English Electric Co. Ltd, 1968-69. DFH, CEng, FIEE. *Publications:* Network for the Nation, 1960; Power Controlled, 1966. *Recreations:* photography, pen-and-ink drawing. *Address:* 23 Balliol House, Manor Fields, Putney Hill, SW15. *T:* 01-788 0583.

**JACKSON, Gordon Noel,** CMG 1962; MBE; HM Ambassador to Ecuador, 1967-70, retired; *b* 25 Dec. 1913; *m* 1959, Mary April Nettlefold, *er d* of late Frederick John Nettlefold and of Mrs Albert Coates; one *s* two *d*. Indian Political Service until 1947; then HM Foreign Service; Political Officer, Sharjah, 1947; transf. to Kuwait, Persian Gulf, 1949; transf. to Foreign Office, 1950; Consul, St Louis, USA, 1953; Foreign Service Officer, Grade 6, 1955; Consul-General: Basra, 1955-57; Lourenço Marques, 1957-60; Benghazi, 1960-63; HM Ambassador to Kuwait, 1963-67. *Publication:* Effective Horsemanship (for Dressage, Hunting, Three-day Events, Polo), 1967. *Address:* c/o Lloyds Bank Ltd, 6 Pall Mall, SW1. *Club:* Travellers'.

**JACKSON, H(arold) Haygarth,** MC; Director and Member, Management Board, Bleachers' Association Ltd, 1948-62; Chairman, North West Regional Board for Industry, 1958-64; Chairman, The Midland Leather Co. Ltd; Director, Manchester Chamber of Commerce, to 1968; Member of Grand Council, Federation of British Industries, to 1965; Vice-Chairman, National Library for the Blind (Northern Branch) to 1964; Member, National Production Advisory Council on Industry to 1964; Member, General Council, British Standards Institute, to 1962; *b* 6 June 1896; *m* 1923, Frieda, *d* of Alderman and Mrs J. A. Barraclough, Rochdale; one *s* one *d*. Served European War, 1914-18: with 6th Bn Manchester Regt, Egypt, Gallipoli, France and Belgium; Mem. of British Military Mission to USA, 1918 (MC 1917; despatches, 1918). Managing Dir, James F. Hutton & Co. Ltd, 1933-40; Executive Mem. of The Cotton Board, 1940-48; Adviser, Control Commission in Germany, 1946; Mem. of Cotton Board Missions to USA, India, Pakistan, Japan, Central African Federation and European countries, 1948-57; Finishing Trades Employer Mem. of Cotton Board, 1949-58; Industrial Mem., Economic Commission for Asia and the Far East, Manila, Philippines, 1953; Chm., United Tanners' Federation, 1958-61; Pres., British Leather Federation, 1963-64. Officer Order of Orange Nassau (Netherlands), 1947; Officer Order of the Crown (Belgium), 1948; Chevalier of the Legion of Honour (France), 1950. *Address:* Highwayside, Talbot Road, Bowdon, Cheshire; Whitecroft Industrial Holdings Ltd, Blackfriars' House, Parsonage, Manchester 3.

**JACKSON, Sir Harold (Warters),** Kt, *cr* 1952; Solicitor; *b* 5 April 1883; *e s* of late Rev. J. Harding Jackson; *m* 1911, Margaret, (*d* 1959), *y d* of late Thomas Jubb; one *s*. *Educ:* Wesley Coll., Sheffield. LLB (London); LLD (Sheffield). Admitted solicitor, 1905; mem. of Sheffield City Council, 1911-67, Alderman, 1928, Lord Mayor, 1930-31, Freeman, 1945; Sheffield Town Trustee. Formerly: Pres. Assoc. of Education Cttees; Mem. Court of Sheffield Univ. *Address:* 19 Slayleigh Lane, Sheffield. *T:* 33883.

**JACKSON, Harry;** *b* 5 July 1892; *s* of John Henry Jackson and Ada Catherine Jackson (*née* Beavan); *m* 1919, Mabel Alice Parkinson; one *s* one *d*; *m* 1957, Nora Richardson Fage. *Educ:* Holt Sch., Liverpool. Midland Bank Ltd, 1908-19; Asst Sec. Guaranty Trust Co. of New York, Liverpool, 1919-24; Barclays Bank Ltd, Liverpool, 1924-52; Pres. Liverpool and District Inst. of Bankers, 1948; served European War, 1914-19 with 9th Bn King's Liverpool Regt and Royal Dublin Fusiliers; Local Govt Service in Wirral, Cheshire, 1925-33 and 1936-53. Vice-Chm. 1953-54, Chm. April 1954, Liquidator Sept. 1954-June 1956, Raw Cotton Commission. *Recreation:* gardening, fishing. *Address:* 3 Thornton House, Thornton Hough, Wirral, Cheshire. *T:* 051-336 3413. *Clubs:* Rembrandt (Liverpool); Cheshire County Cricket.

**JACKSON, Harvey;** Hon. Consulting Surgeon, The National Hospital, Queen Square; Hon. Consulting Neurosurgeon, Westminster Hospital; Hon. Neurological Surgeon, St Thomas' Hospital; Hon. Consulting Surgeon, Acton General Hospital, since 1930; *b* 16 Oct.

1900; *s* of Richard Barlow Jackson and Elizabeth Shepherd; *m* 1930, Freda Mary Frampton; one *s* one *d*. *Educ:* Royal Grammar School, Newcastle upon Tyne; Middlesex Hospital. Hon. Asst Surg., West London Hosp., 1935-38. Past Pres., West London Medico-Chirurgical Soc.; Past Pres., Soc. of Brit. Neurological Surgeons; Fellow of Assoc. of Surgeons; Hunterian Prof. RCS of England, 1947, 1951; Elsberg Lectr, Neurological Soc. of New York, 1960; Visiting Prof. in Neurosurgery, University of Cairo, Guest Lectr, Univ. of Cincinnati, 1959; Lectr, Neurological Soc. of Chicago, 1959; Guest Lectr, Univ. of Santiago de Compostela, Spain, 1969. Past President: Section of Neurology, RSM; Surrey Branch, BMA. *Address:* National Hospital, Queen Square, WC1. *T:* 01-837 3958.

**JACKSON, Gen. Sir Henry Cholmondeley,** KCB 1936 (CB 1919); CMG 1920; DSO 1916; Colonel of Bedfordshire and Hertfordshire Regiment, 1935-47; *b* Cambridge, 12 Aug. 1879; *e s* of late Henry Jackson, OM; *m* 1919, Dorothy Nina, RRC (*d* 1953), 3rd *d* of late Gen. Lord William Seymour. *Educ:* Haileybury; Trinity Coll., Cambridge. Joined 1st Beds Regt 1899; Capt., 1906; Adjutant, 1903-06; Major, 1915; Maj.-Gen. 1930; Lt-Gen. 1935; Gen. 1939; Adjutant Mounted Infantry Sch., Longmoor, 1908-12; PSC; served European War, 1914-18 (despatches eight times, CB, DSO, Bt Col, twice wounded); Commandant Machine Gun Sch., Netheravon, 1924-26; Small Arms Sch. and Machine Gun Sch., 1926; Dir of Military Training, AHQ, India, 1926-30; ADC to HM, 1928-30; Commander 2nd Div., 1931-35; General Officer Commanding-in-Chief, Western Command, 1936-39 and 1940; retired pay, 1939. *Recreation:* hunting. *Address:* West House, Piddletrenthide, Dorchester, Dorset. *Club:* United Service.

**JACKSON, Herbert,** FRIBA; MTPI; architect and planning consultant; in private practice since 1931; *b* 25 June 1909; *s* of John Herbert Jackson; *m* 1930, Margaret Elizabeth Pearson. *Educ:* Handsworth Grammar Sch.; Birmingham Sch. of Architecture. RIBA Bronze Medal, 1928; RIBA Saxon Snell Prizeman, 1930. Mem. RIBA Council, 1956-58; Vice-Pres. RIBA 1960-62; Chm., RIBA Allied Socs Conf., 1960-62. Gov., Birmingham Coll. of Art; Chm. Birmingham Civic Soc., 1960-65; Pres. Birmingham and Five Counties Architectural Assoc., 1956-58; Pres. Royal Birmingham Society of Artists, 1960-62 (Prof. of Architecture, 1961). *Publications:* (jt) Plans (for Minister of Town and Country Planning): S Wales Plan, 1947; W Midlands and N Staffs Plan, 1948. *Recreations:* travelling, reading. *Address:* 14 Clarendon Square, Leamington Spa, Warwicks. *T:* Leamington 24078; 17 Welbeck Street, W1M 7PF. *T:* 01-486 2872/4. *Clubs:* Arts; Union (Birmingham).

**JACKSON, Sir Hugh (Nicholas),** 2nd Bt, *cr* 1913; late Lt R W Fusiliers; *b* 21 Jan. 1881; *s* of 1st Bt and Alice Mary (*d* 1900), *y d* of William Lambarde, JP, DL, of Beechmont, Sevenoaks, Kent; *S* father, 1924; *m* 1931, Violet Marguerite Loftus, *y d* of Loftus St George; one *s* one *d*. *Heir:* *s* Nicholas Fane St George [*b* 4 Sept. 1934; *m* 1961, Jennifer Ann, *d* of F. A. Squire]. *Address:* 38 Oakley Street, SW3.

**JACKSON, Ian (Macgilchrist),** BA Cantab, MB, BChir, FRCS, FRCOG; Obstetric and Gynæcological Surgeon, Middlesex Hospital, 1948; Gynæcological Surgeon: Chelsea Hospital for Women, 1948; King Edward VII Hospital for Officers, 1961; Royal Masonic Hospital, 1963; Consulting Gynæcologist, King Edward VII Sanatorium, Midhurst, 1959; Consultant Obstetrician and Gynæcologist, RAF, 1964; *b* Shanghai, 11 Nov. 1914; *s* of Dr Ernest David Jackson; *m* 1943, Lesley Fenton Bellamy; two *s* one *d*. *Educ:* Marlborough Coll.; Trinity Hall, Cambridge (scholar; double 1st cl. hons, Nat. Sci. tripos pts I, II). London Hospital: open scholarship, 1936; house appointments, 1939; First Asst, Surgical and Obstetric and Gynæcol Depts, 1940-43. Served as Surgical Specialist, RAMC, 1943-47 (Major); Parachute Surgical Team, 224 Para. Field Amb.; Mobile Surgical Unit, 3 Commando Brigade. Royal College of Obstetricians and Gynæcologists: Council, 1951-61, 1962-; Hon. Sec., 1954-61; Chm., Examination Cttee, 1962-65. Hon. Treas., 1966-. Examiner for Univs of Cambridge, Oxford, and London, Conjoint Bd and RCOG. Order of the Star of Africa (Liberia), 1969; Grand Officer of Order of Istiqlal, Jordan, 1970. *Publications:* Surgical Aspects of Medicine (jtly), 1959; Diseases of Women by Ten Teachers (jtly), 1961; British Obstetric and Gynæcological Practice (jtly), 1963; Obstetrics by Ten Teachers (jtly), 1966; numerous contribs to medical literature. *Recreations:* fishing, golf, photography. *Address:* 33 Bryanston Square, W1. *T:* 01-262 6353; 104 Harley Street, W1. *T:* 01-935 1801.

**JACKSON, James Barry;** *see* Barry, Michael.

**JACKSON, Sir John Montrésor,** 6th Bt, *cr* 1815; elected Member of London Stock Exchange, 1948; formerly engaged on development work for Ministry of Aircraft Production; formerly with BBC; *b* Buenos Aires, Argentina, 14 Oct. 1914; *o surv s* of Sir Robert Montrésor Jackson, 5th Bt, and Katherine, *y d* of late John Abrey, The Glen and Barden Park, Tonbridge; *S* father, 1940; *m* 1953, Mrs E. Beatty. *Educ:* Tonbridge Sch.; Clare Coll., Cambridge. BA, 1936; London Stock Exchange, 1937-39; at outbreak of war, 1939, embodied with Territorial Army, RA (AA); released on medical grounds, May 1940. *Recreations:* golf, swimming and rowing. *Address:* Rose Cottage, Charing, Kent.

**JACKSON, John Wharton,** JP; Chairman of Directors, Jackson's (Hurstead) Ltd, Rochdale, Lancs; Director of Era Ring Mills Ltd, Rochdale and Spodden Manufacturing Co., Whitworth; *b* 25 May 1902; *s* of John Jackson and Mary Wharton; *m* 1928, Mary Rigg; two *d*. *Educ:* Shrewsbury. High Sheriff of Radnorshire, 1944-45; JP County of Lancaster, 1952. *Recreation:* golf. *Address:* Brackens, Mottram St Andrew, near Macclesfield, Cheshire. *T:* Prestbury 89277.

**JACKSON, Joseph,** QC 1967; Special Divorce Commissioner, since 1969; *b* 21 Aug. 1924; *s* of late Samuel Jackson and of Hetty Jackson; *m* 1952, Marjorie Henrietta (*née* Lyons); three *d*. *Educ:* Queens' Coll., Cambridge; University Coll., London. MA, LLB Cantab, LLM London. Barrister, 1947, Gibraltar Bar. Chm., Probate and Divorce Bar Assoc., 1968-69. Member: General Council of the Bar, 1969-; Matrimonial Causes Rules Cttee, 1969-. *Publications:* English Legal History, 1951 (2nd edn 1955); Formation and Annulment of Marriage, 1951, 2nd edn, 1969; Rayden on Divorce, 6th edn 1953 to 11th edn 1970; contrib. to Halsbury's Laws of England, Encyclopædia Britannica, Atkin's Encyclopædia of Court Forms, Law Quarterly Review, Modern Law Review, Canadian Bar Review, etc. *Recreations:* gardening, painting, miniature tea-pots. *Address:* Brook House, 28 Uxbridge Road, Stanmore, Middlesex. *T:* 01-954 2039; 1 Mitre Court Buildings, Temple, EC4. *T:* 01-353 0434/2277.

**JACKSON, Prof. Kenneth Hurlstone,** FBA 1957; FSA Scot., 1951; Professor of Celtic Languages, Literatures, History and Antiquities, Edinburgh University, since 1950; *b* 1 Nov. 1909; *s* of Alan Stuart Jackson and Lucy Hurlstone; *m* 1936, Janet Dall Galloway, of Hillside, Kinross-shire; one *s* one *d*. *Educ:* Whitgift Sch., Croydon; St John's Coll., Cambridge (Exhibitioner and Scholar). First Cl. Hons with Distinction, Classical Tripos, 1930 and 1931 (Senior Classic, 1931); BA 1931; First Cl. Hons with Distinction, Archaeology and Anthropology Tripos, 1932; Sir William Brown medals for Greek and Latin verse, 1930 (two), 1931; Allen Research Studentship, 1932-34; research in Celtic at University Colls of North Wales and Dublin. Fellowship at St John's Coll., and Faculty Lectr in Celtic, Cambridge Univ., 1934-39; MA 1935; LittD 1954; Lectureship, 1939, Assoc. Professorship, 1940-49, Professorship, 1949-50, Celtic Languages and Literatures, Harvard Univ. Hon. AM Harvard, 1940. Editor: of the Zeitschrift für Celtische Philologie, 1939; of the Journal of Celtic Studies, 1949-57. Corr. Fellow of Mediæval Acad. of America, 1951; Pres. of Scottish Anthropological and Folklore Soc., 1952-60; Vice-Pres. of Soc. of Antiquaries of Scotland, 1960-63; Mem., Comité Internat. des Sciences Onomastiques, 1955-; Mem. Council for Name Studies in Great Britain and Ireland, 1961-; one of HM Commissioners for Ancient Monuments (Scotland), 1963-. War service in the British Imperial Censorship, Bermuda (Uncommon Languages), 1942-44; in the US censorship, 1944. Hon. DLitt Celt. Ireland, 1958; Hon. DLitt Wales, 1963. Hon. Mem. Mod. Language Assoc. of America, 1958; Hon. Mem. Royal Irish Academy, 1965. *Publications:* Early Welsh Gnomic Poems, 1935; Studies in Early Celtic Nature Poetry, 1935; Cath Maighe Léna, 1938; Scéalta ón mBlascaod, 1939; A Celtic Miscellany, 1951; Language and History in Early Britain, 1953; Contribs to the Study of Manx Phonology, 1955; The International Popular Tale and Early Welsh Tradition, 1961; The Oldest Irish Tradition, 1964; A Historical Phonology of Breton, 1967; The Gododdin, 1969; articles on Celtic Languages, literature, history and folklore in Zeitschrift für Celtische Philologie, Etudes Celtiques, Bulletin of the Bd of Celtic Studies, Antiquity, Journal of Roman Studies, Folklore, Journal of Celtic Studies, Scottish Gaelic Studies, Speculum, Modern Philology, etc. *Recreations:* tennis, walking. *Address:* 34 Cluny Drive, Edinburgh 10. *Club:* Union (Cambridge).

**JACKSON, Hon. Sir Lawrence,** KCMG 1970; Kt 1964; BA, LLB; Judge since 1949 and Chief Justice since 1969, Supreme Court of Western Australia; *b* Dulwich, South Australia, 27 Sept. 1913; *s* of L. S. Jackson; *m* 1937, Mary, *d* of T. H. Donaldson; one *s* two *d*. *Educ:* Fort Street High Sch., Sydney; University of Sydney. *Recreations:* cricket and golf. *Address:* 127 Forrest Street, Peppermint Grove, WA 6011, Australia. *Club:* Weld (Perth, WA).

**JACKSON, Sir Michael (Roland),** 5th Bt, *cr* 1902; MA; MIEE; FIEI; *b* 20 April 1919; *s* of Sir W. D. Russell Jackson, 4th Bt, and Kathleen, *d* of Summers Hunter, CBE, Tynemouth; *S* father 1956; *m* 1st, 1942, Hilda Margaret (marr. diss. 1969), *d* of Cecil George Herbert Richardson, CBE, Newark; one *s* one *d*; 2nd, 1969, Hazel Mary, *d* of Ernest Harold Edwards. *Educ:* Stowe; Clare Coll., Cambridge. Served War of 1939-45; Flight-Lt, Royal Air Force Volunteer Reserve. *Heir: s* Thomas St Felix Jackson, *b* 27 Sept. 1946. *Address:* c/o National Westminster Bank, 291b Oxford Street, W1.

**JACKSON, Mrs Muriel;** *see* Ward-Jackson.

**JACKSON, Oliver James V.;** *see* Vaughan-Jackson.

**JACKSON, Peter (Michael);** *b* 14 Oct. 1928; *s* of Leonard Patterson Jackson; *m* 1961, Christine Thomas. *Educ:* Durham Univ.; University Coll., Leicester. Lecturer, Dept of Sociology, University of Hull, 1964-66. MP (Lab) High Peak, 1966-70. *Recreations:* numismatics, book collecting, ski-ing. *Address:* Cobb Barn, Smalldale, Bradwell, Derbyshire.

**JACKSON, Air Vice-Marshal Ralph Coburn,** CB 1963; Consultant Adviser in Medicine, to RAF, at Central Medical Establishment RAF and to Aviation Department, Board of Trade, since 1966; QHP 1969; *b* 22 June 1914; *s* of Ralph Coburn Jackson and Phillis Jackson (*née* Dodds); *m* 1939, Joan Lucy Crowley; two *s* two *d*. *Educ:* Oakmount Sch., Arnside; Guy's Hosp., London. MRCS 1937; LRCP 1937; MRCPE 1950; FRCPE 1960; MRCP 1968; FRSM. Qualified in Medicine Guy's Hosp., 1937; House Officer appts, Guy's Hosp., 1937-38; commnd in RAF as MO, Nov. 1938; served in France, 1939-40; Russia, 1941; W Africa, 1942-43 (despatches); Sen. MO, 46 Gp for Brit. Casualty Air Evac., 1944-45 (despatches). Med. Specialist, RAF Hosps Wroughton, Aden and Halton, 1946-63 (Consultant in Med., Princess Mary's RAF Hosp. Halton, 1952-63; RAF Hosp., Wegberg, Germany, 1964-66). MacArthur Lectr, Univ. Edinburgh, 1959. Member: Renal Assoc.; Med. Soc. of London; Assurance Med. Soc.; London Topographical Soc.; Aerospace Med. Assoc., USA. Lady Cade Medal, RCS, 1960. *Publications:* chap., The Artificial Kidney, in Recent Advances in Renal Diseases, 1960; chap., The Artificial Kidney, in Recent Advances in the Surgery of Trauma, 1963. Papers, on Acute Renal Failure and The Artificial Kidney, in Lancet, BMJ, Brit. Jl of Clin. Practice, Proc. RSM. *Recreation:* ancient buildings. *Address:* Central Medical Establishment RAF, Kelvin House, Cleveland Street, W1. *T:* 01-636 4651. *Club:* Royal Air Force.

**JACKSON, Sir Richard (Leofric),** Kt 1963; CBE 1958; Director, Security Services Ltd, Securicor Ltd (Joint Vice-Chairman) and Securicor Consultancy Ltd (Chairman), since 1963; *b* 12 July 1902; 3rd *s* of late William Jackson, Barrister-at-Law, of Calcutta; *m* 1930, Mary Elizabeth, *o d* of late Charles Blois Pooley, CIE; one *d*. *Educ:* Cheam Sch.; Eton; Trinity Coll., Cambridge. Called to the Bar, Middle Temple, 1927; Appointed to Staff of Dir of Public Prosecutions, 1933; appointed Sec. of Metropolitan Police Office, 1946; Asst Commissioner, Criminal Investigation Dept, New Scotland Yard, 1953-63; Pres., International Criminal Police Organisation (Interpol), 1960-63 (British Representative, 1957, Mem. Exec. Cttee, 1958). A Mem. of Police Mission to Federation of Malaya, 1949. FRSA 1964. *Publications:* (ed) Criminal Investigation (Hans Gross), 5th edn, 1962; Occupied with Crime, 1967. *Address:* 10 Persfield Mews, Ewell, Surrey. *T:* 01-393 1251. *Club:* Royal Automobile.

**JACKSON, Prof. Richard Meredith,** FBA, 1966; LLD; JP; Downing Professor of the Laws of England since 1966; Fellow, St John's College, Cambridge, since 1946; *b* 19 Aug. 1903; *s* of James Jackson, JP, Northampton and Jenny May Jackson (*née* Parnell); *m* 1st, Lydia Jibourtovitch (marr. diss.); 2nd, 1936, Lenli, *d* of Alexander Tie Ten Quee, Kingston, Jamaica; one *d* (and one *s* decd). *Educ:* Sidcot; Leighton Park; St John's Coll., Cambridge.

Admitted solicitor, 1928. Cambridge Law Sch., LLD 1939; Home Office, 1941-45; Sec. Royal Commn on JPs, 1946-48; Reader in Public Law and Admin., Cambridge, 1950; Member: Royal Commn on Mental Health Services, 1954-57; Deptl Cttee on Children and Young Persons, 1956-60. JP Cambs, 1942. *Publications:* History of Quasi-Contract in English Law, 1936; Machinery of Justice in England, 1940 (5th edn, 1967); Machinery of Local Government, 1958 (2nd edn, 1965); Enforcing the Law, 1967; ed, 3rd edn, Justice of the Peace, by Leo Page, 1967; articles in learned jls. *Recreation:* yacht cruising. *Address:* St John's College, Cambridge. *T:* 61621; 10 Halifax Road, Cambridge. *T:* 58179. *Clubs:* Athenæum; Royal Cruising.

**JACKSON, Comdr Sir Robert (Gillman Allen),** KCVO 1962; Kt 1956; CMG 1944; OBE 1941; Commissioner in Charge, Survey of UN Development System, since 1968; Special Consultant to Administrator, UN Development Programme since 1963; Adviser to President of Liberia since 1962; Advisory Board, Mekong Project, SE Asia, since 1962; Consultant to Volta River Authority, Ghana, since 1962 and Member of Board since 1965; *b* 1911; *m* 1950, Barbara Ward (*see* Lady Jackson); one *s*. RAN, 1929-37; transf. to Malta and RN, 1937; Chief Staff Officer to Gov. and C-in-C, Malta, 1940; Planning Malta Comd Defence Scheme; re-armament of the Fortress; develt Co-ordinated Supply Scheme, 1940 (OBE); Dir-Gen., ME Supply Centre and Principal Asst to UK Minister of State, 1942-45 co-ordn civilian supply ops/mil. ops; develt Aid to Russia Supply route: estab. anti-locust campaign, 1942 (CMG); AFHQ for special duties in Greece, 1944-45; transf. to HM Treasury, 1945; Sen. Dep. Dir-Gen. of UNRRA, 1945-47, and, in 1945, i/c of UNRRA's ops in Europe (inc. 8,500,000 displaced persons); supervised transfer of UNRRA's residual functions t0 WHO, FAO, and assisted in establishment of IRO, and International Children's Emergency Fund, 1947; services recognised by various governments in Europe and Asia; Asst Sec.-Gen. for Co-ordination in the UN, 1948; HM Treasury, for duties with Lord Pres. of Council, 1949; Perm. Sec., Min. of Nat. Development, Australia, 1950-52 (Snowy Mountains Scheme); Adviser to Govt of India on Development Plans, 1952, 1957 and 1962-63, and to Govt of Pakistan, 1952; Chm. of Preparatory Commission for Volta River multi-purpose project, Gold Coast, 1953-56; Chm., Development Commission, Ghana, 1956-61; Organisation of Royal Tours in Ghana, 1959 and 1961. *Address:* United Nations Development Programme, 866 UN Plaza, New York City, NY 10017, USA; Barclays Bank DCO, Oceanic House, Cockspur Street, SW1. *Clubs:* Brooks's; Victoria (Jersey); Melbourne (Victoria).

**JACKSON, Lady (Robert); (Barbara Ward);** author; Schweitzer Professor of International Economic Development, Columbia University, since July 1968; *b* 23 May 1914; *o d* of Walter and Teresa Ward; *m* 1950, Comdr (now Sir) Robert Jackson, *qv*; one *s*. *Educ:* Convent of Jesus and Mary, Felixstowe; Lycée Molière and the Sorbonne, Paris; die Klause, Jugenheim a/d/B, Germany; Somerville Coll., Oxford (Exhibitioner). Hons Degree in Philosophy, Politics and Economics, 1935; Univ. Extension Lecturer, 1936-39; joined staff of The Economist, 1939, as an Asst Editor; Visiting Scholar, Harvard Univ., 1957-68; Carnegie Fellow, 1959-67; Governor of Sadler's Wells and the Old Vic, 1944-53; Governor of BBC, 1946-50; Mem., Pontifical Commn for Justice and Peace, 1967-. Hon. Doctorates: Fordham Univ. and Smith Coll., 1949; Columbia Univ., 1954; Kenyon Coll. and Harvard Univ., 1957; Brandeis Univ., 1961, and others. *Publications:* The International Share-Out, 1938; Turkey, 1941; The West at Bay, 1948; Policy for the West, 1951; Faith and Freedom, 1954; Interplay of East and West, 1957; Five Ideas that Change the World, 1959; India and the West, 1961; The Rich Nations and the Poor Nations, 1962; Spaceship Earth, 1966; Nationalism and Ideology, 1967; The Lopsided World, 1968. *Recreations:* music, reading. *Address:* School of International Affairs, Columbia University, Morningside Heights, New York, NY 10027, USA.

**JACKSON, Rt. Rev. Robert Wyse,** DD; *b* 12 July 1908; *o s* of Richard Jackson and Belinda Hester Sherlock; *m* 1st, 1933, Margaretta Nolan Macdonald; one *s* one *d*; 2nd, 1952, Lois Margery Phair: four *s* one *d*. *Educ:* Abbey Sch., Tipperary; Bishop Foy Sch., Waterford; Trinity Coll., Dublin; Middle Temple; Egerton Hall, Manchester. BA (Hons Law), LLB; MA; LLD; LittD; DD 1961. Barrister, 1932; Curate of St James, Broughton (Dio. Manchester), 1934; Curate-in-charge, Corbally, Diocese of Killaloe, 1937; Rector of St Michael's, Limerick, 1939; Dean of the Cathedral Church of St John the Baptist and St Patrick's Rock, Cashel, 1946-60; Prebendary of Swords in St Patrick's Cathedral, Dublin, 1949-60; Bishop of Limerick, Ardfert and Aghadoe, 1961-70. Mem. Soc. of Antiquaries of Ireland; Water Colour Soc. of Ireland; Godfrey Day Memorial Lectr, Dublin Univ.; MRIA. *Publications:* Pleadings in Tort, 1933; Scenes from Irish Clerical Life in the Seventeenth and Eighteenth Centuries, 1938; Jonathan Swift, Dean and Pastor, 1939, repr. 1970; Swift and his Circle, 1945, repr. 1970; King of the Friday, 1949; Oliver Goldsmith, Essays Towards an Interpretation, 1951; Church of Ireland History, 1600-1932, 1953; The Celtic Cross, an Anthology of Devotion, 1954; An Introduction to Irish Silver, 1964; Voices at the Cross, 1965; The Relationship of Swift and Stella, 1967; The Best of Swift, 1967; Cathedrals of the Church of Ireland, 1970. Contributor to Hermathena, JRSAI; collaborator in: The Legacy of Swift, 1948; Music in Ireland, 1952. *Novels:* Spanish Man Hunt; The Journal of Corinna Brown. *Recreations:* painting, Swiftiana, exploring church silver. *Address:* Vellore, Whitshed Road, Greystones, Co. Wicklow. *T:* 874901; Bishopscove, Camp SO, Co. Kerry. *Clubs:* University, Friendly Brothers (Dublin).

**JACKSON, Mrs Schuyler;** *see* Riding, Laura.

**JACKSON, Thomas;** General Secretary, Union of Post Office Workers, since 1967; *b* 1 April 1925; *s* of George Frederick Jackson and Ethel Hargreaves; *m* 1947, Norma Burrow; one *d*. *Educ:* Jack Lane Elementary Sch. Boy Messenger, GPO, 1939; Royal Navy, 1943; Postman, 1946; Executive Mem., Union of Post Office Workers, 1955; Asst Sec., Union of Post Office Workers, 1964. Mem. Gen. Council of TUC, 1967. A Governor of BBC, 1968. *Recreations:* cooking, photography. *Address:* 50 Leahurst Court, Brighton 6. *T:* 507456.

**JACKSON, Sir Wilfrid Edward Francis,** GCMG 1943 (KCMG 1931; CMG 1919); Governor and Commander-in-Chief, Tanganyika Territory, 1941 to April 1945; *b* 1883; *e s* of late Sir Henry Moore Jackson, GCMG; *m* 1921, Isobel, *d* of late Humphrey Morgan, Donegal, Ireland, and *widow* of Capt. H. H. d'Estamps Vallancey, RFA. *Educ:* Stonyhurst Coll., Blackburn; Lincoln Coll., Oxford; BA. Personal Sec. to Governor of Trinidad, 1905-6;

Private Sec. to Governor and Clerk Executive Council, Bahamas, 1906-7; Asst Collector, Uganda, 1907; Acting District Commissioner, 1911; Acting Asst Chief Sec., 1912; First Asst Sec., 1912; Colonial Sec. and Registrar-General, Bermuda, 1916; Colonial Sec., Barbados, 1921; Mem. Legislative Council; Acting Governor Barbados, May-Oct. 1922, June-Sept. 1924, Aug. 1925-Jan. 1926; Colonial Sec., Trinidad, 1926-29; Acting Governor, Trinidad, April-Nov. 1927, and May-Aug. 1929; Colonial Sec., Gold Coast, 1929-30; Governor and Commander-in-Chief, Mauritius, 1930-37; British Guiana, 1937-41. *Address:* c/o Barclays Bank (DC & O), Capetown, South Africa. *Clubs:* Junior Carlton, East India and Sports.

**JACKSON, Lt-Gen. William Godfrey Fothergill,** OBE 1958; MC 1940, and Bar, 1943; GOC-in-C, Northern Comd, since 1970; *b* 28 Aug. 1917; *s* of late Col A. Jackson, RAMC, Yanwath, Cumberland, and of E. M. Jackson (*née* Fothergill), Brownber, Westmorland; *m* 1946, Joan Mary Buesden; one *s* one *d*. *Educ:* Shrewsbury; RMA, Woolwich; King's Coll., Cambridge, King's medal, RMA Woolwich, 1937. Commnd into Royal Engineers, 1937; served War of 1939-45: Norwegian Campaign, 1940; Tunisia, 1942-43; Sicily and Italy, 1943-44; Far East, 1945; GSO1, HQ Allied Land Forces SE Asia, 1945-48; Instructor, Staff Coll., Camberley, 1948-50; Instructor, RMA, Sandhurst, 1951-53; AA & QMG (War Plans), War Office, during Suez ops, 1956; Comdr, Gurkha Engrs, 1958-60; Col GS, Minley Div. of Staff Coll., Camberley, 1961-62; Dep. Dir of Staff Duties, War Office, 1962-64; Imp. Def. Coll., 1965; Dir, Chief of Defence Staff's Unison Planning Staff, 1966-68; Asst Chief of General Staff (Operational Requirements), MoD, 1968-70. *Publications:* Attack in the West, 1953; Seven Roads to Moscow, 1957; The Battle for Italy, 1967; Battle for Rome, 1969; Alexander of Tunis as a Commander, 1971; contribs to Royal United Service Instn Jl (gold medals for prize essays, 1950 and 1966). *Recreations:* fishing, writing, gardening. *Address:* c/o Glyn, Mills & Co., Holt's Branch, Whitehall, SW1. *Club:* Army and Navy.

**JACKSON, William Theodore,** CBE 1967 (MBE 1946); Director of Post Office Services, Ministry of Public Building and Works, 1969-71, retired; *b* 18 July 1906; *y s* of Rev. Oliver Miles Jackson and Emily Jackson; *m* 1932, Marjorie Campbell; one *s* two *d*. *Educ:* Cheltenham Gram. Sch. Chief Architect, Iraq Govt, 1936-38; Dir, Special Repair Service, Min. of Works, 1939-45; Min. of Public Building and Works, 1946-69; Dir, Mobile Labour Force; Dir of Maintenance; Regional Dir; Dir, Regional Services; Dir, Headquarters Services, 1967-69. *Recreation:* painting. *Address:* 2 Mertonford, Pages Croft, Wokingham, Berks. *T:* Wokingham 814.

**JACOB, Lt-Gen. Sir (Edward) Ian (Claud),** GBE 1960 (KBE 1946; CBE 1942); CB 1944; DL; late RE, Colonel, retired and Hon. Lieutenant-General; a Director, Electrical and Musical Industries, since 1960; Chairman, Matthews Holdings Ltd, since 1970; *b* 27 Sept. 1899; *s* of late Field Marshal Sir Claud Jacob, GCB, GCSI, KCMG; *m* 1924, Cecil Bisset Treherne; two *s*. *Educ:* Wellington Coll.; RMA, Woolwich; King's Coll., Cambridge (BA). 2nd Lieut, Royal Engineers, 1918; Capt. 1929; Bt Major, 1935; Major, 1938; Bt Lt-Col, 1939; Col, 1943. Waziristan, 1922-23. Staff Coll., 1931-32; GSO3 War Office, 1934-36; Bde-Maj., Canal Bde, Egypt, 1936-38; Military Asst Sec., Cttee of Imperial Defence, 1938; Military Asst Sec. to the War Cabinet, 1939-46; retired pay, 1946. Controller of European Services, BBC, 1946; Dir of Overseas Services, BBC, 1947 (on leave of absence during 1952); Chief Staff Officer to Minister of Defence and Deputy Sec. (Mil.) of the Cabinet during 1952; Dir-Gen. of the BBC, 1952-60; Dir, Fisons, 1960-70; Chm., Covent Garden Market Authority, 1961-66; a Trustee, Imperial War Museum, 1966-. CC, E Suffolk, 1960-; JP Suffolk, 1961-69; DL Suffolk, 1964. US Legion of Merit (Comdr). *Address:* The Red House, Woodbridge, Suffolk. *T:* Woodbridge 2001. *Club:* Army and Navy.

**JACOB, Ernest Fraser,** FBA 1946; FSA; FRHistS; MA; DPhil; Fellow and Librarian of All Souls College; *b* 12 Sept. 1894; *s* of late Professor Ernest Henry Jacob and Emma, *d* of late James Fraser, Leeds. *Educ:* Winchester; New College, Oxford. Stanhope Prize, 1920; Gladstone Prize, 1920; Lecturer in Medieval History, King's Coll., London, 1922-24; Lecturer in History and Student of Christ Church, Oxford, 1924-29; Prof. of Medieval History in the University of Manchester, 1929-44; Chichele Prof. of Modern History, Oxford, 1950-61. Prof. Emeritus, 1961. Membre Assesseur, Comité Internat. des Sciences historiques, 1960-; Creighton Lectr, 1951; Mem. of the Church Assembly, 1945-65; Church Comr, 1948-68; served on Archbishops' Commissions: Relations of Church and State, 1932-35; Canon Law, 1944-46; Church Courts, 1952-54; Crown Appointments, 1962-65; Birkbeck Lecturer in Ecclesiastical History, Trinity Coll., Cambridge, 1936-37; Mem. of Royal Commission on Historical Manuscripts; during 1914-18 served with 1st Battalion Hants Regt; Capt. 1917 (wounded twice, despatches). Senior Operations Officer, North West Region (Civil Defence), 1939-41. Hon. LittD Manchester, 1957. *Publications:* Illustrations to the Life of St Alban, 1924; Studies in the Period of Baronial Reform and Rebellion, 1925; (with C. G. Crump) The Legacy of the Middle Ages, 1926; Innocent III and Henry III of England, Cambridge Medieval History; trans of Bémont, Simon de Montfort, 1929; The Register of Archbishop Henry Chichele, 4 vols, 1938-47; Essays in the Conciliar Epoch, 1953; Henry V and the Invasion of France, 1947; (ed and contrib.), Italian Renaissance Studies, 1960; The Fifteenth Century, 1961; Archbishop Henry Chichele, 1967; Essays in Later Medieval History, 1968. *Address:* 205 Woodstock Road, Oxford. *Club:* Athenæum.

**JACOB, Prof. François;** Croix de la Libération; Commandeur de la Légion d'Honneur; Departmental Head, Pasteur Institute; Professor of Cellular Genetics, at the College of France, since 1964; *b* Nancy (Meurthe & Moselle), 17 June 1920; *m* 1947, Lysiane Bloch; three *s* one *d*. *Educ:* Lycée Carnot, France. D en M 1947; D ès S 1954. Pasteur Institute: Asst, 1950; Head of Laboratory, 1956. Charles Léopold Mayer Prize, Acad. des Sciences, Paris, 1962; Nobel Prize for Medicine, 1965. Foreign Member: Royal Danish Acad. of Letters and Sciences, 1962; Amer. Acad. of Arts and Sciences, 1964. Dr *hc* University of Chicago, 1965. *Publications:* various scientific. *Recreation:* painting. *Address:* 28 rue du Dr Roux, Paris 15, France.

**JACOB, Gordon (Percival Septimus),** CBE 1968; DMus; FRCM; Hon. RAM; Composer; Professor of Theory, Composition, and Orchestration, Royal College of Music, retired 1966; Editor of Penguin Musical Scores, 1947-57; *b* 5 July 1895; 7th *s* of late Stephen Jacob, CSI; *m* 1st, 1924, Sidney Wilmot (*d* 1958), *er d* of Rev. A. W. Gray, Ipswich; 2nd, 1959, Margaret Sidney Hannah, *d* of C. A. Gray, Helions Bumpstead; one *s* one *d. Educ:* Dulwich Coll.; Royal College of Music. Served European War, 1914-18; UPS and Queen's Royal West Surrey Regt (Prisoner of War in Germany, April 1917-Dec. 1918); Studied composition at the Royal College of Music under the late Sir Charles V. Stanford; Conducting under Adrian Boult, and Theory under Herbert Howells. Compositions include Orchestral, Choral and Chamber music, many concertos for various instruments, works for Military and Brass Bands, also orchestrations and arrangements. Holder of John Collard Fellowship (Worshipful Company of Musicians), 1943-46; Cobbett Medal for Services to Chamber Music, 1949. *Publications:* Orchestral Technique, a Manual for Students; How to Read a Score; The Composer and his Art; The Elements of Orchestration; most of the works alluded to above; also many other smaller compositions. Contributed to Chambers's Encyclopædia and Encyclopædia Britannica. *Recreations:* gardening, motoring, reading; interested in all forms of art, and in natural history. *Address:* 1 Audley Road, Saffron Walden, Essex. *T:* 2406.

**JACOB, Lieut-Gen. Sir Ian;** *see* Jacob, Lieut-Gen. Sir E. I. C.

**JACOB, Isaac Hai;** A Master of the Supreme Court, Queen's Bench Division, since 1957; Fellow of University College, London, 1966; *b* 5 June 1908; 3rd *s* of late Jacob Isaiah and Aziza Jacob; *m* 1940, Rose Mary Jenkins (*née* Samwell); two *s. Educ:* Shanghai Public Sch. for Boys; London Sch. of Economics; University Coll., London. LLB (1st class Hons), London; Joseph Hume Scholar in Jurisprudence, University Coll., London, 1928 and 1930; Arden Scholar, Gray's Inn, 1930; Cecil Peace Prizeman, 1930. Called to the Bar, Gray's Inn, Nov. 1930. Served in ranks from 1940 until commissioned in RAOC 1942; Staff Capt., War Office (Ord. I), 1943-45; Hon. Lectr in Law, University Coll., London, since 1959; Hon. Visiting Lecturer: Imperial Coll. of Science and Technology, 1963-64; Birmingham Univ., 1964-65; Bedford Coll., 1969-70; Member: Lord Chancellor's (Pearson) Cttee on Funds in Court, 1958-59; Working Party on the Revision of the Rules of the Supreme Court, 1960-65; (Payne) Cttee on Enforcement of Judgment Debts, 1965-69; (Winn) Cttee on Personal Injuries Litigation, 1966-68. Vice-President: Assoc. of Law Teachers; Industrial Law Soc.; Governor, Central London Polytechnic. Adv. Editor, Court Forms; Editor, Annual Practice, 1961-66; Gen. Editor, Supreme Court Practice, 1967-. *Publications:* Law relating to Hire Purchase, 1938; Chitty and Jacob's, Queen's Bench Forms (19th edn), 1965. *Recreations:* walking, painting. *Address:* 16 The Park, Golders Green, NW11. *T:* 01-458 3832. *Club:* Reform.

**JACOB, Rhoda Hannah,** MA Cantab; FRSA; *b* 5 June 1900; *y d* of late Ernest S. and late Lydia J. Brooksby Jacob. *Educ:* Dulwich High School; Sydenham High School, GPDST; Girton Coll., Cambridge (Classical Tripos). Teacher: Queenswood, Clapham Park, 1922-25; Richmond County Sch. for Girls, 1926; Kensington High School, 1926-35; Headmistress: Harrogate Coll., Yorks, 1935-52; Falmouth County High Sch., Cornwall, 1957-65. Archaeological Research Sec. to Sir Charles Walston, 1925; Triple Blue (hockey, netball, tennis); Hockey, County and Territorial (Surrey and South of England). *Recreations:* motoring, reading, archaeology. *Address:* Tregarth, 16 Spernen Wyn Road, Falmouth, Cornwall. *T:* Falmouth 313067.

**JACOB, Very Rev. William Ungoed;** Dean of Brecon Cathedral since 1967; Vicar of St Mary's, Brecon with Battle, since 1967; *b* 6 Oct. 1910; *s* of Wm and L. M. M. Jacob; *m* 1935, Ivy Matilda Hall; one *d. Educ:* Llanelly Gram. Sch.; Llandovery Coll.; Jesus Coll., Oxford; Wycliffe Hall, Oxford. BA 2nd cl. History, 1932; 2nd cl. Theology, 1933; MA 1937. Ordained deacon, 1934; priest, 1935; Curate of Holy Trinity, Aberystwyth, 1934-36; Lampeter, 1936-40; Vicar of Blaenau Ffestiniog 1940-51; Rector of Hubberston, 1951-55; Vicar of St Peter's, Carmarthen, 1955-67; Canon of St David's Cathedral, 1957-67. Rural Dean of Carmarthen, 1958-60; Archdeacon of Carmarthen, 1960-67. Hon. Joint Sec., Council of Churches for Wales, 1960-65. Mem., Coun. for Wales and Mon, 1963-66. Gen. Sec. Church in Wales Prov. Council for Mission and Unity, 1967. *Publications:* Meditations on the Seven Words, 1960; Three Hours' Devotions, 1965. *Recreation:* any form of manual work. *Address:* The Deanery, Brecon, S Wales. *T:* Brecon 3310.

**JACOBS, Brig. John Conrad S.;** *see* Saunders-Jacobs.

**JACOBS, Sir Roland (Ellis),** Kt 1963; Director (retired as Chairman), South Australian Brewing Co. Ltd; Chairman: Executive Trustee & Agency Co. of South Australia Ltd; Director, Mutual Hospital Association Ltd; *b* Adelaide, 28 Feb. 1891; *s* of late S. J. Jacobs, Adelaide; *m* 1917, Olga, *d* of late A. M. Hertzberg; one *s* two *d. Educ:* Geelong Coll., Vic. Past Pres., RSPCA; Pres., Post Graduate Foundation in Medicine; former Mem. Bd of Management: Royal Adelaide Hosp.; Queen Elizabeth Hosp.; Mem. Council: Adelaide Chamber of Commerce (Pres., 1942-43); Crippled Children's Assoc. of SA (past Pres.); Aust. Adv. Council for Physically Handicapped (past Pres.); Dir Mutual Hosp. Assoc. Ltd; President, Meals on Wheels Inc.; Mem., Nat. Council, Aust. Boy Scouts Assoc. *Recreation:* bowls. *Address:* 19 Elm Street, Unley Park, SA 5061, Australia. *Club:* Adelaide (Adelaide).

**JACOBS, Sir Wilfred (Ebenezer),** Kt 1967; OBE 1959; QC 1959; Governor, Antigua, since 1967; *b* 19 Oct. 1919; 2nd *s* of William Henry Jacobs and of late Henrietta Jacobs (*née* Du Bois); *m* 1947, Carmen Sylva, 2nd *d* of Walter A. Knight and late Flora Knight (*née* Fleming); one *s* two *d. Educ:* Grenada Boys' Secondary Sch.; Gray's Inn, London. Called to Bar, Gray's Inn, 1946; Registrar and Additional Magistrate, St Vincent, 1946; Magistrate, Dominica, 1947, and St Kitts, 1949; Crown Attorney, St Kitts, 1952; Attorney-Gen., Leeward Is, 1957-59, and Antigua, 1960. Acted Administrator, Dominica, St Kitts, Antigua, various periods, 1947-60. MEC and MLC, St Vincent, Dominica, St Kitts, Antigua, 1947-60; Legal Draftsman and Acting Solicitor-Gen., Trinidad and Tobago, 1960. Barbados: Solicitor-Gen., and Actg Attorney-Gen., 1961-63; PC and MLC, 1962-63; Dir of Public Prosecutions, 1964; Judge of Supreme Court of Judicature, 1967. KStJ. *Recreations:* swimming, gardening. *Address:* Governor's Residence, Antigua, West Indies. *Clubs:* Oxford and Cambridge University, West Indian (London).

**JACOBS-LARKCOM, Eric Herbert Larkcom,** CBE 1946; *b* 21 Jan. 1895; *s* of Herbert Jacobs, Barrister-at-law; (assumed additional surname of Larkcom by Royal Licence, 1915); *m* 1933, Dorothy Primrose Kerr Tasker; two *d. Educ:* University Coll. Sch. Entered Royal Engineers from RMA, Woolwich, 1916; served European

War, 1914-18, France, 1917-18 (wounded); Staff Coll., Camberley, 1930-31; served War of 1939-45, France 1939-40; China, 1942-45; Col, 1942; retired pay, 1946; i/c Harbin Consulate-Gen. (at Changchun), 1947-48; Consul-Gen. Kunming, 1948-49; Consul, Tamsui, Formosa, 1951-53; Consul, Chiengmai, 1954-58, retired. Mentioned in despatches, 1945, Chinese Cloud and Banner, 1945, American Bronze Star, 1946. *Address:* Curthelar, Trewithian, Portscatho, Cornwall. *Clubs:* United Service; Royal Cornwall Yacht.

**JACOBSEN, Prof. Arne;** Architect; *b* 11 Feb. 1902; *s* of Johan Jacobsen, Merchant, and Pauline (*née* Salmonsen); *m* 1943, Jonna Jacobsen (*née* Mæller); two *c*. *Educ:* The Royal Danish Academy. Has been responsible for many private and public buildings; villas, halls, banks, commercial structures, Royal Hotel, Copenhagen, St Catherine's Coll., Oxford. Central Bank of Denmark, project of Parliament Building Islamabad, Pakistan, etc. Exhibitions: RIBA, London, 1959; Stedelijk Museum, Amsterdam, 1959; Paris, 1961; Zürich, 1962; Hanover, 1962; Vienna, 1963; Dortmund, 1963; Glasgow, 1968. FAIA 1962. Member: Academie Serbe des Sciences et des Arts, Beograd; Akademie der Bildende Künste, Berlin. Hon. Corresp. Mem., RIBA, 1963, etc. Hon. DLitt Oxford, 1966; Hon. LLD Strathclyde, 1968. Awards: Gold Medal of Royal Danish Acad., 1928; Eckersberg Medal, 1936; Prize of Honour, Biennale, São Paulo, Brazil, 1954; C. F. Hansen Medal, 1956; Grand Prix, Architecture d'aujourd'hui, 1960; Akademisk Arkitektforening's Medal of Honour, 1962; The Prince Eugen Medal, Sweden, 1962; RIBA Bronze Medal, 1965. *Publications:* (*relevant*): Bogen om Arne Jacobsen, 1954, 1957 (by Johan Pedersen); Arne Jacobsen (by Tobias Faber), 1964; numerous contributions by writers to Arkitektens and to other learned jls, since 1928, both in Denmark and abroad. *Address:* Strandvej 413, Klampenborg, Denmark. *T:* OR 7010.

**JACOBSON, Sydney,** MC 1944; Editorial Director, International Publishing Corporation Newspapers, since 1968; *b* 26 Oct. 1908; *m* 1938, Phyllis June Buck; two *s* one *d*. *Educ:* Strand Sch., London; King's Coll., London. Asst Editor: Statesman, India, 1934-36; Lilliput Magazine, 1936-39. Served in Army, 1939-45. Special Correspondent, Picture Post, 1945-48; Editor, Leader Magazine, 1948-50; Political Editor, Daily Mirror, 1952-62; Editor, Daily Herald, 1962-64; Editor, Sun, 1964-65; Chairman, Odhams Newspapers, 1968. Member Press Council, 1969. *Recreations'* tennis, walking, reading. *Address:* 6 Avenue Road, St Albans, Herts. *T:* St Albans 53873.

**JACQUES,** family name of **Baron Jacques.**

**JACQUES,** Baron *cr* 1968 (Life Peer), of Portsea Island; **John Henry Jacques;** Chairman of the Co-operative Union Ltd, 1964-70; *b* 11 Jan. 1905; *s* of Thomas Dobson Jacques and Annie Bircham; *m* 1929, Constance White; two *s* one *d*. *Educ:* Victoria Univ., Manchester; Co-operative Coll. Sec-Man., Moorsley Co-operative Society Ltd, 1925-29; Tutor, Co-operative Coll., 1929-42; Accountant, Plymouth Co-operative Soc. Ltd, 1942-45; Chief Executive, Portsea Island Co-operative Soc. Ltd, Portsmouth, 1945-65. *Publications:* Book-Keeping I, II and III, 1940; Management Accounting, 1966; Manual on Co-operative Management, 1969. *Recreations:* walking, snooker, gardening, West-Highland terriers. *Address:* 23 Hilltop Crescent, Cosham, Portsmouth, Hants. *T:* Cosham 75511. *Club:* Co-operative (Portsmouth).

**JACQUOT, General d'Armée Pierre Elie;** Grand Cross of Legion of Honour, 1961; *b* 16 June 1902; *s* of Aimé Jacquot and Marie (*née* Renault); *m* 1929, Lucie Claire Mamet; one *d* (and one *s* killed in action, Algeria, 1962). *Educ:* Saint-Cyr Military Academy, France. Commissioned 30th Chasseur Bn, 1922; Foreign Legion Service, 1925-29; French École de Guerre, 1929-31, Belgian, 1931-33; Capt. 1933; posted to GHQ, Sept. 1939; Comdr 3rd Bn of 109th Inf. Regt, 1940; with André Malraux (alias Col Berger) organised French Resistance in the Corrèze, Dordogne and Lot areas, 1940-44; served in First French Army, 1944-45 (Alsace-Lorraine Bde); Brig.-Gen. 1946; Dep. Chief of Army Staff, 1947; Maj.-Gen. 1950; comd 8th Inf. Div., 1951-54; Lieut-Gen. 1954; High Comr and C-in-C, Indo-China, 1955-56; C-in-C French Forces in Germany, 1956-59; Gen. 1957; Inspector-Gen. of French Land Forces, 1959-61; Commander-in-Chief, Allied Forces Central Europe, 1961-63; Cadre de Réserve, Dec. 1963. *Publications:* Essai de stratégie occidentale, 1953; La Stratégie périphérique devant la bombe atomique, 1954. *Address:* (Winter) 15 Avenue de Villars, Paris 7; (Summer) Vrécourt, 88 Contrexéville, France.

**JAECKEL-BUMBRY, Grace;** Opera singer and Concert singer, as Grace Bumbry; *b* 4 Jan. 1937; *m* 1963, Andreas Jaeckel. *Educ:* Boston Univ.; Northwestern Univ.; Music Academy of the West (under Lotte Lehmann). Debut: Paris Opera, 1960; Vienna State Opera, 1963; Salzburg Festival, 1964; Metropolitan Opera, 1965; La Scala, 1966. Appearances also include: Bayreuth Festival, 1961, 1962, 1963; Royal Opera Covent Garden, London, 1963, 1968. Film, Carmen, 1968. Richard Wagner Medal, 1963. Hon. Dr of Humanities, St Louis Univ., 1968. Has made numerous recordings. *Recreations:* mountain climbing, tennis, sewing, flying, body building, psychology, entertaining. *Address:* Villa Arasio, Montagnola-Lugano, Switzerland.

**JAEGER, Prof. Leslie Gordon;** FRSE 1966; Professor of Civil Engineering, McGill University, since 1966; *b* 28 Jan. 1926; *s* of Henry Jaeger; *m* 1948, Annie Sylvia Dyson; two *d*. *Educ:* King George V Sch., Southport; Gonville and Caius Coll., Cambridge. Royal Corps of Naval Constructors, 1945-48; Industry, 1948-52; University College, Khartoum, 1952-56; Univ. Lectr, Cambridge, 1956-62; Fellow and Dir of Studies, Magdalene Coll., Cambridge, 1959-62; Prof. of Applied Mechanics, McGill Univ., Montreal, 1962-65. Regius Prof. of Engineering, Edinburgh Univ., 1965-66. *Publications:* The Analysis of Grid Frameworks and Related Structures (with A. W. Hendry), 1958; Elementary Theory of Elastic Plates, 1964; Cartesian Tensors in Engineering Science, 1965; various papers on grillage analysis in British, European and American Journals. *Recreations:* golf, curling, contract bridge. *Address:* Faculty of Engineering, McGill University, Montreal 2, Canada. *T:* 392-5971.

**JAFFRAY, Sir William Otho,** 5th Bt, *cr* 1892; *b* 1 Nov. 1951; *s* of Sir William Edmund Jaffray, 4th Bt, and of Anne, *o d* of late Capt. J. Otho Paget, MC, Thorpe Satchville Hall, Leics; *S* father, 1953. *Heir: uncle* Major Hugh Alexander Jaffray [*b* 9 Sept. 1896; *m* 1924, Ruth Eling, *o d* of Col B. E. Spragge, DSO]. *Address:* The Manor House, Priors Dean, Petersfield, Hants. *T:* Hawkley 226.

**JAGAN, Cheddi,** DDS; Guyanese Politician; Leader of Opposition in National Assembly, since 1964; *b* March 1918; *m* 1943; one *s* one *d*. *Educ:* Howard Univ.; YMCA Coll., Chicago (BSc); Northwestern Univ. (DDS). Member of Legislative Council, British Guiana, 1947-53; Minister of Agriculture, Lands and Mines, May-Oct. 1953; Minister of Trade and Industry, 1957-61; (first) Premier, British Guiana, and Minister of Development and Planning, 1961-64. *Publications:* Forbidden Freedom, 1954; Anatomy of Poverty, 1964; The West on Trial, 1966. *Recreations:* swimming, tennis. *Address:* Freedom House, 41 Robb Street, Georgetown, Guyana.

**JAHN, Gunnar;** Norwegian economist and statistician; Chairman Nobel Peace Prize Committee since 1942; *b* 10 Jan. 1883; *s* of Christian Fredrik Jahn and Elisabeth Wexelsen; *m* 1911, Martha Larsen; no *c*. *Educ:* University of Oslo (graduate in Law and in Political Economy); Universities of Berlin, Heidelberg and Paris. Sec. Central Bureau of Statistics, Oslo, 1910-17; Dir, Central Rationing Board, 1918-20; Dir Central Bureau of Statistics, 1920-45; Lectr in statistics, University of Oslo, 1913-20; Minister of Finance, Norway, 1934-35 and 1945; Gov., Bank of Norway, 1946-54. Chairman: Norwegian Jt Cttee of the Research Councils, 1954-60; Economic Assoc. of Norway, 1954-59; Norwegian Whaling Council, 1954-60; Cttee for International Whaling statistics; Member: Acad. of Science in Oslo, 1927-; Econometric Soc.; Statistical Cttee, League of Nations, 1928-30; Statistical Expert Cttee, ILO, 1936-40; UN Statistical Commn, 1946-50. Governor for Norway of Internat. Bank and Fund, 1946-54. Hon. Mem. Internat. Statistical Institute (Vice-Pres. 1947-51); Fellow Royal Statistical Soc., London, 1955-. *Publications:* Types of Houses in Rural Norway, 1920; Statistical Methods, 1937; How to make Trout Flies, 1938; The Longbow, 1938; Miscellany (articles and speeches), 1949; Bank of Norway during 150 years, Part I: 1816-1940. *Recreations:* trout fishing; archery, etc. *Address:* Husebyvegen 12, Smestad, pr Oslo, Norway. *T:* 55 83 30.

**JAHN, Prof. Hermann Arthur,** PhD; Professor of Applied Mathematics, University of Southampton, since 1949; *b* 31 May 1907; *s* of Friedrich Wilhelm Hermann Jahn and Marion May Curtiss; *m* 1943, Karoline Schuler; one *s* one *d*. *Educ:* City Sch., Lincoln; University Coll., London; University of Leipzig. BSc (London) 1928, MSc (London) 1935, PhD (Leipzig) 1935. Davy Faraday Research Laboratory, Royal Instn, London, 1935-41. RAE, Farnborough, 1941-46; University of Birmingham, 1946-48. *Publications:* scientific papers relating mainly to Group Theory and Quantum Mechanics. *Address:* 93 Highfield Lane, Southampton. *T:* Southampton 55039.

**JAKEWAY, Sir (Francis) Derek,** KCMG 1963 (CMG 1956); OBE 1948; Governor and Commander-in-Chief, Fiji, 1964-68; *b* 6 June 1915; *s* of Francis Edward and Adeline Jakeway; *m* 1941, Phyllis Lindsay Watson, CStJ; three *s*. *Educ:* Hele's Sch., Exeter; Exeter Coll., Oxford (BA Hons Mod. Hist.). Colonial Administrative Service, Nigeria, 1937-54, seconded to Seychelles, 1946-49, to Colonial Office, 1949-51; Chief Sec., British Guiana, 1954-59; Chief Sec., Sarawak, 1959-63. KStJ 1964. *Address:* Kingston House, Ebford, near Topsham, Devon.

**JAKOBOVITS, Rabbi Dr Immanuel;** Chief Rabbi of the United Hebrew Congregations of the British Commonwealth of Nations, since 1967; *b* 8 Feb. 1921; *s* of Rabbi Dr Julius Jakobovits and Paula (*née* Wreschner); *m* 1949, Amelia Munk; two *s* four *d*. *Educ:* London Univ. (BA; PhD 1955); Jews' Coll. and Yeshivah Etz Chaim, London. Diploma, 1944; Associate of Jews' Coll. Minister: Brondesbury Synagogue, 1941-44; SE London Synagogue, 1944-47; Great Synagogue, London, 1947-49; Chief Rabbi of Ireland, 1949-58; Rabbi of Fifth Avenue Synagogue, New York, 1958-67. *Publications:* Jewish Medical Ethics, 1959 (NY; 3rd edn 1967); Jewish Law Faces Modern Problems, 1965 (NY); Journal of a Rabbi, 1966 (NY), 1967 (GB); contrib. learned and popular jls in America, England and Israel. *Address:* Adler House, Tavistock Square, WC1. *T:* 01-387 1066.

**JAKOBSON, Prof. Roman;** Samuel Hazzard Cross Professor of Slavic Languages and Literatures and of General Linguistics, Harvard University, since 1949; Institute Professor Massachusetts Institute of Technology, since 1957; *b* Moscow, 11 Oct. 1896; *s* of Osip Jakobson, engineer, and Anna (*née* Wolpert); *m* 1962, Dr Krystyna Pomorska; no *c*. *Educ:* Lazarev Inst. of Oriental Languages, Moscow (AB); Moscow Univ. (AM); Prague Univ. (PhD). Research Assoc., Moscow Univ., 1918-20; Prof. Masaryk University (Brno), 1933-39; Vis. lectr at Univs of Copenhagen, Oslo, Uppsala, 1939-41; Professor: Ecole Libre des Hautes Etudes, New York, 1942-46; Columbia Univ., 1943-49. Hon. MA Harvard, 1949; Hon. doctorates in Letters and Philosophy: Cambridge, 1960; Chicago, 1961; Oslo, 1961; Uppsala, 1963; Mich., 1963; Grenoble, 1966; Nice, 1966; Rome, 1966; Yale, 1967; Prague, 1968; Brno, 1968; Zagreb, 1969; Ohio 1970; in Sciences: New Mexico, 1966; Clark, 1969. Award of Amer. Coun. of Learned Socs, 1960; Medal, Slovak Acad. of Sci., 1968. Mem. of six continental Academies; Hon. Mem. Association phonétique internationale, 1952, Finno-Ugric Soc., 1963, Acad. of Aphasia, 1969; Pres., Permanent Council for Phonetic Sciences, 1955-61; Linguistic Soc. of America, 1956. Vice-Pres., International Cttee of Slavicists, 1966-; Hon. Pres., Tokyo Inst. for Advanced Studies of Language. Chevalier, Légion d'Honneur, 1948. *Publications:* Remarques sur l'évolution phonologique du russe Comparée à celles des autres langues slaves, 1929; Characteristics of the Eurasian Linguistic Affinity (in Russian), 1931; Beitrag sur Allgemeinen Kasuslehre, 1936; Kindersprache, Aphasie und allgemeine Lautgesetze, 1941; (joint) La Geste du Prince Igor, 1948; (joint) Preliminaries to Speech Analysis, 1952; The Kernel of Comparative Slavic Literature, 1953; Studies in Comparative Slavic Metrics, 1952; (joint) Fundamentals of Language, 1956; Morphological Inquiry into Slavic Declension, 1958; Selected Writings, Vol. I (Phonological Studies), 1962; Vol. IV (Slavic Epic Studies), 1966; Vol. II (Word and Language), 1970. *Relevant Publication:* To Honor Roman Jakobson, 1968. *Address:* Boylston Hall, 301, Harvard University, Cambridge, Massachusetts 02138, USA. *T:* 8685619.

**JALLAND, Rev. Trevor Gervase,** DD Oxon, 1941; MA; Head of the Department of Theology, University of Exeter, 1957-62, retired; Lecturer in Theology since 1945, Senior Lecturer, 1956; Member of the Faculty of Theology, University of Oxford, 1944; *b* 14 Oct. 1896; *s* of George Herbert and Mary Mahalah Jalland; *m* 1944, Beatrice Mary, *er d* of late Prof. Alexander Hamilton Thompson, CBE, MA; one *s*. *Educ:* Oundle. Served European War, 1915-19; 2nd Lieut Leicester Yeo., 1916; Capt. acting, 1918; Magdalen

Coll., Oxford (Squire Scholar, Exhibitioner), 1919, 1st Class Theology. Deacon, 1922; Vice-Principal St Stephen's House, Oxford, 1922; Ellerton Prize Essay, 1922; Priest, 1923; Joint Junior Denyer Johnson Scholar, 1925; Asst Chaplain Exeter Coll., 1924; Prox. Acc. Senior Denyer Johnson Schol., 1925; Priest in charge St Luke's, Swindon, 1925-33; Surrogate, 1933; Vicar of St Thomas the Martyr, Oxford, 1933-45; Warden of the Society of Sacred Study, Diocese of Oxford, 1934-45. Bampton Lecturer for 1942; Proctor in Convocation, Dioc. Oxford, 1944-50; Fellow of the Corporation of SS Mary and Nicolas, 1948-50; Proctor in Convocation, Dio. Exeter, 1950-. *Publications:* This our Sacrifice, 1933; The Life and Times of St Leo the Great, 1941; The Church and the Papacy (Bampton Lectures), 1944; The Bible, the Church and South India, 1944; Origin and Evolution of the Christian Church, 1950. Various articles and reviews in Church publications; contributor, Catholic Sermons, 1931, The Office and Work of a Priest, 1937, The Priest as Student, 1939, and Thy Household the Church, 1943; The Apostolic Ministry, 1946. *Recreations:* French bulldogs, foreign bird keeping, motor boating. *Address:* 6a Cranford Avenue, Exmouth, Devon. *T:* Exmouth 5414.

**JAMAICA, Bishop of,** since 1968; **Rt. Rev. John Cyril Emerson Swaby,** CBE 1968; *b* St Andrew, 11 Dec. 1905. *Educ:* Munro Coll.; St Peter's Theological Coll., Jamaica. BA, MA, Univ. of Durham. Deacon and Priest, 1929; Curate, Brown's Town, 1929-32; Actg Rector, St Mary's, Highgate, Jamaica, 1932-38; Rector of St Matthew's, Kingston, Jamaica, 1938-57; Archdeacon of North Middlesex, Jamaica, and Archdeacon of South Middlesex, Jamaica, 1951. Member: Kingston School Board, 1938-57; Diocesan Council; St Peter's Theological College; Hon. Visiting Chaplain, Kingston Public Hosp., 1938-57; Rector of Mandeville Parish Church, 1957-61; Suffragan Bishop of Kingston, Jamaica, 1961-68. *Address:* c/o Church House, Cross Road, Kingston, Jamaica.

**JAMER, Herman Watson;** Agent-General for Atlantic Provinces of Nova Scotia, New Brunswick, Prince Edward Island and Newfoundland, 1958-68; *b* 18 May 1904; of Scottish-English parentage; *m* 1937, Marian Jeannette Dinwoodie; one *s*. *Educ:* Fredericton, New Brunswick, Canada. Ford Motor Company of Canada, 1934-58. Loaned to Ministry of Supply (Technical), 1943-45. District Manager Atlantic Provinces, Ford of Canada, 1948-58. Hon. LLD Mount Allison Univ., NB, 1958. *Recreations:* field and stream; metal and wood working. *Address:* St John West, New Brunswick, Canada. *T:* 1-506 672 2558.

**JAMES,** family name of **Baron James of Rusholme** and **Baron Northbourne.**

**JAMES OF RUSHOLME,** Baron *cr* 1959, of Fallowfield (Life Peer); **Eric John Francis James,** Kt 1956; Vice-Chancellor, University of York, since 1962; *b* 1909; *yr s* of F. W. James; *m* 1939, Cordelia, *d* of late Maj.-Gen. F. Wintour, CB, CBE; one *s*. *Educ:* Taunton's School, Southampton; Queen's Coll., Oxford (Exhibitioner and Hon. Scholar, 1927. Hon. Fellow, 1959). Goldsmiths' Exhibitioner, 1929; BA, BSc 1931; MA, DPhil 1933; Asst Master at Winchester Coll., 1933-45; High Master of Manchester Grammar Sch., 1945-62; Mem. of University Grants Cttee, 1949-59; Chm. of Headmasters' Conference, 1953-54; Mem. Central Advisory Council on Education, 1957-61; Mem. Standing Commission on Museums and Galleries, 1958-61; Chm., Cttee to Inquire into the Training of Teachers, 1970-. Hon. LLD: McGill, 1957; York, Toronto, 1970. Fellow, Winchester Coll., 1963-69. Member: Press Council, 1963-67; Social Science Research Council, 1965-68. *Publications:* (in part) Elements of Physical Chemistry; (in part) Science and Education; An Essay on the Content of Education; Education and Leadership; articles in scientific and educational journals. *Address:* The University, Heslington, York. *Club:* Athenæum.

**JAMES, Wing Comdr Sir Archibald (William Henry),** KBE 1945; MC; *b* 1893; *s* of late H. A. James, of Hurstmonceux Place, Sussex; *m* 1st, 1919, Bridget, *d* of late Murray Guthrie, MP, of Torosay Castle, Isle of Mull; one *s* one *d*; 2nd, 1940, Eugenia, *widow* of Patrick Stirling, younger, of Kippendavie; two *s*. *Educ:* Eton; Trinity Coll., Cambridge. 3rd Hussars and RAF, 1914-26. MP (U) Wellingborough Division of Northants, 1931-45. Parliamentary Private Sec. to R. A. Butler, India Office and Ministry of Labour, 1936-38; Board of Education, 1942; Hon. First Sec. British Embassy, Madrid, 1940-41. *Address:* Kintyre Estate, PO Norton, Rhodesia; Champions Farm, Thakeham, Sussex. *Clubs:* Boodle's, Pratt's.

*See also D. P. James.*

**JAMES, Rev. Canon Arthur Dyfrig,** MA; Vicar of Tilstone Fearnall, Cheshire, since 1956, and of Wettenhale, since 1969; Headmaster of Christ College, Brecon, 1931-56; Member of Governing Body of the Church in Wales, 1933-56; Hon. Chaplain to the Bishop of Swansea and Brecon, 1947-53; Canon of Hay in Brecon Cathedral, 1953-59, Hon. Canon, since 1959; *b* 24 May 1902; *s* of late Very Rev. H. L. James, DD; *m* 1936, Ann Pamela Mary, *d* of late J. S. Pincham; four *s*. *Educ:* Rossall; Jesus Coll., Oxford (Scholar), 1st Class Classical Moderations, 2nd Class Lit. Hum. Sixth Form Master, St Edward's Sch., Oxford, 1925-31; Select Preacher, Oxford, 1952-54; Chaplain to High Sheriff of Breconshire, 1944-45, 1946-47, 1949-51, 1955-57; Asst Inspector of Schools, Diocese of Chester, 1957; Exam. Chaplain to Bishop of Chester, 1958-68; Priest-in-charge of Wettenhall, 1958; part-time Lecturer in Classics, St David's Coll., Lampeter, 1961-62, 1966-68. *Address:* The Vicarage, Tilstone Fearnall, near Tarporley, Cheshire. *T:* Tarporley 449.

**JAMES, Hon. Sir Arthur (Evan),** Kt 1965; DL; **Hon. Mr Justice James;** a Judge of the High Court, Queen's Bench Division, since 1965; *b* 18 May 1816; *s* of John William and Ethel Mary James; *m* 1939, Eileen Brenda (*née* Mills); one *s* three *d*. *Educ:* Caterham Sch.; Jesus Coll., Oxford. BCL (Oxon.) 1939. Harmsworth Scholar, Middle Temple, 1939; Barstow Scholar, Council of Legal Education, 1939. Joined Midland Circuit, 1939. QC 1960; Recorder of Great Grimsby, 1961-63; Recorder of Derby, 1963-65; Dep. Chm., Warwicks Quarter Sessions, 1962-. Mem. Parole Board (Vice-Chm., 1970). DL Co. Warwick, 1967. *Recreation:* gardening. *Address:* Royal Courts of Justice, Strand, WC2.

**JAMES, (Arthur) Walter;** Special Adviser on Education to the Editor-in-Chief, Times Newspapers, since 1969; *b* 30 June 1912; *s* of late W. J. James, OBE; *m* 1st, 1939, Elisabeth (marr. diss. 1956), *e d* of Richard Rylands Howroyd; one *d*; 2nd, 1957, Ann Jocelyn, *y d* of late C. A. Leavy Burton; one adopted *s* two adopted *d*. *Educ:* Uckfield Gram. Sch.; Keble Coll., Oxford (Scholar); 1st Cl. Mod. Hist.; Liddon Student; Arnold Essay Prizeman.

Senior Demy of Magdalen Coll., 1935; Scholar in Mediæval Studies, British School at Rome, 1935; Editorial staff, Manchester Guardian, 1937-46. NFS 1939-45. Contested (L) Bury, Lancs, 1945. Dep. Editor, The Times Educational Supplement, 1947-51, Editor, 1952-69; also Editor, Technology, 1957-60. Member: BBC Gen. Advisory Council, 1956-64; Council of Industrial Design, 1961-66; Council, Royal Society of Arts, 1964; Cttee, British-American Associates, 1964; Governor, Central School of Art and Design, 1966. Woodard Lecturer, 1965. *Publications:* (Ed.) Temples and Faiths 1958; The Christian in Politics, 1962; The Teacher and his World, 1962; A Middle-class Parent's Guide to Education, 1964; (contrib.) Looking Forward to the Seventies, 1967. *Recreation:* golf. *Address:* 5 Norland Square, W11. *T:* 01-727 5065. *Club:* National Liberal.

**JAMES, Basil;** Special Commissioner of Income Tax since 1963; *b* 25 May 1918; *s* of late John Elwyn James, MA (Oxon.), Cardiff, and Mary Janet (*née* Lewis), Gwaelodygarth, Glam; *m* 1943, Moira Houlding Rayner, MA (Cantab.), *d* of late Capt. Benjamin Harold Rayner, North Staffs Regt, and Elizabeth (*née* Houlding), Preston, Lancs; one *s* twin *d. Educ:* Llandovery Coll.; Canton High Sch., Cardiff; Christ's Coll., Cambridge (Exhibnr). Tancred Law Student, Lincoln's Inn, 1936; Squire Law Scholar, Cambridge, 1936. BA 1939; MA 1942. Called to Bar, Lincoln's Inn, 1940. Continuous sea service as RNVR officer in small ships on anti-submarine and convoy duties in Atlantic, Arctic and Mediterranean, 1940-45. King George V Coronation Scholar, Lincoln's Inn, 1946. Practised at Chancery Bar, 1946-63. Mem. of South Wales and Chester Circuit. Admitted to Federal Supreme Court of Nigeria, 1962. *Publications:* contrib. to Atkin's Court Forms and Halsbury's Laws of England. *Recreations:* music, gardening. *Address:* The Mardle, Brockham Green, Betchworth, Surrey. *T:* Betchworth 3113. *Clubs:* RNVR; Bar Music; Bar Yacht.

**JAMES, Cecil;** *see* James, T. C. G.

**JAMES, Cynlais Morgan;** Counsellor and Consul-General, British Embassy, Saigon, since 1969; *b* 29 April 1926; *s* of Thomas James and Lydia Ann James (*née* Morgan); *m* 1953, Mary Teresa, *d* of R. D. Girouard and Lady Blanche Girouard; two *d. Educ:* Trinity Coll., Cambridge. Service in RAF, 1944-47. Cambridge 1948-51. Entered Senior Branch of Foreign Service, 1951; Foreign Office, 1951-53; Third Sec., Tokyo, 1953-56; Second Sec., Rio de Janeiro, 1956-59; First Sec. and Cultural Attaché, Moscow, 1959-62; FO, 1962-65; Paris, 1965-69; promoted Counsellor, 1968. *Recreation:* tennis. *Address:* Brtish Embassy, Saigon. *Club:* Brooks's.

**JAMES, David Pelham,** MBE 1944; DSC 1944; MP (C) North Dorset since 1970; Managing Director, Bow Holdings Ltd; *b* 25 Dec. 1919; *s* of Sir Archibald James, *qv*; *m* 1950, Hon. Jaquetta Digby, *y d* of 11th Baron Digby, KG, DSO, MC, TD; four *s* two *d. Educ:* Eton; Balliol. Served before the mast, Finnish 4-m. barque Viking, 1937-38; Balliol Coll., Oxford, 1938-39. Served War of 1939-45, RNVR, 1939-46; PoW 1943; escaped from Germany to Sweden, 1944. Mem. Antarctic Exped., 1945-46; Polar Adviser, Film Scott of the Antarctic, 1946-48. Joined Burns & Oates Ltd, Publishers, 1951. MP (C) Kemp Town Division of Brighton, 1959-64; Council Mem., Outward Bound Trust, 1948-; Trustee National Maritime Museum, 1953-65. Knight of Malta, 1962. *Publications:* A Prisoner's Progress, 1946; That Frozen Land, 1952; Scott of the Antarctic: The Film, 1950; The Life of Lord Roberts, 1954; (ed) Wavy Navy, 1948; (ed) Outward Bound, 1957; (ed) In Praise of Hunting, 1960. *Recreations:* hunting, stalking. *Address:* Malabar House, Child Okeford, Blandford, Dorset. *T:* Child Okeford 388. *Clubs:* Boodle's, Pratt's.

**JAMES, Air Vice-Marshal Edgar,** CBE 1966; DFC 1945; AFC 1948 (Bar 1959); Executive Director and General Manager, Flight Simulation, Redifon Ltd; *b* 19 Oct. 1915; *s* of Richard George James and Gertrude (*née* Barnes); *m* 1942, Josephine M. Steel; two *s. Educ:* Neath Grammar School. Joined RAF, 1939; commnd; flying instr duties, Canada, until 1944; opl service with Nos 305 and 107 Sqdns, 1944-45. Queen's Commendation for Valuable Service in the Air (1943, 1944, 1956). Empire Flying Sch. and Fighter Comd Ops Staff, until Staff Coll., 1950. Ops Requirements, Air Min., 1951-53; 2nd TAF Germany, 1953-56; comd No 68 Night Fighter Squadron, 1953; CFE, 1956-58; HQ Fighter Comd Staff, 1958-59; Chief Flying Instructor CFS, 1959-61; CO, RAF Leeming, 1961-62; Dir Ops Requirments 1, Min. of Def. (Air Force Dept), 1962-66; Comdr RAF Zambia, Feb.-Sept. 1966. Dep. Controller of Equipment, Min. of Aviation, then Min. of Technology, 1966-69. Wing Comdr 1953; Gp Capt. 1959; Air Cdre 1963; Air Vice-Marshal 1967. AFRAeS. *Recreations:* sailing, golf. *Address:* Overstrand, Riverside Road, Newton Ferrers, Devon. *T:* Newton Ferrers 685; F3 Sloane Avenue Mansions, Sloane Avenue, SW3. *T:* 01-589 6713. *Clubs:* United Service, Royal Air Force.

**JAMES, Edward,** JP Glamorgan; Barrister and Parliamentary Journalist; *b* 20 June 1885; *yr s* of late Thomas James, JP, of Porthcawl, Glam, and Rhoda, *d* of Thomas Evans, of Neath. *Educ:* Porthcawl; Bridgend County Sch. Called to the Bar at Lincoln's Inn, 1922. Began career as a journalist on the Glamorgan Gazette, Bridgend, and afterwards served on editorial staff of Cardiff Western Mail; London Editor of that paper 1914-59, and Chief of Parliamentary Staff 1914-59 (retired); Chm. of the Lobby Journalists of Parliament, 1924-25; Vice-Chm., 1922-23; Chm. of Press Gallery and Cttee Member for twelve years; Chm. Newspaper Conference, 1947 and 1948, Vice-Chm. 1940-47; Vice-Pres. and Council Mem. of the Honourable Society of Cymmrodorion and other Welsh societies; Executive Cttee of Welsh National Eisteddfod for many years; initiated as Bard of Gorsedd of Wales with the title of Ap Baglan, 1935. Jt Organiser, POW Service, Westminster Abbey, 1918; jt sec., Regtl Cttee of London Welsh Anti-Aircraft Regt formed 1939; Mem. of Holborn Borough Council, 1935-65; Alderman, 1945-65; Chm. of Libraries Cttee, 1939-41; again (Vice-Chm.), 1961-62; Member: Law and Parliamentary Cttee, 1943-45; Vice-Chm. 1959, Chm., 1963, Finance Cttee, 1953-65; Chm. Rating and Valuation Cttee, 1949-65; Rating and other Local Govt. Cttees of Assoc. of Municipal Corporations, 1963-. JP Glamorgan, 1936-; FJI; Holborn Soc.; Executive, Holborn Conservative Assoc.; Clwb y Cymry; Liveryman, Stationers' and Newspaper Makers' Soc., Freeman of City of London; Mem. (and London Rep.), Lloyd George Statue Cttee; Empire Games Reception Cttee, 1958. British Legal Party to Canada and USA, 1930; Bronze Medallist of Royal Humane Society. Past Master Kentish Lodge 3021; Past Assistant Grand Dir of Ceremonies. *Publications:* Stirring Deeds in France and Flanders; political essays. *Recreations:* motoring and play-going. *Address:*

Heathlands, Porthcawl, Glamorgan. *T:* Porthcawl 2034; 34 Harlyn Drive, Pinner, Middx. *T:* 01-866 4614.

**JAMES, Edward Foster,** CMG 1968; OBE 1946; HM Diplomatic (formerly Foreign) Service; *b* 18 Jan. 1917; *s* of late Arthur Foster James; *m* 1951, Caroline Warwick Bampfylde, *d* of Hon. Francis Warwick Bampfylde; one *s* two *d*. *Educ:* Chiswick Grammar Sch. Served HM Forces, 1939-46, India, Burma, Malaya, Indonesia; Lieut-Colonel (GSO1) (OBE, despatches twice). Foreign Office, 1947; Rangoon, 1948; Hong Kong, 1951; Foreign Office, 1953; Rome, 1955; Foreign Office, 1958; Berlin, 1960. *Recreations:* gardening, antique collecting. *Address:* Springfield House, West Clandon, Surrey.

**JAMES, Rev. Edwin Oliver,** MA, DLitt (Oxon), PhD (London); Hon. DD St Andrews; FSA; Chaplain, All Souls College, Oxford, since 1960; University Professor of the History and Philosophy of Religion, University of London, 1948-55 (Professor of the Philosophy of Religion in the University of London (King's College), 1945-48); Professor Emeritus, 1955; Fellow of University College, London, 1946; Fellow of King's College, London, 1950; Wilde Lecturer in Natural and Comparative Religion, Oxford University, 1939-42; Examining Chaplain to the Bishop of Wakefield since 1938; Editor of Folklore since 1932; Forwood Lecturer in Philosophy of Religion, University of Liverpool, 1949-50; Visiting Lecturer, University of Amsterdam, 1949; Marburg, 1960; Jordan Bequest Lecturer, 1961; *b* 30 March 1888; *s* of late William and Sophia Mary James; *m* 1911, Clarese Augusta Copeland, LLD; one *s*. *Educ:* University College Sch.; Exeter Coll., Oxford; University College, London. Diploma in Anthropology, University of Oxford; Curate, St Mark's, Low Moor, 1911-13; Curate-in-charge, St Peter's, Hucknall Torkard, 1913-14; Rector of Alvescot and Vicar of Shilton, Oxon, 1914-17; Vicar of St Peter's, Limehouse, 1917-21; Holy Trinity, Reading, 1921-23; St Thomas's, Oxford, 1923-33; Lecturer and Tutor in Anthropology in University of Cambridge, 1928-33; Professor of History and Philosophy of Religion, University of Leeds, 1933-45; Visiting Lecturer in History of Religion, University College of North Wales, 1942, 1943; Examiner in Comparative Religion, University of Durham, 1931-37; Universities of Manchester, London and Sheffield, 1935, Oxford, 1936, 1938, 1939, 1944, 1949, 1952, 1955, 1957, 1958, 1959, 1962, 1963, 1965-67; London (Theol.), 1942-45, 1952 (MTh), since 1947; Wales, 1949-52; TCD, 1960; Manchester, 1953, 1962-64, 1969; Bristol, 1961-63; President: Folklore Society, 1930-32 (Research Medal, 1962); Yorkshire Society for Celtic Studies, 1943-44; Anthropoloical Sect., British Assoc. for the Advancement of Science,, 1952, Member of Council, 1957-62. *Publications:* Primitive Ritual and Belief, 1917; Introduction to Anthropology, 1919; The Stone Age, 1927; The Beginnings of Man, 1928; The Christian Faith in the Modern World, 1930; Origins of Sacrifice, 1933; Christian Myth and Ritual, 1933 (2nd edn 1965); Old Testament in light of Anthropology, 1935; In the Fulness of Time, 1935; Origins of Religion, 1937; Introduction to comparative study of Religion, 1938 (new edn, 1961); The Social Function of Religion, 1940, 2nd edn, 1948 (French translation, 1950); Christianity in England, 1948; The Beginnings of Religion, 1948, 1958 (Spanish translation, 1955; Italian translation, 1968); The Concept of Deity, 1950; Marriage and Society, 1952 (2nd edn 1965); The Nature and Function of Priesthood, 1955 (German translation, 1956); The History of Religions, 1956 (2nd edn 1965); Prehistoric Religion, 1957 (trans. various languages); Myth and Ritual in the Ancient Near East, 1958 (German translation, 1959); French and Italian translations, 1960); The Cult of the Mother goddess, 1959 (French translation, 1959, German translation, 1962); The Ancient Gods, 1959 (French, Italian, German, Polish Spanish, Portuguese translations); Seasonal Feasts and Festivals, 1961 (French translation); Sacrifice and Sacrament, 1962; The Worship of the Sky-god, 1963; Sanctuaries, Shrines and Temples, 1964 (Spanish translation); The Tree of Life, 1966; Christianity and Other Religions, 1967; Creation and Cosmology, 1969. Contributions to Encyclopædia of Religion and Ethics, Dictionary of National Biography, Chambers's Encyclopædia, Encyclopædia Britannica, and scientific and theological journals. *Recreations:* foreign travel, golf. *Address:* Hidsfield House, Cumnor Hill, Oxford. *T:* Cumnor 2040; All Souls College, Oxford. *Club:* Athenæum.

**JAMES, Evan Maitland;** Steward of Christ Church, Oxford, since Oct. 1963 (Acting Steward, 1962-63); *b* 14 Jan. 1911; *er s* of late A. G. James, CBE, and late Helen James (*née* Maitland); *m* 1939, Joan Goodnow, *d* of late Hon. J. V. A. MacMurray, Norfolk, Conn., USA; one *s* two *d*. *Educ:* Durnford; Eton (Oppidan Scholar); Trinity Coll., Oxford. Qualified as Solicitor, 1937. Served War of 1939-45: Ordinary Seaman, 1941; Lieut, RNVR, 1942-46; Clerk of the Merchant Taylors' Company, 1948-62. *Address:* Upwood Park, Abingdon, Berks. *T:* Frilford Heath 253. *Club:* Travellers'.

**JAMES, F(rank) Cyril;** Chevalier de la Légion d'Honneur, 1948; Principal and Vice-Chancellor, McGill University, Canada, 1939-62, Principal Emeritus since 1962; President of the International Association of Universities, 1960-65 (Hon. President since 1965) (Member Executive Board, 1955-); *b* 8 Oct. 1903; *s* of Frank James and Mary Lucy Brown; *m* 1926, Irene L. V. Leeper; (one *d* decd). *Educ:* Oldfield Road Sch.; Hackney Downs Sch., London; LSE, Univ. of London (BCom, 1923); Univ. of Pennsylvania (AM, 1924, PhD, 1926). Has been awarded Hon. Degrees by Universities and Colleges in Europe, Asia, USA and Canada. FRSC 1948. Guggenheim Honour Cup, University of Pennsylvania, 1941. B'nai Brith Humanitarian Award, 1952. Hon. Fellow, London Sch. of Economics, 1960. Clerk in Barclays Bank, London, 1921-23; Instructor in Finance and Transportation, University of Pennsylvania, 1924-27; Asst Professor of Finance, 1927-38, Associate Professor, 1933-35, Professor, 1935-39; Chairman, Grad. Faculty in Social Science, 1936-37; Professor of Finance and Economic History, 1938-39; Professor of Political Economy, McGill Univ., 1939-62; Economist, First Nat. Bank, Chicago, 1937-38; Member: of Council of Education of Province of Quebec, 1940-63; of Exec. Cttee of National Conference of Canadian Universities, 1940-52 (Vice-Pres. 1946-48, Pres. 1948-50); of Executive Council of Assoc. of Universities of British Commonwealth, 1948-51, 1959-62 (Chairman, 1949); of Board of Directors of Canadian University Foundation (Vice-Chairman) 1959-62; Commonwealth Consultant, Inter-University Council, London, 1961-64; of Sub-Cttee on Demobilisation and Rehabilitation, Ottawa, 1940-42; Chairman, Advisory Cttee on Reconstruction, Dominion of Canada, 1941-44; Member University Advisory Board Dept of Veterans Affairs, Ottawa, 1945-50; Vice-

Chairman Counseil d'Orientation Economique, Quebec, 1961-; Chairman of Advisory Board, Lady Davis Foundation, 1947-50; Member Fellowship Cttee, Beaver Club Trust, 1948-50; Trustee, Mackenzie-King Scholarships Foundation, since 1950; Chairman, Joint Hospital Cttee, Montreal, 1942-52; Governor Royal Victoria Hospital, 1940-62; Montreal General Hospital, 1942-62; Montreal Children's Hospital, 1946-60; Hon. President Polish Institute of Arts and Sciences (Canada), 1942-63; Director American Academy of Political and Social Science since 1937, Vice-Pres. since 1952; Pres. World University Service of Canada, 1957-59; Member Board of Directors, The Pulp and Paper Research Inst. of Canada, 1948-62; Montreal City and District Savings Bank, 1953-; Bellairs Research Institute and Bellairs Investment Trust, Barbados, 1955-. Member Exec. Cttee, Oxfam, 1965-, and Hon. Secretary, 1966-. Member: Bd of Govs, Birkbeck Coll., 1967-; Standing Conf. of British Organisations for Aid to Refugees, 1968-; Victor Gollancz Memorial Trust, 1968. Member Canadian Inst. International Affairs; and many economical and historical societies; Phi Beta Kappa. *Publications:* Cyclical Fluctuations in the Shipping and Shipbuilding Industries, 1927; The Economics of Money, Credit and Banking, 1930, 3rd ed., 1940; England Today, A Survey of Her Economic Situation, 1931; The Road to Revival, 1932; The Meaning of Money (with others), 1935; The Economic Doctrines of J. M. Keynes (with others), 1938; The Growth of Chicago Banks, 2 vols, 1938; Economic Problems in a Changing World (with others), 1939; On Understanding Russia, 1959; Formal Programmes of International Co-operation between Universities (with others), 1960; University Autonomy, its Meaning To-day (with others), 1965. *Recreations:* motoring, reading, photography. *Address:* McGill University, Montreal, 2. *TA:* McGill University, Montreal; Univasoc, Paris; Pipers Croft, Devonshire Avenue, Amersham, Bucks. *Clubs:* Athenæum; University, McGill Faculty, Grenadier Guards (Montreal).

**JAMES, Sir Frederick Ernest,** Kt 1941; OBE 1919; Chevalier de l'ordre de Léopold I, 1919; Director, Tata Ltd, London; *b* 1891; *s* of late Rev. G. H. James, Letchworth; *m* 1919, Eleanor May Thackrah, CBE 1945; no *c.* Served European War, 1915-19: General Secretary YMCA, Calcutta, 1920-28; Member Bengal Legislative Council, 1924-28; Political Adviser to United Planters Association and British Commercial Interests in South India, 1929-41; Member Madras Legislative Council and Madras Corporation, 1929-32; Member Indian Central Legislature, 1932-45; Director Board International Rotary, 1934-35; Chairman Commission Rotary International Administration, 1936-37; Representative in New Delhi of Tata Industrial Group, 1941-46; Member Indian Health Survey and Development Cttee, 1944-46; Deputy Chairman and Managing Director, Tata Ltd, London, 1947-62. Member, University College Cttee, 1948- (Treasurer, 1952-62, Vice-Chairman, 1955-62, Hon. Fellow, 1957); President, Westminster Chamber of Commerce, 1959-62 (Chairman, 1953-59); Director Commonwealth Trust; Chairman Finance Cttee Chelsea and Kensington Hospital Group. Contested (L) Sudbury and Woodbridge Parliamentary Division, 1950. *Address:* Yafford, Shorwell, Isle of Wight.

**JAMES, Prof. Ioan Mackenzie,** FRS 1968; MA, DPhil; Savilian Professor of Geometry, Oxford University, since 1970; Fellow of New College, Oxford, since 1970; Editor, Topology, since 1962; *b* 23 May 1928; *o s* of Reginald Douglas and Jessie Agnes James; *m* 1961, Rosemary Gordon Stewart, Fellow of Oxford Centre for Management Studies; no *c.* *Educ:* St Paul's Sch. (Foundn Schol.); Queen's Coll., Oxford (Open Schol.). Commonwealth Fund Fellow, Princeton, Berkeley and Inst. for Advanced Study, 1954-55; Tapp Res. Fellow, Gonville and Caius Coll., Cambridge, 1956; Reader in Pure Mathematics, Oxford, 1957-69, and Senior Research Fellow, St John's Coll., 1959-69. Treasurer, London Math. Soc. 1970-. Gov., St Paul's Schs, 1970-. *Publications:* (ed) The Mathematical Works of J. H. C. Whitehead, 1963; sundry papers in mathematical jls. *Address:* Mathematical Institute, St Giles, Oxford. *T:* Oxford 54295.

**JAMES, Sir Jack;** *see* James, Sir John H.

**JAMES, John Angell,** CBE 1967; MD, FRCP, FRCS; Hon. Consulting Surgeon in Otolaryngology, United Bristol Hospitals, since 1966; President, British Association of Otolaryngologists, 1966; *b* 23 Aug. 1901; *s* of Dr John Angell James, MRCS, LRCP and Emily Cormell (*née* Ashwin), Bristol; *m* 1930, Evelyn Miriam Everard, *d* of Francis Over and Ada Miriam Everard, Birmingham; one *s* two *d.* *Educ:* Bristol Grammar Sch.; University of Bristol; London Hosp.; Guy's Hosp. MB ChB 1st Cl. Hons 1924, Bristol; MBBS London (Hons) 1924; MD 1927; FRCS 1928; FRCP 1965. Res. appts, 1924-28, Bristol and London; Hon. ENT Registrar, Bristol Royal Infirmary, 1928-29; Hon. ENT Surg., Bristol Children's Hosp., 1928-48; Cons ENT Surg., 1948-66; Hon. Asst ENT Surg., later Hon. ENT Surg., Bristol Royal Infirmary, 1929-48; Clin. Tutor, University of Bristol, 1928-55; Lectr and Head of Dept of Otolaryngology, 1955-66; Cons. ENT Surg., United Bristol Hosps, 1948-66. Lt-Col RAMC, 1942-46; Adviser in Otorhinolaryngol., MEF, 1945. Hunterian Prof., RCS Eng. 1962; Semon Lectr in Laryngol., University of London, 1965; James Yearsley Lectr, 1966; Vis. Lectr, Universities of Toronto, Vermont, Cornell, Baylor and Chicago; FRSocMed (Pres. Sect. of Laryngol., 1955); Member: SW Laryngolog. Assoc. (Chm. 1956); Brit. Medical Assoc. (Pres. Sect. of Otolaryngol., 1959. Chm. Bristol Div., 1966-67); Bristol Med.-Chirurg. Soc. (Pres. 1961); Visiting Assoc. of ENT Surgs of G. Brit., 1948 (Pres. 1965-66); Brit. Assoc. of Otolaryngologists, 1942 (Pres. 1966-67); Collegium Oto-Rhino-Laryngologicum Amicitae Sacrum, 1948 (Councillor, 1966-67); Barany Soc. Extern. Examr, University of Manchester, 1964. Jobson Horne Prize, BMA, 1962; Colles Medal, RCSI, 1963; Dalby Prize, RSM, 1963; Sir William Wilde Mem. Lectr Irish Otolaryngol. Soc., 1966; W. J. Harrison Prize in Laryngology, RSM, 1968; Hon. Member: Irish Otolaryngol. Soc.; S Africa Soc. of Otolaryngology. *Publications:* Chapters in: British Surgical Practice, 1951; Diseases of the Ear, Nose and Throat, 1952 (2nd edn 1966); Ultrasound as a diagnostic and surgical tool, 1964; Clinical Surgery, 1966; Ménière's Disease, 1969; articles in learned jls in Eng., USA, Canada and Sweden. *Recreations:* farming (breeding pedigree Guernsey cattle), hunting, sailing, gardening and tennis. *Address:* Sundayshill House, Falfield, near Wotton-under-Edge, Glos; (Consulting rooms) Litfield House, Clifton Down, Bristol 8. *T:* Bristol 33483.

*See also Brig. M. A. James.*

**JAMES, Sir John Hastings, (Sir Jack),** KCVO 1970; CB 1953; Deputy Master and Comptroller of the Royal Mint, and *ex officio* Engraver of HM's Seals, 1957-70; *b* 4 June 1906; *s* of late C. F. James; *m* 1st, 1935, Lady

Ann Florence Cole (marr. diss., 1950), *e d* of 5th Earl of Enniskillen; one *s*; 2nd, 1963, Lady Maryoth, *d* of late Lord Edward Hay, and *widow* of Sir Gifford Fox. *Educ:* Gresham's Sch., Holt; Merton Coll., Oxford. Entered Admiralty, 1929; Imperial Defence Coll., 1938; Under Sec., Admiralty 1948-57; CStJ. *Recreations:* shooting, fishing. *Address:* 221 Cranmer Court, SW3. *T:* 01-589 3845. *Club:* Turf.

**JAMES, Prof. John Ivor Pulsford,** MB, MS London; FRCS; FRCSE; George Harrison Law Professor of Orthopædic Surgery, Edinburgh University, since 1958; Consultant in Orthopædic Surgery to the Navy since 1956; *b* 19 Oct. 1913; *s* of late Stanley B. James and Jessica Heley; *m* 1968, Margaret Eiriol Samuel, MB, ChB; one *s* one *d*. *Educ:* Eggars Grammar Sch., Alton, Hants; University Coll. and Hosp., London, Hampshire County Schol., 1932-38; Ferrière Schol., University Coll., 1935; Goldsmid Schol., University Coll. Hosp., 1935; Magrath Schol., University Coll. Hosp., 1937; Rockefeller Fellowship, 1947-48; Consultant Orthopædic Surgeon, Royal National Orthopædic Hospital, 1946-58; Asst Dir of Studies, Institute of Orthopædics, University of London, 1948-58. Fellow Univ. Coll., London. Hunterian Prof., RCS, 1957; Fellow, British Orthopædic Assoc.; Hon. Mem. Société Française d'Orthopédie et de Traumatologie; Mem. Société Internationale de Chirurgie et de Traumatologie; Corresp. Fellow: Amer. Orthopædic Assoc.; Austr. Orthopædic Assoc.; Hon. Member: Amer. Acad. of Orthopædic Surgeons; Dutch Orthopædic Soc.; Assoc. for Orthopædic Surgery and Traumatology of Jugoslavia; Canadian Orthopædic Assoc. Hon. Fellow, New Zealand Association. Late Temp. Lieut-Col RAMC. Golden Star, Order of Service to the Jugoslav People, 1970. *Publications:* Scoliosis, 1967; articles relating to curvature of the spine and surgery of the hand in medical journals, etc. *Recreations:* sailing and fishing. *Address:* The Princess Margaret Rose Orthopædic Hospital, Fairmilehead, Edinburgh; 2 Regent Terrace, Edinburgh 7.

**JAMES, Rt. Hon. Sir (John) Morrice (Cairns),** PC 1968; KCMG 1962 (CMG 1957); CVO 1961; MBE 1944; British High Commissioner in India, since 1968; *b* 30 April 1916; *s* of late Lewis Cairns James and Catherine, *d* of John Maitland Marshall; *m* 1st, 1948, Elizabeth Margaret Roper Piesse (*d* 1966); one *s* two *d*; 2nd, 1968, Mme Geneviève Sarasin. *Educ:* Bradfield; Balliol Coll., Oxford. Dominions Office, 1939; served Royal Navy and Royal Marines, 1940-45; released as Lieut-Col. Asst Sec., Office of UK High Comr in S Africa, 1946-47; Head of Defence Dept, Commonwealth Relations Office, 1949-51, and of Establishment Dept, 1951-52; Dep. High Comr for the UK, Lahore, 1952-53; attended Imperial Defence Coll., 1954; Dep. High Comr for UK in Pakistan, 1955-56; Asst Under-Sec. of State, Commonwealth Relations Office, 1957. Dep. High Comr for UK in India, 1958-61; British High Commissioner in Pakistan, 1961-66; Dep. Under Sec. of State, CO, 1966-68; Permanent Under-Sec. of State, CO, March-Oct. 1968. *Recreations:* photography, walking and swimming in remote places. *Address:* 2 King George's Avenue, New Delhi, India.

**JAMES, John Richings,** CB 1966; OBE 1956; Professor of Town and Regional Planning, University of Sheffield, since Oct. 1967; *b* 27 Oct. 1912; 2nd *s* of late Henry James, Crook, County Durham, and Florence James; *m* 1946, Elizabeth Emily Frances, 2nd *d* of Dr A. E. Morgan, *qv*; five *d*. *Educ:* Wolsingham Grammar Sch.; King's Coll., London (BA); Inst. of Education. Schoolmaster, 1937-40; Naval Intelligence, 1940-45. Research Officer (Newcastle Regional Office), Min. of Town and Country Planning, 1946-49; Sen. Research Officer (London), Min. of Housing and Local Govt, 1949-58; Dep. Chief Planner, MHLG, 1958-61; Chief Planner, 1961-67. UK Rep. on UN Cttee for Housing, Building and Planning, 1967-; Mem. Panel, Greater London Develt Plan Inquiry, 1970-. *Publications:* Greece (3 vols), 1943-45. Contrib. to Chambers's Encyclopædia (Greece and Greek Towns and Islands). Articles on Land Use: Royal Society of Arts Jl, Royal Geog. Society Jl, etc. *Recreations:* gardening, sports. *Address:* The University, Sheffield 10. *Club:* Athenæum.

**JAMES, Dr John (William),** CB 1970; Deputy Chief Medical Adviser, Department of Health and Social Security, since 1968; *b* 23 March 1907; *s* of Thomas and Sarah James (*née* Sherman); *m* 1st, Dr Margaret Helen Morton (*d* 1953); 2nd, 1955, Jean Bruce Morton, 5th *d* of Dr John Leyden Morton. *Educ:* University Coll. and University Coll. Hosp. Med. School. MRCS, LRCP 1933. Hosp. appts, 1933-40, at: University Coll. Hosp.; Bolingbroke Hosp.; Queen Mary's Hosp., Roehampton; Chapel Allerton Hosp., Leeds; Comr of Med. Services, Min. of Pensions, Northern Region, 1941-53; Sen. Med. Off., Min. of Pensions and Nat. Insce, 1953-62; Princ. Med. Off., 1962-65; Dep. CMO, Min. of Social Security, 1965-68. *Publications:* articles on aspects of medical evidence. *Recreations:* gardening, music, theatre. *Adddress:* Hobarts, Blickling, Norfolk NOR 09Y. *Club:* Oxford and Cambridge University.

**JAMES, John Wynford George,** OBE 1950; FRAeS 1963; MInstT 1954; Member of Board, BEA, since 1964; Operations Director, BEA; *b* 13 Feb. 1911; *s* of William George and Elizabeth James; *m* 1934, Bertha Margaret Joyce Everard; one *s* two *d*. *Educ:* Royal Grammar School, Worcester. Joined Imperial Airways as a pilot, 1933; Capt., Imperial Airways/BOAC, 1935-46; BEA Chief Pilot, 1946. Chm. BALPA, 1943-48; Mem. Board: International Aeradio Ltd, 1956-; College of Air Training; BEA Helicopters Ltd, 1964- (Chm. 1966-); International Helicopters Ltd, 1965-. Governor, College of Air Training, 1959- (Chm. 1959-61, 1963-66, 1968-70). Liveryman, GAPAN, 1960. *Recreations:* golf, gardening, fishing. *Address:* Wynsfield, Mill Lane, Gerrards Cross, Bucks. *T:* Gerrards Cross 4038; Bealine House, Ruislip, Middx. *T:* 01-845 1234. *Club:* Royal Aero.

**JAMES, Brig. Manley Angell,** VC 1918; DSO 1943; MBE 1958; MC; late Gloucestershire Regiment and Royal Sussex Regiment; *b* Odiham, Hants, 12 July 1896; *s* of Dr John Angell and Emily Cormell James; *m* 1928, Noreen Cooper, Bristol; one *s*. *Educ:* Bristol Grammar Sch. Temp. 2nd Lieut Glos. Regt 1914; served in France and Belgium with 8th Glos. Regt, 1915-18 (wounded three times, prisoner of war, despatches, MC, VC, 1915 Star, British War Medal, Victory Medal); Col, 1941; War of 1939-45 (wounded, Africa Star, 1939-45 Star, Italy Star, Defence Medal, 1939-45 war medal); GSO1 54 Div. March-July 1940; BGS 8 Corps. 1940-41; Comd 128 Inf. Bde, 1941-43; Brig. Inf. Middle East, 1943-44; BGS (Trg) Home Forces, 1944-45; Cmd 140 Inf. Bde, July-Oct. 1945; CRO Air HQ BAFO (Germany), 1945-48; Dir of Ground Defence, Air Ministry, 1948-51; retired from army, 1951. Works Defence Officer, Bristol Aeroplane Co. Ltd, 1951-61. psc. DL, Glos., 1957. AFICD. *Recreations:* golf, fishing, cricket, shooting, gardening. *Address:*

Strathmore, Passage Road, Westbury-on-Trym, Bristol. *T:* Bristol 626147. *Club:* Royal Over-Seas League.
*See also J. A. James.*

**JAMES, Sir Morrice;** *see* James, Sir J. M. C.

**JAMES, Noel David Glaves,** OBE 1964; MC 1945; TD 1946; Agent for Clinton Devon Estates since 1961; *b* 16 Sept. 1911; *o s* of late Rev. D. T. R. James, and Gertrude James; *m* 1949, Laura Cecilia (*d* 1970), *yr d* of late Sir Richard Winn Livingstone; two *s* (and one *s* decd). *Educ:* Haileybury Coll.; Royal Agricultural Coll., Cirencester (Gold Medal and Estate Management Prize). In general practice as a land agent, 1933-39. Served War, 1939-46 (MC, despatches); 68 Field Regt RA (TA), France, Middle East, Italy. Bursar, Corpus Christi Coll., Oxford, 1946-51; MA (Oxon.) 1946. Fellow, Corpus Christi Coll., Oxford, 1950-51; Land Agent for Oxford Univ., 1951-61; Estates Bursar and Agent for Brasenose Coll., 1959-61; Fellow, Brasenose Coll., Oxford, 1951-61. President: Land Agents Soc., 1957-58; Royal Forestry Soc. of England and Wales and N Ireland, 1962-64; member: Central Forestry Examination Bd of UK, 1951-; Regional Advisory Cttee, Eastern Conservancy, Forestry Commn, 1951-61; Regional Advisory Cttee, SW Conservancy, Forestry Commission, 1962-; Departmental Cttee on Hedgerow and Farm Timber, 1953; UK Forestry Cttee, 1954-59; Governor Wye Coll., Kent, 1955-61; Governor Westonbirt Sch., 1959-68. FLAS; FRICS (Diploma in Forestry and Watney Gold Medal). Gold Medal for Distinguished Service to Forestry, 1967; Royal Agricultural Coll. Bledisloe Medal for services to agriculture and forestry, 1970. *Publications:* Artillery Observation Posts, 1941; Working Plans for Estate Woodlands, 1948; Notes on Estate Forestry, 1949; An Experiment in Forestry, 1951; The Forester's Companion, 1955 (2nd edn, 1966); The Trees of Bicton, 1969. Many articles on forestry. *Recreations:* forestry, shooting. *Address:* Kitts Hayes, Colaton Raleigh, Sidmouth, Devon. *T:* Colaton Raleigh 321. *Club:* Army and Navy.

**JAMES, Norah C.;** *d* of late John H. Cordner-James. *Educ:* Francis Holland Sch., Baker Street, London; Slade Sch. of Art, where she studied sculpture. Was an organising sec. to the Civil Service Clerical Assoc., Advertising and Publicity Manager to Jonathan Cape, publishers; wrote first novel in 1929; joined ATS as private; invalided out of the ATS, Nov. 1943. *Publications:* Sleeveless Errand, 1929; Hospital; Mighty City; Silent Corridors; Portrait of a Patient; The Uneasy Summer; The Wind of Change; A Sense of Loss; Green Vista; Bright Day Renewed; Sister Veronica Green; Small Hotel; Hospital Angles; Double Take; Point of Return; There Is No Why, etc. *Address:* c/o National Westminster Bank, Swinton House Branch, 322 Gray's Inn Road, WC1.

**JAMES, Philip (Brutton),** CBE 1951; Hon. FMA; Librarian of the Royal Academy of Arts, since 1969; *b* 31 Oct. 1901; *e s* of late Rev. John C. and of Margaretta James; *m* 1926, Bertha, *d* of late Canon Victor L. Whitechurch; one *s* one *d*. *Educ:* Sherborne Sch.; University Coll., London. Sub-Librarian Middle Temple, 1923; entered Victoria and Albert Museum (Library), 1925; Keeper of the Library, 1936; lent to the Ministry of Home Security, 1939-41; Deputy Sec. of CEMA, 1941; Dir of Art, CEMA and The Arts Council of Great Britain, 1942-58; Dir of Waddesdon Manor, Bucks (National Trust, James de Rothschild Bequest), 1958-59; Sec. and Editor of the Museums Association, 1960-64. Knight Comdr, Order of the Aztec Eagle, Mexico; Chevalier de l'Ordre de la Couronne, Belgium; Comdr, Order of the Lion, Finland; Comdr, Order of Merit, Germany. *Publications:* Early Keyboard Instruments, 1930; Children's Books of Yesterday, 1933; (Editor) A Butler's Recipe Book (1719), 1935; English Book Illustration, 1800-1900, 1947; Van Gogh, 1948; Henry Moore on Sculpture, 1966. *Recreation:* music. *Address:* Starveacre, Chalfont Road, Seer Green, Bucks. *T:* Beaconsfield 6665.

**JAMES, Philip Gaved,** CBE 1969; Member of British Railways London Midland Board, since 1969 (part-time); *b* 24 Sept. 1904; *s* of Samuel T. G. James and Frances L. R. James (*née* Richards); unmarried. *Educ:* Amersham Gram. Sch.; London Sch. of Economics. Chartered Accountant. With professional accountancy firms, 1921-34; various posts, London Passenger Transport Bd (later London Transport Exec.), 1934-60; Accounts Officer, 1940; Accountant, 1945; Chief Financial Officer, 1948-60; Chief Accountant, BTC, 1960-62; Financial Controller, Brit. Rlys Bd, 1962-65; Mem. Bd, 1965-69. *Publications:* contribs to various professional accountancy jls. *Recreations:* gardening, hill walking. *Address:* 15 Barham Road, SW20. *T:* 01-946 3989. *Club:* Reform.

**JAMES, Prof. Philip Seaforth;** Professor of English Law, Leeds University, since 1952; *b* 28 May 1914; *s* of Dr Philip William James, MC, and Muriel Lindley James; *m* 1954, Wybetty, *d* of Claas P. Gerth, Enschede, Holland; two *s*. *Educ:* Charterhouse; Trinity Coll., Oxford (MA), Research Fellow, Yale Univ., USA, 1937-38. Called to the Bar, Inner Temple, 1939. Served War of 1939-45, in Royal Artillery, India, Burma (despatches). Fellow of Exeter Coll., Oxford, 1946-49. Visiting Prof. University of Louisville, Kentucky, USA, 1960-61. Chm., Yorks Rent Assessment Panel, 1966-; Assessor to County Court under Race Relations Acts. Governor, Swinton Conservative College, 1970-. *Publications:* An Introduction to English Law, 1950; General Principles of the Law of Torts, 1959; Shorter Introduction to English Law, 1969. Various articles, notes and reviews on legal and biographical subjects. *Recreations:* golf and gardening. *Address:* Leeds University, Leeds 2. *T:* Leeds 31751. *Clubs:* National Liberal; Leeds (Leeds).

**JAMES, Richard Lewis Malcolm,** CMG 1949; *b* 15 June 1897; *s* of R. E. James, solicitor, Cardiff; *m* 1921, Eva Hayes Bates; one *s* one *d*. *Educ:* Cardiff High Sch.; Merthyr Intermediate Sch.; London Univ. Civil Service: War Office, 1914-19; Exchequer and Audit Dept, 1920-42; Treasury, 1942-46; Commissioner for Finance, Newfoundland, 1946-49; Asst Sec., Ministry of Power, 1950-59. *Recreations:* gardening, motoring. *Address:* 14 Cosdach Avenue, Wallington, Surrey. *T:* 01-647 5793.

**JAMES, Robert Leoline,** MA, PhD; Head Master of Harrow, 1953-July 1971; *b* 27 Sept. 1905; 2nd *s* of late Very Rev. H. L. James, DD; *m* 1939, Maud Eliot, *o c* of late W. M. Gibbons, OBE, LLD; two *s*. *Educ:* Rossall Sch.; Jesus Coll., Oxford (Scholar). 1st Class Hon. Classical Mods 1926, 1st Class Lit. Hum. 1928; Asst Master St Paul's Sch., 1928; Housemaster and Upper VIIIth classical master; Headmaster of Chigwell Sch., Essex, 1939-46; High Master of St Paul's Sch., 1946-53. Chm. of Council, Heathfield Sch., 1960. *Publication:* Cicero and Sulpicius, 1933. *Recreations:* fly-fishing and bird-watching. *Address:* The Head Master's, Harrow-on-the-Hill, Middlesex. *Club:* Public Schools.

**JAMES, R(obert) V(idal) Rhodes;** Director, Institute for the Study of International Organisation, University of Sussex, since 1968; *b* 10 April 1933; *y s* of Lieut-Col W. R. James, OBE, MC; *m* 1956, Angela Margaret Robertson, *er d* of late R. M. Robertson; four *d. Educ:* private schs in India; Sedbergh Sch.; Worcester Coll., Oxford. Appointed Asst Clerk, House of Commons, 1955; Senior Clerk, 1961-64. Fellow of All Souls Coll., Oxford, 1965-68. Kratter Prof. of European History, Stanford Univ., Calif., 1968. FRSL 1964; NATO Fellow, 1965. *Publications:* Lord Randolph Churchill, 1959; An Introduction to the House of Commons, 1961 (John Llewelyn Rhys Memorial Prize); Rosebery, 1963 (Royal Society Lit. Award); Gallipoli, 1965; Standardization and Production of Military Equipment in NATO, 1967; Churchill: a study in failure, 1900-39, 1970; (ed) Chips: The Diaries of Sir Henry Channon, 1967; (ed) Memoirs of a Conservative: J. C. C. Davidson's Memoirs and Papers, 1969; (ed) The Czechoslovak Crisis 1968, 1969; Contrib. to: The Suez War, 1967; Essays From Divers Hands, 1967; Churchill: four faces and the man, 1969. *Address:* Dale Cottage, West Burton, near Pulborough, Sussex. *T:* Bury (Sussex) 414; Institute for Study of International Organisation, Stanmer House, University of Sussex, Falmer, near Brighton, Sussex. *T:* Brighton 66755. *Club:* Travellers'.

**JAMES, (Thomas) Cecil (Garside),** CMG 1966; Assistant Under-Secretary of State, Ministry of Defence, since 1968; *b* 8 Jan. 1918; *s* of Joshua James, MBE, Ashton-under-Lyne; *m* 1941, Elsie Williams, Ashton-under-Lyne; one *s* two *d. Educ:* Manchester Grammar Sch.; St John's Coll., Cambridge. Prin. Priv. Sec. to Sec. of State for Air, 1951-55; Asst Sec., Air Min., 1955; Civil Sec., FEAF, 1963-66; Chief of Public Relations, MoD, 1966-68. *Recreation:* golf. *Address:* 12 Dove Park, Hatch End, Mddx.

**JAMES, Thomas Geraint Illtyd,** FRCS; Hon. Surgeon, Central Middlesex Hospital; Late Teacher of Surgery, Middlesex Hospital, and Hon. Surgical Tutor, Royal College of Surgeons of England; *b* 12 July 1900; *s* of late Evan Thomas and Elizabeth James, Barry; *m* 1932, Dorothy Marguerite, *o d* of late David John, Cardiff; two *s. Educ:* Barry, Glam; University Coll., Cardiff; Welsh National Sch. of Medicine; St Mary's Hosp., London; Guy's Hosp., London. BSc Wales, 1921, Alfred Sheen Prize in Anat. and Physiol.; MRCS, LRCP, 1924; MB, ChB, 1925, Maclean Medal and Prize in Obst. and Gynæcol.; FRCSE, 1927; FRCS, 1928; MCh Wales, 1932; FRSocMed; Fellow Association of Surgeons of Great Britian and Ireland; Member: International Society for Surgery; Management Cttee, Leavesden Gp of Hospitals; Corr. Mem. Spanish-Portuguese Soc. of Neurosurgery. Assoc. Examr University of London, 1947; late Mem. and Chm., Court of Examiners RCS of England, 1955; Examr in Surgery, University of Liverpool. Mem. Society of Apothecaries; Freeman of the City of London. Formerly: Ho. phys., Ho. surg. and Resident Surgical Officer, Cardiff Royal Infirmary; Clinical Asst St Mark's, St Peter's and Guy's Hosps, London; Asst to Neurosurg. Dept, London Hosp. *Publications:* in various jls on surg. and neurosurg. subjects. *Recreations:* literature, travelling. *Address:* 1 Freeland Road, W5. *T:* 01-992 2430.

**JAMES, Thurstan Trewartha;** Consultant, Air Affairs; Editor, The Aeroplane, 1945-65, retired; *b* 7 May 1903; *s* of Alfred James, Mining Engr, and Jeanne Hammond Cloutte; *m* 1929, Doris, *o d* of J. Kennedy Allerton, Worthing; one *s* one *d. Educ:* Rugby; Royal School of Mines. After mining in Portugal, 1921, and studying general engineering, worked as fitter in shops at Beardmore's Dalmuir, on first multi-engined all-metal aircraft in this country; joined Short Brothers to work on all-metal flying-boats, 1926. Joined Technical Staff of The Aeroplane, 1929; founded first gliding weekly, The Sailplane and Glider, 1930. Served at Air Ministry and Ministry of Aircraft Production, 1939-45, becoming a Dir of Aircraft Production. Liveryman, Coach Makers' and Coach Harness Makers' Co. Hon. Companion Royal Aeronautical Society, 1965. *Address:* 23 Arundel Road, Kingston-upon-Thames, Surrey. *T:* 01-942 8657. *Clubs:* Royal Aero, Royal Air Force Reserves.

**JAMES, Walter;** *see* James, Arthur Walter.

**JAMES, William Garnet,** OBE 1960; composer and solo pianist; retired as Federal Controller of Music, of the Australian Broadcasting Commission; *b* Ballarat, Vic., Australia, 28 Aug. 1895; *s* of Louisa Chapman, pianist, and Andrew James, publisher; *m* Saffo Arnav, operatic singer. *Educ:* Melbourne Univ. (Scholar); 1st Class Hons in each year for composition and pianoforte playing; came to London in 1914 and studied under Arthur de Greef; played several important concertos with Orchestra at Queen's Hall; from 1915 has performed at Queen's Hall Promenade Concerts, Ballad Concerts, Royal Albert Hall Special Concerts, International Celebrity Concerts, and Provincial Concerts. Compositions: a Ballet produced at the Savoy Theatre, London, 1916, and an Orchestral Suite at the Queen's Hall, etc; Sea Sketches (for piano); Album of 5 pianoforte pieces; The Golden Girl (operetta in one act). Songs: The Sun-God, The Flutes of Arcady, In the Gardens of England, A Warwickshire Wooing, The Sweetest Song, Six Australian Bush Songs, Summer Rain, The Radiant Morn, Madelina, The Showman, Come, gather Roses, I was carried by a Fairy, Moonlit Lake, The First Cuckoo, Sometimes just at Twilight, Cupid's Arrows, Spanish Dances for Piano, When Cupid comes Calling, Six Maori Love Songs, Vol. I Sea Shanties, Skies of Home, Covent Garden, Bush Song at Dawn, Vols I, II, III of Australian Christmas Carols, etc. *Recreations:* tennis, cricket. *Address:* Macleay Regis, Macleay Street, Potts Point, Sydney, NSW 2011, Australia.

**JAMES, Admiral Sir William Milbourne,** GCB, *cr* 1944 (KCB, *cr* 1936; CB 1919); *b* 22 Dec. 1881; *s* of Major W. C. James, 16th Lancers, *o s* of Lord Justice Sir W. M. James and Effie, *d* of Sir J. E. Millais, 1st Bt, PRA; *m* 1915, Dorothy, OBE 1943, *y d* of late Adm. Sir Alexander Duff, GCB, GBE; one *s* (decd). *Educ:* Trinity Coll., Glenalmond; HMS Britannia. Sub-Lieut 1901; Lieut 1902; Commander, 1913; Capt., 1918; Rear-Adm., 1929; Vice-Adm., 1933; Admiral, 1938; Deputy Dir, Royal Naval Staff Coll., Greenwich, 1923-25, Dir, 1925-26; Naval Asst 1st Sea Lord, 1928; Chief of Staff, Atlantic Fleet, 1929-30, Mediterranean Fleet, 1930; Commanding Battle Cruiser Squadron, 1932-34; Lord Commissioner of Admiralty and Deputy Chief of Naval Staff, 1935-38; Commander-in-Chief, Portsmouth, 1939-42; Chief of Naval Information, 1943-44; MP (U) for North Portsmouth, 1943-45. DL Surrey, 1958-65. President Union Jack Services Clubs, 1955-64. *Publications:* The British Navy in Adversity, 1926; Blue Water and Green Fields, 1939; Admiral Sir William Fisher, 1943; Portsmouth Letters, 1946; The British Navies in the Second World War, 1946; The Order of

Release, 1947; The Durable Monument, 1948; Old Oak, 1950; The Sky Was Always Blue, 1951; The Eyes of the Navy, 1955; A Great Seaman, 1956. *Address:* Wynd House, Elie, Fife. *Club:* United Service.

**JAMES, Prof. William Owen,** MA, DPhil; FRS 1952; Senior Research Fellow, Imperial College; London University Professor of Botany, and Head of Department at Imperial College of Science and Technology, 1959-67, now Emeritus Professor; *b* 21 May 1900; *s* of William Benjamin James and Agnes Ursula (*née* Collins); *m* 1928, Gladys Macphail Redfern; two *d. Educ:* Tottenham Grammar Sch.; Universities of Reading and Cambridge. BSc (London); PhD (Cambridge); MA, DPhil Oxon. Research Institute of Plant Physiology, Imperial Coll., 1926-27. Demonstrator in Plant Physiology, Oxford, 1928-55; Reader in Botany, Oxford, 1946-58. Part owner and co-editor of the New Phytologist, 1931-61; Director of Oxford Medicinal Plants Scheme, 1940-52. Member: Vegetable Drugs Cttee of Ministries of Health and Supply, 1940-45; Central Garden Produce Cttee (Ministry of Agriculture). Chairman, Teaching of Biology Cttee, 1962-67. Fellow of Imperial Coll., 1969. Hon. ARCS 1964. Foreign Member: Swedish Royal Academy of Science; Amer. Society of Plant Physiologists; Deutsche botanische Gesellschaft, and Leopoldina. *Publications:* Elements of Plant Biology, 1949; Introduction to Plant Physiology, 6th edn, 1962 (German edn 1965, Spanish edn 1967, Hungarian edn 1969); Plant Respiration, 1953 (Russian edn 1956); Background to Gardening, 1957; (jt) Biology of Flowers, 1935; papers on plant respiration, nutrition, alkaloid synthesis, etc, in botanical and allied journals. *Recreations:* gardening, boating and reading. *Address:* Imperial College of Science and Technology, Prince Consort Road, SW7; 14 Roedean Crescent, SW15. *T:* 01-876 3785.

**JAMES, William Thomas,** OBE 1943; formerly Director of numerous public companies both at home and overseas, mainly associated with British Electric Traction, and also Chairman of many of these; Director: United Transport Co.; United Transport Overseas Ltd; *b* 5 June 1892; *s* of Morgan James, JP, and Mary James, Maesycwmmer Hse, Maesycwmmer, Mon; unmarried. *Educ:* Lewis's Sch., Pengam, Glam. London and Provincial Bank, 1909. Joined family business, 1911-14. Served European War, Glam Yeomanry, 1914-18 (Meritorious Service Medal). Rejoined family business, 1919-22; pioneered road passenger transport in Monmouthshire Valleys, 1923; developed passenger road services in S Wales and Mon, 1923-43. Having sold financial interests in 1932 to British Electric Traction Co. Ltd, joined staff of BET in London as Executive Dir, 1943; Dir of BET, 1947. Chm., Public Transport Assoc., 1951, 1952. Mem. Cttee, set up by Government to consider Rural Bus Services. MInstT. *Recreation:* farming. *Address:* (private) Uplands, Ty-Gwyn Road, Cardiff. *Clubs:* United Service; Cardiff and County (Cardiff); Chepstow; St Pierre Golf and Country.

**JAMESON, (Margaret) Storm,** MA; Hon. LittD (Leeds); Writer; *b* Whitby, Yorks; *d* of William Storm Jameson; *m* Prof. Guy Chapman, *qv*; one *s. Educ:* Leeds Univ. *Publications:* Happy Highways, 1920; Modern Drama in Europe, 1920; The Lovely Ship, 1927; The Voyage Home, 1930; A Richer Dust, 1931; That was Yesterday; A Day Off; No Time Like the Present, 1933; Company Parade, 1934; Love in Winter, 1935; In the Second Year, 1936; None Turn Back, 1936; Delicate Monster, 1937; Civil Journey, 1939; Farewell Night, Welcome Day, 1939; Europe to Let, 1940; Cousin Honoré, 1940; The Fort, 1941; The End of this War, 1941; Then We Shall Hear Singing, 1942; Cloudless May, 1943; The Journal of Mary Hervey Russell, 1945; The Other Side, 1945; Before the Crossing, 1947; The Black Laurel, 1948; The Moment of Truth, 1949; Writer's Situation, 1950; The Green Man, 1952; The Hidden River, 1955; The Intruder, 1956; A Cup of Tea for Mr Thorgill, 1957; A Ulysses Too Many, 1958; A Day Off and other stories, 1959; Last Score, 1961; Morley Roberts: The Last Eminent Victorian, 1961; The Road from the Monument, 1962; A Month Soon Goes, 1963; The Aristide Case, 1964; The Early Life of Stephen Hind, 1966; The White Crow, 1968; (autobiography) Journey from the North, Vol. I 1969, Vol. II 1970. *Recreation:* travelling. *Address:* c/o Macmillan & Co., 4 Little Essex Street, WC2.

**JAMESON, Noel Rutherford,** CBE 1952; Sheepfarmer, New Zealand, since 1919; *b* 24 Dec. 1892; *s* of late James Samuel Jameson; *m* 1927, Olive Catherine Wilson; one *s. Educ:* Wellington Coll.; King's Coll., Auckland. Served European War with NZ Mounted Rifles. Chm., NZ Wool Board, 1945-53; Chm., NZ Wool Commission, 1963-65 (Dep. Chm., 1951-53). *Recreation:* golf. *Address:* 50 Iona Road, Havelock North, Hawkes Bay, New Zealand.

**JAMESON, Air Commodore Patrick Geraint,** CB 1959; DSO 1943; DFC 1940 (and Bar 1942), psa; Royal Air Force, retired, 1960; *b* Wellington, NZ, 10 Nov. 1912; *s* of Robert Delvin Jameson, Balbriggan, Ireland, and Katherine Lenora Jameson (*née* Dick), Dunedin, NZ; *m* 1941, Hilda Nellie Haiselden Webster, *d* of B. F. Webster, Lower Hutt, NZ; one *s* one *d. Educ:* Hutt Valley High Sch., New Zealand. Commissioned in RAF, 1936. War of 1939-45 (despatches 5 times, DFC and Bar, DSO): 46 Squadron, 1936-40, 266 Sqaudron, 1940-41; Wing Commander Flying, Wittering, 1940-42; Wing Commander (Flying), North Weald, 1942-43; Group Capt. Plans, HQ No. 11 Group, 1943-44; 122 Wing in France, Belgium, Holland, Germany and Denmark, 1944-45; Staff Coll., Haifa, 1946; Air Ministry, 1946-48; CFE, West Raynham, 1949-52; Wunsdorf (2nd TAF), 1952-54; SASO, HQ No. II Group, 1954-56; SASO HQ RAF Germany (2nd TAF) 1956-59. Norwegian War Cross, 1943; Netherlands Order of Orange Nassau, 1945; American Silver Star, 1945. *Recreations:* fishing, shooting, sailing, golf. *Address:* Dardistown Castle, Drogheda, Co. Meath, Eire. *Clubs:* Royal Air Force, Royal Air Force Reserves; Royal Air Force Yacht (Hamble); Kildare Street (Dublin).

**JAMESON, Storm;** *see* Jameson, M. S.

**JAMESON, Maj-Gen. Thomas Henry,** CBE 1946 (OBE 1937); DSO 1919; RM, retired; *b* 10 Dec. 1894; *s* of Robert W. Jameson, JP, and Katherine Anne Jameson; *m* 1918, Barbara Adèle Bayley (*d* 1958); one *d. Educ:* Monkton Combe Sch., near Bath, Somerset. Commission in Royal Marines, 1913; served Belgium, France, Gallipoli (despatches) HMS Resolution, HMS Kent, 1914-18; Siberia, 1919 (DSO). War of 1939-45: staff of C-in-C Home Fleet, 15 RM Battalion, Admiralty; Commandant Plymouth, Jan. 1944 and Depot, Deal, June 1944; Commandant Portsmouth Division RM, 1944-46 (CBE); retired, 1946. *Address:* Flete House, Ermington, Devon. *T:* Holbeton 635.

**JAMIESON, Major David Auldjo,** VC 1944; Governor, Australian Agricultural Company since 1952; Director, UK Branch, Australian

Mutual Provident Society, since 1963; one of HM Body Guard, Hon. Corps Gentlemen-at-Arms, since 1968; *b* 1 Oct. 1920; *s* of late Sir Archibald Auldjo Jamieson, KBE, MC; *m* 1st, 1948, Nancy Elwes (*d* 1963), *y d* of Robert H. A. Elwes, Congham, King's Lynn; one *s* two *d*; 2nd, 1969, Joanna, *e d* of Edward Woodall. *Educ:* Eton Coll. Commissioned Royal Norfolk Regt May 1939; served War of 1939-45 (VC); retired, 1948. *Recreations:* shooting, golf. *Address:* The Drove House, Thornham, King's Lynn, Norfolk. *T:* Thornham 206.

**JAMIESON, Lt-Col Harvey Morro Harvey-,** OBE 1969; TD; DL; WS; Secretary and Legal Adviser to The Company of Merchants of the City of Edinburgh since 1946; Member Committee on Conveyancing Legislation and Practice (appointed by Secretary of State for Scotland, 1964); *b* 9 Dec. 1908; *s* of late A. H. Morro Jamieson, OBE, Advocate, Edinburgh, and Isobel, *d* of late Maj.-Gen. Sir Robert Murdoch Smith, KCMG; *m* 1936, Frances, *o c* of late Col. J. Y. H. Ridout, DSO; three *s*; assumed additional surname of Harvey, with authority of Lord Lyon King of Arms, 1958. *Educ:* Edinburgh Acad.; RMC Sandhurst (Prize Cadetship); Edinburgh Univ. (BL). Mem. Queen's Body Guard for Scotland (Royal Company of Archers), 1934-. Commissioned 1st Bn KOSB, 1928; Capt. RARO 1938; Major RA (TA), 1939, to raise 291 HAA Battery RA (TA). Served War of 1939-45, Belgium, Holland and Germany, RA and Staff, Major and Lieut-Col; Comd 3rd Edinburgh HG Bn, 1954-57. France and Germany Star, General Service and Home Defence Medals; Jubilee Medal, 1935; Coronation Medals, 1937 and 1953. DL, County of the City of Edinburgh, 1968. *Publications:* The Historic Month of June, 1953; contrib. to Juridical Review, Scots Law Times and Yachting Monthly. *Address:* The Merchants Hall, Edinburgh EH2 2EP. *T:* 031-225 7202; 4 Moray Place, Edinburgh EH3 6DS. *T:* 031-225 6914; Lechine Cottage, by Lochearnhead, Perthshire. *T:* Lochearnhead 248. *Clubs:* New (Edinburgh); Royal Scottish Automobile (Glasgow); Royal Forth Yacht (Granton).

**JAMIESON, Rear-Adm. Ian Wyndham,** CB 1970; DSC 1945; Chief of Staff to C-in-C Western Fleet since Dec. 1969; *b* 13 March 1920; *s late S. W. Jamieson, CBE; m* 1949, Patricia Wheeler, Knowle, Warwickshire; two *s* one *d*. *Educ:* RNC, Dartmouth. Served War of 1939-45: Anti Submarine Warfare Specialist, 1944. Comdr, 1953; Staff of RN Tactical Sch., 1953-56; HMS Maidstone, 1956-58; Dir, Jt Tactical Sch., Malta, 1958; Capt. 1958; Asst Dir, Naval Intelligence, 1959-61; Comd HMS Nubian and 6th Frigate Sqdn, 1961-64; Dir, Seaman Officers Appts, 1964-66; Comd Britannia RN Coll., Dartmouth, 1966-68; Rear-Adm. 1968; Flag Officer, Gibraltar, and Admiral Superintendent, HM Dockyard, Gibraltar; also NATO Comdr, Gibraltar (Mediterranean Area), 1968-69. *Recreations:* hockey (Scotland and Combined Services), cricket, golf, tennis. *Address:* Ashgrove House, Cross Keys, Sevenoaks, Kent. *T:* Sevenoaks 53473. *Clubs:* Army and Navy, MCC.

**JAMIESON, John Kenneth;** Chairman of Board, Chief Executive Officer and Chairman of Management Committee, Standard Oil Co. (NJ), since Oct. 1969; *b* Canada, 28 Aug. 1910; *s* of John Locke and Kate Herron Jamieson; US citizen; *m* 1937, Ethel May Burns; one *s* one *d*. *Educ:* Univ. of Alberta; Massachusetts Inst. of Technology (BS). Northwest Stellarene Co. of Alberta, 1932; British American Oil Co., 1934; Manager, Moose Jaw Refinery; served War of 1939-45 in Oil Controller's Dept of Canadian Govt; subseq. Manager, Manufrg Dept, British American Oil Co.; joined Imperial Oil Co., 1948: Head of Engrg and Develt Div., Sarnia Refinery, 1949; Asst Gen. Man. of Manufrg Dept, 1950; on loan to Canadian Dept of Defence Production, 1951; Dir, Imperial Oil, 1952, Vice-Pres. 1953; Pres. and Dir, International Petroleum Co., 1959; Vice-Pres., Dir and Mem. Exec. Cttee, Humble Oil & Refining Co., 1961, Exec. Vice-Pres. 1962, Pres. 1963-64; Exec. Vice-Pres. and Dir 1964, Pres. 1965, Jersey Standard. Director: Chase Manhattan Bank; International Nickel Co. of Canada Ltd; Alumni Term Mem., MIT Corp.; Mem. Exec. Cttee of US Council, Internat. Chamber of Commerce; Mem. Bd of Dirs: American Petroleum Inst.; Economic Club of New York; Member: Emergency Cttee for American Trade; Nat. Industrial Pollution Control Council; Business Council; Nat. Petroleum Council; Chairman: United Fund of Greater New York; Community Blood Council of Greater New York Inc. *Address:* 1310 Flagler Drive, Mamaroneck, NY 10543, USA. *T:* 914-698-7837. *Clubs:* Blind Brook (Port Chester); Augusta National Golf (Augusta); Houston Country (Houston); Winged Foot (Mamaroneck); Rosedale (Toronto); International (Washington); Links (New York).

**JAMIESON, Kenneth Douglas,** CMG 1968; Head of Export Promotion Department, Foreign and Commonwealth Office, since 1968; *b* 9 Jan. 1921; *s* of late Rt Hon. Lord Jamieson, PC, KC, Senator of College of Justice in Scotland and Violet Rhodes; *m* 1946, Pamela Hall; two *s* one *d*. *Educ:* Rugby; Balliol Coll., Oxford. War Service: 5th Regt RHA, 1941-45; HQ, RA 7th Armoured Div., 1945-46. Joined Foreign Service, 1946; served in: Washington, 1948; FO, 1952; Lima, 1954; Brussels, 1959; FO, 1961; Caracas, 1963; Dir of Commercial Training, DSAO, 1968. *Address:* 55 Victoria Road, W8. *Club:* St James'.

**JAMIL RAIS, Tan Sri Abdul,** PMN; High Commissioner for Malaysia in the UK since Nov. 1967; *b* 14 Jan. 1912; *s* of Abdul Rais and Saodah; *m*; four *s* six *d* (and one *s* decd). *Educ:* Clifford Sch.; Jesus Coll., Oxford. Joined Govt service, 1932; State Sec., Perlis, 1951-52; State Financial Officer, Selangor, 1954-55; State Sec., Selangor, 1955-56; Chief Minister, Selangor, 1957-59; Sec. to Treasury, 1961-64; Chief Sec. to Malaysian Govt and Sec. to Cabinet, 1964-67. *Recreations:* golf, tennis. *Address:* 45 Belgrave Square, SW1. *T:* 01-245 9221. *Club:* Oxford and Cambridge University.

**JAMISON, Evelyn Mary,** MA Oxon; Hon. Fellow, Lady Margaret Hall, Oxford; FSA; Fellow Royal Historical Society; Corresponding Fellow, Accademia Pontaniana, Naples; *b* 24 Feb. 1877; *d* of Arthur Andrew Jamison, MD, MRCP, and Isabella Green. *Educ:* Francis Holland Sch., Graham Terrace; Lady Margaret Hall, Oxford. Research Fellow Somerville Coll., 1903-06; Bursar and Librarian Lady Margaret Hall, 1907; Asst Tutor, 1917; Vice-Principal and Tutor, Lady Margaret Hall, 1921-37; University Lecturer in History, Oxford, 1928-35. *Publications:* The Norman Administration of Apulia and Capua, 1127-1166, in Papers of the British School at Rome, vol. vi, 1913; Italy before 1250, in Italy Medieval and Modern, 1917; papers on Medieval History of South Italy and reviews in English Historical Review and in Italian and English Journals, 1929-68; S Maria della Strada at Matrice, its History and Sculpture, in Papers of the British Sch. at Rome, vol. xiii, 1938; The Sicilian Norman Kingdom in the Mind of Anglo-Norman

Contemporaries, Annual Italian Lecture, 1938, British Academy; Admiral Eugenius of Sicily, 1957 The Catalogus Baronum, a new edn, Pt II in the press with Istituto storico Italiano per il Medio evo (Fonti per la storia d'Italia), Rome. *Recreations:* study of architecture, formerly travel, climbing and walking. *Address:* 11 Priory Mansions, Drayton Gardens, SW10. *T:* 01-373 8699.

**JAMISON, Dr Robin Ralph,** FRS 1969, CEng, FRAeS, ARIC; Chief Engineer (Research), Rolls Royce Ltd, Bristol Engine Division, since 1965; *b* 12 July 1912; *s* of Reginald Jamison, MD, FRCS, and Eanswyth Heyworth; *m* 1937, Hilda Watney Wilson, Cape Town; two *s* two *d. Educ:* South African Coll.; Univ. of Cape Town. BSc, PhD. S African Govt research grant, 1936-37; research and development of aero engines, Rolls Royce Ltd, 1937-50; Head of Ramjet Dept, Bristol Siddeley Engines Ltd, 1950-62 (Asst Chief Engr, 1956); advanced propulsion res., 1962-65; Chief Engr, Res., 1965-. Visiting Prof., Bath Univ. of Technology, 1969. Herbert Ackroyd-Stuart Prize, RAeS, 1958; Thulin Bronze Medal, Swedish Aero. Soc., 1960; Silver Medal of RAeS, 1965. *Publications:* papers in aeronautical and scientific jls. *Recreations:* sailing, gardening, music. *Address:* 2 The Crescent, Henleaze, Bristol BS9 4RN. *T:* Bristol 62-7083; Rolls Royce Ltd, PO Box 3, Filton, Bristol BS12 7QE. *T:* Bristol 69-3871.

**JANES, Sir Herbert (Charles),** Kt 1954; Founder and Chairman of H. C. Janes Ltd, Builders and Civil Engineers, retired from Chairmanship, July 1962; *b* 10 Oct. 1884; *s* of Charles Walter Janes; *m* 1st, 1911, Edith Brown, Luton; one *s* three *d* (and *er s* killed, RAF, 1943); 2nd, 1944, Hilda Horsfall, Bradford. *Educ:* Luton. Mem. Luton Borough Council, 1942-58; Mayor, 1953-54. Pres. Baptist Men's Movement, 1943; Pres. Mid-Herts Sunday Sch. Union, 1939-45; Pres. Luton and Dunstable Master Builders Assoc., 1945-46; Pres. Beds Union of Baptist and Congregational Churches, 1947-48; Chm. Baptist Missionary Soc., 1949-50; Treas. Baptist Commonwealth Soc., 1946-62. Pres., Baptist Union of Great Britain and Ireland, 1956; Founded: The Janes Trust (from which many charitable bequests have been made); Sir Herbert Janes Village for Old People at Luton, 1958; Green Hills Youth Rendezvous, Worthing, 1962; Green Hills Club for Old People, Luton, 1963. Has travelled considerably. *Recreations:* golf, bridge, travel, cinephotography. *Address:* Apartment 77, Seabright, West Parade, Worthing. *Club:* Royal Commonwealth Society.

**JANES, John Douglas Webster;** Principal Finance Officer and Accountant General (Under-Secretary), Ministry of Housing and Local Government, since 1968; *b* 17 Aug. 1918; *s* of late John Arnold Janes and Maud Mackinnon (*née* Webster); *m* 1943, Margaret Isabel Smith; one *s* two *d. Educ:* Southgate County Sch., Mddx; Imperial Coll. of Science and Technology. 1st cl. BSc (Eng) London, ACGI, DIC. Entered Post Office Engineering Dept, Research Branch, 1939. Served Royal Signals, RAOC, REME, 1939-45: War Office, 1941-45; Major. Min. of Town and Country Planning, 1947; Min. of Housing and Local Govt, 1951; seconded to Min. of Power, 1956-58; HM Treasury, 1960-63; Min. of Land and Natural Resources, 1964-66. *Recreations:* singing, do-it-yourself. *Address:* 136 Waterfall Road, N14. *T:* 01-886 2133.

**JANES, Rev. Maxwell Osborne;** Minister, Crowborough Congregational Church, since 1967; *b* 14 May 1902; *s* of Harry Janes; *m* 1927, Mildred Bertha Burgess; one *s. Educ:* Kilburn Gram. Sch.; University Coll., London; New Coll., London. BA London; BD London. Ordained Congregational Minister, 1927. Minister at: Rectory Road Congreg. Ch., Stoke Newington, 1927-32; Above Bar Congreg. Ch., Southampton, 1932-45; Moderator of Southern Province, Congreg. Union of England and Wales, 1945-50; Gen. Sec., London Missionary Soc., 1950-66; Pres., Congregational Church in England and Wales, 1966-67; Cons. Sec., Congregational Coun. for World Mission, 1966-67. *Publication:* Servant of the Church, 1952. *Recreations:* gardening, philately. *Address:* Windrush, London Road, Crowborough, Sussex. *T:* Crowborough 5729.

**JANES, Maj.-Gen. Mervyn,** MBE 1944; GOC 5th Division since 1970; *b* 1 Oct. 1920; *o s* of W. G. Janes; *m* 1946, Elizabeth Kathleen McIntyre; two *d. Educ:* Sir Walter St John's Sch., London. Commnd 1942; served with Essex Yeo. (104 Regt RHA), 1942-46, Middle East and Italy; psc 1951; served with 3 RHA, 1952-53; 2 Div., BMRA, 1954-55; Chief Instructor, New Coll., RMAS, 1956-57; Batt. Comd, 3 RHA, 1958-60; Asst Army Instructor (GSO1), Imperial Defence Coll., 1961-62; comd 1st Regt RHA, 1963-65; Comdr, RA, in BAOR, 1965-67; DMS2 (MoD(A)), 1967-70. *Recreations:* music, egyptology, ornithology, tennis. *Address:* Upton Lodge, Wealstone Lane, Chester. *T:* 44456. *Club:* Army and Navy.

**JANES, Norman Thomas,** RWS, RE, RSMA; Painter, Etcher and Wood Engraver; *b* Egham, Surrey 1892; *s* of Arthur T. Janes and Ada Louise Croxson, *m* 1925, Barbara Greg, *qv*; one *s* two *d. Educ:* Slade Sch. (drawing and painting); Central Sch. of Arts and Crafts (etching); Royal Coll. of Art. Served in the London Irish Rifles and the Royal Irish Regt, 1914-19; France, 1915-17; joined RAF 1941; served in Middle East for three years (despatches). Exhibited from 1921 at Internat. Soc., Royal Academy, New English Art Club, Goupil Gallery, Society of Wood Engravers and principal provincial galleries; abroad at Florence, Venice, Prague, Chicago, Stockholm, Johannesburg, New York; works purchased for permanent collections of British Museum, Victoria and Albert Museum, Imperial War Museum, Manchester City Gallery, Whitworth Gallery (Manchester), Bradford, Brighton, National Gallery of New Zealand, New York Public Library, Brooklyn Museum, Cincinnati, Pasadena, Brisbane and others. One-man exhibitions: Beaux Arts Gallery, London, 1932 and 1945; Middlesbrough, 1962. *Recreations:* books, garden. *Address:* 70 Canonbury Park South, Canonbury, N1. *T:* 01-226 1925.

**JANNER,** family name of **Baron Janner.**

**JANNER,** Baron *cr* 1970 (Life Peer), of the City of Leicester; **Barnett Janner,** Kt 1961; Solicitor; *b* 1892; *s* of late Joseph and Gertrude Janner, Barry, Glamorgan; *m* 1927, Elsie Sybil Cohen (*see* Lady Janner); one *s* one *d. Educ:* Barry County Sch.; University of S Wales and Mon (Cardiff Coll.) (County Scholarship). BA; Pres. of Students Representative Council; editor of University Magazine; served European War (gassed); ARP Warden in London, War of 1939-45. President: Board of Deputies of British Jews, 1955-64; Assoc. of Jewish Friendly Societies; Zionist Federation of Gt Britain and Ireland; Chm., Anglo-Benelux Parly Gp; Past Chm., now Mem. Exec., Inter-Parly Union, British Gp Chairman, Anglo-Israel Parl. Gp. Chairman, Lords and Commons Solicitors Gp; Vice-Pres. and Mem. Exec. Cttee of Conf. on Jewish

Material Claims against Germany Inc.; Mem. Executive Cttee of Cttee for Jewish Claims on Austria; Mem. Exec., World Zionist Organisation; Vice-Pres., Assoc. of Municipal Corporations; Chairman: Leaseholders' Assoc. of Great Britain, Parliamentary Water Safety Cttee. Contested Cardiff Central, 1929; Whitechapel and St George's, 1930 and 1935; MP (L) Whitechapel and St George's Division of Stepney, 1931-35; joined Labour Party, 1936; MP (Lab), West Leicester, 1945-50, North-West Div. of Leicester, 1950-70; former Mem., House of Commons Panel of Chairmen. Mem. Society of Labour Lawyers; Hon. Rents Adviser to Labour Party. FRSA. Hon. LLD Leeds, 1957. Commander of the Order of Leopold II (Belgium), 1963. *Recreation:* reading. *Address:* 69 Albert Hall Mansions, SW7. *T:* 01-589 8222; Victoria House, Bloomsbury Square, WC1. *T:* 01-405 1311, 01-242 3258; The Jungle, Stone Road, Broadstairs, Kent. *T:* Thanet 61642.

*See also Hon. G. E. Janner, Lord Morris of Kenwood.*

**JANNER, Lady; Elsie Sybil Janner,** CBE 1968; JP; Member of Committee of Magistrates, Inner London, and A Chariman, Juvenile Courts of Inner London; Member, Central Council, Magistrates Courts Committee; *b* Newcastle upon Tyne; *d* of Joseph and Henrietta Cohen; *m* 1927, Barnett Janner (*see* Baron Janner); one *s* one *d. Educ:* Central Newcastle High Sch.; South Hampstead High Sch.; Switzerland. Founder and first Hon. Club Leader, Brady Girls' Club, Whitechapel, 1925 (now Pres., Brady Clubs and Settlement). War of 1939-45: Captain, Mechanised Transp. Corps (Def. Medal). Chm., Bridgehead Housing Assoc., to acquire property for residential purposes for homeless ex-offenders. Mem. Council, Magistrates Assoc. (Mem. Exec. Cttee, Dep. Chm. Road Traffic Cttee, and Past Chm., London Br.); JP, Inner London, 1936; a Visiting Magistrate to Holloway Women's Prison (10 yrs); Dep. Chm., Thames Bench of Magistrates; Mem., Inner London Licensing Cttee. Vice-Pres., Assoc. for Jewish Youth; Hon. Vice-Pres., Fedn of Women Zionists of Gt Brit. and Ire.; Chm. Bd of Deputies, British Jews Educn and Youth Cttee, 1943-66; Chm., United Jewish Educnl and Cultural Org. (internat. body to reconstruct Jewish educn in countries of Europe which had been occupied by Germans), 1947-50; Chm., Jewish Youth Organisations Cttee. Trustee, Mitchell City of London Charity and Educnl Foundn; Mem., former Nat. Road Safety Adv. Council, 1966-68. *Recreations:* tennis, swimming, grandchildren. *Address:* 69 Albert Hall Mansions, SW7. *T:* 01-589 8222; The Jungle, Stone Road, Broadstairs, Kent. *T:* Thanet 61642.

*See also Hon. G.E. Janner, Lord Morris of Kenwood.*

**JANNER, Hon. Greville Ewan;** MP (Lab) Leicester North West since 1970; barrister-at-law; author and journalist; *b* 11 July 1928; *s* of Baron Janner, *qv* and of Lady Janner, *qv*; *m* 1955, Myra Louise Sheink, Melbourne; one *s* two *d. Educ:* Bishop's Coll. Sch., Canada; St Paul's Sch.; Trinity Hall, Cambridge; Harvard Post Graduate Law School. Southern Jr Champion, 100 yds, 1947. Nat. Service: Sgt, RA, BAOR. Pres., Cambridge Union, 1952; Chm., Cambridge Univ. Labour Club, 1952; Internat. Sec., Nat. Assoc. of Labour Students, 1952; Pres., Trinity Hall Athletic Club, 1952. Contested (Lab) Wimbledon, 1955. Chm. of Managers, Brady Clubs, 1960; Founder and Chm., The Bridge in Britain; Jt Hon. Sec., Assoc. for Jewish Youth and Assoc. of Jewish Ex-Servicemen; Mem. Board of Deputies of British Jews and Vice-Chm. of Race Relations Working Party; Pres., Friends of Alyn Home for Crippled Children; Member: Nat. Union of Journalists; Brit. Acad. of Forensic Sciences; Howard League for Penal Reform; Soc. of Labour Lawyers; Fabian Soc., etc. *Publications:* Farming and the Law, 1962; The Lawyer and His World, 1962; The Businessman's Lawyer and Legal Lexicon, 1962; The Retailer's Lawyer, 1963; All You Need To Know About The Law, 1963; Motorists: Know Your Law, 1964; You and the Law, 1964; The Personnel Manager's Lawyer and Employer's Guide to the Law, 1964; Your Office and the Law, 1964; Your Factory and the Law, 1965; The Sales Executive's Lawyer, 1966; Your Property and the Law, 1966; The Director's Lawyer, 1968; The Businessman's Guide to Speech-making and to the Laws and Conduct of Meetings, 1968; Coping With Crime, 1969; Letters of the Law: the Businessman's Encyclopedia of Draft Letters, 1970; The Businessman's Guide to Letterwriting and to the Law on Letters, 1970; The Businessman's Legal Lexicon, 1970; The Business and Professional Man's Lawyer, 1971; The Employer's Lawyer, 1971. *Recreations:* collecting ancient glass; skin diving. *Address:* (home) 2 Linnell Drive, NW11. *T:* 01-455 5157; (chambers) 1 Garden Court, Temple, EC3. *T:* 01-353 5524.

**JANSON, Stanley Eric,** MA, PhD, BSc; Keeper, Department of Astronomy and Geophysics, Science Museum, London, 1967-69, retired; *b* 22 Nov. 1908; *s* of late O. E. Janson and late May Janson (*née* Drucquer); *m* 1939, Irene G. M. Wentworth; two *d. Educ:* Highgate Sch.; Gonville and Caius Coll., Cambridge. BSc 1930, MA 1933, PhD 1934. Assistant to Prof. of Chemistry, University of Cambridge, 1930-35; Asst Keeper, Science Museum Library, 1935; Seconded to Ministry of Supply, 1939-45; Dep. Keeper, Science Museum Library, 1947; Keeper, Dept of Chemistry, 1959-67. *Publications:* various papers on organic chemistry in scientific journals. *Recreations:* gardening, music. *Address:* 68 Tosswill Road, Tahunanui, Nelson, New Zealand.

**JANSZ, Sir (Herbert) Eric,** Kt 1953; CMG 1946; Chairman, Public Service Commission, Ceylon, 1950-60; *b* 1890; Cadet Ceylon Civil Service, 1914; District Judge, Ratnapura, 1925; Asst Settlement Officer, 1928; Settlement Officer, 1938; subsequently Commissioner of Lands, Ceylon, retd 1945. Parly Sec. to Min. of Educn, 1947-48, and to Min. of Finance, 1948-50, Ceylon. *Address:* 55 Ridge Road, N8.

**JANVRIN, Vice-Adm. Sir (Hugh) Richard Benest,** KCB 1969 (CB 1965); DSC 1940; *b* 9 May 1915; *s* of late Rev. Canon C. W. Janvrin, Fairford, Glos.; *m* 1938, Nancy Fielding; two *s. Educ:* RNC, Dartmouth. Naval Cadet, 1929; Midshipman, 1933; Sub-Lt, 1936; Lt, 1937; Qualified Fleet Air Arm Observer, 1938. Served War of 1939-45 (took part in Taranto attack, 1940). In Command: HMS Broadsword, 1951-53; HMS Grenville, 1957-58; RNAS Brawdy, 1958; HMS Victorious, 1959-60. Imperial Defence Coll., 1961; Dir, Tactics and Weapons Policy, Admiralty, 1962-63; Flag Officer, Aircraft Carriers, 1964-66; Dep. Chief of Naval Staff, MoD, 1966-68; Flag Officer, Naval Air Comd, 1968-70. Lieut-Comdr, 1945; Comdr, 1948; Capt., 1954; Rear-Adm., 1964; Vice-Adm. 1967. *Recreation:* gardening. *Address:* Allen's Close, Chalford Hill, near Stroud, Glos. *T:* Brimscombe 2336; Admiral's House, Manor Way, Lee-on-Solent, Hants. *Club:* United Service.

**JANVRIN, Sir Richard;** *see* Janvrin, Sir H. R. B.

**JANZON, Mrs Bengt;** *see* Dobbs, Mattiwilda.

**JARDINE, Sir (Andrew) Rupert (John) Buchanan-**, 4th Bt *cr* 1885; MC 1944; landowner and farmer; *b* 2 Feb. 1923; *s* of Sir John William Buchanan-Jardine, 3rd Bt and of Jean Barbara, *d* of late Lord Ernest Hamilton; *S* father, 1969; *m* 1950, Jane Fiona, 2nd *d* of Sir Charles Edmonstone, 6th Bt; one *s* one *d*. *Educ:* Harrow; Royal Agricultural College. Joined Royal Horse Guards, 1941; served in France, Holland and Germany; Major 1948; retired, 1949. Joint-Master, Dumfriesshire Foxhounds, 1950. JP 1957. Bronze Lion of the Netherlands, 1945. *Recreations:* hunting, shooting and fishing. *Heir: s* John Christopher Rupert Buchanan-Jardine, *b* 20 March 1952. *Address:* Dixons, Lockerbie, Dumfriesshire. *T:* Lockerbie 2508. *Club:* MCC.

**JARDINE, Christopher Willoughby,** CB 1967; Under-Secretary, Board of Trade, since 1962; *b* 5 Aug. 1911; *e s* of Judge Willoughby Jardine, KC; *m* 1940, Anne Eva Katharine, *er d* of Sir George Duckworth-King, 6th Bart; three *d*. *Educ:* Eton (Scholar); King's Coll., Cambridge (Scholar; 1st Cl. Hons. History); and in France and Germany. Asst Principal, Board of Trade, 1934; Principal, 1939; Asst Sec., 1945; Adviser on Commercial Policy, 1962-64; Insurance and Companies Dept, 1964-. Has represented HM Government in many foreign trade negotiations and Conferences. *Address:* 8 St Loo Mansions, Flood Street, SW3. *T:* 01-352 1246. *Club:* MCC.

**JARDINE, Brig. Sir Ian (Liddell),** 4th Bt *cr* 1916; OBE 1966; MC 1945; *b* 13 Oct. 1923; *o s* of Maj.-Gen. Sir Colin Arthur Jardine, 3rd Bt; *S* father 1957; *m* 1948, Priscilla Daphne, *d* of Douglas Middleton Parnham Scott-Phillips, Halkshill, Largs, Ayrshire; two *s* two *d*. *Educ:* Charterhouse. Served War, 1942-45, Coldstream Guards (MC); 2nd Lieut, 1943; Major, 1950; Lt-Col 1964; Col 1968; Brig., 1969. *Heir: s* Andrew Colin Douglas Jardine, *b* 30 Nov. 1955. *Address:* Coombe Place, Meonstoke, Southampton. *T:* Droxford 569.

**JARDINE, James Christopher Macnaughton;** Sheriff Substitute of Stirling, Dunbarton and Clackmannan at Dumbarton, since 1969; *b* 18 Jan. 1930; *s* of James Jardine; *m* 1954, Vena Gordon Kight; one *d*. *Educ:* Glasgow Academy; Gresham House, Ayrshire; Glasgow Univ. (BL). National Service (Lieut RASC), 1950-52. Admitted as Solicitor, in Scotland, 1953. Practice as principal (from 1955) of Nelson & Mackay, and as partner of McClure, Naismith, Brodie & Co., Solicitors, Glasgow, 1956-69. Sec., Glasgow Univ. Graduates Assoc., 1956-66; Mem., Business Cttee of Glasgow Univ. Gen. Council, 1964-67. *Recreations:* boating, photography. *Address:* Sheriff's Chambers, Dumbarton. *T:* Dumbarton 3266. *Club:* Glasgow University College (Glasgow).

**JARDINE, John,** CB 1948; OBE 1919; MD; FRCSE; DPH; FRSE; Chairman General Board of Control for Scotland, 1947-62; *b* 13 Dec. 1881; *s* of John Jardine, Penicuik; *m* 1917, Mary Alexander Hay; one *s* one *d*. *Educ:* George Heriot's Sch.; Edinburgh Univ. Medical Officer for Schools, Midlothian, 1909-24; Medical Officer to Scottish Education Dept, 1924-30; Asst Sec., 1930-43; Principal Asst Sec., 1943-45. *Publications:* numerous. *Recreations:* golf, curling. *Address:* 14 Cobden Crescent, Edinburgh 9. *T:* 031-667 1450. *Club:* New (Edinburgh).

**JARDINE, Lionel Westropp,** CIE 1939; late ICS; *b* 15 Feb. 1895; *s* of late Sir John Jardine, 1st Bt, KCIE, LLD, Godalming; *m* 1922, Marjorie Mildred Woods, Englefield Green, Surrey, one *s* two *d*. *Educ:* Charterhouse (Scholar); Wadham Coll., Oxford (Exhibitioner). Served European War, 1914-18 (despatches, wounded); Political Service, Mesopotamia, 1919-21 (general service medal and bar, Iraq); entered ICS, 1921; NW Frontier, 1924-31 (general service medal, 1931) and 1936-39; Finance Minister, Kashmir State, 1932; Dep. Commissioner, Peshawar, 1936; Revenue and Divisional Commissioner, N-WFP, India, 1938-43 and 1946; Resident for Baroda and the Gujerat States, India, 1943-44; left India, 1947, to join Dr F. N. D. Buchman in the work of Moral Re-armament. *Address:* 4 Balfour Mews, W1Y 5RL. *T:* 01-499 7285. *Club:* Naval and Military.

**JARDINE, Robert Frier,** CMG 1928; OBE 1926; Third Class of the Order of Al Rafidain of Iraq, 1937; *b* 9 June 1894; *s* of late Robert Brown Jardine; *m* 1932, Averil, *o d* of late H. O. Dickin; twin *s* (both Mems of 1960, 1964, 1968 British Olympic Yachting teams). *Educ:* Downing Coll., Cambridge. Commissioned Sept. 1914 from Cambridge Univ. OTC; served European War in Egypt, Gallipoli and Mesopotamia (despatches); in political charge of districts in Northern Iraq and Kurdistan, 1917-21; repatriated Assyrians to their original homes in Hakkiari, 1922; Political Officer to columns in Kurdistan, 1923; Mem. of HMG Delegation to Turkey and League of Nations upon Turkish frontier question, 1924; HM Assessor on League of Nations' Commission in connection with Turco-Iraq frontier, and upon other Commissions, 1925; Administrative Inspector, Mosul Province, 1925-28; Adviser to British Ambassador in Turkey for Tripartite Treaty, 1926; Frontier Commissioner, 1927; Administrative Inspector, Basra Province, 1928-33; Pres. of Commission for settlement of titles to land in Iraq, 1933-36; acted in various capacities in Palestine, 1936-48, including Dir of Settlement and Registration of titles to Land, Civil Aviation, Commissioner for Auqaf, Irrigation, Commissioner of Compensation for Rebellion and War Damages, 1945; Land Settlement and Water Commissioner; Advisory Councillor. During War of 1939-45 assisted with political advice as Lt-Col, Gen. Staff, Jerusalem Bureau. *Publications:* Grammar of Bahdinan Kurmanji (Kurdish), 1922; Gazetteer of Place Names in Palestine and Trans-Jordan, 1941. *Recreation:* yachting. *Address:* Walhampton March, Lymington, Hants. *T:* Lymington 2481. *Clubs:* Royal Lymington Yacht, etc.

**JARDINE, Sir Rupert Buchanan-;** *see* Jardine, Sir A. R. J. B.

**JARDINE of Applegirth, Col Sir William Edward,** 11th Bart, *cr* 1672; OBE 1966; TD; DL; JP; late The KOSB; *b* 15 April 1917; *s* of Sir Alexander Jardine of Applegirth, 10th Baronet, and Winifred Mary Hamilton (*d* 1954), *d* of Major Young, Lincluden House, Dumfries; *S* father, 1942; *m* 1944, Ann Graham, *yr d* of late Lt-Col Claud Maitland, DSO, Gordon Highlanders, of Dundrennan and Cumstoun, Kirkcudbright; two *s*. Mem. of The Queen's Body Guard for Scotland, The Royal Company of Archers. Lt-Col Comd 4/5 KOSB (TA), 1963-67, Bt Col 1967. JP 1962, DL 1970, co. of Dumfries. *Heir: s* Alexander Maule Jardine, *b* 24 Aug. 1947. *Address:* Denbie, Lockerbie, Dumfriesshire. *T:* Carrutherstown 211. *Club:* New, Puffin's (Edinburgh).

**JARDINE-BROWN, Prof. Robert;** Principal of College of Estate Management since 1955 and Dean of Faculty of Urban and Regional Studies, Reading University, since 1967 (on integration of College with University); *b* 16 March 1905; *s* of Walter Falconer Brown, MB, CM, DPH, and Catherine Edith (*née* McGhie); *m* 1938, Ormonde Joan (*née* Butler); two *s*. *Educ:* Ayr Academy; Univs of Glasgow and Edinburgh. MA 1926, LLB 1928, Glasgow; DLitt 1947, Edinburgh. Called to Bar, Middle Temple, 1931; Advocate of Scots Bar, 1945. Has held various posts, incl.: Legal Adviser and Business Man., BBC, 1936-45; Sec., Univ. of Edinburgh, 1945-47. Mem., English Agricultural Wages Board, 1959-; Mem., Scottish Agricultural Wages Board, 1963-. Officer, Order of Orange Nassau. *Publications:* mainly legal and educational in English and American jls. *Recreations:* walking, reading, appreciation of visual art. *Address:* High Point, Riverview Road, Pangbourne, Berks. *T:* Pangbourne 2849. *Clubs:* Chelsea Arts; Royal Cornwall Yacht.

*See also T. W. F. Brown.*

**JARDINE PATERSON, Sir John (Valentine),** Kt 1967; Director, McLeod Russel & Co. Ltd, London, since 1967; *b* 14 Feb. 1920; *y s* of late Robert Jardine Paterson, Balgray, Lockerbie, Dumfriesshire, and Constance Margaret Jardine Paterson (*née* Steel), Dalawoodie, Newbridge, Dumfries; *m* 1953, Priscilla Mignon, *d* of late Sir Kenneth Nicolson, MC, and of Lady Nicolson; one *s* three *d*. *Educ:* Eton Coll.; Jesus Coll., Cambridge. Emergency commn, The Black Watch, RHR, 1939; demobilised and arrived in Calcutta to join Jardine Skinner & Co., 1946 (firm became Jardine Henderson Ltd, 1947); Dir of Jardine Henderson Ltd, 1952-67 (Chm. 1963-67), also Chm. of Braithwaite & Co. (India) Ltd, Indian Cable Co. Ltd, Shalimar Paints Ltd, and Triton Insurance Co. Ltd, 1963-67. Chm., Indian Jute Mills Assoc., 1963; Pres., Bengal Chamber of Commerce and Industry, 1966; Pres., Associated Chambers of Commerce of India, 1966. Mem. Local Bd, Reserve Bank of India, 1965-67. *Recreations:* golf, racing, shooting. *Address:* Norton Bavant Manor, Warminster, Wilts. *T:* Sutton Veny 378. *Clubs:* Bath, Oriental; Bengal, Royal Calcutta Turf (Calcutta).

**JARMAN, Rev. Canon Cyril Edgar;** Canon Residentiary, Chester Cathedral, since 1943; *b* 2 Dec. 1892; *s* of William and Annie Jarman, Cliftonville, Margate; *m* 1928, Alice Josephine, *d* of Canon Stockley, Wolverhampton, Chancellor of Lichfield Cathedral; two *d*. *Educ:* Holy Trinity Sch., Margate; The Theological Coll., Lichfield. Ordained, Lichfield, 1916; Curate, St James', Wednesbury, 1916-22; Curate St Peter's, Wolverhampton, 1922-25; Vicar, St Mary's, Shrewsbury, 1925-37; Vicar, Penkridge, 1937-43; Prebendary of Lichfield Cathedral, 1941-43. Examining Chaplain to Bishop of Chester, 1939-; Chaplain to High Sheriff of Cheshire, 1955. Vice-Dean, 1965. *Recreations:* tennis, walking. *Address:* 9 Abbey Square, Chester. *T:* 20367.

**JARMAN, Air Cdre Lance Elworthy,** DFC 1940; RAF (retired); Director, Engineering Industries Association, since 1958; *b* 17 Aug. 1907; *s* of Hedley Elworthy and Mary Elizabeth Jarman (*née* Chatterway-Clarke); *m* 1940, Elizabeth Evelyn Litton-Puttock; one *s* one *d*. *Educ:* Christchurch High Sch., NZ; Canterbury Coll., NZ. Commissioned, RAF, 1929; No 12 Bomber Sqdn, Andover, 1930; No 14 Bomber Sqdn, Amman, 1931; Officers' Engineering Course, Henlow, 1932; RAF, Abukir, Atbara, Sudan, Cairo, 1935; Maintenance Command, 1938. Served War of 1939-45: Nos 214 and 9 Bomber Sqdns, 1939; Chief Flying Instructor, Nos 11-20 and 23 Operational Training Units, 1940; CO, No 27 OTU, Lichfield, 1941; SASO, No 93 Bomber Gp, 1942; CO, RAF Stations, Kidlington and Wyton, 1943; SASO, No 205 Gp, Italy, 1945, qualified as Pathfinder; OC RAF Stations, Oakington and Abingdon, 1947; Senior Officer Administration, RAF, No 42 Gp, 1949; OC, RAF Jet Training Stations, Full Sutton and Merryfield, 1951; Chief of Staff, Royal Pakistan Air Force, 1952; AO Defence Research Policy Staff, Cabinet Office, 1955; AOA, NATO, Channel and Atlantic Commands, 1957; retired from RAF, 1958. CEng, MIMechE, AFRAeS, MBIM, MAIE. *Publications:* Editor, Engineering Industries Jl. *Recreation:* sailing. *Address:* Merryfield, 42 Murray Road, Northwood, Mddx. *T:* Northwood 24010. *Clubs:* Royal Air Force; Royal Ocean Racing; RAF Yacht (Hamble); Royal New Zealand Yacht Squadron.

**JARRATT, Alexander Anthony,** CB 1968; Managing Director, International Publishing Corporation, since 1970; *b* 19 Jan. 1924; *o s* of Alexander and Mary Jarratt; *m* 1946, Mary Philomena Keogh; one *s* two *d*. *Educ:* Royal Liberty Gram. Sch., Essex; University of Birmingham. War Service, Fleet Air Arm, 1942-46. University of Birmingham, BCom, 1946-49. Asst Principal, Min. of Power, 1949; Priv. Sec. to Perm. Sec., 1951-53; Principal, 1953, and seconded to Treas., 1954-55; Min. of Power: Prin. Priv. Sec. to Minister, 1955-59; Asst Sec., Oil Div., 1959-63; Under-Sec., Gas Div., 1963-64; seconded to Cabinet Office, 1964-65; Secretary to the National Board for Prices and Incomes, 1965-68; Dep. Sec., 1967; Dep. Under Sec. of State, Dept of Employment and Productivity, 1968-70; Dep. Sec., Min. of Agriculture, 1970. Jt Founder and Chm., Hutton Park Preparatory Sch., Essex. *Recreations:* reading, painting, motoring. *Address:* 9 Parkway, Shenfield, Essex. *T:* Brentwood 1753. *Club:* Savile.

**JARRETT, Sir Clifford (George),** KBE 1956 (CBE 1945); CB 1949; Permanent Under-Secretary of State, Department of Health and Social Security (formerly Ministry of Pensions and National Insurance, then Ministry of Social Security), 1964-70; *b* 1909; *s* of George Henry Jarrett; *m* 1933, Hilda Alice Goodchild; one *s* two *d*. *Educ:* Dover County Sch.; Sidney Sussex Coll., Cambridge. BA 1931. Entered Civil Service, 1932; Asst Principal, Home Office, 1932-34, Admiralty, 1934-38; Private Sec. to Parl. Sec., 1936-38; Principal Private Sec. to First Lord, 1940-44; Principal Establishments Officer, 1946-50; a Dep. Sec., Admiralty, 1950-61; Permanent Sec., Admiralty, 1961-64. A Trustee, Nat. Maritime Museum, 1969-. *Address:* Abetone, Yester Road, Chislehurst. *Club:* United University.

**JARRETT, Norman Rowlstone,** CMG 1946; BA (Oxon.); *b* 23 Aug. 1889; *s* of late Arthur E. Jarrett, Netherby Cottage, Anstye, Cuckfield, Sussex; *m* 1st, Doris Griffith; one *s* one *d*; 2nd, Violet, *d* of Rev. W. H. Wilkinson, Warminster. *Educ:* Highgate Sch.; Exeter Coll., Oxford (2nd Class Lit Hum 1912). Cadet FMS Civil Service, 1912; various administrative appointments in Malayan Civil Service, 1913-37; British Adviser, Trengganu, 1937; Food Controller, Malaya, 1939-41; Acting British Resident, Selangor, 1941; interned by Japanese in Singapore, 1942-45; Sec., Assoc. of British Malaya, 1946-53. *Recreations:* gardening, music. *Address:* Anvil Cottage, Lye Green, near Crowborough, Sussex. *T:* Crowborough 4466.

**JARROLD, (Herbert) John,** CBE 1969; MA; JP; Chairman, Jarrold & Sons Ltd, since 1937; *b* 16 Feb. 1906; *s* of late T. H. C. Jarrold, and *g g g s* of John Jarrold, founder of Jarrold & Sons Ltd

(1770); *m* 1932, Catherine Grace Elliott; three *s*. *Educ:* Norwich Sch.; Queens' Coll., Cambridge. Studied printing and bookbinding in Leipzig; joined Jarrold & Sons Ltd, 1927. Councillor, Norwich City Council, 1936-47; Sheriff of Norwich, 1947-49, Alderman, 1949-56. Pres., British Fedn of Master Printers, 1961-62; Chm., Printing, Packaging and Allied Trades Research Assoc., 1964; Pres., Norwich Incorporated Chamber of Commerce, 1965-67. JP Norwich 1949; Lord Mayor of Norwich, 1970-71. *Publications:* many articles on colour reproduction and printing. *Address:* Church Avenue, Norwich NOR 91E. *T:* Norwich 54612. *Club:* National Liberal.

**JARROW, Bishop Suffragan of,** since 1965; **Rt. Rev. Alexander Kenneth Hamilton,** MA; *b* 11 May 1915; *s* of Cuthbert Arthur Hamilton and Agnes Maud Hamilton; unmarried. *Educ:* Malvern Coll.; Trinity Hall, Cambridge; Westcott House, Cambridge. MA 1941. Asst Curate of Birstall, Leicester, 1939-41; Asst Curate of Whitworth with Spennymoor, 1941-45. Chaplain, RNVR, 1945-47. Vicar of S Francis, Ashton Gate, Bristol, 1947-58; Vicar of S John the Baptist, Newcastle upon Tyne, 1958-65; Rural Dean of Central Newcastle, 1962-65. *Publication:* Personal Prayers, 1963. *Recreations:* golf, trout fishing. *Address:* Melkridge House, Gilesgate, Durham. *T:* Durham 3797. *Clubs:* RNVR; Burnham and Berrow Golf; Brancepeth Castle Golf.

**JARVIS, Alan Hepburn;** Chairman, Society of Art Publications, Ottawa, since 1959; *b* 26 July 1915; *s* of Charles Arthur Jarvis and Janet Mackay, Brantford; *m* 1955, Elizabeth Devlin Kingsmill; one *s* two *d*. *Educ:* University of Toronto; University Coll., Oxford; Graduate Sch. of Fine Art, New York Univ. Ministry of Aircraft Production, 1941-45; Priv. Sec. to Sir Stafford Cripps, 1945; Dir of Public Relations, Council of Industrial Design, 1945-47; Dir, Pilgrim Pictures Ltd, 1947-50; Head of Oxford House, Bethnal Green, 1950-55; Dir, National Gallery of Canada, 1955-59. *Publications:* (ed.) Democracy Alive, The Collected Speeches of Sir Stafford Cripps, 1946; The Things We See–Indoors and Out, 1946; (with Sir Gordon Russell) How to Buy Furniture, 1953. *Recreation:* sculpting. *Address:* 541 Manor Road, Rockcliffe, Ont, Canada. *Club:* Rideau (Ottawa).

**JARVIS, Ven. Alfred Clifford,** MA; Archdeacon of Lindsey, and Canon Residentiary of Lincoln Cathedral since 1960; *b* 6 Feb. 1908; *o s* of late A. W. Jarvis; *m* 1937, Mary Dorothea Chapple. *Educ:* Sudbury Grammar Sch.; Fitzwilliam House, Cambridge; Lichfield Theological Coll. Curate of Brightlingsea, 1931; permission to officiate Diocese of Ely, 1936; Vicar of Horningsea, 1937; Chaplain to Fulbourn Mental Hospital, 1937; Rector of Coddenham, 1944-55; Curate in charge of Hemingstone, 1949-52; Hon. Chaplain to Bishop of St Edmundsbury and Ipswich, 1954; Vicar of Elsfield and Beckley, and Curate in charge of Horton cum Studley, 1955-58. Archdeacon of Lincoln, Canon and Preb. of St Mary Crackpool in Lincoln Cathedral, and Rector of Algarkirk, 1958-60. Proctor in Convocation, 1961; Warden of Lincoln Diocesan Assoc. of Readers, 1960. *Recreations:* shooting and fishing. *Address:* The Archdeaconry, Lincoln. *T:* Lincoln 25784. *Clubs:* Oxford and Cambridge University; Flyfishers'.

**JARVIS, Mrs Doris Annie,** CBE 1969; Headmistress, Tower Hamlets Comprehensive Girls' School, since (opening) 1963; *b* 18 April 1912; *d* of William George Mabbitt (killed on active service, 1918) and Ada Marie Mabbitt; *m* 1940, George Harry Jarvis; one *s*. *Educ:* South Hackney Central Sch.; City of London Sch. for Girls; King's Coll., London (BSc); Furzedown Training Coll., London. Commenced teaching in Bethnal Green, E2, Sept. 1935; worked in E London schools and evacuation areas during War period; post-war, taught at Daniel Secondary Sch., E2; Emergency Training College Lecturer, Camden Trg Coll., 1949-50; Headminstress, Wilmot Secondary Girls' Sch., Bethnal Green, E2, 1950-63. *Recreations:* home affairs, reading, walking, gardening; furthering knowledge of education and social work in E London, generally. *Address:* 1a Tolmers Avenue, Cuffley, Herts. *T:* Cuffley 3780.

**JARVIS, Eric William George,** CMG 1961; Judge of the High Court, Rhodesia, since 1963; *b* 22 Nov. 1907; *s* of late William Stokes Jarvis and Edith Mary Jarvis (*née* Langley), both of Essex, England; *m* 1937, Eveline Mavis Smith; one *s* one *d*. *Educ:* Salisbury Boys High Sch. (now Prince Edward Sch.), Salisbury, R; Rhodes Univ., Grahamstown, SA. BA (Hons R Law); LLB; admitted as Advocate High Court of Southern Rhodesia, 1929; appointed Law Officer of Crown, 1934; KC (1949); Solicitor-Gen. for Southern Rhodesia, 1949-55; Attorney-Gen. for Southern Rhodesia, 1955-62. *Recreations:* tennis, golf, bowls. *Address:* (home) 5 Lawson Avenue, Milton Park, Salisbury, Rhodesia. *T:* 82145; (office) PO Box 8050, Causeway, Salisbury. *T:* 26113/4. *Club:* Salisbury (Salisbury, R).

**JASPER, Robin Leslie Darlow,** CMG 1963; HM Consul-General at Naples, since 1967; *b* 22 Feb. 1914; *s* of T. D. Jasper, Beckenham; *m* 1st, 1940, Jean (marr. diss.), *d* of late Brig.-Gen. J. K. Cochrane, CMG; one *d*; 2nd, 1966, Diana Speed (*née* West), two step *d*. *Educ:* Dulwich; Clare Coll., Cambridge. Apprentice, LNER Hotels Dept, 1936-39; Bursar, Dominion Students Hall Trust (London House), 1939-40; RAFVR (Wing Comdr), 1940-46; Principal, India Office (later Commonwealth Relations Officer), 1946; concerned with resettlement of the Sec. of State's Services in India, 1947-48; British Dep. High Commissioner, Lahore, Pakistan, 1949-52; Adviser to London Conferences on Central African Federation, and visited Central Africa in this connection, 1952-53; Counsellor, HM Embassy, Lisbon, 1953-55; visited Portuguese Africa, 1954; Commonwealth Relations Office, 1955-60 (Head of Information Policy Dept, 1958-60); attached to the United Kingdom delegation to the United Nations, 1955 and 1956; British Dep. High Commissioner, Ibadan, Nigeria, 1960-64; Counsellor, Commonwealth Office, 1965-67. *Recreations:* tennis, Rugby fives, wind music, 17th Century Church Sculpture, claret. *Address:* c/o Foreign and Commonwealth Office, SW1. *Clubs:* United University, MCC.

**JASPER, Rev. Canon Ronald Claud Dudley,** DD; Canon Residentiary of Westminster, since 1968; *b* 17 Aug. 1917; *o s* of Claud Albert and late Florence Lily Jasper; *m* 1943, Ethel, *o d* of David and Edith Wiggins; one *s* one *d*. *Educ:* Plymouth Coll.; University of Leeds; College of the Resurrection, Mirfield. MA (with distinction), 1940; DD 1961; FRHistS 1954. Curate of Ryhope, 1940-42; St Oswald's, Durham, 1942-43; Esh, 1943-46; Chaplain of University Coll., Durham, 1946-48; Vicar of Stillington, 1948-55; Succentor of Exeter Cathedral, 1955-60; Lecturer in Liturgical Studies: King's Coll., London, 1960-67 (Reader, 1967-68); Royal School of Church Music, 1970-. Chm., Church of England Liturgical Commn, 1964-. *Publications:* Prayer Book Revision in England, 1800-1900, 1954; Walter Howard Frere: Correspondence and

Memoranda on Liturgical Revision and Construction, 1954; Arthur Cayley Headlam, 1960; The Renewal of Worship (ed), 1965; George Bell: Bishop of Chichester, 1967; The Calendar and Lectionary (ed), 1967; The Daily Office (ed), 1968; contribs to Church Quarterly Review, Jl of Ecclesiastical History, Church Quarterly, London Quarterly. *Recreations:* reading, writing, television. *Address:* 1 Little Cloister, Dean's Yard, Westminster, SW1. *T:* 01-222 4027.

**JAUJARD, Jacques;** Hon. KBE 1953; Hon. CVO 1957; Grand Officier de la Légion d'Honneur, 1946; Médaille de la Résistance; Medal of Freedom; Membre de l'Institut; Conseiller d'Etat; Secrétaire Général des Affaires Culturelles; *b* 3 Dec. 1895. *Educ:* Lycée Condorcet, Paris. Sec. to Paul Painlevé, 1922; Principal Private Sec., 1924-30; Musées Nationaux; Head of Secretariat, 1925; Sec.-Gen., Asst Dir, 1926-39; Dir, 1939-44; during this time brought about many important reforms in the national museums and the Ecole du Louvre. Helped to safeguard Prado collections and Spanish works of art during Spanish Civil War. Organised total evacuation of all French public and some private collections, 1939. As Directeur Général des Arts et des Lettres, 1944-59, has organised many reforms in the national theatres and art schools. Numerous foreign decorations. *Address:* 68 Boulevard Pasteur, Paris 15e. *T:* Ségur 74.08.

**JAUNCEY, Charles Eliot,** QC (Scotland) 1963; Advocate; *b* 8 May 1925; *s* of late Capt. John Henry Jauncey, DSO, RN, Tullichettle, Comrie, and Muriel Charlie, *d* of late Adm. Sir Charles Dundas of Dundas, KCMG; *m* 1948, Jean (marr. diss. 1969), *d* of Adm. Sir Angus Cunninghame Graham, *qv*; two *s* one *d*. *Educ:* Radley; Christ Church, Oxford; Glasgow Univ. BA 1947, Oxford; LLB 1949, Glasgow. Served in War, 1943-46, Sub-Lt RNVR. Advocate, Scottish Bar, 1949; Standing Junior Counsel to Admiralty, 1954; Kintyre Pursuivant of Arms, 1955; Hon. Sheriff-Substitute of Perthshire, 1962. Mem. of Royal Co. of Archers (Queen's Body Guard for Scotland), 1951. *Recreations:* shooting, fishing, genealogy. *Address:* Tullichettle, Comrie, Perthshire. *T:* 349; 11 Forres Street, Edinburgh 3. *T:* 031-225 4612. *Clubs:* New (Edinburgh); Royal (Perth).

**JAWARA, Hon. Sir Dawda Kairaba,** Kt 1966; MP (the Gambia); President of the Republic of the Gambia, since 1970; *b* Barajally, MacCarthy Island Div., 1924. *Educ:* Muslim Primary Sch. and Methodist Boys' Grammar Sch., Bathurst; Achimota Coll. (Vet. School); Glasgow Univ. Veterinary Officer, Kombo St Mary, 1954-60; Dipl. in Trop. Vet. Med., Edinburgh, 1957. Leader of People's Progressive Party, the Gambia, 1960; Minister of Education, 1960-61; Premier, 1962-63; Prime Minister, 1963-70. *Address:* State House, Bathurst, The Gambia.

**JAY, Rt. Hon. Douglas Patrick Thomas,** PC 1951; MP (Lab) North Battersea, since July 1946; *b* 23 March 1907; *s* of Edward Aubrey Hastings Jay and Isobel Violet Jay; *m* 1933, Margaret Christian, *e d* of late J. C. Maxwell Garnett, CBE, ScD; two *s* two *d*. *Educ:* Winchester Coll.; New Coll., Oxford (Scholar). First Class, Litteræ Humaniores; Fellow of All Souls' Coll., Oxford, 1930-37, and 1968-; on the staff of The Times, 1929-33, and The Economist, 1933-37; City Editor of the Daily Herald, 1937-41; Asst Sec., Ministry of Supply, 1941-43; Principal Asst Sec., Bd of Trade, 1943-45; Personal Asst to Prime Minister, 1945-46; Economic Sec. to Treasury, 1947-50; Financial Sec. to Treasury, 1950-51; President, Bd of Trade, 1964-67. Chairman: Common Market Safeguards Campaign, 1970-; London Motorway Action Group, 1968-. Director: Courtaulds Ltd, 1967-70; Trades Union Unit Trust, 1967-; Flag Investment Co., 1968-. *Publications:* The Socialist Case, 1937; Who is to Pay for the War and the Peace, 1941; Socialism in the New Society, 1962; After the Common Market, 1968. *Address:* 12 Well Road, NW3. *T:* 01-435 3192.

**JAY, Rev. Canon Eric George;** Professor of Historical Theology, Faculty of Divinity, McGill University, since 1958; *b* 1 March 1907; *s* of Henry Jay, Colchester, Essex; *m* 1937, Margaret Hilda, *d* of Rev. Alfred W. Webb; one *s* two *d*. *Educ:* Colchester High Sch.; Leeds Univ. BA 1st Cl. Hons Classics, 1929; MA 1930; BD (London) 1937; MTh 1940; PhD 1951. Deacon, 1931; priest, 1932; Curate, St Augustine, Stockport, 1931-34; Lecturer in Theology, King's Coll., London, 1934-47; Curate, St Andrew Undershaft, City of London, 1935-40. Served War as Chaplain in RAFVR 1940-45. Rector, St Mary-le-Strand, 1945-47; Dean of Nassau, Bahamas, 1948-51; Senior Chaplain to the Archbishop of Canterbury, 1951-58; Principal, Montreal Diocesan Theological Coll., 1958-64; Dean Faculty of Divinity, McGill Univ., 1963-70. Fellow of King's Coll., London, 1948; Canon of Montreal, 1960. Hon. DD (Montreal Diocesan Theolog. Coll.), 1964. *Publications:* The Existence of God, 1946; Origen's Treatise on Prayer, 1954; New Testament Greek: an Introductory Grammar, 1958; Son of Man, Son of God, 1965. *Recreations:* reading "thrillers"; watching cricket, Rugby football. *Address:* 570 Milton Street, Montreal 130, Canada.

**JAYAWARDANA, Brig. Christopher Allan Hector Perera,** CMG 1956; CVO 1954; OBE 1944 (MBE 1941); ED 1936; JP; Camp Chief, Boy Scouts' Association of Ceylon; *b* 29 March 1898; 4th *s* of Gate Muhandiram Herat Perera Jayawardana; *m* 1924, Sylvia Dorothy Samarasinhe, *e d* of Mudaliyar Soloman Dias Samarasinhe; one *d* (and one *s* decd). *Educ:* Trinity Coll., Kandy, Ceylon; Keble Coll., Oxford (MA). Sen. Asst Conservator of Forests, Ceylon (retd); Dep. Warden of Wild Life, Ceylon (retd), 1924-29; served War of 1939-45; OC 1st Bn the Ceylon LI, 1938-43; Chief Comr, Ceylon Boy Scouts' Association, 1949-54; Extra Aide de Camp to HE the Governor Gen. of Ceylon, 1949-; Equerry to HM the Queen, during Royal Visit to Ceylon, 1954; Hon. ADC to the Queen, 1954-. Pres., Ceylon Rifle Assoc., 1969-. Awarded Silver Wolf, 1949. FLS, 1924. Carnegie Schol., 1931; Smith-Mundt Schol., 1951; KStJ, 1959 (CStJ, 1954). Diploma of Forestry. *Recreations:* rifle shooting, big game hunting, deep sea fishing, golf, tennis, riding, painting, camping, photography. *Address:* 12 Sukhastan Gardens, Ward Place, Colombo 7, Ceylon. *T:* (home) 91354; (office) 33131. *Clubs:* Corona; Sea Anglers' (Ceylon).

**JAYES, Percy Harris,** MB, BS, FRCS; Plastic Surgeon: St Bartholomew's Hospital, London, since 1952; Queen Victoria Hospital, East Grinstead, since 1948: Consultant in Plastic Surgery to the Royal Air Force, since 1960; Consultant Plastic Surgeon, King Edward VII Hospital for Officers since 1966; Consulting Plastic Surgeon to: Manor House Hospital, London; Chailey Heritage; Seamen's Group of Hospitals; Chelsea Hospital for Women; *b* 26 June 1915; *s* of Thomas Harris Jayes; *m* 1945, Kathleen Mary Harrington (*d* 1963); two *s* one *d*; *m* 1964, Aileen Mary McLaughlin; one *s* one *d*. *Educ:* Merchant Taylors' Sch.; St

Bartholomew's Hosp. Resid. Plastic Surg., EMS Plastic Unit, East Grinstead, 1940-48; Surgeon in Charge, UNRRA Plastic Unit, Belgrade, 1946; Mem. Council, Brit. Assoc. Plastic Surgeons, 1954-64 (Pres., Assoc., 1960). *Publications:* contrib. British Journal of Plastic Surgery, Annals of Royal College of Surgeons and other journals. *Recreation:* tennis. *Address:* Barton St Mary, Lewes Road, East Grinstead. *T:* East Grinstead 23461; 149 Harley Street, W1N 2DE. *T:* 01-935 4444. *Club:* Lansdowne.

**JAYETILEKE, Sir Edward (George Perera),** Kt, *cr* 1951; QC (Ceylon) 1938; *b* 11 Oct. 1888; *s* of John Gratiaen Perera Jayetileke and Maria Perera; *m* 1915, Grace Victoria Abeyesundere; one *s* three *d*. *Educ:* Royal College, Colombo. Called to the Ceylon Bar, 1910; Solicitor-Gen., 1939; Attorney-Gen., 1941; Puisne Justice, 1942; Senior Puisne Justice, 1949; Chm. Judicial Service Commission, 1950-51; Chief Justice, Ceylon, 1950-51. *Recreations:* racing, bridge, horticulture. *Address:* Tilakasthan, Gregory's Road, Colombo 7, Ceylon. *T:* 9440. *Clubs:* Ceylon Turf, Orient (Colombo); Galle Gymkhana (Galle).

**JEANS, Sir Alick (Alexander Grigor),** Kt 1967; TD; JP; Chairman and Managing Director, The Liverpool Daily Post and Echo Ltd; *b* 29 July 1912; *s* of late Allan Jeans; *m* 1939, Jean Mary Plummer; three *s*. *Educ:* Rugby; University Coll., Oxford. Chm., Press Association, 1953-54; Pres., Newspaper Soc., 1959-60. *Address:* Inchbroom, Farr Hall Road, Heswall, Cheshire. *T:* 051-342 2561. *Clubs:* Royal Thames Yacht, Army and Navy; Old Hall, Exchange and Palatine, Racquet, Press (Liverpool).

**JEANS, Isabel;** Actress; *b* London; *d* of Frederick George Jeans; *m* 1st, Claud Rains (marr. diss.); 2nd, Gilbert Edward, *y s* of late Rt Rev. Henry Russell Wakefield, Bishop of Birmingham; no *c*. *Educ:* London. Made first appearance under Sir Herbert Tree's management at His Majesty's; first acting role was at the Garrick as Peggy in The Greatest Wish; went to United States with Granville Barker's Company, playing Titania in A Midsummer Night's Dream and Fanny in Fanny's First Play; on returning to England appeared in musical comedy and then joined the Everyman Repertory Company, playing Fanny, Raina in Arms and the Man, Hypatia in Misalliance, and Olivia in Twelfth Night, and also appeared in a number of Elizabethan and Restoration revivals by the Phœnix Society including Volpone, The Maid's Tragedy, The Jew of Malta, The Old Bachelor, and as Margery Pinchwife in The Country Wife; went to Holland to play Laura Pasquale in At Mr Beam's, and later played Yasmin in Hassan at His Majesty's and Lydia Languish in The Rivals at the Lyric, Hammersmith; since 1924 has appeared as Zelie in The Rat, Nell Gwynne in Mr Pepys, Lady Dare Bellingham in Conflict, Amytis in The Road to Rome, Estelle in Beauty, Crystal Wetherby in The Man in Possession, subsequently playing the same part in New York, Leslie in Counsel's Opinion, Mrs Jelliwell in Springtime for Henry, Lady Coperario in Spring 1600, Lucy Lockit in The Beggar's Opera, Lola in Full House, La Gambogi in The Happy Hypocrite, Alice Galvoisier in Mademoiselle, Susanna Venables in Second Helping, Lady Utterwood in Heartbreak House, Mrs Erlynne in Lady Windermere's Fan; went to New York, Jan. 1948, to play Lucia in Make Way for Lucia; since returning to London has appeared as Madame Arkadina in The Seagull; The Countess in Ardele; Florence Lancaster in The Vortex; Mrs Allonby in A Woman of No Importance; Lady Elizabeth Mulhammer in The Confidential Clerk (created rôle at Edinburgh Festival, 1953, and appeared in it finally at Paris Festival of Dramatic Art, 1954; made first appearance on Television, in this rôle, 1955); Sophie Faramond in the Gates of Summer. In 1957 created rôle of Aunt Alicia in the film Gigi; Duchess of Berwick in Lady Windermere's Fan, 1966; Mrs Malaprop in The Rivals, 1967; Lady Bracknell in The Importance of Being Earnest, Haymarket, 1968; Mme Desmortes in Ring Round the Moon, Haymarket, 1969. Films and TV plays in Hollywood, Paris, Rome and Vienna. *Recreation:* reading historical biographies. *Address:* 66/24 John Islip Street, SW1.

**JEANS, Ronald;** *s* of late Sir Alexander Jeans; *m* 1916, Margaret Evelyn Wise; one *s* one *d*. *Educ:* Loretto. Studied art at the Slade Sch. for a while; then entered business in Liverpool; after some years gave this up for writing; was one of the founders of the Liverpool Playhouse, the second Repertory Theatre in England, in 1911; for this theatre in its early days wrote several plays, and later devoted his whole attention to intimate revues which were produced by André Charlot, C. B. Cochran, Jack Hulbert, etc.; later reverted to plays with Lean Harvest, Can the Leopard?, The Composite Man, Ghost for Sale, and Young Wives' Tale (1949); Count Your Blessings (1951); Grace and Favour, 1954; Double Take, 1958. Founded (with J. B. Priestley) the London Mask Theatre Company, 1938 and revived this company, 1947. *Publications:* Vignettes from Vaudeville; Odd Numbers; The Stage is Waiting; one Dam Sketch After Another; Charlot Revue Sketches, Review of Revues, Sundry Sketches, After Dark, Lean Harvest, Blackout Sketches, Bright Intervals; Writing for the Theatre, 1949. *Address:* 85 Marine Parade, Brighton, Sussex. *Clubs:* Royal Automobile, Dramatists'.

**JEANS, Ursula;** Actress; *b* India; *d* of Major Charles McMinn; *m* 1st, Robin Irvine (*decd*); 2nd, Roger Livesey, *qv*; no *c*. *Educ:* Sacred Heart Convent, Cavendish Square, London. Made first appearance Theatre Royal, Nottingham, 1925, as Sophie Binner in Cobra, after training Royal Academy Dramatic Art, London; first appearance on London stage as Angela in The Firebrand, Wyndham's, 1926, followed by numerous stage successes including Elsie Fraser in The First Mrs Fraser, Haymarket, 1929, Flaemmchen in Grand Hotel, Adelphi, 1931, Sarah Traille in Lovers' Leap, Vaudeville, 1934, Penelope Marsh in Short Story, Queen's, 1935; Alithea in The Country Wife, Old Vic, 1936, etc.; also a season of classical plays at the Old Vic Theatre, 1933-34, Viola in Twelfth Night, Anya in The Cherry Orchard, Anne Bullen in Henry VIII, Mariana in Measure for Measure, Cecily Cardew in The Importance of Being Earnest, Angelica in Love for Love, Miranda in The Tempest; and a further season, 1939, as Kate Hardcastle in She Stoops to Conquer, Petra in The Enemy of the People, Katherine in The Taming of the Shrew; toured as Mary of Magdala in Family Portrait, 1940; Joanna in Dear Brutus, Globe, 1941; toured as Elvira in Blithe Spirit, 1942, as Sara Müller in Watch on the Rhine, 1943 (also at Aldwych, 1943); on tour with ENSA in Dear Brutus, Watch on the Rhine, Springtime for Henry, It Depends What You Mean; Frances in The Banbury Nose, Wyndham's, 1944; with ENSA in Middle and Far East, 1945-46, playing Lady Teazle in School for Scandal and Elizabeth Barrett in The Barretts of Wimpole Street; played Helen in Ever Since Paradise (by J. B. Priestley), New, 1947; Lavinia in The Cocktail Party, Edinburgh Festival, 1949; Mary

Bernard in Man of the World, Lyric (Hammersmith), 1950; toured Italy with Old Vic Co., as Olivia in Twelfth Night, June 1950; Dame Overdo in Bartholomew Fair, Edinburgh Festival, 1950; Old Vic, 1950-51; Olivia in Twelfth Night, Dame Overdo in Bartholomew Fair, Lady Cicely Waynflete in Captain Brassbound's Conversion, Mistress Ford in The Merry Wives of Windsor; Jean Moreland in Third Person, Arts, 1951, and Criterion, 1952; Lady Pounce-Pellott in the Baikie Charivari, Glasgow Citizen's Theatre, 1952; Margaret Bell in The Teddy Bear, St Martin's, 1953; Barbary Leigh in Uncertain Joy, Court Theatre, 1955; Mrs Tarleton in Misalliance, Lyric Theatre (Hammersmith), 1956; Lady Touchwood in The Double Dealer, Edinburgh Festival and Old Vic, 1959; Ivette in the Twelfth Hour, 1964; Lady Markby in An Ideal Husband, Strand, 1965. First appearance on NY stage, 1938, as Pauline Murray in Late One Evening. First film part was in The Gipsy Cavalier. *Films include:* Quinneys, The Flying Fool, Cavalcade, I Lived with You, Woman In The Hall, The Weaker Sex, North West Frontier. *Recreations:* riding, swimming and golf. *Address:* c/o M. C. A. (England) Ltd, 139 Piccadilly, W1.

**JEBB,** family name of **Baron Gladwyn.**

**JEBB, Eglantyne Mary,** CBE 1950; MA Oxon.; Principal of the Froebel Educational Institute, Roehampton, Roehampton Lane, SW15, 1932-55; retired 1955; *b* 22 Dec. 1889; *d* of Rev. Heneage Horsley Jebb and Geraldine Croker Russell. *Educ:* Streatham Coll. for Girls; Lady Margaret Hall, Oxford; Class I, in Hons Sch. of English Language and Literature; trained at S Mary's Coll., Lancaster Gate, W, for London University Teachers' Diploma, 1912-13; Asst English Tutor, Somerville Coll., Oxford, 1913-19; English Lecturer, Education Dept, University of Birmingham, 1919-31; Visiting Lecturer Wellesley Coll., Mass, USA 1928-29. *Address:* Tansey, Wintergreen Lane, Winterbrook, Wallingford, Berks. *Club:* University Women's.

**JEFFARES, Prof. Alexander Norman;** MA, PhD, DPhil; FRSA 1963; FRSL 1965; Professor of English Literature, University of Leeds, since 1957; Head of the Department of English Literature, 1957-64; Chairman of the School of English, 1961-64; *b* 11 Aug. 1920; *s* of late C. Norman Jeffares, Dublin; *m* 1947, Jeanne Agnès, *d* of late E. Calembert, Brussels; one *d*. *Educ:* The High Sch., Dublin; Trinity Coll., Dublin; Oriel Coll., Oxford. Lecturer in Classics, University of Dublin, 1943-44; Lector in English, University of Groningen, 1946-48; Lectr in English, University of Edinburgh, 1949-51; Jury Professor of English Language and Literature, University of Adelaide, 1951-56. Sec., Australian Humanities Research Council, 1954-57; Corresp. Mem. for Great Britain and Ireland, 1958-70; Hon. Fellow, Aust. Acad. of the Humanities, 1970-. Vice-Pres., Film and Television Council of S Aust., 1951-56; Chm., Assoc. for Commonwealth Literature and Language Studies, 1966-68; Dir, Yeats Internat. Summer Sch., Sligo, 1969-. Editor, A Review of English Literature, 1960-67; General Editor: Writers and Critics, 1960-; New Oxford English Series, 1963-; Joint Editor, Biography and Criticism, 1963-; Literary Editor, Fountainwell Drama Texts, 1968-; Editor, Ariel, A Review of Internat. English Literature, 1970-. *Publications:* Trinity Coll., Dublin; drawings and descriptions, 1944; W. B. Yeats: man and poet, 1949 (rev. edition 1962); Maria Edgeworth's Castle Rackrent and other stories, 1953; Seven Centuries of Poetry, 1965 (revised edition 1960); Disraeli's Sybil, 1957; The Scientific Background (with M. Bryn Davies), 1958; Oliver Goldsmith, 1959; Language, Literature and Science, 1959; Oliver St John Gogarty, 1961; The Poetry of W. B. Yeats, 1961; Poems of W. B. Yeats, 1962; Selected Poems of W. B. Yeats, 1962; A Goldsmith Selection, 1963; Cowper, 1963; Selected Prose of W. B. Yeats, 1964; Selected Plays of W. B. Yeats, 1964; Selected Criticism of W. B. Yeats, 1964; George Moore, 1965; In Excited Reverie: A Centenary Tribute to W. B. Yeats (Ed., with G. F. Cross), 1965; Goldsmith's She Stoops to Conquer, 1965; Selected Poetry and Prose of Whitman, 1965; Congreve's The Way of the World and Incognita, 1966; Sheridan's The School for Scandal, 1966; Sheridan's The Rivals, 1967; Congreve's Love for Love, 1967; Fair Liberty was All His Cry: A Tercentenary Tribute to Jonathan Swift 1667-1743, 1967; Swift (Modern Judgements Series), 1968; A Commentary on the Collected Poems of W. B. Yeats, 1968; Farquhar's The Beaux Stratagem, 1970; Farquhar's The Recruiting Officer, 1970; The Circus Animals, 1970. *Recreations:* drawing, motoring. *Address:* 41 Park Lane, Leeds 8. *T:* Leeds 661644. *Clubs:* Athenæum, Royal Commonwealth Society.

**JEFFCOATE, Sir Norman;** *see* Jeffcoate, Sir T. N. A.

**JEFFCOATE, Sir (Thomas) Norman (Arthur),** Kt 1970; Professor of Obstetrics and Gynæcology, University of Liverpool, since 1945; President, Royal College of Obstetricians and Gynaecologists, since 1969 (Vice-President, 1967-69); Obstetrical and Gynæcological Surgeon, Liverpool United Teaching Hospitals and Liverpool Regional Hospital Board; *b* 25 March 1907; *s* of Arthur Jeffcoate and Mary Ann Oakey; *m* 1937, Josephine Lindsay; four *s*. *Educ:* King Edward VI Sch., Nuneaton; University of Liverpool. MB, ChB (Liverpool) 1st class Hons 1929; MD (Liverpool) 1932; FRCS (Edinburgh) 1932; MRCOG 1932; FRCOG 1939. Hon. Asst Surgeon: Liverpool Maternity Hosp., 1932-45; Women's Hosp., Liverpool, 1935-45. Lectures: Blair-Bell Memorial, Royal College of Obst. and Gynaec. 1938; Sir Arcot Mudalier, Univ. of Madras, 1955; Margaret Orford, S African Coll. of Physicians, Surgeons and Gynaecologists, 1969. Joseph Price Orator, Amer. Assoc. of Obstetricians and Gynaecologists, 1966. sims Black Travelling Commonwealth Prof., 1958; Visiting Professor: New York State Univ., 1955; University of Qld, 1964; Univ. of Melbourne, 1964; Univ. of Texas, 1965; Hon. Visiting Obstetrician and Gynæcologist, Royal Prince Alfred Hospital, Sydney, Australia, 1955-. Chairman, Med. Advisory Council of Liverpool Regional Hosp. Bd, 1962-69; President: N of England Obst. and Gynaec. Soc., 1960; Sect. of Obst. and Gynaec., RSM, 1965-66; Liverpool Med. Inst., 1966-67; Vice-Pres. Family Planning Assoc., 1962-; Member: Gen. Med. Council, 1951-61; Clinical Research Bd, MRC, 1961-65; Clinical Trials Sub-Cttee of Safety of Drugs Cttee, 1963-69; Bd of Science and Educn, BMA, 1968-69; Standing Maternity and Midwifery Adv. Cttee, Dept of Health and Social Security (formerly Min. of Health), 1963- (Chm., 1970-); Standing Med. Adv. Cttee and Central Health Services Council, Dept of Health and Social Security, 1969-; Jt Sub-Cttee on Prevention of Haemolytic Disease of the Newborn, 1968- (Chm., 1969-). Hon. Member: Amer. Gynaec. Club; Amer. Assoc. Obst. and Gynaec.; Central Assoc. Obst. and Gynaec.; Assoc. Surg., Ceylon; Obst. and Gynaec. Socs of: Canada, Honolulu, Montreal, Panama, S Africa, Uruguay, Venezuela. *Publications:*

Principles of Gynæcology, 1957 (3rd edn, 1967); communications to medical journals. *Address:* 6 Riversdale Road, Liverpool L19 3QW. *T:* 051-427 1448. *Club:* University (Liverpool).

**JEFFERSON, George Rowland,** CBE 1969; Hon. BSc, CEng, MIMechE, FRAeS; Chairman since 1968 and Managing Director since 1966, Guided Weapons Division, British Aircraft Corporation; *b* 26 March 1921; *s* of Harold Jefferson and Eva Elizabeth Ellen; *m* 1943, Irene Watson-Brown; three *s. Educ:* Grammar Sch., Dartford, Kent. Engrg Apprentice, Royal Ordnance Factory, Woolwich, 1937-42; commnd RAOC, 1942; transf. REME, 1942; served 1942-45, Anti-Aircraft Comd on heavy anti-aircraft power control systems and later Armament Design Dept, Fort Halstead, on anti-aircraft gun mounting development; subseq. Mem. Min. of Supply staff, Fort Halstead, until 1952; joined Guided Weapons Div., English Electric Co. Ltd, 1952; Chief Research Engr, 1953; Dep. Chief Engr, 1958; Dir, English Electric Aviation Ltd, 1961 (on formation of co.); Dir and Chief Exec., British Aircraft Corp. (Guided Weapons) Ltd, 1963 (on formation of Corp.); Dep. Man. Dir, 1964; Mem. Board, British Aircraft Corp. (Operating) Ltd, 1965-; Chm., British Aircraft Corp. (Anti-Tank), 1968-; Director: British Aircraft Corp. (Australia) Pty Ltd, 1968-; British Scandinavian Aviation AB, 1968-. RAeS Gold Medal, 1969. *Address:* Wellesbourne, West End, Ashwell, Herts. *Club:* Army and Navy.

**JEFFERSON, Sir J. A. D.;** *see* Dunnington-Jefferson.

**JEFFERY, Cecil Albert,** CMG 1936; Retired Public Servant; *b* Clyde, New Zealand, 1888; *s* of late Frederick T. D. Jeffery, Clyde, New Zealand; *m* 1917, Lena, *d* of late Matthew Loubere, Westport, New Zealand. *Educ:* Clyde Public Sch. Permanent Head, Prime Minister's Department, New Zealand, 1943-46; Clerk of Executive Council of Dominion of New Zealand and Sec. to Cabinet, 1935-46; and Chief Private Sec. to Prime Minister, 1926-46. *Address:* Dillon Street, Lowry Bay, Wellington, New Zealand.

**JEFFERY, George Henry Padget,** CMG 1965; FASA; Auditor General for South Australia since 1959; Trustee, Savings Bank of South Australia since 1963; *b* 6 June 1907; *s* of late George Frederick Jeffery and late Adelaide Jeffery (*née* Padget), Victor Harbour, S Aust.; *m* 1934, Jean Loudon Watt, *d* of late Thomas Watt, Adelaide; two *s. Educ:* Adelaide High Sch.; Victor Harbour High Sch.; University of Adelaide. Associate, University of Adelaide, 1933; Auditor, SA Public Service, 1936-40, Chief Inspector, 1940-51; Sec., Public Buildings Dept, 1951-53; Chief Executive, Radium Hill Uranium Project, 1953-59; Mem., SA Public Service Board, 1956-59. Pres., SA Div., Aust. Soc. of Accountants, 1965-67. Chm., Royal Commission of Enquiry into Grape Growing Industry, 1965. Member: Parly. Salaries Tribunal, 1966-; Royal Commn on State Transport Services, 1966-67. FASA 1958. *Recreations:* bowls, cricket. *Address:* 49 Anglesey Avenue, St Georges, South Australia 5064, Australia. *T:* 79-2929. *Clubs:* Commonwealth, SA Cricket Association, Glenunga Bowling (Adelaide).

**JEFFERY, Lilian Hamilton,** FBA 1965; FSA 1956; Fellow and Tutor in Ancient History, Lady Margaret Hall, Oxford, since 1952; *b* 5 Jan. 1915; 3rd *d* of Thomas Theophilus Jeffery, MA Cantab., and Lilian Mary (*née* Hamilton). *Educ:* Cheltenham Ladies' Coll.; Newnham Coll., Cambridge. BA (Class. Tripos) 1936; MA 1941; Dipl. in Class. Archæology, 1937; DPhil (Oxon.) 1951. Mem. British Sch. of Archæology, Athens, 1937-; Mem. Soc. for Promotion of Hellenic Studies, 1937-. Nurse in Military Hosp., 1940-41; WAAF (Intelligence), 1941-45. Ed. Annual of British School at Athens, 1955-61. *Publications:* (collab.) Dedications from the Athenian Akropolis, 1948; The Local Scripts of Archaic Greece, 1961; (contrib.) A Companion to Homer, 1962; (contrib.) Perachora ii, 1964; articles in Jl of Hellenic Studies, Annual of Brit. Sch. at Athens, Hesperia, Amer. Jl of Philology, Historia, Philologus, etc. *Recreations:* drawing, photography. *Address:* Lady Margaret Hall, Oxford. *T:* Oxford 54353. *Club:* Service Women's.

**JEFFORD, Barbara Mary,** OBE 1965; Actress; *b* Plymstock, Devon, 26 July 1930; *d* of late Percival Francis Jefford and of Elizabeth Mary Ellen (*née* Laity); *m* 1953, Terence Longdon (marr. diss., 1961); *m* 1967, John Arnold Turner. *Educ:* Weirfield Sch., Taunton, Som. Studied for stage, Bristol and Royal Academy of Dramatic Art (Bancroft Gold Medal). Seasons at Stratford-on-Avon: 1950, 1951, 1953 (Australian and NZ tour with Shakespeare Memorial Theatre Company), 1954; toured NZ with NZ Players' Company in The Lady's Not for Burning, 1954-55; in Tiger at the Gates, London and USA, 1955 and 1956; seasons at the Old Vic: 1956, 1957, 1958, 1959, 1960, 1961, 1962 (attended Baalbek Festival in Lebanon with Old Vic Co., 1957, and toured N America and Canada with same Co. 1958-59). Shakespearian roles include: Isabella in Measure for Measure, 1950 and 1957; Desdemona in Othello, 1953 and 1954; Rosalind in As You Like It, 1953 and 1959; Imogen in Cymbeline, 1956; Beatrice in Much Ado About Nothing, 1956; Portia in The Merchant of Venice, 1956 and 1957; Queen Margaret in Henry VI, 1957; Viola in Twelfth Night, 1949, 1958, 1959 and 1961; Ophelia in Hamlet, 1958 and 1959; Cleopatra, 1965 and 1966. Non-Shakespearian roles include: Andromache in Tiger at the Gates, 1955 and 1956; Beatrice in the Cenci, 1959; Gwendolen Fairfax in The Importance of Being Earnest, 1959 and 1960; Saint Joan, 1960; Lavinia in Mourning becomes Electra, Old Vic, 1961. Tours for Old Vic Company: Ireland and the Provinces, 1960; Russia and Poland, 1961, USA and Canada, 1962, subseq. Germany, Austria, Yugoslavia, Czechoslovakia, Athens and Cairo; then Oxford Playhouse: two plays, one of which, Misalliance, transf. Royal Court and then Criterion; stepdaughter in Pirandello's Six Characters in Search of an Author, Mayfair, 1963. Toured Europe (also appeared Bath Festival, etc.) in Heroines of Shakespeare (solo perf.); Portia in The Merchant of Venice, Helena in A Midsummer Night's Dream, in British Council Tour of S America and Europe, 1964; Ride a Cock Horse, Piccadilly, 1965; Oxford Playhouse, Sept. 1965 to May 1966 (Anthony and Cleopatra, Captain Brassbound's Conversion, Phèdre, The Lady's Not for Burning, Amphitryon 38); Nottingham Playhouse, Oct.-Dec. 1966 (Anthony and Cleopatra, Fill the Stage with Happy Hours); Oxford Playhouse, Jan.-April 1967 (The Balcony, Amphitryon 38); Little Murders, Aldwych, 1967; The Labours of Love, Southampton, 1968 (also performed at University of Victoria, Canada, and on tour of W Africa); As You Desire Me, Yvonne Arnaud, 1968; The Labours of Love, tours Cyprus, Turkey, Rome, 1968, Chile, Argentina, Uruguay, Brazil, 1969, India, Pakistan, Nepal and Far East, 1969-70. *Films:* Ulysses, 1967; A Midsummer Night's Dream, 1967; The Shoes of the Fisherman, 1968; To Love a Vampire, 1970. Has appeared in numerous television and radio plays; Canterbury Tales, TV serial, 1969. *Recreations:* music, swimming, gardening. *Address:* 46 Devonshire Close, W1.

**JEFFORD, Vice-Adm. (Retd), James Wilfred,** CB 1953; CBE 1951 (OBE 1941); *b* 22 March 1901; *o s* of James Harris Jefford; *m* 1926, Dorothy Kate Caswell; one *d. Educ:* HMS Worcester. Sub-Lieut, RIN, 1922; Commander, RIN, 1941; Captain RIN, 1946; Rear-Adm., 1947. Transferred to special list of Royal Navy and appointed Flag Officer commanding Royal Pakistan Navy, on inception of Pakistan, 1947; appointment upgraded to C-in-C, 1950; Vice-Admiral Royal Pakistan Navy, 1953; appointment terminated, 1953; Chm. Penang Harbour Board, 1955-57; Chm. Penang Port Commission, 1956-57; retired 1957. Served European War, 1914-18, as midshipman; War of 1939-45, commanding HMI Ships Indus and Godavar; various staff and shore appointments. *Address:* Pennyroyal, Willey Lane, Sticklepath, near Okehampton, Devon EX20 2NG.

**JEFFREYS,** family name of **Baron Jeffreys.**

**JEFFREYS,** 2nd Baron, *cr* 1952, of Burkham; **Mark George Christopher Jeffreys;** Major, Grenadier Guards; *b* 2 Feb. 1932; *er s* of Capt. Christopher John Darell Jeffreys, MVO, Grenadier Guards (*o s* of 1st Baron; killed in action, 1940) and of Lady Rosemary Beatrice Agar, *y d* of 4th Earl of Normanton; *S* grandfather, 1960; *m* 1st, 1956, Sarah Annabelle Mary (marriage dissolved, 1967), *o d* of Major Henry Claude Lyon Garnett; two *s* two *d*; 2nd, 1967, Anne Louise, *d* of Sir Shirley Worthington-Evans, *qv* and of Mrs Joan Parry. *Educ:* Eton; RMA, Sandhurst. *Heir: s* Hon. Christopher Henry Mark Jeffreys, *b* 22 May 1957. *Address:* Crowood House, Ramsbury, Marlborough, Wilts. *T:* Ramsbury 242. *Club:* Guards.

**JEFFREYS, Anthony Henry,** CB 1961; *b* 13 Aug. 1896; *yr s* of late Major-Gen. H. B. Jeffreys, CB, CMG; *m* 1922, Dorothy Bertha, *d* of late Lieut-Col Edward Tufnell. *Educ:* Eton. Served War of 1914-18 (despatches; wounded); 2nd Lieut RFA, 1915; Lieut 'D' Battery RHA, 1917-19; Staff Captain, GHQ, France, and War Office, 1939-41. Entered Parliament Office, House of Lords, 1919; called to the Bar Inner Temple, 1924. Examiner of Petitions for Private Bills, 1941; Chief Clerk of Cttees and Private Bills and Taxing Officer, 1945; Reading Clerk, House of Lords, 1953; Clerk Asst of the Parliaments, 1959-61, retd. Chm., City of Westminster Boy Scouts' Assoc., 1953-60. *Address:* Doom Bar House, Trebetherick, Wadebridge, Cornwall. *T:* Trebetherick 3380. *Club:* Lansdowne.

**JEFFREYS, Sir Harold,** Kt 1953; FRS 1925; MA Cambridge; DSc Durham; Fellow of St John's College, Cambridge, since 1914; Plumian Professor of Astronomy and Experimental Philosophy, 1946-58; *b* 22 April 1891; *o s* of R. H. and E. M. Jeffreys, Birtley, Durham; *m* 1940, Bertha, *d* of late W. A. Swirles and H. Swirles, Northampton. *Educ:* Armstrong Coll., Newcastle on Tyne; St John's Coll., Cambridge. University Reader in Geophysics, 1931-46. Mathematical Tripos, 1913; Isaac Newton Student, 1914; Smith's Prize, 1915; Adams Prize, 1927; commended, 1923; Buchan Prize of Royal Meteorological Society, 1929. Gold Medal of Royal Astronomical Society, 1937; Murchison Medal of Geological Soc., 1939; Victoria Medal of RGS, 1942; Royal Medal of Royal Society, 1948; Ch. Lagrange Prize, Acad. Royal Sci., Belg., 1948; Bowie Medal, Amer. Geophys. Union, 1952; Copley Medal, Royal Society, 1960; Vetlesen Prize, 1962; Guy Medal, Royal Statistical Society, 1963; Wollaston Medal, Geological Soc., 1964; Pres., Royal Astronomical Soc., 1955-57; Pres. Internat. Seism. Assoc., 1957-60; For. Associate, US Nat. Acad. of Sciences; Accad. dei Lincei, Rome, Acad. Sci. Stockholm, New York Acad. Sci., Amer. Acad. of Arts and Sciences, Acad. Roy. de Belgique; Hon. FRS, NZ; Corresp. Mem. Amer. Geophys. Union; Geolog. Soc. America; RIA. hon. LLD Liverpool, 1953; Hon. ScD Dublin, 1956; Hon. DCL Durham, 1960; Hon. DSc, Southern Methodist Univ., Dallas, 1967. *Publications:* The Earth: Its Origin, History, and Physical Constitution, 1924, 1929, 1952, 1959, 1962, 1970; Operational Methods in Mathematical Physics, 1927, 1931; The Future of the Earth, 1929; Scientific Inference, 1931, 1937, 1957; Cartesian Tensors, 1931, 1953; Earthquakes and Mountains, 1935, 1950; Theory of Probability, 1939, 1948, 1962, 1967; Methods of Mathematical Physics (with B. Jeffreys), 1946, 1950, 1956, 1962; Asymptotic Approximations, 1962, 1968; papers on Astronomy, Geophysics, Theory of Scientific Method, and Plant Ecology. *Address:* 160 Huntingdon Road, Cambridge.

**JEFFREYS, Montagu Vaughan Castelman,** CBE 1953; MA Oxon; Emeritus Professor, University of Birmingham; *b* 16 Dec. 1900; *s* of late Col F. V. Jeffreys, RE, and late Annie Augusta Jeffreys (*née* Barton); *m* 1941, Joan Sheila, *d* of late Col R. D. Marjoribanks; one *s* one *d. Educ:* Wellington Coll.; Hertford Coll., Oxford. Asst Master, Oundle Sch., 1924-27; Lecturer in Education, Armstrong Coll., Newcastle upon Tyne, 1927-32; Lecturer in Educ., University of London Institute of Education, 1932-39; Prof. of Educn in University of Durham, 1939-46. Prof. of Educn in University of Birmingham and Dir of University of Birmingham Inst. of Educn, 1946-64. Pres. Inst. of Christian Educn, 1958-63. Does occasional broadcasting. *Publications:* Play Production: for Amateurs and Schools (3 edns), 1933 (with R. W. Stopford); History in Schools: The Study of Development, 1939; Education–Christian or Pagan, 1946; Kingdom of This World, 1950; Glaucon: an Inquiry into the Aims of Education (2 edns and 3 reprints), 1950; Beyond Neutrality, 1955; Mystery of Man, 1957; Revolution in Teacher Training, 1961; Personal Values in the Modern World, 1962 (rev. Edns 1966, 1968); The Unity of Education, 1966; The Ministry of Teaching, 1967; John Locke, Prophet of Common Sense, 1967; Religion and Morality, 1967; You and Other People, 1969; articles on educational and religious topics in various periodicals. *Address:* Skymers Minor, Minstead, near Lyndhurst, Hants.

**JEFFRIES, Sir Charles Joseph,** KCMG 1943 (CMG 1937); OBE 1928; *b* 1896; *e s* of late C. D. Jeffries, Beckenham, Kent; *m* 1921, Myrtle, *d* of late Dr J. H. Bennett; three *d. Educ:* Malvern Coll.; Magdalen Coll., Oxford (Classical Demy). 2nd Lieut Wilts Regt 1915; Lieut 1917; Invalided from Army, 1917; 2nd Class Clerk, Colonial Office, 1917; Principal, 1920; Asst Sec. and Establishment Officer Colonial Office, 1930-39; Asst Under-Sec. of State, 1939-47; Joint Dep. Under-Sec. of State, Colonial Office, 1947-56; retd 1956. Hon. Sec. Corona Club, 1921-49; Mem. of House of Laity, Church Assembly, 1950-55; a Vice-Pres. of USPG; Sec., Ranfurly Library Service. A Governor of Malvern Coll. *Publications:* The Colonial Empire and its Civil Service, 1938; Creed of Common Sense, 1943; Nebuchadnezzar's Image, 1947; Partners for Progress, 1949; The Colonial Police, 1952; The

Colonial Office (new Whitehall Series), 1956; Joseph in Transit, 1958; Towards the Centre, 1959; Transfer of Power, 1960; Signpost in the Fog, 1961; Proud Record, 1962; Ceylon: The Path to Independence, 1962; (ed) Review of Colonial Research, 1940-60, 1964; Illiteracy: a World Problem, 1967; O.E.G.: a biography of Sir Oliver Ernest Goonetilleke, 1969. *Address:* 1 Brograve Gardens, Beckenham, Kent. *T:* 01-650 1629. *Club:* Royal Commonwealth Society.

**JEFFRIES, Graham Montague;** *see* Graeme, Bruce.

**JEFFS, Ernest Harry;** Editor, The Christian World, 1936-61; *b* 1885; *s* of late Harry Jeffs; *m* 1909, Mary Grantham; two *d. Publications:* Princes of the Modern Pulpit, 1931; The Doctor Abroad, 1933. *Recreations:* reading and walking. *Address:* Gresty Lodge, Station Road, Alsager, Stoke-on-Trent.

**JEFFS, Group Capt. (George) James (Horatio),** CVO 1960 (MVO 1943); OBE 1950; Aviation Consultant; *b* 27 Jan. 1900; *s* of late James Thomas Jeffs, Chilvers Coton, Warwicks; *m* 1921, Phyllis Rosina (*née* Bell); two *s* one *d. Educ:* Kedleston Sch., Derby. Served European War: RNAS, 1916-18; RAF, 1918-19. Air Ministry, 1919-23; Croydon Airport, 1923-34; Heston Airport, 1934-37; Air Ministry, 1937-39. Served War of 1939-45, RAF: Fighter, Ferry, and Transport Commands, Group Captain. Ministry of Transport and Civil Aviation, 1945; Airport Commandant, Prestwick, 1950-57; Airport Commandant, London Airport, 1957-60. Legion of Merit, USA, 1944. *Address:* Pixham Firs Cottage, Pixham Lane, Dorking, Surrey. *T:* 4084. *Club:* Royal Aero.

**JEGER, George;** JP; MP (Lab) Winchester Division of Hampshire, 1945-50, Goole Division of the West Riding of Yorkshire since 1950; *b* 19 March 1903; *m* 1950, Sybil, *d* of late Abraham Prinsky; one *d.* Mayor of Shoreditch, 1937-38; Mem. Shoreditch Boro' Council 1926-40; JP County of London. Sec. Spanish Medical Aid Cttee, 1936-40; Army, 1940-45. Chm., Anglo-Austrian Soc., 1963-. Kt Comdr, Order of Liberation of Spanish Republican Govt (in exile), 1947; Grand Decoration of Honour in Gold (Commander 1st Class) Austria, 1967. *Recreations:* walking, motoring, music, the theatre. *Address:* 2 Parkfields, Putney, SW15. *T:* 01-788 9555.

**JEGER, Mrs Lena (May);** MP (Lab) Holborn and St Pancras South since 1964; *b* 19 Nov. 1915; *e d* of Charles and Alice Chivers, Yorkley, Glos; *m* 1948, Dr Santo Wayburn Jeger (*d* 1953); no *c. Educ:* Southgate County Sch., Middx; Birkbeck Coll., London University (BA). Civil Service: Customs and Excise, Ministry of Information, Foreign Office, 1936-49; British Embassy Moscow, 1947; Manchester Guardian London Staff, 1951-54, 1961-; Mem. St Pancras Borough Council, 1945-59; Mem. LCC for Holborn and St Pancras South, 1952-55. MP (Lab) Holborn and St Pancras South, Nov. 1953-Sept. 1959. Mem., Nat. Exec. Cttee, Labour Party, 1968-. Chm., Govt Working Party on Methods of Sewage Disposal, 1969-. *Publication:* Illegitimate Children and Their Parents, 1951. *Address:* 9 Cumberland Terrace, Regents Park, NW1.

**JEHANGIR, Sir Hirji,** 3rd Bt, *cr* 1908; *b* 1 Nov. 1915; 2nd *s* of Sir Cowasjee Jehangir, 2nd Bt, GBE, KCIE, and Hilla, MBE, *d* of late Hormarji Wadia, Lowji Castle, Bombay; *S* father, 1962; *m* 1952, Jinoo, *d* of K. H. Cama; two *s. Educ:* St Xavier Sch., Bombay; Magdalene Coll., Cambridge. Chairman: Jehangir Art Gallery, Bombay; United Asia Publications; Dir., Coorla Spinning and Weaving Mill. *Heir: s* Jehangir, *b* 23 Nov. 1953. *Address:* Readymoney House, Nepeansea Road, Bombay 6; 24 Kensington Court Gardens, W8. *Clubs:* St James', Crockford's; Willingdon (Bombay).

**JEJEEBHOY, Sir Jamsetjee,** 7th Bt *cr* 1857; *b* 19 April 1913; *s* of Rustamjee J. C. Jamsetjee Jejeebhoy (*d* 1947), and Soonabai Rustomjee Byramjee Jejeebhoy (*d* 1968); *S* cousin, Sir Jamsetjee Jejeebhoy, 6th Bt, 1968, and assumed name of Jamsetjee Jejeebhoy in lieu of Maneckjee Rustomjee Jamsetjee Jejeebhoy; *m* 1943, Shirin Jehangir H. Cama; one *s* one *d. Educ:* St Xavier's Coll., Bombay (BA). Chairman: Sir Jamsetjee Jejeebhoy Charity Funds; Sir J. J. Parsee Benevolent Instn, and other allied charitable instns; Trustee: Sir J. J. Sch. of Arts; Byramjee Jejeebhoy Parsee Charitable Instn; Deccan Coll., Poona, etc. *Heir: s* Rustom Jejeebhoy, b 16 Nov. 1957. *Address:* (residence) Beaulieu, 95 Worli Sea Face, Bombay 18, India. *T:* 453955; (office) Maneckjee Wadia Building, Mahatma Gandhi Road, Fort, Bombay 1. *T:* 251549. *Clubs:* Willingdon Sports, Western India Sports, Turf (all of Bombay).

**JELF, Maj.-Gen. Richard William,** CBE 1948 (OBE 1944); *b* 16 June 1904; *s* of late Sir Ernest Jelf, King's Remembrancer and Master of the Supreme Court; *m* 1928, Nowell, *d* of Major Sampson-Way, RM, Manor House, Henbury; three *s* one *d. Educ:* Cheltenham Coll.; RMA Woolwich. Commissioned Royal Artillery, 1924; Staff Coll., Quetta, 1936; Dep. Dir Staff Duties, War Office, 1946; Imperial Defence Coll., 1948; CRA 2nd Division, 1949; Dep. Chief, Organization and Training Div., SHAPE, 1951; Comdr 99 AA Bde (TA), 1953; Chief of Staff, Eastern Command, 1956; Maj.-Gen., 1957; Commandant, Police Coll., Bramshill, 1957-63; Dir of Civil Defence, Southern Region, 1963-68. ADC to the Queen, 1954. Served North-West Frontier, India (Loe Agra), 1934; NW Europe, 1939-45. *Recreation:* yachting. *Address:* Casella Maria, Clappentail Lane, Lyme Regis, Dorset. *T:* 3284.

**JELLETT, John Holmes,** OBE 1944; DSc, MA, FICE, FIMechE, FRSA; Consulting Engineer in private practice; Consultant to E. W. H. Gifford & Partners since 1966; *b* 20 April 1905; *s* of Henry Holmes Jellett and Beatrice Inez (*née* Smythies); *m* 1937, Frances Sybil Graham; two *s. Educ:* Shrewsbury Sch.; Gonville and Caius Coll., Cambridge. BA 1927, MA 1945; DSc Southampton 1968. Rendel Palmer & Tritton: civil engrg pupil, 1927-30; Asst Engr, 1930-32; Asst Engr, Sir Robert Elliott Cooper, 1932-33; Asst Civil Engr, Civil Engr and Suptg Civil Engr, Dept of CE-in-C, Admty, 1933-46; Temp. Capt., RNVR (Special), 1944-45; Dep. Docks Engr, Docks Engr and Chief Docks Engr, Southampton, 1946-66. Mem. Council, ICE, 1952, Vice-Pres. 1963, Pres. 1968. *Publications:* contribs to Proc. ICE. *Address:* 30 Bassett Wood Drive, Southampton SO2 3PS. *Club:* United Service.

**JELLICOE,** family name of **Earl Jellicoe.**

**JELLICOE,** 2nd Earl, *cr* 1925; **George Patrick John Rushworth Jellicoe,** PC 1963; DSO 1942; MC 1944; Viscount Brocas of Southampton, *cr* 1925; Viscount Jellicoe of Scapa, *cr* 1918; Lord Privy Seal and Minister in Charge, Civil Service Department, since 1970; Leader of the House of Lords since 1970; *b* 4 April 1918; *o s* of Admiral of the Fleet, 1st Earl Jellicoe and late Florence Gwendoline, *d* of Sir Charles Cayzer, 1st Bt; godson of King George V; *S* father, 1935; *m* 1st, 1944, Patricia Christine (marr. diss., 1966), *o d* of Jeremiah O'Kane, Vancouver, Canada; two *s* two *d*; 2nd, 1966, Philippa, *o d* of late Philip Dunne; one *s* two *d*. *Educ:* Winchester; Trinity Coll., Cambridge (Exhibnr). Hon. Page to King George VI; served War of 1939-45, Coldstream Guards, 1 SAS Regt (despatches, DSO, MC, Légion d'Honneur, Croix de Guerre, Greek Military Cross). Entered HM Foreign Service, 1947; served as 1st Sec. in Washington, Brussels, Baghdad (Deputy Sec. General Baghdad Pact). Lord-in-Waiting, Jan.-June 1961; Jt Parly. Sec., Min. of Housing and Local Govt, 1961-62; Minister of State, Home Office, 1962-63; First Lord of the Admiralty, 1963-64; Minister of Defence for the Royal Navy, April-Oct. 1964; Deputy Leader of the Opposition, House of Lords, 1967-70. Chairman: Brit. Adv. Cttee on Oil Pollution of the Sea, 1968-; 3rd Int. Conf. on Oil Pollution of the Sea, 1968. A Governor, Centre for Environmental Studies, 1967-; Pres., National Federation of Housing Societies. *Recreation:* ski-ing. *Heir: s* Viscount Brocas, *qv*. *Address:* Tidcombe Manor, Tidcome, near Marlborough, Wilts. *T:* Oxenwood 225; 97 Onslow Square, SW7. *T:* 01-584 1551. *Club:* Brooks's.

*See also Adm. Sir Charles Madden, Bt.*

**JELLICOE, Ann;** *see* Jellicoe, P. A.

**JELLICOE, Rear-Admiral Christopher Theodore,** CB 1955; DSO 1942; DSC 1939, and Bar, 1943; *b* 20 June 1903; *s* of Rev. T. H. L. Jellicoe and Theodora (*née* Boyd); *m* 1937, Marion Christina Lacy; one *d*. *Educ:* RN Coll., Osborne and Dartmouth. Joined RN 1917; Qualified as Lieut (T), 1930-31; Commander 1939; Commanded destroyers Winchelsea, Southwold and Jackal and served as Staff Officer (Ops) to C-in-C Home Fleet, 1939-43; Captain Dec. 1943; Comd HMS Colombo, 1944; Dep. Dir, Ops Div., Admiralty, 1945-47; Captain in Charge, Sheerness, 1947-48; Naval Asst to First Sea Lord, 1948-50; Comd HM Ships Triumph and Illustrious, 1951-52; idc 1953; Naval ADC to the Queen, 1953; Rear-Adm. 1953; Flag Officer, Admiralty Interview Board, 1955-56; retired 1956. *Address:* Orchard Cottage, Storrington, Sussex. *Club:* Royal Naval (Portsmouth).

**JELLICOE, Geoffrey Alan,** CBE 1961; FRIBA (Dist TP); PPILA; MTPI; Senior Partner of Jellicoe & Coleridge, Architects; *b* London, 8 Oct. 1900; *s* of George Edward Jellicoe; *m* 1936, Ursula, *d* of late Sir Bernard Pares, KBE, DCL. *Educ:* Cheltenham Coll.; Architectural Association. Bernard Webb Student at British School at Rome; RIBA Neale Bursar. Pres., Inst. of Landscape Architects, 1939-49; Hon. Pres. Internat. Fed. of Landscape Architects; Mem. Royal Fine Art Commission, 1954-68; Trustee of the Tate Gallery; Hon. Corr. Mem. American and Venezuelan Societies of Landscape Architects. Gardens for: Sandringham, Royal Lodge (Windsor), Ditchley Park, RHS central area, Wisley, etc; Town Plans for: Guildford, Wellington (Salop), Hemel Hempstead New Town. Arch. Cons. to N Rhodesian Govt, 1947-52. Housing for Basildon, Scunthorpe, LCC; Plymouth Civic Centre; Chertsey Civic Centre; Cheltenham Sports Centre; GLC Comprehensive Sch., Dalston; Durley Park, Keynsham; Grantham Crematorium and Swimming Pool; comprehensive plans for central area, Gloucester, and for Tollcross, Edinburgh; Kennedy Memorial, Runnymede; Plans for Sark, and for Isles of Scilly. *Publications:* Italian Gardens of the Renaissance (joint, 1925); Studies in Landscape Design, Vol. I 1959, Vol. II 1966, Vol. III 1970; Motopia, 1961. *Address:* 19 Grove Terrace, Highgate, NW5. *T:* 01-485 1823; 17 Queen Anne's Gate, SW1.

**JELLICOE, (Patricia) Ann; (Mrs Roger Mayne);** Playwright and Director; *b* 15 July 1927; *d* of John Andrea Jellicoe and Frances Jackson Henderson; *m* 1st, 1950, C. E. Knight-Clarke (marr. diss., 1961); 2nd, 1962, Roger Mayne; one *s* one *d*. *Educ:* Polam Hall, Darlington; Queen Margaret's, York; Central Sch. of Speech and Drama (Elsie Fogarty Prize, 1947). Actress, stage manager and dir, London and provinces, 1947-51; privately commnd to study relationship between theatre architecture and theatre practice, 1949; founded and ran Cockpit Theatre Club to experiment with open stage, 1952-54; taught acting and directed plays, Central Sch., 1954-56. *Plays:* The Sport of My Mad Mother, Royal Court, 1958; The Knack, Arts (Cambridge), 1961, Royal Court, 1962, New York, 1964, Paris, 1967 (filmed, 1965); Shelley, Royal Court, 1965; The Rising Generation, Royal Court, 1967; The Giveaway, Garrick, 1969. *Translations include:* Rosmersholm, Royal Court, 1960; The Lady from the Sea, Queen's, 1961; The Seagull (with Ariadne Nicolaeff), Queen's, 1963; Der Freischütz, Sadlers Wells, 1964. *Principal productions include:* The Sport of My Mad Mother (with George Devine), 1958; For Children, 1959; The Knack (with Keith Johnstone), 1962; Skyvers, 1963; Shelley, 1965. *Publications:* The Sport of My Mad Mother, 1957; Rosmersholm, 1961; The Knack, 1962; Shelley, 1966; Some Unconscious Influences in the Theatre, 1967; The Giveaway, 1970. *Recreations:* sun and sea bathing, the countryside, reading, music, pictures. *Address:* c/o Margaret Ramsay Ltd, 14a Goodwin's Court, St Martin's Lane, WC2.

**JELLINEK, Lionel,** MC 1918; **His Honour Judge Jellinek;** Judge of County Courts, Surrey, since 1958; *b* 30 Nov. 1898; *s* of Robert Jellinek, Company Director, London, and Alice Jellinek (*née* Kennedy); *m* 1923, Lydia, *d* of Ernst Moller, merchant, Oslo; one *d*. *Educ:* Repton; Lincoln Coll., Oxford. Lieut RFA, 1917-19. Called to Bar, Middle Temple, 1923. Art Critic, Sunday Referee, 1926-27. Major RA, 1941-45. Deputy Chm., Essex Quarter Sessions, 1956-58; Chm. Agricultural Land Tribunal, South Eastern Region, 1956-58. Vice-Pres. and Chm. Guildford Symphony Orchestra, 1963. King Haakon VII's Frihets Medal, 1945. *Recreation:* music, especially Chamber Music (viola). *Address:* Yellow Hammers, Shamley Green, Guildford, Surrey. *T:* Bramley 3421. *Club:* United Service.

**JENKIN, (Charles) Patrick (Fleeming),** MA; MP (C) Wanstead and Woodford since 1964; Financial Secretary to the Treasury, since 1970; *b* 7 Sept. 1926; *s* of late Mr and Mrs C. O. F. Jenkin; *m* 1952, Alison Monica Graham; two *s* two *d*. *Educ:* Dragon Sch., Oxford; Clifton Coll.; Jesus Coll., Cambridge. MA (Cantab.) 1951. Served with QO Cameron Highlanders, 1945-48; 1st Class Hons in Law, Cambridge, 1951; Harmsworth Scholar, Middle Temple, 1951; called to the Bar, 1952. Joined Distillers Co. Ltd, 1957. Elected Hornsey Borough Council, 1960; Mem. London Coun. of Social Service, 1963-67. An Opposition front bench spokesman on Treasury, Trade and Economics, 1965; Jt Vice-Chm., Cons. Parly Trade and Power Cttee, 1966; Chm., All Party Parly Group on Chemical Industry, 1968. Governor of Westfield Coll., 1964. *Recreations:* music, sailing. *Address:* 9 Hurst Avenue, Highgate, N6. *T:* 01-340 5538. *Club:* West Essex Conservative.

**JENKIN, Mary Elizabeth,** MBE 1945; *b* 8 Jan. 1892; *d* of Professor C. F. Jenkin and Mrs C. F. Jenkin. *Educ:* Norland Place Sch.; St Paul's Girls Sch.; Oxford High Sch.; Oxford University. Worked in the Intelligence Division, Admiralty, 1916-20. MA Oxon., 1921; held various secretarial posts and travelled in Egypt and India, 1921-27; joined BBC, 1927; Head of the BBC Children's Hour, 1950-53; retd 1953. *Recreations:* acting, painting, reading. *Address:* Southfield House, Painswick, Glos. *Club:* University Women's.

**JENKIN, Patrick;** *see* Jenkin, C. P. F.

**JENKIN, Sir William Norman Prentice,** Kt 1947; CSI 1946; CIE 1931; *b* 11 Aug. 1899. Superintendent, Indian Police Service, 1930; late Deputy Dir, Intelligence Bureau, Home Department, Government of India; Dir of Intelligence, Malaya, 1950-51. *Address:* Sevenoaks Road, Tenterden, Kent.

**JENKIN-JONES, Charles Mark,** CBE 1947; MInstT; CStJ; *b* 2 Nov. 1885; *s* of late Charles and Mable Jenkin-Jones, London; *m* 1913, Violet Olive, *yr d* of late John George and Clara Wood, Hull; one *s* one *d. Educ:* Brighton Coll.; Queen's Coll., Oxford (Open Classical Scholar). Entered Service NE Railway Coy 1908; Superintendent, NE Area, L and NE Rly, 1924; Divisional Gen. Manager, York, 1936-47; Railway Operating Gold Medal, Inst. of Transport, 1934; Visited Palestine to Report on Palestine Railways at request of Government, 1935; Represented British Dock Owners at International Labour Conferences, Geneva, 1928, 1929, 1932; Employers' Delegate at Tripartite Conference on Railway Hours, Geneva, 1939; Major, Engineer and Railway Staff Corps, 1925-36; Vice-Chm. Yorks (E Riding) Agricultural Wages Board, 1932-36; Member of: Tyne Improvement Commission, 1936-47; Governing Body Brighton Coll., 1934-49; Church Schools Coy, London, 1943-54; Mem. of Oxford Univ. Appointments Cttee, 1934-52; Vice-Pres. Oxford Soc., and Pres. of York and District Branch; Mem. York A Group Hospital Management Cttee, 1948-51; Mem. of Leeds Univ. Appointments Board, 1948-52; a Governor of St Peter's Sch., York, 1948-62; Chm., York Coll. for Girls, 1963- (Vice-Chm., 1960-63). Chm., Purey Cust Nursing Home, York, 1953-69. *Address:* Dringcote, Tadcaster Road, York. *T:* York 66348.

**JENKIN PUGH, Rev. Canon Thomas;** *see* Pugh.

**JENKINS, Clive;** *see* Jenkins, D. C.

**JENKINS, (David) Clive;** General Secretary, Association of Scientific, Technical and Managerial Staffs, since 1970 (Joint General Secretary, 1968-70); *b* 2 May 1926; *s* of David Samuel Jenkins and Miriam Harris Jenkins (*née* Hughes); *m* 1963, Moira McGregor Hilley; one *s* one *d. Educ:* Port Talbot Central Boys' Sch.; Port Talbot County Sch.; Swansea Techn. Coll. (evenings). Started work in metallurgical test house, 1940; furnace shift supervisor, 1942; i/c of laboratory, 1943; tinplate night shift foreman, 1945; Mem., Port Talbot Cooperative Soc. Educn. Cttee, 1945; Branch Sec. and Area Treas., AScW, 1946; Asst Midlands Divisional Officer, ASSET, 1947; Transport Industrial Officer, 1949; Nat. Officer, 1954; Gen. Sec., ASSET, 1961-68. Metrop. Borough Councillor, 1954-60 (Chm. Staff Cttee, St Pancras Borough Coun.); Chm., Nat. Jt Coun. for Civil Air Transport, 1967-68. Editor, Trade Union Affairs, 1961-63. *Publications:* Power at the Top, 1959; Power Behind the Screen, 1961; (with J. E. Mortimer) British Trade Unions Today, 1965; (with J. E. Mortimer) The Kind of Laws the Unions Ought to Want, 1968; also pamphlets and essays. *Recreations:* bargaining with employers, organising the middle classes. *Address:* (Home) 16 St Marks Crescent, NW1. *T:* 01-485 4509; (Office) 15 Half Moon Street, W1. *T:* 01-499 4761.

**JENKINS, Elizabeth.** *Educ:* St Christopher School, Letchworth; Newnham College, Cambridge. *Publications:* The Winters, 1931; Lady Caroline Lamb, a Biography, 1932; Harriet (awarded the Femina Vie Heureuse Prize), 1934; The Phoenix' Nest, 1936; Jane Austen, a Biography, 1938; Robert and Helen, 1944; Young Enthusiasts, 1946; Henry Fielding (The English Novelists Series), 1947; Six Criminal Women, 1949; The Tortoise and the Hare, 1954; Ten Fascinating Women, 1955; Elizabeth the Great (biography), 1958; Elizabeth and Leicester, 1961; Brightness, 1963; Honey, 1968. *Address:* 8 Downshire Hill, Hampstead, NW3. *T:* 01-435 4642.

**JENKINS, Sir Evan Meredith,** GCIE, *cr* 1947 (KCIE, *cr* 1944; CIE 1936); KCSI, *cr* 1945 (CSI 1941); *b* 2 Feb. 1896; *s* of late Sir John Lewis Jenkins, KCSI. *Educ:* Rugby; Balliol Coll., Oxford. Served European War, 1914-19; joined Indian Civil Service, 1920, and served in Punjab; Chief Commissioner, Delhi, 1937; Sec., Dept of Supply, 1940-43; Private Sec to the Viceroy and Sec. to the Governor-General (Personal), 1943-45; Governor of the Punjab, 1946-47. *Address:* 24 Ashley Gardens, SW1. *Club:* Travellers'.
*See also Sir Owain Jenkins.*

**JENKINS, Gilbert Kenneth;** Keeper, Department of Coins and Medals, British Museum, since 1965; *b* 2 July 1918; *s* of late Kenneth Gordon Jenkins and of Julia Louisa Jenkins (*née* Colbourne); *m* 1939, Cynthia Mary, *d* of late Dr Hugh Scott, FRS; one *s* two *d. Educ:* All Saints Sch., Bloxham; Corpus Christi Coll., Oxford. Open Classical Scholar (Corpus Christi Coll.), 1936; First Class Honour Mods, 1938. War Service in Royal Artillery, 1940-46 (SE Asia, 1944-46). BA, 1946. Asst Keeper, British Museum, 1947; Dep. Keeper, 1956. An Editor of Numismatic Chronicle, 1964-. Mem., German Archaeology. Inst., 1967; Corresp. Mem., Amer. Numismatic Soc., 1958. Akbar Medal, Numismatic Soc. of India, 1966. *Publications:* Carthaginian Gold and Electrum Coins (with R. B. Lewis), 1963; Coins of Greek Sicily, 1966; Sylloge Nummorum Graecorum (Danish Nat. Museum), part 42, N Africa (ed), 1969; The Coinage of Gela, 1970; articles in numismatic periodicals. *Recreations:* music, cycling. *Address:* 3 Beechwood Avenue, Kew Gardens, Surrey.

**JENKINS, Sir Gilmour;** *see* Jenkins, Sir Thomas G.

**JENKINS, Prof. Harold,** MA, DLitt; Regius Professor of Rhetoric and English Literature, University of Edinburgh, since 1967; *b* 19 July 1909; *s* of late Henry and Mildred Jenkins, Shenley, Bucks; *m* 1939, Gladys Puddifoot; no *c. Educ:* Wolverton Grammar Sch.; University Coll., London. George Smith Studentship, 1930. Quain Student, University Coll., London, 1930-35; William Noble Fellow, University of Liverpool, 1935-36; Lecturer in English, University of the Witwatersrand, South Africa, 1936-45; Lecturer in English, University Coll., London, 1945-46, then Reader in English, 1946-54; Prof. of English, University of London (Westfield Coll.), 1954-67. Visiting Prof., Duke Univ., USA 1957-58. Jt Gen. Editor, Arden Shakespeare, 1958-. *Publications:* The Life and Work of Henry

Chettle, 1934; Edward Benlowes, 1952; The Structural Problem in Shakespeare's Henry IV, 1956; articles in Modern Language Review, Review of English Studies, The Library, Shakespeare Survey, etc. *Address:* 27 Ormidale Terrace, Edinburgh 12.

**JENKINS, Hugh Gater;** MP (Lab) Putney since 1964; *b* 27 July 1908; *s* of Joseph Walter Jenkins and Florence Emily (*née* Gater), Enfield, Middlesex; *m* 1936, Marie (*née* Crosbie), *d* of Sqdn Ldr Ernest Crosbie and Ethel (*née* Hawkins). *Educ:* Enfield Grammar Sch., Personal exploration of employment and unemployment, and political and economic research, 1925-30; Prudential Assce Co., 1930-40. ROC, 1938; RAF: Fighter Comd, 1941; became GCI Controller; seconded to Govt of Burma, 1945, as Dir Engl. Programmes, Rangoon Radio. Nat. Union of Bank Employees: Greater London Organiser, 1947; Res. and Publicity Officer; Ed., The Bank Officer, 1948; British Actors' Equity Assoc.: Asst Sec., 1950; Asst Gen. Sec., 1957-64, now Liaison Officer. Contested (Lab) Enfield West, 1950, Mitcham 1955. Chm., Parly Labour Party Communications and Films Groups. LCC: Mem. for Stoke Newington and Hackney N, 1958-65 (Public Control and Town Planning Cttees). Fabian Soc. lectr and Dir of Summer Schools in early post-war years; Chm., H. Bomb Campaign Cttee, 1954; CND, Aldermaston Marcher, 1957-63; Chm. Victory for Socialism, 1956-60; Mem. Exec. Cttee Greater London Labour Party; Chm. Standing Advisory Council on Local Authorities and the Theatre; Vice-Chm., Theatres Advisory Council; Mem. Arts Council, 1968-. *Publications:* Essays in Local Government Enterprise (with others), 1964. Various pamphlets; contrib. to Tribune, New Statesman, The Times, etc. Occasional broadcasts and lectures on constitutional, theatrical and other subjects. *Recreations:* reading, writing, talking, walking, viewing, listening and occasionally thinking. *Address:* 75 Kenilworth Court, Lower Richmond Road, Putney, SW15. *T:* 01-788 0371.

**JENKINS, Mrs Inez Mary Mackay,** CBE 1943; *b* 30 Oct. 1895; *c* of John Mackay Ferguson; *m* 1923, Frederick Cyril Jenkins; one *s*. *Educ:* Berkhamsted Sch. for Girls; St Hilda's Hall, Oxford. Gen. Sec., National Federation of Women's Institutes, 1919-29; Sec., English Folk Dance and Song Soc., 1931-39; Chief Administrative Officer Women's Land Army (England and Wales), 1939-48; Mem. Central Agricultural Wages Board for England and Wales, 1952-63. *Publication:* History of the Women's Institute Movement of England and Wales, 1953. *Recreations:* gardening, philately. *Address:* White Ends, Rotherfield Greys, Oxon. *T:* Rotherfield Greys 206.

**JENKINS, Ven. (John) Owen;** Archdeacon of Carmarthen and Vicar of Llanfihangel Aberbythick since 1967; *b* 13 June 1906; *m* 1939, Gwladys Margaret Clark Jones, *d* of Ven. D. M. Jones, sometime Archdeacon of Carmarthen. *Educ:* St David's Coll., Lampeter; Jesus Coll., Oxford. Curate of: Cwmamman, 1929-33; Llanelly, 1933-39; Vicar of Spittal with Trefgarn, 1939-48; TCF, 1943-46; Vicar of Llangadock, 1948-60; Canon of St David's, 1957; Rector of Newport, Pembs, 1960-67; Archdeacon of Cardigan, 1962-67. *Address:* The Vicarage, Golden Grove, Carmarthen. *T:* Dryslwyn 306.

**JENKINS, (John) Robin;** *b* Cambuslang, Lanarks, 11 Sept. 1912; *s* of late James Jenkins and of Annie Robin; *m* 1937, Mary McIntyre Wyllie; one *s* two *d*. *Educ:* Hamilton Academy; Glasgow Univ. (MA Hons). Teacher of English: Dunoon Grammar Sch.; Ghazi Coll., Kabul, 1957-59; British Institute, Barcelona, 1959-61; Gaya Coll., Sabah, 1963-68. *Publications:* Happy for the Child, 1953; The Thistle and the Grail, 1954; The Cone-Gatherers, 1955; Guests of War, 1956; The Missionaries, 1957; The Changeling, 1958; Some Kind of Grace, 1960; Dust on the Paw, 1961; The Tiger of Gold, 1962; A Love of Innocence, 1963; The Sardana Dancers, 1964; A Very Scotch Affair, 1968; The Holy Tree, 1969. *Recreation:* travel. *Address:* Southview, 55 Mary Street, Dunoon, Argyll, Scotland. *T:* Dunoon 1497.

**JENKINS, Leslie Augustus Westover;** Chairman of the Forestry Commission, 1965-70; *b* 27 May 1910; *s* of L. C. W. Jenkins; *m* 1936, Ann Barker (*née* Bruce), *d* of R. Hugh Bruce, St John, NB, Canada; no *c*. *Educ:* Lancing Coll. Chm. and Managing Dir, John Wright & Sons (Veneers) Ltd, 1956-59; Dir, Nat. Industrial Fuel Efficiency Service, 1954, Chm. 1968. Man. Dir, I. & R. Morley Ltd, 1959-63; Dir, Restall Brown & Clennell Ltd, 1963; Dir, G. N. Haden & Sons Ltd, 1967. Member: Industrial Coal Consumers Council, 1947-; Brit. Nat. Export Coun., 1964-, a Dep. Chm. 1966-; Vice-Pres., Confedn of Brit. Industry, 1965-68. Pres., Nat. Assoc. Brit. Manufacturers, 1963-65. MInstF 1959; FBIM 1966 (Mem. Bd, 1968-). *Recreations:* yachting, golf. *Address:* Lyneham Lodge, Hook Park, Warsash, Hants. *T:* Locks Heath 3366. *Clubs:* Royal Ocean Racing, Royal Southern Yacht.

**JENKINS, Sir Owain (Trevor),** Kt 1958; Director: Assam & African Investments Ltd; Assam Trading (Holdings) Ltd, etc; Calcutta Electric Supply Corporation; *b* 20 Feb. 1907; 5th *s* of late Sir John Lewis Jenkins, KCSI, ICS; *m* 1940, Sybil Léonie, *y d* of late Maj.-Gen. Lionel Herbert, CB, CVO. *Educ:* Charterhouse; Balliol Coll., Oxford. Employed by Balmer Lawrie & Co. Ltd, Calcutta, 1929; Indian Army, 1939-44; Man. Dir, Balmer Lawrie & Co. Ltd, 1948-58. Pres. of the Bengal Chamber of Commerce and Industry and Pres. of the Associated Chambers of Commerce of India, 1956-57. Mem. (1959) Economic Survey Mission to Basutoland, Bechuanaland and Swaziland. *Address:* Standlands, Petworth, Sussex. *T:* Lodsworth 287. *Clubs:* Oriental, City of London; Bengal (Calcutta).
*See also Sir Evan Jenkins.*

**JENKINS, Ven. Owen;** *see* Jenkins, Ven. J. O.

**JENKINS, Robert Christmas Dewar,** JP; *b* 29 Sept. 1900; *s* of late J. Hamilton Jenkins; *m* 1927, Marjorie, *d* of late Andrew George Houstoun; three *d*. *Educ:* Latymer Upper Sch. Mem. Kensington Borough Council, 1927-68, Leader of Conservative Party of Royal Borough of Kensington, 1945-53; Mem. LCC for Kensington (S), 1934-49; Mayor of Kensington, 1939-45. MP (C) Dulwich Div. of Camberwell, 1951-64. JP County of London, 1946; Alderman of Kensington, 1947. Chairman, Royal Borough of Kensington and Chelsea, 1964-. Hon. Freeman, Royal Borough of Kensington, 1964-. Served in Inns of Court OTC and KRRC, 1918-19. *Recreations:* bridge and phrenology. *Address:* 24 Albemarle, Wimbledon Parkside, SW19. *T:* 01-788 4722. *Clubs:* Carlton, Junior Carlton.

**JENKINS, Robin;** *see* Jenkins, J. R.

**JENKINS, Rt. Hon. Roy Harris,** PC 1964; MP (Lab) Central Southwark, 1948-50, Stechford Division of Birmingham since 1950; Deputy Leader of the Labour Party, since 1970; *b* 11 Nov. 1920; *o s* of late Arthur Jenkins, MP, and of Hattie Jenkins; *m* 1945, Jennifer, *o d* of Sir

Parker Morris, *qv*; two *s* one *d*. *Educ:* Abersychan Grammar Sch.; Balliol Coll., Oxford. Sec. and Librarian, Oxford Union Society; Chairman, Oxford Univ. Democratic Socialist Club; First Class in Hon. Sch. of Philosophy, Politics and Economics, 1941. Served War of 1939-45, in RA, 1942-46; Captain, 1944-46. Contested (Lab) Solihull Div. of Warwicks, at Gen. Election, 1945. Parliamentary Private Sec. to Sec. of State for Commonwealth Relations, 1949-50. Mem. of Staff of Industrial and Commercial Finance Corp. Ltd, 1946-48. Mem. Exec. Cttee of Fabian Soc., 1949-61; Chm., Fabian Soc., 1957-58; Mem. Cttee of Management, Soc. of Authors, 1956-60; Governor, British Film Institute, 1955-58; Dir of Financial Operations, John Lewis Partnership, 1962-64. Minister of Aviation, 1964-65; Home Sec., 1965-67; Chancellor of the Exchequer, 1967-70. Formerly: Dep. Chm. Federal Union; Vice-Pres., Britain in Europe; Dep. Chm., Common Market Campaign; Chm., Labour European Cttee. Pres. of United Kingdom Coun. of the European Movement. Hon. Fellow, Balliol Coll., Oxford. *Publications:* (ed) Purpose and Policy (a vol. of the Prime Minister's Speeches), 1947; Mr Atlee: An Interim Biography, 1948; Pursuit of Progress, 1953; Mr Balfour's Poodle, 1954; Sir Charles Dilke: A Victorian Tragedy, 1958; The Labour Case (Penguin Special), 1959; Asquith, 1964; contrib. to New Fabian Essays, 1952; contrib. to Hugh Gaitskell, A Memoir, 1964; Essays and Speeches, 1967. *Address:* St Amand's House, East Hendred, Berks. *Club:* Brooks's.

**JENKINS, Very Rev. Thomas Edward;** Dean of St Davids since 1957; *b* 14 Aug. 1902; *s* of late David Jenkins, Canon of St Davids Cathedral and Vicar of Abergwili, and of Florence Helena Jenkins; *m* 1928, Annie Laura, *d* of late David Henry, Penygroes, Carms; one *s*. *Educ:* Llandyssul Grammar Sch.; St David's Coll., Lampeter; Wycliffe Hall, Oxford. St David's Coll., Lampeter, BA 1922, BD 1932, Powys Exhibitioner, 1924; Welsh Church Scholar, 1921. Ordained, 1925; Curate of Llanelly, 1925-34; Rector of Begelly, 1934-38; Vicar: Christ Church, Llanelly, 1938-46; Lampeter, 1946-55 (Rural Dean, 1949-54); Canon, St Davids Cathedral, 1951-57; Vicar of Cardigan, 1955-57. *Address:* The Deanery, St Davids, Pembs. *T:* St Davids 202.

**JENKINS, Sir (Thomas) Gilmour,** KCB 1948 (CB 1941); KBE 1944; MC; Director, London and Overseas Freighters Ltd; Chairman: Royal Academy of Music; London Philharmonic Society; Member, London Philharmonic Orchestra Council; Chairman, Seafarers' Education Service; *b* 18 July 1894; *s* of late Thomas Jenkins; *m* 1916, Evelyne Mary, *d* of C. H. Nash; one *s* one *d*. *Educ:* Rutlish Sch.; London Univ. Served European War, RGA (MC and bar); entered Board of Trade, 1919; Asst Sec., 1934; Government Delegate to Maritime Sessions of International Labour Conference Geneva, 1935 and 1936, and Copenhagen, 1945; Principal Asst Sec., Board of Trade, 1937; Second Sec., Ministry of Shipping, 1939; Dep. Dir-Gen., Ministry of War Transport, 1941-46; Permanent Sec., Control Office for Germany and Austria, 1946-47; Joint Permanent Under-Sec. of State, Foreign Office, during 1947; Permanent Sec. to Ministry of Transport, 1947-53; Permanent Secretary to Ministry of Transport and Civil Aviation, 1953-59; Pres. Inst. of Marine Engineers, 1953-54; Pres. Institute of Transport, 1954-55: Pres., International Conference on Safety of Life at Sea, 1960; Pres., International Conference on Pollution of the Sea by Oil, 1954 and 1962; Pres., International Conference on Load Lines, 1966. Hon. FRAM. Grand Officer, Order of Orange Nassau (Netherlands); Comdr with Star, Order of St Olav (Norway); Knight Comdr, Order of George I (Greece); Comdr, Order of the Crown (Belgium). *Publication:* The Ministry of Transport and Civil Aviation, 1959. *Recreation:* music. *Address:* 6 Richardson Walk, Colchester, Essex. *T:* Colchester 74536; 69 Gloucester Crescent, NW1. *T:* 01-485 9111. *Club:* Athenæum.

**JENKINS, Sir William,** Kt 1966; JP; Agent in London for Government of Northern Ireland, 1966-70; *b* 25 July 1904; *m* 1942, Jessie May Watson, Otago, NZ; no *c*. *Educ:* Whitehouse Sch.; Belfast Coll. of Technology. Joined W. H. Brady & Co. Ltd, Bombay, 1931; became Sen. Dir; retd 1956. JP Bombay, 1946; Hon. Presidency Magistrate Bombay, 1948. Dir various joint cos in Bombay. Chm., Gilbert-Ash (NI) Ltd; Divisional Chm., Co-operative Permanent Building Soc.; Director: Belfast Banking Co.; Belfast Bank Executor & Trustee Co.; Arthur Guinness Son & Co. (B) Ltd; Local Dir, Commercial Union Assurance Corp. Ltd. Entered Belfast Corp., 1957; JP Belfast, 1958; High Sheriff, Belfast, 1961; Dep. Lord Mayor, 1962; Lord Mayor of Belfast, 1964, 1965, 1966. Mem. Senate of N Ireland, 1963-66; Mem. Senate of Queen's Univ., 1963-66; Hon. Treas., Queen's Univ., 1965; first recipient of "Community Award" by New Ireland Soc. of Queen's Univ. for outstanding services to community during term as Lord Mayor. Mem. Council of Inst. of Directors, 1967-. *Recreation:* golf. *Address:* Lismachan, 378 Belmont Road, Belfast, N Ireland. *Clubs:* Royal Automobile; Willingdon (Bombay); Ulster Reform (Belfast); Royal Belfast Golf, Fortwilliam Golf.

**JENKINS, William Frank,** CB 1949; CBE 1943; ARCO; *b* 14 May 1889; *m* 1923, Marjorie Newton-Jones. Called to Bar, Gray's Inn, 1922, Dir-Gen. Disposals, Ministry of Supply, 1946; Under-Sec. (Contracts) Ministry of Supply, 1947-53; Principal Finance Officer, UK Atomic Energy Authority, 1954-57, retired. *Address:* Wingfield, Oakleigh Avenue, N20. *T:* 01-445 0275.

**JENKINSON, Sir Anthony Banks,** 13th Bt, *cr* 1661; *b* 3 July 1912; *S* grandfather, 1915; *s* of Captain John Banks Jenkinson (killed European War, Sept, 1914) and Joan, *o d* of late Col Joseph Hill, CB (she *m* 2nd, 1920, Maj.-Gen. Algernon Langhorne, CB, DSO, who died 1945); *m* 1943, Frances, *d* of Harry Stremmel; one *s* two *d*. *Educ:* Eton; Balliol Coll., Oxford. *Heir: s* John Banks Jenkinson, *b* 16 Feb. 1945. *Address:* Bears House, Wentworth, Virginia Water, Surrey. *Clubs:* Oxford and Cambridge, MCC; Bembridge Sailing.

**JENKS, Clarence Wilfred;** Director-General of the International Labour Office, since 1970; Chairman of Board, International Institute of Labour Studies, Geneva, and International Centre for Advanced Technical and Vocational Training, Turin; *b* 7 March 1909; *e s* of late Richard and Alice Sophia Jenks; *m* 1949, Jane Louise, *d* of Frederick S. Broverman, NY City; two *s*. *Educ:* Bootle Secondary Sch.; Liverpool Collegiate Sch.; Gonville and Caius Coll., Cambridge; Geneva Sch. of International Studies. BA 1931; MA 1936; LLD 1953; Cecil Peace Prize, 1928; Pres. of Cambridge Union Soc., 1930; called to the Bar by Gray's Inn, 1936. Mem. of Legal Section of Internat. Labour Office, 1931; Legal Adviser, 1940; Asst Dir-Gen., 1948-64; Dep. Dir-Gen., 1964-67; Principal Dep. Dir-Gen., 1967-70; Adviser to Venezuelan Government on labour legislation, 1938; Mem. ILO Delegns: at UN Monetary and Financial Conference, Bretton Woods, 1944; UN Conf. on International Organisation, San Francisco, 1945. Intergovernmental Copyright Conf., 1952; International Confs on the Peaceful Uses of Atomic Energy, 1955 and 1958; United Nations Conferences on Law of the Sea, 1958 and 1960, Diplomatic Intercourse and Immunities, 1961, Law of Treaties, 1968; at Gen. Assembly and Economic and Social Council of United Nations and other international conferences and cttees; Prof., The Hague Acad. of International Law, 1939, 1950, 1955, and 1966. Member: Institute of International Law; International Academy or Comparative Law; Corresponding Mem., International Academy of Astronautics. Hon. LLD Edinburgh, 1967. *Publications:* The Headquarters of International Institutions, 1945; The International Protection of Trade Union Freedom, 1957; The Common Law of Mankind, 1958; Human Rights and International Labour Standards, 1960; International Immunities, 1961; The Proper Law of International Organisations, 1962; Law, Freedom and Welfare, 1963; The Prospects of International Adjudication, 1964; Space Law, 1965; Law in the World Community, 1967; The World Beyond the Charter, 1968; A New World of Law?, 1969; Social Justice in the Law of Nations, 1970; (ed) The International Labour Code, 1939 and 1952; Constitutional Provisions concerning Social and Economic Policy, 1944; contribs to British Year Book of International Law and other Legal jls. *Recreations:* rowing, swimming, mountain-walking, ski-ing, skating. *Address:* International Labour Office, Geneva, Switzerland. *T:* Geneva 326200; 3 rue de Contamines, Geneva, Switzerland. *T:* Geneva 354235. *Clubs:* Athenæum, Reform; Cosmos (Washington).

**JENKS, Sir Richard Atherley,** 2nd Bt, *cr* 1932; *b* 26 July 1906; *er s* of Sir Maurice Jenks, 1st Bt, and Martha Louise Christabel, *d* of late George Calley Smith; *S* father 1946; *m* 1932, Marjorie Suzanne Arlette, *d* of late Sir Arthur du Cros, 1st Bt; two *s. Educ:* Charterhouse. Chartered Accountant, retired. *Heir: s* Maurice Arthur Brian Jenks [*b* 28 Oct. 1933; *m* 1962, Susan, *e d* of Leslie Allen, Surrey; one *d*]. *Address:* 8 Connaught Place, W2. *T:* 01-723 2540.

**JENKYNS, Henry Leigh;** Under-Secretary, Ministry of Housing and Local Government, since 1969; Chairman, South-East Economic Planning Board, since 1968; *b* 20 Jan. 1917; *y s* of H. H. Jenkyns, Indian Civil Service; *m* 1947, Rosalind Mary Home; two *s* one *d. Educ:* Eton and Balliol Coll., Oxford. War Service in Royal Signals; Lt-Col, East Africa Command, 1944. Treasury, 1945-66; Private Sec. to Chancellor, 1951-53. Treasury Representative in Australia and New Zealand, 1953-56; UK Delegation to OECD, Paris, 1961-63; Asst Under-Sec. of State, DEA, 1966-69. *Recreations:* music, garden, sailing. *Address:* 79 Blue House Lane, Limpsfield, Surrey. *T:* Oxted 3905. *Club:* United University.

**JENNINGS, Sir Albert (Victor),** Kt 1969; Chairman, A. V. Jennings Industries (Australia) Ltd, since 1932; *b* 12 Oct. 1896; *s* of John Thomas Jennings; *m* 1922, Ethel Sarah, *d* of George Herbert Johnson; two *s. Educ:* Eastern Road, Sch., Melbourne. Council Mem., Master Builders Assoc., 1943-; Member: Commonwealth Building Research and Advisory Cttee, 1948-; Manufacturing Industries Adv. Council to Australian Govt, 1962-; Decentralisation and Develt Adv. Cttee to Victorian State Govt, 1965-; Trustee, Cttee for Economic Develt of Australia. Fellow of Aust. Inst. of Building (Federal Pres., 1964-65 and 1965-66). *Recreations:* swimming, golf. *Address:* Ranelagh House, Rosserdale Crescent, Mount Eliza, Victoria 3930, Australia. *T:* 7871350. *Clubs:* Commonwealth (Canberra); Savage (Melbourne).

**JENNINGS, Christopher;** *see* Jennings, R. E. C.

**JENNINGS, (Edgar) Owen,** RWS 1953 (ARWS 1943); ARE 1944; ARCA London 1925; FRSA; Principal, School of Art, Tunbridge Wells, 1934-65; *b* Cowling, Yorks, 28 Dec. 1899; *s* of Wesley Jennings, JP and Ann Elizabeth Hardy; *m* 1929, May, *d* of Arthur Cullingworth; one *s* one *d. Educ:* Sch. of Art, Skipton; Coll. of Art, Leeds; Royal College of Art, London. Examr in Three Dimensional Design for Ministry of Education. Exhibited: Royal Academy, 1925-; RWS, RE, NEAC, Paris Salon, New York, Chicago, Antwerp, Vienna. CEMA and Brit. Coun. Exhibns in England, China, Russia, Poland, etc. Works in: British Museum; Victoria and Albert Museum; Albertina; Brooklyn Museum, New York; Art Inst., Chicago; Public Collections Leeds, Birmingham, Wakefield. Logan Prize Winner, Chicago International, 1930; Silver Medallist, City and Guilds of London Inst.; ATD 1926. Pres., Royal Water-Colour Society Art Club, 1966. *Publications:* contrib. to various art jls (line engravings, wood engravings, watercolours). *Recreations:* reading, drawing. *Address:* Linton, Wilman Road, Tunbridge Wells, Kent. *T:* 20581. *Club:* Chelsea Arts.

**JENNINGS, Elizabeth (Joan);** Author; *b* 18 July 1926; *d* of Dr H. C. Jennings, Oxon. *Educ:* Oxford High Sch.; St Anne's Coll., Oxford. Asst at Oxford City Library, 1950-58; Reader for Chatto & Windus Ltd, 1958-60. FRSL 1961. *Publications:* Poems (Arts Council Prize), 1953; A Way of Looking, poems, 1955 (Somerset Maugham Award, 1956); A Sense of the World, poems, 1958; (ed) The Batsford Book of Children's Verse, 1958; Let's Have Some Poetry, 1960; Every Changing Shape, 1961; Song for a Birth or a Death, poems, 1961; a translation of Michelangelo's sonnets, 1961; Recoveries, poems, 1964; Robert Frost, 1964; Christianity and Poetry, 1965; The Mind Has Mountains, poems, 1966 (Richard Hillary Prize, 1966); Collected Poems, 1967; The Animals' Arrival, poems, 1969; (ed) A Choice of Christina Rossetti's Verse, 1970; also poems and articles in: New Statesman, New Yorker, Botteghe Oscure, Observer, Spectator, Listener, Vogue, etc. *Recreations:* travel in Italy, looking at pictures, continental films, the theatre, conversation. *Address:* 31 Polstead Road, Oxford. *Clubs:* PEN, Society of Authors.

**JENNINGS, Henry Cecil;** Chairman, Co-operative Wholesale Society Ltd, since 1966; Chief Executive Officer, North Eastern Co-operative Society Ltd, since 1970; *b* 2 Jan. 1908; *s* of late Alfred Ernest Jennings and Gertrude Sybil Jennings; *m* 1934, Winifred Evelyn Radford; one *s* decd. *Educ:* Gerard Street Sch., Derby. Inspector of Shops, Derby Co-operative Soc. Ltd, 1947-49; Blackburn Co-operative Soc. Ltd: Grocery Manager and Buyer, 1949-51; Gen. Man., 1951-54; Gen. Man., Darlington Co-operative Soc. Ltd, 1954-70. Dir of Co-operative Insurance Soc. Ltd, 1968-70; Chm., Associated Co-operative Creameries Ltd, 1968-70; Chm., Birtley Distributive Centre, 1964-70. Pres., Co-operative Congress, 1967. *Recreations:* reading, gardening, travel. *Address:* 4 Woodburn Drive, Darlington, Co. Durham. *T:* Darlington 3119.

**JENNINGS, John Charles;** MP (C) Burton-on-Trent Division of Staffordshire since 1955; *b* 10 Feb. 1903; *m* 1927, Berta Nicholson; one *s*. *Educ:* Bede Coll., Durham; King's Coll., Durham Univ. Headmaster. Contested (C), SE Derbyshire, 1950 and 1951. *Recreation:* politics. *Address:* The Elms, Overseal, Burton-on-Trent, Staffs. *T:* Overseal 343.

**JENNINGS, Owen;** *see* Jennings, E. O.

**JENNINGS, Paul (Francis);** writer; *b* 20 June 1918; *s* of William Benedict and Mary Gertrude Jennings; *m* 1952, Celia Blom; three *s* three *d*. *Educ:* King Henry VIII, Coventry, and Douai. Freelance work in Punch and Spectator began while still in Army (Lt Royal Signals); Script-writer at Central Office of Information, 1946-47; Copy writer at Colman Prentis Varley (advertising), 1947-49; on staff of The Observer, 1949-66. Trustee, New Philharmonia Trust. *Publications:* Oddly Enough, 1951; Even Oddlier, 1952; Oddly Bodlikins, 1953; Next to Oddliness, 1955; Model Oddlies, 1956; Gladly Oddly, 1957; Idly Oddly, 1959; I Said Oddly, Diddle I?, 1961; Oodles of Oddlies, 1963; Oddly Ad Lib, 1965; I Was Joking, of Course, 1968; The Living Village, 1968; Just a Few Lines, 1969; For children: The Hopping Basket, 1965; The Great Jelly of London, 1967. *Recreations:* madrigal singing and thinking about writing another vast serious book. *Address:* Hill House, Rectory Hill, East Bergholt, Suffolk.

**JENNINGS, Percival Henry,** CBE 1953; *b* 8 Dec. 1903; *s* of late Rev. Canon H. R. Jennings; *m* 1934, Margaret Katharine Musgrave, *d* of late Brig.-Gen. H. S. Rogers, CMG, DSO; three *d*. *Educ:* Christ's Hospital. Asst Auditor, N Rhodesia, 1927; Asst Auditor, Mauritius, 1931; Auditor, British Honduras, 1934; Dep. Dir of Audit, Gold Coast, 1938; Dep. Dir of Audit, Nigeria, 1945; Dir of Audit, Hong Kong, 1948; Dep. Dir-Gen. of the Overseas Audit Service, 1955; Dir-Gen. of the Overseas Audit Service, 1960-63, retd. *Recreation:* golf. *Address:* Littlewood, Lelant, St Ives, Cornwall. *T:* Hayle 3407. *Clubs:* Royal Commonwealth Society; Penzance; West Cornwall Golf.

**JENNINGS, Sir Raymond (Winter),** Kt 1968; QC 1945; Master, Court of Protection, 1956-70; *b* 12 Dec. 1897; *o s* of late Sir Arthur Oldham Jennings and Mabel Winter; *m* 1930, Sheila, *d* of Selwyn S. Grant, OBE; one *s* one *d*. *Educ:* Rugby; RMC, Sandhurst; Oriel Coll., Oxford (MA, BCL). Served 1916-19 in Royal Fusiliers. Called to Bar, 1922; Bencher of Lincolns Inn, 1951. *Recreation:* fishing. *Address:* Mickleham Cottage, near Dorking, Surrey. *T:* Leatherhead 2552. *Club:* Athenæum.

**JENNINGS, (Richard Edward) Christopher,** MBE 1941; DL; Editor of The Motor, 1946-60; *b* 8 June 1911; *s* of late Lt-Col E. C. Jennings, CBE, DL; *m* 1937, Margaret, *d* of James A. Allan; one *s*. *Educ:* Repton. Served with Riley (Coventry) Ltd, 1931-37. Joined Temple Press as Midland Editor of The Motor, 1937-39. War of 1939-45: Lt Ordnance Mechanical Engineer, 1940; Capt. 1942; Major, 1943; Lt-Col, 1944; served in Western Desert (MBE), Greece, Crete, Syria and Northern Europe. High Sheriff of Carmarthenshire, 1957. DL Carmarthenshire, 1960. Gen. Comr of Income Tax, 1965. director: Trust Houses Ltd, 1960-68; Buckley's Brewery Ltd, 1961; British Automatic Co. Ltd, 1962-68; Teddington Bellows Ltd, 1965. *Publications:* (military) dealing with the fall of Greece and Crete, 1941. *Recreations:* sailing and motoring; interested in preservation of historic ships and vehicles. *Address:* Gelli-deg, Kidwelly, Carmarthenshire. *T:* Ferryside 201. *Clubs:* St James'; Royal Highland Yacht.

**JENNINGS, Prof. Robert Yewdall,** QC 1969; MA, LLB Cantab; Whewell Professor of International Law, University of Cambridge, since 1955; Fellow of Jesus College, Cambridge, since 1939; sometime President of Jesus College; Reader in International Law, Council of Legal Education, since 1959; Member, Institute of International Law; *b* 19 Oct. 1913; *o s* of Arthur Jennings; *m* 1955, Christine, *yr d* of Bernard Bennett; one *s* two *d*. *Educ:* Belle Vue Grammar Sch., Bradford; Downing Coll., Cambridge (Scholar; 1st Cl. Pts I & II, Law Tripos; LLB). Barrister-at-Law, Lincoln's Inn, Hon. Bencher, 1970; Joseph Hodges Choate Fellow, Harvard Univ., 1936-37; Whewell Scholar in Internat. Law, 1936; Asst Lectr in Law, London Sch. of Economics, 1938-39. Served War: Intelligence Corps, 1940-46; Hon. Major, Officers' AER. Senior Tutor, Jesus Coll., 1949-55. Joint Editor: International and Comparative Law Quarterly, 1956-61; British Year Book of International Law, 1960-. *Publications:* The Acquisition of Territory, 1963; articles in legal periodicals. *Address:* Jesus College, Cambridge.

**JENOUR, Sir (Arthur) Maynard (Chesterfield),** Kt 1959; TD 1950; JP; Vice-Lieutenant of Monmouthshire, 1965; Chairman and Joint Managing Director: Aberthaw & Bristol Channel Portland Cement Co. Ltd (Director, 1929); T. Beynon & Co., Ltd (Director, 1938); Chairman, Ruthin Quarries (Bridgend) Ltd (Director 1947); Director: Associated Portland Cement Manufacturers Ltd, 1963; Blue Jacket Motel (Pty) Ltd, Australia, 1964; *b* 7 Jan. 1905; *s* of Brig.-Gen. A. S. Jenour, CB, CMG, DSO, Crossways, Chepstow and Emily Anna (*née* Beynon); *m* 1948, Margaret Sophie (who *m* 1927, W. O. Ellis Fielding-Jones, *d* 1935; three *d*), *d* of H. Stuart Osborne, Sydney, NSW. *Educ:* Eton. Entered business, 1924. Served War of 1939-45, in England and Middle East, Royal Artillery, Major. High Sheriff of Monmouthshire, 1951-52; Pres., Cardiff Chamber of Commerce, 1953-54; Chm. Wales & Mon. Industrial Estates Ltd, 1954-60; Mem. Board, Development Corporation for Wales, 1958-. JP Mon 1946; DL Mon, 1960. KStJ 1969. *Recreations:* walking, gardening, shooting. *Address:* Stonycroft, 13 Ridgeway, Newport, Mon. *T:* Newport 63802. *Clubs:* United Service; Cardiff and County (Cardiff); Monmouthshire County (Newport); Union (Sydney, NSW).

**JENSEN, Dr Johannes Daniel;** Professor of Physics, Heidelberg University, since 1949; *b* 28 June 1906. *Educ:* Hamburg University. Professor of Physics, Hannover Inst. of Technology, 1941. Professor *hc* Hamburg Univ., 1947; Member: Heidelberg Academy of Sciences, 1949; Max Planck Gesellschaft, 1961; Deutsche Akademie der Naturforscher, Leopoldina, Halle, 1964; Nobel Prize for Physics (jtly), 1963. *Publications:* (with Maria Goeppert-Mayer) Elementary Theory of Nuclear Shell Structure, New York, 1955; Editor (with Otto Haxel) Zeitschrift für Physik, 1956-. *Recreation:* physics. *Address:* Philosophenweg 16, Heidelberg, Germany.

**JEPHCOTT, Sir Harry,** 1st Bt *cr* 1962; Kt 1946; MSc (London); FRIC; FPS; Hon. President, late Chairman, Glaxo Group Ltd; Director Metal Box Co. Ltd, 1950-64; *b* 15 Jan. 1891; *s* of late John Josiah Jephcott, Redditch; *m* 1919, Doris Gregory, FPS; two *s*. *Educ:* King Edward's Grammar Sch., Camp Hill, Birmingham; West Ham Technical Coll., London. Called to Bar (Middle Temple), 1925.

Chm. Council, Dept Scientific and Industrial Research, 1956-61; Pres. Royal Inst. of Chemistry, 1953-55; Chm. Assoc. of British Chemical Manufacturers, 1947-52, Pres. 1952-55. Mem. Advisory Council Scientific Policy, 1953-56; Chm. Cttee Detergents, 1953-55. chm. School of Pharmacy, University of London, 1948-69. hon. Fellow, School of Pharmacy, 1966. Governor London Sch. of Economics, 1952-68; Governor North London Collegiate Sch., 1957-. Hon. DSc (Birmingham), 1956. Hon. Fellow Royal Society Med., 1961. *Heir: s* John Anthony Jephcott, BCom [*b* 21 May 1924; *m* 1949, Sylvia Mary, *d* of Thorsten Frederick Relling, Wellington, NZ; two *d*]. *Address:* Weetwood, 1 Cheney Street, Pinner, Middlesex. *T:* 01-866 0305. *Club:* Athenæum.

**JEPSON, Richard Pomfret,** FRCS, FRACS; Professor of Surgery, Adelaide University, Australia, 1958-68; *b* 15 Feb. 1918; *s* of W. N. and L. E. Jepson, Whalley, Lancs; *m* 1951, Mary Patricia Herbert Oliver; five *d*. *Educ:* St Mary's Grammar Sch., Clitheroe, Lancs; Manchester Univ., BSc, MB, ChB. House Surgeon, Manchester Royal Infirmary, 1941-42; Neurosurgical specialist, Major, RAMC, 1942-46; Asst Lecturer, Lecturer and Reader in Surgery, University of Manchester, 1946-54; Prof. of Surgery, University of Sheffield, 1954-58. Hunterian Prof., RCS, 1951; Commonwealth Fund Fellowship, 1951; Research Fellow, Western Reserve Univ., Cleveland, Ohio, 1951-52. Hon. Surgeon: Queen Elizabeth Hosp., 1958-68; Royal Adelaide Hosp., 1958-68 (Hon. Vascular Surgeon, 1968-). *Publications:* articles in physiological and surgical journals. *Recreations:* varied. *Address:* 112 Barnard Street, N Adelaide, S Australia 5006, Australia. *Club:* Adelaide.

**JEPSON, Selwyn;** author and occasional soldier; *o s* of late Edgar Jepson. *Educ:* St Paul's Sch. War of 1939-45, Major, The Buffs, Military Intelligence and SOE. Editorial journalism, 1919. *Publications: novels:* The Qualified Adventurer, 1921; That Fellow MacArthur, 1922; The King's Red-Haired Girl, 1923; Golden Eyes, 1924; Rogues and Diamonds, 1925; Snaggletooth, 1926; The Death Gong, 1928; Tiger Dawn, 1929; I Met Murder, 1930; Rabbit's Paw, 1932; Keep Murder Quiet, 1940; Man Running, 1948; The Golden Dart, 1949; The Hungry Spider, 1950; Man Dead, 1951; The Black Italian, 1954; The Assassin, 1956; Noise in the Night, 1957; The Laughing Fish, 1960; Fear in the Wind, 1964; The Third Possibility, 1965; Angry Millionaire, 1968; Dead Letters, 1970; *short stories:* (with Michael Joseph) Heads or Tails, 1933; *stage play:* (with Lesley Storm) Dark Horizon, 1933; *screen plays:* Going Gay, 1932; For the Love of You, 1932; Irresistible Marmaduke, 1933; Monday at Ten, 1933; The Love Test, 1934; The Riverside Murders, 1934; White Lilac, Hyde Park Corner (Hackett), 1935; Well Done, Henry, 1936; The Scarab Murder, 1936; Toilers of the Sea (adapted and directed), 1936; Sailing Along, 1937; Carnet de Bal: Double Crime on the Maginot Line (English Version), 1938; *television plays:* Thought to Kill, 1952; Dialogue for Two Faces, 1952; My Name is Jones, 1952; Little Brother, 1953; Last Moment, 1953; Forever my Heart, 1953; Leave it to Eve (serial), 1954; The Interloper, 1955; Noise in the Night (USA), 1958; The Hungry Spider, 1964; *radio serial:* The Hungry Spider, 1957; *radio plays:* The Bath that Sang, 1958; Noise in the Night, 1958; Art for Art's Sake, 1959; Small Brother, 1960; Call it Greymail, 1961; Dark Corners, 1963. *Recreation:* painting. *Address:* The Far House, Liss, Hants. *Club:* Savile.

**JEPSON, Stanley;** *b* 1894; *s* of Samuel Jepson, Spalding; *m* Elizabeth, *d* of late Major G. Casswell, Gosberton, Spalding; one *d*. *Educ:* Moulton. Served (Captain) Indian Army, European War, and 3rd Afghan War, 1919; retired 1921; The Yorkshire Post, 1925-27; Editor of the Illustrated Weekly of India, 1928-47. *Publications:* Motor Runs from Bombay, 1934; Big Game Encounters, 1936; The Overland Route from India, 1938; Indian Lenslight, 1947. *Address:* Bentcliffe, St Aubin, Jersey, CI.

**JERITZA, Maria;** Opera and Concert Star; *b* Brno, Czechoslovakia; *m* Irving Seery. *Educ:* Royal Academy of Music, Vienna. Debut, Vienna State Opera, 1918; with Metropolitan Opera Company, New York, and with Vienna State Opera, 1922-49. Recipient of the highest orders and decorations, from: HH the Pope; Republic of Austria; Republic of Italy; and Republic of France. *Publication:* Sunlight and Song. *Address:* c/o Maurice Feldman, Suite 1404, 745 Fifth Avenue, New York, NY 10022, USA.

**JERMYN, Earl; Frederick William John Augustus Hervey;** *b* 15 Sept. 1954; *s* and *heir* of 6th Marquess of Bristol, *qv*.

**JERRAM, Sir (Cecil) Bertrand,** KCMG, *cr* 1947 (CMG 1938); *b* 22 Oct. 1891; *y s* of late C. S. Jerram, Talland, Cornwall. *Educ:* Hillside, Godalming; King's Sch., Canterbury; Pembroke Coll., Cambridge. Entered Levant Consular Service in 1913; employed at Odessa, Kiev, Moscow; arrested and imprisoned by Bolshevik forces at Moscow in 1918; Vice-Consul, Novorossisk, 1919-20; Asst Agent, Moscow and Leningrad, 1923-27; Acting Consul, Bergen, 1927-28; Consul and Chargé d'Affaires ad interim, Tallinn, 1928-30; Commercial Sec., Helsingfors, 1930-33; Commercial Counsellor. Warsaw, 1933-37; Commercial Counsellor to HM Embassy in Spain (at Hendaye), 1937; Asst Agent, Salamanca and Burgos, 1938; Acting Agent at Burgos and HM Chargé d'Affaires in Spain, 1939; Commercial Counsellor to HM Embassy at Buenos Aires, 1939; Minister (Commercial), 1944-45; Minister in Stockholm, 1945-47, Ambassador 1947-48; Minister to Austria, 1948-49; Special Ambassador for Great Britain, Austr. and NZ at inauguration of Gen. Odria as Pres. of Perú, 1950; Ambassador to Chile, 1949-51; retired from the Foreign Service, 1951. Leader of UK Delegation: at Ecosoc Conf., Santiago, 1951; to Plenipotentiary Conf. of Internat. Telecommunications Union, Buenos Aires, 1952. Silver Jubilee Medal, 1935; Coronation Medal, 1937. *Recreation:* travel. *Club:* Athenæum.

**JERRAM, Rear-Adm. Sir Rowland Christopher,** KBE, *cr* 1945 (CBE 1937); DSO 1920; DL; RN, retired; *b* 1890; *s* of late C. S. Jerram, Talland, Cornwall; *m* 1919, Christine E. M. (*d* 1961), *d* of late J. Grigg, Port Looe, Looe, Cornwall; two *s*. Entered RN, 1907; retired list 1945. DL Cornwall, 1958. KStJ. *Address:* Temple Garth, St Cleer, Cornwall.

**JERRAM, Brig. Roy Martyn,** DSO 1940; MC 1918; Legion of Merit (USA); Royal Tank Regiment; retired, 1947; *b* 10 Nov. 1895; *e s* of late Admiral Sir Martyn Jerram, GCMG, KCB; *m* 1926, Monica Gillies; two *s* one *d*. *Educ:* Marlborough. Served European War, Hants Regt, 1914-17; Tank Corps, 1917 (MC); Tank Engineer and GSO 2, Army HQ, India, 1931-35; DAD Mechanisation, War Office, 1937-40; AQMG, GHQ, France, 1940 (DSO); commanded 7th (Army) Bn R Tank Regt 1st Libyan Campaign, 1940-41 (despatches twice, bar to DSO); Comdr 33 Army Tank Bde, 1941-42; DDG Petroleum Warfare Dept, 1943-44; Comdr Assault Training and Development Centre, 1944-45; Control Commission, Germany, 1945-52; Red Cross, Japan, Korea, 1952, 1953. *Address:* Trehane, Trevanson, Wadebridge, Cornwall. *T:* Wadebridge 2523. *Club:* Royal Commonwealth Society.

**JERRARD, Brig. Charles Ian,** CB 1954; CBE 1945; retired 1953; *b* 13 June 1900; *s* of Harry Jerrard, Uplyme, Dorset; *m* 1st, 1931; one *s*; 2nd, 1949, Joan Mary Mathein Mya; one *s* one *d*. *Educ:* Bishop Veseys, Sutton Coldfield; Cadet Coll., Wellington. Commissioned, Indian Army, 1920; Regimental Officer, 1 Bn 12 FF Regt, 1920-25; Adjt Depot,. 12 FF Regt, 1926-28; Staff Coll., Quetta, 1935-36; Brigade Major, Wana Brigade, 1937-38; Company Comdr, RMC Sandhurst, 1938-39; Chief Instructor, 169 OCTU, 1939-40; GSO 2 Ops, 12 Corps 1940-41; GSO 2 14 Indian Div., 1941; GSO 1 Ops 4 Corps, Assam, 1942-43; Commandant 8/12 FF Regt, 1943; Comd 98 Indian Inf. Bde, 1944-47; Operations Waziristan, 1924-37; Assam, Burma, 1942-43; Burma, 1944-45 (CBE, despatches thrice); Burma Anti Dacoit, 1946-47; Acting Maj.-Gen. 1945; Dir Military Training and Education, Pakistan Army, 1948-53; Hon. Brig. 1954. *Recreation:* gardening. *Address:* Solway Cottage, Uplyme, Dorset. *T:* Lyme Regis 2333.

**JERSEY, 9th Earl of,** *cr* 1697; **George Francis Child Villiers;** Viscount Grandison, 1620; Viscount Villiers and Baron Hoo, 1691; *b* 15 Feb. 1910; *e s* of 8th Earl and Lady Cynthia Almina Constance Mary Needham (who *m* 2nd, 1925, W. R. Slessor (*d* 1945); she died 1947), *o d* of 3rd Earl of Kilmorey; *S* father, 1923; *m* 1st, 1932, Patricia Kenneth (who obtained a divorce, 1937; she *m* 2nd, 1937, Robin Filmer Wilson, who *d* 1944; 3rd, 1953, Col Peter Laycock), *o d* of Kenneth Richards, Cootamundra, NSW, and of Eileen Mary (now *widow* of Sir Stephenson Kent, KCB); one *d*; 2nd, 1937, Virginia (who obtained a divorce, 1946), *d* of James Cherrill, USA; 3rd, 1947, Bianca, *er d* of late Enrico Mottironi, Turin, Italy; two *s* one *d*. *Heir: s* Viscount Villiers, *qv*. *Address:* Radier Manor, Longueville, Jersey, Channel Islands. *T:* (Jersey) Central 30002.

**JERSEY, Dean of;** *see* Giles, Very Rev. A. S.

**JERUSALEM, Archbishop in, and Metropolitan,** since 1969; **Most Rev. George Appleton,** MBE 1946; *b* 20 Feb. 1902; *s* of Thomas George and Lily Appleton; *m* 1929, Marjorie Alice, *d* of Charles Samuel Barrett; one *s* two *d*. *Educ:* County Boys' School, Maidenhead; Selwyn Coll., Cambridge; St Augustine's Coll., Canterbury. BA Cantab 1924 (2nd Cl. Math. Trip. pt I, 1st Cl. Theological Trip. pt I); MA 1929. Deacon, 1925; Priest, 1926. Curate, Stepney Parish Church, 1925-27; Missionary in charge SPG Mission, Irrawaddy Delta, 1927-33; Warden, Coll. of Holy Cross, Rangoon, 1933-41; Archdeacon of Rangoon, 1943-46; Director of Public Relations, Government of Burma, 1945-46; Vicar of Headstone, 1947-50; Sec., Conf. of Brit. Missionary Societies, 1950-57; Rector of St Botolph, Aldgate, 1957-62; Archdeacon of London and Canon of St Paul's Cathedral, 1962-63; Archbishop of Perth and Metropolitan of W Australia, 1963-68. *Publications:* John's Witness to Jesus, 1955; In His Name, 1956; Glad Encounter, 1959; On the Eightfold Path, 1961; Daily Prayer and Praise, 1962; Acts of Devotion, 1963; One Man's Prayers, 1967. *Address:* St George's Close, PO Box 1248, Jerusalem.

**JERVIS,** family name of **Viscount St Vincent.**

**JERVIS, Charles Elliott,** OBE 1966; Editor-in-Chief, Press Association, 1954-65; *b* Liverpool, 7 Nov. 1907; *y s* of late J. H. Jervis, Liverpool; *m* 1931, Ethel Braithwaite, Kendal, Westmorland; one *d*. Editorial Asst, Liverpool Express, 1921-23; Reporter, Westmorland Gazette, 1923-28; Dramatic Critic and Asst Editor, Croydon Times, 1928-37; Sub-Editor, Press Assoc., 1937-47; Asst Editor, 1947-54. Pres., Guild of British Newspaper Editors, 1964-65; Mem. of the Press Council, 1960-65. *Address:* Orchard End, Cart Lane, Grange-over-Sands, Lancs. *T:* 2335. *Club:* Press.

**JESSEL,** family name of **Baron Jessel.**

**JESSEL,** 2nd Baron, *cr* 1924, of Westminster; **Edward Herbert Jessel,** Bt, *cr* 1917; CBE 1963; a Deputy Chairman of Committees, and a Deputy Speaker, House of Lords; *b* 25 March 1904; *o s* of 1st Baron, CB, CMG, and Maud (*d* 1965), 5th *d* of late Rt Hon. Sir Julian Goldsmid, Bt, MP; *S* father 1950; *m* 1st, 1935, Lady Helen Maglona Vane-Tempest-Stewart (from whom he obtained a divorce, 1960), 3rd *d* of 7th Marquess of Londonderry, KG, PC, MVO; two *d* (one *s* decd); 2nd, 1960, Jessica, *d* of late William De Wet and Mrs H. W. Taylor, Cape Town. *Educ:* Eton; Christ Church, Oxford (BA). Called to Bar, Inner Temple, 1926. *Address:* 101 Eaton Place, SW1. *T:* 01-235 7210. *Clubs:* Garrick, White's.
*See also G. W. G. Agnew.*

**JESSEL, Sir George,** 2nd Bt, *cr* 1883; MC; JP; late Capt. 5th Buffs; Chairman, Bournemouth and District Water Company, etc; Director, Imperial Continental Gas Association (late Chairman); *b* 28 May 1891; *er s* of 1st Bt and Edith (*d* 1956), 2nd *d* of Rt Hon. Sir Julian Goldsmid, 3rd Bt, MP, *S* father, 1928; *m* 1923, Muriel (*d* 1948), *d* of Col J. W. Chaplin, VC, and *widow* of Major F. Swetenham; one *s*; *m* 1948, Elizabeth, Lady Russell of Liverpool, *d* of late Dr David Ewart, OBE, MD, FRCS, Chichester. *Educ:* Eton; Balliol Coll., Oxford (MA). Served European War, 1914-18 (severely wounded, despatches, MC). JP Kent, 1940; High Sheriff of Kent, 1958. *Heir: s* Charles John Jessel [*b* 29 Dec. 1924; *m* 1956, Shirley Cornelia, *o d* of John Waters, Northampton; two *s* one *d*]. *Address:* Ladham House, Goudhurst, Kent. *T:* Goudhurst 203. *Clubs:* Garrick, Brooks's, Army and Navy.

**JESSEL, Oliver Richard;** Chairman, Jessel Securities Ltd; *b* 24 Aug. 1929; *s* of Comdr R. F. Jessel, DSO, OBE, RN; *m* 1950, Gloria Rosalie Teresa (*née* Holden); one *s* five *d*. *Educ:* Rugby. Founded group of companies, 1954; opened office in City of London, 1960; formed New Issue Unit Trust and other trusts, 1962-68; acquired Wm France Fenwick, 1968, Demerara Co., 1969, Falks, 1970. *Address:* The Grange, Marden, Kent. *T:* Marden 264.
*See also T. F. H. Jessel.*

**JESSEL, Sir Richard (Hugh),** Kt 1960; Chairman and Managing Director, Jessel Toynbee & Co. Ltd, Discount Brokers, 1943-60, retired; *b* 21 Feb. 1896; 2nd *s* of late Sir Charles James Jessel, 1st Bt; *m* 1st, 1923, Margaret Ella (*d* 1953), *d* of late Sir George Lewis, 2nd Bt; two *s* one *d*; 2nd, 1954, Daphne, *widow* of Major T. G. Philipson, MC, the Life Guards, and *d* of late W. B. Gladstone. *Educ:* Eton. Founded Jessel Toynbee & Co., 1922; Limited Co. (private), Chm., 1943; Public Co., 1946; Public Works Commissioner, 1949-60; Exports Credits Guarantee Dept Advisory Council, 1951-60 (Dep. Chm., 1959). Served European War, 1914-18, Lt 2/7 Bn Hants Regt; served War of 1939-45, with Ministry of Economic Warfare, 1939-41; Priority Officer, Air Ministry, 1941-44. *Recreations:* racing, gardening. *Address:* Coney Weston Hall, Bury St Edmunds, Suffolk. *Clubs:* Brooks's, MCC.

**JESSEL, Toby Francis Henry;** MP (C) Twickenham since 1970; Member for Richmond-upon-Thames, GLC, since 1967; Director, Jessel Securities Ltd; *b* 11 July 1934; *y s* of Comdr R. F. Jessel, DSO, OBE, DSC, RN, Lees Court, Matfield, Kent; *m* 1967, Philippa Brigid (BSc Soc), *e d* of Henry C. Jephcott, Cottingham, Yorks; one *d. Educ:* RNC, Dartmouth; Balliol Col., Oxford (MA). Sub-Lt, RNVR, 1954. Conservative Candidate: Peckham, 1964; Hull (North), 1966. Chm., South Area Bd GLC Planning and Transportation Cttee, 1968-70. (Co-opted) LCC Housing Cttee, 1961-65; Councillor, London Borough of Southwark, 1964-66; Hon. Sec. Assoc. of Adopted Conservative Candidates, 1961-66. Mem. Metropolitan Water Bd, 1967-70; Mem., London Airport Consultative Cttee, 1967-; Governor, Mary Datchelor Grammar Sch. 1962-. Whitworth Memorial Prize for Music, 1951. *Recreations:* music, gardening, croquet (Longworth Cup, Hurlingham, 1961), ski-ing. *Address:* Old Court House, Hampton Court, Surrey. *Clubs:* Carlton, Hurlingham.

*See also O. R. Jessel.*

**JESSOP, Joseph Chasser,** MA, PhD (St Andrews); FRHistS 1930; retired as Headmaster, Lossiemouth School (1933-58); *b* 13 Jan. 1892; *s* of Thomas Jessop and Helen Baird Alexander; *m* 1922, Ida Hallsey Bates, Stourbridge; twin *d. Educ:* Montrose Academy; St Andrews Univ., MA (Hons) 1915. Captain of St Andrews Univ. Golf Club; served in India, Egypt, and France as Lt in Black Watch for 3½ years (European War); wounded and gassed in France; after convalescence appointed Chief Education Officer to 4th (Res.) Black Watch. Taught in: Selkirk High Sch.; Hutchesons' Boys' Grammar Sch., Glasgow; Brechin High Sch. *Publications:* Education in Angus: an Historical Survey of Education up to the Act of 1872 from Original and Contemporary Sources, 1931, published under the auspices of the Scottish Council for Research in Education; Teach Yourself Golf, 1950. *Recreation:* golf; three times golf champion of Forfarshire; former amateur record-holder of Eden, St Andrews, Montrose, Edzell, and Moray Golf Courses; three times winner of Montrose, four times winner of Moray, Open Amateur Golf Tournaments. SGU Northern District champion. *Address:* 5 Old Mill Road, Inverness. *T:* Inverness 30480. *Clubs:* Scottish Universities Golfing Society; Moray Golf (Hon. Life Mem.).

**JESSOP, Thomas Edmund,** OBE 1945; MC; MA, BLitt; Hon. LittD (Dublin); Hon. DLitt (Hull); Fellow of the British Psychological Society, Foreign Fellow, Accademia Nazionale dei Lincei (Rome); Médaille d'honneur, Brussels University; Ferens Professor of Philosophy in the University of Hull, 1928-61, Professor Emeritus since 1961; *b* Huddersfield, 10 Sept. 1896; *s* of Newton Jessop; *m* 1930, Dora Anne Nugent Stewart (*d* 1965), MA (Glasgow). *Educ:* Heckmondwike Sch., Leeds Univ.; Oriel Coll., Oxford. Served with Duke of Wellington's West Riding Regt on the Western Front, 1916-18 (twice wounded); Asst Lecturer in Logic and Metaphysics, University of Glasgow, 1925-28; Chm. of E and N Yorks and North Lindsey Adult Education Cttee, 1936-37; Donnellan Lectr, Dublin, 1944; Dunning Trust Lectr, Kingston, Ontario 1948; Visiting Professor: Brussels Univ., 1953; Los Angeles State Coll., 1963; San Francisco State Coll., 1970. Vice-Pres. Methodist Conf., 1955; Member: of World Methodist Council Exec. (1956-66); of Editorial Bd of SCM Press; of Editorial Bd of Archives Internationales d'Histoire des Idées, of Council of Royal Institute of Philosophy, of Institut International de Philosophie, and of Yorks Executive of Royal Society of St George; Chm. of Adult Religious Education Sub-Cttee of Brit. Council of Churches, 1948-61. *Publications:* Lugano and its Environs, 1924; Montreux and Lake of Geneva, 1925; Locarno and its Valleys, 1927; Bibliography of George Berkeley, Bishop of Cloyne, 1934; The Philosophical Background, in France, Companion to French Studies, 1937; Berkeley's Principles of Human Knowledge, 1937; The Scientific Account of Man, in The Christian Understanding of Man, 1938; Bibliography of Hume and of Scottish Philosophy, 1938; part-translator of A Hundred Years of British Philosophy by R. Metz, 1938; Law and Love, a study of the Christian Ethic, 1940; Science and the Spiritual, 1942; The Treaty of Versailles, 1942; Effective Religion, 1944; Education and Evangelism, 1947; The Works of George Berkeley (joint ed.), 1948-57; The Freedom of the Individual in Society, 1948; Reasonable Living, 1948; Berkeley, Philosophical Writings selected and edited, 1952; Social Ethics, 1952; On Reading the English Bible, Peake Lecture, 1958; "Writers and their Work" (British Council): contrib. Berkeley, 1959, Hobbes, 1960; Introduction to Christian Doctrine, 1960; The Christian Morality (Cambridge Open Divinity Lectures), 1960; The Enduring Passion, 1961; Spinoza on Freedom of Thought, 1962; Berkeley, Antologia degli Scritti Filosofici, 1967; contribs to encyclopædias and philosophical periodicals. *Recreation:* gardening. *Address:* 73 Park Avenue, Hull. *T:* 408106.

**JESSUP, Philip C.;** United States teacher and lawyer; Judge of International Court of Justice, 1961-70; Teacher of International Law, Columbia University, 1925-61; Hamilton Fish Professor of International Law and Diplomacy, 1946-61; *b* 5 Jan. 1897; *s* of Henry Wynans and Mary Hay Stotesbury Jessup; *m* 1921, Lois Walcott Kellogg; one *s. Educ:* Hamilton Coll., Clinton, NY (AB 1919); Columbia Univ. (AM 1924, PhD 1927); Yale Univ. (LLB). US Army Exped. Forces, 1918. Parker & Duryea Law Firm, New York, 1927-43. Asst Solicitor, Dept of State, 1924-25; Asst to Elihu Root, Conf. of Jurists, Permanent Court of International Justice, Geneva, 1929; Legal Adviser to American Ambassador to Cuba, 1930; Chm., Div. of Office of Foreign Relief, Dept of State, 1943; Associate Dir, Naval Sch. of Military Government and Administration, 1942-44; Asst Sec. Gen. UNRRA and Bretton Woods Confs, 1943-44; Asst on Judicial Organisation, San Francisco Conf. on UNO, 1945; US Dep. Rep. to Interim Cttee of Gen. Assembly and Security Council, UN, 1948; Deleg. Sessions: UN Gen. Assembly, 3rd, Paris-New York, 1948-49, 4th New York, 1949, 6th, Paris, Nov. 1951-Jan. 1952, 7th New York 1952. Ambassador at Large of USA, 1949-53; Storrs Lectr Yale Univ. Law Sch., 1956; Cooley Lectr, Michigan Univ. Law Sch., 1958. Mem. Curatorium, Hague Acad. of Internat. Law, 1957-68; Trustee: Carnegie Endowment for Internat. Peace, 1937-60; Hamilton Coll., 1958-61; Associate Rockefeller Foundation, 1960-61; Vice-Pres. Institut de droit international, 1959-60. Hon. Mem. Inter-American Institute of International Legal Studies, 1964-. Chm., Chile-Norway Permanent Conciliation Commission, 1958-; Mem. Governing Coun., Inst. for Unification of Private Law, 1964-67, Hon. Mem., 1967-. Hon. President: Amer. Soc. of Internat. Law, 1969-; Amer. Branch,

Internat. Law Assoc., 1970-. Senior Fellow, Council on Foreign Relations (NYC), 1970-71. Hon. LLD: Western Reserve Univ., Trustee: Carnegie Endowment for Internat. Peace, 1937-60; Seoul Nat. Univ., Rutgers Univ., Middlebury Coll., Yale Univ., St Lawrence Univ., Univ. of Michigan; Hon. LCD: Colgate Univ., Union Coll.; Hon. JD Oslo; Doc (*hc*) Univ. of Paris; Hon. LittD, Univ. of Hanoi. Hon. Mem., Academia Mexicana de Derecho International. Hungarian Cross of Merit, Class II; Official Ordem Nacional do Cruzeiro do Sul, Brazil; Grand Officer, Order of the Cedars, Lebanon; Manley O. Hudson Gold Medal of the American Soc. of International Law, 1964. *Publications:* The Law of Territorial Waters and Maritime Jurisdiction, 1927; United States and the World Court, 1929; Neutrality, Its History, Economics and Law, Vol. I, The Origins (with F. Deak), 1935; Vol. IV, Today and Tomorrow, 1936; Elihu Root, 1938; International Problem of Governing Mankind, 1947; A Modern Law of Nations, 1948; Transnational Law, 1956; The Use of International Law, 1959; Controls for Outer Space (with H. J. Taubenfield), 1960. *Address:* Windrow Road, Norfolk, Conn 06058, USA. *Clubs:* Century (New York); Cosmos (Washington).

**JEWELL, Maurice Frederick Stewart,** CBE 1954; JP; DL; *b* 15 Sept. 1885; *s* of Maurice Jewell and Ada Brown; *m* 1911, Elsie May Taylor; one *s* five *d*. *Educ:* Marlborough Coll. Served European War, 1914-19, with Royal Field Artillery; Major 1916. JP 1926, DL 1947, Worcs. *Recreations:* formerly cricket (President of Worcs County Cricket Club until 1954). *Address:* Sufton Cottage, Mordiford, near Hereford. *T:* Barterstree Cross 241. *Club:* Worcestershire (Worcester).

**JEWESBURY, Reginald Charles,** MA; DM Oxon.; FRCP London; Consulting Physician in Paediatrics: St Thomas's Hospital; Victoria Hospital for Children, Chelsea; St Luke's Hospital, Guildford; *b* Ceylon, 1878; *s* of late Charles F. Jewesbury, MRCS, LRCP; *m* Anne C. Oliphant Williamson; two *s*. *Educ:* Westminster Sch.; Christ Church, Oxford; St Thomas's Hospital, Bristowe medal, 1906; Late Physician in charge of Children's Dept, St Thomas's Hospital; Fellow, and Ex-Pres., section for study of Diseases in Children, Royal Society Medicine. Retired. *Address:* 73 Albion Gate, W2. *T:* 01-262 5821. *Club:* United Service.

**JEWKES, John,** CBE 1943; MA; MCom; Director, Industrial Policy Group, since 1969; Economic Adviser, Arthur Guinness, Son and Co. Ltd; *b* June 1902; *m* 1929, Sylvia Butterworth; one *d*. *Educ:* Barrow Grammar Sch.; Manchester Univ. Asst Sec., Manchester Chamber of Commerce, 1925-26; Lecturer in Economics, University of Manchester, 1926-29; Rockefeller Foundation Fellow, 1929-30; Professor of Social Economics, Manchester 1936-46; Stanley Jevons Prof. of Political Economy, Manchester, 1946-48; Prof. of Economic Organisation, Oxford, and Fellow of Merton College, 1948-69, Emeritus Fellow 1969. Visiting Prof., University of Chicago, 1953-54; Visiting Prof., Princeton Univ., 1961. Dir, Economic Section, War Cabinet Secretariat, 1941; Dir-Gen. of Statistics and Programmes, Ministry of Aircraft Production, 1943; Principal Asst Sec., Office of Minister of Reconstruction, 1944; Mem. of Fuel Advisory Cttee, 1945; Independent Mem. of Cotton Industry Working Party, 1946; Mem. of Royal Commission on Gambling, Betting and Lotteries, 1949. Mem. of Royal Commission on Doctors' and Dentists' Remuneration, 1957-60. *Publications:* An Industrial Survey of Cumberland and Furness (with A. Winterbottom); Juvenile Unemployment (with A. Winterbottom); Wages and Labour in the Cotton Spinning Industry (with E. M. Gray); The Juvenile Labour Market (with Sylvia Jewkes); Ordeal by Planning; The Sources of Invention (with David Sawers and Richard Stillerman); The Genesis of the British National Health Service (with Sylvia Jewkes); Value for Money in Medicine (with Sylvia Jewkes); Public and Private Enterprise; New Ordeal by Planning. *Recreation:* gardening. *Address:* Entwood, Red Copse Lane, Boars Hill, Oxford.

**JHABVALA, Mrs R(uth) Prawer;** author; *b* in Germany, of Polish parents, 7 May 1927; *d* of Marcus Prawer and Eleonora Prawer (*née* Cohn); came to England as refugee, 1939; *m* 1951, C. S. H. Jhabvala; three *d*. *Educ:* Hendon County Sch.; Queen Mary Coll., London Univ. Started writing after graduation and marriage, alternating between novels and short stories; occasional original film-scripts, including: Shakespeare-wallah, 1965; The Guru, 1969. *Publications: novels:* To Whom She Will, 1955; The Nature of Passion, 1956; Esmond in India, 1958; The Householder, 1960; Get Ready for Battle, 1962; A Backward Place, 1965; *short story collections:* Like Birds, like Fishes, 1964; A Stronger Climate, 1968. *Recreation:* writing film-scripts. *Address:* 1-A Flagstaff Road, Delhi, India. *T:* 228823.

*See also Prof. S. S. Prawer.*

**JINKS, Prof. John Leonard,** FRS 1970; Professor of Genetics and Head of Department of Genetics, Birmingham University, since 1965; *b* 21 Oct. 1929; *s* of Jack and Beatrice May jinks; *m* 1955, Diana Mary Williams; one *s* one *d*. *Educ:* Longton High Sch., Stoke-on-Trent; Univ. of Birmingham. BSc Botany 1950, PhD Genetics 1952, DSc Genetics 1964, Birmingham. ARC Research Student: Univ. of Birmingham, 1950-52; Carlsberg Labs, Copenhagen; Instituto Sieroterapico, Milan, 1952-53; Scientific Officer, ARC Unit of Biometrical Genetics, Univ. of Birmingham, 1953-59; Harkness Fellow, California Inst. of Technology, 1959-60; Principal Scientific Officer, ARC Unit of Biometrical Genetics, 1960-65; Hon. Lectr 1960-62, Reader 1962-65, Univ of Birmingham. Editor of Heredity, 1960-. FIBiol 1968. *Publications:* Extrachromosomal Inheritance, 1964; (jtly) Biometrical Genetics, 1971; numerous papers and chapters in books on microbial genetics, biometrical genetics and behavioral genetics. *Recreations:* piano, gardening. *Address:* 81 Witherford Way, Selly Oak, Birmingham 29. *T:* 021-472 2008.

**JOCELYN,** family name of **Earl of Roden.**

**JOCELYN, Viscount; Robert John Jocelyn;** *b* 25 Aug. 1938; *e s* and *heir of* 9th Earl of Roden, qv; *m* 1970, Sara Cecilia, *d* of Brig. Andrew Dunlop, Rhodesia. Address: Bryansford, Co. Down, Ireland. *T:* Newcastle (Down) 3469.

**JOEL, Harry Joel;** *b* 4 Sept. 1894; *o s* of Jack Barnato Joel, JP. *Educ:* Malvern Coll. dir, De Beers Consolidated Mines, Ltd, and other Companies. Served European War 1914-18 with 15th Hussars. *Recreations:* racing and shooting. *Address:* 15 Grosvenor Square, W1; Sefton Lodge, Newmarket; Childwick Bury, St Albans, Herts. *Clubs:* Buck's; Jockey (Newmarket).

**JOELSON, F(erdinand) Stephen;** writer on African affairs since 1917; editor, broadcaster and publisher; *b* 3 Jan. 1893; *e s* of late George and Sarah Jane Joelson; *m* 1921, Florence Emily, *er d* of late William and Elizabeth

Buchanan; one *d. Educ:* Cardiff High Sch.; privately and on Continent. Asst manager of rubber estate, E Africa, 1914; POW German E Africa, (Aug.) 1914-17; then Intelligence Officer, GHQ, Dar es Salaam; official interpreter in French, German and Swahili at mil. courts, and liaison officer with Belg. Mil. Mission, GHQ; invalided home; demobilised, 1920. Sec. to internat. businessman; resigned 1924 to found London weekly newspaper East Africa, renamed East Africa and Rhodesia, 1936, and Rhodesia and Eastern Africa, 1966, to mark sympathy with Rhodesian claim for independence. Actively edited journal throughout 43 years until Brit. Govt's imposition of sanctions compelled cessation of publication, 1967. Was Chm. East Africa, Ltd, and Africana, Ltd, which published the newspaper and many vols on Af. affairs. Also Chm., Gold Areas of East Africa, Ltd. Formerly: Gov., Commonwealth Inst.; Vice-Pres. Royal African Society (hon. life Mem. and medallist); Mem. Coun., Royal Commonwealth Soc.; Mem. Grand Council, Royal Over-Seas League, Chm. E African Gp; Mem. Cttee, Royal Commonwealth Soc. for the Blind. Co-founder, with late L. S. Amery, Colonial League, formed to oppose German colonial claims. Rep. Govt of Tanganyika Territory on adv. cttee to E African Office in London, 1925-39; mem. London Cttee of Voice of Kenya throughout its existence. FJI; Mem. Overseas Cttee, Inst. of Journalists; Founder Mem., Commonwealth Writers of Britain; Mem. Council, Anglo-Rhodesian Soc. *Publications:* Tanganyika Territory, 1920; Germany's Claims to Colonies, 1939; compiled Settlement in East Africa, 1927, Eastern Africa Today, 1928, Eastern Africa Today and Tomorrow, 1934, Rhodesia and Eastern Africa, 1958, etc. *Recreations:* reading, writing, book-collecting, travel, watching cricket, gardening, reflecting in a hot bath. *Address:* Westwood, Cotlands, Sidmouth, Devon. *T:* Sidmouth 4753. *Club:* Royal Commonwealth Society.

**JOHANNESBURG, Bishop of,** since 1961; **Rt. Rev. Leslie Edward Stradling,** MA; *b* 11 Feb. 1908; *er s* of late Rev. W. H. Stradling; unmarried. *Educ:* King Edward VII Sch., Sheffield; The Queen's Coll., Oxford; Westcott House, Cambridge. Curate of St Paul's, Lorrimore Square, 1933-38; Vicar of St Luke's, Camberwell, 1938-43; of St Anne's, Wandsworth, 1943-45; Bishop of Masasi, 1945-52; Bishop of South West Tanganyika, 1952-61. Hon. DCL Bishops' Univ., Lennoxville, Canada, 1968. *Publications:* A Bishop on Safari, 1960; The Acts through Modern Eyes, 1963; An Open Door, 1966. *Address:* Bishop's House, Westcliff, Johannesburg, South Africa. *Clubs:* United University; Rand (Johannesburg).

**JOHANNESBURG, Assistant Bishop of;** *see* Pickard, Rt Rev. S. C.

**JOHN, Arthur Walwyn,** CBE 1967 (OBE 1945); FCA; Director, Unigate Ltd, since 1969; *s* of Oliver Walwyn and Elsie Maud John; *m* 1949, Elizabeth Rosabelle, *yr d* of Ernest David and Elsie Winifred Williams; one *s* two *d. Educ:* Marlborough Coll. Mem. Institute of Chartered Accountants, 1934 (Mem. Council, 1965-). Asst to Commercial Manager (Collieries), Powell Duffryn Associated Collieries Ltd, 1936. Joined Army, 1939; served War of 1939-45: commissioned, 1940; War Office, 1941; DAQMG First Army, 1942, and HQ Allied Armies in Italy; AQMG Allied Forces HQ, 1944 (despatches, 1943, 1945). Chief Accountant, John Lewis & Co. Ltd, 1945; Dep. Dir-Gen. of Finance, National Coal Board, 1946; Dir-Gen, of Finance, 1955; Member, NCB, 1961-68; Chm., NCB Coal Products Divn, 1962-68. *Recreations:* golf, gardening. *Address:* Limber, Top Park, Gerrards Cross, Bucks. *T:* Gerrards Cross 84811. *Club:* United Service.

**JOHN, Brynmor Thomas;** MP (Lab) Pontypridd since 1970; *b* 18 April 1934; *s* of William Henry and Sarah Jane John; *m* 1960, Anne Pryce Hughes; one *s* one *d. Educ:* Pontypridd Boys' Grammar Sch.; University Coll., London. LLB Hons 1954. Articled, 1954; admitted Solicitor, 1957; National Service (Officer, Educn Br., RAF), 1958-60; practising Solicitor, Pontypridd, 1960-70. *Recreation:* watching Rugby football. *Address:* Yale Haven, Church Village, Glam. *T:* Newtown Llantwit 2062.

**JOHN, Admiral of the Fleet Sir Caspar,** GCB 1960 (KCB 1956; CB 1952); Chairman, Star and Garter Home, since 1967; Member, Government Security Commission, since 1964; First Sea Lord and Chief of Naval Staff, 1960-63; *b* 22 March 1903; *s* of late Augustus John, OM, RA; *m* 1944, Mary Vanderpump; one *s* two *d. Educ:* Royal Naval College, Dartmouth. Joined Royal Navy, 1916. Served War of 1939-45, Home and Mediterranean Fleets, Captain, 1941; Rear-Adm., 1951; Flag Officer, Commanding Third Aircraft Carrier Squadron and Heavy Squadron, 1951-52; Deputy Controller Aircraft, 1953-54; Vice-Adm. 1954; Flag Officer, Air, 1955-57; Admiral 1957; Vice-Chief of Naval Staff, 1957-60; Principal Naval ADC to the Queen, 1960-62; Admiral of the Fleet, 1962. Chm., Housing Corp., 1964-68. *Address:* 25 Woodlands Road, SW13. *T:* 01-876 5596.

**JOHN, David Dilwyn,** CBE 1961; TD; DSc; Director, National Museum of Wales, Cardiff, 1948-68; *b* 20 Nov. 1901; *e s* of Thomas John, St Bride's Major, Glam; *m* 1929, Marjorie, *d* of J. W. Page, HMI, Wellington, Salop; one *s* one *d. Educ:* Bridgend County Sch.; University Coll. of Wales, Aberystwyth. Zoologist on scientific staff, Discovery Investigations, engaged in oceanographical research in Antarctic waters, 1925-35; awarded Polar Medal. Appointed Asst Keeper in charge of Echinoderms at British Museum (Natural History), 1935; Deputy Keeper, 1948. Joined Territorial Army, 1936; promoted Major, RA, 1942. Hon. LLD Univ. of Wales, 1969. *Publications:* papers, chiefly on Echinoderms, in scientific journals. *Address:* 7 Cyncoed Avenue, Cardiff. *T:* Cardiff 752499.

**JOHN, DeWitt;** Editor, The Christian Science Monitor, 1964-70; *b* 1 Aug. 1915; *s* of Franklin Howard John and Frances DeWitt; *m* 1942, Morley Marshall; one *s* one *d. Educ:* Principia Coll. (BA); University of Chicago (MA); Columbia (MS). Editorial Page Ed., St Petersburg (Fla) Times, 1938-39; Political Writer, Christian Science Monitor (Boston), 1939-42; US Navy, 1942-45 (Bronze Star); Editorial Staff, Christian Science Monitor, 1945-49; associated with Christian Science Cttee on Publication of First Church of Christ, Scientist, Boston, Mass, 1949-64 (Asst Man., 1954-62 and Man. of Cttees on Publication, 1962-64). Authorized teacher of Christian Science, 1964-. *Publication:* The Christian Science Way of Life, 1962. *Address:* Old Concord Road, Lincoln, Mass 01773, USA.

**JOHN, Robert Michael;** British Consul-General, Osaka, Japan, since 1967; *b* 7 May 1924; *s* of E. A. H. John; *m* 1952, Anne Phebe Clifford Smith; two *d. Educ:* Merchant Taylors' Sch., Sandy Lodge. Served Indian Army (9th Jat Regt), 1942-47. Entered HM Foreign (subseq.

Diplomatic) Service, 1950; 2nd Sec., Comr-General's Office, Singapore, 1952-56; 1st Sec. (Commercial), British Embassy, Rio de Janeiro, 1956-60; FO, 1960-64; 1st Sec. (Commercial), subseq. Counsellor (Commercial), British Embassy, Warsaw, 1964-67. *Recreations:* reading, gardening. *Address:* Hyogoken 662, Nishinomiyashi, Kurakuen 2-bancho, 12-27, Japan. *T:* 0798-22-2365; c/o Foreign and Commonwealth Office, SW1. *Club:* Travellers'.

**JOHNES, Herbert J. L.;** *see* Lloyd-Johnes.

**JOHNS, Alun Morris,** MD, FRCOG; Hon. Consulting Gynæcological and Obstetric Surgeon, Queen Charlotte's Hospital, London; *m* 1927, Joyce, *d* of T. Willoughby, Carlton-in-Coverdale, Yorks; one *s* two *d*. *Educ:* Manchester Univ. MB, ChB 1923, MD Manchester (Commend) 1925; FRCOG 1947. Late Consulting Surgeon, Surbiton Hospital and Erith and Dartford Hospitals. Examiner Central Midwives Board; Fellow Royal Society of Medicine; Fellow Manchester Med. Soc.; Fellow Manchester Path. Soc. *Address:* Loosley Row, near Princes Risborough, Bucks. *T:* Princes Risborough 5298.

**JOHNS, Glynis;** actress; *b* Pretoria, South Africa, 5 Oct. 1923; *d* of Mervyn Johns and Alice Maude (*née* Steel-Payne); *m* 1st, Anthony Forwood (marr. diss.); one *s*; 2nd, 1952, David Foster, DSO, DSC and Bar (marr. diss.); 3rd, 1960, Cecil Peter Lamont Henderson; 4th, 1964, Elliott Arnold. *Educ:* Clifton and Hampstead High Schs. First stage appearance in Buckie's Bears, Garrick Theatre, London, 1935. Parts include: Sonia in Judgement Day, Embassy and Strand, 1937; Miranda in Quiet Wedding, Wyndham's, 1938 and in Quiet Weekend, Wyndham's, 1941; Peter in Peter Pan, Cambridge Theatre, 1943; Fools Rush In, Fortune; The Way Things Go, Phœnix, 1950; The King's Mare, Garrick, 1966; Come as You Are, New, 1970; Entered films in 1937. *Films include:* Frieda, An Ideal Husband, Miranda, State Secret, No Highway, The Magic Box, Appointment with Venus, Encore, The Card, Sword and the Rose, Personal Affair, Rob Roy, The Weak and the Wicked, The Beachcomber, Mad About Men; Josephine and Men, The Court Jester, Loser Takes All, The Chapman Report, Mary Poppins. Also broadcasts. *Address:* c/o General Artists Corp., 9025 Wilshire Boulevard, Beverly Hills, Calif, USA.

**JOHNSON;** *see* Croom-Johnson.

**JOHNSON, Alan Campbell;** *see* Campbell-Johnson.

**JOHNSON, Alan Woodworth,** FRS 1965; MA, ScD, PhD, ARCS, DIC, FRIC; Professor of Chemistry and Hon. Director, Agricultural Research Council Unit of Invertebrate Chemistry and Physiology, University of Sussex, since 1968; *b* 29 Sept. 1917; *s* of late James William and Jean Johnson, Forest Hall, Newcastle upon Tyne; *m* 1941, Lucy Ida Celia (*née* Bennett); one *s* one *d*. *Educ:* Morpeth Grammar Sch., Northumberland; Royal College of Science, London. Chemist, Swan, Hunter & Wigham Richardson, Ltd, 1934; Thos Hedley & Co. Ltd, 1935-36; Royal Schol., Imperial Coll. of Science, 1937; BSc, ARCS; PhD, DIC 1940; Research Asst in Organic Chemistry, RCS, 1940-42; Research Chemist, ICI Dyestuffs Div., 1942-46; University of Cambridge: ICI Fellow, 1946-48; Asst Dir of Research in Organic Chemistry, 1948-53; Lecturer in Organic Chemistry, 1953-55; Sir Jesse Boot Prof. of Organic Chemistry and Head of Dept of Chemistry, University of Nottingham, 1955-68; Fellow and Steward, Christ's Coll., Cambridge, 1951-55. Mem., ARC Adv. Cttee on Plants and Soils, 1966-. Vis. Professor: University of Melbourne, 1960; University of Calif, Berkeley, 1962. Meldola Medallist, Royal Inst. of Chemistry, 1946; Lectures: Tilden, Chemical Soc., 1953; Reilly, Univ. Notre Dame, Ind, USA, 1962; Simonsen, Chemical Soc., 1967. Member Council: Royal Society, 1966-67; Chemical Soc., 1955, 1957; Hon. Sec. Chemical Society, 1958-65, Vice-Pres., 1965-. Corday-Morgan Lecturer, India and Ceylon, 1963; Trustee, Uppingham Sch., 1961-66. Hon. DSc, Memorial Univ., Newfoundland. *Publications:* Chemistry of Acetylenic Compounds, Vol. I 1946, Vol. II 1950; numerous papers in chemical and biochemical journals. *Recreations:* tennis, philately. *Address:* School of Molecular Sciences, The University of Sussex, Falmer, Brighton, Sussex. *T:* Brighton 66755.

**JOHNSON, Alvin Saunders,** PhD; President Emeritus of the New School for Social Research, New York City, since 1946; *b* Homer, Nebraska, 18 Dec. 1874; *s* of John Johnson and Edel Marie Bille Johnson; *m* 1904, Margaret Edith Henry; two *s* five *d*. *Educ:* University of Nebraska, AB 1897, AM 1898; Columbia Univ., 1898-1901; PhD 1902. Fellow in Greek, University of Nebraska, 1898; Tutor in Economics, Bryn Mawr, 1901-02; Tutor, Instructor, Asst Professor, Columbia, 1902-6; Professor of Economics, University of Nebraska, 1906-08; of Texas, 1908-10; Associate Professor of Economics, University of Chicago, 1910-11; Professor of Economics, Stanford University, 1911-12; Cornell Univ., 1912-16; Prof. of Political Science, Stanford Univ., 1916-17; Associate Editor, New Republic (NY), 1917-23; Associate Editor, Encyclopædia of the Social Sciences, 1928-34; Dir, New School for Social Research, 1922-46. *Publications:* Rent in Modern Economic Theory, 1902; Introduction to Economics, 1909; The Professor and the Petticoat (a novel), 1914; John Stuyvesant Ancestor and Other Sketches, 1917; Spring Storm (novel), 1936; Pioneer's Progress (autobiography), 1952; The Battle of the Wild Turkey and Other Tales, 1961; A Touch of Color and other Tales, 1963. *Address:* 200 North Broadway, Nyack, NY; 395 Riverside Drive, New York City. *T:* Elmwood 8-0892.

**JOHNSON, Rev. Prof. Aubrey Rodway,** PhD; Emeritus Professor of Semitic Languages, University College of South Wales and Monmouthshire, Cardiff; *b* Leamington Spa, 23 April 1901; *y s* of Frank Johnson, Baptist Minister, and Beatrice Mary Bebb; *m* 1947, Winifred Mary Rowley; two *d*. *Educ:* Newport (Mon) Intermediate Sch.; South Wales Baptist Coll., Cardiff; Universities of Wales (University Coll., Cardiff), London (King's Coll.), Oxford (University Coll.) and Halle-Wittenberg. PhD Wales, 1931; Fellow of the University of Wales, 1931-33; Asst Lecturer and subsequently Lecturer in Semitic Languages, University Coll. of South Wales and Mon, Cardiff, 1934-44, Prof., 1944-66. Dean, Faculty of Theology, University Coll., Cardiff, and Chm. of the Cardiff Sch. of Theology, 1944-65; Dean, Faculty of Theology, University of Wales, 1952-55. Haskell Lectr, Graduate Sch. of Theology, Oberlin, 1951. Pres., Soc. for Old Testament Study, 1956. FBA, 1951. Hon. DD Edinburgh, 1952; Hon. DTheol Marburg, 1963; Hon. teol dr Uppsala, 1968. Burkitt Medal of British Academy, 1961. *Publications:* The One and the Many in the Israelite Conception of God, 1942 (2nd edn, 1961); The Cultic Prophet in Ancient Israel, 1944 (2nd edn revised, 1962);

The Vitality of the Individual in the Thought of Ancient Israel, 1949 (2nd edn revised, 1964); Sacral Kingship in Ancient Israel, 1955 (2nd edn revised, 1967), etc. *Recreation:* gardening. *Address:* The Gate House, Alderley, Wotton-under-Edge, Glos. *T:* Wotton-under-Edge 2145.

**JOHNSON, B. S., (Bryan Stanley William Johnson);** poet, novelist, film director; *b* 5 Feb. 1933; *s* of Stanley Wilfred and Emily Jane Johnson; *m* 1964, Virginia Ann (*née* Kimpton); one *s* one *d*. *Educ:* King's Coll., Univ. of London. First Gregynog Arts Fellow, Univ. of Wales, 1970. Poetry Editor, Transatlantic Review, 1965-. *Films:* (cinema, as dir and writer) You're Human Like the Rest of Them, 1967 (Grand Prix, Tours, 1968; Grand Prix, Melbourne, 1968); Up Yours Too, Guillaume Apollinaire!, 1968; Paradigm, 1969; *Films:* (television, as dir and writer) six documentaries for BBC 2, etc. *Plays:* (as dir) Backwards, and, The Ramp, Mermaid, 1970. *Publications: poetry:* Poems, 1964 (Gregory Award of 1962); *novels:* Travelling People, 1963 (Gregory Award of 1962); Albert Angelo, 1964; Trawl, 1966 (Somerset Maugham Award of 1967); The Unfortunates, 1969; *short stories:* (jointly with Zulfikar Ghose) Statement Against Corpses, 1964; *text* (for photographs by Julia Trevelyan Oman): Street Children, 1964; (ed) The Evacuees, 1968; *play:* (radio) Entry, 1965 (BBC Third Progr.). *Recreations:* Chelsea FC; providing a good home for abandoned paper clips. *Address:* 9 Dagmar Terrace, N1. *T:* 01-226 9033. *Clubs:* Institute of Contemporary Arts, Kismet.

**JOHNSON, Carol Alfred,** CBE 1951; MP (Lab) Lewisham South since Sept. 1959. Admitted a Solicitor, 1933 (Hons). Secretary of the Parliamentary Labour Party, 1943-59. Chairman: Britain and Italy Co-ordinating Cttee; Anglo-Italian Parly Group; Anglo-Tunisian Parly Group; History of Parliament Trust; Jt Hon. Sec., British Council of European Movement. Member Standing Joint Cttee National Parks; Vice-Chm., Commons, Footpaths and Open Spaces Soc.; Pres., Southern Region Ramblers Assoc. Comdr, Italian Order of Merit. *Address:* 19 Melior Court, Shepherds Hill, N6.

**JOHNSON, Celia, (Mrs Peter Fleming),** CBE 1958; Actress; *b* Richmond, Surrey, 18 Dec. 1908; *d* of John Robert Johnson, MRCS, LRCP, and Ethel Griffiths; *m* 1935, Peter Fleming, *qv*; one *s* two *d*. *Educ:* St Paul's Girls' Sch.; abroad. Studied at Royal Academy of Dramatic Art. First appearance on stage as Sarah in Major Barbara, Theatre Royal, Huddersfield, 1928; first London appearance as Currita in A Hundred Years Old, Lyric, Hammersmith; rôles include: Suzette in The Artist and the Shadow, Kingsway, 1930; Loveday Trevelyan in Debonair, Lyric, 1930; Elizabeth in The Circle, Vaudeville, 1931; Phyl in After All, Criterion, 1931. First New York appearance, as Ophelia in Hamlet, Broadhurst, 1931. Betty Findon in Ten Minute Alibi, Embassy and Haymarket, 1933; Anne Hargraves in The Wind and the Rain, St Martin's, 1933; Elizabeth Bennet in Pride and Prejudice, St James's, 1936; Mrs de Winter in Rebecca, Queen's, 1940; Jennifer in The Doctor's Dilemma, Haymarket, 1942; Olga in The Three Sisters, Aldwych, 1951; Laura Hammond in Its Never Too Late, Westminster, 1954; Sheila Broadbent in The Reluctant Debutante, Cambridge Theatre, 1955; Isobel Cherry in Flowering Cherry, Haymarket, 1957; Hilary in The Grass is Greener, St Martin's, 1958; Pamela Puffy-Picq in Chin-Chin, Wyndham's, 1960; Clare Elliot in The Tulip Tree, Haymarket, 1962; Helen Hampster in Out of the Crocodile, Phœnix, 1963; Aline in The Master Builder, National Theatre, 1964; Hay Fever, National Theatre, 1965, Duke of York's, 1968; The Cherry Orchard, Chichester Festival Theatre, 1966. Played St Joan, Old Vic Season, 1948-49, and Viola on Italian tour with Old Vic, 1950. Has appeared in films, including: A Letter from Home; In Which We Serve; Dear Octopus; This Happy Breed; Brief Encounter; The Astonished Heart; I Believe in You; The Holly and the Ivy; The Captain's Paradise; A Kid for Two Farthings; The Good Companions; The Prime of Miss Jean Brodie. *Address:* Merrimoles House, Nettlebed, Oxon.

**JOHNSON, Christopher Hollis,** CBE 1958; DSc; PhD; Director, Explosives Research and Development Establishment, Waltham Abbey (Ministry of Aviation), 1959-64, retired; *b* Reading, Berks, 18 March 1904; *s* of Ernest G. and Agnes M. Johnson; *m* 1st, 1930, Irene Kathleen (*née* Gilbert) (*d* 1963), Farnham, Surrey; no *c*; 2nd, 1966, Mrs Vera G. Lester (*widow*); five step *c*. *Educ:* Reading Sch.; University Coll., London. BSc 1st Cl. Hons (Chemistry), 1925; PhD London, 1927; Ramsay Gold Medal, 1927; DSc London, 1940. Teaching Fellow, Univ. of California, Berkeley, 1927-29; Lectr in Physical Chemistry, Univ. of Bristol, 1930-37; Senior Lectr in Inorganic Chemistry, Univ. of Birmingham, 1937-41; Research Manager, Shell Petroleum Co., 1942-48. Min. of Supply, 1948-59: various posts, the last being: Director, Materials and Explosives Research, Shell-Mex House. *Publications:* contribs to Phil. Mag., Chemical Society, Faraday Society. *Address:* Foxwold, Silford Cross, Bideford, N Devon. *T:* Bideford 4232.

**JOHNSON, Prof. David Hugh Nevil;** Professor of International and Air Law since 1960, and Dean of the Faculty of Laws, since 1968, University of London; *b* 4 Jan. 1920; 2nd *s* of James Johnson and Gladys Mary (*née* Knight); *m* 1952, Evelyn Joan Fletcher. *Educ:* Winchester Coll.; Trinity Coll., Cambridge; Columbia Univ., New York. MA, LLB Cantab. Served Royal Corps of Signals, 1940-46. Called to Bar, Lincoln's Inn, 1950. Asst Legal Adviser, Foreign Office, 1950-53; Reader in Internat. Law, 1953-59, in Internat. and Air Law, 1959-60, Univ. of London. Sen. Legal Officer, Office of Legal Affairs, UN, 1956-57. Registrar, the Court of Arbitration, Argentine-Chile Frontier Case, 1965-68. *Publications:* Rights in Air Space, 1965; articles in legal jls. *Recreation:* gardening. *Address:* 13 Moor Park Road, Northwood, Middx. *T:* Northwood 21388.

**JOHNSON, (Denis) Gordon,** CBE 1969; Chairman and Managing Director, Geo. Bassett Holdings Ltd, since 1964; Chairman: Geo. Bassett & Co. Ltd, Sheffield, since 1955; W. R. Wilkinson & Co. Ltd, Pontefract, since 1961; N. V. de Faam, Holland, since 1964; Drakes Sweets Marketing Ltd, since 1966; Barratt & Co. Ltd, London, since 1968; *b* 8 Oct. 1911; *s* of late Percy Johnson; unmarried. *Educ:* Harrow; Hertford Coll., Oxford (MA). President: Cocoa, Chocolate and Confectionery Alliance, 1964-66; Confectioners' Benevolent Fund, 1967-68; Member: Food Manufacturing Economic Develt Cttee; Council of Confedn of British Industry; Yorks Electricity Bd; Chm., Hallam Conservative Assoc., 1966-69; Hon. Treas., City of Sheffield Conservative Fedn, 1969-. FBIM; Mem., Inst. of Directors. *Publications:* address to British Assoc. (Economics Section), 1964; contributor to: Business Growth (ed Edwards and Townsend), 1966; Pricing Strategy (ed Taylor and Wills).

*Recreations:* philosophy, politics, economics; Pres., Sheffield and Hallamshire Lawn Tennis Club. *Address:* Geo. Bassett & Co. Ltd, PO Box 80, Sheffield S6 2AP. *T:* 349508; 5 Windsor Court, Bents Road, Sheffield S11 9RG. *T:* 367991; 7 Broadbent Street, W1. *T:* 01-629 1642.

**JOHNSON, Dr Donald McIntosh,** MA, MB, BCh Cambridge; MRCS, LRCP; Chairman and Managing Director of Johnson Publications Ltd; *b* 17 Feb. 1903; *s* of late Isaac Wellwood Johnson, Bury, Lancs, and Bertha Louise Hall; *m* 1st, 1928, Christiane Marthe Coussaert, Brussels; one *s*; 2nd, 1947, Betty Muriel Plaisted, Oxford; one *s* one *d*. *Educ:* Cheltenham Coll.; Gonville and Caius Coll., Cambridge; St Bartholomew's Hospital (Entrance Schol.). Qualified as doctor, 1926; barrister-at-law, 1930. Medical Officer, Cambridge University East Greenland Expedn, 1926; Casualty Officer, Metropolitan Hospital, 1926; House Physician, East London Hospital for Children, Shadwell, 1927; Medical Officer to Harrington Harbour Hosp., Internat. Grenfell Assoc., Labrador, 1928-29; General Practitioner, Thornton Heath, Croydon, 1930-37; a Demonstrator of Anatomy, Oxford Univ., 1937-39. Served War in RAMC (Capt. TA), 1939-45. Mem. Croydon Medical Board, Ministry of Labour and National Service, 1951-55; MP (C) Carlisle, 1955-63, (Independent C) 1963-64. *Publications:* A Doctor Regrets, 1948; Bars and Barricades, 1952; Indian Hemp, a Social Menace, 1952; A Doctor Returns, 1956; A Doctor in Parliament, 1958; The British National Health Service: Friend or Frankenstein?, 1962; A Cassandra at Westminster, 1967. *Recreations:* golf, photography. *Address:* 55 Langley Park Road, Sutton, Surrey. *T:* 01-642 6530. *Club:* Oxford and Cambridge University.

**JOHNSON, Dorothy,** CBE 1955; BA; HM Deputy Chief Inspector of Factories, Ministry of Labour, 1947-55, retired; *b* 20 Dec. 1890; *e d* of late Thomas and Emily Johnson. *Educ:* Leeds Univ. Health and Welfare Branch, Min. of Munitions, 1917-21; HM Inspector of Factories, Home Office, 1922; HM Superintending Inspector of Factories, 1942. Called to the Bar, Middle Temple, 1955. *Address:* Poplar Cottage, Hillside Road, Long Ashton, Bristol. *T:* Long Ashton 3312.

**JOHNSON, Maj.-Gen. Dudley Graham,** VC 1919; CB 1939; DSO 1914; MC 1918; *s* of late Capt. William Johnson, Inniskilling Dragoons, and Mrs Rosina Johnson, Oddington, Moreton-in-Marsh, Glos; *b* 13 Feb. 1884; *m* Marjorie (*d* 1950), *o d* of Rev. Arthur George Grisewood, Rector of Daylesford, Chipping Norton; one *s* two *d*. Served Tsingtau, 1914 (despatches, DSO), European War, Gallipoli, 1915, France, 1916-18, Germany, 1919 (VC, bar to DSO, MC); Chief Instructor Small Arms Sch., Hythe, 1919-23; Bt Lt-Col 1924; Chief Instructor, Machine Gun Sch., Netheravon, 1926-28; Lt-Col 1928; Comd 2nd Bn North Staffordshire Regt, 1928-32; Col 1932; Comdr 12th (Secunderabad) Inf. Bde, 1933-36; Comdt, Small Arms Sch., Netheravon, and Officer in charge of Records, Small Arms School Corps, 1936-38; Maj.-Gen., 1938; Comdr of the 4th Division, 1938-40; GOC Aldershot Command, 1940; Inspector of Infantry, 1941; retired, 1944. Col of South Wales Borderers, 1944-49. *Address:* 2 Heathfield Court, Fleet, Hants. *Club:* Army and Navy.

**JOHNSON, Eric Alfred George,** CBE 1953; Chief Engineer, Ministry of Agriculture, Fisheries and Food, since 1949; *b* 3 Sept. 1911; *s* of Ernest George Johnson and Amelia Rhoda Johnson; *m* 1936, Barbara Mary Robin; one *d*. *Educ:* Taunton's Sch., Southampton; UC Southampton. Grad. Engrg, 1931; joined A. P. I. Cotterell & Sons, 1932; served for periods with Great Ouse Catchment Board and Trent Catchment Board, 1933-37; joined Min. of Agriculture, 1937; Regional Engr, 1940; Dep. Chief Engr, 1945. Has specialised in flood control and drainage engineering. *Publications:* papers in ICE and other professional jls. *Recreations:* travel, out-door life. *Address:* 94 Park Avenue, Orpington, Kent. *T:* Orpington 23802.

**JOHNSON, Eric Seymour Thewlis,** MC 1918; *b* 8 Sept. 1897; *e s* of Ernest Johnson, TD, MA, JP. *Educ:* Winchester; Royal Military College, Sandhurst. 2nd Lieut, 16th Lancers, 1916; Lieut 1918-20. Cattle ranching, British Columbia, 1923-30; trained race-horses under National Hunt Rules, in England, 1931-40. War of 1939-45: served with 51st Training Regiment, RAC, and RAC Depot; retired 1945, with rank of Major. MP (C) Blackley Division of Manchester, 1951-64. *T:* (club) 01-499 1261. *Club:* Cavalry.

**JOHNSON, Sir Frederic (Charles),** Kt, *cr* 1952; CB 1946; Receiver for the Metropolitan Police District and Courts, 1945-52; *b* 13 Dec. 1890; *s* of Benjamin Johnson, Leeds; *m* 1916, Constance Annie Ridley; three *s*. *Educ:* Leeds Grammar Sch.; Sidney Sussex Coll., Cambridge. Wrangler, 1912; Natural Sciences Tripos, 1913; entered Home Office, 1913; Asst Under-Sec. of State 1938. *Address:* Hembury Fort House, Honiton, Devon. *T:* Broadhembury 334.

**JOHNSON, George Arthur;** *b* 31 Oct. 1903; *s* of late Arthur Johnson; *m* 1931, Marie Constance Ross-Hurst; no *c*. *Educ:* Christ's Hospital; St Edmund Hall, Oxford. BA Oxon 1st Cl. Modern History, 1925. Asst Editor, The Mail, Madras, 1926-42; Asst Editor, The Statesman, 1942-51; Editor of The Statesman, Calcutta and Delhi, 1951-62, retired. *Address:* 12a Albert Hall Mansions, SW7. *Clubs:* Oriental; Bengal (Calcutta).

**JOHNSON, Maj.-Gen. Sir George Frederick,** KCVO 1957; CB 1951; CBE 1949; DSO 1944; DL; *b* 28 Nov. 1903; *s* of F. P. and F. M. Johnson; *m* 1938, Lady Ida Ramsay, *d* of 14th Earl of Dalhousie; two *s* one *d*. *Educ:* Eton; King's Coll., Cambridge. Commissioned Scots Guards, 1925; psc 1935; GSO1 London District, 1939; served War of 1939-45; Comdr 3rd Bn Scots Guards, 1940; Comdr 201 Guards Brigade, Western Desert, 1942; Comdr 32 Guards Brigade, NW Europe, 1944-45; Lieut-Col commanding Scots Guards, 1945-47; Comdr 1st Guards Brigade, Palestine, 1947-48; Tripoli, 1948-49; Chief of Staff, Scottish Command, 1949-53; GOC, London District, 1953-57, retired. DL Cumberland, 1959; High Sheriff of Cumberland, 1966. *Recreations:* shooting, fishing, ornithology, entomology. *Address:* Castlesteads, Brampton, Cumberland. *T:* Brampton 272. *Club:* Turf.

**JOHNSON, Air Marshal George Owen,** CB 1943; MC; retired 1947; *b* 24 Jan. 1896; *s* of late George Edward Johnson, Woodstock, Ontario, and late Mrs Johnson, Toronto 5, Ontario; *m* 1st, 1924, Jean Eleanor McKay (*d* 1968), Pembroke, Ont; two *d*; 2nd, 1968, Sarah Jane Roberts, RRC. *Educ:* Woodstock, Ontario; RAF Staff Coll., Andover (1927); Imperial Defence Coll. (1937). Lieut, CSCI, Canada, 1913-16; RFC, and RAF 1917-19; Royal Canadian Air Force, 1920-47; AOC, Western Air Command, RCAF, Vancouver, BC, 1938-39; Deputy Chief of Air Staff,

Ottawa, 1939-42; AOC, No. 1 Training Command, RCAF, Toronto, 1942; AOC-in-C, Eastern Air Command, RCAF, Halifax, NS, 1943-45; AOC-in-C RCAF, Overseas, 1945-46. *Address:* 1964 Stanton Avenue, Largo, Florida 33540, USA.

**JOHNSON, Gordon;** *see* Johnson, D. G.

**JOHNSON, Harold Cottam,** CB 1970; CBE 1961 (OBE 1954); Keeper of Public Records 1966-69; *b* 24 July 1903; *e s* of Burley Johnson, Wakefield, and Louisa Cottam; *m* 1929, Esmé Lane; one *s* one *d*. *Educ:* Wakefield Grammar Sch.; University Coll., Oxford (MA). Asst Keeper, Public Record Office, 1927-54; Principal Asst Keeper, 1954-59; Deputy Keeper, 1959-66. Sec., Cttee appointed by British Academy for the preparation of a Dictionary of Medieval Latin, 1935-. Treasurer, Pipe Roll Soc., 1950-69. Mem. Council, Bedford Coll., London, 1969-. FRHistS. *Publications:* Surrey Taxation Returns, Part II, 1931; Register of Henry Chichele, Archbishop of Canterbury, Vol. II (with E. F. Jacob), 1938; Warwickshire Quarter Sessions Records, Vols I to VII (with S. C. Ratcliff), 1935-46; Vol. VIII, 1953; Vol. IX (with N. J. Williams), 1964; Minutes of Proceedings in Wiltshire Quarter Sessions (1563-72), 1949. *Recreations:* music, gardening. *Address:* Hawthorn, 39 Algarth Rise, Pocklington, York. *T:* Pocklington 3103.

**JOHNSON, H(arold) Daintree,** MA, MD; MChir Cantab; FRCS; Hon. Surgeon, Royal Free Hospital, 1947; Senior Lecturer in Surgery, Royal Postgraduate Medical School; lately Member of Court of Examiners, Royal College of Surgeons; Late Examiner in Surgery, University of London; *b* 26 May 1910; *s* of Sir Stanley Johnson, sometime MP, and Lady Johnson (*née* Edith Heather); *m* 1944, Margaret Dixon; one *s* (and one *s* decd). *Educ:* Westminster; Christ's Coll., Cambridge; St Thomas's Hospital. Leverhulme Scholarship in Surgical Research, RCS, 1948. Surgical Registrar, St Thomas's Hosp., 1941; Surg. First Asst, London Hosp., 1942; Surg. Specialist, 224 and 225 Parachute Field Ambs, 6th Airborne Div., RAMC, 1943-46; FRSM; Fellow, Assoc. of Surgeons of Gt Britain and Ireland; Mem., Brit. Soc. of Gastro-enterology; Corr. Mem., Surgical Research Soc. Editor, Surgical Aspects of Medicine, 1959. *Publications:* The Cardia and Hiatus Hernia, 1968; chapters in: Techniques in British Surgery, 1950; Management of Abdominal Operations, 1953 and 1957; Operative Surgery, 1967; Surgery of the Stomach and Duodenum, 1969; papers on various surgical subjects in Brit. Med. J., Lancet, Brit. J. Surg., Gut, Gastroenterol. (USA), Surgery Gynæcology and Obstetrics (USA), Surgery (USA), American J. Surg. (USA), Annals of Surgery (USA), J. thorac. cardiovasc. Surg. (USA), etc. *Recreations:* farming, research. *Address:* 5 Holly Terrace, Highgate Village, N6. *T:* 01-340 3050; Red House Farm, Sible Hedingham, Essex. *T:* Hedingham 201. *Club:* Elizabethan.

**JOHNSON, Prof. Harry Gordon,** FBA 1969; Professor of Economics, London School of Economics, since 1966, and Professor of Economics, University of Chicago, since 1959; *b* 26 May 1923; *s* of Harry H. and Frances L. Johnson; *m* 1948, Elizabeth Scott Serson; one *s* one *d*. *Educ:* University of Toronto Schs; University of Toronto; Cambridge Univ.; Harvard Univ. Various univ. teaching posts, 1943-49; Lectr in Economics, Cambridge Univ., 1950-56; Fellow of King's Coll., Cambridge, 1950-56; Prof. of Economic Theory, Manchester Univ., 1956-59. Vis. Prof., Univ. of Toronto, 1952; Vis. Prof., Northwestern Univ., 1955; Pres. Canadian Political Science Assoc., 1965-66. Hon. LLD: St Francis Xavier Univ., 1965; Univ. of Windsor, Ont, 1966; Queen's Univ., Ont, 1967; Sheffield Univ., 1969; Carleton Univ., 1970. *Publications:* The Overloaded Economy, 1952; International Trade and Economic Growth, 1958; Money, Trade and Economic Growth, 1962; Canada in a Changing World Economy, 1962; The Canadian Quandary, 1963; The World Economy at the Crossroads, 1965; Economic Policies Toward The Less Developed Countries, 1967; Essays in Monetary Economics, 1967; Money in Britain, 1959-1969, 1970; articles on monetary theory, international trade, banking, in various economic jls. *Address:* London School of Economics and Political Science, Houghton Street, Aldwych, WC2.

**JOHNSON, Col Harry Hall,** CIE 1934; MM 1916; IA retired; *b* 18 Aug. 1892; *m* 1930, Marjorie Phyllis Cooke; two *s*. Served European War, 1914-18, France and Belgium (despatches twice, military medal); Third Afghan War, 1919; Operations NW Frontier of India, 1924, 1930 and 1937-38 (despatches). Served in Indian Political Dept, 1930-41: Resident in Waziristan, 1937-38, and HBM's Consul-General, Kashgar, 1938-40. War of 1939-45, service in Burma, China, Ceylon and India including 204 Military Mission to China, 1941-42; Hon. Col 1947. *Address:* Sunny Hill House, Bruton, Som.

**JOHNSON, Ven. Hayman;** Archdeacon of Sheffield since 1963; Chaplain to HM The Queen since 1969; *b* 29 June 1912; *s* of late W. G. Johnson, Exeter; *m* 1943, Margaret Louise Price; one *d*. *Educ:* Exeter Sch.; New Coll., Oxon. Chaplain, RAFVR, 1941-46; Chaplain and Vicar Temporal, Hornchurch, 1953-61; Examining Chaplain to Bishop of Sheffield, 1962. *Address:* 24 Endcliffe Crescent, Sheffield S10 3ED. *T:* 63489.

**JOHNSON, Sir Henry (Cecil),** Kt 1968; CBE 1962; Chairman, British Railways Board, since 1968 (Vice-Chairman, 1967); *b* 11 Sept. 1906; *s* of William Longland and Alice Mary Johnson, Lavendon, Bucks; *m* 1932, Evelyn Mary Morton; two *d*. *Educ:* Bedford Modern Sch. Traffic Apprentice L & NER, 1923-26; series of posts in Operating Dept; Asst Supt, Southern Area, L & NER, 1942; Chief Operating Supt of Eastern Region, BR, 1955; Asst Gen. Man., Eastern Region, Dec. 1955, Gen. Man., 1958; Gen. Man., London Midland Region, BR, 1962, Chm. and Gen. Man., 1963-67. *Recreations:* golf, continuing interest in farming. *Address:* Rowans, Harewood Road, Chalfont St Giles, Bucks. *T:* Little Chalfont 2409; 120 Chiltern Court, Baker Street, NW1.

**JOHNSON, Henry Leslie,** FTI; farmer; *b* 4 March 1904; *s* of Henry and Annie Letitia Johnson, formerly of Macclesfield, Cheshire; *m* 1939, Mabel Caroline Hawkins, Woking, Surrey; one *s* two *d*. *Educ:* Rugby. Joined Courtaulds Ltd, 1922; Dir, 1933-68; Managing Dir, 1935-47. Mem. Warwicks CC; Chm., Mid Warwicks Educn Executive. Pres., Textile Institute, 1942 and 1943. *Address:* Offchurch, Warwicks. *TA* and *T:* Leamington Spa 24293.

**JOHNSON, Howard Sydney;** solicitor; Director, Alliance Building Society; *b* 25 Dec. 1911; *s* of Sydney Thomas Johnson; *m* 1939, Betty Frankiss, actress. *Educ:* Brighton; Highgate. Served War of 1939-45, Africa; invalided out as Major. Joined TA before the war. Mem. of Brighton Town Council, 1945-50. MP (C) Kemptown Div. of Brighton, 1950-Sept. 1959. *Address:* Farm Corner, Ditching,

Sussex. *T:* Hassocks 2526; c/o Howard Johnson & McCabe, 37 East Street, Brighton 1. *T:* Brighton 27173.

**JOHNSON, James,** BA, DPA; MP (Lab) Kingston upon Hull West since 1964; *b* 16 Sept. 1908; *s* of James and Mary Elizabeth Johnson; *m* 1937, Gladys Evelyn Green; one *d*. *Educ:* Duke's Sch., Alnwick; Leeds Univ. BA 1st Cl. Hons Geography, 1931; Diploma in Education, 1932; Diploma in Public Administration (London), 1944. FRGS. Schoolmaster: Queen Elizabeth Grammar Sch., Atherstone, 1931; Scarborough High Sch., 1934; Bablake Sch., Coventry, 1944. Lecturer, Coventry Tech. Coll., 1948-50. MP (Lab) Rugby Div. of Warwicks, 1950-59. Student Adviser, Republic of Liberia, 1960-64. Grand Comdr Order of Star of Africa (Liberia), 1967. *Address:* 70 Home Park Road, SW19. *T:* 01-946 6224. *Club:* Royal Over-Seas League.

**JOHNSON, Air Vice-Marshal James Edgar, (Johnnie Johnson),** CB 1965; CBE 1960; DSO 1943 and Bars, 1943, 1944; DFC 1941 and Bar, 1942; DL; Air Officer Commanding Air Forces Middle East, Aden, 1963-65; retired; Director: Strathmore Diamonds Pty Ltd, South Africa, since 1968; Keir & Cawder Pty Ltd, South Africa, since 1968; *m* Pauline Ingate; two *s*. *Educ:* Loughborough Sch.; Nottingham Univ. Civil Engr and Mem. of RAFVR until 1939; served with 616 Sqdn AAF, 1940-42; 610 Sqdn AAF, 1943; Wing Comdr Flying: Kenley, 1943; 127 Wing, 1944; Officer Comdg: 125 Wing (2nd TAF), 1944-45; 124 Wing (2nd TAF), 1945-46; RCAF Staff Coll., 1947-48; USAF (Exchange Officer), 1948-50; served Korea (with USAF), 1950-51; OC, RAF Wildenrath (2nd TAF), 1952-54; Air Ministry, 1954-57; Officer Commanding, RAF Cottesmore, Bomber Command, 1957-60; idc 1960; Senior Air Staff Officer, No. 3 Group, Bomber Command, Mildenhall, Suffolk, 1960-63. DL Leicester, 1967. Order of Leopold, 1945, Croix de Guerre, 1945 (Belgium); Legion of Merit, 1950, DFC 1943, Air Medal, 1950 (USA). *Publications:* Wing Leader, 1956; Full Circle, 1964. *Recreations:* shooting, golf. *Address:* c/o Lloyds Bank, Melton Mowbray, Leics. *Club:* Royal Air Force.

**JOHNSON, Sir John Paley,** 6th Bt, *cr* 1755; MBE 1945; Lt-Col, RA (retired); *b* 12 June 1907; *s* of Captain Robert Warren Johnson, RN (killed in action, Sept. 1914); *S* cousin, Sir Edward Gordon Johnson, 5th Bt, 1957; *m* 1st, 1929, Carol, *d* of late Edmund Haas, New York, USA; one *s* one *d*; 2nd, 1940, Jasmine, *d* of Hon. Noel Bligh; one *d*; 3rd, 1949, Rosemary, *d* of late Arthur Cohen. *Educ:* Wellington Coll., Berks; Royal Military Academy, Woolwich. Commissioned RA, 1927; resigned, 1930; Mem. of London Stock Exchange, 1930-33; rejoined RA, 1938. Served War of 1939-45 (MBE): Far East, Middle East, Italy. Chief Instructor (Col), Turkish Staff Coll., 1945-49. MFH West Kent Foxhounds, 1958-61. Mem., Kent CC, 1965-. *Publication:* The North American Johnsons, 1963. *Recreations:* show-jumping, hunting, cricket, lawn tennis, royal tennis, squash rackets. *Heir: s* Peter Colpoys Paley Johnson, Capt., RA [*b* 26 March 1930; *m* 1956, Clare, *d* of Nigel Patrick Bruce, BM, BCh; one *s* two *d*]. *Address:* 11 Roebuck House, SW1. *T:* 01-828 4266; Warrigal Farm, Dartford, Kent. *Clubs:* Carlton, United Service, English-Speaking Union, MCC, Royal Automobile.

**JOHNSON, Air Vice-Marshal Johnnie;** *see* Johnson, James Edgar.

**JOHNSON, Lyndon Baines;** President of the United States Nov. 1963-Jan. 1969; *b* Stonewall, Texas, 27 Aug. 1908; *s* of Sam Ealy and Rebekah Baines Johnson; *m* 1934, Claudia Alta (Lady Bird) Taylor; two *d*. *Educ:* Southwest Texas State Teachers Coll. (BS); Georgetown Law Sch. Comdr, USNR, Active Duty, 1941-42 (Silver Star, 1942); resigned Navy commn, 1964. Teacher, Cotulla and Houston, Texas, public schs, 1930-31; Sec. to Congressman Richard Kleberg, 1931-35; Texas Dir of Nat. Youth Administration, 1935-37; elected to 75th Congress, 1937-38 (succ. James B. Buchanan), 10th District of Texas; re-elected 76th-80th Congresses, 1938-48; US Senator, 1949-61; Democratic Minority Leader, 83rd Congress; Democratic Majority Leader, 84th-86th Congresses. Elected Vice-President, 8 Nov. 1960, took office, 20 Jan. 1961; acceded to Presidency, 22 Nov. 1963, on death of President Kennedy; elected President, 3 Nov. 1964; took office 20 Jan. 1965. During Vice-Presidency, Chairman: National Aeronautics and Space Council; President's Cttee on Equal Employment Opportunity; Peace Corps Advisory Council. Hon. LLD: Southwestern Univ., Texas, 1943; Howard Payne Univ., Texas, 1957; Brown Univ., RI, 1959; Bethany Coll., W Va, 1959; Univ. of Hawaii, 1961; Univ. of Philippines, 1961; Gallaudet Coll., DC, 1961; East Kentucky State Coll., 1961; William Jewell Coll., Missouri, 1961; Elon Coll., NC, 1962; Southwest Texas State Teachers Coll., 1962; Wayne State Univ., Mich., 1963; Jacksonville Univ., Fla, 1963; McMurray Coll., Ill., 1963; Univ. of Maryland, 1963; Tufts Univ., Mass, 1963; Univ. of California, 1964; Univ. of Texas, 1964; Swarthmore Coll., Pa, 1964; Syracuse Univ., New York, 1964; Georgetown Univ., DC, 1964; Univ. of Kentucky, 1965; Baylor Univ., Texas, 1965; Howard Univ., DC, 1965; Catholic Univ., DC, 1965; Princeton Univ., 1966; Univ. of Denver, 1966; Texas Technol Coll., 1967; Thomas More Coll., Kentucky, 1968; St Francis Coll., NY, 1968; Texas Christian Univ., 1968; Hon. DCL: Holy Cross Coll., Mass, 1964; Univ. of Michigan, 1964; Univ. of Rhode Island, 1966; Hon. Doctor of Humane Letters: Oklahoma City Univ., 1960; Yeshiva Univ., NY, 1961; Hon. Doctor of Letters: Glassboro State Coll., NJ, 1968; Hon. Doctor of Lit.: St Mary's Coll., Calif., 1962; Hon. Doctor of Political Science: Chulalongkorn Univ., Thailand, 1966. *Publications:* My Hope for America; This America; No Retreat from Tomorrow; To Heal and to Build; The Choices We Face. *Address:* LBJ Ranch, Stonewall, Texas 78671.

**JOHNSON, Most Rev. Martin (Michael),** DD; *b* Toronto, 18 March 1899; *s* of Oliver Johnson and Julia (*née* Radey). *Educ:* St Francis Sch.; St Augustine's Seminary, Toronto (DD). Priest, 1924; Assistant in Churches in Toronto, 1924-28; Chancellor, Archdiocese, Toronto, 1935-54; Rector, St Michael's Cathedral, Toronto, 1935-36; Bishop of Nelson, 1936; Coadjutor Archibishop of Vancouver, 1954, Archbishop, 1964/69. *Address:* 4670 Piccadilly South, West Vancouver, BC, Canada.

**JOHNSON, Dame Monica;** *see* Golding, Dame (Cecilie) Monica.

**JOHNSON, Pamela Hansford, (Rt. Hon. Lady Snow);** writer; *b* London, 29 May 1912; *d* of R. Kenneth and Amy Clotilda Johnson; *m* 1st, 1936, Gordon Stewart; one *s* one *d*; 2nd, 1950, (as Dr Charles Percy Snow), Baron Snow, *qv*; one *s*. *Educ:* Clapham County Secondary Sch. Mem. Société Européenne de Culture; Fellow of Center for Advanced Studies, Wesleyan Univ., Conn., 1961; FRSL. Hon. Fellow: Timothy Dwight Coll., Yale Univ.; Founders

Coll., York Univ., Toronto. Hon. DLitt: Temple Univ., Philadelphia; York Univ., Toronto. *Publications: novels:* This Bed Thy Centre, 1935; Too Dear For My Possessing, 1940; An Avenue of Stone, 1947; A Summer to Decide, 1948; Catherine Carter, 1952; An Impossible Marriage, 1954; The Last Resort, 1956; The Unspeakable Skipton, 1959; The Humbler Creation, 1959; An Error of Judgment, 1962; Night and Silence Who is Here?, 1963; Cork Street, Next to the Hatter's, 1965; The Survival of the Fittest, 1968; The Honours Board, 1970, etc; *criticism:* Thomas Wolfe, 1947; I. Compton-Burnett, 1953; *plays:* Corinth House, 1948 (published 1954); Six Proust Reconstructions, 1958; *translation:* (with Kitty Black) Anouilh's The Rehearsal (Globe Theatre), 1961; *social criticism:* On Iniquity, 1967. *Address:* 85 Eaton Terrace, SW1. *Club:* University Women's.

**JOHNSON, Patrick,** OBE 1945; MA; *b* 24 May 1904; 2nd *s* of A. F. W. Johnson, JP, and F. E. L. Cocking; unmarried. *Educ:* RN Colls, Osborne and Dartmouth; Tonbridge Sch.; Magdalen Coll., Oxford. Fellow and Lecturer in Natural Science, Magdalen Coll., 1928-47, Dean, 1934-38, Vice-Pres., 1946-47. Flying Officer, RAFO, 1929-34; commissioned in RA (TA), 1938; served War of 1939-45, in Middle East and NW Europe, Lt-Col, Asst Dir of Scientific Research, 21st Army Group and comdg No. 2 operational research section. Dir of Studies, RAF Coll., Cranwell, 1947-52; Dean of Inst. of Armament Studies, India, 1952-55; Scientific Adviser to the Army Council, 1955-58; Asst Scientific Adviser, SHAPE, 1958-62; Head of Experimental Develt Unit, Educnl Foundn for Visual Aids, 1962-70. *Recreations:* rowing (rowed against Cambridge, 1927), sailing, shooting. *Clubs:* Reform; Leander; Royal Cruising.

**JOHNSON, Paul (Bede);** author; Editor of the New Statesman, 1965-70; *b* 2 Nov. 1928; *s* of William Aloysius and Anne Johnson; *m* 1957, Marigold Hunt; three *s* one *d. Educ:* Stonyhurst; Magdalen Coll., Oxford. Asst Exec. Editor, Réalités, 1952-55; Editorial Staff, New Statesman, 1955-. Dir, Statesman and Nation Publishing Co., 1965-. *Publications:* The Suez War, 1957; Journey into Chaos, 1958; Left of Centre, 1960; Merrie England, 1964. *Recreations:* mountaineering, painting. *Address:* Copthall, Iver, Bucks. *T:* Iver 350.

**JOHNSON, Philip Cortelyou;** architect, with own firm, since 1953; *b* Cleveland, Ohio, 8 July 1906; *s* of Homer H. Johnson and Louise Pope Johnson. *Educ:* Harvard (AB 1927, *cum laude*). Dir, Dept of Architecture, The Museum of Modern Art, New York, 1932-54; Graduate Sch. of Design, Harvard, 1940-43 (BArch). Has taught and lectured at: Yale Univ.; Cornell Univ.; Pratt Inst. (Dr Fine Arts, 1962). Mem. AIA (New York Chapter); Architectural League, NY. *Publications:* Machine Art, 1934; Mies van der Rohe, 1st edn 1947, 2nd edn 1953; (with Henry-Russell Hitchcock) The International Style, Architecture since 1922, 1932, new edn 1966; (with others) Modern Architects, 1932; Architecture 1949-65, 1966; contributor to Architectural Review. *Address:* (business) Philip Johnson, 375 Park Avenue, New York, NY 10022, USA. *T:* Plaza 1-7440; (home) Ponus Street, New Canaan, Conn. *T:* Woodward 6-0565. *Club:* Athenæum.

**JOHNSON, Richard Stringer,** CBE 1968 (MBE 1945); TD 1954; Chairman, North Thames Gas Board, 1964-70; *b* 18 Jan. 1907; *s* of Percy Harry and Josephine Johnson; *m* 1933, Isabel Alice, *d* of J. N. Hezlett, Coleraine, N Ireland; one *s* one *d. Educ:* Stationers' Company's Sch.; Gonville and Caius Coll., Cambridge. Admitted a Solicitor, 1930; joined Staff of Gas Light and Coke Company, 1935. Served War, RA (TA), 1939-45. Controller of Services, Gas Light and Coke Company, 1946; Dep. Chm., South Eastern Gas Board, 1949; Chm., East Midlands Gas Board, 1956-64. *Address:* Medbourne Manor, near Market Harborough, Leics. *T:* Medbourne Green 224. *Club:* United University.

**JOHNSON, Robert White,** CBE 1962; Director, Cammell Laird & Co. Ltd, 1946-70; Chairman: Cammell Laird & Co. (Shipbuilders and Engineers) Ltd, 1957-68; Cammell Laird (Shiprepairers) Ltd, 1963-68; *b* 16 May 1912; *s* of late Sir Robert (Stewart) Johnson, OBE; *m* 1950, Jill Margaret Preston; two *s* one *d. Educ:* Rossall Sch. Robt Bradford & Co. Ltd (Insurance Brokers), 1931-35. Served War of 1939-45, Provost Marshal's Dept, RAF, becoming Wing Comdr. Director: Patent Shaft & Axletree Co. Ltd, Wednesbury, Staffs, 1946-51; Metropolitan-Cammell Carriage and Wagon Co. Ltd, Birmingham, 1946-64; English Steel Corp. Ltd, Sheffield, 1949-51 and 1954-; North Western Line (Mersey) Ltd, 1964-70; Bradley Shipping Ltd, 1964-70; Coast Lines Ltd; formerly Dir, Scottish Aviation Ltd; Chm. of North West Tugs Ltd, Liverpool, 1951-66; Mem. Mersey Docks and Harbour Board, 1948-; Pt-time Mem. Merseyside and North Wales Electricity Board, 1956-66; Underwriting Mem., Lloyd's, 1937-. Pres., Shipbuilding Employers' Federation, 1958-59. *Recreations:* fishing, shooting, golf. *Address:* Newlands, Croft Drive, Caldy, Cheshire. *T:* 051-625 8712.

**JOHNSON, Sir Ronald (Ernest Charles),** Kt 1970; CB 1962; Secretary, Scottish Home and Health Department, since 1963; *b* 3 May 1913; *o c* of Ernest and Amelia Johnson; *m* 1938, Elizabeth Gladys Nuttall; three *s. Educ:* Portsmouth Grammar Sch.; St John's Coll., Cambridge. Entered Scottish Office, 1935; Principal, Scottish Home Dept, 1940; Asst Sec., 1948; Under-Sec., Scottish Home and Health Dept, 1956-62. Served RNVR on intelligence staff of C-in-C, Eastern Fleet, 1944-45. *Recreations:* church organ, recorders, madrigals. *Address:* 14 Eglinton Crescent, Edinburgh EH12 5DD. *T:* 031-337 7733. *Club:* New (Edinburgh).

**JOHNSON, Stanley,** CBE 1970; FCA; MInstT; Managing Director, British Transport Docks Board, since 1967; *b* 10 Nov. 1912; *s* of late Robert and Janet Mary Johnson; *m* 1940, Sheila McLean Bald; two *s* two *d. Educ:* King George V Sch., Southport. Served as Lieut (S) RINVR, 1942-45. Joined Singapore Harbour Board, 1939; Asst Gen. Man. 1952; Local Chm. 1955; Chm. and Gen. Man. 1958-59; Asst Chief Docks Man. 1960, Chief Docks Man. 1962, Hull; Asst Gen. Man. 1963, Mem. and Dep. Man. Dir 1966, British Transport Docks Board. Member: Exec. Cttee, Dock and Harbour Authorities Assoc., 1967-; UK Nat. Cttee of Internat. Cargo Handling Co-ordination Assoc., 1967-; Alternate Dir, Internat. Assoc. of Ports and Harbours, 1969. *Recreations:* walking, reading, travel. *Address:* The Red House, Bearswood End, Beaconsfield, Bucks. *T:* Beaconsfield 3440. *Club:* United Service.

**JOHNSON, Thomas Frank,** OBE 1919; author; Member, Académie Diplomatique Internationale, Paris, and Institut d'Histoire de l'Emigration politique contemporaine; *s* of Alexander Howard Johnson, East Grinstead; *m* 1921, Evelyn (Rona), *e d* of Charles Welch Lee; one *s. Educ:* Polytechnic; privately France and Germany. Inland Revenue up to 1910;

Education Dept, London County Council, 1910-11; Special Inspector, Public Control Dept, London County Council, 1912-14; volunteer Officer European War, 1914-18, Belgian, French, Roumanian, Russian, Italian, and Bulgarian Fronts; Military Missions to Bulgaria, Roumania, Ukraine, and Poland, 1918-19; Personal Sec. to Dr Nansen, 1921-22; League of Nations Asst High Commissioner for Refugees, 1923-31; Sec. Gen., Nansen International Office for Refugees under League of Nations, 1931-37; Officer RAFVR, Oct. 1939 (France); SE European Manager, BBC, 1942; European Publicity Officer, BBC, 1943. Sec. Gen. of several International Conferences on Refugee Questions, 1922-36; Refugee Settlement Missions to Central Europe and Balkans, 1922-26; Armenian Refugee Settlement Mission, Syria, 1926; Mem. of League Refugee Settlement Commission to Brazil, 1934. Founder, Internat. (Relations) Clubs, 1944, and of Internat. Residential Clubs, 1947 (in suspension pending improved relations with Russia); Comdr Order of St Stanislaus; Officer Order of St Vladimir, and of Star of Roumania. *Publications:* International Tramps; From Chaos to Permanent World Peace, 1938; numerous articles on international affairs. *Recreations:* golf, lawn tennis, cricket. *Address:* Byeways, Frith Hill, Godalming, Surrey. *T:* Godalming 65. *Club:* Allied Circle.

**JOHNSON, Sir Victor Philipse Hill,** 6th Bt, *cr* 1818; *b* 7 May 1905; *s* of Hugh Walters Beaumont Johnson, Kingsmead, Windsor Forest, and Winifred Mena Johnson (*née* Hill, now W. M. Livingstone), Fern Lea, Southampton; *S* cousin, Sir Henry Allen Beaumont Johnson, 5th Bt, 1965; unmarried. *Educ:* Cheltenham Coll. Ranched in BC, Canada, 1926-38. Served with RAF, 1939-45. *Recreations:* gardening, playing at golf. *Heir: kinsman* Cyril Martin Hugh Johnson, *b* (posthumously) 15 Jan. 1905. *Address:* Beach House, 64 Sea Lane, Goring-by-Sea, Worthing, Sussex. *T:* Worthing 43630.

**JOHNSON, Walter Hamlet;** MP (Lab) Derby South since 1970; Executive Assistant, Staff Training; *b* Hertford, 21 Nov. 1917; *s* of John Johnson; *m* 1945. *Educ:* Devon House Sch., Margate. Councillor, Brentford and Chiswick for 6 years. Nat. Treasurer, Transport Salaried Staffs' Assoc. Joined Labour Party, 1945. Contested (Lab) Bristol West, 1955 and South Bedfordshire, 1959, in General Elections; also Acton (Lab), 1968, in by-election. Is particularly interested in welfare services, transport and labour relations. *Recreation:* sport. *Address:* House of Commons, SW1; 10 Melton Street, NW1. *T:* 01-387 2101.

**JOHNSON, Prof. William,** DSc Manchester, CEng, FIMechE; Professor of Mechanical Engineering, University of Manchester Institute of Science and Technology, since 1960; *b* 20 April 1922; *er s* of James and Elizabeth Johnson; *m* 1946, Heather Marie (*née* Thornber); three *s* two *d*. *Educ:* Central Grammar Sch., Manchester; Manchester Coll. of Science and Technology. Served War, Lt REME, UK and Italy, 1943-47. Asst Principal, Administrative Grade, Home Civil Service, 1948-50; Lecturer, Northampton Polytechnic, London, 1950-52; Lectr in Engineering, Sheffield Univ., 1952-56; Senior Lectr in Mechanical Engineering, Manchester Univ., 1956-60; Chm. of Dept of Mechanical Engrg, Univ. of Manchester Inst. of Science and Technology, 1960-69. Hon. Sec., Yorks Br. of IMechE, 1953-56. Editor, Int. J. Mech. Sci. T. Bernard Hall Prize (jt), IMechE, 1965-66 and 1966-67. *Publications:* Plasticity for Mechanical Engineers (with P. B. Mellor), 1962; Mechanics of Metal Extrusion (with H. Kudo), 1962; Slip Line Fields: Theory and Bibliography (with R. Sowerby and J. B. Haddow), 1970; papers in mechanics of solids and metal forming. *Recreation:* walking. *Address:* Dept of Mechanical Engineering, University of Manchester Institute of Science and Technology, Manchester M60 1QD. *T:* 061-236 3311.

**JOHNSON, Sir William Clarence,** Kt 1957; CMG 1952; CBE 1945 (OBE 1939); HM Chief Inspector of Constabulary for England and Wales, 1962-63, retired; *b* 8 May 1899; *m* 1918, Louisa Mary Humphreys; no *c*. *Educ:* Willowfield, Eastbourne. RE, 1914-19; joined Police Service at Portsmouth in 1920 and served in various ranks until 1932 when as Superintendent CID was appointed Chief Constable of Plymouth; Asst Chief Constable of Birmingham, 1936; Chief Constable of Birmingham, 1941-45; one of HM Inspectors of Constabulary, 1945-62; Inspector-Gen. of Colonial Police, 1948-51. Chm., Police Salaries Commission, Malta, 1960. *Recreations:* golf, shooting. *Address:* 5 Elizabeth Court, High Street, Polegate, Sussex. *T:* Polegate 2733. *Club:* Willingdon Golf.

**JOHNSON, William Evelyn Patrick,** AFC 1931; CPA; CEng, FRAeS; Partner, Cleveland and Johnson, Chartered Patent Agents; *b* 7 April 1902; *s* of A. A. Johnson, Sunderland, and Amelia Johnson; *m* 1933, Patricia Margaret Anne Watkins; one *s* one *d*. *Educ:* Gresham's Sch., Holt. Qualified Patent Agent, 1925; commnd RAF, 1926; formed and commanded first Instrument Flight, Central Flying Sch.; made first solo blind flight in world, 1931 (AFC); resumed patent practice, 1932 (Flt Lt, RAFO); became Patent Adviser to Power Jets Ltd, when it was formed by Sir Frank Whittle, 1936; returned RAF on flying duties, 1939, and in Jan. 1940 seconded to Power Jets and continued responsibility for Whittle and kindred gas turbine patents. *Publications:* articles, broadcasts, etc, covering aviation, invention and gas turbines, in UK and abroad. *Recreations:* sailing, flying, controversy. *Address:* 32 Well Walk, Hampstead, NW3. *T:* 01-435 1664. *Club:* Royal Aero.

**JOHNSON, William Harold Barrett;** Commissioner of Inland Revenue since 1965; *b* 16 May 1916; *s* of late William Harold Johnson and Mary Ellen (*née* Barrett); *m* 1940, Susan Gwendolen, *d* of Rev. H. H. Symonds; one *s* one *d*. *Educ:* Charterhouse; Magdalene Coll., Cambridge. Served in Royal Artillery, 1939-45. Entered Inland Revenue Dept, 1945. *Recreations:* cruising under sail, hockey, gardening. *Address:* 45 Granville Park, Lewisham, SE13.

**JOHNSON, William Joseph,** CMG 1936; OBE 1927; *b* 1892; *e s* of late Arthur Benjamin and Barbara Johnson; *m* 1st, 1921, Maud (*d* 1955), 2nd *d* of late Benjamin Woodward, CC, JP; 2nd, 1957, Olga Bryne, 2nd *d* of late John Roch George. Served during European War in E Africa, India, Egypt and Palestine, 1914-20 (despatches); Colonial and Foreign Services, 1914-49; Treas. Palestine Govt and Mem. of Exec. and Advisory Legislative Councils, 1932-40; Chm. of several cttees, in Palestine, on taxation, banking, commerce and industry, agriculture, and transport. Financial Adviser to HM Ambassador at Cairo, 1940-49; HM Govt's representative on British Govt Cotton Buying Commission, 1940, and on Joint Anglo-Egyptian Cotton Commission, 1941. Dir of United Dominions Trust Ltd and certain associated companies, 1949-61. *Address:* Westfield, 91 Bromham Road, Bedford.

**JOHNSON-FERGUSON, Sir Neil (Edward),** 3rd Bt, *cr* 1906; TD; Lt-Col Royal Corps of Signals; Vice-Lieutenant, Dumfriesshire, since 1965; *b* 2 May 1905; *s* of Sir Edward Alexander James Johnson-Ferguson, 2nd Bt, and Hon. Elsie Dorothea McLaren, *d* of 1st Baron Aberconway; *S* father 1953; *m* 1931, Sheila Marion, *er d* of late Col H. S. Jervis, MC; four *s*. *Educ:* Winchester; Trinity Coll., Cambridge (BA). Capt. Lanarks Yeomanry, TA, 1928; Major 1937; Major, Royal Signals, 1939; Lt-Col 1945. DL Dumfriesshire, 1957. American Legion of Merit. *Heir: s* Ian Edward Johnson-Ferguson [*b* 1 Feb. 1932; *m* 1964, Rosemary Teresa, *d* of C. J. Whitehead, The Old House, Crockham Hill, Kent; three *s*]. *Address:* Fairyknowe, Eaglesfield, Dumfriesshire; (seat) Springkell, Eaglesfield, Dumfriesshire.

**JOHNSON-GILBERT, Sir Ian (Anderson),** Kt 1959; CBE 1952; LLD; *b* 23 Oct. 1891; *s* of late Thomas Johnson-Gilbert, Coldoch, Perthshire; *m* 1922, Rosalind Sybil, *d* of Major O. J. Bell, Royal Welch Fusiliers, London; two *s*. *Educ:* Edinburgh Academy. Served European War, 1914-18, Highland Light Infantry, and Pilot Royal Flying Corps. Mem. Town Council, Edinburgh, 1936-60 (Chm. Public Assistance Cttee, 1944-47; Chm. Welfare Cttee, 1949-52). Chm. West Edinburgh Unionist Assoc., 1942-57; Mem. Edinburgh ATC Cttee; Chm. SE Fire Area Jt Cttee (Scotland), 1948-57. Member: Licensing Authority for Public Service Vehicles, Scottish Traffic Area, 1951-58; Nat. Broadcasting Council for Scotland. DL 1944, JP 1944, Edinburgh; Lord Provost of Edinburgh, and Lord Lieutenant of Edinburgh, 1957-60. Hon. LLD Edinburgh Univ., 1959. *Recreation:* golf. *Address:* 3 Ravelston Dykes, Edinburgh 4. *T:* 031-332 1022. *Clubs:* Scottish Conservative, Royal Scots (Edinburgh).

**JOHNSON-MARSHALL, Stirrat Andrew William,** CBE 1954; BArch, FRIBA; architect and industrial designer; partnership: Robert Matthew, Johnson-Marshall & Partners, 1956 (Architects for York University); *b* 1912; *s* of Felix William Norman Johnson-Marshall and Kate Jane Little; *m* 1937, Joan Mary Brighouse; two *s* one *d*. *Educ:* Liverpool Univ. Sch. of Architecture (BArch, 1st Cl. Hons). Served War of 1939-45: Royal Engineers. Dep. County Architect, Herts, 1945-48; Chief Architect, Min. of Education, 1948-56. Mem. Council, RIBA. Part-time Dir, National Building Agency. Past Mem. Welwyn Garden City and Hatfield Development Corporations. Ex-Mem., Medical Research Council. *Publications:* papers to Building Research Congress, 1951, National Union of Teachers, 1951, British Architects Conference, 1953. *Recreations:* sailing and fishing. *Address:* 42/46 Weymouth Street, W1; Cloudsway, New Road, Digswell, Welwyn, Herts. *T:* Welwyn 4159.

**JOHNSON SMITH, Geoffrey;** MP (C) East Grinstead since Feb. 1965; *b* 16 April 1924; *s* of J. Johnson Smith; *m* Jeanne Pomeroy, MD; two *s* one *d*. *Educ:* Charterhouse; Lincoln Coll., Oxford. Served War of 1939-45: Royal Artillery, 1942-47; Temp. Capt. RA, 1946. BA Hons, Politics, Philosophy and Economics, Oxford, 1949. Mem., Oxford Union Soc. Debating Team, USA, 1949. Information Officer, British Information Services, San Francisco, 1950-52; Mem. Production Staff, Current Affairs Unit, BBC TV, 1953-54; London County Councillor, 1955-58; Interviewer, Reporter, BBC TV, 1955-59. MP (C) Holborn and St Pancras South, 1959-64; PPS, Board of Trade and Min. of Pensions, 1960-63; Opposition Whip, 1965-70; a Vice-Chm., Conservative Party, 1965-. *Address:* House of Commons, SW1. *Club:* Travellers'.

**JOHNSTON;** *see* Lawson Johnston.

**JOHNSTON, Hon. Lord; Douglas Harold Johnston,** TD; a Senator of the College of Justice in Scotland since 1961; *b* 1907; *s* of late Joseph Johnston, Advocate, Aberdeen; *m* 1936, Doris Isobel, *d* of late James Kidd, MP; two *s* two *d*. *Educ:* Aberdeen Grammar Sch.; St John's Coll., Oxford; Edinburgh Univ. Called to Bar, Inner Temple, 1931; Scottish Bar, 1932; Advocate-Depute, 1945; QC (Scot.) 1947; Solicitor-Gen. for Scotland, 1947-51. MP (Lab) Paisley, 1948-61. Chm., Royal Fine Art Commission for Scotland, 1965-. Served War of 1939-45. *Address:* Dunosdale, Barnton, Edinburgh. *T:* 031-336 3102.

**JOHNSTON, Alastair McPherson,** QC (Scotland) 1958; BA, LLB; Member of Scottish Law Commission, since 1968; *b* 15 Dec. 1915; *s* of late Rev. A. M. Johnston, BD, Stirling; *m* 1939, Katharine Margaret (Bunty), *d* of Charles Mitchell, Chislehurst; three *s*. *Educ:* Merchiston Castle Sch.; Jesus Coll., Cambridge; Edinburgh Univ. RA (TA), 1939-46 (despatches); Staff Coll., Haifa, 1943; Major 1943. Mem. of Faculty of Advocates, 1946. Sheriff of Dumfries and Galloway, 1966-68. Hon. Fellow, Edinburgh Univ. *Publications:* Jt Editor, 3rd edn of Walton's Law of Husband and Wife, 1951; Jt Editor, 7th edn of Gloag and Henderson's Introduction to Law of Scotland, 1968. *Recreations:* fishing, golf. *Address:* 8 Heriot Row, Edinburgh EH3 6HU. *T:* 031-556 4663. *Club:* New (Edinburgh).

**JOHNSTON, Sir Alexander,** GCB 1962 (CB 1946); KBE 1953; Deputy Chairman: Monopolies Commission, since 1969; Panel on Take-overs and Mergers, since 1970; Director, Industrial and Commercial Finance Corporation, since 1969; *b* 27 Aug. 1905; *s* of Alexander Simpson Johnston and Joan Macdiarmid; *m* 1947, Betty Joan Harris; one *s* one *d*. *Educ:* George Heriot's Sch.; University of Edinburgh. Entered Home Office, 1928; Principal Asst Sec., Office of the Minister of Reconstruction, 1943-45; Under-Sec., Office of Lord Pres. of the Council, 1946-48; Dep. Sec. of the Cabinet, 1948-51; Third Sec., HM Treasury, 1951-58; Chm., Bd of Inland Revenue, 1958-68. *Address:* 18 Mallord Street, SW3. *T:* 01-352 6840. *Club:* Reform.

**JOHNSTON, Alice Crawford,** CBE 1958 (OBE 1942); MA; Social Services Administrator, Women's Royal Voluntary Service, since 1954; *b* 1902; *d* of late Lord Sands, DD, LLD, Senator of Coll. of Justice, Scotland. *Educ:* Queen Margaret's Sch., Scarborough; Lady Margaret Hall, Oxford. Tutor, Bonar Law Coll., Ashridge, 1933-38; Head of WVS Evacuation Dept, 1939-43; Temp. Principal, Ministry of Labour, 1943-44; since then other WVS appointments. Dep. Chm., Nat. Assistance Bd, 1961-64 (Mem. 1948-64); Mem., Royal Commn on Local Govt in Greater London Area, 1957-60. *Publication:* Social Service, The Citizen's Concern, 1938. *Address:* 18 Lennox Gardens, SW1. *T:* 01-589 9771.

**JOHNSTON, Rt. Rev. Allen Howard;** *see* Waikato, Bishop of.

**JOHNSTON, A(nthony) G(ordon) Knox,** CMG 1954; Bahamas Government Liaison Officer, Freeport, Grand Bahama, 1961-67, retired; *b* 21 April 1909; *e s* of late Andrew and Jessie Knox Johnston; *m* 1934, Jean Corstorphine, *o c* of late James Fergusson, Allestree, near

Derby; one *s. Educ:* Derby Sch.; Edinburgh Univ. (MA); Oriel Coll., Oxford. Cadet, Colonial Administrative Service, Northern Rhodesia, 1931; seconded Colonial Office, 1940-41; Clerk of Executive and Legislative Councils, NR, 1943-46; Asst Chief Sec. and Sec. Devel. Authority, 1946-50; Asst Chief Sec. EA High Commission, Nairobi, 1950; acted as Administrator on a number of occasions, 1950-55; Chief Administrative Sec. E Africa High Commn, 1954-58, retd 1958; Dep. Colonial Sec., Bahamas (temp.), 1958; Colonial Sec. (Supernumerary), March 1960-Jan. 1961; Acting Gov., Bahamas, June and July 1960. *Address:* Barclays Bank Ltd, St James's Street, Derby.

**JOHNSTON, Brian (Alexander),** MC 1945; BBC Cricket Correspondent and Commentator; *b* 24 June 1912; *s* of Lt-Col C. E. Johnston, DSO, MC; *m* 1948, Pauline, *d* of Col William Tozer, *qv*; three *s* two *d. Educ:* Eton; New Coll., Oxford (BA). Family coffee business, 1934-39. Served War of 1939-45: in Grenadier Guards; in 2nd Bn throughout, taking part in Normandy Campaign, advance into Brussels, Nijmegen Bridge and Crossing of Rhine into Germany. Joined BBC, 1945; radio and TV: specialises in cricket commentary for TV and radio, interviews, ceremonial commentary (*eg* Funeral of King George VI, 1952; Coronation of Queen Elizabeth II, 1953; Wedding of Princess Margaret, 1960); Let's Go Somewhere feature in In Town Tonight, etc. *Publications:* Let's Go Somewhere, 1952; Armchair Cricket, 1957; Stumped for a Tale, 1965; The Wit of Cricket, 1968. *Recreations:* cricket, theatre and reading newspapers. *Address:* 98 Hamilton Terrace, NW8. *T:* 01-286 2991. *Club:* MCC.

**JOHNSTON, Carruthers Melvill,** CMG 1953; *b* 27 Aug. 1909; *e s* of Leslie Darrell Johnston and Elaine Hudson; *m* 1936, Barbara Mary, *yr d* of George and Gertrude Bonnor; one *s* one *d. Educ:* Shrewsbury Sch.; Brasenose Coll., Oxford (BA) Pres., OUBC, 1931-32. Appointed Cadet, Colonial Administrative Service, Kenya, 1933; Provincial Commissioner, 1951; Minister for African Affairs and Community Development, Kenya, 1957-60. *Address:* Gothic Cottage, Bishops Cleeve, Glos. *Club: Leander Henley-on-Thames* .

**JOHNSTON, Charles Hampton,** QC (Scotland) 1959; MA, LLB; Sheriff-Substitute of Lanarkshire at Glasgow since 1962; *b* 10 April 1919; *s* of John Johnston and Johanna Johnston (*née* Hampton), Edinburgh; *m* 1950, Isobel Ross Young; one *s* one *d. Educ:* Royal High School, Edinburgh; University of Edinburgh. Served War of 1939-45, with 52nd (Lowland) and 51st (Highland) Divs, 1940-46; released with rank of Captain. Advocate, 1947; Chm. Scottish Liberal Party, 1955-56; Standing Junior Counsel, Min. of Works, 1956-59. MA 1940, LLB 1947, Editor, The Student, 1940, Edinburgh. *Publications:* (joint) Agricultural Holdings (Scotland) Acts, 1961, 1970. *Recreation:* pottering about in the country. *Address:* The Grange, 12 Grange Road, Bearsden, Glasgow. *T:* 041-942 0659. *Club:* Strathclyde University Staff (Glasgow).

**JOHNSTON, Sir Charles (Hepburn),** KCMG 1959 (CMG 1953); British High Commissioner, Commonwealth of Australia, since 1965; *b* 11 March 1912; *s* of Ernest Johnston and Emma Hepburn; *m* 1944, Princess Natasha Bagration; no *c. Educ:* Winchester; Balliol Coll., Oxford (1st Class Hon. Mods, 1932, Lit. Hum., 1934). Entered Diplomatic Service, 1936; 3rd Sec., Tokyo, 1939; 1st Sec., Cairo, 1945, and Madrid, 1948; FO, 1951; Counsellor, British Embassy, Bonn, 1955; HM Ambassador in Amman, 1956; Gov. and C-in-C, Aden, 1960-63; High Comr for Aden and Protectorate of South Arabia, 1963; Dep. Under-Sec. of State, Foreign Office, 1963-65. KStJ 1961. *Publication:* The View from Steamer Point, 1964. *Address:* British High Commission, Canberra, ACT; 45 Eaton Square, SW1. *Clubs:* St James', White's.

**JOHNSTON, Rear-Adm. Clarence Dinsmore H.;** *see* Howard-Johnston.

**JOHNSTON, David Alan H.;** *see* Hunter Johnston.

**JOHNSTON, (David) Russell;** MP (L) Inverness since 1964; *b* 28 July 1932; *s* of David Knox Johnston and Georgina Margaret Gerrie Russell; *m* 1967, Joan Graham Menzies. *Educ:* Carbost Public Sch.; Portree High Sch.; Edinburgh Univ. (MA). Commissioned into Intelligence Corps (Nat. Service), 1958; subseq., Moray House Coll. of Educn until 1961; taught in Liberton Secondary Sch., 1961-63. Research Asst, Scottish Liberal Party, 1963-64. Chm., Scottish Liberal Party, 1970- (Vice-Chm., 1965-70); Mem., Royal Commission on Local Govt in Scotland, 1966-69. *Publication:* (pamphlet) Highland Development, 1964. *Recreations:* shinty, badminton. *Address:* 2 Hillside Villas, Inverness. *T:* Inverness 36431. *Club:* Scottish Liberal (Edinburgh).

**JOHNSTON, Denis;** *see* Johnston, (William) Denis.

**JOHNSTON, Douglas Harold;** *see* Johnston, Hon. Lord.

**JOHNSTON, Very Rev. Frederick Mervyn Kieran;** Dean of Cork since 1967; *b* 22 Oct. 1911; *s* of Robert Mills Johnston and Florence Harriet O'Hanlon; *m* 1938, Catherine Alice Ruth FitzSimons; two *s. Educ:* Grammar Sch., Galway; Bishop Foy Sch., Waterford; Trinity Coll., Dublin. BA 1933. Deacon, 1934; Priest, 1936; Curate, Castlecomer, 1934-36; Curate, St Luke, Cork, 1936-38; Incumbent of Kilmeen, 1938-40; Drimoleague, 1940-45; Blackrock, Cork, 1945-58; Bandon, 1958-67; Rector of St Fin Barre's Cathedral and Dean of Cork, 1967. *Address:* The Deanery, Cork. *T:* 42803.

**JOHNSTON, Frederick William;** *b* 22 Dec. 1899; *er s* of late Frederick and Janey Johnston, Terenure, Co. Dublin, Eire; *m* 1928, Eileen Milne, Dublin; one *d. Educ:* St Patrick's Cathedral Grammar Sch. and Mountjoy Sch., Dublin; Dublin Univ. Merchant Navy (2nd mate), 1915-21; entered Dublin Univ. and King's Inns, Dublin, 1922; BA, LLB (TCD), 1925; called to Irish Bar, 1925; Colonial Administrative Service, Uganda, 1926-32; Magistrate, Uganda, 1933-42; Judge of the Supreme Court, Gambia, 1942-47; Puisne Judge, Nigeria, 1947-50; retired 1950; called to English Bar (Middle Temple), 1951; re-appointed Puisne Judge, Nigeria, 1952, retired 1955. *Address:* Lagos, Peel Hall Lane, Ashton, Chester.

**JOHNSTON, Sir Gaston,** Kt 1959; QC (Trinidad); President, Bar Association of Trinidad and Tobago, since 1941; first President, British West Indian Bar Association; *b* 19 Dec. 1874; *s* of late John Israel Johnston and late Laetetia, *d* of Alexandre Tetron; *m* 1900, Julia, *e d* of late William Dugdale; seven *s* four *d* (and two *s* one *d* decd). *Educ:* St Mary's Coll. and Queen Royal College, Port-of-Spain, Trinidad, WI. Admitted to English Bar (Gray's Inn), 1898;

admitted to Bar of Trinidad, WI, 1898; practising from 1898; KC 1921. Mem. of Municipality of Port-of-Spain, 1916-41, serving eleven years as Councillor, fourteen years as Alderman and five times Mayor; served seven years as a nominated mem. of Legislative Council. *Recreations:* chess, bridge. *Address:* 27 St Clair Avenue, Port-of-Spain, Trinidad, West Indies. *T:* 21422. *Club:* Queen's Park Cricket (Port-of-Spain).

**JOHNSTON, George Alexander,** MA, DPhil; *b* Jamaica, 11 Nov. 1888; *e s* of Rev. Robert Johnston, BD; *m* 1919, Pauline Violet, *y d* of late Sir George Roche; one *s* one *d. Educ:* University of Glasgow (MA, 1st cl. Hons Classics and Philosophy, 1912; DPhil, 1918); University of Berlin. Lecturer in Moral Philosophy, St Andrews Univ., 1912-14; Lecturer in Moral Philosophy, Glasgow Univ., 1914-19; served in Macedonia, at the War Office, and GHQ, Palestine and Cairo, 1916-19; Ministry of Labour, 1919-20; International Labour Office, 1920-40; Vis. Prof. of Social Legislation; Columbia Univ., New York, 1931-32; Ministry of Labour, 1940-45; Asst Dir, ILO, 1945-48; Treasurer ILO, 1948-53; Chm. UN Joint Staff Pensions Board, 1951; Sec.-Gen., Govt Training Inst., Istanbul, 1954; Mem. UN Economic Mission to Viet-Nam, 1955-56; Dir ILO London Office, 1956-57. Officer of Order of Orange-Nassau (Netherlands). *Publications:* An Introduction to Ethics, 1915; Selections from the Scottish Philosophy of Common Sense, 1915; The Development of Berkeley's Philosophy, 1923; International Social Progress, 1924; Citizenship in the Industrial World, 1928; Berkeley's Commonplace Book, 1930; The International Labour Organisation: its work for social and economic progress, 1970; articles in periodicals and encyclopædias. *Address:* 4 Chemin des Clochettes, 1206 Geneva, Switzerland.

**JOHNSTON, George Douglas;** Barrister-at-Law; *b* 16 Jan. 1886; *s* of John M. C. and Sophia Johnston; *m* 1922, Elfreda Josephine Wallis (*d* 1966); no *c. Educ:* Westminster; Christ Ch., Oxford (MA, BCL 1st Class). Vinerian Scholar, 1909; Inner Temple: called to the Bar, 1910; Bencher, 1939; Treasurer for 1963. Practised in Chancery Div., 1910-62. Mem. Council of Legal Educn, 1946-63. Sussex Archaeological Soc., 1909 (Council, 1941-); former Vice-Pres., Selden Soc.; FSA 1957. *Publications:* numerous articles in Sussex Notes and Queries (Editor, 1952-). *Recreations:* walking, English topography. *Address;* Stones, Wisborough Green, Billingshurst, Sussex. *T:* Wisborough Green 227.

**JOHNSTON, Henry Butler M.;** *see* McKenzie Johnston.

**JOHNSTON, Maj.-Gen. James Alexander Deans,** OBE 1945; MC 1937; Director of Medical Services, BAOR, 1969-70, retired; *b* 28 Feb. 1911; *s* of Walter Johnston and I. C. Gilchrist; *m* 1940, Enid O. Eldridge; one *s* two *d. Educ:* Glasgow Univ. MB, ChB Glasgow, 1933. House Surgeon, Taunton and Somerset Hosp., 1933-34. Commnd into RAMC, 1934; served in India, 1935-40 (Quetta Earthquake, 1935; Mohmand Ops, 1935; Waziristan Ops, 1936-37); served in NW Europe, 1944-45; SMO during and after liberation of Belsen Concentration Camp, April 1945; ADMS HQ Malaya Comd, 19 Ind. Div. and 2 Br. Inf. Div. in Far East, 1945-47; ADMS Southern Comd, UK, 1947-49; DDMS HQ MELF, 1949-52; ADMS 2 Div., and DDMS HQ BAOR, 1952-57; OC British Military Hosp., Dhekelia, Cyprus, 1957-61; ADG WO, 1961-64; Comdt, Depot and Training Establishment and HQ AER, RAMC, 1964-66; DMS, FARELF, 1966-69. Major 1943; Lt-col 1948; Col 1957; Brig. 1964; Maj.-Gen. 1966. QHP 1967. *Recreations:* swimming, tennis, country pursuits. *Address:* c/o Glyn Mills & Co., Kirkland House, Whitehall, SW1.

**JOHNSTON, James Campbell;** Senior Partner, J. B. Were & Son, Stock and Share Brokers, since 1967 (Partner since 1947); Chairman: Capel Court Corporation Ltd, since 1969; Capel Court Group of Investment Cos, since 1967; *b* 7 July 1912; *s* of late Edwin and Estelle Johnston; *m* 1938, Agnes Emily, *yr d* of late Richard Thomas; two *s* one *d. Educ:* Prince Alfred Coll., Adelaide; Scotch Coll., Melbourne; University of Melbourne. Admitted to Inst. Chartered Accountants, Australia, 1933; joined J. B. Were & Son, 1935; Stock Exchange of Melbourne: Mem., 1947; Mem. Cttee, 1954; Vice-Chm., 1966. *Recreations:* sailing, golf. *Address:* 13 Monaro Road, Kooyong, Victoria, Australia. *T:* 20 2842. *Clubs:* Melbourne, Australian, Athenæum, Naval and Military, Victoria Racing, Royal Melbourne Golf (Melbourne).

**JOHNSTON, Sir John (Baines),** KCMG 1966 (CMG 1962); Deputy Under-Secretary of State, Foreign and Commonwealth Office; *b* 13 May 1918; *e s* of late Rev. A. S. Johnston, Banbury, Oxon; *m* 1969, Elizabeth Mary, *d* of late J. F. Crace; one *s. Educ:* Banbury Grammar Sch.; Queen's Coll., Oxford (Eglesfield Scholar). Served War, 1940-46: Adjt 1st Bn Gordon Highlanders, 1944; DAQMG HQ 30 Corps District, 1945. Asst Principal, Colonial Office, 1947; Principal, 1948; Asst Sec., West African Council, Accra, 1950-51; UK Liaison Officer with Commission for Technical Co-operation in Africa South of the Sahara, 1952; Principal Private Sec. to Sec. of State for the Colonies, 1953; Asst Sec., 1956; Head of Far Eastern Dept, Colonial Office, 1956; transferred to Commonwealth Relations Office, 1957; Dep. High Commissioner in S Africa, 1959-61; British High Commissioner: in Sierra Leone, 1961-63; in the Federation of Rhodesia and Nyasaland in 1963, Rhodesia, 1964-65. *Address:* 16 Kennington Palace Court, Sancroft Street, SE11. *Club:* Oxford and Cambridge University.

**JOHNSTON, Lt-Col John Frederick Dame,** MC 1945; Assistant Comptroller, Lord Chamberlain's Office, since 1964; *b* 24 Aug. 1922; *m* 1949, Hon. Elizabeth Hardinge, *d* of 2nd Baron Hardinge of Penshurst, PC, GCB, GCVO, MC; one *s* one *d. Educ:* Ampleforth. Served in Grenadier Guards, 1941-64. Extra Equerry to the Queen, 1965-. *Address:* Adelaide Cottage, Windsor Home Park, Berks. *T:* Windsor 63106. *Clubs:* Guards, Pratt's, MCC.

**JOHNSTON, Joseph,** MA Dublin, MA Oxon; Fellow since 1913 and Senior Fellow since 1943 of Trinity College, Dublin; Professor of Applied Economics since 1939; *b* 20 Aug. 1890; *s* of John Johnston, Tomagh, Castle Caulfield, Co. Tyrone; *m* 1914, Clara Jane, *d* of late Robert Wilson, Keenagh, Co. Longford; one *s* one *d. Educ:* Royal Sch., Dungannon; Trinity Coll., Dublin; Lincoln Coll., Oxford. BA Dublin (First Class Classics and Ancient History), 1910; BA Oxon. First Class Lit Hum 1912; Albert Kahn Travelling Fellow, 1914-15; Lectr in Ancient History, 1916-32; Barrington Lectr in Economics (extern), 1920-35; Mem. of Agricultural Commn, 1923-24; Mem. of Prices Tribunal, 1926-27; Rockefeller Fellow for Economic Research (in Europe), 1926-27; Mem. of Cttee of Inquiry on Post-Emergency

Agricultural Policy, 1942-45; Mem. Industrial Taxation Cttee, 1953-56; Lectr in Economics, Sch. of Commerce, 1925-32; Lectr in Applied Economics, 1932-39; Representative of Dublin Univ. in Senate of Eire, 1938-43 and 1944-48; nominated Senator, 1951-54. Pres. Statistical and Social Inquiry Soc. of Ireland, 1950-51, 1951-52 and 1952-53. *Publications:* Civil War in Ulster (pamphlet), 1914; A. K. Travelling Fellow Report, 1919; A Groundwork of Economics, 1925; The Nemesis of Economic Nationalism, 1934; Irish Agriculture in Transition, 1951; The Sickness of the Irish Economy (pamphlet), 1957; Why Ireland needs the Common Market, 1962; Irish Economic Headaches: a Diagnosis, 1966; Berkeley's Querist in Historical Perspective, 1970; articles in Economic Jl, also numerous contribs to Hermathena, 1938-53, in interpretation of Bishop Berkeley's Querist, etc. *Recreation:* motoring. *Address:* at 53 Thornhill Road, Mt Merrion, Co. Dublin. *T:* 882348; 39 Trinity College, Dublin. *T:* 72941, ext. 430.

**JOHNSTON, Kenneth Robert Hope;** QC 1953; *b* 18 June 1905; *e s* of Dr J. A. H. Johnston, Headmaster of Highgate Sch., 1908-36, and Kate Winsome Gammon; *m* 1937, Dr Priscilla Bright Clark, *d* of Roger and Sarah Clark, Street, Somerset; one *s* three *d. Educ:* Rugby Sch.; Sidney Sussex Coll., Cambridge Univ.; Harvard Univ., USA. Called to the Bar, Gray's Inn, 1933; Bencher, 1958. RAFVR, 1939-45. *Address:* Nesfield, Three Gates Lane, Haslemere, Surrey. *T:* 3762. *Clubs:* MCC, Oxford and Cambridge University.

**JOHNSTON, Margaret;** *see* Parker, Margaret Annette McCrie J.

**JOHNSTON, Michael Errington;** Under-Secretary, Ministry of Agriculture, Fisheries and Food, since 1970; *b* 22 Jan. 1916; *s* of late Lt-Col C. E. L. Johnston, RA, and late Beatrix Johnston; *m* 1938, Ida Brown; two *d. Educ:* Wellington; Peterhouse, Cambridge (Scholar). BA, 1st cl. Hist. Tripos, 1937; MA 1947. Served War of 1939-45, Rifle Bde (Capt., despatches), Asst Principal, Board of Education, 1938; Principal, 1946; Asst Sec., HM Treasury, 1952, Under-Sec., 1962-68; Under-Sec., Civil Service Dept, 1968-70. *Recreations:* painting and birdwatching. *Address:* 3 The Terrace, Barnes, SW13. *T:* 01-876 5265.

**JOHNSTON, Ninian Rutherford Jamieson,** RSA 1965; architect and town planner in private practice since 1946; *b* 6 March 1912; *s* of John Neill Johnston and Agnes Johnston; *m* 1937, Helen, *d* of Robert Henry Jackson and Jean Patrick Jackson; one *s* two *d. Educ:* Allan Glen's Sch.; Glasgow Sch. of Architecture. Served with Army, 1939-45. BArch 1934; FRIAS 1935; MTPI 1946; FRIBA 1951. *Principal Works:* Pollokshaws Central Redevelopment Area; Woodside Central Redevelopment Area, Glasgow; Hamilton College; Plants for IBM, Olivetti, Geigy, etc; Central Hospitals at Dumfries, Greenock and Rutherglen. Mem. Roy. Fine Art Commission for Scotland, 1969-. *Recreations:* music, painting, gardening. *Address:* 18 Woodlands Terrace, Glasgow C3. *T:* 041-332 9184. *Club:* Art (Glasgow).

**JOHNSTON, Patrick Murdoch,** CBE 1963; HM Diplomatic Service, retired; *b* 5 Oct. 1911; *s* of late Claude Errington Longden Johnston, Lt-Col, Royal Artillery, and Beatrix (*née* Peppercorn); *m* 1936, Beatrice Jean Davidson; one *d. Educ:* Wellington Coll.; Peterhouse, Cambridge. Entered HM Consular Service and appointed Probationer Vice-Consul, Paris, Nov. 1934; transferred to Hamburg, Nov. 1935, Valparaiso, 1936; Vice-Consul, Lima, Nov. 1938; Foreign Service Officer Grade 7 and appointed Consul, Ponta Delgada, Azores, 1945; Consul, Bremen, 1947; Head of Commonwealth Liaison Dept, Foreign Office, 1949; Consul, Denver, Colorado, Dec. 1951, Bordeaux, Nov. 1954; Ambassador to the Republic of Cameroun, 1960-61, to Nicaragua, 1962-63; Consul-Gen., Casablanca, 1963-69. *Recreations:* ski-ing, photography, caravanning, puttering. *Address:* Crown Cottage, Dorchester-on-Thames, Oxon. *T:* Warborough 467. *Club:* Civil Service.

**JOHNSTON, Peter Hope,** CMG 1966; Administrative and Social Affairs Department, Ministry of Overseas Development; *b* 31 Oct. 1915; *s* of late Robert Hope Johnston; *m* 1949, Patricia Cullen; one *s* two *d. Educ:* Summerfields; St Paul's Sch.; Magdalen Coll., Oxford (Maj. Exhibr). BA Oxon. Mem. HMOCS. Joined Tanganyika Govt Service, 1938; District Officer in Provincial Administration, 1938-49; on special duty, African Land Settlement, 1949-51; on special duty, Sec., Special Comr, Constitutional Development, 1952; District Comr, Senior District Officer, 1952-58; Provincial Comr, 1958-62; Courts Integration Adviser, High Court of Tanganyika, 1962-65; retd voluntarily from service of Govt of Tanganyika (Tanzania), 1956. Editor, Jl of Administration Overseas. *Publication:* (ed jtly) The Rural Base for National Development, 1968. *Address:* Bell House, Milton Avenue, near Dorking, Surrey. *T:* Dorking 5611. *Club:* Farmers'.

**JOHNSTON, Robert Smith,** QC (Scotland) 1955; Dean of the Faculty of Advocates of Scotland since 1970; *b* 10 Oct. 1918; *s* of W. T. Johnston, iron merchant, Glasgow; *m* 1943, Joan, *d* of late Col A. G. Graham, Glasgow; one *s* one *d. Educ:* Strathallan, Perthshire; St John's Coll., Cambridge; Glasgow Univ. BA (Hons) Cantab, 1939; LLB (with distinction) Glasgow, 1942. Mem. of Faculty of Advocates, 1942; Advocate-Depute, Crown Office, 1953-55, Home Advocate Depute, 1959-62; Sheriff of Roxburgh, Berwick and Selkirk, 1964-70. Governor, Strathallan Sch. Contested (U) Stirling and Falkirk Burghs General Election, 1959. *Recreation:* golf. *Address:* 4 Brights Crescent, Edinburgh. *T:* 031-667 5260. *Clubs:* Caledonian, Hon. Company of Edinburgh Golfers (Edinburgh).

**JOHNSTON, Robert William Fairfield,** CMG 1960; CBE 1954; MC 1917; TD 1936 (and three Bars, 1947); Assistant Secretary, Ministry of Defence, 1946-62; retired from the Civil Service, 1962; *b* 1 May 1895; *e s* of late Capt. Robert Johnston, Army Pay Dept and Royal Scots; *m* 1922, Agnes Scott, *o c* of late Peter Justice, Edinburgh; one *s*. Entered Civil Service, Dec. 1910: served in War Office, Bd of Trade, Min. of Labour, Home Office, Office of Minister without Portfolio, Min. of Defence, and seconded to FO, as Counsellor in UK Delegation in Paris to NATO and OEEC, 1953-61. Territorial Army, 1910-47; served European War, 1914-18, The Royal Scots (1st, 9th and 16th Battalions) in France, Flanders, Macedonia and Egypt; commissioned 1917; War of 1939-45, Lieut-Col, Comdg 8th Bn Gordon Highlanders, 1940-42, and 100th (Gordons) Anti-Tank Regt, RA, 1942-44, in 51st (Highland) and 2nd (British) Inf. Divs respectively; retired as Lieut-Col TA, Sept. 1947. *Address:* 8 Broad Avenue, Queen's Park, Bournemouth, Hants.

**JOHNSTON, Prof. Ronald Carlyle;** Professor of Romance Philology and Medieval French

Literature, Westfield College, London, since 1961; *b* 19 May 1907; *m*; one *s* three *d*. *Educ:* Ackworth Sch., Yorks; Bootham Sch., York; Merton Coll., Oxford. Travel in France, Germany and Spain, 1929-30. MA Oxon; 1st Cl. Hons Mediaeval and Modern Languages, French, 1929; Docteur de l'Université de Strasbourg, 1935. Asst Master Uppingham Sch., 1930-35; Lectr in French Philology and Old Fr. Lit., Oxford, 1935-45; Fellow of Jesus Coll., Oxford, 1945-48; Professor of French Language and Literature, University of St Andrews, 1948-61. External examiner in French, Universities of Oxford, Cambridge, Edinburgh, Aberdeen, and Manchester. Officier d'Académie. Chevalier de la Légion d'Honneur. *Publications:* Les Poésies lyriques du troubadour Arnaut de Mareuil (Paris), 1935; The Crusade and Death of Richard I (Anglo-Norman Text Soc.), 1961; (with A. Ewert) Selected Fables of Marie de France, 1942; (with D. D. R. Owen) Fabliaux, 1957; reviews in Medium Aevum, Modern Language Review, French Studies, etc. *Recreations:* rough gardening, travel. *Address:* Westfield College, Hampstead, NW3; Taunton House, Freeland, Oxford. *T:* Freeland 276.

**JOHNSTON, Russell;** *see* Johnston, D. R.

**JOHNSTON, Sir Thomas Alexander,** 13th Bt of Caskieben, *cr* 1626; Attorney-at-Law; partner in legal firm of Howell, Johnston, Langford and Finkbohner, Alabama, USA; *b* 7 Sept. 1916; *s* of Sir Thomas Alexander Johnston, 12th Bt and of Pauline Burke, *d* of Leslie Bragg Sheldon, Mobile; *S* father, 1959; *m* 1941, Helen Torrey, *d* of Benjamin Franklin Du Bois; one *s* two *d*. *Educ:* University of Alabama (LLB). Mem., Alabama House of Representatives, 1941-49; Mem., Alabama State Senate, 1949-54; Pres., Mobile Co. Bar Assoc., 1963. *Recreations:* hunting, fishing. *Heir:* *s* Thomas Alexander Johnston, *b* 1 Feb. 1956. *Address:* Howell, Johnston, Langford and Finkbohner, E. A. Roberts Building, Mobile, Alabama, USA.

**JOHNSTON, William,** CMG 1950; retired; *b* 7 Dec. 1890; *s* of James Johnston and Jessie Spence Anderson; *m* 1923, Freda, *d* of late George Nelson, JP, Liverpool; no *c*. *Educ:* Burntisland; Glasgow; privately. Savings Bank, London, 1910; Officer HM Customs and Excise, UK, 1911; Deputy Comptroller Customs, Mauritius, 1920; acted Comptroller Customs and Harbour Master, also MLC on numerous occasions, 1923-31; Collector-Gen., Jamaica, 1932; Colonial Sec. and Financial Sec., British Honduras, 1934-40; administered Government, British Honduras, 1937, 1939, and 1939-40; Comptroller of Customs, Sierra Leone, 1940-42; Dir of Supplies, Sierra Leone, 1942-44; Comptroller of Customs, Tanganyika, 1944-46; Comr of Customs, Kenya and Uganda, 1946-48; Comr, East African Customs and Excise, 1949-51. *Recreations:* golf, etc. *Address:* 77 Alinora Avenue, Goring-by-Sea, Worthing, Sussex. *T:* Worthing 45165.

**JOHNSTON, Ven. William;** Archdeacon of Bradford since 1965; *b* 7 July 1914; *s* of late Dr W. Johnston; *m* 1943, Marguerite Pemberton, 2nd *d* of late H. Macpherson, Headingley Hall, Leeds; no *c*. *Educ:* Bromsgrove Sch.; Selwyn Coll., Cambridge; Westcott House, Cambridge. Asst Curate, S Michael, Headingley, Leeds, 1939-43; Asst Curate, Knaresborough, 1943-45; Vicar of Stourton, Yorks, 1945-49; Vicar of Armley, Leeds, 1949-56; Vicar of S Chad, Shrewsbury, 1956-64. *Address:* 57 Leylands Lane, Bradford 9.

**JOHNSTON, (William) Denis;** Writer, Broadcaster and Professor; *b* Dublin, 18 June 1901; *o s* of late Hon. William John Johnston, Judge of the Supreme Court; *m* 1st, 1928, Shelah Kathleen (marriage dissolved), *d* of John William Richards, Dublin; one *s* one *d*; 2nd, 1945, Betty, *d* of John William Chancellor, Dublin; two *s*. *Educ:* St Andrew's Coll., Dublin; Merchiston, Edinburgh; Christ's Coll., Cambridge (MA, LLM 1926, Pres. of the Union); Harvard Univ., USA (Pugsley Scholar). Barrister Inner Temple and King's Inns, 1925 and Northern Ireland, 1926; Dir, Dublin Gate Theatre, 1931-36; joined British Broadcasting Corporation, 1936; BBC War Correspondent, Middle East, Italy, France and Germany, 1942-45 (despatches); Programme Dir, BBC Television Service, 1946-47. Professor in English Dept, Mount Holyoke Coll., Mass, 1950-60; Guggenheim Fellowship, 1955; Head of Dept of Theatre and Speech, Smith Coll., 1961-66; Visiting Lecturer: Amherst Coll., 1966-67; University of Iowa, 1967-68; Univ. of California, Davis, 1970-71. *Publications: plays:* The Old Lady says 'No!', 1929; The Moon in the Yellow River, 1931; A Bride for the Unicorn, 1933; Storm Song, 1934; The Golden Cuckoo, 1939; The Dreaming Dust, 1940; A Fourth for Bridge, 1948; Strange Occurrence on Ireland's Eye, 1956; The Scythe and the Sunset, 1958; operatic version of Six Characters in Search of an Author (comp. Hugo Weisgall), 1959; *autobiography:* Nine Rivers from Jordan, 1953, operatic version (comp. Hugo Weisgall), 1968; The Brazen Horn, 1969; *biographies:* In Search of Swift, 1959; J. M. Synge, 1965. *Recreation:* sailing. *Address:* Department of English, University of California, Davis, Calif 95616, USA. *Club:* Royal Irish Yacht (Kingstown).

**JOHNSTON-SAINT, Captain Peter Johnston,** MA Cantab; FRSE; FZS; FSA (Scotland); CstJ; Officier Légion d'Honneur; Officer Order of the Spanish Republic; Roumanian Order Meritul Sanitar, 1st Class; late IA; *e s* of late James Saint and Blanche, *d* of late Charles Harcourt Moffatt; *m* Clare (*d* 1967), *e d* of William Mansell MacCulloch, MD, Seigneur of Les Touillets, Guernsey, and Jurat of the Royal Court; two *d*. *Educ:* Rossall; St John's Coll., Cambridge. Served on NW Frontier, India, Egypt, 1908-14, and in France with 1st Indian Cavalry Division, 1914-15 (wounded); Adjt, No. 40 Sqdn and 5th Wing, RFC, 1916; Bde-Maj., Cadet Bde, RAF, 1917-18; retd 1920. Joined Wellcome Research Instn, 1921; Asst Dir, Museum of Medical History, 1934-47. FRSM, 1936-45. Birdwood Medal, RSA, 1927. *Publications:* Jessamine Flowers and Green Leaves, a collection of Poems translated from the Persian, 1925; Outline of a History of Medicine in India, 1927; Green Hills and Golden Sands, on travel in Normandy and Brittany, 1944; Castanets and Carnations, on travel in Spain, 1946; articles in French and English scientific journals. *Recreations:* travelling, writing, sailing. *Address:* c/o Viscountess Sandon, 5 Tregunter Road, SW10. *Clubs:* United Service, Pilgrims; Cercle Interallié (Paris).

*See also Viscount Sandon.*

**JOHNSTONE, VANDEN-BEMPDE-,** family name of **Baron Derwent.**

**JOHNSTONE, Prof. Alan Stewart;** Professor of Radiodiagnosis, University of Leeds, 1948-68, now Emeritus; Director of Radiodiagnosis (General Infirmary, Leeds), United Leeds Hospitals, 1939-68; *b* 12 May 1905; *s* of Dr David A. and Margaret E. Johnstone, The Biggin, Waterbeck, Dumfriesshire; *m* 1934, Elizabeth Rowlett; one *s* one *d*. *Educ:* St Bees Sch.; Edinburgh Univ. Radiologist,

Hammersmith Post-Graduate Hospital, 1935; Radiologist, Leicester Royal Infirmary, 1936-39. Baker Travelling Prof. in Radiology, Coll. of Radiologists of Australasia, 1959. Pres. Radiology Sect., Royal Society of Med., 1959-60; Pres. Thoracic Soc. of Great Britain, 1961-62. *Publications:* contributor to A Text Book of X-ray Diagnosis by British Authors; many in Br. Jl of Radiology, Jl of Faculty of Radiologists, Post Graduate Med. Jl, Edinburgh Med. Jl, Jl of Anatomy. *Recreations:* golf, fly fishing, chess. *Address:* 46 Stanford Road, Rondebosch, Cape Province, South Africa. *T:* Cape Town 653231. *Club:* National Liberal.

**JOHNSTONE, Air Vice-Marshal Alexander Vallance Riddell,** CB 1966; DFC 1940; Deputy Chairman, National Council, TA & VRA, since 1969; *b* 2 June 1916; *s* of late Alex. Lang Johnstone and Daisy Riddell; *m* 1940, Margaret Croll; one *s* two *d*. *Educ:* Kelvinside Academy, Glasgow. 602 (City of Glasgow) Sqdn, AAF, 1934-41; CO RAF Haifa, 1942; Spitfire Wing, Malta, 1942-43 (despatches, 1942); RAF Staff Coll., 1943; OC Fairwood Common, 1943-44; HQ AEAF, 1944; Air Attaché Dublin, 1946-48; OC RAF Ballykelly, 1951-52; OC Air/Sea Warfare Devel. Unit, 1952-54; SASO HQ No. 12 Gp, 1954-55; Founder and First CAS Royal Malayan Air Force, 1957; OC Middleton St George, 1958-60; idc, 1961; Dir of Personnel, Air Min., 1962-64; Comdr, Air Forces, Borneo, 1964-65; AO Scotland and N Ireland, AOC No. 18 Group, and Maritime Air Comdr N Atlantic (NATO), 1965-68. Johan Mengku Negara (Malaya), 1958. *Publications:* Television Series, One Man's War, 1964; Where No Angels Dwell, 1969. *Recreations:* golf, tennis, sailing. *Address:* c/o Bank of Scotland, 1 Waterloo Place, Edinburgh. *Clubs:* Royal Air Force; Conservative (Glasgow).

**JOHNSTONE, Mrs Dorothy (Christian Liddle),** CBE 1955; Commissioner of Customs and Excise since 1964; *b* 5 April 1915; *d* of William Hacket, printer, Peterhead, and Ethel Mary Duncan; *m* 1946, James Arthur Johnstone, *qv*; one *s*. *Educ:* Peterhead Acad.; Aberdeen Univ. Dept of Health for Scotland, 1937; Home Office, 1939; HM Treasury, 1943; Asst Sec., HM Customs and Excise, 1957. *Address:* Flat 3, 18 Buckingham Street, WC2. *T:* 01-930 8782.

**JOHNSTONE, Sir Frederic (Allan George),** 10th Bt, of Westerhall, Dumfriesshire, *cr* 1700; *b* 23 Feb. 1906; *o s* of Sir George Johnstone, 9th Bt and Ernestine (*d* 1955), *d* of Col Porcelli-Cust; *S* father 1952; *m* 1946, Doris, *d* of late W. L. Shortridge; one *s*. *Educ:* Imperial Service Coll. *Heir:* *s* George Richard Douglas Johnstone, *b* 21 Aug. 1948. *Address:* The Drive, Adel, Leeds 6.

**JOHNSTONE, Gerald Ewart,** CB 1959; Principal Assistant Solicitor to the Treasury since 1956; *b* 26 June 1906; *o s* of late Rev. David Ewart Johnstone and late Alice Mary, *e d* of Rt Rev. J. M. Speechly, sometime Bishop of Travancore and Cochin; *m* 1935, Dorothy Betty, *y d* of late Thomas Stone, Exeter. *Educ:* Westminster Sch.; Christ Church, Oxford (BCL). Barrister-at-law, Gray's Inn, 1930; Solicitor's Dept, Min. of Agriculture and Fisheries, 1935-36; Treasury, Solicitor's Dept, 1936-39; Legal Adviser Min. of Economic Warfare, Mem. of Contraband, Enemy Exports and Blockade Cttees and of Cttee on Censorship, 1939-46; Chm. of Bermuda Contraband and Enemy Exports Cttee, 1941; Asst Solicitor to the Treasury, 1946-55; Legal Adviser to Min. of Food, 1954-55; Asst Solicitor to Min. of Agriculture, Fisheries and Food, 1955-56. *Publications:* articles in the Field, Countryman, etc on nature topics. *Recreations:* wild life preservation and watching cricket. *Address:* Nywood, Dunnings Road, East Grinstead, Sussex. *T:* East Grinstead 22194. *Club:* Oxford and Cambridbe University.

**JOHNSTONE, James Arthur;** Commissioner of Inland Revenue since 1964; *b* 29 July 1913; *o s* of Arthur James Johnstone, solicitor, Ayr, and Euphemia Tennant (*née* Fullarton); *m* 1946, Dorothy C. L. Hacket (*see* Mrs Dorothy Johnstone); one *s*. *Educ:* Ayr Academy; Glasgow Univ.; St John's Coll., Cambridge. Entered Inland Revenue Dept, 1936. Sec., Royal Commission on Taxation of Profits and Income, 1952-55. *Address:* Flat 3, 18 Buckingham Street, WC2. *T:* 01-930 8782. *Club:* Reform.

**JOHNSTONE, Kenneth Roy,** CB 1962; CMG 1949; Deputy Director-General of the British Council, 1953-62, retired; Chairman, International Department, British Council of Churches, since 1963; *b* 25 Sept. 1902; 2nd *s* of late Edward Henderson Johnstone and late Stella Fraser; *m* 1944, Mary Pauline, *d* of R. C. Raine. *Educ:* Eton; Balliol Coll., Oxford. Entered HM Diplomatic Service, 1926; served in Warsaw, 1928, Oslo, 1930, Sofia, 1931, and London; seconded to British Council, 1936; resigned to join Welsh Guards, 1939; served War of 1939-45: France, 1940; North Africa, 1942; Staff in Middle East and Greece, 1943-45 (Col). Readmitted to Foreign Service, 1945, and rejoined British Council. Gold Cultural Medal (Italy); Gold Cross of Order of King George I (Greece). *Publications:* translated: Ivo Andric, Bosnian Story, 1959, Devil's Yard, 1962; Djilas, Mountenegro, 1963; Amandos, Introduction to Byzantine History, 1969. *Address:* 4 Priory Crescent, Lewes, Sussex. *T:* Lewes 3738. *Club:* United University.

**JOHNSTONE, Morris Mackintosh O.;** *see* Ord Johnstone.

**JOHNSTONE, Maj.-Gen. Ralph E.;** *see* Edgeworth-Johnstone.

**JOHNSTONE, Maj.-Gen. Reginald Forster,** CB 1958; CBE 1950; *b* 14 May 1904; 3rd *s* of Edwin James Johnstone, Rougham Hall, Suffolk; *m* 1935, Madeline Thornhill, *er d* of E. T. B. Simpson, Walton Hall, Wakefield, Yorks; one *s*. *Educ:* Charterhouse; Pembroke Coll., Cambridge (BA). Commanded 2nd Bn The Royal Scots, 1943-44; commanded 22nd East African Brigade, 1944-46 (Burma); commanded 24th Independent Infantry Brigade, 1947-50; Deputy Dir Military Intelligence, War Office, 1950-53; Deputy Adjutant-Gen., BAOR, 1953-56; Dir of Personal Services, War Office, Sept. 1956-Nov. 1959. Trustee, Imperial War Museum. *Recreations:* shooting, photography, natural history. *Address:* Wood Dalling, Bagshot Road, Bracknell, Berks. *T:* Bracknell 5249. *Club:* United Service.

**JOHNSTONE, R(obert) Edgeworth,** DSc (London); MIChemE; FIMechE; FRIC; Lady Trent Professor of Chemical Engineering, University of Nottingham, 1960-67; *b* 4 Feb. 1900; *e s* of Lieut-Col Sir Walter Edgeworth-Johnstone, KBE, CB; *m* 1931, Jessie Marjorie, *d* of late R. M. T. Greig; two *s* one *d*. *Educ:* Wellington; RMA Woolwich; Manchester Coll. of Technology; University Coll., London. Fellow Salters' Inst. of Industrial Chem., 1926-27. Held various posts at home and abroad with Magadi Soda Co., Trinidad Leaseholds, Petrocarbon, APV Co., Min. of Supply (Royal Ordnance Factories) and UK

Atomic Energy Authority. Vice-Pres., IChemE, 1951; Liveryman, Worshipful Co. of Salters, 1956. *Publications:* (with Prof. M. W. Thring) Pilot Plants, Models and Scale-up Methods in Chemical Engineers, 1957; papers in scientific and engineering jls, especially on distillation, process development and engineering education. *Recreations:* walking, music, philosophy. *Address:* 23 Surrenden Crescent, Brighton BN1 6WE. *T:* Brighton 556845. *Club:* Athenæum.

**JOHNSTONE, Maj.-Gen. Robert Maxwell,** MBE 1954; MC 1942; MA, MD, FRCPE; Postgraduate Medical Dean in the South West Metropolitan Region; *b* 9 March 1914; *s* of late Prof. Emer. R. W. Johnstone, CBE; *m* 1958, Marjorie Jordan Beattie (*d* 1960). *Educ:* Edinburgh Acad.; Craigflower; Fettes Coll.; Christ's Coll., Cambridge; Univ. of Edinburgh. MRCPE 1940; FRCPE 1944; MD Edinburgh 1954; MRCP 1966. Resident House Phys. and Surg., Royal Infirmary, Edinburgh, 1938-39. Sen. Pres., Royal Med. Soc., 1938-39. RMO, 129 Fd Regt RA, 1938-41; Company Comdr, 167 Fd Amb., RAMC, 1941-43; Staff Coll., Haifa, 1943; CO, 3 Fd Amb., 1945-46. Adviser in Medicine: HQ, E Africa Comd, 1950-51; Commonwealth Forces Korea, 1954-55; Officer i/c Med. Division: Cambridge Mil. Hosp., 1955-57; QAMH, Millbank, 1957-59; Prof. of Med., Univ. of Baghdad and Hon. Cons. Phys., Iraqi Army, 1959-63; CO, BMH, Iserlohn, 1963-65; Cons. Phys., HQ, FARELF, 1965-67; Dep. Director of Med. Services: Southern Comd, 1967-68; Army Strategic Comd, 1968-69; retd. CStJ 1969. *Recreations:* music, golf, fishing. *Address:* c/o Royal Bank of Scotland, 4 Shandwick Place, Edinburgh; 12 Thistleworth Close, Osterley, Mddx. *Club:* Athenæum.

**JOHNSTONE, Prof. Thomas Muir;** Professor of Arabic, University of London, since Oct. 1970; *b* 18 Jan. 1924; *s* of Thomas Cunningham Johnstone and Margaret Connolly Johnstone (*née* Muir); *m* 1949, Bernice Jobling; two *s* three *d*. *Educ:* Grove Academy, Broughty Ferry; School of Economics, Dundee. BCom 1944, BA 1954, PhD 1962, London. ICI, Manchester, 1944-57; Lectr in Arabic, School of Oriental and African Studies, 1957; Reader in Arabic, Univ. of London, 1965. Travelled extensively in Eastern Arabia and Oman; Mem., Middle East Comd Expedn to Socotra, 1967. *Publications:* Eastern Arabian Dialect Studies, 1967; articles, mainly on Arabian dialects and modern South Arabian languages, in Bulletin of School of Oriental and African Studies, Jl of Semitic Studies, Mariner's Mirror, Geographical Jl and Encyclopaedia of Islam. *Address:* 24 Comforts Farm Avenue, Hurst Green, Oxted, Surrey. *T:* Oxted 4145.

**JOHNSTONE-BURT, Charles Kingsley,** CB 1950; *b* 14 March 1891; *m* 1917, Mary Younger (*d* 1964); one *s* one *d*. *Educ:* Highgate Sch., London; Durham Univ. BSc in Mechanical Engineering, 1911; BSc in Civil Engineering, 1912. Designer: Grand Trunk Pacific Railway, Winnipeg, Canada, 1913; Sir Wm Arrol & Co. Ltd, Glasgow, 1914-18. Served under Civil Engineer-in-Chief, Admiralty, at Rosyth, Devonport, Portland, Portsmouth, Gibraltar, Ceylon, Singapore Naval Base (in charge of development construction), and Admiralty Headquarters, 1918-39; Asst Civil Engineer-in-Chief, 1939; Deputy Civil Engineer-in-Chief, 1940; Principal Deputy Civil Engineer-in-Chief, 1943, until retirement in 1951. AMICE 1916; MICE 1933. *Address:* West Winds, Kingsway, Craigweil, Bognor Regis, Sussex. *T:* Pagham 3450.

**JOHORE, Sultan of,** since 1959; **HH Ismail,** First Class of the Johore Family Order (DK); Hon. KBE 1937; Hon. CMG 1926; First Class Order of the Crown of Johore (SPMJ); First Class Order Sri Mangku Negara (SMN); *b* 1894; *s* of Maj.-Gen. HH Sir Ibrahim, DK (Darjah Karabat), SPMJ (1st class Order of Crown of Johore), Hon. GCMG, Hon. KBE, Sultan of Johore (*d* 1959); *S* father, 1959; Coronation as Sultan, 1960. *educ:* in England. Major Johore Military and Volunteer Forces. First Class Order of the Crown of Kelantan; also holds some foreign decorations. *Address:* Johore Bahru, via Singapore.

**JOICEY,** family name of **Baron Joicey.**

**JOICEY,** 4th Baron, *cr* 1906; **Michael Edward Joicey;** Bt 1893; *b* 28 Feb. 1925; *s* of 3rd Baron Joicey and Joan (*d* 1967), *y d* of 4th Earl of Durham; *S* father, 1966; *m* 1952, Elisabeth Marion, *y d* of late Lieut-Col Hon. Ian Leslie Melville; two *s* one *d*. *Educ:* Eton; Christ Church, Oxford. *Heir:* *s* Hon. James Michael Joicey, *b* 28 June 1953. *Address:* Etal Manor, Berwick-upon-Tweed, Northumberland. *T:* Crookham 205. *Clubs:* Bath, Lansdowne; Northern Counties (Newcastle upon Tyne).

**JOINT, Sir (Edgar) James,** KCMG 1958 (CMG 1948); OBE 1941; FRGS; HM Ambassador to Republic of Colombia, 1955-60, retired; *b* 7 May 1902; *m* 1st, 1928, Lottie Kerse (*d* 1929); 2nd, 1937, Holly Enid Morgan; three *s*. *Educ:* Fairfield, Bristol; London Univ.; Gonville and Caius Coll., Cambridge. Entered HM Foreign Service, 1923; subseq. served at Mexico City, Montevideo, Beira, Milan, Santos, Léopoldville, Guatemala, San Salvador, Brussels, Buenos Aires and Rome, 1951-55. Chm., Anglo-Colombian Soc., 1960-70. Grand Cross of Boyacá, Colombia, 1960. *Address:* BM/TWVX, WC1.

**JOLL, Prof. James Bysse,** MA; Stevenson Professor of International History, University of London, since 1967; *b* 21 June 1918; *e s* of Lieut-Col H. H. Joll and Alice Muriel Edwards. *Educ:* Winchester; University of Bordeaux; New Coll., Oxford. War Service, Devonshire Regt and Special Ops Exec., 1939-45. Fellow and Tutor in Politics, New Coll., Oxford, 1946-50; Fellow and Sub-Warden, St Antony's Coll., Oxford, 1951-67. Vis. Mem., Inst. for Advanced Study, Princeton, 1954; Vis. Prof. of History, Stanford Univ., Calif., 1958; Vis. Lectr in History, Harvard University, 1962. *Publications:* The Second International, 1955; Intellectuals in Politics, 1960; The Anarchists, 1964. *Recreations:* music, travel. *Address:* London School of Economics and Political Science, Houghton Street, Aldwych, WC2. *T:* 01-405 7686.

**JOLLIFFE,** family name of **Baron Hylton.**

**JOLLIFFE, Christopher;** Director, Science Division, Science Research Council, since 1969 (Director for University Science and Technology, 1965-69); *b* 14 March 1912; *s* of William Edwin Jolliffe and Annie Etheldreda Thompson; *m* 1936, Miriam Mabel Ash. *Educ:* Gresham's Sch., Holt; University Coll., London. Asst Master, Stowe Sch., 1935-37; Dept of Scientific and Industrial Research, 1937-65. *Address:* 8 Broomfield Road, Kew, Richmond, Surrey. *T:* 01-940 4265. *Club:* Athenæum.

**JOLLY, General Sir Alan,** GCB 1968 (KCB 1964; CB 1962); CBE 1955 (OBE 1946); DSO 1944; idc; jssc; psc; Quarter-Master-General, 1966-69; *b* Melbourne, 12 Nov. 1910; *s* of J. M. Jolly; *m* 1939, Margaret Russell. *Educ:* King's Coll. Sch.; RMC Sandhurst. Served NW

Frontier of India, 1936-37 (medal with clasp). Served War of 1939-45 (DSO, OBE). Late Royal Tank Regt. DQMG, BAOR, Oct. 1957-59; GOC 5 Div., 1959-60; GOC 1 Div., 1960-61; Chief of Staff, HQ Southern Comd, 1961-62; VQMG, War Office, 1962-64; Comdr, Far East Land Forces, 1964-66. Colonel Commandant: RAC (RTR Wing), 1964-68; Royal Tank Regt, 1964-69; ADC (General) to The Queen, 1968-69. *Address:* Cherry Court, North Moreton, near Didcot, Berks. *T:* Didcot 2137. *Club:* United Service.

**JOLLY, Hugh R.,** MA, MD, FRCP, DCH; Physician in charge of Pædiatric Department, Charing Cross Hospital, London, since 1965; Visiting Professor of Child Health, Ghana Medical School, since 1966; *b* 5 May 1918; *s* of Canon R. B. Jolly, *qv*; *m* 1944, Geraldine Mary Howard; two *s* one *d. Educ:* Marlborough Coll.; Sidney Sussex Coll., Cambridge; The London Hospital. MB, BChir (Cantab), 1942; (Cantab), 1943; MRCP 1948; DCH (England), 1949; MD (Cantab), 1951 (Raymond Horton-Smith Prize); FRCP 1965. House posts, London Hosp. and N Middlesex Hosp., 1943; Capt., RAMC (Dermatologist), 1944-47; Hosp. for Sick Children, Great Ormond Street, London, 1948-51; Consultant Pædiatrician: Plymouth, 1951-60; Charing Cross Hosp., 1960-; Vis. Consultant, Liverpool Sch. of Tropical Medicine, 1969-. Member: Council, and Overseas Cttee, Brit. Pæd. Assoc.; Overseas Cttee, Save the Children Fund; Council, Western Cerebral Palsy Centre; Exec. Cttee, Brit. Soc. Internat. Health Educn; Tropical Medicine Research Bd, MRC; Jt Cttee, Central and Scottish Health Councils on Vaccination and Immunization; BBC Med. Television Cttee. Vice-Pres., Health Visitor's Assoc. Trustee, London Br., Assoc. for Spina Bifida and Hydrocephalus. Examiner for: RCP; Ghana Med. Sch. Library rep., Pæd. Sect., RSM. On Editorial Board of Brit. Jl Med. Educn. *Publications:* Sexual Precocity, 1955; Diseases of Children, 1964 (2nd edn 1968); contribs (on pædiatric subjects) to: Lancet, Archives Dis. Childr., BMJ, Jl pediatrics, etc. *Recreation:* water ski-ing. *Address:* The Garden House, Warren Park, Kingston Hill, Surrey. *T:* 01-942 7855.

**JOLLY, James Hornby;** Director, Midland Bank Ltd, 1947-67; *b* 26 Feb. 1887; *e s* of William and Ellen Jolly, Preston, Lancashire; *m* 1912, Elizabeth Parkinson; one *d* (one *s* Flying Officer, RAF, missing 1944). *Educ:* Baines's Grammar Sch., Poulton Le Fylde. Chartered Accountant, 1909; Blaenavon Co. Ltd, 1911; Sec., Guest, Keen & Nettlefolds Ltd, 1918; Chm., Guest, Keen & Nettlefolds Ltd, 1947-53; Chm., Guest, Keen Iron & Steel Co. Ltd, 1946-57. *Recreations:* fell-walking, psychic research. *Address:* Langdale, Barnt Green, near Birmingham.

**JOLLY, Rev. Canon Reginald Bradley,** MA; OCF; Canon Emeritus of Worcester Cathedral since 1965 and of Winchester Cathedral since 1947; *b* 1 Oct. 1885; *s* of Rev. John Jolly, Vicar of Thornton, Bradford, and Mary Elizabeth Harding, Leicester; *m* Muriel Ada Crawshaw, Ilkley; three *s* two *d. Educ:* Bradford Gram. Sch.; Emmanuel Coll., Cambridge (Sizar). Deacon, 1909; Priest, 1910; Proctor-in-Convocation for Diocese of Winchester; formerly: Curate of Aston, Birmingham; Vice-Principal of Bishop Wilson Theological Coll., and Vicar of Kirk Michael; Diocesan Chaplain and Hon. Chaplain to the Bishop of Sodor and Man; Diocesan Inspector of Schs; Vicar of St Thomas, Douglas, IOM; Chaplain to the Forces; Metropolitan Sec., CMS; Chaplain to the High Sheriff of Surrey; Vicar of Christ Church, Woking, with St Paul's; Chaplain to the Southern Railway Orphanage; Sec., Guildford Diocesan Bd of Missions; Rector of St Mary's (Mother Church of) Southampton, 1928-45; Rural Dean of Southampton, 1930-45; Vicar, 1945-58, and Rural Dean, 1949-58, of Kidderminster; Hon. Canon of Worcester, 1951-65; Vicar of Overbury with Teddington, with Alstone and Little Washbourne, 1958-64, also Rural Dean of Bredon, 1962-64, retired. Public Preacher, Diocese of Exeter, 1968-. Formerly: Chaplain to Blakebrook County Hosp., Kidderminster; Chaplain to Kidderminster and District Gen. Hosp.; Commissary to Bishop of Armidale and to Archbishop of British Columbia; Proctor-in-Convocation for Diocese of Worcester, 1951 and 1955-61. Joyce of Exmoor Lectr, Dio. of Exeter, 1969. *Recreation:* golf. *Address:* Bessemer Thatch, Berrynarbor, N Devon.

*See also H. R. Jolly.*

**JOLY de LOTBINIÈRE, Lt-Col Sir Edmond,** Kt 1964; President, Eastern Provincial Area Conservative Association, 1969 (Chairman, 1961-65); Chairman, Bury St Edmunds Division Conservative Association since 1953; *b* 17 March 1903; *er s* of late Brig.-Gen. H. G. Joly de Lotbinière, DSO; *m* 1st, 1928, Hon. Elizabeth Alice Cecilia Jolliffe (marr. diss. 1937); two *s*; 2nd, 1937, Helen Ruth Mildred Ferrar (*d* 1953); 3rd, 1954, Evelyn Adelaide (*née* Dawnay), *widow* of Lt-Col J. A. Innes, DSO. *Educ:* Eton Coll.; Royal Military Academy, Woolwich. 2nd Lieut Royal Engineers, 1923; served in India; RARO, 1928; re-employed, 1939. Served War of 1939-45: in Aden, Abyssinian Campaign and East Africa (despatches); Major 1941; Lieut-Col 1943; retired 1945. Chm. and Managing Dir of two private companies manufacturing building materials. Farms 200 acres. *Recreations:* shooting, golf, bridge. *Address:* Horringer Manor, Bury St Edmunds, Suffolk. *T:* Horringer 208. *Clubs:* Carlton, Naval and Military.

*See also S. J. de Lotbinière.*

**JOLY de LOTBINIÈRE, S.;** *see* de Lotbinière.

**JONES;** *see* Armstrong-Jones, family name of Earl of Snowdon.

**JONES;** *see* Griffith-Jones.

**JONES;** *see* Gwynne Jones, family name of Baron Chalfont.

**JONES;** *see* Hope-Jones.

**JONES;** *see* Hugh-Jones.

**JONES;** *see* Lloyd Jones and Lloyd-Jones.

**JONES;** *see* Morris-Jones.

**JONES;** *see* Wansbrough-Jones.

**JONES;** *see* Wynne-Jones.

**JONES,** family name of **Baron Maelor.**

**JONES, Brig. Alan Harvey,** CBE 1955; TD 1947; DL; Secretary, Haydock Park Racecourse, since 1965; Brigadier late RA (TA); *b* 17 April 1910; *s* of late William and Agnes Jones; *m* 1938, Mary Scholfield; one *d. Educ:* King William's Coll., Isle of Man. Commissioned Manchester Regt, 1933; commanded 65th AA Regt, 1942-46 and 96th Army Group, RA, 1951-55. ADC (TA) to the Queen, 1958-63. DL, County Palatine of Lancaster, 1961-. Chm., SSAFA, Manchester Branch, 1957-. *Recreation:* sailing. *Address:* Haydock Park, Newton-le-Willows, Lancs. *T:* Ashton-in-

Makerfield 77124; Ty Plant, Rhosneigr, Anglesey. *T:* Rhosneigr 493. *Clubs:* Naval and Military; St James's (Manchester).

**JONES, Alan Payan P.**; *see* Pryce-Jones.

**JONES, A(lan) Trevor,** MD; FRCP; DPH; Provost of The Welsh National School of Medicine, University of Wales, 1955-Sept. 1969, retired; *b* 24 Feb. 1901; *y s* of Roger W. Jones, MA, JP, Pengam, Glam.; *m* 1931, Gwyneth, *y d* of Edward Evans, Hammersmith; one *s* one *d*. *Educ:* Lewis' Sch., Pengam; University Coll., Cardiff; University Coll., London; University Coll. Hosp., London. MD London 1927; DPH 1929; FRCP 1953. Resident appts, University Coll. Hosp., 1925-28; Dep. Supt, Marylebone Hosp., London, 1928-30; Gen. practice and Hon. Mem. Hosp. Staff, Carmarthen, 1930-34; MOH Carmarthen; MO, Welsh Bd of Health, 1934; Hosp. Officer for Wales, 1937-47; Sen. Admin. MO, Welsh Regional Hosp. Bd, 1947-55; Univ. of Wales Rep., Gen. Med. Council, 1956-69; Vice-Chm., Bd of Govs, United Cardiff Hosps. Commonwealth Fund Travelling Fellow, 1963. Hon. LLD Wales, 1970. *Publications:* Maternal Mortality in Wales, 1937; Survey of Hospital Services of South Wales, 1945; New Medical Teaching Centre, Cardiff, 1966; articles in medical and public health jls. *Recreations:* photography, gardening. *Address:* Windylaw, Graig Road, Lisvane, Cardiff CF4 5UF. *T:* 752481. *Club:* National Liberal.

**JONES, (Albert) Arthur;** MP (C) South Division of Northamptonshire since Nov. 1962; Chairman, Local Government Advisory Committee, Conservative Central Office; estate agent, company director; *b* 23 Oct. 1915; *s* of late Frederick Henry Jones; *m* 1939, Peggy Joyce (*née* Wingate); one *s* one *d*. *Educ:* Bedford Modern Sch. Territorial, Beds Yeomanry, RA, 1938; Middle East with First Armd Div., 1941; captured at Alamein, 1942; escaped as POW from Italy, 600 miles walk to Allied territory. Mem. Bedford RDC, 1946-49; Mem. Bedford Borough Council, 1949-, Alderman, 1957-; Mayor of Bedford, 1957-58, 1958-59; Member: Beds CC, 1956-67; Central Housing Advisory Cttee, 1959-62; Internat. Union of Local Authorities; Vice-Pres., Assoc. of Municipal Corporations, 1963-; Chm. Estates Cttee, Gov. Body of Harpur Charity. Contested (C) Wellingborough Div., 1955. *Address:* 10 Park Avenue, Bedford. *T:* 61810; 1 Little Smith Street, Westminster, SW1.

**JONES, Alec;** *see* Jones, T. A.

**JONES, Allan G.;** *see* Gwynne-Jones.

**JONES, Sir Andrew;** *see* Jones, Sir W. J. A.

**JONES, Arthur;** *see* Jones, (Albert) Arthur.

**JONES, Arthur Davies;** *b* 1897; *s* of late Evan Jones, JP Trimsaran; *m* 1942, Rosemary, 2nd *d* of late Rev. Frank Long-Price, Clearbrook, Llanarthney. *Educ:* Mill Hill; Emmanuel Coll., Cambridge. High Sheriff Carmarthenshire, 1941-42. *Recreations:* hunting, polo, mountaineering, ski-ing. *Address:* Clearbrook Hall, Llanarthney, Carmarthenshire.

**JONES, Maj.-Gen. Sir Arthur Guy S.;** *see* Salisbury-Jones.

**JONES, Arthur R.;** *see* Rocyn-Jones.

**JONES, Brig. Arthur Thomas C.;** *see* Cornwall-Jones.

**JONES, Rt. Hon. Aubrey,** PC 1955; Chairman, Laporte Industries, since 1970; *b* 20 Nov. 1911; *s* of Evan and Margaret Aubrey Jones, Merthyr Tydfil; *m* 1948, Joan, *d* of G. Godfrey-Isaacs, Ridgehanger, Hillcrest Road, Hanger Hill, W5; two *s*. *Educ:* Cyfarthfa Castle Secondary Sch., Merthyr Tydfil; London School of Economics. BSc (Econ.) 1st Cl. Hons, Gladstone Memorial Prizewinner, Gerstenberg Post-grad. Schol., LSE. On foreign and editorial staffs of The Times, 1937-39 and 1947-48. Joined British Iron and Steel Federation, 1949; General Dir, June-Dec. 1955. Served War of 1939-45, Army Intelligence Staff, War Office and Mediterranean Theatre, 1940-46. Contested (C) SE Essex in General Election, 1945 and Heywood and Radcliffe (by-election), 1946; MP (U) Birmingham, Hall Green, 1950-65; Parliamentary Private Sec. to Minister of State for Economic Affairs, 1952, and to Min. of Materials, 1953; Minister of Fuel and Power, Dec. 1955-Jan. 1957; Minister of Supply, 1957-Oct. 1959. Chm., Staveley Industries Ltd, 1964-65 (Dir 1962-65); Director: Guest, Keen & Nettlefolds Steel Company Limited, 1960-65; Courtaulds Ltd, 1960-63. Chm., Nat. Bd for Prices and Incomes, 1965-70. Hon. Fellow, LSE, 1959, Mem., Court of Governors, 1964. Vice-Pres., Consumers' Assoc., 1967-. Hon. DSc Bath, 1968. *Publications:* The Pendulum of Politics, 1946; Industrial Order, 1950. *Address:* Laporte Industries (Holdings) Ltd, Hanover House, 14 Hanover Square, W1R 0BE. *Clubs:* Brooks's, Carlton.

**JONES, Maj.-Gen. Basil Douglas,** CB 1960; CBE 1950; *b* 14 May 1903; *s* of Rev. B. Jones; *m* 1932, Katherine Holberton, *d* of Col H. W. Man, CBE, DSO; one *s* two *d*. *Educ:* Plymouth Coll.; RMC, Sandhurst. 2nd Lieut, Welch Regt, 1924; transferred to RAOC, 1935; Major 1939; served with Australian Military Forces in Australia and New Guinea, 1941-44; Temp. Brig. 1947; Brig. 1955; Maj.-Gen. 1958. ADC to the Queen, 1956-58; Inspector, RAOC, 1958-60, retired. Col Commandant, RAOC, 1963-67. *Recreation:* golf. *Address:* Churchfield, Sutton Courtenay, Abingdon, Berks. *T:* Sutton Courtenay 261.

**JONES, Benjamin Rowland R.;** *see* Rice-Jones.

**JONES, Sir (Bennett) Melvill,** Kt 1942; CBE 1938; AFC 1918; FRC 1939; Hon. FRAeS; Hon. FAIAA; Hon. Fellow, Canadian Aeronautics and Space Institute, 1965; Francis Mond Professor of Aeronautical Engineering, Cambridge University, 1919-52; Fellow of Emmanuel College; Chairman Aeronautical Research Council, 1943-47; *b* 28 Jan. 1887; *s* of Benedict Jones, Barrister-at-law, Liverpool, and Henrietta Melvill; *m* Dorothy Laxton Jotham (*d* 1955), Kidderminster; one *s* one *d* (and one *s* killed in action, War of 1939-45). *educ:* Birkenhead Sch.; Emmanuel Coll., Cambridge. Mechanical Science Tripos, 1909. Aeronautical research at the National Physical Laboratory, 1910-13; Sir W. Armstrong, Whitworth & Co., 1913; Royal Aircraft Establishment, 1914; Armament Experimental Station, Orfordness, 1916; qualified as a pilot and served as observer with No. 48 Sqdn RAF, 1918; Technical Dept Air Ministry, 1918; attached Ministry of Aircraft Production, 1939-45. *Publications:* Aerial Surveying by Rapid Methods, 1925 (jointly with the late Major J. C. Griffiths); Aerodynamic Theory, Vol. 5, Div. N, 1935; various reports of the Aeronautical Research Cttee. *Address:* Lower Watertown, Umberleigh, N Devon. *Club:* Athenæum.

**JONES, Bobby;** *see* Jones, Robert Tyre.

**JONES, Sir Brynmor,** Kt 1968; PhD Wales and Cantab, ScD Cantab, FRIC; Vice-Chancellor, University of Hull, since 1956; *b* Sept. 1903; *o c* of late W. E. Jones, Rhos, Wrexham; *m* 1933, Dora Jones. *Educ:* The Grammar School, Ruabon; University Coll. of North Wales, Bangor (Exhibitioner and Research Scholar); St John's Coll., Cambridge; Sorbonne, Paris. Fellow, Univ. of Wales, 1928-31. Asst Demonstrator, Cambridge, 1930; Lecturer in Organic Chemistry, University of Sheffield, 1931-46; Leverhulme Research Fellowship, 1939; Mem. Extra-Mural Research Team, Min. of Supply, University of Sheffield, 1940-45; G. F. Grant Professor of Chemistry, University Coll. and University of Hull, 1947-56; Dean of Faculty of Science and Dep. Principal, 1949-52, Vice-Principal, 1952-54; Pro-Vice-Chancellor, 1954-56. Sometime Examiner for Univs of St Andrews, London, Leeds, Oxford, Manchester, Edinburgh and the Inst. of Civil Engineers. Chairman, Nat. Council for Educational Technology, 1967-; UGC and Min. of Educn's sub-cttee on Audio-Visual Aids (Report, HMSO, 1965); Univs Council for Adult Educn, 1961-65; Pres., Assoc. for Programmed Learning and Educational Technology, 1969-; Chm., Vis. Grants Cttee to Univ. of Basutoland, Bechuanaland Protectorate and Swaziland, 1965; Member: Kennedy Memorial Trust, 1964-; GMC, 1964-; DSIR Postgraduate Trng Awards Cttee, 1963-65; Univ. Science and Technology Bd (SRC), 1965-68; BBC Further Educn Adv. Council, 1966- (Chm. of Programme Cttee on Higher Educn); Brit. Cttee of Selection for Frank Knox Fellowships to Harvard Univ.; Inter-Univ. Council (and Exec.) for Higher Educn, Overseas; Planning Cttee and Council of Open Univ.; Royal Commn on Higher Educn in Ceylon, 1969-70; University Council, Nairobi; Provisional Council of Univ. of E Africa and of University Coll., Dar es Salaam, 1961-64; Council of University Coll., Dar es Salaam, 1964-68; Provisional Council, Univ. of Mauritius, 1965-67; General Nursing Council, 1960-66; Acad. Adv. Cttee, Welsh Coll. of Advanced Technology 1964-67; East Riding Educn Cttee, 1956-; Hull Chamber of Commerce and Shipping; Council of Chemical Soc., 1945-48, and 1953-56; Senior Reporter, Annual Reports of Chemical Soc., 1948; Pres. Hull Lit. and Philosoph. Soc., 1955-57. Hon. Fellow, St John's Coll., Cambridge; Mem., Court of Universities of Nottingham and Sheffield; Governor: Hymers Coll.; Pocklington Sch. Hon. LLD Wales. *Publications:* numerous papers on Physical Organic and on Organic Chemistry, mainly on kinetics and mechanism of organic reactions and on mesomorphism, in Journal of Chemical Soc. and other scientific periodicals. University of Sheffield Record of War Work, 1939-45. *Recreations:* music, photography and walking. *Address:* The University of Hull. *T:* 408960; 4 Hull Road, Cottingham, East Yorks. *T:* 847246.

**JONES, Charles Mark J.;** *see* Jenkin-Jones.

**JONES, General Sir Charles (Phibbs),** GCB 1965 (KCB 1960; CB 1952); CBE 1945; MC 1940; Governor of Royal Hospital, Chelsea, since 1969; Chief Royal Engineer, since 1967; *b* 29 June 1906; *s* of late Hume Riversdale Jones and Elizabeth Anne (*née* Phibbs); *m* 1934, Ouida Margaret Wallace; two *s*. *Educ:* Portora Royal School; Enniskillen, N Ireland; Royal Military Academy, Woolwich; Pembroke Coll., Cambridge. Commissioned in RE, 1925; service with Royal Bombay Sappers and Miners in India, 1928-34; Adjt of 42nd (EL) Divl Engineers (TA), 1934-39; student at Staff Coll., Camberley, 1939. War of 1939-45: service in BEF, France and Belgium, as Bde Major 127 Inf. Bde, 1940; Instructor at Staff Coll., Camberley, 1940-41; GSO1 at GHQ Home Forces, 1941-42; CRE Guards Armoured Div. in UK and in NW Europe, 1943-44; BGS XXX Corps in NW Europe, 1945. Chief of Staff, Malaya Command UK, 1945-46; BGS HQ Western Command, UK, 1946; idc, 1947; Comdr 2nd Inf. Bde, 1948-50; Dir of Plans, War Office, 1950; GOC 7th Armoured Div., BAOR, 1951-53; Commandant, Staff Coll., Camberley, 1954-56; Vice AG, WO, 1957-58; Dir, Combined Military Planning Staff, CENTO, 1959; GOC, 1st Corps 1960-62; GOC, Northern Command, 1962-63; Master General of the Ordnance, 1963-66; ADC (General) to the Queen, 1965-67. A Governor, Corps of Commissionaires, 1969-. Col Commandant, RE, 1961-; Hon. Col. Engineer and Rly Staffs Corps, RE, T&AVR, 1970-. Order of Leopold, Croix de Guerre (Belgium), 1945. *Recreations:* all games and sports. *Address:* Governor's House, Royal Hospital, Chelsea, SW3. *T:* 01-730 4062. *Club:* Army and Navy.

**JONES, Rev. Canon Cheslyn Peter Montague,** MA; Sir Henry Stephenson Fellow, University of Sheffield, since Oct. 1969; *b* 4 July 1918; *e s* of Montague William and Gladys Muriel Jones; unmarried. *Educ:* Winchester Coll.; New Coll., Magdalen Coll., Oxford. BA 1st cl. Hons Theology, 1939; Senior Demy, Magdalen Coll., 1940-41. Deacon 1941; Priest 1942. Curate of St Peter, Wallsend, 1941-43; St Barnabas, Northolt Park, 1943-46; at Nashdom Abbey, 1946-51; Chaplain, Wells Theological Coll., 1951-52; Librarian, Pusey House, Oxford, 1952-56; Chaplain, Christ Church Cathedral, Oxford, 1953-56; Principal, Chichester Theological Coll., and Chancellor, Chichester Cathedral, 1956-69. Select Preacher, Cambridge Univ., 1962; Bampton Lectr, Oxford Univ., 1970. *Publications:* (Ed) A Manual for Holy Week, 1967; contributions to: Studies in the Gospels, 1955; Studies in Ephesians, 1956; Thirty 20th century hymns, 1960. *Recreations:* travel, music. *Address:* c/o The University, Sheffield S10 2TN.

**JONES, Sir Christopher L.;** *see* Lawrence-Jones.

**JONES, Mrs Colin;** *see* Seymour, Lynn.

**JONES, Daniel,** BEM 1946; MP (Lab) Burnley since Oct. 1959; *b* 26 Sept. 1908; *m* 1932; two *s* one *d*. *Educ:* Ynyshir Council Sch.; NCLC. In coal-mines of Rhondda Valley for 12 years, 1920-32; unemployed for 4 years; in engineering as a SR Engineer, 1937-54; Aircraft Industry, 1939-45 (BEM); full-time Official of the Amalgamated Engineering Union, 1954-59. Mem. British Legion and Ex-Servicemen's Clubs, London, Burnley and Rhondda Valley. *Recreations:* music and walking. *Address:* 124 Marsden Road, Burnley. *T:* Burnley 5638.

**JONES, David,** CBE 1955; *b* Brockley, Kent, 1 Nov. 1895; *s* of James Jones, Holywell, Flintshire, and Alice Ann Bradshaw, Rotherhithe, Surrey; unmarried. Camberwell Sch. of Art, 1910-14; served on West Front with 15th Bn Royal Welch Fusiliers, 1915-18; Westminster Art Sch., 1919-21; became a Roman Catholic, 1921; engravings for the Chester play of The Deluge, The Ancient Mariner, etc., 1924-28; paintings largely in water-colour from 1927 onwards; represented at the Chicago Exhibition, the Venice Biennial Exhibition, the World's Fair, New York, British Art since Whistler, National Gallery, 1940, Six Watercolour Painters of To-day, National Gallery, 1941, the Tate Gallery's Wartime Acquisitions, National Gallery, 1942, one-man exhibition shown by CEMA at various centres in England and Wales, 1944; represented in the two exhibitions: Nine British Contemporaries and Modern British Paintings from the Tate Gallery, shown under the auspices of the British Council in Paris and other capitals, 1945-46; represented at various Festival exhibitions, 1951, and at Biennial International Water-colour Exhibition, Brooklyn, USA, 1952-53; a comprehensive retrospective exhibition shown, under the auspices of the Arts Council, in Wales, in Edinburgh and at the Tate Gallery, 1954-55. Works acquired by Contemporary Art Soc., Tate Gallery, Victoria and Albert and British Museums, National Museum of Wales, Sydney Art Gallery, Toronto Art Gallery, Arts Council, British Council, and by private collectors; Member: Hon. Society of Cymmrodorion; Soc. for Nautical Research. DLitt (*hc*), University of Wales, 1960; FRSL. Hon. Mem. RWS 1961. Gold Medal for Fine Arts, Royal National Eisteddfod of Wales, 1964; Midsummer Prize, Corporation of London, 1968. *Publications:* In Parenthesis, 1937 (New York 1962) (Hawthornden Prize for 1938); The Anathemata, 1952 (New York 1963) (Russell Loines Memorial Award for Poetry, Nat. Inst. of Arts and Letters, New York, 1954); The Wall, 1955 (Harriet Munroe Memorial Prize, 1956); Epoch and Artist: Selected Writings (edited by Harman Grisewood), 1959, New York 1964; The Tribune's Visitation, 1969. *Relevant publication:* Agenda, special issue, June 1967, containing six written pieces, 18 drawings etc., a translation, and critical articles by 12 contributors. *Address:* at Monksdene, 2 Northwick Park Road, Harrow, Middx.

**JONES, David Jeffreys,** CMG 1969; **Hon. Mr Justice Jones;** Puisne Judge, High Court, Uganda, since Dec. 1960; *b* 18 Oct. 1909; *s* of Thomas John and Gwendoline Jones, The Larches, Ystradgynlais, Swansea; unmarried. *Educ:* Maesydderwen Grammar Sch.; Middle Temple. Called to Bar, 1933; practised in London and Wales Circuit to 1938; Sec., Ffynone Estates Co., 1938-43; Asst. Trust Officer, Public Trustee Office, 1943-46; Legal Asst, Control Commission, Germany, 1946-48; Dep. Legal Adviser to Commissioner at Hamburg, 1948-50; Resident Magistrate, Uganda, 1950-55; Sen. Res. Magistrate, Actg. Asst Judicial Adviser, and Chm. Traffic Appeals Tribunal, 1955-60; Acting Chief Justice, June-Oct. 1969; Mem., Judicial Service Commn, 1969-. Awarded Internat. Constantinian Order, 1970. *Recreations:* reading, music, all kinds of sport. *Address:* PO Box 85, High Court, Uganda. *T:* Kampala 56878 and 4730; The Larches, Ystradgynlais, Swansea. *T* Glantawe 2298. *Clubs:* East India and ports; Kampala, Uganda (Uganda).

**JONES, David le Brun;** Under-Secretary, Ministry of Technology (formerly Ministry of Power), since 1968; *b* 18 Nov. 1923; *s* of Thomas John Jones and Blanche le Brun. *Educ:* City of London Sch.; Trinity Coll., Oxford. Asst Principal, Min. of Power, 1947; Principal, MOP, 1952; Asst Sec., Office of the Minister for Science, 1962; Asst Sec., MOP, 1963. *Recreations:* walking, reading, chess. *Address:* 10 Belsize Road, NW6. *T:* 01-722 9774. *Club:* Oxford and Cambridge University.

**JONES, Prof. David Morgan,** MA; Professor of Classics in the University of London (Westfield College) since 1953; *b* 9 April 1915; *m* 1965, Irene M. Glanville. *Educ:* Whitgift Sch.; Exeter Coll., Oxford (Scholar). 1st Class, Classical Hon. Mods, 1936; 1st Class, Lit Hum, 1938; Derby Scholar, 1938; Junior Research Fellow, Exeter Coll., Oxford, 1938-40; Oxford Diploma in Comparative Philology, 1940; Lecturer in Classics, University Coll. of North Wales, 1940-48; Reader in Classics in the University of London (Birkbeck Coll.), 1949-53. *Publications:* papers and reviews in classical and linguistic journals. *Address:* 48 Corringham Road, NW11. *T:* 01-455 7350.

**JONES, D(avid) Prys;** Metropolitan Stipendiary Magistrate since 1969; *b* 7 May 1913; *s* of John William and Ethel Banks Jones; *m* 1940, Joan Wiltshire; one *s* two *d*. *Educ:* Wigan Grammar Sch.; Manchester Univ. LLB (Hons) 1934. Called to Bar, Gray's Inn, 1935; joined Northern Circuit, 1936. Commnd Manchester Regt (TA), 1939; JAG's Dept as Captain, Legal Staff and Major Dep. Judge Advocate, 1944-45. Joined Dir of Public Prosecutions Dept, 1946; Asst Dir of Public Prosecutions, 1966. *Recreations:* music, walking. *Address:* 2 Sefton Road, Croydon, Surrey. *T:* 01-656 9167. *Club:* Royal Over-Seas League.

**JONES, Derek John Claremont;** Counsellor (Hong Kong Affairs), United Kingdom Mission, Geneva, since 1967; *b* 2 July 1927; *er s* of Albert Claremont Jones and Mrs Jones (*née* Hazell); *m* 1st, 1951, Jean Cynthia Withams; one *s* two *d*; 2nd, 1970, Kay Cecile Thewlis. *Educ:* Colston Sch., Bristol; Bristol Univ.; London Sch. of Economics and Political Science. Economic Asst, Economic Section, Cabinet Office, 1950-53; Second Sec., UK Delegn to OEEC/NATO, Paris, 1953-55; Asst Principal, Colonial Office, 1955-57; Principal, Colonial Office, 1957-66; First Secretary, Commonwealth Office, 1966-67. *Recreations:* reading, travel, conversation. *Address:* 5 Avenue de Budé, Geneva, Switzerland. *T:* Geneva 337986.

**JONES, Captain Desmond V.;** *see* Vincent-Jones.

**JONES, Rev. Prof. Douglas Rawlinson;** Lightfoot Professor of Divinity, University of Durham, and Residentiary Canon of Durham Cathedral since 1964; *b* 11 Nov. 1919; *s* of Percival and Charlotte Elizabeth Jones; *m* 1946, Hazel Mary Passmore; three *s* two *d*. *Educ:* Queen Elizabeth's Hosp., Bristol; St Edmund Hall, Oxford; Wycliffe Hall, Oxford. Squire Scholar, 1938; BA 1941; MA 1945; deacon, 1942; priest, 1943. Curate of St Michael and All Angels, Windmill Hill, Bristol, 1942-45; Lectr, Wycliffe Hall, Oxford, 1945-50; Chaplain, Wadham Coll., Oxford, 1945-50; Lectr in Divinity, 1948-50; University of Durham: Lectr, 1951; Sen. Lectr, 1963. *Publications:* Haggai, Zechariah and Malachi, 1962; Isaiah, 56-66 and Joel, 1964; Instrument of Peace, 1965; contrib. to: Peake's Commentary on the Bible, 1962; Hastings' Dictionary of the Bible, 1963; The Cambridge History of the Bible, 1963; articles in Jl of Theolog. Studies, Zeitschrift für die Alttestamentliche Wissenschaft, Vetus Testamentum, Theology, Scottish Jl of Theology. *Recreation:* carpentry. *Address:* 12 The College, Durham. *T:* 4295.

**JONES, Prof. Douglas Samuel,** MBE 1945; FRS 1968; Ivory Professor of Mathematics, University of Dundee, since 1965; *b* 10 Jan. 1922; *s* of late J. D. Jones and B. Jones (*née* Streather); *m* 1950, Ivy Styles; one *s* one *d*. *Educ:* Wolverhampton Grammar Sch.; Corpus Christi Coll., Oxford. DSc Manchester 1957. Flt-Lt, RAFVR, 1941-45. Commonwealth Fund Fellow, MIT, 1947-48; Asst Lectr in Maths, University of Manchester, 1948-51; Lectr 1951-54, Research Prof. 1955, New York Univ.; Sen. Lectr in Maths, Univ. of Manchester, 1955-57; Prof. of Maths, Univ. of Keele, 1957-64. Vis. Prof., Courant Inst., 1962-63. FIMA 1964; FRSE 1967.

*Publications:* Electrical and Mechanical Oscillations, 1961; Theory of Electromagnetism, 1964; Generalised Functions, 1966; Introductory Analysis, vol. 1, 1969, vol 2, 1970; articles in mathematical and physical jls. *Recreations:* walking, photography. *Address:* Department of Mathematics, The University, Dundee DD1 4HN. *T:* Dundee 23181.

**JONES, Douglas V. I.;** *see* Irvine-Jones.

**JONES, Edgar Stafford,** CBE 1960 (MBE 1953); *b* 11 June 1909; *s* of late Theophilus Jones; *m* 1938, Margaret Aldis, *d* of late Henry Charles Askew; one *s* one *d. Educ:* Liverpool Institute High Sch. Mem. of Local Government Service, 1925-34; joined Assistance Board, 1934. Seconded to Air Min., as Hon. Flt-Lt RAFVR, 1943; Hon. Sqdn-Ldr, 1945. Transferred to Foreign Office, 1946; transferred to Washington, 1949; Dep. Finance Officer, Foreign Office, 1953; Head of Finance Dept, Foreign Office, 1957 and Diplomatic Service Administration Office, 1965, retired 1968. *Address:* 27 Cole Park Gardens, Twickenham, Mddx. *T:* 01-892 5435. *Club:* London Welsh Rugby Football.

**JONES, Edmund Angus,** CMG 1963; Director, Mobil Oil Australia Ltd (Managing Director, 1954-65, Chairman, 1962-67); *b* 8 Jan. 1903; *s* of Frederick E. Jones; *m* 1926, Elsie May Townley; two *s* one *d. Educ:* Christchurch Boys' High Sch., NZ; Harvard Business Sch. (Advanced Management Programme). Vacuum Oil Co. Pty Ltd, 1928, Salesman, Christchurch, NZ; Branch Manager, Christchurch, NZ, 1932; Asst Gen. Man., 1935, Gen. Man., 1939, Wellington, NZ; Dir, Melbourne, Australia, 1944; Area Consultant, Standard Vacuum, New York, USA, 1948; Dir, 1951, Man. Dir, 1954, Vacuum Oil Co. Pty Ltd, Melbourne, Australia. *Publications:* various articles on Management. *Recreations:* golf, gardening. *Address:* 4 Lascelles Avenue, Toorak, Victoria 3142, Australia. *T:* 24 5683. *Clubs:* Athenæum (Melbourne), also Rotary, Royal Melbourne Golf, Victoria Racing (all Melbourne).

**JONES, Edward;** *see* Jones, J. E.

**JONES, Air Marshal Sir Edward G.;** *see* Gordon Jones.

**JONES, Sir Edward Martin F.;** *see* Furnival Jones.

**JONES, Rt. Rev. Edward Michael G.;** *see* Gresford Jones.

**JONES, Edward Norton,** CMG 1952; OBE 1940; *b* 28 Jan. 1902; *s* of Daniel Norton Jones; *m* 1940, Cecilia Lucy Shaen (*née* Hamersley). *Educ:* St Paul's Sch., W Kensington; Corpus Christi Coll., Cambridge (BA). Gold Coast: Asst District Comr, 1925; District Commissioner, 1932; Sec. for Social Services, 1943; Dir of Social Welfare and Housing, 1946; Chief Commissioner, Northern Territories, 1948; Sec. for Development and Chm. of Marketing and Development Corporations, 1950; Permanent Sec. to the Ministry of Defence and External Affairs, Gold Coast, 1952; Mem., Public Service Commission, Ghana, 1955-61. *Recreation:* golf. *Address:* Walden, Innhams Wood, Crowborough, Sussex. *Club:* Royal Commonwealth Society.

**JONES, Rt. Hon. Edward Warburton; Rt. Hon. Mr Justice Jones;** PC (N Ireland) 1965; Judge of the High Court of Justice in Northern Ireland, since 1968; *b* 3 July 1912; *s* of late Hume Riversdale Jones and Elizabeth Anne (*née* Phibbs); *m* 1st, 1941, Margaret Anne Crosland Smellie (*d* 1953); three *s*; 2nd, 1953, Ruth Buchan Smellie; one *s. Educ:* Portora Royal School, Enniskillen, N Ireland; Trinity Coll., Dublin. BA (TCD), with First Class Moderatorship, Legal Science, and LLB (TCD) 1935; called to Bar of Northern Ireland, 1936; QC (N Ireland), 1948; called to Bar (Middle Temple), 1964. Junior Crown Counsel: County Down, 1939; Belfast, 1945-55. Enlisted, 1939; commissioned Royal Irish Fusiliers, 1940; Staff Coll., Camberley, 1943; AAG, Allied Land Forces, SEA, 1945; released with Hon. rank Lt-Col, 1946. MP (U) Londonderry City, Parliament of Northern Ireland, 1951-68; Attorney-Gen. for Northern Ireland, 1964-68. Chancellor: Dio. Derry and Raphoe, 1945-64; Dio. Connor, 1959-64; Lay Mem. Court of Gen. Synod, Church of Ireland. Bencher, Inn of Court of NI, 1961. *Recreations:* golf, sailing. *Address:* Hopefield Cottage, Kincora Avenue, Belfast, N Ireland. *T:* 654019; Craig-y-Mor, Trearddur Bay, Anglesey. *T:* Trearddur Bay 406. *Club:* Ulster (Belfast).

**JONES, Eifion,** CMG 1964; OBE 1953; Permanent Secretary, Ministry of Works, Northern Nigeria, 1959-66; Member, Northern Nigerian Development Corporation, 1959-66; retired; *b* Llanelly, Carmarthenshire, 10 June 1912; *s* of I. J. Jones and R. A. Jones (*née* Bassett); *m* 1944, Kathleen, *d* of Donald MacCalman, Argyllshire. *Educ:* Llanelly Grammar Sch.; University Coll., Swansea. BSc (Wales). Executive Engineer, Nigeria, 1942; Senior Executive Engineer, 1951; Chief Engineer, 1954; Dep. Dir of Public Works, Nigeria, 1958. FICE 1957; MIWE 1957. *Recreations:* golf, gardening. *Address:* c/o Barclays Bank Ltd, Llanelly, Carmarthenshire.

**JONES, Eli Stanley,** DD; *b* Clarksville, Maryland, 3 Jan. 1884; *m* 1911, Mabel Lossing; one *d. Educ:* City Coll., Baltimore; Asbury Coll. A Missionary of Methodist Episcopal Church in India, 1907; Pastor of English Church in Lucknow; Superintendent of Lucknow District and Principal of Sitapur Boarding Sch.; Evangelical work for North India Conference, 1917; Evangelist to the educated classes throughout India and the East; spent some months in the sch. of Dr Rabindranath Tagore, Bengal, 1926; elected to Episcopacy, Methodist Episcopal Church, 1928, resigned. *Publications:* The Christ of the Indian Road; Christ at the Round Table; The Christ of Every Road; The Christ of the Mount; Christ and Human Suffering, 1938; Christ and Communism, 1935; Victorious Living, 1936; Christ and Present World Issues, 1937; Along the Indian Road, 1939; Is the Kingdom of God Realism?, 1941; Abundant Living, 1942; The Christ of the American Road, 1944; The Way, 1947; Mahatma Gandhi–an Interpretation, 1948; The Way to Power and Poise, 1949; How to be a Transformed Person, 1951; Growing Spiritually, 1953; Mastery, 1955; Christian Maturity, 1957; Conversion, 1959; In Christ, 1961; The Word Became Flesh, 1963; Victory through Surrender, 1966. *Address:* c/o Methodist Division, World Missions, New York, NY 10027, USA.

**JONES, Rt. Hon. Sir Elwyn;** *see* Jones, Rt Hon. Sir F. E.

**JONES, Prof. Emrys,** MSc, PhD (Wales); FRGS; Professor of Geography, University of London, at London School of Economics, since Oct. 1961; *b* Aberdare, 17 Aug. 1920; *s* of Samuel Garfield and Anne Jones; *m* 1948, Iona Vivien, *d* of R. H. Hughes; two *d. Educ:*

Grammar Sch. for Boys, Aberdare; University Coll. of Wales, Aberystwyth. BSc (1st Class Hons in Geography and Anthropology), 1941; MSc, 1945; PhD, 1947; Fellow of the University of Wales, 1946-47; Asst Lectr at University Coll., London, 1947-50; Fellow, Rockefeller Foundation, 1948-49; Lectr at Queen's Univ., Belfast, 1950-58, Sen. Lectr, 1958. Chm., Regional Studies Assoc.; Mem. Council, Inst. of Brit. Geographers, 1958-60; UN Consultant on urbanisation, 1963. *Publications:* Hon. Editor, Belfast in its Regional Setting, 1952; (jointly) Welsh Rural Communities, 1960; A Social Geography of Belfast, 1961; Human Geography, 1964; Towns and Cities, 1966; Atlas of London, 1968. Articles in geographical, sociological and planning jls. *Recreations:* books, music. *Address:* 4 The Apple Orchard, Hemel Hempstead, Herts. *T:* Hemel Hempstead 52357.

**JONES, Lady (Enid)**; *see* Bagnold, Enid.

**JONES, Eric Kyffin,** CBE 1962 (MBE 1948); Chairman, Welsh Board of Health, 1961-Aug. 1962; *b* 4 Dec. 1896; *s* of Hugh Kyffin Jones and Catherine Jane (*née* Williams); *m* 1920, Helen Roberta Patricia (*née* Montgomery); one *d*. *Educ:* St Margaret's, Liverpool. Home Office, Boy Clerk, 1912; Welsh Board of Health: Principal, 1948; Asst Sec., 1955; Chm. (Under-Sec.), 1961. OStJ 1964. *Address:* 10 Penydre, Rhiwbina, Cardiff. *T:* Cardiff 62421.

**JONES, Sir Eric (Malcolm),** KCMG 1957; CB 1953; CBE 1946; Director, Government Communications Headquarters, Foreign Office, 1952-60, retired; *b* 27 April 1907; *m* 1929, Edith Mary Taylor; one *s* one *d*. *Educ:* King's Sch., Macclesfield. Textile Merchant and Agent, 1925-40. RAFVR 1940-46, Civil Servant, 1946-60; Director: Simon Engineering Ltd; Twyfords Holdings Ltd. Legion of Merit (US), 1946. *Recreations:* ski-ing, golf and gardening. *Address:* Oak Mead, Kemerton, near Tewkesbury, Glos. *T:* Overbury 348.

**JONES, Ernest**; *see* Jones, William Ernest.

**JONES, Ernest Turner,** CB 1953; OBE 1942; MEng; Hon. FAIAA; FRAeS; *b* 7 Jan. 1897; *m* 1921, Millicent Adie Manning; one *s* one *d*. *Educ:* University of Liverpool. Pilot and flying instructor, RFC/RAF, 1915-19. Aerodynamics Dept, Royal Aircraft Establishment, 1923-30; Marine Aircraft Experimental Establishment, Felixstowe, 1930-38; Chief Technical Officer, Aeroplane and Armament Experimental Establishment, Martlesham, 1938-39; Chief Supt, Aeroplane and Armament Experimental Establishment, Boscombe Down, 1939-47; Dir of Instrument Research and Development, Ministry of Supply, 1947-49; Principal Dir of Scientific Research (Air), 1949-55, Dir-Gen. Tech. Development (Air), 1955-58, Dep. Controller (Overseas Affairs), 1958-59, Min. of Supply. Pres. Royal Aeronautical Society, 1956-57. *Publications:* many Research Memoranda published by Aeronautical Research Council. Jl Royal Aeronautical Society (paper in Flight Testing Methods). *Address:* Cross Deep House, 102 Cross Deep, Strawberry Hill, Twickenham, Middx. *T:* 01-892 6208.

**JONES, Evan David,** CBE 1965; FSA 1959; Librarian of the National Library of Wales, 1958-69; *b* 6 Dec. 1903; *e s* of Evan Jones and Jane (*née* Davies), Llangeitho; *m* 1933, Eleanor Anne, *o d* of John Humphrey Lewis, master mariner, Aberystwyth; one *s*. *Educ:* Llangeitho Primary Sch.; Tregaron County Sch.; University Coll. of Wales, Aberystwyth. BA 1926, Hons Welsh, Class 1, History 2a; Sir John Williams Research Student, 1928-29. Archivist Asst, National Library of Wales, 1929-36; Dep. Keeper of MSS and Records, 1936-38, Keeper, 1938-58. Lecturer in Archive Administration, UCW, 1957-58. President: Cambrian Archæological Assoc., 1962-63; New Wales Union, 1965-67; Welsh Harp Soc., 1965-; Cymdeithas Emynau Cymru, 1968-. Chairman: Governors of Welsh Sch., Aberystwyth, 1946-47; Executive Cttee, Urdd Gobaith Cymru, 1954-57; Cambrian Archæological Assoc., 1954-57; Cardigans. Congregational Quarterly Meeting, 1960; Undeb y Cymdeithasau Llyfrau, 1959-61; Welsh Books Centre, 1966-70; Welsh Books Council, 1968-70; Govs, Coll. of Librarianship, Wales, 1968- (Vice-Chm., 1964-68). Mem. Court of Governors: Nat. Museum of Wales, 1958-69; University of Wales; Member: Council of UCW; Congregational Memorial Coll., Swansea; Bala-Bangor Congregational Coll.; Union of Welsh Independents; Council of Brit. Records Assoc., 1958-69; Pantyfedwen Trust, 1958-69; Council of Hon. Soc. of Cymmrodorion; National Eisteddfod Council; Broadcasting Council for Wales; Library Advisory Council (Wales), 1965-69; Hon. Mem. of the Gorsedd (also Mem. Bd and Examr). Editor: NLW Jl, 1958-69; Jl of Merioneth History and Record Soc.; DWB Supplements. *Publications:* Gwaith Lewis Glyn Cothi, 1953; articles in Archæologia Cambrensis, Bulletin of Board of Celtic Studies, and many other journals; contrib. Dictionary of Welsh Biography. *Recreations:* colour photography, walking, gardening. *Address:* Penllerneuadd, North Road, Aberyswyth. *T:* Aberystwyth 7286.

**JONES, Ewan Perrins W.**; *see* Wallis-Jones.

**JONES, Sir Ewart (Ray Herbert),** Kt 1963; FRS 1950; DSc Victoria, PhD Wales, MA Oxon, FRIC; Waynflete Professor of Chemistry, University of Oxford, since 1955; Fellow of Magdalen College; President, Royal Institute of Chemistry, since 1970; *b* Wrexham, Denbighshire, 16 March 1911; *m* 1937, Frances Mary Copp; one *s* two *d*. *Educ:* Grove Park Sch., Wrexham; University Coll. of North Wales, Bangor; Univ. of Manchester. Fellow of Univ. of Wales, 1935-37; Lecturer, Imperial Coll. of Science and Technology, 1938; Reader in Organic Chemistry, University of London, and Asst Prof., 1945; Sir Samuel Hall Prof. of Chemistry, The University, Manchester, 1947-55; Arthur D. Little Visiting Prof. of Chemistry, Massachusetts Institute of Technology, 1952; Karl Folkers Lecturer at Universities of Illinois and Wisconsin, 1957. Mem. Council for Scientific and Industrial Research, and Chm., Research Grants Cttee, 1961-65; Mem. SRC and Chm., Univ. Science and Technology Bd, 1965-69; Mem., Science Bd, 1969-. Tilden Lectr, Chemical Soc., 1949; Pedler Lectr 1959. Meldola Medal, Royal Institute of Chemistry, 1940; Davy Medal, Royal Society, 1966. Fritzsche Award, American Chemical Soc., 1962. Pres., Chemical Soc., 1964-66. Fellow, Imperial Coll., 1967-; Foreign Mem. Amer. Acad. of Arts and Sciences. Hon. DSc: Birmingham; Nottingham; New South Wales; Sussex. *Publications:* scientific papers in Jl of the Chem. Soc. *Address:* Dyson Perrins Laboratory, South Parks Road, Oxford. *T:* Oxford 57809; 6 Sandy Lane, Yarnton, Oxford. *T:* Kidlington 2581. *Club:* Athenæum.

**JONES, Major Francis,** CVO 1969; TD (3 clasps); MA, FSA; DL; Wales Herald Extraordinary since 1963; County Archivist, Carmarthenshire, since 1958; *b* Trevine, Pembrokeshire, 5 July 1908; *s* of James Jones, Grinston, Pembs, and Martha Jones; *m* Ethel

M. S. A., *d* of late J. J. Charles, Trewilym, Pembs; two *s* two *d*. *Educ:* Fishguard County Sch., Pembs. Temp. Archivist of Pembs, 1934-36; Archivist, Nat. Library of Wales, 1936-39. Lt 4th Bn Welch Regt (TA), 1931-39; trans. Pembrokeshire Yeomanry (RA, TA), 1939, Battery Captain; served War of 1939-45: RA (Field), N Africa (despatches), Middle East, Italy; Battery Comdr, and 2nd-in-comd of regt; GSO2 War Histories; Mil. Narrator, Hist. Section, Cabinet Office, 1945-58 (Compiled Official narrative of Sicilian and Italian Campaigns); Battery Comdr, The Surrey Yeomanry, QMR (RA, TA), 1949-56; Mil. Liaison Officer, Coronation, 1953; served on the Earl Marshal's staff, State Funeral of Sir Winston Churchill, 1965; Mem., Prince of Wales Investitute Cttee, 1967-69. Local Sec. and Mem., Cambrian Assoc.; Member: Council, Hon. Soc. of Cymmrodorion; Gorsedd, Royal National Eisteddfod of Wales; Court and Council, Nat. Library of Wales, 1967-; Council, Nat. Museum of Wales; Historical Soc. of the Church in Wales; Carmarthenshire Local History Soc.; Pembrokeshire Records Soc.; Croeso '69 Nat. Cttee; Academie Internationale DiHeraldique; The Heraldry Soc. Trustee, Elvet Lewis Memorial (Gangell), 1967-. Vice-Pres., Carmarthenshire Community Council. DL Carmarthenshire, 1965. Broadcaster (TV and sound radio). Hon. MA Univ. of Wales. OStJ. *Publications:* The Holy Wells of Wales, 1954; The History of Llangunnor, 1965; God Bless the Prince of Wales, 1969; The Princes and Principality of Wales, 1969; (jtly) Royal and Princely Heraldry in Wales, 1969; numerous articles on historical, genealogical and heraldic matters to learned jls. *Recreations:* genealogical research and heraldry, fly-fishing, prowling among ancient ruins. *Address:* Hendre, Springfield Road, Carmarthen. *T:* Carmarthen 7099.

**JONES, Sir Francis Avery,** Kt 1970; CBE 1966; FRCP; Physician, Gastroenterological Department, Central Middlesex Hospital, since 1940; Consultant in Gastroenterology: St Mark's Hospital, since 1950; and to Royal Navy since 1950; *b* 31 May 1910; *s* of Francis Samuel and Marion Rosa Jones; *m* 1934, Dorothea Pfirter; one *s*. *Educ:* Sir John Leman Sch., Beccles; St Bartholomew's Hosp. Baly Research Scholarship, St Bart's, 1936; Julius Mickle Fellowship, University of London, 1952. Goulstonian Lecturer, Royal College of Physicians, 1947; Lumleian Lectr, RCP; Nuffield Lectr in Australia, 1952; First Memorial Lectr, Amer. Gastroenterological Assoc., 1954; Croonian Lectr, RCP, 1969. Examiner: RCP; Univ. of London; Univ. of Leeds. Chairman: Emergency Bed Service; Med. Records Cttee, Dept of Health and Social Security; Member: Med. Sub-cttee, UGC; Management Cttee, King Edward VII Hosp. Fund. Editor of Gut, 1965-70. Hon. Mem., Amer. Proctologic Soc., 1970. Hon. MD Melbourne, 1952. *Publications:* Clinical Gastroenterology (jt author), 2nd edn 1967; Editor of Modern Trends in Gastroenterology First and Second Series, 1952 and 1958. Many articles on Gastroenterology in the Medical Press. *Recreations:* golf; water-side gardening. *Address:* 149 Harley Street, W1N 2DE. *T:* 01-935 4444; Mill House, Nutbourne, Pulborough, West Sussex. *Club:* Athenæum.

**JONES, Francis Edgar,** MBE 1945; FRS 1967; PhD, DSc; FIEE, FRAeS; Managing Director, Mullard Ltd, since 1962; Chairman, Associated Semiconductor Manufacturers Ltd, since 1962; *s* of Edgar Samuel Jones and Annie Maude Lamb; *m* 1942, Jessie Gladys Hazell; four *s* one *d*. *Educ:* Royal Liberty Sch., Romford; King's Coll., London. Demonstrator in Physics, King's Coll., London, 1938-39; at Min. of Aircraft Production Research Estab., finishing as Dep. Chief Scientific Officer, 1940-52; Chief Scientific Officer and Dep. Dir, RAE, Farnborough, 1952-56; Technical Dir, Mullard Ltd, 1956-62. Chairman: Adv. Council on Road Research, 1966-68; Electronic Components Bd, 1967-69; Radio & Electronic Component Manufacturers Fedn, 1967-69; Electronic Valve & Semiconductor Manufacturers Assoc., 1968; Member: Inland Transport Research and Develt Council, 1969; Cttee on Manpower Resources for Sciences and Technology (Chm., Working Group on Migration, 1967); Council for Scientific Policy, 1965-70; Central Adv. Council for Science and Technology, 1966-70; Nat. Defence Industries Council, 1969; Council, IEE, 1965-69; Council, Royal Society, 1968. Fellow, King's Coll., London, 1968. Vis. Prof. of Electrical Engineering, University Coll., London, 1968-. Hon. Fellow, Univ. of Manchester Inst. of Science and Technology, 1970. Hon. DSc: Southampton, 1968; Nottingham, 1968; DUniv Surrey, 1968; Hon. DTech Brunel, 1969. *Publications:* (with R. A. Smith and R. P. Chasmar) The Detection and Measurement of Infrared-Radiation, 1956; articles in Proc. Royal Society, RAeS Jl, Jl IEE, Nature. *Address:* Wendacre, Burton's Way, Chalfont St Giles, Bucks. *T:* Little Chalfont 2228. *Club:* Athenæum.

**JONES, Frank Ernest,** MBE 1947; BSc; CEng, MIEE; Director, Operational Programming, Post Office, Telecommunications. Electrical Industry, 1933-39. Served War of 1939-45, RAFVR. GPO, 1947-; Administrative Staff Coll., 1953; Imperial Defence Coll., 1962. *Address:* Telecommunications Headquarters, 2-12 Gresham Street, EC2. *T:* 01-432 1234.

**JONES, Prof. F(rank) Llewellyn,** CBE 1965; MA, DPhil, DSc Oxon; Vice-Chancellor, University of Wales, since 1969; Principal, University College of Swansea, since 1965 (Vice-Principal, 1954-56 and 1960-62; Acting Principal, 1959-60); *b* 30 Sept. 1907; *er s* of Alfred Morgan Jones, JP, Penrhiwceiber, Glamorgan; *m* 1938, Eileen, *d* of E. T. Davies, Swansea; one *s* (one *d* decd). *Educ:* West Monmouth Sch.; Merton Coll., Oxford. Science Exhibnr 1925; 1st Cl. Nat. Sci. physics, BA 1929; Research Scholar, Merton Coll., 1929, DPhil, MA, 1931; Senior Demy, Magdalen Coll., 1931; Demonstrator in Wykeham Dept of Physics, Oxford, 1929-32; Lecturer in Physics, University Coll. of Swansea, 1932-40; Senior Scientific Officer, Royal Aircraft Establishment, 1940-45; Prof. of Physics, Univ. of Wales, and Head of Dept of Physics, University Coll. of Swansea, 1945-65. Member: Radio Research Board, DSIR, 1951-54; Standing Conference on Telecommunications Research, DSIR, 1952-55; Board of Institute of Physics, 1947-50; Council of Physical Society, 1951-58. Visiting Prof. to Univs in Australia, 1956; Scientific Adviser for Civil Defence, Wales, 1952-59; Senior Sci. Adv., 1959-; Pres., Royal Institution of South Wales, 1958-60; Mem. of Council for Wales and Mon, 1959-63, 1963-; Dir (Part-time), S Wales Gp, BSC, 1968-; Chm., Central Adv. Council for Education (Wales), 1961-64; C. V. Boys' Prizeman, The Physical Soc., 1960; Supernumerary Fellow, Jesus Coll., Oxford, 1965-66, 1969-70. *Publications:* Fundamental Processes of Electrical Contact Phenomena, 1953; The Physics of Electrical Contacts, 1957; Ionization and Breakdown in Gases, 1957, 2nd Edn 1966; The Glow Discharge, 1966; Ionization, Avalanches and Breakdown, 1966; papers in scientific jls on ionization and discharge physics. *Recreations:* railways, walking and gardening. *Address:* Fairwood Lodge, Upper Killay, Swansea. *T:* Swansea 22344. *Club:* Athenæum.

**JONES, Fred,** CBE 1966; Assistant Under-Secretary of State, HM Treasury, since Oct. 1969; *b* 5 May 1920; *s* of late Fred Jones and of Harriet (*née* Nuttall); *m* 1954, Joy (*née* Field); two *s*. *Educ:* Preston Grammar Sch.; St Catherine's Coll., Oxford. Economist, Trades Union Congress, 1951-59; Tutor in Economics and Industrial Relations, Ruskin Coll., Oxford, 1960-62; Economist, National Economic Development Office, 1962-64; Dept of Economic Affairs: Senior Economic Adviser, 1964-66; Asst Sec., 1966-68; Asst Under-Sec. of State, 1968-69. *Recreations:* walking, music, reading. *Address:* 63 Revell Road, Kingston-on-Thames, Surrey. *T:* 01-942 8349.

**JONES, Rt. Hon. Sir (Frederick) Elwyn,** PC 1964; Kt 1964; QC; MP (Lab) West Ham South since 1950 (Plaistow Division of West Ham, 1945-50); *b* 24 Oct. 1909; *s* of Frederick and Elizabeth Jones, Llanelli, Carmarthenshire; *m* 1937, Pearl Binder; one *s* two *d*. *Educ:* Llanelli Grammar Sch.; University of Wales, Aberystwyth; Gonville and Caius Coll., Cambridge (Scholar, MA, Pres. Cambridge Union). Called to Bar, Gray's Inn, 1935, Bencher, 1960; QC 1953; QC (N Ireland) 1958. Major RA (TA); Dep. Judge Advocate, 1943-45; PPS to Attorney-Gen., 1946-51; Attorney General, 1964-70. recorder: of Merthyr Tydfil, 1949-53; of Swansea, 1953-60; of Cardiff, 1960-64; of Kingston-upon-Thames, 1968-. Member of British War Crimes Executive, Nuremberg, 1945. UK Observer, Malta Referendum, 1964. Mem., Inter-Departmental Cttee on the Court of Criminal Appeal, 1964. Mem. of Bar Council, 1956-59. Hon. LLD, University of Wales. Hon. Freeman of Llanelli. FKC 1970. *Publications:* Hitler's Drive to the East, 1937; The Battle for Peace, 1938; The Attack from Within, 1939. *Recreation:* travelling. *Address:* 5 Gray's Inn Square, WC1. *T:* 01-405 4220.
*See also Walter Idris Jones.*

**JONES, Frederick Herbert P.;** *see* Page-Jones.

**JONES, Frederick William F.;** *see* Farey-Jones.

**JONES, Ven. Geoffrey G.;** *see* Gower-Jones.

**JONES, Geoffrey Rippon R.;** *see* Rees-Jones.

**JONES, Air Marshal Sir George,** KBE 1953 (CBE 1942); CB 1943; DFC; RAAF; *b* 22 Nov. 1896; *m* 1919, Muriel Agnes (decd), *d* of F. Stone; one *s* (and one *s* decd). Served Gallipoli and European War, 1914-18 (despatches, DFC); joined RAAF, 1921; Dir Personnel Services, RAAF, 1936-40; Dir of Training, 1940-42; Chief of Air Staff, 1942-52. Dir, Ansett Transport Industries Ltd. *Address:* Flat 10, 104 Cromer Road, Beaumaris, Victoria 3193, Australia. *Club:* Naval and Military (Melbourne).

**JONES, Sir George B. T.;** *see* Todd-Jones.

**JONES, George Lewis;** Coordinator, Senior Seminar in Foreign Policy, US Department of State, since 1964; *b* 18 Jan. 1907; *s* of George Lewis Jones and Emma Little, both of Maryland USA; *m* 1935, Mary Warner Cooke; two *s* one *d*. *Educ:* Univ. of Virginia; Harvard Univ.; Christ's Coll., Cambridge. Clerk to Commercial Attaché, London, 1930-32, Cairo, 1932-34; Asst Trade Comr, Cairo, 1934, Athens, 1935-38; Asst Commercial Attaché, Athens, 1938-41; Third Sec., Cairo, 1941-42; Asst Chief, Div. of Near East Affairs, Dept of State, 1942-46; Second Sec., London, 1946-49; National War Coll., 1949; Policy Planning Staff, Dept of State, 1950; Dir, Office of Near Eastern Affairs, 1950-52; Principal Officer, Tunis, 1952; Counselor, Cairo, 1953; Minister-Counselor, Tehran, 1955; Ambassador to Tunisia, 1956; Asst Sec. of State for Near Eastern and South Asian Affairs, 1959; Minister, American Embassy in London, 1961-64. FZS. *Address:* 1644 Avon Place NW, Washington 20007, USA. *Clubs:* Metropolitan, Chevy Chase (Washington, DC).

**JONES, Geraint Iwan;** *b* 16 May 1917; *s* of Rev. Evan Jones, Porth, Glam; *m* 1st, 1940, M. A. Kemp; one *d*; 2nd, 1949, Winifred Roberts. *Educ:* Caterham Sch.; Royal Academy of Music (Sterndale Bennett Scholar). National Gallery Concerts, 1940-44; played complete organ works of Bach in 16 recitals in London, 1946. Musical dir of Mermaid Theatre performances of Purcell's Dido and Aeneas with Kirsten Flagstad, 1951-53. Formed Geraint Jones Singers and Orchestra, 1951, with whom many Broadcasts, and series of 12 Bach concerts, Royal Festival Hall, 1955; series of all Mozart's piano concertos, Queen Elizabeth Hall, 1969-70. Frequent European engagements, 1947- and regular US and Canadian tours, 1948-. Musical Director: Lake District Festival, 1960-; Kirckman Concert Soc., 1963-. Recordings as organist and conductor; Promenade Concerts; also concerts and recordings as harpsichordist, including sonatas with violinist wife, Winifred Roberts. Grand Prix du Disque, 1959 and 1966. *Recreations:* motoring, photography, antiques, reading. *Address:* Missenden House, Little Missenden, Amersham, Bucks. *T:* Great Missenden 2888.

**JONES, Sir Glyn (Smallwood),** GCMG 1964 (KCMG 1960, CMG 1957); MBE 1944; *b* 9 Jan. 1908; *s* of late G. I. Jones, Chester; *m* 1942, Nancy Madoc, *d* of J. H. Featherstone, CP, South Africa; one *d* (and one *s* decd). *Educ:* King's Sch., Chester; St Catherine's Soc., Oxford Univ. (BA). HM Colonial Service (now HM Overseas Civil Service) N Rhodesia: Cadet, 1931; District Officer, 1933; Commissioner for Native Development, 1950; Acting Development Sec., 1956; Prov. Comr, 1956; Resident Comr, Barotseland, 1957; Sec. for Native Affairs, 1958; Minister of Native Affairs and Chief Comr, 1959; Chief Sec., Nyasaland, 1960-61, Governor, 1961-64; Governor-Gen. of Malawi, 1964-66. KStJ. *Recreations:* shooting, fishing, golf, tennis. *Address:* 38 Calonne Road, Wimbledon, SW19. *Clubs:* Athenæum, Royal Commonwealth Society; Chester City.

**JONES, Griffith Winston Guthrie,** QC 1963; Recorder of Bolton, since 1968; Deputy Chairman of Cumberland Quarter Sessions since 1963; *b* 24 Sept. 1914; second *s* of Rowland Guthrie Jones, Dolgellau, Merioneth; *m* 1959, Anna Maria McCarthy (*d* 1969). *Educ:* Bootham Sch., York; University of Wales; St John's Coll., Cambridge. Called to the Bar, Gray's Inn, 1939. War service in Royal Artillery, 1940-46. *Recreations:* gardening, painting. *Address:* 4 Eaton Road, Cressington Park, Liverpool 19. *T:* 051-427 1969. *Club:* Athenæum (Liverpool).

**JONES, Gwilym Peredur,** MA, LittD (Liverpool); Professor of Economics in the University of Sheffield, 1948-57; Emeritus Professor, 1957; *b* 24 April 1892; *e s* of J. H. and Elizabeth Jones, Birkenhead; *m* 1920, Winifred Agnes Riley, Ulverston, Lancs; two *d*. *Educ:* University of Liverpool. Lord Howard de Walden Fellow in Welsh History, Liverpool

Univ., 1920-23; tutor in History, Economic History and Political Theory for Liverpool Extramural Board, 1920-26; Lecturer in Economic History in University of Sheffield, 1926, Reader, 1946; Sec. to Sheffield Regional Cttee for Adult Education in HM Forces, 1940-46. Vice-Pres., Cumberland and Westmorland Antiq. and Arch. Soc., 1962. *Publications:* The Political Reform Movement in Sheffield (Hunter Arch. Soc. Trans. 1929-30); The Extent of Chirkland, 1391-93, 1933; Workers Abroad, 1939; contrib. to Cambridge Economic History of Europe, Vol. II, 1952; (with Dr A. G. Pool) A Hundred Years of Economic Development, 1940; (with Prof. D. Knoop) The Mediaeval Mason, 1933; also with Prof. D. Knoop, articles in Economic History, Economic History Review, RIBA Journal, etc., on history of building and works on freemasonry, 1932-47; (with Rev. C. M. L. Bouch) The Lake Counties, 1500-1830, 1961. *Recreations:* Welsh studies and fishing. *Address:* Spa House, Witherslack, via Grange-over-Sands, Lancs. *T:* Witherslack 239.

**JONES, Prof. Gwyn,** CBE 1965; Professor of English Language and Literature, University College of South Wales, Cardiff, since 1965; *b* 24 May 1907; *s* of George Henry Jones and Lily Florence (*née* Nethercott); *m* 1928, Alice (*née* Rees). *Educ:* Tredegar Grammar School; University of Wales. Schoolmaster, 1929-35; Lecturer, University Coll., Cardiff, 1935-40; Prof. of Eng. Language and Lit., University Coll. of Wales, Aberystwyth, 1940-64. Dir of Penmark Press, 1939-. Mem. of various learned societies; Pres. of Viking Soc. for Northern Research, 1950-52; Mem. of Arts Council and Chm. of Welsh Arts Council, 1957-67. Fellow, Institut Internat. des Arts et des Lettres, 1960. Knight, Order of the Falcon (Iceland), 1963. *Publications:* A Prospect of Wales, 1948; Welsh Legends and Folk-Tales, 1955; *novels:* Richard Savage, 1935; Times Like These, 1936; Garland of Bays, 1938; The Green Island, 1946; The Flowers Beneath the Scythe, 1952; The Walk Home, 1962; *short stories:* The Buttercup Field, 1945; The Still Waters, 1948; Shepherd's Hey, 1953; *translations:* The Vatnsdalers' Saga, 1942; The Mabinogion, 1948; Egil's Saga, 1960; Eirik the Red, 1961; The Norse Atlantic Saga, 1964; A History of the Vikings, 1968; (ed) Welsh Review, 1939-48; Welsh Short Stories, 1956; contrib. to numerous learned journals. *Recreation:* animals. *Address:* Department of English, University College, Cardiff.

**JONES, Gwyn Owain,** MA, DSc Oxon; PhD Sheffield; Director, National Museum of Wales, since 1968; *b* 29 March 1917; *s* of Dr Abel John Jones, OBE, HMI, and Rhoda May Jones, Cardiff and Porthcawl; *m* 1944, Sheila Heywood; two *d. Educ:* Monmouth Sch.; Port Talbot Secondary Sch.; Jesus Coll., Oxford. Glass Delegacy Research Fellow of University of Sheffield, later mem. of academic staff, 1939-41; Mem. UK Government's Atomic Energy project, 1942-46; Nuffield Foundation Research Fellow at Clarendon Laboratory, Oxford, 1946-49; Reader in Experimental Physics in University of London, at Queen Mary Coll., 1949-53; Prof. of Physics in Univ. of London, and Head of Dept of Physics at Queen Mary Coll., 1953-68; Fellow of Queen Mary Coll. Visiting Prof. Univ. of Sussex, 1964. Mem. Court and Council, Univ. of Wales Inst. of Science and Technology, 1968-; Hon. Professorial Fellow, University Coll., Cardiff, 1969-. *Publications:* Glass, 1956; (in collab.) Atoms and the Universe, 1956; papers on solid-state, glass, low-temperature physics; *novels:* The Catalyst, 1960; Personal File, 1962; Now, 1965. *Address:* National Museum of Wales, Cardiff. *T:* Cardiff 26241. *Club:* Athenæum.

**JONES, Gwyneth;** a Principal Dramatic Soprano, Royal Opera House, Covent Garden, since 1963, Staatsoper Wien since 1966; *b* 7 Nov. 1936; *d* of late Edward George Jones and late Violet (*née* Webster). *Educ:* Twmpath Sec. Mod. Sch., Pontypool, Mon; Royal College of Music, London; Accademia Chigiana, Siena; Zurich Internat. Opera Studio; Maria Carpi Prof., Geneva. Zürich Opera House, 1962-63. Oratorio and recitals as well as opera. Guest Artiste: La Scala, Milan; Berlin State Opera; Munich State Opera; Bayreuth Festival; Tokyo; Zürich; New York; Paris; Marseilles; Monte Carlo; Geneva; Dallas; San Francisco; Los Angeles; Teatro Colon, Buenos Aires; Edinburgh Festival; Welsh National Opera; Rome. Numerous recordings, radio and TV appearances. ARCM. *Address:* Box 380, 8040 Zurich, Switzerland.

**JONES, G(wyneth) Ceris;** Chief Nursing Officer, British Red Cross Society, 1962-70, retired; *b* 15 Nov. 1906; 2nd *d* of late W. R. Jones, OBE, JP, Tre Venal, Bangor, N Wales. *Educ:* Bangor County Sch. for Girls. State Registered Nurse; trained at Nightingale Training Sch., St Thomas' Hosp., 1927-31; Sister Tutor's Certificate, Univ. of London; Diploma in Nursing, Univ. of London. Sister Tutor, St Thomas' Hosp., 1936-39; served with QAIMNS Reserve, 1939-41; Sister-in-charge, Leys School Annexe to Addenbrooke's Hospital, Cambridge, 1941-43; Asst Matron, London Hospital, 1943-47; Matron, Westminster Hospital, 1947-51; London Hospital, 1951-61. *Address:* The Flat, Thelveton Hall, Diss, Norfolk.

**JONES, Gwynoro Glyndwr;** MP (Lab) Carmarthen since 1970; *b* 21 Nov. 1942; *s* of J. E. and A. L. Jones, Minyrafon, Foelgastell, Cefneithin, Carms; *m* 1967, A. Laura Miles; one *s. Educ:* Gwendraeth Grammar Sch.; Cardiff Univ. BSc Econ (Hons) Politics and Economics. Market Research Officer with Ina Needle Bearings Ltd, Llanelli, 1966-67; Economist Section, Wales Gas Bd, 1967-69; Public Relations Officer, Labour Party in Wales, March 1969-June 1970. *Recreations:* sport (played Rugby for both 1st and 2nd class teams). *Address:* 115 Johnston Road, Llanishen, Cardiff. *T:* Cardiff 756195.

**JONES, Harry,** CBE 1955 (OBE 1948; MBE 1945); Foreign Service, retired; *b* 24 July 1894; *s* of Charles Newborn Jones and Harriet Hemingway; *m* 1957, Gwendolen Muriel, *e d* of Ernest MacBeath Kidd, Peterhead, Scotland. *Educ:* Bemrose Sch., Derby. Entered Home Civil Service, 1913; Foreign Office, 1914; released for active service, 1917, 2nd Lieut Northants Regt; returned to Foreign Office, 1919; assimilated to Foreign Service, 1946; Counsellor and Consul General, British Embassy, Washington, 1950-57. *Recreations:* music, photography. *Address:* The Barn, Goose Hill Road, Chester, Conn., USA.

**JONES, Harry,** FRS 1952; BSc, PhD Leeds, PhD Cantab; Professor of Mathematics, Imperial College, London, since 1946, Pro-Rector since 1970; *b* 1905; *m* 1931, Frances Molly O'Neill; one *s* two *d. Educ:* University of Leeds; Trinity Coll., Cambridge. Lecturer at Bristol Univ., 1932-37; Reader in Mathematics, Imperial Coll., 1938-46. *Publications:* (with N. F. Mott) The Theory of the Properties of Metals and Alloys, 1936; Theory of Brillouin Zones and Electronic States in Crystals, 1960; various contributions to scientific journals on Theoretical Physics. *Address:* Imperial College, SW7.

**JONES, Harry Ernest,** CBE 1955; Agent in Great Britain for the Government of Northern Ireland, since 1970; *b* 1 Aug. 1911; *m* 1935, Phyllis Eva Dixon; one *s* one *d*. *Educ:* Stamford Sch.; St John's Coll., Cambridge. Entered Northern Ireland Civil Service, 1934; Min. of Commerce: Principal Officer 1940; Asst Sec. 1942; Perm. Sec. 1955; Industrial Development Adviser to Ministry of Commerce, 1969. FInstD. *Recreation:* fishing. *Address:* 51 Station Road, Nassington, Peterborough, Northants. *T:* Wansford 675; Ulster Office, 11 Berkeley Street, W1X 6BU. *T:* 01-493 0601. *Club:* Royal Commonwealth Society.

**JONES, Henry Arthur,** MA; Vaughan Professor of Education and Head of the Department of Adult Education, University of Leicester, since 1967; *b* 7 March 1917; *er s* of Henry Lloyd Jones; *m* 1942, Molly, 4th *d* of Richard Shenton; two *s*. *Educ:* Chorlton Grammar Sch.; Manchester Univ. George Gissing Prizeman, Manchester Univ., 1936; Graduate Research Fellow, Manchester Univ., 1937, MA 1938. Served War of 1939-45 with Lancs Fusiliers and DLI, 1940-42. Sen. English Master, Chorlton Grammar Sch., 1942-47; Resident Staff Tutor, Manchester Univ., 1947-49; Asst Dir of Extra-Mural Studies, Liverpool Univ., 1949-52, Dep. Dir 1953-57; Principal, The City Literary Institute, 1957-67. Chairman: Assoc. for Adult Education, 1964-67; Education Cttee, Nat. Old People's Welfare Council; Publications, Nat. Inst. of Adult Education. *Publications:* contributes to educational and literary journals. *Address:* Nether House, Great Bowden, Market Harborough, Leics. *T:* Market Harborough 2846.

**JONES, Sir Henry (Frank Harding),** KBE 1965 (MBE 1943); Kt 1956; Chairman: Gas Council, since 1960; British National Committee, World Energy Conference, since 1968; *b* 13 July 1906; *s* of Frank Harding Jones, Housham Tye, Harlow, Essex; *m* 1934, Elizabeth Angela, *d* of J. Spencer Langton, Little Hadham, Herts; three *s* one *d*. *Educ:* Harrow; Pembroke Coll., Cambridge. Served War of 1939-45 with Essex Regt and on staff: France and Belgium, 1939-40; India and Burma, 1942-45. Lieut-Col 1943; Col 1945; Brigadier 1945. Before nationalisation of gas industry was: Deputy Chairman, Watford and St Albans Gas Co., Wandsworth and District Gas Co.; Dir of South Metropolitan, South Suburban and other gas companies. Chm. East Midlands Gas Board, 1949-52; Dep. Chm. Gas Council, 1952-60. Hon. MInstGasE (Pres. 1956-57); MICE; MIChemE; FRSA 1964. Hon. LLD Leeds, 1967; Hon. DSc Leicester, 1970. *Recreations:* fishing, gardening. *Address:* Pathacres, Weston Turville, Aylesbury, Bucks. *T:* Stoke Mandeville 2274. *Clubs:* Athenæum, Bath, MCC.

**JONES, Captain Henry Richmond I.;** *see* Inigo-Jones.

**JONES, Air Commodore Herbert George,** CBE 1942; *b* 26 Nov. 1884; *s* of George Reuben Jones; *m* 1913, Clarisse Lisney West; one *s* one *d*. *Educ:* privately. Joined Royal Army Pay Corps, 1914; Royal Air Force, 1918. Served European War, 1914-18 (despatches twice); War of 1939-45 (despatches twice); retired Nov. 1944. Chartered Sec. *Address:* Lyncroft, Lee-on-Solent, Hants. *T:* Lee-on-Solent 79694.

**JONES, Sir Hildreth G.;** *see* Glyn-Jones.

**JONES, Rev. Professor Hubert C.;** *see* Cunliffe-Jones.

**JONES, Rev. Hugh;** *see* Jones, Rev. R. W. H.

**JONES, Humphrey Lloyd,** CMG 1961; Secretary of the Ashmolean Museum, Oxford, since 1962; *b* 5 April 1910; *s* of Arthur Davis Jones, London; *m* 1938, Edith, *d* of W. H. Tatham, Natal; one *s* two *d*. *Educ:* Westminster (King's Scholar); Christ Church, Oxford (MA). Colonial Administrative Service, Northern Rhodesia, Cadet, 1932; Dist Officer, 1934; Private Sec. to Gov., 1937; Asst Sec., 1948. In 1952: acted as Economic Sec.; MEC and MLC; Chm. Maize Control Bd; Chm. Cold Storage Control Bd; attended Commonwealth Economic Conf. in London as rep. of Northern Rhodesia Govt. Seconded to Federal Govt of Rhodesia and Nyasaland as Under-Sec., 1954; Administrative Sec., Govt of Northern Rhodesia, 1956; MLC; Chm. Whitley Council. Acted as Chief Sec. and Deputy for the Governor on a number of occasions. MEC and MLC, 1961; Minister of Labour and Mines and of Local Government and Social Welfare, Northern Rhodesia Govt, 1961; retired 1962. *Recreations:* travel and photography. *Address:* Ashmolean Museum, Oxford; Bishops Mill, Lucerne Road, Oxford.

**JONES, Prof. Ian C.;** *see* Chester Jones.

**JONES, Ian E.;** *see* Edwards-Jones.

**JONES, Ivan Ellis,** CIE 1944; Principal Classics Master, John Watson's School, Edinburgh, since 1958; *b* 26 June 1903; *s* of James L. Jones, 9 Castlewood Park, Rathmines, Dublin; *m* 1948, Anna, *d* of Peter MacNeil, Eoligarry, Barra; one *s* one *d*. *Educ:* The High Sch., Harcourt Street, Dublin; Trinity Coll., Dublin. Entered Indian Civil Service, 1927; Asst Commissioner in Punjab, 1927; Under-Sec. to Punjab Govt 1929; Deputy Commissioner (Shahpur, Hissar, Multan, Amritsar), 1931-39; Registrar, Co-operative Societies, Punjab, 1940; Dir Food Purchases, Punjab, 1944; Sec. to Govt Punjab Civil Supplies Dept, 1945; Comr Jullundur, 1947; retired from ICS, 1947. Asst Classics Master, Royal High School, Edinburgh, 1949. *Address:* 9 Abbotsford Park, Edinburgh 10. *T:* 031-447 7122.

**JONES, Ivor R.;** *see* Roberts-Jones.

**JONES, Jack L.;** *see* Jones, James Larkin.

**JONES, James;** author; *b* Robinson, Illinois, 6 Nov. 1921; *s* of Ramon Jones and Ada (*née* Blessing); *m* 1957, Gloria Mosolino; one *s* one *d*. *Educ:* Universities of Hawaii and New York. Served with US Army, 1939-44 (bronze star and purple heart). *Publications:* From Here to Eternity, 1951 (National Book Award, US); Some Came Running, 1957; The Pistol, 1959; The Thin Red Line, 1962; Go to the Widow-Maker, 1967; The Ice-Cream Headache, 1968; also numerous short stories. *Recreations:* shooting, skindiving. *Address:* Dell, 750 Third Avenue, New York City 17, NY, USA; 10 Quai d'Orléans, Ile Saint-Louis, Paris 4e, France.

**JONES, James Duncan,** CB 1964; Secretary, Local Government and Development, Department of the Environment, since Oct. 1970; *b* 28 Oct. 1914; *m* 1943, Jenefer Mary Wade; one *s*. *Educ:* Glasgow High Sch.; Glasgow Univ.; University Coll., Oxford. Admiralty, 1941; Ministry of Town and Country Planning: joined 1946; Prin. Priv. Sec., 1947-50; Under-Sec., Min. of Housing and Local Govt, 1958-63; Sec., Local Govt Commn for England, 1958-61; Dep. Sec., Min. of Housing and Local Govt, 1963-66; Dep. Sec., Min. of Transport, 1966-70. Vis. Prof. in Environmental Studies, University College,

London, 1970-. Hon. FRIBA. *Recreations:* reading, looking at buildings, walking. *Address:* 10 Thistle Grove, SW10. *T:* 01-373 2771. *Clubs:* Athenæum; Oxford Union.

**JONES, James Idwal;** *b* 30 June 1900; *s* of James and Elizabeth Bowyer Jones; *m* 1931, Catherine Humphreys; one *s* (one *d* decd). *Educ:* Ruabon Grammar Sch.; Normal Coll., Bangor. Certificated Teacher, 1922. BSc Econ., London Univ. (Externally), 1936. Headmaster, Grango Secondary Modern Sch., Rhosllanerchrugog, near Wrexham, 1938. MP (Lab) Wrexham Div. of Denbighshire, 1955-70. *Publications:* A Geography of Wales, 1938; An Atlas of Denbighshire, 1950; Atlas Hanesyddol o Gymru, 1952 (A Welsh Historical Atlas of Wales); A Geographical Atlas of Wales, 1955; A Historical Atlas of Wales, 1955; A New Geography of Wales, 1960; J. R. Jones (Ramoth), 1967. *Recreations:* photography and landscape painting. *Address:* Maelor, Ponciau, Wrexham, Wales.

**JONES, James Larkin, (Jack),** MBE 1950; General Secretary, Transport and General Workers' Union, since 1969; Deputy Chairman, National Ports Council, since 1967; Member, TUC General Council, since 1968; *b* 29 March 1913; *m* 1938, Evelyn Mary Taylor; two *s*. *Educ:* elementary sch., Liverpool. Worked in engineering and docks industries, 1927-39. Liverpool City Councillor, 1936-39; Coventry District Sec., Transport and General Workers' Union, also District Sec., Confedn of Shipbuilding and Engineering Unions, 1939-55; Midlands Regional Sec., Transport and General Workers' Union, 1955-63, Asst Executive Sec., 1963-69. Mem., Midland Regional Bd for Industry, 1942-46, 1954-63; Chm., Midlands TUC Advisory Cttee, 1948-63. Coventry City Magistrate, 1950-63; Executive Chm., Birmingham Productivity Cttee, 1957-63; Member: Labour Party Nat. Exec. Cttee, 1964-67; Nat. Cttee for Commonwealth Immigrants, 1965-69; Chm., nat. Staff Council, BRS, 1966-; Mem. numerous other joint industrial bodies. Director, Tribune, 1968-. Vis. Fellow, Nuffield Coll., Oxford, 1970-. *Recreation:* walking. *Address:* 74 Ruskin Park House, Champion Hill, SE5. *T:* 01-274 7067; (office) 01-828 7788. *Club:* Tom Mann Trade Union (Coventry).

**JONES, Ven. James William Percy;** Archdeacon of Huntingdon, 1947-55, Canon Emeritus since 1955; *b* 22 April 1881; *s* of late Canon D. Jones; *m* 1917, Judith Efa Bonnor-Maurice (*d* 1959); one *s* one *d* (and one *s* killed in action). *Educ:* Oswestry; Pembroke Coll., Oxford, Queen's Coll., Birmingham, 1904; MA 1907. Hon. CF 1921. Curate: Perry Barr, 1905-08; Nassington with Yarwell, 1908-13 and 1914-15; Llanfechain, 1913-14; Market Harborough, 1915-16. Asst Dir of Religious Education, 1922-32; Rural Dean of Leightonstone, 1930-47; Exam. Chaplain to Bishop of Ely, 1941; Hon. Canon Ely Cathedral, 1941-47, Canon Emeritus, 1954; Vicar of Great Gidding and Little Gidding, 1916-57, with Steeple Gidding, 1926-57. *Recreation:* formerly golf. *Address:* Cae Hywel, Llansantffraid, Montgomeryshire.

**JONES, Jennifer, (Mrs David O. Selznick);** Film actress (US); *b* Tulsa, Okla; *d* of Philip R. Isley and Flora Mae (*née* Suber); *m* 1st, 1939, Robert Walker (marr. diss. 1945); two *s*; 2nd, 1949, David O. Selznick (*d* 1965); one *d*. *Educ:* schools in Okla and Tex; Northwestern Univ., Evanston, Illinois; American Academy of Dramatic Arts, New York City. Films, since 1943, include: The Song of Bernadette; Since You Went Away; Cluny Brown; Love Letters; Duel in the Sun; We Were Strangers; Madame Bovary; Portrait of Jenny; Carrie; Wild Heart; Ruby Gentry; Indiscetion of an American Wife; Beat the Devil; Love is a Many-Splendoured Thing; The Barretts of Wimpole Street; A Farewell to Arms; Tender is the Night; The Idol. Awards include: American Academy of Motion Pictures, Arts and Sciences Award, 1943; 4 other Academy nominations, etc. Medal for Korean War Work. *Address:* 1520 Tower Grove Drive, Beverly Hills, Calif, USA.

**JONES, John Cyril,** CBE 1951; BSc; MICE, FIMechE; Adviser for Technical Education, Colonial Office and Ministry of Overseas Development, 1956-67; *b* 30 Oct. 1899; *s* of John Jones, Swindon, Wilts; *m* 1928, Doris Anne, *d* of A. Tanner, Swindon, Wilts; one *d*. *Educ:* The College, Swindon; Loughborough Coll., Leics. Design and Research asst, GWR Co., 1922-31; Head of Dept, Loughborough Coll., 1931-34; Principal: St Helen's Municipal Coll., 1934-37, Cardiff Tech. Coll., 1937-41, Royal Tech. Coll., Salford, 1941-44; Dir of Educn, The Polytechnic, Regent Street, W1, 1944-56; Adviser for Tech. Educn to Colonial Office, 1956-61, and Dept of Tech. Co-operation, 1961-64. Hon. Sec. Assoc. of Tech. Instns, 1944-56; Hon. Treas. Assoc. of Tech. Instns, 1956-67; Pres., Assoc. of Prins of Tech. Instns, 1951; Mem. Central Advisory Council for Education (Eng.), 1947-56; RAF Educ. Advisory Cttee, 1948-56; Advisory Cttee on Educ. in Colonies, 1953-56; Council for Overseas Colls of Art, Science and Technology, and Council for Tech. Educ. and Training in Overseas Countries, 1949-69. Member: Fulton Commn on Education in Sierra Leone, 1954; Keir Commn on Technical Education in N Rhodesia, 1960. Mem. Council for External Students, University London, 1954-66. Mem. of Council, RSA, 1960-66. Dir Asian Study Tour of Vocational Educ. and Training in the USSR, 1961, 1963; International Bank for Reconstruction and Development Missions to: Pakistan, 1962, 1963; Morocco and Kenya, 1965; Jamaica and Tunisia, 1966; Zambia, Greece, and Guyana, 1968; Cameroun, Tchad, Gabon and Pakistan, 1969; Indonesia, 1970. Mem. International Commn on Tech. Educ. in Sudan, 1966. Officier d'Académie (France), 1950; elected Hon. Mem. City and Guilds of London Inst., 1964. *Publications:* papers on higher technological education and reports on development of technical education in various overseas countries. *Recreations:* books, music, and foreign travel. *Address:* 26 Grand Marine Court, Durley Gardens, Bournemouth BH2 5HS.

**JONES, John Edward; His Honour Judge Jones;** County Court Judge since 1969; *b* 23 Dec. 1914; *s* of Thomas Robert Jones, Liverpool; *m* 1945, Katherine Elizabeth Edwards, SRN, *d* of Ezekiel Richard Edwards, Liverpool; one *s* one *d*. *Educ:* Liverpool Institute High School. ACIS 1939; BCom London 1942; LLB London 1945. Called to Bar, Gray's Inn, 1945; Member of Northern Circuit, 1946; Dep. Chm., Lancs QS, 1966-69. Dep. Chm., Workmen's Compensation (Supplementation) and Pneumoconiosis and Byssinosis Benefit Boards, 1968-69. JP Lancs, 1966. *Address:* India Buildings, Water Street, Liverpool.

**JONES, Air Vice-Marshal John Ernest A.;** *see* Allen-Jones.

**JONES, John Ernest P.;** *see* Powell-Jones.

**JONES, John Harry;** Emeritus Professor, University of Leeds; *b* Wales, 27 July 1881; *m* 1914, Eva (*d* 1955), *d* of late Henry Cuthbertson, Journalist, Newcastle and

Oxford; one *d*. *Educ:* Swansea Grammar Sch.; University Coll., Cardiff; Universities of Leipzig and Berlin. BA first-class Hons in Economics and Political Science, 1903; MA, 1904; Fellow University of Wales, 1904-7; LLD *Hon. Causa*, University of Wales, 1946. Asst Lecturer in Economics, University of Liverpool, 1907-9; Lecturer in Social Economics, University of Glasgow, 1909-19; Prof. of Economics and head of Economics Dept, University of Leeds, 1919-46; OTC, 1915; War Trade Dept, 1915; Ministry of Munitions, 1916-18; of Labour, 1918; Appointed Mem. of Trade Boards, 1919-22; Impartial Mem. West Riding Agricultural Wages Cttee, 1925-46; formerly Mem. of Board of Education Consultative Cttee on Adult Education; Mem. Economic Advisory Council Cttee on the Slaughtering of Livestock, 1930-32 and Cttee on Cattle Diseases, 1932-34; Pres. Section F. of British Association, 1933; Chairman, Nova Scotia Royal Commission of Economic Enquiry, 1934; Mem., Royal Commission on the Geographical Distribution of the Industrial Population, 1937; Mem. Road Research Board; Impartial Mem. Surrey Agricultural Wages Cttee, 1947. Guy Silver Medal, Royal Statistical Society, 1934; Hon. Treas. Royal Statistical Society, 1947-50. *Publications:* The Tinplate Industry, 1914; The Economics of War and Conquest, 1915; Social Economics, 1919; Economics of Private Enterprise, 1926; The Federal Reserve System, 1926; The Economics of Saving, 1934; Editor, The Economics Educator, 1928-29; Report on Road Accidents published for Ministry of Transport by HM Stationery Office, 1946; The Structure of Industry, 1948; Josiah Stamp: Public Servant, 1964, etc. *Club:* National Liberal.

**JONES, Air Marshal Sir John Humphrey E.;** *see* Edwardes Jones.

**JONES, Rev. J(ohn) Ithel;** Principal and Professor of Theology and the Philosophy of Religion at South Wales Baptist College since 1958; *b* 1 Jan. 1911; *s* of David Jones and Elizabeth Catherine Jones; *m* 1938, Hannah Mary Rees. *Educ:* Cyfarthfa Castle Sch., Merthyr Tydfil; University Coll., Cardiff; S Wales Baptist Coll. BA (Wales) 1st cl. hons Philosophy and 2nd cl. hons Welsh; BD (Wales); MA (Wales), Theology. Pastorates: Porthcawl, 1936-40; Horfield, Bristol, 1940-50; Haven Green, Ealing, 1950-57. Moderator, Free Church Federal Coun. of England and Wales, 1963-64; Dean of Divinity for University of Wales, 1964-67; Pres., Baptist Union of Gt Britain and Ireland, 1967-68. Mem. for Wales on Panel of Religious Advisers, ITA and Welsh Cttee, ITA, 1966-69. Lecture tours in USA, Australia, New Zealand. Hon. DD, Eastern, Pa, 1966; Hon. LLD, Baylor, 1966. *Publications:* Colossians, in New Bible Commentary, 1953; Temple and Town, 1961; The Holy Spirit and Christian Preaching, 1967; Facing the New World, 1968. *Recreations:* golf, music, motoring. *Address:* 54 Richmond Road, Cardiff. *T:* Cardiff 29860.

**JONES, Sir (John) Kenneth (Trevor),** Kt 1965; CBE 1956; Legal Adviser to the Home Office since 1956; *b* 11 July 1910; *s* of John Jones and Agnes Morgan; *m* 1940, Menna, *d* of Cyril O. Jones; two *s*. *Educ:* King Henry VIII Grammar Sch., Abergavenny; University Coll. of Wales, Aberystwyth; St John's Coll., Cambridge. Called to the Bar, Lincoln's Inn, 1937. Served Royal Artillery, 1939-45. Entered the Home Office as a Legal Asst, 1945. Mem. of the Standing Cttee on Criminal Law Revision, 1959-. *Address:* 54 Westminster Gardens, SW1. *T:* 01-834 4950. *Club:* Athenæum.

**JONES, Prof. John Kenyon Netherton,** FRS 1957; FRSC 1960; FCIC 1961; Chown Research Professor, Queen's University, Kingston, Ontario, since 1953; *b* 28 Jan. 1912; *m* 1937, Marjorie Ingles Noon; two *s* one *d*. *Educ:* Waverley Grammar Sch., Birmingham; Birmingham Univ. BSc (Hons) 1933; PhD 1936; DSc 1948. Lecturer, Bristol University, 1936-44; Senior Lecturer, Manchester Univ., 1945-48; Reader, Bristol Univ., 1948-53. *Publications:* in Jl of Chem. Soc., Biochem. Jl, Canadian Jl of Chem. *Recreations:* photography, gardening. *Address:* Box 31, Treasure Island, RRI, Kingston, Ontario, Canada. *T:* 613-548-4340.

**JONES, John Morgan,** CB 1964; CBE 1946; Secretary Welsh Department, Ministry of Agriculture, 1944-68; *b* 20 July 1903; *s* of late Richard and Mary Ellen Jones, Pertheirin, Caersws, Montgomeryshire; *m* 1933, Dorothy Morris, *yr d* of late David Morris Wigley, Llanbrynmair, Montgomeryshire, and of Margaret Anne Wigley, Machynlleth; no *c*. *Educ:* Newtown County Sch.; University Coll. of Wales, Aberystwyth. BA 1922; Hons in Econ. 1923, History 1924; MA 1926. Research Staff Dept of Agric. Economics, University Coll. of Wales, 1924-30; Marketing Officer, Min. of Agric. and Fisheries, 1930-35; Registrar Univ. Coll. of Wales, Aberystwyth, 1936; seconded to Min. of Agric. as Minister's Liaison Officer for mid- and south-west Wales, 1940; Chm. Cardigan War Agric. Exec. Cttee, 1943. *Publications:* Economeg Amaethyddiaeth, 1930; articles on rural economics, mainly in Welsh Journal of Agriculture. *Recreations:* walking the hills and gardening. *Address:* Maesnewydd, North Road, Aberystwyth. *T:* Aberystwyth 2507. *Club:* Farmers'.

**JONES, Captain John Murray R.;** *see* Rymer-Jones.

**JONES, Sir John Prichard;** *see* Prichard-Jones.

**JONES, Rev. Prebendary John Stephen Langton;** Residentiary Canon and Precentor of Wells Cathedral, 1947-67, Prebendary, 1967; *b* 21 May 1889; *m* 1921, Jeanne Charlotte Dujardin; three *s* one *d*. *Educ:* Dover College; Jesus College, Cambridge. Asst Curate of Halifax Parish Church, 1914; Asst Curate, Hambleden, Berks, 1919; Vicar of Yiewsley, Middx, 1921; Rector of W Lydford, Taunton, 1939-47. *Address:* 20 Millers Gardens, Wells, Som BA5 2TW.

**JONES, John Walter;** Provost of The Queen's College, Oxford, 1948-62, retired; Hon. Fellow of Emmanuel College, Cambridge, 1949; Hon. Fellow of Queen's College, Oxford, 1962; *b* 21 July 1892; *s* of late William and Hannah Jane Jones, Merthyr Tydfil. *Educ:* Merthyr County Sch.; University Coll. of Wales, Aberystwyth; Emmanuel Coll., Cambridge (Scholar and Research Student). First Class in Law Tripos, Parts I and II; George Long Prize and Yorke Prize, Cambridge; Constitutional Law Prize, Barstow Scholarship and Certificate of Honour of the Inns of Court; Barrister-at-Law of the Inner Temple; Lecturer and Tutor in Law, University of Liverpool, 1920-26; Fellow, Tutor, and Praelector in Law, Queen's Coll., Oxford, 1927-48; University Lecturer in Law, 1937-48; Junior Proctor, 1942-43. *Publications:* Bona Fide Purchase of Goods (Yorke Prize Essay, 1918); Historical Introduction to the Theory of Law, 1940, repr. 1956, 1969; The Law and Legal Theory of the Greeks, 1956; contributions to various legal periodicals. *Recreation:* walking. *Address:* 68 Staunton Road, Headington, Oxford. *T:* Oxford 61315. *Club:* National Liberal.

**JONES, Air Chief Marshal Sir John (Whitworth),** GBE 1954 (CBE 1945); KCB 1949 (CB 1942); psa; retd; *b* 28 Feb. 1896; *s* of Lt-Col Aylmer Jones; *m* 1917, Anne Brown; one *s* decd. *Educ:* Magdalen College Sch., Oxford; St Paul's Sch. Temporary Air Commodore, 1942; Acting Air Vice-Marshal, 1942; Air Cdre, 1943; Air Marshal, 1949; Air Chief Marshal, 1953; Asst Deputy Chief of Staff, SEAC, 1943-45; RAF Dir-Gen of Organisation, Air Ministry, 1945-47; AOC Air Headquarters, Malaya, 1948; Air Officer Commanding-in-Chief Technical Training Command, 1948-52; Mem. for Supply and Organisation, Air Council, 1952-54, retired 1954. Commander, Order of Crown (Belgium). *Address:* 6 Gonville House, Manor Fields, Putney Hill, SW15.

**JONES, Joseph,** CBE 1941; *b* 10 Jan. 1890; *s* of late David E. Jones, Llangollen, Denbighshire; *m* 1919, Gwladys M. (*d* 1961), *d* of Owen Davies, Llanmaes, St Fagans, near Cardiff; (one *d* decd). *Educ:* Llangollen; Cardiff. Joined Glamorgan Constabulary, 1911; Superintendent, 1932; Deputy Chief Constable, 1936; Chief Constable of Glamorgan, 1937-51. Officer Brother Order of St John; King's Police Medal for Distinguished Service, 1947. *Recreations:* bowls, shooting, etc. *Address:* Fron Esgyn, Fron Cysyllte, Llangollen, Denbighshire.

**JONES, Keith M.;** *see* Miller Jones.

**JONES, Hon. Mrs Keith Miller;** *see* Askwith, Hon. Betty E.

**JONES, Sir Kenneth;** *see* Jones, Sir J. K. T.

**JONES, Kenneth (George Illtyd);** QC 1962; Recorder of Wolverhampton since 1966; Deputy Chairman, Herefordshire Quarter Sessions, since 1961; *b* 26 May 1921; *s* of Richard Arthur Jones and late Olive Jane Jones, Radyr, Cardiff; *m* 1947, Dulcie, *yr d* of Thomas William Thursfield and late Winifred Thursfield, Linthorpe, Middlesbrough; one *s* two *d*. *Educ:* Brigg Gram. Sch.; University Coll., Oxford (1939-41, 1945-46), MA; Treas., Oxford Union Society, 1941; served in Shropshire Yeo. (76th Medium Regt RA), 1942-45; Staff Captain, HQ 13th Corps, 1945 (despatches). Called to Bar, Gray's Inn, 1946; joined Oxford Circuit, 1947; Mem. Gen. Council of the Bar, 1961-65, 1968-69; Bencher, Gray's Inn, 1969-. Recorder of Shrewsbury, 1964-66. *Address:* 1 Crown Office Row, Temple, EC4. *T:* 01-353 3372; Treetops, Wantage Road, Streatley, Reading RG8 9LB. *T:* Goring-on-Thames 3234; Cedrwydd, Long Street, Newport, Pembrokeshire.

**JONES, Maj.-Gen. Leonard Hamilton H.;** *see* Howard-Jones.

**JONES, Leonard Ivan S.;** *see* Stranger-Jones.

**JONES, Leslie,** MA; JP; Secretary for Welsh Education, Department of Education and Science, since 1970; *b* Tumble, Carms, 27 April 1917; *y s* of late William Jones, ME and Joanna (*née* Peregrine); *m* 1948, Glenys, *d* of late D. R. Davies, Swansea; one *s* one *d*. *Educ:* Gwendraeth Valley Grammar Sch.; Univ. of Wales. Served with RN, 1940-46 (Lieut RNVR). UC Swansea, 1937-40 and 1946-47 (1st cl. hons Econs); Lectr in Econs, Univ. of Liverpool, 1947-51; Lectr and Sen. Lectr in Econs, UC Cardiff, 1952-65; Dir, Dept of Extra-Mural Studies, UC Cardiff, 1965-69. JP Cardiff 1966. *Publications:* The British Shipbuilding Industry, 1958; articles on maritime, coal, iron and steel industries; industrial economics generally. *Recreations:* walking, gardening. *Address:* The Education Office for Wales, Department of Education and Science, 31 Cathedral Road, Cardiff; 43 Cyncoed Road, Cardiff. *Club:* National Liberal.

**JONES, Lewis;** *see* Jones, George Lewis.

**JONES, Lewis C.;** *see* Carter-Jones.

**JONES, Martin;** Professor Emeritus of Agricultural Botany, University of Newcastle upon Tyne (formerly King's College), since 1962; *s* of J. G. Jones, Ruel Issa, Bow-street, Cardiganshire; *m* 1927, Olwen Elizabeth Watkin; two *s*. *Educ:* University Coll. of Wales, Aberystwyth. Welsh Plant Breeding Station, Aberystwyth, 1920-28; Jealott's Hill Agric. Research Stn, Berks, 1928-37; North of Scotland Coll. of Agriculture, Aberdeen, 1937-47; Prof. of Agricultural Botany, King's Coll., Newcastle upon Tyne, 1947-62. Pres., Brit. Grassland Soc., 1951-52; Pres., Agric. Section of Brit. Assoc., Aberdeen, 1963. Chm. Scientific Advisory Cttee, Sports Turf Research Inst., Bingley, 1948-60. *Address:* Y Winllan, Antaron Avenue, Southgate, Aberystwyth. *T:* Aberystwyth 7781. *Club:* Farmers'.

**JONES, Judge Marvin;** Senior Judge, United States Court of Claims; *b* near Gainsville, Tex.; *s* of Horace K. and Dosia Jones. *Educ:* Southwestern Univ. (AB); University of Tex. (LLB). Chm. Board Legal Examiners, West Texas, 1912-16; served in Congress, 1917-40; Chm. House Cttee on Agriculture, 1931-40. During War of 1939-45, Asst to James F. Byrnes, Dir of Economic Stabilization. Pres. of First Internat. Conf. of 44 nations on Food and Agriculture, Hot Springs, Va., 1943; War Food Administrator (US), 1943-45; Chief Judge US Court of Claims, 1947-64. *Publications:* How War Food Saved American Lives, 1945; Should Uncle Sam Pay–When and Why?, 1963. *Recreation:* fishing. *Address:* (Business) Senior Judge, US Court of Claims, 717 Madison Place, NW, Washington, DC 20005; (Home) Amarillo, Tex. *TA:* Business 382-2768-Washington. *Clubs:* University, National Press, Lawyers (Washington, DC); Amarillo (Amarillo, Texas).

**JONES, Sir Melvill;** *see* Jones, Sir B. M.

**JONES, Mervyn;** *see* Jones, Thomas Mervyn.

**JONES, Mervyn;** author; *b* 27 Feb. 1922; *s* of Ernest Jones and Katharine (*née* Jokl); *m* 1948, Jeanne Urquhart; one *s* two *d*. *Educ:* Abbotsholme School; New York University. Assistant Editor: Tribune, 1955-59; New Statesman, 1966-68; Drama Critic, Tribune, 1959-67. *Publications:* No Time to be Young, 1952; The New Town, 1953; The Last Barricade, 1953; Helen Blake, 1955; On the Last Day, 1958; Potbank, 1961; Big Two, 1962; A Set of Wives, 1965; Two Ears of Corn, 1965; John and Mary, 1966; A Survivor, 1968; Joseph, 1970. *Address:* 9 Hardy Road, SE3. *T:* 01-858 5942.

**JONES, Norman Edward,** CMG 1969; company director; *b* 2 Aug. 1904; *s* of Edward J. Jones; *m* 1928, Mabel Elizabeth Swainson; one *s*. *Educ:* Hamilton and Cooks Hill High Schs, Newcastle, Australia; Newcastle Technical Coll. (Dip.Chem. Hons). Managing Dir, The Broken Hill Proprietary Co. Ltd, 1952-66. Director: The Broken Hill Proprietary Co. Ltd; Australian Paper Manufacturers Ltd; The National Bank of Australasia Ltd; Colonial Mutual Life Assce Soc. Ltd. Pres., The Iron and Steel Institute, 1967-68. Hon. DSc: Univ. of New South Wales; Univ. of Newcastle, NSW. *Recreation:* gardening. *Address:* 136

Kooyong Road, Toorak, Victoria 3142, Australia. *T:* 20 3365. *Clubs:* Melbourne, Australian, Adelaide, Union, Athenæum (Melbourne); Weld (Perth); Newcastle (Newcastle).

**JONES, Norman Stewart C.;** *see* Carey Jones.

**JONES, Captain Oscar Philip,** CVO 1952; OBE 1945; FRGS; FRAeS; *b* 15 Oct. 1898; *s* of Oscar Jones, Beckenham; *m* 1st, 1920, Olive Elizabeth Turner (decd); one *s* decd; 2nd, 1963, Kathleen Jacobs, ARAM, JP, Liverpool. *Educ:* Beckenham, Kent. Served European War, Royal Engineers, 1916-17; Royal Flying Corps and RAF, 1917-19. Berkshire Aviation Tours, 1920-22; Instone Airline, 1922-24; Imperial Airways, 1924-40; Brit. Overseas Airways Corporation, 1940-65; Senior Captain North Atlantic, 1946-55; Special Liaison Officer, BOAC, Worldwide Goodwill and Lecture tours, 1955-65. RAFO and RAFVR, 1924-54. Founder Mem. and Warden, Guild of Air Pilots, 1929 (Deputy Master 1934); Warden, 1954-58; Cumberbach Trophy, 1931; Master Pilot's Certificate, 1935; FAI Gliding Certificate "C", 1939; OC No. 2 ATA Pool, 1940; Flight Capt., Atlantic, 1941; Flight Capt., Landplanes, 1942-45; Air Efficiency Award, 1943; Wing Cmdr, RAFO, 1945. Mem. BOAC "25" Club (Pres. 1952), also Speedbird Club. Flew the Queen, when Princess Elizabeth, to Canada, 1951; Britannia Trophy Award, 1951. Guild Master Pilot's Certificate, 1954. Past Pres., Bull-Terrier Club. *Recreations:* swimming, dog judging (International), light aeroplane flying, riding. *Address:* Squirrels, Spinney Lane, Pulborough, Sussex. *T:* West Chiltington 3140. *Clubs:* Royal Aero, Royal Air Force Reserves; Southern Aero (Shoreham); Scottish Flying; Tiger.

**JONES, Penry;** Head of Religious Broadcasting, BBC, since 1967; *b* 18 Aug. 1922; *s* of Joseph William and Edith Jones; *m* Beryl Joan Priestley; two *d*. *Educ:* Rock Ferry High Sch.; Liverpool Univ. Gen. Sec., YMCA, Altrincham, 1940; Sec., SCM, Southern Univs, 1945; Industrial Sec., Iona Community, 1948; Religious Programmes Producer, ABC Television, 1958; Religious Programmes Officer of ITA, 1964. *Recreations:* climbing, swimming, Rugby football. *Address:* 48 Dartmouth Row, SE10. *T:* 01-692 2117.

**JONES, Brig. Percival de Courcy,** OBE 1953; Chief Secretary, The Royal Life Saving Society, since 1965; *b* 9 Oct. 1913; *s* of P. de C. Jones, Barnsley; *m* 1st, 1947, Anne Hollins (marr. diss., 1951); one *s*; 2nd, 1962, Elaine Garnett. *Educ:* Oundle; RMC, Sandhurst. Commissioned KSLI 1933; Staff Coll., 1942; comd Northamptons, Burma, 1944-45; Staff Coll. Instructor, 1949-50; AA & QMG, 11th Armoured Div., 1951-53; comd 1st KSLI, 1953-55; AQMG, War Office, 1955-58; NATO Defence Coll., 1958-59; Bde Comdr, 1959-62; retd 1962. *Recreations:* ski-ing, shooting, riding. *Address:* Blorenge House, Ashampstead, Berks. *T:* Yattendon 378.

**JONES, Maj.-Gen. Percy George C.;** *see* Calvert-Jones.

**JONES, Sir Peter (Fawcett) Benton,** 3rd Bt *cr* 1919; OBE 1945; *b* 9 Jan. 1911; *s* of Sir Walter Benton Jones, 2nd Bt and Lily Marguerite (*d* 1938), *d* of late James Dixon Fawcett; *S* father, 1967; *m* 1936, Nancy, *o c* of late Warley Pickering; one *s* one *d*. *Educ:* Charterhouse; Trinity Coll., Cambridge (MA). FCA; Chartered Accountant, 1932-39. Served with Army, 1939-45 (despatches); Lieut-Col 1943. United Steel Cos, 1945-70. *Recreations:* shooting, fishing, stalking. *Heir:* *s* Simon Warley Frederick Benton Jones [*b* 11 Sept. 1941; *m* 1966, Margaret Fiona, *d* of David Rutherford Dickson, Ipswich]. *Address:* Irnham, near Grantham, Lincs. *T:* Corby Glen 336. *Club:* Boodle's.

**JONES, Peter Howard,** CB 1968; Assistant Under-Secretary of State, Ministry of Defence, 1964-68; *b* 3 March 1911; *s* of William Howard Jones, MRCS, LRCP, and Mabelle Rose Jones; *m* 1939, Ann Hall; two *d*. *Educ:* St Paul's Sch.; Balliol Coll., Oxford. 1st Cl., Class. Mods and Litt. Hum. Entered Admiralty, 1934; Under-Sec., 1957. *Address:* Holme Hurst, Dedswell Drive, West Clandon, Guildford, Surrey. *T:* Clandon 452.

**JONES, Philip Asterley,** LLB London; Solicitor; Commissioner for Oaths; Principal Lecturer in Law, City of Birmingham Polytechnic; *b* 21 June 1914; *s* of Leonard Asterley Jones, St Albans; *m* 1941, Ruth Florence Davis; two *s* (and one *s* decd). *Educ:* Tonbridge Sch.; Law Society's Sch. of Law. Admitted as Solicitor, 1937. Mem. St Albans City Council, 1938. MP (Lab) Hitchin, 1945-50. Served War of 1939-45; Driver RASC Sept. 1939, 2nd Lieut RASC Dec. 1940, Staff Capt., 1942, DAQMG 1943 (despatches). Lecturer in Law at Law Soc., 1945-51; Asst Sec. Law Soc., 1951; Editor, Solicitors' Journal, 1956-66; Editor, Local Govt Chronicle, 1950-63, Legal Editor, 1963-69. *Publications:* (with Rupert Cross) An Introduction to Criminal Law, 1948, 6th edn, 1968; Cases on Criminal Law, 1949, 4th edn 1968. *Address:* 89 Ferndown Road, Solihull, Warwicks. *T:* 021-705 2646. *Clubs:* New Arts Theatre; Birmingham Press.

**JONES, Philip R. B.;** *see* Bence-Jones.

**JONES, Mrs Rachel (Marianne);** *b* 4 Aug. 1908; *d* of John Powell Jones Powell, solicitor, Brecon, and Kathleen Mamie Powell; *m* 1935, William Edward Jones (*see* Very Rev. William Edward Jones); one *s* three *d*. *Educ:* Princess Helena Coll., Ealing; Bedford Coll., University of London. Subwarden, Time and Talents Settlement, Bermondsey, 1931-32; Member: Bd of Governors, Fairbridge Farm Sch., Western Australia, 1945-49; Council for Wales and Mon, 1959-66; Nat. Governor for Wales of BBC and Chm. of Broadcasting Council for Wales, 1960-65. Member: Governing Body of the Church in Wales; Court and Council of Nat. Museum of Wales; Pres., St David's Diocesan Mothers' Union, 1965-70. *Recreations:* music, gardening. *Address:* Caldey View, Penally, Tenby, Pembrokeshire. *T:* Tenby 3112.

**JONES, Ranald M. H.;** *see* Handfield-Jones.

**JONES, Raymond Edgar;** British Deputy High Commissioner, in South Australia and Northern Territory, since 1967; *b* 6 June 1919; *s* of Edgar George Jones, Portsmouth; *m* 1942, Joan Mildred Clark; one *s* two *d*. *Educ:* Portsmouth Northern Grammar Sch. Entered Admiralty service as Clerical Officer, 1936; joined RAF, 1941; commissioned, 1943; returned to Admty as Exec. Officer, 1946; transf. to Foreign Service, 1948; Singapore, 1949; Second Sec., Rome, 1950; Bahrain, 1952; Rio de Janeiro, 1955; Consul, Philadelphia, 1958; FO, 1961; First Sec., Copenhagen, 1963; Consul, Milan, 1965; Toronto (Dir of British Week), 1966. *Recreations:* music, gardening. *Address:* 44 Stanley Street, Leabrook, S Australia 5068, Australia. *T:* Adelaide 31.9659. *Clubs:* Royal Commonwealth Society; Adelaide (Adelaide).

**JONES, Reginald Ernest,** MBE 1942; Chief Scientific Officer, Ministry of Technology, 1965-69, retired; *b* 16 Jan. 1904; *m* 1933, Edith Ernestine Kressig; one *s* one *d*. *Educ:* Marylebone Gram. Sch.; Imperial Coll. of Science and Technology. MSc, DIC, FIEE. International Standard Electric Corp., 1926-33; GPO, 1933-65 (Asst Engr-in-Chief, 1957). Bronze Star (US), 1943. *Recreations:* music, gardening, walking. *Address:* 22 Links Road, Epsom, Surrey. *T:* Epsom 23625.

**JONES, Reginald Trevor,** CIE 1943; MC 1918; MInstCE 1938; *b* 19 Dec. 1888; *s* of late Trevor Jones, Midland Bank, Carlisle; *m* 1922, Edith Aileen, *d* of late W. Theodore Carr, CBE, MP, Carlisle; one *d*. *Educ:* Malvern Coll. Articled E. Purnell Hooley, MInstCE, 1906-10; joined Indian Service of Engineers, 1912; Chief Engineer and Sec. to Govt, Panjab PWD, 1939; retired Dec. 1943. FInstCE. Capt. 5th Royal Leicestershire Regt, 1914; seconded IA, 1915, attached RE (1st KGO Bengal Sappers and Miners); NWFP, Mesopotamia, Palestine, 1915-19 (despatches, MC). *Address:* Appletrees, Love Lane, Petersfield, Hants. *T:* Petersfield 3573.

**JONES, Reginald Victor,** CB 1946; CBE 1942; FRS 1965; Professor of Natural Philosophy, University of Aberdeen, since 1946; *b* 29 Sept. 1911; *s* of Harold Victor and Alice Margaret Jones; *m* 1940, Vera, *d* of late Charles and Amelia Cain; one *s* two *d*. *Educ:* Alleyn's; Wadham Coll. (Exhibitioner) and Balliol Coll., Oxford. MA, DPhil, 1934; Skynner Senior Student in Astronomy, Balliol, 1934-36. Air Ministry: Scientific Officer, 1936; Air Staff, 1939; Asst Dir of Intelligence, 1941, Dir, 1946; Admiralty: seconded Adm. Res. Lab., 1938-39. Min. of Defence: Consultant, 1948-; Dir of Scientific Intelligence, 1952-53; Mem., Carriers Panel, 1962-63; Chm., Air Defence Working Party, 1963-64. Min. of Labour: Physics Advisory Cttee, 1949-. Min. of Fuel and Power: Chm., Safety in Mines Res. Advisory Bd, 1956-60 (Mem., 1950-56). Home Office: Scientific Adviser, Civil Defence, 1952-. Min. of Supply: Scientific Advisory Council, 1952-55; Chm., Infra-red Cttee, 1950-60. DSIR: Radio Research Bd, 1952-56; Scientific Grants Cttee, 1952-57; General Bd, Nat. Phys Lab., 1951-57, 1961-66. War Office: Scientific Advisory Council, 1963-66. Min. of Aviation: Chm., Electronics Research Council, 1964-67 (Mem., 1960-64). Min. of Technology: Chm., Electronics Research Council, 1967-70; Advisory Council on Calibration and Measurement, 1966-; Visiting Bd, Nat. Phys Lab., 1966-69; Adv. Cttee for Research on Measurements and Standards, 1969-. Dept of Science and Education: Cttee on Universities and Research Estabs, 1965-67; UGC Library Cttee, 1963-67. Royal Society: Chm., Paul Fund Cttee, 1962-; British Nat. Cttee for Scientific Radio, 1961-65; British Nat. Cttee for History of Science, 1966-; Sectional Cttee for Physics, 1967-; Gov., Dulwich Coll., 1966-. Consultant, CCG, 1948-54. Mem. and Chm., Research Adv. Council, BTC, 1949-63. Aberdeen Univ. Ct, 1956-60. Pres., Crabtree Foundation, 1958. Physics Cttee, Nuffield Foundation, 1962-66. Chm., Cttee on University Physics Depts, IPPS, 1962-64. BBC Gen. Adv. Coun., 1964-67. Coun., Soc. of Instrument Technology, 1966-68. Lectures: Poynting, 1961; Brunel, 1962; Kelvin, 1963; Da Vinci, 1963; York, 1964; Tizard, 1964; Joseph Payne, 1965; Cherwell-Simon, 1965; Lees Knowles, 1967-68; Ludwig Mond, 1967-68; Festschrift, Ausschuss für Funkortung, 1955; Kelvin, IEE, 1969; Wilkins, Royal Society, 1969; Vis. Lectr, Amer. Assoc. Advancement of Science, 1962. Rapporteur, European Convention on Human Rights, 1970. Pres., Sect. A, British Assoc., 1971. Jt Editor, Notes and Records of the Royal Society. Hon. Fellow, Wadham Coll., Oxford, 1968. Hon. DSc Strathclyde, 1969. US Medal of Freedom with Silver Palm, 1946; US Medal for Merit, 1947; BOIMA Prize, Inst. of Physics, 1934; Duddell Medal, Physical Soc., 1960; Parsons Medal, 1967. *Address:* Natural Philosophy Department, University of Aberdeen, Aberdeen AB9 2UE. *T:* Aberdeen 40241. *Club:* Athenæum.

**JONES, Sir Reginald Watson;** *see* Watson-Jones.

**JONES, Rhona Mary;** Chief Nursing Officer, St Bartholomew's Hospital, since 1968; *b* 7 July 1921; *d* of late Thomas Henry Jones and late Margaret Evelyn King; single. *Educ:* Liverpool; Alder Hey Children's Hosp.; St Mary's Hosp., Paddington. RSCN 1943; SRN 1945; SCM 1948. Post-Registration Training, and Staff Nurse, Queen Charlotte's Hosp., 1946-48; Ward Sister, 1948-50, Departmental Sister, 1950-52, St Mary's Hosp., Paddington; General Duty Nurse, Canada, 1952-53; Asst Matron, Gen. Infirmary, Leeds, 1953-57; Dep. Matron, Royal Free Hosp., London, 1957-59; Matron, Bristol Royal Hosp., 1959-67. Member: Standing Nursing Adv. Cttee, Central Health Services Coun.; Exec. Cttee, Assoc. Hosp. Matrons, 1963-67, 1968-; Area Nurse Trng Cttee, SW Region, 1965-67; NE Metropolitan Area Nurse Training Cttee, 1969-; E London Group Hosp. Management Cttee, 1969-. Vice-Pres., Bristol Royal Hosp. Nurses League. *Recreations:* reading, travel. *Address:* St Bartholomew's Hospital, West Smithfield, EC1. *T:* 01-606 7777.

**JONES, Air Vice-Marshal Richard Ian,** CB 1960; AFC 1948; psa; pfc; AOC No. 11 (Fighter) Group, Strike Command, 1968-70; *m* 1940, Margaret Elizabeth Wright. *Educ:* Berkhamsted Sch.; Cranwell. Group Captain, 1955; Air Commodore, 1960; Air Vice-Marshal, 1965. Senior Air Staff Officer, Royal Air Force, Germany (Second Tactical Air Force), Command Headquarters, 1959-63; Dir of Flying Training, 1963-64; AOC No. 25 Group, RAF Flying Training Command, 1964-67; SASO, Fighter Command, 1967-68. *Recreations:* golf, ski-ing. *Club:* Royal Air Force.

**JONES, Robert Gerallt;** Warden and Headmaster, Llandovery College, since 1967; *b* 11 Sept. 1934; *s* of Rev. R. E. Jones and Elizabeth Jones, Nefyn, Wales; *m* 1962, Susan Lloyd Griffith; one *s* one *d*. *Educ:* Denstone; University of Wales (University Student Pres., 1956-57). Sen. English Master, Sir Thomas Jones Sch., Amlwch, 1957-60; Lectr in Educn, University Coll., Aberystwyth, 1961-65; Prin., Mandeville Teachers' Coll., Jamaica, 1965-67. Member: Gov. Body, Church in Wales, 1959-; Welsh Acad. (Yr Academi Gymreig), 1959-; Broadcasting Council for Wales; Welsh Arts Council; Univ. Council, Aberystwyth. FRSA. Editor of Impact (the Church in Wales quarterly). *Publications:* Ymysg Y Drain, 1959; Y Foel Fawr, 1960; Cwlwm, 1962; Yn Frawd I'r Eos, 1962; (ed) Fy Nghymru I, 1962; Nadolig Gwyn, 1963; Gwared Y Gwirion, 1966; The Welsh Literary Revival, 1966; Jamaican Landscape, 1969. *Recreations:* freelance TV interviewing, cricket, journalism, writing. *Address:* Llandovery College, Llandovery, Carmarthenshire, Wales.

**JONES, Brig. Robert Llewellyn Jephson,** GC 1940; Commandant Central Ordnance Depot, Branston, 1957-60, retired; *b* 7 April 1905; *s* of Rev. J. D. Jones, and Margaret Noble Jones (*née* Jephson); *m* 1934, Irene Sykes; one *d*.

*Educ:* St Edmund's Sch., Canterbury; RMC, Sandhurst. Commissioned as 2nd Lieut Duke of Wellington's Regt, 1925; served in Singapore and India, 1926-30; served in Royal West African Frontier Force, Adjt, 1930-34; transferred to RAOC, 1936; served War, Malta, Palestine, Egypt, Sudan, Italy, 1939-44 (GC Malta); Col, 1943; Brig., 1954; Deputy Dir of Ordnance Services, Scottish Command, 1954-57. *Address:* Warri Lodge, Chine Walk, Ferndown, Dorset. *Club:* Naval and Military.

**JONES, Air Marshal Sir R(obert) Owen,** KBE, *cr* 1953; CB 1944; AFC; retired; *b* 19 April 1901; *s* of late F. M. and late Mrs Jones; *m* 1928, Betty Hambleton Hood; one *s* one *d. Educ:* Epworth College, Rhyl; Caius Coll., Cambridge. Joined RAF 1924; comd 11 Squadron, 1935-38; British Air Commission, Washington, 1941-43; Ministry of Aircraft Production, 1943-46; Technical Services (Plans) Air Ministry, 1946-47; AOC No. 24 Group, Technical Training Command, 1947; Senior Air Staff Officer, RAF Reserve Command, 1949; AOC No. 24 Group, Technical Training Command, 1949-52; Controller of Engineering and Equipment, Air Ministry, 1952-56. Pres. Instn Mechanical Engineers, 1958-59; Pres., Royal Aeronautical Society, 1961. Commander Legion of Merit (American), 1946. *Recreation:* fishing. *Address:* The Paddock, Westerton, Chichester, Sussex.

**JONES, Robert Tyre, (Bobby);** Attorney-at-Law; Partner in the firm of Jones, Bird, & Howell, Atlanta, USA; *b* Atlanta, Georgia, 17 March 1902; *s* of Robert P. Jones and Clara Thomas; *m* 1924, Mary Malone, Atlanta; one *s* two *d. Educ:* Technical High Sch., and Georgia Inst. of Technology, Atlanta; Harvard; Emory University. Admitted to Georgia Bar, 1928; National Amateur Golf Champion, 1924, 1925, 1927, 1928, 1930; National Open Champion, 1923, 1926, 1929, 1930; awarded Sullivan Memorial Prize, 1930; Open Championship of Great Britain, 1926, 1927, 1930; Amateur Champion Great Britain, 1930. Vice-Pres. Spalding Sales Corp.; Director: The Southern Co.; Canton Textile Mills, Inc.; Jones Mercantile Co. Relieved from active duty as Lieut-Col USAAF at end of War of 1939-45. *Publications:* Down the Fairway, 1927; Golf is My Game, 1960; Bobby Jones on Golf, 1966; Bobby Jones on the Basic Golf Swing, 1969. *Address:* Haas-Howell Building (4th floor), Atlanta, Ga 30303, USA.

**JONES, Rev. (Robert William) Hugh;** Moderator of the West Midland Province of the Congregational Church in England and Wales since 1970; *b* 6 May 1911; *s* of Evan Hugh Jones and Sarah Elizabeth Salmon; *m* 1939, Gaynor Eluned Evans; one *s* one *d. Educ:* Chester Grammar Sch.; Univs of Wales and Manchester; Lancashire Independent College. BA Wales, History and Philosophy. Ordained, 1939; Congregational Church: Welholme, Grimsby, 1939-45; Muswell Hill, London, 1945-49; Warwick Road, Coventry, 1949-61; Petts Wood, Orpington, 1961-69; President, Congregational Church in England and Wales, 1969-70. Frequent broadcaster, radio and TV. *Recreations:* drama, photography. *Address:* 8 Worcester Road, Kenilworth, Warwicks. *T:* Kenilworth 53624. *Club:* National Liberal.

**JONES, R(obin) Huws,** CBE 1969; Principal, National Institute for Social Work Training, since 1961; *b* 1 May 1909; *m* 1944, Enid Mary Horton; one *s* two *d. Educ:* Liverpool Univ. Francis Wood Prizeman, Royal Statistical Society. Lectr, Social Science Dept, Liverpool Univ., 1937-39; Staff Tutor (City of Lincoln) Oxford Univ. Extra-mural Delegacy, 1939-47; Dir of Social Science Courses, University Coll., Swansea, 1948-61. Visiting Prof., University of Minnesota, 1964; Heath Clark Lectr, University of London, 1969; Neely Memorial Lectr, Cleveland, O, 1969. Member: Minister of Health's Long Term Study Group, 1965-69; Cttee on Local Authority and Allied Personal Social Services, 1965-68; NE Metropolitan Reg. Hosp. Bd, 1967-; Home Sec.'s Adv. Council on Child Care, 1968-. Hon. Fellow, Inst. of Social Welfare. *Publications:* contributions to journals. *Address:* 5 Tavistock Place, WC1. *T:* 01-387 3650; Lambfold, High Lorton, Cockermouth, Cumberland.

**JONES, Brigadier Ronald M.;** *see* Montague-Jones.

**JONES, Royston Oscar;** Cervantes Professor of Spanish in the University of London, at King's College, since 1963; *b* 28 Oct. 1925; *s* of David Jones and Gwladys Mary Williams; *m* 1948, Elvira Ranz y Díez de Artázcoz; three *d. Educ:* Neath Grammar Sch.; King's Coll., London. BA Hons First Class, 1946, MA (London) 1949. Asst Lecturer, University of Aberdeen, 1948; Lecturer: University of St Andrews, 1949; King's Coll., London, 1950; Reader and Head of Dept, Queen Mary Coll., London, 1956. *Publications:* Critical edition of Lazarillo de Tormes, 1963; Poems of Góngora, with introduction, 1966. Articles in Mod. Lang. Review, Bulletin of Hispanic Studies, Boletín de la Real Academia, etc. *Recreations:* music, solitude, photography. *Address:* 4 Queen's Road, W5.

**JONES, Sir Samuel Bankole,** Kt 1965; President, Court of Appeal, Sierra Leone, since 1965; *b* 23 Aug. 1911; *s* of Samuel Theophilus Jones, Freetown, and Bernice Janet Jones; *m* 1942, Mary Alexandrina Stuart; three *s* two *d. Educ:* Methodist Boys' High Sch., Freetown; Fourah Bay Coll.; Durham Univ.; Middle Temple, London. MA, BCL, Diploma in Educn (Durham). Barrister-at-Law, 1938; private practice, 1938-49; Police Magistrate, Actg Solicitor Gen., 1949-58; Actg Puisne Judge, 1958-60; Puisne Judge, 1960-63; Chief Justice, Sierra Leone, 1963-65; Acting Governor Gen., Aug.-Nov., 1965. Chm., Fourah Bay Coll. Council, University Coll. of Sierra Leone, 1956-69; Chancellor, Univ. of Sierra Leone, 1969. Member: UNO Commn into death of its late Sec. Gen.; World Habeas Corpus Cttee, World Peace through World Center, 1968. Fellow, Internat. Soc. for Study of Comparative Public Law, 1969. Hon. DCL Durham, 1965. *Recreations:* reading, walking, gardening. *Address:* 8 Kingharman Road, Brookfields, Freetown, Sierra Leone, West Africa. *T:* 5061. *Clubs:* Royal Commonwealth Society (London); Freetown Reform (Freetown).

**JONES, Sir Samuel (Owen),** Kt 1966; FIREE (Aust.), FIE Aust.; Chairman, Standard Telephones & Cables Pty Ltd since 1968 (Managing Director, 1961-69); Managing Director: STC Investments Ltd, since 1962; STC Finance Ltd, since 1966; Chairman: Australian Radio Technical Services and Patents Co. Pty Ltd, since 1962; Australian Telecommunications Development Association, since 1967; Concrete Industries (Monier) Ltd, since 1969; Pink Pages Publicity (WA) Pty Ltd, since 1970; Director: Austral Standard Cables Pty Ltd, since 1962 (Chairman, 1967-69); Cannon Electric (Australia) Pty Ltd, since 1964; Overseas Corporation (Australia) Ltd, since 1969; *b* 20 Aug. 1905; *s* of late John Henry Jones and Eliza Jones (*née* Davies); *m* 1932, Jean, *d* of late J. W. Sinclair; two *d. Educ:* Warracknabeal High Sch.; University of Melbourne. Engineering Branch, PMG's Dept, 1927-39. Lt-Col comdg Divisional Signal Unit, AIF abroad, 1939-41;

CSO Aust. Home Forces, 1941-42; Dir, Radio and Signal Supplies, Min. of Munitions, 1942-45. Technical Manager, Philips Electrical Industries Pty Ltd, 1945-50, Tech. Dir, 1950-61; Chairman, Telecommunication Co. of Aust., 1956-61; Dir, Television Equipment Pty Ltd, 1960-61. National Pres., Aust. Inst. of Management, 1968-70; Councillor, Chamber of Manufactures of NSW, 1968-; Member: Govt's Electronics and Telecommunications Industry Adv. Cttee, 1955-; Export Develt Council, 1969-; Council, Macquarie Univ., 1969-. *Publications:* several technical articles. *Recreations:* bowls, fishing. *Address:* Apartment 11, 321 Edgecliff Road, Edgecliff, NSW 2027, Australia; Mummuga Lodge, Dalmeny, NSW 2537. *Clubs:* Union, Royal Automobile Club of Australia, Royal Sydney Yacht Squadron (all in Sydney); Naval and Military (Melbourne).

**JONES, Stephen Barry;** MP (Lab) Flintshire (East) since 1970; *b* 1938; *s* of Stephen Jones and late Grace Jones, Mancot, Flintshire; *m* 1957, Janet Jones (*née* Davies); one *s*. *Educ:* Hawarden Grammar School; Bangor Coll. of Educn. Head of English Dept, Deeside Secondary School, 1961-66. Regional Field Officer, National Union of Teachers. *Recreations:* tennis, hill-walking. *Address:* 37 Glynne Way, Hawarden, Deeside, Flintshire. *T:* Hawarden 2529.

**JONES, S(tuart) Lloyd;** Chief Executive Officer and Town Clerk of Cardiff, since 1970; *b* 26 Aug. 1917; *s* of Hugh and Edna Lloyd Jones, Liverpool; *m* 1942, Pamela Mary Hamilton-Williams, Heswall; one *s* three *d*. *Educ:* Rydal Sch.; Univ. of Liverpool. Solicitor, 1940; Dep. Town Clerk, Nottingham, 1950-53; Town Clerk of Plymouth, 1953-70. One of Advisers to Minister of Housing and Local Govt on Amalgamation of London Boroughs, 1962; Indep. Inspector, extension of Stevenage New Town, 1964; Mem., Cttee on Public Participation in Planning, 1969. *Address:* 45 Pwllmelin Road, Llandaff, Cardiff. *Clubs:* Reform; Royal Western Yacht Club of England (Plymouth).

**JONES, Sydney,** PhD; Member of Board, British Railways, since 1965 (Director of Research, BR Board, 1962-65); *b* 18 June 1911; *s* of John Daniel Jones and Margaret Ann (*née* Evans); *m* 1938, Winifred Mary (*née* Boulton); two *s* one *d*. *Educ:* Cyfarthfa Castle Grammar Sch.; Cardiff Technical Coll.; Cardiff Univ. Coll.; Birmingham Univ. BSc 1st cl. hons (London) 1932; PhD (London) 1951. General Electric Co., Witton, 1933-36; teaching in Birmingham, 1936-40; Scientific Civil Service at HQ, RRE, Malvern, and RAE, Farnborough, 1940-58; Dir of Applications Research, Central Electricity Generating Board, 1958-61; Technical Dir, R. B. Pullin, Ltd, 1961-62. FIEE 1960; FIMechE 1965; MILocoE 1967. *Publications:* (jtly) Introductory Applied Science, 1942; papers on automatic control. *Recreations:* gardening, cine-photography, house design. *Address:* The White House, Park Chase, Guildford, Surrey. *T:* Guildford 75532. *Club:* Athenæum.

**JONES, Sydney T.;** *see* Tapper-Jones.

**JONES, Rt. Rev. Thomas Edward,** MBE 1956; ThD; *b* 7 March 1903; *s* of Thomas and Charlotte Jones; *m* 1929, Lucy Vincent; one *s* two *d*. *Educ:* Ridley Coll., Melbourne; Australian College of Theology. Deacon, 1927; Priest, 1928; ThL 1928; ThD 1961. Curate of Moreland, 1927-28; Priest-in-Charge of Boggabilla, 1929-32; Victorian Secretary, Bush Church Aid Society, 1932-34; Licentiate to Officiate, Diocese of Sydney, 1934-58; Organising Secretary, Bush Church Aid Society of Australia and Tasmania, 1934-58; Hon. Canon of Sydney, 1956-58; Bishop of Willochra, 1958-69. Coronation Medal, 1953. *Publication:* These Twenty Years: A History of Bush Church Aid Society to 1940. *Address:* c/o Bishop's House, Gladstone, South Australia. *T:* 622057.

**JONES, Thomas E.;** *see* Elder-Jones.

**JONES, (Thomas) Mervyn,** CBE 1961; Chairman of Wales Tourist Board, since 1970; *b* 2 March 1910; *s* of late Rev. Dr Richard Jones and Violet Jones, Llandinam; *m* 1st (marr. diss. 1960); one *s* one *d*; 2nd, 1960, Margaret, *d* of Ernest E. Cashmore, Newport; one *s* one *d*. *Educ:* Newtown Co. Sch.; University Coll. of Wales, Aberystwyth (LLB); Trinity Hall, Cambridge (MA, LLM). Pres. Trinity Hall Law Soc., 1949. Asst Solicitor, Newport Corporation, town Clerk, 1948; Chm., Wales Gas Bd, 1948-70. Chm., Civic Trust for Wales; Member: Board of Management, Welsh National Opera Company; Ashby Cttee on Adult Education, 1953-54; Tucker Cttee on Proceedings before Examining Justices, 1957-58; Council, University of Wales; Council of Industrial Design; Welsh Economic Council, 1965-68; Welsh Council, 1968. Pres., Industrial Assoc., Wales and Mon, 1959-60. *Publications:* Planning Law and the Use of Property; Requisitioned Land and War Works Act, 1945; various titles and articles in Local Govt books and journals. *Recreations:* playing at golf, helping to keep Wales beautiful. *Address:* Dyffryn, Ely Road, Llandaff, Cardiff. *T:* Cardiff 562070. *Club:* Oxford and Cambridge University.

**JONES, Rt. Rev. Thomas Sherwood,** DD; *b* 4 March 1872; one *s* two *d* (and two *s* one *d* decd). *Educ:* London Coll. of Divinity; University of Durham (MA). Hon. DD 1931. Deacon, 1897; Priest, 1898; perpetual curate of St Martin-in-the-Fields, Liverpool, 1903-11; Vicar of: St Cleopas, Toxteth Park, 1911-16; St Mary, Birkenhead, 1916-20; Rector of Middleton, 1920-45; Rural Dean of Middleton, 1920-30; Hon. Canon of Manchester, 1927-30; Canon Emeritus, 1946; Bishop of Hulme, 1930-45. *Address:* Cranford, Aviary Road, Pyrford, near Woking, Surrey. *T:* Byfleet 45158.

**JONES, Tom,** OBE 1962; JP; Regional Secretary for Wales, Transport and General Workers' Union, since 1969 (N Wales and Border Counties, 1953); *b* 13 Oct. 1908; Welsh parents, father coalminer; *m* 1942, Rosa Jones (*née* Thomas); two *s* two *d*. *Educ:* Elem. Sch., Rhos, Wrexham; WEA Studies, Summer Schools. Coalminer, 1922-36 (having left sch. aged 14). Soldier, Spanish Republican Army (Internat. Bde), 1937-38 (captured by Franco Forces, 1938; PoW, 1940; sentenced to death by Franco Authorities, sentence commuted to 30 years imprisonment; released following representations by British Govt which involved a Trade Agreement). Worked in Chem. Industry, 1941-44; became full-time Union Official of T&GWU, 1945; Hon. Sec., RAC of N Wales (TUC) for last 15 years. Member: Welsh Economic Council; Welsh Council (Vice-Chm.); Court of Governors, Univ. of Wales; Welsh Industrial Estates Corp.; Treasurer, N Wales WEA; Governor, Coleg Harlech; Past Mem., Welsh Bd for Industry. JP Flint, 1955. *Recreations:* reading, do-it-yourself hobbies, extra-mural activities. *Address:* Rhoslan, 7 King George Street, Shotton, Deeside, Flintshire. *T:* Connah's Quay 2640.

**JONES, (Trevor) Alec;** MP (Lab) Rhondda West since March 1967; *b* 12 Aug. 1924; *m* 1950,

Mildred M. Evans; one *s*. *Educ:* Porth County Grammar Sch.; Bangor Normal Training Coll. Schoolteacher from 1949. PPS to Minister of Defence for Equipment, 1968-70. Sponsored Divorce Reform Act, 1969. *Address:* 151 Kenry Street, Tonypandy, Rhondda, Wales. *T:* Tonypandy 3472. *Club:* Ystrad Labour (Rhondda).

**JONES, W(alter) Idris,** CBE 1954; BSc Wales, Hon. DSc 1957; PhD Cantab; CEng, MIChemE, FRIC, FIMinE, FInstF; Member (part-time): Government Water Resources Board, 1964-65; Wales Gas Board, since 1964; Director-General of Research National Coal Board, 1946-62; Director General of Research and Development (Coal Processing and Combustion), National Coal Board, 1962-63, retired 1963; *b* Llanelli, Carmarthenshire, 18 Jan. 1900; *s* of Frederick and Elizabeth Jones; unmarried. *Educ:* University Coll. of Wales, Aberystwyth; Gonville and Caius Coll., Cambridge. BSc Hons Chemistry, 1921; Rhondda and Frank Smart Studentships at Gonville and Caius Coll., 1922-26; PhD Cantab 1925; Cambridge Univ. Rugby XV, 1923-25; Wales Rugby XV 1924-25, v. England, France, Ireland and Scotland. ICI (F & SP) Ltd, Billingham, 1926-33; research on methanol and ammonia synthesis, gasification, hydrogenation of coal, etc; Group Manager in Oil Div.: Research Manager, Powell Duffryn Ltd, 1933-46; Vice-Pres., Inst. Chemical Engrs, 1955; Mem. of Council, Inst. Fuel (Pres., 1953-54-55; Treas., 1964); Pres. and Chm. of Council, British Coal Utilisation Research Assoc., 1955-63. Member and Vice-Pres., Hon. Soc. of Cymmrodorion; Member: National Council for Technol. Awards, 1955-62; Court, Univ. of Wales; Court and Council, Univ. of Wales Inst. of Science and Technology; Court and Council, University Coll. of Wales, Aberystwyth, 1957-70 (Vice-Pres., 1963-70); Chm. University of Wales Appointments Board, 1957-68. Mem. Court and Industrial Cttee, Nat. Museum of Wales, 1968-. Mem. Water Advisory Cttee (Wales), 1958-59. Chm., BSI (Solid Fuel Industry Standards Cttee), 1948-63; Chm., London Secretariat, Commonwealth Conf. for Fuel Research, 1961-63; Mem., Parly and Sci. Cttee, 1955-64. RA Cadet Bn, 1918; Major (GI) E Glamorgan Sector, HG. *Publications:* papers in Scientific and Technical jls. *Recreations:* walking, music. *Address:* 9b The Cathedral Green, Llandaff, Cardiff. *T:* Cardiff 563995.

*See also Rt Hon. Sir Frederick Elwyn Jones.*

**JONES, Rev. William David;** Clerk of the General Assembly, The Presbyterian Church of Wales, since 1968; *b* 8 July 1909; British (Welsh); *m* 1939, Gwen Evans, Bala, Merionethshire; two *s* one *d*. *Educ:* UC of N Wales, Bangor (BA); United Theol Coll., Aberystwyth. Ordained, 1936. Minister at: Chwilog, Caern, 1936-45; Bontnewydd, Caern, 1945-50; Edge Lane, Liverpool, 1950-70. Sec., Calvinistic Methodist Orphanage, Bontnewydd, 1945-50. Asst Sec., Gen. Assembly (PCW), 1957-58; Statistician, Gen. Assembly (PCW), 1960-64. Liverpool Presbytery (PCW): Sec., 1951-53; Moderator, 1954. Governor/Manager, Newsham County Schools, Liverpool, 1960-70 (Chm., 1969). Part-time Chaplain, Walton Hosp., Liverpool, 1958-68. *Recreation:* fishing. *Address:* 32 Carstairs Road, Liverpool L6 8NN. *T:* 051-228 4468.

**JONES, Very Rev. William Edward;** Vicar of Penally, 1964-69, retired; *b* 1897; *s* of Captain David Hughes Jones and Elizabeth Jones, Aberystwyth; *m* 1935, Rachel Marianne (*see* Mrs R. M. Jones); one *s* three *d*. *Educ:* St David's Sch., Lampeter; Jesus Coll., Oxford (Mathematical Exhibition). BA 1922; MA 1924. Minor Canon of Brecon Cathedral, 1922-28; Priest-in-Charge, Kondinin, WA, 1928-33; Diocesan Missioner, Swansea and Brecon, 1934-35; Rector St Luke's, Cottesloe, WA, and Rural Dean, 1936-43; Chaplain AMF, 1941-45; Rector St Mary's, West Perth, 1943-49; Canon of St George's, Perth, 1944-49; Dean of Brecon, 1950-64, and Vicar of St Mary's, Brecon, 1950-64; Hon. Canon of Brecon Cathedral, 1964-69. *Recreations:* Rugby football; music, cabinet-making. *Address:* Caldey View, Penally, Tenby, Pembs. *T:* Tenby 3112.

**JONES, William Elwyn Edwards;** *b* 1904; *s* of the Rev. Robert William Jones and Elizabeth Jane Jones, Welsh Methodist Minister; *m* 1936, Dydd, *d* of Rev. E. Tegla Davies; one *s* two *d*. *Educ:* Bootle Secondary Sch.; Festiniog County Sch.; University of Wales. BA (Wales), LLB (London). Admitted Solicitor, 1927; Clerk to the Justices, Bangor Div., Caernarvonshire, 1934. Town Clerk, Bangor, 1939. MP (Lab) Conway Div. of Caernarvonshire, 1950-51. Member: Nat. Parks Commn, 1966-68, Countryside Commn, 1968-; Council and Court of Governors, University Coll. of N Wales. CC Caernarvonshire. *Publications:* Press articles in Welsh and English. *Recreation:* walking. *Address:* 23 Glyngarth Court, Glyngarth, Menai Bridge, Anglesey, N Wales. *T:* Glyn Garth 422.

**JONES, William Emrys,** BSc; Chief Agricultural Adviser, Ministry of Agriculture, Fisheries and Food, since 1967; *b* 6 July 1915; *s* of late William Jones and Mary Ann (*née* Morgan); *m* 1938, Megan Ann Morgan (marr. diss., 1966); three *s*; *m* 1967, Gwyneth George. *Educ:* Llandovery Gram. Sch.; University Coll. of Wales, Aberystwyth. Agricultural Instr, Gloucester CC, 1940-46; Provincial Grassland Adv. Officer, NAAS, Bristol, 1946-50; County Agricultural Officer, Gloucester, 1950-54; Dep. Dir, 1954-57, Dir 1957-59, NAAS, Wales; Sen. Advisory Officer, NAAS, 1959-61; Dir, 1961-66. *Recreations:* golf, shooting. *Address:* 18 Causton Road, N6. *T:* 01-348 2656. *Club:* Farmers'.

**JONES, (William) Ernest,** CBE 1961 (OBE 1945); retired as: Chairman, Southern Regional Board for Industry, 1961-65; Member British Egg Marketing Board, 1961-66; Member (Part-time) Transport Holding Company, 1963-65; *b* 14 April 1895; *s* of Arthur and Constance Jones; *m* 1918, Annie Helen Fall (*d* 1960); one *d*; *m* 1962, Catherine L. Taylor. *Educ:* Renishaw Council Sch. Commenced work at 13 years of age in a boot repairing shop; entered coalmining underground at 14 years of age; employed at Southgate and Cresswell Collieries, Derbyshire, 1910-18; employed at Rossington Colliery, South Yorks, 1918; appointed Branch Official of Mineworkers' Union, 1921; Colliery Checkweighman, 1926; Mem. Doncaster RDC, 1924-39; Mem. West Riding County Council, 1928-42; West Riding Magistrate, 1936; Mem. Executive Cttee of MFGB 1938; Gen. Sec. of Yorks Miners' Assoc., 1939; seconded to act as Regional Labour Dir, Ministry of Fuel and Power, 1942-44; Vice-Pres. of National Union of Mineworkers, 1950; Pres. National Union of Mineworkers, 1954-60, retd; Mem. Gen. Council, TUC, 1950-60; Sec., Miners' International Federation, 1957-60. Member: Radcliffe Cttee on working of the Monetary System; Monopolies Commission, 1959-69; National Savings Cttee, 1961-. Hon. LLD Leeds, 1961. *Recreation:* gardening. *Address:*

Diggers, Moat Lane, Pulborough, Sussex. *T:* Pulborough 2718.

**JONES, Sir (William John) Andrew,** Kt 1943; CMG 1937; *b* 5 Nov. 1889; 2nd *s* of late Rev. J. Jones, formerly Rector of Itton, Chepstow; *m* 1916, Catherine Muriel, 2nd *d* of A. S. Evans, Cowbridge; one *s* one *d. Educ:* Cowbridge Grammar Sch.; Jesus Coll., Oxford. Joined Colonial Administrative Service, 1913; Provincial Commissioner, 1927; Sec. for Native Affairs, 1931; Dep. Governor, 1931, 1932; Chief Commissioner, Northern Territories, Gold Coast; Accredited Representive on three occasions at Sessions of Permanent Mandates Commission; Dep. Chm. West African Governors Conference, 1941; Chief Sec. to resident Minister W Africa, 1942-45; Head of British Food Mission to Canada, 1946-53. *Address:* The Knap House, Ramsbury, Marlborough, Wilts.

**JONES, William Lloyd M.;** *see* Mars-Jones.

**JONES, William Neilson,** MA; Professor Emeritus, University of London since 1948; *b* 1883; *s* of William Beale Jones, London, and Jessie Gilchrist Neilson, Glasgow; *m* 1st, 1912, Mabel Cheveley Rayner (*d* 1948); *m* 2nd, 1957, Margaret, *widow* of Dr J. W. Trevan, FRS, and *d* of late Sir H. Llewellyn Smith, GCB. *Educ:* King's Coll. Sch., London; Emmanuel Coll. (Foundation Scholar), Cambridge. First Class Part I, Natural Science Tripos, Second Class Part II; Lecturer in Botany at University Coll. Reading, 1908; Asst Lecturer in Botany at Bedford Coll., 1913; head of the dept, 1916; Prof. of Botany, Bedford Coll., London, 1920-48; during European War, 1914-18, conducted investigations for the Health of the Munition Workers' Cttee of the Ministry of Munitions, and held commission as Capt. RAF. *Publications:* original scientific investigations in various branches of botany; A Text-book of Plant Biology (with M. C. Rayner, DSc); Plant Chimaras; Problems in Tree Nutrition (with M. C. Rayner); The Growing Plant. *Address:* 169 Woodside Green, SE25. *T:* 01-654 5798.

**JONES, William Tinnion,** MD; Director-General, Health Education Council, since 1969; *b* Maryport, Cumberland, 30 July 1927; *s* of late Ben and Mary Tinnion Jones; *m* 1950, Jennifer Provost Bland, MB; three *d. Educ:* St Bees Sch.; Edinburgh Univ.; London Sch. of Hygiene and Tropical Medicine. MB, ChB Edinburgh, 1950; MD Edinburgh, 1957; DPH London, 1955. Surg. Lt, RNZN (UN Forces, Korea), 1951-54; Med. Dir, Nuffield Industrial Health Survey, Tyneside, 1956-57; Asst MOH, Reading, 1955-56; Med. Adv., Birfield Ltd, 1957-63; Hubert Wyers Travelling Fellow, 1961; Med. Dir (founder) W Midlands Industrial Health Service, 1963-69; Tutor and Lectr in Industrial Health, Univ. of Birmingham, and London Sch. of Hygiene and Tropical Med., 1965-69. *Publications:* articles in several med. jls. *Recreations:* the popular arts in their various forms. *Address:* 63 Crown Street, Harrow-on-the-Hill, Middlesex. *T:* 01-864 1430.

**JONES, Wynn Normington H.,** *see* Hugh-Jones.

**JONES-PARRY, Ernest;** Executive Director: International Sugar Council, 1965-68; International Sugar Organisation, since 1969; *b* 16 July 1908; *o s* of late John Parry and Charlotte Jones, Rhuddlan; *m* 1938, Mary Powell; two *s. Educ:* St Asaph; University of Wales; University of London. MA (Wales) 1932; PhD (London) 1934; FRHistS. Lecturer in History, University Coll. of Wales, 1935-40; Ministry of Food, 1941; Treasury, 1946-47; Asst Sec., Ministry of Food, 1948-57; Under Sec., 1957; Dir of Establishments, Ministry of Agriculture, Fisheries and Food, 1957-61. *Publications:* The Spanish Marriages, 1841-46, 1936; The Correspondence of Lord Aberdeen and Princess Lieven, 1832-1854 (2 vols), 1938-39; articles and reviews in History and English Historical Review. *Recreations:* reading, watching cricket. *Address:* 3 Sussex Mansions, Old Brompton Road, SW7. *T:* 01-589 7979. *Club:* Athenæum.

**JONES-ROBERTS, Kate Winifred,** OBE; *b* 29 Nov. 1889; *d* of Catherine and Rees Roberts, Llys Dorvil, Blaenau Ffestiniog, N Wales; *m* J. Jones-Roberts (*d* 1962), Barrister-at-Law. *Educ:* University Coll. of N Wales, Bangor; Newnham Coll., Cambridge. BA (Wales). JP (Merioneth); Merioneth CC 1939-53; Dep. Chm., Merioneth QS, 1955-64; Chairman: Ffestiniog Bench of Magistrates, 1959-64; Merioneth Magistrates Court Cttee, 1962-64; Merioneth Probation Cttee, 1955-64; Merioneth Appeal Tribunal (Nat. Assistance), 1951-62; N Wales Mental Hosp. Management Cttee, 1948-51; Merioneth Children's Homes, 1948-63; Welsh Tourist Board, 1950-52; Vice-President: University Coll. of N Wales, Bangor, 1956-61; Coleg Harlech, 1949-; Merioneth Historical Soc., 1947-67. Member: University Coun. (Wales), 1949-68; Merioneth Education Cttee, 1939-70; Children and Welfare Cttees of Merioneth CC, 1953-67 (Chm., Children Cttee, 1948-53); Welsh Regional Hosp. Board, 1947-54; Board of British Travel and Holidays Assoc., 1947-53; Advisory Cttee on Child Care, 1948-50; Welsh Jt Education Cttee, 1948-52; Nathan Cttee on Charitable Trusts, 1950-53; Royal Commission on Marriage and Divorce, 1951-55. Tutor, Coleg Harlech, 1960-66. *Address:* Penrhiw, Ffestiniog, N Wales.

**JONZEN, Mrs Karin,** FRBS; Sculptor; *b* London (Swedish parents), 22 Dec. 1914; *d* of U. Löwenadler and G. Munck av Fulkila; *m* 1944, Basil Jonzen (*d* 1967); one *s.* Studied Slade Sch., 1932-36. Slade Dipl. and Scholarship, 1934; Rome Scholarship, 1939. Lectr, Camden Arts Centre, 1969-70. Exhibited: Battersea Park Open Air Exhibn, 1948-51; Leicester Galls; Roland, Browse and Delbanco; Piccadilly Gall.; Royal Academy; New York, 1970; *Work in permanent collections:* V. and A. Museum, also Bradford, Brighton, Glasgow, Melbourne; *official purchases:* Arts Council; Selwyn Coll., Cambridge; Modern Schs in Leics, Cardiff and Hertford; Festival of Britain Exhibition; Southend Art Gall. and Museum. Carving on Guildford Cathedral, 1961; Leverhulme Res. Grant to travel in Greece and Italy, 1962; Life-size Bronze Figure for WHO HQ, New Delhi, 1963, and Bronze Torso for WHO at Geneva, 1965 (both gifts of British Govt); exhibited three works in City of London Festival, 1968 (Madonna and Child purchased for St Mary le Bow, Cheapside, 1969). *Recreation:* music. *Address:* 92a Fordwych Road, NW2. *T:* 01-452 9386.

**JOOSTE, Gerhardus Petrus;** South African Secretary for External Affairs, 1956-66 (Secretary for Foreign Affairs, 1961); retired, 1966; Special Adviser (part-time) on Foreign Affairs to Prime Minister and Minister of Foreign Affairs, since 1966; Chairman, State Procurement Board, since 1968; *b* 5 May 1904; *s* of Nicolaas Jooste and Sofie Jooste (*née* Visser); *m* 1934, Anna van Zyl van der Merwe; one *s* one *d. Educ:* Primary and Secondary Schs, Winburg and Kroonstad; Rondebosch Boys High; Grey Coll., Bloemfontein; Pretoria Univ. Entered Union Public Service, 1924; Priv. Sec. to Hon. N. C. Havenga, Minister of Finance, 1929; Dept of External Affairs, 1934;

Legation Sec. and Chargé d'Affaires *ad interim*, Brussels, 1937-40; Chargé d'Affaires to Belgian Government-in-Exile, 1940-41; transf. to Dept of External Affairs, Pretoria, as Head of Economic Div., 1941-46; Head of Political and Diplomatic Div. of the Dept, 1946-49; Ambassador to US and Permanent Delegate to UN, 1949-54; High Commissioner of the Union of South Africa in London, 1954-56. Mem., Commn of Enquiry regarding Water Matters, 1966-; Mem. (ex officio), Atomic Energy Bd, 1956-66. *Recreations:* golf and hunting. *Address:* (office) Private Bag 316, Pretoria, S Africa; (home) 851 Government Avenue, Arcadia, Pretoria.

**JOPE, Prof. Edward Martyn,** FBA 1965; FSA 1946; Professor of Archæology, The Queen's University of Belfast, since 1963; *b* 25 Dec. 1915; *s* of Edward Mallet Jope and Frances Margaret (née Chapman); *m* 1941, Margaret Halliday; no *c*. *Educ:* Kingswood Sch., Bath; Oriel Coll., Oxford. Staff of Royal Commission on Ancient Monuments (Wales), 1938; Biochemist, Nuffield and MRC Grants, 1940; Queen's Univ., Belfast: Lectr in Archæology, 1949; Reader, 1954; Prof., 1963. Mem. Ancient Monuments Adv. Coun. (NI), 1950; Mem. Royal Commission on Ancient Monuments (Wales), 1963; Pres. Section H, British Assoc., 1965. *Publications:* (ed.) Studies in Building History, 1961; papers in Biochem. Jl, Proc. Royal Society Med., Spectrochemica Acta, Trans. Faraday Soc., Proc. Prehistoric Soc., Antiquaries' Jl, Medieval Archæology, Oxoniensia, Ulster Jl of Archæology, Proc. Soc. of Antiquaries of Scotland, etc. *Address:* 15 Notting Hill, Belfast 9, N Ireland.

**JOPLING, Michael;** *see* Jopling, T. M.

**JOPLING, (Thomas) Michael;** MP (C) Westmorland since 1964; Farmer; *b* 10 Dec. 1930; *s* of Mark Bellerby Jopling, MC, Masham, Yorks; *m* 1958, Gail, *d* of Ernest Dickinson, Harrogate; two *s*. *Educ:* Cheltenham Coll.; King's Coll., Newcastle upon Tyne (BSc Agric.). Mem., Thirsk Rural District Council, 1958-64; Mem. National Council, National Farmers' Union, 1962-64. Jt Sec., Cons. Parly Agric. Cttee, 1966-. *Address:* Ainderby Hall, Thirsk, Yorks. *T:* Sinderby 224; 8 Mylnbeck Court, Windermere, Westmorland. *T:* Windermere 2590. *Clubs:* Carlton, Farmers'.

**JORDAN, Rev. Preb. Hugh;** Curate of St James's, Hereford, and teaching at Hereford High School, since 1969; a Prebendary of St Paul's Cathedral, 1963-69, now Emeritus; *b* 29 Dec. 1906; *m* 1936, Elizabeth Hamilton Lamb, Dublin; two *s* one *d*. *Educ:* Trinity Coll., Dublin; Royal School, Cavan, Eire. School Teacher, 1924-29; Curate, St Kevin's Church, Dublin, 1932-34; Gen. Sec. City of Dublin YMCA, 1934-39; Vicar: St Luke's, Eccleston, St Helens, Lancs, 1939-45; Penn Fields, Wolverhampton, 1945-49; Redland, Bristol (and Lecturer and Tutor, Tyndale Hall, Bristol), 1949-56; Principal, London Coll. of Divinity, 1956-69. *Recreations:* formerly: hockey, soccer, cricket, tennis, athletics and boxing. *Address:* Boylefield Cottage, Clehonger, Hereford. *T:* Madley 579.

**JORDAN, Dr John,** DSO 1940; *b* 18 Oct. 1910; *s* of Andrew and Frances Jordan; *m* 1942; two *s* two *d*. *Educ:* Blackrock Coll., Dublin; University Coll., Dublin. MB, BCh, BAO, National University of Ireland, 1934. House-Surgeon, Mater Misericordiae Hosp., Dublin. General Practice, 5 years; entered Royal Navy, 1937. General Practice in Kildare, 1947-49, then in Emly, 1949-. *Recreations:* general. *Address:* Lisheen, Emly, Co. Tipperary, Ireland.

**JORDAN, Air Marshal Sir Richard Bowen,** KCB 1956 (CB 1947); DFC 1941; psa; RAF retired; *b* 7 Feb. 1902; *s* of late A. O. Jordan, Besford Ct, Worcestershire; *m* 1932, F. M. M. Haines; one *d*. *Educ:* Marlborough Coll.; RAF Coll., Cranwell. Joined RAF, 1921. Late AOC the RAF in India and Pakistan; Air Officer Commanding RAF Gibraltar, 1948-49; Commandant of the Royal Observer Corps, 1949-51; ADC to the King, 1949-51; Air Officer Commanding No. 25 Group, 1951-53; Dir-Gen. of Organisation, Air Ministry, 1953-55; Air Officer Commanding-in-Chief, Maintenance Command, 1956-58, retd. *Address:* The Long House, Ramridge Park, near Andover, Hants.

**JORDAN, Stanley Rupert;** *b* 23 Aug. 1894. Asst in Levant Consular Service, 1919; Trade Commissioner at Durban, 1930; Commercial Secretary at Cairo, 1934; in Dept of Overseas Trade, 1935-36; transferred to Athens, 1936; Commercial Secretary at Angora, 1938; local rank of Commercial Counsellor there, 1940; Minister at Jedda, 1943-45. *Address:* Grantley, Private Bag 716, Gatooma, Rhodesia.

**JORDAN, Prof. Wilbur Kitchener;** Professor of History, Harvard University, since 1946; Williams Professor of History and Political Science, Harvard University, since 1965; *b* 15 Jan. 1902; *s* of William and Emma Shepard Jordan; *m* 1929, Frances Ruml. *Educ:* Oakland City Coll.; Harvard. AB Oakland City Coll., 1923; AM Harvard, 1928; PhD Harvard, 1931. Instructor in History, Harvard Univ., 1931-37; Prof. of History, Scripps Coll., 1937-40; Prof. of History and Gen. Editor, University Press, University of Chicago, 1940-43; Pres., Radcliffe Coll., 1943-60. Sterling Fellow, Harvard Univ., 1930-31; Guggenheim Fellow, 1943. Corres. Fellow, British Acad., 1969. Hon. LHD, Bates Coll., 1944; Hon. DLitt: Oakland City Coll., 1960; Reed Coll., 1967; Hon. LLD: University of Vermont, 1962; Dartmouth Coll., 1965; Hon. LittD, Oxford Univ., 1964. *Publications:* The Development of Religious Toleration in England (4 vols), 1932-40, London; Men of Substance, 1942, Chicago; Philanthropy in England, 1480-1660, 1959, London; The Charities of London, 1480-1660, 1960, London; The Charities of Rural England, 1480-1660, 1961, London; The Social Institutions of Lancashire, 1962, Manchester; The Chronicle and Political Papers of King Edward VI, 1966 (Ithaca, NY and London); Edward VI: The Young King, 1968 (London); Edward IV: the threshold of power, 1970 (London). *Recreation:* farming. *Address:* 3 Concord Avenue, Cambridge, Mass 02138, USA. *Clubs:* Century, Harvard (New York).

**JORDAN MALKIN, Harold;** *see* Malkin, H. J.

**JORDAN-MOSS, Norman,** CMG 1965; Under-Secretary, HM Treasury, since 1968; *b* 5 Feb. 1920; *o s* of Arthur Moss and Ellen Jordan Round; *m* 1965, Kathleen Lusmore; one *s* one *d*. *Educ:* Manchester Gram. Sch.; St John's Coll., Cambridge (MA). Ministry of Economic Warfare, 1940-44; HM Treasury, 1944-; Asst Representative of HM Treas. in Middle East, 1945-48; Principal, 1948; First Sec. (Econ.), Belgrade, 1952-55; Financial Counsellor, Washington, 1956-60; Counsellor, UK Permanent Delegation to OECD, Paris, 1963-66; Asst Sec., HM Treasury, 1956-68. *Recreations:* music, theatre, squash rackets. *Address:* Milton Way, Westcott, Dorking, Surrey. *Club:* Travellers'.

**JORISCH, Mrs Robert;** *see* Lofts, Norah.

**JORY, Philip John,** DSO 1919; retired as Senior Ear, Nose and Throat Surgeon, St George's Hospital, 1958; *b* 1 March 1892; *s* of Rev. J. D. Jory; *m* 1925, Yvonne Moullé; four *s* one *d*. *Educ:* Nelson Coll., NZ; Otago Univ., NZ. NZ Univ. Sen. Schol., 1910; MB, ChB (NZ) 1919; FRCS Eng. 1924. ENT Surgeon: St George's, Mt Vernon, Barnet General, Woodford Jubilee and Harpenden Memorial Hosps. FRSocMed (Former Pres. Otology Section). Served European War, 1914-18 and War of 1939-45 (Col RAMC). *Address:* c/o Glyn, Mills & Co., Kirkland House, Whitehall, SW1; Monksmead, Old Felixstowe, Suffolk. *T:* Felixstowe 4675.

**JOSE, Sir Ivan Bede,** Kt 1963; MC; MB, MS (Adelaide), FRCS (Eng., Edinburgh, and Australasia); Hon. Consultant Surgeon Royal Adelaide Hospital, 1950; Member Medical Board of South Australia, 1963-67; President Australian Post-Graduate Federation in Medicine, 1957-60 and 1965-66 (Governor 1962); Member of Council, University of Adelaide, 1953-65; Chairman, South Australian Division Australian Red Cross, 1964 (Member Executive, 1942); *b* Ningpo, China, 13 Feb. 1893; *s* of late Very Rev. G. H. Jose; *m* Imogen Mervyn, *d* of W. G. Hawkes, Koonoona Station, SA; two *s* one *d*. *Educ:* Privately (Oxford); Queen's Sch., St Peter's Coll., University of Adelaide; London Hosp.; studied surgery, London, Vienna, Paris, and USA. Served European War 1914-18, Egypt, France (despatches MC); Major, 1918; Lt-Col, AAMC, 1931; Squadron-Leader (temp.) RAAF, 1940; Group Capt. 1953, RAAF Reserve. Surgical and Medical Registrar, Adelaide Hosp., 1923-24; Asst Hon. Surgeon, 1925-30; Hon. Surgeon, 1930-50; Dir and Lecturer in Surgery, University of Adelaide, 1936-50, Dean of the Faculty of Medicine, 1948-49; Pres., Royal Australasian Coll. of Surgeons, 1955-57 (Mem. Council, 1943-57); Visiting Urologist, Repatriation Hosp., 1946-63. Pres., SA Branch of BMA, 1954-55. *Publications:* papers in Australian Medical Journal. *Recreations:* cricket, golf, tennis. *Address:* 58 Brougham Place, North Adelaide, South Australia. *Club:* Adelaide (Adelaide).

**JOSEPH, Sir (Herbert) Leslie,** Kt 1952; Chairman: Festival Gardens, Battersea Park, Ltd; Porthcawl Recreations Ltd; Director, Forte's (Holdings) Ltd, etc; *b* 4 Jan. 1908; *s* of David Ernest and Florence Joseph; *m* 1934, Emily Irene, *d* of Dr Patrick Julian Murphy, Cwmbach, Aberdare; two *d*. *Educ:* The King's Sch. Canterbury. Commissioned RE, 1940-46. Chairman: Assoc. Amusement Parks Proprietors Gt Brit., 1949, 1950, 1951; National Amusements Council, 1950-51; Amusement Caterers' Assoc., 1953, 1954; Housing Production Board for Wales, 1952-53. *Recreations:* horticulture and ceramics. *Address:* Coedargraig, Newton, Porthcawl, Glamorganshire. *T:* Porthcawl 2610. *Club:* Naval and Military.

**JOSEPH, Rt. Hon. Sir Keith (Sinjohn),** 2nd Bt, *cr* 1943; PC 1962; MP (C) Leeds North-East since Feb. 1956; Secretary of State, Department of Health and Social Security, since 1970; *b* 17 Jan. 1918; *o c* of Sir Samuel George Joseph, 1st Baronet, and Edna Cicely, *yr d* of late P. A. S. Phillips, Portland Place, W1; *S* father 1944; *m* 1951, Hellen Louise, *yr d* of Sigmar Guggenheimer, NY; one *s* three *d*. *Educ:* Harrow; Magdalen Coll., Oxford. War of 1939-45, served 1939-46; Captain RA; Italian campaign (wounded, despatches). Fellow All Souls Coll., Oxford, 1946-60; barrister, Middle Temple, 1946. Contested (C) Baron's Court, General Election, 1955. PPS to Parly Under-Sec. of State, CRO, 1957-59; Parly Sec., Min. of Housing and Local Govt, 1959-61; Minister of State at Board of Trade, 1961-62; Minister of Housing and Local Govt and Minister for Welsh Affairs, 1962-64. Co-Founder and first Chm., Foundation for Management Education, 1959; Founder and Chm., Mulberry Housing Trust, 1965. Chm., Bovis Ltd, 1958-59; Dep. Chm., Bovis Holdings Ltd, 1964- (Dir, 1951-59); Dir, Gilbert-Ash Ltd, 1949-59. Underwriting Mem., Lloyd's. FIOB. Common councilman of City of London for Ward of Portsoken, 1946, Alderman, 1946-49. Liveryman, Vintners' Company. *Heir: s* James Samuel Joseph, *b* 27 Jan. 1955. *Address:* 23 Mulberry Walk, SW3. *Clubs:* Carlton, MCC.

**JOSEPH, Sir Leslie;** *see* Joseph, Sir H. L.

**JOSEPH, Maxwell;** Chairman: Grand Metropolitan Hotels Ltd; Giltspur Investments Ltd; Norfolk Capital Hotels Ltd; Joint Chairman, Lombard Banking Ltd; Director: Bristol & West Hotels Ltd; Cunard Steam-Ship Co. Ltd; Express Dairy Co. Ltd. *Recreations:* philately (Cape of Good Hope Gold Medallist), gardening. *Address:* 55 Grosvenor Street, W1.

**JOSEPH, Sir Norman;** *see* Joseph, Sir (Samuel) Norman.

**JOSEPH, Sir (Samuel) Norman,** KCVO 1969; Kt 1963; CBE 1953; Director: J. Lyons Co. Ltd since 1948; the Strand Hotels Ltd (Deputy Chairman); Cumberland Hotels Ltd; Chairman, Town and County Catering Co. since 1962; Hon. Catering Adviser, Home Office, since 1953; *b* 12 Dec. 1908; *s* of John and Dora Joseph; *m* 1932, Mina Stern; one *d*. *Educ:* Bedales. Started with J. Lyons and Co. Ltd, 1926. Served War of 1939-45 (despatches twice). Bronze Medal (USA), 1945. *Recreations:* tennis, snooker, bridge. *Address:* Wolsey Spring, George Road, Kingston Hill, Kingston-on-Thames, Surrey. *Clubs:* Hurlingham; Goodwood.

**JOSEPHSON, Dr Brian David,** FRS 1970; Assistant Director of Research, Cambridge University, since 1967; Fellow of Trinity College, Cambridge, since 1962; *b* 4 Jan. 1940. *Educ:* Cardiff High School; Cambridge Univ. BA 1960, MA, PhD 1964, Cantab. New Scientist Award, 1969; Research Corporation Award, 1969. *Publications:* research papers on superconductivity, critical phenomena, etc. *Recreations:* mountain walking, ice skating. *Address:* Cavendish Laboratory, Cambridge. *T:* 0223 54481.

**JOSKE, Percy Ernest,** CMG 1967; **Hon. Mr Justice Joske;** Judge of the Commonwealth of Australia Industrial Court, and of the Supreme Courts of the Australian Capital Territory, the Northern Territory of Australia and Norfolk Island, since 1960; *b* 5 Oct. 1895; *s* of Ernest and Evalyne Joske; *m* 1928, Mavis Connell (*d* 1968); one *s*; *m* 1969, Dorothy Larcombe. *Educ:* Wesley Coll., Melbourne; Melbourne Univ. (MA, LLM). John Madden Exhibitioner and First Class Final Honourman in Laws. QC (Australia) (KC 1944). Editor, Vic. Law Reports, 1936-56; Registrar: Dental Bd of Vic., 1939-58; Dietitians Registration Bd of Vic., 1942-58; Lecturer in Domestic Relations Law, Melbourne Univ., 1948-51. MHR for Balaclava, Australian Parl, 1951-60. Mem., Parly Standing Cttee on Foreign Affairs, Constitution Review, Privileges and Standing Orders; Aust. Deleg. to UN, 1955; Mem. Coun., ANU, 1956-60; Chm., Aust. Commonwealth Immigration Planning Coun., 1959-60. *Publications:* Remuneration of Commission Agents, 1924 (3rd edn 1957); Marriage and Divorce, 1924 (5th edn 1968);

Procedure and Conduct of Meetings, 1936 (4th edn 1963); Insurance Law, 1933 (2nd edn 1948); Sale of Goods and Hire Purchase, 1949 (2nd edn 1961); Partnership, 1957 (2nd edn 1966); Local Government, 1963; Australian Federal Government, 1967. *Recreation:* gardening. *Address:* 119 The Boulevarde, Strathfield, NSW 2135, Australia. *T:* 642 3156. *Clubs:* Royal Automobile of Vic, Melbourne Cricket (Melbourne).

**JOSLIN, Ivy Collin,** BSc; late Headmistress, Francis Holland School, Clarence Gate, NW1; *b* 12 April 1900. *Educ:* Skinners' Company's Sch., London; University Coll., London. Science Mistress, Howell's Sch., Denbigh, 1922-24; Physics Mistress, Southend-on-Sea High Sch., 1924-29; Science Mistress, St Stephen's High Sch., Clewer, 1929-30; Mathematics Mistress, Dame Alice Owen's Sch., London, 1930-33; Headmistress, Derby High Sch., 1933-39; Headmistress, Newcastle on Tyne Church High Sch., 1943-45. *Publications:* Everyday Domestic Science (with P. M. Taylor), 1932; General Science, 1937; The Air Around Us, 1961; Water in the World, 1962; Electricity in Use, 1964. *Recreations:* walking, theatre. *Club:* University Women's.

**JOSLIN, Maj.-Gen. Stanley William,** CB 1951; CBE 1950 (MBE 1936); MA; FIMechE; Chief Inspector of Nuclear Installations, Ministry of Power, 1959-64, retired; *b* 25 March 1899; *m* 1939, Eva Hudson; one *d. Educ:* Hackney Downs Sch.; Royal Military Academy Woolwich; Cambridge Univ. Commissioned 2nd Lieut, Royal Engineers, 1918; served: Germany, 1918-19; India, 1920-23; Nigeria, 1926-28; Singapore, 1937-39; War of 1939-45; NW Europe, 1944-49; transferred to REME, 1943; Maj.-Gen., 1950; Dir of Mechanical Engineering, War Office, 1950-53; retired, 1954. UK Atomic Energy Authority, 1954-59. *Recreations:* walking, ski-ing, music. *Address:* Southern Cottage, Maresfield Park, Uckfield, Sussex. *T:* Uckfield 2933.

**JOSLING, John Francis;** writer on legal subjects; Principal Assistant Solicitor of Inland Revenue, 1965-71; *b* 26 May 1910; *s* of John Richard Josling, Hackney, London, and Florence Alice (*née* Robinson); *m* 1935, Bertha Frearson; two *s* two *d. Educ:* Leyton Co. High Sch. Entered a private Solicitor's office, 1927; articled, 1937; admitted as Solicitor, 1940. Served War of 1939-45 (war stars and medals): RA, 1940-45; JAG's Br, 1945-46. Entered office of Solicitor of Inland Revenue, 1946; Sen. Legal Asst, 1948; Asst Solicitor, 1952. Mem., Law Society. Coronation Medal, 1953. *Publications:* Oyez Practice Notes on Adoption of Children, 1947; Execution of a Judgment, 1948; (with C. Caplin) Apportionments for Executors and Trustees, 1948; Change of Name (edns from 1948); Naturalisation, 1949; Summary Judgment in the High Court, 1950; Periods of Limitation, 1951; (with L. Alexander) The Law of Clubs, 1964; contribs to Simon's Income Tax (2nd edn) and Halsbury's Laws of England vol. 20 (3rd edn); many contribs to Solicitors' Jl and some other legal jls. *Recreations:* music and musical history; Victorian novels; Georgian children and Elizabethan grand-children. *Address:* 55 Downside Road, Sutton, Surrey. *T:* 01-642 7484. *Club:* Civil Service.

**JOSSET, Lawrence;** RE 1951 (ARE 1936); ARCA; Free-lance artist and part-time teacher at Medway College of Arts and Crafts; *b* 2 Aug. 1910; *s* of Leon Antoine Hyppolite and Annie Mary Josset; *m* 1960, Beatrice, *d* of William Alford Taylor. *Educ:* Bromley County Sch. for Boys; Bromley and Beckenham Schs of Art; Royal College of Art (diploma). Engraver's Draughtsman at Waterlow and Son Ltd, Clifton Street, 1930-32; Art Master at Red Hill Sch., East Sutton, near Maidstone, Kent, 1935-36. Mem. of Art Workers' Guild. *Publications:* Mezzotint in colours; Flowers, after Fantin-Latour, 1937; The Trimmed Cock, after Ben Marshall, 1939; Brighton Beach and Spring, after Constable, 1947; Carting Timber and Milking Time, after Shayer, 1948; The Pursuit, and Love Letters, after Fragonard, 1949; Spring and Autumn, after Boucher, 1951; A Family, after Zoffany, 1953; Master James Sayer, 1954; HM The Queen after Annigoni, commissioned by the Times, 1956, and plates privately commissioned after de Lazlo, James Gunn and Oswald Birley. *Recreations:* outdoor sketching, cycling, etc. *Address:* The Cottage, Pilgrims Way, Detling, near Maidstone, Kent.

**JOST, H(ans) Peter,** CBE 1969; DSc; CEng; FIMechE; FIProdE; Managing Director: K. S. Paul Products Ltd, 1955; Centralube Ltd, 1955; Director, Williams Hudson Ltd, 1967; Chairman: Bright Brazing Ltd, 1969; Peppermill Brass Foundry Ltd, 1970; Director of Overseas companies; *b* 25 Jan. 1921; *o s* of late Leo and Margot Jost; *m* 1948, Margaret Josephine, *o d* of late Michael and of Mrs Sara Kadesh, Norfolk Is, S Pacific; two *d. Educ:* City of Liverpool Techn. Coll.; Manchester Coll. of Technology. Apprentice, Associated Metal Works, Glasgow and D. Napier & Son Ltd, Liverpool; Methods Engr, K & L Steelfounders and Engrs Ltd, 1943; Chief Planning Engr, Datim Machine Tool Co. Ltd, 1946; Gen. Man. 1949, Dir 1952, Trier Bros Ltd; Lubrication Consultant: Richard Thomas & Baldwins Ltd, 1960-65; August Thyssen Hütte AG 1963-66. Chairman: Lubrication Educn and Res. Working Gp, Dept of Educn and Science, 1964-65; Cttee on Tribology, Min. of Technology, 1966-; Mem., Adv. Coun. on Technology, 1968-, and Cttee on Terotechnology, 1970-, Min. of Technology. Hon. Associate, Manchester Coll. of Science and Technology, 1962; Hon. MIPlantE, 1969. Hon. DSc Salford, 1970. Sir John Larking Medal 1944, Derby Medal 1955, Liverpool Engrg Soc.; Hutchinson Meml Medal 1952, Silver Medal for Best Paper 1952-53, IProdE. *Publications:* Lubrication (Tribology) Report of DES Cttee, 1966 (Jost Report); various papers in Proc. IMechE, Proc.IProdE, technical jls, etc. *Recreations:* music, opera, gardening, riding. *Address:* Hill House, Wills Grove, Mill Hill, NW7. *T:* 01-959 3355.

**JOULES, Horace,** MD, FRCP; Physician and Medical Director, Central Middlesex Hospital, 1935-65; *b* 21 March 1902; *s* of Richard Edgar and Emily Ann Joules; *m* 1930, Mary Sparrow; two *s* one *d* (and one *s* decd). *Educ:* Cardiff and London Univs. Qualified Middlesex Hosp.; MRCS, LRCP, 1924; MB, BS, 1925; MD (Gold Medal), 1928; MRCP 1928; FRCP 1943; Junior Appointments, Middlesex Hosp., Brompton Hosp., Ancoats Hosp.; Physician, Selly Oak Hosp., Birmingham, 1929; Examiner in Medicine, University of Cambridge and Royal College of Physicians. *Publications:* Ed. Doctors View of War, 1938; articles in medical journals. *Recreations:* gardening, ornithology. *Address:* 20 Templewood Road, Parson's Heath, Colchester, Essex.

**JOWETT, Very Rev. Alfred;** Dean of Manchester since 1964; *b* 29 May 1914; *s* of Alfred Edmund Jowett; *m* 1939, Margaret, *d* of St Clair Benford; one *s* three *d. Educ:* High Storrs Grammar Sch., Sheffield; St Catharine's Coll., Cambridge; Lincoln Theological Coll. BA 1935; Certif. Educn 1936; MA 1959. Deacon 1944; Priest 1945. Curate of St John the

Evangelist, Goole, 1944-47; Sec., Sheffield Anglican and Free Church Council and Marriage Guidance Council, 1947-51; Vicar of St George with St Stephen, Sheffield, 1951-60; Part-time Lecturer, Sheffield Univ. Dept of Education, 1950-60; Vicar of Doncaster, 1960-64; Hon. Canon of Sheffield Cathedral, 1960-64. Select Preacher, Oxford Univ., 1964. Mem., Community Relations Commn, 1968-. *Publication:* (Part-author) The English Church: a New Look, 1966. *Recreations:* theatre, music, walking. *Address:* The Deanery, Prestwich, Manchester M25 8QF. *T:* 061-773 4301.

**JOWETT, Ronald Edward,** CBE 1969; MD, FRCS; Otolaryngologist, Sunderland Hospital Group, since 1925; *b* 5 March 1901; *s* of James and Emma Jowett, Halifax, Yorks; *m* 1929, Lilian Waring, Halifax; two *s*. *Educ:* Heath Sch., Halifax; Leeds Univ.; Leeds Med. Sch. MB, ChB (Hons) Leeds, 1922; Scattergood and Hardwick Prizes; MD Leeds, 1923; DLO, RCP&S London, 1925, MRCP 1933; FRCS 1966. Surgeon, Newcastle upon Tyne Throat, Nose and Ear Hosp., 1937-50. President: Regional Hospitals' Consultants and Specialists Assoc., 1951-53 and 1964-65; Newcastle upon Tyne and Northern Counties Med. Soc., 1955; N of England Otolaryngological Soc., 1955. Mem., Newcastle Regional Hosp. Bd, 1947-69 (Chm. of its Med. Adv. Cttee, 1953-69; Vice-Chm. of the Bd, 1967-69). FRSM. *Publications:* The Injured Workman (with G. F. Walker), 1933; contribs to: Med. Press and Circular, BMJ, Proc. Roy. Soc. Med., Jl of Mental Science, Jl of Laryngology and Otology, Den Norske Turistforenning. *Recreations:* winter sports, making music, fishing. *Address:* White Gates, 80 Queen Alexandra Road, Sunderland, Co. Durham. *T:* Sunderland 68990.

**JOWITT, Edwin Frank,** QC 1969; Deputy Chairman: Rutland Quarter Sessions, since 1967; Derbyshire Quarter Sessions, since 1970; *b* 1 Oct. 1929; *s* of Frank and Winifred Jowitt; *m* 1959, Anne Barbara Dyson; three *s* two *d*. *Educ:* Swanwick Hall Grammar Sch.; London Sch. of Economics. LLB London 1950. Called to Bar, Middle Temple, 1951; Member Midland Circuit. *Recreation:* fell walking. *Address:* 2 Crown Office Row, Temple, EC4. *T:* 01-353 1365.

**JOY, Sir George Andrew,** KBE 1949; CMG 1945; *b* 20 Feb. 1896; 3rd *s* of late George Edward Joy, Ashford, Kent, and Elizabeth Ellen Breakwell, Dublin; *m* 1925, Hettie Claire Wallace (*d* 1966), Sydney, Aust.; one *s*; *m* 1968, Pauline Rhoda Ossorn (*née* Whishaw). *Educ:* Xaverian Coll., Bruges, Belgium. Military Service, 1914-23; entered Colonial Service, 1924; Resident Commissioner, Anglo-French Condominium, New Hebrides, 1928, and Deputy Commissioner, Western Pacific; also Consul for the Hoorn and Wallace Islands. Resident Adviser to Sultans in the Hadhramaut States of Southern Arabia, 1940; Civil Sec. to Govt of Aden, and Comr of Civil Defence, 1942-46; Governor and C-in-C, St Helena and Dependencies, 1946-53; retd 1954. Vice-Pres., Soc. for Physical Research. *Address:* Bay Tree Cottage, Beckley, Rye, Sussex. *T:* Northiam 3204.

**JOY, Michael Gerard Laurie,** CMG 1965; MC 1945; *b* 27 Oct. 1916; *s* of late Frank Douglas Howarth Joy, Bentley, Hants; *m* 1951, Ann Félise Jacomb; one *s* three *d*. *Educ:* Winchester; New Coll., Oxford. Served RA, 1940-46 (MC, wounded). Foreign Office, 1947; Private Sec. to Permanent Under Sec. of State, 1948-50; Saigon, 1950-53; Washington, 1953-55; IDC, 1956; Foreign Office, 1957-59; Counsellor, 1959; Addis Ababa, 1959-62; Stockholm, 1962-64; seconded to Cabinet Office, 1964-66; Foreign Office, 1966-68. *Recreation:* shooting. *Address:* Marelands, Bentley, Hants. *T:* Bentley 3288. *Clubs:* Brooks's, MCC.

**JOYCE, Alec Houghton,** CIE 1943; CBE 1952 (OBE 1938); *b* 5 March 1894; *m* Mary, 2nd *d* of late George Frederick Oates, Roundhay, Leeds; two *s*. Served European War, 1914-19, in France and Russia (Meritorious Service Medal); entered India Office, 1919; Joint Publicity Officer to the India and Burma Round Table Conferences, 1930-32; Personal Asst to the Prime Minister during Monetary and Economic Conference, 1933; on special duty in India and Burma, 1935 and in India, 1936-37. Seconded at various times to No. 10 Downing Street as Actg Chief Press Adviser. Paid official visits to USA and Canada, 1943; to India, 1943; again to India with Cabinet Delegation, 1946; and to USA and all Provs of Canada, 1951; on an official tour of Pakistan, India, and Ceylon, 1951-52; Head of Information Dept Commonwealth Relations Office (Asst Sec.), 1948-Nov. 1954, subseq. employed in charge of branch conducting liaison with UK, Commonwealth, and foreign Press and with BBC; retired, 1957. *Address:* 3 Kaye Moor Road, Sutton, Surrey. *Club:* Devonshire.

**JOYCE, Eileen;** concert pianist; *b* Zeehan, Tasmania; *d* of Joseph and Alice Joyce, Western Australia; *m* 1st (husband killed, War of 1939-45); one *s*; 2nd, Christopher Mann. *Educ:* Loreto Convent, Perth, Western Australia; Leipzig Conservatoire. Studied in Germany under Teichmuller, and later, Schnabel. Concert début in London at Promenade Concerts under Sir Henry Wood. Numerous concert tours, radio performances and gramophone recordings. During War of 1939-45, played in association with London Philharmonic Orchestra, especially in blitzed towns and cities throughout Great Britain. Concerts with: all principal orchestras of the UK; Berlin Philharmonic Orchestra in Berlin; Conservatoire and National Orchestras, France; Concertgebouw Orchestra, Holland; La Scala Orchestra, Italy; Philadelphia Orchestra, Carnegie Hall, New York. Concert tours in: Australia, 1948; SA, 1950; Scandinavia and Holland, 1951; S Amer., Scandinavia and Finland, 1952; Jugoslavia, 1955; NZ, 1958; USSR, 1961; India, 1962; also performed harpsichord in several concerts Royal Albert Hall and Royal Festival Hall. Has contributed to sound tracks of films including: The Seventh Veil, Brief Encounter, Man of Two Worlds, Quartet, Trent's Last Case; appeared in films: Battle for Music, Girl in a Million, Wherever She Goes (autobiographical). *Address:* Chartwell Farm, Westerham, Kent.

**JOYCE, John H.;** Deputy Chairman, Coast Lines Ltd; Director: Belfast Steamship Co. Ltd; Burns & Laird Lines Ltd; Tyne-Tees Steam Shipping Co. Ltd; *b* 6 Oct. 1906. *Address:* Coast Lines Ltd, Reliance House, Water Street, Liverpool 2.

**JOYNSON-HICKS,** family name of **Viscount Brentford.**

**JOYNT, Evelyn Gertrude,** MBE 1967; Major (retired) WRAC; National General Secretary of YWCA of Great Britain since 1968; *b* 5 Sept. 1919; 2nd *d* of late Rev. George Joynt, Dublin. *Educ:* Collegiate Sch., Enniskillen; Banbridge Academy. Joined ATS, 1942; transf. to WRAC, 1952; jsc, WRAC Staff Coll., 1954; served Middle East and Far East; OC Drivers and Clerks Training Wing, WRAC; DAQMG, Eastern Comd; retired 1967. *Address:* 223 Latymer Court, W6. *T:* 01-748 3449. *Clubs:* Service Women's, Soroptomist of Great Britain.

**JUBB, Edwin Charles,** CB 1942; OBE 1925; *b* 1883; *s* of Edwin Charles Jubb, Hull; *m* 1912, Emily Herbert (*d* 1964), *d* of late Charles Powell, Co. Limerick, one *s* one *d* (and one *s* decd). *Educ:* Rossall; Pembroke Coll., Cambridge. 14th Wrangler 1906; Second Class Hons Science Tripos, 1907; entered Civil Service, 1908; Dir of Navy Contracts Admiralty from 1936; retired 1947. *Recreations:* cricket and singing. *Address:* Warren House, Farnham Common, Bucks. *T:* Farnham Common 3952. *Club:* Royal Commonwealth Society.

**JUDD, Charles Wilfred,** CBE 1954; Joint President, United Nations Association (Director-General, 1945-64); *b* 27 Oct. 1896; *o s* of Charles Henry and Isobel Judd; *m* 1927, Helen Osborn Ashcroft, *d* of Rev. Dr Frank Ashcroft, Edinburgh; two *s* one *d. Educ:* Farnham Gram. Sch.; University Coll., London. Served European War, 1914-18: RAMC, Western Front and Italy. Hon. Sec., Nat. Union of Students, 1922-23. League of Nations Union: Sec. British Univs. League of Nations Soc. from formation, 1924-29; Chief Educn Officer, 1929-39; Asst Sec., 1939-43; Sec. and Dir-Gen, 1943-65. Hon. Sec. Geneva Inst. of Internat. Relations, 1929-39; London Internat. Assembly, 1940-45. Part founder and Sec., Coun. for Educn in World Citizenship, 1939-45. World Fedn of United Nations Associations: Mem. Exec. Cttee, 1946-66; Chm., 1955-57; missions to USA, China, India, SE Asia and West Africa. *Publications:* Assault at Arms (with Sir Ronald Adam), 1960; pamphlets and articles on UN affairs. *Recreations:* walking and travelling. *Address:* 42 The Crescent, Belmont, Sutton, Surrey. *T:* 01-642 5017. *Club:* English-Speaking Union.
*See also F. A. Judd.*

**JUDD, Frank Ashcroft;** MP (Lab) Portsmouth West since 1966; *b* 28 March 1935; *s* of Charles Judd, *qv*; *m* 1961, Christine Elizabeth Willington; two *d. Educ:* City of London Sch.; London Sch. of Economics. Pres., UN Student Assoc., 1955. Short Service Commn, RAF, 1957-59. Contested (Lab): Sutton and Cheam, 1959; Portsmouth West, 1964. Sec.-Gen., Internat. Voluntary Service, 1960-66. Jt Sec., Parly Gp for the UN, 1966-; PPS to Minister of Housing, 1967-70; Chm., Parly Labour Party Overseas Aid and Develt Gp; Vice-Chairman: Council for Educn in the Commonwealth, 1966-; Fabian Internat. and Commonwealth Bureau; Pres. Co-ordinating Cttee for Internat. Voluntary Service, 1966-; Member: Parly Select Cttee on Overseas Aid and Develt; Exec. Cttee, Fabian Soc.; British Delegn to Council of Europe and WEU, 1970. Extensive travel, including Mission to UN, 1966 and 1967. Chm., Editorial Bd of Venture. *Publications:* (Jtly) Radical Future; contrib. periodicals, incl. Venture (Chm. Ed. Bd). *Recreation:* walking. *Address:* 42a The Crescent, Belmont, Sutton, Surrey. *T:* 01-643 6103; 5 Palmerston Court, Clarence Parade, Portsmouth. *T:* 24881.

**JUDD, John Basil Thomas;** HM Consul-General at Zagreb, 1961-65; retired; re-employed in the Foreign Office, 1966-69; *b* 12 May 1909; *s* of John Matthews Judd and Helena Beatrice Jenkins; *m* 1939, Cynthia Margaret Georgina, *yr d* of Sir Henry White-Smith, CBE; two *s* one *d. Educ:* The Leys; Downing Coll., Cambridge; Inner Temple (called to the Bar, 1931). Entered Levant Consular Service, 1932; Vice-Consul and 3rd Sec. at Jedda, 1936; Vice-Consul at Casablanca and Tangier, 1939-43; Consul at Tunis and Marseilles, 1943-46; Consul and 1st Sec. at Paris, 1946; Consul at Jerusalem, 1949; Foreign Office, 1951; Consul-Gen. at Valparaiso, 1953; Consul-Gen. and Counsellor, Cairo, 1955-57; Consul-Gen. at Basra, 1957-61. *Recreations:* fishing, theatre and opera. *Address:* 77 Siren Street, Senglea, Malta. *Clubs:* Royal Automobile, St James'.

**JUDD, Nadine;** *see* Nerina, Nadia.

**JUDE, Sir Norman (Lane),** Kt 1965; JP; Member of Legislative Council, Southern District, South Australia, since 1944; *b* 7 April 1905; *o s* of Alexander and Susan Jude, Moseley, Birmingham, Eng.; *m* 1935, Nancy M., *d* of Keith Bowman, Poltalloch, S Aust.; one *s* three *d. Educ:* Stamford Sch., Lincs; Roseworthy Agricultural Coll., SA. Dipl. of Roseworthy Agric. Coll. (RDA). Took up land at Carolside, Naracoorte, SA, as fat lamb and baby beef producer, 1936; mem. Council of SA Stockowners Association, 1938-40. Founded and became first Pres. of SE Fire-Fighting Assoc. Minister of Railways, Minister of Roads and Minister of Local Government, 1953-65; Mem. Aust. Transport Advisory Council, 1953-65; now mem. Subordinate Legislation Cttee. Company Dir. *Recreations:* field shooting, interstate hockey and Rugby football. *Address:* Robin Hill, 109 North-East Road, Collinswood, S Australia 5081, Australia. *T:* Adelaide 65-6000. *Clubs:* Adelaide, Royal Adelaide Golf, Amateur Sports of SA (Patron), Stock Exchange, Tattersall's (Adelaide).

**JUDGE, Edward Thomas,** MA Cantab; Chairman: Darlington & Simpson Rolling Mills Ltd; A. Reyrolle & Co. Ltd; C. A. Parsons and Co.; Reyrolle Parsons; Chairman (non-executive): Dorman Long (Engineering Holdings) Ltd; Dorman Long (Bridge & Engineering) Ltd; Redpath Dorman Long Ltd; Teeside Bridge & Engineering Ltd; T. A. Holdings Ltd; British Structural Steel Co. Ltd; Director: Dorman Long (Africa) Ltd; British International Marine Engineering Co. Ltd; North Sea Marine Engineering Construction Co. Ltd; BPB Industries Ltd; Finance Corp. for Industry Ltd; Pilkington Bros Ltd. *b* 20 Nov. 1908; *o s* of late Thomas Oliver and Florence Judge (*née* Gravestock); *m* 1934, Alice Gertrude Matthews; two *s. Educ:* Worcester Royal Grammar Sch.; St John's Coll., Cambridge. Joined Dorman Long, 1930, and held various appts, becoming Chief Technical Engr, 1937; Special Dir, 1944; Chief Engr, 1945; Dir, 1947; Asst Man. Dir, Dorman Long (Steel) Ltd, 1959; Jt Man. Dir, 1960; Chm. and Gen. Man. Dir, Dorman Long & Co. Ltd, 1961-67. Mem. Exec. and Devel. Cttees of Brit. Iron & Steel Fedn; Gov., Constantine Tech. Coll., Middlesbrough, 1945-; Rep. of Minister of Transport on Tees Conservancy Commn., 1951-; part-time Mem. N Eastern Electricity Bd, 1952-62; Vice-Pres., Iron & Steel Inst., 1958. Pres., British Iron & Steel Federation, 1965, 1966, 1967. Bessemer Gold Medal, Iron and Steel Inst., 1967. *Publications:* technical papers. *Recreation:* fishing. *Address:* Wood Place, Astley Guise, Bletchley, Bucks.

**JUDGE, Harry George,** MA Oxon, PhD London; Principal, Banbury School, since 1967; *b* 1 Aug. 1928; *s* of George Arthur and Winifred Mary Judge; *m* 1956, Elizabeth Mary Patrick; one *s* two *d. Educ:* Cardiff High Sch.; Brasenose Coll., Oxford. Asst Master, Emanuel Sch. and Wallington County Grammar Sch., 1954-59; Dir of Studies, Cumberland Lodge, Windsor, 1959-62; Head Master, Banbury Grammar Sch., 1962-67. Member, Public Schools

Commission, 1966-70. *Publications:* Louis XIV, 1965; contribs on educational and historical subjects to collective works and learned jls. *Address:* Principal's House, Banbury School, Banbury, Oxon.

**JUDGES, Arthur Valentine,** DSc (London); Emeritus Professor, University of London; Fellow of King's College, University of London, since 1957; *b* 14 Feb. 1898; 2nd *s* of late Rev. William Worthington Judges, and late Caroline Susan Judges (*née* Lang); *m* 1927, Kathleen Mitchell, *e d* of late Francis Voltaire Mitchell; two *d. Educ:* St Felix Sch., Felixstowe; Southend-on-Sea High Sch.; King's Coll., London; London Sch. of Economics and Political Science. Served European War, with London Rifle Brigade, Machine-Gun Corps and Tank Corps, 1915-18; Lecturer, London Sch. of Economics and Political Science, 1927-38; Hon. Sec., Council for Preservation of Business Archives, 1934-38; Leverhulme Research Fellow in USA and Canada, 1938-39; Reader in Economic History, University of London, 1938-48; Joint Dir of Royal Historical Society, 1938-45; Ministry of Labour and National Service, 1940-44; Labour Adviser and Asst Sec., Ministry of Production, 1944-45; pt-time mem. of Cabinet Office staff, 1945-53; Professor of the History of Education, King's Coll., London, 1949-65; mem. of Central Advisory Council for Educn in England, 1951-60. Chairman: Editorial Bd, Brit. Jl of Educational Studies, 1952-61; Standing Conference on Studies in Education, 1955-61; Conference of Heads of University Depts of Education, 1959-64; Royal Commission on Education in S Rhodesia, 1962-63. Lecturer, Goldsmiths' Coll., 1965-. *Publications:* books and articles on historical and educational subjects. *Address:* Oliver House, Strand-on-the-Green, W4. *T:* 01-994 1122. *Club:* Athenæum.

**JUKES, E(rnest) Martin,** QC 1954; Barrister-at-Law; Director-General, Engineering Employers Federation, since 1965; *b* 5 Dec. 1909; *s* of Ernest and Hilda Gordon Jukes, Purley, Surrey; *m* 1931, Mary Kinloch (*née* Anderson); two *s* one *d. Educ:* Merchant Taylors' Sch.; St John's Coll., Oxford (MA). Called to the Bar, Jan. 1933; Mem. of the Bar Council, 1952-56 and 1964; Master of the Bench, Middle Temple, 1963; Judge of the Courts of Appeal for Guernsey and Jersey, 1964; Commissioner for Municipal Election Petitions, 1961. Member: Engineering Industry Training Bd (Chm., Supervisor Training Policy Cttee); Council, CBI; First Sec. of State's Nat. Jt Adv. Council. Served War of 1939-45 as Lieut-Col RASC, in UK, France, Germany and Belgium (despatches). *Address:* (home) 35 Trevor Square, SW7. *T:* 01-589 2104. *Clubs:* St James', Flyfishers'.

**JUKES, John Andrew,** CB 1968; Director General (Research and Economic Planning), Ministry of Transport, since 1969; *b* 19 May 1917; *s* of Captain A. M. Jukes, MD, IMS, and Mrs Gertrude E. Jukes (*née* King); *m* 1943, Muriel Child; two *s* two *d. Educ:* Shrewsbury Sch.; St John's Coll., Cambridge; London Sch. of Economics. MA in physics Cambridge, BSc (Econ.) London. Cavendish Laboratory, Cambridge, 1939; Radar and Operational Research, 1939-46; Research Dept, LMS Railway, 1946-48; Economic Adviser, Cabinet Office and Treasury, 1948-54; British Embassy, Washington, DC, 1949-51; Economic Adviser to UK Atomic Energy Authority, 1954-64 and Principal Economics and Programming Office, UKAEA, 1957-64; appointed to Dept Economic Affairs as Dep. Dir Gen., 1964; Dep. Under-Sec. of State, Dept of Economic Affairs, 1967. *Recreations:* ski-ing, walking, gardening. *Address:* 38 Albion Road, Sutton, Surrey. *T:* 01-642 5018. *Club:* Reform.

**JUKES, Richard Starr,** CBE 1969; FCA; Chairman of BPB Industries Ltd, since 1965; *b* 6 Dec. 1906; *s* of late Rev. Arthur Starr Jukes and Mrs Annie Florance Jukes; *m* 1935, Ruth Mary Wilmot; one *s* two *d. Educ:* St Edmund's, Canterbury. Mem. Inst. of Chartered Accountants, 1929. Gyproc Products Ltd: Sec./Accountant, 1934; Dir, 1939; The British Plaster Board (Holdings) Ltd: Dir, 1943; Jt Man. Dir, 1947; Man. Dir, 1954; Dep. Chm., 1962; Chm., 1965 (since Aug. 1965 the company has been known as BPB Industries Ltd). Mem. Council, Inst. of Directors. *Recreation:* golf. *Address:* White House, Watford Road, Northwood, Mddx. *T:* Northwood 24125. *Clubs:* Bath; Island Sailing; Moor Park Golf, Sandy Lodge Golf; Sundsvalls Golfklubb (Sweden); Hillside Golf (Rhodesia).

**JULIAN, Sir (Kenneth) Ivor,** Kt 1958; CBE 1950; Chairman, South-East Metropolitan Regional Hospital Board, 1946-68, retired; *b* 3 Dec. 1895; *s* of late Henry Matthew Julian, Basingstoke, Hants, and late Elizabeth Isabella McKay, Aberdeenshire; *m* 1936, Rosemary Staunton, *d* of late Charles Edgar Terry and late Virginia Constance Terry, Hove; no *c. Educ:* St Anne's Sch., Redhill. Served War of 1914-18 (Army). Chm., Royal Sussex County Hospital, Brighton, 1946-48; Dir of several Companies. Mem. of Bd of Governors of Guy's Hosp. *Recreations:* golf, tennis. *Address:* 4 Ash Close, Dyke Road Avenue, Hove, Sussex. *T:* Brighton 52852. *Club:* Brooks's.

**JULYAN, Lt-Col (retd) William Leopold,** TD; MA Oxon; JP; *b* 7 Dec. 1888; *e s* of Benjamin and Emma Jane Julyan, St Austell, Cornwall; *m* Marie Eileen Phyllis Bennett, LRAM. *Educ:* School of Rural Economy, Oxford; University Coll. Oxford. Distinction in Final Schools of Agriculture and Rural Economy. Served in France and Flanders during European War 1914-18, as Subaltern and Capt. on regimental duties, and as Major and Lt-Col on the Administrative Staff (despatches twice); Lt-Col, Duke of Cornwall's Light Infantry, Territorial Army (retired); employed on staff duties during the war to 1945; commanding 8 Devon/Cornwall HG, 1953-57. Mem. of Gray's Inn, Inns of Court; travelled East African Dependencies and South Africa, 1931, to study agricultural and educational conditions. Warden of the Lord Wandsworth Agricultural Coll., 1922-45; Lecturer for Central Office of Information and for Imperial Institute. Leverhulme Research award, 1952-53. *Publications:* contributions to Educational and Agricultural Journals from time to time. *Recreations:* seeing rural England, interest in bygones of the farm and countryside and rural crafts. *Address:* Cotehele House, St Dominic, Cornwall. *Club:* Royal Commonwealth Society (Life Member).

**JUMA, Midhet;** Order of the Star of Jordan, 1st and 2nd class; Ambassador of the Hashemite Kingdom of Jordan to the Court of St James's, 1967-68; *b* 19 Aug. 1920; *s* of Midhet Juma el-Kurdi, Turkey; *m* 1950, Aida Halim; one *s* one *d. Educ:* Cairo Univ. Attaché, Arab League, Cairo, 1945-47; 1st Sec. and Counsellor, Cairo, 1947-52; Counsellor and Chargé d'Affaires, London, 1952-53; Minister, Pakistan, 1953-55; Chief of Protocol, Royal Palace, Amman, 1956; Under-Sec. of State i/c of Press and Broadcasting, 1956-58; Ambassador: Washington, 1958-59; Morocco, 1959-62;

Bonn, 1962-65; Beirut, 1965-67. Holds many foreign Orders. *Recreations:* politics, reading, swimming, music. *Address:* c/o Ministry of Foreign Affairs, Amman, Jordan. *Clubs:* Travellers', Hurlingham, Clermont, Crockford's.

**JUMA, Sa'ad;** *b* Tafila, Jordan, 21 March 1916; *s* of Mohammed Juma; *m* 1961, Salwa Ghanem, Beirut; two *s* one *d*. *Educ:* Damascus Univ. (L'Essence in Law). Chief of Protocol, Min. of For. Affairs, 1949; Dir of Press, 1950; Sec. to Prime Minister's Office, 1950-54; Under-Sec., Min. of Interior, 1954-57; Governor of Amman, 1957-58; Under-Sec., Min. of For. Affairs, 1958-59; Ambassador: to Iran, 1959-61; to Syria, 1961-62; to USA, 1962-65; Minister of the Royal Court, 1965-67; Prime Minister, 1967; Ambassador to London, 1969-70. Orders of El Nahda (1st Class) and Star of Jordan (1st Class); decorations from Syria, Lebanon, China, Italy, Libya, Malaysia and Ethiopia. *Publication:* Conspiracy and the Battle of Destiny. *Recreations:* reading, music, bridge. *Address:* c/o Ministry of Foreign Affairs, Amman, Jordan. *Clubs:* Travellers', Hurlingham.

**JUNGWIRTH, Sir (William) John,** Kt 1957; CMG, 1948; AASA JP; retired as Permanent Head of Premier's Department, Melbourne, Victoria, 1962; *b* Melbourne, 10 Aug. 1897; British; *m* 1st, 1923, Ruth Powell (*d* 1938); one *s* one *d*; 2nd 1942, Edna Tamblyn; two *s*. *Educ:* Melbourne. Joined Victorian Public Service, 1915; Private Sec. to various Premiers, 1920-32; Permanent Head of Premier's Dept, 1934-62. Past President: YMCA; Methodist Men's Soc. of Victoria; Pres., Board of Management, Prince Henry's Hospital; Chairman: District Trustees, Independent Order of Rechabites; Healesville Wild Life Sanctuary. *Recreations:* bowls, reading. *Address:* 31 Bulleen Road, North Balwyn, Victoria 3104, Australia. *Club:* Royal Automobile of Victoria (Melbourne).

**JUNOR, John;** Editor, Sunday Express, since 1954; Chairman, Sunday Express, 1968; Director, Beaverbrook Newspapers, since 1960; *b* 15 Jan. 1919; *s* of Alexander Junor, Black Isle, Ross and Cromarty; *m* 1942, Pamela Mary Welsh; one *s* one *d*. *Educ:* Glasgow Univ. (MA Hons English). Lt (A) RNVR, 1939-45. Contested (L) Kincardine and West Aberdeen, 1945, East Edinburgh, 1948, Dundee West, 1951; Asst Editor, Daily Express, 1951-53; Dep. Editor, Evening Standard, 1953-54. *Recreations:* golf, tennis, sailing. *Address:* Wellpools Farm, Charlwood, Surrey. *T:* Norwood Hill 370. *Clubs:* Royal Automobile, Royal Southern Yacht; Walton Heath.

**JUPP, Clifford Norman,** CMG 1966; with The Burton Group Ltd, since 1970; *b* 24 Sept. 1919; *s* of Albert Leonard Jupp and Marguerite Isabel (*née* Day Winter); *m* 1945, Brenda (*née* Babbs); one *s* two *d*. *Educ:* Perse Sch., Cambridge; Trinity Hall, Cambridge. Armed Forces, 1940-46. Mem. of HM Foreign and Diplomatic Service, 1946-70; served in: Foreign Office, 1946; Beirut, 1947-49; New York, 1949-51; Foreign Office, 1951-53; Cairo, 1953-56; Kabul, 1956-59; Foreign Office, 1959-61; Brussels, 1961-63; Belgrade, 1963-66; seconded to BoT and Min. of Technology, 1967-70. *Address:* 12 Wallgrave Terrace, SW5. *Clubs:* Royal Automobile, Special Forces.

**JUPP, Kenneth Graham,** MC 1943; QC 1966; Deputy Chairman, Cambridge and Isle of Ely Quarter Sessions, since 1965; *b* 2 June 1917; *s* of Albert Leonard and Marguerite Isabel Jupp; *m* 1947, Kathleen Elizabeth (*née* Richards); two *s* two *d*. *Educ:* Perse Sch., Cambridge; University Coll., Oxford (Sen. Class. Schol.; 1st Cl. Hon. Mods 1938); Lincoln's Inn (Cassel Schol.). Regimental Service in France, Belgium, N Africa and Italy, 1939-43; War Office Selection Board, 1943-46. Called to Bar, 1945. Chm., Independent Schs Tribunal, 1964-67. *Recreations:* sailing, music. *Address:* Farrar's Building, Temple, EC4. *T:* 01-583 9241. *Club:* Garrick.

**JURINAC, (Srebrenka) Sena;** opera singer; Member of Vienna State Opera since 1944; *b* Travnik, Yugoslavia, 24 Oct. 1921; *d* of Ludwig Jurinac, MD, and Christine Cerv. *Educ:* High Sch.; Musical Academy. Made first appearance on stage as Mimi with Zagreb Opera, 1942. Frequent appearances at Glyndebourne Festivals, 1949-56, as well as at the Salzburg Festivals. Regular guest-artist at La Scala and Covent Garden. Principal parts include: Donna Anna and Donna Elvira in Don Giovanni; Elisabeth in Tannhauser; Tosca; Madame Butterfly; Mimi in La Bohème; Marschallin in Der Rosenkavalier; Composer in Ariadne auf Naxos; Elisabeth in Don Carlos; Desdemona in Othello. *Film:* Der Rosenkavalier, 1962. Kammersängerin award, 1951; Ehrenkreuz für Wissenschaft und Kunst, 1961; Grosses Ehrenzeichen für Verdienste um die Republik Oesterreich, 1967. *Address:* c/o Vienna State Opera, Austria.

**JURY, Archibald George,** CBE 1961; FRIBA; FRIAS; City Architect, Glasgow, since 1951; *b* 23 June 1907; *s* of late George John Jury and Mabel Sophie Jury (*née* Fisher); *m* 1931, Amy Beatrice Maw; one *d*. *Educ:* Mount Radford, Exeter; SW School of Art. Architect to Council, Taunton, 1938-40, and 1945. Served War, 1940-45, with Corps of Royal Engineers (rank of Major). Chief Housing Architect, Liverpool, 1946-49; Dir of Housing, Glasgow, 1949-51; Dir of Planning, Glasgow, 1951-66. Organised the building of 80,000 houses, civic buildings and over 100 schools, Glasgow; responsible for the Glasgow Devpt Plan, 1960-80, and implementation of urban renewal programme and official architecture. Several Saltire Soc. awards for best-designed flats in Scotland. Chairman: Technical Panel, Scottish Local Authorities Special Housing Group, 1965-70; Technical Panel, CV Planning Adv. Cttee, 1960-70; Pres., Glasgow Inst. of Architects, 1970. *Publications:* contrib. professional and technical journals. *Recreations:* fishing, painting. *Address:* Buchanan Drive, Newton Mearns, Renfrewshire. *Club:* Royal Scottish Automobile (Glasgow).

**JUSTICE, James Robertson;** *see* Robertson-Justice.

# K

**KABERRY, Sir Donald,** 1st Bt, *cr* 1960; TD; MP (C) North-West Division of Leeds since 1950; *b* 18 Aug. 1907; *m* 1940, Lily Margaret Scott; three *s*. *Educ:* Leeds Grammar Sch. Solicitor (Mem. of Council of The Law Society, 1950-55). Mem. Leeds City Council for 20 years. Pres., Yorks Provincial Area Council of Conservative Party, 1966- (Chm. 1952-56; Dep. Pres. 1956-65); Chm. Association of Conservative Clubs, 1961-; Chm. Board of Governors, United Leeds Hospitals, 1961-. Asst Government Whip, 1951-April 1955; Parliamentary Sec., Board of Trade, April-Oct. 1955; Vice-Chm., Conservative Party,

Oct. 1955-61. Served War of 1939-45, in RA (despatches twice). *Heir:* *s* Christopher Donald Kaberry [*b* 14 March 1943; *m* 1967, Gaenor Elizabeth Vowe, *yr d* of C. V. Peake. *Educ:* Repton Sch.]. *Address:* Adel Willows, Leeds 16. *T:* Leeds 678252. *Clubs:* Carlton, Constitutional; Leeds, Leeds and County Conservative.

**KAGAN, Sir Joseph,** Kt 1970; Chairman of Kagan Textiles Group of Companies; *b* 6 June 1915; *s* of Benjamin and Miriam Kagan; *m* 1943, Margaret Stromas; two *s* one *d. Educ:* High School, Kaunas, Lithuania; Leeds University. BCom hons (Textiles). Founder of 'Gannex'–Kagan Textiles Limited, 1951, since when Chairman and Managing Director. *Recreations:* chess, music. *Address:* Barkisland Hall, Barkisland, Halifax, Yorks. *T:* Elland 4121.

**KAHN,** family name of **Baron Kahn.**

**KAHN,** Baron, *cr* 1965 (Life Peer), of Hampstead; **Richard Ferdinand Kahn,** CBE 1946; FBA 1960; MA; Professor of Economics, Cambridge University, since 1951; Fellow of King's College, Cambridge; *b* 10 Aug. 1905; *s* of late Augustus Kahn. *Educ:* St Paul's Sch. (Scholar); King's College, Cambridge (Scholar). Temporary Civil Servant in various Govt Depts, 1939-46. *Publications:* articles on economic subjects. *Address:* King's College, Cambridge. *T:* Cambridge 53311. *Club:* Royal Automobile.

**KAHN-FREUND, Otto;** FBA 1965; Professor of Comparative Law, University of Oxford, since 1964; *b* 17 Nov. 1900; *s* of Richard and Carrie Kahn-Freund; *m* 1931, Elisabeth (*née* Klaiss); one *d. Educ:* Goethe-Gymnasium, Frankfurt-am-Main; Universities of Frankfurt, Heidelberg, Leipzig, London. Doctor of Laws (Frankfurt) 1925, Master of Laws (London) 1935. Judge in German Courts, 1928-33. Barrister-at-Law (Middle Temple), 1936-; Hon. Bencher, Middle Temple, 1969. Asst Lecturer, Lecturer, and Reader in Law, 1935-51; Professor of Law in the University of London, London Sch. of Economics and Polit. Sci., 1951-64. Co-editor, Modern Law Review; Hon. Pres., Internat. Soc. for Labour Law and Social Legislation; Mem., Royal Commission on Trade Unions and Employers' Assocs, 1965-68. Doctor of Laws (*hc*): Bonn, 1968; Stockholm, 1969; Brussels, 1969. *Publications:* Law of Carriage by Inland Transport, 4th edn, 1965; (Co-editor) Dicey and Morris, Conflict of Laws, 8th edn 1967; English edn of Renner, Institutions of Private Law and their Social Functions, 1949; Co-author, The System of Industrial Relations in Great Britain, 1954; Co-author, Matrimonial Property Law, 1955; Co-author, Law and Opinion in England in the 20th Century, 1959; The Growth of Internationalism in English Private International Law, 1960; Labor Law and Social Security in: American Enterprise in the Common Market, 1960. Numerous articles and notes in legal periodicals. *Recreations:* reading and walking. *Address:* Brasenose College, Oxford. *Club:* Athenæum.

**KAI-SHEK, Chiang;** *see* Chiang Kai-Shek.

**KAI-SHEK, Madame Chiang;** *see* Chiang Kai-Shek.

**KAISER, Philip M.;** Chairman and Managing Director, Encyclopaedia Britannica International Ltd, since 1969; *b* 12 July 1913; *s* of Morris Kaiser and Temma Kaiser (*née* Sloven); *m* 1939, Hannah Greeley; three *s*. *Educ:* University of Wisconsin; Balliol Coll., Oxford (Rhodes Scholar). Economist, Bd of Governors, Fed. Reserve System, 1939-42; Chief, Project Ops Staff, also Chief, Planning Staff, Bd Economic Warfare and Foreign Econ. Admin., 1942-46; Expert on Internat. Organization Affairs, US State Dept., 1946; Exec. Asst to Asst Sec. of Labor in charge of internat. labor affairs, US Dept of Labor, 1947-49; Asst Sec. of Labor for Internat. Labor Affairs, 1949-53; mem., US Govt Bd of Foreign Service, Dept of State, 1948-53; US Govt mem., Governing Body of ILO, 1948-53; Chief, US delegn to ILO Confs, 1949-53; Special Asst to Governor of New York, 1954-58; Prof. and Internat. Relations Dir, Program for Overseas Labor and Industrial Relations, Sch. of Internat. Service, American Univ., 1958-61; US Ambassador, Republic of Senegal and Islamic Republic of Mauritania, 1961-64; Minister, Amer. Embassy, London, 1964-69. Member: US Govt Interdepartmental Cttee on Marshall Plan, 1947-48; Interdepartmental Cttee on Greek-Turkish aid and Point 4 Technical Assistance progs, 1947-49. *Recreations:* walking, swimming, music. *Address:* Encyclopaedia Britannica, 18 Regent Street, SW1. *T:* 01-930 7855. *Club:* St James'.

**KALAT STATE; Major HH Beglar Begi Mir Ahmad Yar Khan,** GCIE 1936; *b* 1904. Ruler of State of Kalat, 1935-38; retired as Khan. *Address:* Kalat, Baluchistan.

**KALDOR, Nicholas,** MA; Hon. Dr (Dijon); FBA 1963; Professor of Economics in the University of Cambridge, since 1966 (Reader in Economics, 1952-65); Fellow of King's College, Cambridge, since 1949; *b* Budapest, 12 May 1908; *s* of late Dr Julius Kaldor; *m* 1934, Clarissa Elisabeth Goldschmidt; four *d*. *Educ:* Model Gymnasium, Budapest; London Sch. of Economics. BSc (Econ.), 1st Class hons, 1930. Asst Lecturer, Lecturer and Reader in Economics, London Sch. of Economics, 1932-47; Rockefeller travelling Fellowship in US, 1935-36; Research Associate (part-time), Nat. Inst. of Economic and Social Research, 1943-45; Chief of Economic Planning Staff, US Strategic Bombing Survey, 1945; Dir, Research and Planning Division, Economic Commission for Europe, Geneva, 1947-49; Mem. of UN group of experts on international measures for full employment, 1949; Mem. of Royal Commission on Taxation of Profits and Income, 1951-55; Adviser on tax reform, Government of India, 1956; Economic Adviser, Economic Commission for Latin America, Santiago, Chile, 1956; Fiscal Adviser, Govt of Ceylon, 1958; Ford Visiting Research Prof., University of Calif., 1959-60; Fiscal Adviser, Government of Mexico, 1960; Economic Adviser, Govt of Ghana, 1961; Fiscal Adviser, Govt of British Guiana, 1961, of Turkey, 1962, of Iran, 1966; Visiting Economist, Reserve Bank of Australia, Sydney, 1963. Special Adviser to the Chancellor of the Exchequer, 1964-68, now Consultant. *Publications:* Quantitative Aspects of the Full Employment Problem in Britain (in Beveridge's Full Employment in a Free Soc.), 1944; (jointly) Statistical Analysis of Advertising Expenditure and Revenue of the Press, 1948; (part author) National and International Measures for Full Employment, 1950; An Expenditure Tax, 1955; Indian Tax Reform, 1956; Essays in Economic Stability and Growth, Essays in Value and Distribution, 1960; Capital Accumulation and Economic Growth (in The Theory of Capital), 1961; Ensayos sobre Desarrollo Económico (Mexico), 1961; Essays on Economic Policy, Vols I, II, 1964; Causes of the Slow Rate of Growth of the United Kingdom, 1966; papers in various economic jls. *Address:* King's College, Cambridge; 2 Adams Road, Cambridge. *T:* Cambridge 59282. *Club:*

Reform.
*See also M. J. Stewart.*

**KALERGI, R. N.**; *see* Coudenhove-Kalergi.

**KALGOORLIE, Bishop of,** since 1967; **Rt. Rev. Denis William Bryant,** DFC 1942; *b* 31 Jan. 1918; *s* of Thomas and Beatrice Maud Bryant; *m* 1940, Dorothy Linda (*née* Lewis); one *d.* *Educ:* Clark's Coll., Ealing; Cardiff Techn. Coll. Joined RAF; Wireless Operator/Air Gunner, 1936; Navigator, 1939; France, 1940 (despatches); Pilot, 1941; commn in Secretarial Br., 1950; Adjt, RAF Hereford, 1950; Sqdn-Ldr i/c Overseas Postings Record Office, Gloucester, 1951; Sqdn-Ldr DP7, Air Min., 1953. Ordinand, Queen's Coll., Birmingham, 1956; Deacon, 1958; Priest, 1959. *Recreations:* squash, tennis, oil painting. *Address:* Bishopsbourne, Kalgoorlie, Western Australia. *T:* Kalgoorlie 329. *Club:* Hannan's (Kalgoorlie).

**KANE, Professor George;** FBA 1968; Professor of English Language and Medieval Literature in the University of London at King's College since 1965; *b* 4 July 1916; *o s* of George Michael and Clara Kane; *m* 1946, Katherine Bridget, *o d* of Lt-Col R. V. Montgomery, MC; one *s* one *d.* *Educ:* St Peter's Coll.; British Columbia University; Toronto Univ.; University Coll., London. BA (University of BC), 1936; Research Fellow, University of Toronto, 1936-37; MA (Toronto), 1937; Research Fellow, Northwestern Univ., 1937-38; IODE Schol., for BC, 1938-39. Served War of 1939-45: Artists' Rifles, 1939-40; Rifle Bde, 1940-46 (despatches). PhD (London), 1946; Asst Lecturer in English, University Coll., London, 1946, Lecturer, 1948, Reader in English, 1953; Prof. of English Language and Literature and Head of English Dept, Royal Holloway College, London Univ., 1955-65. Vis. Prof., Medieval Acad. of America, 1970. Sir Israel Gollancz Memorial Prize, British Acad., 1963; Chambers Memorial Lecturer, University Coll., London, 1965; Public Orator, University of London, 1962-66. Gen. editor of London Edn of Piers Plowman. *Publications:* Middle English Literature, 1951; Piers Plowman, the A Version, 1960; Piers Plowman: The Evidence for Authorship, 1965; articles and reviews. *Recreations:* gardening, fishing. *Address:* Shandon Cottage, Stratton Road, Beaconsfield, Bucks. *T:* Beaconsfield 5396. *Clubs:* Athenæum, Flyfishers'.

**KANSAS CITY, Bishop of,** (RC); *see* Helmsing, Most Rev. Charles H.

**KANTOROWICH, Prof. Roy Herman,** BArch (Witwatersrand), MA (Manchester), ARIBA, MTPI; Professor of Town and Country Planning, University of Manchester, since 1961; *b* Johannesburg, 24 Nov. 1916; *s* of George Kantorowich and Deborah (*née* Baranov); *m* 1943, Petronella Sophie Wissema (violinist, as Nella Wissema); one *s* two *d.* *Educ:* King Edward VII Sch., Johannesburg; University of Witwatersrand. BArch 1939; ARIBA 1940; MTPI 1965 (AMTPI 1946). Post-grad. studies in Housing and Planning, MIT and Columbia Univ., 1939-41; Planning Officer: Vanderbijl Park New Town, 1942-45; directing Cape Town Foreshore Scheme, 1945-48; private practice in Cape Town, in architecture and town planning, 1948-61. Pres., S African Inst. Town Planners, 1960. Formerly Town Planning Consultant to Cape Provincial Admin., and for many cities and towns in S Africa incl. Durban, Pretoria and Port Elizabeth; Cons. for New Town of Ashkelon, Israel, 1950-56. Mem., NW Econ. Planning Coun. 1965-; Mem. Coun., TPI, 1965- (Chm., Educn. Cttee). Buildings include: Civic Centre, Welkom, OFS; Baxter Hall, University of Cape Town; Sea Point Telephone Exchange (Cape Province Inst. of Architects Bronze Medal Award). *Publications:* Cape Town Foreshore Plan, 1948; (with Lord Holford) Durban 1985, a plan for central Durban in its Regional Setting, 1968; contribs to SAArch. Record, Jl TPI and other professional jls. *Recreations:* music, tennis. *Address:* 13 Redclyffe Road, Manchester M20 9JR. *T:* 061-445 9417. *Club:* Northern Lawn Tennis.

**KANU, Victor Sigismond;** High Commissioner for Sierra Leone in London, since 1969; *b* 14 July 1935; *s* of Alpha Kanu and Adama Turay; *m* 1953; one *s* three *d.* *Educ:* Saint Benet's Hall, Oxford Univ. BA (Hons) in Philosophy, Politics and Economics, 1964; MA (Oxford) 1968. Head Master, RC Sch., Lunsar, 1953-59; Admin. Officer, Sierra Leone Govt, 1964-65; Sales Manager, United Africa Co., Sierra Leone, 1965-66; Personnel Officer, Sierra Leone Selection Trust Ltd, 1966-69. *Recreation:* lawn tennis. *Address:* Sierra Leone High Commission, 33 Portland Place, W1. *T:* 01-636 6483.

**KAPITZA, Peter,** FRS 1929; Director of Institute for Physical Problems of Academy of Sciences of the USSR; Editor, Journal of Experimental and Theoretical Physics of Academy of Sciences, USSR; PhD Cantab; FInstPhys; late Royal Society Messel Research Professor; late Director of the Royal Society Mond Laboratory; *b* Kronstadt, Russia, 26 June (old style) 1894; *s* of late Gen. Leonid Kapitza and Olga, *d* of Gen. J. Stebnitsckiy; *m* 1st, late Nadejda, *d* of Cyril Tschernosvitoff; 2nd, Anna, *d* of Professor A. N. Kryloff; two *s.* *Educ:* Secondary Sch., Kronstadt; Petrograd Politechnical Inst. (Faculty of Electrical Engrg). Lecturer, Petrograd Politechnical Inst., 1919-21; Clerk Maxwell Student, Cambridge Univ., 1923-26; Fellow, Trinity Coll., 1925 (Hon. Fellow, 1966). Asst Dir of Magnetic Research, Cavendish Laboratory, Cambridge, 1924-32; Cor. Mem. Acad. of Science of USSR, 1929; For. Mem., Council of French Physical Soc., 1935; Mem. Acad. of Science, USSR, 1939; Hon. Mem. Société des Naturalistes de Moscou, 1935; Fellow, Amer. Physical Soc., 1937; Hon. MInst. Met., 1943; Hon. Mem. and Franklin Medal of Franklin Inst., USA, 1944; Foreign Member: Royal Acad. of Science, Sweden, 1966; Royal Netherlands Acad. of Sciences, 1969; For. Hon. Mem., Amer. Acad. of Arts and Sciences, 1968. Numerous Hon. Doctorates, Fellowships, etc, 1944-. Rutherford Memorial Lectr, 1969. Medal Liege Univ., 1934; State prize for Physics, 1941 and 1943; Faraday Medal of Electr. Engrs 1942. Order of Lenin, 1943, 1944, 1945, 1964; Moscow Defence Medal, 1944; Sir Devaprasad Sarbadhikari Gold Medal, Calcutta Univ., 1955; Hero of Socialist Labour, 1945; Order of the Red Banner of Labour, 1954; Kothenius Gold Medal of German Acad. of Naturalists, 1959; Lomonosov Gold Medal, Acad. of Sciences, USSR, 1959; Great Gold Medal, Exhibn of Economic Achievements USSR, 1962; International Niels Bohr Gold Medal of Dansk Ingeniørvorening, 1964; Rutherford Medal of Inst. of Physics and Physical Soc., England, 1966; Order of the Yugoslav Banner with Ribbon, 1967; Kamerlingh Onnes Gold Medal of Netherlands Soc. for Refrigeration, 1968, etc. *Publications:* Collected Papers, 3 vols, 1964-67; various publications on physics, mainly on magnetism, low temperature and high temperature plasma in scientific journals. *Recreation:* chess. *Address:* The Institute for Physical Problems, Vorobjevskoe Shosse 2, Moscow, B-334, USSR.

**KAPLAN, Prof. Joseph;** Professor of Physics, University of California at Los Angeles (UCLA), 1940-70, now Professor Emeritus; *b* 8 Sept. 1902; *s* of Henry and Rosa Kaplan, Tapolcza, Hungary; *m* 1933, Katherine Elizabeth Feraud; no *c*. *Educ:* Johns Hopkins University, Baltimore, Md, PhD 1927; National Research Fellow, Princeton Univ., 1927-28. University of Calif. at Los Angeles: Asst Prof. of Physics, 1928-35; Associate Prof., 1935-40; Prof., 1940-. Chief, Operations Analysis Section, Second Air Force, 1943-45 (Exceptional Civilian Service Medal, US Air Corps, 1947). Chm., US Nat. Cttee for Internat. Geophysical Year, 1953-64. Fellow: Inst. of Aeronautical Sciences, 1957; Amer. Meteorological Soc., 1970 (Pres., 1963-67). mem. Nat. Acad. of Sciences, 1957; Hon. Mem., Amer. Meteorological Soc., 1967; Vice-Pres., International Union of Geodesy and Geophysics, 1960-63, Pres., 1963-; Hon. Governor, Hebrew Univ. of Jerusalem, 1968. Hon. DSc: Notre Dame, 1957; Carleton Coll., 1957; Hon. LHD: Yeshiva Univ. and Hebrew Union Coll., 1958; Univ. of Judaism, 1959. Exceptional Civilian Service Medal (USAF), 1960; Hodgkins Prize and Medal, 1965. Exceptional Civilian Service Medal, 1969; John A. Fleming Medal, Amer. Geophysical Union, 1970; Commemorative Medal, 50th Anniversary, Amer. Meteorological Soc., 1970; Special Award, UCLA Alumni Assoc., 1970. *Publications:* Across the Space Frontier, 1950; Physics and Medicine of the Upper Atmosphere, 1952; (co-author) Great Men of Physics, 1969; publications in Physical Review, Nature, Proc. Nat. Acad. of Sciences, Jl Chemical Physics. *Recreations:* golf, ice-skating, walking. *Address:* 1565 Kelton Avenue, Los Angeles, Calif 90024, USA. *T:* Granite 38839. *Club:* Cosmos (Washington, DC).

**KAPP, Edmond X.;** artist; *b* London, 5 Nov. 1890; *s* of late E. B. Kapp, London and Bella Wolff, New York; *m* 1st, 1922, Yvonne Cloud, writer; one *d*; 2nd, 1932, Polia Chentoff, artist (*d* 1933); 3rd, 1950, Patricia Greene, writer. *Educ:* Owen's Sch., London; Paris; Berlin University; Christ's Coll., Cambridge (Scholar). BA. Served European War, 1914-19, BEF France; Lieut Royal Sussex Regt; Staff Capt. Spec. Appt Intelligence GHQ (M in D); first one-man shows of drawings and caricatures, Cambridge, 1912, London, 1919; subseq. Exhibitions of paintings, drawings, lithographs at the Leicester Galleries and Wildenstein Gall., London; Brighton; Bath; Birmingham; Manchester; Bradford; Newcastle; Buffalo, USA; Toronto, Canada; UNESCO, Paris; Geneva; Monte Carlo, Milan, etc; represented in National Gallery Exhibition (British Art since Whistler), 1945; invited to exhibit *hors concours* 1st French Biennale Internat., Menton, 1951; Wakefield, York, Harrogate, 1957; invited by Whitechapel Art Gallery, London, to hold 50-year Retrospective Exhibition of paintings and drawings, 1961; Bear Lane Gallery (abstract paintings only), Oxford, 1962; Festival Hall, 1968. Music into Art Programme, BBC TV, 1968. Works acquired by: British Museum; Victoria and Albert Museum; National Portrait Gallery; Imperial War Museum; London Museum; S London Art Gallery, Camberwell; Contemporary Art Soc., London; Perth Museum and Art Gallery, WA; Yale Law Sch. Library, USA (legal portraits as stained-glass windows); Bibliothèque Nationale, Paris; Tel-Aviv Gallery, Israel; Palais de la Paix, Geneva; Fitzwilliam Museum, Cambridge; Ashmolean, Oxford; Manchester; Whitworth (Manchester); Leeds; Birmingham; Bradford; Wakefield; and other provincial galleries; 240 drawings acquired by Barber Inst. of Fine Arts, Birmingham, 1969; also in private collections made by Samuel Courtauld, Sir Kenneth Clark, Sacha Guitry, Sir Hugh Walpole, Daniel de Pass, Jim Ede, etc.; 70 drawings, commnd by the London Philharmonic Orchestra, 1943, and exhibited London and provincial city Art Galleries. The Nations at Geneva, 1934-35, series of twenty-five portraits on the stone, commissioned by British Museum and Nat. Portrait Gallery and acquired for other collections; complete set of Original Lithographs acquired by Buffalo City (Albright) Art Gallery (USA), 1939. Commissioned as Official War Artist, 1940; as Official Artist to UNESCO, Paris, 1946-47 (20 portrait-drawings). Commissioned to make 8 portraits for Gonville and Caius and Christ's Colls., Camb. and Merton Coll., Oxford, 1965-66. *Publications:* Personalities, Twenty-four Drawings (Secker, 1919); Reflections, Twenty-four Drawings (Cape, 1922); Ten Great Lawyers (plates in colour), (Butterworth, 1924); Minims. Twenty-eight Drawings; with Yvonne Cloud, Pastiche: A Music-Room Book (Faber, 1925 and 1926); his work is reproduced in: Modern Drawings (by Campbell Dodgson); History of Caricature (by Bohun Lynch); Encycl. Britannica (XIII edn); From Sickert to 1948 (by John Russell); Things New and Old (by Max Beerbohm); Modern Caricaturists (by H. R. Westwood), etc. *Recreations:* music and nonsense. *Address:* 2 Steele's Studios, Haverstock Hill, NW3. *T:* 01-722 3174.

*See also Helen Kapp.*

**KAPP, Helen;** Director, Abbot Hall, Kendal, 1961-67, retired; *b* London; *d* of late E. B. Kapp, London, and Bella Wolff, New York. *Educ:* Maria Grey Sch.; Slade Sch. of Art; University Coll., London; Paris. Painter and illustrator; one-man shows; London, 1939; Haifa, 1946; Wakefield, 1954; Guide-Lecturer for Arts Council (CEMA) 1940-45; Lecturer for War Office, 1946-48; Lecturer, Extra Mural Dept, London Univ., 1948-51: Dir (formerly Asst) City Art Gallery and Museum, Wakefield, 1951-61. *Publications:* Illustrated: (with Gerald Bullett) Seed of Israel, 1929; (with John Collier) The Scandal and Credulities of John Aubrey, 1931; (with E. S. Rohde) Vegetable Cultivation and Cookery, 1938; (with E. S. Rohde) Rose Recipes, 1939; (with Basil Collier) Take 40 Eggs, 1938; (with Basil Collier) Catalan France, 1939; (with Harold Morland) Satires and Fables, 1945; Toying with a Fancy, 1950. *Recreations:* music, conversation and idleness. *Address:* Lune Cottage, Barbon, Carnforth, Lancs.

*see also Edmond Kapp.*

**KAPPEL, Frederick R.;** Chairman of Board, International Paper Co., since Feb. 1969; *b* Albert Lea, Minnesota, 14 Jan. 1902; *s* of Fred A. Kappel and Gertrude M. Towle Kappel; *m* 1927, Ruth Carolyn Ihm; two *d*. *Educ:* University of Minnesota (BSE). Northwestern Bell Telephone Company: various positions in Minnesota, 1924-33; Plant Engineer, Nebraska, S Dakota, 1934. Plant Operations Supervisor (Exec.) Gen. Staff, Omaha, Nebraska, 1937, Asst Vice-Pres. Operations, 1939, Vice-Pres. Operations and Dir, 1942. Amer. Telephone & Telegraph Co., NY: Asst Vice-Pres. (O & E), Vice-Pres. (Long Lines), Vice Pres. (O & E), 1949. Pres. Western Electric Co., 1954-56; Pres. and Chief Exec. Officer, Amer. Tel. & Tel. Co., 1956-61, Chm. Exec. Cttee, 1967-69. Chm. Board of Dirs, and Chief Exec. Officer, Amer. Tel. & Tel. Co., 1961-67. Director: Amer. Telephone & Telegraph Co., 1956-70. Chase Manhattan Bank, Metropolitan Life Insurance Co., General Foods Corporation; Standard Oil Co. (NJ), 1966-70, Whirlpool Corp., International

Paper Co.; Chase Manhattan Corp.; Boys' Club of America; Acad. of Polit. Sciences; Member: Business Council (Chm., 1963-64); Advisory Board of Salvation Army; US Chamber of Commerce; various societies. Trustee: Presbyterian Hospital; Grand Central Art Galleries, Inc.; Aerospace Corp.; Tax Foundation. Trustee, University of Minnesota Foundation. Holds numerous hon. doctorates and awards, including: Cross of Comdr of Postal Award, France, 1962; Presidential Medal of Freedom, 1964. *Publications:* Vitality in a Business Enterprise, 1960; Business Purpose and Performance. *Recreation:* golf. *Address:* 195 Broadway, New York 7, NY, USA. *T:* 393-1000. *Clubs:* Triangle, Links, University, Economic (New York); Blind Brook (Portchester), Siwanoy Country (Bronxville).

**KARACHI, Archbishop of, (RC),** since 1958; **Most Rev. Mgr. Joseph Cordeiro;** *b* Bombay, India, 19 Jan. 1918. *Educ:* St Patrick's High School; DJ College, Karachi; Papal Seminary, Kandy, Ceylon. Priest, 1946; Asst Chaplain, St Francis Xavier's, Hyderabad, Sind, 1947; Asst Principal, St Patrick's High School, Karachi, 1948; Student at Oxford, 1948; Asst Principal, St Patrick's High Sch., 1950; Principal, Grammar Sch., and Rector, Diocesan Seminary, Quetta, 1952. *Address:* St Patrick's Cathedral, Karachi 3, Pakistan. *T:* 515870.

**KARAJAN, Herbert von;** *see* Von Karajan.

**KARANJA, Dr Josphat Njuguna;** Principal of University College, Nairobi, since 1970; *b* 5 Feb. 1931; *s* of Josphat Njuguna; *m* 1966, Beatrice Nyindombi, Fort Portal, Uganda; one *s* two *d*. *Educ:* Alliance High Sch., Kikuyu, Kenya; Makerere Coll., Kampala, Uganda; University of Delhi, India; Princeton Univ., New Jersey, USA (PhD). Lecturer in African Studies, Farleigh Dickinson Univ., New Jersey, 1961-62; Lecturer in African and Modern European History, University College, Nairobi, Kenya, 1962-63; High Comr for Kenya in London, 1963-70. *Recreations:* golf, tennis. *Address:* University College, Box 30197, Nairobi, Kenya.

**KARIMJEE, Sir Tayabali Hassanali Alibhoy,** Kt 1955; Brilliant Star of Zanzibar (3rd Class); Jubilee Medal of Sultan of Zanzibar; *b* 7 Nov. 1897; *s* of Hassanali A. Karimjee and Zenubbai H. A. Karimjee; *m* 1917, Sugrabai Mohamedali Karimjee; one *d*. *Educ:* Zanzibar and Karachi. Pres., Indian National Association, Zanzibar, 1930 and 1942; Pres. Chamber of Commerce, Zanzibar, 1940 1941, 1942; Mem. Fighter Fund Cttee, 1940-43; Mem. Red Cross Cttee, 1940-45; MLC, Zanzibar, 1933-45. Chm. Board of Directors, Karimjee Jivanjee & Co. Ltd., Karimjee Jivanjee Estates Ltd, Karimjee J. Properties Ltd, International Motor Mart Ltd (Tanganyika), Karimjee Trading Co. (Bombay); Director, Karimjee Jivanjee & Co. (UK) Ltd, London. King George V Jubilee Medal, 1935; Coronation Medals, 1937 and 1953. *Address:* PO Box 51, Karachi, Pakistan. *Clubs:* Royal Commonwealth Society; Royal Over-Seas League; Karachi (Karachi); Cricket of India, WIAA (Bombay).

**KARK, (Arthur) Leslie;** MA (Oxon); FRSA; Author, Barrister; Chairman: Lucie Clayton Secretarial School; Lucie Clayton, Ltd; *b* 12 July 1910; *s* of Victor and Helena Kark, Johannesburg; *m* 1st, 1935, Joan Tetley (marr. diss., 1956); two *d*; 2nd, 1956, Evelyn Gordine (*see* E. F. Kark); one *s* one *d*. *Educ:* Clayesmore; St John's Coll., Oxford. Called to Bar, Inner Temple, 1932; Features Editor of World's Press News, 1933; Editor of Photography, 1934; Public Relations Officer to Advertising Association, 1935; Features Editor News Review, 1936-39; London Theatre Critic, New York Herald Tribune; News Editor, Ministry of Information, 1940. Served War of 1939-45, RAF, 1940-46; Air-gunner; Wing Commander in Command of Public Relations (Overseas) Unit; author, Air Ministry's official book on Air War, Far East. Short stories and novels translated into French. Swedish, German, Polish, etc. Dir, Norman Kark Publications. *Publications:* The Fire Was Bright, 1944; Red Rain, 1946; An Owl in the Sun, 1948; Wings of the Phœnix, 1949; On the Haycock, 1957. *Recreation:* fly-fishing. *Address:* 9 Clareville Grove, SW7. *T:* 01-373 2621; Roche House, Sheep Street, Burford, Oxon. *T:* Burford 3007. *Club:* Savage.

**KARK, Mrs Evelyn Florence,** (*nom de plume* **Lucie Clayton**); Director; *b* 5 Dec. 1928; *d* of Emily and William Gordine; *m* 1956 (Arthur) Leslie Kark, *qv*; one *s* one *d*. *Educ:* privately and inconspicuously. Asst to Editor, Courier Magazine, 1950; became Head of model school and agency (assuming name of Lucie Clayton), 1952; founded Lucie Clayton Sch. of Fashion Design and Dressmaking, 1961, and Lucie Clayton Secretarial Sch., 1966. *Publication:* The World of Modelling, 1968. *Recreations:* talking, tapestry, cooking. *Address:* 9 Clareville Grove, SW7. *T:* 01-373 2621; Roche House, Burford, Oxfordshire. *T:* Burford 3007.

**KARMEL, Alexander D.,** QC 1954; **His Honour Judge Karmel;** Additional Judge, Central Criminal Court, since 1968; *b* 16 May 1904; *s* of Elias Karmel; *m* 1937, Mary, *widow* of Arthur Lee and *d* of Newman Lipton; one *s*. *Educ:* Newcastle upon Tyne Royal Grammar Sch. Barrister-at-law, Middle Temple, 1932; Master of the Bench, 1962; Northern Circuit; Recorder of Bolton, 1962-68. *Recreations:* croquet, golf. *Address:* 28 Addisland Court, Kensington, W14. *T:* 01-603 3725; 5 Essex Court, EC4. *T:* 01-236 4365. *Clubs:* Royal Automobile, Hurlingham.

**KARMEL, David,** CBE 1967; QC 1950; JP; Deputy Chairman, Gloucestershire Quarter Sessions, since 1970; *b* 1907; *s* of Joseph Michael Karmel; *m* 1943, Barbara, *d* of late Sir Montague Burton; one *d*. *Educ:* St Andrews College; Trinity Coll., Dublin. Called to Bar, Gray's Inn, 1928; Mem. of the Northern Circuit; Master of the Bench, Gray's Inn, 1954, Treasurer 1970; Mem. Inner Temple; Mem. of the Bar of Northern Rhodesia. Enlisted King's Royal Rifle Corps, 1939; commissioned in 60th Rifles, Dec. 1940; Capt., 1942; Major, 1943; served War of 1939-45 (wounded thrice), in 1st Bn Western Desert, Tunisia and Italy, 1941-44, and in Jugoslavia, with Mil. Misssion 1944-45. Recorder of Wigan, 1952-62. Mem. Gen. Council of Bar, 1956-60. Steward, British Boxing Bd of Control. Mem. Industrial Disputes Tribunal; Chairman: Cttees of Investigation under Agric. Marketing Act, 1958; Truck Acts Cttee, 1959; Advisory Cttee on Service Candidates, 1963. Mem. indep. panel of Industrial Court, Mem. Cttee on Legal Education of Students from Africa, 1960. Open-cast Referee. JP County of Glos., 1963. *Recreations:* theatre, travelling. *Address:* 1 Brick Court, EC4. *T:* 01-353 0777; 108 Eaton Place, SW1. *T:* 01-235 6159; Great Rissington Hill, Cheltenham, Glos. *T:* Bourton-on-the Water 332. *Clubs:* Beefsteak, Buck's, Travellers', Travellers' (Paris).

**KARMEL, Emer. Prof. Peter Henry,** CBE 1967; Vice-Chancellor, The Flinders University of South Australia, since 1966; Chancellor, University of Papua and New Guinea, since

1969 (Chairman of Interim Council, 1965-69); *b* 9 May 1922; *s* of Simeon Karmel; *m* 1946, Lena Garrett; one *s* five *d*. *Educ:* Caulfield Grammar Sch.; Univ. of Melbourne (BA); Trinity Coll., Cambridge (PhD). Research Officer, Commonwealth Bureau of Census and Statistics, 1943-45; Lectr in Econs, Univ. of Melbourne, 1946; Rouse Ball Res. Student, Trinity Coll., Cambridge, 1947-48; Sen. Lectr in Econs, Univ. of Melbourne, 1949; Prof. of Econs, Univ. of Adelaide, 1950-62; Principal-designate, Univ. of Adelaide at Bedford Park (subseq. Flinders Univ. of SA), 1961-66. Mem., SSRC, 1952-; Mem. Council, Univ. of Adelaide, 1955-69; Vis. Prof. of Econs, Queen's Univ., Belfast, 1957-58; Mem. Commonwealth Cttee: on Future of Tertiary Educn, 1961-65; of Economic Enquiry, 1963-65; Mem., Australian Council for Educnl Research, 1968-; Chm., Cttee of Enquiry into Educn in SA, 1969-. *Publications:* Applied Statistics for Economists, 1957, 1962 (1970 edn with M. Polasek); (with M. Brunt) Structure of the Australian Economy, 1962, 1963, 1966; (with G. C. Harcourt and R. H. Wallace) Economic Activity, 1967 (Italian edn 1969); articles in Economic Record, Population Studies, Jl Royal Statistical Assoc., and other learned jls. *Address:* 40 Westall Street, Hyde Park, South Australia 5061. *T:* 71-8794.

**KARMINSKI, Rt. Hon. Sir Seymour Edward,** PC 1967; Kt 1951; **Rt. Hon. Lord Justice Karminski;** a Lord Justice of Appeal, since 1969; *b* 28 Sept. 1902; *s* of Eugène and Rita Karminski, 82 Portland Place, W1, and Frinton-on-Sea, Essex; *m* 1927, Susan Elizabeth Burney; two *d*. *Educ:* Rugby; Christ Church, Oxford. BA 1923 (1st Class Modern History); MA. Called to Bar, Inner Temple, 1925; Master of the Bench, 1951; KC 1945; Judge of the High Court of Justice (Probate, Divorce and Admiralty Div.), 1951-69. Joined RNVR 1940; Lieut-Cdr 1943. *Recreations:* golf, fishing. *Address:* 32 Pembroke Gardens, W8. *T:* 01-603 5330; Lyncewood, Easton, Woodbridge, Suffolk. *T:* Wickham Market 402. *Club:* Garrick.

**KARP, David;** novelist; *b* New York City, 5 May 1922; *s* of Abraham Karp and Rebecca Levin; *m* 1944, Lillian Klass; two *s*. *Educ:* College of The City of New York. US Army, 1943-46, S Pacific, Japan; College, 1946-48; Continuity Dir, Station WNYC, New York, 1948-49; free-lance motion picture-television writer, 1949-; President: Leda Productions Inc., 1968-; Television-Radio Branch, Writers Guild of America West, 1969-; Member: Editorial Bd, Television Quarterly, 1966-; Council, Writers Guild of America, 1966. Guggenheim Fellow, 1956-57. *Publications:* One, 1953; The Day of the Monkey, 1955; All Honorable Men, 1956; Leave Me Alone, 1957; The Sleepwalkers, 1960; Vice-Pres. in Charge of Revolution (with Murray D. Lincoln), 1960; The Last Believers, 1964; short stories in Saturday Eve. Post, Collier's, Esquire, Argosy, The American, etc; articles and reviews in NY Times, Los Angeles Times, Saturday Review, Nation, etc. *Recreations:* photography, reading. *Address:* 1116 Corsica Drive, Pacific Palisades, Calif 90272, USA. *T:* 459-1623. *Club:* PEN (New York).

**KARRER, Paul;** DrPhil; Professor of Chemistry, University of Zürich, since 1918; Director of Chemical Institute, Zürich, since 1919; *b* Moscow, 21 April 1889; *s* of Paul Karrer and Julie Lerch; *m* 1914, Helena Froelich; two *s*. *Educ:* Wildegg; Lenzburg, Aarau; University of Zürich (DrPhil). Asst, Chemical Institute, University of Zürich, 1911-12; Chemist, Georg-Speyer-Haus, Frankfurt-am-Main, 1912-18. Member, numerous socs and academies, etc. Marcel Benoist Prize (Switzerland); Cannizzaro Prize (Rome); Nobel Prize for Chemistry, 1937. DrMed *hc*; DrPharm *hc*; DrPhil *hc*; Dr rer nat *hc*. *Publications;* Zahlreiche wissenschaftliche Abhandlungen über Kohle hydrate, Alkaloide, Lecithine, Anthocyanidine und insbesondere über Carotinoide, Vitamine (Vit. A, B2, E, K, B1), über Cofermente (Codehydrasen, gelbes Coferment, Codecarboxylase), und Alkaloide (curare); Lehrbuch der organischen Chemie (erschienen in deutscher, englischer, italienischer, französischer, spanischer und japanischer Sprache, 15 Auflagen); Monographie über Carotinoide, 1948. *Address:* Spyristeig 30, Zurich, Switzerland. *T:* Zürich 28.11.20.

**KARSAVINA, Tamara (Mrs H. J. Bruce);** President of the Licentiate Club of the Royal Academy of Dancing, since 1954; *b* 10 March 1885; *d* of Platon Karsavin and Anna (*née* Khomiakova); *m* 1917, H. J. Bruce; one *s*. *Educ:* Imperial Theatre Sch., St Petersburgh, Russia. Artist of the Marinsky Theatre, St Petersburgh, 1902-19, Prima Ballerina: Leading Dancer of Ballets Russes of Serge Diaghilev, 1909-22; guest artist, 1923-29. First London appearance (under name of Tamara Karsavina), in Divertissement, Coliseum, 1909; Armide, in Le Pavillon d'Armide, at first appearance of Imperial Russian Ballet at Covent Garden, 1911; in subsequent years danced frequently in England. Is resident in London. Gold Medal of Order of St Vladimir; Order of the Red Cross; Palmes Académiques; Order of the Emir of Bokhara. Holder of Royal Academy of Dancing Coronation Award for 1954. *Publication:* Theatre Street, 1930. *Recreations:* gardening, interior decoration.

**KARSH, Yousuf,** SM 1968; Portrait Photographer since 1932; *b* Mardin, Armenia-in-Turkey, 23 Dec. 1908; parents Armenian; Canadian Citizen; *m* 1939, Solange Gauthier (*d* 1961); *m* 1962, Estrellita Maria Nachbar. *Educ:* Sherbrooke, PQ Canada; studied photography in Boston, Mass., USA. Portrayed Winston Churchill in Canada's Houses of Parliament, 1941; King George VI, 1943; HM Queen (then Princess) Elizabeth and the Duke of Edinburgh, 1951; HH Pope Pius XII, 1951; also portrayed, among many others: Shaw, Wells, Einstein, Sibelius, Somerset Maugham, Picasso, Eden, Eisenhower, Tito, Eleanor Roosevelt, Thomas Mann, Bertrand Russell, Attlee, Nehru, Ingrid Bergmann, Lord Mountbatten of Burma, Augustus John; seven portraits used on postage stamps of six countries. One man exhibns: Men Who Make our World, Pav. of Canada, Expo. 67; Montreal Mus. of Fine Arts, 1968; Boston Mus. of Fine Arts, 1968; Corning Mus., 1968; Detroit Inst. of Arts, 1969; Corcoran Gall. of Art, Washington, 1969; Macdonald House, London, 1969. Seattle Art Musuem, 1970; Japan (country-wide), 1970; Honolulu, 1970. Vis. Prof. of Fine Arts, Ohio Univ., 1967-69; Photographic Advisor, Internat. Exhibn, Expo '70, Osaka, Japan. Holds seven hon. degrees. Canada Council Medal, 1965; Centennial Medal, 1967. *Publications:* Faces of Destiny, 1947; (co-author) This is the Mass, 1958; Portraits of Greatness, 1959; (co-author) This is Rome, 1960; (co-author) This is the Holy Land, 1961; (autobiog.) In Search of Greatness, 1962; (co-author) These are the Sacraments, 1963; (co-author) The Warren Court; Karsh Portfolio, 1967. *Recreations:* tennis, bird-watching, archæology, music. *Address:* (business) 130 Sparks Street, Ottawa 4, Ontario. *T:* CE.6.7181; Little Wings, Prescott Highway, Ottawa.

**KASSANIS, Basil,** DSc (London), FRS 1966; Virologist, Department of Plant Pathology, Rothamsted Experimental Station, Harpenden, Herts; *b* 16 Oct. 1911; *s* of Zacharias and Helen Kassanis; *m* 1952, Jean Eleanor Matthews; one *s* one *d*. *Educ:* University of Thessaloniki, Greece. Came to Rothamsted Experimental Station as British Council scholar, 1938; appointed to staff, 1943; Senior Principal Scientific Officer, 1961. Research Medal, Royal Agricultural Soc., 1965. *Publications:* scientific papers in various jls. *Recreation:* sculpture. *Address:* 3 Rosebery Avenue, Harpenden, Herts. *T:* 5739.

**KASTLER, Alfred;** French physicist; Director, Atomic Clock Laboratory, Centre national de la Récherche Scientifique, since 1958 (Member, Management Board); *b* 3 May 1902; *s* of Fréderic Kastler and Anna (*née* Frey); *m* 1924, Elise Cosset; two *s* one *d*. *Educ:* Lycée Bartholdi, Colmar; Ecole Normale Supérieure. Taught in Lycées, Mulhouse, Colmar, Bordeaux, 1926-31; Asst at Faculty of Sciences, Bordeaux, 1931-36; Lecturer, Faculty of Science, University of Clermont-Ferrand, 1936-38; Prof., Faculty of Sciences, Bordeaux, 1938-41; Prof. of Physics: Ecole Normale Supérieure, Paris, 1941-; University of Louvain, Belgium, 1953-54. Member: Institut de France; Académie Royale Flamande; Polish Acad. of Science; Deutsche Akademie der Wissenschaften zu Berlin. Hon. Member: Société Française de Physique; Optical Soc. of America; Polish Soc. of Physics. Hon. Doctorates: Louvain, Pisa, Oxford, Edinburgh. Holweck Medal and Prize, Phys. Soc., 1954; Nobel Prize for Physics, 1966. Officier de la Légion d'Honneur; Grand Officier de l'Ordre National du Mérite. *Address:* 1 Rue du Val-de-Grâce, Paris 5e, France.

**KÄSTNER, Erich,** Dr phil; *b* Dresden, 23 Feb. 1899. *Educ:* Universities of Leipzig, Rostock, Berlin. *Publications: novels:* Fabian, 1931 (Eng. trans. Fabian); Drei Männer im Schnee, 1934 (Eng. trans., Three Men in the Snow); Die verschwundene Miniatur, 1935 (Eng. trans. The Missing Miniature); Der kleine Grenzverkehr, 1938 (Eng. trans. A Salzburg Comedy); Notabene 45, 1961; *juvenile novels:* Emil und die Detektive, 1928 (Eng. trans. Emil and the Detectives); Pünktchen und Anton, 1931 (Eng. trans. Anneluise and Anton); Der 35. Mai, 1931 (Eng. trans. The 35th May); Das fliegende Klassenzimmer, 1933 (Eng. trans. The Flying Classroom); Emil und die drei Zwillinge, 1934 (Eng. trans. Emil and the Three Twins); Konferenz der Tiere, 1949 (Eng. trans. The Animals' Conference); Das doppelte Lottchen, 1949 (Eng. trans. Lottie and Lisa); Das Schwein beim Friseur, 1962; Der kleine Mann, 1963 (English trans. The Little Man); Der kleine Mann und die kleine Miss, 1967; *he retold:* Till Eulenspiegel, 1938 (Eng. trans. Till the Jester); Der gestiefelte Kater, 1950 (Eng. trans. Puss in Boots); Münchhausen, 1951 (Eng. trans. Baron Münchhausen); Die Schildbürger, 1954 (Eng. trans. The Simpleton); Don Quichotte, 1956 (Eng. trans. Don Quixote); Gullivers Reisen, 1961; *volumes of poems:* Herz auf Taille, 1928; Lärm im Spiegel, 1929; Ein Mann gibt Auskunft, 1930; Gesang zwischen den Stühlen, 1932; Dr Erich Kästners lyrische Hausapotheke, 1936; Kurz und bündig, Epigramme, 1948; Bei Durchsicht meiner Bücher, 1946; Die dreizehn Monate, 1955; Eine Auswahl, 1956; Probepackung, 1957; (selection, Eng. trans.) Let's Face It, 1963; *juvenile poetry:* Arthur mit dem langen Arm, 1932; Das verhexte Telefon, 1932; *essays:* Der tägliche Kram, 1948; Die kleine Freiheit, 1952; Kästner für Erwachsene, 1966; *plays:* Emil und die Detektive, 1930; Pünktchen und Anton 1932; Zu treuen Händen, 1948; Die Schule der Diktatoren, 1956; *biography:* Als ich ein kleiner Junge war, 1957 (Eng. trans. When I was a Little Boy); Gesammelte Schriften, 1959; Gesammelte Schriften für Erwachsene, 1969. *Address:* Flemingstr. 52, Munich 81, Germany.

**KASTNER, Prof. Leslie James,** MA, ScD Cantab, FIMechE; Professor of Mechanical Engineering, King's College, University of London, since 1955; *b* 10 Dec. 1911; *o s* of late Professor Leon E. Kastner, sometime Prof. of French Language and Literature, University of Manchester, and of Elsie E. Kastner; *m* 1958, Joyce, *o d* of Lt-Col Edward Lillingston, DSO, Belstone, Devon. *Educ:* Dreghorn Castle Sch.; Colinton, Midlothian; Highgate Sch.; Clare Coll., Cambridge (Mechanical Science Tripos). Apprenticeship with Davies and Metcalfe, Ltd, Locomotive Engineers, of Romiley, Stockport, 1930-31 and 1934-36; Development Engineer (mainly employed on steam-jet apparatus and other locomotive accessories), 1936-38; Osborne Reynolds Research Fellowship, University of Manchester, 1938; Lectr in Engineering, University of Manchester, 1941-46; Senior Lectr, 1946-48; Prof. of Engineering, University Coll. of Swansea, University of Wales, 1948-55. Mem. of Council, Institution of Mechanical Engineers, 1954. Graduates' Prize, InstMechE, 1939; Herbert Ackroyd Stuart Prize, 1943; Dugald Clerk Prize, 1956. *Publications:* various research papers in applied thermodynamics and fluid flow. *Address:* 37 St Anne's Road, Eastbourne. *Club:* National Liberal.

**KATENGA-KAUNDA, Reid Willie;** Malawi Independence Medal, 1964; Malawi Republic Medal, 1966; High Commissioner of Malawi in London, since 1969; and concurrently Ambassador to the Holy See, Portugal, Netherlands and Belgium; *b* 20 Aug. 1929; *s* of Gibson Amon Katenga Kaunda and Maggie Talengeske Nyabanda; *m* 1952, Elicy Nyabanda; one *s* three *d* (and one *s* one *d* decd). *Educ:* Ndola Govt Sch., Zambia; Inst. of Public Administration, Malawi; Trinity Coll., Oxford; Administrative Staff Coll., Henley. Sec., Kota Kota Rice Co-op. Soc. Ltd, 1952-62; Dist. Comr, Karonga, Malawi, 1964-65; Sen. Asst Sec., Min. of External Affairs, Zomba, Malawi, 1966; MP and Parly Sec., Office of the President and Cabinet, Malawi, 1966-68; Dep. Regional Chm., MCP, Northern Region, 1967-68; Under Sec., Office of the President and Cabinet, 1968-69. Dep. Chm., Ncheu and Mchinji Inquiry Commn, 1967. *Recreations:* reading, cinema, Association football. *Address:* Malawi High Commission, 47 Great Cumberland Place, W1. *T:* 01-723 6021.

**KATILUNGU, Simon Chikwanda;** High Commissioner for Zambia in London, 1964-67; *b* 1 Nov. 1924; *m* 1952, Anna Chileshe Mwango; two *s* four *d*. *Educ:* Munali Secondary Sch. and Jan. H. Hofmeyr Sch. of Social Work, Johannesburg, SA. Sen. Social Research Asst, 1952-60; Librarian, 1960-61; Politician, 1961-64. *Recreations:* theatre and table tennis. *Address:* c/o Department of Foreign Affairs, Lusaka, Zambia.

**KATIN, Peter Roy;** Concert Pianist; *b* 14 Nov. 1930; *m* 1954, Eva Zweig; two *s*. *Educ:* Henry Thornton Sch.; Westminster Abbey; Royal Academy of Music. First London appearance at Wigmore Hall, 1948. Performances abroad include most European countries, West and East, Turkey, Cyprus, S and E Africa, Rhodesia, Canada, USA. Recordings, Decca,

Everest, Unicorn, HMV, Philips, Lyrita, MFP. Mem. Incorporated Soc. of Musicians (ISM). FRAM, ARCM. *Recreations:* reading, writing, fishing, tape recording. *Address:* c/o Christopher Hunt Ltd, 5 Draycott Place, SW3. *Club:* Arts Theatre.

**KATSINA, Emir of;** *see* Nagogo, Alhaji Hon. Sir Usuman.

**KATZ, Sir Bernard,** Kt 1969; FRS 1952; Professor and Head of Biophysics Department, University College, London, since 1952; *b* Leipzig, 26 March 1911; *s* of M. N. Katz; *m* 1945, Marguerite, *d* of W. Penly, Sydney, Australia; two *s*. *Educ:* University of Leipzig (MD 1934). Biophysical research, University Coll., London, 1935-39; PhD London, and Beit Memorial Research Fellow, 1938; Carnegie Research Fellow, Sydney Hospital, Sydney, 1939-42; DSc London, 1943. Served War of 1939-45 in Pacific with RAAF, 1942-45; Flt-Lt, 1943. Asst Dir of Research, Biophysics Research Unit, University Coll., London, and Henry Head Research Fellow (Royal Society), 1946-50; Reader in Physiology, 1950-51. Lectures: Herter, Johns Hopkins Univ., 1958; Dunham, Harvard Coll., 1961; Croonian, Royal Society, 1961; Sherrington, Liverpool Univ., 1967. A Vice-Pres., Royal Society, 1965, Biological Secretary and Vice-President, 1968-. Mem., Agric. Research Coun., 1967-. Fellow of University Coll., London. FRCP, 1968. Feldberg Foundation Award, 1965; Baly Medal, RCP, 1967; Copley Medal, Royal Society, 1967; Nobel Prize for Medicine, 1970. For. Member: Royal Danish Academy Science and Letters, 1968; Accad. Naz. Lincei, 1968; Amer. Acad. of Arts and Sciences, 1969. *Publications:* Electric Excitation of Nerve, 1939; Nerve, Muscle and Synapse, 1966; The Release of Neural Transmitter Substances, 1969; papers on nerve and muscle physiology in Jl of Physiol., Proc. Royal Society, etc. *Address:* University College, WC1.

**KATZ, Milton;** Director, International Legal Studies, and Henry L. Stimson Professor of Law, Harvard University, since 1954; *b* 29 Nov. 1907; *m* 1933, Vivian Greenberg; three *s*. *Educ:* Harvard Univ. AB 1927; LLB 1931. Anthropological Expedition across Central Africa for Peabody Museum, Harvard, 1927-28; Mem. of Bar since 1932; various official posts, US Government, 1932-39; Prof. of Law, Harvard Univ., 1940-50; served War of 1939-45, with War Production Board and as US Executive Officer, Combined Production and Resources Board, 1941-43, thereafter Lt-Comdr, USNR, until end of war; Dep. US Special Representative in Europe with rank of Ambassador, 1949-50; Chief US Delegation, Economic Commission for Europe, and US Mem., Defense Financial and Economic Cttee under North Atlantic Treaty, 1950-51; Ambassador of the United States and US Special Representative in Europe for ECA, 1950-51; Associate Dir, Ford Foundation, 1951-54, and Consultant, 1954-66. Dir, Internat. Program in Taxation, 1961-63. Fellow Amer. Acad. of Arts and Sciences (Councilor); Trustee: Carnegie Endowment for Internat. Peace (Chm. Bd); World Peace Foundation (Exec. Cttee); Citizens Research Foundation (Exec. Cttee); Inter American Univ. Foundation; Brandeis Univ.; Case Western Reserve Univ.; International Legal Center; Director, Internat. Friendship League; Member: Corp., Boston Museum of Science; Cttee on Foreign Affairs Personnel, 1961-63; Case Inst. of Technology Western Reserve Univ. Study Commn, 1966-67; Panel on Technology Assessment, Nat. Acad. of Sciences, 1968-69; Chm., Cttee on Life Sciences and Social Policy, Nat. Research Council, 1968-. Legion of Merit (US Army), 1945; Commendation Ribbon (US Navy), 1945. *Publications:* Cases and Materials on Administrative Law, 1947; Government under Law and the Individual (co-author and editor), 1957; The Law of International Transactions and Relations (with Kingman Brewster, Jr), 1960; The Things That are Caesar's, 1966; The Relevance of International Adjudication, 1968; articles in legal, business and other jls. *Address:* (business) Harvard Law Sch., Cambridge, Mass, USA; (home) 6 Berkeley Street, Cambridge, Mass, USA.

**KATZ, Mindru;** concert pianist; *b* 3 June 1925; *s* of Bernard Katz and Olga Avramescu; single. *Educ:* Bucharest Royal Academy of Music (under Florica Musicescu). Gave first public recital, 1931; first concert with Bucharest Philharmonic Orchestra, 1947. Subsequently, concert tours in all the continents. Has made numerous recordings. Prizewinner, International Piano Competitions, Berlin, Prague, 1951 and Bucharest, 1953. Emeritus Artist, Rumania, 1953; First Class State Prize, Rumanian People's Republic, 1954. *Recreations:* mountaineering, chess, films, drawing. *Address:* 45 Hanassi Street, Nof-Yam, Israel. *T:* 932415.

**KATZIN, Olga,** Journalist; Pen-name Sagittarius; *b* London, 9 July 1896; *d* of John and Mathilde Katzin; *m* 1921, Hugh Miller, actor; two *s* one *d*. *Educ:* Privately. *Publications:* Troubadours, 1925; A Little Pilgrim's Peeps at Parnassus, 1927; Sagittarius Rhyming, 1940; London Watches, 1941; Targets, 1943; Quiver's Choice, 1945; Let Cowards Flinch, 1947; Pipes of Peace, 1949; Up the Poll, 1950; Strasbourg Geese and Other Verses, 1953; Unaida (with Michael Barsley), play, 1957; The Perpetual Pessimist (with Daniel George), 1963. *Address:* 23 Manor House, Marylebone Road, NW1.

**KAUFMAN, Gerald Bernard;** MP (Lab) Manchester (Ardwick) since 1970; *b* 21 June 1930; *s* of Louis and Jane Kaufman. *Educ:* Leeds Grammar Sch.; The Queen's Coll., Oxford. Asst Gen.-Sec., Fabian Soc., 1954-55; Political Staff, Daily Mirror, 1955-64; Political Correspondent, New Statesman, 1964-65; Parly Press Liaison Officer, Labour Party, 1965-70. *Publications:* How to Live Under Labour (co-author), 1964; The Left (editor), 1966. *Recreations:* travel, going to the pictures. *Address:* 87 Charlbert Court, Eamont Street, NW8. *T:* 01-722 6264.

**KAULBACK, Ronald John Henry,** OBE 1946; publican; *b* 23 July 1909; *er s* of late Lieutenant-Colonel Henry Albert Kaulback, OBE, and Alice Mary, *d* of late Rev. A. J. Townend, CF; *m* 1940, Audrey Elizabeth, 3rd *d* of late Major H. R. M. Howard-Sneyd, OBE; two *s* two *d*. *Educ:* Rugby; Pembroke Coll., Cambridge. In 1933 journeyed through Assam and Eastern Tibet with Kingdon Ward; returned to Tibet, 1935, accompanied by John Hanbury-Tracy, spending eighteen months there in an attempt to discover source of Salween River; 1938 spent eighteen months in Upper Burma hunting and collecting zoological specimens for the British Museum (Natural History); Murchison Grant of Royal Geog. Society, 1937. *Publications:* Tibetan Trek, 1934; Salween, 1938. *Recreations:* shooting, schnorkeling. *Address:* Ardnagashel House, Bantry, Co. Cork, Eire. *T:* Bantry 209.

**KAUNDA, (David) Kenneth;** President of Zambia, since Oct. 1964 (lately Prime Minister, N Rhodesia); Chancellor of the University of Zambia since 1966; *b* 28 April

1924; *s* of David Julizgia and Hellen Kaunda, Missionaries; *m* 1946, Betty Banda; seven *s* two *d*. *Educ:* Lubwa Training Sch.; Munali Secondary Sch. Teacher, Lubwa Training Sch., 1943-44, Headmaster, 1944-47; Boarding Master, Mufulira Upper Sch., 1948-49. African National Congress: District Sec., 1950-52; Provincial Organising Sec., 1952-53; Sec.-Gen., 1953-58; Nat. Pres., Zambia African Nat. Congress, 1958-59; Nat. Pres., United Nat. Independence Party, 1960; Chm., Pan-African Freedom Movement for East, Central and South Africa, 1962; Minister of Local Government and Social Welfare, N Rhodesia, 1962-63. Chm., Organization of African Unity, 1970. Hon. Doctor of Laws: Fordham Univ., USA, 1963; Dublin Univ., 1964; University of Sussex, 1965; Windsor Univ., Canada, 1966; University of Chile, 1966; DUniv York, 1966. *Publications:* Black Government, 1961; Zambia Shall Be Free, 1962; Humanist in Africa, 1966; Humanism in Zambia and its implementation, 1967. *Recreations:* music, table tennis, football, draughts, gardening and reading. *Address:* State House, Lusaka, Zambia.

**KAUNDA, Reid Willie K.**; *see* Katenga-Kaunda.

**KAUNTZE, Ralph,** MBE 1944; MD; FRCP; Physician: to Guy's Hospital since 1948; to Cardiac Department, Guy's Hospital, since 1956; to Royal Masonic Hospital since 1963; Chief Medical Officer, Commercial Assurance Co. Ltd; *b* 5 June 1911; *s* of Charles Kauntze and Edith, *d* of Ralph Bagley; *m* 1935, Katharine Margaret, *yr d* of late Ramsay Moodie; two *s* one *d*. *Educ:* Canford Sch.; Emmanuel Coll., Cambridge; St George's Hosp., London. William Brown Sen. Schol., St George's Hosp. 1932; MRCS, LRCP 1935; MA, MB, BCh Cantab 1937; MRCP 1939; MD Cantab 1946; FRCP 1950. Served, 1939-45, RAMC, chiefly Mediterranean area, Lt-Col O i/c Med. Div. Asst Dir of Dept of Med., Guy's Hosp., 1947-48; Cons. Phys. to High Wycombe War Memorial Hosp., 1948-50; Dir Asthma Clinic, 1948-52, and of Dept of Student Health, 1950-63, Guy's Hosp. Hon. Vis. Phys., Johns Hopkins Hosp., Baltimore, 1958. Examiner in Medicine: RCP; London Univ. Mem. Brit. Cardiac Soc.; Mem. Assoc. of Physicians. *Publications:* contrib. med. jls. *Recreations:* farming, walking. *Address:* Blewbury Manor, near Didcot, Berks. *T:* Blewbury 246.

**KAY, Prof. Andrew Watt;** Regius Professor of Surgery, University of Glasgow, since Oct. 1964; *b* 14 Aug. 1916; of Scottish parentage; *m* 1943, Janetta M. Roxburgh; two *s* two *d*. *Educ:* Ayr Academy; Glasgow Univ. MB, ChB (Hons) with Brunton Memorial Prize, 1939; FRCSEd 1942; MD (Hons) with Bellahouston Gold Medal, 1944; Major Royal Army Medical Corps i/c Surgical Div., Millbank Military Hospital, 1946-48; ChM (Hons) 1949; FRFPS(G), 1956; FRCS, 1960; FRCS (Glasgow), 1967; Consultant Surgeon in charge of Wards, Western Infirmary, Glasgow, 1956-58; Asst to Regius Prof. of Surgery, Glasgow Univ., 1942-56; Prof. of Surgery, University of Sheffield, 1958-64. Sims Travelling Prof., Australasia, 1969; McLaughlin Foundn Edward Gallie Vis. Prof., Canada, 1970. Pres., Surgical Research Soc., 1969-71. Member: Royal Commission on Medical Education, 1965-68; MRC, 1967-; Hon. Mem., The N Pacific Surgical Assoc. Fellow, Royal Australasian Coll. of Surgeons; Hon. Fellow: Norwegian Surgical Assoc., Belgian Surgical Soc. Cecil Joll Prize, RCS, 1969; Gordon-Taylor Lectureship and Medal, 1970. *Publications:* (with R. A. Jamieson, FRCS) Textbook of Surgical Physiology, 1959 (2nd Edn 1964); several papers in medical and surgical jls on gastroenterological subjects. *Recreation:* gardening. *Address:* Ormidale, Grange Avenue, Milngavie, Near Glasgow. *T:* 041-956 3378.

**KAY, Air Vice-Marshal Cyril Eyton,** CB 1958; CBE 1947; DFC 1940; retired as Chief of Air Staff, with the rank of Air Vice-Marshal, RNZAF (1956-58); *b* 25 June 1902; *s* of David Kay and Mary, *d* of Edward Drury Butts; *m* 1932, Florence, *d* of Frank Armfield; two *d*. *Educ:* Auckland, NZ. Joined RAF, 1926, 5 years Short Service Commn; joined RNZAF, 1935, Permanent Commn. As Flying Officer: flew London-Sydney in Desoutter Light aeroplane, 1930 (with Flying Off. H. L. Piper as Co-pilot); first New Zealanders to accomplish this flight; also, as Flying Off. flew a De Havilland-Dragon Rapide (with Sqdn Ldr J. Hewett) in London-Melbourne Centenary Air Race, 1934; then continued over Tasman Sea to New Zealand (first direct flight England-New Zealand). Comdg Officer No 75 (NZ) Sqdn "Wellington" Bombers stationed Feltwell, Norfolk, England, 1940; Air Board Mem. for Supply, RNZAF, 1947; AOC, RNZAF, London HQ, 1950; Air Board Mem. for Personnel, 1953. *Publication:* The Restless Sky, 1964. *Recreation:* golf. *Address:* 25 Clifton Terrace, Wellington, NZ. *T:* 49800 *Club:* Officers' (Wellington, NZ).

**KAY, Prof. Harry,** PhD; Professor of Psychology, University of Sheffield, since 1960; *b* 22 March 1919; *s* of late Williamson T. Kay; *m* 1941, Gwendolen Diana, *d* of Charles Edward Maude; one *s* one *d*. *Educ:* Rotherham Grammar Sch.; Trinity Hall, Cambridge (1938-39, 1946-51). Research with Nuffield Unit into Problems to Ageing, Cambridge, 1948-51; Psychologist of Naval Arctic Expedition, 1949. Lecturer in Experimental Psychology, University of Oxford, 1951-59. Visiting Scientist, National Institutes of Health, Washington, DC, 1957-58. Pro-Vice-Chancellor, University of Sheffield, 1967-. Pres., British Psychological Soc., 1971-72. Hon. Director: MRC Unit, Dept of Psychology, Sheffield; Nat. Centre of Programmed Instruction for Industry, Sheffield. Mem. Social Science Research Council, 1970-. Vernon Prize, 1962. *Publication:* (with B. Dodd and M. Sime) Teaching Machines and Programmed Instruction, 1968. *Recreation:* tennis. *Address:* Department of Psychology, The University, Sheffield 10.

**KAY, Herbert Davenport,** CBE 1946; DSc Manchester, PhD Cantab; FRS 1945; Professor Emeritus, University of Reading; *b* Heaton Chapel, Lancs, 1893; *s* of John Kay and Ellen (*née* Davenport); *m* 1925, Beatrice, *e d* of William Lee, York; four *s*. *Educ:* Manchester Gram. Sch.; Universities of Manchester (University Scholar, 1914), London, Cambridge, Freiburg i/B. Served European War, 1914-18 (wounded, despatches, OBE). Beit Memorial Fellow, 1922; Senior Beit Fellow, 1925; Biochemist, London Hosp., 1925; Prof. of Biochemistry, University of Toronto, 1931; Research Prof. of Biochemistry, University of Reading and Dir National Institute for Research in Dairying, 1933-58; Dir, Twyford Laboratories Ltd, 1959-62. Pres., Section M., British Assoc., 1950; Pres., Studies Commission, Internat. Dairy Fedn, 1950-57. Gold Medallist, Society of Dairy Technology, 1957. Vice-Pres., Soc. of Chem. Industry, 1957-60; Hon. Member: Soc. of Applied Bacteriology; Soc. of Dairy Technology; Royal Agricultural Society; Hon. Fellow, Inst. of Food Science and Technology. Consultant, FAO, Unicef and WHO.

*Publications:* papers in scientific and technical journals. *Recreations:* walking, gardening. *Address:* 2 Christchurch Gardens, Reading. *T:* Reading 81085. *Club:* Athenæum.

**KAY, John Menzies,** MA, PhD, CEng, FIMechE; Director-in-charge, Planning Division, British Steel Corporation, since 1968; *b* 4 Sept. 1920; *s* of John Aiton Kay and Isabel Kay (*née* Menzies). *Educ:* Sherborne Sch.; Trinity Hall Cambridge. University Demonstrator in Chemical Engineering, Cambridge University, 1948; Chief Technical Engineer, Division of Atomic Energy Production, Risley, 1952; Prof. of Nuclear Power, Imperial Coll. of Science and Technology, University of London, 1956; Dir of Engineering Development, Tube Investments Ltd, 1961; Chief Engineer, Richard Thomas & Baldwins Ltd, 1965. *Publications:* Fluid Mechanics and Heat Transfer, 1963; contribs to Proc. of Institution of Mechanical Engineers. *Recreations:* mountaineering, music. *Address:* Church Farm, St Briavels, near Lydney, Glos. *Clubs:* Alpine, Oxford and Cambridge University.

**KAY, Maj.-Gen. Patrick Richard,** MBE 1945; RM; Chief of Staff to Commandant-General, Royal Marines, since 1970; *b* 1 Aug. 1921; *y s* of late Dr and Mrs A. R. Kay, Blakeney, Norfolk; *m* 1944, Muriel Austen Smith; three *s* one *d*. *Educ:* Eastbourne Coll. Commissioned in Royal Marines, 1940; HMS Renown, 1941-43; 4 Commando Bde, 1944-45; Combined Ops HQ, 1945-48; Staff of Commandant-Gen., Royal Marines, 1948-50 and 1952-54; Staff Coll., Camberley, 1951; 40 Commando, RM, 1954-57; Joint Services Amphibious Warfare Centre, 1957-59; Plans Div., Naval Staff, 1959-62; CO, 43 Commando, RM, 1963-65; CO, Amphibious Training Unit, RM, 1965-66; Asst Dir (Jt Warfare) Naval Staff, 1966-67; Asst Chief of Staff to Comdt-Gen. RM, 1968; IDC, 1969. *Recreation:* golf. *Address:* c/o Department of Comdt-General RM, Ministry of Defence (Navy), SW1.

**KAY, Sydney Entwisle,** CBE 1948 (MBE 1918); *b* 18 July 1888. *Educ:* Sutton Valence Sch.; Emmanuel Coll., Cambridge (First Class Hons Mediæval and Modern Languages Tripos). Vice-Consul in Consular Service, 1911; Consul at Stockholm, 1920; Consul-General: Lourenço Marques, 1933-39; Milan, 1939-40; Commercial Counsellor, Lisbon, 1940; Consul-Gen. at Marseilles, 1944; retired, 1948. *Address:* 176 Boulevard Carnot, Nice (AM), France.

**KAY, Very Rev. William,** DSO 1919; MC, MA; Provost of Blackburn Cathedral, 1936-61; *e s* of William Henry Kay, Withnell, Chorley, Lancs; *m* Helen Nora, *d* of late Edgar Brierley, Sandfield, Rochdale; four *d*. *Educ:* Hatfield Coll.; Durham Univ. Late 1st Batt. The Grenadier Guards, and 2nd Batt. The Manchester Regt. (MC and two bars, DSO); Vicar of Cresswell, Derbyshire, 1922-28; Rural Dean of Bolsover, 1928; Rector of Whitwell with Steetley, 1928-29; Vicar of Newark, 1929-36; Hon. Canon of Southwell, 1932-36; Rural Dean of Newark, 1933-36. *Address:* Woodruffe, Brockenhurst, Hants. *T:* 2196.

**KAY-SHUTTLEWORTH,** family name of **Baron Shuttleworth.**

**KAYE, Danny, (Daniel Kominski);** Actor (Stage, Film, TV, and Radio); *b* New York, NY, 18 Jan.; *s* of Jacob Kominski and Clara Memorovsky; *m* 1940, Sylvia Fine; one *d*. Has had various occupations; entertained at parties, in hotels, and in night clubs. Official Permanent Ambassador-at-Large for UNICEF. Played in Straw Hat Review, Ambassador Theatre, New York City, 1939; Lady in the Dark, 1940; Let's Face It, 1941; appeared London Palladium, also provincial tour, Great Britain, 1949; London Palladium, 1955. Has had weekly television show (CBS), 1963-. Since 1943 has appeared successfully in films, including: Up In Arms, 1943; Wonder Man, 1944; Kid from Brooklyn, 1945; The Secret Life of Walter Mitty, 1946; That's Life, 1947; A Song is Born, 1949; The Inspector-General, 1950; On the Riviera, 1951; Hans Christian Andersen, 1952; Knock on Wood, 1954; White Christmas, 1954; The Court Jester, 1956; Merry Andrew, 1957; Me And The Colonel, 1958; Five Pennies, 1959; On the Double, 1960; The Man from The Diner's Club, 1963; The Madwoman of Chaillot, 1968. *Address:* Box 750, Beverly Hills, Calif, USA.

**KAYE, Col Douglas Robert Beaumont,** DSO 1942 (Bar 1945); DL; JP; *b* 18 Nov. 1909; *s* of late Robert Walter Kaye, JP, Great Glenn Manor, Leics; *m* 1946, Florence Audrey Emma, *d* of late Henry Archibald Bellville, Tedstone Court, Bromyard, Herefordshire; one *s* one *d*. *Educ:* Harrow. 2nd Lieut Leicestershire Yeo., 1928; 2nd Lieut 10th Royal Hussars, 1931. Served War of 1939-45: Jerusalem, 1939-41; Cairo and HQ 30 Corps, 1941-42; Lieut-Col comdg 10th Royal Hussars, Africa and Italy, 1943-46 (despatches twice). Bde Major, 30 Lowland Armd Bde (TA), 1947-49; Lieut-Col comdg 16th/5th Queen's Royal Lancers, 1949-51; AA & QMG 56 London Armd Div. (TA), 1952-54; Col Comdt and Chief Instructor, Gunnery Sch., RAC Centre, 1954-56; retd 1956. Master of Newmarket and Thurlow Foxhounds, 1957-59. DL 1963, JP 1961, Cambridgeshire. *Recreations:* hunting, shooting. *Address:* Brinkley Hall, near Newmarket, Suffolk. *T:* Stretchworth 202. *Club:* Cavalry.

**KAYE, Geoffrey John;** Chairman and Managing Director, Pricerite Ltd, since 1966 (Director, 1963); *b* 14 Aug. 1935; *s* of Michael and Golda Kaye; *m* 1968, Susan Ruth Pinkus. *Educ:* Christ College, Finchley. Started with Pricerite Ltd when business was a small private company controlling six shops, 1951; apptd Manager (aged 18) of one of Pricerite Ltd stores, 1953; Supervisor, Pricerite Ltd, 1955; Controller of all stores in Pricerite Ltd Gp, 1958. *Recreations:* football, athletics, golf. *Address:* 6 London House, Avenue Road, St John's Wood, NW8. *Clubs:* Kendal Country, Dyrham Park Country (Hertfordshire).

**KAYE, Sir John Christopher L.;** *see* Lister-Kaye.

**KAYE, Sir Stephen Henry Gordon,** 3rd Bt, *cr* 1923; *b* 24 March 1917; *s* of Sir Henry Gordon Kaye, 2nd Bt and Winifred, *d* of late Walter H. Scales, Verwood, Bradford; *S* father 1956. *Heir: brother* David Alexander Gordon Kaye [*b* 26 July 1919; *m* 1st, 1942, Elizabeth (marr. diss. 1950), *o d* of Capt. Malcolm Hurtley, Baynards Manor, Horsham, Sussex; 2nd, 1955, Adelle, *d* of Denis Thomas, Brisbane, Queensland; one *s* three *d*]. *Address:* 42b Gunter Grove, Chelsea, SW10.

**KAYLL, Wing Commander Joseph Robert,** DSO 1940; OBE 1946; DFC 1940; DL; JP; *b* 12 April 1914; *s* of J. P. Kayll, The Elms, Sunderland; *m* 1940, Annette Lindsay Nisbet; two *s*. *Educ:* Aysgarth; Stowe. Timber trader; joined 607 Sqdn AAF, 1934; mobilised Sept. 1939; Commanding Officer 615 Squadron, 1940; (prisoner) 1941; OC 607 Sqdn AAF 1946. DL Durham, 1956; JP Sunderland, 1962. *Recreation:* yachting. *Address:* Hillside House, Hillside, Sunderland, Co. Durham. *T:* 68935.

*Clubs:* Royal Ocean Racing; Sunderland Yacht; Royal Northumberland Yacht.

**KAYSEN, Prof. Carl;** Director, Institute for Advanced Study, Princeton, NJ, since 1966; *b* 5 March 1920; *s* of Samuel and Elizabeth Kaysen; *m* 1940, Annette Neutra; two *d. Educ:* Philadelphia Public Schs; Overbrook High Sch., Philadelphia; Pa and Harvard Univs. AB Pa 1940; MA 1947, PhD 1954, Harvard. Nat. Bureau of Economic Research, 1940-42; Office of Strategic Services, Washington, 1942-43; Intelligence Office, US Army, 1943-45; State Dept, Washington, 1945. Dep. Special Asst to President, 1961-63. Harvard University, 1947-66: Teaching Fellow in Econs, 1947; Asst Prof. of Economics, 1950-55; Assoc. Prof. of Economics 1955-57; Prof. of Economics, 1957-66; Assoc. Dean, Graduate Sch. of Public Administration, 1960-66; Lucius N. Littauer Prof. of Political Economy, 1964-66; Actg Sen. Fellow, Soc. of Fellows, 1957-58, 1964-65; Syndic, Harvard Univ. Press, 1964-66. sen. Fulbright Res. Schol., LSE, 1955-56. *Publications:* United States *v* United Shoe Machinery Corporation, an Economic Analysis of an Anti-Trust Case, 1956; The American Business Creed (with others), 1956; Anti-Trust Policy (with D. F. Turner), 1959; The Demand for Electricity in the United States (with F. M. Fisher), 1962; The Higher Learning, The Universities, and The Public, 1969; numerous articles on economic theory and applied economics. *Recreations:* squash, tennis. *Address:* Institute for Advanced Study, Princeton, New Jersey 08540, USA.

**KAZAN, Elia;** author; independent producer and director of plays and films; *b* Constantinople, 7 Sept. 1909; *s* of George Kazan and Athena Sismanoglou; *m* 1932, Molly Thacher (*d* 1963); two *s* two *d*; *m* Barbara Loden. Educ: Williams Coll. (AB); 2 years postgraduate work in Drama at Yale. Actor, Group Theatre, 1932-39; first London appearance as Eddie Fuseli in Golden Boy, St James, 1938. Directed *plays:* Skin of Our Teeth, 1942; All My Sons, A Streetcar Named Desire, 1947; Death of a Salesman, 1949; Camino Real, Tea and Sympathy, 1953; Cat on a Hot Tin Roof, 1955; Dark at Top of the Stairs, JB, 1958; Sweet Bird of Youth, 1959; After the Fall, 1964; But For Whom Charlie, 1964; The Changeling, 1964; Four times won best stage Director of Year, 1942, 1947, 1948, 1949. Directed *films:* Streetcar named Desire, 1951; Viva Zapata, 1952; Pinky, 1949; Gentleman's Agreement, 1948 (won Oscar, best Dir); Boomerang, 1947; A Tree Grows in Brooklyn, 1945; On the Waterfront, 1954 (won Oscar, best Dir); East of Eden, 1954; Baby Doll, 1956; A Face in the Crowd, 1957; Wild River, 1960; Splendour in the Grass, 1962; America, America, 1964; The Arrangement, 1969. Three times won Best Picture of Year from New York Film Critics, 1948, 1952, 1955. *Publications:* America, America (novel), 1963; The Arrangement (novel), 1967; magazine articles in New York Times, Theatre Arts, etc. *Recreation:* tennis. *Address:* (business) 1545 Broadway, New York City, NY, USA.

**KAZANJIAN, Varaztad Hovhannes,** CMG 1918; oral and plastic surgeon; retired; Professor Emeritus of Plastic Surgery, Harvard, USA, 1947; Senior Consulting Surgeon: Massachusetts Eye and Ear Infirmary; Massachusetts General Hospital; Boston City Hospital; New England Deaconess Hospital; Mount Auburn Hospital; Beth Israel Hospital and others; *b* Armenia, 18 March 1879; *s* of Hovhannes and Anna Kazanjian; *m* 1923, Marion V. Hanford; one *s* two *d. Educ:* Harvard Univ. (DMD 1905; MD 1921). Member, Harvard Unit Brit. Expeditionary Force, 1915-19; served as Major and surg. specialist for wounds of jaws and face (despatches thrice). Member: State and National Medical and Dental Soc.; Amer. Assoc. Plastic Surgeons (Past Pres.); Amer. Assoc. Plastic and Reconstructive Surgery; American Assoc. of Maxillofacial Surgery (Past Pres.); Amer. Acad. of Ophthalmology and Otolaryngology; Amer. Soc. Oral Surgeons (Past Pres.); Fellow, Amer. Coll. of Surgeons; Internat. Soc. of Surgeons; Boston Surgical Soc. Diplomate, Board of Plastic Surgery. DSc (Hon.) Bowdoin, 1952; Hon. Member: Hellenic Soc. of Oral Surgery, Athens, Greece, 1959; British Assoc. of Plastic Surgeons, 1966; Hon. Fellow in Dental Surgery, RCPGlas. New York University Presidential Citation, 1962. *Publications:* The Surgical Treatment of Facial Injuries (with J. M. Converse, MD); numerous articles on plastic and reconstructive surgery and prosthetic restoration of the face and jaws. *Address:* 191 Clifton Street, Belmont, Mass 02178, USA. *Clubs:* Harvard, Boston (Mass); Faculty (Cambridge, Mass).

**KEAN, Arnold Wilfred Geoffrey;** Principal Assistant Solicitor, Board of Trade, since 1966; *b* 29 Sept. 1914; *s* of late Martin Kean; *m* 1939, Sonja Irene, *d* of Josef Andersson, Copenhagen; two *d. Educ:* Blackpool Gram. Sch.; Queens' Coll., Cambridge (Schol.). 1st cl. 1st div. Law Tripos, Pts I and II; Pres., Cambridge Union, 1935; Wallenberg (Scandinavian) Prize; Commonwealth Fund Fellow, Harvard Law Sch.; Yarborough-Anderson Schol., Inner Temple. Called to the Bar (studentship, certif. of honour, 1939). War of 1939-45, Legal staff of British Purchasing Commn and UK Treas. Delegn in N America. Legal Asst, HM Treasury Solicitor's Dept, 1945; Asst Treas. Solicitor, 1955; Princ. Asst Treas. Solicitor, 1964. Mem., Legal Cttee, Internat. Civil Aviation Organisation, 1954-; UK Deleg. at various internat. confs on maritime and civil aviation law. Tutor in Law, Civil Service Dept Centre for Admin. Studies, 1963-. King Christian X Liberation Medal (Denmark), 1945. *Publications:* articles in Amer. Scholar, Law Quarterly Rev., and in other legal periodicals. *Recreations:* music, stamps, gardening. *Address:* Tall Trees, South Hill Avenue, Harrow, Mddx. *T:* 01-422 5791.

**KEAN, Thomas Alban,** MD; retired; T/Major RAMC (Physician Specialist); Visiting Physician, Belfast City Hospital; Lecturer in Clinical Medicine, Queen's University, Belfast; Medical Specialist, Ministry of Labour, Northern Ireland; Member Northern Ireland hospitals Authority; *b* 19 Aug. 1894; *s* of Thomas Kean, MD, and Delia Ruane; *m* 1927, Mary Molyneaux, *o d* of A. M. Cinnamond; no *c. Educ:* Rockwell; National University, Ireland. *Publications:* The Treatment of Chronic Gastric Ulcer; The Investigation and Treatment of Chronic Diarrhoea; Rheumatoid Arthritis and Gold Salts Therapy, etc. *Recreations:* reading and fishing. *Address:* 22 Derryvolgie Avenue, Belfast. *T:* Belfast 666880.

**KEANE, Major Sir Richard (Michael),** 6th Bt *cr* 1801; farmer; *b* 29 Jan. 1909; *s* of Sir John Keane, 5th Bart, DSO, and Lady Eleanor Hicks-Beach (*d* 1960), *e d* of 1st Earl St Aldwyn; *S* father, 1956; *m* 1939, Olivia Dorothy Hawkshaw; two *s* one *d. Educ:* Sherborne Sch.; Christ Church, Oxford. Diplomatic Correspondent to Reuters 1935-37; Diplomatic Corresp. and Asst to Editor, Sunday Times, 1937-39. Served with County of London Yeomanry and 10th Royal Hussars, 1939-44; Liaison Officer (Major) with HQ

Vojvodina, Yugoslav Partisans, 1944; attached British Military Mission, Belgrade, 1944-45. Publicity Consultant to Imperial Chemical Industries Ltd, 1950-62. *Publications:* Germany: What Next?, (Penguin Special), 1939; Modern Marvels of Science (editor), 1961. *Recreations:* hunting and fishing. *Heir:* *s* John Charles Keane, *b* 16 Sept. 1941. *Address:* Cappoquin House, Cappoquin, County Waterford, Eire. *T:* Cappoquin 11. *Club:* Kildare Street (Dublin).

**KEANE, Mrs Robert; Mary Nesta** (*Nom de plume:* **M. J. Farrell**); *b* 20 July 1905; *d* of Walter Clarmont Skrine and Agnes Shakespeare Higginson; *m*; two *d. Educ:* Privately. (With John Perry) Spring Meeting (play perf. Ambassadors Theatre and New York, 1938); Ducks and Drakes (play perf. Apollo Theatre, 1941); Guardian Angel (play perf. Gate Theatre, Dublin, 1944); Treasure Hunt (play perf. Apollo Theatre, 1949). *Publications:* Young Entry; Taking Chances; Mad Puppettstown; Conversation Piece; Devoted Ladies; Full House; The Rising Tide; Two Days in Aragon, 1941; Loving Without Tears (novel), 1951; Treasure Hunt, 1952. *Address:* Dysert, Ardmore, Co. Waterford, Ireland. *TA:* Ardmore. *T:* Ardmore 5.

**KEARNS, Fred Matthias,** CB 1970; MC 1944; Special assignment to UK Delegation for EEC negotiations, since 1970; *b* 21 Feb. 1921; *er s* of G. H. and Ivy Kearns, Burnley; *m* 1946, Betty Broadbent; one *d. Educ:* Burnley Gram. Sch.; Brasenose Coll., Oxford; RMC Sandhurst. BA (Hons) 1941; MA 1947, Oxon. Commissioned Royal Fusiliers, 1942. Served 8th and 5th Armies, N Africa and Italy, 1942-46; Brigade Major, 167th Inf. Brigade, Trieste, 1946. Asst Principal, Ministry of Agriculture, 1948, Principal 1950; Asst Sec., Min. of Agriculture, Fisheries and Food, 1957; Regional Controller, Northern Region, 1957-60; Head of Finance Division, 1960-63; Head of External Relations Div., 1963-64; External Relations, 1964-68; Meat and Livestock Group 1968-69; Deputy Secretary 1969-70. *Recreations:* fishing, poetry. *Address:* 26 Brookway, Blackheath, SE3. *T:* 01-852 0747. *Club:* Reform.

**KEARNS, Prof. Howard George Henry,** OBE 1954; Professor of Agricultural and Horticultural Science, Bristol University 1957-67, now Emeritus; Dir, Long Ashton Research Station, 1957-67; *b* 13 May 1902; *s* of Henry Kearns and Elizabeth Anne Baker; *m* 1930, Molly Yvonne Cousins. *Educ:* St Paul's Sch., West Kensington; Downing Coll., Cambridge; Wye Coll., University of London. Lecturer in Zoology (Entomology), Bristol Univ., 1926-31; Advisory Entomologist, Long Ashton Research Station, 1931-32; Research Entomologist, 1933-; Reader in Entomology, Bristol Univ., 1950. Particular interests in applied biology, spray techniques and design of spray machinery for temperate and tropical crops. Mem. Ministry Overseas Development's Consultative Panel for Agriculture; Chm., Overseas Pest Control Cttee. *Publications:* contrib. to: Insecticides and Colonial Agricultural Development, 1954; Science and Fruit, 1953; Modern Commercial Fruitgrowing, 1956; articles in learned jls on various aspects of plant protection. *Recreations:* engineering, natural history, photography. *Address:* Clive Weare House, Clewer, Wedmore, Som. *T:* Cheddar 165.

**KEARTON,** family name of **Baron Kearton.**

**KEARTON,** Baron *cr* 1970 (Life Peer), of Whitchurch, Bucks; **Christopher Frank Kearton;** Kt 1966; OBE 1945; FRS 1961; Chairman: Courtaulds Ltd, since 1964; Advisory Committee, Industrial Expansion Act, since 1968; Electricity Supply Research Council since 1960 (Member 1954-); part-time Member UK Atomic Energy Authority, since 1955; Member: Advisory Council on Technology, since 1964; Central Advisory Council for Science and Technology, since 1969; National Economic Development Council, since 1965; Director, Hill Samuel Group, since 1970; *b* 17 Feb. 1911; *s* of Christopher John Kearton and Lilian Hancock; *m* 1936, Agnes Kathleen Brander; two *s* two *d. Educ:* Hanley High Sch.; St John's Coll., Oxford. Joined ICI, Billingham Division, 1933. Worked in Atomic Energy Project, UK and USA, 1940-45. Joined Courtaulds Ltd, i/c of Chemical Engineering, 1946; Dir 1952; Dep. Chm., 1961-64. Visitor, DSIR, 1955-61, 1963-68. Chm., Industrial Reorganisation Corp., 1966-68. Member: Windscale Accident Cttee, 1957; Tropical Products Inst. Cttee, 1958-; Special Advisory Group, British Transport Commn, 1960. Chm., Heavy Organic Chemical Section, Soc. of Chemical Industry, 1961-62; Hon. Fellow: St John's Coll., Oxford, 1965; Manchester Coll. of Sci. and Techn., 1966; Comp. TI, 1965; Hon. MIChemE 1968; Hon. LLD Leeds, 1966; Hon. DSc: Bath, 1966; Aston in Birmingham, 1970; Reading, 1970. FRSA 1970. *Address:* The Old House, Whitchurch, Near Aylesbury, Bucks. *T:* Whitchurch 232.

**KEARTON, Prof. William Johnston,** DEng, FIMechE, MRINA; Emeritus Professor, Liverpool University, since 1958; *b* 26 March 1893; *s* of Christopher and Dinah Kearton; *m* 1917, Janet Miller; one *d* decd. *Educ:* University of Liverpool. Commenced practical training with Vickers, Sons, and Maxim, at the Naval Construction Works, Barrow-in-Furness, 1909; Vickers Scholar, 1913. Lecturer in Engineering, Liverpool Univ., 1919-37; Senior Lecturer in Mechanical Engineering, Liverpool Univ., 1937-47; Dean of the Faculty of Engineering, Liverpool Univ., 1948-53; Harrison Prof. of Mechanical Engineering, Liverpool University, 1947-58, retd. *Publications:* Steam Turbine Theory and Practice, 1922; (Jt) Alignment Charts, 1924; Turbo-Blowers and Compressors, 1926; (Joint) Turbo-Gebläse und Kompressoren, 1929; Steam Turbine Operation, 1931; papers in Proc. Inst. of Mech. Engineers. *Recreations:* various. *Address:* 51 Radnor Drive, Wallasey, Cheshire. *T:* 051-639 1852.

**KEATING, Brigadier Harold John Buckler,** CBE 1945; ED 1945; *b* 15 March 1893; *s* of Col John B. Keating, OBE; *m* 1915, Gwladys M. Weston; two *s* one *d. Educ:* Portland, Maine, USA. Joined Permanent Force of Canadian Army, 1912; retired 1922; Investment Business, 1922-39. Canadian Army Active, 1939; Dep. Q-M-G, National Defence HQ, Ottawa; retired, 1946. *Recreations:* fishing, tennis, hunting. *Address:* Kenall, Wolfville, Nova Scotia.

**KEATING, Henry Reymond Fitzwalter;** author; *b* 31 Oct. 1926; *s* of John Hervey Keating and Muriel Marguerita Keating (*née* Clews); *m* 1953, Sheila Mary Mitchell; three *s* one *d. Educ:* Merchant Taylors' Sch.; Trinity Coll., Dublin. Journalism, 1952-60; Crime Reviewer for The Times, 1967. Chm. Crime Writers' Assoc., 1970-71. *Publications:* Death and the Visiting Firemen, 1959 (paperback, 1962); Zen there was Murder, 1960 (paperback, 1963); A Rush on the Ultimate, 1961 (paperback, 1966); The Dog it was that Died, 1962 (paperback, 1966); Death of a Fat God, 1963 (paperback, 1967); The Perfect Murder, 1964 (paperback, 1968); Is Skin-Deep, Is Fatal, 1965 (paperback,

1968); Inspector Ghote's Good Crusade, 1966 (paperback, 1968); Inspector Ghote Caught in Meshes, 1967 (paperback, 1969); Inspector Ghote Hunts the Peacock, 1968; Inspector Ghote Plays a Joker, 1969; Inspector Ghote Breaks an Egg, 1970; The Strong Man, 1971. *Recreation:* not quite going to India. *Address:* 35 Northumberland Place, W2. *T:* 01-229 1100.

**KEATING, John; (Seān Ceitinn)**; RHA; Hon. RA; Hon. RSA; Painter; *b* Limerick, 29 Sept. 1889; *s* of Joseph Keating and Anne Hannan; *m* 1919, May, *d* of John Walsh, Eadstown, County Kildare; two *s*. *Educ:* St Munchin's Coll., Limerick. At twenty went to Dublin, having won a Scholarship in Art at the Dublin Metropolitan Sch. of Art; spent four years in Aran, off the west coast of Ireland; came back to Dublin and won the Taylor Scholarship in Painting; worked with Sir William Orpen in London until 1916; returned to Ireland in that year. *Recreations:* reading and idling. *Address:* Ait an Cuain, Rathfarnham, Co. Dublin. *T:* 904957.

**KEATINGE, Sir Edgar (Mayne)**, Kt 1960; CBE 1954; *b* 3 Feb. 1905; *s* of late Gerald Francis Keatinge, CIE; *m* 1930, Katharine Lucile Burrell; one *s* one *d*. *Educ:* Rugby Sch.; School of Agriculture, S Africa. Diploma in Agriculture, 1925. S African Dept of Agriculture, 1926-29; farming Suffolk, 1932-39. Served War of 1939-45 with RA. Resigned with rank of Lieut-Col. West African Frontier Force, 1941-43; Commandant Sch. of Artillery, West Africa, 1942-43; CC West Suffolk, 1933-45. Parliamentary Candidate, Isle of Ely, 1938-44; MP (C) Bury St Edmunds, 1944-45; JP Wilts 1946; Chm. Wessex Area Nat. Union of Conservative Assocs, 1950-53; Mem. Panel, Land Tribunal, SW Area. Gov. of Sherborne Sch. *Recreations:* travel, shooting. *Address:* Teffont, Salisbury, Wilts. *T:* Teffont 224. *Clubs:* Carlton, Boodle's.

**KEAY, Sir Lancelot Herman**, KBE 1947 (OBE 1934); MArch Liverpool; City Architect and Director of Housing, Liverpool, 1925-48; *b* 3 Aug. 1883; 2nd *s* of late Henry William Keay, JP, Elms-Meade, Eastbourne; *m* 1920, Iris, *er d* of late E. G. Stone, Clifton, Guernsey; two *d*. *Educ:* Eastbourne Coll.; Brighton Sch. of Art. Held architectural appointments at Norwich and under Corporations of Birmingham and Liverpool; served in Royal Engineers during European War with 34th Div. in France and as CRE Kantara Area, Egypt; in Liverpool responsible for erection of over 35,000 houses and flats, and for effecting rebuilding of slum areas and for four re-development schemes comprising 850 acres in centre of City; Senior Partner of firm of Sir Lancelot Keay, Basil G. Duckett and Partners, Chartered Architects, 80 Wimpole Street, W1; First Chairman: Bracknell New Town Development Corporation; Basildon New Town Development Corporation; Member: Housing Advisory Cttee, 1936-57; Advisory Council on Building and Civil Engineering Research and Development, 1947-57. Past Pres. RIBA, 1946-48. *Publications:* Frequent contributor to Technical Journals. *Address:* 22 Hyde Park Gardens, W2. *Clubs:* Athenæum, Arts.

**KEEBLE, (Herbert Ben) Curtis**, CMG 1970; Minister (Commercial), UK High Commission, Canberra, since 1968; *b* 18 Sept. 1922; *s* of Herbert Keeble and Gertrude Keeble, BEM; *m* 1947, Margaret Fraser; three *d*. *Educ:* Clacton County High Sch.; London University. Served Royal Irish Fusiliers, 1942-47. Entered HM Foreign (subsequently Diplomatic) Service, 1947; served in Djakarta, 1947-49; Foreign Office, 1949-51; Berlin, 1951-54; Washington, 1954-58; Foreign Office, 1958-65; Counsellor, Berne, 1965-68. *Recreation:* sailing. *Address:* c/o Foreign and Commonwealth Office, SW1. *Club:* Travellers'.

**KEEBLE, Major Robert**, DSO 1940; MC 1945; TD 1946; Director, Associated Portland Cement Manufacturers Ltd; engaged in cement manufacture; Managing Director, G. & T. Earle Ltd; Director, Nottinghamshire Gypsum Products Ltd; Manager, Hull Savings Bank; *b* 20 Feb. 1911; *s* of late Edwin Percy and Alice Elizabeth Keeble; unmarried. *Educ:* King Henry VIII's Sch., Coventry. Commanded Royal Engineer Field Company; Territorial Army Commission, passed Staff Coll., Camberley, 1939; Freeman of City of London and Liveryman of Company of Fanmakers; served in War of 1939-45 (despatches twice, twice wounded, DSO, MC, 1939-45 Star, African Star, France-Germany Star and Defence Medal, TD). Member institute Directors; Inst. Quarrying. Governor, Hull Univ. Hon. Brother, Hull Trinity House. *Recreations:* fired in rifle team winning Lord Wakefield Shield for TA, 1939; sailing. *Address:* 15 Marsham Court, Westminster, SW1. *T:* 01-834-8831. *Clubs:* Royal Automobile; East India and Sports.

**KEEBLE, Thomas Whitfield**; HM Diplomatic Service; Minister, British Embassy, Madrid, since 1969; *b* 10 Feb. 1918; *m* 1945, Ursula Scott Morris; two *s*. *Educ:* Sir John Deane's Grammar Sch., Cheshire; St John's Coll., Cambridge (MA); King's Coll., London (PhD). Served, 1940-45, in India, Persia, Iraq and Burma in RA (seconded to Indian Artillery), Captain. Asst Principal, Commonwealth Relations Office, 1948; Private Sec. to Parliamentary Under Sec. of State; Principal, 1949; First Sec., UK High Commn in Pakistan, 1950-53, in Lahore, Peshawar and Karachi; seconded to Foreign Service and posted to UK Mission to the United Nations in New York, 1955-59; Counsellor, 1958; Head of Defence and Western Dept, CRO, 1959-60; British Dep. High Comr in Ghana, 1960-63; Head of Econ. Gen. Dept, CRO, 1963-66; Minister (Commercial), British Embassy, Buenos Aires, 1966-67; Hon. Research Associate, Inst. of Latin American Studies, Univ. of London, 1967-68. *Publications:* articles in Bulletin of Hispanic Studies. *Recreations:* golf, Spanish literature, bird watching. *Address:* c/o Foreign and Commonwealth Office, King Charles Street, SW1. *Club:* Oxford and Cambridge University.

**KEEGAN, Denis Michael**; Director: Radio and Television Retailers' Association; Electrical Appliance Association Ltd; Barrister-at-Law; *b* 26 Jan. 1924; *o s* of Denis Francis Keegan and Mrs Duncan Campbell; *m* 1st, 1951, Pamela Barbara (marriage dissolved), *yr d* of late Percy Bryan, Purley, Surrey; one *s*; 2nd, 1961, Marie Patricia, *yr d* of late Harold Jennings; one *s*. *Educ:* Oundle Sch.; Queen's University, Kingston, Ontario, Canada (BA). Served RN Fleet Air Arm, 1944-46 (petty officer pilot). Called to Bar, Gray's Inn, 1950; practised law in Nottingham; Mem. Nottingham City Council, 1953-55, resigned. MP (C) Nottingham Sth, 1955-Sept. 1959. *Recreations:* reading, talking, golf. *Address:* April Wood, St Mary's Road, Ascot, Berks. *T:* Ascot 22919.

**KEEL, Jonathan Edgar**, CB 1956; retired; *b* 21 Feb. 1895; *s* of Wm Keel, JP and Elizabeth Keel; *m* 1927, Olga Constance Pointing; one *s*. *Educ:* Middlesbrough High Sch. Inland Revenue as second division clerk, 1912; transferred to Tax Dept as Surveyor of Taxes,

1916; transferred to Air Ministry with rank of Principal, 1938; went to USA as Dir of Finance and Administration of British Air Commission, 1940; Asst Sec., 1941; Ministry of Aircraft Production, 1944; Min. of Civil Aviation, 1946; Under Sec., 1948; in charge of Safety and General Dept, 1948-53; UK Rep. on Coun. of Internat. Civil Aviation Org., Montreal, 1953-57; retd from Public Service, 1957. *Recreations:* gardening and golf. *Address:* 5 Redcroft Walk, Cranleigh, Surrey. *T:* Cranleigh 3282.

**KEELE, Prof. Cyril Arthur;** Director, Rheumatology Research Department, Middlesex Hospital Medical School, London, since 1968; *b* 23 Nov. 1905; 2nd *s* of Dr David and Jessie Keele; *m* 1942, Joan Ainslie, *er d* of Lieut-Col G. A. Kempthorne; three *s*. *Educ:* Epsom Coll.; Middlesex Hospital Medical Sch. MRCS, LRCP 1927; MB, BS (London) 1928; MRCP 1929; MD London 1930; FRCP 1948; FFARCS 1958. Medical Registrar, Middlesex Hosp., 1930-32; Demonstrator and Lectr in Physiology, 1933-38; Lectr in Pharmacology, 1938-49; Reader in Pharmacology and Therapeutics, 1949-52, at Middlesex Hospital Medical Sch.; Prof. of Pharmacology and Therapeutics, Univ. of London, 1952-68. *Publications:* Recent Advances in Pharmacology (with Prof. J. M. Robson), 1956; Samson Wright's Applied Physiology, 11th edn (with Prof. E. Neil); (with Dr D. Armstrong) Substances producing Pain and Itch, 1964. Papers in scientific journals on the control of sweating, analgesic drugs and chemical factors producing pain. *Address:* Middlesex Hospital Medical School, W1P 9PG. *T:* 01-636 8333.

**KEELEY, Thomas Clews,** CBE 1944; MA; physicist; Fellow of Wadham College, Oxford, 1924-61, Sub-Warden, 1947-61, retired; *b* 16 Feb. 1894; *s* of T. F. Keeley, Erdington, Birmingham. *Educ:* King Edward's School, Birmingham; St John's Coll., Cambridge (Scholar). Royal Aircraft Establishment, 1917-19. Oxford from 1919. Fellow of the Institute of Physics. *Recreations:* photography, travel. *Address:* Wadham College, Oxford. *T:* 42564. *Club:* English-Speaking Union.

**KEELING, Cyril Desmond Evans;** Under-Secretary, Ministry of Agriculture, Fisheries and Food; *b* 13 April 1921; *s* of late Cyril F. J. Keeling, MC, and Susan Evans Keeling; *m* 1947, Megan Miles; one *d*. *Educ:* Southend High Sch., Peterhouse, Cambridge. Parts I and II, Economics, Cambridge, 1939-41 and 1945-46. Served 1941-45 in Infantry (wounded, despatches): Adjutant 5th Bn Wilts Regt, 1944-45. Research, LSE, 1946; Ministry of Works, 1947; Sec. Historic Buildings Council, 1953-57; Private Sec. to Minister, 1957-60; Asst Sec., 1960; Dir, Treasury Centre for Administrative Studies, 1963-65; Under-Sec., Treasury, and Dir of Training, 1965-68; Under-Sec., Civil Service Dept, 1968-69; study at London Graduate Business Sch., 1970. Fellow-Commoner, Emmanuel Coll., Cambridge, Michaelmas 1969. *Recreation:* gardening. *Address:* Headlong Hill, Stokesheath Road, Oxshott, Surrey. *T:* Oxshott 2616. *Club:* United University.

**KEELING, Edward Allis;** *b* 1885; *m* 1920, Countess Magda Gaetani d'Aragona (*d* 1945), Rome. *Educ:* Eton; Christ Church, Oxford; Third Sec., Diplomatic Service, 1913-19; Second Sec., 1919-20; First Sec., 1920; Counsellor of Embassy, Brazil, 1931; Minister to Venezuela, 1932-36; British Consul-Gen. with rank of Minister at Tangier, 1936-39. *Address:* Palazzo Lovatelli, Rome. *Clubs:* Travellers', Beefsteak, Pratt's.

**KEELING, Sir John (Henry),** Kt 1952; Director, Safeguard Industrial Investments Ltd, 1953-69 (Chairman, 1953-66); Vice-Chairman, Bowater Paper Corp. Ltd, 1945-67; Chairman, West Riding Worsted and Woollen Mills Ltd, 1944-62 (Director, 1962-68); *b* 18 Aug. 1895; *s* of John Henry Keeling and Mary, *d* of Edward P. Allis, Milwaukee, Wisconsin; *m* Dorothy *d* of Dr Morgan I. Finucane and Jane Sheridan; three *s* one *d*. *Educ:* Summerfields, St Leonards, and Oxford; Eton. Queen's Royal West Surrey Regt Territorials, 1914-18, when transferred to Coldstream Guards. In 1923 founded London and Yorkshire Trust Ltd (with Reginald E. Cornwall), Dir (Past Chm.). Min. of Aircraft Prod., 1940-45; Dir-Gen. Aircraft Distrib., 1943-45; Dep. Chm., BEA, 1947-65. *Address:* Hurst House, Sedlescombe, Sussex. *T:* 340; Grosvenor House, Park Lane, W1. *T:* 01-499 2987. *Club:* White's.

**KEELY, Eric Philipps,** CBE 1950; Director, National Sulphuric Acid Association Ltd, 1959-67; *b* 11 Aug. 1899; *s* of late Erasmus Middleton Keely, Nottingham; *m* 1942, Enid Betty Curtis; two *d*. *Educ:* Highgate Sch. Served European War, 1917-18, Lancashire Fusiliers; Ministry of Agriculture and Fisheries, 1930; Food (Defence Plans) Dept, Board of Trade 1937; Ministry of Food, 1939; seconded to Govt of India, 1943-44; Under-Sec., Ministry of Food, 1952; Under-Sec., Ministry of Agriculture, Fisheries and Food, 1955-59. *Address:* Wilderness Cottage, Oxted, Surrey. *T:* Oxted 3907. *Club:* Travellers'.

**KEEN, Sir Bernard (A.),** Kt 1952; FRS 1935; DSc; Fellow of University College, London; *b* 1890; *m* Elsie Isabelle Cowley (*d* 1956); two *s*. *Educ:* University Coll., London. Andrews Scholar, 1908; Trouton Research Scholar, 1911; Carey Foster Res. Prizeman, 1912; Soil Physicist, Rothamsted, 1913; Suffolk Regt (Gallipoli and Palestine), 1914-17; Research Dept, Woolwich Arsenal, 1918; returned to Rothamsted, 1919; Dir, Imperial Institute of Agricultural Research, India, 1930-31; Pres., Royal Meteorological Soc., 1938 and 1939; Vice-Pres., Institute of Physics, 1941-43; Cantor Lecturer, Royal Society of Arts, 1942; formerly Asst Dir and Head of Soil Physics Dept, Rothamsted Experimental Station, 1919-43; Scientific Adviser Middle East Supply Centre, Cairo, 1943-45; adviser on rural development, Palestine, 1946; Chm. of UK Govt Mission to W Africa on production of vegetable oils and oil seeds, 1946; adviser to E African Governments on agricultural policy and research needs, 1947; mem., Scientific Council for Africa, 1950-54; Chm. of Governors, E African Tea Research Inst., 1951-54. Broadcast talks to schools on science of agriculture and gardening, 1928-41; Dir, E African Agriculture and Forestry Research Organisation, 1947-55; Scientific Adviser, Baird and Tatlock (London) Ltd, 1955-63; mem., Scientific Panel Colonial Development Corp., 1955-63; Mem., Forest Products Res. Bd, DSIR, 1957-59. Travelled extensively in USA, S Africa, India, E and W Africa, Middle East, Bulgaria and Australia, to examine and report on the scientific, technical, and administrative problems in agriculture. *Publications:* The Physical Properties of the Soil, 1931; The Agricultural Development of the Middle East, 1946; various papers in scientific and agricultural journals. *Address:* 72 Eaton Square, SW1. *Clubs:* Athenæum, Farmers'.

**KEEN, Patrick John,** CMG 1968; MBE 1944; retired; *b* 30 June 1911; *s* of Brig. P. H. Keen,

CB; *m* 1st, 1940, Joyce (*d* 1954), *d* of E. Seth-Ward; two *s* one *d* (and one *s* decd); 2nd, 1958, Anne Cunitia, *d* of Capt. J. A. A. Morris, RN. *Educ:* Haileybury Coll.; RMC Sandhurst. Hampshire Regt, 1931; Indian Political Service, 1931-47; served with 2/13th FF Rifles, 1939-43; HM Diplomatic Service, 1948-68; served in Afghanistan, Pakistan, Cyprus and British Guiana; retd, 1968. *Address:* Saxted House, Emsworth, Hants. *T:* Emsworth 2302. *Club:* United Service.

**KEENE, Air Vice-Marshal Allan L. A. P.;** *see* Perry-Keene.

**KEENE, Sir Charles (Robert),** Kt 1969; CBE 1950; JP; Alderman, City of Leicester, 1945-70; Managing Director, Kingstone Ltd; *b* 21 Sept. 1891; *s* of late C. E. Keene; *m* 1st, 1921, Ruth Stocks (*d* 1949); two *s* (one *s* decd); 2nd, 1952, Hetty Swann. Mem. Leicester City Council, 1926-70; Dep. Regional Comr (N Midland Region), 1941-44; Chm., Leicester City Town-Planning Cttee, 1942-53, Slum Clearance Cttee, 1952-62, and Educn Cttee, 1953-62. High Bailiff, Leicester, 1935-36, Lord Mayor, 1953-54. Pro-Chancellor, Univ. of Leicester; Chairman: Governors of Leicester Colls of Art and Technology, 1927-69; City of Leicester Polytechnic; Charles Keene Coll. of Further Education, 1961-70; Council of University of Leicester; Governors, Gateway Sch., 1928-68. Hon. Freeman, City of Leicester, 1962. Hon. LLD Leicester Univ., 1963. *Address:* Gaulby, Leicestershire. *T:* Billesdon 215.

**KEENE, Mary Frances Lucas,** DSc, MB, BS (London); FRCS; President, Royal Free Hospital School of Medicine; Professor Emeritus in Anatomy, University of London; Lecturer at Royal Free Hospital School of Medicine; Past President of the Medical Women's Federation; Past President of the Anatomical Society of Great Britain and Ireland; Vice-President, The Medical Protection Society; late Examiner in Anatomy, Universities of London and Bristol: Conjoint Board, England; University of South Wales, and to Royal College of Surgeons, England; *d* of late G. J. Lucas of Milton Court, near Gravesend; *m* 1916, Richard F. (*decd*), *s* of late Henry Keene. *Educ:* Eversley, Folkestone; London (RFH) School of Medicine for Women. Took Degree, London Univ., Bachelor of Medicine and Bachelor of Surgery, 1911; Lecturer in Embryology and Senior Demonstrator in Anatomy at above Medical School, 1914; Lecturer and Head of Department (same school), 1919. *Publications:* various papers in scientific journals. *Recreations:* gardening, reading, beginning painting. *Address:* Newhaven, The Droveway, St Margaret's Bay, Dover, Kent. *T:* St Margaret's Bay 2138.

**KEENE, Vice-Adm. Philip R.;** *see* Ruck Keene.

**KEENLEYSIDE, Hugh Llewellyn,** CC (Canada) 1969; consultant; *b* 7 July 1898; *s* of Ellis William Keenleyside and Margaret Louise Irvine; *m* 1924, Katherine Hall Pillsbury, BA, BSc; one *s* three *d*. *Educ:* Langara School and Public Schools, Vancouver, BC; University of British Columbia (BA); Clark University (MA, PhD). Holds several hon. degrees in Law, Science. Instructor and Special Lecturer in History, Brown University, Syracuse Univ., and University of British Columbia, 1923-27; Third Sec., Dept of External Affairs, 1928; Second Sec., 1929; First Sec. and First Chargé d'Affaires, Canadian Legation, Tokyo, 1929; Dept of External Affairs and Prime Minister's Office, 1936; Chm, Board of Review to Investigate charges of illegal entry on the Pacific Coast, 1937; Sec., Cttee in charge of Royal Visit to Canada, 1938-39; Counsellor, 1940; Asst Under-Sec. of State for External Affairs, 1941-44; Mem. and Sec., Canadian Section, Canada-United States Permanent Joint Board on Defence, 1940-44. Acting Chm., 1944-45; Mem. North-West Territories Council, 1941-45; Mem., Canada-United States Joint Economic Cttees, 1941-44; Mem., Special Cttee on Orientals in BC; Mem., Canadian Shipping Board, 1939-41; Mem., War Scientific and Technical Development Cttee, 1940-45; Canadian Ambassador to Mexico, 1944-47; Deputy Minister of Resources and Development and Comr of Northwest Territories, 1947-50; Head of UN Mission of Technical Assistance to Bolivia, 1950; Dir-Gen., UN Technical Assistance Administration, 1950-58; Under-Sec. for Public Administration, UN, 1959. Chairman: BC Power Commn, 1959-62; BC Power and Hydro Authy, 1962-69. Vice-Pres. National Council of the YMCAs of Canada, 1941-45; Vice-Chm., Canadian Youth Commission, 1943-45; Head of Canadian Deleg. to UN Scientific Conf. on Conservation and Utilization of Resources, 1949. Life Mem., Asiatic Soc. of Japan; one of founders and mem. of first Board of Governors of Arctic Institute of North America; Vice-Chm., Board of Governors, Carleton Coll., 1943-50; Pres. Assoc. of Canadian Clubs, 1948-50; Mem. Bd of Trustees, Clark Univ., 1953-56; Mem. Senate, University of British Columbia, 1963-69. Haldane Medal, Royal Inst. of Public Administration, 1954; First recipient Vanier Medal, Inst. of Public Admin. of Canada, 1962. Hon. Life Mem., Canadian Association for Adult Education; Mem. Board of Governors, Canadian Welfare Council; Member: Canadian National Cttee of World Power Conference; BC Energy Bd; Adv. Bd (BC), Canada Permanent Cos; Hon. Mem., Bd of Dirs, Resources for the Future; Dir, Toronto-Dominion Bank. Chancellor, Notre Dame Univ., Nelson, BC, 1969-. Dir and Fellow, Royal Canadian Geographic Soc., FRHistS, FRGS. *Publications:* Canada and the United States, 1929, revised edn 1952; History of Japanese Education (with A. F. Thomas), 1937; International Aid: a summary, 1966; various magazine articles. *Recreations:* reading, outdoor sports, cooking, poker. *Address:* 3470 Mayfair Drive, Victoria, BC, Canada. *T:* 592-9331.

**KEENLYSIDE, Francis Hugh;** Managing Director, Manica Trading Co. Ltd; Editor, the Alpine Journal; *b* 7 July 1911; *s* of late Capt. Cecil A. H. Keenlyside and Gladys Mary (*née* Milne); *m* 1935, Margaret Joan, *d* of late E. L. K. Ellis; two *s* two *d*. *Educ:* Charterhouse; Trinity Coll., Oxford. 1st class Hons in Philosophy, Politics and Economics, 1933, Whitehead Travelling Student. Entered Administrative Class, Home Civil Service, 1934; Principal Private Sec. to four successive Ministers of Shipping and War Transport, 1939-43; Asst Sec. in charge of Shipping Policy Div., 1943; Asst Manager, Union Castle, 1947; Dep. Leader, British delegation to Danube Conf., Belgrade, 1948; Gen. Manager, Union Castle, 1953; Asst Managing Dir, Union-Castle, 1956-60; Shipping Adviser, Suez Canal Users Assoc., 1957. Mem., Gen. Council of Chamber of Shipping, 1953-60; Chevalier (1st Cl.) of Order of St Olav (Norway), 1948; Officer of Order of George I (Greece), 1950; King Christian X Liberty Medal (Denmark), 1946. *Publications:* contrib. to mountaineering jls, etc. *Recreation:* mountaineering. *Address:* Odiham Priory, Hants. *T:* Odiham 289. *Clubs:* Travellers', Alpine.

**KEENS, Philip Francis,** OBE 1966; Deputy Chairman, Trustee Savings Bank Association, since 1966 (Chairman Southern Area, 1967); Chairman, London Trustee Savings Bank, since 1964 (Vice-Chairman, 1958); *b* 18 June 1903; *s* of Sir Thomas Keens; *m* 1930, Sylvia Irene Robinson (*d* 1970); one *s* one *d*. *Educ:* Tettenhall Coll., Staffs. Incorporated Accountant, 1925; Chartered Accountant, 1957. Partner, Keens, Shay, Keens & Co., London, 1926-67; Trustee, Luton Trustee Savings Bank, 1934 (Chairman, 1949-64). Past Master, Worshipful Co. of Feltmakers. *Recreation:* golf. *Address:* Kimpton Grange, near Hitchin, Herts. *T:* Kimpton 205. *Clubs:* City Livery; The Club (St Austell, Cornwall).

**KEEPING, Charles William James;** artist, book designer and Fine Art Lecturer since 1952; Visiting Lecturer in Art, Croydon College of Art, since 1963; *b* 22 Sept. 1924; *s* of Charles Keeping and Eliza Ann Trodd; *m* 1952, Renate Meyer; three *s* one *d*. *Educ:* Frank Bryant Sch., Kennington; Polytechnic, Regent Street. Apprenticed to printing trade, 1938; served as telegraphist, RN, 1942-46; studied for Nat. Diploma of Design at Polytechnic, London, 1946-52; Vis. Lectr in Art, Polytechnic, 1956-63. Illustrated over 100 books, drawings for wall murals, television and advertising. MSIA. Kate Greenaway Medal 1967, Hon. Book Award 1969, Library Assoc. *Publications:* Black Dolly, 1966; Shaun and the Carthorse, 1966; Charley Charlotte and the Golden Canary, 1967; Alfie and the Ferryboat, 1968; Joseph's Yard, 1969 (also filmed for TV); Through the Window, 1970 (also filmed for TV). *Recreations:* talking, walking, driving ponies. *Address:* 16 Church Road, Shortlands, Bromley BR2 0HP. *T:* 01-460 7679. *Club:* Nash House.

**KEESEY, Walter Monckton,** OBE; MC; ARCA; ARIBA (retired); Hon. FIBD; Hon. Vice-President, RBSA; architect and etcher; *b* 16 June 1887; *s* of Rev. G. W. Keesey; *m* J. H. Swinglehurst (*d* 1963), Kendal, Westmorland; one *d*. *Educ:* Caterham; St Olave's; Royal College of Art, Architectural Assoc. Staff, 1913-25; Brit. Institution Scholar; served Royal Engineers, 1914-19 (Major, MC). Lately HMI Ministry of Educn. Hon. Life Mem., BFCAA; Pres., Cheltenham Group, 1961. *Principal Works:* Caterham Memorial Hall, etc., various domestic jobs. *Publications:* Architectural Drawing; various papers, etc. *Recreation:* golf. *Address:* Yew Tree Cottage, Epperstone, Notts. *T:* Lowdham 2545. *Club:* Chelsea Arts.

**KEETON, George Williams,** FBA 1964; Barrister-at-law; Professor of English Law: University of Notre Dame, since 1969; Brunel University, since 1969; Principal, London Institute of World Affairs, since 1938; *b* 22 May 1902; *o s* of John William and Mary Keeton; *m* 1st, 1924, Gladys Edith Calthorpe; two *s*; 2nd, Kathleen Marian Willard. *Educ:* Gonville and Caius Coll., Cambridge (Foundation Scholar in Law); Gray's Inn (Bacon Scholar). BA, LLB, with first class hons, 1923; MA, LLM, 1927; LLD 1932. Called to Bar, 1928; Editor, The Cambridge Review, 1924; Reader in Law and Politics, Hong Kong Univ., 1924-27; Senior Lecturer in Law, Manchester Univ., 1928-31; Reader in English Law, University Coll., London, 1931-37; Prof. of English Law, 1937-69; Dean, Faculty of Laws, 1939-54; Vice-Provost, 1966-69. Hon. LLD (Sheffield), 1966. *Publications:* The Development of Extraterritoriality in China, 1928; The Austinian Theories of Law and Sovereignty (with R. A. Eastwood, LLD), 1929; The Elementary Principles of Jurisprudence, 1930, 2nd edn 1949; Shakespeare and his Legal Problems, 1930; The Problem of the Moscow Trial, 1933; The Law of Trusts, 1st Edn 1934, 9th edn 1967; An Introduction to Equity, 1st edn 1938, 5th edn 1960; National Sovereignty and International Order, 1939; Making International Law Work (with G. Schwarzenberger, PhD), 1st edn 1939, 2nd edn 1946; The Speedy Return (novel), 1938; Mutiny in the Caribbean (novel), 1940; The Case for an International University, 1941; Russia and Her Western Neighbours (with R. Schlesinger), 1942; China, the Far East, and the Future, 1st edn 1942, 2nd edn 1949; A Liberal Attorney-General, 1949; The Passing of Parliament, 1952; Social Change in the Law of Trusts, 1958; Case Book on Equity and Trusts, 1958; Trial for Treason, 1959; Trial by Tribunal, 1960; Guilty but Insane, 1961; The Modern Law of Charities, 1962; The Investment and Taxation of Trust Funds, 1964; Lord Chancellor Jeffreys, 1964; The Norman Conquest and the Common Law, 1966; Shakespeare's Legal and Political Background, 1967; (with L. Sheridan) Equity, 1970; Government in Action, 1970; numerous contributions to periodicals. *Address:* Picts Close, Picts Lane, Princes Risborough, Bucks. *T:* 94; School of Law, Notre Dame University, Ind, USA.

**KEEVIL, Colonel Sir Ambrose,** Kt 1952; KBE 1962 (CBE 1944; MBE 1918); MC 1917 (Bar 1918); DL; President (formerly Chairman), Fitch Lovell Ltd and Chairman various other companies; *b* 1893; *s* of late Clement Keevil; *m* 1918, Dorothy Pearsall, *d* of Arthur Andrews, JP, Southfields, Ryde, I of W; one *s* one *d*. *Educ:* University College Sch.; France. Served European War, 1914-19, with Royal Munster Fusiliers; retired 1921. Chm. Wholesale Produce Merchants Assoc.; Pres. Metropolitan Market Clerks Benevolent Institution, 1934-36; Chm. London Provision Exchange, 1938-39; Chm. Albert & Victoria Hospital Aid Soc., 1938-40; Master Worshipful Co. of Poulters, 1938-39, 1958-59. Chm. Co-ord Cttee of Produce and Provision Exchanges of UK, 1938-41; Chm. London Area Cttee, Ministry of Food, 1939-42 and Chm. Co-ord. Cttee London, Southern, Eastern and South Eastern Areas, Min. of Food, 1941-42. Mil. Mem. Surrey T & AFA, 1940-50 and 1952-. Comdr Home Guard Sector of London Dist, 1942-45 and Surrey E Sector, 1952-55; Chm. E Surrey Conservative Assoc., 1945-51 (Pres. 1951-); Hon. Treas, Union of Cons. Assocs for Kent, Surrey and Sussex, 1947-60, Vice-Pres., 1960-; Vice-Chm. Cons. Central Board of Finance, 1953-61; Chm. Surrey Playing Fields Association, 1952-; Chairman of Governors: Reedham School, Purley, 1963; Moor Park Coll., 1964-; Governor, Royal Wanstead School, 1963-68. President: East Surrey Horse Society and Hunter Trials, 1955-; Surrey Small Bore Rifle Association, 1965-68. Chairman: Surrey Rifle Association, 1967-69; Swinton Coll. Education Cttee, 1960-69; Springfield Group Hospital Management Cttee, 1964-68. Life Vice-Pres., Greater London Area Conservative Assoc. DL Surrey, 1944; High Sheriff, Surrey, 1956-57. Chevalier Ordre de Mérite Agricole (France), 1939; Chevalier Legion of Honour, 1956. *Recreations:* people, horses, and dogs. *Address:* Bayards, Warlingham, Surrey. *T:* Upper Warlingham 4256. *Clubs:* Bath, MCC, City Livery.

**KEEWATIN, Bishop of,** since 1969; **Rt. Rev. Hugh Vernon Stiff;** *b* 15 Sept. 1916; unmarried. *Educ:* Univ. of Toronto (BA); Trinity Coll., Toronto (LTh). BD General Synod; Hon. DD, Trinity Coll., Toronto. *Address:* Box 118, Kenora, Ontario, Canada. *T:* 468-7011.

**KEGGIN, Air Vice-Marshal Harold,** CB 1967; CBE 1962; LDS; Director of Dental Services, Royal Air Force, 1964-69, retired; *b* 25 Feb. 1909; *y s* of John and Margaret Keggin, Port Erin, Isle of Man; *m* 1935, Margaret Joy (*née* Campbell); one *s* two *d*. *Educ:* Douglas High Sch.; University of Liverpool. Dental Officer, RAF, commissioned, 1932; Flt Lieut 1934; Sqdn Ldr 1939; Wing Comdr 1942; Gp Capt. 1954; Air Cdre 1958; Air Vice-Marshal 1964. QHDS 1958-69. *Recreations:* golf, fishing. *Address:* Rosecroft, 7 Cotlands, Sidmouth, Devon EX10 8SP. *T:* Sidmouth 4790.

**KEIGHLEY, Frank;** Regional Director, West Midlands and Wales Regional Board, National Westminster Bank Ltd; Director: North Central Finance Ltd; Rank Organisation Ltd, and 5 Subsidiaries; Fellow of Institute of Bankers; *b* 19 March 1900; *e s* of late Wm L. Keighley; *m* 1926, Mary, *e d* of late J. K. Wilson; one *s*. *Educ:* Northern Institute, Leeds. Entered Union of London & Smiths Bank (which was amalgamated with National Provincial Bank in 1918) as Junior Clerk, 1915; retired as Chief General Manager, Dec. 1961. *Address:* Little Court, 88 Fulmer Drive, Gerrards Cross, Bucks. *T:* Gerrards Cross 84117.

**KEIGHLY-PEACH, Captain Charles Lindsey,** DSO 1940; OBE 1941; RN retired; *b* 6 April 1902; *s* of late Admiral C. W. Keighly-Peach, DSO; *m* 1st, V. B. Cumbers; one *s* one *d*; *m* 2nd, Beatrice Mary Harrison. *Educ:* RN Colleges, Osborne and Dartmouth. Midshipman, 1919; Sub-Lieut 1922; Lieut 1924; 3 Squadron, RAF, 1926; HMS Eagle (402 Sqdn), 1927; H/M S/M M2, 1929; HMS Centaur, 1930; Lieut-Cdr 1932; HMS Glorious (802 Sqdn), 1932; RN Staff Coll., Greenwich, 1934; SOO to RA Destroyers, 1935; HMS London, 1937; Commander, 1938; RN Air Station Lee-on-Solent, 1939; HMS Eagle, 1940-41; Naval Assistant (Air) to 2nd Sea Lord, 1941-44; Capt. 1943; RN Air Station, Yeovilton, 1944-45; Comdg HMS Sultan, Singapore, 1945-47; in command HMS Troubridge and 3rd Destroyer Flot. Med., 1947-49; Dir Captain, Senior Officer's War Course, RN, 1949-51; Asst Chief Naval Staff (Air) on loan to Royal Canadian Navy, 1951-53, Vice-Chm., S Norfolk Conservative Assoc. *Recreations:* golf, gardening. *Address:* Empton House, Brockdish, Diss, Norfolk. *T:* Hoxne 273. *Clubs:* Royal Over-Seas League; Norfolk (Norwich).

**KEIGHTLEY, Gen. Sir Charles (Frederic),** GCB 1953 (KCB 1950; CB 1943); GBE 1957 (KBE 1945; OBE 1941); DSO 1944; DL; President: British Legion South West Area and Dorset County; St John Ambulance Association and Brigade, Dorset; Vice-President, Royal Victoria Patriotic Fund Corporation; *b* 24 June 1901; *s* of late Rev. C. A. Keightley; *m* 1932, Joan Lydia, *d* of late Brig.-Gen. G. N. T. Smyth Osbourne, CB, CMG, DSO, Ash, Iddesleigh, N Devon; two *s*. *Educ:* Marlborough Coll.; RMC, Sandhurst. 5th Dragoon Guards, 1921; served in Palestine, Egypt and India; Adjutant 5th Royal Inniskilling Dragoon Guards, 1930-33; Staff Coll., 1934-35; Staff Officer to Dir Gen., TA, 1936; Bde Major, Cairo Cav. Bde, 1937-38; Instructor Staff Coll., Camberley, 1938-40; Served War of 1939-45 (despatches thrice); AAQMG 1st Armoured Div. in France, 1940; Comd 30th Armd Bde, 1941-42; Comd 6th Armoured Div. in Tunisia, 1942-43; Comd 78th Div. in Italy, 1943-44; Comdg V Corps in Italy and Austria, 1944-45; DMT, War Office, 1946-47; Milit. Sec. to Sec. of State for War, 1948; C-in-C, BAOR, 1948-51; C-in-C Far East Land Forces, 1951-53; C-in-C, Middle East Land Forces, 1953-57; ADC Gen. to the Queen, 1953-56; Governor and C-in-C of Gibraltar, 1958-62. Kermit Roosevelt Lecturer to the USA, 1957. Col 5th Royal Inniskilling Dragoon Guards, 1947-57; Col Comdt, RAC (Cavalry Wing), 1958-68. Governor, Allhallows Sch. DL Dorset, 1970. American Legion of Merit, 1942; Grand Officer, Legion of Honour, 1958. KStJ. *Recreations:* gardening, fishing, shooting. *Address:* White Kennels, Tarrant Gunville, Dorset. *Clubs:* Cavalry, Lansdowne.

**KEIGWIN, Richard Prescott,** MA Cantab; *b* Colchester, 8 April 1883; 4th *s* of Charles David and Louisa Keigwin. *Educ:* Colet Court; Temple Grove; Clifton; Peterhouse, Cambridge (Classical Exhibitioner); France and Germany. Mod. Lang. master, Royal Naval Coll., Osborne; served European War, 1914-18, as Lieut RNVR (Belgian Order of Leopold); Editor, The Granta, 1919; housemaster at Clifton, 1920-35; Warden of Wills Hall, University of Bristol, 1935-45; President, Old Cliftonian Society, 1957-59. Danish Order of the Dannebrog; King Christian X's Frihedsmedaille; Hans Christian Andersen Prize, Copenhagen, 1964. *Publications:* Lanyard Lyrics; Lyrics for Sport; The Jutland Wind; Kaj Munk (some examples of his work); In Denmark I was born; new translations of Hans Andersen; Five Plays by Kaj Munk; English libretto of Carl Nielsen's Opera Saul and David; numerous other verse and prose translations from the Danish; contributions to periodicals in England, Denmark and America. *Recreations:* cricket, etc.; (represented Cambridge Univ. at cricket, rackets, hockey, Association football). *Address:* The Old Forge, Polstead, Suffolk.

**KEILLER, Brian Edwin,** CMG 1961; Farmer (dairy and pig) 1930-59; now retired; *b* Bulls, NZ, 18 July 1901; *s* of E. Keiller, Bulls, NZ, and Muriel Kathrine Waitt; *m* 1932, Helena Maude Harcourt; two *s* one *d*. *Educ:* Wanganui Collegiate Sch., Wanganui, NZ. Dep. Chm. from its inception of Nat. Pig Industry Council, also Chm. Wellington Dist Pig Council (15 yrs), retd, 1953; original Mem. NZ Horse Soc., 1951 (Hon. Treas., 1955-); Mem. Council, Royal Agric. Society, 1942- (Chm. 1945-52); Hon. Life Mem. Royal Agric. Society of England; Treas., Manawatu Agric. and Pastoral Assoc., 1951- (Mem., 1933, Chm., 1942-51). Mem. Wellington Harbour Bd, 1947- (Chm. 1957-61); Pres. Harbours Assoc. of NZ, 1957-61. Chairman: Watson Bros Ltd; Abraham Seed & Produce Co. Ltd, 1963-; Everyday Products Pty Co., 1966; Dir, Barnard and Abraham Ltd. Pres. Wanganui Old Boys' Assoc., 1951-55 (centenary, 1954); Governor: Massey Agric. Coll., 1954-63; Chm. Exec. Cttee, Nga Taura Girls' Sch.; 1959-; Chm., Carnot Sch. for Girls, 1951-. Held various offices in Manawatu. War of 1939-45: Home Guard and Chm. Manawatu Primary Production Council. Coronation Medal, 1953. *Recreations:* golf (Chm. Greens Research Cttee of NZ Golf Council, retd 1956), ski-ing, fishing. *Address:* Atawhai-iti, 88 Te Awe Awe Street, Palmerston North, New Zealand. *T:* 80655. *Clubs:* Wellington (Wellington); Manawatu, Manawatu Golf (Pres. and Treasurer); Palmerston North.

**KEIR, Mrs David;** *see* Cazalet-Keir, T.

**KEIR, Sir David Lindsay,** Kt 1946; MA Oxon; Hon. DCL Oxon; Hon. LLD Glasgow, Dublin, New Brunswick, Queen's, Kingston and Queen's, Belfast; Hon. DLitt Sussex; Hon. Fellow of University College, Balliol and New College, Oxford; Hon. ARIBA; *b* 22 May 1895; *er s* of Rev. William Keir; *m* 1930, Anna Clunie, *yr d* of R. J. Dale, Montreal; one *s* one *d*. *Educ:* Glasgow Univ.; New Coll., Oxford. Served in King's Own Scottish Borderers, 1915-19. Fellow, 1921-39, Dean, Estates Bursar, University Coll., Oxford; University Lecturer in English Constitutional History, 1931-39; Pres. and Vice-Chancellor, The Queen's Univ., Belfast, 1939-49; Master of Balliol Coll., Oxford, 1949-65. Exchange tutor, Harvard Univ., 1923-24; Donnellan Lecturer, Trinity Coll., Dublin, 1942; Vice-Pres., Ulster Soc. for Irish Historical Studies, 1942; Mem., Official War History Cttee and Chm. NI War History Cttee, 1947-49; Pres. Scottish History Soc., 1958-62; Chm., NI Educn Advisory Council, 1948-49; Pres., Assoc. of Technical Instns, 1955-57; Pres., Assoc. of Educl Instns, 1958; Vice-Chm. Council, Benenden Sch.; Chairman: Cttee on Med. Educn, Malaya, 1953; Advisory Cttees on higher educn E Africa, 1955 and 1958, technical educn Nigeria, 1958 and N Rhodesia, 1960; Chm., Advisory Cttee (later Council) on Overseas Colls, 1954-64; Adviser to Govt of Iraq on University of Baghdad, 1956; Mem. Council, Royal College, Nairobi, 1954-63, and Provl Council of University of E Africa, 1962-63; Trustee, Nuffield Provincial Hosps Trust, 1941-62. Chm., NI Regional Hosps Council, 1942-49; Chm., 1941-49. Vice-Pres., 1949-, NI Council for Orthopædic Development; Chm. Govs, United Oxford Hosps, 1950-58; Chm., NI Planning Advisory Bd, 1943-49; Chm., Ulster Young Farmers' Clubs, 1942-48. Hon. Member: Royal Society of Ulster Architects; Oxfordshire Soc. of Architects. Mem. Council, Festival of Britain, 1951; Chm., CEMA (NI), 1943-49; Chm., Oxford Subscrip. Concerts, 1951-64; Trustee, Oxford Union, 1956-69; Hon. Treas., OURFC 1935-39; Pres., Queen's Univ. RFC, 1940-41; Trustee, R. V. Stanley's Match, 1949-. *Publications:* Cases in Constitutional Law (with F. H. Lawson), 1928 (5th edn 1967); The Constitutional History of Modern Britain, 1938 (9th edn 1968). *Recreations:* sailing, walking, gardening. *Address:* Hillsborough, Boar's Hill, Oxford. *T:* Oxford 35219.

**KEIR, Thelma C.;** *see* Cazalet-Keir.

**KEIRSTEAD, Burton Seely;** Professor of Economics, University of Toronto, since 1954; *b* 17 Nov. 1907; *s* of late Wilfred Currier Keirstead; *m* 1933, Marjorie Stella Brewer; one *s* one *d*. *Educ:* Fredericton Grammar Sch.; University of New Brunswick; Exeter Coll., Oxford (Rhodes Scholar, 1928). LLD hc University of NB, 1949. Prof. of Economics and Political Science, Univ. of New Brunswick, 1931-42; Visiting Professor at University of Arizona, 1937-38; McGill University: Bronfman Professor of Economics and Political Science, 1942-46; Dow Professor of Economics, 1946-54; Chairman, Dept. of Economics and Politics, 1947-50; Chairman, Social Sciences Group, 1951-54; represented Oxford v. Cambridge at ice-hockey, 1930. Fell. Roy. Soc. Canada; sometime mem., Bd of Editors, Canadian Journal of Economics and Political Science; Mem. Roy. Economic Soc., Canadian Economics Assoc.; sometime member Conseil Supérieur du Travail, Quebec; political commentator, Canadian Broadcasting Corporation. Hon. LLD, Mount Allison Univ., 1969. *Publications:* The Essentials of Price Theory, 1942; The Economic Effects of the War on the Maritime Provinces of Canada, 1944; The Theory of Economic Change, 1948 (Japanese edn 1955); An Essay on the Theory of Profits and Income Distribution, 1953; Canada in World Affairs, Vol. VII (1951-53), 1955; Capital, Interest and Profits, 1959 (Japanese edn 1966); The Canadian Economy: Selected Readings (ed. with Deutsch, Levitt and Will), 1961; The Federal Shipping Service, 1962 (2nd edn. 1966); contributions to Canada After the War (ed. Brady and Scott), 1943; The British Commonwealth at War (ed. Elliott and Hall), 1943; Encyclopēdie Française, Tome IX, 1963; International Encyclopedia of the Social Sciences, 1967; Encyclopædia Britannica, 1971 edn; various articles on economic and political subjects, and some detective fiction and short stories. *Recreations:* fishing, swimming. *Address:* 432 Charlotte Street, Fredericton, NB, Canada; (winter) c/o Development Bank, Bridgetown, Barbados, West Indies. *Clubs:* Faculty (Montreal); Faculty (Toronto).

**KEITH,** family name of **Countess of Kintore.**

**KEITH, David;** *see* Steegmuller, Francis.

**KEITH, Hon. Henry Shanks,** QC (Scotland) 1962; Sheriff of Roxburgh, Berwick and Selkirk, since 1970; *b* 7 Feb. 1922; *s* of late Baron Keith of Avonholm, PC (Life Peer); *m* 1955, Alison Hope Alan Brown; four *s* (including twin *s*) one *d*. *Educ:* Edinburgh Academy; Magdalen Coll., Oxford (MA); Edinburgh Univ. (LLB). War of 1939-45 (despatches); commnd Scots Guards, Nov. 1941; served N Africa and Italy, 1943-45; released, 1945 (Capt.). Advocate, Scottish Bar, 1950; Barrister, Gray's Inn, 1951. Standing Counsel to Dept of Health for Scotland, 1957-62. Mem. Scottish Valuation Adv. Coun., 1957-; Mem. Law Reform Cttee for Scotland, 1964-; Mem. Panel of Arbiters: European Fisheries Convention, 1964-; Convention for Settlement of Investment Disputes, 1968-. *Recreations:* sailing, golf. *Address:* 33 Heriot Row, Edinburgh 3. *T:* 031-225 6013. *Club:* New (Edinburgh).

**KEITH, John Lucien,** CBE 1951 (OBE 1943); London Representative of University of Ife, Nigeria, since 1962; *b* 22 May 1895; *s* of George Keith, Engineer and Director of S American Telephone Companies; unmarried. *Educ:* Ecole Closelet, Lausanne; Hertford Coll., Oxford (MA). British South Africa Co., N Rhodesia, 1918-25; District Officer, Colonial Service, N Rhodesia, 1925-37; Acting Dir of African Education, N Rhodesia, 1930-31; African Research Survey, Chatham House, 1937-39; Colonial Office, 1939; Dir of Colonial Scholars and head of Student Dept, Colonial Office, 1941-56, retd. Adviser on Students' Affairs, W Nigeria Office, London, 1957-62. Official missions to British West Africa, 1947, BWI, 1947, Malaya and Hong Kong, 1948, British East Africa and Mauritius, 1951, North America and British West Indies, 1954, British East and Central Africa, 1955, Ghana, 1957, Nigeria, 1960, and Zambia, 1964, for Independence celebrations. *Recreations:* travelling and reading. *Address:* 175 Ashley Gardens, SW1. *T:* 01-834 4671.

**KEITH, Sir Kenneth (Alexander),** Kt 1969; Chairman: Hill, Samuel & Co. Ltd, Merchant Bankers; Deputy Chairman, British European Airways; *b* 30 Aug. 1916; *er s* of Edward Charles Keith, Swanton Morley House, Norfolk; *m* 1st, 1946, Hon. Ariel Olivia Winifred Baird (marr. diss., 1958), 2nd *d* of 1st Viscount Stonehaven, PC, GCMG, DSO; one *s* one *d*; 2nd, 1962, Mrs Nancy Hayward, Manhasset, New York. *Educ:* Rugby Sch. Trained as a Chartered Accountant. 2nd Lt Welsh Guards, 1939; Lt-Col 1945; served in North Africa, Italy, France and Germany (despatches, Croix de Guerre with Silver Star). Asst to Dir Gen. Political Intelligence Dept, Foreign Office, 1945-46. Chm., Philip Hill Investment Trust Ltd; Director: Eagle Star Insurance Co. Ltd; Beecham Group Ltd; The Times Newspapers Ltd, and other companies. Mem. NEDC, 1964; Chairman: Economic Planning Council for East Anglia, 1965-70; City Liaison Panel; Gov., Nat. Inst. of Economic and Social Research; Council Mem., Manchester Business Sch. *Recreations:* shooting, and farming. *Address:* 80 Eaton Square, SW1. *T:* 01-730 4000; The Wicken House, Castleacre, Norfolk. *T:* Castleacre 225. *Clubs:* White's, Pratt's; Racquet and Tennis (New York).

*See also Sir Rupert Mackeson, Bt.*

**KEITH, Robert Farquharson,** OBE 1948; Assistant Under-Secretary of State (Director of Establishments), Department of Employment and Productivity (formerly Ministry of Labour), since 1965; *b* 22 June 1912; *s* of Dr Robert Donald Keith and Mary Lindsay (*née* Duncan), Turriff, Aberdeenshire; *m* 1958, Jean Abernethy (*née* Fisher); one *s*. *Educ:* Fettes; Caius Coll., Cambridge. Indian Civil Service, 1937-47; Dep. Comr, Upper Sind Frontier, 1945-47; Home Civil Service, Min. of Labour, 1948-. *Address:* 6 Strathray Gardens, NW3. *T:* 01-435 4226. *Club:* Caledonian.

**KEITH-JONES, Maj.-Gen. Richard,** CB 1968; MBE 1947; MC 1944; Group Personnel and Training Manager, Mardon Packaging International Ltd, since 1969; *b* 6 Dec. 1913; *o s* of late Brig. Frederick Theodore Jones, CIE, MVO, VD; *m* 1938, Margaret Ridley Harrison; three *d*. *Educ:* Clifton Coll.; Royal Military Academy Woolwich. Commissioned into Royal Artillery, 1934; served in UK, 1934-42; 1st Airborne Div., 1943-44; War Office, 1944-47; Palestine and Egypt, 1st Regt RHA, 1947-49; Instructor Staff Coll., Camberley, 1949-52; Military Asst to F-M Montgomery, 1953-55; CO 4th Regt, RHA, 1955-57; Senior Army Instructor, JSSC, 1957-59; Dep. Comdr 17 Gurkha Div., Malaya, 1959-61; Student, Imperial Defence Coll., 1962-63; Military Adviser, High Comr, Canada, 1963-64; GOC 50 (Northumbrian) Div. (TA), 1964-66; Comdt, Jt Warfare Establishment, 1966-68; retd 1969. Col Comdt RA, 1970-. *Recreations:* cricket, fishing, shooting, golf. *Address:* c/o Lloyd's Bank Ltd, Cox's & King's Branch, 6 Pall Mall, SW1; The White House, Brockley, Backwell, Bristol BS19 3AU. *Clubs:* East India and Sports, MCC.

**KEITH-LUCAS, David,** MA, DSc; FIMechE, FRAeS; Professor of Aircraft Design, Cranfield Institute of Technology (formerly College of Aeronautics, Cranfield), since 1965; Pro Vice-Chancellor, Cranfield Institute of Technology, since 1970; *b* 25 March 1911; *s* of late Keith Lucas, ScD, FRS, and Alys (*née* Hubbard); *m* 1942, Dorothy De Bauduy Robertson; two *s* one *d*. *Educ:* Gresham's Sch., Holt; Gonville and Caius Coll., Cambridge. BA (Mech Sci Tripos, 2nd Class Hons) 1933; MA 1956; FRAeS 1948; FIMechE 1949. Apprenticed 1933-35, design team 1935-39, C. A. Parsons & Co. Ltd; Chief Aerodynamicist, Short Bros Ltd, 1940-49; Short Bros & Harland Ltd: Chief Designer, 1949-58; Technical Dir, 1958-64; Dir of Research, 1964-65. Mem. of Senate, Queen's Univ., Belfast, 1955-65. Pres., Royal Aeronautical Society, 1968; Mem., Council, Air Registration Board, 1967-. Hon. DSc Queen's Univ., Belfast, 1968. *Publications:* The Shape of Wings to Come, 1952; The Challenge of Vertical Take-Off (lects IMechE), 1961-62; The Role of Jet Lift (lect. RAeS), 1962. *Recreations:* youth organisations, small boats. *Address:* Cranfield Institute of Technology, Bedford. *T:* Cranfield 1551. *Clubs:* Athenæum, Royal Aero.

**KEKWICK, Alan,** MA, MB, BCh, FRCP; Professor of Medicine, University of London; Physician, Middlesex Hospital, W1; Director, Institute of Clinical Research and Experimental Medicine, Middlesex Hospital; *b* 12 April 1909; 2nd *s* of John Kekwick and Catherine Lesslie Curror-Prain; *m* 1939; one *s*; *m* 1949, Elizabeth Dorothy Forster Shackleton; one *s* one *d*. *Educ:* Charterhouse Sch.; Emmanuel Coll., Cambridge; Middlesex Hosp. Medical Sch. Qualified medical practitioner, 1933; RMO Middlesex Hosp., 1936-39; Leverhulme Research Scholar, 1939-41; Lt-Col (Temp.) RAMC, 1943-45; ex-Censor and Senior Censor RCP; Examiner in Medicine and Physiology, Makerere Coll., Uganda, University Coll. of West Indies, University Coll. Ibadan, Baghdad Univ., London and other English Univs. Hon. Librarian and Mem. of Council, Royal Society Medicine, 1951; Member: Med. Research Soc. and Physiological Soc., New York Acad. of Sciences and Internat. Soc. of Internal Medicine; Hosp. Cttee King Edward VII Hosp. Fund; Bd of Management, Medical Insurance Agency. Mem. Senate and Academic Council, University of London. *Publications:* papers on dehydration, blood transfusion, including continuous drip blood transfusion, on wound shock, on nutritional problems including those in Bantu natives and obesity. *Address:* Pitts Folly, Hadlow, Kent. *Clubs:* Athenæum; Maidstone.

**KEKWICK, Prof. Ralph Ambrose,** FRS 1966; Professor of Biophysics, University of London, since 1966; Member Staff, Lister Institute, since 1940 (Head, Division of Biophysics, since 1943); *b* 11 Nov. 1908; 2nd *s* of late Oliver A. and Mary Kekwick; *m* 1933, Barbara, 3rd *d* of W. S. Stone, DD, New York; one *d*. *Educ:* Leyton County High Sch.; University Coll., London. BSc 1928; MSc 1936; DSc 1941. Bayliss-Starling Scholar, University Coll. London, 1930-31. Commonwealth Fund Fellow, New York and Princeton Univs, 1931-33. Lectr in Biochemistry University Coll. London, 1933-37. Rockefeller Fellow, University of Uppsala, Sweden, 1935; MRC Fellow, Lister Inst., 1937-40. Reader in Chemical Biophysics, University of London, 1954-66. Oliver Memorial Award for Blood Transfusion, 1957. *Publications:* MRC Special Report "Separation of protein fractions from human plasma" (with M. E. Mackay), 1954. Papers on physical biochemistry and hæmatology, mostly in Biochemical Jl and Brit. Jl of Hæmatology. *Recreations:* music, gardening and bird watching. *Address:* 31 Woodside Road, Woodford Wells, Essex. *T:* 01-504 4264.

**KELBURN, Viscount of; Patrick Robin Archibald Boyle;** television director/producer; with Yorkshire Television, since 1968; *b* 30 July 1939; *s* and *heir* of 9th Earl of Glasgow, *qv*. *Educ:* Eton; Paris Univ. National Service in Navy; Sub-Lt, RNR, 1959-60. Worked in Associated Rediffusion Television, 1961, since when has worked at various times for Woodfall Film Productions; Asst on Film Productions, 1962-64; Asst Dir in film industry, 1962-67. *Recreations:* ski-ing, theatre. *Address:* 111 Gloucester Terrace, W2. *T:* 01-723 3348.

**KELCEY, Air Vice-Marshal Alick F.;** *see* Foord-Kelcey.

**KELF-COHEN, Reuben,** CB 1950; Economics writer and consultant; Director and Secretary, Radio Industry Council, 1960-66; *b* Leeds, 29 Sept. 1895; *m* 1922, Edith Florence Kelf (*d* 1964); one *d*. *Educ:* Manchester Grammar Sch.; Wadham Coll., Oxford (Classical Scholar). Gaisford Greek Verse Prize, 1915; Lothian Historical Essay Prize, 1920; 1st Class Hons (History), 1920; 1st class Hons (Economics) London Univ., 1931. Served European War,

1914-18, Royal Field Artillery (wounded). Entered Bd of Educn, 1920; Tutorial Class Tutor, London Univ., 1924-39; Board of Trade, 1925-41; Petroleum Dept, 1941-42; Principal Asst Sec. (Gas and Electricity), Ministry of Fuel and Power, 1942-45; Under-Sec., Ministry of Fuel and Power, 1946-55; Dir, East Indian Produce Co. 1955-59. Vis. Lectr, St Andrews Univ., 1970. Freeman of the City of London; Liveryman of the Company of Horners; Chm., First Div. Pensioners. FRSA 1970. *Publications:* Knights of Malta, 1920; Nationalisation in Britain, 1958; Twenty Years of Nationalisation: The British Experience, 1969; articles on economic subjects. *Recreations:* cycling, bridge, bowls, sea voyages. *Address:* 14 Harold Road, Upper Norwood, SE19. *T:* 01-653 1086. *Club:* Savage.

**KELL, Joseph;** *see* Burgess, Anthony.

**KELLAR, Alexander James,** CMG 1961; OBE 1948; attached War Office since 1941; *b* 26 June 1905; *er s* of James Dodds Ballantyne Kellar and Florence Maud Kellar (*née* Coveney). *Educ:* George Watson's Coll.; Edinburgh Univ. (MA, LLB). Sen. Pres., Students' Representative Council; Commonwealth Fund Fellow, Yale (Mem. Elizabethan Club) and Columbia (AM Internat. Law and Relations); called to Bar, Middle Temple, 1936. Asst Sec., Brit. Employers' Confedn, 1938-41; Employers' (Substitute) Delegate, Governing Body of ILO, 1940. Mem. Army Officers' Emergency Reserve, 1938. *Recreations:* riding, travel. *Address:* Grey Walls, Friston, Sussex. *T:* East Dean 3294. *Club:* Royal Automobile.

**KELLAR, Prof. Robert James,** CBE 1968 (MBE 1943); MB, ChB, FRCSEd, FRCPEd, FRCOG; Professor of Obstetrics and Gynæcology, University of Edinburgh. *Educ:* Univ. of Edinburgh; MB, ChB, 1931; MRCPEd, 1934, FRCSEd, 1935; FRCOG, 1945; FRCPEd, 1946. Univ. of Edinburgh: Annandale Gold Medal for Clinical Surgery, Wightman Prize for Clinical Medicine, Murchison Prize for Medicine (halved), Buchanan Prize for Midwifery and Diseases of Women, 1931, Simpson Prize for Obstetrics, 1932; Lister Prize for Surgery, 1934; Freeland Barbour Fellowship in Obstetrics; Leckie Mactier Research Fellow, 1934-35; Beit Memorial Research Fellow, 1935-37. Formerly: Reader in Obstetrics and Gynæcology, University of London, British Post-Graduate Medical Sch.; Asst, Obstetrical Unit, University Coll. Hosp.; Tutor in Clinical Gynæcology, House Surgeon Out-patients Department and to Prof. of Midwifery, Royal Infirmary, Edinburgh. Lt-Col, Royal Army Medical Corps; Officer in charge of a Surgical Div. (despatches, MBE). Mem. Council, RCOG, 1963. Hon. Fellow Amer. Assoc. of Obst. and Gynæcol. *Address:* Department of Obstetrics and Gynæcology, 39 Chalmers Street, Edinburgh, 3; 27 Hope Terrace, Edinburgh 9.

**KELLAS, Arthur Roy Handasyde,** CMG 1964; Ambassador to Southern Yemen, since 1970; *b* 6 May 1915; *s* of Henry Kellas and Mary Kellas (*née* Brown); *m* 1952, Katharine Bridget, *d* of Sir John Le Rougetel, *qv*; two *s* one *d*. *Educ:* Aberdeen Grammar Sch.; Aberdeen Univ.; Oxford Univ.; Ecole des Sciences Politiques. Passed into Diplomatic Service, Sept. 1939. Commissioned into Border Regt, Nov. 1939. War of 1939-45: Active Service with 1st Bn Parachute Regt and Special Ops, Af. and Gr, 1941-44 (despatches twice). Third Sec. at HM Embassy, Tehran, 1944-47; First Sec. at HM Legation, Helsingfors, 1948-50; First Sec. (press) at HM Embassy, Cairo, 1951-52; First Sec. at HM Embassy, Baghdad, 1954-58; Counsellor, HM Embassy, Tehran, 1958-62; Imperial Defence Coll., 1963-64; Counsellor, HM Embassy and Consul-Gen., Tel Aviv, 1964-65; Ambassador to Nepal, 1966-70. *Recreations:* reading, riding, boxing. *Address:* British Embassy, Aden, PRSY. *Club:* United University.

**KELLEHER, Dame Joan,** DBE 1965; Hon. ADC to the Queen, 1964-67; Director, Women's Royal Army Corps, 1964-67; *b* 24 Dec. 1915; *d* of late Kenneth George Henderson, Stonehaven; *m* 1970, Brig. M. F. H. Kelleher, OBE, MC, late RAMC. *Educ:* privately at home and abroad. Joined ATS, 1941; commissioned ATS, 1941; WRAC, 1949. *Recreations:* golf and gardening. *Address:* c/o Midland Bank, 123 Chancery Lane, WC2.

**KELLER, René;** Head of Department for International Organisation, Foreign Ministry of Switzerland, since 1971; *b* 19 May 1914; *s* of Jacques Keller and Marie (*née* Geiser); *m* 1942, Marion (*née* Werder); one *s* two *d*. *Educ:* Geneva; Trinity Coll., Cambridge. Vice-Consul, Prague, 1941-45; 2nd Sec. of Legation, The Hague, 1947-50; 1st Sec., London, 1950-54; Head of News Dept, Berne, 1954-56; 1st Counsellor, Swiss Embassy, Paris, 1957-60; Ambassador to Ghana, Guinea, Liberia, Mali and Togo, 1960-62; Ambassador to Turkey, 1962-65; Head of Perm. Mission of Switzerland to Office of UN and Internat. Organisations, Geneva, 1966-68; Ambassador of Switzerland to UK, 1968-71. *Recreations:* golf, sailing. *Address:* Département politique fédéral, 3003 Berne, Switzerland. *Club:* Travellers'.

**KELLER, Prof. Rudolf Ernst,** MA Manchester; DrPhil Zürich; Professor of German Language and Medieval German Literature, University of Manchester, since 1960; *b* 3 Feb. 1920; *m* 1947, Ivy Sparrow; two *d*. *Educ:* Kantonsschule Winterthur, Switzerland; University of Zürich. Teacher at Kantonsschule Winterthur, 1944-46; Asst, 1946-47, Asst Lecturer, 1947-49, University of Manchester; Lecturer in German, Royal Holloway College, University of London, 1949-52; Sen. Lecturer, 1952-59, Reader in German, 1959-60, Dean of Faculty of Arts, 1968-70, University of Manchester. *Publications:* Die Ellipse in der neuenglischen Sprache als semantisch-syntaktisches Problem, 1944; Die Sprachen der Welt, 1955 (trans. Bodmer: The Loom of Language); German Dialects, Phonology and Morphology with Selected Texts, 1961; articles in learned periodicals. *Recreations:* reading, travel. *Address:* 11a Rathen Road, Manchester 20. *T:* 061-445 6952.

**KELLETT, Alfred Henry,** CBE 1965; Chairman, South Western Areas, National Coal Board, 1967-69, retired; *b* 2 Aug. 1904; British; *m* 1934, Astrid Elizabeth (*née* Hunter); one *s* three *d*. *Educ:* Rossall Sch.; Universities of Cambridge and Birmingham. Man. Dir, Washington Coal Co. Ltd, 1940-47; Area Gen. Man., NCB Durham Div., 1950-59; Dep. Chm., Durham Div., 1960; Chm., South Western Div., NCB, 1961-67. CStJ. *Recreation:* travel. *Address:* Pent House, Benenden, Cranbrook, Kent. *Club:* Lansdowne.

**KELLETT, Elaine;** *see* Kellett, M. E.

**KELLETT, Maj.-Gen. (Retd) Gerald,** CB 1959; CBE 1957; *b* 24 Oct. 1905; *s* of Surgeon Rear-Adm. L. H. Kellett, RN; *m* 1941, Elizabeth Bridges; one *s* one *d*. *Educ:* Bedford Sch.; RMA Woolwich. Commissioned 2nd Lt Royal Artillery, 1925, Capt. 1937, Major 1942, Lt-

Col 1948, Col 1951, Brig. 1955, Maj.-Gen. 1957. Dir of Inspectorate of Armaments, 1954-56; Dir-Gen. of Artillery, War Office, 1957-60; retired from Army, Jan. 1961. *Recreations:* golf and sailing. *Address:* Rendham Road, Saxmundham, Suffolk. *T:* Saxmundham 2194.

**KELLETT, (Mary) Elaine;** MP (C) Lancaster, since 1970; *b* 8 July 1924; *d* of late Walter Kay; *m* 1945, Charles Norman Kellett (decd); three *s* one *d. Educ:* Queen Mary Sch., Lytham; The Mount, York; St Anne's Coll., Oxford (post-graduate distinction in welfare diploma). Contested (C): Nelson and Colne, 1955; South-West Norfolk, March and Oct. 1959; Buckingham, 1964, 1966. Camden Borough Council: Alderman, 1968-; Vice-Chm., Housing Cttee, 1968-; Chm., Welfare Cttee, 1969. Called to Bar, Middle Temple, 1964. Lay Mem., Press Council, 1964-68. Governor, East Anglian Girls' Sch., 1963; Mem. Union European Women, 1956; Delegate to Luxemburg, 1958. No 1 Country Housewife, 1960; Christal MacMillan Law Prize, 1963. *Recreations:* gardening, stamp collecting. *Address:* The Beeches, Aughton, Halton, Lancaster. *Clubs:* English-Speaking Union, Farmers'.

**KELLETT, Sir Stanley Everard,** 6th Bt *cr* 1801; *b* 1911; *s* of Francis Stanley Kellett (*d* 1955) (2nd *s* of 3rd Bt); *S* Kinsman, Sir Henry de Castres Kellett, 5th Bt, 1966; *m* 1938, Audrey Margaret Phillips; one *s* one *d. Heir: s* Stanley Charles Kellett [*b* 1940; *m* 1962, Lorraine May, *d* of F. Winspear]. *Address:* 33 Caroma Avenue, Kyeemagh, New South Wales, Australia.

**KELLEY, Mrs Joanna Elizabeth;** Assistant Director of Prisons (Women) since 1967; *b* 23 May 1910; *d* of late Lt-Col William Beadon, 51st Sikhs; *m* 1934, Harper Kelley (*d* 1962); no *c. Educ:* Hayes Court; Girton Coll., Cambridge (MA). Souschargé, Dept of Pre-History, Musée de l'Homme, Paris, 1934-39; Mixed Youth Club Leader, YWCA, 1939-42; Welfare Officer, Admiralty, Bath, 1942-47; Prison Service, 1947-; Governor of HM Prison, Holloway, 1959-66. FSA. Hon. Fellow Girton Coll., Cambridge, 1968. Hon. LLD Hull Univ., 1960. *Publication:* When the Gates Shut, 1967. *Recreations:* travel, walking and reading. *Address:* c/o Prison Dept, Home Office, 89 Eccleston Square, SW1.

**KELLEY, Richard;** MP (Lab) Don Valley Division of West Riding of Yorks since Oct. 1959; *b* July 1904. *Educ:* Elementary Sch. Councillor, West Riding of Yorks County Council for ten years; a Trade Union Secretary for ten years. Mem. of the National Union of Mineworkers. *Address:* 23 St Lawrence Road, Dunscroft, West Riding, Yorks.

**KELLGREN, Prof. Jonas Henrik,** FRCS, FRCP; Professor of Rheumatology, University of Manchester, since 1953; a Pro-Vice-Chancellor since 1969; *b* 11 Sept. 1911; *s* of Dr Harry Kellgren and Vera (*née* Dumelunksen); *m* 1942, Thelma Marian Reynolds; four *d. Educ:* Bedales Sch.; University Coll., London. MB, BS, 1934; FRCS 1936; FRCP 1951. Junior clinical appointments, University Coll. Hosp., 1934-42 (Beit Memorial Fellow 1938-39); served War, 1942-46, as surgical and orthopædic specialist, RAMC; Mem. Scientific Staff, Med. Research Council, Wingfield Morris Orthopædic Hosp., Oxford, Chronic Rheumatism, University of Manchester, 1947. Pres. Heberden Soc., 1958-59. *Publications:* numerous articles in medical and scientific jls. *Recreation:* landscape painting. *Address:* 163 Palatine Road, Manchester 20. *T:* 061-445 1568.

**KELLIHER, Sir Henry (Joseph),** Kt 1963; Managing Director (Founder), Dominion Breweries Ltd since 1929; *b* March 1896; *s* of Michael Joseph Kelliher; *m* 1917, Evelyn J., *d* of R. S. Sproule; one *s* four *d. Educ:* Clyde Sch. dir, Bank of New Zealand, 1936-42. Founded League of Health of NZ Youth, 1934 (objective, Free milk scheme for NZ children, in which it succeeded); purchased Puketutu Island, 1938; established Puketutu Ayrshire Stud, 1940, Aberdeen Angus Stud, 1942, Suffolk Stud, 1946; Thoroughbred and Standard Bred Studs, 1969. Founded: Kelliher Art Trust, 1961; Kelliher Charitable Trust, 1963. KStJ 1960. *Publications:* New Zealand at the Cross Roads, 1936; Why your £ buys Less and Less, 1954. *Recreations:* gardening, riding. *Address:* Puketutu Island, Manukau Harbour, Auckland, New Zealand. *T:* 543733.

**KELLOCK, Hon. Roy Lindsay,** QC; Counsel, Messrs Blake, Cassels and Graydon, Toronto; *b* Perth, Ontario, 12 Nov. 1893; *s* of James F. and Annie M. Kellock; *m* 1932, Elinor Harris; one *s* one *d. Educ:* Harbord Collegiate; McMaster Univ.; Osgoode Hall. Called to Bar of Ontario, 1920; KC (Canada) 1934. Joined Mason, Foulds, Davidson & Kellock, 1920; Justice, Court of Appeal for Ontario, 1942; Judge, Supreme Court of Canada, 1944-58, retd. Chancellor, McMaster University, Hamilton, Canada, 1955-60. Hon. LLD, McMaster, 1950. Hon. DCL, Acadia, 1952. *Address:* 25 King Street W, Toronto, Ontario, Canada. *Clubs:* National Toronto Hunt.

**KELLOCK, Thomas Oslaf,** QC 1965; Director, Legal Division, Commonwealth Secretariat; *b* 4 July 1923; *s* of late Thomas Herbert Kellock, MA, MD, MCh Cambridge, FRCS LRCP; *m* 1967, Jane Ursula, *d* of late Arthur George Symonds, Osmington, Dorset. *Educ:* Rugby; Clare Coll., Cambridge. Sub-Lieut (Special Branch), RNVR, 1944-46. Called to the Bar, Inner Temple, 1949. Contested (L) Torquay, 1959. S Kensington, 1966 and March 1968. *Recreation:* travelling. *Address:* 91 Warwick Avenue, W9. *T:* 01-286 0986. *Clubs:* National Liberal, Reform.

**KELLOW, Kathleen;** *see* Hibbert, Eleanor.

**KELLY, Sir Arthur (John),** Kt 1961; CBE 1950; *b* 17 Nov. 1898; *yr s* of John Kelly, Hodge Bower, Shropshire; *m* 1928, Florence Mary Smyth, *yr d* of John Smyth, Belfast. *Educ:* Bridgnorth; Shrewsbury. Served European War, 1917-19: RFC 12 Sqdn and RAF Army of Occupation, Germany. Temp. Asst, Min. of Labour, Whitehall, 1919-22; Asst Principal, Min. of Labour, N Ireland, 1922; Principal, Cabinet Offices, N Ireland, 1940; Asst Sec., 1941; seconded as N Ireland Govt Liaison Officer at Home Office, Whitehall, 1943; Permanent Sec., Min. of Labour N Ireland, 1956; Sec. to the Cabinet and Clerk of the Privy Council of Northern Ireland, 1957-63, retd. *Recreation:* golf. *Address:* 6 Cherryhill, Malone Road, Belfast. *Clubs:* Royal Commonwealth Society; Malone Golf (Belfast).

**KELLY, Basil;** *see* Kelly, J. W. B.

**KELLY, Brig. George Alexander,** CB 1946; *b* 24 Aug. 1888; *s* of John J. Kelly, Roscommon; *m* 1923, Sydney Russell Stanley; one *d. Educ:* Castleknock Coll., Dublin; Royal Veterinary Coll. of Ireland. Commissioned RAVC 1911; Bt Lieut-Col 1935; ADVS India, 1936-39; DDV and RS MEF. Served France, 1914-16, Waziristan, 1919 (despatches); Middle East Force, 1940-42 (despatches); WO, Dir Army Vet. and Remount Services, 1943-47; retd, 1947; formerly Col Commandant Royal Army

Veterinary Corps. *Address:* 35 Hill Drive, Hove 4, Sussex.

**KELLY, Sir Gerald (Festus),** KCVO, *cr* 1955; Kt, *cr* 1945; PPRA 1954 (PRA 1949; RA 1930; ARA 1922); RHA 1914; Hon. RSA; Hon. FRIBA; Hon. LLD (Cambridge and TCD); Mem. Royal Fine Art Commission, 1938-43; *b* 1879; *o s* of Rev. F. F. Kelly; *m* 1920, Lilian, 5th *d* of S. Ryan. *Educ:* Eton; Trinity Hall, Cambridge. The State Portraits of the King and the Queen, 1945. Pictures in many public collections. Membre correspondant de la section de peinture de l'Académie des Beaux Arts de l'Institut de France, 1953; Académico Correspondiente de la Réal Academia de Bellas Artes de San Fernando, Madrid, 1953. Commander of Legion of Honour, 1950; Commander of Order of Oranje Nassau, 1953. *Address:* 117 Gloucester Place, Portman Square, W1. *T:* 01-935 0148. *Club:* The Club.

**KELLY, Rev. Canon John Norman Davidson,** DD; FBA, 1965; Principal of St Edmund Hall, Oxford, since 1951; Vice-Chancellor, Oxford University, Sept.-Oct. 1966 (Pro-Vice-Chancellor, 1964-66); *b* 13 April 1909; *s* of John and Ann Davidson Kelly. *Educ:* privately; Glasgow Univ.; Queen's Coll., Oxford (Ferguson Scholar; Hertford Scholar; 1st Cl. Hon. Mods, Greats and Theology); St Stephen's House. Deacon, 1934; priest, 1935; Curate, St Lawrence's, Northampton, 1934; Chaplain, St Edmund Hall, Oxford, 1935; Vice-Principal and Trustee, 1937. Select Preacher (Oxford), 1944-46, 1959, 1961, 1962; Speaker's Lectr in Biblical Studies, 1945-48; University Lecturer in Patristic Studies, 1948; Select Preacher (Cambridge), 1953; Chm. Cttee of Second Internat. Conf. on Patristic Studies, Oxford, 1955; Proctor in Convocation of Canterbury representing Oxford University, 1958-64; Paddock Lecturer, General Theological Seminary, New York, 1963; Chm. Archbishop's Commn on Roman Catholic Relations, 1964-68; accompanied Archbishop of Canterbury on his visit to Pope Paul VI, 1966; Mem., Academic Council, Ecumenical Theological Inst., Jerusalem, 1966-. In the War of 1939-45 did part-time work at Chatham House and collaborated in organizing the Oxford Leave Courses for United States, Allied, and Dominions Forces. Canon of Chichester and Prebendary of Wightring, 1948, Highleigh, 1964. Took lead in obtaining Royal Charter, new statutes and full collegiate status for St Edmund Hall, 1957. Mem. governing bodies of St Stephen's House, Royal Holloway Coll., London, King's Sch., Canterbury. Hon. DD Glasgow, 1958; Hon. Fellow, Queen's Coll., Oxford, 1963. *Publications:* Early Christian Creeds, 1950; Rufinus, a Commentary on the Apostles' Creed, 1955; Early Christian Doctrines, 1958; The Pastoral Epistles, 1963; The Athanasian Creed, 1964; The Epistles of Peter and of Jude, 1969. *Recreations:* squash rackets, cinema, travel. *Address:* Principal's Lodgings, St Edmund Hall, Oxford. *T:* Oxford 41039. *Clubs:* Athenæum, Royal Automobile.

**KELLY, (John William) Basil,** QC (N Ireland) 1958; Attorney-General for Northern Ireland since 1968; MP (U) Mid-Down, Parliament of Northern Ireland, since 1964; *b* 10 May 1920; *o s* of late Thomas William Kelly and late Emily Frances (*née* Donaldson); *m* 1957, Pamela, *o d* of late Thomas Colmer and Marjorie Colthurst. *Educ:* Methodist Coll., Belfast; Trinity Coll., Dublin. BA (Mod.) Legal Science, 1943; LLB (Hons) 1944. Called to Bar: of Northern Ireland, 1944; Middle Temple, 1970. Senior Crown Counsel: Co. Fermanagh, 1965-66; Co. Tyrone, 1966-67; Co. Armagh, 1967-68. *Recreations:* golf, music. *Address:* White Gates, Ballymenoch, Holywood, Co. Down. *T:* Holywood 2842. *Club:* Ulster Reform (Belfast).

**KELLY, Kenneth Linden;** Secretary-General of the Automobile Association, 1954-63; *b* 5 Dec. 1913; *s* of Herbert Linden Kelly and Alice Maud Gray; *m* 1939, Betty Joan Roe; two *d*. *Educ:* Kingston Grammar School. Served War of 1939-45 in RAOC, Europe and Middle East; Actg Dep. Dir of OS Middle East Forces, 1945 (Col.). Chm., Governors of Kingston Grammar School. Associate Institution of Highway Engineers; Associate Inst. of Transport. FRSA 1955. MIMI 1956. Royal Order of the Phœnix, Greece, 1963. *Address:* 13 Magdalene House, Manor Fields, Putney Hill, SW15. *T:* 01-788 4308. *Clubs:* Royal Irish Automobile (Dublin); Kingston Rowing (Vice-Pres.); Remenham (Henley).

**KELLY, Dr Mervin J.;** Consultant to Chairman of the Board, International Business Machines, 1961-65 and 1968-70 (Consultant to the President, 1959-61); Consultant to president of Bausch & Lomb Inc., 1959-62; *b* 14 Feb. 1894; *s* of Joseph Fenemore Kelly and Mary Etta Kelly (*née* Evans); *m* 1917, Katharine Milsted; one *s* one *d*. *Educ:* University of Missouri (BS); University of Kentucky (MS); University of Chicago (PhD). Western Elec. Co. Research Physicist, 1918-25. Bell Telephone Labs: Research Physicist, 1925-34; Development Dir of Transmission Instruments and Electronics, 1934-36; Dir of Research, 1936-44; Exec. Vice-Pres., 1944-51; Pres., 1951-59. Mem. Nat. Acad. of Sciences, 1945; Mem. Amer. Philosophical Soc. 1952; For. Mem. Swedish Royal Acad. of Sciences, 1956. Hon. Degrees: DEng University of Missouri, 1936; DSc University of Kentucky, 1946; LLD University of Pa, 1954; DEng New York Univ., 1955; DEng Polytechnic Inst. of Brooklyn, 1955; DSc University of Pittsburgh, 1957; Dr University of Lyons, 1957; Dr Eng. Wayne State Univ., 1958; DSc Case Inst. of Tech., 1959; Dr Eng. Princeton Univ., 1959. Presidential Certificate of Merit, 1947; US Air Force Assoc. Trophy, 1953; Industrial Research Institute Medal, 1954; Christopher Columbus Internat. Communication Prize, 1955; Air Force Exceptional Service Award, 1957; James Forrestal Medal, Nat. Security Industrial Assoc., 1958; John Fritz Medal Award, 1959; Stevens Honor Award, Stevens Inst. of Technology, 1959; Golden Omega Award, 1960; Hoover Medal Award, 1961. Chicago Alumni Medal, 1959; Mervin J. Kelly Award in Telecommunications (by Amer. Inst. Elec. Engrs) for 1960. *Publications:* numerous in scientific and tech. jls of USA. *Recreations:* golf and gardening. *Address:* (office) International Business Machines, 590 Madison Avenue, New York, NY 10022, USA. *T:* (212) 753-1900; (home) 2 Windemere Terrace, Short Hills, New Jersey 07078, USA. *T:* (201) 3793319. *Club:* University (New York).

**KELLY, Richard Barrett Talbot,** MBE; MC; RI 1924; late RA; retired as Art Master, Rugby School, 1966; *b* 20 Aug. 1896; *s* of late R. Talbot Kelly, RI, RBC and Lilias Fisher Lindsay; *m* 1924, Dorothy, *d* of late Edgar Bundy, ARA, RI; one *s* one *d*. *Educ:* Rugby; Royal Military Academy, Woolwich. Served in Royal Artillery, 1915-29; European War, France, 1915-18, (MC, despatches), India, 1919-22; retired from Army, 1929; War of 1939-45 (MBE): Chief Instructor at War Office Sch. of Military Camouflage. Exhibitor at Royal Academy, RI, Paris Salon, and all important Municipal Galleries, as well as in Canada; various display designs for museums and exhibitions; Design Consultant, Pavilion of the Natural Scene, Festival of Britain, 1951;

designed displays in new Museum of Natural History, Kampala, Uganda, 1964. Lectured on Art and taught in USA by invitation, 1968. *Publication:* The Way of Birds, 1937; Paper Birds, Birds of Mountain & Moor (Puffin Books); Illustrations for Sea Birds (King Penguin); Bird Life and the Painter. *Recreation:* study of bird life. *Address:* 22 St Philip's Road, Stoneygate, Leicester. *T:* 37143.

**KELLY, Sir Robert (McErlean);** Kt 1969; JP; Chairman, Celtic FA Co. Ltd, since 1947 (Director, 1932); *b* 17 Oct. 1902; *s* of James Kelly, JP; *m* 1933, Marie Josephine Reilly; no *c. Educ:* St Aloysius Coll., Glasgow; St Joseph's Coll., Dumfries. President: Scottish Football League for six years; Scottish Football Assoc. for four years (Vice-Pres. for four years). *Recreations:* reading, gardening. *Address:* Marisdale, East Kilbride Road, Burnside, Rutherglen, Scotland. *T:* 041-634 4078.

**KELLY, Sir Theo,** Kt 1966; OBE 1958; JP; Chairman and Managing Director, Woolworths (Australia and New Zealand); *b* 1907; *m* 1944, Nancy Margaret Williams; two *s* two *d.* War of 1939-45; RAAF, 1942-44, Wing Comdr. Dir, RAAF Canteen Services, 1946-59. General Manager: Woolworths Ltd (NZ), 1932; Woolworths (Australia and NZ), 1945. Pres., Retail Traders Assoc. of NSW; Mem. Board, Reserve Bank of Australia; Exec. Life Mem., Australian Council of Retailers; Director: Australian National Travel Assoc.; Aust. Mutual Life Assurance Co. Trustee, National Parks and Wildlife Foundn. Mem. Board, Royal North Shore Hosp.; Fellow, Senate, Univ. of Sydney. FAIM. JP NSW, 1946. *Recreations:* tennis, boating. *Address:* 22d Vaucluse Road, Vaucluse, Sydney, NSW, Australia. *T:* 370077; (office) Woolworths Ltd, 534 George Street, Sydney, NSW. *Clubs:* Royal Prince Alfred Yacht; Royal Sydney Yacht Squadron, Royal Motor Yacht, American, Australian Golf (all in Sydney).

**KELLY, Sir William Theodore;** *see* Kelly, Sir Theo.

**KELSEY, Mrs Denys E. R.;** *see* Grant, Joan.

**KELSEY, Emanuel;** Solicitor and Parliamentary Officer to the Greater London Council, 1964-70; *b* 16 Feb. 1905; *s* of late Emanuel and Margaret Kelsey, Blyth, Northumberland; *m* 1934, Dorothy, *d* of late Alexander Mitchell-Smith, Bathgate, Scotland; one *s* one *d. Educ:* King Edward VI School, Morpeth. Legal Asst, Min. of Agric. and Fisheries, and Commissioners of Crown Lands, 1929; Sen. Asst, Parly Dept, LCC, 1931; Dep. Solicitor and Parly. Officer, LCC, 1962; Solicitor and Parly Officer, LCC, 1964. Hon. Solicitor to Royal Society for the Prevention of Accidents, 1964-70. *Recreations:* painting, reading, bridge. *Address:* Monk's Rest, Arterberry Road, Wimbledon, SW20. *T:* 01-946 2564.

**KELSEY, Julian George;** Under-Secretary, Ministry of Agriculture, Fisheries and Food, since 1969; *b* 28 Aug. 1922; *s* of William and Charlotte Kelsey, Dulwich; *m* 1944, Joan (*née* Singerton); one *d. Educ:* Brockenhurst County School. Clerk, Lord Chancellor's Dept, 1939; War Service, 1941-46: Captain, Lancs Fusiliers and RAC; SOE and Force 136; comdg No 11, Searcher Party Team, Burma. Exec. Officer, Central Land Board, 1948; Asst Principal, MAFF, 1951; Private Sec. to Perm. Sec. 1954, and Parly Sec. 1955; Principal 1955; Asst Sec. 1962. *Recreations:* gardening, tennis, travel. *Address:* 13 Hillside Gardens, Barnet, Herts. *T:* 01-449 6961. *Club:* Special Forces.

**KELSICK, Osmund Randolph,** DFC 1944; President and Managing Director of Antigua Holdings Ltd (owning and operating The Blue Waters Beach Hotel and Half Moon Bay Hotel); Antigua Land Development Co. Ltd; Chairman: Antigua Dairies Ltd; Caribbean Consultants Ltd; Bottlers (Antigua) Ltd; Director: Caribbean Tobacco Co. (Antigua) Ltd; T. H. Kelsick Ltd (Montserrat); Caribbean Travel Association; Air Commonwealth (Canada) Ltd; President, Caribbean Hotel Association; *b* 21 July 1922; *s* of T. H. Kelsick; *m* 1950, Doreen Avis Hodge; one *s* (and one *s* decd); two step *d. Educ:* private preparatory sch.; Montserrat Grammar Sch.; Oxford Univ. (Devonshire Course). RAF, Fighter Pilot, 1940-46. ADC and Personal Sec. to Governor of the Leeward Islands, 1946-47; District Commissioner, Carriacou, 1947-51; Asst Chief Sec., Governor's Office, Grenada, 1951-52; Asst Administrator and Administrator, St Vincent, 1952-57. In 1956 seconded for short periods as Asst Trade Commissioner for British West Indies, British Guiana and British Honduras in UK, and Executive Sec. of Regional Economic Cttee in Barbados. Chief Sec., Leeward Islands, 1957-60. *Recreations:* fishing, gardening, tennis. *Address:* Blue Waters Beach Hotel, Antigua, Leeward Islands, West Indies. *Clubs:* West Indian (London); New (Antigua).

**KELSO, Maj.-Gen. J. E. U.;** *see* Utterson-Kelso.

**KELWAY, Colonel George Trevor,** CBE 1963; TD 1941; DL, JP; District Registrar, HM High Court of Justice in Pembrokeshire and Carmarthenshire, 1940-62; Deputy Chairman, Pembrokeshire Quarter Sessions, since 1960; *b* 30 March 1899; *yr s* of late George Stuart Kelway, Milford Haven, Ch. de la Légion d'Honneur, Ch. de l'Ordre de Léopold, &c.; *m* 1931, Gwladys, *d* of late Joseph Rolfe, Goodig, Burry Port, Carm., formerly High Sheriff of Carmarthenshire; one *d. Educ:* Warminster; St Edmund Hall, Oxford. Served European War, 1914-18, and War of 1939-45; Comdg Pembrokeshire Hy. Regt RA (TA), 1927-35; formerly Hon. Col. Pembs Coast Regt, 424 and 425 (Pembs.) Regts RA (TA), and The Pembroke Yeomanry, 1943-58; Chm. Pembs T & AFA, 1945-60. Admitted a Solicitor, 1922. Chm. Pembs Conservative Assoc., 1950-60; Pres. Wales & Mon Cons. Party, 1957 and 1961; Mem. Lloyd's, 1942-; an original Mem. Milford Haven Conservancy Bd, 1958-. DL 1948, JP 1957, Pembrokeshire; High Sheriff, 1958. Provincial Grand Master, S Wales (Western Div.). *Recreation:* golf. *Address:* Cottesmore, near Haverfordwest, Pembrokeshire. *T:* Haverfordwest 2282. *Club:* Pembrokeshire (Haverfordwest).

**KEM** (pseudonym of Kimon Evan Marengo); Political Cartoonist and Journalist; *b* Zifta, Egypt, 4 Feb. 1906; 2nd *s* of Evangelo Tr. Marango and Aristea *d* of Capt. John Raftopoulo, Lemnos; *m* 1954, Una O'Connor; two *s. Educ:* privately, publicly and personally and from time to time attended such seats of learning as the Ecole des Sciences Politiques, Paris, Exeter Coll., Oxford, etc. Edited and Illustrated Maalesh, a political weekly published simultaneously in Cairo and Alexandria, 1923-31; in summer of 1928 represented a group of Newspapers at International Press Conference, Cologne; has travelled extensively; a fluent linguist, has command of English, French, Greek, Italian, and Arabic and understands a few other languages. *Publications:* In French: Oua Riglak! 1926; Gare les Pattes! 1929; Alexandrie, Reine de la Méditerranée, 1928. In English: Toy Titans, International politics in verse and pictures, 1937; Lines of Attack,

1944. In Arabic: Adolf and his donkey Benito, 1940; now a free-lance, contributing to newspapers and periodicals all over the world. *Recreations:* swimming, riding, drawing, and castigating politicians. *Address:* Farleigh House, Farleigh Wallop, near Basingstoke, Hants; 9 Cullum Street, EC3. *TA:* Marengo, London. *T:* 01-623 6631.

**KEMBALL, Prof. Charles,** FRS 1965; MA, ScD Cantab; FRIC; MRIA; FRSE; Professor of Chemistry, Edinburgh University, since 1966; *b* 27 March 1923; *s* of late Charles Henry and of Janet Kemball; *m* 1956, Kathleen Purvis, *o d* of late Dr and Mrs W. S. Lynd, Alsager, Cheshire; one *s* two *d. Educ:* Edinburgh Academy; Trinity Coll., Cambridge (Sen. Schol.). First Class Hons in Natural Sciences Tripos, Pt I, 1942, Pt II, 1943. Employed by Ministry of Aircraft Production in Dept of Colloid Science, University of Cambridge, 1943-46; Fellow of Trinity Coll., 1946-54; Commonwealth Fund Fellow, Princeton Univ., 1946-47; Junior Bursar of Trinity Coll., 1949-51; Asst Lectr, 1951-54; Univ. Demonstrator in Physical Chemistry, 1951-54; Professor of Physical Chemistry, Queen's Univ., Belfast, 1954-66 (Dean of the Faculty of Science, 1957-60, Vice-Pres., 1962-65). Meldola Medal, 1951, Royal Inst. of Chemistry; Corday-Morgan Medal, Chemical Soc., 1958; Ipatieff Prize, American Chemical Soc., 1962; Vice-Pres., Royal Institute of Chemistry, 1959-61. *Publications:* contributions to various scientific jls. *Recreations:* bridge, gardening, golf. *Address:* 5 Hermitage Drive, Edinburgh EH10 6DE. *Clubs:* Athenæum, English-Speaking Union.

**KEMBALL-COOK, Brian Hartley,** MA Oxon; Headmaster, Bedford Modern School, since 1965; *b* 12 Dec. 1912; *s* of Sir Basil Alfred Kemball-Cook, KCMG, CB, and Lady Nancy Annie Kemball-Cook (*née* Pavitt); *m* 1947, Marian, *d* of R. C. R. Richards, OBE; three *s* one *d. Educ:* Shrewsbury Sch. (Sidney Gold Medal for Classics); Balliol Coll., Oxford (Scholar). First Class Classical Honour Mods, 1933; First Class, Litt. Hum., 1935. Sixth Form Classics Master, Repton Sch., 1936-40. Intelligence Corps, 1940-46 (despatches); Regional Intelligence Officer and Political Adviser to Regional Comr, Hanover, 1946; Principal, Min. of Transport, 1946-47. Sen. Classics Master, Repton Sch., 1947-56; Headmaster, Queen Elizabeth's Grammar Sch., Blackburn, 1956-65. Mem. Education Panel, Boy Scouts' Assoc., 1963; Chm. and Dir, Bedfordshire Musical Festival, 1967. Croix de Guerre with Palm, 1946. *Publication:* Ed. Shakespeare's Coriolanus, 1954. *Recreations:* mountaineering, music. *Address:* 182 Bromham Road, Bedford. *T:* Bedford 52510. *Clubs:* Alpine, Climbers.

**KEMMER, Prof. Nicholas,** FRS 1956; FRSE 1954; MA Cantab, DrPhil Zürich; Tait Professor of Mathematical Physics, University of Edinburgh, since 1953; *b* 7 Dec. 1911; *o s* of late Nicholas P. Kemmer and of late Barbara Kemmer (*née* Stutzer; later Mrs Barbara Classen); *m* 1947, Margaret, *o d* of late George Wragg and of Nellie (now Mrs C. Rodway); two *s* one *d. Educ:* Bismarckschule, Hanover; Universities of Göttingen and Zürich. DrPhil Zürich, 1935; Imperial Coll., London: Beit Scientific Research Fellow, 1936-38. Demonstrator, 1938. Mem. of UK Govt Atomic Energy Research teams in Cambridge and Montreal, 1940-46; University Lecturer in Mathematics, Cambridge, 1946-53 (Stokes Lecturer since 1950). Hughes Medal, Royal Society, 1966. *Publications:* The Theory of Space, Time and Gravitation, 1959 (trans. from The Russian of V. Fock, 1955); What is Relativity?, 1960 (trans from the Russian, What is the theory of Relativity?, by Prof. L. D. Landau and Prof. G. B. Rumer, 1959); papers in scientific jls on theory of nuclear forces and elementary particles. *Address:* 35 Salisbury Road, Edinburgh EH16 5AA. *T:* 031-667 2893.

**KEMP,** family name of **Viscount Rochdale.**

**KEMP, Athole Stephen Horsford,** OBE 1958 (MBE 1950); Secretary-General, Royal Commonwealth Society, since 1967 (Deputy Secretary-General, 1964-67); *b* 21 Oct. 1917; *o s* of late Sir Joseph Horsford Kemp, CBE, KC, LLD, and Mary Kemp; *m* 1940, Alison, *yr d* of Geoffrey Bostock, FCA; two *s* one *d. Educ:* Westminster Sch.; Christ Church, Oxford (MA). Commissioned RA, 1939; seconded Colonial Admin. Service, 1940-41; POW Far East (Thailand-Burma Railway), 1942-45. Colonial Administrative Service and HMOCS, Malaya 1940-64; Sec. to Govt, Fedn of Malaya, 1955-57. Dep. Perm. Sec., Prime Minister's Dept, Fedn of Malaya, 1957-61; seconded to Malaysian High Commn in London, 1961-64. Comdr, Order of Defender of the Realm (JMN) (Malaysia), 1958. *Address:* Lockey House, Langford, near Lechlade, Glos. *T:* Filkins 239. *Clubs:* Royal Automobile, Royal Commonwealth Society.

**KEMP, Charles,** CMG 1957; CBE 1951; retired as UK Senior Trade Commissioner and Economic Adviser to UK High Commissioner in South Africa (1953-58); *b* Whitstable, Kent, 25 Oct. 1897; *e s* of late Capt. Alfred and Elizabeth Kemp; *m* 1924, Helen Beatrice Stowe (*d* 1957); one *s. Educ:* Christ's Hospital; London University. HM Office of Works, 1915; served European War (wounded 1917); rejoined HM Office of Works, 1917; Dept of Overseas Trade, 1918; Asst to UK Trade Comr in E Africa, 1920; Trade Comr Grade III, 1931; Winnipeg, 1935; Cape Town, 1937; Trade Comr, Grade II, 1942, Grade I and transferred to Johannesburg, 1946. *Address:* 57 Hedge Row, Brighton Beach, Durban, South Africa. *Clubs:* Royal Commonwealth Society; Pretoria (Pretoria); Durban (Durban).

**KEMP, Charles Edward;** retired as Headmaster of Reading School; *b* 18 Nov. 1901; *e s* of Frederick Kemp, Salford, Lancs; *m* 1927, Catherine Mildred, *e d* of W. H. Taggart, IOM; two *s. Educ:* Manchester Grammar School (Foundation Scholar); Corpus Christi Coll., Oxford (open Scholar), Goldsmith Exhibitioner, 1922; 1st Class Maths, 1923. Master, Manchester Grammar Sch., 1923-30; Master, Royal Naval Coll., Dartmouth, 1930-34; Headmaster: Chesterfield Sch., 1934-39; Reading Sch., 1939-66. *Address:* Maple House, Wantage Road, Streatley, Berks. *T:* Goring-on-Thames 2679.

**KEMP, Rear-Adm. Cuthbert Francis,** CB 1967; ADC 1965; Chief Service Manager, Westland Helicopters, 1968-69; *b* 15 Sept. 1913; *s* of A. E. Kemp, Willingdon; *m* 1947, Margaret Law, *d* of L. S. Law, New York; two *s. Educ:* Victoria Coll., Jersey. Joined RN, 1931; RN Engrg Coll., 1936. Served in HMS Ajax and Hood; Pilot, 1939. Served War of 1939-45: carriers and air stations at home and abroad; Naval Staff, Washington, 1945-47; Fleet Engr Officer, E Indies, 1950-52; qual. Staff Coll., 1956; Admty, 1957-59; qual. Canadian Nat. Defence Coll., 1962; Supt RN Aircraft Yard, Belfast, 1962-65; Rear-Adm., Engineering, Staff of Flag Officer, Naval Air Command, 1965, retd 1967. *Recreations:* cricket, squash, shooting. *Address:* Beech House, Marston Magna, Som. *T:* Marston Magna 563. *Clubs:* Army and Navy; Royal Naval (Portsmouth).

**KEMP, Very Rev. Eric Waldram,** MA Oxon, DD; Dean of Worcester, since 1969; Canon and Prebendary of Caistor in Lincoln Cathedral, since 1952; *b* 27 April 1915; *o c* of Tom Kemp and Florence Lilian Kemp (*née* Waldram), Grove House, Waltham, Grimsby, Lincs; *m* 1953, Leslie Patricia, 3rd *d* of late Rt Rev. K. E. Kirk, sometime Bishop of Oxford; one *s* four *d*. *Educ:* Brigg Grammar Sch., Lincs; Exeter Coll., Oxford; St Stephen's House, Oxford. Deacon 1939; Priest 1940; Curate of St Luke, Southampton, 1939-41; Librarian of Pusey House, Oxford, 1941-46; Chaplain of Christ Church Oxford, 1943-46; Actg Chap., St John's Coll., Oxford, 1943-45; Fellow, Chaplain, Tutor, and Lectr in Theology and Medieval History, Exeter Coll., Oxford, 1946-69. Exam. Chaplain: TO Bp of Mon, 1942-45; to Bp of Southwark, 1946-50; to Bp of St Albans, 1946-69; to Bp of Exeter, 1949-69; to Bp of Lincoln, 1950-69. Proctor in Convocation for University of Oxford, 1949-69. Bp of Oxford's Commissary for Religious Communities, 1952-69; Chaplain to the Queen, 1967-69. Hon. Provincial Canon of Cape Town, 1960-; Bampton Lecturer, 1959-60. FRHistS 1951. *Publications:* (contributions to) Thy Household the Church, 1943; Canonization and Authority in the Western Church, 1948; Norman Powell Williams, 1954; Twenty-five Papal Decretals relating to the Diocese of Lincoln (with W. Holtzmann), 1954; An Introduction to Canon Law in the Church of England, 1957; Life and Letters of Kenneth Escott Kirk, 1959; Counsel and Consent, 1961; The Anglican-Methodist conversations: A Comment from within, 1964; (ed) Man: Fallen and Free, 1969. Contrib. to English Historical Review, Jl of Ecclesiastical History. *Recreations:* music, travel. *Address:* The Deanery, 15 College Green, Worcester. *T:* Worcester 23501. *Club:* National Liberal.

**KEMP, Maj.-Gen. Geoffrey Chicheley,** CB 1942; MC; *b* 28 Dec. 1890; *s* of Brig.-Gen. G. C. Kemp, CB, CMG; *m* 1927, Isabel Rosemary Gore Graham (*d* 1960); three *d*. *Educ:* private and RMA, Woolwich. Joined RFA, 1910; Capt., 1916; Major, 1929; Bt Lieut-Col, 1934; Lieut-Col, 1937; Col, 1938; Maj.-Gen., 1941; served European War, France and Belgium (wounded twice, despatches, MC); Major Inst. in Gunnery (Art.) School of Artillery, 1929-32; Brig.-Comdr (temp. Brig.), 1938-40; Comdr Orkney and Shetland Defences, 1939-42; Pres. War Office Selection Boards in this country and in Middle East, 1943; retired 1946; Col Commandant, RA, 1948. *Recreations:* all forms of sport, *Address:* Thurston Lodge, North Berwick, East Lothian. *T:* North Berwick 2204. *Club:* Army and Navy.

**KEMP, Sir Leslie (Charles),** KBE 1957 (CBE 1948); BScEng; FICE, MIEE, ACGI; *b* 22 April 1890; *s* of John Charles Kemp, London; *m* 1st, 1918, Millicent Constance (marr. diss., 1959), *d* of late Thomas Maitland; two *s*; 2nd, 1961, Melina Enriquez. *Educ:* Forest Hill House School; London Univ. BScEng 1st Cl. Hons, 1910. Engineer with Fraser and Chalmers, Erith, 1910-14. Served as captain in RGA, France, 1914-19. Contract Engineer, English Electric Co., 1919-23; Technical Adviser, Power and Traction Finance Co., 1923-25; Midlands Branch Manager, English Electric Co., 1924-26; Man. Dir, Athens Piraeus Electricity Co., 1926-41; Manager, Asmara War (land plane repair) base, Asmara, Eritrea, 1942-43; Dep. Regional Dir, Middle East, BOAC, 1943-44; Vice-Chm and Managing Director, Athens Piraeus Electricity Co., 1944-55; Vice-Chairman: Société Générale Hellenique, 1957-; General Develt Corp., Athens, 1960-. Citizen (Feltmaker) and Freedom of City of London, 1956. Cross of Commander of Royal Order of George I of Greece, 1951. *Recreations:* yachting and golf. *Address:* 12 Queen Amalia Avenue, Athens, Greece. *Clubs:* Junior Carlton, Royal Thames Yacht; Royal Yacht Squadron (Cowes); Royal Corinthian Yacht (Burnham-on-Crouch); Royal Hellenic Yacht (Greece).

**KEMP, Oliver,** CMG 1969; OBE 1960; *b* 12 Sept. 1916; *s* of Walter Kemp; *m* 1940, Henrietta Taylor; two *s*. *Educ:* Wakefield Grammar Sch.; Queen's Coll., Oxford. MA Oxon (Lit. Hum.). Served in HM Forces, 1939-45. Apptd Officer in HM Foreign Service, 1945; served in Moscow, Egypt, Indonesia, Yemen, Laos and Foreign Office, 1946-62. HM Chargé d'Affaires in Yemen, 1957-58; First Secretary and Head of Chancery in Laos, 1958-60. HM Ambassador to Togo (and Consul-General), 1962-65; Deputy Head of the United Kingdom Delegation to the European Communities, Luxembourg, 1965-67; Ambassador to Mongolia, 1967-68. *Recreations:* music, reading, languages, golf, gardening, travel. *Address:* Thornton-le-Dale, North Yorks. *T:* Thornton 368.

**KEMP, Lt-Comdr Peter Kemp,** OBE 1963; RN (retd); FSA, FRHistS; Head of Naval Historical Branch and Naval Librarian, Ministry of Defence, 1950-68; Editor of Journal of Royal United Service Institution, 1957-68; *b* 11 Feb. 1904; *e s* of Henry and Isabel Kemp; *m* 1st, 1930, Joyce, *d* of Fleming Kemp; 2nd, 1949, Eleanore, *d* of Frederick Rothwell; two *d* (and one *s* decd). *Educ:* Royal Naval Colleges, Osborne and Dartmouth. Served in submarines till 1928 (invalided); Naval Intelligence Division, 1939-45. Asst Editor, Sporting and Dramatic, 1933-36; Member: Editorial Staff, The Times, 1936-39 and 1945-50; Council of Navy Records Society; Editorial Adv. Board of Military Affairs (US). *Publications:* Prize Money, 1946; Nine Vanguards, 1951; HM Submarines, 1952; Fleet Air Arm, 1954; Boys' Book of the Navy, 1954; HM Destroyers, 1956; Famous Ships of the World, 1956; Victory at Sea, 1958; Famous Harbours of the World, 1958; (with Prof. C. Lloyd) Brethren of the Coast, 1960; History of the Royal Navy, 1969. Regiment Histories of: Staffordshire Yeomanry; Royal Norfolk Regiment; Middlesex Regiment; King's Shropshire Light Infantry; Royal Welch Fusiliers. Books on sailing. Children's novels. Edited: Hundred Years of Sea Stories; Letters of Admiral Boscawen (NRS); Fisher's First Sea Lord Papers, Vol. I (NRS), 1960, Vol. II (NRS), 1964. *Recreations:* sailing, golf. *Address:* 51 Market Hill, Maldon, Essex. *T:* Maldon 2609. *Clubs:* United Service; West Mersea Yacht.

**KEMP, Thomas Arthur,** MD; FRCP; Physician, St Mary's Hospital, since 1947, Paddington General Hospital since 1950; *b* 12 Aug. 1915; *s* of late Fred Kemp and Edith Peters; *m* 1942, Ruth May Scott-Keat; one *s* one *d*. *Educ:* Denstone Coll.; St Catharine's Coll., Cambridge (Exhibitioner); St Mary's Hospital, London (Scholar). MB, BChir 1940; MRCP 1941; FRCP 1949; MD 1953. Examiner in Medicine, Universities of London and Glasgow. FRSM (Jt Hon. Sec., 1961-67). Mem. Med. Soc. of London. Served in Middle East, 1944-47. Lt-Col RAMC Officer i/c Medical Division. Pres. Brit. Student Health Assoc., 1962-63; Chm. Brit. Student Tuberculosis Foundation, 1963-65. *Publications:* papers in medical journals. *Recreations:* Rugby football, Cambridge (1936) (Rep. CURUFC on RU Cttee, 1953-), England (Captain 1948); cricket and other games. *Address:* 104 Harley Street, W1. *T:* 01-

935 6155; 2 Woodside Road, Northwood, Middx. *T:* Northwood 21068. *Club:* Hawks (Cambridge).

**KEMPE, John William Rolfe;** Headmaster of Gordonstoun since 1968; *b* 29 Oct. 1917; *s* of late William Alfred Kempe and Kunigunda Neville-Rolfe; *m* 1957, Barbara Nan Stephen, *d* of Dr C. R. Huxtable, FRCS, MC, Sydney, Australia; two *s* one *d*. *Educ:* Stowe; Clare Coll., Cambridge (Exhibitioner in Mathematics). 1st cl. Maths Tripos I; 2nd cl. Economics Tripos II. Served war of 1939-45, RAFVR Training and Fighter Command; CO 153 and 255 Night Fighter Squadrons. Board of Trade, 1945; Firth-Brown (Overseas) Ltd, 1946-47; Head of Maths Dept, Gordonstoun, 1948-51; Principal, Hyderabad Public Sch., Deccan, India, 1951-54; Headmaster, Corby Grammar School, Northants, 1955-67. Exploration and mountaineering, Himalayas, Peru, 1952-56; Member: Cttee, Mount Everest Foundation, 1956-62; Cttee, Brathay Exploration Group; Cttee, Brathay Field Studies Centre. FRGS. *Publications:* Articles in Alpine Jl, Geographical Jl, Sociological Review. *Recreations:* philosophy, travel. *Address:* Gordonstoun School, Elgin, Moray. *Club:* Alpine.

**KEMPE, Rudolf;** Artistic Director since 1964, and Principal Conductor for life, 1970, Royal Philharmonic Orchestra; Artistic Director, Tonhalle Orchestra, Zürich, since 1965; Generalmusikdirektor, Münchener Philharmoniker, München, since 1967; also long contracts with Royal Opera, Covent Garden; *b* 14 June 1910; *m* Elisabeth (*née* Lindermeier) four *d* (one *s* decd). *Educ:* State Orchestra Sch., Dresden. Principal Oboist and Repetitor, Gewandhaus, Leipzig, 1929-36; started conducting in Leipzig, 1936; Dir of Music, State Orchestra, Dresden, 1949; General Musikdirektor, München Staatsoper, 1952-54. Subseq. Conductor Salzburg Festival, 1955, 1959, 1962, Edinburgh Festival, 1956, 1959, 1961, and Bayreuth, 1960, 1961, 1962, 1963, 1967, also conducted for many great orchestras of the world and in famous opera houses. Chief Conductor, Royal Philharmonic Orchestra, 1961-63, Artistic-Dir, 1964-. Broadcasts and recordings. *Address:* Duernbach/Tegernsee, Bavaria. *T:* Tegernsee 7248.

**KEMPFF, Wilhelm Walter Friedrich;** pianist and composer; *b* Jüterbog, Berlin, 25 Nov. 1895. *Educ:* Viktoria Gymnasium, Potsdam; Berlin University and Conservatoire (studied under H. Barth and Robert Kahn). Professor and Director of Stuttgart Staatliche Hochschule für Musik, 1924-29, since when has made concert tours throughout the world. Has made numerous recordings. Mem. of Prussian Academy of Arts. Mendelssohn Prize, 1917; Swedish Artibus et Litteris Medal, etc. *Compositions include:* two symphonies; four operas; piano and violin concertos; chamber, vocal and choral works. *Publication:* Unter dem Zimbelstern, Das Werden eines Musikers (autobiog.), 1951. *Address:* 8193 Ammerland, Oberbayern, Germany; c/o Ibbs & Tillett, 124 Wigmore Street, W1.

**KEMPSTER, Michael Edmund Ivor,** QC 1969; *b* 21 June 1923; *s* of late Rev. Ivor T. Kempster, DSO; *m* 1949, Sheila, *d* of Dr T. Chalmers, KiH, Inverness; two *s* two *d*. *Educ:* Mill Hill Sch.; Brasenose Coll., Oxford (MA, BCL). Royal Signals, 1943-46. Called to Bar, Inner Temple, 1949. *Recreations:* fishing, hare-hunting. *Address:* Queen Elizabeth Building, Temple, EC4. *T:* 01-353 4789.

**KEMSLEY,** 2nd Viscount *cr* 1945, of Dropmore; **(Geoffrey) Lionel Berry;** Bt 1928; Baron 1936; *b* 29 June 1909; *e s* of 1st Viscount Kemsley, GBE and Mary Lilian (*d* 1928), *d* of Horace George Holmes; *S* father, 1968; *m* 1933, Lady Helen Hay, OStJ, *e d* of 11th Marquess of Tweeddale; four *d*. *Educ:* Marlborough; Magdalen Coll., Oxford. Served War of 1939-45. Capt. Grenadier Guards; invalided out of Army, 1942. MP (C) Buckingham Div. of Bucks, 1943-45. Dep. Chm., Kemsley Newspapers Ltd, 1938-59. Master of Spectacle Makers' Co., 1949-51, 1959-61. CC Northants, 1964-70; High Sheriff of Leicestershire, 1967. FRSA; CStJ. *Heir: b* Hon. Denis Gomer Berry, TD [*b* 11 July 1911; *m* 1st, 1934, Rosemary Leonora de Rothschild (marr. diss., 1942); two *d*; 2nd, 1947, Mrs Pamela Grant, *d* of late Lord Richard Wellesley; one *s* one *d*]. *Address:* Thorpe Lubenham, Market Harborough, Leics. *T:* Market Harborough 2629. *Clubs:* Guards, Carlton, Bath, Turf, Pratt's.

*See also Hon. A. G. Berry.*

**KEMSLEY, Sir Colin Norman T.;** *see* Thornton-Kemsley.

**KENDALL, Arthur Wallis,** MS, FRCS; Surgeon to King's College Hospital and to Queen Elizabeth Hospital for children; *b* 3 Dec. 1904; *s* of Dr John Arthur Kendall; *m* 1930, Verna, *d* of late Sir John Winthrop Hackett, KCMG; two *s* two *d*. *Educ:* Barnard Castle Sch.; King's Coll., London. Lecturer in Surgery and Surgical Pathology, King's Coll. Hospital; Examiner in Surgery, University of London and Soc. of Apothecaries. Mem. of Court of Examiners, RCS. Served during war of 1939-45 as Surgeon Capt. RNVR (VRD). *Publications:* various medical. *Recreation:* golf. *Address:* 23 Margin Drive, Wimbledon, SW19. *Club:* Savile.

**KENDALL, Prof. David George,** FRS 1964; MA Oxon; Professor of Mathematical Statistics, University of Cambridge, and Fellow of Churchill College, since Oct. 1962; *b* 15 Jan. 1918; *s* of Fritz Ernest Kendall and Emmie Taylor, Ripon, Yorks; *m* 1952, Diana Louise Fletcher; two *s* four *d*. *Educ:* Ripon GS; Queen's Coll., Oxford. Fellow Magdalen Coll., Oxford, and Lectr in Mathematics, 1946-62. Vis. Lectr, Princeton Univ., USA, 1952-53. Guy Medal in Silver of Royal Statistical Soc., 1955. Mem. Internat. Statistical Inst.; Mem. Coun., Royal Society, 1968-69. *Address:* Churchill College, Cambridge.

**KENDALL, Denis;** *see* Kendall, W. D.

**KENDALL, Edward Calvin,** PhD; Visiting Professor in Chemistry, James Forrestal Research Center, Princeton University, since 1951; Emeritus Professor of Physiologic Chemistry, University of Minnesota (Mayo Foundation), since 1951; *b* 8 March 1886; *s* of George Stanley Kendall and Eva Frances (*née* Abbott); *m* 1915, Rebecca Kennedy; one *s* one *d* (and two *s* decd). *Educ:* Columbia Univ., USA. BS 1908, MS 1909, PhD 1910, Alexander Hamilton Award (Columbia Univ.), 1961. Research chemist (thyroid gland), Parke Davis and Co., Detroit, 1910-11; St Luke's Hosp., New York City, 1911-14; Mayo Clinic: Head of Section on Biochemistry, 1914, Prof. of Physiologic Chemistry, 1921. Isolated active constituent of thyroid gland, 1914; investigations on glutathione resulting in its preparation in crystalline form and determination of its structure, 1926-30; undertook investigation of adrenal cortex, 1930; (with Dr L. H. Sarett) cortisone was prepared, 1948. Hon. doctor of science: University of Cincinnati, Yale Univ., Western

Reserve Univ., Williams Coll., National Univ. of Ireland, Columbia Univ. Mem. many societies, both American and foreign. Holds various American awards for research, from 1921; (jointly) Nobel Prize for Physiology and Medicine, 1950. Gold Medal for Scientific Achievement, American Med. Assoc., 1965. *Publications:* Thyroxine, 1929. Numerous articles in scientific journals. *Recreations:* chess, outdoor activities. *Address:* 3 Queenston Place, Princeton, New Jersey, USA. *Club:* Nassau (Princeton).

**KENDALL, James;** MA; DSc (Edinburgh); LLD (Glasgow); FRS 1927; Professor of Chemistry, University of Edinburgh, 1928-59, retired (Dean of the Faculty of Science, 1953-54 and 1957-59); Vice-President, British Association for the Advancement of Science, 1951; *b* Chobham, Surrey, 30 July 1889; *s* of William Henry Kendall and Rebecca Pickering; *m* 1st, 1915, Alice (*d* 1955), *d* of Thomas Tyldesley, Victoria, BC; one *s* two *d*; 2nd, 1955, Jane Bain, *d* of late Malcolm Steven, Auckingill, Caithness. *Educ:* Farnham Grammar Sch.; University of Edinburgh; Nobel Institute, Stockholm. Prof. of Chem., Columbia University New York City, 1913-26; Professor of Chem., Washington Square Coll., New York Univ., 1926-28; Dean of the Graduate Sch., New York Univ., 1927-28; Visiting Professor, Stanford Univ., 1919 and 1923; University of Calif, 1923; Pennsylvania State Coll., 1927; Chm., New York Section, American Chemical Soc., 1925; Hon. Member, American Institute of Chemists; Lieut, US Naval Reserve, 1917-19; Lieut-Comdr, 1924-26. Pres. Royal Society of Edinburgh, 1949-54 (General Sec., 1936-46). *Publications:* At Home among the Atoms, 1929; Breathe Freely!, 1938; Young Chemists and Great Discoveries, 1939; Great Discoveries by Young Chemists, 1953; Humphry Davy, Pilot of Penzance, 1954; Michael Faraday, Man of Simplicity, 1955; contributions to scientific journals in the field of inorganic and physical chemistry; revisions of chemistry textbooks of Alexander Smith. *Address:* 200 Colinton Road, Edinburgh EH14 1BP. *T:* 031-443 5318. *Clubs:* Century, Chemists' (New York); New (Edinburgh).

**KENDALL, Maurice George,** MA, ScD; FBA 1970; Chairman, Scientific Control Systems Ltd; Fellow: American Statistical Association; Econometric Society; Institute of Mathematical Statistics; London Graduate School of Business Studies; *b* 6 Sept. 1907; *s* of late John Roughton Kendall and Georgina Kendall; *m* 1st, 1933, Sheila Frances Holland Lester; two *s* one *d*; 2nd, 1947, Kathleen Ruth Audrey Whitfield; one *s*. *Educ:* Central Sch., Derby; St John's Coll., Cambridge (Wrangler 1929). Entered Administrative Class, Civil Service, 1930; Ministry of Agriculture, 1930-41; Statistician, Chamber of Shipping, 1941-49 and Jt Asst Gen. Manager, 1947-49; Professor of Statistics in the University of London 1949-61. Fellow, British Computer Soc.; Treasurer, Institut International de Statistique; ex-President: Royal Statistical Soc.; Operational Research Soc.; Inst. of Statisticians; Hon. Mem., Market Research Soc. Gold Medal, Royal Statistical Society, 1968. DUniv Essex, 1968. *Publications:* (with G. Udny Yule) An Introduction to the Theory of Statistics; (with Alan Stuart) The Advanced Theory of Statistics; Contributions to Study of Oscillatory Time-Series; Rank Correlation Methods; (ed) The Sources and Nature of the Statistics of the United Kingdom; (with W. R. Buckland) A Dictionary of Statistical Terms; A Course in Multivariate Analysis; The Geometry of n Dimensions; (with Alison G. Doig) A Bibliography of Statistical Literature; (with P. A. Moran) Geometrical Probability; various papers on theory of statistics and applications to economics and psychology. *Recreation:* sleeping. *Address:* 49-57 Berners Street, W1. *T:* 01-580 5599; 1 Frank Dixon Close, SE21. *T:* 01-693 6076.

**KENDALL, (William) Denis,** FIMechE; MIAE; MIPE; Chartered Engineer; *b* Halifax Yorks, 27 May 1903; *yr s* of J. W. Kendall, Marton, Blackpool; *m* 1952, Margaret Hilda Irene Burden. *Educ:* Trinity Sch.; Halifax Technical Coll. MP (Ind.) Grantham Division of Kesteven and Rutland, 1942-50; Mem., War Cabinet Gun Bd, 1941-45 (decorated). Cadet in Royal Fleet Auxiliary; Asst to Chief Inspector, Budd Manufacturing Corp., Philadelphia, Pa, 1923; Dir of Manufacturing, Citroen Motor Car Co., Paris, 1929-38; Managing Director, British Manufacture and Research Co., Grantham, England, 1938-45, and Consultant to Pentagon, Washington, on high velocity small arms. Executive Vice-Pres., Brunswick Ordnance Corp., New Brunswick, NJ, 1952-55 (also Dir and Vice-Pres. Ops, Mack Truck Corp.); Pres. and Director: American MARC, Inc., 1955-61 (manufacturers of Diesel Engines, who developed and produced the world's first Diesel outboard engine, and also electric generators, etc), Inglewood, Calif; Dynapower Systems Corp. (Manufacturers of Electro-Medical equipment), Santa Monica, Calif, 1961-. Mem. President's Council, American Management Assoc. Mem. Worshipful Co. of Clockmakers, Freeman City of London, 1943; Governor of King's Sch., Grantham, 1942-52. Chevalier de l'Ordre du Ouissam Alouite Cherifien. Mason. Society of Friends (Quakers). *Address:* 1319 North Doheny Drive, Los Angeles, Calif 90069, USA. *T:* Crestview 66506; 115 Preston New Road, Marton, Blackpool, England. *Clubs:* National Liberal; Royal Norfolk and Suffolk Yacht (Lowestoft); Riviera Country, Cave des Rois (Los Angeles, Calif); United British Services.

**KENDALL, William Leslie;** General Secretary, Civil and Public Services Association (formerly Civil Service Clerical Association), since 1967; *b* 10 March 1923; *m* 1943, Irene Canham; one *s* one *d*. Clerk Insurance Cttee, 1937-41. RAF 1941-46. Entered Civil Service, 1947; Civil Service Clerical Association: held hon. posts; Asst Sec., 1952; Dep. Gen. Sec., 1963. Sec., Civil Service Alliance, 1967; Mem., CS Nat. Whitley Council; Mem., TUC Non-Manual Workers Adv. Cttee; Governor, Ruskin Coll. *Recreations:* reading, some marginal political activity. *Address:* (home) 4 Portal Close, Royal Circus, West Norwood, SE27. *T:* 01-670 4881; (office) CPSA, 215 Balham High Road, SW17. *T:* 01-672 1299.

**KENDALL-CARPENTER, John MacGregor Kendall;** Headmaster, Eastbourne College, since 1970; *b* 25 Sept. 1925; *s* of C. E. Kendall-Carpenter and late F. F. B. Kendall-Carpenter (*née* Rogers); *m* 1955, Iris Anson; three *s* two *d*. *Educ:* Truro Sch.; Exeter Coll., Oxford. Fleet Air Arm, Pilot RNVR, 1943-45. Oxford, 1947-51; Asst Master, Clifton Coll., 1951-61, and Housemaster, 1957-61; Headmaster, Cranbrook School, Kent, 1961-70. Member: Air Cadet Council; Air League Council; Chm., Air League Education Cttee; Schools Mem., Rugby Football Union Cttee. (Member or Captain: Oxford Univ. Rugby XV, 1948-50, England Rugby XV, 1948-54). *Recreation:* outdoor activities. *Address:* Headmaster's House, The College, Eastbourne, Sussex. *T:* Eastbourne 23136. *Club:* Vincent's (Oxford).

**KENDON, Donald Henry,** CBE 1961; FIEE, FIMechE; Chairman Merseyside and North Wales Electricity Board, 1954-62, retired; *b* 9

Aug. 1895; *s* of Samuel and Ellen Susan Kendon; *m* 1923, Katharine Grace Honess; five *s*. *Educ:* Goudhurst, Kent; King's Coll., University of London. BSc (Eng.) Hons. Served European War, 1914-19, in RE and RAF. Electrical Engineer with Edmundson's Electricity Corp., Ltd, 1921-34; General Manager: Cornwall Electric Power Co., 1934-39; Shropshire, Worcestershire and Staffordshire Electric Power Co., 1939-48; Dep. Chairman, Midlands Electricity Board, 1948-54; Member: Central Electricity Authority, 1956, 1957; Electricity Council. *Address:* Quedley, Flimwell, via Wadhurst, Sussex.

**KENDREW, Maj.-Gen. Sir Douglas (Anthony),** KCMG 1963; CB 1958; CBE 1944; DSO 1943 (Bar 1943, 2nd Bar 1944, 3rd Bar 1953); Governor of Western Australia since 1963; *b* 22 July 1910; *er s* of Alexander John Kendrew, MC, MD, Barnstaple, North Devon; *m* 1936, Nora Elizabeth, *d* of John Harvey, Malin Hall, County Donegal; one *s* one *d*. *Educ:* Uppingham Sch. 2nd Lieut Royal Leicestershire Regt, 1931; Capt. 1939; Major 1941; served War of 1939-45: Bde Major, N Africa, 1942; comd 6th Bn York and Lancaster Regt. N Africa and Italy, 1943; Bde Comd. Italy, Middle East and Greece, 1944-46; Commandant, Sch. of Infantry, Rhine Army, 1946-48; Commandant Army Apprentice Sch., Harrogate, 1948-50; Chief of Staff, NID, 1950-52; Bde Comd. 29 Brit. Inf. Bde, Korea, 1952-53; idc 1954; Brig. Administration HQ Northern Comd, 1955; GOC Cyprus Dist, and Dir of Ops, 1956-58; Dir of Infantry, War Office, 1958-60; Head of British Defence Liaison Staff, Australia, 1961-63. Col, Royal Leicestershire Regt, 1963-64. Hon. Col, SAS Regt, RWAR Australia, 1965. Hon. LLD Univ. of WA, 1969. KStJ 1964. *Recreations:* Rugby football (played for England 10 times, Capt. 1935; toured NZ and Australia, 1930; Army XV, 1932-36); golf and fishing. *Address:* Government House, Perth, Western Australia 6000, Australia. *Clubs:* Army and Navy, United Hunts.

**KENDREW, John Cowdery,** CBE 1963; ScD; FRS 1960; Fellow of Peterhouse, Cambridge, since 1947; Deputy Chairman of Medical Research Council Laboratory for Molecular Biology, Cambridge; Member, Council for Scientific Policy, since 1965, Deputy Chairman 1970; *b* 24 March 1917; *s* of late Wilfrid George Kendrew, MA, and Evelyn May Graham Sandberg. *Educ:* Dragon Sch., Oxford; Clifton Coll., Bristol; Trinity Coll., Cambridge. Scholar of Trinity Coll., Cambridge, 1936; BA 1939; MA 1943; PhD 1949; ScD 1962. Min. of Aircraft Production, 1940-45; Hon. Wing Comdr, RAF, 1944. Reader at Davy-Faraday Laboratory at Royal Instn, London, 1954-68. Sec.-Gen., European Molecular Biology Conf., 1970. Pres., Internat. Union for Pure and Applied Biophysics, 1969-. Hon. Mem., American Soc. of Biological Chemists, 1962; Foreign Hon. Mem., Amer. Acad. of Arts and Sciences, 1964; Leopoldina Academy, 1965; Hon. Fellow: Inst. of Biology, 1966; Weizmann Inst., 1970. Herbert Spencer Lecture, University of Oxford, 1965; Crookshank Lecture, Faculty of Radiologists, 1967; Procter Lecture, Internat. Soc. of Leather Chemists, 1969. Hon. DSc: University of Reading, 1968; University of Keele, 1968. (Jointly) Nobel Prize for Chemistry, 1962; Royal Medal of Royal Society, 1965. *Publications:* The Thread of Life, 1966; scientific papers in Proceedings of Royal Society, etc. *Address:* Peterhouse, Cambridge; The Guildhall, 4 Church Lane, Linton, Cambs CB1 6JX. *T:* 545 *Club:* Athenæum.

**KENDRICK, John Bebbington Bernard;** Chief Inspector of Audit, Ministry of Housing and Local Government, 1958-65, retired; *b* 12 March 1905; 3rd *s* of late John Baker Kendrick and Lenora Teague, Leominster, Herefordshire; *m* 1932, Amelia Ruth, 4th *d* of late James Kendall, Grange-over-Sands; two *s*. *Educ:* Leominster Grammar Sch.; King's Sch., Chester; Queen's Coll., Oxford (MA). Called to Bar, Middle Temple. Asst District Auditor, 1926; Deputy District Auditor, 1946; District Auditor, 1953; Deputy Chief Inspector of Audit, 1958. *Recreation:* fell walking. *Address:* Green Acres, Old Hall Road, Calgarth, Windermere, Westmorland. *T:* Windermere 3705.

**KENDRICK, Sir Thomas Downing,** KCB, *cr* 1951; FBA; FSA; Hon. DLitt (Durham and Oxford); Hon. LittD (Dublin); Hon. ARIBA; Director and Principal Librarian of British Museum, 1950-59, retired; *b* 1895; *m* 1st, 1922, Helen Kiek (*d* 1955); *m* 2nd, 1957, Katharine Elizabeth Wrigley. Keeper of Brit. Antiquities, Brit. Museum, 1938-50. Hon. Fellow Oriel Coll., Oxford. Mem. Royal Commn of 1851; Foreign Mem. Royal Swedish Acad. of Letters, History and Antiquities; Mem. German Archæological Inst. *Publications:* The Lisbon Earthquake, 1956; Saint James in Spain, 1960; Great Love for Icarus, 1962; Mary of Agreda, 1967. *Address:* Organford Farm House, near Poole, Dorset. *Club:* Athenæum.

**KENILWORTH,** 2nd Baron, *cr* 1937, of Kenilworth; **Cyril Davenport Siddeley,** CBE 1951; TD 1942; Lord of the Manor of Kenilworth; *b* 27 Aug. 1894; *e s* of 1st Baron and Sara Mabel Goodier (*d* 1953); *S* father 1953; *m* 1919, Marjorie Tennant, *d* of late Harry Firth; one *s* one *d*. *Educ:* St Lawrence Coll., Ramsgate. Formerly Lieut-Col and Hon. Col 7th Bn Royal Warwickshire Regt (TA); served European War, 1914-19, France and Belgium (despatches twice, 1914-15 Star); War of 1939-45, France, 1940 (despatches). Vice-Chm. and Chm. Coventry and Warwicks Hosp., 1925-29; DL Warwicks, 1942-67; Sheriff of Warwicks, 1944-45; Master Coachmakers and Coach harness makers of London, 1956-57; a Manager Coventry Trustee Savings Bank; formerly Chm. Coventry Diocesan Bd of Finance. Pres. Queen Victoria Memorial Hosp., Nice, 1961-64. *Recreation:* motoring. *Heir:* *s* Hon. John Davenport Siddeley, *qv*. *Address:* Hotel Metropole, Monte Carlo, Monaco.

**KENNABY, Very Rev. Noel Martin;** Dean of St Albans and Rector of the Abbey Church since 1964; Commissary, Jamaica, 1950-67; *b* 22 Dec. 1905; *s* of Martin and Margaret Agnes Kennaby; *m* 1st, 1933, Margaret Honess Elliman; 2nd, 1937, Mary Elizabeth Berry. *Educ:* Queens' Coll., Cambridge; Westcott House, Cambridge. BA 1928; MA 1932. Deacon 1929, priest 1930, Diocese of Guildford; Curate of Epsom, 1929-32; in charge of Christ Church, Scarborough, 1932-36; Vicar of St Andrew's, Handsworth, 1936-42; Tynemouth, 1942-47; Surrogate from 1942; Rural Dean of Tynemouth, 1943-47; Provost and Vicar of Newcastle upon Tyne, 1947-61; Rural Dean of Newcastle upon Tyne, 1947-61; Senior Chaplain to the Archbishop of Canterbury, 1962-64; Hon. Canon, Newcastle Cathedral, 1962-64. *Publication:* To Start You Praying, 1951. *Address:* The Deanery, Sumpter Yard, St Albans, Herts. *Club:* United University.

**KENNAN, George Frost;** Professor, Institute for Advanced Study, Princeton, NJ, since 1956; Professor, Princeton University, NJ, since

1963; *b* 16 Feb. 1904; *m* 1931, Annelise Sorensen; one *s* three *d*. *Educ:* Princeton Univ. (AB); Seminary for Oriental Languages, Berlin. Foreign Service of the USA; many posts from 1926-52; US Ambassador to the USSR, 1952-53; Institute for Advanced Study, Princeton, 1953-61; George Eastman Visiting Prof., Oxford Univ., 1957-58; Reith Lecturer, BBC, 1957; US Ambassador to Yugoslavia, 1961-63. Hon. LLD: Dartmouth and Yale, 1950; Colgate, 1951; Notre Dame, 1953; Kenyon Coll., 1954; New School for Social Research, 1955; Princeton, 1956; University of Michigan and Northwestern, 1957; Brandeis, 1958; Wisconsin, 1963; Harvard, 1963; Denison, 1966; Rutgers, 1966; Hon. DCL Oxford, 1969. Benjamin Franklin Fellow, RSA, 1968. President: Nat. Inst. of Arts and Letters, 1965-68; Amer. Acad. of Arts and Letters, 1968-. *Publications:* American Diplomacy, 1900-50, 1951 (US); Realities of American Foreign Policy, 1954 (US); Amerikanisch Russische Verhältnis, 1954 (Germany); Soviet-American Relations, 1917-20; Vol. I, Russia Leaves the War, 1956 (National Book Award; Pulitzer Prize 1957); Vol. II, The Decision to Intervene, 1958; Russia, the Atom and the West, 1958; Soviet Foreign Policy, 1917-1941, 1960; Russia and the West under Lenin and Stalin, 1961; On Dealing with the Communist World, 1964; Memoirs, 1925-1950, 1967 (National Book Award 1968; Pulitzer Prize 1968); From Prague after Munich: Diplomatic Papers 1938-1940, 1968; Democracy and the Student Left, 1968. *Club:* Century (New York City).

**KENNARD, Sir George Arnold Ford,** 3rd Bt *cr* 1891; Midland Representative for Cement Marketing Co.; *b* 27 April 1915; *s* of Sir Coleridge Kennard, 1st Bt; *S* brother, 1967; *m* 1st, 1940, Cecilia Violet Cokayne Maunsel (marriage dissolved, 1958); one *d*; 2nd, 1958, Jesse Rudd Miskin, *d* of Hugh Wyllie. *Educ:* Eton. Commissioned 4th Queen's Own Hussars, 1939; served War of 1939-45 (despatches twice), Egypt, Greece (POW Greece); comd Regt, 1955-58; retired, 1958. Joined Cement Marketing Co., 1967. *Recreations:* hunting, shooting, fishing. *Heir:* none. *Address:* Hook Norton, Banbury, Oxon. *T:* Hook Norton 308. *Club:* Cavalry.

**KENNAWAY, Sir John (Lawrence),** 5th Bt, *cr* 1791; *b* 7 Sept. 1933; *s* of Sir John Kennaway, 4th Bt and Mary Felicity, *yr d* of late Rev. Chancellor Ponsonby; *S* father 1956; *m* 1961, Christina Veronica Urszenyi, MB, ChB (Cape Town); one *s* two *d*. *Educ:* Harrow; Trinity Coll., Cambridge. *Heir:* *s* John Michael Kennaway, *b* 17 Feb. 1962. *Address:* Escot, Ottery St Mary, Devon.

**KENNEDY,** family name of **Marquess of Ailsa.**

**KENNEDY**; *see* Mackenzie-Kennedy.

**KENNEDY, Sir Albert (Henry),** Kt 1965; Chairman, Securicor (Ulster) Ltd; Managing Director, Styletype Printing Ltd, Glengormley, Co. Antrim; *b* 11 May 1906; *s* of Joseph and Catherine Kennedy; *m* 1st, 1931, Elizabeth Freeborn (decd); two *d*; 2nd, 1942, Muriel Lucile Hamilton; one *d* (and one step-*s* one step-*d*). Joined Royal Ulster Constabulary, 1924; District Inspector, 1936; County Inspector, 1951; Deputy Commissioner, Belfast, 1954; Deputy Inspector General, 1957; Inspector General, Jan. 1961-Jan. 1969. Has studied police methods in N and S America, Africa, ME and various European countries. King's Police Medal, 1947. *Recreations:* reading, golf, light gardening; general interest in sporting activities. *Address:* 11 Bladon Drive, Belfast 9. *Clubs:* Malone Golf, Clandeboye Golf (Ulster). *T:* Belfast 667500.

**KENNEDY, Alfred James,** DSc (London), PhD (London), CEng, MIEE, MIMM, FIM, FInstP; Director, The British Non-Ferrous Metals Research Association, London, since 1966; *b* 6 Nov. 1921; *m* 1950, Anna Jordan; no *c*. *Educ:* Haberdashers' Aske's Hatcham Sch.; University Coll., London. BSc (Physics) 1943. Commissioned R Signals, 1944; Staff Major (Telecommunications) Central Comd, Agra, India, 1945-46 and at Northern Comd, Rawalpindi, 1946-47; Asst Lectr in Physics, UCL 1947-50; Res. Fellow, Davy-Faraday Lab. of Royal Institution, London, 1950-51; Royal Society, Armourers' and Brasiers' Research Fellow in Metallurgy (at Royal Institution), 1951-54; Head of Metal Physics Sect., BISRA, 1954-57; Prof. of Materials and Head of Dept. of Materials, Coll. of Aeronautics, Cranfield, 1957-66. Pres., Inst. of Metals, 1970-71 (Mem. Council, 1968-); Member: Metallurgy Cttee, CNAA, 1965-; Instn of Metallurgists, 1968-; Inst. of Physics, 1968-. Pres., Brit. Soc. of Rheology, 1964-66; a Governor, Nat. Inst. for Agric. Engrg, 1966-. *Publications:* Processes of Creep and Fatigue in Metals, 1962; The Materials Background to Space Technology, 1964; Creep and Stress Relaxation in Metals (English edn), 1965; (ed) High Temperature Materials, 1968; some eighty research papers and articles, mainly on physical aspects of deformation and fracture in crystalline materials, particularly metals. *Recreations:* music, painting. *Address:* The Old Bakehouse, Weston Underwood, Olney, Bucks. *T:* Olney 345. *Club:* Athenæum.

**KENNEDY, Archibald E. C.**; *see* Clark-Kennedy.

**KENNEDY, Daisy;** Violinist (Australian); *b* Burra, South Australia, 1893; *d* of J. A. Kennedy, Headmaster, Norwood, Adelaide; *m* 1924, John Drinkwater (*d* 1937); one *d*; two *d* by former marriage to Benno Moiseiwitsch, CBE. *Educ:* Elder Scholar, University Conservatorium, Adelaide. Left Adelaide for Prague, 1908; studied with Prof. Sevcik; later entered Meisterschule, Vienna, under same Prof., and held a Scholarship during 2nd year; made début in Vienna, 1911, and in London at Queen's Hall with Prof. Sevcik the same year; played at principal concerts at Queen's Hall, (Royal) Albert Hall, and throughout United Kingdom; has given many recitals at Wigmore Hall, Æolian Hall, and Grotrian Hall since début; toured Australia and New Zealand, 1919-20; début in Æolian Hall, New York, Nov. 1920; second tour, 1925; has given first performances of many violin works in London; appeared in recitals and with orchestra in Prague, Vienna and Budapest, and also played on the Radio several times in each city 1931; formed the Kennedy Trio with Lauri and Dorothy Kennedy, 1932; recital in Egypt, 1933. *Address:* 208 Rivermead Court, Hurlingham, SW6. *T:* 01-736 4379.

**KENNEDY, David Matthew;** American Banker; Secretary of the Treasury, USA, since 1969; *b* Randolph, Utah, 21 July 1905; *s* of George Kennedy and Katherine Kennedy (*née* Johnson); *m* 1925, Lenora Bingham; four *d*. *Educ:* Weber Coll., Ogden, Utah (AB); George Washington Univ., Washington, DC (MA, LLB); Stonier Grad. Sch. of Banking, Rutgers Univ. (grad.). Technical Asst to Chm. of Bd, Federal Reserve System, 1930-46; Vice-Pres. in charge of bond dept, Continental Illinois Bank and Trust Co., Chicago, 1946-53, full Vice-Pres., 1951, Pres., 1956-58, Chm. Bd and Chief Exec. Officer, 1959- (temp. resigned, Oct. 1953-Dec. 1954, to act as special Asst to Sec. of Treas., in Republican Admin.); after return to Continental Ill Bank, still advised Treasury (also under Democrat Admin.). Chm. of a Commission: (apptd by President Johnson) to improve drafting of Federal budget, 1967; (apptd by Mayor of Chicago) for Economic and Cultural Develt of Chicago, 1967. Again in Govt, when nominated to Nixon Cabinet, Dec. 1968. Director (past or present) of many corporations and companies including: Internat. Harvester Corp.; Abbott Laboratories; Swift & Co.; Pullman Co.; Nauvoo Restoration Inc.; Member of numerous organizations; Trustee: Univ. of Chicago; George Washington Univ.; Brookings Instn, etc. Holds hon. doctorates. *Address:* Department of the Treasury, 15th Street and Pennsylvania Avenue, NW, Washington, DC 20220, USA; (home) 33 Meadow View Drive, Northfield, Ill 60093, USA. *Clubs:* Union League, Commercial Executives (Chicago); Old Elm Country (Fort Sheridan, Ill); Glenview Country, etc.

**KENNEDY, Douglas Neil,** OBE 1952 (MBE); Vice-President, English Folk Dance and Song Society; President, Folk Lore Society, 1964-65; *b* Edinburgh, 1893; *s* of John Henderson Kennedy and Patricia Grieve Thomson, *g s* of David Kennedy the Scottish singer; *m* 1914, Helen May Karpeles; two *s*. *Educ:* George Watson's Coll., Edinburgh; Imperial College of Science. Served London Scottish prior to and during European War, 1914-18, and received his commission in that regiment; MBE for War services, and retired with the rank of Captain; served War of 1939-45, RAF, 1940-45. Demonstrator in the Department of Botany, Imperial Coll., 1919-24; Organising Dir, English Folk Dance Society (on the death of its founder Cecil J. Sharp), 1924. *Publications:* England's Dances, 1950; English Folk-dancing Today and Yesterday, 1964; other works relating to traditional dance and song. *Address:* 10 Downside Crescent, NW3. *T:* 01-794 3228.

**KENNEDY, Frank Robert,** CMG 1947; OBE 1937; *b* 9 Nov. 1895; *s* of late Rev. R. J. Kennedy; *m* 1917, Ethel Florence Jennett (*d* 1970); one *s* two *d*. *Educ:* Weymouth Coll.; Queens' Coll., Cambridge (BA). Served European War, 1914-18, 16th Middlesex Regt, 1914-16; Machine Gun Corps, 1916-19; Colonial Administrative Service, Uganda, 1920; District Officer, 1932; Deputy Provincial Commissioner, 1939; Development and Welfare Sec. and Adviser on Native Affairs, 1944; Sec. for African Affairs, 1946; retd 1948; Trusteeship Dept, United Nations, 1949-52. *Address:* Long Corner, Menin Way, Farnham, Surrey. *T:* Farnham 6357.

**KENNEDY, Sir James (Edward),** 5th Bt *cr* 1836; farmer; *b* 18 Jan. 1898; *s* of Sir John Charles Kennedy, 3rd Bt (*d* 1923) and Maude (*d* 1939), *d* of Sir James Macaulay Higginson; *S* brother, 1968. *Educ:* Malvern Coll. *Recreation:* shooting. *Heir: cousin* Captain Derrick Edward de Vere Kennedy [*b* 5 June 1904; *m* 1st, 1926, Phyllis Victoria (marr. diss. 1945), *d* of late Gordon Fowler; two *s* one *d*; 2nd, 1945, Barbara Mary (*d* 1959), *d* of late William Shepherd]. *Address:* Johnstown Kennedy, Rathcoole, Co. Dublin. *T:* Celbridge 289203.

**KENNEDY, Prof. John (Stodart),** FRS 1965; Deputy Chief Scientific Officer, Agricultural Research Council, and Professor of Animal Behaviour in the University of London, Imperial College Field Station, Ascot; *b* 19 May 1912; *s* of James John Stodart Kennedy, MICE, and Edith Roberts Kennedy (*née* Lammers); *m* 1st, 1936, Dorothy Violet Bartholomew (divorced, 1946); one *s*; 2nd, 1950, Claude Jacqueline Bloch (*widow, née* Raphäel); one step *s*, one *s* one *d*. *Educ:* Westminster Sch.; University Coll., London. BSc (London) 1933. Derby Res. Schol., University Coll., London, 1933-34; Locust investigator for Imperial Inst. of Entomology, University of Birmingham, 1934-36, Anglo-Egyptian Sudan, 1936-37; MSc (London) 1936; Avebury Research Student, London Sch. of Hygiene and Trop. Med., 1937-38; PhD (Birmingham) 1938; Rockefeller Malaria Res. Lab., Tirana, Albania, 1938-39; Wellcome Entomolog. Field Labs, Esher, Surrey, 1939-42; Res. Officer, Middle East Anti-Locust Unit, 1942-44; Chem. Defence Exptl. Station, Porton, Wilts, 1944-45; ARC Unit of Insect Physiology, Cambridge, 1946-67; DSc (London) 1956; Sen. Prin. Sci. Officer, 1962. Fellow University Coll., Cambridge, 1966. Fellow University Coll., London, 1967. Pres. Royal Entomological Society, 1967-69. *Publications:* numerous research papers and review articles on the biology of locusts, mosquitos and greenfly. *Recreations:* domestic. *Address:* 43 Upper Redlands Road, Reading, Berks. *T:* Reading 84864.

**KENNEDY, Ludovic Henry Coverley;** writer and broadcaster; *b* Edinburgh, 3 Nov. 1919; *o s* of Captain E. C. Kennedy, RN (killed in action, 1939, while commanding HMS Rawalpindi against German battle-cruisers Scharnhorst and Gneisenau), and of Rosalind, *d* of Sir Ludovic Grant, 11th Bt of Dalvey; *m* 1950, Moira Shearer King (*see* Moira Shearer); one *s* three *d*. *Educ:* Eton; Christ Church, Oxford (MA). Served War, 1939-46: Midshipman, Sub-Lieut, Lieut, RNVR. Priv. Sec. and ADC to Gov. of Newfoundland, 1943-44. Librarian, Ashridge (Adult Education) Coll., 1949; Rockefeller Foundation Atlantic Award in Literature, 1950; Winner, Open Finals Contest, English Festival of Spoken Poetry, 1953; Editor, feature, First Reading (BBC Third Prog.), 1953-54; Lecturer for British Council, Sweden, Finland and Denmark, 1955; Introducer of feature, Profile, in ATV's Sunday Afternoon, 1955-56; Lecturer for British Council in Belgium and Luxembourg, 1956; Newscaster, Independent Television News, 1956-58. Introducer of AR's feature On Stage, 1957. Member of Council of Navy Records Society, 1957-60. Contested (L) Rochdale in Parly by-elect., 1958 and Gen. elec., 1959. Introducer of AR's, This Week, 1958-59. Pres. Nat. League of Young Liberals, 1959-61. Chm. BBC features: Your Verdict, 1962; Your Witness, 1967-68; Commentator: BBC's Panorama, 1960-63; Television Reporters Internat., 1963-64 (also Prod.). Introducer, BBC's Time Out, 1964-65, World at One, 1965-66. Mem., Liberal Party Council, 1965-67. Presenter: Lib. Party's Gen. Election Television Broadcasts, 1966; The Middle Years, ABC, 1967; The Nature of Prejudice, ATV, 1968; Face the Press, Tyne-Tees, 1968-69; 24 Hours, BBC, 1969-. Pres., Sir Walter Scott Club, Edinburgh, 1968-69. *Films include:* The Sleeping Ballerina; The Singers and the Songs; Scapa Flow, etc. *Publications:* Sub-Lieutenant, 1942; Nelson's Band of Brothers, 1951; One Man's Meat, 1953; Murder Story (play, with essay on Capital Punishment), 1956; play: Murder Story (Cambridge Theatre), 1954; Ten Rillington Place, 1961; The Trial of Stephen Ward, 1964; Very Lovely People, 1969. *Recreations:* fishing, shooting, golf. *Address:* c/o A.D. Peters, 10 Buckingham Street, WC2. *Clubs:* St James', MCC.

**KENNEDY, Mrs Ludovic;** *see* Shearer, Moira.

**KENNEDY, Hon. Sir Robert,** Kt 1949; MA, LLM, FRIH(NZ); Judge of Supreme Court of New Zealand, 1929-50; Royal Commissioner Orakei Native Reserves; Chairman Royal

Commission on Waterfront Industry; Commission on Police Conduct; *b* Southland, NZ, 18 May 1887; *o s* of John James Kennedy and Agnes Dow; *m* Alice Denniston Troup. *Educ:* Southland Boys' High Sch. (dux); Victoria Coll., New Zealand Univ. (Junior and Senior Univ. Scholar, First Class Hons). Jacob Joseph Research Scholar in Arts and Law; First Junior and First, with distinction, Senior Civil Service, 1906; admitted as Barrister and Solicitor, 1909. *Recreations:* fishing and gardening. *Address:* Whitelee, Waikanae, NZ.

**KENNEDY, William Quarrier,** FRS 1949; retired as Professor of Geology, University of Leeds (1945-67), now Emeritus; Director of Research Institute of African Geology in the University of Leeds, 1955-67; *b* 30 Nov. 1903; *s* of John Gordon Kennedy and Peterina Webster; *m* 1st, 1933, Elizabeth Jane Lawson McCubbin; one *s* two *d*; 2nd, 1962, Sylvia Margaret Greeves; one *s* one *d*. *Educ:* Glasgow High Sch.; Glasgow Univ.; University of Zürich. Geologist and senior geologist in the geological survey of Great Britain, 1928-45. Leader of the British Ruwenzori Expedition, 1951-52; Scientific Dir, Royal Society's expedition to Tristan da Cunha, 1962. Clough Medal, 1966; Lyell Medal, 1967. *Publications:* various in scientific journals. *Address:* Loseberry, Kirkpark Road, Elie, Fife.

**KENNEDY SHAW, W. B.;** *see* Shaw.

**KENNER, George Wallace,** FRS 1964; PhD, ScD Cantab; MSc Manchester; Heath Harrison Professor of Organic Chemistry, Liverpool University, since 1957; *b* Sheffield, 16 Nov. 1922; *s* of Professor James Kenner, *qv*; *m* 1951, Jillian Gervis, *d* of Angus K. Bird, Cambridge; two *d*. *Educ:* Manchester Grammar Sch.; Manchester Univ. Holder of DSIR Senior Award at Christ's Coll., Cambridge, 1944-46; Research Fellow of Trinity Hall, Cambridge, 1946-49; University Demonstrator, Cambridge, 1946-53; Rockefeller Foundation Fellow, Eidgenössische Technische Hochschule, Zürich, 1948-49; Staff Fellow of Trinity Hall, 1949-57; University Lecturer, 1953-57. Chemical Society, Tilden Lecturer, 1956; Meldola Medal, 1951; Corday-Morgan Medal, 1957. *Publications:* papers in Jl Chem. Soc. and Tetrahedron. *Recreations:* sailing, walking. *Address:* The Robert Robinson Laboratories, Oxford Street, Liverpool 7. *T:* 051-709 6022.

**KENNER, James,** FRS 1925; DSc (London); PhD (Heidelberg); Fellow of Queen Mary College, London; Emeritus Professor of Technological Chemistry in the University of Manchester; formerly Professor of Organic Chemistry, Pure and Applied, University of Sydney, Australia; *b* Morpeth, 1885; *m* 1918, Annie Moore, *d* of Dr S. Mathews (*see s* G. W. Kenner). *Educ:* Universities of London and Heidelberg. On Staff Sheffield Univ., 1909; Military and Munition Service, 1914-19. *Publications:* papers in Proc. and Trans Chem. Society; Berichte der deutschen chemischen Gesellschaft; Tetrahedron, Nature, Chemistry and Industry; Annual Reports of the Chemical Society; Society of Chemical Industry. *Address:* Hescott House, Lyndhurst Road, Didsbury, Manchester.

**KENNET,** 2nd Baron; *see* Young, Wayland.

**KENNEY, Edward John,** FBA 1968; Fellow, Director of Studies in Classics, and Librarian of Peterhouse, Cambridge, since 1953; Reader in Latin Literature and Textual Criticism, University of Cambridge, since 1967; *b* 29 Feb. 1924; *s* of George Kenney and Emmie Carlina Elfrida Schwenke; *m* 1955, Gwyneth Anne, *d* of late Henry Albert Harris. *Educ:* Christ's Hospital; Trinity Coll., Cambridge. BA 1949, MA 1953. Served War of 1939-45: Royal Signals, UK and India, 1943-46; commissioned, 1944, Lieut 1945. Porson Schol., 1948; Craven Schol., 1949; Craven Student, 1949; Chancellor's Medallist, 1950. Asst Lectr, Univ. of Leeds, 1951-52; Research Fellow, Trinity Coll., Cambridge, 1952-53; Asst Lectr, Univ. of Cambridge, 1955-60, Lectr, 1966-70; Tutor, Peterhouse, 1956-62, Senior Tutor, 1962-65. Jt Editor, Classical Quarterly, 1959-65. James C. Loeb Fellow in Classical Philology, Harvard Univ., 1967-68; Sather Prof. of Classical Literature, Univ. of California, Berkeley, 1968. *Publications:* P. Ouidi Nasonis Amores etc (ed), 1961; (with Mrs P. E. Easterling) Ovidiana Graeca (ed), 1965; (with W. V. Clausen, F. R. D. Goodyear, J. A. Richmond) Appendix Vergiliana (ed), 1966; articles and reviews in classical jls. *Recreations:* cats and books. *Address:* Peterhouse, Cambridge CB2 1RD. *T:* Cambridge 50256.

**KENNEY, Reginald;** Principal, Harper Adams Agricultural College since 1962; *b* 24 Aug. 1912; *m* 1946, Sheila Fay De Sa; two adopted *d*. *Educ:* King Edward VII School, Lytham St Anne's; Leeds Univ.; West of Scotland Agric. Coll. Warden and Lectr, Staffs Farm Inst., 1937-38; Asst County Agric. Educn Officer, Beds CC, 1938-42 (seconded Beds WAEC, 1939-42); Lectr in Farm Management and Animal Husbandry, University of Reading, 1942-48; Principal, Dorset Farm Inst., 1948-62. *Publication:* Dairy Husbandry, 1957. *Recreations:* swimming, mountains. *Address:* Principal's House, Harper Adams Agricultural College, Newport, Shropshire. *T:* Newport Salop 3233. *Club:* Farmers'.

**KENNEY, (William) John;** United States lawyer; member of firm of Sullivan, Shea & Kenney; *b* Oklahoma, 16 June 1904; *s* of Franklin R. Kenney and Nelle Kenney (*née* Torrence); *m* 1931, Elinor Craig; two *s* two *d*. *Educ:* Lawrenceville Sch., New Jersey; Stanford Univ (AB); Harvard Law Sch. (LLB). Practised law in San Francisco, 1929-36; Head of oil and gas unit, Securities and Exchange Commission, 1936-38; practised law in Los Angeles, 1938-41; Special Asst to Under-Sec. of the Navy; Chm. Navy Price Adjustment Board, General Counsel, 1941-46; Asst Sec. of the Navy, 1946-47; Under-Sec. of the Navy, 1947-49; Minister in charge of Economic Cooperation Administration Mission to the United Kingdon, 1949-50; Deputy Dir for Mutual Security, resigned 1952. Chairman: Democratic Central Cttee of DC, 1960-64; DC Chapter, American Red Cross. Director: Riggs National Bank; Merchants Transfer and Storage Co. (both of Washington DC); Trustee, Meridian House Foundn, Washington, DC. *Address:* 78 Kalorama Circle, NW, Washington, DC 20008; (office) Ring Building, Washington, DC 20036, USA. *Clubs:* Pacific Union (San Francisco); California (Los Angeles); Alibi, Metropolitan, Chevy Chase, Burning Tree (Washington).

**KENNY, Sean;** Designer; Associate Director, Mermaid Theatre, since 1968; *b* 23 Dec. 1932; *s* of Thomas J. Kenny and Nora Gleeson; *m* 1967, Judy Huxtable. *Educ:* St Flannan's Coll., Ireland; School of Architecture, Dublin. Designer of sets for stage productions: Shadow of a Gunman, 1957; Bloomsday, Hamlet, 1958; Coriolanus, Sugar-in-the-Morning, Lock up your Daughters, The Hostage, Cock-a-Doodle-Dandy, Glimpse of the Sea, 1959; Julius Caesar, Treasure Island, The Lily White Boys, Henry V, Great Expectations, Oliver!, Laughing Academy,

Here is the News, Tchin-Tchin, 1960; Why the Chicken, The Devils, Altona, The Miracle Worker, Arms and the Man, Stop the World . . ., Romeo and Juliet, 1961; Blitz, King Priam, Uncle Vanya, 1962; Pickwick, Beggar's Opera, Hamlet, Uncle Vanya, 1963; Maggie May, 1964; Flying Dutchman, Roar of the Greasepaint . . ., 1965; Four Musketeers! 1967; Gulliver's Travels (also adapter and director), 1968; Les Noces (Royal Swedish Ballet Co. Stockholm), Uncle Vanya (Haifa), Lock Up Your Daughters, 1969. Sets for TV and films: Windmill near a Frontier, 1960; The Plow and the Stars, 1961; I Thank a Fool, 1962. Architecture and interior design: Quinn House, Londonderry, 1953; Theatre, Casino de Liban, 1965; University of Sussex Fine Arts Centre Theatre, 1969; Canadian World Exhibition, Montreal, 1967; Gyrotron Spectacular Ride; Section 1, British Pavilion; New Winter Garden Theatre, Drury Lane, 1969-70; Mobile Theatre for Welsh Theatre Co., 1967; Casino de Paris, Dunes Hotel, Las Vegas, 1967; Irish Pavilion, 57th Street, New York City, 1968. Tony Award for sets for Oliver!, 1963. *Address:* 13 Manette Street, W1. *T:* 01-437 4286.

**KENRICK, Brig. Harry Selwyn,** CB 1945; CBE 1941; ED 1941; Superintendent-in-Chief, Auckland Hospitals, 1946-61; retired; *b* 7 Aug. 1898; *s* of late W. G. K. Kenrick, Stipendiary Magistrate, Auckland, NZ, and Beatrice Thom; *m* 1926, Lorna Winifred Dick; two *d*. *Educ:* Waitaki; Oamaru, NZ; Otago Univ., NZ; Edinburgh Univ. MB, ChB (NZ), 1924; FRCS (Edinburgh), 1926; practised as consulting Obstetrician and Gynæcologist in Auckland, NZ, 1928-39. Served as infantry officer with NZ Division in France, 1916-18 (wounded); maintained interest in Territorial work and on outbreak of war, 1939, appointed ADMS Northern Command; went overseas, 1940, in command of a NZ Field Ambulance; ADMS, NZ Division, 1940 (despatches for services in Greece and CBE for Service as Senior Medical Officer in Battle for Crete, also Greek Military Cross for this); formerly Col Commandant, RNZAMC and Hon. Surgeon to the Governor-General of NZ; DMS, NZEF (CB). *Address:* 90 Symonds Street, Auckland 1, New Zealand. *Clubs:* Northern, Officers (Auckland, NZ).

**KENSINGTON,** 7th Baron *cr* 1776; **William Edwardes;** Baron Kensington (UK) 1886; Lieutenant-Colonel Guides Cavalry, Indian Army; *b* 15 May 1904; *s* of 6th Baron and Mabel Carlisle (*d* 1934), *d* of George Pilkington, Stoneleigh, Woolton; *S* father 1938. *Educ:* Eton; RMC. *Heir:* *n* Hugh Ivor Edwardes [*b* 24 Nov. 1933; *m* 1961, Juliet Elizabeth Massy Anderson; two *s* one *d*]. *Address:* Mardan, PO Bromley, Rhodesia. *Club:* Cavalry.

**KENSINGTON, Suffragan Bishop of,** since 1964; **Rt. Rev. Ronald Cedric Osbourne Goodchild;** *b* 17 Oct. 1910; *s* of Sydney Osbourne and Dido May Goodchild; *m* 1947, Jean Helen Mary (*née* Ross); one *s*; four *d*. *Educ:* St John's School, Leatherhead; Trinity Coll. (Monk Schol.); Cambridge; Bishops' Coll., Cheshunt. 2nd Cl. Hist. Tripos Parts I and II, 1931, Dealtry Exhibn. 1932, 3rd Class Theol. Tripos, 1932, Asst Master, Bickley Hall Sch., Kent, 1932-34; Curate, Ealing Parish Church, 1934-37; Chap. Oakham Sch., 1937-42. Chap. RAFVR, 1942-46 (despatches), Warden St Michael's House, Hamburg, 1946-49; Gen. Sec. SCM in Schools, 1949-53; Rector St Helen's Bishopsgate with St Martin Outwich, 1951-53; Vicar of Horsham, Sussex, 1953-59; Surrogate and Rural Dean of Horsham, 1954-59; Archdeacon of Northampton and Rector of Ecton, 1959-64. Examiner, Religious Knowledge, Southern Univs Jt Bd, 1954-58; Examining Chaplain to Bishop of Peterborough, 1959. Chairman Christian Aid Dept, British Council of Churches, 1964. Mem. of Convocation, 1959. *Publication:* Daily Prayer at Oakham School, 1938. *Recreations:* tennis, golf, cricket, photography. *Address:* 19 Campden Hill Square, W8. *T:* 01-727 9818. *Club:* United Services.

**KENSWOOD,** 2nd Baron, *cr* 1951; **John Michael Howard Whitfield;** *b* 6 April 1930; *o s* of 1st Baron Kenswood; *S* father, 1963; *m* 1951, Deirdre Anna Louise, *d* of Colin Malcolm Methven, Errol, Perthshire; four *s* one *d*. *Educ:* Trinity Coll. Sch., Ontario; Harrow; Grenoble Univ.; Emmanuel Coll., Cambridge (BA). *Heir:* *s* Hon. Michael Christopher Whitfield, *b* 3 July 1955. *Address:* Manor Farm, Roch, Haverfordwest, Pembrokeshire. *T:* Camrose 359.

**KENT, Arthur William,** CMG 1966; OBE 1950; Chief Executive, Transport Holdings of Zambia Ltd; *b* 22 March 1913; *s* of Howard and Eliza Kent; *m* 1st, 1944, Doris Jane (*née* Crowe; marr. diss., 1958); one *s* one *d*; 2nd, 1958, Mary (*née* Martin). Deputy City Treasurer, Nairobi, 1946-48, City Treasurer, 1948-65. FIMTA; FCA. *Address:* PO Box 2404, Lusaka, Zambia. *T:* (office) 74295, (home) 50731. *Clubs:* East India and Sports; Muthaiga Country (Nairobi); Ndola; Lusaka Sports.

**KENT, Sir Harold Simcox,** GCB 1963 (KCB 1954; CB 1946); Standing Counsel to Church Assembly since 1964; *b* 11 Nov. 1903; *s* of late P. H. B. Kent, OBE, MC; *m* 1930, Zillah Lloyd; one *s* (one *d* decd). *Educ:* Rugby School; Merton Coll., Oxford. Barrister-at-law, 1928; Parliamentary Counsel to the Treasury, 1940; HM Procurator-General and Treasury Solicitor, 1953-63. *Address:* 36 Whitehall, SW1. *T:* 01-930 1234; Oak Meadow, Broad Campden, Glos. *T:* Campden 421. *Club:* Oxford and Cambridge University.

**KENT, Percy Edward,** DSc, PhD, FRS, FGS; Chief Geologist, British Petroleum Co. Ltd, since 1966; Adrian Visiting Fellow, University of Leicester, since 1967; *b* 18 March 1913; *s* of Edward Louis Kent and Annie Kate (*née* Woodward); *m* 1940, Margaret Betty Hood, JP; two *d*. *Educ:* West Bridgford Gram. Sch.; Nottingham Univ. 1st cl. hons BSc London 1934; PhD 1941; DSc 1959; FRS 1966. RAFVR, 1941-46 (despatches, 1944). Legion of Merit (USA), 1946. Geologist to E African Archæological Expedn (L. S. B. Leakey), 1934-35. Joined Anglo Iranian Oil (later BP), 1936; responsible for geological survey work in UK, Iran, E Africa, Papua, Canada and Alaska, for BP, 1946-60; managerial duties in BP, 1960-65. Pres. Yorks Geol Soc., 1964-66; Chm., Petroleum Exploration Soc. of Great Britain, 1966; Member: Council, Royal Soc., 1968-69; Council for Science Policy, 1968-. Murchison Medal, Geological Soc. of London, 1969. *Publications:* many papers on stratigraphy and structural geology, Britain and abroad. *Recreations:* walking, gardening, landscape painting, choral singing. *Address:* 38 Rodney Road, West Bridgford, Nottingham. *T:* Nottingham 23-13-55. *Club:* Geological Society Club.

**KENT, Rockwell;** *b* Tarrytown, New York, 21 June 1882; *s* of Rockwell and Sara Holgate Kent; *m* 1st, Kathleen Whiting; two *s* three *d*; 2nd, Frances Lee; 3rd, Sally Johnstone. *Educ:* Columbia Univ. Architect, painter, wood-engraver, lithographer, writer, traveller, editor, illustrator, carpenter, fisherman, dairy farmer. Hon. Member: Acad. of Fine Arts of USSR; Soc. of Typographic Arts; Internat.

Longshoremen's and Warehousemen's Union; Mem., Nat. Inst. of Arts and Letters. Lenin Peace Prize, 1967. *Publications:* Wilderness, 1919; Voyaging, 1924; N by E, 1930; Rockwellkentiana, 1933; Salamina, 1935; This is My Own, 1940; It's Me O Lord (Autobiography); Of Men and Mountains, 1959; Rockwell Kent's Greenland Journal, 1963; miscellaneous reviews, essays, etc. *Address:* Au Sable Forks, New York, USA.

**KENT, Ronald Clive,** CB 1965; Deputy Under-Secretary of State, Ministry of Defence since 1967; *b* 3 Aug. 1916; *s* of Dr Hugh Braund Kent and Margaret Mary Kent; *m* 1965, Mary Moyles Havell; one step-*s* one step-*d*. *Educ:* Rugby Sch.; Brasenose Coll., Oxford. Air Ministry, 1939; Royal Artillery, 1940-45; Air Ministry, 1945-58; Asst Under-Sec. of State, Air Min., 1958-63, Min. of Defence, 1963-67. *Address:* 16 St Bernards, Chichester Road, Croydon, Surrey. *Club:* Royal Automobile.

**KENT-HUGHES, Hon. Sir Wilfred;** *see* Hon. Sir W. S. K. Hughes.

**KENTNER, Louis;** Concert Pianist and Composer; *b* Silesia, 19 July 1905; *s* of Julius and Gisela Kentner; *m* 1931, Ilona Kabos (marr. diss. 1945); *m* 1946, Griselda Gould, *d* of late Evelyn Suart; no *c*. *Educ:* Budapest, Royal Academy of Music (at age of 6) under Arnold Szekely, Leo Weiner, Zoltan Kodaly. Concert début Budapest at age of 15; awarded a Chopin prize, Warsaw, a Liszt prize, Budapest. Has given concerts in most European countries; toured South Africa, Far East, New Zealand, Australia, S America; 6 tours of USA; three tours of USSR. First world performance, Bartok 2nd Piano Concerto, Budapest, and first European performance, Bartok 3rd Piano Concerto, London, 1946; many first performances of Kodaly and Weiner's Piano works. Came to England, 1935; naturalised British, 1946; since residence in England played much modern British music. Played numerous troop concerts during War of 1939-45. Has made many gramophone recordings. Pres., Liszt Society. Hon. RAM 1970. *Publications:* Three Sonatinas for Piano, 1939; two essays in Liszt Symposium, 1967. *Recreations:* reading, chess playing. *Address:* 1 Mallord Street, Chelsea, SW3.

**KENWORTHY,** family name of **Baron Strabolgi.**

**KENWORTHY, Cecil;** Registrar of Probate and Divorce Division of High Court of Justice, since 1968; *b* 22 Jan. 1918; *s* of John T. and Lucy Kenworthy; *m* 1944, Beryl Joan Willis; no *c*. *Educ:* Manchester and Bristol Grammar Schools. Entered Principal Probate Registry, 1936. *Publication:* (co-editor) supplements to Rayden on Divorce, 1967, 1968. *Address:* 7 Arlington House, EC1R 1XB. *T:* 01-837 6166.

**KENYA, Archbishop of,** since 1970; **Most Rev. Festo Habakkuk Olang';** *b* 11 Nov. 1914; *m* 1937, Eseri D. Olang'; four *s* eight *d*. *Educ:* Alliance High School. Teacher, 1936-43; ordained 1945; consecrated Assistant Bishop of Mombasa in Namirembe Cathedral, by Archbishop of Canterbury, 1955; Bishop of Maseno, 1961. *Address:* PO Box 502, Nairobi, Kenya. *T:* 20207.

**KENYATTA, Jomo;** (First) President of the Republic of Kenya since Dec. 1964; Prime Minister, also Minister for Internal Security and Defence, and Foreign Affairs, Kenya, since 1963; *b* (approximately) 1889; *m*; four *s* four *d*. *Educ:* Church of Scotland Mission, Kikuyu, Kenya; London School of Economics, Great Britain. General Sec., Kikuyu Central Assoc., 1922. Founded first African-owned journal, Mwigwithania, 1928; sent by Kenya Africans to Britain to press case for Independence; travelled extensively in Europe: represented Ethiopia at the League of Nations, briefly, during war; Pres., first Pan-African Congress, Manchester, Gt Britain, 1945; Pres., Kenya African Union, 1947-52; imprisoned and detained by British, 1952-61; elected *in absentia,* while in restriction at Lodwar, Pres., Kenya African National Union, 1960; MLC 1962; Minister of State for Constitutional Affairs and Economic Planning, 1962. Hon. LLD: University of E Africa, 1965; Manchester Univ., 1966. *Publications:* Facing Mt Kenya; Kenya, The Land of Conflict; My People of Kikuyu; Harambee. *Address:* PO Box 30510, Nairobi, Kenya. *T:* Nairobi 27411; Ichaweri, Gatundu, Kenya.

**KENYON,** family name of **Baron Kenyon.**

**KENYON,** 5th Baron, *cr* 1788; **Lloyd Tyrell-Kenyon,** Bt 1784; Baron of Gredington, 1788; JP, DL; FSA; Captain late Royal Artillery, TA; *b* 13 Sept. 1917; *o s* of 4th Baron and Gwladys Julia (*d* 1965), *d* of late Col H. R. Lloyd Howard, CB; *S* father, 1927; *m* 1946, Leila Mary, *d* of Comdr J. W. Cookson, RN, Strand Hill, Winchelsea, and *widow* of Lt Hugo Peel, Welsh Guards; three *s* one *d*. *Educ:* Eton; Magdalene Coll., Cambridge. BA (Cambridge), 1950. 2nd Lt Shropshire Yeo. 1937; Lt RA, TA, retired (ill-health) 1943 with hon. rank of Capt. Director: Lloyd's Bank Ltd, 1962- (Chm. North West Bd); National Provident Institution, 1962. President: University Coll. of N Wales, Bangor, 1947-; Nat. Museum of Wales, 1952-57. Trustee, Nat. Portrait Gall., 1953-, Chm., 1966-; Chairman: Wrexham Powys and Mawddach Hosp. Management Cttee, 1960-; Friends of the Nat. Libraries, 1962-; Flint Agricultural Exec. Cttee, 1964-. Member: Standing Commn on Museums and Galleries, 1953-60; Welsh Regional Hosp. Bd, 1958-63; Council for Professions Supplementary to Medicine, 1961-65; Royal Commn on Historical MSS, 1966-; Bd of Governors, Welbeck Coll. Chief Comr for Wales, Boy Scouts' Assoc., 1948-65. DL Co. Flint, 1948; CC Flint, 1946 (Chm., 1954-55). Hon. LLD Wales, 1958. *Heir: s* Hon. Lloyd Tyrell-Kenyon, *b* 13 July 1947. *Address:* Gredington, Whitchurch, Salop. *TA:* Hanmer 330. *T:* Hanmer 330. *Clubs:* Cavalry, Beefsteak.

**KENYON, Alec Hindle,** CEng, FIEE; Chairman, East Midlands Electricity Board, 1965-69, retired; *b* 11 June 1905; *s* of late William Kenyon, Accrington, Lancs; *m* 1932, Elizabeth Mary Wollaston; one *s* one *d*. *Educ:* Bootham Sch., York. Accrington Corp., Northampton Electric Light & Power Co., and North Eastern Electricity Supply Co.; Liaison Officer, North Eastern Electricity Board, 1948-59; Dep. Chm., East Midlands Electricity Board, 1959-64. Chm., North Eastern Centre, Instn of Electrical Engineers, 1955-56. *Recreations:* walking and gardening. *Address:* 8 Oakwood, Hexham, Northumberland.

**KENYON, Sir Bernard,** Kt 1962; Clerk of the Peace and County Council of West Riding of Yorkshire, 1943-69, retired; *b* 28 June 1904; *s* of late Harry Kenyon, Penzance, Cornwall; *m* 1936, Doreen Mary, *d* of late Lawrence Richmond, CBE; one *s* two *d*. *Educ:* Taunton Sch., Taunton; Sidney Sussex Coll., Cambridge. Dep. Clerk of the West Riding County Council, 1941-43. *Address:* Hall Cliffe House, Horbury, Yorks. *T:* Horbury 302. *Club:* Union.

**KENYON, Clifford,** CBE 1966; JP; farmer; *b* 11 Aug. 1896; *m* 1922, Doris Muriel Lewis, Herne Hill, London; three *s* two *d*. *Educ:* Brighton Grove Coll., Manchester; Manchester Univ. Joined Labour Party, 1922; Mem. Rawtenstall Council, 1923; Mayor, 1938-42, resigned from Council, 1945. MP (Lab) Chorley Div. of Lancs, 1945-70. *Address:* Scarr Barn Farm, Crawshawbooth, Rossendale, Lancs. *T:* Rossendale 5703.

**KENYON, Kathleen Mary,** CBE 1954; MA; DLitt, DLit, LHD, FBA; FSA; Principal of St Hugh's College, Oxford since 1962; *b* 5 Jan. 1906; *e d* of late Sir Frederic G. Kenyon, GBE, KCB. *Educ:* St Paul's Girls' Sch.; Somerville Coll., Oxford. Asst at excavations, British Assoc's expedition to Zimbabwe, S Rhodesia, 1929, Verulamium, 1930-35, Joint Expedition to Samaria, Palestine, 1931-34; Dir, excavations at Jewry Wall site, Leicester, 1936-39, Viroconium, Salop, 1936-37, the Wrekin, Salop, 1939; Southwark, 1945-48; Breedon-on-the-Hill, Leics, 1946; Sutton Walls, Herefords, 1948-51; Sabratha, Tripolitania, 1948-49, -51; Jericho, Jordan, 1952-58; Jerusalem, Jordan, 1961-67. Sec., University of London Inst. of Archæology, 1935-48; acting Dir, 1942-46; Sec., Council for British Archæology, 1944-49; Lecturer in Palestinian Archæology, University of London, Institute of Archæology, 1948-62; Dir, British Sch. of Archæology in Jerusalem, 1951-66. Divisional Comdt and Sec., Hammersmith Div., British Red Cross Soc., 1939-42; Dir, Youth Dept British Red Cross Soc., 1942-45. Norton Lecturer, Archæological Institute of America, 1959; Schweich Lecturer, British Academy, 1963. Hon. Fellow, Somerville Coll., 1960. Trustee, British Museum, 1965. Hon. DLitt Exon. *Publications:* Verulamium Theatre Excavations, 1935; Excavations at Viroconium, 1940; Excavations on the Wrekin, 1943; Excavations at the Jewry Wall Site, Leicester, 1948; Excavations at Breedon-on-the-Hill, Leicester, 1950; Beginning in Archæology, 1952; Excavations at Sutton Walls, Herefordshire, 1954; Digging Up Jericho, 1957; contributor to Samaria–Sebaste, 1, 1942 and 3, 1958; Excavations at Jericho I, 1960 and II, 1965; Archæology in the Holy Land, 1960; Amorites and Canaanites, 1966; Jerusalem in the Light of Recent Discoveries, 1967; Royal Cities of the Old Testament, 1970. *Recreation:* gardening. *Address:* St Hugh's College, Oxford; Old Brands Lodge, Terriers, High Wycombe, Bucks. *T:* High Wycombe 21089. *Club:* University Women's.

**KEOGH, Charles Alfred,** FRCS; Hon. Consulting Surgeon, Ear, Nose and Throat Department, The London Hospital and Medical Coll. *Educ:* London Hosp. Comdr of Royal Norwegian Order of St Olaf, 1943. *Address:* 21 The Lodge, Kensington Park Gardens, W11.

**KEPPEL,** family name of **Earl of Albemarle.**

**KEPPEL-COMPTON, Robert Herbert,** CMG 1953; *b* 11 Dec. 1900; *s* of late J. H. Keppel-Compton, Southampton; *m* 1930, Marjorie, *yr d* of late Rev. W. B. Preston; one *s* one *d*. *Educ:* Oakham Sch.; Sidney Sussex Coll., Cambridge. BA, LLB Cantab. Entered Colonial Administrative Service, 1923. Dep. Provincial Commissioner, 1945; Development Sec., 1946; Provincial Commissioner, Nyasaland, 1949-55; retired from Colonial Service, 1955. *Address:* Higher Leigh, Kingsbridge, Devon.

**KER;** *see* Innes-Ker, family name of **Duke of Roxburghe.**

**KER, Douglas R. E.;** *see* Edwardes-Ker.

**KER, Frederick Innes,** CBE 1943; MEIC; Hon. President of the Canadian Daily Newspapers Association; *s* of late Ven. John Ker, DD, LLD, and Mary Thomson Cousins, Montreal; *m* 1919, Amy (*decd*), *d* of late F. N. Southam, OBE, Montreal; three *s* one *d*. *Educ:* Montreal High Sch.; McGill Univ. Civil Engineer, 1909-21; entered Journalism, 1921. Pres. Canadian Daily Newspapers Assoc., 1930; Editor and Publisher, The Hamilton Spectator, Hamilton, Ont, 1930-51; Pres. Canadian Press, 1946-48. Delegate to various Imperial Press Conferences, 1930-; Hon. Life Mem., Commonwealth Press Union. Chm. National Press Cttee on War Finance, 1940-46. An Hon. Governor of McMaster Univ., Hamilton, Ont. *Publications:* Canada and Intra-Empire co-operation, 1938; Press Promotion of War Finance, 1946. *Recreations:* yachting, golf, curling. *Address:* Malahide House, Port Talbot, RR1 Fingal, Ont, Canada. *Clubs:* University, Montreal (Montreal); Hamilton Golf (Hamilton).

**KER, K(eith) R(eginald) Welbore,** OBE 1964; Consul-General, Cape Town, since 1970; *b* 8 Aug. 1913; *s* of late Reginald Arthur Ker and Morna, *d* of Welbore MacCarthy, sometime Bishop of Grantham; *m* 1954, Marisa (*née* Ummarino), formerly Lo Bianco; three *s* two *d* (one step *s* one step *d*). *Educ:* Malvern Coll. Business, 1932-39. Served in HM Army, 1939-46, Major 1945 (despatches). Apptd British Consul, Bolzano, 1946; Second Sec., Rio de Janeiro, 1948; transf. to Stockholm, 1950; to Singapore, 1951; acting Consul, Hanoi, 1952; First Sec., Belgrade, 1953-55; transf. to Rangoon, 1956; to Saigon, 1957; to FO, 1957; to Hamburg, 1958; to Bonn, 1959; HM Consul-Gen., Hanover, 1961-64; First Sec., 1965-67, Counsellor, 1967-69, Lisbon. *Recreations:* walking, tennis, collecting water-colour drawings. *Address:* c/o Cox's & King's Branch, Lloyds Bank Ltd, 6 Pall Mall, SW1. *Club:* Naval and Military.

**KER, Neil Ripley,** FBA 1958; Reader in Palæography, Oxford University, 1946-68, Reader Emeritus since 1968; Fellow of Magdalen College, 1946-68, Emeritus Fellow, since 1970; *b* 28 May 1908; *s* of Robert MacNeil Ker and Lucy Winifred Strickland-Constable; *m* 1938, Jean Frances, *d* of Brig. C. B. Findlay; one *s* three *d*. *Educ:* Eton Coll.; Magdalen Coll., Oxford. BLitt (Oxon), 1933; Lecturer in Palæography, Oxford, 1936-46; James P. R. Lyell Reader in Bibliography, Oxford, 1952-53; Sandars Reader in Bibliography, Cambridge, 1955. Sir Israel Gollancz Mem. Prize, British Acad., 1959; Edwards Lecturer, Glasgow, 1960. Hon. DLitt (Reading), 1964. *Publications:* Medieval Libraries of Great Britain, 1941 (2nd edn 1964); Pastedowns in Oxford Bindings, 1954; Catalogue of Manuscripts containing Anglo-Saxon, 1957; English Manuscripts in the Century after the Norman Conquest, 1960; Medieval Manuscripts in British Libraries: I, London, 1969; Ed. The Parochial Libraries of the Church of England, 1959; articles and reviews in Medium Aevum, etc. *Recreation:* mountain walking. *Address:* 22 London Street, Edinburgh EH3 6NA.

**KERANS, Comdr John Simon,** DSO 1949; RN retired; *b* 30 June 1915; *m* 1946, Stephanie Campbell Shires; two *d*. *Educ:* RN Coll., Dartmouth. Cadet and Midshipman, HMS Rodney, Home Fleet, 1932-33; Midshipman and Sub-Lt HMS Cornwall, 1933-35; RN Coll., Greenwich, 1935-37; China Station, 1937-39. Served War of 1939-45: Staff, Chief of Intelligence Staff, Far East, Hong Kong and

Singapore, 1939; HMS Naiad, Home and Medit. Stations, 1940-42; Staff Officer (Intelligence), Staff C-in-C, Medit. and Levant, 1942-43; 1st Lt, HMS Icarus, N Atlantic, 1943-44; Staff, C-in-C, Portsmouth, 1944; i/c HMS Blackmore (Lt-Comdr) 1944; Security Intelligence, Hong Kong, 1947; on loan to Malayan Police, Kuala Lumpur, 1948; Asst Naval Attaché, Nanking, 1949, joined frigate Amethyst after her attack by Communist forces (DSO), 1949; Comdr Dec. 1949; RN Staff Course, Greenwich, 1950; Head Far East Section, Naval Intelligence Admiralty, 1950-52; i/c HMS Rinaldo, 1953-54; Brit. Naval Attaché, Bangkok, Phnom Penh, Ventiane, Saigon and Rangoon, 1954-55; Sen. Officers' Technical Course Portsmouth, 1957; retired RN, 1958. MP (C) The Hartlepools, 1959-64. *Address:* 26 Riddlesdown Avenue, Purley CR2 1JG. *T:* 01-660 3614. *Clubs:* Naval and Military; Littlehampton Sailing; 1900.

**KERBY, Captain Henry Briton,** MP (C) for West Sussex (Arundel and Shoreham Division) since March 1954; *b* 11 Dec. 1914; *m* 1947, Enid, *d* of late Judge M. F. P. Herchenroder, CMG, CBE; two *d. Educ:* on Continent, and Highgate Sch. Regular Army, 1933-37; Hon. Attaché, Diplomatic Service, Brit. Legation, Riga, 1939-40; Actg Brit. Consul, Malmö, Sweden, 1940; specially employed under War Office, 1941-45. Contested Spelthorne (L), 1945, and Swansea (West) (C), 1951. Mem. of Parliamentary Delegation to Denmark, 1955, Israel, 1957, USSR, 1957, 1959, Nationalist China (Formosa), 1958, Federation of Rhodesia and Nyasaland, 1961. Member: Southampton Univ. Court, 1959-63; University of Sussex Court, 1961-68. FRGS 1962. Commander's Cross of Order of Polonia Restituta (Poland); Haakon VII Cross (Norway); Christian X pro Dania Medal (Denmark); Knight's Cross, 1st Cl. of Order of White Rose (Finland); Comdr, Royal Yugoslav Order of St Sava. *Address:* Hobbs Farm House, Yapton, Arundel, Sussex. *T:* Middleton-on-Sea 2012.

**KERENSKY, Dr Oleg Alexander,** CBE 1964; FRS 1970; Partner, Freeman Fox & Partners, Consulting Engineers, since 1955; *b* 16 April 1905; *s* of late Alexander F. Kerensky and of Olga (*née* Baronovsky); *m* 1928, Nathalie (*d* 1969), *d* of James and Dorothy Bely; one *s. Educ:* Russia, later small private sch. in England; Northampton Engrg Coll. (now The City Univ.). Jun. Asst, Oxford CC, 1926; Dorman Long & Co.: Asst Engr, Bridge Design Office, 1927-30, construction of Lambeth Bridge, 1930-32; Sen. Design Engr, Bridge Dept, 1932-37; Chief Engr and Sub-Agent: on construction of Wandsworth Bridge, Holloway Bros (London) Ltd, 1937-40; on Avonmouth Oil Jetty, 1940-43; Chief Engr, Mulberry Harbours, N Wales, 1943-45; Sen. Designer, Holloway Bros (London) Ltd, 1945-46; Principal Bridge Designer, Freeman Fox & Partners, 1946-55. Hon. Dr of Science, City Univ., 1967. *Publications:* numerous papers in learned jls. *Recreations:* bridge, croquet, swimming. *Address:* 72 Elizabeth Street, SW1. *T:* 01-235 7173. *Clubs:* Athenæum, Hurlingham.

**KERLE, Rt. Rev. Ronald Clive;** *see* Armidale, Bishop of.

**KERLEY, Peter James,** CVO 1952; CBE 1951; MD, FRCP, FFR, DMRE; Emeritus Consultant, X-Ray Department, Westminster Hospital; Emeritus consultant Adviser to Ministry of Health on radiology; Emeritus Consultant Radiologist to: King Edward VII Sanatorium, Midhurst; The National Heart Hospital; Ministry of Aviation; late Hon. Editor of the Journal of Faculty of Radiologists; President, Radiology Section, Royal Society of Medicine, 1939-40; President, Faculty of Radiologists, 1952-55; Röntgen Award, 1944; Examiner in radiology: Royal College of Physicians; University of Leeds; Faculty of Radiologists, University of Liverpool; *b* Dundalk, Ireland, 27 Oct. 1900; *s* of Michael and Matilda Kerley; *m* 1929, Olivia MacNamee, Enniskillen; two *d. Educ:* University Coll., Dublin (MB 1923 and MD 1932); University of Vienna (Diploma, 1924); Cambridge Univ. (DMRE 1925). Major RAMC 1939-44. FRSM; Hon. Fellow: Amer. Coll. of Radiology; Australasian Coll. of Radiology; Faculty of Radiologists of Ireland; Radiological Soc. of Chicago; Radiological Soc. of Toronto. OStJ 1958. *Publications:* Recent Advances in Radiology, 2nd Edn; (with Shanks) A Text-Book of Radiology in 6 vols; also various articles on diseases of the Chest and Digestive Tract. *Recreations:* golf, fishing. *Address:* 10 Upper Wimpole Street, W1. *T:* 01-935 1918; 9 Heath Rise, SW15. *Clubs:* Buck's, White's, Travellers'; Royal Wimbledon Golf.

**KERMACK, Stuart Grace,** CBE 1955; *b* 11 April 1888; 2nd *s* of Henry Kermack, Advocate; *m* 1922, Nell P., *y d* of Thomas White, SSC; two *s* one *d. Educ:* Edinburgh Academy; Fettes Coll.; Edinburgh Univ. MA, LLB, Edinburgh Univ.; Scots Bar, 1911; served European War, RFA (TF) Capt., Gallipoli, Egypt, Palestine; Judge in Sudan, 1918-19; Judicial Service, Palestine, 1920-30; Lecturer in Jurisprudence, Edinburgh Univ., 1933-36; Sheriff-Substitute of Lanarks at Glasgow, 1936-55; Sheriff-Substitute of Renfrew and Argyll at Oban, 1955-62. King Haakon VII Liberty Cross, 1948. *Publications:* Criminal Procedure in Palestine, 1927; Law of Scotland: Sources and Juridical Organisation, 1933; Contributions to Juridical Review, Stair Society's Sources of Scots Law, etc. *Address:* An Sealladh, Connel, Argyll.

*See also S. O. Kermack.*

**KERMACK, Stuart Ogilvy;** Sheriff Substitute of Inverness, Moray, Nairn and Ross and Cromarty at Elgin and Nairn, since 1965; *b* 9 July 1934; *s* of Stuart Grace Kermack, *qv*; *m* 1961, Barbara Mackenzie, BSc; three *s* one *d. Educ:* Glasgow Academy; Jesus Coll., Oxford; Glasgow Univ.; Edinburgh Univ. BA Oxon (Jurisprudence), 1956; LLB Glasgow, 1959. Elected to Scots Bar, 1959. *Publications:* articles in legal journals. *Recreation:* hill walking. *Address:* 7 Findhorn, Forres, Moray. *T:* Findhord 317.

**KERMODE, Air Vice-Marshal Alfred Cotterill,** CBE 1956 (OBE 1944); MA; CEng; FRAeS; Royal Air Force; retired; Aeronautical adviser to Sir Isaac Pitman & Sons Ltd, 1961; *b* 30 Jan. 1897; *s* of late Rev. S. A. P. Kermode, Isle of Man, and late Lucy Emma (*née* Lynam); *m* 1946, Rose Price Nowell (*née* Roberts); three *s. Educ:* Dragon Sch., Oxford; Oundle Sch. (Scholar); Clare Coll., Cambridge (Scholar). Served European War as Pilot in RNAS and RAF, 1916-19. Experimental flying (as technical observer), RAE, Farnborough, 1921-23; entered RAF Educl Service, 1923; served at schs of tech. trng, Cranwell and Halton, 1923-36; Sch. of Aeronautical Engineering, Henlow, 1936-38; RAF Coll., Cranwell, 1938-39; served War of 1939-45, as Chief Ground Instructor: Central Flying Sch., Upavon, 1940-41; No. 3 BFTS, Oklahoma, USA, 1941-42; ECFS, Hullavington, 1942-46; Sen. Tutor (Aeronautical Science and Engineering), RAF Coll., Cranwell, 1946-48; Comd Educn Officer: Far East Air Force, 1948-51; Maintenance Comd, 1951-52;

Technical Training Command, 1952-55; Dir of Educational Services, Air Ministry 1955-60; retired, 1960. ADC to the Queen, 1953-56. *Publications:* Mechanics of Flight, 1930; Flight without Formulae, 1938; The Aeroplane Structure, 1938; (co-author) Hydrofoils, 1966. *Recreations:* Cine-photography, writing, dramatic production, travel, gardening. *Address:* Staplewood, Nether Wallop, Hants. *T:* Wallop 333.

**KERMODE, Prof. John Frank,** MA; Lord Northcliffe Professor of Modern English Literature, University College, London, since 1967; *b* 29 Nov. 1919; *s* of late John Pritchard Kermode and late Doris Pearl Kermode; *m* 1947, Maureen Eccles (marr. diss. 1970); twin *s* and *d. Educ:* Douglas High Sch.; Liverpool Univ. BA 1940; War Service (Navy), 1940-46; MA 1947; Lecturer, King's Coll., Newcastle, in the University of Durham, 1947-49; Lecturer in the University of Reading, 1949-58; John Edward Taylor Prof. of English Literature in the University of Manchester, 1958-65; Winterstoke Prof. of English in the University of Bristol, 1965-67. Co-editor, Encounter, 1966-67. FRSL 1958. Mem. Arts Council, 1968-; Chm., Poetry Book Soc., 1968-. *Publications:* (Ed.) Shakespeare. The Tempest (Arden Edition), 1954; Romantic Image, 1957; John Donne, 1957; The Living Milton, 1960; Wallace Stevens, 1960; Puzzles & Epiphanies, 1962; The Sense of an Ending, 1967; Continuities, 1968, etc; contrib. Review of Eng. Studies, Partisan Review, New York Review, New Statesman, etc. *Address:* University College, WC1. *T:* 01-387 7050. *Club:* Garrick.

**KERNOFF, Harry,** RHA 1935; Professional Artist, Portrait, Landscape and Mural; *b* London, 9 Jan. 1900; *s* of Isaac Kernoff (Russian Jewish) and Katherine A'Barbanelle (Old Spanish Jewish Stock), family migrated to Dublin, May 1914. *Educ:* Elementary Sch., London; Metropolitan Sch. of Art, Dublin. All Ireland Taylor Art Scholarship, 1923; Exhibited yearly RHA, from 1926; 16 One-man Exhibitions in Dublin Yearly, 1926-58; 1 Ex. Gieves Gallery, London, 1931; One-man Show, White Gallery, 1938; 1 Ex. Castlebar, Co. Mayo, 1947; Exhibited Mural at Royal Academy, 1931, and in Paris, Chicago, New York, Amsterdam, Cork, Glasgow and Wales 1953, etc.; 80 small oils, Toronto, 1965. *Work in public collections:* 3 Pictures in Belfast Art Gallery (1 water colour, 2 woodcuts); 2 Oil Paintings Municipal Gallery, Dublin (Street Scene, Brazen Head); 2 Oil Paintings Limerick Art Gallery; 2 Oil Paintings in Waterford Art Gall.; Oil Painting in Castlebar Gallery, 1947; 3 Oils in Killarney Art Gallery; 1 Oil in Monaco. Pictures in World's Fair, Glasgow, 1938; and World's Fair, New York, 1939; Oil, Killarney Landscape, in Irish Legation, Washington, 1959-63; Oil, Irish Volunteer, purchased by Irish Government, 1946; Oil, Turf-Girl, Tel-Aviv, 1950; Oil, Thomas Ashe, Teacher's Club, 1953; Oil, Berkeley Univ., Calif, USA, 1966; 2 Portraits, National Gall. of Ireland, 1968. 10 works, Arts Festival in Nova Scotia, 1957; Ex. Ritchie Gall., (NS), Dublin, 1958 (oils, pastels, water colours); Ex. Lugano, 1964; Exhibn Robertstown, Kildare, 1968 (40 portraits from James Joyce to Brendan Behan). Paintings in many private collections. Sold Portraits (in 1965) of: James Joyce (USA); W. B. Yeats (England); James Stephen; Brendan Behan; Oliver St John Gogarty (USA); Sean O'Casey, etc. Interested in Modern Movements in Art. Mem. Royal Dublin Society, 1947-. *Publications:* 1 Colour Reprod. in Twelve Irish Artists, 1940; Ltd Ed. Book of Woodcuts (220 signed and numbered copies), 1942; Book of New-Woodcuts (Ltd Ed. 300 signed), 1944, (Ltd Ed. 400 signed and numbered), 1951; Calendar for Egan's Tullamore, 1952; Calendar for Cherry-Tree, Dublin, 1955; Woodcuts in Ireland of the Welcomes, 1955. 12 Woodcuts in New Irish Poets, USA, 1948; Woodcuts in Bi. Cen. Guinness Harp, 1959; 6 Oils, Dublin Scenes, in Irish Tatler, 1959; (new 4 colour print, 16″ × 16″) A Bird Never Flew on One Wing, 1961; New Colour Prints, Old Claddagh, Galway, 1962. Illustrated: Centenary Books, 1946-; Storyteller's Childhood, 1947; Tinker Boy, 1955. *Recreations:* swimming, verse. *Address:* 13 Stamer Street, Dublin 8, Ireland. *T:* Dublin 751675. *Club:* United Arts (Dublin).

**KERR,** family name of **Marquess of Lothian** and **Baron Teviot.**

**KERR, Mrs Anne Patricia, (Mrs R. W. Kerr)**; *b* 24 March 1925; *d* of late Arnold Bersey and Kathleen (*née* Mitchell); *m* 1st, 1944, James Doran Clark; one *s*; 2nd, 1960, Russell Whiston Kerr, *qv. Educ:* St Paul's Girls' Sch. Served with WRNS, 1943-45. Worked in theatre, films, TV and radio as an actress, interviewer and broadcaster. Mem. of London CC, 1958-61 and 1961-65. MP (Lab) Rochester and Chatham, 1964-70. *Recreations:* travel, theatre, camping. *Address:* 37 Popes Avenue, Twickenham, Middx. *T:* 01-894 4343.

**KERR, Archibald Brown,** CBE 1968 (OBE 1945); TD; Surgeon i/c Wards, Western Infirmary, Glasgow, since 1954; Lecturer in Clinical Surgery, University of Glasgow, since 1946; *b* 17 Feb. 1907; *s* of late Robert Kerr and Janet Harvey Brown; *m* 1940, Jean Margaret, *d* of late John Cowan, MBE; two *d. Educ:* High Sch. and University of Glasgow. BSc 1927; MB, ChB 1929; FRFPSGlas. 1933; FRCSEd 1934; FRCSGlas. 1962. Asst to Prof. Path. Glasgow Univ., 1931-33; Surg. to Out-Patients, West. Infirm. Glasgow, 1932-39. Served in 156 (Lowland) Field Amb. and as Surgical Specialist, Officer in Charge of Surgical Div. and Col Comdg No. 23 (Scottish) Gen. Hosp., 1939-45. Surg. to Royal Alexandra Infirmary, Paisley, 1946-54; Asst Surg., West. Infirm., Glasgow, 1945-54. Pres. Royal Medico-Chirurgical Society of Glasgow, 1951-52; Pres., Royal College of Physicians and Surgeons of Glasgow, 1964-66. Mem., Western Regional Hosp. Bd. Periods on Council of RCPS Glasgow and RCS Edinburgh. *Publications:* contribs to Med. and Surg. Jls. *Recreation:* golf. *Address:* 9 Kirklee Road, Glasgow, W2. *T:* 041-339 2878. *Clubs:* College (University of Glasgow), Royal Scottish Automobile.

**KERR, Clark;** Professor of Industrial Relations, University of California at Berkeley, since 1945; Director, Carnegie Fund Study on Future of Higher Education, since 1967; *b* 17 May 1911; *s* of Samuel W. and Caroline Clark Kerr; *m* 1934, Catherine Spaulding; two *s* one *d. Educ:* Swarthmore Coll. (AB); Stanford Univ. (MA); University of Calif., Berkeley (PhD). Actg Asst Prof., Stanford Univ., 1939-40; Asst Prof., later Assoc. Prof., University of Washington, 1940-45; Prof., Dir, Inst. of Industrial Relations, University of Calif., Berkeley, 1945-52; Chancellor, University of Calif. at Berkeley, 1952-58; Pres., University of Calif, 1958-67. Govt service with US War Labor Board, 1942-45. Mem. Pres. Eisenhower's Commn on Nat. Goals, President Kennedy and President Johnson Cttee on Labor-Management Policy; Contract Arbitrator for: Boeing Aircraft Co. and Internat. Assoc. of Machinists, 1944-45; Armour & Co. and United Packinghouse Workers, 1945-47, 1949-52; Waterfront Employers' Assoc. and Internat.

Longshoremen's and Warehousemen's Union, 1946-47, etc. Member: Amer. Acad. of Arts and Sciences; Royal Economic Society; Amer. Econ. Assoc.; Nat. Acad. of Arbitrators, etc. Phi Beta Kappa, Kappa Sigma. Trustee, Rockefeller Foundation, 1960-; Chm., Armour Automation Cttee, 1959-, Hon. LLD: Swarthmore, 1952; Harvard, 1958; Princeton, 1959; Notre Dame, 1964; Chinese Univ. of Hong Kong, 1964; Rochester, 1967; Hon. DLitt, Strathclyde, 1965; Hon. DHC, Bordeaux, 1962, etc. *Publications:* Unions, Management and the Public (Jt), 1948 (rev. edn 1960); Industrialism and Industrial Man (jtly), 1960 (rev. edn 1964); The Uses of the University, 1963; Labor and Management in Industrial Society, 1964; Marshall, Marx and Modern Times, 1969; contribs to American Economic Review, Review of Economics and Statistics, Quarterly Jl of Economics, etc. *Recreation:* gardening. *Address:* 8300 Buckingham Drive, El Cerrito, Calif 94530, USA. *T:* 5244930. *Club:* Bohemian.

**KERR, Dr David Leigh;** *b* 25 March 1923; *s* of Myer Woolf Kerr and Paula (*née* Horowitz); *m* 1st, 1944, Aileen Baddington (marr. diss. 1969); two *s* one *d*; 2nd, 1970, Margaret Dunlop. *Educ:* Whitgift Sch., Croydon; Middlesex Hosp. Med. Sch., London. Hon. Sec., Socialist Medical Assoc., 1957-63; Hon. Vice-Pres., 1963-. LCC (Wandsworth, Central), 1958-65, and Coun., London Borough of Wandsworth, 1664-68. Contested (Lab) Wandsworth, Streatham (for Parlt), 1959; MP (Lab) Wandsworth Central, 1964-70. Family Doctor, Tooting, 1946-. Member: Royal Society of Medicine; Inter-departmental Cttee on Death Certification and Coroners. Governor, British Film Inst., 1966-. *Recreations:* gardening, photography, squash. *Address:* 222 Norbury Avenue, Thornton Heath, Surrey CR4 8AJ. *T:* 01-764 7654.

**KERR, Deborah Jane (Deborah Kerr Viertel);** Actress; *b* 30 Sept. 1921; *d* of Capt. Arthur Kerr-Trimmer; *m* 1st, 1945, Sqdn Ldr A. C. Bartley (marr. diss., 1959); two *d*; 2nd, 1960, Peter Viertel. *Educ:* Northumberland House, Clifton, Bristol. Open Air Theatre, Regent's Park, 1939, Oxford Repertory, 1939-40; after an interval of acting in films, appeared on West End Stage; Ellie Dunn in Heartbreak House, Cambridge Theatre, 1943; went to France, Belgium, and Holland for ENSA, playing in Gaslight, 1945. *Films:* Major Barbara, 1940; Love on the Dole, 1940-41; Penn of Pennsylvania, 1941; Hatter's Castle, 1942; The Day Will Dawn, 1942; Life and Death of Colonel Blimp, 1942-43; Perfect Strangers, 1944; I See a Dark Stranger, 1945; Black Narcissus, 1946; The Hucksters and If Winter Comes, 1947 (MGM, Hollywood); Edward My Son, 1948; Please Believe Me, 1949 (MGM, Hollywood); King Solomon's Mines, 1950; Quo Vadis, 1952; Prisoner of Zenda, Julius Caesar, Dream Wife, Young Bess (MGM), 1952; From Here to Eternity, 1953; The End of the Affair, 1955; The Proud and Profane, The King and I, 1956; Heaven Knows, Mr Allison, An Affair to Remember, Tea and Sympathy, 1957; Bonjour Tristesse, 1958; Separate Tables, The Journey, Count Your Blessings, 1959; The Sundowners, The Grass is Greener, The Naked Edge, The Innocents, 1961; The Chalk Garden, The Night of the Iguana, 1964; Casino Royale, 1967; Eye of the Devil, Prudence and the Pill, 1968; The Arrangement, 1970. New York Stage: Tea and Sympathy, 1953. *Address:* c/o MGM Studios, Culver City, Calif, USA.

**KERR, Donald Frederick,** CVO 1961; OBE 1960; Controller (Overseas), Central Office of Information, since 1963; *b* 20 April 1915; *s* of Dr David Kerr, Cheshire; *m* 1942, Elizabeth Hayward; two *s* one *d*. *Educ:* Sydney High Sch.; University of Sydney (BEcon). Served RAF (Navigator), SEAC, 1942-46. Deputy Director: British Information Services, New Delhi, 1947-53; UK Information Service, Ottawa, 1953-55; UK INformation Service, Toronto, 1955-56; Dir, UK Information Service in Canada, Ottawa, 1956-59; Dir, British Information Services in India, New Delhi, 1959-63; on secondment, Dir of Information, Commonwealth Secretariat, Sept. 1969-Sept. 1970. *Recreation:* golf. *Address:* 36 Murray Road, Wimbledon, SW19. *Clubs:* Royal Automobile; Royal Wimbledon Golf.

**KERR, Francis Robert Newsam,** OBE 1962; MC 1940; farmer since 1949; Vice Lieutenant of Berwickshire since 1970; *b* 12 Sept. 1916; *s* of Henry Francis Hobart Kerr and Gertrude Mary Kerr (*née* Anthony); *m* 1941, Anne Frederica Kitson; two *s* one *d*. *Educ:* Ampleforth College. Regular Officer, The Royal Scots, 1937-49; TA 1952-63; retired as Lt-Col. Member Berwickshire County Council, 1964-. *Recreations:* country pursuits. *Address:* Blanerne, Duns, Berwickshire. *T:* Cumledge 222. *Clubs:* Farmers'; Royal Scots (Edinburgh).

**KERR, Captain Frank Robison,** DSO 1915; MB ChB (Melbourne); DPH (Melbourne); MD (Melbourne); RAMC, SR; late Dep. Dir of Health for Victoria, Commonwealth Dept of Health, retired; Registrar, Anti-Cancer Council of Victoria; *b* Melbourne, Australia, 5 April 1889; *s* of John H. Kerr, Paymaster, Treasury, Melbourne; *m* 1916, Myrtle, *d* of John M'Meekin, Mortlake, Victoria; two *s* one *d*. *Educ:* Camberwell Grammar Sch. and Wesley Coll., Melbourne; Queen's Coll., University of Melbourne. Rhodes Scholar, Victoria, 1913; proceeded to Oxford (University Coll.), 1913-14, there studied physiology; served European War, 1914-19 (despatches, DSO, for splendid devotion to duty in peril of his own life at Cuinchy, Sept. 1915); Mem. of Royal Society of Australia. Congregational. *Publications:* Inquiry into Morbidity Statistics of Victorian State School Teachers, 1923; Inquiry into the Health of Workers in Gasmaking Plants, 1927; Foundations: The Building of a Man, 1939; Days after To-morrow, 1944; articles in scientific journals. *Recreations:* triple blue, Melbourne, in cricket, football, athletics; 5 miles cross-country champion, Victoria, 1910, etc; formerly hiking, mountaineering. *Address:* 48 Wentworth Avenue, Canterbury, Melbourne, Vic. 3126, Australia. *T:* 839094. *Club:* Melbourne Cricket (Melbourne).

**KERR, Sir Hamilton (William),** 1st Bt, *cr* 1957; MA; *b* 1 Aug. 1903; *s* of Henry S. Kerr, Long Island, New York, and Olive Grace (who *m* 2nd, 1909, 3rd Baron Greville, OBE), *d* of J. Grace of Leybourne Grange, Kent. *Educ:* Eton; Balliol Coll., Oxford; MA Oxon and Cantab. Oxford Running Blue, half mile; worked on Daily Mail and Daily Telegraph. Flying Officer No. 909 (County of Essex) balloon Sqdn AAF, 1939; Flt Lt, 1941. MP (C), Oldham, 1931-45. Parliamentary Private Sec. to Mr Duff Cooper when First Lord of the Admiralty; Parliamentary Private Sec. to Captain H. H. Balfour, Under-Sec. of State for Air, 1942-45; Parliamentary Sec. Ministry of Health, 1945; Parliamentary Private Sec. to Mr Harold Macmillan when Minister of Defence, 1954, when Sec. of State for Foreign Affairs, 1955 and when Chancellor of Exchequer, 1955-56; MP (C) Cambridge, 1950-66. Delegate to Consultative Assembly of

Council of Europe, Strasbourg, 1952. Chancellor, Primrose League, 1961-63. Master, Worshipful Company of Pattenmakers, 1966-67. Mem. St John's Coll., Cambridge. Chevalier de la Légion d'Honneur, 1960. *Recreations:* tennis, painting. *Address:* 71 Westminster Gardens, Marsham Street, SW1; The Mill House, Whittlesford, Cambridge. *Clubs:* Carlton, Brooks's.

**KERR, Maj.-Gen. Sir (Harold) Reginald,** KBE, *cr* 1946; CB 1945; MC 1918; MInstT; psc; *b* 22 April 1897; *s* of H. F. Kerr; *m* 1921, Helen Margaret, *d* of B. M. Tuckett; two *s*. *Educ:* Bedford Sch.; Royal Military College, Sandhurst. Commissioned 1914 in ASC and served as a Regimental Officer and on the staff in France and Flanders, 1914-19, and subsequently on the Staff with the army of occupation in Germany until 1920. Was Instructor at Royal Military College, 1924-28; Adjutant, RASC Training Coll., 1929-30; Student Staff Coll., 1931-32; Staff Officer, Sudan, 1934; Staff Officer, 3rd Div., 1935-36; Chief Instructor at Royal Army Service Corps Training Centre, 1937-39; Instructor in the Senior Wing Staff Coll., 1939-40; Dep. Quartermaster-Gen., British Army Staff, Washington, June 1941-Nov. 1942; Maj.-Gen. i/c Administration, Eastern Command, Dec. 1942-May 1943; Dir of Supplies and Transport, War Office, 1943-46; Maj.-Gen. i/c Administration, Far East Land Forces, 1946-48; retd 1949. Divisional Manager, British Road Services, Midland Div., 1949-54; Chm. and Gen. Manager, British Waterways, 1955-62; Consultant, British Waterways Board, 1963. Col Comdt, RASC, 1949-59. *Recreation:* four-in-hand driving. *Address:* Timber Lodge, Lyme Regis, Dorset. *T:* Lyme Regis 2772. *Club:* Army and Navy.

**KERR, Lt-Col Sir Howard,** KCVO 1948 (CVO 1942; MVO 1929); CMG 1935; OBE 1922; Equerry to Duke of Gloucester, 1924-46, Comptroller, 1946-50, Extra Equerry since 1950; *s* of late Capt. Walter Raleigh Kerr, *g s* of Lord Robert Kerr, and of Annabel, *d* of Hon. James Jackson Jarves, Boston, Mass.; *m* Christina, *d* of late Arthur Ram, of Ramsfort, County Wexford; three *s*. *Educ:* Lower Canada Coll., Montreal; Trinity Coll., Cambridge. Joined 11th Hussars, 1914; served European War, 1914-19; ADC to Viscount Fitzalan of Derwent, Lord Lieutenant of Ireland, 1921-22; Private Chamberlain to the Pope, 1928. Accompanied Duke of Gloucester on Garter Mission to Japan, 1929, and on visit to Australasia, 1934-35; was Personal Asst to HRH with BEF in France, 1939-40, and accompanied HRH on visits to Gibraltar, 1941 and 1942; Chief of Staff to HRH on tour of Middle East Forces and India and Ceylon, 1942. Temporarily attached to US Army in France, Belgium and Holland in 1944. Retired pay, 1950. Life Governor Queen Mary's Hospital; Mem. Board of Govs, Royal Nat. Orthopædic Hosp. (Dep. Chm., 1957-60). A Fellow in Perpetuity of the Metropolitan Museum of New York, 1954; Associate of Yale Univ., USA. Councillor Shardlow Rural District Council, Derbs, 1954-57. Royal Humane Society of Canada's Medal for Life Saving; Chevalier of the Order of Belgium; Order of the Sacred Treasure of Japan. *Recreations:* hunting and boxing; played for England, The United Services, Lower Canada Coll. and St John's Sch., Montreal, at Ice Hockey. *Address:* The Dower House, Melbourne, near Derby. *T:* Melbourne (Derbs) 2696; Flat 133, Grosvenor House, Park Lane, W1. *T:* 01-499 6363. *Clubs:* Buck's, Bath, Hurlingham, White's.

**KERR, John Robert,** CMG 1966; **Hon. Mr Justice Kerr;** Judge of Commonwealth Industrial Court since 1966; Deputy President: Trade Practices Tribunal, since 1966; Copyright Tribunal, since 1969; Judge of Supreme Court of Australian Capital Territory since 1966; Judge of Courts of Marine Inquiry since 1967; *b* 24 Sept. 1914; *s* of late H. Kerr, Sydney; *m* 1938, Alison, *d* of F. Worstead, Sydney; one *s* two *d*. *Educ:* Fort Street Boys' High Sch.; Sydney Univ. (LLB). Admitted NSW Bar, 1938. Served War of 1939-45: 2nd AIF, 1942-46; Col, 1945-46. Princ., Australian Sch. of Pacific Admin., 1946; Organising Sec., S Pacific Commn, 1946-47; QC (NSW) 1953; Mem. NSW Bar Coun., 1960-64; Vice-Pres., 1962-63, Pres., 1964, NSW Bar Assoc.; Vice-Pres., 1962-64, Pres., 1964-66, Law Coun. of Australia; presided at 3rd Commonwealth and Empire Law Conf., Sydney, 1965; Pres., Industrial Relations Soc. of Australia, 1964-66; Pres., NSW Marriage Guidance Coun., 1961-62; Mem. Bd of Coun. on New Guinea Affairs, 1964-; Mem. Med. Bd of NSW, 1963-66; Pres., Law Assoc. for Asia and Western Pacific, 1966-. Hon. Life Mem., Law Soc. of England and Wales, 1965; Hon. Mem., Amer. Bar Assoc., 1967-. *Publications:* various papers and articles on industrial relations, New Guinea affairs, organisation of legal profession, etc. *Address:* Ingalara, 62 Kissing Point Road, Turramurra, NSW 2074, Australia. *T:* 44-1462. *Club:* Union (Sydney).

**KERR, Lt-Col Sir L. W. H.;** *see* Kerr, Lt-Col Sir Howard.

**KERR, Michael Robert Emmanuel,** QC 1961; practising barrister; *b* 1 March 1921; *s* of Alfred Kerr; *m* 1952, Julia, *d* of Joseph Braddock; two *s* one *d*. *Educ:* Aldenham Sch.; Clare Coll., Cambridge. Served War, 1941-45: (Pilot; Flt-Lt). BA Cantab (1st Cl. Hons Law) 1947; called to Bar, Lincoln's Inn, 1948, Bencher 1968; MA Cantab 1952. Governor, Aldenham Sch., 1959. Deputy Chm., Hants Quarter Sessions, 1961. Member: Bar Council, 1968; Senate, 1969. *Publication:* McNair's Law of the Air, 1953, 1965. *Recreations:* travel, ski-ing, music. *Address:* 51 Bedford Gardens, W8. *T:* 01-727 3180; 4 Essex Court, Temple, EC4. *T:* 01-353 6771.

**KERR, Sir Reginald;** *see* Kerr, Sir (H.) R.

**KERR, Robert Reid,** TD; BA, LLB; Sheriff-Substitute of Stirling, Dumbarton and Clackmannan at Falkirk, since 1969; *b* 7 May 1914; *s* of James Reid Kerr, sugar refiner, and Olive Rodger; *m* 1942, Mona Kerr; three *d*. *Educ:* Cargilfield; Trinity Coll., Glenalmond; Oxford Univ.; Glasgow Univ. Sheriff-Substitute: of Inverness, Moray, Nairn and Ross and Cromarty at Fort William, 1952-61; of Aberdeen, Kincardine and Banff at Banff, 1961-69. *Address:* Kinneil House, Old Polmont, Stirlingshire.

**KERR, Russell (Whiston);** MP (Lab) Feltham (Middlesex) since 1966; Air Charter Executive; *b* 1 Feb. 1921; *s* of Ivo W. and Constance Kerr, Australia; *m* 1st, 1946, Shirley W. N. Huie; one *s* one *d*; 2nd, 1960, Anne P. Clark (*née* Bersey) (*see* Mrs A. P. Kerr); no *c*. *Educ:* Shore Sch., Sydney; University of Sydney. BEcon 1941. RAAF Aircrew, 1942-46; operational service with Bomber Comd Pathfinder Force, flying Lancaster Bombers over Germany (Flying Officer/Navigator). Returned to England to live, 1948. Contested (Lab): Horsham, Sussex, 1951; Merton and Morden, 1959; Preston North, 1964. Director, Tribune, 1969-; Chm., Tribune group of Mps, 1969-70. Nat. Exec. Mem., ASTMS, 1964-. *Publications:* articles in various radical and TU jls. *Recreations:*

cricket, golf, walking, talking. *Address:* 12/13 Cannon Row, SW1. *T:* 01-839 3115. *Clubs:* Feltham Ex-Servicemen's, Putney Workingmen's.

**KERR, Mrs Russell Whiston;** *see* Kerr, Mrs A. P.

**KERR, William Alexander B.;** *see* Blair-Kerr.

**KERRIDGE, Sir Robert (James),** Kt 1962; Managing Director, Kerridge Odeon; Director of over 50 companies; *b* 29 Oct. 1901; British; *m* 1922, Phyllis Elizabeth Roland; three *s* two *d.* *Educ:* Christchurch, NZ. Qualified in Accountancy, 1920; Principal, Kerridge Commercial Coll., 1920-29. Engaged in transport and newspaper business for a number of years. Acquired first theatre, 1920; subseq. numerous theatres, and controlling interest of NZ Theatres Ltd (W. R. Kemball); also took over: Fullers Theatre Corp. Ltd, John Fuller & Sons Ltd; J. C. Williamson Picture Corp. Ltd; company now directs well over 100 theatres and some merchandising companies. CStJ. Cavaliere Dell'Ordine Al Merito Della Repubblica (Italy), 1958. *Recreations:* farming, golf, fishing. *Address:* 1 Judge Street, Parnell 1, Auckland N2, NZ. *T:* 44091. *Club:* Auckland (New Zealand).

**KERRIGAN, Daniel Patrick,** QC 1966; *b* 14 Jan. 1909; *s* of Patrick and Margaret Kerrigan; *m* 1936, Margaret (*née* Thomson); two *s.* *Educ:* Perth Academy; Edinburgh Univ. Called to the Bar, Middle Temple, 1933. War Service, RNVR, 1939-46. *Publications:* (jtly) Hill and Kerrigan Law of Housing; (jtly) Hill and Kerrigan Town and Country Planning Act, 1947; (jtly) Kerrigan and James Town and Country Planning Act, 1954; (jtly) Kerrigan and McDonald Land Commission Act, 1967; titles in Halsbury's Statutes and Halsbury's Laws. *Address:* 5 Pump Court, Temple, EC4; Homestead, Postling, Hythe, Kent.

**KERRIN, Very Rev. Richard Elual,** MA; Dean of Aberdeen and Orkney, 1956-69; Rector of St John's Episcopal Church, Aberdeen, since 1954; *b* 4 July 1898; *s* of Rev. Daniel Kerrin and Margaret Kerrin; *m* 1925, Florence Alexandra, *d* of Captain J. Reid; one *s.* *Educ:* Robert Gordon's Coll., Aberdeen; University of Aberdeen (MA); Edinburgh Theological Coll. (Luscombe Scholar). Ordained deacon, 1922; priest, 1923. Curate, Old St Paul, Edinburgh, 1922-25; Rector, Inverurie, 1925-37; Rector, Holy Trinity, Stirling, 1937-47; Rector, Fraserburgh, 1947-54; Canon of Aberdeen, 1954-56. *Address:* The Rectory, 15 Ashley Road, Aberdeen. *T:* Aberdeen 51527.

**KERRY, Bishop of, (RC),** since 1969; **Most Rev. Eamonn Casey,** DD; *b* Firies, Co. Kerry, 23 April 1927; *s* of John Casey and late Helena (*née* Shanahan). *Educ:* St Munchin's Coll., Limerick; St Patrick's Coll., Maynooth. LPh 1946; BA 1947. Priest, 1951. Curate, St John's Cath., Limerick, 1951-60; Chaplain to Irish in Slough; set up social framework to re-establish people into new environment; started social welfare scheme; set up lodgings bureau; savings scheme, 1960-63; invited by Cardinal Heenan to place Catholic Housing Aid Soc. on national basis; founded Family Housing Assoc.; Dir, British Council of Churches; Trustee, Housing the Homeless Central Fund; Founder-Trustee of Shelter (Chm. 1968); Mem. Council, Nat. Fedn of Housing Socs; Mem., Commn for Social Welfare; Founder Mem., Marian Employment Agency; Founder Trustee, Shelter Housing Aid Soc., 1963-69. *Publication:* (with Adam Fergusson) A Home of Your Own. *Recreations:* music, theatre, concerts, films when time, conversation, motoring. *Address:* The Bishop's House, Killarney, Co. Kerry, Ireland. *T:* Killarney 31168.

**KERRY, Knight of;** *see* FitzGerald, Sir G. P. M.

**KERSHAW,** family name of **Baron Kershaw.**

**KERSHAW,** 4th Baron, *cr* 1947; **Edward John Kershaw;** Chartered Accountant; *b* 12 May 1936; *s* of 3rd Baron and Katharine Dorothea Kershaw (*née* Staines); *S* father, 1962; *m* 1963, Rosalind Lilian Rutherford; two *d.* *Educ:* Selhurst Grammar Sch., Surrey. Entered RAF Nov. 1955, demobilised Nov. 1957. Admitted to Inst. of Chartered Accountants in England and Wales, Oct. 1964. Partner in Roberts, McLennan & Co., and Atkins, Yates & Co., Chartered Accountants, Woking, Surrey, 1967-, and Watling & Hirst, Chartered Accountants, Chichester, Sussex. *Recreations:* swimming, tennis, cricket, classical music, chess. *Heir:* *u* Hon. Donald Arthur Kershaw [*b* 1915; *m* 1942, Barbara Edith Ford; two *s*]. *Address:* 21 Trelawne Drive, Cranleigh, Surrey.

**KERSHAW, J(ohn) Anthony,** MC 1943; MP (C) Stroud Division of Gloucestershire, since 1955; Parliamentary Under-Secretary of State, Foreign and Commonwealth Office, since Oct. 1970; Barrister-at-Law; *b* 14 Dec. 1915; *s* of Judge J. F. Kershaw, Cairo and London, and of Anne Kershaw, Kentucky, USA; *m* 1939, Barbara, *d* of Harry Crookenden; two *s* two *d.* *Educ:* Eton; Balliol Coll., Oxford (BA). Called to the Bar 1939. Served War, 1940-46: 16th/5th Lancers. Mem. LCC, 1946-49; Westminster City Council, 1947-48. Parly Sec., Min. of Public Building and Works, June-Oct. 1970. *Address:* The Tithe Barn, Didmarton, Badminton, Glos. *Club:* White's.

**KERSHAW, Philip Charles Stones; His Honour Judge Kershaw;** Deputy Chairman, Lancashire Quarter Sessions, since 1961; *b* 9 April 1910; *s* of Joseph Harry and Ethel Kershaw; *m* 1935, Michaela Raffael; one *s* one *d.* *Educ:* Stonyhurst Coll.; Merton Coll., Oxford. Called to the Bar, Gray's Inn, 1933; practised Northern Circuit until Aug. 1939. Served in Army, 1939-45 (Major). Resumed practice, 1945-61. *Address:* Fountain House, East Beach, Lytham, Lancs. *T:* Lytham 6072. *Club:* Portico Library (Manchester).

**KERSHAW, Raymond Newton,** CMG 1947; MC; *b* 3 May 1898; *s* of G. W. Kershaw, Wahroonga, Sydney, Australia; *m* 1925, Hilda Mary, *d* of W. J. Ruegg, JP; two *s* one *d.* *Educ:* Sydney High Sch.; Sydney Univ.; New Coll., Oxford; Sorbonne. Served European War, 1914-18, with AIF in France, 1917-18 (MC); Rhodes Scholar for NSW, 1918; Mem. of Secretariat, League of Nations, Geneva, 1924-29; Adviser to the Governors, Bank of England, 1929-53; Member: E African Currency Bd, 1932-53; W African Currency Bd, 1943-53, Palestine Currency Bd, 1943-52, Burma Currency Board, 1946-52; Adviser to Commonwealth Development Finance Co., 1953-55; a Gen. Comr of Income Tax for City of London, 1956-65; a London Director: Commercial Banking Co. of Sydney, 1956-66 (Chm., London Bd, 1964-66); Bank of NZ, 1955-68 (Chm. London Bd, 1963-68); Australian Mutual Provident Soc., 1955-70. *Address:* Warren Row, near Wargrave, Berks. *T:* Littlewick Green 2708.

**KERSHAW, Prof. William Edgar,** VRD; Professor of Biology, University of Salford, since 1966. *Educ:* Manchester University. MB, ChB, 1935; MRCS LRCP, 1936; DTM&H Eng. 1946; MD 1949; DSc 1956. Chalmers Memorial Gold Medal, Royal Society of Tropical Medicine and Hygiene, 1955.

Formerly: Surgeon Captain, RNR; Demonstrator in Morbid Anatomy, Manchester Univ.; Leverhulme Senior Lectr in Med. Parasitology, Liverpool Sch. of Trop. Med. and Liverpool Univ.; Walter Myers and Everett Dutton Prof. of Parasitology and Entomology, Liverpool Univ., 1958-66. *Address:* 27 Rodney Street, Liverpool 1. *T:* 051-709 4758.

**KERTESZ, Istvan;** General Music Director, Opernhaus Köln, Germany, since 1964, Opera Director since 1969; *b* Budapest, Hungary, 28 Aug. 1929; *s* of Miklos Kertesz and Margit Kertesz (*née* Muresian); *m* 1951, Edith Kertesz (*née* Gabry); two *s* one *d.* *Educ:* Acad. Franz Liszt, Budapest; Accad. Santa Cecilia, Rome. Prin. Conductor, Philharmonic Orch., Györ, 1953-55; Conductor, State Opera House, Budapest, 1955-57; Gen. Mus. Dir, Augsburg Opera House, 1958-63; Conductor, Salzburg Festival, 1961-64; Principal Conductor, London Symphony Orchestra, 1965-68. Festivals: Salzburg, Edinburgh, Lucerne, Vienna, Bath, Spoleto, Gulbenkian, Lisbon, Montreux, Israel, Adelaide, German-Mozart, Osaka, Vienna, Ravinia Park. Tours: USA, with Hamburg Radio-Orch., 1963; Switzerland, and World Tour with LSO, 1964, 1966. Has conducted with over eighty leading orchestras all over the world, including LSO, RPO, Vienna Philharmonic Berlin Philharmonic, Concertgebouw of Amsterdam, Orchestre de la Suisse Romande, and Israel Philharmonic. Operas: Covent Garden, Teatro Colon, La Scala. Prof., Salzburg, Summer-Acad. for conducting, 1964. Hon. Master degrees for conducting: Budapest, 1953; Rome, 1958 (*cum laude*); Premio D'Atri, Rome, 1958. Has made many prize-winning recordings. *Recreations:* cars, boats, skiing, reading. *Address:* Köln, Germany.

**KESWICK, David Johnston,** CMG 1946; JP; *b* 6 July 1901; *s* of Henry Keswick and Ida Wynifred Johnston; *m* 1928, Nony Barbara Pease (*d* 1969); three *d.* *Educ:* Eton Coll.; Trinity Coll., Cambridge. Asst Private Sec. to Governor-Gen. of New Zealand, 1924-27; Private Sec. to Sir Thomas Inskip, KC, MP, Attorney-Gen. 1927-29; Samuel Montagu & Co., Bankers, 1930-39 and from demobilisation. Commissioned KOSB Sept. 1939; employed on staff duties; demobilised, 1946. Mem., Royal Company of Archers (Queen's Body Guard for Scotland). JP Dumfriesshire 1958. *Recreations:* all country pursuits, painting. *Address:* Cowhill, Dumfries. *T:* Newbridge 304. *Clubs:* Boodle's; New (Edinburgh).

*See also J. H. Keswick, W. J. Keswick.*

**KESWICK, John Henry,** CMG 1950; Director: Matheson & Co. Ltd, London (Chairman, 1966-70); Jardine, Matheson & Co. Ltd, Hong Kong; Barclays Bank Ltd; Yorkshire Bank Ltd (Deputy Chairman); Hongkong and Shanghai Banking Corporation (London Committee); Sun Alliance and London Insurance Ltd; Chairman, China Association; President, Sino-British Trade Council; *b* 1906; *s* of late Henry Keswick; *m* 1940, Celia Clare Mary Alice Elwes; one *d.* *Educ:* Eton; Trinity Coll., Cambridge. Hon. Treas., National Association of Youth Clubs. *Address:* 5 Chester Place, NW1; Matheson & Co. Ltd, 3 Lombard Street, EC3. *T:* 01-626 6555. *Clubs:* Boodle's, Buck's, White's.

*See also D. J. Keswick, W. J. Keswick.*

**KESWICK, William Johnston;** Director; Matheson & Co. Ltd; Bank of England; Hudson's Bay Company (Governor, 1962-65); Director of British Petroleum Co. Ltd; *b* 6 Dec. 1903; *s* of late Major Henry Keswick of Cowhill Tower, Dumfries, Scotland; *m* 1937, Mary, *d* of late Rt Hon. Sir Francis Lindley, PC, GCMG; three *s* one *d.* *Educ:* Winchester Coll.; Trinity Coll., Cambridge. Dir of Jardine, Matheson & Co. Ltd (Hong Kong and Far East); Chm. of various public companies in Far East; Chm., Shanghai Municipal Council of late International Settlement; Mem., Royal Commission on Taxation of Profits and Income; Brigadier Staff Duties 21 Army Gp; Mem., Royal Company of Archers. Trustee, National Gallery 1964-. *Recreations:* shooting, fishing. *Address:* Theydon Priory, Theydon Bois, Essex. *T:* Theydon Bois 2256; Glenkiln, Shawhead, Dumfries, Scotland. *Clubs:* White's, Boodle's.

*See also D. J. Keswick, J. H. Keswick.*

**KETTLEWELL, Comdt Dame Marion M.,** DBE 1970 (CBE 1964); Director, WRNS. 1967-70, retired; *b* 20 Feb. 1914; *d* of George Wildman Kettlewell, Bramling, Virginia Water, Surrey, and Mildred Frances (*née* Atkinson), Belford, Northumberland. *Educ:* Godolphin Sch., Salisbury; St Christopher's Coll., Blackheath. Worked for Fellowship of Maple Leaf, Alta, Canada, 1935-38; worked for Local Council, 1939-41; joined WRNS as MT driver, 1941; commnd as Third Officer WRNS, 1942; Supt WRNS on Staff of Flag Officer Air (Home), 1961-64; Supt WRNS Training and Drafting, 1964-67. *Recreations:* needlework, walking, and country life. *Address:* 38 Rochester Row, SW1.

*See also R. W. Kettlewell.*

**KETTLEWELL, Richard Wildman,** CMG 1955; Colonial Service, retired 1962; Consultant to Hunting Technical Services, since 1963; *b* 12 Feb. 1910; *s* of George Wildman Kettlewell and Mildred Frances Atkinson; *m* 1935, Margaret Jessie Palmer; one *s* one *d.* *Educ:* Clifton Coll.; Reading and Cambridge Univs. BSc 1931; Dip. Agric. Cantab 1932; Associate of Imperial Coll. of Tropical Agriculture (AICTA), 1933. Entered Colonial Agricultural Service, 1934; appointed to Nyasaland. Served War of 1939-45 (despatches) with 2nd Bn King's African Rifles, 1939-43; rank of Major. Recalled to agricultural duties in Nyasaland, 1943; Dir of Agriculture, 1951-59; Sec. for Natural Resources, 1959-61; Minister for Lands and Surveys, 1961-62. *Address:* Orchard Close, Overnorton, Chipping Norton, Oxon. *T:* Chipping Norton 2407. *Club:* MCC.

*See also Comdt Dame M. M. Kettlewell.*

**KEVILLE, Sir (William) Errington,** Kt 1962; CBE 1947; *b* 3 Jan. 1901; *s* of William Edwin Keville; *m* 1928, Ailsa Sherwood, *d* of late Captain John McMillan; three *s* two *d.* *Educ:* Merchant Taylors'. Pres., Chamber of Shipping, 1961 (Vice-Pres. 1960, Mem. of Council, 1940-); Chairman: Gen. Coun. of British Shipping, 1961; International Chamber of Shipping, 1963-68; Cttee of European Shipowners, 1963-65; Member: Executive Council of Shipping Federation Ltd, 1936-68; National Maritime Board, 1945-68; Mem. of Cttee of Lloyd's Register of Shipping, 1957-68; Director: Shaw Savill & Albion Co. Ltd, 1941-68 (former Dep. Chm.); National Bank of New Zealand Ltd, 1946-; Economic Insurance Co. Ltd, 1949-68 (Chm., 1962-68); National Mortgage & Agency Co. of NZ Ltd, 1950-68; British Maritime Trust Ltd, 1959- (Chm. 1962-68); Furness Withy & Co. Ltd, 1950-68 (Chm., 1962-68); Chm., Air Holdings Ltd, 1968-69. *Recreations:* walking, golf, history. *Address:* Lunces Hall, Wivelsfield, Haywards Heath, Sussex. *T:* Wivelsfield Green 381. *Club:* Bath.

**KEWISH, John Douglas,** CB 1958; TD 1944; DL; Head of the County Courts Branch in the Lord

Chancellor's Department; *b* 4 May 1907; *s* of late John James Kewish, Birkenhead; *m* 1934, Marjorie Phyllis, *d* of late Dr Joseph Harvey, Wimbledon; one *s* one *d*. *Educ:* Birkenhead Sch. Admitted a Solicitor, 1931. Served TA, 1928-45; served 1939-44, with 4th Bn Cheshire Regt (UK, France and Belgium); commanded 4th Bn, 1940-44; commanded depots, The Cheshire Regt and The Manchester Regt and 24 Machine Gun Training Centre, 1944-45. Hon. Col 4th Bn Cheshire Regt, 1947-62. Chm., Cheshire T & AFA, 1951-59. Chm., Liverpool Shipwreck and Humane Soc., 1953-60. Mem. Civil Judicial Statistics Cttee, 1966-68. DL Cheshire, 1952. *Address:* Southlea, Hollybank Road, West Byfleet, Surrey. *T:* Byfleet 42548.

**KEY, Maj.-Gen. Berthold Wells,** CB 1947; DSO; MC; psc; IA (retired); *b* 19 Dec. 1895; *s* of late Dr J. M. Key; *m* 1917, Aileen Leslie (*d* 1951), *d* of late Col E. L. Dunsterville, RE; (one *s* killed in action in Italy) two *d*. *Educ:* Dulwich Coll. Joined 45th Rattrays Sikhs, IA, 1914; European War, 1914-19. Mesopotamia (wounded, MC); Afghanistan, 1919; NWF of India, 1930 (despatches); NWF Waziristan, 1936-37 (despatches, DSO); SE Asia, 1941-45; Comd, 2nd (Royal) Bn The Sikh Regt; Comd, 8 Ind. Bde, 1940-41; Comd 11 Ind. Div. 1942; ADC to the King, 1945-47; Comd, Rawalpindi Dist, 1946; Comd, Lahore Dist, 1947. *Recreation:* golf. *Address:* Naini, St George's Road, Sandwich, Kent.

**KEY, Sir Charles (Edward),** KBE 1956 (CBE 1946); CB 1952; *b* 22 March 1900; *s* of late E. T. and late F. M. Key, Tunbridge Wells; *m* 1st, 1935, Doris May Watkins (decd); no *c*; 2nd, 1953, Annie Elizabeth King. *Educ:* St John's, Tunbridge Wells. War Office, 1915-60: Assistant Secretary, 1942; Director of Finance, 1949-54; Deputy Under-Secretary of State, War Office, 1954-60, retired. Medal of Freedom with bronze palm (USA), 1946; Officer Order of Orange-Nassau (Netherlands), 1947. *Address:* The Cottage, Highfield Road, East Grinstead, Sussex. *T:* East Grinstead 25321. *Club:* Reform.

**KEY, Maj.-Gen. Clement Denis,** MBE 1945; RAOC, retired; *b* 6 June 1915; *s* of late William Clement Key, Harborne, Birmingham; *m* 1941, Molly, *d* of late F. Monk, Kettering, Northants; two *s*. *Educ:* Seaford Coll. Commnd in RAOC, 1940; served in: England, 1940-44; France, Belgium, Burma, Singapore, 1944-48; Staff Coll., Camberley, 1945; England, 1948-51; USA, 1951-54; England, 1954-59; jssc 1954; Belgium, 1959-61; War Office, 1961-64; Dep. Dir of Ordnance Services, War Office, 1964-67; Dep. Dir of Ordnance Services, Southern Comd, 1967; Comdr, UK Base Organisation, RAOC, 1968-70; retd, 1970. Hon. Col, RAOC (T&AVR). *Recreations:* rowing, gardening. *Address:* 104 Maidenhead Road, Stratford-upon-Avon, Warwicks. *T:* Stratford-upon-Avon 4345. *Club:* Naval and Military.

**KEY, Rt. Rev. John M.;** *see* Truro, Bishop of.

**KEY, Sir Neill C.;** *see* Cooper-Key.

**KEYES,** family name of **Baron Keyes.**

**KEYES,** 2nd Baron, *cr* 1943, of Zeebrugge and of Dover; **Roger George Bowlby Keyes;** Bt, *cr* 1919; RN, retired; *b* 14 March 1919; 2nd *s* of Admiral of the Fleet Baron Keyes, GCB, KCVO, CMG, DSO and Eva Mary Salvin Bowlby, Red Cross Order of Queen Elisabeth of Belgium, *d* of late Edward Salvin Bowlby, DL, of Gilston Park, Herts, and Knoydart, Inverness-shire; *S* father 1945; *m* 1947, Grizelda Mary, 2nd *d* of late Lieut-Col William Packe, DSO; three *s* two *d*. *Educ:* King's Mead Sch., Seaford; RNC, Dartmouth. *Heir: s* Hon. Charles William Packe Keyes, *b* 8 Dec. 1951. *Address:* Leith Hill Place, Dorking, Surrey. *T:* Dorking 6236.

**KEYNES, Lady; (Lydia Lopokova);** *b* Russia, 21 Oct. 1892; *d* of Vassili Lopokoff, Leningrad, and Constanzia Douglas; *m* 1925, 1st and last Baron Keynes, CB, FBA (*d* 1946), Fellow and Bursar of King's Coll., Cambridge. *Educ:* Imperial Ballet Sch., St Petersburgh. First stage appearance, Marinsky Theatre, St Petersburg, 1901; solo parts in Imperial Russian Ballet; Opera, Paris, 1910; Winter Garden Theatre, New York, 1911; as an actress, several parts in New York, 1914-16; subsequently with Diaghileff's Russian Ballet, New York and London; The Lilac Fairy in Diaghileff's revival of The Sleeping Princess, 1921. Created rôle of Mariuccia in Massine's Les Femmes de Bonne Humeur, 1917, and with Leonide Massine, The Can-Can Dancers in La Boutique Fantasque, 1919; Camargo Society, 1930-32; Vic-Wells Ballet, 1932-33; (Lady) Olivia in Twelfth Night, Old Vic, 1933; Nora Helmer in A Doll's House, 1934; Hilda Wangel in The Master Builder, 1936; Celimene in The Misanthrope, 1937; Mem. of Council, Arts Council of GB, Aug. 1946-49. *Address:* Tilton, Firle, Sussex.

**KEYNES, Sir Geoffrey (Langdon),** Kt 1955; MA, MD Cantab; Hon. LLD Edinburgh; Hon. DLitt: Oxford, Cambridge; Birmingham; Sheffield; Reading; FRCP, FRCS England, FRCS Canada, FRCOG; Hon. Fellow, Pembroke College, Cambridge; Hon. Librarian and late Member of Council Royal College of Surgeons; Hunterian Trustee, 1958; Consulting Surgeon: St Bartholomew's Hospital; New End Endocrine Clinic and City of London Truss Society; a Trustee of the National Portrait Gallery, 1942-66, Chairman, 1958-66; *b* Cambridge, 25 March 1887; 2nd *s* of late John Neville Keynes; *m* 1917, Margaret Elizabeth, *d* of late Sir George Darwin, KCB; four *s*. *Educ:* Rugby Sch.; Pembroke Coll., Cambridge (Foundation Scholar); 1st Class Natural Science Tripos, 1909; Entrance Scholar, St Bartholomew's Hospital, 1910; Brackenbury Surgery Scholar and Willett Medal Operative Surgery, 1913; House Surgeon St Bartholomew's Hospital, 1913; Lieut RAMC, 1914; Major RAMC; Surgical Specialist, BEF (despatches); Chief Asst St Bartholomew's Hospital, 1920; Hunterian Prof., RCS, 1923, 1929, 1945; Cecil Joll Prize, RCS, 1953; Harveian Orator, RCP, 1958; Fitzpatrick Lectr, RCP, 1966; Wilkins Lectr, Royal Society, 1967; Osler Orator and Gold Medal, 1968. Actg Air Vice-Marshal, Sen. Cons. Surg., RAF, 1939-45. Sir Arthur Sims Commonwealth Travelling Professor, 1956. Hon. Foreign Corresp. Mem. Grolier Club, New York; Hon. Mem., Mod. Lang. Assoc., 1966; formerly Pres. Bibliographical Soc. of London; Hon. Fellow American Association Surgeons; Hon. Freeman, Soc. of Apothecaries, 1964; Hon. Fellow, Royal Society of Medicine, 1966. Hon. Gold Medal, RCS, 1969. *Publications:* Blood Transfusion, 1922, 1949; many articles in medical journals; Bibliographies of John Donne, 1914, 1932 and 1958; William Blake, 1921, 1953; Sir Thomas Browne, 1924 and 1968; William Harvey, 1928 and 1953; Jane Austen, 1929; William Hazlitt, 1931; John Evelyn, 1937 and 1968; John Ray, 1950; Rupert Brooke, 1954 and 1959; Robert Hooke, 1960; Siegfried Sassoon, 1962; edited Writings of William Blake, 1925, 1927, 1957 and 1966; of Sir Thomas Browne, 1928, 1964, 1968, of Izaak Walton, 1929, etc.; Compiled William Blake's Illustrations to the Bible,

1957; Blake Studies 1949 and 1970; Bibliotheca Bibliographici (cat. of his library), 1964; William Blake, Poet, Printer, Prophet, 1964; Life of William Harvey, 1966 (James Tait Black Memorial Prize). *Address:* Lammas House, Brinkley, Newmarket, Suffolk. *T:* Stetchworth 268. *Club:* Roxburghe.
*See also R. D. Keynes, S. J. Keynes.*

**KEYNES, Richard Darwin,** FRS 1959; MA, PhD, ScD Cantab; Director of ARC Institute of Animal Physiology, Babraham, since 1965 (Head of Physiology Department and Deputy Director, 1960-64); Extraordinary Fellow of Churchill College, since 1961; Fellow of Eton; *b* 14 Aug. 1919; *e s* of Sir Geoffrey Keynes, *qv*; *m* 1945, Anne Pinsent Adrian, *e d* of 1st Baron Adrian, *qv*; four *s*. *Educ:* Oundle Sch. (Scholar); Trinity Coll., Cambridge (Scholar). Temporary experimental officer, HM Anti-Submarine Establishment and Admiralty Signals Establishment, 1940-45. 1st Class, Nat. Sci. Tripos Part II, 1946; Michael Foster and G. H. Lewes Studentships, 1946; Research Fellow of Trinity Coll., 1948-52; Gedge Prize, 1948; Rolleston Memorial Prize, 1950. Demonstrator in Physiology, University of Cambridge, 1949-53; Lecturer, 1953-60; Fellow of Peterhouse, 1952-60; a Vice-Pres., Royal Society, 1965-68. Dr *hc* Univ. of Brazil, 1968. *Publications:* papers in Journal of Physiology, Proceedings of Royal Soc., etc. *Recreations:* sailing, gardening. *Address:* 3 Herschel Road, Cambridge. *T:* 53107; Primrose Farm, Wiveton, Norfolk. *T:* Cley 317. *Club:* Athenæum.
*See also S. J. Keynes.*

**KEYNES, Stephen John;** Director: Charterhouse Japhet & Thomasson Ltd, since 1965; Sun Life Assurance Society Ltd, since 1966; Member, Independent Television Authority, since 1969; *b* 19 Oct. 1927; 4th *s* of Sir Geoffrey Keynes, *qv*; *m* 1955, Mary, *o d* of Senator the Hon. Adrian Knatchbull-Hugessen, *qv*; three *s* two *d*. *Educ:* Oundle Sch.; King's Coll., Cambridge (Foundn Scholar). MA Cantab. Served with Royal Artillery, 1949-51. Partner, J. F. Thomasson & Co., Private Bankers, 1961-65. Mem. Cttee and Treas., Islington and North London Family Service Unit, 1956-; Mem. Adv. Cttee, Geffrye Museum, 1964-. *Recreations:* gardening, good living. *Address:* 16 Canonbury Park South, Islington, N1. *T:* 01-226 8170; White Hart Cottage, Brinkley, Newmarket, Suffolk. *T:* Stetchworth 223; Pot Ing Farm, Gunnerside, Swaledale, Richmond, Yorks. *Club:* City of London.
*See also R. D. Keynes.*

**KEYS, Prof. Ivor Christopher Banfield,** MA, DMus Oxon; FRCO; Hon. RAM; Professor of Music, University of Birmingham, since 1968; *b* 8 March 1919; *er s* of Christopher Richard Keys, Littlehampton, Sussex; *m* 1944, Margaret Anne Layzell; two *s* two *d*. *Educ:* Christ's Hospital, Horsham; Christ Church, Oxford. FRCO 1935; music scholar and asst organist, Christ Church Cathedral, Oxford, 1938-40 and 1946-47. Served with Royal Pioneer Corps, 1940-46. Lecturer in Music, Queen's University of Belfast, 1947, Reader, 1950, Sir Hamilton Harty Professor of Music, QUB, 1951-54; Prof. of Music, Nottingham Univ., 1954-68. Pres., Royal College of Organists, 1968-. *Publications:* Sonata for Violoncello and Pianoforte; Completion of Schubert's unfinished song Gretchens Bitte; Concerto for Clarinet and Strings; Prayer for Pentecostal Fire (choir and organ); The Road to the Stable (3 Christmas songs with piano); Magnificat and Nunc Dimittis (choir and organ); (Book) The Texture of Music: Purcell to Brahms, 1961. Reviews of Music, in Music and Letters, and of books, in Musical Times. *Recreation:* bridge. *Address:* Barber Institute of Fine Arts (Department of Music), Birmingham.

**KHAMA, Sir Seretse M.,** KBE 1966 (OBE 1963); first President, Republic of Botswana, since 1966; Prime Minister of Bechuanaland, 1965-66; *b* 1 July 1921; *s* of Sekgoma and Tebogo Khama; *m* 1948, Ruth Williams; three *s* one *d*. *Educ:* Fort Hare, University of South Africa (BA); Balliol Coll., Oxford; Inner Temple. Bechuanaland: MEC, 1961; Pres., Democratic Party, 1962; MLA, 1965. Chancellor, University of Botswana, Lesotho and Swaziland, 1967-70. Hon. DPhil, 1967. Hon. LLD, Fordham Univ., New York, 1965. Hon. Fellow, Balliol Coll., Oxford, 1969. *Address:* Gaborone, Botswana.

**KHAN, Vice-Adm. Afzal Rahman,** Sitara-i-Quaid-i-Azam 1958; Hilal-i-Quaid-i-Azam 1961; Hilal-i-Pakistan 1964; Hilal-i-Jurat 1965; Chairman, Ark Ocean Lines Ltd; *b* 20 March 1921; *s* of late Abdur Rahman Khan, landlord, Gurdaspur District; *m* 1944, Hameeda Khan; one *s* two *d*. *Educ:* Baring High Sch., Batala; Govt Coll., Lahore. Joined Indian Mercantile Marine Trng Ship Dufferin, 1936; entered Royal Indian Navy, 1938; Actg Sub-Lieut 1940; Lieut 1942; Lieut-Comdr 1947; Comdr 1950; Captain 1953; Cdre 1958; Rear-Adm. 1959; Vice-Adm. 1961. War of 1939-45: active service, HM Ships in Atlantic, Mediterranean and N Sea and in Royal Indian Navy ships in Indian Ocean and Burma Coast. After Independence in 1947, comd various ships and shore estabs of Pakistan Navy and held other sen. appts; Specialist in Gunnery; psc, jssc; C-in-C, Pakistan Navy, 1959; retd from Navy, 1966. Minister for Defence, Pakistan, 1966-69. Order of Humayun (Iran), 1961; Legion of Merit (US), 1960 and 1964. *Recreations:* shooting, deep-sea fishing, tennis, golf, study of naval history. *Address:* The Anchorage, 27b South Central Avenue, 8th South Street, Karachi, Pakistan. *T:* 541550; Premier Insurance Building, Wallace Road, Karachi. *Clubs:* Sind, Gymkhana (Karachi).

**KHAN, Field-Marshal Mohammad Ayub,** (Hon.) GCMG 1960; NPk; HJ; President of Pakistan, 1958-69; *b* Rehana; *m* Zubeida Khatoon; four *s* three *d*. *Educ:* Aligarh Moslem Univ.; Royal Military Coll., Sandhurst. Commissioned, 1928. Served War of 1939-45. Col, 1947; Maj.-Gen. and first Commander, East Pakistan Division, 1948; Adjutant-Gen., 1950; General and first Pakistani Commander-in-Chief of Pakistan Army, 1951; Minister of Defence, Pakistan, 1954-55; Chief Martial Law Administrator and Supreme Commander of all Armed Forces, 1958; Field-Marshal, 1959. *Publication:* Friends Not Masters, a Political Autobiography, 1967. *Recreations:* riding, shooting, reading, golf and horticulture. *Address:* Rawalpindi, Pakistan.

**KHAN, Sir Muhammad Zafrulla;** *see* Zafrulla Khan.

**KHAN, Gen. Yahya;** *see* Yahya Khan, Gen. Agha Muhammad.

**KHORANA, Prof. Har Gobind;** Sloan Professor of Chemistry and Biology, Massachusetts Institute of Technology, since 1970; *b* Raipur, India, 9 Jan. 1922; *s* of Shri Ganpat Rai and Shrimata Krishna (Devi); *m* 1952, Esther Elizabeth Sibler; one *s* two *d*. *Educ:* Punjab Univ. (BSc, MSc); Liverpool Univ. (PhD, Govt of India Student). Post-doctoral Fellow of Govt of India, Federal Inst. of Techn., Zurich, 1948-49; Nuffield Fellow, Cambridge Univ., 1950-52; Head, Organic Chemistry Group, BC Research Council, 1952-60. Univ.

of Wisconsin: Co-Dir, Inst. for Enzyme Research, 1960-70; Prof., Dept of Chemistry, 1962-70; Conrad A. Elvehjem Prof. in the Life Sciences, 1964-70. Visiting Professor: Rockefeller Inst., NY, 1958-60; Stanford Univ., 1964; Harvard Med. Sch., 1966. Has given special or memorial lectures in USA, Poland, Canada, Switzerland, UK and Japan. Fellow: Chem. Inst. of Canada; Amer. Assoc. for Advancement of Science; Amer. Acad. of Arts and Sciences; Overseas Fellow, Churchill Coll., Cambridge; Member: Nat. Acad. of Sciences; Deutsche Akademie der Naturforscher Leopoldina. Hon. Dr Science, Chicago, 1967. Merck Award, Chem. Inst. Canada, 1958; Gold Medal for 1960, Professional Inst. of Public Service of Canada; Dannie-Heinneman Preiz, Germany, 1967; Remsen Award, Johns Hopkins Univ., ACS Award for Creative Work in Synthetic Organic Chemistry, Louisa Gross Horwitz Award, Lasker Foundn Award for Basic Med. Research, Nobel Prize for Medicine (jtly), 1968. *Publications:* Some Recent Developments in the Chemistry of Phosphate Esters of Biological Interest, 1961; numerous papers in Biochemistry, Jl Amer. Chem. Soc., etc. *Recreations:* hiking, swimming. *Address:* Department of Biology, Massachusetts Institute of Technology, Cambridge, Mass 02139, USA.

**KHRUSHCHEV, Nikita Sergeyevich;** Hero of the Soviet Union; Hero of Socialist Labour (3); Order of Lenin (6); Order of Red Banner of Labour; Order of Suvorov (1st and 2nd cl.); Order of Kutuzov (1st cl.); Order of Great Patriotic War (1st cl.); *b* Kalinovka, near Kursk, 17 April 1894. *Educ:* Industrial Institute, Donetsk; Moscow Industrial Acad. Joined Communist Party, 1918; fought in Civil War, 1918-20; Sec., Moscow City Party Cttee, 1932-34; elected to Central Cttee of Communist Party, 1934-; Sec., Moscow Regional and Moscow City Cttees, 1935-38; responsible for industrialisation programme and construction of Moscow subway; designated Mem. of Supreme Soviet by Krasnaya Presnya district of Moscow, 1937; First Sec., Communist Party of the Ukraine, 1938-49; full mem. of the political bureau, 1938-49, and Mem. of the Presidium of CPSU Central Cttee, 1949-. Organised guerrilla defence of the Ukraine, 1941, given rank of Lieut-Gen. During War of 1941-45, Mem. of the military councils of the Kiev Special Military District, the South-Western direction, the Stalingrad, Southern and first Ukrainian fronts. Chm. Ukraine Council of Ministers, 1947; transf. back to Moscow Regional Cttee, 1949, Sec. of the Central Cttee, 1949-53; First Sec. of Central Cttee of Communist Party, 1953-64; Chm. of Council of Ministers of USSR, 1958-64; Serp i Molot (Sickle and Hammer) gold medal (3); Laureate of Internat. Lenin Peace Prize. *Publications:* For Durable Peace and Peaceful Co-existence, 1958; Let us Live in Peace and Friendship, 1959; For Victory in Peaceful Competition with Capitalism, 1959; A World Without Arms–A World Without War (speeches and interviews), 1960; Peace and Happiness for the Peoples, 1960; For Peace, for Disarmament, for Freedom of the Peoples, 1960; The Foreign Policy of the Soviet Union, 1961; Communism–Peace and Happiness for Peoples, 1962; Construction of Communism in the USSR and the Development of Agriculture (7 vols) 1962-63; The Noble Mission of Literature and Art, 1963; To Prevent War and to Safeguard Peace, 1963. Several vols of speeches (Eng. trans), 1959-61 (London). *Address:* Moscow, USSR.

**KIDD, Franklin,** CBE 1950; FRS 1944; MInstR; FRSA; MA Cantab, DSc London; Director of Food Investigation, Department of Scientific and Industrial Research, 1947-57, retired; *b* 1890, *e s* of late Benjamin Kidd, author of Social Evolution, The Science of Power, etc; *m* 1920, Mary Nest, *d* of late John Owen, Rt Rev. the Lord Bishop of St Davids. *Educ:* Tonbridge Sch.; St John's Coll., Cambridge; Fellow of St John's Coll., 1913-19, 1950-58. 12 months in Australia and NZ reporting to Govts on organisation of food research, 1927; Chm. Royal Commission (South Africa) to enquire into precooling of Deciduous Fruit, 1936; Chm. of Food Group of Soc. of Chemical Industry, 1936-38; Supt, Low Temperature Research Station, Cambridge, 1934-47. Mem. Board of Governors, Nat. Coll. of Food Technology, 1950; Mem. Nat. Council for Technological Awards, Board of Studies in Technologies other than Engineering, 1955; Kamerlingh Onnes Gold Medallist, 1963. *Publications:* Papers in various scientific journals and Food Investigation Special Reports; also Almond in Peterhouse and other Poems, 1950; The Peopled Earth in Five Movements, 1964. *Recreations:* fishing, bee-keeping. *Address:* Appleby Cottage, 24 Woodlands Road, Great Shelford, Cambs. *T:* Shelford 2138.

**KIDD, Frederic William,** CIE 1943; KPM 1931, indian Police (retired); *b* 1 Sept. 1890; *s* of late F. W. Kidd, MD, 17 Lower Fitzwilliam Street, Dublin, Ireland; *m* 1924, Margaret Blake Loveday; one *s* one *d*; *m* 1956, Helen Beatrice Woods (*née* Blake). *Educ:* Tipperary Grammar Sch.; Trinity Coll., Dublin. Indian Police, 1911; various posts in Bengal Province; Deputy Commissioner Calcutta Police, 1919-28; Supt of Police, Midnapore, 1929-31; Darjeeling, 1932-33; Dacca, 1935-37; Central Intelligence Officer, Calcutta, 1938-39; Deputy Director, Intelligence Bureau, Home Dept, Govt of India, 1940-44. *Address:* Lower Coach House, Westwell, Tenterden, Kent. *T:* Tenterden 3110.

**KIDD, Margaret Henderson, (Mrs Margaret Macdonald),** QC (Scotland), 1948; Sheriff of Perth and Angus since 1966 (of Dumfries and Galloway, 1960-66); *b* 14 March 1900; *e d* of late James Kidd, Solicitor, Linlithgow (sometime MP (U) for W Lothian), and late J. G. Kidd (*née* Turnbull); *m* 1930, Donald Somerled Macdonald (*d* 1958), WS Edinburgh; one *d*. *Educ:* Linlithgow Acad.; Edinburgh Univ. Admitted to the Scottish Bar, 1923; contested (U) West Lothian, 1928. Keeper of the Advocates' Library, 1956-69; Editor Court of Session Reports in Scots Law Times. Vice-Pres. British Federation of University Women, Ltd. *Address:* 5 India Street, Edinburgh. *T:* 031-225 3867.

**KIDSON, Harold Percy,** MA, BSc (NZ); late Rector, Otago Boys' High School, Dunedin, New Zealand; retired 1948; *b* 11 June 1887; *s* of Charles and Christiana Kidson; *m* 1914, Dorothy Owen; two *d*. *Educ:* Nelson Coll., NZ; Canterbury University Coll., NZ; Sorbonne, Paris. Asst Master at Nelson Coll., Christchurch Boys' High School, NZ, Mathematical Sch., Rochester, England; Inspector of Secondary Schs, Department of Education, New Zealand; Principal Hutt Valley High Sch.; Formerly Pres. New Zealand Secondary Schs Association, and Mem. Otago Univ. Council. *Recreations:* fly-fishing, silviculture. *Address:* Wanaka, Otago, NZ.

**KIDWELL, Raymond Incledon,** QC 1968; *b* 8 Aug. 1926; *s* of Montague and Dorothy Kidwell; *m* 1951, Enid, *d* of Edmund Rowe; two *s*. *Educ:* Whitgift Sch.; Magdalen Coll.,

Oxford. RAFVR, 1944-48. BA (Law) 1st cl. 1950; MA 1951; BCL 1st cl. 1951; Vinerian Law Schol., 1951; Eldon Law Schol., 1951; Arden Law Schol., Gray's Inn, 1952; Birkenhead Law Schol., Gray's Inn, 1955. Called to Bar, 1951; Lectr in Law, Oriel Coll., Oxford, 1952-55; Mem., Winn Commn on Personal Injuries, 1966-68; Mem., Bar Coun., 1967-. *Address:* Sanderstead House, Rectory Park, Sanderstead, Surrey. *T:* 01-657 4161.

**KIESINGER, Kurt Georg;** Member of Bundestag, 1949-58 and since 1969; Chancellor of the Federal Republic of Germany, 1966-69; *b* 6 April 1904; *m* Marie-Luise Schneider; one *s* one *d*. *Educ:* Tübingen Univ.; Berlin Univ. Lawyer. minister-Pres., Baden-Württemberg 1958-66; Pres., Bundesrat, 1962-63. Chm., Christian Democratic Group, 1958. Member: Consultative Assembly, Council of Europe, 1958 (Vice-Pres.); WEU Assembly, 1958; Central Cttee, Christian Democratic Party (Chm., 1967-). DIuris *hc:* Univ. of Cologne, 1965; New Delhi; Maryland, Coimbra. Grand Cross, Order of Merit, German Federal Republic; Grand Cross, Order of Merit, Italian Republic; Grand Officier de la Légion d'Honneur, Palmes Académiques. *Address:* Nassestrasse 2, 53 Bonn, West Germany.

**KILBRACKEN,** 3rd Baron, *cr* 1909, of Killegar; **John Raymond Godley,** DSC 1945; writer and cameraman; *b* 17 Oct. 1920; *er s* of 2nd Baron, CB, KC, and Elizabeth Helen Monteith, *d* of Vereker Monteith Hamilton and *widow* of Commander N. F. Usborne, RN; *S* father 1950; *m* 1943, Penelope Anne (marr. diss., 1949), *y d* of Rear-Adm. Sir C. N. Reyne, KBE; one *s* (and one *s* decd). *Educ:* Eton; Balliol Coll., Oxford (MA). Served in RNVR (Fleet Air Arm), as air pilot, 1940-46; entered as naval airman, commissioned 1941; Lieut-Commdr 1944; commanded Nos 835 and 714 Naval Air Sqdns. A reporter for many US, UK and foreign journals, from 1948; cameraman (TV and stills), from 1962. Joined Parly Liberal Party, 1960; transferred to Labour, 1966. *Publications:* Even For An Hour (poems), 1940; Tell Me The Next One, 1950; The Master Forger, 1951; Living Like a Lord, 1955; A Peer behind the Curtain, 1959; Shamrocks and Unicorns, 1962; Van Meegeren, 1967; (ed.) Letters from Early New Zealand, 1951. TV documentaries: The Yemen, 1964; Morgan's Treasure, 1965; Kurdistan, 1966. *Recreations:* none. *Heir: s* Hon. Christopher John Godley [*b* 1 Jan. 1945; *m* 1969, Gillian Christine, *yr d* of Lt-Comdr S. W. Birse, RN retd, Alverstoke]. *Address:* Killegar, Cavan, Ireland. *T:* Killeshandra 9.

*See also Hon. W. A. Godley.*

**KILBRANDON, Hon. Lord; Charles James Dalrymple Shaw;** Senator of College of Justice in Scotland and Lord of Session, since 1959; Member, Commission on the Constitution, since 1969; *b* 15 Aug. 1906; *s* of James Edward Shaw, DL, County Clerk of Ayrshire, and Gladys Elizabeth Lester; *m* 1937, Ruth Caroline Grant; two *s* three *d*. *Educ:* Charterhouse; Balliol Coll., Oxford; Edinburgh Univ. Admitted to Faculty of Advocates, 1932, Dean of Faculty, 1957; QC (Scotland) 1949; Sheriff of Ayr and Bute, 1954-57; Sheriff of Perth and Angus, 1957; Chancellor of Dioceses of Moray, Ross and Caithness, and Argyll and the Isles; Chairman: Standing Consultative Council on Youth Service in Scotland, 1960-68; Departmental Cttee on Treatment of Children and Young Persons, 1964; Scottish Boundary Commission, 1963; Scottish Law Commn, 1965; Bd of Management, Royal Infirmary, Edinburgh, 1960-68. Hon. LLD Aberdeen, 1965; Hon. DSc (Soc. Sci.) Edinburgh, 1970. hon. Fellow, Balliol Coll., Oxford, 1969. *Address:* 2 Blackie House, Lady Stair's Close, Edinburgh 1. *T:* 031-225 6928; Kilbrandon House, Balvicar, by Oban. *T:* Balvicar 239. *Clubs:* New, Royal Highland Yacht (Oban).

**KILBURN, Prof. Tom,** FRS 1965; Professor of Computer Science, University of Manchester, since 1964; *b* 11 Aug. 1921; *o s* of John W. and Ivy Kilburn, Dewsbury; *m* 1943, Irene (*née* Marsden); one *s* one *d*. *Educ:* Wheelwright Grammar Sch., Dewsbury; Sidney Sussex Coll., Cambridge; Manchester Univ. MA Cambridge 1944. Telecommunications Research Estab., Malvern, 1942-46. Manchester Univ., 1947-; PhD 1948; Lecturer, 1949; Senior Lecturer, 1951; DSc 1953; Reader in Electronics, 1955; Prof. of Computer Engineering, 1961. MIEE 1954. *Publications:* papers in Jl of Instn of Electrical Engineers, etc. *Address:* 11 Carlton Crescent, Urmston, Lancs. *T:* Urmston 3846.

**KILDARE, Marquess of; Gerald FitzGerald;** Major late 5th Royal Inniskilling Dragoon Guards; Managing Director, CSE Aviation Ltd; *b* 27 May 1914; *o s* of 7th Duke of Leinster, *qv*; *m* 1st, 1936, Joane (who obtained a divorce, 1946), *e d* of late Major McMorrough Kavanagh, MC, Borris House, Co. Carlow; two *d*; 2nd, 1946, Anne Eustace Smith; two *s*. *Educ:* Eton; Sandhurst. *Heir: s* Earl of Offaly, *qv*. *Recreations:* flying, fishing, shooting. *Address:* Langston House, Chadlington, Oxford. *T:* Chadlington 436. *Clubs:* Cavalry; Kildare Street (Dublin).

**KILDARE and LEIGHLIN, Bishop of,** (RC), since 1967; **Most Rev. Patrick Lennon,** DD; *b* Borris, Co. Carlow, 1914. *Educ:* Rockwell Coll., Cashel; St Patrick's Coll., Maynooth. BSc 1934; DD 1940. Prof. of Moral Theology, St Patrick's Coll., Carlow, 1940; Pres., St Patrick's Coll., 1956-66; Auxiliary Bishop and Parish Priest of Mountmellick, 1966-67. *Address:* Bishop's House, Carlow. *T:* Carlow 41217.

**KILÉNYI, Edward A.;** Professor of Music, Florida State University; *b* 7 May 1911; *s* of Edward Kilényi and Ethel Frater; *m* 1945, Kathleen Mary Jones; two *d*. *Educ:* Budapest; since childhood studied piano with Ernö Dohnányi; Theory and conducting Royal Academy of Music. First concert tour with Dohnányi (Schubert Centenary Festivals), 1928; concert tours, recitals, and soloist with Principal Symphony Orchestras, 1930-39, in Holland, Germany, Hungary, Roumania, France, Scandinavia, North Africa, Portugal, Belgium; English debut, 1935, with Sir Thomas Beecham in Liverpool, Manchester, London; tours, 1940-42, and 1946-, US, Canada, Cuba. Columbia and Remington Recordings internationally distributed. Served War of 1939-45, Capt. US Army, European theatre of operations. *Address:* c/o Florida State University, Tallahassee, Fla 32306, USA.

**KILFEDDER, James Alexander;** MP (UU) North Down since 1970; Barrister-at-Law; *b* 16 July 1928; *yr s* of late Robert and Elizabeth Kilfedder; unmarried. *Educ:* Model Sch. and Portora Royal Sch., Enniskillen, NI; Trinity Coll., Dublin (BA); King's Inn, Dublin. Called to English Bar, Gray's Inn, 1958; Mem., SE Circuit. MP (UU) Belfast West, 1964-66. *Recreation:* walking in the country. *Address:* 7 Gray's Inn Square, WC1. *T:* 01-405 6226; 5 Paper Buildings, Temple, EC4. *T:* 01-353 3724; Eastonville, Donaghadee Road, Millisle, NI. *T:* Donaghadee 3222.

**KILHAM ROBERTS, Denys,** OBE 1946; MA; Barrister-at-Law; Consultant, Society of Authors (previously Secretary-General); *b* 2 April 1903; *m* 1st, Elizabeth Hume Bone; one *d*; 2nd, Mary, *o d* of Dr T. K. Maclachlan, *qv*. *Educ:* St Paul's Sch.; Magdalene Coll., Cambridge. Called to Bar, Inner Temple, 1928. Has edited numerous periodicals and miscellanies. *Publications:* Titles to Fame, 1937; Straw in the Hair, 1938; The Centuries' Poetry 5 vols 1938-54; Stories of W. W. Jacobs, 1959; contribs on legal and literary subjects, wine and racing, to British and foreign books and periodicals. *Recreation:* bully-baiting. *Address:* Restharrow, Lombard, Lanteglos-by-Fowey, Cornwall; 84 Drayton Gardens, SW10.

**KILLALOE, Bishop of, (RC),** since 1967; **Most Rev. Michael Harty;** *b* Feb. 1922; *s* of Patrick Harty, Lismore, Toomevara, Co. Tipperary, Ireland. *Educ:* St Flannan's Coll., Ennis, Ire.; St Patrick's Coll., Maynooth, Ire.; University Coll., Galway. Priest, 1946; Prof., St Flannan's Coll., Ennis, 1948; Dean, St Patrick's Coll., Maynooth, 1950; Asst Priest, dio. Los Angeles, 1954. LCL, DD (Hon.); Hon. Dipl. in Educn. *Address:* Westbourne, Ennis, Co. Clare, Ireland. *T:* Ennis 21638.

**KILLALOE, KILFENORA, CLONFERT and KILMACDUAGH, Bishop of,** since 1957; **Rt. Rev. Henry Arthur Stanistreet,** DD (*jure dig*), Dublin University, 1958; *b* 19 March 1901; *s* of late Rev. Precentor A. H. Stanistreet; *m* 1938, Ethel Mary Liversidge; one *d*. *Educ:* Trent Coll., Derbyshire; St Columba's Coll., Rathfarnham; Trinity Coll., Dublin (MA). Ordained 1924. Curate, Clonmel with Innislonagh, 1924-27; Curate in charge, Corbally and Chaplain, Roscrea Hospital, 1927-30; Rector: Templeharry with Borrisnafarney, 1930-31; Roscrea, 1931-43; Surrogate, 1931; Rural Dean, Ely O'Carroll, 1933-43; Canon, Killaloe, 1940-43; Dean of Killaloe Cathedral, 1943-57; Prebendary, Killaloe, Rural Dean, O'Mullod, Rector, St Flannan with O'Gonnilloe and Castletownarra, 1943-57; Rural Dean, Traderry, 1949-57; Prebendary, St Patrick's Cathedral, Dublin, 1955-57. *Address:* Clarisford, Killaloe, Co. Clare, Eire. *T:* Killaloe 7. *Club:* University (Dublin).

**KILLANIN,** 3rd Baron, *cr* 1900; **Michael Morris,** Bt, *cr* 1885; MBE 1945; TD 1945; MRIA, MInstT; Author, Film Producer; *b* 30 July 1914; *o s* of late Lieut-Col Hon. George Henry Morris, Irish Guards, 2nd *s* of 1st Baron, and Dora Maryan [who *m* 2nd, 1918, Lieut-Col Gerard Tharp, Rifle Brigade (*d* 1934)], *d* of late James Wesley Hall, Melbourne, Australia; *S* uncle, 1927; *m* 1945, Mary Sheila Cathcart, MBE 1946, *o d* of Rev. Canon Douglas L. C. Dunlop, MA, Kilcummin, Galway; three *s* one *d*. *Educ:* Eton; Sorbonne, Paris; Magdalene Coll., Cambridge. BA 1935; MA 1939; formerly on Editorial Staff, Daily Express; Daily Mail, 1935-39; Special Daily Mail War Correspondent Japanese-Chinese War, 1937-38. Political Columnist Sunday Dispatch, 1938-39. Served War of 1939-45 (MBE, TD), KRRC (Queen's Westminsters); Brigade Maj. 30 Armd Bde, 1943-45. Director: Irish Shell and BP Ltd; Bovril (Ireland) Ltd (Chm.); Four Provinces Films; Lombard Bank (Ireland) Ltd (Chm.), etc. President: Olympic Council of Ireland; Incorporated Sales Managers' Association (Ireland), 1955-58; Galway Chamber of Commerce, 1952-53; Chm. of the Dublin Theatre Festival, 1958-70. member: Council Irish Red Cross Soc.; Cttee RNLI; Internat. Olympic Cttee (Vice-Pres., 1968-); Cultural Adv. Cttee to Minister for External Affairs; Nat. Monuments of Ireland Advisory Council (Chm., 1961-65); International Association of Art Critics; Irish National Hunt Steeplechase Cttee; first President, Irish Club, London, 1947-65; Trustee, Irish Sailors and Soldiers Land Trust; Hon. Consul-General for Monaco, in Ireland. Knight of Honour and Devotion of Sovereign Order of Malta, 1948; Finnish Order of Olympic Merit, 1952; Star of Italy, 1958; Comdr Order of The Grimaldi, Monaco, 1961; Austrian Olympic Medal, 1965. *Films:* (with John Ford) The Rising of the Moon; Gideon's Day; Young Cassidy; Playboy of the Western World; Alfred the Great. *Publications:* Contributions to British, American and European Press; Four Days; Sir Godfrey Kneller; Shell Guide to Ireland (with Prof. M. V. Duignan). *Heir: s* Hon. George Redmond Fitzpatrick Morris, [*b* 26 Jan. 1947. *Educ:* Ampleforth; Trinity Coll., Dublin]. *Address:* 30 Lansdowne Road, Dublin. *T:* 63362; St Annins, Spiddal, County Galway. *T:* Spiddal 3. *Clubs:* Garrick, Beefsteak; Stephen's Green (Dublin); Royal Irish Yacht (Dun Laoghaire); County (Galway).

**KILLBY, Leonard Gibbs,** CMG 1946; BA, BSc (Oxon); *b* 1883; *y s* of late James and Anne Killby; *m* 1926, Marjorie Mayson, *e d* of late Sir Mayson Beeton, KBE; no *c*, *Educ:* Brentwood Sch., Essex; New Coll., Oxford (Scholar). BA 1904, 1st Class Hons, School of Natural Science (Chemistry); Demonstrator in Chemistry, Christ Church, 1904-6; BSc (Oxon) 1907; on staff of City and Guilds of London Institute Department of Technology, 1906-20; succeeded Sir Philip Magnus as Superintendent of the Dept, 1914; served European War, 1915-18, first in France and subsequently attached Ministry of Munitions Chemical Warfare Dept, Capt. General List (despatches); Sec., Empire Cotton Growing Corporation, 1920-44, Dir, 1944-47. *Recreations:* gardening, photography. *Address:* Little Orchard, Charlbury, Oxford.

**KILLEARN,** 2nd Baron, *cr* 1943; **Graham Curtis Lampson;** *b* 28 Oct. 1919; *er s* of 1st Baron Killearn, PC, GCMG, CB, MVO, and his 1st wife (*née* Rachel Mary Hele Phipps) (*d* 1930), *d* of W. W. Phipps; *S* father, 1964; is *heir-pres.* to cousin, Sir Curtis George Lampson, 3rd Bt, *qv*; *m* 1946, Nadine Marie Cathryn, *o d* of late Vice-Adm. Cecil Horace Pilcher, DSO; two *d*. *Educ:* Eton Coll.; Magdalen Coll., Oxford (MA). Major, RARO, Scots Guards. US Bronze Star. *Heir: half-b* Capt. Hon. Victor Miles George Aldous Lampson, RARO, lately Scots Guards, *b* 9 Sept. 1941. *Address:* 5 Wilton Place, SW1. *T:* 01-235 6906. *Clubs:* Anglo-Belgian; MCC.

*See also Lord Eliot.*

**KILLEY, Professor Homer Charles;** Professor of Oral Surgery, University of London, since 1959; Hon. Consultant in Oral Surgery, and Head of Department of Oral Surgery, Eastman Dental Hospital, since 1959; Hon. Consultant, Westminster Hospital Teaching Group; *b* 5 May 1915; *s* of Thomas H. Killey and Marguerite Killey (*née* Parker); *m* 1940, Phoebe (*née* James); one *s*. *Educ:* King William's Coll., Isle of Man. KCH, LDSRCS, 1937; HDD Edinburgh, 1939; FDSRCS, 1948; Guy's Hospital, MRCS, LRCP, 1950; FDSRCS (Edinburgh) 1961. Consultant in oral and maxillo-facial surgery, Maxillo-facial Unit, Rooksdown House, Basingstoke, also Consultant in Oral Surgery, Holy Cross Hosp., Haslemere, Queen Mary's Hosp., Roehampton, and Aldershot Gen. Hosp., 1950-59. Hon. Civilian Lecturer in Maxillo-facial Injuries, Royal Army Dental Corps Depot, Aldershot, 1950-; Legg Memorial Lecturer, 1967. Member: Board of Dental Studies, University of London; British Assoc. of Head and Neck Oncologists; Associate

Mem. British Assoc. of Plastic Surgeons; Fellow, Internat. Assoc. of Oral Surgeons; FZS; FICS; FRSM; Foundn Fellow Brit. Assoc. of Oral Surgeons; Fellow, RSH. *Publications:* (jointly) Fractures of the Facial Skeleton, 1955; chapters in: Holdsworth's Cleft Lip and Palate, 3rd Edn, 1963; Morrant's Modern Trends in Dental Surgery, 1963; Hamilton Bailey's Emergency Surgery, 8th Edn, 1967; Fractures of Middle Third of the Facial Skeleton, 1965; The Impacted Wisdom Tooth (Killey and Kay), 1965; Benign Cystic Lesions of the Jaws (Killey and Kay), 1966; Fractures of the mandible, 1967; The Prevention of Complications in Dental Surgery (Killey and Kay), 1969; contrib. to learned jls. *Recreations:* reading and music. *Address:* Institute of Dental Surgery, Eastman Dental Hospital, Gray's Inn Road, WC1. *T:* 01-837 7251.

**KILLIAN, James Rhyne,** Jr; Chairman of Corporation, Massachusetts Institute of Technology, USA; *b* 24 July 1904; *s* of James R. and Jeannette R. Killian; *m* 1929, Elizabeth Parks; one *s* one *d*. *Educ:* Trinity Coll. (Duke Univ.), Durham, North Carolina; Mass Institute of Technology, Cambridge, Mass (BS). Asst Managing Editor, The Technology Review, MIT, 1926-27; Managing Editor, 1927-30; Editor, 1930-39; Exec. Asst to Pres., MIT, 1939-43; Exec. Vice-Pres., MIT, 1943-45; Vice-Pres., MIT, 1945-48; 10th Pres. of MIT, 1948-59 (on leave 1957-59); Special Asst to Pres. of United States for Science and Technology, 1957-59; Mem., 1957-61, Chm. 1957-59, Consultant-at-large, 1961-, President's Science Advisory Cttee; Mem., President's Bd of Consultants on Foreign Intelligence Activities, 1956-59 (Chm., 1956-58); Mem. of President's Commission on National Goals, 1960; Chm., President's Foreign Intelligence Advisory Board, 1961-63. Mem., Bd of Trustees: Alfred P. Sloan Foundation and Mitre Corporation; Pres. Bd of Trustees, Atoms for Peace Awards, Inc., 1959-69; Mem., Bd of Visitors, Tulane Univ., 1960-69; Trustee: Institute for Defense Analyses, Inc., 1959-69 (Chm., 1956-57, 1959-61); Mount Holyoke Coll.; Boston Museum of Science; US Churchill Foundation; Chm. Carnegie Commn on Educl TV, 1965-67; Director: General Motors Corp.; Polaroid Corp.; Amer. Tel. & Tel. Co.; Cabot Corp.; Corp. for Public Broadcasting; Fellow Amer. Acad. of Arts and Sciences; Hon. Mem., Amer. Soc. for Engrg Educn; Mem., Nat. Acad. of Engineering; Moderator, Amer. Unitarian Assoc., 1960-61; President's Certificate of Merit, 1948; Certificate of Appreciation, 1953, and Exceptional Civilian Service Award, 1957, Dept of the Army; Public Welfare Medal of the Nat. Acad. of Sciences, 1957; Officier Légion d'Honneur (France), 1957. Gold Medal Award, Nat. Inst. of Social Sciences, 1958; World Brotherhood Award, Nat. Conf. of Christians and Jews, 1958; Award of Merit, Amer. Inst. of Cons. Engineers, 1958; Washington Award, Western Soc. of Engineers, 1959; Distinguished Achievement Award, Holland Soc. of NY, 1959; Gold Medal of Internat. Benjamin Franklin Soc., 1960; Good Govt Award, Crosscup-Pishon Post, American Legion, 1960; Hoover Medal, 1963. Hon. degrees: ScD: Middlebury Coll., 1945; Bates Coll., 1950; University of Havana, 1953; University of Notre Dame, Lowell Technological Inst., 1954; Columbia Univ., Coll. of Wooster, Ohio, Oberlin Coll., 1958; University of Akron, 1959; Worcester Polytechnic Inst., 1960; University of Maine, 1963; DEng: Drexel Inst. of Tech., 1948; University of Ill., 1960; University of Mass., 1961; LLD: Union Coll., 1947; Bowdoin Coll., Northeastern Univ., Duke Univ., 1949; Boston Univ., Harvard Univ., 1950; Williams Coll., Lehigh Univ., University of Pa, 1951; University of Chattanooga, 1954; Tufts Univ., 1955; University of Calif. and Amherst Coll., 1956; College of William and Mary, 1957; Brandeis Univ., 1958; Johns Hopkins Univ., New York Univ., 1959; Providence Coll., Temple Univ. 1960; University of S Carolina, 1961; Meadville Theological Sch., 1962; DAppl Sci., University of Montreal, 1958; EdD, Rhode Island Coll., 1962; HHD, Rollins Coll., 1964. *Address:* 77 Massachusetts Avenue, Cambridge, Mass 02139, USA. *Clubs:* Algonquin, Odd Volumes, St Botolph, Union, (Boston); The Century, University (New York); Metropolitan (Washington).

**KILLICK, Brig. Sir Alexander Herbert,** Kt 1956; CBE 1944; DSO 1919; MC; *b*. 10 Feb. 1894; *m* 1920, Mary Catherine, *d* of Ira Wentzel, Bellwood, Penn., USA; one *s* one *d*. *Educ:* Dulwich Coll.; Exeter Coll., Oxford (MA); Staff Coll., Camberley (psc). Served European War 1914-19 (despatches, DSO, MC, Order of Nile of Egypt); retired (RARO) 1932. Sec., Royal Institution of Chartered Surveyors, 1932-59; Hon. Mem., 1959-; Sec.-Gen., Internat. Fedn of Surveyors, 1934-38. War of 1939-45: recalled to Colours (RARO); Gen. Staff, War Office, 1939-40; Joint Sec. (Mil.), Army Council Secretariat, WO, 1941-45, retd 1945; Hon. Brig. 1945. Mem., Mining Qualifications Bd, Min. of Power, 1959-62; Pres. Coll. of Estate Management, 1960-61; Director: London Merchant Securities and associated companies; Sanitas Trust; Invergordon Distillers (Holdings); Trustee, Max Rayne Foundation; Mem., Professional Classes Aid Council; Freeman, Worshipful Company of Farmers. *Address:* Carlton House, 33 Duke Street, W1M 5DF. *T:* 01-935 3555. *Clubs:* Army and Navy, St Stephen's.

**KILLICK, John Edward,** CMG 1966; Assistant Under-Secretary of State, Foreign and Commonwealth Office, since 1968; *b* 18 Nov. 1919; *s* of Edward William James Killick and Doris Marjorie (*née* Stokes); *m* 1949, Lynette du Preez (*née* Leach); no *c*. *Educ:* Latymer Upper Sch.; University Coll., London; Bonn Univ. Served with HM Forces, 1939-46: Suffolk Regt, W Africa Force and Airborne Forces. Foreign Office, 1946-48; Control Commn and High Commn for Germany (Berlin, Frankfurt and Bonn), 1948-51; Private Sec. to Parly Under-Sec., Foreign Office, 1951-54; British Embassy, Addis Ababa, 1954-57; Canadian Nat. Def. Coll., 1957-58; Western Dept, Foreign Office, 1958-62; Imp. Def. Coll., 1962; Counsellor and Head of Chancery, British Embassy, Washington, 1963-68. *Recreations:* golf, tennis, sailing. *Address:* 17 Park Road, Limpsfield, Oxted, Surrey. *Clubs:* Royal Commonwealth Society, Royal African Society.

**KILMAINE,** 6th Baron, *cr* 1789; **John Francis Archibald Browne,** Bt 1636; CBE 1956; Secretary of the Pilgrim Trust, 1945-67; a Trustee: the Historic Churches Preservation Trust; The Dulverton Trust (Secretary, 1953-66); High Steward of the Borough of Harwich; Chairman of the Oxford Society; a Governor of the Thomas Wall Trust; Chairman: Charities Investment Managers Ltd; Rochester Diocesan Advisory Committee for the care of Churches, since 1970; *b* 22 Sept. 1902; *e s* of 5th Baron and Lady Aline Kennedy (*d* 1957), *d* of 3rd Marquess of Ailsa; *S* father 1946; *m* 1930, Wilhelmina Phyllis, *o d* of Scott Arnott, Tanners, Brasted, Kent; one *s* two *d*. *Educ:* Winchester; Magdalen Coll., Oxford, MA. On staff of British Xylonite Co. Ltd, 1925-29; Administrative Sec. to University Coll., Southampton, 1930-33; Sec. of the

Oxford Society, 1933-40. served War of 1939-45 as Lt-Col RASC and on Staff, 1940-45 (despatches twice). *Heir:* s Hon. John David Henry Browne [*b* 2 April 1948. *Educ:* Eton]. *Address:* The Mount House, Brasted, Kent. *Club:* Travellers'.

**KILMANY, Baron,** *cr* 1966 (Life Peer), of Kilmany; **William John St Clair Anstruther-Gray;** 1st Bt, *cr* 1956; PC 1962; MC 1943; DL; *b* 1905; *o s* of late Col W. Anstruther-Gray, MP, DL, JP, of Kilmany; *m* 1934, Monica Helen, OBE 1946, JP, *o c* of late Geoffrey Lambton, 2nd *s* of 4th Earl of Durham; two *d.* *Educ:* Eton; Christ Church, Oxford, MA (Hons). Lieut, Coldstream Guards, 1926-30; served Shanghai Defence Force, 1927-28; rejoined Sept. 1939 and served N Africa, France, Germany, etc with Coldstream Guards and Lothians and Border Horse; Major, 1942; MP (U) for North Lanark, 1931-35; up to Sept. 1939 Parly Private Sec. to Rt Hon. Sir John Colville, MP, Sec. of State for Scotland, and previously to the Financial Sec. to the Treasury, and to Sec. for Overseas Trade; Asst Postmaster-Gen., May-July 1945; Crown nominee for Scotland on Gen. Medical Council, 1952-65. Contested (U) Berwick and East Lothian, 1951-66. Chm. of Ways and Means and Dep. Speaker, House of Commons, 1962-64 (Dep. Chm., 1959-62); Chm. Conservative Members' 1922 Cttee, 1964-66. Elected Mem. National Hunt Cttee, 1948; Mem., Horserace Betting Levy Bd, 1966-. DL Fife, 1953. *Address:* Kilmany, Cupar, Fife. *T:* Gauldry 247. *Clubs:* Carlton, Guards, Brooks's, Turf, Jockey; New (Edinburgh).
*See also A. C. Macnab of Macnab.*

**KILMARNOCK,** 6th Baron, *cr* 1831; **Gilbert Allan Rowland Boyd,** MBE 1945; Chairman, Harris and Dixon, Ltd; Chairman, Baltic Mercantile & Shipping Exchange, 1965-67 (Vice-Chairman 1963-65); Hon. Lieutenant-Colonel RA (TA), (retired); late Hertfordshire Yeomanry; Chief of the Clan Boyd; *b* 15 Jan. 1903; *yr s* of 21st Earl of Erroll; *S* to Barony of brother, 22nd Earl of Erroll, 1941; assumed surname of Boyd instead of Hay, 1941; *m* 1st, 1926, Hon. Rosemary Guest (marriage dissolved, 1955; she *m* 2nd, 1955, John Berger), *er d* of 1st Viscount Wimborne; two *s* two *d*; 2nd, 1955, Denise, *o c* of late Major Lewis Coker and of Mrs T. E. Fenlon; two *s.* *Educ:* Cheltenham Coll. Served War of 1939-45, N Africa and Italy with 1st Div. as DAAG, 1943-44 (despatches, MBE). Asst Military Sec. to Supreme Allied C-in-C Mediterranean Theatre, 1945. Deputized for Lord High Constable of Scotland at Coronation of HM the Queen, 1953. Pres. Inst. of Chartered Shipbrokers, 1959-62; Pres. London Chamber of Commerce, 1961-63. Chief of the Scottish Clans Assoc. of London, 1962. A Freeman of the City of London; A Liveryman of the Worshipful Company of Shipwrights. President: Sino-British Trade Council, 1961-63; Royal Caledonian Schools, Bushey, Herts, 1964-. *Recreations:* shooting, gardening. *Heir:* *s* Hon. Alastair Ivor Gilbert Boyd, Lieutenant Irish Guards, retired [*b* 11 May 1927; *m* 1954, Diana Mary (marr. diss. 1970), *o d* of D. Grant Gibson. Served Palestine, 1947-48]. *Address:* 28 Eaton Terrace, SW1. *T:* 01-730 8393. *Clubs:* White's, Pratt's.

**KILMORE, Bishop of, (RC),** since 1950; **Most Rev. Austin Quinn,** DD; *b* Brookley, Co. Armagh, 15 March 1892. *Educ:* St Patrick's Coll., Armagh; Maynooth Coll. Ordained, 1915; DD (Maynooth) 1920. Prof. in All Hallows Coll., Dublin, 1917-26; Curate in Archdiocese of Armagh, 1926-40; Administrator, Cathedral, Armagh, 1940-43; Parish Priest of St Peter's, Drogheda, Archdeacon of Cathedral Chapter, and Vicar General of Archdiocese of Armagh, 1943-50. *Address:* Bishop's House, Cullis, Cavan, Ireland. *T:* Cavan 55.

**KILMORE and ELPHIN and ARDAGH, Bishop of,** since 1959; **Rt. Rev. Edward Francis Butler Moore,** DD; *b* 1906; *s* of Rev. W. R. R. Moore; *m* 1932, Frances Olivia Scott; two *s* two *d.* *Educ:* Trinity Coll., Dublin (MA, PhD, DD). Deacon, 1930; Priest, 1931; Curate, Bray, 1930-32; Hon. Clerical Vicar, Christ Church Cathedral, Dublin, 1931-35; Curate, Clontarf, 1932-34; Incumbent, Castledermot with Kinneagh, 1934-40; Greystones, Diocese of Glendalough, 1940-49; Chaplain to Duke of Leinster, 1934-40; Rural Dean, Delgany 1950-59; Canon of Christ Church, Dublin, 1951-57; Archdeacon of Glendalough, 1957-59. *Recreations:* tennis, golf, fishing. *Address:* See House, Cavan, Ireland. *Club:* University (Dublin).

**KILMOREY,** 5th Earl of, *cr* 1822; **Francis Jack Richard Patrick Needham;** Viscount Kilmorey, 1625; Viscount Newry and Mourne, 1822; *b* 4 Oct. 1915; *er s* of Major Hon. Francis Edward Needham, MVO, Gren. Guards (*d* 1955) and of Blanche Esther Combe; *S* uncle, 1961; *m* 1941, Helen Bridget, *y d* of Sir Lionel Faudel-Phillips, 3rd and last Bt; three *s.* *Educ:* Stowe; RMC, Sandhurst. 2nd Lt Gren. Gds, 1935. Served War of 1939-45 (wounded): Europe and N Africa; Major 1943. *Recreations:* shooting, fishing. *Heir:* *s* Viscount Newry and Morne (*see under* Needham, Richard Francis). *Address:* Via San Leonardo 32, Florence, Italy. *T:* Florence 220284. *Club:* Turf.
*See also Earl of Jersey.*

**KILMUIR, Countess of;** *see* De La Warr, Countess.

**KILNER, Cyril;** Assistant Editor, Doncaster Gazette, since 1952; *b* 5 Sept. 1910; *s* of Bernard Kilner and Edith Annie (*née* Booker); *m* 1949, Joan Siddons; one *s* one *d.* *Educ:* Mexborough Grammar School. Army War Service in Royal Tank Regt, 1940-45. Reporter, Barnsley Independent, 1927-30; Reporter, Sports Editor, Sub-Editor, Barnsley Chronicle, 1931-47; Reporter, Sub-Editor, Yorkshire Evening News (Doncaster edn), 1947-52. Member: The Press Council, 1968-; Nat. Exec. Council, NUJ, 1958- (Pres., 1969). *Recreations:* Rugby, cricket, table tennis, athletics. *Address:* Cranford, 159 Boothferry Road, Goole, Yorks. *T:* Goole 3774. *Club:* London Press.

**KILNER BROWN, Hon. Sir Ralph;** *see* Brown.

**KILPATRICK, Rev. George Dunbar;** Dean Ireland's Professor of Exegesis of Holy Scripture, Oxford, since 1949; Fellow of the Queen's College, Oxford; Fellow of University College, London, since 1967; *b* Coal Creek, Fernie, BC, Canada, 15 Sept. 1910; *o c* of late Wallace Henry and Bessie Kilpatrick; *m* 1943, Marion, *d* of Harold Laver and Dorothy Madeline Woodhouse; one *s* three *d.* *Educ:* Ellis Sch., BC; St Dunstan's Coll.; University Coll., London; Oriel Coll., Oxford (Scholar); University of London, Granville Scholar, 1931; BA Classics (1st Class), 1932; University of Oxford, BA Lit. Hum. (2nd Class), 1934, Theology (2nd Class), 1936, Junior Greek Testament Prize, 1936, Senior Greek Testament Prize, 1937, Junior Denyer and Johnson Scholarship, 1938, BD 1944; Grinfield Lecturer, 1945-49; DD 1948; Schweich Lecturer, 1951; Deacon 1936; Priest 1937; Asst Curate of Horsell, 1936; Tutor, Queen's Coll., Birmingham, 1939; Asst Curate of Selly Oak, 1940; Acting Warden of Coll. of the Ascension,

Birmingham, 1941; Rector of Wishaw, Warwicks, and Lecturer at Lichfield Theological Coll., 1942; Head of Dept of Theology and Reader in Christian Theology, University Coll., Nottingham, 1946. Vice-Pres., British and Foreign Bible Soc., 1958. *Publications:* The Origins of the Gospel according to St Matthew, 1946; The Trial of Jesus, 1953; Remaking the Liturgy, 1967. Editor: The New Testament in Greek, British and Foreign Bible Society's 2nd edn, 1958; contributions to periodicals. *Recreation:* reading. *Address:* The Queen's College and 27 Lathbury Road, Oxford. *T:* Oxford 58909.

**KILPATRICK, Dr George Gordon Dinwiddie,** DSO 1919; ED 1950; BA, DD; LLD; DCL; Principal, United Theological College, Montreal, 1938-43 and again, 1945-55, retired; Assistant Minister of St Andrews United Church, Toronto, since Sept. 1955; *b* 12 April 1888; *s* of Thomas Buchanan Kilpatrick and Anna Orr; *m* 1920, Ruth McGillivray Fotheringham; three *s* one *d*. *Educ:* Grammar Sch., Aberdeen, Scotland; The Collegiate, Winnipeg; Toronto Univ.; Knox Theological Coll., Toronto; New Coll., Edinburgh. Travelling Scholarship to Germany, 1913-14; Asst Minister Westminster Presbyterian Church, Toronto; Canadian Expeditionary Force (42nd Bn Royal Highlanders) 1915-19, (DSO, despatches, two medals); Minister St Andrew's Presbyterian Church, Ottawa, 1919-25; Minister Chalmers United Church, Ottawa, 1925-29; Minister Melrose Church, The United Church of Canada, 1929-38. Dir of Education, Canadian Army (rank–Col), 1943-Dec. 1945. The DD has been conferred by 4 Colleges. *Recreations:* golf, fishing, squash, badminton, etc. *Address:* 133 Eastbourne Avenue, Toronto. *Clubs:* Royal Montreal Curling, McGill University Faculty (Montreal).

**KILPATRICK, Sir William (John),** KBE 1965 (CBE 1958); Chairman: Guardian Assurance Group; Business Equipment Group Ltd; *b* 27 Dec. 1906; *s* of late James Park Scott Kilpatrick, Scotland; *m* 1932, Alice Margaret Strachan; one *s* three *d*. *Educ:* Wollongong, NSW. Sqdn Ldr, RAAF, 1942-45. Pastoral interests, Victoria. Mem., Melbourne City Council, 1958-64. Chm. Cancer Service Cttee, Anti-Cancer Coun. of Vic., 1958-; Dep. Nat. Pres., Nat. Heart Foundn of Aust., 1960-64; Chm., Finance Cttee, Nat. Heart Foundn of Aust., 1960-; Pres. Aust. Cancer Soc., 1961-64; World Chm., Finance Cttee, Internat. Union Against Cancer, 1961-; Ldr Aust. Delegn to 8th Internat. Cancer Congr, Moscow, 1962. Nat. Chm. Winston Churchill Mem. Trust, 1965; Pres., The ESU of the Commonwealth (Vic. Br.), 1968. *Recreations:* golf, swimming. *Address:* 8 Hopetoun Road, Toorak, Victoria 3142, Australia. *T:* 20 5206. *Clubs:* Naval and Military, Victorian Golf, VRC, VATC (all Melbourne); Commonwealth (Canberra).

**KILROY, Dame Alix;** *see* Meynell, Dame Alix.

**KILVINGTON, Frank Ian;** Headmaster of St Albans School since 1964; *b* West Hartlepool, 26 June 1924; *e s* of H. H. Kilvington; *m* 1949, Jane Mary, *d* of Very Rev. Michael Clarke, *qv*; one *s* one *d*. *Educ:* Repton (entrance and foundn scholar); Corpus Christi, Oxford (open class. scholar). 2nd cl. Lit Hum, 1948; MA 1950. Served War of 1939-45: RNVR, 1943-46 (Lt); West Africa Station, 1943-45; RN Intelligence, Germany, 1945-46. Westminster School: Asst Master, 1949-64; Housemaster of Rigaud's House, 1957-64. Chm., St Albans Marriage Guidance Council, 1968. *Publication:* A Short History of St Albans School, 1970. *Recreations:* music, local history. *Address:* Abbey Gateway, St Albans, Herts. *T:* St Albans 55702. *Club:* Public Schools.

**KIMBALL, Major Lawrence;** *b* 1900; *s* of Marcus Morton Kimball; *m* 1st, 1927, Kathleen Joan (marr. diss., 1946), *o surv d* of late H. R. Ratcliff of Stanford Hall, Loughborough; one *s* one *d*; 2nd, Gillian, *d* of late W. S. Tresawna, Leven House, Abergavenny, and *widow* of Capt. John Waterman. *Educ:* abroad; Caius Coll., Cambridge. Barrister-at-Law, Gray's Inn, 1926; MP (U) Loughborough Div. of Leics, 1931-45; High Sheriff of Rutland 1931. Lt PAO Leics Yeo., 1929; Capt. 67th LAA Regt, RA, 1939; Major 1940. *Address:* Down House, Redlynch, Salisbury, Wilts. *T:* Downton 347. *Clubs:* St James', Carlton. *See also M. R. Kimball.*

**KIMBALL, Marcus Richard;** MP (C) Gainsborough Division of Lincolnshire since Feb. 1956; *b* 18 Oct. 1928; *s* of Major Lawrence Kimball, *qv*; *m* 1956, June Mary Fenwick; two *d*. *Educ:* Eton; Trinity Coll., Cambridge. Contested Derby South, Gen. Election, 1955. Privy Council Rep., Council of RCVS, 1969. Jt Master and Huntsman: Fitzwilliam Hounds, 1950-51 and 1951-52; Cottesmore Hounds, 1952-53, 1953-54, 1955-56 (Jt Master, 1956-58). Chm., British Field Sports Soc., 1966. Lt Leics Yeo. (TA), 1947; Capt., 1951. Mem. Rutland CC, 1955. *Address:* Great Easton Manor, Market Harborough, Leics. *T:* Rockingham 333; Altnaharra, Lairg, Sutherland. *T:* Altnaharra 224; 70 Cranmer Court, Sloane Avenue, SW3. *T:* 01-536 3257. *Clubs:* Buck's, Pratt's.

**KIMBER, Sir Charles Dixon,** 3rd Bt, *cr* 1904; *b* 7 Jan. 1912; *o surv s* of Sir Henry Dixon Kimber, 2nd Bt, and Lucy Ellen, *y d* of late G. W. Crookes; *S* father 1950; *m* 1st, 1933, Ursula (marr. diss., 1949), *er d* of late Ernest Roy Bird, MP; three *s*; 2nd, 1950, Margaret Bonham (marr. diss., 1965), Writer; one *s* one *d*. *Educ:* Eton; Balliol Coll., Oxford (BA). *Heir: s* Timothy Roy Henry Kimber [*b* 3 June 1936; *m* 1960, Antonia Kathleen Brenda, *d* of Francis John Watkin Williams, *qv*; two *s*].

**KIMBER, Gurth,** CMG 1952; *b* 19 Jan. 1906; *s* of late R. J. Kimber; *m* 1943, Joan, *d* of late Roy Gibson and of Mrs Emily Gibson, Ditton Grange, Surbiton; two *d*. *Educ:* Perse; Clare Coll., Cambridge. Appointed Dominions Office, 1928; Asst UK Government Representative, Canberra, 1934-35; Official Sec., United Kingdom High Commissioner's Office, Canberra, 1946-50; Dep. High Commissioner for the UK, Bombay, 1952-54; Counsellor, British Embassy, Dublin, 1956-60; British Dep. High Commissioner, Canberra, 1962-65; retired, 1966. *Recreation:* sailing. *Address:* 14 Stoke Road, Nayland, Suffolk.

**KIMBERLEY,** 4th Earl of, *cr* 1866; **John Wodehouse;** Bt, 1611; Baron Wodehouse, 1797; Lt Grenadier Guards; *b* 12 May 1924; *o s* of 3rd Earl and Margaret (*d* 1950), *d* of late Col Leonard Howard Irby; *S* father 1941; *m* 1st, 1945; 2nd, 1949; one *s*; 3rd, 1953; two *s*; 4th, 1961; one *s*. *Educ:* Eton; Cambridge. *Heir: s* Lord Wodehouse, *qv*. *Clubs:* Guards, Bath.

**KIMBERLEY and KURUMAN, Bishop of,** 1961-65 and since 1968; **Rt. Rev. Philip William Wheeldon,** OBE 1946; *b* 20 May 1913; *e s* of late Alfred Leonard Wheeldon and late Margaret Proctor Wheeldon (*née* Smith); *m* 1966, Margaret Redfearn. *Educ:* Clifton Coll., Bristol; Downing Coll., Cambridge; Westcott House Theological Coll. BA 1935, MA 1942. Deacon, 1937; Priest, 1938; Farnham Parish Church, Dio. Guildford, 1937-39; Chaplain to the Forces, 1939-46; Chaplain, 1st Bn

Coldstream Guards, 1939-42; Senior Chaplain, 79th Armoured Div., 1942-43; Dep. Asst Chaplain-Gen. 12th Corps, 1943-45; 8th Corps, 1945-46; Hon. Chaplain to the Forces, 1946-; Domestic Chaplain to Archbishop of York, 1946-49, Hon. Chaplain, 1950-54; General Sec., CACTM, 1949-54; Prebendary of Wedmore II in Wells Cathedral, 1952-54; Suffragan Bishop of Whitby, 1954-61; Bishop of Kimberley and Kuruman, 1961-65; resigned, 1965; an Asst Bishop, Dio. Worcester, 1965-68. *Recreations:* music and sport. *Address:* Bishopsgarth, Bishop's Avenue, Kimberley, CP, S Africa. *Clubs:* St James', Royal Automobile.

**KIMBLE, George (Herbert Tinley),** PhD; retired; *b* 2 Aug. 1908; *s* of John H. and Minnie Jane Kimble; *m* 1935, Dorothy Stevens Berry; one *s* one *d*. *Educ:* Eastbourne Grammar Sch.; King's Coll., London (MA); University of Montreal (PhD). Asst Lecturer in Geography, University of Hull, 1931-36; Lecturer in Geography, University of Reading, 1936-39. Served War as Lt and Lt-Comdr, British Naval Meteorological Service, 1939-44. Prof. of Geography and Chm. Dept of Geography, McGill Univ., 1945-50; Sec.-Treasurer, Internat. Geographical Union, 1949-56; Chm., Commn on Humid Tropics, Internat. Geog. Union, 1956-61. Dir, Amer. Geog. Soc., 1950-53; Dir, Survey of Tropical Africa, Twentieth Century Fund, NY, 1953-60. Chm., Dept of Geography, Indiana Univ., 1957-62; Prof. of Geography, Indiana Univ., 1957-66; Research Dir, US Geography Project, Twentieth Century Fund, 1962-68. Rushton Lecturer, 1952; Borah Lecturer, University of Idaho, 1956; Haynes Foundn Lectr, University of Redlands, 1966; Visiting Prof., University of Calif. (Berkeley), 1948-49; Stanford Univ., 1961; Stockholm Sch. of Economics, 1961. *Publications:* Geography in the Middle Ages, 1938; The World's Open Spaces, 1939; The Shepherd of Banbury, 1941; (co-author) The Weather, 1943 (Eng.), 1946 (Amer.), (author) 2nd (Eng.) edn, 1951; Military Geography of Canada, 1949; The Way of the World, 1953; Our American Weather, 1955; Le Temps, 1957; Tropical Africa (2 vols), 1960; Tropical Africa (abridged edition), 1962; (with Ronald Steel) Tropical Africa Today, 1966. (Ed. for Hakluyt Soc.) Esmeraldo de Situ Orbis, 1937; (Ed. for American Geographical Soc. with Dorothy Good) Geography of the Northlands, 1955; articles in: Geog. Jl, Magazine, Review; Canadian Geog. Jl; Bulletin Amer. Meteorological Soc.; The Reporter; Los Angeles Times; The New York Times Magazine. *Recreations:* music, gardening. *Address:* La Marine de Davia, Ile-Rousse, Corsica.

**KIMMINS, Lt-Gen. Sir Brian Charles Hannam,** KBE 1956 (CBE 1944); CB 1946; DL; retired; *b* 30 July 1899; *s* of late Dr Charles William Kimmins and Dame Grace Kimmins, DBE; *m* 1929, Marjory, *d* of late Lt-Col W. J. Johnston, CBE, Lesmurdie, Elgin, Scotland; one *s* two *d*. *Educ:* Harrow; RMA, Woolwich. Commissioned RA 1917; served France and Flanders, 1918; in RHA in India, 1920-26; RHA in Egypt, 1926-28; ADC to Lord Lloyd, High Commissioner for Egypt and the Sudan, 1928-29; Adjutant RMA, Woolwich, 1930-33; Bde Major 147 Inf. Bde (TA), 1935-37; Staff Coll., Minley Manor, 1938-39; GSO 2 HQ, BEF, France, 1939-40: Instructor Staff Coll., 1940-41; GSO 1 ops GHQ Home Forces, 1941; DDMT War Office, 1941-42; BGS Southern Command, 1942; CRA Guards Armoured Div., 1943; Director of Plans, SEAC, 1944; Asst Chief of Staff, HQ, SACSEA, 1945; Chief of Staff HQ Combined Operations, 1946; Dir of Quartering, War Office, 1947-50; GOC, Home Counties District and 44th Div. TA, 1950-52; Dir, Territorial Army and Cadets, 1952-55; GOC Northern Ireland District, 1955-58. Col Comdt, Royal Artillery, 1955-64. DL, Somerset, 1968. Legion of Merit degree of Comdr (USA), 1946. Legion of Honour degree of Officer, Croix de Guerre (France), 1949. OStJ 1959. *Recreations:* fishing, golf. *Address:* Lamb Cottage, South Petherton, Somerset. *Club:* Army and Navy.

**KIMPTON, Lawrence Alpheus;** Assistant to Chairman of the Board, Standard Oil Co. (Ind), since 1969 (Executive since 1960, Director since 1958, Vice-President 1963), *b* 7 Oct. 1910; *s* of Carl Edward Kimpton and Lynn (*née* Kennedy); *m* 1943, Marcia Drennon (*d* 1963). *Educ:* Stanford Univ., Stanford, Calif. (AB, MA); Cornell Univ., Ithaca, NY (PhD). Hon. DSc, Beloit Coll., 1952; Hon. LLD of several univs; 24th Hon. Stanford Fellow, 1959. Deep Springs Coll., Calif: Instructor, 1935-36; Dean and Dir, 1936-41; Dean, College of Liberal Arts, Prof. of Mathematics and Philosophy, University of Kansas City, 1942-43; University of Chicago: Chief Admin. Officer, Atomic Bomb Project, 1943-44; Prof. of Philosophy and Education, 1944-46; Academic Vice-Pres., Prof. of Philosophy and Education, 1946-47; Vice-Pres. in Charge of Development, 1950-51; Chancellor and Prof. of Philosophy, 1951-60; Dean of Students, Prof. of Philosophy, Stanford Univ., 1947-50; Trustee: Museum of Science and Industry, 1961; Robert A. Taft Inst. of Government, 1961-; Newberry Library, 1962-. *Recreations:* boating, reading. *Address:* 910 S Michigan Avenue, Chicago, Illinois 60680, USA. *T:* 856-6530. *Clubs:* Chicago, Commercial, Commonwealth, Economic, Tavern, Wayfarers' Chicago Yacht (Chicago); Bohemian (San Francisco).

**KINAHAN, Adm. Sir Harold (Richard George),** KBE 1949 (CBE 1942); CB 1945; retired; *b* 4 June 1893; *s* of Vice-Adm. R. G. Kinahan, Belfast; *m* 1919, Mary Kathleen Downes (*d* 1970) Two *d* *Educ:* RN Colls, Osborne and Dartmouth. Entered RNC, Osborne, 1906; Lt 1914; Comdr 1927; Capt. 1934; Rear-Adm. 1943; Vice-Adm. 1947; Adm. 1950. DPS, Admiralty, 1944-46; Flag Officer Comdg 1st Cruiser Sqdn, Mediterranean Fleet, 1946-47; Vice-Pres., 1947-49, Pres., 1949-50, Ordnance Board; Pres., RNC, Greenwich, 1950-52; retired list, 1952. *Address:* Severnridge, Almondsbury, Glos. *Club:* United Service.

**KINAHAN, Sir Robert (George Caldwell),** Kt 1961; ERD 1946; DL; JP; Chairman: Charrington Kinahan Ltd (Managing Director, Lyle & Kinahan Ltd, 1956); Inglis & Co. Ltd; The Ulster Brewery Ltd; E. T. Green Ltd; Ulster Folk Museum; Ulster Bank Ltd; Director: United Breweries Ltd; Charrington United Breweries Ltd; Gallaher Ltd; *b* 24 Sept. 1916; *s* of Henry Kinahan, Lowwood, Belfast; *m* 1950, Coralie I., *d* of Capt. C. de Burgh, *qv*; two *s* three *d*. *Educ:* Stowe Sch., Buckingham. Vintners' Scholar (London), 1937. Served Royal Artillery, 1939-45, Capt. Councillor, Belfast Corporation, 1948; JP Co. Antrim, 1950, DL 1962; High Sheriff: Belfast, 1956; Co. Antrim, 1969. MP (N Ireland), Clifton constituency, 1958-59. Lord Mayor of Belfast, 1959-61. Hon. LLD (Belfast) 1962. *Recreations:* tennis, family life. *Address:* Castle Upton, Templepatrick, Co. Antrim. *T:* Templepatrick 466. *Club:* Ulster (Belfast).

**KINDERSLEY,** family name of **Baron Kindersley.**

**KINDERSLEY,** 2nd Baron, *cr* 1941, of West Hoathly; **Hugh Kenyon Molesworth Kindersley,** CBE 1945 (MBE 1941); MC 1918; Director:

Lazard Brothers & Co. Ltd, since 1965 (Chairman, 1953-64; Managing Director, 1927-64); Cierva Rotocraft Co. Ltd; *b* 1899; *s* of 1st Baron Kindersley, GBE, and Gladys Margaret Beadle; *S* father 1954; *m* 1921, Nancy Farnsworth, *d* of Dr Geoffrey Boyd, Toronto; one *s* two *d*. *Educ:* Eton. Served European War, Scots Guards, 1917-19 (MC). War of 1939-45, Scots Guards, temporary Brig. (MBE, CBE). Chairman: Rolls Royce Ltd, 1956-68; Guardian Royal Exchange Assurance Ltd, 1968-69; Governor, Royal Excahnge Assurance, 1955-69; Dir, Bank of England, 1947-67. Chm., Review Body on Doctors' and Dentists' Remuneration, 1962-70. Hon. FRCS, 1959. High Sheriff of the County of London, 1951. Mem., Court of Patrons, RCS, 1960. Comdr, Royal Order of St Olav of Norway, 1958. *Heir: s* Hon. Robert Hugh Molesworth Kindersley, Lt, Scots Guards [*b* 18 Aug. 1929; *m* 1954, Venice Marigold (Rosie), *d* of late Capt. Lord (Arthur) Francis Henry Hill; three *s* one *d*. *Educ:* Eton; Trinity Coll., Oxford; Harvard Business Sch., USA. Served in Malaya, 1949]. *Address:* Ramhurst Manor, Near Tonbridge, Kent. *T:* Hildenborough, 2174; 16 Bryanston Court, George Street, W1. *T:* 01-262 6900. *Clubs:* White's.

*See also Sir Napier Crookenden, Hon. J. P. Philipps.*

**KING,** family name of **Earl of Lovelace.**

**KING, Albert Leslie,** MBE 1945; *b* 28 Aug. 1911; *s* of late William John King and of Elizabeth Mary Amelia King; *m* 1938, Constance Eileen Stroud; two *d*. *Educ:* University Coll. Sch., Hampstead. Joined Shell-Mex and BP Statistical Dept, 1928. Joined Territorial Army, 1939; Major, RA, 1944. Manager, Secretariat, Petroleum Board, 1947; Manager, Trade Relations Dept, Shell-Mex and BP Ltd, 1948; Gen. Manager: Administration, 1954; Sales, 1957; Operations, 1961; apptd Dir, 1962, Managing Dir, 1963-66. Dep. Dir-Gen., BIM, 1966-68. FACCA 1965. Hon. JDipMA, 1965. *Address:* Highlands, 50 Waggon Road, Hadley Wood, Barnet, Herts. *T:* 01-449 6424. *Clubs:* Reform, MCC.

**KING, Alexander,** CBE 1948; Director-General for Scientific Affairs, OECD, since 1968; *b* Glasgow, 26 Jan. 1909; *s* of J. M. King; *m* 1933, Sarah Maskell Thompson; three *d*. *Educ:* Highgate Sch.; Royal College of Science, London (DSc); University of Munich. Demonstrator, 1932, and later Senior Lecturer, until 1940, in physical chemistry, Imperial Coll. of Science; Dep. Scientific Adviser, Min. of Production, 1942; Head of UK Scientific Mission, Washington, and Scientific Attaché, British Embassy 1943-47; Head of Lord President's Scientific Secretariat, 1947-50; Chief Scientific Officer, Dept of Scientific and Industrial Research, 1950-56; Dep. Dir, European Productivity Agency, 1956-61. Leader Imperial Coll. Expedition to Jan Mayen, 1938; Harrison Prize of Chemical Soc., 1938; Gill Memorial Prize, Royal Geographical Society, 1938, mem. Council, 1939-41; Hon. Sec. Chemical Soc., 1948-50. *Publications:* various chemistry textbooks, and papers in Journal of The Chemical Soc., Faraday Soc., etc. *Address:* 168 Rue de Grenelle, Paris VII, France. *Club:* Athenæum.

**KING, Sir Alexander Boyne,** Kt 1944; CBE 1937; DL 1947; LLD 1957; JP; director of cinema companies, *b* Glasgow, 1888; *s* of late James L. King and late Mrs King; *m* 1919, Helen (*d* 1965), *d* of late John Craig, Glasgow; two *d*. *Educ:* Rutland Crescent Sch., Glasgow. Entered Theatrical Profession, 1900, and Cinematograph Industry, 1913; Past President, Cinematograph Exhibitors' Assoc. (1949-50). Chairman: Films of Scotland Cttee; Grants Sub-Cttee Scottish Advisory Cttee to Army Benevolent Fund; Appeals Cttee, IXth British Commonwealth Games, Edinburgh, 1970. KStJ 1964. Officier de la Légion d'Honneur, 1961. *Recreations:* golf, fishing. *Address:* Tigh-na-Righ, The Grove, Whitecraigs, Giffnock, Glasgow; 309 Sauchiehall Street, Glasgow C2. *TA:* Kenafilm Glasgow. *T:* (office) 041-332 8668; (home) 041-638 1000. *Clubs:* Royal Scottish Automobile (Glasgow); Royal and Ancient (St Andrews); Western Gailes, Nairn, Old Troon Golf.

**KING, Alison;** Director/Administrator, Premises, Women's Royal Voluntary Service, since 1969. Flight-Capt., Operations, Air Transport Auxiliary, 1940-45. Dir, Women's Junior Air Corps, 1952-58; Gen. Sec., NFWI, 1959-69. Chm., British Women Pilots' Assoc., 1956-64. *Publication:* Golden Wings, 1956. *Recreations:* writing, painting in oils. *Address:* 87 Kenilworth Court, Putney, SW15. *T:* 01-788 4087. *Club:* Royal Aero.

**KING, Sir Anthony (Highmore),** Kt 1962; CBE 1953; Senior Master and Queen's Remembrancer, 1960-62; Queen's Coroner and Attorney, Master of the Crown Office and Registrar of the Court of Criminal Appeal, 1946-62; *b* 22 April 1890; 2nd *s* of Sir George Anthony King; *m* 1934, Winifride Botterell McConnell; no *c*. *Educ:* Winchester Coll.; Corpus Christi Coll., Oxford. Barrister-at-Law, Inner Temple, 1913. Served European War, 1914-18: France; Lt East Surrey Regt. Asst Registrar, Court of Criminal Appeal, 1933. Master, Scriveners' Company, 1933 and 1947. Hon. Liveryman, Glass-Sellers' Company, 1966. *Address:* Polyapes, Eaton Park Road, Cobham, Surrey. *T:* Cobham (Surrey) 2256. *Club:* United University.

**KING, Prof. Basil Charles;** Professor of Geology, Bedford College, University of London, since 1956; *b* 1 June 1915; *s* of Charles William Argent King; *m* 1939, Dorothy Margaret Wells; two *s* two *d*. *Educ:* King Edward VI Sch., Bury St Edmunds; Durham Univ.; London Univ. Demonstrator, Bedford Coll., London, 1936-38; Chemist and Petrologist, Geological Survey of Uganda, 1938-46; Mineralogist, Geological Survey of Nigeria, 1946-48; Senior Lecturer, University of Glasgow, 1948-56. FRSE 1950. Bigsby Medal, Geological Soc., 1959; André Dumont Medal, Société Géologique de Belgique, 1967. *Publications:* geological publications on E Africa, Nigeria, Bechuanaland and Scotland. *Address:* 5 Wentworth Way, Pinner, Middlesex. *T:* 01-866 5210.

**KING, Dr Brian Edmund;** Director, Wool Industries Research Association, since 1967; *b* 25 May 1928; *s* of Albert Theodore King and Gladys Johnson; *m* 1952, Thelma Margaret Lane; two *s*. *Educ:* Pocklington Sch.; Leeds Univ. TMM (Research) Ltd, 1952-57; British Oxygen, 1957-67. *Recreation:* swimming. *Address:* Stone Weald, Manor Close, Bramhope, Leeds LS16 9HQ. *T:* Arthington 2146.

**KING, Cecil Edward,** CMG 1956; HM Diplomatic Service, retired 1970; *b* 27 March 1912; *s* of John Stuart King and Thérèse (*née* Dubied); *m* 1944, Isabel Haynes; two *s* one *d*. *Educ:* King Edward VII Sch., Sheffield; Charterhouse; Queen's Coll., Oxford. Appointed Vice-Consul in HM Consular Service, 1934; served in Europe, North and South America, 1934-61; HM Ambassador, Yaoundé, 1961-63; Minister for Trusteeship

Affairs at the UK Mission to the UN, 1963-65; Asst Under-Sec. of State, Foreign Office, 1965-67; Ambassador to the Lebanon, 1967-70. *Address:* c/o National Westminster Bank Ltd, 208-209 Piccadilly, W1. *Club:* Travellers'.

**KING, Cecil (Harmsworth)**; *b* 20 Feb. 1901; *e surv s* of Sir Lucas White King, CSI, and Geraldine Adelaide Hamilton, *d* of Alfred Harmsworth, barrister of the Middle Temple; *m* 1st, 1923, Agnes Margaret, *d* of the Rev. Canon G. A. Cooke, DD, Regius Prof. of Hebrew, Oxford, and Canon of Christ Church; three *s* one *d*; 2nd, 1962, Dame Ruth Railton, *qv. Educ:* Winchester; Christ Church, Oxford (2nd class hons history). Dir, Daily Mirror, 1929; Dep. Chm., Sunday Pictorial, 1942; Chairman: Daily Mirror Newspapers Ltd and Sunday Pictorial Newspapers Ltd, 1951-1963; International Publishing Corp., 1963-68; The Reed Paper Group, 1963-68; Wall Paper Manufacturers, 1965-67; British Film Institute, 1948-52; Newspaper Proprietors' Assoc., 1961-68; Nigerian Printing & Publishing Co., 1948-68; Butterworth & Co. Ltd, 1968. Director: Reuters, 1953-59; Bank of England, 1965-68. Part-time Mem., National Coal Board, 1966-69. Mem., National Parks Commn, later Countryside Commn, 1966-69. Gold Badge for services to City of Warsaw. *Publications:* The Future of the Press, 1967; Strictly Personal, 1969. *Recreations:* travel and reading. *Address:* The Pavilion, Hampton Court, East Molesey, Surrey.

**KING, Charles Andrew Buchanan,** CMG 1961; MBE 1944; Head of West European Division, Overseas Department, London Chamber of Commerce, since 1968; Chairman, Premier Sauna Ltd; *b* 25 July 1915; *s* of late Major Andrew Buchanan King, 7th Argyll and Sutherland Highlanders and of Evelyn Nina (*née* Sharpe). *Educ:* Wellington Coll.; Magdalene Coll., Cambridge (MA). Vice-Consul: Zürich, 1940, Geneva, 1941; Attaché, HM Legation, Berne, 1942; transf. to FO, 1946; 2nd Sec., Vienna, 1950; transf. to FO 1953; to Hong Kong, 1958; to FO 1961; retired from HM Diplomatic Service, 1967. *Recreations:* ski-ing, travel. *Address:* 19 Archery Close, W2. *Club:* Bath.

**KING, Charles Martin M.** ; *see* Meade-King.

**KING, Sir (Clifford) Robertson,** KBE 1960 (CBE 1954); Director, Pirelli-General Cable Works Ltd, since 1963 (Chairman, 1963-66); Chairman, Electricity Council, 1959-61, retired; *b* 6 Feb. 1895; *s* of William and Edith L. King, Ilkeston, Derbs; *m* 1926, Dorothy V. N. Latimore, Ilkeston; one *s* one *d. Educ:* Ilkeston Secondary Sch.; Heanor Technical Sch. Served European War, 1914-18, with Sherwood Foresters and as a commissioned Officer with Northumberland Fusiliers. Joined Derbs and Notts Electric Power Co., 1919; Dep. Gen. Man. of Derbs and Notts, Leicester and Warwick, and associated Companies within the Midland Counties Group, 1936, General Manager, 1940-48; Chm., The East Midlands Electricity Board, 1948-57; Mem. of the British Electricity Authority, 1950-51, and of Central Electricity Authority, 1956-57; Chm. Nat. Inspection Council for Electrical Installation Contracting, 1956-58; Dep. Chm. Central Electricity Generating Board, 1957-59; Chm. Electrical Development Assoc., 1955-56. *Recreations:* cricket, football, hockey. *Address:* (private) Riverside House, Borrowash, near Derby.

**KING, Rev. Cuthbert,** CIE 1946; MA Oxon; ICS (retired); *b* 27 Jan. 1889; *s* of Rev. E. G. King, DD, and Mary, *d* of Rt Rev. B. F. Westcott, Durham; *m* 1921, Elsie Vivienne (*née* Harris), MBE 1946, K-I-H (1st Cl.) 1936 (*d* 1960). *Educ:* Sherborne Sch.; Christ Church, Oxford; Göttingen; Trinity Coll., Dublin. Indian Civil Service (Punjab), 1913-47; last appointments as Commissioner of Multan, Lahore and Rawalpindi Divs. On Military Service, IARO, 1917-20. Mem. of Order of Cloud and Banner (Chinese), 1945. Deacon, 1949; Priest, 1950. *Recreations:* golf, literature, languages, art. *Address:* 3 Canford House, Canford Cliffs, Poole, Dorset.

**KING, Cyril Lander,** QC; Called to the Bar, Middle Temple, 1919; KC 1937; Bencher, 1943. *Address:* New Court, Temple, EC4.

**KING, E(dward) J(ohn) Boswell,** CBE 1942; MC; *s* of late Edward Charles King; *m* 1935, Edith (*d* 1949), *e d* of late Arthur Milan Beckwith, Belleville, Illinois, USA. *Educ:* Christ's Hospital. Entered service of London County Council, 1930; Chief Asst Public Assistance Dept 1932; Dir of London County Council Rest Centres, 1941-42; Chief Officer of Supplies, London County Council, 1943-51; Mem. Board of Trade Furniture Production Cttee, 1944-48; appointed by Uganda Government to report on administration of supplies and stores, 1954-55. First Fellow and First Pres., Inst. of Public Supplies. *Publications:* Public Supplies, 1954; The Blue Pheasant, 1958; Lost Girl, 1959. *Recreations:* photography, painting for pleasure. *Address:* c/o Midland Bank Ltd, 194 Strand, WC2. *Club:* Athenæum.

**KING, Very Rev. Edward Laurie;** Dean of Cape Town since 1958; *b* 30 Jan. 1920; *s* of William Henry and Norah Alice King; *m* 1950, Helen Stuart Mathers, MB, BCh; two *s* three *d. Educ:* King's Coll., Taunton; University of Wales (BA). Deacon, 1945; priest, 1946, Monmouth; Associate in Theology (S Af.). Curate of Risca, 1945-48; Diocese of Johannesburg, 1948-50; Rector of Robertson, Cape, 1950-53; Rector of Stellenbosch, 1953-58. *Recreations:* cricket, reading. *Address:* The Deanery, Upper Orange Street, Cape Town, South Africa. *T:* 45-2609. *Club:* City.

**KING, Adm. Edward Leigh Stuart,** CB 1940; MVO 1925; *b* 1889; *e s* of C. J. S. King of Chardstock; *m* 1917, Lilian Alice (*d* 1944), *d* of Edward Strickland, Clifton; no *c.* Served in HMS Repulse during Prince of Wales' African and S American Tour, 1925; Dir of Plans, Admiralty, 1933-35; Chief of Staff to Commander-in-Chief, Home Fleet, 1938; ADC to the King, 1938; commanded a Cruiser Sqdn, 1940-41; a Lord Commissioner of the Admiralty and an Asst-Chief of Naval Staff, 1941-42; Principal Naval Liaison Officer to Allied Navies, 1943; retired, 1944. DL Cornwall, 1953. *Address:* Ruan Minor, Helston, Cornwall. *Club:* United Service.

**KING, Evelyn Mansfield,** MA; MP (C) South Dorset since 1964; *b* 30 May 1907; *s* of Harry Percy King and Winifred Elizabeth Paulet; *m* 1935, Hermione Edith, *d* of late Arthur Felton Crutchley, DSO; one *s* two *d. Educ:* Cheltenham Coll.; King's Coll., Cambridge; Inner Temple. Cambridge Univ. Correspondent to the Sunday Times, 1928-30; Asst Master Bedford Sch., 1930; Headmaster and Warden, Clayesmore Sch., 1935-50; Gloucestershire Regt 1940; Acting Lt-Col 1941. MP (Lab) Penryn and Falmouth Div. of Cornwall, 1945-50; Parliamentary Sec., Ministry of Town and Country Planning, 1947-50. Resigned from Labour Party, 1951, and joined Conservative Party; contested (C) Southampton (Itchen), 1959. *Publications:* (with J. C. Trewin) Printer to the House, Biography of Luke Hansard, 1952.

*Recreations:* farming, riding. *Address:* Embley Manor, near Romsey, Hants. *T:* Romsey 2342; 11 Barton Street, SW1. *T:* 01-222 4525; Athelhampton, Dorset.
*See also R. G. Cooke.*

**KING, Francis Henry,** FRSL; Author; *b* 4 March 1923; *o s* of Eustace Arthur Cecil King and Faith Mina Read. *Educ:* Shrewsbury; Balliol Coll., Oxford. *Publications: novels:* To the Dark Tower, 1946; Never Again, 1947; An Air That Kills, 1948; The Dividing Stream, 1951 (Somerset Maugham Award, 1952); The Dark Glasses, 1954; The Widow, 1957; The Man on the Rock, 1957; So Hurt and Humiliated (short stories), 1959; The Custom House, 1961; The Japanese Umbrella (short stories), 1964 (Katherine Mansfield Short Story Prize, 1965); The Last of the Pleasure Gardens, 1965; The Waves Behind the Boat, 1967; The Brighton Belle (short stories), 1968; A Domestic Animal, 1970; *Poetry:* Rod of Incantation, 1952; *general* (ed); Introducing Greece, 1956; Japan, 1970. *Address:* 17 Montpelier Villas, Brighton BN1 3DG. *T:* Brighton 29645. *Clubs:* Reform, PEN.

**KING, Maj.-Gen. Frank Douglas,** MBE 1953; Commandant, Royal Military College of Science, since 1969; *b* 9 March 1919; *s* of Arthur King, Farmer, and Kate Eliza (*née* Sheard), Brightwell, Berks; *m* 1947, Joy Emily Ellen Taylor; one *s* two *d*. *Educ:* Wallingford Gram. Sch. Joined Army, 1939; commnd into Royal Fusiliers, 1940; Parachute Regt, 1943; dropped Arnhem, Sept. 1944 (wounded, POW); Royal Military College of Science (ptsc), 1946; Staff Coll., Camberley (psc), 1950; comd 2 Parachute Bn, Middle East, 1960-62; comd 11 Infantry Bde Gp, Germany, 1963-64; Military Adviser (Overseas Equipment), 1965-66; Dir, Land/Air Warfare, MoD, 1967-68; Dir, Military Assistance Overseas, MoD, 1968-69. *Recreations:* golf, gardening, flying. *Address:* Shrivenham House, Shrivenham, Berks. *T:* Shrivenham 266. *Club:* Army and Navy.

**KING, Frederick Ernest,** FRS 1954; MA, DPhil, DSc Oxon; PhD London; Scientific Adviser to British Petroleum Co. Ltd since 1959; *er s* of late Frederick and of Elizabeth King, Bexhill, Sussex. *Educ:* Bancroft's Sch.; University of London; Oriel Coll., Oxford. Ramsay Memorial Fellow, 1930-31; Demonstrator, Dyson Perrins Laboratory, 1931-34; University Lecturer and Demonstrator in Chemistry, Oxford Univ., 1934-48, and sometime lecturer in Organic Chemistry, Magdalen Coll. and Balliol Coll.; Sir Jesse Boot Prof. of Chemistry, University of Nottingham, 1948-55; Dir in charge of research, British Celanese Ltd, 1955-59. Fellow Queen Mary Coll., 1955. *Publications:* scientific papers mainly in Jl of Chem. Soc. *Recreations:* mountaineering, gardening. *Address:* c/o British Petroleum Co. Ltd, Britannic House, Moor Lane, EC2. *T:* 01-920 7457; 360 The Water Gardens, W2; Glyde's Farm, Ashburnham, Sussex. *Club:* Athenæum.

**KING, Sir Geoffrey Stuart,** KCB, *cr* 1953 (CB 1943); KBE, *cr* 1946; MC; Civil Service, retired; *s* of late Charles James Stuart King, Chardstock, Devon; *m* 1920, Ethel Eileen May, *yd* of late D. C. M. Tuke, Chiswick House. Sec. Assistance Bd, 1944-48; Dep. Sec., Ministry of National Insurance, 1949-51; Permanent Sec., Ministry of Pensions and National Insurance, 1953-55 (Ministry of National Insurance, 1951); retired, 1955. *Address:* Oliver's Farm, Ash, near Sevenoaks, Kent.

**KING, Mrs Grace M. H.;** *see* Hamilton-King.

**KING, Maj.-Gen. Harold Francis Sylvester,** CB 1952; CBE 1949 (MBE 1940); retired; *b* 16 Oct. 1895; *m* 1919, Bertha Eveleen Alldred one *d*. *Educ:* Forest Sch., Walthamstow, E17. Served European War, 1914-18 (France). RFA 1915; RAOC, 1926; served War of 1939-45 (Middle East and Persia); Lt-Col 1942; Col 1948; Brig. 1950; Maj.-Gen. 1950; Inspector, Royal Army Ordnance Corps, 1950-53, retired 1953. Hon. Col, RAOC Supplementary Reserve, 1954-55. *Address:* 45 Woodland Way, Petts Wood, Kent. *T:* Orpington 5575.

**KING, Hilary William,** CBE 1964 (MBE 1944); HM Diplomatic Service; Foreign and Commonwealth Office, since 1968; *b* 10 March 1919; *s* of Dr W. H. King, Fowey, Cornwall; *m* 1947, Dr Margaret Helen Grierson Borrowman; one *s* three *d*. *Educ:* Sherborne; Corpus Christi Coll. Cambridge. Served War of 1939-45 (MBE). Apptd Mem. Foreign (subseq. Diplomatic) Service, Nov. 1946. A Vice-Consul and Acting Consul in Yugoslavia, 1947-48; apptd 2nd Sec., 1947; transferred to Foreign Office, 1949; promoted 1st Sec., 1950; transf. to Vienna as a Russian Sec., 1951; 1st Sec., Washington, 1953; transf. Foreign Office, 1958; Commercial Counsellor, Moscow, 1959; acted as Chargé d'Affaires, 1960; Ambassador (and Consul-Gen.) to Guinea, 1962-65; St Antony's Coll., Oxford, Oct. 1965-June 1966; Counsellor of Embassy, Warsaw, 1966-67. *Recreation:* sailing. *Address:* Nutcombe, Nutcombe Lane, Hindhead, Surrey. *T:* Hindhead 4174. *Clubs:* Royal Over-Seas League; Royal Fowey Yacht.

**KING, Rt. Hon. Horace Maybray,** PC 1965; MP Itchen Division of Southampton; Speaker of the House of Commons since Oct. 1965 (Chairman of Ways and Means and Deputy Speaker, 1964-65); *b* 25 May 1901; *s* of John William and Margaret Ann King; *m* 1st, 1924, Victoria Florence Harris (*d* 1966); one *d*; 2nd, 1967, Una Porter. *Educ:* Norton Council Sch.; Stockton Secondary Sch.; King's Coll., University of London. BA 1st Class Hons 1922, PhD 1940. Head of English Dept, Taunton's Sch., Southampton, 1930-47; Headmaster, Regent's Park Secondary Sch., 1947-50. MP (Lab): Test Div. of Southampton, 1950-55; Itchen Div. of Southampton, 1955-65 (when elected Speaker). Fellow, King's Coll., London; Hon. FRCP. Hon. DCL Durham, 1968; Hon. LLD: Southampton, 1967; London, 1967; Bath Univ. of Technology, 1969; Hon. DSocSci Ottawa, 1969. Hants County Hon. Alderman; Freeman of Southampton and Stockton-on-Tees. *Publications:* Selections from Macaulay, 1930; Selections from Homer, 1935; (ed) Sherlock Holmes Stories, 1950; Parliament and Freedom, 1953; State Crimes 1967; Songs in the Night, 1968; Before Hansard, 1968. *Recreations:* music and the entertainment of children. *Address:* Speaker's House, SW1; 37 Manor Farm Road, Southampton. *T:* Southampton 55884. *Club:* Athenæum.

**KING, Ivor Edward,** CB 1961; CBE 1943; CEng, MRINA; Royal Corps of Naval Constructors; Director of Dockyards, Admiralty, 1958-61; *b* 1899; *s* of John and Minnie Elizabeth King, Pembroke Dock; *m* 1923, Doris, *d* of John and Catherine Hill, Lee, SE; three *d*. *Educ:* Royal Naval College, Greenwich. Formerly Manager, HM Dockyards, Portsmouth, Malta, Sheerness and Bermuda. Constructor Capt. to Commander-in-Chief, Mediterranean, 1942-44. Served War, 1942-44 (CBE). Vice-Pres., Royal Institution of Naval Architects. *Recreation:* golf. *Address:* 10 Combe Park, Bath BA1 3NP. *T:* Bath 23047.

**KING, Sir James Granville Le Neve,** 3rd Bt, *cr* 1888; TD; *b* 17 Sept. 1898; *s* of Sir John Westall King, 2nd Bt, and Frances Rosa (*d* 1942), *d* of John Neve, Oaken, Staffs; *S* father 1940; *m* 1928, Penelope Charlotte, *d* of late Capt. E. Cooper-Key, CB, MVO, RN; one *s* two *d*. *Educ:* Eton; King's Coll., Cambridge. *Heir: s* John Christopher King [*b* 1933; *m* 1958, Patricia Monica, *o d* of late Lt-Col Kingsley Foster and of Mrs Foster, Hampton Court Palace; one *s* one *d*]. *Address:* The Old Vicarage, King's Somborne, Hants. *Club:* Travellers'.

*See also Sir Neill Cooper-Key.*

**KING, Prof. James Lawrence;** Regius Professor of Engineering, University of Edinburgh, since 1968; *b* 14 Feb. 1922; *s* of Lawrence Aubrey King and Wilhelmina Young McLeish; *m* 1951, Pamela Mary Ward Hitchcock; one *s* one *d*. *Educ:* Latymer Upper Sch.; Jesus Coll., Cambridge; Imperial Coll., London. Min. of Defence (Navy), 1942-68. *Recreations:* golf, walking. *Address:* 2 Arboretum Road, Edinburgh EH3 5PD. *T:* 031-552 3854.

**KING, Prof. Jeffrey William Hitchen,** MSc, FICE, FIStructE; Professor of Civil Engineering, Queen Mary College, University of London, since 1953; *b* 28 Sept. 1906; *s* of George and Edith King, Wigan; *m* 1930, Phyllis Morfydd Harris, *d* of Rev. W. Harris; one *s* one *d*. *Educ:* Ashton-in-Makerfield Grammar Sch.; Manchester Univ. Engineer and Agent to Cementation Co. Ltd, British Isles, Spain and Egypt, 1927-36; Research Engineer, Michelin Tyre Co. 1936-37; Lecturer in Civil Engineering, University Coll., Nottingham, 1937-47; Reader in Civil Engineering, Queen Mary Coll., London, 1947-53. Governor, Queen Mary Coll., 1962-65; Mem., Academic Board and Vice-Chm., Civil Engineering Cttee of Regional Advisory Council for Higher Technological Education; formerly mem., Research Cttee, Chm., Concrete Specification Cttee and Cttee on Accelerated Testing of Concrete, Instn of Civil Engineers. Mem. BSI Cttees, CEB/4/4, CEB/21. FRSA. *Publications:* papers in Journals of Instn of Civil Engineers, Instn of Structural Engineers, and Inst. of Mine Surveyors, and in various technical periodicals. *Recreations:* many and varied. *Address:* 99 Malford Grove, E18. *T:* 01-989 2648; Queen Mary College, Mile End Road, E1. *T:* 01-980 4811.

**KING, John George Maydon,** CMG 1959; OBE 1953 (MBE 1945); retired from Colonial Agricultural Service; *b* 26 Jan. 1908; 2nd *s* of late Harold Edwin and Elizabeth Lindsay King, Durban, Natal, SA; *m* 1938, Françoise Charlotte de Rham (*d* 1966), Lausanne; two *s*. *Educ:* University Coll. Sch. (Preparatory); Oundle Sch.; London Univ. (Wye Coll.); Cambridge Univ. (Colonial Office Schol., Cambridge Univ. and Imperial Coll. of Tropical Agric.). Appointed to Colonial Agricultural Service as Agricultural Officer, Tanganyika, 1932-46; seconded to Cambridge Univ. as Lecturer in Tropical Agric. to Colonial Services Courses, 1946-48; Dir of livestock and Agricultural Services, Basutoland, 1948-54; Dir of Agriculture, Uganda, 1954-60, Swaziland, 1960-63; Regional Manager, Lower Indus Project, Hyderabad-Sind, 1964-66. *Recreations:* fishing and shooting; photography. *Address:* Karibu, En Frasses, 1882 La Barboleusaz sur Gryon, Vaud, Switzerland. *T:* 025 59725; c/o Mrs Leigh, 11 King's Close, Henley-on-Thames. *Clubs:* Reform, Farmers'; Phyllis Court (Henley-on-Thames).

**KING, Sir John Richard D.;** *see* Duckworth-King.

**KING, Laurence (Edward);** FRIBA; FRSA; FSA (Scotland); Architect; Senior Partner and Founder of firm of Laurence King and Partners, Chartered Architects; Tutor at Royal College of Art, 1936-39 and 1946-51; Lecturer at Royal College of Art, 1951-58; *b* 28 June 1907; *o s* of late Frederick Ernest King and Flora King (*née* Joyner); unmarried. *Educ:* Brentwood Sch.; University of London. Architectural Education under late Prof. Sir Albert Richardson at University of London, 1924-29; entered private practice in 1933. Served in the Army during 1939-45 War, principally in Middle East; rank, Major. Commenced Architectural practice again in 1946. Architect for the United Westminster Schools, Grey Coat Hospital, Eastbourne and Framlingham Colleges. Re-built: Grey Coat Hospital, 1955; Wren's Church of St Magnus, London Bridge, 1951; Wren's Church of St Mary-le-Bow (Bow Bells) (completed, 1964); Walsingham Parish Church, rebuilt after destruction by fire in 1961, completed 1964; at present engaged on designing, building, and completing several churches in New Housing areas. Has undertaken work for the following religious communities: Nashdom Abbey; Malling Abbey; Burnham Abbey; St John's Convent, Clewer. Architect for St James' Church, Marden Ash, completed 1958; St Mary's Church, South Ruislip, completed 1959; St Nicholas, Fleetwood, 1961; Ascension Church, Chelmsford, 1962; St Mary and St Nicholas, Perivale, 1965; St Mary, Hobs Moat, Solihull, 1967; St Michael, Letchworth, 1967; St John's, North Woolwich, 1968; St James, Leigh-on-Sea, 1969; appointed Architect to Blackburn Cathedral, 1962; appointed Consulting Architect for Exeter Cathedral, 1965; Architect for various Houses, Halls and Schools, etc, including work at Brentwood School, Sutton Valence School, Emanuel School, Wandsworth, Westminster City School, Queen Anne's School, Caversham; The Coopers' Co. and Coborn School; numerous Church interior decoration and furnishing schemes including High Altar and furnishings for Eucharistic Congress, 1958; Architect for restoration of various ancient Churches, particularly in London, Middx, Essex, Suffolk, Norfolk, Herts, Notts, Kent; Architect in association with late A. B. Knapp-Fisher; FRIBA for extensions to the Queen's Chapel of the Savoy for Royal Victorian Order. Mem. Archbishop's Commn in connection with repair of churches, 1951-52; Hon. Cons. Architect for Historic Churches Preservation Trust; Member: Church Assembly; Council for Care of Churches; Council of Worship and Arts Assoc. Freeman, City of London. Liveryman: Worshipful Co. of Barbers; Worshipful Co. of Needlemakers. *Publications:* Sanctuaries and Sacristies; and various articles and reviews in magazines and periodicals. *Recreations:* the visual arts, the theatre, travel. *Address:* (Home) The Wayside, Shenfield Common, Brentwood, Essex. *T:* Brentwood 438; (Office) 9 Gower Street, WC1. *T:* 01-580 6752. *Clubs:* Athenæum, Boodle's, City Livery, Art Workers' Guild.

**KING, Sir Louis,** Kt 1969; CMG 1962; CVO 1963; Under-Secretary, Secretary to Minister of Health and Clerk of Executive Council, South Australian Government, 1961-69, retired; *b* 15 April 1904; *s* of late Ernest and Mary C. King; *m* 1938, Audrey Cleve Sutton; no *c*. *Educ:* Adelaide High Sch. Entered Public Service of South Australia, 1920; Sec., Agent General for South Australia in London, 1938-46; Sec., Minister of Agriculture, 1947-54; Sec. to Premier and Sec. to Minister of

Immigration, 1954-61. *Recreations:* bowls and gardening. *Address:* 12 Fortrose Street, Glenelg, SA 5045, Australia. *T:* 95-3519.

**KING, Sir Peter (Alexander)**, 7th Bt *cr* 1815; Company Director; *b* 13 Nov. 1928; *s* of Sir Alexander William King, 6th Bt and Dorothy Alice (*d* 1961), *d* of H. W. Champion; *S* father, 1969; *m* 1957, Jean Margaret, *d* of Christopher Thomas Cavell, Deal; one *s* one *d*. *Educ:* Cliftonville Coll.; Cranbrook School. *Recreations:* fishing and all sports. *Heir: s* Wayne Alexander King, *b* 2 Feb. 1962. *Address:* Charlestown, 365 London Road, Upper Deal, Deal, Kent. *T:* Deal 4855. *Clubs:* Royal Marine Association, Headquarters (Portsmouth).

**KING, Philip;** playwright and actor; *b* 1904. First play produced, 1940. *Plays include:* Without the Prince, 1940; Come to the Fair, 1940; See How They Run, 1944; (with Falkland L. Cary) Crystal Clear, 1945; On Monday Next . . ., 1949; (with Anthony Armstrong) Here We Come Gathering, 1951; As Black as She's Painted, 1952; Serious Charge, 1953; (with Falkland L. Cary), Sailor Beware, 1955; Watch It Sailor, 1961; Pools Paradise, 1961; (with Falkland L. Cary), Rock-A-Bye, Sailor, 1962; How Are You, Johnnie, 1963; (with Falkland L. Cary), Big Bad Mouse, 1966; I'll Get My Man, 1966. *Address:* 3 Woodland Way, Withdean, Brighton BN1 8BA. *T:* Brighton 505675. *Clubs:* Constitutional, Savage.

**KING, Ralph Malcolm MacDonald,** OBE 1968; Colonial Service, retired; Legal Draftsman to Government of Northern Nigeria, 1963 and to Northern States of Nigeria, 1967; *b* 8 Feb. 1911; *s* of Dr James Malcolm King and Mrs Norah King; *m* 1948, Rita Elizabeth Herring; two *s* one *d*. *Educ:* Tonbridge Sch. Solicitor (Hons) 1934. Asst to Johnson, Stokes and Master, Solicitors, Hong Kong, 1936-41. Commissioned Middx Regt, 1941; prisoner of war, 1941-45; demobilised, 1946. Colonial Legal Service, 1947; Legal Officer, Somaliland, 1947; Crown Counsel, Somaliland, 1950. Called to Bar, Gray's Inn, 1950. Solicitor-General, Nyasaland, 1953; Attorney-General, Nyasaland, 1957-61. Disbarred at his own request and since restored to Roll of Solicitors, in April 1961. *Recreations:* tennis, walking. *Address:* c/o Ministry of Justice, Private Mail Bag 2072, Kaduna, Nigeria; St John's Lodge, Burgh Hill, Hurst Green, Etchingham, Sussex. *Club:* Royal Over-Seas League.

**KING, Richard Brian Meredith,** CB 1969; MC 1944; Deputy Secretary, Ministry of Overseas Development, since 1968; *b* 2 Aug. 1920; *s* of late Bernard and of Dorothy King; *m* 1944, Blanche Phyllis Roberts; two *s* one *d*. *Educ:* King's Coll. Sch., Wimbledon. Air Ministry, 1939; Min. of Aircraft Prod., 1940. Army 1940-46: Major, N Irish Horse; N Af. and Ital. campaigns (MC, Cassino). Min. of Supply, 1946; Asst Principal, Ministry of Works, 1948; Principal, 1949; Asst Regional Dir (Leeds), 1949-52; seconded Treas., 1953-54; Prin. Priv. Sec. to Minister of Works, 1956-57; Asst Sec., 1957; seconded Cabinet Off., 1958 (Sec. of Commonwealth Educn. Conf. (Oxford), 1959; Constitutional Confs: Kenya, 1960; N Rhodesia, Nyasaland and Fed. Review, 1960; WI Fedn, 1961); Dept of Tech. Co-op, on its formation, 1961; Min. of Overseas Develt, on its formation, 1964; Under-Sec., 1964; Dep. Sec., 1968. *Recreations:* music, lawn tennis, gardening, doing-it-himself. *Address:* Field House, Leigh Hill Road, Cobham, Surrey. *T:* Cobham 2713.

**KING, Maj.-Gen. Robert Charles Moss,** CB 1955; DSO 1945; OBE 1944; retired; *b* 6 June 1904; *s* of Robert Henry Curzon Moss King, ICS and Mrs King; *m* 1940, Elizabeth Stuart Mackay (*d* 1966); two *d*. *Educ:* Clifton Coll.; RMC, Camberley. 2nd Lieut, W Yorks Regt, 1924; Capt. 1935. Served War of 1939-45: India, Malaya, Java, Assam and Burma (despatches). Maj.-Gen. 1955. GOC Home Counties District and 44th (HC) Infantry Division TA, Deputy Constable Dover Castle, 1954-56; Dir of Quartering, War Office, 1957-58. *Recreations:* shooting and fishing. *Address:* c/o Coutts & Co., 440 Strand, WC2.

**KING, Sir Robertson;** *see* King, Sir C. R.

**KING, Dame Ruth;** *see* Railton, Dame R.

**KING, Sydney Percy,** OBE 1965; JP; District Organiser, National Union of Agricultural and Allied Workers, since 1946; Chairman of Sheffield Regional Hospital Board, since 1969 (Member since 1963); *b* 20 Sept. 1916; *s* of James Edwin King and Florence Emily King; *m* 1944, Millicent Angela Prendergast; two *d*. *Educ:* Brockley Central School. Member: N Midland Regional Board for Industry (Vice-Chm. 1949); E Midland Economic Planning Council, 1965; Kesteven Water Board (Chm. 1963); E Midlands Gas Board, 1970. JP 1956, Alderman 1967, Kesteven. *Recreations:* reading, music, talking. *Address:* 49 Robertson Drive, Sleaford, Lincs. *T:* Sleaford 2056.

**KING, Thomas Jeremy, (Tom);** MP (C) Bridgwater since March 1970; Parliamentary Private Secretary to Minister for Posts and Telecommunications, since 1970; *b* 13 June 1933; *s* of J. H. King, JP; *m* 1960, Jane, *d* of Robert Tilney, *qv*; one *s* one *d*. *Educ:* Rugby; Emmanuel Coll., Cambridge (MA). National service, 1952-53: commnd Somerset Light Inf., 1952; seconded to KAR; served Tanganyika and Kenya; Actg Captain 1953. Cambridge, 1953-56. Joined E.S. & A. Robinson Ltd, Bristol, 1956; various positions up to Divisional Gen. Man., 1964-69. *Recreations:* cricket, ski-ing. *Address:* House of Commons, SW1.

**KING, Air Vice-Marshal Walter MacIan,** CB 1961; CBE 1957; Retired, 1967; *b* 10 March 1910; *s* of Alexander King, MB, ChB, DPH, and Hughberta Blannin King (*née* Pearson); *m* 1946, Anne Clare Hicks; two *s*. *Educ:* St Mary's Coll., Castries, St Lucia, BWI; Blundell's Sch., Tiverton, Devon. Aircraft Engineering (Messers Westland Aircraft Ltd, Handley-Page Ltd, Saunders-Roe Ltd), 1927-33; joined Royal Air Force, 1934; Overseas Service: No 8 Sqdn, Aden, 1935-37; South-east Asia, 1945-47; Middle East (Egypt and Cyprus), 1955-57. Student: RAF Staff Coll., 1944; Joint Services Staff Coll., 1947; IDC, 1954. Directing Staff, RAF Staff Coll., 1957-58; Comdt, No 16 MU, Stafford, 1958-60; Dir of Equipment (B), Air Ministry, 1961-64; Air Cdre Ops (Supply), HQ's Maintenance Command, during 1964; Senior Air Staff Officer, RAF Maintenance Command, 1964-67. *Recreations:* swimming (rep. RAF in inter-services competition, 1934); dinghy sailing. *Address:* 1a Oswald Road, Edinburgh 9.

**KING, William Charles Holland,** FRBS; *b* 5 Oct. 1884; *s* of Charles Holland and Martha King, Cheltenham; *m* Constance, *e d* of A. J. Bagley; two *d*. *Educ:* Cheltenham Grammar Sch.; Royal Academy Schs, London (Landseer Schol.). Exhibitor at Royal Academy and other exhibitions, 1910-. *Works:* Busts of Louise, Dowager Duchess of Beaufort; 10th Duke of Beaufort; 8th Earl of Bessborough; 9th Earl of Bessborough; Viscount Peel; Hon. Windham Baring; Lady Ulrica Baring; Sir Max Waechter; Lady Max Waechter; Hon. Desmond

Ponsonby; F-M Sir Henry Wilson; P. A. Laszlo de Lombos; Mrs H. A. Rose; Mrs Lynch; Evelyn d'Alroy; Dr Paula Machado of Rio de Janeiro; Mrs E. Barrett; the late Sir Robert Mond; Garden Statuary at Bessborough, Ireland, and Canford Manor, Dorset; Figure-heads for yachts for Lord Tredegar and Mr Lionel de Rothschild; Memorials to late King Edward at Bagshot, Baron Carlo de Tuyll at Horton, Glos, Gen. Sir F. Maude, Sir Peile Thompson, Bt, Capt. Gordon Duff at Drummuir, Col E. Barrett at Farnham, Silvester Horne at Whitfields (London), Rev. Kirkpatrick at St Augustine's, Kilburn, Earl of Carnarvon at Campo Santo, Genoa, E. Grace at Westcliffe; Panel and Statues of co-Founders All Souls Coll., Oxford; War Memorials: Men of SE & C Railway at Dover, Wolverhampton, Latimer, etc. Formerly Pres. Royal Society of British Sculptors. RBS Gold Medal for Distinguished Services to Sculpture. *Address:* The House of St Francis, Whitwell, Ventnor, IOW.

**KING-HALL, Magdalen, (Mrs Patrick Perceval-Maxwell)**; *b* 22 July 1904; *yr d* of late Admiral Sir George King-Hall and Lady King-Hall; *m* 1929, Patrick Perceval-Maxwell; two *s* one *d*. *Educ:* Downe House; St Leonard's Sch. *Publications:* The Diary of a Young Lady of Fashion, 1925; I think I remember, 1927; The Well-meaning Young Man (with L. King-Hall), 1930; Gay Crusaders, 1934; Maid of Honour, 1936; Jehan of the Ready Fists, 1936; Lady Sarah, 1939; Sturdy Rogue, 1941; Somehow Overdone, 1942; Lord Edward, 1943; Life and Death of the Wicked Lady Skelton, 1944; How Small a Part of Time, 1946 (published in USA as The Lovely Lynchs, 1947); Lady Shane's Daughter, 1947; Tea at Crumbo Castle, 1948; The Fox Sisters, 1950; The Edifying Bishop, 1951; The Venetian Bride, 1954; Hag Khalida, 1954; 18th Century Story, 1956; The Story of the Nursery, 1958; The Noble Savages, 1962. *Address:* c/o Mrs Walker, St Columb's Movillle, Co. Donegal, Eire. *T:* Moville 32.

**KING-HAMILTON, Myer Alan Barry,** QC 1954; **His Honour Judge King-Hamilton;** an additional Judge of the Central Criminal Court since 1964; *b* 9 Dec. 1904; *o s* of Alfred King-Hamilton; *m* 1935, Rosalind Irene Ellis; two *d*. *Educ:* Bishop's Stortford Grammar Sch.; Trinity Hall, Cambridge (BA 1927, MA 1929; Pres. Cambridge Union Soc., 1927). Called to Bar, Middle Temple, 1929; served War of 1939-45, RAF, finishing with rank of Squadron Leader; served on Finchley Borough Council, 1938-39 and 1945-50. Recorder of Hereford, 1955-56; Recorder of Gloucester, 1956-61; Recorder of Wolverhampton, 1961-64; Dep. Chm. Oxford County Quarter Sessions, 1955-64, 1966-; Leader of Oxford Circuit, 1961-64. Elected Bencher, Middle Temple, 1961. Elected to General Council of Bar, 1958. Freeman of City of London. *Recreations:* cricket, gardening, the theatre. *Address:* Central Criminal Court, Old Bailey, EC4. *Clubs:* Constitutional; MCC.

**KING-HARMAN, Captain Robert Douglas,** DSO 1941; DSc and Bar; Royal Navy; *b* Barbadoes, BWI, 18 Aug. 1891; 2nd *s* of Sir C. A. King-Harman, KCMG (*d* 1939), and Lady Constance King-Harman (*d* 1961), Ouse Manor, Sharnbrook, Bedfordshire; *m* 1st, 1916, Lily Moffatt (marr. diss., 1926; she *d* 1966); one *s*; 2nd, 1927, Elizabeth Lilian Bull. *Educ:* Royal Naval Coll., Dartmouth. Entered Navy, 1904; served in destroyers, Grand Fleet and Dover Patrol, 1914-18; at Jutland; DSC given for his part in HMS Swift in action between destroyers Swift and Broke and German destroyers, 1917; the bar to DSC was for minesweeping after the Armistice of 1918; retired 1928 and entered Singapore Pilotage; returned to Navy, Sept. 1939 and served until 1946; retired from Singapore Pilotage, 1948. *Address:* Jakins, Great Gransden, Huntingdonshire. *T:* Great Gransden 346. *Club:* Naval and Military.

**KING-HELE, Desmond George,** FRS 1966; Deputy Chief Scientific Officer, Space Department, Royal Aircraft Establishment, Farnborough, since 1968; *b* 3 Nov. 1927; *s* of S. G. and B. King-Hele, Seaford, Sussex; *m* 1954, Marie Thérèse Newman; two *d*. *Educ:* Epsom Coll.; Trinity Coll., Cambridge. BA (1st cl. hons Mathematics) 1948; MA 1952. At RAE, Farnborough, from 1948, working on space research from 1955. Mem., International Academy of Astronautics, 1961; FIMA; FRAS. *Publications:* Shelley: His Thought and Work, 1960, 2nd edn 1971; Satellites and Scientific Research, 1960; Erasmus Darwin, 1963; Theory of Satellite Orbits in an Atmosphere, 1964; Space Research V, 1965; Observing Earth Satellites, 1966; (ed) Essential Writings of Erasmus Darwin, 1968; The End of the Twentieth Century?, 1970; numerous papers in Proc. Royal Society, Nature, Keats-Shelley Memor. Bull., New Scientist, and other scientific and literary jls. *Recreations:* tennis, walking, reading. *Address:* 3 Tor Road, Farnham, Surrey. *T:* Farnham 4755.

**KING-MARTIN, Brig. John Douglas,** CBE 1966; DSO 1957; MC 1953; Deputy Commander, HQ Eastern District, 1968-70, retired; *b* 9 March 1915; *s* of late Lewis King-Martin, Imperial Forest Service; *m* 1940, Jeannie Jemima Sheffield Hollins, *d* of late S. T. Hollins, CIE; one *s* one *d*. *Educ:* Allhallows Sch.; RMC Sandhurst. Commnd 1935; 3rd Royal Bn 12 Frontier Force Regt, IA, 1936; Waziristan Ops, 1936-37; Eritrea, Western Desert, 1940-42; Staff Coll., Quetta, 1944; Bde Maj., 1944-46; GSO 2, Indian Inf. Div., 1946-47; transf. to RA, 1948; Battery Comdr, 1948-50, 1951-54; Korea, 1952-53; CO, 50 Medium Regt, RA, 1956-57; Suez, Cyprus, 1956-57; Coll. Comdr, RMA Sandhurst, 1958-60; Dep. Comdr and CRA, 17 Gurkha Div., 1961-62; Comdr, 17 Gurkha Div., 1962-64; Comdr, Rhine Area, 1964-67. Lieut-Col 1956; Brig. 1961. ADC to The Queen, 1968-70. *Recreations:* golf, cricket, painting, photography. *Address:* White House Farm, Polstead, Suffolk. *T:* Boxford 327. *Clubs:* East India and Sports, XL.

**KING MURRAY, Ronald;** *see* Murray, Ronald K.

**KING-REYNOLDS, Guy Edwin;** Headmaster, Dauntsey's School, West Lavington, since Sept. 1969; *b* 9 July 1923; *er s* of Dr H. E. King Reynolds, York; *m* 1st, 1947, Norma Lansdowne Russell (*d* 1949); 2nd, 1950, Jeanne Nancy Perris Rhodes; one *d*. *Educ:* St Peter's Sch., Yorks; Emmanuel Coll., Cambridge (1944-47). Served RAF, 1942-44. BA 1946, MA 1951. Asst Master, Glenhow Prep. Sch., 1947-48; Head of Geography Dept, Solihull Sch., Warwickshire, 1948-54; family business, 1954-55; Head of Geography, Portsmouth Grammar Sch., 1955-57; Solihull School: Housemaster, 1957-63, Second Master, 1963-69. JP, Co. Borough of Solihull, 1965-69. Part-time Lecturer in International Affairs, Extra-Mural Dept, Birmingham Univ.; Chm., Solihull WEA. LRAM (speech and drama) 1968; FRGS 1951. *Recreations:* drama (director and actor); director of semi-professional theatre company, touring professional theatres at home and abroad; fashion design, travel, living in Italy, squash racquets. *Address:* Headmaster's House,

Dauntsey's School, West Lavington, Wilts. *T:* Lavington 3382.

**KING-TENISON,** family name of **Earl of Kingston.**

**KINGDOM, Thomas Doyle,** CB 1959; Controller, Government Social Survey Department, 1967-70, retired; *b* 30 Oct. 1910; *er s* of late Thomas Kingdom; *m* 1937, Elsie Margaret, *d* of L. C. Scott, MBE, Northwood; two *d. Educ:* Rugby; King's Coll., Cambridge (MA). Entered Civil Service as Asst Principal, Inland Revenue, 1933; transferred to Unemployment Assistance Board, 1934; Principal, 1937; Asst Sec., 1943; seconded to HM Treasury as Dep. Dir of Organisation and Methods, 1945-49; Under-Secretary: National Assistance Board, 1955-66; Min. of Social Security, 1966-67. Chm., Royal Inst. of Public Administration, 1965-66. *Publication:* Improvement of Organisation and Management in Public Administration, 1951. *Address:* 2 Grosvenor Road, Northwood, Mddx HA6 3HJ. *T:* Northwood 22006. *Club:* United University.

**KINGHORN, Squadron Leader Ernest;** *b* 1 Nov. 1907; *s* of A. Kinghorn, Leeds; *m* 1942, Eileen Mary Lambert Russell; two *s* (one *d* decd). *Educ:* Leeds, Basel and Lille Universities. Languages Master Ashville Coll., Doncaster Grammar Sch. and Roundhay Sch., Leeds. Served in Intelligence Branch, RAF. British Officer for Control of Manpower, SHAEF, and Staff Officer CCG. MP (Lab) Yarmouth Division of Norfolk, 1950-51, Great Yarmouth, 1945-50. *Address:* 59 Queens Avenue, Hanworth, Middx.

**KINGMAN, John Frank Charles;** Professor of Mathematics in the University of Oxford, since 1969; *b* 28 Aug. 1939; *er s* of Frank Edwin Thomas Kingman and Maud Elsie Harley; *m* 1964, Valerie Cromwell; one *s. Educ:* Christ's Coll., Finchley; Pembroke Coll., Cambridge. MA, ScD Cantab; Smith's Prize, 1962. Fellow of Pembroke Coll., Cambridge, 1961-65. Asst Lectr in Mathematics, 1962-64, Lectr, 1964-65, Univ. of Cambridge; Vis. Lectr, Univ. of Western Australia, 1963; Reader in Mathematics and Statistics, 1965-66, Prof. 1966-69, Univ. of Sussex; Vis. Prof., Stanford Univ., USA, 1968. Mem., Brighton Co. Borough Council, 1968-. Mem., Internat. Statistical Inst., 1967; Fellow, Inst. of Mathematical Statistics (USA), 1968. Junior Berwick Prize (London Math. Soc.), 1967. *Publications:* Introduction to Measure and Probability (with S. J. Taylor), 1966; The Algebra of Queues, 1966; papers in mathematical and statistical jls. *Address:* St Cross College, Oxford; 8 Montpelier Villas, Brighton, Sussex. *Club:* Oxford and Cambridge University.

**KINGS NORTON,** Baron *cr* 1965, of Wotton Underwood (Life Peer); **Harold Roxbee Cox,** Kt 1953; PhD, DIC, FIMechE, FRAeS; Chairman: Sidney-Barton Ltd, since 1968; Berger Jenson & Nicholson Ltd, since 1967; Supramar AG, since 1969; Metal Box Co., 1961-67 (Director, 1957-67, Deputy Chairman, 1959-60); Director: Dowty Rotol, since 1968; Ricardo & Co. (Engineers) 1927 Ltd, since 1965; David Rendel Ltd, since 1967; British Printing Corporation, since 1968; Hoechst UK, since 1970; Chairman: Council for National Academic Awards; Air Registration Board; Chancellor, Cranfield Institute of Technology; *b* 6 June 1902; *s* of late William John Roxbee Cox, Birmingham; *m* 1927, Marjorie, *e d* of late E. E. Withers, Northwood; two *s. Educ:* Kings Norton Grammar Sch.; Imperial Coll. of Science and Technology (Schol.). Engineer on construction of Airship R101, 1924-29; Chief Technical Officer, Royal Airship Works, 1931; Investigations in wing flutter and stability of structures, 1931-35; Lectr in Aircraft Structures, Imperial Coll., 1932-38; Principal Scientific Officer. Aerodynamics Dept, RAE, 1935-36; Head of Air Defence Dept, RAE, 1936-38; Chief Technical Officer, Air Registration Board, 1938-39; Supt of Scientific Research, RAE, 1939-40; Dep. Dir of Scientific Research, Ministry of Aircraft Production, 1940-43; Dir of Special Projects Ministry of Aircraft Production, 1943-44; Chm. and Man. Dir Power Jets (Research and Development) Ltd, 1944-46; Dir National Gas Turbine Establishment, 1946-48; Chief Scientist, Min. of Fuel and Power, 1948-54; Chm. Gas Turbine Collaboration Cttee, 1941-44, 1946-48; Mem. Aeronautical Research Council, 1944-48, 1958-60; Chm., Coun. for Scientific and Industrial Research, 1961-65; Past Pres. Royal Aeronautical Soc.; Pres., Royal Institution, 1969. Fellow of Imperial Coll. of Science and Technology, 1960. R38 Memorial Prize, 1928; Busk Memorial Prize, 1934; Wilbur Wright Lecturer, 1940; Wright Brothers Lecturer (USA), 1945; Hawksley Lecturer, 1951; James Clayton Prize, 1952; Thornton Lectr, 1954; Parsons Memorial Lectr, 1955; Handley Page Memorial Lectr, 1969. Hon. DSc: Birmingham, 1954; Cranfield Inst. of Technology, 1970; Hon. DTech Brunel, 1966; Hon. LLD CNAA, 1969. Medal of Freedom with Silver Palm, USA, 1947. *Publications:* numerous papers on theory of structures, wing flutter, gas turbines, civil aviation and airships. *Address:* 3 Upper Harley Street, NW1. *T:* 01-935 3167; Mill Cottage, Locks Lane, Wantage, Berks. *T:* Wantage 3806. *Clubs:* Athenæum, Royal Automobile.

**KINGSALE,** 35th Baron *cr* 1223 (by some reckonings 30th Baron); **John de Courcy;** Baron Courcy and Baron of Ringrone; Premier Baron of Ireland; Political Journalist, Kilbrittain Newspapers, since 1968; *b* 27 Jan. 1941; *s* of Lieutenant-Commander the Hon. Michael John Rancé de Courcy, RN (killed on active service, 1940), and Joan (*d* 1967), *d* of Robert Reid; *S* grandfather, 1969. *Educ:* Stowe; Universities of Paris and Salzburg. Short service commission, Irish Guards, 1962-65. At various times before and since: law student, property developer, film extra, white hunter, bingo caller, etc. *Recreations:* shooting, food and drink, and redheads. *Heir: cousin* Nevinson Russell de Courcy [*b* 21 July 1920; *m* 1954, Nora Lydia, *yr d* of James Arnold Plint; one *s* one *d*]. *Address:* Grove Farm, Bourton, Gillingham, Dorset. *T:* Bourton 498. *Club:* Guards'.

**KINGSBOROUGH, Viscount; Robert Charles Henry King-Tenison;** *b* 20 March 1969; *s* and *heir* of 11th Earl of Kingston, *qv.*

**KINGSFORD, Reginald John Lethbridge,** CBE 1963; MA; Fellow of Clare College, Cambridge, since 1949; *b* 10 Sept. 1900; *o s* of late Rev. R. L. Kingsford and late Gertrude Rodgers; *m* 1927, Ruth, *o d* of late W. F. A. Fletcher, Biggleswade; one *s. Educ:* Sherborne Sch. (scholar); Clare Coll., Cambridge (scholar). General Manager, Cambridge Univ. Press, London, 1936-48; Sec. to the Syndics of the Cambridge University Press, 1948-63. Mem. of Council, Publishers' Association, 1940-53; Pres. of Publishers' Association, 1943-45; Mem. Governing Body of Sherborne Sch. *Publication:* The Publishers' Association, 1896-1946, 1970. *Recreations:* books, travel. *Address:* 2 Barrow Close, Cambridge. *T:* 52963. *Club:* United University.

**KINGSLEY, J(ohn) Donald;** Special Representative for Middle East Affairs, The Ford Foundation, since 1968; *b* 25 March 1908; *s* of John H. and Carolyn Donaldson Kingsley; *m* 1st, 1930, Alice W. Boyd (marr. diss.); one *d*; 2nd, 1946, Ruth Caplan; one *s* one *d*. *Educ:* Syracuse Univ. (MA, PhD); London Sch. of Economics; University of Louisville (LLD). Prof. of Politics, Antioch Coll., 1933-42; Asst Regional Dir, US War Manpower Commn, 1943-44; Dep. Exec. Dir, US War Manpower Commn, 1945; Dep. Dir, Office of War Mobilization and Reconversion, 1946; Programme Co-ordinator, The White House, 1947; Asst Federal Security Administrator, 1948; Dir-Gen., International Refugee Organization, 1949-52; Agent-Gen., United Nations Korean Reconstruction Agency, 1951-53; Administrator, Paris Refugee Reparations Fund, 1949-58; The Ford Foundation: Resident Rep. (W Africa), 1959-63; Dir for ME and Africa, 1963-68. *Publications:* Public Personnel Administration (with W. E. Mosher), 1936, 1940; Representative Bureaucracy, 1944. *Recreations:* painting, sailing. *Address:* PO Box 2379, Beirut, Lebanon. *Clubs:* Overseas Press (New York); Ikoyi (Lagos); Capitol Democratic (Washington).

**KINGSLEY, Sir Patrick (Graham Toler),** KCVO 1962 (CVO 1950); Secretary and Keeper of the Records of the Duchy of Cornwall since 1954 (Assistant Secretary, 1930-54); *b* 1908; *s* of late Gerald Kingsley; *m* 1947, Priscilla Rosemary, *o d* of late Capt. Archibald A. Lovett Cameron, RN; three *s* one *d*. *Educ:* Winchester; New Coll., Oxford. OUCC 1928-30 (Capt. 1930), OUAFC 1927 and 1929. Served War of 1939-45 with Queen's Royal Regt. *Address:* 10 Buckingham Gate, SW1; Brookhill House, Cowfold, Sussex.

**KINGSMILL, Lieut-Col William Henry,** DSO 1943; MC 1940; Grenadier Guards, Retired; *b* 1 Dec. 1905; *s* of late Lieut-Col Andrew de Portal Kingsmill, DSO, OBE, MC, DL; *m* 1st, 1929, Aileen Kyrle Smith (from whom he obtained a divorce); 2nd, 1939, Diana Ivy, *widow* of Lieut-Col Guy Kingston Olliver; no *c*. *Educ:* Eton; RMC, Sandhurst. Joined Grenadier Guards 1925; transferred to RARO 1929; Dir of Cos., 1932-39; rejoined Grenadier Guards, Aug. 1939. Served France and Belgium, 1939-40 (MC); North Africa 8th Army, 1942-43; Italy, 1943-44 (DSO); commanded 6th Bn Grenadier Guards, 1943-44. MP (C) Yeovil Div. of Somerset, 1945-51. Chm. of companies; company dir, 1946-. *Recreations:* golf, tennis, shooting, yachting. *Address:* Sydmonton Court, Burghclere, near Newbury, Berks. *T:* Burghclere 332; 7 Cheyne Gardens, SW3. *T:* 01-352 5419. *Clubs:* Guards, White's.

**KINGSTON,** 11th Earl of, *cr* 1768; **Barclay Robert Edwin King-Tenison,** Bt 1682; Baron Kingston, 1764; Viscount Kingsborough, 1766; Baron Erris, 1800; Viscount Lorton, 1806; formerly Lieutenant, Royal Scots Greys; *b* 23 Sept. 1943; *o s* of 10th Earl of Kingston and Gwyneth, *d* of William Howard Evans (who *m* 1951, Brig. E. M. Tyler, DSO, MC, late RA; she *m* 1963, Robert Woodford); *S* father 1948; *m* 1965, Patricia Mary, *o d* of E. C. Killip, Llanfairfechan, N Wales; one *s* one *d*. *Educ:* Winchester. *Heir:* *s* Viscount Kingsborough, *qv*. *Address:* Kilronan, Cholderton, near Salisbury, Wilts. *Club:* Cavalry.

**KINGSTON (JAMAICA), Archbishop of, (RC),** since 1967; **Most Rev. John McEleney,** SJ, DD; PhD, MA; *b* 13 Nov. 1895; *s* of Charles McEleney and Bridget McEleney (*née* McGaffigan). *Educ:* Woburn Public Sch.; Weston Coll.; Boston Coll. Entered Soc. of Jesus at Yonkers, New York; classical studies at St Andrew on Hudson, 1920-21; Philosophy, Weston Coll. (MA), 1921-23. Teacher Ateneo de Manila, 1923-27; Theology, 1927-31; formerly: Rector, Shadowbrook Jesuit Novitiate, Lenox, Mass; Rector, Prep. Sch., Fairfield, Conn; Tutor Ateneo de Manila Jesuit Coll., Manila; Provincial New England Province Soc. of Jesus, 1944-50. Consecrated Bishop, 1950; Vicar Apostolic of Jamaica, 1950; Bishop of Kingston (Jamaica), 1956-67. Hon. Dr of Laws: Fairfield Univ., 1951; Boston Coll., 1968. *Address:* (Chancery Office and Residence) 21 Hopefield Avenue, Kingston 6, Jamaica. *T:* (Chancery) 79915; (Residence) 76282. *Club:* American (Jamaica).

**KINGSTON (ONTARIO), Archbishop of, (RC),** since 1967; **Most Rev. Joseph Lawrence Wilhelm,** DD, JCD; *b* Walkerton, Ontario, 16 Nov. 1909. *Educ:* St Augustine's Seminary, Toronto; Ottawa Univ., Ottawa, Ont. Ordained priest, Toronto, 1934. Mil. Chaplain to Canadian Forces, 1940-46 (MC, Sicily, 1943). Auxiliary Bishop, Calgary, Alberta, 1963-66. *Address:* Archbishop's House, Kingston, Ont, Canada.

**KINGSTON-UPON-THAMES, Bishop Suffragan of,** since 1970; **Rt. Rev. Hugh William Montefiore,** MA, BD; *b* 12 May 1920; *s* of late Charles Sebag-Montefiore, OBE, and Muriel Alice Ruth Sebag-Montefiore; *m* 1945, Elisabeth Mary Macdonald Paton, *d* of late Rev. William Paton, DD, and Mrs Grace Paton; three *d*. *Educ:* Rugby Sch.; St John's Coll., Oxford. Served during war, 1940-45; Capt. RA (Royal Bucks Yeo). Deacon 1949, priest 1950. Curate, St George's, Jesmond, Newcastle, 1949-51; Chaplain and Tutor, Westcott House, Cambridge, 1951-53; Vice-Principal, 1953-54; Examining Chaplain: to Bishop of Newcastle, 1953-; to Bishop of Worcester, 1957-60; to Bishop of Coventry, 1957-; to Bishop of Blackburn, 1966-; Fellow and Dean of Gonville and Caius Coll., 1954-63; Lectr in New Testament, Univ. of Cambridge, 1959-63; Vicar of Great Saint Mary's, Cambridge, 1963-70; Canon Theologian of Coventry, 1959-; Hon. Canon of Ely, 1969-. *Publications:* To Help You To Pray, 1958; Josephus and the New Testament, 1962; Beyond Reasonable Doubt, 1962; Awkward Questions on Christian Laove, 1964; A Commentary on the Epistle to the Hebrews, 1964; Truth to Tell, 1966; Mixed Marriage and Re-marriage, 1966; My Confirmation Notebook, 1968; The Question Mark, 1969; contributor to The Historic Episcopate, 1954; Soundings, 1962; Thomas and the Evangelists, 1962; God, Sex and War, 1963; The Responsible Church, 1966; (ed) We must Love One Another or Die, 1966; (ed) Sermons from Great St Mary's, 1968; Journeys in Belief, 1968; contribs to New Testament and Theological jls. *Recreation:* walking. *Address:* White Lodge, 23 Bellerne Road, Wandsworth Common, SW17. *T:* 01-672 6697. *Club:* Royal Commonwealth Society.

*See also Prof. W. D. M. Paton.*

**KINGSTON-UPON-THAMES, Archdeacon of;** *see* Robb, Ven. P. D.

**KINGSTON-McCLOUGHRY, Air Vice-Marshal Edgar James,** CB 1950; CBE 1943; DSO 1918; DFC 1918; AFRAeS; retired; *b* 10 Sept. 1896; *s* of late James Kingston-McCloughry, N Adelaide, SA; *m* 1924, Freda, 2nd *d* of late Sir Alfred Lewis, KBE; two *d*. *Educ:* Trinity Coll., Cambridge (MA); Adelaide Univ. Fellow of South Australian Sch. of Mines and Industries, 1914; entered Army, 1914; Lieut Engineer, 1915; Capt. Flying Corps, 1917; served

European War, 1914-18; Egypt, 1916 (DSO, DFC and bar); psa 1928; qualified RAF Staff Coll., 1929; qualified Camberley Staff Coll., 1935; Asst Comdt, RAF Coll., Cranwell, 1938; AOC No 44 Group, 1942; Head Planner, Air Operations, AEAF, 1943-44 (Overlord); Air Mem. Govt of India Frontier Defence Cttee, 1945; Air Mem. C-in-C India Reorganisation Cttee of Armed Forces, 1945-46; Senior Air Staff Officer, RAF, India Command, April 1946; AOC No 18 Group and Senior Air Officer Scotland, Jan. 1947; SASO, HQ, Fighter Comd 1948-50; AOC No 38 Group, 1950; Chief Air Defence Officer, Ministry of Defence, 1951-53, retired 1953. Member: RIIA; Inst. for Strategic Studies. *Publications:* Winged Warfare, 1937; War in Three Dimensions, 1949; The Direction of War, 1955; Global Strategy, 1957; Defence, 1959; The Spectrum of Strategy, 1963. *Address:* Fordel Croft, Glenfarg, Perthshire. *T:* Glenfarg 308. *Club:* Oxford and Cambridge University.

**KININMONTH, William Hardie,** PRSA, FRIBA, FRIAS; Senior Partner, Sir Rowand Anderson, Kininmonth and Paul, architects, Edinburgh and Forres; Member, Royal Fine Arts Commission for Scotland, 1952-65; *b* 8 Nov. 1904; *s* of John Kininmonth and Isabella McLean Hardie; *m* 1934, Caroline Eleanor Newsam Sutherland; one *d*. *Educ:* George Watson's Coll., Edinburgh. Architectural training in Edinburgh Coll. of Art, London Univ. and in offices of Sir Edwin Lutyens, Sir Rowand Anderson and Paul, and Wm N. Thomson; entered partnership Rowand Anderson and Paul, 1933; served War of 1939-45: RE 1940, North Africa, Sicily and Italy; resumed architectural practice, 1945; buildings for Edinburgh Univ., Renfrew Air Port and Naval Air Station, Edinburgh Dental Hospital, Town Hall, churches, banks, hospitals, schools, housing, etc. Saltire and Civic Trust Awards. Appointed: 1955, Adviser to City of Edinburgh, for development of Princes Street; 1964, to design new Festival Theatre and Festival Centre. Pres., Royal Scottish Academy, 1969- (formerly Treas. and then Sec.); Pres. Edinburgh Architectural Association, 1951-53; Member: Council RIBA, 1951-53; Council Royal Incorp. of Architects in Scot., 1951-53; Board, Edinburgh Coll. of Art, 1951-, Board Merchant Co. of Edinburgh, 1950-52. Edinburgh Dean of Guild Court, 1953-. *Address:* 16 Rutland Square, Edinburgh. *T:* 031-229 5515, 5516, 5517; The Lane House, 46a Dick Place, Edinburgh. *T:* 031-667 2724. *Clubs:* Scottish Arts, New (Edinburgh).

**KINLOCH, Sir Alexander (Davenport),** 12th Bt of Gilmerton, *cr* 1685; Major Special Reserve Grenadier Guards; *b* 17 Sept. 1902; *s* of Brig.-Gen. Sir David Kinloch, 11th Bt, and Elinor Lucy (*d* 1943), *d* of Col Bromley Davenport of Capesthorne, Cheshire; *S* father 1944; *m* 1st, 1929, Alexandra (marr. diss., 1945), *d* of Frederick Y. Dalziel, New York; two *d*; 2nd, 1946, Anna (marr. diss., 1965), *d* of late Thomas Walker, Edinburgh; one *s* three *d*; 3rd, 1965, Ann, *d* of Group Capt. F. L. White and Mrs H. R. White, London; one *s*. *Educ:* Eton. Mem. of Queen's Body Guard for Scotland (Royal Company of Archers). *Heir: s* David Kinloch, *b* 5 Aug. 1951. *Address:* Gilmerton House, North Berwick, East Lothian. *Clubs:* White's New (Edinburgh).

*See also Hon. H. W. Astor, Baron Brownlow, Baron Grantley.*

**KINLOCH, Sir John,** 4th Bt, of Kinloch, *cr* 1873; John Swire & Sons, Ltd, London; *b* 1 Nov. 1907; *e s* of Sir George Kinloch, 3rd Bt, OBE, and Ethel May (*d* 1959), *y d* of late Major J. Hawkins; *S* father 1948; *m* 1934, Doris Ellaline, *e d* of C. J. Head, Shanghai; one *s* two *d*. *Educ:* Charterhouse; Magdalene Coll., Cambridge. Served with British Ministry of War Transport as their repr. at Abadan, Persia, and also in London. *Recreations:* shooting, golf. *Heir: s* David Oliphant Kinloch, CA [*b* 15 Jan. 1942; *m* 1968, Susan Minette, *y d* of Maj.-Gen. R. E. Urquhart, *qv*]. *Address:* Northlands, Warnham, Sussex. *T:* Oakwood Hill 223; 6 Pensioners' Court, Charterhouse, EC1. *T:* 01-253 1143. *Clubs:* Oriental; Royal and Ancient.

**KINLOSS,** 12th Baroness *cr* 1602; **Beatrice Mary Grenville Freeman-Grenville** (surname changed by Lord Lyon King of Arms, 1950); *b* 1922; *e d* of late Rev. Hon. Luis Chandos Francis Temple Morgan-Grenville, Master of Kinloss; *S* grandmother, 1944; *m* 1950, Dr Greville Stewart Parker Freeman-Grenville, FSA, FRAS (name changed from Freeman by Lord Lyon King of Arms, 1950), Capt. late Royal Berks Regt, *er s* of late Rev. E. C. Freeman; one *s* two *d*. *Heir: s* Master of Kinloss, *qv*. *Address:* North View House, Sheriff Hutton, Yorks. *T:* Sheriff Hutton 447. *Club:* Royal Commonwealth Society.

**KINLOSS, Master of; Hon. Bevil David Stewart Chandos Freeman-Grenville;** *b* 20 June 1953; *s* of Dr Greville Stewart Parker Freeman-Grenville, FSA, Capt. late Royal Berks Regt, and of 12th Baroness Kinloss. *qv*.

**KINMONTH, Prof. John Bernard;** Surgeon and Director of Surgical Unit, St Thomas' Hospital, and Professor of Surgery in the University of London, since 1955; Consultant in Vascular Surgery to the RAF, since 1958; *b* 9 May 1916; *s* of Dr George Kinmonth; *m* 1946, Kathleen Margaret, *d* of Admiral J. H. Godfrey, *qv*; two *s* two *d*. *Educ:* Dulwich Coll.; St Thomas's Hosp. Medical Sch. House Surgeon, Resident Asst Surgeon, etc, St Thomas' Hosp., 1938-43. Wing Comdr, Surgical Specialist, RAFVR, 1944-47. Research Asst, St Bartholomew's Hosp., 1947-48; Research Fellow, Harvard Univ., 1948-49; Asst Surgeon, St Bartholomew's Hosp., 1950-54. Arris and Gale Lecturer, 1951, Hunterian Prof., 1954, RCS; Sir Arthur Sim's Commonwealth Travelling Professor, 1962. Past Pres., European Soc. Cardiovascular Surgery; Vice-Pres. Internat. Cardiovascular Soc.; Member: University of London Cttee on Colleges Overseas in Special Relations; Surgical Research Soc.; Physiological Soc. Consultant Adviser in Surgery to Min. of Health. Hon. Prof. Universidad Peruana Cayetano Heredia, 1968. Hon. Member: Brazilian Soc. Angiology; Internat. Soc. Lymphology. *Publications:* Vascular Surgery, 1962; (Chapters in) British Surgical Practice, 1950; articles on gen. and cardiovascular surgery and physiology in scientific journals. *Recreations:* sailing, the opera, gardening. *Address:* 70 Ladbroke Road, W11. *T:* 01-727 6045; St Thomas' Hospital, SE1. *T:* 01-928 9292. *Clubs:* Royal Cork Yacht, Royal Cruising, Irish Cruising, Cruising Association.

**KINNAIRD,** family name of **Baron Kinnaird.**

**KINNAIRD,** 12th Baron *cr* 1682; **Kenneth FitzGerald Kinnaird,** KT 1957; KBE 1946; Baron Kinnaird of Inchture, 1682; Baron Kinnaird of Rossie (UK), 1860; LLD (Hon.) St Andrews; late Captain Scottish Horse; Lord Lieutenant of County of Perth, 1942-60; Lord High Commissioner to General Assembly of Church of Scotland, 1936-38; Member Royal Company of Archers, Queen's Body Guard for Scotland; *b* 31 July 1880; *s* of 11th Baron and Mary Alma (*d* 1923), *d* of Sir Andrew Agnew,

8th Bart; *S* father, 1923; *m* 1903, Frances Victoria (*d* 1960), *y d* of late T. H. Clifton, Lytham Hall, Lancs; two *s* one *d* (and two *d* decd). *Educ:* Eton; Trinity Coll., Cambridge. Served with Scottish Horse, European War, 1914-18. Chm. Scottish Branch Brit. Red Cross Soc., 1935-56; Chm. Perth (East) Agricultural Cttee, 1939-47. Mem. Jt County Council of Perth and Kinross, 1925-61. *Heir: s* Master of Kinnaird, *qv*. *Address:* Rossie Priory, Inchture, Perthshire. *T:* Inchture 246. *Clubs:* Travellers'; New (Edinburgh). *See also Most Rev. H. R. Gough.*

**KINNAIRD, Master of; Hon. Graham Charles Kinnaird;** Flying Officer RAFVR; *b* 15 Sept. 1912; *e s* of 12th Baron Kinnaird, *qv*; *m* 1st, 1938, Nadia (who obtained a decree of divorce, 1940), *o c* of H. A. Fortington, Isle of Jethou, Channel Islands; 2nd, 1940, Diana, *yr d* of R. S. Copeman, Roydon Hall, Diss, Norfolk; four *d* (one *s* decd). *Educ:* Eton. Demobilised RAF, 1945. *Address:* Rossie Priory, Inchture, Perthshire. *T:* Inchture 246; Durham House, Durham Place, SW3. *Clubs:* Brooks's, Pratt's; New (Edinburgh).

**KINNELL, Rev. Gordon,** BD, FKC; Rector of Westmill, 1955-63, retired; Provost of St Andrew's Cathedral, Aberdeen, 1932-55; *b* 2 May 1891; *s* of Samuel and Elizabeth Kinnell; *m* 1928, Annie, 2nd *d* of Harry Dunford; one *s* one *d*. *Educ:* Ipswich Middle Sch.; King's Coll., London. Curate of: St Andrew's, Battersea, 1915-20; Christ Church, Clapton, 1920-23; Asst Diocesan Supernumerary in Diocese of Glasgow and Galloway, 1923; Rector of All Saints, Bearsden, 1923-31; Rector of S James, Cupar, Fife, 1931-32; Warden of Scottish Society of Reparation, 1937-39; Examining Chaplain to Bishop of Aberdeen, 1940; Hon. Canon of Christ Church Cathedral, Hartford, Conn, 1951; Hon. Canon of St Andrew's Cathedral, Aberdeen, 1956. *Recreation:* golf. *Address:* 5 Southview Road, Danbury, Essex.

**KINNOCK, Neil Gordon;** MP (Lab) Bedwellty, since 1970; Member, Welsh Hospital Board, since 1969; Tutor Organiser in Industrial and Trade Union Studies, Workers' Educational Assoc. since 1966; *b* 28 March 1942; *s* of Gordon Kinnock, Labourer, and Mary Kinnock (*née* Howells), Nurse; *m* 1967, Glenys Elizabeth Parry; one *s*. *Educ:* Lewis Sch., Pengam; University Coll., Cardiff. BA in Industrial Relations and History, UC, Cardiff (Chm. Socialist Soc., 1962-65; Pres. Students' Union, 1965-66). *Recreations:* male voice choral music, reading, walking, children; supporting Cardiff City AFC and Blackwood RFC. *Address:* 1 Chestnut Grove, Y Bryn, Pontllanfraith, Mon. *T:* Blackwood 3401. *Clubs:* Llanarth Workingmen's, Blackwood RFC.

**KINNOULL,** 15th Earl of, *cr* 1633; **Arthur William George Patrick Hay;** Viscount Dupplin and Lord Hay, 1627, 1633, 1697; Baron Hay (Great Britain), 1711; *b* 26 March 1935; *o surv. s* of 14th Earl and Mary Ethel Isobel Meyrick (*d* 1938); *S* father 1938; *m* 1961, Gay Ann, *er d* of Sir Denys Lowson, 1st Bt, *qv*; one *s* two *d*. *Educ:* Eton. Chartered Land Agent, 1960; Mem., Agricultural Valuers' Assoc., 1962. Fellow, Chartered Land Agents' Soc., 1964. Pres., National Council on Inland Transport, 1964. Mem. of Queen's Body Guard for Scotland (Royal Company of Archers), 1965. Junior Cons. Whip, House of Lords, 1966-68. *Heir: s* Viscount Dupplin, *qv*. *Address:* 15 Carlyle Square, SW3; Pier House, Seaview, IoW. *Clubs:* Turf, Lansdowne, Pratt's, MCC.

**KINROSS,** 3rd Baron *cr* 1902, of Glasclune; **John Patrick Douglas Balfour;** author and journalist; *b* 25 June 1904; *er s* of 2nd Baron and Caroline Elsie (*d* 1969), *d* of Arthur H. Johnstone-Douglas, DL; *S* father 1939; *m* 1938, Angela Mary (from whom he obtained a divorce, 1942), *o d* of late Capt. George Culme-Seymour. *Educ:* Winchester; Balliol Coll., Oxford (BA 1925). Worked on editorial staffs of various newspapers; travelled extensively in Middle East, Africa and elsewhere. Served RAFVR MEF, 1940-44 (despatches); First Sec. and Dir Publicity Section, British Embassy, Cairo, Egypt, 1944-47. *Publications:* (as Patrick Balfour): Society Racket, 1933; Grand Tour, 1934; Lords of the Equator, 1937; The Ruthless Innocent, 1950; The Orphaned Realm, 1951; (as Lord Kinross) Within the Taurus, 1954; The Century of the Common Peer, 1954; Europa Minor, 1956; Portrait of Greece, 1956; The Candid Eye, 1958; The Kindred Spirit, 1959; The Innocents at Home, 1959; Atatürk: The Rebirth of a Nation, 1964; Portrait of Egypt, 1966; The Windsor Years, 1967; Between Two Seas, 1968. *Recreation:* cooking. *Heir: b* Lt-Col Hon. David Andrew Balfour [*b* 29 March 1906; *m* 1st, 1936, Araminta (from whom he obtained a decree of divorce, 1941), *d* of Lt-Col W. E. Peel, DSO; one *d*; 2nd, 1948, Helen (*d* 1969), *d* of late Alan Hog, Edinburgh; one *s* (*b* 1 Oct. 1949)]. *Address:* 4 Warwick Avenue, W2. *Clubs:* Travellers', Beefsteak.

**KINROSS, John Blythe,** CBE 1967 (OBE 1958); Deputy Chairman, Industrial & Commercial Finance Corp. Ltd, since 1964; *b* 31 Jan. 1904; *s* of late John Kinross, RSA, architect, and late Mary Louisa Margaret Hall; *m* 1st, 1930; one *s* two *d*; 2nd, 1943, Mary Elizabeth Connon; one *s* two *d*. *Educ:* George Watson's Coll., Edinburgh. Manager Issue Dept, Gresham Trust, until 1933 when started business on own account as Cheviot Trust (first Issuing House to undertake small issues). Joined Industrial & Commercial Finance Corp. Ltd at inception, 1945; Gen. Man., 1948; Exec. Dir, 1961; Dep. Chm., 1964. Mem. Finance Cttee, Royal College of Surgeons, 1956-; Hon. Financial Adviser to Royal Scottish Academy, 1950-. Founded Mary Kinross Charitable Trust, 1957 (includes Good Companions Workshops Ltd, Student Homes Ltd and various med. res. projects). Chairman: Scottish Industrial Finance Ltd; London Atlantic Investment Trust Ltd; Tanker Charter Co. Ltd; Director: Ship Mortgage Finance Co. Ltd; Estate Duties Investment Trust Ltd; Equity Income Trust Ltd; House of Fraser Ltd; Imperial Investments Ltd; Scottish Ontario Investment Co. Ltd; Investment Trust of Guernsey Ltd and other companies. Hon. RSA, 1957; Hon. FFARCS, 1961. *Recreation:* farming. *Address:* 23 Cumberland Terrace, NW1. *T:* 01-935 8979; Little Hyde, Chipperfield, Kings Langley, Herts. *T:* Kings Langley 2317; (office) 01-628 4040. *Club:* Athenæum.

**KINSEY, Joseph Ronald,** JP; MP (C) Perry Barr Division of Birmingham since 1970; *b* 28 Aug. 1921; *s* of Walter and Florence Annie Kinsey; *m* 1953, Joan Elizabeth Walters; one *d*. *Educ:* Birmingham elementary and C of E schools. Shop management trng; served RAF ground staff, 1940-47; GPO telephone engr, 1947-57; started own business, florists, horticultural and fruit shop, 1957. JP Birmingham, 1962. *Address:* 68 Grange Road, Birmingham 24. *T:* 021-373 4606.

**KINSLEY, Rev. Prof. James,** MA, PhD, DLitt; Professor of English Studies and Head of Department of English Studies, University of Nottingham, since 1961; *b* Borthwick, Midlothian, 17 April 1922; *s* of late Louis Morrison Kinsley, Gorebridge; *m* 1949, Helen,

2nd *d* of late C. C. Dawson, Dewsbury; two *s* one *d*. *Educ:* Royal High Sch., Edinburgh; Edinburgh Univ.; Oriel Coll., Oxford. MA Edinburgh and James Boswell Scholar, 1943; BA Oxford (1st cl. Hons Sch. of Eng. Lang. and Lit.), 1947; PhD Edinburgh, 1951; MA Oxford, 1952; DLitt Edinburgh, 1959. Served with RA, 1943-45 (Captain). Lectr in English, University Coll. of Wales, 1947-54; Prof. of English Language and Literature in Univ. of Wales (at Swansea), 1954-61; Dean, Faculty of Arts, Univ. of Nottingham, 1967-70. William Will Memorial Lecture, 1960 (publ.); Gregynog Lectr, Aberystwyth, 1963. Editor, Renaissance and Modern Studies, Nottingham Miscellany, 1961-68; Gen. Editor: Oxford English Novels, 1967-; Oxford English Memoirs and Travels, 1969-. Vice-Pres., Tennyson Soc., 1963-. Ordained deacon 1962, priest 1963; Public Preacher, Southwell Diocese, 1964. FRSL 1959; FRHistS 1961. *Publications:* (ed) Lindsay, Ane Satyre of the Thrie Estaits, 1954; Scottish Poetry: A Critical Survey, 1955; (ed) W. Dunbar: Poems, 1958; (ed) John Dryden: Poems, 4 vols, 1958; (ed) Lindsay, Squyer Meldrum, 1959; (ed) Robert Burns: Poems and Songs, 1959; (ed) Dryden, The Works of Virgil, 1961; (ed with Helen Kinsley) Dryden, Absolom and Achitophel, 1961; (ed) John Dryden: Poetical Works, 1962; (ed) John Dryden: Selected Poems, 1963; (with J. T. Boulton) English Satiric Poetry: Dryden to Byron, 1966; (ed) J. Galt, Annals of the Parish, 1967; (ed) Robert Burns: Poems and Songs, 3 vols, 1968; (ed) The Oxford Book of Ballads, 1969; (textual Editor) The Novels of Jane Austen, 5 vols, 1970-71; (ed with George Parfitt) Dryden's Criticism, 1970; (with Helen Kinsley) Dryden: The Critical Heritage, 1971. Contribs to Encyclopædia Britannica, Review of English Studies, Medium Aevum, Modern Language Review, etc. *Recreations:* carpentry, gardening, folk-song. *Address:* 17 Elm Avenue, Beeston, Nottingham. *T:* Nottingham 257438.

**KINTORE, Countess of** (12th in line), *cr* 1677; **(Ethel) Sydney Keith;** Lady Keith of Inverurie, 1677 (Scotland); *b* 20 Sept. 1874; *e d* of 10th Earl of Kintore, KT, PC, GCMG (*d* 1930); *S* brother, 11th Earl of Kintore, 1966; officially recognised by the name of Keith and Chief of the name of Keith by warrant of Lord Lyon King of Arms, 1966; *m* 1905, John Baird (*e s* of Sir Alexander Baird of Urie), Visc. Stonehaven (*cr* 1938), PC, GCMG, DSO (*d* 1941); one *s* (and one *s* killed, Bomber Command, War of 1939-45) two *d* (and one *d* decd). *Heir: s* 2nd Viscount Stonehaven, *qv. Address:* Rickerton House, Stonehaven, Kincardineshire. *T:* Stonehaven 2756. *Club:* English-Speaking Union.

**KIPARSKY, Prof. Valentin Julius Alexander,** MA, PhD; Finnish writer and Professor, Helsinki; *b* St Petersburg, 4 July 1904; *s* of Professor René Kiparsky and Hedwig (*née* Sturtzel); *m* 1940, Aina Dagmar, MagPhil, *d* of Rev. Matti Jaatinen and Olga (née Jungmann); one *s*. *Educ:* St Annen-Schule, St Petersburg; St Alexis Sch., Perkjärvi, Finland; Finnish Commercial Sch., Viipuri, Finland; Helsinki Univ.; Prague Univ.; and research work in different countries. Helsinki University: Junior Lectr, 1933, Sen. Lectr, 1938, actg Prof., 1946, Prof., 1947 and again, 1963. Visiting Prof., Indiana Univ., Bloomington, USA, 1952, Minnesota Univ., USA, 1961-62; Prof. of Russian Language and Literature, University of Birmingham, 1952-55, when he returned to Finland; Prof. of Slavonic Philology, Freie Univ., Berlin, 1958-63. Co-Editor: Slavistische Veröffentlichungen (W Berlin), 1958-; Scando-Slavica (Copenhagen), 1963-. Lt Finnish Army, 1939-40, 1941-42; Translator and Interpreter to Finnish Govt, 1942-44; Director: Finnish Govtl Inst. for studies of USSR, 1948-50; Osteuropa-Institut, W Berlin, 1958-63. Mem., Societas Scientiarum Fennica; Finn. Acad.; Corresp. Member: Akad. der Wissenschaften und der Literatur, Mainz; Internat. Cttee of Slavists. Comdr of the Finnish Lion, 1954. *Publications:* Die gemeinslavischen Lehnwörter aus dem Germanischen, 1934; Fremdes im Baltendeutsch, 1936; Die Kurenfrage, 1939; Suomi Venäjän Kirjallisuudessa, 1943 and 1945; Venäjän Runotar, 1946; Norden i den Ryska Skönlitteraturen, 1947; Wortakzent der russischen Schriftsprache, 1962; Russische historische Grammatik I, 1963; English and American Characters in Russian Fiction, 1964; Russische historische Grammatik II, 1967; numerous articles in various languages in learned jls. *Recreation:* cycling. *Address:* Maurinkatu 8-12 C 37, Helsinki, Finland.

**KIPPING, Sir Norman (Victor),** GCMG 1966; KBE 1962; Kt 1946; JP; Director: Joseph Lucas (Industries) Ltd; Pilkington Bros Ltd; *b* 11 May 1901; *y s* of P. P. and Rose E. Kipping, London; *m* 1928, Eileen Rose; two *s* one *d*. *Educ:* University Coll. Sch.; Birkbeck Coll., London. Research Dept, GPO, 1920-21, as jun. engineer; Internat. Western Electric Co., 1921-26; Standard Telephones & Cables Ltd, 1926-42, finally as works manager; Head of Regional Div., Min. of Production, 1942-45; Under-Sec. Bd of Trade, 1945; Dir-Gen., FBI, 1946-65; retired 1965 on formation of Confedn of British Industry. Dir, Brit. Overseas Fairs Ltd from foundation, 1953 (Chm. 1958-66). FIEE, FIPE (Chm. Council, 1940-41). Chm. Coun. University Coll. Sch.; President: Consultative Council of Professional Management Orgs; Anglo-Finnish Soc. Past Sec., Anglo-Amer. Coun. on Productivity; past Member: Br. Productivity Coun.; Dollar Exports Coun.; Export Coun. for Europe; Brit. Nat. Export Coun.; Nat. Prod. Advisory Council; Fulton Cttee on Civil Service. Led missions for FBI to India, Japan, Nigeria and for HM Govt to Zambia. Hon. Fellow, BIM (Elbourne Lectr, 1965). Hon. DSc (Loughborough, 1966). Commander: Order of Dannebrog (Denmark), 1948; Order of the Lion (Finland), 1959; Order of Merit of the Italian Republic, 1962; Order of Vasa (Sweden), 1962. *Publication:* The Suez Contractors, 1969. *Recreations:* shooting, gardening. *Address:* Fosters, Wykeham Rise, Totteridge, N20. *T:* 01-445 4054. *Club:* East India and Sports.

**KIRALFY, Prof. Albert Kenneth Roland;** Professor of Law, King's College, London, since 1964; *b* Toronto, 5 Dec. 1915; *s* of Bolossy Kiralfy, Theatrical Impresario, and Helen Dawnay; *m* 1960, Roberta Ann Routledge; no *c*. *Educ:* Streatham Grammar Sch.; King's Coll., London Univ. LLB 1935, LLM 1936, PhD 1949, London. Called to the Bar, Gray's Inn, 1947. King's Coll., London: Asst Lectr, 1937-39 and 1947-48; Lectr, 1948-51; Reader, 1951-64; Vice-Dean of Law, 1966-68. Vis. Prof., Osgoode Hall Law Sch., Toronto, 1961-62; Exchange Scholar, Leningrad Law Sch., Spring 1964. Dir, Comparative Law Course, Luxembourg, Aug. 1968. Mem. Editorial Bd, Internat. and Comparative Law Quarterly, 1956-. *Publications:* The Action on the Case, 1951; The English Legal System, 1954 (and later edns; 4th edn 1967); A Source Book of English Law, 1957; Potter's Historical Introduction to English Law, (4th edn) 1958; (with Dr G. Jones) Guide to Selden Society Publications, 1960; Translation of Russian Civil Codes, 1966; chapter, English Law, in Derrett, Introduction to Legal Systems, 1968.

*Recreations:* travel, reading, languages. *Address:* 25 Woodhayes Road, Wimbledon, SW19. *T:* 01-946 6113.

**KIRBY, Sir Arthur (Frank),** GBE 1969 (KBE 1957); CMG 1945; MInstT; Chairman, National Ports Council, since 1967; *b* Slough, 13 July 1899; *s* of George and Lily Maria Kirby; *m* 1935, Winifred Kate, *d* of Fred Bradley, Waterloo Park, Liverpool; one *d*. *Educ:* Sir William Borlase's Sch., Marlow; London Sch. of Economics. Entered Service GWR 1917; returned 1919 after serving with London Rifle Brigade and 2nd Rifle Brigade; special training for six years with GWR; entered Colonial Service, Asst Sec., Takoradi Harbour, Gold Coast, 1928; Traffic Manager, Gold Coast Railway, 1936; Asst Supt of the Line, Kenya and Uganda Railways and Harbours, 1938; Gen. Man., Palestine Railways and Ports Authority and Dir Gen. Hejaz Railway, 1942-48; Supt of the Line, E African Railways and Harbours, 1949-50; Asst Comr for Transport, E Africa High Commn, 1951-52; Actg Comr for Transport, 1952-53; Gen. Manager, East African Railways and Harbours 1953-57; Commissioner for East Africa, London, 1958-63; Chm., British Transport Docks Board, 1963-67; Pres., Shipping and Forwarding Agents Inst., 1966. Dep. Chairman: Royal Commonwealth Society, 1965-68; Gt Ormond Street Children's Hosp., 1963-69; Governor: National Hosp. for Nervous Diseases, 1966-69; Woking Staff Coll. Mem. Council, Royal Society of Arts. Chm., Palestine Assoc. OStJ. *Address:* 6 Baltimore Court, The Drive, Hove, Sussex BN3 3PR.

**KIRBY, Dennis,** MVO 1961; MBE 1955; General Manager, Irvine Development Corporation, since 1967; *b* 5 April 1923; *s* of William Ewart Kirby and Hannah Kirby; *m* 1943, Mary Elizabeth Kilby; one *d*. *Educ:* Hull Grammar Sch.; RNC Greenwich; Queen's Coll., Cambridge. Lt (A) RNVR (fighter pilot), 1940-46. Colonial Service, Sierra Leone: Asst Colonial Sec., 1946-49; District Comr, 1950-58; Special Duty, 1959; Dep. Financial Sec., 1960; Perm. Sec., 1961-62; 1st Sec., UK Diplomatic Service, 1962; General Manager East Kilbride Development Corp., 1963-68. *Publication:* Careers in New Town Building, 1970. *Recreations:* shooting, fishing, ski-ing, squash. *Address:* 17 Ottoline Drive, Troon, Ayrshire. *T:* Troon 1449. *Clubs:* Caledonian; Royal Naval Volunteer Reserves (Scotland) (Glasgow).

**KIRBY, Gwendolen Maud,** MVO; Matron, The Hospital for Sick Children, Great Ormond Street, 1951-69; *b* 17 Dec. 1911; 3rd *d* of late Frank M. Kirby, Gravesend, Kent. *Educ:* St Mary's Sch., Calne, Wilts. State Registered Nurse: trained at Nightingale Training Sch., St Thomas' Hosp., SE1. 1933-36; The Mothercraft Training Soc., Cromwell House, Highgate, 1936; State Certified Midwife: trained at General Lying-in Hosp., York Road, Lambeth, 1938-39; Registered Sick Children's Nurse: trained at the Hospital for Sick Children, Great Ormond Street, WC1, 1942-44. Awarded Nightingale Fund Travelling Scholarship, 1948-49, and spent 1 year in Canada and United States. Mem. of Gen. Nursing Council, 1955-65. *Address:* 15 Essex Road, Gravesend, Kent.

**KIRBY, Sir James (Norman),** Kt 1962; CBE 1956; MIProdE; Chairman: James N. Kirby group of companies since 1924; International Products Ltd and subsidiaries; Champion Spark Plug Co. (Australia) Pty Ltd; Wales Unit Investment Pty Ltd (subsid. of Bank of NSW); Reinsurance Co. of Australasia Ltd; Director: Dow Chemical (Australia) Ltd; Mutual Life & Citizens' Ltd; Qantas Airways Ltd; Australian General Electric Pty Ltd; Australian General Electric (Appliances) Pty Ltd; Australia & New Guinea Corp. Ltd; *b* 15 June 1899; *s* of Louis Kirby, Melbourne; *m* 1926, Agnes Anne Wessler; two *s*. *Educ:* Sydney. Mem., Manufacturing Industries Advisory Council; Pres., Electrical & Radio Development Assoc. of NSW; Dir, National Heart Foundation of Aust.; Governor, Science Foundation for Physics within University of Sydney; Life Governor, Australian Inst. of Management; Mem., Industrial Design Council of Australia. *Recreations:* golf, fishing. *Address:* 205 Salisbury Road, Camperdown, NSW 2050, Australia. *T:* LA 0455. *Clubs:* Royal Sydney Yacht Squadron, Australian Golf, NSW, American National (all in Australia).

**KIRBY, Air Cdre John Lawrance,** CB 1946; CBE 1943; JP; DL; RAF; *b* 1899; *s* of Wilson Kirby, York; *m* 1941, Rachel Margaret Cunningham, *y d* of R. G. Smith; two *s* three *d*. *Educ:* Archbishop Holgate's Sch., York. JP Grimsby, 1951; DL Lincs, 1952. *Address:* Utterby Close, Louth, Lincs. *T:* North Thoresby 240.

**KIRBY, Hon. Sir Richard (Clarence),** Kt 1961; Chief Judge, Commonwealth Court of Conciliation and Arbitration since 1956 (Judge, 1947); (first) President, Commonwealth Conciliation and Arbitration Commission, since 1956; *b* 22 Sept. 1904; *s* of Samuel Enoch Kirby and Agnes Mary Kirby, N Queensland; *m* 1937, Hilda Marie Ryan; two *d*. *Educ:* The King's Sch., Parramatta; University of Sydney (LLB). Solicitor, NSW, 1928; called to Bar, 1933; served AIF, 1942-44; Mem. Adult Adv. Educl Council to NSW Govt, 1944-46; Judge, Dist Court, NSW, 1944-47; Mem. Austr. War Crimes Commn, 1945, visiting New Guinea, Morotai, Singapore, taking evidence on war crimes; Australia Rep. on War Crimes, Lord Mountbatten's HQ, Ceylon, 1945; Royal Commissioner on various occasions for Federal, NSW and Tasmanian Govts, 1945-47; Actg Judge Supreme Court of NSW, 1947; Austr. Rep., UN Security Council's Cttee on Good Offices on Indonesian Question, 1947-48, participating in Security Council Debates, Lake Success, USA; Chm. Stevedoring Industry Commn, 1947-49. *Recreations:* horse racing and breeding. *Address:* 10 Myrnong Crescent, Toorak, Vic 3142, Australia; 451 Law Courts Place, Melbourne, Vic 3000; 75 Elizabeth Street, Sydney, NSW 2000. *T:* Sydney 289717. *Clubs:* Athenæum, Victoria Racing, Victoria Amateur Turf, Moonee Valley Racing and Mornington Racing, Victoria Golf (Melbourne).

**KIRBY, Walter,** CIE 1945; BSc (Birmingham); retired; *b* 6 Dec. 1891; *m* 1st, 1920, Lily Watkins (*d* 1957); two *d*; 2nd, 1961, Violet Eveline Harris. *Educ:* Birmingham Univ. (BSc 1919). Past Pres. Mining Geological and Metallurgical Institute of India. Joined Dept of Mines in India as Junior Inspector of Mines, 1921; Senior Inspector, 1925-38; Chief Inspector of Mines in India, 1938-46; retired, 1946. *Address:* 4 Haddington Street, The Range, Toowoomba, Queensland 4350, Australia.

**KIRCHEIS, John Reinhardt;** Chairman, Mobil Oil Co. Ltd and Mobil Holdings Group since 1969; *b* 4 April 1916; *s* of J. R. Kircheis III and Thelba Deibeet; *m* 1940, Jean Ohme; two *d*. *Educ:* Buena Vista College. Teacher and Prin., Bode Public Schools, 1937; Account Analyst, General Motors Corp., 1940; Lt-Comdr, USNR, 1942; various assignments, Mobil Oil

Corp., 1946; Vice-Pres. and Area Manager, Mobil Europe Inc., 1966; Man. Dir, Mobil Oil Co. Ltd, 1968. *Recreations:* golf, fishing, music. *Address:* Mobil Oil Co. Ltd, Mobil House, 54-60 Victoria Street, SW1. *Clubs:* Directors', Royal Automobile, New Century.

**KIRCHNER, Bernard Joseph,** CBE 1944; *b* 1894; *er s* of Alexander and Teresa Kirchner; *m* 1st, 1924, Vivienne Mary (*d* 1949), *y d* of late Lt-Col T. P. Ffrench, IA, and step-*d* of late Ray Knight, ICS; two *d*; 2nd, 1957, Margaret Jane, *o d* of late T. M. Upton, and *widow* of G. W. F. Brown. *Educ:* Imperial Coll. of Science, London Univ. European War, 1914-18, France and Flanders, Artists' Rifles, South Staffs Regt and RAF (wounded, 1914 Star, Gen. Service and Victory Medals). Joined The Statesman, Calcutta, 1922; Mgr The Englishman, 1928-30; Man. Editor Delhi office of The Statesman, 1932-41, and 1946-48; Dir, 1940; London Agent, The Statesman, 1948-54; Mem. of Nat. Service Advisory Cttee, Delhi, 1939-41; Chief Press Adviser, Govt of India, 1941-44; Vice-Chm. Ex-Services Assoc., India, 1946; Delhi Corresp., The Times, 1946-47. Mem. Council of Commonwealth Press Union; Pres. London Assoc. of British Empire Newspapers Overseas, 1953-54. Silver Jubilee Medal, 1935. *Address:* 13 Spencer Road, East Molesey, Surrey.

**KIRK, Adam Kennedy;** retired; *b* 24 March 1893; *s* of John and Mary Kirk, Melbourne; *m* 1921, Freda Minnie Matthews; one *d* (one *s* killed, RAF). *Educ:* public schs, Melbourne. Served with Australian Forces, 1914-18 (Anzac Decoration; 1914-18 medals): landing at Gallipoli, 1915. Founder, Kirk & Co. (Tubes) Ltd (now part of American combine). Past Mem., local Coun. (Chm., 1946-47); Past Mem., Surrey CC; Sheriff of London, 1960-61; Master, Poulters' Co.; Past Master, Joiners' and Ceilors' Co.; Freeman and Liveryman, Founders' Co. MIM; MInst British Foundrymen; MInstBE; MRSH. OStJ; Grand Officer, Republic of Tunisia; Lion of Finland; Nepal Decoration. *Recreations:* racehorse owner, cricket, Rugby football, golf. *Address:* Oakdene, Ladyegate Road, Dorking, Surrey. *Clubs:* Devonshire, Eccentric, City Livery, United Wards; Ascot, Goodwood, Epsom, Fontwell.

**KIRK, Alexander Comstock;** US Ambassador (retired); *b* 26 Nov. 1888; *s* of James Alexander Kirk and Clara Comstock. *Educ:* Yale; Harvard; Ecole Libre des Sciences Politiques. American Embassy, Berlin, 1915; American Legation, The Hague, 1917. Amer. Commission to negotiate peace, Paris, 1918-19; Asst to Sec. of State, 1919; Amer. Embassy, Tokyo, 1920; Amer. Legation, Peking, 1922; Amer. Embassy, Mexico City, 1924; Dept of State, Washington, DC, 1925; Amer. Embassy, Rome, 1928-38; Chargé d'Affaires, Moscow, 1938, Berlin, 1939; Minister-Counsellor, Rome, 1940; Envoy Extraordinary and Minister Plenipotentiary to Egypt and Saudi Arabia, 1941; Ambassador to Govt of King of Hellenes, 1943; US Rep., Advisory Council for Italy, 1944; US Adviser to Supreme Allied Comdr-in-Chief Mediterranean Theatre; Ambassador to Italy, 1944; retired, 1946. *Address:* 4630 Calle Altivo, Tucson, Arizona 85718, USA.

**KIRK, Geoffrey Stephen,** DSC 1945; FBA 1959; Fellow of Trinity Hall, Cambridge, since 1946; Professor of Classics, Yale University, since 1965; *b* 3 Dec. 1921; *s* of Frederic Tilzey Kirk, MC and Enid Hilda (*née* Pentecost); *m* 1950, Barbara Helen Traill; one *d*. *Educ:* Rossall Sch.; Clare Coll., Cambridge. Served War in Royal Navy, 1941-45; commissioned 1942; Temp. Lt, RNVR, 1945. Took Degree at Cambridge, 1946; Research Fellow, Trinity Hall, 1946-49; Student, Brit. Sch. at Athens, 1947; Commonwealth Fund Fellow, Harvard Univ., 1949-50; Official Fellow, Trinity Hall, 1950-65; Cambridge University: Asst Lecturer in Classics, 1951; Lecturer in Classics, 1952-61; Reader in Greek, 1961-65. Visiting Lecturer, Harvard Univ., 1958; Sather Prof. of Classical Literature, University of California, Berkeley, 1968-69. LittD (Cambridge) 1965; MA (Yale) 1965. *Publications:* Heraclitus, the Cosmic Fragments, 1954; (with J. E. Raven) The Presocratic Philosophers, 1958; The Songs of Homer, 1962 (abbrev., as Homer and the Epic, 1965); Euripides, Bacchae, 1970; Myth, 1970; articles in classical, archæological and philosophical journals. *Recreation:* sailing. *Address:* 2 Latham Close, Cambridge. *T:* Cambridge 57314.

**KIRK, Geoffrey William,** CMG 1959; Ambassador to El Salvador, 1960-67; *b* 9 Aug. 1907; *o s* of Percy R. Kirk and Alice H. York; *m* 1935, Maria Annunziata Montrezza; no *c*. *Educ:* Mill Hill Sch.; London Univ. Mem. of HM Foreign Service. First Sec., Panama, 1948-50; Prague, 1950-53; Commercial Counsellor, HM Embassy, The Hague, 1953-60. Hon. Comdr, Order of Orange-Nassau (Netherlands), 1958. *Address:* c/o Midland Bank, 10 Newgate Street, EC1. *Club:* Reform.

**KIRK, Grayson Louis;** President Emeritus, Columbia University; *b* 12 Oct. 1903; *s* of Traine Caldwell Kirk and Nora Eichelberger; *m* 1925, Marion Louise Sands; one *s*. *Educ:* Miami Univ. (AB); Clark Univ. (AM); Ecole Libre des Sciences Politiques, Paris, 1928-29. PhD University of Wisconsin, 1930. Prof. of History, Lamar Coll., Beaumont, Tex, 1925-27; Social Science Research Coun. Fellowship (chiefly spent at London Sch. of Economics), 1936-37; Instructor in Political Science, 1929-30, Asst Prof., 1930-36, Associate Prof., 1936-38, Prof., 1938-40, University of Wisconsin; Associate Prof. of Government, Columbia Univ., 1940-43; Head, Security Section, Div. of Political Studies, US Dept of State, 1942-43; Mem. US Delegn Staff, Dumbarton Oaks, 1944; Exec. Officer, Third Commn, San Francisco Conf., 1945. Research Associate, Yale Inst. of Internat. Studies, 1943-44; Prof. of Government, Columbia Univ., 1943-47; Prof. of Internat Relations, Acting Dir of Sch. of Internat. Affairs, and Dir of European Inst., 1947-49. Appointed Provost in Nov. 1949, and also Vice-Pres in July 1950; became acting head of Columbia in President Eisenhower's absence on leave, March 1951; Pres. and Trustee of Columbia Univ., 1953-68; Bryce Prof. of History of Internat. Relations, Columbia, 1959-. Trustee: Greenwich Savings Bank; Carnegie Foundation for the Advancement of Teaching; Inst. of Internat. Education; Asia Soc.; The Asia Foundation; French Inst.; Lycée Français of NY; Hon. Trustee, United Coll. of Hongkong. member: American Political Science Assoc.; Academy of Political Science (Dir); American Philosophical Soc.; Pilgrims of the US; Council on Foreign Relations (Pres.); American Soc. for Internat. Law; Amer. Acad. of Arts and Sciences; Amer. Soc. of French Legion of Honour (Pres.). Director: Mobil Oil Co.; International Business Machines Corporation; Dividend Shares Inc.; Nation-Wide Securities Co. Inc.; Japan Soc.; Belgian-Amer. Educl Foundn, Inc.; France-America Soc.; Consolidated Edison Co. of NY Inc. Hon. LLD: Miami Univ., 1950; 1951: Waynesburg Coll., Brown Univ.; Union Coll.; 1953: University of Puerto Rico; Clark Univ.; Princeton Univ.; New York Univ.; University of Wisconsin; Columbia, Jewish Theol.

Seminary of America; 1954: Syracuse Univ.; Williams Coll.; University of Pennsylvania; Harvard Univ.; Washington Univ.; St Louis; Central Univ., Caracas; University of the Andes, Merida, Venezuela; Univ. of Zulia, Maracaibo, Venezuela; University of Delhi, India; Thamasset Univ., Bangkok; 1956: Johns Hopkins Univ., Baltimore; Amherst; 1958: Dartmouth Coll.; Northwestern Univ., University of Tennessee, 1960; Hon. LHD, University of N Dakota, 1958; Hon. PhD, University of Bologna, 1951; Dr of Civil Law, University of King's Coll., Halifax, Nova Scotia, 1958; LLD: St Lawrence Univ., 1963; University of Denver, 1964; University of Notre Dame, 1964; Bates Coll., 1964; Waseda Univ., Japan, 1965; University of Michigan, 1965; University of Sussex, 1966. Associate KStJ 1959. Comdr, Order of Orange-Nassau, 1952; Hon. KBE, 1955; Grand Officer, Order of Merit, of the Republic, Italy, 1956; Commandeur Légion d'Honneur, France, 1956. Medal of the Order of Taj, Iran, 1961; Grand Cross, Order of George I (Greece), 1965; Order of the Sacred Treasure, 1st Class (Japan), 1965; Comdr, Ordre des Palmes Académiques (France), 1966. *Publications:* Philippine Independence, 1936; Contemporary International Politics (with W. R. Sharp), 1940; (with R. P. Stebbins) War and National Policy, Syllabus, 1941; The Study of International Relations in American Colleges and Universities, 1947. *Address:* Columbia Univ., New York, NY 10027, USA. *T:* 280-4256. *Clubs:* Athenæum; Columbia University, Century, University, Union, Men's Faculty (New York); Cosmos (Washington).

**KIRK, Rt. Hon. Herbert Victor,** PC (N Ireland), 1942; Minister of Finance, Government of Northern Ireland, since 1965; MP Windsor Division of Belfast, Parliament of Northern Ireland, since 1956; *b* 5 June 1912; *s* of Alexander and Mary A. Kirk; *m* 1944, Gladys A. Dunn; three *s. Educ:* Queen's Univ., Belfast (BComSc). Minister of Labour and Nat. Insce, Govt of N Ireland, 1962-64; Minister of Education, 1964-65. FCA 1940. JP Co. Borough Belfast. *Recreation:* golf. *Address:* 57 Bawnmore Road, Belfast 9, Northern Ireland. *T:* 666523. *Club:* Reform (Belfast).

**KIRK, James Balfour,** CMG 1941; MB, ChB; FRCP; DPH; DTM and H; retired; *b* 7 April 1893; *s* of John A. G. Kirk, Falkirk, and Jessie Y. Rintoul, also of Falkirk; *m* 1917, Jane C., *d* of Hume Purdie, LDS, Edinburgh; three *d. Educ:* Falkirk High Sch.; George Watson's Coll., Edinburgh; Edinburgh Univ. (Vans Dunlop Scholar). Private, 9th Bn Royal Scots, Aug.-Dec. 1914; 2nd Lt, RFA 1914-16; Lt RAMC, 1917-20 (1914-15 Star, Victory and General Service Medals); Medical Officer of Health, Port Louis, Mauritius, 1922-26; Acting Dir, Medical and Health Dept, Mauritius, 1926-27; Dir, Medical and Health Dept, Mauritius, 1927-41; Dir of Medical Services, Gold Coast, 1941-44; Dir, Health Div. Greece Mission, UNRRA, 1945; Chief Medical Officer, Central Headquarters, Displaced Persons Operation UNRRA, Germany, Aug. 1945-Feb. 1946; Temp. MO, Min. of Health, 1946-62. *Publications:* Public Health Practice in the Tropics, 1928; Hints on Equipment and Health for Intending Residents in the Tropics, 1926; Practical Tropical Sanitation, 1936; numerous articles on public health and medical subjects. *Recreations:* gardening, golf, photography. *Address:* 16 Brook Lane, Haywards Heath, Sussex. *T:* Lindfield 2185.

**KIRK, John Henry,** CBE 1957; Professor of Marketing (with special reference to horticulture), Wye College, since 1965; *b* 11 April 1907; *s* of William Kirk, Solicitor; *m* 1946, Wilfrida Margaret Booth; two *s. Educ:* Durban High Sch., S Africa; Universities of S Africa, Cambridge, North Carolina and Chicago. Ministry of Agriculture (from 1934, as economist and administrator); Under-Sec., 1959-65. *Publications:* Economic Aspects of Native Segregation, 1929; Agriculture and the Trade Cycle, 1933. Contributions to Journals of Sociology, Economics and Agricultural Economics. *Recreation:* gardening. *Address:* Burrington, Cherry Gardens, Wye, Ashford, Kent. *T:* Wye 640.

**KIRK, Peter Michael;** MP (C) Saffron Walden since March 1965; Parliamentary Under-Secretary of State, Ministry of Defence, since 1970; *b* 18 May 1928; *er s* of Rt Rev. Kenneth Escott Kirk, sometime Bishop of Oxford; *m* 1950, Elizabeth Mary, *d* of late R. B. Graham; three *s. Educ:* Marlborough; Trinity Coll., Oxford; Zürich Univ. Pres., Oxford Union, 1949. Journalist in Glasgow, London, USA, and Foreign Correspondent world-wide. MP (C) Gravesend Div. of Kent, 1955-64; Parliamentary Under-Sec. of State, War Office, 1963-64; Parliamentary Under-Sec. of State for Defence for the Army, Ministry of Defence, April-Oct. 1964. UK Delegn to Council of Europe, 1956-63, 1966-; Chairman: Non-Represented Nations Cttee, Council of Europe, 1959-61; Gen. Affairs Cttee, WEU, 1960-63; Budgetary and Administrative Cttee, WEU, 1968-69; Political Affairs Cttee, Council of Europe, 1969-. Mem. Carshalton UDC, 1952-55. *Publications:* One Army Strong?, 1958; various newspaper articles. *Recreations:* walking, listening to music. *Address:* Cootes Farm, Steeple Bumpstead, near Haverhill, Suffolk. *T:* Steeple Bumpstead 388. *Clubs:* Brooks's, Bath.

**KIRKALDY, Prof. Harold Stewart,** CBE 1958; MA, LLB; Fellow since 1944, Vice-President and Bursar, 1965-70, of Queens' College, Cambridge; *b* 27 Dec. 1902; *s* of late David and Anne Kirkaldy; unmarried. *Educ:* Grove Academy, Broughty Ferry; University of Edinburgh. Called to Bar, Middle Temple, 1928; Asst Sec. British Employers' Confederation, 1929-39; Gen. Sec. Iron and Steel Trades Employers' Assoc., 1939-45; Prof. of Industrial Relations, Cambridge Univ., 1944-63, Emeritus Prof. since 1967. Mem. of British Delegation at International Labour Conference, 1929-44; Mem., Cttee of Experts on Application of Internat. Labour Conventions, 1946-; Mem., 1946- (Chm., 1958-) Administrative Bd of Staff Pensions Fund of Internat. Labour Office; Chm. of UN Joint Staff Pensions Board, 1960-62; Chm. of various Wages Councils under Wages Councils Act, 1946-62; Chm. for Eastern Region of Minister of Labour's Compensation Appeal Tribunal, 1949-59; Chm., Cambridge and District Employment Cttee, 1957-69; Mem. of Industrial Disputes Tribunal, 1952-59; Chm. of Courts of Arbitration under Industrial Courts Act, 1958-62; Chm. of Commissions of Inquiry under Wages Councils Act, 1949-62; Chm. of Bd of Inquiry into Trinidad Oil Industry, 1955; Chm. of BBC Arbitration Tribunal, 1958; Pres. of Mauritius Trade Disputes Arbitration Tribunal, 1959; Chm. of Industrial Disputes Tribunal, Isle of Man, 1960; Mem. Cttee on Remuneration of Ministers and Members of Parliament, 1963-64; Dep. Chm., Nat. Incomes Commn, 1962-65. Perin Memorial Lecturer, Jamshedpur, India, 1946. *Address:* 31a The Strand, Walmer, Deal, Kent. *Club:* Oxford and Cambridge.

**KIRKALDY, Prof. John Francis,** DSc (London); FGS; Professor of Geology, Queen Mary College, University of London, since 1962; *b*

14 May 1908; *o s* of late James and Rose Edith Kirkaldy, Sutton, Surrey; *m* 1935, Dora Muriel, *e d* of late Grimshaw Heyes Berry, Enfield, Middlesex; four *d*. *Educ:* Felsted Sch.; King's Coll., London. 1st Cl. Special Hons BSc (Geol.) 1929; MSc 1932; DSc 1946. Demonstrator in Geology, King's Coll., 1929-33; Asst Lectr in Geology, University Coll., London, 1933-36; Lectr in Geology, King's Coll., London, 1936-47. War Service with Meteorological Branch, RAF, Sqdn Ldr, 1939-45. Reader in Geology and Head of Dept, Queen Mary Coll., 1947-62. FKC 1970. Daniel Pidgeon Fund, Geol. Soc., 1935; Foulerton Award, Geologists' Assoc., 1947. *Publications:* Outline of Historical Geology (with A. K. Wells), 1948 (and subseq. edns); General Principles of Geology, 1954 (and subseq. edns); Rocks and Minerals in Colour, 1963. Papers in Quart. Jl Geol. Soc.; Proc. Geol. Assoc., Geol. Mag., etc. *Recreations:* gardening, Scottish country dancing. *Address:* Department of Geology, Queen Mary College, Mile End Road, E1. *T:* 01-980 4811. *Club:* Geological Society's.

**KIRKBRIDE, Sir Alec Seath,** KCMG 1949 (CMG 1942); Kt 1946; CVO 1954; OBE 1932; MC; Ambassador in Libya, 1954, retired (Minister, 1951-54); Director of the British Bank of the Middle East, since 1956; *b* 19 Aug. 1897; *m* 1st, 1921, Edith Florence James (*d* 1966); three *s*; 2nd, 1967, Ethel Mary James. Military Service, 1916-21; British Rep., Es Salt, Transjordan, 1921; Junior Asst Sec., Palestine Govt, 1922, Asst Sec., 1926; Asst British Resident, Transjordan, 1927; District Commissioner, Galilee and Acre, 1937; British Resident, in Transjordan, 1939; Minister to the Hashemite Kingdom of the Jordan, 1946; representative of HM Government to Permanent Mandates Commission, Geneva, 1936, 1938, and 1939. *Publication:* A Crackle of Thorns, 1956. *Address:* 264 Leigham Court Road, SW16.

**KIRKCONNELL, Watson,** SM (Canada) 1969; MA; PhD; DLitt; DPEc; LLD; LHD; DèsL; DCL; President Emeritus, Acadia University, Wolfville, Nova Scotia, Canada; *b* Port Hope, Ontario, Canada, 1895; 2nd *s* of T. A. Kirkconnell, BA, LLD, and Bertha Watson; *m* 1st, 1924, Isabel (*d* 1925), *e d* of James Peel; twin *s*; 2nd, 1930, Hope, *d* of Andrew Kitchener; three *d*. *Educ:* Queen's Univ., Kingston (University medallist in classics); Lincoln Coll., Oxford. FRSC (Lorne Pierce Medal, 1942). Mem., Sch. of Slavonic and E European Studies, Univ. of London. President: Canadian Authors' Assoc., 1942; Baptist Fedn of Canada, 1953; Chm., Humanities Research Council of Canada, 1944. Mem. several foreign learned societies; Knight (Officers' Cross), Order of Polonia Restituta; Knight Comdr, Order of the Falcon (Iceland); Medal of Honour, PEN Club of Hungary; Gold Medal of Freedom, Hungarians in Exile, 1964. *Publications:* Victoria County Centennial History, 1921; International Aspects of Unemployment, 1923; European Elegies, 1928; The European Heritage, 1930; The North American Book of Icelandic Verse, 1930; The Tide of Life and other Poems, 1930; The Magyar Muse, 1933; The Eternal Quest, 1934; A Canadian Headmaster, 1935; Canadian Overtones, 1935; A Golden Treasury of Polish Lyrics, 1936; The Death of Buda (from the Magyar of Arany), 1936; Primer of Hungarian, 1938; Titus, the Toad, 1939; Canada, Europe, and Hitler, 1939; The Ukrainian Canadians and the War, 1940; The Flying Bull, and other Tales, 1940; Canadians All, 1941; Twilight of Liberty, 1941; Seven Pillars of Freedom, 1944; National Minorities in the USSR, 1946; Red Foe of Faith, 1946; (with S Marion) The Quebec Tradition, 1946; (with A. S. P. Woodhouse) The Humanities in Canada, 1947; The Celestial Cycle, 1952; The Mod at Grand Pré, 1955; Pan Tadeusz (from the Polish of Mickiewicz), 1961; (with C. H. Andrusyshen) The Ukrainian Poets, 1963; (with C. H. Andrusyshen) Complete Poetical Works of Taras Shevchenko, 1964; The Theme of Samson Agonistes in World Literature, 1964; Centennial Tales, and Other Poems, 1965; A Slice of Canada, Memoirs, 1966; The Fifth Quarter-Century, 1968; Awake the Courteous Echo, 1970. *Address:* Acadia University, Wolfville, Nova Scotia, Canada.

**KIRKE, Rear-Adm. David Walter,** CB 1967; CBE 1962 (OBE 1945); Director, Brim Exports Ltd; Business Consultant, Training Partnerships Ltd; *b* 13 March 1915; *s* of late Percy St George Kirke and late Alice Gertrude, *d* of Sir James Gibson Craig, 3rd Bt; *m* 1st, 1936, Tessa O'Connor (marr. diss., 1950); one *s*; 2nd, 1956, Marion Margaret Gibb; one *s* one *d*. *Educ:* RN Coll., Dartmouth. China Station, 1933-35; Pilot Training, 1937; served War of 1939-45, Russian Convoys, Fighter Sqdns; loaned RAN, 1949-50; Chief of Naval Aviation, Indian Navy, New Delhi, 1959-62. Rear-Adm. 1965; Flag Officer, Naval Flying Training, 1965-68; retired, 1968. MBIM, 1967. *Recreation:* golf. *Address:* Lismore House, Pluckley, Kent. *T:* Pluckley 439. *Club:* Naval and Military.

**KIRKLAND, Edward Chase;** Professor Emeritus of American History, Bowdoin College; *b* 24 May 1894; *s* of Edward and Mary Chase Kirkland; *m* 1924, Ruth Stevens Babson; one *s*. *Educ:* Dartmouth Coll. (AB); Harvard Univ. (MA, PhD). Private 1st Cl., US Ambulance Corps with the French Army, 1917-19 (Croix de Guerre, 1918). Instructor: Dartmouth Coll., 1920-21; Mass Inst. of Technology, 1922-24; Professor: Brown Univ., 1924-30; Bowdoin Coll., 1930-55. Visiting Prof., University of Wisconsin, 1951; Commonwealth Lecturer, University Coll., London, 1952; Pitt Prof. of Amer. History and Instns, Cambridge Univ., 1956-57. Hon. LittD: Dartmouth Coll., 1948; Princeton Univ., 1957; Bowdoin Coll., 1961. *Publications:* The Peacemakers of 1864, 1926; History of American Economic Life, 1st edn 1932, 4th edn 1969; Men, Cities and Transportation: A Study in New England History (2 vols), 1948; Business on the Gilded Age, The Conservatives' Balance Sheet, 1952; Dream and Thought in the Business Community, 1860-1900, 1956; Industry Comes of Age; Business, Labor, and Public Policy, 1860-1897, 1961; Charles Francis Adams, Jun., 1835-1915: The Patrician at Bay, 1965. *Recreations:* gardening, walking. *Address:* Thetford Center, Vernmont 05075, USA; c/o Pembroke College, Cambridge.

**KIRKLEY, (Howard) Leslie,** CBE 1966; Director of Oxfam (Oxford Committee for Famine Relief); *b* Manchester, 1911. *Educ:* Manchester Central High Sch. Associate of the Chartered Inst. of Secretaries (ACIS). Worked in local government in Manchester until War of 1939-45 (during which he was engaged in relief work in Europe). Served on the UK Cttee for World Refugee Year and was also Chm. of the Publicity Sub-Cttee. Founder and Hon. Sec. of the Leeds and District European Relief Cttee; Gen. Sec. (later Dir), Oxford Cttee for Famine Relief, 1951. Pres., Gen. Conf., Internat. Council of Voluntary Agencies, 1968-71. Hon. MA: Oxford, 1969; Leeds, 1970. Knight Comdr of the Order of St Sylvester (conferred by HH the Pope), 1963; holds other foreign decorations. *Address:* Oxfam, 274 Banbury Road, Oxford. *T:* Oxford 56777.

**KIRKMAN, Gen. Sir Sidney Chevalier,** GCB, 1951 (KCB, 1949; CB 1944); KBE 1945 (CBE 1943; OBE 1941); MC; retired; *b* 29 July 1895; *s* of late J. P. Kirkman, Bedford; *m* 1932, Carol Amy Erskine Clarke; two *s*. *Educ:* Bedford Sch.; RMA, Woolwich. Served European War, 1914-18 (wounded twice, MC, despatches). Staff Coll. Camberley, 1930-32. Served War of 1939-45: Brig. RA, 8th Army, 1942; Comd 50 (N) Div., 1943; Comd British 13th Corps in Italy, 1944; GOC-in-C Southern Comd 1945; Comd 1 Corps BLA, 1945; Dep. Chief of Imperial Gen. Staff, 1945-47; Quartermaster-Gen. to the Forces, 1947-50; Mem. of Army Council, 1945-50; Col Comdt RA, 1947-57; Special Financial Representative in Germany, 1951-52; Dir Gen. of Civil Defence, 1954-60; Chm. Central Fire Brigades Advisory Council for England and Wales, 1957-60. *Address:* The White House, West Side, Wimbledon Common, SW19. *Club:* Army and Navy.

**KIRKMAN, William Patrick;** Secretary, University of Cambridge Appointments Board, since 1968; Fellow, University College, Cambridge; *b* 23 Oct. 1932; *s* of Geoffrey Charles Aylward Kirkman and Bertha Winifred Kirkman; *m* 1959, Anne Teasdale Fawcett; two *s* one *d*. *Educ:* Churcher's Coll., Petersfield, Hants; Oriel Coll., Oxford. 2nd cl. hons, mod. langs, 1955; MA 1959; MA (Cantab) by incorporation, 1968. Editorial staff: Express & Star, Wolverhampton, 1955-57; The Times, 1957-64 (Commonwealth staff, 1960-64, Africa Correspondent, 1962-64). Asst Sec., Oxford Univ. Appointments Cttee, 1964-68. Trustee, Sir Halley Stewart Trust. *Publications:* Unscrambling an Empire, 1966; contributor to: International Affairs, African Affairs, etc. *Recreations:* broadcasting, gardening, church activities, writing. *Address:* 19 High Street, Willingham, Cambridge CB4 5ES. *T:* Willingham 393. *Club:* Royal Commonwealth Society.

**KIRKPATRICK, Rev. Canon Herbert Francis;** Hon. Canon of Ely Cathedral, since 1964; Archdeacon of Ely, 1947-61; Examining Chaplain to Bishop of Bath and Wells, 1944-60, to Bishop of Ely since 1947; retired; *b* 31 July 1888; *s* of late Very Rev. A. F. Kirkpatrick, DD. *Educ:* Marlborough Coll.; Jesus Coll., Cambridge (Rustat Scholar). BA; Lady Kay Scholar; 2nd Cl. Classical Tripos: 2nd Cl. Theological Tripos; MA; Cuddesdon Theological Coll., 1912-13. Deacon, 1913; Priest, 1914; Curate S John Evangelist, Middlesbrough, 1913-16; Cockington, Torquay, 1916-19; Vicar of All Saints', Cambridge, 1919-22; Principal of the Missionary Coll. of S Peter and S Paul, Dorchester, Oxon, 1922-47; Commissary to the Bishop of Labuan and Sarawak, 1938-48; Officiating Curate in charge of Launton, 1940-44; Rector of Bathwick with Woolley, Bath, 1944-47; Lecturer at Cuddesdon Coll., Oxford, 1941-43; Prebendary of Combe II in Wells Cathedral, 1945-47. *Address:* 44 Tunwell's Lane, Great Shelford, Cambridge CB2 5LJ. *T:* Shelford 3181.

**KIRKPATRICK, Air Vice-Marshal Herbert James,** CB 1957; CBE 1945; DFC 1941; RAF (retired); *b* 30 Oct. 1910; *s* of late Maj.-Gen. Charles Kirkpatrick, CB, CBE, IA, Larchwood, Pitlochry, Perthshire, and of Elsie Isobel, *d* of H. J. H. Fasson, ICS; *m* 1937, Pamela Evelyn Darvill, *d* of Lt-Col H. D. Watson, IA, retired, Colchester; three *s* two *d*. *Educ:* Cheltenham Coll.; Trinity Coll., Oxford (MA). Mem. Oxford Univ. Air Sqdn, 1929-32; entered RAF, 1933; served in India, 1933-35; Instructor and Adjutant OU Air Sqdn, 1936-39; served War of 1939-45 (despatches twice, DFC, CBE): Air Staff Fighter Comd, 1939-40; served in Bomber Comd, 1941-45, and in Transport Comd, 1946-48; Instructor at RAF Staff Coll., 1949-51; Chief Instructor, RAF Flying Coll., 1951-53; Imperial Defence Coll., 1954; Dir of Operational Requirements (A), 1955-57; ACAS (Op. Req.), 1957; Chief of Staff, 2nd Allied Tactical Air Force, 1957-60; Air Officer Commanding No 25 Group, 1961-63; idc; psa; pfc; cfs*. *Address:* c/o Lloyds Bank (Cox's and King's Branch), 6 Pall Mall, SW1; 51 Lexden Road, Colchester, Essex. *T:* Colchester 5448. *Club:* Royal Air Force.

**KIRKPATRICK, Sir Ivone Elliott,** 11th Bt, *cr* 1685; *b* 1 Oct. 1942; *s* of Sir James Alexander Kirkpatrick, 10th Bt and Ellen Gertrude, *o d* of Captain R. P. Elliott, late RNR; *S* father 1954. *Educ:* Wellington Coll., Berks; St Mark's Coll., University of Adelaide. *Heir:* *b* Robin Alexander Kirkpatrick, *b* 19 March 1944.

**KIRKUP, James;** travel writer, poet, novelist, playwright, translator, broadcaster; *b* 23 April 1923; *o s* of James Harold Kirkup and Mary Johnston. *Educ:* South Shields High Sch.; Durham Univ. (BA). FRSL 1962. Atlantic Award in Literature (Rockefeller Foundation), 1950; Gregory Fellow in Poetry, University of Leeds, 1950-52. Visiting Poet and Head of English Dept, Bath Academy of Art, Corsham Court, Wilts, 1953-56; Lectr in English, Swedish Ministry of Education, Stockholm, 1956-57; Prof. of Eng. Lang. and Lit., University of Salamanca, 1957-58, of English, Tohoku Univ., Sendai, Japan, 1958-61; Lecturer in English Literature, University of Malaya in Kuala Lumpur, 1961-62; Literary Editor, Orient/West Magazine, Tokyo, 1963-64; Prof., Japan Women's Univ., 1964-; Poet in Residence and Visiting Prof., Amherst Coll., Mass, 1968-; Prof. of English Literature, Nagoya Univ., 1969-. President: Poets' Soc. of Japan, 1969. Blackmore Soc., 1970. Mabel Batchelder Award, 1968. *Plays performed:* Upon this Rock (perf. Peterborough Cathedral), 1955; Masque, The Triumph of Harmony (perf. Albert Hall), 1955; The True Mistery of the Nativity, 1957; The Physicists (Eng. Trans.), 1963; The Meteor (Eng. trans.); *television plays performed:* The Peach Garden, Two Pigeons Flying High, etc. Contributor to BBC, The Listener, The Spectator, Times Literary Supplement, Time and Tide, New Yorker, Botteghe Oscure, etc. *Publications:* The Drowned Sailor, 1948; The Cosmic Shape, 1947; The Creation, 1950; The Submerged Village, 1951; A Correct Compassion, 1952; A Spring Journey, 1954; Upon This Rock, 1955; The Dark Child (Eng. trans.), 1955; Ancestral Voices (Eng. trans.), 1956; The Radiance of the King (Eng. trans.), 1956; The True Mistery of the Nativity, 1957; The Descent into the Cave, 1957; The Only Child (autobiog.), 1957; Memoirs of a Dutiful Daughter (Eng. trans.), 1958; The Girl from Nowhere (Eng. trans.), 1958; Sorrows, Passions and Alarms, 1959; The Prodigal Son (poems), 1959; It Began in Babel (Eng. trans.), 1961; The Captive (Eng. trans.), 1962; Sins of the Fathers (Eng. trans.), 1962; The Gates of Paradise (Eng. trans.), 1962; These Horned Islands, A Journal of Japan, 1962; The True Mistery of the Passion, 1962; The Love of Others (novel), 1962; Refusal to Conform, 1963; Tropic Temper: a Memoir of Malaya, 1963; The Heavenly Mandate (Eng. trans.), 1964; Daily Life of the Etruscans (Eng. trans.), 1964; The Little Man (Eng. trans.), 1966; The Little Man and The Little Miss (Eng. trans.), 1969; The Tales of Hoffmann (Eng. trans.), 1966; Michael Kohlhaas (Eng. trans.), 1966; Japan Industrial, 1964-65 (2 vols); Daily Life in the French Revolution, 1964; Tokyo, 1965; England, Now, 1965; Japan, Now, 1966; A Dream of Africa (Eng. trans.), 1967; Frankly Speaking,

I-II, 1968; Paper Windows: Poems from Japan, 1968; Bangkok, 1968; One Man's Russia, 1968; Filipinescas, 1968; Streets of Asia, 1969; Japan Physical, 1969; Aspects of the Short Story, 1969; Shepherding Winds (anthol.), 1969; Songs and Dreams (anthol.), 1970; White Shadows, Black Shadows: Poems of Peace and War, 1970; Hong Kong, 1970; Japan Behind the Fan, 1970; The Eternal Virgin (Eng. trans of Valéry's La Jeune Parque), 1970. *Recreation:* standing in shafts of sunlight. *Address:* 5-13 Nakayama-Cho, Mizuhoku, Nagoya, Japan. *T:* 851-0034; Amherst College, Amherst, Mass 01002, USA.

**KIRKWOOD,** family name of **Baron Kirkwood.**

**KIRKWOOD,** 3rd Baron *cr* 1951, of Bearsden; **David Harvie Kirkwood;** Lecturer in Metallurgy, Sheffield University, since 1962; *b* 24 Nov. 1931; *s* of 2nd Baron Kirkwood and of Eileen Grace, *d* of Thomas Henry Boalch; *S* father, 1970; *m* 1965, Judith Rosalie, *d* of late John Hunt; two *d. Educ:* Rugby; Trinity Hall, Cambridge (MA, PhD). *Heir: b* Hon. James Stuart Kirkwood [*b* 19 June 1937; *m* 1965, Alexandra Mary, *d* of late Alec Dyson; two *d*]. *Address:* 56 Endcliffe Hall Avenue, Sheffield. *T:* Sheffield 63107.

**KIRKWOOD, Prof. Kenneth,** MA; Rhodes Professor of Race Relations, University of Oxford, since 1954; *b* Benoni, Transvaal, 1919; *s* of late Thomas Dorman Kirkwood and Lily Kirkwood (*née* Bewley); *m* 1942, Deborah Burton, *d* of late Burton Ireland Collings and Emily Frances Collings (*née* Loram); three *s* three *d.* BA; BSc Rand. Captain, South African Engineer Corps, War of 1939-45; served in East Africa, North Africa and Italy (despatches). Lecturer, University of the Witwatersrand, 1947; Lecturer, University of Natal, 1948-51; Fellowship, University of London (Inst. of Commonwealth Studies, 1952); Carnegie Travelling Fellowship, USA, 1953; Senior Research Officer, Inst. of Colonial Studies, Oxford Univ., 1953; Organiser of Institute for Social Research, University of Natal, 1954. Chm. Regional Cttee, S African Inst. of Race Relations in Natal, 1954; UK Rep. SA Inst. of Race Relations, 1955. Investigation on behalf UNESCO into trends in race relations in British Non-Self-Governing Territories of Africa, 1958; Visiting Prof. of Race Relations (UNESCO), University Coll. of Rhodesia and Nyasaland, 1964; composed memorandum on meaning, and procedure for further study of 'racial discrimination,' for UN Div. of Human Rights, 1966-67; Mem., Africa Educational Trust, Oxfam, etc, 1955-. *Publications:* The Proposed Federation of the Central African Territories, 1952; other booklets and articles on race relations and international affairs; contributions to revision of Lord Hailey's An African Survey, 1957, and 2nd edn, Vol. VIII, Cambridge History of the British Empire, 1963; Britain and Africa, 1965; Editor, St Antony's Papers: African Affairs, number 1, 1961; number 2, 1963; number 3, 1969. *Address:* St Antony's College, Oxford. *T:* Oxford 55867.

**KIRKWOOD, Sir Robert (Lucien Morrison),** Kt 1959; Chairman: Sugar Manufacturers' Association of Jamaica, since 1945; West Indies Sugar Association, 1946-58, and since 1961; Citrus Growers Association, 1944-60; *b* Yeo, Fairy Cross, N Devon, 9 Jan. 1904; *e s* of late Major John Hendley Morrison Kirkwood, DSO, sometime MP for Southend Div. of Essex, and Gertrude Agnes, *e d* of Sir Robert Park Lyle, 1st and last Bt, Eaton Place, SW1; *m* 1925, Sybil Attenborough, Hartford House, Nottingham; one *s* two *d. Educ:* Wixenford; Harrow; Le Rosey (Switzerland). Joined Tate & Lyle, 1922; Managing Dir, The United Sugar Company, 1929-36; Dir Yorks Sugar Co., 1928-36 and Central Sugar Co. (Peterborough), 1929-36; joined Board of Tate & Lyle, 1935; Man. Dir, West Indies Sugar Co., Jamaica, 1937; Dir, Caroni Ltd, Trinidad, 1937. MLC Jamaica, 1942-62. Rep. Jamaica on Colonial Sugar Cttee, 1937-. Rep. West Indies at Internat. Sugar Confs, 1953, 1956, 1958, 1961, 1965, 1968. Pres. Sugar Club of New York, 1965-66; Chm. International Sugar Council, 1966. Mem. various Govt Bds and Cttees in Jamaica. *Recreations:* gardening, golf and good food. *Address:* Craigton, Irish Town, Jamaica, West Indies. *T:* Irish Town 224; (in England: Haven House, Sandwich. *T:* 2428). *Clubs:* White's, Queen's; St George's (Sandwich); The Brook (New York); Jamaica (Kingston).

**KIRSTEIN, Lincoln Edward;** Director: School of American Ballet; New York City Ballet Company; Chairman, American Dressage Institute; *b* Rochester, NY, 4 May 1907; *s* of Louis E. Kirstein and Rose Stein; *m* 1941, Fidelma Cadmus; no *c. Educ:* Harvard Coll. Edited Hound & Horn, 1927-34; founded School of American Ballet, 1934; founded and directed American Ballet Caravan, 1936-41; Third US Army (Arts, Monuments and Archives Section), 1943-45. Editor, The Dance Index, 1941-47. *Publications:* Dance, A Short History of Theatrical Dancing, 1935; Blast at Ballet, 1938; Ballet Alphabet, 1940; Drawings of Pavel Tchelitchew, 1947; Elie Nadelman Drawings, 1949; The Dry Points of Elie Nadelman, 1952; What Ballet is About, 1959; Three Pamphlets Collected, 1967; The Hampton Institute Album, 1968; Movement and Metaphor: four centuries of ballet, 1970; *verse:* Rhymes of a PFC (Private First Class), 1964; *monographs:* Gaston Lachaise, 1935; Walker Evans, 1938; Latin American Art, 1942; American Battle Art, 1945; Henri Cartier-Bresson, 1946; Dr William Rimmer, 1946; Elie Nadelman, 1948; Pavel Tchelitchew, 1964; *edited:* The Classic Dance, Technique and Terminology, 1951; William Shakespeare: A Catalogue of the Works of Art in the American Shakespeare Festival Theater, 1964. *Address:* New York State Theater, Lincoln Center, New Yor, NY 10023, USA. *T:* 799.2256.

**KIRTON, Robert James,** CBE 1963; MA, FIA; Director, Equity and Law Life Assurance Society, Ltd since 1944 (General Manager, 1939-66; Actuary, 1947-66); Chairman, Equity and Law Unit Trust Managers Ltd, since 1969; *b* 13 July 1901; *er s* of late Albert William Kirton, Ealing, Middlesex; *m* 1931, Isabel Susan, *y d* of late Henry Hosegood, JP, Bristol; two *s* two *d. Educ:* Merchant Taylors' Sch.; Peterhouse, Cambridge. Scottish Widows' Fund and Life Assurance Soc., 1923-32; Scottish Amicable Life Assce Soc., 1932-38; Equity and Law Life Assce, Soc. Ltd, 1938-. Chm., Life Offices' Assoc., 1945-47; Chm. Royal UK Beneficent Assoc., 1958-; Hon. Treas., Nat. Coun. of Social Service, 1962-; Trustee, Charities Official Investment Fund, 1962-; Governor, London Sch. of Economics, 1963-; Vice-Chm., St Peter's Hosp., 1967-; Mem. Council, Bath Univ. of Technology, 1967-; Mem., Buitengewoon Lid, Actuarial Genootschap, Holland, 1949. Silver Medal, Institute of Actuaries, 1966. *Publications:* contrib. Jl Inst. Actuaries, Trans. Faculty of Actuaries (with A. T. Haynes). *Recreations:* walking, ski-ing and squash rackets. *Address:* Byron Cottage, North End Avenue, NW3. *T:* 01-455 0464. *Clubs:* Athenæum, Bath.

**KIRWAN, (Archibald) Laurence Patrick,** CMG 1958; TD; BLitt Oxon; Director and Secretary, Royal Geographical Society, since 1945; *b* 1907; 2nd *s* of Patrick Kirwan, Cregg, County Galway, Ireland, and Mabel Norton; *m* 1st, 1932, Joan Elizabeth Chetwynd; one *d*; 2nd, 1949, Stella Mary Monck. *Educ:* Wimbledon Sch.; Merton Coll., Oxford. Asst Dir of the Archaeological Survey of Nubia, Egyptian Dept of Antiquities, 1929-34; Field Dir, Oxford Univ. Expeditions to Sudan, 1934-37; Tweedie Fellowship in Archæology and Anthropology, Edinburgh Univ., 1937-39. Boston and Philadelphia Museums, 1937; Exploratory journeys, Eastern Sudan and Aden Protectorate, 1938-39. TARO Capt., General Staff, 1939; Major, 1941; Lieut-Col 1943; Joint Staffs, Offices of Cabinet and Ministry of Defence, 1942-45; Hon. Lt-Col, 1957. Editor, Geographical Journal, 1945-; Pres., Brit. Inst. of History and Archæology in East Africa, 1961-. Pres. (Section E), British Assoc. for the Advancement of Science, 1961-62; Member: Court of Arbitration, Argentine-Chile Frontier Case, 1965-68 (Leader, Field Mission, 1966); Min. of Transport Adv. Cttee on Landscape Treatment of Trunk Roads, 1968-; UN Register of fact-finding experts, 1968-; Court, Exeter Univ., 1969-; a Governor, Imperial Coll. of Science and Technology, 1962-; Fellow, University Coll., London. Hon. Member: Geographical Societies of Paris, Vienna, Washington; Inst. of Navigation. Knight Cross of the Order of St Olav, Norway. *Publications:* Excavations and Survey between Wadi-es-Sebua and Adindan, 1935 (with W. B. Emery); Oxford University Excavations at Firka, 1938; The White Road (polar exploration), 1959; papers on archæology, historical and political geography, exploration, in scientific and other publications. *Recreation:* travelling. *Address:* Royal Geographical Society, SW7. *T:* 01-589 0648. *Club:* Athenæum.

**KIRWAN, Geoffrey Dugdale,** CB 1945; CMG 1954; MC 1918; *b* 17 Oct. 1896; *s* of late G. R. Kirwan, South Shields; *m* 1st, 1929, Mary, *d* of R. A. Morrow (marr. diss., 1948); two *s* one *d*; 2nd, 1950, Diana, *e d* of late Dr R. L. E. Downer. *Educ:* South Shields High Sch.; Repton; University Coll., Oxford. Commissioned Royal Garrison Artillery, 1915; served in France, 1915-18; Staff Captain V Corps Heavy Artillery, 1918; entered Home Office, 1919; Asst Sec. to Royal Commission on Police Powers and Procedure, 1928-29; Sec. of Cttee of Inquiry into London Motor Coach Services, 1932; ARP Dept of Home Office, 1935-39; Ministry of Home Security, 1939-45; Home Office, 1945; Control Office for Germany and Austria, 1945-47; Foreign Office (German Section), 1947-54. Sec. and Comptroller General, National Debt Office, 1954-61. A Vice-Pres., Trustee Savings Banks Association, 1961-. Coronation Medal, 1953. *Address:* Oast Cottage, 17 Nargate Street, Littlebourne, Canterbury, Kent. *T:* Littlebourne 383.

**KIRWAN, Laurence;** *see* Kirwan, A. L. P.

**KIRWAN-TAYLOR, Harold George,** MA, MB, BCh Cantab; FRCS; *b* 14 April 1895; *s* of Alfred George Taylor and Mary Kirwan; *m* 1926, Elizabeth Mary (marriage dissolved, 1946), *d* of late J. R. J. Neild; one *s* three *d*. *Educ:* Epsom Coll.; Trinity Coll., Cambridge. Hon. Consulting Obstetric and Gynæcological Surgeon: St George's Hospital; War Memorial Hospital, Woolwich; Hon. Consulting Gynæcological Surgeon, Royal National Orthopædic Hospital; Hon. Cons. Surg., The General Lying-in Hospital, Lambeth; late Lectr on Obstetrics and Gynæcology, St George's Hospital; late Obstetric Consultant, Borough of Woolwich and Bexley Heath. Late Examiner: University of Cambridge; University of Durham; Society of Apothecaries; Conjoint Board and Central Midwives Board. Served European War, 1914-18, as Surgeon Probationer RNVR and later as Surgeon Royal Navy. Served 1940-43, MEF (despatches), as Lieut-Col, with short period as Temporary Consulting Surgeon, MEF; 1943-45, service in BNAF and Italy, retiring with rank of Hon. Col AMS. Late Prospective Conservative Candidate E Woolwich and Royal Borough of Kingston. *Publications:* various articles in medical journals. *Recreations:* shooting, fishing, riding, golf, farming. *Address:* Denne, Mersham, near Ashford, Kent. *T:* Aldington 278. *Club:* Boodle's.

**KISCH, John Marcus,** CMG 1965; Assistant Secretary, Ministry of Overseas Development, since 1968; *b* 27 May 1916; *s* of late Sir Cecil Kisch, KCIE, CB, and late Myra Kisch; *m* 1951, Gillian Poyser; four *d*. *Educ:* Rugby Sch.; King's Coll., Cambridge. Asst Principal, Board of Inland Revenue, 1938; Asst Principal, Colonial Office, 1939. Served Royal Corps of Signals, 1939-45. Principal, Colonial Office, 1945; seconded E Africa High Commission, 1951; Kenya Govt 1952; Asst Sec., Colonial Office, 1956; seconded CRO, 1964; transferred Min. of Defence, 1965; Asst Sec., MoD (Navy Dept), 1965-68. *Recreations:* tennis, croquet. *Address:* Hatchford Corner, Cobham, Surrey. *T:* Cobham 2138. *Clubs:* United University, Reform.

**KISCH, Royalton;** Artistic Director, Cork Street Gallery; conductor of symphony concerts; *b* London, 20 Jan. 1919; *s* of late E. Royalton Kisch, MC and Pamela Kisch; *m* 1940, Aline, *d* of Bruce Hylton Stewart and late M. F. (Molly) Hylton Stewart; one *s* two *d*. *Educ:* Wellington Coll., Berks; Clare Coll., Cambridge. Has conducted Royal Festival Hall concerts with London Philharmonic Orchestra, London Symphony Orchestra, Philharmonia Orchestra, Royal Philharmonic Orchestra, etc. Guest conductor to Hallé Orchestra, Birmingham Symphony Orchestra, etc. Has also conducted concerts in Europe with Paris Conservatoire Orchestra, Palestine Symphony Orchestra, Florence Philharmonic Orchestra, Athens State Symphony Orchestra, Pasdeloup Orchestra of Paris, Royal Opera House Orchestra of Rome, San Carlo Symphony Orchestra of Naples, Vienna Symphony Orchestra, etc. Has broadcast on BBC with London Symphony Orchestra, Royal Philharmonic Orchestra, and Philharmonia Orchestra. Gramophone recordings for Decca. Specialist in English and French paintings of 20th century. Member: Friends of Tate Gallery; Inst. of Contemporary Arts. *Recreations:* good food and wine. *Address:* 2 Edwardes Square, Kensington, W8. *T:* 01-937 8867. *Club:* Hurlingham.

**KISSEN, Hon. Lord; Manuel Kissen;** a Senator of the College of Justice in Scotland since 1963; *b* 2 May 1912; *er s* of Lewis and Annie Kissen; *m* 1964, Mrs Victoria Solomons, *widow* of Professor Edward Solomons, New York, USA. *Educ:* Hutchesons' Boys' Grammar Sch., Glasgow; Glasgow Univ. (MA, LLB). Solicitor, 1934. Served with RAF, 1940-45 (despatches). Admitted to Faculty of Advocates, 1946; Standing Junior Counsel in Scotland to Min. of Labour and to Min. of Nat. Insurance, 1948-55. QC (Scotland) 1955. Chm. National Health Service Tribunal (Scotland), 1962-63; Chm. Law Reform Cttee for Scotland, 1964-. Mem., Restrictive

Practices Court, 1966-. Hon. LLD Glasgow, 1968. *Address:* 22 Braid Avenue, Edinburgh 10. *T:* 031-447 3000. *Clubs:* National Liberal; Scottish Liberal (Edinburgh).

**KISSEN, Manuel;** *see* Kissen, Hon. Lord.

**KISSINGER, Prof. Henry Alfred;** Bronze Star (US); Assistant to the President of the United States for National Security Affairs, since 1968; Professor of Government, Harvard University, since 1962; Faculty Member, Center for International Affairs, Harvard; Director: Harvard International Seminar; Harvard Defense Studies Program, since 1958; *b* 27 May 1923; *s* of Louis Kissinger and Paula (*née* Stern); *m* 1949, Anne Fleischer (marr. diss. 1964); one *s* one *d*. *Educ:* George Washington High Sch., NYC; Harvard Univ., Cambridge, Mass (AB, MA, PhD). Teaching Fellow, Harvard Univ., 1950-54; Study Director: Council on Foreign Relations, 1955-56: Rockefeller Bros Fund, 1956-58; Associate Professor of Govt, Harvard Univ., 1958-62. Consultant to various government agencies. *Publications:* A World Restored: Castlereagh, Metternich and the Restoration of Peace, 1957; Nuclear Weapons and Foreign Policy, 1957 (Woodrow Wilson Prize, 1958; citation, Overseas Press Club, 1958); The Necessity for Choice: Prospects of American Foreign Policy, 1961; The Troubled Partnership, 1965; Problems of National Strategy: A Book of Readings (ed), 1965; American Foreign Policy, 1969; articles in Foreign Affairs, Harper's Magazine, The Reporter, New York Times Sunday Magazine, etc. *Address:* The White House, Washington, DC, USA. *T:* 456-1414. *Clubs:* Century, Harvard (New York); Cosmos, Federal City, Metropolitan (Washington); St Botolph (Boston).

**KISTIAKOWSKY, Prof. George Bogdan;** Professor of Chemistry, Harvard University, since 1938 (Deputy Chairman, 1947-50); Special Assistant to the President of the USA for Science and Technology, 1959-61; Member Advisory Board to US Arms Control and Disarmament Agency, 1962-68, etc; Vice-President, National Academy of Sciences, since 1965; *b* Kiev, Ukraine, 18 Nov. 1900; *s* of Bogdan Kistiakowsky and Mary Berenstam; came to USA, 1926; naturalized citizen, 1933; *m* 1st, 1926, Hildegard Moebius (marriage dissolved 1942); one *d*; 2nd, 1945, Irma E. Shuler (marriage dissolved, 1962); 3rd, 1962, Elaine Mahoney. *Educ:* University of Berlin (DPhil). Fellow and Staff Mem. Chem. Dept, Princeton, 1926-30; Asst Prof., 1930-33, Associate Prof., 1933-38, Harvard. On leave from Harvard to: Nat. Defense Research Cttee, 1940-43; Los Alamos Lab., 1944-45. Mem. National Acad. of Sciences, etc; Hon. Fellow, Chem. Soc., London; Foreign Mem. Royal Society, London, 1960. Hon. DSc: Harvard Univ., 1955; Williams Coll., 1958; Oxford Univ., 1959; University of Pennsylvania, 1960; University of Rochester, 1960; Carnegie Inst. of Technology, 1961; Princeton Univ., 1962; Case Institute, 1962; Columbia Univ., 1967. Medal for Merit, USA, 1946; King's Medal for Services in the Cause of Freedom, 1948; Willard Gibbs Medal, 1960; Medal of Freedom (awarded by Pres. Eisenhower), 1961; George Ledlie Prize, Harvard Univ., 1961; Nat. Medal of Science (awarded by Pres. Johnson), 1967; Peter Debye Award, 1968; Theodore William Richards, 1968, and several other awards. *Publications:* Photochemical Processes, 1929; numerous articles. *Address:* 12 Oxford Street, Cambridge, Mass 02138, USA. T: University 617-495-4083.

**KITCHEN, Sir Geoffrey,** Kt 1963; TD; Chairman: Pearl Assurance Co. Ltd, since 1956; Manor Developments Ltd, since 1967; United British Securities Trust Ltd, since 1965; London and Holyrood Trust Ltd, since 1964; Second United British Securities Trust Ltd, since 1965; Director: Companhia de Seguros, "Portugal"; Monarch Fire Insurance Co. (USA); London Weekend Television Ltd; Montagu Trust Ltd; Pearl Insurance Co. of South Africa Ltd; Royal Garden Hotel (Oddenino's) Ltd; Trans-Oceanic Trust Ltd; Cavenham Confectionery; *b* 20 Dec. 1906; *m* 1946, Joan Aistrope. *Educ:* Bradford Grammar Sch.; St John's Coll., Oxford (MA). Entered Pearl Assurance Co. Ltd, 1934; Dir, 1948; Dep. Chm., 1952. Served War of 1939-45, RA, with 8th Army in Middle East and Italy (despatches); Lt-Col. Governor, St Mary's Hosp., 1958-63; Life Associate, British Red Cross Soc. Chm. Industrial Life Offices' Assoc., 1958-59. Freeman, City of London; Liveryman and Mem. Court, Worshipful Co. of Gunmakers, Master 1969; Liveryman, Guild of Air Pilots and Air Navigators. Pres. of Appeals, National Playing Fields Association, 1965, 1966. *Recreations:* shooting, golf and tennis. *Address:* Ghyll Manor, Rusper, Sussex. *T:* Rusper 288; Flat 141, Grosvenor House, W1. *T:* 01-499 6363. *Clubs:* Carlton, City of London, Portland; Sky (New York).

**KITCHENER of Khartoum** and of Broome; 3rd Earl, *cr* 1914; **Henry Herbert Kitchener,** TD; Viscount, *cr* 1902, of Khartoum; of the Vaal, Transvaal, and Aspall, Suffolk; Viscount Broome, *cr* 1914, of Broome, Kent; Baron Denton, *cr* 1914, of Denton, Kent; late Major, Royal Corps of Signals; *b* 24 Feb. 1919; *er s* of Viscount Broome (*d* 1928) and Adela Mary Evelyn, *e d* of late J. H. Monins, Ringwould House, near Dover; *S* grandfather, 1937. *Educ:* Sandroyd Sch.; Winchester Coll.; Trinity Coll., Cambridge. *Heir:* *b* Hon. Charles Eaton Kitchener [*b* 11 March 1920; *m* 1959, Ursula Hope Luck; one *d*]. *Address:* 56 Elm Park Road, SW3. *T:* 01-352 5468; 435 Chester Road, Hartford, Northwich, Cheshire. *T:* Sandiway 3287. *Club:* Brooks's.

**KITCHING, Maj.-Gen. George,** CBE 1945; DSO 1943; Canadian Military Forces, retired; Director: A. Bradshaw & Son; Empire Club of Canada; Co-ordinator, Duke of Edinburgh's Award in Canada, since 1967; Executive Director, Canadian National Committee, United World Colleges, since 1969; *b* 1910; *m* 1946, Audrey Calhoun; one *s* one *d*. *Educ:* Cranleigh; Royal Military College. 2nd Lieut Glos Regt, 1930. Served War of 1939-45 with Royal Canadian Regt, in Sicily, Italy and North-West Europe; commanding Canadian Infantry Brigade, 1943; actg Maj.-Gen., 1944 (despatches, DSO, CBE). Subseq. Vice-Chief of General Staff at Army Headquarters, Ottawa; Chairman of the Canadian Joint Staff in London, 1958-62. GOC Central Command, Canada, 1962-65, retd. Commander: Order of Orange Nassau (Netherlands); Military Order of Italy; Order of Merit (US). *Address:* 3 Riverside Crescent, Toronto 3, Ont, Canada. *Clubs:* National (Toronto); Rideau Golf.

**KITCHING, John Alwyne,** OBE 1947; FRS 1960; ScD (Cambridge); PhD (London); Professor of Biology, University of East Anglia, since 1963; Dean of School of Biological Sciences, 1967-70; *b* 24 Oct. 1908; *s* of John Nainby Kitching; *m* 1933, Evelyn Mary Oliver; one *s* three *d*. *Educ:* Cheltenham Coll.; Trinity Coll., Cambridge. BA 1930, MA 1934, ScD 1956; PhD London. Lecturer: Birkbeck Coll., London, 1931; Edinburgh Univ., 1936; Bristol Univ., 1937; Rockefeller Fellow, Princeton

Univ., 1938; Research in aviation-medical problems under Canadian Nat. Research Council, 1939-45; Reader in Zoology, University of Bristol, 1948-63. *Publications:* contrib. Jl of Experimental Biol., Jl of Ecology, Jl of Animal Ecology, etc. *Recreations:* travel, gardening, small boats. *Address:* University of East Anglia, University Plain, Norwich NOR 88C; 29 Newfound Drive, Cringleford, Norwich.

**KITCHING, Wilfred,** CBE 1964; retired as General of The Salvation Army (1954-63) and from Chairmanship of various Salvation Army Companies, etc; *b* 22 Aug. 1893; *s* of late Commissioner Theodore Kitching, CBE; *m* 1929, Kathleen Bristow. *Educ:* Friern Barnet Grammar Sch. Corps and Divisional Officer, 1915-25, 1929-39; National Sec. for Salvation Army Bands 1925-29, National Young People's Sec. 1939-45; Field Sec., 1945-46; Chief Sec. for Australia, 1946-48. Territorial Leader for Sweden, 1948-51. British Commissioner, Officer responsible for Evangelical and Red Shield Services in Great Britain and Ireland, 1951-54. *Publications:* A Goodly Heritage (autobiography); numerous instrumental and vocal compositions published by The Salvation Army. *Recreation:* music. *Address:* International Headquarters, 101 Queen Victoria Street, EC4. *T:* 01-236 5222; 9 Crofton Park Avenue, Cooden, Bexhill-on-Sea, Sussex.

**KITSON,** family name of **Baron Airedale.**

**KITSON, Geoffrey Herbert,** OBE 1948; TD; DL; company director; *b* 22 June 1896; *s* of Henry Herbert Kitson, Leeds; *m* 1923, Kathleen Mary Alexandra, *d* of James Paul, Bramhope; three *s* one *d*. *Educ:* Charterhouse. Mem. Leeds City Council, 1930-38; as Chm. Leeds Corp. Gas Cttee, was Pres. Brit. Commercial Gas Assoc., 1931; Dir, Leeds Permanent Building Soc., 1934; Pres. Leeds Chamber of Commerce, 1935-36. Pro-Chancellor, University of Leeds; Chm., Theatre and Opera House (Leeds) Ltd. DL W Riding of Yorks, 1963. Hon. LLD Leeds Univ., 1963. Hon. Col 249 (W Riding Artillery) Regt RA, 1957-63. *Recreations:* shooting, gardening. *Address:* West Lawn, Linton, Wetherby, Yorks. *T:* Wetherby 2950. *Club:* Leeds (Leeds).

**KITSON, Sir George (Vernon),** KBE 1957 (CBE 1946); *b* 10 Feb. 1899; *s* of late George Kitson, Wakefield; *m* 1935, Phoebe, *yr d* of late John Owen George, Hirwaun, Glamorganshire; no *c*. *Educ:* Queen Elizabeth Grammar Sch., Wakefield; Clare Coll., Cambridge (MA). Served RFC and RAF, 1917-19; entered HM Consular Service in China, 1922; Vice-Consul at Peking, Shanghai, Canton, Mukden, Harbin, Chungking; Consul at Hankow, Swatow, Chefoo, Peking, Shanghai, Nanking; Chinese Sec. at HM Embassy, Chungking, 1942-45; Counsellor, FO, 1945-47; Deputy High Commissioner for the UK at Bombay, 1947-50; Counsellor, Office of Commissioner General for SE Asia, Singapore, 1951-52; HM Consul-General at Milan, 1952-58; retired 1959. High Sheriff of Breconshire, 1968-69. *Recreations:* gardening, fishing. *Address:* Llais-yr-Afon, Crickhowell, Breconshire. *T:* Crickhowell 298.

**KITSON, Captain James Buller,** DSO 1916; Royal Navy, retired; *b* Dec. 1883; *s* of Rev. J. Buller Kitson, Rector of Lanreath; *m* 1913, Hon. Frances Margaret Palmer Howard (*d* 1958), *e d* of late R. J. B. Howard and late Baroness Strathcona and Mount Royal; two *s* two *d*. Joined RN 1898; Lieut 1905; Commander, 1917; served European War, including Jutland Bank (despatches, DSO); retired list, 1925; Captain, retired, 1928. *Address:* Lower Farm, Madehurst, near Arundel, Sussex; Fursecroft, George Street, W1. *Clubs:* United Service; Royal Yacht Squadron.

**KITSON, Timothy Peter Geoffrey;** MP (C) Richmond, Yorkshire, since 1959; *b* 28 Jan. 1931; *s* of Geoffrey H. and Kathleen Kitson; *m* 1959, Diana Mary Fattorini; one *s* two *d*. *Educ:* Charterhouse; Royal Agricultural College, Cirencester. Farmed in Australia, 1949-51. Member: Thirsk RDC, 1954-57; N Riding CC, 1957-61. Parliamentary Private Sec. to Parliamentary Sec. to Minister of Agriculture; An Opposition Whip, 1967. *Recreations:* shooting, hunting, racing. *Address:* Leases Hall, Leeming Bar, Northallerton, Yorks. *T:* Bedale 180.

**KITSON CLARK, George Sidney Roberts,** MA; LittD (Cambridge); Reader in Constitutional History, Cambridge, 1954-67, retired, 1967; Fellow of Trinity College, Cambridge, since 1922; University Lecturer, Cambridge University, since 1929; Praelector, Trinity College, since 1953; *b* 14 June 1900; 2nd *s* of Lieut-Col Edwin Kitson Clark and Georgina, *d* of late George Parker Bidder, QC. *Educ:* Shrewsbury, Trinity Coll., Cambridge. Lecturer, Trinity Coll., Cambridge, 1928; Tutor, 1933-45; founded Cambridge University Educational Films Council, 1947, and helped to found British University Film Council, 1948 (first Chm., 1948-51); Visiting Lecturer University of Pennsylvania, Pa, 1953-54; Chm., Faculty Bd of History, Cambridge Univ., 1956-58; Ford's Lecturer, Oxford Univ., 1959-60; Maurice Lecturer, King's Coll., London, 1960; George Scott Visiting Fellow, Ormond Coll., University of Melbourne, 1964; Birkbeck Lecturer, Cambridge, 1967. Hon. DLitt: Durham; E Anglia. *Publications:* Peel and the Conservative Party, 1929 (new edn 1965); Sir Robert Peel (Great Lives Series), 1936; The English Inheritance, 1950; Ainslie Memorial Lecture, 1953; The Romantic Element 1830-1850 (in Studies in Social History, ed J. H. Plumb), 1955; The Kingdom of Free Men, 1957; Guide for Research Students working on Historical subjects, 1958; The Making of Victorian England, 1962; An Expanding Society: Britain 1830-1900, 1967; The Critical Historian, 1967; articles in Trans Royal Historical Soc., Economic History Review, Journal of Modern History (Chicago), The Historical Journal (Cambridge), etc. *Address:* Trinity College, Cambridge. *T:* Cambridge 58201. *Club:* Athenæum.

**KITTERMASTER, F. R.,** BA; Headmaster, The King's School, Worcester, 1942-59; *b* 26 Oct. 1899; *s* of F. J. Kittermaster, Rugby School; *m* 1930, Meriel Greenstock; one *d*. *Educ:* Rugby Sch.; RMA Woolwich. BA London, 1941. Royal Field Artillery, 1918-21; Prince of Wales's College, Dehra Dun, India, 1921-27; Duke of York's Sch., Dover, 1927-28; Canford Sch., 1928-42. *Publication:* The Victory March, 1921. *Recreations:* ski-ing, gardening, lobster catching. *Address:* c/o Old Farmhouse, Compton Abbas, Shaftesbury, Dorset. *Clubs:* Free Foresters, Butterflies, Harlequins.

**KITTO, Rt. Hon. Sir Frank (Walters),** PC 1963; KBE 1955; Chancellor, University of New England, since 1970; *b* 30 July 1903; *s* of late James W. Kitto, OBE, Austinmer, New South Wales; *m* 1928, Eleanor, *d* of late Rev. W. H. Howard; four *d*. *Educ:* North Sydney High Sch.; Sydney Univ. BA 1924; Wigram Allen Scholar, G. and M. Harris Scholar and Pitt Cobbett Prizes in Faculty of Law, and LLB first class hons, 1927; called to Bar of NSW,

1927. KC (NSW), 1942. Challis Lecturer in Bankruptcy and Probate, Sydney Univ., 1930-33; Justice of the High Court of Australia, 1950-70. Mem. Council, University of New England, 1967-, Deputy Chancellor, 1968-70. *Address:* University of New England, Armidale, NSW 2351, Australia. *Club:* Australian (Sydney).

**KITTO, H. D. F.,** FBA, 1955; FRSL 1957; Professor of Greek, University of Bristol, 1944-62, Emeritus since 1962; *b* 1897; *s* of late H. D. Kitto, Stroud, Glos; *m* 1928, Ann Kraft; one *s* one *d*. *Educ:* Crypt Grammar Sch., Glos; St John's Coll., Cambridge. Asst to Professor of Greek and then Lecturer in Greek, University of Glasgow, 1921-44. Visiting Prof., Cornell Univ., 1954; Brandeis Univ., 1959; Sather Professor, University of California, 1960-61; Ziskind Prof., Brandeis Univ., 1962-63; Regents' Professor, University of California (Santa Barbara), 1963-64. Hon. D-ès-lettres, Aix-Marseille, 1961. *Publications:* In the Mountains of Greece, 1933; Greek Tragedy, 1939, 3rd edn 1961; The Greeks (Pelican), 1951; Form and Meaning in Drama, 1956; Sophocles: Dramatist and Philosopher, 1958; Sophocles' Antigone, Electra and Oedipus Rex (translated into English verse), 1962; Poiesis, 1966; articles and reviews in Classical journals. *Recreations:* music and Greek. *Address:* 9 Southfield Road, Bristol 6.

**KITTS, Sir Francis (Joseph),** Kt 1966; Mayor of Wellington, New Zealand, since 1956; *b* 1914. Elected to: Wellington City Council, 1950; Wellington Harbour Board, 1950; Wellington Hospital Board, 1950. MP for Wellington Central, 1954-60. *Address:* City Offices, Wellington; 25a Shannon Street, Wellington, New Zealand.

**KLARE, Hugh John,** CBE 1967; Secretary, Howard League for Penal Reform, since 1950; *b* Berndorf, Austria, 22 June 1916; *yr s* of F. A. Klare; *m* 1946, Eveline Alice Maria, *d* of Lieut-Col Rankin. *Educ:* privately. Came to England, 1932. Served War of 1939-45: volunteered for Army, 1939; served in Middle East and Europe; Major. Dep. Dir, Economic Organisation Br., Brit. Control Commn for Germany, 1946-48; seconded to Coun. of Europe as Dep. Head, Div. of Crime Problems, 1959-61; Member of Council: Internat. Soc. of Criminology, 1960-66; Inst. for Study and Treatment of Delinquency, 1964-66; Nat. Assoc. for Care and Resettlement of Offenders, 1966-. Chm. Planning Cttee, Brit. Congress on Crime, 1966. *Publications:* Anatomy of Prison, 1960; (ed and introd) Changing Concepts of Crime and its Treatment, 1966; (ed jtly) Frontiers of Criminology, 1967; numerous articles. *Recreation:* travel. *Address:* Flat 23, Thorncliffe Court, King's Avenue, SW4.

**KLECZKOWSKI, Alfred Alexander Peter,** MD Cracow, PhD London; FRS 1962; Biochemist, Department of Plant Pathology, Rothamsted Experimental Station, Harpenden, Herts, since 1946; *b* 4 Dec. 1908; *s* of Alfred and Isabella Kleczkowski; *m* 1932, Janina Helen Mirzynski; one *d*. *Educ:* Cracow Univ., Cracow, Poland. Worked at Rothamsted Experimental Station, Harpenden, Herts, from 1939, at first as a voluntary worker (schols and grants); Beit Memorial Res. Fellow, 1943-45; on staff of Rothamsted Experimental Station, 1946-; Sen. Principal Scientific Officer, 1961. *Publications:* articles in various scientific jls. *Recreations:* various. *Address:* 7 Grasmere Avenue, Harpenden, Herts. *T:* Harpenden 4252.

**KLEFFENS, Eelco Nicolaas van;** Netherlands Minister of State (life), 1950; *b* Heerenveen (Netherlands), 17 Nov. 1894; *m* 1935, Margaret Helen Horstman. *Educ:* University of Leyden. Adjusted shipping questions arising out of European War for Netherlands, 1919; Mem. Secretariat League of Nations, 1919-21; Sec. to directorate of Royal Dutch Petroleum Co., 1921-23; deputy-chief of legal section, Netherlands Ministry for Foreign Affairs, 1923-27; deputy-chief of diplomatic section, 1927-29; chief of diplomatic section, 1929-39; appointed Minister to Switzerland and Netherlands representative with League of Nations, 1939; Minister for Foreign Affairs of the Netherlands, 1939-46; Minister without portfolio and Netherlands representative on Security Council and Economic and Social Council of UN, 1946-47; Netherlands Ambassador to the United States of America, 1947-50; Minister to Portugal, 1950-56; Permanent Representative of Netherlands on NATO Council and OEEC (Paris), 1956-58; Chief Representative in UK of High Authority of European Coal and Steel Community, 1958-67; Pres., IX Session United Nations General Assembly. Pres., Arbitral Tribunal established under Bonn-Paris Agreements, 1952-54, by France, Germany, UK, USA. Holds several hon. degrees; Corresponding Mem., Netherlands and Portuguese Academy of Sciences; Mem. of Curatorium, Hague Academy of International Law, 1947-68; Hon. Member, Amer. Soc. of Internat. Law. Grand Cross: Orange-Nassau (Netherl.); Legion of Honour (France); St Gregory (Holy See); Christ (Portugal), *et al. Publications:* The Relations between the Netherlands and Japan in the Light of International Law, 1605-1919, 1919; The Rape of the Netherlands, 1940; Sovereignty in International Law, 1953; Hispanic Law until the end of the Middle Ages, 1968; articles in periodicals. *Address:* Casal de Sta. Filomena, Almoçagême, Colares, Portugal. *Clubs:* St James' (London); Haagsche (The Hague); Eça de Queiroz (Lisbon); Century (New York).

**KLEIN, Bernat;** Chairman and Managing Director, Bernat Klein Design Consultation ltd, since 1966; *b* 6 Nov. 1922; *s* of Lipot Klein and Serena Weiner; *m* 1951, Margaret Soper; one *s* two *d*. *Educ:* Senta, Yugoslavia; Bezalel Sch. of Arts and Crafts, Jerusalem; Leeds Univ. Designer to: Tootal, Broadhurst, Lee, 1948-49; Munrospun, Edinburgh, 1949-51; Chm. and Man. Dir, Colourcraft, 1952-62; Man. Dir of Bernat Klein Ltd, 1962-66. Exhibitions of paintings: E-SU, 1965; Alwyn Gall., 1967; O'Hara Gall., 1969. *Publication:* Eye for Colour, 1965. *Recreations:* reading, tennis, walking. *Address:* High Sunderland, Galashiels, Selkirkshire. *T:* Selkirk 3358.

**KLEINWORT, Sir Alexander Santiago,** 2nd Bt, *cr* 1909; *b* 31 Oct. 1892; *e s* of Sir Alexander D. Kleinwort, 1st Bt; *S* father, 1935; *m* 1938, Yvonne, *d* of late John Bloch. *Educ:* St John's Coll., Oxford. *Heir: b* Ernest Greverus Kleinwort, *qv*. *Address:* 15 First Avenue, Hove, Sussex. *T:* Hove 71752.

*See also Air Chief Marshal Sir D. C. S. Evill.*

**KLEINWORT, Cyril Hugh;** Chairman; Kleinwort, Benson, Lonsdale Ltd, since 1968; Kleinwort, Benson Ltd, since 1966; Joint Vice-Chairman, Commercial Union Assurance Co.; Chairman, Committee on Invisible Exports; Deputy Chairman, British National Export Council; *b* 17 Aug. 1905; *s* of Sir Alexander D. Kleinwort, 1st Bt; *m* 1933, Elisabeth Kathleen Forde; three *d*. *Educ:* privately. Served as Lieut-Commander, RNVR, 1939-45. *Recreations:* hunting, ski-ing, yachting. *Address:* 20 Cheyne Walk, SW3. *T:* 01-352

4047; Sezincote, Moreton-in-Marsh, Glos. *T:* Blockley 444.

**KLEINWORT, Ernest Greverus;** Director, Kleinwort, Benson, Lonsdale Ltd (Chairman, 1961-68); *b* 13 Sept. 1901; *s* of late Sir Alexander Drake Kleinwort, 1st Bt, and late Etienette, Lady Kleinwort (*née* Girard); *heir-pres.* to Sir Alexander S. Kleinwort, 2nd Bt, *qv*; *m* 1932, Joan Nightingale, MBE, JP, *d* of late Prof. Arthur William Crossley, CMG, CBE, FRS, LLD, DSc; one *s* one *d. Educ:* Jesus Coll., Cambridge. Partner Kleinwort Sons & Company, 1927-47. RAFVR, 1942-45. Actg Chm. of Kleinwort, Sons & Co. Ltd, 1947-61; Chm. Kleinwort Benson Ltd, 1961-66; Member: Accepting Houses Cttee, 1945-66; Internat. Board of Trustees, World Wildlife Fund, 1967-; Council, Wildfowl Trust, 1967-. *Recreations:* landscaping and development of his garden, hunting, swimming. *Address:* Heaselands, Haywards Heath, Sussex; 50 South Audley Street, W1; Quarterdeck, Boscobel, St Mary, Jamaica, West Indies.

**KLEMPERER, Otto;** musical conductor; *b* Breslau, Germany, 14 May 1885; *s* of Nathan and Ida Klemperer; *m* 1919, Johanna Geissler; one *s* one *d. Educ:* Conservatory, Frankfurt and Berlin. Conductor: German National Theatre, Prague, 1907-10; Hamburg Opera House, 1910-13; Barmen Opera, 1913-15; Strasbourg Opera, 1915-17; Cologne, 1917-24, Gen. Music Dir, 1923-24; Wiesbaden, 1924-27; First Conductor, Berlin State Opera and Philharmonic Choir, 1927-33; Dir Los Angeles Philharmonic, 1933-39; since then Guest-Conductor in US, Canada, South America, Australia, Europe, Israel, Soviet Union; conducted concerts in the Festival Hall, 1954, 1955, 1956, 1957, 1958, and 1960-; Covent Garden, 1961, 1962, 1963, 1969. Appointed (for Principal Conductor of Philharmonia Orchestra of England, 1959, but when Philharmonia Orchestra disbanded, became Hon. Pres. and Principal Conductor for Life of New Philharmonia Orch. Nikisch Prize, Leipzig, 1966. LLD, Occidental Coll., Calif. and University of California, Los Angeles, 1937. Goethe Medal, Berlin, 1933; Grand Medal of Merit with Star, Federal Republic of Germany, 1958, Order of Merit, 1967. *Publications:* Minor Recollections, 1964 (publ. London); Symphony in Two Movements, 1962 (publ. London); Symphony No 2, 1970 (publ. London); songs (publ. Mainz, Germany). *Address:* Dufourstrasse 104, 8008 Zürich, Switzerland.

**KLETZKI, Paul, (Paul Klecki);** conductor since 1929; composer; Musical Director and Conductor of Dallas Symphony Orchestra, since 1958; *b* Lodz, Poland, 21 March 1900; *m* 1928, Celine H. Woodtli. *Educ:* Warsaw Univ.; Conservatorium; Berlin Academy of Music. Professor, Conservatoire de Musique, Lausanne, 1940-45 (now Hon. Prof.). Has been conducting all over Europe, 1945-; Conductor, Suisse Romande Orchestra, 1958-70; also made tours to Australia and Latin America. *Publications:* symphonies, orchestral works and chamber music.

**KLIBANSKY, Raymond,** MA, PhD; Frothingham Professor of Logic and Metaphysics, McGill University, Montreal, since 1946; Visiting Professor of History of Phislosphy, Université de Montréal, since 1947; General Editor, Corpus Platonicum Medii Aevi, British Academy, since 1936; *b* Paris, 15 Oct. 1905; *s* of late Hermann Klibansky. *Educ:* Paris; Odenwald Sch.; Univs of Keil, Hamburg, Heidelberg. PhD, 1929; MA Oxon by decree, 1936. Asst, Heidelberg Acad., 1927-33; Lecturer in Philosophy: Heidelberg Univ., 1931-33; King's Coll., London, 1934-36; Oriel Coll., Oxford, 1936-48; Dir of Studies, Warburg Inst., Univ. of London, 1947. Forwood Lectr in Philosophy of Religion, Univ. of Liverpool, 1938-39; Cardinal Mercier Prof. of Philosophy, Univ. of Louvain, 1956; Vis. Prof., Univ. of Rome, 1961. Temp. Civil Servant, FO, 1941-46. President: Inst. Internat. de Philosophie, Paris, 1966-; Canadian Soc. for History and Philosophy of Science. Coresp. Mem., Heidelberg Acad., 1964-. FRHistSoc; Fellow, Académie Internationale d'Histoire des Sciences, Paris; Hon. Fellow, Warburg Inst., Univ. of London. Joint Editor: Magistri Eckardi Opera Latina, 1933-36; Philosophy and History, 1936; Mediaeval and Renaissance Studies, 1941-61. Editor: Philosophical Texts, 1951-62; Philosophy and World Community, 1957-66; Philosophy in the Mid-Century, 1958-59; Contemporary Philosophy, 1968-69. *Publications:* Ein Proklos-Fund und seine Bedeutung, 1929; Heidelberg Acad. edn of Opera Nicolai Cusani, 1929-33; The Continuity of the Platonic Tradition, 1939; (with E. Panofsky and F. Saxl) Saturn and Melancholy, 1964; articles in Jahresberichte d., Heidelberger Akademie, Proceedings of British Acad., Enciclopedia Italiana, and elsewhere. *Address:* McGill University, Montreal, Canada; Oriel College, Oxford.

**KLINGHOFFER, Clara;** painter; *b* Szezerzec, near Lemberg, Austria; *d* of S. Klinghoffer and Anna Stark; *m* Joseph Willem Ferdinand Stoppelman, an American author and journalist of Dutch birth; one *s* one *d. Educ:* Slade Sch., University Coll., London; Central Sch. of Arts and Crafts. First exhibition of drawings and paintings at Hampstead Art Gallery; subsequent one-man shows in: Leicester Galleries, Redfern Gallery (1923, 1926, 1932 and 1938); Royal Glasgow Institute of the Fine Arts, 1962; Royal Academy, London, 1933, 1962; Scottish Academy, 1963. Also exhibited repeatedly in other London Galleries and in numerous provincial shows. Had works at: numerous New English Art Club Exhibitions; Women's International Exhibitions; Whitechapel Art Gallery; Contemp. Portrait Soc., London, 1961, 1963; Royal Society of Portrait Painters, 1964, 1966, 1968. Three one-man shows in Amsterdam and The Hague. Also exhibited in: Stockholm, Paris, Venice (Bi-Annual), Toronto, New York; Wildenstein Gallery, London, 1947, 1961, 1963; one-man shows at 460 Park Avenue Gallery, 1941; New Sch. for Social Research, 1951; Juster Gallery, New York, 1958; Fairleigh Dickinson Univ., Rutherford, NJ, 1958. connected with Pittsburgh (USA–Carnegie International); Instituto Mexicano-Norteamericano, Mexico City, 1969. Member of New English Art Club; Board Mem., Artists' Equity, New York, 1953, re-elected on Board, 1956, 1957. Works in permanent collections: Tate Gallery, London; City Art Gallery, Manchester; The Art Gallery and Industrial Museum, Aberdeen; Stoke-on-Trent Museum; British Museum (Print Room); Victoria and Albert Museum (Print Room); Brisbane Art Gallery; Contemporary Art Society; also in many private collections in England, France, Holland, Mexico, Canada and United States. *Recreations:* music and literature. *Address:* (studio) 800 Riverside Drive, New York, NY 10032, USA. *T:* Wadsworth 7-3220.

**KLUG, Aaron,** FRS 1969; PhD (Cantab); Member of Scientific Staff of Medical Research Council at MRC Laboratory of Molecular Biology, Cambridge, since 1962; Fellow of Peterhouse, since 1962; *b* 11 Aug. 1926; *s* of Eliezer Klug and Bella Silin; *m* 1948,

Liebe Bobrow, Cape Town, SA; two *s*. *Educ:* Durban High Sch.; Univ. of the Witwatersrand (BSc); Univ. of Cape Town (MSc). Junior Lecturer, 1947-48; Research Student, Cavendish Laboratory, Cambridge, 1949-52; Rouse-Ball Research Studentship, Trinity Coll., Cambridge, 1949-52; Colloid Science Dept, Cambridge, 1953; Nuffield Research Fellow, Birkbeck Coll., London, 1954-57; Dir, Virus Structure Research Group, Birkbeck Coll., 1958-61. Foreign Hon. Mem., Amer. Acad. of Arts and Sciences, 1969. *Publications:* papers in scientific jls. *Recreations:* reading, gardening. *Address:* 70 Cavendish Avenue, Cambridge. *T:* 48959.

**KLYNE, Prof. William;** MA Oxon, DSc London, PhD Edinburgh; Professor of Chemistry, Westfield College, University of London, since Oct. 1960; *b* 23 March 1913; *s* of late Carl Adolphe Klein and Ivy Adkin, Enfield, Middx; *m* 1949, Dr Barbara Evelyn Clayton; one *s* one *d*. *Educ:* Highgate Sch.; New Coll., Oxford. Asst in Medical Chemistry, University of Edinburgh, 1936-39, Lecturer, 1939-47; Lecturer in Biochemistry, Postgrad. Med. Sch. of London, 1947-52; Reader in Biochemistry, London, 1952-60. Mem. Editorial Board, Biochemical Journal, 1949-55. Hon. Sec., Chemical Soc., 1966-. *Publications:* Practical Chemistry for Medical Students, 1946; Chemistry of Steroids, 1957; (ed 3 vols with Prof. P. B. D. de la Mare) Progress in Stereochemistry, 1954-62; contrib. to chemical and biochemical journals. *Address:* 19 Malcolm Road, SW19. *T:* 01-946 4194; Bay View, Studland, Swanage, Dorset BH19 3AS. *T:* Studland 325. *Club:* Athenæum.

**KNAPP-FISHER, Rt. Rev. E. G.;** *see* Pretoria, Bishop of.

**KNARESBOROUGH, Bishop Suffragan of,** since 1965; **Rt. Rev. John Howard Cruse,** MA; *b* 15 Feb. 1908; *s* of George Thomas Cruse; *m* 1942, Ethne, *d* of Winslow Sterling-Berry, MB; no *c*. *Educ:* Roborough Sch.; Jesus Coll., Cambridge; Wycliffe Hall, Oxford. 2nd Class Economics Tripos, 2nd Class Theological Tripos, MA, Jesus Coll. Curate of St John, Southall, 1932; Curate of Christ Church, Folkestone, 1934; Vicar of St Paul's, South Harrow, 1936; Vicar of Holy Trinity, Cambridge, 1942 (Chaplain to the Cambridge Pastorate); Exam. Chaplain to Bishop of Sodor and Man; Proctor in Convocation, 1948; Provost of Sheffield, 1949. *Publication:* Marriage, Divorce and Repentance, 1949. *Recreations:* fishing and sailing. *Address:* 8 Weetwood House, 240 Otley Road, Leeds 16. *T:* Leeds 53116.

**KNATCHBULL,** family name of **Baron Brabourne.**

**KNATCHBULL-HUGESSEN, Hon. Adrian Norton,** QC; LLD; Barrister, Bar of Province of Quebec; Member of Senate, Canada, 1937-67; *b* 5 July 1891; *y s* of first Baron Brabourne, PC; *m* 1922, Margaret, *o d* of G. H. Duggan, Montreal; four *s* one *d*. *Educ:* Eton; McGill Univ., Montreal. Admitted to Quebec Bar, and joined the present firm of Smith, Davis, Anglin, Laing, Weldon and Courtois, 1914; served in Canadian Heavy Artillery, 1916-19, spending one year at the front; contested St Lawrence St George div. of Montreal, 1935; Dir, Canadian Marconi Company, International Paints (Canada) Ltd; Chancellor of Anglican Diocese of Montreal, 1946-66; Bâtonnier of Bar of Prov. of Quebec, 1960-61. *Recreations:* golf, ski-ing. *Address:* 4306 Montrose Avenue, Westmount, Montreal, Canada. *TA:* Fleural, Montreal. *Clubs:* University, Royal Montreal Golf, Royal St Lawrence Yacht (Montreal); Rideau (Ottawa).

**KNATCHBULL-HUGESSEN, Sir Hughe Montgomery,** KCMG, 1936 (CMG 1920); *b* 26 March 1886; *s* of late Rev. R. B. Knatchbull-Hugessen and Rachel Mary, *d* of late Sir Alexander Montgomery, Bt; *m* Mary, *d* of late Brig.-Gen. Sir R. G. Gordon-Gilmour, Bt, CB, CVO, DSO; one *d* (and one *d* decd). *Educ:* Eton; Balliol, Oxford. Foreign Office, 1908; attached to British Delegation at Peace Conference, Jan. 1919; First Sec. in HM Diplomatic Service, 1919; Counsellor, 1926; Counsellor HM Embassy, Brussels, 1926-30; British Minister to the Baltic States, 1930-34; British Minister in Teheran, 1934-36; Ambassador in China, 1936-37; Ambassador to Turkey, 1939-44; Ambassador in Brussels and Minister to Luxembourg, 1944-47. *Publications:* Diplomat in Peace and War, 1949; Kentish Family, 1960. *Address:* The Red House, Barham, near Canterbury, Kent. *Club:* Anglo-Belgian.

**KNEALE, Sydney James,** CBE 1963 (OBE 1944); HM's First Deemster and Clerk of the Rolls, 1958-69; Deputy Governor of the Isle of Man; *b* 3 July 1895; *s* of William Henry Kneale, Douglas, Isle of Man; *m* 1928, Margaret Alexandra Burnett; two *s* (and one *d* decd). *Educ:* Douglas Higher Grade and Eastern District Secondary Schs. Served European War in ranks and as commissioned officer, 6th Kings Liverpool Rifles, 1914-19. Admitted to Manx Bar, 1921; Asst Island Comr of Sea Scouts, 1929-45; Lt-Col First Battalion Manx Home Guard, 1940-44; Chm. Isle of Man Sea Cadet Corps, 1944-69; HM's Attorney-General, 1944-57; HM's Second Deemster, 1957-58. Coronation Medal, 1953. *Publications:* Notes for Isle of Man Justices of the Peace, 1956; Manx Coroners, 1958. *Recreations:* golf, Association football, rugby, cricket. *Address:* Vicarage Road, Braddan, Isle of Man. *T:* Douglas 5637. *Club:* Manx Automobile (Douglas).

**KNEALE, Prof. William Calvert,** FBA 1950; White's Professor of Moral Philosophy, University of Oxford, and Fellow of Corpus Christi College, 1960-66; *b* 22 June 1906; *s* of late William Kneale; *m* 1938, Martha Hurst, Fellow of Lady Margaret Hall, Oxford; one *s* one *d*. *Educ:* Liverpool Institute; Brasenose Coll., Oxford (Classical Scholar). Senior Hulme Scholar, Brasenose Coll., 1927, studied in Freiburg and Paris; Asst in Mental Philosophy, University of Aberdeen, 1929; Asst Lecturer in Philosophy, Armstrong Coll., Newcastle upon Tyne, 1931; Lecturer in Philosophy, Exeter Coll., Oxford, 1932; Fellow, 1933-60; Senior Tutor, 1945-50; Emeritus Fellow, 1960. War of 1939-45, temp. Civil Servant, Ministry of Shipping (later War Transport). Hon. LLD Aberdeen, 1960; Hon. Fellow, Brasenose Coll., Oxford, 1962, and Corpus Christi Coll., Oxford, 1966; Hon. DLitt Durham, 1966. *Publications:* Probability and Induction, 1949; (with M. Kneale) The Development of Logic, 1962; On Having a Mind, 1962; articles in Mind, Proceedings of Aristotelian Society, etc. *Address:* Colton House, Burnsall, near Skipton, Yorks. *T:* Burnsall 248.

**KNEBWORTH, Viscount; John Peter Michael Scawen Lytton;** *b* 7 June 1950; *s* and *heir* of 4th Earl of Lytton, *qv*. *Educ:* Downside.

**KNELL, Rt. Rev. E. H.;** *see* Reading, Suffragan Bishop of.

**KNIGHT, Most Rev. Alan John;** *see* West Indies, Archbishop of.

**KNIGHT, Sir Allan Walton,** Kt 1970; CMG 1960; MIE (Aust.); Commissioner, The Hydro-Electric Commission, Tasmania, Australia, since 1946; *b* 26 Feb. 1910; *s* of late Mr and Mrs G. W. Knight, Lindisfarne, Tasmania; *m* 1936, Margaret Janet Buchanan; two *s* one *d*. *Educ:* Hobart Technical Coll.; University of Tasmania. Diploma of Applied Science, 1929; BSc 1932; ME 1935; BCom 1946. Chief Engineer, Public Works Dept, Tasmania, 1937-46. Mem., Australian Univs Commn, 1966. Peter Nicol Russel Medal, Instn of Engrs of Australia, 1963; William Kernot Medal, Univ. of Melbourne, 1963. *Recreation:* royal tennis. *Address:* 64 Waimea Avenue, Hobart, Tasmania 7005, Australia. *T:* Hobart 51498. *Club:* Tasmanian (Hobart).

**KNIGHT, Prof. Bert Cyril James Gabriel,** DSc London; Professor of Microbiology, University of Reading, 1951-69, Emeritus since 1969; *b* 4 Feb. 1904; *s* of late Cyril Fennel Knight and Kate Knight (*née* Gabriel); *m* 1st, 1929, Doris, *d* of late G. D. Kemp; one *d*; 2nd, 1944, Frideswide, *d* of late Dr H. F. Stewart; two *s* two *d* (and one *s* decd). *Educ:* Reigate Grammar Sch.; University Coll., London. BSc (Chemistry), University Coll., London, 1925; MSc 1927; DSc 1938. Worked on problems of bacterial physiology at London Hosp., 1929-34, and at Middlesex Hosp., 1934-38, in Medical Research Council Unit for Bacterial Chemistry. Halley Stewart Research Fellow, 1934-38; Biochemist, Lister Institute of Preventive Medicine, Serum Dept, Elstree, 1939-43; Wellcome Research Laboratories, Beckenham (Depts of Biochemistry and Bacteriology), 1943-50. Joint Editor, Journal of General Microbiology, 1946-70. Visiting Commonwealth Prof., New York Univ. Medical Sch., Nov. 1947-Jan. 1948. *Publications:* Bacterial Nutrition, 1936; Growth Factors in Microbiology, 1945; (trans. with J. Stewart) Stendhal's The Life of Henry Brulard, 1959. Papers in: Biochem. Jl, British Journal of Experimental Pathology, Journal Chem. Soc., Jl Gen. Microbiol., Bull. Soc. Chim. biol., etc. Harvey Lecture, NY, 1947; William Henry Welch Lecture, NY, 1948. *Recreations:* 18th-20th century French and English literature, walking in mountains and Paris. *Address:* 28 Park Parade, Cambridge CB5 8AL.

**KNIGHT, Charles,** VPRWS 1961 (RWS 1935; ARWS 1933); ROI 1933; Landscape Painter and Designer; Vice-Principal, Brighton College of Art and Crafts, 1959-67, retired; *b* 27 Aug. 1901; *s* of Charles and Evelyn Mary Knight; *m* 1934, Leonora Vasey; one *s*. Art training, Brighton Coll. of Art; Royal Academy Schools, London (Turner Gold Medal); works in permanent collections, London, British Museum, Victoria and Albert Museum, Sheffield, Leeds, Hull, Oxford, Brighton, Hove, Eastbourne, Preston, etc; regular exhibitor RA, 1924-. Illustrated monograph by Michael Brockway, 1952. *Address:* Chettles, 34 Beacon Road, Ditchling, Sussex. *T:* Hassocks 3998.

**KNIGHT, Eric John Percy Crawford Lombard;** Joint Chairman since 1965 and Managing Director since 1947, Lombard Banking Ltd; Chairman, Lombank Ltd (Managing Director, 1951-68), etc; *b* 17 Aug. 1907; *yr s* of late Herbert John Charles and Mary Henrietta Knight; *m* 1933, Peggy Julia (*née* Carter); one *s* one *d*. *Educ:* Ashford Gram. Sch. Served War of 1939-45, RAF. British Mercedes Benz; Bowmaker Ltd; established Lombard Banking, 1947. *Recreations:* breeding of thoroughbreds and racing; tennis, Association football. *Address:* The White House, Sanderstead Village, Surrey. *T:* 01-657 2021; c/o Churchill Stud, Lingfield, Surrey. *T:* 2662. *Clubs:* Caledonian, Royal Automobile; Royal Scottish Automobile (Glasgow).

**KNIGHT, Esmond Pennington;** actor; *b* 4 May 1906; 3rd *s* of Francis and Bertha Knight; *m* 1st, 1929, Frances Clara (marr. diss.); one *d*; 2nd, 1946, Nora Swinburne, *qv*. *Educ:* Willington Prep. Sch.; Westminster. Made first appearance on stage at Pax Robertson's salon in Ibsen's Wild Duck, 1925; Old Vic., 1925-27; Birmingham Repertory Co., 1927-28; Contraband, Prince's Theatre; To What Red Hell, Wyndham's, 1928; The Children's Theatre; Fashion, Kingsway; Maya, Studio des Théâtres des Champs-Elysées, Paris, 1929; Art and Mrs Bottle, Royalty; Hamlet, Queen's, 1930; Salome, Gate; Waltzes from Vienna, Alhambra, 1931; Wild Violets, Drury Lane, 1932; Three Sisters, Drury Lane; Streamline, Palace, 1934; Wise Tomorrow, Lyric; Van Gogh, Arts Theatre Club; Night Must Fall, Cambridge Theatre, 1936; The Insect Play, Little; The King and Mistress Shore, Little, 1937; Crest of the Wave, Tour; Twelfth Night, Phœnix, 1938; in management with Wilson Barrett, King's, Hammersmith and Edinburgh, 1939; Peaceful Inn, Duke of York's; Midsummer Night's Dream, Open Air, 1940. Joined RNVR (HMS King Alfred, Drake, Excellent, Prince of Wales); discharged from Navy as a result of being blinded in HMS Prince of Wales during action with Bismarck, 1941. Returned to stage in Crisis in Heaven, March 1945; shared lead with Evelyn Laye in The Three Waltzes, Princes. Season of plays with travelling Repertory Theatre, King's, Hammersmith, 1946; The Relapse, 1947; Memorial Theatre, Stratford-on-Avon, 1948-49; Caroline (by Maugham), Arts Theatre Club; Old Vic Co., Edinburgh Festival, 1950, in Bartholomew Fair by Ben Jonson; Who is Sylvia, Criterion, 1950; Sir Laurence Olivier's Festival Season, St James's Theatre, 1951; Heloise, Duke of York's; Montserrat, Lyric; Bermuda Festival (Bermuda); Emperor's Clothes (New York); Age of Consent; Bell, Book and Candle, Phœnix, 1955; The Caine Mutiny, Hippodrome, 1956; The Country Wife, Adelphi, 1957; The Russian, Lyric, Hammersmith, 1958; A Piece of Silver (Cheltenham), 1960; The Lady from the Sea, Queen's, 1961; Becket, Taming of the Shrew, Aldwych, 1961; Two Stars for Comfort, Garrick, 1962; Last Old Vic Season, 1962-63; Season, Mermaid, 1965; Edinburgh Festival: Winter's Tale, and Trojan Women 1966; Getting Married, Strand, 1967; Greenwich Theatre: Martin Luther King; Spithead. *Films:* Romany Love, 77 Park Lane, The Ringer, Pagliacci, Waltzes from Vienna, Black Roses (Ufa, Berlin), What Men Live By, The Bermondsey Kid, The Blue Squadron, Girls Will Be Boys, Dandy Dick, Someday, Crime Unlimited, Contraband, The Silver Fleet, Half-Way House, King Henry V, A Canterbury Tale, Black Narcissus, Hamlet, Red Shoes, Gone to Earth, The River, 1950, Helen of Troy (Rome), 1954, The Dark Avenger, Ratcliffe in Olivier's Richard III, The Sleeping Prince, On Secret Service, Battle of the V1; Sink the Bismarck; The Spy Who Came in From the Cold; Anne of a Thousand Days; Where's Jack, 1968. Assisted in making several Natural History films. Has appeared frequently on BBC and Independent Television, notably in Dickens and Ibsen and in Dr Finlay's Casebook. *Publications:* Seeking the Bubble (Autobiography), 1943; Story in Blackwood's, Jan. 1942; various articles in daily and weekly Press. *Recreation:* painting. *Address:* 35 Bywater Street, Chelsea, SW3. *T:* 01-589 1611. *Club:* Savage.

**KNIGHT, Geoffrey Cureton,** MB, BS London; FRCS; Consulting Neurological Surgeon in London, since 1935; Senior Neurological Surgeon, West End Hospital for Neurology and Neurosurgery; Neurological Surgeon, British Postgraduate Medical School of London and Teacher of Surgery, University of London; Neurological Surgeon: Queen Elizabeth Hospital for Children; Runwell Hospital, Wickford; Surgeon in Charge, SE Metropolitan Regional Neurosurgical Centre; Visiting Neurological Surgeon: St Augustine's Hospital, Canterbury; Oakwood Hospital, Maidstone; Hellingly Hospital, Eastbourne; *b* 4 Oct. 1906; *s* of Cureton Overbeck Knight; *m* 1933, Betty, *d* of Francis Cooper Havell, London; two *s*. *Educ:* Brighton Coll.; St Bartholomew's Hosp. Medical Sch. Brackenbury Surgical Schol. St Bart's Hosp., 1930. Ho. Surg. and Chief Asst, Surgical Professorial Unit at St Bart's Hosp.; Demonstrator in Physiology, St Bart's Hosp. Medical Sch.; Leverhulme Research Scholar, Royal College of Surgeons, 1933-35; Mackenzie Mackinnon Research Scholar, 1936-38; Bernard Baron Research Scholar, 1938; Hunterian Prof., 1935-36 and 1963. FRSocMed; Fellow Soc. Brit. Neurological Surgeons; Fellow Med. Soc. London. Neurological Surg. Armed Forces of Czecho-Slovakia, 1941; Hon. Fellow, Czecho-Slovak Med. Soc., Prague, 1946; Officer, Order of the White Lion of Czecho-Slovakia, 1946. *Publications:* contrib. med. jls on aetiology and surgical treatment of diseases of the spine and nervous system and the surgical treatment of mental illness. *Recreations:* gardening, swimming. *Address:* 7 Aubrey Road, Campden Hill, W8. *T:* 01-727 7719 (Sec., 01-935 7549). *Club:* Hurlingham.

**KNIGHT, Geoffrey Egerton,** CBE 1970; Director, British Aircraft Corporation Ltd, since 1964; Chairman: British Aircraft Corporation (Filton) Ltd; British Aircraft Corporation (Weybridge) Ltd; British Aircraft Corporation (USA) Inc.; Director, British Aircraft Corporation (Australia) Pty Ltd; Joint Deputy Chairman, BNEC Committee for Exports to USA; *b* 25 Feb. 1921; *s* of Arthur Egerton Knight and Florence Gladys Knight (*née* Clarke); *m* 1947, Evelyn Bugle; two *d*. *Educ:* Stubbington House; Brighton Coll. Royal Marines, 1939-46. Read for Bar, Middle Temple, while working for Instn of Production Engrs; joined Aircraft Div. of Bristol Aeroplane Co. Ltd, 1953; Commercial Dir, Bristol Aircraft Ltd, 1956; Commercial Man., British Aircraft Corp. Ltd, 1960. *Address:* 33 Smith Terrace, SW3. *T:* 01-352 5391. *Clubs:* Boodle's, Hurlingham.

**KNIGHT, Prof. (George) Wilson,** CBE 1968; MA Oxon; FRSL; FIAL; Professor of English Literature, Leeds University, 1956-62, now Emeritus (Reader in English Literature, Leeds University, 1946-56); *b* 19 Sept. 1897; *s* of George Knight and Caroline L. Jackson; unmarried. *Educ:* Dulwich Coll.; St Edmund Hall, Oxford. Served European War, Middle East; Master at Seaford House, Littlehampton, 1920, and St Peter's, Seaford, 1921; St Edmund Hall, 1922-23; Honour Sch. of English Language and Literature, 1923; Chess, Oxford *v* Cambridge, 1923; Master at Hawtreys, Westgate-on-Sea, 1923-25, and Dean Close Sch., Cheltenham, 1925-31; Chancellors' Prof. of English, Trinity Coll., University of Toronto, 1931-40; Master at Stowe, Buckingham, 1941-46. Stage: Shakespearian productions at Hart House Theatre, Toronto, 1931-40; produced and acted in: Hamlet, Rudolf Steiner Hall, London, 1935; This Sceptred Isle, Westminster Theatre, London, 1941; productions (Agamemnon, Athalie, Timon of Athens) and performances (Timon, Lear, Othello, Shylock) at Leeds Univ., 1946-60. Lectured in Jamaica for British Council and University Coll. of West Indies, 1951; Visiting Lecturer to University of Cape Town, 1952; Byron Foundation Lecture, University of Nottingham, 1953; Mem. of Delegation to the University of Munich, 1957; Clark Lectures, Cambridge, 1962; Festival Seminars, Stratford (Ont), 1963, 1967; lectured at University of Chicago, 1963; City of London Sch. Lecture. BBC talks and readings on Shakespeare and Byron, 1963-64; joint-petitioner, Byron Memorial (Westminster Abbey, 1969). Mem., Internat. Adv. Cttee, World Shakespeare Congress, Vancouver, 1971. Pres., Devonshire Assoc., 1971; Hon. Vice-Pres., Spiritualist Assoc. of Great Britain, 1955. Hon. Fellow St Edmund Hall, Oxford, 1965; Hon. LittD Sheffield, 1966; Hon. DLitt Exon, 1968. *Publications:* Myth and Miracle, 1929; The Wheel of Fire, 1930; The Imperial Theme, 1931; The Shakespearian Tempest, 1932; The Christian Renaissance, 1933; Principles of Shakespearian Production, 1936; Atlantic Crossing, 1936; The Burning Oracle, 1939; This Sceptred Isle, 1940; The Starlit Dome, 1941; Chariot of Wrath, 1942; The Olive and the Sword, 1944; The Dynasty of Stowe, 1945; Hiroshima, 1946; The Crown of Life, 1947; Christ and Nietzsche, 1948; Lord Byron: Christian Virtues, 1952; Laureate of Peace, 1954; The Last of the Incas, 1954 (play, first prod. Sheffield, 1954); The Mutual Flame, 1955; Lord Byron's Marriage, 1957; The Sovereign Flower, 1958; The Golden Labyrinth, 1962; Ibsen, 1962; Shakespearian Production, 1964; The Saturnian Quest, 1965; Byron and Shakespeare, 1966; Shakespeare and Religion, 1967; Poets of Action, 1967; Gold-Dust, 1968; Neglected Powers, 1970; (ed) W. F. Jackson Knight, Elysion, 1970; also contribs to: John Masefield, OM, ed G. Handley-Taylor, 1960; Times Literary Supplement, The Yorkshire Post, Review of English Studies, Essays in Criticism, Twentieth Century, etc. *Address:* c/o National Westminster Bank, Exeter.

**KNIGHT, Gerald Hocken,** MA, MusB Cantab; DMus Lambeth; FRCM; FRCO (Choirmaster's Diploma); FRSCM; Archbishop of Canterbury's Diploma in Church Music; Director of the Royal School of Church Music since 1952 (Associate-Director, 1947-52); Hon. Organist to Archbishop of Canterbury, since 1953; *b* 27 July 1908; *o s* of Alwyne and Edith Knight, Wyngarvey, Par, Cornwall. *Educ:* Truro Cathedral Sch.; Peterhouse, Cambridge (Choral Exhibitioner); College of St Nicolas, Chislehurst; Royal College of Music. Asst Organist, Truro Cathedral, 1922-26; Peterhouse, Cambridge, 1926-29; John Stewart of Rannoch Scholar in Sacred Music, Cambridge Univ.; Organist and Choirmaster, St Augustine's, Queen's Gate, South Kensington, 1931-37; Tutor, College of St Nicolas, Chislehurst, 1932-38; Organist and Master of the Choristers, Canterbury Cathedral, 1937-52; Warden and Fellow of College of St Nicolas, Canterbury, 1945-52; External Examiner, Yorks Trg Colls Exam. Bd, 1937-41; Airman, RAF, 1942-43; Education Officer, Royal Air Force, 1943-45. Mem., House of Laity, Church Assembly, 1945-55; Mem., Archbishops' Psalter Revision Commission, 1958-63. Hon. Fellow: St Michael's Coll., Tenbury, 1953; Westminster Choir Coll., Princeton, New Jersey, USA, 1965. Hon. RAM; Hon. FTCL. *Publications:* Accompaniments (with J. Eric Hunt) to Merbecke's Communion Service, 1933; Music for Dorothy L. Sayers' plays, The Zeal of Thy

House, 1937, and The Devil to Pay, 1939. Jt Musical Editor, Hymns Ancient and Modern, revised 1950; Jt Editor, The Treasury of English Church Music, 1965; (ed) The Revised Parish Psalter, 1967. *Address:* Addington Palace, Croydon CR9 5AD. *T:* 01-654 7676. *Club:* Athenæum.

**KNIGHT, Air Vice-Marshal Glen Albyn Martin,** CB 1961; CBE 1956; *b* 10 Sept. 1903; *e s* of Lt-Col G. A. Knight, OBE, VD, Melbourne, Australia; *m* 1933, Janet Elizabeth Warnock, *o d* of Peter Crawford, Dargavel, Dumfriesshire; two *d. Educ:* Scotch Coll., Melbourne, Australia; Melbourne Univ. MB, BS, 1927; Diploma in Laryngology and Otology (RCP & S), 1937. House Surgeon and Physician, Alfred and Children's Hospitals, Melbourne; joined Medical Branch, RAF, 1932. War Service: South Africa, Malta (despatches), Italy; PMO Desert Air Force. Principal Medical Officer, 2nd Tactical Air Force, 1956-57; Dep. Dir-Gen. of Medical Services, Royal Air Force, 1958-61, retired, 1961. QHS 1959-61. *Recreation:* golf. *Address:* Craig Gowan, Laurieston Road, Gatehouse-of-Fleet, Kirkcudbrightshire. *T:* Gatehouse 417.

**KNIGHT, Harold Murray,** DSC 1945; Deputy Governor and Deputy Chairman of Board, Reserve Bank of Australia, since 1968; *b* 13 Aug. 1919; *s* of W. H. P. Knight, Melbourne; *m* 1951, Gwenyth Catherine Pennington; four *s* one *d. Educ:* Scotch Coll., Melbourne; Melbourne Univ. Commonwealth Bank of Australia, 1936-40. AIF (Lieut), 1940-43; RANVR (Lieut), 1943-45. Commonwealth Bank of Australia, 1946-55; Asst Chief, Statistics Div., Internat. Monetary Fund, 1955-59; Reserve Bank of Australia, 1960-. *Publication:* Introducción al Analisis Monetario (Spanish), 1959. *Address:* 39 Hull Road, Beecroft, NSW 2119, Australia. *T:* 84.1969.

**KNIGHT, Jasper Frederick,** FCA; Director, Unilever Ltd and Unilever NV, 1958-70; Chairman, Warwick Securities, since 1970; *b* 3 Oct. 1909; *er s* of late Jasper Webb Knight and Esther Austin Knight (*née* Low); *m* 1935, Elizabeth Margaret, *o d* of late Dr Andrew Wilson and Margaret Wilson (*née* Kintrea); two *s* one *d. Educ:* Eton; Exeter Coll., Oxford. BA 1930. Articled Peat Marwick Mitchell & Co., London, 1931. ACA 1934; FCA 1960. Finance Dir, then Principal Asst Sec., Ministry of Food, 1939-45. Asst Chief Accountant, Unilever Ltd, 1945-48; Chief Accountant, 1948-52; various positions in Unilever in Germany and England, 1952-57; Chm. Van den Berghs & Jurgens Ltd, 1957-58. Part-time Member: Iron and Steel Board, 1964-65; National Board for Prices and Incomes, 1965-67; Council, Inst. of Chartered Accountants, 1966-70. Hon. Treasurer, Wycombe Div. Cons. Assoc., 1970-. Jt Master, Old Berkeley Beagles, 1967-. Medal of Freedom (Silver Palm) (US), 1945. JDipMA, 1965. *Recreations:* beagling, boating and gardening. *Address:* Little Colstrope, Hambleden, Henley-on-Thames, Oxon. *T:* Hambleden 306. *Clubs:* Lansdowne, Leander, London Rowing.

**KNIGHT, Mrs Jill,** MBE 1964; MP (C) Edgbaston since 1966; *m* 1947, Montague Knight; two *s. Educ:* Fairfield Sch., Bristol; King Edward Gram. Sch., Birmingham. Mem., Northampton County Borough Council, 1956-66. *Recreations:* music, reading, tapestry work, theatre-going. *Address:* 84 Courtenay Street, SE11. *T:* 01-735 3431. *Club:* Constitutional.

**KNIGHT, Very Rev. Marcus;** Dean of Exeter since Dec. 1960; *b* 11 Sept. 1903; *e s* of late Mark Knight, Insurance Manager; *m* 1931, Claire L. Hewett, MA, *o d* of late Charles H. Hewett, Bank Dir; two *s. Educ:* Christ's Hosp.; University of London; Birkbeck Coll. (BA Hons); King's Coll. (BD Hons); Fellow of King's Coll.; Union Theological Seminary, New York; STM 1930. Curacies at Stoke Newington and Ealing; Priest-Vicar of Exeter Cathedral; Vicar of Cockington, 1936-40; Vicar of Nuneaton; RD of Atherstone, 1940-44; Examining Chaplain to Bishop of Coventry, 1944; Canon of St Paul's, 1944-60, Precentor, 1944-54, Chancellor, 1954-60. Hon. Sec. Church of England Council for Education, 1949-58; Chapter Treas., St Paul's, 1950-60; Church Commissioner, 1968. *Publications:* Spiritualism, Reincarnation, and Immortality, 1950; (part author) There's an Answer Somewhere, 1953; many papers and reviews. *Recreations:* reading, travel. *Address:* The Deanery, Exeter. *T:* Exeter 72697.

**KNIGHT, Richard James,** MA; JP; Headmaster of Monkton Combe School since 1968; *b* 19 July 1915; *s* of Richard William Knight; *m* 1953, Hilary Marian, *d* of Rev. F. W. Argyle; two *s* one *d. Educ:* Dulwich Coll. (Scholar); Trinity Coll., Cambridge (Scholar). 1st class Hons Classical Tripos Pt I, 1936, Part II, 1937. Asst Master, Fettes Coll., Edinburgh, 1938-39. Served War of 1939-45 in Gordon Highlanders, Capt. Asst Master and Housemaster, Marlborough Coll., 1945-56; Headmaster of Oundle Sch., 1956-68. JP Bath, 1970. *Recreations:* cricket and other games. *Address:* Headmaster's House, Monkton Combe School, Bath.

**KNIGHT, William Arnold,** CMG 1966; OBE 1954; Controller and Auditor-General of Uganda, 1962-68; *b* 14 June 1915; *e s* of late William Knight, Llanfairfechan, and of Clara Knight; *m* 1939, Bronwen Parry; one *s* one *d. Educ:* Friars' Sch., Bangor; University Coll. of North Wales (BA Hons). Entered Colonial Audit Dept as an Asst Auditor, 1938; service in Kenya, 1938-46; Mauritius, 1946-49; Sierra Leone, 1949-52; British Guiana, 1952-57; Uganda, 1957-68. *Recreations:* fishing and gardening. *Address:* Neopardy Mills, near Crediton, Devon. *T:* Crediton 2513. *Club:* East India and Sports.

**KNIGHTLEY;** *see* Finch-Knightley.

**KNIGHTS, Lionel Charles,** MA, PhD; King Edward VII Professor of English Literature, University of Cambridge, since 1965; Fellow, Queens' College, Cambridge, since 1965; *b* 15 May 1906; *s* of C. E. and Lois M. Knights; *m* 1936, Elizabeth M. Barnes; one *s* one *d. Educ:* grammar schs; Selwyn Coll., and Christ's Coll., Cambridge Univ. Lecturer in English Literature, Manchester Univ., 1933-34, 1935-47; Prof. of English Lit. in the University of Sheffield, 1947-52; Winterstoke Prof. of English, Bristol Univ., 1953-64; Andrew Mellon Visiting Prof., University of Pittsburgh, 1961-62; Mem. of editorial board of Scrutiny, a Quarterly Review, 1932-53. Docteur (*hc*) de l'Univ. de Bordeaux, 1964; Hon. DUniv York, 1969. *Publications:* Drama and Society in the Age of Jonson, 1937; Explorations: Essays in Literary Criticism, 1946; Shakespeare's Politics, Shakespeare Lecture, British Academy, 1957; Some Shakespearean Themes, 1959; An Approach to Hamlet, 1960; (ed with Basil Cottle), Metaphor and Symbol, 1961; Further Explorations, 1965, etc. *Address:* Queens' College, Cambridge.

**KNIGHTS, Maj.-Gen. Robert William,** CB 1969; CBE 1960; GOC Southern Command, Australia, 1966-69, retired; *b* 24 June 1912; *s* of late William James Knights, Canberra, Australia; *m* 1937, Betty Adrienne, *d* of late George Leonard Davis, Sale, Victoria, Australia; one *s* two *d. Educ:* Telopea Park High Sch., Canberra; Royal Military College, Duntroon, Canberra. Lt, Australian Staff Corps, 1932; Adj., CMF, 1933-39. Served War of 1939-45: Middle East and Australia, Lt-Col, 1943. Staff, RMC, Duntroon, 1945-47; AHQ, 1947-49; Joint Services Staff Coll., UK, 1949; seconded Dept of Defence, 1950-51; Dir of Personnel Administration, AHQ, Melbourne, 1951-54; Brig., 1954; idc, 1957; Maj.-Gen., 1958; Head of Australian Joint Services Staff, London, 1958-59; Extra Gentleman Usher to the Queen, 1958-60; GOC, W Comd, Aust., 1960; Comdt, RMC, Duntroon, 1960-61; Chm., Joint Planning Cttee, Dept of Defence, Australia, 1962-63. QMG, AHQ, Australia, 1964-66. *Address:* 128 Empire Circuit, Yarralumla, ACT 2600, Australia. *Clubs:* Naval and Military (Melbourne); Commonwealth (Canberra).

**KNILL, Sir Stuart,** 3rd Bt, *cr* 1893; *b* 11 April 1886; *s* of Sir John Knill, 2nd Bt, and Edith (*d* 1944), *d* of John Hardman Powell; *S* father, 1934; *m* 1st, 1910, Lucy (who obtained a divorce, 1937; she *d* 1952), *d* of Capt. T. H. Willis; one *s*; 2nd, 1941, Ruth Evelyn, *d* of Archibald Barnes; two *s* one *d.* Served European War, Machine Gun Corps, 1914-18; RAF Pilot Officer, 1940-41, then invalided. *Heir: s* John Kenelm Stuart Knill [*b* 8 April 1913; *m* 1951, Violette Maud Florence Barnes; two *s*]. *Address:* 19 Council Houses, Edingworth, Axbridge, Somerset.

[*But his name does not, at the time of going to press, appear on the Official Roll of Baronets.*

**KNOLLYS,** family name of **Viscount Knollys.**

**KNOLLYS,** 3rd Viscount, of Caversham, *cr* 1911; **David Francis Dudley Knollys;** Baron *cr* 1902; *b* 12 June 1931; *s* of 2nd Viscount Knollys, GCMG, MBE, DFC, and Margaret, *o d* of Sir Stuart Coats, 2nd Bt; *S* father 1966; *m* 1959, Hon. Sheelin Virginia Maxwell (granted, 1959, title, rank and precedence of a baron's *d,* which would have been hers had her father survived to succeed to barony of Farnham), *d* of late Lt-Col Hon. Somerset Maxwell, MP and late Mrs Remington Hobbs; three *s* one *d. Educ:* Eton. Lt, Scots Guards, 1951. *Heir: s* Hon. Patrick Nicholas Mark Knollys, *b* 11 March 1962. *Address:* Bramerton Grange, Norwich NOR 06W. *T:* Surlingham 266.

**KNOPF, Alfred A.;** publisher; Chairman Alfred A. Knopf, Inc., 201 East 50th Street, New York 22, NY; *b* 12 Sept. 1892; *s* of Samuel Knopf and Ida Japhe; *m* 1st, 1916, Blanche Wolf (*d* 1966); one *s*; 2nd, 1967, Helen Norcross Hedrick. *Educ:* Mackenzie Sch.; Columbia Coll. AB (Columbia), 1912; Pres., Alfred A. Knopf, Inc., NYC, 1918-57 (Chm. of the Board, 1957-); Director, Random House, Inc. Gold Medal, Amer. Inst. of Graphic Arts, 1950; C. A. Pugsley Gold Medal for conservation and preservation, 1960; Alexander Hamilton Medal, Columbia Coll., 1966. Hon. LHD: Yale, 1958; Columbia, 1959; Bucknell, 1959; William and Mary, 1960; Lehigh, 1960; Michigan, 1969; Hon. LLD (Brandeis), 1963; Hon. DLitt: Adelphi, 1966; Chattanooga, 1966. *Address:* (home) Purchase, NY 10577, USA. *TA:* KSP KNOPF.

**KNOTT, Lt-Gen. Sir Harold (Edwin),** KCB 1963 (CB 1961); OBE 1945; MA; MD; DPH; *b* 15 May 1903; *s* of Arthur Knott; *m* 1929, Dora Georgina, *d* of Dr J. Bradley; four *s* one *d. Educ:* King's Hosp., Dublin; Trinity Coll., Dublin. MA, MD Dublin, 1935; DPH (London) 1936. Comnd, 1929; served in India, 1930-35; Egypt, BLA, India, 1938-47; Col, and Comdt Army Sch. of Health, 1949-53; Brigadier: Dep. Dir Army Health, Northern Army Group, 1953-55; DDMS, West Africa, and ADMS, Ghana, 1955-57; ADMS, Aldershot Dist, 1957-58; Maj.-Gen., DDMS, Eastern Command, 1958-61; Lt-Gen, 1961; DGAMS, 1961-65, retired, 1965. QHP 1960-65. Hon. LLD (Dublin) 1961. CStJ 1962. *Recreation:* golf. *Address:* La Belle Hougue, Fauvic, Grouville, Jersey, Channel Islands. *T:* Jersey East 185. *Clubs:* Army and Navy; Dublin University (Dublin); Victoria, Royal Jersey Golf (Jersey).

**KNOTT, Air Vice-Marshal Ronald George,** CB 1967; DSO 1944; DFC 1943; AFC 1955; Air Officer in charge of Administration, Headquarters Air Support Command, RAF, since 1970; *b* 19 Dec. 1917; *s* of late George Knott and of Edith Rose Knott; *m* 1941, Hermione Violet (*née* Phayre); three *s* one *d. Educ:* Borden Grammar Sch., Sittingbourne, Kent. No 20 Sqdn RAF, 1938-40; No 5 Flight IAFVR, 1940-41; HQ Coast Defence Wing, Bombay, 1942; No 179 Sqdn, 1943-44; No 524 Sqdn, 1944-45; RAF, Gatow (Ops), 1949-50; OC, RAF Eindhoven, 1950-51; HQ 2nd TAF, 1951-52; RAF Staff Coll., 1952; Flying Trng Comd, 1953-55; Chief Flying Instructor, Central Flying Sch., 1956-58; Air Plans, Air Min., 1959; OC, RAF Gutersloh, 1959-61; ACOS Plans, 2 ATAF, 1962-63; Defence Res. Policy Staff Min. of Def. 1963; DOR2 (RAF), Min. of Def., 1963-67; SASO, HQ NEAF Cyprus, 1967-70. *Recreations:* squash, gardening, painting, building. *Address:* HQ Air Support Command, RAF, Upavon, Pewsey, Wilts. *Club:* Royal Air Force.

**KNOWELDEN, Prof. John,** MD, MRCP, DPH, JP; Professor of Preventive Medicine and Public Health, University of Sheffield, since 1960; *b* 19 April 1919; *s* of Clarence Arthur Knowelden; *m* 1946, Mary Sweet; two *s. Educ:* Colfe's Grammar Sch., Lewisham; St George's Hosp. Med. Sch.; London Sch. of Hygiene and Trop. Med.; Johns Hopkins Sch. of Public Health, Baltimore. Surg. Lt, RNVR, 1942-46. Rockefeller Fellowship in Preventive Med., 1947-49; Lectr in Med. Statistics and Mem., MRC Statistical Research Unit, 1949-60. Editor, Brit. Jl of Preventive and Social Medicine, 1959-. Formerly Hon. Sec., Sect. of Epidemiology, Royal Society Medicine and Chm., Soc. for Social Medicine; Mem., WHO Expert Advisory Panel on Health Statistics. *Publications:* (with Ian Taylor) Principles of Epidemiology, 2nd edn, 1964; papers on clinical and prophylactic trials and epidemiological topics. *Recreations:* photography, gardening. *Address:* 258 Dobcroft Road, Sheffield S11 9LJ. *T:* Sheffield 363130.

**KNOWLAND, William Fife;** Newspaper Publisher; *b* 26 June 1908; *s* of Joseph Russell and Ellie (Fife) Knowland; *m* 1926, Helen Davis Herrick; one *s* two *d. Educ:* University of California, Berkeley, Calif (AB 1929). Pres., Publisher and Editor, Oakland, Calif, Tribune, 1933-; Member: California State Assembly, 1933-35; California State Senate, 1935-39; Republican National Cttee, 1938; Chm. Republican Nat. Exec. Cttee, 1941-42. Served War with US Army, from private to Major, 1942-45 (serving in Europe). On service overseas when apptd US Senator to fill unexpired term; elected for six-year term, 1946; re-elected, 1952; Chm. Republican Policy Cttee (Senate), 1953; Senate Republican Leader, 1953-59. Hon. LLD (holds several hon. degrees in the USA). *Address:* Oakland Tribune, 401 13th Street, Oakland,

California 94604, USA. *T:* 273-2200. *Clubs:* Mason (Scottish 33°), Native Sons of the Golden West, Elks, Eagles, Moose, Athenien-Nile; Bohemian (San Francisco).

**KNOWLES, Rev. David;** *see* Knowles, Rev. Michael Clive.

**KNOWLES, Rt. Rev. Donald Rowland,** OBE 1951; Assistant Bishop of Nassau and the Bahamas, *b* 14 July 1898; *s* of Frederick F. and Addie A. Knowles, Long Island, Bahamas; *m* 1933, Carolyn Elizabeth Knowles; two *s. Educ:* Boys' Central School, Nassau; St Paul's College, Burgh, Lincs; Hatfield College, Durham. BA (Hons Theol.) First Class. Government Service, Nassau, 1915-19. Deacon, 1923; Priest, 1924. Curate, Andros Is., Diocese of Nassau, 1923-25; Priest-in-Charge: Long Cay, Acklins, Crooked Islands, and Inagua, 1925-35; Eleuthera, 1935-38; Rector, St Matthew's Nassau, 1938-53; Canon, 1944; Archdeacon of Bahamas, 1951; Bishop of Antigua, 1953-69. *Address:* PO Box 5695, Nassau, NP, Bahamas.

**KNOWLES, Air Vice-Marshal Edgar,** CB 1965; CBE 1959 (MBE 1944); BSc; FRAeS; Director of Educational Services, RAF, 1960-67, retired; *b* 11 Sept. 1907; *o s* of Ernest Knowles and Annie Collins, Bradford; *m* 1935, Jane, *er d* of William Griffiths and Annie Evans, Coedely; two *d. Educ:* Colne Grammar; University Coll. and King's Coll., London. Sen. Science Master, Harrogate Grammar Sch., 1929-35; entered RAF Educl Service, 1935; served at Sch. of Tech. Trg, Halton, 1935-40; Air Ministry, 1940-43; Senior Education Officer, Middle East, 1943-47; Air Ministry, 1947-48; HQ, 23 Group, 1948-50; Command Educn Officer, Transport Comd, 1950-51; Dir of Studies, RPAF Cadet College, Risalpur, Pakistan, 1951-52; Dep. Dir of Educnl Services, Air Ministry, 1952-53; Principal Education Officer, Halton, 1953-55; Command Educn Officer, Tech. Trg Comd, 1955-60; ADC to the Queen, 1956-60. Group Capt. 1952; Air Cdre, 1959; Air Vice-Marshal, 1960. Chm., Bucks County Branch, SS & AFA. Governor: Garnet Coll.; John Colet Sch. *Address:* 5 Dobbins Lane, Wendover, Bucks. *T:* Wendover 2216. *Club:* Royal Air Force.

**KNOWLES, Sir Francis (Gerald William),** 6th Bt, *cr* 1765; FRS 1966; Professor of Anatomy, King's College, London, since Oct. 1967; *b* 9 March 1915; *s* of Sir Francis Howe Seymour Knowles, 5th Bt, and Kathleen Constance Averina, *d* of William Lennon; *S* father 1953; *m* 1948, Ruth Jessie, *widow* of Pilot Officer R. G. Hulse, RAF, and *d* of late Rev. Arthur Brooke-Smith; one *s* three *d* (of these one *s* one *d* are twins). *Educ:* Radley; Oriel Coll., Oxford. BA 1936; MA and DPhil 1939; DSc 1963. Oxford Univ. Naples Schol., 1937; Royal Society Browne Fund Bermuda Schol., 1949; Nuffield Foundation Schol., 1953. Head of Biology Dept, Marlborough Coll., 1938-58; Lectr in the Dept of Anatomy, Birmingham Univ., 1958-63; Prof. of Comparative Endocrinology, Birmingham Univ., 1967 (Reader, 1963-67). *Publications:* Man and Other Living Things, 1945 (2nd edn, 1960); The Living Organism, 1948; Biology and Man, 1950; Diagrams of Human Biology, 1950; Freshwater and Saltwater Aquaria, 1953; (co-author) Endocrine Control in Crustaceans, 1959; (co-author) Animal Hormones, 1966. Research publications on neuroendocrinology. *Recreation:* travel. *Heir: s* Charles Francis Knowles, *b* 20 Dec. 1951. *Address:* Avebury Manor, Avebury, Wilts. *T:* Avebury 203. *Club:* Athenæum.

**KNOWLES, John;** Solicitor; Assistant Public Trustee, 1956-60, retired 1960; *b* 8 March 1898. *Educ:* Abingdon Sch.; Pembroke Coll., Oxford (BA). Served with Lancs Fusiliers in European War, 1917-19; Qualified as Solicitor, 1925. A Chief Administrative Officer, Public Trustee Office, 1955. *Address:* c/o The Public Trustee Office, Kingsway, WC2.

**KNOWLES, Joshua Kenneth,** CBE 1953; General Secretary, National Farmers' Union, 1945-70; *b* 4 Dec. 1903; *s* of Robert Dixon Knowles and Annie Rawcliffe, Greenmount, Lancs; *m* 1928; one *s. Educ:* The Old College, Windermere; Midland Agricultural Coll., Sutton Bonnington, Loughborough (now Nottingham Univ.). Farming, 1922-45, at Morley, Derbyshire. Derbyshire Council Deleg., NFU, 1933-43; Vice-Pres., NFU, 1943; Pres., NFU, 1944. Liveryman, Co. of Farmers. *Recreation:* fishing. *Address:* 3 Manor Way, Holyport, Maidenhead, Berks. *T:* Maidenhead 21729. *Clubs:* City Livery, Farmers', Royal Automobile.

**KNOWLES, Maurice Baxendale,** CBE 1952; late Government Actuary's Department; *b* 6 Nov. 1893; *m* 1919, Lilla Shepherdson (decd); one *s* one *d. Educ:* Bridlington Sch. Served European War, 1914-18, in 3 London Regt and RFC. *Address:* 164 Foxley Lane, Purley, Surrey.

**KNOWLES, Rev. Michael Clive** (in religion **David**), OSB, MA, LittD, FBA, FSA; *b* 1896; *o s* of late Harry Herbert and Carrie Knowles, Studley, Warwicks. *Educ:* Downside; Christ's Coll., Cambridge; Collegio Sant' Anselmo, Rome. Entered novitiate at Downside, 1914; Priest, 1922; Editor of Downside Review, 1930-34; Fellow of Peterhouse, Cambridge, 1944-63; University Lecturer in History, 1946; Prof. of Medieval History, 1947-54; Regius Prof. of Modern History, 1954-63. Pres. of the Royal Historical Society, 1956-60. Ford's Lecturer in English History, Oxford, 1948-49; British Academy Raleigh Lecturer, 1949; Creighton Lecturer, London, 1956; Sarum Lecturer, Oxford, 1964-65; Hon. Mem. Royal Irish Academy, 1955; Mem. Pontifical Hist. Institute, Rome; Corresp. Mem. Monumenta Germaniæ Historica, 1965; Hon. Fellow: Christ's Coll., Cambridge, 1958; Peterhouse, Cambridge, 1963. Hon. DD Cambridge, 1969; Hon. DLitt: Oxford, 1952; Leicester, 1962; LittD Kent, 1969; Bristol, 1956; DLit London, 1963; DUniv York, 1969. *Publications:* The Monastic Order in England, 1940 (revised 1963); The Religious Houses of Medieval England, 1940 (enlarged edn with R. N. Hadcock, 1953); The Religious Orders in England: vol I, 1948; vol. II, 1955; vol. III, 1959; The Monastic Constitutions of Lanfranc, 1951; The Episcopal Colleagues of Archbishop Thomas Becket, 1951; Monastic Sites from the air (with J. K. St Joseph), 1952; Charterhouse (with W. F. Grimes), 1954; The English Mystical Tradition, 1961; Saints and Scholars, 1962; The Evolution of Medieval Thought, 1962; The Historian and Character, 1963; Great Historical Enterprises, 1963; From Pachomius to Ignatius, 1966; What is Mysticism?, 1967; Christian Monasticism, 1969; The Christian Centuries, 1969; Thomas Becket, 1970; articles in Downside Review, English Historical Review, Cambridge Historical Review and Journal of Ecclesiastical History. *Address:* 9 Old House Close, Church Road, Wimbledon, SW19. *T:* 01-946 0010; The Old Cottage, Linch, Liphook, Hants. *T:* Milland 227. *Club:* Athenæum.

**KNOX,** family name of **Earl of Ranfurly.**

**KNOX, Col Bryce Muir,** MC 1944 and Bar, 1944; TD 1947; Vice-Lieutenant, County of Ayr, since 1970; Chairman, W. & J. Knox Ltd; Director, Lindustries Ltd; *b* 4 April 1916; *s* of late James Knox, Kilbirnie; *m* 1948, Patricia Mary Dunsmuir; one *s* one *d*. *Educ:* Stowe; Trinity Coll., Cambridge. Served with Ayrshire (ECO) Yeomanry, 1939-45, N Africa and Italy; CO, 1953-56; Hon. Col 1969. Member, Royal Company of Archers. *Recreation:* foxhunting. *Address:* Kersland, Monkton, Ayrshire. *T:* Symington 231. *Club:* Cavalry.

**KNOX, Collie;** author and journalist; *s* of late Edmund Francis Vesey Knox, KC, MP, Shimnah, Newcastle, Co. Down; *m* 1944, Gwendoline Frances Mary (marriage dissolved, 1948), *yr d* of late I. Davidson Mitchell. *Educ:* Rugby; RMC, Sandhurst. Regular Commission in Queen's Royal Regiment. Seconded to RFC. Served European War, 1914-18 (wounded, 1916, when pilot); Captain on staff at War Office and in India, Uganda, Anglo-Egyptian Sudan. Served with Regt during Irish Rebellion at Londonderry and Co. Cork; on staff of GOC London Air Defences, 1917, at Horse Guards; on staff of late Lord Lloyd when Gov. of Bombay; on staff of late Sir Geoffrey Archer during his whole terms of office when Gov. of Uganda and Gov.-Gen. of the Sudan; Bimbashi (Lt-Col) in Sudan Defence Force, 1925. Entered Fleet Street, in 1928 on Daily Express; joined Daily Mail as Special Columnist, 1933, until War broke out; rejoined Daily Mail as Columnist, March 1945; resigned from Daily Mail, Oct. 1955; Feature writer for Newnes & Pearson Publications and Daily Mirror Group, till 1963; Special London Columnist and drama critic of Morning Telegraph, New York, 1955-; was first radio columnist-critic. Has written 14 books, 30 songs (lyrics). Contributed during War of 1939-45 to Ministry of Information, and to Service Publications; on Special Duties; Dir of Public Relations, ENSA, Drury Lane Theatre, WC2, 1943-45. *Publications:* It Might Have Been You (autobiography), 1938; Collie Knox Calling, 1937; Draw Up Your Chair, 1938; Collie Knox Again, 1938; Collie Knox Re-Calls, 1940; Heroes All, 1941; Atlantic Battle, 1941; For Ever England, 1943; The Un-Beaten Track, 1944; People of Quality, 1947; It Had To Be Me, 1947; We Live and Learn, 1951; Steel at Brierley Hill (A Centenary History of Round Oak Steelworks), 1957. *Recreations:* lyric-writing, golf, lawn tennis, motoring. *Address:* The Small House, 40a Sussex Square, Brighton, Sussex. *T:* Brighton 62461. *Clubs:* Garrick, Royal Automobile.

**KNOX, David Laidlaw;** MP (C) Leek Division of Staffordshire since 1970; *b* 30 May 1933; *s* of J. M. Knox, Lockerbie and Mrs C. H. C. Knox (*née* Laidlaw), Greencroft, Lockerbie, Dumfriesshire. *Educ:* Lockerbie Academy; Dumfries Academy; London Univ. (BSc (Econ) Hons). Management Trainee, 1953-56; Printing Executive, 1956-62; O&M Consultant, 1962-70. Contested (C): Stechford, Birmingham, 1964 and 1966; Nuneaton, March 1967. *Recreations:* association football, reading. *Address:* The Flat, Consall Hall, Wetley Rocks, Stoke on Trent; Greencroft, Lockerbie, Dumfriesshire. *T:* Lockerbie 2428.

**KNOX, Edmund George Valpy;** *b* 1881; *e s* of late Rt Rev. E. A. Knox, DD, and Ellen Penelope, *d* of Dr Valpy French, Bishop of Lahore; *m* 1st, 1912, Christina Frances (*d* 1935), *y d* of Dr E. L. Hicks, Bishop of Lincoln; one *s* one *d*; 2nd, 1937, Mary Eleanor Jessy, *d* of Ernest Howard Shepard, *qv*. *Educ:* Rugby; Corpus Christi Coll., Oxford. Hon. MA, Oxford; Fellow Institute of Journalists. Staff of Punch, 1921; Editor, 1932-49. Leslie Stephen Lecture, 1951. Pen-name Evoe. Served in Lincs Regt, 1914-19 (wounded at Passchendaele). *Publications:* The Brazen Lyre; A Little Loot; Parodies Regained; These Liberties; Fiction As She Is Wrote; An Hour from Victoria; Fancy Now; It Occurs to Me; Gorgeous Times; Quaint Specimens; Awful Occasions; Poems of Impudence; I'll Tell the World; Wonderful Outings; Here's Misery; Blue Feathers; This Other Eden; Things That Annoy Me; Slight Irritations; Folly Calling; (ed) Anthology of Humorous Verse; Adventures of a School. Articles in several encyclopaedias. *Recreations:* reading and writing. *Address:* 110 Frognal, Hampstead, NW3. *Club:* Athenæum.

**KNOX, Sir Edward (Ritchie),** Kt 1956; MC 1918; Partner, Harrison, Knox and Leslie, 1922-59, retired; Director: CSR Co. Ltd, 1923-64 (Chairman, 1933-59); Commercial Banking Co. of Sydney Ltd, 1928-64 (Chairman, 1939-59); United Insurance Co. Ltd, 1930-64 (Chairman, 1942-53); Perpetual Trustee Co. Ltd, 1935-64; CSR Chemicals, 1948-64 (Chairman, 1948-61); *b* 27 Nov. 1889; *er s* of Thomas Forster and Amy Hope Knox, Sydney; *m* 1923, Barbara Mary, 2nd *d* of H. P. Owen, Sydney; one *s* one *d*. *Educ:* Sydney Church of England Grammar Sch.; Sydney Grammar Sch. Clerk, Dalgety & Co. Ltd, Sydney, 1908-12; pastoral pursuits, 1913-14, and 1919-21. Served with RFA, 1915-18. Accountancy, 1922-56; FCA Aust. 1936. *Recreations:* golf and fly-fishing. *Address:* 22 Victoria Road, Bellevue Hill, NSW 2023, Australia. *Clubs:* Union, Royal Sydney Golf (Sydney).

**KNOX, Gen. Sir Harry (Hugh Sidney),** KCB 1935 (CB 1919); DSO 1917; *b* 5 Nov. 1873; 4th *s* of late Vesey Ed. Knox, Shimnah, Newcastle, Co. Down; *m* 1904, Grace Una (*d* 1954), *d* of Rev. R. A. Storrs, Rector, Shanklin, Isle of Wight; one *d*. *Educ:* St Columba's Coll., Rathfarnham, Dublin. 5th RI Rifles, 1890-93; Northants Regt, 1893-1919: served Samana, Tirah, and NW Frontier, India, 1897-98 (medal, 3 clasps); Uganda Protectorate with Uganda Rifles, 1900-01; Adj. 1st Batt. Northants Regt, 1902-05; Staff Coll., Quetta, 1908-09; Gen. Staff AHQ, India, 1911-14; BEF, France, 1915-19; Gen. Staff HQ V Army Corps, 1915; GSO I 15th Scottish Div., 1915-17; Brig.-Gen. Gen. Staff XV Army Corps, 1917-19, commanding 29th Div. (temp.) Aug. 1918 (wounded, despatches seven times; Brevet Lt-Col, Brevet Col, DSO, CB, Croix de Guerre, Officier Legion of Honour, Officier, Couronne Belge); acting Maj.-Gen., Gen. Staff, First Army, 6 Feb.-7 March 1919; Maj.-Gen. 1926; Commanded 3rd Infantry Brigade, Bordon, 1923-26; Dir of Military Training, War Office, 1926-30; commanded 3rd Div., 1930-32; ADC to the King, 1925-26; Lt-Gen. 1932; Lt of Tower of London, 1933-35; Gen., 1936; Adj. Gen. to the Forces, 1935-37; retired pay, 1938; Governor of Royal Hospital, Chelsea, 1938-43; Col Northants Regt, 1931-43. *Recreations:* gardening, shooting, fishing. *Address:* Hillborough Cottage, Highcliffe, Hants. *T:* Highcliffe 3465. *Club:* United Service.

**KNOX, Prof. Henry Macdonald;** Professor of Education, The Queen's University of Belfast, since 1951; *b* 26 Nov. 1916; *e s* of Rev. R. M. Knox, Edinburgh, and J. E. Church; *m* 1945, Marian, *yr d* of N. Starkie, Todmorden; one *s* one *d*. *Educ:* George Watson's Coll., Edinburgh; University of Edinburgh. MA 1938; MEd 1940; PhD 1949. Served as Captain, Intelligence Corps, commanding a wireless intelligence section, Arakan sector of Burma, and as instructor, War Office special wireless training wing, 1940-46. Lecturer in Education,

University Coll. of Hull, 1946; Lecturer in Education, University of St Andrews, 1949; sometime Examiner in Educn, Universities of Leeds, Sheffield, Aberdeen, Glasgow and Ireland (National); occasional Examiner, Universities of Edinburgh, Dublin and Bristol. Dean of Faculty of Education, QUB. Member: Advisory Board for Postgraduate Studentships in Arts Subjects, Ministry of Education for N Ireland; N Ireland Council for Educl Research. Formerly Member: Advisory Council on Educn for N Ireland; Senior Certificate Examination Cttee for N Ireland. *Publications:* Two Hundred and Fifty Years of Scottish Education, 1696-1946, 1953; John Drury's Reformed School, 1958; Introduction to Educational Method, 1961; Schools in Europe (ed W. Schultze): Northern Ireland, 1969; numerous articles in educational journals. *Address:* 69 Maryville Park, Belfast BT9 6LQ. *T:* 665588.

**KNOX, Henry Murray Owen,** OBE 1944; Senior Partner, Oxley, Knox & Co., Stock-jobbers, retired, 1965; *b* 5 March 1909; *yr s* of late Brig.-Gen. and Mrs H. O. Knox; *m* 1932, Violet Isabel (*d* 1962), *yr d* of late Mr and Mrs Frank Weare, The Dell, Tunbridge Wells, Kent; two *s*; *m* 1963, Mrs E. M. Davidson. *Educ:* Charterhouse; Trinity Coll., Oxford (MA Hons Law). Joined Oxley, Knox & Co., 1930; Partner, 1931. Served War of 1939-45, Queen's Own Royal West Kent Regt (despatches, wounded, OBE); various appts. Staff, ending in Col "A" Organisation, HQ 21 Army Group. Master, Skinners' Company, 1951-52. Stock Exchange Council, 1948-64; Dep. Chm., Stock Exchange, 1958-64. Chm., House of Sears Holdings and other companies. Governor: Tonbridge Sch.; Sutton's Hosp. in Charterhouse. *Recreations:* golf, gardening. *Address:* 49 Whitelands House, Cheltenham Terrace, SW3. brooklands, Manwood Road, Sandwich, Kent. *Clubs:* Boodle's, Garrick.

**KNOX, Most Rev. James Robert;** *see* Melbourne, Archbishop of, (RC).

**KNOX, Mrs Jean M.;** *see* Swaythling, Lady.

**KNOX, John;** Chief Scientific Officer, Ministry of Technology, since 1965; Head of Materials Division, since 1968; *b* 11 March 1913; *s* of William Knox and Mary Mure Ferguson; *m* 1942, Mary Blackwood Johnston; one *s* one *d*. *Educ:* Lenzie Acad.; Glasgow Univ. (Kitchener's Schol.; MA). Business Management Trng, 1935-39; joined RAE, 1939; Op. Research with RAF, 1939-45; Asst Chief Scientific Adviser, Min. of Works, 1945-50; Dep. Dir and Dir, Intelligence Div., DSIR, 1950-58; Dep. Dir (Industry), DSIR, 1958-64; Asst Controller, Min. of Technology, 1964-65; Head of External Research and Materials Div., Min. of Technology, 1965-68. *Publications:* occasional articles on operational research, management of research and development, impact of automation. *Recreation:* golf. *Address:* Brackenridge, 14 The Broad Walk, Northwood, Middlesex. *T:* Northwood 21788. *Club:* Athenæum.

**KNOX, Prof. Joseph Alan Cruden;** Professor of Physiology in the University of London, at Queen Elizabeth College, since 1954; *b* 23 March 1911; *s* of Dr Joseph Knox; *m* 1945, Elsa Margaret Henry; one *d*. *Educ:* Aberdeen Grammar Sch.; Glasgow High Sch.; Glasgow Univ. MB, ChB (Glasgow) 1935; MD (Hons) 1948; House Surgeon and Physician, Glasgow Royal Infirmary, 1935-36; Asst to Prof. of Physiology, Glasgow Univ., 1936-40; Lecturer in Physiology: Glasgow Univ., 1940-44; King's Coll., London, 1944-48; Senior Lecturer, King's Coll., 1948-54. Mem. of Physiological Soc., 1941; Mem. of British Biophysical Soc., 1960. *Publications:* papers in Jl of Physiology, British Heart Jl, etc. *Recreations:* reading, gramophone, gardening. *Address:* 129 Northumberland Road, North Harrow, Harrow, Middlesex HA2 7RB. *T:* 01-866 6778.

**KNOX, Sir Malcolm;** *see* Knox, Sir T. M.

**KNOX, Robert,** MA, MD, FRCP, FRCPath; Emeritus Professor of Bacteriology, University of London (Professor of Bacteriology, Guy's Hospital Medical School, 1949-69); *b* 1904; *s* of Dr Robert Knox, radiologist; *m* 1936, Bessie Lynda Crust; three *d*. *Educ:* Highgate; Balliol Coll., Oxford (Classical Scholar); St Bartholomew's Hosp. 1st Class Hon. Mods, 1924, 2nd Class Lit Hum, 1926; BA Oxford, 1927; MRCS, LRCP, 1932; MB, BS London, 1932; MD 1934; MRCP 1934; FCPath, 1964. house Physician and Chief Asst St Bartholomew's Hosp., 1932-35; MA Cambridge 1935; Demonstrator in Pathology, University of Cambridge, 1935-37; Mem. of Scientific Staff, Imperial Cancer Research Fund, 1937-39; Dir of Public Health Laboratories (Med. Research Council) at Stamford, 1939, Leicester 1940, and Oxford, 1945; MA Oxford, 1945. Fellow Royal Society Medicine; Member: Pathological Soc.; Soc. of Gen. Microbiology; Assoc. of Clinical Pathologists. *Publications:* on bacteriological subjects in medical and scientific journals. *Recreation:* coxed Oxford Univ., 1925. *Address:* Bracken, Woodland Way, Kingswood, Surrey. *Club:* Athenæum.

**KNOX, Sir Robert Wilson,** Kt 1934; company director; *b* 17 May 1890; *s* of late Hon. William Knox; *m* 1914, Ivy Victoria Clarke; one *s* one *d*. *Educ:* Melbourne Church of England Grammar Sch. Pres. Melbourne Chamber of Commerce, 1928-31, and Associated Chamber of Commerce of Australia, 1934-36; Chm., Australian National Cttee, Internat. Chamber of Commerce, 1933-36; consultant to Australian Delegation Ottawa Conference, 1932; First Federal Pres. Australian Assoc. British Manufacturers, 1929; Dir, Dunlop Rubber Co. Ltd, and other industrial companies; Commissioner Australian Red Cross Soc., Egypt, France. *Recreation:* golf. *Address:* Greenknowe Court, Toorak, Victoria 3142, Australia. *TA:* Knox, Melbourne. *Clubs:* Melbourne, Australian (Melbourne).

**KNOX, Sir (Thomas) Malcolm,** Kt 1961; Principal, University of St Andrews, 1953-66; Hon. Fellow, Pembroke College, Oxford, 1950; Hon. LLD Edinburgh, Pennsylvania and Dundee; Hon. DLitt Glasgow; *b* Birkenhead, Cheshire, 28 Nov. 1900; *e s* of James Knox, MA, and Isabella Russell Marshall, Tillicoultry, Clackmannan; *m* 1st, Margaret Normana McLeod Smith (*d* 1930), Tarbert, Harris; 2nd, Dorothy Ellen Jolly, Thornton-le-Fylde, Lancs; no *c*. *Educ:* Mostyn House, Parkgate, Cheshire; Bury Grammar Sch.; Liverpool Institute; Pembroke Coll., Oxford. Entered business of Lever Brothers Ltd as Sec. to 1st Lord Leverhulme, 1923; various executive and secretarial positions in firms managing Lever Brothers' West African interests, 1925-31; Lecturer in Philosophy, Jesus Coll., Oxford, 1931-33; Fellow and Tutor, 1933-36; Lecturer in Greek Philosophy, Queen's Coll., Oxford, 1934-36; Prof. of Moral Philosophy, University of St Andrews, 1936-53, Dep. Principal, 1951-52. Acting Principal, 1952-53. Gifford Lecturer, University of Aberdeen, 1965-66 and 1967-68. Chm. Govs of Morrison's Acad., Crieff, 1946-62; Chm. Advisory Council on Education in Scotland, 1957-61; Mem. Catering Wages Commission, 1943-46; Mem. Nat. Reference

Tribunal for the Coal Industry of Great Britain, 1943-56; Mem. Review Body on Doctors' and Dentists' Remuneration, 1962-65. *Publications:* Translation, with commentary, of Hegel's Philosophy of Right, 1942, Hegel's Early Theological Writings, 1948, and Hegel's Political Writings, 1964; Action, 1968; A Layman's Quest, 1969; articles and reviews in periodicals. *Address:* 19 Victoria Terrace, Crieff, Perthshire. *T:* 2808.

**KNOX JOHNSTON, A. G.;** *see* Johnston.

**KNOX-SHAW, Thomas,** CBE 1954; MC; MA; Hon. ARIBA; Fellow of Sidney Sussex College (Master, June 1945-June 1957); 2nd *s* of late C. T. Knox-Shaw; *b* 27 Nov. 1886. *Educ:* Blundell's Sch., Tiverton; Sidney Sussex Coll., Cambridge (Mathematical Scholar); 4th Wrangler, 1908; Class I Div. II in Part II Mathematical Tripos, 1909; Fellow, 1909; Coll. Lecturer, 1914; Tutor, 1919-29; University Lecturer in Mathematics, 1926-29; Mem. of the Council of the Senate, 1920-24, 1925-30, 1945-50; Treasurer of the University of Cambridge, 1929-45; Cambridge City Councillor, 1944-52; Chm., United Cambridge Hospitals, 1948-55. During European War, 1914-18, served as Adjutant 1st Battalion York and Lancaster Regt, and on Infantry Brigade Staffs in France and Salonica (MC, Belgian Croix de Guerre, despatches thrice). *Recreation:* golf. *Address:* Sidney Sussex College, Cambridge. *Clubs:* Oxford and Cambridge; Hawks, University Pitt (Cambridge).

**KNUDSEN, Semon Emil;** President, Ford Motor Company, 1968-69; *b* 2 Oct. 1912; *o s* of William S. and Clara Euler Knudsen; *m* 1938, Florence Anne McConnell; one *s* three *d*. *Educ:* Dartmouth Coll.; Mass Inst. of Technology. Joined General Motors, 1939; series of supervisory posts; Gen. Man., Detroit Diesel Div., 1955; Gen. Man., Pontiac Motor Div., 1956; Gen. Man., Chevrolet Motor Div., 1961; Dir of General Motors and Gp Vice-Pres. i/c of all Canadian and overseas activities, 1965; Exec. Vice-Pres. with added responsibility for domestic non-automotive divs, 1966, also defense activities, 1967; resigned from Gen. Motors Corp., 1968. *Recreations:* golf, tennis, deepsea fishing, hunting. *Address:* Bingham Road, Birmingham, Michigan 48010, USA. *Clubs:* Detroit, Detroit Athletic, Yondotega (Detroit); Bloomfield Hills Country (Mich).

**KNUTSFORD,** 4th Viscount *cr* 1895; **Thurstan Holland-Hibbert,** Bt 1853; Baron, 1888; Barrister; *b* 19 June 1888; *e s* of 3rd Viscount and Ellen (*d* 1949), *e d* of Sir Wilfrid Lawson, 2nd Bt of Brayton, Cumberland; *S* father, 1935; *m* 1912, Viola Mary (*d* 1964), *d* of Thomas Meadows Clutterbuck, Putteridge Bury, Herts; one *s* one *d*. *Educ:* Eton; Cambridge Univ., BA. Called to Bar, Inner Temple, 1914; late Royal Scots Greys; Master of Avon Vale Foxhounds, 1924-33; Joint Master VWH (Cirencester) 1935. *Heir: s* Hon. Julian Thurstan Holland-Hibbert, *qv*. *Address:* Munden, Watford, Herts.

*See also Lord D. Malise Graham.*

**KOCH, Ludwig,** MBE 1960; Author and Lecturer; *b* 13 Nov. 1881; *m* 1912, Nellie Sylvia Herz; one *s* one *d*. *Educ:* Frankfurt A. M.; Paris; Milan. Violinist, pupil of Prof. Hugo Heermann, 1890-1902; Lieder and Oratorio Singer, pupil of Clara Sohn, Johannes Meschaert and Jean de Reszke, 1905-14; responsible for repatriation of Allied Prisoners of War, 1918-19; Delegate for the occupied zone in Germany, 1919-25; Syndic of the City of Frankfurt A. M. for Publicity, Propaganda and Exhibition, 1926-28; Creator and Organiser of International Music Exhibition, Music in the Life of Nations, 1927; Dir of the Culture Dept of German Gramophone, Odeon and Parlophone Company, 1928-35; first outdoor recording of Songs of Wild Birds; Originator of Sound-Books; since 1936 in this country as Naturalist, Author of Sound-Books, Lectr, Broadcasts and Synchroniser of Nature Films, 1948-51; joined BBC with his famous collection of bird and animal sounds for purpose of completing the library and making it available to the public. Grosse Verdienstkreuz des Verdienstorden der Bundesrepublik Deutschland, 1962. *Publications:* Songs of Wild Birds (with E. M. Nicholson), 1936; More Songs of Wild Birds (with E. M. Nicholson), 1937; Hunting by Ear (with Michael Berry and D. W. E. Brock), 1937; Animal Language (with Julian Huxley), 1938; Memoirs of a Birdman, 1955; Bird Song (text and recording by Ludwig Koch), 1960. (ed) Encyclopedia of British Birds, 1955. *Address:* Bird Cottage, 39 Walton Avenue, South Harrow, Mddx.

**KODICEK, Egon Hynek,** MD Prague, PhD Cantab; FIBiol; Director of Dunn Nutritional Laboratory, Medical Research Council and University of Cambridge, since 1963; *b* 3 Aug. 1908; *s* of Emma and Samuel Kodicek, MD; *m* 1936, Jindriska E. M. Hradecká, MD, DOMS; two *d*. *Educ:* Charles Univ., Medical Sch., Prague; Trinity Coll., Cambridge. MD Prague, 1932; Diploma of Specialist for Internal Diseases and Metabolic Disorders, Prague, 1938; PhD Cantab., 1942. Charles Univ., Prague: clinical and experimental research work in Endocrinology, and Nutrition, 1932-39; Demonstrator, Dept of Internal Medicine, 1932-34; Asst-Physician, 1934-38; Physician-in-Charge, Endocrinological Outpatient Unit, Dept of Internal Medicine, 1938-39. Scholar of Soc. for Protection of Science and Learning, 1939; Mem. Scientific Staff, MRC, 1947-. Vis. Lectr, Harvard, Yale, Columbia and University of California, 1952, 1958; Lectr, under Nicolaysen Scheme, University of Oslo, 1964. Mem. Cttee of Biochemical Soc., 1961-65; Mem. Council of Nutrition Soc., 1964-67, 1968-; Hon. Mem., Amer. Inst. of Nutrition, 1969-. *Publications:* scientific papers in Biochemical Jl, Jl of General Microbiology, and other British and foreign scientific jls. *Address:* Dunn Nutritional Laboratory, Milton Road, Cambridge. *T:* Cambridge 63356; 11 Bulstrode Gardens, Cambridge. *T:* Cambridge 57321.

**KOECHLIN, Patricia Rosemary,** OBE 1956; Member of British Show Jumping Team; *b* 22 Nov. 1928; *d* of late Capt. Eric Hamilton Smythe, MC, Légion d'Honneur, and late Frances Monica Smythe (*née* Curtoys); *m* 1963, Samuel Koechlin, Switzerland; two *d*. *Educ:* St Michael's Sch., Cirencester; Talbot Heath, Bournemouth. Show Jumping: first went abroad with British Team, 1947; Leading Show Jumper of the Year, 1949, 1958 (with T. Edgar), and 1962; European Ladies' Championship: Spa, 1957; Deauville, 1961; Madrid, 1962; Hickstead, 1963; Harringay: BSJA Spurs, 1949, 1951, 1952, 1954 (Victor Ludorum Championship), 1953 and 1954; Harringay Spurs, 1953; Grand Prix, Brussels, 1949, 1952 and 1956. Ladies' record for high jump (2 m. 10 cm.) Paris, 1950; won in Madrid, 1951. White City: 1951 (Country Life Cup); 1953 (Selby Cup). Was Leading Rider and won Prix du Champion, Paris, 1952; Leading Rider, etc, Marseilles, 1953; Individual Championship, etc, Harrisburg, Penn, USA, 1953; Pres. of Mexico Championship, New York, 1953; Toronto (in team winning Nations Cup), 1953; Lisbon (won 2 events), Grand Prix, Madrid, and Championship, Vichy, 1954;

Grand Prix de Paris and 3 other events, 1954; Bruxelles Puissance and new ladies' record for high jump (2m. 20 cm.), Leading Rider of Show, 1954; BHS Medal of Honour, Algiers Puissance and Grand Prix, 4 events in Paris, 4 events at White City including the Championship, 1955; Grand Prix and Leading Rider of Show and 4 other events, Brussels, 1956; Grand Prix Militaire and Puissance, Lucerne; Mem. British Equestrian Olympic Team, Stockholm (Show Jumping Bronze Medal), 1956; IHS National Championship, White City; Leading Rider and other events, Palermo, 1956; won 2 Puissance events, Paris, 1957; BSJA, 1957; Ladies' National Championship in 1954-59 and 1961 and 1962 (8 times); Daily Mail Cup, White City, 1955, 1957, 1960, 1962; Mem. winning British Team, White City: 1952, 1953, 1956, 1957; Amazon Prize, Aachen, 1958; Queen's Cup, Royal Internat. Horse Show, White City, 1958; Preis von Parsenn, Davos, 1957, 1958, 1959; Championship Cup, Brussels Internat. Horse Show, 1958; Lisbon Grand Prix, 1959; Olympic Trial, British Timken Show, and Prix de la Banque de Bruxelles at Brussels, 1959. Lucerne Grand Prix; Prince Hal Stakes, Country Life and Riding Cup, White City; Pembroke Stakes, Horse Show Cttee Cup, and Leading Rider, Dublin (all in 1960). Mem. British Olympic Team in Rome, 1960. Copenhagen Grand Prix; Amazon Prize, Aachen; John Player Trophy, White City; St Gall Ladies Championship (all in 1961); Saddle of Honour and Loriners' Cup, White City, 1962; British Jumping Derby, Hickstead, 1962. Hon. Freeman, Worshipful Co. of Farriers, 1955; Freeman of the City of London, 1956; Hon. Freeman, Worshipful Company of Loriners, 1962; Yeoman, Worshipful Company of Saddlers, 1963. *Publications:* (as Pat Smythe): Jump for Joy; Pat Smythe's Story, 1954; Pat Smythe's Book of Horses, 1955; One Jump Ahead, 1956; Jacqueline rides for a Fall, 1957; Three Jays against the Clock, 1957; Three Jays on Holiday, 1958; Three Jays go to Town, 1959; Horses and Places, 1959; Three Jays over the Border, 1960; Three Jays go to Rome, 1960; Three Jays Lend a Hand, 1961; Jumping Round the World, 1962; Florian's Farmyard, 1962; Flanagan My Friend, 1963; Bred to Jump, 1965; Show Jumping, 1967; (with Fiona Hughes) A Pony for Pleasure, 1969; A Swiss Adventure, 1970. *Recreations:* tennis, swimming, music, ski-ing, sailing, all sports, languages. *Address:* Sudgrove House, Miserden, near Stroud, Glos. *T:* Miserden 360; Im Steinacker, 4149 Burg-im-Leimental, BE, Switzerland. *T:* Basle 751411. *Club:* Lansdowne.

**KOELLE, Vice-Adm. (retired) Sir Harry (Philpot)**, KCB 1959 (CB 1957); *b* 16 Aug. 1901; *s* of late Rev. C. Philpot Koelle, Rector of Wickford, Essex, and Durley, Hampshire; *m* 1st, 1930, Enid (*d* 1942), *d* of C. F. Corbould Ellis, JP, Reading; one *d*; 2nd, 1948, Elizabeth Anne, *d* of late Sir Philip Devitt, 1st and last Bt; two *d*. *Educ:* Rossall; RN Colleges, Osborne and Dartmouth. Joined RN 1915. Served HMS Bellerophon and Renown, 1917-18. Served War of 1939-45: HMS Royal Soverign and Duke of York; Deputy Dir of Manning, Admiralty, 1945-48. Dir of Welfare and Service Conditions, Admiralty, 1953-55; Command Supply Officer, Plymouth, 1955-57; Dir-General Supply and Secretariat Branch, Admiralty, 1957-60. Comdr 1938; Capt. 1948; Rear-Adm. 1955; retired 1960. *Recreation:* racing. *Address:* Mill House, Thornford, near Sherborne, Dorset. *Club:* Army and Navy.

**KOENIGSBERGER, Prof. Franz**, DSc, DrIngEh; FIMechE; Professor of Machine Tool Engineering, University of Manchester Institute of Science and Technology, since 1961; *b* 9 Nov. 1907; *s* of Hans and Margaret Koenigsberger; *m* 1934, Lilli Gertrude Kate (*née* Schlesinger); one *s* one *d*. *Educ:* Goethe-Schule, Berlin; Technische Hochschule, Berlin-Charlottenburg. Research Asst for Machine Tools, Technische Hochschule, Berlin-Charlottenburg, 1931-32; Draughtsman and Designer of machine tools, 1932-35; Chief Designer and Chief Engr, Machine Tool Dept, Ansaldo SA, Genoa, 1936-38; Chief Mech. Engr, Cooke & Ferguson Ltd, Manchester, 1939-47; Lectr in Mech. Engrg, 1947-54; Sen. Lectr in Prod. Engrg, 1954-57; Reader in Machine Tools and Prod. Processes, The Manchester Coll. of Science and Technoloy, 1957-61. Jt Editor-in-Chief, Internat. Jl for Machine Tool Design and Research. Pres. Manchester Assoc. of Engineers, 1965-66; Pres., Internat. Inst. of Prod. Engrg Research (CIRP), 1965-66. Thomas Lowe Gray Prize, 1944, and Water Arbitration Prize, 1951, of Instn of Mech. Engrs; Constantine Medal, 1956, and Butterworth Medal, 1961, of Manchester Assoc. of Engineers. *Publications:* Design for Welding, 1948; Welding Technology, 1949 (1953, 1961); Spanende Werkzeugmaschinen, 1961; Design Principles of Metal Cutting Machine Tools, 1964; (with J. T. Lusty) Machine Tool Structures, 1970; (with C. Ruiz) Design for Strength and Production, 1970; papers in Proceedings Institution Mechanical Engineers, The Production Engineer, Welding Jl, British Welding Jl. *Recreations:* music, photography. *Address:* 15 Peel Moat Road, Heaton Moor, Stockport SK4 4PL. *T:* 061-432 4677.

**KOENIGSBERGER, Prof. Helmut Georg**, MA, PhD; Professor of Early Modern European History, Cornell University, USA, since 1966; *b* 24 Oct. 1918; *s* of late Georg Felix Koenigsberger, chief architect, borough of Treptow, Berlin, Germany, and of late Käthe Koenigsberger (*née* Born); *m* 1961, Dorothy M. Romano; two *d* (twins). *Educ:* Adams' Grammar Sch., Newport, Shropshire; Gonville and Caius Coll., Cambridge. Asst Master: Brentwood Sch., Essex, 1941-42; Bedford Sch., 1942-44. Served War of 1939-45, Royal Navy, 1944-45. Lecturer in Economic History, QUB, 1948-51; Senior Lecturer in Economic History, University of Manchester, 1951-60; Prof. of Modern History, University of Nottingham, 1960-66. Visiting Lecturer: Brooklyn Coll., New York, 1957; University of Wisconsin, 1958; Columbia University, 1962; Washington Univ., St Louis, 1964. Sec., Internat. Commn for the History of Representative and Parliamentary Institutions, 1955-. *Publications:* The Government of Sicily under Philip II of Spain, 1951, new edn, as The Practice of Empire, 1969; The Empire of Charles V in Europe (in New Cambridge Modern History II), 1958; Western Europe and the Power of Spain (in New Cambridge Modern History III), 1968; Europe in the Sixteenth Century (with G. L. Mosse), 1968; Estates and Revolutions, 1970; The Habsburgs and Europe, 1516-1660, 1971; contrib. to historical journals. *Recreations:* playing chamber music, sailing, travel. *Address:* Department of History, Cornell University, Ithaca, New York 14850, USA.

**KOESTLER, Arthur**, MInstPI, FRSL; author; *b* Budapest, Hungary, 5 Sept. 1905; *o s* of Henrik and Adela Koestler; *m* 1935, Dorothy Asher, Zürich; divorced 1950; no *c*; *m* 1950, Mamaine Paget; divorced 1953; no *c*; *m* 1965, Cynthia Jefferies. *Educ:* University of Vienna. Foreign Correspondent in Middle East, Paris, Berlin, 1926-31; Mem. of Graf Zeppelin Arctic Expedition, 1931; travels in Russia and Soviet

Central Asia, 1932-33; covering the Spanish Civil War for News Chronicle, London, 1936-37; imprisoned by General Franco; served 1939-40 in French Foreign Legion and 1941-42 in British Pioneer Corps. Fellow, Centre for Advanced Study in the Behavioural Sciences, Stanford, 1964-65. Hon. LLD Queen's Univ., Kingston, Ont, 1968. Sonning Prize, 1968. *Publications:* Spanish Testament, 1938; The Gladiators, 1939; Darkness at Noon, 1940; Scum of the Earth, 1941; Arrival and Departure, 1943; The Yogi and the Commissar, 1945; Twilight Bar, 1945; Thieves in the Night, 1946; Insight and Outlook, 1948; The God that Failed (with others), 1949; Promise and Fulfilment, 1949; The Age of Longing, 1950; Arrow in the Blue, 1952; The Invisible Writing, 1954; The Trail of the Dinosaur, 1955; Reflections on Hanging, 1956; The Sleepwalkers, 1959; The Lotus and the Robot, 1960; Suicide of a Nation? (ed), 1963; The Act of Creation, 1964; The Ghost in the Machine, 1967; Drinkers of Infinity, 1968; (ed with J. R. Smythies) Beyond Reductionism–New Perspectives in the Life Sciences: The Alpbach Symposium 1968, 1969. *Relevant Publications:* Arthur Koestler, by John Atkins, 1956; Arthur Koestler, Das Literarische Werk, by Peter Alfred Huber, Zürich, 1962. *Recreations:* canoeing, chess, good wine. *Address:* c/o A. D. Peters, 10 Buckingham Street, WC2.

**KOHAN, Major Charles Mendel,** OBE, MA; Barrister-at-Law, retired; *b* 15 Nov. 1884; *y s* of M. Kohan and *g s* of G. J. Bloomfield, Chapel-en-le-Frith, Derbyshire; *m* 1932, Ethel May Ashford. *Educ:* Manchester Grammar Sch.; Trinity Coll., Cambridge (Open Scholarship for History; Hons, Parts I and II, Historical Tripos; Chancellor's Medal for English Verse). Asst Sec. to the Royal Statistical Society, 1909-14. Served in Royal Artillery, 1914-19 (Western Front), and on the General Staff, Headquarters, Fourth Army, BEF, 1918-19 (OBE); called to Bar, Inner Temple, 1919; late Hon. Sec. Mansion House Council on Health and Housing; Commission in Army Emergency Reserve, Sept., 1939; transferred to Offices of the War Cabinet, 1942; an Official Historian in the Cabinet Secretariat, 1944-52; Dir, New Health Trust, 1952. *Publications:* History of the Second World War (Civil Series): Works and Buildings, 1952. Miscellaneous contributions to the Press. *Recreations:* fishing, motoring, amateur drama. *Address:* 2 Penn Mead, Penn, Bucks. *T:* Penn 2719. *Clubs:* Royal Automobile, United and Cecil.

**KOHLER, Foy David;** Professor, Center for Advanced International Studies, University of Miami, since 1967; *b* 15 Feb. 1908; *s* of Leander David Kohler and Myrtle McClure; *m* 1935, Phyllis Penn. *Educ:* Toledo and Ohio State Univs, Ohio. US Foreign Service: posts include (1932-): Amer. Emb., London, 1944; Adviser to US Mem., 2nd Session of Council of UN Relief and Rehabilitation Admin., Montreal, Can., Sept. 1944; 1st Sec. Amer. Emb., Moscow, 1947; Counselor, 1948; Minister, Oct. 1948; Chief, Internat. Broadcasting Div., Dept of State, 1949; VOA 1949; Asst Administr, Internat. Information Admin, 1952; Policy Planning Staff, Dept of State, 1952; Counselor, Amer. Emb., Ankara, Turkey, 1953-56; detailed ICA, 1956-58; Deputy Asst Sec. of State for European Affairs, 1958-59; Asst Sec. of State, 1959-62; US Ambassador to USSR, 1962-66; Deputy Under-Sec. of State for Political Affairs, United States, 1966-67; Career Ambassador, USA, 1966-67 (Career Minister, Foreign Service of USA, 1959). Holds honorary doctorates. *Publication:* Understanding the Russians: a citizen's primer, 1970. *Recreations:* golf, badminton, ping-pong. *Address:* 215 Golf Club Circle, Village of Tequesta, Jupiter, Fla 33458, USA.

**KOHLER, Irene;** pianist; Professor, Trinity College of Music, London; *b* London. *Educ:* Royal College of Music. Studied with Arthur Benjamin (Challen Medal, Danreuther Prize, etc); travelling scholarship to Vienna; studied there with Edward Steuermann and Egon Wellesz. BMus; Hon. FTCL, GRSM, LRAM, ARCM. First professional engagement, Bournemouth, 1933, resulting in engagement by BBC; played at first night of 40th Promenade Season, 1934. First foreign tour (recitals and broadcasts), Holland, 1938. During War of 1939-45 gave concerts for the Forces in this country and toured France and Belgium, also India and Burma, under auspices of ENSA; subsequently played in many countries of Europe and made tours. Eugene Goossens selected her for first European performance of his Phantasy Concerto. She gave 3 concerts at the Festival Hall in Festival of Britain Year, 1951. Canadian American Tour, 1953; World Tour, 1955-56; African Tour, 1958; 2nd African Tour, 1959; Bulgarian Tour, 1959; 2nd World Tour, 1962; Czechoslovakian Tour, 1963. Film appearances include: Train of Events, Odette, Secret People, Lease of Life, and a documentary for the Ministry of Information. *Address:* 28 Castelnau, SW13. *T:* 01-748 5512.

**KOHOBAN-WICKREME, Alfred Silva,** CVO 1954; Member Ceylon Civil Service; Secretary to the Cabinet, since 1968; *b* 2 Nov. 1914; *m* 1941, Mona Estelle Kohoban-Wickreme. *Educ:* Trinity Coll., Kandy; University Coll., Colombo. BA (Hons) London, 1935. Cadet, Ceylon Civil Service, 1938; served as Magistrate, District Judge, Asst Govt Agent etc, until 1948; Chief Admin. Officer, Ceylon Govt Rly, 1948; Asst Sec., Min. of Home Affairs, 1951; attached to Ceylon High Commissioner's Office in UK, May-July, 1953; Dir of Social Services and Commissioner for Workmen's Compensation, Ceylon, 1953; Conservator of Forests, Ceylon, 1958; Port Commissioner, Ceylon, 1959; Postmaster General and Dir of Telecommunications, Dec. 1962; Permanent Sec., Ministry of: Local Govt and Home Affairs, April 1964; Cultural Affairs and Social Services, June 1964; Ministry of Communications, 1965. Organised the Queen's Tour in Ceylon, April 1954 (CVO). *Recreations:* sports activities, particularly Rugby football, tennis and cricket. *Address:* 6 Kalinga Place, Jawatta Road, Colombo 5, Ceylon. *T:* (office) 25337, (residence) 86385.

**KOHT, Paul;** Ambassador of Norway to the Court of St James's since 1968; *b* 7 Dec. 1913; *s* of Dr Halvdan Koht and Karen Elisabeth (*née* Grude); *m* 1938, Grete Sverdrup; two *s* one *d*. *Educ:* University of Oslo. Law degree, 1937. Entered Norwegian Foreign Service, 1938; held posts in: Bucharest, 1938-39; London, 1940-41; Tokyo, 1941-42; New York, 1942-46; Lisbon, 1950-51; Mem. Norwegian Delegn to OEEC and NATO, Paris, and Perm. Rep. to Coun. of Europe, 1951-53; Dir General of Dept for Econ. Affairs, Min. of For. Affairs, Oslo, 1953-56; Chargé d'Affaires, Copenhagen, 1956-58; Ambassador to USA, 1958-63; Ambassador to Fed. Republic of Germany, 1963-68. Comdr, Order of St Olav; Comdr 1st Class, Order of Dannebrog; Grand Cross, Order of Merit (Federal Republic of Germany). *Address:* 10 Palace Green, W8. *T:* 01-937 2247.

**KOKOSCHKA, Oskar,** CBE 1959; artist and writer; *b* Pöchlarn, Austria, 1 March 1886; *m*

Olda (*née* Palkovsky); British subject since 1947. *Educ:* Vienna Sch. of Industrial Art. Worked in Vienna from 1905; in Berlin, 1910, joined group of expressionist painters; first one-man exhibn, Paul Cassirer's Gall., 1910; contrib. to Der Sturm. Served as Cavalry Officer, Russian and Italian fronts, 1915-17 (wounded). Prof. Acad. of Art, Dresden, 1919-24; travelled throughout Europe, North Africa and Near East, painting landscapes and panoramic views of cities, 1924-31; returned to Vienna, 1931; to Prague, 1934, became a Czech citizen; works included in Nazi exhibn of "Degenerate Art", Munich, 1937; to England, 1938; Founder, Internat. Summer Acad. of Fine Arts, Salzburg, and has taught there since 1953. Has held one-man exhibns in Austria, Germany, Italy, Holland, France, Switzerland, USA, etc.; in Great Britain: Tate Gallery, 1962; Marlborough Fine Art Galleries, 1967, 1969. Order of Merit of Federal Republic of Germany, 1956. Winner of the Rome Prize, 1960; Erasmus Prize (jt), 1960; Hon. DLitt Oxon, 1963. Freedom of Vienna, Salzburg and Pöchlarn. *Works include:* portraits, landscapes, illustrations, compositions (politically symbolic works, etc.). *Publications:* A Sea ringed with Visions (short stories), 1962; *Plays:* Mörder, Hoffnung der Frauen, 1907; Der brennende Dornbusch, Hiob, 1911; Orpheus and Eurydice, 1916, etc. *Relevant Publication:* Oskar Kokoschka: The Artist and his Time, by J. P. Hodin, 1966. *Address:* 1844 Villeneuve, Vaud, Switzerland.

**KOLBUSZEWSKI, Professor Janusz,** DSc (Eng), PhD, DIC, FICE; Professor of Transportation and Environmental Planning and Head of Department, University of Birmingham, since 1965 (Professor of Highway and Traffic Engineering, 1959-64, of Transportation, 1964-65); *b* 18 Feb. 1915; *s* of Jan Alexander and Bronislawa Kolbuszewski; *m* 1946, Marie-Louise Jasinska; one *s* one *d*. *Educ:* Technical University of Lwow, Poland (DiplIng); Imperial Coll. of Science and Technology, University of London. PhDEng, London, 1948; DIC 1948; DSc(Eng), London, 1968. Lecturer, Technical Univ. of Lwow, Poland, until 1939. Served War of 1939-45: Polish, French and British Armies. Imperial Coll. Science and Technology, London, 1945-48; Prof., Dir of Studies, Polish University Coll., London, 1948-50; Lecturer, Sen. Lecturer, Reader, in charge of Graduate Schs in Foundation Engrg and in Highway and Traffic Engineering, University of Birmingham, 1951-59. Member: Civil Engrg and Aero Cttee, SRC, 1967; Research Cttee, ICE, 1966. Governor, Birmingham Coll. of Arts. Hon. Mem., Midlands Soc. for Soil Mechanics and Foundn Engrg. Lister Prize, Midland Branch of IStructE, 1953; Nusey Prize, Soc. of Engineers, London, 1967. *Publications:* various scientific papers on Geometry, Perspective, Soil Mechanics, Foundations and Highway Engineering, Transportation and Planning. *Recreations:* travelling, oil painting. *Address:* 87 Wellington Road, Edgbaston, Birmingham 15. *T:* 021-440 0343.

**KOLHAPUR, Maharaja of; Maj.-Gen. HH Sir Shahaji Chhatrapati,** (adopted these names in lieu of those of Vikramsinha Rao Puar, on succeeding); GCSI, 1947 (KCSI, 1941); *b* 4 April 1910. Formerly Maharaja of Dewas (Senior Branch); succeeded as Maharaja of Kolhapur, 1947; State merged with Bombay, 1949. Appointed Major and Hon. ADC to HM King Emperor George VI, 1946; Hon. Maj.-Gen. Indian Army, 1962. *Address:* Kolhapur, Maharashtra, India.

**KOLLER, Prof. Pius Charles,** PhD, DSC; Professor Emeritus, University of London, since 1969 (Professor of Cytogenetics, Institute of Cancer Research, University of London, 1954-69, retired); *b* 3 April 1904; *m* 1946, Anna Edith Olsen, Denmark; three *d*. *Educ:* Universities of Budapest, Cambridge and Edinburgh. PhD Budapest, 1926; DSc Edinburgh, 1934. Rockefeller Fellow, Pasadena, Calif, 1936-37; Lecturer, University of Edinburgh, 1938-44; Research Cytologist, Royal Cancer Hospital, 1944-46, and Chester Beatty Research Inst., 1946-54. *Publications:* Chromosomes and Genes; Chromosome Breakage: a chapter in Progress in Biophysics; numerous scientific papers in Jl of Genetics, Heredity, Brit. Jl of Cancer etc. *Recreations:* music, reading. *Address:* 68 Rosemont Road, W3. *T:* 01-992 6440.

**KOMINSKI, Daniel;** *see* Kaye, Danny.

**KONOVALOV, Sergey,** MA Oxon, BLitt Oxon; Professor of Russian in the University of Oxford, 1945-67, now Emeritus; Emeritus Fellow of New College, Oxford; *b* Moscow, 31 Oct. 1899; *s* of Alexander Konovalov, Minister of Trade and Industry in Russian Provisional Government of 1917, and of Nadejda Vtorov; *m* 1949, Janina Ryzowa. *Educ:* Classical Lycée, Moscow; Exeter Coll., Oxford (Diploma in Economics and Political Science 1921, BLitt 1927; MA 1936). Professor of Russian Language and Literature, University of Birmingham, 1929-45; Lecturer in Slavonic Studies, University of Oxford, 1930-45; Hon. Lecturer at University of London (Sch. of Slavonic Studies), 1931-32, 1940-41. Mem. Internat. Cttee of Slavists, 1958-68. *Publications:* Anthology of Contemporary Russian Literature, 1932; editor and contributor Birmingham Russian Memoranda, 1931-40; co-editor Birmingham Polish Monographs, 1936-39, and Bibliographies of Research Work in Slavonic Countries, 1932-34; article Soviet Union in Encyclopædia Britannica Year-Book, 1941; Russo-Polish Relationsan Historical Survey (in collaboration), 1945; editor of Blackwell's Russian Texts, and of the OUP's Russian Readers and Oxford Slavonic Papers, Vols I-XIII, 1950-67. *Address:* 175 Divinity Road, Oxford.

**KOO, Vi Kyuin Wellington;** Judge of International Court of Justice, 1957-67 (Vice-President, 1964-67); *b* 1888. *Educ:* Columbia Univ. (Doctor of Philosophy). Sec. to Pres. of China; Councillor in Foreign Office; Minister to USA, 1915; attended Peace Conference as China's Plenipotentiary, and later as Head of the Chinese Delegation, 1919; Chinese delegate to the Assembly and China's representative on the Council of the League of Nations at Geneva, 1920-22; Chinese Minister to Great Britain, 1921; Plenipotentiary to Washington Conference, 1921-22; Minister of Foreign Affairs, Peking, 1922-24; Finance Minister, 1926; Prime Minister and Minister of Foreign Affairs, 1926-27; Mem. on the International Court of Arbitration at the Hague, 1927-57; Minister of Foreign Affairs, China, 1931; Chinese Assessor to the Commission of Inquiry of the League of Nations, 1932; Chinese Minister to France, 1932-35; Chinese Ambassador to France, 1936-41; Chinese Ambassador in London, 1941-46; Chinese representative on the Council of the League of Nations at Geneva, 1932-34; Delegate 13th and 14th Assemblies of League of Nations and to the Special Assembly of the League of Nations, 1932-33; Delegate to the World Monetary and Economic Conference, London, 1933; Delegate to Conference for Reduction and Limitation of Armaments, at

Geneva, 1933; Chief Delegate to Assemblies of League of Nations, 1935-36 and 1938; Delegate to sessions of League Coun., 1937-39 (Pres. 96th); Chief Deleg. to Brussels Conference, Nov. 1937; Special Envoy to coronation of His Holiness Pius XII; Ambassador Extraordinary to 800th Anniversary of Foundation of Portugal, 1940; Chinese Ambassador in Washington, 1946-56; Senior Advisor to General Chiang Kai-Shek, 1956-57, 1967-. *Publications:* Status of Aliens in China, 1912; Memorandum presented to Lytton Commission (3 volumes), 1932. *Recreations:* ski-ing, tennis, golf, fishing. *Address:* 1185 Park Avenue, New York, NY 10028, USA.

**KOOTENAY, Bishop of,** since 1966; **Rt. Rev. Edward Walter Scott;** *b* Edmonton, Alberta; *s* of Tom Walter Scott and Kathleen Frances Ford; *m* 1942, Isabel Florence Brannan; one *s* three *d*. *Educ:* Univ. of British Columbia; Anglican Theological Coll. of BC. Vicar of St Peter's, Seal Cove, 1943-45; SCM Secretary, Univ. of Manitoba, 1945-49; Staff of St John's Coll., Winnipeg, 1947-48; Rector: St John the Baptist, Fort Garry, 1949-55; St Jude's, Winnipeg, 1955-60; Dir, Diocesan Council for Social Service, Diocese of Rupertsland, and Priest Dir of Indian Work, 1960-64; Associate Sec., Council for Social Service, Anglican Church of Canada, 1964-66. *Recreation:* carpentry. *Address:* 1429 Alta Vista, Kelowna, BC, Canada. *T:* 762 2923.

**KOPAL, Prof. Zdenek;** Professor of Astronomy, University of Manchester, since 1951; *b* 4 April 1914; 2nd *s* of Prof. Joseph Kopal, of Charles University, Prague, and Ludmila (*née* Lelek); *m* 1938, Alena, *o d* of late Judge B. Muldner; three *d*. *Educ:* Charles University, Prague; University of Cambridge, England; Harvard Univ., USA. Agassiz Research Fellow, Harvard Observatory, 1938-40; Research Associate in Astronomy, Harvard Univ., 1940-46; Lecturer in Astronomy, Harvard Univ., 1948; Associate Prof., Mass Institute of Technology, 1947-51. Vice-Pres., Foundation Internationale du Pic-du-Midi; Mem. Internat. Acad. of Astronautical Sciences, New York Acad. of Sciences; Chm., Cttee for Lunar and Planetary Exploration, Brit. Nat. Cttee for Space Research; Mem. Lunar-Planetary Cttee, US Nat. Space Bd. Editor-in-Chief, Astrophysics and Space Science, 1968-; Editor: Icarus (internat. jl of solar system); The Moon (internat. jl of lunar studies), 1969-. Gold Medal, Czechoslovak Acad. of Sciences, 1969. *Publications:* An Introduction to the Study of Eclipsing Variables, 1946 (US); The Computation of Elements of Eclipsing Binary Systems, 1950 (US); Tables of Supersonic Flow of Air Around Cones, 3 vols, 1947-49 (US); Numerical Analysis (London), 1955; Astronomical Optics (Amsterdam), 1956; Close Binary Systems, 1959; Figures of Equilibrium of Celestial Bodies, 1960; The Moon, 1960; Physics and Astronomy of the Moon, 1962; Photographic Atlas of the Moon, 1965; An Introduction to the Study of the Moon, 1966; The Measure of the Moon, 1967; (ed) Advances in Astronomy and Astrophysics, 1968. Over 180 original papers on astronomy, aerodynamics, and applied mathematics in publications of Harvard Observatory, Astrophysical Journal, Astronomical Journal, Astronomische Nachrichten, Monthly Notices of Royal Astronomical Society, Proc. Amer. Phil. Soc., Proc. Nat. Acad. Sci. (US), Zeitschrift für Astrophysik, etc. *Recreation:* mountaineering. *Address:* Greenfield, Parkway, Wilmslow, Cheshire. *T:* Wilmslow 22470.

**KOREA, Diocese of;** divided in 1965 into the two dioceses of Seoul, *qv* and Taejon, *qv*.

**KORNBERG, Prof. Arthur;** Professor of Biochemistry, Stanford University, and Head of Department of Biochemistry, since 1959; *b* Brooklyn, 3 March 1918; *s* of Joseph Kornberg and Lena Katz; *m* 1943, Sylvy R. Levy; three *s*. *Educ:* College of the City of New York (BSc 1937); University of Rochester, NY (MD 1941). Strong Memorial Hospital, Rochester, 1941-42; National Insts of Health, Bethesda, Md, 1942-52; Guest Research Worker, New York Univ., 1946, Washington Univ., 1947, University of California, 1951; Professor of Microbiology, Washington Univ., and Head of Dept of Microbiology, 1953-59. Commissioned Officer, US Public Health Service, 1942; Medical Dir, 1951. MNAS; MAAS; Mem. Amer. Phil Soc. Foreign Mem., Royal Soc., 1970. Paul Lewis Award in Enzyme Chemistry, 1951; Nobel Prize (joint) in Medicine, 1959. Hon. LLD, City Coll. of New York, 1960; Hon. DSc, University of Rochester, 1962; Hon. LHD, Yeshiva Univ., 1962. *Publications:* articles in scientific jls. *Address:* 365 Golden Oak Drive, Alpine Hills, Portola Valley, Calif, USA; Stanford University School of Medicine, Palo Alto, Calif.

**KORNBERG, Prof. Hans Leo,** MA, DSc Oxon, PhD Sheffield; FRS 1965; FIBiol; Professor of Biochemistry, University of Leicester, since 1960; *b* 14 Jan. 1928; *o s* of Max Kornberg and Margarete Kornberg (*née* Silberbach); *m* 1956, Monica Mary (*née* King); twin *s* two *d*. *Educ:* Queen Elizabeth Grammar Sch., Wakefield; University of Sheffield. Commonwealth Fund Fellow of Harkness Foundation, at Yale University and Public Health Research Inst., New York, 1953-55; Mem. of scientific staff, MRC Cell Metabolism Res. Unit, University of Oxford, 1955-60; Lecturer of Worcester Coll., Oxford, 1958-61; Res. Associate of University of Calif, Berkeley, 1954, of Harvard Med. Sch., Boston, 1958; Visiting Instructor, Marine Biological Lab., Woods Hole, Mass, 1964, 1965, 1966; Vis. Prof., Univ. of Miami, 1970-. Member: SRC, 1967- (Chm., Science Bd, 1969-); UGC Biol. Sci. Cttee, 1967-. Colworth Medal of Biochemical Soc., 1965. CIBA Lecturer, Rutgers, NJ, 1968. *Publications:* (with Sir Hans Krebs) Energy Transformations in Living Matter; articles in scientific jls. *Recreations:* cooking and conversation. *Address:* 2 Woodland Avenue, Stoneygate, Leicester LE2 3HG. *T:* 704466.

**KÖRNER, Stephan,** FBA 1967; JurDr, PhD; Professor of Philosophy, University of Bristol, since 1952; Dean, Faculty of Arts, 1965-66; Pro-Vice-Chancellor, since 1968; *b* Ostrava, Czechoslovakia, 26 Sept. 1913; *o s* of Emil Körner and Erna (*née* Maier); *m* 1944, Edith Laner, BSc, JP; one *s* one *d*. *Educ:* Classical Gymnasium; Charles' Univ., Prague; Trinity Hall, Cambridge. Army Service, 1936-39, 1943-46. Lectr in Philosophy, University of Bristol, 1946; Visiting Prof. of Philosophy: Brown Univ., 1957; Yale Univ., 1960; Texas Univ., 1964; Indiana Univ., 1967. President: Brit. Soc. for Philosophy of Science, 1965; Aristotelian Soc., 1967; Internat. Union of History and Philosophy of Science, 1969. Editor, Ratio, 1961-. *Publications:* Kant, 1955; Conceptual Thinking, 1955; The Philosophy of Mathematics, 1960; Experience and Theory, 1966; Kant's Conception of Freedom (British Acad. Lecture), 1967; What is Philosophy?, 1969; Categorial Frameworks, 1970. Editor of Observation and Interpretation, 1957; contribs to Mind, Aristotelian Soc. Proc. and other philosophical periodicals. *Recreation:* walking. *Address:* 10 Belgrave Road, Bristol 8; University of Bristol. *T:* Bristol 33036.

**KOSSOFF, David;** actor; designer-illustrator; *b* 24 Nov. 1919; *s* of Louis and Anne Kossoff, both Russian; *m* 1947, Margaret (Jennie) Jenkins; two *s. Educ:* elementary sch.; Northern Polytechnic. Commercial Artist, 1937; Draughtsman, 1937-38; Furniture Designer, 1938-39; Technical Illustrator, 1939-45. Began acting, 1943; working as actor and illustrator, 1945-52, as actor and designer, 1952-. BBC Repertory Company, 1945-51. Took over part of Colonel Alexander Ikonenko in the Love of Four Colonels, Wyndham's, 1952; Sam Tager in The Shrike, Prince's, 1953; Morry in The Bespoke Overcoat, and Tobit in Tobias and the Angel, Arts, 1953; Prof. Lodegger in No Sign of the Dove, Savoy, 1953; Nathan in The Boychik, Embassy, 1954 (and again Morry in The Bespoke Overcoat); Mendele in The World of Sholom Aleichem, Embassy, 1955, and Johannesburg, 1957; one-man show, One Eyebrow Up, The Arts, 1957; Man on Trial, Lyric, 1959; Stars in Your Eyes, Palladium, 1960; The Tenth Man, Comedy, 1961; Come Blow Your Horn, Prince of Wales, 1962; one-man show, Kossoff at the Prince Charles, 1963, later called A Funny Kind of Evening (many countries); Enter Solly Gold, Mermaid, 1970; own Bible storytelling programmes on radio and TV, as writer and teller, 1964-66. Has appeared in many films. Won British Acad. Award, 1956. Elected MSIA 1958. FRSA 1969. *Play:* Big Night for Shylock, 1968. *Publication:* Bible Stories retold by David Kossoff, 1968. *Recreations:* conversation, watching other actors work. *Address:* 15 Hayes Crescent, NW11.

**KOSTELANETZ, André;** orchestra conductor; *b* Leningrad, Russia; *s* of Nachman Kostelanetz and Rosalie Dimscha; *m* 1938, Lily Pons, *qv. Educ:* St Peter's Sch.; St Petersburg Conservatory of Music. Hon. MusD: Albion Coll., Albion, Mich, 1939; Cincinnati Conservatory of Music, 1945. Came to United States 1922, naturalised 1928. For many years conducted own shows over Columbia Broadcasting System; directed music for several motion pictures; selected by radio editors of US and Canada for Fame Award as leading conductor for several years running. Made overseas tours conducting soldier orchestras organized and trained by him, N Africa, Persian Gulf, Italian Theatre, summer 1944; China, Burma, India and European theatres, winter 1944-45. Regular guest conductor with all leading orchestras in US (New York Philharmonic, Boston Symphony, Philadelphia Orchestra, San Francisco Symphony, etc), Canada, S America and Europe. Inaugurated Special Non-Subscription Concerts of New York Philharmonic Orchestra, 1953. Records with his own orchestra for Columbia Records. Awarded Asiatic-Pacific ribbon by Army for overseas services. *Address:* c/o Columbia Broadcasting System, 485 Madison Avenue, New York, NY 10022, USA.

**KOSYGIN, Alexei Nikolaevich;** Hero of Socialist Labour; Order of Lenin (four times); Order of Gold Star "Hammer and Sickle"; Order of the Red Banner; Chairman, Council of Ministers of the Union of Soviet Socialist Republics, since 1964; Member, Politburo of the Central Committee of the Communist Party since 1966 (also Member, 1948-52); *b* 1904. *Educ:* Leningrad Textile Institute; Leningrad Co-operative Technical Sch. Worker in Irkutsk Regional Co-operative Union and other co-op. organisations, 1924-29; Shop Superintendent, Zhelyabov Factory, Leningrad, 1935-37; Dir, October Textile Mills, Leningrad, 1937-38; Chm. Leningrad City Council, 1938-39; Deputy to Supreme Soviet, 1938; People's Commissar of Textile Industry, 1939-40; Vice-Chm. Council of People's Commissars of the USSR, 1940-46; Chm. Council of People's Commissars of RSFSR, 1943-46; Vice-Chm., Council of Ministers of the USSR, 1946-60; Minister: of Finance, 1948; of Light Industry, 1949-54; Chm., State Planning Commission, 1959-60; a First Vice-Chm., 1960-64, Council of Ministers of USSR. Mem. of Communist Party, 1927-; Mem. Central Cttee, of Communist Party, 1939-; Candidate Mem., Politburo of Central Cttee of Communist Party 1946-48; Mem. of the Presidium, 1952-53 and 1957-66. *Address:* Council of Ministers, The Kremlin, Moscow, USSR.

**KOTCH, Mrs John Keith;** *see* Purden, R. L.

**KOTELAWALA, Col Rt. Hon. Sir John (Lionel),** PC 1954; CH 1956; KBE 1948; *m*; one *d. Educ:* Christ's Coll., Cambridge; Royal College, Colombo. Mem. State Council, 1931; Minister for Communications and Works, 1935; Minister for Transport and Works, 1947; Prime Minister and Minister of Defence and External Affairs, Ceylon, 1953-56. LLD University of Ceylon. Grand Cross, Legion of Honour (France), 1954; Grand Cross, Order of Merit (Italy), 1954; Grand Cross, Order of Rising Sun (Japan), 1954; Grand Cross, Order of Merit (Germany), 1955; Grand Cross, Order of White Elephant (Thailand), 1955. *Publication:* An Asian Prime Minister's Story, 1956. *Recreations:* polo, tennis, riding. *Address:* Brogues Wood, Biddenden, Kent; Ratmalana, Ceylon. *Clubs:* Orient, Royal Aero, No 10 (Institute of Directors); Sinhalese Sports; Eighty.

**KOTHAVALA, Tehmasp Tehmul,** CIE 1943; retired; *b* 6 Feb. 1893; *s* of Tehmul R. Kothavala; *m* 1918, Shernaz Munchershaw Disana; two *s* one *d. Educ:* Baroda and St Xavier's Colls. Graduated, 1915; MA 1916; BSc 1916; joined Bombay Civil Service, 1919; Sec. to Government Bombay Revenue Dept, 1936; Collector, Bijapur, 1938; Revenue Officer, Loyd Barrage, Sind, 1939; Collector, Sukkur, 1940; Sec., Provincial Transport Authority and Motor Transport Controller for the Province of Bombay, from 1941; Settlement Commissioner, Dir Land Records and Inspector-Gen. of Registration for the Province of Bombay, 1948-50. Adviser to HH the Maharaja of Kolahpur, 1954; Public Relations Adviser, Wandleside National Conductors, 1964. *Recreations:* riding, shooting, natural history. *Address:* Yeravda, Poona. *Clubs:* Willingdon Sports (Bombay); Western India Turf, Poona (Poona).

**KOTSOKOANE, Joseph Riffat Larry;** Permanent Secretary and Head of the Diplomatic Service, Lesotho, since 1969; *b* 19 Oct. 1922; *s* of Basotho parents, living in Johannesburg, South Africa; *m* 1947, Elizabeth (*née* Molise); two *s* three *d.* BSc (SA); BSc Hons (Witwatersrand); Cert. Agric. (London). Development Officer, Dept of Agric., Basutoland, 1951-54; Agric. Educn Officer i/c of Agric. Sch. for junior field staff, 1955-62; Agric. Extension Officer i/c of all field staff of Min. of Agric., 1962-63; Princ. Agric. Off. (Dep. Dir), Min. of Agric., 1964-66; High Comr for Lesotho, in London, 1966-69; Ambassador to Germany, Holy See, Rome, France, and Austria, 1968-69. Guest of Min. of Agric., Netherlands, 1955; studied agric. educn, USA (financed by Carnegie Corp. of NY and Ford Foundn), 1960-61; FAO confs in Tunisia, Tanganyika and Uganda, 1962 and 1963; travelled extensively to study and observe methods of agric. administration, 1964; meetings on nutrition, Berlin and Hamburg, 1966; diplomatic trainee, Brit.

Embassy, Bonn, 1966. *Recreations:* golf, tennis, amateur dramatics, photography, debating, reading, travelling. *Address:* Ministry of Foreign Affairs, PO Box 527, Maseru, Lesotho, Southern Africa.

**KOZYGIN**; *see* Kosygin.

**KRABBE, Col Clarence Brehmer,** OBE 1918; DL; *b* 1886; *s* of Charles Krabbé, Buenos Aires; *m* 1915, Joan Alison (*d* 1968), *d* of Col A. Evans-Gordon, IA; one *s* (killed 1940) one *d*. *Educ:* Dulwich Coll.; Trinity Coll., Oxford. Served European War, 1914-19, with Berks Yeomanry and RFC, Gallipoli and France (despatches). Col Berks Home Guard, 1943-45. Chm., Royal Berks Hosp., 1942-48; Chm., S Berks Conservative Assoc., 1946-52; Vice-Chm., Berks T & AF Assoc., 1950-54; Mem., Oxford Regional Hosp. Bd, 1947-62 (Vice-Chm. 1951-62). Mem., Board of Governors, Oxford United Hosps, 1953-57; Mem. of Reading and District Hosp. Management Cttee (Chm., 1948-50), 1948-66; Mem. St Birinus Hosp. Management Cttee, 1962-66. DL Berks, 1946. High Sheriff of Berks, 1952-53. *Recreations:* curling, gardening. *Address:* Calcot Green, near Reading, Berks. *T:* Reading 27428.

**KRAMRISCH, Stella,** PhD; Professor in the Art of South Asia, University of Pennsylvania, Philadelphia, Pa, USA, since 1950; Curator of Indian Art, Philadelphia Museum of Art since 1954; formerly Professor of Indian Art in the University of Calcutta; Editor, Journal of the Indian Society of Oriental Art; *d* of Jacques Kramrisch, scientist, and Berta Kramrisch; *m* 1929, Laszlo Neményi (*d* 1950). *Educ:* Vienna University. Lecturer on Indian Art, Courtauld Institute of Art, University of London, 1937-40. *Publications:* Principles of Indian Art, 1924; Vishnudharmottara, 1924; History of Indian Art, 1929; Indian Sculpture, 1932; Asian Miniature Painting, 1932; A Survey of Painting in the Deccan, 1937; Indian Terracottas, 1939; Kantha, 1939; The Hindu Temple, 1946; Arts and Crafts of Travancore, 1948; Dravida and Kerala, 1953; Art of India, 1954; Indian Sculpture in the Philadelphia Museum of Art, 1960; The Triple Structure of Creation, 1962; The Art of Nepal, 1964; Unknown India: Ritual Art in Tribe and Village, 1968. *Address:* University of Pennsylvania, Pa 19355, USA.

**KRATOVIL, Bohuslav G.,** PhD; author; formerly politician and ambassador; *b* 21 Oct. 1901; *s* of V. A. Kratovil; *m* 1946, Helene Gut-Schenk (*d* 1956); one *s*. *Educ:* Universities of Prague, Brno and Paris. Official of Czechoslovak Ministry of Education, 1930-39; War Cross, 1939; in prison in Germany, 1939-45; Mem. of Parliament, Czechoslovakia, 1945-46; Czechoslovak Ambassador in London, 1947-49; Czechoslovak Ambassador to India, 1949-51 (resigned his appointment because of political disagreements with the Czechoslovak Government; granted asylum in Great Britain and subsequently British citizenship). Name inscribed in Golden Book of Jerusalem. *Publications:* Translations into Czech from different languages of various works on Psychology and Pedagogy and original publications on Pedagogy, 1925-35; The Position of the Intelligentsia in the Post-War Period, 1946; Czechoslovak Cultural Traditions, 1946; Czechoslovak-British Relations, 1947; articles on internat. policy in British, Continental and Indian papers (Observer, Central European Observer, Indian News Chronicle, Daily Mail, Manchester Guardian, etc), 1951-69. *Recreations:* tennis, and water sports.

**KRAUS, Otakar;** operatic singer; *b* Prague, 1909; *m* Maria Graf; one *s*. *Educ:* privately; in Prague and in Milan. Engaged as Principal Baritone, National Opera House, Bratislava; subsequently at: Opera House, Brno; State Opera House, Prague; Royal Opera House, Covent Garden. Has also appeared with Carl Rosa Opera, English Opera Group, at Glyndebourne, Bayreuth, Aldeburgh, Vienna State Opera, Munich, Venice, (Scala) Milan, Nederlandsche Opera, Amsterdam. *Address:* 223 Hamlet Gardens, W6. *T:* 01-748 7366.

**KRAUSE, Madame Otto;** *see* Lehmann, Lotte.

**KREBS, Sir Hans (Adolf),** Kt 1958; FRS 1947; FRCP; MD Hamburg, 1925; MA Cantab, 1934; Research Scientist in the Nuffield Department of Clinical Medicine, Radcliffe Infirmary, Oxford, and Supernumerary Fellow of St Cross College, Oxford, since 1967; Visiting Professor of Biochemistry, Royal Free Hospital School of Medicine, since 1967; *b* 25 Aug. 1900; *e s* of late Georg Krebs, MD, and Alma Davidson, Hildesheim, Germany; *m* 1938, Margaret Cicely, *d* of J. L. Fieldhouse, Wickersley, Yorks; two *s* one *d*. *Educ:* Universities of Göttingen, Freiburg i. B., Munich, Berlin. Asst Kaiser Wilhelm Institut f. Biologie, Dept of Prof. O. H. Warburg, Berlin-Dahlem, 1926-30; Privatdozent f. int. Medizin, Freiburg, 1932; Rockefeller research student, Cambridge, 1933-34; Demonstrator in Biochemistry, Cambridge, 1934-35; Lecturer in Pharmacology, University of Sheffield, 1935-38; Lecturer i/c Dept of Biochemistry, University of Sheffield, 1938-45; Prof., 1945-54. Whitley Prof. of Biochemistry, and Fellow of Trinity Coll., Oxford, 1954-67. Hon. Degrees from Universities of Chicago, Freiburg, Paris, Glasgow, Sheffield, London, Berlin (Humboldt), Jerusalem, Leicester, Leeds, Granada, Pennsylvania, Wales and Bordeaux. Hon. Mem. Belgian Royal Academy of Medicine, 1962; Hon. Fellow, Nat. Inst. of Sciences of India, 1956; Correspondent étranger, Académie Nationale de Médicine, Paris, 1952; Foreign Hon. Mem., Amer. Acad. of Arts and Sciences, 1957; Mem., Amer. Philosophical Soc., 1960; Foreign Associate, Amer. Nat. Acad. of Science, 1964; (Jointly) Nobel Prize for Medicine, 1953; Royal Medal, Royal Society, 1954; Gold Medal of Netherlands Soc. for Physics, Medical Science, and Surgery, 1958; Copley Medal of Royal Society, 1961. Gold Medal, RSM, 1965. *Publications:* Papers on biochemical subjects in scientific journals. *Address:* Nuffield Department of Clinical Medicine, Radcliffe Infirmary, Oxford; 27 Abberbury Road, Oxford.

**KREISEL, Prof. Georg,** FRS 1966; Professor of Logic and the Foundations of Mathematics, Stanford University, Stanford, California, USA; *b* 15 Sept. 1923. Distinguished for his work in mathematical logic and investigations into the foundations of mathematics. *Address:* Department of Philosophy, Stanford University, Stanford, California 94305, USA; 27240 Moody Road, Los Altos Hills, California 94022, USA.

**KREMER, Michael,** MD; FRCP; Neurologist, Middlesex Hospital, W1, since 1946; Physician, National Hospital, Queen Square, WC1, since 1967; Hon. Consultant Neurologist to St Dunstan's, since 1966; Hon. Consultant in Neurology to the Army, since 1969; *b* 27 Nov. 1907; *s* of W. and S. Kremer; *m* 1933, Lilian Frances (*née* Washbourn); one *s* two *d*. *Educ:* Middlesex Hosp. Medical Sch. BSc 1927; MD 1932; FRCP 1943. *Recreations:* music, reading, photography. *Address:* 121

Harley Street, W1. *T:* 01-935 4545. *Clubs:* Athenæum, Royal Automobile.

**KRESTIN, David,** MD (London), BS, MRCP; Consulting Physician, London Jewish Hospital; Medical Specialist, Ministries of Pensions and of National Insurance; late Physician with charge of Out-Patients, Dreadnought Hospital; Medical Registrar, Prince of Wales' Hospital; Lecturer in Medicine, N-E London Post-Graduate Medical College; *b* London; *s* of Dr S. Krestin; *m* Ruth Fisher; one *s*. *Educ:* University of London; London Hosp. Medical Coll.; University of Pennsylvania. Anatomy prize, London Hosp.; MRCS, LRCP 1922; MB, BS London 1923, Hons Medicine and Surgery; MD London 1926, MRCP 1926. Clinical Asst, House Surg., House Physician, Medical Registrar and First Asst, London Hosp.; Rockefeller Medical Fellowship, 1928-29; Fellow in Pathology, Henry Phipps Institute, University Penna; Yarrow Research Fellow, London Hosp. *Publications:* Pulsation in Superficial Veins, Lancet, 1927; The Seborrhœic facies in Post-Encephalitic Parkinsonism, Quart. Jour. Med., 1927; Congenital Dextrocardia and Auric. Fibrillation, Brit. Med. Jour., 1927; Latent Pulmonary Tuberculosis, Quart. Journ. Med., 1929; Glandular Fever, Clinical Journal, 1931 and other medical papers. *Recreation:* fishing. *Address:* 93 Harley Street, W1. *T:* 01-935 8787; 14 Spaniards End, NW3. *T:* 01-455 1500.

**KRETZMER, Herbert;** Theatre Critic, Daily Express, London, since 1961; *b* Kroonstad, OFS, S Africa, 5 Oct. 1925; *s* of William and Tilly Kretzmer; *m* 1961, Elisabeth Margaret Wilson; one *s* one *d*. *Educ:* Kroonstad High Sch.; Rhodes Univ., CP. Entered journalism, 1946, writing weekly cinema newsreel commentaries and documentary films for African Film Productions, Johannesburg. Reporter and entertainment columnist, Sunday Express, Johannesburg, 1951-54; feature writer and columnist, Daily Sketch, London, 1954-59; Columnist, Sunday Dispatch, London, 1959-61. As lyric writer, contributed weekly songs to: That Was The Week . ., Not So Much A Programme . ., BBC 3. Wrote lyrics for Ivor Novello Award song Goodness Gracious Me, 1960; Our Man Crichton, Shaftesbury Theatre, 1964 (book and lyrics); The Four Musketeers, Drury Lane, 1967 (lyrics); *film:* Can Heironymus Merkin Ever Forget Mercy Humppe And Find True Happiness?, 1969 (lyrics); has also written lyrics for other films, and for TV programmes. *Publications:* Our Man Crichton, 1965; (jointly) Every Home Should Have One, 1970. *Recreations:* watching Association football matches and bullfights. *Address:* 55 Lincoln House, Basil Street, SW3. *T:* 01-589 2541.

**KRIPS, Josef;** Conductor Emeritus, San Francisco Symphony Orchestra; Permanent Guest Conductor, Vienna State Opera, since 1931; *b* Vienna, 8 April 1902; *s* of Dr Josef Krips and Luise Seitz; *m* 1947, Mitzi Wilheim; *m* 1969, Harrietta Freün von Prochazka. *Educ:* Acad. of Music, Vienna. Studied under Eusebius Mandyczewsky and Felix von Weingartner. Made début as conductor, Vienna, 1921; with Vienna Volksoper under Weingartner, 1921-24; Chief of Opera Dept: Stadttheater, Aussig ad Elbe, 1924-25; Stadttheater, Dortmund, 1925-26; Dir-Gen. of Music, Staatstheater, Karlsruhe, 1926-33; Permanent Conductor, Vienna State Opera, 1933-38; Prof. at Vienna Acad. of Music, 1935-38; Conductor, Opera, Belgrade and Philharmonic, 1938-39; under Hitler, no permission to conduct, 1939-45; reorganised musical life in Vienna in Opera, concerts and Hofkapelle, 1945; opened Salzburg Festival, 1946 and appeared there, 1946-50 and 1969; Conductor in chief: London Symphony Orchestra, 1950-54; Buffalo Philharmonic Orchestra, 1954-63; San Francisco Symphony Orchestra, 1963-70. Toured: Mexico, 1953, 1954; Switzerland, 1955; Australia, 1955, 1959; NZ, 1959; Japan, 1968; also USA, Canada, Israel, etc. Guest Conductor at Rome, Paris, Copenhagen, Moscow, Leningrad, Budapest, Berlin, Munich, Strasbourg, Bordeaux, Nice, Basle, Zürich, USA, Israel, etc, and frequently in Great Britain (London Symphony, London Philharmonic, Royal Philharmonic, Hallé, Liverpool Philharmonic Orchestras). Vice-Pres., Anglo-Austrian Soc., 1962-. Mem., Soc. of Music Friends, Vienna, 1962-; Hon. Member: Gustav Mahler Soc., 1962-; Vienna State Opera, 1968. Hon. Citizen, City and County of San Francisco, 1970. Ring of UN, 1947; Nicolai Medal, Vienna Philharmonic Orchestra, 1947; Bruckner Medal (European), 1953; Bruckner Medal, Amer. Bruckner Soc., 1956; Chancellor's Medal, Univ. of Buffalo, 1961; Vienna Ring of Honour, 1962; Mozart Ring, Austria, 1965; Grosses silbernes Ehrenzeichen, Austria, 1967. *Address:* 6 Riant-Château, Montreux, Vaud, Switzerland.

**KRISH, Mrs Felix;** *see* Moiseiwitsch, Tanya.

**KRISHNA, Sri,** CIE 1942; DSc (London), PhD, FRIC, FNI; late Scientific Adviser to High Commission of India and Scientific Liaison Officer, London; Deputy Director, Council of Scientific and Industrial Research, New Delhi, India, 1952; Vice-Pres. and Director of Research, Forest Research Institute, Dehra Dun, UP, India, 1950; Biochemist since 1928; *b* 6 July 1896; *s* of M. Mohan; *m* 1925, Usha Khanna (*d* 1929); (one *s* decd). *Educ:* Forman Coll., Lahore; Government Coll., Lahore; Queen Mary Coll., London; King's Coll., London. Prof. of Chemistry, University of the Punjab, Lahore, 1925-28. *Publications:* numerous scientific. *Recreations:* tennis, etc. *Address:* 62 Perryn Road, Acton, London, W3; 88 Rajpur Road, Dehra Dun, UP, India.

**KRISHNA MENON, Vengalil Krishnan;** Indian Statesman and Lawyer; Member, Lok Sabha, for Midnapore, West Bengal, since 1969; Senior Counsel, Supreme Court of India, at New Delhi; Chairman, Indian Academy of International Law and Diplomacy; *b* 3 May 1896; *s* of late K. Krishna Kurup and late Lakshmi Kutty Amma, Malabar, India; unmarried. *Educ:* Municipal Sch., Tellicherry; Zamoris Coll., Calicut; Presidency Coll. and Law Coll., Madras; London Sch. of Economics; University Coll., London; Middle Temple, London; King's Inns, Dublin. Lecturer, National Univ., Adyar, Madras, 1919-23. Degrees in Arts, Science and Law, and Diploma in Education, London Univ. Practised at the Bar. Joined Indian National Congress, from which he resigned 1966. Has been teacher, journalist and publicist. President: India League, 1947- (Sec., 1927-47); Indian Soc. of Internat. Law. Borough Councillor, St Pancras, 1934-47; parliamentary candidate (Lab.), Dundee, 1938-41. High Commissioner for India, 1947-52, and formerly Indian Ambassador to the Republic of Ireland. Rep. India at UN General Assembly, Lake Success, 1946; visited various European capitals as Pandit Nehru's personal envoy, 1947. Called to Irish Bar, 1952. Rep. India at UN Gen. Assembly annually, 1952-62. Mem. of Indian Parliament (Council of States), 1953-57; Lok Sabha, 1957-67, 1969-. cabinet Minister without Portfolio, 1956-57; Minister for Defence, 1957-62; Minister of Defence Production (for a short period), 1962.

Hon. LLD: Glasgow; Saugor; Osmania; Utkal; DLitt, Mysore; Hon. Fellow, LSE, 1960. First Award of Padma Vibushan, 1954. *Publications:* (with Ellen Wilkinson) Condition of India; first editor Pelican Books; editor Twentieth Century Library; several pamphlets and articles. *Address:* c/o Lawyers' Chambers, Supreme Court of India, New Delhi, India. *Clubs:* India (London); Gymkhana (New Delhi).

**KRISTENSEN, Prof. Thorkil;** Director, Institute for Development Research, Copenhagen, since 1969; Secretary-General, Organisation for Economic Co-operation and Development, 1960-69; Professor of Commercial and Industrial Economics, in School of Advanced Commercial Studies, Copenhagen, since 1947; *b* Denmark, 9 Oct. 1899; *m* 1931, Ellen Christine Nielsen; one *s* one *d. Educ:* School of Commerce; People's Coll., Askov; University of Copenhagen (Cand. polit.). Dipl. Polit. and Econ. Sciences, 1927. Lectr in High Sch. of Commerce, Aarhus, and in University of Copenhagen, 1927-38; Prof. of Commercial and Industrial Economics: University of Aarhus, 1938-47; Sch. of Advanced Commercial Studies, Copenhagen, 1947-60; Sec.-Gen., Organisation for Economic Co-operation and Develt, 1960-69. Mem., Danish Parliament, 1945-60; Minister of Finance, 1945-47 and 1950-53; Mem. Finance Cttee, 1947-49 and 1953-60; Mem. Consultative Assembly of Council of Europe, 1949-50; Mem. Foreign Affairs Cttee, 1953-60; Mem. Nordic Council, 1953-60; Mem. Acad. of Technical Sciences; Pres. Foreign Policy Soc., 1948-60; Pres. Nat. Anti-Unemployment Fedn, 1956-60; Mem. Assurance Council, 1958-60; Mem. Institute of History and Economics. DrSc Pol *hc* (Ankara), 1962. *Publications:* several, on finance, 1930-39; The Food Problem of Developing Countries, 1968. Editor of: De europaeiske markedsplaner (European Markets–Plans and Prospects), 1958; The Economic World Balance, 1960, etc. *Address:* Odinsvej 18, 3460 Birkerød, Denmark.

**KRISTIANSEN, Erling (Engelbrecht),** Knight Commander, Order of Dannebrog; Royal Danish Ambassador to the Court of St James's since 1964; concurrently accredited to Ireland; *b* 31 Dec. 1912; *s* of Kristian Engelbrecht Kristiansen, Chartered Surveyor, and Andrea Kirstine (*née* Madsen); *m* 1938, Annemarie Selinko, novelist; one *s. Educ:* Herning Gymnasium; University of Copenhagen (degree awarded equiv. of MA Econ). Postgraduate Studies, Economics and Internat. Relations, Geneva, Paris, London, 1935-37. Sec.-Gen., 1935, Pres. 1936, of the Fédération Universitaire Internationale pour la Société des Nations. Danish Civil Servant, 1941; served with: Free Danish Missions, Stockholm, 1943; Washington, 1944; London, 1945; joined Danish Diplomatic Service and stayed in London until 1947; Danish Foreign Ministry, 1947-48; Head of Denmark's Mission to OEEC, Paris, 1948-50; Sec. to Economic Cttee of Cabinet, 1950-51; Asst Under-Sec. of State, 1951; Dep. Under-Sec. of State (Economic Affairs), Danish For. Min., 1954-64. Grand Officier, Légion d'Honneur; Kt Comdr: Order of St Olav; Order of White Rose of Finland; Star of Ethiopia; Knight Grand Cross, Icelandic Falcon; Comdr, Order of Northern Star of Sweden. *Publication:* Folkeforbundet (The League of Nations), 1938. *Recreations:* ski-ing, fishing and other out-door sports, modern languages. *Address:* 1 Cadogan Square, SW1. *T:* 01-235 4291.

**KROHN, Dr Peter Leslie,** FRS 1963; Professor of Endocrinology, University of Birmingham, 1962-66; *b* 8 Jan. 1916; *s* of Eric Leslie Krohn and Doris Ellen Krohn (*née* Wade); *m* 1941, Joanna Mary French; two *s. Educ:* Sedbergh; Balliol Coll., Oxford. BA 1st Cl. Hons Animal Physiol, 1937; BM, BCh Oxon, 1940. Wartime Research work for Min. of Home Security, 1940-45; Lectr, then Reader in Endocrinology, University of Birmingham, 1946-53; Nuffield Sen. Gerontological Research Fellow and Hon. Prof. in University, 1953-62. *Publications:* contrib. to scientific jls on physiology of reproduction, transplantation immunity and ageing. *Recreations:* ski-ing, mountain walking. *Address:* La Forêt, St Mary, Jersey, Channel Islands. *T:* West 287.

**KRUSIN, Stanley Marks,** CB 1963; Second Parliamentary Counsel, since 1970; *b* 8 June 1908; *m* 1937; one *s* one *d. Educ:* St Paul's Sch.; Balliol Coll., Oxford. Called to the Bar, Middle Temple, 1932. Served RAFVR, Wing Comdr, 1944. Dep. Sec., British Tabulating Machine Co. Ltd, 1945-47. Entered Parliamentary Counsel Office, 1947; Parliamentary Counsel, 1953-69. *Address:* 31 Platt's Lane, NW3. *T:* 01-435 3141. *Club:* Reform.

**KUBELIK, Rafael;** conductor and composer; *b* Bychory, Bohemia, 29 June 1914; *s* of Jan Kubelik, violinist, and Marianne (*née* Szell); *m* 1942, Ludmila Bertiova, (*decd*), violinist; one *s*; *m* 1963, Elsie Morrison, singer. *Educ:* Prague Conservatoire. Conductor, Czech Philharmonic Society, Prague, 1936-39; Musical Director of Opera, Brno, Czechoslovakia, 1939-41; Musical Dir, Czech Philharmonic Orchestra, 1941-48; Musical Dir, Chicago Symphony Orchestra, 1950-53; Musical Dir of the Covent Garden Opera Company, 1955-58; Chief Conductor of Bayerischer Rundfunk, München, 1961-. Guest Conductor, North and South America, Europe, Australia. Festivals at Edinburgh, Salzburg, Lucerne, Vienna, Zürich and Amsterdam. Concerts and tours with Vienna Philharmonic Orchestra and Concertgebouw Orchestra; Compositions include: 4 operas; 2 symphonies with chorus; 4 string quartets; 1 violin concerto; 1 cello concerto; 1 cantata; Requiems: Pro Memoria Uxoris; Libera Nos; Quattro Forme per Archi; songs; piano and violin music. *Address:* Kastanienbaum, Hans im Sand, Switzerland.

**KUBRICK, Stanley;** producer, director, script writer; *b* 26 July 1928; *s* of Dr Jacques L. Kubrick and Gertrude Kubrick; *m* 1958, Suzanne Christiane Harlan; three *d. Educ:* William Howard Taft High Sch.; City Coll. of City of New York. Joined Look Magazine, 1946. At age of 21 made Documentary, Day of the Fight; made Short for RKO, Flying Padre. *Feature Films:* Fear and Desire, 1953 (at age of 24); Killer's Kiss, 1954; The Killing, 1956; Paths of Glory, 1957; Spartacus, 1960; Lolita, 1962; Dr Strangelove or How I Learned to Stop Worrying and Love the Bomb, 1964; 2001: A Space Odyssey, 1968. *Recreations:* literature, music, public affairs. *Address:* Box 123, Boreham Wood, Herts.

**KÜCHEMANN, Dietrich,** CBE 1964; Dr rer nat; FRS 1963; FRAeS, FIMA; FAIAA; Head of Aerodynamics Department, Royal Aircraft Establishment, Farnborough, since 1966; *b* Göttingen, Germany, 11 Sept. 1911; *s* of Rudolf Küchemann and Martha Egener; *m* 1936, Helga Janet Praefcke; one *s* two *d. Educ:* Oberrealschule, Göttingen; Göttingen and München Univs. Aerodynamic research at: Aerodynamische Versuchsanstalt, Göttingen, 1936-46; Royal Aircraft Establishment, Farnborough, Hants, 1946-. *Publications:* Aerodynamics of Propulsion, 1953; Progress in Aeronautical Sciences (Ed.) vols 1-9, 1961-.

Contrib. to Incompressible Aerodynamics, 1960; Prandtl's Strömungslehre, 6th edn, 1965. Articles chiefly in: Jl Fluid Mechs, ZAMM, Jl RAeS, Jl Aeron. Sci., Aeron. Quart., Luftfahrtforschg., Zeitschr. Flugw., Progress in Aeron. Sci., Repts and Mem. of ARC. *Recreation:* music. *Address:* Steding, 32 Echo Barn Lane, Farnham, Surrey. *T:* Farnham, Surrey, 4947.

**KUHN, Heinrich Gerhard,** FRS 1954; DPhil, MA; Reader in Physics, Oxford University, since 1955; Fellow of Balliol College since 1950; *b* 10 March 1904; *s* of Wilhelm Felix and Martha Kuhn; *m* 1931, Marie Bertha Nohl; two *s. Educ:* High Sch., Lueben (Silesia); Universities of Greifswald and Goettingen. Lecturer in Physics, Goettingen Univ., 1931; Research at Clarendon Laboratory, Oxford, 1933; Lecturer, University Coll., Oxford, 1938; work for atomic energy project, 1941-45; University Demonstrator, Oxford, 1945-55. Dr *hc* Aix-Marseille, 1958. Holweck Prize, 1967. *Publications:* Atomspektren, 1934 (Akad. Verl. Ges., Leipzig); Atomic Spectra, 1962, 2nd edn 1970; articles on molecular and atomic spectra and on interferometry. *Address:* 25 Victoria Road, Oxford. *T:* 55308.

**KUIPER, Gerard Peter;** Director of Lunar and Planetary Laboratory, University of Arizona, since 1961; *b* 7 Dec. 1905; *s* of G. Kuiper and Anna de Vries-Kuiper; *m* 1936, Sarah Parker Fuller; one *s* one *d. Educ:* University of Leyden, Netherlands. PhD Leyden 1933. Post-doctoral Fellow, University of California, 1933-35; Lecturer, Harvard Univ., 1935-36; Prof. of Astronomy, University of Chicago, 1936-; Dir Yerkes observatory, University of Chicago, and McDonald obs., University of Texas, 1947-49 and 1957-60. Civilian war service, 1943-45. Principal Investigator on NASA's Ranger Program, 1963-66. Janssen Medal of French Astronomical Soc. (for discovery of satellites of Uranus and Neptune); Rittenhouse Medal (for his theory of origin of solar system). Member: Nat. Acad. of Sciences, Amer. Acad. of Arts and Sciences; Internat. Astronomical Union; Amer. Astronomical Soc.; Astronomical Soc. of the Pacific; Royal Astronomical Society of London (Associate); Netherlands Soc. of the Sciences (For. Mem.), Royal Netherlands Academy of Sciences (For. Mem.). Comdr, Order of Orange Nassau (Netherlands). *Publications:* (Ed.) The Atmospheres of the Earth and Planets, 1949, 2nd edn, 1952; (Ed.) The Solar System, 4 vols, 1953-60; (Ed.) Stars and Stellar Systems, 6 vols, 1960-65; Atlases of the Moon issued by him and his staff: Photographic Lunar Atlas, 1960 (Chicago); Orthographic Lunar Atlas, and Rectified Lunar Atlas, 1961-63 (Arizona); Consolidated Lunar Atlas, 1965-; contributions to Astrophysical Journal, etc. *Recreations:* photography, travel. *Address:* Lunar and Planetary Laboratory, University of Arizona, Tucson, Arizona, USA.

**KUNCEWICZ, Mrs Witold;** *see* Herlie, Eileen.

**KUNERALP, Zeki;** Turkish Ambassador to the Court of St James's, 1964-66 and since 1969; *b* Istanbul, 5 Oct. 1914; *s* of Ali Kemal Kuneralp and Sabiha, *d* of Mustafa Zeki Pasha; *m* 1943, Necla Ozdilci; two *s. Educ:* Univ. of Berne. DrIuris 1938. Entered Diplomatic Service, 1940: served Bucharest, Prague, Paris, Nato Delegn and at Min. of Foreign Affairs, Ankara; Asst Sec.-Gen. 1957; Sec.-Gen. 1960; Ambassador to Berne, 1960, to Court of St James's, 1964-66; Sec.-Gen. at Min. of Foreign Affairs, Ankara, 1966-69. Mem., Hon. Soc. of Knights of the Round Table. Holds German, Greek, Italian, Papal, Jordanian, Iranian and National Chinese orders. *Recreations:* reading, ballet. *Address:* Turkish Embassy, 69 Portland Place, W1. *Clubs:* National Liberal, Hurlingham, Travellers'.

**KUROSAWA, Akira;** Japanese film director; *b* 1910. *Educ:* Keika Middle School. Assistant Director, Toho Film Co., 1936. Directed first film, Sugata Sanshiro, 1943. *Films include:* Sugata Sanshiro, Ichiban Utsukushiku, Torano Owofumu Otokotachi, Rashomon (1st Prize, Venice Film Festival), Hakuchi, Ikiru, The Seven Samurai, Living, Kakushi Toride no San Akunin, The Hidden Fortress, Throne of Blood, Yojimbo, The Bad Sleep Well, Tsubaki Sanjuro, Tengoku To Jigoku, Red Beard, 1965. *Address:* 1755 Nichome Matsubara-Machi, Setagaya-Ku, Tokyo, Japan. *T:* Tokyo (328) 4380.

**KURTI, Nicholas,** FRS 1956; MA Oxon; DrPhil (Berlin); FInstP; Professor of Physics, Clarendon Laboratory, University of Oxford, since 1967; Vice-President, Royal Society, 1965-67; *b* 14 May 1908; *s* of late Charles Kürti and Margaret Pintér, Budapest; *m* 1946, Georgiana, *d* of late Brig.-Gen. C. T. Shipley and of Mrs Shipley, Oxford; two *d. Educ:* Minta-Gymnasium, Budapest; University of Paris (Licence ès sci. phys.); University of Berlin (DrPhil). Asst, Techn Hochschule Breslau, 1931-33; Research Position, Clarendon Laboratory, Oxford, 1933-40; UK Atomic Energy Project, 1940-45; University Demonstrator in Physics, Oxford, 1945-60; Reader in Physics, Oxford, 1960-67; Senior Research Fellow, Brasenose Coll., 1947-67; Professorial Fellow, 1967-. Buell G. Gallagher Visiting Prof., City Coll., New York, 1963; Vis. Prof., University of Calif, Berkeley, 1964. A Governor, College of Aeronautics, Cranfield, 1953-69. Member: Electricity Supply Research Council; Advisory Cttee for Scientific and Technical Information, 1966-68; Chm., Adv. Cttee on Measurement and Standards, Min. of Technology, 1969-. Member: Council, Royal Soc., 1964-67; Council, Soc. Française de Physique, 1957-60, 1970-; Council, Inst. of Physics and Physical Soc., 1969-. Foreign Hon. Member: Amer. Acad. Arts and Sciences, 1968; Hungarian Acad. of Sciences, 1970. Holweck Prize (British and French Physical Socs), 1955; Fritz London Award, 1957; Hughes Medal, Royal Soc., 1969. *Publications:* (jointly) Low Temperature Physics, 1952. Papers in scientific periodicals on cryophysics and magnetism; articles in the New Chambers's Encyclopædia. *Address:* 38 Blandford Avenue, Oxford OX2 8DZ. *T:* 56176; Clarendon Laboratory, Oxford OX1 3PU. *T:* 59291. *Club:* Athenæum.

**KURZ, Prof. Otto,** FBA 1962; Professor of the History of the Classical Tradition with special reference to the Near East, University of London, since 1965; *b* 26 May 1908; *s* of Dr Maximilian Kurz and Anna Kurz; *m* 1937, Hilde (*née* Schuller); one *d. Educ:* University of Vienna. Librarian, Warburg Institute, 1944-65. Visiting Lecturer, Hebrew Univ., Jerusalem, 1964; Slade Prof. of Fine Arts, Oxford, 1970-71. Hon. Fellow: Associazione Francesco Francia, Bologna; Raccolta Vinciana, Milan. *Publications:* contributions to learned journals. *Address:* The Warburg Institute, Woburn Square, WC1.

**KUSCH, Prof. Polykarp;** Professor of Physics since 1949, and Vice-President and Dean of Faculties since 1969, Columbia University, New York, NY; *b* Germany, 26 Jan. 1911; *s* of John Matthias Kusch and Henrietta van der Haas; *m* 1935, Edith Starr McRoberts (*d* 1959); three *d*; *m* 1960, Betty Jane Pezzoni;

two *d*. *Educ:* Case Institute of Technology, Cleveland, Ohio (BS); University of Illinois, Urbana, Ill. (MS, PhD). Asst, University of Ill, 1931-36; Research Asst, University of Minnesota, 1936-37; Instr in Physics, Columbia Univ., 1937-41; Engr, Westinghouse Electric Corp., 1941-42; Mem. Tech. Staff, Div. of Govt Aided Research, Columbia Univ., 1942-44; Mem. Tech. Staff, Bell Telephone Laboratories, 1944-46; Assoc. Prof. of Physics, Columbia Univ., 1946-49; Chm., Dept of Physics, Columbia Univ., 1960-63 (Exec. Officer, 1949-52); Exec. Dir, Columbia Radiation Laboratory, Columbia Univ., 1952-60. Member: Nat. Acad. of Sciences, US; American Philosophical Soc. Hon. DSc: Case Institute of Technology, 1955; Ohio State Univ., 1959; Colby Coll., 1961; University of Ill, 1961. (Jointly) Nobel Prize in Physics, 1955. *Publications:* technical articles in Physical Review and other Journals. *Address:* 450 Riverside Drive, New York, NY 10027, USA. *T:* 662-8120.

**KUSTOW, Michael David;** Artistic Controller, Institute of Contemporary Arts, since 1970 (Director, 1967-70); *b* 18 Nov. 1939. *Educ:* Haberdashers' Aske's; Wadham Coll., Oxford (BA Hons English). Festivals Organiser, Centre 42, 1962-63; Royal Shakespeare Theatre Company: Dir, RSC Club, Founder of Theatreground, Editor of Flourish, 1963-67. *Publications:* Punch and Judas, 1964; The Book of US, 1968; Guillaume Apollinaire: I Wonder, 1971. *Recreations:* inland waterways, yoga. *Address:* 47 Downshire Hill, NW3. *T:* 01-435 3266.

**KWAN, Sir Cho-Yiu,** Kt 1969; CBE 1965 (OBE 1959); Member of Executive Council, Government of Hong Kong, since 1961; Solicitor, Senior Partner of C. Y. Kwan & Co., Hong Kong; *b* 10 July 1907; *s* of Kwan Yick Chow and Yue Kam; *m* 1934, Chow Wai Fun; two *s* two *d*. *Educ:* Diocesan Boys' Sch.; University Coll., London Univ. Vice-Pres., Standing Mil. Court, Hong Kong, 1946. Pres., Law Society, Hong Kong, 1950-51; Dep. Comr of Civil Aid Services, 1951-66; Mem., Urban Council, 1956-61; MLC, 1959-66. Chm. Council, Chinese Univ. of Hong Kong, 1963-; Mem. Court, Univ. of Hong Kong; Vice-Chm. and a Founder, Hong Kong Housing Soc.; Chm. or Mem. of Cttee of a number of social, charitable and educational institutions. Hon. Doctor of Laws (Chinese Univ. of Hong Kong), 1964. *Address:* 8 Shouson Hill Road, Hong Kong. *T:* 92537. *Clubs:* Chinese, Country, Royal Jockey (Hong Kong).

**KYDD, Ronald Robertson,** BA; LLB; Advocate; Sheriff-Substitute of Fife and Kinross at Cupar and Kinross since 1960; *b* 21 Feb. 1920; *yr s* of Arthur Robertson Kydd, manufacturer, Dundee, and of Elizabeth Munro Stevenson; *m* 1951, Margaret Virginia, *e d* of Andrew St Clair Jameson, WS, Edinburgh; two *d*. *Educ:* Dundee High Sch.; Dalhousie Castle Sch.; Fettes Coll.; Trinity Hall, Cambridge (Open Scholar; BA); Edinburgh Univ. (Thow Scholar in Scots Law; LLB with Dist.). Passed Advocate (admitted to Faculty of Advocates in Scotland), 1945; in practice at Scottish Bar, 1945-56; Sheriff-Substitute of Fife and Kinross at Dunfermline and Kinross, 1956-60. *Recreations:* golf, gardening. *Address:* Middle Balado House, Kinross. *T:* Kinross 2236. *Clubs:* New (Edinburgh); Royal and Ancient (St Andrews); Honourable Company of Edinburgh Golfers.

**KYLE, Elisabeth, (Agnes M. R. Dunlop);** novelist and writer of books for children; *d* of late James Dunlop, Ronaldshaw Park, Ayr; unmarried. *Publications:* first novel published 1932; since then she has had about fifty books published, in Britain and America (also in translations); The Begonia Bed, 1934; Orangefield, 1938; The Mirrors of Versailles, 1939; Broken Glass, 1940; The White Lady, 1941; But We Are Exiles, 1942; The Pleasure Dome, 1943; The Skaters' Waltz, 1944; Carp Country, 1946; Mally Lee, 1947; A Man of Talent, 1948; Douce, 1950; The Tontine Belle, 1951; Conor Sands, 1952; Forgotten as a Dream, 1953; The Regent's Candlesticks, 1954; A Stillness in the Air, 1956; The Other Miss Evans, 1958; Oh Say, Can You See?, 1959; Return to the Alcazar, 1962; Mirror Dance, 1970; *children's books:* Visitors from England, 1941; Vanishing Island, 1942; Behind the Waterfall, 1944; The Seven Sapphires, 1944; Holly Hotel, 1945; Lost Karin, 1946; The Mirrors of Castle Doone, 1947; West Wind, 1948; The House on the Hill, 1949; The Provost's Jewel, 1950; The Lintowers, 1951; The Captain's House, 1952; The Reiver's Road, 1953; The House of the Pelican, 1954; Caroline House, 1955; Run to Earth, 1957; Queen of Scots, 1957; Maid of Orleans, 1957; The Money Cat, 1958; The Eagle's Nest, 1961; Girl with a Lantern, 1961; Girl With An Easel, 1963; Girl With A Pen, 1964; Girl With A Song, 1964; Victoria, 1964; Girl with a Destiny, 1965; The Boy who asked for More, 1966; Love is for the Living, 1966; High Season, 1968; Queen's Evidence, 1969; The Song of the Waterfall, 1969. *Recreations:* music, travel, collecting antiques. *Address:* 10 Carrick Park, Ayr, Scotland. *T:* Ayr 63074.

**KYLE, Air Chief Marshal Sir Wallace (Hart),** GCB 1966 (KCB 1960; CB 1953); CBE 1945; DSO 1944; DFC 1941; Air Officer Commanding-in-Chief, Strike Command, 1968 (Bomber Command, 1965-68); retired, 1968; *b* 22 Jan. 1910; *s* of A. Kyle, Kalgoorlie, Western Australia; *m* 1941, Molly Rimington (*née* Wilkinson); three *s* one *d*. *Educ:* Guildford Sch., WA; RAF Coll., Cranwell. 17 Sqdn, 1930-31; Fleet Air Arm, 1931-34; Flying Instructor, 1934-39; served War of 1939-45; Bomber Command, 1940-45; Staff Coll., 1945-47; Middle East, 1948-50; ADC to King George VI, 1949; Asst Commandant, RAF Coll., Cranwell, 1950-52; Dir of Operational Requirements, Air Ministry, 1952-54; AOC Malaya, 1955-57; ACAS (Op. Req.), 1957-59. AOC-in-C Technical Training Command, 1959-62; VCAS, 1962-65. ADC to the Queen, 1952-56. Air Marshal, 1961; Air Chief Marshal, 1964; Air ADC to the Queen, 1966-68. *Recreations:* cricket, squash, golf. *Address:* Kingswood, Tiptoe, Hordle, Hants. *Club:* Royal Air Force.

**KYNCH, Prof. George James,** ARCS, DIC, PhD (London); FIMA; Professor of Mathematics at the Institute of Science and Technology and in the University of Manchester, since 1957; *b* 26 Oct. 1915; *s* of Vincent Kynch; *m* 1944, Eve, *d* of Edward A. Robinson; one *s* two *d*. *Educ:* Selhurst Grammar Sch.; Imperial Coll. of Science, London. BSc in physics, 1936, and mathematics, 1936; PhD 1939; Sir John Lubbock Memorial Prize, 1936. Demonstrator at Imperial Coll., 1937; Lecturer at Birmingham Univ., 1942-52; Prof. of Applied Mathematics, University Coll. of Wales, Aberystwyth, 1952-57. *Publications:* Mathematics for the Chemist, 1955; articles in scientific jls. *Recreations:* caravanning, dry stone wall-building, civic society. *Address:* Rectory Cottage, Ford Lane, Northenden, Manchester 22; University of Manchester Institute of Science and Technology, Sackville Street, Manchester 1.

**KYRLE POPE, Rear-Adm. Michael Donald,** CB 1969; MBE 1946; joined aviation industry,

Hawker Siddeley Dynamics Ltd, 1970; *b* 1 Oct. 1916; *e s* of Comdr R. K. C. Pope, DSO, OBE, RN retd, and Mrs A. J. Pope (*née* Macdonald); *m* 1947, Angela Suzanne Layton; one *s* one *d*. *Educ:* Wellington Coll., Berks. Joined RN, 1934; China Stn, 1935-37; Submarine Service, 1938; Mediterranean, HMS Oswald, 1939; POW, Italy and Germany, 1940-45; HMS Vanguard, 1946-47; Admty Operation Div., 1949; HMS Warrior, 1950; Brit. Jt Services Mission, Washington, 1951-53; HMS Eagle, 1953; Naval Intell., Germany, 1955-57; RAF Staff Coll., Bracknell, 1957-58; Staff (Intell.) C-in-C, Far East Stn, 1958-60; idc 1961; Sen. Naval Off., Persian Gulf, 1962-64; MoD (Naval Intell.), 1965-67; Chief of Staff to C-in-C Far East, 1967-69; retd 1970. Comdr 1951; Capt. 1958; Rear-Adm. 1967. *Recreations:* country pursuits, walking, shooting, sailing. *Address:* Hopfields House, Westmill, Buntingford, Herts. *Club:* Army and Navy.

*See also J. E. Pope.*

# L

**LABOUCHERE, Sir George (Peter),** GBE 1964; KCMG 1955 (CMG 1951); *b* 2 Dec. 1905; *s* of late F. A. Labouchere; *m* 1943, Rachel Katherine, *d* of Hon. Eustace Hamilton-Russell. *Educ:* Charterhouse Sch.; Sorbonne, Paris. Entered Diplomatic Service, 1929. Served in Madrid, Cairo, Rio de Janeiro, Stockholm, Nanking, Buenos Aires. UK Deputy-Commissioner for Austria, 1951-53; HM Minister, Hungary, 1953-55; Ambassador to Belgium, 1955-60; Ambassador to Spain, 1960-66. Retired, 1966. Member of Council, Friends of the Tate Gallery; Mem., dilettanti Society; FRSA. *Recreations:* shooting, fishing, Chinese ceramics, contemporary painting and sculpture. *Address:* Dudmaston, Bridgnorth, Shropshire. *Clubs:* St James', Pratt's, Beefsteak.

**LABOUISSE, Henry (Richardson);** Executive Director, United Nations Children's Fund (UNICEF), since 1965; lawyer, US; *b* New Orleans, La., 11 Feb. 1904; *s* of Henry Richardson Labouisse; *m* 1935, Elizabeth Scriven Clark (*d* 1945); one *d*; *m* 1954, E. D. Curie (*see Eve Curie*). *Educ:* Princeton Univ. (AB); Harvard Univ. (LLB). Attorney-at-Law, NYC, 1929-41. Joined US State Dept, 1941; Minister Economic Affairs, US Embassy, Paris, 1945; Chief, Special Mission to France of Economic Co-operation Administration, 1951-54; Director, UN Relief and Works Agency for Palestine Refugees, 1954-58; Consultant, International Bank for Reconstruction and Development, 1959-61 (Head of IBRD Mission to Venezuela, 1959); Director, International Co-operation Admin., 1961-62; US Ambassador to Greece, 1962-65. Hon. LLD: University of Bridgeport, 1961; Princeton Univ., 1965; Lafayette Coll., 1966; Tulane Univ., 1967. *Address:* UNICEF, United Nations, New York, NY 10017, USA.

**LABOUISSE, Mrs H. R.;** *see* Curie, Eve.

**LACEY, Daniel;** *see* Lacey, W. D.

**LACEY, Gerald,** CIE 1942; BSc; FCGI; FICE; Chartered Civil Engineer; Consultant, Sir M. Macdonald and Partners, since 1950; *b* 26 July 1887; 3rd *s* of late Thomas Stephen Lacey, MInstCE; *m* 1918, Elsie Ann, *d* of Charles Willford, ISO, PWD; two *s*. *Educ:* Westminster City Sch.; City and Guilds and mechanical engineering, Central Tech. Coll., 1904-07; Bramwell medallist; BSc Engineering, 1st Class Hons, London Univ.; early training with G. H. Hill and Sons, Consulting Engineers, Westminster, Thames Conservancy and Chiswick Urban District Council; Assistant Engineer, Indian Service of Engineers, 1910; Military Service attached 1st KGO Sappers and Miners, 1917-19; 3rd Afghan War, 1919; Under-Secretary to Government, PWD, 1924-27; Irrigation Research Officer and Prof. Civil Engineering, Roorkee Coll., 1928-32; Superintending Engineer, 1934; Member of Council Inst. of Civil Engineers, 1940; Chief Engineer Eastern Canals. Irrigation Branch PWD, UP, 1941; retired 1942; Lieut-Colonel Corps of Indian Engineers, 1942-44; Prof. Civil Engineering, Roorkee Coll., March 1945; Principal Roorkee Coll., Dec. 1945; retired, Dec. 1946; Member: Colonial Office East Africa Rice Mission, 1948; British Honduras Rice Mission, 1949; Abyan Mission (Aden Protectorate), 1951; British Guiana Mission, 1953; Co-Director FAO, UN Training Centre and Study Tour on Irrigation and Drainage, held in USSR 1956; Aden Protectorate, 1957. Drainage and Irrigation Adviser, part-time, CO, 1950-58. Awarded Telford Gold Medal of InstCE, 1958. *Publications:* Papers in Procs. Inst. of CE, 1930, 1934, 1946 and 1958. *Address:* Cottage on the Links, Steepways, Hindhead, Surrey. *T:* Hindhead 742. *Club:* East India and Sports.

**LACEY, Janet,** CBE 1960; Acting Director, Family Welfare Association, 1969; Director, Christian Aid Department, British Council of Churches, 1952-May 1968, retired; *b* 25 Oct. 1903; *d* of Joseph Lacey, Property Agent, and Elizabeth Lacey. *Educ:* various schools, Sunderland; Drama Sch., Durham. YWCA, Kendal, 1926; General Secretary, YMCA/YWCA Community Centre, Dagenham, 1932; YMCA Education Secretary, BAOR, Germany, 1945; Youth Secretary, British Council of Churches, 1947. *Publications:* A Cup of Water, 1970; series booklets, Refugees, Aid to Developing Countries, Meeting Human Need with Christian Aid, 1956-64. *Recreations:* theatre, music, reading, crosswords. *Address:* Flat 8. Leslie Court, Strutton Ground, SW1. *T:* 01-222 4573.

**LACEY, Walter Graham,** CSI 1947; CIE 1939; *b* 17 July 1894; *s* of late Rev. R. L. Lacey, Exmouth; *m* 1920, Helen Frances Joan Pell-Smith; two *s*. *Educ:* Bedford Sch.; Balliol Coll., Oxford. Served in European War, Bedfordshire Regt and Machine Gun Corps, 1914-19; Indian Civil Service, 1919-47. *Publication:* The Census of Bihar and Orissa, 1931. *Address:* Compton Beeches, Compton, Winchester. *T:* Twyford (Hants) 3218. *Club:* Oxford Union.

**LACEY, (William) Daniel,** CBE 1961; Head of Architects and Building Branch, Department of Education and Science, since 1969; *b* 8 Jan. 1923; *s* of Ivor Ewart and Mary Lacey; *m* 1946, Julie Ellen (*née* Chandler); no *c*. *Educ:* Bishop Gore's Grammar Sch., Swansea. FRIBA 1967; Associate TPI 1949. Assistant Architect, Herts County Council, 1946-55; Assistant County Architect, Notts County Council, 1955-58; County Architect, Notts County Council, 1958-64; Chief Architect, Dept of Educn and Science, 1964-69. Awarded Gran Premio Con Menzione Speciale at Milan Triennale Exhibition, 1960. *Publications:* various papers in Architectural Journals. *Recreation:* gardening. *Address:* c/o Department of Education and Science, Curzon Street, W1. *T:* 01-493 7070.

**LACHMAN, Harry;** impressionist Painter; film director; *b* La Salle, Illinois, 29 June 1886; *m* 1927 (in France), Quon Tai, Chinese concert singer. *Educ:* La Salle High Sch.; High School at Ann Arbor. Orphan at age of ten. Made his own way by selling newspapers, waiting on table at college; Cover Artist, Saturday Evening Post, Colliers, McCall's Cosmopolitan Magazines; went to France with his savings, 1912, and painted for the first time in his life; three months later had two pictures accepted and hung in the Salon Nationale, Paris; since then has shown in various American Exhibitions, England, Spain, and Paris Salons; four paintings bought by the French Government for the Musée du Luxembourg, the National Museum of France; decorated with the cross of the Legion of Honor for services rendered 1914-20 and for artistic achievements; managed the Metro-Goldwyn Studio in Nice, 1927; directed pictures in England for Paramount, 1929: Under the Greenwood Tree, The Outsider, Aren't We All, Down Our Street; directed pictures in France for Paramount, 1930: La Belle Marinière, La Couturière de Luneville, Mistigri; went to Hollywood to direct for Fox, 1932: Face in the Sky, Paddy the Next Best Thing, Charlie Chan at the Circus, Baby Take a Bow (first Shirley Temple starring picture), The Man Who Lived Twice, The Devil is Driving, It Happened in Hollywood, Our Relations, No Time to Marry, George White Scandals, Charlie Chan in Rio, Murder Over New York, Dead Men Tell; went to England to direct for Fox, 1939: They Came By Night, 1942. Discovered: Rita Hayworth, Merle Oberon, Margot Graham, Binnie Barnes, Phyllis Calvert, Jean Gabin. After 30 years returned to painting and exhib. in Kammer Galls, New York; exhib. Los Angeles, 1959. Has been painting in Spain, Morocco, Italy and France. Represented in: Chicago Art Institute; Luxembourg Museum, Paris; Min. of Beaux Arts, Paris; Museum of Modern Art, Rome, etc. Chevalier de l'Ordre des Arts et des Lettres France, 1967; Most Honoured Citizen of Los Angeles; Knight of Mark Twain. *Recreation:* fishing. *Address:* 718 N Beverly Drive, Beverly Hills, Calif 90210, USA.

**LACK, David,** FRS 1951; MA, ScD; Director, Edward Grey Institute of Field Ornithology, Oxford, since 1945; Fellow of Trinity College, Oxford, since 1963; *b* 16 July 1910; *s* of H. Lambert Lack, MD, FRCS; *m* 1949, Elizabeth Silva; three *s* one *d*. *Educ:* Gresham's Sch., Holt; Magdalene Coll., Cambridge. Zoology master, Dartington Hall Sch., 1933-40. Army Operational Research Group, 1940-45. *Publications:* The Life of the Robin, 1943; Darwin's Finches, 1947; Robin Redbreast, 1950; The Natural Regulation of Animal Numbers, 1954; Swifts in a Tower, 1956; Evolutionary Theory and Christian Belief, 1957; Enjoying Ornithology, 1965; Population Studies of Birds, 1966; Ecological Adaptations for Breeding in Birds, 1968. *Recreation:* home help. *Address:* Edward Grey Institute of Field Ornithology, Oxford.

**LACK, Henry Martyn,** RE 1948 (ARE 1934); ARCA 1933; Artist; Member of Epigraphic Survey, Oriental Institute, University of Chicago, at Luxor, Egypt, 1968; *b* 5 Dec. 1909; *s* of Arthur Henry Lack, Bozeat, Northants, and Laura Sophia Keyston; *m* 1941, Phyllis Mary Hafford, Leicester; no *c*. *Educ:* Wellingborough Sch.; Leicester College of Art (Royal Exhibition); Royal College of Art. Member of Sakkarah Expedition (Egypt), 1934-36. Master: Christ's Hospital, Horsham, 1937-46; Northampton School of Art, 1947; Tutor, Engraving School, RCA, South Kensington, 1947-53; Senior Master, Hastings School of Art, 1953-68, Acting Principal part 1968. Served War of 1939-45 (Captain), in North Africa, Sicily, Italy and Middle East, 1942-46. Represented by prints in BM and V&A; Works purchased by Contemporary Art Soc., British Council, Univ. of Reading, S London Art Gallery. Has exhibited widely abroad through the British Council and at home at Royal Academy and Royal Society of Painter-Etchers and Engravers, etc. *Recreations:* travel, gardening. *Address:* 17 White Rock, Hastings, Sussex.

**LACK, Victor John Frederick,** FRCP, FRCS; FRCOG; retired. *Educ:* London Hospital. Examiner: Universities of Oxford and Cambridge and Central Midwives' Board; Midwifery and Diseases of Women Conjoint Board, London; late Lectr in Midwifery and Diseases of Women, Birmingham Univ.; Asst Obst. Queen Elizabeth Hosp., Birmingham; Obst. Regist., Ho. Surg. and Ho. Phys. London Hosp. Obstetrical and Gynæcological Surgeon, London Hospital; Cons. Obstetrician Greenwich Borough Council Maternity Home; Gynæcologist King George's Hosp., Ilford; Obst. and Gyn. Surgeon, Royal Bucks Hosp., Aylesbury. FRSM (Mem. Obst. Sect.); a Vice-Pres., RCOG, 1955-. *Publications:* (jointly) Ten Teachers of Midwifery and Diseases of Women. Contrib. to medical jls. *Address:* Elm House, Loughton, Bletchley, Bucks. *T:* Shenley Church End 243.

**LACON, Sir George Vere Francis,** 7th Bt, *cr* 1818; *b* 25 Feb. 1909; *s* of Sir George Haworth Ussher Lacon, 6th Bt and Vere Valerie Florence Eleanore (*d* 1916), *o d* of late H. S. H. Lacon, Ormesby Hall, Norfolk; *S* father 1950; *m* 1935, Hilary Blanche (marriage dissolved, 1956) *yr d* of C. J. Scott, Adyar, Walberswick; two *s*; *m* 1957, Kathlyn, *d* of late E. Pilbrow, London. *Educ:* Eton. *Heir:* *s* Edmund Vere Lacon [*b* 3 May 1936; *m* 1963, Gillian, *o d* of J. H. Middleditch, Wrentham, Suffolk; one *d*]. *Address:* Cliff House, Southwold, Suffolk.

**LA COUR, Leonard Francis,** MBE 1952; FRS 1970; Principal Senior Scientific Officer, John Innes Institute, since 1970; *b* 28 July 1907; *o c* of Francis La Cour and Maud (*née* Coomber); *m* 1935, Anne Wilkes; no *c*. *Educ:* Merton Sch., Surrey; Sen. Exper. Officer 1948, Chief Exper. Officer 1956, John Innes Institute. Hon. MSc East Anglia, 1969. *Publications:* (with C. D. Darlington) The Handling of Chromosomes, 5th edn 1969; various research articles in scientific jls. *Recreation:* gardening. *Address:* 24 Cranleigh Rise, Eaton, Norwich NOR 54D.

**LACRETELLE, J. de;** *see* de Lacretelle.

**LACY, Sir Hugh Maurice Pierce,** 3rd Bt, *cr* 1921; *b* 3 Sept 1943; *s* of Sir Maurice John Pierce Lacy, 2nd Bt, and of his 2nd wife, Nansi Jean, *d* of late Myrddin Evans, Bangor, Caernarvonshire; *S* father, 1965. *Educ:* Aiglon Coll., Switzerland. *Heir:* *b* Patrick Bryan Finucane Lacy, *b* 18 April 1948. *Address:* The White House, Instow, Bideford, N Devon. *T:* Instow 61.

**LADAS, Mrs Diana Margaret;** Head Mistress, Heathfield School, Ascot, since Sept. 1965; *b* 8 Feb. 1913; *er d* of late Bertram Hambro and Mrs Charles Boyle; *m* 1945, Alexis Christopher Ladas (marriage dissolved, 1955); one *s*. *Educ:* Downe House Sch.; Girton Coll., Cambridge. Before the war, Sec. in Geneva, Malta and London. During War of 1939-45, worked as temp. asst Principal in Min. of Economic Warfare, Board of Trade and Political Warfare executive in Cairo. Transferred to UNRRA, worked in Athens, Washington and London; on the staff of

British Information Services, in New York, 1948-50. Began teaching at Westminster Tutors, 1955; joined staff of Heathfield Sch., 1958; Dep. Head of Moira House Sch., 1959, Head Mistress, 1960; Vice-Principal of Queen's Gate Sch., 1962-65. *Recreations:* gardening and travelling. *Address:* Heathfield School, Ascot; 19 Selwood Terrace SW7. *T:* 01-373 0768.

**LAFERTÉ, Hon. Hector,** QC 1919; BA; LLL; LLD; *b* St Germain de Grantham, Drummond Co., 8 Nov. 1885; *s* of Joseph Laferté and Georgiana Jeanne Tessier; *m* 1911, Irène Senécal, St Césaire, PQ. *Educ:* Seminary, Nicolet; Laval Univ. Called to Bar, 1909; Mem. of the Council of the Bar; was lawyer for the bootmakers at the time of the strike 1913; is legal adviser for many corporations, and also of several Labour Unions; elected to Legislative Assembly for Drummond 1916, 1919, 1923, 1927 and 1931; Dep. Speaker of the Legislative Assembly and Chm. of Cttees, 1923; first Pres. of the Liberal Federals Club, Quebec; attended convocation of Canadian and American Barristers in London and Paris, 1924; Speaker of the Legislature of Quebec, 1928; Minister of Col., Game and Fisheries, 1929; Life mem. of Société Zoologique of Quebec since 1933; Legislative Council of Quebec, and Pres. of the Council, 1934; Leader of Opposition of Legislative Council, 1936, and again 1945; Pres. of Council, 1940 and 1960-66; Liberal Catholic. *Address:* 41 St Louis Street, Quebec, Canada.

**LAFFAN, Robert George Dalrymple;** Fellow of Queens' College, Cambridge; *b* 21 Oct. 1887; *s* of Edward Sidney Laffan, ICS, *s* of Lt-Gen. Sir Robert Laffan, KCMG, and Gertrude, *d* of Gen. Hew Prendergast, late RE; *m* 1st, 1923, Katharine (*d* 1937), *d* of George Frederick Bindloss; no *c*; 2nd, 1939, Hon. Mabel (*d* 1968), *d* of 1st Baron Chalmers and *widow* of Sir M. Stevenson, KCMG. *Educ:* Eton; Balliol Coll., Oxford (Scholar). Pres. of the Oxford Union Soc., 1909; 1st Class, Modern History, 1910; Fellow of Queens' Coll., Cambridge, 1912; Asst Curate of St Olave's, York, 1912-13; Temporary Chaplain to the Forces, 1914-18; attached to Serbian Army, 1916-18; Order of St Sava (Yugoslavia) 3rd class, 1919; Select Preacher, Cambridge, 1922, Oxford, 1930-31; Examining Chaplain to the Bishop of Wakefield, 1928-33; University Lecturer, Cambridge, 1927-53; Tutor of Queens', 1931-35; Bursar, 1935-39; received into Catholic Church, 1933; served in R. Institute of International Affairs (wartime organisation), 1939-43; Research Dept Foreign Office, 1943-46; Italo-Yugoslav Boundary Commission, 1946. *Publications:* The Serbs, Guardians of the Gate, 1918; Select Documents of European History, 1930; Translation of Pasquet's Origins of the House of Commons; The Crisis over Czechoslovakia, 1951; contributor to Cambridge Medieval History and to the History of the Peace Conference of Paris. *Address:* White Shutters, Exlade Street, near Woodcote, Reading, Berks. *T:* Checkendon 316. *Clubs:* Royal Over-Seas League, MCC.

**LAFITTE, Prof. François;** Professor of Social Policy and Administration, University of Birmingham, since Oct. 1959; *b* 3 Aug. 1913; *s* of Françoise Lafitte and adopted *s* of late Havelock Ellis; *m* 1938, Eileen (*née* Saville). (one *s* decd). *Educ:* Collège Municipal, Maubeuge; George Green's Sch., Poplar; St Olave's Grammar Sch., Southwark; Worcester Coll., Oxford. Research and translating for Miners' Internat. Fed., 1936-37; on research staff, and subseq. Dep. Sec., PEP, 1938-43; on editorial staff of The Times, as special writer on social questions, 1943-59; Chm. of PEP research groups on health services, 1943-46, on housing policy, 1948-51. Dean of Faculty of Commerce and Social Science, Birmingham, Univ., 1965-68. Member: Home Office Advisory Council on the Treatment of Offenders, 1961-64; Adv. Cttees Social Science Research Council, 1966-69; UK Nat. Commn for UNESCO, 1966-69; Redditch New Town Corp., 1964-. *Publications:* The Internment of Aliens, 1940; Britain's Way to Social Security, 1945; Family Planning in the Sixties, 1964; (part author) Socially Deprived Families in Britain, 1970; many PEP Planning monographs; contributed to British Journal of Delinquency, Eugenics Review, Chambers's Encyclopædia. etc. *Address:* The University, Birmingham 15. *T:* 021-472 1301; 77 Oakfield Road, Birmingham 29. *T:* 021-472 2709. *Clubs:* Royal Society of Medicine (London); University (Birmingham).

**LAGDEN, Alderman Godfrey William;** Director: Elm Park Petrol & Oil Supplies Ltd, since 1958; Preflor Ltd, since 1968; *b* 12 April 1906; *s* of Augustine William and Annie Lagden; *m* 1935, Dorothy Blanche Wheeler. *Educ:* Richmond Hill Sch., Richmond, Surrey. Sun Insurance Office, London, 1931-34; IBM (United Kingdom) Ltd, 1934-. MP (C) Hornchurch, 1955-66. *Recreations:* cricket, water polo, boxing, and dog breeding. *Address:* St Austell, 187 Southend Arterial Road, Hornchurch, Essex. *T:* Ingrebourne 42770. *Clubs:* Constitutional, Wig and Pen, Spanish.

**LAGERKVIST, Pär (Fabian);** PhD; Swedish Dramatist, Poet, Novelist; *b* 23 May 1891; *s* of Anders Johan Lagerquist and Johanna (*née* Blad); *m* 1st, 1918, K. D. J. Sorensen (marriage dissolved, 1925); 2nd, 1925, E. L. Hallberg, *widow* of Gösta Sandels. *Educ:* University of Uppsala. First book, and some poems, published 1912; visited Paris and was influenced by movements in modern painting, 1913; first play, 1917; theatre critic for Stockholm newspaper Svenska Dagbladet, 1919; subs. visited France and Italy frequently; dramatisation of Bödeln (The Hangman) given in London, 1935. Mem. Swedish Acad. of Lit., 1940; Hon. PhD Gothenburg, 1941; Nobel Prize for Literature, 1951. *Publications:* between 30 and 40 books; several plays and poetry. (Trans.); Guest of Reality (vol. incl. also The Eternal Smile and The Hangman). Eng. 1936; The Dwarf (novel), (US) 1945, (Eng.) 1954; Barabbas (novel), (US) 1951, (Eng.) 1952 (trans. many langs., dramatized and filmed, 1952); The Eternal Smile and other Stories, (US) 1954; The Marriage Feast and other Stories, (Eng.) 1955; The Sibyl (novel), (US and Eng.), 1958; The Death of Ahasuerus (US and Eng.), 1962; Two of his plays, The Man Without a Soul, and Let Man Live, have been included in Scandinavian Plays of the Twentieth Century, 1944, 1951; Midsummer Dream in the Workhouse (play), London, 1953; Pilgrim at Sea (novel), (US and Eng.), 1963; The Holy Land (novel), (US and Eng.), 1966; Mariamne (novel) (US and Eng.), 1968. *Address:* Lidingö, Sweden; c/o Random House Inc., 201 East 50th Street, New York, NY 10022, USA; c/o Albert Bonniers Förlag, 605 Madison Avenue, New York, NY 10022, USA.

**LAGHZAOUI, Mohammed;** Ouissam El Ouala (1st class) and Commander of the Order of the Crown, Morocco; Moroccan Ambassador to the Court of St James's, since 1969; *b* Fez, Morocco, 27 Sept. 1906; *m* 1940, Kenza Bouayad; three *s* three *d*. *Educ:* Moulay Idriss Coll., Fez. Founded many commercial and industrial companies; Chm., Société marocaine des Transports Laghzaoui. During French Protectorate over Morocco, he was

Mem. Government's Council (many times Chm.); one of principal Signatories to Act of Independence, 1944; Dir-Gen. of Nat. Security (apptd by late Mohammed V), 1956-60. Then, as Dir-Gen. of Office chérifien des Phosphates (first nat. mining concern) he promoted production and export; later, he was responsible for Office marocain des Phosphates, and Coordinator of Nat. Mining and Industrial Cos. In charge of four ministries: Industry, Mining, Tourism and Handicraft, and was Pres. of Afro-Asiatic Assoc. for Economic Development, 1966-69. Holds foreign orders. *Recreations:* bridge, football. *Address:* Kent Holme, 44 Bishop's Avenue, N2; Route de Suissi, Rabat, Morocco. *Clubs:* Boodle's Hurlingham.

**LAGOS, Archbishop of, (RC),** since 1965; **Most Rev. John Kwao Amuzu Aggey,** DD, OON; *b* 5 March 1908. *Educ:* St Gregory's Coll., Lagos. Auxiliary Bishop of Lagos, 1957. Chairman: Bishops' Conference of Nigeria; Welfare Dept, Catholic Secretariat. Mem., Curia for Propaganda Fide, 1968-. *Address:* Holy Cross Cathedral, PO Box 8, Lagos, Nigeria. *T:* 20672.

**LAHORE, Bishop of,** since 1968; **Rt. Rev. Inayat Masih;** *b* 14 Sept. 1918; *m* 1952, Farkhanda; one *d. Educ:* Punjab Univ., Lahore; Bishop's Coll., Calcutta; Serampore Univ. Curate, Holy Trinity cum Lahore Cathedral Parish, 1947-50; Vice-Princ., St John's Divinity Sch., Narowal, Dio. of Lahore, 1950-52; Priest i/c Pattoki District, 1952-53; higher studies in USA, 1953-55; Priest i/c Gojra District, Lahore Dio., 1955-59; Exec. Sec., West Pakistan Christian Coun., 1959-65; Archdeacon of Lahore, 1965-68. *Recreations:* reading, badminton. *Address:* Bishopsbourne, Cathedral Close, The Mall, Lahore, Pakistan. *T:* Lahore 53790.

**LAIDLAW, William Allison,** MA, LittD; Professor of Classics in the University of London, Queen Mary College, 1949-64, now Emeritus Professor; *b* 15 July 1898; *s* of James and Sarah A. Laidlaw. *Educ:* Wesley Coll., Dublin; Trinity Coll., University of Dublin. Classical Foundation Scholar, Vice-Chancellor's Medallist in Latin, Vice-Chancellor's Prize for Latin Prose; Senior Moderator in Classics and in Mental and Moral Science, 1922; Lecturer in Classics and Philosophy, University of W. Australia, 1923-28; Student of British Sch., Athens, 1929; Asst Lecturer in Classics, University Coll., Southampton, 1929-31; Lecturer in Latin, University of St Andrews, 1931-46; Reader in Classics, University of London, Queen Mary Coll., 1946-49; Ford Visiting Prof. of Classics, University of Ibadan, 1964-65. *Publications:* A History of Delos, 1933; The Prosody of Terence, 1938; Latin Literature, 1951; contribs to: Oxford Classical Dictionary, 1949; Fifty Years of Classical Scholarship, 1954, Chambers's Encyclopædia: articles, notes, reviews in various classical journals. *Recreations:* music, gardening. *Address:* Minvale, St Anthony's Road, Blundellsands, Liverpool L23 8TN. *T:* 051-924 1279.

**LAILEY, John Raymond N.;** *see* Nicholson-Lailey.

**LAINE, Cleo, (Mrs Clementina Dinah Dankworth);** vocalist; *b* 28 Oct. 1927; British; *m* 1st, 1947, George Langridge (marr. diss. 1957); one *s*; 2nd, 1960, John Philip William Dankworth, *qv*; one *s* one *d*. Joined Dankworth Orchestra, 1953. Melody Maker and New Musical Express Top Girl Singer Award, 1956; Moscow Arts Theatre Award for acting role in Flesh to a Tiger, 1958; Top place in Internat. Critics Poll by Amer. Jazz magazine, Downbeat, 1965. Lead, in Seven Deadly Sins, Edinburgh Festival and Sadler's Wells, 1961; acting roles in Edin. Fest., 1966, 1967. Many appearances with symphony orchestras performing Façade (Walton) and other compositions. Frequent TV appearances. *Recreation:* painting. *Address:* The Old Rectory, Wavendon, near Bletchley, Buckinghamshire. *T:* Woburn Sands 3151.

**LAING, Prof. John Archibald,** PhD; MRCVS; Courtauld Professor of Animal Husbandry and Veterinary Hygiene, at Royal Veterinary College, University of London, since 1959; *b* 27 April 1919; *s* of late John and Alexandra Laing; *m* 1946, June Margaret Lindsay Smith, *d* of Hugh Lindsay Smith, Downham Market; one *s* two *d*. *Educ:* Johnston Sch. Durham; Royal (Dick) School of Veterinary Studies, Edinburgh University; Christ's Coll. Cambridge. BSc(Edinburgh); MRCVS; PhD Cantab. Aleen Cust Scholar, Royal Coll. of Veterinary Surgeons. Research Officer, Ministry of Agriculture, 1943-46; Asst Veterinary Investigation Officer, 1946-49; Lecturer in Veterinary Science, 1949-51, Senior Lecturer in Veterinary Medicine, 1951-57, Reader in Veterinary Science, 1957-59, university of Bristol. Anglo-Danish Churchhill Fellowship, University of Copenhagen, 1954; Vis. Prof., Univ. of Queensland and John Thompson Memorial Lectr, 1970. Consultant to FAO, UN, 1955-56; Representative of FAO in Dominican Republic, 1957-58; Consultant to UNESCO in Central America, 1963-65; Mem., British Agricultural Mission to Peru, 1970. Editor, British Veterinary Journal. Sec., Perm. Cttee, Internat. Congress on Animal Reproduction; Member: Governing Body, Houghton Poultry Research Station. Treasurer, University Fedn for Animal Welfare. Governor, Mount Grace Sch., 1967-70. *Publications:* Fertility and Infertility in the Domestic Animals, 1955, 2nd edn 1970; papers on animal breeding and husbandry in various scientific journals. *Address:* Lower Meadow, Ayot St Lawrence, Welwyn, Herts. *T:* Codicote 413. *Club:* Farmers'.

**LAING, Sir (John) Maurice,** Kt 1965; Chairman, John Laing Construction Ltd; Deputy Chairman, John Laing & Son Ltd; Director: Bank of England; Rolls-Royce Ltd; *b* 1 Feb. 1918; *s* of Sir John Laing, *qv*; *m* 1940, Hilda Violet Richards; one *s*. *Educ:* St Lawrence Coll., Ramsgate. Joined firm as pupil, 1935. RAF, 1941-45. Member: UK Trade Missions to Middle East, 1953, and to Egypt, Sudan and Ethiopia, 1955; Bd of Trade Adv. Coun. on Overseas Construction, 1956-59; Export Gp for Constructional Industries, 1957-59 (Chm.); Min. of Works Nat. Consultative Council, 1959-60; Economic Planning Bd, 1961; Export Guarantees Adv. Council, 1959-63; Nat. Jt Adv. Council to Min. of Labour, 1960-66; Min. of Transport Cttee of Inquiry into Major Ports of Gt Brit. (Rochdale Cttee), 1961-62; Nat. Economic Develt Council, 1962-66. Vice-Pres., Fedn of Civil Engrg Contractors, 1960- (Chm. 1959-60); President: British Employers Confederation, 1964-65; Pres. Confedn of British Industry, 1965-66, Vice-Pres., 1966-. Visiting Fellow, Nuffield Coll., 1965-; A Governor: Administrative Staff Coll., 1966; Nat. Inst. of Economic and Social Research, 1964-. Hon. LLD University of Strathclyde, 1967. Has keen interest in Church activities at home and abroad. *Recreation:* sailing. *Address:* Reculver, Totteridge, N20. *Clubs:* Royal Automobile; Royal Yacht Squadron, Royal Ocean Racing, Royal Burnham Yacht (Burnham-on-Crouch), etc.

**LAING, Sir John (William),** Kt 1959; CBE 1951; President John Laing and Son Ltd, since 1957;

*b* 24 Sept. 1879; *s* of John Laing, Sebergham, Cumberland; *m* 1910, Beatrice, *y d* of William Harland, Chartered Accountant, Stockton on Tees; two *s*. *Educ:* Carlisle Grammar Sch. Director, Grosvenor-Laing Holdings Ltd; Member: Building Research Cttee (Chm. 1945); Nat. House Builders' (Vice-Chm.); Registration Council (Chm. Specification Cttee); Inst. of Builders (Fellow, Mem. Council); Fedn of Civil Engr Contractors (Past Mem. Cttee); British Standards Instn (Mem. Standing Cttee). Pres. London Bible Coll. Vice-Pres. British and Foreign Bible Soc.; Vice-Pres. Crusaders' Union; Chm. Inter-Varsity Fellowship Trust Ltd; Vice-Pres. Fact and Faith Films. *Address:* Fair Holme, Marsh Lane, Mill Hill, NW7. *Club:* National.

*See also Sir John Maurice Laing, Sir W. K. Laing.*

**LAING, Sir Kirby;** *see* Laing, Sir W. K.

**LAING, Malcolm Buchanan,** CMG 1945; OBE 1939; Commissioner for Local Government, British Guiana, 1938-51; retired; *b* 17 April 1890; *y s* of late John Bridges Laing, Wickham, Hants; *m* 1916, Marjory (*d* 1953), *widow* of John Bourke and *er d* of Dr F. A. Neal; one *s*; *m* 1954, Mary Treadwell. *Educ:* Forest Sch., Essex. Entered Colonial Civil Service 1914, British Guiana; Protector of Immigrants, 1920; Liaison Officer to Parliamentary Commission, 1926; Private Sec. to Governor of British Guiana, 1929; Liaison Officer to West Indian Sugar Commission, 1929; District Commissioner, 1932; MLC 1935; Liaison Officer to West India Royal Commission, 1939; acted as Colonial Sec., British Guiana, 1943, 1944, 1945. *Recreations:* tennis, golf and fishing. *Address:* 19 Arundel Road, Worthing, Sussex. *Club:* Royal Commonwealth Society.

**LAING, Sir Maurice;** *see* Laing, Sir J. M.

**LAING, Percy Lyndon,** CMG 1970; retired as Commissioner of Works, NZ; Chairman: NZ Natural Gas Corporation; Vocational Training Council; *b* 12 July 1909; *s* of Percy William and Jessie Laing, Dunedin, NZ; *m* 1937, Mabel Collis Wood; one *s*. *Educ:* Otago Boys' High Sch.; Univ. of Canterbury, NZ. Chief Designing Engineer, NZ Min. of Works, 1951-55; Dir. of Roading (Highways), 1959-62; Comr of Works, 1965-69, retd. Pres. NZ Inst of Engineers, 1962. *Publications:* contribs to engineering jls, etc. *Recreations:* golf, fishing. *Address:* 124 Trelissick Crescent, Wellington 4, New Zealand. *T:* 796678. *Club:* Wellington (Wellington, NZ).

**LAING, Scott;** *see* Laing, W. J. S.

**LAING, (William James) Scott;** Chief, Sales Section, UN Secretariat, since 1969; *b* 14 April 1914; *er s* of late William Irvine Laing and Jessie C. M. Laing (*née* Scott); *m* 1952, Isabelle Mary Durrant-Fox; two *s* one *d*. *Educ:* George Watson's Coll., Edinburgh Univ. Appointed to Dept of Overseas Trade, 1937; Asst to Commercial Counsellor, British Embassy, Buenos Aires, 1938; Second Sec. (Commercial), Buenos Aires, 1944; First Sec. (Commercial), Helsinki, 1947; Consul, New York, 1950; Consul-Gen. (Commercial), New York, 1954; Counsellor (Commercial), Brussels and Luxembourg, 1955; Consultant to UN Secretariat, Financial Policies and Institutions Section, 1958, African Training Programme, 1960. Editor, UN Jl, 1964. *Publications:* reports and articles on international commerce and finance. *Address:* 444 East 52nd Street, New York, NY 10022, USA.

**LAING, Sir (William) Kirby,** Kt 1968; JP, MA, FICE, FIOB; Chairman, The Laing Group of Cos, since 1957; *b* 21 July 1916; *s* of Sir John Laing, *qv*; *m* 1939, Joan Dorothy Bratt; three *s*. *Educ:* St Lawrence Coll., Ramsgate; Emmanuel Coll., Cambridge. Served with Royal Engineers, 1943-45. John Laing & Son Ltd: Pupil, 1937; Joint Man. Dir, 1946. President: London Master Builders Assoc., 1957; Reinforced Concrete Assoc., 1960; Nat. Fedn of Building Trades Employers, 1965, 1967. Chm., Nat. Jt Council for Building Industry, 1968-. Member: DSIR Joint Cttee on Soils, 1958-61; BRS Building Ops and Economics Cttee, 1960-66; MPBW Nat. Consultative Cttee, 1965-67; Board of Govs, St Lawrence Coll., 1961; Court of Govs, The Polytechnic of Central London, 1963-. *Publications:* papers in Proc. ICE and other jls concerned with construction. *Recreation:* sailing. *Address:* Sabie House, Marsh Lane, NW7. *Clubs:* Oxford and Cambride University; Royal Southern Yacht; Royal Engineers Yacht.

**LAIRD, Edgar Ord,** CMG 1969; MBE 1958; HM Diplomatic Service; Foreign and Commonwealth Office, since 1970; *b* 16 Nov. 1915; *s* of late Edgar Balfour Laird; *m* 1940, Heather Lonsdale Forrest; four *d*. *Educ:* Rossall; Emmanuel Coll., Camb. Surveyor, Uganda Protectorate, 1939. Served Army, 1939-46 (Major). Appointed to Malayan Civil Service, 1947; Sec. to Government, Federation of Malaya, 1953-55; Sec. for External Defence, Federation of Malaya, 1956; Sec., Federation of Malaya Constitutional Commission, 1956-57; Dep. Sec., Prime Minister's Dept, Federation of Malaya, 1957. Appointed to Commonwealth Relations Office, 1958; First Sec. (Finance), Office of British High Comr, Ottawa, Canada, 1960-63; High Comr in Brunei, 1963-65; Dep. High Comr, Kaduna, 1965-69; RNC Greenwich, 1969-70. *Recreations:* music, tennis. *Address:* c/o Foreign and Commonwealth Office, SW1. *Club:* Royal Commonwealth Society.

**LAIRD, Hon. Melvin R.;** Secretary of Defense, USA, since Jan. 1969; *b* 1 Sept. 1922; *s* of Melvin R. Laird and Helen Laird (*née* Connor); *m* 1945, Barbara Masters; two *s* one *d*. *Educ:* Carleton Coll., Northfield, Minn. Enlisted, US Navy, 1942, commissioned, 1944; served in Third Fleet and Task Force 58 (Purple Heart and other decorations). Elected: to Wisconsin State Senate, 1946 (re-elected, 1948); to US Congress, Nov. 1952 (83rd through 90th; Chm., House Republican Conf., 89th and 90th). Various awards from Assocs, etc (for med. research, polit. science, public health, nat. educn). *Publications:* A House Divided: America's Strategy Gap, 1962. Editor: The Conservative Papers, 1964; Republican Papers, 1968. *Recreations:* golf, fishing, playing electronic organ. *Address:* 3E880, The Pentagon, Washington, DC 20301, USA. *T:* Oxford 5-5261 (USA). *Clubs:* Kenwood Country, Burning Tree (Washington, DC).

**LAITHWAITE, Prof. Eric Roberts;** Professor of Heavy Electrical Engineering, Imperial College of Science and Technology, London, since Oct. 1964; *b* 14 June 1921 ; *s* of Herbert Laithwaite; *m* 1951, Sheila Margaret Gooddie; two *s* two *d*. *Educ:* Kirkham Gram. Sch.; Regent Street Polytechnic; Manchester Univ. RAF, 1941-46 (at RAE Farnborough, 1943-46). BSc 1949, MSc 1950. Manchester Univ.: Asst Lectr, 1950-53; Lectr, 1953-57; Sen. Lectr, 1957-64; PhD 1957; DSc 1964. Pres., Assoc. for Science Educn, 1970. S. G. Brown Award and Medal of Royal Society, 1966; Prof. of Royal Instn, 1967-70. *Publications:* Propulsion without Wheels, 1966; Induction

Machines for Special Purposes, 1966; The Engineer in Wonderland, 1967; many papers in Proc. IEE (7 premiums) and other learned jls. *Recreations:* entomology, gardening. *Address:* The Circles, Wentworth Close, Ditton Hill, Surbiton, Surrey. *T:* 01-398 3919.

**LAITHWAITE, Sir (John) Gilbert,** GCMG 1953 (KCMG 1948); KCB 1956; KCIE 1941 (CIE 1935); CSI 1938; Director, Inchcape Overseas Ltd, since 1969 (Deputy Chairman Inchcape & Co. Ltd, 1960-64; Director 1964-69); Chairman: Bedford Life Assurance Co. Ltd; Bedford General Insurance Co. Ltd; UK Committee of Federation of Commonwealth Chambers of Commerce; *b* 5 July 1894; *e s* of late J. G. Laithwaite, formerly of the Post Office Survey. *Educ:* Clongowes; Trinity Coll., Oxford (Scholar). Hon. Fellow, Trinity Coll., Oxford, 1955. Served in France with 10th Lancs Fusiliers, 1917-18 (wounded); appointed to India Office, 1919; Principal, 1924; specially attached to Prime Minister (Mr Ramsay MacDonald) for 2nd Indian Round Table Conference, Sept.-Dec. 1931; Secretary, Indian Franchise (Lothian) Committee, Jan.-June 1932; Secretary, Indian Delimitation Cttee, Aug. 1935-Feb. 1936; Private Secretary to the Viceroy of India (Marquess of Linlithgow), 1936-43, and a Secretary to the Governor-General 1937-43; Assistant Under-Secretary of State for India, 1943; an Under-Secretary (Civil) of the War Cabinet, 1944-45; Deputy Under-Secretary of State for Burma, 1945-47, for India, 1947, for Commonwealth Relations, 1948-49; Ambassador, 1950-51 (United Kingdom Representative, 1949-50) to the Republic of Ireland; High Commissioner for the UK in Pakistan, 1951-54; Permanent Under-Secretary of State for Commonwealth Relations, 1955-59. Vice-Chm., Commonwealth Inst., 1963-66; Governor, Queen Mary Coll., Univ. of London, 1959-; Trustee, Hakluyt Soc., 1958- (Pres., 1964-69); Vice-Pres., Royal Central Asian Soc., 1967- (Chm. Council, 1964-67); Vice-Pres., RGS, 1969 (Pres., 1966-69); Mem. Standing Commn on Museums and Galleries, 1959-. A Freeman of the City of London, 1960. Renter Warden, Tallowchandlers' Co., 1969. Hon. LLD Dublin, 1957. Kt of Malta, 1960. *Publications:* The Laithwaites, Some Records of a Lancashire Family; etc. *Address:* c/o National and Grindlay's Bank Ltd, 13 St James's Square, SW1. *Clubs:* Travellers', United University, City of London.

**LAKE, Captain Sir Atwell Henry,** 9th Bt, *cr* 1711; CB 1945; OBE 1919; US Legion of Merit degree of Commander, 1945; RN retired; *b* 13 Feb. 1891; *s* of late Admiral Atwell Peregrine Macleod Lake; *S* cousin, 1924; *m* 1922, Kathleen Marion, *d* of late Alfred Morrison Turner, Broughton, West Derby, Liverpool; three *s*. Served European War, 1914-18, in HMS Lion; present at Battle of Jutland; War of 1939-45, Chief of Staff to Commander-in-Chief, Portsmouth, with rank of Commodore, 1939-42; Chief of Naval Staff, New Zealand, and First Member of Naval Board with rank of Commodore, 1942-45. Formerly ADC to King George VI. *Heir: s* Atwell Graham Lake, *b* 1923. *Address:* Hedgerow Cottage, Barnsfold Lane, Rudgwick, Sussex. *T:* Rudgwick 534.

**LAKER, Frederick Alfred;** Chairman and Managing Director, Laker Airways Ltd, since 1966; *b* 6 Aug. 1922; British; *m* 1968, Rosemary Belfrage Black. *Educ:* Simon Langton Sch., Canterbury. Short Brothers, Rochester, 1938-40; General Aircraft, 1940-41; Air Transport Auxiliary, 1941-46; Aviation Traders, 1946-60; British United Airways, 1960-65; Laker Airways (International) Ltd, 1966-. *Recreations:* horse breeding, racing, sailing. *Address:* New Manor Farm, East Clandon, Surrey. *T:* (office) 01-668 2471, Crawley 27181. *Clubs:* Eccentric, Little Ships.

**LAKIN, Charles Ernest,** MD London; FRCP, FRCS; Consulting Physician Middlesex Hospital; Advisory Physician Golden Square Throat Hospital; late Physician London Fever Hospital; late Medical Referee to HM Treasury; Hon. Librarian Medical Society of London; ex-President Section of Medicine, Royal Society of Medicine; late Examiner in Medicine in Universities of Cambridge, London and Birmingham; Lumleian Lecturer, Royal College of Physicians; Lettsomian Lecturer Medical Society of London; Lecturer in Medical Pathology, Middlesex Hospital Medical School; *b* 1878. *Educ:* Middlesex Hospital. Fellow Royal Society of Medicine; late Senior Censor Royal College of Physicians; President Medical Society of London; Pathologist Middlesex Hospital and Addington Park War Hospital; Clinical Assistant Hospital for Children, Great Ormond Street; Demonstrator in Anatomy, Middlesex Hospital, and Clinical Assistant in Dermatological Department; First Entrance Scholarship, Broderip and Freeman Scholarships, Middlesex Hospital. *Publications:* contributions on Medicine and Pathology to medical journals. *Address:* West Stow Hall, Bury St Edmunds, Suffolk. *T:* Culford 288.

**LAKIN, Sir Henry,** 3rd Bt, *cr* 1909; *b* 8 Oct. 1904; *s* of Sir Richard Lakin, 2nd Bt, and Mildred Alice (*d* 1960), *d* of G. J. Shakerley; *S* father, 1955; *m* 1927, Bessie, *d* of J. D. Anderson, Durban; one *s* (one *d* decd). *Educ:* Eton; Jesus Coll., Cambridge. BA 1926. *Heir: s* Michael Lakin [*b* 28 Oct. 1934; *m* 1st, 1956, margaret (marr. diss., 1963), *d* of Robert Wallace, Co. Armagh; 2nd, 1965, Felicity-Ann, *d* of A. D. Murphy, Kenya]. *Address:* Torwood, PO Mooi River, Natal, S Africa.

**LAKING, George Robert,** CMG 1969; Secretary of Foreign Affairs and Permanent Head, Prime Minister's Department, New Zealand, since 1967; *b* Auckland, NZ, 15 Oct. 1912; *s* of R. G. Laking; *m* 1940, Patricia, *d* of H. Hogg; one *s* one *d*. *Educ:* Auckland Grammar Sch.; Auckland Univ.; Victoria Univ. of Wellington (LLB). Prime Minister's and Ext. Affairs Depts, 1940-49; New Zealand Embassy, Washington: Counsellor, 1949-54; Minister, 1954-56. Dep. Sec. of Ext. Affairs, Wellington, NZ, 1956-58; Acting High Comr for NZ, London, 1958-61, and NZ Ambassador to European Economic Community, 1960-61; New Zealand Ambassador, Washington, 1961-67. *Recreation:* golf. *Address:* Ministry of Foreign Affairs, Wellington, New Zealand. *T:* 44-560.

**LAL, Shavax Ardeshir,** CIE 1941; Advocate, High Court, Bombay; *b* 12 Nov. 1899; *s* of Ardeshir Edulji Lal, Nasik, Bombay Presidency; *m* 1933, Coomi, *d* of N. N. Master; three *d*. *Educ:* Fergusson College and Law College, Poona. Practised law, 1926-30; joined Bombay Judicial Service, 1930; transferred to Legal Department, Bombay, 1930; Assistant Secretary to Government of Bombay, Legal Department, 1932-36; nominated member and Secretary of Council of State, 1936-46; Secretary to Government of India, Ministry of Law, 1947-48; Secretary to Governor-General of India, 1948-50; Secretary to President of India, 1950-54. *Address:* Windcliffe, Pedder Road, Bombay, India.

**LALOUETTE, Marie Joseph Gerard; Hon. Mr Justice Lalouette;** Senior Puisne Judge, Supreme Court, Mauritius, since 1967; *b* 24

Jan. 1912; 3rd *s* of late Henri Lalouette and Mrs H. Lalouette; *m* 1942, Jeanne Marrier d'Unienville; four *s* two *d*. *Educ:* Royal Coll., Mauritius; Exeter Coll., Oxford; London School of Economics; Middle Temple. District Magistrate, Mauritius, 1944; Electoral Commissioner, 1956; Addl. Subst. Procureur-General, 1956; Master, and Registrar, Supreme Court, 1958; Assistant Attorney-General, 1959; Solicitor-General, 1960; Puisne Judge, 1961. *Publications:* Digest of Decisions of Supreme Court of Mauritius, 1926-43; The Mauritius Digest to 1950; A First Supplement to the Mauritius Digest, 1951-55; A Second Supplement to the Mauritius Digest, 1956-60. *Recreations:* music, gardening. *Address:* 4 Barry Street, Curepipe, Mauritius. *T:* Curepipe 801.

**LAMARQUE, Walter Geoffrey,** MBE 1947; Head of East Africa Department, Ministry of Overseas Development, since 1965; *b* 12 Feb. 1913; *s* of late Charles and Elma Lamarque, West Byfleet, Surrey; *m* 1945, Patricia Aikman; two *s* one *d*. *Educ:* Marlborough Coll.; Oriel Coll., Oxford (Scholar). 1st Class Classical Mods, 1934; 2nd Class Lit.Hum., 1936. Indian Civil Service, 1936-47; served in Madras Presidency, and in Government of India at New Delhi and Calcutta. Joined Board of Trade, 1947; UK Trade Commissioner, Melbourne, Australia, 1947-50; Karachi, 1951-55. Joined Commonwealth Relations Office, 1957; First Secretary (Finance), UK High Commission Office, Ottawa, 1957-60; British Deputy Commissioner, Enugu, Nigeria, 1960-63; Africa Economic Department, CRO, 1963-65. *Recreations:* fox-hunting, golf. *Address:* The Parsonage House, Fyfield, Ongar, Essex. *T:* Fyfield 262. *Club:* Oxford and Cambridge University.

**LAMB,** family name of **Baron Rochester.**

**LAMB, Albert, (Larry Lamb);** Editor, The Sun, since 1969; Director, News of the World Organisation, since 1970; *b* 15 July 1929; *m* Joan Mary Denise Grogan; two *s* one *d*. *Recreations:* fell-walking, cricket, deep-sea fishing. *Address:* 16 Cedar Court, Wimbledon Common, SW19.

**LAMB, Albert Thomas,** MBE 1953; DFC 1945; Diplomatic Service Inspector, since 1968; *b* 23 Oct. 1921; *s* of R. S. Lamb and Violet Lamb (*née* Haynes); *m* 1944, Christina Betty Wilkinson; one *s* two *d*. *Educ:* Swansea Grammar Sch. Served RAF 1941-46. FO 1938-41; Embassy, Rome, 1947-50; Consulate-General, Genoa, 1950; Embassy, Bucharest, 1950-53; FO 1953-55; Middle East Centre for Arabic Studies, 1955-57; Political Residency, Bahrain, 1957-61; FO 1961-65; Embassy, Kuwait, 1965; Political Agent in Abu Dhabi, 1965-68. *Recreations:* gardening, tennis. *Address:* 25 Sondes Place Drive, Dorking, Surrey. *T:* Dorking 3400. *Club:* Travellers'.

**LAMB, Air Commodore George Colin,** CBE 1966; AFC 1947; Officer Commanding, Royal Air Force Lyneham, since 1969; *b* 23 July 1923; *s* of George and Bessie Lamb, Hornby, Lancaster; *m* 1945, Nancy Mary Godsmark; two *s*. *Educ:* Lancaster Royal Grammar School. War of 1939-45: commissioned, RAF, 1942; flying duties, 1942-53; Staff Coll., 1953; Air Ministry, special duties, 1954-58; OC No 87 Sqdn, 1958-61; Dir Admin. Plans, MoD, 1961-64; Asst Comdt, RAF Coll., 1964-65; Dep. Comdr, Air Forces Borneo, 1965-66; Fighter Command, 1966; MoD (Dep. Command Structure Project Officer), 1967; HQ, Strike Command, 1967-69. *Recreation:* international Rugby football referee. *Address:* 15 Rushington Avenue, Maidenhead, Berks. *T:* Maidenhead 22624. *Club:* Royal Air Force.

**LAMB, Rev. John,** CVO 1952 (MVO 1947); Parish Minister of Crathie, Aberdeenshire, 1937-63; Domestic Chaplain to the Queen, in Scotland, 1952-64, Extra Chaplain since 1964; *b* 31 Jan. 1886; *s* of Rev. John Lamb, West Kilbride, Ayrshire; *m* 1912, Catharine Smith Hendrie, *d* of Rev. George S. Hendrie, Dalmellington, Ayrshire; one *s* one *d*. *Educ:* Hutchesons' Grammar Sch. and High Sch., Glasgow; Glasgow Univ. (MA), Edinburgh Univ. (BD, DD 1953, Glover Scholar). Parish Minister of Fyview, Aberdeenshire, 1912; of Hyndland, Glasgow, 1923. Domestic Chaplain to King George VI, in Scotland, 1937-52, to the Queen, 1952-64; Chaplain attached 51st Division (6th and 7th Black Watch), European War, 1914-18. *Recreations:* angling, gardening, hill walking. *Address:* Kincairney, Auchterarder, Perthshire. *Club:* Scottish Conservative (Edinburgh).

**LAMB, Prof. John;** James Watt Professor of Electrical Engineering, University of Glasgow, since Sept. 1961; *b* 26 Sept. 1922; *m* 1947, Margaret May Livesey; two *s* one *d*. *Educ:* Accrington Grammar Sch.; Manchester Univ. BSc (1st class Hons) Manchester Univ. 1943; Fairbairn Prizeman in Engineering; MSc 1944, PhD 1946, DSc 1957, Manchester. Ministry of Supply Extra-Mural Res., 1943-46. Assistant Lecturer, 1946-47, Lecturer, 1947-56, Reader, 1956-61, in Electrical Engineering at Imperial Coll. (London Univ.); Assistant Director, Department of Electrical Engineering, Imperial Coll., 1958-61. Pres., British Soc. of Rheology, 1970. AMIEE 1953; FInstP 1960; Fellow, Acoustical Society of America, 1960; FRSE 1968. *Publications:* numerous in Proc. Royal Society, Trans Faraday Society, Proc. Instn Electrical Engineers, Proc. Physical Society, Journal Acoustical Society of America, Quarterly Reviews of Chem. Society, Nature, Phys. Review, Journal of Polymer Science, Vol. IIa. Contrib.: (The Theory and Practice of Ultrasonic Propagation) to Principles and Practice of Non-destructive Testing (ed) J. H. Lamble), 1962; (Dispersion and Absorption of Sound by Molecular Processes) to Proc. International School of Physics "Enrico Fermi" Course XXVII (ed D. Sette), 1963; (Thermal Relaxation in Liquids) to Physical Acoustics, Vol. II (ed W. P. Mason), 1965. *Recreations:* squash, wine-making, music. *Address:* Royston, 10 Crown Road North, Glasgow W2. *T:* 041-339 2101.

**LAMB, Hon. Kenneth Henry Lowry;** Director, Public Affairs, British Broadcasting Corporation, since 1969; *b* 23 Dec. 1923; *y s* of 1st Baron Rochester, CMG; *m* 1952, Elizabeth Anne Saul; one *s* two *d*. *Educ:* Harrow; Trinity Coll., Oxford (MA). President of the Union, Oxford, 1944. Instructor-Lieut, Royal Navy, 1944-46. Lecturer, then Senior Lecturer in History and English, Royal Naval Coll., Greenwich, 1946-53. Commonwealth Fund Fellow in United States, 1953-55. Joined BBC in 1955 as a Talks Producer (Sound); became a Television Talks Producer, 1957, and then Chief Assistant, Current Affairs, TV talks, 1959-63; Head of Religious Broadcasting, BBC, 1963-66; Secretary to the BBC, 1967-68. *Recreations:* cricket, walking. *Address:* 25 South Terrace, Thurloe Square, SW7. *T:* 01-584 7904. *Clubs:* National Liberal; Royal Fowey Yacht.

*See also Baron Rochester.*

**LAMB, Larry;** *see* Lamb, A.

**LAMB, Sir Lionel (Henry),** KCMG 1953 (CMG 1948); OBE 1944; HM Diplomatic Service, retired; *b* 9 July 1900; *s* of late Sir Harry Lamb, GBE, KCMG; *m* 1927, Jean Fawcett (*née* MacDonald); one *s*. *Educ:* Winchester; Queen's Coll., Oxford. Appointed HM Consular Service in China, Dec. 1921; Consul (Gr. II), 1935; served Shanghai, 1935-37, Peking, 1937-40; Consul (Gr. I), 1938; Superintending Consul and Assistant Chinese Secretary, Shanghai, 1940; transferred to St PaulMinneapolis, 1943; Chinese Counsellor, HM Embassy, Chungking, 1945; HM Minister, Nanking, 1947-49; Chargé d'Affaires, Peking, China, 1951-53; Ambassador to Switzerland, 1953-58, retired. *Address:* St Cross House, Winchester.

**LAMB, Lynton Harold;** FRSA 1953; FSIA 1948; Painter, Book Illustrator, Designer; Production Adviser, Oxford University Press (the Publisher); on Staff, The Slade School of Fine Art, since 1950; Lecturer on Methods and Materials, Painting School, Royal College of Art, since 1956; *b* 15 April 1907; *s* of Rev. Frederick Lamb; *m* 1933, Barbara Grace Morgan, *d* of Rev. J. H. Morgan; two *s*. *Educ:* Kingswood Sch., Bath; LCC Central School of Arts and Crafts. Served as Camouflage Staff Officer, 1940-45. Member, London Group; President Society of Industrial Artists, 1951-53. Architectural decorations in various mediums for Orient Liners, 1935-50; first exhibition of paintings, Storran Gallery, 1936; designed Commemorative Binding for lectern Bible, St Giles Cathedral, 1948, and for Coronation Bible, 1953. Adjudicator, National Book League's Exhibition of Book Design, 1950; participant in Arts Council's Exhibition of Painting for 1951 Festival of Britain. Designed the £1 (International Philatelic Art Society award, 1960), 10/-, 5/- and 2/6 postage stamps for new reign, 1955, and air mail stamp, 1957; Designed Purcell Memorial, Royal Festival Hall, London, 1959; Member: Art Panel, The Arts Council, 1951-54; Council of Industrial Design, 1952-55; National Advisory Committee on Art Examinations, 1953-58; Graphic Panel, National Council for Diplomas in Art and Design, 1962; External Examiner (Fine Art), University of Reading, for Diplomas of Scottish Central Art Institutions, 1962, 1963, and Liverpool College of Art, 1965-68. Co-editor with Prof. Quentin Bell of Oxford Paperbacks, Handbooks for Artists; Contributor to Oxford Illustrated Old Testament, 1968. *Publications:* The Purpose of Painting, 1936; County Town, 1950; Preparation for Painting, 1954 (Penguin edition, 1960); Cat's Tales, 1959; Drawing for Illustration, 1962; Death of a Dissenter, 1969; Materials and Methods of Painting, 1970; contrib. to Chambers's Journal, Signature, Motif, etc. *Recreation:* village cricket. *Address:* Sandon, near Chelmsford, Essex. *T:* Chelmsford 71141.

**LAMB, His Honour Percy,** QC; MA; an Official Referee of the Supreme Court of Judicature, 1959-69; Chancellor of the Diocese of Rochester since 1954; *b* 26 Sept. 1896; *s* of Thomas Lamb and Bertha (*née* Poole); *m* 1923, Constance White; one *s* two *d*. *Educ:* Mill Hill School. Served European War, 1914-18, HAC (Lieut); Queen Victoria's Own Corps of Guides, Frontier Force (Captain), 1918-22, Afghanistan, 1919 (Medal and Clasp). Called to the Bar by Gray's Inn, 1923, Bencher, 1947; KC 1949; Treasurer, Gray's Inn, 1962. Recorder of Faversham, 1948-50, of Rochester, 1950-59; First and only Chairman, Inns of Court Executive Council, 1962-67. Commissioner of Assize, Oxford Circuit, 1965, Midland Circuit, 1966. *Publications:* (jointly: Lamb and Evans) Law and Practice of Town and Country Planning, 1950; A Guide to Rating Practice and Procedure, 1951 (2nd edition, 1956) (3rd edition, 1963); Lamb's Encyclopædia of Housing, 1957. *Recreations:* lawns and painting. *Address:* Roughwood, Chislehurst, Kent. *T:* 01-467 1527.

**LAMB, Captain William John,** CVO 1947; OBE 1944; RN retired; *b* 26 Dec. 1906; *s* of late Sir Richard Amphlett Lamb, KCSI, CIE, ICS, and Kathleen Maud Barry; *m* 1948, Bridget, *widow* of Lieut-Commander G. S. Salt, RN; two *d*. *Educ:* St Anthony's, Eastbourne; RNC Osborne and Dartmouth. Commander, 1941; Staff of C-in-C Mediterranean Fleet, 1940-42; Staff of C-in-C, Eastern Fleet, 1942-44; Executive Officer, HMS Vanguard, 1945-47; Deputy Director of Naval Ordnance, 1948-50; Comd HMS Widemouth Bay and Captain (D) 4th Training Flotilla, Rosyth, 1951-52; Commanding Admiralty Signal and Radar Establishment, 1952-54; Commanding HMS Cumberland, 1955-56. *Recreation:* sailing. *Address:* Westons, Bank, Lyndhurst, Hampshire. *T:* Lyndhurst 2620. *Clubs:* United Service, Royal Cruising.

**LAMB, Prof. Willis E(ugene), Jr;** Ford Professor of Physics, Yale University, since 1962; Fellow, Branford College, Yale University, 1963; *b* Los Angeles, California, USA, 12 July 1913; *s* of Willis Eugene Lamb and Marie Helen Metcalf; *m Ursula Schaefer*. *Educ:* Los Angeles High Sch.; University of California (BS, PhD). Columbia Univ.: Instructor in Physics, 1938-43, Associate, 1943-45, Assistant Professor, 1945-47, Associate Professor, 1947-48, Professor of Physics, 1948-52; Professor of Physics, Stanford Univ., California, 1951-56; Wykeham Professor of Physics and Fellow of New Coll., University of Oxford, 1956-62. Morris Loeb Lecturer, Harvard Univ., 1953-54; Lecturer, University of Colorado, Summer, 1959; Visiting Professor, Tata Institute of Fundamental Research, Bombay, 1960; Guggenheim Fellow, 1960-61; Visiting Professor, Columbia Univ., 1961; Fulbright Lecturer, University of Grenoble, Summer, 1964. MNAS, 1954. Hon. DSc Pennsylvania, 1954; MA (by decree), Oxford, 1956; Hon. MA Yale, 1961; Hon. Fellow, Institute of Physics and Physical Society, 1962; Res. Corp Award, 1954; Rumford Medal, American Academy of Arts and Sciences, 1953; (jointly) Nobel Prize in Physics, 1955; Guthrie Award, The Physical Society, 1958; Yeshiva University Award, 1962; Hon. LHD Yeshiva, 1965. *Publications:* contributions to The Physical Review, Physica, Science, Journal of Applied Physics, etc. *Recreation:* sailing. *Address:* Sloane Physics Laboratory, Yale University, New Haven, Connecticut 06520, USA.

**LAMBART,** family name of **Earl of Cavan.**

**LAMBART, Julian Harold Legge;** *b* 7 May 1893; *s* of late Brig.-General E. A. Lambart, CB, RA, and late Mary Louisa, *d* of Sir James Walker, 2nd Bt, of Sand Hutton; *m* 1948, Margaret, *widow* of Sir Walford Davies. *Educ:* Eton Coll.; King's Coll., Cambridge. Served European War, 1914-18, as Capt. RFA (Croix de Guerre). Assistant Master at Eton, 1919; Lower Master, 1945-59; Vice-Provost, 1959-67. *Recreations:* travel and architecture. *Address:* 1 Abbotts Road, Winchester, Hants. *T:* Winchester 2347.

**LAMBART, Sir Oliver Francis,** 2nd Bt *cr* 1911; Lieut late RASC; *b* 6 April 1913; *s* of 1st Bt and Kathleen Moore-Brabazon; *S* father, 1926. *Heir:* none. *Address:* Beau Parc, Co. Meath. *Club:* Turf.

**LAMBERT,** family name of **Viscount Lambert.**

**LAMBERT,** 2nd Viscount, *cr* 1945, of South Molton, **George Lambert,** TD; *b* 27 Nov. 1909; *e s* of 1st Viscount Lambert, PC; *S* father, 1958; *m* 1939, Patricia Mary, *d* of J. F. Quinn; one *d* (one *s* decd). *Educ:* Harrow Sch.; New Coll., Oxford. War of 1939-45: TA, Lieut-Colonel 1942. MP (L.Nat.) South Molton Division, Devon, July 1945-Feb. 1950. (Nat. L-C) Torrington Division, Devon, 1950-58. Formerly Chm. Governors, Seale-Hayne Agricultural Coll., Newton Abbot, Devon. Life Vice-Pres., National Federation of Young Farmers' Clubs, 1970. DL Devon, 1969-70. *Recreation:* golf. *Heir: b* Hon. Michael John Lambert [*b* 29 Sept. 1912; *m* 1939, Florence Dolores, *d* of late Nicholas Lechmere Cunningham Macaskie, QC; three *d*]. *Address:* House of Lords, SW1. *Club:* Carlton.
*See also Hon. Margaret Lambert.*

**LAMBERT, Sir Anthony (Edward),** KCMG 1964 (CMG 1955); HM Ambassador to Portugal, 1966-70; *b* 7 March 1911; *o s* of late R. E. Lambert, Pensbury House, Shaftesbury, Dorset; *m* 1948, Ruth Mary, *d* of late Sir Arthur Fleming, CBE; two *d. Educ:* Harrow; Balliol Coll., Oxford (Scholar). Entered HM Foreign (subseq. Diplomatic) Service, 1934, and served in: Brussels, 1937; Ankara, 1940; Beirut and Damascus, 1942; Brussels, 1944; Stockholm, 1949; Athens, 1952; HM Minister to Bulgaria, 1958-60; HM Ambassador to: Tunisia, 1960-63; Finland, 1963-66. *Address:* 28 Victoria Road, W8. *Club:* Brooks's.

**LAMBERT, Charles Ernest,** CMG 1953; Assistant Secretary Colonial Office, 1947-61; *b* 28 Aug. 1900; *s* of late John and late Mary Eleanor Lambert; *m* 1929, Constance Gray; one *s. Educ:* Aske's Haberdashers' Hampstead Sch. On Military Service, 1918-19. Appointed Colonial Office, 1923; Registrar, UK High Commission in Canada, 1928-32 (on secondment); Assistant Principal, 1937; Principal, 1941; Assistant Secretary, 1947. Visited W. Africa as Sec. Civil Service Salaries Commn, 1945-46, similarly for E. Africa, 1947. Accompanied the then Secretary of State for the Colonies on a visit to Central Africa, 1950. *Address:* Holmwood, Ballinger Road, South Heath, Great Missenden, Bucks. *T:* Great Missenden 2696.

**LAMBERT, Ven. Charles Henry,** MA; Archdeacon of Lancaster, 1959-66, Emeritus, 1966; Vicar of St Cuthbert's, Lytham, 1960-66; Senior Examining Chaplain to Bishop of Blackburn; *b* 13 Jan. 1894; *s* of Henry and Frances Ann Lambert; *m* 1920, Dorothy Ellen Birch; three *s* one *d. Educ:* Primary Schools; privately; Leeds Univ.; Cuddesdon Coll. BA 1916; MA 1932; deacon 1917; priest 1918; Curate of Redcar, 1917-20; of Guisborough, 1920-22; Rector of St Denys with St George, York, 1922-24; Vicar of Royston, Yorks, 1924-28; Rector of St Clement, York, 1928-34; Warden of Whalley Abbey, 1934-45; Director of Religious Education, diocese of Blackburn, 1934-46; Canon of Blackburn, 1934-46; Archdeacon of Blackburn, 1946-59; Proctor in Convocation, 1929-34, York, 1935-45, Blackburn. OCF 1941-44; Archbishops' Visitor to RAF, 1944-45; Rural Dean of Whalley, 1942-45. *Publications:* Go Ye, . . . . Teach, 1939; Whalley Abbey, Yesterday and To-Day, 1948. *Recreations:* reading, walking, keenly interested in all outdoor sports. *Address:* 71a Upper Church Road, Weston-super-Mare, Somerset. *T:* Weston-super-Mare 27851.

**LAMBERT, Sir Edward (Thomas),** KBE 1958 (CBE 1953); CVO 1957; retired from Foreign Service, 1960; *b* 19 June 1901; *s* of late Brig. and Mrs T. S. Lambert; *m* 1936, Rhona Patricia Gilmore; one *s* one *d. Educ:* Charterhouse and Trinity Coll., Cambridge. Member of HM Diplomatic (formerly Foreign) Service. Entered Far Eastern Consular Service, 1926; served at Bangkok, Batavia, Medan, Curaçao, and The Hague. Consul-General, Geneva, 1949-53, Paris, 1953-59. Commandeur, Légion d'Honneur, 1957. *Recreations:* reading and travel. *Address:* Crag House, Aldeburgh, Suffolk. *T:* 2296.

**LAMBERT, Eric Thomas Drummond,** CMG 1969; OBE 1946; retd, 1968; *b* 3 Nov. 1909; *s* of late Septimus Drummond Lambert. *Educ:* Royal Sch., Dungannon; Trinity Coll., Dublin. Indian (Imperial) Police, 1929-47: Political Officer for Brahmaputra-Chindwin Survey, 1935-36, and Tirap Frontier Tract, 1942; District Comr, Naga Hills, 1938. Served with Chinese Vth Army, Indo-Burma Front, 1942; Chief Civil Liaison Officer XXXIII Corps, XIVth Army, 1944; FCO, 1947-68, with service in SE Asia, W Africa, S America, Nepal, Afghanistan. King's Police Medal, 1943; Chinese Armed Forces Distinguished Service, 1st Order, 1st class, 1943. *Publications:* Assam (jointly with Alban Ali), 1943; articles in jls of RGS and Royal Siam Soc.; Man in India. *Recreations:* golf, historical research, lecturing. *Address:* Drumkeen, Glenamuck, Carrickmines, Co. Dublin. *T:* 893169. *Club:* Stephen's Green (Dublin).

**LAMBERT, Frank,** CBE 1948; MA; *b* London, 4 June 1884; *m* 1929, Dorothy Elizabeth, *d* of Major E. H. Beeton, OBE, RAMC. *Educ:* St Olave's Grammar Sch.; Christ's Coll., Cambridge. Assistant Curator, Guildhall Museum, London, 1908-24; served with Essex and Suffolk Regiments, 1916-19; Curator, Stoke-on-Trent Art Gallery and Museums, 1924-27; Director, Leeds City Art Gallery, 1927-31; Extension Lecturer, London Univ., 1920-24; Extension Lecturer, Leeds Univ., 1927-31; Director, Walker Art Gallery, Liverpool, 1932-52; Sydney Jones Lecturer in Art, Liverpool Univ., 1937-38; President, North-Western Federation of Museums, 1941; President, Museums Association, 1946-48. *Publications:* papers in Archæologia, The Studio and other journals. *Address:* 49 Bath Street, Southport, Lancs.

**LAMBERT, Sir Greville Foley,** 9th Bt, *cr* 1711; *b* 17 Aug. 1900; *s* of late Lionel Foley Lambert, 4th *s* of 6th Bt; *S* cousin (Sir John Foley Grey), 1938; *m* 1932, Edith Roma, *d* of Richard Batson; three *d. Educ:* Rugby Sch. Chartered Accountant. *Heir: kinsman,* John Hugh Lambert [*b* 31 May 1910; *m* 1947, Edith Davies; one *s*]. *Address:* 1 Linden Court, Hampton Lane, Solihull, Warwickshire.
[*But his name does not, at the time of going to press, appear on the Official Roll of Baronets.*]

**LAMBERT, Guy William,** CB 1942; BA; *b* 1 Dec. 1889; 2nd *s* of late Col J. A. Lambert, Brookhill, Claremorris, Co. Mayo, and Grace, *e d* of late W. D. Fane, Fulbeck Hall, Lincs; *m* 1917, Nadine, *y d* of late Wilson Noble, Park Place, Henley-on-Thames; one *s* two *d. Educ:* Cheltenham Coll.; St John's Coll., Oxford. Higher Div. Clerk, War Office, 1913; Private Secretary to Sir C. Harris, KCB, Assistant Financial Secretary, 1915; Private Secretary to H. W. Forster, Financial Secretary, 1916; Chevalier, Légion d'Honneur, 1920; Principal Private Secretary to successive Secretaries of State for War, Rt Hon. Sir L. Worthington-Evans Bt, GBE, and Rt Hon. T. Shaw, CBE, 1926-29; Assistant Under-Secretary of State for War, 1938-51. President Society for Psychical Research, 1955-58. Fellow, Irish Genealogical Research Soc., 1970. Silver Jubilee Medal, 1935; Coronation Medal, 1937.

*Address:* Flat 7, 86 Elm Park Gardens, SW10. *T:* 01-352 3686. *Clubs:* Athenæum, Leander, London Rowing.
*See also Sir A. C. W. Drew.*

**LAMBERT, Harold George;** Under-Secretary, Ministry of Agriculture, Fisheries and Food, 1964-70; *b* 8 April 1910; *s* of late Rev. David Lambert; *m* 1934, Winifred Marthe, *d* of late Rev. H. E. Anderson, Farnham, Surrey; two *s*. *Educ:* King Edward's Sch., Birmingham; Corpus Christi Coll., Cambridge (MA); Imperial College of Science, London. Entered Ministry of Agriculture and Fisheries, 1933; Private Secretary to Second Secretary and Parliamentary Secretary, 1936-39; Assistant Secretary, 1948. *Recreations:* music, art, travel. *Address:* 22 Queen Anne's Grove, Bedford Park, W4. *T:* 01-994 3901. *Club:* Royal Commonwealth Society.

**LAMBERT, Maj.-Gen. Harold Roger,** CBE 1941; DSC 1916; RM, retired; *b* 26 Jan. 1896; *y s* of late G. B. Lambert, PWD, Madras, India; *m* 1918, Ruth Noel St Clair (*d* 1955), *d* of late Rev. Dr W. St Clair Tisdall, DD; (one *s*, Lieut RN, DSC and bar, missing, presumed killed, 1943); *m* 1955, Elizabeth Lois King-Church. *Educ:* Dulwich Coll. 2nd Lieut RM, 1913; Captain 1917; served in European War, 1914-19 (DSC); Instructor of Musketry, China Squadron, 1920-22; qualified Royal Naval Staff Coll., Greenwich, 1924-25; Staff Officer (Intelligence) East Indies Station, 1926; Staff Coll., Camberley, 1927-28; awarded King George Prize Scholarship for 1927 and 1928; Plans Division of Naval Staff, Admiralty, 1929-32 and 1933-36; a Member of UK Delegation to London Naval Conference of 1936; Senior Officer RM, on Staff of C-in-C, Portsmouth, 1936-38; commanded RM Field Formations in Orkneys, Norway, Iceland, Middle East and Sicily, 1939-44; Maj.-Gen. 1942; ADC to the King, 1943; Comdt Portsmouth Div. RM, 1944; 1939-43 Star, Africa Star, Italy Star; reitred 1944. Chm., St Birinus Gp. Hosps Management Cttee, 1951-61; Member: Oxon CC, 1955-61; Rural Dist Council, Henley, 1958-61. *Address:* 27 Victoria Hill, Eye, Suffolk. *T:* Eye 313.

**LAMBERT, Jack Walter,** CBE 1970; DSC 1944; Literary and Arts Editor, The Sunday Times; Member of the Arts Council, since 1968; *b* 21 April 1917; *o s* of Walter and Ethel Lambert; *m* 1940, Catherine Margaret, *e d* of Alfred Read, CBE; one *s* two *d*. *Educ:* Tonbridge Sch. Served with Royal Navy in Atlantic, Arctic and North Sea (Light Coastal Forces), 1940-46 (Ordinary Seaman; Lieut-Commander). Joined Sunday Times as Assistant Literary Editor, 1948. Member: Nat. Council, British Drama League; Drama Adv. Cttee, British Council (Chm. 1968-69); Arts Council: Mem. Drama Panel (Chm. 1968-); Theatre Enquiry, 1967-69; Vice-Chm., New Activities Cttee, 1969-70; Chm., Computer Booking Working Party, 1969-; Cttee, Royal Literary Fund. Governor, British Inst. of Recorded Sound, 1966-69. *Publications:* Penguin Guide to Cornwall, 1939; The Bodley Head Saki (ed.), 1963; much occasional writing and broadcasting on literature, opera and the theatre. *Recreation:* singing lieder. *Address:* 30 Belsize Grove, NW3. *T:* 01-722 1668. *Clubs:* Garrick, Beefsteak.

**LAMBERT, John Henry;** Head of United Nations (Political) Department, Foreign and Commonwealth Office (formerly Foreign Office), since 1967; *b* 8 Jan. 1921; *s* of Col R. S. Lambert, MC, and Mrs H. J. F. Mills; *m* 1950, Jennifer Ann (*née* Urquhart); one *s* two *d*. *Educ:* Eton Coll.; Sorbonne; Trinity Coll., Cambridge. Grenadier Guards, 1940-45 (Captain). Appointed 3rd Secretary, HM Embassy, The Hague, 1945; Member of HM Foreign Service, 1947; FO, 1948; 2nd Secretary, Damascus, 1951; 1st Secretary, 1953; FO, 1954; Dep. to UK Representative on International Commn for Saar Referendum, 1955; Belgrade, 1956; Head of Chancery, Manila, 1958; UK Delegation to Disarmament Conference, Geneva, 1962; FO, 1963; Counsellor, Head of Chancery, Stockholm, 1964. *Recreations:* tennis, golf. *Address:* 16 Woodfall Street, SW3. *T:* 01-730 3222. *Clubs:* Travellers', MCC; Hurlingham, Royal St George's Golf.

**LAMBERT, Hon. Margaret (Barbara),** CMG 1965; PhD; British Editor-in-Chief, German Foreign Office Documents, since 1951; *b* 7 Nov. 1906; *yr d* of 1st Viscount Lambert, PC. *Educ:* Lady Margaret Hall, Oxford; London School of Economics. BA 1930, PhD 1936. Served during War of 1939-45 in European Service of BBC. Assistant Editor British Documents on Foreign Policy, 1946-50; Lecturer in Modern History, University College of the South-West, 1950-51; Lecturer in Modern European History, St Andrews University, 1956-60. *Publications:* The Saar, 1934; When Victoria began to Reign, 1937; (with Enid Marx) English Popular and Traditional Art, 1946, and English Popular Art, 1952. *Address:* 39 Thornhill Road, Barnsbury Square, N1. *T:* 01-607 2286; 1 St Germans, Exeter.

**LAMBERT, Richard Stanton,** MA; Supervisor of Educational Broadcasts, Canadian Broadcasting Corporation, 1943-60; *b* 25 Aug. 1894; *s* of late Richard Cornthwaite Lambert and Lilian Lambert, London; *m* 1918, Kate Elinor, *d* of Sydney T. Klein; one *s* one *d*; *m* 1944, Joyce, *d* of Edward Morgan. *Educ:* Repton; Wadham Coll., Oxford (classical scholar). Joined staff of The Economist, 1916; served with the Friends' Ambulance Unit, 1916-18; Lecturer to University Tutorial Classes, Sheffield, 1919; Staff Tutor for Tutorial Classes, University of London, 1924; Head of Adult Education Section, BBC, 1927; Editor, The Listener, 1928-39; Member of Commission on Educational and Cultural Films, 1929-33; of Governing Body of British Film Institute, 1933-40; Vice-Chairman, British Institute of Adult Education, 1936-39; Education Adviser to Canadian Broadcasting Corporation, 1940-43, 1960-61. Couns. to UNESCO on media of mass communication, 1946. *Publications:* The Prince of Pickpockets, 1930; A Historian's Scrapbook, 1932; The Railway King, 1934; When Justice Faltered, 1935; (jointly with Harry Price) The Haunting of Cashen's Gap, 1935; The Innocence of Edmund Galley, 1936; The Universal Provider, 1938; Propaganda, 1938; The Cobbett of the West, 1939; Ariel and all his Quality, 1940; Home Front, 1940; Old Country Mail, 1941; For the Time is at Hand, 1946; The Adventure of Canadian Painting, 1947; Franklin of the Arctic, 1949; The Fortunate Traveller, 1950; North for Adventure, 1953; Exploring the Supernatural, 1955; Redcoat Sailor, 1956; Trailmaker, 1957; The Great Heritage, 1958; The Twentieth Century, 1960; School Broadcasting in Canada, 1962; Mutiny in the Bay, 1963; Renewing Nature's Wealth (Ontario Forests), 1967; Greek and Roman Myths and Legends, 1967. Edited (jointly) Memoirs of the Unemployed, 1933; For Filmgoers Only, 1934; Grand Tour, 1935; Art in England, 1938; translated and printed Vida's Game of Chess, 1921; Walafrid Strabo's Hortulus, 1923, and Plays of Roswitha, 1922-23; ed. and printed Sir John Davies' Orchestra or a Poeme of Dancing, 1922. *Recreation:* fishing.

**LAMBERT, His Honour Robert,** JP; County Court Judge, Circuit No 3 (Cumberland), 1968-70; *b* 28 May 1908; *e s* of late R. F. W. Lambert, Preston; *m* 1936, Doris Mary, *d* of late Robert Casson, Preston; two *s* two *d*. *Educ:* Preston Grammar Sch.; London Univ. (LLB). Called to Bar, Lincoln's Inn, 1931; Tancred Student, 1929, George V Coronation Scholar and Buchanan Prizeman, 1931 (all of Lincoln's Inn). Practised Manchester and Northern Circuit. War of 1939-45: Sqdn-Leader, RAF (VR); served UK, Iceland and NW Europe, Coastal Command and JAG's Staff. Dep. Chairman, Lancashire County QS, 1961-62; Chairman, Agric. Land Tribunal, Lancs-Yorks area, 1962; Dep. Chairman, Mental Health Review Tribunal, Manchester region, 1960-62; Chairman, Preston (South) Conservative Association, 1954-62. JP, Co. Lancaster and Preston Borough, 1960, Co. Westmorland, 1969. *Publication:* Ebb Tide (play), 1930. *Recreations:* amateur play production, small-boat cruising. *Address:* Wavertree Lodge, Bowness-on-Windermere, Westmorland. *T:* Windermere 2345.

**LAMBERT, Dr Royston James;** Headmaster of Dartington Hall School and Director of Dartington Research Unit into the Sociology of Education since 1969; *b* 7 Dec. 1932; *s* of Albert Edward Lambert and Edith Alice Tyler; unmarried. *Educ:* Barking Abbey Sch.; Sidney Sussex Coll., Cambridge; Magdalen Coll., Oxford. Open Exhibitioner, Magdalen Coll., Oxford, 1951; Major Scholar, Sidney Sussex Coll., Cambridge, 1954; Hentsch Prize, 1954. 1st class Hist. Tripos Pt I (dist), 1954, 1st class Pt II 1955, MA 1959, PhD 1960, Cantab; BA Oxon, 1955. Bachelor Schol., Sidney Sussex Coll., Cambridge, 1956-58, Research Fellow, 1958-61; Nuffield Senior Sociological Schol., LSE, 1961-64; Ehrman Fellow, King's Coll., Cambridge, 1962-69. Founded and directed Research Unit into Boarding Education, 1964-68; directed research for Public Schools Commn, 1966-68; directed research for Home Office into Approved School system, 1968-. Founded Boarding Schools Assoc., 1966. *Publications:* Sir John Simon and English Social Administration, 1963; Nutrition in Britain 1950-1960, 1964; The State and Boarding Education, 1966; The Hothouse Society, 1968; New Wine in Old Bottles?: Studies in integration in the Public Schools, 1968; Manual to the Sociology of the School, 1970; contribs in: The Public Schools (G. Kalton, 1966); Religious Education (ed. P. Jebb, 1968); The Progressive School (ed. M. Ash, 1968); Appendix to the First Report of the Public Schools Commission; pamphlets on education, and articles in learned journals on social and administrative history, sociology and education. *Recreations:* restoring paintings; herbaceous borders; Bavarian Rococo; Victorian Gothic; Irish setters. *Address:* Highcross House, Dartington Hall, Totnes, Devon. *T:* Totnes 3630; 2 St Olaves, Murchington, Chagford, Devon. *T:* Chagford 3492.

**LAMBERT, Victor Albert George,** CB 1957; CBE 1951 (OBE 1944); Director, Lansing Bagnall Ltd; Chairman: Modern Materials Management Ltd; J. E. Shay Ltd; *b* 24 May 1897; *m* 1929, Kathleen Florence Browne, Colchester; one *s* (decd). *Educ:* Colchester Technical Coll. Served Royal Horse Artillery, Near East, 1914-19. Royal Ordnance Factories: Assistant Director, 1939; Deputy Director (Engineering), 1941; Director (Guns), 1942. Deputy Director-General Housing Supplies, 1945, Director-General, 1946; Director-General of Armaments Production, Ministry of Supply, 1947-57. FIMechE. *Recreations:* gardening and golf. *Address:* Bayford, St Paul's Road, Dorking, Surrey. *T:* Dorking 2588. *Clubs:* National Liberal, City Livery.

**LAMBERT, Prof. Victor Francis,** MD, ChM, FRCS, FRCSE; Professor of Oto-laryngology, Manchester University, 1947-64; Professor Emeritus, 1964; Director, English Sewing Cotton Co., 1947-68; *b* 12 Aug. 1899; *s* of James and Ann Lambert; *m* 1st, 1930, Myra (*d* 1950), *d* of William and Eva Farnworth, Bolton, Lancs; one *s* one *d*; 2nd, 1954, Margaret, *d* of John and Beatrice Norris, Whalley Range, Manchester; one *d*. *Educ:* Bolton Sch.; Manchester Univ. Inns of Court OTC, Royal Artillery, 1917-19. Formerly: Director of Department of Oto-laryngology, Manchester Royal Infirmary; Christie Hospital and Holt Radium Inst.; Laryngologist, Christie Hospital and Holt Radium Inst.; Consultant to Department of Education of the Deaf, University of Manchester; Cons. Surgeon, Manchester Victoria Memorial Jewish Hospital. Hon. Laryngologist, Royal Manchester College of Music; Pres. Sect. of Laryngology, RSM, 1954-55; Chairman Richard Arkwright Educ. Scholarship; Governor of Bolton School; President, Old Boltonians Association, 1962; Member Manchester Regional Hosp. Board, 1951-60; former Member Court of examiners, RCS of England and Edinburgh; Examiner, National University of Ireland; President: N of England Oto-laryngological Soc., 1950 (Hon. Life Mem.); Manchester Surgical Society, 1955-56; British Assoc. Oto-laryngologists, 1960-64; Manchester Medical Soc., 1963-64; Semon Lecture, 1959; Guest Lecturer, Canadian Medical Society, British Columbia Div., 1963; Watson Williams Memorial Lecture, University of Bristol, 1964. MB, ChB (Victoria Univ., Manchester), 1923; FRCSEd 1927; FRCS Eng (*ad eund.*) 1949; ChM (Victoria Univ., Manchester) 1932; MD 1940. Jobson Horne Memorial Prize, 1963. *Publications:* papers and articles in Journal of Laryngology and Otology; Proc. Royal Society Med.; Anatomical Society of Great Britain; Medical Press; Manchester Univ. Med. Sch. Gazette; Clinical Journal; BMJ Journal of Anatomy. *Recreations:* golf and music. *Address:* (home) Erlesdene Garden Cottage, Green Walk, Bowdon, Cheshire. *T:* 061-928 4144; 46 The Downs, Altrincham, Cheshire.

**LAMBERT, Maj.-Gen. William Harold,** CB 1954; CBE 1944; *b* 29 May 1905; *s* of late Brig.-General T. S. Lambert, CB, CMG, and late Geraldine Rachel (*née* Foster); *m* 1933, Rachel Nina Maxwell; two *d*. *Educ:* The New Beacon, Sevenoaks; Charterhouse; RMC Sandhurst. Commissioned 1924; Lieut, 1926; ADC to GOC-in-C Western Command, India, 1929-31; Adjut 1st E. Lancs Regt, 1932-35; Adjut Depot, E. Lancs Regt, 1936-37; Captain, 1937; psc 1938; GSO3 War Office, 1939-40; GSO2, 44 Div. 1940-41; GSO1 44 Div. 1941-42; OC4 Royal West Kent Regt, 1942-43; GSO1 Instructor, Staff Coll., Haifa, 1943-44; BGS 13 Corps, Feb.-Nov. 1944; Comdt 13 Inf. Bde, 1944-45; BGS 30 Corps Dist., 1945-46; Assistant Comdt Staff Coll., Camberley, 1946-47; idc 1948; DDSD(A) War Office, 1948-52; Comdt 18 Inf. Bde March-Sept. 1952 and Jan.-Aug. 1953; Comdt 1 Malay Inf. Bde, 1952-53; Comdt 1st Federal Div., Malaya, 1953-55; Director, Personnel Administration, War Office, 1955-58, retired. *Recreation:* sailing. *Address:* Little Redlap, near Dartmouth, Devon. *T:* Dartmouth 2679. *Club:* United Service.

**LAMBIE, David;** MP (Lab) Ayrshire Central since 1970; *b* 13 July 1925; *m* 1954, Netta May

Merrie; one *s* four *d. Educ:* Kyleshill Primary Sch.; Ardrossan Academy; Glasgow University; Geneva University. BSc, DipEd. Teacher, Glasgow Corp., 1950-70. Chm., Glasgow Local Assoc., Educnl Inst. for Scotland, 1958-59; Chm., Scottish Labour Party, 1964; Chief Negotiator on behalf of Scottish Teachers in STSC, 1969-70. FEIS, 1970. *Recreation:* football. *Address:* 11 Ivanhoe Drive, Saltcoats, Ayrshire, Scotland. *T:* Saltcoats 4843. *Clubs:* Bute and North Ayrshire Constituency Labour Social (Saltcoats).

**LAMBO, Prof. Thomas Adeoye,** OBE 1961; MD, DPM; FRCPE; JP 1968; Vice-Chancellor, University of Ibadan, since 1968; *b* 29 March 1923; *s* of Chief D. B. Lambo, The Otunbade of Igbore, Abeokuta, and Madam F. B. Lambo, The Iyalode of Egba Christians; *m* 1945, Dinah Violet Adams; three *s. Educ:* Baptist Boys' High Sch., Abeokuta; Univs of Birmingham and London. From 1949, served as House Surg. and House Phys., Birmingham, England; Med. Officer, Lagos, Zaria and Gusau; Specialist, Western Region Min. of Health, 1957; Consultant Psychiatrist, UCH Ibadan; Sen. Specialist, Western Region Min. of Health, Neuro-Psychiatric Centre, 1960; Prof. of Psychiatry and Head of Dept of Psychiatry and Neurology, Univ. of Ibadan, 1963-68; Dean, Medical Faculty, Univ. of Ibadan, 1966-68. Member: Scientific Council for Africa (Chm., 1965); Expert Adv. Panel on Mental Health, WHO, 1959-; UN Perm. Adv. Cttee on Prevention of Crime and the Treatment of Offenders (Chm.); Exec. Cttee, World Fedn for Mental Health, 1964; Scientific Adv. Panel, Ciba Foundn, 1966; WHO Adv. Cttee on Med. Research; Scientific Cttee on Advanced Study in Developmental Sciences; Vice-Chm., UN Adv. Cttee on Application of Science and Technology to Development, 1970; Co-Chm., Internat. Soc. for Study of Human Development, 1968; Chm., West African Examinations Council, 1969, etc. Hon. DSc Ahmadu Bello, 1967. *Publications:* (jtly) Psychiatric Disorders Among the Yorubas, 1961; monographs, and contribs to medical and other scientific jls. *Recreation:* tennis. *Address:* University of Ibadan, Ibadan, Nigeria. *T:* (office) 23248, (home) 21165.

**LAMBOOY, Maj.-Gen. Albert Percy,** CB 1950; OBE 1946; *b* 30 Nov. 1899; *s* of Theodore Lambooy; *m* 1926, Doris (decd); two *d. Educ:* Queen Elizabeth's Sch., Crediton; RMA Woolwich. Commissioned 2nd Lieut from RMA Woolwich, 1919; Captain, 1932; Major, 1938; Temp. Colonel, 1943; Lieut-Colonel, 1946; Colonel, 1946; Temp. Brigadier, 1946; Maj.-General, 1949. Dep. Director of Artillery, Ministry of Supply, 1942-45; Dep. Chief Engineer, Armaments Design, 1945-48; Director General of Artillery, Ministry of Supply, 1948-53; retired 1953. *Recreations:* golf and theatre. *Address:* 10 Paulton's House, Paulton's Square, SW3. *Clubs:* United Service; Chislehurst Golf.

*See also Sir William Esplen, Bt.*

**LAMBRICK, Hugh Trevor,** CIE 1944; Fellow of Oriel College, Oxford; *b* 20 April 1904; 2nd *s* of late Rev. C. M. Lambrick; *m* 1948; Gabrielle Margaret (*d* 1968), *yr d* of late H. H. Jennings; two *s. Educ:* Rossall; Oriel Coll., Oxford (1st Cl. Hons. Mod. Hist. 1926). Entered ICS 1927; Assistant Commissioner in Sind, 1931; Deputy Commissioner, Upper Sind Frontier, 1934; Collector of Sholapur, 1936; Superintendent of Census, Sind, 1939; Secretary to Governor of Sind, 1941; Civil Adviser to Chief Administrator of Martial Law, Sind, 1942; Special Commissioner for Sind, 1943-46; retired 1947; Spalding Senior Res. Fellow, Oriel Coll., Oxford, 1947. Treasurer, 1951-55, Res. Fellow, 1955. *Publications:* Sir Charles Napier and Sind, 1952; John Jacob of Jacobabad, 1960; History of Sind, Vol. I, 1964. Numerous articles on Historical and Archæological subjects in Journal of Sind Historical Society since 1935 (President, 1940-43); Census of India, 1941, Vol. XII; Sind (Official). *Recreation:* music. *Address:* Pickett's Heath, Boars Hill, Oxford. *Club:* East India and Sports.

**LAMBTON,** family name of **Earldom of Durham.**

**LAMBTON, Prof. Ann Katharine Swynford,** OBE 1942; FBA 1964; BA, PhD, DLit, Professor of Persian, University of London, since 1953; *b* 8 Feb. 1912; *d* of late Hon. George Lambton, Press Attaché, British Embassy (formerly Legation), Tehran, 1939-45; Senior Lecturer in Persian, School of Oriental and African Studies, 1945-48; Reader in Persian, University of London, 1948-53. PhD London, 1939; DLit London, 1953. *Publications:* Three Persian Dialects, 1938; Landlord and Peasant in Persia, 1953; Persian Grammar, 1953; Persian Vocabulary, 1964; The Persian Land Reform 1962-66, 1969. *Address:* c/o School of Oriental and African Studies, University of London, WC1. *T:* 01-580 9021.

**LAMBTON, Antony Claud Frederick (Viscount Lambton,** Courtesy title by which he was known when his father was Earl of Durham); MP (C) Berwick upon Tweed Division of Northumberland since 1951; Parliamentary Under-Secretary of State, Ministry of Defence, since 1970; *b* 10 July 1922; *s* of 5th Earl of Durham (*d* 1970) (whose title he disclaimed), and Diana (*d* 1924), *o d* of Granville Farquhar; *m* 1942, Belinda, *d* of Major D. H. Blew-Jones, Westward Ho!, North Devonshire; one *s* five *d.* Parliamentary Private Secretary to the Foreign Secretary, 1955-57. *Heir to disclaimed peerages: s* Hon. Edward Richard Lambton, *b* 19 Oct. 1961. *Address:* The Garden House, Lambton Castle, Fence Houses, Co. Durham.

**LAMING, Very Rev. Frank Fairbairn;** Provost of St Andrew's Cathedral, Inverness, since 1966; *b* 24 Aug. 1908; *s* of William John Laming and Maude Elizabeth (*née* Fairbairn); *m* 1939, Ruth Marion, *d* of Herbert William Pinder and Rose Marion (*née* Price). *Educ:* King Edward VI Sch., Retford; The Theological Coll., Edinburgh. In business, 1925-33; Edinburgh Theological Coll., 1933-36; Luscombe Scholar, 1936; Durham LTh, 1936. Deacon, 1936; Priest, 1937; Assistant Priest, Christ Church, Glasgow, 1936-39; Priest in Charge, St Margaret, Renfrew, 1939-44; Rector, Holy Trinity Church, Motherwell, 1944-53; Rector and Provost of St Mary's Cathedral, Glasgow, 1953-66. *Recreations:* woodworking, gardening, fishing. *Address:* St Andrew's Lodge, 15 Ardross Street, Inverness. *T:* 33535.

**LAMOND, James Alexander,** MP (Lab) Oldham (East) since 1970; JP; *b* Durrelton, Perthshire, 29 Nov. 1928; *s* of Alexander N. G. Lamond and Christina Lamond (*née* Craig); *m* 1954, June Rose Wellburn; three *d. Educ:* Burrelton Sch.; Coupar Angus Sch. Apprentice Draughtsman, 1944-49; Draughtsman, 1949-70. Aberdeen City Council: Mem., 1959-70 (Chm., Transport Cttee, 1963-67; Chm., Finance Cttee, 1967-70). Lord Provost of Aberdeen, 1970-; Lord Lieutenant of the County of the City of Aberdeen, 1970-. Mem. DATA (Draughtsman's Union), 1944- (Chm., No 1 Divisional Council of DATA, 1968-70); Pres., Aberdeen Trades Council, 1969. JP, Aberdeen. *Recreations:* golf, travel, reading, thinking. *Address:* 20 Beechgrove Terrace,

Aberdeen. *T:* Aberdeen 51074. *Clubs:* Labour (Oldham); Trades Council (Aberdeen).

**LAMOND, Sir William,** Kt, *cr* 1936; *b* 21 July 1887; *s* of late Thomas Lamond and Jane MacDonald; *m* 1914, Ethel Speechly (*d* 1939); one *s*; *m* 1946, Norah Aitken. *Educ:* Harris Academy, Dundee. Joined Royal Bank of Scotland, Meigle, 1902; Bank of Bombay, 1907; Managing Governor, Imperial Bank of India, 1934; Managing Director, Imperial Bank of India, 1935-45; Member Indian Central Banking Enquiry Cttee, 1930-31; President, Indian Institute of Bankers, 1943-45. *Address:* 23 Rivermead Court, Hurlingham, SW6. *Clubs:* Oriental; Bengal (Calcutta).

**LAMONT, William Dawson,** MA, DPhil; *b* Prince Edward Island, Canada, 3 Feb. 1901; 4th *s* of Rev. Murdoch Lamont, Rothiemurchus, Inverness-shire, and Euphemia Ann Hume; *m* 1930, Ann Fraser, *d* of Dr David Christie, Glasgow; no *c*. *Educ:* Glasgow Univ. (Edward Caird Medallist; First Class in Moral and Mental Philosophy 1924, Euing Fellow and Ferguson Scholar 1924); Balliol Coll., Oxford. Assistant in Moral Philosophy, University of Glasgow, 1926, and Lecturer, 1929; Professor of Philosophy, University of Cairo, 1942. Principal of Makerere Coll., East Africa, 1946-49. Served with Clyde River Patrol and as Naval Intelligence Liaison Officer, West Scotland, 1939-42. Hon. Secretary Anglo-Egyptian Union, 1944; Vice-Chairman Cairo Group of RIIA, 1944. FSA Scot. 1968. HonDLitt, University of East Africa, 1965. *Publications:* Introduction to Green's Moral Philosophy, 1934; Principles of Moral Judgement, 1946; The Value Judgement, 1955; The Early History of Islay, 1966; Ancient and Mediæval Sculptured Stones of Islay, 1968; articles (on philosophical subjects) in Mind, Proceedings of the Aristotelian Society, Philosophy; (on historical subjects) in Scottish Studies, Proceedings of the Royal Irish Academy. *Recreations:* walking, sailing. *Address:* 37 Kirklee Road, Glasgow W2. *T:* 041-339 5399.

**LAMPE, Rev. Professor Geoffrey William Hugo,** MC 1945; DD; FBA 1963; Regius Professor of Divinity, Cambridge University, since 1970; Fellow of Gonville and Caius College, since 1960; *b* 13 Aug. 1912; *s* of late B. M. Lampe and Laura M. Lampe; *m* 1938, Elizabeth Enid Roberts; one *s* one *d*. *Educ:* Blundell's Sch.; Exeter Coll., Oxford (scholar, MA); Queen's Coll., Birmingham. Ordained, 1937; Curate of Okehampton, 1937-38; Assistant Master, King's Sch., Canterbury, 1938-41; Chaplain to the Forces, 1941-45; Fellow and Chaplain of St John's Coll., Oxford, 1943-53; Professor of Theology, Birmingham Univ., 1953-59; Dean of the Faculty of Arts, 1955-59; Vice-Principal, 1957-60; Ely Prof. of Divinity, Cambridge Univ., 1959-70. DD 1953, Hon. DD, Edinburgh, 1959; Teol. Dr (*hc*) Lund, 1965. Hon. Canon of Birmingham Cathedral, 1957-59. *Publications:* Aspects of the New Testament Ministry, 1948; The Seal of the Spirit, 1951; Reconciliation in Christ, 1956; (ed) Justification by Faith, 1954; I Believe, 1960; (ed) A Patristic Greek Lexicon, vol. 1, 1961–vol. 5, 1969; (ed) The West from the Fathers to the Reformation (Cambridge History of the Bible), 1969; various essays in symposia and articles in theological journals. *Address:* Gonville and Caius College, Cambridge; The Black Hostelry, Ely.

**LAMPLOUGH, Maj.-Gen. Charles Robert Wharram,** CBE 1945; DSC 1918; DL; JP; Royal Marines, retired; *b* 10 June 1896; *s* of late Robert Lamplough and Louisa Lamplough, Scarborough; *m* 1921, Doris Mary Ford; one *d*. *Educ:* Warwick Sch. Served European War, 1914-18: joined Royal Marines, 1914, and served in Mediterranean and in Grand Fleet, Dardanelles and Zeebrugge (DSC). Served, 1919-39, in HM ships in various waters and held instructional and staff appointments at home and in Far East. Served War of 1939-45 on Naval Staff, Admiralty, and in 1943 returned to Far East as Maj.-General on staff of Supreme Allied Commander, SEAC (CBE). ADC to King George VI, 1946; Maj.-General Commanding Plymouth Group, Royal Marines, 1946-49; retired, 1949; Hon. Colonel Comdt, Plymouth Group Royal Marines, 1953-57. DL Devonshire, 1966; JP County of Devon, 1954. *Address:* Falklands, 32 Salterton Road, Exmouth, Devon. *T:* Exmouth 3648.

**LAMPLUGH, Rt. Rev. Kenneth E. N.;** *see* Southampton, Suffragan Bishop of.

**LAMPLUGH, Maj.-Gen. Stephen,** CB 1954; CBE 1943; retired 1955; Past Director of Civil Defence, Northern Region (Newcastle upon Tyne), 1955-64; *b* 25 May 1900; *s* of late George William Lamplugh, FRS, Driffield, Yorks; *m* 1938, Mary Lewis, *d* of A. H. Vesey, Suddon Grange, Wincanton, Somerset; one *s* one *d*. *Educ:* St Albans; RMA, Woolwich. 2nd Lieut RE, 1919; Major, 1938; Lt-Col (temp.), 1940; Brigadier (temp.), 1942; Maj.-Gen. (temp.), 1945 and 1952; Colonel, 1945; Brigadier, 1947; Maj.-General, 1953. Served Near East, 1922-23; NW Frontier, 1930; France, 1939-40 (despatches); psc 1937. Commander Rhine District, BAOR, 1952-55, retired 1955. Chairman Joint War Office Treasury Cttee, 1955. *Recreations:* normal. *Address:* Lower Mead, Middle Ridge Lane, Corton Denham, Sherborne, Dorset. *T:* Corton Denham 249.

**LAMPSON,** family name of **Baron Killearn.**

**LAMPSON, Sir Curtis George,** 3rd Bt, *cr* 1866, FRGS, FZS; Member of British Institute of Plastics; *b* 23 Jan. 1890; *s* of 2nd Bt and Sophia, *d* of Manuel Van Gelderen; *S* father, 1899; *m* 1921, Maud Lawton (*d* 1960), *d* of Alfred Wrigley, Bolton, Lancs; one *d*. *Educ:* Charterhouse. Explored French Central W. Africa and Libyan Desert; visited Poland, Lithuania, Latvia and Estonia, under auspices of respective Governments to study Agrarian Reform and Vilna Question; lectured on both subjects throughout Great Britain and USA; 1st Lieut Somerset LI, 1914-16; Captain, Motor Transport in Egypt, 1916-18; Lecturer on Travel; broadcaster on art and travel, Great Britain and USA; author of The Life of Edward Jenner, adapted for television; contributed to Sunday Times, New York Times, Cape Times, XIX Century and After, Daily Express, Accountancy, etc.; various articles syndicated in USA and Canada; contributed also to leading British, S African and Canadian farming periodicals on bovine matters, particularly those appertaining to non-pulmonary tuberculosis among human beings. *Recreations:* literary. *Heir: cousin,* 2nd Baron Killearn, *qv*. *Address:* 2 The Square, Burwash, Sussex. *T:* Burwash 574.

**LANCASTER, Bishop of, (RC),** since 1962; **Rt. Rev. Brian C. Foley;** *b* Ilford, 25 May 1910. *Educ:* St Cuthbert's Coll., Ushaw; Gregorian Univ., Rome. Priest, 1937; Assistant Priest, Shoeburyness; subseq. Assistant Priest, Romford; Parish Priest, Holy Redeemer, Harold Hill, and Holy Cross, Harlow. Canon of Brentwood Diocese, 1959. *Address:* Bishop's House, Cannon Hill, Lancaster.

**LANCASTER, Suffragan Bishop of,** since 1955; **Rt. Rev. Anthony Leigh Egerton Hoskyns-**

**Abrahall;** *b* 13 Oct. 1903; *s* of Bennet Hoskyns-Abrahall, CBE, and Edith Louise (*née* Tapp); *m* 1937, Margaret Ada Storey; two *s* one *d*. *Educ:* RNC Osborne and Dartmouth; Westcott House Theological Coll., Cambridge. Left RN, 1929; ordained, 1931; Curate, St Mary's, Portsea, 1931-33; Chaplain, Shrewsbury Sch., 1933-36; Curate, St Wilfrid's, Harrogate, 1936-39; Chaplain, Tower of London, 1939; Chaplain, RNVR, 1939-45; Vicar, St Michael's, Aldershot, 1945-54; Rural Dean of Aldershot, 1949-54; Provost, Northern Chapter of Woodard Schools, 1964. *Recreations:* fishing, shooting, cricket. *Address:* Pedder's Wood, Scorton, near Preston, Lancs PR3 1BD. *T:* Garstang 2300. *Clubs:* United Service; MCC.

**LANCASTER, Archdeacon of;** *see* Gower-Jones, Ven. G.

**LANCASTER, Col Claude Granville;** Chairman, The Bestwood Co. Ltd; *b* 1899. *Educ:* Eton, RMC. Royal Horse Guards, 1918; served Sherwood Foresters, 1939-43 (despatches). Hon. Colonel, 112th Regt, RAC (Foresters). MP(C) Fylde, 1938-50, South Fylde, 1950-70. *Address:* 11 St Leonard's Terrace, SW3. *T:* 01-730 9272; Kelmarsh Hall, Northampton. *T:* Maidwell 276; Langford Grove, Maldon, Essex. *T:* Maldon 3567. *Club:* White's.

**LANCASTER, Brig. Edmund Henry,** CB 1936; Indian Army, retired; *b* 1881; *s* of William Henry Lancaster, Epsom; *m* 1905, Alice (*d* 1966), *d* of Charles J. Grahame; one *s* one *d*. *Educ:* United Services Coll., Westward Ho! Queen's Royal West Surrey Regt, 1900; 25th Cavalry (FF) Indian Army, 1902-05; Indian Army Service Corps, 1905-30; Colonel DDS and T, AHQ, India, 1930-32; Inspector RIASC Services, India, 1932-36; served NWFP, 1908 (despatches, medal with clasp); European War, 1914-18 (despatches, medals); Iraq, 1920 (medal with clasp). *Address:* c/o National and Grindlays Bank, 13 St James's Square, SW1.

**LANCASTER, Dame Jean,** DBE 1963; *b* 11 Aug. 1909; *d* of late Richard C. Davies; *m* 1967, Roy Cavander Lancaster. *Educ:* Merchant Taylors' Sch., Crosby, Lancashire. Director, Women's Royal Naval Service, 1961-64. *Address:* 2 Fair Meadow, Rye Hill, Rye, Sussex.

**LANCASTER, Vice-Admiral Sir John (Strike),** KBE 1961; CB 1958; retired 1962; *b* 26 June 1903; *s* of George Henry Lancaster; *m* 1927, Edith Laurie Jacobs; two *d*. *Educ:* King Edward VI Sch., Southampton. Joined RN, 1921; Commander, 1940; Captain, 1951; Rear-Admiral, 1956; Vice-Admiral, 1959. Served War of 1939-45: HMS Gloucester; RN Barracks, Portsmouth; Persian Gulf; HMS Ocean. Rear-Admiral Personnel, Home Air Command, Lee-on-the-Solent, 1956; Director-General of Manpower, 1959-62; Chief Naval Supply and Secretariat Officer, 1959-62. *Recreation:* gardening. *Address:* Moorings, Western Way, Alverstoke, Hants. *Club:* Army and Navy.

**LANCASTER, Osbert,** CBE 1953; Artist and Writer; *b* 4 Aug. 1908; *o s* of late Robert Lancaster and Clare Bracebridge Manger; *m* 1933, Karen (*d* 1964), 2nd *d* of late Sir Austin Harris, KBE; one *s* one *d*; *m* 1967, Anne Scott-James. *Educ:* Charterhouse; Lincoln Coll., Oxford; Slade Sch. Hon. ARIBA. Cartoonist Daily Express since 1939; Foreign Office (News Dept), 1940; Attached to HM Embassy, Athens, 1944-46; Sydney Jones Lecturer in Art, Liverpool Univ., 1947. Adviser to GLC Historic Buildings Bd, 1969-. Governor King Edward VII Sch., King's Lynn. Hon. DLitt: Birmingham Univ., 1964; Newcastle-upon-Tyne, 1970. Fellow, University College, London, 1967. Theatre Décors: Pineapple Poll, Sadler's Wells, 1951; Bonne Bouche, Covent Garden, 1952; Love in a Village, English Opera Group, 1952; High Spirits, Hippodrome, 1953; Rake's Progress, Edinburgh (for Glyndebourne), 1953; All's Well That Ends Well, Old Vic, 1953; Don Pasquale, Sadler's Wells, 1954; Coppelia, Covent Garden, 1954; Napoli, Festival Ballet, 1954; Falstaff, Edinburgh (for Glyndebourne), 1955; Hotel Paradiso, Winter Garden, 1956; Zuleika, Saville, 1957; L'Italiana in Algeri, Glyndebourne, 1957; Tiresias, English Opera Group, 1958; Candide, Saville, 1959; La fille mal gardée, Covent Garden, 1960; She Stoops to Conquer, Old Vic, 1960; La Pietra del Paragone, Glyndebourne, 1964; Peter Grimes, Bulgarian National Opera, Sofia, 1964; L'Heure Espagnole, Glyndebourne, 1966; The Rising of the Moon, Glyndebourne, 1970. *Publications:* Progress at Pelvis Bay, 1936; Our Sovereigns, 1936; Pillar to Post, 1938; Homes, Sweet Homes, 1939; Classical Landscape with Figures, 1947; The Saracen's Head, 1948; Drayneflete Revealed, 1949; Façades and Faces, 1950; Private Views, 1956; The Year of the Comet, 1957; Etudes, 1958; Here, of All Places, 1959; Signs of the Times, 1961; All Done From Memory (Autobiog.), 1963; With an Eye to the Future (Autobiog.), 1967; Temporary Diversions, 1968; Sailing to Byzantium, 1969; Recorded Live, 1970. *Recreation:* topography. *Address:* 12 Eaton Square, SW1. *Clubs:* St James', Pratt's, Beefsteak, Garrick.

**LANCE, Ven. John Du Boulay,** MC 1945; MA; Archdeacon of Wells and Canon of Wells Cathedral, since 1963; *b* 14 March 1907; *s* of Rev. Arthur Porcher Lance and Harriet Agatha Lance, Buckland St Mary, Somerset; *m* 1936, Lena Winifred Clifford; one *s*. *Educ:* Marlborough; Jesus Coll., Cambridge; Cuddesdon Theological Coll. Assistant Curate, St Peter, Wolverhampton, 1930-34; Missioner, Trinity Coll., Oxford. Mission, Stratford, 1934-36; Vicar of Bishops Lydeard, 1936-47. Chaplain to the Forces, 1941-46 (despatches). Vicar of St Andrew's, Taunton, 1947-57; Preb. of Wells, 1951-63; Rector of Bathwick, Bath, 1957-63. Proctor in Convocation, 1959-64; Diocesan Adviser in Christian Stewardship, 1961-67; Warden, Abbey Retreat House, Glastonbury, 1965-. *Address:* 6 The Liberty, Wells, Somerset. *T:* Wells 2224. *Club:* Hawks (Cambridge).

**LANCHBERY, John Arthur,** FRAM; Principal Conductor, Royal Ballet, since 1959; *b* London, 15 May 1923; *s* of William Lanchbery and Violet (*née* Mewett); *m* 1951, Elaine Fifield (divorced 1960); one *d*. *Educ:* Alleyn's Sch., Dulwich; Royal Academy of Music. Henry Smart Composition Scholarship, 1942. Served, Royal Armoured Corps, 1943-45. Royal Academy of Music, 1945-47; Musical Director, Metropolitan Ballet, 1948-50; Sadler's Wells Theatre Ballet, 1951-57; Royal Ballet, 1957-. ARAM 1953; Bolshoi Theatre Medal, Moscow, 1961. *Publications:* Arrangements and Compositions of Ballets include: Pleasuredrome, 1949; Eve of St Agnes (BBC commission), 1950; House of Birds, 1955; La Fille Mal gardée, 1960; The Dream, 1964; Don Quixote, 1966; Giselle, 1968; La Sylphide, 1970. *Recreations:* walking, reading. *Address:* 11 Marlborough Street, Chelsea, SW3. *T:* 01-584 1927. *Club:* Garrick.

**LANCHESTER, Elsa;** Actress; *d* of James Sullivan and Edith Lanchester; *m* 1929, Charles Laughton (*d* 1962); became American Citizen, 1950. *Educ:* Privately. Started the

Children's Theatre, Charlotte Street, Soho, 1918; first appearance on stage, 1922; afterwards played at Lyric, Hammersmith, in The Way of the World, 1924, in The Duenna, 1924 and in Riverside Nights, 1926; first appearance in New York at Lyceum Theatre, 1931; joined Old Vic-Sadler's Wells company, 1933; was Peter Pan, Palladium, 1936; was in They Walk Alone, New York, 1941; 5th Year, 1946, as star of Turnabout Theatre, Los Angeles, California; Turn About Theatre, nightly continuously, from 1941. Acted in The Party, London, 1958. Has appeared in films including The Constant Nymph, Potiphar's Wife, The Private Life of Henry VIII, David Copperfield, Bride of Frankenstein, Naughty Marietta, The Ghost Goes West, Rembrandt, Vessel of Wrath, Ladies in Retirement, Son of Fury, Passport to Destiny, Lassie Come Home, Spiral Staircase, Razor's Edge, The Big Clock, The Inspector General, The Secret Garden, Come to the Stable, Buccaneer Girl, The Glass Slipper, Witness for the Prosecution, Bell, Book and Candle, Mary Poppins, That Darn Cat, Blackbeard's Ghost. Television series, The John Forsythe Show. *Publication:* Charles Laughton and I, 1938. *Recreation:* wild flowers. *Address:* 9405 Brighton Way, Beverly Hills, Calif 90210, USA.

**LAND, Edwin Herbert;** US physicist and inventor; Founder Chairman of Board, President, and Director of Research, Polaroid Corporation, Cambridge, Massachusetts; Visiting Institute Professor, Massachusetts Institute of Technology, since 1956; Member, Board of Trustees, Ford Foundation, since 1967; *b* Bridgeport, Connecticut, 7 May 1909; *s* of Harry M. and Matha G. Land; *m* 1929, Helen Maislen; two *d*, *Educ:* Norwich Acad.; Harvard, Founded Polaroid Corporation, 1937. War of 1941-45, in charge of research into development of weapons and materials, and cons. on missiles to US Navy. Invented polarizer for light in form of extensive synthetic sheet; also camera which produces complete photograph immediately after exposure, 1947. Member: President's Foreign Intelligence Adv. Bd; Nat. Commn on Technology, Automation, and Economic Progress, 1965-66; Carnegie Commn on Educational TV, 1966-67; William James Lectr on Psychology, Harvard, 1966-67. Awards include: Hood Medal and Progress Medal, RPS; Cresson Medal and Potts Medal, Franklin Inst.; Scott Medal, Philadelphia City Trusts; Rumford Medal, Amer. Acad. of Arts and Sciences, 1945; Holley Medal, Amer. Soc. Mech. Engrs, 1948; Duddell Medal, British Physical Soc., 1949. Presidential Medal of Freedom, 1963; Nat. Medal of Science, 1967. Mem., President's Science Adv. Cttee, USA. Fellow: Photographic Soc. of America; Amer. Acad. of Arts and Sciences (Past Pres.); Royal Photographic Society; Nat. Acad. of Science, etc. Hon. Fellow: Royal Microscopical Society, and many other American and foreign learned bodies. ScD (Hon.) Harvard Univ., 1957, and holds many other hon. doctorates in science and law. *Publications:* contributions Journal Opt. Soc. America, Amer. Scientist, Proceedings of Nat. Acad. of Science. *Recreations:* music, horseback riding. *Address:* 163 Brattle Street, Cambridge, Mass, USA. *T:* Univ. 4-6000; 730 Main Street, Cambridge, Mass. *Clubs:* Harvard (NY and Boston); Century Association (New York); St Botolph, Harvard Faculty (Boston); Cosmos (Washington, DC).

**LAND, Frank William,** Professor of Education, University of Hull, since 1961; *b* 9 Jan. 1911; *s* of Charles and Mary Land; *m* 1937, Nora Beatrice Channon; two *s* one *d*. *Educ:* King's Coll., University of London. Assistant Master, The Grammar School, Hampton-on-Thames, 1933-37; Mathematics Lecturer: College of St Mark and St John, Chelsea, 1937-39; Birkbeck Coll., London, 1939-40. Instructor Lieut, Royal Navy, 1940-46. Vice-Principal, College of St Mark and St John, Chelsea, 1946-49; Senior Lecturer, University of Liverpool, 1950-61. Chairman, Association of Teachers in Colleges and Departments of Education, 1956-57. *Publications:* Recruits to Teaching, 1960; The Language of Mathematics, 1961. *Recreations:* gardening, walking. *Address:* 60 Hull Road, Cottingham, Yorks.

**LAND, Rev. W. Leslie,** MA Cantab; BLitt, MA, DipTheol, Oxon. *Educ:* Anthony Gell Grammar Sch., Wirksworth, Derbyshire; Christ's Coll., Cambridge; Mansfield Coll., Oxford. Schoolmaster, 1924-44; Headmaster Seaford Coll., 1935-44. Ordained 1944; Minister, Melbourne Hall Evangelical Free Church, Leicester, 1947-61. *Recreations:* music, golf, tennis. *Address:* 16 Brooklyn Avenue, Worthing, Sussex.

**LANDA, Hon. Abram,** CMG 1968; LLB; Agent-General for New South Wales in London since 1965; *b* 10 Nov. 1902; *s* of late D. Landa, Belfast; *m* 1930, Perla, *d* of late L. Levy; one *s* one *d*. *Educ:* Christian Brothers' Coll., Waverley, NSW; University of Sydney. Solicitor, 1927-. MLA for Bondi, NSW, 1930-32 and 1941-65; Minister for Labour and Industry, 1953-56; Minister for Housing and Co-operative Societies, 1959-65; Minister for Housing, NSW, 1956-65. Past Member Senate, University of Sydney; Past Trustee, NSW Public Library. *Recreation:* swimming. *Address:* 56 Strand, WC2. *Clubs:* Royal Automobile; Tattersall's (Sydney).

**LANDALE, David Fortune;** Director: The Royal Bank of Scotland (Chairman 1955-65); The British Investment Trust Ltd; *b* 7 Nov. 1905; *e s* of late David Landale, Dalswinton, Dumfries, and Mildred Sophia Fortune; *m* 1st, 1929, Louisa (*d* 1956), *y d* of late Charles William Forbes, Callendar House, Falkirk; one *s* three *d*; 2nd, 1957, Beatrice, *widow* of K. Lund. *Educ:* Eton Coll.; Balliol Coll., Oxford. Managing Director Jardine Matheson & Co. Ltd (Hong Kong, China and Japan), 1945-51. Unofficial Member: Executive Council, Hong Kong, 1946-51; Legislative Council, Hong Kong, 1946-50. Served War of 1939-45, Lieut, RNVR, 1940-43; Minister of War Transport Representative in the Middle East, 1944-45. Member, Review Body on Doctors' and Dentists' Remuneration, 1967-70. Member The Queen's Body Guard for Scotland, The Royal Company of Archers. *Address:* Dalswinton, Dumfries, Scotland. *T:* Auldgirth 208. *Clubs:* Boodle's, Pratt's; New (Edinburgh).

*See also Rear-Adm. J. D. Treacher.*

**LANDALE, Russell Talbot;** HM Consul-General, Amsterdam, since 1969; *b* 25 Oct. 1911; 3rd *s* of W. H. Landale; *m* 1938, Margaret Myfanwy George; two *d* (one *s* decd). *Educ:* Berkhamsted Sch.; Wiesbaden Konservatorium; Dresden Commercial Coll.; Institut de Touraine, Tours. British Tabulating Machine Co. (now ICL), 1933-39; HM Forces, 1940/46; Diplomatic Service, 1946-. *Recreations:* music (including composing), writing, riding, fishing. *Address:*

British Consulate-General, Herengracht 460, Amsterdam, Netherlands. *T:* 220982; 22 Arterberry Road, Wimbledon, SW20. *T:* 01-946 5427. *Clubs:* Junior Carlton, Canning; Groote, Industriele (Amsterdam).

**LANDAU, Muriel Elsie, (Mrs Samuel Sacks);** Hon. Cons. Gynæcologist, Elizabeth Garrett Anderson Hospital, London Jewish Hospital and Marie Curie Hospital; *b* 21 Jan. 1895; *d* of Marcus and Caroline Landau; *m* 1922, Dr Samuel Sacks; four *s*. *Educ:* Dame Alice Owen's Sch., (Foundation Schol., Owen's Leaving Exhibn, Isabel Thorne Entrance Schol. to London Sch. of Medicine); London School of Medicine; Royal Free Hospital. During student career won prizes in Anatomy, Surgery (incl. Gant Medal for operative surgery), Gynæcology, Venereology and diseases of Ear, Nose and Throat; MRCS, LRCP 1918; Helen Prideaux Post Graduate Prize, 1918; MB, BS London 1918; FRCS, 1920; MD London 1921. Various resident hosp. appts, 1918-21; Royal Free Hospital; Tite Street Children's Hosp.; Hosp. for Women, Soho Sq.; Queen Charlotte's Hosp., RMO; Registrar, Hosp. for Women, 1921-22; Asst Surg. Eliz. Garrett Anderson Hosp., 1922, subseq. Sen. Surg.; Surg., Marie Curie Hosp., 1926; Sen. Gynæcologist, London Jewish Hosp., 1929. *Publications:* Women of Forty, 1956; contrib. Lancet. *Recreations:* cooking, gardening. *Address:* 37 Mapesbury Road, NW2. *T:* 01-452 6381.

**LANDAU, Rom,** FRGS; Author, Sculptor; *b* 17 Oct. 1899; Professor of Islamic and North African Studies, University of the Pacific, 1952-67 (and American Academy of Asian Studies, San Francisco, 1952-58). Mem., Executive Cttee of World Congress of Faiths, London, 1936-44; RAF Liaison Officer, Air Gunner, 1939-41; Senior Specialist Middle East Div. of Ministry of Information, 1941; Mem. of Arab. Cttee, Political Intelligence Dept. of F.O. 1941-44; lectured Princeton, Yale, Columbia, Harvard, Stanford and other American Universities, 1952-53. A Rom Landau Collection (of his MSS) made at University of Syracuse (New York), 1964; a Rom Landau Moroccan Collection made at University of the Pacific (California) 1967. Dir, Peace Corps, Area Studies, Morocco Project 1, 1962-63. Hon. LHD University Pacific, 1967. Comdr of Ouissam Alaouite Order (Morocco), 1956. *Publications:* Minos the Incorruptible, 1925; Pilsudski, Hero of Poland, 1929; Paderewski, 1934; God is my Adventure, 1935 (revised and brought up to date, Paperback, 1964); Seven, 1936; Thy Kingdom Come, 1937; Search for Tomorrow, 1938; Arm the Apostles, 1938; Love for a Country, 1939; Of No Importance, 1940; We Have Seen Evil, 1941; Hitler's Paradise, 1941; The Fool's Progress, 1942; Islam Today (co-edited with Prof. A. J. Arberry and contributed the chapter on Saudi Arabia), 1943; Letter to Andrew, 1943 (3rd ed.); The Brother Vane, 1944; The Wing, 1945; Sex, Life and Faith, 1946; The Merry Oasis, 1947; Odysseus, 1948; Human Relations, 1949; Personalia, 1949; Invitation to Morocco, 1950; The Beauty of Morocco, 1951; The Sultan of Morocco, 1951; Moroccan Journal, 1952; The Moroccan Problem (in the Year Book of World Affairs), 1952; Morocco (survey written for and publ. by Carnegie Endowment for Internat. Peace, New York), 1952; Portrait of Tangier, 1952; Among the Americans, 1954; France and the Arabs (for Can. Inst. of Internat. Affairs), 1954; The Arabesque–The Abstract Art of Islam, 1955; Moroccan Drama 1900-1955, 1956; An Outline of Moroccan Culture, 1957; Mohammed V, King of Morocco, 1957; Arab Contribution to Civilization, 1958; Islam and the Arabs, 1958; The Philosophy of Ibn Arabi, 1959; Morocco–Independent, 1961; The Arab Heritage of Western Civilization, 1962; Hassan II, King of Morocco, 1962; The Moroccans–Yesterday and Today, 1963; History of Morocco in the Twentieth Century (in Arabic), 1963; Morocco: Marrakesh, Fez, and Rabat, 1967; The Kasbas of Southern Morocco, 1969; Al Hassan al Thani Malik al Maghrib (in Arabic), 1969; The Alaovites: the cultural contribution of King Hassan II, 1970. *Recreations:* the countryside, talking to dogs. *Address:* c/o Allen & Unwin, 40 Museum St, WC1; Marrakesh, Morocco.

**LANDER, Frank Patrick Lee,** OBE 1944; MD, FRCP; Consulting Physician, Royal Free Hospital, since 1937, Brompton Hospital and Putney Hospital since 1939; *b* 1906; *e s* of Edward Lee and Alice Mary Lander, Morecambelake, Dorset; *m* 1932, Dorothy Briggs; two *s*. *Educ:* Dover Coll.; Middlesex Hospital. Medical Registrar: Middlesex Hospital, 1931, Brompton Hospital, 1934. Lt-Col, RAMC, 1941-45: North Africa, Sicily and Italy (despatches). Examiner in Medicine, University of London, University of Cambridge, University Coll., of the West Indies, and Royal College of Physicians. Formerly Censor, and Senior Censor, Royal College of Physicians. *Publications:* various articles in leading medical journals. *Recreation:* fishing. *Address:* 11 Wimpole Street, W1. *T:* 01-580 2955. *Club:* Savile.

**LANDON, Alfred Mossman;** Independent Oil Producer: *b* 9 Sept. 1887; *s* of John Manuel Landon and Anne Mossman; *m* 1915, Margaret Fleming (*d* 1918); one *d*; *m* 1930, Theo Cobb; one *s* one *d*. *Educ:* University of Kansas. Republican State Chm., 1928; Governor of Kansas, 1933-37; Republican nominee for Pres. of United States, 1936; Delegate to Eighth International Conference, Lima, Peru, 1938; Chm. Kansas Delegation Republican Nat. Convention, 1940, 1944, and 1948; Mem. Methodist Church; Member, Kansas Bar; Member, Phi Gamma Delta; Mason, Elks, Odd Fellows. *Recreations:* horseback riding, fishing, bridge. *Address:* 521 Westchester Road, Topeka, Kansas 66606, USA. *T:* 233-4136.

**LANDON, Howard Chandler Robbins;** author and music historian; *b* 6 March 1926; *s* of William Grinnell Landon and Dorothea LeBaron Robbins. *Educ:* Aiken Preparatory Sch.; Lenox Sch.; Swarthmore Coll.; Boston Univ., USA (BMus). European rep. of Intercollegiate Broadcasting System, 1947; founded Haydn Soc. (which recorded and printed music of Joseph Haydn), 1949; became a Special Correspondent of The Times, 1957 and contrib. to that newspaper until 1961. Visiting Prof., Queen's Coll., NYC, 1969; Regents Prof. of Music, Univ. of California (Davis), 1970. Hon. DMus Boston Univ., 1969. *Publications:* The Symphonies of Joseph Haydn, 1955 (London) (2nd edn, 1970); The Mozart Companion (co-ed with Donald Mitchell), 1956 (London); The Collected Correspondence and London Notebooks of Joseph Haydn, 1959 (London); Essays on Eighteenth-Century Music, 1969 (London); Ludwig van Beethoven: a documentary study, 1970 (London); critical edn of the 107 Haydn Symphonies, (completed) 1968; scholarly edns of eighteenth-century music (various European publishing houses). *Recreations:* swimming, cooking, walking. *Address:* 51011 Buggiano Castello (Pistoia), Italy. *T:* 0572/52269.

**LANE, David William Stennis Stuart;** MP (C) Cambridge, since Sept. 1967; Parliamentary Private Secretary to Minister of State for Employment and Productivity, since 1970; *b* 24 Sept. 1922; *s* of Hubert Samuel Lane, MC; *m* 1955, Lesley Anne Mary Clauson; two *s*. *Educ:* Eton: Trinity Coll., Cambridge. Yale Univ. Served War of 1939-45 (Navy). British Iron and Steel Federation, 1948 (Sec., 1956); Shell International Petroleum Co., 1959-67. Called to the Bar, Middle Temple, 1955. Chm., N Kensington Cons. Assoc., 1961-62. Contested (C) Lambeth (Vauxhall), 1964, Cambridge, 1966. *Recreations:* walking, golf, cricket. *Address:* 40 Chepstow Place, W2; 5 Spinney Drive, Great Shelford, Cambridge. *Clubs:* Junior Carlton, MCC.

**LANE, Hon. Dame Elizabeth (Kathleen),** DBE 1965; **Hon. Mrs Justice Lane;** a Judge of the High Court, Probate, Divorce and Admiralty Div., since 1965; *b* 9 Aug. 1905; *o d* of late Edward Alexander Coulborn and late Kate May Coulborn (*née* Wilkinson); *m* 1926, Henry Jerrold Randall Lane, *qv*; one *s* decd. *Educ:* Malvern Girls Coll. and privately. Barrister, Inner Temple, 1940; Master of the Bench, 1965. Mem. of Home Office Committee on Depositions in Criminal Cases, 1948. An Asst Recorder of Birmingham, 1953-61; Chm. of Birmingham Region Mental Health Review Tribunal, 1960-62; Recorder of Derby, 1961-62; Commissioner of the Crown Court at Manchester, 1961-62; Judge of County Courts, Circuit 38 (Edmonton, etc.), 1962-65; Acting Dep. Chm., London Sessions, 1965. *Recreations:* tennis, travel, needlework. *Address:* The Royal Courts of Justice, Strand, WC2; (private) 4 King's Bench Walk, Temple, EC4.

**LANE, Ernest Olaf,** DFC 1943; AFC 1945; Solicitor to the Metropolitan Police since 1965; *b* 26 April 1916; *s* of James and Margaret Beatrice Lane; *m* 1949, Nancy Eileen Fairbairn; one *d*. *Educ:* University of Sydney, NSW (LLB). Private practice, 1938-39. Pilot, RAAF, 1940-45. Solicitor's Dept, New Scotland Yard, 1946-; apptd Head of Dept, 1965. *Recreation:* golf. *Address:* Grey Cottage, Whitmoor Vale, near Hindhead, Surrey. *T:* Hindhead 880. *Clubs:* St Stephen's; MCC; Hindhead Golf.

**LANE, Frank Laurence,** CBE 1961; Chairman: Elder Dempster Lines Ltd, 1963; *b* 1912; *s* of late Herbert Allardyce Lane, CIE, and Hilda Gladys Duckie Lane (*née* Wraith); *m* 1938, Gwendolin Elizabeth Peterkin; one *s* one *d*. *Educ:* Wellington Coll., Berks; New Coll., Oxford. Mansfield & Co. Ltd, Singapore and Penang, 1934-42; BOAC, UK and USA, 1942-45; Mansfield & Co. Ltd, Singapore, 1945-61; Elder Dempster Lines Ltd, Liverpool, 1962-. *Recreations:* golf, fishing. *Address:* Oldany, Croft Drive East, Caldy, Wirral, Cheshire. *T:* 051-625 5759. *Club:* East India and Sports.

**LANE, Hon. Sir Geoffrey Dawson,** Kt 1966; AFC 1943; **Hon. Mr Justice Geoffrey Lane;** Judge of the High Court of Justice, Queen's Bench Division, since 1966; *b* 17 July 1918; *s* of late Percy Albert Lane, Lincoln; *m* 1944, Jessie, *d* of Donald Macdonald; one *s*. *Educ:* Shrewsbury; Trinity Coll., Cambridge. Served in RAF, 1939-45; Sqdn-Leader, 1942. Called to Bar, Gray's Inn, 1946; Bencher 1966. QC 1962. JP Rutland, 1958-66; Dep. Chm., Rutland QS., 1958-66, Chm. 1962-66; Dep. Chm., Beds. QS, 1960-66; Recorder of Bedford, 1963-66. Mem., Parole Board, 1970-. *Address:* Royal Courts of Justice, Strand, WC2.

**LANE, H(enry) J(errold) Randall,** CBE 1963; Legal Adviser to the British Council, 1940-64; retired; *b* 29 April 1898; *e s* of Henry Lane, Polegate House, Cranleigh, Surrey; *m* 1926, Elizabeth Kathleen Coulborn (*see* Dame Elizabeth Lane); one *s* decd. *Educ:* privately; Manchester Univ. Served as cadet in Merchant Fleet Aux., 1916-17 and in Canadian Army Med. Corps, 1917-19. Lived in Canada and Italy, 1919-26. MA 1929, but remained at Manchester Univ. for a further year's research. Admitted a student of Inner Temple, 1936; called to Bar, 1944. Lectr in Eng. Lang. and Lit. Extra-Mural Dept, Leicester Univ. Coll., 1930-40; Dir, British Inst. of Milan (British Council), 1940; returned to England as Legal Officer (British Council); title of post changed to that of Legal Adviser, 1944. Legal Chairman, London Rent Assessment Cttees (Lord Chancellor's Panel), 1966-70; Chm., Brent and Harrow Rent Tribunal, 1970-. Mem. Comparative Law Cttee of British Inst. of Internat. and Comparative Law, 1959-64. *Recreations:* tennis, walking, travel. *Address:* 4 King's Bench Walk, Temple, EC4. *T:* 01-353 1317. *Club:* Reform.

**LANE, Jane, (Mrs Andrew Dakers);** author; (Elaine) *y d* of late Mason Kidner; *m* 1937, Andrew Dakers; one *s*. Adopting pseudonym of Jane Lane (maiden name of maternal grandmother), wrote first novel at age of seventeen. *Publications:* Undaunted, 1934; Be Valiant Still, 1935; King's Critic, 1935; Prelude to Kingship, 1936; Come to the March, 1937; Sir Devil May Care, 1937; You Can't Run Away, 1940; England for Sale, 1943; He Stooped to Conquer, 1944; Gin and Bitters, 1945; His Fight is Ours, 1946; London Goes to Heaven, 1947; Parcel of Rogues, 1948; Fortress in the Forth, 1950; Dark Conspiracy, 1952; The Sealed Knot, 1952; The Lady of the House, 1953; Thunder on St Paul's Day, 1954; The Phœnix and the Laurel, 1954; Conies in the Hay, 1957; Command Performance, 1957; Queen of the Castle, 1958; Ember In the Ashes, 1960; Sow the Tempest, 1960; Farewell to the White Cockade, 1961; The Crown for a Lie, 1962; A State of Mind, 1964; The Wind through the Heather, 1965; From the Snare of the Hunters, 1968; The Young and Lonely King, 1969; The Questing Beast, 1970. In addition to these: *books for children:* The Escape of the King, 1950; The Escape of the Prince, 1951; Desperate Battle, 1953; The Escape of the Queen, 1957; The Escape of the Duke, 1960; The Escape of the Princess, 1962; The Trial of the King, 1963; The Return of the King, 1964; The March of the Prince, 1965; The Champion of the King, 1966; *biographies and history:* King James the Last, 1943; Titus Oates, 1949; Puritan, Rake and Squire, 1950; The Reign of King Covenant, 1957; Cat among the Pigeons, 1959. *Recreations:* riding and embroidery. *Address:* Kingsbury, 97 Sea Road, Angmering-on-Sea, Sussex.

**LANE, Margaret;** Novelist, biographer, journalist; *b* 23 June 1907; *o d* of late H. G. Lane; *m* 1st, 1934, Bryan (marr. diss. 1939), *e s* of Edgar Wallace; 2nd, 1944, 15th Earl of Huntingdon, *qv*; two *d*. *Educ:* St Stephen's, Folkestone; St Hugh's Coll., Oxford (MA). Reporter, Daily Express, 1928-31; special correspondent: in New York and for International News Service, USA, 1931-32: for Daily Mail, 1932-38. President: Women's Press Club, 1958-60; Dickens Fellowship, 1959-61, 1970. *Publications:* Faith, Hope, No Charity (awarded Prix Femina-Vie Heureuse), 1935; At Last the Island, 1937; Edgar Wallace: The Biography of a Phenomenon, 1938; Walk Into My Parlour, 1941; Where Helen Lies, 1944;

The Tale of Beatrix Potter, 1946; The Brontë Story, 1953; A Crown of Convolvulus, 1954; A Calabash of Diamonds, 1961; Life With Ionides, 1963; A Night at Sea, 1964; A Smell of Burning, 1965; Purely for Pleasure, 1966; The Day of the Feast, 1968. *Address:* Blackbridge House, Beaulieu, Hants: A15 Albany, Piccadilly, W1.

**LANE, Hon. Mrs Miriam;** *see* Rothschild, Hon. Miriam.

**LANE, Prof. Ronald Epey,** CBE 1957; Emeritus Nuffield Professor of Occupational Health, University of Manchester (Professor, 1945-65); *b* 4 July 1897; *s* of E. E. Lane. *m* 1924, Winifred E. Tickner; one *s* one *d. Educ:* Simon Langton Sch. Canterbury; Guy's Hospital. Served European War, RFC, 1915-19. Guy's Hospital, 1919-24, qualified, 1923; General Medical practice, 1925-27; MRCP, 1925. Medical Officer, Chloride Elec. Storage Co. Ltd, 1928; Physician, Salford Royal Hospital, 1935; FRCP, 1938; Milroy Lecturer (Royal College of Physicians), 1947, McKenzie Lecturer, 1950. Mem. of various Govt Advisory Cttees. *Publications:* original papers on Lead Poisoning, Medical Education, Occupational Health and Universities, in Lancet, BMJ, Brit. Jl of Industrial Med., Jl of Industrial Hygiene and Toxicology, etc. *Recreations:* golf, fishing. *Address:* 3 Daylesford Road, Cheadle, Cheshire. *T:* 061-428 5738. *Club:* Athenæum.

**LANE, Rear-Admiral (Retd) Walter Frederick Boyt,** CB 1960; DSC 1941; MIMechE; MIMarE; Director of Marine Engineering, Admiralty, 1958-61; *b* 7 Feb. 1909; *s* of W. H. Lane, Freshwater, I of W; *m* 1931, Anne Littlecott; one *s. Educ:* RN Engineering Coll., Devonport. Eng.-in-Chief, Admiralty, Bath, 1957; Rear-Adm., 1957. Director, Fairfields (Eng.) Co., Glasgow. *Recreations:* tennis, painting. *Address:* Foxleaze, Limpley Stoke, Wilts. *Club:* Army and Navy.

**LANE, Sir William Arbuthnot,** 2nd Bt *cr* 1913; CBE 1954; *b* 7 July 1897; *o s* of Sir Arbuthnot Lane, 1st Bart; *S* father, 1943; *m* 1937, Fritzi, *yr d* of Capt. F. Szamvald; one *d. Educ:* Winchester Coll. Served European War, 1914-18; Dresser, Anæsthetist and Ambulance Driver, France, 1915-16; joined RFC, 1917; RAF Airship Pilot, 1918; War of 1939-45, RAFVR, 1940; Staff Captain and DAPM to Provost Marshal of the UK, 1941-45. Metropolitan Special Constabulary, 1926; Commandant Y Div., 1947; Comdt-in-C. Metropolitan Special Constabulary, 1950-58, retd. Director: Lothbury Estates Ltd. OStJ. *Address:* 72 Drayton Gardens, SW10. *T:* 01-373 2497. *Club:* Royal Air Force.

**LANE FOX, Col Francis Gordon Ward;** Vice-Lieutenant of West Riding of Yorkshire since 1968; Royal Horse Guards, 1919-46, retired; *b* 14 Oct. 1899; *s* of late C. Ward Jackson; assumed surname of Lane Fox in lieu of that of Jackson, by deed poll, 1937; *m* 1929, Hon. Marcia Agnes Mary, *e d* of 1st and last Baron Bingley, PC (*d* 1947); two *s* one *d. Educ:* Eton; RMC, Sandhurst. West Riding of Yorkshire: JP 1948; DL 1952; CC 1949, CA 1955. KStJ 1965. Officer Order of the Crown, with Palm, and Croix de Guerre, with Palm (Belgium), 1946. *Address:* Bramham Park, Boston Spa, Yorkshire. *T:* Boston Spa 2114; Kingsley Mill, Black Torrington, Beaworthy, Devon. *T:* Black Torrington 209. *Clubs:* Turf, Cavalry; Yorkshire (York).

**LANE-POOLE, Charles Edward;** *b* 1885; *s* of late Stanley Lane-Poole, and Charlotte Bell Wilson; *m* 1911, Ruth Pollexfen; three *d. Educ:* St Columba's Coll. Dublin; Forest Sch., Nancy. South African Forest Dept, 1906; Conservator of Forests, Sierra Leone, 1910; Western Australia, 1917; commissioned by Commonwealth Govt to report on Forests of Papua and New Guinea, 1922; Forestry Adviser Commonwealth Govt, 1925; Inspector-Gen. of Forests of the Commonwealth of Australia, 1927-45; Consulting Forester Sydney, 1946; represented Commonwealth at the 1920 Empire Forestry Conference in London; Vice-Chm. of the Third Empire Forestry Conference in 1928 in Australia; represented the Commonwealth at Fourth Empire Conference, in S Africa, Chm. Silvicultural Cttee, 1935; reported on eucalypt plantations of S Africa, 1935. *Publications:* Trees, Shrubs and Climbers of Sierra Leone; Kiln Drying of Jarrah; Forest Resources of Papua and New Guinea; Forests of Norfolk Island; Forest Policy for Capital Territory and Jervis Bay; Forests and Water; Statistical Methods, Forest Problems. *Address:* Flat 38 Selsdon, 16 Macleay Street, Potts Point, Sydney, NSW 2011, Australia. *Clubs:* Alpine (Canberra); University (Sydney).

**LANE-POOLE, Vice-Admiral Sir Richard Hayden Owen,** KBE, *cr* 1944 (OBE 1919); CB 1936; *b* 1 April 1883; *s* of Stanley Lane-Poole, Author and Oriental scholar, and Charlotte Wilson, Ballymoney, Co. Antrim; *m* Sigrid, *d* of Col E. H. Haig; one *d. Educ:* France; Bedford Sch. Commanded Cambrian, 1927-29; RN Coll., Greenwich, 1929-31; Commodore commanding S American division, 1932-33; Commodore, Devonport, 1934-35; commanded HM Australian Squadron, 1936-38; retired list, 1939; War of 1939-45, served as Commodore of Convoys and Dir of Demagnetisation. Hon. DLitt, University of New England, Australia, 1962. *Recreations:* fishing and shooting. *Address:* Spyway, Armidale, NSW, Australia. *Club:* United Service.

**LANESBOROUGH,** 9th Earl of *cr* 1756; **Denis Anthony Brian Butler;** DL; Baron of Newtown-Butler, 1715; Viscount Lanesborough, 1728; Major, Leicestershire Yeomanry (RA); *b* 28 Oct. 1918; *er s* of 8th Earl and Grace Lilian, *d* of late Sir Anthony Abdy, 3rd Bt; *S* father 1950; *m* 1939, Bettyne Ione (marriage dissolved, 1950), *d* of late Sir Lindsay Everard; one *d* (and one *d* decd). *Educ:* Stowe. Leicestershire Yeomanry; Lieutenant, 1939; Major, RAC, TA (TD), 1945. DL Leicester, 1962. JP 1967. *Heir: kinsman,* Comdr Terence Brinsley John Danvers Butler, RN; *b* 7 March 1913. *Address:* Swithland Hall, Loughborough. *T:* Rothley 2001.

**LANG, Air Vice-Marshal Albert Frank,** CB 1946; MBE 1919; AFC 1936; *b* 1895; *m* 1920, Martha Eiluned Roberts; one *d.* Joined RFC, 1912; Dir of Signals, Air Commission, Washington, 1941-45; Controller of Signals Equipment, British Air Commission, Washington, 1945; retired, 1946. *Address:* 1223 Garden Street, Santa Barbara, Calif 93104, USA.

**LANG, Col Bertram John,** CB 1919; CMG 1918; DSO 1916; late Argyll and Sutherland Highlanders; President, South African War Veterans Association, since 1967; *b* London, 14 Jan. 1878; 2nd *s* of late Basil Lang, Advocate-Gen., Bombay, and late Mrs Basil

Lang, *d* of Colonel Trenchard Haggard, RA; *m* 1st, 1904, Mrs Montgomery Bartlett (*decd*); 2nd, 1924, Mrs Ruby Julia Hunter (*decd*); one *s*; 3rd, 1951, Catherine Macdonald (*d* 1964), Hougharry, N. Uist, Outer Hebrides. *Educ:* Harrow; Royal Military College, Sandhurst. Joined 1st Batt. Argyll and Sutherland Highlanders, 1898; served in South African War (Queen's medal with 5 clasps); Adjutant 3rd Vol. Batt. Argyll and Sutherland Highlanders and 4th (TF) Batt. Leicestershire Regiment, 1905-11; passed into Staff Coll., Camberley, 1913; went out to France with Expeditionary Force, 10 Aug. 1914, as Staff Capt., Boulogne Base; served on Staff of HQ L of C as DAQMG; at GHQ as DAQMG; with 8th Corps HQ as AQMG; and 7th Div. as AA and QMG; served in France, Aug. 1914-Nov. 1917, and in Italy, Nov. 1917 to end of war (despatches seven times, CB, CMG, DSO, BT Lt-Col, 1914 Star, French Croix de Guerre with Palm, and Officier Mérite Agricole; Officer of the Order of the Crown of Italy. Italian Croce di Guerra); AQMG Army HQ, India, 1930-34; retired, 1934. *Clubs:* Army and Navy, Royal Automobile.

**LANG, Prof. David Marshall,** MA, PhD, DLit, LittD; Professor of Caucasian Studies in the University of London since 1964; Warden of Connaught Hall, University of London, since 1955; *b* 6 May 1924; *s* of Dr David Marshall Lang, Medical Practitioner, Bath, and Mrs May Rena Lang; *m* 1956, Janet, *d* of George Sugden, Leeds; two *s* two *d*. *Educ:* Monkton Combe Sch.; St John's Coll., Cambridge. Actg Vice-Consul, Tabriz, 1944-46; 3rd Sec., British Embassy, Tehran, 1946; Research Fellow, St John's Coll., Cambridge, 1946-52; Lectr in Georgian, School of Oriental and African Studies, University of London, 1949-58; Senior Fellow, Russian Inst., Columbia Univ., 1952-53; Reader in Caucasian Studies, University of London, 1958-64; Vis. Prof. of Caucasian Languages, University of California, Los Angeles, 1964-65. Hon. Sec., Royal Asiatic Society, 1962-64. Hon. Dr Philological Sciences, Tbilisi State Univ. *Publications:* Studies in the Numismatic History of Georgia in Transcaucasia, 1955; Lives and Legends of the Georgian Saints, 1956; The Wisdom of Balahvar, 1957; The Last Years of the Georgian Monarchy, 1957; The First Russian Radical; Alexander Radishchev, 1959; A Modern History of Georgia, 1962; Catalogue of the Georgian Books in the British Museum, 1962; The Georgians, 1966; The Balavariani, 1966; Armenia, Cradle of Civilization, 1970; articles in Bulletin of School of Oriental and African Studies, Encyclopædia Britannica, etc. *Recreations:* music, foreign travel. *Address:* (Office) School of Oriental and African Studies, University of London, WC1. *T:* (Home) 01-387 6181. *Clubs:* Athenæum; Leander.

**LANG, Lt-Gen. Sir Derek (Boileau),** KCB 1967 (CB 1964); DSO 1944; MC 1941; Secretary, University of Stirling, since 1970; *b* 7 Oct. 1913; *s* of Lt-Col C. F. G. Lang and Mrs Lumsden Lang (*née* M. J. L. Forbes); *m* 1st, 1942, Massey Dawson; one *s* one *d*; 2nd 1953, A. L. S. Shields (*d* 1970); 3rd 1969, Mrs E. H. Balfour. *Educ:* Wellington Coll.; RMA, Sandhurst. Commnd, The Queen's Own Cameron Highlanders, 1933; Adjutant, TA, 1938; Chief Instructor, Battle Sch., 1944; Comdt, Sch. of Infty, 1945; Staff, Australia, 1949-51; GSO1, War Office, 1951-53; Chief Instructor, Sch. of Infantry Tactical Wing, 1953-55; AAG, War Office, 1955-57; Comd Infty Bde (153-TA), 1958-60; Chief of Staff, Scottish Comd, 1960; Gen. Officer Commanding, 51st Highland Div. and District, Perth, 1962-64; Dir of Army Training, 1964-66; GOC-in-C, Scottish Command, 1966-68 Governor of Edinburgh Castle, 1966-69. *Recreations:* golf, shooting, photography. *Address:* University of Stirling, Stirling. *Clubs:* Naval and Military; Hon. Co. of Edinburgh Golfers (Muirfield).

*See also J. M. Hunt.*

**LANG, Rev. Gordon;** Nonconformist Minister; Member of Board, Cwmbran New Town Corporation, since 1955; *b* Monmouth, 1893; *e s* of T. W. Lang, JP; *m* 1916, Emilie Anne, *d* of J. W. Evans, Leechpool, Chepstow; one *s* one *d*. *Educ:* Monmouth Grammar Sch.; Cheshunt. MP (Lab) Oldham, 1929-31; Stalybridge and Hyde Div. of Ches., 1945-51. Hon. Chaplain to Showmen's Guild of Great Britain and Ireland; Chairman: Parliamentary Federal Group; Proportional Representation Soc.; Hon. Sec. United Europe Movement; Vice-Pres. International Youth Bureau; Mem. Council of Hansard Soc.; Exec. Mem. Internat. Union of Parliamentarians. Criminologist. *Publications:* Biography of Mr Justice Avory, 1935; Modern Epistles, 1952; Mind Behind Murder, 1960; fiction and many works and papers on Applied Psychology and Criminology. *Address:* Wyecliffe, Chepstow, Mon. *T:* Chepstow 2462. *Clubs:* Authors', National Labour.

**LANG, Sir John (Gerald),** GCB 1954 (KCB 1947; CB 1946); *b* 20 Dec. 1896; *s* of late George and Rebecca Lang, Woolwich; *m* 1922, Emilie J. (*d* 1963), *d* of late Henry S. Goddard, Eastbourne; one *d*. *Educ:* Aske's Haberdashers' Sch., Hatcham. Second Div. Clerk, Admiralty, 1914; Royal Marine Artillery, Lt, 1917-18; Returned to Admiralty: Asst Principal, 1930; Principal, 1935; Asst Sec., 1939; Principal Asst Sec., 1942; Under-Sec., 1946; Sec., Admiralty, SW1, 1947-61. Chm. Bettix Ltd, 1961-70. Principal Adviser on Sport to the Government, 1964-, and Dep. Chm., Sports Council, 1965-. Mem. Bd of Govs, Bethlem Royal Hosp. and Maudsley Hosp., 1961-70; Treasurer, RINA, 1969-; Vice-Pres., Royal Naval Assoc. *Recreations:* gardening, motoring. *Address:* 2 Egmont Park House, Walton-on-the-Hill, Tadworth, Surrey. *T:* Tadworth 2200. *Clubs:* Royal Automobile, Samuel Pepys (Pres. 1965).

**LANG, John Russell,** CBE 1963; Deputy Chairman, The Weir Group Ltd; *b* 8 Jan. 1902; *s* of Chas Russell Lang, CBE; *m* 1934, Jenny (*d* 1970), *d* of Sir John Train, MP, of Cathkin, Lanarkshire; four *d* (one *s* decd). *Educ:* Loretto Sch., Musselburgh; France and USA. Dir, G. & J. Weir Ltd, 1930-67. Chairman, Weir Housing Corp., 1946-66. President, Scottish Engineering Employers' Association, 1963-64. Mem., Toothill Cttee and EDC for Mec. Eng. Lt-Col 277 Field Regt, RA (TA), 1937. *Recreations:* hunting, shooting, golf. *Address:* The White House of Milliken, Brookfield, Renfrewshire. *T:* Johnstone 20898. *Clubs:* Lansdowne, Farmers'; Western (Glasgow). Prestwick Golf.

**LANG, Hon. John Thomas;** former Premier of New South Wales; *b* Sydney, 21 Dec. 1876; *m d* of late Mrs Bertha Macnamara, Sydney; five *c*. Mayor of Auburn two years; MLA Granville, 1913-20, Parramatta, 1920-27, and Auburn, 1927-46; Colonial Treasurer, 1920-22; Premier and Treasurer of New South Wales, 1925-27, and 1930-32; MHR for Reid, 1946-49. *Publication:* The Turbulent Years, 1970. *Address:* 36 Nithsdale Street, Sydney, NSW 2000, Australia.

**LANG, Rt. Rev. Leslie Hamilton,** MA, Hon. CF; *b* 27 May 1889; *s* of Alex. Lang, CMG, and Mary Susan Lang; *m* 1918, Janette Catharine Todd (*d* 1964); two *s Educ:* Repton; Trinity Coll., Cambridge. Curate of Portsea, 1915-17; Chaplain to Forces, 1917-18; Domestic Chaplain to Archbishop of York, 1918; Chaplain to Returned Soldiers in Diocese of Edmonton, Canada, 1919-20; Vicar of All Saints, Swanscombe, 1920-22; Warden of Trinity Coll. Mission and Vicar of St George's Camberwell, 1922-27; Vicar of Kingston-upon-Thames, 1927-34; Rural Dean of Kingston, 1932-34; Canon Residentiary of Winchester and Diocesan Missioner, 1934; Bishop of Woolwich, 1936-47; Archdeacon of Lewisham, 1936-47; Canon Residentiary of Winchester Cathedral, Archdeacon of Winchester and Asst Bishop, 1947-62. Select Preacher Cambridge Univ., 1937. *Recreations:* golf, fishing. *Address:* The Friary, 19 St Cross Road, Winchester, Hants.

**LANGDON, Alfred Gordon,** CMG 1967; CVO 1966; Commissioner of Police, Jamaica, since 1964 (Deputy Commissioner, 1962-64); *b* 3 July 1915; *s* of Wilfred James Langdon and Norah (*née* Nixon); *m* 1947, Phyllis Elizabeth Pengelley; one *s* two *d. Educ:* Munro Coll., Jamaica. Berkhampstead Sch., Herts. Bank of Nova Scotia, Kingston, Jamaica, 1933-37; Jamaica Infantry Volunteers, 1937-39; Jamaica Constabulary Force, 1939-. Queen's Police Medal for Distinguished Service, 1961. *Recreations:* fishing, tennis, swimming. *Address:* Police Headquarters, Kingston, Jamaica. *T:* 77703 or 68008. *Club:* Kingston Cricket.

**LANGDON, David,** FRSA, FSIA; Cartoonist and Illustrator; Member of Punch Table; regular contributor to Punch since 1937, to The New Yorker since 1952; *b* 24 Feb. 1914; *er s* of late Bennett and Bess Langdon; *m* 1955, April Sadler-Phillips; two *s* one *d. Educ:* Davenant Gram. Sch., London. Architect's Dept, LCC, 1931-39; Executive Officer, London Rescue Service, 1939-41; served in Royal Air Force, 1941-46; Squadron Leader, 1945. Editor, Royal Air Force Jl, 1945-46. Creator of Billy Brown of London Town for LPTB. Cartoonist to Sunday Mirror, 1948-. *Publications:* Home Front Lines, 1941; All Buttoned Up, 1944; Meet Me Inside, 1946; Slipstream (with R. B. Raymond), 1946; The Way I See It, 1947; Hold Tight There!, 1949; Let's Face It, 1951; Wake Up and Die (with David Clayton), 1952; Look at You, 1952; All in Fun, 1953; Laugh with Me, 1954; More in Fun, 1955; Funnier Still, 1956; A Banger for a Monkey, 1957; Langdon At Large, 1958; I'm Only Joking, 1960; Punch with Wings, 1961; How to Play Golf and Stay Happy, 1964; David Langdon's Casebook, 1969; Let's Be Broad-Based (with Dennis Rooke), 1964; Camper Beware! (with Dennis Rooke), 1965; (with George Mikes): Down with Everybody!, 1951; Shakespeare & Myself, 1952; Über Alles, 1953; Eight Humorists, 1954; Little Cabbages, 1955; Italy for Beginners, 1956; How to Unite Nations, 1963. *Recreation:* golf. *Address:* 73 Grosvenor Street, W1. *T:* 01-493 8501; White House, Widmer End, Bucks. *T:* Holmer Green 2221. *Clubs:* Savage, Toby, Royal Automobile.

**LANGDON, Michael;** Principal Bass Soloist, Royal Opera House, Covent Garden, since 1951; *b* 12 Nov. 1920; *s* of Henry Langdon, Wednesfield Road, Wolverhampton; *m* 1947, Vera Duffield, Norwich; two *d. Educ:* Bushbury Hill Sch., Wolverhampton. First Principal Contract, Royal Opera House, Covent Garden, 1951; first Gala Performance, before Queen Elizabeth II (Gloriana), 1953; Grand Inquisitor in Visconti Production of Don Carlos, 1958; debut as Baron Ochs (Rosenkavalier), 1960; first International Engagement (Hamburg), 1961; first Glyndebourne Festival, 1961; since then, has appeared in international performances in Paris, Berlin, Aix-en-Provence, San Francisco and Los Angeles, 1962; Lausanne, Geneva, Vienna and Budapest, 1963; Zürich, New York, 1964; Geneva, Marseilles, 1965; Seattle, Buenos Aires; Gala Performances, 1967, 1969. *Recreations:* swimming, walking and Association football (now only as spectator). *Address:* 49 Banstead Road South, Sutton, Surrey. *T:* 01-642 0385. *Club:* Savage.

**LANGDON, Air Commodore William Frederick,** CBE 1950; RAF retired; Director of British Atlantic Committee, 1955; *b* 11 Feb. 1898; *s* of late William Frederick Langdon, Sunningdale, Berks; *m* 1925, Eneid Mary Eleanor, *d* of late Major E. J. W. Platt, Llanfairfechan, N Wales; no *c. Educ:* City of London Sch. Served European War, with Royal Naval Div., 1915-19 (wounded); served with Army, Iraq, 1919-23; trans. to RAF, 1923; 14 Sqdn, Palestine, 1925; attached RAuxAF, 1926-31; 30 Sqdn RAF Mosul, 1933-35; Air Min., 1936-39; served War of 1939-45, Wing Comdr 1940. Middle East, 1943; Group Capt. 1943; Asst Air Attaché, Ankara, 1943-45. Air Cdre, 1952; SASO 41 Grp, 1952-55; retired, 1955. Freeman, City of London, 1919. *Recreations:* lawn tennis, travel, shooting. *Address:* 2 Grosvenor Court, 99 Sloane Street, SW1. *T:* 01-235 1609. *Clubs:* White's, RAF, Queen's.

**LANGDON-DAVIES, John,** MBE; Author; *b* 1897; *s* of late Rev. Guy Langdon-Davies; *m* 1st, 1918, Constance, *d* of D. H. Scott, FRS; two *s*; 2nd, 1933, Elizabeth Barr; one *d*; 3rd, 1949, Patricia Kipping; three *s* one *d. Educ:* Tonbridge Sch. (New Judd Schol.); St John's Coll., Oxford (Smythe Exhibitioner, Kent County Senior Scholar and Sir Thomas White Scholar). Did not take a degree. Lectured throughout USA annually, 1924-36; War Corresp. in Spain, 1936-38; in Finnish War, 1940. Hon. Comdt of South-Eastern Army Fieldcraft Sch., 1941-44. Founder of Foster-Parents Scheme for European children; Inventor and Ed. Jackdaw collections of historical documents for Schs, 1963-. Science Correspondent of various daily newspapers, 1936-48. *Publications:* New Age of Faith, 1925; Short History of Women, 1928; Dancing Catalans, 1929; Man and His Universe, 1930; Science and Common Sense, 1931; Inside the Atom, 1934; How Wireless Came, 1935; Short History of the Future, 1936; Behind the Spanish Barricades, 1937; Air Raid, 1939; Finland, the First Total War, 1940; Nerves versus Nazis, 1940; Fifth Column, 1940; Home Guard Warfare, 1941; Home Guard Training Manual, 1941; Home Guard Fieldcraft Manual, 1942; American Close Up, 1943; Life-Blood, 1945; British Achievement in the Art of Healing, 1946; Conquer Fear, 1948; Russia Puts the Clock Back, 1949; NPL Jubilee Book of the National Physical Laboratory, 1951; Westminster Hospital, 1719-1948, 1952; Gatherings from Catalonia, 1958; Sex, Sin and Sanctity, 1954; Seeds of Life, 1955; (with E. J. Dingwall) The Unknown is It Nearer?, 1956; Man the Known and Unknown, 1961; Carlos the Bewitched (as John Nada), 1963; Cato Street Conspiracy (as John Stanhope), 1963. *Address:* Holly Place, Shoreham, near Sevenoaks, Kent. *T:* Otford 3874.

**LANGDON-DOWN, Barbara;** *see* Littlewood, Lady (Barbara).

**LANGFORD,** 9th Baron, *cr* 1800; **Colonel Geoffrey Alexander Rowley-Conwy,** OBE 1943; RA, retired; Constable of Rhuddlan Castle and Lord of the Manor of Rhuddlan; *b* 8 March 1912; *s* of late Major Geoffrey Seymour Rowley-Conwy (killed in action, Gallipoli, 1915), Bodrhyddan, Flints, and of Bertha Gabrielle Rowley-Conwy, JP (now of Bodrhyddan), *d* of late Lieutenant Alexander Cochran, Royal Navy, Ashkirk, Selkirkshire; *S* kinsman 1953; *m* 1st, 1939, Ruth St John (marriage dissolved, 1956), *d* of late Albert St John Murphy, The Island House, Little Island, County Cork; 2nd, 1957, Grete, *d* of Col E. T. C. von Freiesleben, formerly Chief of the King's Adjutants Staff to the King of Denmark and now of Snekkersten, Denmark; one *s*. *Educ:* Marlborough; RMA Woolwich. Served War of 1939-45, with RA; Singapore, (POW escaped) and Burma, 1941-45 (despatches, OBE); Lt-Col 1945; Colonel (Hon.), 1967. *Heir:* *s* Hon. Owen Grenville Rowley-Conwy, *b* 27 Dec. 1958. *Address:* Bodrhyddan, Rhuddlan, Flints. *Club:* Naval and Military.

**LANGFORD-HOLT, Sir John (Anthony),** Kt 1962; Lieutenant-Commander RN (Retired); MP (C) Shrewsbury Division of Salop since 1945; *b* 30 June 1916; *s* of late Ernest Langford-Holt and Mrs Christine Langford-Holt; *m* 1953, Flora Evelyn Innes Stuart (marr. diss. 1969); one *s* one *d*. *Educ:* Shrewsbury Sch. Joined RN and Air Branch (FAA), 1939. Sec. of Conservative Parl. Labour Cttee, 1945-49; Chm., Anglo-Austrian Soc., 1960-63; Member: Commonwealth Parliamentary Association; Interparliamentary Union, and other Internat. Bodies; Parliamentary and Scientific Cttee; Chairman: Ferro Metal and Chemical Corp. Ltd; Tretol Ltd; Vice-Chm., Authority Investments Ltd; Director: James North & Sons; James North Export Ltd. Freeman and Liveryman of City of London; Mem. Court, Company of Horners. *Address:* 13 Butcher Row, Shrewsbury; 409 Frobisher House, Dolphin Square, SW1. *T:* 01-834 3800. *Club:* United Hunts.

**LANGFORD-SAINSBURY, Air Vice-Marshal Thomas Audley,** CB 1945; OBE 1940; DFC; AFC and 2 bars; Royal Air Force, retired; *b* 23 Nov. 1897; *s* of Emma and Thomas Hugh Langford-Sainsbury, Bath; *m* 1918, Maude Hamilton Russell-Mortimer; one *d*; *m* 1948, Dorothy (Prescott) Goodwin; one *d*. *Educ:* Radley Coll., Berks. Joined Royal Flying Corps, 1916; Wing Comdr, Royal Air Force, 1939; Group Capt., 1941; Air Commodore, 1944; Temp. Air Vice-Marshal, 1944; retired, 1949. OStJ 1964. *Recreations:* cricket and shooting. *Address:* Oakley Hay, Vincent Road, Selsey, Sussex. *T:* Selsey 2481. *Club:* Royal Air Force.

**LANGHAM, Sir John (Charles Patrick),** 14th Bt, *cr* 1660; *b* 30 June 1894; *s* of Sir (Herbert) Charles Arthur Langham, 13th Bt, and Ethel Sarah (*d* 1951), *e d* of Sir William Emerson Tennent, 2nd Bt (*ext*); *m* 1930, Rosamond Christabel, MBE 1969, *yr d* of Arthur Rashleigh, Holy Well House, Malvern Wells, Worcs; one *s*. *Educ:* Rugby Sch.; Royal Military College, Sandhurst. *Heir:* *s* James Michael Langham [*b* 24 May 1932; *m* 1959, Marion, *d* of O. Barratt, Tanzania; two *s* one *d*]. *Address:* Tempo Manor, Co. Fermanagh, Ireland.

**LANGKER, Sir Erik,** Kt 1968; OBE 1949; Artist; *b* 3 Nov. 1898; *s* of Christian and Elizabeth Langker; *m* 1929, Alice, *d* of Robert Pollock; one *s* one *d*. *Educ:* Fort St Boys' High Sch.; Julian Ashton Art Sch.; Royal Art Society Sch.; studied under Sir William Ashton. Exhibited widely throughout Commonwealth and America. Assoc. Mem. 1926, Fellow 1928, Pres. 1946, Royal Art Soc. NSW; President: Art Gall. of NSW, 1958-; Sydney Arts Foundation, 1969; Captain Cook Trust; La Perouse Trust; Foundation President: Nat. Opera of Australia; Opera Guild of NSW; North Shore Historical Soc. Chairman: Independent Theatre Ltd, 1946-; North Side Arts Festival; Member: Winston Churchill Meml Trust; State Adv. Coun. for Technical Educn; Trustee, Children's Library and Craft Movement, etc.; *Publication:* Australian Art Illustrated, 1947. *Recreations:* music, hiking. *Address:* Lombardy, 8 Eastview Street, Wollstonecroft, NSW 2065, Australia. *T:* 43-1209. *Club:* Savage (NSW).

**LANGLEY, Brig. Charles Ardagh,** CB 1962; CBE 1945; MC 1916 (Bar, 1918); Managing Director, UKRAS (Consultants) Ltd, since 1969; *b* 23 Aug. 1897; *s* of late John Langley, CBE, Under Sec. of State, Egyptian Govt, 1922; *m* 1st, 1920, V. V. M. Sharp (*d* 1931); one *s* one *d*; 2nd, 1936, M. J. Scott; two *d*. *Educ:* Cheltenham Coll.; Royal Military Academy, Woolwich. Served European War: commissioned Royal Engineers, 1915; France, 1916, served in field co. and as Adjutant to divisional engineers (MC and Bar; despatches three times). Subseq. took course of higher military engineer training, including one year at Cambridge Univ.; Railway Training Centre, Longmoor, 1922-27; seconded to Great Indian Peninsular Railway, 1927-33, in connection with electrification of Bombay-Poona main line, including construction of power station at Kalyan; Railway Trg Centre, Longmoor, 1933-38; various appointments, including Chief Instructor of Railways, War Office, 1938-40; War of 1939-45: responsible for initial transportation developments in Middle East; later formed Transportation Trg Centre for raising and training Docks and Inland Water Transport troops of Indian Engineers. Dep. Quartermaster-Gen. (Movements and Transportation), Allied Land Forces, South East Asia Command, 1943-45 (despatches, CBE); Commandant, Transportation Trg Centre, Longmoor, 1946. Inspecting Officer of Railways, 1946-58, Chief Inspecting Officer, 1958-63, Min. of Transport. Consultant, British Railways Bd, 1963-66; Projects Manager, UKRAS (Consultants) Ltd, 1966-69. Pres. Junior Institution of Engineers, 1961-62. MInstT. *Publications:* several military text books on transportation. *Recreation:* gardening. *Address:* Beeches, Little Austins, Farnham, Surrey. *T:* Farnham 5712. *Club:* United Service.

**LANGLEY, Brig. George Furner,** CBE 1958; DSO 1919; State Film Appeal Censor, Victoria; *b* 1 May 1891; *s* of Jabez and Fanny Langley; *m* 1918, Edmée Mary, *d* of late P. Plunkett, Cairo; two *d*. *Educ:* Melbourne Univ., BA, Diploma of Educn; FACE. Enlisted, Dec. 1914; 2nd Lt 1915; served Gallipoli, Torpedoed SS Southland, Evacuation; Gallipoli; transferred Imperial Camel Corps Jan. 1916; appointed CO 1st Battalion ICC Sept. 1916, commanded 1st Bn ICC to 30 June 1918, then commanded 14th Australian Light Horse; T/Command 5th A. L. H. Brigade Jan. 1919-Sept. 1919 (DSO, Serbian Order of White Eagle, despatches four times); commanded 20th ALH Regt and 4th ALH Regt of CMF; comd an Inf. Bde in 2 AIF, War of 1939-45; OStJ; ED; Red Cross Com. for Australia at Australia House, 1944-46. Formerly Principal, Melbourne High Sch. *Address:* 22 Munro Street, Armadale, Victoria 3143, Australia. *T:* BY 3953. *Club:* Naval and Military (Melbourne).

**LANGLEY, Vice-Admiral Gerald Maxwell Bradshaw,** CB 1948; OBE 1919; *b* 1895; *s* of Admiral Gerald Charles Langley. *Educ:*

Wellington. Joined Royal Navy, 1914; served European War, 1914-19; in Fleet Air Arm, 1923-39; Capt., 1936; Dir of Gunnery, Naval Staff, 1941-43; Chief Naval Staff Officer, Supreme Allied Command, South-East Asia, 1943-44; Rear-Admiral, 1946; Ministry of Defence, 1946-49; Vice-Adm. (retd), 1949. *Address:* Agecroft Mill, Milland, Liphook, Hants.

**LANGLEY, Noel A.;** Author-Playwright; *B* Durban, SA, 25 Dec. 1911; *m* 1937, Naomi Mary Legate (marriage dissolved, 1954); three *s* two *d*; *m* 1959, Pamela Deeming. *Educ:* Durban High Sch.; University of Natal, SA. Plays produced in London: Queer Cargo; For Ever; Edward My Son (with Robert Morley); Little Lambs Eat Ivy; Cage Me a Peacock; The Burning Bush; The Land of Green Ginger, 1966; The Snow Queen, 1967. Plays produced in New York: Farm of Three Echoes, 1939; The Walrus and the Carpenter, 1941. Films: Maytime, 1936 (USA); The Wizard of Oz, 1938 (USA); They Made Me a Fugitive, 1946; Cardboard Cavalier, Adam and Evalyn, 1948; Trio, Tom Brown's School Days, 1950; Scrooge, 1951; Ivanhoe (USA), Pickwick Papers (adaptation and direction), 1952; Knights of the Round Table (USA), 1953; Our Girl Friday (Adventures of Sadie) (screenplay and direction); Trilby and Svengali (screenplay and direction); Vagabond King (USA), 1954; The Search for Bridey Murphy (screenplay and direction), 1957. *Publications:* Cage Me a Peacock, 1935; There's a Porpoise Close Behind Us, 1936; Hocus Pocus, 1941; Land of Green Ginger, 1937; The Music of the Heart, 1946; The Cabbage Patch, 1947; Nymph in Clover, 1948; The Inconstant Moon, 1949; Tales of Mystery and Revenge, 1950; The Rift in the Lute, 1952; Where Did Everybody Go?, 1960; An Elegance of Rebels, 1960; The Loner, 1967; My Beloved Teck, 1970. (Jointly) There's a Horse in My Tree, Somebody's Rocking My Dream Boat, Cuckoo in the Dell. *Address:* Route 1, Box 1170, Virginia Beach, Va 23456, USA.

**LANGLEY MOORE, D.;** *see* Moore, Doris L.

**LANGMAN, Sir John Lyell,** 3rd Bt, *cr* 1906; *b* 9 Sept. 1912; *o s* of Sir Archibald Langman, 2nd Bt, CMG, North Cadbury Court, Somerset, and late Eleanor Katherine, 2nd *d* of 1st Baron Lyell; *S* father 1949; *m* 1936, Pamela, *o d* of Capt. Spencer Kennard; two *d* (one *d* decd). *Educ:* Eton; Christ Church, Oxford. Dir Newman Hender & Co. *Heir:* none. *Address:* Perrotts Brook House, near Cirencester, Glos. *T:* North Cerney 283. *Club:* Lansdowne.

**LANGRISHE, Capt. Sir Terence Hume,** 6th Bt, *cr* 1775; *b* 9 Dec. 1895; *s* of Sir Hercules Robert Langrishe, 5th Bt, and Helen, (*d* 1955), *d* of Rt Hon. Fitzwilliam Hume-Dick, Humewood, Co. Wicklow; *S* father, 1943; *m* 1926, Joan Stuart, *e d* of Major Ralph Grigg, late 18th Hussars; three *s*. *Educ:* Eton. Served European War as Lt Irish Guards, attached to RFC/RAF; War of 1939-45 as Capt. in the Intelligence Corps. *Heir:* *s* Hercules Ralph Hume Langrishe, 9th Lancers [*b* 17 May 1927; *m* 1955, Hon. Grania Wingfield, *o d* of Visc. Powerscourt, *qv*; one *s* three *d*]. *Address:* Knocktopher Abbey, Co. Kilkenny. *Clubs:* Royal Yacht Squadron (Cowes); Kildare Street (Dublin); Bembridge Sailing (Bembridge).

**LANGTON;** *see* Temple-Gore-Langton.

**LANGTON, Bernard Sydney,** CBE 1966; Alderman, Manchester City Council, 1963, Magistrate, 1961; Trustee, Young Volunteer Force Foundation, since 1967, and Chairman of its Advisory Council since 1968; *b* 1 Aug. 1914; *s* of Leon and Theresa Langton; *m* 1942, Betty Siroto; two *d*. *Educ:* Blackpool Grammar Sch.; Manchester Univ. Manchester City Council, 1945- (past Chm., Watch Cttee, Rivers Cttee); Mem., Police Council Great Britain, 1956-67; Governor, Police Coll., 1956-67; Mem., Police Adv. Board, 1957-67; Mem., Race Relations Board, 1966-68; Chm., Manchester Port Health Authority, 1957-; Mem., Gen. Adv. Coun. of ITA, 1969. *Recreations:* gardening, theatre, music. *Address:* 5 Pine Road, Didsbury, Manchester M20 0UY. *T:* 061-445 1669.

**LANGTON, Sir Henry (Algernon),** Kt 1964; DSO 1945; DFC 1943; DL; Owner and Manager of a stud since 1948; *b* 9 Feb. 1914; *s* of Rev. A. C. M. Langton and Mrs Langton (*née* Calley); unmarried. *Educ:* St John's Sch., Leatherhead. Taught at Corchester. Corbridge-on-Tyne, 1933-35; Bombay Burmah Trading Corp., 1935-36; teaching, 1936-38; Metropolitan Police Coll., and Police Force, 1938-41; Royal Air Force, 1941-48; Pilot in Bombers, Actg Wing Comdr, 1944. Mem. Wiltshire CC, 1955; Chm. Finance Cttee, 1959-68; Chm. of Council, 1968; Chm. Wessex Area Conservative Assoc., 1963-66. DL Wilts., 1968. *Recreation:* shooting.

**LANSDOWNE,** 8th Marquess of (GB), *cr* 1784; **George John Charles Mercer Nairne Petty-Fitzmaurice,** 29th Baron of Kerry and Lixnaw, 1181; Earl of Kerry, Viscount Clanmaurice, 1723; Viscount FitzMaurice and Baron Dunkeron, 1751; Earl of Shelburne, 1753; Baron Wycombe, 1760; Earl of Wycombe and Viscount Calne, 1784; PC 1964; DL; *b* 27 Nov. 1912; *o s* of Major Lord Charles George Francis Mercer Nairne, MVO (killed in action, 1914; 2nd *s* of 5th Marquess), and Lady Violet Mary Elliot (she *m* 2nd, 1916, Baron Astor of Hever, *qv*), *d* of 4th Earl of Minto; *S* cousin, 1944; *m* 1st, 1938, Barbara, (*d* 1965), *d* of Harold Stuart Chase, Santa Barbara, Calif; two *s* one *d* (and one *d* decd); 2nd, 1969, Mrs Polly Carnegie, *d* of Viscount Eccles, *q v*. *Educ:* Eton: Christ Church, Oxford. Sec. Junior Unionist League for E Scotland, 1939. Served War of 1939-45, Capt. Royal Scots Greys 1940, formerly 2nd Lt Scottish Horse (TA); Major 1944; served with Free French Forces (Croix de Guerre, Légion D'Honneur); Private Sec. to HM Ambassador in Paris (Rt Hon. A. Duff Cooper). 1944-45. Lord-in-Waiting to the Queen, 1957-58; Joint Parliamentary Under-Sec. of State, Foreign Office, 1958-62; Minister of State for Colonial Affairs, 1962-64, and for Commonwealth Relations, 1963-64. Mem. Royal Company of Archers (Queen's Body Guard for Scotland); JP, Perthshire, 1950; DL Wilts, 1952. Patron of two livings. Chm., Victoria League in Scotland, 1952-56; Inter-Governmental Cttee on Malaysia, 1962. Pres., Franco-British Soc. Prime Warden, Fishmongers' Company, 1967-68. *Heir:* *s* Earl of Shelburne, *qv*. *Address:* Bowood, Calne, Wilts; Meikleour House, Perthshire. *Clubs:* Turf, Beefsteak; New (Edinburgh).

*See also Baroness Nairne, Duke of St Albans.*

**LAPOINTE, Lt-Col Hon. Hugues,** PC (Canada) 1949; QC; Lieutenant-Governor of Quebec since 1966; *b* Rivière-du-Loup, Quebec, 3 March 1911; *s* of Rt Hon. Ernest Lapointe, PC, QC, Minister of Justice at Ottawa, and Emma Pratte; *m* 1938, Lucette, *d* of Dr and Mrs R. E. Valin, Ottawa. *Educ:* University of Ottawa (BA 1932); Laval Univ., Quebec (LLL 1935). Mem. of Quebec Bar, July 1935. Served War of 1939-45, Overseas, with Regt de la Chaudière. Elected (L) to House of Commons, Lotbinière County Constituency, 1940, 1945, 1949, 1953. Delegate to Gen. Assembly, UN:

Paris, Sept. 1948; Lake Success, April 1949; Lake Success, Sept. 1950 (Vice-Chm. Canadian Delegation). Parliamentary Asst to Minister of National Defense, 1945, to Sec. of State for External Affairs, 1949; Solicitor-Gen. of Canada, 1949; Minister of Veterans Affairs, Aug. 1950; Postmaster Gen., 1955; Agent-Gen. for Quebec in the United Kingdom, 1961-66. Hon. LLD University of Ottawa, 1954. Croix de Guerre avec palme. KStJ 1966; Kt Grand Cross, Sovereign and Milit. Order of Malta, 1966. Is a Roman Catholic. *Address:* Residence of the Lieutenant-Governor, 1010 St Louis Road, Quebec 6, Canada. *Clubs:* Garrison (Quebec); Rideau (Ottawa).

**LAPSLEY, Air Marshal Sir John (Hugh),** KBE 1969 (OBE 1944); CB 1966; DFC 1940; AFC 1950; Head of British Defence Staff and Defence Attaché, Washington, since 1970; *b* 24 Sept. 1916; *s* of late Edward John Lapsley, Bank of Bengal, Dacca, and Norah Gladis Lapsley; *m* 1942, Jean Margaret MacIvor; one *s* one *d. Educ:* Wolverhampton Sch.; Royal Air Force Coll., Cranwell. Served in Fighter Squadrons in UK, Egypt and Europe, 1938-45; psc 1946; Air Ministry Directorate of Policy, 1946-48; Commander No 74 Fighter Squadron and Air Fighting Development Squadron, 1949-52; HQ Fighter Command Staff, 1952-54; 2nd TAF Germany, 1954-58; Ministry of Defence Joint Planning Staff, 1958-60; Deputy Chief of Staff Air, 2nd Allied TAF, 1960-62; IDC, 1963; Secretary to Chiefs of Staff Cttee and Director of Defence Operations Staff, Ministry of Defence, 1964-66; No 19 Group, RAF Coastal Comd, 1967-68; AOC-in-C, RAF Coastal Commnad, 1968-69. *Recreations:* golf, sailing. *Club:* Royal Air Force.

**LARCOM, Sir (Charles) Christopher (Royde),** 5th Bt, *cr* 1868; Partner in Grieveson, Grant & Co., Stockbrokers, since 1960; *b* 11 Sept. 1926; *s* of Sir Philip Larcom, 4th Bt, and Aileen Monica Royde (*née* Colbeck); *S* father, 1967; *m* 1956, Barbara Elizabeth, *d* of Balfour Bowen; four *d. Educ:* Radley; Clare Coll., Cambridge. (Wrangler, 1947; BA, 1947; MA, 1951). Served RN (Lieutenant), 1947-50. Articled to Messrs Spicer and Pegler (Chartered Accountants), 1950-53; ACA 1954; FCA 1965; joined Grieveson, Grant and Co., 1955; Member, The Stock Exchange, London, 1959. *Recreations:* sailing, music. *Address:* Butlers, Hatfield Peverel, nr Chelmsford, Essex. *T:* Hatfield Peverel 508. *Club:* Bath.

**LARKCOM, Eric Herbert Larkcom J.;** *see* Jacobs-Larkcom.

**LARKIN, Alfred Sloane,** CIE 1944; *b* 11 June 1894; *s* of late George Larkin, Ballsbridge, Co. Dublin; *m* 1925, Phyllis, *d* of late Thomas Hodson, Wainfleet, Lincs; one *s. Educ:* High Sch., Dublin; Trent Coll., Derbyshire; Trinity Coll., Dublin. Entered Indian Civil Service, 1921; late Additional Member, Board of Revenue, Government of Bengal. *Address:* 3 Ashburnham Road, Eastbourne, Sussex.

**LARKIN, John Cuthbert,** MA; Headmaster, Wyggeston School, Leicester, 1947-69, retired; *b* 15 Oct. 1906; *s* of J. W. Larkin; *m* 1933, Sylvia Elizabeth Pilsbury; one *s* three *d. Educ:* King Edward VI Sch., Nuneaton; Downing Coll., Cambridge. Assistant Master, Shrewsbury Sch., 1928-45; Headmaster, Chesterfield Grammar Sch., 1946-47. *Recreations:* cricket, gardening. *Address:* Groves Cottage, Summers Lane, Totland Bay, Isle of Wight. *T:* Freshwater 2506.

**LARKIN, Philip (Arthur),** MA; FRSL; poet and novelist; Librarian of the University of Hull, since 1955; *b* 9 Aug. 1922; *o s* of Sydney and Eva Emily Larkin. *Educ:* King Henry VIII Sch., Coventry; St John's Coll., Oxford. Has held posts in different libraries since 1943. Jazz correspondent for the Daily Telegraph, 1961-. Vis. Fellow, All Souls Coll., Oxford, 1970-71. The Queen's Gold Medal for Poetry, 1965. Hon. DLit, Belfast; Hon. DLitt, Leicester. *Publications:* The North Ship (poems), 1945; Jill (novel), 1946 (rev. edition, 1964); A Girl in Winter (novel), 1947; The Less Deceived (poems), 1955; The Whitsun Weddings (poems), 1964; All What Jazz (essays), 1970. *Address:* c/o The University of Hull, Hull, Yorks.

**LARKING, Lt-Col Sir (Charles) Gordon,** Kt 1970; CBE 1951; Chartered Accountant; *b* 31 Aug. 1893; *s* of late Charles Larking, Norwich; *m* 1917, Kathleen Ethel Pank (*d* 1970), Norwich; two *s* one *d. Educ:* Norwich. Served European War, 1914-19, Royal Fusiliers, Royal Sussex, MGC (Egypt and France); War of 1939-45, commanded 8th Bn E. Surrey Regt, 1939-42; British Legion: National Chairman, 1947-50 (visited Malaya, Burma, Australia, New Zealand, Kenya, Uganda, Tanganyika, S Africa, Canada and US); National Treasurer, 1962-70. Member of Maidstone Town Council, 1922-; Mayor, 1931-32, 1944-45, 1950-51; Hon. Freeman, 1948. *Recreations:* cricket and football. *Address:* Pear Patch, Loose, Maidstone.

**LARKING, Sir Gordon;** *see* Larking, Sir C. G.

**LARMOR, Sir Graham;** *see* Larmor, Sir J. G.

**LARMOUR, Edward Noel,** CMG 1966; British High Commissioner to Jamaica, since 1970; Ambassador (non-resident) to Haiti, since 1970; *b* 25 Dec. 1916; *s* of Edward and Maud Larmour, Belfast, N Ireland; *m* 1946, Nancy, 2nd *d* of Thomas Bill; one *s* two *d. Educ:* Royal Belfast Academical Institution; Trinity Coll., Dublin (Scholar); Sydney Univ., NSW. Royal Inniskilling Fusiliers, 1940; Burma Civil Service, 1942; 14th Punjab Regt, 1943; Civil Affairs Staff (Burma), 15th Ind. Corps, 1944-45; Dep. Secretary to Governor of Burma, 1947; Commonwealth Relations Office, 1948; on staff of British High Commissioner in New Zealand, 1950-54; on staff of Comr-General for UK in SE Asia, 1954-57; Asst Secretary CRO, 1957; on staff of British High Comr in Australia, 1961-64; Asst Under-Secretary of State, 1964; British Dep. High Comr in Nigeria, 1964-68; Dep. Chief of Administration, FCO, 1968-70. *Recreations:* cricket, golf, music. *Address:* 68 Wood Vale, N10. *T:* 01-444 9744. *Club:* Royal Commonwealth Society.

**LARSEN, Roy Edward;** Vice Chairman of Board since 1969 (Director, 1933, President, 1939-60, Chairman, Executive Committee, 1960-69), of Time Incorporated; *b* 20 April 1899; *s* of Robert Larsen and Stella Belyea; *m* 1927, Margaret Zerbe; three *s* one *d. Educ:* Boston Latin Sch.; Harvard Univ. Circulation Manager, Time, 1922; Vice-President, Time Inc., 1927-39; Publisher Life, 1936-46. Overseer Harvard Univ., 1940-46, 1953-59; Chairman National Citizens Commn for Public Schools, 1949-56; Chairman of the Board of the Fund for the Advancement of Education, 1955-67; Member President's Cttee on Education Beyond the High School; Trustee, Ford Foundation, 1957-69; Trustee and Vice-President, New York Public Library. Chevalier, French Legion of Honour, 1950. Hon. LLD: Marietta Coll., 1946; Bucknell Univ., 1950; New York Univ., 1952; Harvard, 1953; Dartmouth Coll., 1954; Boston Univ., 1956; Hon. LHD, Kalamazoo Coll., 1951; Hon. LittD, Oberlin Coll., 1958. hon. Phi Beta

Kappa, 1957. *Address:* Time Inc., Time & Life Building, Rockefeller Center, New York, NY 10020, USA. *T:* Judson 6-1212; 4900 Congress Street, Fairfield, Conn 06431, USA. *Clubs:* Harvard, Century, River, University, Links (New York).

**LARSON, Frederick H.,** DFM 1943; Agent General for Province of Saskatchewan, Canada, in London since Dec. 1967; *b* 24 Nov. 1913; *s* of Herman B. and Martha C. Larson; *m* 1941, Dorothy A. Layng; one *s*. *Educ:* University of Saskatchewan. Observer, RCAF, 1941-43. Member for Kindersley, Parliament of Canada, 1949-53; Delegate to UN, Paris, 1952. Ten years in oil and gas business, production refining and sales, domestic and offshore; eight years in financial trust business, representing financial interests, Canada amd Jamaica; three years in construction and engineering; agricultural interests, Saskatchewan. *Recreation:* golf. *Address:* Saskatchewan House, 28 Chester Street, SW1. *T:* 01-235 1871. *Clubs:* Travellers', Royal Automobile.

**LARTIGUE;** *see* Cools-Lartigue.

**LASBREY, Rt. Rev. Bertram,** MA, DD. *Educ:* Bedford Sch.; St Catherine's Coll., Cambridge; Ridley Hall, Cambridge. Deacon, 1904; Priest, 1905; Curate of St Andrew, Auckland, 1904-07; Chaplain, Weymouth Coll., 1907-11; Curate of St John, Melcombe Regis, 1907-11; Vicar of St Gabriel, Bishop Wearmouth, 1911-22; Bishop on the Niger, 1922-45; Assistant Bishop of Worcester and Rector of St Andrew's and All Saints with St Helen's, St Albans and St Michael's, Worcester, 1946-Jan. 1953. Hon. Canon of Worcester Cathedral, 1946-53; Public Preacher in the Diocese of Southwell, 1953-62. *Address:* Homes of St Barnabas, Dormans, Lingfield, Surrey.

**LASCELLES,** family name of **Earl of Harewood.**

**LASCELLES, Viscount; David Henry George Lascelles;** *b* 21 Oct. 1950; *s* and *heir* of 7th Earl of Harewood, *qv*.

**LASCELLES, Rt. Hon. Sir Alan Frederick,** PC 1943; GCB 1953 (KCB 1944; CB 1937); GCVO 1947 (KCVO 1939; MVO 1926); CMG 1933; MC; MA; Past Director, The Midland Bank; Director, Royal Academy of Music; Private Secretary to the Queen, 1952-53; Keeper of the Queen's Archives, 1952-53 (of the King's Archives, 1945-52); *b* 11 April 1887; *s* of Hon. F. C. Lascelles; *m* 1920, Hon. Joan Thesiger, *e d* of 1st Viscount Chelmsford; two *d* (one *s* decd). *Educ:* Marlborough Coll.; Trinity Coll., Oxford (Hon. Fellow, Trinity Coll., Oxford, 1948). Served in France with Bedfordshire Yeomanry, 1914-18; Captain, 1916; ADC to Lord Lloyd, when Governor of Bombay, 1919-20; Assistant Private Secretary to Prince of Wales, 1920-29; Secretary to Governor General of Canada, 1931-35; Assistant Private Secretary to King George V, 1935, and to King George VI, 1936-43, Private Secretary, 1943-52. Chairman, The Pilgrim Trust, 1954-60; Chairman, Historic Buildings Council for England, 1953-63; LLD (Hon.) Bristol and Durham; Hon. DCL (Oxon), FRAM (Hon.). *Address:* Kensington Palace, W8. *Clubs:* Brooks's, MCC.

*See also Viscount Chandos.*

**LASCELLES, Daniel Richard,** CBE 1962; *b* 18 Sept. 1908; 4th *s* of Councillor A. Lascelles, JP, Darlington; *m* 1941, Mildred Joyce Burr; two *s* one *d*. *Educ:* Durham Sch.; St John's Coll., Cambridge. Called to Bar, Inner Temple, 1930; Sarawak Administrative Service, 1932; Circuit Judge, Sarawak, 1948; Colonial Legal Service, 1951; Acting Puisne Judge, 1951; Puisne Judge of Supreme Court of Sarawak, North Borneo and Brunei, 1952-62; retired, Sept. 1962. Legal Chairman Pensions Appeal Tribunals, 1964; Chairman, Medical Appeal Tribunals, 1967; Member, Mental Health Review Tribunal, 1967. *Recreations:* shooting, gardening, golf, tennis. *Address:* Galsworthy House, Middleton Tyas, Richmond, Yorks.

**LASCELLES, Sir Francis (William),** KCB 1954 (CB 1937); MC; MA; Clerk of the Parliaments, 1953-58; *b* 23 March 1890; *s* of late Lieut-Colonel H. A. Lascelles, Woolbeding, Midhurst; *m* 1924, Esmée Marion, *d* of late C. A. Bury, Downings, Co. Kildare; two *s*. *Educ:* Winchester; Christ Church, Oxford. Served in European War, 1914-19 with Sussex Yeomanry (wounded, MC). *Address:* The Low Hall, Hackness, Scarborough. *Club:* Athenæum.

**LASCELLES, Maj.-Gen. Henry Anthony,** CB 1967; CBE 1962 (OBE 1945); DSO 1944; *b* 10 Jan. 1912; *s* of Edward Lascelles and Leila Kennett-Barrington; *m* 1941, Ethne Hyde Ussher Charles. *Educ:* Winchester; Oriel Coll., Oxford (BA). Served War of 1939-45: Egypt, North Africa, Sicily and Italy, rising to second in command of an armoured brigade. Instructor, Staff Coll., Camberley, 1947-49; GSO 1, HQ 7th Armoured Div., BAOR, 1949-52; Comdg Officer 6th Royal Tank Regt, BAOR, 1952-55; Instructor NATO Defence Coll., 1955-56; Brigadier Royal Armoured Corps HQ 2nd Infantry Div., BAOR, 1956-57; National Defence Coll., Canada, 1958-59; BGS Military Operations, War Office, 1959-62; Chief of Staff, HQ Northern Ireland Command, 1962-63; Maj.-General, General Staff, Far East Land Forces, 1963-66. Director-General, Winston Churchill Memorial Trust, 1967-. *Recreations:* squash, tennis, golf, music, gardening. *Address:* Manor Farm Cottage, Hedgerley Green, Bucks. *T:* Gerrards Cross 83582. *Club:* United Service.

**LASCELLES, Mary Madge,** FBA 1962; Fellow of Somerville College, 1932-60, Hon. Fellow 1967; *b* 7 Feb. 1900; *d* of William Horace and Madeline Lascelles. *Educ:* Sherborne School for Girls; Lady Margaret Hall, Oxford. Research Studentship, Westfield Coll., 1923; Assistant Lecturer, Royal Holloway Coll., 1926; Somerville College: Tutor in English Language and Literature, 1931; Fellow, 1932-60; Vice-Principal, 1947-60; University Lecturer in English Literature, 1960-66; Reader, 1966-67. *Publications:* Jane Austen and her Art, 1939; Shakespeare's Measure for Measure, 1953; contributions to learned journals, etc. *Address:* 3 Stratfield Road, Oxford. *T:* Oxford 57817. *Club:* University Women's.

**LASDUN, Denys Louis,** CBE 1965; FRIBA; Architect (own private practice); *b* 8 Sept. 1914; *s* of Norman Lasdun and Julie Abrahams; *m* 1954, Susan Bendit; two *s* one *d*. *Educ:* Rugby Sch.; Architectural Assoc. Served with Royal Engineers, 1939-45 (MBE). Practised with Wells Coates, Tecton and Fry, Drew. Hoffman Wood Professor of Architecture, University of Leeds, 1962-63. Works include: housing schemes and schools for Bethnal Green and Paddington; new store for Peter Robinson, Strand; luxury flats at 26 St James's Place (RIBA Bronze Medal, London Architecture, 1960); Royal College of Physicians (RIBA Bronze Medal, London Architecture, 1964; Civic Trust Award, Class I, 1967); new Fitzwilliam College and Chapel, and Christ's College extension, Cambridge; new University of East Anglia (Civic Trust

Award, Group A, 1969) and work for the Universities of London, Leicester (Civic Trust Award, Group A, 1969) and Liverpool; Royal Instn of Chartered Surveyors, Parliament Square; National Theatre, South Bank. Hon. Fellow, American Institute of Architects, 1966. *Publications:* contributions to architectural and other papers. Lectures given in UK, USA, Spain, Portugal and Norway. *Address:* 25 Dawson Place, W2. *T:* 01-486 4761.

**LASH, Rt. Rev. William Quinlan;** Assistant Bishop of Truro, Hon. Canon of St Mary's Cathedral, Truro, since 1962; Vicar of St Clement, since 1963; *b* 5 Feb. 1905; *s* of Nicholas Alleyne and Violet Maud Lash. *Educ:* Tonbridge Sch., Emmanuel Coll., Cambridge; Westcott House. BA 1927; MA 1932; Deacon, 1928; Priest, 1929; Curate, S Mary's Church, Portsea, 1928-32; Christa Seva Sangha, Poona, 1932; Acharya, Christa Prema Seva Sangha, Poona, 1934-49, 1953-61; Bishop of Bombay, 1947-61. *Publications:* Approach to Christian Mysticism, 1947; The Temple of God's Wounds, 1951. *Address:* The Vicarage, St Clement, Truro, Cornwall. *T:* Truro 4605.

**LASKEY, Denis Seward,** CMG 1957; CVO 1958; Ambassador to Rumania since 1969; *b* 18 Jan. 1916; *s* of F. S. Laskey; *m* 1947, Perronnelle Mary Gemma, *d* of late Col Sir Edward Le Breton, MVO; one *s* three *d. Educ:* Marlborough Coll.; Corpus Christi Coll., Oxford. 3rd Secretary, Diplomatic Service, 1939; FO, Sept. 1939-June 1940; served in Army, 1940-41; FO, 1941-46; Berlin, 1946-49; Member UK Delegation to UN, New York, 1949-53; FO, 1953-59; Private Secretary to Secretary of State for Foreign Affairs, 1956-59; Minister, HM Embassy, Rome, 1960-64; Under-Secretary, Cabinet Office, 1964-67; Minister, HM Embassy, Bonn, 1967-68. *Recreations:* ski-ing, fishing, golf. *Address:* c/o Foreign and Commonwealth Office, SW1. *Clubs:* Junior Carlton; Leander (Henley-on-Thames).

**LASKEY, Francis Seward,** MC; *b* 1886; *m* 1915, Elaine Dorothie Nancie, *d* of William Procter Dilworth; two *s* (and one *s* killed in action, 1943). *Educ:* Merchant Taylors' Sch.; Oriel Coll., Oxford. Called to Bar, 1913; Recorder: Poole, 1939-41; Salisbury, 1941-61; served European War, 1914-19 (MC). *Address:* Queen Elizabeth Building, Temple, EC4. *T:* Central 5432. *Clubs:* Athenæum, Junior Carlton, Leander.

**LASKI, Marghanita; (Mrs J. E. Howard);** *b* 24 Oct. 1915; *d* of late Neville J. Laski, QC, m 1937, John Eldred Howard; one *s* one *d. Educ:* Ladybarn House Sch., Manchester; Somerville Coll., Oxford. Novelist, critic, journalist. *Publications:* Love on the Supertax (novel), 1944; The Patchwork Book (anthology), 1946; To Bed with Grand Music (pseudonymous novel), 1946; (ed) Stories of Adventure, 1947; (ed) Victorian Tales, 1948; Tory Heaven (novel), 1948; Little Boy Lost (novel), 1949; Mrs Ewing, Mrs Molesworth, Mrs Hodgson Burnett (criticism), 1950; The Village (novel), 1952; The Victorian Chaise-Longue (novel), 1953; The Offshore Island (play), 1959; Ecstasy: A study of some secular and religious experiences, 1961; Domestic Life in Edwardian England, 1964; (ed, with E.G. Battiscombe) A Chaplet for Charlotte Yonge, 1965; The Secular Responsibility (Conway Memorial Lecture), 1967; Jane Austen and her World, 1969. *Address:* c/o David Higham Associates, 76 Dean Street, W1.

**LASKY, Melvin Jonah,** MA; Editor, Encounter Magazine, since 1958; *b* New York City, 15 Jan. 1920; *s* of Samuel Lasky and Esther Lasky (*née* Kantrowitz); *m* 1947, Brigitte Newiger; one *s* one *d. Educ:* City Coll. of New York (BSS); Univ. of Michigan (MA); Columbia Univ. Literary Editor, The New Leader (NY), 1942-43; US Combat Historian in France and Germany, 1944-45; Capt., US Army, 1946; Foreign Correspondent, 1946-48; Editor and Publisher, Der Monat (Berlin), 1948-58; Co-Editor, Encounter Magazine (London), 1958-; Editorial Director, Library Press, NY, 1970-. Univ. of Michigan, Sesquicentennial Award, 1967. *Publications:* Reisenotizen und Tagebucher, 1958; Africa for Beginners, 1962; Utopia and Revolution, 1971; contributor to: America and Europe, 1951; New Paths in American History, 1965; Sprache und Politik, 1969; (ed) The Hungarian Revolution, 1957. *Address:* c/o Encounter, 25 Haymarket, SW1. *T:* 01-839 4561. *Club:* Garrick.

**LAST, Prof. Raymond Jack,** FRCS; Professor of Applied Anatomy, and Warden, Royal College of Surgeons, 1949-70; *b* 26 May 1903; English. *Educ:* Adelaide High Sch., Australia. MB, BS (Adelaide), 1924; Medical practice S. Australia, 1927-38; arrived London, 1939; Surgeon, EMS, Northern Hospital, N21, 1939-40. OC Abyssinian Medical Unit, Hon. Surgeon to Emperor Haile Selassie I, also OC Haile Selassie Hospital, Surgeon to British Legation, Addis Ababa, 1941-44; returned to London, Lieut-Colonel, RAMC, 1945; ADMS, British Borneo, 1945-46. Anatomical Curator and Bland Sutton Scholar, RCS, 1946; FRCS 1947; Adviser to Central Government of Pakistan on organization and conduct of primary FRCS instruction, Colombo Plan, 1961. *Publications:* Anatomy, Regional and Applied, 4th edn, 1966; Wolff's Anatomy of Eye and Orbit, 6th edn, 1968; Aids to Anatomy, 12th edn, 1962. Contrib. to Journals of Surgery; various articles. *Address:* 15a Sunshine Flats, Upper Gardens, St Julian's, Malta GC.

**LATEY, Hon. Sir John (Brinsmead),** Kt 1965; MBE 1943; QC 1957; **Hon. Mr Justice Latey;** Judge of the High Court of Justice, Probate, Divorce and Admiralty Division, since 1965; *b* 7 March 1914; *s* of William Latey, *qv; m* 1938, Betty Margaret (*née* Beresford); one *s* one *d. Educ:* Westminster; Christ Church, Oxford. MA (Hon. Sch. Jurispr.). Called to the Bar, 1936. Served in Army during War, 1939-45, mainly in MEF (Lieut-Colonel, 1944-). General Council of the Bar, 1952-56, 1957-61 and 1964- (Hon. Treasurer, 1959-61). Master of the Bench of the Middle Temple, 1964. Chairman, Lord Chancellor's Cttee on Age of Majority, 1965-67. Dep. Chairman, Oxfordshire QS, 1966. *Publications:* (Asst Ed.) Latey on Divorce, 14th edn, 1952; Halsbury's Laws of England (Conflict of Laws: Husband and Wife), 1956. *Recreations:* golf, bridge, chess. *Address:* 33 Pembroke Gardens, W8. *T:* 01-603 6760. *Club:* Oxford and Cambridge.

**LATEY, William,** CBE 1965 (MBE 1918); QC 1950; Special Divorce Commissioner, 1952-64 (Continuously); *b* 12 Feb. 1885; *y s* of late John Latey, Editor of the Penny Illustrated Paper, 1860-1900 and later of The Illustrated London News, also of The Sketch, and of late Constance Latey; *m* 1912, Anne Emily, *d* of late Horace G. Brinsmead; two *s. Educ:* Mercers' Sch. Writer and journalist; FJI 1915. War correspondent, Daily Chronicle, 1914-15; on Secretariat, Ministry of Munitions, Gun and Tank Supply, 1916-18; called to the Bar, 1916 (Oxford Circuit); practising since 1919, mainly in Probate and Divorce. War of 1939-45, Temple ARP Control Cttee and City Warden. Member General Council of the Bar, 1935-52; Chairman, Legal Board of National Marriage Guidance Council, till 1966; Member

Archbishops' Commission on Law of Nullity of Marriage, 1950-54; HM Commissioner of Assize on various occasions, 1952-60; President, Medico-Legal Society, 1956-57; Member Councils of Law-Reporting, 1947-67, International Law Association, British Institute of International Law. Bencher of the Middle Temple, 1947; Lenten Reader, 1961; Treasurer, 1966. Freeman of the City of London. *Publications:* Latey on Divorce; Probate and Conflict on Laws (Husband and Wife) in Halsbury's Laws of England, 1932; Family Law in Jenks' Civil Law Digest, 1947; The Tide of Divorce, 1970; and numerous other legal publications. *Recreations:* chess, golf. *Address:* New Court, Temple, EC4. *T:* 01-353 1487. *Clubs:* Athenæum, Savage. *See also Hon. Sir J. B. Latey.*

**LATHAM,** family name of **Baron Latham.**

**LATHAM,** 2nd Baron *cr* 1942, of Hendon; **Dominic Charles Latham;** *b* 20 Sept. 1954; *s* of Hon. Francis Charles Allman Latham (*d* 1959) and of Gabrielle, *d* of Dr S. M. O'Riordan; *S* grandfather, 1970. *Heir: yr* twin *b* Anthony Latham, *b* 20 Sept. 1954. *Address:* 7 Bellvue Street, Maroubra, Sydney, NSW, Australia.

**LATHAM, Arthur Charles;** MP (Lab) Paddington North since Oct. 1969; *b* Leyton, 14 Aug. 1930; *m* 1951, Margaret Latham; one *s* one *d. Educ:* Romford Royal Liberty Sch.; Garnett Coll. of Educn. Lectr in Further Educn, Southgate Technical Coll., 1967-. Mem., Havering Council (formerly Romford Borough Council) 1952- (Alderman, 1962-). Contested (Lab): Woodford, 1959; Rushcliffe, Notts, 1964. Mem., NE Regional Metropolitan Hosp. Bd, 1966-. *Recreations:* bridge, chess, cricket. *Address:* House of Commons, SW1; 17 Tudor Avenue, Gidea Park, Romford, Essex.

**LATHAM, E(dward) Bryan,** CBE 1964; MM 1915; Chairman, James Latham Ltd, Timber Importers, Leeside Wharf, London, E5, since 1951 (Director, 1921, Managing Director, 1939); Chairman, Nigerian Hardwood Co. Ltd, London, since 1951; *b* 7 May 1895; *s* of late E. Locks Latham, The Towers, Theydon Bois, Essex, and late Emily Latham (*née* Chappell); *m* 1927, Anne Arnot Duncan, Newton of Lathrisk, Fife; two *s. Educ:* Felsted, Essex. Served European War, 1914-18 (MM): France, Indian Frontier, Palestine; Lieut, 17th London Regt, later Captain, 19 Punjabi Regt. Governor Metropolitan Hosp., London, 1930-40; Chm., Nat. Sawmilling Assoc., 1942-43; Pres. Timber Trade Fedn of UK, 1945-47; Governing Council, Commonwealth Forestry Association, 1945- (Chm., 1961; Vice-Pres., 1964-70); Gen. Council, British Standards Inst., 1946-48; Mem. Education Cttee, FBI, 1956-; Founder-Pres., Inst. of Wood Science, 1956-58, Mem. Council, 1959-; Mem. Forestry Commn, 1957-63. Mem. British Delegs to Commonwealth Forestry Confs: London, 1947; Ottawa, 1952; to 5th World Forestry Congress, Seattle, 1960; Hon. Pres. Univ. of Edinburgh Forestry Assoc., 1962-63; Vice-Pres., Timber Research and Development Assoc. (TRADA), 1963-69 (Chm., 1943-44; Mem. Council, 1943-70); Pres., Timber Trade Benevolent Soc.; Member: Business Archives Council, 1962-68; Furniture and Timber Industry Training Board, 1965-; F.Inst. of Wood Science, London, 1957-70; F.Forest History Foundation, Yale Univ., 1959-70; FRSA 1961. Mem. Royal Horticultural Soc., Surrey; Pres. Launceston Agric. Soc., 1967. *Publications:* Victorian Staffordshire Portrait Figures, 1953; Timber: Its Development and Distribution, 1957; Wood from Forest to Man, 1964; History of the Timber Trade Federation of the UK, 1965; Territorial Soldiers War, 1967; Trebartha, the House by the Stream: a Cornish history, 1970. Contributor to: Encyclopædia Britannica, Empire Forestry Review, Wood, Timber Trades Journal, Unasylva (FAO), etc. *Recreations:* fishing, riding, natural history, gardening; collector of Victorian Staffordshire Portrait figures. *Address:* Trebartha House, near Launceston, Cornwall. *T:* Coad's Green 336. *Clubs:* United Service, Royal Automobile.

**LATHAM, Gustavus Henry,** LLD, JP; Chairman and Managing Director, Whitehead Iron and Steel Co. Ltd, 1938-64 and other Companies; Director, Richard Thomas & Baldwins Ltd, 1964, retired (Deputy Chairman, 1955-64); Past Chairman: British Iron & Steel Corporation Ltd; British Steel Corporation Ltd; President, University College of South Wales and Monmouthshire, 1955-60; Past President British Iron and Steel Federation; Founder President, Newport and District Metallurgical Society, 1934; Vice-President Iron and Steel Institute; late Member of the Iron and Steel Board; *b* 29 Dec. 1888; *s* of Henry Charles Latham, Stoke-on-Trent, and Emma Fairall, Buxton; *m* 1916, Gwladys Gwen, *d* of Engr Rear-Admiral J. A. Lemon; one *s* one *d. Educ:* Secondary, High School and Technical Coll., Longton, Staffs. With L. & N.W. Railway for special training in Transport, 1901-04; joined L. D. Whitehead, Tredegar, to study and develop Continuous Rolling Mills for steel trade, 1905; started up first Semi-Continuous Rolling Mill in England and Europe, 1907; General Manager and Deputy Chairman Whitehead Iron and Steel Co. Ltd, 1931; appointed by Control Cttee set up by Bank of England as Managing Director Richard Thomas & Co. Ltd, 1939-45; Technical Adviser for steel trade for Finance Corporation for Industry, 1944; and to late Governor of the Bank of England (Lord Norman); Past President British Iron and Steel Research Association. Member Newport Harbour Commissioners, 1941-64; Governor, Newport and Monmouthshire College of Technology; Chairman, Newport Council, Order of St John, 1951-68. KStJ. *Recreation:* continuous hot and cold rolling of steel. *Address:* Fields House, Newport, Mon. *T:* 65743.

**LATHAM, Sir Joseph,** Kt 1960; CBE 1950; Chairman, Metal Industries Ltd, since 1968; Managing Director, Engineering Group, Thorn Electrical Industries, Ltd, since 1970; Director: George Wimpey and Co. Ltd; Black & Decker Ltd; Black & Decker Manufacturing Co., USA; *b* 1 July 1905; *s* of John and Edith Latham, Prestwich, Lancs; *m* 1932, Phyllis Mary Fitton; one *s* one *d. Educ:* Stand Grammar Sch. Chartered Accountant, 1926; Liaison Officer, Lancashire Associated Collieries, 1935; Director and Secretary, Manchester Collieries Ltd, 1941; Director-General of Finance, National Coal Board, 1946-55; Finance Member, NCB, 1955-56; Deputy Chairman, NCB, 1956-60. Vice-Chm., AEI, 1964-65, Dep. Chm., 1965-68, Man. Dir, 1967-68. Mem., ECGD, Advisory Council, 1964-69; Chm., Economic Development Cttees, Food Processing and Chocolate & Sugar Confectionery Industries, 1965-66. *Address:* Ovington, The Mount, Leatherhead, Surrey. *T:* Leatherhead 2433. *Clubs:* Royal Automobile; Effingham Golf.

**LATHAM, Sir Richard Thomas Paul,** 3rd Bt, *cr* 1919, of Crow Clump; *b* 15 April 1934; *s* of Sir (Herbert) Paul Latham, 2nd Bt, and Lady Patricia Doreen Moore (*d* 1947), *o d* of 10th Earl of Drogheda; *S* father, 1955; *m* 1958,

Marie-Louise Patricia, *d* of Frederick H. Russell, Vancouver, BC; two *d. Educ:* Trinity Coll., Cambridge (MA). *Address:* Maple Springs Farm, RR 3, Mission City, BC, Canada. *Club:* Cavalry.

**LATHBURY, General Sir Gerald (William),** GCB 1962 (KCB 1956; CB 1950); DSO 1943; MBE 1940; DSC (USA) 1944; Governor of Gibraltar, 1964-69; *b* 14 July 1906; *m* 1942, Jean Thin; two *d. Educ:* Wellington Coll.; Royal Military Coll., Sandhurst, 1924-25; gazetted to Oxfordshire and Buckinghamshire Light Infantry, 1926; Gold Coast Regt, 1928-33; Staff Coll., 1937-38; served throughout War of 1939-45 in France and Belgium, North Africa, Sicily, Italy and North-West Europe; Palestine, 1945-46; Imperial Defence Coll., 1948; GOC 16 Airborne Division (TA), 1948-51; Commandant, Staff Coll., Camberley, 1951-53; Vice-Adjutant-General, War Office, 1954; Commander-in-Chief, East Africa, 1955-57; Director-General of Military Training, War Office, 1957-60; General Officer Commanding-in-Chief, Eastern Command, 1960-61; Quartermaster-General to the Forces, 1961-65; ADC General to the Queen, 1962-65. Colonel, West India Regt, 1959; Jamaica Regt, 1962-68; Colonel Comdt, 1st Green Jackets, 43rd and 52nd, 1961-65; Colonel Comdt, The Parachute Regt, 1961-65. *Club:* Brooks's.

**LATHE, Prof. Grant Henry;** Professor of Chemical Pathology, University of Leeds, since 1957; *b* 27 July 1913; *s* of Frank Eugene and Annie Smith Lathe; *m* 1st, 1938, Margaret Eleanore Brown; one *s*. 2nd, 1950, Joan Frances Hamlin; one *s* two *d. Educ:* McGill Univ.; Oxford Univ. ICI Research Fellow: Dept. of Biochemistry, Oxford Univ., 1946; Dept. of Chemical Pathology, Post Graduate Medical School of London, 1948; Lecturer in Chemical Pathology, Guy's Hospital Medical School, 1948; Biochemist, The Bernhard Baron Memorial Research Laboratories, Queen Charlotte's Maternity Hospital, London, 1949. *Publications:* papers in medical and biochemical journals. *Recreations:* skating, listening to music. *Address:* 14 Lidgett Park Road, Leeds 8. *T:* 66-1507.

**LATIMER, Sir (Courtenay) Robert,** Kt 1966; CBE 1958 (OBE 1948); Registrar, Kingston Polytechnic, Surrey; *b* 13 July 1911; *er s* of late Sir Courtenay Latimer, KCIE, CSI; *m* 1944, Elizabeth Jane Gordon (*née* Smail); one *s* one *d. Educ:* Rugby; Christ Church, Oxford. ICS, 1934 (Punjab); IPS, 1939; Vice-Consul, Bushire, 1940-41; Sec. Foreign Publicity Office, Delhi, 1941-42; Sec. Indian Agency Gen., Chungking, 1944; in NW Frontier Prov., as Asst Political Agent N Waziristan, Dir of Civil Supplies, Sec. to Governor and District Comr, Bannu, 1942-43 and 1945-47. HM Overseas Service, 1948; served in Swaziland, 1948-49; Bechuanaland Protectorate, 1951-54; Office of High Comr for Basutoland, the Bechuanaland Protectorate and Swaziland, as Asst Sec., 1949-51; Sec. for Finance, 1954-60; Chief Sec., 1960-64; Minister, British Embassy, Pretoria, 1965-66. *Recreations:* tennis, golf, photography. *Address:* Queen Anne House, Westwood Place, Normandy, Surrey.

**LATNER, Prof. Albert Louis;** Professor of Clinical Biochemistry, University of Newcastle upon Tyne, since 1963, and Director of Cancer Research Unit, since 1967; Consultant Chemical Pathologist, Royal Victoria Infirmary, Newcastle upon Tyne, since 1948; *b* 5 Dec. 1912; *s* of Harry Latner and Miriam Gordon; *m* 1936, Gertrude Franklin. *Educ:* Imperial College of Science and University College, London; University of Liverpool. ARCSc, 1931; MSc (London) 1933; DIC, 1934; MB, ChB (Liverpool) 1939; MD (Liverpool) 1948; FRIC 1953; MRCP 1956; DSc (Liverpool) 1958; FRCPath 1964; FRCP 1964. Lectr in Physiology, Univ. of Liverpool, 1933-36 and 1939-41; Pathologist in RAMC, 1941-46; Sen. Registrar, Postgrad. Medical Sch., 1946-47; Lectr in Chem. Pathol., King's Coll., Univ. of Durham, 1947-55; Reader in Medical Biochemistry, Univ. of Durham, 1955-61; Prof. of Clin. Chem., Univ. of Durham, 1961-63. Chm. Assoc. of Clinical Biochemists, 1958-61 (Pres., 1961-63); Mem., Editorial Bd of Clinica Chimica Acta, 1960-68; Titular Member, Section of Clinical Chemistry, International Union of Pure and Applied Chemistry, 1967-. *Publications:* (co-author) Isoenzymes in Biology and Medicine, 1968; Chapter on Metabolic Aspects of Liver Disease in Metabolic Disturbances in Clinical Medicine (ed G. A. Smart), 1958; Chapters on Chemical Pathology and Clinical Biochemistry in British Encyclopædia of Med. Practice, Med. Progress (ed Lord Cohen of Birkenhead), 1961, 1962, 1964, 1966 and 1968; Chapter on Isoenzymes in Recent Advances in Clinical Pathology, Series IV, 1964; Section on Isoenzymes in Advances in Clinical Chemistry (ed C. P. Stewart), 1966. Contributions to Medical and Scientific Journals dealing with liver disease, pernicious anæmia, the serum proteins in disease and isoenzymes. *Recreations:* art, photography, gardening. *Address:* Ravenstones, Rectory Road, Gosforth, Newcastle upon Tyne NE3 1XP. *T:* Gosforth 858020. *Club:* Savage.

**LATTER, Maj.-Gen. John Cecil,** CBE 1944; MC; DL; *b* 6 May 1896; *o s* of late Dr Cecil Latter, Folkestone, Kent, and of late Ruth Beechey; unmarried. *Educ:* Cheltenham Coll. (Scholar); Trinity Coll., Oxford (Scholar). Served European War, 1914-18, 2/5 Lancs Fusiliers and Staff (MC). Diplomatic Service, 1919-21; resigned to take up permanent commission in Regular Army; psc, 1933; AAG, GHQ, BEF, Nov. 1939-June 1940 (despatches); Deputy Military Secretary (B), War Office, Aug. 1940-Jan. 1943; Deputy Military Secretary, GHQ Middle East Forces, Jan.-Dec. 1943; DAG, GHQ, Middle East Forces, Dec. 1943-July 1944; DA and QMG, 5th AA Group, July 1944-March 1945; Deputy Director, TA and Army Cadet Force, 1945-47; Colonel, 1944; retired 1947 (hon. Maj.-General); Secretary, Leeds Univ. Appointments Board, 1948-52; Chairman Combined Cadet Force Association, 1952-55; Assistant Director-General, Leeds Centenary Musical Festival, 1958. DL West Riding, 1952. *Publications:* edited (and partly wrote) Cadet Training Manual, for British National Cadet Association, 1933; The History of the Lancashire Fusiliers, 1914-18, 1949. *Address:* Riverside Cottage, Naburn, York YO1 4RR. *Club:* Army and Navy.

**LATTIMORE, Owen;** Professor of Chinese Studies, Leeds University, 1963-70, now Professor Emeritus; Director, Page School of International Relations, 1938-50 and Lecturer in History to 1963, Johns Hopkins University, USA; *b* Washington, DC, 29 July 1900; *s* of David Lattimore and Margaret Barnes; *m* 1926, Eleanor, (*d* 1970), *d* of Dr T. F. Holgate, Evanston, Ill.; one *s. Educ:* St Bees Sch., Cumberland; Research Student at Harvard Univ., 1929. Early childhood in China; returned to China, 1919; engaged in business in Tientsin and Shanghai, 1920; Journalism in Tientsin, 1921; business in Tientsin and Peking with Arnhold and Co., 1922-25; travelled in Mongolia, 1926; in Chinese Turkestan, 1927; studied in America, 1928, 1929; travelled in

Manchuria, as Fellow of Social Science Research Council, 1929-30; Research work in Peiping, as Fellow of Harvard-Yenching Institute, 1930-31; Research Fellow, Guggenheim Foundation, Peking, 1931-33; travelled in Mongolia, 1932-33; editor, Pacific Affairs, 1934-41; research work in China and Mongolia, 1934-35, 1937; Political Adviser to Generalissimo Chiang Kai-Shek, 1941-42; Director, Pacific Operations, Office of War Information, San Francisco, 1943; accompanied Vice-President Wallace in Siberia and China, 1944; economic consultant, American Reparations Mission in Japan, 1945; UN Technical Aid Mission, Afghanistan, 1950; Visiting Lecturer: Ecole Pratique des Hautes Etudes, Sorbonne, 1958-59; University of Copenhagen, 1961. Travelled in Soviet Central Asia, 1960, Mongolia, 1961, 1964, 1966. Chichele Lecturer, Oxford, 1965. DLitt Glasgow, 1964. Awarded Cuthbert Peek Grant by Royal Geographical Society for travels in Central Asia, 1930; gold medallist, Geographical Society of Philadelphia, 1933; Patron's Medal, Royal Geographical Society, 1942; FRGS; Fellow, Royal Asiatic Society; Member: Royal Central Asian Society; American Historical Society; American Philosophical Society; For. Member, Academy of Sciences, Mongolian People's Republic; Hon. Member, American Geographical Society, etc. *Publications:* The Desert Road to Turkestan, 1928; High Tartary, 1930; Manchuria: Cradle of Conflict, 1932; The Mongols of Manchuria, 1934; Inner Asian Frontiers of China, 1940; Mongol Journeys, 1941; Solution in Asia, 1945; China, A Short History (with Eleanor Lattimore), 1947; The Situation in Asia, 1949; Sinkiang, Pivot of Asia, 1950; Ordeal by Slander, 1950; Nationalism and Revolution in Mongolia, 1955; Nomads and Commissars, 1962; Studies in Asian Frontier History, 1962; Silks, Spices and Empire (with Eleanor Lattimore), 1968; contributor to periodicals. *Recreation:* cycling. *Address:* c/o Arnold & Porter, 1229 Nineteenth Street, Washington DC 20036, USA.

**LATTIN, Francis Joseph,** CMG 1953; Barrister-at-law; *b* 23 March 1905; *s* of John Lattin, Morland, Westmorland; *m* 1934, May Sadler, Harrogate; one *s* (and one *s* decd). *Educ:* Appleby Grammar Sch.; Durham Univ. (MA); Cambridge Univ.; called to Bar, Gray's Inn. Assistant District Officer, Colonial Administrative Service, Uganda, 1930; Deputy Controller of Prices and Military Contracts, Kenya, 1942; Development Comr, Uganda, 1949. MLC 1949, MEC 1951, Uganda; Mem. East African Legislative Assembly, 1951; London Representative, Uganda Electricity Board, 1952. Bursar, Grey Coll., Durham, 1963-68. *Publications:* (jointly) Economic Survey of Western Uganda, 1951; articles on various aspects of colonial development. *Recreation:* interest in all outdoor sports. *Address:* Howfoot, Pooley Bridge, Penrith, Cumberland. *Club:* Royal Commonwealth Society.

**LATYMER,** 7th Baron, *cr* 1431; **Thomas Burdett Money-Coutts;** Chairman: Investment Trust Corporation and of London Cttee of Ottoman Bank; Anglo-American Securities Corporation; North Atlantic Securities Corporation; Vice-Chairman Middlesex Hospital; Director, Coutts & Co.; *b* 6 Aug. 1901; *e s* of 6th Baron and Hester Frances, 4th *d* of late Maj.-Gen. John Cecil Russell, CVO; *S* father 1949; *m* 1925, Patience, *d* of late W. Courtenay-Thompson and Mrs Herbert Money; one *s* two *d*. *Educ:* Radley; Trinity Coll., Oxford. Served War of 1939-45. OStJ. *Heir:* *s* Hon. Hugo Neville Money-Coutts [*b* 1 March 1926; *m* 1st, 1951, Penelope Ann Clare (marr. diss., 1965), *yr d* of late T. A. Emmet and of Baroness Emmet of Amberley; two *s* one *d*; 2nd, 1965, Jinty, *d* of P. G. Calvert, London]. *Address:* 45 Green Street, W1. *Clubs:* Carlton, St James', MCC.

**LAUDENBACH, Pierre;** *see* Fresnay, Pierre.

**LAUDER, Sir George Andrew Dick-,** 12th Bt, *cr* 1688; *b* 17 Nov. 1917; *s* of Lt-Col Sir John North Dalrymple Dick-Lauder, 11th Bt, and of Phyllis, *d* of late Brig.-Gen. H. A. Iggulden, CIE; *S* father 1958; *m* 1945, Hester Marguerite, *y d* of late Lt-Col G. C. M. Sorell-Cameron, CBE, Gorthleck House, Gorthleck, Inverness-shire; two *s* two *d*. *Educ:* Stowe; RMC. 2nd Lt Black Watch, 1937; served War of 1939-45, Palestine, Somaliland, Middle East (52nd Commandos), Sudan, Crete (pow); Major, 1945. *Publication:* Let Soldiers Lust (novel), 1963; Our Man for Ganymede, 1969. *Heir:* *s* Piers Robert Dick-Lauder, *b* 3 Oct. 1947. *Address:* 22 Garscube Terrace, Murrayfield, Edinburgh EH12 6BQ. *T:* 031-337 1734. *Club:* Puffins (Edinburgh).

**LAUDERDALE,** 17th Earl of, *cr* 1624; **Patrick Francis Maitland;** Baron Maitland, 1590; Viscount Lauderdale, 1616; Viscount Maitland, Baron Thirlestane and Boltoun, 1624; Bt of Nova Scotia, 1680; Hereditary Bearer of the National Flag of Scotland, 1790 and 1952; Company Director; Industrial Consultant; Consultant in Economic Geography; *b* 17 March 1911; *s* of Reverend Hon. Sydney G. W. Maitland and Ella Frances (*née* Richards); *S* brother, 1968; *m* 1936, Stanka, *d* of Professor Milivoje Lozanitch, Belgrade Univ.; two *s* two *d*. *Educ:* Lancing Coll., Sussex; Brasenose Coll., Oxford. BA Hons Oxon, 1933; Journalist 1933-59. Appts include: Balkans and Danubian Corresp., The Times, 1939-41; Special Corresp. Washington, News Chronicle, 1941; War Corresp., Pacific, Australia, New Zealand, News Chronicle, 1941-43. Foreign Office, 1943-45. MP (U) for Lanark Div. of Lanarks, 1951-Sept. 1959 (except for period May-Dec. 1957 when Ind. C). Founder and Chairman, Expanding Commonwealth Group, House of Commons, 1955-59; re-elected Chairman, Nov. 1959. Editor of The Fleet Street Letter Service, and of The Whitehall Letter, 1945-58. Mem., Coll. of Guardians of National Shrine of Our Lady of Walsingham, Norfolk, 1955-. President, The Church Union, 1956-61. FInstD. FInstPI. *Publications:* European Dateline, 1945; Task for Giants, 1957. *Heir:* *s* The Master of Lauderdale, Viscount Maitland, *qv*. *Address:* 10 Ovington Square, SW3. *T:* 01-589 7451. *Clubs:* Travellers'; Conservative (Glasgow); Caledonian, Puffins (Edinburgh).

**LAUDERDALE, Master of;** *see* Maitland, Viscount.

**LAUGHTON, Prof. Eric;** Firth Professor of Latin in the University of Sheffield since 1952; *b* 4 Sept. 1911; 2nd *s* of Rev. G. W. Laughton; *m* 1938, Elizabeth Gibbons; one *s* one *d*. *Educ:* King Edward VII Sch., Sheffield; St John's Coll., Oxford (open classical scholar). Asst in Humanity Dept, University of Edinburgh, 1934-36; University of Sheffield: Asst Lecturer in Classics, 1936; Lecturer in Classics, 1939; Senior Lecturer, 1946; Public Orator, 1955-68; Pro-Vice-Chancellor, 1968. Service in Intelligence Corps, South East Asia, 1943-45. *Publications:* verse translation of Papyrus (17th-century Latin poem by J. Imberdis), 1952; The Participle in Cicero, 1964. Articles and reviews in various classical journals. *Recreations:* walking, music. *Address:*

4 Park Lane, Sheffield 10. *T:* 64244. *Club:* University (Sheffield).

**LAURENCE, Peter Harold,** MC 1944; Counsellor (Commercial), Paris, since 1970; *b* 18 Feb. 1923; *s* of late Ven. George Laurence, MA, BD and late Alice (*née* Jackson); *m* 1948, Elizabeth Aïda Way; two *s* one *d. Educ:* Radley Coll.: Christ Church, Oxford. 60th Rifles. 1941-46 (Major). Entered Foreign Service, 1948; Western Dept, FO, 1948-50; Athens, 1950-53; Asst Political Adviser, Trieste, 1953-55; 1st Sec., Levant Dept, FO, 1955-57; Prague, 1957-60; Cairo, 1960-62; North and East African Dept, FO, 1962-65; Personnel Dept, DSAO, 1965-67; Counsellor, 1965; Political Adviser, Berlin, 1967-69. Visiting Fellow, All Souls Coll., 1969-70. *Address:* c/o Foreign and Commonwealth Office, SW1. *T:* 01-930 8440. *Club:* United University.

**LAURENT, Sir Edgar,** Kt 1952; CMG 1943; MD; Member of Executive and Legislative Councils, Mauritius. *Address:* c/o Executive Council, Port Louis, Mauritius.

**LAURIE, Lt-Col George H. F. P. V.;** *see* Vere-Laurie.

**LAURIE, Maj.-Gen. Sir John Emilius,** 6th Bt, *cr* 1834; CBE 1940; DSO 1916; *b* 12 Aug. 1892; *S* father 1936; *m* 1922, Evelyn Clare, *o d* of late Lt-Col L. J. Richardson-Gardner, 14th Hussars; one *s* two *d.* Served European War, 1914-18 (despatches 5 times, DSO and bar, Chevalier Légion d'Honneur); commanded 6th (Morayshire) Bn Seaforth Highlanders, 1918-19, and 2nd Bn Seaforth Highlanders, 1934-38; Comdr, Tientsin Area, British Troops in China, 1939-40 (despatches); 157 Inf. Bde., France, 1940 (CBE); 52nd (Lowland) Div., 1941-42; Combined Operations Training Centre, Inveraray; retired 1945; Col, Seaforth Highlanders, 1947-57. *Heir: s* Robert Bayley Emilius Laurie [*b* 8 March 1931; *m* 1968, Laurelie, *er d* of Sir Reginald Williams, Bt, *qv*]. *Address:* Woodlands, Westonbirt, near Tetbury, Glos. *Clubs:* Army and Navy, Caledonian, MCC.

**LAURIE, Prof. Malcolm Vyvyan,** CBE 1969 (OBE 1946); MA; DipFor; Professor of Forestry, University of Oxford, 1959-68; Emeritus Fellow of St John's College, Oxford; *b* 30 Aug. 1901; *s* of late Malcolm Laurie, DSc, FRSE and late Helena Agnes Laurie (*née* Phillips); *m* 1956, Margery Catherine Jackson. *Educ:* Edinburgh Academy; Sedbergh Sch.; King's Coll., Cambridge. BA Hons 1923; DipFor 1925; MA 1930. Indian Forest Service, 1925; served in various posts in Madras Province, 1925-35; Central Silviculturist, Forest Research Institute, Dehra Dun, UP, 1935-40; Dep. Dir, Timber Supplies, Dept of Supply, New Delhi, 1940-43; Director, Timber Supplies, New Delhi, 1943-46; retired from Indian Forest Service, 1946; Chief Research Officer, Forestry Commission, 1946-59. Mem., Natural Environment Research Council, 1965-68. Fellow, Soc. of Foresters. *Recreations:* gliding, flying. *Address:* 11 Chadlington Road, Oxford. *T:* Oxford 58520. *Clubs:* Royal Over-Seas League, Royal Commonwealth Society; Surrey Gliding (Lasham, Hants); Oxford Gliding (Weston-on-the-Green).

**LAURIE, Col Vernon Stewart,** CBE 1964 (OBE 1945); TD; DL; *b* 23 Feb. 1896; *o s* of Lt-Col R. M. Laurie, DSO, TD, DL, late of Ford Place, Stifford, Essex; *m* 1922, Mary, 2nd *d* of Selwyn R. Pryor, late of Plaw Hatch, Bishop's Stortford, Herts; one *s* one *d. Educ:* Eton; Christ Church, Oxford. Served European War, 1914-18; Essex RA (TF); 2 Lt 1914, Lt 1915, Capt. 1918, France, Egypt and Palestine (despatches twice). Served War of 1939-45: Lt-Col comdg 147 Essex Yeomanry, RA, 1939-42; 107 LAA Regt RA, 1942-44; 22 LAA Regt RA, 1944-45; N Africa, Malta and Italy. Hon. Col Essex Yeomanry, 1956-60. Actg Master Essex Union Foxhounds, 1946-48, Jt Master, 1956-57. DL Essex, 1946; High Sheriff, Essex, 1950. Master Saddlers Co., 1955 and 1958. Mem. London Stock Exchange, 1921-; Chm., Brit. Empire Securities & General Trust. *Recreation:* foxhunting. *Address:* The Old Vicarage, South Weald, Brentwood, Essex. *T:* Brentwood 1358. *Clubs:* Oxford and Cambridge University, MCC.

**LAUTERPACHT, Elihu,** QC 1970; Fellow of Trinity College, Cambridge, since 1953; Lecturer in Law, University of Cambridge, since 1958; *b* 13 July 1928; *o s* of late Sir Hersch Lauterpacht, QC and Rachel Steinberg; *m* 1955, Judith Maria, *er d* of Harold Hettinger; one *s* two *d. Educ:* Phillips Acad., Andover, Mass; Harrow; Trinity Coll., Cambridge (Entrance Schol.). 1st cl. Pt II of Law Tripos and LLB; Whewell Schol. in Internat. Law, 1950; Holt Schol. 1948 and Birkenhead Schol. 1950, Gray's Inn; called to Bar, 1950. Joint Sec., Interdepartmental Cttee on State Immunity, 1950-52; Asst Lectr in Law, Univ. of Cambridge, 1953; Sec., Internat. Law Fund, 1955; Dir of Research, Hague Academy of Internat. Law, 1959-60; Vis. Prof. of Internat. Law, Univ. of Delhi, 1960. Editor: British Practice in International Law, 1955-; International Law Reports, 1960-. Comdr, Order of Merit, Chile, 1969. *Publications:* Jerusalem and the Holy Places, 1968; various articles on international law. *Address:* Trinity College, Cambridge. *T:* Cambridge 58201; 3 Essex Court, Temple, EC4. *T:* 01-353 2624; 7 Herschel Road, Cambridge. *T:* Cambridge 54707. *Club:* Athenæum.

**LAUWERYS, Prof. Joseph Albert;** Director, Atlantic Institute of Education, Nova Scotia, and Professeu Associé, Sorbonne, since 1970; Professor of Comparative Education in University of London Institute of Education, 1947-70, now Emeritus Professor; *b* 7 Nov. 1902; *s* of Henry and Louise Lauwerys (*née* Nagels); *m* 1931, Waltraut Dorothy Bauermeister; three *s. Educ:* Ratcliffe Coll., Leicester; Bournemouth Sch.; King's Coll., London Univ. BScGen, 1st Cl. Hons 1927; Special BSc 1st Cl., Chemistry, 1928; Associate of Institute of Chemistry, 1928; Fellow, 1942. Special Physics BSc, 1929; Science Master, Stirling House, Bournemouth; Sen. Physics Master, Christ's Hosp., Horsham, 1928-32; Lectr in Methods of Science, Inst. of Educn, 1932-41. Reader in Educn, 1941-46. Joint Editor, World Year Book of Education, 1947-70. Rockefeller Foundation, Consultant in Education, 1937; Visiting Professor: Teachers' Coll., Columbia Univ., 1939 and 1951; University of Indiana, 1952; University of Southern Calif., 1953, 1955, 1957, 1959, 1961; University of Michigan, 1954; Kyushu Univ., Japan, 1956; University of Cape Town and Witwatersrand, 1958; International Christian Univ., Tokyo, 1959; University of Chile, 1962; University of Concepción, 1964 and 1965; University of Bahia, 1966; University of Ankara, 1968. Centennial Prof., American University of Beirut, 1967. Dir Commission of Enquiry, Conference of Allied Ministers of Education, 1945; Consultant to UNESCO, 1946-48. Hon. Prof. Univ. of Ankara. DSc (Ghent), 1946; DLit (London), 1958. Chm. Internat. New Educn Fellowship. Comdr, Ordre des Palmes Académiques, 1961. *Publications:* Education and Biology, 1934; Chemistry, 1938; Film in the School, 1936; Film and Radio as

Educational Media, 1939; Educational Problems in the Liberated Countries, 1946; The Roots of Science, 1947; The Enterprise of Education, 1955; Morals, Democracy and Education, 1958; (with H. C. Barnard) Handbook of British Educational Terms, 1963; Essays in Comparative Education (3 vols), 1969; numerous textbooks, articles, reviews and papers including contrib. to Chambers's Encyclopædia, Encyclopædia Britannica, etc. *Recreations:* walking, chess. *Address:* Aston House, Chilworth, Surrey. *T:* Bramley 2040.

**LAVER, Frederick John Murray;** Member, Post Office Corporation, since 1969; *b* 11 March 1915; *er s* of Clifton F. Laver and Elsie Elizabeth Palmer, Bridgwater; *m* 1948, Kathleen Amy Blythe; one *s* two *d. Educ:* Plymouth Coll. BSc London. Entered PO Engrg Dept, 1935; PO Research Stn, 1935-51; Radio Planning, 1951-57; Organization and Efficiency, 1957-63; Asst Sec., HM Treasury, 1963-65; Chief Scientific Officer, Min. of Technology, 1965-68; Director, National Data Processing Service, 1968-70. Mem. Council: IEE, 1966-69; British Computer Soc., 1969-; Nat. Computing Centre, 1966-68, 1970-; IEE Electronic Divl Bd, 1966-69, 1970-. CEng, FIEE; FBCS. *Publications:* Electric Power, 1957; Electrons at Work, 1957; Waves, 1959; Energy, 1962; Introducing Computers, 1965; several scientific papers. *Recreations:* reading, writing, lecturing. *Address:* 8 Hillcrest Road, Loughton, Essex. *T:* 01-508 1014. *Club:* Oxford and Cambridge University.

**LAVER, James,** CBE 1951; Hon. RE; FRSA, FRSL; retired as Keeper, Departments of Engraving, Illustration and Design, and of Paintings, Victoria and Albert Museum, London (1938-59); author; *b* Liverpool, 14 March 1899; *o s* of A. J. Laver, Liverpool; *m* 1928, Bridget Veronica, *d* of Martin Turley, Bray, Ireland; one *s* one *d. Educ:* Liverpool Institute; New Coll., Oxford. 2nd Lt King's Own (Royal Lancaster) Regiment, 1918. *Publications:* Cervantes (Newdigate Prize Poem), 1921; His Last Sebastian, 1922; Portraits in Oil and Vinegar, 1925; The Young Man Dances, 1925; A Stitch in Time, 1927; Design in the Theatre (with George Sheringham), 1927; The Circle of Chalk (translation), 1928, (produced by Mr Basil Dean at the New Theatre, 1929); Memoirs of Harriet Wilson, 1929; History of British and American Etching, 1929; Love's Progress, 1929; Nineteenth Century Costume, 1929; Macrocosmos, 1929; Etchings of Arthur Briscoe, 1930; Whistler, 1930; Eighteenth Century Costume, 1931; Nymph Errant, 1932 (produced by C. B. Cochran as a musical comedy at the Adelphi Theatre, 1933); Wesley, 1932; Works of Charles Churchill, 1933; Ladies' Mistakes, 1933; Stage Designs by Oliver Messel, 1933; Background for Venus, 1934; Winter Wedding, 1934; Forty Drawings by Horace Brodzky, 1935; Laburnum Tree (short stories), 1935; Tommy Apple, 1935; Panic Among Puritans, 1936; Tommy Apple and Peggy Pear, 1936; Vulgar Society (James Tissot), 1936; The House that Went to Sea (children's play), at Liverpool Repertory Theatre, 1936; French Painting and the Nineteenth Century, 1937; Taste and Fashion, 1937; The Heart was not Burned (play), Gate Theatre Studio, 1938; Swiss Family Robinson (children's play with Sir Barry Jackson), Birmingham Repertory Theatre, 1938; Poems of Baudelaire, 1940; Adventures in Monochrome, 1941; Nostradamus, 1942; Ladies of Hampton Court, 1942; Fashions and Fashion-Plates, 1943; XIXth Century French Posters, 1944; Isabella's Pageant, 1947; British Military Uniforms, 1948; Homage to Venus, 1949; Style in Costume, 1949; The Changing Shape of Things: Dress, 1950; Titian, 1950; Children's Costume in the Nineteenth Century, 1951; Tudor Costume, 1951; The Fertile Image, 1951; Drama: Its Costume and Décor, 1951; The Pleasures of Life: Clothes, 1953; The First Decadent, 1954; Victorian Vista, 1954; London as it is, 1954-55; Fragonard, 1956; Costume (Junior Heritage), 1956; Edwardian Promenade, 1958; Between the Wars, 1961; Costume, 1963; Museum Piece, 1963; Costume in the Theatre, 1964; Women's Dress in the Age of Jazz, 1964; The Age of Optimism, 1966; Victoriana, 1966; The Dandies, 1968; Modesty in Dress, 1969; A Concise History of Costume, 1969; English Sporting Prints, 1970. *Address:* 4/10 The Glebe, SE3. *Clubs:* Beefsteak, Chelsea Arts (Hon.).

**LAVER, William Scott,** CBE 1962; HM Diplomatic Service, retired; *b* 7 March 1909; *s* of Robert John Laver, Latchingdon, Essex, and Frances Lucy (*née* Pasmore), Windsor; *m* 1969, Marjorie Joan Hall, Chislehurst, Kent. *Educ:* St Dunstan's Coll., Catford; Downing Coll., Cambridge. Dept of Overseas Trade, 1932; Asst to Commercial Counsellor: Brussels, 1934, Rome, 1936; Commercial Sec., Rio de Janeiro, 1940; Commercial Sec., Cairo, 1946; Foreign Office, 1950-51; Financial Sec., Bahrain, 1951; Political Agent, Bahrain, 1951-52; Counsellor (Economic), Belgrade, 1954; Counsellor (Commercial), Oslo, 1958-62; Ambassador to Congo Republic, Gabon, Republic of Chad, and Central African Republic, 1962-66. *Recreations:* music, walking. *Address:* Flat 30, Mapledene, Kemnal Road, Chislehurst, Kent. *Club:* Royal Automobile.

**LAVERICK, Elizabeth,** PhD, CEng, FIEE, FInstP, SMIEEE (US); Technical Director, Elliott-Automation Radar Systems Ltd, since 1969; *b* 25 Nov. 1925; *d* of William Rayner and Alice Garland; *m* 1946 (marr. diss. 1960); no *c. Educ:* Dr Challoner's Grammar Sch., Amersham; Durham Univ. Research at Durham Univ., 1946-50; Section Leader at GEC, 1950-53; Microwave Engineer at Elliott Bros, 1954; Head of Radar Research Laboratory of Elliott-Automation Radar Systems Ltd, 1959; Jt Gen. Manager, Elliott-Automation Radar Systems Ltd, 1968-69. President, Women's Engineering Soc., 1967-69; Governor: Boreham Wood Coll. of Further Educn; Hatfield Polytechnic; Member: IEE Electronics Divisional Bd, 1967-70; Council IEE, 1969-70; Council, Inst. of Physics and Physical Soc., 1970-; DEP Adv. Cttee on Women's Employment, 1970-; Mem., representing IEE, Nat. Electronics Council Working Party on Recruitment of Engineers for Electronics Industry. Hon. Fellow, UMIST, 1969. *Publications:* contribs to IEE and IEEE Jls. *Recreations:* music, gardening. *Address:* Arden, Watford Road, Radlett, Herts. *T:* Radlett 4841.

**LAVERS, Sydney Charles Robert;** *b* 4 June 1898; *m* 1915; one *s* two *d. Educ:* Oxford Street Board Schs, Plymouth, Devon. Miner prior to European War; served 3½ years in HM Forces. Returned to mines; became miners' official. Mem. of Parish Council at Birtley, 1927; RDC at Chester-le-Street, 1927; Durham CC since 1934; MP (Lab) for Barnard Castle Div. of Durham, 1945-50. Chairman: Northern Clubs Federation Brewery Ltd; Nat. Assoc. of Clubs Breweries Ltd. *Address:* 10 Station Road, New Penshaw, Houghton-le-Spring, Co. Durham.

**LAVILLA, Teresa;** *see* Berganza, Teresa.

**LAVIN, Mary, (Mrs M. MacDonald Scott);** Writer; *b* East Walpole, Mass, USA, 11 June 1912; *m* 1st, 1942, William Walsh, MA, NUI; three *d*; 2nd, 1969, Michael MacDonald Scott. *Educ:* National Univ. of Ireland, Dublin (Graduate, MA; Hon DLitt, 1968). Mem. of Irish Academy of Letters. Guggenheim Fellow 1959, 1961, 1962. *Publications:* Tales from Bective Bridge (short stories, awarded James Tait Black Memorial Prize), 1942 (London, 1943); The Long Ago (short stories), 1944; The House in Clewe Street (novel), 1945. At Sally Gap (Boston), 1946; The Becker Wives, 1946; Mary O'Grady (novel), 1950; Patriot Son (short stories), 1956; A Single Lady (short stories); A Likely Story (short novel), 1957; Selected Stories, 1959 (New York); The Great Wave (short stories), 1961; Stories of Mary Lavin, 1964; In the Middle of the Fields (short stories), 1966; Happiness (short stories), 1969. *Address:* The Abbey Farm, Bective, Navan, Co. Meath. *T:* Navan 21243; Mews Eleven, Lad Lane, Rere Fitzwilliam Place, Dublin. *T:* 63031.

**LAVINGTON, Cyril Michael,** MBE 1946; Deputy-Chairman, Dorset Quarter Sessions, since 1962; Recorder of Barnstaple since 1964; *b* 21 June 1912; *e s* of Cyril Claude Lavington, MB, BS of Bristol and Nora Vernon Lavington; *m* 1950, Frances Anne (marr. diss. 1968), *d* of Colston Wintle, MD, of Bristol; one *s*. Barrister-at-Law, Middle Temple, 1936; Western Circuit, Wilts QS. Joined Army, 1939; Major, DAA and QMG, 1 GRTD, N Africa, 1943; DAAG 37 Mil. Miss. to Yugoslav Army of Nat. Liberation, 1944; DAAG 3 Corps, Greece, 1945 (despatches twice, MBE). Returned to practice, 1946. *Recreations:* sailing, gardening. *Address:* Albion Chambers, E, Bristol 1. *T:* 22927; 2 Kings Bench Walk, Temple, EC4. *T:* 01-353 1746; 19 Lansdown Crescent, Bath. *T:* 63528. *Clubs:* Royal Yachting Association; Bar Yacht; Royal Cornwall Yacht (Falmouth).

**LAVINGTON EVANS, L. G.,** *see* Evans, L. G. L.

**LAVOIPIERRE, Jacques Joseph Maurice;** Judge of the Supreme Court, Mauritius, 1956-65; Attorney-General, Mauritius, 1960-64; (after new constitution came into force, reverted to private practice); *b* 4 April 1909; 3rd *s* of Antoine Lavoipierre and Elisa la Hausse de Lalouvière; *m* 1939, Pauline Koenig; two *s* one *d*. *Educ:* Royal Coll., Mauritius; King's Coll., London (LLB); Middle Temple. Magistrate, Mauritius, 1944; Civil Comr, 1946; Magistrate, Industrial Court, 1949; Master and Registrar, Supreme Court, 1952; Substitute Procureur and Advocate-Gen., 1954. QC (Mauritius), 1961. Coronation Medal, 1953. *Clubs:* Mauritius Turf, Grand Sable (Mauritius).

**LAVRIN, Prof. Janko (John),** MA; Professor of Slavonic Languages, University of Nottingham, 1923, Emeritus Professor since 1953; *b* 10 Feb. 1887; *s* of John Lavrin and Gertrude (*née* Golobich), both Slovene; *m* 1928, Nora (*née* Fry); two *s*. *Educ:* Austria, Russia, and partly in Scandinavia. Began as journalist in Russia, 1910; Russian war correspondent, 1915-17. During War of 1939-45, attached to BBC (European service) as broadcaster and language superviser. Public lecturer. *Publications:* Aspects of Modernism, 1935; An Introduction to the Russian Novel, 1942; Dostoevsky, 1943 (repr. 1968); Tolstoy, 1944 (repr. 1968); Pushkin and Russian Literature, 1947 (repr. 1968); Nietzsche, 1948; From Pushkin to Mayakovsky, 1948; Ibsen, 1950 (repr. 1968); Nikolai Gogol, 1951 (repr. 1968); Goncharov, 1954 (repr. 1968); Russian Writers, 1954; Lermontov, 1959; Tolstoy (in German), 1961; Dostojevsky (in German), 1963; Literature and the Spirit of the Age (in Slovene), 1968; Russia, Slavdom and the Western World, 1969. *Recreations:* travels, mountaineering. *Address:* 28 Addison Gardens, W14. *T:* 01-603 8347. *Club:* PEN.

**LAW,** family name of **Barons Coleraine** and **Ellenborough.**

**LAW, Alfred Noel,** CMG 1947; MC 1918; retired; *B* 1895; *s* of late Frank Law; *m* 1937, Kathleen, *d* of A. Fishkin, Newcastle upon Tyne; one *d*. *Educ:* Northampton Sch.; Hertford Coll., Oxford. Served European War, 1914-19, with 4th Battalion Northamptonshire Regiment. Entered Colonial Service (Palestine), 1920; District Commissioner, Haifa, Palestine, 1942-48; Chief Sec., British Administration, Somalia, 1948-50; Dep. Dir of Education (Administration), Uganda, 1950-53; Ministry of Education, Labour and Lands, Nairobi, Kenya, 1954-57. *Address:* 53 Weedon Road, Northampton.

**LAW, Anastasia, (Mrs Nigel Law),** cbe 1918; *d* of late M. Mouravieff, Imperial Russian Ambassador in Rome; *m* 1st, 1907, Sir Milne Cheetham (who obtainded a divorce, 1923); one *s*; 2nd, 1929, Nigel Walter Law. Dame of Grace of Order of St John of Jerusalem. *Address:* High Trees, Chalfont St Peter, Bucks.

*See also Sir N. J. A. Cheetham.*

**LAW, Sir Charles Ewan,** Kt *cr* 1937; *b* 16 Feb. 1884; *s* of Charles Woodin and Janet Eliza Law; *m* 1909, Madeleine (*d* 1967), *yr d* of Albert Lagier, Perroy, Vaud, Switzerland; two *s* two *d*. *Educ:* High Sch., Croydon; Pembroke Coll., Cambridge. Called to Bar, Middle Temple, 1905; Burma Bar, 1905; Crown Counsel, Kenya, 1922; Resident Magistrate, Jamaica, 1925; Judge, Kingston Court, Jamaica, 1927; Puisne Judge, Uganda, 1930; Chief Justice, Zanzibar, 1934-39; Mem., Court of Appeal for Eastern Africa, 1930-39; Chief Justice, Northern Rhodesia, 1939; Mem., Rhodesian (conjoint) court of Appeal, 1939; retired, 1945. Chm. Brighton and Area Rent Tribunal, 1946-49; Chm. Medical Appeal Tribunal, London Region (Industrial Injuries), 1948-57. Special Divorce Commissioner (Matrimonial Causes), 1949-57. JP Sussex, 1947. Order of the Brilliant Star of Zanzibar (2nd class), 1939. *Address:* 84 Offington Lane, Worthing, Sussex. *T:* Worthing 61756.

*See also Eric J. E. Law.*

**LAW, Eric John Ewan; Hon. Mr Justice Law;** Justice of Appeal, Court of Appeal for East Africa, since 1965; *b* 10 June 1913; *er s* of Sir Charles Ewan Law, *qv*; *m* 1948, Patricia Constance Elizabeth, *d* of C. W. S. Seed, CBE; two *s* one *d*. *Educ:* Wrekin Coll.; St Catharine's Coll., Cambridge (Exhibitioner), MA (Hons). Called to Bar, Middle Temple, 1936. War Service, 1939-42: E Yorks Regt and KAR, Capt. Asst Judicial Adviser to Govt of Ethiopia, 1942-44; Crown Counsel, Nyasaland, 1944-53; Resident Magistrate, Tanganyika, 1953-55; Senior Resident Magistrate, 1955-56; Asst Judge, Zanzibar, 1956-58; Judge, Tanganyika, 1958-64. *Recreations:* fishing, sailing. *Address:* c/o Court of Appeal for East Africa, PO Box 30187, Nairobi, Kenya. *Clubs:* Nairobi, Flyfishers' (Kenya); Dar es Salaam Yacht (Tanzania).

**LAW, Frank William,** MA, MD, BChir Cantab, FRCS, FRSM, LRCP; KStJ; Consulting Ophthalmic Surgeon, Guy's Hospital; Consulting Surgeon, Moorfields Eye Hospital;

Hon. Visiting Ophthalmologist, Johns Hopkins Hospital, Baltimore; Consulting Ophthalmic Surgeon, Royal Hospital, Chelsea, and King Edward VII Hospital for Officers; Treas. and Past Pres. Ophth. Soc. of UK; Councillor and late Master Oxford Ophth. Congress; Vice-Pres. Internat. Assoc. for Prevention of Blindness; Chm., Ophth. Nursing Board; Mem. Ophth. Hosp. Cttee, Order of St John; British Mem. Council, European Ophth. Soc.; Membre, Soc. Française d'Ophth.; Membre d'Honneur, Soc. Belge d'Ophth.; Hon. Mem., Greek Ophth. Soc., Pan-American Medical Assoc. and American Acad. Ophth.; American Medical Assoc.; Canadian Ophth. Soc.; Past Master, Company of Spectacle Makers, and Freeman of the City of London; Consultant in Ophthalmology, Ministry of Pensions; Member, Medical Supplies Working Party, Ministry of Health; Member of Ophth. Advisory Panel, Ministry of Labour; Medical Assessor, Min. of Nat. Insurance; *b* Isleworth, 1898; *y s* of late Thomas Law and Emma Janet MacRae; *m* 1929, Brenda, *d* of Edwin Thomas; one *s* one *d*. *Educ:* St Paul's Sch.; St John's Coll., Cambridge; Middlesex Hosp. Served European War, France and Flanders, 1917-19, Royal Field Artillery; Capt. Lady Margaret Boat Club, 1922; Spare Man for Varsity Boat and Trial Cap, 1922; rowed 2 for Cambridge, 1923; Late Consultant to the Army in Ophthalmology and Surgeon to Queen Alexandra Military Hosp., Millbank; Past Pres. and Councillor, Faculty of Ophthalmologists; Sec. Gen., International Ophth. Congress, 1950; Past Mem. International Ophthalmological Council. *Publications:* Ultra-Violet Therapy in Eye Disease, 1934; articles in Brit. Jl of Ophthalmology, Transactions of Ophthalmological Society, and other Med. Jls. *Recreations:* music, fishing, shooting. *Address:* 36 Devonshire Place, W1. *T:* 01-935 1055; Baldersby Cottage, Chipperfield. *T:* 01-544 2905. *Clubs:* Athenæum, Leander, MCC, Savage.

**LAW, Adm. Sir Horace (Rochfort),** KCB 1967 (CB 1963); OBE 1950; DSC 1941; Commander-in-Chief, Naval Home Command, and Flag Officer, Portsmouth Area, since 1970; First and Principal Naval Aide-de-Camp to the Queen, since 1970; *b* 23 June 1911; *s* of S. Horace Law, MD, FRCSI, and Sybil Mary (*née* Clay); *m* 1941, Heather Valerie Coryton; two *s* two *d*. *Educ:* Sherborne Sch. Entered Royal Navy, 1929; gunnery specialist, 1937. Served War of 1939-45 (DSC): AA Cruisers: Cairo, 1939; Coventry, 1940; Cruiser Nigeria, 1942; Comdr 1946; Capt. 1952; comd HMS Centaur, 1958 and Britannia, RN Coll., 1960; Rear-Adm. 1961; Vice-Adm. 1965; Flag Officer Sea Training, 1961-63; Flag Officer, Submarines, 1963-65; Controller of the Navy, 1965-69. *Recreations:* tennis, sailing, gardening. *Address:* Cell Cottage, Sheet, Petersfield, Hants. *T:* Petersfield 3757. *Club:* Royal Ocean Racing.

**LAW, Col Hugh Francis d'Assisi Stuart,** DSO 1940; OBE 1956; MC; TD; DL; *b* 29 Jan. 1897; *s* of late Hugh Alexander Law; *m* 1928, Susan Rosemary Dacre, *e d* of Sir George Clerk, 9th Bt of Penicuik; two *s* one *d*. *Educ:* Shrewsbury; RMC Sandhurst. 2nd Lt Irish Guards, 1915; with Irish Guards, France and Flanders, 1915-18; Acting Capt., 1916; attached General Headquarters, Intelligence, 1916; Capt., 1918 (wounded, MC); with Irish Guards Army of Occupation of Rhineland; ADC to GOC 22nd Army Corps, 1919; ADC Governor and C-in-C, Malta, 1921; with Irish Guards, Turkey, 1922-24; retired, 1931; Brevet Major, Irish Guards, Regular Army Reserve of Officers; Major 5th Bn Border Regt, 1932; Lt-Col, 1938; Col (Temp.) 1941; Commanding 5th Bn Border Regt, 1938-41; served France and Belgium, 1940 (DSO) and in Middle East, 1943-45. Comdr Sub-District of South-West Scotland, 1941-43; Comdr Sub-Area of the Lebanon, 1943-45; Comdr Cyprus, 1945; Sec., Army Cadet Force in Scotland, 1948-65. DL Co. of Midlothian, 1965. *Recreations:* shooting, fishing, riding, gardening. *Address:* Barony House, Lasswade, Midlothian. *T:* Lasswade 3217. *Clubs:* Guards; New (Edinburgh).

**LAW, Margaret Dorothy,** OBE 1951; MA; Consultant Editor, Chambers's Encyclopædia; *d* of Thomas Robert Evans, Shrewsbury, and Dorothy, *d* of late David Davies; *m* 1925, George Edward, *s* of late Rev. William Law, Vicar of Rotherham; two *s*. *Educ:* St Leonards Sch., St Andrews; Girton Coll., Cambridge. Dir of Encyclopædia Britannica, 1925-43; Managing Editor Chambers's Encyclopædia, 1943-63; Mem. Cambridge Univ. Women's Appts Board, 1959-66. *Recreations:* swimming and reading. *Address:* Courtup Hill, Maplehurst, Sussex. *T:* Cowfold 429.

**LAW, Phillip Garth,** CBE 1961; MSc, FAIP; Vice-President, Victoria Institute of Colleges, since 1966; Director of the Antarctic Division, Department of External Affairs, Australia, and Leader of the Australian National Antarctic Research Expeditions (ANARE), 1949-66; *b* 21 April 1912; *s* of Arthur James Law and Lillie Lena Chapman; *m* 1941, Nellie Isabel Allan; no *c*. *Educ:* Hamilton High Sch.; Ballarat Teachers' Coll.; Melbourne Univ. Science master, State secondary schs, Vic., 1933-38; Tutor in Physics, Newman Coll., Melbourne Univ., 1940-47; Lectr in Physics, 1943-48. Research Physicist and Asst Sec. of Scientific Instrument and Optical Panel of Austr. Min. of Munitions, 1940-45. Sen. Scientific Officer, ANARE, 1947-48; cosmic ray measurements in Antarctica and Japan, 1948; Expedition relief voyages to Heard I. and Macquarie I., 1949, 1951, 1952, 1954. Australian observer with Norwegian-British-Swedish Antarctic Exped., 1950; Leader of expedition: to establish first permanent Australian station in Antarctica at Mawson, MacRobertson Land, 1954; which established second continental station at Davis, Princess Elizabeth Land, 1957; which took over Wilkes station from USA, 1959; to relieve ANARE stations and to explore coast of Australian Antarctic Territory, annually, 1955-66. Founder's Gold Medal of Royal Geographical Soc., 1960; Chm., Australian Nat. Cttee for Antarctic Research; Member: Council of Melbourne Univ., 1959-; Council, La Trobe Univ., 1964-; Pres., Royal Soc. of Victoria, 1967, 1968. Trustee, Science Museum, Melbourne, 1968-. Hon. DAppSc (Melbourne). *Publications:* (with John Bechervaise) ANARE, 1957; Ed series of ANARE scientific reports; numerous papers on Antarctica and education. *Recreations:* tennis, ski-ing, skin diving, music, photography. *Address:* 16 Stanley Grove, Canterbury, Vic 3126, Australia. *T:* 82-5630. *Clubs:* University (Sydney); Melbourne, Kelvin, Melbourne Cricket, Royal South Yarra Lawn Tennis (Melbourne).

**LAWDER, Rear-Adm. Keith Macleod,** CB 1948; OBE 1919; Associate of the Chartered Institute of Secretaries; *b* 1893; *s* of F. E. Lawder; *m* 1918; two *d* (one *s* decd). *Educ:* Fettes Coll., Edinburgh. Joined Royal Navy, 1910; served European War, 1914-18 and War of 1939-45; retired, 1949. *Address:* Brook Cottage, South Zeal, Okehampton, Devon

EX20 2QB. *T:* Whiddon Down 308. *Club:* Climbers'.

**LAWES, Sir John (Claud Bennet),** 4th Bt, *cr* 1882; *b* 9 Sept. 1898; *er s* of Sir John Lawes-Wittewronge, 3rd Bt, and Helena Ramsey (*d* 1961), *d* of Henry Ramsey Cox of Folkestone; relinquished surname of Wittewronge by deed poll, 1951; *S* father, 1931; *m* 1st, 1928, Kathleen Marjorie Livingstone (*d* 1938), *er d* of Gerald Tylston Hodgson; one *s*; 2nd, 1938, Naomi Constance Helen, *y d* of Lancelot Wykeham Badnall; one *d*. *Educ:* Blundell's Sch., Tiverton. *Heir: s* John Michael Bennet Lawes, *b* 24 Oct. 1932. *Address:* Le Clos Du Coudré, St Pierre du Bois, Guernsey, CI.

**LAWLER, Wallace Leslie;** *b* 15 March 1912; *s* of Stephen Lawler and Elizabeth Lawler (*née* Taylor); *m* 1943, Catherine Leticia (*née* Durcan); two *s* two *d*. *Educ:* St Paul's, Worcester; privately at Malvern. Founded Public Opinion Action Assoc., 1943. Contested Parly seats: Dudley, 1955; Perry Barr, 1959; Handsworth, 1964; Ladywood, 1966; MP (L) Ladywood Div. of Birmingham, June 1969-1970. First Liberal Councillor for 28 years, Birmingham City Council, 1962; re-elected, 1965 and 1968 (Leader of Council's Liberal Gp, 1968-); Vice-Chm., 1967, Vice-Pres., 1968, of the Liberal Party. Hon. Sec., Homeless Bureau, 1956-. *Publications:* Pensions for All, 1958; The Truth About Cathy, 1968. *Recreations:* politics, reading, camping. *Address:* 39 Tenbury Road, Birmingham 14. *T:* 021-444 1636. *Club:* National Liberal.

**LAWLEY, Edgar Ernest,** CBE 1961; Chairman: Adderley Trading Co. (Pty) Ltd of S Africa; Afstral Investment Co. (Pty) Ltd of S Africa; Denton Heath Trading Co. Ltd; Jacobs Production & Distributing Co. Ltd; Jacobs (P & D) Sales Ltd; Lawley Estates Ltd; Chairman, West End Branch, Yorkshire Insurance Co.; Joint Founder and Chairman, Lawley Group Ltd (now Allied English Potteries Ltd), resigned 1952; Underwriter of Lloyd's; Member Council and Trustee, Wright-Fleming Institute; Vice-President St Mary's Medical School; Member Council, Royal Society of Arts; Member, General Council, King Edward's Hospital Fund for London; Chairman: Regent Street Association, 1947-49; St Mary's Hospital Medical School Centenary Appeal, 1956-57; St Mary's Hospital, 1957-64 (Vice-Chairman, 1945-57); *s* of Ernest Henry Lawley and Anne Elizabeth Jones; *m* Violet Victoria (*d* 1970), *d* of Arthur and Mary Moore; one *d*. *Educ:* King Edward's High Sch., Birmingham; Jena, Germany. *Recreation:* walking. *Address:* 41 Green Street, Mayfair, W1. *T:* 01-629 7551. *Club:* Devonshire.

**LAWLOR, John,** CVO 1969; Deputy Assistant Commissioner, Metropolitan Police, New Scotland Yard; *b* 16 March 1906; *s* of William and Janet Lawlor, Liverpool; *m* 1934, Ethel Guimaraes-Hackett; one *s* one *d*. *Educ:* St Margaret's Sch., Anfield, Liverpool. Joined Metropolitan Police, 1929; served principally in West End; passed through the ranks; apptd Comr No 1 Dist, 1964; on re-organisation of the Force in 1968, became responsible for Uniformed Police opns throughout Metropolitan Police Dist, with specific responsibilities for commanding Police action in connection with ceremonial events, demonstrations, and public order. *Recreations:* sport generally, football and fishing in particular. *Address:* 15 Pickhurst Rise, West Wickham, Kent. *T:* 01-777 1671.

**LAWLOR, Prof. John James;** Professor of English Language and Literature, University of Keele, since 1950; *b* 5 Jan. 1918; *o s* of Albert John and Teresa Anne Clare Lawlor, Plymouth; *m* 1941, Thelma Joan Weeks, singer; one *s* three *d*. *Educ:* Devonport High Sch.; Magdalen Coll., Oxford. BA Hons English Cl. I, 1939; MA 1946. Service in Devonshire Regt, 1940-45; Asst Chief Instructor, 163 Artists' Rifles OCTU, 1943-44; CMF, 1944-45. Sen. Mackinnon Scholar, Magdalen Coll., 1946; Sen. Demy, 1947; Lectr in English, Brasenose and Trinity Colls, 1947-50; University Lectr in Eng. Lit., Oxford, 1949-50. Fellow of Folger Shakespeare Library, Washington, DC, 1962. Toured Australian and NZ Univs and visited Japan, 1964. Ziskind Visiting Prof., Brandeis Univ., Mass., 1966. Mem. Internat. Consultative Cttee, Internat. Assoc. of University Profs. of English; Contrib. Mem. Medieval Academy of America; Gov., Oswestry Sch.; Pres., N Staffs Drama Assoc.; Mem. Western Area Cttee, Brit. Drama League; Vice-Pres., The Navy League; FSA. *Publications:* The Tragic Sense in Shakespeare, 1960; Piers Plowman, an Essay in Criticism, 1962; The Chester Mystery Plays (with Rosemary Sisson), perf. Chester, 1962; The Vision of Piers Plowman, commnd, Malvern, 1964; (ed) Patterns of Love and Courtesy, 1966; (with W. H. Auden) To Nevill Coghill from Friends, 1966; Chaucer, 1968; (ed). The New University, 1968. Articles on medieval and modern literature in various journals and symposia. *Recreations:* travel, book-collecting, any sort of sea-faring. *Address:* 14 Church Plantation, Keele, Staffs. *T:* Keele Park 397. *Clubs:* Athenæum, National Liberal.

**LAWRENCE,** family name of **Baron Lawrence** and of **Baron Trevethin and Oaksey.**

**LAWRENCE,** 5th Baron *cr* 1869; **David John Downer Lawrence;** Bt 1858; *b* 4 Sept. 1937; *s* of 4th Baron Lawrence and of Margaret Jean, *d* of Arthur Downer, Kirdford, Sussex; *S* father, 1968. *Educ:* Bradfield College. *Address:* c/o Bird & Bird, 2 Gray's Inn Square, WC1.

**LAWRENCE, Alfred Kingsley,** RA 1938 (ARA 1930); RP 1947; Figure Painter; *b* Southover, Lewes, Sussex. *Educ:* Armstrong Coll., Newcastle upon Tyne; Royal College of Art, South Kensington. ARCA Travelling Scholarship, 1922. 19th Batt. Northumberland Fusiliers, 1914-18 (despatches); Prix de Rome Scholar, 1923; works: (Mural) The Altruists, Wembley Basilica, 1924; Building Pons Ælii, Newcastle; Queen Elizabeth Commissions Sir Walter Raleigh to discover unknown lands AD 1584, St Stephen's Hall, Houses of Parliament; Committee of Treasury of Bank of England, 1928, and other mural paintings in new Bank of England; County Hall, Chelmsford; The Resurrection, Altarpiece, Church of St James, Beckenham, Kent, etc.; other works: Return of Persephone, Cornish Venus, Leda, etc. Portrait painter, portrait draughtsman. Mem. of Faculty of Painting, British Sch. at Rome, 1926-50; Founder Mem. Council Abbey Scholarships for Mural Painting, 1926-53; Mem. Jury of award, Internat. Exhibition: Ghent, 1929; Carnegie Inst., Pittsburgh, USA, 1936. *Recreation:* the theatre. *Address:* 30 Holland Park Road, Kensington, W14. *T:* 01-937 8879. *Clubs:* Arts, Garrick, Chelsea Arts.

**LAWRENCE, Arnold Walter,** MA; FSA; Professor of Archæology, University College of Ghana, and Director, National Museum of Ghana, 1951-57; Secretary and Conservator, Monuments and Relics Commission of Ghana, 1952-57; Laurence Professor of Classical

Archæology, Cambridge University, 1944-51, and Fellow of Jesus College; *b* 2 May 1900; *s* of T. R. Lawrence; *m* 1925, Barbara Thompson; one *d*. *Educ:* City of Oxford Sch.; New Coll., Oxford. Student, British Schs of Athens and Rome; Ur excavations, 1923; Craven Fellow, 1924-26; Reader in Classical Archæology, Cambridge Univ., 1930; Corr. Mem., German Archæological Institute; literary executor of T. E. Lawrence, 1935; Military Intelligence, Middle East, 1940; Scientific Officer, Coastal Command, RAF, 1942; Ministry of Economic Warfare, 1943; lectured in Latin America, 1948; Leverhulme Research Fellow, 1951. *Publications:* Later Greek Sculpture and its Influence, 1927; Classical Sculpture, 1929; Herodotus, Rawlinson's translation revised and annotated, 1935; Greek Architecture (Pelican History of Art), 1957, rev. edn 1967; Trade Castles and Forts of West Africa, 1963, abr. as Fortified Trade Posts: the English in West Africa, 1968, etc. Ed T. E. Lawrence by his Friends, 1937; Letters to T. E. Lawrence, 1962, etc. *Recreation:* going to and fro in the earth and walking up and down in it. *Address:* c/o Barclays Bank, 68 Lombard Street, EC3.

**LAWRENCE, Bernard Edwin,** CBE 1957; Chief Education Officer, County of Essex, 1939-65, retired; Dean of the College of Preceptors, 1958-68; *b* 3 Jan. 1901; *s* of late Albert Edward and Emma Lawrence; *m* 1925, Dorothy Rosa Collings; two *s* one *d*. *Educ:* Sir Joseph Williamson's Sch., Rochester; Worcester Coll., Oxford. BA Oxon double first class Hons 1922; MA 1930; PhD, University Coll. London, 1934. Asst Master: George Green's Sch., 1923-25; Skinners' Sch., 1925-28; Lecturer: Goldsmiths' Coll., 1928-35; Birkbeck Coll., 1930-35; Asst Dir of Education, Essex, 1936-39; Chairman: Educational Commission to Uganda and Kenya, 1961; Nat. Inst. of Adult Educn, 1964-69. Pres. Assoc. of Chief Educn. Officers, 1957-58. Chevalier de la Légion d'Honneur, 1958. *Publications:* occasional contribs to Educational Jls and to Proceedings of London Mathematical Society and Mathematical Gazette. *Recreation:* gardening. *Address:* Chapel House, Ingatestone, Essex.

**LAWRENCE, Sir David (Roland Walter),** 3rd Bt, *cr* 1906; late Captain, Coldstream Guards, 1951; *b* 8 May 1929; *er s* of Sir Roland Lawrence, 2nd Bt, MC, and Susan, 3rd *d* of late Sir Charles Addis, KCMG; *S* father 1950; *m* 1955, Audrey, Duchess of Leeds, *yr d* of Brig. Desmond Young. *Educ:* Radley; RMC Sandhurst. *Heir: b* Clive Wyndham Lawrence [*b* 6 Oct. 1939; *m* 1966, Sophia Annabel Stuart, *d* of Hervey Stuart Black, Balfron, Stirlingshire]. *Address:* Cannon Platt, Pinkneys Green, near Maidenhead.

**LAWRENCE, Dennis George Charles,** OBE 1963; Under-Secretary, Ministry of Posts and Telecommunications, since 1969; *b* 15 Aug. 1918; *s* of George Herbert and Amy Frances Lawrence; *m* 1946, Alida Jantine, *d* of late Willem van den Berg, The Netherlands. *Educ:* Haberdashers' Aske's Hatcham School. Entered Civil Service as Clerical Officer, Min. of Transport, 1936; Exec. Officer 1946; Asst Principal, Central Land Board, 1947; Principal, 1949; GPO, 1953; Asst Sec. 1960; Sec., Cttee on Broadcasting, 1960-62; Asst Sec., GPO, 1962; Under-Sec., GPO, 1969. *Recreation:* walking. *Address:* Monks Ford, Monk Sherborne, Hants. *T:* Monk Sherborne 193.

**LAWRENCE, Evelyn M.,** BSc (Econ.) London, PhD; **(Mrs Nathan Isaacs)**; *b* 31 Dec. 1892; *d* of Samuel and Mary Lawrence, Walton-on-Thames; *m* 1950, Nathan Isaacs, OBE (*d* 1966). *Educ:* Tiffins Sch., Kingston-on-Thames; Stockwell Training Coll.; London Sch. of Economics, University of London. Teacher in LCC schs, 1913-24; BSc Econ. 1st cl. Hons 1923; Ratan Tata and Metcalfe scholar, London Sch. of Economics, 1924-26; on staff of Malting House Sch., Cambridge, 1926-28; Commonwealth Fund scholar, USA, 1929; Chief Social Worker, London Child Guidance Clinic, 1929-30; Lecturer in Education, National Training Coll. of Domestic Subjects, 1931-43. Dir, National Froebel Foundation, and Editor, Froebel Foundation Bulletin, 1943-63. Hon. Sec. British Psychological Soc., Education Section, 1931-34; Mem. of Council of Eugenics Soc., 1949-59. *Publications:* The Relation between Intelligence and Inheritance, 1931. Editor: Friedrich Froebel and English Education, 1952. *Recreations:* walking, gardening, music. *Address:* Grove Cottage, Owletts Lane, Ashurst Wood, East Grinstead, Sussex. *T:* Forest Row 2728. *Club:* Cowdray.

**LAWRENCE, Sir Frederick,** Kt 1963; OBE 1957; JP; *b* 23 Sept. 1889; *s* of Isaac Lawrence, London; *m* 1921, Gertrude, *d* of Asher Simons; one *d*. *Educ:* LCC Sch. Founder, Chairman and Managing Director of: Fredk Lawrence Ltd, London, W2; B. Maggs & Co., Bristol; Maggs Furniture Industries Ltd; Chm., Croydon Estates Ltd, 1935-. Served in 1914-18 War with RE (Signals). Mem. LCC, 1946-65; Mem., NW Metropolitan Regional Hosp. Bd, 1950-66; Mem. Bd of Govs, St Mary's Hosp., Paddington, 1948; Pres., Paddington (S) Cons. and Unionist Assoc., 1962; Mem., Paddington Borough Council, 1934-65; Alderman, 1942; Dep. Mayor, 1942-44; Mayor, 1944-45; Dep. Leader, 1945-65; Dep. Chm. LCC, 1953-54; Mem., Bow St Magistrates' Panel, 1954-64; Chm. Paddington Gp Hosp. Management Cttee, 1948-60; Member: House Cttee, St Mary's Hosp.; Council, Wright-Fleming Inst. for Microbiology, 1961; British Post-graduate Medical Fedn, 1953-65; Vice-Pres., Anti-Tuberculosis League of Israel. JP, Co. London, 1943. *Recreations:* Association football, golf; dancing. *Address:* 77 Albion Gate, Hyde Park, W2. *T:* 01-723 6964. *Clubs:* Coombe Hill Golf, Potters Bar Golf.

**LAWRENCE, Geoffrey Charles,** CMG 1963; OBE 1958; Temporary Principal, Ministry of Overseas Development, since 1966; *b* 11 Nov. 1915; *s* of Ernest William Lawrence; *m* 1945, Joyce Acland Madge, *d* of M. H. A. Madge, MC. *Educ:* Stationers' Company's Sch.; Brasenose Coll., Oxford. Served 1939-46, Middlesex Yeo. and Brit. Mil. Administration of Occupied Territories (Major). HM Overseas Civil Service (Colonial Administrative Service). Administrative Officer, Somaliland Protectorate, 1946; Asst Chief Sec., 1955; Financial Sec., 1956; Financial Sec., Zanzibar and Mem. of East African Currency Board, 1960-63; Temp. Principal, Colonial Office, 1964-66. *Address:* c/o Barclays Bank Ltd, 42 Coombe Lane, SW20. *Club:* East India and Sports.

**LAWRENCE, Sir John (Waldemar),** 6th Bt, *cr* 1858; OBE 1945; Editor of Frontier since 1957; *b* 27 May 1907; *s* of Sir Alexander Waldemar Lawrence, 4th Bt, and Anne Elizabeth Le Poer (*née* Wynne); *S* brother, Sir Henry Eustace Waldemar Lawrence, 5th Bt, 1967; *m* 1948, Jacynth Mary (*née* Ellerton); no *c*. *Educ:* Eton; New Coll., Oxford (MA, Lit. Hum.). Personal Asst to Dir of German Jewish Aid Cttee, 1938-39; with BBC as European Intelligence Officer and European Services Organiser, 1939-42; Press Attaché, HM Embassy, USSR, 1942-45; became freelance writer, 1946. Officer, Order of Orange Nassau, 1950. *Publications:* Life in

Russia, 1947; Russia in the Making, 1957; A History of Russia, 1960; The Hard Facts of Unity, 1961; Russia (Methuen's Outlines), 1965; Soviet Russia, 1967; Russians Observed, 1969. *Recreations:* travelling, reading. *Heir: b* George Alexander Waldemar Lawrence [*b* 22 Sept. 1910; *m* 1949, Olga, *d* of late Peter Schilovsky; one *s* two *d*]. *Address:* 24 St Leonard's Terrace, SW3. *T:* 01-730 8033. *Club:* Athenæum.

**LAWRENCE, Marjorie Florence;** dramatic soprano; Professor of Voice and Director of Opera Workshop, Southern Illinois University, Carbondale, Illinois, since 1960; Professor of Voice, Newcomb College, Tulane University, New Orleans, Louisiana, 1956-60; *b* Dean's Marsh, Vic., Australia; *d* of William Lawrence and Elizabeth Smith; *m* 1941, Dr Thomas Michael King, New York. *Educ:* privately. Studied voice with Mme Cécile Gilly, Paris, Louis Bachner, New York. Début with Monte Carlo Opera Co., as Elizabeth in Tannhäuser, 1932; début with Paris Grand Opera Co., as Ortrud in Lohengrin, 1932; début with Metropolitan Opera Co., as Brüennhilde in Die Walküre, 1935. Has appeared with Chicago, St Louis, and San Francisco opera companies, and in the Teatro Colon of Buenos Aires and Palacio de Belles Artes, Mexico City; has sung with leading symphony orchestras of the world. Stricken with infantile paralysis in Mexico City, June 1941; although unable to walk, made "come-back" as Venus in Tannhäuser at Metropolitan Opera, 1942, and as Isolde in Tristan und Isolde at Metropolitan Opera, 1943: in 1944 made a 50,000-mile troop concert tour of Australia and the South West Pacific; 1945, made two troop concert tours of England, Belgium, Germany, and France, and sang at Buckingham Palace for the King and Queen; 1946, returned to the Paris Opera. FRSA 1969. Hon. DHL Ohio, 1969. Légion d'Honneur (France). *Publication:* Interrupted Melody, The Story of My Life (New York, Australia and New Zealand, London), 1949 (made into film, 1955; repr. 1969). *Address:* Metropolitan Opera Association, New York, NY 10023, USA.

**LAWRENCE, Michael Hugh;** Clerk of the Overseas Office, House of Commons, since 1967; *b* 9 July 1920; *s* of late Hugh Moxon Lawrence and of Mrs. L. N. Lawrence; *m* 1948, Rachel, *d* of Humphrey Gamon, Gt Barrow, Cheshire; one *s* two *d*. *Educ:* Highgate; St Catharine's Coll., Cambridge. Served Indian Army, 1940-45. Indian Civil Service, 1945-46; Asst Clerk, House of Commons, 1947; Senior Clerk, 1948; Deputy Principal Clerk, 1962. *Recreations:* beagling, lawn tennis, looking at churches. *Address:* 11 Vine Court Road, Sevenoaks, Kent. *T:* Sevenoaks 54972.

**LAWRENCE, Lt-Col Richard Travers,** CIE 1934; MC; Indian Army, retired; late Secretary to Governor of Punjab; *b* 7 July 1890; *m* 1st, 1933, Elisabeth Margaret (*d* 1937), *d* of Maj.-Gen. G. H. Addison, CB, CMG, DSO; two *d*; 2nd, 1940, Beryl Mary Dru, *d* of Dr Drury Pennington. Commissioned, 1910; Indian Army, 1911; Capt., 1915; Major, 1927; Lt-Col, 1936; retired, 1939. *Address:* Westdown, The Ridgeway, Guildford. *T:* Guildford 4730. *Club:* United Service.

**LAWRENCE, Robert Leslie Edward,** OBE 1944; ERD 1952; MInstT; Chairman and General Manager, London Midland Region of British Railways, since 1968; *b* 29 Oct. 1915; *s* of late Robert Riach Lawrence; *m* 1940, Joyce Marjorie (*née* Ricketts); one *s* one *d*. *Educ:* Dulwich Coll. Served War of 1939-45 (despatches, 1942, 1945), RE; 2nd Lt; Col 1945; Lt-Col, Engr and Rly Staff Corps RE (TA). Traffic Apprentice, LNER, 1934; Headquarters, LNER, 1938; appts in operating depts, 1946-59; London Midland Region: Divisional Man., 1959; Line Man., 1961; Asst Gen. Man., 1963; Gen. Man., Sundries Div., British Railways, 1967. Mem., Nat. Freight Corporation, 1969-. Past Pres., Rly Students Assoc. Liveryman, Co. of Loriners. Freeman, City of London. OStJ. Legion of Merit (US), 1945. *Recreations:* swimming, Rugby football. *Address:* 2 Alexandra Road, Watford, Herts. *T:* Watford 29458; Clifford Cottage, Porthcurno, Cornwall. *T:* Sennen 297. *Clubs:* United Service, public Schools.

**LAWRENCE, Samuel Chave;** *b* 9 June 1894; *s* of late John Lawrence, DLit, Prof. of English, Tokyo Univ.; *m* 1st, 1917, Dorothy Austen Storey (*d* 1943); two *d;* 2nd, 1955, Lucia Rosa de Maria. *Educ:* Collège Classique Cantonal, Lausanne; Universities of Tokyo and Berlin. Enlisted Queen's Westminster Rifles, Aug. 1914; 2nd Lt Leicestershire Regt 1915; Lt 1917; Consular Service, 1919; Vice-Consul, Washington, 1920; Cologne, 1924; Acting Consul, Mainz, 1925; Vice-Consul, Naples, 1926; Chicago, 1929; Consul (local rank), Santos, 1931; Acting Consul-Gen., São Paulo, in 1931; Consul at Pará, 1934; Chargé d'Affaires, Tegucigalpa, 1938; Consul, Curacao, 1939; Consul-Gen. (local rank) Duala, 1943; Consul, Turin, 1946-48, retd. *Recreation:* photography. *Address:* corso Matteotti 24A/37, Rapallo, Italy.

**LAWRENCE, Sydney,** CBE 1961 (OBE 1951; MBE 1941); an Inspector of Constabulary for England and Wales, 1962-70; seconded as Commandant, Police College, Oct. 1963-Oct. 1966; *b* 18 Jan. 1905; *s* of Herbert and Margaret Lawrence; *m* 1929, Gladys Gregory; one *s*. *Educ:* Eccles Gram. Sch., Lancs. Articled clerk to City Treasurer Salford Corporation, 1922-26; joined Salford City Police, 1926, and left when Dep. Chief Constable, 1945; Chief Constable, Reading, 1945-48; Chief Constable, Kingston upon Hull, 1948-62. Pres. Assoc. of Chief Police Officers, 1960-61. Queen's Police Medal for Distinguished Service, 1955. *Address:* Many Waters, De La Warr Parade, Bexhill-on-Sea, Sussex. *T:* Bexhill 377. *Clubs:* Royal Commonwealth, St John, Civil Service.

**LAWRENCE, Air Vice-Marshal Thomas Albert,** CB 1945; Director and Secretary-Treasurer, Found Bros Aviation Ltd, Grand Bend, Ont., Canada; *b* 1895; *s* of K. J. Lawrence; *m* 1921, Claudine Audrey Jamieson. AOC, NW Air Comd, Canada, 1944-47, retd; Legion of Merit (USA). *Address:* 581 Avenue Road, Toronto 7, Ont., Canada.

**LAWRENCE, Vernon,** CBE 1959 (OBE 1942); JP; DL; Clerk of the County Council and Clerk of the Peace for Monmouthshire, 1937-66; also Clerk of the Lieutenancy; Hon. Secretary, Welsh Counties' Committee, 1949-66; *b* 29 Sept. 1899; *s* of William John and Annie Maud Lawrence; *m* 1919, Gertrude Mary Thomas (*d* 1969), Maesteg, Glam; one *s* one *d*. *Educ:* privately and University of S Wales and Monmouthshire; Cardiff Law Sch. Private Sec., 1919-29; Solicitor's Articled Clerk and Principal Clerk, Glamorgan County Council, 1929-32; Asst County Solicitor and Asst County Prosecuting Solicitor, Glamorgan, 1933-34; County Solicitor and County Prosecuting Solicitor, 1934-37. County ARP Controller for Monmouthshire, 1939-45. Mem., Welsh Advisory Cttee for Civil Aviation; Pres., Rent Assessment Panel for Wales. Mem., Tribunal of Inquiry into

Aberfan Disaster, 1966-67. Former Chm., Law Cttee, Soc. of Clerks of the Peace of Counties and Clerks of County Councils. DL, County of Monmouth, 1965. *Recreations:* golf, gardening, motoring. *Address:* Greenover, Castleton, near Cardiff. *T:* Castleton 264. *Clubs:* Royal Aero; Monmouthshire County (Newport); Newport Golf.

**LAWRENCE, Sir William,** 4th Bt, *cr* 1867; Senior Executive, Wilmot Breeden, Ltd; Major east Surrey Regiment; *b* 14 July 1913; *er s* of Sir William Matthew Trevor Lawrence, 3rd Bt, and Iris Eyre (*d* 1955), *y d* of late Brig.-Gen. E. M. S. Crabbe, CB; *S* father, 1934; *m* 1940, Zoë (marr. diss., 1945), *yr d* of H. S. S. Pether, Stowford, Headington, Oxford; *m* 1945, Pamela, *yr d* of J. E. Gordon, Beechbank, Bromborough, Cheshire; one *s* two *d. Educ:* Bradfield Coll. *Recreation:* gardening. *Heir: s* William Fettiplace Lawrence, *b* 23 Aug. 1954. *Address:* The Knoll, Walcote, near Alcester, Warwicks. *T:* Great Alne 303. *Club:* Royal Automobile.

**LAWRENCE, W(illiam) Russell,** MA, LLB; Barrister-at-Law; Senior Master of the Supreme Court, Queen's Bench Division, and Queen's Remembrencer, since 1970 (Master, since 1951); *b* 14 Feb. 1903; 3rd and sole *surv. s* of late George Lawrence, Barrister-at-Law, and late Maria Hannah Russell; *m* 1st, 1940, Gertrude Emily Helene (*d* 1948), *d* of Carl Sanders; one *d*; 2nd, 1951, Barbara Mary Constance, *o d* of William Heathcote Morphett; one *s* one *d. Educ:* The Abbey Sch., Tipperary; Christ's Coll., Cambridge. Called to Bar, Gray's Inn, Jan. 1927; joined North Eastern circuit, Nov. 1927; practised in London and on NE circuit; Asst Recorder of Newcastle upon Tyne, 1946-51; Recorder of Pontefract, 1950-51; Mem. of the Hendon Borough Council, 1947-51. Served War of 1939-45, Territorial Army 99th HAA Regt RA; active service in ranks until commissioned, May 1940; active service in UK, Iraq, India, and with Middle East Forces as Dep. Judge Advocate (Major), office of Judge Advocate General of the Forces. Mem. Civil Judicial Statistics Cttee, 1966-68. *Recreations:* lawn tennis, golf, gardening. *Address:* 5 Dunstan Road, NW11. *T:* 01-455 7341; Royal Courts of Justice, Strand, WC2. *T:* 01-405 7641. *Clubs:* Junior Carlton, Queen's Club.

**LAWRENCE-JONES, Sir Christopher,** 6th Bt *cr* 1831; Medical Adviser to British Petroleum Co. Ltd; *b* 19 Jan. 1940; *s* of Commander B. E. Jones, RN (*d* 1958) (*yr s* of Sir Lawrence Jones, 4th Bt), and Margaret Louise, *d* of late Geoffrey Montague Cookson; *S* uncle, Sir Lawrence Jones, 5th Bt, MC, 1969; *m* 1967, Gail, *d* of C. A. Pittar, FRCS, Auckland, NZ; one *s. Educ:* Sherborne; Gonville and Caius Coll., Cambridge; St Thomas' Hospital. MA Cantab 1964; MB, BChir Cantab 1964; DIH Eng. 1968. *Recreation:* sailing. *Heir: s* Mark Christopher Lawrence-Jones, *b* 28 Dec. 1968. *Address:* Silwood House, London Road, Ascot, Berks. *Club:* Royal Society of Medicine.

**LAWRENCE-WILSON, Harry Lawrence;** Under-Secretary, Ministry of Technology, since 1969; *b* 18 March 1920; *s* of late H. B. Wilson and of Mrs May Wilson, Biddenden, Kent; *m* 1945, Janet Mary Gillespie; two *s* one *d. Educ:* Cranbrook Sch.; Worcester Coll., Oxford. Served Indian Army, 1940-46. Colonial Office, 1946-47; MoD, 1947-66; Cabinet Office, 1967-69. Asst Principal, 1947; Principal, 1948; Assistant Secretary, 1956; Under-Secretary, 1961. *Address:* 22 Marlborough Crescent, Riverhead, Sevenoaks, Kent.

**LAWRIE, James Haldane;** Chairman, Air Transport Licensing Board, since 1971 (Member, since 1965; Deputy Chairman, 1968-70); Managing Director, Gleneagles Productions Ltd; General Administrator, D'Oyly Carte Opera Trust Ltd; Chairman, Phœnix Opera; *b* 28 March 1907; *e s* of late Allan James Lawrie, KC, and late Ethel Annette Lawrie, *d* of Judge Richard Adams, QC. *Educ:* Newlands, Seaford, Sussex; Fettes Coll., Edinburgh (Open Schol.); University Coll., Oxford (Open Schol.). Lloyds Bank Ltd, 1930-37; Secretary, 1937-45, London Manager, 1940-45, National Bank of New Zealand Ltd; Chm., British Overseas Banks Assoc., 1944-45; Vice-Pres. British Bankers' Assoc., 1944-45; Council London Chamber of Commerce, 1944-48; Gen. Man., 1945-48, Industrial and Commercial Finance Corp. Ltd; Chm. and Man. Dir, National Film Finance Co. Ltd, 1948-49, when it became National Film Finance Corp.; Man. Dir, National Film Finance Corp., 1949-53; since 1953, film producer and theatrical Manager, including 59 Theatre Company; Chm. English Opera Group, 1950-60; Member BBC General Advisory Council, 1952-59; Chm. British Film Academy, 1958-59; Vice-Chm., Touring Opera, 1958; Sec., Soc. of Film and Television Arts, 1959-61; Member: Plant Cttee on Distribution and Exhibition of Cinematograph Films, 1949; Hutton Cttee on Purchase Tax, 1952. *Address:* Flat 2, 24 Palace Court, W2. *T:* 01-727 8349. *Club:* Savile.

**LAWS, Group Capt. Frederick Charles Victor,** CB 1946; CBE 1944 (OBE 1919); President Fairey Air Surveys Ltd; *b* 29 Nov. 1887; *yr s* of late William Laws, Thetford; *m* Grace, *d* of late Samuel Withers; one *d.* Served Coldstream Guards, 1905-12, RFC and RAF, 1912-33, retired; returned active list, 1939-46; reverted to retired list, 1946. Served European War, 1914-18 (despatches); Air Component BEF, 1939-40 (despatches); Air Ministry Air Staff Officer for the development of Air Photography, 1940-46; Managing Director, Race Finish Recording Co., 1946-63. Master Worshipful Company Coach and Coach Harness Makers, 1955; Upper Freeman, Guild of Air Pilots, 1956. FRPS, 1920; President Photogrametric Society, 1955-57 (Vice-President, 1952); Presidents Medal, 1958; Hon. Member, 1962. Chairman National Cttee for Photogrametry, 1955-63. Legion of Merit, Degree of Officer (USA), 1945; Legion of Honour; Croix de Guerre (1939-45), with Palm (France). *Address:* 22 Dukes Lodge, Holland Park, W11. *T:* 01-727 9761. *Club:* Royal Air Force.

**LAWSON,** family name of **Baron Burnham.**

**LAWSON, Charles,** QC 1961; Recorder of Gloucester, since 1968; *b* 23 Feb. 1916; 2nd *s* of Barnet Lawson, London; *m* 1943, Olga Daphne Kay; three *d. Educ:* Grocers' Company Sch.; University College, London. LLB 1937. Served War of 1939-45: in Army, 1940-46; Major, Royal Artillery. Recorder, Burton-upon-Trent, 1965-68. Bencher, Inner Temple, 1968. *Recreations:* golf, music. *Address:* 40 Hyde Park Gate, SW7. *T:* 01-584 7394; Mayes Green Cottage, Ockley, Surrey. *T:* Forest Green 317.

**LAWSON, Frederick Henry,** DCL 1947; FBA 1956; Part-time Lecturer in Law, University of Lancaster, since 1964; *b* Leeds, 14 July 1897; *s* of Frederick Henry Lawson and Mary Louisa Austerberry; *m* 1933, Elspeth, *yr d* of late Captain Alexander Webster, Kilmarnock; one *s* two *d. Educ:* Leeds Grammar Sch. Hastings Exhibitioner in Classics (Hon. Scholar), Queen's Coll., Oxford, 1915; Akroyd Scholar, 1915. Served European War, 1916-18. 1st Class, Final Hon. School of Modern History, 1921; 1st Class, Final Hon. School of Jurisprudence, 1922. Barrister-at-Law, Gray's Inn, 1923; Lecturer in Law, University Coll., Oxford, 1924-25, Christ Church, 1925-26, CCC, 1925-26 and 1927-30; Junior Research Fellow, Merton Coll., Oxford, 1925-30, official Fellow and Tutor in Law, 1930-48. Studied at Göttingen, 1926-27; University Lecturer in Byzantine Law, 1929-31; All Souls Reader in Roman Law, 1931-48; Temp. Principal in Ministry of Supply, 1943-45; Prof. of Comparative Law, and Fellow of Brasenose Coll., Oxford, 1948-64. Visiting Prof., Univ. of California, 1953; Thomas M. Cooley Lectr, Univ. of Michigan Law Sch., 1953; Joint Editor Journal of Comparative Legislation and International Law, 1948-52, of International and Comparative Law Quarterly, 1952-55; Senior Editor, Journal of Society of Public Teachers of Law, 1955-61; Member International Social Science Council, 1952-58; Lecturer in Roman Law, Council of Legal Education, 1954-58 (Reader, 1958-64); Visiting Lecturer, New York University School of Law, 1956, 1959, 1962, 1965; Visiting Professor, University of Pennsylvania Law School, 1959 (Spring Semester); University of Michigan Law School, 1959 (Fall Semester); University of Houston, 1967-68. Mem. Internat. Acad. of Comparative Law, 1958-; Sec.-Gen., Internat. Assoc. of Legal Science, 1964-69. Hon. Doctor: Louvain, 1958; Paris, 1964; Ghent, 1968; Hon. Dr jur. Frankfurt; Hon. LLD Glasgow, 1960. *Publications:* (with Sir D. L. Keir) Cases in Constitutional Law, 1st edn 1928, 5th edn 1967; Negligence in the Civil Law, 1950; The Rational Strength of English Law (Hamlyn Lectures), 1951; A Common Lawyer looks at the Civil Law (Thomas M. Cooley Lectures), 1955; An Introduction to the Law of Property, 1958; (with D. J. Bentley) Constitutional and Administrative Law, 1961; The Oxford Law School, 1850-1965, 1968; The Roman Law Reader, 1969; much re-editing, including Buckland and McNair, Roman Law and Common Law, 2nd edn 1952; various articles on Roman and Comparative Law. *Address:* High Cliff, Eden Park, Lancaster.

**LAWSON, George McArthur;** MP (Lab) Motherwell Division of Lanarkshire since April 1954; *b* Edinburgh, 11 July 1906; *s* of Alexander Lawson and Euphemia Gordon McPherson McArthur; *m* 1939, Margaret Robertson Munro; two *s* (and one *s* decd). *Educ:* St Bernard's; North Merchiston elementary schools. Staff tutor with National Council of Labour Colleges, 1937-40; West of Scotland Organiser with NCLC, 1940-50. Secretary, Edinburgh Trades Council, 1950-54. An Opposition Whip, 1959-64; Government Whip, 1964; Dep. Chief Government Whip, 1966-67. *Address:* Brooklyn, 37 Burnblea Street, Hamilton, Lanarkshire. *T:* Hamilton 21691.

**LAWSON, Lieut-Colonel Harold Andrew Balvaird,** MVO 1963; Rothesay Herald since 1939; Lyon Clerk and Keeper of the Records of the Court of the Lord Lyon, 1929-66; *b* 19 Oct. 1899; 2nd *s* of late Dr Charles Wilfrid Lawson, Edinburgh; *m* 1934, Kathleen Alice, *o d* of Alexander Banks, of Banks & Co., Printers; one *d. Educ:* George Watson's Coll.; Edinburgh Univ. Joined RA, 1916; 2nd Lieut, 1919; RA (TA), 1924; Major, 1936; Lieut-Colonel, 1939; Unicorn Pursuivant, 1929-39. OStJ 1968. *Recreations:* golf, badminton. *Address:* Lyon Office, HM Register House, Edinburgh. *T:* 031-556 7255.

**LAWSON, Sir Henry (Brailsford),** Kt 1963; MC 1917; Director, the Industrial and General Trust Ltd; retired as Chief Legal Adviser and a Deputy Chief General Manager, Lloyds Bank Ltd, 1963 (Mem. Southern Regional Bd, 1963); *b* 19 Feb. 1898; *s* of H. P. Lawson; *m* 1930, Mona Lilian, *e d* of Dr B. Thorne Thorne; three *s* one *d. Educ:* Lancing Coll.; Trinity Coll., Cambridge (BA, LLB). Member Council, 1943, Vice-President, 1961-62, President, 1962-63, of Law Society. *Address:* Churchmead, Pirbright, Surrey. *T:* Brookwood 4133.

**LAWSON, Hugh McDowall,** BScEng London; CEng, FICE, FIMunE; Deputy City Engineer, Nottingham, since 1948; *b* Leeds, 13 Feb. 1912; *s* of late John Lawson, Pharmaceutical Chemist; *m* 1937, Dorothy, *d* of late Rev. T. H. Mallinson, BA; two *s. Educ:* Nottingham High Sch.; University Coll., Nottingham. Served in Royal Engineers, 1940-44. MP (Common Wealth) Skipton Div. of Yorks, 1944-45. Contested (Common Wealth) Harrow West Div., 1945; (Lab) Rushcliffe Div., 1950; (Lab) King's Lynn Div., 1955. *Address:* 45 Hazel Grove, Mapperley, Nottingham NG3 6DQ. *T:* 65241.

**LAWSON, Air Vice-Marshal Ian Douglas Napier,** CB 1965; CBE 1961; DFC 1941, Bar 1943; RAF, retired; Regional Sales Manager, Western Europe, British Aircraft Corporation, since 1969; *b* 11 Nov. 1917; *y s* of late J. L. Lawson and of Ethel Mary Lawson (*née* Ludgate); *m* 1945, Dorothy Joyce Graham Nash; one *s* one *d. Educ:* Brondesbury Coll.; Polytechnic, Regent Street. Aircraft Industry, 1934-39. Joined RAFVR 1938. Served War of 1939-45 (despatches thrice): Bomber Comd, 1940-41; Middle East Comd, 1941-45. Permanent Commission, 1945. Bomber Comd, 1945-46; Staff Coll., 1946; Air Ministry, 1946-49; Transport Comd, 1949-50; Middle East Comd, 1950-52; JSSC, 1953; Ministry of Defence, 1953-56; Flying Coll., Manby, 1956-57; Transport Comd, 1957-62; Air Forces Middle East, 1962-64; Commandant, RAF Coll., Cranwell, 1964-67; Asst Chief Adviser (Personnel and Logistics), MoD, 1967-69. MBIM. US Legion of Merit. *Recreations:* gardening, motor sport. *Address:* The Red Cottage, Shere, Guildford, Surrey. *T:* Shere 2409. *Club:* Royal Air Force.

**LAWSON, John,** CB 1955; *b* 10 Nov. 1893; *y s* of late Thomas Lawson, Clapham; *m* 1933, Millicent Mary, *y d* of late Samuel White, Taunton, and *widow* of Lieut-Colonel T. W. Bullock. *Educ:* Dulwich Coll.; Merton Coll., Oxford (Postmaster). Served European War, 1914-18, Sherwood Foresters. 1st Class Lit. Hum. Oxford, 1920; MA. Admiralty, 1921; Principal Assistant Secretary, 1945; Under Secretary, Admiralty, 1948-56. *Address:* 2 Sefton House, Terminus Road, Bexhill-on-Sea, Sussex. *T:* 1997.

**LAWSON, Sir John Charles Arthur Digby,** 3rd Bt, *cr* 1900; DSO 1943; MC 1940; Lieutenant-Colonel 11th Hussars, retired; Chairman, Fairbairn Lawson Ltd, Leeds, and subsidiary companies; *b* 24 Oct. 1912; *e s* of Sir Digby Lawson, Bt, TD, JP, and late Mrs Gerald Wallis (*née* Iris Mary Fitzgerald); *S* father 1959; *m* 1st, 1945, Rose (marr. diss., 1950), *widow* of Pilot Officer William Fiske, RAF, and *er d* of late D. C. Bingham and late Lady Rosabelle Brand; 2nd, 1954, Tresilla Ann Eleanor (de Pret Roose), *d* of Major E. Buller Leyborne Popham, MC; one *s. Educ:* Stowe; RMC, Sandhurst. Served War of 1939-45 (despatches twice, MC, DSO). Comd Inns of Court Regt, 1945-47; retired, 1947. Colonel, 11th Hussars (PAO), 1965-69; Hon. Col, The Royal Hussars (POW), 1969. Legion of Merit (US). *Heir: s* Charles John Patrick Lawson, *b* 19 May 1959. *Address:* Littlethorpe House, Ripon, Yorks. *T:* Ripon 2170. *Clubs:* Cavalry, MCC.

**LAWSON, Neil,** QC 1955; a Law Commissioner since 1965; Recorder of Folkestone, since 1962; *b* 8 April 1908; *s* of late Robb Lawson and Edith Marion Lawson (*née* Usherwood); *m* 1933, Gweneth Clare (*née* Wilby); one *s* one *d*. Called to Bar, Inner Temple, 1929. RAFVR, 1940-45. Foreign decorations: DK (Dato' Peduka Kerubat), 1959, DSN (Dato' Setia Negara), 1962, PSMB (Dato' Sri Mahota), 1969, Brunei. *Recreations:* literature, music, the country. *Address:* 30a Heath Drive, Hampstead, NW3.

**LAWSON, Nigel;** journalist; *b* 11 March 1932; *s* of Ralph Lawson and Joan Elisabeth, *e d* of Bernard Davis; *m* 1955, Vanessa Mary Addison, 2nd *d* of late Felix Addison Salmon; one *s* three *d*. *Educ:* Westminster; Christ Church, Oxford (Scholar). 1st class hons PPE, 1954. Served with Royal Navy (Sub-Lt RNVR), 1954-56. Mem. Editorial Staff, Financial Times, 1956-60; City Editor, Sunday Telegraph, 1961-63; Special Assistant to Prime Minister (Sir Alec Douglas-Home), 1963-64; Financial Times columnist and BBC broadcaster, 1965 Editor of the Spectator, 1966-70. Chm., Coningsby Club, 1963-64. Contested (C), Eton and Slough, 1970. *Address:* 24 Hyde Park Gate, SW7. *T:* 01-584 7978. *Clubs:* Carlton, Garrick, Political Economy.

**LAWSON, Colonel Sir Peter Grant,** 2nd Bt, *cr* 1905; *b* 28 July 1903; *s* of 1st Bt and Sylvia (*d* 1962), *y d* of Charles Hunter, Selaby Hall, nr Darlington; *S* father, 1919; *m* 1940, Virginia, *d* of Sidney B. Dean, St Paul, Minn, USA, and Mrs Northup Dean, Burghfield, Berks. 2nd Lieut RHG, 1925; Lieut, 1927; Captain, 1934; Major, 1942; Lieut-Colonel, 1948; Colonel, 1952; retired, 1954. Served War of 1939-45 (despatches). *Heir:* none. *Address:* Venards House, North Gorley, Fordingbridge, Hampshire. *T:* Fordingbridge 3104.

**LAWSON, Sir Ralph Henry,** 4th Bt, *cr* 1841; *b* 27 Sept. 1905; *s* of Sir Henry Joseph Lawson, 3rd Bt, and Ursula Mary, *o c* of late Philip John Canning Howard, Corby Castle, Carlisle; *S* father, 1947; *m* 1st, 1935, Lilyan Mary (*d* 1968), *e d* of Sir Edmund Chaytor, 6th Bt, and of Isabel, Lady Chaytor; two *d*; 2nd, 1970, Mrs Helen Beresford Petre. *Educ:* Ampleforth. *Recreations:* all field sports. *Heir: b* William Howard Lawson [*b* 15 July 1907; *m* 1933, Joan Eleanor, *d* of late Major Arthur Cowie Stamer, CBE; three *s* one *d*]. *Address:* Brough Hall, Catterick, Yorks.

**LAWSON, Sir William (Halford),** Kt 1962; CBE 1948; FCA; formerly Senior Partner in Binder, Hamlyn & Company, Chartered Accountants; *b* 21 March 1899; *s* of late H. P. Lawson; *m* 1931, Susan Elisabeth Bray; three *s* three *d*. *Educ:* Lancing; Trinity Coll., Cambridge. Pres., Institute of Chartered Accountants, 1957-58. Delegate on Austrian Treaty Commission in Vienna, 1947. Member: Transport Arbitration Tribunal, 1948-57; Purchase Tax (Valuation) Cttee, 1952; Royal Commission on Local Government in Greater London, 1957-60; Cttee to enquire into Company Law, 1959-62; Board of Trade Companies Act Accountancy Advisory Cttee, 1955-68; Chairman: (part-time) Iron and Steel Holding and Realisation Agency, 1962-67; Taxation Cttee, CBI, 1965-69; Arbitral Bodies for remuneration of Teachers, 1965-69; Min. of Technology (formerly BoT) Adv. Cttee under Local Employment Acts, 1966-; Review Bd for Government Contracts, 1969-. *Address:* Sands Lodge, Leigh Lane, Farnham, Surrey. *Clubs:* City of London, United University.

**LAWSON JOHNSTON,** family name of **Baron Luke.**

**LAWSON JOHNSTON, Hon. Hugh de Beauchamp,** TD 1951; DL; Vice-Chairman and Joint Managing Director, Bovril Ltd, since 1967; *b* 7 April 1914; *yr s* of 1st Baron Luke of Pavenham, KBE, and *b* of 2nd Baron Luke, *qv*; *m* 1946, Audrey Warren, *d* of late Colonel F. Warren Pearl and late Mrs A. L. Pearl; three *d*. *Educ:* Eton; Chillon Coll.; Corpus Christi, Cambridge. BA 1934, MA (Cantab), 1938. With Bovril Ltd, 1935. Territorial Service with 5th Bn Beds and Herts Regt, 1935-; Captain, 1939, and throughout War. Director: Bovril Ltd; Argentine Estates of Bovril Ltd; Tribune Investment Trust Ltd (Chm.); Marmite Ltd (Chm.); Bovril Group Marketing Ltd (Chm.). Chm. of Cttees, United Soc. for Christian Literature. High Sheriff of Bedfordshire, 1961-62; DL Beds, 1964. *Recreations:* hunting, walking, gardening, photography. *Address:* 20 Chelsea Square, SW3. *T:* 01-352 5059; Melchbourne Park, Bedfordshire. *T:* Riseley 282. *Club:* City of London.

**LAWSON-TANCRED, Sir Henry,** 10th Bt, *cr* 1662; JP; *b* 12 Feb. 1924; *e surv. s* of Major Sir Thomas Lawson-Tancred, 9th Bt, and Margery Elinor (*d* 1961), *d* of late A. S. Lawson, Aldborough Manor; *S* father, 1945; *m* 1950, Jean Veronica (*d* 1970), 4th and *y d* of late G. R. Foster, Stockeld Park, Wetherby, Yorks; five *s* one *d*. *Educ:* Stowe; Jesus Coll., Cambridge. Served as Pilot in RAFVR, 1942-46. JP West Riding, 1967. *Heir: s* Andrew Peter Lawson-Tancred, *b* 18 Feb. 1952. *Address:* Aldborough Manor, Boroughbridge, Yorks. *T:* Boroughbridge 2716.

**LAWTHER, Barry Charles Alfred,** CIE 1931; *b* 25 Aug. 1888. Indian Police Service in Punjab and NWF Province; retired 1934; Ministry of Home Security, 1941-42. *Address:* c/o National & Grindlay's Bank Ltd, 13 St James's Square, SW1. *Club:* Royal Commonwealth Society.

**LAWTHER, Sir William,** Kt, *cr* 1949; JP; Past President National Union of Mineworkers; Past President Trades Union Congress; Past Secretary Miners' International; *b* Northumberland, 1889; *m* 1915, Lottie Laws (*d* 1962). *Educ:* Colliery Sch.; Central Labour Coll., London. Contested S Shields, 1922-23-24; MP (Lab) Barnard Castle, 1929-31; Durham CC, 1925-29; Member National Labour Party Exec. Cttee, 1923-26. TUC General Council, 1935-54. Chevalier of the Legion of Honour. *Recreation:* enjoyment in watching others enjoy themselves. *Address:* 6 Grange Close, Marden, Cullercoats, North Shields, Northumberland. *T:* North Shields 72589.

**LAWTON, Frank Dickinson;** Solicitor, Department of Employment and Productivity, since 1967; *b* 14 July 1915; *o s* of F. W. Lawton, CB, OBE, and Elizabeth Mary Lawton; *m* 1943, Margaret Joan, *o d* of Frederick Norman Reed; one *s* two *d*. *Educ:* Epsom Coll.; Law Society's Sch. of Law. Solicitor (hons), 1937. Entered Solicitor's Dept, Ministry of Labour, 1939; seconded to Treasury, Solicitor's Dept, 1940; returned to Solicitor's Dept, Ministry of Labour, 1947; Assistant Solicitor, 1959; Solicitor, Min. of Labour (now Dept of Employment and

Productivity), Oct. 1967. Mem. Court of Assts, Scriveners' Co. (Master, 1970-71; Mem. Examination Cttee, 1967-). *Address:* 22 Shirley Avenue, Cheam, Surrey. *T:* 01-642 3452. *Club:* Athenæum.

**LAWTON, Hon. Sir Frederick (Horace),** Kt 1961; **Hon. Mr Justice Lawton;** Judge of the High Court of Justice (Queen's Bench Division) since 1961; *b* 21 Dec. 1911; *o s* of William John Lawton; *m* 1937, Doreen (*née* Wilton); two *s*. *Educ:* Battersea Grammar Sch.; Corpus Christi Coll., Cambridge (Hon. Fellow, 1968). Barrister, 1935. Served with London Irish Rifles, 1939-41; invalided out of Army, 1941, and returned to practice at the Bar. QC 1957; Recorder of City of Cambridge, 1957-61; Dep. Chm., Cornwall QS, 1968-. Member: Bar Council, 1957-61; Departmental Cttee on Proceedings before Examining Justices, 1957-58; Standing Cttee on Criminal Law Revision, 1959-; Inter-departmental Cttee on Court of Criminal Appeal, 1964-65. Presiding Judge, Western Circuit, 1970-. President, British Academy of Forensic Sciences, 1964. *Address:* Netherstone, Promenade de Verdun, Purley, Surrey, CR2 3LN. *T:* 01-660 1931; Mordryg, Stoptide, Rock, near Wadebridge, Cornwall. *T:* Trebetherick 3375. *Club:* Garrick.

**LAWTON, Harold Walter,** MA; Docteur de l'Université de Paris; Officier d'Académie; Emeritus Professor, University of Sheffield, since 1964; *b* Stoke-on-Trent, 27 July 1899; *y s* of late William T. C. and Alice Lawton; *m* 1938, Bessie, *y d* of T. C. Pate; two *s* one *d*. *Educ:* Middle Sch., Newcastle under Lyme; Rhyl Grammar Sch.; Universities of Wales and Paris. BA Hons (Wales) 1921; MA (Wales) 1923; Fellow University of Wales, 1923-26; Docteur de l'Univ. de Paris, 1926. University College, Southampton: Lecturer in French, 1926-37; Professor of French, 1937-50; Dean of Faculty of Arts, 1945-49; University of Sheffield: Professor of French, 1950-64; Warden of Ranmoor House, 1957-63; Deputy Pro-Vice-Chancellor, 1958-61; Pro-Vice-Chancellor, 1961-64. Médaille d'Argent de la Reconnaissance Française, 1946; Officier d'Académie, 1948. *Publications:* Térence en France au XVIe Siècle: éditions et traductions (Paris), 1926; Handbook of French Renaissance Dramatic Theory, 1950; J. du Bellay, Poems, selected with introduction and notes, 1961; articles and reviews to British and French periodicals. *Recreations:* walking, drawing. *Address:* Ranmoor Cottage, Ffordd-y-Wylan, Rhosneigr, Anglesey, North Wales. *T:* Rhosneigr 552.

**LAWTON, Philip Charles Fenner,** CBE 1967; DFC 1941; Member of British European Airways Corporation since 1964, Commercial and Sales Director since 1947; Chairman, BEA Airtours, since 1969; *b* Highgate, London, 18 Sept. 1912; *o s* of late Charles Studdert Lawton and late Mabel Harriette Lawton; *m* 1941, Emma Letitia Gertrude, *y d* of late Lieut-Colonel Sir Henry Kenyon Stephenson, 1st Bt, DSO, and Frances, Hassop Hall, Bakewell, Derbyshire; one *s* one *d*. *Educ:* Westminster Sch. Solicitor, 1934-39. Joined AAF, 1935. Served War of 1939-45 (despatches twice, Group Captain): Pilot with 604 Aux. Sqdn (night fighters), 1939-41; Staff Officer HQ, Fighter Command, 1942; Station Commander, RAF Predannock; RAF Portreath; RAF Cranfield and Special Duties for Inspector-General, RAF, 1943-45. LLB Hons Degree, 1933; MInstT 1955. *Recreations:* track sports, flying, golf. *Address:* 7 Ladbroke Terrace, W11. *T:* 01-727 8564; North Springs, Fittleworth, Sussex. *T:* Fittleworth 367. *Club:* RAF Reserves.

**LAXNESS, Halldor Kiljan;** Icelandic writer; *b* 23 April 1902; *s* of Gudjon Helgason and Sigridur Halldorsdottir, Iceland; *m* 1st, Ingibjörg Einarsdottir; one *s*; 2nd, Audur Suensdottir; two *d*. Awarded Nobel literary prize, 1955; Sonning Prize, 1969. *Publications:* (many of which have been translated into English): The Great Weaver of Cashmere, 1927; Salka Valka, 1934; Independent People (an epic), 1939; The Atom Station, 1947 (English trans. 1961); Happy Warriors, 1956 (English trans. 1958); World Light, 1969, etc. Translations into Icelandic: Farewell to Arms by Ernest Hemingway; Candide by Voltaire, etc. *Address:* Reykjavik, Iceland.

**LAYBOURNE, Rear-Adm. Alan Watson,** CB 1955; CBE 1944 (OBE 1942); DL; a Governor and Almoner of Christ's Hospital; County Vice-President, Sussex, St John Ambulance Brigade; *b* 29 Nov. 1898; *s* of late William Watson Laybourne, Liverpool; *m* 1926, Helen, *d* of late George Gorrie Burnett, Toronto; one *s* one *d*. *Educ:* Christ's Hospital. Joined RN (Supply and Secretariat Branch), Jan. 1916. Served European War, 1916-19: Grand Fleet (Jutland), Mesopotamia; North Atlantic Convoys; served War of 1939-45: Scapa; Eastern Fleet and in USA (OBE, CBE). Promoted Comdr 1936, Actg Capt. 1942. Capt. 1947; Rear-Adm. 1952; retired 1955, Clerk to the Dean and Chapter of Durham, 1955-69. DL, Durham, 1967. OStJ 1968. *Recreation:* shooting. *Address:* 2 Vicar's Close, Chichester, Sussex. *T:* Chichester 89219. *Clubs:* Naval and Military; Royal Naval (Portsmouth).

*See also P. J. Liddell.*

**LAYCOCK, Leslie Ernest,** CBE 1967 (OBE 1960); JP; Company Director; Chairman, Leeds Regional Hospital Board since 1963; President, Leeds & Holbeck Building Society, since 1969 (Vice-President, 1967-69); *b* 14 Sept. 1903; *s* of Ernest Bright Laycock and Margaret Ann Laycock; *m* 1931, Hilda Florence, *d* of Christopher Ralph Carr; two *s*. *Educ:* Uppingham Sch.; Leeds Univ. (BCom). President, Leeds and District Woollen Manufacturers Assoc., 1937-39; Vice-President, Assoc. of British Chambers of Commerce, 1962- (Past Pres., Leeds Chamber; Past Chm, Assoc. of Yorks Chambers); Chairman: Governors, Leeds Coll. of Commerce, 1948-69; W Riding Br. of Inst. of Directors, 1959-; Advisory Cttee to Leeds Prison, 1961-; Harrogate (White Rose) Theatre Trust Ltd, 1961-65 (Pres., 1965-); Member Ct and Council, Leeds Univ., 1953-. Civil Defence Director Operations, W Riding, 1958-68. JP Leeds, 1952-. *Recreations:* tennis, badminton, sailing, bridge. *Address:* The Gables, Rayleigh Road, Harrogate. *T:* Harrogate 66219. *Clubs:* United Service; Leeds (Leeds); Club, Sports (Harrogate).

**LAYE, Evelyn;** actress; singer; *b* London, 10 July 1900; *o d* of Gilbert Laye and Evelyn Froud; *m* 1st, 1926, Sonnie Hale (from whom she obtained a divorce, 1931); 2nd, 1934, Frank Lawton (*d* 1969). *Educ:* Folkestone; Brighton. Made first appearance on stage, Theatre Royal, Brighton, 1915, as Nang-Ping in Mr Wu. First London appearance in The Beauty Spot, Gaiety, 1918; first big success in title-role of The Merry Widow, Daly's, 1923; subsequently starred in London in Madame Pompadour, Daly's, 1923; The Dollar Princess, Daly's, 1925; Cleopatra, Daly's, 1925; Betty in Mayfair, Adelphi, 1925; Merely Molly, Adelphi, 1926; Princess Charming, Palace, 1927; Lilac Time, Daly's, 1927; Blue Eyes, Piccadilly, 1928; The New Moon, Drury Lane, 1929; Bitter Sweet, His Majesty's, 1930; Helen!, Adelphi, 1932; Give Me A Ring,

Hippodrome, 1933; Paganini, Lyceum, 1937; Lights Up, Savoy, 1940; The Belle of New York, Coliseum, 1942; Sunny River, Piccadilly, 1943; Cinderella, His Majesty's, 1943; Three Waltzes, Prince's, 1945; Cinderella, Palladium, 1948; Two Dozen Red Roses, Lyric, 1949; Peter Pan, Scala, 1953; Wedding in Paris, Hippodrome, 1954-56; Silver Wedding, Cambridge, 1957; The Amorous Prawn, Saville/Piccadilly, 1959-62; Never Too Late, Prince of Wales, 1964; The Circle, Savoy, 1965; Strike A Light!, Piccadilly, 1966; Let's All Go Down the Strand, Phoenix, 1967; Charlie Girl, Adelphi, 1969; Phil the Fluter, Palace, 1969. First New York appearance in Bitter Sweet, Ziegfeld Theatre, 1929; subsequently on Broadway in Sweet Aloes, Booth, 1936; Between the Devil, Majestic, 1937. Film début in silent production, The Luck of the Navy, 1927. Films include: One Heavenly Night (Hollywood), 1932; Waltz Time, 1933; Princess Charming, 1934; Evensong, 1935; The Night is Young (Hollywood), 1936; Make Mine A Million, 1959; Theatre of Death, 1967; Within and Without, 1969. Numerous broadcasts and television appearances. *Publication:* Boo, to my Friends (autobiography), 1958. *Address:* c/o Film Rights Ltd, Hammer House, 113 Wardour Street, W1V 4EH.

**LAYFIELD, Frank Henry Burland Willoughby,** QC 1967; *b* 9 Aug. 1921, Toronto; *s* of late H. D. Layfield; *m* 1965, Irene Patricia, *d* of Captain J. D. Harvey, RN (retired); one **d.** *Educ:* Sevenoaks Sch. Army, 1940-46. Called to the Bar, Gray's Inn, 1954. Chm., Inquiry into Greater London Development Plan, 1970. *Publications:* (with A. E. Telling) Planning Applications, Appeals and Inquiries, 1953; (with A. E. Telling) Applications for Planning Payments, 1955; Engineering Contracts, 1956. *Recreations:* walking, tennis. *Address:* 2 Mitre Court Buildings, Temple, EC4. *T:* 01-353 2246.

**LAYMAN, Captain Herbert Francis Hope,** DSO and Bar, 1940; RN; *b* 23 March 1899; *s* of Major F. H. Layman, 11th Hussars; *m* 1934, Elizabeth, *o d* of Rear-Admiral A. P. Hughes; one *s* one *d. Educ:* Haileybury. Grand Fleet, 1918; Fleet Signal Officer, Home Fleet, 1933-36. Director of Radio Equipment, Admiralty, 1949-51; Commanded HMS Hotspur, 1939-41; HMS Rajah, 1945-46; Royal Naval Air Station, Culham, Oxon, 1947-48; Chief of Staff to Commander-in-Chief, The Nore, 1951-53; retired, 1953. Mem. Gen. Council, Tennis and Rackets Association. *Publications:* articles on sport. *Address:* Cleve House, Blewbury, Didcot, Berks. *Club:* United Service.

**LAYTON,** family name of **Baron Layton.**

**LAYTON,** 2nd Baron *cr* 1947, of Danehill; **Michael John Layton;** Board Member and Managing Director (Commercial), British Steel Corporation, since 1967; *b* 28 Sept. 1912; *s* of Walter Thomas, 1st Baron Layton, and Eleanor Dorothea (*d* 1959), *d* of Francis B. P. Osmaston; *S* father, 1966; *m* 1938, Dorothy, *d* of Albert Luther Cross, Rugby; one *s* one *d. Educ:* St Paul's Sch.; Gonville and Caius Coll., Cambridge. BA Mech. Scis Cantab, 1934; MIMechE. Student Apprentice, British Thomson Houston Co. Ltd, Rugby (specialised in Industrial Admin), 1934-37; Student Engr, Goss Printing Co., Chicago, 1937-39; Works Man. and Production Engr, Ibbotson Bros & Co. Ltd, Sheffield, Manufacturing 25-pounder armour piercing shot, 1939-43; Gen. Man., two armoured car production plants, Rootes Ltd, Birmingham, 1943-46; Mem. Control Commn for Germany in Metallurgy Br. and latterly in Econ. Sub-Commn, assisting at formation of OEEC, 1946-48; Head of Internat. Relations Dept of British Iron and Steel Fedn, 1948-55; Sales Controller, 1956, Dir, 1960, Asst Man. Dir, 1965-67, Man. Dir, 1967, The Steel Co. of Wales Ltd. *Heir: s* Hon. Geoffrey Michael Layton [*b* 18 July 1947; *m* 1969, Viviane, *y d* of François Cracco, Belgium]. *Address:* 45 Westleigh Avenue, Putney, SW15. *T:* 01-788 3530. *Clubs:* Reform, Hurlingham.

**LAYTON, Dr (Lieut-Colonel) Basil Douglas Bailey,** CD 1958; Principal Medical Officer, International Health, Department of National Health and Welfare, Canada, since 1956; *b* 8 Aug. 1907; *s* of David Bailey Layton and Mary Eliza Merrick; *m* 1938, Marion Marie McDonald; three *s* one *d. Educ:* University of Toronto Medical Sch. (MD); Harvard University School of Public Health (MPH). Postgrad. medical study, 1931-36; medical practice, 1936-42. RCAMC, 1942-46: service in Canada, UK, and NW Europe. Dept of National Health and Welfare, 1946-. Certified Specialist, Public Health, Royal Coll. of Phys and Surgs, Canada, 1951; postgrad. public health studies, Harvard School of Public Health, 1951-52. Canadian Army (Militia), RCAMC, 1949-58; retired Lt-Col, OC No 10 Medical Co., RCAMC(M). Mem. Canadian Delegn to 11th-22nd World Health Assemblies, Head of Delegn to 15th, 16th. Alternate to Canadian Mem., 1957-59, Mem. (Canada) 1962-65, 1968-71, Chm., 1963-64, of Exec. Board, WHO. Vice-President American Public Health Assoc., 1962-63; Vice-President, Harvard Public Health Alumni Assoc., 1961-63, President, 1963-64. Delta Omega (Beta Chapter) Hon. PH Fraternity, 1952. Fellow, American Public Health Assoc., 1957. France-Germany Star, Defence, Canada War Services and Victory Medals, 1946. *Publications:* scientific articles in Canadian Medical Assoc. Journal, Canadian Public Health Assoc. Journal, etc. *Address:* (business) Brooke Claxton Building, Ottawa, Ontario. *T:* 992-4197; (home) 211 Sunnyside Avenue, Ottawa, Ontario. *T:* 233-9295.

**LAYTON, Paul Henry; His Honour Judge Layton;** Deputy Chairman, Inner London Quarter Sessions, since 1965; *b* Walsall, 11 July 1905; *s* of Frank George Layton, MRCS, LRCP, and Dorothea Yonge; *m* 1950, Frances Evelyn Weekes, Ottawa; two *s. Educ:* Epsom Coll.; St John's Coll., Cambridge (MA). Called to Bar, Inner Temple, 1929; Joined Oxford Circuit, 1930; Recorder of Smethwick, 1952-64; Dep. Chm., Staffs QS, 1955-65; Chm., Agricultural Land Tribunal, W Midlands, 1955-65; Mem., Mental Health Review Tribunal, Birmingham Region, 1960-65; Recorder of Walsall, 1964-65. Served War of 1939-45, AAF and RAF. *Recreation:* gardening. *Address:* 70A Leopold Road, SW19. *T:* 01-946 0865. *Club:* Reform.

**LAYTON, Thomas Arthur;** writer on wine and food; editor; wine merchant; *b* 31 Dec. 1910; *s* of late T. B. Layton, DSO, FRCS, and of Edney Sampson; *m* 1935, Eleanor de P. Marshall; one *s* one *d. Educ:* Bradfield Coll., Berks. Vintners' Co. Travelling Schol., 1929. Public Relations Officer, Wine Trade, 1951. Pres., Circle of Wine Tasters, 1936. *Publications:* Choose Your Wine, 1940 (rewritten, 1959); Table for Two, 1942; Restaurant Roundabout, 1944; Five to a Feast, 1948; Wine's my Line, 1955; Choose Your Cheese, 1957; Winecraft, 1959; Wines and Castles of Spain, 1959; Wines of Italy, 1961; Vignes et Vins de France (trans.), 1962; Choose Your Vegetables, 1963; Modern Wines, 1964; A Year at The Peacock, 1964;

Cheese and Cheese Cookery, 1967; Wines and Chateaux of the Loire, 1967; Cognac and Other Brandies, 1968; Wines and People of Alsace, 1969. Editor: Wine Magazine, 1958-60; Anglo-Spanish Journal (Quarterly), 1960-. *Recreations:* wine, travelling in Spain. *Address:* Grindfield, Uckfield, Sussex. *T:* Chelwood Gate 284.

**LAZARUS, Peter Esmond;** Under-Secretary, Railways, Ministry of Transport, since 1968; *b* 2 April 1926; *er s* of late Kenneth M. Lazarus and Mary R. Lazarus (*née* Halsted); *m* 1950, Elizabeth Anne Marjorie Atwell, *e d* of Leslie H. Atwell, OBE; three *s*. *Educ:* Westminster Sch.; Wadham Coll., Oxford (Open Exhibition). Served RA, 1945-48. Entered Ministry of Transport, 1949; Secretary, London and Home Counties Traffic Advisory Cttee, 1953-57; Private Secretary to Minister, 1961-62; Asst Sec., 1962; Under-Sec., 1968. Chm., Assoc. of First Div. Civil Servants, 1969-. *Recreations:* music, reading. *Address:* 12 Buckingham Mansions, West End Lane, NW6. *T:* 01-435 3086. *Club:* Reform.

**LAZARUS, Robert Stephen,** QC; National Insurance Commissioner, since 1966; *b* 29 Oct. 1909; *s* of Solomon and Mabel Lazarus; *m* 1938, Amelia (*née* Isaacs); two *d*. *Educ:* Marlborough Coll.; Caius Coll., Cambridge. Called to the Bar, at Lincoln's Inn, 1933; QC 1958. Member Bar Council, 1960-64; Member Legal Aid Cttee, 1961-66. Bencher, 1964. Served with RASC, 1940-46; Staff Coll., 1944; AJAG, HQ Allied Land Forces, SE Asia, 1945. *Recreations:* music and golf. *Address:* Sherwood, Lucastes Lane, Hayward's Heath, Sussex. *T:* Hayward's Heath 3046.

**LAZELL, Henry George Leslie;** Hon. President, Beecham Group Ltd (Chairman, 1958-68; President, 1968-70); Chairman, Beecham Incorporated, since 1962; *b* 23 May 1903; *e s* of late Henry William Lazell and late Ada Louise Pickering; *m* 1928, Doris Beatrice Try; one *s*. *Educ:* LCC Elementary Sch. Left school at age of 13; various clerical employments until 1930; Accountant, Macleans Ltd, 1930; Secretary, 1930; Director and Secretary, 1936; Secretary, Beecham Group Ltd, 1939; Managing Director, Macleans Ltd, and Director, Beecham Group Ltd, 1940; Managing Director, Beecham Group Ltd, 1951; Director, ICI Ltd, 1966-68. Member of Association of Certified and Corporate Accountants, 1929, Fellow, 1965; Associate, Chartered Institute of Secretaries, 1930, Fellow, 1934. *Recreations:* sailing, theatre-going, reading. *Address:* The Princess, Hamilton, Bermuda. *Club:* Thirty.

**LEA, Christopher Gerald,** MC; a Metropolitan Magistrate since 1968; *b* 27 Nov. 1917; *y s* of late George Percy Lea, Franche, Kidderminster, Worcs; *m* 1952, Susan Elizabeth Dorrien Smith, *d* of Major Edward Pendarves Dorrien Smith, Greatwood, Restronguet, Falmouth, Cornwall; two *s* one *d* (and one *d* decd). *Educ:* Charterhouse; RMC, Sandhurst. Commissioned into XX The Lancashire Fusiliers, 1937, and served with Regt in UK until 1939. Served War of 1939-45 (despatches, MC): with Lancashire Fusiliers, No 11 Special Air Service Bn, and Parachute Regt in France, Italy and Malaya. Post-war service in Indonesia, Austria and UK; retired, 1948. Called to Bar, Inner Temple, 1948; Oxford Circuit. Mem. Nat. Assistance Bd Appeal Tribunal (Oxford Area), 1961-63; Mem. Mental Health Review Tribunal (Oxford Region), 1962-68. Dep. Chm., Berks QS, 1968-. *Address:* Simms Farm House, Mortimer, Berkshire. *T:* Mortimer 360. *Clubs:* English-Speaking Union; Island Sailing.
*See also Sir G. H. Lea.*

**LEA, Sir Frederick (Measham),** Kt 1966; CB 1960; CBE 1952 (OBE 1944); DSc; FRIC; Hon. ARIBA; Hon. FIOB; Director of Building Research, Department of Scientific and Industrial Research, 1946-65; *s* of late Measham Lea, CIE, OBE; *m* 1938, Eleanor, *d* of Frank James. *Educ:* King Edward VI Sch., Birmingham; Univ. of Birmingham. Admiralty, 1922-25; Building Research Station, 1925-65; Guest Research Associate, Nat. Bureau of Standards, Washington, DC, USA, 1928-29; Mem. of Council, Royal Inst. of Chemistry, 1943-46, 1948-51; Pres. Internat. Council for Building Research, 1955-57, 1959-62. Hon. Mem., Amer. Concrete Inst. Walter C. Voss Award, American Society for Testing and Materials, 1964. *Publications:* Chemistry of Cement and Concrete (3rd edn 1970); (with J. T. Crennel) Alkaline Accumulators, 1928; many papers in scientific and technical journals. *Address:* Pond Cottage, Potten End, Berkhamsted, Herts. *T:* Berkhamsted 3974. *Club:* Reform.

**LEA, Lt-Gen. Sir George (Harris),** KCB 1967 (CB 1964); DSO 1957; MBE 1950; Head of British Defence Staff, Washington, 1967-70; *b* 28 Dec. 1912; *s* of late George Percy Lea, Franche, Kidderminster, Worcs; *m* 1948, Pamela Elizabeth, *d* of Brig. Guy Lovett-Tayleur; one *s* two *d*. *Educ:* Charterhouse; RMC, Sandhurst. Commnd into Lancashire Fusiliers, 1933, and served with Regt in UK, China and India until 1940. Served War of 1939-45 with Lancashire Fusiliers and Parachute Regt in India, N Africa, Italy and NW Europe. Post-war service: Regtl duty and on staff with Parachute Regt, Royal Marine Commando Bde and SAS Regt in UK, China and Malaya. Post-war staff appts in Allied Command Europe (SHAPE) and as Dep. Military Secretary (War Office); Comd 2nd Inf. Bde Group, 1957-60; GOC 42 (Lancs) Div. and North-West District, 1962-63; Comdr Forces, Northern Rhodesia and Nyasaland, 1963-64; Director of Borneo Operations and Commander Land Forces, Borneo, 1965-66. Colonel of The Lancashire Fusiliers, 1965-68; Dep. Colonel for Lancashire, The Royal Regt of Fusiliers, 1968-. *Address:* 36 Drayton Gardens, SW10; c/o Lloyds Bank Ltd, Cox's & King's Branch, 6 Pall Mall, SW1. *Club:* Army and Navy.

**LEA, Sir Thomas Claude Harris,** 3rd Bt, *cr* 1892; *b* 13 April 1901; *s* of Sir Sydney Lea, 2nd Bt, and Mary Ophelia, *d* of Robert Woodward, of Arley Castle, Worcs; *S* father, 1946; *m* 1st, 1924, Barbara Katherine (*d* 1945), *d* of Albert Julian Pell, Wilburton Manor, Isle of Ely; one *s* four *d*; 2nd, 1950, Diana, *d* of Howard Thompson, Coton Hall, Bridgnorth, Salop. *Educ:* Lancing Coll.; Clare Coll., Cambridge. Served War of 1939-45: joined RNVR 1940 as Sub-Lieut; Lieut-Commander 1943; Commander, 1945; demobilised, 1946. *Recreations:* fishing, shooting, ornithology. *Heir:* *s* Thomas Julian Lea, [*b* 18 Nov. 1934; *m* 1970, Gerry Valerie, *d* of late Captain Gibson C. Fahnestock and of Mrs David Knightly, Brockenhurst, Hants]. *Address:* Coneybury, Bayton, near Kidderminster, Worcs. *TA:* Bayton, Worcs. *T:* Clows Top 323.

**LEA-COX, Maj.-Gen. Maurice,** CB 1952; CBE 1946 (OBE 1941); *b* 8 Feb. 1898; *s* of Charles and Lizzie Maria Lea-Cox; *m* 1st, 1923, Joyce (*née* Duchesne); one *s* one *d*; 2nd, 1949, Ivy May Ashley (*née* Biggs). *Educ:* Eastbourne Coll.; RMA, Woolwich. 2nd Lieut, RA, 1916; Lieut, 1917; Captain, 1929; Bt Major, 1937; Major, 1938; Acting Lieut-Colonel, 1940;

Colonel, 1944; transf. RAOC, 1945; Brig., 1948; Maj.-Gen., 1951. Served European War, France, Belgium, 1916-18 (British War and Victory Medals); NW Frontier (Mohmand), 1933 (Medal and Clasp); despatches, 1934; NW Frontier (Mohmand), 1935 (Clasp), France, 1940, AQMG 1940; Dep. Director Warlike Stores, DOS (W) War Office, 1941; DDOS (W) War Office, 1946; Commandant, BAOR, 1947; DOS BAOR, 1948; Commander, Mechanical Transport Organisation, 1951-April 1954, retired. Legion of Merit, USA, 1945. *Recreation:* sport. *Address:* Brae Cottage, Compton, Surrey. *T:* Godalming 6785.

**LEA SMITH,** family name of **Baron Dudley.**

**LEACH, Archibald A.;** *see* Grant, Cary.

**LEACH, Arthur Gordon,** CIE 1933; late Indian Civil Service; *b* 16 March 1885; *s* of A. F. Leach, Charity Commissioner; *m* 1914, Margaret Sydney Woods (*d* 1969); one *s* one *d*. *Educ:* Bradfield Coll.; New Coll., Oxford. Entered Indian Civil Service 1909; served in Madras as Sub-Collector, Special Settlement Officer, Collector and Sec. to Government in the Public Works and Labour Dept; retd 1934; Mem. Legislative Assembly, Delhi, 1933; IARO attached 9th Gurkha Rifles, 1917-19. *Address:* Cuttmill Rise, Puttenham, Guildford. *T:* Elstead 3147.

**LEACH, Bernard (Howell),** CBE 1962; Founder and Director of The Leach Pottery, St Ives, Cornwall, since 1920; *b* 5 Jan. 1887; *o s* of Andrew John Leach, Puisne Judge, Straits Settlements; *m* 1st, 1909, Edith Muriel, *o d* of Dr William Evans Hoyle, Dir of the Nat. Museum of Wales, Cardiff; two *s* three *d*; 2nd, 1936, Laurie Cookes; one adopted *s*; 3rd, 1955, Janet Darnell, American potter. *Educ:* Beaumont Coll.; Slade Sch. of Art. Studied at Slade Sch. of Art, 1903; practised etching; went to Japan, 1909, studied pottery under Kenzan VI; returned to England, started The Leach Pottery at St Ives, Cornwall; revisited Japan and Korea, 1934-35; exhibited widely in England and abroad, and taught many students; lectured across USA, sponsored by Inst. of Contemp. Art, 1950, 1953, 1960; revisited Japan as guest of Nat. Craft Soc. Exhibitions: with Shoji Hamada, at Gallerie de France, Paris, 1964; Caracas, 1966; Crane Kalman Gall., London, 1967; Tokyo, Osaka, Okinawa and London, 1969. Visited Venezuela and Columbia on Lectures and Exhibns for Brit. Council, 1966. Retrospective Exhibns: Arts Council, London, 1961; Tokyo, 1961. Amer. Ceramic Soc., Binns Medal for 1950. Hon. DLitt Exeter, 1961. Order of the Sacred Treasure (Japan), 2nd Class, 1966. Freedom of the Borough of St Ives, 1968. *Publications:* A Potter's Book, 1940; A Potter's Portfolio, 1951; Japan Diary (in Japanese), 1953-54; (Eng. trans A Potter in Japan, 1960); Kenzan and His Tradition, 1966; (with J. P. Hodin) Bernard Leach: a potter's work, 1967. *Recreations:* cricket, tennis. *Address:* The Leach Pottery, St Ives, Cornwall. *T:* St Ives 6398.

**LEACH, Charles Harold,** CBE 1963; MA, FCA; retired; *b* 2 May 1901; *s* of late John Herbert Charles Leach; *m* 1928, Nora Eunice Ashworth; two *s*. *Educ:* Manchester Grammar Sch.; Brasenose Coll., Oxford. Articled Clerk, W. Bolton and Co., Manchester, 1923-26; Asst Sec., Alliance and Dublin Consumers Gas Co., Dublin, 1927-39; Gen. Manager and Sec., Liverpool Gas Co., Liverpool, 1939-49; Gen. Manager, Liverpool Group, North Western Gas Board, 1949-55; Chm., Southern Gas Board, 1956-61; Chm., West Midlands Gas Board, 1961-66. OStJ 1961. *Recreation:* bridge, previously lacrosse (Half Blue OU). *Address:* 6 Western Avenue, Branksome Park, Poole, Dorset.

**LEACH, Edmund Ronald,** MA Cantab, PhD London; Provost of King's College, Cambridge, since 1966; University Reader in Social Anthropology since 1957; *b* 11 Nov. 1910; *s* of late William Edmund Leach; *m* 1940, Celia Joyce, *d* of late Henry Stephen Guy Buckmaster; one *s* one *d*. *Educ:* Marlborough Coll.; Clare Coll., Cambridge (Exhibnr). Served War of 1939-45, Burma Army. Commercial Asst, Butterfield & Swire, Shanghai, 1932-37; Graduate Student, LSE, 1938-39, 1946-47; Lectr, later Reader, in Social Anthrop., LSE, 1947-53; Lectr, Cambridge, 1953-57. Anthropological Field Research: Formosa, 1937; Kurdistan, 1938; Burma, 1939-45; Borneo, 1947; Ceylon, 1954, 1956. Fellow of King's Coll., Cambridge, 1960-66; Fellow, Center for Advanced Study in Behavioral Sciences, Stanford, 1961; Sen. Fellow, Eton Coll., 1966-. Mem., Social Science Research Council, 1968-. Vice-Pres., Royal Anthrop. Inst., 1964-66, 1968-70 (Curl Essay Prize, 1951, 1957; Rivers Medal, 1958; Henry Myers Lectr, 1966); Chm. Assoc. of Social Anthropologists, 1966-70; Pres. British Humanist Assoc., 1970-; Malinowski Lectr, 1959; Reith Lectr, 1967. Foreign Hon. Mem., Amer. Acad. of Arts and Sciences, 1968. *Publications:* Social and Economic Organization of the Rowanduz Kurds, 1940; Social Science Research in Sarawak, 1950; Political Systems of Highland Burma, 1954; Pul Eliya: A Village in Ceylon, 1961; Rethinking Anthropology, 1961; A Runaway World?, 1968; Genesis as Myth, 1970; Lévi-Strauss, 1970; Editor and contributor to various anthrop. symposia; numerous papers in Man, Journal of the Royal Anthropological Institute, American Anthropologist, South Western Journal of Anthropology, Daedalus, European Archives of Sociology, New Society, Current Anthropology, etc.; various articles in Encyclop. Britannica, Internat. Encyclop. of the Social Sciences. *Recreations:* ski-ing, travel. *Address:* Provost's Lodge, King's College, Cambridge. *T:* Cambridge 50411. *Club:* United University.

**LEACH, Norman,** CMG 1964; Under-Secretary, Ministry of Overseas Development, since 1964; *b* 8 March 1912; *s* of W. M. Leach. *Educ:* Ermysted's Gram. Sch., Skipton in Craven, Yorks; St Catharine's Coll., Cambridge (Scholar). 1st Class Hons, Pts I and II English Tripos, 1933 and 1934; Charles Oldham Shakespeare Schol., 1933. Asst Principal, Inland Revenue Dept, 1935; Under-Secretary: Ministry of Pensions and National Insurance, 1958-61; Dept of Technical Co-operation, 1961-64. *Address:* 45 Morpeth Mansions, Morpeth Terrace, SW1. *T:* 01-834 2774. *Club:* Reform.

**LEACH, Sir Ronald (George),** Kt 1970; CBE 1944; Senior Partner in firm of Peat, Marwick, Mitchell & Co., Chartered Accountants; *b* 21 Aug. 1907; *s* of William T. Leach, 14 Furze Croft, Hove; *m* Margaret Alice Binns. *Educ:* Alleyn's. Dep. Financial Sec. to Ministry of Food, Sept. 1939-June 1946. Member: Cttee on Coastal Flooding, 1953; Inquiry into Shipping, 1967-70; Chairman: Consumer Cttee for GB (Agricultural Marketing Acts, 1931-49), 1958-67; BoT Companies Act Accountancy Advisory Cttee. Pres. Inst. of Chartered Accountants in England and Wales, 1969-70. *Address:* Waterlane Farm, Headcorn, Kent. *T:* Headcorn 249; 37 Lowndes Street, W1. *T:* 01-235 8670. *Clubs:* Athenæum, Beefsteak.

**LEACH, Thomas Stephen,** CMG 1959; MC 1916; Chief Inspector of Fisheries, Ministry of Agriculture, Fisheries and Food, 1948-61, retired; *b* 20 Sept. 1896; *s* of Henry Robert Leach, Rickmansworth, Herts; *m* 1921, Eileen Isabel, *d* of Sir Rowland Whitehead, 3rd Bt, Wallingford, Berks; two *s* one *d. Educ:* Aldenham. Joined 18th Royal Fusiliers, 1914; commissioned, 1916, 14th Hampshire Regt (MC). Joined Min. of Agriculture and Fisheries, 1919. *Recreations:* fishing and gardening. *Address:* Stockbridge Cottage, Tilford, Surrey. *T:* Frensham 2348.

**LEADBEATER, Howell;** Under-Secretary since 1968 and Controller of Supplies since 1967, Ministry of Public Building and Works; *b* 22 Oct. 1919; *s* of late Thomas and Mary Ann Leadbeater; *m* 1946, Mary Elizabeth Roberts; two *s* one *d. Educ:* Pontardawe Grammar Sch.; University College of Wales, Swansea. Army Service, 1940-46: Adjt 11th E African Divl Signals. Asst Principal, Min. of Works, 1948, Principal, 1949; Asst Sec., 1958. *Address:* Milk Wood, Stokesheath Road, Oxshott, Surrey. *T:* Oxshott 2614.

**LEADBETTER, David Hulse,** CB 1958; Assistant Under Secretary of State, Department of Education and Science, 1964-68 (Under Secretary, Ministry of Education, 1953-64); *b* 14 Aug. 1908; *s* of late Harold Leadbetter; *m* 1933, Marion, *d* of late Horatio Ballantyne, FRIC, FCS; two *s* three *d. Educ:* Whitgift; Merton Coll., Oxford. Entered Board of Education, 1933. *Address:* Stenson, Vicarage Road, Southborough, Kent. *T:* Tunbridge Wells 28833.

**LEADBITTER, Edward;** MP (Lab) The Hartlepools, since 1964; *b* 18 June 1919; *s* of Edward Leadbitter, Easington, Durham; *m* 1940, Phyllis Irene Mellin, Bristol; one *s* one *d. Educ:* State Schs; Teachers' Training Coll. Served War, 1939-45, with RA; commissioned 1943; War Office Instructor in Gunnery. Joined Labour Party, 1938; Pres., Hartlepools Labour Party, 1958-62. Became Teacher Member: West Hartlepool Borough Council; NUPE; Town Planning and Finance Cttees; Chm., Industrial Development Cttee. Organizer of Exhibition on History of Labour Movement, 1956. *Address:* 30 Hylton Road, Hartlepool, Co. Durham.

**LEADBITTER, Sir Eric Cyril Egerton,** KCVO, *cr* 1951 (CVO 1937); Kt, *cr* 1946; *b* 8 June 1891; *y s* of late T. F. Leadbitter of Warden, near Hexham, Northumberland; *m* W. Irene, *d* of late Frederick Lloyd. *Educ:* Shrewsbury. Entered Public Trustee Office, 1910; Royal Naval Reserve, 1917-19; Asst Principal, Treasury, 1919; Private Sec. to Controller of Establishments, 1919-21; Private Sec. to Permanent Sec., 1921-28; Senior Clerk, Privy Council Office, 1928-34; Dep. Clerk of the Council, 1934-42; Clerk, 1942-51. *Publications:* Rain before Seven, 1915; The Road to Nowhere, 1916; Perpetual Fires, 1918; Shepherd's Warning, 1920; Dead Reckoning, 1922; The Evil that Men Do, 1923. *Address:* Oak Lodge, Bayhall Road, Tunbridge Wells.

**LEADBITTER, Jasper Michael,** OBE 1960; HM Consul-General, Hanover, since 1969; *b* 25 Sept. 1912; *s* of late Francis John Graham Leadbitter, Warden, Northumberland, and Teresa del Riego Leadbitter; *m* 1942, Anna Lisa Hahne Johansson, Stockholm, Sweden; one *d. Educ:* Shrewsbury and Dresden. Press Attaché, Stockholm, 1945; established in Foreign Service, 1947; Foreign Office, 1947; Panama, 1948; Actg Consul-Gen., Detroit, 1952; First Sec. (Information), Buenos Aires, 1953 and Helsinki, 1956; Foreign Office, 1958; HM Consul and, later, 1st Sec. at Léopoldville, Congo, Dec. 1959 and at Brazzaville, 1961; Dep. Permanent UK Representative to Council of Europe and Consul at Strasbourg, March 1962; HM Consul-Gen., Berlin, Nov. 1963-66; Consul, Palermo, 1966-69. *Recreations:* travel, golf. *Address:* 38 Jubilee Place, Chelsea, SW3; Sycamore, Overstrand, Norfolk. *Clubs:* Hurlingham, Public Schools.

**LEAHY, John Henry Gladstone;** HM Diplomatic Service; Head of Personnel Services Department since 1969; *b* 7 Feb. 1928; *s* of late William Henry Gladstone and late Ethel Leahy; *m* 1954, Elizabeth Anne Pitchford; two *s* two *d. Educ:* Tonbridge Sch.; Clare Coll., Cambridge; Yale University. RAF, 1950-52; FO, 1952-54 (Asst Private Sec. to Minister of State, 1953-54); 3rd, later 2nd Sec., Singapore, 1955-57; FO, 1957-58; 2nd, later 1st Sec., Paris, 1958-62; FO, 1962-65; Head of Chancery, Tehran, 1965-68; Counsellor, FCO, 1969. Member of Livery, Skinners' Co., 1954. *Recreations:* golf, tennis, squash. *Address:* 15 Ernle Road, Wimbledon, SW20. *T:* 01-946 1511. *Clubs:* Royal Automobile; Royal Wimbledon Golf.

**LEAK, Hector,** CBE 1942; *b* 23 July 1887; *s* of late Dr Hector Leak and Miriam A. Bagott, Winsford, Cheshire; *m* 1916, Kathleen (*d* 1948), *d* of Capt. W. H. Ridgway, Birkenhead; four *s. Educ:* Berkhamsted Sch.; Caius Coll., Cambridge (Major Scholar). 9th Wrangler, 1908; BA 1909; entered Board of Trade, 1911; served on secretariat of International Conference on Safety of Life at Sea, 1914, of Imperial Conference, 1930, and of UK Delegation to International Monetary and Economic Conference, 1933; Asst Sec., 1932; Dir of Statistics, 1946; Adviser on Statistics, Board of Trade, 1948-51; Guy Medal, Royal Statistical Soc., 1939; Mem. of Council Royal Statistical Soc., 1933-49; Pres., 1941; Mem. of Internat. Institute of Statistics, 1937. *Publications:* Papers read before Royal Statistical Society. *Recreations:* bowls, gardening. *Address:* Bracondale, 8 Brook Barn Way, Worthing. *T:* Worthing 41091.

**LEAKE, Hugh Martin-,** ScD (Cambridge); *b* 28 Oct. 1878; *s* of late William Martin Leake, Ceylon; *m* 1914, Lois Millicent Frieda Bloxam; one *s* (elder son killed in action). *Educ:* Dulwich; Christ's Coll., Cambridge. Biologist, Bihar Indigo Planters' Association, 1901-4; Economic Botanist to Govt United Provinces, India, 1904-19; Dir of Agriculture, United Provinces, 1919-23; services to Egyptian Government, 1919; Sudan Government, 1923-24; Principal, Imperial Coll. of Tropical Agriculture, Trinidad, 1924-27. Agric. Editor, Internat. Sugar Jl, 1932-63. *Publications:* The Foundations of Indian Agriculture; Land Tenure and Agricultural Production in the Tropics; Unity, National and Imperial; Recent Advances in Agricultural Plant Breeding (with Dr H. H. Hunter); Things not Generally Said; numerous papers in scientific journals. *Recreation:* rifle shooting. *Address:* Wardington House, Wardington, near Banbury, Oxon.

**LEAKE, Sidney Henry,** OBE 1918; retired, 1958, as Chairman and Senior Managing Director of Lewis's Investment Trust, Ltd and its Associated Companies, including Selfridge's; Chairman, Water Valley Estates Ltd, Mazabuka, Zambia and Entre Rios (Pvt) Ltd, Bromley, Rhodesia, since 1963; *b* 31 May 1892; *s* of Henry and Elizabeth Leake; *m* 1924, Gertrude Elizabeth, *d* of Albert Burnell; two *s* one *d. Educ:* Model Sch. and Teachers' Training Coll., York. Ministry of Munitions, 1915-19, including service with Mil. Mission in

Russia, 1917; War Office, 1919; Colonial Office, 1920; Crosse & Blackwell, 1921-23; joined Lewis's, 1923: Gen. Manager; Director; Managing Director; Dep. Chm. *Recreations:* golf, gardening. *Address:* Entre Rios, Bromley, Rhodesia. *Club:* Salisbury (Rhodesia).

**LEAKEY, Maj.-Gen. (retd) Arundell Rea,** CB 1967; DSO 1945; MC 1941 (Bar 1942); Director and Secretary, Wolfson Foundation, since 1968; *b* 30 Dec. 1915; parents British; *m* 1950, Muriel Irene Le Poer Trench; two *s*. *Educ:* Weymouth Coll.; Royal Military Coll., Sandhurst. Command of 5th Royal Tank Regt, 1944; Instructor at Staff Coll., Camberley, 1951-52; Comdr, 1st Arab Legion Armoured Car Regt, 1954-56; Instructor (Col), Staff Coll., Camberley, 1958-60; Comdr, 7th Armoured Brigade, 1961-63; Dir-Gen. of Fighting Vehicles, 1964-66; GOC Troops in Malta and Libya, 1967-68; retired 1968. Czechoslovakian Military Cross, 1944. *Recreations:* squash, tennis. *Address:* Hurnlea, Goodworth Clatford, Andover, Hants. *Club:* United Service.

**LEAKEY, Louis Seymour Bazett,** MA, PhD, DSc (*hc*) Oxford; LLD (*hc*) California University, 1963; FBA 1958; FGS, DSc (*hc*) University of East Africa, 1965; LLD (*hc*) Guelph University, 1969; FRAI; Hon. Director of the National Centre of Pre-History and Palæontology, Nairobi; Curator of the Coryndon Memorial Museum, Nairobi, Kenya, 1945-61, Hon. Keeper of Palæontology and Pre-history, 1961, 1962; General Secretary of the Pan-African Congress on Pre-history, 1947-51 (President, 1955-59); also handwriting expert to CID Nairobi, 1943-51; *b* Kabete, 7 Aug. 1903; *er s* of late Canon H. Leakey, of CMS Kabete, Kenya; *m* 1st, 1928, H. Wilfrida, 3rd *d* of late Henry Avern, Reigate, Surrey; one *s* one *d*; 2nd, Mary Douglas, *o d* of late Erskine E. Nicol; three *s*. *Educ:* Weymouth Coll.; St John's Coll., Cambridge. Corresp. Mem. Zool. Soc. Mem. of Brit. Museum E African Expedition to Tanganyika Territory, 1924; Leader of E African Archæological Research Expeditions, 1926-27, 1928-29, 1931-32, 1934-35; Member of Govt Cttee to report on Kikuyu Land Tenure, 1929. Cuthbert Peek prize from RGS 1933; Andrée Medal of Swedish Geographical Soc., 1933; Fellow of St John's Coll., Cambridge, 1929-34; Leverhulme Research Fellow, 1933-35; Jane Ellen Harrison Memorial Lecturer, 1934; Munroe Lecturer, Edinburgh Univ., 1936; research into customs of Kikuyu tribe for Rhodes Trustees, 1937-39. Officer in charge special branch 6 of CID Nairobi, Sept. 1939-Aug. 1945. Hon. (part-time) Curator, Coryndon Museum, 1941-45; Mem. Bd of Trustees, Royal Kenya Nat. Parks, 1948-62. Trustee: Kenya Wild Life Soc., 1957; Motor Mart Trust, 1957; Vice-Pres. and Chm. Cttee of E African Kennel Club, 1957; Judge of Grand Challenge Class of E African Kennel Club Dog Show, 1958; Pres. E African Kennel Club, 1959-60; Pres. South African Archæological Soc., 1960-61; Herbert Spencer Lectr, Oxford Univ., 1960-61; Huxley Memorial Lectr, Birmingham Univ., 1961; Regent's Lectr, Univ. of California, 1963; Siliman Lectr, Yale, 1963-64; George R. Miller Prof., Univ. of Illinois, Urbana, 1965. Rivers Memorial Medal of Royal Anthrop. Inst., 1952; Henry Stopes Memorial Medal of Geological Association, 1955; Hubbard Medal of Nat. Geographic Soc. 1962 (jointly with Mrs Leakey); Viking Medal of Wenner-Gren Foundation, 1962; Swedish Vega Medal, 1963; Royal Medal, Royal Geog. Soc., London, 1964; Richard Hopper Day Memorial Medal, Acad. of Natural Sciences of Philadelphia, 1964. Haile Selassie Award (jointly), 1968; Welcome Medal, Royal African Soc., 1968; Science Medal, Acad. for Biological Sciences, Italy, 1968; Prestwich Medal, Geol. Soc. of London, 1969 (jointly with Dr M. D. Leakey); André Dumont Medal, Royal Geological Soc. of Belgium, 1969. Hon. Fellow, St John's Coll., Cambridge, 1966. Prof. at Large of Cornell Univ., 1966-; Andrew D. White Prof. at Large, Cornell Univ., 1968. Hon. Prof. of Human Anatomy and Histology, Nairobi Coll., 1969. Hon. Life Member: New York Acad. of Science, 1962; the Explorers' Club, 1964. Commander, Nat. Order of Senegal, 1968. *Publications:* New Classification of Bow and Arrow in Africa in the JRAI, 1930; The Stone-age Cultures of Kenya, 1931; Adam's Ancestors, 1934 (revised edition, 1953); The Stone-age Races of Kenya, 1935; Stone-age Africa, 1936; Kenya Contrasts and Problems, 1936; White African, 1937; A Contribution to the Study of the Tumbian Culture in Kenya (with W. E. Owen), 1945; Tentative Study of the Pleistocene Sequence and Stone-Age Cultures of NE Angola, 1949; Olduvai Gorge, 1952; Mau Mau and the Kikuyu, 1952; Animals in Africa (with Ylla), 1953; Defeating Mau Mau, 1954; The Pleistocene Fossil Suidæ of East Africa, 1958; First Lesson in Kikuyu, 1959; Olduvai Gorge, 1951-61, vol I: Unveiling Man's Origins (with V. Goodall), 1968; Animals of East Africa, 1969; articles in scientific journals; contributions to Encyclopædia Britannica, to Chambers's Encyclopædia and to The World Encyclopædia. *Recreations:* reading; tropical fish aquaria. *Address:* PO Box 15028, Langata, Nairobi, Kenya.

**LEAN, David,** CBE 1953; film director; *b* 25 March 1908; *s* of Francis William le Blount Lean and Helena Annie Tangye; *m*; one *s*; *m* 1949, Ann Todd, *qv* (marr. diss. 1957); *m* 1960, Mrs Leila Matkar. *Educ:* Leighton Park Sch., Reading. Entered film industry as number board boy, 1928; edited and did commentary for Gaumont Sound News and British Movietone News; then edited Escape Me Never, Pygmalion, 49th Parallel, etc. Co-directed, with Noel Coward, In Which We Serve. *Directed:* This Happy Breed, Blithe Spirit, Brief Encounter, Great Expectations, Oliver Twist, The Passionate Friends, Madeleine, The Sound Barrier (British Film Academy Award, 1952), Hobson's Choice, Summer Madness (Amer. title Summertime), The Bridge on the River Kwai, Lawrence of Arabia (US Academy Award, 1963, Italian silver ribbon, 1964), Doctor Zhivago, Ryan's Daughter. Officier de l'Ordre des Arts et des Lettres, France, 1968.

**LEAN, (Edward) Tangye,** CBE 1952; Director, External Broadcasting, BBC, 1964-67 (Assistant Director, 1952-64); *b* 23 Feb. 1911; 2nd *s* of Francis William le Blount Lean and Helena Anne Tangye; *m* Doreen Myra Sharp; two *s* one *d*. *Educ:* Leighton Park; University Coll., Oxford. Editor, The Isis, 1932-33. Junior Leader Writer, News Chronicle, 1934, Leader Page Editor, 1936; Govt work in England and Scandinavia, 1939-40. Talks Asst, BBC German Service, 1941; News Commentator, 1942; Editor, BBC French Service for Europe, 1943; West European Services Dir, 1945; Principal Asst to Controller European Services, 1946; Editor, European Services, 1947; Controller, European Services, 1949. Mem. British Sch. at Athens. *Publications:* Of Unsound Mind, 1931; Spirit of Death, 1932; Storm in Oxford, 1933; Voices in the Darkness, 1943; A Study of Toynbee, 1947; The Napoleonists, 1970. *Recreation:* taking a long view, preferably from Greece. *Address:* 89 Albert Street, NW1.

**LEAN, Tangye;** *see* Lean, (Edward) T.

**LEAR, Cyril James;** Editor, News of the World, since 1970; *b* 9 Sept. 1911; *s* of R. H. Lear, Plymouth; *m* Marie Chatterton; five *s* one *d*. *Educ:* Hoe Grammar Sch., Plymouth. Served War of 1939-45: Rifleman, Queen's Westminsters; Major, Royal Berks Regt. Western Morning News, 1928-32; Torquay Times, 1932-34; Daily Mail, 1934-38; Daily Telegraphy, 1938-39; News of the World, 1946-: Features Editor, Asst Editor, Dep. Editor. *Recreations:* shooting, fishing, gardening. *Address:* News of the World, 30 Bouverie Street, EC4. *T:* 01-353 3030.

**LEARMONT, Captain Percy Hewitt,** CIE 1946; RIN retired; *b* 25 June 1894; *s* of late Capt. J. Learmont, OBE, DL, JP, Penrith and Skinburness, Cumberland; *m* 1926, Doris Orynthia, *e d* of E. G. Hartley, Dunoon, Argyll; one *s* one *d*. *Educ:* HMS Conway. Served European War, HMS Alsatian, 1914-17; HMS Ceres, 1917-19; joined RIN, 1919; Comdr, 1935; Extended Defence Officer, Calcutta, 1939-41; Capt. Superintendent, HMI Dockyard, Bombay, 1941-42; in command HMIS Bahadur, 1942-43; Capt., 1942; Naval Officer-in-Charge, Calcutta, 1943-45; in command HMIS Akbar, 1945; HMIS Kakauri, 1946; retired, 1946. *Address:* Crofters, Curry Rivel, Langport, Somerset. *T:* Curry Rivel 317. *Club:* Royal Commonwealth Society.

**LEAROYD, Wing Comdr Roderick Alastair Brook,** VC 1940; RAF; *b* 5 Feb. 1913; *s* of late Major Reginald Brook Learoyd and Marjorie Scott Boadle. *Educ:* Wellington Coll. *Address:* 18 Queen's Mews, W2.

**LEASK, Lt-Gen. Sir Henry (Lowther Ewart Clark),** KCB 1970 (CB 1967); DSO 1945; OBE 1957 (MBE 1945); GOC Scotland and Governor of Edinburgh Castle, since 1969; *b* 30 June 1913; *s* of Rev. James Leask, MA; *m* Zoë de Camborne, *d* of Col W. P. Paynter, DSO, RHA; one *s* two *d*. 2nd Lt Royal Scots Fusiliers, 1936. Served War of 1939-45 in Mediterranean and Italy; GSO 1942; Bde Major Inf. Bde 1943; 2nd in Comd and CO, 8 Bn Argyll and Sutherland Highlanders, 1944-45; Comd 1st Bn London Scottish, 1946-47; Gen. Staff Mil. Ops, WO, 1947-49; Instr Staff Coll., 1949-51; Comd 1st Bn The Parachute Regt, 1952-54; Comdt, Tactical Wing Sch. of Inf., 1957-58; Comd Infantry Bde, 1958-61; Dep. Mil. Sec. to Sec. of State for War, 1962-64; GOC 52 Lowland Div., 1964-66; Dir of Army Training, MoD (Army), 1966-69. Brig. 1961, Maj.-Gen. 1964, Lt-Gen. 1969. Col of the Royal Highland Fusiliers, 1964-69; Col Comdt, Scottish Div. of Infantry, 1968-. *Recreations:* shooting and fishing. *Address:* Gogar Bank House, Edinburgh. *Club:* Army and Navy.

**LEASK, Air Vice-Marshal Kenneth Malise St Clair Graeme,** CB 1945; MC 1918; MIMechE; RAF (retired); *b* 30 Oct. 1896; *s* of late John Leask, MB, CM, Boardhouse, Birsay, Orkney; *m* 1923, Lydia Alexandrovna, *d* of Alexander N. Modestoff of Tver (Kalinin); one *d*. *Educ:* St Bees Sch.; Victoria Coll., Jersey. 2nd Lt Devon Regt 1914; seconded to Machine-Gun Corps 1915 and to RFC 1916, and trained as pilot: with BEF France in Nos 42, 41 and 84 Sqdns, 1916, Lt 1917, Capt. 1917, regular Army commission in Devonshire Regt (MC and Bar). Permanent Commission in RAF as Flight Lt, 1919; at HQ Southern Area and Inland Area, 1919-20; in No. 208 Squadron, Egypt and Turkey as Flight Comdr, 1921-23; in Directorate of Intelligence, Air Ministry, 1923-26; Squadron Leader, 1925; Senior Officers' Course, Sheerness, 1926; Officers' Long Engineering Course, 1926-28; CTO No. 4 Apprentices Wing, Halton, 1928-29; CTO Aircraft Depot, Karachi, India, 1929-32; OC No. 60 Squadron, Kohat, 1932-33; Wing Comdr 1933; Senior Engineer Staff Officer, HQ, RAF, India, 1933-34; Senior Engineer Staff Officer HQ ADGB and Bomber Command, 1935-40 (despatches); Group Capt., 1938; AOC No. 43 Group as Acting Air Commodore, 1940, and as Acting Air Vice-Marshal, 1942; Air Commodore and Air Vice-Marshal, 1946; Air Officer Commanding No. 24 Group, RAF, 1944-47. Dir-Gen. of Engineering, Air Ministry, 1947-49. *Recreation:* photography. *Address:* Per Ardua, Vache Lane, Chalfont St Giles, Bucks.

**LEASOR, (Thomas) James;** author; Director: Pagoda Films Ltd, since 1959; Jason Love Ltd, since 1964; *b* 20 Dec. 1923; *s* of late Richard and Christine Leasor, Erith, Kent; *m* 1951, Joan Margaret Bevan, Barrister-at-law, *o d* of late Roland S. Bevan, Crowcombe, Somerset; three *s*. *Educ:* City of London Sch.; Oriel Coll., Oxford. Kentish Times, 1941-42. Served in Army in Burma, India, Malaya, 1942-46, Capt. Royal Berks Regt. Oriel Coll., Oxford, 1946-48, BA 1948; MA 1952; edited The Isis. On staff Daily Express, London, 1948-55, as reporter, then columnist (William Hickey), foreign correspondent, feature writer; editorial advisor to women's magazines, Geo. Newnes and C. A. Pearson Ltd, 1955-69. Contrib. to many American and British magazines, newspapers and periodicals; scriptwriter for TV series The Michaels in Africa. OStJ. *Publications: Novels:* Not Such a Bad Day, 1946; The Strong Delusion, 1951; NTRNothing to Report, 1955; Passport to Oblivion, 1964; Spylight, 1966; Passport in Suspense, 1967; Passport for a Pilgrim, 1968; They Don't Make Them Like That Any More, 1969; A Week of Love, 1969; Never had a Spanner on Her, 1970; Love-all, 1971; *non-fiction:* Author by Profession, The Monday Story, 1951; Wheels to Fortune, The Serjeant Major, 1954; The Red Fort; (with Kendal Burt) The One That Got Away, 1956; The Millionth Chance, 1957; War at the Top, 1959; (with Peter Eton) Conspiracy of Silence, 1959; Bring Out Your Dead, 1961; Rudolf Hess: The Uninvited Envoy, 1961; Singapore: The Battle that changed the World, 1968. Also others under pseudonyms. *Recreations:* sports cars, collecting 18th-century sporting prints. *Address:* Swallowcliffe Manor, Salisbury, Wilts. *T:* Tisbury 248; Casa do Zimbro, Praia da Luz, Lagos, Algarve, Portugal. *Clubs:* Garrick, East India and Sports, Savile, Press, PEN.

**LEATHAM, Dr Aubrey (Gerald),** FRCP; Physician: St George's Hospital since 1954; National Heart Hospital since 1956; Dean, Institute of Cardiology, 1962-69; *b* 23 Aug. 1920; *s* of Dr H. W. Leatham, Godalming and Kathleen Pelham Burn, Nosely Hall, Leicester; *m* 1954, Judith Augustine Savile Freer; one *s* three *d*. *Educ:* Charterhouse; Trinity Hall, Cambridge; St Thomas' Hospital. BA Cambridge 1941; MB, BChir 1944; MRCP 1945; FRCP 1957. House Phys., St Thomas' Hosp., 1944; RMO, Nat. Heart Hosp., 1945; Phys., RAMC, 1946-47; Sherbrook Research Fellow, Cardiac Dept, and Sen. Registrar, London Hosp., 1948-50; Asst Dir, Inst. of Cardiology, 1951-54. Goulstonian Lectr, RCP, 1958. R. T. Hall Travelling Prof., Australia and NZ, 1963. Member: Brit. Cardiac Soc.; Sociedad Peruana de Cardiologia, 1966; Sociedad Colombiana de Cardiologia, 1966. Royal Order of Bhutan, 1966. *Publications:* Auscultation of the Heart and Phonocardiography, 1970; articles in

Lancet, British Heart Jl, etc, on auscultation of the heart and phonocardiography, artifical pacemakers, coronary artery disease, etc. *Recreations:* ski-ing and ski-touring, mountain walking, tennis, racquets, gardening, photography. *Address:* 75 Albert Drive, SW19. *T:* 01-788 5759; 45 Wimpole Street, W. *T:* 01-935 5295; Rookwood Lane House, West Wittering, Sussex. *T:* W Wittering 3331. *Club:* Hurlingham.

**LEATHART, Air Cdre James Anthony,** CB 1960; DSO 1940; Manager, Machinery Division, Cleanacres Ltd; *b* 5 Jan. 1915; *s* of P. W. Leathart, BSc, MD, Ear, Nose and Throat Specialist, Liverpool; *m* 1939, E. L. Radcliffe, Birkenhead; two *s* one *d*. *Educ:* St Edward's, Oxford; Liverpool Univ. Joined Auxiliary Air Force (610 County of Chester Squadron), 1936; transferred RAF, 1937; Chief of Staff Headquarters, 12 Group, RAF, 1959-61; Dir of Operational Requirements, Air Ministry, 1961-62, retd. Oct. 1962. *Recreations:* fly-fishing, motoring, ornithology, gardening. *Address:* Wortley Farmhouse, Wotton-under-Edge, Glos. *T:* Wotton-under-Edge 2312.

**LEATHEM, John Gaston,** JP; Headmaster of Taunton School, 1945-66; *b* 14 May 1906; *s* of late J. G. Leathem, MA, ScD, fellow and senior bursar of St John's Coll., Cambridge, and Annie Muir (*née* McMullan), Belfast. *Educ:* Marlborough Coll.; St John's Coll., Cambridge. Pres. Cambridge Union, 1929. Housemaster, St Lawrence Coll., Ramsgate, 1929; Asst Master, Marlborough Coll., 1932; Headmaster, King Edward VII Sch., King's Lynn, 1939; Marlborough Town Council, 1938; JP King's Lynn, 1941; Somerset Education Cttee, 1946-55; Somerset County Council, 1952-55. JP Somerset 1953; Chm. Juvenile Bench, 1959-68; Chm., Bench, 1968. *Recreations:* foreign travel, walking, hockey, fives. *Address:* 8 Parkfield Road, Taunton, Somerset. *T:* Taunton 5385. *Clubs:* Royal Over-Seas League; Somerset County (Taunton); Jesters.

**LEATHER, Sir Edwin (Hartley Cameron),** Kt 1962; Director: William Baird Ltd; William Baird Textiles Ltd; Hill Samuel & Co. Ltd (Western Board Chairman); Leather Cartage Co.; Micro Plastics Co. Ltd; Gilson Manufacturing Co., Canada; broadcaster; *b* 22 May 1919; *s* of Harold H. Leather, MBE, Hamilton, Canada, and Grace C. Leather (*née* Holmes); *m* 1940, Sheila A. A., *d* of Major A. H. Greenlees, Hamilton; two *d*. *Educ:* Trinity College Sch., Canada; Royal Military Coll., Kingston, Canada. Served War of 1939-45 with Canadian Army, UK and in Europe, 1940-45. Contested (C) South Bristol, 1945; MP (C) N Somerset, 1950-64. Exec. Cttee: British Commonwealth Producers Organisation, 1960-63; British Caribbean Assoc.; Chairman: Horder Centres for Arthritics, 1962-65; Nat. Union, Cons and Unionist Assocs, 1969- (Vice-Chm. 1967-69); Mem., Nat. Executive Cttee, and Central Board of Finance, Conservative Party, 1963-; Governor, Yehudi Menuhin Sch., and Menuhin Orchestra. Canadian Legion rep. on Exec. Cttee of Brit. Commonwealth Ex-Servicemen's League, 1954-63; Pres., Institute of Marketing, 1963-67. Chm., Bath Festival Soc., 1960-65, Trustee 1965-. Lay reader, in Church of England. Mem. Council, Imp. Soc. of Knights Bachelor, 1969-. FRSA 1969. Hon. Mem. Nat. Inst. Social Sciences, NY. Medal of Merit, Royal Canadian Legion. *Address:* 55 Melton Court, SW7. *T:* 01-589 3922; Eden Park, Batheaston, Somerset. *T:* Bath 88024. *Clubs:* Carlton; Constitutional (Bristol); Hamilton (Hamilton).

**LEATHER, Ted;** *see* Leather, Sir E. H. C.

**LEATHERLAND,** Baron, *cr* 1964, of Dunton (Life Peer); **Charles Edward Leatherland,** OBE 1951; JP; DL; Treasurer and Member of Council, University of Essex, since foundation; *b* 18 April 1898; *e s* of John Edward Leatherland, Churchover, Warwicks; *m* 1922, Mary Elizabeth, *d* of Joseph Henry Morgan, Shareshill, Staffs; one *s* one *d*. *Educ:* Harborne, Birmingham; University Extension Courses. Asst Editor, Daily Herald, until retirement, 1963. Served European War, 1914-19 (despatches, MSM); enlisted, 1914; served in France, Belgium, Germany; Company Sgt Major, Royal Warwicks Regt; Essex TA Assoc., 1946-68, and E Anglian TA Assoc., 1968. Chm., Essex County Council, 1960-61 (Vice-Chm. 1952-55 and 1958-60); CA Essex, 1946-68. Dep. Chm., Epping Magistrates Bench. JP (Essex) 1944; DL (Essex) 1963. Mem. Bd of Basildon Development Corporation, 1967-. Addtl Mem., Monopolies Commn, to consider newspaper mergers, 1969. Chm., E Counties Regional Council of the Labour Party, 1950-66. *Publications:* (part author) The Book of the Labour Party, 1925; Labour Party pamphlets; contribs on local govt affairs in Municipal Jl and general press; essays on economic and social subjects (4 Prince of Wales gold medals, 1923 and 1924). *Recreations:* formerly fox hunting, now walking. *Address:* 19 Starling Close, Buckhurst Hill, Essex. *T:* Buckhurst 3164.

**LEATHERS,** family name of **Viscount Leathers.**

**LEATHERS,** 2nd Viscount, *cr* 1954; **Frederick Alan Leathers;** Baron Leathers, 1941; Chairman: Wm Cory & Son, Ltd; Cory Mann George Ltd; R. & J. H. Rea, Ltd; Smit and Cory International Port Towage Ltd; Hull Blyth & Co. Ltd; Rea Ltd; St Denis Shipping Co. Ltd; Director: Afsa Ltd; Laporte Industries Ltd; Laporte Industries (Holdings) Ltd; Guardian Cement Co. Ltd; New Zealand Cement Holdings Ltd; Tunnel Cement Ltd; *b* 4 April 1908; *er s* of 1st Viscount Leathers, PC, CH, LLD; *S* father, 1965; *m* 1940, Elspeth Graeme, *yr d* of late Sir Thomas (Alexander) Stewart; two *s* two *d*. *Educ:* Brighton Coll.; Emmanuel Coll., Cambridge (MA (hons) in Economics). Mem. of Baltic Exchange; Underwriting Member of Lloyd's. Member: Court of Worshipful Company of Shipwrights; Court of Watermen's and Lightermen's Company; Fellow Institute of Chartered Shipbrokers; FRPSL; MInstPet. *Heir: s* Hon. Christopher Graeme Leathers [*b* 31 Aug. 1941; *m* 1964, Maria Philomena, *yr d* of Michael Merriman, Charlestown, Co. Mayo; one *s* one *d*]. *Address:* Hills Green, Kirdford, Sussex. *T:* Kirdford 202; 9 Kingston House North, Princes Gate, SW7. *T:* 01-589 8678. *Clubs:* United University, Royal Automobile.

**LEATHES, Maj.-Gen. Reginald Carteret de Mussenden,** CB 1960; MVO 1947; OBE 1952; Colonel Commandant, Royal Marines, since 1971; *b* 19 Sept. 1909; *s* of late Major Carteret de M. Leathes; *m* 1939, Marjorie Mary Elphinston; three *s* one *d*. *Educ:* Imperial Service Coll. 2nd Lt, Royal Marines, 1928; HMS Resolution, 1931-33; ADC to Governor of Queensland, 1935-37; 1st Bn Royal Marines, 1940-43; 42 Commando RM, 1943-44; GSO1 HQ, SACSEA, 1944-45; GSO1 HQ, Land Forces Hong Kong, 1945-46; HMS Vanguard, 1947; RN Staff Coll., 1947-49; 45 Commando RM, 1950-52; Comdt Amphibious Sch., RM, 1952-55; Col GS Staff Comdt Gen., RM, 1956; idc 1957, ADC to the Queen, 1957-58. Chief of Staff to Comdt Gen., RM, 1958-60; Maj.-Gen. Commanding Royal Marines, Portsmouth, 1961-62. Retired, 1962. Officer Order of Phoenix (Greece), 1933; Chevalier Legion of Honour and Croix de Guerre (France), 1945;

Officer Order of Cloud and Banner (China), 1945. *Recreations:* fishing, ski-ing. *Address:* Oaklands, Highbrook, Ardingly, Sussex. *T:* Ardingly 295. *Club:* United Service.

**LEAVEY, John Anthony,** BA; Deputy Chairman, Smith & Nephew Associated Companies Ltd; Chairman, wilson (Connolly) Holdings Ltd; Director, BIA Direct Mail Ltd; *b* 3 March 1915; *s* of George Edwin Leavey and Marion Louise Warnock; *m* 1952, Lesley Doreen, *d* of Rt Hon. Sir Benjamin Ormerod, *qv. Educ:* Mill Hill Sch.; Trinity Hall, Cambridge. Served War, 1939-46; 5th Royal Inniskilling Dragoon Guards. MP (C) Heywood and Royton Div. of Lancashire, 1955-64. *Recreation:* fishing. *Address:* c/o 2 Temple Place, Victoria Embankment, WC2. *Club:* Carlton.

**LEAVIS, Frank Raymond,** PhD; Hon. Visiting Professor of English, University of York, 1965; Hon. Fellow of Downing College, Cambridge, 1962-64 (Fellow, 1936-62); University Reader in English, 1959-62; Editor of Scrutiny, a Quarterly Review, 1932-53; *b* 14 July 1895; *s* of Harry Leavis; *m* 1929, Queenie Dorothy Roth; two *s* one *d. Educ:* Perse Sch.; Emmanuel Coll., Cambridge (Scholar). Historical Tripos and English Tripos; research and university teaching; one of the founders of Scrutiny, 1932. Cheltenham Lectr, 1968; Vis. Prof., Univ. of Wales, 1969; Churchill Prof. Dept of English, Bristol Univ., 1970. Hon. Mem. Amer. Acad. of Arts and Sciences, 1963. Hon. LittD: Leeds, 1965; York, 1967; Hon LlD Aberdeen, 1970. *Publications:* Mass Civilization and Minority Culture, 1930; D. H. Lawrence, 1930; New Bearings in English Poetry, 1932; For Continuity, 1933; Culture and Environment (with Denys Thompson), 1933; Revaluation: Tradition and Development in English Poetry, 1936; Education and the University, 1943; The Great Tradition: George Eliot, James and Conrad, 1948; The Common Pursuit, 1952; D. H. Lawrence: Novelist, 1955; Two Cultures?: The Significance of C. P. Snow, 1962; Retrospect of Scrutiny, 1963; Anna Karenina and Other Essays, 1967; (comp.) A Selection from Scrutiny, 1968; (with Q. D. Leavis) Lectures in America, 1969; English Literature in Our Time and the University, 1969; (with Q. D. Leavis) Dickens the Novelist, 1970. Editor, Towards Standards of Criticism, 1933; Determinations, 1934; Mill on Bentham and Coleridge, 1950. *Address:* 12 Bulstrode Gardens, Cambridge.

**LE BAILLY, Vice-Adm. Louis Edward Stewart Holland,** CB 1969; OBE 1952; Deputy Chief of the Defence Staff (Intelligence), since 1971; *b* 18 July 1915; *s* of Robert Francis Le Bailly and Ida Gaskell Le Bailly (*née* Holland); *m* 1946, Pamela Ruth Berthon; three *d. Educ:* RNC Dartmouth. HMS Hood, 1932; RNEC, 1933-37; HMS Hood, 1937-40; HMS Naiad, 1940-42; RNEC, 1942-44; HMS Duke of York, 1944-46; Admiralty, 1946-50; HMS Bermuda, 1950-52; RNEC, 1955-58; Admiralty: Staff Officer to Dartmouth Review Cttee, 1958; Asst Engineer-in-Chief, 1958-60; Naval Asst to Controller of the Navy, 1960-63; IDC, 1963; Dep. Dir of Marine Engineering, 1963-67; Naval Attaché, Washington, DC, and Comdr, British Navy Staff, 1967-69; Director of Service Intelligence, MoD, 1970-71. FIMechE; MInstPet; MIMarE. *Publications:* contrib. to RUSI Jl. *Recreation:* ski-ing. *Address:* c/o Barclays Bank, 36 Curzon Street, Mayfair, W1. *Club:* United Service.

**LE BAS, Air Vice-Marshal Michael Henry,** CB 1969; CBE 1966; DSO 1944; AFC 1954; Director General of Personal Services (RAF), Ministry of Defence, since 1969; *b* 28 Sept. 1916; *s* of R. W. O. Le Bas and Florence Marrs; *m* 1945, Moyra Benitz; one *s* one *d. Educ:* St George's Coll., Buenos Aires; Malvern Coll. Joined RAF, 1940; 234 Sqdn Fighter Comd, 1941; 601 Sqdn Malta and Western Desert, 1942-43; 242 Sqdn Malta, Italy, Middle East, 1943-44; comdg 241 Sqdn Italy, 1944; RAF Staff Coll., 1948-51; HQ 2 TAF and RAF Wildenrath, 1951-54; Sch. of Land Air Warfare, 1954-56; Suez, 1956; OC, RAF Coningsby, 1959-61; HQ Bomber Comd, 1961-63; SASO, Air Forces Middle East, 1963-66; AOC No. 1 Group, Bomber Command, 1966-68; AOC No. 1 (Bomber) Gp, Strike Comd, 1968. *Recreations:* golf, tennis, shooting, photography. *Address:* c/o Midland Bank, Oakham, Rutland. *Club:* Royal Air Force.

**LEBETER, Fred;** Keeper, Department of Transport and Mining, Science Museum, 1953-67; *b* 27 Dec. 1903; *e s* of Arthur Lebeter, Mining Engineer, and Lucy Wilson; *m* 1926, Sybil Leah, *o d* of Henry Ward; one *d. Educ:* Rotherham and Bridgnorth Gram. Schs; Birmingham Univ. BSc 1925; MSc (Research on Classification of British Coals) 1926. Manager, Magnesite Mines and Works, Salem, S India, 1926-31; Lecturer in Mining, Heanor Mining Sch., 1931-33; Sen. Lectr in Mining, Chesterfield Tech. Coll., 1933-37; Asst Keeper, Science Museum, 1937-39; Dep. Chief Mining Supplies Officer, Min. of Fuel and Power, 1939-47; Asst Keeper, Science Museum, 1947-49, Dep. Keeper, 1949-53. Consultant on Mine Ventilation and Underground Transport, 1931-; Mem. Council Nat. Assoc. of Colliery Managers (Midland Br.), 1935-37; Adviser to Coal Commission, Germany, on Mining Supplies, 1944; UK rep. to European Coal Organisation, 1945-47. United Kingdom delegate to European Coal Organisation, Paris, 1946. Mem., Industrial Cttee, National Museum of Wales, 1959-67. Retired 1967. *Publications:* contributor of many technical articles to Colliery Engineering, Mine and Quarry Engineering, historical articles in Zeitschrift für Kunst und Kultur im Bergbau, etc. *Recreations:* sport and gardening. *Address:* Gay Bowers, Cliff Road, Seaford, Sussex. *T:* Seaford 4751.

**LEBLANC, Rt. Rev. Camille André;** Chaplain at Caraquet Hospital; *b* Barachois, NB, 25 Aug. 1898. *Educ:* Collège Sainte-Anne, Church Point, NS; Grand Séminaire Halifax, NS. Priest, 1924; Subseq. Curé at Shemogue and the Cathedral of Nôtre Dame de l'Assomption, Moncton; Bishop of Bathurst, 1942-69. *Address:* c/o Caraquet Hospital, Caraquet, NB, Canada.

**LEBLOND, Prof. C(harles) P(hilippe),** MD, PhD, DSc; FRSC 1951; FRS 1965; Professor of Anatomy, McGill University, Canada, since 1948; *b* 5 Feb. 1910; *s* of Oscar Leblond and Jeanne Desmarchelier; *m* 1936, Gertrude Elinor Sternschuss; three *s* one *d. Educ:* Sch. St Joseph, Lille, France; Univs. of Lille, Nancy, Paris, Montreal. L-ès-S, Nancy 1932; MD Paris 1934; PhD Montreal 1942; DSc Sorbonne 1945. Asst in Histology, Med. School, Univ. of Paris, 1934-35; Rockefeller Fell., Sch. of Med., Yale Univ., 1936-37; Asst, Laboratoire de Synthèse Atomique, Paris, 1938-40; McGill Univ.: Lectr in Histology and Embryology, 1941-42; Asst Prof. of Anatomy, 1942-43; Assoc. Prof. of Anatomy, 1946-48; Prof. of Anatomy, 1948-; Chm. of Dept of Anatomy, 1957-. Mem. Amer. Assoc. of Anatomists, etc. Many special lectures and honours, etc. *Publications:* over 200 articles in anatomical journals. *Recreation:* country. *Address:* (home) 68 Chesterfield Avenue, Westmount 217, PQ, Canada. *T:* 486-4837; (office) Department of Anatomy, McGill University. *T:* 392-4931.

**le BROCQUY, Louis,** FSIA 1960; painter since 1939; *b* Dublin, 10 Nov. 1916; *s* of Albert le Brocquy, MA, and Sybil Staunton; *m* 1st, 1938, Jean Stoney (marr. diss., 1948); one *d*; 2nd, 1958, Anne Madden Simpson; two *s*. *Educ:* St Gerard's Sch., Wicklow, Ireland. Self-taught. Founder-mem. of Irish Exhibn of Living Art, 1943; Visiting Instructor, Central Sch. of Arts and Crafts, London, 1947-54; Visiting Tutor, Royal Coll. of Art, London, 1955-58. Mem., Irish Council of Design, 1963-65. Dir, Kilkenny Design Workshops, 1965-. Represented Ireland, Venice Biennale (awarded internat. prize), 1956. Work exhibited in "50 Ans d'Art Moderne", Brussels, 1958; Marzotto, 1962-63, 1968-69; Pittsburgh Internat., 1961-62, 1964-65; Recklinghausen, 1966, 1967; "Art Vivant", Fondation Maeght, 1967, 1968; Rijeka, 1968, 1970; Biennale, Tokyo, 1970-71. One Man Shows: Leicester Galleries, London, 1948; Gimpel Fils, London, 1947, 1949, 1951, 1955, 1956, 1957, 1959, 1961, 1966, 1968; Waddington Galleries, Dublin, 1951; Robles Gallery, Los Angeles, 1960; Gallery Lienhard, Zürich, 1961; Dawson Gallery, Dublin, 1962, 1966, 1969; Municipal Gallery of Modern Art, Dublin, 1966; Ulster Gallery, Belfast (retrospective), 1966-67; Gimpel-Hanover, Zürich, 1969. Public Collections possessing work include: Albright Museum, Buffalo; Arts Council, London; Carnegie Inst., Pittsburgh; Chicago Arts Club; Detroit Inst. of Art; Dublin Municipal Gallery; Fort Worth Center, Texas; J. H. Hirshhorn Foundation, NY; Fondation Maeght, St Paul; Leeds City Art Gallery; Museo de Arte Moderna, São Paolo; Tate Gallery; Ulster Museum, Belfast; V. & A. Museum. RHA 1950-69. Hon. DLitt Dublin, 1962. Commandeur du Bontemps de Médoc et des Graves, 1969. *Illustrated work:* The Táin, trans. Thomas Kinsella, 1969; The Playboy of the Western World, Synge, 1970. *Address:* c/o Gimpel Fils, 50 South Molton Street, W1.

**LE CARRÉ, John;** *see* Cornwell, David John Moore.

**LE CHEMINANT, Peter;** Assistant Secretary, Ministry of Technology (formerly Ministry of Power), since 1968; *b* 29 April 1926; *s* of William Arthur Le Cheminant; *m* 1959, Suzanne Elisabeth Horny; three *s*. *Educ:* Holloway Sch.; London Sch. of Economics. Sub-Lt, RNVR, 1944-47. Min. of Power, 1949, 1952-62 and 1963-64 (Asst Private Sec. to Minister of Power, 1954-55); Cabinet Office, 1950-52 and 1964-65; UK Delegn to ECSC, 1962-63; Private Sec. to Prime Minister, 1965-68. *Recreation:* water sports. *Address:* 87 Manor Road North, Hinchley Wood, Esher, Surrey.

**LE CHEMINANT, Air Vice-Marshal Peter de Lacey,** CB 1968; DFC 1943, and Bar, 1951; Commandant Joint Warfare Establishment, Ministry of Defence, 1968-70; *b* 17 June 1920; *s* of Lieut-Colonel Keith Le Cheminant and Blanche Etheldred Wake Le Cheminant (*née* Clark); *m* 1940, Sylvia, *d* of J. van Bodegom; one *s* two *d*. *Educ:* Elizabeth Coll., Guernsey; RAF Coll., Cranwell. Flying posts in France, UK, N Africa, Malta, Sicily and Italy, 1940-44; comd No. 223 Squadron, 1943-44; Staff and Staff Coll. Instructor, 1945-48; Far East, 1949-53; comd No. 209 Sqn, 1949-51; Jt Planning Staff, 1953-55; Wing Comdr, Flying, Kuala Lumpur, 1955-57; jssc 1958; Dep. Dir of Air Staff Plans, 1958-61; comd RAF Geilenkirchen, 1961-63; Dir of Air Staff Briefing, 1964-66; SASO, HQ FEAF, 1966-67, C of S, 1967-68. *Recreations:* golf, swimming, shooting. *Address:* c/o Ministry of Defence, Whitehall, SW1. *Club:* Royal Air Force.

**LECHIN-SUAREZ, Brigadier General Juan,** Condor de los Andes, Guerrillero José Miguel Lanza, Mérito Aeronautico, Mérito Naval (Bolivia); Bolivian Ambassador to the Court of St James's and to the Netherlands since 1970; *b* 8 March 1921; *s* of Juan Alfredo Lechín and Julia Suárez; *m* 1947, Ruth Varela; one *s* three *d*. *Educ:* Bolivian Military College. Chief of Ops, Bolivian Army HQ, 1960-61; Military and Air Attaché, Bolivian Embassy, Bonn, 1962-63; Comdr, Bolivian Army Fifth Inf. Div., 1964; Pres., Bolivian State Mining Corp. (with rank of Minister of State), 1964-68; Comdr, Bolivian Army Third Inf. Div., 1969. Mem., Internat. Tin Research Council, 1970-. Das Grosse Verdienstcreuz (Fed. Rep. Germany). *Recreations:* tennis, swimming. *Address:* Bolivian Embassy, 106 Eaton Square, SW1. *T:* 01-235 4248.

**LECHMERE, Sir Berwick (Hungerford),** 6th Bt, *cr* 1818; JP; Land Agent; *b* 21 Sept. 1917; *s* of Sir Ronald Berwick Hungerford Lechmere, 5th Bt, and of Constance Marguerite (*née* Long); *S* father, 1965; *m* 1954, Norah Garrett Elkington; no *c*. *Educ:* Charterhouse; Magdalene Coll., Cambridge. High Sheriff of Worcs, 1962, JP, 1966. FRICS, FLAS. *Heir: cousin* Reginald Anthony Hungerford Lechmere [*b* 24 Dec. 1920; *m* 1956, Anne Jennifer Dind; three *s* one *d*]. *Address:* Severn End, Hanley Castle, Worcester. *T:* Upton-on-Severn 2130.

**LECKIE, John,** CB 1955; Deputy Secretary, Ministry of Technology, since 1964; *b* 2 Sept. 1911; *o s* of late Alexander M. Leckie; *m* 1937, Elizabeth Mary Murray Brown; two *s*. *Educ:* Hamilton Academy; Glasgow Univ. (MA, BSc). Entered Administrative Class, Home Civil Service, by competitive examination, 1934; Customs and Excise Dept, 1934; transferred to Board of Trade, 1940; Head of Board of Trade Delegation, Washington, USA, 1943-45; Adviser on Commercial Policy, 1950; Under-Secretary, Board of Trade, 1950-60; Second Secretary, Board of Trade, 1960-64. *Address:* Mackery End, Moor Lane, Rickmansworth, Herts. *T:* Rickmansworth 73218.

**LECKIE, Air Marshal Robert,** CB 1943; DSO 1917; DSC 1916; DFC 1918; retired; *o s* of late Samuel Leckie, Glasgow; *m* Bernice, *y d* of Mrs Douglas O'Kane, La Plata, Maryland, USA. *Educ:* Glasgow. Joined RNAS 1915; served in North Sea, European War, 1914-18 (despatches, DSC, DFC, DSO); Lieut-Colonel 1st Central Ontario Regt; commanded No. 1 Canadian Wing, RCAF; Director of Flying Operations, Canadian Air Board, 1920; Member Canadian Air Board, 1921-22; Boys' Training Wing, Halton (RAF), 1922; RN Staff Coll., England, 1922-23; HQ Staff Coastal Comd, 1923-25; commanded: (RAF) HMS Hermes (Aircraft Carrier), 1925-27; (RAF) HMS Courageous (Aircraft Carrier), 1927-29; RAF Station, Bircham Newton, 1929-31; at RAF Marine Experimental Station, Felixstowe, England, 1931; commanded: 210 Flying Boat Squadron, 1931; RAF Station, Pembroke Dock, 1931-33; RAF Station, Hendon, 1933-35; Supt RAF Reserve, i/c Elem. Civil Flying Schools, 1933-35; ADC to the King, 1936; Director of Training, Air Ministry, 1935-38; commanded RAF Medit. (HQ Malta), 1938-39; to Canada as Director of Training, RCAF, 1940; Member Air Council for Training, RCAF, 1940; Acting Chief of Air Staff, RCAF, 1943; Chief of Air Staff, RCAF, 1944; retired, 1947. Order of Polonia Restituta, 1st Class (Poland); US Legion of Merit, Degree of Commander; Order of White Lion, Class II (Czechoslovakia); Commandeur de la Légion d'Honneur (France). *Publications:*

various articles, magazines and service journals. *Recreations:* golf, hunting and fishing. *Clubs:* Royal Air Force; Gatineau Fish and Game.

**LECKONBY, William Douglas,** CBE 1967; Collector of Customs and Excise, London, 1963-67, retired; *b* 23 April 1907; *m* 1933; one *d. Educ:* Hymers Coll., Hull. Entered Customs and Excise, 1928; subsequently held various posts in that department. *Address:* Ebor, Withyham Road, Groombridge, Sussex. *T:* Groombridge 481.

**LECKY, Arthur Terence,** CMG 1968; *b* 10 June 1919; *s* of late Lieut-Colonel M. D. Lecky, DSO, late RA, and late Bertha Lecky (*née* Goss); *m* 1946, Jacqualine, *d* of late Dr A. G. Element; three *s. Educ:* Winchester Coll.; Clare Coll., Cambridge (1938-39). Served RA, 1939-46. FO (Control Commission for Germany), 1946-49; FO, 1950-54; Vice-Consul, Zürich, 1954-56; FO, 1957-61; First Secretary, The Hague, 1962-64, FCO (formerly FO), 1964-70, retired. *Address:* Harthill House, Godshill, Fordingbridge, Hants. *T:* Fordingbridge 2070.

**LECLERC, Maj.-Gen. Pierre Edouard,** CBE 1943; MM; ED; CD; *b* 20 Jan. 1893; *s* of late Pierre Leclerc, Civil Engineer, Montreal; *m* 1st, 1918, Esther (*d* 1956), *d* of Capt. Olsen Norlie, Bergen, and Arundal, Norway; one *d*; 2nd, 1958, Germaine, *d* of late Robert Sarra-Bournet, Montreal. *Educ:* Mont St Louis Coll., Montreal; Methodist Institute, Westmount, PQ. Joined Canadian Expeditionary Force, 1915, as Sapper; commissioned, 1916; qualified Canadian Militia Staff Course, 1935; commanded 5th Canadian Infantry Bde, 1940 (overseas); Maj.-General, 1942; GOC 7th Canadian Div., 1942; GOC Canadian and Newfoundland Army Forces, Newfoundland, Oct. 1943; retired from Canadian Army, 1945. Mem., Sir Arthur Currie Branch, Montreal, Quebec, The Royal Canadian Legion, 1945. Hon. Colonel Le Regt de Joliette, 1955-; Hon. President Canadian Corps Association, 1956. *Address:* 5045 MacDonald Avenue, Apartment 4, Montreal 248, Quebec, Canada. *Clubs:* Canadian (Montreal); Royal Commonwealth Society (Montreal Branch).

**LECONFIELD,** 6th Baron; *see under* Egremont, 1st Baron.

**LEDERBERG, Prof. Joshua,** PhD; Professor and Executive Head, Department of Genetics, School of Medicine, Stanford University, USA, since 1959; *b* Montclair, NJ, USA, 23 May 1925; *s* of Zwi H. and Esther Lederberg (*née* Goldenbaum); *m* 1968, Marguerite Stein Kirsch, MD. *Educ:* Stuyvesant High Sch., NYC; Columbia Coll. (BA); Yale Univ. (PhD). Assistant Professor of Genetics, University of Wisconsin, 1948; Associate Professor, 1950; Professor, 1954. Shared in discoveries concerning genetic re-combination, and organization of genetic material of bacteria, contributing to cancer research; discovered a method of artificially introducing new genes into bacteria in investigation of hereditary substance. Member: National Academy of Sciences, United States, 1957. ScD (*hc*): Yale Univ.; Columbia Univ.; Univ. of Wisconsin; MD (*hc*), Univ. of Turin. (Jointly) Nobel Prize in Medicine, 1958. *Publications:* contribs to learned journals on genetics, bacteria and general biological problems; weekly column on Science and Man, Washington Post, 1966-. *Address:* Department of Genetics, Stanford University, Stanford, California 94305, USA. *T:* 415-3211200.

**LEDGER, Claude Kirwood,** CBE 1943; retired; *b* Hereford, 1 Jan. 1888; 3rd *s* of Rev. Charles George Ledger and Isabel Mary Kirwood; *m* 1919, Elsie (*née* Litton); two *s* two *d. Educ:* Christ's Hospital; Hereford Cathedral Sch.; Wadham Coll., Oxford (BA 1911); Hannover and Marburg; Paris; Gray's Inn. Modern Languages Master at Leighton Park Sch., Reading, 1911-12, and at Haberdashers' Aske's Boys' Sch., Cricklewood, 1912-13; Vice-Consul, Antwerp, 1914; New York, 1914-20; Chargé d'Affaires, Dominican Republic, 1920-22; Consul, Belgian and French Congo, 1922-24; Madeira and Azores, 1924-31; Acting Consul-General, Monrovia, 1926-27; Consul, Bordeaux, 1931-37; Havre, 1937-40; Consul-General, Strasbourg, 1940; Lourenço-Marques, 1940-44; Léopoldville, 1944-46; Strasbourg, 1946-48; Tetuan, Spanish Morocco; retired, 1948. Coronation Medal, 1937. *Recreation:* philately. *Address:* 2 Castleway, Steyning, Sussex BN3 4FG.

**LEDGER, Sir Frank, (Joseph Francis),** Kt 1963; Company Director (engineering etc.); *b* 29 Oct. 1899; *s* of Edson and Annie Frances Ledger; *m* 1923, Gladys Muriel Lyons; one *s* two *d. Educ:* Perth Boys' Sch., Perth, WA. Chairman of Directors: J. & E. Ledger Pty Ltd; J. & E. Ledger Sales Pty Ltd; Ledger Electrics Pty Ltd (formerly C. A. Hine & Co. Pty Ltd); Governing Director, Ledger Investments; Chairman of Directors, S Australian Insurance Co.; Director: Chamber of Manufrs Insurance Co.; ARC Engineering Co.; Winget Moxey (WA) Pty Ltd; Lake View and Star Ltd; Member, Past Chairman, WA Branch of Inst. of Directors (London); Chairman, WA Government Industrial Development Advisory Cttee; President, Royal Commonwealth Society (WA Branch); Past President: WA Chamber of Manufacturers; WA Employers Federation; Ironmasters Assoc. (WA); Metal Industries Assoc. (WA); Inst. of Foundrymen (WA); Past Vice-President, Associated Chamber of Manufacturers (Canberra). *Recreations:* golfing, sailing. *Address:* (office) 231-249 Pier Street, Perth, Western Australia; (home) 2 The Esplanade, Peppermint Grove, Western Australia. *Clubs:* Weld, Perth, Royal Freshwater Bay Yacht, Cottesloe Golf; WA Turf, WA Trotting Association, WA Cricket Association (all in Perth, WA).

**LEDGER, Sir Joseph Francis;** *see* Ledger, Sir Frank.

**LEDGER, Ronald Joseph;** *b* 7 Nov. 1920; *s* of Arthur and Florence Ledger; *m* 1946, Madeleine Odette de Villeneuve; three *s* one *d. Educ:* Skinners Grammar Sch., Tunbridge Wells; Nottingham Univ. Toolroom Engineer, 1938-42. Served RAF, 1942-47, fitter, Leading Aircraftsman; India three years. Univ. of Nottingham, 1947-49 (Diploma in Social Science); Staff Training Officer, Enfield Highway Co-op. Society, 1949; Business Partner, 1950, Company Director, 1953, Employment Specialists. Mem. Herts CC, 1952-54. Contested (Lab) Rushcliffe Div. of Nottingham, 1951; MP (Lab and Co-op) Romford, 1955-70. Director: Enfield Electronics (CRT) Ltd, 1958; London Co-operative Society Ltd, 1961. Chairman, Hairdressing Council, 1966-. Proprietor, Halland Hotel, Seaview, Isle of Wight. *Recreations:* tennis, cricket, golf, snooker. *Address:* The Boat House, Pier Road, Seaview, Isle of Wight. *T:* Seaview 2222. *Clubs:* Sandown and Shanklin Golf, Ryde Golf, Enfield Golf.

**LEDINGHAM, Colonel George Alexander,** DSO 1940; MC; *b* 8 March 1890; *e s* of late Alexander

Ledingham, SSC, Advocate in Aberdeen; *m* 1918, Ethel Curtis Thomson (marr. diss., 1952); one *d*. Served European War (despatches, MC, wounded); commanded 98th (Surrey and Sussex Yeomanry QMR) Field Regt, RA, 1937-42 (despatches twice, DSO); Colonel, 1942; Commander Military Government, South Brabant, on liberation, 1944, and Province of Westphalia occupation, 1945; Secretary-General United Nations War Crimes Commission, 1945-48. *Recreations:* riding, shooting; played Rugby football for Scotland, 1913; captained United Services *v* South Africans, 1917. *Address:* Peplow, Private Bag J 185, Umtali, Rhodesia. *Club:* Salisbury (Salisbury, Rhodesia).

**LEDINGHAM, Prof. John Marshall,** MD, FRCP; Consultant Physician, The London Hospital, since 1954; Professor of Experimental Medicine, University of London, at London Hospital Medical College, since 1964 (University Reader in Medicine, 1953-64); *b* 1916; *s* of late Prof. Sir John C. G. Ledingham, CMG, FRS, of The Lister Institute, London, and of Lady Barbara Ledingham; *m* 1950, Josephine, *d* of late Matthew and Jane Metcalf, Temple Sowerby, Westmorland; two *s*. *Educ:* Whitgift Sch.; University College, London; The London Hospital. BSc (London) First Class Hons in Physics, 1936; MRCS, LRCP, 1942; MD (London) Gold Medal, 1951, FRCP, 1957. Service in RAMC as Graded Clinical and Experimental Pathologist, in UK, France, Middle and Far East, 1942-47. Lectr in Medicine, 1948. Editor, Dep. Chm. and Chm. Editorial Bd, Clinical Science, 1965-70. *Publications:* numerous scientific, mainly in field of hypertension and renal disease, 1938-. *Address:* 41 Dollis Avenue, N3. *T:* 01-346 1531.

**LEDUC, Paul,** BA, LLD; Barrister; *b* 28 Jan. 1889; *s* of Napoléon Leduc and Joséphine Béliveau; *m* 1917, Gabrielle Belcourt; one *s* one *d*. *Educ:* Collège Ste Marie, Montreal; Seminary of Quebec; Laval Univ. Called Quebec Bar, 1911; Practised Quebec until 1915, then moved to Ottawa; called Ontario Bar, 1916; practised law Ottawa, 1916-34, when retired from practice upon joining cabinet; MLA for Province of Ontario for the Riding of Ottawa East, 1934-40; Minister of Mines for Ontario, 1934-40; Attorney-General for Ontario, April to October 1937; Registrar Supreme Court of Canada, 1940-58. QC (Quebec), 1927; (Ontario), 1934. *Recreation:* reading. *Address:* 200 Rideau Terrace, Ottawa, Canada.

**LEDWIDGE, William Bernard John,** CMG 1964; HM Ambassador to Finland since 1969; *b* 9 Nov. 1915; *s* of late Charles Ledwidge and Eileen O'Sullivan; *m* 1948, Anne Kingsley (marr. diss. 1970); one *s* one *d*. *Educ:* Cardinal Vaughan Sch.; King's Coll., Cambridge; Princeton Univ., USA. Commonwealth Fund Fellow, 1937-39; served War of 1939-45: RA 1940; Indian Army, 1941-45. Private Secretary to Permanent Under-Secretary, India Office, 1946; Secretary, Frontier Areas Cttee of Enquiry, Burma, 1947; Foreign Office, 1947-49; British Consul, St Louis, USA, 1949-52; First Secretary, British Embassy, Kabul, 1952-56; Political Adviser British Military Govt, Berlin, 1956-61; Foreign Office, 1961-65; Minister, Paris, 1965-69. *Recreations:* golf, bridge, chess. *Address:* British Embassy, Helsinki, Finland. *Club:* Travellers'.

**LEE, Rt. Rev. Albert William;** Archdeacon of Vryheid and Zululand, 1928-35; Bishop of Zululand, 1935-46. *Publications:* Charles Johnson of Zululand, 1930; Once Dark Country; Zulu Knight-errant. *Address:* Cascades, Eshowe PO, Zululand, South Africa.

**LEE, Maj.-Gen. Alec Wilfred,** CB 1946; MC 1915; retired; *b* 20 Aug. 1896; *s* of late Wilfred Lee, Heathfield, Nailsea, Somerset; *m* 1938, Mary Alison Horn (*d* 1939); *m* 1947, Pamela Blanche Hammick, MBE (*d* 1969), *yr d* of late Capt. S. F. Hammick; *m* 1970, Margaret Lyndsey Norman, Te Puke, New Zealand. *Educ:* Clifton Coll. Commissioned S Stafford Regt, 1914; served France and Italy, 1915-19 (despatches 6 times); Captain, 1923; Bt Major, 1932; psc; Directing Staff, Staff Coll., 1933-36; Bt Lt-Col, 1936; transferred Royal Irish Fusiliers, 1937; Col, 1939; Brig., 1940; served France, 1939-40 (despatches); Libya, 1942-43; D/Comdr British Army Staff, Washington, 1944-47; Temp. Maj.-Gen., 1944; ADC to King, 1946-47. Colonel: S Stafford Regt, 1954-59; The Staffordshire Regt (The Prince of Wales's), 1959-61; retired, 1947. Commander Legion of Merit (USA). *Publications:* articles for Encyclopædia Britannica. *Recreations:* sailing, fishing, polo, travel. *Address:* Red Poulden, Tisbury, Wilts. *T:* Tisbury 287. *Clubs:* Naval and Military; Royal Dart Yacht; Cruising Association.

**LEE, Sir Arthur (James),** KBE 1966 (CBE 1959); MC and Bar (1939-45); Company Director; National President, Returned Services League, Australia, since 1960 (State President, 1954-60); *b* 30 July 1912; *s* of Arthur James and Kathleen Maud Lee; *m* 1945, Valerie Ann Scanlan; three *s* one *d*. *Educ:* Collegiate School of St Peter, Adelaide. Company Director, Lee's Hotels Ltd; Chm. Trustees, World War Two Services Welfare Fund, S Australia; Trustee, Australian War Memorial; Chm., Regional Cttees Services Canteen Fund, S Australia. *Recreation:* golf. *Address:* 148 Grant Avenue, Toorak Gardens, SA 5065, Australia. *T:* 35106. *Clubs:* Adelaide, Naval and Military, Royal Adelaide Golf (Adelaide).

**LEE, Arthur Michael,** DSC 1941; QC 1961; **His Honour Judge Lee;** Judge of County Courts, Circuit 53, since 1962; Deputy Chairman Hampshire Quarter Sessions, since 1960; *b* 22 Aug. 1913; *s* of Edward Cornwall Lee and Katherine Sybil Lee (*née* Wilberforce); *m* 1940, Valerie Burnett Georges Drake-Brockman; two *s*. *Educ:* Horris Hill Preparatory Sch.; Winchester Coll. (Scholar); Brasenose Coll. (Heath Harrison Exhibitioner), Oxford. Honours Degree in Philosophy, Politics and Economics, 1935, in Law, 1936. Called to Bar, Middle Temple (Harmsworth Exhibitioner), 1937. Served War of 1939-45, RNVR: served in destroyers, Atlantic convoys; Lieut, 1939; Lieut-Commander, 1943; Acting Commander, 1945. Returned to practice at the Bar, Jan. 1946; Recorder of Penzance, 1960-62. Chairman Governors, Horris Hill Sch., Newbury, 1964. *Publications:* ed Shawcross on Motor Insurance, 1947; ed Shaw on Evidence in Criminal Cases, 1950. *Recreations:* golf, fishing. *Address:* The Manor Farm House, Easton, Winchester, Hants. *T:* Itchen Abbas 277. *Club:* Athenæum.

**LEE, Air Vice-Marshal Arthur Stanley Gould,** MC 1917; retired; *b* 31 Aug. 1894; *s* of late Arthur Lee, Nottinghamshire; *m* 1st, 1916, Gwyneth (*d* 1951), *d* of late Robert Lewis, Cheshire; one *d*; 2nd, 1953, Fay, *widow* of Sqdn-Leader M. R. Atkinson (killed air operations, 1942). Served European War, 1914-18: Sherwood Foresters, RFC (46 Fighter Sqn), RAF; Air Headquarters, Iraq, 1925-27; psa 1928; No. 10 (B) Squadron, 1929-30; Air Ministry (Air Staff), 1931-34; idc 1935; commanded RAF Station, Hornchurch (54, 65 and 74 Fighter Sqns), 1935-37; Group Captain, 1938; Air

Commodore, 1942; Air Vice-Marshal, 1945; Chief Instructor, Turkish Air Force Staff Coll., 1937-40; SAO, British Air Forces, Greece, 1941 (despatches, Order of King George I of Greece, with crossed swords); Deputy SASO, Middle East HQ, 1941-42; SASO, No. 12 Group, Fighter Command, 1943-44 (despatches); Chief of Air Section, British Armistice Control Commn, Roumania, 1944; Chief of British Military-Air Mission to Marshal Tito, Yugoslavia, 1945; retired, 1946. Chm., Anglo-Turkish Soc., 1958-62, Vice-Pres., 1962-. Order of Partisan Star, Yugoslavia, 1970. *Publications:* Special Duties in the Balkans and the Near East, 1946; The Royal House of Greece, 1948; Crown against Sickle (story of King Michael of Roumania), 1950; The Empress Frederick Writes to Sophie, Crown Princess of Greece (edited), 1955; Helen, Queen Mother of Roumania, 1956; The Son of Leicester, 1964; The Flying Cathedral (S. F. Cody), 1965; No Parachute (RFC, 1917), 1968; Open Cockpit, 1969; and some fiction. *Address:* 52 Queen's Gate Terrace, SW7. *T:* 01-584 0929. *Club:* Royal Air Force.

**LEE, Mrs Asher;** *see* Lee, Mollie Carpenter.

**LEE, Air Chief Marshal Sir David (John Pryer),** GBE 1969 (KBE 1965; CBE 1947; OBE 1943); CB 1953; UK Military Representative to NATO, 1968-71; *b* 4 Sept. 1912; *s* of late John Lee, Byron Crescent, Bedford; *m* 1938, Denise, *d* of late Louis Hartoch; one *s* one *d*. *Educ:* Bedford Sch.; RAF Coll., Cranwell. NWFP, India, 1933-36; Central Flying Sch., Upavon, 1937; RAF Examining Officer, Supt. of Reserve, 1938-39; Bomber Command, Hemswell, 1939-40; RAF Staff Coll. (student), 1942; Deputy Director Plans, Air Ministry, 1943-44; OC 904 Fighter Wing, Batavia, Java, 1945-46; Directing Staff, RAF Staff Coll., 1948-50; Deputy Director Policy, Air Ministry, 1951-53; OC RAF Scampton, Lincs, 1953-55; Secretary, Chiefs of Staff Cttee, Ministry of Defence, 1956-59; AOC, AFME (Aden), 1959-61; Comdt, RAF Staff Coll., 1962-65; Air Member for Personnel, MoD, 1965-68. *Address:* Danemore Cottage, South Godstone, Surrey.

**LEE, Sir Desmond;** *see* Lee, Sir H. D. P.

**LEE, Edward,** MSc, PhD; Deputy Controller (R), Ministry of Technology, since 1965; *b* 2 March 1914; *s* of Thomas and Florence Lee; *m* 1942, Joan Pearson; three *d*. *Educ:* Consett Grammar Sch.; Manchester Univ.; Pembroke Coll., Cambridge. Admiralty Research Laboratory, 1939-46; Ministry of Defence, 1946-48; Dept of Physical Research, Admiralty, 1948-51; Admiralty Research Laboratory, 1951-55; Dir of Operational Research, Admty, 1955-58; Dep. Dir, Nat. Physical Laboratory, 1958-60; Director, Stations and Industry Div., DSIR, 1960-65. *Publications:* scientific papers. *Recreations:* golf, gardening. *Address:* 8 Courtlands Avenue, Hampton, Middlesex. *T:* 01-979 1081. *Club:* Athenæum.

**LEE, (Edward) Stanley,** FRCS; Senior Surgeon Westminster Hospital; late Director of Surgical Studies, Westminster Medical School; Consultant in Surgery of Neoplastic Diseases, Queen Alexandra Military Hospital; Surgeon: Guildford Radiotherapy Centre; St Luke's Nursing Home for the Clergy; *b* 1907. *Educ:* Westminster Hospital. MB, BS 1931; FRCS, 1933; MS London, 1936. Past Member of Court of Examiners, Royal College of Surgeons, England, 1953-59; Member: Grand council British Empire Cancer Campaign; Internat. Union against Cancer; Mem. Nat. Cttee, Assoc. of Head and Neck Oncologists of GB. FRSM; Fellow, Assoc. of Surgeons. Hon. Mem. Faculty of Radiologists; Mem. British Institute of Radiology. *Publications:* contributions to medical literature, etc. *Address:* 61 Harley Street, W1. *T:* 01-637 2117; Westminster Hospital, SW1. *Club:* Athenæum.

**LEE, Rt. Hon. Sir Frank (Godbould),** PC 1962; GCMG 1959 (CMG 1946); KCB 1950; Master of Corpus Christi College, Cambridge, 1962-June 1971; Hon. Fellow, Downing College, Cambridge; Fellow, London Graduate School of Business Studies, since 1966; *b* 26 Aug. 1903; *o s* of Joseph G. and Florence Lee, Brentwood, Essex; *m* 1937, Kathleen Mary Harris; three *d*. *Educ:* Brentwood Sch.; Downing Coll., Cambridge. Entered CS, 1926; Colonial Office, 1926-40; served in Nyasaland, 1931-33; Imperial Defence Coll., 1938; transferred Treasury, 1940; Treasury Delegation, Washington, 1944-46; transferred Ministry of Supply, 1946, Dep. Secretary, 1947; Minister at Washington, 1948; Permanent Secretary: Board of Trade, 1951-59; Min. of Food, 1959-61; Treasury (Joint), 1960-62; retired, Oct. 1962. Mem. Council, Univ. of E Anglia; Governor, LSE; Chm. Governors, Leys Sch., Cambridge. Hon. LLD, London. *Recreation:* walking. *Address:* The Master's Lodge, Corpus Christi College, Cambridge. *T:* 55345; Newnham Path, Church Rate Walk, Cambridge. *Clubs:* MCC; Hawks (Cambridge).

**LEE, Rt. Hon. Frederick,** PC 1964; MP (Lab) Newton Division of Lancashire, since 1950 (Hulme Division of Manchester, 1945-50); *b* 3 Aug. 1906; *s* of Joseph Wm and Margaret Lee; *m* 1938; one *d*. *Educ:* Langworthy Road Sch. Engineer. Chairman: Works Cttee, Metro-Vickers Ltd, Trafford Park, Manchester; National Cttee, Amal. Engineering Union, 1944-45; formerly: Member Salford City Council; Parliamentary Private Secretary to Chancellor of Exchequer; Parliamentary Secretary, Ministry of Labour and National Service, 1950-51; Minister of Power, 1964-66; Secretary of State for the Colonies, 1966-67; Chancellor of the Duchy of Lancaster, 1967-69. *Address:* Sunnyside, 52 Ashton Road, Newton-le-Willows, Lancs.

**LEE, George Russell,** CMG 1970; Acting Assistant Director, Ministry of Defence, since 1967; *b* 11 Nov. 1912; *s* of Ernest Harry Lee and Alice Mary Lee (*née* Russell); *m* 1947, Annabella Evelyn (*née* Dargie); one *s* one *d*. *Educ:* Birkenhead Sch., Cheshire. WO and MoD, 1940-. *Address:* 30 Christ Church Crescent, Radlett, Herts. *T:* Radlett 5914.

**LEE, Sir (George) Wilton,** Kt 1964; TD 1940; Chairman of Arthur Lee & Sons Ltd and Group of Companies, since 1949, Managing Director, 1949-68 and since 1970; *b* 8 April 1904; *e s* of Percy W. Lee, Tapton Holt, Sheffield; *m* 1934, Bettina Stanley, *e d* of Colonel R. B. Haywood, TD; three *s*. *Educ:* Uppingham Sch.; Queens' Coll., Cambridge. TA, 1922-40; Major RE, 1935. Twelve months American steel mills; Member Exec. Cttee, BISF, 1953-67 (Joint Vice-President, 1966-67); Chairman, British Independent Steel Producers' Assoc., 1967-69; Mem. Iron and Steel Advisory Cttee, 1967-; Chm. S Yorks Industrialists' Council; Director: The Glover Group Ltd; Jonas Woodland & Sons Ltd; Chm., S Yorks Board of Eagle Star Insurance Co. Ltd. Master Cutler, 1950-51. Chm. City of Sheffield Cons. and Nat. Lib. Fedn., 1959-70; Mem. Exec. Cttee of Yorks Provincial Area. Town Trustee of the City of Sheffield; JP, 1950-64. Vice-Consul for Norway. *Recreations:* golf, shooting, fishing. *Address:* Birkett House, Lindrick Common, near Worksop,

Nottinghamshire. *T:* Dinnington 2810. *Clubs:* Golfers'; Sheffield (Sheffield); Royal and Ancient.

**LEE, Sir (Henry) Desmond (Pritchard),** Kt 1961; MA; Senior Research Fellow, University College, Cambridge; *b* 30 Aug. 1908; *s* of Rev. Canon Henry Burgass Lee; *m* 1935, Elizabeth, *d* of late Colonel A. Crookenden, CBE, DSO; one *s* two *d. Educ:* Repton Sch. (George Denman Scholar); Corpus Christi Coll., Cambridge (Entrance Scholar). 1st Class Part 1 Classical Tripos, 1928; Foundation Scholar of the College; 1st Class Part 2 Classical Tripos, 1930; Charles Oldham Scholar; Fellow of Corpus Christi Coll., 1938, Life Fellow, 1948-68; Tutor, 1935-48; University Lecturer in Classics, 1937-48. Member of the Council of the Senate, 1944-48; Regional Commissioner's Office, Cambridge, 1941-44. Headmaster of Clifton Coll., 1948-54; Headmaster of Winchester Coll., 1954-68. Mem. Anderson Cttee on Grants to Students, 1958-59; Chm., Headmasters' Conference, 1959-60, 1967. Hon. DLitt (Nottingham), 1963. *Publications:* Zeno of Elea: a Text and Notes (in Cambridge Classical Studies), 1935; Aristotle, Meteorologica (Loeb Classical Library), 1952; Plato, Republic (Penguin Classics), 1955; Plato, Timæus (Penguin Classics), 1965. *Address:* 8 Barton Close, Cambridge. *Club:* Athenæum.

**LEE, Col Tun Sir Henry Hau Shik,** SMN 1959 (Federation of Malaya); KBE 1957 (CBE 1948); JP; Chairman: Development & Commercial Bank Ltd; China Press Ltd; Board of Governors of Lady Templer Hospital; Council of Elders of Malayan Chinese Association; Director: Golden Castle Finance Corporation, Berhad (Chairman) and Singapore; Hong Leong Finance Co Ltd; International Telephone & Telegraph Corporation; President: Royal Commonwealth Society; Selangur Kwang Tung Association; Federation of Kwang Tung Association; All Malaya Kochow Association; Wine and Food Society; Federation of Malaya Golf Association; Golf Association of Malaysia; Selangor Miners' Club, 1938- (Hon. Member); Vice-President: Malayan Zoological Society; sole Proprietor of H. S. Lee Tin Mines, Malaya; *b* 19 Nov. 1901; *e s* of late K. L. Lee; *m* 1st, 1922 (wife *d* 1926); one *s*; 2nd, 1929, Choi Lin (*née* Kwan); four *s* two *d* (and one *s* decd). *Educ:* Queen's Coll., Hongkong; Univ. of Cambridge. BA (Cantab) 1923. War of 1939-45; Chief of Passive Defence Forces, Kuala Lumpur, 1941; Col in Allied Armed Forces, 1942-45. Co-founder, Alliance Party, 1952; Minister of Transport, 1953-56; Minister of Finance, 1956-59. Past Chairman: Federal Finance Cttee, and other political cttees. Member, Standing Sub-Cttee of MCA; Past President: Oxford and Cambridge Soc.; Royal Commonwealth Soc.; Selangor Chinese Chamber of Commerce; Kuen Cheng Girls' Sch.; All Malaya Chinese Mining Assoc.; Associated Chinese Chambers of Commerce, Malaya and Singapore; United Lee's Assoc.; Selangor MCA; Sen. Golfers' Soc., Malaya, 1957-58, 1960-63; Fedn Malaya Red Cross Soc.; Fedn Malaya Olympic Council; Past Member: KL Sanitary Board; Council FMS Chamber of Mines; Council of State, Selangor; Malayan Union Advisory Council; Tin Advisory Cttee; Chinese Tin Mines Rehabilitation Loans Board; War Damage Commn; Federal Finance Cttee; Malayan Tin Delegn to all Internat. Tin Meetings; Fed. Leg. Council, 1948-57; Fed. Exec. Council, 1948-57; Dir, Ops. Cttee, 1948-55. Alliance Exec. Cttee and Alliance Nat. Council, 1953-59; Merdeka Mission to London, 1956; Financial Mission to London, 1957; Mem. Cabinet, 1957-59. JP, Kuala Lumpur, 1938. Hon. Mem. various clubs in Malaysia; Mem., British Assoc. of Malaysia; Member, Four Hundred Club, London. FREconS (Eng.). *Recreations:* riding, golf, tennis. *Address:* 22 Jalan Langgak Golf, Kuala Lumpur, Malaysia. *Clubs:* Selangor; Singapore Island Country; Royal and Ancient Golf (St Andrews).

**LEE, Rt. Hon. Jennie,** PC 1966; Director of Tribune; Member of Central Advisory Committee on Housing; Member, National Executive Committee, Labour Party, 1958- (Chairman, 1967-68); *b* 3 Nov. 1904; *d* of a Fifeshire miner; *m* 1934, Rt Hon. Aneurin Bevan, PC, MP (*d* 1960). *Educ:* Edinburgh Univ. MA, LLB. MP (Lab) North Lanark, 1929-31, Cannock, 1945-70. Parly Sec., Ministry of Public Building and Works, 1964-65; Parly Under-Sec. of State, Dept of Education and Science, 1965-67, Minister of State, 1967-70. *Publications:* Tomorrow is a New Day, 1939; Our Ally, Russia, 1941; This Great Journey, 1963. *Address:* 65 Chester Row, SW1.

[*Created a Baroness (Life Peeress), 1970, as Baroness Lee of Asheridge.*]

**LEE, John Michael Hubert;** Barrister-at-Law; *b* 13 Aug. 1927; *s* of Victor Lee, Wentworth, Surrey, and late Renee Lee; *m* 1960, Margaret Ann, *d* of James Russell, ICS, retired, and Kathleen Russell; one *s* one *d. Educ:* Reading Sch.; Christ's Coll., Cambridge (Open Exhibnr Modern Hist.; MA). Administrative Officer, Colonial Service, Ghana, 1951-58; Principal Assistant Secretary, Min. of Communications. On staff of BBC, 1959-65. Called to the Bar, Middle Temple, 1960; Midland Circuit. MP (Lab) Reading, 1966-70. *Publications:* articles in Fabian Commonwealth magazine Venture; chapter in the Radical Future (ed Whitaker), 1967. *Recreations:* gardening, tennis, walking. *Address:* 2 Dr Johnson's Buildings, EC4. *Clubs:* Royal Over-Seas League; Reading Workingmen's.

**LEE KUAN YEW,** Hon. CH, 1970; Prime Minister, Singapore, since 1959; *b* 16 Sept. 1923; *s* of Lee Chin Koon and Chua Jim Neo; *m* 1950, Kwa Geok Choo; two *s* one *d. Educ:* Raffles Coll., Singapore; Cambridge Univ. (double first Law Tripos, Star for special distinction). Barrister-at-law, Middle Temple; Hon. Bencher, Middle Temple. Hon Fellow, Fitzwilliam Coll., Cambridge. *Recreation:* golf. *Address:* Prime Minister's Office, Singapore 6. *T:* 31155.

**LEE, Laurie,** MBE 1952; poet and author; *b* 26 June 1914; *m* 1950, Catherine Francesca Polge; one *d. Educ:* Slad Village Sch.; Stroud Central Sch. Travelled Mediterranean, 1935-39; GPO Film Unit, 1939-40; Crown Film Unit, 1941-43; Publications Editor, Ministry of Information, 1944-46; Green Park Film Unit, 1946-47; Caption Writer-in-Chief, Festival of Britain, 1950-51. *Publications:* The Sun My Monument (Poems), 1944; Land at War (HMSO), 1945; (with Ralph Keene) A Film in Cyprus, 1947; The Bloom of Candles (Poems), 1947; The Voyage of Magellan, 1948; My Many-Coated Man (Poems), 1955; A Rose for Winter, 1955; Cider With Rosie (autobiography), 1959; Pocket Poets (Selection), 1960; The Firstborn, 1964; As I Walked Out One Midsummer Morning (autobiography), 1969. *Recreations:* indoor sports, music, travel. *Address:* 49 Elm Park Gardens, SW10. *T:* 01-352 2197.

**LEE, Manfred B.;** co-author with Frederic Dannay, *qv*, under pseudonym Ellery Queen. *Publications:* Roman Hat Mystery, 1929; French Powder Mystery, 1930; Dutch Shoe

Mystery, 1931; Greek Coffin Mystery, Tragedy of X, Egyptian Cross Mystery, Tragedy of Y, 1932; American Gun Mystery, Tragedy of Z, Siamese Twin Mystery, Drury Lane's Last Case, 1933; The Chinese Orange Mystery, Adventures of Ellery Queen, 1934; Spanish Cape Mystery, 1935; Halfway House, 1936; Door Between, 1937; Devil to Pay, Challenge to the Reader, Four of Hearts, 1938; Dragon's Teeth, 1939; New Adventures of Ellery Queen, 1940; 101 Years' Entertainment, 1941; Calamity Town, The Detective Short Story (a Bibliography), Sporting Blood, 1942; There was an Old Woman, Female of the Species, 1943; Misadventures of Sherlock Holmes, 1944; The Murderer is a Fox, Case Book of Ellery Queen, Rogues' Gallery, 1945; To the Queen's Taste, The Queen's Awards, 1946, 1946; The Queen's Awards, 1947, 1947; Murder by Experts, 1947; 20th Century Detective Stories, Ten Days' Wonder, The Queen's Awards, 1948, 1948; The Queen's Awards, 1949. Cat of Many Tails, 1949; Double, Double, The Queen's Awards 5th Series, The Literature of Crime, 1950; Queen's Quorum, 1951; The Origin of Evil, 1951; The Queen's Awards, 6th Series, 1951; Calendar of Crime, The King is Dead, The Queen's Awards, 7th Series, 1952; The Scarlet Letters, The Queen's Awards, 8th Series, 1953; The Glass Village, Ellery Queen's Awards, 9th Series, 1954; Queen's Bureau of Investigation, Ellery Queen's Awards, 10th Series, 1955; Inspector Queen's Own Case, Ellery Queen's Awards, 11th Series, 1956; In The Queen's Parlor, Ellery Queen's Awards, 12th Series, 1957; The Finishing Stroke, Ellery Queen's 13th Annual, 1958; Ellery Queen's 14th Annual, Ellery Queen's 1960 Anthology, 1959; Ellery Queen's 1961 Anthology, Ellery Queen's 15th Mystery Annual, 1960; Ellery Queen's 16th Mystery Annual, 1962; The Quintessence of Queen, 1962; To Be Read Before Midnight, 1963; The Player on the Other Side, 1963; Ellery Queen's Mystery Mix No 18, 1963; And on the Eighth Day, 1964; Ellery Queen's Double Dozen, No 19, 1964; Queens Full, 1965; Ellery Queen's 20th Anniversary Annual, 1965; The Fourth Side of the Triangle, 1965; Ellery Queen's Crime Carousel, 1966; Face to Face, 1967; Ellery Queen's All-Star Line-up, 1967; Poetic Justice, 1967; Ellery Queen's Mystery Parade, 1968; QED: Queen's Experiments in Detection, 1968; The House of Brass, 1968; Cop Out, 1969; Elllery Queen's Murder Menu, 24th Mystery Annual, 1969; Ellery Queen's Minimysteries, 1969; The Last Woman in His Life, 1970. (Joint) Ellery Queen, Junior juvenile mysteries. Joint author of Radio and Television Programs: The Adventures of Ellery Queen; Joint editor of Ellery Queen's Mystery Magazine. *Address:* Roxbury, Connecticut, USA.

**LEE, May B.**; *see* Stott, May, Lady.

**LEE, Mollie Carpenter, (Mrs Asher Lee)**; Editor, Woman's Hour, BBC, since 1967; *d* of Louis Hales and Florence (*née* Carpenter); *m* 1934, Asher Lee, OBE; one *d*. *Educ:* Sittingbourne Co. Sch.; King's Coll., London Univ.; School of Slavonic Studies. BBC News Dept, External Services, 1943; BBC Woman's Hour, 1959. *Publications:* The Cat and The Medal, 1936; A Debt, 1949; Home for the Night, 1951; So Many Zeros, 1961; (Ed.) Woman's Hour: a Selection, 1967, 1969. *Recreations:* writing, cooking, theatre-going, travelling in France, making historical and literary pilgrimages. *Address:* 12 Malcolm Road, Wimbledon, SW19. *T:* 01-946 6391.

**LEE, Rt. Rev. Paul Shun Hwan**; *see* Seoul (Korea), Bishop of.

**LEE, Roger Malcolm**; *b* 18 March 1902; *s* of late Lennox B. Lee; *m* 1935, Cecily Grace (*d* 1956), *d* of late Major Guy Mellor and of Mrs Mellor; two *s* one *d*. *Educ:* Eton; Pembroke Coll., Cambridge. In commerce in Argentine, 1927-29, and in India, 1930. Director of industrial companies in England and overseas, since 1933; Chairman, The Calico Printers' Association Ltd, 1947-64; Chairman, Lancashire Cotton Corporation, 1955-64. *Address:* How Caple Court, Hereford. *T:* How Caple 202. *Club:* Canning.

**LEE, Stanley**; *see* Lee, (Edward) S.

**LEE, Tsung-Dao**; Enrico Fermi Professor of Physics at Columbia University, USA, since 1964; *b* 25 Nov. 1926; 3rd *s* of C. K. and M. C. Lee; *m* 1950, Jeannette H. C. Chin; two *s*. *Educ:* National Chekiang Univ., Kweichow, China; National Southwest Associated Univ., Kunming, China; University of Chicago, USA. Research Associate: University of Chicago, 1950; University of California, 1950-51; Member, Inst. for Advanced Study, Princeton, 1951-53. Columbia University: Asst Professor, 1953-55; Associate Professor, 1955-56; Professor, 1956-60; Member, Institute for Advanced Study, Princeton, 1960-63; Columbia Univ.: Adjunct Professor, 1960-62; Visiting Professor, 1962-63; Professor, 1963-. Nobel Prize for the non-conservation of parity (with C. N. Yang), 1957; Albert Einstein Award in Science, 1957; Member, National Academy of Sciences, 1964. Hon. Dr Science, Princeton Univ., 1958. *Publications:* mostly in Physical Review. *Address:* Department of Physics, Columbia University, New York, New York 10027, USA.

**LEE, William Alexander**, CBE 1920; Chevalier of Legion of Honour; Knight Officer of Order of the Crown of Italy; Director then Chairman, Mining Association of Great Britain, until 1954; *b* 1886; *s* of William Allan Lee, Grantham; *m* 1914, Edith Lydia, *d* of William Henry Grimwood, Willesden; two *s* two *d*. *Educ:* Royal Grammar Sch., Newcastle upon Tyne; London Univ. BA, BSc. Barrister, Inner Temple; entered Board of Trade, 1907; Secretary of Coal Mines Dept, 1918-19. *Publications:* Thirty Years in Coal, 1954; contributions to Historical Review of Coal Mining, 1925; etc. *Address:* White Croft, Littleworth Road, Esher, Surrey. *Club:* Junior Carlton.

**LEE, Rev. W(illiam) Walker**; Chairman of the Bolton and Rochdale District of the Methodist Church since 1957; President, Conference of the Methodist Church, 1965; Chairman, Leeds District of Methodist Church since Sept. 1966; *b* 1909; *s* of Matthew and Florence Lee; *m* 1935, Laura Annie Linsley; one *d*. *Educ:* King James I Grammar Sch., Bishop Auckland; Hartley Victoria Theological Coll., Manchester. Minister: Redditch Methodist Circuit, 1931-35; Birmingham Mission, 1935-40; Leeds Mission, 1940-44; Superintendent: Wednesbury Mission, 1944-49; Bolton Mission, 1949-57. Member of Methodist Delegation in Conversations between Church of England and Methodist Church, 1955-63. Hon. MA (Manchester). *Recreation:* gardening. *Address:* 281 Otley Road, West Park, Leeds 16. *T:* Leeds 53546.

**LEE, Sir Wilton**; *see* Lee, Sir G. W.

**LEE-BARBER, Rear-Adm. John**, CB 1959; DSO 1940 and Bar 1941; Admiral Superintendent, HM Dockyard, Malta, 1957-59, retired; *b* 16 April 1905; *s* of Richard Lee-Barber,

Herringfleet, Nr Great Yarmouth; *m* 1939, Suzanne, *d* of Colonel Le Gallais, ADC, MC, La Moye, Jersey, CI; two *d. Educ:* Royal Naval Colleges, Osborne and Dartmouth. Service in destroyers and in Yangtze gunboat until 1937; CO Witch, 1937-38; CO Griffin, 1939-40-41; Commander, 1941; CO Opportune, 1942-44; 2nd in Command, HMS King Alfred, 1945; CO, HMS St James, 1946-47; Captain, 1947; Senior Officer Reserve Fleet, Harwich, 1948-49; Naval Attaché, Chile, 1950-52; CO Agincourt and Captain D4, 1952-54; Commodore, Inshore Flotilla, 1954-56; Rear-Admiral, 1957. Polish Cross of Valour, 1940. *Recreation:* sailing. *Address:* Bracken Hile, La Moye, Jersey. *T:* Jersey Central 42116. *Club:* Royal Ocean Racing.

**LEE HOWARD, Leon Alexander,** DFC 1944; Editor, Daily Mirror, 1961-71; *b* 18 June 1914; *m* 1951, Sheila Psyche Black, *qv*; one step *d. Educ:* privately. Served War of 1939-45: RAF Coastal Command, 1940-43; RAF Operational Film Production Unit, 1943-45. Editor: Woman's Sunday Mirror, 1955-59; Sunday Pictorial, 1959-61. *Publications: fiction: as Leigh Howard:* Crispin's Day, 1952; Johnny's Sister, 1954; Blind Date, 1955; *as Alexander Krislov:* No Man Sings, 1956. *Recreation:* journalism. *Address:* c/o Barclays Bank Ltd, Africa House, Kingsway, WC2.

**LEE POTTER, Air Marshal Sir Patrick (Brunton),** KBE 1958 (CBE 1953; OBE 1946); MD (Sheffield) 1936; *b* 15 March 1904; *s* of Samuel Lee Potter and Isabella Henrietta Handyside; *m* 1933, Audrey Mary Pollock; two *s. Educ:* Epsom Coll.; Sheffield Univ. MB, ChB 1928. Joined RAF Medical Branch, 1928; DTM & H, 1931; DPH 1934; MD 1936. OC RAF Institute of Pathology, 1939; served War of 1939-45: Middle East and Air Ministry (despatches twice, OBE); OC 21 Mobile Field Hospital, 1940-42; Air Ministry, 1943-45; psa 1947; DMS, RNZAF, 1948-50; Director Hygiene and Research, Air Ministry, 1951-53; PMO, Bomber Command, 1953-55; PMO, MEAF, 1955-57; Director General, RAF Medical Services, 1957-62. Air Vice-Marshal, 1956. QHS 1953-62. KStJ. *Publication:* RAF Handbook of Preventive Medicine, 1947. *Recreation:* golf. *Address:* North Cottage, Braunton, Devon. *Club:* Royal Air Force.

**LEECH, Clifford;** Professor of English in University of Toronto since 1963; *b* 16 Jan. 1909; *s* of Edmund John Leech and Laura Mary Cumming; *m* 1961, Gabriele Anspach. *Educ:* Clapham Coll.; Queen Mary Coll. (Univ. of London). Assistant Lecturer in English: University College of Swansea, 1933-36; Univ. of Durham, 1936-50; seconded to British Council in Turkey and Middle East, 1941-45; Principal of St Cuthbert's Society, Durham, 1946-52; Senior Lecturer in English, Univ. of Durham, 1950-54; Prof. of English Language and Literature, Univ. of Durham (Durham Division) 1954-63; Foyle Res. Fellow, The Shakespeare Institute, 1952; Visiting Lectr, Free Univ. of Berlin, 1953; Research Fellow, Folger Shakespeare Lib., 1958; Commonwealth Prestige Fellow to Univ. of NZ, 1967. Fellow, Royal Soc. of Canada, 1969. Dr (*hc*), Univ. of Clermont-Ferrand, 1962; Hon. DLitt Acadia Univ., NS, 1969. *Publications:* Mildmay Fane's Raguaillo d'Oceano and Candy Restored, 1938; Shakespeare's Tragedies and Other Studies in Seventeenth Century Drama, 1950; John Webster: a Critical Study, 1951; A School of Criticism (inaugural lecture), 1955; John Ford and the Drama of his Time, 1957; The John Fletcher Plays, 1962; Shakespeare: The Chronicles, 1962; O'Neill, 1963; Webster: The Duchess of Malfi, 1963; John Ford, 1964; Twelfth Night and Shakespearian Comedy, 1965; Comedy in the Grand Style (W. D. Thomas Memorial Lecture), 1966; Tragedy (The Critical Idiom), 1969; The Dramatist's Experience with Other Essays in Literary Theory, 1970; ed Marlowe (Twentieth Century Views), 1964; Shakespeare: The Tragedies, 1965; The Two Noble Kinsmen, 1966; The Two Gentlemen of Verona, 1969. General Editor, The Revels Plays, 1958-. Contributions to Studies in Honor of T. W. Baldwin, 1958; Studies in English Drama presented to Baldwin Maxwell, 1962; Essays on Shakespeare and Elizabethan Drama in Honor of Hardin Craig, 1962; A Book of Masques in Honour of Allardyce Nicoll, 1967; Imagined Worlds: Essays on some English Novels and Novelists in Honour of John Butt, 1968; The Morality of Art: Essays presented to G. Wilson Knight by his Colleagues and Friends, 1969; Studies in English Literature, Indian Jl of English Studies, Tulane Drama Review, Review of English Literature, University of Toronto Quarterly, Shakespeare Survey, Review of English Studies, Mod. Lang. Review, Durham Univ. Jl, Shakespeare Quarterly, Jl of English and Germanic Philology, E. L. H., Essays in Criticism, Cambridge Jl, Mod. Lang. Notes, Die Neuren Sprachen, Shakespeare-Jahrbuch, Philological Quarterly, Etudes Anglaises, Critical Quarterly, Stratford-upon-Avon Studies, etc. *Recreations:* films, theatres, people. *Address:* University College, Toronto, Canada. *Club:* National Liberal.

**LEECH-PORTER, Maj.-Gen. John Edmund,** CB 1950; CBE 1945 (OBE 1944); OStJ; *b* 1896; *s* of Henry Leech-Porter, Winchester. *Educ:* Imperial Service Coll., Windsor. 2nd Lt RMA, 1914; served European War, 1914-19. Major, 1934; Lt-Col, 1941; Actg Brig., 1942-45; served in Sicily, 1943, and NW Europe, 1944-45; Commanding Plymouth Group, Royal Marines, 1949-51; retired list, 1951. Comdr Order of Leopold II with Palm; Croix de Guerre with Palm. *Recreations:* fishing, shooting, golf. *Address:* Neathern Brock, Tavistock, Devon.

**LEECHMAN, Hon. Lord; James Graham Leechman;** a Senator of the College of Justice in Scotland since 1965; *b* 6 Oct. 1906; *s* of late Walter Graham Leechman, solicitor, Glasgow, and late Barbara Louisa Leechman (*née* Neilson); *m* 1935, Margaret Helen Edgar; two *d. Educ:* High Sch. and Univ., Glasgow. MA 1927; BSc 1928; LLB 1930. Admitted to Membership of Faculty of Advocates, 1932; Advocate-Depute, 1947-49; KC 1949; Clerk of Justiciary, 1949-64; Solicitor-Gen. for Scotland, 1964-65. *Recreation:* golf. *Address:* 626 Queensferry Road, Edinburgh EH4 6AT. *T:* 031-336 2713.

**LEECHMAN, Barclay,** CMG 1952; OBE 1941; Executive Director, Tanganyika Sisal Growers' Assoc., 1959-66; Chairman, Transport Licensing Authority, Tanganyika, 1956-59; Member for Social Services, Tanganyika, 1948-55; retired from Colonial Service, 1956; *b* Eastbourne, 28 Sept. 1901; *e s* of late Alleyne Leechman, MA, FLS, FCS, Bexhill, and late of Colonial Civil Service and late Jean Macmaster Leechman; *m* 1933, Grace, 4th *d* of late Frederick William Coller, Cape Town, SA; no *c. Educ:* Oundle Sch. Cadet, Colonial Administrative Service, Tanganyika, 1925; Asst District Officer, 1928; District Officer, 1937; Dep. Provincial Commissioner, 1944; Labour Commissioner, 1946. Seconded as Sec. of East African Economic Council, Nairobi, 1940-41, and Dir of Economic Control, Aden, 1943-45. Pres. Fedn of Tanganyika Employers, 1964-66

(Vice-Pres., 1959-63). Fellow, Ancient Monuments Soc. *Publications:* occasional light articles in various publications. *Recreations:* books and music. *Address:* c/o National and Grindlay's Bank, 13 St James's Square, SW1. *Clubs:* Reform, Lansdowne, Farmers'; City (Cape Town).

**LEECHMAN, James Graham;** *see* Leechman, Hon. Lord.

**LEEDS, Bishop of, (RC),** since 1966; **Rt. Rev. William Gordon Wheeler,** MA Oxon; *b* 5 May 1910; *o s* of Frederick Wheeler and Marjorie (*née* Upjohn). *Educ:* Manchester Gram. Sch.; University Coll. and St Stephen's House, Oxford; Beda Coll., Rome. Curate, St Bartholomew's, Brighton, 1933; Curate, St Mary and All Saints, Chesterfield, 1934; Asst Chaplain, Lancing Coll., 1935. Received into Roman Catholic Church at Downside, 1936; Beda Coll., Rome, 1936-40; ordained priest, 1940; Asst, St Edmund's, Lower Edmonton, 1940-44; Chaplain of Westminster Cathedral and Editor of Westminster Cathedral Chronicle, 1944-50; Chaplain to the Catholics in the University, London, 1950-54, and Ecclesiastical Adviser to the Union of Catholic Students, 1953-60; Privy Chamberlain to HH The Pope, 1952; Hon. Canon of Westminster, 1954, Administrator of Cathedral, 1954-64; Coadjutor Bishop of Middlesbrough, 1964-66. Created Domestic Prelate to HH Pope Pius XII, 1955; Conventual Chaplain to the British Association of the Sovereign and Military Order of Malta, 1958. *Publications:* Edited and contributed to Homage to Newman, 1945; Richard Challoner, 1947; The English Catholics, etc. Contribs to Dublin Review, The Tablet, etc. *Address:* Eltofts House, Carr Lane, Thorner, Leeds. *Club:* Athenæum.

**LEEDS, Auxiliary Bishop of, (RC);** *see* Moverley, Rt Rev. Gerald.

**LEEDS, Archdeacon of;** *see* Page, Ven. A. C.

**LEEDS, Sir George (Graham Mortimer),** 7th Bt *cr* 1812; *b* 21 Aug. 1927; *s* of Sir Reginald Arthur St John Leeds, 6th Bt, and of Winnaretta, *d* of late Paris Eugene Singer; *S* father, 1970; *m* 1954, Nicola (marr. diss. 1965), *d* of Douglas Robertson McBean, MC; three *d. Educ:* Eton. Formerly Captain, Grenadier Guards. *Heir: cousin* Christopher Anthony Leeds, *b* 31 Aug. 1935. *Address:* Roche Bois, Mont ès Tours, St Aubin, Jersey.

**LEEK, James,** CBE 1941; lately Director BSA Co. Ltd, BSA Guns Ltd, BSA Motor Cycles Ltd; Ariel Motors Ltd, Birmingham; Monochrome Ltd; Triumph Engineering Co. Ltd, Coventry; President Birmingham Chamber of Commerce, 1949; *b* 12 Sept. 1892; *s* of Richard Harley and Annie Leek; *m* 1917, Kathleen Louise, *d* of J. E. Riley, Manufacturer, Bradford; one *s. Educ:* Newport Grammar School, Newport. *Address:* Sandown, Banbury Road, Stratford-on-Avon, Warwicks. *T:* Stratford-on-Avon 3590.

**LEEPER, Richard Kevin;** Chairman of The Lep Group Ltd and its principal subsidiary companies since 1956; *b* 14 July 1894; *s* of late William John Leeper of Stranorlar, Co. Donegal; *m* 1916, Elizabeth Mary Fenton; two *s. Educ:* Sligo Gram. Sch.; London Univ. Served in Army, European War, 1914-18; Dir of Transport, MAP, 1940-45. Engaged in shipping and forwarding in Yugoslavia, 1920-32; Managing Dir of Lep Transport Ltd and Chief Executive of the Lep Group of Companies, 1932. KHS; MInstT. order of St Sava (Yugoslavia), 1930. *Address:* Sunlight Wharf, Upper Thames Street, EC4. *T:* 01-236 5050; Holly Wood House, West Byfleet, Surrey. *T:* Byfleet 42537. *Club:* United Service.

**LEES, Air Marshal Sir Alan,** KCB, *cr* 1946 (CB 1943); CBE 1942; DSO 1937; AFC; *b* 23 May 1895; *e s* of late Maurice Lees, Park Bridge, Ashton-under-Lyne; *m* 1930, Norah Elizabeth, *y d* of late John Thomson, West Hartlepool; two *s* one *d. Educ:* Wellington Coll., Berks; RMC, Sandhurst. Served European War, 1914-18, with RFC; Iraq, 1923-26; NWFP, 1933-37; Air Officer Commanding-in-Chief, Reserve Command, 1946-49; retired list, 1949. *Address:* Home Close, Highclere, Newbury, Berks. *Clubs:* Royal Air Force, Queen's.

**LEES, Prof. Anthony David,** FRS 1968; Senior Principal Scientific Officer and Professor of Insect Physiology, Agricultural Research Council at Imperial College Field Station, Ascot; *b* 27 Feb. 1917; *s* of Alan Henry Lees, MA and Mary Hughes Bomford; *m* 1943, Annzella Pauline Wilson; one *d. Educ:* Clifton Coll., Bristol; Trinity Hall, Cambridge (Schol.). BA 1939; PhD (Cantab) 1943; ScD 1966. Mem., ARC Unit of Insect Physiology at Zoology Dept, Cambridge, 1945-67; Lalor Fellow, 1956; Vis. Prof., Adelaide Univ., 1966; Hon. Lectr, London Univ., 1968. *Publications:* scientific papers. *Recreations:* gardening, fossicking. *Address:* Wells Lane Corner, Sunninghill, Ascot, Berks. *T:* Ascot 20732.

**LEES, David,** CBE 1963; Rector, The High School of Glasgow, since 1950; *b* 12 Aug. 1910; *s* of late David Lees and Margaret W. Lees, Airdrie; *m* 1935, Olive, *d* of Arthur and Alice Willington, Montreal; one *s* two *d. Educ:* Airdrie Academy; Glasgow, McGill and London Univs. MA (Hons) Glasgow, 1930; MA in Education, McGill, 1932; BA (Hons) London, 1945. Principal Teacher of Classics, Campbeltown Gram. Sch., 1933-46; Rector, Elgin Academy, 1946-49; Dir of Education, Roxburghshire, 1949-50. *Recreation:* bridge. *Address:* Oaklea, 16 Larch Road, Glasgow, S1. *T:* 041-427 0322. *Clubs:* Lanarkshire County (Hamilton); Campbeltown (Argyll).

**LEES, Rear-Adm. Dennis Marescaux,** CB 1951; DSO 1940; *b* 28 Jan. 1900; *s* of Captain J. Lees, Royal W Kent Regt, and Gemma Lees (*née* Marescaux); *m* 1934, Daphne May Burnett; three *s. Educ:* Ludgrove Preparatory Sch.; RN Colls Osborne and Dartmouth. Fleet Gunnery Officer, Med. Fleet, 1934-36; in command HMS Calcutta, 1940-41, HMS Black Prince, 1943-45; Chief of Staff, Home Fleet, 1945-46; Dir of Naval Ordnance, 1946-49; Chief of Staff, Portsmouth, 1949-51; Dep. Chief of Naval Personnel (personal services), 1951-53; retired list, 1953. Greek War Cross, 1941; American Legion of Merit, 1945; French Croix de Guerre, 1948; French Legion of Honour, 1948. *Recreations:* cricket, golf, shooting. *Address:* 21 Selsey Avenue, Southsea, Hants. *T:* Portsmouth 33283. *Club:* United Service.

**LEES, Geoffrey William;** Headmaster, St Bees School, since 1963; *b* 1 July 1920; *o s* of late Mr F. T. Lees and of Mrs Lees, Manchester; *m* 1949, Joan Needham, *yr d* of late Mr and late Mrs J. Needham, Moseley, Birmingham. *Educ:* King's Sch., Rochester; Downing Coll., Cambridge. Royal Signals, 1940-46 (despatches): commissioned 1941; served in NW Europe and Middle East, Captain. 2nd Class Hons English Tripos, Pt I, 1947; History Tripos, Part II, 1948; Asst Master, Brighton Coll., 1948-63. Leave of absence in Australia, Asst Master, Melbourne Church of England Gram. Sch., 1961-62. *Recreations:* reading, games, walking. *Address:* St Bees School, Cumberland. *T:* St Bees 263. *Clubs:* MCC; Hawks', Union (Cambridge).

**LEES, Sir Hereward;** *see* Lees, Sir W. H. C.

**LEES, Lt-Col Lawrence Werner Wyld;** *b* 11 Sept. 1887; *s* of late Rev. George Wyld Lees, Clifford, York, and Anna Werner, Dublin; *m* 1915, Gwendolen, *d* of late R. T. Daniell, Colchester; one *s* one *d*. *Educ:* privately. Commissioned in Militia, Special Reserve, RA and RAF, 1906-21; served in France and East Africa, 1915-17; Dep. Asst Dir, War Office, 1917, and at Air Ministry, 1918; mem. of London and Liverpool Corn Trade Associations, 1924; of British Exec. Cttee Internat. Chamber of Commerce and British spokesman at Copenhagen Conference, 1939. High Sheriff of Shropshire, 1944-45. *Address:* 66 Wellington Road, Nantwich, Cheshire. *T:* Nantwich 5922.

**LEES, Roland James;** Deputy Director (Equipment), Royal Aircraft Establishment, since 1966; *b* 3 Dec. 1917; *s* of Roland John Lees and late Ada Bell (*née* Jeavons), Stourbridge, Worcs; *m* 1948, Esmé Joyce, *d* of late Alfred Thomas Hill, Malvern Link, Worcs; no *c*. *Educ:* King Edward's Sch., Stourbridge; St John's Coll., Cambridge. BA Cantab 1939; BSc London 1939; MA Cantab 1942. Dir, Scientific Research Electronics and Guided Weapons, Min. of Supply, 1955-56; Head of Airborne Radar Dept, RRE, 1957-58; Head of Instruments and Electrical Engrg Dept, RAE, 1959-62; Dir, Signals Research and Development Establishment, 1963-65. Assessor to Lord Mountbatten, Inquiry into Prison Security, 1966. *Address:* Fairoaks, Frensham Vale, Lower Bourne, Farnham, Surrey. *T:* Frensham 3146.

**LEES, Air Marshal Sir Ronald Beresford,** KCB 1961 (CB 1946); CBE 1943; DFC; retired as C-in-C, RAF, Germany, 1963-65; *b* 27 April 1910; *s* of John Thomas and Elizabeth Jane Lees; *m* 1931, Rhoda Lillie Pank; one *s* one *d*. *Educ:* St Peter's Coll., Adelaide, Australia. Joined Royal Australian Air Force, 1930; transferred Royal Air Force, 1931. ADC to the Queen, 1952-53 (to King George VI, 1949-52); AOC No 83 Gp, 2nd TAF in Germany, 1952-55; Asst Chief of Air Staff (Operations), 1955-58; SASO, Fighter Command, 1958-60; Dep. Chief of the Air Staff, 1960-63; Air Marshal, 1961. *Address:* Jelbra, RMB 367, Albury, NSW 2640, Australia. *Club:* Royal Air Force.

**LEES, Stanley Lawrence,** MVO 1952; Under-Secretary, Ministry of Transport, since 1966; *b* 1911; *yr s* of Dr Charlie Lees and Eveleen Lees, Tunbridge Wells; *m* 1938, Audrey, *d* of A. E. Lynam, Oxford; two *s* two *d*. *Educ:* Rugby Sch.; New Coll., Oxford. Solicitor, 1936; Solicitor's Office, Inland Revenue, 1936; Secretaries' Office, Inland Revenue, 1943; Royal Navy, 1944; HM Treasury, 1946; Under-Sec., 1958; Dir of Organisation and Methods, 1959-66. *Address:* 3 Malbrook Road, Putney, SW15. *T:* 01-788 6732.

**LEES, Sir Thomas (Edward),** 4th Bt, *cr* 1897; landowner; *b* 31 Jan. 1925; 2nd *s* of Sir John Victor Elliott Lees, 3rd Bt, DSO, MC, and Madeline A. P. (*d* 1967), *d* of Sir Harold Pelly, 4th Bt; *S* father 1955; *m* 1949, Faith Justin, *d* of G. G. Jessiman, OBE, Great Durnford, Wilts; one *s* three *d*. *Educ:* Eton; Magdalene Coll., Cambridge. Served War in RAF; discharged 1945, after losing eye. Magdalene, Cambridge, 1945-47; BA Cantab. 1947 (Agriculture). Since then has farmed at and managed South Lytchett estate. JP 1951, CC 1952, High Sheriff 1960, Dorset. *Recreations:* field sports, sailing. *Heir: s* Christopher James Lees, *b* 4 Nov. 1952. *Address:* Post Green, Lytchett Minster, Poole, Dorset. *T:* Lytchett Minster 317. *Clubs:* Farmers', Royal Cruising.

**LEES, Sir Thomas Harcourt Ivor,** 8th Bt *cr* (UK) 1804, of Black Rock, County Dublin; *b* 6 Nov. 1941; *s* of Sir Charles Archibald Edward Ivor Lees, 7th Bt, and of Lily, *d* of Arthur Williams, Manchester; *S* father, 1963. *Heir: kinsman* John Rutherfoord d'Olier-Lees [*b* 17 Sept. 1887; *m* 1923, Margery, *d* of Thomas H. Scott; three *s* two *d*].

**LEES, Walter Kinnear P.;** *see* Pyke-Lees.

**LEES, Sir (William) Hereward (Clare),** 2nd Bt, *cr* 1937; retired as Director, Bleachers' Association Ltd; Director, Manchester District Board of Martin's Bank; *b* 6 March 1904; *o s* of Sir William Clare Lees, 1st Bt, OBE, LLD, and Kathleen (*d* 1967), *d* of John Nickson, Liverpool; *S* father, 1951; *m* 1930, Dorothy Gertrude, *d* of Francis Alexander and Gertrude Florence Lauder; one *s* one *d*. *Educ:* Leys Sch., Cambridge. *Heir: s* William Antony Clare Lees, *b* 14 June 1935. *Address:* Ardeevin, Chapel-en-le-Frith, Stockport, Cheshire. *Club:* St James's (Manchester).

**LEES-MILNE, James;** author; *b* 6 Aug. 1908; *er s* of George Crompton Lees-Milne, Crompton Hall, Lancs and Wickhamford Manor, Worcs; *m* 1951, Alvilde, formerly wife of 3rd Viscount Chaplin and *d* of late Lt-Gen. Sir Tom Molesworth Bridges, KCB, KCMG, DSO; no *c*. *Educ:* Eton Coll.; Magdalen Coll., Oxford. Private Sec. to 1st Baron Lloyd, 1931-35; on staff, Reuters, 1935-36; on staff, National Trust, 1936-66; Adviser on Historic Buildings to National Trust, 1951-66. 2nd Lieut Irish Guards, 1940-41 (invalided). FRSL 1957. *Publications:* The National Trust (ed), 1945; The Age of Adam, 1947; National Trust Guide: Buildings, 1948; Tudor Renaissance, 1951; The Age of Inigo Jones, 1953; Roman Mornings, 1956 (Heinemann Award, 1956); Baroque in Italy, 1959; Baroque in Spain and Portugal, 1960; Earls of Creation, 1962: Worcestershire: A Shell Guide, 1964; St Peter's, 1967; English Country Houses: Baroque 1685-1714, 1970; Another Self, 1970. *Recreations:* walking, sightseeing. *Address:* Alderley Grange, Wotton-under-Edge, Glos. *T:* Wotton-under-Edge 2161. *Club:* Brooks's.

**LEESE, Lt-Gen. Sir Oliver William Hargreaves,** 3rd Bt, *cr* 1908; KCB 1943 (CB 1942); CBE 1940; DSO 1916; *b* 27 Oct. 1894; *e s* of 2nd Bt and Violet Mary (*d* 1947), 4th *d* of late Albert G. Sandeman; *S* father, 1937; *m* 1933, Margaret Alice (*d* 1964), *o d* of late Cuthbert Leicester-Warren. *Educ:* Ludgrove; Eton. Served European War, 1914-18 (wounded three times, DSO, despatches twice); Adj. 3rd Bn Coldstream Guards, 1920-22; Adj. OTC Eton, 1922-25; Staff Coll., Camberley, 1927-28; Bde Major, 1st Guards Brigade, 1929-32; DAA and QMG London District, 1932-33; Gen. Staff Officer, 2nd Grade, The War Office, 1935-36; commanded 1st Bn Coldstream Guards, 1936-38; Gen. Staff Officer, 1st Grade, Staff Coll., Quetta, 1938-40; Brigadier, 20th Guards Brigade, 1940; Dep. Chief of the Gen. Staff BEF, 1940; Brigadier, 29th Independent Brigade Group, 1940; Comdr West Sussex Div., 1941; Comdr, 15th (Scottish) Div., Comdr Guards Armoured Div., 1941; Commanding 30th Corps, 1942; Comdr, 8th Army, 1944; C-in-C Allied Land Forces South-East Asia, 1944-45; GOC-in-C Eastern Command, 1945-46; retired, 1946. Dep. Lt County of Salop, 1947. Hon. Col Shropshire Yeo., 1947-62; JP 1949-63; High Sheriff of Salop, 1958. Pres. Combined Cadet Force Assoc., 1950. Lt, Tower of London, 1954. Pres. Warwickshire County Cricket Club, 1959; Nat. Pres., British Legion, 1962-70; Pres. Shropshire County Cricket Club, 1962; Chm., Old Etonian Assoc., 1964 (Pres.,

1946); Pres. MCC, 1965-66; Pres. Cricket Soc., 1969. *Heir:* b Alec William Leese, b 1909. *Address:* Worfield House, Bridgnorth, Salop. *T:* Worfield 250 and 259. *Club:* Turf.

**LEETE, Leslie William Thomas,** CBE 1965 (MBE 1952); Chief Officer of the London Fire Brigade, 1962-70; *b* 18 Dec. 1909; *o s* of William Leete and Maud Evelyn Leete (*née* Cain), Luton, Beds; *m* 1941, Isabel, *yr d* of William Peover, Batchacre Hall, Adbaston, Salop; one *d*. *Educ:* Bedford Sch. Hat manufacturer, 1928-39. London Fire Brigade, 1939-: Senior Staff Officer: London Region, National Fire Service, 1944-48; London Fire Brigade, 1948-52; Dep. Chief Officer, London Fire Brigade, 1952-62. Mem. Instn of Fire Engineers. *Recreations:* cabinet-making, gardening. *Address:* 3 Lansdowne Road, Luton, Beds. *Club:* Royal Automobile.

**LE FANU, Admiral of the Fleet Sir Michael,** GCB 1968 (KCB 1963; CB 1960); DSC 1941; Chief of Naval Staff and First Sea Lord, 1968-70; *b* 2 Aug. 1913; *s* of Capt. H. B. Le Fanu, Royal Navy; *m* 1943, Prudence, *d* of late Adm. Sir Vaughan Morgan, KBE, CB, MVO, DSC; two *s* one *d*. Served in HM Ships Aurora, Howe and US 3rd/5th Fleets, 1939-45. Commanded HMS Eagle, 1957-58; Third Sea Lord and Controller of the Navy, 1961-65; C-in-C Middle East, 1965-68. Hon. Elder Brother of Trinity House, 1969. US Bronze Star, 1945. *Address:* 17 Stonehill Road, SW14. *T:* 01-876 1477.

**LE FANU, Mrs W. R.;** *see* Maconchy, Elizabeth.

**LE FEVRE, Prof. Raymond James Wood,** PhD, DSc London; FRS; FRIC; FRACI; FAA; Professor of Chemistry, since 1946 and Head of the School of Chemistry, since 1948, in the University of Sydney; *b* 1 April 1905; *s* of Raymond James and Ethel May Le Fèvre; *m* 1931, Catherine Gunn Tideman; one *s* one *d*. *Educ:* Isleworth County Sch.; Queen Mary Coll., University of London. Lecturer in Organic Chemistry, University Coll., London, 1928; Reader, 1939; Chemical Adviser to RAF and RAAF in UK, Far East, and Australia, 1939-44; Asst Dir R & D (Armament Chemistry), Ministry of Aircraft Production, London, 1944; Head, Chem. Dept, RAE Farnborough, 1944-46; Trustee, Mitchell Library, Sydney, 1947; Mem., Development Council NSW University of Technology, 1948-50; Trustee, Museum of Applied Arts and Science, Sydney, 1947-. Foundation Fellow, Austr. Acad. of Science, 1953. Liversidge Lecturer, 1960; Masson Lecturer, ANZAAS, 1967; Pres., Royal Society NSW, 1961. Pres. NSW Br., Royal Aust. Chem. Inst. Smith Medal, Royal Aust. Chem. Inst., 1952. Coronation Medal, 1953. Fellow, Queen Mary Coll., London, 1962. *Publications:* Dipole Moments, 3rd edn 1953; Molecular Polarizability and Refractivity, 1965; Establishment of Chemistry within Australian Science, 1968; about 400 papers on chemical research topics, mostly in Jl Chem. Soc., Trans. Faraday Soc., Austr. Jl Chem., etc. *Recreation:* pleasant work. *Address:* 6 Aubrey Road, Northbridge, Sydney, NSW 2063, Australia. *T:* 951018.

**le FLEMING, Sir Frank Thomas,** 10th Bt, *cr* 1705; *b* 27 Dec. 1887; *s* of Sir William Hudleston le Fleming, 9th Bt, and Martha, *d* of John Kelland, Crwys Morchard, Devon; *S* father 1945; *m* 1921, Isabel Annie Fraser, *d* of late James Craig, Manaia, NZ; three *s*. *Educ:* Napier Boys' High Sch., NZ. Served European War, 1914-18, in Engineer Corps. Landowner. *Heir: s* William Kelland le Fleming [*b* 27 April 1922; *m* 1948, Noveen Avis, *d* of C. C. Sharpe, Rukuhia, Hamilton, NZ; three *s* three *d*]. *Address:* Rydal Lovat, Auroa Road, PD Manaia, Taranaki, NZ. *T:* 41 Manaia.

**LEFSCHETZ, Prof. Solomon,** PhD; ME; HB Fine Research Professor Emeritus, Princeton University; Professor, National University of Mexico, since 1944; *b* Moscow, 3 Sept. 1884; *m* 1913, Alice Berg Hayes. *Educ:* Ecole Centrale, Paris; Clark Univ., Worcester, Mass. With Westinghouse Electric & Manufacturing Co., Pittsburgh, 1907-10; Instructor of Maths, Nebraska Univ., 1911-13; University of Kansas: Instructor of Maths, 1913-16; Asst Prof., 1916-19; Assoc. Prof., 1919-23; Prof., 1923-25; Princeton University: Assoc. Prof., 1925-28; Prof., 1928-32; HB Fine Research Prof., 1933-53; Chm. Dept of Mathematics, 1945-; Exchange Prof., Mexico City, 1945-46, 1947. Member: Nat. Acad. of Sciences; Amer. Math. Soc., (Pres. 1935-36); Math. Assoc. of Amer.; Amer. Philos. Soc.; Royal Society (For. Mem.); Acad. des Sciences de Paris (Associate Mem.), etc. Holds several hon. degrees. Decoration Aztec Eagle, 1964. Bordin Prize, French Academy, 1919; Bôcher Prize, Amer. Math. Soc., 1924; Feltrinelli Prize, Accad. dei Lincei, 1956. *Publications:* L'Analyse Situs et la géométrie algébrique, 1924; Surfaces et variétés algébriques, 1927; Topology, 1930; Algebraic Topology, 1942; Introduction to Topology, 1949; Algebraic Geometry, 1952; Differential Equations: geometric theory, 1958; editor, Annals of Mathematics. *Address:* 11 Lake Lane, Princeton, NJ 08540, USA.

**LE GALLAIS, Sir Richard (Lyle),** Kt 1965; Member, Panel of Chairmen, Industrial Tribunals for England and Wales, since 1968; *b* 15 Nov. 1916; *s* of late William Le Gallais and Mrs Cory; *m* 1947, Juliette Forsythe; two *s*. *Educ:* Victoria Coll., Jersey; Inns of Court Sch. of Law. Called to Bar, 1939; Dep. Asst JAG (SEAC) 1945. Pres. War Crimes Tribunal, Singapore, 1946 (Lt-Col). Advocate, Royal Court, Jersey, 1947; Resident Magistrate, Kenya, 1949; Sen. Res. Magistrate and Acting Puisne Judge, N Rhodesia, 1958; Chief Justice, Aden, 1960-67. *Recreations:* gastronomy, music. *Address:* Bainly House, Gillingham, Dorset. *T:* Bourton 373.

**LE GALLIENNE, Eva;** Theatrical Producer, Director and Actress; *b* London, England, 11 Jan. 1899; *d* of Richard Le Gallienne and Julie Norregaard. *Educ:* College Sévigné, Paris, France. Début Prince of Wales Theatre, London, in The Laughter of Fools, 1915; New York Début in The Melody of Youth, 1916; appeared in NY and on tour, in Mr Lazarus, season of 1916-17; with Ethel Barrymore in The Off Chance, 1917-18; Not So Long Ago, 1920-21; Liliom, 1921-22; The Swan, 1923; Hannele in The Assumption of Hannele, by Hauptmann, 1923; Jeanne d'Arc, by Mercedes de Acosta, 1925; The Call of Life, by Schnitzler, 1925; The Master Builder, by Henrik Ibsen, 1925-26. Founder and Director Civic Repertory Theatre, NY, 1926; played in Saturday Night, The Three Sisters, Cradle Song, 2x2–5, The First Stone, Improvisations in June, The Would-Be Gentleman, L'Invitation au Voyage, The Cherry Orchard, Peter Pan, On the High Road, The Lady from Alfaqueque, Katerina, The Open Door, A Sunny Morning, The Master Builder, John Gabriel Borkman, La Locandiera, Twelfth Night, Inheritors, The Good Hope, Hedda Gabler, The Sea Gull, Mlle. Bourrat, The Living Corpse, Women Have Their Way, Romeo and Juliet, The Green Cockatoo, Siegfried, Allison's House, Camille, Liliom (revival), Dear Jane, Alice in Wonderland, L'Aiglon, 1934; Rosmersholm, 1935; Uncle Harry, 1942; Cherry Orchard, 1944; Thérèse,

1945; Elizabeth I in Schiller's Mary Stuart, Phœnix Theatre, NYC, 1958; toured in same, 1959-60; Elizabeth the Queen, 1961-62; The Sea Gull, 1963; Ring Around the Moon, 1963; The Mad Woman of Chaillot, 1964; The Trojan Women, 1964; Exit the King, 1967. Man. Dir of Amer. Repertory Theatre, which did six classic revivals in repertory, NY, 1946 and 1947; Dir The Cherry Orchard, Lyceum Theatre, NY, 1967-68. Hon. MA (Tufts Coll.), 1927, and several honorary doctorates from 1930. Member Actors' Equity Assoc. and Managers' Protective Assoc.; Founder National Woman's Party. Has won various awards; Gold Medal, Soc. Arts and Sciences, 1926; Am. Acad. of Arts and Letters medal for good speech, 1945; Cross of St Olav (Norway), 1961. *Publications:* At 33 (autobiography), 1934; Flossie and Bossy, (NY) 1949, (London) 1950; With A Quiet Heart, 1953; A Preface to Hedda Gabler, 1953; The Master Builder, a new translation with a Prefatory Study, 1955; trans. Six Plays by Henrik Ibsen, 1957 (NYC); trans. The Wild Duck and Other Plays by Henrik Ibsen, 1961 (NYC); The Mystic in the Theatre: Eleonora Duse, 1966 (NYC and London); articles for New York Times, Theatre Arts Monthly, etc. *Recreations:* gardening, painting. *Address:* Weston, Conn 06880, USA.

**LEGARD, Capt. Sir Thomas (Digby),** 14th Bt, *cr* 1660; Captain Royal Artillery; *b* 16 Oct. 1905; *e s* of Sir D. A. H. Legard, 13th Bt; *S* father, 1961; *m* 1935, Mary Helen, *e d* of late Lt-Col E. G. S. L'Estrange Malone; three *s. Educ:* Lancing; Magdalene Coll., Cambridge. *Heir: s* Charles Thomas Legard [*b* 26 Oct. 1938; *m* 1962, Elizabeth, *d* of John M. Guthrie, High House, East Ayton, Scarborough; two *s* one *d*]. *Address:* Scampston Hall, Malton, Yorks. *T:* Rillington 224. *Club:* MCC.

**LEGENTILHOMME, Général Paul Louis,** Hon. KCB, *cr* 1946; *b* at Valognes, Department of Manche (Normandy), 26 March 1884; *m* 1947, Marjorie M., *widow* of Comdr C. J. Smith, RN, and *o d* of late Alderman Sir Charles McRea. *Educ:* College of Le Havre. Military Sch. of St Cyr, 1905-7; Sub-Lt in the Colonial Infantry, 1907; Lt, 1909; Capt., 1915; Major, 1925; Lt-Col, 1928; Col, 1934; Général de brigade, 1938; Général de division, 1941; Général de Corps d'Armée, 1943; Général d'Armée, 1947; has served in Syria, in Indo-China, in Madagascar, and passed French, Staff Coll. and Centre des Hautes Etudes Militaires before the war; C-in-C in French Somaliland, 1938; C-in-C allied forces in French and British Somaliland, 1940; on 16 June, 1940 informed Foreign Office of his decision to carry on fight with Great Britain till victory, but was obliged to give in at Jibuti and escaped by night, 1 Aug. 1940, to join General de Gaulle; GOC Free French Forces in Sudan for operations against Erythrea, 1941; in command of allied forces operating in Syria and took Damascus, 1941; Haut Commissaire de France pour les possessions de l'Océan Indien et Gouvernement Général de Madagascar, 1942-43; Commissioner for National Defence, French Cttee of National Liberation, 1943: Commandant la 3ème Région Militaire, Rouen, 1944-45; Military Governor of Paris, 1945-47; retired 1947; Member, Assembly of French Union, 1952. Decorations: French: Médaille Militaire, Grande Croix de la Légion d'Honneur, Croix de la Libération, Croix de Guerre 1914-18 and 1939-45, etc. American: Commander of Legion of Merit. Belgian: Grand Officier de l'Ordre de la Couronne and Croix de Guerre. Czechoslovakian: Grand Officier du Lion Blanc. Brazilian: Grand Officier de l'Ordre de la Croix du Sud. Polish: Virtutis Militaris, 3rd Class. *Address:* Logio de la Plage, 06 Villefranche O/Mer, France.

**LEGER, (Marie-René) Alexis Saint-Leger** (*pseudonym* St-John Perse); Grand Officier de la Légion d'Honneur; Commandeur des Arts et des Lettres; poet; *b* Guadeloupe, 31 May 1887; *s* of Amédée Leger, lawyer; *m* 1958, Dorothy Milburn Russell, USA. *Educ:* Universities of Bordeaux and Paris. Joined French Foreign Service, 1914; Sec., French Embassy, Peking, 1916-21; Chef de Cabinet, Ministry of Foreign Affairs, 1925-32; Counsellor, 1925; Minister, 1927; Ambassadeur de France and Sec.-Gen., Min. of Foreign Affairs, 1933-40. Left France for America, 1940. Consultant on French Literature, Library of Congress, 1941-45. Member: Amer. Acad. of Arts and Letters; Bayerischen Akademie Der Schönen Künste. Doctor (*hc*), Yale University. Hon. Mem., Modern Language Assoc. Grand Prix National des Lettres, Paris, 1959. Nobel Prize for Literature, 1960. Hon. Mem. American Academy of Arts and Sciences, 1963. KCVO (Hon.), 1927; GBE (Hon.), 1938; KCB (Hon.), 1940. *Publications:* Anabase, 1924 (Eng. trans., 1930, rev. edn, 1938, 1949); Eloges, 1911 (Eng. trans., 1944, rev. edn, 1956); La Gloire des Rois, 1925; Exil, 1944 (Eng. Trans., 1949); Vents, 1946 (Eng. trans., Winds, 1953); Amers, 1957 (Eng. trans., Seamarks, 1958); Chronique, 1960 (Eng. trans., 1961); Oiseaux, 1962 (Eng. trans., 1963); Pour Dante, 1965. *Address:* 1621, 34th Street, NW Washington, DC 20007, USA; Les Vigneaux, 83 Giens, France.

**LÉGER, His Eminence Cardinal Paul Emile;** *b* Valleyfield, Quebec, Canada, 26 April 1904; *s* of Ernest Léger and Alda Beauvais. *Educ:* Ste-Thérèse Seminary; Grand Seminary, Montreal. Seminary of Philosophy, Paris, 1930-31; Seminary of Theology, Paris, 1931-32; Asst Master of Novices, Paris, 1932-33; Superior Seminary of Fukuoka, Japan, 1933-39; Prof., Seminary of Philosophy, Montreal, 1939-40; Vicar-Gen., Diocese of Valleyfield, 1940-47; Rector, Canadian Coll., Rome, 1947-50; consecrated bishop in Rome and apptd to See of Montreal, 1950; elevated to Sacred Coll. of Cardinals and given titular Church of St Mary of the Angels, 1953; Archbishop of Montreal, 1950-67; resigned to work as a missionary in Africa. Has several hon. doctorates both from Canada and abroad. Holds foreign decorations. *Address:* 1071 Cathedral Street, Montreal 3, PQ, Canada.

**LEGG, Allan Aubrey R.;** *see* Rowan-Legg.

**LEGGATE, John Mortimer,** MB, ChB, FRCS; Dean of the Faculty of Medicine, University of Liverpool, 1953-69, retired; *b* 7 April 1904; *s* of late Dr James Leggate, Liverpool; *m* 1936, Grace, *d* of late Rev. John Clark, Newport, Fife; one *s. Educ:* Liverpool Coll.; University of Liverpool. Gladstone Divinity Prize, 1923; Pres., Guild of Undergraduates, University of Liverpool, 1927-28; MB, ChB (Hons) 1929; MRCS, LRCP, 1929; FRCS, 1933; John Rankin Fellow in Anatomy, 1929-30. Resident Surgical Officer and Surgical Tutor, Liverpool Royal Infirmary, 1932; Prof. of Surgery, Moukden Med. Coll. (Manchuria), 1933-41 and 1946-49; Resident Asst Surgeon, David Lewis Northern Hosp., Liverpool, 1941-43. Served War of 1939-45, Major, RAMC, comdg Field Surgical Unit, D Day Landing, 1944 (despatches); OC Surgical Div. of a Gen. Hosp. in India, 1945-46; demobilised, 1946 (Hon. Lt-Col). Sen. Registrar in Neuro-Surgical Unit at Walton Hosp., Liverpool, 1950-51. *Publications:* Spontaneous separation of gall-bladder, 1948; contrib. to medical journals.

*Recreation:* fishing. *Address:* 19 Skipton Avenue, Banks Road, Southport, Lancs. *Club:* University (Liverpool).

**LEGGATT, Maj.-Gen. Charles St Quentin Outen Fullbrook-,** CBE 1945; DSO 1914; MC; *b* 16 Aug. 1889; *m* 1917, Mary Katharine, *d* of late Col G. H. Bittleston, RA, of Ashleigh, Whitchurch, Devon; two *d. Educ:* Bath Coll.; RMC, Sandhurst. Entered Army, 1909; Capt., 1915; Bt Maj., 1918; Major, 1924; Lt-Col, 1932; Col, 1936; served European War, 1914-18 (wounded twice, despatches four times, DSO, Military Cross, Bt Maj.); commanded 2nd Bn Royal Berks Regt, 1932-36; Instructor Senior Officers' Sch., Sheerness, 1936-39; Comdr Inf. Brigade, TA, 1939-41; Div., 1941-42; Tunisia, 1943-44; 61 Area, Ancona, N Italy, 1944-46; retired pay, 1946. Officier Légion d'Honneur, 1947. *Address:* c/o Barclays Bank Ltd, King Street, Reading, Berks.

**LEGGE,** family name of **Earl of Dartmouth.**

**LEGGE, Maj.-Gen. (Retd) Stanley Ferguson,** CBE 1952; Master General of the Ordnance, Australia, 1954-57; *b* 24 April 1900; *s* of late Lt-Gen. J. G. Legge, CB, CMG; *m* 1929, Joyce Y. Walker, Melbourne, Aust.; one *s* one *d* (and one *d* decd). *Educ:* Melbourne Gram. Sch.; St Paul's, London. Lt, Aust. Staff Corps, 1920; various postings; DAQMG, 7 Aust. Div., AIF, 1940; held various positions in Middle East, Australia, New Guinea, Solomon Islands, until 1946; QMG 1953. *Address:* 459 Glenferrie Road, Kooyong, Melbourne, Vic., Australia.

**LEGGE-BOURKE, Major Sir (Edward Alexander) Henry,** KBE 1960; DL; MP (C) Isle of Ely, since 1945; *b* 16 May 1914; *o s* of late N. W. H. Legge-Bourke, Coldstream Guards, and Lady Victoria Forester; *m* 1938, Catherine Jean, 3rd *d* of Col Sir Arthur Grant, DSO, 10th Bt of Monymusk; two *s* one *d. Educ:* Eton; RMC, Sandhurst. 2nd Lt RHG 1934; served War of 1939-45 (wounded). Chm., 1922 Cttee, 1970-. Chm. Grant Production Co. Ltd. DL Cambridgeshire, 1955. *Publications:* Defence of the Realm, 1949; Master of the Offices, 1950; The King's Guards, Horse and Foot, 1951; The Queen's Guards, 1965. *Address:* 9 Wilbraham Place, SW1. *Club:* Carlton.

**LEGGETT, Douglas Malcolm Aufrère,** MA, PhD, DSc; FRAeS; FIMA; Vice-Chancellor, University of Surrey, since 1966; *b* 27 May 1912; *s* of George Malcolm Kent Leggett and Winifred Mabel Horsfall; *m* 1943, Enid Vida Southall; one *s* one *d. Educ:* Rugby Sch.; Edinburgh Univ.; Trinity Coll., Cambridge. Wrangler, 1934; Fellow of Trinity Coll., Cambridge, 1937; Queen Mary Coll., London, 1937-39; Royal Aircraft Establishment, 1939-45; Royal Aeronautical Society, 1945-50; King's Coll., London, 1950-60; Principal, Battersea Coll. of Technology, 1960-66. *Publications:* contrib. to scientific and technical jls. *Address:* Southlands, Fairoak Lane, Oxshott, Surrey. *T:* Oxshott 3061.

**LEGGETT, Sir Frederick William,** KBE 1951; Kt 1941; CB 1933; *b* 23 Dec. 1884; *s* of late F. J. Leggett and Frances Mary, *d* of William Murphy, Huntingdon; *m* 1st, Edith Guinevere (*d* 1949), *d* of Henry Kitson, Woodford; one *s* three *d*; 2nd, Beatrice Melville, *d* of Joseph Roe. *Educ:* City of London and Strand Schs; King's Coll., London. Entered Civil Service, 1904; Private Sec. to Parliamentary Sec., Board of Trade, 1915; to Minister of Labour, 1917; Asst Sec. Ministry of Labour, 1919; Under-Sec., 1939; Chief Industrial Commissioner, 1940-42; Mem. of Government Mission of Inquiry into Industrial Conditions in Canada and United States, 1926. Brit. Govt Member of Governing Body of ILO, 1932-44, Chm., 1937-38; Dep. Sec. Ministry of Labour and National Service, 1942-45. Member: British Reparations Mission, Moscow, 1945; Anglo-American Cttee of Inquiry into Palestine, 1946; Docks Emergency Cttee, 1949; Cttee on London Transport, 1956-57; Chairman: London and S-E Regional Board for Industry, 1947-48; London Docks Disputes Inquiry Cttee, 1950; Building Apprenticeship and Training Council, 1953; Bldg and Civil Engrg Holidays Management Bd, 1946-; Industrial Relations Adviser, Anglo-Iranian Oil Co., 1947-60. Vice-Pres. Royal Coll. of Nursing, 1948-. *Address:* Downside Lodge, West Kingston, Sussex. *T:* Rustington 6074. *Club:* Reform.

**LEGH,** family name of **Baron Newton.**

**LEGH, Charles Legh Shuldham Cornwall-,** AEA; *b* 10 Feb. 1903; *er s* of late Charles Henry George Cornwall Legh, of High Legh Hall, Cheshire, and late Geraldine Maud, *d* of Lt-Col Arthur James Shuldham, Royal Inniskilling Fusiliers; *m* 1930, Dorothy, *er d* of late J. W. Scott, Seal, Sevenoaks; one *s* two *d.* Served 1939-45 with AAF and RAF. JP Cheshire, 1938; High Sheriff, 1939; DL and CC 1949. Chairman, Cheshire Police Authority, 1957-. *Address:* High Legh House, Knutsford, Cheshire. *T:* Lymm 2303. *Club:* Carlton.

**LEGH, Major Hon. Sir Francis (Michael),** KCVO 1968 (CVO 1967; MVO 1964); Major (retired), Grenadier Guards; Treasurer since 1962 and Private Secretary since 1959, to the Princess Margaret; also Equerry to Queen Elizabeth the Queen Mother, since 1956 (Assistant Private Secretary and Equerry, 1956-59); *b* 2 Aug. 1919; 3rd *s* of 3rd Baron Newton and Hon. Helen Winifred Meysey-Thompson (*d* 1958); *m* 1948, Ruadh Daphne, *o c* of late Alan Holmes Watson; one *s* one *d. Educ:* Eton; Royal Military College, Sandhurst. Served War of 1939-45 (despatches); Italy, 1943-45; GSO2, Military Mission to Greece. *Recreations:* shooting, golf. *Address:* 13 The Boltons, SW10. *T:* 01-373 8787. *Clubs:* White's, Brooks's, Guards, Pratt's.

**LE GOY, Raymond Edgar Michel;** Under-Secretary, Board of Trade (Civil Aviation Division) since 1968; *b* 1919; *e s* of J. A. S. M. N. and May Le Goy; *m* 1960, Ernestine Burnett, Trelawny, Jamaica; two *s. Educ:* William Ellis Sch.; Gonville and Caius Coll., Cambridge (MA). 1st cl. hons. Hist. Tripos. Sec. Cambridge Union, 1939. Served Army, 1940-46: Staff Captain, HQ E Africa, 1944; Actg Major, 1945. LPTB, 1947; Min. of Transport, 1947; UK Shipping Adviser in Japan, 1949-51; in Far East and SE Asia, 1951; Asst Secretary: MoT, 1958; Min. of Aviation, 1959; Bd of Trade, 1966. *Publication:* The Victorian Burletta, 1953. *Recreations:* theatre, music, race relations. *Address:* 199 Goldhurst Terrace, NW6. *T:* 01-624 7023. *Clubs:* National Liberal, Players'.

**LE GRICE, Very Rev. F(rederick) Edwin,** MA; Dean of Ripon, since 1968; *b* 14 Dec. 1911; *s* of Frederick and Edith Le Grice; *m* 1940, Joyce Margaret Hildreth; one *s* two *d. Educ:* Paston Sch., North Walsham; Queens' Coll., Cambridge; Westcott House, Cambridge. BA (2nd class hons Mathematics, 2nd class hons Theology) 1934; MA 1946. Asst Curate: St Aidan's, Leeds, 1935-38; Paignton, 1938-46; Vicar of Totteridge, N20, 1946-58; Canon Residentiary and Sub-Dean of St Albans Cathedral, 1958-68; Examining Chaplain to the Bishop of St Albans, 1958-68. *Address:* The Minster House, Ripon, Yorks. *T:* Ripon 3615.

**LEHMANN, Andrew George;** Managing Director, Linguaphone Institute Ltd, since 1968; *b* 1922; British; *m* 1942, Alastine Mary, *d* of late K. N. Bell; two *s* one *d*. *Educ:* Dulwich Coll.; The Queen's Coll., Oxford. MA, DPhil Oxon. Served with RCS and Indian Army, 6th Rajputana Rifles. Asst lecturer and lecturer, Manchester Univ., 1945-51; Prof. of French Studies, University of Reading, 1951-68; Dean of Faculty of Letters, University of Reading, 1960-66. Visiting Prof. of Comparative Literature, University of Mainz, 1956. Mem., Hale Cttee on University Teaching Methods, 1961. Mem., Anglo-French Permanent Mixed Cultural Commission, 1963-68. Adviser: Chinese Univ. of Hong Kong, 1964; Haile Selassie I Univ., Ethiopia, 1965. Member: Hong Kong Univ. Grants Cttee, 1966; Academic Planning Board, New Univ. of Ulster, 1966. Associated Prof., University of Warwick, 1968. *Publications:* The Symbolist Aesthetic in France, 1950 and 1967; Sainte-Beuve, a portrait of the Critic, 1962; A Social History of Modern France, 1969; articles in various periodicals and learned reviews. *Recreations:* music, travel, gardening. *Address:* 3 Hanover Terrace, NW1. *T:* 01-723 8215.

**LEHMANN, Beatrix;** Actress; *b* 1 July 1903; 3rd *d* of late Rudolph Chambers Lehmann. *Educ:* home; Paris. Trained for stage at Royal Academy of Dramatic Art. First professional engagement, Sidney in The Bill of Divorcement on a tour of South Coast Village Halls. First London appearance, Lyric Theatre, Hammersmith, 1924, as Peggy in The Way of the World; subsequently played numerous West End parts. Appearances include: Lavinia in Mourning Becomes Electra; Abbie in Desire Under the Elms; Mrs Alving in Ghosts; Family Reunion; No Sign of the Dove; Blood Wedding; Waltz of the Toreadors; Garden District; Lady Macbeth in Macbeth (Old Vic); Miss Bordereau in The Aspern Papers; A Cuckoo in the Nest; Marfa Kabanova in The Storm (Old Vic); Hecuba (Mermaid); The Night I Chased the Women with an Eel; Peer Gynt, Chichester, 1970. Entered films, 1935. Appears on TV. *Publications:* two novels; a number of short stories. *Recreations:* swimming and history. *Address:* c/o International Famous Agency, 11/12 Hanover Street, W1.

**LEHMANN, Prof. Hermann,** MD, PhD, ScD, FRCP, FRIC, FRCPath; Professor of Clinical Biochemistry, Cambridge University, since 1967; University Biochemist to Addenbrooke's Hospital, Cambridge, and Hon. Director, MRC Abnormal Haemoglobin Unit (WHO Reference Centre for Abnormal Haemoglobins), University Department of Biochemistry, Cambridge, since 1963; Fellow of Christ's College, Cambridge, since 1965; *b* 8 July 1910; *s* of Paul Lehmann, Publisher, and Bella Lehmann (*née* Apelt); *m* 1942, Benigna Norman-Butler; one *s* two *d* (and one *s* decd). *Educ:* Kreuzschule, Dresden; Universities of Freiburg-i-B, Frankfurt, Berlin, Heidelberg. MD (Basle) 1934; Research Asst, Heidelberg, 1934-36; Research Student: Sch. of Biochem., also Christ's Coll., Cambridge, 1936-38. PhD (Cambridge), 1938; Beit Memorial Fellow for Med. Res., 1938-42. RAMC 1943-47. Colonial Med. Research Fellow for Malnutrition and Anæmia, Makerere Coll., Uganda, 1947-49; Cons. Pathologist, Pembury Hosp., Kent, 1949-51; Sen. Lectr, (Reader, 1959), Chem. Pathol. St Bart's, Hosp., 1951-63. Rockefeller Travelling Fellowship to USA, 1954. Hon. Prof., University of Freiburg-i-B, 1964-. Has various academic honours and Hon. Corresp. Memberships. *Publications:* Man's Haemoglobins (with R. G. Huntsman), 1966; articles in sci. jls. *Address:* 22 Newton Road, Cambridge. *Club:* Athenæum.

**LEHMANN, John Frederick,** CBE 1964; FRSL; President, Royal Literary Fund, since 1966; Editor of the London Magazine from its foundation to 1961; Managing Director of John Lehmann Ltd from its foundation to 1952; Founder and Editor of New Writing and of Orpheus; *b* 2 June 1907; *s* of late Rudolph Chambers Lehmann and Alice Marie Davis. *Educ:* Eton (King's Scholar); Trinity Coll., Cambridge. Partner and Gen. Manager, The Hogarth Press, 1938-46; Advisory Editor, The Geographical Magazine, 1940-45. Editor, New Soundings (BBC Third Programme), 1952, The London Magazine, 1954. Chm. Editorial Advisory Panel, British Council, 1952-58; Vis. Prof., Univ. of Texas, 1970; Pres. Alliance Française in Great Britain, 1955-63; Officer, Gold Cross, Order of George I (Greece), 1954, Comdr, 1961; Officier Légion d'Honneur, 1958; Grand Officier, Etoile Noire, 1960; Officier, Ordre des Arts et des Lettres, 1965. Prix du Rayonnement Français, 1961. *Publications:* A Garden Revisited, 1931; The Noise of History, 1934; Prometheus and the Bolsheviks, 1937; Evil Was Abroad, 1938; Down River, 1939; New Writing in Europe, 1940; Forty Poems, 1942; The Sphere of Glass, 1944; Shelley in Italy, 1947; The Age of the Dragon, 1951; The Open Night, 1952; The Whispering Gallery (Autobiography I), 1955; I Am My Brother (Autobiography II), 1960; Ancestors and Friends, 1962; Collected Poems, 1963; Christ the Hunter, 1965; The Ample Proposition (Autobiography III), 1966; A Nest of Tigers, 1968; In My Own Time (condensed one-volume autobiography), 1969 (USA); Holborn, 1970; Editor: Poems from New Writing, 1946, French Stories from New Writing, 1947, The Year's Work in Literature, 1949 and 1950, English Stories from New Writing, 1950, Pleasures of New Writing, 1952; The Chatto Book of Modern Poetry, 1956 (with C. Day Lewis); The Craft of Letters in England, 1956; Modern French Stories, 1956; Coming to London, 1957; Italian Stories of Today, 1959; Selected Poems of Edith Sitwell, 1965; (with Derek Parker) Edith Sitwell: selected letters, 1970. *Recreations:* aquatic and literary. *Address:* 85 Cornwall Gardens, SW7. *Clubs:* Garrick, Bath, Eton Viking.

**LEHMANN, Lotte;** Opera, Concert and Radio Singer (Soprano), retired; *b* Perleberg, Germany, 27 Feb. 1888; *d* of Carl Lehmann and Marie Schuster; *m* Otto Krause (*d* 1939). *Educ:* Royal Academy of Music, Berlin. Has sung in opera and concert in the principal cities of Europe, USA, South America, Australia, New Zealand. Hon. Pres., Music Acad. of West, Santa Barbara, Calif.; Hon. mem. Vienna State Opera; Hon. mem. Music Academy, Vienna. Medals: Legion of Honour, France; Golden Palm, France; Golden Medal, Sweden; Golden Medal, Austria; Golden Medal, Germany; Rings of Honour: Viennese Philharmonic Orchestra; Soloists of Vienna Opera House; Ring of City of Vienna. Holds four doctorates in music and humane letters. *Publications:* Eternal Flight (novel); Midway in my Song (biography); More than Singing (song interpretation); My Many Lives (book on opera); Five Operas and Richard Strauss, 1964 (Eng. edn as: Singing with Richard Strauss). *Address:* 4565 Via Huerto, Hope Ranch, Santa Barbara, Calif 93105, USA. *T:* Santa Barbara 93105.

**LEHMANN, Rosamond Nina;** 2nd *d* of R. C. Lehmann and Alice Davis; *m* 1928, Hon. Wogan Philipps (*see* 2nd Baron Milford); one *s* (and one *d* decd). *Educ:* privately; Girton Coll.,

Cambridge (scholar). *Publications:* Dusty Answer, 1927; A Note in Music, 1930; Invitation to the Waltz, 1932; The Weather in the Streets, 1936; No More Music (play), 1939; The Ballad and the Source, 1944; The Gypsy's Baby, 1946; The Echoing Grove, 1953; The Swan in the Evening, 1967. *Recreations:* reading, music. *Address:* 70 Eaton Square, SW1.

**LEHRER, Thomas Andrew;** writer of songs since 1943; Lecturer in Political Science, Massachusetts Institute of Technology, since 1962; *b* 9 April 1928; *s* of James Lehrer and Anna Lehrer (*née* Waller). *Educ:* Harvard Univ.; Columbia Univ. AB 1946, MA 1947, Harvard Univ. Student (mathematics, especially probability and statistics) till 1953. Part-time teaching at Harvard, 1947-51. Theoretical physicist at Baird-Atomic, Inc., Cambridge, Massachusetts, 1953-54. Entertainer, 1953-55, 1957-60. US Army, 1955-57. Lecturer in Business Administration, Harvard Business Sch., 1961; Lecturer: in Education, Harvard Univ., 1963-66; in Psychology, Wellesley Coll., 1966. *Publications:* Tom Lehrer Song Book, 1954; Tom Lehrer's Second Song Book, 1968; contrib. to Annals of Mathematical Statistics, Journal of Soc. of Industrial and Applied Maths. *Recreation:* piano. *Address:* P.O. Box 121, Cambridge, Massachusetts 02138, USA. *T:* Eliot-4-7708.

**LEICESTER,** 5th Earl of, *cr* 1837; **Thomas William Edward Coke,** MVO 1937; Viscount Coke, 1837; Major Scots Guards (retired); Extra Equerry to the Queen since 1952 (to King George VI, 1937-52); DL Norfolk; *b* 16 May 1908; *o surv s* of 4th Earl and Marion Gertrude (*d* 1955), *d* of late Colonel Hon. W. R. Trefusis; *S* father 1949; *m* 1931, Lady Elizabeth Yorke, CVO, 1965, Lady of the Bedchamber to the Queen, since 1953, *o d* of 8th Earl of Hardwicke; three *d. Educ:* Eton; RMC Sandhurst. Joined Scots Guards in 1928; Captain, 1938; Major, 1945; served War of 1939-45; ADC to Field Marshal Earl Wavell, 1941. Equerry to the Duke of York (later King George VI), 1934-37. Lieut-Colonel Home Guard, 1952-56; Hon. Colonel, 1st Cadet Battalion, Royal Norfolk Regt. Local Director, Royal Insurance Co. Member Board of Governors, Gresham's School, Holt. President: Royal Norfolk Agricultural Assoc., 1958; CLA, Norfolk Branch, 1958-61. Royal Order of George I, Greece, 1963. *Heir: cousin* Anthony Louis Lovel Coke, RAF [*b* 11 Sept. 1909; *m* 1st, 1934, Moyra Crossley (marr. diss., 1947); two *s* one *d*; 2nd, 1947, Vera Haigh, Salisbury, Rhodesia]. *Address:* Holkham Hall, Norfolk. *Clubs:* Brooks's, Turf, MCC.
*See also Baron Glenconner, Major T. C. Harvey.*

**LEICESTER, Bishop of,** since 1953; **Rt. Rev. Ronald Ralph Williams,** MA, DD; *b* 14 Oct. 1906; *s* of Rev. Ralph Williams and Mary, *d* of Joseph Sayers; *m* 1934, Cicely Maud, *o d* of Edward Glanville Kay, Enfield; no *c. Educ:* Judd Sch., Tonbridge; Gonville and Caius Coll., Cambridge; Ridley Hall, Cambridge. 2nd Class, Division I, English Tripos Part I, Cambridge, 1926; 1st Class Theological Tripos, Part I, 1927; 1st Class with distinction, Part II, 1928; Carus Greek Testament Prize, 1927; Scholefield Greek Testament Prize, 1928; Archbishop Cranmer Prize, 1932; Hulsean Preacher, 1934. Tutor, St Aidan's Coll., Birkenhead, 1928-29; Curate, Leyton Parish Church, 1929-31; Chaplain, Ridley Hall, Cambridge, 1931-34; Examining Chaplain to Bishop of Chelmsford, 1931; Home Education Secretary, CMS, 1934-40; Religious Division, Ministry of Information, 1940-45 (Director, 1943-45); Lieut MOI Home Guard; Commissary to Bishop of Tasmania, 1944; Examining Chaplain to Bishop of Durham, 1945; Principal, St John's Coll., Durham, 1945-53; Hon. Canon Durham Cathedral, 1953-54; Proctor in Convocation of York, 1950. President Queen's Coll., Birmingham, 1957-63; Visitor, Ridley Hall, Cambridge, 1957. Entered House of Lords, 1959. *Publications:* Religion and the English Vernacular, 1940; The Strife Goes On, 1940; The Christian Religion, 1941; Authority in the Apostolic Age, 1950; The Perfect Law of Liberty, 1952; The Acts of the Apostles, 1953; Reading Through Hebrews, 1960; The Word of Life, 1960; Take thou Authority, 1961; The Bible in Worship and Ministry, 1962; Letters of John and James (Commentary), 1965; What's right with the C. of E., 1966. *Recreations:* golf, walking, climbing. *Address:* Bishop's Lodge, Leicester. *T:* Leicester 708985. *Clubs:* United University, Alpine, English-Speaking Union; Leicestershire (Leicester).

**LEICESTER, Assistant Bishops of;** *see* Horstead, Rt Rev. J. L. C. and Smith, Rt Rev. Thomas Geoffrey S.

**LEICESTER, Provost of;** *see* Hughes, Very Rev. John Chester.

**LEICESTER, Archdeacon of;** *see* Cole, Ven. Ronald Berkeley.

**LEICESTER, James,** MSc, MScTech, PhD, FRIC; Principal, Northern Polytechnic, London, N7. since 1961; *b* 23 Dec. 1915; *o s* of late James Leicester, Lancs; *m* 1943, Doris Waugh; two *s. Educ:* Cowley Sch., St Helens; Sheffield Univ. BSc (Hons. Chemistry) Sheffield, 1936; MSc Sheffield, 1937; MScTech, Manchester, 1939; PhD London, 1952. Demonstrator, Manchester Univ., 1937-40; Chemical Inspectorate, Ministry of Supply, 1940-45; Lecturer, Medway College of Technology, 1946-47; Lecturer and Senior Lecturer, Woolwich Polytechnic, 1948-56; Head of Dept of Chemistry, Northampton College of Advanced Technology, London, 1956-61. Member Court, City Univ. *Recreation:* map collecting. *Address:* 28 Broomfield Road, Bexleyheath, Kent. *T:* Crayford 21758.

**LEICESTER-WARREN, Lieut-Colonel John Leighton Byrne,** TD 1945; Land Owner; Vice-Lieutenant of Cheshire, since 1968; *b* 25 Sept. 1907; *s* of Cuthbert and Hilda Leicester-Warren; *heir-pres.* to *cousin* Sir M. J. B. Leighton, 11th Bt, *qv*; unmarried. *Educ:* Eton; Magdalen Coll., Oxford. BA 1928, MA 1933. Barrister-at-law, Inner Temple, 1933; N Wales and Chester Circuit, 1935-39. Served War of 1939-45, Cheshire Yeomanry and Staff 6 Cavalry Bde, GSO 3 Athens Area, 1940; captured 1941, POW; ADJAG (War Crimes) BAOR, 1946; Lieut-Colonel Comdg Cheshire Yeomanry, 1949-52. JP 1948, DL 1955, Cheshire; High Sheriff of Cheshire, 1965. *Address:* Tabley House, Knutsford, Cheshire. *T:* Knutsford 3021. *Club:* Pratt's.

**LEIGH,** family name of **Baron Leigh.**

**LEIGH,** 4th Baron *cr* 1839; **Rupert William Dudley Leigh;** TD; DL; JP; *b* 14 March 1908; *o s* of late Major Hon. Rupert Leigh; *S* uncle, 1938; *m* 1931, Anne, *d* of Ellis Hicks Beach, Witcombe Park, Glos; four *s. Educ:* Eton; RMC, Sandhurst. 11th Hussars, 1928-36; Royal Gloucestershire Hussars, 1937-44 (Lieut-Colonel, 1st RGH, 1943). Served with Notts (Sherwood Rangers) Yeomanry in NW Europe, 1944-45. High Steward of Sutton

Coldfield; Member, National Hunt Cttee; Joint Master, North Warwickshire Foxhounds, 1961-65. President, BSJA, 1968-. CStJ 1969. *Heir: s* Hon. John Piers Leigh [*b* 11 Sept. 1935; *m* 1957, Cecilia Poppy, *y d* of late Robert Cecil Jackson, Redlynch, Wilts; one *s* one *d*]. *Address:* Stoneleigh Abbey, Kenilworth, Warwickshire. *T:* Kenilworth 53981. *Club:* Cavalry.

**LEIGH, Archibald Denis,** MD, FRCP; Consultant Physician, Bethlem Royal and Maudsley Hospitals since 1949; Secretary-General, World Psychiatric Association, since 1966; Hon. Consultant in Psychiatry to the British Army, since 1969; Lecturer, Institute of Psychiatry; *b* 11 Oct. 1915; *o s* of Archibald Leigh and Rose Rushworth; *m* 1941, Pamela Parish; two *s* three *d*. *Educ:* Hulme Grammar Sch.; Manchester Univ.; University of Budapest. Manchester City Schol. in Medicine, 1932; BSc 1936; MB, ChB (1st class hons) 1939; Dauntesey Med. Sen. Schol., Prof. Tom Jones Exhibitioner in Anatomy; Sidney Renshaw Jun. Prize in Physiol.; Turner Med. Prize; John Henry Agnew Prize; Stephen Lewis Prize; Prize in Midwifery; MRCP 1941; MD (Manchester), 1947; FRCP, 1955. RAMC, 1940-45 (Lt-Col); Adviser in Neurology, Eastern Army, India. 1st Assistant, Dept of Neurology, London Hospital; Nuffield Fellow, 1947-48; Clinical Fellow, Harvard Univ., 1948. Recognised Clinical Teacher, London Univ.; Founder European Society of Psychosomatic Research; Editor-in-Chief and Founder, Journal of Psychosomatic Res.; Editorial Bd, British Journal of Psychiatry, Japanese Journal of Psychosomatic Med., Medicina Psychosomatic, Behaviour Therapy; Examiner in Psychological Med., Edinburgh Univ., 1958-65; Examiner, DPM (Conjt Bd). Governor, Bethlem Royal and Maudsley Hospitals, 1956-62; President Sect. of Psychiatry, Royal Society Med., 1967-68. Member: Parole Board of England; Deutschen Gesellschaft für Psychiatrie und Nervenheilkun; Hon. Mem., Italian Psychosomatic Soc. Beattie Smith Lecturer, Melbourne Univ., 1967. *Publications:* (trans. from French) Psychosomatic Methods of Painless Childbirth, 1959; The Historical Development of British Psychiatry, Vol. I, 1961; Bronchial Asthma, 1967; chapters in various books; papers on neurology, psychiatry, history of psychiatry and psychosomatic medicine. *Recreations:* shooting, fishing, collecting. *Address:* 152 Harley Street, W1. *T:* 01-935 8868; The Grange, Otford, Kent. *T:* Otford 3427.

**LEIGH, His Honour Christopher Thomas Bowes,** OBE 1944; TD 1943; Hon. Lt-Col RA; County Court Judge 1962-70; *b* 3 Jan. 1905; 2nd *s* of His Honour Thomas Bowes Leigh, BSc, formerly County Court Judge of Manchester, and Marta Leigh, Wilmslow; *m* 1936, Vida Mary, *d* of H. R. and Mary Brunt, Staffordshire; no *c*. *Educ:* Cheltenham Coll. (Scholar); Queen's Coll., Oxford (Scholar). Hons in Classics and Law. Called to Bar, Gray's Inn, 1928; practised on Northern Circuit. Commissioned 7th Bn Lancashire Fusiliers (TA), 1926; Major, 1935. Served War of 1939-45: at first with 39th (LF) SL Regt; transferred to RA, 1942; served N Africa and Italy, commanding 105 and 12th LAA Regts, RA. Chairman, Agricultural Land Tribunal for Yorkshire and Lancashire, 1947-62. *Recreations:* racquets, tennis, golf. *Address:* 60 King Street, Manchester. *T:* 061-834 6876. *Clubs:* Vincent's (Oxford); Manchester Tennis and Racquet.

**LEIGH, Sir John,** 2nd Bt, *cr* 1918; *b* 24 March 1909; *s* of Sir John Leigh, 1st Bt, and Norah Marjorie, CBE (*d* 1954); *S* father 1959; *m* 1959, Ariane, *d* of late Joseph Wm Allen, Beverly Hills, California, and *widow* of Harold Wallace Ross, NYC. *Educ:* Eton; Balliol Coll., Oxford. *Heir: b* Eric Leigh [*b* 13 April 1913; *m* 1st, 1934, Joan Fitzgerald Lane (marr. diss., 1939); one *s*; 2nd, 1939, Mary Babette Jaques; one *s* one *d*]. *Address:* 23 Quai du Mont Blanc, Geneva, Switzerland. *T:* 31 53 63. *Clubs:* St James'; Travellers' (Paris).

**LEIGH, Ralph Alexander,** FBA 1969; LittD; Reader in French, University of Cambridge, since 1969; Fellow of Trinity College, Cambridge, since 1952 (Senior Research Fellow, 1969); *b* London, 6 Jan. 1915; *m* 1945, Edith Helen Kern; one *s* one *d*. *Educ:* Raine's Sch. for Boys, London; Queen Mary Coll., Univ. of London; Univ. of Paris (Sorbonne). BA London 1st class hons. 1936; Diplôme de l'Université de Paris, 1938. Served War, 1941-46: RASC and Staff; CCG; Lieut (ERE list) 1942; Major, 1944. Lecturer in Dept of French: Univ. of Edinburgh, 1946; Cambridge Univ., 1952. LittD (Cambridge) 1968. *Publications:* Correspondance Complète de Jean Jacques Rousseau, vols i-xiv, 1965-1970 (in progress); contribs to Revue de littérature comparée; Modern Language Review; French Studies; Studies on Voltaire; The Library, etc. *Recreation:* book-collecting. *Address:* 12 Porson Road, Cambrdige. *T:* Cambridge 57166; Trinity College, Cambridge.

**LEIGH-PEMBERTON, John,** AFC 1945; Artist painter; *b* 18 Oct. 1911; *s* of Cyril Leigh-Pemberton and Mary Evelyn Megaw; *m* 1948, Doreen Beatrice Townshend-Webster. *Educ:* Eton. Studied Art, London, 1928-31. Past Member Royal Institute of Painters in Oils and other Societies. Served 1940-45 with RAF as Flying Instructor. Series of pictures for Coldstream Guards, 1950. Festival Almanack, 1951, for Messrs Whitbread; Royal Progress, 1953, for Shell Mex & BP Ltd. Works in public and private collections, UK and America; decorations for ships: City of York, City of Exeter, Britannic, Caledonia, Corfu, Carthage, Kenya, Uganda. Many series of paintings, chiefly of natural history subjects, for Midland Bank Ltd. *Publications:* A Book of Garden Flowers, 1960; A Book of Butterflies, Moths and other Insects, 1963; British Wildlife, Rarities and Introductions, 1966; Garden Birds, 1967; Sea and Estuary Birds, 1967; Heath and Woodland Birds, 1968; Vanishing Wild Animals of the World, 1968; Pond and River Birds, 1969; African Mammals, 1969; Australian Mammals, 1970; North American Mammals, 1970; Birds of Prey, 1970. *Address:* 5 Roehampton Gate, Roehampton, SW15. *T:* 01-876 3332.

**LEIGHTON OF ST MELLONS,** 2nd Baron, *cr* 1962; **John Leighton Seager;** Bt 1952; *b* 11 Jan. 1922; *er s* of 1st Baron Leighton of St Mellons, CBE, JP, and of Marjorie, *d* of William Henry Gimson, Breconshire; *S* father, 1963; *m* 1953, Elizabeth Rosita, *o d* of late Henry Hopgood, Cardiff; two *s* one *d* (and one *d* decd). *Educ:* Caldicott Sch.; The Leys Sch., Cambridge. *Heir: s* Hon. Robert William Henry Leighton Seager, *b* 28 Sept. 1955. *Address:* Shamal, Highlight Lane, Barry, Glam.

**LEIGHTON, Clare,** RE 1934; *b* 1899; *d* of late Marie Connor Leighton, and late Robert Leighton. *Educ:* privately; Brighton School of Art; Slade School. Elected Member of Society of Wood Engravers, 1928; First prize International Engraving Exhibition, Art Institute of Chicago, 1930; Fellow National Acad. of Design, New York; Member, Society of American Graphic Arts; Member, National Inst. of Arts and Letters, USA, 1951. Prints purchased for permanent collection of British Museum, Victoria and Albert Museum, National Gallery of Canada, Museums of Boston, Baltimore, New York, etc. Designed: 33 stained glass windows for St Paul's Cathedral, Worcester, Mass; 12 plates for Josiah Wedgwood & Sons Ltd. *Publications:* Illustrated with wood engravings the following books: Thomas Hardy's The Return of the Native, 1929; Thornton Wilder's The Bridge of San Luis Rey, 1930; The Sea and the Jungle, 1930; Wuthering Heights, 1931; E. Madox Roberts's The Time of Man, 1943; North Carolina Folk Lore, 1950; Woodcuts: examples of the Work of Clare Leighton, 1930; The Trumpet in the Dust, 1934; Writer: How to do Wood Engraving and Woodcuts, 1932; Wood Engraving of the 1930's, 1936; Tempestuous Petticoat, 1948; written and illustrated: The Musical Box, 1932; The Farmer's Year, 1933; The Wood That Came Back, 1934; Four Hedges, 1935; Country Matters, 1937; Sometime, Never, 1939; Southern Harvest, 1942; Give us this Day, 1943; Where Land meets Sea, 1954. *Address:* Woodbury, Connecticut, USA.

**LEIGHTON, Margaret;** actress; *b* 26 Feb. 1922; *d* of George Leighton and Doris Evans; *m* 1947, Max Reinhardt (marr. diss.), *qv*; *m* 1957, Laurence Harvey (marr. diss., 1961), *qv*; *m* 1964, Michael Wilding, *qv*. *Educ:* C of E Coll., Birmingham. Joined Birmingham Repertory Company, 1938, and remained for season; with Travelling Repertory Company and touring for CEMA and ENSA, 1940; re-joined Birmingham Rep. Co., 1941. Old Vic Theatre Co., 1944; season 1944-45: Arms and the Man; Peer Gynt; Richard III; Uncle Vanya; with Old Vic Co. on European Tour, season 1945-46: Henry IV parts 1 and 2; Arms and the Man; six weeks season in New York; season 1946-47: Cyrano de Bergerac; An Inspector Calls; King Lear; The Alchemist; Richard II; played in Old Vic production of King Lear in Paris. Played in A Sleeping Clergyman, Criterion, 1947; Philadelphia Story, Duchess, 1949; The Cocktail Party, New, 1950; Three Sisters, Aldwych, 1951; Memorial Theatre, Stratford-upon-Avon, 1952; The Apple Cart, Haymarket, 1953; The Confidential Clerk, Edinburgh Festival and Lyric, 1953; Separate Tables, St James's, 1954-56 and in New York from 1956; Variation on a Theme, Globe, 1958; Much Ado about Nothing, New York, 1959; The Wrong Side of the Park, Cambridge Theatre, 1960; The Lady from the Sea, Queen's, 1961; The Night of the Iguana, 1961, Tchin Tchin, 1962, The Chinese Prime Minister, 1964, New York; Cactus Flower, Lyric, 1967; Little Foxes, New York, 1968; Antony and Cleopatra, Chichester Festival, 1969; Girlfriend, Apollo, 1970. *Films include:* Bonnie Prince Charlie; The Winslow Boy; Under Capricorn; The Elusive Pimpernel; The Astonished Heart; Calling Bulldog Drummond; Home at Seven; The Holly and the Ivy; The Good Die Young; The Constant Husband; The Teckman Mystery; Carrington, VC; A Novel Affair; The Passionate Stranger; The Sound and the Fury; The Waltz of the Toreadors; The Loved One, 1965; Seven Women, 1966; The Mad Woman of Chaillot, 1968. *Address:* London International, 11 Hanover Street, W1.

**LEIGHTON, Sir Michael (John Bryan),** 11th Bt, *cr* 1693; *b* 8 March 1935; *o s* of Colonel Sir Richard Tihel Leighton, 10th Bt, and Kathleen Irene Linda, *o d* of Maj. A. E. Lees, Rowton Castle, Shrewsbury; *S* father 1957. *Educ:* Stowe; Tabley House Agricultural Sch.; Cirencester Coll. *Heir: cousin* Lieut-Colonel John Leighton Byrne Leicester-Warren, *qv*. *Address:* Loton Park, Shrewsbury.

**LEINSDORF, Erich;** orchestral and operatic conductor; *b* Vienna, 4 Feb. 1912; *s* of Ludwig Julius Leinsdorf and Charlotte (*née* Loebl); *m* 1939, Anne Frohnknecht (marr.diss. 1968); three *s* two *d*; *m* 1968, Vera Graf. *Educ:* University of Vienna; State Academy of Music, Vienna (dipl.). Assistant conductor: Salzburg Festival, 1934-37; Metropolitan Opera, NY, 1937-39; Chief Conductor, German operas, 1939-43; Conductor, Rochester Philharmonic, 1947-56; Director, NYC Opera, 1956; Music Cons. Director, Metropolitan Opera, 1957-62; Music Director, Boston Symphony Orchestra, 1962-69. Director, Berkshire Music Center, Berkshire Music Festival, 1963-69; guest appearances with Philadelphia Orchestra, Los Angeles, St Louis, New Orleans, Minneapolis, Concertgebouw Amsterdam, Israel Philharmonic, London Symphony, New Philharmonia, San Francisco Opera, Bayreuth, Holland and Prague Festivals, BBC. Records many symphonies and operas. Member Executive Cttee, John F. Kennedy Center for Performing Arts. Fellow, American Academy of Arts and Sciences. Holds hon. degrees. *Publications:* transcriptions of Brahms Chorale Preludes; contribs. to Atlantic Monthly, Saturday Review, New York Times, High Fidelity. *Address:* London Symphony, New Philharmonia, 320 West 56th Street, New York, NY 10019, USA.

**LEINSTER,** 7th Duke of, *cr* 1766; **Edward FitzGerald;** Baron of Offaly, 1205; Earl of Kildare, 1316; Viscount Leinster (Great Britain), 1747; Marquess of Kildare, 1761; Earl of Offaly, 1761; Baron Kildare, 1870; Premier Duke, Marquess, and Earl, of Ireland; Captain, late Argyll and Sutherland Highlanders; late 2nd Lieut Irish Guards and Lieut 8th Battalion West Riding Regt; *b* 6 May 1892; *s* of Gerald, 5th Duke, and Hermione, *d* of 1st Earl of Feversham; *S* brother, 1922; *m* 1st, 1913, May (from whom he obtained a decree of divorce, 1930; she *d* 1935), *d* of late Jesse Etheridge; one *s*; 2nd, 1932, Mrs Clare van Neck (Rafaelle Kennedy, who obtained a divorce, 1946), *d* of Mrs J. H. Patterson, New York; 3rd, 1946, Mrs Theodore Wessel (*d* 1960); 4th, 1965, Mrs Vivien Conner; ONE step *s*. Served European War, 1914-17 (wounded). *Heir: s* Marquess of Kildare, *qv*. *Address:* c/o Lloyds Bank Ltd, 38 High Street, Banstead, Surrey.

**LEIR, Rear-Admiral Ernest W.,** DSO 1916; Legion of Honour, 1917; Royal Navy, retired; *b* 1883; *s* of Rev. C. E. Leir of Ditcheat, Somerset; *m* 1st, 1905, Muriel Amyatt (*d* 1937), *o d* of Rev. E. Amyatt-Burney, and *g d* of Rev. Edward Burney of the Royal Academy, Gosport; two *s* one *d*; 2nd, 1938, Gwendolen Iliffe, *o d* of late Brig.-General J. A. Gibbon, CMG. *Educ:* King's Sch., Bruton. Entered navy, 1898; served as midshipman on China Station, 1899-1902; took part in the relief of the Legations in Pekin, 1900; Lieut, 1903; attached to the Submarine Service; specially promoted to Commander, for services in the Bight of Heligoland action, Aug. 1914 (DSO for services rendered in overseas submarine work, despatches); Captain of the Dockyard, Dep.-Superintendent and King's Harbour-master at Chatham, 1923-24; Senior Naval Officer in the Persian Gulf, 1924-26; Captain, Reserve Flotilla, Portsmouth, 1926-27; Captain-in-Charge and King's Harbour-master, Portland, 1929-31; Naval ADC to the King, 1931; retired list, 1931. Commodore of Convoys during War of 1939-45 (despatches).

*Address:* South Hill House, Ditcheat, Shepton Mallet, Somerset.

**LEISHMAN, Frederick John,** CVO 1957; MBE 1944; Deputy Chairman and Chief Executive, The Hill Samuel Group (SA) Ltd; Director, Hill, Samuel & Co. Ltd; *b* 21 Jan. 1919; *s* of Alexander Leishman and Freda Mabel (*née* Hood); *m* 1945, Frances Webb, Evanston, Illinois, USA; two *d*. *Educ:* Oundle; Corpus Christi, Cambridge. Served RE, 1940-46, and with Military Government, Germany, 1945-46; Regular Commission, 1945; resigned, 1946. Joined Foreign Service, 1946; FO, 1946-48; Copenhagen, 1948-51; Civil Service Selection Board, 1951; Assistant Private Secretary to the Foreign Secretary, 1951-53; First Secretary, Washington, 1953-58; First Secretary and Head of Chancery, British Embassy, Teheran, 1959-61; Counsellor, 1961; HM Consul-General, Hamburg, 1961-62; Foreign Office, 1962-63. *Recreations:* golf, fishing. *Address:* Willowvale, PO Bryanston, Johannesburg, South Africa. *Clubs:* Travellers'; London Scottish Rugby Football; Hawks (Cambridge); Royal Ashdown Forest Golf; Rand (Johannesburg); Bryanston Country, Glendower Golf (SA).

**LEITCH, George,** CB 1963; OBE 1945; Deputy Under-Secretary of State, Ministry of Defence, since 1965; *b* 5 June 1915; *er s* of late James Simpson and Margaret Leitch; *m* 1942, Edith Marjorie Maughan; one *d*. *Educ:* Wallsend Grammar Sch.; King's Coll., University of Durham. Research and teaching in mathematics, 1937-39. War Service in Army (from TA), 1939-46 (despatches, OBE): Lieut-Colonel in charge of Operational Research in Eastern, then Fourteenth Army, 1943-45; Brigadier (Dep. Scientific Adviser, War Office), 1945-46; entered Civil Service, as Principal, 1947; Ministry of Supply, 1947-59 (Under-Secretary, 1959); War Office, 1959-64 (Asst Under-Secretary of State). Ministry of Defence, 1964-65 (Asst Under-Secretary of State). Commonwealth Fund Fellow, 1953-54. Hon. DSc (Durham), 1946. *Recreations:* swimming, gardening. *Address:* 73 Princes Way, Wimbledon, SW19. *T:* 01-788 4658. *Club:* Reform.

**LEITCH, Isabella,** OBE 1949; MA, DSc; retired as Director Commonwealth Bureau of Animal Nutrition (1940-60); *b* 13 Feb. 1890; 3rd *d* of John Leitch and Isabella McLennan. *Educ:* Peterhead Academy; Aberdeen Univ. MA (Hons Mathematics and Natural Philosophy), 1911; BSc, 1914; research in Genetics and Physiology at Copenhagen Univ., 1914-19; DSc 1919. Staff of Rowett Research Institute, 1923-29; Staff of Imperial (now Commonwealth) Bureau of Animal Nutrition, 1929. Hon. LLD (Aberdeen), 1965. *Publications:* (with Frank E. Hytten) The Physiology of Human Pregnancy, 1964; also contributions on genetics, physiology, and nutrition in MRC Special Report Series and scientific journals, etc. *Recreation:* hill-climbing. *Address:* 30 Ashgrove Road West, Aberdeen. *T:* Aberdeen 43697. *Clubs:* Farmers'; Strathcona (Bucksburn, Aberdeen).

**LEITCH, William Andrew,** CB 1963; First Parliamentary Draftsman to Government of Northern Ireland since 1956; *b* 16 July 1915; *e s* of Andrew Leitch, MD, DPH, Castlederg, Co. Tyrone, and May, *d* of W. H. Todd, JP, Fyfin, Strabane, Co. Tyrone; *m* 1939, Edna Margaret, *d* of David McIlvennan, Solicitor, Belfast; one *s* two *d*. *Educ:* Methodist Coll., Belfast; Queen's Univ., Belfast; London Univ. (LLB). Admitted Solicitor, NI, 1937; Asst Solicitors Dept, Ministry of Finance, NI, 1937-43; Asst Parliamentary Draftsman, 1944-56. Hon. LLM, Queen's Univ., Belfast, 1967. *Publications:* A Handbook on the Administration of Estates Act (NI), 1955, 1957; (jointly) A Commentary on the Interpretation Act (Northern Ireland) 1954, 1955. Articles in: Irish Law Times; Northern Ireland Legal Quarterly; American Bar Assoc. Journal, etc. *Recreations:* fishing, golf, reading, carpentry. *Address:* 53 Kensington Road, Belfast 5. *T:* Belfast 654784. *Club:* Royal Commonwealth Society.

**LEITH,** family name of **Baron Burgh.**

**LEITH, Sir R. Ian A. F.;** *see* Forbes-Leith.

**LEITH-BUCHANAN, Sir George Hector Macdonald,** 6th Bt, *cr* 1775; JP; *b* 30 Jan. 1889; *s* of 5th Bt and Maude Mary (*d* 1956), *d* of late Alexander Grant; *S* father, 1925; *m* 1933, Barbara Leshure. *Heir: cousin,* Charles Alexander James Leith-Buchanan, *b* 1 Sept. 1939. *Address:* Drummakill, Alexandria, Dunbartonshire.

**LEITHEAD, James Douglas;** Export Planning and Development Division, Board of Trade, since 1968; *b* 4 Oct. 1911; *s* of late William Leithead, Berwick-on-Tweed; *m* 1936, Alice, *d* of Thomas Wylie, Stirling, Scotland; one *s*. *Educ:* Bradford Grammar Sch. Accountant, 1927-32; ACA 1932; FCA 1960; Chartered Accountant, 1932-39. Lecturer Bradford Technical Coll., 1934-39; Secretarial Assistant, Midland (Amalgamated) District (Coal Mines) Scheme, 1939-42; Ministry of Supply, 1942-45; Board of Trade, 1945-64; HM Diplomatic Service, 1965-68. British Trade Commissioner: Australia, 1950-63; New Zealand, 1963-67. Vice-Pres., W Australian Branch of Royal Commonwealth Soc., 1957-63. *Recreation:* golf. *Address:* 48 Eaton Road, Appleton, Berks; Board of Trade, 1 Victoria Street, SW1.

**LEJEUNE, C. A.; (Mrs E. Roffe Thompson);** Film Critic to the Observer, 1928-60; Broadcaster and Television script writer; *b* Manchester; *m* E. Roffe Thompson; one *s*. *Educ:* Manchester Univ. Hon. DLitt, Durham Univ., 1961. *Publications:* Cinema; Chestnuts in Her Lap; Thank You for Having Me; *television adaptations:* Sherlock Holmes Series; The Three Hostages; Clementina; *original television play:* (with son, Anthony Lejeune) Vicky's First Ball; completed Angela Thirkell's posthumous novel Three Score and Ten. *Address:* Lane End, Pinner Hill, Middlesex.

**LEJEUNE, Maj.-General Francis St David Benwell,** CB 1949; CBE 1944; *b* 1 March 1899; 2nd *s* of late J. F. P. Lejeune, Bedford; *m* 1927, Joyce Mary, *d* of late Charles E. Davies, Hampton Court; one *s* one *d*. *Educ:* Bedford; RMA, Woolwich. 2nd Lieut, RA, 1917; served European War, 1914-18, France and Belgium (despatches); seconded RAF, Somaliland and Iraq Operations, 1920-24; GSO 3 War Office, 1929; Asst Military Attaché, Washington, 1932-34; Special Mission in Spain, 1938-39. War of 1939-45 served in Italy and Burma (despatches); Maj.-General, 1944; Chief of Staff AA Command, Comdr AA Group, 1944; Director Technical Training, War Office, 1946; President Ordnance Board, 1947; retired, 1949; International Staff, NATO, 1952-62; psc; pac. *Address:* Casa do Rouxinol, Rua Joaquim Ereira, Cascais, Portugal. *T:* 281447.

**LE MARCHANT, Sir Denis,** 5th Bt, *cr* 1841; *b* 28 Feb. 1906; *er s* of Brigadier-General Sir Edward Thomas Le Marchant, 4th Bt, KCB, CBE, JP, DL, and Evelyn Brooks (*d* 1957), *er d* of late Robert Millington Knowles, JP, DL, Colston Bassett Hall, Nottinghamshire; *S* father, 1953; *m* 1933, Elizabeth Rowena, *y d* of late Arthur Hovenden Worth; two *s* one *d.* *Educ:* Radley. High Sheriff, Lincolnshire, 1958. *Heir: s* Peter Edward Le Marchant [*b* 11 June 1934. *Educ:* Eton; Oxford]. *Address:* Hungerton Hall, Grantham, Lincolnshire. *T:* Knipton 244.

**LE MARCHANT, Spencer;** MP (C) High Peak Division of Derbyshire since 1970; *b* 15 Jan. 1931; *s* of Alfred Le Marchant and Turdis Le Marchant (*née* Mortensen); *m* 1955, Lucinda Gaye Leveson Gower; two *d. Educ:* Eton. National Service and Territorial Commissions, Sherwood Foresters. Mem., Stock Exchange, 1954-; Partner, L. Messel & Co., 1961-. Mem., Westminster City Council, 1956-71; contested (C) Vauxhall, 1966. *Address:* Hillside, Chinley, Derbyshire. *T:* Chinley 520; 508 Frobisher House, Dolphin Square, SW1. *Club:* White's.

**LEMASS, Seán Francis;** *b* Dublin, 15 July, 1899; *m* 1924, Kathleen Hughes; one *s* three *d. Educ:* Christian Brothers' Schools. Participated in Easter Week Rising, 1916, and taken prisoner at GPO; served again with IRA on renewal of hostilities; taken prisoner and interned until the Truce of 1921; remained with IRA after the Anglo-Irish Treaty; taken prisoner on capture of Four Courts garrison during first week of Civil War, July 1922, but escaped; appointed to IRA Headquarters staff; again taken prisoner, Dec. 1922, and interned. Managing Director, The Irish Press, Ltd, 1948-51. Minister for Industry and Commerce, Ireland, 1932-39, 1941-48, 1951-54 and 1957-59; Minister for Supplies, 1939-45; Tánaiste (Deputy Prime Minister), 1945-48, 1951-54 and 1957-59; Taoiseach (Prime Minister), 1959-67. TD, Dublin South, 1924-48, Dublin South (Central), 1948-69. Chairman: United Breweries of Ireland; Ronald Lyon Estates (Ireland), 1966-; Irish Security Services, 1968-; MacDonagh and Boland, 1966-; Unidare Ltd; Director: Electrical Industries of Ireland Ltd; Ryans Tourist Holdings Ltd; Waterford Glass Ltd. Hon. degrees: LLD: New Rochelle (New York), 1953; Villanova (Philadelphia), 1963; University of Dublin, 1965; DEconSc, National Univ. of Ireland, 1954. Grand Cross of Order of Gregory the Great, 1948; Grand Cross of Order of Merit of Federal Republic of Germany, 1962. *Address:* Hillside Drive, Rathfarnham, Dublin.

**LE MASURIER, Sir Robert (Hugh),** Kt 1966; DSC 1942; Bailiff of Jersey since 1962; *b* 29 Dec. 1913; *s* of William Smythe Le Masurier and Mabel Harriet Briard; *m* 1941, Helen Sophia Sheringham; one *s* two *d. Educ:* Victoria Coll., Jersey. MA 1935; BCL 1936. Sub-Lieut RNVR, 1939; Lieut RNVR, 1943; Lieut-Commander RNVR, 1944. Solicitor-General, Jersey, 1955; Attorney-General, Jersey, 1958. *Recreations:* sailing, carpentry. *Address:* Greencourt, Green Street, St Helier, Jersey. *Clubs:* Royal Ocean Racing; St Helier Yacht, United (Jersey).

**le MAY, Reginald Stuart,** PhD (Cantab); Hon. Member, Siam Society; retired; *b* 6 January 1885; *s* of Herbert le May and Harriet Jane Newman; *m* 1916, Dorothy Madeline Castle; one *d. Educ:* Framlingham Coll. Confidential Clerk to Consul-General, Zürich, 1903-04; Asst Master, Framlingham Coll., 1907; Consular Service, Siam, 1907; Vice-Consul, Chiengmai, 1915, Bangkok, 1917; Acting Consul-General, Saigon, 1920, resigned, 1922; Economic Adviser to Siamese Government, 1922-23; Editor of Official Journal, The Record; responsible for spread of Rural Credit Societies throughout Siam; Pembroke Coll., Cambridge, 1934-37 (PhD 1937). President, Society of Old Framlinghamians, 1947. Has lectured to learned societies for 40 years to interpret East to West; his collection of Buddhist Art from Siam exhibited at Cambridge, Oxford and London (India House); part is now in the British Museum. Silver Medallist, RSA. *Publications:* The Stamps of Siam, 1920; An Asian Arcady–Northern Siam, 1926; Siamese Tales, Old and New, 1930 (re-published 1958); The Coinage of Siam, 1932 (re-published 1961); The Economic Conditions of North-Eastern Siam, 1932; The Ceramic Wares of North-Central Siam, 1933; Buddhist Art in Siam, 1938 (re-published Tokyo, 1963); The Culture of South-East Asia, 1954 (2nd edn 1956, 3rd edn 1964; special Indian edn 1962, with foreword by late Pandit Nehru; German edn 1968); Response to Beauty, 1954; Records of the le May Family in England (1630-1950), 1958; contributions on SE Asia to Burlington Magazine, Indian Art and Letters, Asian Review, Oriental Art, Chambers's New Encyclopædia. *Recreations:* football (Capt. of School); cricket (Kent 2nd XI); golf (Bangkok championship); bridge (Kent County champion with late Lieut-Colonel Stopford, 1947 and 1950); ballet and art exhibitions. *Address:* Southview Guest House, 21 Rusthall Road, Tunbridge Wells, Kent. *Club:* West Kent (Tunbridge Wells).

**LE MAY, Group Captain William Kent,** CBE 1943 (OBE 1942); RAF; *b* 29 June 1911; *s* of Percy Kent and Kate Le May (decd); *m* 1938, Greta Lettice Violet Blatchley; two *s* two *d. Educ:* Tonbridge Sch.; Agricultural Coll., Wye. Aux. Air Force, 1931-40, No. 500 County of Kent Squadron; permanent commission, 1946; retired, 1961. *Address:* Moat Farm, Ash, nr Canterbury, Kent. *T:* Ash 313. *Club:* Royal Air Force.

**LEMBERG, (Max) Rudolf,** FRS 1952; FAA 1954 (Vice-President, 1957); PhD (Breslau); Director of Biochemical Laboratories and Assistant Director Institute of Medical Research, The Royal North Shore Hospital, Sydney, NSW, since 1935; *b* 19 Oct. 1896; *s* of Justizrat Dr Arthur Lemberg and Margarethe (*née* Wendriner); *m* 1924, Hanna (Adelheid) Claussen. *Educ:* Johannes Gymnasium, Breslau, Silesia; Universities of Breslau, Munich, Heidelberg. PhD (Dr phil.) Breslau, 1921; habilitation as Lecturer (Privatdozent), Heidelberg Univ., 1930; Rockefeller Foundation Fellow, Sir William Dunn Institute of Biochemistry, Cambridge, 1930-31; Privatdozent, Heidelberg Univ. and Asst at Chemical Inst., 1931-33; Academic Assistance Council (now Society for Protection of Science and Learning) Fellow, Sir William Dunn Institute of Biochemistry, Cambridge, 1933-35. Member, Advisory Research Cttee of Australian National Health and Med. Research Council, 1948-59; H. G. Smith Medal of Royal Australian Chemical Inst., 1948; Professor Emeritus, Heidelberg Univ., 1956. Visiting Professor, University of Pennsylvania, Philadelphia, 1966. Foreign Member, Heidelberg Acad. Science, 1956; Hon. Member: Accad. Anatomico-Chirurgica Perusina, 1959, and of several scientific societies in Australia and the United States. Hon DSc, Sydney, 1970. James Cook Medal of the Royal Society of New South Wales, 1965, etc; Britannica Australia Award, 1966. *Publications:* The Disintegration of Haemoglobin in the Animal Body, in Perspectives in Biochemistry, 1937; Hematin Compounds and Bile Pigments (with J. W. Legge) (New York and London), 1949; Haematin Enzymes, Papers and Discussions of IUB Symposium, Canberra, 1959 (ed with J. E. Falk amd R. K. Morton), (London) 1961.

Numerous publications in Biochemical Journal, Proc. of Royal Society, Annual Review of Biochemistry (prefatory chap., 1965), Biochimica et Biophysica Acta, Australian Journal of Experimental Biology and Medical Science, etc. *Recreations:* bushwalking, motoring; relations of religion and science; work for international peace. *Address:* Boundary Road, Wahroonga, NSW 2076, Australia. *T:* JW 3714.

**LE MESURIER, Captain Edward Kirby,** CBE 1961; MVO 1935; RN; Secretary, National Rifle Association, 1953-68; *b* 11 Dec. 1903; *s* of Captain Charles Edward Le Mesurier, CB, RN, and Florence Kirby; *m* 1930, Eleanor Marion Esther Churchill; one *s* two *d. Educ:* RN Colleges. Served War of 1939-45 (despatches). *Address:* Glentworth, Coombe, Wotton-under-Edge, Glos. *T:* 3227.

**LEMIEUX, Most Rev. (M.) Joseph;** Apostolic Pro-Nuncio to India, since 1969; *b* Quebec City, 10 May 1902; *s* of Joseph E. Lemieux and Eva (*née* Berlinguet). *Educ:* College of St Anne de la Pocatière; Dominican House of Studies, Ottawa; College of Angelico, Rome; Blackfriars, Oxford. Missionary to Japan, 1930; Parish Priest, Miyamaecho, Hakodate, Japan, 1931-36; First Bishop of Sendai, 1936; resigned, 1941; Administrator of Diocese of Gravelbourg, Sask., 1942; Bishop of Gravelbourg, 1944-53; Archbishop of Ottawa, 1953-67; Apostolic Nuncio to Haiti, 1967-69. *Address:* Apostolic Nunciature, New Delhi, India.

**LEMIEUX, Prof. Raymond Urgel,** SM (Canada), 1968; FRS 1967; Professor of Organic Chemistry, University of Alberta, since 1961; *b* 16 June 1920; *s* of Octave Lemieux; *m* 1948, Virginia Marie McConaghie; one *s* five *d* (and one *s* decd). *Educ:* Edmonton, Alberta. BSc Hons (Chem.) Alta, 1943; PhD (Chem.) McGill, 1946. Research Fellow, Ohio State Univ., 1947; Asst Professor, Saskatchewan Univ., 1948-49; Senior Research Officer, National Research Council, 1949-54; Professor, Ottawa Univ., 1954-61. FRSC 1955. Chem. Inst. of Canada Medal, 1964; C. S. Hudson Award, American Chem. Society, 1966. Hon. DSc, New Brunswick Univ., 1967. *Publications:* over 100 research papers mainly in area of carbohydrate chemistry in Canadian Journal of Chemistry, etc. *Recreations:* golf, curling, fishing. *Address:* 7602119th Street, Edmonton, Alberta, Canada. *T:* 439-6275. *Clubs:* University of Alberta Faculty, Mayfair Golf and Country (Edmonton).

**LEMMON, Cyril Whitefield,** FRIBA, AIA; Architect, Honolulu, Hawaii (Private Practice), since 1946; *b* Kent, 27 Oct. 1901; *s* of T. E. Lemmon and Catherine Whitefield; *m* 1st, 1921, Ethel Belinda Peters, artist (marr. diss., 1936); no *c*; 2nd, 1938, Rebecca Robson Ramsay; two *d. Educ:* University of Pennsylvania, Philadelphia, Pa. Fifth-year Studio Instructor and Lecturer in the School of Architecture, University of Liverpool, 1933-36; Consulting Architect to Government of India for Rebuilding of Quetta, 1936; Consulting Architect to MES for all military buildings in India, 1938. Lieut-Colonel, Royal Indian Engineers, 1941; Director of Civil Camouflage in India, 1943; GSO 1, GHQ, India and 11th Army Group, 1943-44. President, Hawaii Chapter, AIA, 1950. Exhibited paintings in Salon des Tuileries, Paris, 1933; travel in United States, Mexico, Europe, N Africa and Asia. Public Lectures on Architecture and Painting. *Publications:* contributions to professional journals on Architecture. *Recreations:* golf, swimming. *Address:* 1410 Kapiolani Boulevard, Honolulu, Hawaii; (business) 1501 First National Bank Building, Honolulu, Hawaii. *Clubs:* Kiwanis, Oahu Country, etc. (Honolulu).

**LEMNITZER, General Lyman L.,** DSM (US Army) (with 3 Oak Leaf Clusters); DSM (US Navy); DSM (US Air Force); Silver Star; Legion of Merit (Officer's Degree); Legion of Merit; Supreme Allied Commander, Europe, 1963-69; Commander-in-Chief, US European Command, 1962-69; *b* Pennsylvania, 29 Aug. 1899; *s* of late William L. Lemnitzer; *m* 1923, Katherine Mead Tryon; one *s* one *d. Educ:* Honesdale High Sch.; US Military Academy. Duty with troops, Instructor at Army Schools, etc., 1920-40; War Plans Division, War Dept General Staff, 1941; Comdg General, 34th Anti-Aircraft Artillery Bde, and Allied Force HQ England, as Asst Chief of Staff for Plans and Ops, 1942 (2nd in Command, Secret Submarine Mission to contact friendly French Officials in N Africa); served in Europe and N Africa, 1942-45; with Joint Chiefs of Staff, 1945-47; Dep. Comdt National War Coll., 1947-49; Asst to Secretary of Defence, 1949-50; Head of US Delegation to Military Cttee of the Five (Brussels Pact) Powers. London; Student, Basic Airborne Course, Fort Benning, 1950; Comdg General 11th Airborne Div., 1951, 7th Infantry Div. (in Korea), 1951-52; DCS (Plans and Research), 1952-55; Comdg General Far East and 8th US Army, 1955; C-in-C, Far East and UN Commands, and Governor of Ryukyu Is, 1955-57; Vice-Chief of Staff, 1957-59, Chief of Staff, 1959-60, US Army; Chairman Joint Chiefs of Staff, 1960-62. Holds several hon. doctorates. Hon. CB and Hon. CBE (Great Britain); Grand Cross, Order of Merit (Germany), 1969; and numerous other foreign Orders and decorations. *Recreations:* golf, fishing, photography, interested in baseball, correspondence with his many friends around the world. *Address:* 3286 Worthington Street, NW, Washington, DC 20015, USA.

**LEMON, Sir (Richard) Dawnay,** Kt 1970; CBE 1958; QPM 1964; Chief Constable of Kent since 1962; *b* 1912; *o s* of late Lieut-Colonel F. J. Lemon, CBE, DSO, and of Mrs Laura Lemon; *m* 1939, Sylvia Marie Kentish; one *s* one *d* (and one *d* decd). *Educ:* Uppingham Sch.; RMC, Sandhurst. Joined West Yorks Regt, 1932; retired 1934. Metropolitan Police, 1934-37; Leicestershire Constabulary, 1937-39; Chief Constable of East Riding of Yorkshire, 1939-42; Chief Constable of Hampshire and Isle of Wight, 1942-62. *Recreations:* cricket, golf, shooting. *Address:* Chief Constable's House, County Police Headquarters, Maidstone. *T:* Maidstone 55854. *Clubs:* Naval and Military, MCC; Royal Yacht Squadron, Cowes (hon.).

**LENANTON, Lady;** *see* Oman, C. M. A.

**LENDRUM, Prof. Alan Chalmers,** MA, MD, BSc, ARPS; FRCPath; Professor of Pathology, University of St Andrews, 1947-67, University of Dundee since 1967; *b* 1906; *yr s* of late Rev. Dr Robert Alexander Lendrum and Anna, *e d* of late James Guthrie of Pitforthie, Angus; *m* 1934, Elizabeth Bertram, *e d* of late Donald Currie, BA, LLB; two *s* one *d. Educ:* High Sch., Glasgow; Ardrossan Acad.; University of Glasgow. Asst to Sir Robert Muir, MD, FRS, 1933; Lecturer in Pathology, University of Glasgow. Visiting Prof. of Pathology, Yale, 1960. Hon. For. Mem. Argentine Soc. of Normal and Pathological Anatomy. Hon. Fellow, and ex-Pres., Inst. Med. Lab. Tech. Capt. RAMC (TA) retd. *Publications:* (co-author) Recent Advances in Clinical Pathology, 1948; Trends in Clinical Pathology, 1969; publications in medical journals. *Address:* Invergowrie House, Dundee. *T:* Dundee 66666.

**LE NEVE FOSTER, F.;** *see* Foster, Fermian Le N.

**LENNARD, Sir Richard Barrett-;** *see* Lennard, Sir T. R. F. B.

**LENNARD, Lt-Col Sir Stephen Arthur Hallam Farnaby,** 3rd Bt, *cr* 1880; late Scots Guards; formerly President, S. H. Lennard and Co. Ltd, Investment Dealers, Vancouver, BC (retired); *b* 31 July 1899; *o s* of Lt-Col Sir Henry Arthur Hallam Farnaby Lennard, 2nd Bt, and Beatrice (*d* 1948), *d* of Albemarle Cator, Woodbastwick Hall, Norfolk; *S* father, 1928; *m* 1st, 1928, Mary Isabel (*d* 1970), *er d* of Lawrence Bruce Latimer, Vancouver, BC; 2nd, 1970, Margaret Jean, *widow* of Group Captain William Neville Cumming, OBE, DFC, RAF, and *o d* of Daniel Hockin, Vancouver, BC. *Educ:* Winchester; RMC, Sandhurst. Lt Scots Guards, 1918-25; residing in Vancouver since 1925. Served War of 1939-45, with BEF, France, 1940; MEF and 8th Army, 1941-42; Persia and Iraq, 1943, and India, 1943-45; latterly on the Staff, retiring with rank of Lt-Col, 1945. 1939-45 Star and N African Star with 8th Army Clasp. *Recreations:* shooting, fishing and golf. *Heir:* none. *Address:* Glenhead, Whonnock, BC. *T:* 462-7277. *Clubs:* Carlton; Vancouver (Vancouver).

**LENNARD, Sir (Thomas) Richard (Fiennes) Barrett-,** 5th Bt, *cr* 1801; OBE 1970; Vice-President of Norwich Union Life Insurance Society and Vice-Chairman of Norwich Union Fire Insurance Society Ltd; Chairman, East Anglian Trustee Savings Bank; Director: Scottish Union & National Insurance Co.; Maritime Insurance Co. Ltd; *b* 12 Dec. 1898; *s* of 4th Bt and Lepel Julia (*d* 1959), *d* of late Rev. Henry Thornton Pearse; *S* father, 1934; *m* 1922, Kathleen Finora, *d* of late Hon. John Donohoe FitzGerald; one *d. Educ:* Brighton Coll.; Clare Coll., Cambridge. KStJ. *Heir: cousin,* Rev. Hugh Dacre Barrett-Lennard [*b* 27 June 1917. *Educ:* Radley. Served War of 1939-45 (despatches), Capt. Essex Regt. Is a Priest of London Oratory]. *Address:* Horsford Manor, near Norwich. *Clubs:* Royal Automobile; Leander; Norfolk (Norwich).

**LENNIE, Douglas;** *b* 30 March 1910; *e s* of Magnus S. Lennie; *m* 1941, Rhona Young Ponsonby; two *s. Educ:* Berkhamsted Sch.; Guy's Hospital, LDS, RCS, 1934; Northwestern University, Chicago, DDS, 1938. served War of 1939-45, Temporary Surg. Lt-Comdr (D) RNVR; formerly Surgeon Dentist to Queen Mary. *Address:* 7 Knightsbridge Court, Sloane Street, SW1. *T:* 01-235 3763.

**LENNON, Dennis,** CBE 1968; MC 1942; Senior Partner, Dennis Lennon & Partners, since 1950; *b* 23 June 1918; British; *m* 1948, Else Bull-Andersen; three *s. Educ:* Merchant Taylors' Sch.; University Coll., London. Served Royal Engineers, 1939-45 (despatches): 1st, 7th, 6th Armd Divs; captured in France 1940, later escaped; 7th Armd Div., N Africa; 6th Armd Div., Italy. Dir, Rayon Industry Design Centre, 1948-50; private practice, 1950-. Main Work: Jaeger shops; London Steak Houses; co-ordinator of interior, RMS Queen Elizabeth II; Chalcot Housing Estate, Hampstead. FRIBA, FSIA, FRSA. *Recreations:* arts and design. *Address:* Hamper Mill, Watford, Herts. *T:* Watford 34445. *Club:* Royal Thames Yacht.

**LENNON, Prof. (George) Gordon;** Dean of the Faculty of Medicine, University of Western Australia, Perth, since 1967; *b* 7 Oct. 1911; *s* of J. Lennon, 21 Camperdown Road, Aberdeen; *m* 1940, Barbara Brynhild (*née* Buckle); two *s. Educ:* Aberdeen Academy; Aberdeen Univ. MB, ChB Aberdeen, 1934; served in hospital posts in Aberdeen, Glasgow, London, Birmingham; MRCOG 1939; FRCOG 1952; MMSA 1943; ChM (Hons) Aberdeen, 1945. Served War of 1939-45, Sqdn-Ldr in charge of Surgical Div., RAFVR, 1942-46. First Asst, Nuffield Dept of Obstetrics and Gynæcology, Radcliffe Infirmary (University of Oxford), 1946-51; Prof. of Obstetrics and Gynæcology, Univ. of Bristol, 1951-67. Visiting Professor: Iraq and Turkey, 1956; South Africa and Uganda, 1958; Iran, 1965. *Publications:* Diagnosis in Clinical Obstetrics; articles in British Medical Journal, Proceedings of the Royal Society of Medicine, Journal of Obstetrics and Gynæcology of the British Empire, etc. *Recreation:* golf. *Address:* Dean's Office, Victoria Square, Perth, WA 6000, Australia.

**LENNON, Most Rev. Patrick;** *see* Kildare and Leighlin, Bishop of, (RC).

**LENNOX;** *see* Gordon-Lennox and Gordon Lennox.

**LENNOX, Robert Smith;** Lord Provost of Aberdeen since May 1967; *b* 8 June 1909; *m* 1963, Evelyn Margaret; no *c. Educ:* St Clement Sch., Aberdeen. *Address:* 7 Gillespie Crescent, Ashgrove, Aberdeen. *T:* Aberdeen 43862.

**LENNOX-BOYD,** family name of **Viscount Boyd of Merton.**

**LENSKI, Lois;** *b* Springfield, Ohio, 14 Oct. 1893; *d* of Richard C. H. Lenski and Marietta Young; *m* 1921, Arthur S. Covey; one *s. Educ:* Ohio State Univ., Columbus; Art Students' League, NY; Westminster School of Art, London. Artist, painter; writer and illustrator of children's books. Hon. Doctor of Humane Letters, Women's Coll., University of North Carolina, USA 1962; Hon. LittD: Wartburg Coll., Iowa, 1959; Capital Univ., Ohio 1966; Southwestern Coll., Winfield, Kan, 1968. Regina Medal, Catholic Library Assoc., 1969; Special Children's Collection Silver Medallion, Univ. of Southern Mississippi, 1969. *Publications:* Skipping Village; A Little Girl of 1900; Jack Horner's Pie; Alphabet People; Two Brothers and their Animal Friends; Two Brothers and their Baby Sister; Spinach Boy; The Wonder City; Washington Picture Book; Benny and his Penny; Grandmother Tippytoe; Arabella and her Aunts; The Little Family; Johnny Goes to the Fair; The Little Auto; Surprise for Mother; Gooseberry Garden; Sugar Plum House; Little Baby Ann; The Easter Rabbit's Parade; The Little Sail Boat; Phebe Fairchild Her Book; A-Going to the Westward; The Little Airplane; Bound Girl of Cobble Hill; Susie Mariar (repr. 1968); Ocean-Born Mary; The Little Train; Blueberry Corners; Indian Captive: The Story of Mary Jemison; Animals for Me; The Little Farm; Bayou Suzette; Davy's Day; Puritan Adventure; Let's Play House; Spring is Here; Strawberry Girl (awarded Newbery Medal, 1946); The Little Fire Engine; Blue Ridge Billy; Surprise for Davy; Judy's Journey (awarded Child Study Assoc. Award for 1947); Mr and Mrs Noah; Now It's Fall; Boom Town Boy, 1948; Cowboy Small; Cotton in My Sack, 1949; Texas Tomboy, 1950; I Like Winter, 1950; Prairie School, 1951; Papa Small, 1951; We Live in the South; Peanuts for Billy Ben; We are Thy Children; Hymn Book for Boys and Girls, 1952; On a Summer Day; Mama

Hattie's Girl, 1953; Project Boy; We Live in the City; Songs of Mr Small; Corn-Farm Boy, 1954; San Francisco Boy; A Dog Came to School, 1955; We Live by the River; Berries in the Scoop; Songs of the City; Big Little Davy; Flood Friday, 1956; Houseboat Girl; Davy and His Dog, 1957; Little Sioux Girl, 1958; I went for a Walk, 1958; At our House, 1959; Coal Camp Girl, 1959; When I Grow Up, 1960; We Live in the Country, 1960; Davy Goes Places, 1961; Policeman Small, 1962; We Live in the Southwest, 1962; Shoo-Fly Girl, 1963; The Life I Live: Collected Poems, 1965; We Live in the North, 1965; High-Rise Secret, 1966; To Be a Logger, 1967; Debbie and her Grandma, 1967; Lois Lenski's Christmas Stories, 1968; Deer Valley Girl, 1968; Debbie Herself, 1969; Debbie and her Family, 1969; Debbie and her Dolls, 1970; Debbie Goes to Nursery School, 1970. *Address:* Lutean Shores, Tarpon Springs, Florida 33589, USA.

**LEON, His Honour Henry Cecil,** MC 1942; County Court Judge, 1949-67; *b* 19 Sept. 1902; *y s* of late J. A. Leon and late Mrs Leon, of 4 Cleveland Gardens, Bayswater, W2; *m* 1st, 1935, Lettice Mabel (*d* 1950), *o d* of late H. D. Apperly and of Mrs Apperly, late of Chalfont St Peter, Bucks; no *c*; 2nd, 1954, Barbara Jeanne Ovenden (*née* Blackmore); one step *s*. *Educ:* St Paul's Sch.; King's Coll., Cambridge. Called to the Bar, 1923. Served War 1939-45, 1/5 Queen's Regt. *Publications,* under pseudonym Henry Cecil: *fiction:* Full Circle, 1948; The Painswick Line, 1951; No Bail for the Judge, 1952; Ways and Means, 1952; Natural Causes, 1953; According to the Evidence, 1954; Brothers in Law, 1955 (filmed 1957); Friends at Court, 1956; Much in Evidence, 1957; Sober as a Judge, 1958; Settled out of Court, 1959; Alibi for a Judge, 1960; Daughters in Law, 1961; Unlawful Occasions, 1962; Independent Witness, 1963; Portrait of a Judge and Other Stories, 1964; Fathers in Law, 1965; The Asking Price, 1966; A Woman Named Anne, 1967; No Fear or Favour, 1968; Tell You What I'll Do, 1969; *non-fiction:* Brief to Counsel, 1958; Not Such an Ass, 1961; Tipping the Scales, 1964; Know About English Law, 1965; A Matter of Speculation, 1965; The English Judge (Hamlyn Lectures), 1970; a number of short stories and articles; under pseudonym Clifford Maxwell: I Married the Girl, 1960. *Plays:* Brothers in Law (with Ted Willis), 1959; Settled Out of Court (with William Saroyan), Strand, 1960; Alibi for a Judge (with Felicity Douglas and Basil Dawson), Savoy, 1965; According to the Evidence (with Felicity Douglas and Basil Dawson), Savoy, 1967; No Fear or Favour, 1967; Hugo (with C. E. Webber), 1969; A Woman Named Anne, Duke of York's, 1970; *TV Series:* with Frank Muir and Denis Norden: Brothers in Law, Mr Justice Duncannon; numerous radio plays. *Address:* 6 Gray's Inn Square, Gray's Inn, WC1. *T:* 01-242 7595. *Clubs:* Garrick, Lansdowne.

**LEON, Sir John (Ronald),** 4th Bt, *cr* 1911; Actor (stage name, John Standing); *b* 16 Aug. 1934; *er s* of 3rd Bt and of Kay Hammond, *qv*; *S* father, 1964; *m* 1961, Jill, *d* of Jack Melford; one *s*. *Educ:* Eton. Late 2nd Lt, KRRC. *Plays include:* Darling Buds of May, Saville, 1959; leading man, season, Bristol Old Vic, 1960; The Irregular Verb to Love, Criterion, 1961; Norman, Duchess, 1963; So Much to Remember, Vaudeville, 1963; The Three Sisters, Oxford Playhouse, 1964; See How They Run, Vaudeville, 1964; The Importance of Being Earnest, Haymarket 1968. Seasons at Chichester Theatre, 1966, 1967. *Films:* The Wild and the Willing, 1962; Iron Maiden, 1962; King Rat, 1964; Walk, Don't Run, 1965. *Recreation:* painting. *Heir:* *s* Alexander John Leon, *b* 3 May 1965. *Address:* 9 Luna Street, SW10. *T:* 01-352 9350.

**LEON, Prof. Philip,** MA Oxon; Professor of Classics, University of Leicester, 1954-60, retired; Professor Emeritus, 1966; *b* 10 April 1895; *s* of Meyer and Taube Leon; *m* 1st, 1927, Mariette Eileen Soman (*d* 1941); two *d*; 2nd, 1948, Elizabeth Palmer Elliott; one *s*. *Educ:* Manchester Grammar Sch.; New Coll., Oxford. Asst Lecturer at University Coll., London, Dept of Latin, 1921-23; Lecturer in charge of Dept of Classics, University Coll., Leicester, 1923-54. Visiting Prof., University Coll. of Rhodesia and Nyasaland, Salisbury, 1961-63. *Publications:* The Ethics of Power, 1935; The Philosophy of Courage, 1939; Plato, 1939; Body, Mind and Spirit, 1948; The Professors, 1955; (trans.) Gandhi to Vinoba, 1957; Beyond Belief and Unbelief, 1965; The Gospel according to Judas, 1968. Contrib. to Mind, Philosophy, The Hibbert Jl, Classical Quarterly, The Listener, Time and Tide, etc. *Recreations:* tennis, walking, climbing, swimming, chess, mathematics. *Address:* 42 Stoughton Road, Leicester LE2 2EB. *T:* Leicester 704355.

**LEON TROUT, Sir H.;** *see* Trout, Sir H. L.

**LEONARD, Dick;** *see* Leonard, Richard Lawrence.

**LEONARD, Rt. Rev. Graham Douglas;** *see* Willesden, Bishop Suffragan of.

**LEONARD, (Hamilton) John,** QC 1969; Commissioner, Central Criminal Court, since 1969; *b* 28 April 1926; *s* of late Arthur Leonard and Jean Leonard, Poole, Dorset; *m* 1948, Doreen Enid, *yr d* of late Lt-Col Sidney James Parker, OBE, and late May Florence Parker, Sanderstead, Surrey; one *s* one *d*. *Educ:* Dean Close Sch., Cheltenham; Brasenose Coll., Oxford (MA). Coldstream Guards (Captain), 1944-47. Called to Bar, Inner Temple, 1951; South-Eastern Circuit. 2nd Junior Prosecuting Counsel to the Crown at Central Criminal Court, 1964-69; Dep. Chm., Surrey QS, 1969. Mem., General Council of the Bar, 1970-. *Recreations:* books, music. *Address:* 6 King's Bench Walk, Temple, EC4. *T:* 01-353 1696; Fieldend, Harps Oak Lane, Merstham, Surrey. *T:* Merstham 4472. *Club:* Lansdowne.

**LEONARD, James Charles Beresford Whyte,** MA Oxon; **His Honour Judge Leonard;** barrister Inner Temple, 1928; Bencher 1961; Chairman of Statutory Committee of Pharmaceutical Society of Great Britain, 1962-65; Deputy Chairman of Quarter Sessions: Oxfordshire, since 1962; Inner London, since 1965; Middlesex, since 1969; *b* 1905; *s* of Hon. J. W. Leonard, KC; *m* 1939, Barbara Helen, *d* of late Capt. William Incledon-Webber; two *s* one *d*. *Educ:* Clifton Coll.; Christ Church, Oxford. Served 1940-45, with RAF. Recorder of Walsall, Staffs, 1951-64; Junior Counsel to Ministry of Agriculture, Fisheries and Food, Forestry Commission and Tithe Redemption Commission, 1959-64; Dep. Chm., Co. of London OS. 1964-65. *Address:* 1 Paper Buildings, Temple, EC4 *T:* 01-583 1870; Cross Trees, Sutton Courtenay, Berks. *T:* Sutton Courtenay 230.

*See also Lord Delvin.*

**LEONARD, John;** *see* Leonard, H. J.

**LEONARD, Richard Lawrence, (Dick Leonard);** MP (Lab) Romford since 1970; *b* 12 Dec. 1930; *s* of Cyril Leonard, Pinner, Mddx, and late Kate Leonard (*née* Whyte); *m* 1963, Irène, *d* of Dr Ernst Heidelberger, Courbevoie, France, and of Dr Gertrud Heidelberger, Bad

Godesberg, Germany. *Educ:* Ealing Grammar Sch.; Inst. of Education, London Univ.; Essex Univ. (MA). School teacher, 1953-55. Contested (Lab) Harrow (West), 1955. Dep. Gen. Sec., Fabian Society, 1955-60; journalist and broadcaster, 1960-68; Sen. Research Fellow (Social Science Research Council), Essex Univ., 1968-70. *Publications:* Guide to the General Election, 1964; Elections in Britain, 1968; contrib.: Guardian, Sunday Times, New Society, Encounter, etc. *Recreations:* walking, neglecting the garden. *Address:* 16 Albert Street, NW1.

**LEONARD-WILLIAMS, Air Vice-Marshal Harold Guy,** CB 1966; CBE 1946; retired; *b* 10 Sept. 1911; *s* of late Rev. B. G. Leonard-Williams; *m* 1937, Catherine Estelle, *d* of late G. A. M. Levett; one *d*. *Educ:* Lancing Coll.; RAF Coll., Cranwell. 58 Sqdn, 1932-33; 208 Sqdn, Middle East, 1933-36; No 17 Signals Course, 1936-37; Instructor, RAF Coll., 1937-38; Advanced Air Striking Force, France, 1939-40 (despatches, 1940); Air Min. (Signals), 1940-43; Chm., Brit. Jt Communications Bd, 1943-46; RAF Staff Coll., 1947; Dep. CSO, RAF Middle East, 1947-50; Jt Services Staff Coll., 1950-51; CO Radio Engrg Unit, 1951-53; Dep. Dir Signals, Air Min., 1953-56; Sen. Techn. Staff Off., 90 Signals Gp, 1956-57; Dir of Signals, Air Min., 1957-59; Comdt No 1 Radio Sch., 1959-61; Comd. Electronics Off., Fighter Comd., 1961-63; AOA, HQ Far East Air Force, and AOC, HQ Gp, 1963-65; Dir-Gen. of Manning (RAF), Air Force Dept, 1966-68. Warden, St Michael's Cheshire Home, Axbridge. Officer, Legion of Merit (US), 1945. *Recreations:* gardening, boating, do-it-yourself. *Address:* Open-barrow, Barrows Park, Cheddar, Somerset. *T:* Cheddar 474. *Club:* Royal Air Force.

**LE PATOUREL, Brig. Herbert Wallace,** VC 1943; Director, Harveys of Bristol, since 1969; *b* 20 June 1916; *yr s* of late Herbert Augustus Le Patourel (Attorney-General for Guernsey) and Mary Elizabeth Daw; *m* 1949, Babette Theresa Beattie; two *d*. *Educ:* Elizabeth Coll., Guernsey. Bank Clerk, 1934-37; 2nd Lt Royal Guernsey Militia, 1936; transferred to The Hampshire Regt, 1937; served War of 1939-45 (despatches, VC); Instructor at Staff Coll., Quetta, 1945-47; Instructor, School of Infantry, Warminster, 1948-50; Parachute Regt, 1950-53; CO, 5th Bn The Royal Hampshire Regt TA, 1954-67; GSO1. British Joint Services Mission, Washington, DC, 1958-60; Dep. Comdr, Ghana Army, 1960-61; Dep. Comdr, 43 Div./District, 1961-62; retired 1962. Executive Asst to the Directors of Showerings Vine Products and Whiteways Ltd, 1965-69. *Recreations:* sailing, horses. *Address:* Vine House, Bishop Sutton, Bristol. *T:* Chew Magna 345. *Club:* Army and Navy.

**LE PATOUREL, John Herbert,** MA, DPhil Oxon; Docteur *hc* Caen; Research Professor of Medieval History, University of Leeds, since 1970; Archivist to Royal Court of Guernsey since 1946; *b* Guernsey, 29 July 1909; *er s* of late H. A. Le Patourel (HM Attorney-Gen. for Guernsey) and Mary Elizabeth Daw; *m* 1939, Hilda Elizabeth Jean Bird, BA, FSA; three *s* one *d*. *Educ:* Elizabeth Coll., Guernsey; Jesus Coll., Oxford (King Charles I Scholar); Goldsmiths' Company's Senior Student, 1931-33. Asst Lecturer, Dept of History, University Coll., London, 1933; Lecturer, 1936; Reader in Medieval History, University of London, 1943; Prof. of Medieval History, 1945-70, and Dir, Graduate Centre for Medieval Studies, 1967-70, Univ. of Leeds. leverhulme Research Fellow, 1950-51. Pres., Leeds Philosophical and Literary Soc., 1966-68; Vice-President: Thoresby Soc. (Pres. 1949-55); Royal Horticultural Soc., 1968-70; Hon. Vice-Pres., Yorkshire Archæological Soc. (Pres., 1965-69). *Publications:* The Medieval Administration of the Channel Islands, 1199-1399, 1937; The Building of Castle Cornet, Guernsey, 1958; The Manor and Borough of Leeds, 1066-1400, 1957; articles, etc, in English and French historical periodicals, publications of Channel Island societies, etc. *Address:* The University, Leeds 2; Westcote, Hebers Ghyll Drive, Ilkley, Yorks. *T:* Ilkley 4406.

**LE-POER-TRENCH,** family name of **Earl of Clancarty.**

**LEPPARD, Raymond John;** conductor, harpsichordist, composer; *b* 11 Aug. 1927; *s* of A. V. Leppard. *Educ:* Trinity Coll., Cambridge. Fellow of Trin. Coll., Cambridge, Univ. Lecturer in Music, 1958-68; Musical Dir, English Chamber Orchestra, 1960. Hon. Keeper of the Music, Fitzwilliam Museum, 1963. Conductor: Covent Garden, Sadlers Wells, Glyndebourne, and abroad. *Publications:* realisations of Monteverdi: Il Ballo delle Ingrate, 1958; L'Incoronazione di Poppea, 1962; L'Orfeo, 1965; Realisations of Francesco Cavalli: Messa Concertata, 1966; L'Ormindo, 1967; La Calisto, 1969; Magnificat 1970; British Academy Italian Lecture, 1969, procs Royal Musical Assoc. *Recreations:* music, theatre, books, friends. *Address:* 16 Hamilton Terrace, NW8. *T:* 01-286 0504. *Clubs:* Brooks's, Beefsteak.

**LE QUESNE, Charles Martin,** CMG 1963; Ambassador to Algeria, since 1968; *b* 10 June 1917; *s* of C. T. Le Quesne, QC; *m* 1948; three *s*. *Educ:* Shrewsbury; Exeter Coll., Oxford. Served in Royal Artillery, 1940-45. Apptd HM Foreign Service, 1946; 2nd Sec. at HM Embassy, Baghdad, 1947-48; 1st Secretary: Foreign Office, 1948-51, HM Political Residency, Bahrain, 1951-54; attended course at NATO Defence Coll., Paris, 1954-55; HM Embassy, Rome, 1955-58; Foreign Office, 1958-60; apptd HM Chargé d'Affaires. Republic of Mali, 1960, subsequently Ambassador there, 1961-64; Foreign Office, 1964-68. *Recreations:* gardening, sailing, bridge. *Address:* Beau Désert, St Saviour's, Jersey, Channel Islands. *T:* Jersey-Eastern 876. *Clubs:* Reform; Royal Channel Islands Yacht.

*See also J. G. Le Quesne, L. P. Le Quesne.*

**LE QUESNE, John Godfray,** QC 1962; Deputy Chairman of Quarter Sessions, County of Lincoln (Parts of Kesteven), since Dec. 1963; Judge of Courts of Appeal of Jersey and Guernsey, since 1964; *b* 1924; 3rd *s* of late C. T. Le Quesne, QC; *m* 1963, Susan Mary Gill; two *s* one *d*. *Educ:* Shrewsbury Sch.; Exeter Coll., Oxford (MA). Pres. of Oxford Union, 1943. Called to bar, Inner Temple, 1947; Master of the Bench, Inner Temple, 1969; admitted to bar of St Helena, 1959. Chm. of Council, Regent's Park Coll., Oxford, 1958-. *Recreations:* music, walking. *Address:* 1 Harcourt Buildings, Temple, EC4. *T:* 01-353 3731. *Club:* Reform.

*See also C. M. Le Quesne, L. P. Le Quesne.*

**LE QUESNE, Prof. Leslie Philip,** DM, MCh, FRCS; Professor of Surgery, Middlesex Hospital Medical School and Director, Department of Surgical Studies, Middlesex Hospital, since 1963; *b* 24 Aug. 1919; *s* of late C. T. Le Quesne, QC; *m* 1969, Pamela Margaret, *o d* of Dr A. Fullerton, Batley, Yorks. *Educ:* Rugby; Exeter Coll., Oxford; Middlesex Hosp. Med. Sch. Jun. Demonstrator, Path. and Anat., 1943-45; House Surgeon, Southend Hosp. and St Mark's Hosp., 1945-47. Appointments at

Middlesex Hospital: Asst, Surgical Professorial Unit, 1947-52; Asst Dir, Dept of Surgical Studies, 1952-63; Surgeon, 1960-63. Editor, Post Graduate Med. Jl, 1951-52. Arris and Gale Lectr, RCS, 1952; Baxter Lectr, Amer. Coll. Surgs, 1960. Examr in Surgery, Universities London, Glasgow, Birmingham and Khartoum. Chm., The British Jl of Surgery. Moynihan Medal, 1953. *Publications:* medical articles and contribs to text books; Fluid Balance in Surgical Practice, 2nd edn, 1957. *Recreations:* sailing, reading. *Address:* 104 Harley Street, W1. *T:* 01-935 4321. *Club:* Royal Burnham Yacht.

*See also C. M. Le Quesne, J. G. Le Quesne.*

**LERMON, Norman,** QC 1966; *b* 12 Dec. 1915; *s* of late Morris and Clara Lermon; *m* 1939, Sheila Veronica Gilks; one *d. Educ:* Clifton Coll.; Trinity Hall, Cambridge. Joined Royal Fusiliers, 1939; commnd into S Wales Borderers, 1940; served in 53 (W) and 11th Armoured Divs; Staff Officer Ops (Air) 8th Corps, France, Holland and Germany; Major, 1945; NW Europe 1946 (despatches). Called to the Bar, 1943; South-Eastern Circuit. *Recreations:* golf, reading. *Address:* 2 Harcourt Buildings, Temple, EC4. *T:* 01-353 4746. *Club:* Liphook Golf.

**LERNER, Alan Jay;** American playwright-lyricist; *b* 31 Aug. 1918; *s* of Joseph J. and Edith Lerner. *Educ:* Bedales Sch., Hampshire, England; Choate Sch., Wallingford, Conn, USA; Harvard Univ., USA. Wrote screen play, An American in Paris. Wrote book and lyrics for Brigadoon, Paint Your Wagon, My Fair Lady, Gigi (film), Camelot, On a Clear Day, Coco, etc. *Address:* 745 Fifth Avenue, New York, NY 10022, USA.

**LERNER, Max;** Author; Syndicated newspaper column appears New York Post, Los Angeles Times and elsewhere; Professor of American Civilization and World Politics, Brandeis University, USA, since 1949; Ford Foundation research project on European unity, 1963-64; *b* 20 Dec. 1902; *s* of Benjamin Lerner and Bessie Podel; *m* 1st; two *d* (and one *d* decd); 2nd, 1941, Edna Albers; three *s. Educ:* Yale Univ. (BA); Washington Univ., St Louis (MA); Robert Brookings Graduate Sch. of Economics and Government (PhD). Encyclopædia of Social Sciences, 1927, managing editor; Sarah Lawrence Coll., 1932-36, Prof. of Social Science; Harvard, 1935-36, Prof. of Government; Prof. of Political Science, Williams Coll., 1938-43; Ford Foundation Prof. of Amer. Civilization, Sch. of Internat. Studies, University of Delhi, 1959-60; Editor of the Nation, 1936-38; Editorial Director PM, 1943-48; Columnist for the New York Star, 1948-49. *Publications:* It is Later Than You Think, 1938, rev. edn, 1943; Ideas are Weapons, 1939; Ideas for the Ice Age, 1941; The Mind and Faith of Justice Holmes, 1943. Public Journal, 1945; Actions and Passions, 1949; America as a Civilization, 1957; The Unfinished Country, 1959; Education and a Radical Humanism, 1962; The Age of Overkill, 1962; Tocqueville and American Civilization, 1969; (ed) Essential Works of John Stuart Mill, 1961; (ed) Tocqueville, Democracy in America, 1966; Life and Thought of Thomas Jefferson, 1969. *Address:* 445 E 84th Street, New York, NY 10028, USA.

**LE ROUGETEL, Sir John Helier,** KCMG, *cr* 1946 (CMG 1943); MC, 1917 and bar 1918; *b* 19 June 1894; *s* of Daniel Le Rougetel; *m* 1925, Mary Penrose-Thackwell; one *s* one *d. Educ:* Rossall; Magdalene Coll., Cambridge (Hon. Fellow 1952). Army, 1914-19. Entered Diplomatic Service, 1920; served at Vienna, Budapest, Ottawa, Tokyo, Peking, The Hague, Bucharest, Moscow, Shanghai, and at Foreign Office; Ambassador to Persia, 1946-50; Ambassador to Belgium, 1950-51. High Commissioner for the UK in South Africa, 1951-55; retired from Foreign Service, 1955. *Recreations:* fishing, golf. *Address:* Borovere Cottage, Alton, Hants.

*See also A. R. H. Kellas.*

**LESLIE,** family name of **Earl of Rothes.**

**LESLIE, Lord; Ian Lionel Malcolm Leslie;** *b* 10 May 1932; *o s* of 20th Earl of Rothes, *qv*; *m* 1955, Marigold, *o d* of Sir David M. Evans Bevan, 1st Bt, *qv*; two *s. Educ:* Eton. Sub-Lt RNVR, 1953. *Heir:* *s* Master of Leslie, *qv*. *Address:* Tanglewood, West Tytherley, Salisbury, Wilts. *Club:* Travellers'.

**LESLIE, Master of; James Malcolm David Leslie;** *b* 4 June 1958; *s* of Lord Leslie, *qv*.

**LESLIE, Doris, (Lady Fergusson Hannay);** novelist and historian; *m* Sir Walter Fergusson Hannay (*d* 1961). *Educ:* London; Brussels; studied art in Florence. Served in Civil Defence, 1941-45. Woman of the Year for Literature (Catholic Women's League), 1970. *Publications: novels:* Full Flavour; Fair Company; Concord in Jeopardy; Another Cynthia; House in the Dust; Folly's End; The Peverills; Peridot Flight; As the Tree Falls; Paragon Street; The Marriage of Martha Todd; A Young Wives' Tale; *biographical studies:* Royal William (Life of William IV); Polonaise (Life of Chopin); Wreath for Arabella (Life of the Lady Arabella Stuart); That Enchantress (Life of Abigail Hill, Lady Masham); The Great Corinthian (Portrait of the Prince Regent); A Toast to Lady Mary (Life of Lady Mary Wortley Montagu); The Perfect Wife (Life of Mary Anne Disraeli, Viscountess Beaconsfield), 1960; I Return (The Story of François Villon), 1962; This for Caroline (Life of Lady Caroline Lamb), 1964; The Sceptre and the Rose (marriage of Charles II and Catherine of Braganza) 1967; The Rebel Princess (Life of Sophia Dorothea, wife of George I), 1970. *Address:* c/o A. P. Watt & Son, 26/28 Bedford Row, WC1.

**LESLIE, Mrs D. G.;** *see* Erskine-Lindop, A. B. N.

**LESLIE, Rt. Rev. Ernest Kenneth;** *see* Bathurst, (NSW), Bishop of.

**LESLIE, Sir Francis (Galloway),** KCVO 1965 (CVO 1956); Physician in Ordinary HRH the late Princess Royal, 1951-65; *b* 10 April 1902; *e s* of late Lewis Francis Leslie, OBE, Haslemere; *m* 1929, Enid Mary, *o d* of Arthur Powell Simon, London; one *s* one *d. Educ:* Shrewsbury Sch.; Trinity Coll., Cambridge; The London Hospital. BA Cantab 1923; MRCS, LRCP, 1927; DCH Eng. 1943; MA Cantab 1959. Gen. Practitioner: Chichester, Sussex, 1928-36; London, 1937-39; Eton, Windsor (Mem. Eton Coll., Medical Board), 1941-44; Gen. Physician, London, 1944-. War of 1939-45, Lt, RAMC (Dep. Med. Specialist i/c Female Personnel), Aldershot Comd, 1939-40. Past Pres. Hunterian Soc., 1958-59. *Recreations:* various. *Address:* 24 Napier Avenue, Hurlingham, SW6. *T:* 01-736 4105.

**LESLIE, Rear-Adm. George Cunningham,** CB 1970; OBE 1944; Domestic Bursar and Fellow of St Edmund Hall, Oxford, since 1970; *b* 27 Oct. 1920; 4th *s* of Col A. S. Leslie, CMG, WS, Kininvie, and Mrs M. I. Leslie (*née* Horne); *m* 1953, Margaret Rose Leslie; one *s* three *d. Educ:* Uppingham. Entered RN, 1938; War service in HMS York, Harvester, Volunteer and Cassandra, 1939-45; comd HMS: Wrangler, 1950-51; Wilton, 1951; Surprise, 1954-55; Capt. Fishery Protection Sqdn, 1960-62; Cdre HMS Drake, 1964-65; comd HMS Devonshire, 1966-67; Flag Officer, Admiralty Interview Bd, 1967-68; NATO HQ, Brussels, 1968-70. Comdr 1952; Capt. 1958; Rear-adm. 1968; retired 1970. *Recreations:* sailing, golf, painting, country pursuits. *Address:* c/o Clydesdale Bank, 88 Princes Street, Edinburgh.

**LESLIE, Gilbert Frank; His Honour Judge Leslie;** Judge of County Courts (Circuit 42, Bloomsbury and Marylebone, previously Circuits 14 and 46), since 1960; Acting Deputy Chairman, Inner London Area Sessions, since 1965; *b* 25 Aug. 1909; *e s* of late F. L. J. Leslie, JP and late M. A. Leslie (*née* Gilbert), Harrogate; *m* 1947, Mary Braithwaite, MD, JP, *e d* of late Col W. H. Braithwaite, MC, TD, DL and Mrs E. M. Braithwaite, Harrogate; three *d. Educ:* St Christopher Sch., Letchworth; King's Coll., Cambridge (MA). Called to the Bar, Inner Temple, 1932; joined North-Eastern Circuit. Served War of 1939-45; Private Sherwood Foresters, 1939; commissioned West Yorkshire Regt, 1940; on Judge-Advocate-General's staff from Nov. 1940; finally ADJAG, HQ BAOR; released Nov. 1945 (Hon. Lt-Col). Asst Recorder, Newcastle upon Tyne City Quarter Sessions, 1954-60, Sheffield City Quarter Sessions, 1956-60; Recorder of Pontefract, 1958-60; Recorder of Rotherham, 1960; Dep. Chm., West Riding Quarter Sessions, 1960-63. A Dep. Chm., Agricultural Lands Tribunal (Yorkshire Area), 1958-60; Mem. Board of Faculty of Law and Court of Governors, Sheffield Univ., 1958-61. *Publications:* articles in legal and other periodicals. *Recreation:* gardening. *Address:* Ottways, 26 Ottways Lane, Ashtead, Surrey. *T:* Ashtead 74191. *Club:* Reform.

**LESLIE, Harald Robert;** *see* Birsay, Hon. Lord.

**LESLIE, Ian (William) Murray,** OBE 1954; Editor of Building (formerly The Builder), 1948-70; Vice-Chairman, The Builder Ltd, since 1970; *b* 13 March 1905; 2nd *s* of John Gordon Leslie, MB, CM, Black Isle, Inverness, and Agnes Macrae, Kintail, Wester Ross; *m* 1929, Josette, 2nd *d* of late André Dèlétraz, actor, Paris, and Mme Hachard; one *s. Educ:* St Paul's (foundation scholar); Crown and Manor Boys' Club, Hoxton. Joined editorial staff of The Builder, 1926; Associate Editor, 1937. Mem. Council, National Assoc. of Boys' Clubs, 1944-54; Chm. London Federation of Boys' Clubs, 1945-50; Mem. Metropolitan Juvenile Courts panel, 1947-61; made survey (with John B. Perks) of Canadian construction industry for The Builder, 1950; organized £1000 house, architectural competition for The Builder, 1951; made survey of housing, South Africa and Rhodesia, for The Builder, 1954. Associate RICS; Hon. Mem. of Art Workers' Guild. Hon. ARIBA; Hon. FIOB. *Recreations:* watching cricket; sleep. *Address:* 4 Catherine Street, Aldwych, WC2. *T:* 01-836 6251. *Clubs:* Savage, Architectural Association, MCC.

**LESLIE, James Campbell,** OBE 1943; MA, BSc(Agr); Livestock Consultant; *m* 1926; one *d. Educ:* Stonehaven Mackie Acad.; Aberdeen Univ.; North of Scotland Coll. of Agriculture, Teacher of Science, Mathematics and Agriculture, Annan Acad., Dumfriesshire; Lectr in Agriculture, Leeds Univ.; Organiser of Agricultural Educn to the Lindsey (Lincs) CC; Organiser of Agricultural Education to the Cambridgeshire County Council; Principal, Essex Institute of Agriculture, Chelmsford; Executive Officer, Essex War Agricultural Cttee; Dep. Gen. Sec., National Farmers' Union; Agricultural Adviser, Edmundsons Electricity Corporation, Ltd; Agricultural Adviser British Oil and Cake Mills Ltd, retired. *Publications:* contributed to various Agricultural Journals and Weekly Papers and the Scientific Cyclopædia of Agriculture. *Address:* Lightoaks, Fryerning, Ingatestone, Essex. *Clubs:* Chelmsford, Chelmsford Golf.

**LESLIE, Sir (John Randolph) Shane,** 3rd Bt, *cr* 1876; LLD (Notre Dame University, USA); Member Irish Academy; Author and Professor; *b* 1885; *er s* of Sir John Leslie, 2nd Bt, CBE, and Léonie Blanche (*d* 1943), *d* of Leonard Jerome of New York; *S* father, 1944; *m* 1912, Marjorie (*d* 1951), *y d* of Henry C. Ide, of Vermont, USA, late Gov.-Gen. of the Philippines and US Ambassador to Spain; two *s* one *d*; *m* 1958, Iris, *y d* of C. M. Laing, barrister, Bury Knowle, Headington, Oxford. *Educ:* Eton; King's Coll., Cambride (MA). Knight Comdr of St Gregory. *Publications:* Songs of Oriel; The Isle of Columcille; The End of a Chapter, 1916; Verses in Peace and War; The Oppidan, 1922; Life of Cardinal Manning; Life of Sir Mark Sykes, 1922; Doomsland, 1923; Memoir of Brig.-Gen. Gordon Shephard; Masquerades, 1924; An Anthology of Catholic Poets, 1925; The Cantab; George the Fourth, 1926; The Skull of Swift, 1928; The Greek Anthology, 1929; The Anglo-Catholic, 1929; A Ghost in the Isle of Wight, 1929; Memoir of J. E. C. Bodley, 1930; The Epic of Jutland, 1930; Sublime Failures, 1932; The Oxford Movement, 1933; Poems and Ballads, 1933; The Passing Chapter, 1934; The Script of Jonathan Swift and other Essays, 1935; American Wonderland, 1936; Men were Different: Studies in Late Victorian Biography, 1937; Sir Evelyn Ruggles-Brise, 1938; The Film of Memory, 1938; The Life of Mrs Fitzherbert, 1939; Letters of Mrs Fitzherbert, 1940; From Cabin Boy to Archbishop, 1942; Letters of Cardinal Vaughan to Lady Herbert of Lea, 1943; The Irish Tangle for English Readers, 1946; Salutation to Five, 1951; Memoir of Cardinal Gasquet, 1954; Shane Leslie's Ghost Book, 1955; Long Shadows, 1966. *Recreations:* Irish archæology and forestry. *Heir: s* John Norman Ide Leslie, *b* 6 Dec. 1916. *Address:* 16b Palmeira Court, Hove, Sussex.

**LESLIE, Hon. John Wayland;** Flight Lieutenant late RAFVR (invalided 1943); *b* 16 Dec. 1909; 2nd *s* of 19th Earl of Rothes; *m* 1932, Coral Angela, *d* of late G. H. Pinckard, JP, Combe Court, Chiddingfold; one *s* one *d. Educ:* Stowe Sch.; Corpus Christi Coll., Cambridge. Mem. of Royal Company of Archers (Queen's Body Guard for Scotland). Mem. Clothworkers' Co. *Recreations:* shooting, fishing, stalking. *Address:* East Kintrockat, Brechin, Angus. *T:* Brechin 2739. *Clubs:* Brooks's; New (Edinburgh).

**LESLIE, Samuel Clement,** CBE 1946; Consultant on information policy to Location of Offices Bureau; retired as Head of the Information Division of the Treasury, 1959; Member, Northern Ireland Development Council, 1955-65; *b* Perth, Western Australia, 15 July 1898; *m* 1924, Doris Frances Falk; one *s* two *d. Educ:* Melbourne C of E Gram. Sch.; Melbourne Univ. (MA); Balliol Coll., Oxford (Rhodes Scholar, DPhil). Post-graduate work in philosophy; Lecturer in Philosophy, University Coll. of North Wales, 1922-23; Senior Lecturer in Philosophy, Melbourne Univ., 1924-25; accompanied Mr S. M. Bruce (Australian Prime Minister) to Imperial Conference of 1926; remained in Britain and entered business; Publicity Manager to Gas Light & Coke Co., 1936-40; Director of Public Relations, Ministry of Supply, 1940, Home Office and Ministry of Home Security, 1940-43; Principal Asst Sec., Home Office, etc., 1943-45; Dir, Council of Industrial Design, 1945-47. *Publication:* Front Line 1940-41, 1942 (official publication, anon.). *Address:* 5a View Road, N6. *Club:* Reform.

**LESLIE, Sir Shane;** *see* Leslie, Sir John R. S.

**LESLIE MELVILLE,** family name of **Earl of Leven and Melville.**

**LESOTHO, Bishop of,** since 1950; (diocese known as Basutoland, 1950-66); **Rt. Rev. John Arthur Arrowsmith Maund,** MC 1946; *b* 1909; *s* of late Arthur Arrowsmith and Dorothy Jane Maund, Worcester, England; *m* 1948, Catherine Mary Maurice, Bromley, Kent; no *c. Educ:* Worcester Cathedral King's Sch.; Leeds Univ.; Mirfield Theological Coll. BA Leeds 1931; Asst Priest, All Saints and St Laurence, Evesham, Worcs, 1933-36; Asst Priest, All Saints, Blackheath, London, 1936-38; Asst Priest, Pretoria Native Mission, Pretoria, South Africa, 1938-40; CF 1940-46 (despatches, 1942); Asst Priest, Pretoria Native Mission, in charge Lady Selborne, Pretoria, 1946-50. Fellow Royal Commonwealth Society. *Recreation:* horse riding. *Address:* Bishop's House, Box 87, PO Maseru, Lesotho. *T:* Maseru 2426.

**LESSER, Most Rev. Norman Alfred;** *see* New Zealand, Primate and Archbishop of.

**LESSING, Mrs Doris (May);** author; *b* Persia, 22 Oct. 1919; *d* of Captain Alfred Cook Tayler and Emily Maude McVeagh; lived in Southern Rhodesia, 1924-49; *m* 1st, 1939, Frank Charles Wisdom (marr. diss., 1943); one *s* one *d*; 2nd, 1945, Gottfried Anton Nicholas Lessing (marr. diss., 1949); one *s*. *Publications:* The Grass is Singing, 1950; This Was the Old Chief's Country, 1951; Martha Quest, 1952; Five, 1953 (Somerset Maugham Award, Soc. of Authors, 1954); A Proper Marriage, 1954; Retreat to Innocence, 1956; Going Home, 1957; The Habit of Loving, 1957; A Ripple from the Storm, 1958; Fourteen Poems, 1959; In Pursuit of the English, 1960; The Golden Notebook, 1962; A Man and Two Women (short stories), 1963; African Stories, 1964; Landlocked, 1965; Particularly Cats, 1966; The Four-Gated City, 1969; Briefing for a Descent into Hell, 1971; *play:* Play with a Tiger, 1962. *Address:* c/o Curtis Brown, 13 King Street, Covent Garden, WC2.

**LESTANG, Sir M. C. E. C. N. de;** *see* Nageon de Lestang.

**LESTER, Richard;** Film Director; *b* 19 Jan. 1932; *s* of Elliott and Ella Young Lester; *m* 1956, Deirdre Vivian Smith; one *s* one *d. Educ:* Wm Penn Charter Sch.; University of Pennsylvania (BSc). Television Director: CBS (USA), 1951-54; AR (Dir TV Goon Shows), 1956. Directed The Running, Jumping and Standing Still Film (Acad. Award nomination; 1st prize San Francisco Festival, 1960). *Feature Films directed:* It's Trad, Dad, 1962; Mouse on the Moon, 1963; A Hard Day's Night, 1964; The Knack, 1964 (Grand Prix, Cannes Film Festival); Help, 1965 (Best Film Award and Best Dir Award, Rio de Janeiro Festival); A Funny Thing Happened on the Way to the Forum, 1966; How I won the War, 1967; Petulia, 1968; The Bed Sitting Room, 1969 (Gandhi Peace Prize, Berlin Film Festival). *Recreations:* composing, playing popular music. *Address:* Twickenham Film Studios, St Margaret's, Twickenham, Mddx.

**LESTER SMITH, Ernest;** *see* Smith, E. L.

**LESTOR, Joan;** MP (Lab) Eton and Slough since 1966; *b* Vancouver, British Columbia, Canada, 13 Nov. 1931. *Educ:* Blaenavon Secondary Sch., Monmouth; William Morris Secondary Sch., Walthamstow; London Univ. Diploma in Sociology; nursery nurses' diploma. Nursery Sch. Teacher, 1959-66. Member: Wandsworth Borough Council, 1958-68; LCC, 1962-64; Exec. Cttee of the London Labour Party, 1962-65; Nat. Exec., Labour Party, 1967-. Contested (Lab) Lewisham West, 1964. Parly Under-Sec., Dept of Educn and Science, Oct. 1969-June 1970. Chm. Council, Nat. Soc. of Children's Nurseries, 1969-70. *Recreations:* theatre, reading, playing with children. *Address:* House of Commons, SW1; 121c Castelnau SW13. *T:* 01-748 0261.

**L'ESTRANGE, Laurence Percy Farrer,** OBE 1958; HM Ambassador to the Republic of Honduras since 1969; *b* 10 Sept. 1912; *s* of late S. W. L'Estrange and Louie Knights L'Estrange (*née* Farrer); *m* 1933, Anne Catherine (*née* Whiteside); two *s. Educ:* Shoreham Grammar Sch., Shoreham, Sussex; Univ. of London. Employed at HM Embassy, Caracas, 1939, and Acting Vice-Consul, 1941 and 1942. Resigned and joined RAF, 1943-46. HM Vice-Consul, Malaga, 1946; Second Sec., San Salvador, 1949; Chargé d'Affaires, 1952; Vice-Consul, Chicago, 1953; First Sec. (Commercial): Manila, 1954; Lima, 1958; Chargé d'Affaires, 1961; seconded to Western Hemisphere Exports Council, in charge of Latin American Div., 1962; HM Consul, Denver, 1963; Counsellor (Commercial), Lagos, 1967. *Recreations:* golf, riding, sailing, fishing and shooting. *Address:* c/o British Embassy, Tegucigalpa, Republic of Honduras (PO Box 290). *T:* 2-0479. *Club:* Royal Automobile.

**LETCHWORTH, Thomas Edwin,** CMG 1959; Colonial Administrative Service, retired; *b* 1 April 1906; *m* 1936, Marjorie Danvers Bayliffe, *d* of late Col A. D. Bayliffe, CMG. *Educ:* Downside; Christ's Coll., Cambridge. Winning Cambridge crews, 1927, 1928 (stroke). Administrative Service, Nigeria, 1928; seconded Gambia, 1943-45; Resident, Bornu Province, 1955-58; retired, 1959. *Address:* Quarr Coach House, Sway, near Lymington, Hants SO4 0EB. *T:* Sway 593. *Clubs:* Royal Commonwealth Society; Leander, Royal Lymington Yacht.

**LETHAM, James;** Treasurer and General Manager, Bank of Scotland, 1966-70. Director, since 1967; *b* 6 Aug. 1907; *s* of Robert Letham, Ironfounder, Airdrie, and Bethia McHutchison; *m* 1935, Williamina Margaret Robb (*d* 1969); one *s. Educ:* Airdrie and Glasgow High Schs. Entered service of Bank of Scotland, 1923; Asst Treasurer, 1955; Dep. Treasurer, 1965. Director: North West Securities Ltd. Pres., Inst. of Bankers in Scotland; Chm., Cttee of Scottish Bank General Managers, 1968-70. Mem. of Court, Heriot-Watt Univ., 1966-; Vice-Pres. and Dir, Edinburgh Chamber of Commerce and Manufactures; Member: British Computer Soc. (papers on Computer Accountancy to professional and commercial bodies); Organising Cttee for British Commonwealth Games, 1970; Exec. Cttee, Scottish Council (Develt and Industry), 1967-69; Board, Forth Ports Authority; Scottish Regional Council, CBI. Hon. DLitt, Heriot-Watt, 1970. *Recreations:* golf, curling and gardening. *Address:* The Dykes, 89 Ravelston Dykes, Edinburgh 12. *T:* 031-337 7749. *Clubs:* Caledonian; Caledonian (Edinburgh).

**LETHBRIDGE, Captain Sir Hector (Wroth),** 6th Bt, *cr* 1804; *b* 26 Aug. 1898; *s* of Sir Wroth Periam Christopher Lethbridge, 5th Bart, and Alianore (*y d* of late Edward Chandos Pole, Radbourne Hall, Derby, and Lady Anne Chandos Pole, *d* of 5th Earl of Harrington); *S* father, 1950; *m* 1946, Diana, *widow* of Major John Vivian Bailey, The Royal Scots Fusiliers, and *er d* of Lt-Col Frank Noel, Hopton Hall, Great Yarmouth; one *s* one *d*. *Educ:* Radley. Served European War, 1914-18: Officers Cadet Bn, 1916; commissioned, The Rifle Brigade, 1917; France, 1917-18 (POW); India, 1919-20; RARO, 1920; recalled, 1939; served War of 1939-45, in Gold Coast, 1941; invalided home, 1941; demobilized, 1945. *Recreations:* tennis, shooting, golf. *Heir:* *s* Thomas Periam Hector Noel Lethbridge, *b* 17 July 1950. *Address:* Long Sutton House, Langport, Somerset. *T:* Long Sutton 284. *Clubs:* Junior Carlton; Somerset County (Taunton).

**LETHBRIDGE, Thomas Charles,** MA, FSA; *b* 23 March 1901; *s* of Ambrose Y. Lethbridge and Violet Murdoch; *m* 1st, 1923, Sylvia Frances Robertson (marriage dissolved, 1944); one *s* one *d* (and one *s* decd); 2nd, 1944, Mina Elizabeth Leadbitter. *Educ:* Wellington Coll.; Trinity Coll., Cambridge. Cambridge Expedition to Jan Mayen, 1921, to East Greenland, 1923; Excavator for Cambridge Antiquarian Soc., 1925-56; Hon. Keeper, Anglo-Saxon Collections, University Museum of Archæology and Ethnology, Cambridge; Cambridge Expedition to Baffin Bay etc, 1937. Hon. Mem., Cambridge Antiquarian Soc., 1957. Served War of 1939-45, RNVSR, NID, Major HG. *Publications:* Merlin's Island, 1945; Herdsmen and Hermits, 1950; Boats and Boatmen, 1952; Coastwise Craft, 1952; The Painted Men, 1954; Gogmagog, 1957; Ghost and Ghoul, 1962; Witches, 1962; Ghost and Divining-rod, 1963; ESP, 1965; A Step in the Dark, 1967; The Monkey's Tail, 1969; numerous papers and monographs on Anglo-Saxon, Scottish and Eskimo archæology. *Recreations:* boats, natural history, water-colour painting, curiosity. *Address:* Hole House, Branscombe, Seaton, Devon. *T:* Branscombe 229.

**LE TOCQ, Eric George;** Counsellor, Foreign and Commonwealth Office, since 1968; *b* 20 April 1918; *s* of Eugene Charles Le Tocq; *m* 1946, Betty Esdaile; two *s* one *d*. *Educ:* Elizabeth Coll., Guernsey; Exeter Coll., Oxford (MA). Served War of 1939-45: commissioned in Royal Engineers, 1939; North Africa, 1942-43; Italy, 1943; Austria and Greece; major. Taught Modern Languages and Mathematics at Monmouth Sch., 1946-48; Assistant Principal, Commonwealth Relations Office, 1948; Karachi, 1948-50; Principal, 1950; Dublin, 1953-55; Accra, 1957-59; Assistant Secretary, 1962; Adviser on Commonwealth and External Affairs, Entebbe, 1962; Deputy High Commissioner, Uganda, 1962-64; Counsellor, British High Commission, Canberra, 1964-67. *Recreations:* golf and gardening. *Address:* c/o Foreign and Commonwealth Office, SW1.

**LETSON, Major-General Harry Farnham Germaine,** CB 1946; CBE 1944; MC; ED; CD; *b* Vancouver, BC, 26 Sept. 1896; *e s* of late J. M. K. Letson, Vancouver, BC; *m* 1928, Sally Lang Nichol; no *c*. *Educ:* McGill Univ.; University of British Columbia; University of London. BSc (UBC) 1919; PhD (Eng) London, 1923. Active Service Canadian Army, 1916-19; Associate Professor Mechanical and Electrical Engineering, University of BC, 1923-36; Chairman of Board, Letson and Burpee, Ltd, 1936-39; President Tormag Transmissions Ltd; on Active Service Canadian Army, 1939-46; Adjt-General Canadian Army, 1942-44; Commander of Canadian Army Staff in Washington, 1944-46; Secretary to Governor-General of Canada, 1946-52; Adviser on Militia, Canadian Army, 1954-58, retired. Hon. Colonel British Columbia Regt, 1963. LLD (University of BC), 1945. *Recreations:* fishing, shooting. *Address:* 474 Lansdowne Road, Ottawa, Canada. *Clubs:* Rideau, Country (Ottawa); Vancouver (Vancouver, BC).

**LETTS, Charles Trevor;** Marine Underwriter at Lloyd's since 1948; Deputy Chairman of Lloyd's, 1966 (entered Lloyd's, 1924; Member, 1941; Cttee, 1964-67); *b* 2 July 1905; *o s* of late Charles Hubert and Gertrude Letts; *m* 1942, Mary R. (Judy), *o d* of late Sir Stanley and late Lady (Hilda) Woodwark; two *s* one *d*. *Educ:* Marlborough Coll. Served RNVR, Lieut-Commander, 1940-45. Member Cttee: Lloyd's Underwriters' Assoc., 1960- (Chairman, 1963-64); Lloyd's Register of Shipping (Chairman, Yacht Sub-Cttee, 1967-); Salvage Association. *Recreations:* sailing (Vice-Commodore, Lloyd's Yacht Club), golf. *Address:* Bearwood, Holtye, Edenbridge, Kent. *T:* Cowden 472. *Clubs:* Royal Ocean Racing; Bosham Sailing.

**LETTS, Winifred M.;** *y d* of late Rev. E. F. Letts, MA; *m* 1926, W. H. F. Verschoyle. *Educ:* St Anne's, Abbots Bromley; Alexandra Coll., Dublin. Contributions in prose and verse to the Spectator, Cornhill, Punch, Yale Review, etc; two plays, Eyes of the Blind, and The Challenge, performed at Abbey Theatre, Dublin; 3 act play, Hamilton & Jones, Gate Theatre, Dublin, 1941. *Publications:* Songs from Leinster (new edn illus., 1944); Hallowe'en and Poems of the War; More Songs from Leinster; Diana Dethroned; The Rough Way; Christina's Son; Naughty Sophia; other books for children; Corporals' Corner; Saint Patrick, the Travelling Man, 1932; Knockmaroon, 1933; Pomona & Co., 1934; Pomona's Island; The Gentle Mountain, 1938. *Recreations:* hunting wild flowers, gardening. *Address:* Beech Cottage, Killiney, Co. Dublin.

**LEVEEN, Jacob;** senior member, University College, Cambridge; Keeper of Department of Oriental Printed Books and Manuscripts, British Museum, 1953-56; retired; now engaged upon cataloguing the Hebrew manuscripts in the University Library, Cambridge; *b* 24 Dec. 1891; *o surv. c* of late David and Rose Leveen; *m* 1928, Violet Egerton (marr. dissolved, 1963), *yr d* of late Capt. George Egerton Pearch; one *s* decd. *Educ:* Jews' Coll.; University Coll., London (Prizeman in Greek, and Hollier Scholar in Hebrew); School of Oriental and African Studies (BA with First Class Honours in Arabic; Ouseley Scholar in Arabic). Entered British Museum, 1914; Deputy Keeper, Dept of Oriental Printed Books and Manuscripts, 1944. War Service, 1916-20. *Publications:* Part IV of Catalogue of Hebrew and Samaritan Manuscripts in British Museum, 1935; The Hebrew Bible in Art (Schweich Lectures in Biblical Archæology, British Academy), 1944; (ed) A Digest of Commentaries on the Babylonian Talmud, British Museum, 1961; studies in the text of the Psalms (in Journal of Theological Studies and *Vetus Testamentum*); occasional articles and reviews in learned, art and popular journals. *Recreations:* walking, talking, music, art and literature. *Address:* 5 Brookside, Cambridge. *T:* 50619. *Club:* Athenæum.

**LEVEN,** 13th Earl of, **and MELVILLE,** 14th Earl of, *cr* 1641. **Alexander Robert Leslie Melville,** Baron Melville, 1616; Baron

Balgonie, 1641; Earl of Melville, Viscount Kirkcaldie, 1690; Lord Lieutenant of Nairnshire since 1969; *b* 13 May 1924; *e s* of 13th Earl and Lady Rosamond Sylvia Diana Mary Foljambe, *d* of 1st Earl of Liverpool; *S* father, 1947; *m* 1953, Susan, *er d* of Lieut-Colonel R. Steuart-Menzies of Culdares, Arndilly House, Craigellachie, Banffshire; two *s* one *d*. *Educ:* Eton. ADC to Governor General of New Zealand, 1951-52. Formerly Capt. Coldstream Guards; retired, 1952. DL, County of Nairn, 1961; Convener, Nairn CC, 1970. *Heir:* *s* Lord Balgonie, *qv*. *Address:* Glenferness House, Nairn. *T:* Glenferness 202. *Clubs:* Guards, Pratt's.

**LEVER,** family name of **Viscount Leverhulme.**

**LEVER, Rt. Hon. Harold,** PC 1969; MP (Lab) Cheetham Division of Manchester since 1950 (formerly Exchange Division, 1945-50, when Division's boundaries altered and new constituency of Cheetham constituted); *b* Manchester, 15 Jan. 1914; *s* of late Bernard and Bertha Lever; *m* 1962, Diane, *d* of Saleh Bashi; three *d* (and one *d* from late wife). *Educ:* Manchester Grammar Sch. Called to Bar, Middle Temple, 1935. Promoted Defamation Act, 1952, as a Private Member's Bill. Joint Parliamentary Under-Secretary, Dept of Economic Affairs, 1967; Financial Sec. to Treasury, Sept. 1967-69; Paymaster General, 1969-70. Chm., Public Accounts Cttee, 1970. *Address:* House of Commons, SW1.

*See also Sir L. M. Lever.*

**LEVER, Sir Leslie Maurice,** Kt 1970; JP; Solicitor since 1927; *b* 29 April 1905; *e s* of late Bernard Lever amd Mrs Bertha Lever; *m* 1939, Ray Rosalia, JP, Lancs, *o c* of Dr Leonard Levene, formerly RAMC, Leicester; one *s* one *d*. *Educ:* Elementary Sch.; Manchester Grammar Sch.; University of Leeds. LLB (Hons) 1925; Solicitor (Hons) 1927; senior partner in firm of solicitors, Leslie M. Lever & Co.; Commissioner for Oaths, 1933. CC Manchester, 1932-; Alderman, 1949-; Lord Mayor of Manchester, 1957-58; JP 1957 (Chairman Manchester Magistrates). MP (Lab) Ardwick Div. of Manchester, 1950-70. Governor: Manchester Univ.; Salford Univ.; Manchester Grammar Sch.; President: Manchester and Salford (East) Corps, St John Ambulance Bde; N Western Counties Horticultural Soc.; N Western Brass Bands Federation; Assoc. of Lancastrians in London, 1968-69; Patron Manchester and Salford Savings Bank; Member Council, Lancashire and Cheshire Industrial Development Assoc.; Hon. Life Member Dunkirk Veterans' Assoc.; Life Vice-President, Navy League, 1960-; President, India League; President, Manchester and District Liaison Cttee of all Ex-Servicemen's Assocs, Army, Navy and Air Force, in the area; Hon. President, Manchester Branch Brit. Limbless Ex-Servicemen's Assoc. (BLESMA) and Hon. Secretary All Party Parliamentary Cttee. Past Chairman, Manchester Univ. Settlement. Hon. Solicitor to various organisations. Holds or has held office as President or Vice-President in various local organisations to do with welfare, sports, etc. Mem., Nat. Council, Royal Institute for the Deaf, 1961. A representative of British Parliament at World Interparliamentary Convention, Brussels, 1961. Vice-President: Disabled Drivers' Assoc.; British Assoc. at Manchester, 1962. Patron, National Assoc. of Education Welfare Officers. FRSA 1935 (former President, NW Centre). Coronation Medal, 1953. Knight Grand Cross, Order of St Gregory the Great, 1968 (Kt Comdr, 1960). Associate Serving Brother, O St John, 1967. Hon. LLD (Leeds), 1963. *Recreations:* reading and social work. *Address:* 16 John Dalton Street, Manchester 2. *T:* 061-832 5841-4. *Club:* Manchester Press (Hon. Life Member).

*See also Rt Hon. Harold Lever.*

**LEVER, Rt. Hon. Norman Harold;** *see* Lever, Rt. Hon. Harold.

**LEVER, Sir Tresham (Joseph Philip),** 2nd Bt, *cr* 1911; *b* 3 Sept. 1900; *o c* of 1st Bt and Beatrice Hilda (*d* 1917), 3rd *d* of late Philip Falk, Kensington Palace Gardens; *S* father, 1924; *m* 1st, 1930, Frances Yowart (*d* 1959), *yr d* of late Lindsay Hamilton Goodwin and *widow* of Cecil Parker, Walton Hall, Lancs; one *s*; 2nd, 1962, Pamela, Lady Malcolm Douglas-Hamilton, *o d* of late Lieut-Colonel the Hon. Malcolm Bowes Lyon. *Educ:* Harrow; University College, Oxford. MA (Hons Hist.). Called to Bar, 1925. Contested (C) S Hackney, 1929. High Sheriff of Leics, 1962-63. Member Council, Brontë Society, 1963-. Equipped and furnished Brontë Memorial Chapel, St Michael and All Angels, Haworth, 1964. *Publications:* Profit and Loss, 1933; The Life and Times of Sir Robert Peel, 1942; The House of Pitt: a Family Chronicle, 1947; Godolphin, his Life and Times, 1952; The Letters of Lady Palmerston (ed), 1957; The Herberts of Wilton, 1967; articles in Times Literary Supp., History To-day, etc. *Recreations:* shooting, fishing. *Heir:* *s* Tresham Christopher Arthur Lindsay Lever [*b* 9 Jan. 1932; *m* 1970, Susan Mary, *d* of Prof. J. A. Nicholson, Enniscoe, Crossmolina, Co. Mayo. *Educ:* Eton; Trinity Coll., Cambridge]. *Address:* Lessudden, St Boswells, Roxburghshire. *T:* St Boswells 2746; Cullerne House, Findhorn, Forres, Morayshire. *T:* Findhorn 254. *Clubs:* Carlton, St James', Beefsteak; New (Edinburgh).

**LEVERHULME,** 3rd Viscount, *cr* 1922, of the Western Isles; **Philip William Bryce Lever,** TD; Baron, *cr* 1917; Bt, *cr* 1911; Knight of Order of St John of Jerusalem; Major, Cheshire Yeomanry; Lord Lieutenant of City and County of Chester since 1949; Advisory Director of Unilever Ltd; *b* 1 July 1915; *s* of 2nd Viscount and Marion, *d* of late Bryce Smith of Manchester; *S* father, 1949; *m* 1937, Margaret Ann, *o c* of John Moon, Tiverton; three *d*. *Educ:* Eton; Trinity Coll., Cambridge. Hon. Air Commodore 663 Air OP Squadron, RAuxAF; Hon. Air Commodore 610 (County of Chester) Squadron, Royal Auxiliary Air Force; Hon. Colonel, Cheshire Yeomanry. Pres. Council, Liverpool Univ., 1957-63, Sen. Pro-Chancellor, 1963-66. Member: National Hunt Cttee, 1961 (Steward, 1965-68); Council of King George's Jubilee Trust; Chairman, Exec. Cttee Animal Health Trust, 1964. Hon. FRCS 1970. Hon. LLD Liverpool. *Recreations:* shooting, hunting. *Heir:* none. *Address:* Thornton Manor, Thornton Hough, Wirral, Cheshire; Badanloch, Kinbrace, Sutherland; 62 Grosvenor House, W1. *Clubs:* Boodle's; Jockey.

**LEVERSEDGE, Leslie Frank,** CMG 1955; Economic Secretary to Northern Rhodesia Government, 1956-60, retired; *b* 29 May 1904; *s* of F. E. Leversedge, UP, India; *m* 1945, Eileen Melegueta Spencer Payne; two *s* three *d*. *Educ:* St Paul's Sch., Darjeeling, India; St Peter's Sch., York; St John's Coll., Cambridge; Inner Temple, London. Cadet in Colonial Administrative Service, Northern Rhodesia, Dec. 1926; District Officer, Dec. 1928; Provincial Commissioner, Jan. 1947; Senior Provincial Commissioner, Dec. 1948. Development Secretary to Northern Rhodesia Government, 1951-56. MLC 1951; MEC 1951. *Recreations:* hockey, squash rackets. *Address:* Earley House, Petham, Canterbury, Kent. *T:* Petham 285.

**LEVESON, Lord; Granville George Fergus Leveson Gower;** *b* 10 Sept. 1959; *s* and *heir* of 5th Earl Granville, *qv*.

**LEVESON GOWER,** family name of **Earl Granville.**

**LEVESQUE, Most Rev. Louis;** *see* Rimouski, Archbishop of, (RC).

**LEVEY, Michael Vincent,** MVO 1965; MA Oxon and Cantab; Keeper of the National Gallery, since 1968; *b* 8 June 1927; *s* of O. L. H. Levey and Gladys Mary Milestone; *m* 1954, Brigid Brophy, *qv*; one *d*. *Educ:* Oratory Sch.; Exeter Coll., Oxford. Served with Army, 1945-48; commissioned, KSLI, 1946, and attached RAEC, Egypt. Asst Keeper, Nat. Gall., 1951-66, Dep. Keeper, 1966-68. Slade Prof. of Fine Art, Cambridge, 1963-64; Supernumerary Fellow, King's Coll., Cambridge, 1963-64. *Publications:* Six Great Painters, 1956; National Gallery Catalogues: 18th Century Italian Schools, 1956; The German School, 1959; Painting in 18th Century Venice, 1959; From Giotto to Cézanne, 1962; Room-to-Room Guide to National Gallery, 1964, new edn 1969; Dürer, 1964; The Later Italian Paintings in the Collection of HM The Queen, 1964; Canaletto Paintings in the Royal Collection, 1964; Tiepolo's Banquet of Cleopatra (Charlton Lecture, 1962), 1966; Rococo to Revolution, 1966; Bronzino (The Masters), 1967; Early Renaissance, 1967 (Hawthornden Prize, 1968); Fifty Works of English Literature We Could Do Without (co-author), 1967; Holbein's Christina of Denmark, Duchess of Milan, 1968; A History of Western Art, 1968; Painting at Court (Wrightsman Lectures), 1970; contributions Burlington Magazine, etc. *Address:* 185 Old Brompton Road, SW5. *T:* 01-373 9335.

**LEVI, Prof. Edward Hirsch;** President, University of Chicago, since Nov. 1968 and Professor of Law, since 1945; *b* 26 June 1911; *s* of Gerson B. Levi and Elsa B. Levi (*née* Hirsch); *m* 1946, Kate Sulzberger; three *s*. *Educ:* Univ. of Chicago; Yale Univ. Law Sch. Univ. of Chicago: Asst Prof. of Law, 1936-40; Dean of the Law School, 1950-63; Provost, 1963-68. Special Asst to Attorney-Gen., Washington, DC, 1940-45; 1st Asst, War Div., Dept of Justice, 1943; 1st Asst, Anti-trust Div., 1944-45; Chm., Interdeptl Cttee on Monopolies and Cartels, 1944; Counsel, Subcttee on Monopoly Power Judiciary Cttee, 81st Congress, 1950; Member: White House Task Force on Educn, 1966-67; White House Central Gp in Domestic Affairs, 1964; Citizens Commn on Graduate Medical Educn, 1965; Sloan Commn on Cummunications, 1970; Nat. Commn on Productivity, 1970. Benjamin N. Cardozo Lectr, 1969. Hon. degrees: LHD, Hebrew Union Coll.; LLD: Univ. of Michigan; Univ. of California at Santa Cruz; Univ. of Iowa; Jewish Theological Seminary of America; Brandeis Univ.; Lake Forest Coll.; Univ. of Rochester; Loyola Univ. *Publications:* Introduction to Legal Reasoning, 1949; Four Talks on Legal Education, 1952; Point of View, 1969; Elements of the Law (ed, with Roscoe Steffen), 1936; Gilbert's Collier on Bankruptcy (ed, with James W. Moore), 1937. *Address:* 5801 South Ellis Avenue, Chicago, Ill 60637, USA. *T:* Midway 3-0800 (Area Code 312).

**LÉVI-STRAUSS, Claude,** Officier de la Légion d'Honneur, 1964; Professor, Collège de France, since 1959; Director of Studies, Ecole pratique des hautes études, Paris, since 1950; *b* 28 Nov. 1908; *s* of Raymond Lévi-Strauss and Emma Lévy; *m* 1st, 1932, Dina Dreyfus; 2nd, 1946, Rose-Marie Ullmo; one *s*; 3rd, 1954, Monique Roman; one *s*. *Educ:* Lycée Janson-de-Sailly, Paris; Sorbonne. Prof., Univ. of São Paulo, Brazil, 1935-39; Vis. Prof., New School for Social Research, NY, 1941-45; Cultural Counsellor, French Embassy, Washington, 1946-47; Assoc. Curator, Musée de l'Homme, Paris, 1948-49. Corresp. Member: Royal Acad. of Netherlands; Norwegian Acad.; British Acad.; Nat. Acad. of Sciences, USA; Amer. Museum of Natural History; Amer. Philos. Soc.; Royal Anthrop. Inst. of Great Britain; London Sch. of African and Oriental Studies. Hon. Dr: Brussels, 1962; Oxford, 1964; Yale, 1965; Chicago, 1967. *Publications:* La Vie familiale et sociale des Indiens Nambikwara, 1948; Les Structures élémentaires de la parenté, 1949 (The Elementary Structures of Kinship, 1969); Race et histoire, 1952; Tristes Tropiques, 1955 (A World on the Wane, 1961); Anthropologie Structurale, 1958 (Structural Anthropology, 1964); Le Totémisme aujourd'hui, 1962 (Totemism, 1963); La Pensée sauvage, 1962 (The Savage Mind, 1966); Le Cru et le Cuit, 1964 (The Raw and the Cooked, 1970); Du Miel aux cendres, 1967; L'Origine des manières de table, 1968; *relevant publication:* Conversations with Lévi-Strauss (ed G. Charbonnier), 1969. *Address:* 2 rue des Marronniers, 75 Paris 16, France. *T:* 288-34-71.

**LEVINGE, Major Sir Richard Vere Henry,** 11th Bt, *cr* 1704; MBE 1941; *b* 30 April 1911; *o s* of 10th Bt and Irene Marguerite (who *m* 2nd, 1916, Major R. V. Buxton), *d* of late J. H. C. Pix of Bradford; *S* father, 1914; *m* 1935, Barbara Mary, 2nd *d* of late George J. Kidston, CMG; two *s* three *d*. *Educ:* Eton; Balliol Coll., Oxford (Domus Exhibition). Assistant Managing Director, A. Guinness Sons & Co. (Dublin) Ltd to 1968. War Service, 1939-45: Lovat Scouts and Staff (despatches Burma 1945). *Recreations:* shooting, fishing. *Heir: s* Richard George Robin Levinge, *b* 18 Dec. 1946. *Address:* Grangehill, Sandyford, Co. Dublin; Clohamon House, Ferns, Co. Wexford. *Clubs:* Flyfishers'; Kildare Street (Dublin).

**LEVIS, Maj.-Gen. Derek George,** OBE 1951; QHP 1969; Deputy Director of Medical Services, Southern Command, since 1970; *b* 24 Dec. 1911; *er s* of late Dr George Levis, Lincoln; *m* 1938, Doris Constance Tall; one *d*. *Educ:* Stowe Sch.; Trinity Coll., Cambridge; St Thomas' Hospital, London. BA Cantab 1933; MRCS, LRCP 1936; MB, BChir (Cantab), 1937; DPH 1949. Commnd into RAMC, 1936; house appts, St Thomas' Hospital, 1936-37; served in: China, 1937-39; War of 1939-45 (1939-45 Star, Pacific Star, France and Germany Star, Defence and War Medal): Malaya and Java, 1939-42; Ceylon, 1942-43; NW Europe, 1944-45; qualified as specialist in Army Health, RAM Coll., 1949; Asst Director Army Health, HQ British Troops Egypt, 1949-51; Deputy Asst Dir Army Health, HQ British Commonwealth Forces, Korea, 1952-53 (Korean Co. Medal and UN Medal); Asst Dir Army Health: Malaya Comd, 1953-55 (Gen. Service Medal, Clasp Malaya, despatches); War Office, 1956-58; Deputy Director, Army Health, HQ, BAOR, 1958-62; Comdt Army School of Health, 1962-66; Director of Army Health, Australian Military Forces, Melbourne, 1966-68; Dep. Director Army Health, HQ Army Strategic Comd, 1968; Director of Army Health, MoD (Army), 1968-70. OStJ 1968. *Publications:* contribs to Journal RAMC and Proc. Royal Society Med. *Recreations:* fishing, gardening. *Address:* Dial House, Navenby, Lincoln.

**LÉVIS MIREPOIX, Duc de; Antoine;** Commandeur de la Légion d'Honneur, Croix de Guerre, Grand Croix de l'Ordre d'Adolphe de Nassau; author; Member of the French Academy since 1953; Mainteneur de l'Académie des Jeux floraux de Toulouse; Commandeur, Ordre des Palmes Académiques; *b* 1 Aug. 1884; *s* of Henri and Henriette de Chabannes La Palice; *m* 1911, Nicole de Chaponay; one *s*. *Educ:* Lycée de Toulouse; Sorbonne (Licencié en philosophie). Lecturer for the Alliance française; President of Mission Maria Chapdeleine, Canada; President, Cincinnati de France; Vice-President, France Amérique; President, France Canada Institut. *Publications:* Le Seigneur Inconnu; Montségur; Philippe Auguste et ses trois femmes; Sainte Jeanne de France, fille de Louis XI; François Ier; La France de la Renaissance; Les Guerres de Religion (Grand Prix Gobert de l'Académie Française), 1948; Le cœur secret de Saint Simon; La Politesse (with M. de Vogüé); Le Siècle de Philippe le Bel; Aventures d'une famille française; Misère et Grandeur le l'Individualisme français; Le roi n'est mort qu'une fois. *Heir: s* Charles Henri, Marquis de Lévis Mirepoix [*b* 4 Jan. 1912; *m*; one *s* one *d*]. *Address:* 30 Rue de Berri, Paris; Léran, Ariège. *Clubs:* Jockey (Vice-President), Union, Interallié (Paris).

**LEVITT, Walter Montague,** of Lincoln's Inn, Barrister-at-Law; MD, FRCP, FFR, DMRE Cambridge; Deputy Chairman, Metropolitan Traffic Commissioners, since 1969 (Deputy Commissioner, 1967-69); Hon. Consulting Radiotherapist, since 1945, St Bartholomew's Hospital, London; Late Director, Department of Radiotherapy, London Clinic; Hon. Associate Editor of the British Journal of Radiology; Member of Minister of Labour's Advisory Panel in Radiology; Hon. Physician in charge, Department of Radiotherapy, St George's Hospital; late Medical Officer in charge of Radiotherapeutic Department, St Bartholomew's Hospital; Foundation Fellow, and vice-President and Chairman of Therapeutic Cttee, Faculty of Radiologists, 1940-43; Vice-President, Royal Society of Medicine, and President, Section of Radiology, 1945-46; late Hon. Medical Secretary, British Institute of Radiology; late Lecturer in X-Ray Therapy for Diploma in Radiology, University of Cambridge; Member of Clinical Research Cttee, British Empire Cancer Campaign; Delegate to International Cancer Congress, Atlantic City, 1939; *b* 1900; *e s* of Lewis and Caroline Levitt, Rathmines, Co. Dublin; *m* 1929, Sonia Esté Nivinsky, BSc, MRCS, DPH; no *c*. *Educ:* High Sch., Dublin; University College, Dublin (Medical Scholar and First Class Exhibitioner); Cambridge and Frankfurt on Main. Gold Medallist, Mercers Hospital, 1922; Demonstrator of anatomy, 1920-21, and of pathology, 1921; Hon. Secretary Section of Radiology, International Cancer Conference, London, 1928; Hon. Secretary Radiology Section, British Medical Association Centenary Meeting, London, 1932; Fellow, Royal Society of Medicine. Freeman, City of London, Livery of Apothecaries, 1956. *Publications:* Deep X-Ray Therapy in Malignant Disease (with Introduction by Lord Horder), 1930; completed and edited Knox's Text Book of X-Ray Therapeutics, 1932; Handbook of Radiotherapy for Senior and Post-graduate students, 1952; Short Encyclopædia of Medicine for Lawyers, 1966; Section on X-Ray therapy in Bourne and Williams' Recent Advances in Gynæcology, 1952; Chapter on Reticulosis and Reticulosarcoma (with R. Bodley Scott) in British Practice in Radiotherapy, 1955; Section on Diseases of the Blood in Paterson's Treatment of Malignant Disease by X-Rays and Radium, 1948; various articles on medico-legal subjects. *Address:* 10 Old Square, Lincoln's Inn, WC2. *T:* 01-242 3892; Gray's Inn Chambers, Gray's Inn, WC1. *T:* 01-242 5226. *Clubs:* Oxford and Cambridge; University (Dublin).

**LEVY, Aaron Harold,** BA, MD, CM, FRCS; Consulting Surgeon, Moorfields Eye Hospital; Consulting Ophthalmic Surgeon, British Home and Hospital for Incurables and St Monica's Hospital, etc; Consulting Ophthalmic Surgeon, Willesden General Hospital, London Jewish Hospital, and Putney Hospital; *b* Montreal; *m* 1908, Lena (*d* 1965), *d* of I. Samuel, JP, Cardiff; one *s* one *d*. *Educ:* McGill Univ., Montreal; St Bartholomew's Hospital. Late Ophthalmic Surgeon, Tooting Military Hospital, Mitcham Military Hospital; Captain, RAMC; Fellow of the Royal Society of Medicine; Member of the Royal Institution; Fellow of the Royal Geographical Society. *Publications:* various artices on Ophthalmic Medicine and Surgery. *Address:* 7 St Agnes Court, 6 Porchester Terrace, Bayswater, W2. *T:* 01-723 2678. *Clubs:* Royal Societies, Roehampton.

**LEVY, Benn Wolfe,** MBE; dramatist; *b* March 1900; *o s* of late Octave G. Levy and Nannie Levy, *gs* of late Hon. L. W. Levy, Sydney, NSW, Australia; *m* 1933, Constance Cummings, *qv*; one *s* one *d*. *Educ:* Repton; University College, Oxford. Royal Air Force, 1918. Publisher, 1923; Royal Navy, War of 1939-45. MP (Lab) Eton and Slough Division of Bucks, 1945-50. Arts Council Executive, 1953-61. *Publications:* This Woman Business; A Man with Red Hair (from the novel by Hugh Walpole); Mud and Treacle; Mrs Moonlight; Art and Mrs Bottle; The Devil; Topaze (from the French of Marcel Pagnol); Evergreen; Hollywood Holiday (with John van Druten); Springtime for Henry; Madame Bovary (from the French dramatization); The Poet's Heart; Young Madame Conti (adapted, from German of Bruno Frank, with Hubert Griffith); The Jealous God; Clutterbuck; Return to Tyassi; Cupid and Psyche; The Rape of the Belt; The Tumbler; Public and Confidential; The Marriage. *Address:* 66 Old Church Street, Chelsea, SW3. *T:* 01-352 0437. *Club:* Garrick.

**LEVY, Sir Bruce;** *see* Levy, Sir (E.) B.

**LEVY, Sir (Enoch) Bruce,** Kt 1953; OBE 1950; retired, 1951; *b* 19 Feb. 1892; *s* of William and Esther Ann Levy; *m* 1925, Phyllis R., *d* of G. H. Mason; no *c*. *Educ:* Primary Sch.; Banks Commercial Coll.; Victoria University College (BSc). Brought up on farm to age 18; appointed Dept Agriculture, 1911; agrostologist to 1937; charge seed-testing station. Ecological studies Grasslands and indigenous vegetative cover of NZ; transferred to DSIR, 1937, and appointed Director Grasslands Division; Director Green-keeping Research; Chairman NZ Institute for Turf Culture (Life Mem. 1957); Official Rep. International Grassland Conference, Great Britain, 1937, Netherlands, 1949; Lecture tour, Great Britain, 1949-50; Member: Rotary International; Grassland Assoc. (Life Mem. 1951); NZ Animal Production Society (Life Mem. 1961); Manawatu Catchment Board; Central Standing Cttee, Soil Conservation; Trustee, Grassland Memorial Trust (Chm. 1966-68). Life Member NZ Royal Agric. Society, 1956. Hon. Dr of Science, University of NZ; R. B. Bennett Empire Prize, 1951 (Royal Society of Arts, London). *Publications:* Grasslands of New Zealand, 1943 (revised and enlarged, 1951, 1955 and 1970); Construction, Renovation and Care of the Bowling Green, 1949; Construction, Renovation and Care of the Golf Course, 1950. 150 scientific papers in popular and scientific journals in NZ and overseas. *Recreations:* bowling, gardening. *Address:* 217 Fitzherbert Avenue, Palmerston North, New Zealand. *T:* 80-803 Palmerston North.

**LEVY, Sir Ewart Maurice,** 2nd Bt *cr* 1913; *b* 10 May 1897; *o s* of Sir Maurice Levy, 1st Bt; *S* father, 1933; *m* 1932, Hylda (*d* 1970), *e d* of late Sir Albert Levy; one *d*. *Educ:* Harrow. High Sheriff of Leicestershire, 1937; served, 1940-45, Royal Pioneer Corps, Lieut-Colonel, 1944; BLA, 1944-45 (despatches). JP Co. Leicester. *Heir:* none. *Address:* Great Glen House, Great Glen, Leicestershire; 25 Farm Street, W1. *Club:* Reform.

**LEVY, Hyman,** MA, DSc, FRSE; Professor of Mathematics, Imperial College of Science and Technology, SW, 1923-54; Emeritus Professor, 1954; Head of Department of Mathematics and Mechanics, 1946; Dean of Royal College of Science, 1946-52; Fellow, Imperial College, 1955; *b* Edinburgh, 7 March 1889. *Educ:* George Heriot's Sch., Edinburgh; Universities of Edinburgh, Oxford, and Göttingen. Graduated at Edinburgh, First Class Hons, Mathematics and Physics, 1911; awarded Ferguson Scholarship, 1851 Exhibition, Carnegie Research Fellowship; Member of Aerodynamics Research Staff of the National Physical Laboratory, 1916-20; Assistant Professor of Mathematics at Royal College of Science, 1920-23; Member of Council of London Mathematical Society, 1929-33; Vice-President, 1931-32; Chairman Science Advisory Cttee of Labour Party, 1924-30. Hon. ARCS. *Publications:* Aeronautics in Theory and Experiment; Science in Perspective; Science in the Changing World; The Universe of Science, 1932; Science in Edwardian England; Makers of the Modern Spirit, Newton, 1933; Science in an Irrational Society; The Web of Thought and Action; Numerical Studies in Differential Equations, 1934; Thinking, 1935; Elements of the Theory of Probability, 1936; A Modern Philosophy, 1937; Modern Science, 1939; Science, Curse or Blessing? 1940; Social Thinking, 1945; Literature in an Age of Science, 1953; Jews and the National Question, 1957; Finite Difference Equations, 1958; Journeys in Belief, 1968; several mathematical text-books and a number of original memoirs on mathematical and aeronautical subjects; numerous articles on science and scientific philosophy in weekly and monthly periodicals. *Recreations:* scientific and political journalism, chess. *Address:* 25 Home Park Road, SW19. *T:* 01-946 7379.

**LEWEN, John Henry;** one of HM Inspectors of Diplomatic Estalishments, since 1970; *b* 6 July 1920; *s* of Carl Henry Lewen and Alice (*née* Mundy); *m* 1945, Emilienne Alette Julie Alida Galant; three *s*. *Educ:* Christ's Hospital; King's Coll., Cambridge (MA). Royal Signals, 1940-45 (Capt.). HM Foreign (subseq. Diplomatic) Service, 1946; HM Embassy: Lisbon, 1947-50; Rangoon, 1950-53; FO, 1953-55; HM Embassy: Rio de Janeiro, 1955-59; Warsaw, 1959-61; FO, 1961-63; Head of Chancery, HM Embassy, Rabat, 1963-67; Consul-General, Jerusalem, 1967-70. OStJ 1969. *Recreations:* singing, sailing. *Address:* c/o Foreign and Commonwealth Office, SW1. *Club:* Travellers'.

**LEWES, Suffragan Bishop of,** since Nov. 1959; **Rt. Rev. James Herbert Lloyd Morrell;** Canon and Prebend of Heathfield in Chichester Cathedral since 1959; Provost of Lancing (Southern Division Woodard Schools), since 1961; *b* 12 Aug. 1907; *s* of George Henry and Helen Adela Morrell. *Educ:* Dulwich Coll; King's Coll., London; Ely Theological Coll. Deacon, 1931; Priest, 1932; Curate of St Alphage, Hendon, 1931-35; Curate of St Michael and All Angels, Brighton, 1935-39; Bishop of Chichester's Chaplain for men, 1939-41; Lecturer for The Church of England Moral Welfare Council, 1941-44; Vicar of Roffey, 1944-46; Archdeacon of Lewes, 1946-59. Fellow of King's Coll., London, 1960. *Publications:* Four Words (broadcast talks to the Forces), 1941; The Heart of a Priest, 1958; A Priest's Notebook of Prayer, 1961; The Catholic Faith Today, 1964. *Recreations:* walking, camping, photography. *Address:* 83 Davigdor Road, Hove BN3 1RA. *T:* Brighton 733971. *Club:* English-Speaking Union.

**LEWES, Archdeacon of;** *see* Booth, Ven. David Herbert.

**LEWES, John Hext,** OBE 1944; Lord Lieutenant of Cardiganshire, since 1956; *b* 16 June 1903; *s* of late Colonel John Lewes, RA, and of Mrs Lewes (*née* Hext); *m* 1929, Nesta Cecil, *d* of late Captain H. Fitzroy Talbot, DSO, RN; one *s* two *d*. *Educ:* RN Colleges Osborne and Dartmouth. Sub-Lieut, 1923, Lieut, 1925; specialised in Torpedoes, 1928; Commander, 1939; commanded: HMS Shikari, Intrepid, 1941-42 (despatches); Ameer, 1944-45 (despatches); retired 1947, with war service rank of Captain, RN. Now farming. KStJ 1964. *Address:* Llanllyr, nr Lampeter, Cardiganshire. *T:* Aeron 323. *Club:* United Service.

**LEWEY, Hon. Sir Arthur Werner,** Kt 1954; QC (Jamaica), 1939; MA (Cantab); *b* 2 Sept. 1894; *s* of late Arthur Lewey and Frances Helena Moorcroft Williams; *m* 1928, Kitty, *y d* of late Trevelyan Arnold Pope; one *s*. *Educ:* St Pauls; Trinity Hall, Cambridge. Gazetted Middlesex Regt, 1914, and served in Egypt, Flanders, Gallipoli, and Palestine (wounded twice); served with Territorial Army (8th Bn, Middlesex Regt), 1920-29; Called to Bar, Inner Temple, 1920, and joined South-Eastern Circuit; entered Colonial Service, 1929; Police Magistrate, Gambia, 1930; Crown Counsel, Kenya, 1932; Solicitor-General, Uganda, 1936; Attorney-General, Jamaica, 1939; Attorney-General, Gold Coast, 1943-48; Legal Adviser to the Resident Minister, West Africa (Viscount Swinton), 1944, and to West African Council, 1946; a Justice of Appeal, West African Court of Appeal, 1948-51 and Rhodesia and Nyasaland Court of Appeal, 1952; Chief Justice, N Rhodesia, 1952-55; Member, Judicial Commission on Central African Federation, 1952; A Federal Justice of the Supreme Court of the Federation of Rhodesia and Nyasaland, 1955-58, retired; acted as Chief Justice of the Federation for various periods. *Address:* Little Stodham House, Liss, Hampshire. *Clubs:* United Service, MCC.

**LEWIN, Capt. Duncan;** *see* Lewin, Capt. E. D. G.

**LEWIN, Captain (Edgar) Duncan (Goodenough),** CB 1958; CBE 1953; DSO 1941; DSC 1939; Royal Navy, retired; Sales Director, Hawker Siddeley Aviation Ltd, since 1968; *b* 9 Aug. 1912; *s* of Captain G. E. Lewin, RN; *m* 1943, Nancy Emily Hallett, Tintinhull, Somerset; one *s* one *d*. *Educ:* RN Coll., Dartmouth. Cadet, HMS Royal Oak, 1930; specialized in flying, 1935. Served in HMS Ajax, River Plate action, 1939; Comd 808 Squadron in HMS Ark Royal, 1941; served staff of Admiral Vian in Mediterranean and Pacific, 1944-45. Comd HMS Glory, in Korean waters, 1952-53; Director of Air Warfare, Admiralty, 1953-54; Comd HMS Eagle, 1955; Director of Plans, Admiralty, 1956-57; retired from Navy and joined Board of Blackburn's, 1957. AFRAeS 1958. *Recreations:* tennis and gardening. *Address:* 116 Priory Lane, Roehampton, SW15. *T:* 01-876 9740. *Club:* United Service.

**LEWIN, George Ronald;** Editor, Hutchinson Publishing Group; *b* 11 Oct. 1914; *s* of late Frank Lewin, Halifax; *m* 1938, Sylvia Lloyd Sturge; two *s* one *d,* (and one *s* decd). *Educ:* Heath Sch., Halifax; The Queen's Coll., Oxford (Hastings Scholar, 1st Class Hon. Mods, 1st Class Lit. Hum., Goldsmiths' Exhibitioner). Editorial Assistant, Jonathan Cape Ltd, Publishers, 1937. Served in Royal Artillery, N Africa and NW Europe (despatches), 1939-45. Producer, BBC Home Talks Dept, 1946; Chief Asst, Home Service, 1954; Head, 1957; Chief, 1963. Retired 1965. *Publications:* Rommel: as military commander, 1968; (ed) Freedom's Battle, vol.3, the War on Land 1939-45, 1969; numerous articles and reviews on military history. *Address:* Woodmancote, West Byfleet, Surrey. *T:* Byfleet 45146. *Club:* Oxford and Cambridge.

**LEWIN, Vice-Adm. Terence Thornton,** MVO 1958; DSC 1942; Vice-Chief of the Naval Staff, since 1971; *b* Dover, 19 Nov. 1920; *m* 1944, Jane Branch-Evans; two *s* one *d. Educ:* The Judd Sch., Tonbridge. Joined RN, 1939; War Service in Home and Mediterranean Fleets in HMS Valiant, HMS Ashanti in Malta Convoys, N Russian Convoys, invasion N Africa and Channel (despatches); comd HMS Corunna, 1955-56; Comdr HM Yacht Britannia, 1957-58; Captain (F) Dartmouth Training Squadron and HM Ships Urchin and Tenby, 1961-63; Director, Naval Tactical and Weapons Policy Division, MoD, 1964-65; comd HMS Hermes, 1966-67; Asst Chief of Naval Staff (Policy), 1968-69; Flag Officer, Second-in-Comd, Far East Fleet, 1969-70. Rear-Adm., 1968; Vice-Adm., 1970. *Recreations:* golf; formerly athletics and Rugby football (rep. RN at both, 1947-48). *Address:* Pitfields, Blackham, Tunbridge Wells, Kent.

**LEWIN, Walpole Sinclair;** Consultant Neurological Surgeon to Addenbrooke's Hospital, Cambridge, since 1955; *b* 20 Aug. 1915; *s* of Eric Sinclair Lewin, London; *m* 1947, Marion Cumming; one *s* one *d. Educ:* University College, and University College Hospital, London. MRCS, LRCP 1939; MB, BS 1939; MS (London) 1942; FRCS 1940; MA (Cantab) 1970. University College First Entrance Exhibn, 1934; Magrath Clin. Schol., and Atkinson Morley Surgical Schol., 1939; Leverhulme Research Grant, RCS, 1947. Sometime House Physician, House Surgeon, Cas., Surgical Officer, Harker Smith Surgical Registrar, University College Hospital; First Assistant, Nuffield Department of Surgery, Oxford; Clinical Lecturer in Neurosurgery, University of Oxford; Assistant Neurological Surgeon, Radcliffe Infirmary, Oxford, 1949-61; Consultant Neurological Surgeon to Army. Hunterian Professor, RCS, 1948; Erasmus Wilson Demonstrator, RCS, 1965; Mem. Council, RCS, 1970-. Ruscoe Clarke Lectr, Birmingham, 1967. Fellow: Assoc. of Surgeons; Royal Society of Med.; Society of British Neurological Surgeons; Member, BMA; Chm., Central Cttee, Hosp. Med. Services, 1968-; Vice-Chairman, Joint Consultants Cttee, 1967-. Mem., Central Health Services Council, 1966-. Served Army, 1942-47; Lieut-Colonel, RAMC; OC Surgical Div., MEF. Fellow: University Coll. London; Darwin Coll., Cambridge. *Publications:* The Management of Head Injuries, 1966. Section, British Surgical Progress, 1958. Papers to Medical Journals on Neurosurgical subjects. *Recreations:* tennis, gardening. *Address:* Martins Lodge, 4 Babraham Road, Cambridge. *T:* Cambridge 48843; (Addenbrooke's Hospital), Cambridge 45151. *Club:* Athenæum.

**LEWIS,** family name of **Barons Brecon, Essendon** and **Merthyr.**

**LEWIS, Maj.-Gen. Alfred George,** CBE 1969; Director General, Fighting Vehicles and Engineer Equipment, since 1970; *b* 23 July 1920; *s* of Louis Lewis; *m* 1946, Daye Neville, *d* of Neville Greaves Hunt; two *s* two *d. Educ:* St Dunstan's Coll.; King's Coll., London. Served War of 1939-45, India and Burma. Commanded 15th/19th Hussars, 1961-63; Dir, Defence Operational Requirements Staff, MoD, 1967-68; Dep. Comdt, Royal Mil. Coll. of Science, 1968-70. *Recreations:* shooting, golf, sailing. *Address:* Chipstead, Dinorben Avenue, Fleet, Hants. *T:* Fleet 5271. *Club:* Cavalry.

**LEWIS, A(lfred) Neville;** *see* Lewis, Neville.

**LEWIS, Sir Allen (Montgomery),** Kt 1968; **Hon. Mr Justice Lewis;** Chief Justice of West Indies Associated States Supreme Court since 1967; *b* 26 Oct. 1909; *s* of George Ferdinand Montgomery Lewis and Ida Louisa (*née* Barton); *m* 1936, Edna Leofrida Theobalds; three *s* two *d. Educ:* St Mary's Coll., St Lucia. LLB Hons (external) London, 1941. Admitted to practice at Bar of Royal Court, St Lucia (later Supreme Court of Windward and Leeward Islands), 1931; called to English Bar, Middle Temple, 1946; in private practice, Windward Islands, 1931-59; Acting Magistrate, St Lucia, 1940-41; Acting Puisne Judge, Windward and Leeward Islands, 1955-56; QC 1956; Judge: of Federal Supreme Court, 1959-62; of British Caribbean Court of Appeal, 1962; of Court of Appeal, Jamaica, 1962-67; Acting President, Court of Appeal, 1966; Acting Chief Justice of Jamaica, 1966. MLC, St Lucia, 1943-51; Member, Castries Town Council, 1942-56 (Chairman six times); President W Indies Senate, 1958-59. Served on numerous Government and other public cttees; rep. St Lucia, Windward Islands, and W Indies at various Conferences; Director, St Lucia Branch, British Red Cross Society, 1955-59; President, Grenada Boy Scouts' Assoc., 1967; Comr for reform and revision of laws of St Lucia, 1954-58. Served as President and/or Cttee Member, cricket, football and athletic associations, St Lucia, 1936-59. Coronation Medal, 1953. *Publication:* Revised Edition of Laws of St Lucia, 1957. *Recreations:* gardening, swimming. *Address:* Chief Justice's Chambers, St George's, Grenada. *T:* 2040; Mount Wheldale, St George's, Grenada. *T:* 2391. *Clubs:* West Indian, Grenada Golf.

**LEWIS, Vice-Admiral Andrew Mackenzie,** CB 1967; Second Sea Lord and Chief of Naval Personnel, since 1970; *b* 24 Jan. 1918; *m* 1943, Rachel Elizabeth Leatham; two *s. Educ:* Haileybury. Director of Plans, Admiralty, 1961-63; in command of HMS Kent, 1964-65; Director-General, Weapons (Naval), 1965-68; Flag Officer, Flotillas, Western Fleet, 1968-69. *Address:* Coleman's Farm, Finchingfield, Braintree, Essex. *T:* Great Bardfield 391. *Club:* United Service.

**LEWIS, Anthony;** *see* Lewis, J. A.

**LEWIS, Prof. Anthony Carey,** CBE 1967; Principal of the Royal Academy of Music, since 1968; *b* 1915; *s* of late Colonel Leonard Carey Lewis, OBE, and Katherine Barbara Lewis; *m* 1959, Lesley, *d* of Mr and Mrs Frank Lisle Smith. *Educ:* Wellington; Peterhouse, Cambridge (Organ Schol.). MA, MusB

Cantab; Hon. MusD Birmingham; Hon. RAM; joined music staff of BBC, 1935; director Foundations of Music and similar programmes; responsible many revivals 16th-18th century music; War of 1939-45, served MEF; planned and supervised music in BBC Third Programme, 1946; Peyton-Barber Professor of Music, University of Birmingham, 1947-68, and Dean of the Faculty of Arts, 1961-64. President, Royal Musical Association, 1963-69; Chairman: Music Advisory Panel, Arts Council of Great Britain, 1954-65; Music Advisory Cttee, British Council, 1967-; Founder and General Editor, Musica Britannica; Hon. Secretary, Purcell Society; Chairman, Purcell-Handel Festival, 1959; Governor, Wellington Coll. *Compositions include:* Psalm 86 (Cambridge, 1935); A Choral Overture (Queen's Hall, 1937); City Dances for Orchestra (Jerusalem, 1944); Trumpet Concerto (Albert Hall, 1947); Three Invocations (Birmingham, 1949); A Tribute of Praise (Birmingham, 1951); Horn Concerto (London, 1956); Canzona for Orchestra, Homage to Purcell (Birmingham, 1959). Conductor many recordings, especially Purcell and Handel. *Publications:* research: A Restoration Suite (Purcell and others), 1937; Venus and Adonis (Blow), 1939; Matthew Locke, 1948; Libera me (Arne), 1950; Coronation Anthems (Blow), 1953; Apollo and Daphne (Handel), 1956; Odes and Cantatas (Purcell), 1957; Anthems (3 vols), (Purcell), 1959-62; Fairy Queen (Purcell), 1966; Athalia (Handel), 1967. Editor, English Songs Series; numerous contributions on musical subjects to various periodicals. *Address:* Royal Academy of Music, Marylebone Road, NW1.

**LEWIS, Sir Arthur;** *see* Lewis, Sir W. A.

**LEWIS, Arthur William John;** MP (Lab) North Division of West Ham since 1950 (Upton Division West Ham, 1945-50); Ex-Trade Union Official (National Union of General and Municipal Workers); *b* 21 Feb. 1917; *s* of late J. Lewis; *m* 1940, Lucy Ethel Clack; one *d*. *Educ:* Elementary Sch.; Borough Polytechnic. Shop steward of his Dept of City of London Corporation at 17; Vice-Chairman of TU branch (City of London NUGMW) at 18; full-time London district official NUGMW 1938-48; Member of London Trades Council and Holborn City Trades Council, various joint industrial councils, Government cttees, etc. Formerly Member Exec. Cttee, London Labour Party; Chairman Eastern Regional Group of Labour MPs, 1950-; Member Eastern Regional Council of Labour Party and Exec. Cttee of that body, 1950-. Served in the Army. *Recreations:* swimming, motoring, boxing, general athletics. *Address:* 1 Doveridge Gardens, Palmers Green, N13.

**LEWIS, Sir Aubrey Julian,** Kt 1959; MD, FRCP; Professor of Psychiatry, University of London, 1946-66; *b* Adelaide, South Australia, 8 Nov. 1900; *s* of George Lewis, Adelaide; *m* 1934, Hilda Stoessiger, MD, FRCP (*d* 1966); two *s* two *d*. *Educ:* Christian Brothers' Coll., Adelaide; University of Adelaide. Medical Registrar, Adelaide Hospital, 1924-26; Rockefeller Medical Fellow, 1926-28; Clinical Director, Maudsley Hospital, 1936-48; President Section of Psychiatry, RSM, 1946; Consultant in Psychological Medicine British Post-Graduate Medical Sch., 1932-45; Civilian Consultant in Psychiatry, RAF, 1945-67. Manson Lecturer, British Institute Philosophy, 1949; Maudsley Lecturer, RMPA, 1951; Bradshaw Lecturer, RCP, 1957; Galton Lecturer, Eugenics Society, 1958; Hobhouse Lecturer, University College, London, 1960; Bertram Roberts Lecturer, Yale, 1960; Maurice Bloch Lecturer, 1962; Harveian Orator, RCP, 1963; Linacre Lectr, Cambridge, 1967; Mapother Lectr, Inst. of Psychiatry, 1969. Member American Philosophical Society. Ambuj Nath Bose Prize, RCP, 1968. Hon. DSc, Belfast; Hon. LLD, Toronto. *Publications:* Inquiries in Psychiatry, 1967; The State of Psychiatry, 1967; articles on medical topics. *Address:* Caversham Lodge, Barnes, SW13. *Club:* Athenæum.

**LEWIS, Bernard,** FBA 1963; BA, PhD, FRHistS; Professor of History of the Near and Middle East, University of London, since 1949; *b* London, 31 May 1916; *s* of H. Lewis, London; *m* 1947, Ruth Hélène, *d* of late Overretsagfører M. Oppenhejm, Copenhagen; one *s* one *d*. *Educ:* Wilson Coll.; The Polytechnic; Universities of London and Paris. Derby Student, 1936. Asst Lecturer in Islamic History, Sch. of Oriental Studies, University of London, 1938. Served RAC and Intelligence Corps, 1940-41; attached to Foreign Office, 1941-45. Visiting Prof. of History, University of Calif, Los Angeles, 1955-56, Columbia Univ., 1960 and Indiana Univ., 1963; Class of 1932 Lectr, Princeton Univ., 1964; Vis. Mem., Inst. for Advanced Study, Princeton, New Jersey, 1969. *Publications:* The Origins of Ismā'īlism, 1940; Turkey Today, 1940; British contributions to Arabic Studies, 1941; Handbook of Diplomatic and Political Arabic, 1947, 1956; Land of Enchanters, 1948 (ed); The Arabs in History, 1950 (4th rev. edn, 1966); Notes and Documents from the Turkish Archives, 1952; The Emergence of Modern Turkey, 1961 (rev. edn, 1968); The Kingly Crown (translated from Ibn Gabirol), 1961; co-ed. with P. M. Holt, Historians of the Middle East, 1962; Istanbul and the Civilization of the Ottoman Empire, 1963; The Middle East and the West, 1964; The Assassins, 1967; co-ed., Encyclopædia of Islam, 1956-; articles in learned journals. *Address:* School of Oriental and African Studies, University of London, WC1. *T:* 01-580 9021. *Club:* Athenæum.

**LEWIS, Bernard; His Honour Judge Bernard Lewis;** a County Court Judge since 1966; *b* 1906; 3rd *s* of late Solomon and Jeannette Lewis, London; *m* 1934, Harriette, *d* of late I. A. Waine, Dublin, London and Nice; one *s*. *Educ:* Trinity Hall, Cambridge (MA). Called to the Bar, Lincoln's Inn, 1929. Mem. S-E Circuit. Hon. Mem., Central Criminal Court Bar Mess. *Recreations:* revolver shooting, bricklaying. *Address:* Trevelyan House, Arlington Road, St Margaret's, Middx. *Clubs:* Reform; Ham and Petersham Rifle and Pistol.

**LEWIS, Cecil Arthur,** MC; Author; *b* Birkenhead, 29 March 1898; *m* 1921 (marriage dissolved, 1940); one *s* one *d*; *m* 1942 (marriage dissolved, 1950; no *c*); *m* 1960. *Educ:* Dulwich Coll.; University Coll. Sch.; Oundle. Royal Flying Corps, 1915 (MC, despatches twice); Manager Civil Aviation, Vickers, Ltd, 1919; Flying Instructor to Chinese Government, Peking, 1920, 1921; one of four founders of BBC, Chm. of Programme Board, 1922-26; Varied Literary Activities: stage, screen (first two adaptations of Bernard Shaw's plays to screen, 1930-32), and television plays (Nativity, Crucifixion and Patience of Job, 1956-59) and production connected therewith. RAF, 1939-45. Sheep farming, South Africa, 1947-50. United Nations Secretariat, New York, radio and television, 1953-55. Commercial television, London, 1955-56. Daily Mail, 1956-66; retd. *Publications:* Broadcasting From Within, 1924; The Unknown Warrior, trans. from French of Paul Raynal, 1928; Sagittarius Rising, 1937; The Trumpet is Mine, 1938; Challenge to the

Night, 1938; Self Portrait: Letters and Journals of the late Charles Ricketts, RA (Editor), 1939; Pathfinders, 1943; Yesterday's Evening, 1946; Farewell to Wings, 1964. *Address:* c/o National Westminster Bank, 97 Strand, WC2.

**LEWIS, Cecil D.**; *see* Day-Lewis.

**LEWIS, Brig. Sir Clinton (Gresham),** Kt 1941; OBE 1928; *b* 25 Nov. 1885; *s* of J. Hardwicke Lewis, late of Veytaux, Switzerland; *m* 1916, Lilian Eyre (*d* 1962), *d* of late Rev. Walter Wace; one *s* one *d* (and one *s* decd). *Educ:* privately, Montreux, Switzerland. Royal Military Acad., Woolwich, 1903-04 (Sword of Honour); Commission RE 1904; joined Survey of India, 1907; in charge Miri Mission Survey, NE Frontier, 1911-12; served European War, 1914-18 (despatches, Bt Major); Afghan War, 1919; Indo-Afghan Boundary Commission, 1919; with Turco-Iraq frontier delimitation commission, 1927; Surveyor-Gen. of India, 1937-41; employed with Ord. Survey, 1942-45. Hon. Sec. RGS, 1944-46, Vice-Pres. 1946-50. Founders' Gold Medal RGS 1937. *Publication:* (co-editor) first edition The Oxford Atlas, 1951. *Recreations:* climbing, tennis. *Address:* 10 Gainsborough Gardens, Hampstead, NW3. *T:* 01-435 4478.

*See also Lt-Col W. G. Hingston.*

**LEWIS, Dan,** FRS 1955; PhD; DSc; Quain Professor of Botany, London University, since 1957; *b* 30 Dec. 1910; *s* of Ernest Albert and Edith J. Lewis; *m* 1933, Mary Phœbe Eleanor Burry; one *d*. *Educ:* High Sch., Newcastle-under-Lyme, Staffs; Reading University (BSc); PhD, DSc (London). Research Scholar, Reading Univ., 1935-36; Scientific Officer, Pomology Dept, John Innes Hort. Inst., 1935-48; Head of Genetics Dept, John Innes Horticultural Institution, Bayfordbury, Hertford, Herts, 1948-57. Rockefeller Foundation Special Fellowship, California Inst. of Technology, 1955-56; Visiting Prof. of Genetics, University of Calif., Berkeley, 1961-62; Royal Society Leverhulme Vis. Prof., University of Delhi, 1965-66. Pres., Genetical Soc., 1968-; Mem., UGC, 1969-. *Publications:* Editor, Science Progress; scientific papers on Genetics and Plant Physiology. *Address:* 50 Canonbury Park North, N1. *T:* 01-226 9136.

**LEWIS, Alderman David John,** JP; Practising Architect; Lord Mayor of Liverpool, 1962-63; *b* 29 April 1900; Welsh; *m* 1919, Margaret Elizabeth Stubbs; no *c*. *Educ:* Aberystwyth Univ.; Faculty of Architecture, Liverpool Univ. Elected to Liverpool City Council, 1936; Alderman, 1952; Chm. Educn Cttee, 1961-62; Past Chm. Royal Liverpool Philharmonic Soc.; Chm. Liverpool Welsh Choral Union; Pres. Liverpool Male Voice Soc.; Chm. Merseyside Youth Orchestra; Acting Chm. British Council, Liverpool. JP Liverpool. *Recreations:* music, county cricket, football (Rugby), reading biography. *Address:* Spunholme, Greenhill Road, Allerton, Liverpool 18. *T:* 051-427 7194. *Clubs:* Lyceum, Masonic, Press (Liverpool).

**LEWIS, David Thomas,** CB 1963; Professional Fellow, University College of Wales, Aberystwyth, since 1970; *b* 27 March 1909; *s* of Emmanuel Lewis and Mary (*née* Thomas), Breconshire, Wales; *m* 1st, 1934, Evelyn (*née* Smetham); one *d*; 2nd, 1959, Mary (*née* Sadler). *Educ:* Brynmawr County Sch.; University Coll. of Wales, Aberystwyth. BSc (Wales), 1st Class Hons In Chemistry, 1930; PhD (Wales), 1933; DSc (Wales), 1958. Senior Chemistry Master, Quakers' Yard Secondary Sch., 1934-38; Asst Lecturer, University Coll., Cardiff, 1938-40. Various scientific posts finishing as Principal Scientific Officer, Ministry of Supply, Armaments Research Establishment, 1941-47; Senior Superintendent of Chemistry Div., Atomic Weapons Research Establishment. Aldermaston, 1947-60; Govt Chemist, 1960-70. FRIC 1940; FRSH 1964. Dawes Memorial Lectr, 1965. Scientific Governor, British Nutrition Foundn, 1967; Member: British National Cttee for Chemistry (Royal Society), 1961-; British Pharmacopœia Commission, 1965-. *Publications:* Ultimate Particles of Matter, 1959; Mountain Harvest (Poems), 1964. Analytical Research Investigations in learned Jls; Scientific Articles in Encyclopædias, Scientific Reviews, etc. *Recreations:* writing, fishing, shooting. *Address:* University College of Wales, Aberystwyth, Wales.

**LEWIS, Mrs Dorothy;** *see* Lewis, Mrs M. D.

**LEWIS, E(dward) Daly; His Honour Judge Daly Lewis;** Judge of County Courts (Circuit 17, Lincolnshire) since 1960; *b* 14 Nov. 1908; *s* of Ernest Edward Lewis, MD, Weymouth Street, W1; *m* 1941, Nancy Ruth, *d* of Harold Margetson, Wingham, near Canterbury; two *d*. *Educ:* Harrow; Magdalen Coll., Oxford (MA). Called to Bar, Middle Temple, 1932; Midland Circuit. Joined RE (TA), 1938. Served War of 1939-45: Major, 1942; GSO2 Southern Command, DAAG War Office, 1943; Allied Force HQ in N Africa and Italy, 1944-45. Chm. Agricultural Land Tribunal for Yorks, 1954-60. Chm. Quarter Sessions for Parts of Holland, 1961; Dep. Chm., Quarter Sessions for Parts of Kesteven, 1962. *Recreations:* walking, golf. *Address:* Kettlethorpe Hall, near Lincoln. *T:* Torksey 279.

**LEWIS, Sir Edward (Roberts),** Kt 1961; Member of London Stock Exchange since 1925; Chairman: Decca Ltd; The Decca Record Co. Ltd; The Decca Navigator Co. Ltd; Decca Radar Ltd; Reid & Sigrist Ltd; *b* 19 April 1900; *s* of late Sir Alfred Lewis, KBE; *m* 1923, Mary Margaret Hutton (*d* 1968), *d* of late Rev. George Dickson Hutton; one *s* (and one *s* decd). *Educ:* Rugby Sch.; Trinity Coll., Cambridge. Gold Albert Medal (RSA) 1967. *Address:* 23 Rutland Gate, SW7. *T:* 01-584 7330; Bridge House Farm, Felsted, Essex. *T:* Felsted 349. *Club:* United University.

**LEWIS, Eiluned;** Writer; 2nd *d* of late Hugh Lewis, MA Cantab, JP, and Eveline Lewis, MA, JP, Glan Hafren, Newtown, Montgomeryshire; *m* 1937, Graeme Hendrey, MIEE; one *d*. *Educ:* Levana, Wimbledon; Westfield Coll., University of London. Editorial Staff, News-Chronicle; Editor's Asst, Sunday Times, 1931-36. *Publications:* Dew on the Grass (Book Guild gold medal), 1934; (with Peter Lewis) The Land of Wales, 1937; The Captain's Wife, 1943; In Country Places, 1951; The Leaves of the Tree, 1953; Honey Pots and Brandy Bottles, 1954; Selected Letters of Charles Morgan, with Memoir, 1967; and two books of verse; regular contributor to Country Life. *Address:* Snatts Hill, Bletchingley, Surrey.

**LEWIS, Captain Henry E.,** CBE 1942; RN (retired); *b* 24 Sept. 1889; *s* of W. C. Lewis, Plymouth, Devon; *m* 1911, E. E. Rice, Plympton, Devon; one *d*. *Educ:* Plymouth. *Recreations:* tennis, etc. *Address:* 8 Fastnet House, South Parade, Southsea PO5 2JG. *T:* Portsmouth 31768.

**LEWIS, Henry Gethin,** DL, JP; Chairman and Managing Director of private companies; *b* 31

Oct. 1899; *e s* of late Henry Gethin Lewis, LLD, JP, High Sheriff of Glamorgan, 1920-21, Porthkerry, Glamorgan; *m* 1925, Gwendolen Joan, 5th *d* of T. W. David, JP, Ely Rise, Cardiff; one *s* two *d*. *Educ:* Shrewsbury Sch.; Trinity Coll., Oxford (MA). Served European War 2nd Lt RAF with 48 Sqdn, 1918, BEF France (POW). Called to the Bar, Inner Temple, 1925. RAFVR, 1939-45, Sqdn-Ldr 1943. JP 1957, DL 1961, High Sheriff of Glamorgan, 1958. Chief Comr for Wales, St John Ambulance Bde, 1958-66; KStJ; Mem., Welsh Hosp. Bd, 1958-64, and Mem. Bd of Governors, United Cardiff Hosps, 1958-64. *Address:* Cliffside, Penarth, Glamorgan. *T:* Penarth 707096. *Clubs:* Royal Air Force; Leander (Henley-on-Thames); Cardiff and County (Cardiff).

**LEWIS, H(erbert) J(ohn) Whitfield,** CB 1968; Chief Architect, Ministry of Housing and Local Government, since Sept. 1964; *b* 9 April 1911; *s* of Herbert and Mary Lewis; *m* 1963, Pamela (*née* Leaford); one *s* three *d*. *Educ:* Monmouth Sch.; Welsh Sch. of Architecture. Associate with Norman & Dawbarn, Architects and Consulting Engineers; in charge of housing work, 1945-50; Principal Housing Architect, Architects Dept, London County Council, 1950-59; County Architect, Middlesex County Council, 1959-64. FRIBA; MTPI, DisTP 1957. *Recreations:* sailing, electronics. *Address:* 8 St John's Wood Road, NW8.

**LEWIS, Prof. Hywel David,** MA, BLitt; Professor of History and Philosophy of Religion, in the University of London, since 1955; *b* 21 May 1910; *s* of Rev. David John and Rebecca Lewis, Waenfawr, Cærnarvon; *m* 1943, Megan Elias Jones, MA (*d* 1962), *d* of J. Elias Jones, Bangor; *m* 1965, K. A. Megan Pritchard, *d* of T. O. Pritchard, Pentrefoelas. *Educ:* University Coll., Bangor; Jesus Coll., Oxford. Lecturer in Philosophy, University Coll., Bangor, 1936; Senior Lecturer, 1947; Prof. of Philosophy, 1947-55; President: Mind Association, 1948-49, Aristotelian Soc., 1962-63; Chm. Council, Royal Inst. of Philosophy; Soc. for the Study of Theology, 1964-66; President: Oxford Soc. for Historical Theology, 1970-71; London Soc. for Study of Religion, 1970-72; Editor, Muirhead Library of Philosophy; Editor, Religious Studies; Leverhulme Fellow, 1954-55; Visiting Professor: Brynmawr Coll., Pa, USA, 1958-59; Yale, 1964-65; University of Miami, 1968; Boston Univ., 1969; Robert McCahan Lectr, Presbyterian Coll., Belfast, 1960; Wilde Lectr in Natural and Comparative Religion, University of Oxford, 1960-63; Edward Cadbury Lectr, University of Birmingham, 1962-63; Visiting Lectr, Centre for the Study of World Religions, Harvard, 1963; Ker Lectr, McMaster Divinity Coll., Ont, 1964; Owen Evans Lectr, University Coll., Aberystwyth, 1964-65; Firth Memorial Lectr, University of Nottingham, 1966; Gifford Lectr, University of Edinburgh, 1966-68; L. T. Hobhouse Memorial Lectr, University of London, 1966-68. Elton Lectr, George Washington Univ., 1969; Otis Memorial Lectr, Wheaton Coll., 1969. Commemoration Preacher, University of Southampton, 1958; Commemoration Lectr, Cheshunt Coll., Cambridge, 1960, and Westminster Coll., 1964. Fellow of King's Coll., London, 1963; Dean of the Faculty of Theology in the University of London, 1964-68; Dean of the Faculty of Arts, King's Coll., 1966-68, and Faculty of Theology, 1970-72. Sec. Philosophical Section of Guild of Graduates, University of Wales; Mem., Advisory Council for Education (Wales), 1964-67. Mem., Gorsedd of Bards. Hon. DD St Andrews. *Publications:* Morals and the New Theology, 1947; Morals and Revelation, 1951; Contemporary British Philosophy, Vol. III (ed), 1956; Our Experience of God, 1959; Freedom and History, 1962; Clarity is not Enough (ed), 1962; Teach yourself the Philosophy of Religion, 1965; World Religions (with R. L. Slater), 1966; Dreaming and Experience, 1968; The Elusive Mind, 1969; Gwerinaeth, 1940; Y Wladwriaeth a'i Hawdurdod (with Dr J. A. Thomas), 1943; Ebyrth, 1943; Diogelu Diwylliant, 1945; Crist a Heddwch, 1947; Dilyn Crist, 1951; Gwybod am Dduw, 1952; contributions to Mind, Proc. of Aristotelian Society, Philosophy, Ethics, Hibbert Jl, Philosophical Quarterly, Analysis, Efrydiau Athronyddol, Llenor, Traethodydd, etc. *Address:* 1 Normandy Park, Normandy, near Guildford, Surrey.

**LEWIS, Sir Ian (Malcolm),** Kt 1964; QC (Nigeria) 1961; MA Cantab, LLB; a Justice of the Supreme Court of Nigeria since 1966; *b* 14 Dec. 1925; *s* of late Prof. Malcolm M. Lewis, MC, MA, LLB, and Eileen (*née* O'Sullivan); *m* 1955, Marjorie, *d* of W. G. Carrington; one *s*. *Educ:* Clifton Coll.; Trinity Hall, Cambridge (Scholar, 1st cl. hons Law Tripos Pt 2, and LLB). Served with RAFVR, 1944-47. Called to Bar, Middle Temple, 1951; pupil of R. W. Goff (now Mr Justice Goff), 1951. Western Circuit, 1951; Crown Counsel, Nigeria, 1953; Northern Nigeria: Solicitor-Gen., 1958; Dir of Public Prosecutions, 1962; Attorney-Gen. and Minister in the Government of Northern Nigeria, 1962-66. MEC, 1962-66; Adv. Coun. on the 1962-66; of Mercy, House of Assembly, 1962-66. Mem. of Nigerian Bar Council, 1962-66; Mem. of Nigerian Council of Legal Education, 1962-66; Chancellor of the Diocese of Northern Nigeria, 1964-66; Assoc. Mem. Commonwealth Parly Assoc. *Recreations:* swimming (Capt. Cambridge Univ. Swimming and Water Polo, 1949); bridge; sailing; trying to find chapels in Wales where Grandfather "Elfed" (late Rev. H. Elvet Lewis, CH, DD) had not preached. *Address:* Supreme Court, Lagos, Nigeria; 10 Southfield Road, Westbury-on-Trym, Bristol. *T:* Bristol 626942. *Clubs:* Royal Commonwealth Society; Hawks (Cambridge); Clifton, Constitutional (Bristol); Lagos Yacht.

**LEWIS, Ivor Evan Gerwyn; Hon. Mr Justice Lewis;** Puisne Judge, High Court of Uganda; *b* 1904; *er s* of late Dr Lionel H. Lewis, Porth, Glamorgan; *m* 1940, Winifred M. Hill; one *s*. *Educ:* Malvern Coll. Solicitor of the Supreme Court of Judicature, 1929; practised in UK and Straits Settlements. Called to the Bar, Gray's Inn, 1945 (Hons). Magistrate, Singapore, 1937; Registrar, High Court, Zanzibar, 1937; Resident Magistrate, 1938-46; Crown Counsel, 1947-48; Uganda, 1948. *Recreations:* cricket, golf and the Turf. *Address:* 21 Carlton Place, Porthcawl, Glam. *Clubs:* East India and Sports; Kampala (Uganda).

**LEWIS, Prof. Jack;** Professor of Chemistry, University of Cambridge, since 1970; *m* 1951, Elfreida Mabel (*née* Lamb); one *s* one *d*. *Educ:* Barrow Grammar Sch. BSc London 1949; PhD Nottingham 1951; DSc London 1961; MSc Manchester 1964. Lecturer: Univ. of Sheffield, 1953-56; Imperial Coll., London, 1956-57; Lecturer-Reader, University Coll., London, 1957-62; Prof. of Chemistry: Univ. of Manchester, 1962-67; UCL, 1967-70. *Publications:* papers, mainly in Jl of Chem. Soc. *Address:* Chemistry Department, University Laboratories, Lensfield Road, Cambridge.

**LEWIS, J(ack) Haydon,** CMG 1958; OBE 1955; Commissioner of Prisons, Kenya, 1951-59, retired; *b* 18 Oct. 1904; British; *m* 1935, Doris

Gwendoline; one step-*s*. *Educ:* Plumtree Sch., S Rhodesia; Rhodes Univ., S Rhodesia; Cambridge Univ. Cadet, Kenya, 1931; District Officer, 1934; District Commissioner, 1949; Senior District Commissioner, 1950. *Recreations:* cricket, golf. *Address:* Hill Rise, The Lane, West Mersea, Essex. *Club:* West Mersea Yacht (Hon. Sec.).

**LEWIS, Sir John Duncan;** *see* Orr-Lewis.

**LEWIS, Sir John (Todd),** Kt 1970; OBE 1946; JP; Chairman: Davenports CB & Brewery (Holdings) Ltd since 1952; Midland Caledonian Investment Trust Ltd, since 1951; Director: Wellington Tube Holdings Ltd since 1959; Express & Star (Wolverhampton) Ltd since 1964, and other Companies; *b* 25 July 1901; *s* of George Lewis; *m* 1st, 1926, Lydia Mary Hall (*d* 1961); no *c*; 2nd, 1965, Marjorie Jean Hardy. *Educ:* Wolverhampton Gram. Sch. Qual. as Chartered Accountant, 1924. Partner in Agar, Bates, Neal & Co., 1925-62. Life Governor, Birmingham Univ., 1956-; Chm. Birmingham Regional Hospital Bd, 1963-70. JP, Wolverhampton, 1950. *Recreation:* golf. *Address:* Clos des Pins, Gorey, Jersey. *T:* Jersey East 207. *Club:* Golfers.

**LEWIS, Ven. John Wilfred;** Archdeacon of Hereford and Canon Residentiary of Hereford Cathedral since 1970; Prebendary of Colwall in Hereford Cathedral since 1948; *b* 25 Sept. 1909; *e s* of Fritz and Ethel Mary Lewis; *m* 1938, Winifred Mary Griffin; one *s* two *d*. *Educ:* privately; Gonville and Caius Coll., Cambridge. History Tripos Pt I Cl. II, 1932; BA 1933; MA, 1937; Steel Studentship (University), 1933; Exhibitioner, 1933-34; Westcott House, 1934; Deacon, 1935; Priest, 1936; Asst Dir of London Diocesan Council for Youth, 1935-37; Head of Oxford House, 1937-40; Vicar of Kimbolton, 1940-46; Rector of Cradley, 1946-60; Archdeacon of Ludlow, 1960-70; Rector of Wistanstow, 1960-70; Dir of Hereford Diocesan Council of Education, 1943-63. *Recreations:* walking, sailing. *Address:* The Archdeacon's House, The Close, Hereford. *T:* Hereford 2873.

**LEWIS, (Joseph) Anthony;** Chief London Correspondent, New York Times, since 1965; *b* 27 March 1927; *s* of Kassel Lewis and Sylvia Lewis (*née* Surut), NYC; *m* 1951, Linda, *d* of John Rannells, NYC; one *s* two *d*. *Educ:* Horace Mann Sch., NY; Harvard Coll. (BA). Sunday Dept, New York Times, 1948-52; Reporter, Washington Daily News, 1952-55; Legal Corresp., Washington Bureau, NY Times, 1955-64; Nieman Fellow, Harvard Law Sch., 1956-57. Governor, Ditchley Foundation; Mem., US-UK Commn, London. Pulitzer Prize for Nat. Correspondence, 1955 and 1963; Heywood Broun Award, 1955. Hon. DLitt, Adelphi Univ. (NY), 1964. *Publications:* Gideon's Trumpet, 1964; Portrait of a Decade: The Second American Revolution, 1964; articles in American law reviews. *Recreation:* dinghy sailing. *Address:* Canonbury House, N1. *T:* 01-226 3461; Deep Bottom Cove, West Tisbury, Mass 02575, USA. *Clubs:* Garrick; Century (NY); Federal City (Washington).

**LEWIS, Kenneth;** MP (C) Rutland and Stamford since 1959; Chairman, Conservative Back Bench Labour Committee, 1963-64; *b* 1 July 1916; *s* of William and Agnes Lewis, Jarrow; *m* 1948, Jane, *d* of Samuel Pearson, of Adderstone Mains, Belford, Northumberland; one *s* one *d*. *Educ:* Jarrow; Edinburgh Univ. Labour Manager, R. & W. Hawthorn Leslie Co. Ltd, 1939-41. Served War of 1939-45. RAF, 1941-46; Flight-Lt, Staff, SHAEF; Air Ministry. Co. of London Electric Supply Co. Ltd, 1946-48; Chm. Business and Holiday Travel Ltd. Contested (C) Newton-le-Willows, 1945 and 1950, Ashton-under-Lyne, 1951. CC Middx, 1949-51; Mem. NW Metropolitan Hosp. Management Cttee, 1949-62; Hon. Treas., Commonwealth and Continental Church Soc. Trustee, Uppingham Sch. *Recreations:* music, painting, travelling. *Address:* 96 Green Lane, Northwood, Middx. *T:* Northwood 23354; Dale Cottage, Preston, Rutland. *Clubs:* Junior Carlton, Pathfinder, St Stephen's.

**LEWIS, Maj.-Gen. Kenneth Frank Mackay,** CB 1951; DSO 1944; MC 1918; retired; Chairman, Earl Haig Memorial Homes; *b* 29 Jan. 1897; *s* of Frank Essex Lewis and Anne Florence Mackay; *m* 1930, Pamela Frank Menzies Pyne; two *s*. *Educ:* privately. Commissioned 2nd Lt RH & RFA, 1916; served with 9th Scottish Div., France and Belgium, 1916-18; ADC to GOC Lowland Div., 1921; ADC to GOC. Upper Silesia Force, 1922; Iraq Levies, 1923-25; Adjutant, Portsmouth and IOW, 1926-29; Royal West African Frontier Force, Nigeria Regt, 1929-30; Colchester, 1930-33; India, School of Artillery, 1933-37; Military Coll. of Science, UK, 1938; School of Artillery, Larkhill, 1939-41; CO 7th Survey Regt, 1942; CO 185 Field Regt, 1943; CRA 43 and 49 Divisions, 1944 and 1945; CCRA Palestine, 1947 and 1948; BRA Western Command, UK, 1948; GOC 4th Anti-Aircraft Group, 1949-50; Dir of Royal Artillery, War Office, Dec. 1950-54; retired, 1954; Col Comdt RA, 1957-62. OStJ 1955. Order of Leopold, Croix de Guerre (Belgium). *Recreations:* shooting, fishing, sailing. *Address:* Stamps and Crows, Layer Breton, near Colchester. *T:* Birch 220. *Club:* Army and Navy.

**LEWIS, Leonard,** QC 1969; *b* 11 May 1909; *e s* of Barnet Lewis; *m* 1939, Rita Jeanette Stone; two *s* one *d*. *Educ:* Grocer's Company Sch.; St John's Coll., Cambridge (Major Schol.). Wrangler, Wright's Prizeman, MA Cantab; BSc 1st class Hons London. Called to Bar, 1932 and started to practise. Served War of 1939-45, RAF. *Recreations:* squash racquets, tennis. *Address:* East Park House, Newchapel, near Lingfield, Surrey. *T:* Lingfield 114.

**LEWIS, Prof. Leonard John,** CMG 1969; BSc; DipEd; Professor of Education, with special reference to Education in Tropical Areas, in the University of London, since 1958; *b* 28 Aug. 1909; of Welsh-English parentage; *s* of Thomas James Lewis and Rhoda Lewis (*née* Gardiner); *m* 1940, Nora Brisdon; one *s* (and one *s* decd). *Educ:* Lewis Sch., Pengam; University Coll., of South Wales and Monmouth (BSc); University of London Institute of Education (DipEd). Lecturer, St Andrew's Coll., Oyo, Nigeria, 1935-36; Headmaster, CMS Gram. Sch., Lagos, Nigeria, 1936-41; Education Sec., CMS Yoruba Mission, 1941-44; Lectr, University of London Institute of Education, 1944-48; Editorial staff, Oxford Univ. Press, 1948-49; Prof. of Educn and Dir of Institute of Educn, University Coll. of Ghana, 1949-58. Nuffield Visiting Prof., University of Ibadan, 1966. Coronation Medal, 1953. *Publications:* Equipping Africa, 1948; Henry Carr (Memoir), 1948; Education Policy and Practice in British Tropical Areas, 1954; (ed and contrib.) Perspectives in Mass Education and Community Development, 1957; Days of Learning, 1961; Education and Political Independence in Africa, 1962; Schools, Society and Progress in Nigeria, 1965; The Management of Education (with A. J. Loveridge), 1965. *Recreations:* music, walking. *Address:* Fishers Vane, Fishers Hill, Woking, Surrey. *T:* Woking 63030.

**LEWIS, Alderman Mrs (Mary) Dorothy,** CBE 1961 (MBE 1953, OBE 1957); JP; Lord Mayor of Cardiff, 1960-61; *b* 5 Jan. 1894; *d* of George and Helena Lovell; *m* 1917, David Aubrey Lewis (*d* 1946); one *s*. *Educ:* Severn Road Sch.; Canton High Sch., Cardiff. Foundation Mem., first Branch of Conservative Women, Cardiff (formed after women granted parliamentary vote), Sept. 1919; Hon. Officer of Cardiff Conservative and Unionist Assoc. 1924-, and Life Vice-Pres. of Cardiff West Assoc.; Mem., Cardiff City Council, May 1944-. Holder of Souvenir Cert. for vol. work for St Dunstans; Souvenir Brochure for vol. services, Glamorgan Welfare for Troops Cttee, 1946. Vice-Pres. Weights and Measures Admin. for Gt Britain, 1960. JP 1946. OStJ 1962. *Recreations:* reading, charitable social work. *Address:* Birchgrove Cottage, Caerphilly Road, Cardiff. *T:* Cardiff 60378.

**LEWIS, Prof. Morris Michael;** Professor Emeritus, University of Nottingham, since 1963; Director, Institute of Education, 1947-63, and Professor of Education, 1956-63; *b* 27 June 1898; *m* 1921, Hilda Winifred Maizels (Hilda Lewis, novelist); one *s*. *Educ:* University Coll., London. University Scholarship in English; Morley Medallist in Eng. Lit.; BA 1st Cl. Hons English; MA Educ, with Distinction; PhD. Senior English Master, Newport Gram. Sch., 1918-19, William Ellis Sch., 1919-24; Lecturer, University Coll., Nottingham, 1924-29, Sen. Lecturer, 1929-40; Vice-Principal, Goldsmiths' Coll., London, 1940-47. Chairman: Soc. of Teachers of Speech and Drama, 1942-57; Dept of Educn and Science Cttee on Educn of Deaf Children. Fellow British Psychological Soc. *Publications:* Infant Speech (Internat. Library of Psych.) 1936, 2nd edn 1951; Language in School, 1942; Language in Society, 1948; The Importance of Illiteracy, 1953; How Children Learn to Speak, 1957; Language, Thought and Personality, 1963; Language and Personality in Deaf Children, 1968; Language and the Child, 1969; papers on education and psychology in various journals. *Address:* 38 Wollaton Hall Drive, Nottingham. *T:* Nottingham 76417.

**LEWIS, Neville,** RP; Artist; Member New English Art Club; *b* Cape Town, 8 Oct. 1895; *s* of Rev. A. J. S. Lewis, Cape Town; *m* 1st, 1916, T. M. C. Townshend; two *s* one *d*; 2nd, 1932, Vera Player; one *s* one *d*; 3rd, 1955, Countess Rosa Cécile, *d* of late Prince zu Solms-Baruth and of H. H. Princess zu Solms-Baruth, Mariental, SW Africa; one *s* one *d*. *Educ:* South African Coll. Sch., Cape Town; Slade Sch. of Fine Arts, University of London. Served European War, France, Belgium, Italy; worked some years in South Africa, painting native life; painted portraits Spain, USA and England; offical War Artist SA Forces, 1940-43. Pictures have been acquired by National Gallery of British Art (Tate Gallery), Galleria Nacional del Arte Moderno (Madrid), Imperial War Museum, Corporation Galleries: Oldham, Manchester, Liverpool, Sheffield, Belfast, Leeds, Bradford, Birmingham etc.; SA National Gallery, Cape Town, Johannesburg, Durban. Has painted portraits of the following: Sir Winston Churchill, Air-Marshal Tedder, Solly Joel, HM King of Spain (late Alfonso XIII), HM King of Greece (late George II), The Earl of Athlone, Princess Alice, and Field-Marshals Smuts, Montgomery and Alexander, Sobhuza II, King of the Swazis, State President of SA Republic, etc. *Publication:* Studio Encounters, 1963. *Address:* 42 Rowan Street, Stellenbosch, South Africa. *Clubs:* Chelsea Arts; Stellenbosch (S Africa).

*See also T. L. T. Lewis.*

**LEWIS, Norman;** author; *s* of Richard and Louise Lewis. *Educ:* Enfield Gram Sch. Served War of 1939-45, in Intelligence Corps. *Publications:* Sand and Sea in Arabia, 1938; Samara, 1949; Within the Labyrinth, 1950; A Dragon Apparent, 1951; Golden Earth, 1952; A Single Pilgrim, 1953; The Day of the Fox, 1955; The Volcanoes Above Us, 1957; The Changing Sky, 1959; Darkness Visible, 1960; The Tenth Year of the Ship, 1962; The Honoured Society, 1964; A Small War Made to Order, 1966; Every Man's Brother, 1967. *Address:* c/o William Heinemann Ltd, 15-16 Queen Street, W1.

**LEWIS, Prof. Norman Bache,** MA, PhD; retired; *b* 8 Nov. 1896; *o s* of G. D. and L. A. Lewis, Newcastle-under-Lyme; *m* 1928, Julia, *o d* of John and Catherine Wood, Riddlesden, Keighley; one *d* (one *s* decd). *Educ:* Boys' High Sch., Newcastle-under-Lyme (foundation scholar); University of Manchester (Jones scholar). Served European War in RFA, 1917-19. Manchester University: Hovell and Shuttleworth Prizes in History, 1919; BA in History Hons Cl I and graduate scholarship in History, 1921; Research Fellowship in History, 1922. University of Sheffield: Lecturer in Dept of Modern History, 1924; Senior Lecturer in Mediæval History, 1946; Reader in Mediæval History, 1955; Prof. of Mediæval History in the University of Sheffield, 1959-62, Emeritus Prof., 1962. *Publications:* articles in historical journals. *Recreations:* music and walking. *Address:* 8 Westcombe Park Road, SE3. *T:* 01-858 1763.

**LEWIS, Percival Cecil; Hon. Mr Justice Lewis;** Puisne Judge of Supreme Court of the Windward and Leeward Islands since 1956; Justice of Appeal of the West Indies Associated States Supreme Court, since 1967; *b* St Vincent, 14 Aug. 1912; *s* of late Philip Owen Lewis; *m* 1936, Gladys Muriel Pool; one *s* one *d*. *Educ:* St Vincent Intermediate Sch.; St Vincent Gram. Sch. Called to Bar, Middle Temple, 1936. Practised in Uganda and St Vincent; Registrar and Additional Magistrate, St Lucia, 1940; Magistrate, Dominica, 1943; Crown Attorney, St Vincent, 1945; Crown Attorney, St Lucia, 1952; Attorney-Gen., Leeward Islands, 1954. *Recreations:* gardening and swimming. *Address:* c/o Supreme Court, PO Box 80, St George's, Grenada, Windward Islands, West Indies.

**LEWIS, Peter Tyndale;** Deputy Chairman, John Lewis Partnership, since 1970; *b* 26 Sept. 1929; *s* of Oswald Lewis and Frances Merriman Lewis (*née* Cooper); *m* 1961, Deborah Anne Collins; one *s* one *d*. *Educ:* Eton; Christ Church, Oxford. National Service, Coldstream Guards, 1948-49; MA (Oxford) 1953; called to Bar (Middle Temple) 1956; joined John Lewis Partnership, 1959. Mem. Council, Industrial Soc., 1968-; Vice-Chm., Retail Distributors' Assoc., 1970. *Address:* 34 Victoria Road, W8. *T:* 01-937 2662.

**LEWIS, Richard,** CBE 1963; FRAM, FRMCM, LRAM; Concert and Opera Singer, Tenor; *b* of Welsh parents; *m* 1963, Elizabeth Robertson; one *s* (and one *s* by a previous *m*). *Educ:* Royal Manchester Coll. of Music (schol.; studied with Norman Allin); RAM. As a boy won many singing competitions in N England; Gold Medals of Assoc. Bd exams, 1935, 1937. Served in RCS during war and whilst so doing sang in Brussels and Oslo. English début in leading rôle of Britten's Opera The Rape of Lucretia at Glyndebourne, where he has appeared each season since 1947; several opera, concert, recital appearances, Edinburgh Festival; created parts: Troilus in Sir William Walton's Opera Troilus and Cressida; Mark in The

Midsummer Marriage, and Achilles in King Priam, both Operas by Michael Tippett; sang in first perf. of Stravinsky's Canticum Sacrum, under composer's direction, Venice Festival; sang Aaron in first British performance of Schoenberg's opera Moses and Aaron at Covent Garden. Recitalist and oratorio singer, particularly in name part of Elgar's The Dream of Gerontius. In addition to appearance at Glyndebourne is a guest artist at Covent Garden, San Francisco, Chicago, Vienna State Opera and Berlin State Opera Houses; début Teatro Colon, Buenos Aires, 1963. Sings frequently on the Continent and has made several tours of America; also toured Australia and New Zealand, 1957, 1964. Leading part in first American presentation of Cherubini's Opera, Medea, San Francisco, USA, 1958, where he has now appeared for ten seasons; Has appeared with leading European and American orchestras, etc including the New York Philharmonic, Chicago Symphony, San Francisco Symphony, and Philadelphia Orchestras, etc. Has made numerous recordings and appearances on radio and television. *Recreations:* private film making, tennis, golf. *Address:* Casuarina, Harrington Sound, Bermuda.

**LEWIS, Maj.-Gen. (retd) Robert Stedman,** CB 1946; OBE 1942; late IA; *b* 20 March 1898; *s* of Sidney Cooke Lewis, MInstCE, and Mary Anne Jane Lewis Lloyd; *m* 1925, Margaret Joan Hart; one *s* one *d*. *Educ:* Amesbury Sch., Bickley Hall, Kent; Bradfield Coll., Berks; Royal Military Academy, Woolwich. 2nd Lt RFA 1915; Seconded to RFC in 1916 and 1917 and served as a pilot in France in 100 Squadron RFC; served in France with RFA, 1918; proceeded to India with RFA, 1919; Seconded to Indian Army Ordnance Corps, 1922, and permanently transferred to Indian Army, 1925, with promotion to Capt.; Major, 1933; Bt Lt-Col 1937; Lt-Col 1940; Col 1944; employed at General Headquarters, India, 1939; Dir of Ordnance Services (India), 1945; retired, 1948. High Sheriff of Radnorshire, 1951. *Address:* Y Neuadd, Rhayader, Radnorshire. *T:* Rhayader 227.

**LEWIS, Capt. Roger Curzon,** DSO 1939; OBE 1944; RN retired; *b* 19 July 1909; *s* of late F. W. and K. M. Lewis; *m* 1944, Marguerite Christiane, *e d* of late Capt. A. D. M. Cherry, RN, retd; two *s*. *Educ:* Royal Naval Coll., Dartmouth. HMS Sowestoft, Africa Station, 1927-29; HMS Vivien and HMS Valentine, 6th Flotilla Home Fleet, 1930-32; Qualifying Lt T 1933; HMS Enterprise, East Indies Station, 1935-37; Staff of HMS Vernon, 1938-39; HMS Florentino, 1939-40; HMS Rodney, 1940-42; Staff of Comdr-in-Chief Mediterranean, 1942-45; Superintendent of Torpedo Experimental Establishment, Greenock, 1950-55; Capt. of the Dockyard and Queen's Harbourmaster, Chatham, 1955-58; retired, 1959. *Address:* Corner Hall, West Hyde, near Rickmansworth, Herts.

**LEWIS, Roland Swaine,** FRCS; Senior Consultant Surgeon to the ENT Department, King's College Hospital, since 1968 (Consultant Surgeon, 1946-68); Consultant ENT Surgeon: to Mount Vernon Hospital and The Radium Institute since 1947; to Norwood and District Hospital, since 1948; *b* 23 Nov. 1908; *s* of Dr William James Lewis, MOH, and Constance Mary Lewis, Tyrwaun, Ystalyfera; *m* 1936, Mary Christianna Milne (Christianna Brand); one adopted *d*. *Educ:* Epsom Coll.; St John's Coll., Cambridge; St George's Hospital. BA Cantab 1929; FRCS 1934; MA Cantab 1945; MB BCh Cantab 1945. Surgical Chief Asst, St George's Hospital, 1935. Major, RAMC (ENT Specialist), 1939-45. *Publications:* papers to medical journals. *Recreations:* ornithology, fishing. *Address:* 152 Harley Street, W1N 1HH. *T:* 01-935 8868; (home) 88 Maida Vale, W9. *T:* 01-624 6253.

**LEWIS, Ronald Howard;** MP (Lab) Carlisle since 1964; *b* 16 July 1909; *s* of Oliver Lewis, coal miner; *m* 1937, Edna Cooke; two *s*. *Educ:* Elementary Sch. and Cliff Methodist Coll. Left school at 14 years of age and worked in coal mines (Somerset; subseq. Derbyshire, 1930-36); then railways (LNER Sheds, Langwith Junction); left that employment on being elected to Parliament. Mem., Blackwell RDC 1940- (twice Chm.); Derbyshire CC, 1949-; Mem. Bd of Directors, Pleasley Co-operative Soc. Ltd, 1948- (Pres. 1952). Mem. NUR. Methodist Local Preacher. *Recreations:* walking, football, gardening. *Address:* 1 The Crescent, Langwith Junction, Mansfield, Notts. *T:* Shirebrook 460.

**LEWIS, Saunders,** MA; Welsh writer and dramatist; *b* 15 Oct. 1893; *s* of Rev. Lodwig Lewis and Mary Margaret Thomas; *m* 1924, Margaret Gilcriest; one *d*. *Educ:* privately; Liverpool Univ. *Publications:* Critical works, plays, novels, verse, etc., works on Welsh economic and political conditions in the Welsh language. Translations of plays have been presented on stage and television in English, German, and Spanish. *Address:* 158 Westbourne Road, Penarth, Glam.

**LEWIS, Thomas Loftus Townshend,** FRCS; Consultant Obstetric and Gynæcological Surgeon at Guy's Hospital, Queen Charlotte's Maternity Hospital and Chelsea Hospital for Women, since 1948; *b* 27 May 1918; *e s* of Neville Lewis, *qv*, and his first wife, Theodosia Townshend; *m* 1946, Kathleen Alexandra Ponsonby Moore; five *s*. *Educ:* Diocesan Coll., Rondebosch, S Africa; St Paul's Sch.; Cambridge Univ.; Guy's Hospital. BA Cantab (hons in Nat. Sci. Tripos), 1939; MB, BChir Cantab, 1942. FRCS 1946; MRCOG 1948; FRCOG 1961. House Appointments Guy's Hospital, 1942-43; Gold Medal and Prize in Obstetrics, Guy's Hospital, 1942. Volunteered to join South African Medical Corps, 1944; seconded to RAMC and served as Capt. in Italy and Greece, 1944-45. Returned to Guy's Hospital; Registrar in Obstetrics and Gynæcology, 1946, Obstetric Surgeon, 1948; Surgeon, Chelsea Hosp. for Women, 1950; Surgeon, Queen Charlotte's Maternity Hosp., 1952. Examiner in Obstetrics and Gynæcology: University of Cambridge, 1950; University of London, 1954; Royal College of Obstetricians and Gynæcologists, 1952; London Soc. of Apothecaries, 1955; University of St Andrews, 1960. Hon. Sec. and Mem. Council Royal College of Obstetricians and Gynæcologists, 1955-68; Mem. Council Obstetric Section, Royal Society of Med., 1953-. Guest Prof. to Brisbane, Australia, Auckland, New Zealand, 1959, Johns Hopkins Hosp., Baltimore, 1966; Litchfield Lectr, University of Oxford, 1968; Sims-Black Prof. to Australia, NZ and Rhodesia, 1970. *Publications:* Progress in Clinical Obstetrics and Gynæcology, 2nd edn 1964; Diseases of Women, 11th edn (jointly), 1964; Obstetrics, 11th edn (jointly), 1966; Queen Charlotte's Textbook of Obstetrics, 9th edn (jointly), 1965. Contributions to: Lancet, BMJ, Practitioner, Proc. Roy. Soc. Med., Encyclopædia Britannica Book of the Year (annual contrib.), etc. *Recreations:* ski-ing, sailing, tennis, golf, croquet, water ski-ing, underwater swimming, photography, staying on the Isle of Elba. *Address:* 109 Harley Street, W1. *T:* 01-935 5855; (home) 13 Copse Hill, Wimbledon, SW20. *T:* 01-946 5089. *Clubs:* Royal Wimbledon Golf; United Hospitals Rugby Football (ex-Pres.).

**LEWIS, Wilfrid Bennett,** CC (Canada) 1967; CBE 1946; FRS 1945; FRSC 1952; MA; PhD; Senior Vice-President, Science, Atomic Energy of Canada Ltd, since 1963; *b* 24 June 1908; *s* of Arthur Wilfrid Lewis and Isoline Maud Steavenson; unmarried. *Educ:* Haileybury Coll., Herts; Gonville and Caius Coll., Cambridge. Cavendish Laboratory, Cambridge, research in Radio-activity and Nuclear Physics, 1930-39; Research Fellowship, Gonville and Caius Coll., 1934-40; University Demonstrator in Physics, 1934; University Lecturer in Physics, 1937; lent to Air Ministry as Senior Scientific Officer, 1939; Chief Superintendent Telecommunications Research Establishment, Ministry of Aircraft Production, 1945-46; Dir of Division of Atomic Energy Research, National Research Council of Canada, 1946-52; Vice-Pres. Research and Development, Atomic Energy of Canada, Ltd, 1952-63. Canadian Representative United Nations Scientific Advisory Cttee, 1955-. Fellow American Nuclear Soc., 1959 (Pres., 1961). Hon. DSc: Queen's Univ., Kingston, Ontario, 1960; University of Saskatchewan, 1964; McMaster Univ., Hamilton, Ontario, 1965; Dartmouth Coll., New Hampshire, 1967; McGill Univ., Montreal, 1969; Hon. LLD: Dalhousie Univ., Halifax, Nova Scotia, 1960; Carleton Univ., Ottawa, 1962; Trent Univ., Peterborough, Ont, 1969. Amer. Medal of Freedom, with Silver Palms, 1947. First Outstanding Achievement Award, Public Service of Canada, 1966; Atoms for Peace Award (shared), 1967; Can. Assoc. of Physicists 25th anniversary special Gold Medal, 1970. *Publications:* Electrical Counting, 1942; articles in Wireless Engineer, 1929, 1932 and 1936; papers in Proc. Royal Society A. 1931, 1932, 1933, 1934, 1936, 1940; etc. *Recreations:* walking, sailing. *Address:* 13 Beach Avenue, Deep River, Ontario, Canada. *T:* 584-3561.

**LEWIS, Sir (William) Arthur,** Kt; PhD, BCom (London); MA (Manchester); Professor of Public and International Affairs, Princeton University, since 1963, on leave of absence as President, Caribbean Development Bank, 1970-72; Chancellor, University of Guyana, since 1966; *b* 23 Jan. 1915; 4th *s* of George F. and Ida Lewis, Castries, St Lucia; *m* 1947, Gladys Jacobs; two *d. Educ:* St Mary's Coll., St Lucia; London Sch. of Economics. Lecturer at London Sch. of Economics, 1938-47; Reader in Colonial Economics, University of London, 1947; Stanley Jevons Prof. of Political Economy, University of Manchester, 1948-58; Principal, University Coll. of the West Indies, 1959-62; Vice-Chancellor, University of the West Indies, 1962-63. Assigned by United Nations as Economic Adviser to the Prime Minister of Ghana, 1957-58; Dep. Man. Dir, UN Special Fund, 1959-60. Temp. Principal, Board of Trade, 1943, Colonial Office, 1944; Consultant to Caribbean Commn, 1949: Mem. UN Group of Experts on Under-developed Countries, 1951; Part-time Mem. Board of Colonial Development Corporation, 1951-53; Mem. Departmental Cttee on National Fuel Policy, 1951-52; Consultant to UN Economic Commission for Asia and the Far East, 1952; to Gold Coast Govt, 1953: to Govt of Western Nigeria, 1955. Mem. Council, Royal Economic Soc., 1949-58; Pres. Manchester Statistical Soc., 1955-56. Hon. LHD (Columbia); Hon. LLD (Toronto, Wales, Williams, Bristol, Dakar, Leicester, Rutgers, Brussels); Hon. LittD (WI); Hon. Fellow, LSE; For. Fellow Amer. Acad. of Arts and Sciences; Mem., Amer. Phil. Soc.; Hon. Fellow Weitzmann Inst. *Publications:* Economic Survey, 1918-1939, 1949; Overhead Costs, 1949; The Principles of Economic Planning, 1949; The Theory of Economic Growth, 1955; Politics in West Africa, 1965; Development Planning, 1966; Reflections on the Economic Growth of Nigeria, 1968; Some Aspects of Economic Development, 1969; articles in technical, economic and law jls. *Address:* Caribbean Development Bank, Bridgetown, Barbados.

**LEWIS, William Edmund Ames,** OBE 1961; Charity Commissioner since 1962; *b* 21 Sept. 1912; *s* of late Ernest W. Lewis, FRCSE, Southport, Lancashire; *m* 1939, Mary Elizabeth, *e d* of late C. R. Ashbee; two *s* one *d*. *Educ:* Merchant Taylors', Great Crosby; Emmanuel Coll., Cambridge. Barrister-at-law, Inner Temple, 1935. Entered Charity Commission, 1939; Asst Commissioner, 1953-61; Sec., 1961-69. Served in RAF, 1941-46. *Recreations:* music, painting. *Address:* 33 Pembridge Square, W2. *T:* 01-727 5574. *Club:* Oxford and Cambridge.

**LEWIS, Wilmarth Sheldon,** FSA, FRSA, FRSL; Hon. MA (Yale 1937); Hon. LittD (Brown, 1945, Rochester, 1946, Delaware, 1961, Cambridge 1962); LHD (Trin. Coll., Hartford, 1950, Bucknell 1958); DLitt (NUI, 1957); LLD (Yale 1965); Yale Medal, 1965; Editor Yale Edn of Horace Walpole's Correspondence since 1933; *b* 14 Nov. 1895; *s* of Azro N. and Miranda Sheldon Lewis; *m* 1928, Annie Burr Auchincloss (*d* 1959). *Educ:* Thacher Sch.; Yale Univ. (BA 1918). Served European War as 2nd Lt 144 Field Artillery, 1917-19; War of 1939-45 as Chief, Central Information Div., Office of Strategic Services, 1941-43; Research Assoc., Yale Univ., 1933-38; Fellow of Yale Univ., 1938-64; Fellow Amer. Acad. of Arts and Sciences; Mem., Amer. Philosoph. Soc. Chairman: Yale Library Assoc., 1933-45; Librarian's Council, Library of Congress, 1941-47; John Carter Brown Library Assoc., 1943-46; Hon. Fellow, Pierpont Morgan Library, 1970. Trustee: Institute for Advanced Study, Princeton, 1945-; Thacher Sch., 1940-46, 1954-; Brooks Sch., 1946-49; Miss Porter's Sch., 1941-65; Watkinson Library, 1941-; Redwood Library, 1946-; Henry Francis duPont (Winterthur) Museum, Delaware, 1954-; John Carter Brown Library, 1955-; Heritage Foundn, 1962–; John F. Kennedy Library, 1964-; Mem. Commission: on National Portrait Gallery (Washington), 1964-; National Coll. of Fine Arts, 1958-. Donald F. Hyde Award (Princeton), 1968. *Publications:* Tutor's Lane, 1922; Three Tours Through London, 1748, 1776, 1797 (Colver Lectures, Brown Univ.), 1941; The Yale Collections, 1946: Collector's Progress, 1951; Horace Walpole's Library (Sandars Lectures), 1957; Horace Walpole (A. W. Mellon Lectures), 1960; One Man's Education, 1967. Editor: A Selection of Letters of Horace Walpole, 1926, 1951; Horace Walpole's Fugitive Verses, 1931; (with Ralph M. Williams) Private Charity in England, 1747-57, 1938; Yale Edition of Horace Walpole's Correspondence, 34 vols, 1937-71, with completion (50 vols) about 1980. *Address:* Farmington, Conn. USA; Hammersmith Farm, Newport, RI. *Clubs:* Athenæum (London); Century, Grolier, Yale (New York); Tavern (Boston); Metropolitan (Washington); Pacific Union (San Francisco).

**LEWISHAM, Viscount; William Legge;** *b* 23 Sept. 1949; *er s* and *heir* of 9th Earl of Dartmouth, *qv. Educ:* Eton; Christ Church, Oxford. Secretary, Oxford Union Soc., 1969. *Address:* 40a Hill Street, W1. *Clubs:* Turf, Bath.

**LEWISHAM, Dean of;** *see* Davies, Very Rev. I. G.

**LEWISHAM, Archdeacon of;** *see* Hayman, Ven. William Samuel.

**LEWISON, Peter George Hornby;** Chairman, National Dock Labour Board, since Aug. 1969; *b* 5 July 1911; *s* of George and Maud Elizabeth Lewison; *m* 1937, Lyndsay Sutton Rothwell; one *s* one *d*. *Educ:* Dulwich; Magdalen Coll., Oxford. Labour Manager, Dunlop Rubber Co., Coventry, 1935-41; Min. of Supply (seconded), 1941-44; RNVR (Lieut, Special Br.), 1944-46. Personnel Management Adviser, Min. of Labour, 1946-47; Personnel Manager, British-American Tobacco Co. Ltd, 1947-68, retd. *Recreations:* music, cricket, squash, bird-watching. *Address:* Court Hill House, East Dean, Chichester. *T:* Singleton 200. *Club:* MCC.

**LE WITT, Jan;** painter, poet and designer; *b* 3 April 1907; *s* of Aaron Le Witt and Deborah (*née* Koblenz); *m* 1939, Alina Prusicka; one *s*. *Educ:* Czestochowa. Began artistic career as self-taught designer in Warsaw, 1927; first one-man exhibn of his graphic work, Soc. of Fine Arts, Warsaw, 1930. Co-author and illustrator of children's books, publ. several European langs. Settled in England, 1937; Brit. subject, 1947-; at head of Le Witt-Him partnership, 1933-54. During War of 1939-45 executed (in partnership) a series of murals for war factory canteens, posters for Min. of Inf., Home Office, GPO, etc. Co-designer of murals for Festival of Britain, 1951, and Festival Clock, Battersea Park. First one-man exhibn, Zwemmer Gall., London, 1947; subseq. Hanover Gall. London, 1951; in Rome, 1952; Zwemmer Gall., 1953; New York, 1954; Milan, 1957; Paris, 1960; Grosvenor Gall., London, 1961; Paris, 1963; Musée d'Antibes, 1965; Salon d'Automne, Paris, 1963; Salon de Mai, Paris, 1964; Warsaw (retrosp.), 1967; Venice (retrosp.) (organised by City of Venice), 1970. In 1955 when at top of his profession, he gave up graphic design to devote himself entirely to painting. *Works at:* Musée National d'Art Moderne, Paris; Nat. Museum, Jerusalem; Nat. Museum, Warsaw; Musée d'Antibes; Museum and Art Gall., Halifax; City Art Gall., Middlesbrough; British Council; Contemp. Art Soc., London; and in private collections. Represented in collective exhibns in Tate Gall., London, and many foreign galleries. Other artistic activities: décors and costumes for Sadler's Wells Ballet; glass sculptures Venice (Murano); tapestry designs, Aubusson. Gold Medal, Vienna, 1948; Gold Medal Triennale, Milan, 1954; Mem., Alliance Graphique Internationale, 1948-60; Mem., Exec. Council, Société Européenne de Culture, Venice, 1961-. *Publication:* Vegetabull, 1956 (London and New York); Contribs to Poetry Review; Adam; Comprendre, etc. *Recreations:* music, natural history. *Relevant Publication:* Sir Herbert Read, Jean Cassou, Pierre Emmanuel and John Smith (jointly), Jan Le Witt, 1970. *Address:* (studio) 22 Holland Park Avenue, W11. *T:* 01-727 8709; (private) 117 Ladbroke Road, Holland Park, W11. *T:* 01-229 1570. *Club:* PEN.

**LEWITTER, Prof. Lucjan Ryszard;** Professor of Slavonic Studies, University of Cambridge, since 1968; *b* 1922; *m*. *Educ:* schools in Poland; Perse Sch., Cambridge; Christ's Coll., Cambrdige. PhD 1951. Univ. Asst Lectr in Polish, 1948; Fellow of Christ's Coll., 1951; Dir of Studies in Modern Languages, 1951-64; Tutor, 1960-68; Univ. Lectr in Slavonic Studies (Polish), 1953-68. *Publications:* articles in learned jls. *Address:* Department of Slavonic Studies, Sidgwick Avenue, Cambridge CB3 9DA. *T:* Cambridge 56411. *Club:* United University.

**LEWTHWAITE, Raymond,** CMG 1955; OBE 1945; Medical Research Adviser, Ministry of Overseas Development, 1964-68; retired; *b* 18 Nov. 1894; *s* of late Charles A. Lewthwaite, Kendal; *m* 1926, Gladys (*d* 1964), *d* of Harry Johnson, Kendal; one *s* one *d*. *Educ:* Kendal Sch.; Magdalen Coll., Oxford; Middlesex Hosp. (Leopold Hudson prizeman). Served European War, 1916-19, Lt Border Regt; Capt. 1919-23. BA 1922; MA 1930; BM, BCh, 1925; DM 1930; North Persian Forces Memorial Medal for Medical Research, 1936; MRCP 1939; FRCP 1948. Institute for Medical Research, Malaya: Research Student, 1926, Senior Pathologist, 1931; Dir 1945. Field Dir, Med. Res. Council's Scrub-typhus Commission, South-East Asia Command, 1944-45. Dir of Colonial Medical Research, Colonial Office, 1949-61; Medical Research Adviser, Dept of Technical Co-operation, 1961-64. Assessor, Tropical Medicine Research Bd. *Publications:* sundry articles on tropical diseases, especially typhus group of fevers, in medical literature. Contributor to Modern Practice in Infectious Fevers. *Recreations:* reading and music. *Address:* 121 Erskine Hill, NW11. *T:* 01-458 3713.

**LEWTHWAITE, Sir William Anthony,** 3rd Bt, *cr* 1927; Solicitor of Supreme Court since 1937; Partner in Southall & Co., London; *b* 26 Feb. 1912; *e s* of Sir William Lewthwaite, 2nd Bt, JP, and Beryl Mary Stopford (*d* 1970), *o c* of late Major Stopford Cosby Hickman, JP, DL, of Fenloe, Co. Clare; *S* father, 1933; *m* 1936, Lois Mairi, *o c* of late Capt. Robertson Kerr Clark and Lady Beatrice Minnie Ponsonby, *d* of 9th Earl of Drogheda (who *m* 2nd, 1941, 1st Baron Rankeillour, PC; she *d* 1966); two *d* (*er* adopted) (and one *d* decd). *Educ:* Rugby; Trinity Coll., Cambridge, BA. Signalman Royal Corps of Signals, 1942-43; Lt, Grenadier Guards, 1943-46. Mem. Council, Country Landowners Association, 1949-64. Mem. Cttee: Westminster Law Society; Brooks's Club. *Heir:* *b* Brig. Rainald Gilfrid Lewthwaite, MC, Scots Guards [*b* 21 July 1913; *m* 1936, Margaret Elizabeth, MBE, *yr d* of Harry Edmonds, New York; two *s* one *d* (and one *d* decd). Defence and Military Attaché, HM Embassy, Paris, 1964-68, retd]. *Address:* 3 Culford Mansions, SW3. *T:* 01-589 0765.

**LEY, Arthur Harris,** FRIBA, AADip, FIStructE, CompRAeS; Senior Partner, Ley Colbeck & Partners, Architects; *b* 24 Dec. 1903; *s* of late Algernon Sydney Richard Ley, FRIBA, and Esther Eliza Harris; *m* 1935, Ena Constance Riches; one *d*. *Educ:* Westminster City Sch.; AA Coll. of Architecture. Architect for: Principal London Office Barclays Bank DCO; Head Office Nat. Mutual Life Assce. Soc.; Palmerston Hse, EC2; Baltic Hse, EC3; Hqrs Marine Soc.; Hqrs SBAC; Hqrs RAeS; Hqrs Instn Struct. Engrs; York Hall, Windsor Gt Park; Aircraft Research Assoc. Estab., Bedford. Factories and Office Blocks for: Vickers-Armstrongs, at Barrow, etc.; British Aircraft Corporation at Weybridge and Hurn; Wallpaper Manufrs Ltd; Sir Isaac Pitman & Sons; Decca Radar Ltd; Ever Ready Co.; also Office Block, Vancouver. Banks for: Nat. Provincial; Barclays; Bank of Scandinavia; Swiss-Israel Trade Bank. Hospitals: Watford and Harrow. Schools: London, Hertfordshire and Surrey. Mem. Council: Architects Registr Coun. of UK, 1958-60; Instn Struct. Engrs, 1951-54; London Chamber of Commerce, 1955-; Liveryman: Worshipful Co. of Paviors (Master, 1962), and of Upholders (Master, 1966); Freeman, City of London; Sheriff 1964-65, and Mem. Court of Common Council, City of London, 1964-; Churchwarden of St Mary-le-Bow. Grand Officer of the Order of Merit

(Chile). *Publications:* contributions to journals and technical press. *Address:* Palmerston House, 51 Bishopsgate, EC2. *T:* 01-588 7282: Mixbury, Weybridge, Surrey. *T:* Weybridge 42701. *Clubs:* City Livery (Pres., 1968-69), Guildhalll, Anglo-Belgian, United Wards (Pres., 1961).

**LEY, Francis Douglas,** MBE 1961; TD; DL; JP; Managing Director: Ley's Malleable Castings Co. Ltd; Ewart Chainbelt Co. Ltd; Chairman, Ley's Foundries and Engineering Ltd; *b* 5 April 1907; *yr s* of Major Sir Gordon Ley, 2nd Bt (*d* 1944); *heir-pres.* to brother, Sir Gerald Gordon Ley, 3rd Bt, *qv*; *m* 1931, Violet Geraldine Johnson; one *s* one *d*. *Educ:* Eton; Magdalene Coll., Cambridge (MA). JP 1939, DL 1957, Derbyshire. High Sheriff of Derbyshire, 1956. *Address:* Shirley House, Brailsford, Derbyshire. *T:* Brailsford 327. *Club:* Cavalry.

**LEY, Sir Gerald Gordon,** 3rd Bt, *cr* 1905; TD; Captain, 1st Derbyshire Yeomanry; *b* 5 Nov. 1902; *e s* of Major Sir Henry Gordon Ley, 2nd Bt, and late Rhoda Lady Ley, *d* of Herbert Prodgers, Kington St Michael, Chippenham; *S* father 1944; *m* 1st, 1936, Rosemary Catherine Cotter (marr. diss. 1956), *d* of late Captain Duncan Macpherson, Royal Navy; three *d*; 2nd, 1958, Grace Foster (marr. diss. 1968). *Educ:* Eton; Oxford Univ., BA Agriculture. Manages estates in Cumberland; High Sheriff of Cumberland, 1937. Lord of the Manors of Lazonby, Kirkoswald, Staffield and Glassonby. Served Duke of Lancaster's Own Yeomanry, 1927-39; War Service, 1939-40; 1st Derbyshire Yeomanry, 1940-45. *Recreations:* fishing, salmon in particular; shooting. *Address:* Lazonby Hall, nr Penrith, Cumberland. *TA:* Lazonby, Cumberland. *T:* Lazonby 218.

*See also F. D. Ley.*

**LEYLAND, Norman Harrison;** Director, Warwick Securities, since 1970; Investment Bursar, Brasenose College, Oxford; *b* 27 Aug. 1921; *m* J. I. McKillop; one *s* two *d*. *Educ:* Manchester Grammar Sch.; Brasenose Coll., Oxford. Dir, Oxford Centre for Management Studies, 1965-70. Chm., Consumers' Cttee for Great Britain, 1967-70. Fellow, Brasenose Coll., Oxford, 1948-. *Address:* Brasenose College, Oxford. *Club:* Lansdowne.

**LEYLAND, Peter;** *see* Pyke-Lees, W. K.

**LEYLAND, Sir V. E. N.;** *see* Naylor-Leyland.

**LEYTON, Dr Nevil;** *see* Leyton, Dr R. N. A.

**LEYTON, Dr (Robert) Nevil (Arthur);** Consulting Physician, Specialising in Migraine, since 1950; *b* 15 June 1910; *s* of Prof. A. S. F. Leyton, MD, DSc, FRCP, and Mrs H. G. Leyton, MD; *m* 1943, Wendy (*d* 1960), *er d* of Tom and Dylis Cooper; one *s*. *Educ:* private; Gonville and Caius Coll., Cambridge; Westminster Hospital (entrance Schol.). BA (Cantab) Double Hons Natural Sciences Tripos, 1932; MA 1938. Ho. Phys. and Surg., Westminster Hospital, 1937. Served with RAF, 1943-46, and with 601 Squadron RAuxAF, 1947-57; retired rank Squdn Leader. FRSocMed, 1946. Registrar (Med.), St Stephen's Hospital, 1947-50; Hon. Cons Physician to Migraine Clinic, Putney Health Centre, 1950-; Hon. Cons. in migraine to Royal Air Forces Assoc., 1947-; Hon. Cons Physician to Wendy Leyton Memorial Migraine Centre, Harley Street, 1961-; Sen. Medical Adviser, International Migraine Foundn, 1961-; Consulting Physician to Kingdom of Libya, 1968-69. President, 601 Squadron RAuxAF Old Comrades Assoc., 1963-. Air Force Efficiency Medal, 1954. *Publications:* Migraine and Periodic Headache, 1952 (USA, 1954); Headaches, The Reason and the Relief, 1955 (USA); Migraine, 1962; Migraine, Modern Concepts and Preventative Treatment, 1964. Contrib.: Lancet, British Medical Journal, Medical World and Journal, Lancet (USA), etc. *Recreations:* travel, riding, horse racing, lawn tennis (Cambridge Univ. Blue, 1933), squash racquets. *Address:* 49 Harrington Gardens, SW7.

**LI, Choh-Ming;** Vice-Chancellor, The Chinese University of Hong Kong, since 1964; Professor of Business Administration, University of California, Berkeley, on leave since 1964; *b* 17 Feb. 1912; *s* of Kanchi Li and Mewching Tsu; *m* 1938, Sylvia Chi-wan Lu; two *s* one *d*. *Educ:* Univ. of California at Berkeley (MA, PhD). Prof. of Economics, Nankai and Southwest Associated and Central Univs in China, 1937-43; Dep. Dir-Gen., Chinese Nat. Relief and Rehabilitation Admin. (CNRRA), 1945-47; China's chief deleg. to UN Releif and Rehabilitation Confs and to UN Econ. Commn for Asia and Far East, 1947-49; Chm., Board of Trustees for Rehabilitation Affairs, Nat. Govt of China, 1949-50; Expert on UN Population Commn and Statistical Commn, 1952-57; Lectr, Assoc. Prof., and Prof. of Business Admin., and Dir of Center for Chinese Studies, Univ. of California (Berkeley), 1951-63. Hon. Dr of Laws: Hong Kong, 1967; Michigan, 1967; Marquette, 1969; Western Ontario, 1970; Hon. Dr Social Science, Pittsburgh, 1969. Hon. CBE 1967. *Publications:* Economic Development of Communist China, 1959; Statistical System of Communist China, 1962; (ed) Industrial Development in Communist China, 1964; (ed) Asian Workshop on Higher Education, 1969. *Recreations:* tennis, calligraphy. *Address:* The Vice-Chancellor's Residence, The Chinese University of Hong Kong, Shatin, New Territories, Kowloon, Hong Kong. *Clubs:* American, Country (Hong Kong).

**LIARDET, Maj.-Gen. Henry Maughan,** CB 1960; CBE 1945 (OBE 1942); DSO 1945; DL; *b* 27 Oct. 1906; *s* of late Maj.-Gen. Sir Claude Liardet, KBE, CB, DSO, TD, DL; *m* 1933, Joan Sefton, *d* of Major G. S. Constable, MC, JP; three *s*. *Educ:* Bedford School. 1st Commission for Territorial Army, 1924, Royal Artillery; Regular Commission, Royal Tank Corps, 1927; service UK, India, Egypt, 1927-38; Staff Coll., Camberley, 1939; War of 1939-45: War Office, 1939-41; active service in Egypt, N. Africa, Italy, 1941-45; General Staff appointments, command of Regiment and Brigade (despatches twice); idc, 1955; Chief of Staff, British Joint Services Mission (Army Staff), Washington, DC, 1956-58; ADC to the Queen, 1956-58; Director-General of Fighting Vehicles, WO, 1958-61; Deputy Master-General of the Ordnance, War Office, 1961-64, retired. Colonel Comdt, Royal Tank Regt, 1961-67. Dir, British Sailors' Soc., 1961. DL Sussex, 1964. West Sussex CC, 1964. *Recreations:* shooting, gardening. *Address:* Warningcamp House, Arundel, Sussex. *T:* Arundel 3233. *Club:* Army and Navy.

**LIBBY, Dr Willard Frank;** Professor of Chemistry, University of California, since 1959; Director, Institute of Geophysics, since 1962; *b* 17 Dec. 1908; *s* of Ora Edward Libby and Eva May (*née* Rivers); *m* 1940, Leonor Hickey (marr. diss. 1966); twin *d*; *m* 1966, Leona Marshall. *Educ:* Grammar and High Sch., nr Sebastopol, California; Univ. of California, Berkeley. BS, 1931; PhD, 1933. Instr of Chemistry, Univ. of California, 1933-38; Asst Prof., 1938-45; Associate Prof., 1945;

Prof., Enrico Fermi Inst. for Nuclear Studies, Univ. of Chicago, 1945-54; Research Associate, Geophysics Lab., Carnegie Instn, 1954-59; Atomic Energy Commission: Mem., 1954-59; Cttee of Sen. Reviewers, 1945-52; Gen. Advisory Cttee, 1950-54, 1960-63; Member: Plowshare Advisory Cttee, 1959-; Advisory Board of Guggenheim Memorial Foundn, 1959-; Edit. Board, Science, 1962-70. Director, Douglas Aircraft Co., 1963-67. Member: Air Resources Board, State of California, 1967-; President's Task Force on Air Pollution, 1969-70; US-Japan Cttee on Scientific Co-operation, 1970-. Holds hon. doctorates in Science. Nobel Prize for Chemistry, 1960. Has received numerous awards from universities and scientific institutions. Member: National Academy of Science; Royal Swedish Academy of Science, American Phil. Society; American Academy of Arts and Sciences; Heidelberg Academy Science; Fellow, Amer. Nuclear Soc.; Corres. Fellow, British Acad.; Mem. several professional societies and fraternities. *Publications:* Radiocarbon Dating, 1952 (3rd edn, 1965); author of numerous articles appearing principally in scientific journals (Journal American Chemistry Society, Phys. Review, Proc. National Academy Science, Journal Geophys. Research, Science, etc.). *Recreations:* swimming, golf. *Address:* (office) Department of Chemistry, University of California, Los Angeles, California 90024, USA. *T:* 825-1968. *Club:* Cosmos (Washington, DC); Explorer's (Los Angeles).

**LICHFIELD,** 5th Earl of, *cr* 1831; **Thomas Patrick John Anson;** Viscount Anson and Baron Soberton, 1806; *b* 25 April 1939; *s* of Viscount Anson (Thomas William Arnold) (*d* 1958) and Princess Georg of Denmark (*née* Anne Fenella Ferelith Bowes-Lyon); *S* grandfather, 1960. *Educ:* Harrow Sch.; RMA, Sandhurst. Joined Regular Army, Sept. 1957, as Officer Cadet; Grenadier Guards, 1959-62 (Lieut). Now Photographer. *Heir: kinsman* Geoffrey Rupert Anson [*b* 28 Jan. 1929; *m* 1957, Verna Grace Hall; three *s* one *d*]. *Address:* 20 Aubrey Walk, W8. *T:* 01-727 4468; (seat) Shugborough Hall, Stafford. *T:* Little Haywood 454. *Club:* Guards.

**LICHFIELD, Bishop of,** since 1953; **Rt. Rev. Arthur Stretton Reeve,** DD (Lambeth), 1953; DD (Leeds), 1956; *b* 11 June 1907; *s* of Rev. Arthur and Mrs Violet Inez Reeve; *m* 1936, Flora Montgomerie (*née* McNeill); one *s* two *d*. *Educ:* Brighton Coll. (Exhibitioner); Selwyn Coll., Cambridge (Scholar); Westcott House, Cambridge. 1st class Theological Tripos, 1928, 2nd class Theological Tripos, 1929; BA 1929, MA 1933; rowed in Cambridge Univ. crew, 1930. Curate of Putney, 1930-32; Domestic Chaplain to Bishop of Winchester and Joint Hon. Secretary, Winchester Diocesan Council of Youth, 1932-36; Vicar of Highfield, Southampton, 1936-43; Vicar of Leeds, 1943-53; Rural Dean of Leeds, 1943-53; Proctor in Convocation for Diocese of Ripon, 1945-53; Hon. Canon of Ripon Cathedral, 1947-53; Chaplain to the Queen, 1952-53 (to King George VI, 1945-52). Hon. Fellow, Selwyn Coll., Cambridge, 1955-. *Address:* Bishop's House, The Close, Lichfield. *T:* Lichfield 2251. *Clubs:* Athenæum; Leander (Henley on Thames).

**LICHFIELD, Dean of;** *see* Holderness, Rt Rev. G. E.

**LICHINE, Mme David;** *see* Riabouchinska, Tatiana.

**LICHINE, David;** Choreographer; *b* 25 Dec. 1910; *m* 1942, Tatiana Riabouchinska, *qv*; one *d*. *Educ:* in France. De Basil Champs-Elysées Ballet and then Marquis de Cuevas Ballet, 1932-49. Choreography: over 25 ballets. Last Ballets seen in London: La Création, La Rencontre (Ballets des Champs-Elysées); Infanta, Enchanted Mill (de Cuevas); Symphonic Impressions, Concerto Grosso, Graduation Ball, Nutcracker (London Festival Ballet). *Address:* 965 Oakhurst Drive, Los Angeles 49, California, USA.

**LICKLEY, Robert Lang,** BSc; DIC; CEng; FRAeS; FIMechE; Assistant Managing Director, Hawker Siddeley Aviation Ltd, since 1965 (Director, 1963-); *b* Dundee, 19 Jan. 1912. *Educ:* Dundee High Sch.; Edinburgh Univ.; Imperial Coll. Formerly: Professor of Aircraft Design, College of Aeronautics, Cranfield; Managing Director, Fairey Aviation Ltd, Hayes, Middlesex; Chief Executive, Hawker-Blackburn Division, HSA Ltd, 1963-65. *Recreation:* golf. *Address:* c/o Hawker Siddeley Aviation Ltd, Richmond Road, Kingston-upon-Thames, Surrey.

**LIDBURY, Sir Charles,** Kt, *cr* 1941; Director of Westminster Bank Ltd, and of Westminster Foreign Bank Ltd, 1935-62; *b* 30 June 1880; *s* of Frank Albert Lidbury; *m* 1909, Mary (*d* 1939), *d* of George Moreton, Kinderton Hall, Middlewich, Cheshire; two *d*. General Manager Westminster Foreign Bank Ltd, 1928-47; General Manager, Westminster Bank Ltd, 1927-30; Chief General Manager Westminster Bank Ltd, 1930-47; President of Institute of Bankers, 1939-46. *Address:* Winter Field, Melbury Abbas, Shaftesbury, Dorset. *T:* Shaftesbury 2274. *Clubs:* Reform, National Liberal.

**LIDBURY, Sir David John,** KCMG 1948 (CMG 1941); CB 1943; DSO 1916; *b* 3 Oct. 1884; *e s* of late E. A. Lidbury, CBE; *m* 1923, Ethel (*d* 1942), *d* of late Charles Norbury; one *d*; *m* 1944, Alice (*d* 1952), *d* of late Matthew S. Morrison. *Educ:* Llandovery Sch.; Hertford Coll., Oxford. Assistant Surveyor, General Post Office, 1908. Served European War, 1914-18 (despatches, DSO); Controller, Money Order Department, 1929-34; Controller Post Office Savings Bank, 1934-35; Director of Army Postal Services to 1935; Assistant Secretary, Headquarters, GPO, 1935-38; Director, London Postal Region GPO, 1938; Principal Assistant Secretary, Ministry of Home Security, 1939-40; Assistant Director-General, GPO, 1941-47. President, 1st Commn at Postal Union Congresses at Buenos Aires (1939) and Paris (1947). Vice-President Exec. Commn of Universal Postal Union, 1947-52. Chairman, Commmn on Gold Coast Civil Service, 1950. Chairman East African Salaries Commission, 1953-54; Commissioner, Staff Revision Posts and Telegraphs Dept, Nigeria, 1955-56. Commander Order of Aviz (Portugal), 1917. *Address:* Flat 7, 37 Adelaide Crescent, Hove, Sussex. *T:* Brighton 731369.

**LIDBURY, John Towersey,** FRAeS; Deputy Managing Director, Hawker Siddeley Group Ltd, since 1970 (Director, 1960); Deputy Chairman and Managing Director, Hawker Siddeley Aviation Ltd, since 1963; Deputy Chairman: Hawker Siddeley Dynamics Ltd, since 1970; High Duty Alloys Ltd, since 1970; Deputy President, Society of British Aerospace Companies, 1970-71 (Member Council, since 1959); *b* 25 Nov. 1912; *m* 1939, Audrey Joyce (*née* Wigzell); one *s* two *d*. *Educ:* Owen's Sch. Joined Hawker Aircraft Ltd, 1940; Secretary, 1948, Director, 1951, General Manager, 1953; Director and General Manager, Hawker Aircraft (Blackpool) Ltd, 1956; became Joint Managing Director

Hawker Siddeley Aviation Ltd, 1959, Director and Chief Exec., 1961; Managing Director, Hawker Aircraft Ltd, and of Folland Aircraft Ltd, 1959, Chairman of both companies, 1961. Director: A. V. Roe & Company Ltd, 1959-; Whitworth Gloster Aircraft Ltd, 1959-; Hawker Siddeley Internat. Ltd, 1963-. Vice Pres. 1968-69, Pres. 1969-70, Soc. of British Aerospace Companies Ltd (formerly Soc. of British Aircraft Constructors Ltd). JP Kingston-upon-Thames, 1952-62. *Address:* 18 St James's Square, SW1. *T:* 01-930 2064. *Clubs:* Royal Aero; Richmond Golf.

**LIDDELL,** family name of **Baron Ravensworth.**

**LIDDELL, Dr Donald Woollven;** FRCP 1964; Head of Department of Psychological Medicine, King's College Hospital; Physician to Bethlem and Maudsley Hospitals; *b* 31 Dec. 1917; *m* 1954, Emily (*née* Horsfall); one *s* one *d*. *Educ:* Aldenham Sch.; London Hospital. MRCP 1941; Neurological training as RMO, The National Hospital, Queen Square, 1942-45; Psychiatric training, Edinburgh and Maudsley Hospital. Medical Superintendent, St Francis Hospital, Haywards Heath, 1957-61. *Publications:* contrib. Journal of Mental Science, Journal of Neurology, Psychiatry and Neuro-surgery, American Journal of Mental Diseases, Journal of Social Psychology. *Address:* 49 Bury Walk, SW3.

**LIDDELL, Edward George Tandy,** FRS 1939; MD, BCh, MA, Oxon; *b* 25 March 1895; *m* 1923, Constance Joan Mitford, *y d* of late Dr B. M. H. Rogers; three *s* one *d*. *Educ:* Summer Fields; Harrow; Trinity Coll., Oxon; St Thomas' Hospital. 1st class Physiology Finals, Oxford, 1918; Asst Serum Dept, Lister Institute, 1918; Senior Demy, Magdalen Coll., Oxford, 1918; BM Oxon, 1921; Fellow of Trinity Coll., Oxford, 1921-40; University Lecturer in Physiology, Oxford Univ., 1921-40; Waynflete Professor of Physiology, Oxford, 1940-60; Professor Emeritus, 1960; Fellow of Magdalen Coll., 1940-60, Emeritus Fellow, 1970. *Publications:* Papers, various since 1923, on physiology of central nervous system, published in Journal Physiol., Brain, Proc. Royal Society, Quarterly Journal of Experimental Physiology; assistant author of Sherrington's Mammalian Physiology, 1929; Reflex Activity of the Spinal Cord, 1932 (jointly); The Discovery of Reflexes, 1960. *Recreation:* FRHS. *Address:* 69 Old High Street, Headington, Oxford.

**LIDDELL, (John) Robert;** author; *b* 13 Oct. 1908; *e s* of late Major J. S. Liddell, CMG, DSO, and Anna Gertrude Morgan. *Educ:* Haileybury Coll.; Corpus Christi Coll., Oxford. Lecturer in Universities of Cairo and Alexandria, 1942-51, and assistant professor of English, Cairo Univ., 1951; Head of English Dept, Athens Univ., 1963-68. *Publications:* The Last Enchantments, 1948; The Rivers of Babylon, 1959; An Object for a Walk, 1966; The Deep End, 1968; Stepsons, 1969, and other novels; A Treatise on the Novel, 1947; Aegean Greece, 1954; The Novels of I. Compton-Burnett, 1955; Byzantium and Istanbul, 1936; The Morea, 1958; The Novels of Jane Austen, 1963; Mainland Greece, 1965. *Address:* c/o Barclays Bank, High Street, Oxford.

**LIDDELL, Peter John,** DSC 1944; MA; FZS; farmer; *b* 2 June 1921; *s* of Comdr Lancelot Charles Liddell, OBE, RN, and Rosalie Liddell (*née* Ballantyne); *m* 1st, 1948, Dorothy Priscilla Downes; two *s* one *d*; 2nd, 1960, Helen Ann, *d* of Rear-Adm. A. W. Laybourne, *qv*. *Educ:* Ampleforth; Wadham Coll., Oxford (MA). Served RNVR, 1940-46 (DSC). Mem., Cumberland River Board, 1954-65; Chm., Cumberland River Authority, 1970- (Mem. 1964; Vice-Chm. 1967-70); Vice-Chm., Assoc. of River Authorities, 1969- (Chm. Fisheries Cttee, 1967-); Chm. Internat. Adv. Gp, Internat. Salmon Foundn, NYC, 1970-; Vice-Pres., Inst. of Fisheries Management, 1969-; Pres., River Eden and District Fisheries Assoc., 1970- (Chm. 1956-70). Mem. Exec. Cttee: Central Coun. of Physical Recreation; Salmon and Trout Assoc.; Atlantic Salmon Res. Trust Ltd; Cumberland and Westmorland Playing Fields Assoc.; many other adv. or local bodies. Mem., The Sports Council, 1969-; Dep. Chm., Northern Adv. Coun. for Sport and Recreation; Vice-Chm., Standing Conf. of Northern Sport and Recreation, 1967-. Churchill Fellow, 1968. Freeman: City of Newcastle upon Tyne, 1953; City of London, 1969. *Publications:* articles in various jls, yearbooks, etc. *Recreations:* fishing, shooting, watching cricket. *Address:* Moorhouse Hall, Warwick-on-Eden, Carlisle. *T:* Wetheral 60356; 30d Cadogan Square, SW1. *T:* 01-584 4660. *Clubs:* White's, Beefsteak, Naval, MCC; County (Carlisle); International Fario (Paris).

**LIDDELL, Robert;** *see* Liddell, J. R.

**LIDDERDALE, David William Shuckburgh,** CB 1963; Clerk Assistant, House of Commons, since 1962; *b* 30 Sept. 1910; *s* of late Edward Wadsworth and Florence Amy Lidderdale; *m* 1943, Lola, *d* of late Rev. Thomas Alexander Beckett, Tubbercurry and Ballinew; one *s*. *Educ:* Winchester; King's Coll., Cambridge (MA). Assistant Clerk, House of Commons, 1934. Served War of 1939-45, The Rifle Brigade; active service, N Africa and Italy. Senior Clerk, 1946, Fourth Clerk at the Table, 1953, Second Clerk Assistant, 1959, House of Commons. Joint Secretary Autonomous Sect. of Secretaries-General of Parliaments (Inter-Parliamentary Union), 1946-54. Temporarily attached to Consultative Assembly of Council of Europe during sessions, 1949-53. *Publications:* The Parliament of France, 1951; (with Lord Campion) European Parliamentary Procedure, 1953. *Recreation:* walking. *Address:* 46 Cheyne Walk, SW3. *T:* 01-352 0432. *Clubs:* Travellers', MCC.

**LIDDLE, Major Donald Ross;** *b* 11 Oct. 1906; *s* of Thomas Liddle, Bonnington, Edinburgh; *m* 1933, May, *d* of R. Christie, Dennistoun, Glasgow; one *s* two *d*. *Educ:* Allen Glen's School, Glasgow. Served War of 1939-45 with RAOC, Burma and India; Major, 1944. DL, County of Glasgow, 1963; Lord Provost of Glasgow, 1969. *Address:* 15 Riddrie Crescent, Glasgow E3. *Club:* Conservative (Glasgow).

**LIENHOP, Hon. Sir John,** Kt, *cr* 1952; former Member of the Legislative Council for Bendigo, Victoria; pastoralist; *b* Bendigo, 1898. *Educ:* State Sch., Kangaroo Flat. Formerly Wool Growers' representative, State Wool Council. Chairman War-time Location of Industries Cttee; Minister for Public Works and Decentralisation, 1942-45; Minister for Electrical Undertakings and Mines, 1947-48; for two years was Government Leader in the Legislative Council; Agent-General for Victoria (in London), 1950-56. Chairman Bendigo Jockey Club. *Address:* 28 Wallace Avenue, Toorak, Victoria 3142, Australia. *Club:* Athenæum (Melbourne).

**LIESCHING, Sir Percivale,** GCMG 1951 (KCMG 1944; CMG 1932), KCB 1947; KCVO 1953; *b* 1895; *m* 1924, Georgina, *d* of late James Williamson, Tunbridge Wells; three *d*. *Educ:* Bedford Sch.; Brasenose Coll., Oxford, MA.

Served European War, 1914 and 1917-18 (despatches); East African Expeditionary Force, 1916; appointed to the Colonial Office, 1920; transferred to the Dominions Office, 1925; seconded to staff of High Commissioner for the United Kingdom in Canada, 1928-32; Political Secretary, Office of the High Commissioner for the United Kingdom in S. Africa, 1933-35; Official Secretary, Office of the High Commissioner for the United Kingdom in Australia, 1936-38; Assistant Under-Secretary of State, Dominions Office, 1939-42; Second Secretary, Board of Trade, 1942-46; Permanent Secretary, Ministry of Food, 1946-48; Permanent Under-Secretary of State, Commonwealth Relations Office, 1949-55; High Commissioner for the UK in South Africa, and High Commissioner for Basutoland, Bechuanaland Protectorate, and Swaziland, 1955-58. *Address:* The Lodge, 10 Broadwater Down, Tunbridge Wells, Kent. *T:* Tunbridge Wells 27341. *Club:* Travellers'.

*See also J. P. Hayes.*

**LIFAR, Serge;** Dancer, Choreographer, Writer; Director, Institut Chorégraphique, since 1947; Professeur de Chorélogie, Sorbonne; lately Maître de Ballet, Professeur, Théâtre National de l'Opéra, Paris; *b* Kieff, South Russia, 2 April 1905. Pupil of Bronislava Nijinska, 1921; joined Diaghileff company, Paris, 1923; studied under Cecchetti. First London appearance, in Cimarosiana and Les Fâcheux, Coliseum, 1924. Choreographer (for first time) of Stravinsky's Renard, 1929; produced Prométhée, Opera House, Paris, 1929. Cochran's 1930 Revue, London Pavilion, 1930; returned to Paris, produced and danced in Bacchus and Ariadne, Le Spectre de la Rose, Giselle, and L'Après-midi d'un Faune, 1932; Icare, David Triomphant, Le Roi Nu, 1936; Alexandre le Grand, 1937; arranged season of Ballet at the Cambridge, London, 1946; Choreographer of Noces Fantastiques, Romeo et Juliette (Prokofiev), 1955. Prix de l'Académie Française. *Publications:* Traditional to Modern Ballet, 1938; Diaghilev, a biography, 1940; A History of Russian Ballet from its Origins to the Present Day (trans. 1954); The Three Graces, 1959; Ma Vie, 1965 (in Eng., 1969). *Address:* Villa des Lauriers, Palais de Provence, Cannes, France.

**LIFFORD,** 8th Viscount *cr* 1781; **Alan William Wingfield Hewitt;** *b* 11 Dec. 1900; 2nd but *o surv. s* of Hon. George Wyldbore Hewitt (*d* 1924; 7th *s* of 4th Viscount Lifford) and Elizabeth Mary, *e d* of late Charles Rampini, DL, LLD, Advocate; *S kinsman* 1954; *m* 1935, Alison Mary Patricia, *d* of T. W. Ashton, The Cottage, Hursley, nr Winchester; one *s* three *d*. *Educ:* Winchester; RMC, Sandhurst. Lieut late Hampshire Regt. *Heir:* *s* Hon. Edward James Wingfield Hewitt, *b* 27 Jan. 1949. *Address:* Field House, Hursley, Hants. *T:* Hursley 3.

*See also Sir Anthony Swann, Bt.*

**LIGHTBOUND, Rt. Rev. Aloysius Anselm;** Member Order of St Benedict; Titular Abbot of St Augustine's, Canterbury; Abbot of Belmont, 1948-53, resigned. *Address:* St Mary's Priory, 22 Church Road, Harrington, Cumberland.

**LIGHTHILL, Dr (Michael) James;** FRS 1953; FRAeS; Lucasian Professor of Mathematics, University of Cambridge, since 1969; a Secretary and Vice-President of the Royal Society, 1965-69; *b* 23 Jan. 1924; *s* of E. B. Lighthill; *m* 1945, Nancy Alice Dumaresq; one *s* four *d*. *Educ:* Winchester Coll.; Trinity Coll., Cambridge. Aerodynamics Division, National Physical Laboratory, 1943-45; Fellow, Trinity Coll., Cambridge, 1945-49; Senior Lecturer in Maths, University of Manchester, 1946-50; Beyer Professor of Applied Mathematics, University of Manchester, 1950-59; Director, Royal Aircraft Establishment, Farnborough, 1959-64; Royal Society Research Prof., Imperial College, 1964-69. Chairman, Academic Advisory Cttee, University of Surrey, 1964; Member: Advisory Council on Technology, 1964; Natural Environment Research Council, 1965-70; Shipbuilding Inquiry Cttee, 1965; First President, Institute of Mathematics and its Applications, 1964-66. FRAeS 1961. Foreign Member: American Academy of Arts and Sciences, 1958; American Philosophical Soc., 1970. Hon. Fellow American Inst. of Aeronautics and Astronautics, 1961. Hon. DSc: Liverpool, 1961; Leicester, 1965; Strathclyde, 1966; Essex, 1967; Princeton, 1967; East Anglia, 1968; Manchester, 1968; Bath, 1969; St Andrews, 1969; Surrey, 1969. Royal Medal, Royal Society, 1964; Gold Medal, Royal Aeronautical Society, 1965, etc. Comdr Order of Léopold, 1963. *Publications:* Introduction to Fourier Analysis and Generalised Functions; articles in Royal Society Proc. and Trans., Quarterly Journal of Mechanics and Applied Maths, Philosophical Magazine, Journal of Aeronautical Sciences, Quarterly Journal of Maths, Aeronautical Quarterly, Communications on Pure and Applied Mathematics, Proc. Cambridge Philosophical Society, Journal of Fluid Mechanics, Reports and Memoranda of Aeronautical Research Council. Contrib. to Modern Developments in Fluid Dynamics: High Speed Flow; High Speed Aerodynamics and Jet Propulsion; Surveys in Mechanics; Laminar Boundary Layers. *Recreations:* music and swimming. *Address:* Department of Mathematics, Cambridge. *Club:* Athenæum.

**LIGHTMAN, Harold,** QC 1955; Master of the Bench of Lincoln's Inn; General Commissioner of Income Tax, Lincoln's Inn; *b* 8 April 1906; *s* of Louis Lightman, Leeds; *m* 1936, Gwendoline Joan, *d* of David Ostrer, London; three *s*. *Educ:* City of Leeds Sch.; privately. Accountant, 1927-29. Barrister, Lincoln's Inn, 1932. Home Guard, 1940-45. Defence Medal, 1946. Liveryman, Company of Glovers, 1960. *Recreations:* walking, reading. *Address:* Stone Buildings, Lincoln's Inn, WC2. *T:* 01-242 3840. *Club:* Royal Automobile.

**LIGHTON, Sir Christopher Robert,** 8th Bt, *cr* 1791; MBE 1945; *b* 30 June 1897; *o s* of 7th Bt and Helen (*d* 1927), *d* of late James Houldsworth, Coltness, Lanarkshire; *S* father, 1929; *m* 1st 1926, Rachel Gwendoline (marr. dissolved, 1953), *yr d* of late Rear-Admiral W. S. Goodridge, CIE; two *d*; 2nd, 1953, Horatia Edith, *d* of A. T. Powlett, Godminster Manor, Bruton, Somerset; one *s*. *Educ:* Eton Coll.; RMC. Late The King's Royal Rifle Corps; rejoined the Army in Aug. 1939 and served War of 1939-45. *Heir:* *s* Thomas Lighton, *b* 4 Nov. 1954. *Address:* Elphinstone House, North Berwick, East Lothian.

**LIGHTWOOD, Reginald,** MD; FRCP; Consulting Physician to The Hospital for Sick Children, Great Ormond Street, London, and Consulting Paediatrician to St Mary's Hospital, London, since 1963; President, British Pædiatric Association, 1959-60; Fellow of Royal Society of Medicine; Hon. Fellow American Academy of Pediatrics; Hon. Member, Swedish and Portuguese Paediatric Societies; Corresponding Member of Société de Pédiatrie de Paris and of the American Pediatric Society; *b* 1898; *s* of late John M. Lightwood, Barrister-at-Law, and Gertrude (*née* Clench); *m* 1937, Monica Guise Bicknell, *d* of Laurance G. Ray; two *s*. *Educ:* Monkton Combe Sch., Bath. Served European War in Royal Artillery, 1917-19. Jelf Medal and Alfred Hughes Memorial Prize, King's Coll., London, 1919; MD (London), 1924, FRCP 1936. Hon. Medical Staff: Westminster Hospital, 1933-39 (resigned); Hospital for Sick Children, Great Ormond Street, London, 1935-63; St Mary's Hospital, London, 1939-63; Prof. of Pediatrics, American University of Beirut, 1964 and 1965, and Civilian Consultant to Royal Jordanian Army Medical Service; Prof. of Paediatrics and Child Health, University Coll. of Rhodesia, 1966-69. Kenneth Blackfan Memorial Lecturer, Harvard Medical Sch., 1953; Visiting Prof. of Pediatrics: Boston Univ., 1966; Univ. of Calif, Los Angeles, 1969. *Publications:* Textbooks: Pædiatrics for the Practitioner (ed jtly with Prof. W. Gaisford); Sick Children (with Dr F. S. W. Brimblecombe and Dr D. Barltrop); scientific papers and articles on pædiatrics in medical journals, textbooks, etc. *Address:* Hillfoot Farm, Beenham, near Reading, Berks. *T:* Woolhampton 3342. *Club:* Bath.

**LILEY, Prof. Albert William,** CMG 1967; PhD; FRSNZ; Professor in Perinatal Physiology, New Zealand Medical Research Council Postgraduate School of Obstetrics and Gynæcology, University of Auckland; *b* 12 March 1929; *s* of Albert Harvey Liley; *m* 1953, Helen Margaret Irwin, *d* of William Irwin Hunt; two *s* three *d*. *Educ:* Auckland Grammar Sch.; University of Auckland; University of Otago; Australian National Univ.; Columbia Univ. BMedSc 1952; MB, ChB (UNZ) 1954; PhD (ANU) 1957; Dip. Obst. (UA) 1962; FRSNZ 1964. Research Schol. in Physiology, ANU, 1955-56. Sandoz Research Fellow in Obstetrics, Postgrad. Sch. of Obstetrics and Gynæcology, 1957-58; NZMRC Research Fellow in Obstetrics, 1959-. United States Public Health Service Internat. Research Fellowship, 1964-65. *Publications:* numerous articles in physiological, obstetric and pædiatric journals. *Recreations:* farming, forestry. *Address:* 19 Pukenui Road, Epsom, Auckland 3, New Zealand. *T:* 656-433.

**LILFORD,** 7th Baron, *cr* 1797; **George Vernon Powys;** *b* 8 Jan. 1931; *s* of late Robert Horace Powys (*g g grandson* of 2nd Baron) and of Vera Grace Bryant. Rosebank, Cape, SA; *S* kinsman, 1949; *m* 1st, 1954, Mrs Eve Bird (marr. diss.); 2nd, 1957, Anuta Merritt (marr. diss., 1958); 3rd, 1958, Norma Yvonne Shell (marr. diss., 1961); 4th, 1961, Mrs Muriel Spottiswoode (marr. diss., 1969); two *d*; 5th, 1969, Margaret Penman. *Educ:* St Aidan's Coll., Grahamstown, SA; Stonyhurst Coll. *Recreations:* shooting, boating, cricket. *Heir: cousin*, Frank Lilford Powys [*b* 1902; *m* 1929, Gertrude Frances Elizabeth, *d* of G. G. F. Meyer; one *s*]. *Address:* Bowerswood House, Nateby, near Garstang, Lancs; (Seat) Bank Hall, Preston, Lancs.

**LILIENTHAL, David Eli;** Business Executive; Author; *b* Morton, Ill., 8 July 1899; *s* of Leo Lilienthal and Minna Rosenak; *m* 1923, Helen Marian Lamb; one *s* one *d*. *Educ:* DePauw Univ. (AB, LLD); LLB Harvard, 1923. Admitted Illinois bar, 1923; practised law, Chicago, 1923-31; Wisconsin Public Service Commn, 1931; Director, Tennessee Valley Authority, 1933 (Chairman 1941-46); Chairman, State Dept Board of Consultants on international control of atomic energy, 1946; Chairman, US Atomic Energy Commn, 1946-50; Chairman, Development and Resources Corporation, 1955-; Member of: Delta Upsilon, Delta Sigma Rho, Sigma Delta Chi, Phi Beta Kappa, American Academy of Arts and Sciences. Trustee: The Twentieth Century Fund; Education and World Affairs Inc.; Freedom Award, 1949; Public Welfare Medal of National Academy of Science, 1951. Holds Hon. Doctorates from Institutions in USA; also foreign awards. *Publications:* TVA–Democracy on the March, 1944; This I Do Believe, 1949; Big Business: A New Era, 1953; The Multinational Corporation, 1960; Change, Hope and the Bomb, 1963; The Journals of David E. Lilienthal, Vols I and II, 1964; Vol. III, 1966; Vol. IV, 1969; Management: a Humanist Art, 1967; articles in miscellaneous periodicals. *Recreations:* gardening, small-boat sailing. *Address:* (home) 88 Battle Road, Princeton, NJ 08540, USA; (office) One Whitehall Street, New York, NY 10004, USA. *Clubs:* Century Association (New York).

**LILLEY, Francis James Patrick;** *b* 24 July 1907; *s* of Francis John Charles Lilley; *m* 1937, Agnes Crossley Mackay, Glasgow; two *s*. *Educ:* Bellahouston Academy. Served with Argyll and Sutherland Highlanders, 1934-40; with 12th Battalion City of Glasgow Home Guard, 1941-45; Lieut-Colonel, 1942. Elected to Glasgow Corporation, 1957; has served on education and municipal transport cttees. Chairman, F. J. C. Lilley Ltd group of cos, civil engineering and public works contractors, etc. MP (C) Kelvingrove Division of Glasgow, 1959-64; PPS to Minister of Power, 1960-64, to Minister of Pensions, 1964. *Recreations:* golf and yachting. *Address:* 5 Le Boulevard, La Rocque, Jersey, CI. *T:* Jersey East 715. *Clubs:* Constitutional; Conservative (Glasgow); Royal Scottish Motor Yacht.

**LILLICRAP, Harry George;** Senior Director, Customer Services (formerly Senior Director, Planning), Post Office, since 1967; *b* 29 June 1913; *s* of late Herbert Percy Lillicrap; *m* 1938, Kathleen Mary Charnock; two *s*. *Educ:* Erith County Sch.; University College, London. BSc (Eng) 1934. Post Office Engineering Dept, 1936-50; Principal, Post Office, 1951; Assistant Secretary, 1958; Under-Secretary, 1964; Director of Radio Services, 1964-67. *Address:* Thornhurst, Felbridge, East Grinstead, Sussex. *T:* East Grinstead 25811.

**LILLIE, Beatrice, (Lady Peel);** actress; *b* Toronto, 19 May 1898; *d* of John Lillie, Lisburn, Ireland, and Lucie Shaw; *m* 1920, Sir Robert Peel, 5th Bt (*d* 1934); (one *s* killed on active service 1942). *Educ:* St Agnes' Coll., Belleville, Ontario. First appearance, Alhambra, 1914; at the Vaudeville, Prince of Wales's etc., 1915-22; in The Nine O'Clock Revue, Little Theatre, 1922; first New York appearance, Times Square Theatre, in André Charlot's Revue, 1924; in Charlot's Revue at Prince of Wales's, 1925; in New York, 1925-26; at The Globe and The Palladium, 1928; This Year of Grace, New York, 1928; Charlot's Masquerade, at the Cambridge, London, 1930; New York; 1931-32; at the Savoy and London Palladium, 1933-34; New York, 1935; Queen's, London, 1939; Big Top, Adelphi, 1940; Troops: Africa, Italy, etc., 1942-45; Seven Lively Arts, Ziegfeld, New York, 1945; Better Late, Garrick, London, 1946; appeared in television and radio programmes, England and America, 1946-47; Inside USA, New York, 1948, subs. on tour for one year, USA; returned to London (cabaret), 1950 and June 1951. Solo artiste at several Royal performances; appeared in NY television, 1951-52; produced one-woman show, Summer Theatre, 1952; subs. on tour and produced show in Broadway, Oct. 1952-June 1953. Radio and TV, London, July-Aug. 1953. Road tour in US of this production, Sept. 1953-June 1954; London, 1954-55. An Evening with Beatrice

Lillie, Globe, AEWBL, Florida, Feb and March, 1956; 2nd one-woman show, Beasop's Fables, USA, June-Sept. 1956; Ziegfeld Follies, New York, 1957; Auntie Mame, Adelphi, London, 1958. Appeared in films: Exit Smiling, 1927; Doctor Rhythm, 1938; On Approval, 1944; Around the World in Eighty Days, 1956; Thoroughly Modern Millie, 1967. Free French Liberation Medal, N. Africa, 1942, also African Star and George VI Medal, Donaldson. Award, USA, 1945, also Antoinette Perry Award, New York, 1953, and many others. *Recreation:* painting. *Address:* 55 Park Lane, W1; Drayton Manor, Staffs.

**LILLIE, Very Rev. Henry Alexander,** MA; Dean of Armagh since 1965; *b* 11 May 1911; *s* of David William Lillie and Alicia Lillie (*née* Morris), Carrick-on-Shannon; *m* 1942, Rebecca Isobel, *yr d* of Andrew C. Leitch, Homelea, Omagh, Co. Tyrone; one *d. Educ:* Sligo Grammar Sch.; Trinity Coll., Dublin. BA 1935, MA 1942. Junior Master, Grammar Schools: Elphin, 1932; Sligo, 1932-34. Deacon, 1936; Curate Asst, Portadown, 1936-41; Incumbent of: Milltown, 1941-47; Kilmore, 1947-52; Armagh, 1952-65; Armagh Cathedral: Prebendary of Tynan, 1952-60; Treas., 1960-61; Chancellor, 1961; Precentor, 1961-65; Dean and Keeper, 1965-. Keeper of Armagh Public Library, 1965. *Recreations:* reading, fishing, gardening. *Address:* The Library, Abbey Street, Armagh. *T:* Armagh 3142.

**LILLIE, John Adam;** QC; LLD; Sheriff of Fife and Kinross; *b* 25 July 1884; *e s* of Thomas Lillie and Ellen Harper Tait. *Educ:* Brockley's Acad., Broughty Ferry; Aberdeen Grammar Sch.; University of Aberdeen (MA 1906); University of Edinburgh (LLB 1910). Admitted to Faculty of Advocates, 1912; called to English Bar, 1921; Lecturer on Mercantile Law, University of Edinburgh, 1928-47; KC (Scotland) 1931; Member Royal Commn on Workmen's Compensation, 1938; Sheriff of Fife and Kinross, 1941. Chairman for Scotland Board of Referees under Income Tax Acts, 1942-45; Chairman for Scotland and NI of British Motor Trade Assoc. Price Protection Cttee, 1949-52; Legal Commissioner and Dep. Chairman, General Board of Control for Scotland, 1944-62; Convener of the sheriffs, 1960-65; Hon. LLD Aberdeen, 1967. *Publications:* The Mercantile Law of Scotland (6th edn, 1965); Articles in Green's Encyclopædia of the Law of Scotland on Company Law, and Sale of Goods; The Northern Lighthouses Service, 1965. *Address:* 85 Great King Street, Edinburgh. *T:* 031-556 1862. *Club:* Scottish Liberal (Edinburgh).

**LIM, Sir Han-Hoe,** Kt, *cr* 1946; CBE 1941; Hon. LLD (Malaya); MB, ChB (Edinburgh); JP; Pro-Chancellor, University of Malaya, 1949-59; *b* 27 April 1894; 2nd *s* of late Lim Cheng Sah, Singapore; *m* 1920, Chua Seng Neo; two *s* two *d. Educ:* St Andrew's Sch. and Raffles Institution; University of Edinburgh. RMO North Devon General Hospital, with charge of Military Auxiliary Hospital, 1919; Municipal Commissioner, Singapore, 1926-31; Member of Legislative Council, Straits Settlements, 1933-42, and its Finance Cttee, 1936-42; Member of Exec. Council, Straits Settlements, 1939-42; Member of Advisory Council, Singapore, 1946-48; Member of Exec. Council, Singapore, 1948-50. Member of Council, King Edward VII College of Medicine, Singapore, 1930-42; Member of Public Services Commission, Singapore, 1952-56. *Recreations:* tennis, chess. *Address:* 758 Mountbatten Road, Singapore. *T:* 40655. *Clubs:* Garden, Singapore Chinese Recreation (Singapore).

**LIMBU;** *see* Rambahadur Limbu.

**LIMENTANI, Prof. Uberto;** Professor of Italian, University of Cambridge, since 1962; Fellow of Magdalene College, Cambridge; *b* Milan, 15 Dec. 1913; *er s* of Prof. Umberto Limentani and Elisa Levi; *m* 1946, Barbara Hoban; three *s. Educ:* University of Milan (Dr in Giurispr., Dr in Lettere); University of London (PhD); University of Cambridge (MA). Commentator and script-writer Italian Section, BBC European Service, 1939-45. Lector 1945, Assistant Lecturer, 1948, Lecturer, 1952, in Italian, University of Cambridge. Corresp. Member Accademia Letteraria Ital. dell'Arcadia, 1964. *Publications:* Stilistica e Metrica, 1936; Poesie e Lettere Inedite di Salvator Rosa, 1950; L'Attività Letteraria di Giuseppe Mazzini, 1950; La Satira nel Seicento, 1961; The Fortunes of Dante in Seventeenth Century Italy, 1964; (ed.) The Mind of Dante, 1965. Co-editor yearly review, Studi Secenteschi (founded 1960); an ed. of Italian Studies. Transl.: E. R. Vincent's Ugo Foscolo Esule fra gli Inglesi, 1954. Several contrib. on Italian Literature to: Encyclopædia Britannica; Cassell's Encyclopædia of Literature; Italian Studies; La Bibliofilia; Giornale Storico della Letteratura Italiana; Amor di Libro; Studi Secenteschi; Il Pensiero Mazziniano; Bollettino della Domus Mazziniana; Il Ponte; Cambridge Review; Modern Language Review. *Recreations:* walking in the Alps, fencing, photography. *Address:* 17 St Barnabas Road, Cambridge. *T:* Cambridge 58198.

**LIMERICK,** 6th Earl of, *cr* 1803 (Ire.); **Patrick Edmund Pery,** MA, CA; Baron Glentworth, 1790 (Ire.); Viscount Limerick, 1800 (Ire.); Baron Foxford, 1815 (UK); Director: Kleinwort, Benson Ltd; Robert Benson, Lonsdale & Co. Ltd; Airlease International Management Ltd; Commercial Bank of Australia Ltd (London Advisory Board); *b* 12 April 1930; *e s* of 5th Earl of Limerick, GBE, CH, KCB, DSO, TD, and Angela Olivia (*see* Angela Countess of Limerick); *S* father, 1967; *m* 1961, Sylvia Rosalind, MA (Oxon), *er d* of Maurice S. Lush, *qv*; two *s* one *d. Educ:* Eton; New Coll., Oxford. A Dep. Chm., BNEC Cttee for Middle East Trade; Mem. Council, London Chamber of Commerce. CA 1957. *Heir: s* Viscount Glentworth, *qv. Address:* Chiddinglye, West Hoathly, East Grinstead, Sussex. *T:* Sharpthorne 214; 30 Victoria Road, W8. *T:* 01-937 0573.

**LIMERICK, Angela Countess of,** GBE 1954 (DBE 1946; CBE 1942); **Angela Olivia;** *b* 27 Aug. 1897; *yr d* of late Lt-Col Sir Henry Trotter, KCMG, CB; *m* 1926, Hon. Edmund Colquhoun Pery, later 5th Earl of Limerick, GBE, CH, KCB, DSO, TD (*d* 1967); two *s* one *d. Educ:* North Foreland Lodge, Broadstairs; London Sch. of Economics. Vice-Chm. of the Council, British Red Cross Soc.; Vice-Chm., League of Red Cross Societies; Chm., Standing Commission, International Red Cross; served as VAD at home and overseas, 1915-19; Poor Law Guardian, 1928-30; on Kensington Borough Council, 1929-35, Chm of Maternity and Child Welfare and Public Health Cttees; Mem. for South Kensington on LCC, 1936-46; Privy Council rep. on Gen. Nursing Council for England and Wales, 1933-50; Mem. of Royal Commn on Equal Pay, and of various Govt Cttees; Dep. Chm. of War Organization BRCS and Order of St John, 1941-47. Hon. LLD Manchester Univ., 1945, Leeds Univ., 1951. DStJ, 1952. Commander's Gold Cross, Order of Merit, Republic of Austria, 1959. Red Cross Decorations; Médaille de Vermeil, French Red Cross, 1945; Silver Medal, American Red

Cross, 1946; Gold Medal (1st class), Belgian Red Cross, 1946; First Class Medal, German Red Cross, 1954; Gold Medal of Merit, Swedish Red Cross, 1957; Gold Medal, Greek Red Cross, 1959; Gold Medal, Turkish Red Crescent, 1959. *Address:* Chiddinglye, West Hoathly, East Grinstead, Sussex. *T:* Sharpthorne 214.

*See also Earl of Limerick and P. F. Thorne.*

**LIMERICK, Bishop of, (RC),** since 1958; **Most Rev. Henry Murphy,** DD; *b* 19 May 1912; *s* of Patrick Murphy and Mary Nash. *Educ:* St Patrick's Coll., Maynooth. BSc 1932; DD 1938 (Maynooth, postgraduate studies). Ordained Priest 1936. Prof., St Munchin's Coll., Limerick, 1938-58. *Address:* Kilmoyle, North Circular Road, Limerick, Ireland. *T:* Limerick 44974.

**LIMERICK, Dean of;** *see* Talbot, Very Rev. M. J.

**LIN YUTANG,** MA (Harvard), PhD (Leipzig), LittD (Elmira and Rutgers, USA); Author; *b* 10 Oct. 1895; *s* of Lin Chiseng and Yang Sunming; *m* 1919, Lian Tsulfeng; three *d*. *Educ:* St John's Univ., Shanghai; Harvard Univ. Prof. of English at Peking Univ., 1923-26; Sec. of Min. of Foreign Affairs, 1927; Chancellor, Nanyang Univ., Singapore, 1954-55. *Publications:* My Country and My People, 1935; History of the Press and Public Opinion, 1936; Importance of Living, 1937; Wisdom of Confucius (Modern Library), 1938; Moment in Peking, 1939; With Love and Irony, 1940; A Leaf in the Storm, 1941; Wisdom of China and India, 1942; Between Tears and Laughter, 1943; The Vigil of a Nation, 1945; The Gay Genius, 1947; Chinatown Family, 1948; Wisdom of Laotse, 1948; (compiled and edited) The Wisdom of China, 1949; Peace is in the Heart, 1950; On the Wisdom of America, 1950; Widow, Nun and Courtesan, 1951; Famous Chinese Short Stories, 1952; The Vermillion Gate, 1953; The Unexpected Island, 1955; Lady Wu, 1956; The Secret Name, 1959; From Pagan to Christian, 1960; Importance of Understanding, 1961; Imperial Peking: Seven Centuries of China, 1961; The Red Peony, 1961; The Pleasures of a Nonconformist, 1962; Juniper Loa, 1963; The Flight of the Innocents, 1964; The Chinese Theory of Art, 1967. Edited: The Wisdom of Laotse; The Wisdom of Confucius, 1959. *Recreation:* fishing. *Address:* William Heinemann Ltd, 15-16 Queen Street, Mayfair, W1.

**LINCOLN, Bishop of,** since 1956; **Rt. Rev. Kenneth Riches,** DD, STD; *b* 20 Sept. 1908; *s* of Capt. A. G. Riches; *m* 1942, Kathleen Mary Dixon, JP 1964; two *s* one *d*. *Educ:* Royal Gram. Sch., Colchester; Corpus Christi Coll., Cambridge. Curate of St Mary's, Portsea, 1932-35; St John's, East Dulwich, 1935-36; Chaplain and Librarian, Sidney, Sussex Coll., Cambridge, 1936-42; Examining Chaplain to Bishops of Bradford and Wakefield, 1936; Editorial Sec., Cambridgeshire Syllabus, 1935; Editor, Cambridge Review, 1941-42; Rector of Bredfield with Boulge, Suffolk, and Dir of Service Ordination Candidates, 1942-45; Principal of Cuddesdon Theological Coll., Oxford, and Vicar of Cuddesdon, 1945-52; Hon. Canon of Portsmouth Cathedral, 1950-52; Bishop Suffragan of Dorchester, Archdeacon of Oxford and Canon of Christ Church, 1952-56. Select Preacher University of Cambridge, 1941, 1948, 1961, and 1963. University of Oxford, 1954-55. Mem. Archbishops' Commission on Training for the Ministry, 1942; Sec. of Theol. Commn on the Church of Faith and Order Movement. Visiting Lecturer the General Theological Seminary, New York, 1956 and 1962. Hon. Fellow of Sidney Sussex Coll., Cambridge, 1958. Chm., Central Advisory Council for the Ministry, 1959-65. *Recreations:* gardening, antiques, and country Life. *Address:* The Bishop's House, Lincoln. *T:* 25430.

**LINCOLN, Assistant Bishop of;** *see* Clarkson, Rt Rev. G. W.; Healey, Rt Rev. K.; Otter, Rt Rev. A.

**LINCOLN, Dean of;** *see* Fiennes, Very Rev. Hon. O. W. T. -W.

**LINCOLN, Archdeacon of;** *see* Smith, Ven. Arthur Cyril.

**LINCOLN, Sir Anthony (Handley),** KCMG 1965 (CMG 1958); CVO 1957; Ambassador to Venezuela, 1964-69; *b* 2 Jan. 1911; *s* of late J. B. Lincoln, OBE; *m* 1948, Lisette Marion Summers; no *c*. *Educ:* Mill Hill Sch.; Magdalene Coll., Cambridge (BA). Prince Consort and Gladstone Prizes, 1934. Appointed Asst Principal, Home Civil Service, 1934; subsequently transferred to Foreign Service; served in Foreign Office; on UK Delegation to Paris Peace Conf., 1946, and in Buenos Aires. Counsellor, and Head of a Dept of Foreign Office, 1950. Dept. Sec.-Gen., Council of Europe, Strasbourg, France, 1952-55; Counsellor, British Embassy, Copenhagen, 1955-58; British Ambassador to Laos, 1958-60; HM Minister to Bulgaria, 1960-63; Officer Order of Orange Nassau, 1950; Comdr Order of Dannebrog, 1957. *Publication:* Some Political and Social Ideas of English Dissent, 1937. *Recreations:* country pursuits. *Clubs:* St James', Reform.

**LINCOLN, Anthony Leslie Julian,** QC 1968; Practising Barrister, Writer and Broadcaster; *b* 7 April 1920; *s* of Samuel and Ruby Lincoln. *Educ:* Highgate; Queen's Coll., Oxford (Schol., MA). Served Somerset Light Inf. and RA, 1941-45. Called to Bar, 1949. Vice-Princ., Working Men's Coll., 1955-60; Chm. and Trustee, Harrison Homes for the Elderly, 1963-; Chm., Working Men's Coll. Corp., 1969-; Trustee, Fund for Research into Ageing Process. *Publications:* (Ed.), Lord Eldon's Anecdote Book, 1960; regular contribs to Observer, Spectator and other jls. *Recreations:* fishing, cricket, walking. *Address:* 9 Paultons Sq., Chelsea, SW3. *T:* 01-352 0519; Heale Park Cottage, Upper Woodford, Salisbury, Wilts; 2 Hare Court, Temple, EC4. *T:* 01-353 0076. *Clubs:* Beefsteak, United University.

**LINCOLN, Fredman Ashe,** QC 1947; MA, BCL; Captain RNVR; Recorder of Gravesend since 1967; Master of the Bench, Inner Temple, since 1955; Master of the Moots, 1955-64, and 1968-70; *s* of Reuben and Fanny Lincoln; *m* 1933, Sybil Eileen Cohen; one *s* one *d*. *Educ:* Hoe Gram. Sch., Plymouth; Haberdashers' Aske's Sch.; Exeter Coll., Oxford, 1928; called to Bar, Inner Temple, Nov. 1929; joined RNV(S)R, 1937; served in Royal Navy (RNVR), Sept. 1939-May 1946; Mediterranean, 1943, with commandos in Sicily and Italy at Salerno landings, 1943; assault crossing of Rhine, March 1945 (despatches twice); Renter Warden of Worshipful Company of Plaisterers, 1946-47, Master, 1949-50; Freeman and Liveryman of City of London; fought general election 1945 (C) Harrow East Div. (Middx.); Chm. Administrative Law Cttee of Inns of Court Conservative Association, 1951; Mem. Exec., Gen. Council of the Bar, 1957-61. Vice-Pres., RNR Officers' Club; Chm., London Flotilla, *Publications:* The Starra, 1939; Secret Naval Investigator, 1961. *Recreations:* yachting, tennis. *Address:* 2 Harcourt Buildings, Temple,

EC4. *T:* 01-353 7202. *Clubs:* United Service, Royal Automobile, MCC, Naval; Royal Corinthian Yacht (Burnham-on-Crouch and Cowes); Bar Yacht.

**LINCOLN, Air Cdre Philip Lionel,** CB 1945; DSO 1918; MC 1916; late RAF; late Chairman, R. Passmore & Co.; *b* 20 Jan. 1892; *s* of Philip Passmore Lincoln and Louisa Baxter; *m* 1916, Kathleen Daisy Shepherd (*d* 1965); two *s*. *Educ:* Framlingham Coll. Entered family business R. Passmore & Co., 1910, partner 1913; Pres., Building Industry Distributors, 1948. 2nd Lt Northumberland Fusiliers, 1914; Capt. 1915; Major, 1917; Lt-Col 1918; served France and Italy (wounded twice, despatches, MC, DSO); demobilised 1919. Flying Officer AAF Balloon Branch; Squadron Leader to Command No. 902 Squadron, 1938; Wing Comdr 1939; Group Capt. 1940; Air Commodore, 1941. *Address:* 2 Church Lane, Bearsted, Maidstone, Kent. *T:* Maidstone 37106.

**LIND-SMITH, Gerard Gustave; His Honour Judge Lind-Smith;** Judge of County Courts (Warwickshire), since 1967; *b* 1903; *o s* of C. F. Lind-Smith, Liverpool; *m* 1928, Alexandra Eva, *e d* of Lt-Col J. C. Kirk, CBE, Monmouthshire; three *d*. *Educ:* Wellington Coll.; University Coll., Oxon. Called to Bar, Inner Temple, 1928. JP and Dep. Chm. Ches. QS, 1957, Chm., 1961-68. Recorder of Birkenhead, 1958-59; County Court Judge (Birmingham), 1959-66. *Address:* Pitt House, Wellesbourne, Warwick. *T:* 345. *Club:* English-Speaking Union.

**LINDBERGH, Anne Spencer Morrow;** author, United States; *b* 1906; *d* of Dwight Whitney Morrow and Elizabeth Reeve Morrow (*née* Cutter); *m* 1929, Col Charles Augustus Lindbergh, *qv*; three *s* two *d* (and one *s* decd). *Educ:* Miss Chapin's Sch., New York City; Smith Coll., Northampton, Mass (two prizes for literature). Received Cross of Honour of United States Flag Association for her part in survey of air route across Atlantic, 1933; received Hubbard Gold Medal of National Geographical Soc. for work as co-pilot and radio operator in flight of 40,000 miles over five continents, 1934. Hon. MA, Smith Coll., Mass., 1935. *Publications:* North to the Orient, 1935; Listen, the Wind, 1938; The Wave of the Future, 1940; The Steep Ascent, 1944; Gift from the Sea, 1955; The Unicorn, 1958; Dearly Beloved, 1963; Earth Shine, 1970. *Address:* c/o Harcourt, Brace & Co., 383 Madison Avenue, New York, NY 10017, USA.

**LINDBERGH, Col Charles Augustus,** AFC, DSC; Special Adviser on technical matters to Chief of Staff, US Air Force; nominated Brigadier-General by Mr Eisenhower; *b* Detroit, 4 Feb. 1902; *s* of late Charles Augustus Lindbergh and Evangeline Lodge Land; *m* 1929, Anne (*see* Anne Lindbergh), *d* of late Dwight W. Morrow; three *s* two *d* (and one *s* decd). *Educ:* University of Wisconsin. Enrolled in Flying Sch., Lincoln, Nebraska, 1922; flew alone from New York to Paris, 1927; flew from America to Copenhagen via Greenland, Iceland and the Shetland Isles, 1933, with a view to establishing a Transatlantic air route. *Publication:* The Spirit of Saint Louis, 1953 (Pulitzer Prize, 1954). *Relevant publication:* The Hero, Charles A. Lindbergh: The Man and the Legend, by Kenneth S. Davis, 1960. *Address:* Scott's Cove, Darien, Conn, USA.

**LINDEN, Anya;** Ballerina, Royal Ballet, 1958-64; *b* 3 Jan. 1933; English; *d* of George Charles and Ada Dorothea Eltenton; *m* 1963, Hon. John Sainsbury, *qv*; two *s* one *d*. *Educ:* Berkeley, Calif; Sadler's Wells Sch. Entered Sadler's Wells Sch., 1947; promoted to 1st Company, 1951; became Soloist, 1952. Principal rôles in the ballets: Copelia; Sylvia; Prince of Pagodas; Sleeping Beauty; Swan Lake; Giselle; Cinderella; Agon; Solitaire; Noctambules; Fête Etrange; Symphonic Variations; Invitation; Firebird; Lady and the Fool; Antigone. *Recreation:* drawing. *Address:* c/o Royal Opera House, Covent Garden, WC2.

**LINDESAY-BETHUNE,** family name of **Earl of Lindsay.**

**LINDGREN,** family name of **Baron Lindgren.**

**LINDGREN,** Baron, *cr* 1961, of Welwyn Garden City (Life Peer); **George Samuel Lindgren, DL;** *b* 11 Nov. 1900; *s* of George William Lindgren, Islington, London; *m* 1926, Elsie Olive, *d* of Frank Reed, Chishill, Herts; one *s*. *Educ:* Hungerford Road LCC Elementary Sch. LNER Railway clerk. Mem. National Executive Cttee of Railway Clerks' Association, 1933-46; Chm. London Trades Council 1938-42. Mem. of Welwyn Garden City UDC, 1927-45; of Herts County Council, 1931-49; re-elected, 1952. Dep. Regional Commissioner, Midland Region, 1942-45. MP (Lab) Wellingborough Div. of Northamptonshire, 1945-Sept. 1959; Parly Sec. to: Ministry of: National Insurance, 1945-46; Civil Aviation, 1946-50; Town and Country Planning, 1950-51; Housing and Local Govt, Jan.-Oct. 1951; Joint Parly Sec., Min. of Transport, 1964-66; Parly Sec., Min. of Power, 1966-70. Treasurer, Transport Salaried Staffs Assoc., 1956-61. DL Herts, 1966. *Recreation:* swimming. *Address:* 4 Attimore Close, Welwyn Garden City. *T:* Welwyn Garden 22669.

**LINDISFARNE, Archdeacon of;** *see* Bates, Ven. Mansel Harry.

**LINDLEY, Sir Arnold (Lewis George),** Kt 1964; DSc; CGIA, FIMechE, FIEE; Chairman, Engineering Industry Training Board, since 1964; Deputy-Chairman, Motherwell Bridge (Holdings) Ltd, 1965; *b* 13 Nov. 1902; *s* of George Dilnot Lindley; *m* 1927, Winifred May Cowling (*d* 1962); one *s* one *d*; *m* 1963, Mrs Phyllis Rand. *Educ:* Woolwich Polytechnic. Chief Engineer BGEC, South Africa, 1933; Director: East Rand Engineering Co., 1943; BGEC, S Africa, 1945; Gen. Manager Erith Works, GEC, 1949; GEC England, 1953; Vice-Chm. 1959, Managing Dir, 1961-62, Chm., 1961-64, of GEC; retd. Chairman: BEAMA, 1963-64; Internat. Electrical Assoc., 1962-64. President, Instn of Mechanical Engineers, 1968-; Member: Council, City and Guilds of London Inst., 1969-; Council, City University, 1969-. Appointed by Govt to advise on QE2 propulsion turbines, 1969. *Recreations:* sailing and golf. *Address:* The Crest, Raggleswood, Chislehurst, 1969-; Council, City University, 1969-. *T:* 01-467 2159. *Clubs:* Chislehurst Golf; Medway Yacht.

**LINDLEY, Bryan Charles;** Director, Electrical Research Association, since 1968; *b* 30 Aug. 1932; *m* 1956, Joan Mary McGill; one *s*. *Educ:* Reading Sch.; University Coll., London. BSc (Eng) 1954; PhD 1960; FIMechE 1968; FIEE 1968; FInstP 1968; FInstD 1968. National Gas Turbine Establishment, Pyestock, 1954-57; Hawker Siddeley Nuclear Power Co. Ltd, 1957-59; C. A. Parsons & Co. Ltd, Nuclear Research Centre, Newcastle upon Tyne, 1959-61; International Research and Development Co. Ltd, Newcastle upon Tyne, 1962-65; Man., R&D Div., C. A. Parsons & Co. Ltd, Newcastle upon Tyne, 1965-68; Dir, ERA Patents Ltd, 1968. *Publications:* articles on plasma physics, electrical and mechanical engineering, management science, impact of technological innovation, etc, in learned jls. *Recreations:* literature, ski-ing. *Address:* 11 Badingham Drive, Fetcham Park, Leatherhead, Surrey. *T:* Leatherhead 2237. *Club:* Number Ten.

**LINDLEY, Prof. Dennis Victor;** Professor and Head of Department of Statistics, University College, London, since 1967; *b* 25 July 1923; *s* of Albert Edward and Florence Louisa Lindley; *m* 1947, Joan Armitage; one *s* two *d*. *Educ:* Tiffin Boys' Sch., Kingston-on-Thames; Trinity Coll., Cambridge. MA Cantab 1948. Min. of Supply, 1943-45; Nat. Physical Lab., 1945-46 and 1947-48; Statistical Lab., Cambridge Univ., 1948-60 (Dir, 1957-60); Prof. and Head of Dept of Statistics, UCW, Aberystwyth, 1960-67. Vis. Prof., Chicago and Stanford Univs, 1954-55, Harvard Business Sch., 1963. Guy Medal (Silver), Royal Statistical Soc., 1968. Fellow, Inst. Math. Statistics; Fellow, American Statistical Assoc.; Mem., Internat. Statistical Inst. *Publications:* (with J. C. P. Miller) Cambridge Elementary Statistical Tables, 1953; Introduction to Probability and Statistics (2 vols), 1965; contribs to Royal Statistical Soc., Biometrika, Annals of Math. Statistics. *Address:* 8 Hill Close, NW11. *T:* 01-455 4822.

**LINDNER, Doris Lexey Margaret;** sculptress; *b* 8 July 1896. *Educ:* Norland Place, London; St Martin's Art School; Frank Calendron Animal Sch.; British Academy, Rome. Modelled animals for Royal Worcester Porcelain Co. for over 40 years. Has made bronzes of Horses; also carved in stone, wood, concrete etc. *Recreation:* bridge. *Address:* Studio Cottage, Broad Campden, Glos. *T:* Campden 608.

**LINDO, Sir (Henry) Laurence,** Kt 1967; CMG 1957; High Commissioner for Jamaica in London, since 1962; Ambassador to France, since 1966, to Federal Republic of Germany, since 1967; *b* 13 Aug. 1911; *e s* of Henry Alexander and Ethel Mary Lindo (*née* Gibson); *m* 1943, Holly Robertson Clacken; two *d*. *Educ:* Jamaica Coll., Jamaica; Keble Coll., Oxford. Rhodes Scholar, 1931; OUAC 1934. Inspector of Schools, Jamaica, 1935; Asst Information Officer, 1939-43; asst Sec., Colonial Secretariat, 1945; Principal Asst Sec., 1950. Administrator, Dominica, Windward Islands, 1952-59. Actg Governor, Windward Islands, 1957 and 1959; Governor's Sec., Jamaica, 1960-62. *Address:* 48 Grosvenor Street, W1. *Clubs:* Travellers', West Indian.

**LINDON, Sir Leonard (Charles Edward),** Kt 1964; MS, FRCS, FRCSE, FRACS; Hon. Surgeon and Neuro-Surgeon, Royal Adelaide Hospital; Associate Lecturer in Surgery, University of Adelaide; *b* Adelaide, 8 Feb. 1896; *s* of late J. H. Lindon, Adelaide; *m* 1921, Jean, *d* of late Dr H. Marten; two *s* one *d*. *Educ:* Geelong Gram. Sch.; St Peter's Coll., Adelaide; Universities of Adelaide and Oxford; London and Guy's Hospitals. Rhodes Scholar 1918. MB, BS 1919; MRCS LRCP 1920; FRCSEd 1922; FRCS 1922; MS Adelaide 1923; FRACS 1929. Served European War, 1914-18: Private, AIF, 1914-16; served War of 1939-45; Lt-Col, Australian Army Medical Corps, AIF, 1939-41 (despatches). Pres., Royal Australasian Coll. of Surgeons, 1959-61 (Vice-Pres., 1957-59); Mem., BMA (Pres. South Australian Branch, 1934-35). *Address:* 222 Brougham Place, North Adelaide, South Australia; 178 North Terrace, Adelaide, South Australia. *Club:* Adelaide (Adelaide, SA).

**LINDOP, Audrey Beatrice Noël E.;** *see* Erskine-Lindop, A. B. N.

**LINDSAY,** family name of **Earl of Crawford** and **Baron Lindsay of Birker.**

**LINDSAY,** 14th Earl of, *cr* 1633; **William Tucker Lindesay-Bethune;** Lord Lindsay of The Byres, 1445; Baron Parbroath, 1633; Viscount Garnock; Baron Kilbirny, Kingsburne, and Drumry, 1703; Representative Peer, 1947-59; late Major, Scots Guards; Member of Queen's Body Guard for Scotland, Royal Company of Archers; *b* 28 April 1901; *s* of 13th Earl and Ethel (*d* 1942), *d* of W. Austin Tucker, Boston, USA; assumed addtl surname of Bethune, 1939; *S* father, 1943; *m* 1925, Marjory, DStJ, *d* of late Arthur J. G. Cross and Lady Hawke; two *s* two *d*. Served War of 1939-45 (wounded); retd pay, 1947. Hon. Col, Fife and Forfar Yeomanry/Scottish Horse, 1957-62. Zone Comr for Northern Civil Defence Zone of Scotland, 1963-69. Pres., Shipwrecked Fishermen and Mariners Royal Benevolent Soc., 1966-. DL Co. of Fife. KStJ. *Heir: s* Viscount Garnock, *qv*. *Address:* Lahill, Upper Largo, Fife. *T:* Upper Largo 251; 6 Denbigh House, Hans Place, SW1. *Clubs:* Guards; New (Edinburgh).

**LINDSAY OF BIRKER,** 2nd Baron, *cr* 1945; **Michael Francis Morris Lindsay;** Professor and Chairman of Far Eastern Programme in School of International Service, The American University, Washington, DC; *b* 24 Feb. 1909; *e s* of 1st Baron Lindsay of Birker, CBE, LLD, and Erica Violet (*née* Storr) (*d* 1962); *S* father 1952; *m* 1941, Li Hsiao-li, *d* of Col Li Wen-chi of Lishih, Shansi; one *s* two *d*. *Educ:* Gresham's Sch., Holt; Balliol Coll., Oxford. Adult education and economic research work in S Wales, 1935-37; Tutor in Economics, Yenching Univ., Peking, 1938-41; Press Attaché, British Embassy, Chungking, 1940. Served War of 1939-45, with Chinese 18th Group Army, 1942-45. Visiting Lecturer at Harvard Univ., 1946-47; Lecturer in Economics, University Coll., Hull, 1948-51; Senior Fellow of the Dept of International Relations, Australian National Univ., Canberra, 1951-59 (Reader in International Relations, 1959): Visiting Prof., Yale Univ., 1958. *Publications:* Educational Problems in Communist China, 1950; The New China, three views, 1950; China and the Cold War, 1955; Is Peaceful Co-existence Possible?, 1960; articles in learned journals. *Recreations:* wireless, tennis. *Heir: s* Hon. James Francis Lindsay, *b* 29 Jan. 1945. *Address:* c/o School of International Service, The American University, Washington 16, DC, USA; 6812 Delaware Street, Chevy Chase 15, Md, USA.

**LINDSAY, Master of; Anthony Robert Lindsay;** *b* 24 Nov. 1958; *s* and *heir* of Lord Balniel, *qv*.

**LINDSAY, Maj.-Gen. Courtenay Traice David,** CB 1963; Director-General of Artillery, War Office, 1961-64, retired; *b* 28 Sept. 1910; *s* of late Courtenay Traice Lindsay and Charlotte Editha (*née* Wetenhall); *m* 1934, Margaret Elizabeth, *d* of late William Pease Theakston, Huntingdon; two *s*. *Educ:* Rugby Sch.; RMA Woolwich. 2nd Lt RA, 1930. Mem., Ordnance Board (Col), 1952; Dir of Munitions, British Staff (Brig.), Washington, 1959; Maj.-Gen. 1961. *Address:* Huggits Farm, Stone-in-Oxney, Tenterden, Kent. *Club:* Royal Automobile.

**LINDSAY, Sir Daryl;** *see* Lindsay, Sir E. D.

**LINDSAY, Donald Dunrod;** Headmaster Malvern College, 1953-71; *b* 27 Sept. 1910; *s* of Dr Colin Dunrod Lindsay, Pres. BMA 1938, and Mrs Isabel Baynton Lindsay; *m* 1936, Violet Geraldine Fox; one *s* one *d*. *Educ:* Clifton Coll., Bristol; Trinity Coll., Oxford. Asst Master, Manchester Gram. Sch., 1932;

Asst Master, Repton Sch., 1935; temp. seconded to Bristol Univ. Dept of Education as lecturer in History, 1938; Senior History Master, Repton Sch., 1938-42; Headmaster Portsmouth Gram. Sch., 1942-53. Chm., Headmasters' Conference, 1968. *Publications:* A Portrait of Britain Between the Exhibitions, 1952; A Portrait of Britain, 1688-1851, 1954; A Portrait of Britain Before 1066, 1962. *Recreations:* walking, theatre, music. *Address:* Headmaster's House, Malvern College, Worcs. *T:* Malvern 4472; (from Aug. 1971) 34 Belgrave Road, Seaford, Sussex.

**LINDSAY, Maj.-Gen. (Retd) Edward Stewart,** CB 1956; CBE 1952 (OBE 1944); DSO 1945; Assistant Master General of Ordnance, 1961-64; Deputy Controller, Ministry of Supply, 1957-61; *b* 11 July 1905; *s* of Col M. E. Lindsay, DSO, DL, Craigfoodie, Dairsie, Fife; *m* 1933, Margaret, *d* of late Gen. Sir Norman Macmullen, GCB, CMG, CIE, DSO; two *d* (one *s* decd). *Educ:* Harrow Sch.; Edinburgh Univ. (BSc). 2nd Lt, RA 1926; served War of 1939-45, NW Europe (OBE, DSO); despatches, 1946; Col 1949; Brig. 1953; Maj.-Gen. 1955; Prin. Staff Officer to High Comr, Malaya, 1954-56. Comdr Legion of Merit, USA, 1947. *Address:* Hill Cottage, Eversley, Hants. *T:* Eversley 3107. *Club:* Army and Navy.

**LINDSAY, Sir (Ernest) Daryl,** Kt 1956; LLD; Chairman of Council, Australian National Art Gallery, Canberra; Director, National Gallery of Victoria, Australia, 1941-56, retired; *b* 31 Dec. 1889; *s* of Robert Charles Lindsay, MD, and Jane Elizabeth Lindsay; *m* 1922, Joan A'Beckett, *d* of Mr Justice Weigall, Supreme Court of Victoria; no *c*. *Educ:* Creswick State Sch.; Creswick Gram. Sch. Bank clerk from 1907; pastoral pursuits, NSW, Queensland and Vic., 1908-14. Served European War, 1915-18 (war service medals); official War Artist, Med. Section, Queens Hosp., Sidcup, Kent (for Facial Restoration), 1918-19. Studied at Slade Sch. of Art, University of London, 1919; followed profession of painting. Australia, 1919-39; Keeper of the Prints, Nat. Gallery of Vic., 1939; appointed Dir of Gallery, 1941. Mem., Cttee of Aust. Art Advisory Board; Mem., Nat. Capital Devel. Commn; Overseas Vice-Pres., National Trust for Scotland. ARWS 1937; medals for services to Art, 1952, 1956; Queen's Medal, 1955. Rep. by oil paintings and water colours, drawings, etc. in all Australian Nat. Galleries and at Victoria and Albert Museum, London. Hon. LLD Australian National Univ., Canberra. *Publications:* (with Lady Lindsay) The Story of the Red Cross, 1940; Historical Record of the Felton Bequests; The Leafy Tree, My Family, 1965. *Recreation:* farming. *Address:* Mulberry Hill, Baxter, Vic 3418, Australia. *T:* Baxter 8-7292. *Clubs:* Melbourne, Victoria Racing (Melbourne).

**LINDSAY, Rt. Rev. Hugh;** Auxiliary Bishop of Hexham and Newcastle, (RC), and Titutlar Bishop of Chester-le-Street, since 1969; *b* 20 June 1927; *s* of William Stanley Lindsay and Mary Ann Lindsay (*née* Warren). *Educ:* St Cuthbert's Grammar Sch., Newcastle upon Tyne; Ushaw Coll., Durham. Priest 1953. Asst Priest; St Lawrence's, Newcastle upon Tyne, 1953; St Mathew's, Ponteland, 1954; Asst Diocesan Sec., 1953-59; Diocesan Sec., 1959-69; Chaplain, St Vincent's Home, West Denton, 1959-69. *Recreation:* walking. *Address:* St Vincent's Home, The Roman Way, West Denton, Newcastle upon Tyne NE15 7LT. *T:* Lemington 67-9481.

**LINDSAY, Jack;** author, *b* Melbourne, Australia, 1900; *s* of late Norman Lindsay; *m* 1958, Meta Waterdrinker; one *s* one *d*. *Educ:* Queensland Univ., BA, FRSL. Soviet Badge of Honour, 1968. *Publications:* Fauns and Ladies (Poems); Marino Faliero (Verse Drama); Hereward (Verse drama); Helen Comes of Age (Three verse plays); Passionate Neatherd (Poems); William Blake, Creative Will and the Poetic Image, an Essay; Dionysos; The Romans; The Anatomy of Spirt; Mark Antony; John Bunyan; Short History of Culture; Handbook of Freedom; Song of a Falling World; Byzantium into Europe; Life of Dickens; Meredith; The Romans were Here; Arthur and his Times; A World Ahead; Daily Life in Roman Egypt; Leisure and Pleasure in Roman Egypt; Men and Gods on the Roman Nile; Origins of Alchemy; Cleopatra; The Clashing Rocks; translations of Lysistrata, Women in Parliament (Aristophanes), complete works of Petronius, Love Poems of Propertius, A Homage to Sappho, Theocritos, Heronadas, Catullus, Ausonius, Latin Medieval Poets, I am a Roman; Golden Ass; Edited Metamorphosis of Aiax (Sir John Harington, 1956;) Loving Mad Tom (Bedlamite Verses); Parlement of Pratlers (J. Eliot, 1593); Blake's Poetical Sketches; Into Action (Dieppe), a poem; Russian Poetry, 1917-55 (selections and translations); Memoirs of J. Priestley; *novels:* Cressida's First Lover; Rome for Sale; Cæsar is Dead, Storm at Sea; Last Days with Cleopatra; Despoiling Venus; The Wanderings of Wenamen; Come Home at Last; Shadow and Flame; Adam of a New World; Sue Verney; 1649; Lost Birthright; Hannibaal Takes a Hand; Brief Light; Light in Italy; The Stormy Violence; We Shall Return; Beyond Terror; Hullo Stranger; The Barriers are Down; Time to Live; The Subtle Knot; Men of Forty-Eight; Fires in Smithfield; Betrayed Spring; Rising Tide; Moment of Choice; The Great Oak; Arthur and His Times; The Revolt of the Sons; The Way the Ball Bounces; All on the Never-Never (filmed as Live Now–Pay Later); Masks and Faces; Choice of Times; Thunder Underground; *history:* 1764; The Writing on the Wall; *autobiography;* Life Rarely Tells; The Roaring Twenties; Fanfrolico and After; Meetings with Poets; *Art-criticism;* The Death of the Hero; Life of Turner; Cézanne. *Recreation:* anthropology. *Address:* Castle Hedingham, Halstead, Essex.

**LINDSAY, Hon. James;** *b* 16 Dec. 1906; *yr s* of 27th Earl of Crawford and Balcarres; *m* Bronwen, *d* of late Lord Howard de Walden; three *s* one *d*. *Educ:* Eton; Magdalen Coll., Oxford. Contested (C) Bristol South-East, 1950 and 1951; MP (C) N Devon, 1955-Sept. 1959. *Address:* Througham Slad, Bisley, Stroud, Glos. *T:* Bisley 221. *Club:* Travellers'.

**LINDSAY, Sir James Harvey Kincaid Stewart,** Kt 1966; Chairman, The Metal Box Company of India Ltd, Calcutta; *b* 31 May 1915; *s* of Arthur Harvey Lindsay and Doris Kincaid Lindsay; *m* 1948; one *s* one *d*. *Educ:* Highgate Sch. Joined Metal Box Co. Ltd, 1934; joined Metal Box Co. of India Ltd; Man. Dir, 1961; Chm., 1967. President: Bengal Chamber of Commerce and Industry; Associated Chambers of Commerce and Industry of India, 1965-66. Director: Indian Oxygen Co., 1966; Westinghouse, Saxby Farmer Ltd, 1966. Pres., Calcutta Management Association, 1964; Pres., All India Management Assoc., 1964-69; Mem. of Governing Body: India Inst. of Management, Calcutta, 1964; Administrative Staff Coll. of India, 1965; Indian Institutes of Technology, 1966; National Council of Applied Economic Research, 1966; All-India Board on Management Studies, 1964; Indian Inst. of Foreign Trade, 1965; National Council on Vocational and Allied Trades, 1963. *Recreations:* music, golf, riding, table tennis.

*Address:* Christmas Cottage, Lower Shiplake, near Henley-on-Thames, Oxon. *T:* Wargrave 2856. *Clubs:* Oriental, Public Schools; Bengal (Calcutta); Delhi Gymkhana (New Delhi).

**LINDSAY, John Vliet;** Mayor of New York City (elected as Republican-Liberal, Nov. 1965, re-elected as Liberal-Independent, Nov. 1969); *b* 24 Nov. 1921; *s* of George Nelson and Eleanor (Vliet) Lindsay; *m* 1949, Mary Harrison; one *s* three *d. Educ:* St Paul's Sch., Concord, NH; Yale Univ. BA 1944; LLB 1948. Lt US Navy, 1943-46. Admitted to: NY Bar, 1949; Fed. Bar, Southern Dist NY, 1950; US Supreme Court, 1955. Counsel of law firm of Webster, Sheffield, Fleischman, Hitchcock & Chrystie, NYC, 1953-55; Exec. Asst to US Attorney Gen., 1955-57; Mem., 86th-89th Congresses, 17th Dist, NY, 1959-65. *Publications:* Journey into Politics, 1967; The City, 1970. *Address:* (home) Gracie Mansion, East End Avenue, New York, NY 10028, USA. *T:* (office) 566-1000.

**LINDSAY, Kenneth;** *b* 16 Sept. 1897; *s* of George Michael Lindsay and Anne Theresa Parmiter; unmarried. *Educ:* St Olave's; Worcester Coll., Oxford. Served European War, HAC, 1916-18; Pres., Oxford Union, 1922-23; Leader, First Debating Visit to Amer. Univs. Barnett Research Fellow, Toynbee Hall, 1923-26; Councillor and Guardian, Stepney, 1923-26; Dir of Voluntary Migration Societies, Dominions Office, 1929-31; First Gen. Sec. Political and Economic Planning, 1931-35; MP (Ind. Nat.) Kilmarnock Burghs, 1933-45; MP (Ind.) Combined English Universities, 1945-50; Civil Lord of the Admiralty, 1935-37; Parliamentary Sec., Board of Education, 1937-40; Founder of Youth Service, and of CEMA (now Arts Council); a Vice-Pres., Educational Interchange Council (Ex-Chm.); Ex-Chm. National Book League; Dir, Anglo-Israel Assoc.; Vis. Prof. at many Amer. Univs. Contested Oxford, Harrow and Worcester. *Publications:* Social Progress and Educational Waste; English Education; Eldorado–An Agricultural Settlement: Towards a European Parliament; European Assemblies. *Recreations:* Association Football, Oxford University, 1921-22; Corinthians; cricket, Authentics. *Address:* 48 Basildon Court, Devonshire Street, W1. *T:* 01-486 2178. *Club:* Athenæum.

**LINDSAY of Dowhill, Sir Martin (Alexander),** 1st Bt *cr* 1962, of Dowhill; CBE 1952; DSO 1945; Representer of Baronial House of Dowhill, 22nd in derivation from Sir William Lindsay, 1st of Dowhill, 1398; *b* 22 Aug. 1905; *s* of late Lt-Col A. B. Lindsay, 2nd KEO Gurkhas; *m* 1st, 1932, Joyce (marr. diss., 1967), *d* of late Major Hon. Robert Lindsay, Royal Scots Greys; two *s* one *d*; 2nd, 1969, Lœlia, Duchess of Westminster, *o d* of 1st Baron Sysonby, PC, GCB, GCVO, Treasurer to HM King George V. *Educ:* Wellington Coll.; RMC, Sandhurst. 2nd Lt Royal Scots Fusiliers, 1925. Served Army 1925-36 and 1939-45. Active service on staff Norway 1940 (despatches), and 1st Bn The Gordon Highlanders, 51st Highland Div., July 1944-May 1945 (despatches, wounded, DSO); demobilised as Lt-Col; seconded 4th Bn Nigeria Regt, 1927; travelled West to East Africa through Ituri Forest, Belgian Congo, 1929; Surveyor to British Arctic Air-Route Expedition to Greenland (King's Polar Medal), 1930-31; Leader British Trans-Greenland Expedition, 1934; Prospective National Unionist Candidate, Brigg Div., 1936-39; MP (C) Solihull Div. of Warwicks, 1945-64. DL for County of Lincoln, 1938-45; Chm., West Midlands Area of Conservative and Unionist Associations, 1949-52; Murchison Grant, Royal Geographical Society; Gold Medallist, French Geographical Soc.; Medallist Royal Belgian Geographical Soc.; André Plaque, Royal Swedish Soc. for Geography and Anthropology; Hon. Member Royal Belgian Geographical Soc.; a Mem. of the Queen's Body Guard for Scotland (Royal Company of Archers); Gold Staff Officer, Coronation, 1953. *Publications:* Those Greenland Days, 1932; The Epic of Captain Scott, 1933; Sledge, 1935; So Few Got Through: the Diary of an Infantry Officer, 1946; Three Got Through: Memoirs of an Arctic Explorer, 1947; The House of Commons (Britain in Pictures), 1947; Shall We Reform "the Lords"?, 1948. *Heir: s* Ronald Alexander Lindsay [*b* 6 Dec. 1933; *m* 1968, Nicoletta, *yr d* of Capt. Edgar Storich, Italian Navy, retd; one *s*]. *Address:* The Old Vicarage, Send, near Woking, Surrey. *T:* Ripley 3157. *Club:* Boodle's.

**LINDSAY, Sir William,** Kt 1963; CBE 1956; DL; *b* 22 March 1907; *er s* of late James Robertson Lindsay, Tower of Lethendy, Meikleour, Perthshire, and late Barbara Coupar, *d* of late Sir Charles Barrie; *m* 1936, Anne Diana, *d* of late Arthur Morley, OBE, KC; one *s* two *d. Educ:* Trinity Coll., Glenalmond; Christ Church, Oxford. BA 1928, MA 1931; Barrister-at-Law, Inner Temple, 1931. Dir, Royal Caledonian Schs, 1934-; Admin Officer, HM Treas., 1940-45. Member: Cuckfield UD Council, 1946-67 (Chm. 1951-54); Mid-Sussex Water Bd, 1946-60 (Chm. 1952-60); E Sussex CC, 1949- (Ald. 1957, Chm. 1961-64); Nat. Health Exec. Coun. for E Sussex, 1954-66; Hailsham Hospital Management Cttee, 1956-68; National Parks Commn, 1961-68, Countryside Commn, 1968-; Chairman: E Grinstead Conservative Assoc., 1948-51 and 1957-59; Sussex Co. Cons. Org., 1951-53 and 1958-59; Vice-Chm., 1951-54 and 1957-60 and Hon. Treas. 1960-69 of SE Area of Nat. Union of Cons. and Unionist Assocs.; Mem. Nat. Exec. Cttee of Conservative Party, 1952-54 and 1957-69. DL Sussex, 1970-. Dir, Mid Sussex Water Co., 1961-. *Address:* Wickham Farm, Haywards Heath, Sussex. *T:* Haywards Heath 371. *Club:* Bath.

**LINDSAY, Sir William O'Brien,** KBE 1955; Partner in Messrs Hamilton, Harrison and Mathews, Advocates, Nairobi; *b* Kent, 8 Oct. 1909; *s* of Col M. E. Lindsay, DSO, Craigfoodie House, Dairsie; *m* 1st, 1937, Janey Sevilla Glass Hooper (marr. diss., 1962); one *s* two *d*; 2nd, 1962, Elizabeth Sturman; one *d. Educ:* Harrow; Balliol Coll., Oxford (BA). Barrister, Gray's Inn. Sudan Political Service: Asst Dist Comr, 1932; Comdt, Administrators and Police Sch., 1936; Legal Dept, Dep. Asst Legal Sec., 1938; Police Magistrate, Khartoum, 1939-41; Chief Censor, Port Sudan, 1940; Bimbashi, Sudan Defence Force, 1942. Cyrenaica: Pres. of Courts, 1943. Judge of the High Court, Sudan, 1944; Dep. Legal Sec., 1948; Chief Justice, 1950; Acting Legal Sec., 1953-54; Mem. Executive Council, Chief Justice (Independent Judiciary), 1954-55. Retired as Chief Justice of the Sudan, Sept. 1955. Chief Representative, Petroleum Development (Oman) Ltd in Muscat and Oman, 1955-58. *Recreations:* cricket, football, squash, boxing. *Address:* PO Box 30181, Nairobi, Kenya.

**LINDSAY-HOGG, Sir William (Lindsay),** 3rd Bt *cr* 1905; Chairman, Roebuck Air Charter Ltd, since 1970 (Managing Director, 1967-70); *b* 12 Aug. 1930; *s* of Sir Anthony Henry Lindsay-Hogg, 2nd Bt and Frances (*née* Doble; she *d* 1969); *S* father, 1968; *m* 1961, Victoria Pares (marr. diss. 1968); one *d. Educ:* Stowe. Hereditary Cavaliere d'Italia. *Recreations:* riding, skiing. *Heir: uncle* Edward William

Lindsay-Hogg [*b* 23 May 1910; *m* 1st, 1936, Geraldine (marr. diss. 1946), *d* of E. M. Fitzgerald; one *s*; 2nd, 1957, Kathleen Mary, *widow* of Captain Maurice Cadell, MC and *d* of James Cooney]. *Address:* 4 Marlborough Gate House, Elms Mews, W2. *T:* 01-723 6206. *Club:* No 10.

**LINDSAY-REA, R.;** *see* Rea.

**LINDSELL, Herbert George,** CB 1952; retired public official; *b* 17 May 1903; *er s* of Henry George and Elizabeth Lindsell; *m* 1924, Dorothy, *d* of John and Mildred Watts; one *s*. *Educ:* elementary and secondary schs. Board of Trade, 1918-32; Import Duties Advisory Cttee, 1932-39; Principal, 1939; Ministry of Supply, 1939-; Asst Sec., 1941; Under-Sec., 1950-59; Principal Officer (Establishments), UKAEA, 1959-63, retd; Consultant to UKAEA, 1963-70. *Address:* 105 Holland Road, Hove 2, Sussex. *T:* Brighton 734893; Wheelers Bank, Blackboys, Sussex. *T:* Framfield 279.

**LINDSELL, Lt-Gen. Sir Wilfrid Gordon,** GBE 1946 (KBE 1940; OBE 1919), KCB 1943 (CB 1942); DSO 1918; MC; retd pay, 1945; *b* 29 Sept. 1884; *s* of Col Robert F. Lindsell, CB, and Kathleen, *d* of Richard Eaton of Mitchelstown, Ireland; *m* 1st, 1916, Marjorie (*d* 1957), OBE 1946; *d* of Adm. Swinton C. Holland, of Langley House, Chichester; two *d*; 2nd, 1958, Evelyn Nairn Butler, Hobart, Tasmania. *Educ:* Birkenhead Sch.; Victoria Coll., Jersey; Royal Military Academy, Woolwich. 2nd Lt Royal Artillery, 1903; Lt 1906; Capt. 1914; Major, 1918; Bt Lt-Col 1927; Bt Col and Col, 1931; served European War, 1914-18, as ADC to CRA 7th Div.; Staff-Capt. RA 7th Div.; Bde Major RA 62nd Div.; GSO, RA, 8 Corps (despatches four times, DSO, OBE, MC, Croix de Guerre Française); DAAG War Office, 1920; Instructor DAA and QMG. School of Military Administration, 1921-23; Instructor DAQMG Staff Coll., Camberley, 1925-28; GSO1 War Office, 1930-33; Commandant Senior Officers' Sch., Sheerness, 1934-35; Dep. Military Sec., War Office, 1935-36; Comdr, Royal Artillery, 4th Div., 1937-38; Maj.-Gen. in charge of Administration, Southern Command, 1938-39; Quartermaster-Gen. of BEF; Temp. Lt-Gen., 1940; Lt-Gen. 1941; Lt-Gen. in charge of Administration in the Middle East, 1942-43; Principal Administrative Officer to the Indian Command, 1943-45 (despatches thrice, KBE, KCB, GBE, American Order of Merit, degree of Commander). LLD (Hon.) Aberdeen Univ. *Publications:* Military Organisation and Administration, 29th edition; A and Q or Military Administration in War, 3rd edition. *Address:* Flat 6, 169 Queen's Gate, SW7. *Club:* Army and Navy.

**LINDSEY,** 14th Earl of, *cr* 1626, and **ABINGDON,** 9th Earl of, *cr* 1682; **Richard Henry Rupert Bertie;** Baron Norreys, of Rycote, 1572; *b* 28 June 1931; *o s* of Hon. Arthur Michael Bertie, DSO, MC (*d* 1957) and Aline Rose (*d* 1948), *er d* of George Arbuthnot-Leslie, Warthill, Co. Aberdeen, and *widow* of Hon. Charles Fox Maule Ramsay, MC; *S* cousin, 1963; *m* 1957, Norah Elizabeth Farquhar-Oliver, *yr d* of Mark Oliver, OBE, Edgerston, Jedburgh, Roxburghshire; two *s* one *d*. *Educ:* Ampleforth. Lieut, Royal Norfolk Regt (Supplementary Reserve of Officers), 1951. Underwriting Member of Lloyd's, 1958. High Steward of Abingdon, 1963. *Heir: s* Lord Norreys, *qv*. *Address:* Hunsdonbury, Hunsdon, Ware, Hertfordshire. *T:* Stanstead Abbots 297; 8 Little Grosvenor Court, Pavilion Road, SW1. *T:* 01-235 6844. *Club:* Turf.

**LINDSEY, Archdeacon of;** *see* Jarvis, Ven. Alfred Clifford.

**LINDT, Auguste Rudolph,** LLD; Ambassador of Switzerland to India and Nepal, since 1969; *b* Berne, Switzerland, 5 Aug. 1905. Studied law at Universities of Geneva and Berne. Special correspondent of several European newspapers, in Manchuria, Liberia, Palestine, Jordan, the Persian Gulf, Tunisia, Roumania and Finland, 1932-40. Served in Swiss Army, 1940-45. Special delegate of International Cttee of the Red Cross at Berlin, 1945-46. Press Attaché, 1946, Counsellor, 1949, Swiss Legation in London. Switzerland's Permanent Observer to the United Nations (appointed 1953) and subseq. Minister plenipotentiary (1954); appointments connected with work of the United Nations: Chairman Exec. Board of UNICEF, 1953 and 1954; President, UN Opium Conference, 1953; Head of Swiss Delegation to Conference on Statute of International Atomic Energy Agency, held in New York, 1956. United Nations High Commissioner for Refugees (elected by acclamation), Dec. 1956-60; Swiss Ambassador to USA, 1960-63; Delegate, Swiss Fed. Council for Technical Co-operation, 1963-66; Swiss Amassador to Soviet Union and Mongolia, 1966-69, on leave as International Red Cross Comr-Gen. for Nigeria-Biafra relief operation, 1968-69. Hon. DrUniv Geneva, 1960; Hon. Dr, Coll. of Wilmington, Ohio, 1961. *Publication:* Special Correspondence with Bandits and Generals in Manchuria, 1933. *Address:* Embassy of Switzerland, New Delhi, India.

**LINEHAN, Prof. Patrick Aloysius,** OBE 1969; DSc, MAgr, ARCScI; Senior Principal Scientific Officer, Field Botany Division, Ministry of Agriculture, Northern Ireland, 1948-69; Professor of Agricultural Botany, The Queen's University of Belfast, 1951-69; *b* 7 March 1904; *s* of late Senator Thomas Linehan, Ballinvarrig, Whitechurch, Co. Cork; *m* 1933, Teresa Josephine Gilmore (*d* 1966); two *s* (one *d* decd). *Educ:* Christian Brothers' Coll., Cork; Royal College of Science for Ireland; National University of Ireland; University of Cambridge. Research Demonstrator, Plant Breeding, University College, Dublin, 1927. Queen's Univ., Belfast: Asst, Dept of Agricultural Botany, 1930; Lecturer, 1944; Reader, 1950; Dean of Faculty of Agriculture, 1965-68. Min. of Agriculture for N Ireland: Research Asst, Seed Testing and Plant Disease Div., 1930; Dep. Head, Field Botany Div., 1938; Dep. Principal Officer (war-time), 1943; Principal Scientific Officer, Field Botany Div., 1946. President International Seed Testing Assoc., 1960-62; former President British Grassland Society, 1954. *Publications:* scientific papers on grassland research, mainly in Journal of British Grassland Society; papers on seed research in Proc. International Seed Testing Assoc. *Recreation:* fishing. *Address:* 46 Ailesbury Road, Belfast BT7 3FH. *T:* Belfast 648013.

**LINES, Walter;** President, Lines Brothers Ltd (Chairman 1920-62); *b* 10 March 1882; *s* of Joseph Lines and Jane Lines (*née* Fitzhenry); *m* 1922, Henrietta Katherine Hendrey (*d* 1970); two *s* two *d*. *Educ:* Owen's Sch., EC1; Camden School of Art. Joined G. & J. Lines Ltd, 1896, Managing Director, 1908. Served European War, 1914-18: Honourable Artillery Company and RFA (Captain), France and Italy. Founded Lines Bros Ltd, with brothers W. J. and A. E. Lines, 1919. Was formerly Chairman and Managing Director, Lines Bros Ltd, and subsidiary Companies, Great Britain, Canada, Australia, New Zealand, S Africa, France, West Germany; Chairman Hamley Bros Ltd, Regent Street. Hon. Life President,

Regent Street Assoc.; FRSA. *Address:* Leigh Place, Godstone, Surrey.

*See also W. M. Lines.*

**LINES, (Walter) Moray,** CBE 1969; Chairman, Lines Brothers Ltd, since 1962 (Joint Managing Director, 1962-70); Chairman, British Toy Manufacturers Association, since 1968; *b* 26 Jan. 1922; *er s* of Walter Lines, *qv*; *m* 1955, Fiona Margaret Denton; three *s* one *d*. *Educ:* Gresham Sch. Joined Board of Lines Bros Ltd, 1946. *Address:* Selsfield House, nr East Grinstead, Sussex. *T:* Turner's Hill 226.

**LINFOOT, Dr Edward Hubert,** MA, DPhil, DSc (Oxon); ScD (Cantab); John Couch Adams Astronomer in the University of Cambridge and Assistant Director of the University Observatory, 1948-70; *b* 8 June 1905; *s* of late George E. Linfoot; *m* 1935, Joyce, *o d* of James and Ellen Dancer; one *s* one *d*. *Educ:* King Edward VII Sch., Sheffield; Balliol Coll., Oxford. Oxford Junior Mathematical Scholar, 1924; Senior Mathematical Scholar, 1928; Goldsmiths' Senior Student, 1926; J. E. Procter Visiting Fellow, Princeton Univ., USA, 1929; Tutor in Mathematics, Balliol Coll., 1931; Asst Lecturer in Math., Bristol Univ., 1932, Lecturer, 1935. *Publications:* Recent Advances in Optics, 1955; Qualitätsbewertung optischer Bilder, 1960; Fourier Methods in Optical Image Evaluation, 1964; papers in scientific journals. *Recreations:* music, chess, gardening. *Address:* 7 Sherlock Road, Cambridge. *T:* Cambridge 56513.

**LINFORD, Alan C.;** *see* Carr Linford.

**LING, Prof. Arthur George,** FRIBA; PPTPI; architect and town planner in practice with Arthur Ling and Associates; Special Professor of Environmental Design, University of Nottingham, since 1969; *b* 20 Sept. 1913; *s* of George Frederick Ling and Elsie Emily (*née* Wisbey); *m* 1939, Marjorie Tall; one *s* three *d*. *Educ:* Christ's Hospital; University College, London (Bartlett School of Architecture). BA (Architecture), London. Architect in Office of E. Maxwell Fry and Walter Gropius, 1937-39; Structural Engineer with Corporation of City of London (Air raid shelters and War debris clearance), 1939-41; Member town planning team responsible for preparation of County of London Plan, 1943, under direction of J. H. Forshaw and Sir Patrick Abercrombie, 1941-45; Chief Planning Officer, London County Council, 1945-55; Head of Department of Town Planning, University College, London Univ., 1947-48; Sen. Lecturer in Town Planning, 1948-55; City Architect and Planning Officer, Coventry, 1955-64; Prof. and Head of Dept of Architecture and Civic Planning, Univ. of Nottingham, 1964-69. Visiting Professor: University of Santiago, Chile, 1963; Univ. of NSW, Australia, 1969; Chancellor Lectures, Univ. of Wellington, NZ, 1969. Joint Architect for Development Plan for University of Warwick. Cons. Architect Planner, Runcorn New Town Corporation. Former Chairman, Board of Chief Officers, Midlands Housing Consortium; Vice-Chairman, Town Planning Commn, International Union of Architects; Past President, Town Planning Inst.; Past Vice-Pres., RIBA; Member, Sports Council; Vice-Chm., E Midlands Sports Council. RIBA Dist. in Town Planning, 1956; Silver Medallist (Essay), 1937; Hunt Bursary, 1939. Fellow University College, London, 1967. *Publications:* Contrib. to professional journals on architecture and town planning. *Address:* 11 Salthouse Lane, Beeston, Nottinghamshire.

**LING, Maj.-Gen. Fergus Alan Humphrey,** CB 1968; CBE 1964; DSO 1944; DL; *b* 5 Aug. 1914; 3rd *s* of John Richardson and Mabel Ling; *m* 1940, Sheelah Phyllis Sarel; two *s* three *d*. *Educ:* Stowe Sch.; Royal Military Coll., Sandhurst. Comd 2nd/5th Queen's, 1944; GSO 1 (Ops), GHQ, Middle East, 1945-46; British Liaison Officer, US Infantry Centre, 1948-50; Comd Regt Depot, Queen's Royal Regt, 1951; Directing Staff, Staff Coll., Camberley, 1951-53; comd 5th Queen's, 1954-57; Asst Military Secretary, War Office, 1957-58; comd 148 North Midland Brigade (TA), 1958-61; DAG, HQ, BAOR, 1961-65; GOC: 54 (East Anglian) Division/District, 1965-67; East Anglian District, 1967-68; Eastern District, 1968-69. Dep. Col, The Queen's Regt, 1969-. DL Surrey, 1970-. *Recreations:* homes and gardens, country pursuits. *Address:* Grove Cottage, Shalford, near Guildford, Surrey. *T:* Guildford 61567. *Clubs:* Army and Navy, MCC.

**LINGHAM, Brig. John,** CB 1948; DSO 1944; MC 1916; *b* 27 June 1897; *s* of Windeyer George Lingham; *m* 1924, Juliet Judd (*d* 1943); two *d*; *m* 1945, Jean Chisholm. *Educ:* City of London Sch.; Royal Military Coll., Sandhurst; Staff Coll., Camberley. Joined the Northamptonshire Regt, 1915; served European War, 1914-18, France, Mesopotamia, Egypt, Palestine, 1916-18; Pilot attached RAF, 1919. Served War of 1939-45, commanding 4th Bn Northamptonshire Regt, 1940-42; commanding 197 Infantry Bde, 1942-44; France, Belgium, Germany, 1944-45; retired from Army, 1949; Control Commission, Germany, 1945; Land Commissioner, Lower Saxony, 1948, North Rhine–Westphalia, 1951; Consul-General, 1952; retired 1954. Colonel, The Northamptonshire Regt, 1956-60. *Recreation:* fishing. *Address:* 7 Fairlawn Close, Claygate, Surrey. *T:* Esher 65287.

**LINK, Edwin Albert;** inventor, airman, ocean engineer; Director and Chief Marine Consultant, Ocean Systems Inc.; *b* 26 July 1904; *s* of Edwin A. Link and Katherine Link; *m* 1931, Marion Clayton; two *s*. *Educ:* Binghamton and Lindsley Schools. Aviator, 1927-; President, founder, Link Aviation Inc., 1935-53; President, General Precision Equipment Corp., 1958-59. Director: First City National Bank, Binghamton; Mohawk Airlines. Inventor Link Aviation Trainers. Founder, Link Foundation, 1953. Awarded Exceptional Service Medal, USAF; Wakefield Medal, RAeS, 1947; also varied awards from American organisations; holds honorary doctorates from Tufts University, Syracuse Univ. and Hamilton Coll.; Hon. DSc, Florida Inst. of Technology, 1970. *Publications:* Simplified Celestial Navigation (with P. V. H. Weems), 1940; articles on diving development and research in National Geographic magazines. *Address:* 10 Avon Road, Binghamton, NY 13905, USA.

**LINKLATER, Eric,** CBE 1954; TD; DL; LLD (Aberdeen), 1946; *b* 1899; *o s* of late Robert Linklater, of Dounby, Orkney; *m* 1933, Marjorie, *y d* of late Ian MacIntyre; two *s* two *d*. *Educ:* Aberdeen Grammar Sch.; Aberdeen Univ. Sometime private in The Black Watch; studied medicine; MA, 1925; assistant editor, The Times of India, Bombay, 1925-27; assistant to Professor of English Literature, Aberdeen, 1927-28; Commonwealth Fellow in United States of America, 1928-30; Major, RE, commanding Orkney Fortress RE, 1939-41; in Directorate of Public Relations, War Office, 1941-45; Rector of Aberdeen Univ., 1945-48; Temp. Lieut-Colonel, Korea, 1951. DL Ross and Cromarty, 1968. *Publications:* White Maa's Saga, 1929; Poet's Pub, 1929 (filmed, 1949); A Dragon Laughed, 1930; Juan in America, 1931; Ben Jonson and King James, 1931; The Men of Ness, 1932; Mary Queen of Scots, 1933; The Crusader's Key, 1933; Magnus Merriman, 1934; The Revolution, 1934; Robert the Bruce, 1934; The Devil's in the News, 1934; Ripeness is All, 1935; The Lion and the Unicorn, 1935; God Likes Them Plain, 1935; Juan in China, 1937; The Sailor's holiday, 1937; The Impregnable Women, 1938; Judas, 1939; The Man on My Back, 1941; The Cornerstones, 1941; The Raft *and* Socrates Asks Why, 1942; The Great Ship *and* Rabelais Replies, 1944; Crisis in Heaven (play), 1944; The Wind on the Moon (awarded Carnegie Medal), 1944; Private Angelo, 1946 (filmed 1949); The Art of Adventure, 1947; Sealskin Trousers, 1947; The Pirates in the Deep Green Sea, 1949; Love in Albania (play), 1949; A Spell for Old Bones, 1949; Mr Byculla, 1950; The Campaign in Italy, 1951; Laxdale Hall, 1951 (filmed, 1953); The Mortimer Touch (play), 1952; A Year of Space, 1953; The House of Gair, 1953; The Faithful Ally, 1954; The Ultimate Viking, 1955; The Dark of Summer, 1956; A Sociable Plover, 1957; Karina with Love, 1958; Position at Noon, 1958; Breakspear in Gascony (play), 1958; The Merry Muse, 1959; Edinburgh, 1960; Roll of Honour, 1961; Husband of Delilah, 1962; A Man Over Forty, 1963; The Prince in the Heather, 1965; Orkney and Shetland, 1965; The Conquest of England, 1966; A Terrible Freedom, 1966; The Survival of Scotland, 1968; The Stories of Eric Linklater, 1968; (with Edwin Smith) Scotland, 1968; The Royal House of Scotland, 1970; John Moore's England, 1970; Fanfare for a Tin Hat, 1970. *Address:* Pitcalzean House, Easter Ross, Ross-shire. *Clubs:* Savile; New (Edinburgh).

**LINKS, Mrs J. G.;** *see* Lutyens, Mary.

**LINLEY, Viscount; David Albert Charles Armstrong-Jones;** *b* 3 Nov. 1961; *s* and *heir* of 1st Earl of Snowdon, *qv*, and *s* of HRH the Princess Margaret.
*See under Royal Family.*

**LINLITHGOW,** 3rd Marquess of, *cr* 1902; **Charles William Frederick Hope,** MC 1945; Earl of Hopetoun, 1703; Viscount Aithrie, Baron Hope, 1703; Baron Hopetoun (UK) 1809; Baron Niddry (UK), 1814; Bt (Scotland), 1698; Captain (retired), 19th (Lothians and Border Horse) Armoured Car Company, Royal Tank Corps (Territorial Army); Lord Lieutenant of W Lothian, since 1964; Director, Eagle Star Insurance Co. Ltd; *b* 7 April 1912; *er s* of 2nd Marquess of Linlithgow, KG, KT, PC and Doreen Maud, CI 1936, Kaisar-i-Hind Medal 1st Class (*d* 1965), 2nd *d* of Rt Hon. Sir F. Milner, 7th Bt; *S* father 1952; *m* 1st, 1939, Vivien (*d* 1963), *d* of Capt. R. O. R. Kenyon-Slaney, and of Lady Mary Gilmour; one *s* one *d*; 2nd, 1965, Judith, *widow* of Esmond Baring. *Educ:* Eton; Christ Church, Oxford. Lieut, Scots Guards R of O; served War of 1939-45 (prisoner, MC). *Heir: s* Earl of Hopetoun, *qv*. *Address:* Hopetoun House, South Queensferry, West Lothian. *T:* South Queensferry 317. *Clubs:* Turf, White's.
*See also Baron Glendevon, Countess of Pembroke, Maj.-Gen. G. E. Prior-Palmer.*

**LINNELL, Prof. Wilfred Herbert,** MSc, DSc, PhD, FRIC, FPS; retired as Dean of the School of Pharmacy, University of London (1956-62); Professor of Pharmaceutical Chemistry, 1944-62; Professor Emeritus, 1962; Fellow of School of Pharmacy, University of London, 1962; *b* Sandbach, Cheshire, 1894; *s* of John Goodman and Evelyn Pring Linnell; *m* 1927, Margery, *d* of R. H. Hughes, Streetly; one *s*. *Educ:* Stockport Grammar Sch.; University of Durham; Lincoln Coll., Oxford; Armstrong Coll., Durham Univ., 1919-23; awarded the Earl Grey Memorial Fellowship, which was held at Lincoln Coll., Oxford; Governor, Chelsea College of Science and Technology. Research Chemist at HM Fuel Research Station, 1924-26; Examiner to the Pharmaceutical Society for Statutory Examinations since 1927; Corresp. étranger de l'Acad. Royale de Médecine de Belgique; Corresp. étranger de l'Acad. de Pharmacie de France. *Publications:* original contribs to science, published in the Journal of the Chemical Society, Journal of Society of Chemical Industry, and Journal of Pharmacy and Pharmacology. *Recreation:* sailing. *Address:* 103 Park Avenue, Ruislip, Middlesex.

**LINNETT, John Wilfrid,** FRS 1955; MA, DPhil (Oxon); Professor of Physical Chemistry, University of Cambridge, since 1965; Master of Sidney Sussex College, since 1970; *b* 3 Aug. 1913; *s* of late Alfred Thirlby Linnett and Ethel Mary Linnett (*née* Ward); *m* 1947, Rae Ellen Libgott; one *s* one *d*. *Educ:* King Henry VIII Sch., Coventry; St John's Coll., Oxford (Hon. Fellow, 1968). Henry Fellow, Harvard Univ., 1937-38; Junior Research Fellow, Balliol Coll., Oxford, 1939-45; Lectr, Brasenose Coll., Oxford, 1944-46; Fellow of Queen's Coll., Oxford, 1945-65; University Demonstrator in Chemistry, Oxford, 1944-62; Reader in Inorganic Chemistry, Oxford, 1962-65; Fellow, Emmanuel Coll., Cambridge, 1965-70. Council, Faraday Society, 1956-58, Vice-President, 1959-61, 1965-67, and 1969-; Council, Chemical Society, 1960-62; Hon. Secretary Chemical Society, 1962. Visiting Professor, University of California, 1964, 1970; Victor Emmanuel Visiting Professor, Cornell Univ., 1966; Visiting Lecturer, University of Minnesota, 1967. JP City of Oxford, 1964-65. Coventry Award of Merit, 1966. *Publications:* Wave Mechanics and Valency, 1960; The Electronic Structure of Molecules, a New Approach, 1964; scientific papers in Proc. Royal Society, Trans. Faraday Society, Journal Chemical Society, and other scientific journals. *Recreation:* cricket. *Address:* The Master's Lodge, Sidney Sussex College, Cambridge. *T:* Cambridge 55860. *Club:* Athenæum.

**LINSLEY, Ven. Stanley Frederick;** Archdeacon of Cleveland and Canon of Bilton, since 1965; Vicar of Harome since 1967; Rector of North and South Otterington, 1965-67; Chaplain to the Queen since 1964; *b* 19 Oct. 1903; *o s* of Frederick Linsley, Driffield, Yorks; *m* 1950, Joan, *d* of Horace Mulliner, Ellerdine, Shropshire; one *s* one *d*. *Educ:* Bridlington Sch.; Lichfield Theological Coll. Vicar of N Ormesby, Middlesbrough, 1932; Vicar of Tunstall, Stoke on Trent, 1937; Vicar of Cannock, Lichfield, 1943; Prebendary of Lichfield Cathedral, 1945; Canon Missioner and Warden of Retreat House, Shallowford, Diocese of Lichfield, 1946; Vicar of Sambrook, Salop, 1951. General Director of Industrial Christian Fellowship and Vicar of Guild Church of St Katherine Cree, London, 1954; Vicar of Guild Church of St Botolph, Aldersgate, 1956; Vicar of Kidderminster, 1958; Rural Dean of Kidderminster, 1959; Rector of Thwing and Wold Newton, 1963-65. Proctor in Convocation, Lichfield, 1946-51. *Publications:* contributions to theological journals. *Recreation:* agriculture. *Address:* Harome Vicarage, York. *T:* Helmsley 394.

**LINSTEAD, Sir Hugh (Nicholas),** Kt 1953; OBE 1937; Chairman, macarthy's Pharmaceuticals Ltd, *b* 3 Feb. 1901; *e s* of late Edward Flatman Linstead and Florence Evelyn Hester; *m* 1928, Alice Winifred Freke; two *d*. *Educ:* City of

London Sch.; Pharmaceutical Society's Sch. (Jacob Bell Scholar); Birkbeck Coll. Pharmaceutical chemist; barrister-at-law, Middle Temple, 1929. MP (C) Putney Div. of Wandsworth, 1942-64. Secretary: Pharmaceutical Society of Great Britain, 1926-64; Central Pharmaceutical War Cttee, 1938-46; Pres., Internat. Pharmaceutical Fedn, 1953-65; Member, Medical Research Council, 1956-64; Chairman and Vice-Chairman, Joint Negotiating Cttee (Hospital Staffs), 1946-48; Member Poisons Board (Home Office), 1935-57; Chairman: Wandsworth Group Hospital Cttee, 1948-53; Parliamentary and Scientific Cttee, 1955-57; Library Cttee, House of Commons, 1963-64; Franco-British Parliamentary Relations Cttee, 1955-60; Conservators of Wimbledon and Putney Commons. Member: Central Health Services Council (Min. of Health), 1951-66; Departmental Cttee on Homosexual Offences and Prostitution; Departmental Cttee on Experiments on Animals. Parliamentary Charity Comr for England and Wales, 1956-60. Comr for Training Scout Officers, Boy Scouts' Assoc., 1932-41; Hon. LLD: British Columbia, 1956; Toronto, 1963; Hon. Member American and Canadian Pharmaceutical Assocs, British Dental Assoc. and other societies; Corresponding Member Académie de Médecine de France and Académie de Pharmacie de Paris; Warden of the Farriers' Company. Commandeur de la Légion d'Honneur; Officier de la Santé Publique (France); Kt Comdr Al Merito Sanitario (Spain). *Address:* 22 Rodway Road, SW15. *Club:* Savage.

**LINTERN, Bernard Francis;** journalist; *b* 26 Nov. 1908; *e s* of late Rev. F. G. Lintern and Beatrice Golding; *m* 1931, Mary, *e d* of late Arthur Watts. *Educ:* Chigwell; University of London. Editor of Discovery, and Associate-editor of Television, 1932-34; Associate-editor of Industria Britanica, 1934; Editorial Director, Lawrence H. Tearle Publications, Cape Town and Johannesburg, 1950-60; Editor of The Stethoscope and Pharmacy News, Director, Marketing Publications Ltd, 1961-63. Seaman, RN, 1940; Lieut, RNVR, 1942; Combined Operations, 1941; attached, Fleet Air Arm, 1942-46, transferred to Supplementary Reserve. *Address:* 194 Russell Court, Woburn Place, WC1. *Clubs:* RNVR; Southern African Naval Officers'; Wig and Pen.

**LINTON, Sir Andrew,** KBE 1964 (CBE 1953); Chairman, New Zealand Dairy Board, 1956-68 (formerly Deputy Chairman); *b* 1893; Scottish; *m* 1922, Catherine Shaw; one *s* two *d*. *Educ:* Otago and Southland. Elected NZ Dairy Board, 1935. Chairman: Dairy Research Institute (18 years); NZ Veterinary Council, 1947-57; NZ Superannuation Board (Dairy), 1952; formerly Member: NZ Meat Producers' Board, 1958-69; NZ Agricultural Council; NZ Trade Promotion Council; NZ Export Shipping Council; Director: Freezing Co., 1941-69; Trustee Co., 1958-69; member of many local bodies; Chairman of Dairy Companies, etc. *Address:* Glenavon, Greytown, Wairarapa, New Zealand. *Club:* Wellesley (Wellington, NZ).

**LINTON, Prof. David Leslie;** Professor of Geography, University of Birmingham, since Oct. 1958; *b* 12 July 1906; *m* 1929, Vera Cicely Tebbs; three *s* one *d*. *Educ:* Haberdashers' Aske's Sch.; University of London, King's Coll. Demonstrator in Geography and Geology, University of London, 1927-29; Lecturer in Geography, University of Edinburgh, 1929-45; Professor of Geography, University of Sheffield, 1945-58; William Evans Visiting Professor, University of Otago, 1959. Served War with RAF (Photographic Intelligence), as Sqdn Leader, 1940-45. Hon. Editor of Geography, the Quarterly Journal of the Geographical Association, 1945-65 and Pres., 1964; Mem. Deutsche Akademie Leopoldina, 1961; Pres., Inst. of British Geographers, 1962, Geographical Assoc., 1964. Murchison Award, Royal Geographical Soc., 1943. *Publications:* Structure, Surface and Drainage in South-East England (with S. W. Wooldridge), 1955; Sheffield and its Region (Ed.), 1956; papers in geographical journals. *Address:* 75 Wellington Road, Edgbaston, Birmingham 15. *T:* 021-440 2476.

**LINTOTT, Sir Henry,** KCMG 1957 (CMG 1948); Director: The Metal Box Company, since 1968; Glaxo Group Ltd; *b* 23 Sept. 1908; *s* of late Henry John Lintott, RSA, and of Edith Lunn; *m* 1949, Margaret Orpen; one *s* one *d*. *Educ:* Edinburgh Acad.; Edinburgh Univ.; King's Coll., Cambridge. Entered Customs and Excise Dept, 1932; Board of Trade, 1935-48; Dep. Secretary-General, OEEC, 1948-56. Dep. Under-Secretary of State, Commonwealth Relations Office, 1956-63; British High Commissioner in Canada, 1963-68.

**LINZEE, Captain Robert Gordon Hood,** CB 1944; CBE 1944 (OBE 1940); Royal Navy, retired; *b* 1900; *o s* of Alexander Grosvenor Linzee; *m* 1929, Hon. Ellinor Aileen Cecil Craig, *d* of 1st Viscount Craigavon; one *s*; *m* 1946, Elizabeth, *widow* of Rear-Admiral Philip Mack. *Educ:* West Downs, Winchester; Royal Naval Coll., Osborne. *Clubs: United Service, MCC.*

**LIPMANN, Fritz (Albert),** MD, PhD; Professor of Biochemistry, Rockefeller University, since 1965 (Rockefeller Institute, 1957-65); Head of Biochemical Research Laboratory, Mass. General Hospital, 1941-57; Professor of Biological Chemistry, Harvard Medical School, 1949-57; *b* Koenigsberg, Germany, 12 June 1899; *s* of Leopold Lipmann and Gertrud Lachmanski; *m* 1931, Elfreda M. Hall; one *s*. *Educ:* Universities of Koenigsberg, Berlin, Munich. MD Berlin, 1924; PhD Koenigsberg, Berlin, 1927. Research Asst, Kaiser Wilhelm Inst., Berlin and Heidelberg, 1927-31; Research Fellow, Rockefeller Inst. for Medical Research, New York, 1931-32; Research Assoc., Biological Inst. of Carlsberg Foundation, Copenhagen, 1932-39; Res. Assoc., Dept of Biological Chem., Cornell University Med. Sch., NY, 1939-41; Res. Fellow in Surgery, 1941-43, and Associate in Biochemistry, 1943-49, Harvard Medical Sch.; Prof. of Biological Chemistry, Mass. General Hospital, 1949-57. Carl Neuberg Medal, 1948; Mead Johnson and Co. Award, 1948. Hon. MD, Marseilles, 1947; Hon. DSc: Chicago, 1953; Sorbonne, 1966; Harvard, 1967; Hon. Doc. Humane Letters: Brandeis, 1959; Albert Einstein College of Medicine of Yeshiva Univ., 1964; Nobel Prize in Medicine and Physiology, 1953; National Medal of Science, 1966. Member : National Academy of Sciences, American Association for Advancement of Science, American Chemical Society, Society of Biological Chemists, Harvey Society, Biochem. Society, Society of American Microbiologists; Fellow Danish Royal Academy of Sciences; Fellow, NY Academy Science; Foreign Member Royal Society, 1962. *Publications:* articles in German, American and English journals. *Address:* (office) The Rockefeller University, New York, NY 10021, USA; (home) 150 East 18th Street, New York, NY 10003, USA.

**LIPPMANN, Walter;** writer; *b* 23 Sept. 1889; *s* of Jacob Lippmann and Daisy Baum; *m* 1st, 1917, Faye Albertson; no *c*; 2nd, 1938, Helen Byrne Armstrong. *Educ:* Harvard (AB). Associate Editor, New Republic, 1914-17; Assistant to Secretary of War, June-Oct., 1917; Captain, Military Intelligence, USA, 1918; Secretary of organisation directed by Colonel E. M. House to prepare data for Peace Conference; Editor, New York World, till 1931; special writer New York Herald Tribune Syndicate, 1931-62; syndicated by Washington Post and Los Angeles Times Syndicate, 1963; former Member Board of Overseers of Harvard Univ. Holds numerous Hon. Degrees. Overseas Press Club of America "Best Press Interpretation of Foreign News", 1953, 1955, 1960; Pulitzer Prize International Reporting, 1962; George Foster Peabody Television Award for Outstanding Contrib. to International Understanding, 1962; Medal of Freedom (US), 1964; Gold Medal for Essays and Criticism, American Inst. of Arts and Letters, 1965. Member of Institute of Arts and Letters; American Academy of Arts and Letters; Senator, Phi Beta Kappa; Comdr, Legion of Honor; Officer Order of Crown of Leopold; Commander, Order of Orange-Nassau (Netherlands); Knight Cross First Class, Order of St Olav (Norway). *Publications:* A Preface to Politics; Drift and Mastery; Stakes of Diplomacy; The Political Scene; Liberty and the News; Public Opinion; The Phantom Public; American Inquisitors; Men of Destiny; A Preface to Morals; The US in World Affairs, Vol. I, 1932; Interpretations; The US in World Affairs, Vol. II, 1933; The Method of Freedom, 1934; The New Imperative, 1935; The Good Society, 1937; US Foreign Policy; Shield of the Republic, 1943; US War Aims, 1944; The Cold War, 1947; The Public Philosophy, 1955; The Communist World and Ours, 1959; The Coming Tests With Russia, 1961; Western Unity and the Common Market, 1962. *Recreations:* golf, tennis. *Address:* 28 East 63rd Street, New York, NY 10021, USA. *Clubs:* Harvard, Century, River (New York); Cosmos, Metropolitan, Tavern (Boston); National Press (Washington, DC).

**LIPSCOMB, Maj.-Gen. Christopher Godfrey,** CB 1961; DSO and Bar 1945; Chief of Joint Services Liaison Organisation, BAOR, Bonn, 1958-61, retired; *b* 22 Dec. 1907; *s* of Godfrey Lipscomb and Mildred Agnes (*née* Leatham); *m* 1937, Ellen Diana Hayward; two *s*. *Educ:* Charterhouse; Sandhurst. Commissioned into Somerset Light Infantry, 1928; seconded Nigerian Regt, Royal West African Frontier Force, 1933-39; Commanded 4th Somerset LI, 1944-46; Staff Coll., 1947; AA&QMG, SW District, 1948-50; Comd 19 Inf. Bde, 1950-53; Commandant Senior Officers' Sch., 1954-56; Comd Hanover District, BAOR, 1957-58. *Address:* Crockerton House, Warminster, Wilts.

**LIPSCOMB, Air Vice-Marshal (retired) Frederick Elvy,** CB 1958; CBE 1953; *b* 2 Sept. 1902; *s* of late Arthur Bossley Lipscomb, St Albans; *m* 1931, Dorothy May (*d* 1964), *d* of Frederick Foskett, Berkhamsted, Herts; no *c*. *Educ:* Aldenham Sch.; Middlesex Hospital. MRCS LRCP 1927; DTM&H (Eng.), 1933; DPH (London) 1934. commnd RAF 1927; psa 1946. Served Aden, Malta, Palestine; War of 1939-45, Mediterranean and West Africa (despatches thrice). Director of Hygiene and Research, Air Ministry, 1950; Principal Medical Officer, Far East Air Force, 1951-54; Dep. Director General RAF Medical Services, 1954-55; Principal Medical Officer, Home Command, 1955-57. KHP 1952; QHP 1952-57. CStJ 1952. *Publications:* Tropical Diseases section, Conybeare's Textbook of Medicine, 6th to 9th edns. Contributions to British Medical Journal, RAF Quarterly, etc. *Address:* 79 Perry Street, Wendover, Bucks.

**LIPSEY, Prof. Richard George;** Sir Edward Peacock Professor of Economics, Queens University, Kingston, Ontario, since 1970; *b* 28 Aug. 1928; *s* of R. A. Lipsey and F. T. Lipsey (*née* Ledingham); *m* 1960, Diana Louise Smart; one *s* two *d*. *Educ:* Univ. of British Columbia (BA 1st Cl. Hons 1950); Univ. of Toronto (MA 1953); LSE (PhD 1957). Dept of Trade and Industry, British Columbia Provincial Govt, 1950-53; LSE: Asst Lectr, 1955-58; Lectr, 1958-60; Reader, 1960-61; Prof. 1961-63; Univ. of Essex: Prof. of Economics, 1963-70; Dean of School of Social Studies, 1963-67. Vis. Prof., Univ. of California at Berkeley, 1963-64. Economic Consultant, NEDC, 1961-63; Editor, Review of Economic Studies, 1960-64; Member of Council: Social Science Research Council, 1966-69; Royal Economic Soc., 1968-. *Publications:* An Introduction to Positive Economics, 1963, 2nd edn 1967; Economics (with P. O. Steiner), 1966, 2nd edn 1969; An Introduction to a Mathematical Treatment of Economics (with G. C. Archibald), 1967; articles in learned jls on many branches of theoretical and applied economics. *Recreations:* skiing, fishing, walking. *Address:* 16 Market Street, Gananoque, Ontario, Canada.

**LIPSON, Prof. Henry Solomon,** FRS 1957; Professor of Physics, University of Manchester Institute of Science and Technology, since 1954; *b* 11 March 1910; *s* of Israel Lipson and Sarah (*née* Friedland); *m* 1937, Jane Rosenthal; one *s* two *d*. *Educ:* Hawarden Grammar Sch.; Liverpool Univ. BSc 1930, MSc 1931, DSc 1939 (Liverpool); MA Cambridge, 1942; MSc Tech., Manchester, 1958; Oliver Lodge Scholar, Liverpool, 1933; Senior DSIR Grant, Manchester, 1936. Junior Scientific Officer, National Physical Lab., 1937; Asst in Crystallography, Cambridge, 1938; Head of Physics Dept, Manchester College of Technology, 1945. President Manchester Literary and Philosophical Society, 1960. Visiting Professor of Physics: University of Calcutta, 1963-64; Technion, Haifa, 1969. *Publications:* The Interpretation of X-ray Diffraction Photographs (with Drs Henry and Wooster), 1951; Determination of Crystal Structures (with Dr Cochran), 1953; Fourier Transforms and X-Ray Diffraction (with Prof. Taylor), 1958; Optical Transforms: Their Preparation and Application to X-ray Diffraction Problems (with Prof. Taylor), 1964; Optical Physics (with Dr Lipson), 1968; The Great Experiments in Physics, 1968; Interpretation of X-ray Powder Diffraction Patterns (with Dr Steeple), 1970; papers in Royal Society Proceedings, Acta Crystallographica, etc. *Recreations:* tennis, D-I-Y. *Address:* 22 Cranmer Road, Manchester 20. *T:* 061-445 4517.

**LIPTON, Marcus,** CBE 1965 (OBE 1949); MP (Lab) Brixton Division of Lambeth, since 1945; *b* 29 Oct. 1900; *s* of late Benjamin Lipton and of Mary Lipton, Sunderland. *Educ:* Hudson Road Council Sch.; Bede Grammar Sch., Sunderland; Merton Coll., Oxford (Goldsmiths' Company Exhibitioner) MA. Barrister-at-law, Gray's Inn, 1926. Councillor, Stepney Borough Council, 1934-37. Contested (Lab) Brixton, 1935. Alderman, Lambeth Borough Council, 1937-56. JP County of London. Private, TA, 1939; Lieut-Colonel, 1944. Councillor, Binfield Parish Council, 1955-59. President: Brixton Labour Party; Cowley Operatic Society; Brixton Branch,

British Legion; Southern Sunday Football League; Chairman, Anglo-Nepalese and Anglo-Bulgarian Parliamentary Groups. *Recreation:* giving advice. *Address:* 50 Wiltshire Road, SW9. *T:* 01-274 3942.

**LISBURNE,** 8th Earl of, *cr* 1776; **John David Malet Vaughan;** Viscount Lisburne and Lord Vaughan, 1695; barrister-at-law; *b* 1 Sept. 1918; *o s* of 7th Earl of Lisburne; *S* father, 1965; *m* 1943, Shelagh, *er d* of late T. A. Macauley, 1266 Redpath Crescent, Montreal, Canada; three *s. Educ:* Eton; Magdalen Coll., Oxford (BA, MA). Called to Bar, Inner Temple, 1947. Captain, Welsh Guards. Dep. Chm., Westward Television Ltd; Dir, British Home Stores Ltd. *Heir: s* Viscount Vaughan, *qv. Address:* 90 New Bond Street, W1; 22 York House, Kensington Church Street, W8. *T:* 01-937 3043; High Ridge, Bembridge, IoW. *T:* 220; Plas Treflyn, Tregaron, Cardiganshire. *T:* Tregaron 334. *Clubs:* Turf, Pratt's.

**LISLE,** 7th Baron, *cr* 1758; **John Nicholas Horace Lysaght;** *s* of late Hon. Horace G. Lysaght and Alice Elizabeth, *d* of Sir John Wrixon Becher, 3rd Bt; *b* 10 Aug. 1903; *S* grandfather, 1919; *m* 1st, 1928, Vivienne (who obtained a divorce, 1939; she *died* 1948), *d* of Rev. M. Brew; 2nd, 1939, Mary Helen Purgold. *Heir: b* Horace James William Lysaght [*b* 1908; *m* 1st, 1930, Joanna Mary (marr. diss., 1951), *d* of late Dr J. S. Nolan, Bedwas, Mon; four *s*; 2nd, 1953, Vyrna, *d* of J. Jones, Pontypool; two *d*].

**LISSMANN, Hans Werner,** FRS 1954; Reader, Department of Zoology, Cambridge, since 1966, and Director, Sub-Department of Animal Behaviour, since 1969; Fellow of Trinity College, Cambridge, since 1955; *b* 30 April 1909; *s* of Robert and Ebba Lissmann; *m* 1949, Corinne Foster-Barham; one *s. Educ:* Kargala and Hamburg. Dr.rer.nat., Hamburg, 1932; MA, Cantab, 1947. Asst Director of Research, Dept of Zoology, Cambridge, 1947-55; Lecturer, 1955-66. *Address:* Department of Zoology, Downing Street, Cambridge; 9 Bulstrode Gardens, Cambridge. *T:* 56126.

**LISTER;** *see* Cunliffe-Lister, family name of Earl of Swinton.

**LISTER, Arthur,** FRCS; Senior Ophthalmic Surgeon, London Hospital, 1948-70; Opthalmic Surgeon, Moorfields Eye Hospital, 1946-70; retired; *b* 12 Feb. 1905; *s* of Arthur Hugh Lister, Physician, and Sybil (*née* Palgrave); *m* 1937, Margaret Emily Pryor; three *s* two *d. Educ:* Lancing Coll.; Trinity Coll., Cambridge; London Hospital. BA Cambridge, 1927; MRCS, LRCP 1930; FRCS 1933; MB, BCh, Cambridge, 1934. House Surgeon and Senior Resident Officer, Moorfields Hospital, 1934-36; Asst Surgeon, Moorfields Hospital, 1939; Asst Ophth. Surgeon, London Hospital, 1939. Served War of 1939-45: Temp. Major (Ophthalmic Specialist), 1940; Temp. Lieut-Colonel, 1944; Adviser in Ophthalmology, 21 Army Group, NW Europe, 1944-45; Adviser in Ophthalmology, ALFSEA, 1945-46; demobilised, 1946. *Publications:* contributions to British Journal of Ophthalmology, Ophthalmic Literature, Trans. Ophthalmic Society UK, and Proc. Royal Society of Med. *Recreations:* fishing, gardening, model railway. *Address:* (home) 89 Hamilton Terrace, NW8. *T:* 01-286 5732; (professional) 56 Wimpole Street, W1. *T:* 01-935 6305.

**LISTER, Sir (Charles) Percy,** Kt 1947; DL; Past Chairman and Managing Director: R. A. Lister and Co. Ltd, Dursley; United Kingdom Commercial Corp., 1940-45; Director: Sir W. G. Armstrong Whitworth (Engineers) Ltd; Hawker Siddeley Group Ltd; *b* 15 July 1897; 3rd *s* of late Charles Ashton Lister, CBE; *m* 1953, Mrs Geraldine Bigger, Portstewart, Ulster. *Educ:* Mill Hill; RMC, Sandhurst. 18th QMO Royal Hussars. member: Capital Issues Cttee, 1946-47; Dollar Exports Councils, 1949-64; Iron and Steel Board, 1953-58. DL County of Gloucester, 1960. *Recreations:* hunting, yachting, golf. *Address:* Stinchcombe Hill House, Dursley, Glos. *TA* and *T:* Dursley 2030. *Club:* Cavalry.

**LISTER, Lieut-Colonel Frederick Hamilton,** DSO 1916; late of HM's Body Guard of the Honourable Corps of Gentlemen-at-Arms; late Royal Artillery; *b* 5 Dec. 1880; *yr s* of late Sir T. Villiers Lister, KCMG, and Lady Lister (sister of 10th Lord Belhaven and Stenton); *m* 1921, Mildred (*d* 1952), *yr d* of late Duncan Cameron, Springfield, Canterbury, NZ. *Educ:* Radley Coll.; RMA, Woolwich. Joined Royal Artillery, 1900; Captain, 1911; Major, 1915; Bt Lieut-Colonel, 1918; Lieut-Colonel, 1927; seconded for service in the Punjab Frontier Force, 1902-11; graduated at the Staff Coll., 1914; posted to General Staff, Aug. 1914; served European War and in South Russia, 1914-20 (despatches, DSO, Croix de Guerre, Bt Lieut-Colonel, Officer of Order of Leopold of Belgium, Order of St Vladimir of Russia); GSO 1 British Mission, Belgian GHQ, 1917; GSO 1 GHQ, British Forces, France, 1917-18; GSO i/c British Mission, 1st French Army, 1918; GSO 1 Supreme War Council, Versailles, 1918-19; GSO 1 Paris Peace Conference, 1919; GSO 1 British Mission to General Denikin in South Russia, 1919-20; Accompanied French operations in Rif Mountains in Morocco, 1926; retired pay, 1931. FRGS, FRHS. *Address:* 47 Whitelands House, Chelsea, SW3. *T:* 01-730 7007. *Clubs:* Brooks's, Geographical, Shikar.

**LISTER, Ven. John Field,** MA; Archdeacon of Halifax since 1961; *b* 19 Jan. 1916; *s* of Arthur and Florence Lister. *Educ:* King's Sch., Worcester; Keble Coll., Oxford; Cuddesdon Coll., Oxford. Asst Curate, St Nicholas, Radford, Coventry, 1939-44; Asst Curate, St John Baptist, Coventry, 1944-45; Vicar of St John's, Huddersfield, 1945-54; Vicar of Brighouse, 1954-; Asst Rural Dean of Halifax, 1955-61; Hon. Canon of Wakefield Cathedral, 1961, Canon, 1968. Chaplain to the Queen, 1966-. *Address:* The Vicarage, Brighouse, Yorkshire. *T:* Brighouse 4032. *Club:* National.

**LISTER, Laurier;** Theatrical Director and Manager, since 1947; Director, Yvonne Arnaud Theatre, Guildford (appointed 1964); *b* 22 April 1907; *s* of George Daniel Lister and Susie May Kooy. *Educ:* Dulwich Coll. Trained as actor at Royal Academy of Dramatic Art, 1925-26; appeared in Noël Coward's Easy Virtue, 1926; with Bristol Repertory Company, 1926-27; three seasons with Stratford-upon-Avon Festival Company, and also toured Canada and the USA with them, 1927-29; spent a year in S Africa with Olga Lindo's Company, 1930; Death Takes a Holiday, Savoy, 1931; The Lake, Westminster and Piccadilly, 1933; Visited Finland with Sir Nigel Playfair's Company, 1933; Hervey House, His Majesty's, 1934; This Desirable Residence, Criterion, 1935; Parnell, New, 1936; People of our Class, New, 1938; The Flashing Stream, Lyric, 1938; also in New York, Biltmore, 1939. Served in RAF, 1940-45. Wrote, with Dorothy Massingham, The Soldier and the Gentlewoman, Vaudeville, 1933; with Hilda Vaughan, She Too Was Young, Wyndham's and New, 1938. Organized Poetry Recitals at the Lyric, Hammersmith, and Globe, 1946-47. Devised, directed and (except for the first two) presented under his own management, the following intimate revues: Tuppence Coloured, Lyric, Hammersmith, and Globe, 1947-48; Oranges and Lemons, Lyric, Hammersmith, and Globe, 1948-49; Penny Plain, St Martin's, 1951-52; Airs on a Shoestring, Royal Court, 1953-55; Joyce Grenfell Requests the Pleasure, Fortune and St Martin's, 1954-55, later, in New York, Bijou, 1955; Fresh Airs, Comedy, 1956. Directed plays in USA, 1957 and 1958; appointed Artistic Director to Sir Laurence Olivier's Company, 1959; Dear Liar (directed and presented) and The Art of Living (Director), Criterion, 1960; J. B., Phœnix, 1961 (Dir. and presented); Asst to Sir Laurence Olivier at Chichester Festivals, 1962, 1963. *Publications:* She Too Was Young, 1938; The Apollo Anthology, 1954. *Recreations:* gardening, travelling. *Address:* c/o National Westminster Bank Ltd, 57 Aldwych, WC2.

**LISTER, Sir Percy;** *see* Lister, Sir C. P.

**LISTER-KAYE, Sir John (Christopher Lister),** 7th Bt, *cr* 1812; Director: Bath and Portland Group; Soil Fertility Dunns Ltd, since 1950; *b* 13 July 1913; *s* of Sir Lister Lister-Kaye, 6th Bt and Emily Mary Lister-Kaye (*d* 1944); *S* father, 1962; *m* 1942, Audrey Helen Carter; one *s* one *d. Educ:* Oundle; Loughborough Coll. *Heir: s* John Philip Lister Lister-Kaye, *b* 8 May 1946. *Address:* Woodsome, Bannerdown, Bath, Somerset. *T:* Bath 88036. *Club:* Farmers'.

**LISTON, James Malcolm,** CMG 1958; Medical Adviser, Ministry of Overseas Development, since 1964; *b* 1909; *m* 1935, Isobel Prentice Meiklem, Edinburgh; one *s* one *d. Educ:* Glasgow High Sch.; Glasgow Univ. MB, ChB, Glasgow, 1932; DTM & H Eng., 1939; DPH University of London, 1947; FRCP Glasgow, 1963. Medical Officer, Kenya, 1935; Director of Medical and Health Services, Sarawak, 1947-52; Deputy Director of Medical Services, Hong Kong, 1952-55; Director of Medical Services, Tanganyika, 1955-59; Permanent Secretary to Ministry of Health, 1959-60; Deputy Chief Medical Officer: Colonial Office, 1960-61; Dept of Tech. Co-op., 1961-62; Chief Medical Adviser, Dept of Tech. Co-op., 1962-64. *Address:* Ministry of Overseas Development, Eland House, Stag Place, Victoria, SW1; (home) Honeybrae, Nine Mile Burn, Midlothian. *Clubs:* Athenæum, Royal Societies.

**LISTON, Rt. Rev. James Michael;** *see* Auckland, Bishop of, (RC).

**LISTON-FOULIS, Sir Ian P.,** 13th Bt, *cr* 1634; Language Teacher, Madrid, since 1966; *b* 9 Aug. 1937; *s* of Lieut-Colonel James Alistair Liston-Foulis, Royal Artillery (killed on active service, 1942), and of Mrs Kathleen de la Hogue Moran; *S cousin,* Sir Archibald Charles Liston Foulis, 1961. *Educ:* Stonyhurst Coll.; Cannington Farm Inst., Somerset (Dip. Agr.); Madrid (Dip. in Spanish). National Service, 1957-59; Argyll and Sutherland Highlanders, Cyprus, 1958 (Gen. Service Medal). Language Teacher Estremadura and Madrid, 1960-61; Trainee, Bank of London and South America, 1962; Trainee, Bank of London and Montreal (in Nassau, 1963, Guatemala City, 1963-64, Managua, Nicaragua, 1964-65); Toronto (Sales), 1965-66. *Recreations:* long-distance running, swimming, walking, climbing, travelling, foreign languages and customs, reading, history.

**LISTOWEL,** 5th Earl of, *cr* 1822; **William Francis Hare,** PC 1946; GCMG 1957; Baron Ennismore, 1800; Viscount Ennismore, 1816; Baron Hare (UK), 1869; Chairman of Committees, House of Lords, since 1965; *b* 28 Sept. 1906; *e s* of 4th Earl and Hon. Freda Vanden-Bempde-Johnstone (*d* 1968), *y d* of 2nd Baron Derwent; *S* father, 1931; *m* 1st, 1933, Judith (marr. diss., 1945), *o d* of R. de Marffy-Mantuano, Budapest; one *d*; 2nd, 1958, Stephanie Sandra Yvonne Wise (marr. diss., 1963), Toronto; one *d*; 3rd, 1963, Mrs Pamela Read; two *s* one *d. Educ:* Eton; Balliol Coll., Oxford. PhD London Univ. Lieut, Intelligence Corps; Whip of Labour Party in House of Lords, 1941-44; Parliamentary Under-Secretary of State, India Office, and Deputy Leader, House of Lords, 1944-45; Postmaster-General, 1945-47; Secretary of State for India, April-Aug. 1947; for Burma, 1947-Jan. 1948; Minister of State for Colonial Affairs, 1948-50; Joint Parliamentary Secretary, Ministry of Agriculture and Fisheries, 1950-51; Member (Lab) LCC for East Lewisham, 1937-46, for Battersea North, 1952-57. Governor-General of Ghana, 1957-60. *Publications:* The Values of Life, 1931; A Critical History of Modern Æsthetics, 1933 (2nd edn, as Modern Æsthetics: an Historical Introduction, 1967). *Heir: s* Viscount Ennismore, *qv. Address:* 7 Constable Close, Wildwood Road, NW11. *Club:* Athenæum.
*See also Viscount Blakenham, Baron Grantley, Earl of Iveagh, Captain Sir Clive Milnes-Coates.*

**LITCHFIELD, Jack Watson,** FRCP; Physician since 1946, and Physician in charge of Cardiac Department since 1947, St Mary's Hospital, W2; Physician, King Edward Memorial Hospital, W13, since 1947; *b* 7 May 1909; *s* of H. L. Litchfield, Ipswich; *m* 1941, Nan, *d* of A. H. Hatherly, Shanghai; two *s* one *d. Educ:* Ipswich Sch.; Oriel Coll., Oxford (Scholar); St Mary's Hospital. Theodore Williams Schol. in Physiology, 1929, in Pathology, 1931; Radcliffe Schol. in Pharmacology, 1932; BA (2nd class hons) 1930; BM, BCh 1933; University schol. at St Mary's Hospital Medical Sch., 1931; MRCP 1936; FRCP 1947. Medical Registrar: St Mary's Hospital, 1936; Brompton Hospital, 1938; Physician, King Edward Memorial Hosp., W13, 1947-69. Served in RAMC in N Africa, Italy, etc (despatches), Lt-Col i/c Medical Div. FRSocMed; Member Assoc. of Physicians of Great Britain and Ireland. *Publications:* papers on various subjects in medical journals. *Recreations:* gardening, walking. *Address:* 104 Harley Street, W1. *T:* 01-935 6155; 111 Highview Road, W13. *T:* 01-997 2826.

**LITCHFIELD, Captain John Shirley Sandys,** OBE 1943; RN; *b* 27 Aug. 1903; *e s* of late Rear-Admiral F. S. Litchfield-Speer, CMG, DSO, and late Cecilia Sandys; *m* 1939, Margaret, *d* of late Sir Bertram Portal, KCB, DSO, and late Hon. Lady Portal; one *s* two *d. Educ:* St Aubyns, Rottingdean; RN Colleges Osborne and Dartmouth. Midshipman and Lieut in HMS Renown during Royal Cruise to India and Japan, 1921-22 and to Australia and NZ, 1927; Yangtse river gunboat, 1929-31; RN Staff Coll., 1935; comd naval armoured trains and cars, Palestine, 1936 (despatches); Staff Officer (Ops) to C-in-C Mediterranean, 1937-38; comd HMS Walker, 1939, HMS Norfolk 1943, HMS Tyne, 1946-47 and HMS Vanguard, 1951-53; Naval SO, Supreme War Council, 1939; Joint Planning Staff, 1940; SO (O) Western Approaches, 1941; Russian Convoys and N. Africa landings, 1941-43; planning staff, Normandy ops, 1944; Combined Chiefs of Staff, Washington, 1945; National War College of US, 1947-48; Dep. Director Naval Intelligence, 1949-50; idc 1951; Director of Ops, Admiralty, 1953-54; retired 1955. CC Kent, 1955-58. MP (C) Chelsea, 1959-66.

*Address:* Snowfield, Bearsted, Kent. *Clubs:* United Service, MCC.

**LITHGOW, Sir William (James),** 2nd Bt of Ormsary, *cr* 1925; DL; Shipbuilder; Chairman: Lithgows Ltd; Scott Lithgow Drydocks Ltd; G. M. Hay & Co. Ltd; Caledonia Joinery Co. Ltd; Kingston Marine Technology Ltd; Lithgow Housing Co. Ltd; Vice-Chairman, Scott Lithgow Ltd; Director: Bank of Scotland; Western Ferries Ltd; Lithgow Group Ltd, and associated cos; *b* 10 May 1934; *o s* of Colonel Sir James Lithgow, 1st Bt of Ormsary, GBE, CB, MC, TD, DL, JP, LLD, and Gwendolyn Amy, *d* of late John Robinson Harrison of Scalesceugh, Cumberland; *S* father, 1952; *m* 1964, Valerie Helen (*d* 1964) 2nd *d* of late Denis Scott, CBE, and of Mrs Laura Scott; *m* 1967, Mary Claire, *d* of Colonel F. M. Hill, CBE; one *s one d. Educ:* Winchester Coll. Member: Board of Clyde Port Authority; Exec. Cttee, Scottish Council Develt and Industry; Scottish Regional Council of CBI. Hon. President Students Assoc. and Member Court, University of Strathclyde, 1963-69. MRINA. Member, Queen's Body Guard for Scotland (Royal Company of Archers). DL Renfrewshire, 1970. *Recreations:* shooting, photography. *Heir: s* James Frank Lithgow, *b* 13 June 1970. *Address:* Drums, Langbank, Renfrewshire. *T:* Langbank 606; Ormsary, By Lochgilphead, Argyllshire. *T:* Ormsary 212. *Clubs:* Western, Royal Scottish Automobile (Glasgow).

**LITTEN, Maurice Sidney,** RP 1968; portrait painter; *b* 3 May 1919; *s* of Sidney Mackenzie Litten and Margaret Lawson; *m* 1958, Alma Jean Thomson; one *s. Educ:* Skinners' Company's Sch.; St Martin's Sch. of Art; Goldsmiths' Sch. of Art. Served RAMC, 1939-46; 1st prize All India Services Art Exhbn, 1942. Exhibits at Royal Academy, Royal Soc. of Portrait Painters, Royal Soc. of British Artists. Principal commissions include: HM the Queen and HRH the Duke of Edinburgh for RMCS, 1954; Countess Bathurst; Maharanee of Cooch Behar; Sir Anthony Elkins; Arthur Wintner; Marchioness of Donegal; Lord Shawcross, 1970. *Recreations:* music, swimming, sailing. *Address:* Studio 6, 49 Roland Gardens, SW7. *T:* 01-373 0653. *Club:* Chelsea Arts.

**LITTLE, Sir Alexander;** *see* Little, Sir R. A.

**LITTLE, Admiral Sir Charles James Colebrooke,** GCB 1945 (KCB 1935; CB 1919); GBE 1942; *b* Shanghai, 14 June 1882; *s* of Louis Stromeyer Little, FRCS, BA, FRAS; *m* 1st, 1908, Rothes Beatrix (*d* 1939), *d* of Colonel Sir Charles Leslie, 7th Bt; one *d*; 2nd, 1940, *cousin* Mary Elizabeth (Bessy), JP Sussex, *d* of late Ernest Muirhead Little, FRCS. *Educ:* Britannia, Dartmouth (1897). Specialised in Submarine Branch, 1903; commanded: H4, A7, B7, C5, C10, D1; Hibernia, 1907; St Vincent, 1910; HMS Fearless and Grand Fleet Submarine Flotilla, 1916-18 (CB civil); in command of HMS Cleopatra in the Baltic, 1919 (CB military); Director of Trade Div. Naval Staff, 1920-22; Member of British Delegation to the Washington Naval Conference, 1921; Captain of the Fleet, Mediterranean Station, 1922-24; SSO, RN War Coll., 1924-26; in command of HMS Iron Duke, 1926-27; Director Royal Naval Staff Coll., 1927-30; Rear-Admiral Second Battle Squadron, 1930-31; Rear-Admiral Submarines, 1931-32; Lord Commissioner of Admiralty and Deputy Chief of Naval Staff, 1932-35; Vice-Admiral, 1933; Commander-in-Chief, China Station, 1936-38; Admiral, 1937; a Lord Commissioner of the Admiralty and Chief of Naval Personnel, 1938-41; Head of British Joint Staff Mission in Washington, 1941-42; Commander-in-Chief, Portsmouth, 1942-45. Ex-Trustee of the National Maritime Museum; Ex-President, British Legion S. Area; Vice-President, Royal United Service Institution; Vice-President, Navy Records Society. Grand Officer Legion of Honour, Bronze medal, Royal Humane Society, Grand Cross Orange Nassau, Legion of Merit (Comdr), Grand Cross of St Olav. *Address:* The Old Mill, Ashurst, near Steyning, Sussex. *T:* Partridge Green 461. *Clubs:* Army and Navy, Pilgrims.

**LITTLE, John Eric Russell,** OBE 1961 (MBE 1943); Counsellor, British Embassy, Brussels, since 1970; *b* 29 Aug. 1913; *s* of William Little and Beatrice Little (*née* Biffen); *m* 1945, Christine Holt; one *s* one *d. Educ:* Strand Sch. Served in FO, 1930-40, and in Army, 1940-41. Transferred to Minister of State's Office, Cairo, 1941, and seconded to Treasury. Returned to FO and appointed to British Middle East Office, 1946. Transferred to FO, 1948; Consul, Milan, 1950 (acting Consul-General, 1951, 1952); Bahrain as Asst Political Agent, 1952 (acting Politcal Agent, 1953, 1954, 1955); 1st Secretary, Paris, 1956; Asst Finance Officer, Foreign Office, 1958; HM Consul-General: Basra, 1962-65; Salonika, 1965-70. *Recreations:* walking, reading. *Address:* c/o Midland Bank Ltd, 16 Regent Street, SW1. Politcal

**LITTLE, John Philip Brooke B.;** *see* Brooke-Little.

**LITTLE, Prof. Kenneth Lindsay;** Professor of Social Anthropology, Edinburgh University, since 1965; *b* 19 Sept. 1908; *e s* of late J. Muir Little, Liverpool; *m* 1957, Iris May Cadogan; one *s* one *d. Educ:* Liverpool Coll.; Selwyn Coll., Cambrdige; Trinity Coll., Cambridge (William Wyse Student). MA Cantab 1944; PhD London 1945. Lectr in Anthropology, LSE, 1946; Reader in Social Anthropology, Edinburgh Univ., 1950. *Publications:* Negroes in Britain, 1948; The Mende of Sierra Leone, 1951; West African Urbanization, 1967. *Recreation:* squash racquets. *Address:* 45 Braid Farm Road, Edinburgh 10.

**LITTLE, Sir (Rudolf) Alexander,** KCB, *cr* 1950 (CB 1946); *b* 23 May 1895; *s* of Charles Little; *m* 1925, Margaret Macnaughton; three *d. Educ:* Oundle; Caius Coll., Cambridge. Served European War, 1915-18; entered General Post Office, 1920; Director GPO, Scotland, 1942-44; Director of Postal Services, GPO, 1944-47, Dep. Director-General, 1947-49; Director-General, GPO, 1949-55, retired. *Recreation:* gardening.

**LITTLEJOHN COOK, George Steveni;** Counsellor and Consul-General, Bangkok, Thailand, since 1969; *b* 29 Oct. 1919; *s* of William Littlejohn Cook, OBE, and of late Xenia Steveni, BEM; *m* 1st, 1949, Marguerite Teresa Bonnaud; one *d*; 2nd, 1964, Thereza Nunes Campos. *Educ:* Wellington Coll.; Trinity Hall, Cambridge. Served with 2nd Bn Cameronians (Scottish Rifles), 1939-46, rank of Capt.; POW Germany; Political Intelligence Dept, Foreign Office, 1945-46. Entered Foreign Service, 1946; Third Secretary, Foreign Office, 1946-47; Second Secretary, Stockholm, 1947-49; Santiago, Chile, 1949-52; First Secretary, 1950; Foreign Office, 1952-53; Chargé d'Affaires, Phnom-Penh, 1953-55; Berne, 1956-58; Director of British Information Service in Brazil, 1959-64; Head of Information Depts, FO (and FCO), 1964-69. *Recreations:* painting, sailing, ski-ing. *Address:* British Embassy, Bangkok, Thailand. *Clubs:* Brooks's, Travellers', Royal Automobile.

**LITTLER, Emile;** Theatrical Impresario, Producer, Author and Company Director; *b* Ramsgate, Kent, 9 Sept. 1903; *s* of F. R. and Agnes Littler; *m* 1933, Cora Goffin (actress). *Educ:* Stratford-on-Avon. Served apprenticeship working on stage of the Theatre; was Asst Manager of Theatre in Southend, 1922; subsequently worked as Asst Stage Manager, Birmingham Rep. Theatre; in US, 1927-31; became Manager and Licensee of Birmingham Rep. Theatre for Sir Barry Jackson, Sept. 1931. Personally started in Management, Sept. 1934; theatrical productions include: Victoria Regina; 1066 and All That; The Maid of the Mountains; The Night and the Music; Claudia; The Quaker Girl; Lilac Time; Song of Norway; Annie Get Your Gun; Zip Goes a Million; Blue for a Boy; Love from Judy; Affairs of State; Book of the Month; Hot Summer Night; Signpost to Murder; The Right Honourable Gentleman; Latin Quarter; The Impossible Years; 110 in the Shade, Student Prince; Desert Song; Annual Pantomimes in London and big cities of British Isles. Director: Eagle Star Insurance Co.; Cambridge Theatre; Chairman: Emile Littler Ltd; Somerset Films Ltd; London Entertainments Ltd; Theatres' National Cttee; President, Society West End Theatre Managers, 1964-67, 1969-70; A Governor, Royal Shakespeare Theatre, Stratford-on-Avon. Prominent play-doctor and race-horse owner. *Publications:* (jointly): Cabbages and Kings; Too Young to Marry; Love Isn't Everything; and 100 Christmas Pantomimes. *Recreations:* tennis, swimming, racing. *Address:* Palace Theatre, Shaftesbury Avenue, W1. *T:* 01-734 9691/2; Downmere, Poynings, Sussex. *Clubs:* Royal Automobile, Royal Aero, Clermont.

**LITTLER, Prince,** CBE 1957; Chairman and Managing Director: Stoll Theatres Corporation Ltd; Associated Theatre Properties (London) Ltd; Theatre Royal, Drury Lane, Ltd; Chairman, Moss Empire Ltd; Director: Associated Television Ltd; Independent Television Corporation; *b* Ramsgate, Kent, 25 July 1901; *s* of F. R. and Agnes Littler; *m* 1932, Nora Delany. *Educ:* Stratford-on-Avon. For many years has presented Musical Comedies and Pantomimes in London, including Jack and the Beanstalk, Drury Lane, 1936; Cinderella, Coliseum, 1937; Brigadoon, Her Majesty's, 1950; Carousel, Drury Lane, 1951; Tea House of the August Moon, Her Majesty's, 1955; No Time for Sergeants, Her Majesty's, 1956; and over 200 Pantomimes in the Provinces. Member Council Theatrical Managers' Assoc.; Vice-President: Society of West End Theatre Managers; Denville Home for Aged Actors and Actresses; Variety Artistes Benevolent Fund. *Address:* Cranbourn Mansions, Cranbourn Street, WC2.

**LITTLER, William Brian,** CB 1959; MSc, PhD; Chemist-in-Charge, Quality Assurance Directorate (Materials), Royal Ordnance Factory, Bridgwater, since 1969; *b* 8 May 1908; *s* of William Littler, Tarporley, Ches; *m* 1937, Pearl Davies, Wrexham; three *d. Educ:* Grove Park, Wrexham; Manchester Univ.; BSc (1st Class), Chemistry, 1929; MSc, 1930; PhD, 1932; Beyer Fellow, 1930-31. Joined Res. Dept, Woolwich, 1933; loaned by Min. of Supply to Defence Res. Bd, Canada; Chief Supt, Cdn Armament Research and Devel. Establishment, Valcartier, Quebec, 1947-49; Supt of Propellants Research, Explosives Research and Devel. Estab., Waltham Abbey, 1949-50; in industry (Glaxo Laboratories Ltd, Ulverston), 1950-52; Dir of Ordnance Factories (Explosives), Min. of Supply, 1952-55; Principal Dir of Scientific Research (Defence), Ministry of Supply, 1955-56; Dir-Gen. of Scientific Research (Munitions), Ministry of Supply, 1956-60; Dep. Chief Scientist, Min. of Defence (Army), 1960-65; Minister, and Head of Defence R&D Staff, British Embassy, Washington, DC, 1965-69. *Publications:* Papers on Flame and Combustion in Proc. Royal Society and Jour. Chem. Soc. *Recreations:* golf, swimming. *Address:* The Old School House, Catcott, near Bridgwater, Som.

**LITTLETON,** family name of **Baron Hatherton.**

**LITTLEWOOD, Lady (Barabara);** Consultant with Barlows, Solicitors, of Guildford; Lay Member of the Press Council, since 1968; *b* 7 Feb. 1909; *d* of Dr Percival Langdon-Down, Teddington; *m* 1934, Sir Sydney Littlewood (*d* 1967); one *s. Educ:* Summerleigh Sch., Teddington; King's Coll., London, (BSc). Admitted solicitor, 1936. Pres. West Surrey Law Soc., 1952-53; Mem. Home Office Departmental Committees on: the Summary Trial of Minor Offences, 1954-55; Matrimonial Proceedings in Magistrates' Courts, 1958-59; Financial Limits prescribed for Maintenance Orders made in Magistrates' Courts, 1966-68. Pres., Nat. Fedn of Business and Professional Women's Clubs of Gt Brit. and N Ire., 1958-60; Pres. Internat. Fedn of Business and Professional Women, 1965-68. JP Middx, 1950-. *Recreation:* occasional golf. *Address:* 26 St Margarets, London Road, Guildford, Surrey. *T:* Guildford 4348. *Club:* Arts Theatre.

**LITTLEWOOD, Rear-Adm. Charles,** CB 1954; OBE 1942; retired; *b* 1 Jan. 1902; *s* of Alfred Littlewood, Croydon, Surrey; *m* 1924, Doris Helen, *d* of William Mackean, London, SW16; no *c. Educ:* Falconbury Sch. (Preparatory), Purley; RN Colls Osborne and Dartmouth. Entered RN 1915; Midshipman, Emperor of India, 1918; Lt (E) RNEC Keyham, 1924; served in Ramillies, Concord, Erebus, Admiralty Experimental Station, 1924-32; Engineer Officer; HMS Ardent, 1932-34; HMS Apollo, 1934-36; Comdr (E) 1936; Flotilla Eng. Officer, HMS Kempenfelt, 1936-38; Manager Engineering Dept, Malta Dockyard, 1938-44; Actg Capt. (E) 1942; Capt (E) 1945; Eng. Officer in HMS Howe, Brit. Pacific Fleet, served at Okinawa Operation, 1944-46; Asst Engineer in Chief, 1946-49; Manager Engineering Dept, Rosyth Dockyard, 1949-52; Rear-Admiral, 1952; Asst Dir of Dockyards, 1952-55, retd 1955. *Address:* Woodlands, Bransgore, near Christchurch, Hants. *T:* Bransgore 540.

**LITTLEWOOD, James;** Deputy Director, Department for National Savings, since 1967; *b* Royton, Lancashire, 21 Oct. 1922; *s* of late Thomas and Sarah Littlewood; *m* 1950, Barbara Shaw; two *s* one *d. Educ:* Manchester Grammar Sch.; St John's Coll., Cambridge (Scholar, MA). Army (Captain), 1942-46. Asst Principal, HM Treasury, 1947; Private Sec. to Financial Sec., 1949-50; Principal, 1950; Civil Service Selection Bd, 1951-52; Sec. to Cttee on Administrative Tribunals and Enquiries, 1955-57; Colombo Plan Conf. Secretariat, 1955 and 1959. Asst Sec., 1962; Under Sec., 1969. *Recreations:* golf, bridge. *Address:* 143 Green Dragon Lane, N21. *T:* 01-360 5457.

**LITTLEWOOD, Joan (Maud);** Artistic Director, Theatre Workshop, since 1945. *Educ:* London. Productions (at Theatre Royal, Stratford and subseq. in West End) include: A Taste of Honey, Wyndham's, 1959; The Hostage, Wyndham's, 1959-60; Make Me an Offer, New, 1959-60; Fings Ain't Wot They Used T'Be, Garrick, 1960-61; Oh What a Lovely War, Wyndham's, 1963; A Kayf up

West, Theatre Royal, Stratford, 1964; (Dir.) Henry IV, Edinburgh Fest., and Oh, What a Lovely War, Broadway, 1964; MacBird, Stratford E, 1967 and Mrs Wilson's Diary (also Criterion), 1967; Forward, Up Your End, Theatre Royal, Stratford, 1970. (Film) Dir., Sparrers Can't Sing, 1963. Centre Culturel Internationale, Tunisia, 1965, 1966. Medal for Excellent Perf., Berlin, 1958; Olympic Award for Theatre, Taormina, 1959. *Recreation:* theatre. *Address:* c/o Theatre Royal, Stratford, E15.

**LITTLEWOOD, John Edensor,** MA, Cambridge; Hon. DSc, Liverpool; Hon. LLD, St Andrews; Hon. ScD Cambridge; FRS, FRAS; Hon. FIMA; Fellow of Trinity College, Cambridge, since 1908; Rouse Ball Professor of Mathematics in University of Cambridge, 1928-50; Fellow of the Cambridge Philosophical Society; Royal Medallist of the Royal Society, 1929, Sylvester Medallist, 1944; Copley Medallist, 1958; De Morgan Medallist, London Mathematical Society, 1939, Senior Berwick Prize, 1960; Corr. Member, French and Göttingen Academies; Former Member Royal Dutch, Royal Danish and Royal Swedish Academies; *b* Rochester, 9 June 1885. *Educ:* St Paul's Sch.; Trinity Coll., Cambridge (Scholar); Bracketed Senior Wrangler, 1905; Richardson Lecturer in Victoria Univ. of Manchester, 1907-10; Lecturer of Trinity Coll., 1910-28; Cayley Lecturer in the University of Cambridge, 1920-28. *Publications:* papers in various scientific journals. *Address:* Trinity College, Cambridge. *TA:* Cambridge 58201.

**LITTMAN, Mark,** QC 1961; Deputy Chairman, British Steel Corporation, since 1970; Director: Rio Tinto-Zinc Corporation Ltd, since 1968; Commercial Union Assurance Co. Ltd, since 1970; *b* 4 Sept. 1920; *s* of Jack and Lilian Littman; *m* 1965, Marguerite Lamkin, USA. *Educ:* Owen's Sch.; London Sch. of Economics; The Queen's Coll., Oxford. BScEcon. 1939; MA Oxon 1941. Served RNVR, Lieut, 1941-46. Called to Bar, Middle Temple, 1947; practised, as Barrister-at-law, 1947-67; Mem., General Council of the Bar, 1968-. *Address:* 79 Chester Square, SW1. *Club:* Reform.

**LIVERMAN, John Gordon,** OBE 1956; Under-Secretary, Ministry of Technology (formerly Ministry of Power), since 1964; *b* London, 21 Oct. 1920; *s* of late George Gordon Liverman and of Hadassah Liverman; *m* 1952, Peggy Earl; two *s* one *d. Educ:* St Paul's Sch.; Trinity Coll., Cambridge (BA). Served with RA, 1940-46. Asst Principal, Min. of Power, 1947, Principal, 1948; Volta River Preparatory Commission, Accra, 1953; Treasury, 1956; Asst Sec., Min. of Power, 1957; Office of Minister for Science, 1961. *Address:* 11 Linkfield Lane, Redhill, Surrey. *Club:* Royal Commonwealth Society.

**LIVERMORE, Harry;** Lord Mayor of Liverpool, 1958-59; *b* 17 Oct. 1908; *m* 1940, Esther Angelman; one *s* one *d. Educ:* Royal Grammar Sch., Newcastle on Tyne; Durham Univ. Solicitor; qualified, 1930; practises in Liverpool. Former Alderman, Liverpool City Council; late Chm., Royal Liverpool Philharmonic Soc.; Chm., Liverpool Everyman Theatre, Ltd; Dep. Chm., Merseyside Arts Assoc. *Recreations:* music, golf. *Address:* 18 Burnham Road, Liverpool 18. *T:* 051-724 2144.

**LIVERPOOL,** 5th Earl of, *cr* 1905 (2nd creation); **Edward Peter Bertram Savile Foljambe;** Baron Hawkesbury, 1893; Viscount Hawkesbury, 1905; *b* posthumously, 14 Nov. 1944; *s* of Captain Peter George William Savile Foljambe (killed in action, 1944) and of Elizabeth Joan (who *m* 1947, Major Andrew Antony Gibbs, MBE, TD), *d* of late Major Eric Charles Montagu Flint, DSO; *S* great uncle, 1969; *m* 1970, Lady Juliana Noel, *e d* of Earl of Gainsborough, *qv. Educ:* Shrewsbury School. *Heir: great uncle* Hon. Victor Alexander Cecil Savile Foljambe, *b* 19 Jan. 1895. *Address:* 10 Reece Mews, SW7. *Club:* Turf.

**LIVERPOOL, Archbishop of, (RC),** and Metropolitan of Northern Province with Suffragan Sees, Hexham, Lancaster, Leeds, Middlesbrough and Salford, since 1964; **Most Rev. George Andrew Beck,** AA; *b* 28 May 1904; 2nd *s* of late P. T. Beck, journalist. *Educ:* Clapham Coll. and St Michael's Coll., Hitchin. Priest, 1927; BA Hons (History), London, 1934. Staff St Michael's Coll., Hitchin, until 1941, Headmaster, 1941-44; Headmaster, The Becket Sch., Nottingham, 1944-48. Consecrated Titular Bishop of Tigia and Coadjutor Bishop of Brentwood by Cardinal Griffin, 1948; Bishop of Brentwood, 1951-55; Bishop of Salford, 1955-64. Chm. Catholic Education Council, 1949-. *Publications:* Assumptionist Spirituality, 1936; The Family and the Future, 1948; (ed. with A. C. F. Beales) Eng. translation of Gonella's The Papacy and World Peace, 1944; (ed.) The English Catholics 1850-1950, 1950; occasional contributions to the Tablet and Clergy Review. *Address:* Archbishop's House, Woolton, Liverpool L25 6DE. *T:* 051-428 1233. *Clubs:* Athenæum, Royal Automobile.

**LIVERPOOL, Bishop of,** since 1966; **Rt. Rev. Stuart Yarworth Blanch;** *b* 1918; *s* of William Edwin and Elizabeth Blanch; *m* 1943, Brenda Gertrude Coyte; one *s* four *d. Educ:* Alleyns Sch., Dulwich. Employee of Law Fire Insurance Soc. Ltd, 1936-40; Navigator in RAF, 1940-46; St Catherine's Soc., Oxford, 1946-49; Curate of Highfield, Oxford, 1949-52; Vicar of Eynsham, Oxon., 1952-57; Vice-Principal of Wycliffe Hall, Oxford, 1957-60; Oriel Canon of Rochester and Warden of Rochester Theological Coll., 1960-66. *Address:* Bishop's Lodge, Woolton Park, Woolton, Liverpool L25 6DT. *T:* (Home) 051-428 2020; (office) 051-709 7593.

**LIVERPOOL, Auxiliary Bishops of, (RC);** *see* Gray, Rt Rev. Joseph, Harris, Rt Rev. Augustine.

**LIVERPOOL, Assistant Bishop of;** *see* Baker, Rt Rev. W. S.

**LIVERPOOL, Dean of;** *see* Patey, Very Rev. E. H.

**LIVERPOOL, Archdeacon of;** *see* Wilkinson, Ven. H. S.

**LIVESEY, Rev. Herbert;** *b* 6 June 1892; *e s* of late Walter Livesey, and Alice, *d* of Christopher Wigglesworth, Lancs. *Educ:* Accrington Grammar Sch.; St Edmund Hall, Oxford, MA, Dip Anthropology, LTh Durham, FRAI. Lt South Lancs Regt (now the Lancs Regt) (wounded); Asst Priest, Wigton, Cumberland; Chaplain and Tutor Lincoln Theological Coll.; Chaplain to Bishop of Newcastle upon Tyne; Sub-warden, St Saviour's Coll., Carshalton: Sub-warden, Diocesan House, Carshalton; Asst Priest St Martin in the Fields; Head of Cambridge Univ. Settlement, 1936-39; Warden of Connaught Hall, University of Southampton and Dir of Theological Studies, 1939-57. *Address:* Barclays Bank, Accrington, Lancs.

**LIVESEY, Roger;** Actor; *b* 25 June 1906; *s* of Samuel Livesey and Mary Catherine Livesey (*née* Edwards); *m* 1936, Ursula Jeans, *qv*. *Educ:* Westminster City Sch. First stage appearance, St James's, 1917; West End parts, 1920-26; subsequently toured in W Indies and two seasons in S Africa, then continued London appearances; joined Old Vic-Sadler's Wells Company Sept. 1932, remaining there until May 1934; Alfred in Martine and Fontaney in The Poet's Secret, Ambassadors, 1933; Harold Parker in Meeting at Night, Globe, 1934; Jim Milburn in Sour Grapes, Apollo, 1934; Hsieh-Ping-Kuei in Lady Precious Stream, Little, 1934; Frank Burdon in Storm in a Teacup, Royalty, 1936; first stage appearance in New York as Mr Horner in The Country Wife, Henry Miller Theatre, 1936; Frank Burdon in Storm Over Patsy, Storm in a Teacup, Guild, 1937; Sir Richard Furze in Spring Meeting, Ambassadors, London, 1938; Dr Stockman in An Enemy of the People and Petruchio in The Taming of the Shrew, Old Vic, 1939; Anthony Anderson in The Devil's Disciple, Piccadilly, 1940; Matey in Dear Brutus, Globe, 1941; toured as Kurt Müller in Watch on the Rhine, and appeared in the same part at the Aldwych, 1943; Philip in The Fifth Column, Theatre Royal, Glasgow, 1944; Lt-Gen. Hume Banbury in The Banbury Nose, Wyndhams, 1944; toured Middle and Far East for ENSA in Dear Brutus, Watch on the Rhine, and Springtime for Henry; William in Ever Since Paradise, New, 1947; Hoerderer in Crime Passionel, Lyric, Hammersmith, 1948; George Bernard in Man of the World, Lyric, Hammersmith, 1950; toured Italy as Sir Toby Belch in Old Vic production of Twelfth Night, June 1950; Justice Overdo in Ben Jonson's Bartholomew Fair, Edinburgh Festival, 1950; 1950-51 Festival Season at reopened Old Vic: Sir Toby Belch in Twelfth Night, Justice Overdo in Bartholomew Fair, Chorus in Henry V, Captain Brassbound in Captain Brassbound's Conversion, Sir John Falstaff in The Merry Wives of Windsor; Hank Moreland in Third Person, Arts, 1951, and Criterion, 1952; Professor Mortimer in The Mortimer Touch, Duke of York's, 1952; Charley Delaney in The Teddy Bear, St Martin's, 1953; Marcus McLeod in Keep in a Cool Place, Saville, 1954; Stephen Leigh in Uncertain Joy, Royal Court, 1955; John Tarleton in Misalliance, Lyric, Hammersmith, 1956; Marcus Heatherington in A Lodging for a Bride, Westminster, 1960; Captain Shotover in Heartbreak House, Wyndhams, 1961; Inspector Gates in Kill Two Birds, St Martin's, 1962; Earl of Caversham in An Ideal Husband, Strand, 1965. Has played in numerous films including The Life and Death of Colonel Blimp, I Know Where I'm Going, A Matter of Life and Death, Vice Versa, That Dangerous Age, Green Grow the Rushes, The Master of Ballantrae, League of Gentlemen, No My Darling Daughter, Of Human Bondage. TV appearances include: The Winslow Boy, Amphitryon 38, The Canvas Rainbow, Adam's Apple, All Our Yesterdays, The Master Builder, The Entertainer, The Physicists. *Recreations:* golf, swimming, cricket, tinkering. *Address:* c/o MCA (England) Ltd, 139 Piccadilly, W1. *T:* 01-629 7211. *Clubs:* Royal Automobile, Stage Golfing Society.

**LIVINGSTON, James Barrett,** DSC 1942; Director: Rockware Group Ltd.; Rockware Glass Ltd. (Joint Managing Director, 1951-60; Managing Director, 1960-69; Vice-Chairman, 1967-69); *b* 13 Sept. 1906; *yr s* of late Capt. David Liddle Livingston and Ruth Livingston, Bombay and Aberdour; *m* 1933, Joyce Eileen, *fourth d* of late Arthur and Lilian Birkett, Clements Inn and Southwold; one *s* one *d*. *Educ:* HMS Worcester. Served War of 1939-45, RN: Staff Officer (Ops) 10th Cruiser Sqdn, Norwegian Campaign, North Russian and Malta Convoys (despatches 1943); Ops Div. Admiralty, 1943-45 (Comdr). Joined Rockware Group of Cos, 1945; Exec. Director, British Hartford-Fairmont Ltd, 1947. Director: Portland Glass Co. Ltd, 1956-69; Jackson Bros (Knottingley) Ltd, 1968-69 (Chm.); Burwell, Reed & Kinghorn Ltd, 1962; Blewis & Shaw (Plastics) Ltd, 1960; Automotated Inspection Machinery Ltd, 1962-69; Garston Bottle Co. Ltd, 1966-69 (Chm.); Forsters Glass Co. Ltd, 1967-69; also other Glass and Associated Companies. Member: Bd of Govs, Charing Cross Hospital, 1956 (Chm., Medical School Council, 1967-); Council, Glass Manufacturers' Fedn 1967 (Pres. 1970-71); Nat. Cttee, Assoc. of Glass Container Manufacturers, 1959-69 (Vice-Pres.); Nat. Jt Industrial Council 1959-69; Court of Ironmongers' Co., 1946 (Master, 1960-61); Adv. Cttee to Faculty of Materials Technology, Sheffield University, 1969; Council CBI, 1970; Council, Royal College of Art, 1970. *Recreations:* golf, racket re-strings, gardening. *Address:* (home) Ferroners, Beaconsfield, Bucks. *T:* Beaconsfield 3853; (office) Rockware Avenue, Greenford, Middlesex. *T:* 01-578 4353.

**LIVINGSTON, Air Marshal Sir Philip C.,** KBE *cr* 1950 (CBE 1946); CB 1948; AFC 1942; retired; FRCS; FRCSE, LRCP, DPH, DOMS; *b* 2 March 1893; *y s* of Clermont Livingston, Cleveland, Vancouver Island, BC, Canada; *m* 1920, Lorna Muriel, *o d* of C. W. Legassicke Crespin, London, Eng.; one *s* (and one *s* decd). *Educ:* Jesus Coll., Cambridge; London Hosp. Served European War, 1914-17, RNVR 4th Destroyer Flotilla, 1915; 10th Cruiser Sqdn, 1916. Qualified Jan. 1919; joined RAF, 1919, as MO; served India, Iraq, Far East; Consultant in Ophthalmology, 1934-46; Dep. Dir RAF Medical Services, 1947; Dir-Gen., 1948-51. Chadwick Prize and Gold Medal for researches in applied physiology, 1938. CStJ. *Publications:* Montgomery, Moynihan, and Chadwick Lectures, 1942-45; *autobiography:* Fringe of the Clouds, 1962; many papers on subjects connected with vision. *Recreation:* rowing (rowed 3 in winning Cambridge Univ., Crew, march 1914). *Address:* Maple Bay, RR1, Duncan, BC, Canada.

**LIVINGSTON-HERBAGE, Julian;** *see* Herbage.

**LIVINGSTONE, Archibald Macdonald,** CIE 1941; MC; MA, BSc (Agric.) Edinburgh. FRSA. Served European War, 1914-18; Major RFA (MC). Agricultural Marketing Adviser India and Burma (CIE) 1934-41. Lately Senior Marketing Officer, Ministry of Agriculture and Fisheries; retired, 1955. *Address:* 92 Marine Parade, Napier, New Zealand.

**LIVINGSTONE, James,** CMG 1968; OBE 1951; Controller, Overseas A Division, British Council, since 1969; *b* 4 April 1912; *e s* of late Angus Cook Livingstone, sometime Provost of Bo'ness, Scotland, and Mrs Jean Fraser Aitken Wilson Livingstone; *m* 1945, Dr Mair Eleri Morgan Thomas, MB, ChB, BSc, DPH, FRCPath, *e d* of late John Thomas, DSc, Harlech and Mrs O. M. Thomas, Llanddewi Brefi and Wilmslow; one *d* (one *s* decd). *Educ:* Bo'ness Acad.; Edinburgh Univ.; Moray House Trng Coll., Edinburgh. Adult Educn and School Posts, Scotland and Egypt, 1936-42; British Coun. Service, Egypt and Iran, 1942-45; Middle East Dept, 1945-46; Asst Rep., Palestine, 1946-48; Dep. Dir, Personnel Dept, 1949; Dir, Personnel Dept, 1956; Controller, Establishments Div., 1962. *Recreations:* photography, exploring the West Highlands and Islands. *Address:* 21 Park Avenue, Golders Green, NW11. *T:* 01-455

7600; Tan-yr-allt, Llangeitho, Cards. *Club:* Royal Commonwealth Society.

**LIVINGSTONE, James Livingstone,** MD, FRCP; Retired; Consulting Physician: King's College Hospital; Brompton Hospital; St Dunstan's; *b* 8 May 1900; *m* 1935, Janet Muriel Rocke; two *s* one *d. Educ:* Worksop Coll., Notts; King's Coll., University of London; King's Coll. Hospital. MRCS, LRCP, 1922; MB, BS 1923; MRCP 1925; MD London 1925; FRCP 1933. RAF, 1918-19. Fellow of King's Coll., London. Member: Assoc. of Physicians of Gt Britain; Thoracic Soc. *Publications:* Bronchitis and Broncho-pneumonia in Brit. Encyc. of Med. Practice, 2nd edn; Modern Practice in Tuberculosis, 1952; jt editor contributions to medical journals. *Recreations:* golf, fishing. *Address:* 11 Chyngton Road, Seaford, Sussex. *Club:* Seaford Golf.

**LLANDAFF, Bishop of;** *see* Wales, Archbishop of.

**LLANDAFF, Assistant Bishop of;** *see* Hughes, Rt Rev. Thomas Maurice.

**LLANDAFF, Dean of;** *see* Phillips, Very Rev. G. L.

**LLANDAFF, Archdeacon of;** *see* Williams, Ven. J. F.

**LLEWELLYN, Sir David (Treharne),** Kt 1960; Captain, late Welsh Guards; Director: James Howell & Co. Ltd; Howells Garages Ltd; Thameside Radio Ltd; *b* Aberdare, 17 Jan. 1916; 3rd *s* of Sir David Richard Llewellyn, 1st Bt, LLD, JP, and of Magdalene Anne (*d* 1966), *yr d* of late Rev. Henry Harries, DD, Porthcawl; *m* Joan Anne Williams, OBE, 2nd *d* of R. H. Williams, Bonvilston House, Bonvilston, near Cardiff; two *s* one *d. Educ:* Eton; Trinity Coll., Cambridge. BA 1938. Served War of 1939-45; enlisted Royal Fusiliers, serving in ranks; commissioned Welsh Guards; North-West Europe, 1944-45. Contested (Conservative) Aberavon Div. of Glamorgan, 1945. MP (C) Cardiff, North, 1950-Sept. 1959; Parliamentary Under-Sec. of State, Home Office, 1951-52 (resigned, ill-health). Mem. of the Broadcasting Council for Wales (B.B.C.), 1960-61; Member Welsh Advisory Cttee for Civil Aviation, 1961-62. Has travelled in Europe (including USSR), America and Canada. Mem. Nat. Union of Journalists. *Publication:* Nye: The Beloved Patrician. *Address:* The Old Rectory, Yattendon, Newbury, Berks.

**LLEWELLYN, Dr Donald Rees;** Vice-Chancellor, University of Waikato, since 1964; *b* 20 Nov. 1919; *s* of late R. G Llewellyn, Dursley; *m* 1943, Ruth Marian, *d* of late G. E. Blandford, Dursley; one *s* one *d. Educ:* Dursley Grammar Sch.; Univ. of Birmingham. BSc 1st cl. hons Chem. 1941, DSc 1957, Birmingham; DPhil Oxon 1943. Research Fellow, Cambrdige Univ., 1944-46; Lectr in Chemistry, UC of N Wales, 1946-49; ICI Research Fellow, University Coll., London, 1949-52; Lectr in Chemistry, UCL, 1952-57; Prof. of Chemistry and Dir of Labs, Univ. of Auckland, 1957-64; Asst Vice-Chancellor, Univ. of Auckland, 1962-64. FRIC 1952; FNZIC 1957; FRSA 1960. *Publications:* numerous papers on application of stable isotopes in Jl Chem. Soc. and others. *Recreations:* hockey, squash, tennis, showjumping (FEI Judge), photography. *Address:* Cambrdige Road, Hamilton, RD3, New Zealand. *T:* 69-172. *Club:* Hamilton (NZ).

**LLEWELLYN, Dr Frederick John;** Vice-Chancellor of Exeter University since 1966; *b* 29 April 1915; *er s* of R. G. Llewellyn, Dursley, Glos.; *m* 1939, Joyce, *d* of late Ernest Barrett, Dursley; one *s* one *d. Educ:* Dursley Gram. Sch.; University of Birmingham. BSc, 1st Cl. Hons Chemistry, 1935; PhD, 1938; DSc, 1951 (Birmingham); FRIC, 1944, FNZIC, 1948; FRSA, 1952; FRSNZ, 1964. Lecturer in Chemistry, Birkbeck Coll., 1939-45; Dir, Min. of Supply Research Team, 1941-46; ICI Research Fellow, 1946-47; Prof. of Chemistry, Auckland Univ. Coll., 1947-55; Vice-Chancellor and Rector, University of Canterbury, Christchurch, NZ, 1956-61; Chairman: University Grants Cttee (NZ), 1961-66; N Zealand Broadcasting Corp., 1962-65; NZ Coun. of Adult Educn, 1961-66; NZ Commonwealth Scholarships and Fellowships Cttee, 1961-66; Mem. Senate, University of New Zealand, 1956-60; Mem. Council of Scientific and Industrial Research, 1957-61, 1962; Mem. NZ Atomic Energy Cttee, 1958; Mem. NZ Cttee on Technical Education, 1958-66; Member Council: Royal Society, 1961-63; Assoc. of Commonwealth Univs, 1967-; Member: Inter-University Council for Higher Education Overseas, 1967-; British Council Cttee for Commonwealth Univ. Interchange, 1968-; Representative of UK Universities on Council of Univ. of Ahmado Bello, Nigeria, 1968-. Chm., Northcott Theatre Bd of Management, 1966-. Hon. LLD Canterbury 1962; Hon. LLD Victoria Univ. of Wellington, 1966. *Publications:* Crystallographic papers in Jl of Chemical Soc., London, and in Acta Crystallographica. *Recreations:* photography and travel. *Address:* The University, Exeter. *T:* Exeter 77911. *Club:* Athenæum.

**LLEWELLYN, Col Sir Godfrey;** *see* Llewellyn, Col Sir R. G.

**LLEWELLYN, Lt-Col (Hon.) Henry Morton,** CBE 1953 (OBE 1944); MA; late Warwicks Yeomanry; Chairman: Whitbread Wales Ltd; Davenco (Engineers) Ltd; South Wales Board, Eagle Star Assurance Co.; Director: Whitbread International Ltd; Cardiff Malting Co. Ltd; Chepstow Racecourse Co. Ltd; Member: South Wales Regional Board, Lloyds Bank; Wales Tourist Board, since 1969; Vice-Chairman, Civic Trust for Wales; *b* 18 July 1911; 2nd *s* of Sir David Llewellyn, 1st Bt, and *heir-pres.* to Lt-Col Sir Rhys Llewellyn, 2nd Bt, *qv*; *m* 1944, Hon. Christine Saumarez, 2nd *d* of 5th Baron de Saumarez; two *s* one *d. Educ:* Oundle; Trinity Coll., Cambridge (MA). Steward: Nat. Hunt Cttee, 1948-51; Jockey Club, 1969. Jt Master Monmouthshire Hounds, 1952-57, 1963-65; Riding Captain winning Brit. Olympic Show-Jumping Team, Helsinki, 1952; Chm., Brit. Show Jumping Assoc., 1967-69. Royal Humane Soc. medal for life-saving, 1956. DL Monmouthshire, 1952, JP 1954-68, High Sheriff 1966. US Legion of Merit, 1945. *Recreations:* show jumping, hunting and steeplechasing. *Address:* Llanvair Grange, near Abergavenny, Monmouth. *T:* Nantyderry 389. *Club:* Cavalry.

**LLEWELLYN, John Charles,** JP; **His Honour Judge Llewellyn;** a Judge of County Courts, since 1965; a Deputy Chairman, Inner London Area Sessions, since 1965; *b* 11 Feb. 1908; *o s* of late J. E. Llewellyn, Letchworth, Herts; *m* 1937, Rae Marguerite Cabell Warrens, *d* of Lt-Col E. R. C. Warrens, DSO, Froxfield, Hants; one *s* two *d. Educ:* St Christopher Sch., Letchworth; Emmanuel Coll., Cambridge (MA, LLB). Barrister, Inner Temple, 1931; Master of the Bench, Inner Temple, 1963. Common Law Counsel to PO, 1960-65; Recorder of King's Lynn, 1961-65. Mem. Gen. Council of the Bar, 1956-60, and 1961-65; Chm. Jt Advisory Council, Carpet Industry of

Gt Brit., 1958-; Dep. Chm. Agric. Land Tribunal (Eastern Region), 1959-65; JP Greater London, 1965-. *Recreation:* riding. *Address:* Bulford Mill, Braintree, Essex. *T:* 616; 2 Temple Gardens, EC4. *T:* 01-353 7907. *Clubs:* Athenæum, Boodle's.

**LLEWELLYN, Lt-Col Sir Rhys,** 2nd Bt, *cr* 1922; late Welsh Guards; *b* 9 March 1910; *e s* of Sir David Llewellyn, 1st Bt, LLD, and Magdalene (*d* 1966), *d* of Rev. H. Harries, DD, Porthcawl; *S* father, 1940; unmarried. *Educ:* Oundle; Trinity Coll., Cambridge, MA. Master of Talybont Foxhounds, 1936-40; Supplementary Reserve of Officers, Welsh Guards, June 1939; War of 1939-45 (France and Germany, despatches); Regular Army Reserve of Officers, 1945-61. High Sheriff of Glamorgan, 1950-51. Comdr, Order of St John of Jerusalem. *Publications:* Breeding to Race, 1965; many articles on Thoroughbred breeding, etc. *Heir:* *b* Lt-Col Henry Morton Llewellyn, *qv*. *Address:* 100 Arlington House, St James's, SW1. *T:* 01-499 3666.
*See also Sir Donald Forsyth Anderson.*

**LLEWELLYN, Richard;** *see* Lloyd, R. D. V. L.

**LLEWELLYN, Col Sir (Robert) Godfrey,** 1st Bt *cr* 1959; Kt 1953; CB 1950; CBE 1942 (OBE 1927); MC 1918; TD; DL; JP; Chairman Welsh Hospital Board, 1959-65; Director of Companies; Chairman of the Wales and Monmouthshire Conservative and Unionist Council, 1949-56, President, 1958, 1962, 1966, 1967, 1968, 1969; President, National Union of Conservative and Unionist Associations, 1962 (Vice-Chairman 1952-53, Chairman 1954-55); Chairman Glamorgan TA and AFA, 1953-58; *b* 13 May 1893; *y s* of Robert William Llewellyn, DL, JP, Cwrt-Colman, Bridgend and Baglan Hall, Briton-Ferry, Glamorgan; *m* 1920, Frances Doris (*d* 1969), *d* of Rowland S. Kennard, JP, Little Harrow, Christchurch, Hants; one *s* one *d*. *Educ:* Royal Naval Colls, Osborne and Dartmouth. Joined Royal Navy, 1906; Midshipman, 1910; Sub-Lt 1913; resigned, 1914; served European War, with Montgomeryshire Yeomanry Cavalry to 1917 when attached Royal Welch Fusiliers; commanded Brigade Signal Troop 6th Mounted Brigade, 1917-18. Captain 1918; 4th Cavalry Division Signal Squadron, 1918 (despatches twice, MC); Commanded 53rd Div. Signals (TA), 1920-29; Major, 1920; Bt Lt-Col, 1924; Lt-Col 1925; Bt Col 1928; Dep. Chief Signal Officer, Western Command, 1929-37; retired, 1937; Hon. Col 53rd Div. Signals, Royal Corps Signals, 1929-33. Col i/c Administration, Home Guard and Home Guard Adviser, S Wales District, 1940-44; Hon. Col 38th Div. Royal Corps Signals, 1941-49; Col Commandant Glamorgan Army Cadet Force, 1943-49; formerly Hon. Col 16th (Welsh) Battalion The Parachute Regt, TA. JP Neath Borough, 1925. Pres. of the Bath and West Show, 1956; Chm. of Organising Cttee Empire and Commonwealth Games, 1958. DL Glamorgan, 1936; DL Mon., 1960; JP Glamorgan County, 1934; High Sheriff: of Glamorgan, 1947-48, of Monmouth, 1963-64. KStJ 1969. *Recreations:* yachting, shooting, fishing, racing. *Heir:* *s* Captain Michael Rowland Godfrey Llewellyn, Grenadier Guards R of O. [*b* 15 June 1921; *m* 1st, 1946, Bronwen Mary (marriage dissolved, 1951), *d* of Sir (Owen) Watkin Williams-Wynn, 8th Bt; 2nd, 1956, Janet Prudence, *y d* of Lt-Col Charles Thomas Edmondes, DL, JP, Ewenny Priory, Bridgend, Glam; three *d*. *Educ:* Harrow; RMC Sandhurst]. *Address:* Tredilion Park, Abergavenny, Mon. *T:* 405. *Clubs:* Carlton, Pratt's, United Service; Royal Thames Yacht, Royal Automobile; Cardiff and County (Cardiff).

**LLEWELLYN, Rt. Rev. William Somers;** *see* Lynn, Suffragan Bishop of.

**LLEWELLYN JONES, Frank;** *see* Jones, F. Ll.

**LLEWELYN, Brig. Sir (Charles) Michael D.;** *see* *Venables-Llewelyn.*

**LLEWELYN-DAVIES,** family name of **Baron Llewelyn-Davies** and **Baroness Llewelyn-Davies of Hastoe.**

**LLEWELYN-DAVIES,** Baron, *cr* 1963 (Life Peer); **Richard Llewelyn-Davies,** MA, FRIBA; MTPI; Professor of Urban Planning in the University of London, at University College, since 1969 (Professor of Architecture, 1960-69); Member, Royal Fine Art Commission, since 1961; in private practice as Planner, and Senior Partner, Llewelyn-Davies, Weeks, Forestier-Walker & Bor; *b* 24 Dec. 1912; *s* of Crompton Llewelyn Davies and Moya Llewelyn Davies (*née* O'Connor); *m* 1943, Patricia (*see* Baroness Llewelyn-Davies of Hastoe); three *d*. *Educ:* privately; Trinity Coll., Cambridge; Ecole des Beaux Arts, Paris; Architectural Association. Architect, LMS Railways, 1942-48. Director: Investigation into Functions and Design of Hospitals; Division of Architectural Studies, Nuffield Foundation, London, 1953-60; First Pres., World Soc. for Ekistics, 1965; Chm., The Centre for Environmental Studies, 1967-; Mem., RIBA Council and Board of Architectural Education. Consulting Architect: to Times Publishing Co. Ltd for new offices at Printing House Square; for rebuilding of London Stock Exchange; for many hosps in the UK and overseas. Other projects include: Master Planner, Memorial Teaching Hosp., Memorial Univ., Newfoundland, 1967-; Tate Gallery Extensions; new village at Rushbrooke, Suffolk (West Suffolk Award, 1957); Nuffield diagnostic centre and maternity hosp. at Corby, Northants (RIBA Bronze Medal, 1957); Master Plan for Washington New Town, Co. Durham, 1966; Master Plan for new city of Milton Keynes, 1967-. Hon. Fellow, American Institute of Architects, 1970. *Publications:* (jointly) Studies in the Functions and Design of Hospitals, 1955; (jointly) Building Elements, 1956; (jointly) The Design of Research Laboratories, 1960; contributions to Nature, Journal of RIBA, Architects' Journal, Architectural Review, Architectural Record, Jl Town Planning Inst., Jl Royal Inst. of Chemistry. *Address:* 36 Parkhill Road, NW3. *T:* 01-485 6576. *Club:* Brooks's.

**LLEWELYN-DAVIES OF HASTOE,** Baroness *cr* 1967, of Hastoe (Life Peer); **Patricia Llewelyn-Davies;** A Baroness-in-Waiting (Government Whip), since 1969; Director, Africa Educational Trust, 1960-69; *b* 16 July 1915; *d* of Charles Percy Parry and Sarah Gertrude Parry (*née* Hamilton); *m* 1943, Richard Llewelyn-Davies (now Baron Llewelyn-Davies, *qv*); three *d*. *Educ:* Liverpool Coll., Huyton; Girton Coll., Cambridge. Civil Servant, 1940-51 (Min. of War Transp., FO, Air Min., CRO). Contested (Lab) Wolverhampton S-W, 1951, Wandsworth Cent., 1955, 1959. Hon. Sec., Lab. Parly Assoc., 1960-69. Member: Bd of Govs, Hosp. for Sick Children, Gt Ormond Street, 1955-67 (Chm. Bd, 1967-69); Court, Univ. of Sussex, 1967-69. *Address:* 36 Parkhill Road, NW3. *T:* 01-485 6576.

**LLOYD,** family name of **Barons Lloyd** and **Lloyd of Hampstead.**

**LLOYD,** 2nd Baron, *cr* 1925, of Dolobran; **Alexander David Frederick Lloyd,** MBE 1945;

DL; Captain Welsh Guards (Reserve); Director: Lloyds Bank Ltd; National and Grindlay's Bank Ltd, and other companies; Deputy Chairman, National Bank of New Zealand, 1969, Chairman since 1970; Member, White Fish Authority and Herring Board since 1963; *b* 30 Sept. 1912; *o s* of 1st Baron and Hon. Blanche (*d* 1969) (late Maid of Honour to Queen Alexandra), *d* of late Hon. F. C. Lascelles; *S* father, 1941; *m* 1942, Lady Victoria Jean Marjorie Mabel Ogilvy, *e d* of 11th Earl of Airlie; one *s* two *d*. *Educ:* Eton; Cambridge (MA). Served in British Council prior to War of 1939-45; served War of 1939-45 in Palestine, Syria and NW Europe. Pres. Navy League, 1948-51; Mem. LCC, 1949-51. Lord in Waiting to King George VI, Oct. 1951-Feb. 1952, to the Queen until Dec. 1952; Jt Under-Sec. of State for Home Dept with responsibility for Welsh Affairs, Nov. 1952-Oct. 1954; Parliamentary Under-Sec. of State for the Colonies, Oct. 1954-Jan. 1957. Pres. Commonwealth and British Empire Chambers of Commerce, 1957-61. Board of Governors, London Sch. of Hygiene and Tropical Medicine. DL Herts 1963. *Recreations:* shooting, fishing. *Heir: s* Hon. Charles George David Lloyd, *b* 4 April 1949. *Address:* Clouds Hill, Offley, Hitchin, Herts. *T:* Offley 350. *Clubs:* White's, Royal Automobile.

**LLOYD OF HAMPSTEAD,** Baron *cr* 1965 (Life Peer); **Dennis Lloyd;** Quain Professor of Jurisprudence in the University of London (University College), since 1956; *b* 22 Oct. 1915; 2nd *s* of Isaac and Betty Lloyd; *m* 1940, Ruth Emma Cecilia Tulla; two *d*. *Educ:* University Coll. Sch.; University Coll., London; Gonville and Caius Coll., Cambridge. LLB (London) 1935; BA 1937, MA 1941, LLD 1956 (Cantab). Called to Bar, 1936; Yorke Prize, 1938; in practice in London, 1937-39 and 1946-. Served War of 1939-45 in RA and RAOC, Liaison Officer (DADOS) with Free French Forces in Syria and Lebanon, 1944-45. Reader in English Law, University Coll., London, 1947-56; Fellow of University Coll., London; Hon. Legal Adviser to Assoc. of Univ. Teachers; Dean of Faculty of Laws, University of London, 1962-64; Head of Dept of Law, University Coll.; Member: Law Reform Cttee; Consolidation Bills Cttee; Joint Cttee on Theatre Censorship; Conseil de la Fédération Britannique de l'Alliance Française; Chairman: Nat. Film Sch. Cttee; Planning Cttee for Nat. Film Sch.; Chm. of Governors, Nat. Film School, 1970-; Governor, British Film Inst. *Publications:* Unincorporated Associations, 1938; Rent Control, 1st edition, 1949, 2nd edition, 1955; Public Policy: A Comparative Study in English and French Law, 1953; United Kingdom: Development of its Laws and Constitution, 1955; Business Lettings, 1956; Introduction to Jurisprudence, 1st edn, 1959, 2nd edn, 1965; The Idea of Law, 1964, rev. imps, 1968, 1970, Japanese trans., 1969; Law (Concept Series), 1968; contrib. to periodicals. *Recreations:* painting, listening to music. *Address:* 6 Pump Court, Temple, EC4. *T:* 01-236 3938; 18 Hampstead Way, NW11. *T:* 01-455 0954. *Club:* Athenæum.

**LLOYD, Rev. (Albert) Kingsley;** President of the Conference of the Methodist Church, 1964; *b* 1903; *s* of Rev. Albert Lloyd; *m* 1926, Ida Marian (*née* Cartledge) (*d* 1969); one *s* one *d*. *Educ:* Kingswood Sch., Bath; Richmond Coll., Surrey (University of London). Methodist Circuit Minister: London, Bedford, Cambridge, 1926-52; Chm., London N Dist, 1951-53. Secretary, Dept of Connexional Funds of the Methodist Church, 1952-69. Chairman: Methodist Ministers' Housing Soc.; Finance Cttee, British Council of Churches, Christian Aid. Visitor and Chm. of Governors, Kingswood Sch. Wesley Historical Soc. Lectr, 1968. *Recreations:* gardening, fishing. *Address:* 13 High Street, Orwell, Royston, Herts.

**LLOYD, Anthony (John Leslie),** QC 1967; Barrister-at-law; Attorney-General to HRH The Prince of Wales, since 1969; *b* 9 May 1929; *o s* of Edward John Boydell Lloyd and Leslie Johnston Fleming; *m* 1960, Jane Helen Violet, *er d* of C. W. Shelford, Chailey Place, Lewes, Sussex. *Educ:* Eton (Schol.); Trinity Coll., Cambridge (Maj. Schol.). National Service, 1st Bn Coldstream Guards, 1948; Montague Butler Prize, Cambridge, 1950; Sir William Browne Medal, 1951. Choate Fellow, Harvard, 1952; Fellow of Peterhouse, 1953. Called to Bar, Inner Temple, 1955. Trustee, Crafts Centre of Great Britain, 1967; Member: Educn Cttee, ILEA, 1969-70; Formation Cttee, Polytechnic of the South Bank, 1970-. *Recreations:* music, carpentry; formerly running (ran for Cambridge in Mile, White City, 1950). *Address:* 68 Strand-on-the-Green, Chiswick, W4. *T:* 01-994 7790; Ludlay, Berwick, Sussex. *T:* Alfriston 204. *Club:* Brooks's.

**LLOYD, Prof. Antony Charles;** Professor of Philosophy, Liverpool University, since 1957; *b* 15 July 1916; *s* of Charles Mostyn Lloyd and Theodosia Harrison-Rowson. *Educ:* Shrewsbury Sch.; Balliol Coll., Oxford. Asst to Prof. of Logic and Metaphysics, Edinburgh Univ., 1938-39 and 1945; served in Army, 1940-45; Lecturer in Philosophy, St Andrews Univ., 1946-57. *Publications:* Chapters in Cambridge History of Later Ancient Philosophy; articles in philosophical journals. *Address:* The University, Liverpool 3.

**LLOYD, Dr Brian Beynon;** Director, Oxford Polytechnic, since 1970; *b* 23 Sept. 1920; *s* of David John Lloyd, MA Oxon and Olwen (*née* Beynon); *m* 1949, Reinhold Johanna Engeroff; four *s* three *d* (inc. twin *s* and *d*). *Educ:* Newport High Sch.; Winchester Coll. (Schol.); Balliol Coll., Oxford (Domus and Frazer Schol.). Special Certif. for BA (War) Degree in Chem., 1940; took degrees BA and MA, 1946; Theodore Williams Schol. and cl. I in Physiology, 1948; DSc 1969. Joined Oxford Nutrition Survey after registration as conscientious objector, 1941; Pres., Jun. Common Room, Balliol, 1941-42; Chm., Undergraduate Rep. Coun., 1942; Biochemist: SHAEF Nutrition Survey Team, Leiden, 1945; Nutrition Survey Group, Düsseldorf, 1946. Fellow of Magdalen by exam. in Physiology, 1948-52, by special election, 1952-70; Senior Tutor, 1963-64; Vice-Pres., 1967 and 1968; Senior Research Officer, later Univ. Lectr, Univ. of Oxford, 1948-70; Senior Proctor, 1960-61. Vis. Physiologist, New York, 1963. Pres., Section I, British Assoc. for the Advancement of Science, 1964-65. Chm. of Govs, Oxford Coll. of Technology, 1963-69; Chm. of Dirs, Oxford Gallery, 1967-. *Publications:* Gas Analysis Apparatus, 1960; (jt ed) The Regulation of Human Respiration, 1962; Cerebrospinal Fluid and the Regulation of Respiration, 1965; articles in physiological and biochemical jls. *Recreations:* Klavarskribo, Correggio, haemoglobin, the analysis of running records. *Address:* 13 Charlbury Road, Oxford. *T:* Oxford 55310.

**LLOYD, (Charles) Christopher;** author, historian; *b* 2 Sept. 1906; *s* of E. S. Lloyd, CSI, and M. Young; *m* 1938, Katharine Brenda Sturge; one *s* one *d*. *Educ:* Marlborough; Lincoln Coll., Oxford. Lecturer: Bishop's Univ., Quebec, 1930-34; Royal Naval Coll., Dartmouth, 1934-45; Lectr, 1945-66, Prof. of

History, 1962-66, Royal Naval College, Greenwich; retired, 1967. *Publications:* The Navy and the Slave Trade, 1949; The Nation and the Navy, 1961; Medicine and the Navy, 1961; William Dampier, 1966; The British Seaman, 1968; Mr Barrow of the Admiralty: a Life of Sir John Barrow, 1764-1848, 1970, etc. *Recreation:* gardening. *Address:* Pilgrims House, Knockholt, Kent. *T:* Knockholt 3104. *Club:* Travellers'.

**LLOYD, Charles William,** MA; JP; Master, Dulwich College, since 1967; *b* 23 Sept. 1915; *s* of late Charles Lloyd and late Frances Ellen Lloyd, London; *m* 1939, Doris Ethel, *d* of late David Baker, Eastbourne; one *s* one *d* (and one *d* decd). *Educ:* St Olave's Sch.; Emmanuel Coll., Cambridge. Asst Master Buckhurst Hill Sch., 1938-40. War Service with RA, 1940-46 (despatches). Asst Master Gresham's Sch., Holt, 1946-51; Headmaster, Hutton Gram. Sch., near Preston, 1951-63; Headmaster, Alleyn's Sch., London, 1963-66. *Publication:* Contrib. to Domesday Geography of SE England (Surrey) ed. by H. C. Darby. *Recreations:* golf, sailing and gardening. *Address:* Elm Lawn, Dulwich Common, SE21.

**LLOYD, Christopher;** *see* Lloyd, Charles C.

**LLOYD, Maj.-Gen. Cyril,** CB 1948; CBE 1944 (OBE 1943); TD 1945 (2 bars); psc: Director-General, City and Guilds of London Institute, 1949-67, Consultant, since 1968; Hon. Executive Principal, West Dean College, 1969; Vice-Chairman, Associated Examining Board for General Certificate of Education; *b* 1906; *s* of late A. H. Lloyd. *Educ:* Brighton Grammar Sch.; London and Cambridge Univs. First Class in Mathematics, Physics, Divinity. Fellow of Institute of Physics; FRGS; MRST; Lecturer and Teacher; Research Worker in Science; Sussex Territorials (RA), 1929-39; Major, 1939; BEF, 1939-40 (despatches); General Staff, Canadian Army, 1940-42 (despatches, OBE); served various overseas theatres; a Dep Chief of Staff, 21 Army Group, 1943-45; Invasion of Europe (despatches, CBE), 1944-45; Dir-Gen. of Army Education and Training, 1945-49; Member: Council of Boy Scouts Assoc.; Coun. Assoc. of Techn. Institutions, 1961-64; Central Adv. Coun. for Educn (England) and Adv. Cttee on Educn in Colonies, 1949-53; Adv. Coun. on Sci. Policy (Jt Enquiry on Technicians, 1962-65; Bd, Internat. Centre for Advanced Technical and Vocational Trg (Turin); Council for Tech. Education and Training for Overseas Countries; Regional Adv. Coun. for Higher Technological Educn (London); Parly and Scientific Cttee; Nat. Adv. Coun. for educn in Industry and Commerce, 1945-68; Southern Regional Council for Further Educn; Vice-Pres. Brit. Assoc. for Commercial and Industrial Educn (Chm. 1955-58); Industrial Trg Coun., 1958-64; Central Trg Council and its General Policy Cttee, 1964-68; Chm., Governing Body, National Institute of Agricultural Engineering; Schools Broadcasting Council for the UK, 1962-65; W Sussex Educn Cttee; Coun. Rural Industries Bureau; Chm., Cttee on Scientific Library Services; Chm. Governors, Crawley Coll. of Further Educn; Vice-Pres., Crawley Planning Gp; Chief Officer, Commonwealth Tech. Trg Week, 1961; Treas., 1963 Campaign for Educn; Mem. Coun. for Educl Advance; Trustee, Industrial Trg Foundn; Pres., Roffey Park Management Inst. Governor, Imperial Coll.; Mem. Delegacy, City and Guilds Coll.; Liveryman, Goldsmiths' Co. and Freeman of City of London; FRSA. *Publications:* booklets: British Services Education, 1950; Human Resources and New Systems of Vocational Training and Apprenticeship, 1963; contrib. to jls. *Recreations:* the countryside and sailing. *Address:* The Pheasantry, Colgate, Horsham, Sussex; West Dean House, Chichester, Sussex. *Club:* Athenæum.

**LLOYD, Major Sir (Ernest) Guy (Richard),** 1st Bt *cr* 1960; Kt 1953; DSO 1917; DL; late Administrator J. and P. Coats, Ltd, Glasgow (retired 1938); *b* 7 Aug. 1890; *e s* of late Major E. T. Lloyd, late Bengal Civil Service; *m* 1918, Helen Kynaston, *yr d* of late Col E. W. Greg, CB; one *s* three *d* (and one *d* decd). *Educ:* Rossall; Keble Coll., Oxford, MA. Served European War, 1914-18 (despatches, DSO); War of 1939-45, 1940. MP (U) East Renfrewshire, Scotland, 1940-Sept. 1959. DL, Dunbartonshire, 1953. *Recreations:* fishing and gardening. *Heir: s* Richard Ernest Butler Lloyd [*b* 6 Dec. 1929; *m* 1955, Jennifer, *e d* of Brig. Ereld Cardiff, CB, CBE; three *s*. *Educ:* Wellington Coll.; Hertford Coll., Oxford]. *Address:* Rhu Cottage, Carrick Castle, Lochgoilhead, Argyll. *Club:* Carlton.

*See also Sir A. M. A. Denny, Bt, Sir Robert Green-Price, Bt.*

**LLOYD, Francis Nelson,** CBE 1970; Chairman F. H. Lloyd Holdings Ltd; Director of Lloyds Bank since 1956; *b* 13 Aug. 1907; *s* of Daniel Charles Lloyd and Alice Hilda Lloyd, Bolton; *m* 1937, Pamela Mary Langley; two *s* two *d*. *Educ:* Charterhouse; Trinity Coll., Oxford. Graduated in Natural Science, 1928. With F. H. Lloyd & Co., Steel Founders, 1928-39; served in TA, RAOC, 1939-40; Man. Dir F. H. Lloyd & Co., 1941-69. Chm., Steel Castings Res. and Trade Assoc. Mem., Iron and Steel Adv. Cttee, 1967-. *Recreations:* golf and tennis. *Address:* Clyde House, Tinacre Hill, Wightwick, Wolverhampton. *T:* Wolverhampton 62604.

**LLOYD, Rt. Hon. Geoffrey William,** PC 1943; MP (C) Sutton Coldfield since 1955 (King's Norton Division of Birmingham, 1950-55); *b* 17 Jan. 1902; *e s* of late G. W. A. Lloyd, Andover House, Newbury. *Educ:* Harrow Sch.; Trinity Coll., Cambridge (MA); Pres. of the Cambridge Union, 1924. Contested (C) SE Southwark, 1924, Ladywood, 1929; Private Sec. to Rt Hon. Sir Samuel Hoare (Sec. of State for Air), 1926-29; Private Sec. to Rt Hon. Stanley Baldwin, 1929-31; MP (U) Ladywood Div. of Birmingham, 1931-45; Parliamentary Private Sec. to Rt Hon. Stanley Baldwin (Lord Pres. of the Council), 1931-35, (Prime Minister), 1935; Parliamentary Under-Sec., Home Office, 1935-39; Sec. for Mines, 1939-40; Sec. for Petroleum, 1940-42; Chm. Oil Control Board, 1939-45; Minister in charge of Petroleum Warfare Dept 1940-45, and Parliamentary Secretary (Petroleum) Ministry of Fuel and Power, 1942-45; Minister of Information, 1945; a Governor of BBC, 1946-49; Minister of Fuel and Power, 1951-55; Minister of Education, 1957-Oct. 1959; President Birmingham Conservative and Unionist Association. *Address:* 77 Chester Square, SW1. *Clubs:* Brooks's, Carlton, Pratt's; Conservative (Birmingham).

**LLOYD, George Peter,** CMG 1965; Chief Secretary, Fiji, since 1966; *b* 23 Sept. 1926; *er s* of late Sir Thomas Ingram Kynaston Lloyd, GCMG, KCB; m 1957, Margaret Harvey; two *s* one *d*. *Educ:* Stowe Sch.; King's Coll., Cambridge. Lieut, KRRC, 1945-48; ADC to Governor of Kenya, 1948; Cambridge, 1948-51 (MA; athletics blue); District Officer, Kenya, 1951-60; Principal, Colonial Office, 1960-61; Colonial Secretary, Seychelles, 1961-66. *Address:* Chief Secretary's Office, Suva, Fiji. *Clubs:* Oxford and Cambridge; Muthaiga (Nairobi, Kenya).

**LLOYD, Major Sir Guy;** *see* Lloyd, Major Sir E. G. R.

**LLOYD, Guy Vaughan,** JP; Vice-Lieutenant of Carmarthenshire, since 1968; *b* 12 Aug. 1901; *y* and *o surv s* of late H. Meuric Lloyd, JP, and late Mrs Lloyd, Cynghordy, Llandovery; *m* 1948, Katherine, *d* of late A. Kenney Tyrer, Lower Carden Hall, Cheshire; one *s. Educ:* Malvern Coll.; New Coll., Oxford. JP 1950, DL 1965, Carmarthenshire. *Recreations:* farming, fishing. *Address:* Cynghordy, Llandovery, Carmarthenshire. *T:* Cynghordy 202.

**LLOYD, Very Rev. Henry Morgan,** DSO 1941; OBE 1959; MA; Dean of Truro and Rector of St Mary, Truro, since 1960; *b* 9 June 1911; *y s* of late Rev. David Lloyd, Weston-super-Mare, Somerset; *m* 1962, Rachel Katharine, *d* of late J. R. Wharton, Haffield, nr Ledbury; one *d. Educ:* Canford Sch.; Oriel Coll., Oxford; Cuddesdon Theological Coll. Deacon, 1935; priest, 1936; Curate of Hendon Parish Church, Middlesex, 1935-40. Served War as Chaplain RNVR, 1940-45. Principal of Old Rectory Coll., Hawarden, 1946-48; Secretary of Central Advisory Council of Training for the Ministry, 1948-50; Dean of Gibraltar, 1950-60. *Recreations:* walking and archæology. *Address:* The Deanery, Truro. *Club:* Royal Commonwealth Society (Fellow).

**LLOYD, Dame Hilda Nora,** DBE, *cr* 1951; Emeritus Professor of Obstetrics and Gynæcology at Queen Elizabeth Hospital and University of Birmingham; Senior Surgeon, Women's Hospital and Maternity Hospital, Birmingham; *b* 11 Aug. 1891; *d* of John Shufflebotham and Emma Jenkins; *m* 1930, Bertram A. Lloyd (*d* 1948); no *c*; *m* 1949, Baron Rose, FRCS. *Educ:* King Edward's High School for Girls, Birmingham; University of Birmingham (BSc 1914, MB, ChB 1916); London Hospital. MRCS, LRCP 1918; FRCS 1920; FRCOG 1936; FRSM; President RCOG, 1949-52; Member Med. Women's Federation. retired, 1954. *Recreations:* mountaineering, gardening. *Address:* Baysham Orchard, Ross-on-Wye, Hereford. *Clubs:* Cowdray, VAD Ladies.

**LLOYD, Air Chief Marshal Sir Hugh Pughe,** GBE, *cr* 1953 (KBE, *cr* 1942; CBE 1941); KCB, *cr* 1951 (CB 1942); MC; DFC; retired; Hon. LLD (Wales); *b* 1895; *m* Kathleen, *d* of late Maj. Robert Thornton Meadows, DSO, MD; one *d.* Served European War, 1914-18, with Army and RAF (DFC, MC); War of 1939-45 (CBE, CB, KBE); Air ADC to the King, 1940-41; AOC Malta, 1941-42; Senior Instructor Imperial Defence Coll., 1946-47; C-in-C, Air Command Far East, 1947-49; AOC-in-C Bomber Command, 1950-53; retired 1953. Master Peshawar Vale Hounds, 1934-36. Order of Legion of Merit (USA), 1944; Officier Légion d'Honneur, 1944. *Publication:* Briefed to Attack, 1949. *Address:* Peterley Manor Farm, Great Missenden, Bucks. *T:* 2959.

**LLOYD, Huw Ifor,** OBE 1921; MC 1916; MA; Barrister-at-law, Gray's Inn; *b* 21 Nov. 1893; *s* of late I. T. Lloyd, Chelsea, and Aberdovey, Merionethshire; *m* 1919, Jessie, *d* of late T. C. Watson, DL, JP, Milton House, Morley, Yorks; one *d. Educ:* City of London Sch.; Emmanuel Coll., Cambridge (Exhibitioner), President Cambridge Union Society; History Tripos. Served European War, 1914-18, with 2nd Northamptonshire Regt in France and with 6th King's Own Royal Lancaster Regt in Mesopotamia; Military Governor and Political Officer, Baqubah, 1919-20; prisoner in Arab hands, Aug.-Sept. 1920; Assistant Adviser Ministry of Interior, 1921-23; Administrative Inspector, Iraq, 1923-30; attached as local expert to the British Delegation to the League of Nations, Geneva, respecting the Turko-Iraq Boundary, 1925-26; Judge of Civil Courts, Iraq, and Additional Member, Court of Cassation, 1930; President Civil and Criminal Courts, S. Iraq, 1931-38; Iraq Government Delegate to Round Table Conference on Palestine, London, 1939; served on Staff of General Wavell in Middle East, 1939-41; Director-General of Date Assoc., Iraq, 1939-46; Controller of Foreign Property, Iraq, 1939-41; Economic Adviser, Iraq Government, 1941-46; Trade Commr, Iraq Government in India, 1942; Controller of Cereals in Iraq, 1942; Iraq Government Delegate to UN Food and Agricultural Conf., Hot Springs, 1943; Asst Delegate Iraq Government to UN Conf., San Francisco, 1945; Legal Adviser: Iraq Government Deleg. to UN Conf., Lake Success, 1947; Iraq Embassy in London, 1947-58. *Publications:* The Geography of the Mosul Boundary in RGS Journal, 1926; reviews, and articles in Journals and Newspapers. *Address:* New Court, Temple, EC4; 50 Wood Vale, SE23.

**LLOYD, Ian Stewart;** MP (C) Langstone Division of Portsmouth since 1964; Economic Adviser, British and Commonwealth Shipping, since 1956 (Director of Research, 1956-64); Chairman: International Shipping Information Services Ltd; ISIS Computer Services; *b* 30 May 1921; *s* of Walter John Lloyd and Euphemia Craig (now Mrs C. S. Richards); *m* 1951, Frances Dorward Addison, *d* of late Hon. W. Addison, CMG, OBE, MC, DCM; three *s. Educ:* Michaelhouse; University of the Witwatersrand; King's Coll., Cambridge. President, Cambridge Union, and Leader, Cambridge tour of USA, 1947; MA 1951; MSc 1952. Econ. Adviser, Central Mining and Investment Corporation, 1949-52; Member, SA Board of Trade and Industries, 1952-55; Director, Acton Soc. Trust, 1956. Chairman, UK Cttee and Vice-Chairman, International Exec., International Cargo Handling Co-ordination Assoc., 1961-64. Member, UK Delegation, Council of Europe, Western European Union, 1968. *Publications:* contribs to SA Journal of Economics and Journal of Industrial Economics. *Recreations:* yachting, ski-ing, good music. *Address:* Bakers House, Priors Dean, Petersfield, Hants. *Clubs:* Brooks's; Royal Cork Yacht, Royal Yacht Squadron.

**LLOYD, Ifor Bowen,** QC 1951; **His Honour Judge Ifor Lloyd;** Judge of the County Courts since 1959, Circuit 45 (Wandsworth) since 1964 (Willesden, 1959-60, West London, 1960-64); Bencher of the Inner Temple, 1959; *b* 9 Sept. 1902; *er s* of late Rev. Thomas Davies Lloyd and Mrs Margaret Lloyd; *m* 1938, Naomi, *y d* of late George Pleydell Bancroft; one *s* one *d. Educ:* Winchester (Exhibitioner); Exeter Coll., Oxford (Scholar). BA Oxford (Mod. Hist.), 1924; called to Bar, Inner Temple, 1925; Yarborough Anderson scholar, 1926; Midland Circuit; President, Hardwicke Society, 1929. Liberal Candidate, Burton Division of Staffordshire, 1929, Chertsey Division of Surrey, 1931. Member General Council of the Bar, 1950, 1957. *Address:* 11 King's Bench Walk, Temple, EC4. *T:* 01-353 1729; Francis Taylor Building, Temple, EC4. *T:* 01-353 9942. *Club:* Reform.

**LLOYD, James Monteith,** CMG 1961; Permanent Secretary, Jamaica, since 1962; *b* 24 Nov. 1911; *s* of late Jethro and Frances Lloyd; *m* 1936, Mavis Anita Frankson; two *s* two *d. Educ:* Wolmer's High Sch., Jamaica. Called to Bar, Lincoln's Inn, 1948. Jamaica: entered Public Service as Asst, Registrar-General's

Dept, 1931 (2nd Class Clerk, 1939, 1st Class Clerk, 1943, Asst Registrar-General, 1947); Asst Secretary, Secretariat, 1950; Principal Asst Secretary, Secretariat, 1953 (seconded to Grenada on special duty, Dec. 1955-May 1956); Permanent Secretary, Jamaica, 1956; Administrator, Grenada, 1957-62. Coronation Medal, 1953; Jamaica Independence Medal, 1962. *Recreations:* cricket, tennis, golf. *Address:* Ministry of External Affairs, Kingston, Jamaica. *Clubs:* Jamaica; Constant Spring Golf; Kingston CC; YMCA.

**LLOYD, John Davies Knatchbull,** OBE 1957; MA; FSA; DL; JP; *b* 28 April 1900; *e s* of late John Maurice Edward Lloyd, Plas Trefaldwyn, Montgomery, Barrister-at-law, and Alice Norton, *yr d* of late Maj.-Gen. Charles Stirling Dundas (of Dundas), Bengal Artillery; unmarried. *Educ:* Winchester; Trinity Coll., Oxford. Secretary to the Council for the Preservation of Rural Wales, 1929-46; Secretary to Powysland Club, 1937-67; Mayor of Montgomery, 9 years, 1932-38, 1961, 1962; Commission in RAFVR, 1940; High Sheriff, Montgomeryshire, 1940; Chairman: Montgomeryshire Health Executive Council, 1948-51; Montgomeryshire Joint Planning Cttee, 1953-55; County Library Cttee, 1957; Member: Historic Buildings Council for Wales, 1953; Ancient Monuments Board for Wales, 1954 (Chairman, 1959); Board of Celtic Studies, University of Wales, 1957; Council, National Museum of Wales; Royal Commn on Ancient Monuments (Wales), 1967; Chairman, St Asaph Diocesan Faculty Advisory Cttee, 1961. JP 1934, DL 1960, County of Montgomery. Hon. LLD Wales, 1969. Editor, Archæologia Cambrensis, 1956-69. *Publications:* various articles in Archæologia Cambrensis and in Montgomeryshire Collections (publication of Powysland Club); A Guide to Montgomery (published by the Corporation, 1936, 1948 and 1961); (Editor) Montgomeryshire Handbook (published by C. Council, 1949, 1958 and 1963). *Recreations:* music, archæology. *Address:* Bron Hafren, Garthmyl, Montgomery, N Wales. *T:* Berriew 261. *Club:* Brooks's.

**LLOYD, John Owen,** CBE 1965; HM Ambassador to Laos since 1970; *b* 7 Feb. 1914; *s* of George Thomas Lloyd; *m* 1940, Ellen Marjorie Howard Andrews; one *s* one *d*. *Educ:* Marlborough; Clare Coll., Cambridge. Probationer Vice-Consul, Tokyo, 1937; Acting Vice-Consul, Hankow, 1940-41; served at Tokyo, 1941; Vice-Consul, 1943; on staff of HM Special Commission, Singapore, 1946; transferred to Foreign Office, 1948; Foreign Office Representative, Canadian National Defence Coll., 1952; First Secretary (Commercial), Paris, 1953-56; First Secretary, Office of Comr-Gen., Singapore, 1957; Counsellor, Office of the Commissioner-General, Singapore, 1958-60; Foreign Service Inspector, 1960-63; Consul-General: Osake Kobe, 1963-67; San Francisco, 1967-70. *Publication:* A Governor's Sermons (trans. of Governor of Osaka Prefecture Gisen Sato's work), 1967. *Recreations:* tennis, sailing. *Address:* c/o Foreign and Commonwealth Office, SW1. *Clubs:* Oxford and Cambridge University; Bohemian, Pacific Union (San Francisco).

**LLOYD, Prof. John Raymond;** Principal, Architectural Association School of Architecture, since 1966; *b* 20 Aug. 1927; *s* of W. R. Lloyd; *m* 1957, Berit Hansen; one *s* two *d*. *Educ:* Wellington Sch., Somerset; AA School of Architecture. AA Dipl. 1953; ARIBA 1954; MNAL 1960. Private practice and Teacher, State School of Arts and Crafts, Oslo, 1955-60 and 1962-63; First Year Master, AA School of Architecture, 1960-62; Dean, Faculty of Arch., and Prof. of Arch., Kumasi Univ. of Science and Technology, 1963-66. *Publications:* Tegning og Skissing; ed world Architecture, Vol. I Norway, Vol. III Ghana; Shelter in Society: Norwegian Laftehus. *Recreations:* sailing, ski-ing. *Address:* Architectural Association School of Architecture, 34 Bedford Square, WC1. *T:* 01-636 0974.

**LLOYD, Rt. Hon. (John) Selwyn (Brooke),** PC 1951; CH 1962; CBE 1945 (OBE 1943); TD; QC 1947; DL; MP (C) Wirral Division of Cheshire since 1945; *b* 28 July 1904; *s* of late J. W. Lloyd, MRCS, LRCP, Hoylake, and Rodney Street, Liverpool; *m* 1951, Elizabeth Marshall (marr. diss., 1957); one *d*. *Educ:* Fettes; Magdalene Coll., Cambridge. President Cambridge Union, 1927; Barrister Gray's Inn and Northern Circuit, 1930; a Master of the Bench, Gray's Inn, 1951. Service Throughout War in Army, 2nd Lieut (TA) June 1939; Captain, Jan. 1940; Major, July 1940; Lieut-Colonel, 1942; Colonel, 1943; Brigadier, 1944. Served as General Staff Officer on HQ Second Army from its formation to surrender of Germany; returned to Bar, Aug. 1945; Recorder of Wigan, 1948-51; Minister of State, FO, Oct. 1951-54; Minister of Supply, Oct. 1954-April 1955; Minister of Defence, April-Dec. 1955; Secretary of State for Foreign Affairs, 1955-60; Chancellor of the Exchequer, July 1960-62; Lord Privy Seal and Leader of the House of Commons, 1963-64. Member: Commn on the Constitution, 1969-; NEDC, 1962-. Director: Sun Alliance and London Insurance Ltd; Alliance Assurance Co. Ltd; English & Caledonian Investment Co. Ltd; Rank Organisation Ltd. Produced Selwyn Lloyd Report, 1963 (for Conservative Party Organisation). President, National Union of Conservative and Unionist Associations, 1965-66. Chm., Young Volunteer Force Foundn, 1970-. DL City and County of Chester, 1963-. Hon. LLD Sheffield Univ., 1955, Liverpool Univ., 1957; Hon. DCL, Oxford, 1960; Hon. Fellow, Magdalene Coll. Legion of Merit, Degree of Commander, USA, 1946. *Address:* 32 Queens Road, Hoylake, Cheshire. *T:* Hoylake 4191; St James's Court, SW1. *Clubs:* Carlton, Turf.

**LLOYD, Air Vice-Marshal Kenneth Buchanan,** CB 1949; CBE 1943; AFC 1918; RAF (retired); *b* 8 Nov. 1897; *s* of late Major T. W. Lloyd; *m* 1924, Nellie Sanforth, *d* of late C. J. H. Jefferies; one *s*. *Educ:* St Bees; Royal Military Coll., Sandhurst; Royal Welsh Fusiliers; seconded RFC, 1914-18; RAF, 1918-49. Served War of 1939-45 (despatches); AOC, Iceland, 1942-43; AOC, Malta, 1944-47; SASO, HQ, Coastal Command, 1947-49; retired, 1949. *Address:* Brocket Hall, Welwyn, Herts.

**LLOYD, Rev. Kingsley;** *see* Lloyd, Rev. A. K.

**LLOYD, Martin,** MA (Cantab); Warden, Missenden Abbey Adult Education College, since 1966; *b* 1908; 2nd *s* of late Thomas Zachary Lloyd, Edgbaston, Birmingham; *m* 1943, Kathleen Rosslyn, *y d* of late Colonel J. J. Robertson, DSO, Wick, Caithness; two *s* two *d*. *Educ:* Marlborough Coll.; Gonville and Caius Coll., Cambridge (1st Class Parts I and II Mod. Languages Tripos). Asst Master, Rugby Sch., 1930-40; on military service, 1940-44. Headmaster of Uppingham Sch., 1944-65. *Address:* The Abbey Farm, Great Missenden, Bucks. *T:* Great Missenden 2329.

**LLOYD, Norman,** FRSA, ROI, 1935; Landscape Painter; *b* 16 Oct. 1895; *s* of David Lloyd and Jane Ogilvie; *m* 1923, Edith Eyre-Powell. *Educ:*

Hamilton and Sydney Art School, Australia. Exhibitioner Royal Academy and Royal Institute of Oil Painters; Salon des Artistes Français, Paris; Laureat du Salon Mention Honorable, 1948; Silver Medal, Portrait Salon, Paris, 1956; Palmes, Acad. Française, 1957. Member Société des Artistes Français, Paysagistes; Member Internat. Assoc. of Plastic Arts, 1962. *Recreation:* travel. *Address:* 63 Marlborough Place, NW8. *T:* 01-624 6384.

**LLOYD, Colonel Pen;** *see* Lloyd, Colonel Philip H.

**LLOYD, Peter,** CBE 1957; Head of British Defence Research and Supply Staff, Canberra, since 1969; *b* 26 June 1907; *s* of late Godfrey I. H. Lloyd and late Constance L. A. Lloyd; *m* 1st, 1932, Nora K. E. Patten; one *s* one *d*; 2nd, 1951, Joyce Evelyn Campbell. *Educ:* Gresham's Sch.; Trinity Coll., Cambridge (MA). Industrial Research in Gas Light and Coke Co., London, 1931-41; Royal Aircraft Establishment, 1941-44; Power Jets (Research and Development), 1944-46. National Gas Turbine Establishment, Pyestock, 1946-60, Deputy Director, 1950; Dir-Gen. Engine R&D, Mins of Aviation and Technology, 1961-69. FRAeS, FInstF. *Publications:* various papers in scientific and technical journals. *Recreations:* mountaineering, fishing, gardening. *Address:* 89 Endeavour Street, Red Hill, Canberra, ACT, Australia. *Clubs:* Athenæum, Alpine.

**LLOYD, Colonel Philip Henry, (Pen),** CBE 1968; TD; DL; JP; Farmer, Landowner and Company Director; *b* 7 April 1905; *s* of late Samuel Janson Lloyd, JP; *m* 1943, Monica, *d* of W. C. Beasley-Robinson, and *widow* of H. R. Murray-Philipson, MP; no *c. Educ:* Oundle. Chairman: Breedon and Cloud Hill Lime Works Ltd; Breedon General Services Ltd; British Tar Products Ltd; Director, Cavendish Syndicate; Adv. Dir, Nottingham Local District, Barclays Bank, 1969-; Hon. Manager of Leicester Trustee Savings Bank; Member: County Councils Assoc.; Member: Local Authorities Mutual Investment Trust; Local Authorities Management Services and Computer Cttee; Chairman, Leicestershire CC; Governor: Brooksby Agricultural Coll.; Wyggeston Hospital; Member: East Midlands Economic Planning Council; Inter-Departmental Cttee on Coroners and Death Certification; Library Advisory Council (England); Board of Visitors, Gartree Prison (Chairman); Leicestershire Agricultural Exec. Cttee; Landowners' Standing Conference, Ironstone; Worshipful Company of Farmers. Military Member Territorial and Auxiliary Forces Assoc., 1950-70. Vice-Chairman, Leicester and County Mission for the Deaf. DL Leicestershire, 1950; High Sheriff of Leicestershire, 1957; CA, 1960. Farming approximately 800 acres. Hon. MA, Loughborough Univ. of Technology, 1969. *Recreations:* Hunting (Joint Master Fernie Fox Hounds, 1946-62), shooting, breeding Springer spaniels, golf, tennis. *Address:* Stone House, Blaston, Market Harborough, Leics. *T:* Hallaton 234. *Clubs:* Boodle's; Leicestershire (Leicester).

**LLOYD, Lieut-Colonel Reginald Broughton,** IMS retired; late Imperial Serologist and Chemical Examiner to Government of India, and Professor of Serology and Immunology, School of Tropical Medicine and Hygiene, Calcutta; *b* 31 Aug. 1881; *e s* of late Rev. L. W. Lloyd, MA; *m* 1912; Elizabeth (*d* 1961), *e d* of late Rev. J. W. Pratt, MA. *Educ:* Emmanuel Coll., Cambridge (Scholar); The London Hospital; MA Cambridge (1st Cl. Nat. Science Trip. Parts I and II), MB, BChir, 1907; Price Entrance Scholar, Anat. and Phys. Schol., Med. Schol.; Duckworth Nelson Prize for Med. and Surg., Wynne Baxter Prize for Medical Jurisprudence. *Publications:* Scientific papers on blood transfusion, medico-legal analysis of bloodstains and on the serology of tropical diseases. *Recreations:* fishing and gardening. *Address:* 91 Cooden Drive, Bexhill-on-Sea.

**LLOYD, Rhys Gerran,** CBE 1953; QC, 1961; JP; Barrister-at-law; *b* 12 Aug. 1907; *s* of late J. G. Lloyd, Kilgerran, Pembrokeshire; *m* 1940, Phyllis Mary, *d* of late Ronald Shepherd, JP, Chilworth, Hants; two *d. Educ:* Sloane Sch.; Selwyn Coll., Cambridge (science scholar). MA Cantab; BSc London. Gray's Inn, 1939; Middle Temple, 1955; admitted to S Rhodesian Bar, 1962. Wartime service in scientific research Departments of Air Ministry and MAP, 1939-46. Royal Commn on Awards to Inventors, 1946. Contested (L) Anglesey, General Election, 1959. Director: Martonair International Ltd; Terrapin International Ltd; Aladdin Industries Ltd; Inter-Nation TV Trust Ltd; Target Unit Trust Managers (Wales) Ltd. Governor: Bembridge Sch.; Twickenham College of Technology. Chairman, Liberal Party Law Panel, 1965–; Member, Lord Sainsbury's Cttee on relationship of Drug Industry and National Health Service, 1965-67. Hon. Treasurer, Welsh Liberal Party, 1967-. Hon. Fellow, Selwyn Coll., Cambridge, 1967-. JP Surrey, 1954. *Publication:* Kerly's Law of Trade Marks and Trade Names, 8th edn, 1960; Halsbury's Trade Marks, Trade Names and Designs (3rd edn), 1962. *Recreation:* tennis. *Address:* Bracondale, Claremont Lane, Esher, Surrey. *Clubs:* Reform, Royal Commonwealth Society, Eighty, City Livery.

**LLOYD, Richard Dafydd Vivian Llewellyn, (Richard Llewellyn);** author; *b* Wales; *m* 1952, Nona Theresa Sonsteby (marr. diss., 1968), Chicago. *Educ:* St David's, Cardiff; London. Coalmining; studied hotel management in Italy; film writing and producing; Captain, The Welsh Guards, 1942. *Publications:* (as Richard Llewellyn) How Green Was My Valley, 1939; None but the Lonely Heart, 1943, new completed edn, 1968; A Few Flowers for Shiner, 1950; A Flame for Doubting Thomas, 1954; Mr Hamish Gleave, 1956; The Flame of Hercules, 1957; Warden of the Smoke and Bells, 1958; Chez Pavan, 1959; A Man in a Mirror, 1961; Up, Into the Singing Mountain, 1963; Sweet Morn of Judas' Day, 1964; Down Where the Moon is Small, 1966; The End of the Rug, 1968; But We Didn't Get the Fox, 1970. Has also written for the younger reader. *Plays:* Poison Pen, 1937; Noose, 1947; The Scarlet Suit, 1962. *Recreations:* economics, anthropology, photography. *Address:* c/o Michael Joseph Ltd, 26 Bloomsbury Street, WC1. *Club:* Guards.

**LLOYD, Maj.-Gen. Richard Eyre,** CB 1959; CBE 1957 (OBE 1944); DSO 1945; late RE, retired, Sept. 1962; Arms Control and Disarmament Research Unit, Foreign and Commonwealth Office, since 1966; *b* 7 Dec. 1906; *s* of late Lieut-Colonel W. E. Eyre Lloyd; *m* 1939, Gillian, *d* of Rear-Admiral J. F. C. Patterson, *qv;* one *s* two *d. Educ:* Eton; Pembroke Coll. (Cambridge). 2nd Lieut in Royal Engineers, 1927. Served War of 1939-45 on Staff, also with RE in North West Europe; Lieut-Colonel 1942; Colonel, 1951; Brigadier, 1955; Maj.-Gen., 1957. Chief of Staff, Middle East Land Forces, 1957-59; Director of Military Intelligence, 1959-62. Colonel Comdt, Intelligence Corps, 1964-69. *Recreations:* sailing, ski-ing. *Address:* 56 Gloucester

Terrace, W2. *T:* 01-723 7507. *Club:* United Service.

**LLOYD, Rt. Hon. Selwyn;** *see* Lloyd, Rt Hon. John Selwyn Brooke.

**LLOYD, Prof. Seton Howard Frederick,** CBE 1958 (OBE 1949); Archæologist; Emeritus Professor of Western Asiatic Archæology, University of London; *b* 30 May 1902; *s* of John Eliot Howard Lloyd and Florence Louise Lloyd (*née* Armstrong); *m* 1944, Margery Ulrica Fitzwilliams Hyde; one *s* one *d*. *Educ:* Uppingham; Architectural Assoc. ARIBA 1926; Asst to Sir Edwin Lutyens, PRA, 1926-28; excavated with Egypt Exploration Society, 1928-30; excavated in Iraq for University of Chicago Oriental Institute, 1930-37; excavated in Turkey for University of Liverpool, 1937-39; FSA 1938; Technical Adviser, Government of Iraq; Directorate-General of Antiquities, 1939-49, Director British Institute of Archæology, Ankara, Turkey, 1949-61; Prof. of Western Asiatic Archæology, Univ. of London, at the Inst. of Archæology, 1962-69. Hon. MA (Edinburgh), 1953. FBA 1955. *Publications:* Mesopotamia (London), 1936; Sennacherib's Aqueduct at Jerwan, (Chicago), 1935; The Gimilsin Temple (Chicago), 1940; Presargonid Temples (Chicago), 1942; Ruined Cities of Iraq (Oxford), 1942; Twin Rivers, (Oxford), 1942; Foundations in the Dust (London), 1947; Early Anatolia (Pelican), 1956; Art of the Ancient Near East (London), 1961; Mounds of the Ancient Near East (Edinburgh), 1963; Highland Peoples of Anatolia (London), 1967; Excavation Reports and many articles in journals. *Recreation:* shooting. *Address:* Woolstone Lodge, Faringdon, Berkshire. *T:* Uffington 248. *Club:* Athenæum.

**LLOYD, Brigadier Thomas Ifan,** CBE 1957; DSO 1944; MC 1940; retired; *b* 20 March 1903; *s* of late Rev. David Lloyd, Vicar of St Paul's, Weston-super-Mare, Somerset; *m* 1927, Irene Mary, *d* of Andrew Fullerton, CB, CMG, FRCS, of Belfast, N. Ireland; one *s* one *d*. *Educ:* Westminster Sch.; RMA, Woolwich. Commissioned into the Corps of Royal Engineers as Second Lieut, 1923; concluded military career as Dep. Engineer-in-Chief (Brigadier), War Office, 1955-57. *Publications:* Twilight of the Railways–What Roads they'll Make!, 1957. Paper, Instn Civil Engineers, 1955. *Recreations:* golf, bridge. *Address:* 24 Grove Road, Merrow, Guildford, Surrey. *T:* Guildford 75428. *Club:* Royal Commonwealth Society.

**LLOYD, Prof. William Arnold de Gorges;** Professor of Education in the University of Cambridge since 1959; Fellow of Trinity College; Chairman, Cambridge Schools Classics Project, Nuffield Foundation, 1965-68; *b* 20 May 1904; *s* of Jonathan and Mary G. Lloyd, Meifod; *m* 1st, 1929, Margaret Elizabeth Manley; three *d*; 2nd, 1952, Daphne Stella Harris; two *s* one *d*. *Educ:* Sidcot Sch., Somerset; Birmingham Univ. (Flounders Scholar); Institut J. J. Rousseau, Geneva; Sorbonne. MA Birmingham 1936; PhD Cambridge, 1946. Schoolmaster in primary, technical and grammar schools, 1926-32 and 1938-44; director of adult education, 1934-38; Lecturer in Education, Selly Oak Colleges, 1933-34; University of Nottingham, 1946-52; Prof. of Education, Dean of the Faculty and Dep. Chairman of the Institute of Social Research, University of Natal, 1952-56; Senior Prof. of Education, University of the Witwatersrand, 1956-59. Travelling fellowship for Universities of Italy, Switzerland and France, 1956; Carnegie fellowship for Universities of USA, 1957; British Council travel grant to visit English universities, 1958; Commissioner to report on technical education in France, 1959. Fellow of Haverford Coll., Pennsylvania, 1959. Consultant, curricula in Education, European University, Council of Europe, 1966-68. Associate editor, Journal of Conflict Resolution, Chicago, 1956-. Editor, Pædagogica Europaea, 1964-. *Publications:* God in the experience of men, 1938; God in the experience of youth, 1940; Quaker Social History, 1950; Creative Learning, 1953; Education and Human Relations, 1957; The Old and the New Schoolmaster, 1959; The Principles and Practice of Education, 1964; (ed) International Dictionary of Educational Terms, vol I, England and Wales, 1970. *Recreations:* Quaker and family history; cabinet-making; book-binding. *Address:* 17 Brookside, Cambridge. *T:* Cambridge 55271; Withersfield House, Withersfield, West Suffolk.

**LLOYD, William Ernest,** MD, FRCP; Consulting Physician, Westminster Hospital, Brompton Hospital for Diseases of the Chest, and Bolingbroke Hospital. *Educ:* St Bartholomew's Hospital. Senior Scholar in Anatomy, Physiology and Chemistry; MB, BS (London), 1923; MD (London) 1925 (Univ. Gold Medal); MRCS 1921; FRCP 1934. Examiner in Medicine, Conjoint Board; Fellow Royal Society of Med.; Fellow Med. Soc. London. *Publications:* contrib. to Medical journals. *Address:* Innisfree, Coppice Drive, Roehampton, SW15.

**LLOYD, Wynne Llewelyn,** CB 1962; MA (Cantab); HM Chief Inspector of Schools (Wales) since 1952; *b* 25 Jan. 1910; *s* of late Captain D. Ll. Lloyd, OBE, and E. A. Lloyd, Birchgrove, Pontardulais; *m* 1934, Kathleen Isobel Ormrod, Manchester; one *d*. *Educ:* Gowerton; Trinity Hall, Cambridge. Geographical Tripos, Parts I and II, Economics Tripos, Part II; Prizeman and Exhibitioner of Trinity Hall, 1930. Assistant Master, William Hulme's Grammar Sch., Manchester; Extra-mural Tutor, University College, Swansea; successively Asst Inspector, HM Inspector and Staff Inspector, Welsh Dept, Ministry of Education. Member: School Broadcasting Council of the UK; Schools Council for Curriculum and Examinations; Council, University Coll. of South Wales and Monmouthshire; Hon. Member, Royal Cambrian Acad., 1955. *Publications:* Vol. VI of Social and Economic Survey of Swansea and District, 1940; contrib. to Pioneers of Welsh Education, 1964, and to various journals. *Recreation:* gardening. *Address:* Llain, Dimlands, Llantwit Major, Glam. *T:* Llantwit Major 361. *Club:* Oxford and Cambridge University.

**LLOYD-BAKER, Olive Katherine Lloyd,** CBE 1958; JP; *b* 1902; *d* of Capt. Michael G. Lloyd-Baker (killed in action, 1916) and late Blanche Verney, *d* of 18th Baron Willoughby de Broke, Compton Verney, Warwickshire. *Educ:* St James's, West Malvern. Member RDC, 1930-64; CC, 1943-51. County Chairman, NFU, 1942-43; County Chairman, CLA, 1953-56. Chairman Stroud Conservative Assoc., 1956-58, President, 1958-61. Prospective Conservative Candidate, West Glos, 1957-59. Landowner. JP Glos 1943; High Sheriff, Glos, 1970-71. *Recreations:* walking, collecting. *Address:* Hardwicke Court, Gloucester. *T:* Hardwicke 212. *Club:* Farmers'.

**LLOYD DAVIES, John Robert;** *see* Davies.

**LLOYD-DAVIES, Oswald Vaughan,** Surgeon: Middlesex Hospital since 1950; St Mark's

Hospital for diseases of the Colon and Rectum since 1935; Consulting Surgeon, Connaught Hospital; formerly Surgeon, Hampstead General Hospital; *b* 13 Jan. 1905; *s* of late Rev. Samuel Lloyd-Davies, BA; *m* 1939, Menna (*d* 1968), *d* of late Canon D. J. Morgan, MA; one *s* one *d*; *m* 1970, Rosamund Mary Ovens. *Educ:* Caterham Sch.; Middlesex Hospital Medical Sch., London Univ. MRCS, LRCP, 1929; MB, BS (London) 1930; FRCS 1932; MS (London) 1932. Fellow Royal Society of Med. (Past Pres. sect. of proctology); Fellow Assoc. of Surgeons of Great Britain and Ireland; Member, Harveian Society. *Publications:* various chapters in, British Surgical Practice; articles on colon, rectal and liver surgery. *Recreations:* croquet, gardens, fishing. *Address:* 16 Devonshire Place, W1. *T:* 01-935 2825; Townsend Close, Ashwell, Herts. *T:* Ashwell 386.

**LLOYD DAVIES, Trevor Arthur,** MD; FRCP; Senior Medical Inspector of Factories, Department of Employment and Productivity (formerly Ministry of Labour), since 1961; *b* 8 April 1909; *s* of Arthur Lloyd Davies and Grace Margret (*née* Bull). *Educ:* Woking Grammar Sch.; St Thomas's Hospital, SE1. MRCS, LRCP 1932; MB, BS London (gold medal and hons in surgery, forensic med., obst. and gynæc.); MRCP 1933; MD London 1934; FRCP 1952. Resident Asst Physician, St Thomas's Hospital, 1934-36; Prof. of Social Medicine, University of Malaya, 1953-61. QHP 1968-. *Publications:* The Practice of Industrial Medicine, 2nd edn, 1957. Numerous papers on industrial and social medicine, in Lancet and Medical Journal of Malaya. *Recreations:* gardening, carpentry and bricklaying. *Address:* 65 Vandon Court, Petty France, SW1; The Birk, Barrington, Cambridgeshire. *Club:* Athenæum.

**LLOYD-ELEY, John,** QC 1970; Barrister, Middle Temple; *b* 23 April 1923; *s* of Edward John Eley; *m* 1946, Una Fraser Smith; two *s*. *Educ:* Xaverian Coll., Brighton; Exeter Coll., Oxford. Barrister, Middle Temple, 1951; Mem., Bar Council, 1969. *Recreations:* farming, travel. *Address:* 1 Hare Court, Temple, EC4. *T:* 01-353 5324; Luxfords Farm, East Grinstead. *T:* East Grinstead 21583.

**LLOYD GEORGE,** family name of **Earl Lloyd George of Dwyfor** and **Viscount Tenby.**

**LLOYD GEORGE OF DWYFOR,** 3rd Earl, *cr* 1945; **Owen Lloyd George;** Viscount Gwynedd, 1945; an Underwriting Member of Lloyd's; *b* 28 April 1924; *s* of 2nd Earl Lloyd George of Dwyfor, and Roberta Ida Freeman, 5th *d* of Sir Robert McAlpine, 1st Bt; *S* father, 1968; *m* 1949, Ruth Margaret, *o d* of Richard Coit; two *s* one *d*. *Educ:* Oundle. Welsh Guards, 1942-47. European War, 1944-45. Formerly Captain Welsh Guards. Chm. Cavalier Securities Ltd; Director: Bland Payne Ltd; Bland Welch (UK) Ltd. Carried the Sword at Investiture of HRH the Prince of Wales, Caernarvon Castle, 1969. *Heir: s* Viscount Gwynedd, *qv*. *Recreations:* shooting, tennis. *Address:* 43 Cadogan Square, SW1; Brimpton Mill, near Reading, Berks. *Clubs:* White's, City of London, Pratt's.

**LLOYD GEORGE OF DWYFOR, Frances, Countess; (Frances Louise),** CBE 1918; BA (London Classics Hons); Private Secretary to Rt Hon. D. Lloyd George, 1913-43; *d* of John and Louise Stevenson, Worthing; *m* 1943, 1st Earl Lloyd George of Dwyfor, PC, OM. *Educ:* Clapham High Sch.; Royal Holloway Coll. *Publications:* Makers of the New World, 1922; The Years that are Past, 1967. *Address:* Farm Cottage, Churt, Surrey.

**LLOYD-HUGHES, Sir Trevor Denby,** Kt 1970; *b* 31 March 1922; *er s* of late Elwyn and Lucy Lloyd-Hughes, Bradford, Yorks; *m* 1950, Ethel Marguerite Durward, *o d* of late J. Ritchie, Dundee and Bradford; one *s* one *d*. *Educ:* Woodhouse Grove Sch., Yorks; Jesus Coll., Oxford (MA). Commissioned RA, 1941; served with 75th (Shropshire Yeomanry) Medium Regt, RA, in Western Desert, Sicily and Italy, 1941-45. Asst Inspector of Taxes, 1948; freelance journalist, 1949; joined staff of Liverpool Daily Post, 1949; Political Corresp., Liverpool Echo, 1950, Liverpool Daily Post, 1951. Press Secretary to the Prime Minister, 1964-69; Chief Information Adviser to Govt, 1969-70. Member of Circle of Wine Writers, 1961. *Recreations:* yoga, playing the Spanish guitar, walking, travel. *Address:* Mead Cottage, Byers Lane, South Godstone, Surrey. *T:* South Godstone 2128. *Club:* Reform.

**LLOYD-JOHNES, Herbert Johnes,** TD 1950; FSA; *b* 9th Dec. 1900; *e s* of Herbert Thomas Lloyd-Johnes, MC, and Georgina Mary Lloyd-Johnes, Dolaucothy, Co. Carmarthen; *m* 1942, Margaret Ruth Edgar (Lieut, FANY, War of 1939-45); two *d*. *Educ:* St Andrews, Eastbourne; Malvern. Spent much of his time in Poland, 1931-39; Member British Military Mission to Poland, 1939; a Senior British Liaison Officer to Polish Forces, 1940-46. Chairman: Historic Buildings Council for Wales (Mem. 1955-); Welsh Folk Museum Cttee, 1953-55; Rural Industries Cttee for Monmouth and Glamorgan, 1955-66; Member Ct and Council: Nat. Library of Wales, 1948; Nat. Museum of Wales, 1949; Member Court of Governors of University of Wales, 1952; Governor University College of S Wales and Monmouth, Cardiff. Major RA, TA, Pembroke and Cardigan. Cross For Valour (Poland), 1939. *Publications:* (with Sir Leonard Twiston-Davies) Welsh Furniture, 1950. Contributor to several learned journals. *Recreation:* reading. *Address:* Fosse Hill, Coates, near Cirencester, Glos. *T:* Kemble 279. *Club:* Boodle's.

**LLOYD JONES, Cyril Walter,** CIE 1925; FCGI; MICE; *b* 6 March 1881; *e s* of late Richard Lloyd Jones; *m* 1907, Edith Kathleen, *d* of Frederick Penty; two *s* two *d*. *Educ:* Aske's Sch.; Imperial College of Science. Chief Engineer, HEH Nizam's State Railway Board, 1913; Agent, 1919; Managing Director, 1930; English Agent, 1941; retired. *Address:* Roundhay, Pit Farm Road, Guildford, Surrey.
*See also R. F. Lloyd Jones, C. P. Scott.*

**LLOYD JONES, David Elwyn,** MC 1945; Assistant Under-Secretary of State, Department of Education and Science, since 1969; *b* 20 Oct. 1920; *s* of Daniel Lloyd Jones and late Blodwen Lloyd Jones (*née* Evans); *m* 1955, Mrs E. W. Gallie (*widow* of Ian Gallie), *d* of Prof. Robert Peers, *qv*; no *c* (one step *s*). *Educ:* Ardwyn Grammar Sch., Aberystwyth; University College of Wales, Aberystwyth (BA, 1st class Hons). War of 1939-45: British Army, 1941; commissioned, Indian Army, 1942; served 1st Bn, The Assam Regt, in Burma Campaign, 1942-46 (Major, MC). Entered Ministry of Education, 1947. Principal Private Sec. to Chancellor of the Duchy of Lancaster, 1960-61; Asst Sec., Min. (later Dept) of Educn and Science, 1961-69. Hon. Sec., Assam Regt Assoc., 1948-. *Recreation:* golf. *Address:* 5 Playfair Mansions, Queen's Club Gardens, W14. *T:* 01-385 0586. *Clubs:* MCC, Roehampton.

**LLOYD-JONES, David Trevor,** VRD 1958; Chairman, Caernarvonshire Quarter Sessions, since 1970; *b* 6 March 1917; *s* of Trevor and

Anne Lloyd Jones, Holywell, Flints; *m* 1958, Anstice Elizabeth, *d* of William Henry Perkins, Whitchurch; one *s* one *d*. *Educ:* Holywell Grammar School. Banking, 1934-39 and 1946-50; Barrister-at-law, 1951; Prosecuting Counsel to Post Office (Wales and Chester Circuit), 1961-66; Dep. Chm., Caerns QS, 1966-70; Legal Mem., Mental Health Appeal Tribunal (Wales Area), 1960-; Dep. Chm., Agricultural Land Tribunal (Wales Area), 1968-. Served War of 1939-45, RNVR and RNR, Atlantic, Mediterranean and Pacific; Lt-Comdr, RNR. *Recreations:* golf, music. *Address:* 1 Dr Johnson's Buildings, Temple, EC4. *T:* 01-353 7972; 39 White Friars, Chester. *T:* Chester 20480. *Clubs:* Naval; Royal Liverpool Golf.

**LLOYD-JONES, Hon. Sir (Harry) Vincent,** Kt 1960; **Hon. Mr Justice Lloyd-Jones;** a Judge of the High Court of Justice, Probate, Divorce and Admiralty Division, since 1960; *b* 16 Oct. 1901; 3rd *s* of late Henry Lloyd-Jones; *m* 1933, Margaret Alwena, *d* of late G. H. Mathias; one *s* one *d*. *Educ:* St Marylebone Grammar Sch. (Old Philological); University Coll., London; Jesus Coll., Oxford. Exhibitioner English Language and Literature, Jesus Coll., Oxford, 1921; BA (Eng. Lang. and Lit.) 1923; BA (Jurisprudence) 1924; MA 1927. President Oxford Union Society, (Summer Term) 1925. Member Oxford Union Debating Team in USA, 1925. Called to Bar by Inner Temple, 1926, Master of the Bench, 1958; practised Common Law Bar; Wales and Chester Circuit; QC 1949. Recorder of Chester, 1952-58; Recorder of Cardiff, 1958-60. Hon. Fellow: Jesus Coll., Oxford, 1960; University Coll., London, 1962. Dep. Chairman, Boundary Commission for Wales. *Recreations:* reading, walking. *Address:* 24 Vincent Square, SW1. *T:* Victoria 5109; Royal Courts of Justice, WC2. *Club:* Reform.

**LLOYD-JONES, Prof. Hugh;** *see* Lloyd-Jones, Prof. P. H. J.

**LLOYD-JONES, Prof. (Peter) Hugh (Jefferd);** FBA 1966; Regius Professor of Greek in the University of Oxford and Student of Christ Church since 1960; *b* 21 Sept. 1922; *s* of Major W. Lloyd-Jones, DSO, and Norah Leila, *d* of F. H. Jefferd, Brent, Devon; *m* 1953, Frances Elisabeth Hedley; two *s* one *d*. *Educ:* Lycée Français du Royaume Uni, S. Kensington; Westminster Sch.; Christ Church, Oxford. Served War of 1939-45, 2nd Lieut, Intelligence Corps, India, 1942; Temp. Captain, 1944. 1st Cl. Classics (Mods), 1941; MA 1947; 1st Cl., LitHum, 1948; Chancellor's Prize for Latin Prose, 1947; Ireland and Craven Schol., 1947; Fellow of Jesus Coll., Cambridge, 1948-54; Asst Lecturer in Classics, University of Cambridge, 1950-52, Lecturer, 1952-54; Fellow and E. P. Warren Praelector in Classics, Corpus Christi Coll., Oxford, 1954-60; J. H. Gray Lecturer, University of Cambridge, 1961; Visiting Prof., Yale Univ., 1964-65, 1967-68; Sather Prof. of Classical Literature, Univ. of California at Berkeley, 1969-70. Fellow, Morse Coll., Yale Univ. Hon. Mem., Greek Humanistic Soc., 1968. Hon. DHL Chicago, 1970. *Publications:* Appendix to Loeb Classical Library edn of Aeschylus, 1957; Menandri Dyscolus (Oxford Classical Text), 1960; Greek Studies in Modern Oxford, 1961; (trans.) Paul Maas, Greek Metre, 1962; (ed) The Greeks, 1962; Tacitus (in series The Great Historians), 1964; (trans.) Aeschylus: Agamemnon, The Libation-Bearers, and The Eumenides, 1970; The Justice of Zeus, 1970; contributions to periodicals. *Recreations:* cats, watching cricket. *Address:* Christ Church, Oxford. *T:* Oxford 48737; Gateways, Harberton Mead, Oxford. *T:* Oxford 62393.

**LLOYD JONES, Richard Francis,** MA (Cantab), FICE, AFRAeS; Partner in Norman and Dawbarn, Architects and Consulting Engineers, since 1938; *b* 18 April 1908; *e s* of Cyril Walter Lloyd Jones, *qv*; *m* 1938, Hester, *d* of late Henry Alan Ritchie; one *s* two *d*. *Educ:* Oundle; Trinity Coll., Cambridge. Assistant Engineer with Rendel, Palmer and Tritton, Consulting Engineers, 1929; Assistant to Resident Engineer, Royal Dock Approaches, Approaches Improvement Scheme, 1932; Assistant Engineer, Norman & Dawbarn, 1934. Served in Royal Navy, 1942-45. Served on London Airport Advisory Panel, 1946. *Address:* Shepherds' Close, Munstead, Godalming, Surrey. *T:* Godalming 1561. *Club:* Oxford and Cambridge University.

**LLOYD-JONES, Sir Vincent;** *see* Lloyd-Jones, Sir H. V.

**LLOYD MEAD, William Howard;** *see* Mead.

**LLOYD-MOSTYN,** family name of **Baron Mostyn.**

**LLOYD OWEN, Maj.-Gen. David Lanyon,** DSO 1945; OBE 1954; MC 1942; President, Regular Commissions Board, since 1969; *b* 10 Oct. 1917; *s* of late Capt. Reginald Charles Lloyd Owen, OBE, RN; *m* 1947, Ursula Evelyn, *d* of late Evelyn Hugh Barclay, and of Hon. Mrs Barclay, MBE, JP; three *s*. *Educ:* Winchester; RMC, Sandhurst. 2nd Lieut, The Queen's Royal Regt, 1938. Comdr, Long Range Desert Group, 1943-45. Military Asst to High Commissioner in Malaya, 1951-53; Comdg 1st Queen's, 1957-59; Comdr 24 Infantry Bde Group, 1962-64; GOC Cyprus District, 1966-68; GOC Near East Land Forces, 1968-69. Knight of Malta, 1946. *Publication:* The Desert My Dwelling Place, 1957. *Address:* The Old Rectory, Newton Flotman, Norwich, Norfolk. *T:* Swainsthorpe 468. *Club:* United Service.

**LLOYD PHILLIPS, Ivan,** CBE 1963 (OBE 1959); *b* Cambridge, June 1910; *er s* of late Rev. A. Lloyd Phillips, formerly Vicar of Ware, Herts; *m* 1941, Faith Macleay, *o c* of late Brig.-Gen. G. M. Macarthur Onslow, CMG, DSO, Camden, New South Wales; one *s*. *Educ:* Worksop Coll.; Selwyn Coll., Cambridge; Balliol Coll., Oxford. Appointed Colonial Administrative Service, 1934; served in: Gold Coast, 1934-38; Palestine, 1938-47; District Commissioner, Gaza-Beersheba, 1946-47; Colonial Office, 1947-48; Cyprus, 1948-51; Commissioner, Nicosia-Kyrenia, 1950-51; Singapore, 1951-53; Commissioner-General's Office, 1951-52; Dep. Secretary for Defence, 1952-53; Malaya, 1953-62; Secretary to Chief Minister and Minister for Home Affairs, 1955-57; Secretary, Ministry of the Interior, 1957-62. Secretary, Oxford Preservation Trust, 1962-65; Inst. of Commonwealth Studies, Oxford Univ., 1965-70. Chairman, Oxfordshire Playing Fields Assoc., 1966. Commander, Order of Defender of the Realm (Malaysia), 1958. *Address:* Cranmer Cottage, Dorchester-on-Thames, Oxford. *T:* Warborough 294. *Club:* Travellers'.

**LLOYD-ROBERTS, George Charles,** MChir; FRCS; Consultant Orthopædic Surgeon, St George's Hospital, since 1957; Consultant Orthopædic Surgeon, The Hospital for Sick Children, Great Ormond Street, since 1955; Consultant in Paediatric Orthopaedics to the RAF, since 1970; *b* 23 Nov. 1918; *e s* of Griffith and Gwendoline Lloyd-Roberts; *m* 1947, Catherine Lansing Ray (marr. diss. 1967), *widow* of Edward Lansing Ray, St Louis, Missouri; one *s* two *d*. *Educ:* Eton Coll.; Magdalene Coll., Cambridge. BA, MB, BChir

(Cantab), 1943, MChir (Cantab), 1966; FRCS, 1949. Graded Surgical Specialist, RAMC, 1944, Surgeon, Yugoslav and Italian Partisan Forces. Late 1st Assistant, Orthopædic Dept, St George's Hospital, 1954; Clinical Research Assistant, Royal National Orthopædic Hospital, 1952; Nuffield Fellow in Orthopædic Surgery, 1952. Robert Jones Gold Medal of British Orthopædic Assoc., 1953. *Publications:* (Ed.) Orthopædic Surgery, 1968; articles on orthopædic subjects in medical journals. *Recreations:* fishing, shooting. *Address:* 9 Cheyne Place, SW3. *T:* 01-352 5622; (Private Consulting Room), St George's Hospital, SW1. *Club:* Boodle's.

**LLOYD WEBBER, William Southcombe;** *see* Webber, W. S. L.

**LLOYD-WILLIAMS, Dorothy Sylvia,** MA (Cantab); Headmistress King Edward VI High School for Girls, Birmingham, 1953-64; *b* 2 Aug. 1901; *d* of late J. J. Lloyd-Williams, MA Oxon, and Ellen Augusta Crawley Vincent. *Educ:* Moreton Hall Sch., Shropshire; Girton Coll., Cambridge. Assistant mistress, Queen Mary's High Sch. for Girls, Walsall, 1924-26; Assistant mistress, Belvedere Sch., GPDST, Liverpool, 1926-29; Head of Science Dept, Roedean Sch., Brighton, 1929-40; Senior house mistress, Roedean Sch., Brighton, 1935-53. Member of Council, University of Birmingham. *Recreations:* reading, foreign travel, walking. *Address:* Brynele, Bwlchllan, Lampeter, Cardiganshire. *Club:* University Women's.

**LLOYD-WILLIAMS, Commander Hugh,** DSO 1941; VRD; CEng; MInstCE; FIEE; RNVR (retired); *b* 29 Aug. 1900; *s* of late Dr H. Lloyd-Williams, JP, Waenfawr, Caernarvonshire; *m* 1st, 1927, Emmy Lund (*d* 1933); two *s*; 2nd, 1935, Anne Marie Lomsdalen; one *d*. *Educ:* Mill Hill Sch.; Glasgow Univ., BSc (Eng). Served student apprenticeship with British Thomson Houston Co., Rugby; Sub-Area Engineer, 1948-57; joined Metropolitan Electric Supply Co. Ltd, 1925; District Manager, London Electricity Board, 1958-65. Joined London Division, RNVR in 1924; DSO for successful action against enemy submarine whilst in command of HMS Arbutus, 1941. *Address:* Brynmeredydd, Waenfawr, Caernarvon. *T:* Waenfawr 265. *Clubs:* Old Milhillians; Royal Welsh Yacht (Caernarvon).

**LLOYD-WILLIAMS, Katharine Georgina,** CBE 1956; MD London; FFARCS; Consultant Anæsthetist to Royal Free Hospital Group, retired 1960; *b* 14 Feb. 1896; *d* of John Jordan Lloyd-Williams, MA Oxon, and Ellen Augusta Crawley Vincent. *Educ:* Queen Anne's Sch., Caversham; Bedford Physical Training Coll.; London (Royal Free Hospital) School of Medicine for Women. President, University of London Athletic Union (Women), 1922-23; Fellow, 1st Board of Faculty of Anæsthetists, RCS, 1948-53; President, Med. Women's Federation, 1958-59; Dean of Faculty of Med., University of London, 1956-60; Dean of Royal Free Hospital School of Medicine, 1945-62. Past President (now Hon. Fellow), Anæsth. Section of Royal Society of Med., 1956; Past President, Anæsth. Section, BMA Annual Meeting, 1946; Member GMC, 1961-; Member NW Metropolitan Reg. Hospital Board, 1948-63; Visitor for King Edward VII Hospital Fund and Member King's Fund Aux. Cttee; Member Board of Management, Royal Med. Benevolent Fund and its Case Cttee, 1962-69. *Publications:* Anæsthesia and Analgesia in Labour, 1934; contrib. medical and dental journals. *Recreations:* travel, walking, gardening. *Address:* 8 Rosslyn Mansions, Goldhurst Terrace, NW6. *T:* 01-624 6486; Brynele, Bwlchllan, Lampeter, Cardiganshire. *T:* Aeron 466. *Club:* University Women's.

**LOANE, Most Rev. Marcus Lawrence;** *see* Sydney, Archbishop of.

**LOBB, Howard Leslie Vicars,** CBE 1952; FRIBA, AIStructE, FRSA, FGS; Senior Partner Howard V. Lobb and Partners, Architects and Town Planning Consultants; *b* 9 March 1909; *e s* of late Hedley Vicars Lobb and Mary Blanche (*née* Luscombe); *m* 1949, Charmian Isobel (*née* Reilly); three *s*. *Educ:* privately; Regent Street Polytechnic School of Architecture. During War of 1939-45, Architect to various ministries: subseq. built numerous schools for County Authorities; HQ of City and Guilds of London Inst., W1; British Pavilion Brussels International Exhibition, 1958; Cons. Architect for Hunterston Nuclear Power Station, Ayrshire; Dungeness Nuclear Power Station; Newcastle Racecourse; Newmarket Rowley Mile, for Jockey Club; Car park, Savile Row, for City of Westminster. Chairman Architectural Council, Festival of Britain, and later Controller (Constr.) South Bank Exhibition. Member RIBA Council and Executive, 1953-56; Life Vice-Pres. (formerly Chm.), London Group of Building Centres; Chm., architects' Registr. Council, UK, 1957-60; Hon. Secretary, Architects' Benevolent Society. Freeman of City of London; Member Court, Masons' Company. *Publications:* contrib. various Arch. Journals, Reviews, etc. *Recreations:* sailing, gardening, colour photography, model railways. *Address:* 12 Gower Street, WC1. *T:* 01-636 8575; Blackhill, Esher, Surrey. *T:* Esher 63092. *Clubs:* Arts; Royal Corinthian Yacht (Vice-Cdre 1960-63); Royal London Yacht; Island Sailing (Cowes); Tamesis (Teddington) (Cdre, 1954-57).

**LOCH,** family name of **Baron Loch.**

**LOCH,** 3rd Baron *cr* 1895, of Drylaw; **George Henry Compton Loch;** Major late 11th Hussars; *b* 3 Feb. 1916; *s* of 2nd Baron and Lady Margaret Compton (*d* 1970), *o d* of 5th Marquess of Northampton; *S* father 1942; *m* 1st, 1942, Leila Mary Grace Isabel Hill Mackenzie (marr. diss., 1946), Grafton House, The Avenue, Worcester Park; one *d*; 2nd, 1946, Mrs Betty Castillon du Perron (marr. diss., 1952); 3rd, 1952, Joan Dorothy Hawthorn Binns. *Educ:* Eton; RMC, Sandhurst. *Heir:* *b* Hon. Spencer Douglas Loch, MC 1945 [*b* 1920; *m* 1948, Hon. Rachel, *yr d* of Group Captain H. L. Cooper, AFC, and of Baroness Lucas and Dingwall (Nan Ino Herbert-Cooper who *d* 1958); two *s* one *d*. *Educ:* Wellington Coll.; Trinity Coll., Cambridge. Major Grenadier Guards; called to Bar, 1948]. *Address:* 51 Lennox Gardens, SW1. *T:* 01-584 2293.

**LOCH, Colonel John Carysfort,** CBE 1929; Member of the Royal Company of Archers, the Queen's Body Guard for Scotland; *b* Jamon Damoh District, CP, India, 25 Dec. 1877; *s* of Lieut-Colonel John Lowis Loch and Lucy Proby; *m* 1st, 1901, Violet Francis, *d* of Lieut-General Jenkin Jones; two *s* one *d* (and one *d* decd); 2nd, 1933, Helen Gladys Montgomery, *widow* of Spencer C. Thomson. *Educ:* Wellington Coll.; Sandhurst. Commissioned Unattached List for Indian Army, 1897; Attached 1st Bn Norfolk Regt 7th DCO Rajputs, 1898-1901; 1/3 QAO Gurkha Rifles, 1901-20; raised and commanded 1st Bn Nayar Bde, 1903-07; Commandant (Officiating) Nayar Brigade, 1907; raised and commanded 2/130 Baluchis, 1918-20; commanded 4/39 Garhwal Rifles, 1920; 3/152 Punjaubis, 1920-21; Kumaon

Rifles, 1921-25; Officiating AAG Army HQ India, 1924-25; Director Military Prisons in India, 1925-29; retired, 1929; Chief Commandant, Mysore State Forces, 1929-35; served China, 1900-01 (medal and 2 clasps); European War, 1914-18, Mesopotamia (Staff) (despatches, brevet of Lieut-Colonel); Waziristan, 1920-21; Mahsud, 1920; Member, American Military Order of the Dragon (1901). *Recreations:* fishing, colour photography. *Address:* Pilgrims Progress, St Boswells, Roxburghshire. *T:* St Boswells 2262. *Clubs:* Army and Navy, Victory Ex-Service; Royal Bombay Yacht (Bombay).

**LOCK, (Cecil) Max,** FRIBA (Dis. TP), AADip, MTPI; Head of Max Lock & Partners; *b* 29 June 1909; *s* of Cecil William Best Lock and Vivian Cecil Hassell. *Educ:* Berkhamsted Sch.; Architectural Assoc., London. Entered private practice, 1933; (firm established as Max Lock 1933, Max Lock Group 1944, Max Lock & Associates 1950, Max Lock & Partners 1954); entered partnership with Geoffrey Easton, Gerald King and Laurence Perlston, 1954; Member Watford Borough Council, 1936-40; on staff of AA School of Architecture, 1937-39; Head of Hull School of Architecture, 1939; Leverhulme Research Schol. (carried out a Civic Diagnosis of Hull). Surveys and plans by Max Lock Group for: Middlesbrough, 1946; The Hartlepools, 1948; Portsmouth District, 1949; Bedford, 1951; by Max Lock and Partners, Surveys and plans for amman, Aqaba (Jordan), 1954-55; Town Plans for development of Iraq at Um Qasr, Margil and Basrah, 1954-56; New Towns at El Beida, Libya, 1956, and Sheikh Othman, Aden, 1960. Survey and plan for the Capital City and Territory of Kaduna for Government of Northern Nigeria, 1965-66. British Town Centre redevelopment plans include: Sevenoaks; Sutton Coldfield; Salisbury; Brentford; redevelopment of new central housing communities at Oldham; development of Woodley Airfield, Reading. Visiting Professor: Dept of City Planning, Harvard Univ., 1957; University of Rio de Janeiro, 1960; Guest Chairman, 5th Australian National Planning Congress, 1960. Member Council, TPI, 1946-50 and 1961-63. *Publications:* The Middlesbrough Survey and Plan, 1946; The Hartlepools Survey and Plan, 1948; The Portsmouth and District Survey and Plan, 1949; Bedford by the River, 1952; The New Basrah, 1956; Kaduna, 1917-1967-2017: A Survey and Plan of the Capital Territory for the Government of Northern Nigeria, 1967; contribs to RIBA Journal, TPI Journal, Town Planning Review, etc. *Recreations:* music, pianist. *Address:* 7 Victoria Square, SW1. *T:* 01-834 7071. *Club:* Reform.

**LOCK, Mrs John;** *see* Gērin, Winifred.

**LOCK, Max;** *see* Lock, C. M.

**LOCKE, Arthur D'Arcy, (Bobby Locke);** professional golfer; *b* Germiston, Transvaal, 20 Nov. 1917; *s* of Charles James Locke; *m* 1943, Lillian, *d* of N. le Roux, Montagu; one *d*. *Educ:* Benoni High Sch. Won Open and Amateur South African Championships, 1935; won Irish, Dutch and New Zealand Open Championships, 1938; French Open Championship, 1952-53; British Open Championship, 1949, 1950, 1952, 1957. Member Professional Golfers' Association (London). Served War of 1939-45, Middle East and Italy as Pilot, South African Air Force. *Publication:* Bobby Locke on Golf, 1953. *Club:* Ohenimuri Golf and Country (Johannesburg).

**LOCKE, Bobby;** *see* Locke, A. D'A.

**LOCKE, Hon. Charles Holland,** MC, QC; Judge, Supreme Court of Canada, 1947-62, retired; *b* Morden, Manitoba, 16 Sept. 1887; *s* of Judge Corbet Locke, QC, and Esther Alice Locke (*née* Holland), both of Morden, Manitoba; *m* 1916, Marie Amelie, *d* of late Clayton M. Weiss; one *s* two *d*. *Educ:* Morden Public Sch.; read Law with Arnold W. Bowen, Morden, and A. B. Hudson, KC, Winnipeg. Called to Bar of Manitoba, 1910; British Columbia, 1928; Ontario, 1962; KC Manitoba, 1923, in BC 1936; QC Ontario, 1962. Served in France with 61st Battery, Canadian Field Artillery (MC). *Address:* (office) 77 Metcalfe Street, Ottawa, Ontario, Canada.

**LOCKE, John Howard;** Assistant Under-Secretary of State, Department of Employment and Productivity, since 1968; *b* 26 Dec. 1923; *s* of Percy Locke and Josephine Locke (*née* Marshfield); *m* 1948, Eirene Sylvia Sykes; two *d*. *Educ:* Hymers Coll., Hull; Queen's Coll., Oxford. Ministry of Agriculture, Fisheries and Food, 1945-65; Under-Secretary: Cabinet Office, 1965-66; MoT, 1966-68. *Address:* 4 Old Palace Terrace, The Green, Richmond-on-Thames, Surrey. *T:* 01-940 1830; Old Box Trees, East Preston, Sussex.

**LOCKETT, Richard Jeffery,** CBE 1949; Chairman, Wm & Jno Lockett (Wines & Spirits) Ltd, since 1962; *b* 16 Sept. 1907; *s* of Richard Cyril Lockett and Beatrice (*née* Bell); *m* 1939, Mary Edna Crist, Oakland, California; one *s* one *d*. *Educ:* Winchester Coll.; Christ Church, Oxford. Sugar Planter and Cotton Merchant, Peru, 1928-50; responsible for procurement Peruvian Cotton for Ministry of Supply, 1941-45; Chairman, British Chamber of Commerce, Peru, 1943-44. Director: Cunard Steam Ship Co. Ltd, 1952-68; Royal Insurance Co. Ltd, 1954-; Combined English Mills (Spinners) Ltd, 1961-64; Matthew Clark & Sons (Holdings) Ltd, 1962-. Permanent Delegate of Peru to International Sugar Council, 1960-. High Sheriff of Cheshire, 1967-68. *Recreations:* shooting, fishing, gardening. *Address:* The Lodge, Malpas, Cheshire. *T:* Malpas 469. *Clubs:* Carlton; Palatine (Liverpool).

**LOCKHART;** *see* Bruce Lockhart.

**LOCKHART, Sir Allan R. E.;** *see* Eliott Lockhart.

**LOCKHART, Sir Muir Edward S.;** *see* Sinclair-Lockhart.

**LOCKHART, Gen. Sir Rob (McGregor Macdonald),** KCB 1946 (CB 1944); CIE, 1942; MC; Indian Army (retired); *b* 1893; 3rd *s* of late R. Bruce Lockhart, formerly of Eagle House, Sandhurst, Berks; *m* 1918, Margaret Amy, *yr d* of late Col Sir R. Neil Campbell, KCMG, IMS; one *s* three *d*. *Educ:* Marlborough Coll.; RMC, Sandhurst; Staff Coll., Camberley. Commissioned ULIA, 1913; joined 51st Sikhs FF, March 1914. Acting governor, NWFP (India) Jan.-Aug. 1947. C-in-C IA, Aug.-Dec. 1947; retired 1948. Dir of Ops, Malaya, Dec. 1951-Feb. 1952; Dep. Dir, Feb. 1952-March 1953. Dep. Chief Scout, Boy Scouts' Association, 1951-61; Pres., Greater London Central Scout County (Boy Scouts' Assoc.). Order of Star of Nepal (2nd Class), 1946. *Address:* c/o Lloyds Bank Ltd, Cox's & King's Branch, 6 Pall Mall, SW1.

**LOCKHART, Robert Douglas,** MB, ChB, MD, ChM; LLD; FSAScot, FRSE; Hon. Curator, Anthropology Museum (Cultural), University of Aberdeen; Regius Professor of Anatomy, University of Aberdeen, 1938-Sept. 1965;

Dean of the Faculty of Medicine, 1959-62; *b* 7 Jan. 1894; *s* of William Lockhart and Elizabeth Bogie. *Educ:* Robert Gordon's Coll., Aberdeen; University, Aberdeen. Ho. Surg. Aberdeen Royal Infirmary; Surgeon-Probationer, RNVR, 1916; Surgeon-Lt, RN 1918; Lecturer in Anatomy, Aberdeen Univ., 1919; Prof. of Anat., Birmingham Univ. 1931; Past Pres., Anatomical Soc. of Great Britain and Ireland. *Publications:* Chapter, Ways of Living, in Man and Nature, 1926; Myology Section in Cunningham's Anatomy, 1964; Living Anatomy–photographic atlas, 1963; Anatomy of the Human Body, 1969; contributor to Kodak Med. Film Library, 1933; Structure and Function of Muscle, 1960. *Recreations:* roses and rhododendrons. *Address:* 25 Rubislaw Den North, Aberdeen. *T:* Aberdeen 37833.

**LOCKHART, Stephen Alexander,** CMG 1960; OBE 1949; HM Diplomatic Service, retired 1965; re-employed in Foreign and Commonwealth Office; *b* 19 March 1905; *o s* of late Captain Murray Lockhart, RN, Milton Lockhart, and of Leonora Rynd; *m* 1944, Angela Watson; two *s* two *d*. *Educ:* Harrow; Jesus Coll., Cambridge. Served Lisbon, 1940-43; Ministry of Information, 1943; Press Attaché, Lisbon, 1944, Brussels, 1945; First Sec. (Information), Brussels, 1946-51; Foreign Office, 1951; First Sec., Buenos Aires, 1952-55; UK Rep., Trieste, 1955-57; HM Consul-Gen., Leopoldville, and in French Equatorial Africa, 1957-60; HM Consul-Gen., Zurich, 1960-62; HM Ambassador to Dominican Republic, 1962-65. *Recreations:* swimming, bridge. *Address:* 71 Chester Square, SW1. *Club:* Travellers'.

**LOCKHART-MUMMERY, Hugh Evelyn,** MD, MChir; FRCS; Consultant Surgeon: St Mark's Hospital since 1951; St Thomas' Hospital since 1960; King Edward VII's Hospital for Officers since 1968; HM Household since 1969; *b* 28 April 1918; *s* of John Percy Lockhart-Mummery, FRCS; *m* 1946, Elizabeth Jean Crerar, *d* of Sir James Crerar, KCSI, CIE; one *s*. *Educ:* Stowe Sch.; Trinity Coll., Cambridge; Westminster Hosp. Med. Sch. MB, BCh 1942; FRCS 1943; MChir 1950; MD 1956. Served RAF, 1943-46. Examr in Surgery, Univ. of London, 1965; Pres., Sect. of Proctology, RSM, 1966. Hon. Fellow, (French) Académie de Proctologie, 1961. *Publications:* chapters in surgical textbooks; articles on surgery of the colon and rectum in Brit. jls. *Recreations:* golf, fishing. *Address:* 5 Hereford Square, SW7. *T:* 01-373 3630; 149 Harley Street, W1N 2DE. *T:* 01-935 4444. *Club:* Royal Automobile.

**LOCKLEY, Ven. Harold;** Archdeacon of Loughborough and Vicar of All Saints, Leicester, since 1963; Senior Examining Chaplain to Bishop of Leicester since 1951; Lecturer in Divinity, University of Leicester; *b* 16 July 1916; *s* of Harry and Sarah Elizabeth Lockley; *m* 1947, Ursula Margaret, *d* of Rev. Dr H. Wedell and Mrs G. Wedell; three *s*. *Educ:* Loughborough Coll. (Hons Dip. Physical Education); London University; Westcott House, Cambridge. BA Hons 1937, BD Hons 1943, MTh 1949, London Univ.; PhD 1955, Nottingham Univ. Chaplain and Tutor, Loughborough Coll., 1946-51; Vicar of Glen Parva and South Wigston, 1951-58. Proctor in Convocation of Canterbury, 1960-63; Canon Chancellor of Leicester Cathedral, 1958-63. *Publications:* Editor, Leicester Cathedral Quarterly, 1960-63. *Recreations:* walking and foreign travel. *Address:* 1 Knighton Grange Road, Leicester. *T:* Leicester 707328. *Clubs:* English-Speaking Union, National Liberal.

**LOCKLEY, Ronald Mathias;** author and naturalist; *b* 8 Nov. 1903. *Publications:* Dream Island, 1930; The Island Dwellers; Island Days; The Sea's a Thief; Birds of the Green Belt; I Know an Island; A Pot of Smoke; Early Morning Island; The Way to an Island; Shearwaters; Dream Island Days; Inland Farm; Birds of the Sea; Islands Round Britain; The Island Farmers; Letters from Skokholm; The Golden Year; The Cinnamon Bird; The Charm of the Channel Islands; The Nature-Lovers Anthology; Travels with a Tent in Western Europe; (with John Buxton) Island of Skomer; Puffins: (with Rosemary Russell) Bird Ringing; The Seals and the Curragh; Gilbert White; (with James Fisher) Sea-Birds; Pembrokeshire; The Bird-Lover's Bedside Book; The Private Life of the Rabbit; Britain in Colour; Wales; Grey Seal, Common Seal; Animal Navigation; Traveller's Guide to the Channel Islands; The Book of Bird-Watching; The Island; The Naturalist in Wales, etc. *Address:* c/o E. P. S. Lewin and Partners, 7 Chelsea Embankment, SW3.

**LOCKSPEISER, Sir Ben,** KCB 1950; Kt 1946; FRS 1949; FIMechE, FRAeS; Director and Scientific Adviser, Staveley Industries Ltd; Director, Ricardo & Co. (Engineers 1927) Ltd; *b* 9 March 1891; *s* of late Leon and Rose Lockspeiser, London; *m* 1920, Elsie Shuttleworth (*d* 1964); one *s* two *d*; *m* 1966, Mary Alice Heywood. *Educ:* Grocers' Sch.; Sidney Sussex Coll., Cambridge (Hon. Fellow); Royal School of Mines. MA; Hon. DSc Oxford; Hon. DEng Witwatersrand; Hon. DTech, Haifa; Aeronautical Research at Royal Aircraft Establishment, Farnborough, 1920-37; Head of Air Defence Dept, RAE, Farnborough, 1937-39; Asst Dir of Scientific Research, Air Ministry, 1939; Dep. Dir of Scientific Res., Armaments, Min. of Aircraft Production, 1941; Dir of Scientific Research, Ministry of Aircraft Production, 1943; Dir-Gen. of Scientific Research, Ministry of Aircraft Production, 1945; Chief Scientist to Ministry of Supply, 1946-49; Sec. to Cttee of Privy Council for Scientific and Industrial Research, 1949-56; retired 1956. President: Engineering Section of British Association, 1952; Johnson Soc., 1953-54; Council European Organization for Nuclear Research, 1955-57; Mem. Council British Association for the Advancement of Science. Chm., Govs of Farnborough Technical Coll., 1957-68. Medal of Freedom (Silver Palms), 1946. *Recreations:* music, gardening. *Address:* Birchway, Waverley Road, Farnborough, Hants. *T:* Farnborough, Hants, 43021. *Club:* Athenæum.

**LOCKWOOD, James Horace;** *b* 25 May 1888; *s* of George Henry Lockwood, Woollen and Worsted Cloth Manufacturer, of Huddersfield. admitted a Solicitor, 1912; Captain RFA (T) European War; Pres., Bradford Law Soc., 1929; MP (C) Shipley Div. of Yorks, 1930-35; has taken a great interest in Bankruptcy Law Reform; Chm of Directors of Wm Fison and Co. Ltd, and a Dir of other companies in the cloth manufacturing and merchanting industry. *Recreations:* shooting and sailing. *Address:* 5 and 6 Stuart Court, Prince of Wales Mansions, Harrogate, Yorks. *T:* Harrogate 3780; Scutcheon House, Far Sawrey, Ambleside. *Clubs:* Union (Bradford); The Club (Harrogate).

**LOCKWOOD, Lt-Col John Cutts,** CBE 1960; TD; JP; *s* of late Colonel John Lockwood and Mrs Lockwood, Kingham, Oxon. Served European War, 1914-18, in Essex Regt and Coldstream Guards; War of 1939-45, with Essex Territorials; Staff Captain in JAG Dept; later Legal Officer to SHAEF Mission to Denmark, and with them in Copenhagen,

1945. MP (C) Central Hackney, 1931-35; Romford, 1950-55. Barrister, Middle Temple; Mem. of Hon. Co. of Basket-makers and Freeman of the City of London. Mem. of the House of Laity Church Assembly. Order of Dannebrog (Denmark). *Recreation:* gardening. *Address:* Bishops Hall, Lambourne End, Essex. *T:* 01-500 2016. *Club:* Royal Automobile.

**LOCKWOOD, Sir Joseph (Flawith),** Kt 1960; Chairman: Electric and Musical Industries, Ltd and subsidiaries since 1954; Industrial Reorganisation Corporation, since 1969 (Member, since 1966); Director: The Beecham Group, since 1966; Smiths Industries Ltd (previously S. Smith & Sons (England) Ltd), since 1959; Hawker Siddeley Group, since 1963; British Domestic Appliances Ltd, since 1966 (Chairman, 1966-70), and other cos; *b* 14 Nov. 1904. Manager of flour mills in Chile, 1924-28; Technical Manager of Etablissements, Henry Simon Ltd, in Paris and Brussels, 1928-33; Director, 1933; Dir Henry Simon Ltd, Buenos Aires, Chm. Henry Simon (Australia) Ltd, Dir Henry Simon (Engineering Works) Ltd, etc, 1945, Chm. and Managing Dir, Henry Simon Ltd, 1950; Dir, National Research Development Corporation, 1951-67; Member: Engineering Advisory Council, Board of Trade, 1959; Export Council for Europe, 1961-63; Export Credits Guarantee Adv. Council, 1963-67; Council Imperial Soc. of Knights Bach. Director: Racecourse Holdings Trust Ltd, 1969; Metropolitan & Country Racecourse Management & Holdings Ltd, 1969. Hon. Treasurer British Empire Cancer Campaign, 1962-67; Chm., Royal Ballet Sch. Endowment Fund, 1960-; Chm. Governors, Royal Ballet Sch.; Governor, Central Sch. of Speech and Drama (Chm., Governors, 1965-68); Member: Arts Council, 1967-; South Bank Theatre Board, 1968-. Comp. IEE; Comp. IERE. *Publications:* Provender Milling–the Manufacture of Feeding Stuffs for Livestock, 1939; Flour Milling (trans. into various languages), 1945. *Address:* 33 Grosvenor Square, W1. *Club:* Carlton.

**LOCKWOOD, Margaret Mary;** Actress; *b* Karachi, India, 15 Sept. 1916; (*née* Margaret Lockwood); *m* Rupert W. Leon (marr. diss.); one *d*. *Educ:* Sydenham Girls' High Sch. Studied for Stage under Italia Conti and at Royal Academy of Dramatic Art. Appeared in: *plays:* Family Affairs; Miss Smith; *films:* Lorna Doone; Case of Gabriel Perry, 1934; Midshipman Easy; Jury's Evidence; Amateur Gentleman, 1935; Irish for Luck; Beloved Vagabond; Street Singer, 1936; Who's Your Lady Friend; Owd Bob; Bank Holiday, 1937; The Lady Vanishes; A Girl Must Live; Stars Look Down; Night Train to Munich, 1939; Quiet Wedding, 1940; Alibi; Man in Grey, 1942; Dear Octopus; Give Us The Moon; Love Story, 1943; Place of One's Own; I'll Be Your Sweetheart, 1944; Wicked Lady; Bedelia, 1945; Hungry Hill; Jassy, 1946; The White Unicorn, 1947; Look Before You Love, 1948; Cardboard Cavalier; Madness of the Heart, 1949; Highly Dangerous, 1950; Laughing Anne, 1952; Trent's Last Case, 1952; Trouble in the Glen, 1954; Cast A Dark Shadow, 1955. Named top money-making Star in Britain by motion Picture Poll; Motion Picture Herald Fame Poll, 1945 and 1946; Winner Daily Mail Film Award, 1945-46, 1946-47 and 1947-48. Stage tour in Private Lives, 1949; Peter Pan, 1949-50, 1950-51 and 1957-58; Pygmalion, 1951; Spider's Web, Savoy, 1954-56; Subway in the Sky, Savoy, 1957; And Suddenly It's Spring, Duke of York's, 1959-60; Signpost to Murder, Cambridge Theatre, 1962-63; Every Other Evening, Phœnix, 1964-65; An Ideal Husband, Strand, 1965 and Garrick, 1966; The Others, Strand, 1967; On a Foggy Day, St Martin's, 1969; Lady Frederick, Vaudeville, 1970. BBC (TV) series (with daughter Julia) The Flying Swan, March-Sept. 1965; Yorkshire TV series, Julia Stanford, QC, 1971. *Recreations:* crossword puzzles and swimming. *Address:* c/o Herbert de Leon, 30 South Audley Street, W1.

**LOCKWOOD, Walter Sydney Douglas,** CBE 1962 (OBE 1948); FRAeS; MIProdE; *b* 4 Jan. 1895; *s* of Walter Lockwood, Thetford, Norfolk; *m* 1924, Constance Rose, *d* of T. F. Bayliss, Norwich. *Educ:* Thetford Sch.; Bristol Univ. Served European War, 1914-18: Gloucester Regt, France and Belgium (Belgian Croix de Guerre; despatches; wounded). Joined design staff of Sir W. G. Armstrong Whitworth Aircraft Ltd, 1921; became Works Man., 1944. Armstrong Whitworth Aircraft: Works Dir, 1950; Dir and Gen. Man., 1955; Man. Dir, 1960; Man. Dir, Whitworth Gloster Aircraft Ltd (when Armstrong Whitworth Aircraft and Gloster Aircraft Companies merged), 1961-63 (when Co. dissolved); Dir, Hawker Siddeley Aviation Ltd, 1961-64, retired. Mem. Coun., SBAC, 1960. *Address:* Wayside, Abbey Road, Leiston, Suffolk.

**LOCMARIA, Marquis du P.;** *see* Parc-Locmaria.

**LODER,** family name of **Baron Wakehurst.**

**LODER, Sir Giles Rolls,** 3rd Bt, *cr* 1887; *b* 10 Nov. 1914; *o s* of late Capt. Robert Egerton Loder, *s* of 2nd Bt, and late Muriel Rolls, *d* of J. Rolls-Hoare; *S* grandfather, 1920; *m* 1939, Marie, *o d* of Captain Symons-Jeune, Runnymede House, Old Windsor; two *s*. *Educ:* Eton; Trinity Coll., Cambridge (MA). High Sheriff of Sussex, 1948-49. FLS. *Recreations:* sailing, horticulture. *Heir: s* Edmund Jeune Loder [*b* 26 June 1941; *m* 1966, Penelope Jane, *d* of Ivo Forde, Cranleigh, Surrey; one *d*]. *Address:* Leonardslee, Horsham, Sussex. *T:* Lower Beeding 305. *Clubs:* Junior Carlton; Royal Yacht Squadron.

**LODER, Sir Louis (Francis),** Kt 1962; CBE 1953; retired; *b* 30 Dec. 1896; *s* of James Edward Loder and Marie Dorthea Loder (*née* Jensen); *m* 1924, Jean Arnot Maxwell; three *s*. *Educ:* Wesley Coll., Melbourne; Queen's Coll., University of Melbourne. Chief Engineer, Country Roads Board, Vic., 1928-40; Chm., 1940-44; Dir-Gen., Commonwealth Dept of Works, 1944-61. DEng, Perth, 1948. *Publications:* Papers in Proceedings of Institution of Engineers, Australia. *Recreation:* tennis. *Address:* PO Box 214, Healesville, Victoria 3777, Australia. *T:* Healesville 786. *Club:* Royal Automobile (Victoria).

**LODGE, Henry Cabot;** Politician, US; President Nixon's Special Representative to the Vatican, since 1970; *b* 5 July 1902; *s* of George Cabot Lodge and Mathilda Elizabeth Frelinghuysen Davis; *g s* of late Henry Cabot Lodge, Senator (US); *m* 1926, Emily Sears; two *s*. *Educ:* Middx Sch., Concord, Mass.; Harvard (AB *cum laude*; LLD). Boston Transcript, New York Herald Tribune, 1923-32. Thrice elected US Senator from Massachusetts. Harvard Overseer. Senate author of the Lodge-Brown Act which created Hoover Commission; Chm., resolutions cttee, Republican National Convention, 1948; US Senate Foreign Relations Cttee. Campaign Manager of effort to win Republican nomination for Gen. Eisenhower, 1951-52; Mem. President's Cabinet and US Rep. to UN, 1953-60. Republican nominee for Vice-Pres., USA, 1960. Dir-Gen., Atlantic Inst., Paris, 1961-63; Ambassador to Vietnam, 1963-64, 1965-67, to Federal Republic of Germany,

1968-69. US Representative at Vietnam Peace Talks, Paris, Jan.-Nov. 1969. Began War Service as Major United States Army, with first American tank detachment in Brit. 8th Army, Libya, 1942 (citation); resigned from Senate for further Army service (first Senator to do so since the Civil War); Italy, 1944; Lt-Col S France, Rhine and S Germany, 1944-45 (Bronze Star, US, 1944, Legion of Merit, 1945, Légion d'Honneur and Croix de Guerre with palm, France, 1945). Maj.-Gen., US Army Reserve. Has been awarded numerous Hon. Degrees; Sylvanus Thayer Medal, West Point; Theodore Roosevelt Assoc. Medal. Holds some foreign decorations. *Publications:* articles for Atlantic Monthly, Collier's, Life, Reader's Digest, Saturday Evening Post. *Address:* 275 Hale Street, Beverly, Mass 01915, USA.

**LODGE, Thomas C. S.**; *see* Skeffington-Lodge.

**LODGE, Tom Stewart,** CBE 1967; Director of Research and Statistics, Home Office, since 1969; *b* 15 Dec. 1909; *s* of George Arthur and Emma Eliza Lodge, Batley, Yorks; *m* 1936, Joan McFadyean (*d* 1961); one *d. Educ:* Batley Grammar Sch.; Merton Coll., Oxford. BA Hons Maths 1931, MA 1934; FIA 1939. Prudential Assurance Co., 1931-43; Min. of Aircraft Production, 1943-46; Admty as Superintending Actuary, 1946-50; Statistical Adviser, Home Office, 1950; Statistical Adviser and Dir of Research, Home Office, 1957. *Publications:* articles in British and French jls. *Address:* Chaddesley, Slines Oak Road, Woldingham, Surrey. *T:* Woldingham 3245. *Clubs:* Royal Automobile, Civil Service.

**LOEHNIS, Sir Clive,** KCMG 1962 (CMG 1950); Commander RN (retired); *b* 24 Aug. 1902; *s* of H. W. Loehnis, Barrister-at-Law, Inner Temple; *m* 1929, Rosemary Beryl, *d* of late Major Hon. R. N. Dudley Ryder, 8th Hussars; one *s* one *d. Educ:* Royal Naval Colls, Osborne, Dartmouth and Greenwich. Midshipman, 1920; Lt, 1924; qualified in signal duties, 1928; Lt-Comdr, 1932; retired, 1935; AMIEE 1935. Re-employed in Signal Div. Admiralty, 1938; Comdr on retd List, 1942; Naval Intelligence Div., 1942; demobilised and entered Foreign Office, 1945; Dep. Dir, Government Communications Headquarters, 1952-60; Dir, Government Communications HQ, 1960-64. Dep. Chm., Civil Service Selection Bd, 1967-70. *Address:* 12 Eaton Place, SW1. *T:* 01-235 6803. *Clubs:* White's, MCC.
*See also Baron Remnant.*

**LOEWE, Frederick;** composer; concert pianist; *b* Vienna, 10 June 1901; *s* of Edmund Loewe, actor. Began career as concert pianist playing with leading European orchestras; went to US, 1924; first musical, Salute to Spring, produced in St Louis, 1937; first Broadway production, Great Lady, 1938; began collaboration with Alan Jay Lerner, *qv,* in 1942, since when has written music for: Day Before Spring, 1945; Brigadoon, 1947 (1st musical to win Drama Critics' Award); Paint Your Wagon, 1951 (best score of year); My Fair Lady, 1956 (many awards); Gigi (film), 1958 (Oscar); Camelot, 1960. DMus *hc* Univ. of Redlands, Calif; Dr of Fine Arts *hc* Univ. of NYC. *Address:* c/o ASCAP, 575 Madison Avenue, New York, NY 10022, USA. *Clubs:* Players' Lambs (New York); Palm Springs Racquet.

**LOEWEN, Gen. Sir Charles (Falkland),** GCB 1957 (KCB 1954; CB 1945); KBE 1951 (CBE 1944); DSO 1945; late RA; *b* 17 Sept. 1900; *s* of late Charles J. Loewen, MA, Vancouver, Canada, and Edith Loewen; *m* 1928, Kathleen, *d* of late Maj.-Gen. J. M. Ross; two *s. Educ:* Haileybury Coll.; Royal Military College, Kingston, Canada. 2nd Lt RFA 1918; Capt. 1931; Bt Major, 1937; Major, 1938; Bt Lt-Col 1939; Col 1942; Maj.-Gen. 1944; Lt-Gen. 1950; Gen. 1954. Served War of 1939-45, in Norway (despatches) and in Italy (despatches); comd: 1st Inf. Div., 1944-45; 6th Armd Div., 1946; 1st Armd Div., 1947; Northumb. Dist and 50th (Inf.) Div. (TA), 1948-49; GOC-in-C Anti-Aircraft Command, 1950-53; GOC-in-C, Western Command, April-Sept. 1953; C-in-C Far East Land Forces, 1953-56; Adjutant-Gen. to the Forces, 1956-59; ADC Gen. to the Queen, 1956-59. Col Comdt, RA, 1953-63. Hon. DSc Mil., Roy. Mil. Coll. Canada, 1966. Comdr Legion of Merit (US), 1945. *Recreations:* shooting, fishing, boating. *Address:* 13969 Trites Road, Surrey, BC, Canada. *Clubs:* Army and Navy; Vancouver (Vancouver).

**LOEWENSTEIN-WERTHEIM-FREUDENBERG, Hubertus Friedrich, Prince of,** Dr iur, LittD (*hc*); Commander's Cross of German Order of Merit, 1968; Special Adviser, German Government, Press and Information Office, since 1960; Member of Parliament, 1953-57; *b* Schoenwoerth Castle, near Kufstein, Tirol, 14 Oct. 1906; *y s* of Prince Maximilian Loewenstein-Wertheim-Freudenberg and Constance, *y d* of 1st Baron Pirbright, PC; *m* 1929, Helga Maria Mathilde v. d. Schuylenburg; three *d. Educ:* Gymnasium at Gmunden and Klagenfurt, Austria; Universities at Munich, Hamburg, Geneva, and Berlin. Referendar Berlin Kammergericht, 1928, Doctor iuris utriusque, Hamburg, 1931; member of Catholic Centre Party, 1930; leader of Republican Students, and Republican Youth, Berlin, 1930; Prussian delegate to Munich, 1932; left Germany, 1933; returned 1946; Visiting Prof. of Hist. and Gov. to USA and Canada of the Carnegie Endowment for International Peace, 1937-46; Lecturer in History, University of Heidelberg, during 1947. Publisher and editor, Das Reich, Saarbrücken, 1934-35; Founder of American Guild for German Cultural Freedom, 1936; Founder and leader, German Action movement, 1949-. Southern German Editor, Die Zeit, 1952-53; Hon. DLitt Hamline Univ., 1943. Grand Cross of Athos, 1966; Commendatore, Order of Merit (Italy), 1970. *Publications:* The Tragedy of a Nation, 1934; After Hitler's Fall, Germany's Coming Reich, 1934; A Catholic in Republican Spain, 1937; Conquest of the Past, autobiography (till 1933), 1938; On Borrowed Peace, autobiography (1933 to 1942), 1942; The Germans in History, 1945; The Child and the Emperor: a Legend, 1945; The Lance of Longinus, 1946; The Eagle and the Cross, 1947; Deutsche Geschichte, 1950; Stresemann, biography, 1953; Die römischen Tagebücher des Dr von Molitor, 1956; (co-author Volkmar von Zuehlsdorff) Das deutsche Schicksal 1945-1957, 1957; (same co-author) NATO, The Defence of the West, 1963; Towards The Further Shore (autobiography), 1968; contributions to (previous to 1933) Berliner Tageblatt, Vossische Zeitung, etc; (after 1933) Spectator, Nineteenth Century Review, Contemporary Review, American Mercury, Atlantic Monthly, New York Herald Tribune, Commonweal, American Scholar, Social Science, Die Tat, Die Zeit, etc. *Recreations:* swimming, riding. *Address:* c/o Prince Leopold zu Löwenstein, 209 Coleherne Court, SW5.

**LOEWY, Raymond Fernand;** Industrial Designer; Chairman: Raymond Loewy, William Snaith, Inc., since 1961, consultant designers to US and foreign Corporations; Compagnie de l'Esthétique Industrielle, Paris; Lecturer: Massachusetts Institute of Technology; Harvard Graduate School of

Business Administration; *b* Paris, 5 Nov. 1893; *s* of Maximillian Loewy and Marie Labalme; naturalized citizen of US 1938; *m* 1948, Viola Erickson; one *d*. *Educ:* Chaptal Coll., Paris; Paris Univ.; Ecole de Lanneau (grad. eng.). Began as Fashion Illustrator, 1919; Art Director, Westinghouse Electric Co. 1929; started private organization of Industrial Design, 1929. Served as Capt. Corps of Engineers attached to Gen. Staff, 5th Army, France, 1914-18; Liaison Officer, AEF (Officer Legion of Honour, Croix de Guerre, with 4 citations; Interallied Medal); Comdr, Fr. Legion of Honour, 1959. Hon. RDI 1937; FRSA 1942; Fellow American Soc. of Industrial Designers; Advisor, Coll. of Arch., University of South Calif; American Design Award, 1938; Hon. Doctor of Fine Arts, University of Cincinnati, 1956; Member: Society of Automotive Engineers; Amer. Soc. Mech. Engrs; Adv. Board on Vocational Educn, Bd of Educn, NYC; Assoc. Mem. Soc. of Naval Arch. and Marine Engrs; Vice-Pres. French Chamber of Commerce of the US, 1958. Mem., President's Cttee on Employment of the Handicapped, 1965-; Habitability Consultant to NASA Apollo Saturn Application program, 1967-; also perm. 1975 advance stations for 60 to 100 astronauts. *Publications:* The Locomotive–its Esthetics, 1937; Never Leave Well Enough Alone (autobiography), 1951 (trans. various langs). Contrib. to trade jls and magazines. *Address:* 900 Fifth Avenue, NYC, USA; Château de la Cense, near Paris; Tierra Caliente, Palm Springs, Calif; (Office) 110 E 59th Street, NYC; 39 Avenue d'Iéna, Paris, France. *Clubs:* Racquet, Tennis (Palm Springs, Calif), NY Athletic.

**LOFTS, Norah, (Mrs Robert Jorisch)**; *b* 27 Aug. 1904; *d* of Isaac Robinson and Ethel (*née* Garner); *m* 1st, 1931, Geoffrey Lofts (decd); one *s*; 2nd, 1949, Dr Robert Jorisch. *Educ:* West Suffolk County Sch. *Publications:* I Met a Gypsy, 1935; White Hell of Pity, 1937; Out of This Nettle, 1939; Road to Revelation, 1941; Jassy, 1944; Silver Nutmeg, 1947; Women of the Old Testament, 1949; A Calf for Venus, 1949; The Luteplayer, 1951; Bless This House, 1954; Queen in Waiting, 1955; Afternoon of An Autocrat, 1956; Scent of Cloves, 1958; Heaven In Your Hand, 1959; The Town House, 1959; The House at Old Vine, 1961; The House at Sunset, 1963; The Concubine, 1964; How Far to Bethlehem?, 1965; Lovers All Untrue, 1970; (with M. Weiner), Eternal France, 1969; The Lost Ones, 1969; The King's Pleasure, 1970. *As Peter Curtis:* You're Best Alone, 1939; Dead March in Three Keys, 1940; Lady Living Alone, 1944; The Devil's Own, 1959. *Address:* Northgate House, Bury St Edmunds, Suffolk. *T:* Bury St Edmunds 2680.

**LOFTUS, Viscount; Charles John Tottenham;** Instructor of French, Martingrove CI, Toronto; *b* 2 Feb. 1943; *e s* and *heir* of 8th Marquess of Ely, *qv*; *m* 1969, Judith Marvelle, *d* of Dr J. J. Porter, FRSC, Calgary, Alberta. *Educ:* Trinity Coll. Sch., Port Hope, Ont; Ecole Internationale de Genève; Univ. of Toronto (MA). *Address:* 557 The East Mall, Islington, Ont, Canada. *T:* 416-622-0137.

**LOFTUS, Col Ernest Achey,** OBE 1928; TD 1929; DL; MA (TCD), BSc Econ. (London), LCP, FRGS, FRSA, MRST; Member RSL; an Education Officer in service of Northern Rhodesian Government (now Zambia) from 1963; *b* 11 Jan. 1884; *s* of Capt. William Loftus, Master Mariner, Kingston-upon-Hull; *m* 1916, Elsie, *er d* of Allen Charles Cole, West Tilbury, Essex; two *s*. *Educ:* Archbishop Holgate's Gram. Sch., York; Trinity Coll., Dublin. Senior Geography Master, Palmer's Sch., Grays, Essex, 1906-19; Asst Dir of Educn, Southend-on-Sea, 1920-22; Headmaster, Barking Abbey Sch., 1922-49; coined term 'Health Science' and drew up first syllabus of work (London Univ.) in that subject, 1937; an Educn Officer in Kenya, 1953-60, in Nyasaland, 1960-63; formed two Cadet Corps and raised four Territl Units in Co. Essex; served with The Essex Regt 1910-29; European War in Gallipoli 1915, Egypt 1916, France 1918; Staff Officer for Educn to Independent Force (Kent) 1917; Lt-Col Commanding 6th Essex Regt, 1925-29; Mem. Essex Territorial Army Association 1925-29; Brevet Col, 1929; served in War of 1939Pioneer Corps, 1939-42, commanding No. 13 (Italian) Group in France and No. 31 Group in London, etc.; Founder Hon. Sec. Essex County Playing Fields Association, 1925-29; Hon. Organiser or Sec. various Appeals, in Essex. Mem. Standing Cttee Convocation, London Univ., 1944-53, and Bedell of Convocation, 1946-53. A chm. Nat. Assistance Board, 1949-53; Mem. Exec. Cttee Essex Playing Fields Assoc., 1925-53; Mem. Thurrock UDC 1946-53, Vice-Chm. 1951-52; Controller, Civil Defence, Thurrock area, 1951-53. Freeman, City of Kingston-upon-Hull, 1968. For some years a Governor, The Strand Sch. (Brixton), Palmer's Sch. (Grays), etc. DL 1929, Essex. Mason, 1915-; Rotarian (Pres., Barking, 1935), 1930-. *Publications:* Education and the Citizen; History of a Branch of the Cole Family; Growls and Grumbles; A History of Barking Abbey (with H. F. Chettle); A Visual History of Africa; A Visual History of East Africa; and brochures for the East African Literature Bureau. Contributor of feature articles in London Daily and Weekly Press, etc. on Education; author of 8 scenes of Barking Pageant, 1931, and of Elizabethan scene in Ilford Pageant of Essex, 1932. *Recreations:* historical and genealogical research. *Address:* (temp.) PO Box 655, Lusaka, Zambia; Polwicks, West Tilbury, Essex. *Club:* Royal Commonwealth Society.

**LOGAN, Donald Arthur,** CMG 1965; HM Ambassador to Bulgaria, since 1970; *b* 25 Aug. 1917; *s* of late Arthur Alfred Logan and Louise Anne Bradley; *m* 1957, Irène Jocelyne Angèle, *d* of Robert Everts (Belgian Ambassador at Madrid, 1932-39) and Alexandra Comnène; one *s* two *d*. *Educ:* Solihull. Fellow, Chartered Insurance Institute, 1939. War of 1939-45: commissioned, RA, Sept. 1939; Major, 1942; British Army Staff, Washington, 1942-43; Germany, 1945. Joined HM Foreign (subseq. Diplomatic) Service, Dec. 1945; Foreign Office, 1945-47; HM Embassy, Tehran, 1947-51, as First Sec. (Commercial); Foreign Office, 1951-53; Asst Political Agent, Kuwait, 1953-55; Asst Private Sec. to Sec. of State for Foreign Affairs, 1956-58; HM Embassy, Washington, 1958-60; HM Ambassador to Guinea, 1960-62; Foreign Office, 1962-64; Information Counsellor, British Embassy, Paris, 1964-70. Vice-Pres., Internat. Exhibitions Bureau, Paris, 1963-67. *Address:* British Embassy, Sofia, Bulgaria. *Clubs:* St James', White's, Royal Automobile.

**LOGAN, Sir Douglas (William),** Kt 1959; DPhil, MA, BCL, Hon. DCL Western Ontario; Hon. LLD: Melbourne, Madras, British Columbia, Hong Kong, Liverpool, McGill; Hon. FDSRCS; Hon. ARIBA; Principal of the University of London since 1948; President, British Universities Sports Federation; *b* Liverpool, 27 March 1910; *yr s* of Robert Logan and Euphemia Taylor Stevenson, Edinburgh; *m* 1st, 1940, Vaire Olive Wollaston (from whom he obtained a divorce); two *s*; 2nd, 1947, Christine Peggy Walker; one *s* one *d*. *Educ:* Liverpool Collegiate Sch.; University

Coll., Oxford (Open Classical Scholar). First Classes: Hon. Mods 1930, Lit. Hum. 1932, Jurisprudence, 1933; Oxford Univ. Senior Studentship, 1933; Henry Fellowship Harvard Law Sch., 1935-36; Asst Lecturer, LSE, 1936-37; Barstow Scholarship, 1937; called to Bar, Middle Temple, 1937; Fellow of Trinity Coll., Cambridge, 1937-43; Principal, Ministry of Supply, 1940-44; Clerk of the Court, University of London, 1944-47. Rede Lecturer, 1963. Hon. Fellow London Sch. of Economics, 1962; Fellow, Wye Coll.; Hon. Bencher, Middle Temple, 1965; Hon. Mem., Pharmaceutical Soc. Vice-Chm., Association of Commonwealth Univs, 1961-67 (Chm. 1962-63; Hon. Treasurer, 1967-68); Vice-Chm., Athlone Fellowship Cttee; Dep. Chm., Commonwealth Scholarships Commn; Member: Marshall Scholarships Commn, 1961-67; Exec. Cttee and Admin. Bd, British Institute in Paris; Nat. Theatre Bd, 1962-68; a Governor, Old Vic and Bristol Old Vic; a Trustee, City Parochial Foundation, Mem., 1953-67; Member: Anderson Cttee on Grants to Students, 1958-60; Hale Cttee on Superannuation of Univ. Teachers, 1958-60; Northumberland Cttee on Recruitment to the Veterinary Profession, 1962-64; Madden Working Party on the Superannuation of Univ. Teachers, 1965-68. Mem. British Delegation to 1st, 2nd, 3rd, and 4th Commonwealth Educn Confs, Oxford, 1959, Delhi, 1962, Ottawa, 1964, and Lagos 1968; Commonwealth Medical Conf. Edinburgh, 1965. Chevalier de l'Ordre de la Légion d'Honneur. *Address:* The University of London, Senate House, WC1E 7HU. *T:* 01-636 8000. *Club:* Athenæum.

**LOGAN, Lt-Col Harry Tremaine;** MC; MA; Professor Emeritus of Classics, University of British Columbia, retired; *b* Londonderry, Nova Scotia, 5 March 1887; *yr s* of Rev. John A. Logan, DD; *m* 1916, Gwyneth, *v d* of Sir James A. H. Murray, Editor, Oxford English Dictionary; one *s* one *d* (*er s* died of wounds, Normandy, 1944). *Educ:* BC Elementary Schs; Vancouver High Sch.; McGill; (Rhodes Scholar) St John's Coll., Oxford. Instructor in Classics, McGill Coll. of BC, 1913-15; Lt 72nd Seaforth Highlanders of Canada, 1915; served in Belgium and France in Canadian Machine Gun Corps, 1916-18 (despatches, MC); prepared Official History Canadian Machine Gun Corps, 1919; Mem. Classics Dept, University of British Columbia, 1915-36; Head, 1949-54; Special Lectr in Classics, 1954-67. Principal, Prince of Wales Fairbridge Farm Sch., 1936-45; Sec., The Fairbridge Soc., London, 1946-49. Mem., University of British Columbia Senate, 1930-48 and 1954-60; Board of Governors, 1941-45. Hon. LLD, University of British Columbia, 1965. *Publication:* Tuum Est, A History of the University of British Columbia, 1958. *Recreation:* gardening. *Address:* The University of British Columbia, Vancouver, BC, Canada.

**LOGAN, Lt-Col John,** TD 1945; Vice-Lieutenant, Stirlingshire, since 1965; *b* 25 May 1907; *s* of Crawford William Logan and Ada Kathleen Logan (*née* Kidston); *m* 1937, Rosaleen Muriel O'Hara (*d* 1967); one *s* one *d*. *Educ:* Eton Coll., Windsor. British American Tobacco Co. Ltd (China), 1928-32; Imperial Tobacco Co. (of Great Britain and Ireland) Ltd, 1932-39. POW in Germany, 1940-45 (Capt., 7th Argyll and Sutherland Hdrs). Imperial Tobacco Co. (of Great Britain and Ireland) Ltd, 1946-67. DL Stirlingshire, 1956. *Recreations:* shooting, fishing, golf. *Address:* Wester Craigend, Stirling. *T:* Stirling 5025. *Club:* Western (Glasgow).

**LOGAN, Thomas Moffat,** CBE 1963; retired as Under-Secretary, National Assistance Board, 1966; *b* 21 June 1904; *s* of late John Logan, builder and contractor, Carluke, Lanarkshire; *m* 1947, Freda Evelyn Andrew; no *c*. *Educ:* Hamilton Academy. Carluke Parish Council 1922; Relieving Officer, Lanark County Council, 1929; National Assistance Board: Area Officer, 1934; Asst Principal, 1942, Principal, 1945; Asst Sec., (Head of Organization and Methods), 1955; Under-Sec., 1964. *Recreations:* gardening, do-it-yourself, dancing. *Address:* Castlehill House, Castlehill Road, Carluke, Lanarkshire. *T:* Carluke 3591.

**LOGAN, William Philip Dowie,** MD, PhD, BSc, DPH, FRCP; Director, Division of Health Statistics, WHO, since 1961; *b* 2 Nov. 1914; *s* of late Frederick William Alexander Logan and late Elizabeth Jane Dowie; *m* 1941, Pearl Mabel Piper, four *s* two *d* (and one *s* decd). *Educ:* Queen's Park Sch., Glasgow; Universities of Glasgow and London. RAF Med. Branch, 1940-46 (Squadron Leader). Hospital appointments in Glasgow, 1939-40 and 1946. Gen. practice in Barking, Essex, 1947-48; General Register Office, 1948-60 (Chief Medical Statistician, Adviser on Statistics to Ministry of Health, Head of WHO Centre for Classification of Diseases, and Member, WHO panel of experts on Health Statistics). *Publications:* contribs on epidemiology, vital and health statistics, in offical reports, and medical jls. *Address:* Division of Health Statistics, WHO, Geneva, Switzerland.

**LOGSDON, Geoffrey Edward,** CBE 1962; TD 1950; Clerk to Worshipful Company of Mercers since 1952; *b* 24 July 1914; *o s* of Edward Charles Logsdon; *m* 1st, 1943, Marie Carolinne Dumas (*d* 1957); one *s* one *d*; 2nd, 1958, Barbara Joyce Bird. *Educ:* City of London Sch. Admitted Solicitor, 1937; Legal Asst, Mercers' Company, 1945-52; Commissioned RA (TA), 1938. Served War of 1939-45: Malta, Middle East and UK. Lt-Col Comd 458 (M) HAA Regt (Kent) RA, TA, 1949-52. Clerk to: Jt Grand Gresham Cttee; Governors of St Paul's Schs; The City and Metropolitan Welfare Charity; Mem. City of London Savings Cttee. *Address:* Mercers' Hall, Ironmonger Lane, EC2. *T:* 01-606 5652; St Eloi, World's End Lane, Chelsfield, Kent. *T:* Farnborough 53065.

**LÖHR, Marie;** *b* Sydney, NSW, 28 July 1890; *d* of late Kate Bishop and Lewis J. Löhr; *m* Anthony Leyland Val Prinsep (whom she divorced, 1928; he died 1942); one *d*. *Educ:* Greycoat Sch. Made her first appearance on the stage at Sydney in The World Against Her, 1894; first appearance on the London stage at the Garrick, in Shockheaded Peter, and The Man who Stole the Castle, 1901; played with the Kendals, Sir Beerbohm Tree, and Sir John Hare; Manageress of the Globe Theatre, 1918-25, when she produced amongst other plays, Nurse Benson, A Voice from the Minaret, L'Aiglon, A Marriage of Convenience, etc. Has played many stage parts in the West End since then. Successes include: (Noël Coward's) Waiting in the Wings; The Silver Wedding; Ring Round the Moon; Treasure Hunt. Has also appeared on Television. Entered films in Aren't We All, 1932, and has appeared frequently. *Recreations:* golf, dancing, reading, music. *Address:* Flat 8, 199 Sussex Gardens, W2.

**LOMAS, Kenneth,** MP (Lab) Huddersfield West, since 1964; *b* 16 Nov. 1922; *s* of George Lomas and Rhoda Clayton; *m* 1945, Helen Wilson; two *s* one *d*. *Educ:* Ashton-under-Lyne Elementary and Central Schs. Served with

Royal Marines and RM Commando Group, 1942-46 (Sergeant). Central Office, Union of Shop, Distributive and Allied Workers, 1937-55; Asst Regional Organiser Blood Transfusion Service, 1955-64. PPS to Minister of Technology, 1969-70. JP Ches, 1961. *Recreations:* arguing, watching football, reading. *Address:* 20 Kingston Road, Handforth, Wilmslow, Cheshire. *T:* Wilmslow 24787.

**LOMAX, Maj.-Gen. Cyril Ernest Napier,** CB 1944; CBE 1941; DSO 1918; MC; *b* 28 June 1893; *s* of late Capt. and Adjutant D. A. N. Lomax, 41st (The Welch) Regt; *m* 1927, Constance Turberville Williams (*d* 1967); one *d*; *m* 1968, Mrs Edith May Mulcahy. *Educ:* Marlborough; RMC, Sandhurst. Served European War, 1914-19 (despatches five times, DSO and bar, MC, Italian War Cross); commanded 2nd Bn The Welch Regt, 1936-39; served Middle East, 1941 (second bar to DSO, CBE), in command 16th Inf. Brigade; Burma and on E Frontier, India (CB), in command 26th Indian Div.; GOC East Anglian District, 1946-48; Pres. No 1 Regular Commns Bd, 1948-49. Col The Welch Regt, 1949-58. *Address:* White Gates, Sea Lane, Ferring, Sussex. *T:* Worthing 43858.

**LOMAX, Sir John Garnett,** KBE 1953 (MBE 1928); CMG 1944; MC 1917; HM Diplomatic Service, retired; *b* Liverpool, 27 Aug. 1896; *s* of Rev. Canon Edward Lomax and Bessie Garnett; *m* 1922, Feridah Yvette Krajewski; two *s*. *Educ:* Liverpool Coll.; Liverpool Univ. Served European War, France, Belgium, India, and Egypt; Driver, RFA (West Lancs), 1915, Lt 1916. HM Vice-Consul, New Orleans, 1920, Chicago, 1921; Vice-Consul and 2nd Sec. HM Legation, Bogota, 1926-30; 2nd Commercial Sec. HM Embassy, Rio de Janeiro, 1930; transferred to HM Embassy, Rome, 1935; HM Commercial Agent, Jerusalem, 1938; Commercial Counsellor, HM Embassy, Madrid, 1940; HM Legation, Berne, 1941; Commercial Counsellor at Angora, 1943; Minister (commercial), British Embassy, Buenos Aires, 1946-49; Ambassador to Bolivia, 1949-56. *Publication:* The Diplomatic Smuggler, 1965. *Recreations:* golf, sailing, riding, shooting. *Address:* Tanterfyn, Llaneilian, Anglesey; 803 Nelson House, Dolphin Square, SW1. *Clubs:* Reform, Royal Automobile.

**LOMAX, Michael Roger T.;** *see* Trappes-Lomax.

**LOMBE, Vice-Adm. Sir Edward Malcolm E.;** *see* Evans Lombe.

**LONDESBOROUGH,** 9th Baron, *cr* 1850; **Richard John Denison;** *b* 2 July 1959; *s* of John Albert Lister, 8th Baron Londesborough, TD, AMICE, and of Elizabeth Ann, *d* of late Edward Little Sale, ICS; *S* father, 1968. *Address:* Dragon House, Edgioak, Redditch, Worcs.

**LONDON, Bishop of,** since 1961; **Rt. Rev. and Rt. Hon. Robert Wright Stopford,** PC 1961; CBE 1949; FKC 1965; DD (Lambeth) 1957; *b* 20 Feb. 1901; *s* of John William Stopford; *m* 1st, 1935, Winifred Sophia (who *d* by enemy action, 1942), *d* of William Morton; two *s*; 2nd, 1945, Kathleen Mary, *d* of Harold Holt; one *d*. *Educ:* Liverpool Coll.; Hertford Coll., Oxford (Scholar); 1st Class Hons Classical Mods, 1922; BA 1st Class Hons School Mod. Hist. 1924, MA 1927; Hon. Fellow, 1956. Asst Master, Highgate Sch., 1924-25; Senior History Master, Oundle Sch., 1925-34, and Housemaster, 1926-34. Ordained, 1932; Asst Chaplain, 1932-34; Principal: Trinity Coll., Kandy, Ceylon, 1935-41; Achimota Coll., Gold Coast, 1941-45; Rector of Chipping Barnet, 1946-48; Moderator of the Church Training Colls, 1947-55; Gen. Sec. of the National Soc. and Sec. of the Church Assembly Schs Council, 1952-55; Suffragan Bishop of Fulham, 1955-56; Bishop of Peterborough, 1956-61. Chaplain to the Queen, 1952-55; Hon. Canon of Canterbury, 1951-56; Episcopal Sec., Lambeth Conference, 1958; Chm., Church of England Board of Education, 1958-; Jt Chairman, Anglican-Methodist Unity Commission, 1967-69; Select Preacher, Oxford, 1959, Cambridge, 1963. Dean of HM Chapels Royal, 1961-; Prelate of the Order of the British Empire, 1961-; Prelate, Imperial Soc. of Knights Bachelor, 1967-. Hon. FCP 1965. Freeman, City of London, 1965; Hon. Freeman, Grocers' Company, 1967. Churchill Fellow, Westminster Coll., Fulton, Mo, 1969. Hon. DCL, Durham, 1951; Hon. DD: London, 1965; Westminster Coll., Fulton, Missouri, 1966; College of William and Mary, Virginia, 1968. *Publications:* Play Production (with M. V. C. Jeffreys); The Anglican Communion (with others); Church, School and Life; No Man Liveth unto Himself. *Address:* Fulham Palace, SW6. *T:* 01-736 5821. *Clubs:* Athenæum, Royal Over-Seas League.

**LONDON, Assistant Bishops of;** *see* Craske, Rt Rev. F. W. T., Patterson, Rt Rev. C. J., sansbury, Rt Rev. C. K.

**LONDON, Archdeacon of;** *see* Woodhouse, Ven. S. M. F.

**LONDONDERRY,** 9th Marquess of, *cr* 1816; **Alexander Charles Robert Vane-Tempest-Stewart;** Baron Londonderry, 1789; Viscount Castlereagh, 1795; Earl of Londonderry, 1796; Baron Stewart, 1814; Earl Vane, Viscount Seaham, 1823; *b* 7 Sept. 1937; *s* of 8th Marquess of Londonderry and Romaine (*d* 1951), *er d* of Major Boyce Combe, Great Holt, Dockenfield, Surrey; *S* father 1955; *m* 1958, Nicolette, *d* of Michael Harrison, Netherhampton, near Salisbury, Wilts; one *s* two *d*. *Educ:* Eton. *Heir:* *s* Viscount Castlereagh, *qv*. *Address:* Wynyard Park, Billingham-on-Tees, Co. Durham. *T:* Stockton-on-Tees 66667.

**LONG,** family name of **Viscount Long.**

**LONG,** 4th Viscount, *cr* 1921, of Wraxall; **Richard Gerard Long;** *b* 30 Jan. 1929; *s* of 3rd Viscount and Gwendolyn (*d* 1959), *d* of Thomas Reginald Hague Cook; *S* father, 1967; *m* 1957, Margaret Frances, *d* of Ninian B. Frazer; one *s* two *d*. *Educ:* Harrow. Wilts Regt, 1947-49. Vice-Pres., Wilts British Legion; Pres., Bath Gliding Club. *Heir:* *s* Hon. James Richard Long, *b* 31 Dec. 1960. *Address:* Steeple Ashton Manor, Trowbridge, Wilts. *T:* Keevil 234. *Club:* Carlton.

**LONG, His Honour Athelstan Charles Ethelwulf,** CMG 1968; CBE 1964 (MBE 1959); Administrator of the Cayman Islands, since 1968; *b* 2 Jan. 1919; *s* of Arthur Leonard Long and Gabrielle Margaret Campbell (historical writer and novelist as Marjorie Bowen); *m* 1948, Edit Mäjken Zadie Harriet Krantz, *d* of late Erik Krantz, Stockholm; two *s*. *Educ:* Westminster Sch.; Brasenose Coll., Oxford. Served War of 1939-45: commnd into RA, 1940; seconded 7th (Bengal) Battery, 22nd Mountain Regt, IA, 1940; served Malaya; POW as Capt., 1942-45. Cadet, Burma Civil Service, 1946-48; Colonial Admin. Service (N Nigeria), 1948; Sen. District Officer, 1958; Resident, Zaria Province, 1959; Perm. Sec., Min. of Animal Health and Forestry, 1959; started new Min. of Information as Perm. Sec., 1960; Swaziland: appointed Govt Sec.,

1961; Chief Sec., 1964; Leader of Govt business in Legislative Council and MEC, 1964-67; HM Dep. Comr, 1967-68. Chm. Governing Council, Waterford Sch., 1963-. *Recreations:* travel, golf, reading. *Address:* Government House, Grand Cayman, Cayman Islands, West Indies; 8 Spring Terrace, Richmond, Surrey. *T:* Richmond 2175.

**LONG, Sir Bertram,** Kt 1957; MC; TD; Senior Registrar Principal Probate Registry, 1953-64 (Registrar, 1935-53); *b* 12 Sept. 1889; *s* of William Long, Horley, Surrey; *m* 1st, 1919, Beatrix Frederica Frances Mackay (who obtained a divorce, 1933; *d* 1958), *yr d* of late Sir Walter Grindlay Simpson, 2nd Bt of Strathavon and Balabraes, Ayton, NB (one *s* killed in action 1945); 2nd, 1940, Eleanora Carroll (*d* 1946), *o d* of late Dr and Mrs Dudley Morgan, Washington, DC; 3rd, 1947, Joan, *er d* of Walter Littleton. *Educ:* Dulwich Coll.; Worcester Coll., Oxford (MA). Called to Bar, Inner Temple, 1912; served with Oxfordshire and Buckinghamshire Light Infantry (TA), 1910-21, and 1924-31; mobilised, 1914-19, served France, Belgium, Italy (MC and Bar, 1914-15 Star, despatches thrice), TD 1928, served again with Oxfordshire and Buckinghamshire LI (TA), 1939-44; attached RAF, 1940-44; served France, Ireland; Lieut-Colonel; TED 1951. *Recreations:* walking, golf. *Address:* 23 Beechwood Crescent, Eastbourne, Sussex. *T:* Eastbourne 26501. *Club:* Athenæum.

**LONG, Ernest,** CBE 1962; Member of Central Electricity Generating Board and of Electricity Council, 1957-62; *b* 15 Aug. 1898; *er s* of late John H. Long, Carlisle; *m* 1923, Dorothy Phœbe, *y d* of late John Nichol, Carlisle; one *s*. *Educ:* Carlisle Grammar Sch. Town Clerk's Dept and City Treasurer's Dept, Carlisle Corporation, 1915-25; articled to City Treasurer, Carlisle. Served RFC and RAF, 1917-19. Chief Audit Asst, Croydon Corporation, 1928-30; Dep. City Treasurer, Coventry, 1930-35; Borough Treasurer: Luton, 1935-36, Finchley, 1936-42; City Treasurer, Newcastle upon Tyne, 1942-44; Secretary, Institute of Municipal Treasurers and Accountants, 1944-48 (Hon. Fellow, and Collins Gold Medallist, 1927); Dep. Chief Accountant, British Electricity Authority, 1948-51; Secretary, British (later Central) Electricity Authority, 1951-57. fellow, Member of Council (1947-), President (1960), Chartered Inst. of Secretaries. Member: Colonial Local Government Advisory Panel, 1948-53; Departmental Cttee on Legal Aid in Criminal Proceedings, 1964-66; Chartered Accountant (Society Gold Medallist, 1924). *Publications:* various articles and lectures on accountancy and public administration. *Recreations:* golf, crosswords. *Address:* Rivermead, Wetheral, Carlisle. *T:* Wetheral 60505. *Clubs:* Royal and Ancient (St Andrews); Golfers', Border (Carlisle).

**LONG, Air Vice-Marshal Francis William,** CB 1946; DL; *b* 1899; *s* of Rev. F. P. Long, Oxford; *m* 1921, Doreen Langley, *d* of Rev. F. L. Appleford; one *d*. *Educ:* Lancing Coll. Joined RAF 1918; member Schneider Trophy Team, 1931. AOC No. 23 Gp, Flying Training Command, 1952-53; retd, 1953. DL Herts, 1963. *Address:* 19 Marina Court, Douglas Avenue, Exmouth, Devon. *T:* Exmouth 6320.

**LONG, Gerald;** General Manager, Reuters Ltd, since 1963; Chairman, Visnews Ltd, since 1968; *b* 22 Aug. 1923; *o s* of Fred Harold Long and Sabina Long (*née* Walsh); *m* 1951, Anne Hamilton Walker; two *s* three *d*. *Educ:* St Peter's Sch., York; Emmanuel Coll., Cambridge. Army Service, 1943-47. Joined Reuters, 1948; served as Reuter correspondent in Germany, France and Turkey, 1950-60; Asst General Manager, 1960. Commander, Royal Order of the Phœnix (Greece), 1964. *Recreation:* cooking. *Address:* 17 Southwood Avenue, Highgate, N6. *T:* 01-340 4543. *Club:* Reform.

**LONG, Hubert Arthur,** CBE 1970; Deputy Secretary, Exchequer and Audit Department, since 1963; *b* 21 Jan. 1912; *s* of Arthur Albert Long; *m* 1937, Mary Louise Parker; three *s*. *Educ:* Taunton's Sch., Southampton. Entered Exchequer and Audit Department, 1930. *Address:* 48 Hayes Lane, Bromley, Kent. *T:* 01-460 4251.

**LONG, Ven. John Sanderson,** MA; Archdeacon of Ely, Hon. Canon of Ely and Rector of St Botolph's, Cambridge, since 1970; *b* 21 July 1913; *s* of Rev. Guy Stephenson Long and late Ivy Marion Long; *m* 1948, Rosamond Mary, *d* of Arthur Temple Forman; one *s* three *d*. *Educ:* St Edmund's Sch., Canterbury; Queen's Coll., Cambridge; Cuddesdon Theological Coll. Deacon, 1936; Priest, 1937; Curate, St Mary and St Eanswythe, Folkstone, 1936-41. Chaplain, RNVR, 1941-46. Curate, St Peter-in-Thanet, 1946; Domestic Chaplain to the Archibishop of Canterbury, 1946-53; Vicar of: Bearsted, 1953-59; Petersfield with Sheet, 1959-70; Rural Dean of Petersfield, 1967-70. *Recreations:* walking, gardening. *Address:* St Botolph's Rectory, Summerfield, Cambrdige CB3 9HE. *T:* Cambridge 50684.

**LONG, Olivier;** Ambassador; Director-General, GATT, since 1968; *b* 1915; *s* of Dr Edouard Long and Dr Marie Landry; *m* 1946, Francine Roels; one *s* two *d*. *Educ:* Univ. de Paris, Faculté de Droit et Ecole des Sciences Politiques; Univ. de Genève. PhD Law, 1938; PhD Pol. Sc., 1943. Swiss Armed Forces, 1939-43; International Red Cross, 1943-46; Swiss Foreign Affairs Dept, Berne, 1946-49; Washington Embassy, 1949-53; Div. of Commerce, Berne, 1954; Govt Delegate for Trade Agreements, 1955-66; Head of Swiss Delegn to EFTA, 1960-66; Ambassador to UK and Malta, 1967-68. Prof., Graduate Inst. of Internat. Studies, Geneva, 1962-. *Publications:* several on political sciences and trade policies. *Recreations:* music, reading, ski-ing, swimming. *Address:* General Agreement on Tariffs and Trade, Villa le Bocage, Palais des Nations, CH-1211 Geneva 10, Switzerland. *T:* (022) 34-60-11.

**LONG, Sir Ronald,** Kt 1964; Solicitor; *b* 5 Sept. 1902; *s* of Sydney Richard and Kate Long; *m* 1931, Muriel Annie Harper; one *s* two *d*. *Educ:* Earls Colne Grammar Sch.; The School, Stamford, Lincs. President, The Law Society, 1963-64; Member, Criminal Injuries Compensation Board, 1964. *Recreations:* fishing, golf, gardening. *Address:* Ayletts Farm, Halstead, Essex. *T:* Halstead 2072. *Club:* Junior Carlton.

**LONG, Captain Rt. Hon. William Joseph,** PC (N Ireland) 1966; JP; Minister of Education, Northern Ireland, since May 1969; MP (Unionist) Ards, Parliament of Northern Ireland, since 1962; *b* 23 April 1922; *s* of James William Long and Frederica (Walker); *m* 1942, Dr Elizabeth Doreen Mercer; one *s*. *Educ:* Friends' Sch., Great Ayton, Yorks; Edinburgh Univ.; RMC, Sandhurst. Served Royal Inniskilling Fusiliers, 1940-48. Secretary: NI Marriage Guidance Council, 1948-51; NI Chest and Heart Assoc., 1951-62. Parliamentary Secretary, Min. of Agriculture, NI, 1964-66; Sen. Parliamentary Secretary, Min. of Development, NI, Jan.-Oct. 1966; Minister of Educn, 1966-68; Minister of Home

Affairs, Dec. 1968-March 1969; Minister of Develt, March 1969-May 1969. *Recreations:* cricket, horticulture, angling, sailing, model engineering, aviation. *Address:* Lisvarna, Warren Road, Donaghadee, Co. Down. *T:* Donaghadee 2538.

**LONGBOTTOM, Charles Brooke;** *b* 22 July 1930; *s* of late William Ewart Longbottom, Forest Hill, Worksop; *m* 1962, Anita, *d* of G. Trapani, Sorrento, Italy, and Mrs Basil Mavroleon, 49 Grosvenor Square, W1; one *d*. *Educ:* Uppingham. Contested (C) Stockton-on-Tees, 1955. Parliamentary Private Secretary to Mr Iain Macleod, Leader of the House, 1961-63. MP (C) York, 1959-66. Barrister, Inner Temple, 1958; Chairman, Austin & Pickersgill, Shipbuilders, Sunderland, 1966-; Dep. Chairman, Bartram & Sons; Director: Seascope Holdings Ltd; Seascope Ltd; Seascope Insurance Services Ltd. Chairman, Ariel Foundation, 1960-. Member: General Advisory Council, BBC, 1965-; Community Relations Commn, 1968-. *Recreations:* shooting, golf and racing. *Address:* 34 Bryanston Square, W1. *T:* 01-262 6499. *Clubs:* White's, Carlton; Yorkshire (York).

**LONGDEN, Gilbert James Morley,** MBE 1944; MA (Cantab), LLB; MP (C) South West Hertfordshire since 1950; *b* 16 April 1902; *e s* of late Lieut-Colonel James Morley Longden, and of late Kathleen, *d* of George Blacker Morgan, JP; unmarried. *Educ:* Haileybury; Emmanuel Coll., Cambridge. Secretary ICI (India) Ltd, 1930-36; travelled throughout Asia (Middle and Far East) and in North and South America. Student at University of Paris, 1937. Called up from AOER into DLI, 1940; served with 2nd and 36th Divisions in Burma campaigns. Adopted Parliamentary Candidate for Morpeth, 1938; contested (C) Morpeth, 1945. UK Representative to Council of Europe, 1953-54; United Kingdom Delegate to 12th and 13th Sessions of United Nations; Vice-Pres., British Atlantic Cttee; Chm., Great Britain-East Europe Centre; Member, Exec. Cttees: British Council; 1922 Cttee. Hon. Sec., Nat. Adv. Council on Educn. *Publications:* A Conservative Philosophy, 1947; (jointly) One Nation, 1950; (jointly) Change is our Ally, 1954; A Responsible Society, 1959; (jointly) One Europe, 1969. *Recreations:* reading, riding. *Address:* 89 Cornwall Gardens, SW7. *T:* 01-584 5666. *Club:* Travellers'.

**LONGDEN, Maj.-General Harry Leicester,** CB 1947; CBE 1944 (OBE 1940); late The Dorsetshire Regt; psc; *b* 1900. 2nd Lieut Dorset Regt, 1919; Major, 1938. Served War of 1939-45, France and North-West Europe (despatches, OBE, CBE, CB). Temp. Maj-General, 1946; retired pay, 1948. *Address:* 4a Mortonhall Road, Edinburgh 9.

**LONGDEN, Henry Alfred,** CEng, FICE, FIMinE, MIMM; FGS; Chairman and Chief Executive, Cementation Co. Ltd, since 1963 (Dep. Chm. and Chief Exec., 1961); Director: J. Samuel White & Co. Ltd; Trafalgar House Investments Ltd; *b* 8 Sept. 1909; *s* of late Geoffrey Appleby Longden and late Marjorie Mullins; *m* 1935, Ruth, *d* of Arthur Gilliat, Leeds; one *s* four *d*. *Educ:* Oundle; Birmingham Univ. (BSc Hons). Served in Glass Houghton and Pontefract Collieries, 1930; Asst Gen. Manager, Stanton Ironworks Co., 1935; Gen. Manager, Briggs Colliers Ltd, 1940; Director: Blackwell Colliery Co., 1940; Briggs Collieries Co., 1941; New Hucknell Colliery Co., 1941; Area Gen. Manager, 1947, and Production Dir, 1948, NE Div., NCB; Dir-Gen., Production, NCB, 1955; Chm., W Midlands Div., NCB, 1960. President: Instn of Mining Engineers, 1958; Engineering Industries Assoc., 1965; Member: Engineering Industry Trg Bd, 1967; Confedn of British Industry, 1968. *Publication:* Cadman Memorial Lecture, 1958. *Recreations:* Rugby football, cricket, tennis, shooting, fishing, sailing. *Address:* South Hawke, Woldingham, Surrey. *T:* Woldingham 2245. *Club:* Royal Automobile.

**LONGE, Desmond Evelyn;** MC 1944; President and Chairman, Norwich Union Insurance Group, 1964 (Vice-President, 1963); Chairman: Norwich Union Life Insurance Society, 1964; Norwich Union Fire Insurance Society Ltd, 1964; Maritime Insurance Co. Ltd, 1968; Scottish Union and National Insurance Co., 1968; East Coast Grain Silos Ltd, 1962; Napak Ltd, 1969; Euripco (UK) Ltd, 1962; D. E. Longe & Co. Ltd, 1962; *b* 8 Aug. 1914; *y s* of late Rev. John Charles Longe, MA, Spixworth Park, Norfolk; *m* 1944, Isla (*née* Bell); one *s* one *d*. *Educ:* Woodbridge Sch., Suffolk. Director, Schiedam Insurance Co. of Amsterdam; Member: British Railways (Eastern) Board; BNEC Aust. Cttee. A Church Commissioner, 1970-. Croix de Guerre avec Palme (French), 1944. *Recreations:* travel and riding. *Address:* Woodton Grange, Bungay, Suffolk. *T:* Woodton 260. *Clubs:* Special Forces, MCC; Norfolk County (Norwich).

**LONGFORD,** 7th Earl of, *cr* 1785, **Francis Aungier Pakenham,** PC 1948; Baron Longford, 1759; Baron Silchester (UK), 1821; Baron Pakenham (UK), 1945; Leader of the House of Lords, 1964-68; Lord Privy Seal, 1966-68; Member, The Pilgrims Society; *b* 5 Dec. 1905; 2nd *s* of 5th Earl of Longford, KP, MVO; *S* brother (6th Earl) 1961; *m* 1931, Elizabeth (*see* Countess of Longford); four *s* three *d* (and one *d* decd). *Educ:* Eton; New Coll., Oxford, MA. 1st Class in Modern Greats, 1927. Tutor, University Tutorial Courses, Stoke-on-Trent, 1929-31; Cons. Party Economic Res. Dept, 1930-32. Christ Church, Oxford: Lecturer in Politics, 1932; Student in Politics, 1934-46, and 1952-64. Prospective Parliamentary Labour Candidate for Oxford City, 1938. Enlisted Oxford and Bucks LI (TA), May 1939; resigned commission on account of ill-health, 1940. Personal assistant to Sir William Beveridge, 1941-44; a Lord-in-Waiting to the King, 1945-46; Parliamentary Under-Secretary of State, War Office, 1946-47; Chancellor of the Duchy of Lancaster, 1947-48; Minister of Civil Aviation, 1948-51; First Lord of the Admiralty, May-Oct. 1951; Lord Privy Seal, 1964-65; Secretary of State for the Colonies, 1965-66. Chairman: The National Bank Ltd, 1955-63; Sidgwick and Jackson, 1970-. Chairman: Nat. Youth Employment Council, 1968-; Inquiry into Youth Services in Inner London, 1970-; Council, Royal Holloway Coll., 1969-. *Publications:* Peace by Ordeal (The Anglo-Irish Treaty of 1921), 1935; Born to Believe (an autobiography), 1953; (with Roger Opie), Causes of Crime, 1958; The Idea of Punishment, 1961; Five Lives, 1964; Humility, 1969; (with Thomas P. O'Neill) Eamon De Valera, 1970. *Heir: s* Hon. Thomas Frank Dermot Pakenham (does not use title, Lord Silchester) [*b* 14 Aug. 1933; *m* 1964, Valerie, *y d* of McNair Scott, Huish House, Old Basing, Hants; one *s* two *d*. *Educ:* Ampleforth; Magdalen Coll., Oxford]. *Address:* Bernhurst, Hurst Green, Sussex. *T:* Hurst Green 248; 18 Chesil Court, Chelsea Manor Street, SW3. *T:* 01-352 7794. *Club:* Athenæum.

*See also Lady Antonia Fraser, A. D. Powell.*

**LONGFORD, Countess of; Elizabeth Pakenham;** *b* 30 Aug. 1906; *d* of late N. B. Harman, FRCS,

108 Harley Street, W1, and of Katherine (*née* Chamberlain); *m* 1931, Hon. F. A. Pakenham (*see* 7th Earl of Longford); four *s* three *d* (and one *d* decd). *Educ:* Headington Sch., Oxford; Lady Margaret Hall, Oxford (MA). Lectr for WEA and Univ. Extension Lectr, 1929-35. Contested (Lab) Cheltenham, 1935, Oxford, 1950; candidate for King's Norton, Birmingham, 1935-43. Member: Rent Tribunal, Paddington and St Pancras, 1947-54; Cranbrook Cttee on Maternity Services, 1958-60; Labour Party Youth Cttee, 1962. Trustee, National Portrait Gall., 1968-; Mem. Adv. Council, V&A Museum, 1969-. Hon. DLitt Sussex 1970. *Publications:* (as Elizabeth Pakenham): Points for Parents, 1956; Catholic Approaches (ed), 1959; Jameson's Raid, 1960; weekly articles for Daily Express, 1954-56; (as Elizabeth Longford) Victoria RI, 1964 (James Tait Black Memorial Prize for Non-Fiction, 1964); Wellington: Years of the Sword, 1969 (Yorkshire Post Prize); weekly articles for Sunday Times, 1961-63. *Recreations:* gardening, reading. *Address:* Bernhurst, Hurst Green, Sussex. *T:* Hurst Green 248; 18 Chesil Court, Chelsea Manor Street, SW3. *T:* 01-352 7794.

*See also Lady Antonia Fraser.*

**LONGFORD, Elizabeth;** *see* Longford, Countess of.

**LONGHURST, Henry Carpenter;** journalist, author, broadcaster, etc; *b* 18 March 1909; *s* of Henry William Longhurst, JP, and Mrs Constance Longhurst, Bedford; *m* 1938, Claudine Marie Sier; one *s* one *d*. *Educ:* Charterhouse (scholar); Clare Coll., Cambridge (BA Econ). Captain Cambridge Univ. Golf team, 1930 (and in USA 1931). Journalist: Sunday Times, etc since 1932. MP (Nat. C) Acton Division of Middlesex, 1943-45. Journalist of the Year Special Award, 1969. *Publications:* Candid Caddies, 1936; Golf, 1937; It Was Good While it Lasted, 1941; I Wouldn't Have Missed It, 1946; You Never Know Till You Get There, 1950; Golf Mixture, 1952; Round in Sixty-Eight, 1953; The Borneo Story, 1957; Adventure in Oil, 1959; Spice of Life, 1963; Only on Sundays, 1964; Never on Weekdays, 1968. *Recreations:* golf, shooting, fishing, travel. *Address:* Clayton Windmills, Hassocks, Sussex. *Clubs:* Bath, Boodle's, Garrick.

**LONGLAND, Austin Charles,** CBE 1959; QC 1946; *b* 1888; *o s* of Rev. Charles Boxall Longland, MA; *m* 1915, Sybil, 3rd *d* of Rev. John Coker Egerton, MA; no *c*. *Educ:* Radley Coll.; Merton Coll., Oxford (Postmaster, MA). Barrister, Inner Temple, 1914; Bencher, 1955; Oxford Circuit. Served France and Macedonia, 1914-19, Wiltshire Regt (despatches). Referee Contributory Pensions Acts, 1927, Family Allowances Act, 1947; Vice-Chairman, Oxfordshire Quarter Sessions, 1947-54; Comr Agricultural Marketing Acts Inquiries 1948, 1950, 1951; Council Radley Coll., 1934-65 (Vice-Chairman 1949-59); Chairman House Cttee, Maida Vale Hospital, 1949-54. *Address:* Clanfield House, 16 Park Crescent, Abingdon, Berks. *T:* Abingdon 278; 4 Paper Buildings, Temple, EC4. *T:* 01-353 9568. *Club:* Athenæum.

**LONGLAND, Cedric James,** MVO 1949; Surgeon, Glasgow Royal Infirmary, since 1954; *b* 30 Sept. 1914; *s* of Frank Longland; *m* 1945, Helen Mary Cripps; three *d*. *Educ:* Monkton Combe Sch. MB, BS (Hons in Medicine) London, 1937; House Surgeon and Demonstrator of Pathology, St Bartholomew's Hosp.; FRCS, 1939; MS London, 1949. 1 Airborne Division; Lieut RAMC 1942, Temp. Major, RAMC, 1943; SMO Bermuda Command, 1945; First Assistant, Surgical Professorial Unit, St Bartholomew's Hospital, 1947; Assistant Surgical Professorial Unit, University College Hospital, 1951. Bronze Cross (Holland), 1945. *Publications:* articles in Lancet and British Journal of Surgery. *Recreations:* lawn tennis, sailing. *Address:* 11 Campbell Drive, Bearsden, Dunbartonshire. *T:* 041-942 0798.

**LONGLAND, Sir Jack;** *see* Longland, Sir J. L.

**LONGLAND, Sir John Laurence, (Sir Jack),** Kt 1970; Director of Education, Derbyshire, 1949-70; *b* 26 June 1905; *e s* of late Rev. E. H. Longland and late Emily, *e d* of Sir James Crockett; *m* 1934, Margaret Lowrey, *y d* of late Arthur Harrison, Elvet Garth, Durham; two *s* two *d*. *Educ:* King's Sch., Worcester; Jesus Coll., Cambridge (Rustat Exhibitioner and Scholar). 2nd Class, 1st Part Classical Tripos, 1925; 1st Class, 1st Division, Historical Tripos, Part II, 1926; 1st Class with special distinction, English Tripos, 1927; Charles Kingsley Bye-Fellow at Magdalene Coll., Cambridge, 1927-29; Austausch-student, Königsberg University, 1929-30; Lecturer in English at Durham Univ., 1930-36; Director of the Community Service Council for Durham County, 1937-40; Regional Officer of National Council of Social Service, 1939-40; Deputy Education Officer, Hertfordshire, 1940-42; County Education Officer, Dorset County Council, 1942-49; Athletic Blue; President, Cambridge Univ. Mountaineering Club, 1926-27; Member of Mount Everest Expedition, 1933; British East Greenland Expedition, 1935; President, Climbers' Club, 1945-48 and Hon. Member, 1964; Vice-President Alpine Club, 1960-61. Member: Colonial Office Social Welfare Advisory Cttee, 1943-48; Development Commission, 1948-; Advisory Cttee for Education in RAF, 1950-57; Advisory Cttee for Education in Germany, 1950-57; Central Advisory Council for Education in England and Wales, 1948-51; National Advisory Council on the Training and Supply of Teachers, 1951-; Children's Advisory Cttee of the Independent Television Authority, 1956-60; Wolfenden Ctte on Sport, 1958-60; Outward Bound Trust Council, 1962-. Central Council of Physical Recreation Council and Executive, 1961-; Electricity Supply Industry Training Board, 1965-66; Royal Commn on Local Govt, 1966-69; The Sports Council, 1966-; Countryside Commn, 1969-; President: Assoc. of Education Officers, 1960-61; British Mountaineering Council, 1962-65; Chairman: Mountain Leadership Training Board, 1965-; Council for Environmental Education, 1968-. *Publications:* literary and mountaineering articles in various books and journals. *Recreations:* mountain climbing and walking. *Address:* Bridgeway, Bakewell, Derbyshire. *T:* Bakewell 2252. *Clubs:* Savile, Alpine, Achilles.

**LONGLEY, Sir Norman,** Kt 1966; CBE 1954; Chairman, James Longley (Holdings) Ltd, Building and Civil Engineering Contractors, Crawley, Sussex; Chairman, Construction Training Board, since 1964; *b* 14 Oct. 1900; *s* of Charles John Longley and Anna Gibson Marchant; *m* 1925, Dorothy Lilian Baker; two *s* one *d*. *Educ:* Clifton. West Sussex County Council, 1945-61, Alderman 1957-61. President: National Federation of Building Trades Employers, 1950; International Federation of Building and Public Works Contractors, 1955-57. Hon. Fellow, Institute of Builders. Hon. DSc Heriot-Watt, 1968. Coronation Medal, 1953. *Recreation:* horticulture. *Address:* The Beeches, Crawley, Sussex. *T:* Crawley 20253. *Club:* Royal Automobile.

**LONGLEY-COOK, Vice-Adm. Eric William,** CB 1950; CBE 1943; DSO 1945; *b* 6 Oct. 1898; *s* of late Herbert William Cook and late Alice Longley; *m* 1st, 1920, Helga Mayre Lowles (*d* 1962); one *d*; 2nd, 1965, Elizabeth, *widow* of Sir Ulick Temple Blake, 16th Baronet. *Educ:* Osborne and Dartmouth. Served at sea European War, 1914-18 and War of 1939-45 (despatches thrice). Rear-Adm., 1948; Vice-Adm., 1951; Dir of Naval Intelligence, 1948-51; retired, 1951. Formerly: Man. Dir, Fairfield Shipbuilding & Engineering Co., London; Dir, Lithgow Group; Member: Cttee, Lloyd's Register; Amer. Bureau of Ships; a Gen. Comr of Income Tax; a Governor, Bishop Otter Coll. Légion d'Honneur and Croix de Guerre, 1943. *Recreations:* golf, gardening. *Address:* Gathorne Cottage, West Lavant, near Chichester, Sussex. *Clubs:* United Service; Royal Yacht Squadron.

**LONGMAN, Mark Frederic Kerr;** Chairman: Longman Holdings Ltd; Longman Group Ltd; The Fine Art Society Ltd; Envopak Ltd; Chairman of the National Book League; President of the Publishers Association; *b* 12 Nov. 1916; *s* of Henry Kerr Longman and Margot Amy Cecil Russell; *m* 1949, Lady Elizabeth Mary Lambart, *d* of 10th Earl of Cavan; three *d*. *Educ:* Eton; Trinity Coll., Cambridge (BA). Joined staff of Longmans Green & Co. Ltd, 1938. Served in Army, in Africa and Europe, 1939-46; Captain, City of London Yeomanry. Rejoined Longmans Green & Co. Ltd, 1946; Dir, 1947. Mem. Council, Publishers' Assoc., 1963, Treas., 1967; Jt Hon. Treas., English-Speaking Union, 1964-70; Dep. Chairman, Nat. Book League, 1965. Director, Pearson Longman Ltd (formerly S. Pearson Publishers Ltd), 1968. *Address:* 22 Grosvenor Square, W1. *T:* 01-493 3775; Bishopstone House, Salisbury, Wiltshire. *T:* Coombe Bissett 345. *Clubs:* Beefsteak, Buck's, Pratt's, Travellers', White's.

**LONGMORE, Air Chief Marshal Sir Arthur Murray,** GCB 1941 (KCB 1935; CB 1925); DSO 1919; *b* 1885; *m* 1st, 1913, Marjorie (*d* 1959), *o c* of late W. J. Maitland, CIE; two *s* (and one killed in action, 1943) one *d*; 2nd, 1960, Enid, *widow* of Lt-Col Geoffrey Bolster, and *d* of late Col M. R. de B. James. Late Lt-Comdr Royal Navy; served European War, France, Battle of Jutland and Italy, 1914-19 (despatches, DSO; officer Order of Crown of Belgium, Chevalier Legion of Honour, French Croix de Guerre, Italian Order of St Maurice and St Lazarus, Italian Croix de Guerre); Grand Cross of Royal Order of George I of Greece with swords; Greek War Cross. Commandant RAF Coll., Cranwell, 1929-33; Air Officer Commanding Inland Area, 1933-34; Coastal Area, renamed Coastal Command, RAF, 1934-36; Commandant Imperial Defence Coll., 1936-38; AOC-in-C, Training Command, 1939; Mem. British Air Mission to Australia and NZ, 1939; Member of UK delegation to Pacific Defence Conference, New Zealand, 1939; AOC-in-C, RAF, Middle East, 1940-41; Inspector-General of the Royal Air Force, 1941; retired list, 1942; Vice-Chairman, Imperial War Graves Commn, 1954-57. *Publication:* From Sea to Sky, 1947. *Address:* Little Trees, Broomfield Park, Sunningdale, Berks. *Clubs:* Royal Over-Seas League; Royal Yacht Squadron (Cowes).
*See also W. J. M. Longmore, G. A. Worth.*

**LONGMORE, Brigadier John Alexander,** CB 1957; CBE 1946 (MBE 1927); TD; DL (Herts); Solicitor; *b* 7 May 1899; *s* of late Colonel Sir Charles Elton Longmore, KCB, VD, TD, DL, Porthill House, Hertford; *m* 1925, Marguerite Madeleine, *d* of late Major John Edward Chapman Mathews, and *g d* of Sir Richard Quain, Bt; one *s* two *d*. *Educ:* Harrow. Served European War with Coldstream Guards, 1917-19. 1st Bn Herts Regt, 1919-42 (which Bn he comd, 1939-42, and of which Bn he was Hon. Col, 1952-61). Brigadier, and Dep. Director Home Guard and Territorial Army, War Office, 1942-46. Admitted Solicitor, 1922. Sometime Vice-Chairman and Hon. Treasurer, now Vice-President, Army Cadet Force Assoc.; Chairman T&AFA for Co. of Hertford, 1953-64; Life Governor of Haileybury and Imperial Service Coll. *Recreation:* gardening. *Address:* Great Amwell House, Ware, Herts. *T:* Stanstead Abbotts 415; Point Head, Chapel Point, Mevagissey, Cornwall. *T:* Mevagissey 2217. *Clubs:* Guards; Royal Cornwall Yacht.

**LONGMORE, William James Maitland;** Director, Bank of London & South America Ltd, since Dec. 1960; *b* 6 May 1919; 2nd *s* of Air Chief Marshal Sir Arthur Murray Longmore, *qv*; *m* 1941, Jean, *d* of 2nd Baron Forres of Glenogil; three *d*. *Educ:* Eton Coll. Royal Air Force, 1938-46 (Wing Comdr). Balfour, Williamson & Co. Ltd, 1946- (Chairman, 1967-). Dep. Chairman, BNEC for Latin America, 1966-. *Recreations:* shooting, sailing. *Address:* Gracious Pond Farm, Chobham, Surrey. *T:* Long Cross 332. *Club:* Royal Yacht Squadron.

**LONGMUIR, Very Rev. James Boyd,** TD 1950; Hon. DD; Moderator of the General Assembly of the Church of Scotland, May 1968-May 1969; Secretary of the General Administration Committee and Secretary to the Moderator of the General Assembly; Principal Clerk of General Assembly of the Church of Scotland, 1955-69; Chaplain to the Queen since 1957; Dean of the Chapel Royal, since 1969; Chaplain to HM Bodyguard for Scotland (Royal Company of Archers), since 1969; *b* 26 April 1907; *s* of William Longmuir and Margaret Lohoar Boyd; *m* 1934, Bethia Liddell, *d* of Rev. Thomas MacGregor; one *s* one *d*. *Educ:* Dalziel High Sch.; Glasgow Univ. (MA and BL). Ordained to Swinton Parish, 1934. Scoutmaster 9th Berwickshire, and District Commissioner of Scouts, 1951. Commissioned Royal Army Chaplains Dept (TA), 1938; mobilised 1939; served in France, attached 4th Gordons, 1940; Italy, 5 Corps Troops, RE, 1944; SCF 5 Corps Troops; Staff Chaplain, HQ British Troops, Austria, 1945 (despatches). Clerk to Presbytery of Duns, 1949-53; Minister at Chirnside, 1952-61; Dep. Clerk of General Assembly, 1953. Governor of Esdaile; Trustee of Iona Cathedral; Chairman, Chalmers Lectureship Trust; General Trustee, Church of Scotland. Mem., Commn on the Constitution, 1969. Hon. DD, Edinburgh, 1967. *Publications:* Simprim Church and Parish, 1947; Editor, Cox's Practice and Procedure in the Church of Scotland (5th edn), 1964. *Recreations:* history and gardening. *Address:* 1 Lygon Road, Edinburgh 9. *T:* 031-667 5175. *Clubs:* New, Caledonian (Edinburgh).

**LONGRIGG, Brigadier Stephen Hemsley,** OBE 1927; DLitt (Oxon); *b* 7 Aug. 1893; *s* of W. G. Hemsley Longrigg; *m* 1922, Florence, *d* of Henry Aitken Anderson, CSI, CIE; two *s* one *d*. *Educ:* Highgate Sch.; Oriel Coll., Oxford. Served Royal Warwickshire Regt, European War and after, 1914-21 (Major, 1918). Govt of Iraq, 1918-31; Inspector-Gen. of Revenue, 1927-31; Iraq Petroleum Co., 1931-51; War of 1939-45: Gen. Staff, GHQ, Cairo, 1940-41; Chief Administrator of Eritrea, 1942-44, Brigadier, 1940-45. Governor of Highgate Sch., 1946, Chairman of Governors, 1954-65. Chairman, British Petroleum Employers'

Cttee for International Labour Affairs, 1946-51. Vice-President, Royal Central Asian Society; Member Council, Royal Institute of International Affairs, 1956; Lecture tours: Scandinavia, 1952; Germany, 1954; US and Canada, 1956 and annually, 1959-66. Visiting Professor: Columbia Univ., Summer, 1966; University of Colorado, 1967. Order of the Rafidain (Iraq), 1931; Lawrence of Arabia Medallist, 1962; Sir Richard Burton Memorial Medallist, 1969. *Publications:* Four Centuries of Modern Iraq, 1925; Short History of Eritrea, 1945; Iraq, 1900 to 1950, 1953; Oil in the Middle East, 1954 (3rd edn 1968); Syria and Lebanon under French Mandate, 1958; (in collaboration) Iraq, 1958; The Middle East, a Social Geography, 1963 (2nd edn 1970). *Address:* 58 Chancellor House, Tunbridge Wells, Kent. *T:* Tunbridge Wells 21900. *Clubs:* Athenæum, East India and Sports.

**LONGSTRETH-THOMPSON, Francis,** OBE 1948; BScEng London, FRICS, MICE; Past President and Member Council of Town Planning Institute, 1924-57; Planning Consultant in private practice, 1914-44; County Planning Adviser for Essex, 1944-55; Member Executive Committee, Council for the Preservation of Rural England; *b* 3 May 1890; *s* of Francis Thompson and Emma Florence Pepler (*née* Mills); changed his surname by deed poll, from Thompson to Longstreth-Thompson in 1964; *m* 1st, 1913, Mildred Grace Corder (*d* 1963); one *s* three *d*; 2nd, 1964, Olga Mary Radcliff. *Educ:* Bootham Sch., York; University College, University of London. Chadwick Gold Medallist in Municipal Engineering (University College, London); articled to Messrs Stothert and Pitt of Bath and W. T. Douglass, MInstCE, of Westminster; Asst Engineer Port of London Authority, 1912-13; Resident Engineer on Ridham Dock for Rendel, Palmer and Tritton, 1913-14; work in France for Friends War Victims Relief Cttee, 1917-18; Asst Architect Housing, Ministry of Health, 1919-21; in private practice as Town Planning Consultant in Westminster, 1922-44; Adviser to Witwatersrand and Pretoria Jt Town Planning Cttee (S Africa), 1934-39; and (with Prof. Thornton White) to Govt of Union of South Africa, in connection with Foreshore Reclamation Scheme at Cape Town, 1940; Member Advisory Cttee, appointed by LCC in 1930 in connection with proposed Charing Cross Bridge; Consultant for numerous Regional and Town Planning Schemes in England, Newfoundland, South Africa and Southern Rhodesia, 1923-40! appointed in 1943 by Minister of Town and Country Planning to prepare a planning scheme for Merseyside; Chairman Technical Cttee of Advisory Cttee for London Regional Planning; Member Terminal Railway Station Commission, Durban, 1948; Chairman County Planning Officers Society, 1947-54; Member Planning Cttee, County Councils Assoc., 1946-55. Coronation Medal, 1953. *Publications:* Site Planning in Practice, 1923; Cape Town Foreshore Scheme, 1940; Merseyside Plan, 1944; numerous Regional Planning Reports; articles on Town Planning, Encyclopædia of Local Government Law, 1940, and elsewhere. *Recreations:* books, sketching, The Times Crossword. *Address:* Bobbins, Hawksdown, Walmer, Kent. *T:* Deal 2904. *Club:* Athenæum.

**LONGUET-HIGGINS, Prof. Hugh Christopher,** FRS 1958; DPhil (Oxon); Royal Society Research Professor, University of Edinburgh, since 1967; *b* 11 April 1923; *e s* of late Rev. H. H. L. Longuet-Higgins. *Educ:* Winchester (schol.); Balliol Coll., Oxford (schol., MA). Research Fellow of Balliol Coll., 1946-48; Lecturer and Reader in Theoretical Chemistry, University of Manchester, 1949-52; Prof. of Theoretical Physics, King's Coll., University of London, 1952-54; FRIC; John Humphrey Plummer Professor of Theoretical Chemistry, University of Cambridge, 1954-67; Fellow of Corpus Christi Coll., 1954-67, Life Fellow 1968; Hon. Fellow, Balliol Coll., Oxford, 1969. Warden, Leckhampton House, 1961-67; Harrison Memorial Prizeman (Chemical Society), 1950. Editor of Molecular Physics, 1958-61. Foreign Associate, US National Academy of Sciences, 1968. *Publications:* papers on theoretical physics, chemistry and biology in scientific journals. *Recreations:* music and arguing. *Address:* 26 Dundas Street, Edinburgh 3.

**LONGUET-HIGGINS, Michael Selwyn,** FRS 1963; Royal Society Research Professor, University of Cambridge, since 1969; *b* 8 Dec. 1925; *s* of late Henry Hugh Longuet and Albinia Cecil Longuet-Higgins; *m* 1958, Joan Redmayne Tattersall; two *s* two *d*. *Educ:* Winchester Coll. (Schol.); Trinity Coll., Cambridge (Schol.). (BA). Admiralty Research Lab., Teddington, 1945-48; Res. Student, Cambridge, 1948-51; PhD Cambridge, 1951; Rayleigh Prize, 1951; Commonwealth Fund Fellowship, 1951-52; Res. Fellow, Trinity Coll., Cambridge, 1951-55. Nat. Inst. of Oceanography, 1954-69. Visiting Professor: MIT, 1958; Institute of Geophysics, University of California, 1961-62; Univ. of Adelaide, 1964. Prof. of Oceanography, Oregon State Univ., 1967-69. *Publications:* papers in applied mathematics, esp. seismology and physical oceanography, dynamics of sea waves and currents, etc. *Recreations:* music, gardening, mathematical toys. *Address:* 1 Long Road, Cambridge.

**LONGWORTH, Sir Fred,** Kt 1966; DL; retired Trade Union Secretary; Vice-Chairman, Lancashire County Council, since 1967 (Chairman, 1964-67); *b* 15 Feb. 1890; *s* of James and Cresina Longworth; *m* 1916, Mary Smith. *Educ:* Tyldesley Upper George Street County Sch. Mem., Tyldesley UDC, 1940-70 (Chm., 1948-49, 1961-62); Mem., Lancs CC, 1946-; CA, 1952; Mem., Educn Cttee, County Councils Assoc.; Mem., Council and Court, Lancaster Univ. DL Lancs 1968. *Recreations:* reading, music, politics, education. *Address:* 30 Crawford Avenue, Tyldesley, near Manchester. *T:* Atherton 2906.

**LONGWORTH, Rt. Rev. Tom,** DD; *b* Jan. 1891; *s* of late Thomas Longworth, JP, Oak Hill, Whalley, Lancs; *m* 1926, Dorothy, *er d* of Rev. Frank Conyers Hardy, Vicar of Edensor, Derbyshire; one *d*. *Educ:* Shrewsbury Sch.; University Coll., Oxford; Cuddesdon Coll. BA 1914; MA 1927; DD (Lambeth), 1949. Deacon, 1915; priest, 1916; Rector of Guisborough, 1927-35; Vicar of Benwell, 1935-39; Bishop Suffragan and Archdeacon of Pontefract and Canon of Wakefield, 1939-49; Bishop of Hereford, 1949-61. Mem. House of Lords, 1956-61. *Address:* Wye House, Compton, near Winchester, Hants. *T:* Twyford 3109.

**LONSDALE,** 7th Earl of (UK), *cr* 1807; **James Hugh William Lowther,** Viscount and Baron Lowther, 1797; Bt 1764; *b* 3 Nov. 1922; *er s* of Anthony Edward, Viscount Lowther (*d* 1949), and Muriel Frances, Viscountess Lowther (*d* 1968), 2nd *d* of late Sir George Farrar, Bt, DSO, and Lady Farrar; *S* grandfather, 1953; *m* 1st, 1945; one *s* one *d*; 2nd, 1954; one *s* two *d*; 3rd, 1963, Nancy Ruth, *d* of late Thomas Cobbs, Pacific Palisades, Calif; one *s*. *Educ:* Eton. Armed Forces, 1941-46; RAC and East Riding Yeo. (despatches, Capt.). Structural engineering, 1947-50. Farmer, forester, and director of associated and local companies in Cumberland and Westmorland; Director: International Life Insurance Co. (UK) Ltd; Border TV and NE Housing Assoc.; Chm., Northern Adv. Council for Sport and Recreation; Member: Minister's Hill Farming Adv. Cttee; Westmorland AEC; Northern Region Economic Planning Council; Councils of CLA and TGO; Court of Newcastle Univ.; President: NW Area British Legion; NW Div. YMCA; Cumberland and Westmorland NPFA; local agricultural societies, etc. *Heir: s* Viscount Lowther, *qv. Address:* Askham Hall, Penrith, Cumberland. *T:* Hackthorpe 208; 33 Westminster Gardens, SW1. *Clubs:* Carlton, National Sporting; Northern Counties (Newcastle upon Tyne).

**LONSDALE, Lt-Col Arthur H.;** *see* Heywood-Lonsdale.

**LONSDALE, Maj.-Gen. Errol Henry Gerrard,** CB 1969; MBE 1942; Appeals Secretary, British Olympic Association; Transport Officer-in-Chief (Army) 1966-69; *b* 26 Feb. 1913; 2nd *s* of Rev. W. H. M. Lonsdale, Arlaw Banks, Barnard Castle; *m* 1944, Muriel Allison, *d* of E. R. Payne, Mugswell, Chipstead; one *s* one *d. Educ:* Westminster Sch.; St Catharine's Coll., Cambridge (MA). 2nd Lt, RASC, 1934; Lt 1936; Capt. 1941; Maj. 1946; Bt Lt-Col 1952; Lt-Col 1953; Col 1957; Brig. 1961; Maj-Gen. 1966. Sudan Defence Force, 1938-43 (despatches); CRASC, 16 Airborne Div., 1947-48; AA & QMG, War Office, 1951-53; CRASC, 1st Commonwealth Div. Korea, 1953-54; 1st Federal Div., Malaya, 1954-56 (despatches); Asst Chief of Staff Logistics, Northern Army Group, 1957-60; DDST, 1st Corps, 1960-62; Comdr, RASC Training Centre, 1962-64; Inspector, RASC, 1964-65; ADC to the Queen, 1964-66; Inspector, RCT, 1965-66; psc; jssc. Col Comdt, RCT, 1969-. Hon. Colonel: 160 Regt RCT(V), 1969-; 562 Para Sqdn RCT(V), 1969-. MInstT, 1966. Chm. Modern Pentathlon Assoc. of Great Britain, 1967. *Recreations:* modern pentathlon, golf, photography, driving. *Address:* Arlaw Banks, Godalming, Surrey. *T:* Hascombe 233. *Clubs:* East India and Sports, MCC.

**LONSDALE, Dame Kathleen,** DBE 1956; FRS 1945; DSc; formerly Professor of Chemistry and Head of Department of Crystallography, University College, London, now Emeritus; *b* 28 Jan. 1903; 10th and *y c* of late Harry Frederick Yardley and late Jessie Cameron; *m* 1927, Thomas J. Lonsdale, MSc, PhD, FInstP; one *s* two *d. Educ:* Bedford Coll., London Univ. Research Asst to late Sir Wm Bragg, OM, 1922-27 and 1937-42; Amy Lady Tate Scholar, 1927-29 (at Leeds Univ.); Leverhulme Research Fellow, 1935-37; Dewar Fellow, Royal Institution, 1944-46; Special Research Fellow, US Federal Health Service, 1947; Fellow of University Coll. Vis. Prof., Michigan State Univ., 1958; Distinguished Vis. Prof.: Ohio State Univ., 1969; Harvard Univ., 1970. Vice-Pres., Royal Society, 1960-61; Pres., British Association, 1967-68, Hon. Sec., 1960-64, Pres., Section A, 1966-67. Pres., Internat. Union of Crystallography, 1966. Mem. Court, Univ. of Essex; Governor and Fellow, Bedford Coll., London Univ. Hon. DSc: Wales, 1960; Leicester, Manchester, 1962; Lancaster, 1967; Kent, 1968; Oxford, 1969; Bath, 1969; Hon. LLD: Leeds, 1967; Dundee, 1968. Hon. Fellow: Lucy Cavendish Coll., Cambridge; Somerville Coll., Oxford, 1969. Davy Medal, Royal Society, 1957. *Publications:* Structure factor tables, 1936; Crystals and X-rays, 1949; International Tables for X-ray Crystallography, Vol. I, 1952; Vol. II, 1959; Vol. III, 1962; Quakers Visit Russia, 1952; Removing the Causes of War (Swarthmore Lecture), 1953; Is Peace Possible? (Penguin Special), 1957; I believe . . . (Eddington Lecture), 1964; many papers in scientific periodicals, from 1925 onwards. *Address:* 125a Dorset Road, Bexhill-on-Sea, Sussex. *T:* Bexhill 3405.

**LOOKER, Sir Cecil (Thomas),** Kt 1969; Principal Partner, Ian Potter & Co., Sharebrokers, since 1967 (Partner, 1953); Chairman, Stock Exchange of Melbourne, since 1966; Chairman, Australian United Corporation; Director of various other companies; *b* 11 April 1913; *s* of Edward William and Martha Looker; *m* 1941, Jean Leslyn Withington; one *s* two *d. Educ:* Fort Street Boys' High Sch., Sydney; Sydney Univ. (BA). Apptd to Commonwealth Public Service, 1937; Private Sec. to Prime Minister (Rt Hon. now Sir Robert Menzies), 1939-41. War of 1939-45: RANVR, 1942-45. Resigned Commonwealth Public Service, 1946, and joined Ian Potter & Co. Elected: Cttee of Stock Exchange of Melbourne, 1962; Pres., Australian Associated Stock Exchanges, 1968. Apptd by Dept of Territories as Dir of Papua and New Guinea Development Bank, 1966; Chm., Exec. Cttee, Duke of Edinburgh's Third Commonwealth Study Conf., Aust., 1966-68. *Recreation:* farming. *Address:* 26 Tormey Street, North Balwyn, Victoria 3104, Australia. *T:* 857-9316. *Clubs:* Australian, Royal Automobile Club of Victoria (Melbourne).

**LOOMBE, Claude Evan,** CMG 1961; Chairman, British Bank of the Middle East, since 1967; *b* 9 Aug. 1905; *yr s* of late Arthur Thomas Loombe and Catherine Jane Jermy; *m* 1936, Zoë Isabella, *o d* of late R. D. Hotchkis, MD, and of Penelope, *d* of late Alexander Ionides; three *d.* Entered Chartered Bank, 1925; service in Ceylon, China and India; seconded to Min. of Finance, Iraq Govt, 1941-45. Entered service of Bank of England as an Adviser, 1945; Adviser to the Governors, 1964-65; retired 1965; Chm., British Bank of the Middle East (Morocco), SA; Member: Kuwait Currency Bd, 1960-69; Jordan Currency Bd, 1948-65; Sudan Currency Bd, 1956-60; Libyan Currency Commn, 1952-56; London Cttee, Hongkong and Shanghai Banking Corp. Vice-Pres., Middle East Assoc. Cons., British Aircraft Corp. Iraqi Order of Al-Rafidain, 4th Class, 1946; Jordan Independence Order, 2nd Class, 1961; Order of Jordanian Star (1st Class), 1965. *Address:* Flowermead, Maori Road, Guildford, Surrey. *T:* Guildford 75172. *Club:* Oriental.

**LOOSLEY, Stanley George Henry,** MC 1944; MA Cantab; JP Glos; Headmaster of Wycliffe College, 1947-67; *b* 18 July 1910; *s* of Harold D. and Edith M. Loosley; *m* 1938, Margaret Luker; two *s* one *d. Educ:* Wycliffe Coll.; St John's Coll., Cambridge. Asst Master, Wycliffe Coll., 1934-39; War of 1939-45, RA, Sept. 1939-Oct. 1945; Major OC 220 Field Battery, 1941 (despatches, MC); NW Europe Campaign, 1944; sc; Bde Major RA 43 Div., 1945; Senior Asst Master, Wycliffe Coll., 1945-47. *Recreations:* travel, educational design. *Address:* Brillings Cottage, Chalford Hill, Stroud, Glos. *T:* Brimscombe 3505. *Club:* Royal Over-Seas League.

**LOPES,** family name of **Baron Roborough.**

**LOPOKOVA, Lydia;** *see* Keynes, Lady.

**LORANT, Stefan;** *b* 22 Feb. 1901; *m* 1963, Laurie Robertson; two *s. Educ:* Evangelical Gymnasium, Budapest; Academy of Economics, Budapest; Harvard University

(MA 1961). Editor: Das Magazin, Leipzig, 1925; Bilder Courier, Berlin, 1926; Muenchner Illustrierte Presse, 1927-33; Picture Post, 1938-40; Founder of Lilliput, Editor, 1937-40. Hon. LLD, Knox Coll., Galesburg, Ill., 1958. *Publications:* I Was Hitler's Prisoner, 1935; Lincoln, His Life in Photographs, 1941; The New World, 1946; F.D.R., a pictorial biography, 1950; The Presidency, a pictorial history of presidential elections from Washington to Truman, 1951; Lincoln: a picture story of his life, 1952; rev. and enl. edn 1969; The Life of Abraham Lincoln, 1954; The Life and Times of Theodore Roosevelt, 1959; Pittsburgh, the story of an American city 1964; The Glorious Burden: the American Presidency, 1968. *Address:* Farview, Lenox, Mass 01240, USA. *T:* Lenox 637-0666.

**LORD, Alan;** Commissioner of Inland Revenue since 1969; *b* 12 April 1929; *er s* of Frederick Lord and Anne Lord (*née* Whitworth), Rochdale; *m* 1953, Joan Ogden; two *d. Educ:* Rochdale; St John's Coll., Cambridge. Entered Inland Revenue, 1950; Private Sec. to Dep. Chm. and to Chm. of the Board, 1952-54; HM Treasury, 1959-62; Principal Private Sec. to First Secretary of State (then Rt Hon. R. A Butler), 1962-63. *Address:* 22 Greystone Park, Sundridge, Sevenoaks, Kent. *T:* Westerham 3657. *Club:* Reform.

**LORD, Cyril,** LLD (Hon.); Chairman and Managing Director, Cyril Lord Ltd, 1945-68; Director, numerous Companies in Great Britain, Northern Ireland, and South Africa, 1945-68; *b* 12 July 1911; *m* 1st, 1936, Bessie Greenwood (marr. diss. 1959); two *s* two *d*; 2nd, 1960, Shirley Stringer. *Educ:* Central Sch., Manchester; Manchester Coll. of Technology (Associate), and University. Dir of Hodkin & Lord Ltd, 1939; Technical Adviser to the Cotton Board, England, 1941. Hon. LLD Florida Southern Coll., 1951. *Recreations:* yachting, tennis. *Address:* c/o Bank of Nassau, Nassau, Bahamas; 3B Carefree Apartments, Nassau. *Clubs:* Royal Automobile, Royal Aero; Royal Corinthian (Cowes); Ballyholme Yacht (N Ire.).

**LORD, Sir Frank,** KBE 1962 (OBE 1945); Kt 1954; MA; DL; JP, County of Lancaster; JP, County Borough of Oldham; formerly Mayor of Oldham; Master, Farriers' Company, 1962-63; Past Chm., Oldham and District Hospital Management Committee; President Oldham Conservative Association; Member Court of Assistants, Paviors' Co.; High Sheriff, 1963, DL, 1968, County Palatine of Lancaster; *b* 3 May 1894; *s* of Joseph Lord, Oldham; *m* 1923, Rosalie Jeannette, *d* of Clement Joseph Herent, Bruxelles; two *s. Address:* Parkfield, Werneth Hall Road, Oldham, Lancs; 3 Lord Court, Clayhall, Ilford, Essex. *Clubs:* City Livery, Carlton.

**LORD, Maj.-Gen. Wilfrid Austin,** CB 1954; CBE 1952; MEng, CEng; FIMechE; FIEE; REME, retired; *b* 20 Sept. 1902; *s* of late S. Lord, Rochdale and Liverpool; *m* 1937, Mabel, *d* of late T. Lamb, York and Carlisle; one *s. Educ:* Birkenhead Institute; Liverpool Univ. Formerly RAOC, Lt 1927; Capt. 1933; Major 1935; Local Lt-Col 1940, Col 1947; Temp. Brig. 1949; Temp. Maj.-Gen. 1950; Maj.-Gen. 1950; Dir Mechanical Engineers, GHQ, ME Land Forces, 1950-53; Dir, Mechanical Engineering, War Office, 1954-57; retired, 1957. Col Comdt REME, 1957-63. *Address:* Redfields Home Farmhouse, Church Crookham, Hants. *T:* Crondall 543.

**LORD, William Burton Housley;** Deputy Chief Scientist (Army), Ministry of Defence, since 1968; *b* 22 March 1919; *s* of Arthur James Lord and Elsie Lord (*née* Housley); *m* 1942, Helena Headon Jaques; two *d. Educ:* King George V Sch., Southport; Manchester Univ.; London Univ. (External MSc); Trinity Coll., Cambridge (MA). Enlisted Royal Fusiliers, wartime commn S Lancs Regt, 1941-46. Cambridge Univ., 1946. Entered Civil Service, 1949; joined Atomic Weapons Res. Estab., 1952; Head of Metallurgy Div., AWRE, 1958; moved to MoD, 1964; Asst Chief Scientific Adviser (Research), 1965. *Publications:* papers on metallurgy in learned jls. *Recreations:* amateur radio (callsign G5NU); various water sports. *Address:* Linden Mews, The Mount, Christchurch Road, Reading, Berks. *T:* Reading 81200.

**LOREN, Sophia;** film actress; *b* 20 Sept. 1934; *d* of Ricardo Scicolone and Romilda Villani; *m* 1957, Carlo Ponti, film producer (marriage annulled in Juarez, Mexico, Sept. 1962; marriage in Paris, France, April 1966); one *s. Educ:* parochial sch. and Teachers' Institute, Naples. First leading role in, Africa sotto i Mari, 1952; acted in many Italian films, 1952-55; subsequent films include: The Pride and the Passion; Boy on a Dolphin; Legend of the Lost; The Key; Desire under the Elms; Houseboat; The Black Orchid; That Kind of Woman; It Started in Naples; Heller in Pink Tights; The Millionairess; Two Women; A Breath of Scandal; Madame sans Gêne; La Ciociara; El Cid; Boccaccio 70; Five Miles to Midnight; Yesterday, Today and Tomorrow; The Fall of the Roman Empire; Marriage, Italian Style; Operation Crossbow; Lady L; Judith; A Countess from Hong Kong; Arabesque; Sunflower. Award (for Black Orchid) Venice Film Festival, 1958. *Address:* Palazzo Colonna, Piazza d'Aracoeli 1, Rome, Italy.

**LORENZ, Prof. Dr Konrad,** MD, DPhil; Director of Max-Planck-Institut für Verhaltenphysiologie, since 1961 (Vice-Director, 1954); *b* 7 Nov. 1903; *s* of Prof. Dr Adolf Lorenz and Emma Lorenz (*née* Lecher); *m* 1927, Dr Margarethe Lorenz (*née* Gebhardt); one *s* two *d. Educ:* High Sch., Vienna; Columbia Univ., New York; Univ. of Vienna. Univ. Asst at Anatomical Inst. of University of Vienna (Prof. Hochstetter), 1928-35; Lectr in Comparative Anat. and Animal Psychol., University of Vienna, 1937-40; University Lectr, Vienna, 1940; Prof. of Psychol. and Head of Dept, University of Königsberg, 1940; Head of Research Station for Physiology of Behaviour of the Max-Planck-Inst. for Marine Biol., 1951. Hon. Prof., University of Münster, 1953 and München, 1957. Mem., Pour le Mérite for Arts and Science; Hon. Member: Assoc. for Study of Animal Behaviour, 1950; Amer. Ornithol. Union, 1951, etc; For. Mem., Royal Society, 1964. For. Assoc. Nat. Acad. of Sciences, USA, 1966. Hon. degrees: Leeds, 1962; Basel, 1966; Yale, 1967; Oxford, 1968; Chicago, 1970. Gold Medal, Zoological Soc., New York, 1955; City Prize, Vienna, 1959; Gold Boelsche Medal, 1962; Austrian Distinction for Science and Art, 1964; Prix Mondial, Cino de Duca, 1969. *Publications:* King Solomon's Ring, 1952; Man Meets Dog, 1954; Evolution and Modification of Behaviour, 1965; On Aggression, 1966; Studies in Animal and Human Behaviour, 1970; articles in Tierpsychologie, Behaviour, etc. *Address:* 8131 Seewiesen, Max-Planck-Institut für Verhaltensphysiologie, Germany. *T:* Feldafing 8121.

**LORIMER, Hew Martin,** RSA; FRBS; Sculptor; Treasurer Royal Scottish Academy, since 1963; Representative in Fife of National Trust for Scotland; *b* 22 May 1907; 2nd *s* of late Sir

Robert Stodart Lorimer, KBD, Hon. LLD, ARA, RSA, architect, and of Violet Alicia (*née* Wyld); *m* 1936, Mary McLeod Wylie (*d* 1970), 2nd *d* of H. M. Wylie, Edinburgh; two *s* one *d*. *Educ:* Loretto; Magdalen Coll., Oxford; Edinburgh Coll. of Art. Andrew Grant Scholarship, 1933 and Fellowship, 1934-35; travelled in France, Italy and Sicily; studied under late Eric Gill, ARA, 1935, and practised in Edinburgh. Sculptor in charge of work on National Library of Scotland, Edinburgh, himself designing and executing the 7 allegorical figures, 1952-55; Our Lady of the Isles, South Uist, 1955-57; St Francis, Dundee, 1957-59. *Recreations:* music, travel, home. *Address:* Kellie Castle, Pittenweem, Fife. *T:* Arncroach 211. *Club:* Scottish Arts (Edinburgh).

**LORING, Sir (John) Nigel,** KCVO 1964 (CVO 1953); MRCS, LRCP; Apothecary to the Household of Queen Elizabeth the Queen Mother, 1953, and to the Household of the Duke of Gloucester, 1959-66 (to the Household of King George VI and to that of The Princess Elizabeth and The Duke of Edinburgh, 1949-52; to that of Queen Mary, 1949-53; to HM Household, 1952-64); now in private practice only; *b* 31 Aug. 1896; *s* of late Nele Loring, Market Drayton, Salop; *m* 1932, Sylvia, 2nd *d* of late Col Blakeney-Booth, Billingham Manor, IoW; one *d* (and one *d* decd). *Educ:* RNC Osborne; Tonbridge Sch.; St Thomas's Hospital. Served European War 1914-19, RNR (Dover Patrol); War of 1939-45, Flight Lt 1941, Sqdn Ldr 1942 (despatches). Past Pres. of the Chelsea Clinical Soc.; Freeman, Worshipful Society of Apothecaries, London. *Recreations:* eighteenth century furniture, music. *Address:* 4 Woden House, Goring-on-Thames, Oxon. *T:* Goring-on-Thames 2922.

**LORING, Sir Nigel;** *see* Loring, Sir J. N.

**LORNE, Marquess of; Ian Campbell;** *b* 28 Aug. 1937; *e s* and *heir* of 11th Duke of Argyll, *qv*; *m* 1964, Iona Mary, *d* of Capt. Sir Ivar Colquhoun, *qv*; one *s*. *Educ:* Glenalmond; McGill Univ., Montreal. *Heir:* *s* Earl of Campbell, *qv*. *Address:* Grasmere, Rhinebeck, NY, USA.

**LOS ANGELES, Bishop of,** since 1948; **Rt. Rev. Francis Eric Irving Bloy,** DD, STD; *b* Birchington, Isle of Thanet, Kent, England, 17 Dec. 1904; *s* of Rev. Francis Joseph Field Bloy and Alice Mary (*née* Poynter); *m* 1929, Frances Forbes Cox, Alexandria, Va; no *c*. *Educ:* University of Arizona; University of Missouri (BA); Georgetown Univ. of Foreign Service; Virginia Theological Seminary (BD). Rector, All Saints Ch., Reisterstown, Maryland, 1929-33; Assoc. rector, St James-by-the-Sea, La Jolla, Calif, 1933-35, rector, 1935-37; Dean, St Paul's Cathedral, Los Angeles, Calif, 1937-48. Awarded DD degree, Occidental Coll., Los Angeles, 1942, and STD degree, Ch. Divinity Sch. of the Pacific, Berkeley, Calif, 1948. Pres., Hosp. of Good Samaritan, Los Angeles; Pres., Standing Cttee, Diocese of Los Angeles, 1946-48; Pres., Church Federation of Los Angeles, 1946-47; Mem. Nat. panel of Nat. Arbitration Assoc., Bd of Directors Los Angeles Chapter, Amer. Red Cross; deleg. to Reg. Conf. on UNESCO; Bd mem., Univ. Religious Conf.; mem. Advisory Council Graduate Sch. of Religion, University of S Calif, Los Angeles; mem. Ch. Extension Soc., FAM, KT, Gr. Chaplain DeMolay. Board of Trustees, Occidental Coll., Los Angeles; member of Board of Trustees: California Coll. in China; Church Divinity Sch. of the Pacific; Gen. Theological Seminary, New York. *Publications:* contributions Arts and Church Magazines. *Recreations:* fishing, landscape painting; has a private pilot's licence. *Address:* 1220 W 4th Street, Los Angeles, Calif 90054, USA. *Clubs:* University, Jonathan (Los Angeles); California.

**LOSEY, Joseph;** Film Director; *b* 14 Jan. 1909; *s* of Joseph Walton Losey and Ina Higbee; *m*; two *s*. *Educ:* Dartmouth Coll., New Hampshire; Harvard Univ. Resident in England from 1952. Directed first Broadway play, 1932; subseq. productions include: (with Charles Laughton) Galileo Galilei, by Bertholt Brecht, NY and Hollywood, 1947; (with Wilfrid Lawson) The Wooden Dish, London, 1954; short films from 1938; radio from 1942; first feature film, The Boy with Green Hair, 1948; Hollywood films include: The Dividing Line; The Prowler; films since 1952 include: Time Without Pity; Blind Date; The Criminal; The Damned; Eve; The Servant; King and Country; Modesty Blaise; Accident; Boom; Secret Ceremony; Figures in a Landscape. Guest Prof., Dartmouth Coll., NH, 1970. Chevalier de l'Ordre des Arts et des Lettres. *Recreations:* work, drink. *Address:* c/o Robin Fox, International Famous Agency Ltd, 11/12 Hanover Street, W1. *T:* 01-629 8080; c/o George Litto, George Litto Agency Inc., 9000 Sunset Boulevard, Los Angeles, Calif 90069, USA. *T:* 278-0017.

**LOTEN, Harold Ivens,** MBE 1950; JP; retired; *b* 28 June 1887; *s* of Arthur Richard and Caroline Loten; *m* 1914, Hilda Mary, *d* of John S. Kemp; two *d* (one *s* killed on active service, RNVR). *Educ:* St Bede's Sch., Hornsea. Served 1st Bn HAC Infantry, 1917-18. Sheriff of City and County of Kingston upon Hull, 1943-44, JP East Riding of Yorks, 1945; Pres. Hull Incorp. Chamber of Commerce and Shipping, 1946 and 1947. Manager, Midland Bank Ltd, Silver Street, Hull, 1937-49. Chm. Council and Pro-Chancellor, University of Hull, 1950-. Chairman: Governors, Hornsea County Schs; Hull Braves' Guild; Hornsea Holiday Home; Fellow, Institute of Bankers. Lay Preacher, 65 years. Hon. LLD (Hull), 1956. *Recreations:* gardening and reading. *Address:* Briar Garth, Atwick Road, Hornsea, E Yorks. *T:* Hornsea 3138.

**LOTH, David;** Editor and Author; *b* St Louis, Missouri, 7 Dec. 1899; *s* of Albert Loth and Fanny Sunshine. *Educ:* University of Missouri. Staff of New York World, 1920-30; Editor and Publisher The Majorca Sun, 1931-34; NY Times, 1934-41; US Govt Information Services, 1941-45; Information Dir, Planned Parenthood Federation of America, 1946-51; Acting Nat. Dir, 1951; Information Dir, Columbia Univ. Bicentennial, 1953-54; Assoc. Nieman Fellow, Harvard Univ., 1957-58; Lecturer, Finch Coll., 1961-65. Senior Editor-Writer, High Sch. Geog. Project of Assoc. of Amer. Geographers, 1967-68. Consultant, Psychological Corp., 1969-. Contributor to various English, American, and Australian publications. *Publications:* The Brownings; Lorenzo the Magnificent; Charles II; Philip II; Public Plunder; Alexander Hamilton; Lafayette; Woodrow Wilson; Chief Justice; A Long Way Forward; Swope of GE; The Erotic in Literature; Pencoyd and the Roberts Family; Crime Lab.: How High is Up; The City Within a City; Crime in Suburbia; The Marriage Counselor; Gold Brick Cassie. Co-author: American Sexual Behaviour and the Kinsey Report; Report on the American Communist; For Better or Worse; Peter Freuchen's Book of the Seven Seas; The Frigid Wife; The Emotional Sex; Ivan Sanderson's Book of Great Jungles. *Address:* Putnam Green 6B, Greenwich, Conn 06830, USA.

**LOTHIAN,** 12th Marquess of *cr* 1701; **Peter Francis Walter Kerr;** Lord Newbattle, 1591; Earl of Lothian, 1606; Baron Jedburgh, 1622; Earl of Ancram, Baron Kerr of Nisbet, Baron Long-Newton and Dolphingston, 1633; Viscount of Brien, Baron Kerr of Newbattle, 1701; Baron Ker (UK), 1821; DL; Parliamentary Under-Secretary of State, Foreign and Commonwealth Office, since 1970; *b* 8 Sept. 1922; *s* of late Captain Andrew William Kerr, RN, and Marie Constance Annabel, *d* of Capt. William Walter Raleigh Kerr; *S* cousin, 1940; *m* 1943, Antonella, *d* of late Maj.-Gen. Sir Foster Newland, KCMG, CB, and Mrs William Carr, Ditchingham Hall, Norfolk; two *s* four *d*. *Educ:* Ampleforth; Christ Church, Oxford. Lieut, Scots Guards, 1943. Mem. Brit. Delegation to UN Gen. Assembly, 1956-57; UK Delegate, Council of Europe and WEU, 1959. PPS to Foreign Sec., 1960-63; a Lord-in-Waiting, 1962-64; Joint Parliamentary Sec., Min. of Health, April-Oct. 1964. Past Mem., Departmental Cttee on Homosexual Offences and Prostitution. Mem., Queen's Body Guard for Scotland (Royal Company of Archers); Comdt Special Constabulary, Roxburgh, Selkirk and Berwickshire, 1954. DL, Roxburgh, 1962. Hon. Pres., Maltese Nobility, 1952; Kt, SMO Malta. *Heir:* *s* Earl of Ancram, *qv*. *Address:* Melbourne Hall, Derby. *T:* Melbourne 3; Monteviot, Ancrum, Roxburghshire. Ancrum 288; 54 Upper Cheyne Row, SW3. *Clubs:* Boodle's, Beefsteak; New (Edinburgh).

**LOTON, Sir Ernest Thorley,** Kt 1965; JP (WA); *b* Perth, Western Australia, 26 Dec. 1895; *s* of E. W. Loton, Perth; *m* 1927, Grace M., *d* of H. Smith; two *s*. *Educ:* Hale Sch., Perth, WA. Mem. Council, Royal Agric. Soc. of W Australia since 1923 (Pres. 1932-33 and 1941-46); Hon. Org. Sec., Aust. Soc. Breeders of British Sheep, 1925-26 (Vice-Chm., 1926-53; Chm., 1953-55; Fed. Pres., 1949-50); Mem. Bd of Govs, Hale Sch., Perth, 1934-57 (Chm., 1947-57); Foundation Mem., Faculty of Agriculture, University of Western Australia, 1936-54; Mem., Commonwealth Banking Corporation, 1960-63. Formerly Chairman: Westralian Farmers Co-operative Ltd; Co-operative Federation of WA; Westralian Farmers' Superphosphate Ltd; Kleen-heat Gas Pty, Ltd; Dir, WA Trustee & Exec. Company, 1952 (Chm. 1960); Mem., Swan Road Board, 1929-61 (Chm., 1931-61); Pres. Swan-Guildford Shire, 1961-62. Formerly Dir, Cuming Smith and Mt Lyell Farmers' Fertilizers Ltd. *Address:* 7 Jutland Parade, Dalkeith, Western Australia. *Club:* Weld (Perth, Western Australia).

**LOTT, Air Vice-Marshal Charles George,** CB 1955; CBE 1944; DSO 1940; DFC 1940; Royal Air Force, retired; *b* 28 Oct. 1906; *s* of late Charles Lott, Sandown; *m* 1936, Evelyn Muriel Little; two *s* one *d*. *Educ:* Portsmouth Junior Technical Sch. Joined Royal Air Force as Aircraft Apprentice, 1922; learned to fly at Duxford in No 19 Squadron, 1927-28; Sergeant, 1928; Commissioned 1933 and posted to No 41 Squadron; Iraq, 1935-38; HQ No 11 Gp, 1938-39; Commanded No 43 Squadron, 1939-40 (DFC, wounded, DSO); Temp. Wing Comdr, 1941; HQ 13 Group, 1940-42; Sector Comdr, Fighter Command, 1952; Acting Group Capt. 1942; Temp. Group Captain 1944; RAF Delegation (USA), 1944-45; Group Captain 1947; Air Commodore, 1954; Air Vice-Marshal, 1956; Dir Air Defence, SHAPE, 1955-57; Commandant, Sch. of Land/Air Warfare, Old Sarum, Wilts, 1957-59. Retd 1959. *Club:* Royal Air Force.

**LOTT, Frank Melville,** CBE 1945; DDS, MScD, PhD; retired; formerly Professor and Chairman of the Prosthodontics Department, University of Southern California, USA; *b* 9 Nov. 1896; *s* of Charles Lott, Uxbridge, Ont.; *m* 1933, Mabel Maunder Martin; one *s* one *d*. *Educ:* Toronto, Ont. Prof., Prosthetic Dentistry, University of Toronto. Dir-Gen. Dental Services, Canadian Forces, 1939-46; Col Comdt Royal Canadian Dental Corps. *Publications:* Bulletins of Canadian Dental Research Foundation and papers to dental congresses and journals. *Recreations:* photography, fishing, hunting. *Address:* 1628 Brae Burn Road, Altadena, Calif 91001, USA. *T:* Sycamore 1-1313.

**LOTZ, Dr Kurt;** German business executive; Chairman Board of Management, Volkswagenwerk AG, since 1968 (Deputy Chairman, 1967-68); Chairman Board of Directors, Audi NSU Auto Union AG, since 1969; *b* 18 Sept. 1912; *m* Elizabeth Lony; two *s* one *d*. *Educ:* August-Vilmar-Schule, Homberg. Joined Police Service, 1932; Lieut 1934. Served Luftwaffe (Gen. Staff; Major), 1942-45. Employed by Brown Boveri & Cie, Dortmund, 1946; Head of Business Div., Mannheim, 1954; Dir 1957; Chm. 1958-67; Mem. Board of Directors in parent company, Baden, Switzerland, 1961; Managing Director, 1963-67. Member: Presidium, Bundesverband der Deutschen Industrie; Exec. Council, Verband der Automobilindustrie; Cttee, Stifterverband für die Deutsche Wissenschaft; Deutsche Atomkommission; Trustee, Volkswagenwerk Foundn. Mem., Rotary Internat. Hon. Senator, Heidelberg Univ., 1963; Hon. Prof., Technische Universität Carolo Wilhelmina, Brunswick, 1970. Dr rer. pol. *hc* Wirtschaftshochschule (Inst. of Economics) Mannheim, 1963. *Recreations:* hiking, hunting. *Address:* Volkswagenwerk, 3180 Wolfsburg, Germany.

**LOUDON, John Hugo;** Jonkheer (Netherlands title); Knight in the Order of the Netherlands Lion, 1953; Grand Officer, Order of Orange-Nassau, 1965; KBE (Hon.) (Gt Brit.), 1960; Officer, Légion d'Honneur, 1963; holds other decorations; Chairman: NV Koninklijke Nederlandsche Petroleum Mij. (Royal Dutch Petroleum Co.), since 1965; Internat. Adv. Cttee for Chase Manhattan Bank, since 1965; Shell Petroleum NV, The Hague, since 1966; Dir Shell Petroleum Co. Ltd; Chairman, Board, Atlantic Institute, since 1969; Member, Board of Trustees, Ford Foundation, since 1966; *b* 27 June 1905; *s* of Jonkheer Hugo Loudon and Anna Petronella Alida Loudon (*née* van Marken); *m* 1931, Baroness Marie Cornelie van Tuyll van Serooskerken; three *s* (and one *s* decd). *Educ:* Netherlands Lyceum, The Hague; Utrecht Univ., Holland. Doctor of Law, 1929. Joined Royal Dutch/Shell Group of Cos, 1930; served in USA, 1932-38; Venezuela, 1938-47 (Gen. Man., 1944-47); Man. Dir, 1947-52, Pres., 1952-65, Royal Dutch Petroleum Co.; Principal Dir, Bataafse Petroleum Maatschappij NV, and Man. Dir the Shell Petroleum Co. Ltd, 1947-65; Senior Man. Dir, Royal Dutch Shell Gp, 1957-65, retired; former Chm. and Man. Dir, Shell Internat. Petroleum Co. Ltd; former Chairman: Shell Oil Co. (New York); Shell Caribbean Petroleum Co. (New York); Bataafse Internationale Petroleum Maatschappij NV; former Director: Cia Shell de Venezuela Ltd; Shell Western Holdings Ltd; Bataafse Internationale Chemie Mij. NV; Shell Internat. Chemical Co. Ltd. *Recreations:* golf, yachting. *Address:* 35 Grosvenor Square, W1. *T:* 01-629 0305; Koekoeksduin, Aerdenhout, Holland. *T:* Haarlem 241210. *Clubs:* White's; Royal Yacht Squadron.

**LOUDOUN, Countess of** (13th in line) *cr* 1633; **Barbara Huddleston Abney-Hastings;** Lady Campbell Baroness of Loudoun, 1601; Lady Tarrinzean and Mauchline, 1638; the 3 English baronies of Botreaux 1368, Stanley 1456, and Hastings 1461, which were held by the late Countess, are abeyant, the Countess and her sisters being *co-heiresses*; *b* 3 July 1919; assumed by deed poll, 1955, the surname of Abney-Hastings in lieu of that of Griffiths; *S* mother, 1960; *m* 1st, 1939 (marr. diss., 1945), Capt. Walter Strickland Lord; one *s*; 2nd, 1945, Capt. Gilbert Frederick Greenwood (*d* 1951); one *s* one *d*; 3rd, 1954, Peter Griffiths (who assumed by deed poll the surname of Abney-Hastings in lieu of his patronymic, 1958); three *d*. *Heir: s* Lord Mauchline, *qv*. *Address:* Loudoun Castle, Galston, Ayrshire.

**LOUDOUN, Donaldson;** Metropolitan Magistrate since 1961; Barrister-at-law; *b* 30 Jan. 1909; *m* 1st, 1933, Irene Charpentier; one *s* two *d*; 2nd, 1949, Clare Dorothy Biggie. Called to the Bar, Gray's Inn, 1934. Served War of 1939-45: BEF, 1939-40; Captain, Intelligence Corps (Parachute Section), 1944; Major, 1945; served in France, 1944; Belgium, 1945. *Recreation:* golf. *Address:* 2 Clifton Road, Wimbledon.

**LOUGH, Prof. John;** Professor of French, University of Durham (late Durham Colleges), since 1952; *b* 19 Feb. 1913; *s* of Wilfrid Gordon and Mary Turnbull Lough, Newcastle upon Tyne; *m* 1939, Muriel Barker; one *d*. *Educ:* Newcastle upon Tyne Royal Grammar Sch.; St John's Coll., Cambridge; Sorbonne. Major Schol., St John's Coll., 1931; BA, First Cl. Hons Parts I and II Mod. and Medieval Langs Tripos, 1934; Esmond Schol. at British Inst. in Paris, 1935; Jebb Studentship, Cambridge, 1936; PhD 1937, MA 1938, Cambridge. Asst (later Lectr), Univ. of Aberdeen, 1937; Lectr in French, Cambridge, 1946. Hon. Dr, Univ. of Clermont, 1967. *Publications:* Locke's Travels in France, 1953; An Introduction to Seventeenth Century France, 1954; Paris Theatre Audiences in the 17th and 18th centuries, 1957; An Introduction to Eighteenth Century France, 1960; Essays on the Encyclopédie of Diderot and D'Alembert, 1968; The Encyclopédie in 18th Century England and other studies, 1970; The Encyclopédie, 1971; (ed) selected philosophical writings of Diderot, 1953; (ed) selected articles from the Encyclopédie, 1954; articles on French literature and ideas in 17th and 18th centuries in French and English learned jls. *Address:* 1 St Hild's Lane, Gilesgate, Durham. *T:* Durham 3034.

**LOUGHBOROUGH, Lord; Peter St Clair-Erskine;** *b* 31 March 1958; *s* and *heir* of 6th Earl of Rosslyn, *qv*.

**LOUGHBOROUGH, Archdeacon of;** *see* Lockley, Ven. Harold.

**LOUGHLIN, Dame Anne,** DBE 1943 (OBE 1935); General Secretary, Tailors and Garment Workers Trade Union, 1948-53; *b* 28 June 1894. *Educ:* Leeds. General organiser, 1916-48; General Council, Trades Union Congress, 1929 (Pres. 1943). Retired. *Address:* 5 Victoria House, 84 King's Avenue, SW4.

**LOUGHLIN, Charles William;** MP (Lab) Gloucestershire West since 1959; trade union official; *b* 16 Feb. 1914; *s* of late Charles Loughlin, Grimsby; *m* 1945, May, *d* of David Arthur Dunderdale, Leeds; one *s* (one *d* decd). *Educ:* St Mary's Sch., Grimsby; National Council of Labour Colls. Area Organiser, Union of Shop, Distributive and Allied Workers, 1945-. Parly Sec., Min. of Health, 1965-67; Jt Parly Sec., Min. of Social Security, then Dept of Health and Social Security, 1967-68; Parly Sec., Min. of Public Building and Works, 1968-70. *Address:* Staunton, Coleford, Glos. *T:* Coleford 3378.

**LOUGHRAN, James;** Principal Conductor, BBC Scottish Symphony Orchestra, since 1965; *b* 30 June 1931; *s* of James and Agnes Loughran; *m* 1961, Nancy (*née* Coggon); two *s*. *Educ:* St Aloysius' Coll., Glasgow; Bonn, Amsterdam and Milan. 1st Prize, Philharmonia Conducting Competition, 1961. Asst Conductor, Bournemouth Symphony Orchestra, 1962; Associate Conductor, Bournemouth Symphony Orchestra, 1964. *Address:* BBC, Queen Margaret Drive, Glasgow W2. *T:* 041-339 8844.

**LOUSADA, Anthony (Baruh);** Partner of Stephenson Harwood & Tatham, Solicitors; *b* 4 Nov. 1907; *s* of Julian George Lousada and Maude Reignier Conder; *m* 1st, 1937, Jocelyn (marriage dissolved, 1960), *d* of Sir Alan Herbert, *qv*; one *s* three *d*; 2nd, 1961, Patricia, *d* of C. J. McBride, USA; one *s* one *d*. *Educ:* Westminster; New Coll., Oxford. Admitted Solicitor, 1933. Min. of Economic Warfare, 1939-44; Min. of Production and War Cabinet Office, 1944-45. Member: Coun., Royal College of Art, 1952- (Hon. Fellow, 1957; Sen. Fellow., 1967; Vice-Chm., 1960-67; Treas., Nov. 1967-); Cttee, Contemp. Art Soc., 1955- (Vice-Chm., 1961-); Fine Arts Cttee, British Council (visited Japan on behalf of Council, 1970, to set up exhibn of sculpture by Barbara Hepworth); GPO Adv. Cttee on Stamp Design, 1968; Council, Friends of Tate Gallery, 1958- (Hon. Treasurer, 1960-65); Trustee, Tate Gallery, 1962- (Vice-Chm., 1965-67; Chm., 1967-69); Mem., GLC Arts and Recreation Cttee, 1970. Officer, Order of Belgian Crown, 1945. *Recreations:* painting, sailing. *Address:* The Tides, Chiswick Mall, W4. *T:* 01-994 2257. *Clubs:* City of London; London Corinthian Sailing.

**LOUTH,** 16th Baron, *cr* 1541, **Otway Michael James Oliver Plunkett;** *b* 19 Aug. 1929; *o s* of Otway Randal Percy Oliver Plunkett, 15th Baron, and Ethel Molly, *d* of Walter John Gallichen, Jersey, Channel Islands; *S* father, 1950; *m* 1951, Angela Patricia Culinane, Jersey; three *s* two *d*. *Heir: s* Hon. Jonathan Oliver Plunkett, *b* 4 Nov. 1952. *Address:* Gardone, Holmfield Avenue, St Brelade, Jersey, Channel Islands; c/o R. H. Beauchamp & Orr, 5 Foster Place, Dublin.

**LOUTIT, John Freeman,** CBE 1957; FRS 1963; MA, DM, FRCP; External Scientific Staff MRC, Radiobiology Unit; *b* 19 Feb. 1910; *s* of John Freeman Loutit, Perth, WA; *m* 1941, Thelma Salusbury; one *s* two *d*. *Educ:* C of E Grammar Sch., Guildford, W Australia; Univs of W Australia, Melbourne, Oxford, London. Rhodes Scholar (W Australia), 1930; BA Oxon 1933, BM, BCh Oxon 1935. Various appointments, London Hosp., 1935-39; MA (Oxon) 1938; Director, South London Blood Supply Depot, 1940-47; DM Oxon, 1946; Dir, Radiobiological Research Unit, AERE Harwell, 1947-69. FRCP 1955. VMD (*hc*) Stockholm, 1965. Officer, Order of Orange-Nassau (Netherlands) 1951. *Publications:* Irradiation of Mice and Men, 1962; Tissue Grafting and Radiation (jointly), 1966; articles in scientific journals. *Recreations:* cricket, gardening. *Address:* Green Farm, Milton Lane, Steventon, Berks. *T:* Steventon 279.

**LOVAT,** 17th Baron *cr* before 1440 (*de facto* 15th Baron, 17th but for the Attainder); **Simon Christopher Joseph Fraser,** DSO 1942; MC; TD; DL; JP; 24th Chief of Clan Fraser; *b*

9 July 1911; *s* of 16th Baron and Hon. Laura Lister (*d* 1965), 2nd *d* of 4th Baron Ribblesdale; *S* father, 1933; *m* 1938, Rosamond, *o d* of Sir Delves Broughton, 11th Bt; four *s* two *d*. *Educ:* Ampleforth; Magdalen Coll., Oxford, BA. Lt, Scots Guards, 1934-37, retd. Served War of 1939-45: Capt. Lovat Scouts, 1939; Lt-Col 1942; Brig. Commandos, 1943 (wounded, MC, DSO, Order of Suvarov, Légion d'Honneur, Croix de Guerre avec palme); Under-Sec. of State for Foreign Affairs, 1945. Awarded LLD (Hon.) by Canadian universities. Owns about 190,000 acres. *Heir:* *s* Master of Lovat, *qv*. *Address:* Beaufort Castle, Beauly, Inverness-shire.
*See also Earl of Eldon, Rt Hon. Hugh Fraser, Sir Fitzroy Maclean, Bt, Baron Reay.*

**LOVAT, Master of; Hon. Simon Augustine Fraser;** *b* 28 Aug. 1939; *s* of 17th Baron Lovat, *qv*. *Educ:* Ampleforth Coll. Lt Scots Guards, 1960. *Address:* Beaufort Castle, Beauly, Inverness-shire.

**LOVE, Enid Rosamond, (Mrs G. C. F. Whitaker);** Head of Educational Programmes, Yorkshire Television Ltd, since 1968; *b* 15 May 1911; *d* of late Cyril Maurice Love and late Louise Gaston (*née* Harrison), Reading, Berks; *m* 1965, Geoffrey Charles Francis Whitaker. *Educ:* Royal Masonic Sch. for Girls; University of London (Bedford Coll. and Institute of Historical Research). Teaching in various public and grammar schs, 1934-44; Head Mistress, County Grammar Sch. for Girls, Wokingham, Berks, 1944-49. Joined BBC, 1949, as Regional Education Officer for School Broadcasting Council; Asst Head of Sch. Broadcasting (Sound), 1951-56. Asst Head of School Broadcasting (Television), BBC, 1956-59; Head of School Broadcasting, Associated-Rediffusion Ltd, 1959-63; Head Mistress, Sydenham Sch., 1963-68. *Publications:* occasional contributions to educational journals. *Recreations:* reading, walking, foreign travel. *Address:* 9 Welburn Avenue, Leeds 16, Yorks.

**LOVE, Robert John McNeill,** MS, London; FRCS; FACS; FICS; late Demonstrator of Anatomy and Physiology, late Surgical Assistant, London Hospital; Consulting Surgeon: Royal Northern Hospital; Metropolitan Hospital; Mildmay Mission Hospital; West End Hospital for Nervous Diseases; City of London Maternity Hospital; late Chairman, Court of Examiners, Erasmus Wilson Demonstrator, and Hunterian Professor, late member of Council, Royal College of Surgeons; Fellow, Royal Society of Medicine; Fellow, Association of British Surgeons; Member, Barbers' Company; *b* Plymouth, Devon, 2 May 1891; *s* of Alderman Joseph Boyd Love, JP, and Elizabeth Caroline Coleman; *m* 1930, Dorothy Borland (*d* 1961), Plymouth; one *d* (one *s* decd); *m* 1963, Rhoda Evelyn MacKie. *Educ:* Taunton Sch.; London Hospital. Qualified as doctor, 1914; commission in Royal Army Medical Corps, 1915; served at Gallipoli, in India, and Mesopotamia; returned to London Hospital and held resident appointments. *Publications:* Minor Surgery, 3rd edn, 1947; A Short Practice of Surgery (jointly), 14th edn, 1968; Surgery for Nurses (jointly), ninth edition, 1965; The Appendix, 1947; many articles in Medical Press. *Recreations:* phillumery, shooting; Hon. Commissioner Boy Scouts. *Address:* Sewards Farm, Brickendon, Hertford. *T:* Bayford 271. *Clubs:* East India and Sports; Hertford Constitutional.

**LOVEDAY, Alan (Raymond);** Solo Violinist; Professor at the Royal College of Music since 1955; an Associate Leader, London Bach Orchestra, since 1968; *b* 29 Feb. 1928; *s* of Leslie and Margaret Loveday; *m* 1952, Ruth Stanfield; one *s* one *d*. *Educ:* privately; Royal College of Music (prizewinner). Made debut at age of 4; debut in England, 1946; has given many concerts, broadcasts, and made TV appearances, in this country and abroad, playing with all leading conductors and orchestras; repertoire ranges from Bach (which he likes to play on an un-modernised violin), to contemporary music. Hon. ARCM 1961. *Recreations:* tennis, golf, chess, bridge. *Address:* 82 Porchester Terrace North, Bayswater, W2. *T:* 01-723 9188.

**LOVEDAY, Rt. Rev. David Goodwin;** *see* Dorchester, Suffragan Bishop of.

**LOVEGROVE, Geoffrey David,** QC 1969; *b* 22 Dec. 1919; *s* of late Gilbert Henry Lovegrove; *m* 1959, Janet, *d* of John Bourne; one *s* two *d*. *Educ:* Haileybury; New College, Oxford (MA). Called to the Bar, Inner Temple, 1947; Dep. Chairman, W Sussex Quarter Sessions, 1965. *Address:* 1 King's Bench Walk, Temple, EC4.

**LOVELACE,** 5th Earl of, *cr* 1838; **Peter Axel William Locke King;** Baron King and Ockham, 1725; Viscount Ockham, 1838; *b* 26 Nov. 1951; *s* of 4th Earl and of Manon Lis, *d* of Axel Sigurd Transo, Copenhagen, Denmark; *S* father, 1964. *Address:* Torridon House, Torridon, Ross-shire.

**LOVELACE, Lt-Col Alec,** CMG 1958; MBE 1941; MC; *b* 1907; *m* 1948, Eleanor, *d* of W. E. Platt. *Educ:* Dorchester Grammar Sch.; University College of the South-West, Exeter; Birkbeck Coll., University of London. Served War of 1939-45 in Army (Lt-Col), Education Officer, Mauritius, 1946; Civil Commissioner, 1949; Administrator, Antigua, 1954; Defence Officer, The West Indies, 1958; Administrator of Dominica, Windward Islands, 1960-64, retired. CStJ. *Address:* Honeysellers, North Street, Winchelsea, Sussex.

**LOVELL, Sir (Alfred Charles) Bernard,** Kt 1961; OBE 1946; FRS 1955; Professor of Radio Astronomy, University of Manchester, and Director of Jodrell Bank Experimental Station, Cheshire, now Nuffield Radio Astronomy Laboratories, since 1951; *b* 31 Aug. 1913; *s* of G. Lovell, Oldland Common, Gloucestershire; *m* 1937, Mary Joyce Chesterman; two *s* three *d*. *Educ:* Kingswood Grammar Sch., Bristol; University of Bristol. Assistant Lecturer in Physics, University of Manchester, 1936-39; Telecommunication Research Establishment, 1939-45. Physical Laboratories, University of Manchester and Jodrell Bank Experimental Station, Cheshire; Lecturer, 1945, Senior Lecturer, 1947, Reader, 1949, in Physics. Reith Lecturer, 1958; Condon Lecturer, 1962; Guthrie Lecturer, 1962; Halley Lecturer, 1964; Queen's Lecturer, Berlin, 1970. Member: Aeronautical Research Council, 1955-58; Science Research Council, 1965-70. Pres., Royal Astronomical Soc., 1969. Hon. Fellow, Society of Engineers, 1964; Hon. Foreign Member American Academy of Arts and Sciences, 1955; Hon. Life Member, New York Academy, 1960; Hon. Member, Royal Swedish Academy, 1962. Hon. LLD: Edinburgh, 1961; Calgary, 1966; Hon. DSc: Leicester, 1961; Leeds, 1966; London, 1967; Bath, 1967; Bristol, 1970; Hon. FIEE, 1967. Duddell Medal, 1954; Royal Medal, 1960; Daniel and Florence Guggenheim International Astronautics Award, 1961; Ordre du Mérite pour la Recherche et l'Invention, 1962; Churchill Gold Medal, 1964; Maitland Lecturer and Silver Medallist, Institution of Structural Engineers, 1964. *Publications:*

Science and Civilisation, 1939; World Power Resources and Social Development, 1945; Radio Astronomy, 1951; Meteor Astronomy, 1954; The Exploration of Space by Radio, 1957; The Individual and The Universe, (BBC Reith Lectures, 1958); The Exploration of Outer Space (Gregynog Lectures, 1961); Discovering the Universe, 1963; Our Present Knowledge of the Universe, 1967; (ed. with T. Margerison) The Explosion of Science: The Physical Universe, 1967; The Story of Jodrell Bank, 1968. Many Publications in Physical and Astronomical journals. *Recreations:* cricket, gardening, music. *Address:* The Quinta, Swettenham, Cheshire. *T:* Lower Withington 254. *Club:* Athenæum.

**LOVELL, Sir Bernard;** *see* Lovell, Sir A. C. B.

**LOVELL, Reginald,** DSc (Manchester); PhD (London); MRCVS; DVSM; Professor of Veterinary Bacteriology, University of London, at Royal Veterinary College, London, NW1, 1953-64; Professor Emeritus, since 1964; *b* 2 Jan. 1897; *s* of late Sidney and Mary Lovell, Wyke Regis; *m* Alice M. Orrell, MB, ChB (*d* 1969), *d* of late W. W. Orrell, OBE, Rochdale; one *s. Educ:* Hardye's Sch., Dorchester; Royal Veterinary Coll., Manchester Univ. QO, Dorset Yeomanry, 1914-19; Demonstrator in Bacteriology, University of Manchester, 1925-27; Research Asst and Lecturer in London Sch. of Hygiene and Tropical Medicine, 1927-33. Reader in Bacteriology, 1933, then Deputy Director of the Research Institute in Animal Pathology. President, Comparative Medicine Sect., Royal Society Med., 1949-50; Almroth-Wright Lecturer, 1951; Dalrymple-Champneys Cup and Medal, 1951; Hon. Treasurer Society Gen. Microbiology, 1951-61, President, 1961-63; Distinguished visiting lecturer, Michigan State Univ., USA, 1955; Benjamin Ward Richardson Lecturer, 1956. Ford Foundation Visiting Professor, University of Ibadan, 1964. Member of Council, RCVS, 1953-65. John Henry Steel Mem. Medal, 1965. *Publications:* The Aetiology of Infective Diseases, 1959; lectures, addresses, papers, etc, on Bacteriology, animal and human diseases in J. Path. Bact., J. comp. Path., Lancet and other learned journals. *Recreation:* books. *Address:* 4 Brookside Close, Kilmington, Axminster, Devon. *T:* Axminster 2765.

**LOVELOCK, Douglas Arthur;** Under-Secretary (Contracts), Ministry of Technology, since 1968; *b* 7 Sept. 1923; *s* of late Walter and Irene Lovelock; *m* 1961, Valerie Margaret (*née* Lane); one *s* one *d. Educ:* Bec Sch., London. Entered Treasury, 1949; Min. of Supply, 1952; Private Sec. to Permanent Sec., 1953-54; Principal, 1954; Private Sec. to successive Ministers of Aviation (Rt Hon. Peter Thorneycroft and Rt Hon. Julian Amery), 1961-63; Asst Sec., 1963; Under-Sec., 1968. *Recreations:* walking, gardening, outdoor activities generally. *Address:* 13 Court Avenue, Old Coulsdon, Surrey. *T:* Downland 55211.

**LOVELY, Percy Thomas;** Member of Court of Common Council; Deputy of Tower Ward; Sheriff of the City of London, 1950; *b* 12 Dec. 1894; *s* of late Thomas Lovely; *m* 1919, Ethel Ada Rust (*d* 1970); five *d. Educ:* King's Coll., London. Volunteered for RNVR, 1914 (Prisoner of War, 1914-18). Underwriting Member of Lloyd's, 1948-; Director of Messrs. Ellis & Co., 1949-. Member of the Worshipful Companies of: Bakers (Ct), Glaziers (Master, 1963), Horners (Ct), Innholders, Painter Stainers and Basketmakers (1925-, Prime Warden, 1950); Past Master, Parish Clerks' Company; Past Master, Guild of the Freemen of the City of London (Master, 1958-). Churchwarden of St Margaret Pattens, London; Life Governor: St Bartholomew's Hospital, Bridewell Royal Hospital, Queen Elizabeth Training College for the disabled; Hon. Treasurer, British Section: Council of European Municipalities; Council of Commonwealth Municipalities. FRSA. *Recreations:* travel, golf, chess. *Address:* Kings-Leigh, Westmoreland Road, Bromley, Kent. *T:* 01-460 4898. *Clubs:* City Livery (President, 1949-50), United Wards, Guild of Freemen, Entre Nous (Past President).

**LOVEMORE, Wing Commander Robert Baillie,** DSO 1919; RAFVR; late 3rd Battalion London Regiment (Royal Fusiliers), RFC and RAF; *e s* of late W. B. Lovemore, JP, of Swaziland; *m* Gwendolen Amy, *o d* of late H. C. Edwards, England; one *s. Educ:* Michaelhouse, Natal. Served European War, 1914-18 (despatches twice, DSO). Served as pilot Air Mail Lines, Union Airways, South African Airways and Wilson Airways (Kenya). Established and commanded E. African flying training scheme, 1939-40; 117 Squadron, Middle East Command, 1940-41; Comd No. 7, and subs. No. 6, Air Schools in Training Command, Union of South Africa, 1942-46. *Address:* Blythe Glade, P.O. Emerald Hill, Port Elizabeth, S. Africa; c/o Port Elizabeth Club.

**LOVERIDGE, Arthur John,** CMG 1954; OBE 1947; Lecturer, London University Institute of Education, 1959; *b* 1904; *e s* of late C. W. Loveridge, CB; *m* 1932, Marjorie Gertrude Coleman, Shepperton; one *d. Educ:* Emanuel Sch.; St John's Coll., Cambridge; Middle Temple. In Business, 1926-29; appointed Colonial Administrative Service, 1929. Chief Comr Gold Coast Colony, 1950, Northern Territories, 1953, Ashanti, 1954; retired 1956. Member of Commission of Enquiry into Disturbances in Sierra Leone, 1956, Uganda, 1960. *Publication:* (with L. J. Lewis), The Management of Education, 1965. *Recreations:* golf and dialectics. *Address:* Bird's Elm, Lower Road, Bookham, Surrey. *T:* Bookham 2369. *Club:* Travellers'.

**LOVERIDGE, Joan Mary,** OBE 1968; Matron and Superintendent of Nursing, St Bartholomew's Hospital, 1949-67; *b* 14 Aug. 1912; *d* of William Ernest Loveridge. *Educ:* Maidenhead, Berkshire. Commenced training, 1930, Royal National Orthopædic Hospital, W1; St Bartholomew's Hospital, 1933-37; Radcliffe Infirmary, Oxford, Midwifery Training, 1937-38; Night Sister, Ward Sister, Matron's Office Sister, Assistant Matron, St Bartholomew's Hospital. *Address:* Third Acre, 3 Wisborough Gardens, Wisborough Green, Sussex. *Club:* Cowdray.

**LOVERIDGE, John Warren,** JP; MP (C) Hornchurch since 1970; Principal of St Godric's College since 1954; farmer and landowner; *b* 9 Sept. 1925; *s* of C. W. Loveridge and Emily (Mickie), *d* of John Malone; *m* 1954, Jean Marguerite (JP, S Westminster), *d* of E. J. Chivers; three *s* two *d. Educ:* St John's Coll., Cambridge (MA). Contested (C) Aberavon, 1951, Brixton (LCC), 1952; Mem. Hampstead Borough Council, 1953-59. Treasurer Hampstead Conservative Assoc., 1959-65, and Trustee, 1965-. JP West Central Division, 1963. FRAS; MRIIA. *Recreations:* shooting, historic houses and early furniture; golf (Pres., Axe Cliff Golf Club). *Address:* The White House, 82 Fitzjohn's Avenue, Hampstead, NW3. *T:* 01-435 2684; Bindon Manor, Axmouth, near Seaton, Devon. *T:* Seaton 234. *Clubs:* Carlton, Hurlingham.

**LOVETT, Maj.-General Osmond de Turville,** CB 1947; CBE 1945; DSO 1943, and Bar 1944; late 2nd Gurkha Rifles; retired; *b* 1898; *s* of William Edward Turville Lovett, Tamworth, Dunster; *m* 1940, Eleanor Barbara, *d* of late Albert Leslie Wright, late of Butterley Hall, Derbyshire; no *c*. *Educ:* Blundells, Tiverton; Cadet Coll., Wellington, India. 2nd Lieut, Indian Army, 1917; served European War, 1914-18, India, Mesopotamia; NW Persia, 1919-21 (wounded); transferred 2nd Gurkhas, 1919; Major, 1936; War of 1939-45, 10th Army, transferred to 8th Army, Middle East Forces (wounded); Central Mediterranean Force; Brigadier, 1943; temp. Maj.-General, 1945; retired, 1948. Farming. *Recreations:* polo, tennis, fishing. *Address:* c/o Standard Bank of South Africa, Mooi River, Natal, South Africa; c/o Lloyds Bank (Cox's and King's Branch), 6 Pall Mall, SW1. *Club:* United Service.

**LOVETT, Robert Abercrombie;** Banker, United States; *b* 14 Sept. 1895; *s* of Robert Scott Lovett and Lavinia Chilton (*née* Abercrombie); *m* 1919, Adèle Quartley Brown; one *s* (one *d* decd). *Educ:* Yale Univ. (BA), 1918; law study, Harvard, 1919-20; course in business administration, Harvard Grad. Schools, 1920-21. Clerk, National Bank of Commerce, NY City, 1921-23; employee, Brown Brothers & Co., 1923; partner, 1926; continued in successor firm, Brown Brothers Harriman & Co. until 1940. Served as Special Asst to Secretary of War, and as Asst Secretary of War for Air in charge of Army Air Program, 1940-45. Under-Secretary of State, 1947-49; Deputy Secretary of Defence, 1950-51; Secretary of Defence, 1951-Jan. 1953. Readmitted Brown Brothers Harriman & Co., March 1953. Director: Los Angeles & Salt Lake Railroad Co.; Oregon Short Line Railroad Co.; Oregon-Washington Railroad & Navigation Co.; Union Pacific Railroad Co.; Union Pacific Corp.; Columbia Broadcasting System Inc.; Freeport Sulphur Co. Member, NY Investment Cttee, Royal Globe Insurance Companies. Trustee, Carnegie Institution of Washington. Life Member of Corporation of Massachusetts Institute of Technology. Holds hon. degrees. Served (pilot to Lieut-Commander) US Naval Air Service, March 1917-Dec. 1918 (Navy Cross, DSM). Grand Cross of the Order of Leopold II (Belgium), 1950; Presidential Medal of Freedom, USA, 1963. *Address:* Locust Valley, Long Island, NY 11560, USA. *Clubs:* Century, Yale, Links (New York); Creek (Locust Valley); Metropolitan (Washington, DC).

**LOVICK, Albert Ernest Fred;** Chairman, 1964-68, Director, 1950-68 and since 1969, Co-operative Insurance Society Ltd; Director, CWS Ltd since 1949; *b* 19 Feb. 1912; *s* of late Arthur Alfred Lovick and late Mary Lovick (*née* Sharland); *m* 1934, Florence Ena Jewell; no *c*. *Educ:* Elementary Sch., Eastleigh, Hants; Peter Symonds, Winchester. Hearne & Partner, rating surveyors, 1928; Eastleigh Co-operative Society, 1929-33; Harwich, Dovercourt and Parkeston CS, 1933-35; Managing Secretary, Basingstoke CS, 1935-49. During War of 1939-45, government cttees. Member, Basingstoke Borough Council, 1946-49. Chairman: South-Western Wool Assoc. Ltd; Centratours Ltd; Ten Acres & Stirchley Co-op. Soc. Ltd, Birmingham. Member, Export Credits Guarantees Advisory Council, 1968-. Fellow, Co-operative Secretaries Assoc.; FCIS. *Recreations:* golf, gardening. *Address:* 1 Miller Street, Manchester, 4; Coedway, Bristol Road, Stonehouse, Glos. *T:* Stonehouse 167. *Club:* Royal Commonwealth Society.

**LOW,** family name of **Baron Aldington.**

**LOW, Alan Roberts;** Governor, Reserve Bank of New Zealand, since 1967; *b* 11 Jan. 1916; 4th *s* of Benjamin H. Low and Sarah Low; *m* 1940, Kathleen Mary Harrow; one *s* two *d*. *Educ:* Timaru Main Sch.; Timaru Boys' High Sch.; Canterbury University College. MA 1937. Joined Reserve Bank of New Zealand, 1938; Economic Adviser, 1951; Asst Governor, 1960; Deputy Governor, 1962; Governor, 1967. Army Service, 1942-44; on loan to Economic Stabilisation Commission, 1944-46. *Publications:* contributions to Economic Record. *Recreations:* gardening, music, reading. *Address:* 83 Penrose Street, Lower Hutt, New Zealand. *T:* 699-526. *Club:* Wellington (NZ).

**LOW, David Morrice,** FRSL; Writer; *b* 14 Sept. 1890; *o c* of late D. M. Low; *m* 1st, 1915, Heather Belle (*d* 1953), *d* of late Major A. T. Hancocks, DL, JP, Wolverley Court, Worcestershire; 2nd, 1956, Dorothy Margaret, *d* of R. W. Butters, Bury St Edmund's. *Educ:* Westminster Sch. (scholar); Oriel Coll., Oxford (scholar); 1st Class Mods, 1911; 2nd Class Lit. Hum., 1914; BA 1914; MA 1915; Assistant Master, Marlborough Coll., 1914-18; Westminster Sch., 1919-21; Rector of Kelvinside Academy, Glasgow, 1921-29; temp. Junior Asst Air Ministry, 1941-43; temp. Senior Assistant Foreign Office, 1943-45. Classical Lecturer and Sub-Dean Arts Faculty, King's Coll., London, 1945-57. Chairman, English Association, 1959-64. *Publications:* Kelvinside Academy, 1878-1928; Gibbon's Journal, 1929; Edward Gibbon, 1937; London is London, 1949; Norman Douglas, A Selection, 1955; A Century of Writers, 1855-1955, 1955; Essays and Studies Collected for the English Association, 1955; Gibbon's The Decline and Fall, abridged, 1960; Trends in English Pronunciation, 1960; contributor to: Cambridge Biblio. of English Literature; Encyclopædia Britannica; Encyclopædia Amer.; *trans:* N. Ginzburg, Voices in the Evening, 1963; Family Sayings, 1967; E. Patti, Roman Chronicle, 1965; *novels:* Twice Shy, 1933; This Sweet Work, 1935. *Address:* 115 Chatsworth Court, Pembroke Road, W8. *Club:* Garrick.

**LOW, Sir Francis,** Kt, *cr* 1943; *b* 19 Nov. 1893; *s* of late Francis Low, Finzean, Aberdeenshire, and Janet Harper; *m* 1926, Margaret H. Adams; two *s* one *d*. *Educ:* Robert Gordon's Coll., Aberdeen. Joined Aberdeen Free Press, 1910; commissioned 4th Bn Gordon Highlanders, 1916; served in Mesopotamia with 6th Bn Hampshire Regt, 1917-19; Intelligence Staff I Corps, 1918; Special Service Officer, GHQ Mesopotamian Expeditionary Force, 1919; Chief Reporter, Aberdeen Free Press, 1920; Sub-Editor, Times of India, 1922; Editor, Evening News of India, 1923; News Editor, Times of India, 1925; Assistant Editor, 1926; Editor, 1932-48; London Editorial Representative, 1948-53; Chairman, St Dunstan's War Appeal Cttee, Bombay, 1940-46; President, Bombay YMCA, 1943-48; Vice-President, Bombay Branch Royal Asiatic Society, 1944-48; Chairman, India Section, Empire Press Union, 1946-48; Leader, Indian delegation, Sixth Imperial Press Conference, London, 1946; FJI; President: Commonwealth Correspondents' Assoc., 1951; London Association of British Empire Newspapers Overseas, 1952-53; Hon. Secretary, East India Assoc., 1954-66; Vice-President, Royal Society for India, Pakistan and Ceylon; Chairman Cttee of Management, YMCA Indian Student Hostel, London; President, Woking Division Conservative Association, Chairman, 1957-60; President,

London District, The Boys' Brigade, 1954-67. *Publications:* Struggle for Asia, 1955; articles on visits to the N. Africa, Malaya, and Burma war theatres, 1940-44. *Recreations:* golf and hill climbing. *Address:* High Gardens, Hook Heath, Woking, Surrey. *T:* Woking 63211. *Clubs:* Athenæum; Royal Bombay Yacht, Willingdon Sports (Bombay).

**LOW, Graeme Campbell;** Puisne Judge, High Court, Uganda, 1950-54, retired; *b* 1902. *Educ:* Charterhouse; Magdalen Coll., Oxford. Called to the Bar, Inner Temple, 1926; Resident Magistrate, Uganda, 1935. Served War of 1939-45. *Address:* c/o Barclays Bank, 27 Regent Street, SW1.

**LOW, Sir James (Richard) Morrison-,** 3rd Bt, *cr* 1908; DFH, CEng, MIEE; Director, Osborne & Hunter Ltd, Glasgow and Kirkcaldy, since 1956 (Electrical Engineer with firm, 1952-); *b* 3 Aug. 1925; *s* of Sir Walter John Morrison-Low, 2nd Bt and Dorothy Ruth de Quincey Quincey (*d* 1946); *S* father 1955; *m* 1953, Ann Rawson Gordon; one *s* three *d. Educ:* Ardvreck; Harrow; Merchiston. Served Royal Corps of Signals, 1943-47; demobilised with rank of Captain. Faraday House Engineering Coll., 1948-52. *Recreations:* shooting, piping. *Heir: s* Richard Walter Low, *b* 4 Aug. 1959. *Address:* Kilmaron Castle, Cupar, Fife. *T:* Cupar 2248. *Clubs:* Royal and Ancient Golf (St Andrews); Royal Scottish Pipers Society (Edinburgh).

**LOW, Mabel Bruce,** RBA 1919; artist; *d* of late Dr Robert Bruce Low, CB, MD; *m* 1933, Alexander Chisholm. *Educ:* Westminster School of Art; Edinburgh School of Art; Dresden. Colour print purchased by Contemporary Art Society for British Museum, 1939, and by Sunderland Corporation, 1940; Water Colours purchased by Bournemouth Corporation, 1940, 1953, 1961 and 1966. Past President, Southbourne Art Society. Vice-President, Society of Women Artists. *Address:* 14 Burford Court, Manor Road, Bournemouth, Hants. *T:* Bournemouth 23815.

**LOWE, Group Captain Cyril Nelson,** MC, DFC; BA Cambridge; late OC, RAF Station, Amman, Trans Jordan; *b* 7 Oct. 1891; *s* of Rev. C. W. Nelson Lowe, MA; *m* Ethel Mary Watson; one *s* two *d. Educ:* Dulwich Coll.; Pembroke Coll., Cambridge. Rugby Blue at Cambridge, 1911-12-13; first played for England v S. Africa in 1913, and subsequently gained 25 International Caps; Commission Aug. 1914 in ASC, and qualified for 1914 Star; seconded to Royal Flying Corps, 1916; No. 11 Squadron RFC France, 1916-17; 24 Squadron RFC, France, 1918 (MC, DFC). *Address:* Little Brook, Burrow Hill, Chobham, Surrey.

**LOWE, Sir David,** Kt 1962; CBE 1950; Chairman: Elvingston Estates Ltd, since 1962; British Society for the Promotion of Vegetable Research; *b* 12 May 1899; *s* of late Provost David Lowe, Musselburgh; *m* 1932, Katherine Cecile Jane, *d* of late Roderick Ross, CVO, CBE, Edinburgh; three *d. Educ:* Musselburgh Grammar Sch. President, National Farmers' Union of Scotland, 1948-49; President, Edinburgh Chamber of Commerce and Manufactures, 1958-60 and 1962-63; Governor, Edinburgh and East of Scotland College of Agriculture. Chairman: David Lowe & Sons Ltd, 1943-63; Thomson & Mathieson Ltd, 1959-65; Livingston Development Corporation (New Town), 1962-65; Scottish Horticultural Advisory Cttee, 1961-69. Director, National Seed Development Organisation Ltd. Member: Agricultural Research Council, 1954-64 (Dep. Chairman, 1958-64); Agricultural Marketing Development Exec. Cttee, 1962-68; Cinematograph Films Council, 1958-63. Chairman, Scottish Agric. & Horti. Apprenticeship Scheme, 1949-. Vice-President, Scottish Council Development & Industry, 1963-68. Trustee, Scottish Country Industries Development Trust, 1960-66. Hon. DSc Edinburgh, 1966. FRSE 1961; Fellow, Royal Agricultural Socs, 1970. *Recreation:* plant breeding. *Address:* Elvingston, Gladsmuir, East Lothian. *T:* Longniddry 2128. *Club:* Royal Aero.

**LOWE, David Nicoll,** OBE 1946; MA, BSc; FRSE; Secretary, Carnegie United Kingdom Trust, 1954-70; *b* 9 Sept. 1909; *s* of George Black Lowe and Jane Nicoll, Arbroath, Angus; *m* 1939, Muriel Enid Bryer, CSP; one *s* three *d. Educ:* Arbroath High Sch.; St Andrews Univ. (Kitchener Scholar). MA 1931; BSc (1st Class Hons Botany) 1934; President Union, 1933-34; President Students' Representative Council, 1934-35; Founder President, University Mountaineering Club: Asst Secretary British Assoc. for the Advancement of Science, 1935-40, Secretary 1946-54. War Cabinet Secretariat, 1940-42 and 1945-46; Ministry of Production, 1942-45. Joint Hon. Secretary, Society of Visiting Scientists, 1952-54; Member Executive Cttee, Scottish Council of Social Service. Contributor to Annual Register, 1947-59. Chairman, Scottish Congregational Coll., 1961-68. Member, Countryside Commn for Scotland, 1968-. *Recreations:* those of his family and gardening. *Address:* Caddam, Perth Road, Crieff, Perthshire. *Club:* Athenæum.

**LOWE, Air Vice-Marshal Douglas Charles,** DFC 1943; AFC 1946; Senior Air Staff Officer, Near East Air Force, since 1969; *b* 14 March 1922; *s* of John William Lowe; *m* 1944, Doreen Elizabeth (*née* Nichols); one *s* one *d. Educ:* Reading School. Joined RAF, 1940; No 75 (NZ) Sqdn, 1943; Bomber Comd Instructors' Sch., 1945; RAF Coll., Cranwell, 1947; Exam. Wing CFS, 1950; Air Min. Operational Requirements, 1955; OC No 148 Sqdn, 1959; Exchange Officer, HQ SAC, USAF, 1961; Stn Comdr Cranwell, 1963; idc 1966; DOR 2 (RAF), MoD (Air), 1967. *Recreations:* gardening, domestic odd-jobbing, photography, theatre, music. *Address:* Westland Cottage, Manor House, Byfleet, Surrey. *T:* Byfleet 43171. *Club:* Royal Air Force.

**LOWE, Douglas Gordon Arthur,** QC 1964; Barrister-at-Law; Recorder of Lincoln, since 1964; Deputy Chairman, Warwickshire QS, since 1965; *b* 7 Aug. 1902; *o s* of Arthur John Lowe; *m* 1930, Karen, *e d* of Surgeon Einar Thamsen; one *s. Educ:* Highgate Sch.; Pembroke Coll., Cambridge (Exhibitioner, MA). Called to the Bar, Inner Temple, 1928; Bencher, Inner Temple, 1957. Councillor, Hampstead Borough Council, 1940-44; Governor, Highgate Sch., 1939- (Chairman, 1965-); Chairman, Oxford Mental Health Tribunal, 1962-64. Member, Criminal Injuries Compensation Board, 1965-. *Publication:* (with Sir Arthur Porritt) Athletics, 1929. *Recreations:* lawn tennis, golf, gardening; formerly athletics, cricket, association football and Eton fives. (President Cambridge Univ. Athletic Club; Assoc. Football amd Athletics Blue; winner Olympic 800 meters, 1924 and 1928; Hon. Secretary Amateur Athletic Assoc., 1931-38). *Address:* Yeomans, Wellington Avenue, Virginia Water, Surrey; 12 King's Bench Walk, Temple, EC4. *T:* 01-353 7008. *Clubs:* Carlton; MCC; Achilles; Hawks (Cambridge).

**LOWE, Air Vice-Marshal Sir Edgar (Noel),** KBE 1962 (CBE 1945); CB 1947; Director General of Supply Co-ordination, Ministry of Defence, since 1966 (Inspector General of Codification and Standardisation, 1964); *b* 1905; *s* of late Albert Henry Lowe, Church Stretton, Shropshire; *m* 1948, Mary McIlwraith, *o d* of George M. Lockhart, Stair House, Stair, Ayrshire; one *s* one *d.* Served India, 1934-38; psa 1939; served in France 1939-40 (despatches); Air Commodore, Director of Organisation (Forecasting and Planning), Air Ministry, 1945-47; idc 1949; ADC to the King, 1949-52, to the Queen, 1952-57; Directing Staff, RAF Staff Coll., Bracknell, 1950-51; Director of Organisation, Air Ministry, 1951-53; Deputy Asst Chief of Staff (Logistics), SHAPE, 1953-56; Senior Air Staff Officer, HQ No. 41 Group, RAF, 1956-58; AOC No. 40 Group, RAF, 1958-61; Director-General of Equipment, Air Ministry, 1961-64. *Address:* Wyndford, 97 Harestone Hill, Caterham, Surrey. *T:* Caterham 45757. *Club:* Royal Air Force.

**LOWE, Sir (Francis) Gordon,** 2nd Bt, *cr* 1918; Director Gordon Lowes Ltd; Lawn Tennis Journalist; *b* Edgbaston, 21 June 1884; *e s* of Rt Hon. Sir Francis William Lowe, 1st Bt, PC, MP; *S* father, 1929; *m* 1926, Honor Dorothy, *d* of late Lieut-Colonel H. S. Woolrych; one *s.* *Educ:* Charterhouse; Clare Coll., Cambridge. Gained International distinction at Lawn Tennis over a period of 25 years; has won innumerable championships, at home and abroad; was a member of the British team which brought the Davis Cup back from Australia in 1912; represented England against Spain in 1921, against Italy in 1922 and against Poland in 1925; reached semi-final of singles at Wimbledon 1911 and 1923; was in the final of the doubles with the late A. H. Lowe in 1914 and 1921; won covered Court Championship of the World, 1920; joined Indian Army Reserve of Officers in 1916, and went to Mesopotamia, 1917-19 (despatches). *Heir: s* Francis Reginald Gordon Lowe [*b* 8 Feb. 1931; *m* 1961, Francesca Cornelia Steinkopf; two *s.* *Educ:* Stowe; Clare Coll., Cambridge]. *Address:* 8 Seymour Walk, SW10. *T:* 01-352 6925; (business) Gordon Lowes Ltd, 173-174 Sloane Street, SW1. *T:* 01-235 8484/5/6. *Clubs:* Queen's, All England Lawn Tennis.

**LOWE, Sir Gordon;** *see* Lowe, Sir (Francis) Gordon.

**LOWE, John Eric Charles,** MVO 1965; MBE 1937; *b* 11 Aug. 1907; 6th *s* of late John Frederick Lowe; *m* 1935, Trudy (*née* Maybury); one *s* two *d.* *Educ:* Burghley Road Sch., Highgate. Vice-Consul, Jibuti, 1930-37, Harar, 1940; Political Officer, Aden Protectorate, 1940; served in HM Forces, Somaliland and Ethiopia, 1941-46; Senior Asst, Foreign Office, 1947-49; Acting Consul, Suez, 1949; Vice-Consul, Beira, 1950; Vice-Consul, Hamburg, 1951 and Frankfurt, 1953; 2nd Secretary, Helsinki, 1953; Political Agent's Representative, Mina-Al-Ahmadi (Kuwait), 1956; Vice-Consul, Leopoldville, 1959; Consul, Khartoum, 1962; Consul-General, Basra, 1965-67; retired, Sept. 1967. Order of the Two Niles (Sudan), 1965. *Recreations:* gardening, golf, sailing. *Address:* Fairview, New Road, Rotherfield, Sussex. *T:* Rotherfield 651.

**LOWE, John Evelyn,** MA, FSA; Director, The Weald and Downland Open Air Museum, West Dean, Sussex, since 1969; *b* 23 April 1928; *s* of late Arthur Holden Lowe; *m* 1956, Susan Helen Sanderson; two *s* one *d.* *Educ:* Wellington Coll., Berks; New Coll., Oxford. Victoria and Albert Museum, Dept of Woodwork, 1953-56; Deputy Story Editor, Pinewood Studios, 1956-57; Victoria and Albert Museum: Dept of Ceramics, 1957-61; Assistant to the Director, 1961-64; Dir, City Museum and Art Gall., Birmingham, 1964-69. *Publications:* articles on the applied arts and foreign travel. *Recreations:* reading and fishing. *Address:* Duffryn, Liphook, Hants. *T:* Liphook 3104.

**LOWELL, Robert (Traill Spence), Jr,** AB; poet and playwright; Professor of Literature, Essex University, since 1970; *b* Boston, Mass, USA, 1 March 1917; *s* of Robert Traill Spence and Charlotte (*née* Winslow); *m* one *d.* *Educ:* Kenyon Coll., Ohio; Harvard Univ. Awarded the American Academy of Arts and Letters Prize and Pulitzer Prize, 1947; Guggenheim Fellowship and Consultant in poetry, Library of Congress, 1947-48; Vis. Fellow, All Souls Coll., Oxford, 1970. guinness Poetry Award, National Book Award, 1959. Member of American Academy of Arts and Letters. *Publications:* Land of Unlikeness, 1944; Lord Weary's Castle, 1946; The Mills of the Kavanaughs, 1951; Life Studies: New Poems and an Autobiographical Fragment, 1959; Imitations, 1961; For the Union Dead, 1964; Old Glory (play), 1966 (US 1965); Benito Cereno (London 1967); Near the Ocean (poems), 1967; The Voyage (poems), 1968; Prometheus Bound (trans.), 1970. *Address:* 15 West 67th Street, New York, USA; University of Essex, Wivenhoe Park, Colchester, Essex.

**LOWENFELD, Margaret Frances Jane,** MRCS, LRCP; Director of Training (formerly Physician-in-Charge), The Institute of Child Psychology; *b* London, 4 Feb. 1890; *d* of Henry Lowenfeld and Alice E. Evens. *Educ:* Cheltenham Ladies' Coll. Entered London School (Royal Free Hospital) of Medicine for Women, 1912; Intermediate MB, BS, 1914; MRCS, LRCP, 1918; House Surgeon, South London Women's Hospital, 1918; MO, British Typhus Unit, Poland, MO to American YMCA working with Polish Army and POW Dept, and Secretary, European Student Relief, Warsaw, for students at work in reestablishment of Universities, 1919-23; Medical Research Scholarship and Muirhead Scholarship, held 1923-24 at Royal Hospital for Sick Children, Glasgow, for work on Acute Rheumatism and Social Conditions; Alfred Langton Research Scholarship; Obstetric Dept, Royal Free Hospital, 1924-25. Founded Institute of Child Psychology, 1928; Consultant Columbia University. Research in Contemporary Cultures, New York, 1950. Member of Medical Women's Federation; Member RMPA. Fellow British Psychological Society; FRSM; Member, International Council of Psychologists. *Publications:* Play in Childhood, 1935, repr. 1969; The Lowenfeld Mosaic Test, 1954. Contributions, since 1939, to Journal of Mental Science, American Journal of Orthopsych., American Journal Psychotherapy, Proc. RSM, Lancet, etc. *Address:* 92 Harley Street, W1. *T:* 01-935 3469; Eastwing, Cherry Orchards, Cholesbury, Tring, Herts.

**LOWENSTEIN, Prof. Otto Egon,** FRS 1955; FRSE; DSc (Glasgow); PhD (Birmingham); DrPhil (Munich); Mason Professor of Zoology and Comparative Physiology, Birmingham University, since 1952; *b* 24 Oct. 1906; *s* of Julius Lowenstein and Mathilde Heusinger. *Educ:* Neues Realgymnasium, Munich; Munich Univ. Asst, Munich Univ., 1931-33; Research Scholar, Birmingham Univ., 1933-37; Asst Lecturer, University College, Exeter, 1937-38; Lecturer, Glasgow Univ., 1938-52. President: Assoc. for the Study of Animal Behaviour, 1961-64; Section D, British Assoc., 1962; Institute of Biology, 1965-67; Member

Council, Royal Society, 1968-69. *Publications:* Revision of 6th edn of A Textbook of Zoology (Parker and Haswell), Vol. I; The Senses, 1966. Scientific papers on Sensory Physiology in various learned journals. *Recreations:* music, travel, painting. *Address:* Dept of Zoology and Comparative Physiology, The University, Birmingham, 15. *T:* 021-472 1301, Ext. 108.

**LOWMAN, Rev. Canon Edward (Sydney Charles);** Canon Residentiary of Portsmouth Cathedral 1962-69, now Honorary Canon; *b* 20 Feb. 1908; *s* of William Sydney George Lowman and Margaret Ellen Lowman (*née* Ford); *m* 1947, Betty Margaret (*née* Jolly); one *d. Educ:* Ashford Grammar Sch., Kent; King's Coll., London; Bishops' Coll., Cheshunt. Royal Air Force, 1924-28. Deacon, 1938; Priest, 1939; Curate of Heckmondwike, Yorks, 1938-41; Curate of Bray, Berks, 1941-45; Vicar of Bray, Berks, 1945-57; Cathedral Chaplain, Portsmouth, 1958-62. *Address:* Semaphore House, Battery Row, Portsmouth. *T:* Portsmouth 20470. *Club:* Royal Naval (Portsmouth).

**LOWNDES, Brigadier Montacute W. W. S.;** *see* Selby-Lowndes.

**LOWREY, Air Comdt Dame Alice,** DBE 1960; RRC 1954; Matron-in-Chief, Princess Mary's Royal Air Force Nursing Service, 1959-63 (retired); *b* 8 April 1905; *d* of William John Lowrey and Agnes Lowrey (formerly Walters). *Educ:* Yorkshire; Training Sch., Sheffield Royal Hospital. Joined PMRAFNS, 1932; served in Iraq and Aden. Principal Matron: HQ, MEAF and FEAF, 1956-58; HQ, Home Command and Technical Training Command, 1958-59. Air Commandant, 1959. Officer Sister Order of St John, 1959. *Address:* c/o Midland Bank, Northwood, Middlesex.

**LOWRY, Laurence Stephen,** RA 1962 (ARA 1955); RBA 1934; Hon. MA (Manchester); Hon. LLD (Manchester) 1961; Member National Society; Member London Group; *b* Manchester, 1 Nov. 1887; *o s* of late R. S. M. Lowry and Elizabeth Hobson, Manchester. Exhibited, Paris Salon d'Automme and many places abroad; One Man Shows: Lefevre Gallery, 1939, 1943, 1945, 1948, 1951, 1953, 1956, 1958, 1963, 1964; Sheffield Art Gallery, 1962; Retrospective Exhibition, Tate Gallery, 1966; Stone Gallery, Newcastle, 1967; Official purchases: Tate Gallery; Royal Scottish Academy; Contemporary Art Society; Glasgow, Liverpool, Birmingham, Manchester, Stoke, Aberdeen, Salford, Leeds, Leicester, Nottingham, Southampton; Ministry of Information; Ministry of Works; British Council; Arts Council; Royal Academy (Chantrey Bequest). BBC Television Film, 1957. *Address:* The Elms, Stalybridge Road, Mottram in Longdendale, Cheshire.

**LOWRY, Mrs Noreen Margaret (Nina);** Metropolitan Stipendiary Magistrate, since 1967; *b* 6 Sept. 1925; *er d* of John Collins, MC, Little Arnewood House, Sway, Hants; *m* 1st, 1950, Edward Lucas Gardner, QC (marr. diss., 1962); one *s* one *d*; 2nd, 1963, Richard John Lowry, *qv*; one *d. Educ:* Bedford High Sch.; Birmingham Univ. LLB Birmingham, 1947. Called to the Bar, Gray's Inn, 1948. Criminal practice on S Eastern Circuit, Central Criminal Court, Inner London Sessions, etc., practising as Miss Nina Collins. *Recreations:* theatre, sun-bathing, cooking. *Address:* 44 Upper Mall, W6. *T:* 01-748 7773.

**LOWRY, Mrs Richard;** *see* Lowry, Mrs N. M.

**LOWRY, Richard John,** QC 1968; Barrister-at-law since 1949; *b* 23 June 1924; *s* of Geoffrey Charles Lowry, OBE, TD, and Margaret Spencer Lowry; *m* 1963, Noreen Margaret Lowry, *qv*; one *d. Educ:* St Edward's Sch.; University College, Oxford. RAF, 1943; qualified as pilot and commnd, 1944; No. 228 Group Staff Officer, India, 1945; Flt-Lieut, 1946. University College, Oxford, 1942-43 and 1946-48; BA, 1948, MA 1949. Called to Bar, Inner Temple, 1949. Member, General Council of Bar, 1965-69. Dep. Chm., Herts QS, 1968. *Recreations:* theatre, swimming, fossicking; formerly rowing (Oxford Univ. wartime VIII, 1943). *Address:* 3 Temple Gardens, Temple, EC4. *T:* 01-353 1662; 44 Upper Mall, W6. *T:* 01-748 7773. *Clubs:* Garrick; Leander (Henley-on-Thames).

**LOWRY, Robert Lynd Erskine; Hon. Mr Justice Lowry;** Judge of the High Court of Justice in Northern Ireland, since 1964; *b* 30 Jan. 1919; *o s* of late William Lowry (Rt Hon. Mr Justice Lowry) and Catherine Hughes Lowry, 3rd *d* of Rev. R. J. Lynd, DD; *m* 1945, Mary Audrey, *o d* of John Martin, 43 Myrtlefield Park, Belfast; three *d. Educ:* Royal Belfast Academical Institution; Jesus Coll., Cambridge. Entrance Exhibn. (Classics); Scholar, 1939; 1st Class Classical Tripos, Part I, 1939, Part II 1940; MA 1944. Served HM Forces, 1940-46; Tunisia, 1942-43 with 38 Irish Inf. Bde; commissioned Royal Irish Fusiliers, 1941; Major, 1945; Hon. Colonel, 7th Bn Royal Irish Fusiliers, 1969- (5th Bn, 1967-68). Called to the Bar of N Ireland, 1947; Bencher of the Inn of Court, 1955-; QC (N Ireland), 1956. Counsel to HM Attorney-General, 1948-56; Member Departmental Cttees on Charities, Legal Aid and Registration of Title; Dep. Chrmn., Boundaries Commission (NI) 1964-; Chairman: Interim Boundary Commission (NI Constituencies), 1967; Permanent Boundary Commn, 1969-. Governor, Royal Belfast Academical Institution and Richmond Lodge School; Chairman Governing Bodies Assoc. (NI), 1965. *Recreations:* golf, showjumping (Chm., SJAI Executive, 1970). *Address:* White Hill, Crossgar, Co. Down. *T:* Crossgar 397. *Club:* Ulster (Belfast).

**LOWRY-CORRY,** family name of **Earl of Belmore.**

**LOWRY-CORRY, Lt-Col Sir Henry (Charles),** Kt, *cr* 1954; MC 1916; DL 1946; Vice Lieutenant in the County of Suffolk, 1957-64; Chairman West Suffolk County Council, 1950-57; *b* 20 Feb. 1887; *er s* of Colonel the Hon. H. W. Lowry-Corry, Edwardstone, Suffolk; *heir pres.* to 8th Earl of Belmore, *qv*; *m* 1920, Betty, *d* of Colonel D. J. Proby, Elton Hall, Peterborough; two *s* two *d. Educ:* Eton; RMA, Woolwich. Served in RHA and RFA, 1906-35; served European War, 1914-18; retired as Major; served War of 1939-45, in TA, as Lieut-Colonel, Middle East. Chairman: Suffolk T & AFA, 1947-53; West Suffolk CC, 1950-57. *Address:* Edwardstone Hall, Boxford, Suffolk. *T:* Boxford 233. *Club:* United Service. *See also General Sir Michael Carver.*

**LOWSON, Sir Denys (Colquhoun Flowerdew),** 1st Bt, *cr* 1951; MA (Oxon); FCIS; *b* 22 Jan. 1906; *o s* of late J. G. Flowerdew Lowson, JP, PhD, Balthayock, Perthshire, and Adelaide, *d* of Col Courtenay Scott; *m* 1936, Patricia, OStJ, *yr d* of 1st Baron Strathcarron, PC, KC, LLD; one *s* two *d. Educ:* Winchester; Christ Church, Oxford (Hons in History and Law). Called to Bar, Inner Temple, 1930; Member Royal Company of Archers (Queen's Body Guard for Scotland), 1948; Sheriff of City of London, 1939; Member for Coleman Street, Court of Common Council, 1940; Alderman City of London, Vintry Ward, 1942-68; transferring to the Ward of Bridge Without on becoming Senior Alderman of the City of London, 1968; one of HM Lieutenants for City of London, 1942; Lord Mayor of London, 1950-51 (Festival of Britain year). A Church Commissioner for England, 1948-62; Life Governor and Almoner of St Bartholomew's Hospital and Chairman, Finance Cttee, Governor of Bridewell and Bethlem Hospitals, and of the Royal Hospitals, Vice-President, St Mary's Hospital, Paddington to 1948 and reappointed to Board of St Bartholomew's Hospital under National Health Act, 1948-67; Hon. Treasurer, Princess Louise Kensington Hospital for Children, 1938-48, and Vice-President, League of Mercy to 1948; Master of Worshipful Company of Glaziers, 1947-48, of Worshipful Company of Loriners, 1950, of Gold and Silver Wyre Drawers, 1951; Hon. Member Court of Assistants, Haberdashers Company, 1951; Prime Warden, Shipwrights Company, 1955-56; Past Grand Warden, United Grand Lodge of England; Vice-President St John Ambulance Bde (Prince of Wales No. 1 District), and Dep. Commissioner, No. 1 District, 1944-66; Member Exec. Council, Lord Mayor's National Flood and Tempest Distress Fund, 1953; Original Member, Victoria (Australia) Promotion Cttee, 1956; Chairman: Commonwealth Producers' Organisation, 1957; British section, Council of European Municipalities; Governor, The Honourable The Irish Society, 1958-61; President, British Philatelic Assoc., Ltd, 1958-61; Vice-President, Royal Over-Seas League, 1959; President, Chartered Institute of Secretaries, 1962-63. Hon. Colonel 290 Regt, City of London RA, 1950; a member of London County Council for cities of London and Westminster, 1949-52; a life Governor of University College, Dundee, and of Royal Shakespeare Theatre; High Steward of Stratford-upon-Avon, 1952; Hon. Freeman, Cities of London (Ontario), Nanaimo (Vancouver Is.), Granby (Quebec), Halifax (Nova Scotia), and Lewes (Sussex). KJStJ; Order of Mercy; Grand Officer Order of Orange Nassau (Netherlands); Kt Commander Royal Order of the Dannebrog (Denmark); Kt Commander, with Star, Royal Order of St Olaf (Norway); Kt Commander of the Lion of Finland. *Recreations:* shooting, shot for Oxford against Cambridge (Chancellor's Plate), Harvard and Yale; travelling and philately. *Heir: s* Ian Patrick Lowson, OStJ, *b* 4 Sept. 1944. *Address:* Brantridge Park, Balcombe, Sussex; 56 Gresham Street, EC2. *T:* 01-606 7131. *Clubs:* Bath, Bucks, MCC; St James's (Montreal)

*See also Earl of Kinnoull.*

**LOWTHER,** family name of **Earl of Lonsdale** and **Viscount Ullswater.**

**LOWTHER, Viscount; Hugh Clayton Lowther,** *b* 27 May 1949; *s* and *heir* of 7th Earl of Lonsdale, *qv.*

**LOWTHER, Capt. Hon. Anthony George,** MBE 1954; DL; *b* 23 Sept. 1925; *yr s* of Viscount Lowther (*d* 1949); granted 1954, title, rank and precedence of an earl's son which would have been his had his father survived to succeed to earldom of Lonsdale; *m* 1958, Lavinia, *o c* of late Thomas H. Joyce, San Francisco, California; one *s* three *d. Educ:* Eton; RMA, Sandhurst. Joined Army, 1943; 2nd Lieut, 12th Royal Lancers, 1946; served in Egypt, 1946; Palestine, 1946-47; Malaya, 1951-54; Captain, 1952; retired 1954. Managing Dir, Whitbysteads Hill Farms Ltd; Director: Lakeland Investments Ltd; Lowther Builders Ltd; Carlisle (New) Racecourse Co. Ltd. Chm., Cumbria Police Authority; CC Westmorland, 1960 (Mem., Cumberland River Authority); DL 1964, High Sheriff 1964, Westmorland. Dep. Master 1956, Jt Master 1957, Ullswater Foxhounds. *Address:* Whitbysteads, Askham, Penrith, Cumberland. *T:* Hackthorp 284. *Clubs:* White's, National Sporting; Cumberland County (Carlisle).

**LOWTHER, Sir Guy;** *see* Lowther, Sir (W.) G.

**LOWTHER, Col John George,** CBE 1953; DSO 1919; MC; TD; DL; JP Northants; *b* 1885; 2nd *s* of late G. W. Lowther of Swillington House, Leeds, and *b* of late Lieut-Colonel Sir C. B. Lowther, 4th Bt, CB, DSO; *m* 1911, Hon. Lilah White, *er d* of 3rd Baron Annaly; two *s* one *d. Educ:* Winchester. 2nd Lieut, Yorkshire Hussars, 1904; joined 11th Hussars, 1905; retired as Captain, 1919; served with Northamptonshire Yeomanry in European War (DSO, MC, despatches twice); Major in Northamptonshire Yeomanry, 1919; Major Commanding NY Armoured Car Coy, 1921; Col, 1928; Commanded 4th Bn Northamptonshire Regt, 1924-28, 1939-40; Infantry D. and M. School, 1940-41; Hon. Colonel 1st Northants Yeomanry, 1931-50; Sector Comdr, Home Guard, 1942-50; Joint Master of Pytchley Hounds, 1923-40 and 1949-60; County Councillor (Northants), 1939-49; County Alderman, 1949-70. Chairman, Little Bowden Justices (Petty Sessional Court), 1942-59. *Recreation:* hunting. *Address:* 2 Wesley Street, W1. *T:* 01-935 0741; Guilsborough Court, Northampton. *T:* Guilsborough 208. *Club:* Buck's.

*See also Lieut-Colonel Sir W. G. Lowther, Bt.*

**LOWTHER, Lt-Col Sir (William) Guy,** 5th Bt, *cr* 1824; OBE 1952; DL; retired; one of HM Body Guard of the Honourable Corps of Gentlemen-at-Arms since 1962; *b* 9 Oct. 1912; *o s* of Lieut-Colonel Sir Charles Bingham Lowther, 4th Bt, CB, DSO, and Marjorie Noel (*d* 1925), *d* of Thomas Fielden, MP, of Grimston, Yorks; *S* father, 1949; *m* 1939, Grania Suzanne Douglas, *y d* of late Major Douglas Campbell, of Blythswood, and the Hon. Mrs Douglas Campbell; one *s* one *d. Educ:* Winchester; RMC, Sandhurst. 2nd Lieut, 8th Hussars, 1932; served Palestine, 1936 (despatches); War of 1939-45, in W. Desert (prisoner); Captain, 1941; Major, 1945; Lieut-Colonel, 1951; Staff Coll., 1947; Staff appointment, 1948 and 1949. Served Korea, 1950-51, Lieut-Colonel comd 8th Hussars (despatches); commanding BAOR, 1952-53; retired Jan. 1954. Comr, St John Ambulance Bde for Denbighshire, 1966. High Sheriff 1959, DL 1969, Denbighshire. CStJ. *Heir: s* Charles Douglas Lowther [*b* 22 Jan. 1946; *m* 1969, Melanie Musgrave, *d* of late R. C. Musgrave and of Mrs J. S. H. Douglas, Ravensheugh, Selkirk]. *Address:* Erbistock Hall, near Wrexham. *T:* Overton 244. *Club:* Cavalry.

*See also Colonel J. G. Lowther.*

**LOWTHER CLARKE, Rev. William Kemp;** *see* Clarke.

**LOWTHIAN, George Henry,** CBE 1963 (MBE 1949); General Secretary, Amalgamated Union of Building Trade Workers, since 1951; Part-time Member, British Transport Docks Board, since 1963; *b* 30 Jan. 1908; *s* of Ernest and Margaret Lowthian; *m* 1933, Florence Hartley; one *s* one *d. Educ:* Creighton Sch., Carlisle. Branch Secretary, 1930-45; District Secretary, 1934-45; Exec. Council, 1940-45; Divisional Secretary, 1945-50; TUC General Council, 1951-, Chairman, 1963-64; Chairman, Industrial Training Council, 1960-62; Chairman, Board of Directors, Industrial Training Service, 1965-. *Recreations:* photography, motoring. *Address:* 17 Holly Way, Mitcham, Surrey. *T:* 01-764 2200.

**LOYD, Christopher Lewis,** MC 1943; Landowner; *b* 1 June 1923; 3rd and *o surv s* of late Arthur Thomas Loyd, OBE, JP, Lord Lieutenant of Berkshire, Lockinge, Wantage, Berks, and Dorothy, *d* of late Paul Ferdinand Willert, Headlington, Oxford; *m* 1957, Joanna, *d* of Captain Arthur Turberville Smith-Bingham, Evans Close, Malmesbury, Wilts; two *s* one *d*. *Educ:* Eton; King's Coll., Cambridge (MA). Served 1942-46, with Coldstream Guards, Captain. ARICS 1952, FRICS 1955. Mem., Jockey Club. JP 1950, DL 1954, Berks; High Sheriff of Berkshire, 1961. *Address:* Lockinge, Wantage, Berkshire. *T:* East Hendred 265. *Clubs:* Boodle's, Buck's.

**LOYD, Sir Francis Alfred,** KCMG 1965 (CMG 1961); OBE 1954 (MBE 1951); Warden, Dominion Students Hall Trust; *b* 5 Sept. 1916; *s* of Major A. W. K. Loyd, Royal Sussex Regt; *m* 1946, Katharine Layzell Layzell; two *d*. *Educ:* Eton; Trinity Coll., Oxford (MA). District Officer, Kenya, 1939; Mil. Service, E Africa, 1940-42; Private Secretary to Governor of Kenya, 1942-45; HM Consul, Mega, Ethiopia, 1945; District Comdr, Kenya, 1947-55; Commonwealth Fund Fellowship to USA, 1953-54; Provincial Commissioner, 1956; Permanent Secretary, Governor's Office, 1962-63; HM Commissioner for Swaziland, 1964-68. *Recreations:* golf, fishing. *Address:* London House, Mecklenburgh Square WC1. *T:* 01-837 8888; 53 Park Road, Aldeburgh, Suffolk. *Club;* East India and Sports.

**LOYD, Gen. Sir Henry Charles,** GCVO 1965 (KCVO 1947); KCB 1943 (CB 1941); DSO 1918; MC; DL; Colonel of Coldstream Guards, 1945-66; *b* 1891; *s* of late Edward Henry Loyd; *m* 1922, Lady Moyra Brodrick, *y d* of 1st Earl of Midleton, KP, PC; one *s* one *d*. Served European War, 1914-18 (despatches, MC, DSO); commanded 3rd Batt. Coldstream Guards, 1929-32; Officer Commanding Coldstream Guards Regt and Regimental District, 1932-34; General Staff Officer, 1st Grade, War Office, 1934-36; Brigadier, General Staff, British Troops in Egypt, 1936-38; Commander 1st Infantry Brigade (Guards), 1938-39; Commander 2nd Division, 1939-40; Chief of General Staff, Home Forces, 1941-42; GOC-in-C Southern Command, 1942-43; General 1946; GOC London District, 1944-47; retired pay, 1947. DL Norfolk, 1954. *Address:* Mettingham Pines, Bungay, Suffolk. *T:* Bungay 2516. *Club:* Guards.

**LOYNES, John Barraclough de;** *see* de Loynes.

**LUARD, (David) Evan (Trant);** Fellow of St Antony's College, Oxford, since 1957; *b* 31 Oct. 1926; *s* of Colonel T. B. Luard, DSO, RM, Blackheath. *Educ:* Felsted; King's Coll., Cambridge (Maj. Schol.). Factory worker, 1949-50; HM Foreign Service, 1950-56; served in Hong Kong, Peking, London; resigned, 1956. Oxford City Councillor, 1958-61. MP (Lab) Oxford, 1966-70; Delegate, UN General Assembly, 1967-68; Parly Under-Sec., Foreign and Commonwealth Office, 1969-70. *Publications:* (part author) The Economic Development of Communist China, 1959 (2nd edn 1961); Britain and China, 1962; Nationality and Wealth, 1964; (ed) The Cold War, 1965; (ed) First Steps to Disarmament, 1966; (ed) The Evolution of International Organisations, 1967; Conflict and Peace in the Modern International System, 1968; (ed) The International Regulation of Frontier Disputes, 1970; articles in The China Quarterly, World Politics, World Today, The Annals. *Recreations:* music, painting. *Address:* St Antony's College, Oxford. *T:* 57534.

**LUARD, Evan;** *see* Luard, D. E. T.

**LUARD, Commander William Blaine,** OBE 1945; RN (retired); Naval Officer, Author and Inventor; *b* 2 Jan. 1897; *e s* of late Major William Du Cane Luard, RE, and late Maud, *d* of Sir Robert Blaine; *m* 1929, May Gladys Hayes. *Educ:* Mowden Sch., Brighton; RN Colleges, Osborne and Dartmouth. Invalided, 1917, as a Sub-Lieut. Contributor to numerous publications. Co-inventor, Addison-Luard Course and Distance Calculator; Sestral-Luard Navigator, and other navigational devices. Rejoined 1940; special duties (Croix de Guerre and palm, OBE). Co-inventor four devices in production during war. President Little Ship Club, 1944-54; Chairman, Cornwall Sea Fisheries Cttee, 1947-67. Special Study of French and English Fisheries. FIN. *Publications:* A Celtic Hurly-Burly, 1931; All Hands, 1933; Yachtsman's Modern Navigation and Practical Pilotage, 1933; Conquering Seas, 1935; Wild Goose Chase, 1936; ABC of Blue Water Navigation, 1936; Northern Deeps, 1937; Changing Horizons, 1946; Where the Tides Meet, 1948; The Little Ship Navigator, 1950 (rev. 1966, 1970). *Recreations:* yachting, cruising. *Address:* Trelour, Mawnan Smith, near Falmouth, Cornwall. *T:* Mawnan Smith 328. *Clubs:* United Service, Royal Yacht Squadron (Naval Member), Royal Cruising, Royal Ocean Racing, Little Ship; Royal Fowey Yacht (Fowey); Royal Cornwall Yacht (Falmouth); Ocean Cruising.

**LUBBOCK,** family name of **Baron Avebury.**

**LUBBOCK, Sir Alan,** Kt 1963; MA, FSA; *b* 13 Jan. 1897; 6th *s* of Frederic Lubbock, Ide Hill, Kent; *m* 1918, Helen Mary, *d* of late John Bonham-Carter, Adhurst St Mary, Petersfield; two *s*. *Educ:* Eton; King's Coll., Cambridge. Served in Royal Artillery, 1915-19 and 1939-45. Fellow of King's, 1922-28. Hants County Council, 1932 (Alderman 1939, Vice-Chairman 1948, Chairman 1955-67); JP (Hants) 1935; DL; High Sheriff of Hants, 1949-; Member: National Parks Commission, 1954-61; Royal Commission on Common Land, 1955; War Works Commission, 1959-64. Chairman: Council, Southampton Univ., 1957-69 (Pro-Chancellor, 1967); County Councils Assoc., 1965-69 (Vice-Chairman 1963); Nat. Foundn for Educnl Research, 1967. Hon. LLD Southampton, 1969. *Publication:* The Character of John Dryden, 1925. *Address:* Adhurst St Mary, Petersfield, Hants. *T:* Petersfield 3043. *Clubs:* Oxford and Cambridge; Leander; Hampshire (Winchester).

**LUBBOCK, Christopher William Stuart;** a Master of the Supreme Court (Queen's Bench Division), since 1970; *b* 4 Jan. 1920; 2nd *s* of late Captain Rupert Egerton Lubbock, Royal Navy; *m* 1947, Hazel Gordon, *d* of late Gordon Chapman; one *s* one *d*. *Educ:* Charterhouse; Brasenose Coll., Oxford. Served 1939-46, RNVR. Called to Bar, Inner Temple, 1947. *Recreation:* chatting to railway men, nurserymen, and music publishers. *Address:* Great Horkesley, Essex. *Clubs:* Brooks's, Pratt's.

**LUBBOCK, Eric Reginald;** Vice-President, Liberal Party, since 1963; *b* 29 Sept. 1928; *s* of Hon. Maurice Fox Pitt Lubbock and Hon. Mary Katherine Adelaide Stanley; *cousin* and *heir-pres.* to 3rd Baron Avebury, *qv; m* 1953, Kina Maria, *d* of Count Joseph O'Kelly de Gallagh and Mrs I. D. Bruce; two *s* one *d*. *Educ:* Upper Canada Coll.; Harrow Sch.; Balliol Coll., Oxford (BA Engineering; boxing blue). Welsh Guards (Gdsman, 2nd Lieut), 1949-51;

Rolls Royce Ltd, 1951-56; Grad. Apprentice; Export Sales Dept; Tech. Assistant to Foundry Manager. Management Consultant, Production Engineering Ltd, 1953-60; Nominee Director of several associate companies, Charterhouse Group Ltd, 1960. MP (L) Orpington, 1962-70; Liberal Whip in House of Commons, 1963-70. Consultant: Morgan-Grampian Ltd, 1970-; Miles Roman Ltd, 1970-. AMIMechE. *Recreations:* listening to music, reading, golf, darts. *Address:* High Elms House, Downe, Orpington, Kent. *Club:* National Liberal.

**LUBBOCK, Roy;** *b* 1 Oct. 1892; *s* of Frederic Lubbock and Catherine Gurney; *m* 1919, Yvonne Vernham; two *s*. *Educ:* Eton (Scholar); King's Coll., Cambridge (Exhibitioner, scholar); Fellow of Peterhouse, Cambridge and University Lecturer in Engineering, 1919-60; Bursar of Peterhouse, 1929-31 and 1940-45, Tutor, 1934-40. *Address:* Riding Oaks, Hildenborough, Tonbridge, Kent.

**LUCAN,** 7th Earl of, *cr* 1795; **Richard John Bingham;** Bt 1632; Baron Lucan, 1776; Baron Bingham (UK), 1934; *b* 18 Dec. 1934; *e s* of 6th Earl of Lucan, MC; *S* father, 1964; *m* 1963, Veronica, *d* of late Major C. M. Duncan, MC, and of Mrs J. D. Margrie; one *s* two *d*. *Educ:* Eton. Lieut (Res. of Officers) Coldstream Guards. *Heir: s* Lord Bingham, *qv*. *Address:* 46 Lower Belgrave Street, SW1. *T:* 01-730 0534.
*See also Duke of Abercorn, Earl Alexander of Tunis, J. H. Bevan.*

**LUCAS,** family name of **Baron Lucas of Chilworth.**

**LUCAS OF CHILWORTH,** 2nd Baron *cr* 1946, of Chilworth; **Michael William George Lucas;** *b* 26 April 1926; *er s* of 1st Baron and Sonia, *d* of Marcus Finkelstein, Libau, Latvia; *S* father, 1967; *m* 1955, Ann-Marie, *o d* of Ronald Buck, Southampton; two *s* one *d*. *Educ:* Peter Symond's Sch., Winchester. Served with Royal Tank Regt. MIMI; AMBIM. *Heir: s* Hon. Simon William Lucas, *b* 6 Feb. 1957. *Address:* c/o Barclays Bank Ltd, Manchester Street, Southampton. *Clubs:* Royal Automobile; Royal Southern Yacht.
*See also Hon. I. T. M. Lucas.*

**LUCAS OF CRUDWELL, Baroness** (10th in line) *cr* 1663 **and DINGWALL, Lady** (6th in line) *cr* 1609; **Anne Rosemary Palmer;** *b* 28 April 1919; *er d* of Group Captain Howard Lister Cooper, AFC, and Baroness Lucas and Dingwall; *S* mother, 1958; is a *co-heir* to Barony of Butler; *m* 1950, Major the Hon. Robert Jocelyn Palmer, MC, JP, late Coldstream Guards; 3rd and *e surv s* of 3rd Earl of Selborne, *qv*; two *s* one *d*. *Heir: er s* Hon. Ralph Matthew Palmer, *b* 7 June 1951. *Address:* The Old House, Wonston, Winchester, Hampshire.

**LUCAS, Claude Arthur,** TD 1950; Chairman Board of Governors, Hospital for Sick Children, Great Ormond Street, WC, 1953-67; *b* 5 Feb. 1894; *s* of late Sir Arthur Lucas; *m* 1928, Dorothy Hope, OBE 1950, *y d* of late Maj.-Gen. Sir John Hanbury-Williams, GCVO, KCB, CMG; no *c*. *Educ:* Wellington Coll.; University Coll., Oxford (MA). Served European War, 1914-18, 1/5 Hampshire Regt, NW Frontier, India, 1919; War of 1939-45, Middlesex Regt, Capt., seconded to Provost. Chartered Accountant; ACA 1925, FCA 1959; Mem. of Board, Hospital for Sick Children, 1921 (Vice-Chm., 1948); Member: House Cttee, Westminster Hosp. (Parkwood), Auxiliary Hosp. and Convalescent Home, 1921-63; Asthma Research Council, 1950- (Hon. Treas., 1950-60); Teaching Hosps Assoc., 1953-57 (a Dep. Chm.); Inst. of Child Health, 1955-67; Chm., London Postgraduate Hospitals Cttee, 1960-61 (Dep.-Chm., 1959-60). *Address:* 25 Melton Court, SW7. *T:* 01-589 8683. *Club:* United University.

**LUCAS, Colin Anderson,** BA; FRIBA; Architect; *b* London, 1906; 2nd *s* of late Ralph Lucas, Engineer, and late Mary Anderson Juler; *m* 1930, Dione Narona Margaris (marr. diss.), *d* of Henry Wilson; two *s*; *m* 1952, Pamela Margaret, *e d* of late Sir Gerald Campbell, GCMG; *Educ:* Cheltenham Coll.; Trinity Coll., Cambridge; Cambridge Univ. Sch. of Architecture. In practice in London, 1928-; Founder Mem. of Mars (Modern Architectural Research Group). *Publications:* works published in England, America and Continent. *Recreations:* sailing, ski-ing, travel. *Address:* 2 Queen's Grove Studios, Queen's Grove, NW8.

**LUCAS, Dr Cyril Edward,** CMG 1956; FRS 1966; Director of Fisheries Research, Scotland (Department of Agriculture and Fisheries for Scotland) and Director Marine Laboratory Aberdeen, 1948-70; *b* Hull, Yorks, 30 July 1909; *o s* of Archibald and late Edith Lucas, Hull; *m* 1934, Sarah Agnes, *o d* of late Henry Alfred and Amy Rose; two *s* one *d*. *Educ:* Grammar Sch., Hull; University Coll., Hull. BSc (London) 1931, DSc (London) 1942. FRSE 1939; Vice-Pres., 1962-64; Neill Prize, 1960. Research Biologist, University Coll., Hull, 1931; Head of Dept of Oceanography, University Coll., Hull, 1942. UK Expert or Delegate to various internat. confs on Marine Fisheries and Conservation, 1948-, and Chm. of research cttees in connexion with these; Chm., Consultative and Liaison Cttees, Internat. Council for Exploration of Sea, 1962-67; Member: Adv. Cttee on Marine Resources Research, FAO, 1964- (Chm. 1966-); Council for Scientific Policy, 1969-. *Publications:* various scientific, particularly on marine plankton and fisheries research in Bulletins of Marine Ecology (Joint Editor), Jl of Marine Biological Assoc., etc and various international jls. *Address:* 16 Albert Terrace, Aberdeen AB1 1XY. *T:* Aberdeen 25568.

**LUCAS, David K.;** *see* Keith-Lucas.

**LUCAS, Donald William;** Fellow of King's College, Cambridge, 1929, and Director of Studies in Classics, 1935-65; University Lecturer in Classics, 1933-69; P. M. Laurence Reader in Classics, 1952-69; *b* 12 May 1905; *s* of Frank William Lucas and Ada Ruth Blackmur; *m* 1933, Mary Irene Cohen; one *s* one *d*. *Educ:* Colfe's Gram. Sch.; Rugby; King's Coll., Cambridge. War of 1939-45: FO, 1940-44. *Publications:* The Greek Tragic Poets, 1950; Aristotle Poetics, 1968; *translations* (from Euripides): Bacchae, 1930; Medea, 1949; Ion, 1949; Alcestis, 1951; Electra, 1951; Joint Editor, Classical Quarterly, 1953-59; articles and reviews in classical journals and Encyclopædia Britannica. *Recreations:* travel and reading. *Address:* 39 Bridle Way, Grantchester, Cambs. *T:* Trumpington 3108; Pwllymarch, Llanbedr, Merioneth. *T:* Llanbedr 208.

**LUCAS, Maj.-Gen. (Retd) Geoffrey,** CB 1957; CBE 1944; *b* 19 Oct. 1904; *s* of Henry Lucas, Mossley Hill, Liverpool; *m* 1927, Mabel Ellen, *d* of Dr George Henry Heald, Leeds; one *s* one *d*. *Educ:* Liverpool High Sch.; RMC, Sandhurst. Commissioned, 1925, in Royal Tank Corps; Staff Coll., Camberley, 1938; served War of 1939-45 in Italy and Greece; DQMG, BAOR, 1947-50; Dep. Dir Personnel Admin, War Office, 1950-53; Dep. Fortress Comd, Gibraltar, 1953-56; Maj.-Gen. i/c Admin, FARELF, 1957; retired, 1958.

*Address:* Newbold House, Linkway, Camberley, Surrey. *T:* Camberley 5544.

**LUCAS, Hon. Ivor Thomas Mark;** British Deputy High Commissioner, Kaduna, Nigeria, since 1969; *b* 25 July 1927; 2nd *s* of George William Lucas, 1st Baron Lucas of Chilworth, and Sonia (*née* Finkelstein); *m* 1954, Christine Mallorie Coleman; three *s*. *Educ:* St Edward's Sch., Oxford; Trinity Coll., Oxford (MA). Served in Royal Artillery, 1945-48 (Captain). BA Oxon 1951. Entered Diplomatic Service, 1951; Middle East Centre for Arabic Studies, Lebanon, 1952; 3rd, later 2nd Sec., Bahrain, Sharjah and Dubai, 1952-56; FO, 1956-59; 1st Sec., British High Commn, Karachi, 1959-62; 1st Sec. and Head of Chancery, British Embassy, Tripoli, 1962-66; FO, 1966-68; Counsellor, British Embassy, Aden, 1968-69 (Chargé d'Affaires, Aug. 1968-Feb. 1969). *Recreations:* music, cricket, tennis. *Address:* 63 Parkside, Vanbrugh Park, SE3. *T:* 01-858 1658. *Club:* Royal Commonwealth Society.

**LUCAS, Major Sir Jocelyn (Morton),** 4th Bt *cr* 1887; KBE 1959; MC; late 4th Battalion Royal Warwickshire Regt; *b* 27 Aug. 1889; 2nd *s* of Sir Edward Lingard Lucas, 3rd Bt and Mary Helen (*d* 1915), *d* of Henry Chance, Sherborne, Warwick; *S* father, 1936; *m* 1st, 1933, Edith (*d* 1956), *d* of late Very Rev. David Barry Cameron, DD, JP, Dundee, and *widow* of Sir Trehawke Herbert Kekewich, Bt, Peamore, Devon; 2nd, 1960, Mrs Thelma Grace de Chair, *d* of Harold Dennison Arbuthnot, Field Place, Compton, Surrey. *Educ:* Eton; Royal Military Coll., Sandhurst. Joined 4th (Special Reserve Bn) Royal Warwicks Regt, 1919; served European War, 1914-19 (wounded, prisoner, MC) Oct. 1914, subseq. ADC to Gen. Sir Sydney Lawford, Army of Occupation, Cologne; Vice-Pres., Royal Over-Seas League and Chm. of the Hospitality Cttee, 1938-; welfare liaison officer for Dominion troops, London District, 1940-48; founder and Chm. Allies Welcome Cttee, 1940-50; also of Returned Prisoners of War Advice Cttee, 1944-48. MP (C) Portsmouth, South, 1939-66; Member: Parly delegn to France, 1946 and 1957; Commonwealth Conf., Ottawa, 1952; led delegn to Denmark, 1955, to Sweden, 1962, and to France for 50th Anniversary of Anglo-French Condominion of the New Hebrides. Has hunted several packs of hounds; served as part-time auxiliary fireman, 1938-42 (Section Leader); broken back and other injuries while fire fighting; Chm. Empire War Memorial Fund (St Paul's); a Governor and Mem. Council of Royal Veterinary Coll. and on Cttee of Kennel Club; Pres. Pitt Street Settlement; Chm. British Sportsman's Club, 1957-68; was responsible for legalisation of fishing on Serpentine, 1942 and holds Fishing Licence No. 1 for the Royal Parks; holds RAC Pilot's Certificate 893. Comdr, Order of Orange-Nassau. Czechoslovak Military Medal of Merit, 1st Class. *Publications:* Hunt and Working Terriers; Pedigree Dog Breeding; The Sealyham Terrier; the New Book of the Sealyham; Simple Doggie Remedies, etc. *Recreations:* travel, all equestrian and field sports, breeding pedigree dogs. *Heir: cousin* Thomas Edward Lucas [*b* 16 Sept. 1930; *m* 1958, Charmian, *d* of Col J. S. Powell; one *s*]. *Address:* 14 Clabon Mews, Cadogan Square, SW1. *T:* 01-589 3076; Michelmersh Court, Romsey, Hants. *T:* Braishfield 270/289. *Clubs:* Carlton, Bath, Kennel, United Hunts, MCC.

**LUCAS, Percy Belgrave,** DSO 1943 and Bar 1945; DFC 1942; Chairman: GRA Property Trust Ltd (Managing Director, 1957-65); GRA and White City (Manchester) Association Ltd; Greyhound Racing Association Ltd; White City Stadium Ltd; New Cross Greyhounds Ltd; GRA (Caterers) Ltd; Stamford Bridge Stadium Ltd; Athlon Sports Ltd; Director: Catford Stadium Ltd; Stowe School Ltd; *b* Sandwich Bay, Kent, 2 Sept. 1915; *y s* of late Percy Montagu Lucas, Prince's, Sandwich, form. of Filby House, Filby, Norfolk; *m* 1946, Jill Doreen, *d* of Lt-Col A. M. Addison, Ascot; two *s* (and one *s* decd). *Educ:* Stowe; Pembroke Coll., Cambridge. Editorial Staff, Sunday Express, 1937-40. Joined RAFVR, 1939; Commanded: 249 (Fighter) Sqdn, Battle of Malta, 1942; 616 (Fighter) Sqdn, 1943; Coltishall Wing, Fighter Command, 1943; 613 Sqdn, North-West Europe, 1944-45; Fighter Command, HQ Staff, 1942; Air Defence of Great Britain HQ Staff, 1944; demobilised with rank of Wing Comdr, 1946. Contested (C) West Fulham, 1945; MP (C) Brentford and Chiswick, 1950-59. Capt. Cambridge Univ. Golf team, 1937; Pres. Hawks Club, Cambridge, 1937; English International Golf team, 1936, 1948, 1949 (Capt. 1949); British Walker Cup team, 1936, 1947, 1949 (Capt. 1949). President: Golf Foundation Ltd, 1963-66; Nat. Golf Clubs Advisory Assoc., 1963-69; Assoc. of Golf Clubs Secretaries, 1968-. Member: General Advisory Council, BBC, 1962-67; Council, National Greyhound Racing Soc. of Great Britain; AAA Cttee of Inquiry, 1967; Exec. Cttee, General Purposes and Finance Cttee; Central Council of Physical Recreation; Management Cttee, Crystal Palace Nat. Sports Centre, 1961-; Vice-Patron, Amateur Athletic Assoc.; British Olympic Assoc. Gov., Stowe Sch. Croix de Guerre, 1945. *Recreations:* golf, shooting, photography. *Address:* GRA Property Trust Ltd, White City, Wood Lane, W12. *T:* 01-743 0152; Sparrow Hall, Titchwell, King's Lynn, Norfolk. *Clubs:* Bath; Sandy Lodge Golf; Walton Health Golf; Prince's Golf; Royal West Norfolk Golf.

**LUCAS, Prof. Raleigh Barclay;** Professor of Oral Pathology, University of London, since 1954; Consultant Pathologist, Royal Dental Hospital of London, since 1950; *b* 3 June 1914; *s* of H. Lucas; *m* 1942, Violet Sorrell; one *d* (one *s* decd). *Educ:* George Watson's Coll.; Univ. of Edinburgh. MB, ChB (Edinburgh) 1937; DPH 1939; MD 1945; MRCP 1946; FCPath 1963. Asst Bacteriologist, Edinburgh Royal Infirmary, 1939-40; Pathologist, Stoke Mandeville Hosp. and Royal Buckinghamshire Hospital, 1947-49; Reader in Pathology, University of London, 1950-54. Examiner in Pathology and Bacteriology for dental degrees, Univs of London, Birmingham, Sheffield and Wales. Served War of 1939-45, Major RAMC; FRSocMed; Fellow and Past Pres., Royal Medical Society; Mem. Pathological Soc. of Great Britain and Ireland; Mem. BMA. *Publications:* Bacteriology for Students of Dental Surgery (jointly), 1954; Pathology of Tumours of the Oral Tissues, 1964; various articles in medical and scientific journals. *Address:* Department of Pathology, Royal Dental Hospital, WC2. *T:* 01-930 8831.

**LUCAS, Prof. Wilfrid Irvine,** MA (Bristol), DrPhil (Heidelberg); Professor of German, University of Southampton, since 1954; *b* 12 Dec. 1905; *m* 1930, Emmeli, *d* of Prof. Ludolph Brauer, Univ. of Hamburg; two *s* two *d*. *Educ:* Bristol Gram. Sch.; University of Bristol. Lecturer in English, University of Heidelberg, 1927-31; Lecturer in German, University of Southampton, 1931; Dean, Faculty of Arts, 1952-56; Public Orator, 1953, 1955; Dep. Vice-Chancellor, 1957-59. Mem., University Grants Cttee, 1964-69. *Publications:* (ed.) Bergengruen's Das Hornunger Heimweh and other stories, 1957; revised and enlarged Twentieth Century of Robertson's History of

German Literature, 1959; various articles and reviews. *Recreation:* photography. *Address:* 6 Highfield Close, Southampton SO2 1QZ. *T:* Southampton 54204. *Club:* Royal Commonwealth Society.

**LUCAS-TOOTH, Sir Hugh;** *see* Munro-Lucas-Tooth.

**LUCE, Rev. Arthur Aston,** DD; LittD; MC; Chancellor, St Patrick's Cathedral, Dublin, since 1936; Precentor since 1952; Captain late 12th Royal Irish Rifles; Senior Fellow, Trinity College Dublin; Professor of Moral Philosophy, 1934-49; retired 1949; Berkeley Professor of Metaphysics, 1953; Member, Royal Irish Academy; *b* 21 Aug. 1882; *s* of Rev. J. J. Luce, Vicar, St Nicholas, Gloucester; *m* 1918, Lilian Mary Thompson (*d* 1940); two *s*. *Educ:* Eastbourne Coll.; Trinity Coll., Dublin. Fellow, Trinity Coll., Dublin, 1912; served with 12th Royal Irish Rifles, 1915-18. Litt D (*hc*) Queen's Univ., Belfast, 1953. *Publications:* Monophysitism Past and Present, 1920; Bergson's Doctrine of Intuition, 1922; Berkeley and Malebranche, 1934; Berkeley's Philosophical Commentaries (Commonplace Book), 1944; Berkeley's Immaterialism, 1945; The Works of George Berkeley, Vol. I, 1948, Vol. IV, 1950, Vol. VII, 1955, Vol. VIII, 1956, Vol. IX, 1957; The Life of George Berkeley, 1948; Sense without Matter, 1954; Teach yourself Logic, 1958; Fishing and Thinking, 1959; (ed.) The Book of Durrow, 1961; The Dialectic of Immaterialism, 1963; several articles on Berkeley. *Recreations:* salmon and trout angling. *Address:* Ryslaw, Bushy Park Road, Dublin. *T:* 905572. *Club:* University (Dublin).

**LUCE, Rev. Canon Harry Kenneth;** Headmaster, Durham School, 1932-58, retired; Examining Chaplain to Bishop of Birmingham since 1924; Hon. Canon of Durham since 1942; Canon Emeritus, since 1965; *b* 20 July 1897; *s* of Edmund and Margaret Eleanor Luce, Brighton; *m* 1925, Norah, *o d* of late Sir Sydney Chapman, KCB, CBE; three *d*. *Educ:* Eton (Scholar); King's Coll., Cambridge (Scholar); Westcott House, Cambridge. Bell Univ. Scholar, 1st class Classical Tripos Pt I, 1920; 2nd class Theological Tripos Pt II, 1921; BD Cambridge, 1933. Deacon, 1921; Priest, 1922; Curate of Holy Trinity, Cambridge, 1921; Master of King's Scholars in Westminster Sch., 1922-29; Headmaster, King Edward VI Sch., Southampton, 1929-32. *Publications:* S Matthew's Gospel in English for Schools; S Mark's Gospel in English for Schools; A Modern Confirmation Manual; The Creed of a Schoolboy; St Luke's Gospel, in Cambridge Greek Testament; Lift up your Hearts; St Luke's Gospel in English for Schools; St Luke's Gospel, in Cambridge Bible; The Courage of God; The Acts of the Apostles, in English for Schools; To the School at War, 1944; The Life of Christ in the Four Gospels, 1953; St Paul, 1957; To Believe and to Do, 1959; Jesus of Nazareth, 1961; The Religions of Mankind, 1961. *Recreations:* gardening, music. *Address:* 36 Highland Road, Charlton Kings, Cheltenham, Glos. *T:* Cheltenham 21048.

**LUCE, Mrs Henry Robinson, (Clare Boothe);** playwright and author since 1933; *d* of William F. and Ann Snyder Boothe; *m* 1st, 1923, George Tuttle Brokaw; 2nd, 1935, Henry Robinson Luce (*d* 1967). *Educ:* St Mary's Sch., Garden City, Long Island; The Castle, Tarrytown, New York. Associate Editor Vogue, 1930; Associate Editor Vanity Fair, 1931-32; Managing Editor Vanity Fair, 1933-34. Mem. of Congress from 4th District of Connecticut, 1943-47. United States Ambassador to Italy, 1953-57. Holds hon. doctorates. Dame of Magistral Grace, SMO Malta; Kt Gr Cross, Order of Merit, Italy. *Publications:* Stuffed Shirts, 1933; Europe in the Spring (English Title–European Spring), 1940; (ed) Saints For Now, 1952; *plays:* Abide with Me, 1935; The Women, 1936; Kiss the Boys Goodbye, 1938; Margin for Error, 1939; Child of the Morning, 1952; articles to magazines. *Address:* Honolulu, Hawaii, USA.

**LUCE, Admiral Sir (John) David,** GCB 1963 (KCB 1960; CB 1957); DSO 1940, and Bar, 1944; OBE 1942; Chief of Naval Staff and First Sea Lord, 1963-66; *b* 23 Jan. 1906; *s* of late Adm. John Luce, CB; *m* 1935, Mary Adelaide Norah Whitham; two *s*. *Educ:* RNC Dartmouth. Joined Submarines, 1927; Commanded HM Submarine H 44, 1936; Rainbow, 1939-40; Cachalot, 1940-41; Capt., 1945; RN Air Station, Ford, 1946-48; Dep. Dir, Plans Div., Admiralty, 1948-51; in comd of HMS Liverpool, 1951-52; HMS Birmingham, 1952-53; Dir of Royal Naval Staff Coll., 1953-54; Rear-Adm., 1955; Naval Sec. to the First Lord of the Admiralty, 1954-56; Flag Officer (Flotillas), Home Fleet, 1956-58; Vice-Adm. 1958; Flag Officer, Scotland, 1958-59; Adm., 1960; C-in-C, Far East Station, 1960-62; First C-in-C of British Forces in the Far East, 1962-63, and UK Military Adviser to SEATO. Pres. Royal Naval Assoc. *Recreations:* tennis, golf. *Address:* c/o Lloyds Bank Ltd, Devizes, Wilts; Monastery Garden, Edington, Westbury, Wilts. *Clubs:* Army and Navy, Royal Over-Seas League (Chm. Central Council).

**LUCE, Reginald William,** CB 1947; MBE 1937; MSM; *b* 1893; *s* of P. J. Luce, Jersey, CI. *Educ:* Modern Sch., Jersey; Paris; King's Coll., London. Entered Civil Service by open competition, 1912, and appointed to Board of Trade. Served throughout European War, 1914-18, in Middx Yeomanry and RHA (MSM 1916). Sec. to BoT Cttee on Patent Law, 1929-31; to Bot Cttee on Trade Mark Law, 1932-33; Sec. to London Conf. of Industrial Property Union, 1934; to BoT Cttee on International Copyright, 1936; transferred to Min. of Labour and National Service, 1939; Asst Sec., Min. of Labour and National Service, 1942-45; seconded to Foreign Office as Chief, Manpower Div. Control Commn for Germany, 1945-48; Manpower Adviser to UK High Comr for Germany, 1949; Comr for Schleswig-Holstein, 1950-52; Counsellor (Labour), British Embassy, Paris, 1953-56; Adviser to Govt of Mauritius on Employment situation and wages of sugar plantation workers, 1957-58; to Govts of Windward Islands, on establishment of Employment Services, 1963 and 1965. *Address:* 266 Cooden Drive, Bexhill-on-Sea, Sussex. *T:* Cooden 3391.

**LUCE, Sir William (Henry Tucker),** GBE 1961 (KBE 1956; OBE 1947); KCMG 1957 (CMG 1954); Personal Representative of the Foreign and Commonwealth Secretary for Persian Gulf Affairs, since 1970; Political Resident in the Persian Gulf, 1961-66; *b* 25 Aug. 1907; *s* of late Adm. John Luce, CB; *m* 1934, Margaret, *d* of late Adm. Sir Trevylyan Napier, KCB; one *s* one *d*. *Educ:* Clifton Coll.; Christ's Coll., Cambridge. Sudan Political Service, 1930; Private Sec. to Governor-Gen., 1941-47; Dep. Governor, Equatoria Province, 1950; Governor, Blue Nile Province, and Dir of Sudan Gezira Board, 1951; Adviser to the Gov.-Gen. of the Sudan on Constitutional and External Affairs, 1953-56; Governor and C-in-C, Aden, 1956-60. Director: Eastern Bank, 1966-70; Tilbury Overseas Contractors, 1967-70; Gray Mackenzie, 1967-70. Chm., Anglo-

Arab Assoc., 1968. *Address:* Brook House, Fovant, near Salisbury, Wilts. *T:* Fovant 254. *Club:* Bath.

**LUCET, Charles (Ernest);** French Ambassador to the United States since Oct. 1965; *b* Paris, 16 April 1910; *s* of Louis Lucet and Madeleine Lucet (*née* Zoegger); *m* 1931, Jacqueline Bardoux; one *s* one *d. Educ:* University of Paris. Degree in law, also degree of Ecole Libre des Sciences Politiques. French Embassy, Washington, 1935-NOv. 1942; then joined Free French movement and was apptd to its mission in Washington; attached to Foreign affairs Commissariat in Algiers, 1943; First Sec., Ankara, 1943-45; Asst Dir for Middle Eastern Affairs, Foreign Affairs Min., Paris, 1945-46; First Counsellor: Beirut, 1946; Cairo, 1949; Dept Head of Cultural Relations Div. of Foreign Affairs Min., Paris, 1950-53; rank of Minister Plenipotentiary, 1952; Mem. French Delegn to UN, serving as Dep. Permanent Rep. to UN and to Security Council, 1953-55; Minister Counsellor, French Embassy, Washington, 1955-59; Dir of Political Affairs, Foreign Affairs Min., Paris, 1959-65. Commandeur de la Légion d'Honneur; Commandeur de l'Ordre National du Mérite; holds foreign decorations. *Address:* French Embassy, 2221 Kalorama Road, NW, Washington, DC 20008, USA. *T:* DU 7.2666.

**LUCEY, Most Rev. Cornelius;** *see* Cork, Bishop of, (RC).

**LUCEY, Rear-Adm. Martin Noel,** DSC 1944; Admiral President, RNC Greenwich, since Oct. 1970; *b* 21 Jan. 1920; *s* of A. N. Lucey; *m* 1947, Barbara Mary Key; two *s* one *d. Educ:* Gresham's Sch., Holt. Entered RN, 1938. Served War of 1939-45: qualif. in navigation, 1944; "N" 10th Destroyer Sqdn, 1944. Comdr, 1953; Mem. NATO Defence Coll., 1954; Captain, 1961; Captain "F7" HMS Puma, 1964; Cdre, Sen. Naval Officer, West Indies, 1968; Rear-Adm., 1970. *Recreation:* painting. *Address:* Admiral's House, RNC, Greenwich, SE10.

**LUCIE-SMITH, (John) Edward (McKenzie);** poet and art critic; *b* Kingston, Jamaica, 27 Feb. 1933; *s* of John Dudley Lucie-Smith and Mary (*née* Lushington); unmarried. *Educ:* King's Sch., Canterbury; Merton Coll., Oxford (MA). Settled in England, 1946. Education Officer, RAF, 1954-56; subseq. worked in advertising and as free-lance journalist and broadcaster. FRSL. *Publications:* A Tropical Childhood and other poems, 1961 (jt winner, John Llewellyn Rhys Mem. Prize; winner, Arts Coun. Triennial Award); (ed, with Philip Hobsbaum) A Group Anthology, 1963; Confessions and Histories, 1964; (with Jack Clemo, George MacBeth) Penguin Modern Poets 6, 1964; (ed) Penguin Book of Elizabethan Verse, 1965; What is a Painting?, 1966; (ed) The Liverpool Scene, 1967; (ed) A Choice of Browning's Verse, 1967; (ed) Penguin Book of Satirical Verse, 1967; Thinking about Art, 1968; Towards Silence, 1968; Movements in Art since 1945, 1969; (ed) British Poetry Since 1945, 1970; (ed) A Primer of Experimental Verse, 1970; (ed with S. W. Taylor) French Poetry: the last fifteen years, 1970; (jt author, with Patricia White) Art in Britain, 69-70, 1970; contribs to Times, Sunday Times, Listener, Spectator, New Statesman, Encounter, London Magazine. etc. *Recreations:* classical and near eastern antiquities; malice. *Address:* 24 Sydney Street, SW3. *T:* 01-352 2555.

**LUCKER, Sydney Charles;** *b* 5 Jan. 1897; *m* 1920, Florence Hardy (*d* 1966); one *d.* Editorial Advisor, National Sunday School Union's Business Dept, 1959-61 (Gen. Manager and Editor, 1939-59); Editor, Sunday School Chronicle, 1930-59; Editor, Graded Teacher Series of Lesson Helps (Quarterlies and Annuals), 1940-59; Chief London Correspondent, Religious News Service (USA), 1938-65; Chm., Religious Weekly Press Group, 1953-54; previous journalistic appointments at Bournemouth, Torquay and London. *Publication:* Answers to Life's Questions, 1939. *Recreation:* photography. *Address:* 24 Aynhoe Road, W14. *T:* 01-603 2344. *Club:* Royal Commonwealth Society.

**LUCKHOO, Hon. Sir Edward Victor,** Kt 1970; QC (Guyana); Hon. Mr Justice Luckhoo; Chancellor and Pres. of Court of Appeal, Guyana; *b* Guyana (when Br. Guiana), 24 May 1912. *Educ:* New Amsterdam Scots Sch.; Queen's Coll., Guyana; Oxford Univ. (BA). Barrister-at-Law. Began career in magistracy as acting Magistrate, Essequibo District, 1943. *Address:* Court of Appeal, Georgetown, Guyana.

**LUCKHOO, Hon. Sir Joseph (Alexander),** Kt 1963; Judge, Court of Appeal, Jamaica, since 1967; lately Chief Justice of Guyana, during 1966 (and of British Guiana, 1960-66); *b* 8 June 1917; *e s* of late Joseph Alexander Luckhoo, KC and Irene Luckhoo; *m* 1964, Leila Patricia Singh; two *s. Educ:* Queen's Coll., British Guiana; University Coll., London; Middle Temple. BSc London, 1939. Barrister, Middle Temple, 1944; practised at Bar, British Guiana. Crown Counsel, British Guiana, 1949; Legal Draftsman, 1953; acted as Solicitor Gen., British Guiana, 1952, 1954 and 1955; Puisne Judge, British Guiana, 1956; Acting Chief Justice, 1959; Chief Justice, 1960. Chm. Judicial Service Commission, 1961. *Publications:* Editor: Law Reports of British Guiana, 1956-58; British Guiana section of West Indian Reports, 1958-61, Jamaica section, 1970. *Recreations:* watching cricket and tennis; table tennis. *Address:* Judges' Chambers, Court of Appeal, Kingston, Jamaica. *Club:* West Indian.

**LUCKHOO, Sir Lionel (Alfred),** KCMG 1969; Kt 1966; CBE 1962; QC (Guyana) 1954; Ambassador of Guyana to Venezuela, since 1970; *b* 2 March 1914; 2nd *s* of late Edward Alfred Luckhoo, OBE, Solicitor, and Evelyn Luckhoo; *m* Sheila Chamberlin; two *s* three *d. Educ:* Queen's Coll., Georgetown, Brit. Guiana; Middle Temple, London. MLC, 1949-51; Mem. State Coun., 1952-53; Minister without Portfolio, 1954-57; Mem. Georgetown Town Coun., 1950-64; Mayor, City of Georgetown, 1954, 1955, 1960, 1961 (Dep. Mayor three times); High Comr in UK, for Guyana, May 1966-70; for Barbados, Nov. 1966-70; Ambassador of Guyana and Barbados, to Paris, Bonn and The Hague, 1967-70. Pres., MPCA Trade Union, Brit. Guiana, 1949-52; Pres. of several Unions; has served on Commns of Enquiry, Public Cttees, Statutory Bodies, Legal Cttees, Drafting Cttees, Disciplinary Cttees, etc. Head of Luckhoo & Luckhoo, Legal Practitioners. Mem. of the Magic Circle. *Publication:* (jtly) The Fitzluck Theory of Breeding Racehorses. *Recreations:* cricket, horse-racing. *Address:* Embassy of Guyana, Caracas, Venezuela. *Clubs:* West Indian, Crockford's, Twenty-one.

**LUCRAFT, Frederick Hickman,** CBE 1952; *b* 10 May 1894; *s* of late Frederick Thomas Lucraft, Customs and Excise Dept; *m* 1927, June, *d* of John Freeman Wright, Dover; one *s* one *d. Educ:* Grocers' Company's Sch. Entered Inland Revenue, 1913. Served European War, King's Own Royal Lancaster Regt, 1914-17. Railway Traffic Establishment, 1917-19;

Inter-allied Railway Commn, Cologne SubCommn, 1919-22; demobilised with rank of Capt., 1922. Regional Services Dir, Min. of Fuel and Power, North-Western Region, 1942-45; Dep. Accountant and Comptroller Gen., Inland Revenue, 1945-47; Special Comr of Income Tax, Clerk to the Special Commissioners and Inspector of Foreign Dividends, Inland Revenue, 1947-59; HM Treasury, 1959-60. *Address:* 100 Dean Court Road, Rottingdean, Brighton, Sussex. *T:* Brighton 34195.

**LUDBROOK, Dr Samuel Lawrence,** CMG 1970; FRCP; Medical Adviser to Auckland Branch of the New Zealand Crippled Children Society; *b* 20 Aug. 1895; *e s* of H. S. Ludbrook, Ohaewai, Bay of Islands, NZ; *m* 1928, Ailsa Hannah Burns; three *s. Educ:* Wanganui Collegiate Sch.; Otago Univ. Medical Sch. MB, ChB, 1919; MRCP 1924. Auckland Hosp., 1920; Royal Northern Hosp., London, 1922; St George's Hosp., London, 1923; SMO, Shadwell Children's Hosp., 1924-25; Hon. Physician, Auckland Hosp., NZ, 1926, Senior Paediatrician, 1930, Hon. Cons. Paediatrician, 1952. Foundation Fellow, Royal Australasian Coll. of Physicians, 1939; FRCP 1950. *Publications:* sundry articles in medical jls. *Recreation:* horticulture. *Address:* 165 Mellons Bay Road, Howick, New Zealand. *Clubs:* Northern, Auckland University (Auckland).

**LUDLOW-HEWITT, Air Chief Marshal Sir Edgar Rainey,** GCB, *cr* 1946 (KCB, *cr* 1933; CB 1928); GBE, *cr* 1943; CMG 1919; DSO 1918; MC; DL; *b* 1886; *s* of Rev. Thomas Arthur Ludlow-Hewitt of Clancoole, Bandon, Co. Cork, and Minety, Wilts; *m* 1923, Albinia Mary, *d* of Major Edward Henry Evans-Lombe of Marlingford Hall, Norwich, and *widow* of Capt. Francis Clerke, Coldstream Guards. *Educ:* Radley; Sandhurst. 1st Bn Royal Irish Rifles, 1905-14; Royal Flying Corps, 1914; served European War, 1914-19 (CMG, DSO, MC, despatches six times, Legion of Honour), Bt Major, Royal Irish Rifles, 1915; Comd 10th Bde RAF, 1918; Chief Staff Officer, Headquarters RAF in France, 1918-19; Commandant Royal Air Force Staff Coll., 1926-30; Air Officer Commanding Iraq Command, 1930-32; Dir of Operations and Intelligence, Air Ministry, 1933-35; Air Officer Commanding RAF, India, 1935-37; AOC-in-C, Bomber Comd, 1937-40; Inspector-Gen. of the RAF, 1940-45; retd 1945. Air ADC to the King, 1921-23; Principal Air ADC to the King, 1943-45. Chm. Board of Governors, College of Aeronautics, 1945-53; Pres., Southern Area British Legion, 1946-51. DL Wilts 1953. *Address:* Westbrook House, Bromham, Chippenham, Wilts. *T:* Bromham 345.
*See also Sir J. E. L. Clerke, Bt.*

**LUDOVICI, Capt. Anthony M.,** late RFA; author; *b* 1882; *s* of late Albert and Marie Ludovici, London; *m* 1920, Elsie F. Buckley (*d* 1959). *Educ:* privately and abroad, but chiefly by his mother. Started life as an artist; illustrated various books; was for some time private sec. to late Auguste Rodin; ultimately left art for literature; lectured in London and elsewhere on Friedrich Nietzsche's philosophy, art, politics, etc; translated various foreign works, including six vols of Nietzsche's philosophy; served European War, 1914-19; fought at Armentières and the Somme; attached Intelligence Staff, War Office, April 1917; GSO3, March 1919; demobilised, Oct. 1919. Mem., Soc. of Authors. *Publications:* Who is to be Master of the World?, 1909; Nietzsche: His Life and Works, 1910; Nietzsche and Art, 1911; A Defence of Aristocracy, 1915; Man's Descent from the Gods, 1921; The False Assumption of Democracy, 1921; Woman: A Vindication, 1923; Lysistrata, 1924; Reminiscences of Rodin, 1926; Man, an Indictment, 1927; A Defence of Conservatism, 1927; The Night-Hoers, 1928; The Sanctity of Private Property, 1932; The Secret of Laughter, 1932; Health and Education through Self-Mastery, 1933; Violence, Sacrifice and War, 1933; Creation or Recreation, 1934; The Choice of a Mate, 1935; The Future of Woman, 1936; The Truth about Childbirth, 1937; English Liberalism, 1939; The Four Pillars of Health, 1945; Enemies of Women, 1947; The Child: An Adult's Problem, 1948; The Quest of Human Quality, 1952; Religion for Infidels, 1960; The Specious Origins of Liberalism, 1967; *novels:* Mansel Fellowes, 1918; Catherine Doyle, 1919; Too Old for Dolls, 1920; What Woman Wishes, 1921; The Goddess that Grew Up, 1922; French Beans, 1923; The Taming of Don Juan, 1924. *Recreations:* painting, conversation. *Address:* 197 Henley Road, Ipswich, Suffolk. *Club:* Naval and Military.

**LUFT, Rev. Hyam Mark,** MA, MLitt; JP; Headmaster, Merchant Taylors' School, Crosby, since April 1964; *b* 1913; *s* of I. M. Luft, Liverpool; *m* 1943, Frances, *er d* of F. Pilling, CBE; two *s* one *d. Educ:* Liverpool Institute; St John's Coll., University of Durham (Foundation Scholar). BA (1st Cl. Classics) 1934; Dip. TPT 1935; MA 1937; MLitt 1953. Deacon, 1937; Priest, 1938. Asst Priest, Liverpool Diocese, 1937-56; Asst Master, Merchant Taylors' Sch., Crosby, 1941-56; Headmaster, Blackpool Grammar Sch., 1956-64. Pres., Literary and Philosophical Soc. of Liverpool, 1953-54; Mem., Religious Education Commn, 1967-. Fellow-Commoner, Emmanuel Coll., Cambridge, 1968. JP Lancs, 1968-. *Publication:* History of Merchant Taylors' School, Crosby, 1620-1970, 1970. *Recreations:* lakeland walking, classical research and lecturing. *Address:* 44 St Michael's Road, Liverpool 23. *T:* 051-924 6034. *Club:* Public Schools.

**LUGG, Group Captain Sidney,** CBE 1944; CEng; FIEE, FInstD, FIERE; Director of Vacuum Reflex Ltd, since 1956; RAF 1922-52, retired; *b* 20 May 1906. *Educ:* Bournemouth Secondary Sch. Officer, Legion of Merit (US), 1944. *Recreation:* cricket. *Address:* Casita, 16 Smithambottom Lane, Purley, Surrey. *T:* 01-660 7105.

**LUKE,** 2nd Baron *cr* 1929, of Pavenham; **Ian St John Lawson Johnston,** TD; DL; JP; *b* 7 June 1905; *e s* of 1st Baron and Hon. Edith Laura (*d* 1941), *d* of 16th Baron St John of Bletsoe; *S* father, 1943; *m* 1932, Barbara, *d* of Sir FitzRoy Hamilton Anstruther-Gough-Calthorpe, 1st Bt; four *s* one *d. Educ:* Eton; Trinity Coll., Cambridge, MA. Chairman: Bovril Ltd; Argentine Estates of Bovril Ltd; Virol Ltd; Electrolux Ltd; Director: Ashanti Goldfields Corporation Ltd; Lloyds Bank Ltd; National Provident Institution; Bedfordshire Building Society; IBM United Kingdom Ltd and other companies; Hon. Col 5th Bn Beds Regt, 1947-62; OC 9th Bn Beds and Herts Regt, 1940-43; Chairman: Area Cttee for National Fitness in Herts and Beds, 1937-39; London Hospitals Street Collections Cen. Cttee, 1943-45; Beds TAA, 1943-46; Duke of Gloucester's Red Cross and St John Fund, 1943-46; National Playing Fields Assoc.; an Hon. Sec., Assoc. of British Chambers of Commerce, 1944-52; Mem. of Church Assembly (House of Laity), 1935; Mem., International Olympic Cttee, 1952-; President: Incorporated Sales Managers Assoc., 1953-56; Advertising Assoc., 1955-58; Outdoor Advertising Council, 1957; Operation Britain Organisation, 1957-62; London Chamber of Commerce, 1952-55. MFH Oakley

Hunt, 1947-49. CC, DL, JP, Bedfordshire. *Heir:* *s* Hon. Arthur Charles St John Lawson Johnston [*b* 13 Jan. 1933; *m* 1959, Silvia Maria, *yr d* of Don Honorio Roigt and Doña Dorothy Goodall de Roigt; one *s* two *d*]. *Address:* Odell Castle, Beds. *T:* Harrold 240. *Club:* Carlton.

*See also Hon. H. de B. Lawson Johnston, Sir I. J. Pitman.*

**LUKE, Hon. Sir Emile Fashole,** KBE 1969 (CBE 1959); Speaker of the House of Representatives, Sierra Leone, since 1968; *b* 19 Oct. 1895; *s* of late Josiah Thomas Steven Luke and late Dorcas Evangeline Luke; *m* 1929, Sarah Christina Jones-Luke (decd); two *s* one *d*. *Educ:* Wesleyan Methodist High Sch.; Fourah Bay Coll.; Lincoln's Inn. Civil Servant, 1913-19; practised Law, 1926-44; City Councillor, Freetown, 1940-44; Asst Police Magistrate, 1944-45; Police Magistrate, 1945-51; Senior Police Magistrate, 1951; Actg Judge, Bathurst, Gambia, 1953; Actg Puisne Judge, 1951-54; Puisne Judge, Sierra Leone, 1954-59, retired; Acting Chief Justice, in Sierra Leone and Gambia, on various occasions between 1956 and 1968, and Appeal Court Justice on several occasions, 1960-68. Chief Scout, Scouts Assoc., Sierra Leone, 1969 (awarded the Silver Wolf). *Recreations:* tennis and walking. *Address:* 67 Motor Road, Wilberforce, PO Box 228, Freetown, Sierra Leone. *T:* Freetown 3502. *Clubs:* Royal Commonwealth Society; Freetown Dinner (Freetown).

**LUKE, Eric Howard Manley,** CMG 1950; FRCSE 1922; FRACS 1932; retired; *b* 18 Aug. 1894; *s* of Sir Charles Luke; *m* 1923, Gladys Anne, *d* of Col J. J. Esson, CMG; one *s* two *d*. *Educ:* Wellington Coll.; Otago Univ.; Edinburgh Univ. MB, ChB, Otago Univ., NZ, 1920; senior surgeon, Wellington Hospital, NZ, 1925-50; Thoracic Surgeon, East Coast Hospitals, 1942-50; Chm. of Council, British Medical Association, NZ Branch, 1944-49; President BMA, NZ Branch, 1950. Has a citrus orchard. *Recreations:* formerly Rugby; now bowls and gardening. *Address:* Keri Keri, Bay of Islands, NZ. *Club:* Wellington (Wellington, NZ).

**LUKE, Sir Kenneth George,** Kt 1962; CMG 1954; JP 1945; Chairman and Managing Director: K. G. Luke Group Industries Ltd; Concentric Engineering Pty Ltd; Luke and Singer Pty Ltd; Chairman: F. L. Hudson & Co.; Terry Engineering; Director, Mercantile Mutual Insurance Co. Ltd; *b* 11 Nov. 1898; *s* of George Edwin Luke, Somerset, England; *m* 1939, Valda Letitia, *d* of Louis John A. Richardson, Melbourne, Vic.; one *d*. *Educ:* Melbourne and Ballarat, Vic. Hon. Consultant Dept of Supply, Australia. Public service includes holding of various offices in naval and civil clubs and assocs; Life Governor many hosps of all denominations; holds several records and championships in breeding Poll Hereford cattle and Dorset Horn sheep; Life Member, Councillor and Mem. Cttees, Royal Agricultural Society. *Recreations:* interested in football, cricket, motor cycling, yachting, lawn tennis, golf, bowls, racing (breeder of bloodstock). *Address:* K. G. Luke Group Industries Ltd, 505 St Kilda Road, Melbourne, Victoria 3004, Australia. *T:* (business) 26.3654; (private) 81.3662. *Clubs:* Savage, Green Room (Melbourne).

**LUKE, Sir Stephen (Elliot Vyvyan),** KCMG 1953 (CMG 1946); Director: E. D. Sassoon Banking Co. Ltd; Pirelli Ltd; Television Recordings Ltd, and other companies; *b* 26 Sept. 1905; *o c* of late Brigadier-General Thomas Mawe Luke, CBE, DSO; *m* 1st, 1929, Helen Margaret Reinold; two *s*; 2nd, 1948, Margaret Stych; one *d*. *Educ:* St George's Sch., Harpenden; Wadham Coll., Oxford. Asst Clerk, House of Commons, 1930; Asst Principal, Colonial Office, 1930; Asst Private Sec. to successive Secs of State, 1933-35; seconded to Palestine Administration, 1936-37; Sec., Palestine Partition Commission, 1938; Under-Sec., Cabinet Office, 1947-50; Asst Under-Sec. of State, Colonial Office, 1950-53; Comptroller for Development and Welfare in the West Indies, and British Co-Chm. of Caribbean Commn, 1953-58; Comr for preparation of WI Federal Organisation, 1956-58; Senior Crown Agent for Oversea Governments and Administrations, 1959-68; Interim Comr for the West Indies, May 1962-68; Mem. Exec. Cttee, W India Cttee, 1969-. Chm., Board of Governors, St George's Sch., Harpenden, 1963-68. First Class Order of Laila Jasa (PSLJ) (Brunei), 1966. *Recreation:* gardening. *Address:* Lyewood House, Ropley, Hants. *T:* Ropley 2283. *Club:* Oxford and Cambridge University.

**LUKE, William Edgell;** Chairman since 1959 and Managing Director since 1949, Lindustries Ltd (formerly the Linen Thread Co. Ltd) and associated companies at home and abroad; Director, Powell Duffryn Ltd, since 1966; *b* 9 June 1909; *s* of George Bingley Luke and Violet Edgell; *m* 1933, Muriel Aske Haley (marr. diss. 1969); one *s* one *d*; *m* 1970, Anne, *d* of late Charles Reid. *Educ:* Old Hall, Wellington; Kelvinside Academy, Glasgow. Served War of 1939-45: Major, Intelligence Corps, S Africa and Central America. Mem. Grand Coun., FBI, 1947- (Chm. Scottish Council, 1957) (FBI is now CBI); Mem. Coun. of Aims of Industry, 1958-; Chm. Industrial Advisers to the Blind Ltd, 1963-67; Chm., UK-S Africa Trade Assoc., 1963-; Mem., Brit. Nat. Export Council, and Chm., BNEC Southern Africa Cttee for Exports to Southern Africa, 1965-68; Trustee, South Africa Foundation. Master, Worshipful Company of Makers of Playing Cards, 1958. *Recreations:* golf, water ski-ing, music and travel. *Address:* Tudor Cottage, South Stoke, Oxon; Trevor House, 100 Brompton Road, SW3. *T:* 01-584 6161. *Clubs:* Royal Thames Yacht, Travellers'; Ulster (Belfast); Racquet and Tennis (New York); Western Province (Cape Town).

**LUMBY, Henry,** CBE 1957; DL, JP; Chairman of Lancashire County Council since 1967; *b* 9 Jan. 1909; *m* 1936, Dorothy Pearl Watts; two *s*. *Educ:* Merchant Taylors' Sch., Crosby. Served War of 1939-45 (POW, 1942-45). Mem. of Northern Stock Exchange. Mem., Lancs CC, 1946; Alderman, 1956; Leader of Conservative Gp, Lancs CC, 1965-; DL 1965, JP 1951, Lancashire. *Recreation:* gardening. *Address:* The Dawn, Dark Lane, Ormskirk, Lancs. *T:* Ormskirk 2030.

**LUMLEY,** family name of **Earl of Scarbrough.**

**LUMLEY, Air Cdre Eric Alfred,** CBE 1948; MC 1918; MD, BCh, DPH, DTM&H; RAF retired; lately Medical Officer to RAF Recruiting Centre, Birmingham; *b* 7 Dec. 1891; *s* of Joseph Alfred Lumley and Henrietta Lumley (*née* Barnes), Tullamore, King's County, Ireland; *m* 1920, Elsie Clift (*d* 1969), Redcar, Yorks; one *s* two *d*. *Educ:* Wesley Coll., Dublin; Dublin Univ. MB, BCh, BAO (Univ. of Dublin), 1914; LM Rotunda, 1914; DPH (London), 1930; DTM&H (London), 1946; MD (Dublin), 1948; Capt. RAMC, 1914-18 (MC); service with 8/10 Gordon Highlanders, No. 138 Field Amb., 36th (Ulster) Divisonal Artillery, etc. Joined RAF, 1919; Group Capt. 1928; Air Cdre 1946; served in Egypt, Iraq (2 tours), Aden (2 tours), as well as home appts, 1919-38; War of 1939-45; PMO British Forces in Aden, 1938-40; OC, RAF

Hosp., Ely, 1940-42; SMO Nos 27 & 28 Groups RAF, 1942-44; PMO Fighter Comd, 1944-46; PMO, RAF in India and Royal Indian Air Force, 1946-47; RAF Rep. on Govt of India Cttee (Roy. Cttee) on Integration of Medical Services of Indian Armed Forces, 1947; retd from RAF, 1950. Public Health Service MO, 1950-52; Civilian MO employed by Air Ministry, 1952-65. *Publications:* various, in BMJ, Jl Indian Med. Assoc. and Sports India. *Recreations:* cricket, golf, billiards, trout and salmon fishing. *Address:* Gindle's Cottage, Walmersley, Bury, Lancs. *T:* 061-764 2529.

**LUMLEY-SAVILE,** family name of **Baron Savile.**

**LUMSDEN, Dr David James;** Fellow and Organist, New College, Oxford, since 1959; Lecturer in the Faculty of Music, Oxford; *b* Newcastle upon Tyne, 19 March 1928; *m* 1951, Sheila Daniels; two *s* two *d. Educ:* Dame Allan's Sch., Newcastle upon Tyne; Selwyn Coll., Cambridge. Organ scholar, Selwyn Coll., Cambridge, 1948-51; BA Class I, 1950; MusB (Barclay Square Prize) 1951; MA 1955; DPhil 1957. Asst Organist, St John's Coll., Cambridge, 1951-53; Res. Student, 1951-54; Organist and Choirmaster, St Mary's, Nottingham, 1954-56; Founder/Conductor, Nottingham Bach Soc., 1954-59; Rector Chori, Southwell Minster, 1956-59; Dir of Music, Keele, 1958-59; Prof. of Harmony, Royal Academy of Music, 1959-61. Conductor, Oxford Harmonic Soc., 1961-63; Founder/Conductor, Oxford Univ. Madrigal Soc., 1962-; Pres., Inc. Assoc. of Organists, 1966-68; Hugh Porter Lectr, Union Theological Seminary, NY, 1967; Conductor, Oxford Sinfonia, 1967. *Publications:* An Anthology of English Lute Music, 1954; Thomas Robinson's Schoole of Musicke, 1603, 1970; Articles in: The Listener; The Score; Music and Letters: Galpin Soc. Jl; La Luth et sa Musique; La Musique de la Renaissance, etc. *Recreations:* reading, theatre, cinema, television, gardening, camping, photography, travel, etc. *Address:* New College, Oxford. *T:* Oxford 48451; 8 New College Lane, Oxford. *T:* Oxford 41769.

**LUND, John Walter Guerrier,** FRS 1963; DSc, PhD; Botanist, at Windermere Laboratory of Freshwater Biological Association, since 1945; Deputy Chief Scientific Officer; *b* 27 Nov. 1912; *s* of George E. Lund and Kate Lund (*née* Hardwick); *m* 1949, Hilda M. Canter; one *s* one *d. Educ:* Sedbergh Sch.; Univs of Manchester and London. Demonstrator in Botany, Univ. of Manchester, also Queen Mary Coll. and Chelsea Polytechnic, Univ. of London, 1935-38; Temp. Lectr in Botany, Univ. of Sheffield, 1936; PhD (London) 1939; Staff Biologist, W Midland Forensic Science Laboratory, Birmingham, 1938-45; DSc (London) 1951. *Publications:* papers and articles in scientific jls, symposium vols, etc. *Recreation:* gardening. *Address:* Ellerbeck, Ellerigg Road, Ambleside, Westmorland. *T:* Ambleside 2369.

**LUND, Sir Thomas (George),** Kt 1958; CBE 1948; Director-General, International Bar Association, since 1969; *b* 6 Jan. 1906; *s* of late Kenneth Fraser Lund, MA, MB, Cowper Cottage, Mundesley, Norfolk; *m* 1931, Catherine Stirling, *d* of late Arthur John Audsley; one *d. Educ:* Westminster Sch. Admitted a Solicitor, 1929; Asst Solicitor, The Law Soc., 1930; Asst Sec., 1937; Secretary-General, 1939-69; Treas., Internat. Bar Assoc., 1950-69; Chm. Board of Management, College of Law, 1962, 1969; Sec-Gen., International Legal Aid Assoc., 1963-; Dir, Solicitors' Benevolent Assoc., 1949-69; Member: British Council; Professional Classes Aid Council; Past Master, Worshipful Co. of Solicitors of the City of London; Liveryman, Worshipful Co. of Cordwainers. Past Pres., British Academy of Forensic Sciences. Dir, Law Fire Insurance Soc. Ltd. *Publications:* The Solicitors Act, 1941, 1943; contributed many articles to English and American legal jls. *Recreations:* foreign travel, motoring, gardening. *Address:* International Bar Association, 14 Waterloo Place, SW1; 1 Bryanston Court, George Street, W1; Brass Tacks, Biddenden, Kent. *Club:* Athenæum.

**LUNN, Sir Arnold,** Kt 1952; Hon. DPhil (Zürich), 1954; Citoyen d'honneur of Chamonix, France, 1952; Grand Cross of Isabel la Catolica, Spain, 1959; *b* Madras, 18 April 1888; *e s* of late Sir Henry Lunn; *m* Lady Mabel (*d* 1959), *d* of late Rev. Hon. John Stafford Northcote, Chaplain to HM, and *sister* of 3rd Earl of Iddesleigh; two *s* one *d*; *m* 1961, Phyllis, *d* of late O. N. Holt-Needham. *Educ:* Harrow; Balliol Coll., Oxford. Sec., Oxford Union Soc.; Edited the Isis. Ex-President Ski Club of Great Britain, Founder and Ex-President of Alpine Ski, Kandahar Ski and Oxford Univ. Mountaineering Clubs; Mem. Cttee, Internat. Ski Federation, 1943-49; Chm., International Downhill Ski-racing Cttee, 1946-49; invented and obtained Olympic recognition for the modern Slalom race. During war of 1939-45, Press Correspondent Balkans, Chile, Peru. Lectured: in USA; for British Council, Spain, Rome, Malta; Lowell Lectr, Harvard Univ., 1960. Attached to Ministry of Information (SP), War Office, June 1941; to Amer. High Comr in Germany, April-July 1953. *Publications:* Guide to Montana, 1907; Oxford Mountaineering Essays (ed.), 1912; The Englishman in the Alps, 1912; The Harrovians, 1913; Ski-ing, 1913; The Alps (Home Univ. Library), 1914; Was Switzerland Pro-German? (*non de plume* Sutton Croft), 1918; Loose Ends, 1919; Auction Piquet (*nom de plume* Rubicon), 1920; Cross Country Ski-ing, 1920; The Alpine Ski Guides (Bernese Oberland), 1920; Alpine Ski-ing, 1921; Roman Converts, 1924; Ski-ing for Beginners, 1924; The Mountains of Youth, 1925; A History of Ski-ing, 1927; Things that have Puzzled Me, 1927; Switzerland (Kit-bag Travel Books), 1927; John Wesley, 1928; The Flight from Reason, 1930; The Complete Ski-runner, 1930; Family Name, 1931; Venice (Kitbag Travel Books), 1932; (with Rev. R. A. Knox) Difficulties, 1932; The Italian Lakes and Lakeland Cities, 1932; Within the Precincts of the Prison, 1932; (with C. E. M. Joad) Is Christianity True?, 1933; Public School Religion, 1933; Now I See, 1933; A Saint in The Slave Trade, 1934; (with Prof. J. B. S. Haldane, FRS) Science and the Supernatural, 1935; Within that City, 1936; Spanish Rehearsal, 1937; Communism and Socialism, 1938; Whither Europe?, 1940; Come What May: An Autobiography, 1940; And the Floods Came, 1942; Mountain Jubilee, 1943; The Good Gorilla, 1943; Switzerland and the English, 1944; The Third Day, 1945; Is the Catholic Church Anti-Social? (with G. G. Coulton), 1946; Switzerland in English Prose and Poetry, 1947; Mountains of Memory, 1948; The Revolt against Reason, 1950; The Cradle of Switzerland, 1952; The Story of Ski-ing, 1952; Zermatt and the Valais, 1955; Memory to Memory, 1956; Enigma, 1957; A Century of Mountaineering, 1957; The Bernese Oberland, 1958; And Ever New, 1958; The Swiss and their Mountains, 1963; The Englishman on Ski, 1963; The New Morality (with Garth Lean), 1964; The Cult of Softness (with Garth Lean), 1965; Matterhorn Centenary, 1965; Unkilled for So Long (memoirs), 1967; (with Garth Leon) Christian Attack, 1969; The Kandahar Story, 1969; contributed to Encyclopædia Britannica;

Editor Georgian Stories, 1922, 1924, 1925; Editor British Ski Year Book since 1919. *Address:* c/o Ski Club of Great Britain, 118 Eaton Square, SW1. *Clubs:* Athenæum, Alpine (Hon. Mem.).

*See also P. N. Lunn.*

**LUNN, Peter Northcote,** CMG 1957; OBE 1951; serving in Foreign and Commonwealth Office; *b* 15 Nov. 1914; *e s* of Sir Arnold Lunn, *qv*; *m* 1939, Hon. (Eileen) Antoinette, *d* of 15th Visc. Gormanston; three *s* three *d. Educ:* Eton. Joined RA, 1940; served 1940-46 (Malta, Italy and BAOR); entered FO, 1947; Vienna, 1948-50; Berne, 1950-53; Germany, 1953-56; London, 1956-57; Bonn, 1957-62; Beirut, 1962-67. Mem., Brit. International Ski team, 1931-37, Capt. 1934-37; Capt. British Olympic Ski team, 1936. *Publications:* High-Speed Skiing, 1935; Evil in High Places, 1947; A Skiing Primer, 1948. *Clubs:* Ski Club of Great Britain, Prince's Water Ski.

**LUNS, Dr Joseph Marie Antoine Hubert;** Officer, Order of Orange-Nassau; Hon. GCMG; Minister of Foreign Affairs, The Netherlands, since 1952; *b* 28 Aug. 1911; *m* Baroness E. C. van Heemstra; one *s* one *d. Educ:* sec. schs, Amsterdam and Brussels; universities of Leyden, Amsterdam, London and Berlin. Attaché of Legation, 1938; 2nd Sec., 1942; 1st Sec., 1945; Counsellor, 1949. Served in: Min. for For. Affairs, 1938-40; Berne, 1940-41; Lisbon, 1941-43; London, at Netherlands Min. for For. Affairs, 1943-44, and at Netherlands Embassy, 1944-49; Netherlands Delegn to UN, NY, 1942-52. MP (Second Chamber, Netherlands), July-Oct. 1956 and March-June 1959. Hon. Fellow, London Sch. of Economics. Prix Charlemagne, Aachen, 1967; Gustav Stresemann Medal, 1968. Hon. degree from Harvard. Holds numerous foreign orders. *Publications:* The Epic of The Royal Netherlands Navy; articles on Royal Netherlands Navy in Dutch and foreign jls., and articles on international affairs in International Affairs, La Revue Politique, and others. *Recreation:* swimming. *Address:* Plein 1813 No 2, The Hague, The Netherlands. *T:* (office) 614941. *Clubs:* Haagsche, De Witte (Netherlands).

**LUNT, Alfred;** actor; *b* Milwaukee, 1892; *m* Lynn Fontanne, *qv. Educ:* Carroll Coll., Waukesha. First appearance, Castle Square Theatre, Boston, 1913; toured with Margaret Anglin, 1914; with Mrs Langtry in vaudeville; Claude Estabrook in Romance and Arabella, New York, 1917; Clarence in Clarence, 1919-21; Charles II in Sweet Nell of Old Drury, 1923; The Guild Theatre, 1925-29; first appearance in London as von Echardt in Caprice at St James's Theatre; leading parts in: Reunion in Vienna, New York, 1931, London, 1934; Design for Living; Point Valaine; The Taming of the Shrew; Idiots' Delight; Amphitryon 38, New York and London, 1938; The Pirate, New York, 1943; There Shall Be No Night, New York and London, 1943; Quadrille, London, 1952; The Great Sebastians, New York, 1956; The Visit, London, 1960, etc; Dir Theatre Guild, 1935-. Presidential Medal of Freedom, 1964; Kt White Rose, Finland. Holds hon. degrees, incl. Hon. DLitt, Milwaukee, 1930. Emmy Award. *Club:* Players' (New York).

**LUNT, Rt. Rev. Francis Evered;** *b* 15 Oct. 1900; *e s* of late Francis Bryan Lunt; *m* 1938, Helen Patricia, *y d* of late Alfred Bolton; three *d. Educ:* University Coll., Durham (LTh 1923); London Coll. of Divinity. Deacon, 1925; Priest, 1927; Curate of St Andrew and St Mary, Maidenhead, 1925-31; St Barnabas, Cambridge, 1931-34; licensed to officiate, Diocese of Ely, 1933-43; Chaplain, Downing Coll., Cambridge and Cambridge Pastorate, 1934-43; Hon. Fellow, Downing Coll., 1966-; MA Cambridge, 1939; Senior Chaplain to Oxford Pastorate and Rector of St Aldate, Oxford, 1943-51; Dean of Bristol, 1951-57; Bishop Suffragan of Stepney, 1957-68. MA Oxford (Oriel Coll.), 1945. Select Preacher, Univ. of Cambridge, 1943 and 1962; Surrogate, 1943; Examining Chaplain to Bishop of Oxford, 1946-51, to Bishop of Portsmouth, 1949-51. Mem. Council, Ridley Hall, Cambridge, 1950-. *Address:* Ridgeway House, Felpham, Sussex. *Club:* Athenæum.

**LUNT, Maj.-Gen. James Doiran,** CBE 1964 (OBE 1958); Vice-Adjutant-General, Ministry of Defence, since 1970; *b* 13 Nov. 1917; *s* of Brig. W. T. Lunt, MBE, Camberley, Surrey; *m* 1940, Muriel, *d* of late A. H. Byrt, CBE, Bournemouth; one *s* one *d. Educ:* King William's Coll., IOM; RMC, Sandhurst. 2nd Lieut, Duke of Wellington's Regt, 1937; served with 4th Bn Burma Rifles, 1939-41; Burma Campaign, 1942; Indian Military Academy, 1942-44; Staff Coll., Camberley, 1945; GSO2 Trieste, 1946-48; transf. to 16/5th Queen's Royal Lancers, 1949; served with Arab Legion, 1952-55; jssc 1956; comd 16/5th Queen's Royal Lancers, 1957-59; idc 1961; comd Fed. Regular Army, Aden, 1961-64; Dir of Admin. Planning (Army), MoD, 1964-66; Defence Adviser to British High Commissioner, India, 1966-68; Chief of Staff, Contingencies Planning, SHAPE, 1969-70. Order of Independence (Jordan), 1956; Commander, Order of South Arabia, 1964. *Publications:* Charge to Glory, 1961; Scarlet Lancer, 1964; The Barren Rocks of Aden, 1966; Bokhara Burnes, 1969; From Sepoy to Subedar, 1970. *Recreations:* golf, fishing, riding, writing. *Address:* c/o Cox's & King's, 6 Pall Mall, SW1. *Clubs:* Cavalry, Flyfishers'.

**LUNT, Rev. Canon Ronald Geoffrey,** MC 1943; MA, BD; Chief Master, King Edward's School, Birmingham, since 1952; *b* 25 June 1913; *s* of late Rt Rev. G. C. L. Lunt, DD, Bishop of Salisbury; *m* 1945, Veslemoy Sopp Foss, Oslo, Norway; one *s* two *d. Educ:* Eton (King's Scholar); The Queen's Coll., Oxford (Scholar, 1st class Lit. Hum.); Westcott House, Cambridge. Assistant Master, St George's Sch., Harpenden, 1935; Haberdashers' Sch., Hampstead, 1936-37; Deacon, 1938; Priest, 1939; Master in Orders at Radley Coll., Abingdon, 1938-40; CF 1940-45; Middle East, 1941-44 (MC); CF 3rd class, SCF 1 Airborne Division, 1945; Headmaster, Liverpool Coll., 1945-52. Won Cromer Greek Prize, 1937; Page Scholar to USA, 1959; Select Preacher: University of Cambridge, 1948, 1960, Oxford, 1951-53. Chm., Birmingham Council of Churches, 1957-60; Hon. Canon, Birmingham Cathedral, 1969. Life Governor, Queen's Coll., Birmingham, 1954. Pres., Incorporated Assoc. of Head Masters, 1962. Mem., Press Council, 1964-69. BD (Oxon), 1967. *Publications:* Edition of Marlowe's Dr Faustus, 1937, Edward II, 1938; contrib. to Arts v. Science, 1967; articles in Theology, Hibbert Journal, and other journals. *Recreations:* travel, gardening. *Address:* King Edward's School, Birmingham 15. *T:* 021-472 1672, 021-472 0652. *Club:* University Staff (Birmingham).

**LURGAN,** 4th Baron *cr* 1839; **William George Edward Brownlow;** *b* 22 Feb. 1902; *o s* of 3rd Baron and Lady Emily Julia Cadogan (*d* 1909), *d* of 5th Earl Cadogan, KG; *S* father, 1937. *Educ:* Eton; Oxford. *Heir: cousin* John Desmond Cavendish Brownlow, *b* 1911. *Address:* c/o The Chase Manhattan Bank, 1

Mount Street, W1. *Clubs:* Turf; Ulster (Belfast).

**LURIA, Prof. Salvador Edward;** Sedgwick Professor of Biology, Massachusetts Institute of Technology, since 1964; *b* 13 Aug. 1912; *s* of David Luria and Ester Sacerdote; *m* 1945, Zella Hurwitz; one *s*. *Educ:* Turin Univ. (MD 1935). Res. Fellow, Inst. of Radium, Paris, 1938-40; Res. Asst, Columbia Univ. Medical School, NY, 1940-42; Guggenheim Fellow, Vanderbilt and Princeton Univs, 1942-43; Instructor in Bacteriology, Indiana Univ., 1943-45, Asst Prof., 1944-47, Associate Prof. 1947-50; Prof. of Bacteriology, Illinois Univ., 1950-59; Prof. and Chm. of Dept of Microbiology, MIT, 1959-64. Fellow of Salk Inst. for Biol Studies, 1965-. Associate Editor, Jl Bacteriology, 1950-55; Editor: Virology, 1955-; Biological Abstracts, 1958-62; Member: Editorial Bd, Exptl Cell Res. Jl, 1948-; Advisory Bd, Jl Molecular Biology, 1958-64; Hon. Editorial Advisory Bd, Jl Photochemistry and Photobiology, 1961-. Lecturer: Univ. of Colorado, 1950; Jesup, Notre Dame, 1950; Nieuwand, Notre Dame 1959; Dyer, Nat. Insts of Health, 1963. Member: Amer. Phil Soc.; Amer. Soc. for Microbiology (Pres. 1967-68); Nat. Acad. of Scis; Amer. Acad. of Arts and Scis; AAAS; Soc. Genetic Microbiology; Genetics Soc. of America; Amer Assoc. Univ. Profs; Sigma Xi. Prizes: Lepetit, 1935; Lenghi, 1965; Louisa Gross Horowitz of Columbia University; Nobel Prize for Physiology or Medicine (jtly), 1969. Hon. ScD: Chicago, 1967; Rutgers, 1970; Indiana, 1970. *Recreation:* sculpting. *Address:* 48 Peacock Farm Road, Lexington, Mass 02173, USA.

**LUSAKA, Archbishop of, (RC),** since 1969; **Most Rev. Emanuel Milingo;** *b* 13 June 1930; *s* of Yakobe Milingo Chilumbu and Tomaide Lumbiwe Miti. *Educ:* Kachebere Seminary, Malawi; Pastoral Inst., Rome; University Coll., Dublin. Curate: Minga Parish, Chipata Dio., 1958-60; St Mary's Parish, 1960-61; Chipata Cathedral, 1963-64; Parish Priest, Chipata Cathedral, 1964-65; Sec. for Communications at Catholic Secretariat, Lusaka, 1966-69. *Recreation:* music. *Address:* PO Box RW3, Lusaka, Zambia. *T:* Lusaka 62232.

**LUSH, Sir Archibald (James),** Kt 1969; retired as Chief Inspector of Schools (Monmouthshire); *b* 15 Sept. 1900. *Educ:* Tredegar Grammar Sch.; Jesus Coll., Oxford. *Publication:* The Young Adult in South Wales, 1939. *Address:* Tremon, The Close, Gilwern, Abergavenny, Mon. *T:* Gilwern 671.

**LUSH, Maurice Stanley,** CB 1944; CBE 1942; MC 1916; *b* 23 Nov. 1896; *s* of late Hubert Stanley Lush; *m* 1930, Diana Ruth, *d* of late Charles Alexander Hill; one *s* two *d*. *Educ:* Tonbridge Sch.; RMA, Woolwich. European War, RA, 1915-19 (MC and Bar); Egyptian Army, 1919-22; Sudan Political Service from 1919; Secretary HM Legation, Addis Ababa, 1919-22; District Commissioner, Sudan, 1922-26; Assistant Civil Secretary Sudan Government, 1926-29; Private Secretary to Governor-General of Sudan, 1929-30; Dep. Governor, Sudan, 1930-35; Sudan Agent, Cairo, 1935-38; Governor, Northern Province, Sudan, 1938-41. War of 1939-45 recalled from RARO as Brig.; Deputy Chief Political Officer, Ethiopia, 1941-42; Military Administrator, Madagascar, 1942; Deputy Chief Civil Affairs Officer British Military Administration, Tripolitania, 1942-43; Executive Commissioner and Vice-President, Allied Commission, Italy, 1943-46; Resident representative for Germany and Austria of Intergovernmental Cttee on Refugees, 1946-47; Chief of Mission in Middle East, IRO, 1947-49; Special Representative for Middle East of IRO, 1949-51; Rep. Anglo-Saxon Petroleum Co., Libya, 1952-56; Man. Dir, Pakistan Shell Oil Co. Ltd, 1956-59. Member, Overseas Cttee, British and Foreign Bible Soc. Order of the Nile, 3rd Class; Officer, Legion of Merit US, 1945; Comdr Order of Knights of Malta, 1945. *Recreation:* gardening. *Address:* Brantridge Forest, Balcombe, Haywards Heath, Sussex. *T:* Handcross 333. *Club:* Athenæum.

*See also Earl of Limerick.*

**LUSHINGTON, Sir Henry Edmund Castleman,** 7th Bt *cr* 1791; *b* 2 May 1909; *s* of Sir Herbert Castleman Lushington, 6th Bt and Barbara Henrietta (*d* 1927), *d* of late Rev. William Greville Hazlerigg; *S* father, 1968; *m* 1937, Pamela Elizabeth Daphne, *er d* of Major Archer R. Hunter, Wokingham, Berks; one *s* two *d*. *Educ:* Dauntsey's Sch. Served War of 1939-45, Flt-Lieut, RAFVR. Metropolitan Police, 1935-58; retired as Superintendent. *Recreations:* gardening, golf. *Heir:* *s* John Richard Castleman Lushington [*b* 28 Aug. 1938; *m* 1966, Bridget Gillian Margaret, *d* of Colonel John Foster Longfield, Crowthorne, Berks; two *s*]. *Address:* Carfax, Crowthorne, Berkshire. *T:* Crowthorne 2819. *Clubs:* MCC; East Berks Golf.

**LUSTGARTEN, Edgar;** author, journalist, broadcaster; *b* 3 May 1907; *s* of Joseph and Sara Lustgarten; *m* 1932, Joyce (*née* Goldstone); no *c*. *Educ:* Manchester Grammar Sch.; St John's Coll., Oxford. Pres., Oxford Union, 1930. Practising Barrister, 1930-40; Radio Counter-Propaganda, 1940-45; BBC Staff Producer, 1945-48; Organiser: BBC Television Programme, In The News, 1950-54; ATV Television Prog., Free Speech, 1955-61; Chm., ATV Television Prog., Fair Play, 1962-65; Narrator, BBC Focus Prog., 1965-68. Solo Broadcaster in many BBC series of Famous Trials, 1952-. *Publications: novels:* A Case to Answer, 1947; Blondie Iscariot, 1948; Game for Three Losers, 1952; *studies in true crime:* Verdict in Dispute, 1949; Defender's Triumph, 1951; The Woman in the Case, 1955; The Business of Murder, 1968. *Address:* c/o Curtis Brown Ltd, 13 King Street, WC2.

**LUSTY, Sir Robert (Frith),** Kt 1969; Managing Director, Hutchinson Publishing Group Ltd, and associated imprints (also Chairman until 1965); Director, Geographia Ltd; *b* 7 June 1909; *o s* of late Frith Lusty; *m* 1st, 1939, Joan Christie (*d* 1962), *y d* of late Archibald Brownlie, Glasgow; 2nd, 1963, Eileen, *widow* of Dr Denis Carroll. *Educ:* Society of Friends' Co-educational Sch., Sidcot. Joined editorial staff The Kent Messenger, 1927; abandoned journalism for publishing and entered production and editorial departments Messrs Hutchinson and Company, 1928; appointed manager associated company, Messrs Selwyn & Blount, 1933; left in 1935 to join Michael Joseph Ltd, on its formation, resigned as Deputy Chairman, 1956, to rejoin the Hutchinson Group; a Governor of the BBC, 1960-68 (Vice-Chairman, 1966-68); Member Council of Publishers' Assoc., 1955-61; Chairman: National Book League, 1949-51 and of its 1951 Festival Cttee; Soc. of Bookmen, 1962-65. Liveryman Stationers' Co., 1945; Freeman of City of London. A Governor and Councillor, Bedford Coll. FRSA 1969. *Address:* 4 Turner's Wood, NW11. *T:* 01-455 5709. *Club:* Garrick.

**LUTTIG, Dr Hendrik Gerhardus;** Ambassador of Republic of South Africa to the Court of St James's since 1967; *b* 26 Oct. 1907; *s* of David and Susanna Luttig; *m* 1939, Dr Marie van Castricum; one *s* one *d*. *Educ:* Wepener High Sch., SA; Grey University College, SA (MA); Leiden Univ., Holland (DLitt et Phil). Became Principal of a leading correspondence college in South Africa. MP for Mayfair, Johannesburg, 1949; served on Public Accounts Cttee and various other select cttees; Ambassador to Vienna, 1965-67. *Recreation:* golf. *Address:* South African Embassy, Trafalgar Square, WC2N 5DP. *T:* 01-930 4488. *Clubs:* Devonshire, Travellers', Eccentric, Hurlingham, MCC; Wimbledon Golf, Swinley Forest Golf (Ascot), Wyke Green Golf (Osterley); HERE XVII (Cape Town); Windsor Park Golf (Johannesburg).

**LUTTRELL, Lieut-Colonel Geoffrey Walter Fownes,** MC 1945; JP; Liaison Officer, Ministry of Agriculture, since 1965; Vice-Lieutenant of Somerset, since 1968; *b* 2 Oct. 1919; *s* of late Geoffrey Fownes Luttrell of Dunster Castle, Somerset; *m* 1942, Hermione Hamilton, *er d* of late Capt. Cecil Gunston, MC, and of Lady Doris Gunston. *Educ:* Eton; Exeter Coll., Oxford. Served War of 1939-45, with 15th/19th King's Royal Hussars, 1940-46; North Somerset Yeomanry, 1952-57; Lt-Col 1955. Member: National Parks Commn, 1962-66; SW Electricity Bd, 1969-. DL Somerset, 1958-68; High Sheriff of Somerset, 1960; JP 1961. *Address:* Court House, East Quantoxhead, Bridgwater, Somerset. *T:* Holford 242. *Clubs:* Cavalry, Flyfishers'.

**LUTYENS, (Agnes) Elisabeth, (Mrs Edward Clark),** CBE 1969; musician, composer; *b* London, 1906; 3rd *d* of late Sir Edwin Landseer Lutyens, OM, KCIE, PRA, LLD and of late Lady Emily Lutyens; *m* 1st, 1933, Ian Herbert Campbell Glennie (marr. diss.); one *s* twin *d*; 2nd, 1942, Edward Clark (*d* 1962); one *s*. *Compositions include:* The Pit, a dramatic scene (for tenor, bass, women's chorus, and orchestra); 3 Symphonic Preludes for orchestra; String Quartet No. 6; O Saisons, O Châteaux (Rimbaud) (for soprano and strings); String Trio; Viola Concerto; Six Chamber Concertos; Valediction for clarinet and piano, 1954; Four Nocturnes, 1954; 6 Tempi for 10 Instruments, 1957; Music for Orchestra, I, II, III; Quincunx for Orchestra, 1959; Wind Quintet, 1961; Symphonies for Solo Piano, Wind, Harps and Percussion, 1961; The Country of the Stars (cantata), 1963; Hymn of Man, 1965; The Valley of Hatsu-se, 1966; Akapotik Rose, 1966; And Suddenly It's Evening, 1967; The Numbered, opera, 1966; Time Off? Not a ghost of a chance, charade in 4 scenes and 3 interruptions; Isis and Osiris, lyric drama, 1969; Novenaria (for orchestra), 1969. Also music for numerous films and radio features. City of London Midsummer Prize, 1969. *Address:* 13 King Henry's Road, NW3. *T:* 01-722 8505.

*See also Mary Lutyens.*

**LUTYENS, Mary, (Mrs J. G. Links);** Writer since 1929; *b* 31 July 1908; *y d* of late Sir Edwin Lutyens, OM, KCIE, PRA, and late Lady Emily Lutyens; *m* 1st, 1930, Anthony Sewell (marr. diss. 1945; decd); one *d*; 2nd, 1945, J. G. Links, OBE. *Educ:* Queen's Coll., London; Sydney, Australia. *Publications: fiction:* Forthcoming Marriages, 1933; Perchance to Dream, 1935; Rose and Thorn, 1936; Spider's Silk, 1939; Family Colouring, 1940; A Path of Gold, 1941; Together and Alone, 1942; So Near to Heaven, 1943; And Now There is You, 1953; Week-End at Hurtmore, 1954; The Lucian Legend, 1955; Meeting in Venice, 1956; *for children:* Julie and the Narrow Valley, 1944; *autobiography:* To Be Young, 1959; *edited:* Lady Lytton's Court Diary, 1961; (for Krishnamurti) Freedom from the Known, 1969; The Only Revolution, 1970; The Penguin Krishnamurti Reader, 1970; The Urgency of Change, 1971; *biography:* Effie in Venice, 1965; Millais and the Ruskins, 1967; also numerous serials, afterwards published, under pseudonym of Esther Wyndham; contribs to Apollo and The Cornhill. *Recreations:* reading, cinema-going. *Address:* 2 Hyde Park Street, W2. *T:* 01-262 0455.

*See also Elisabeth Lutyens.*

**LUTZ, Marianne Christine;** Headmistress, Sheffield High School for Girls (Girls' Public Day School Trust), since 1959; *b* 9 Dec. 1922; *d* of Dr H. Lutz. *Educ:* Wimbledon High Sch., GPDST; Girton Coll., Cambridge (Schol.); University of London. Asst Mistress (History) at: Clergy Daughters' Sch., Bristol, 1946-47; South Hampstead High Sch., GPDST, 1947-59. Member: History Textbooks Panel for W Germany (under auspices of FO and Unesco); Diocesan Educn Council and other educational advisory bodies; Ct and Professional Cttee, Univ. of Sheffield; Historical Assoc.; Headmistresses' Assoc.; Schnauzer Club of Great Britain. *Publications:* several in connection with Unesco work and Historical Assoc. *Recreations:* travel, crosswords, books, opera, art and theatre. *Address:* Flat A, 8 Summerfield, Broomhill, Sheffield, S10 3DD.

**LUXFORD, John Hector,** CMG 1953; Chairman War Pensions Appeal Board for New Zealand, 1951-65; *b* Palmerston North, New Zealand, 28 May 1890; *y s* of W. L. Luxford, JP; *m* Laura Dagmar, *y d* of John Otton, Numerella, Bega, New South Wales; two *s*. *Educ:* Wanganui Collegiate Sch., NZ. Admitted Solicitor of the Supreme Court of NZ, 1913; admitted Barrister of the Supreme Court of NZ, 1919; served in NZ Expeditionary Forces, attaining rank of Major (despatches); subsequently posted to Reserve of Officers, NZ Military Forces, with rank of Major; Stipendiary Magistrate, 1928; Chief Judge of Western Samoa, 1929-35; Stipendiary Magistrate, Wellington, 1935-41; Principal Stipendiary Magistrate, Auckland, NZ, 1941-51. Mayor of Auckland, NZ, 1953-56. Chairman, Transport Licensing Appeal Authority, Air Services Licensing Appeal Authority, 1966-68; Chm., No 2 town and Country Planning Appeal Board, 1968-. *Publications:* With the Machine Gunners in France and Palestine, 1922 (an official history of the NZ Machine Gun Corps); Liquor Laws of New Zealand, 3rd edn 1964; Police Law in New Zealand, 3rd edn 1966; Real Estate Agency in New Zealand, 4th edn 1964; Commercial Law in New Zealand, 2nd edn 1961; Domestic Proceedings, 1956, 2nd edn 1970. *Address:* Bega, 35 Orakei Road, Remuera, Auckland 5, NZ. *Club:* Northern (Auckland).

**LUXTON, William John,** CBE 1962; Director, The London Chamber of Commerce, since 1964 (Secretary since 1958); Director, Federation of Commonwealth Chambers of Commerce, since Nov. 1958; *b* 18 March 1909; *s* of late John Luxton; *m* 1942, Megan, *d* of late John M. Harries; one *s* one *d*. *Educ:* Shebbear Coll., N Devon; London Univ. Wallace Brothers & Co. Ltd (merchant bankers), 1926-38. Called to the Bar, Lincoln's Inn, 1938; Chancery Bar, 1938-40. Served with Royal Armoured Corps, 1940-45. Legal Parliamentary Secretary, Association of British Chambers of Commerce, 1947-53; Secretary Birmingham Chamber of Commerce, 1953-58. Organised Federation of Commonwealth Chambers of Commerce Congresses at canberra, 1960, London, 1962, Port of Spain, 1964, London, 1968, Hong Kong 1970. *Address:* Abbots Lodge,

Abbotswood, Guildford, Surrey. *T:* Guildford 63439. *Club:* Gresham.

**LUYT, Sir Richard (Edmonds),** GCMG 1966 (KCMG 1964; CMG 1960); KCVO 1966; DCM 1942; Vice-Chancellor and Principal, University of Cape Town, since 1968; *b* 8 Nov. 1915; *m* 1st, 1948, Jean Mary Wilder (*d* 1951); one *d;* 2nd, 1956, Eileen Betty Reid; two *s*. *Educ:* Diocesan Coll., Rondebosch, Cape, SA; Univ. of Cape Town (BA); Trinity Coll., Oxford (MA). Rhodes Scholar from S Africa, 1937. Entered Colonial Service and posted to N Rhodesia, 1940; War Service, 1940-45: with Mission 101, in Ethiopia, 1941; remained in Ethiopia with British Military Mission, for remainder of War. Returned to N Rhodesia, Colonial Service, 1945; transferred to Kenya, 1953; Labour Commissioner, Kenya, 1954-57; Permanent Secretary to various Ministries of the Kenya Government, 1957-60; Secretary to the Cabinet, 1960-61; Chief Secretary, Northern Rhodesia, 1962-64; Governor and C-in-C, British Guiana, 1964-66, until Guyana Independence; Governor-General of Guyana, May-Oct. 1966. *Recreations:* gardening, sport, particularly Rugby (Oxford Blue, 1938) and cricket (Oxford Captain 1940) (also played for Kenya at cricket). *Address:* University of Cape Town, Rondebosch, Cape, South Africa. *Clubs:* Royal Commonwealth Society; Nairobi (Kenya); Civil Service (Cape Town).

**LWOFF, Prof. André;** Commandeur de la Légion d'Honneur, 1966 (Officier, 1960; Chevalier, 1947); Médaille de la Résistance, 1946; Directeur de l'Institut de Recherches Scientifiques sur le Cancer, since 1968; Professor of Microbiology, Faculté des Sciences, Paris, 1959-68, and Head of Department of Microbial Physiology, Pasteur Institute, since 1938; *b* Ainay-le-Château, Allier, France, 8 May 1902. *Educ:* (Fac. des Sciences et de Méd.) Univ. of Paris. MD (Paris) 1927; DSc (Paris) 1932. With the Pasteur Institute, 1921-. Foreign Member of the Royal Society (London), 1958; also Hon. or Foreign Member of American Academies, etc; Pres., Internat. Assoc. of Societies of Microbiology, 1962. Vis. Prof., Albert Einstein Coll. of Medicine, New York, 1964. Holds hon. doctorates in science and law at British and other foreign univs. Awarded several prizes and medals from 1928 onwards, both French and foreign, for his work; Nobel Prize for Medicine (jointly), 1965; Einstein Award, 1967. *Publications:* L'Evolution physiologique, Collection de microbiologie, Hermann éd., 1944 (Paris); Problems of Morphogenesis in Ciliates, The Kinetosomes in Development, Reproduction and Evolution, 1950 (New York); Biological Order, 1962, MIT. *Recreation:* painting. *Address:* 69 Avenue de Suffren, Paris 7e. *T:* Suffren 27-82; BP no 8, 94 Villejuif, France.

**LYALL, Mrs Gavin;** *see* Whitehorn, Katharine E.

**LYALL, William Chalmers,** MBE 1952; HM Consul-General, Genoa, since 1969; *b* 6 Aug. 1921; *s* of John Brown Lyall and Margaret Angus Leighton Stevenson Lyall; *m* 1948, Janet Lawson McKechnie; two *s* one *d. Educ:* Kelty Public and Beath Secondary schools. Min. of Labour, 1940-48; HM Forces, 1941-47; FO, 1948; Hankow, 1948-51; São Paulo, 1952-53; Manila, 1953-55; FO, 1955-57; Caracas, 1957-60; Bahrain, 1960-64; FO, 1964-65; DSAO, 1965-68; FCO, 1968-69. *Recreations:* music, photography. *Address:* Villa Medici, Via S Bartolomeo degli Armeni 11, Genoa, Italy. *T:* 881397. *Clubs:* Union, Propeller (Genoa).

**LYALL GRANT, Maj.-Gen. Ian Hallam,** MC 1944; Director General, Systems Co-ordination, Ministry of Defence, since 1970; *b* 4 June 1915; *s* of Col H. F. Lyall Grant, DSO; *m* 1951, Mary Jennifer Moore; one *s* two *d. Educ:* Cheltenham Coll.; RMA, Woolwich; Cambridge Univ. (MA). Regular Commission, RE, 1935; service in: India, Burma and Japan, 1938-46 (MC; twice mentioned in despatches); Cyprus and Egypt, 1951-52; Imperial Defence Coll., 1961; Aden, 1962-63; Comdt, Royal School of Mil. Engineering, 1965-67; Maj.-Gen. 1966; Dep. QMG, 1967-70, retired 1970. *Recreations:* sailing, ski-ing, fishing, shooting, paintings. *Address:* Kingswear House, Kingswear, S Devon. *T:* Kingswear 359. *Club:* United Service.

**LYCETT, Brigadier Cyril Vernon Lechmere,** OBE 1921; BA; *b* 14 May 1894; *s* of A. E. Lechmere and J. M. Lycett; *m* 1921, Alexandra Sandika Camarioto; two *d. Educ:* King Edward VI Sch., Birmingham; Trinity Coll., Cambridge (Scholar). Entered army, Royal Engineers (SR) 1914; served European War, 1914-18 (despatches twice, OBE). Transferred Royal Corps of Signals, 1922; Chairman Wireless Telegraphy Board, 1938-42; served War of 1939-45; Director of Signal Intelligence, India and SEAC, 1945-46, retired 1946. Sec. Royal Horticultural Soc., 1946-56. *Address:* 3700 Los Feliz Boulevard, Apt 20, Los Angeles, California 90027, USA.

**LYDDON, William Derek Collier;** Chief Planning Officer, Scottish Development Department, since 1967; *b* 17 Nov. 1925; *s* of A. J. Lyddon, CBE, and E. E. Lyddon; *m* 1949, Marian Louise Kaye Charlesworth, *d* of Prof. J. K. Charlesworth, *qv*; two *d. Educ:* Wrekin Coll.; University College, London. BA (Arch.) 1952; ARIBA 1953; DipTP 1954; AMTPI 1963. Depute Chief Architect and Planning Officer, Cumbernauld Development Corporation, 1962; Chief Architect and Planning Officer, Skelmersdale Development Corporation, 1963-67. *Recreations:* walking, reading. *Address:* 38 Dick Place, Edinburgh 9. *T:* 031-667 2266.

**LYDFORD, Air Marshal Sir Harold Thomas,** KBE 1954 (CBE 1945); CB 1948; AFC; Commander of Legion of Merit, USA; *b* 1898; *m* Isabel Broughton Smart. Wing Commander, 1937; Group Captain, 1942; Air Commodore, 1946; Air Vice-Marshal, 1947; Air Marshal, 1953; Director of Organisation, Air Ministry, 1941; Member RAF delegation, Washington, DC, 1942-44; Air Officer Commanding No. 28 Group, 1944; Air Officer Commanding, British Forces, Aden, 1945-48; Comdt-General RAF Regiment, 1948-50; AOC No. 18 Group, Coastal Command, and Senior Air Force Officer in Scotland, 1950-52; Air Officer Commanding-in-Chief, Home Command, 1952-March 1956, retired. Chairman National Council, Royal Air Forces Assoc. *Address:* Merchiston, Hare Hatch, Twyford, Berks. *Clubs:* United Service, Royal Air Force.

**LYELL,** family name of **Baron Lyell.**

**LYELL, 3rd Baron** *cr* 1914, of Kinnordy; **Charles Lyell;** Bt, 1894; *b* 27 March 1939; *s* of 2nd Baron, VC (killed in action, 1943), and Sophie, *d* of Major S. W. and Lady Betty Trafford; *S* father, 1943. *Educ:* Eton; Christ Church, Oxford. 2nd Lieut Scots Guards, 1957-59. CA Scotland. *Heir:* none. *Address:* 20 Petersham Mews, SW7. *T:* 01-584 9419; Kinnordy House, Kirriemuir, Angus. *T:* Kirriemuir 2848. *Club:* Turf.

**LYELL, Hon. Sir Maurice (Legat),** Kt 1962; QC 1954; **Hon. Mr Justice Lyell;** Judge of the

Queen's Bench Division, High Court of Justice, since 1962; *b* 28 July 1901; 7th *s* of Alexander Lyell, Gardyne Castle, Angus; *m* 1937, Veronica Mary Luard (*d* 1950); one *s* one *d* (and one *d* decd); *m* 1955, Hon. Katharine, *y d* of 1st Viscount Runciman of Doxford, and *widow* of 4th Baron Farrer. *Educ:* Trinity Coll., Glenalmond; Keble Coll., Oxford (MA). Called to Bar, Inner Temple, 1926; Bencher, 1960. Dir of Press Censorship, Min. of Information, 1940-45. Gen. Council of Bar, 1953-57, 1958-62. Joint Master, with wife, of Aldenham Harriers. *Publication:* Law of Income Tax relating to Non-residents and Foreign Income, 1930. *Recreation:* idling. *Address:* Royal Courts of Justice, Strand, WC2; Puddephats, Markyate, Herts. *T:* Markyate 317.

**LYGON,** family name of **Earl Beauchamp.**

**LYLE,** family name of **Baron Lyle of Westbourne.**

**LYLE OF WESTBOURNE,** 2nd Baron *cr* 1945, of Canford Cliffs; **Charles John Leonard Lyle;** Bt, 1932; JP; Director, Messrs Tate & Lyle Ltd, since 1954, Managing Director, 1929-54; *b* 8 March 1905; *S* father, 1954; *m* 1927, Joyce Jeanne, *er d* of Sir (Joseph) John Jarvis, 1st Bt; no *c. Educ:* Harrow Sch.; Pembroke Coll., Cambridge (BA). Dep. Dir, Sugar Div., Min. of Food, 1939-50. JP Surrey, 1951-. *Recreations:* travel, lawn tennis. *Heir:* none. *Address:* Bakersgate, Pirbright, Woking, Surrey. *T:* Worplesdon 2120.

**LYLE, Sir Gavin Archibald,** 3rd Bt *cr* 1929; *b* 14 Oct. 1941; *s* of late Ian Archibald de Hoghton Lyle and of Hon. Lydia Yarde-Buller (who *m* 1947, as his 2nd wife, 13th Duke of Bedford; marr. diss. 1960; now Lydia Duchess of Bedford), *d* of 3rd Baron Churston; *S* grandfather, 1946; *m* 1967, Suzy Cooper; two *s. Heir: s* Ian Abram Lyle, *b* 25 Sept. 1968. *Address:* Burrow Hill Farm, Chobham, Surrey.

**LYLE, Sir Ian D.,** Kt 1959; DSC; President of Tate & Lyle Ltd (Chairman 1954-64); *b* 1907; *s* of late Colonel Arthur Lyle, OBE, TD, Barrington Court, Ilminster, Somerset; *m* 1935, Julia Margaret (*d* 1962), *d* of David McWhirter McKechnie, South Africa; one *s* two *d. Educ:* Shrewsbury Sch.; St John's Coll., Oxford. *Address:* Tate & Lyle Ltd, 21 Mincing Lane, EC3; Barrington Court, Ilminster, Somerset. *T:* South Petherton 243. *Club:* Royal Thames Yacht.

**LYLE, James Duncan,** MB, BS, MRCS, LRCP; retired; *b* 1887; *o s* of late James Lyle, Hunter's Quay, Argyllshire; *m* 1918, Irene Violet, *o d* of late Henry Alabaster, Eastbourne; one *d.* James Anderson Prize in Clinical Medicine; late Emergency Officer, late assistant anæsthetist, London Hospital. *Address:* c/o Mrs G. T. Hesketh, 41 Hanover Gate Mansions, Park Road, NW1. *T:* 01-723 4889.

**LYLE, John Oliver;** Chairman, Tate & Lyle Ltd since 1964; *b* 26 April 1918; *o s* of late Sir Oliver Lyle and of Lilian Isobel, Lady Lyle (*née* Spicer); *m* 1944, Lydia Joan Mildred (marr. diss. 1948); one *d*; *m* 1960, Jill Margaret Pilkington (*née* Skinner); one *s* one *d. Educ:* Uppingham; Clare Coll., Cambridge. Joined HAC 1939; Lieut, RA; transferred RAF for flying duties, 1942, 26 and 234 Squadrons. Joined Tate & Lyle Ltd, 1945; appointed to Board, 1951. *Address:* Rotherhurst, Rotherfield, Sussex. *T:* Rotherfield 648; 25 Catherine Place, SW1. *T:* 01-834 2773.

**LYLE, Thomas Keith,** CBE 1949; MA, MD, MChir (Cantab); FRCP, FRCS; Consulting Ophthalmic Surgeon: King's College Hospital (Ophthalmic Surgeon, 1938-69); Moorfields Eye Hospital (Ophthalmic Surgeon, 1936-69); National Hospital, Queen Square (Ophthalmic Surgeon, 1936-69); Director, Orthoptic Department, Moorfields Eye Hospital, 1947-69; Dean of Institute of Ophthalmology, British Post-graduate Medical Federation of University of London, 1959-67; Teacher of Ophthalmology, University of London; *b* 26 Dec. 1903; *s* of late Herbert Willoughby Lyle, MD, FRCS, Fircliff, Portishead, Somerset; *m* 1949, Jane Bouverie, *e d* of late Major Nigel Maxwell, RA, and of Mrs Maxwell, Great Davids, Kingwood, Henley-on-Thames; one *s* three *d. Educ:* Dulwich Coll.; Sidney Sussex Coll., Cambridge (Exhib.); King's College Hospital (Burney Yeo Schol.). Todd medal for Clinical Medicine; House Physician, House Surg., Sen. Surg. Registrar; First Asst Neurol. Dept, King's Coll. Hosp., 1929-33; House Surgeon, Royal Westminster Ophth. Hosp., 1934. Civilian Consultant in Ophth., RAF, 1948-; Consultant in Ophth. Dept of Civil Aviation, Board of Trade; Hon. Consultant in Ophth., BALPA. Examiner in Ophthalmology: Bristol Univ., 1947-50; RCS, 1949-55; FRCS (Ophthalmology), 1958-66; FRCSE (Ophthalmology), 1960; Mem. Coun., Faculty of Ophthalmologists, 1946-, Pres., 1965-68, and Rep. on Council of RCS, 1958-63; Past Mem., International Council of Ophthalmology; Mem. Court of Assts, Soc. of Apothecaries, Junior Warden, 1960; Senior Warden, 1961; Master, 1962-63. Mem., Ophthalmic Hosp. Cttee Of St John; Order of St John, Deputy Hospitaller, 1960-69; Hospitaller, 1969-; Member Council: Med. Protection Soc.; Royal London Soc. for the Blind; Past Pres., Internat. Strabismological Assoc.; Treas., British Orthoptic Board. Member: Ophth. Soc. UK, Pres. 1968-70; Orthoptists Bd, Council for Professions Supplementary to Medicine; Soc. Franc. d'Ophthalmologie; FRSocMed (Vice-Pres. Ophth. Section, Pres. United Services Section, 1964-66); Hon. Mem. Ophth. Socs of Australia and New Zealand. Chas H. May Memorial Lectr, New York, 1952; Doyne Memorial Lectr, Oxford, 1953; Alexander Welch Lectr, 1965. Nettleship Medal, 1959. Served RAFVR, 1939-46, Temp. Air Cdre Cons. in Ophth. RAF overseas (despatches). CStJ 1956; KStJ 1960; Kt, Order of Holy Sepulchre, 1970. *Publications:* (co-ed with Sylvia Jackson) Practical Orthoptics in the Treatment of Squints, 1937, 5th edn (co-ed with K. C. Wybar) 1967; (co-ed with Hon. G. J. O. Bridgeman) Worth's Squint by F. B. Chavasse, 9th edn 1959; (co-ed with A. G. Cross) May and Worth's Diseases of the Eye, 13th edn 1968; (co-ed with late H. Willoughby Lyle) Applied Physiology of the Eye, 1958; articles in British Jl Ophth., Lancet, BMJ, Med. Press and Circular, etc, chapters in Sorsby's Modern Trends in Ophthalmology, 1948, in Stallard's Modern Practice in Ophthalmology, 1949 and in Rob and Rodney Smith's Operative Surgery, 1958. *Recreations:* lawn tennis, riding, ski-ing. *Address:* 6 Chesterfield Street, Mayfair, W1. *T:* 01-944 2481; Cherrycroft, Kingwood, nr Henley-on-Thames, Oxon. *T:* Rotherfield Greys 234. *Clubs:* Bath, Royal Air Force, Royal Automobile.

**LYMBERY, Robert Davison,** QC 1967; Barrister-at-Law; Recorder of Grantham since 1965; Chairman: Rutland Quarter Sessions, since 1966; Bedfordshire Quarter Sessions, since 1969; *b* 14 Nov. 1920; *s* of Robert Smith Lymbery and late Louise Lymbery; *m* 1952, Pauline Anne, *d* of John Reginald and Kathleen Tuckett; three *d. Educ:* Gresham's Sch.; Pembroke Coll., Cambridge. Served Army, 1940-46; commissioned 17/21 Lancers, 1941; Middle East, Italy, Greece (Royal Tank Regt),

1942-46, Major. Pembroke Coll., 1939-40, 1946-48 (MA, LLB 1st class hons). Foundation Exhibn. 1948; called to Bar, 1949; Harmsworth Law Scholar, 1949; practice on Midland Circuit, 1949-. Dep. Chm., Rutland QS, 1962-66, Beds QS, 1961-69; Chm. Stevenage New Town Licensed Premises Cttee, 1966-. *Recreations:* golf, cricket, motoring, gardening. *Address:* 2 Crown Office Row, Temple, EC4. *T:* 01-353 1365; Park Lodge, Knebworth, Herts. *T:* Knebworth 3308. *Club:* Hawks (Cambridge).

**LYMER, Brigadier Rymel Watts,** CBE 1945 (MBE 1943); DSO 1943; TD 1951; DL; *b* 1909; *s* of late Charles Richard Lymer, Chorley, Lancs; *m* 1st, Shelagh Dorham (*d* 1954), *d* of late Frederick Dearden, Upton, Cheshire; two *s* one *d*; 2nd, 1957, Edna, *d* of late Evan Dixon Robinson, Chorley, Lancs, and *widow* of George William Harper. *Educ:* William Hulme's Sch. Served War of 1939-45: France, Middle East, Sicily, Italy and NW Europe (despatches thrice, MBE, DSO, CBE). ADS & T, 1942, AQMG, 1943, Eighth Army; Brig. 'Q', 21st Army Group, 1944. Hon. Col 42 Lancs Div. RASC, 1949-54; Vice-Chm. E Lancs T & AFA, 1959-68; Mem., Lancs and Cheshire TA&VRA, 1968-. A Governor of Lyme Green Settlement for Paraplegics, Macclesfield. Managing Director, North British Chemical Co. Ltd, 1946-58. Retired from Manchester Stock Exchange, Sept. 1965. DL Lancs, 1961. *Recreations:* Territorial Army and travel. *Address:* Chynalls, Mobberley, Cheshire. *T:* Mobberley 2100. *Club:* St James's (Manchester).

**LYMINGTON, Viscount; Oliver Kintzing Wallop;** Lieut RNVR (retired); *b* 14 Jan. 1923; *s* of 9th Earl of Portsmouth, *qv*; *m* 1st, 1952, Maureen (marr. diss. 1954), *o d* of Lt-Col Kenneth B. Stanley; 2nd, 1954, Ruth Violet, *yr d* of late Brig.-General G. C. Sladen, CB, CMG, DSO, MC; one *s* two *d*. *Educ:* Eton. *Address:* Barton House, Bridford, near Exeter, Devon.

**LYMPANY, Miss Moura,** FRAM 1948; concert pianist; *b* Saltash, Cornwall, 18 Aug. 1916; British; *d* of John and Beatrice Johnstone; *m* 1944, Lt-Col Colin Defries (marr. diss. 1950); *m* 1951, Bennet H. Korn, American Television Executive (marr. diss. 1961); one *s* decd. *Educ:* Belgium, Austria, England. First public performance at age of 12, 1929, at Harrogate, playing Mendelssohn G Minor Concerto. Won second prize out of 79 competitors at Ysaye International Pianoforte Competition at Brussels, 1938. Has played in USA, Canada, South America, Australia, New Zealand, India, and all principal European countries. Records for HMV and Decca. *Recreations:* travelling and reading. *Address:* 18 East 68th Street, New York, NY 10021, USA.

**LYNAM, Jocelyn Humphrey Rickman,** MA (Oxon); Headmaster Dragon School, Oxford, 1933-65; *b* 27 June 1902; *s* of Alfred Edmund and Mabel Agnes Lynam; *m* 1965, Barbara Frearson. *Educ:* The Dragon School, Oxford; Rugby (Scholar); Hertford Coll. (Exhibitioner), Oxford. Asst master at The Dragon School, 1925; Joint Headmaster, 1933. Served on Council of Incorporated Association of Preparatory Schools, 1936-38, 1940-42, 1944-46, 1949-51, 1953-55, 1958-. Chairman of Council of IAPS, 1941 and 1942. *Recreations:* gardening; formerly cricket (Rugby School XI) and hockey (Oxford Univ., 1925). *Address:* 6 Chadlington Road, Oxford. *Club:* Vincent's (Oxford).

**LYNCH, Rev. Prebendary Donald MacLeod,** MA; Chief Secretary of the Church Army since 1960; Prebendary of Twiford in St Paul's Cathedral, since 1964; Chaplain to the Queen, since 1969; *b* 2 July 1911; *s* of Herbert and Margaret Lynch; *m* 1st, 1941, Ailsa Leslie Leask; three *s* one *d*; 2nd, 1963, Jean Wileman. *Educ:* City of London Sch.; Pembroke Coll., Cambridge; Wycliffe Hall, Oxford. Curate, Christ Church, Chelsea, 1935; Tutor, Oak Hill Theological Coll., 1938; Curate, St Michael's, Stonebridge Park, 1940; Minister, All Saints, Queensbury, 1942; Vicar, St Luke's, Tunbridge Wells, 1950; Principal, Church Army Training Coll., 1953. *Recreations:* reading and gardening. *Address:* 185 Marylebone Road, NW1. *T:* 01-262 3211. *Club:* Union (Cambridge).

**LYNCH, John;** Taoiseach (Head of Government of Ireland) since Nov. 1966; Teachta Dala (TD) for Cork, Parliament of Ireland, since 1948; *b* 15 Aug. 1917; *y s* of Daniel Lynch and Norah O'Donoghue; *m* 1946, Mairin O'Connor. *Educ:* Christian Brothers' Schools, N Monastery, Cork; University College, Cork; King's Inns, Dublin. Entered Civil Service (Dept of Justice), 1936; called to Bar, 1945; resigned from Civil Service, became Mem. Munster Bar and commenced practice in Cork Circuit, 1945. Parly Sec. to Govt and to Minister for Lands, 1951-54; Minister for: Education, 1957-59; Industry and Commerce, 1959-65; Finance, 1965-66. Alderman, Co. Borough of Cork, 1950-57; Mem. Cork Sanatoria Board and Cttee of Management, N Infirmary, Cork, 1950-51 and 1955-57; Mem. Cork Harbour Comrs, 1956-57; Vice-Pres., Consultative Assembly of Council of Europe, 1958; Pres., Internat. Labour Conf., 1962. Hon. LLD: Dublin, 1967; Nat. Univ. of Ireland, 1969. Grand Cross, Order of the Crown (Belgium), 1968. *Address:* 21 Garville Avenue, Rathgar, Dublin 6, Ireland.

**LYNCH, Patrick,** MA; Associate Professor of Political Economy, University College, Dublin, since 1966; Chairman, Aer Lingus, since 1954; *b* 5 May 1918; *s* of Daniel and Brigid Lynch, Co. Tipperary and Dublin; *m* Mary Crotty (*née* Campbell). *Educ:* Catholic Univ. Sch., Dublin; Univ. Coll., Dublin; Peterhouse, Cambridge. Fellow Commoner, Peterhouse, 1956. Entered Irish Civil Service, 1941; Asst Sec. to Govt, 1950; Univ. Lectr in Econs, UC Dublin, 1952. Has lectured in Econs in Dublin Univ., UC Cork, Magee Univ., LSE and delivered many Thomas Davis lectures from Radio Eireann. Has acted as economic consultant to OECD, Council of Europe, Dept of Finance, Dublin, Gulbenkian Inst., Lisbon. Directed surveys sponsored by Irish Govt with OECD into long-term Irish educnl needs, 1965, and into requirements of Irish economy in respect of scientific res., develt and technology, 1966; estab. Science Policy Res. Centre in Dept of Applied Econs, UC Dublin, 1969. Mem., Statistical and Social Inquiry Soc. of Ireland; Mem., various Irish Govt Commns and Cttees, 1952-; Chm., Medico-Social Research Board, 1966-; Mem., Higher Educn Authority, 1968-; Mem. Ed. Board: Economic and Social Review; University Review; European Teacher; Chm., Nat. Library of Ireland Soc., 1969; Chm., Irish Anti-Apartheid Movement, 1969; Mem., Irish Assoc. for Civil Liberty. *Publications:* Planning for Economic Development in Ireland, 1959; (with J. Vaizey) Guinness's Brewery in the Irish Economy, 1960; (jtly) Economics of Educational Costing, 1969; (with Brian Hillery) Ireland in the International Labour Organisation, 1969; (jt ed) Economic Development Planning, 1969; essays in various symposia, etc; articles in Administration, The Bell, Encycl. Britannica, Econ. History Review, Irish Hist. Studies, Irish Jl of Educn, Statist, Studies, University

Review, etc. *Address:* University College, Dublin 4, Ireland. *T:* Dublin 694866. *Clubs:* University (Dublin); Royal Irish Yacht.

**LYNCH-BLOSSE, Sir David Edward,** 16th Bt *cr* 1622; with George Allen & Unwin Ltd, since 1960; *b* 24 Nov. 1925; *s* of Hely Richard Lynch-Blosse (*d* 1928), and Evangeline Margaret Victoria, *d* of late Charles William Maitland Hudson; *S* uncle, 1969; *m* 1950, Elizabeth, *er d* of Thomas Harold Payne, Welwyn Garden City; one *s* two *d. Educ:* Marlborough; Jesus College, Oxford. Administrative Officer, Northern Nigeria, 1950-59. *Heir: s* Richard Hely Lynch-Blosse, *b* 26 Aug. 1953. *Address:* 38 Elmwood, Welwyn Garden City, Herts.

**LYNCH-ROBINSON, Sir Niall (Bryan),** 3rd Bt *cr* 1920; DSC 1941; late Lieut RNVR; Deputy Chairman, Leo Burnett LPE Ltd; *b* 24 Feb. 1918; *s* of Sir Christopher Henry Lynch-Robinson, 2nd Bt and Dorothy (*d* 1970), *d* of Henry Warren, Carrickmines, Co. Dublin; *S* father 1958; *m* 1940, Rosemary Seaton, *e d* of Mrs M. Seaton Eller; one *s* one (adopted) *d. Educ:* Stowe. Sub-Lieut 1939, Lieut 1940, RNVR; served War of 1939-45 (DSC, Croix de Guerre). *Recreations:* fishing, gardening. *Heir: s* Dominick Christopher Lynch-Robinson, *b* 30 July 1948. *Address:* The Old Parsonage, East Clandon, Surrey.

**LYNDE, Professor Carleton J.,** BA, PhD; Professor of Physics, Teachers' College, Columbia University, 1924-39; Professor Emeritus, since 1939; *b* Mitchell, Ontario, 1 Sept. 1872; *m*; one *s. Educ:* University of Toronto, AB; University of Chichago, PhD. Science Master, Auburn, NY, High Sch., 1896-99; Instructor in Physics, University High Sch., Chicago, 1899-1906; Professor of Physics, Washington and Jefferson Coll., Washington, Pa, 1906-07; Prof. of Physics, Macdonald Coll., PQ, Canada, 1907-24. *Publications:* Effect of Pressure on Surface Tension; Home Waterworks; Osmosis in Soils: the soil acts as a Semipermeable Membrane; On Osmosis in Soils: the Efficiency of the Soil Constituents as Semipermeable Membranes; On a New Method of Measuring the Capillary Lift of Soils; Physics of the Household: an elementary text-book for students of household science; Laboratory Manual on Physics of the Household; Hydraulic and Pneumatic Engineering for Boys; Light Experiments for Boys; Experimental Glass-Blowing for Boys; Everyday Physics; A Laboratory Course in Everyday Physics; Science Experiences with Home Equipment; Science Experiences with Inexpensive Equipment; Science Experiences with Ten-Cent Store Equipment. *Recreations:* formerly tennis, golf, fishing. *Address:* 809 Carlton Towers, 470 Third Street, St Petersburg, Florida 33701, USA.

**LYNE, Arthur W.,** OBE 1939; *b* 21 July 1884; one *d. Educ:* Kettering Road Elementary Sch., Northampton. Boot and Shoe Operative until 1914. Served War of 1914-18 with Northants Regt as Sergeant. Officer National Union Boot and Shoe Operative, 1919. A Chairman, Northampton Borough Council, 1920-64; Mayor of Borough, 1938 and 1939; Hon. Freeman of Borough, 1958. JP Northampton Borough, 1923-64. MP (Lab) for Burton-on-Trent, 1945-50. *Address:* 52 Greenfield Road, Northampton. *T:* Northampton 42079.

**LYNE, Air Vice-Marshal Michael Dillon,** CB 1968; AFC (two Bars); AFRAeS; Director-General of Training, Royal Air Force, since 1970; *b* 23 March 1919; *s* of late Robert John Lyne, Winchester; *m* 1943, Avril Joy Buckley, *d* of late Lieut-Colonel Albert Buckley, CBE, DSO; two *s* two *d. Educ:* Imperial Service Coll.; RAF Coll., Cranwell. Commissioned and joined No 19 Fighter Squadron, July 1939; Merchant Ship Fighter Unit, 1941; Egypt, 1943 (AFC); Comdg No 54 Fighter Squadron, 1946-48; RAF Coll., Cranwell, 1950-52; RAF Flying Coll., 1953-56; Directing Staff, RAF Staff Coll., 1956-58; Comdg RAF Wildenrath, 1958-60; Air Attaché, Moscow, 1961-63; Commandant, Royal Air Force Coll., Cranwell, 1963-64; Imperial Defence Coll., 1965; Air Officer Commanding No 23 Group, RAF Flying Training Command, 1965-67; Senior RAF Instructor, Imperial Defence Coll., 1968-69. *Recreations:* ski-ing, photography, fell walking, gardening. *Address:* Far End, Far Lane, Coleby, Lincoln. *T:* Navenby 468. *Clubs:* United Service, Royal Air Force.

**LYNES, Rear-Adm. Charles Edward,** CMG 1919; *b* 1875; *s* of late Edward Lynes, MD, JP, Coventry; *m* 1954, Muriel Vaughan. Entered Royal Navy, 1893; retired list, 1930. *Address:* Brown Ridge, Long Crendon, Aylesbury, Bucks. *Club:* United Service.

**LYNN, Suffragan Bishop of,** since 1963; **Rt. Rev. William Somers Llewellyn;** *b* 16 Aug. 1907; *s* of Owen John and Elizabeth Llewellyn; *m* 1947, Innis Mary, *d* of Major Arthur Dorrien-Smith, Tresco Abbey, Isles of Scilly; three *s. Educ:* Eton; Balliol and Wycliffe Hall, Oxford. BA 1929; diploma in Theology (with dist.) 1934; MA 1937. Priest, 1936; Curate of Chiswick, 1935-37; Vicar of Badminton, with Acton Turville, 1937-49. CF 1940-46; served with Royal Gloucestershire Hussars in Egypt and Western Desert, and as Senior Chaplain with 8th Army HQ, Canal Area and East Africa; Vicar of Tetbury with Beverston, 1949-61; Rural Dean of Tetbury, 1955-61; Archdeacon of Lynn, 1961-. Appointed first Suffragan Bishop of Lynn, 1963. *Address:* Archdeacon's House, Stiffkey, Wells-next-the-Sea, Norfolk. *T:* Binham 347.

**LYNN, Archdeacon of;** *see under* Lynn, Suffragan Bishop of.

**LYNN, Prof. Richard;** Research Professor in Psychology, at the Economic and Social Research Institute, Dublin, from 1967; *b* 20 Feb. 1930; *s* of Richard and Ann Lynn; *m* 1956, Susan Maher; one *s* two *d. Educ:* Bristol Grammar Sch.; King's Coll., Cambrdige. Lectr in Psychology, Univ. of Exeter, 1956-67; Prof. of Psychology, Dublin Economic and Social Research Inst., 1967-71. *Publications:* Attention, Arousal and the Orientation Reaction, 1966; The Irish Braindrain, 1969; The Universities and the Business Community, 1969; Personality and National Character, 1970; Introduction to Personality, 1970; articles on personality and social psychology. *Address:* 6 Palmerston Road, Dublin 6, Ireland. *T:* 975408. *Club:* Arts (Dublin).

**LYNN, Wilfred;** Director: National Westminster Bank Ltd (Outer London Board); North Central Finance Ltd; *b* 19 May 1905; *s* of late Wilfred Crosland Lynn and Alice Lynn; *m* 1936, Valerie, *e d* of late B. M. A. Critchley; one *s* one *d* (twins). *Educ:* Hull Grammar Sch. Entered National Provicial Bank Ltd, 1921; Joint General Manager, 1953; Chief General Manager, 1961; retired, 1965. *Recreation:* golf. *Address:* Godden Way, Blackhall Lane, Sevenoaks, Kent. *T:* Sevenoaks 61255.

**LYNNE, Gillian;** director, choreographer, dancer, actress; *b* 20 Feb. 1926; *d* of Leslie Pyrke and late Barbara Pyrke (*née* Hart); *m*

1948, Patrick St John Back (marr. diss., but close friends). *Educ:* Baston-Bromley, Kent; Arts Educnl School. Leading soloist, Sadlers Wells Ballet, 1944-51; star dancer, London Palladium, 1951, 1952, 1953; film, Master of Ballantrae, 1952; lead in Can-Can, London Coliseum, 1954-55; Becky Sharp in Vanity Fair, Windsor, 1956; guest principal dancer, Covent Garden, Sadlers Wells Aida, Samson and Delilah, 1957; Tannhauser, Covent Garden; ballerina in Chelsea at Nine, 1958; title role in Puss in Boots, Frou Frou in The Merry Widow, 1959; lead in New Cranks, 1959; Wanda, Rose Marie, Cinderella, Out of My Mind, lead in revue, 1960-61; staged revue England Our England, Princes, 1961; leading lady, 5 Past Eight Show, Edinburgh, 1962; choreographed first ballet Owl and the Pussycat, Western Theatre Ballet, 1962; Queen of the Cats, London Palladium, 1962-63; directed revue Round Leicester Square, 1963; conceived, directed, choreographed and starred in modern dance revue Collages, Edinburgh Fest., 1963, transf. to Savoy; chor. 1st film Wonderful Life, 1963-64; chor. musical films Every Day's a Holiday and Three Hats for Lisa, 1964; chor. musicals The Roar of the Greasepaint and Pickwick, Broadway, 1965; dir., chor. The Match Girls, Globe, 1966; chor. Flying Dutchman, Covent Garden, 1966; dir., chor. Bluebeard, Sadlers Wells, 1966; chor. and staged musical nos in Half a Sixpence (film), 1966-67; How Now Dow Jones, Broadway, 1967; chor. Midsummer Marriage, 1968 and The Trojans, 1969, Covent Garden; chor. new ballet Breakaway, Scottish Theatre Ballet, 1969; Phil the Fluter, Palace, 1969; dir. new prod. Bluebeard, Sadlers Wells Opera, London Coliseum, 1969; dir. and chor. musical Love on the Dole, Nottingham Playhouse, 1970; chor. new ballet Bat-Dor Co., Israel, 1970; has also appeared in or choreographed TV shows inc. Peter and the Wolf, 1958 (narr. and mimed all 9 parts); Puck, Midsummer Night's Dream, 1958; Val Doonican Shows, 1970; prod and devised TV Noël Coward and Cleo Laine Specials, 1968. *Publications:* articles in Dancing Times. *Address:* 40 Rowan Road, W6. *T:* 01-603 9470. *Club:* Pickwick.

**LYON**; *see* Bowes-Lyon.

**LYON, Alexander Ward;** MP (Lab) York since 1966; *b* 15 Oct. 1931; *s* of Alexander Pirie and Doris Lyon; *m* 1951, Hilda Arandall; two *s* one *d*. *Educ:* West Leeds High Sch.; University Coll., London. RASC, 1954-56. Called to Bar, 1954; practised NE Circuit from 1956. Contested (Lab) York, 1964. Addtl PPS to the Treasury Ministers, 1969; PPS to Paymaster General, 1969. Methodist Local Preacher; Member: Select Cttees on Parly Comr and on Race Relations; British Council of Churches; Connexional Cttee, Christian Citizenship of Methodist Church; Younger ~ Cttee on Intrusions into Privacy. *Address:* 218 London Road, Twickenham, Middlesex. *T:* 01-892 2852.

**LYON, Hugh;** *see* Lyon, P. H. B.

**LYON., (Percy) Hugh (Beverley),** MC, MA; *b* 14 Oct. 1893; *s* of late P. C. Lyon, CSI; *m* 1920, Nancy Elinor (*d* 1970), *d* of Wm Richardson, Guisborough and Sandsend; three *d*. *Educ:* Rugby Sch.; Oriel Coll., Oxford. Served with 6th Bn the Durham Light Infantry, 1914-19; Captain, 1917; MC 1917; wounded, 1918; prisoner of war, May 1918. Newdigate Prize Poem, 1919; BA and MA 1919; 1st class Final School Lit. Hum., 1921. Asst Master, Cheltenham Coll., 1921-26; Rector of the Edinburgh Academy, 1926-31; Headmaster of Rugby Sch., 1931-48; Director, Public Schools Appointments Bureau, 1950-61. *Publications:* Songs of Youth and War, 1917; Turn Fortune, 1923; The Discovery of Poetry, 1930. *Address:* Springhill, Amberley, Stroud, Glos. *T:* Amberley 2275. *Club:* English-Speaking Union.

**LYON, Robert,** MA (Dunelm); RBA; RP; retired as Principal, Edinburgh College of Art (1942-60); *b* 18 Aug. 1894; 3rd *s* of Charles Lyon, Elgin, and Grace Mortimer Wood, Yorkshire; *m* 1924, Mabel Sansome Morrison, Blundellsands; one *s*. *Educ:* Royal College of Art, London; British School at Rome. Served with King's Liverpool Regt, 1914-19; Lecturer in Fine Art and Master of Painting, King's Coll., Newcastle-on-Tyne (Univ. of Durham), 1932; Mem. Soc. Mural Painters; professional practice includes Mural Painting. Exhibitor: Royal Society of Portrait Painters; Royal Academy and New English Art Club. *Recent work includes:* murals for Western General Hosp., Edinburgh, and King's College Hosp. Dental Dept. *Recreation:* fishing. *Address:* Little Downgate, Punnetts Town, Heathfield, Sussex. *T:* Rushlake Green 433.

**LYON-DALBERG-ACTON,** family name of **Baron Acton.**

**LYONS, Bernard,** CBE 1964; JP; Deputy Chairman and Joint Managing Director of United Drapery Stores Ltd; *b* 30 March 1913; *m* 1938, Lucy Hurst; three *s* one *d*. *Educ:* Leeds Grammar Sch. Chm., Glanfield Securities Ltd. Chm., Yorkshire Conciliation Cttee, Race Relations Bd, 1968-. Mem., Leeds City Council, 1951-65. President, Leeds Jewish Representative Council, 1954-68. JP Leeds, 1960. *Recreation:* farming. *Address:* Wigton House, Wigton Lane, Leeds 17. *T:* Leeds 685978; 24 St James's Place, SW1. *T:* 01-499 4838.

**LYONS, Dennis John,** CEng, FRAeS; Director of Road Research Laboratory since 1965; *b* 26 Aug. 1916; *s* of late John Sylvester Lyons and of Adela Maud Lyons; *m* 1939, Elisabeth, *d* of Arnold and Maria Friederika Müller Haefliger, Weggis, Switzerland; five *s* two *d*. *Educ:* Grocers' Company School; Queen Mary Coll., London Univ. (Fellow, 1969). Aerodynamics Dept, Royal Aircraft Estabt, 1937; RAFVR, 1935-41; Aerodynamics Flight Aero Dept, RAE, 1941-51; Head of Experimental Projects Div., Guided Missiles Dept, RAE, 1951; Head of Ballistic Missile Group, GW Dept, 1956; Head of Weapons Dept, RAE, Chief Scientific Officer, 1962. Pres. OECD Road Research Unit, 1968-70. Hon. Mem., Instn Highway Engineers. *Publications:* papers in scientific jls. *Recreations:* ski-ing, pottery-making, philately. *Address:* Summerhaven, Gough Road, Fleet, Hants. *T:* 4773.

**LYONS, Edward,** LLB; MP (Lab) Bradford East since 1966; *b* 17 May 1926; *s* of late A. Lyons and of Mrs S. Taylor; *m* 1955, Barbara, *d* of Alfred Katz; one *s* one *d*. *Educ:* Roundhay High Sch.; Leeds Univ. LLB (Hons) 1951. Served Royal Artillery, 1944-48; Combined Services Russian Course, Cambridge Univ., 1946; Interpreter in Russian, Brit. CCG, 1946-48. Called to Bar, Lincoln's Inn, 1952. Practises on NE Circuit. Contested (Lab) Harrogate, 1964. Sec., British Parly Delegn to Soviet Union, 1968; PPS at Treasury, 1969-70. Special emissary of Internat. Commn of Jurists to S African Govt, 1969. Member: Soc. of Labour Lawyers; Fabian Soc.; United Nations Assoc. *Recreations:* history, family, talking, walking. *Address:* House of Commons, SW1; 38 Park Square, Leeds. *T:* 23601; 11 King's Bench Walk, Temple, EC4. *T:* 01-353

3337; 4 Primley Park Lane, Leeds 17. *T:* 685351.

**LYONS, Hon. Dame Enid Muriel,** GBE 1937; retired 1962; Member Australian Broadcasting Commission, 1951 (Board of Control, 1951-62); Hon. Fellow College of Nursing, Australia (FCNA), 1951; an original Vice-President, Australian Elizabethan National Theatre Trust, 1954; *b* Leesville, Tasmania, 9 July 1897; *d* of William Charles Burnell; *m* 1915, Rt Hon. Joseph Aloysius Lyons, PC, CH (*d* 1939); five *s* six *d*. *Educ:* State Sch.; Teachers' Training Coll., Hobart. Vice-Pres. of Executive Council, Australia, 1949-51; first woman member of Federal Cabinet; MHR for Darwin, Tasmania, 1943-51; first woman MHR; re-elected at general elections, 1946, 1949. Newspaper columnist, 1951-54. *Publications:* So We Take Comfort (autobiography); The Old Haggis (collection). *Address:* Home Hill, Middle Road, Devonport, Tasmania.

**LYONS, Eric (Alfred),** OBE 1959; FRIBA; DistTP; architect in private practice since 1945; *b* 2 Oct. 1912; *s* of Benjamin and Caroline Lyons; *m* 1944, Catherine Joyce Townsend; two *s* two *d*. *Educ:* The Polytechnic Sch. of Architecture. DistTP, RIBA, 1961; Architecture Award, RIBA, 1966; Mem. RIBA Coun., 1960-63, 1964-; Vice-Pres., RIBA, 1967, 1968; eleven awards for Good Design in Housing by Min. of Housing and Local Govt; five awards by Civic Trust. In partnership with G. Paulson Townsend, 1945-50; Partner, Eric Lyons & Partners, 1963-. Consultant Architect to Span Developments Ltd. FSIA. Hon. Fellow, Amer. Inst. of Architects. *Principal works:* housing at Blackheath, Ham, Cambridge, Weybridge, etc; Architect/Planner for New Ash Green Village, Kent, 1965-69; other work includes housing and schools for various local authorities. *Recreations:* music, drama. *Address:* Mill House, Bridge Road, Hampton Court, Surrey. *T:* 01-979 6656.

**LYONS, Prof. Francis Stewart Leland,** MA, PhD, LittD Dublin; FRHistS; MRIA; Master of Eliot College, University of Kent, since 1969; Professor of Modern History, University of Kent at Canterbury, since 1964; *b* 11 Nov. 1923; *e s* of Stewart Lyons and Florence May Leland; *m* 1954, Jennifer Ann Stuart McAlister; two *s*. *Educ:* Dover Coll.; Trinity Coll., Dublin. Lecturer in History, University Coll., Hull, 1947-51; Fellow of Trinity Coll., Dublin, 1951-64. *Publications:* The Irish Parliamentary Party, 1951; The Fall of Parnell, 1960; Internationalism in Europe, 1815-1914, 1963; John Dillon: a biography, 1968; Ireland since the Famine, 1970; articles and reviews in various historical jls. *Recreations:* walking, squash rackets, revisiting Ireland. *Address:* Eliot Lodge, 8 St Stephen's Hill, Canterbury, Kent. *T:* Canterbury 69615. *Club:* University (Dublin).

**LYONS, Hamilton;** Sheriff Substitute of Renfrew and Argyll, and Ayr and Bute, since 1968; *b* 3 Aug. 1918; *s* of Richard Lyons and Annie Cathro Thomson; *m* 1943, Jean Cathro Blair; two *s*. *Educ:* Gourock High Sch.; Greenock High Sch.; Glasgow Univ. BL (Glasgow) 1940. Practised as Solicitor, Greenock, until 1966; Sheriff Substitute of Inverness, Moray, Nairn and Ross and Cromarty at Stornoway and Lochmaddy, 1966-68. Member: Coun. of Law Soc. of Scotland, 1950-66 (Vice-Pres., 1962-63); Law Reform Cttee for Scotland, 1954-64; Cttee of Inquiry on Children and Young Persons, 1961-64; Cttee of Inquiry on Sheriff Courts, 1963-67; Sheriff Court Rules Coun., 1952-; Scottish Probation Adv. and Trng Coun., 1959-69. *Recreation:* sailing. *Address:* 14 Cloch Road, Gourock. *T:* Gourock 32566. *Club:* Royal Gourock Yacht.

**LYONS, Isidore Jack,** CBE 1967; Chairman, William Whiteley Ltd; Deputy Chairman: Alexandre Ltd; British Bank of Commerce Ltd; Deputy Chairman and Joint Managing Director, Glanfield Securities Ltd; Joint Managing Director: Bridge End Properties Ltd; Brooks Bros Ltd; Yorkshire & City Properties Ltd; Director, United Drapery Stores Ltd; Director of other companies; *b* 1 Feb. 1916; *s* of Samuel H. Lyons and Sophia Niman; *m* 1943, Roslyn Marion Rosenbaum; two *s* two *d*. *Educ:* Leeds Grammar Sch. Chm., Leeds Triennial Musical Festival, 1955; Dep. Chm., Joint Palestine appeal, 1957; Chm., Federation of Jewish Relief Organisations, 1958; Dep. Chm., Governors of Carmel Coll., 1961-69; Jt Chm., London Symphony Orchestra Trust, 1963; Chm., Shakespeare Exhibn (quater-centenary celebrations Stratford-upon-Avon), 1964; Mem. Exec. Cttee, Royal Acad. of Dancing, 1964; Mem., Canadian Veterans' Assoc., 1964; Mem. Pilgrims, 1965; Mem. Ct of York Univ., 1965; Life Trustee, Shakespeare Birthplace Trust, 1967. *Recreations:* music, the arts and swimming. *Address:* Blundell House, 2 Campden Hill, W8. *T:* 01-727 2750. *Club:* Carlton.

**LYONS, James,** OBE 1964; FDSRCSE; FFDRCSIre; Dental Surgeon in private practice; Hon. Consultant Dental Surgeon to Northern Ireland Hospitals Authority since 1952; Member N Ireland Health Services Bd, 1948-66; Member of the General Dental Council, 1956-61; *b* 4 June 1887; *s* of Richard Lyons, Sligo; *m* 1916, Kathleen Arnold, *d* of George Myles, Crieff, Scotland; two *s* one *d*. *Educ:* Clevedon Sch., Somerset; Royal Coll. of Surgeons, Edinburgh. LDS 1912; FDS 1951, RCS Edinburgh; FFD 1963, RCS, Ireland. Hon. Dental Surgeon to Royal Victoria Hospital, Belfast, 1927-51; Lectr on Dental Materia Medica, at Dental Sch. of Queen's Univ., Belfast, 1935-52. Mem. British Dental Assoc. (Pres. N Ireland Branch, 1939-41). *Recreations:* photography, motoring. *Address:* Fountain House, Donegall Place, Belfast, NI. *T:* Belfast 23052.

**LYONS, Sir James (Reginald);** JP; Airport Manager, Cardiff Airport, since 1955; *b* 15 March 1910; *s* of James Lyons; *m* 1937, Doreen Mary Fogg; one *s*. *Educ:* Howard Gardens High Sch.; Cardiff Technical Coll. Served War of 1939-45: Royal Tank Regt, 1940-46 (1939-45 Star, Africa Star, Italy Star, Defence Medal, War Medal of 1939-45). Civil Service, 1929-65: Post Office, Min. of Supply, Min. of Aviation. Local Govt, 1965-; Mem., Wales Tourist Bd. glamorgan CC; Cardiff City Council: Councillor, 1949-58; Alderman, 1958-; Lord Mayor of Cardiff, 1968-69. JP Cardiff, 1966-. OStJ. *Recreations:* Rugby football, swimming, tennis. *Address:* 101 Minehead Avenue, Sully, Glam. *T:* Sully 403. *Club:* Civil Service.

**LYONS, Most Rev. Patrick Francis;** *see* Sale, Bishop of, (RC).

**LYONS, Brig. Richard Clarke,** CIE 1946; MC; *b* 4 June 1893; *m* 1920, Francis Emily Gavin (*d* 1969), *d* of late Col A. L. Lindesay; two *s* one *d*. *Educ:* Rugby; RMA Woolwich. Royal Artillery, 1914-27; Indian Army, 1927; Chief Inspector of Armaments, India, 1942; Ordnance Consulting Officer for India (India Office), 1945; retired, 1948. Served European War, 1914-18 (wounded, MC, despatches).

*Address:* 32 Apsley Road, Clifton, Bristol BS8 2SS. *T:* Bristol 36909. *Club:* Army and Navy.

**LYONS, Rudolph,** QC 1953; **His Honour Judge Lyons;** Recorder of Liverpool and Judge of the Crown Court at Liverpool, since 1970; *b* 5 Jan. 1912; *er s* of late G. Lyons, Leeds; *m* 1936, Jeannette, *yr d* of late Philip Dante; one *s* two *d*. *Educ:* Leeds Grammar Sch.; Leeds Univ. (LLB). Called to Bar, Gray's Inn, 1934; Mem., Gen. Council of the Bar, 1958; Master of the Bench, Gray's Inn, 1961-. Recorder of: Sunderland, 1955-56; Newcastle upon Tyne, 1956-61; Sheffield, 1961-65; Leeds, 1965-70. Commr, Central Criminal Court, 1962-70; Commr of Assize, 1969; Leader of N Eastern Circuit, 1961-70; Solicitor-Gen., 1961-65, Attorney-Gen., 1965-70, County Palatine of Durham. *Recreation:* horticulture. *Address:* (home) 8 Brookside, Alwoodley, Leeds 17. *T:* Leeds 683274; St George's Hall, Liverpool 1. *Clubs:* National; Sheffield (Sheffield).

**LYONS, Thomas;** MP (N Ireland) North Tyrone since 1943; farmer; *b* 18 Feb. 1896; *s* of J. J. Lyons, JP, farmer, Newtownstewart, Co. Tyrone, and Elizabeth McFarland, Ballinamallaght, Donemana, Co. Tyrone; *m* 1927, Clarice E. Kiss, Croydon, Sydney, Australia; two *s* one *d*. *Educ:* Albert Agricultural Coll., Glasnevin, Dublin. Enlisted 1915, in N Irish Horse, served European War, France, with that Regt until transferred, 1917, to Royal Irish Fus. (wounded). Went to Australia, 1922; returned N Ireland, 1939; entered politics as result of by-election, Aug. 1943; Dep. Speaker and Chm. of Ways and Means, House of Commons, N Ireland, 1955-. *Address:* Riversdale, Newtownstewart, Co. Tyrone. *T:* Newtownstewart 258. *Club:* Tyrone County (Omagh).

**LYONS, Sir William,** Kt 1956; Chairman and Chief Executive: Jaguar Cars Ltd, Coventry; Daimler Co. Ltd; Chairman: Guy Motors Ltd; Coventry Climax Engines Ltd; a Deputy Chairman, British Leyland Motor Corporation; *b* Blackpool; *m*; two *d* (one *s* decd). Past President: Soc. of Motor Manufrs and Traders, 1950-51; Motor Industry Research Assoc., 1954; Motor Trades Benevolent Fund, 1954; Fellowship of the Motor Industry (FMI). RDI 1954; FRSA 1964. Hon. DTech Loughborough, 1969. *Address:* Jaguar Cars Ltd, Browns Lane, Coventry. *T:* Allesley 2121.

**LYSAGHT,** family name of **Baron Lisle.**

**LYSTER, Anthony St George,** CSI 1943; Indian Service of Engineers, retired; *b* 13 March 1888; *e s* of Major Charles Bybie Lyster, Newsholme, West Malvern, Worcs; *m* 1921, Dorothy Prideaux, 2nd *d* of Dr John Delpratt Harris, 45 Southernhay, Exeter; two *s*. *Educ:* Harrow Sch.; Pembroke Coll., Cambridge. Asst Engineer Public Works Dept Punjab, India, 1911. Served in Mesopotamia and Persia, 1915-19 (two medals, despatches). Chief Engineer and Sec. for Irrigation to Punjab Govt, 1940-43; Pres. Punjab Engineering Congress, 1942; retired, 1943. Jubilee Medal, 1935; Coronation Medal, 1937; Civil Defence Long Service Medal. *Recreations:* Attendance at Rowing Regattas and travel. *Address:* Southernhay, Cliff Road, Sidmouth, Devon. *T:* Sidmouth 2852. *Club:* Royal Over-Seas League.

**LYTHALL, Basil Wilfrid,** CB 1966; MA; a Member of Admiralty Board of Defence Council; Chief Scientist (Royal Navy), and Deputy Controller for Research and Development, since 1964; *b* 15 May 1919; *s* of Frank Herbert Lythall and Winifred Mary (*née* Carver); *m* 1942, Mary Olwen Dando; one *s*. *Educ:* King Edward's Sch., Stourbridge; Christ Church, Oxford. Joined Royal Naval Scientific Service, 1940; Admiralty Signal and Radar Establishment, 1940-53; Admiralty Research Laboratory, 1954-57; Asst Dir of Physical Research, Admty, 1957-58; a Dep. Chief Scientist, Admty Signal and Radar Estabt (later Admty Surface Weapons Estabt), 1958-60; first Chief Scientist of Admty Underwater Weapons Estabt, Portland, 1960-64. *Publications:* occasional articles in learned jls. *Recreations:* walking, music. *Address:* 48 Grove Way, Esher, Surrey. *T:* 01-398 2958. *Club:* Athenæum.

**LYTHGO, Wilbur Reginald,** OBE 1964; Counsellor, British Embassy, Washington, DC, and Consul-General, since 1968; *b* 7 June 1920; *yr s* of late Alfred and of Marion Lythgo, Monkton, Ayrshire; *m* 1943, Patricia Frances Sylvia Smith; two *s*. *Educ:* Palmer's Sch., Grays, Essex. Joined Home Office, 1937. Served in RASC, 1939-41 and Indian Army, 1941-46. Rejoined Home Office, 1946; British Information Services, New Delhi, 1948-54; UK High Commn, New Delhi, 1956-59; British High Commn, Ottawa, 1962-66; Head of Office Services and Supply Dept, DSAO, 1966-68. *Address:* 5205 Lawn Way, Kenwood, Chevy Chase, Md 20015, USA. *T:* 301-656-1629.

**LYTHGOE, Prof. Basil,** FRS 1958; Professor of Organic Chemistry, Leeds University, since 1953; *b* 18 Aug. 1913; 2nd *s* of Peter Whitaker and Agnes Lythgoe; *m* 1946, Kathleen Cameron, *er d* of H. J. Hallum, St Andrews; two *s*. *Educ:* Leigh Grammar Sch.; Manchester Univ. Asst Lectr, Manchester Univ., 1938; Univ. Lectr, Cambridge Univ., 1946. Fellow of King's Coll., Cambridge, 1950. *Publications:* papers on chemistry of natural products, in Jl of Chem. Soc. *Recreation:* mountaineering. *Address:* 113 Cookridge Lane, Leeds 16. *T:* Leeds 678837.

**LYTHGOE, Sir James,** Kt 1951; CBE 1945; Hon. MA Manchester, 1948, Hon. LLD Manchester, 1970; *b* 21 Oct. 1891; *s* of James Clare Lythgoe; *m* 1918, Dorothy May Ashworth; one *s* one *d*. *Educ:* Cheadle Hulme Schs; Stand Grammar Sch. Ex-Treasurer of the City, Manchester. Mem. Council, Inst. of Municipal Treasurers and Accountants, 1942-51 (Pres., 1947-48); Member: Rushcliffe Cttees (Nurses and Midwives Salaries), 1941-47; National Savings, 1941-43; Central Health Service Whitley Council, 1949-51; Home Office Cttees on Police Extraneous Duties, 1950, and Police Pensions, 1951; Colonial Office Advisory Panel on Local Govt, 1951; Hon. Treas., Hallé Concerts Soc., 1952-60; Interdepartmental Cttee on Concentration of Slaughter Houses, 1953; Departmental Cttee to review Salmon and Freshwater Fisheries Act, 1957; Public Works Loans Bd, 1956-68; Manchester Regional Hosps Bd, 1951-66 (Chm., 1962-66); Manchester Univ. Coun.; Feoffee Chetham's Hosp. Sch. and Library; Trustee, Municipal Mutual Insurance Ltd. *Publications:* various, on local government, public administration and finance. *Recreations:* golf, photography. *Address:* 34 Carrwood Road, Wilmslow, near Manchester. *T:* Wilmslow 3234. *Club:* National Liberal.

**LYTTELTON,** family name of **Viscount Chandos** and of **Viscount Cobham.**

**LYTTLETON, Raymond Arthur,** FRS; MA, PhD (Cantab); Professor of Theoretical Astronomy, and Fellow of St John's College, University of Cambridge; *o s* of William John Lyttleton and Agnes (*d* of Patrick Joseph Kelly), Warley Woods, near Birmingham, formerly of Ireland; *m* Meave Marguerite, *o d* of F. Hobden, Parkstone, formerly of Shanghai; no *c*. *Educ:* King Edward's Grammar Sch., Five Ways; King Edward's Sch., Birmingham; Clare Coll., Cambridge. Wrangler; Tyson Medal for Astronomy. Jane Eliza Procter Visiting Fellowship, Princeton Univ., USA, 1935-37; Exptl Officer, Min. of Supply, 1940-42; Technical Asst to Scientific Adviser to the Army Council, War Office, 1943-45. Lectr in Mathematics, 1937-59, Reader in Theoretical Astronomy, 1959-69, Univ. of Cambridge. Jacob Siskind Vis. Prof., Brandeis Univ., USA, 1965-66; Vis. Prof., Brown Univ., USA, 1967-68; Halley Lectr, Oxford Univ., 1970. Mem. of Council, Royal Society, 1959-61; Geophysical Sec. of Royal Astronomical Soc., 1949-60 and Mem. of Council, 1950-61, 1969-; Vice-Pres., 1955-56, 1960-61; Fellow, 1934-. Hopkins Prize (for 1951) of Cambridge Philosophical Soc.; Gold Medallist of Royal Astronomical Soc., 1959; Royal Medallist of Royal Society, 1965. *Publications:* The Comets and their Origin, 1953; The Stability of Rotating Liquid Masses, 1953; The Modern Universe, 1956; Rival Theories of Cosmology, 1960; Man's View of the Universe, 1961; Mysteries of the Solar System, 1968; (Play) A Matter of Gravity (produced by BBC, 1968); papers on astrophysics, cosmogony, physics, dynamics, and geophysics in Proc. Royal Soc., Monthly Notices of Royal Astron. Soc., Proc. Cambridge Philosophical Soc., etc. *Recreations:* golf, motoring, music; wondering about it all. *Address:* 165 Huntingdon Road, Cambridge. *T:* 54910; St John's College, Cambridge. *T:* 61621.

**LYTTON,** family name of **Earl of Lytton.**

**LYTTON,** 4th Earl of, *cr* 1880; **Noel Anthony Scawen Lytton,** OBE 1945; Viscount Knebworth, 1880; Baron Lytton, 1866; Baron Wentworth, 1529; Bt 1838; *b* 7 April 1900; *s* of 3rd Earl of Lytton, OBE, and 16th Baroness Wentworth (*d* 1957); *S* father 1951; *m* 1946, Clarissa Mary, *er d* of late Brig.-General C. E. Palmer, CB, CMG, DSO, RA, and of Mrs Palmer, Christchurch, Hants; two *s* three *d*. *Educ:* Downside; RMC, Sandhurst. Lieut, Rifle Bde, 1921, attached King's African Rifles, 1922-27; Captain Rifle Brigade, 1936; Staff Captain, War Office, 1937; Major, 1938; served War of 1939-45 (temp. Lieut-Colonel) in North Africa, Italy, Greece and Austria; retired, 1946. Farmer, 1959-; author. *Publications:* The Desert and the Green (autobiography), 1957; Wilfrid Scawen Blunt (biog.), 1961; Mickla Bendore (novel), 1962; Lucia in Taormina (novel), 1963; The Stolen Desert (history), 1966. *Recreations:* travel, riding, letter-writing. *Heir:* *s* Viscount Knebworth, *qv*. *Address:* Lillycombe, Porlock, Somerset. *T:* Porlock 353.

*See also Earl of Balfour, Baron Cobbold, Hon. C. M. Woodhouse.*

**LYTTON SELLS, Arthur Lytton,** MA (Cambridge), Docteur de l'Université de Paris, Lauréat de l'Académie française; Officier d'Académie; *b* Edgbaston, Birmingham, England, 28 May 1895; *s* of Arthur Sells and Elizabeth Whittaker; *m* 1929, Iris Esther, MA, *d* of F. T. Robertson, JP, formerly editor of Adelaide Advertiser, Adelaide, South Australia; one *s*. *Educ:* King Edward VII School, Sheffield; Univs of Cambridge and Paris. Scholar of Sidney Sussex Coll., Cambridge, 1914-15, 1919-21; served HAC, 1918-19; Lectr, Cambridge, 1923-29; Univ. Lectr in French, 1929; Prof. of French, Durham Univ., 1930-51; Prof. of English Literature, Padua Univ., 1946; Prof. of French and Italian at Indiana Univ., 1951; Research Prof. Emer., 1965. Vis. Prof., Assumption Coll., Worcester, Mass., 1967, Wake Forest Univ., N Carolina, 1970-. *Publications:* Les Sources françaises de Goldsmith, 1924, awarded Prix Bordin of the French Academy; The Early Life of J. J. Rousseau, 1929; Molière and La Mothe le Vayer, 1933; The History of Francis Wills, 1935; (with I. E. Sells) Key to Manual of French Tr. & Comp., 1937; Contribution to France, ed by R. L. G. Ritchie, 1937; Earth of the Tarentines, 1940; Hérédia's Hellenism, 1942; The Italian Influence in English Poetry, 1954; Animal Poetry in French and English Literature, 1955; (ed) The Military Memoirs of James II, 1962; The Paradise of Travellers, 1964. *Recreations:* walking, photography. *Address:* Dunster House, The Avenue, Durham. *T:* 2525. *Club:* Athenæum.

**LYVEDEN,** 5th Baron *cr* 1859; **Sydney Munro Vernon;** retired; *b* 21 Nov. 1888; *s* of Cecil Sydney Archibald Vernon (*g s* of 1st Baron) (*d* 1944) and Jessie Jane (*d* 1942), *d* of John Munro; *S* kinsman, 1969; *m* 1st, 1912, Ruby Shandley (*d* 1932); one *s* three *d* (and one *d* decd); 2nd, 1959, Gladys, *widow* of John Cassidy. *Educ:* Northland Private Boarding School. *Recreations:* bowling and motoring. *Heir:* *s* Hon. Ronald Cecil Vernon [*b* 10 April 1915; *m* 1938, Queenie Constance, *d* of Howard Ardern; three *s*]. *Address:* 2a Main Road, Day's Bay, Wellington, New Zealand. *T:* 86-86. *Clubs:* Petone Working Men's and Literary Institute; Central Bowling; Royal Automobile and AA Motor.

# M

**MAAZEL, Lorin;** symphony conductor; *b* 6 March 1930; *s* of Lincoln Maazel and Marie Varencove; *m* 1st, 1952, Miriam Sandbank; two *d*; 2nd, 1969, Israela Margalit. *Educ:* Pittsburgh University. Début as a conductor at age of 8, as violinist a few years later; by 1941 had conducted foremost US Orchestras, including Toscanini's NBC; since 1952, over 500 concerts in Europe and performances at major festivals, including Edinburgh, Bayreuth and Salzburg; in USA: conducted Boston Symphony, New York Philharmonic, Philadelphia Orchestra, and at Metropolitan, 1960 and 1962. Several world tours, including Latin America, Australia, USSR and Japan. Musical Director of Deutsche Oper Berlin and Berlin Radio Symphony Orchestra, 1965. Has made numerous recordings. Hon. Dr of Music, Pittsburgh Univ., 1965. *Address:* Deutsche Oper Berlin, Richard-Wagner-Strasse 10, 1 Berlin 10.

**MABBOTT, John David,** CMG 1946; President of St John's College, Oxford, 1963-69; *b* 18 Nov. 1898; *s* of late Walter John and Elizabeth Mabbott; *m* 1934, Doreen Roach. *Educ:* Berwickshire High Sch.; Edinburgh Univ.; St John's Coll., Oxford. Asst Lectr in Classics, Reading Univ., 1922; Asst Lectr in Philosophy, Univ. Coll. of North Wales, 1923; John Locke Scholar, Univ. of Oxford, 1923; Fellow of St John's Coll., Oxford, 1924-63, Hon. Fellow 1969, and Tutor, 1930-63. *Publications:* The State and the Citizen, 1948; An Introduction to Ethics, 1966; contribs to Philosophy, Proc. Aristotelian Soc., Classical Quarterly, Mind. *Address:* Wing Cottage, Mill Lane, Islip, Oxon. *T:* Kidlington 2360.

**MABON, (Jesse) Dickson;** MP (Lab and Co-op), Greenock, since Dec. 1955; *b* 1 Nov. 1925; *s* of Jesse Dickson Mabon and Isobel Simpson Montgomery; *m* 1970, Elizabeth *o d* of William Zinn, *qv*. *Educ:* Possilpark, Cumbrae, North Kelvinside Schools. Worked in coalmining industry before Army service, 1944-48. MB, ChB (Glasgow), 1954; Visiting Physician, Manor House Hospital, London, 1958-64. President: Glasgow University Union, 1951-52; Scottish Union of Students, 1954-55; Chairman: Glasgow Univ. Labour Club, 1948-50; National Assoc. of Labour Students, 1949-50; contested: (Lab) Bute and N Ayrshire, Gen. Election, Oct. 1951; (Lab and Co-op) W Renfrewshire, Gen. Election, May 1955. Political columnist, Scottish Daily Record, 1955-64. Joint Parly Under-Sec. of State for Scotland, 1964-67; Minister of State, Scottish Office, 1967-70. *Recreations:* theatre, golf. *Address:* 90 Colston Road, Bishopbriggs, Glasgow; House of Commons, SW1.

**MABY, (Alfred) Cedric,** CBE 1962; Consul-General at Zurich since 1968; *b* 6 April 1915; 4th *s* of late Joseph Maby, Penrose, Monmouthshire; *m* 1944, Anne-Charlotte, *d* of Envoyén Elnar Modig, Stockholm; one *s* two *d*. *Educ:* Cheltenham; Keble Coll., Oxford. Joined HM Consular Service, 1939. Served at Peking, 1939, Chungking, 1940, Tsingtao, 1941, Istanbul, 1943, Angora, 1944, Buenos Aires, 1946, Caracas, 1949, Singapore, 1954; Counsellor and Consul-General, Peking, 1957-59 (Chargé d'Affaires, 1957 and 1958); Deputy Consul-General, New York, 1959-62; Counsellor (Commercial) at Vienna, 1962-64; Asst Sec., Min. of Overseas Development, 1964-67. *Address:* Cae Canol, Penrhyn-Deudraeth, Merioneth.

**McADAM, Prof. Sir Ian (William James),** Kt 1966; OBE 1957; FRCS, FRCSE; Professor of Surgery, Makerere University College, University of East Africa, since 1957; Consultant Surgeon to Uganda Government and to Kenyatta Hospital, Kenya, since 1957; *b* 15 Feb. 1917; *s* of W. J. M. McAdam and Alice Culverwell; *m* 1st, 1939, Hrothgarde Gibson (marr. diss. 1961); one *s* two *d*; 2nd, 1967, Lady (Pamela) Hunt, *née* Medawar. *Educ:* Plumtree Sch., S Rhodesia; Edinburgh Univ. MB, ChB 1940; FRCSE 1945. Univ. teaching appts, Cambridge Anatomy Sch., 1940 and Dept of Surgery, Edinburgh, 1942; Wilkie Surgical Research Fellow, 1942; Clinical Tutor, Royal Infirmary, Edinburgh, 1942; Surgical Specialist, Uganda, 1946; Senior Consultant, Uganda, 1959. FRCS 1966. *Publications:* various papers in medical jls. *Recreations:* golf, cricket. *Address:* Makerere University College Medical School, PO Box 7072, Kampala, Uganda. *T:* Kampala 56216.
*See also Sir Peter Medawar.*

**MACADAM, Sir Ivison (Stevenson),** Kt 1955; CVO 1953 (MVO 1937); CBE 1935 (OBE 1919); FRSE; MIMechE; Editor, The Annual Register of World Events; *b* 18 July 1894; 2nd *s* of late Col W. Ivison Macadam, FRSE, Professor of Chemistry, Edinburgh; *m* 1934, Caroline Ladd, *e d* of late Elliott Corbett, Portland, Oregon, USA; two *s* two *d*. *Educ:* Melville Coll., Edinburgh; King's Coll., London; Christ's Coll., Cambridge. Member of Council and Delegacy and Fellow of King's Coll., London. Served European War, 1914-19, City of Edinburgh (Fortress) Royal Engineers; Officer commanding Royal Engineers, Archangel, North Russian Expeditionary Force (despatches thrice). Asst Dir-Gen. and Principal Asst Sec., Min. of Information, 1939-41; Sec. and Dir-Gen., Royal Inst. of Internat. Affairs, 1929-55. A Founder and Trustee of the National Union of Students; Mem. Council, King George's Jubilee Trust; Pres., NE (Cromer) Area, Co. of Norfolk St John Ambulance Bde; a Dep. Pres., Victoria League. CStJ. *Address:* 16 Upper Belgrave Street, SW1. *T:* 01-235 4417; Runton Old Hall, Cromer, Norfolk. *T:* Cromer 2425. *Clubs:* Athenæum; Norfolk (Norwich).

**McADAM, Prof. Robert,** BSc, PhD, CEng, FIMinE, FRSE; Hood Professor of Mining Engineering, Heriot-Watt University, Edinburgh, since 1967; *b* 15 March 1906; *y s* of William McAdam, Broomieknowe, Midlothian; *m* 1933, Winifred Julia, *o d* of T. W. Dixon, Edinburgh; one *s*. *Educ:* Lasswade Secondary Sch.; Univ. of Edinburgh. Practical experience in coal mines in Scotland and gold mines in India; Tait research worker on Mine Ventilation, 1930. Sen. Lectr in Mining, Heriot-Watt Coll., Edinburgh, 1931-48; Hood Prof. of Mining, Univ. of Edinburgh and Heriot-Watt Coll., Edinburgh, 1948-67. Carried out research work on errors affecting mine surveying operations, production of oil from coal, geophysical prospecting, and mine rescue work. *Publications:* Colliery Surveying, 1953, 1963; Mine Rescue Work, 1955; Mining Explosives, 1958; numerous papers on mining and scientific subjects in Trans of IMinE, Inst. Mining Surveyors, and in technical press. *Address:* Allermuir, Captains Road, Edinburgh EH17 8DT. *T:* 031-664 2770.

**MacADAM, William,** MA, BSc, MD, FRCP; Professor of Medicine and Clinical Medicine, University of Leeds, 1932-46, Emeritus Professor since 1946; Hon. Consultant Physician, General Infirmary, Leeds; *b* 10 Dec. 1885; *s* of Archibald MacAdam, Corstorphine; *m* Irene M. H. Tincker, MB, ChB; two *s* one *d*. *Educ:* Glasgow Univ. MB, ChB Hons, with Brunton Memorial Prize, 1909. Formerly: Consulting Physician: United Leeds Hosp. Board; Leeds Regional Hosp. Board; Hon. Physician: General Hosp., Halifax; Clayton Hosp., Wakefield; General Hosp., Skipton; Lectr in Pathology and in Metabolic Medicine, Univ. of Leeds; McCunn and Carnegie Research Scholar, Univ. of Glasgow; Pres., British Gastro-Enterological Soc., FRCP, 1932; Fellow, BMA, 1959. *Publications:* numerous contribs and papers in various scientific and medical jls. *Address:* 24 Park Square, Leeds. *T:* Leeds 28441. *Club:* Leeds (Leeds).

**McADAM CLARK, James;** *see* Clark, James McAdam.

**McADDEN, Sir Stephen (James),** Kt 1962; CBE 1959; MP (C) Southend East since 1950; Director: Butlins Construction Co. Ltd; Camden Chemical Co. Ltd; Four Circle Development Co. Ltd; Copthall Holdings Ltd; Reid Walker Advertising Ltd; *b* 3 Nov. 1907; *s* of William John McAdden and Elizabeth (*née* Mulhern); *m* 1951, Doris Hearle, *d* of Walter and Ethel Gillies, Leytonstone, and *widow* of Captain William Hearle, RAC. *Educ:* Salesian Sch., Battersea. Comd Hackney Bn, Home Guard, Lt-Col. Councillor: Hackney Borough Council, 1937-45; Woodford Borough Council, 1945-48; Essex County Council, 1947-48. Chairman: West Toxteth (Liverpool) Junior Imperial League, 1929-31, Hackney Branch, 1932-35; Grand Prior, Primrose League, 1955-58. Trustee Liverpool Victoria Friendly Society; National Pres. and Chm., Music Users Assoc.; Vice-Pres., National Chamber of Trade. *Recreations:* tennis, cricket, debating. *Address:* 552 Woodgrange Drive, Thorpe Bay, Essex. *T:* Southend-on-Sea 88421; House of Commons, SW1. *Clubs:* Constitutional, St Stephen's, Farmers';

Alexandra Yacht (Southend), Thorpe Bay Yacht.

**McADOO, Rt. Rev. Henry Robert;** *see* Ossory, Ferns and Leighlin, Bishop of.

**MACAFEE, Prof. Charles Horner Greer,** CBE 1961; DL; Emeritus Professor of Midwifery and Gynæcology, The Queen's University, Belfast, since 1963 (Professor, Oct. 1945-Oct. 1963, retired); Member of Senate; *b* 23 July 1898; *s* of Rev. Andrew Macafee, BA, and A. H. Macafee, MBE, JP; *m* 1930, Margaret Crymble (*d* 1968), *d* of Prof. C. G. Lowry; two *s* one *d*. *Educ:* Omagh Academy; Foyle Coll., Londonderry. MB, BCh, BAO, First Class Hons, 1921; FRCS 1927; FRCSI 1927; Foundation Fellow, 1929, and Mem. Council, RCOG; Past Pres., Ulster Obstetrical and Gynæcological Soc.; Chm. Adv. Cttee on the Maternity Services in Northern Ireland; Past Pres., Ulster Medical Soc.; Vice-Pres., RCOG, 1961-64; formerly Mem. Northern Ireland Hospitals Authority; formerly External Examiner: Oxford, Dublin, Glasgow and Leeds; Lichfield Lectr, Oxford, 1955; Sims-Black Travelling Prof. to Rhodesia and S Africa, RCOG, 1956; William Meredith Fletcher Shaw Memorial Lectr, London, 1961. DL, County Down, 1969. Hon. DSc Leeds, 1961. Blair Bell Memorial Medal, RSM, 1965; Eardley Holland Medal, RCOG, 1965. *Publications:* contributed to: Modern Trends in Obstetrics and Gynæcology; Modern Trends in British Surgery; many contribs to Jl of Obstetrics and Gynæcology, British Empire; Proc. RSocMed; Ulster Medical Jl. *Recreation:* gardening. *Address:* Stramore Lodge, 142 Warren Road, Ballywilliam, Donaghadee, Co. Down, Northern Ireland. *Club:* English-Speaking Union.

**MACAFEE, Colonel John Leeper Anketell,** CBE 1964; RM; Director of Naval Security since 1961; *b* 24 July 1915; *s* of late Thomas Boyd Macafee, BA, Clonallen, Armagh, Northern Ireland, and late Muriel Kathleen Macafee; *m* 1939, Mary Ruth Noel Lewis, *d* of late Comdr G. J. W. Lewis, Green Court, Bredhurst, Kent; two *d*. *Educ:* Campbell Coll., Belfast. Entered RM (2nd Lieut), 1934; HMS Hood, 1937; PT Course, 1938; HMS Royal Sovereign, 1938-40; Naval Provost Marshal, Mediterranean Fleet, 1940-42; 3rd Bn RM, 1942-43; 44 Commando, RM, 1943-44; Holding Commando (overseas) (CO), 1944-45; HQ RM (Devon), 1945-46; Staff Coll., Camberley, 1947; Staff of Comdt General, RM, Admiralty, 1948-49; Instructor, Staff Coll., Camberley, 1950-52; Staff Officer (Intelligence) S Atlantic, 1953-55; Joint Services Amphibious Warfare Centre, 1955-57; 42 Commando RM (CO), 1957-59; HQ, RM, Plymouth, 1959; Fleet RM Officer, Mediterranean Fleet, 1960; Deputy Director, Naval Intelligence, 1961. ADC to the Queen, 1963-64. *Recreations:* tennis, gardening, carpentry. *Address:* Grove House, Bredhurst, Gillingham, Kent. *T:* Medway 32316.

**McALISTER, Mrs J. A.;** *see* McAlister, Mary A.

**McALISTER, Mary A., (Mrs J. Alexander McAlister),** CBE 1968; *d* of late Charles McMackin and Winifred (*née* Deeney); *m* 1927, J. Alexander McAlister; four *d*. *Educ:* Franciscan Convent, Glasgow. Nurse by profession (fevers); trained Knightswood Hospital, Glasgow, 1923-26. Served during War of 1939-45, Civil Nursing Reserve and ultimately Postal Censorship. Member Glasgow Corporation (Labour), 1945-48; Convener, Health and Welfare Cttee, 1952-55. Formerly Member: Standing Advisory Cttee on Local Authority Services; Western Region Hospitals Board; General Nursing Council for Scotland; Central Midwives Board. JP Glasgow, 1947-51. MP (Lab) Kelvingrove Div. of Glasgow, March 1958-Sept. 1959. Hon. Pres., Royal College of Nursing (Glasgow Branch), 1956-58. Member: National Assistance Board, 1961-; Supplementary Benefits Commn, 1966-67 (Dep. Chm., 1967). *Address:* 22 North Gardner Street, Glasgow W1. *T:* 041-339 1606.

**McALISTER, Samuel,** CBE 1944; retired banker; *b* 10 May 1896; *s* of late Francis McAlister, Dunlaoghaire, Co. Dublin, Ireland; *m* 1927, Jessie A., *er d* of late Fred Smith, CBE, JP, Pollard Hall, Gomersal, Yorks; two *s* one *d*. *Educ:* Wesley Coll., Dublin. Served European War, 1914-19, RN. Chm., British Chamber of Commerce in Brazil, 1941-44; Vice-Pres., Brazilian Bankers' Assoc., Rio de Janeiro, 1950-54. *Address:* Ashcroft, 114 Ashley Road, Walton-on-Thames, Surrey.

**McALLISTER, Reginald Basil,** CMG 1966; CVO 1963; JP; retired; Finance Manager for Trustees, Australian Country Party since 1966; *b* 8 May 1900; *s* of Basil William and Beatrice Maud McAllister; *m* 1951, Joyce Isabel Roper; no *c*. *Educ:* Brisbane Primary and Secondary State Schools. Clerk, Railway Dept, Brisbane, 1916; secretarial duties, Parlt House, Brisbane, and Sec. to Speaker, 1924-26; reporter, State Reporting Bureau, Parlt House, 1926-33; Sec. to Premier of Queensland, 1933-37 (accompanied Premier on missions to: UK AND Canada, 1934; UK and Europe, 1936; UK Internat. Sugar Conf., 1937); Asst Under-Sec., Premier and Chief Secretary's Dept, 1938; Official Sec., Qld Govt Offices, London, 1943-48 (actg Agent-Gen. on many occasions); resumed former duties in Brisbane, 1948; Clerk of Exec. Council of Qld, 1941-43, 1951-66; Under-Sec., Premier's Dept, and Chm., State Stores Board, 1962-66; acted as Sec. to Cabinet on many occasions; retd 1966. President: Qld Br., Royal Commonwealth Soc.; Australian-Asian Soc.; Chairman: Royal Academy of Dancing (Ballet); Appeal Cttee, Australian Red Cross Soc.; Mem. Coun., RGS; Mem. State Coun., Boy Scouts' Assoc. Dep. Chm., Bd of Dirs, Warana Spring Festival, 1965-. Liveryman, Farriers' Co.; Freeman, City of London; JP 1933. *Recreations:* golf, fishing, gardening, rotary activities. *Address:* 34 Scott Road, Herston, Brisbane, Queensland. *T:* 56-5361. *Clubs:* Queensland Turf, Masonic, Tattersall's, Queensland Lawn Tennis, Royal Automobile (all Queensland).

**McALPINE, Douglas,** MD, FRCP; Emeritus Consultant Physician to the Middlesex Hospital; *b* 19 Aug. 1890; *s* of late Sir Robert McAlpine, 1st Bt, and late Florence Palmer; *m* 1917, Elizabeth Meg Sidebottom (*d* 1941); one *s* one *d*; *m* 1945, Diana, *d* of late Bertram Plummer; one *s*. *Educ:* Cheltenham; Glasgow Univ.; Paris. MB, ChB, Glasgow, 1913; joined RAMC, Aug. 1914; served France till 1915; Aug. 1915, joined Navy as Surgeon Lt, RN; served afloat until 1918 (despatches); elected to staff of several London Hospitals; became Neurologist to Middlesex Hospital, 1924; FRCP 1933. Late Brig. RAMC; Cons. Neurol. MEF, India Comd and SEAC, 1941-45 (despatches). *Publications:* Multiple Sclerosis: a Reappraisal (jointly), 1965; various papers in medical jls. *Recreations:* fishing, shooting, golf. *Address:* Lovells Mill, Marnhull, Dorset.

*See also R. D. C. McAlpine.*

**McALPINE, Sir Edwin;** *see* McAlpine, Sir R. E.

**McALPINE, Hon. John Kenneth,** CMG 1970; Chairman, New Zealand Ports Authority, since 1969; *b* 21 July 1906; *s* of Walter Kenneth and Gwendolin Marion McAlpine; *m* 1934, Lesley Ruth Hay; one *s* two *d*. *Educ:* Christ's Coll., Christchurch, New Zealand. MP Selwyn, NZ, 1946-66. Mem. Tawera CC, 1927-63; Pres., Canterbury Federated Farmers, 1945-47. Mem. Bd: Arthur's Pass National Park, 1942-; Lyttleton Harbour, 1937-54 (Chm., 1942-45); Canterbury Univ., 1950-60; Canterbury Agricultural Univ., 1959- (Chm., 1967-). Minister: Railways, Marine, and Printing, 1954-66; Transport and Civil Aviation, 1957-66; Labour, 1956-58. Chairman: NZ Holiday Travel, etc, 1966-; South Island, NZ, Promotion Bd, 1937-; Canterbury Progress League, 1937-. *Recreations:* Rugby football, long distance running, gardening, skiing. *Address:* 41 Innes Road Christchurch 5, New Zealand. *T:* 558057. *Club:* Christchurch (NZ).

**McALPINE, Robert Douglas Christopher,** CMG 1967; Counsellor, British Embassy, Mexico City, since 1965; *b* 14 June 1919; *s* of Dr Douglas McAlpine, *qv*; *m* 1943, Helen Margery Frances Cannan; two *s* one *d* (and one *d* decd). Educ: Winchester; New Coll., Oxford. RNVR, 1939-46. Entered Foreign Service, 1946. FO, 1946-47; Asst Private Sec. to Sec. of State, 1947-49; 2nd Sec. and later 1st Sec., UK High Commn at Bonn, 1949-52; FO, 1952-54; Lima, 1954-56; Moscow, 1956-59; FO, 1959-62; Dep. Consul-Gen., New York, 1962-65; Counsellor, 1962. *Recreations:* sailing, ski-ing, tennis, shooting, fishing. *Address:* British Embassy, Mexico City, Mexico. *Club:* Travellers'.

**McALPINE, Sir (Robert) Edwin,** Kt 1963; Partner, Sir Robert McAlpine & Sons, since 1928; Chairman: The Nuclear Power Group Ltd; The Dorchester Hotel Ltd, since 1967; *b* 23 April 1907; *s* of William Hepburn McAlpine and Margaret Donnison; *m* 1930, Ella Mary Gardner Garnett; three *s* one *d*. *Educ:* Oundle. Joined Sir Robert McAlpine & Sons, 1925. *Recreations:* breeding race horses, farming, travel, golf, theatre. *Address:* Benhams, Fawley Green, Henley-on-Thames, Oxon. *T:* Hambleden 246. *Clubs:* Garrick, Caledonian. *See also Sir T. G. B. McAlpine, Bt.*

**McALPINE, Sir Robin,** Kt 1969; CBE 1957; Chairman, Sir Robert McAlpine & Sons Ltd, since 1967; *b* 18 March 1906; *s* of late Sir (Thomas) Malcolm McAlpine, KBE, and late Lady (Maud) McAlpine; *m* 1st, 1939, Nora Constance (*d* 1966), *d* of F. H. Perse; 2nd, 1970, Mrs Philippa Nicolson. *Educ:* Charterhouse. Pres., Federation of Civil Engineering Contractors. *Recreation:* owner and breeder of racehorses. *Address:* Aylesfield, Alton, Hants. *Club:* Jockey.

**McALPINE, Sir Thomas (George Bishop),** 4th Bt *cr* 1918; Director of Sir Robert McAlpine & Sons; *b* 23 Oct. 1901; *s* of William Hepburn McAlpine (2nd *s* of 1st Bt) and Margaret Donnison, *d* of T. G. Bishop; *S* kinsman, Sir (Alfred) Robert McAlpine, 3rd Bt, 1968; *m* 1st, 1934, Doris Frew (*d* 1964), *d* of late D. C. Campbell and *widow* of W. E. Woodeson; 2nd, 1965, Kathleen Mary, *d* of late Frederick Best and *widow* of Charles Bantock Blackshaw; no *c*. *Educ:* Warriston; Rossall Sch. Joined firm of Sir Robert McAlpine on leaving school; eventually became a partner and director; retired from the partnership, 1966. *Recreations:* farming, photography, travel. *Heir:* *b* Sir (Robert) Edwin McAlpine, *qv*. *Address:* The Torrs, Portling, Dalbeattie, Kirkcudbrightshire. *T:* Rockcliffe 229. *Club:* Royal Automobile.

**MacANDREW,** family name of **Baron MacAndrew.**

**MacANDREW,** 1st Baron *cr* 1959; **Charles Glen MacAndrew;** PC 1952; Kt 1935; TD; DL; JP; Hon. LLD (St Andrews); Member of Racecourse Betting Control Board, 1938-61; *b* 13 Jan. 1888; *s* of F. G. MacAndrew; *m* 1918, Lilian Cathleen Curran (from whom he obtained a divorce 1938); one *s* one *d*; *m* 1941, Mona, *d* of J. A. Ralston Mitchell, Perceton House, by Irvine; one *d*. *Educ:* Uppingham; Trinity Coll., Cambridge. MP (U) Ayr and Bute, Kilmarnock Div., 1924-29; MP (U) Partick Div., Glasgow, 1931-35; Dep. Chm. of Ways and Means, House of Commons, May-July 1945 and March 1950-Oct. 1951; MP (U) Bute and Northern div. of Ayr and Bute, 1935-59; Dep. Speaker of the House of Commons, 1951-59; Chm. of Ways and Means, 1951-59. Commanded Ayrshire Yeomanry, 1932-36; Hon. Col, 1951-55; DL, JP, Ayrshire. OStJ. *Heir:* *s* Hon. Colin Nevil Glen MacAndrew [*b* 1 Aug. 1919; *m* 1943, Ursula, *yr d* of Capt. Joseph Steel, Lockerbie, Dumfriesshire; two *s* one *d*. *Educ:* Eton; Trinity Coll., Cambridge]. *Address:* The White House, Monkton, Ayrshire. *T:* Prestwick 77872; 28 Empire House, Thurloe Place, SW7. *T:* 01-589 6066. *Clubs:* Carlton; Royal Yacht Squadron (Cowes); Royal and Ancient Golf (St Andrews).

**MacANDREW, Lt-Col James Orr,** TD; DL; Ayrshire Yeomanry; *b* 22 June 1899; *s* of F. G. MacAndrew, Knock Castle, Largs; *m* 1944, Eileen, *o d* of Robin Butterfield; one *d*. *Educ:* Trinity Coll., Glenalmond; Trinity Hall, Cambridge. Served European War, 1914-18, joined RFC 1917; War of 1939-45. Hon. Col Ayrshire Yeomanry, 1955-60. MP (U) Ayr and Bute South Ayrshire Div., 1931-35. Jt Master, Eglinton foxhounds, 1939-40. DL Ayrshire, 1966. *Address:* South Park, Ayr. *T:* Ayr 64783. *Clubs:* Carlton, Boodle's.

**MACARA, Sir (Charles) Douglas,** 3rd Bt, *cr* 1911; *b* 19 April 1904; *s* of 2nd Bt and Lillian Mary, *d* of John Chapman, of Boyton Court, East Sutton, Kent; *S* father, 1931; *m* 1926, Quenilda (marr. diss. 1945), *d* of late Herbert Whitworth, St Anne's-on-Sea; two *d* (one *s* decd). *Heir:* *b* John Keith Macara [*b* 29 Oct. 1905; *m* 1948, J. F. M. Bennett (*d* 1956) (*née* Stonor)]. *Address:* Cheltenham Gold Cup Restaurant, Bandon, Co. Cork, Ireland.

**McARDLE, Michael John Francis,** MB, BS (Hons, London), FRCP; Physician for Nervous Diseases, Guy's Hospital; Physician, National Hospital for Nervous Diseases, Queen Square, WC1; Consulting Neurologist, Kingston Hospital and St Teresa's Maternity Hospital, Wimbledon, SW19; *b* 1909; *s* of Andrew McArdle; *m* 1955, Maureen MacClancy. *Educ:* Wimbledon Coll.; Guy's Hospital; Paris. Entrance Scholarship, Arts, Guy's Hospital. Medical Registrar, Guy's Hospital; Asst Medical Officer, Maudsley Hospital. Rockefeller Travelling Fellow in Neurology, 1938. War of 1939-45, Temp. Lt-Col, RAMC and Adviser in Neurology, 21st Army Group. *Publications:* papers on neurological subjects in medical journals. *Recreation:* golf. *Address:* 121 Harley Street, W1. *T:* 01-935 0244; 35 Marryat Road, Wimbledon, SW19. *T:* 01-946 4149.

**MacARTHUR, Mrs Charles;** *see* Hayes, Helen.

**MacARTHUR, (David) Wilson,** MA; author and freelance journalist; *b* 29 Aug. 1903; *s* of Dr Alex. MacArthur, MB, CM; *m* 1956, Patricia Knox Saunders; two *s*. *Educ:* The Academy, Ayr; Glasgow Univ. (MA Hons Eng. Lang. and Lit.). Fiction Editor, Daily Mail and Evening News, London, 1935. Travelled widely in Europe, America and Africa, 1929-39 (over 500 short stories and innumerable articles). Served War of 1939-45, RNVR. Overland by car London to S Africa, 1947, and again 1949-50. Settled in S Rhodesia, 1947; engaged in tree-farming as well as writing, broadcasting, etc. Publications Officer, Rhodesian Instn of Engineers; Editor: The Rhodesian Engineer; The RTA Jl. *Publications:* Yellow Stockings, 1925; Lola of the Isles, 1926; Mystery of the "David M", 1929; Landfall, 1932; Quest of the Stormalong, 1934; Carlyle in Old Age, 1934; They Sailed for Senegal, 1938; Convict Captain, 1939; The Royal Navy, 1940; The North Patrol, 1941; The Road to the Nile, 1941; East India Adventure, 1945; The Young Chevalier, 1947; The River Windrush, 1946; The River Fowey, 1948; The River Conway, 1952; The River Doon, 1952; Auto Nomad in Sweden, 1948; Traders North, 1951; Auto Nomad in Barbary, 1950; Auto Nomad Through Africa, 1951; Auto Nomad in Spain, 1953; The Desert Watches, 1954; Simba Bwana, 1956; The Road from Chilanga, 1957; Zambesi Adventure, 1960; Harry Hogbin, 1961; Death at Slack Water, 1962; The Valley of Hidden Gold, 1962; Guns for the Congo, 1963; A Rhino in the Kitchen, 1964; The Past Dies Hard, 1965; under pseudonym of David Wilson, The Search for Geoffrey Goring, 1962; Murder in Mozambique, 1963. *Address:* PO Box 411, Marandellas, Rhodesia. *T:* Marandellas 241319.

**MacARTHUR, Ian;** MP (C) Perth and East Perthshire since 1959; Associate Director, J. Walter Thompson Co. Ltd (joined firm, 1947); *b* 17 May 1925; *yr s* of late Lt-Gen. Sir William MacArthur, KCB, DSO, FRCP; *m* 1957, Judith Mary, *d* of late Francis Gavin Douglas Miller; three *s* three *d*. *Educ:* Cheltenham Coll.; The Queen's Coll., Oxford (Scholar, MA). Contested (U), Greenock Gen. Election, May 1955, also by-election, Dec. 1955; Mem., Conservative and Unionist Nat. Exec. Cttee, 1953; Hon. Pres., Scottish Young Unionists, 1962-65. Introduced, as Private Member's Bill, Law Reform (Damages and Solatium) (Scotland) Act, 1962. An Asst Government Whip, 1962-63; a Lord Comr of the Treasury, 1963-64; Opposition Scottish Whip, 1964-65. Personal Asst to the Prime Minister, Rt Hon. Sir Alec Douglas-Home, Kinross and W Perthshire By-Election, Nov. 1963. Hon. Mem., Inst. of Practitioners in Advertising, 1963. Served War of 1939-45, with RN and RNVR, 1943-46 (Flag Lieut to C-in-C Portsmouth, 1946). *Address:* Strone House, Bridge of Cally, Perthshire. *T:* Bridge of Cally 272. *Clubs:* Naval; New (Edinburgh); Puffin's (Edinburgh); Royal County (Perth).

**MacARTHUR, Neil,** DL; *b* 20 March 1886; *s* of John MacArthur, Castleton, Glassary, Argyll; *m* 1916, Mary MacArthur, *d* of Capt. Malcolm Campbell, Ibrox, Glasgow; one *s* one *d*. *Educ:* Lochgilphead Sch.; Glasgow Univ. Qualified as Solicitor, 1911. Served European War, 1914-18, with 4th Bn QO Cameron Highlanders, and RAF (despatches). Lt-Col 1927; Bt Col 1931. DL Inverness-shire, 1954. Hon. Sheriff Substitute of Inverness, Moray, Nairn, and Ross and Cromarty. Director: Deltenne (Ceylon) Tea Estates Ltd, Highland Haulage Ltd. *Recreations:* shooting, fishing, golf. *Address:* Milnfield, Inverness. *T:* Inverness 33439. *Clubs:* Caledonian (Edinburgh); Highland (Inverness).

**MacARTHUR, Wilson;** *see* MacArthur, D. W.

**MACARTHUR-ONSLOW, Maj.-Gen. Sir Denzil,** Kt 1964; CBE 1951; DSO 1941; ED; *b* 5 March 1904; *s* of late F. A. Macarthur-Onslow; *m* 1st, 1927, Elinor Margaret (marriage dissolved, 1950), *d* of late Gordon Caldwell; three *s* one *d*; 2nd, 1950, Dorothy, *d* of W. D. Scott; one *s* one *d*. *Educ:* Tudor House Sch., Moss Vale; King's Sch., Parramatta, New South Wales. Commissioned Australian Field Artillery, 1924. Served War of 1939-45 in Middle East and New Guinea (despatches thrice, DSO). Gen. Officer Commanding 2nd Div. Australian Military Forces, 1954-58; Citizen Forces Mem. of Australian Mil. Board, 1958-60. *Address:* Mount Gilead, Cambelltown, New South Wales; Camden Park, Menangle, New South Wales, Australia. *Clubs:* Australian, Royal Sydney Golf, Australasian Pioneers (Sydney, NSW).

**MACARTNEY, Carlile Aylmer;** FBA 1965; MA, DLitt, Oxon; sometime Foreign Member of Hungarian Academy of Sciences; *b* 1895; *s* of late Carlile Henry Hayes Macartney; *m* Nedella, *d* of late Col Dimitri Mamarchev, Bulgarian Army; no *c*. *Educ:* Winchester (scholar, Pitt Exhibitioner); Trinity Coll., Cambridge (scholar). Served European War, 1914-18; HBM Vice-Consul (acting), Vienna, 1921-25; with Encyclopædia Britannica, 1926-28; Intelligence Dept, League of Nations Union, 1928-36; Research Dept, Foreign Office, 1939-46; Montagu Burton Prof. of International Relations, Edinburgh Univ., 1951-57; Research Fellow, All Souls Coll., Oxford, 1936-65. *Publications:* The Social Revolution in Austria, 1926; Survey of International Affairs for 1925, Part II (with other authors) 1927; The Magyars in the Ninth Century, 1930 (2nd edn 1968); National States and National Minorities, 1934 (2nd edn 1968); Hungary (Modern World Series), 1934 (Hungarian edn, revised, 1936); Hungary and her Successors, 1937 (2nd edn 1965); Studies in the Earliest Hungarian historical sources, I-VIII, 1933-52; Problems of the Danube Basin, 1942 (Hungarian translation, 1943); The Mediæval Hungarian Historians, 1953; Oct. 15th, 1957 (2nd edn rev. 1961); (with A. W. Palmer) Independent Eastern Europe, 1961; Hungary: A Short History, 1962; The Habsburg Empire 1790-1918, 1969; Maria Theresa and the House of Austria, 1969; The Habsburg and Hohenzollern Powers, 1969; contribs to Encyclopædia Britannica, 13th and 14th edns, Chambers's Encyclopædia, and to British and Central European Reviews; translations. *Recreation:* travel. *Address:* Hornbeams, Boars Hill, near Oxford. *T:* Oxford 35224.

**MACARTNEY, Sir John Barrington,** 6th Bt *cr* 1799, of Lish, Co. Armagh; dairy farmer; *b* 21 Jan. 1917; *s* of John Barrington Macartney (3rd *s* of Sir John Macartney, 3rd Bt; he *d* 1951) and Selina Koch, Hampton, Mackay, Qld, Australia; *S* uncle, Sir Alexander Miller Macartney, 5th Bt, 1960; *m* 1944, Amy Isobel Reinke; one *s*. *Heir: s* John Ralph Macartney, *b* 24 July 1945. *Address:* Golden Hills, Glastonbury, via Gympie, Queensland, Australia.

**MACAULAY, Lt-Col Archibald Duncan Campbell,** OBE 1961; Secretary, All England Lawn Tennis Club, Wimbledon, 1946-63; *b* 27 Sept. 1897; *o s* of late Major and Mrs A. Macaulay; unmarried. *Educ:* King's Sch., Canterbury. Served with The Buffs European War, 1914-18 in France, afterwards transferring to Indian Army, 7th Bn Gurkha Rifles, retiring in 1924. Referee and manager of many lawn tennis tournaments in United Kingdom, 1923-39; served with Royal Army Service Corps, 1939-45. *Publication:* Behind the Scenes at Wimbledon, 1965. *Address:* Spinaway Cottage, Slindon, near Arundel, Sussex. *T:* Slindon 308. *Clubs:* United Service; All England Lawn Tennis (Wimbledon).

**MACAULAY, Sir Hamilton,** Kt 1960; CBE 1956; *b* 1901; *s* of late Hugh Stevenson Macaulay, Glasgow; *m* 1930, Marjorie Slinger, *d* of late Francis Gill, Litton, Yorks. *Educ:* Calder HG Sch., Glasgow. Served War of 1939-45 (despatches), Lt-Col. Pres., Chittagong Chamber of Commerce, 1953-54, 1956-57 and 1959-60; Dep. Pres., Assoc. Chambers of Commerce of Pakistan, 1953-54. Chm., Chittagong Branch UK Assoc. of Pakistan, 1955-56 and 1959-60. Director, Rivers Steam Navigation Co. (Holdings) Ltd, London. *Recreation:* golf. *Address:* The Cottage, Harpers Road, Ash, Surrey. *Club:* Oriental.

**MACAULAY, Janet Stewart Alison,** MA; Headmistress of St Leonards and St Katharines Schools, St Andrews, 1956-70; *b* 20 Dec. 1909; 3rd *d* of late Rev. Prof. A. B. Macaulay, DD, of Trinity Coll., Glasgow. *Educ:* Laurel Bank Sch., Glasgow; Glasgow Univ.; Somerville Coll., Oxford. BA Oxon 1932; BLitt Oxon 1934; MA Oxon 1936. Asst Mistress, Wycombe Abbey Sch., Bucks, 1933-36; Sutton High Sch. (GPDST), Sutton, Surrey, 1937-45; Headmistress, Blackheath High Sch. (GPDST), 1945-Dec. 1955. *Address:* Grampian Cottage, Kincraig, Inverness-shire.

**MACAULAY, Hon. Leopold,** QC (Canada); BA, LLB; Barrister; Vice-President, Canadian Red Cross Society; Counsel, Thomson and Rogers; *b* Peterboro, Ont., 25 Nov. 1887; *s* of Robert Macaulay and Agnes Giroux, Canadians; *m*; two *s* one *d*; *m* 1963, Kathleen H. Sherk, Midland, Mich., USA. *Educ:* Lindsay Public Sch.; Harbord Collegiate, Toronto; Univ. of Toronto; Osgoode Hall, Toronto. Provincial Sec. and Registrar of the Province of Ontario, Canada, 1930-31; Minister of Highways, Ontario, 1931-34, and Minister of Public Works, 1934; Pres. Univ. of Toronto Alumni Fedn, 1937-38; Conservative Mem. for South York Riding, Ont., 1926-43; retired 1943; Chm. National Council, Red Cross, Canada, 1951-52; Chm. Board of Regents, Victoria Univ., Toronto, 1951-58. *Recreations:* golf, curling, etc. *Address:* 95 River View Drive, Toronto 12, Canada. *Clubs:* Rosedale Golf, National.

**McAULIFFE, Gen. Anthony Clement,** DSC (US); DSM (US) (with Oak Leaf Cluster); Silver Star; Legion of Merit and Bronze Star Medal; US Army retired; Vice-President, American Cyanamid Company, 1956-64, retired; *b* 2 July 1898; *s* of John J. and Alice K. McAuliffe; *m* 1920, Helen Willet Whitman; one *s* one *d*. *Educ:* US Military Academy, West Point, NY. Passed through grades 2nd Lt to Gen. in US Army, 1918-56. Combat operations, War of 1939-45, European Theatre as Dep. Div. Comdr and Acting Div. Comdr of 101st Airborne Div. and as Div. Comdr of 103rd Infantry Div.; retired, 1956. DSO and Bar (British), 1945 also decorations from governments of France, Belgium, Holland and Luxembourg. *Recreations:* golf, poker and bridge. *Address:* 2101 Connecticut Avenue, Washington 8, DC 20008, USA.

**McBAIN, Alexander Richardson,** CB 1946; OBE 1968; Under-Secretary, Ministry of Supply, Jan. 1946-Dec. 1948, re-employed Oct. 1949; late Chairman, Southern Gas Board, 1952-55; *b* 1887; *s* of Alexander McBain, Glasgow; *m* 1925, Winifred Alice, *d* of William Winton Davies. *Educ:* Glasgow High Sch. and Technical Coll. *Address:* Cherrygarth, Hillfield Square, Chalfont St Peter, Bucks. *T:* Gerrards Cross 84209.

**MACBEATH, Prof. Alexander Murray,** PhD (Princeton, NJ); MA (Cantab); FRSE; Mason Professor of Pure Mathematics, University of Birmingham, since 1962; *b* 30 June 1923; *s* of late Prof. Alexander Macbeath, CBE; *m* 1951, Julie Ormrod, Lytham St Anne's; two *s*. *Educ:* Royal Belfast Academical Inst.; Queen's Univ., Belfast; Clare Coll., Cambridge. Entrance Schol., Dixon Prize in Maths, Purser Studentship, 1st class hons in Maths, BA, QUB. Temp. post with Foreign Office, 1943-45. Cambridge, 1945-48; Maj. Entrance Schol., Wrangler Math. Tripos, Part II, dist. Part III, BA, Owst Prize. Commonwealth Fund Fellowship, Princeton, NJ, 1948-50; Smith's Prize, 1949; PhD Princeton, 1950. Research Fellow, Clare Coll., Cambridge, 1950-51; MA Cambridge, 1951. Lectr in Maths, Univ. Coll. of North Staffordshire, 1951-53; Prof. of Maths, Queen's Coll., Dundee, 1953-62. Vis. Prof., California Inst. of Technology, 1966-67. *Publications:* Elementary Vector Algebra, 1964; papers in: Jl London Mathematical Soc.; Proc. London Math. Soc.; Proc. Cambridge Philosophical Soc.; Quarterly Jl of Mathematics; Annals of Mathematics; Canadian Jl of Mathematics. *Recreation:* swimming. *Address:* 51 Shakespeare Drive, Shirley, Solihull, Warwickshire.

**McBEATH, Rear-Admiral John (Edwin Home),** CB 1957; DSO 1940; DSC 1941; DL; retired, 1958; *b* 27 Sept. 1907; *er s* of late Mr and Mrs J. H. McBeath, Natal, S Africa; *m* 1952, Hon. Janet Mary Blades, *y d* of 1st Baron Ebbisham, GBE; one *s* one *d*. *Educ:* Massachusetts, USA; Hilton Coll., Natal, S Africa. Entered Royal Navy, 1923; Comdr 1941; Captain, 1945; Rear-Admiral, 1955. During War of 1939-45 commanded destroyers in North Sea, Atlantic, Arctic, Mediterranean (despatches). HM Naval Base, Singapore, 1945-48; Comd First Destroyer Flotilla, Mediterranean Fleet, 1948-50; Chief of Staff to Flag Officer Commanding Reserve Fleet, 1950-52; Commodore, Royal Naval Barracks, Devonport, 1953-55; lent to RNZN, 1955; Chief of Naval Staff and First Member Naval Board, RNZN, 1955-58. Hon. Commodore, Sea Cadet Corps, 1958-. DL Surrey, 1968. Order of Merit (France), 1939. *Address:* Woodbury House, Churt, Surrey. *T:* Headley Down 2275. *Club:* United Service.

**MacBETH, George Mann;** verse-writer; *b* Scotland, 1932; *s* of George MacBeth and Amelia Morton Mary Mann; *m* 1955, Elizabeth Browell Robson. *Educ:* New Coll., Oxford (read Classics and Philosophy). Joined BBC, 1955; Producer, Overseas Talks Dept, 1957; Producer, Talks Dept, 1958; Editor: Poet's Voice, 1958-65; New Comment, 1959-64; Poetry Now, 1965-. Sir Geoffrey Faber Memorial Award (jointly), 1964. *Publications: poems:* A Form of Words, 1954; The Broken Places, 1963; A Doomsday Book, 1965; The Colour of Blood, 1967; The Night of Stones, 1968; A War Quartet, 1969; The Burning Cone, 1970; Poems 1958-1969, 1971; *anthologies:* The Penguin Book of Sick Verse, 1963; (with J. Clemo and E. Lucie-Smith) Penguin Modern Poets VI, 1964; The Penguin Book of Animal Verse, 1965; (with notes) Poetry, 1900-1965, 1967; The Penguin Book of Victorian Verse, 1968; *children's books:* Jonah and the Lord, 1969; The Dark Wind, 1970. *Recreation:* motoring. *Address:* c/o BBC, Broadcasting House, W1.

**McBRIDE, Neil;** MP (Lab) Swansea East since 1963; *b* Neilston, Renfrewshire, Scotland, 13 April 1910; *e s* of late Neil McBride, Senior, of Neilston; *m* 1937, Delia, 3rd *d* of late James Maloney, Paisley; no *c*. *Educ:* St Thomas' Sch., Neilston; continuation classes; National Council of Labour Colleges. Brass finisher; last employers, John Brown & Co. (Clydebank) Ltd. Formerly Member Paisley

Corporation. Contested (Lab): Perth and Perth East, 1951, High Peak, Derbyshire, 1955. Asst Govt Whip, 1966-69; a Lord Comr, HM Treasury, Oct. 1969-1970; Opposition Whip, 1970-. *Recreations:* travel, reading, spread of Socialism. *Address:* 116 Eaton Road, Brynhyfryd, Swansea, Glam.

**McBRIDE, Rt. Hon. Sir Philip Albert Martin,** PC 1959; KCMG 1953; *b* 18 June 1892; *s* of late Albert J. McBride, Adelaide; *m* 1914, Rita I., *d* of late E. W. Crews, Kooringa, South Australia; two *s* (and one *s* decd). *Educ:* Burra Public Sch., South Australia; Prince Alfred Coll. MHR for Grey, South Australia, 1931-34; for Wakefield, S Australia, 1946-; Member of Senate for S Australia, 1937-43; Minister without Portfolio assisting Minister for Commerce, March-Aug. 1940; Minister: for the Army and for Repatriation, Aug.-Oct. 1940; for Supply and Development, Oct. 1940-June 1941; for Munitions, 1940-41; Mem. Australian Advisory War Council, Aug.-Oct. 1941; Mem. Economic Cabinet, 1939-40, and War Cabinet, 1940-41; Dep. Leader of Opposition in Senate, 1941-43; Minister for the Interior, 1949-50; Acting Minister for Defence, April-Oct. 1950; Minister: for Defence, 1950-58; for the Navy and for Air, May-July 1951; Leader of Australian Govt Delegn to Defence Conf., London, 1951. *Recreation:* tennis. *Address:* c/o House of Representatives, Adelaide, S Australia. *Clubs:* Adelaide (Adelaide); Australian (Melbourne).

**MacBRIDE, Sean;** Senior Counsel, Irish Bar; *b* 26 Jan. 1904; *s* of late Major John MacBride and late Maud Gonne; *m* 1926, Catalina Bulfin; one *s* one *d*. *Educ:* St Louis de Ganzague, Paris, Mount St Benedict, Gorey, Co. Wexford, Ireland. Was a journalist for a number of years before being called to Irish Bar, 1937; Irish correspondent for Havas and some American and South African papers before War of 1939-45. Called to Bar, 1937; called to Inner Bar, 1943; holds record of having become a Senior Counsel in a shorter period of time than any other living member of the Bar; defended many sensational capital cases and had an extensive practice in High Court and Supreme Court. Founder, 1936, and Leader of political party, Clann na Poblachta (Republican Party). Member of Dail Eireann, 1947-58; Minister for External Affairs, Eire, 1948-51. Pres., Council of Foreign Ministers of Council of Europe, 1950; Vice-Pres., OEEC, 1948-51; declined portfolio, June 1954, on ground of inadequate parliamentary representation; delegate to Council of Europe from Ireland, 1954. Trustee, Internat. Prisoners of Conscience Fund; Mem. Exec., Pan-European Union; Mem., European Round Table; Mem., Ghana Bar; International Congress of Jurists, New Delhi, 1958 and Rio de Janeiro, 1962; Chairman: Irish Assoc. of Jurists; Amnesty International; International Peace Bureau, Geneva; late Chm., Irish Section, Internat. Commn of Jurists (Sec.-Gen. of the Commn, 1963-70). *Publications:* Civil Liberty, 1948 (pamphlet); Our People–Our Money, 1951. *Recreation:* sailing. *Address:* Roebuck House, Clonskea, Dublin, 14. *T:* Dublin 973225; 2 Quai du Cheval-Blanc, Geneva, Switzerland.

**McBURNEY, Charles Brian Montagu,** FBA 1966; FSA, MA, ScD; Reader in Prehistory, University of Cambridge, since 1967; Fellow and Director of Studies in Archæology and Anthropology, Corpus Christi College, Cambridge, since 1962; *b* 18 June 1914; *s* of Henry McBurney and Dorothy Lilian (*née* Rundall); *m* 1953, Anne Francis Edmonstone Charles; two *s* one *d*. *Educ:* privately; King's Coll., Cambridge (BA 1937). Research Fellow, King's Coll., Cambridge, 1940-53, PhD; Univ. Lectr in Archæology, 1953-67. Hon. Corresp. Mem. Istituto Italiano di Paleontologia Umana, Rome; British Rep. Société Préhistorique Française. Knight of Order of the Dannebrog (First Class), 1961. *Publications:* (with R. W. Hey) Prehistory and Pleistocene Geology of Cyrenaican Libya, 1955; The Stone Age of Northern Africa, 1960; The Haua Fteah (Cyrenaica) and the Stone Age of the SE Mediterranean, 1967; articles on early prehistory of Iran, Libya, Central and SW Europe, and Britain in Proc. Prehistoric Soc., Jl of Royal Anthropological Inst., L'Anthropologie, Encyclopædia Britannica, etc. *Recreations:* trout fishing, walking, travelling. *Address:* 5 Grange Road, Cambridge. *T:* Cambridge 51385. *Club:* Oxford and Cambridge University.

**McBURNEY, Air Vice-Marshal Ralph Edward,** CBE 1945; CD; RCAF, retired; Chief, Technical Information Service, National Research Council, Ottawa, since 1960; President, International Federation for Documentation; *b* Montreal, Quebec, 17 Aug. 1906; *s* of Irville Albert and Lilian McBurney, Saskatoon, Sask.; *m* 1931, Gertrude Elizabeth Bate, Saskatoon; two *s* one *d*. *Educ:* Univs of Saskatchewan and Manitoba. BSc (EE); Commenced flying training as a cadet in RCAF, 1924; Pilot Officer, 1926; employed on Forest Fire Patrols and photographic mapping; Course in RAF School of Army Co-operation and tour as Instructor in RCAF School of Army Co-operation, 1931; Course at RAF Wireless School, Cranwell, and tour as Signals Adviser at Air Force HQ, Ottawa, 1935-36; RAF Staff Coll., Andover, 1939; Dir of Signals, AFHQ, Ottawa, 1939-42; CO, RCAF Station, Trenton, Ont., 1943; CO, RCAF Station, Dishforth, Yorks, 1943; Air Cdre 1944; Base Comdr of 61 Training Base, and later, 64 Operational Base in No. 6 (RCAF) Bomber Group of Bomber Comd; SASO of the Group, Dec. 1944. AOC RCAF Maintenance Comd, 1945-46; Senior Canadian Air Force Liaison Officer, London, 1946-48; AOC Air Materiel Comd, RCAF, Ottawa, 1948-52. *Address:* 2022 Sharon, Ottawa, Ontario, Canada.

**McCABE, Alasdair;** Managing Director, Educational Building Society; Editor, Irish Year Book. MP (SF) South Sligo, 1918-22; Member Dail Eireann for Mayo East and Sligo County, 1921-23; Leitrim and Sligo, 1923-24. Commandant Army, 1921-23. *Recreation:* golf. *Address:* 33 Oakley Road, Ranelagh, Dublin. *T:* 974335.

**MacCABE, Brian Farmer,** MC and Bar, 1942; Chairman: FCB International Inc. (New York), since 1969; Foote, Cone & Belding Ltd (London), since 1948; FCB International Ltd, since 1969; Director, Foote, Cone & Belding Communications Inc. (New York), since 1953; *b* 9 Jan. 1914; *s* of late James MacCabe and Katherine MacCabe (*née* Harwood); *m* 1940, Eileen Elizabeth Noel Hunter; one *s*. *Educ:* Christ's Coll., London. Executive, C. R. Casson Ltd, 1934-40. Major, RTR (Sqdn Comd, Alamein; Instructor Turkish Staff Coll., Ankara), 1940-45. World-wide Advertising Manager, BOAC, 1945-47. Dir and Sen. Vice-Pres., Foote, Cone & Belding Inc., 1953-. Mem. Council: Inst. of Practitioners in Advertising, 1951-; Advertising Assoc., 1952-; Internat. Marketing Programme, 1965-. Mem., Reith Commn on Advertising, 1962-66; Pres., Inst of Practitioners in Advertising, 1963-65; Member: Promotion Cttee, BNEC, 1965-68; Marketing Cttee, Ashridge Management Coll., 1965-; Advertising Standards Authority, 1969-; Appeals Cttee, Olympic and Commonwealth Games, 1952-;

Management Cttee, British Sports Assoc. for the Disabled, 1962-65; Nat. Council, Brit. Polio Fellowship, 1959-65. Royal Humane Soc. Medal for saving life at sea, 1934; awards for services to advertising, 1957-. *Recreations:* finalist: (800 metres) Olympic Games, Berlin, 1936; (880 yards) British Commonwealth Games, Sydney, 1938; golf, tennis, fishing, painting. *Address:* Somerford, Penn Road, Beaconsfield, Bucks. *T:* Beaconsfield 3365.

**McCABE, Most Rev. Thomas;** *see* Wollongong, NSW, Bishop of, (RC).

**McCALL, Sir Alexander,** Kt 1947; MD, ChB; Fellow London Medical Society and Hunterian Society. MB, ChB, 1906; MD Glasgow (high commend.), 1909; late Asst Pathologist, London Homoeopathic Hosp.; Clinical Asst, West End Hosp. for Diseases of the Nervous System; Asst Physician, City of Glasgow Fever and Smallpox Hospitals. *Publications:* Diazo-Reaction and Bacilluria in Enteric Fever. *Address:* 30a Wimpole Street, W1. *T:* 01-935 7311.

**McCALL, Charles James,** ROI 1949; DA (Edinburgh); artist-painter; *b* 24 Feb. 1907; *s* of late William McCall, Edinburgh; *m* 1945, Eloise Jerwood, *d* of F. Ward, Bickley, Kent. *Educ:* Edinburgh Univ.; Edinburgh College of Art. RSA Travelling Schol., 1933; Edinburgh College of Art: Travelling Schol., 1936 (Fellow, 1938). Studied in many art galleries in Europe; also in studios in Paris. Returned to London in 1938, exhibiting RA, NEAC, London Group, etc. Commissioned, RE 1940; at end of war taught drawing and painting at Formation College. Has exhibited regularly in London; one-man shows held at: Leicester Galleries, 1950 and 1953; Victor Waddington Galleries, Dublin, 1951; Duveen Graham Galleries, New York, 1955 and 1957; Crane Galleries, Manchester, 1955; Klinkhoff Gallery, Montreal, 1958 and 1960; Whibley Gallery, London, 1963; Federation of British Artists, 1965; Ash Barn Gallery, Stroud, 1965, 1969; Eaton's Gallery, Winnipeg, Canada, 1966. Painter of portraits, landscapes, interiors with figures, and of contemporary life. NEAC 1957. Lord Mayor's Art Award, 1963. *Recreations:* music, literature, travel. *Address:* 1a Caroline Terrace, SW1. *T:* 01-730 8737.

**McCALL, Charles Patrick Home,** MBE 1944; TD 1946; DL; Clerk of the Peace, Clerk of the County Council, and Clerk of the Lieutenancy, Lancashire; *b* 22 Nov. 1910; *s* of late Charles and Dorothy McCall; *m* 1934, Anne, *d* of late Samuel Brown, Sedlescombe, Sussex; two *s* one *d*. *Educ:* St Edward's Sch., Oxford. Served 1939-45; Substantive Major TA. Hon. Lt-Col. *Recreations:* travel, walking, swimming, gardening. *Address:* (office) County Hall, Preston. *T:* Preston 54868; (home) Ribby Wood, Wrea Green, near Preston. *T:* Kirkham 2336. *Club:* Royal Automobile.

**McCALL, Adm. Sir Henry William Urquhart,** KCVO 1953; KBE 1951; CB 1949; DSO 1942; retired; *b* 11 June 1895; *s* of Henry John McCall, Largs, Ayrshire, and Isobel Alston McCall (*née* Dykes); *m* 1926, Helen Mary Leycester; two *d*. *Educ:* RN Colleges, Osborne and Dartmouth. Entered RNC Osborne, 1908; Lieut 1917; Comdr 1931; Capt. 1937; Naval Attaché, Buenos Aires, 1938-40; comd HMS Dido, 1940-42; Chief of Staff to Head of British Admiralty Delegn, Washington, 1943; comd HMS Howe, 1944-46; Rear-Adm. 1946; Senior British Naval Officer, Middle East, 1946-48; Flag Officer Destroyers, Mediterranean Fleet, 1949-50; Vice-Adm. 1950; Vice-Adm. Commanding Reserve Fleet, 1950-53; Adm. 1953; Retd Sept. 1953. *Address:* Doiley Hill Farm, Hurstbourne Tarrant, near Andover, Hants. *T:* Hurstbourne Tarrant 229. *Club:* Naval and Military.

**McCALL, John Armstrong Grice,** CMG 1964; Principal Administrative Officer, East Kilbride Development Corporation, since 1967; *b* 7 Jan. 1913; 2nd *s* of Rev. Canon J. G. McCall; *m* 1951, Kathleen Mary Clarke; no *c*. *Educ:* Glasgow Academy; Trinity Coll., Glenalmond; St Andrews Univ.; St John's Coll., Cambridge. MA 1st class hons Hist. St Andrews, 1935. Colonial Administrative Service (HMOCS), Nigeria, 1935-67; Cadet, 1936; Class I, 1956; Staff Grade, 1958. Chairman, Mid-Western Nigeria Development Corporation, Benin City, 1966-67, retired 1967. *Recreations:* golf, walking. *Address:* Burnside, West Linton, Peeblesshire. *T:* West Linton 488. *Clubs:* Caledonian; Royal and Ancient (St Andrews).

**McCALL, John Donald;** Chairman, Consolidated Gold Fields Ltd, since Oct. 1969; *b* 1 Feb. 1911; *s* of late Gilbert Kerr McCall; *m* 1942, Vere Stewart Gardner; one *s* one *d*. *Educ:* Clifton Coll.; Edinburgh Univ. Gold Mining industry, S Africa, 1930-37. Served War of 1939-45: commissioned, Gordon Highlanders. Joined Consolidated Gold Fields Ltd, London, 1946 (Dir, 1959; Jt Dep. Chm., 1968). *Recreations:* gardening, golf. *Address:* 93 Eaton Place, SW1. *T:* 01-235 8627; Heydon Place, Heydon, near Royston, Hertfordshire. *T:* Crishall 289. *Club:* Caledonian.

**McCALL, Kenneth Murray;** Lord Lieutenant of Dumfriesshire since 1970; *b* 21 Dec. 1912; *s* of late Major William McCall, DL; *m* 1938, Christina Eve Laurie; two *s* two *d*. *Educ:* Merchiston Castle School. *Recreations:* shooting, golf. *Address:* Caitloch, Moniaive, Thornhill, Dumfriesshire. *T:* Moniaive 211.

**McCALLUM, Archibald Duncan Dugald,** FRSA 1969; TD 1950; Headmaster, Strathallan School, since 1970; *b* 26 Nov. 1914; *s* of late Dr A. D. McCallum and Mrs A. D. McCallum; *m* 1950, Rosemary Constance, *widow* of Sqdn Ldr John Rhind, RAF, and *d* of William C. Thorne, OBE, Edinburgh; two *s* (one step *s*). *Educ:* Fettes Coll., Edinburgh; St John's Coll., Cambridge (Classical Sizar). Asst Master and Housemaster, Fettes Coll., 1937-39, 1945-51. Served War of 1939-45 (despatches): Home Forces, India, and Burma. Second Master, Strathallan Sch., 1951-56; Headmaster: Christ Coll., Brecon, 1956-62; Epsom Coll., 1962-70. *Recreations:* Rugby football, golf, reading. *Address:* Strathallan School, Forgandenny, Perthshire. *T:* Bridge of Earn 232.

**McCALLUM, Brig. Frank,** CIE 1947; OBE 1936; MC 1923; DL; *b* 11 March 1900; *s* of late Lt-Col D. McCallum, RASC, Edinburgh; *m* 1932, Sybilla Mary de Symons, *d* of late Gen. Sir George Barrow, GCB, KCMG; one *s* (and one *s* decd). *Educ:* George Watson's Coll.; RMC. Commissioned 1918; Brig. 1943. ADC to GOC-in-C Eastern Comd, India, 1928-29; Staff Coll., Quetta, 1934-35; Bde Major, Razmak, 1936-39; GSO2 Meerut Dist, 1940-41; served in Iraq, Persia, Western Desert, and Syria, 1941-46; GSO1, 8 Indian Div., 1941-43; Bde Comd, 1943-46; BGS Northern Comd, India, 1946-47; Dir Staff Duties, Army HQ, Pakistan, 1947. Served 3rd Afghan War, 1919; NWF, 1920-21 and 1923 (MC); NWF, 1936 (OBE) and 1937-39; despatches 7 times, 1936-46; retd 30 May 1948. Asst Regional Food Officer, North Midland Region, 1948-51; Regional Sec. Country Landowners Assoc. for

Lincs, Notts, and Derbs, 1951-65; CC Kesteven, Lincolnshire, 1952-, Alderman, 1964-. DL Lincolnshire, 1965. Syrian Order of Merit, 1st Class, 1945-46. *Address:* Westborough Grange, near Newark, Notts. *T:* Long Bennington 285.

**McCALLUM, Mrs John;** *see* Withers, Googie.

**MacCALLUM, Sir Peter,** Kt 1953; MC; MSc (NZ and Melbourne), MA, MB, ChB(Ed), MD (hc Melbourne), DPH, FRCP(Ed), FRS(Ed), FRACP; MCPA; Professor Emeritus, University of Melbourne, 1951; *b* 1885; *s* of Peter MacCallum, Christchurch, NZ; *m* 1st, 1919, Bella Dytes McIntosh (*d* 1927), DSc, MA, *d* of late George Cross, Timaru, NZ; three *d*; 2nd, 1928, Ursula Lillie (*d* 1941), *d* of late Archdeacon T. Grace, of Blenheim, NZ; one *s*; 3rd, Frieda Maud (*d* 1953), *d* of late Rev. A. D. Davies, Camperdown, Victoria. *Educ:* Christ's Coll. and Canterbury Univ. Coll., Christchurch, NZ; University of Edinburgh. Lecturer in Pathology Univ. and Royal Colls, Edinburgh; Prof. of Pathology, University of Melbourne, 1925-50! Hon. Dir Clinical Studies, 1948-52; Chm.: Australian Red Cross, 1951-58; Australian National Research Council, 1948-51; Australian Coll. of Dentistry, Melbourne, 1941-63; Executive Anti-Cancer Council of Victoria, 1945-63; Pres. BMA (Vic. Branch), 1946; Pres. Victorian Cancer Congress, 1960; Chm. Consultative Council on Tuberculosis, 1945-48; Member: Dental Bd of Vic., 1928-33; University Council, 1931-50 and 1953-61; Med. Bd of Vic., 1945-63. Royal Commn on Bundaberg Fatalities, 1928. Served European War, 1914-18, Capt. RAMC(SR) 1915-19, France and Belgium (MC); War of 1939-45, Lt-Col AAMC, Dir of Pathology. *Publications:* articles on Pathology and Medical Education; Advisory Report to Govt of Western Australia on Medical School establishment. *Recreation:* fishing. *Address:* 91 Princess Street, Kew, Victoria 3101, Australia.

**McCALLUM, Ronald Buchanan;** Master, Pembroke College, Oxford, 1955-67; Principal of St Catharine's, Cumberland Lodge, Windsor Great Park, since 1967; *b* 28 Aug. 1898; 4th *s* of late Andrew Fisher McCallum and of Catherine Buchanan Gibson, Paisley; *m* 1st, 1932, Ischar Gertrude Bradley (*d* 1944), Wallasey, Ches; two *d*; 2nd, 1950, Evelyn Margaret, *er d* of Sir Douglas Veale, *qv*; two *s* one *d*. *Educ:* Paisley Grammar Sch.; Trinity Coll., Glenalmond; Worcester Coll., Oxford. Lt Labour Corps, BEF, France, 1917-19. 1st Cl. Hons School of Modern History, Oxford, 1922. Procter Visiting Fellow to Princeton Univ., 1923. Lectr in History, Glasgow Univ., 1924; Fellow of Pembroke Coll., Oxford, 1925; Statutory Comr for Univ. of St Andrews, 1953-58. Member: Oxford City Council, 1958-67; Council of Reading Univ., 1957-67; Chm. Adv. Cttee for Univ. of Dundee, 1964-66. Hon. Fellow: Worcester Coll., Oxford, 1961; Pembroke Coll., Oxford, 1968. Hon. LLD, Dundee, 1967. *Publications:* Life of Asquith, 1936; Public Opinion and the Last Peace, 1944; Britain and France, 1944; (with Alison Readman) The General Election of 1945, 1947; Supplementary Chapter to Halévy, History of the English People, Vol. IV; The Liberal Party from Earl Grey to Asquith, 1963. *Address:* Cumberland Lodge, The Great Park, Windsor, Berks. *Clubs:* United University, National Liberal.

**McCANCE, Sir Andrew,** Kt 1947; FRS 1943; DL; DSc; LLD; Hon. President (formerly Chairman and Managing Director), Colvilles Ltd; President, Clyde Alloy Steel Co. Ltd; Chairman, Colville Clugston Shanks Ltd; *b* 30 March 1889; *yr s* of John McCance; *m* 1936, Joya Harriett Gladys Burford (*d* 1969); two *d*. *Educ:* Morrison's Academy, Crieff; Allan Glen's Sch., Glasgow; Royal School of Mines, London. Asst Armour Manager, W. Beardmore & Co., 1910-19; Founder and Man. Dir, Clyde Alloy Steel Co. Ltd, 1919-30; DSc (London Univ.), 1916; Bessemer Medallist, 1940; Past President: Iron and Steel Inst.; Glasgow and West of Scotland Iron and Steel Inst.; Inst. of Engineers and Shipbuilders in Scotland: President: British Iron and Steel Federation, 1957, 1958; Instn of Works Managers, 1964-67. Chm., Mechanical Engineering Research Board, DSIR, 1952-58. DL Lanarkshire. Hon. DSc, Strathclyde, 1965. *Publications:* several papers in Technical Society jls. *Address:* 27 Broom Cliff, Newton Mearns, Glasgow. *T:* 041-639 5115. *Clubs:* Athenæum; Scottish Automobile (Glasgow).

**McCANCE, Robert Alexander,** CBE 1953; FRS 1948; Professor of Experimental Medicine, Medical Research Council and University of Cambridge, 1945-66; Director, MRC Infantile Malnutrition Research Unit, Mulago Hospital, Kampala, 1966-68; Fellow of Sidney Sussex College; *b* near Belfast, Northern Ireland, 9 Dec. 1898; *s* of Mary L. Bristow and J. S. F. McCance, linen merchant, Belfast; *m* 1922, Mary L. MacGregor (*d* 1965); one *s* one *d*. *Educ:* St Bees Sch., Cumberland; Sidney Sussex Coll., Cambridge. RN Air Service and RAF, 1917-18; BA (Cambridge), 1922; Biochemical Research, Cambridge, 1922-25; qualified in medicine King's Coll. Hosp., London, 1927; MD (Cambridge), 1929; Asst Physician i/c biochemical research, King's Coll. Hosp., London; FRCP 1935; Goulstonian Lectr, RCP, 1936; Humphrey Rolleston Lectr, RCP, 1953; Groningen Univ. Lectr, 1958; Leonard Parsons Lectr, Birmingham Univ., 1959; Lumleian Lectr, RCP, 1962. Reader in Medicine, Cambridge Univ., 1938; War of 1939-45, worked on medical problems of national importance; visited Spain and Portugal on behalf of British Council, 1943, South Africa, 1965; i/c Medical Research Council Unit, Germany, 1946-49. Hon. FRCOG; Hon. Member: Assoc. of American Physicians; American Pediatric Soc.; Swiss Nutrition Soc.; Brit. Pædiatric Assoc. Gold Medal, West London Medico-Chirurgical Soc., 1949. Conway Evans Prize, RCP and Royal Society, 1960; James Spence Medal, Brit. Pæd. Assoc., 1961. Hon. DSc Belfast, 1964. *Publications:* Medical Problems in Mineral Metabolism (Goulstonian Lectures), 1936; (jointly) The Chemical Composition of Foods; An Experimental Study of Rationing; (jointly) Breads White and Brown; numerous papers on the physiology of the newborn animal. *Recreations:* mountaineering, cycling, photography. *Address:* 4 Kent House, Sussex Street, Cambridge CB1 1PH.

**McCANDLISH, Maj.-Gen. John Edward Chalmers,** CB 1946; CBE 1942 (OBE 1941); CEng; MIEE 1961; psc; *b* 11 Oct. 1901; *s* of late E. J. McCandlish, WS; *m* 1st, 1924, Margaret Storey, JP (marr. diss.), *d* of late Rev. C. E. Julian; one *s*; 2nd, 1950, Pauline, *d* of late P. L. Squirrell, MC; one *d*. *Educ:* Wellington Coll.; RMA, Woolwich; Staff Coll., Camberley. 2nd Lt Royal Engineers, 1921; Major 1938; Col 1944; served War of 1939-45 (despatches five times, OBE, CBE, CB; Order of the House of Orange, 2nd class); Maj.-Gen. 1947; Dir of Personnel Administration, War Office, 1946-49; retired, 1949. Colonial Development Corp., 1949-56; Chief Executive, Scottish Electrical Training Scheme, 1957-68. Hon. Col, 80 (S) Port Regt RCT (TA), 1962-67. Master, RE Draghounds, 1930-32. *Address:*

The White House, Buckland, Faringdon, Berks. *T:* Buckland 268. *Club:* Army and Navy.

**McCANN, Hugh James;** Secretary, Department of External Affairs, Dublin, since 1963; *b* 8 Feb. 1916; *e s* of late District Justice Hugh Joseph McCann, BL, and late Sophie McCann, Dublin; *m* 1950, Mary Virginia Larkin, Washington, DC, USA; four *s* one *d*. *Educ:* Belvedere Coll., Dublin; London Sch. of Economics, Univ. of London. Served in Dept of Lands, Dublin, and in Dept of Industry and Commerce, Dublin; Commercial Sec., London, 1944-46; First Sec., Dept of External Affairs, Dublin, 1946-48; Counsellor, Irish Embassy, Washington, DC, 1948-54; Irish Minister to Switzerland and Austria, 1954-56; Asst Sec., Dept of External Affairs, Dublin, 1956-58; Irish Ambassador at the Court of St James's, 1958-62. *Recreations:* golf, tennis, swimming, winter sports and photography. *Address:* Frankfield, Mart Lane, Foxrock, Co. Dublin. *Clubs:* Royal Dublin Society, St Stephen's Green (Dublin).

**McCANN, Most Rev. James,** MA; PhD; DD; *b* Grantham, Lincs, 31 Oct. 1897; *s* of James W. and Agnes McCann; *m* 1924, Violet, *d* of James and Mary Henderson, Ballymena, Ireland; no *c*. *Educ:* Royal Belfast Academical Institution; Queen's University, Belfast (BA); Trinity College, Dublin (MA, PhD, DD). Ecclesiastical History Prizeman (1st), 1917; Elrington Theological Prizeman (1st), 1930; ordained 1920; held curacies at Ballymena, Ballyclare, Cavan, Oldcastle; Rector of Donaghpatrick, 1930-36; St Mary's, Drogheda, 1936-45; Canon of St Patrick's Cathedral, Dublin, 1944-45; Bishop of Meath, 1945-59; Archbishop of Armagh and Primate of All Ireland, 1959-69. Hon. LLD QUB, 1966. *Publication:* Asceticism: an historical study, 1944. *Recreations:* music, reading. *Address:* The Cliff, Larne, Co. Antrim, N Ireland. *Club:* University (Dublin).

**McCANN, John,** CBE 1966; MP (Lab) Rochdale, since Feb. 1958; *b* 4 Dec. 1910; *s* of John and Margaret McCann; *m* 1939, Alice Nolan; one *s* one *d*. *Educ:* Beech Street Elementary Sch. Diesel engineer. Councillor, Eccles, 1945; Alderman, 1952; Mayor of Eccles, 1955-56. Contested (Lab) Rochdale, 1955; an Opposition Whip, 1961-64; Vice-Chamberlain of the Household, 1966-67; a Lord Commissioner of the Treasury, 1964-66 and 1967-69. *Recreations:* public works; watching Rugby; archery. *Address:* 7 School Road, Barton, Eccles, Lancs. *T:* Eccles 4024.

**McCANN, His Eminence Cardinal Owen;** *see* Cape Town, Cardinal Archbishop of.

**McCARRON, Edward Patrick;** Barrister-at-Law; Peace Commissioner. *Educ:* O'Connell Schs, Dublin; University Coll., Dublin. Called to Irish Bar, King's Inns, 1914. Late Senior Auditor Local Government Board for Ireland; Permanent Sec., Dept of Local Government and Public Health, Irish Free state, 1922-36; Registrar-Gen., 1926-36; retd, 1936; Director: Hibernian Fire & General Insurance Co. Ltd; Waterford Ironfounders Ltd; Masser-Waterford Ironfounders Ltd; Dublin Savings Bank; Irish Pensions Trustees Ltd. *Address:* Anerley, Cowper Road, Rathmines, Dublin. *T:* Dublin 971742. *Club:* St Stephen's Green (Dublin).

**McCARTHY, Donal John,** CMG 1969; Imperial Defence College, 1970; *b* 31 March 1922; *s* of Daniel and Kathleen McCarthy; *m* 1951, Rosanna Parbury; three *s*. *Educ:* Holloway Sch.; London Univ. Served Royal Navy, 1942-46. Foreign Office, 1946; Middle East Centre for Arab Studies, 1947-48; 3rd and 2nd Sec., Brit. Embassy, Jedda, 1948-51; 2nd Sec., Political Div., Brit. Middle East Office, 1951-55; 1st Sec., FO, 1955-58; Asst Polit. Agent, Kuwait, 1958-60; Brit. High Commn, Ottawa, 1960-63; FO, 1963-64; Counsellor, Brit. High Commn, Aden, and Polit. Adviser to C-in-C Middle East, 1964-67; Head of Aden Dept, FO, 1967-68, of Arabian Dept, FCO, 1968-70. *Recreations:* music, skiing, being idle. *Address:* 29a Frognal, NW3. *T:* 01-794 5600; Glenculloo Lodge, Killoscully, Newport, Tipperary, Ireland. *T:* Silvermines 21. *Clubs:* Travellers', Royal Automobile, Ski Club of Great Britain.

**McCARTHY, Sir Edwin,** Kt 1955; CBE 1952; Chairman, Commonwealth Economic Committee, 1964-67; *b* 30 March 1896; *s* of late Daniel and Catherine McCarthy, Melbourne, Australia; *m* 1938, Marjorie Mary, *d* of George and Alice Graham, Sydney; one *s* one *d*. *Educ:* Christian Brothers' Coll., Melbourne; Melbourne Univ. Joined Australian Commonwealth Govt Service; Sec., Dept of Commerce, 1945-50. Austr. Shipping representative in USA, 1941-44; also during this period engaged in other work associated with war activities in USA and UK; Australian Comptroller-Gen. of Food, 1945-46. Dep. High Comr for Australia in the United Kingdom, 1950-58; Australian Ambassador to the Netherlands, 1958-62 and to Belgium, 1959-62; Australian Ambassador to the European Economic Community, 1960-64. *Recreation:* golf. *Address:* 12 Lowndes Square, SW1. *Clubs:* Athenæum; University (Sydney).

**McCARTHY, Eugene Joseph;** US Senator, Minnesota, since 1959; *b* 29 March 1916; *s* of Michael J. and Anna Baden McCarthy; *m* 1945, Abigail Quigley McCarthy; one *s* three *d*. *Educ:* St John's Univ., Collegeville (BA); Univ. of Minnesota (MA). Teacher in public schools, 1935-40; Coll. Prof. of Econs and Sociology, and civilian techn. Asst in Mil. Intell. for War Dept, 1941-48; US Representative in Congress of 4th District, Minnesota, 1949-59. Democrat. Holds hon. degrees. *Publications:* Frontiers in American Democracy, 1960; Dictionary of American Politics, 1962; A Liberal Answer to the Conservative Challenge, 1964; The Limits of Power, 1967; contribs to Saturday Review, Commonweal, Atlantic. *Address:* 100 Imperial Drive, West St Paul, Minn., USA; 3525 Woodley Road, NW, Washington, DC.

**McCARTHY, John Haydon,** CB 1963; Controller, Central Office, Department of Health and Social Security (formerly Ministry of Pensions and National Insurance), Newcastle upon Tyne, since 1956; *b* 1914; 3rd *s* of late Lt-Comdr Jeremiah and Mrs Margaret McCarthy, Walton-on-Thames; *m* 1947, Mary, *e d* of Ebenezer Barclay, Lanark; three *s*. *Educ:* St Joseph's (de la Salle) Coll., London. Entered GPO, 1931; transferred Home Office, 1936; Min. of Nat. Insce, 1945; Under-Sec., 1956. *Recreation:* sea fishing. *Address:* 3 Front Street, Whitley Bay, Northumberland. *T:* 20206.

**McCARTHY, Mary, (Mrs James West);** writer; *b* 21 June 1912; *m* 1933, Harold Johnsrud; *m* 1938, Edmund Wilson; one *s*; *m* 1946, Bowden Broadwater; *m* 1961, James Raymond West. *Educ:* Annie Wright Seminary; Vassar Coll. Theatre critic, Partisan Review, 1937-57, Editor, Covici Friede, 1937-38; Instructor, Bard Coll., 1945-46; Instructor, Sarah Lawrence Coll., 1948. Lectures and broadcasts, 1952-65. Horizon award, 1948; Guggenheim Fellow, 1949-50, 1959-60; National Academy of Arts and Letters award, 1957. *Publications:* The Company She Keeps,

1942; The Oasis, 1949; Cast a Cold Eye, 1950; The Groves of Academe, 1952; A Charmed Life, 1955; Venice Observed, 1956; Sights and Spectacles, 1956; Memories of a Catholic Girlhood, 1957; The Stones of Florence, 1959; On the Contrary, 1962; The Group, 1963 (filmed 1966); Vietnam, 1967; Hanoi, 1968; The Writing on the Wall and Other Literary Essays, 1970; essays, journalism, short stories and reviews in the New Yorker, Partisan Review, Horizon, The New York Review of Books, The Observer, etc. *Address:* 141 Rue de Rennes, Paris, France.

**McCARTHY, Ralph;** Managing Director, Neilson McCarthy; last Editor of The Star, London, until its demise, Oct. 1960; *b* 30 Nov. 1906; 3rd *s* of late James McCarthy and Margaret McCarthy, Gourock; *m* 1933, Nan Graham, MA (*d* 1966); two *s* one *d. Educ:* Gourock; Greenock High Sch. Reporter, Glasgow Evening Times, 1926; Sub-editor, Daily Express, 1929; Asst Editor, Sunday Express, 1933; News Chronicle: Features Editor, 1936; Asst Editor, 1938; Northern Editor, 1949; Dir, 1955; Editor and Dir, The Star, March 1957. *Address:* 24 Bruton Place, W1X 7AB. *Club:* Caledonian.

**McCARTHY, Rt. Hon. Sir Thaddeus (Pearcey),** PC 1968; Kt 1964; **Rt. Hon. Mr Justice McCarthy;** Judge of the Court of Appeal of New Zealand since 1963; *b* 24 Aug. 1907; *s* of Walter McCarthy, Napier, merchant; *m* 1938, Joan Margaret Miller; one *s* two *d* (and one *d* decd). *Educ:* St Bede's Coll., Christchurch, New Zealand; Victoria Univ. Coll., Wellington. Master of Laws (1st Class Hons) 1931. Practised as Barrister and Solicitor until 1957 when appointed to Supreme Court. Chairman: Royal Commn on State Services, 1961-62; Winston Churchill Memorial Trust, 1966; Royal Commissions: on Salary and Wage Fixing Procedures in the State Services, 1968; on Social Security, 1969; on Horse Racing, Trotting and Dog Racing, 1969. Served War of 1939-45 in MEF with 22 Bn 2 NZEF; later as DJAG, 2 NZEF. *Recreations:* golf, fishing. *Address:* 9 Wadestown Road, Wellington, New Zealand. *T:* 45-379. *Club:* Wellington (Wellington, NZ).

**McCARTNEY, Hugh;** MP (Lab) Dunbartonshire East since 1970; *b* 3 Jan. 1920; *s* of John McCartney and Mary Wilson; *m* 1949, Margaret; one *s* two *d. Educ:* Royal Technical Coll., Glasgow; John Street Senior Secondary School. Apprentice in textile industry, 1934-39; entered aircraft engrg industry, Coventry, 1939; joined Rolls Royce, Glasgow, 1941; joined RAF as aero-engine fitter, 1942 and resumed employment with Rolls Royce, 1947; representative with company (now one of GKN group) specialising in manufacture of safety footwear, 1951; retained by company as a consultant. Joined Ind. Labour Party, 1934; joined Labour Party, 1936. Town Councillor, 1955-; CC and Magistrate, 1965-. *Recreation:* spectating at football matches and athletic meetings (political activities permitting). *Address:* 63g Townhead, Kirkintilloch, Glasgow. *T:* 041-776 4292.

**McCAUGHEY, Sir (David) Roy,** Kt 1963; CMG 1956; grazier; former Chairman New South Wales Board of Elder, Smith, Goldsbrough Mort Ltd, with which is amalgamated The Commonwealth Wool & Produce Co. Ltd; *b* Jerilderie, NSW, 2 Oct. 1898; *s* of David and Lucilla McCaughey, Coree, Jerilderie; *m* 1944, Gwendoline Patricia Camille, *d* of Walter Thomas Phelan, Ireland; no *c. Educ:* Geelong Grammar Sch., Vic., Australia. Served War 1914-18, in AIF and BEF; 2nd Lt RFA, 1918. *Address:* Box 131, GPO Sydney, NSW 2001, Australia; The Astor Flats, Macquarie Street, Sydney, NSW 2002, Australia. *T:* 27-2143 and 20-138; Coonong, Urana, NSW 2645. *Clubs:* Australian, Union (Sydney); Australian, Melbourne (Melbourne).

**McCAULEY, Air Marshal Sir John Patrick Joseph,** KBE 1955 (CBE 1943); CB 1951; *b* 18 March 1899; *s* of late John and Sophia McCauley; *m* 1926, Murielle Mary, *d* of late John Burke, and of Maude Burke; one *s* two *d. Educ:* St Joseph's Coll., Sydney; RMC, Duntroon; Melbourne Univ. (BCom 1936). Grad. RMC 1919; Aust. Staff Corps, 1919-23; RAAF, 1924-; passed RAF Staff Coll., 1933; Flying Instructor's Course, Central Flying Sch., RAF, 1934; Dir Trg, RAAF HQ Melbourne, 1937-38; CO 1 Flying Trg Sch. 1939; CO 1 Eng. Sch., 1940; CO RAAF Stn Sembawang, Malaya, 1941-42; CO RAAF Stn, Palembang 11, Sumatra, 1942; SASO RAAF Darwin, 1942; Air Cdre Ops, 2nd TAF France and Germany, 1944; DCAS, 1946-47; Chief of Staff, BCOF, Japan, 1947-49; AOC E Area, 1949-53; CAS, RAAF, 1954-57, retd. *Recreations:* tennis, golf. *Address:* 10 Onslow Gardens, Greenknowe Avenue, Potts Point, Sydney, Australia. *Clubs:* Naval and Military (Melbourne); Imperial Service (Sydney).

**McCAUSLAND, Lucius Perronet T.;** *see* Thompson-McCausland.

**McCLEAN, Mrs Douglas;** *see* Hale, Kathleen.

**McCLEAN, Rt. Rev. (John) Gerard;** *see* Middlesbrough, Bishop of, (RC).

**McCLELLAND, William,** CB 1923; OBE; MIEE; retired; *b* 1873; *m* 1898, Isabella Shepherd (*d* 1933), Manchester; two *s* one *d. Educ:* Manchester. Asst to C. H. Wordingham, MICE, Consulting Engineer, 1901-03; Electrical Engineer, Admiralty, on design and inspection of Warship Construction, 1903-06; Electrical Engineering Asst to Dir of Dockyards, Admiralty, 1906-18; Dir of Electrical Engineering, Admiralty, SW1; Principal Electrical Adviser to Board of Admiralty, 1919-34; responsible for designs and equipment of electrical installations in all HM ships; served on Defence Cttees; Ex-Hon. Treas. and Mem. Council of Instn of Electrical Engineers; Gen. Board of National Physical Laboratory, 1930-36; responsible for repair of electrical installations in all HM ships during the war in 1914-18; also for electrical equipment for many naval bases and emergency dockyards. *Publication:* The Applications of Electricity in Warships. *Address:* 76 Marine Court, St Leonards-on-Sea, Sussex. *T:* Hastings 639.

**McCLELLAND, William Grigor;** Director, Manchester Business School, since 1965, Professor of Business Administration, since 1967 and Dean, Faculty of Business Administration, since 1968, University of Manchester; *b* 2 Jan. 1922; *o c* of Arthur and Jean McClelland, Gosforth, Newcastle upon Tyne; *m* 1946, Diana Avery, *y d* of William Harold and Etha Close; two *s* two *d. Educ:* Leighton Park; Balliol Coll., Oxford. First Class PPE, 1948. Friends' Ambulance Unit, 1941-46. Man. Dir, 1949-65, and Chm., 1966-, Laws Stores Ltd, Gateshead; Sen. Res. Fellow in Management Studies, Balliol Coll., 1962-65; Dep. Chm., Nat. Computing Centre, 1966-68; Member: The Consumer Council, 1963-66; Economic Planning Council, Northern Region, 1965-66; NEDC, 1969-; Economic Development Cttee for the Distributive Trades; NEDC Cttee on Management Educn; Council, Royal Econ. Soc.; Chm., Centre for Business Research; Governor: Nat. Inst. of

Econ. and Social Research; Leighton Park Sch., 1952-60 and 1962-66; Treas., International Fellowship of Reconciliation, 1954-65; Trustee, 1956-, and Chm., 1965-, Joseph Rowntree Charitable Trust; Elder, Soc. of Friends, 1958-62. FBIM (Mem. Council). *Publications:* Studies in Retailing, 1963; Costs and Competition in Retailing, 1966; (ed) Quakers Visit China, 1957; Editor, Jl of Management Studies, 1963-65. *Recreation:* tennis. *Address:* Manchester Business School, 26 Hilton Street, Manchester 1. *Club:* Reform.

**McCLEMENS, John Henry; Hon. Mr Justice McClemens;** Justice of the Supreme Court of New South Wales since 1951; *b* 7 March 1905; *m* Joan Raymunde Delaney (Principal, Petersham Girls' High Sch.), *d* of M. B. Delaney; one *s* one *d. Educ:* N Sydney Boys' High Sch.; Sydney Univ. (BA, LLB). Admitted Solicitor, Supreme Court of NSW, 1929; Barrister, 1930. Large practice in workmen's compensation and industrial cases; KC 1945; practised largely in Common Law and Appeal work until appt to Bench. Chm. Bd of Management, Mater Misericordiæ Gen. Hosp., N Sydney; Former Pres. Prisoners Aid Assoc. (NSW); Mem. Adv. Cttee, Dept of Criminology, Sydney Univ.; rep. Australia at UN Conventions on Crime and Treatment of Offenders; Former Pres., Australian Prison After-Care Council; former Chm., Australian Council of National Trusts. Australian Governmental participant, United Nations Seminar on the Role of the Police in the Protection of Human Rights, Canberra, 1963; KCSG 1960. *Publications:* Report of Royal Commission on Callan Park Mental Hospital, 1961; contribs to Australian Law Jl, Sydney Law Review, Australian Jl of Criminology, Social Service (Review). *Recreation:* gardening. *Address:* Judges' Chambers, Supreme Court, Sydney, NSW, Australia. *Club:* University (Sydney).

**MACCLESFIELD,** 7th Earl of *cr* 1721; **George Loveden William Henry Parker;** Baron Parker, 1716; Viscount Parker, 1721; Lord Lieutenant of County of Oxford, 1954-63; *b* 24 May 1888; *g s* of 6th Earl, and *o c* of Viscount Parker (*d* 1895) and Carine Agnes (*d* 1919), *d* of late Pryse Loveden, Gogerddan, Cardigan (she *m* 2nd, 1897, Capt. L. W. Matthews, 5th Dragoon Guards); *S* grandfather, 1896; *m* 1909, Lilian Joanna Vere, *d* of Major Charles Boyle, The Priory, Great Milton, Oxon; two *s*. Chm., Oxfordshire CC, 1937-. *Heir: s* Viscount Parker, *qv. Address:* Shirburn Castle, Watlington, Oxon. *Club:* Royal Yacht Squadron (Cowes).

**MACCLESFIELD, Archdeacon of;** *see* House, Ven. F. H.

**McCLINTIC, Mrs Guthrie;** *see* Cornell, Katharine.

**McCLINTOCK-BUNBURY,** family name of **Baron Rathdonnell.**

**McCLOUGHRY, Air Vice-Marshal Edgar J. K.;** *see* Kingston-McCloughry.

**McCLOY, John Jay,** DSM (US); Partner, Milbank Tweed, Hadley & McCloy, since 1961; Director and Chairman Executive Committee, Squibb Beech-Nut Inc.; Chairman of Board of the Council on Foreign Relations, Inc.; *b* 31 March 1895; *s* of John Jay McCloy and Anna May Snader; *m* 1930, Ellen Zinsser; one *s* one *d. Educ:* Amherst Coll. (AB); Harvard Univ. (LLB). Admitted to New York bar, 1921; mem. of law firm of Cravath, de Gersdorff Swaine & Wood, New York City, 1929-40; expert cons. to Sec. of War, 1940; The Asst Sec. of War, 1941-45; Chm. of The Combined Civil Affairs Cttee of Combined Chiefs of Staff; mem. of law firm of Milbank, Tweed, Hope, Hadley & McCloy, NY City, 1945-47; Pres. International Bank for Reconstruction and Development, Washington, DC, 1947-49; US Military Governor and US High Comr for Germany, Frankfurt, Germany, 1949-52; Mem. State Dept Cttee on Atomic Energy, 1946-47; Counsel, Milbank, Tweed, Hope & Hadley, 1961; Adviser to President Kennedy on Disarmament, 1961; Chairman: Co-ordinating Cttee of the US on Cuban Crisis, 1962-63; Gen. Adv. Cttee on Arms Control and Disarmament; The Salk Inst., La Jolla, Calif; Atlantic Institute, 1966-68. Mem., President's Commn on the Assassination of President Kennedy; Mem., American and NY Bar Assocs; Mem., Bar Assoc. of City of New York. Past Chm. and Trustee, Ford Foundation. Director: Allied Chemical Corp.; The Chase Manhattan Bank (Chm. 1953-60); Dreyfus Corp., NYC; retired Director: Metropolitan Life Insurance Co.; Westinghouse Electric Corp.; American Telephone & Telegraph Co. Hon. Trustee: Bd of Trustees, Amherst Coll., Mass (Chm.); Lenox Hill Hosp.; Johns Hopkins Univ.; Trustee, Deerfield Acad.; Treasurer, Amer. Sch. of Classical Studies, Athens; Mem., Bd of Overseers to visit Center for Internat. Studies, Harvard Univ. Capt. FA, AEF. Holds numerous hon. degrees both in US and abroad, also Civic Hons. US Presidential Medal of Freedom and Distinguished Service Medal; Grand Officer of Legion of Honour (France); Grand Officer of Order of Merit of the Republic (Italy); Grand Cross of Order of Merit (Federal Republic of Germany). *Publication:* The Challenge to American Foreign Policy, 1953. *Recreations:* tennis and fishing. *Address:* 1 Chase Manhattan Plaza, New York, NY 10005, USA. *Clubs:* Brook, Links, University, Century, Anglers, Wall Street, Ausable (NY City); Metropolitan (Washington).

**McCLURE, Ivor Herbert,** DSO 1918; 2nd *s* of late Rev. Canon Edmund McClure; *m* 1925, Beatrice Eliott-Drake, *e d* of late Rev. H. M. Eliott-Drake Briscoe, MA, formerly Rector of Burnham Thorpe and Rural Dean of Burnham; one *s* one *d*; *m* 1950, Mabel James Orr, Bow Cottage, Charmouth, Dorset, *y d* of late James Angus, Ochiltree House, Ayrshire. *Educ:* Eton; Harrow; Clare Coll., Cambridge (BA). Served European War, 1914-19 (despatches five times, DSO, 1914 Star). Asst Dir, Cardiff Station, BBC, 1926, Head of Aviation Dept, Automobile Assoc., 1929; Chm., Aviation Section, London Chamber of Commerce, 1934; Operational Adviser, Dir of Civil Aviation, Air Min., 1935; Dir of Operational Services and Intelligence, Dept of Civil Aviation, Air Min., 1937; Asst Sec. Gen. for Air Navigation, Provisional Internat. Civil Aviation Organization (later ICAO), 1945; retd, 1949. *Address:* Sutton, County Brome, Quebec, Canada. *Clubs:* Oxford and Cambridge University, Royal Automobile.

**McCLUSKEY, John Herbert,** QC (Scotland) 1967; *b* 12 June 1929; *s* of Francis John McCluskey, Solicitor, and Margaret McCluskey (*née* Doonan); *m* 1956, Ruth Friedland; two *s* one *d. Educ:* St Bede's Grammar Sch., Manchester; Holy Cross Acad., Edinburgh; Edinburgh Univ. Harry Dalgety Bursary, 1948; Vans Dunlop Schol., 1949; Muirhead Prize, 1949; MA 1950; LLB 1952. Sword of Honour, RAF Spitalgate, 1953. Admitted Faculty of Advocates, 1955; Standing Jun. Counsel to Min. of Power

(Scotland), 1963; Advocate-Depute, 1964. *Recreations:* golf, swimming. *Address:* 12 Moray Place, Edinburgh. *T:* 031-447 3880.

**MacCOLL, James Eugene,** JP; MP (Lab) Widnes Division of Lancashire since 1950; *b* 27 June 1908; *y s* of late Hugo MacColl and Maude Macarthy, Sunderland. *Educ:* Sedbergh Sch.; Balliol Coll., Oxford (Exhibitioner); Univ. of Chicago. Librarian, Oxford Union, 1930; Commonwealth Fund Fellow, 1930-32; Barrister, Inner Temple, 1933; Co-opted Mem., LCC Education Cttee, 1936-46; Paddington Metropolitan Borough Council, 1934 (Mayor of Paddington, 1947-49); JP County of London, 1938. Jt Parly Sec., Min. of Housing and Local Govt, 1964-69. Research Asst, Polit. and Economic Planning Trust, 1945-50; Chm.'s Panel, London Juvenile Courts, 1946-64; Hemel Hempstead New Towns Corporation, 1946-50; Domestic Coal Consumers Council, 1947-50. *Publications:* (with E. C. R. Hadfield) Pilot Guide to Political London, 1945; British Local Government, 1948; articles in Political Quarterly, Fortnightly, Public Administration. *Address:* 21 Randolph Road, W9. *T:* 01-286 4347.

**MacCOLL, René;** author; Chief Foreign Correspondent, The Daily Express, 1959-69; *b* 12 Jan. 1905; *yr s* of Dugald Sutherland MacColl and Andrée Zabé; *m* 1st, 1928, Helen (*d* 1945), *o d* of Walter Edwards, Boyertown, Pa, USA; one *s* one *d*; 2nd, 1946, Margaret Hermione, *e d* of Lt-Col Kenneth H. Bruce, DSO, and Lorna Burn-Murdoch. *Educ:* University College Sch., London; Lincoln Coll., Oxford. Sec. to late Van-Lear Black, Baltimore, Md, 1926-29 (with whom flew on his pioneering flights, incl. London-Capetown-London, Jan.-Apr. 1929). Reporter on Baltimore Sun, 1927-28; joined Daily Telegraph, 1929 (Correspondent in Spanish Civil War, Franco side, 1939). Press Liaison, RAFVR (Sqdn Ldr) in France, 1939-40: Dir, Press and Radio Div., British Information Services, New York, 1941-45. Washington Correspondent, Daily Express, 1946-48; Paris Correspondent, 1949-50; Chief American Correspondent, 1951-52; Roving Reporter, 1953-58. *Publications:* A Flying Start, 1939; Assignment Stuffed Shirt, 1952; Just Back from Russia, 1955; Roger Casement: A New Judgement, 1956; Deadline and Dateline, 1956; Land of Ghengis Khan, 1963. *Recreation:* numismatics. *Address:* Clock Lodge, Crowborough, Sussex. *T:* Crowborough 61364. *Clubs:* Garrick; National Press (Washington, DC).

**McCOLVIN, Lionel Roy,** CBE 1951; FLA; Librarian, City of Westminster Public Libraries, 1938-61; *b* Newcastle on Tyne, 30 Nov. 1896; 2nd *s* of late John Andrew McColvin, artist; *m* 1922, Mary Carter; two *s* two *d*. *Educ:* Croydon. Reference Librarian, Croydon Public Libraries, to 1921; Dep. Librarian, Wigan Public Libraries, 1921-24; Chief Librarian, Ipswich Public Libraries, 1924-31; Chief Librarian, Hampstead Public Libraries and Curator of the Keats House and Museum, Hampstead, 1931-38; Fellow and Hons Diplomate of Library Assoc.; Councillor, 1925-, Pres., 1952 (Hon. Sec., 1934-51), Library Assoc.; visited USA to study library administration on behalf of the Library Assoc., 1936, Middle East, Australia, NZ and USA, 1946-47, Germany, 1950 and 1956, Sweden, Norway, etc; Pres., Soc. of Municipal and County Chief Librarians, 1953-; Vice-Pres., Internat. Fedn of Library Assocs; Mem. Exec. Cttee of Nat. Central Library, UNESCO; Nat. Cooperating Body for Libraries, Cen. Music Library, Brit. Council Advisory Panel on Books and Libraries, etc. *Publications:* Music in Public Libraries, 1924; The Theory of Book Selection, 1925; Euterpe or the future of art, 1926; Library Extension Work and Publicity, 1927; How to Find Out, 1933, new edn 1947; How to Use Books, 1933, new edn 1947; How to Enjoy Music, 1934; How to Enjoy Plays, 1934; Library Stock and Assistance to Readers, 1936; Libraries and the Public, 1937; Music Libraries (with Harold Reeves), 1937-38; Library Staffs, 1939; The Public Library System of Great Britain, 1942; British Libraries (with J. Revie), 1946; Public Libraries in Australia, 1947; Library Extension (for UNESCO), 1950; The Personal Library, 1953; Reference Library Stock, 1952; The Chance to Read, 1956; Library Service for Children (for UNESCO), 1957; Ed. 'Librarian' Subject Guide to Books, 1958. *Recreations:* music, painting, letter-writing, talking. *Address:* 17 Seymour Court, Eversley Park Road, N21.

**McCOMB, James Ellis,** CBE 1964; DFC 1940; General Manager, Cwmbran New Town Development Corporation, since 1962; *b* 19 April 1909; *er s* of late D. K. McComb, TD, JP; *m* 1939, Sonia, *d* of late Col H. J. Decker, TD; one *d*. *Educ:* Stowe Sch. Served War of 1939-45: comd 611 Fighter Sqdn AAF, 1939-40; RAF Staff Coll., 1942; 8th USAF Liaison, 1942; COSSAC Cover Plan, Invasion Europe, 1943; Air Liaison, C-in-C Allied Navies, 1944; SHAEF, 1944-45. Solicitor, 1932; Allen & Overy, City of London, 1933-36; Lancs CC, 1936-48; Dep. Clerk of Peace, Lancs, 1946-48; Gen. Man., Welwyn Garden City and Hatfield New Towns, 1949-62. *Recreations:* gardening, painting. *Address:* Catsash House, Christchurch, Newport, Mon. *T:* Caerleon 385. *Club:* RAF Reserves.

**McCOMBE, Lt-Col Gault,** DSO 1917; OBE 1945; Director, Anaconda American Brass Ltd; *b* Armagh, Northern Ireland, 26 March 1885; *s* of Alexander McCombe, MA, Trinity Coll., Dublin, and Eliza Browne McCombe; *m* 1917, Marjorie, *d* of George Orme, Ottawa, Ont., Canada; one *d* (and one *d* decd). *Educ:* Montreal High Sch. Bank of Montreal, 1903-10; Gault McCombe & Co., 1910-14; served European War (despatches four times, wounded thrice): 1st Canadian Div., Flanders, 1915-18. Commanded Royal Montreal Regt, 1917-18. Joined Anaconda American Brass Ltd, 1922. Chm. Montreal Rehabilitation Cttee, 1941-45. *Recreations:* fishing, golf. *Address:* Dunara, Como, Province of Quebec, Canada. *T:* 236-5356. *Clubs:* St James's (Montreal); Rideau (Ottawa); Toronto (Toronto); Whitlock Golf (Hudson Heights).

**McCONE, John A.;** US business executive; Chairman, Hendy International Co., since 1969; *b* 4 Jan. 1902; *s* of Alexander J. McCone and Margaret McCone (*née* Enright); *m* 1938, Rosemary Cooper (*d* 1961); no *c*; *m* 1962, Mrs Theiline Pigott (widow). *Educ:* Univ. of California, Coll. of Engineering. Began as construction engineer, Llewellyn Iron Works; supt Consolidated Steel Corp., 1929; Exec. Vice-Pres. and Dir, 1933-37; Pres. of Bechtel-McCone Corp., Los Angeles, 1937-45; Pres. and Dir, California Shipbuilding Corp., 1941-46; Joshua Hendy Corp., Joshua Hendy Iron Works, 1945-58; Mem. President's Air Policy Commn, 1947-48; Dep. to Sec. of Defense, March-Nov. 1948; Under Sec. of US Air Force, 1950-51. Chm., US Atomic Energy Commn, 1958-61; Dir, Central Intelligence Agency, 1961-65. Chm., Joshua Hendy Corp., 1961-69; holds hon. degrees from Univs and colls in the US. *Recreation:* golf. *Address:* (home) 1100 Oak Grove Avenue, San Marino, Calif 91108, USA; Norcliffe, The Highlands,

Seattle, Washington; (office) 612 South Flower Street, Los Angeles, Calif 90017. *T:* Madison 9-3631. *Clubs:* California (Los Angeles); Valley Club of Montecito, Los Angeles Country (Los Angeles); Pacific Union (San Francisco); Burning Tree, Metropolitan, F Street, Chevy Chase (Washington, DC); The Links, Blind Brook (NYC); Cypress Point (Pebble Beach, Calif); Seattle Golf.

**McCONNELL, Adams Andrew,** MA, MCh (Hon.) Dublin; FRCSI; Hon. FRCS; Regius Professor of Surgery, Dublin University, 1946-61; Surgeon Richmond Hospital, Dublin; Consulting Surgeon to Dr Steeven's Hospital, Dublin, National Children's Hospital, Dublin, Stewart Institution, Palmerstown, Co. Dublin; Consulting Neurological Surgeon to the Royal Victoria Eye and Ear Hospital, Dublin; FRSM; Hon. Fellow Trinity College, Dublin; Ex-President and Emeritus Member, Society of British Neurological Surgeons; late Professor of Surgery and Ex-President RCS in Ireland; *b* 1884; *s* of Dr Andrew McConnell, Belfast; *m* 1st, 1914, Nora (*d* 1968), *d* of S. P. Boyd, DL, Dublin; 2nd, 1969, Gladys Danefield, *d* of David Hopkins, Dublin. *Educ:* Royal Academical Institution, Belfast; Trinity Coll., Dublin. First Prizeman in Anatomy and Physiology, Trinity Coll.; Medical Scholar in Anatomy and Institutes of Medicine. First Senior Moderator (large Gold Medal) in Natural Science; Demonstrator in Zoology and Physiology; Asst to Prof. of Anatomy, Trinity Coll., 1910-12; Anæsthetist and Lectr on Anæsthetics, Sir Patrick Dun's Hosp., Dublin, 1909-10; Anæsthetist Incorporated Dental Hosp., 1910-12; Fellow (Pres. 1946, 1947) Royal Academy of Medicine in Ireland; Ex-Pres. Dublin Univ. Biological Assoc.; Hon. member: Société de Neuro-Chirurgie de Langue Française; Nordisk Neurokirurisk Förening; La Real Academia Nacional de Medicina; Asociación Española de Neuropsiquiatria; late Lectr on Applied Anatomy Trinity Coll., Dublin. *Publications:* many papers on neurosurgery to medical journals. *Address:* Conna, Shankill, Co. Dublin. *T:* Dublin 851607. *Clubs:* Royal Societies; University, Friendly Brothers (Dublin).

**McCONNELL, Albert Joseph,** MA, ScD, Hon. DSc (Belfast), Hon. ScD (Columbia); Hon. Fellow of Oriel College, Oxford; Provost of Trinity College, Dublin, since 1952; *b* 19 Nov. 1903; *s* of Joseph McConnell; *m* 1934, Hilda (*d* 1966), *d* of late Francis McGuire. *Educ:* Ballymena Acad.; Trinity Coll., Dublin (Scholar, First Math. Moderator and Univ. Student); Univ. of Rome. Dr of Univ. of Rome, 1928; Mem. of Royal Irish Academy, 1929; ScD (Dublin), 1929; Fellow of Trinity Coll., Dublin, 1930-52; Chm., Governing Board of Sch. of Theoretical Physics, and Mem. Council of Dublin Inst. for Advanced Studies; Lectr in Maths, Trinity Coll., Dublin, 1927-30; Prof. of Natural Philosophy, Univ. of Dublin, 1930-57; Vis. Prof., Univ. of Alexandria, 1946-47; Special Univ. Lectr, Univ. of London, 1949. *Publications:* Applications of the Absolute Differential Calculus, 1931; papers on relativity, geometry and dynamics in various mathematical jls; Joint-editor of the Mathematical Papers of Sir W. R. Hamilton. *Address:* Provost's House, Trinity College, Dublin. *T:* Dublin 772941. *Clubs:* Athenæum, East India and Sports; Dublin University (Dublin).

**McCONNELL, Gerard Hamilton,** CB 1967; Assistant Under-Secretary of State, Home Office, since 1957; Principal Finance Officer, since 1967; *b* 22 Jan. 1913; *s* of late J. McConnell and of Mrs E. McConnell; *m* 1939, Dorothy Margaret Drummond Wilson; two *d.* *Educ:* Manchester Grammar Sch.; St John's Coll., Cambridge. Scottish Home Dept, 1936-46 (Royal Air Force, 1942-44); Home Office, 1946; Asst Sec., 1948. *Address:* 35 Roundwood Park, Harpenden, Herts. *T:* 4157. *Club:* Athenæum.

**McCONNELL, Comdr Sir Robert Melville Terence,** 3rd Bt, *cr* 1900; VRD; RNVR (retired); *b* 7 Feb. 1902; *s* of Sir Joseph McConnell, 2nd Bt, and Lisa (*d* 1956), *d* of late Jackson McGown; *S* father, 1942; *m* 1st, 1928, Rosamond Mary Elizabeth (marr. diss., 1954), *d* of James Stewart Reade, Clonmore, Lisburn, Co. Antrim; three *s* one *d*; 2nd, 1967, Mrs Alice A. M. Hills. *Educ:* Glenalmond; St John's Coll., Cambridge; College of Estate Management, London. Partner R. J. McConnell and Co., estate agents, Belfast. *Heir: s* Robert Shean McConnell, *b* 23 Nov. 1930. *Address:* Quoilequay House, Downpatrick, N Ireland. *T:* Downpatrick 20634.

**McCONNELL, Rt. Hon. Robert William Brian,** PC (N Ireland) 1964; President of the Industrial Court of Northern Ireland, since 1968; *b* 25 Nov. 1922; *s* of late Alfred E. McConnell, Belfast; *m* 1951, Sylvia Elizabeth Joyce Agnew; two *s* one *d. Educ:* Sedbergh Sch.; Queen's Univ., Belfast (BA, LLB). Called to Bar of Northern Ireland, 1948. MP (U) for South Antrim, N Ire. Paret, 1951-68; Dep. Chm. of Ways and Means, N Ire. Parlt, 1962; Parly Sec. to Min. of Health and Local Govt for N Ireland, 1963; Minister of Home Affairs for Northern Ireland, 1964-66; Minister of State, Min. of Develt, 1966-67; Leader of the House of Commons, N Ire., 1967-68. *Recreation:* fishing. *Address:* Aughnahough, Lisburn, Co. Antrim, Northern Ireland. *T:* Lisburn 3432.

**McCONNELL, William Samuel,** DA (RCS); FFA, RCS; late Senior Anaesthetist, Guy's Hospital, retired; *b* 22 April 1904; *s* of late James McConnell, BA, MB, BCh; *m* 1932, Olive, *d* of late Capt. L. E. Stannard; two *s.* *Educ:* Emanuel Sch., London; Univ. of London. Guy's Hospital Medical Sch.: MRCS, LRCP, 1927; MB, BS (London), 1929; DA (RCS), 1935; FFA, RCS, 1948. Anaesthetist to Guy's Hospital, 1935. Temp. Lt-Col RAMC: Adviser in Anaesthetics, Southern Army, India Comd, 1942-45. Hon. Visiting Anaesthetist, Johns Hopkins Hosp., Baltimore, Md, 1955. *Publications:* articles on anaesthesia in professional jls. *Address:* 55 Chartfield Avenue, SW15. *Club:* Athenæum.

**MacCONOCHIE, John Angus,** MBE 1943; MInstT; Chairman of Furness Withy & Co. Ltd since 1968 (Director since 1964); Deputy Chairman, Shaw Savill & Albion Co. Ltd, since 1968; *b* 12 April 1908; *m* 1938, Peggy, *d* of late Robert Gunson Martindale, MA, Worthing, Sussex; one *s* one *d. Educ:* Royal Caledonian Schools, Bushey, Herts. Joined Shaw Savill Line, 1927. Seconded to Min. of War Transport, 1942; served on Staff of Resident Minister for W Africa, Accra; Min. of War Transport Rep. in Gold Coast (MBE); London, 1944; Min. HQ with 21 Army Group; subseq. Paris, Marseilles, Naples. Returned to Shaw Savill Line, 1945: New Zealand, 1949; subseq. Manager for Australia; Gen. Manager for New Zealand, 1953; returned to Britain, 1958; Dir, 1957. Chairman: Royal Mail Lines, 1968; Johnston Warren Lines, 1968-70; Director: Economic Insurance, 1967 (Chm. 1969); British Maritime Trust, 1967 (Chm., 1968); Cairns Noble & Co. Ltd, 1967; Pacific Steam Navigation Co. Ltd, 1967; Pacific Maritime Services, 1967; Houlder Bros & Co.

Ltd, 1967; Whitehall Insurance Co. Ltd, 1967; Manchester Liners Ltd, 1968; Air Holdings Ltd, 1968; Standard Ship-Owners' Mutual War Risk Assoc. Ltd; Standard Steamship Owners' Protection & Indemnity Assoc. Ltd. Member: Coun., Chamber of Shipping; Coun. of Management, Ocean Travel Development (Chm.); Exec. Coun., Shipping Fedn Ltd; Cttee, NZ Society (PP); Coun., Fedn of Commonwealth Chambers of Commerce (a NZ Rep.); British Ship Adoption Soc. (Chm.); BNEC Cttee for Exports to NZ (Jt Dep. Chm.); BIM; Inst. of Directors, English Speaking Union; Royal Inst. of Internat. Affairs; Hon. Mem. NZ Co. Master Mariners. *Address:* Red Gables, Cleardown, Woking, Surrey. *T:* Woking 61123. *Club:* Bath.

**McCORMACK, Most Rev. John;** *see* Meath, Bishop of, (RC).

**McCORMACK, John William;** Member US House of Representatives 1927-70; House Majority Leader (Democrat) 1955-70 (with exception 4 years Democrat Whip); Speaker, 1962-70; lawyer; *b* Boston, Mass., 21 Dec. 1891; *s* of Joseph H. McCormack and Mary E. O'Brien; *m* 1920, M. Harriet Joyce. *Educ:* public schools. Admitted Massachusetts Bar, 1913, practised law, Boston, firm of McCormack & Hardy; Mem. Mass Const. Conv., 1917-18, House of Representatives, 1920-22, State Senate, 1923-26. Holds hon. degrees. Kt of Malta, 1st class; Kt Comdr, with star, St Gregory the Great. *Address:* 726 Columbia Road, Boston, Mass, USA.

**McCORMACK, Percy Hicks,** FIA; General Manager and Actuary, Provident Mutual Life Assurance Association, 1938-51, Director, 1951-66; *b* 23 Aug. 1890; *s* of late Martin McCormack, formerly of Knutsford, Cheshire, and Elizabeth Ann, *d* of Edmund Hicks; *m* 1926, Marjorie Vera Stewart, *d* of Charles A. Norris, Frittenden; two *s*. *Educ:* Bickerton, Birkdale; Liverpool Univ. Joint Asst Actuary, Provident Mutual Life Assurance Assoc., 1920; Joint Actuary, 1928; Consulting Actuary, London, Midland & Scottish Railway Co. and British Railways (Midland Region), 1938-55; Dir, London & Lomond Investment Trust Ltd, 1938-68. *Publications:* contribs to jls on actuarial and other subjects. *Address:* 5 Brymon Court, Montagu Square, W1. *Club:* Athenæum.

**McCORMICK, John Ormsby,** CMG 1965; MC 1943; HM Consul-General in Lyons since 1967; *b* Dublin, 7 Feb. 1916; *s* of Albert Victor McCormick and Sarah Beatty de Courcy; *m* 1955, Francine Guieu (*née* Paris); one *d* one step *s*. *Educ:* The Leys Sch., Cambridge; New Coll., Oxford. BA Hon. Mods and Greats (Oxford), 1938. Passed Competitive Exam. for Consular Service, 1939, and appointed Asst Officer, Dept of Overseas Trade. Served War of 1939-45, in Royal Corps of Signals, Africa, Sicily, Germany, 1940-45. 2nd Sec. (Commercial), British Embassy, Athens, 1945-47; FO, London, 1948-50; 1st Sec., UK High Commn, Karachi, 1950-52; Consul, New York, 1952-54; transferred to Washington, 1954-55; NATO Defence Coll., 1955; Asst Head, SE Asia Dept, FO, 1956-59; Foreign Service Officer, Grade 6, 1959; Counsellor (Commercial), British Embassy, Djakarta, 1959-62; Corps of Inspectors, FO, 1962-64; Counsellor (Commercial), British Embassy, Ankara, 1965-67. *Recreations:* golf, sailing, philosophy. *Address:* British Consulate-General, 24 rue Childebert, Lyon 2e, France; Oldfort, Newcastle, Co. Wicklow, Ireland. *Club:* Travellers'.

**McCORQUODALE,** family name of **Baron McCorquodale of Newton.**

**McCORQUODALE OF NEWTON,** 1st Baron *cr* 1955, of Newton-le-Willows; **Malcolm Stewart McCorquodale,** PC 1945; KCVO 1965; *b* 29 March 1901; 2nd *s* of late Norman McCorquodale, Winslow Hall, Bucks; *m* 1st, 1931, Winifred (*d* 1960), *d* of late J. O. M. Clark; two *d*; 2nd, 1962, Hon. Mrs Gibb. *Educ:* Harrow; Christ Church, Oxford (scholar, MA). MP (Nat C) Sowerby Div. of Yorks, 1931-45; Parly Sec., Min. of Labour and National Service, 1942-45; MP (C) Epsom Div. of Surrey, Nov. 1947-55. Served War of 1939-45, RAFVR. Chm., McCorquodale & Co. Ltd, and other printing companies till 1942, and again 1945-67, Pres., 1968-; Director: United Kingdom Provident Institution; Bank of Scotland Ltd, etc; Pres., British Employers' Confederation, 1960 (Vice-Pres. 1955). Governor of Harrow School, 1962, Chm., 1964-. *Heir:* none. *Address:* 30 Jay Mews, SW7; Cotswold Park, Cirencester, Glos. *Clubs:* Carlton, Royal Automobile.
*See also Baron Cranworth.*

**McCORQUODALE, Mrs Barbara;** *see* Cartland, Barbara H.

**McCOWAN, Sir Hew Cargill,** 3rd Bt, *cr* 1934; *b* 26 July 1930; *s* of Sir David James Cargill McCowan, 2nd Bt and Muriel Emma Annie, *d* of W. C. Willmott; *S* father, 1965. *Heir: b* David William Cargill McCowan, *b* 28 Feb. 1934. *Address:* Maebelo, Estrade de Logoa Agul, Malveisa de Serra, Lisbon, Portugal.

**McCOWEN, Alec, (Alexander Duncan McCowen);** actor; *b* 26 May 1925; *s* of Duncan McCowen and Hon. Mrs McCowen. *Educ:* Skinners' Sch., Tunbridge Wells. RADA, 1941; Repertory: York, Birmingham, etc, 1943-50. West End Plays: Escapade, 1952; The Matchmaker, 1954; The Count of Clérambard, 1955; The Caine Mutiny Court Martial, 1956; Look Back in Anger, 1957; The Elder Statesman, 1958. Old Vic Seasons, 1959-61: Touchstone, Ford, Richard II, Mercutio, Oberon, Malvolio; Dauphin in St Joan; Algy in The Importance of Being Earnest. Royal Shakespeare Company, 1962-63: Antipholus of Syracuse in The Comedy of Errors; Fool, in King Lear; Father Fontana in The Representative, Aldwych, 1963; Thark, Garrick, 1965; The Cavern, Strand, 1965; After the Rain, Duchess, 1967, Golden Theatre, NY, 1967; Hadrian VII, Birmingham, 1967, Mermaid, 1968, New York, 1969; Hamlet, Birmingham, 1970; The Philanthropist, Royal Court, 1970. *Recreations:* music, gardening. *Address:* Flat 3, 172 Kensington Church Street, W8. *T:* 01-229 5799.

**McCOY, William Frederick,** QC; Senior Crown Prosecutor for the City of Belfast, 1949-67; retired; *s* of late William and C. L. McCoy, Fivemiletown, Co. Tyrone; *m* 1940, Margaret Edna Earls; two *s*. *Educ:* Clones High Sch. Admitted Solicitor of Supreme Court of Judicature, Ireland, 1907; called to Irish Bar, 1920; joined NW Circuit and, on establishment of Northern Ireland, became member of Circuit of N Ireland; Resident Magistrate, City of Belfast, 1937-43; called to Inner Bar, 1939, Bencher, 1942. MP (U) South Tyrone, Northern Ireland House of Commons, 1945-65. Elected Speaker Northern Ireland House of Commons, Jan. 1956; resigned April 1956. *Recreations:* hunting and shooting. *Address:* Knockballymore, Magheraveely, Co. Fermanagh. *T:* Newtownbutler 211. *Clubs:* Northern Counties (Londonderry); Tyrone County (Omagh).

**McCRACKEN, Esther Helen;** writing for stage and screen; Member of Court, Newcastle University; Member, Alnwick and Rothbury Hospital Management Committee; *b* 25 June 1902; *d* of Henry Armstrong and Maud Clapham; *m* 1st, 1926, Lt-Col Angus Murray McCracken, DSO, MC, RA (died of wounds in Italy, 1943); two *d*; 2nd, 1944, Mungo Campbell, *qv*; (one *d* decd). *Educ:* Central Newcastle High Sch. War of 1939-45, discharged from WRNS, 1942, on compassionate grounds. Eight years with Newcastle Repertory Theatre Company; Playhouse, Newcastle, 1929-; fairly regular broadcasting of own songs, sketches, etc (and other people's), 1935-; first attempt at writing short story, The Willing Spirit, published by Daily Herald, 1936, quickly followed by broadcast version and then by stage version produced by herself, acted by YWCA team and winning Drama Festival at Old Vic; first 3-act play, Quiet Wedding, Richmond Theatre, spring 1938, Wyndham's, Oct. 1938; Counter Attraction, Richmond, 1938; White Elephants, Richmond, 1940; Quiet Weekend, Wyndham's, 1941; Living Room, Garrick Theatre, 1943; No Medals, Vaudeville, 1944; Cry Liberty, Vaudeville, 1950. *Publications:* The Willing Spirit (1-Act Play), 1937; Behind the Lace Curtains (1-Act Play), 1937; North Country Lullaby (Song), 1937; Quiet Wedding (3-Act Play), 1938; Living Room; Quiet Weekend. *Recreations:* reading, writing, sailing. *Address:* Rothley Lake, Hartburn, Morpeth, Northumberland. *T:* Scots Gap 255. *Club:* English-Speaking Union.

**McCRAITH, Col Patrick James Danvers,** MC 1943; TD; DL; Solicitor and Notary Public; *b* 21 June 1916; *s* of late Sir Douglas McCraith; *m* 1946, Hon. Philippa Mary Ellis, *yr d* of 1st and last Baron Robins, KBE, DSO, of Rhodesia and Chelsea; one *s* one *d*. *Educ:* Harrow. Served 1939-45 with Sherwood Rangers Yeomanry, N Africa and NW Europe (three times wounded); raised and commanded Yeomanry Patrol of Long Range Desert Group, 1940-41; commanded Sherwood Rangers Yeomanry, 1953-57; Bt Colonel, 1958. Hon. Col, "B" (Sherwood Rangers Yeomanry) Sqdn, Royal Yeomanry Regt, 1968-. High Sheriff of Nottinghamshire, 1963; DL Notts, 1965. *Address:* Cranfield House, Southwell, Notts. *T:* Southwell 2129. *Clubs:* Pratt's, MCC; Nottinghamshire (Nottingham).

**McCREA, William Hunter,** FRS 1952; MA; PhD, ScD (Cambridge); BSc (London); FRSE, FRAS, MRIA; Research Professor of Theoretical Astronomy, University of Sussex, since 1966; *b* Dublin, 13 Dec. 1904; *er s* of late Robert Hunter McCrea; *m* 1933, Marian Nicol Core, 2nd *d* of late Thomas Webster, JP, Burdiehouse, Edinburgh; one *s* two *d*. *Educ:* Chesterfield Grammar Sch.; Trinity Coll., Cambridge (Scholar); University of Göttingen. Wrangler, Rayleigh Prizeman, Sheepshanks Exhibitioner, and Isaac Newton Student, of Cambridge Univ.; Rouse Ball Travelling Student, and Rouse Ball Senior Student, of Trinity Coll.; Comyns Berkeley Bye-Fellow, Gonville and Caius Coll., Cambridge, 1952-53. Lecturer in Mathematics, Univ. of Edinburgh, 1930-32; Reader in Mathematics, Univ. of London, and Assistant Prof., Imperial Coll. of Science, 1932-36; Prof. of Mathematics: Queen's Univ., Belfast, 1936-44; Univ. of London (Royal Holloway Coll.), 1944-66. Visiting Prof. of Astronomy: Univ. of California, 1956; Case Inst. of Technology, 1964; Consulting Astronomer, Kitt Peak National Observatory, Arizona, 1965; Royal Society Exchange Visitor to USSR, 1960, 1968; For. Visiting Prof. of American Astronomical Soc. and Vis. Prof., Berkeley Astronomy Dept, 1967; first occupant, Chaire Georges Lemaître, Louvain Univ., 1969. Visiting Lecturer: Univ. of Liège, 1960 (British Council); Technische Hochschule, Aachen, 1962; York Univ., 1965; Lectures: Harland, Univ. of Exeter, 1970; Larmor, QUB, 1970. Temp. Princ. Experimental Officer, Admty, 1943-45; Commnd RAFVR (Training Branch), 1941-45. Mem., Governing Board of School of Theoretical Physics, Dublin Institute for Advanced Studies, 1940-50; Governor: Royal Holloway Coll., 1946-49; Ottershaw Sch., 1947-52; Barclay Sch. for Partially Sighted Girls, 1949-66; Mem. Adv. Council, Coll. of Aeronautical and Automobile Engineering, 1958-. Secretary of Section A of British Assoc., 1935-39; President Section A, 1966. Joint Editor of The Observatory, 1935-37. Pres., Royal Astronomical Soc., 1961-63 (Sec., 1940-49; Foreign Correspondent, 1968-). Keith Prize, RSE, 1939-41. Hon. DSc: National Univ., Ireland, 1954; QUB, 1970. Fellow Imperial Coll., 1967. *Publications:* Relativity Physics, 1935; Analytical Geometry of Three Dimensions, 1942; Physics of the Sun and Stars, 1950; trans. A. Unsöld's The New Cosmos, 1969; various papers and reviews in mathematical and astronomical journals. *Address:* 87 Houndean Rise, Lewes, Sussex. *Club:* Athenæum.

**McCREERY, Henry Edwin Lewis,** QC 1965; Deputy Chairman: Cornwall Quarter Sessions, since 1966; Devon Quarter Sessions, since 1967; Recorder of Salisbury, since 1969; *b* 26 July 1920; *s* of late Rev. William John McCreery, BD, and late Anne Cullen McCreery; *m* 1945, Margaret Elizabeth Booth; two *d*. *Educ:* St Andrew's Coll., Dublin; Trinity Coll., Dublin. RAF, 1942-47. Called: Irish Bar King's Inns, 1943; English Bar, Middle Temple, 1946. *Recreation:* gardening.

**McCRIE, John Gibb,** OBE 1945; TD 1947; Hon. Lecturer in the History of Medicine, University of Sheffield, since 1962; Member, Hon. Consultant Staff, United Sheffield Hospitals, since 1968; (part-time) Associate Dean of Faculty of Medicine, University of Nottingham; *b* 24 Nov. 1902; *o c* of C. G. McCrie and J. W. Gibb, Edinburgh; *m* 1947, Margaret Isabella, *d* of Walter Forrest and Margaret Logan. *Educ:* George Watson's Coll., Edinburgh; Univ. of Edinburgh. MB, ChB (1st Class Hons), Edinburgh, 1925; MRCPE 1928; FRCPE 1931; Lectr in Medicine, Univ. of Edinburgh, 1931-46; Asst Physician, Royal Infirmary, Edinburgh, 1936-38; Physician, and Dep.-Director of the Medical Unit, Edinburgh Municipal Hospitals, 1938-46; Senior Administrative Officer, School of Medicine, University of Leeds, 1946-47; Dean of the Faculty of Medicine, University of Sheffield, 1947-68. Former Member, Sheffield Regional Hospital Board and Board of Governors, United Sheffield Hospitals; former Hon. Consultant (Adviser in Medical Teaching), United Sheffield Hospitals; former (Co-opted) Mem., N Midlands (Sheffield) Faculty, Coll. of General Practitioners. Representative of Univ. of Sheffield on GMC; Vice-Pres., and Chm. Coun., Assoc. for Study of Medical Education; Pres., S Yorks Branch, British Red Cross Society. Hon. Lt-Col, RAMC (TA). Served War of 1939-45 with BEF, 1940, and BNAF and CMF, 1942-45 (Lieut-Colonel, Acting Colonel). *Publications:* various papers on clinical subjects in medical jls. *Address:* 7 Ranmoor Crescent, Sheffield, S10 3GU. *T:* Sheffield 301265. *Club:* Sheffield (Sheffield).

**McCRINDLE, Major John Ronald,** CMG 1950; OBE 1919; MC; Chairman Breaches Commission International Air Transport Association, 1959-68; *b* 29 Nov. 1894; *s* of J. R. Ronald McCrindle, MB, CM, Kingston, Jamaica; *m* 1st, 1921, Odette, *d* of J. F. Feder, New York; one *s*; 2nd, 1932, Susan Ertz, *qv*. *Educ:* Jamaica Coll.; Glasgow Univ.; Harvard Univ. 2nd Lieut, Gordon Highlanders TF, Aug. 1914; seconded Royal Flying Corps, Nov. 1914; served France, Mesopotamia, Egypt, Palestine (OBE, MC, despatches thrice); Permanent Commission, Royal Air Force, 1919; Commanded London-Paris Communication Squadron during Peace Conference, 1919; Asst to British Air Representative in Paris on Council of Ambassadors, Marshal Foch's Cttee and Aeronautical Adv. Cttee, 1919-22; Mission of Supreme Council of Peace Conference to Bucharest and Budapest, 1919; retired, 1922. Called to Bar, Lincoln's Inn, 1927; practised Chancery Bar, 1927-35; Managing Director, British Airways Ltd, 1935-40; Dep. Director-General, BOAC, 1940-47; Adviser on international affairs to BOAC, 1948-58; Managing Director (External Affairs) BOAC, 1947-48; Member of the Board, 1946-58. Mem. Exec. Cttee International Air Transport Assoc., 1945-58; Adviser: UK Delegn, Chicago Civil Aviation Conference, 1944; Civil Aviation Conference, Bermuda, 1946; other internat. aviation confs, 1944-58. Officer of the Crown (Belgium); Commander of Order of Orange Nassau; Officer of Legion of Honour; Commander, 2nd Class of Order of Vasa (Sweden). *Address:* 17 Sloane Court West, SW3. *T:* 01-730 6361; Lossenham Manor, Newenden, Hawkhurst, Kent. *T:* Northiam 2196. *Clubs:* Athenæum, United Service.

**MacCRINDLE, Robert Alexander,** QC 1963; Practising Barrister since 1952; *b* 27 Jan. 1928; *s* of F. R. MacCrindle; *m* 1959, Pauline Dilys, *d* of Mark S. Morgan; one *s* one *d*. *Educ:* Girvan High Sch.; King's Coll., London; Gonville and Caius Coll., Cambridge. LLB London, 1948. Served RAF, 1948-50, Flt-Lt. LLB Cantab, Chancellor's Medal, 1951. Called to Bar, Gray's Inn, 1952; Junior Counsel to Board of Trade (Export Credits), 1961-63. *Publication:* McNair's Law of the Air, 1953. *Recreation:* golf. *Address:* 24 St Paul's Place, Canonbury, N1. *T:* 01-226 9094; 4 Essex Court, Temple, EC4. *T:* 01-353 6771.

**McCRINDLE, Robert Arthur;** MP (C) Billericay since 1970; *b* 19 Sept. 1929; *o s* of Thomas Arthur and Isabella McCrindle; *m* 1953, Myra Anderson; two *s*. *Educ:* Allen Glen's Coll., Glasgow. Chairman, Fenchurch Life & Pensions Brokers Ltd; Director, Fenchurch Group Brokers. Contested: Dundee (East), 1959; Thurrock, 1964. *Address:* 26 Ashburnham Gardens, Upminster, Essex. *T:* Upminster 27152.

**McCRONE, Robert Watson,** MC 1916; BSc, MICE; *b* 6 Feb. 1893; *s* of Edward McCrone, Craigallion, Kilmacolm, Renfrewshire; *m* 1934, Enid Marie, *d* of B. W. Just, Bristol; three *d*. *Educ:* Merchiston Castle Sch., Edinburgh; Royal College of Science and Technology, Glasgow; Glasgow Univ. Served European War, 1914-18, in Royal Engineers, 51st Highland Div. (despatches, MC); Croix de Guerre, France, 1918. One of the founders in 1923 of Metal Industries Group of Companies; Man. Dir and then Chm. until 1955; Dir, British Oxygen Co. Ltd, 1933-63; Chm. of Dir of many other industrial concerns until 1963. Past Mem. East of Scotland Electricity Board. Formerly Governor Royal College of Science and Technology, Glasgow; formerly member of Lloyd's. *Recreations:* farming, riding, yachting. *Address:* Pitliver, by Dunfermline, Fife. *T:* Limekilns 232. *Club:* Farmers'.

**McCROSTIE, Hugh Cecil,** DSO 1919; Director and Chief Secretary, Scottish Omnibuses Group of Companies, 1934-62; *b* 1897; *y s* of Hugh McCrostie, Strath Tummel and Edinburgh, and Agnes Watson Hutchison; *m* 1934, Doris Harcourt, Bebington, Cheshire; four *d*. *Educ:* George Watson's Coll.; Edinburgh Univ. (BCom). Member of Institute of Chartered Accountants of Scotland and of Institute of Transport. Served Royal Scots and Tank Corps, 1915-20, 2nd Lieut–Captain France, Belgium and North (Baltic) Russia (seriously wounded, despatches, DSO, Orders of St Anne 2nd Class and St Stanislas 2nd Class of Russia). Lieut–Major 7/9th (Highlanders) Bn, The Royal Scots, TA, 1920-31; Major, TARO, 1931-39; served War, 1939-42, Major, DAAG, 4th Corps, NWEF, and 5th Corps, TD, (bar); Lieut-Colonel Commanding 1st Edinburgh Home Guard Bn, 1954-57. *Recreations:* country pursuits. *Address:* 27b Greenhill Gardens, Edinburgh 10. *T:* 031-447 3848. *Club:* Caledonian United Service (Edinburgh).

**McCRUM, Michael William,** MA; Head Master of Eton, since 1970; *b* 23 May 1924; 3rd *s* of Captain C. R. McCrum, RN (retired) and of Ivy Hilda Constance (*née* Nicholson); *m* 1952, Christine Mary Kathleen, *d* of Sir Arthur fforde, *qv*; three *s* one *d*. *Educ:* Horris Hill, Newbury; Sherborne Sch.; Corpus Christi Coll., Cambridge. Entrance Scholar to CCC, Dec. 1942. Served RN, 1943-45 (Sub-Lt RNVR, Dec. 1943). CCC, Cambridge, 1946-48; Part I, Class. Tripos, First Class, 1947; Part II, First Class, with distinction, 1948. Asst Master, Rugby School, Sept. 1948-July 1950 (Lower Bench Master, 1949-50); Fellow CCC, Cambridge, 1949; Second Tutor, 1950-51; Tutor, 1951-62; Member, Council of the Senate, University of Cambridge, 1955-58, General Board of Faculties, 1957-62; Headmaster, Tonbridge School, 1962-70. *Publication:* (with A. G. Woodhead) Select Documents of the Principates of the Flavian Emperors AD 68-96, 1961. *Address:* The Cloisters, Eton College, Windsor, Berks. *Clubs:* Athenæum, Public Schools; Hawks (Cambridge).

**McCULLAGH, Sir Crawford;** *see* McCullagh, Sir (J.) C.

**McCULLAGH, Sir (Joseph) Crawford,** 2nd Bt *cr* 1935; *b* 25 Sept. 1907; *s* of Sir Crawford McCullagh, 1st Bt, PC (N Ireland), DL, and Margaret Craig, CBE (*d* 1944), *d* of William Brodie, Bolton-le-Moors; *S* father, 1948; *m* 1937, Elizabeth Green. *Educ:* Campbell Coll., Belfast. Ex-Councillor Belfast Corporation, Clifton Ward. *Recreation:* aviculture. *Heir:* none. *Address:* Lismara, Whiteabbey, Co. Antrim. *T:* Whiteabbey 2220. *Clubs:* Constitutional; Royal Ulster Yacht (Bangor, Co. Down); North of Ireland Cricket and Football (Belfast).

**McCULLOUGH, Donald;** *see* McCullough, W. D. H.

**McCULLOUGH, Thomas Warburton,** CB 1962; OBE 1954; HM Chief Inspector of Factories,

Ministry of Labour, 1958-63; *b* 13 March 1901; *o s* of late Robert McCullough and Emma Warburton, *d* of Thomas Rigby; *m* 1928, Lisette Hunter, *d* of late Henry George Gannaway; one *s*. *Educ:* Ballymena Academy; Glasgow Univ.; Middle Temple. BSc 1925. Engineering training, Glasgow, 1917-25; Valuation Dept, Ministry of Finance, Belfast, 1925; joined Factory Dept, Home Office, 1926. Member Joint Advisory Cttee on Conditions in Iron Foundries, 1947; Hon. Adviser Scottish Industrial Groups Advisory Council, 1951-53; Chairman of numerous Joint Standing Cttees, 1950-56. Member: Home Office Inter-Departmental Cttee on Accidents in the Home, 1954-57; National Industrial Safety Cttee, 1954-57, Executive Cttee, 1958-63, Royal Society for Prevention of Accidents; Industrial Grants Cttee, Dept of Scientific and Industrial Research, 1958-63; Nuclear Safety Advisory Cttee, 1960-63; Technical Adviser (Safety), The United Steel Companies Ltd, 1963-67. Hon. Life Member, Royal Society for Prevention of Accidents, 1963; Hon. Fellow, Institution of Industrial Safety Officers, 1964; Hon. Adviser (Safety) British Steel Corp. (formerly British Iron and Steel Fedn), 1964-; Pres., London Construction Safety Group, 1963-. Silver Medal, L'Institut National de Sécurité, Paris, 1961; Industrial Safety Award, RoSPA, 1970. *Publications:* sundry contribs to literature of accident prevention in industry. *Recreation:* fly-fishing. *Address:* 69 Walsingham Road, Hove, Sussex. *Club:* Flyfishers'.

**McCULLOUGH, (William) Donald (Hamilton),** MA; Advertising and Public Relations Consultant, Writer and Broadcaster; *s* of late Rev. W. C. McCullough, BA, LLB, St Margaret's Manse, Hawick; *m* Nan, *yr d* of late Captain H. L. Watts-Jones, RN; three *s* two *d*. *Educ:* Watson's Coll.; Edinburgh Univ. RAFVR, 1939-40. *Publications:* How to Run a Brains Trust, 1947; with Fougasse: Aces Made Easy, 1934; You Have Been Warned, 1935; Many Happy Returns, 1936; Fancy Meeting You, 1947; Question Mark, 1949; with Ernest Clegg: Countryman County Maps, 1946. *Recreations:* golf, sailing. *Address:* Flagstaff House, Burnham Overy Staithe, Norfolk. *TA* and *T:* Burnham Market 248. *Clubs:* Bath; Brancaster Golf.

**McCUNN, Peter Alexander;** Director, Cable & Wireless Ltd; *b* 11 Nov. 1922; *m* 1943, Margaret Prescott; three *s*. *Educ:* Mexborough Grammar Sch.; Edinburgh University. Commnd W Yorks Regt, 1942; served in Normandy, Malta, Italy; left Army, Nov. 1946 (Captain). Joined Cable & Wireless, 1947; Director: Cable & Wireless/Western Union International Inc. of Puerto Rico, 1968; Cable & Wireless, 1969; Nigerian External Telecommunications Ltd, 1969; Sierra Leone External Telecommunications Ltd, 1969. *Recreations:* music, gardening, swimming, cricket, Association football (now non-active). *Address:* Wychelms, 14 Lime Walk, Pinkneys Green, Maidenhead, Berks. *T:* Maidenhead 24308, (office) 01-242 4433. *Club:* Royal Commonwealth Society.

**McCUTCHEON, Sir Osborn;** *see* McCutcheon, Sir W. O.

**McCUTCHEON, Sir (Walter) Osborn,** Kt 1966; FRAIA; Senior Partner, Bates, Smart & McCutcheon, Melbourne (Architects, Engineers and Town Planners) since 1951 (Partner, 1926-); *b* 8 April 1899; *s* of W. B. McCutcheon, Solicitor, Melbourne; *m* 1928, Mary, *d* of A. A. Buley; two *s* one *d*. *Educ:* Wesley Coll., Melbourne; Univ. of Melbourne. Mem. Faculty, Melbourne Univ. School of Architecture; Director, Arch., Melbourne Technical Sch., 1930-39; Member Council, Royal Victoria Inst. of Architecture, 1930-45 (Pres., 1940-42; Mem. Board of Arch. Educn, 1933-39, 1940-42, 1953-57); Pres., Building Indust. Congr. of Victoria, 1934-36; Member Council, RAIA, 1941-42; Chief Architect, Engineers HQ, US Army, SW Pacific Area, 1942-44; Controller of Planning etc to Australian Commonwealth Govt, 1944-46; resumed private practice, 1946. Mem. various cttees; assessor of sundry competitions. Mem., National Capital Planning Cttee, Nat. Capital Develt Commn, 1967-. Gold Medal, RAIA, 1965. Hon. LLD, Monash Univ., 1968. *Publications:* articles in Architecture in Australia, etc. *Recreations:* sailing, reading. *Address:* (office) 366 St Kilda Road, Melbourne, Victoria, Australia. *T:* Melbourne 69-6131; (home) Keraboit, Baden Powell Drive, Mount Eliza, Victoria, Australia. *T:* Mount Eliza 71479. *Clubs:* Melbourne, Savage (Melbourne); Peninsula Country Golf, Davey's Bay Yacht, Mornington Yacht.

**McDAVID, Sir Edwin Frank,** Kt, *cr* 1953; CMG 1948; CBE 1942 (MBE 1933); retired; *b* 26 Oct. 1895; *s* of late E. N. McDavid, Company Secretary, and Elizabeth McDavid; *m* 1920, Elma Hildred Delph; no *c*. *Educ:* Queen's Coll., British Guiana. Served with Fitzpatrick, Graham and Co., Chartered Accountants, 1914-20; Secretary, Excess Profits Tax Board of Assessment, British Guiana, 1920; Chief Accountant, British Guiana Govt Railway and Steamer Services, 1923; acted as Man. Dir of above Services, 1928; Deputy Colonial Treas., British Guiana, 1929; Commissioner of Income Tax, 1929-53; Financial Secretary (formerly Colonial Treasurer) amd Member of Executive and Legislative Councils, 1935-53; Chairman: British Guiana Rice Marketing Board, 1939-46; British Guiana Rice Development Co., 1952-60; President, State Council, 1953; MEC, MLC, Minister of Lands and Agriculture, 1954-57. Managing Director, Demerara Mutual Life Assurance Society Ltd, 1960-62 (Chairman, 1957-59). Chairman, British Guiana Public Library, 1941-61; Hon. Colonel British Guiana Volunteer Force, 1954-62. *Address:* c/o The Royal Bank of Canada, West End Branch, Cockspur Street, SW1.

**MacDERMOT, The, (Charles J.),** styled Prince of Coolavin; *b* 20 Feb. 1899; 2nd and *e surv. s* of late Charles E., The MacDermot, and Caroline MacDermot; *m* 1954, Felicity, *d* of Edward T. MacDermot, MA, JP, Lillycombe, Porlock, Somerset. *Educ:* Stonyhurst Coll.; Trinity Coll., Dublin. *Heir:* *b* Sir Dermot F. MacDermot, *qv*. *Address:* Coolavin, Ballaghaderreen, Co. Roscommon.

**MacDERMOT, Brian (Charles),** CBE 1966; MVO 1961; HM Ambassador and Consul-General to Paraguay since 1968; *b* 29 Jan. 1914; *m* 1949, Mary Arden Hunter; seven *s* two *d*. Probationer Vice-Consul, Peking, China, 1936; served at: Hankow, China, 1939-40; Kobe, Japan, 1940-41; Kunming, South China, 1942; Vice-Consul, Shiraz, Persia, 1943; Paris, 1944, promoted Consul, 1945; Foreign Office, 1946; Consul, Beirut, 1948; First Secretary, Belgrade, 1950; First Secretary, Berne, 1951, acted as Chargé d'Affaires, 1951, 1952, 1953; transferred to Foreign Office, 1954; transferred to Holy See, 1955, acted as Chargé d'Affaires, 1958, 1959, 1960 and 1961; HM Consul-General, Oporto, 1962-68. *Address:* The Old Rectory, St James, Shaftesbury, Dorset.

**MacDERMOT, Sir Dermot (Francis),** KCMG 1962 (CMG 1954); CBE 1947; *b* 14 June 1906; 2nd *surv. s* of late Charles Edward, The MacDermot, Prince of Coolavin; *m* 1934, Betty Steel; three *s. Educ:* Stonyhurst Coll.; Trinity Coll., Dublin, LLD *jure dignitatis,* 1964. Joined HM Consular Service in 1929 and served in Tokyo, Yokohama, Kobe and Osaka in Japan, Manila (Philippines), Tamsui (Formosa), New Orleans, and in the Foreign Office. Appointed a Counsellor in the Foreign Office, 1947; Inspector, HM Foreign Service, 1951; HM Minister to Roumania, 1954-56; HM Ambassador to Indonesia, 1956-59; Assistant Under-Secretary, Foreign Office, 1959-61; HM Ambassador to Thailand, 1961-65. *Recreations:* golf, tennis. *Address:* Gates House, Tal-Virtu Road, Rabat, Malta GC.
*See also The MacDermot.*

**MACDERMOT, Niall,** OBE 1944; QC 1963; barrister-at-law; *b* 10 Sept. 1916; *s* of late Henry MacDermot, KC, Dublin; *m* 1940, Violet Denise Maxwell (marr. diss. 1966); one *s*; *m* 1966, Ludmila Benvenuto. *Educ:* Rugby Sch.; Corpus Christi Coll., Cambridge; Balliol Coll., Oxford. Served in Intelligence Corps, 1939-46; GSO1 HQ 21 Army Group, 1944-45. MP (Lab) Lewisham North, Feb. 1957-59, Derby North, April 1962-1970; Mem. Exec., London Labour Party, 1958-62. Dep. Chm., Beds QS, 1961-64, 1969-; Recorder of Newark-on-Trent, 1963-64. Master of the Bench, Inner Temple, 1970-. Financial Sec., Treasury, 1964-67; Minister of State, Min. of Housing and Local Govt, 1967-68. Hon. Treasurer, Justice, 1968-. Trustee of Tate Gall., 1969-. *Publication:* (with M. D. Van Oss) The Lands Tribunal, 1950. *Address:* 2 Crown Office Row, Temple, EC4.

**MacDERMOTT,** Baron (Life Peer), *cr* 1947, of Belmont; **John Clarke MacDermott,** PC 1947, PC (Northern Ireland), 1940; MC; LLD; Lord Chief Justice of Northern Ireland since 1951; *b* 12 April 1896; *s* of late Rev. John and Lydia Allen MacDermott, Belmont, Belfast; *m* 1926, Louise Palmer, *o d* of Rev. J. C. Johnston, MA, DD; two *s* two *d. Educ:* Campbell Coll., Belfast; Queen's Univ. of Belfast. Foundation Scholar, 1914. Served European War in France: Lieut, 51st Bn MGC (MC). LLB First Class Honours, 1921; Victoria Prizeman and Exhibitioner, King's Inns, Dublin; called to Irish Bar, 1921; Lecturer in Jurisprudence, Queen's Univ. of Belfast, 1931-35; appointed to determine Industrial Assurance Disputes in Northern Ireland, 1929-38; KC (Northern Ireland), 1936; MP (U) Queen's University of Belfast, Parliament of Northern Ireland, 1938-44; Governor, Campbell Coll., 1934-59; Chairman Joint Select Cttee on Road and Rail Transport in Northern Ireland, 1939; Sept. 1939, Major RA; Minister of Public Security for Northern Ireland, June 1940-Nov. 1941; Attorney-General, 1941-44; Judge, High Court of Justice, Northern Ireland, 1944-47; a Lord of Appeal in Ordinary, 1947-51; Chairman, National Arbitration Tribunal, Northern Ireland, 1944-46; Bencher Inn of Court of Northern Ireland; Hon. Bencher Gray's Inn, 1947. Hamlyn Lectures on Protection from Power, 1957; Chairman Commission on Isle of Man Constitution, 1958. Pro-Chancellor, Queen's Univ. of Belfast, 1951-69. Hon. LLD: QUB, 1951; Edinburgh, 1958; Cambridge, 1968. *Address:* Glenburn, Cairnburn Road, Belfast 4. *T:* Belfast 63361. *Clubs:* Athenæum; Ulster (Belfast).

**McDERMOTT, Geoffrey Lyster,** CMG 1957; Diplomat and Author; retired from Foreign Service, 1962; *b* 7 Oct. 1912; *o s* of late Captain J. W. McDermott, CIE, and Mrs G. E. McDermott; *m* 1st, 1937, Ruth Mary, *d* of late Sir Arthur Fleming, CBE; one *s* one *d*; 2nd, 1947, Elizabeth Marion Robertson; two *s* (and one step *s*). *Educ:* Marlborough Coll. (scholar); King's Coll., Cambridge. Scholar in Mod. Langs at King's, 1930; 1st class hons both parts of Mod. Langs tripos, 1931 and 1933. Entered Diplomatic Service, 1935; 3rd Sec., FO, 1935; Sofia, 1938; 2nd Sec., Ankara, 1941; FO, 1943; 1st Sec., FO, 1944; Cairo, 1946; Santiago, 1948; Chargé d'Affaires there, 1949, 1950, 1951; Counsellor and Head of Permanent Under-Secretary's Dept in the Foreign Office, 1953-56; Minister HM Foreign Service, employed in Foreign Office, 1956-58; Political Representative with Middle East Forces, Cyprus, 1958-61; HM Minister in Berlin, 1961-62. FRSA 1958. *Publications:* Berlin: Success of a Mission?, 1963; The Eden Legacy and the Decline of British Diplomacy, 1969; Leader Lost: a biography of Hugh Gaitskell, 1970; numerous articles. *Recreations:* walking, motoring, and the arts. *Address:* 22 Queen Street, W1X 7PJ. *T:* 01-499 1466; The Old Rectory, Ripple, near Tewkesbury, Glos. *T:* Upton-upon-Severn 2444. *Clubs:* Boodle's, Garrick.

**McDIARMID, Hugh;** *see* Grieve, C. M.

**MACDIARMID, Niall Campbell;** Deputy Chairman, Vickers Ltd, since 1970; *b* 7 June 1919; *y s* of Sir Allan Campbell Macdiarmid, and Grace Buchanan (*née* McClure); *m* 1946, Patricia Isobel Mackie-Campbell, *yr d* of Geordie Osmonde Lorne Campbell and Jessie Isobel (*née* Mackie); three *d. Educ:* Uppingham Sch.; Magdalen Coll., Oxford. Served War of 1939-45 with The Argyll and Sutherland Highlanders (despatches three times). Managing Director, The Stanton Ironworks Co. Ltd (later Stanton and Staveley Ltd), 1957-62, Chm., 1962-64; Chm., Stewarts and Lloyds Ltd, 1964-69; Dir, The United Steel Companies Ltd, 1964-67; Man. Dir, Northern and Tubes Group, BSC, 1967-70. Member: Iron and Steel Board, 1961-67; BSC, 1967-70; E Midlands Gas Board, 1962-67; Pres., Iron and Steel Inst., 1969-70. Trustee of Uppingham School (Chairman, 1967-); Trustee, Duke of Edinburgh's Award Scheme, 1963-. *Recreations:* shooting, golf. *Address:* Stibbington Hall, Wansford, Peterborough PE8 6LP. *T:* Wansford 322. *Club:* Caledonian.

**MACDONA, Brian Fraser,** CBE 1967; Director, Barclays Bank DCO and Barclays Export Finance Co. Ltd, since 1964; *b* 26 Jan. 1901; *o s* of late G. Bagot Macdona, Streatham, and Hannah Mary (*née* Gomersall); *m* 1923, Elsie May, *d* of late E. W. Fellgate, Ealing; no *c. Educ:* Modern Sch., Streatham. FIB 1951. Jun. Clerk, Van den Berghs Ltd, 1915-17; joined Barclays Bank Ltd, Head Office, 1917; served in Suffolk, 1920-22; attached Barclays Bank (Dominion, Colonial and Overseas), London, Sudan, S Africa, Rhodesia, E Africa, 1927-29; transf. in 1929 to that bank and appointed Bank Manager at Nairobi, Mombasa, Eldoret and Kampala, 1929-37; Supt, E African Brs and Local Dir's Asst, Nairobi, 1937; Local Dir, E Africa, 1942-45, Egypt, Sudan and Libya, 1945-48; Asst Gen. Man., Head Office,

London, 1948; Gen. Man. 1951; Sen. Gen. Man. 1959-64. Dir, Bank of London & Montreal Ltd, 1964-70. Served as govt nominee, various projects, and as office-bearer, numerous assocs, cttees, bds, etc in E Africa and Egypt. Hon. Treasurer: 20th Congress, IGU, 1964; Brit. Inst. History and Archaeology in E Africa, 1965-; Royal African Soc., 1951-53 (Vice-Chm. of Council, 1953-65, Chm. 1965-); Mem. Council: Mount Everest Foundn, 1964-69; RSA, 1965 (Jt Treas. 1968-); Hakluyt Soc., 1967-; RGS, 1960-70 (Hon. Treas. 1970-); Internat. Students Trust, 1961 (Dep. Chm. of Govs, 1964-); Royal Commonwealth Soc., 1960-69 (Chm., 1969-). Personal Asst to Chief Scout of Commonwealth, 1965. Gov., Victoria Coll., Alexandria, 1945-. Mem. Adv. Commn: of FBI, on possibilities of Nigerian Industrialisation, 1961; of Western Hemisphere Export Council, on British Exports and W Indies Industrialisation, 1962. Has lectured on African affairs in N America and UK. Visited Africa and the Caribbean frequently from 1950, also Moscow, Australasia and the Americas. Liveryman, Scriveners' Co., 1955-; Freeman, City of London, 1955. Lord Mayor's medal for services to export, 1964. Hon. FRGS 1967. *Recreations:* motoring, watching cricket, admiring other people gardening, writing and talking about Africa and Commonwealth problems. *Address:* Square Cottage, East Road, St George's Hill, Weybridge, Surrey. *T:* Weybridge 42115. *Clubs:* Overseas Bankers, City Livery, MCC, Royal Commonwealth Society; Nairobi, Kenya Kongonis (Kenya); Kampala (Uganda).

**MACDONALD,** family name of **Barons Macdonald** and **Macdonald of Gwaenysgor.**

**MACDONALD,** 7th Baron *cr* 1776; **Alexander Godfrey Macdonald of Macdonald,** MBE 1944; TD; Lord Lieutenant since 1952, and Convener since 1968 (Vice-Convener, 1952), of the County of Inverness; *b* 27 June 1909; *e s* of Hon. Godfrey Evan Hugh Macdonald, and Helen, *e d* of Meyrick Bankes, and *g d* of late Meyrick Bankes, Winstanly Hall, Lancs; *S* grandfather, 1947; *m* 1945, Anne, *o d* of late Alfred Whitaker and of Mrs Maclachlan; two *s* one *d*. *Educ:* Eton; Magdalene Coll., Cambridge, MA. JP and a CC for Inverness-shire; late Major QO Cameron Highlanders. Member of: Agricultural Advisory Cttee for Skye (Chm.), 1950-52; Skye Hospital Board of Management (Chairman); North of Scotland Hydro-Electric Board (part-time), 1961, and Consultative Council (Chairman); Chairman, Inverness-shire Unionist Assoc., 1945-50; President, Association of County Councils in Scotland, 1958-60. Grand Master Mason of Scotland, 1953-57. *Heir:* *s* Hon. Godfrey James Macdonald [*b* 28 Nov. 1947; *m* 1969, Claire, *e d* of Cdre Thomas Catlow, CBE]. *Address:* Ostaig House, Isle of Skye. *Clubs:* Boodle's; New (Edinburgh); Highland (Inverness).

**MACDONALD OF GWAENYSGOR,** 2nd Baron *cr* 1949, of Gwaenysgor, Flint; **Gordon Ramsay Macdonald;** Chief Executive in UK of Hayek Consultancy Group; *b* 16 Oct. 1915; *er s* of 1st Baron Macdonald of Gwaenysgor, PC, KCMG; *S* father, 1966; *m* 1941, Leslie Margaret Taylor; three *d*. *Educ:* Manchester Univ. MA, Economics and Commerce. Served War, 1940-46; Army, Major, Artillery; GSO2 Operations and Intelligence (despatches, Burma). Board of Trade, 1946-53: Principal, 1946-47; UK Trade Comr, Canberra, ACT, 1947-53. With Tube Investments Ltd, and Man. Dir TI (Export) Ltd, 1953-64; Chief Exec., Telecommunications Group, Plessey Co., 1964-67. *Recreations:* golf, chess. *Heir:* *b* Hon. Kenneth Macdonald [*b* 3 Feb. 1921; m 1952, Maureen Margaret Watson-Allan; two *d*]. *Address:* The Lodge, Pyebush Lane, Beaconsfield, Bucks. *T:* Beaconsfield 4081.

**MACDONALD of Sleat** (Btcy); *see under* Bosville Macdonald.

**MACDONALD, Adam Davidson,** MA, MSc, MD; retired as Leech Professor of Pharmacology in the University of Manchester, Sept. 1964; *b* Perth, Scotland, 17 Oct. 1895; *s* of Robert Macdonald, schoolmaster; *m* 1927, Helen Muriel Anderson, Edinburgh; one *s* two *d*. *Educ:* High School of Dundee; Univ. of Edinburgh (Neill Arnott Scholar and Goodsir Fellow). Demonstrator in Physiology, Univ. of Edinburgh; Lectr in Experimental Physiology and Reader in Pharmacology, Univ. of Manchester. *Publications:* various papers in physiological and pharmacological journals. *Recreations:* golf, gardening. *Address:* 2 Broadway Avenue, Cheadle, Cheshire. *T:* 061-428 2435.

**McDONALD, Alexander Forbes,** DL; Chairman, The Distillers Company Ltd, since Oct. 1967 (Deputy Chairman, 1964-67); Chairman Council, Scotch Whisky Association, since 1967; *b* 14 Aug. 1911; *s* of late Angus McDonald and late Christina Jane Forbes; *m* 1937, Ethel Marjorie, *d* of late Theodore Crawford, MC, and late Sarah Anne Mansfield; two *s* two *d*. *Educ:* Hillhead Sch.; Glasgow Univ. BL Glasgow 1933. Chartered Accountant, 1934. DL, County of City of Edinburgh, 1963. *Address:* 6 Oswald Road, Edinburgh. *T:* 031-667 4246. *Club:* Bath.

**McDONALD, Alexander Hugh,** FBA 1967; MA, PhD; LittD; Fellow of Clare College and Lecturer in Ancient History, Cambridge University, since 1952; *b* 19 May 1908; *s* of Rev. William and Mary McDonald; *m* 1941, Joan Urey, *d* of Sir Martin and Ada McIlrath. *Educ:* Auckland Grammar Sch.; Auckland Univ. Coll., NZ; Clare Coll., Cambridge. Univ. of NZ: BA, Sen. Schol. in Greek, 1928; MA, Double First in Latin and Greek, Travelling Scholarship in Arts, 1929; Clare Coll., Cambridge: Exhibitioner, First in Classical Tripos, Part II, 1932; Research at Göttingen Univ., 1933; Senior Research Student, Clare Coll., 1934; PhD (Cambridge) 1936. Lecturer in Ancient History, Nottingham University Coll., 1934-38; Sydney Univ., Australia: Reader in Ancient History, 1939-44; Acting Prof. of Latin, 1945, Prof. of Ancient World History, 1945-51; Editor, Current Affairs Bulletin, Australian Army, 1943-46; News Commentator, ABC, 1943-51; Liaison Officer (NSW) for Colonial Service appointments, 1946-51. Acting Prof. of Ancient History, Chicago Univ., 1954; Sen. Tutor, 1954-57, and Steward, 1963-65, Clare Coll., Cambridge. Mem. Inst. Advanced Study, Princeton, NJ, 1966; Vice-President, Roman Society, 1967; Chairman Archæol. Faculty, British School at Rome, 1967; Pres., Cambridge Philological Soc., 1968-70. Hon. LLD Glasgow, 1948; Hon. LittD Auckland, 1967. *Publications:* Japanese Imperialism, 1944; (ed) Trusteeship in the Pacific, 1948; (ed) Oxford Text of Livy, 1937, Vol. V, 1965; Republican Rome, 1966; papers and reviews in Jl of Roman Studies; reviews in Classical Review. *Recreations:* squash racquets, golf, theatre. *Address:* Clare College,

Cambridge. *T:* Cambridge 58681. *Clubs:* Devonshire, Authors'; New South Wales, University (Sydney).

**McDONALD, Prof. Alexander John,** MA (Cantab), LLB, WS: Professor of Conveyancing, University of Dundee (formerly Queen's College), since 1955 (Dean of the Faculty of Law, 1958-62, 1965); *b* 15 March 1919; *o s* of late John McDonald, and Agnes Mary Stewart McDonald; *m* 1951, Doreen Mary, *o d* of late Frank Cook, OBE; two *s* two *d. Educ:* Cargilfield Sch.; Fettes Coll. (open scholar); Christ's Coll., Cambridge (Classical Exhibn, BA 1942); Edinburgh Univ. (Thow Schol. and John Robertson Prize in Conveyancing; LLB with dist., 1949). Admitted as Solicitor and Writer to the Signet, 1950; Lectr in Conveyancing, Edinburgh Univ., 1952-55; Registrar of the Diocese of Brechin, 1963-. Member firm of Dickie, Gray, McDonald & Fair, WS, Dundee. *Address:* 4 Middlebank Crescent, Dundee. *T:* Dundee 66049.

**MACDONALD, Alistair;** Member of Lord Chancellor's Department; consultant to Royal Institute of Public Administration, since 1970; *b* 23 July 1912; 2nd *s* of late Reginald James Macdonald and Dorothy Bolden; *m* 1941, Myra Jones; one *s* six *d. Educ:* King's Sch., Bruton. Called to the Bar, Inner Temple, 1935. Served in RAF, 1940-45; Air Staff (Intelligence), 1943-45 (despatches). Legal Assistant, Law Officers Dept, 1948; Legal Sec. to Law Officers of the Crown, 1950-58; Secretary, The Council on Tribunals, 1958-70. *Address:* Luxford's, Lewes Road, East Grinstead, Sussex. *T:* East Grinstead 23365.

**MacDONALD, Alistair Archibald,** MA, LLB; Sheriff Substitute of Caithness, Sutherland, Orkney and Zetland at Lerwick, since 1961, and at Kirkwall since 1968; *b* 8 May 1927; *s* of James and Margaret MacDonald; *m* 1950, Jill Russell; one *s* one *d. Educ:* Broughton Sch.; Edinburgh Univ. Called to Scottish Bar, 1954. President: Shetland Council of Social Service; Fedn of Highlands and Islands Councils of Social Service; Mem., Scottish Rural Develt Cttee; Civil Defence Controller for Zetland. *Address:* West Hall, Shetland Islands. *Club:* Aberdeen University.

**MACDONALD, Alistair H.;** *b* 18 May 1925. *Educ:* Dulwich Coll.; Enfield Technical Coll.; Corpus Christi Coll., Cambridge. MP (Lab) Chislehurst, 1966-70. Councillor, Chislehurst and Sidcup UDC, 1958-62; Alderman, London Borough of Bromley, 1964-68. *Address:* 79 Oakdene Avenue, Chislehurst, Kent BR7 6DZ. *T:* 01-857 8219.

**MACDONALD, Allan Ronald,** CMG 1953; *b* 21 Dec. 1906; *s* of Major Ronald Macdonald and Elizabeth Blair Macdonald (*née* Coats); *m* 1st, 1937, Katherine May Hodson; two *s*; 2nd, 1954, Dr Mary Shaw (*d* 1956). *Educ:* Fettes Coll., Edinburgh; St John's Coll., Cambridge. Ceylon Civil Service, 1929-48; Establishment Sec., Uganda, 1948-51; Colonial Sec., Sierra Leone, 1951-56; Mem. of Lidbury Commn on Gold Coast Public Service, 1951; Chm., Public Service Commn: Kenya, 1956-64; Fedn of South Arabia, 1965-67. *Address:* c/o Hongkong and Shanghai Bank, 9 Gracechurch Street, EC3. *Club:* Oxford and Cambridge University.

**McDONALD, Air Comdt Ann Smith,** ARRC 1958; QHNS 1970; Matron-in-Chief Princess Mary's Royal Air Force Nursing Service, since Sept. 1970; *b* 21 Oct. 1914; *d* of late Archibald McDonald and late Mrs McDonald. *Educ:* Queen's Park Sch., Glasgow. SRFN, Belvidere Hosp. Glasgow, 1935; SRN, Victoria Infirmary, Glasgow, 1939. Joined PMRAFNS, 1941; Matron, 1959; Senior Matron, 1966; Principal Matron, 1968 (having served in Hospitals and Med. Centres in UK, West Africa, India, Aden, Germany). QHNS 1970-OStJ 1960. *Address:* Ministry of Defence NSB(RAF), 1-6 Tavistock Square, WC1. *T:* 01-387 5040 (Ext. 203). *Club:* Royal Air Force.

**MACDONALD, Archibald J. F.,** JP; *b* 2 May 1904; *s* of late Dr G. B. D. Macdonald, MB, ChM, and late Beatrice B. Macdonald; *m* 1945, Hon. Elspeth Ruth Shaw, *y d* of 2nd Baron Craigmyle; two *s. Educ:* Chatswood Grammar Sch., Australia; Royal Australian Naval Coll. Joint Chief Executive, Management Research Groups, London, 1937-40; Secretary, Paint Industry Export Group, 1940-49; Dir and Sec., Wartime Paint Manufacturers' Assoc., 1943-45; Dir, Robert Bowran & Co. Ltd, 1949-53; Vice-Chm., Joseph Freeman Sons & Co. Ltd, 1954-66. MP (L) Roxburgh and Selkirk, 1950-51. Member Visiting Cttee, Wormwood Scrubs and Pentonville Prisons. JP County of London. Hampstead Borough Councillor, 1962-65. *Recreations:* tennis, golf. *Address:* 22 Heath Drive, Hampstead, NW3. *T:* 01-435 2317. *Clubs:* Reform, Garrick.

**MACDONALD, Maj.-Gen. Arthur Leslie,** CB 1969; OBE 1953; GOC Northern Command, Australian Military Forces, since 1970; *b* 30 Jan. 1919; *s* of late Arthur Leslie MacDonald, Yaamba, Queensland; *m* 1940, Joan Bevington, *d* of late Sidney Brady, Brisbane, Queensland; one *d. Educ:* The Southport School, Southport, Queensland; Royal Military College, Duntroon, ACT. Regtl and Staff appts, Aust., ME and New Guinea, 1940-44; Instructor, Staff Coll., Camberley, 1944-45; CO 3rd Bn, The Royal Australian Regt, Korea, 1953-54; Dir of Mil. Ops, AHQ, 1955-56; Senior Aust. Planner, SEATO, Bangkok, 1957-58; Commandant, Jungle Training Centre, Canungra, 1959-60; Dir of Staff Duties, AHQ, 1960-61; Imperial Defence Coll., 1962; Dep. Commander, 1st Div., 1963-64; Commander, Papua and New Guinea Comd, 1965-66; Dep. Chief of the General Staff, 1966-67; Commander Australian Force, Viet Nam, 1968-69; Adjutant-Gen. and 2nd Mil. Mem. of Mil. Board, AMF, 1969-70. *Recreations:* golf, swimming. *Address:* HQ Northern Command, Brisbane, Queensland 4000, Australia. *Clubs:* Imperial Service (Sydney); Commonwealth (Canberra); Papua (Port Moresby).

**McDONALD, Air Marshal Sir Arthur (William Baynes),** KCB 1958 (CB 1949); AFC 1935; CEng, FRAeS 1959; DL; retired; *b* 14 June 1903; *s* of late Dr Will McDonald, OBE, Antigua, BWI; *m* 1928, Mary Julia Gray, Hindhead, Surrey; two *s* two *d. Educ:* Epsom Coll.; Peterhouse, Cambridge (MA). Joined RAF, 1924; served in Singapore, 1933-35; in Air Ministry, 1939-40; Fighter Command, 1941. Appointed Air Defence Commander, Ceylon, 1942; Air Officer Training, Air HQ, India, 1943-44; Air Officer Commanding No. 106 Group, 1945-46; Comdt RAF Staff Coll., Bulstrode and later Andover, 1947-48; Student Imperial Defence Coll., 1949; OC Aeroplane and Armament Experimental Establishment, under the Ministry of Supply, 1950-52; Director-General of Manning, Air Ministry,

1952-55; Commander-in-Chief, Royal Pakistan Air Force, 1955-57; AOC-in-C, RAF Technical Training Comd, 1958-59; Air Mem. for Personnel, Air Council, 1959-61, retired 1962. DL Hampshire, 1965. *Recreations:* sailing (rep. Great Britain in Olympic Games, 1948), ski-ing. *Address:* Five Oaks, Woodside, Lymington, Hants. *Clubs:* Royal Air Force; Royal Lymington Yacht; RAF Sailing Association.

**MACDONALD of Sleat, Miss Celia Violet Bosville,** CBE 1937; *b* Thorpe Hall, Bridlington, 28 Jan. 1889; *d* of Sir Alexander Wentworth Macdonald Bosville Macdonald of the Isles, 14th Bt, and 21st Chief of Sleat. *Educ:* home. At one time Scoutmaster and Commissioner for Girl Guides in E Riding, Yorks; OBE in 1919 for War Work; in 1921 joined Lady Frances Ryder in her private scheme for hospitality for Dominion Students, and became Chairman of The Dominions Fellowship Trust formed out of that work in 1948. Retired 1961. Coronation Medal, 1953. Hon. MA Oxford, 1959. *Recreations:* music, travelling. *Address:* 90 Whitelands House, Cheltenham Terrace, SW3.

**MACDONALD, Prof. Donald Farquhar;** Professor of Modern Social and Economic History, University of Dundee, since 1967 (University of St Andrews, 1955-67); *b* 3 June 1906; 3rd *s* of Donald Macdonald and Annabella Mackenzie; *m* Jeannette Eileen Bickle; one *s*. *Educ:* Dingwall Academy; Aberdeen Univ.; Balliol Coll., Oxford. University Lecturer, Aberdeeen Univ. and University Coll., Exeter, 1934-41; Ministry of Supply and Ministry of Labour and National Service, 1941-43; Secretary (later General Manager), National Assoc. of Port Employers, 1943-55. *Publications:* Scotland's Shifting Population, 1770-1850, 1937; The State and the Trade Unions, 1960; The Age of Transition, 1967, etc. *Recreation:* golf. *Address:* University of Dundee. *Club:* Oxford and Cambridge University.

**MACDONALD, Air Vice-Marshal Donald Malcolm Thomas,** CB 1952; RAF retired; *b* 15 Aug. 1909; *s* of late D. P. Macdonald, Tormore, Isle of Skye; *m* 1938, Kathleen Mary de Vere, *d* of late J. T. Hunt, Oxford; one *s* four *d*. *Educ:* Westminster School. Joined Royal Air Force, 1930. Dir-Gen. of Personal Services, Air Min., 1957-58; Dir-Gen. of Manning, Air Min., 1958-61, retd 1961. Mem. Crofters Commn, 1962-65. *Address:* Tarland House, Nairn, Inverness-shire. *Club:* Highland (Inverness).

**McDONALD, (Edward) Lawson,** MA, MD Cantab; FRCP; Physician, and Physician to the Cardiac Department, London Hospital, since 1960, to National Heart Hospital, since 1961; Lecturer to the Institute of Cardiology, since 1961; Hon. Consultant Cardiologist, Canadian Red Cross Memorial Hospital, Taplow, since 1960; *b* 1918; *s* of Charles Seaver McDonald, Belfast, NI; *m* 1953, Ellen Greig, *o d* of James Macdonald Rattray, Boston, Mass; one *s*. *Educ:* Felsted Sch.; Clare Coll., Cambridge; Middlesex Hospital; Harvard Univ. House appointments Middlesex Hospital, 1942-43. Temp. Surgeon-Lt, RNVR, 1943-46; served War of 1939-45, in N Atlantic and Normandy Campaigns. RMO, Nat. Heart Hosp., 1946-47; Asst Registrar, Inst. of Cardiology, 1947-48; Med. Registrar, Middlesex Hosp., 1948-49; studied in Stockholm, 1949; Asst to Prof. of Medicine, Middlesex Hosp., 1949-52; Rockefeller Travelling Fellow in Medicine, 1952-53; Asst in Medicine, Med. Dept, Peter Bent Brigham Hosp., Boston, Mass. and Research Fellow in Medicine, Harvard Univ., 1952-53; Clinical and Research Asst, Dept of Cardiology, Middlesex Hosp., 1953-55; Asst Dir, Inst. of Cardiology and Hon. Asst Physician, Nat. Heart Hosp., 1955-61. Visiting Lecturer: Univ. of Toronto, Queen's Univ., Kingston, Ont; Univ. of Bombay; University of Barcelona, Eliseo Migoya Inst. of Cardiology, Bilbao, Spain; Istanbul Univ., Turkey; Univs of Chicago, Cincinnati and Kansas; Harvard Univ.; Mayo Foundation, USA; Univs of Belgrade, Ljubljana and Zagreb, Yugoslavia; Nat. Univ. of Cordoba, Argentine; Univ. of Chile, and Catholic Univ., Santiago; nat. Univ. of Colombia; Nat. Inst. of Cardiology, Mexico; Nat. Univ. of Mexico; University of San Marcos and University of Cayetano Heredia, Peru; Nat. Univ. of Venezuela. From 1961, has addressed numerous heart societies in Europe, Canada, USA, and South America; St Cyres Lecturer, 1966. Member: British Cardiac Soc.; Assoc. of Physicians of Great Britain and Ireland, and other societies; FACC; Corresp. Mem. or Hon. Mem. of various socs of Cardiology or Angiology in S America. Hon. Fellow, Turkish Med. Soc.; Mem., Italian Soc. of Cardiology. Editorial Bd, New Istanbul Contribution to Clinical Science. *Publications:* (ed) Pathogenesis and Treatment of Occlusive Arterial Disease, 1960; Medical and Surgical Cardiology, 1969; numerous contribs to learned jls; also papers and addresses. *Recreations:* ski-ing and sailing. *Address:* 9 Upper Wimpole Street, W1M 7TD. *T:* 01-935 7101; 9 Bentinck Mansions, Bentinck Street, W1. *T:* 01-935 0868; The Trippet, Old Bosham, near Chichester, Sussex. *T:* Bosham 2373. *Club:* Bath.

**MACDONALD, Maj.-Gen. Harry,** CB 1940; CIE 1946; DSO 1918; DL Inverness-shire, 1948; Hon. Sheriff Substitute, Inverness, Moray, Nairn and Ross and Cromarty, 1949; *b* 3 May 1886; *s* of late John Macdonald, Redcliff, Portree, Isle of Skye, and late Anne Marjory Walker; *m* 1934, Sheila Mairi Adelaide, *d* of late Brig.-Gen. Sir Walter C. Ross, KBE, Cromarty; three *d*. *Educ:* Fettes Coll., Edinburgh; RMC Sandhurst. Joined Indian Army, 1906; served European War, 1914-19 (despatches five times, Bt Major, DSO, Croix de Guerre avec palmes); graduated at Staff Coll., Camberley, 1919; Gen. Staff, War Office, 1920-24; Major, 1921; Bt Lt-Col, 1929; Lt-Col, 1932; Col 1935; Maj.-Gen., 1940; Gen. Staff Officer, Western Command, India, 1928-31; Commandant, Probyn's Horse (5th KEO Lancers) Indian Army, 1933-35; Gen. Staff Officer, 1st Grade, Lahore District, 1935-36; commanded 1st (Risalpur) Cavalry Bde, India, 1936-39; Maj.-Gen. Cavalry, India, 1939-40; Comd, Meerut District, India, 1940-43; retd, 1943; re-employed as Chief Civil Liaison Officer and Dep. Dir of Recruiting, N Area, India, 1943-46; retired, 1946. *Recreations:* shooting, fishing, polo. *Address:* Redcliff, Portree, Isle of Skye. *T:* Portree 14. *Club:* Cavalry.

**MACDONALD, Sir Herbert (George deLorme),** KBE 1967 (OBE 1948); JP (Jamaica); retired government officer (Jamaica); company director; sportsman; President Organising Committee, IX Central American and Caribbean Games, 1962, and 8th British Empire and Commonwealth Games, 1966 (compiled and edited history); Chairman, National Sports Ltd (a Government body owning and operating National Stadium and Sports Centre), 1960-67, now President (specially created post); Director: Prospect Beach Ltd; Macdonald Ltd; *b* Kingston, 23 May 1902; *s* of late Ronald Macdonald, JP, planter, and late Louise (*née* Alexander). *Educ:* Wolmer's Boys' Sch., Jamaica; Northeast High Sch., Philadelphia, USA. Clerical and planting activities, 1919-43. Published Sportsman Magazine (with late Sir Arthur Thelwell). Accompanied Jamaica's team to World Olympics, London, 1948, and (as Manager) to Helsinki, 1952, Melbourne, 1956; Chef de Mission, WI Olympic Team to Rome, 1960; Deleg., Tokyo, 1964. Chief Liaison Officer, BWI Central Lab. Org. (USA), 1943-55; Pres., Jamaica Olympic Assoc., 1940-44 and 1956-58; Pres., WI Olympic Assoc. (from inception), 1958-61 (when Polit. Fedn was broken up). Past Pres. etc, various Jamaican sporting assocs and boards; Mem. Exec. Cttee Pan American Sports Organisation which controls Pan American Games; Exec. Sec., Jamaica Tercentenary Celebrations Cttee, 1955. Mem. Bd of Trustees, Wolmer's Sch. Diploma of Merit, 1966 Internat. Olympic Cttee, 1968. Is an Anglican. *Recreations:* all sports; stamp collecting (athletic stamps); represented Jamaica in football and tennis *v* foreign teams, 1925-32. *Address:* (home) 206 Mountain View Avenue, Kingston 6, Jamaica. *T:* 78213. *Clubs:* (Life Mem., past Hon. Sec.) Kingston Cricket (Kingston, Jamaica); Constant Spring Golf.

**MacDONALD, Ian,** MC 1945; QC (Scot.) 1964; *b* 26 May 1921; *s* of H. J. and J. M. MacDonald; *m* 1946, Elizabeth de Vessey Lawson; one *s* one *d*. *Educ:* Colston's Sch., Bristol; Edinburgh Univ. (MA, LLB). Served 1939-46: Royal Tank Regt (Capt.). TA Lothians and Border Horse, later Queen's Own Lowland Yeomanry, 1948-62. Called to Bar, 1952. *Recreation:* sport. *Address:* 16 Mayfield Terrace, Edinburgh. *T:* 031-667 5542. *Club:* Caledonian United Service and Northern (Edinburgh).

**MACDONALD, Ian Wilson,** MA; DLitt; CA; Chairman, Lloyds and Scottish Ltd; Deputy Chairman National and Commercial Banking Group Ltd; Director: Lloyds Bank Ltd; Royal Bank of Scotland Ltd (formerly Chairman, and Chairman National Commercial Bank of Scotland Ltd); Member, National Research Development Corporation; *b* Old Cumnock, Ayrshire, 28 May 1907; *s* of late Rev. Alexander B. Macdonald, BD, PhD, Dron, Perthshire, and late Dr Mary B. W. Macdonald; *m* 1933, Helen Nicolson, MA; one *s* two *d*. *Educ:* Perth Academy; Edinburgh Academy; Glasgow Univ. Prof. of Accountancy, Univ. of Glasgow, 1938-50. Partner in Kerr Macleod and Macfarlan, CA, Glasgow, 1933-53. Mem. Cttee of Investigation into Port Transport Industry, 1945; Member Court of Inquiry into Omnibus Industry, 1946, Shipbuilding Industry, 1947, Railwaymen's Wages and Hours of Work, 1947; Arbitrator, Nigerian Railways Labour dispute, 1948; Mem. Gen. Claims Tribunal, 1943-58. Mem. Cttee of Inquiry: Fishing Industry, 1957-60; Ports and Harbours, 1961-62. Member: S Scotland Electricity Board, 1956-61; National Ports Council, 1963-67. *Recreations:* shooting, fishing. *Address:* 24 Hermitage Drive, Edinburgh. *Clubs:* Caledonian; New (Edinburgh).

**MACDONALD, Ishbel A.;** *see* Peterkin, I. A.

**McDONALD, Iverach;** Associate Editor, The Times, since Jan. 1967; Director, The Times Ltd, since 1968; *b* 23 Oct. 1908; *s* of Benjamin McDonald, Strathcool, Caithness, and Janet Seel; *m* 1935, Gwendoline, *o d* of Capt. Thomas R. Brown; one *s* one *d*. *Educ:* Leeds Gram. Sch.; on Continent (language study). Asst Editor, Yorkshire Post, 1933; sub-editor, The Times, 1935; correspondent in Berlin, 1937; diplomatic correspondent 1938; Asst Editor, 1948; Foreign Editor, 1952; Managing Editor, 1965. War of 1939-45: Capt., Gen. Staff, 1939-40; travelled extensively in Soviet Union, Far East and America; reported all allied conferences after the war, including San Francisco, 1945, Paris, 1946 and 1947, Moscow, 1947, Colombo, 1950, and Bermuda, 1953. *Address:* 64 Bryanston Court, W1. *T:* 01-262 5277. *Club:* Garrick.

**McDONALD, Sir James,** KBE 1967 (CBE 1956; OBE 1948); British Consul (Hon.), Portland, Oregon USA, since 1938; President, McDonald Dock Co.; Managing Partner: Macdon & Co.; Kermac Investment Co.; Director: Hawaiian Flour Mills Inc.; Western Transportation Co.; Waterway Terminals Co.; Chairman, Benjamin D. Dagwell Foundation; *b* 23 July 1899; *s* of late James McDonald, Renfrew, Scotland; *m* 1933, Anne, *d* of late Peter Kerr, Portland, Ore, USA; one *s* two *d*. *Educ:* Allen Glen's Sch., Glasgow. Lt, RFC, 1917-19. Partner McDonald Gattie & Co., 1927-67; Pres., Norpac Shipping Co., 1940-67. *Recreations:* walking, farming. *Address:* 11626 SW Military Lane, Portland, Ore, USA. *T:* 636-4775; Inchinnan Farm, Rt 1, Box 1405, Wilsonville, Ore, USA. *T:* 625-6914. *Clubs:* Boodle's, Arlington, University, Racquet (Portland, Ore.).

**MacDONALD, Mrs J. G.;** *see* Sinclair, I. S.

**MACDONALD, Prof. James Alexander,** BSc (Agric.), PhD (Edinburgh), DSc (St Andrews); Professor of Botany, University of St Andrews, since 1961; *b* 17 June 1908; *s* of late James Alexander and Jessie Mary Macdonald; *m* 1935, Constance Mary Simmie; one *d*. *Educ:* Inverness Royal Academy; Edinburgh Univ. Asst Lecturer in Botany, East of Scot. Coll. of Agriculture, 1932-35; St Andrews University: Lecturer in Botany, 1935-52; Senior Lecturer, 1952-60; Dean, Faculty of Science, 1967-69. Pres., Botanical Soc. of Edinburgh, 1955-57; FRSE 1940 (Council Mem., 1956-59); Vice-Pres. RSE, 1961-64. *Publications:* Introduction to Mycology, 1951; scientific papers in Trans Brit. Mycol. Soc., Annals Applied Biol., Mycologia, Proc. and Trans Royal Soc. Edinburgh. *Recreations:* golf, fishing, philately. *Address:* The Cottage, Boarhills, St Andrews, Fife. *T:* Boarhills 272. *Club:* Royal & Ancient (St Andrews).

**MACDONALD, John B(arfoot),** DDS, MS, PhD; Executive Director, Committee of Presidents, Universities of Ontario, since 1968; Professor of Higher Education, University of Toronto, since 1968; *b* 23 Feb. 1918; *s* of Arthur A. Macdonald and Gladys L. Barfoot; *m*; two *s* one *d*; *m* 1967, Liba Kucera; two *d*. *Educ:* Univ. of Toronto, University of Illinois, Columbia Univ. DDS (with hons) Toronto, 1942; MS (Bact) Ill, 1948; PhD (Bact) Columbia, 1953. Lectr, Prev. Dentistry, University of Toronto, and private practice, 1942-44. Canadian Dental Corps, 1944-46 (Capt.) Instr, Bacteriol, University of Toronto, and private practice, 1946-47; Res. Asst, Univ. of Illinois, 1947-48; Kellogg Fellow and Canadian Dental Assoc. Res. Student, Columbia Univ., 1948-49; University of Toronto: Asst Prof. of Bacteriol., 1949-53; Assoc. Prof. of Bacteriol., 1953-56; Chm., Div. of Dental Res., 1953-56; Prof. of Bacteriol., 1956; Cons. in Dental Educn, University of BC, 1955-56; Dir, Forsyth Dental Infirmary, 1956-62 (Cons. in Bacteriol., 1962); Prof. of Microbiol., Harvard Sch., of dental Med., 1956-62 (Dir of Postdoctoral Studies, 1960-62); President, Univ. of British Columbia, 1962-67. Consultant: Dental Med. Section of Corporate Research Div. of Colgate-Palmolive Co., 1958-62; Donwood Foundn, Toronto, 1967-;

Science Council of Canada, 1967-69; Addiction Research Foundn of Ontario, 1968-. Chm., Commn on Pharmaceutical Services of the Canadian Pharmaceutical Assoc., 1967-; Consultant, Nat. Inst. of Health, 1968-; Mem., Dental Study Sect., Nat. Inst. of Health, 1961-65; Councillor-at-Large, Internat. Assoc. for Dental Research, 1963-, Pres. 1968-69. Fellow, Mem. or Chm. of numerous assocs. etc, both Canadian and international. FACD 1955; Hon. FICD 1965. Hon. AM, Harvard Univ., 1956; Hon. LLD: Univ. of Manitoba, 1962; Simon Fraser Univ., 1965; Hon DSc Univ. of British Columbia, 1967. *Publications:* Dental Education in British Columbia, 1961; Higher Education in British Columbia and a Plan for the Future, 1962, etc.; numerous contribs to learned jls. *Recreations:* golf, tennis. *Address:* Committee of Presidents, 230 Bloor Street West, Toronto, Canada. *T:* 920-6865. *Clubs:* University, University of BC Faculty, Vancouver (Vancouver); Faculty, University of Toronto (Toronto).

**MACDONALD, Air Commodore John Charles,** CB 1964; CBE 1957; DFC 1940 (Bar 1942); AFC 1941; Aviation Consultant; *b* 25 Dec. 1910; *s* of late Robert Macdonald; *m* 1952, Gladys Joan, *d* of John Hine, Beaminster, Dorset; two *s*. *Educ:* Berkhamsted Sch.; RAF Cadet Coll., Cranwell. Commissioned RAF, 1930. Served War of 1939-45 in Bomber Command; POW Stalag Luft III, 1942-45, escaped April 1945. Commanded RAF Akrotiri during Suez campaign; UK National Military Representative, SHAPE, 1959-61; Comdr RAF East Africa, 1961-64; Min. of Defence, 1964; retd, 1964. Chevalier, Légion d'Honneur, 1958; Croix de Guerre, 1958. *Recreations:* golf, sailing, shooting. *Address:* 35 Hare Hill Close, Pyrford, Surrey. *T:* Byfleet 42932. *Clubs:* Royal Automobile, Hunts.

**MACDONALD, Maj.-Gen. (retd) John Frederick Matheson,** CB 1959; DSO 1951; OBE 1945; *b* 7 Nov. 1907; *e s* of late Major Eric William Macdonald, Ringmer, Sussex; *m* 1st, 1933, Joan Drayson (*d* 1961), *d* of late Norval H. Prentis, East Bergholt, Suffolk; one *s*; 2nd, 1964, Kathleen Flora, *widow* of Lieut-Col D. W. Mac L. Prinsep, Skinner's Horse. *Educ:* Marlborough Coll.; Royal Military Coll., Sandhurst. 2nd Lt KOSB 1927; Lt (Adjt) 1 KOSB 1935-37; Lt-Col 1 KOSB, 1944; Lt-Col (GSO1) HQ 3 Brit. Inf. Div., 1944-45, France, Belgium, Germany. Lt-Col (AQMG) West Africa Comd, 1948-49; Lt-Col 1 KOSB, Hong Kong and Korea, 1949-51; Lt-Col 1949; Brig. 28 British Commonwealth Brigade, Korea, 1951-52; Brig. 31 Lorried Inf. Brigade, Germany, 1952-54; Imperial Defence Coll., 1955; Brig. 1956; Maj.-Gen., Chief of Staff Scottish Command, 1957-1958; Maj.-Gen. 1957; GOC 52 (Lowland) Division/District, 1958-61; retired, 1961. Hon. Col 4/5 Bn KOSB, TA, 1962-67. County Comr, Boy Scouts, Suffolk, 1962-67. Chevalier, Order of Leopold, with Palm, and Croix de Guerre, 1940, with Palm, 1947 (Belgium); Officer, Legion of Merit, USA, 1953. *Address:* The Grange, Elmswell, Bury St Edmunds, Suffolk. *T:* Elmswell 270. *Club:* Army and Navy.

**McDONALD, Hon. Sir John (Gladstone Black),** Kt 1957; retired from Parliament of Victoria, Australia; *b* 6 Dec. 1898; *s* of Donald McDonald, Falkirk, Scotland; *m* 1932, Mary Cosser Trotter; one *s* two *d*. *Educ:* Camelon, Scotland. MLA for Shepparton, Victoria, 1936-55. Minister for Water Supply and Minister for Electricity, 1943-45; Minister for Lands etc., 1947-48; Leader of the Opposition, 1945-47; Premier and Treasurer, 1950-52. Served in 37th Bn AIF, in France, 1916-18. Chm. of Directors, Shepparton Preserving Co.; Director: Goulburn and Murray Television Co.; Farmers Co-operative Fertilisers Euroa Ltd. *Address:* P.O. Box 101 Shepparton, Vic., Australia. *T:* 31 Shepparton East.

**McDONALD, Lawson;** *see* McDonald, E. L.

**MacDONALD, Rt. Hon. Malcolm John,** OM 1969; PC 1935; Special Representative of HM Government in Africa, 1966-69; Chancellor of the University of Durham, since 1970; *b* Lossiemouth, Morayshire, 1901; *s* of late J. Ramsay and Margaret MacDonald; *m* 1946, Mrs Audrey Fellowes Rowley; one *d*. *Educ:* Bedales Sch., Petersfield; Queen's Coll., Oxford, MA. Mem. of LCC, 1927-30. Contested (Lab) Bassetlaw Div., 1923, 1924; MP (Lab) Bassetlaw Div. of Notts, 1929-31 (National Labour), 1931-35; MP (National Government) Ross and Cromarty, 1936-45; Parliamentary Under-Sec., Dominions Office, 1931-35; Sec. of State for Dominion Affairs, 1935-38 and 1938-39; Sec. of State for Colonies, 1935 and 1938-40; Minister of Health, 1940-41; United Kingdom High Comr in Canada, 1941-46; Gov.-Gen. of the Malayan Union and Singapore, May-July 1946; Gov.-Gen. of Malaya, Singapore and British Borneo, 1946-48; Special Ambassador at inauguration of Indonesian Republic, 1949; Comr-Gen. for the UK in South-East Asia, 1948-55; High Commissioner for the UK in India, 1955-60. Governor and C-in-C, Kenya, 1963; Governor-Gen. Kenya, 1963-64; British High Comr in Kenya, 1964-65; British Special Representative in East and Central Africa, 1963-66; Special Envoy to Sudan, Nov. 1967, and to Somalia, Dec. 1967. Leader of British Delegation and Co-Chm., International Conference on Laos, 1961-62. Rhodes Trustee, 1948-57; Chancellor of the University of Malaya, 1949-61; Visitor, University Coll., Kenya, 1963-64; UK Representative on South-East Asia Defence Treaty Council, 1955. Hon. Fellow, Queen's Coll., Oxford. Doctor of Laws and Doctor of Letters, *hc*: various North American Univs and Univs of Hanoi, Hong Kong, Singapore and Malaya. Freeman of City of Singapore, 1955; Freeman, Burgh of Lossiemouth, 1969. *Publications:* Down North, 1945; The Birds of Brewery Creek, 1947; Borneo People, 1956; Angkor, 1958; Birds in my Indian Garden, 1961; Birds in the Sun, 1962; Treasure of Kenya, 1965; People and Places, 1969. *Recreations:* ornithology, collecting, ski-ing. *Address:* Raspit Hill, Ivy Hatch, Sevenoaks, Kent. *Clubs:* Brooks's; Royal Island (Singapore).

**MACDONALD, Mrs Margaret;** *see* Kidd, Margaret Henderson.

**MACDONALD, Patrick Donald,** CMG 1953; CVO 1963; Chairman, Public and Police Service Commissions, Fiji, since 1966; *b* 21 July 1909; *s* of late Major E. W. Macdonald and Amy Beatrice Cavalier; *m* 1937, Delia Edith, 5th *d* of Capt. R. W. Travers, RN (retired); one *s* twin *d*. *Educ:* Marlborough Coll.; St John's Coll., Cambridge. BA 1931. Cadet officer, Gilbert and Ellice Islands Colony, 1932; Administrative Officer, 1936; Sec. to Government, 1935-36 and 1938-39; Asst Sec., Western Pacific High Commission, 1940-42; Asst Colonial Sec., Trinidad and Tobago, 1942-45. Fiji: Administrative Officer, Grade II, 1946, Grade I, 1947; Asst Colonial Sec., 1946-49; Colonial Secretary, Governor's Deputy and Acting Governor: Leeward Islands, 1950-57; Colonial Sec. and Acting Governor, Fiji, 1957-66. *Recreations:* swimming and deep-sea fishing. *Address:* The Public Service Commission, PO Box 2035, Suva, Fiji.

**MACDONALD, Sir Peter (George),** Kt 1963; DL; Hon. Life President, United Biscuits Ltd (Chairman, 1948-67) and McVitie & Price Ltd (Chairman, 1947-64); Director: Guardian Assurance Co. Ltd, London; Caledonian Insurance Co. and other companies; *b* 20 Feb. 1898; *s* of William Macdonald, Darnaway, Forres, and Annie Cameron; *m* 1929, Rachel Irene, *d* of Rev. Dr Robert Forgan; one *s* two *d*. *Educ:* Forres Academy; Edinburgh Univ. Served European War, 1914-18, with Scottish Horse, Black Watch, RGA, and Lovat Scouts. Served with Home Guard, 1940-45; Regional Deferment Officer, Bd of Trade, Edinburgh and SE Scotland; Mem., Edinburgh and dist local Emergency Reconstruction Panel (chm. Food Section); Staff Officer on Scottish Regional Comr's Staff: Mem. London Council, Inst. of Directors (formerly Chm., Scottish Br.); WS 1927. JP Edinburgh, 1935. DL Edinburgh, 1966. *Recreations:* fishing, shooting, golf. *Address:* 18 Hermitage Drive, Edinburgh. *T:* 031-447 1256. *Clubs:* Caledonian, Flyfishers'; Conservative (Edinburgh).

**MacDONALD, Robert,** CBE 1965; Sheriff-Substitute of Dumfries and Galloway at Dumfries, 1965-70; *s* of John Robert MacDonald and Isabella Sinclair; *m* 1948, Elizabeth Grant, JP. *Educ:* Wick High Sch.; Edinburgh Univ. Grad. Law with dist., Edinburgh 1930. Procurator-Fiscal, Glasgow, 1951-65; Lectr in Law, Glasgow Univ., 1946-52; Examiner in Law to Law Soc. of Scotland, 1960-65; Examiner in Medical Jurisprudence, Law Faculty, Glasgow Univ. *Address:* Maryfield, Auldgirth, Dumfries. *T:* Auldgirth 225. *Clubs:* Royal Over-Seas League; Royal Scottish Automobile, Glasgow University College (Glasgow).

**McDONALD, Robert Howat,** MC 1944; QC (Scotland) 1957; Sheriff of Ayr and Bute since 1966; *b* 15 May 1916; *s* of Robert Glassford McDonald, and Roberta May Howat, Paisley, Renfrewshire; *m* 1949, Barbara Mackenzie, *d* of John Mackenzie, Badcaul, Ross-shire; no *c*. *Educ:* John Neilson Institution, Paisley. MA (Glasgow) 1935; LLB (Glasgow) 1937; admitted Faculty of Advocates, 1946. Served with KOSB, 1939-46. Mem., Criminal Injuries Compensation Board, 1964-; Chm., Mental Welfare Commission for Scotland, 1965-; Vice-Chm., Gen. Nursing Council for Scotland, 1963-. *Recreations:* golf, fishing. *Address:* 5 Doune Terrace, Edinburgh EH3 6EA. *T:* 031-225 3586. *Club:* Caledonian (London).

**MACDONALD, Maj.-Gen. Ronald Clarence,** CB 1965; DSO 1944 and Bar, 1945; OBE 1953; Director, Griffin Farms Ltd, Wilts; *b* 1 Aug. 1911; 2nd *s* of late Col C. R. Macdonald, CMG; *m* 1939, Jessie Ross Anderson; one *s* one *d*. *Educ:* Rugby; RMC, Sandhurst. Royal Warwicks Regt: Commissioned, 1931; Comdr 2nd Bn, 1945-46; Comdr 1st Bn, 1953-55; Bn Comdr, France, Germany Campaign, 1944-45; Mil. Asst to CIGS, 1946-49; GSO1, HQ, West Africa Comd, 1950-53; Col Gen. Staff, SHAPE, 1955-56; Comdr 10th Inf. Bde Gp, 1956-59; DDI, War Office, 1959-60; Chief of Staff, HQ Middle East Comd, 1960-62; Dep. Chief of Staff, Headquarters, Allied Land Forces, Central Europe, 1962-65; retired, 1965. Col Royal Warwicks Fusiliers, 1963-68; Dep. Col (Warwicks), The Royal Regt of Fusiliers, 1968-. *Recreation:* golf. *Address:* Grassmead, Beanacre, near Melksham, Wilts. *Club:* Army and Navy.

**MACDONALD, Air Vice-Marshal Somerled Douglas,** CB 1951; CBE 1945; DFC 1920; retired; *b* 1899; *s* of late Dr D. Macdonald, of Glen Urquhart, Inverness-shire; *m* 1949, Hon. Margaret Anne, *d* of 2nd Baron Trent, KBE. *Educ:* George Watson's Coll., Edinburgh. Served European War, 1914-19: joined RFC, 1917, transferred to RAF, 1918; served in Mesopotamia and Persia; served in Iraq and ME (Egypt), 1924-27, and 1936-37; attached HQ Sudan Defence Force, 1937-39; served War of 1939-45: commanded 3 Wing (Sudan), 263 Wing (Palestine), 213 Wing (Lebanon), 217 Wing (Persia), and Bomber detachment in Iraq during rebellion, 1941; SASO No. 9 (Fighter) Group, Fighter Comd, 1944; SASO No. 12 (Fighter) Group, 1945; AOC No. 11 (Fighter) Group, 1946-48; Assistant Chief of Air Staff (Training), 1948; Inspector-Gen. of Air Training, Western Union, 1950. Head of Air Training Advisory Group, NATO, 1952-54, retired. *Address:* Ballaig House, by Crieff, Perthshire. *Clubs:* White's, Caledonian, Royal Air Force.

**MACDONALD, Rt. Rev. Thomas Brian;** Coadjutor Bishop of Perth, Western Australia, since 1964; *b* 25 Jan. 1911; *s* of Thomas Joseph Macdonald, MD, and Alice Daisy Macdonald; *m* 1936, Audrey May Collins; three *d*. *Educ:* Mercers' Sch., Holborn, EC. Licentiate of Theology 1932, Aust. Coll. of Theol. Deacon 1934, priest 1935, Diocese of Ballarat, Vic.; Deacon in charge of All Saints, Ballarat, 1934; Priest in charge of Landsborough, 1935; Rector of Williams, Dio. of Bunbury, 1935-39; Rector of Manjimup, WA, 1939-40. Chaplain, Australian Imperial Forces, 1941-44 (despatches). Rector of Christ Church, Claremont, Dio. of Perth, 1944-50; Chaplain of Collegiate Sch. of St Peter, Adelaide, S Australia, 1950-58; Dean of Perth, Western Australia, 1959-61; Archdeacon of Perth, 1961-63. Administrator, Diocese of Perth during 1963 and 1969. *Recreations:* golf, tennis. *Address:* 10 King's Park Avenue, Crawley, WA6009, Australia. *T:* 21.7541. *Clubs:* Naval, Military and Air Force of WA, Weld (Perth).

**MACDONALD, Air Vice-Marshal Thomas Conchar,** CB 1962; AFC 1942; MD (retired); *b* 6 Aug. 1909; *s* of John Macdonald, MA, BSc, and Mary Jane Conchar; *m* 1937, Katharine Cairns Frew. *Educ:* Hermitage Sch.; Glasgow High Sch.; University of Glasgow; MB, ChB 1932; MD 1940; DPH (London) 1949. Joined RAF Medical Br., 1933; served in Iraq, Egypt and England, before 1939. War service included RAF Inst. of Aviation Med., Farnborough, as Asst to Consultant in Applied Physiology, 1939-41; USA and Canada, 1941-42; DPMO (Flying) Fighter Command, 1942-45; Far East, 1945-46 (despatches, AFC). Post-war appts include: PMO 2nd TAF (Germany), 1951-53; Dir of Hygiene and Research, Air Min., 1953-56 (Chm. Aero-Medical Panel of Advisory Gp for Research and Develt (AGARD) of NATO); PMO, Bomber Command, 1956-58; PMO Middle East Air Force, 1958-61; PMO Technical Training Command, RAF, 1961-66. Air Vice-Marshal, 1961. QHP 1961-66; CStJ 1961. *Publications:* contributions to various med. jls. *Recreations:* sailing, fishing. *Address:* Wakeners Wood, Midhurst Road, Haslemere, Surrey. *T:* Haslemere 3685. *Club:* Royal Air Force.

**MACDONALD, Hon. Sir Thomas (Lachlan),** KCMG 1963; High Commissioner for New Zealand in London, 1961-68; New Zealand Ambassador to the European Economic Community, 1961-67; New Zealand Ambassador to Ireland, 1966-68; *b* 14 Dec. 1898; *s* of Thomas Forsaith and Margaret Ann Macdonald; *m* 1925, Elsie Ann Stuart; one *d*. *Educ:* South Sch. and Southland Boys' High

Sch., Invercargill, NZ. Union Steamship Co. of New Zealand Ltd, 1915-18. Served NZ Mounted Rifles, Egypt and Palestine, 1918-19. Farming in New Zealand, 1919-37 and 1945-55. MP for Mataura, NZ, 1938-46; MP for Wallace, NZ, 1946-57. Min. of Defence, 1949-57, and of External Affairs, 1954-57. Served overseas, North Africa, 2nd NZEF, 1940-43. *Recreations:* tramping, photography, swimming, gardening. *Address:* 10 Kotare Street, Waikanae, New Zealand.

**McDONALD, Hon. Sir William (John Farquhar),** Kt 1958; Speaker, Legislative Assembly, State of Victoria, Australia, 1955-67; MP, electorate of Dundas, 1947-52, 1955-70; *b* 3 Oct. 1911; *s* of John Nicholson McDonald and Sarah McDonald (*née* McInnes); *m* 1935, Evelyn Margaret Koch; two *d*. *Educ:* Scotch Coll., Adelaide, South Australia. Served AIF, 1939-45, Capt. Councillor, Shire of Kowree, 1946-61. Minister of Lands, Soldier Settlement, and for Conservation, 1967-70. Trustee, Shrine of Remembrance, 1955-70. Pres., Poll Shorthorn Soc. of Aust.; Trustee, Royal Agricultural Soc. of Victoria, 1968- (Mem. Exec. Council, 1967-70). *Address:* Brippick, Neuarpurr, Vic., Australia. *T:* Neuarpurr 5. *Clubs:* Hamilton (Hamilton, Victoria); Australian, Naval and Military (Melbourne).

**MACDONALD, Air Chief Marshal Sir William (Laurence Mary),** GCB 1965 (KCB 1959; CB 1956); CBE 1946; DFC 1940; *b* 10 Aug. 1908; *s* of William Stephen Macdonald, Co. Cork; *m* 1939, Diana (*d* 1964), *d* of late Nicholas Challacombe; one *s* one *d*. *Educ:* Castleknock Coll., Eire. Joined RAF 1929; Group Capt., 1942; Air Commodore, 1944; Air Vice-Marshal, 1954; Air Marshal, 1960; Air Chief Marshal, 1963. Served War of 1939-45, France, Belgium, Holland, Germany (despatches twice, DFC, CBE). Comdt, Central Flying Sch., 1946-47; Exchange Officer with USAF, USA, 1948-50; Dep. Dir of Plans (Jt Planning), Air Min., 1952; AOC, RAF, Singapore, 1952-54; Asst Chief of Air Staff (Intelligence), 1954-58; Comdr-in-Chief, Middle East, Air Force, 1958-62, and Administrator of the Sovereign Base Areas of Akrotiri and Dhekilia, Cyprus, 1960-62; Air Sec., Ministry of Defence (formerly Air Ministry), 1962-66. Air ADC to the Queen, 1965-66. Governor, Oratory Sch. Vice-Pres., RAF Assoc. Chevalier, Legion of Honour; Croix de Guerre; Star of Jordan 1st Class. *Address:* Quarry House, Yateley, Hants. *T:* 3283. *Club:* East India and Sports.

**MACDONALD-BUCHANAN, Major Sir Reginald (Narcissus),** KCVO 1964 (CVO 1952); MBE 1942; MC 1917; *b* May 1898; *m* 1922, Hon. Catherine Buchanan, *o c* of 1st Baron Woolavington, GCVO; two *s* two *d*. Joined Scots Guards from RMC, Sandhurst, 1916. Served European War (MC); retired, 1926. Chairman: James Buchanan & Co. Ltd; W. P. Lowrie & Co. Ltd, 1939-70; Director: Buchanan-Dewar Ltd, 1939-69; Distillers Co. Ltd, 1930-69. Mem. Council, King Edward VII's Hosp. for Officers (Chm., House and Finance Cttee 1947-69, Vice-Pres. and Treasurer, 1969). Mem. Racecourse Betting Control Bd, 1949-59; Steward of Jockey Club, 1950-51-52; Pres. Hunter's Improvement and Nat. Light Horse Breeding Soc., 1950-51, 1951-52, 1965-66. Master, Worshipful Co. of Distillers, 1952. DL Northamptonshire; High Sheriff, Northamptonshire, 1939; Pres. Northamptonshire County Agricultural Soc., 1951. Joint Master, Pytchley Hounds, 1934-39 and 1946-49; Rejoined Scots Guards, 1939; ADC to Field-Marshal Sir John Dill, 1940-43; served BEF, France, 1940; War Office, 1940-41; British Joint Staff Mission, Washington, 1941-43 (MBE); France and Belgium, 1944-45 when demobilised (despatches, US Bronze Star Medal). *Address:* Cottesbrooke Hall, Northampton. *T:* Creaton 232; 49 Grosvenor Square, W1. *T:* 01-629 4237; Scatwell, Ross-shire. *T:* Scatwell 244; Egerton House, Newmarket. *T:* Newmarket 2151. *Clubs:* Turf, Guards; Royal Yacht Squadron (Cowes); Muthaiga (Nairobi).

**McDONALD SCOTT, Mrs Michael;** *see* Lavin, Mary.

**MACDONALD-SMITH, Sydney,** CMG 1956; Assistant Manager, Arthur Guinness Son & Co. (Park Royal) Ltd; *b* 9 July 1908; *s* of late John Alfred Macdonald-Smith, MB, ChB, FRCSE; *m* 1st, 1935, Joyce (*d* 1966), *d* of Austen Whetham, Bridport, Dorset; one *s* one *d*; 2nd, 1968, Winifred Mary Atkinson, JP, *widow* of Captain T. K. W. Atkinson, RN. *Educ:* Nottingham High Sch.; New Coll., Oxford. Entered Colonial Administrative Service, Nigeria, 1931; Controller of Imports, 1945; Director of Supplies, 1947; Under-Sec., Gold Coast, 1949; Permanent Sec. Ministry of Communications and Works, 1950; Chief Regional Officer, Northern Territories, 1954-57; retired Nov. 1957. *Recreation:* gardening. *Address:* Woodman's, Westbourne, Emsworth, Hants. *T:* Emsworth 2943.

**McDONAUGH, James,** CBE 1970 (OBE 1965); British Council Representative in Germany, since 1966; *b* 26 July 1912; *s* of late Edward McDonaugh and late Christina, *d* of William Bissell; *m* 1944, Mary-Eithnē Mitchell, *d* of James Vyvyan Mitchell; three *s* two *d*. *Educ:* Royal Grammar Sch., Worcester; St Edmund Hall, Oxford (Exhibitioner, MA). Asst Master, Ampleforth Coll., 1935-40; War Service, 1940-45; Lecturer, Graz and Innsbruck Univs, 1947-50; Asst Rep., British Council, Austria, 1950-54; Representative, Malta, 1954-58; Dep. Counsellor (Cultural), Bonn, 1958-59; Dep. Rep., Germany, 1958-61; Dir Specialist Tours Dept, 1961-65; Asst Controller, Education Div., 1965. *Address:* c/o The British Council, Cologne, Hahnenstrasse 6, W Germany.

**MacDONELL of Glengarry, Air Cdre Aeneas Ranald Donald,** CB 1964; DFC 1940; Hereditary 22nd Chief of Glengarry; *b* 15 Nov. 1913; *e s* of late Ranald MacDonell of Glengarry, CBE; *m* 1940, Diana Dorothy, *yr d* of late Richard Henry Keane, CBE; two *s* one *d*. *Educ:* Hurstpierpoint Coll.; Royal Air Force Coll., Cranwell. No. 54 Fighter Sqdn, 1934; Fleet Air Arm, 1935-37; Flying Instructor, 1938-39; Air Ministry, 1939-40; No. 64 Fighter Sqdn, 1940-41; POW, 1941-45; Ministry of Defence, 1946-47; HQ Flying Training Command, 1947-49; Chief Flying Instructor, RAF Coll., Cranwell, 1949-51; Ministry of Defence, 1952-54; Senior RAF Instructor, Joint Services Staff Coll., 1954-56; Air Attaché, Moscow, 1956-58; Dir of Management and Work Study, Ministry of Defence, Air Force Dept, 1960-64, retd. *Recreations:* ciné photography, flying, art, shooting. *Address:* Rockwood, Fairwarp, Uckfield, Sussex. *T:* Nutley 2301. *Clubs:* Royal Air Force; Puffins' (Edinburgh).

**McDONNELL,** family name of **Earl of Antrim.**

**McDONNELL, Denis Lane,** OBE 1945; **His Honour Judge McDonnell;** County Court Judge since 1967; *b* 2 March 1914; *o c* of late David McDonnell, LLD and Mary Nora (*née* Lane), Riversdale, Sundays Well, Cork and Fairy Hill, Monkstown, Co. Cork and *gs* of Denny Lane, poet and Young Irelander; *m* 1940, Florence Nina (Micky), *d* of late Lt-Col Hugh T. Ryan, DSO and Clare Emily (*née*

Conry), Castle View, Ballincollig, Co. Cork; three *d* (and one *s* one *d* decd). *Educ:* Christian Brothers' Coll., Cork; Ampleforth Coll.; Sidney Sussex Coll., Cambridge (MA). Served in RAFVR, Equipment and Admin. and Special Duties Branches, 1940-45 in UK and with No. 84 Gp in NW Europe (Wing Comdr). Called to Bar, Middle Temple, 1936; Bencher, 1965. Practised at Bar, 1938-40 and 1946-67. *Publications:* Kerr on Fraud and Mistake (7th edn, with J. G. Monroe), 1952; titles on Carriers and Civil Aviation in Encyclopædias of Forms and Precedents and Court Forms and Precedents; articles in British Tax Review. *Recreations:* family life, listening to music, golf. *Address:* Stanmore House, Silverdale Road, Burgess Hill, Sussex. *T:* Burgess Hill 2158. *Clubs:* Piltdown Golf, Rye Golf, Woking Golf, Royal Cinque Ports Golf.

**McDOUALL, John Crichton,** CMG 1966; HM Overseas Civil Service, retired; *b* 26 April 1912; *s* of late Rev. Crichton Willoughby McDouall; *m* 1946, Kathleen Glover Moir, *d* of late A. B. Moir, Taikoo, Hong Kong; one *s* two *d*. *Educ:* Monkton Combe Sch.; Jesus Coll., Cambridge; Birmingham Univ. Colonial Administrative Service, Hong Kong, 1934-39; served War of 1939-45, Hong Kong RNVR and POW; Brit. Mil. Administration, Hong Kong, 1945-46; Administrative Service, Hong Kong, 1946-52; Chief Social Welfare Officer, Fedn of Malaya, 1952-57; Sec. for Chinese Affairs, Hong Kong, 1957-67; retired, 1967. Coronation Medal, 1953. *Address:* The Old School, Souldern, Bicester, Oxfordshire. *T:* Fritwell 217.

**MACDOUGALL, Maj.-Gen. Alastair Ian,** CBE 1943; DSO 1919; MC; *s* of late Col James William Macdougall, Edinburgh; *b* 1888; *m* 1922, Constance, *d* of late S. St Barb Emmott, Havant, Hants; (one *s* died of wounds, 1945) one *d*. *Educ:* Wellington Coll.; RMC, Sandhurst. Served European War, 1914-19 (despatches, MC, DSO, Brevet Major, Brevet Lt-Col); commanded Royal Scots Greys, 1928-32; Comdr 6th (Midland) Cavalry Brigade TA 1932-34; Instructor (Class Y) Senior Officers' Sch., Sheerness, 1934; Gen. Staff, War Office, 1936-39; Area Comdr 1939; Maj.-Gen., Gen. Staff, 1940; DCGS 1940; District Comdr, 1940-44; ADC to the King, 1939-44; retired, 1944. Chm., Argyll TA Assoc., 1946-55. *Address:* Home Close, Beaulieu, Hants. *T:* 284. *Club:* Army and Navy.

**McDOUGALL, Archibald,** MA, BCL; Attorney at Law and pastoralist, USA; *b* Hobart, 5 Aug. 1903; 2nd *s* of late Emeritus Prof. Dugald Gordon McDougall and Helen Ione Atkinson; *m* 1932, Corinne Margaret Cunningham Collins, Mobile, Alabama, and Washington, DC, USA. *Educ:* Hutchins Sch., Hobart; University of Tasmania; Balliol Coll., Oxford; Columbia Univ., New York. BA Tasmania, and Rhodes Scholar, 1924; 1st Class Final Honour Sch. of Jurisprudence, 1926; Proxime Accessit Vinerian Law Scholarship, 1927; 2nd Class Examination for BCL 1927; Commonwealth Fund Fellowship, 1927-29; US Senate Legislative Counsel's Office, Washington, DC 1928; Harmsworth Law Scholarship, 1929; Lecturer in Law, Victoria Univ. of Manchester, 1931-35; called to Bar, Middle Temple, 1932; Mem. of Northern Circuit; practised in Chancery Div. of High Court and in Chancery of County Palatine of Lancaster, 1932-35; Examiner in Law, London Univ., 1934-35; 1936-40 Legal Adviser to Iraqi Ministry for Foreign Affairs, Baghdad, and Prof. of Int. Law at Iraqi Law Sch.; Delegate of Iraq at 17th Assembly of League of Nations, 1936; 1940 travelled extensively through India, Burma, Malaya, NEI, and Australia; Counsel, British Purchasing Commission, New York, 1940-41; Head, Non-Ferrous Metals Div., British Raw Materials Mission, Washington, DC, and UK Staff of Combined Raw Materials Board, 1941-43; Combined Production and Resources Board (UK Staff), Washington, DC, 1944-45; Head of UK Economic Group, US Dept of Commerce and British Embassy, Washington, DC, to Aug. 1946; Legal Counsellor, British Embassy, Cairo, 1946-49; Asst Legal Adviser, Foreign Office, 1949-50. Dep. Comr of Forfeited and Delinquent Lands, 1964-. Pres., Berkeley County Bar Assoc., 1964-65. *Publications:* Modern Conveyancing, 1936; and articles in British Year book of International Law. *Recreation:* motoring. *Address:* Oban Hall, Gerrardstown, West Virginia 25420, USA. *T:* Area Code 304, 229-5400.

**MacDOUGALL of MacDougall, Madam; (Coline Helen Elizabeth);** 30th Chief of Clan MacDougall, 1953; *b* 17 Aug. 1904; *e d* of Col Alexander J. MacDougall of MacDougall, 29th Chief, and Mrs Coline Edith MacDougall of MacDougall; *m* 1949, Leslie Grahame-Thomson (*see under* MacDougall, Leslie Grahame); resumed surname of MacDougall of MacDougall on succession to Chiefship, 1953. *Educ:* St James's, West Malvern. Served WRNS (Second Officer), 1941-46. *Address:* Dunollie Castle, Oban, Argyll. *T:* Oban 2012.

**MacDOUGALL, Brig. David Mercer,** CMG 1946; MA; *b* 1904. *Educ:* St Andrews Univ. Cadet Hong Kong Administrative Service, 1928; seconded to Colonial Office as asst principal, Feb. 1937-March 1939; seconded Hong Kong Dept of Information and Sec. Far Eastern Bureau of British Ministry of Information, Oct. 1939; Colonial Office, 1942; British Embassy, Washington, DC, 1943; Dir British Political Warfare Mission, San Francisco, Dec. 1943; Colonial Office, 1944; Brig. Chief Civil Affairs Officer, Hong Kong, 1945; Colonial Sec., Hong Kong, 1946-49; retired, 1949; Order of the Brilliant Star (China), 1946. *Address:* c/o The Crown Agents, 4 Millbank, SW1.

**MacDOUGALL, Sir Donald;** *see* MacDougall, Sir G. D. A.

**MacDOUGALL, Sir (George) Donald (Alastair),** Kt 1953; CBE 1945 (OBE 1942); FBA 1966; Head of Government Economic Service, and Chief Economic Adviser to the Treasury, since 1969; *b* 26 Oct. 1912; *s* of late Daniel Douglas MacDougall, Glasgow, and late Beatrice Amy Miller; *m* 1937, Bridget Christabel Bartrum; one *s* one *d*. *Educ:* Kelvinside Acad., Glasgow; Shrewsbury Sch.; Balliol Coll., Oxford. George Webb Medley Junior (1934) and Senior (1935) Scholarships in Political Economy; Asst Lecturer (later Lecturer) in Economics, University of Leeds, 1936-39; First Lord of the Admiralty's Statistical Branch, 1939-40; Prime Minister's Statistical Branch, 1940-45 (Chief Asst, 1942-45). Work on Reparations and German Industry, Moscow and Berlin, 1945; Mem. of Heavy Clothing Industry Working Party, 1946; Official Fellow of Wadham Coll., Oxford, 1945-50, Domestic Bursar, 1946-48, Hon. Fellow, 1964-; Econ. Dir, OEEC, Paris, 1948-49; Faculty Fellow, Nuffield Coll., 1947-50, Professorial Fellow, 1951-52, Official Fellow, 1952-64, First Bursar, 1958-64, Hon. Fellow, 1967-; Nuffield Reader in Internat. Economics, Oxford Univ., 1951-52; Chief Adviser, Prime Minister's Statistical Branch, 1951-53; Visiting Prof., Australian Nat. Univ., 1959; MIT Center for Internat. Studies, New Delhi, 1961; Dir, Investing in Success Equities, Ltd, 1959-62; Economic Dir, NEDC, 1962-64; Mem.

Turnover Tax Cttee, 1963-64; Dir-Gen., Dept of Economic Affairs, 1964-68. mem. Council, Royal Econ. Soc., 1950- (Hon. Sec., 1958-70; Vice-Pres., 1970-). Hon. LLD Strathclyde, 1968. *Publications:* (part author) Measures for International Economic Stability, UN, 1951; The World Dollar Problem, 1957; (part author) The Fiscal System of Venezuela, 1959; The Dollar Problem: A Reappraisal, 1960; contrib. to Britain in Recovery, 1938, Lessons of the British War Economy, 1951, and to various economic and statistical jls. *Address:* 19 Park Town, Oxford. *T:* Oxford 55794. *Club:* Reform.

**MacDOUGALL, Air Cdre Ian Neil,** CBE 1964; DFC 1942; Military Liaison, Rolls-Royce (Composite Materials) Ltd, since 1970; *b* 11 June 1920; *s* of late Archibald MacDougall, Colonial Service, and Helen Grace (*née* Simpson); *m* 1944, Dorothy Eleanor, *d* of late John Frankland; one *s* one *d*. *Educ:* Morrison's Academy, Crieff; RAF Coll., Cranwell. Commnd Sept. 1939; served in Fighter Sqdns in Battle of Britain, Syrian and Western Desert Campaigns, Malta and in invasions of Sicily and Normandy; War Studies Lectr at RAF Coll., 1948-50 and USAF Academy, Colorado, 1956-58; Asst Air Attaché, Paris, 1950-53; Chief Flying Instructor, RAF Coll., 1953-56; Supt of Flying, Boscome Down, 1959-62; comd RAF Fighter Stn, Binbrook, 1962-64; SASO 38 Gp, 1964-67; comd Zambian Expedn and Zambian Oil Lift, 1965-66; Air Attaché, Paris, 1967-69; jssc, psc, pfc, cfs; retd Dec. 1969. *Recreation:* fishing. *Address:* Ringtail Cottage, Lower Morton, Thornbury, Glos. *T:* Thornbury 2037. *Club:* Royal Air Force.

**MacDOUGALL, Leslie Grahame,** RSA 1946 (ARSA 1937); FRIBA 1937 (ARIBA 1926); PPRIAS; FSA (Scotland); Architect; *b* Edinburgh, 14 Aug. 1896; *s* of late Patrick William Thomson, Edinburgh; *m* 1st, 1933, Barbara Mary Henderson (against whom he obtained decree of divorce (undefended) 1943); 2nd, 1949, Coline Helen Elizabeth (*see* Madam MacDougall of MacDougall), *e d* of late Col A. J. MacDougall of MacDougall, CMG. Assumed the surname of MacDougall in lieu of Grahame-Thomson on accession of his wife to Chiefship of Clan MacDougall, 1953. *Educ:* Merchiston Castle Sch.; Edinburgh Univ. and School of Architecture, Edinburgh Coll. of Art. Served Great War, 1914-18, HLI and Army Pay Dept, Overseas with Egyptian Expeditionary Force, 1917-19; Edinburgh Coll. of Art, 1920-26; entered office of late Sir Robert Lorimer, KBE, ARA, RSA, as pupil, 1921; commenced private practice, 1926; works: National Bank of Scotland new head office, Caledonian Insurance Company's new head office, Reid Memorial Church, Edinburgh, Fairmilehead Parish Church, Moncur Memorial Church, Isle of Stronsay, Orkney, Christ's Church, Oban, other Banks and Churches, Domestic and Hotel work. *Publications:* papers in Quarterly of Royal Incorporation of Architects in Scotland. *Recreations:* foreign travel, hill-climbing, gardening. *Address:* Dunollie Castle, Oban, Argyll. *T:* Oban 2012; 6 Ainslie Place, Edinburgh, 3. *T:* 031-225 8129. *Clubs:* Savage, Caledonian, New (Edinburgh), Scottish Arts; Royal Highland Yacht.

**McDOUGALL, Richard Sedgwick,** CBE 1957; FCA; Chairman, Building Research Station Steering Committee, 1967-70; *b* 29 May 1904; *o s* of late R. E. C. McDougall and Evelyn Mary, *d* of Richard Sedgwick; *m* 1929, Margaret Sylvia, *d* of late John Charles Denmead; two *d*. *Educ:* Haileybury Coll. County Treasurer, Hertfordshire County Council, 1939-57; General Manager, Stevenage Development Corporation, 1957-67. Member: Weeks Cttee on Army Works Services, 1956-57; Colonial Secretary's Advisory Cttee on Local Govt, 1950-; North West Metropolitan Regional Hosp. Bd, 1963-68. For British Govt, visited Sierra Leone, 1950, Nyasaland, 1954, Fiji Islands, 1957, and Kenya, 1967. *Recreations:* painting, golf. *Address:* 56 The Shimmings, Boxgrove Road, Guildford, Surrey. *T:* Guildford 69702.

**McDOWALL, Robert John Stewart,** DSc, MD, MRCP; FRCP (Edinburgh); Professor Emeritus in the University of London since 1959; Professor of Physiology, 1923-59, and Dean of Faculty of Medicine and Fellow of King's College, London; Vice-Chairman Medical Advisory Committee and Founder Member, Asthma Research Council; Formerly Examiner for Universities of London, Leeds, Durham, Manchester, Aberdeen, St Andrews, Edinburgh, Sheffield, Bristol, West Indies, Nigeria, RCP, RCS, in India, Egypt, Australasia, and Eire; *b* 1892; *s* of Robert McDowall, Auchengaillie, Wigtonshire, and Fanny Grace Stewart; *m* 1st, 1921, Jessie (*d* 1963), *yr d* of Alexander Macbeth, JP, Pitlochry, Perthshire; two *d*; 2nd, 1964, Dr Jean Rotherham, *d* of Col Ewan Rotherham, TD, DL (Warwickshire). *Educ:* Watson's Coll., Edinburgh; University of Edinburgh (Gold Medal for MD thesis). Assistant and Lecturer in Physiology, University of Edinburgh, 1919-21; Lectr, Experimental Physiology and Experimental Pharmacology, Univ. of Leeds, 1921-23; Lectr in Applied Physiology, London Sch. of Hygiene, 1927-29. Ellis prizeman, 1920; Parkin prizeman, RCP, Edinburgh, 1930; Gunning Victoria Jubilee Cullen Prize, RCP, Edinburgh, 1938; Arris and Gale Lectr, RCS, 1933; Oliver Sharpey Lectr, RCP, 1941; medal of honour, University of Ghent, 1951. Hon. Fellow: Amer. Acad. of Allergy, 1953; Soc. Française d'Allergie, 1957; European Acad. of Allergy; Finnish Acad. of Allergy. Pres., 4th European Congress of Allergy, 1959; Hon. Mem., British Soc. of Allergy; Extraordinary Mem., British Cardiac Soc. Has been Resident House Physician, Edinburgh Royal Infirmary, and Clinical Tutor in Medicine, Univ. of Edinburgh; served with RAMC, European War, 1914-18, also 1940-41; became DADMS for British Forces in Palestine, Syria, and Cilicia; President, Physiology Sect. British Assoc., 1936; Chairman Board of Intermediate Medical Studies and of Physiology, University of London. *Publications:* Clinical Physiology; The Science of Signs and Symptoms in relation to Modern Diagnosis and Treatment, 4 editions; Handbook of Physiology, 13 editions; The Control of the Circulation of the Blood, 1938, 1957; The Whiskies of Scotland, 1967; Editor, The Mind, by various authors; Sane Psychology, 6 reprints; Anatomy and Physiology for students of Physiotherapy (with Smout) and numerous scientific papers. *Recreations:* chess, curling (1st President, Hampstead Curling Club; 1st President, London Watsonian Curling Club; President, Province of London; Captained England against Scotland, 1966 and 1969); golf (Ex-Captain, Life Mem. and Director, Hampstead Golf Club). *Address:* 34 Park Drive, NW11. *T:* 01-455 2858.

*See also J. K. Rotherham.*

**McDOWALL, Roger Gordon,** CIE 1935; *b* 9 Nov. 1886; *s* of Rev. William McDowall, MA, and Jessie Crocket; *m* 1913, Martha Law Howie; one *s*. *Educ:* Duncow; Dumfries Academy; Glasgow Univ.; Christ Church, Oxford. Entered Indian Civil Service, 1911; Assistant Commissioner in Burma, 1911-16; Assistant

Secretary to Government of Burma, 1916-19; Registrar of Chief Court (and later of High Court), Rangoon, 1920-23; Deputy Commissioner, Bassein, 1923-27; Tharrawaddy, 1927-28; Finance Secretary to Government of Burma, 1929-32; Reforms Secretary to Government of Burma, 1932-37; Secretary tp the Governor of Burma, 1937-39; retired, 1941. *Recreation:* gardening. *Address:* Old Mill, Dunlop, Ayrshire. *T:* Dunlop 277.

**McDOWELL, Sir Frank (Schofield),** Kt 1967; Chairman of Directors, McDowell Ltd, since 1935; *b* 8 Aug. 1889; *s* of John McDowell; *m* 1912, Ethel Sophia Perrott; six *s* one *d*. *Educ:* Petersham Public School. Grand Master: United Grand Lodge of NSW Freemasons, 1947-49; Mark Master Masons NSW, 1946-48; Inspector General, 33rd Rose Croix SE Central District NSW, 1967. *Recreations:* bowls, garden, swimming. *Address:* Melrose, 157 Ewos Parade, Cronulla, Sydney, NSW, Australia. *T:* 5235115. *Clubs:* (President) All Nations, (Patron) Retailers (Sydney); (Patron) South Cronulla Bowling.

**McDOWELL, Sir Henry (McLorinan),** KBE 1964 (CBE 1959); Chairman, Rhodesian Board, Barclays Bank DCO, since 1969; Director, Anglo-American Corporation Rhodesia Ltd, and other companies, since 1965; *b* Johannesburg, S. Africa, 10 Dec. 1910; *s* of John McDowell and Margaret Elizabeth Bingham; *m* 1939, Norah, *d* of Walter Slade Douthwaite; one *s* one *d*. *Educ:* Witwatersrand Univ.; Queen's Coll., Oxford; Yale Univ. Served War of 1939-45, 1 Bn Northern Rhodesia Regt, East Africa and South-East Asia, 1940-44. Entered HM Colonial Service (Cadet, Northern Rhodesia), 1938; Clerk, Legislative and Executive Councils, 1945; Assistant Secretary, 1950; Deputy Financial Secretary, 1952. Imperial Defence College, 1948; seconded Colonial Office, 1949. Economic and Financial Working Party, in preparation for federation of Rhodesias and Nyasaland, 1953; Federal Treasury, 1954; Secretary, Ministry of Transport, 1955; Secretary, Federal Treasury, 1959-63. Chairman: Council of the University Coll. of Rhodesia and Nyasaland, 1968; Ranche House Coll., Salisbury; Mem., governing bodies, educational institutions, Rhodesia. *Recreations:* tennis, reading. *Address:* 6 Malcolm House, Blakiston Street, Salisbury, Rhodesia. *Clubs:* Salisbury, Salisbury Sports (Salisbury).

**MACDUFF, Earl of; David Charles Carnegie;** *b* 3 March 1961; *s* and *heir* of 3rd Duke of Fife, *qv*.

**MACE, Cecil Alec,** MA Cantab, DLit London; Emeritus Professor of Psychology, University of London, since 1961; Hon. Fellow, Birkbeck Coll.; Hon. Fellow, British Psychological Society; *b* 22 July 1894; *s* of Walter and Mary Mace, Norwich; *m* 1922, Marjorie, *d* of Harris Lebus; two *s*. *Educ:* King Edward VI Middle Sch.; City of Norwich Sch.; Queens' Coll., Cambridge. Lectr, University Coll., Nottingham, 1922-25; Lectr, Univ. of St Andrews, 1925-32; Reader, Bedford Coll., Univ. of London, 1932-44; Prof. of Psychology, Birkbeck Coll., Univ. of London, 1944-61. Tarner Lectr, Trinity Coll., Cambridge, 1940-41; Manson Lectr, Royal Inst. of Philosophy, 1965. Hon. Mem. Aristotelian Soc. (Pres., 1948-49); Pres. Psychological Section, British Assoc. 1951; Pres., British Psychological Soc., 1952-53. *Publications:* The Psychology of Study, 1932 (Rev. paperback edns 1968, 1970); The Principles of Logic, 1933; Incentives: Some Experimental Studies, 1935; Articles in Times Lit. Supp., Encyclopædia Britannica, Chambers's Encyclopædia and Encyclopedia of Philosophy; Ed. and Contrib., British Philosophy in the Mid Century, 1957 (rev. edn, 1966); various articles and papers in Proc. Aristotelian Society, British Journal of Psychology, and other journals of Philosophy and Psychology. For some years Editor of Methuens Manuals of Psychology and of the Pelican Psychology Series. *Address:* 105 Roebuck House, Palace Street, SW1. *T:* 01-828 2764; Vale Farm, Hollesley, Woodbridge, Suffolk. *T:* Shottisham 258.

**McELDERRY, Samuel Burnside Boyd,** CMG 1935; *b* 7 Oct. 1885; *s* of late Thomas McElderry and late Alice Knox of Ballymoney, Co. Antrim; *m* 1913, Mildred Mary Orme; three *d*. *Educ:* Campbell Coll., Belfast; Trinity Coll., Dublin. Eastern Cadet, 1909; Hong Kong Administrative Service, 1909-28; Deputy Chief Secretary, Tanganyika, 1929-33; Chief Secretary, Zanzibar, 1933-40; retired 1940; attached to office of High Commissioner for Basutoland, Bechuanaland Protectorate and Swaziland (Pretoria and Cape Town), 1940-45; temporarily employed Colonial Office, 1945-46. Member of Council, Royal Commonwealth Society for Blind, 1951-70; Royal National Institute for Blind, 1958-70. *Address:* Fircroft, 19 Kivernell Road, Milford-on-Sea, Lymington, Hants.

*See also W. Wenban-Smith.*

**McELENEY, Most Rev. John;** *see* Kingston (Jamaica), Archbishop of, (RC).

**McELHONE, Francis;** MP (Lab) Gorbals Division of Glasgow since Oct. 1969; *b* Glasgow, 5 April 1929; *m* 1958, Helen Brown; two *s* two *d*. *Educ:* St Bonaventure's Secondary Sch., Glasgow. Fruit merchant, Glasgow. Member, Glasgow CC, for Hutchesontown Ward, 1963-; JP Glasgow 1966, Senior Magistrate 1968, Police Judge 1969. Trustee, Easterhouse Youth Project, 1968-. *Address:* House of Commons, SW1; 164 Nithsdale Road, Glasgow S1.

**McELLIGOTT, James,** MA, LLD; Secretary, Department of Finance, 1927-53; Governor, Central Bank of Ireland, 1954-60; President of Economic and Social Research Institute; *b* Tralee, Co. Kerry, 1893; *m* 1927, Annie Gertrude, *d* of James Fay, of Edenderry, Offaly. *Educ:* University College, Dublin, National University of Ireland; BA (hons) Classics, 1913; MA Economics, 1917. Passed for Indian Civil Service; left Service for financial journalism; Managing Editor, The Statist, London, 1921; returned to Ireland as Financial Adviser to Irish Government, 1923, and acted on many important Commissions and Cttees. *Publications:* papers, economic and financial subjects. *Recreation:* travelling. *Address:* Central Bank of Ireland, Dublin.

**McELLIGOTT, Neil Martin;** Metropolitan Magistrate at Old Street Magistrates Court, EC1, since 1961; *b* 21 March 1915; *s* of Judge E. J. McElligott, KC, Limerick; *m* 1939, Suzanne, *d* of late Air Chief Marshal Sir Arthur Barratt, KCB, CMG, MC, DL; one *d*. *Educ:* Ampleforth. Served in Royal Air Force, 1935-45. Called to Bar, Inner Temple, 1945, South Eastern Circuit, Recorder of King's Lynn, 1961. *Recreations:* hunting, racing, fishing, gardening. *Address:* Stone Cottage, Abthorpe, nr Towcester, Northants. *T:* Silverstone 310.

**McELROY, Neil H.;** Chairman, The Procter & Gamble Co., since 1959; *b* 30 Oct. 1904; *s* of Malcolm Ross McElroy and Susan Hosler McElroy; *m* 1929, Mary Camilla Fry; one *s* two *d*. *Educ:* Harvard Coll. Joined The Procter & Gamble Co., Cincinnati, Ohio, 1925;

Advertising Dept, 1925; Manager, Promotion Dept, 1929-40; Manager, Advertising and Promotion, 1940-43; Dir, and Vice-Pres. in charge Advertising, 1943-46; Vice-Pres., Gen. Man., 1946-48; Pres., 1948-57. Secretary of Defense, USA, 1957-59. Dir, Gen. Electric Co., Chrysler Corp.; Dir, Equitable Life Assurance Soc. of the United States. Dir, Atlantic Council of US; Mem., Exec. Cttee, The Business Council; Chm., Cttee on Univ. Resources, Harvard Univ.; Mem. of 2 Harvard visiting cttees; Member: United Negro Coll. Fund Council; Cttee for Corporate Support of American Univs; Nat. Adv. Council, Girl Scouts of America; Exec. Cttee, Cincinnati Inst. of Fine Arts. Trustee, National Safety Council; Founding Mem., Business Cttee for the Arts, Inc.; Pres., Board of Overseers, Harvard Univ., 1963-66; Chairman: Council for Financial Aid to Education, 1963-66; White House Conference on Education, 1954-55; Pres., Soap and Detergent Assoc., 1950; various positions, Nat. Industrial Conf. Bd, 1953-64. Holds several Hon. degrees. Medal of Freedom (USA), 1959. *Address:* P.O. Box 599, Cincinnati, Ohio, USA. *Clubs:* Cincinnati Country, Commonwealth, Commercial (Pres., 1960-61), Camargo, Queen City (Cincinnati); Links, 29 (New York); Chevy Chase, 1925 F Street (Washington, DC); Bohemian (San Francisco); Harvard (Boston and New York).

**MacENTEE, Seán;** Member, Dáil Eireann for Dublin South (East), retired May 1969; Member, Council of State; Tánaiste (Deputy Prime Minister), 1959-65; Minister for Health, 1957-65 (of Social Welfare, 1958-61); a consulting electrical engineer, registered patent agent, company director, etc.; *b* 1889; *e s* of James MacEntee, TC, Belfast; *m* Margaret, *d* of late Maurice Browne, of Grange-Mockler, Co. Tipperary; one *s* two *d*. *Educ:* St Malachy's Coll., Belfast; Belfast College of Technology. Participated in Irish insurrection, 1916; tried by General Court-Martial, May 1916, and sentenced to death (sentence afterwards commuted to penal servitude for life); imprisoned in Dartmoor, Lewes and Portland prisons and released under General Amnesty, June 1917; MP (SF) South Monaghan, Dec. 1918; Member of National Executive Cttee of Irish Volunteers and Irish Republican Army, 1917-21; served with Irish Republican Army, 1916-21; contested County Dublin, Aug. 1923, Dec. 1924; TD (Representative Fianna Fail) Co. Dublin, June 1927; re-elected Sept. 1927, 1932, and 1933; TD Dublin Townships, 1937-48, and Dublin SE, since 1948; Minister for Finance, Irish Free State, 1932-37, and Eire, 1937-39; Minister for Industry and Commerce, Eire, 1939-41; Minister for Local Government and Public Health, Eire, 1941-46; for Local Government, 1946-48; Minister for Finance, Republic of Ireland, 1951-54. LLD (*hc*) NUI. Kt Grand Cross, Pian Order. *Publications:* Poems (1918); Episode at Easter, 1966. *Address:* Leeson Park, Dublin. *T:* 972227; Tignacille, Dunquin, Co. Kerry. *Club:* Irish (London).

**MacEOIN, Lt-Gen. Seán;** *b* County Longford, 30 Sept. 1893; *e s* of Andrew MacEoin and Catherine Treacy, Kilshruley, Ballinalee, Co. Longford; *m* 1922, Alice Christina, *e d* of Mr Cooney, Gurteen House, Killashee, Co. Longford. *Educ:* Ballinalee National School; correspondence course. Co. Captain Irish Volunteers at 21 years of age, 1914-17; Batt. Commander 1st Batt. Longford Brigade Irish Volunteers, 1917-20; Vice-Brigadier Longford Brigade, 1920-21; OC 1st Midland Divison rank Comdt General, 1921-22; GOC Western Command rank Maj.-Gen., 1922-23; GOC Athlone Command, 1923-24; GOC Reformed Western Command, 1924-25; GOC Curragh Training Camp, 1925-27; Quartermaster-General, 1927-29; Chief of Staff, 1928-29; resigned June 1929; Lt-Gen. 1929 (R of O); Dáil Deputy, 1921-23; seconded motion for Ratification Treaty between Great Britain and Ireland, 1921; Member of the Dáil for Athlone-Longford, 1929-65; Minister for Justice, 1948-51; Minister for Defence, March-June 1951, and 1954-57. Candidate Presidential Elections, 1945-59. Retired active politics, 1965. Grand Cross and Commander Merit, Argentine, 1957; Silver Sword of Light, Ireland, 1965. *Recreations:* hunting, golf. *Address:* Cloncoosc, Stillorgan Road, Donnybrook, Dublin.

**McEVOY, Air Chief Marshal Sir Theodore Newman,** KCB 1956 (CB 1951); CBE 1945 (OBE 1941); *b* 21 Nov. 1904; *s* of late Rev. C. McEvoy, MA, Watford; *m* 1935, Marian, *d* of late W. A. E. Coxon, Cairo; one *s* one *d*. *Educ:* Haberdashers' School; RAF Coll., Cranwell. Served with Fighter Squadrons and in Iraq, 1925-36; psa 1937; Air Ministry, 1938-41; commanded Northolt, 1941; Group Captain Operations, HQ Fighter Command, 1942-43; SASO No. 11 Group, 1943; SASO No. 84 Group, 1944 (despatches); Air Ministry (DST), 1945-47; idc 1948; AOC No. 61 Group, 1949-50; Assistant Chief of Air Staff (Training), 1950-53; RAF Instructor, Imperial Defence Coll., 1954-56; Chief of Staff, Allied Air Forces, Central Europe, 1956-59; Air Secretary, Air Ministry, 1959-62; Air ADC to the Queen, 1959-62; retired, 1962. Director, Common Cause; Vice-President, British Gliding Assoc.; Chairman, Society for Italic Handwriting. Commander Order of Polonia Restituta (Poland), 1942. *Recreations:* gliding, golf. *Address:* Parkfield, Farthing Green Lane, Stoke Poges, Bucks. *Club:* Royal Air Force.

**McEWAN, Geraldine, (Mrs Hugh Cruttwell);** actress; Member, National Theatre Company; *b* 9 May 1932; *d* of Donald and Norah McKeown; *m* 1953, Hugh Cruttwell, *qv*; one *s* one *d*. *Educ:* Windsor County Girls' School. Acted with Theatre Royal, Windsor, 1949-51; Who Goes There, 1951; Sweet Madness, 1952; For Better For Worse, 1953; Summertime, 1955; Stratford-on-Avon, 1956: Love's Labours Lost; The Member of the Wedding, Royal Court Theatre, 1957; The Entertainer, Palace, 1957-58; Stratford-on-Avon, 1958: Pericles; Twelfth Night; Much Ado About Nothing; 1961: Much Ado About Nothing; Hamlet; School for Scadal, Haymarket, and USA, 1962; The Private Ear, and The Public Eye, USA, 1963; Loot, 1965; National Theatre, 1965 onwards: Armstrong's Last Goodnight; Love For Love; A Flea in Her Ear; The Dance of Death; Edward II; Home and Beauty; Rites; The Way of the World; The White Devil; Guys and Dolls. *Address:* 93 Abingdon Road, W8. *T:* 01-937 9726.

**M'EWEN, Ewen,** MScEng; CEng, FIMechE, MAmSocME; Vice-Chairman (Engineering), Joseph Lucas Ltd, since 1967; *b* 13 Jan. 1916; *e s* of Clement M'Ewen and Doris Margaret Pierce-Hope; *m* 1938, Barbara Dorrien, *d* of W. F. Medhurst; two *s* one *d*. *Educ:* Merchiston; University Coll., London. BSc (Eng) 1st class Hons, 1935; Head Memorial Medallist and Prizeman, 1935; Graduate Apprentice David Brown & Sons (Huddersfield) Ltd, 1935-37, Research Engineer, 1937-40, Asst Works Manager, 1940-42; served War of 1939-45, 1942-46: Lt-Col 1943; Lt-Col (Hon. Col) REME (TARO); Asst Dir, Dept of Tank Design, 1943-46; Asst Chief Engineer, Fighting Vehicles Design Dept, 1946-47; Prof. of Agricultural Engineering, King's Coll., Univ. of Durham, Newcastle upon Tyne, 1947-

54, and Reader in Applied Mechanics, 1952-54; Dir Armament R and D Establishment, Fort Halstead, 1955-58; Dir of Engineering, Massey Ferguson Ltd, 1958-63; Dep. Man. Dir, 1963, Man. Dir, 1965-67, Hobourn Group Ltd. Commanded REME 50 (N) Infantry Div. (TA), 1949-52. Hon. Col Durham Univ. OTC, 1955-60. Mem. Council, Instn of Mech. Engs, 1961- (Vice-Pres., 1970-). Fellow University Coll., London, 1965. Liveryman, Glaziers Company. *Publications:* papers and articles in Technical Press. *Recreation:* sailing. *Address:* 45 Pearce Avenue, Poole, Dorset BH14 8EG. *T:* Parkstone 2067; Joseph Lucas Ltd, Great King Street, Birmingham 19. *T:* 021-554 5252. *Clubs:* Athenæum; Parkstone Yacht (Poole).

**McEWEN, Sir James Napier Finnie,** 2nd Bt, *cr* 1953; *b* 14 Dec. 1924; *s* of Sir John Helias Finnie McEwen, 1st Bt; *S* father, 1962; *m* 1958, Clare, *d* of J. E. W. G. Sandars, *qv*; three *d*. *Educ:* Eton. Served War of 1939-45 with Grenadier Guards in France. *Heir: b* Robert Lindley McEwen [*b* 23 June 1926; *m* 1954, Brigid Cecilia Laver; two *s* four *d*]. *Address:* Bardrochat, Colmonell, Ayrshire. *Club:* New (Edinburgh).

**McEWEN, Rev. Professor James Stevenson,** DD; Professor of Church History, University of Aberdeen, since 1958; *b* 18 Feb. 1910; *s* of Rev. Thomas McEwen and Marjorie Bissett; *m* 1945, Martha M. Hunter, Auchendrane, Alexandria; two *s*. *Educ:* George Watson's Coll., Edinburgh Univ. Ordained Church of Scotland, 1940; held parishes at Rathen, Hawick and Invergowrie; Lecturer in Church History at University of Edinburgh, 1953. *Publication:* The Faith of John Knox, 1961. *Address:* 8 Westfield Terrace, Aberdeen. *T:* Aberdeen 25413.

**McEWEN, Rt. Hon. John,** PC 1953; CH 1969; Minister for Trade and Industry, Australia, since 1963 (Minister for Trade, 1956-63); Deputy Prime Minister since 1958 (Acting Prime Minister at frequent periods from 1959-70; Prime Minister, 19 Dec. 1967-10 Jan. 1968); Leader of the Australian Country Party; Member of the House of Representatives for Murray since 1949; *b* Chiltern, Victoria, 29 March 1900; *s* of David James McEwen and Amy Ellen Porter; *m* 1st, 1921, Annie Mills, DBE 1966 (*d* 1967), *d* of John McLeod, Tongala, Victoria; 2nd, 1968, Mary Eileen, *d* of Patrick Aloysius Byrne, Adelaide. Enlisted Australian Imperial Forces, 1918; farmer at Stanhope, Victoria, since 1919; MHR Echuca, 1934-37, Indi, 1937-49; Minister for the Interior, Australia, 1937-39; Minister of External Affairs, 1940; Minister for Air and Civil Aviation, 1940-41; Member War Cabinet, 1940-41; Member War Advisory Council, Australia, 1941-45; Member Australian Delegation, UNCIO, San Francisco, 1945; Minister for Commerce and Agriculture, Australia, Dec. 1949-56. *Address:* Stanhope, Victoria, Australia. *Club:* Melbourne (Melbourne).

**MacEWEN, Malcolm;** Editor, RIBA Journal, since 1964; Head of Publishing services, Royal Institute of British Architects, since 1966; *b* 24 Dec. 1911; *s* of late Sir Alexander MacEwen and of Lady (Mary Beatrice) MacEwen; *m* 1st, 1937, Barbara Mary Stebbing, BSc (*d* 1944); one *d*; 2nd, 1947, Mrs Ann Maitland Wheeler (*née* Radford), ARIBA, AMTPI; one *d* (and two step *d*). *Educ:* St Salvator's Sch., St Andrews; Rossall Sch.; Aberdeen Univ.; Edinburgh Univ. (MA, LLB; Editor, The Student). Lost leg in motor cycle accident, 1933. Practised as Solicitor, Inverness, 1937-41; Member (Lab) Ross and Cromarty CC, 1938-40; became journalist, 1941; wrote for Daily Worker, mainly as Parliamentary Correspondent, 1944-56; Asst Editor, Architects' Jl, 1956-60. Head of RIBA Information Services, 1960-66. Broadcaster and writer on town planning and architectural subjects. *Recreations:* walking, riding. *Address:* 31a Tanza Road, NW3. *T:* 01-435 2138.

**McEWIN, Hon. Sir (Alexander) Lyell,** KBE 1954; President, Legislative Council, South Australia, since 1967; *b* 29 May 1897; *s* of late A. L. McEwin; *m* 1921, Dora Winifred, *d* of late Mark Williams, Blyth; four *s* one *d*. *Educ:* State Sch.; Prince Alfred Coll., Adelaide. Engaged in farming at Hart, near Blyth, since 1912; Sec., Blyth Agric. Bureau, 1920-26, Pres., 1927-36; Life Mem. State Advisory Bd of Agric., 1930, Chm., 1935-37; Mem. Agric. Settlement Cttee, 1931; Mem. Debt Adjustment Cttee, 1933; Producers' representative for SA on Federal Advisory Cttee for Export Mutton and Beef, prior to appt of Australian Meat Bd, 1934. Entered Legislative Council of South Australian Parliament as Member for Northern District, 1934; Chief Secretary, Minister of Health, and Minister of Mines, 1939-65; Leader of Opposition in Legislative Council, 1965-67. Councillor, Hart Ward of Hutt and Hill Rivers' District Council, 1932-35; transferred to Blyth Dist Council, 1935-53; retired. Member South Australian Rifle Assoc., 1925 (Chairman, 1948-). Chief, Royal Caledonian Society (SA), 1959-68. *Recreation:* bowls. *Address:* Parliament House, Adelaide, South Australia. *T:* 513241; 93 First Avenue, St Peters, South Australia. *T:* 63, 3698.

**McEWIN, Hon. Sir Lyell;** *see* McEwin, Hon. Sir A. L.

**MACEY, John Percival,** CBE 1969; FRICS, FIHM; Director of Housing to the Greater London Council; *b* 3 Dec. 1906; *s* of Edward Macey; *m* 1931, Jill, *d* of Joseph Gyngell; one *s* one *d*. *Educ:* Varndean Grammar Sch., Brighton. Entered LCC service, 1926; Principal Asst, Housing Dept, 1948-51; Dep. Housing Manager, City of Birmingham, 1951-54; Housing Manager, City of Birmingham, 1954-63; Director of Housing to LCC, 1964. President: Inst. of Housing, 1957 and 1963; Inst. of Housing Managers, 1969. Served with Royal Engineers, 1939-45 (despatches); retired with rank of Major. *Publications:* (joint author) Housing Management; numerous papers to professional bodies and journals on housing and allied subjects. *Recreations:* motoring, walking, gardening. *Address:* Ravenscroft, Horseshoe Lane East, Merrow, Guildford, Surrey. *T:* Guildford 73749.

**McFADYEAN, Sir Andrew,** Kt, *cr* 1925; *b* 23 April 1887; *e s* of late Sir John McFadyean; *m* 1913, Dorothea Emily, *y d* of late Charles Kean Chute; one *s* three *d*. *Educ:* University College School., London; University College, Oxford (Scholar); First Class Final Honour School, Lit. Hum., 1909. Entered Treasury, 1910, by open competition; Private Secretary, 1913, to Mr Masterman and successively to Mr Montagu, Mr Acland, Sir John Bradbury, Mr McKinnon Wood, Sir Hardman Lever and Mr Stanley Baldwin; accompanied Sir H. Lever to USA on special financial mission, 1917; Treasury representative, Paris, Sept. 1919-Jan. 1920; Sec. to British Delegn Reparation Commn, 1920-22; Gen. Sec. to Reparation Commn, 1922-24, and Sec. to Dawes Cttee, 1924; Comr of Controlled Revenues, Berlin, 1924-30; Member, Executive National Liberal Federation, 1933-36; Joint Treasurer, Liberal Party Organisation, 1936-48, Pres., 1949-50; Vice-Pres., 1950-60; Pres., Free Trade Union, 1948-59; Vice-Pres., Liberal Internat., 1954-

67; Vice-Pres., Anglo-Israel Assoc. (Chm. Council, 1950-60). Mem. Council, Royal Inst. of Internat. Affairs, 1933-67, President, 1970. Contested (L) City of London, 1945; Finchley, 1950. *Publications:* Reparation Reviewed, 1930; The Liberal Case, 1950; Recollected in Tranquility, 1964; trans. Count Coudenhove-Kalergi's The Totalitarian State Against Man, 1938, Europe Must Unite, 1939. *Address:* 21 Cavendish Close, NW8. *T:* 01-286 5268. *Club:* Travellers'.

*See also Prof. S. E. Finer.*

**McFADZEAN,** family name of **Baron McFadzean.**

**McFADZEAN,** Baron, *cr* 1966 (Life Peer), **William Hunter McFadzean;** Kt 1960; Chairman, British Insulated Callender's Cables Ltd, since 1954 (Managing Director, 1954-61); a Deputy Chairman, Midland Bank, since 1968 (Director, since 1959); Deputy Chairman, RTZ/BICC Aluminium Holdings Ltd, since 1967; *b* Stranraer, 17 Dec. 1903; *s* of Henry and Agnes McFadzean, Stranraer; *m* 1933, Eileen, *e d* of Arthur Gordon, Blundellsands, Lancs.; one *s* one *d,* one adopted *d. Educ:* Stranraer Academy and High Sch.; Glasgow Univ. Served articles with McLay, McAllister & McGibbon, Chartered Accountants, Glasgow, 1922-27; qualified as Chartered Accountant, 1927; with Chalmers Wade & Co., 1927-32; joined British Insulated Cables Ltd, as Accountant, 1932 (Financial Secretary, 1937; Exec. Manager, 1942); on amalgamation of British Insulated Cables Ltd and Callender's Cable & Construction Co. Ltd, in 1945, appointed to Board of British Insulated Callender's Cables Ltd as Exec. Director (Dep. Chairman, 1947; Chief Exec. Director, 1950); Chairman British Insulated Callender's Construction Co. Ltd, 1952-64; Chm., British Insulated Callender's (Submarine Cables) Ltd, 1954; Director: Anglesey Aluminium Ltd, 1968-; Midland Bank Executor and Trustee Co., 1959-67; English Electric Co., 1966-68; Steel Co. of Wales Ltd, 1966-67; Canadian Imperial Bank of Commerce, 1967; Canada Life Assurance Co., 1969-. Pres. FBI, 1959-61; Mem. Council, CBI, 1965-. Chairman: Council of Industrial Fedns of EFTA, 1960-63; Export Council for Europe, 1960-64 (Hon. Pres. 1964-); Commonwealth Export Council, 1964-66; British Nat. Export Council, 1964-66 (Pres. 1966-68); President: Brit. Electrical Power Convention, 1961-62; Brit. Nuclear Forum, 1964-66; BNEC, 1966-68; Coal Trade Benevolent Assoc., 1967-68; Electrical and Electronics Industries Benevolent Assoc., 1968. Vice-President: Middle East Assoc., 1965; City of London Soc., 1965; British/Swedish Chamber of Commerce, 1963. Member: Council, Inst. of Directors, 1954; Min. of Labour Adv. Bd on Resettlement of Ex-Regulars, 1957-60; Bd of Trade Adv. Council on ME Trade, 1958-60; Shipping Adv. Panel, 1962-64; Ct of British Shippers' Council, 1964 (Pres., 1968); Council, Foreign Bondholders, 1968; Anglo-Danish Soc., 1965 (Chm., 1969). Adv. Cttee, Queen's Award to Industry, 1965-67 (Chm. 1970). FRSA 1967. CompIEE 1956. JDipMA 1965. Commander Order of Dannebrog, 1964. *Address:* 87 Whitehall Court, SW1. *T:* 01-930 3160; Garthland, Woldingham, Surrey. *T:* Woldingham 3222. *Club:* Carlton.

**McFALL, David (Bernard),** RA 1963 (ARA 1955); Sculptor; Master of Sculpture, City and Guilds of London Art School, Lambeth, since 1956; *b* 21 Dec. 1919; *s* of David McFall and Elizabeth McEvoy. *Educ:* Art Schools, Birmingham, Lambeth and Royal College of Art. Official Commissions: Unicorns (pair, 12 ft, gilt-bronze) mounted on roof of Bristol New Council House, known as The Bristol Unicorns, 1950; Finials (pair, carved, Portland stone, 10 ft), Zodiac Clock (8 ft, carved stone and cast aluminium), Bronze Portrait Bust (Alderman Frank Sheppard), 1955, same building; Festival of Britain, Boy and Foal (carved stone 5 ft), 1951, now at Missenden Abbey, Bucks. Pocahontas (bronze), 1956; Bust (bronze, Lord Methuen), 1956; Head of Ralph Vaughan Williams, OM (bronze) in Royal Festival Hall, 1957; 8 ft Statues of St Bride and St Paul in St Bride's Church, Fleet Street; Bronze Head of Sir Winston Churchill, in Grocers Hall, 1958; 8 ft 6 ins Bronze Figure of Sir Winston Churchill, 1959 (Woodford Green); Lord Balfour, House of Commons, 1962; Bust (bronze) Lord Brabazon of Tara (Royal Institution); Memorial to Sir Albert Richardson, PPRA, for Crypt of St Paul's Cathedral; Crucifixion (Portland stone), Church of Our Lady of Lourdes, Thames-Ditton; bust (bronze, Lord Ridley) for Univ., Newcastle upon Tyne; The Golden Gazelle, Abu Dhabi, Trucial States; bronze figure of Sir Winston Churchill, trophy for Dame Felicity Peake Essay Prize; The Black Horse for LTB Victoria Line, 1968; stone freize on Wm Whitfield's extension to Inst. of Chartered Accountants, London, 1969. Official purchase: The Bullcalf (Chantrey Bequest), 1943. Has exhibited at Royal Academy yearly since 1943. *Recreations:* swimming, cycling. *Address:* (studio) The Forge, 77 Kennings Way, SE11; (residence) 118 Kennington Park Road, SE11. *T:* 01-735 4848; 41 Salisbury Road, Seaford, Sussex. *T:* Seaford 4346.

**McFARLAND, Sir Basil (Alexander Talbot),** 2nd Bt, *cr* 1914; CBE 1954; ERD 1954; HM Lieutenant for the City of Londonderry, since 1939; *b* 18 Feb. 1898; *o c* of Sir John McFarland, 1st Bt, and Annie, 2nd *d* of late John Talbot, Terryglass, County Tipperary; *S* father, 1926; *m* 1st, 1924, Annie Kathleen (*d* 1952), 2nd *d* of late Andrew Henderson, JP, of Parkville, Whiteabbey, Belfast; one *s* (one *d* decd); 2nd, 1955, Mary Eleanor, 2nd *d* of late William Dougan, Londonderry. *Educ:* Neuwied-on-Rhine, Germany; Brussels; Bedford Sch. High Sheriff, Londonderry, 1930, 1931, 1932, 1933, 1934, 1935, 1936, 1937, 1938 and 1952; Mayor of Londonderry, 1939, 1945, 1946, 1947, 1948, 1949, 1950. Formerly ADC (Additional) to The Queen. Member: Northern Ireland Air Advisory Council, 1946-65; Londonderry Port & Harbour Commissioners (Chairman, 1952-67); London Midland Area Board, British Transport Commission, 1955-61; Director: Belfast Banking Co. Ltd; Belfast Bank Executors Trustee Co.; Donegal Railways Co.; Local Dir Commercial Union Assurance Co.; R. C. Malseed & Co. Ltd; Chairman: Sir Alfred McAlpine & Son (Northern Ireland) Ltd; Londonderry & Lough Swilly Railway Co.; Lanes (Derry), Ltd; J. W. Corbett & Sons; A. Thompson & Co. Ltd; Londonderry Gaslight Co.; Trustee of Magee University College, 1962-65; Comr of Irish Lights. Original Member, NI Unemployment Assistance Board, to 1939. Served War of 1914-18, Artists Rifles, 1918; War of 1939-45, Overseas with 9th Londonderry HAA Regt (despatches); Chm., T&AFA (Co. Londonderry), 1947-62; Hon. Col, 9th Londonderry HAA Regt RA (TA); Pres., NI TA&VR Assoc., 1968-70. Irish Rugby International, 1920-22. Hon. Freeman of City of Londonderry since 1944. CStJ. *Heir: s* John Talbot McFarland [*b* 3 Oct. 1927; *m* 1957, Mary Scott, *er d* of late Dr W. Scott Watson, Londonderry; two *s* two *d*]. *Address:* Aberfoyle, Londonderry. *T:* 2881. *Clubs:* Bath; Ulster (Belfast), Kildare Street (Dublin), Northern Counties (Londonderry).

**MacFARLANE, Donald,** CBE 1963; HM Diplomatic Service, retired; *b* 26 Oct. 1910; *s* of late Donald MacFarlane, CIE; *m* 1933, Jean Carmen, *d* of late Charles Young, Pitt Manor, Winchester; one *s* decd. *Educ:* Stowe; Queens' Coll., Cambridge. Lamson Paragon Supply Co. Ltd, 1932-39. Served in RA and Intelligence Corps, 1939-46 (despatches); North Africa, Sicily, Italy and France; Colonel, head of Anglo-Greek Information Services, Athens, 1945-46. First Secretary, Foreign Service, 1946; British Embassy, China, 1946-49; Foreign Office, 1949-52; British Embassy: Rio de Janeiro, 1952-55; Counsellor (Commercial), washington, 1955-58; Lisbon, 1958-60; HM Consul-General, Frankfurt-am-Main, 1960-64, Naples, 1964-67; Head of Nationality and Treaty Dept, FCO, 1967-70. *Recreations:* fishing, ski-ing. *Address:* 27 Lennox Gardens, SW1. *Clubs:* Travellers', Flyfishers'.

**MACFARLANE, George Gray,** CB 1965; BSc; Dr Ing (Dresden); Controller (Research), Ministry of Aviation Supply (formerly Ministry of Technology), since 1967; *b* 8 Jan. 1916; *s* of late John Macfarlane, Airdrie, Lanarks; *m* 1941, Barbara Grant, *d* of Thomas Thomson, Airdrie, Lanarks; one *s* one *d*. *Educ:* Airdrie Academy; Glasgow Univ.; Technische Hochschule, Dresden, Germany. On scientific staff, Air Ministry Research Establishment, Dundee and Swanage, 1939-41; Telecommunications Research Establishment (TRE), Malvern, 1941-60; Deputy Chief Scientific Officer (Individual Merit Post), 1954-60; Deputy Director, National Physical Laboratory, 1960-62; Director, Royal Radar Establishment, 1962-67. Hunter Mem. Lecturer, IEE, 1966. Hon. LLD Glasgow. *Publications:* papers in IEE, Proc. Phys. Society, Phys. Review. *Recreations:* golf, sailing. *Address:* Red Tiles, Orchard Way, Esher, Surrey. *T:* Esher 63778. *Club:* Athenæum.

**McFARLANE, Prof. Ian Dalrymple,** MBE 1946; Professor of French Literature, Oxford, since 1971; *b* 7 Nov. 1915; *s* of James Blair McFarlane and Valérie Edith Liston Dalrymple; *m* 1939, Marjory Nan Hamilton; one *s* one *d*. *Educ:* Lycée St-Charles, Marseilles; Tormore Sch., Upper Deal, Kent; Westminster Sch.; St Andrews Univ. MA 1st class Hons St Andrews, 1938; Carnegie Research Scholar, 1938-39. Served 1st Bn Black Watch, RHR, 1940-45. Apptd Lectr in French, Cambridge Univ., 1945; Gonville and Caius Coll.: elected Fellow, 1947; appointed Senior Tutor, 1956; Prof. of French Language and Literature, St Andrews, 1961-70. Member, Scottish Cert. of Educn Examination Board, 1964; Member Academic Planning Board, University of Stirling, 1964-67; Mem. Cttee on Research and Develt in Modern Languages, 1966. Doctor of Univ. of Paris, 1950. *Publications:* Critical edn of M Scève's Délie, 1966; various, in learned periodicals. *Recreations:* cricket, music. *Address:* Department of French, University of Oxford.

**MACFARLANE, Janet Alston,** MA, LLD (St Andrews); Headmistress of St Leonards and St Katharines Schools, St Andrews, Fife, 1938-55; *e c* of late Charles Macfarlane, JP, Hutton Avenue, West Hartlepool, Co. Durham. *Educ:* Dundee High Sch.; St Andrews Univ. Senior French Mistress, Cheltenham Ladies' Coll., 1927; Vice-Principal, 1931-38; Acting Principal, May-Dec. 1936. *Address:* 33 Town Wall, Hartlepool, Co. Durham. *T:* Hartlepool 4304.

**MACFARLANE, Robert Gwyn,** CBE 1964; FRS 1956; MD; FRCP; Member of External Staff, Medical Research Council, Sir William Dunn School of Pathology, Oxford, since 1967; Fellow, All Souls College, Oxford, since 1963; *b* 26 June 1907; *o c* of Robert Gray and Eileen Macfarlane; *m* 1936, Hilary, *o c* of H. A. H. and Maude Carson; four *s* one *d*. *Educ:* Highfield Sch., Liphook, Hants; Cheltenham Coll.; St Bartholomew's Hospital, London. MRCS, LRCP, 1933; MB, BS (London), 1933; MD (London), Gold Medal, 1938; MA (Oxford), 1948; FRCP 1960. Sir Halley Stewart Research Fellow, 1935; Asst Clinical Pathologist, Postgrad. Medical School, London, 1936; Asst Bacteriologist, Wellcome Physiological Research Lab., 1939. Major, RAMC, 1944, attached Mobile Bacteriological Research Unit, Normandy and NW Europe. Director, Medical Research Council Blood Coagulation Research Unit, Churchill Hospital, Oxford, 1959-67; Professor of Clinical Pathology, Oxford Univ., 1964-67, now Emeritus (Reader in Haematology, 1957-64); Clinical Pathologist, Radcliffe Infirmary, Oxford, 1941-67. Vice-President, Haemophilia Society, 1955. *Publications:* (with R. Biggs) Human Blood Coagulation and its Disorders (3rd edn, 1962); papers, chapters in books and encyclopædias on haematological and pathological subjects. *Address:* Park Cottage, Ramsden, Oxford. *Club:* United University.

**MACFARLANE, Robert Mafeking,** CMG 1954; MP (L) (New Zealand) for Christchurch Central from 1946 (for Christchurch South, 1936-46); *b* Christchurch, NZ, 17 May 1901; *m* 1932, Louisa E., *d* of T. F. Jacobs, Woolston. *Educ:* Christchurch, NZ. Secretary, Christchurch Labour Representation Cttee, 1929; Member Christchurch City Council for many years (Mayor, 1938-41). Chairman Metropolitan Transport Licensing Authority. Formerly Senior Opposition Whip, and Speaker, New Zealand Parliament. Served War of 1939-45 with Second New Zealand Expeditionary Force. *Address:* 19 Stenness Avenue, Christchurch, SW1, New Zealand.

**McFARLANE, Stuart Gordon,** CMG 1933; *b* 4 May, 1885; *s* of late J. J. McFarlane, Malden, Victoria; *m* Grace (decd), *d* of late Alfred McDermott, Orange, NSW; one *s*; *m* 1958, Evelyn (decd), *widow* of Hon. J. A. Perkins, MP. Asst Secretary (Finance), Commonwealth Treasury, 1926-32; Asst Secretary (Administrative) Treasury, 1932-35; also Secretary to Australian Loan Council and Secretary to National Debt Commission, 1932-36; Official Secretary, Australia House, 1936-37; Secretary to Commonwealth Treasury, 1938-48; Mem. of Commonwealth Bank Board, 1938-45; Mem. of Commonwealth Bank Advisory Council, 1945-48. Mem. of Overseas Telecommunications Commn (Australia), 1946-48; Exec. Director of International Monetary Fund; also International Bank for Development, Washington, 1948-50. *Address:* 22 Dampier Crescent, Canberra, ACT 2603, Australia. *Club:* Australian (Sydney).

**MacFARQUHAR, Sir Alexander,** KBE, *cr* 1952; CIE 1945; Director of Personnel, United Nations, 1962-67; *b* 6 Nov. 1903; *s* of Roderick MacFarquhar; *m* 1929, Berenice Whitburn; one *s*. *Educ:* Aberdeen Univ. (MA 1st class Hons Classics); Emmanuel Coll., Cambridge. Entered ICS 1926; Deputy Commissioner, Ferozepore, 1930; Deputy Commissioner, Amritsar, 1933; Settlement Officer, Amritsar, 1936; Deputy Secretary, Government of India, 1941; Deputy Director-General, Directorate-General of Supply, Government of India, 1943; Dir-Gen. Disposals, India, 1946; Commerce and Education Sec. Govt of Pakistan, 1947-51. Resident Rep. to Pakistan of UN Technical Assistance Board, 1952; Regional Rep. to Far East, of UN Technical Assistance Board, Bangkok, 1955; UN Secretary General's Special Adviser for Civilian Affairs in the Congo, 1960. *Address:* Ottershaw, Beverley Lane, Coombe Hill, Kingston-upon-Thames, Surrey.

*See also R. L. MacFarquhar.*

**MacFARQUHAR, Roderick Lemonde;** research scholar and freelance journalist; *b* 2 Dec. 1930; *s* of Sir Alexander MacFarquhar, *qv; m* 1964, Emily Jane Cohen; one *d. Educ:* Fettes Coll.; Oxford Univ. (BA); Harvard Univ. (AM). Specialist on China, Daily Telegraph (and later Sunday Telegraph), 1955-61; Founding Editor, China Quarterly, 1959-68; Rockefeller Grantee, 1962; Reporter, BBC TV programme Panorama, 1963-64. Associate Fellow, St Antony's Coll., Oxford, 1965-68. Mem., Editorial Bd, New Statesman, 1965-69; Ford Foundation Grant, 1968; Senior Research Fellow, Columbia Univ., 1969. Contested (Lab): Ealing South, 1966; Meriden, March 1968. *Publications:* The Hundred Flowers, 1960; The Sino-Soviet Dispute, 1961; Chinese Ambitions and British Policy (Fabian Pamphlet), 1966; (ed) China under Mao, 1966; articles in Foreign Affairs, The World Today, Atlantic Monthly, Pacific Affairs, Commentary, etc. *Recreations:* reading, listening to music, travel. *Address:* 187 Queen's Gate, SW7.

**Mac FEELY, Most Rev. Anthony;** *see* Raphoe, Bishop of, (RC).

**McFETRICH, Cecil,** OBE 1949; Managing Director: Austin & Pickersgill Ltd, since 1969 (Jt Man. Dir, 1968-69); Bartram & Sons Ltd, since 1964; Ward & Davidson Ltd; Chairman, Sunderland Structural Steel Ltd; Director: Coachwork Repairs & Painting Co. Ltd; Sunderland and Shields Building Soc., etc; *b* 17 Jan. 1911; *y s* of Archibald B. and Hannah B. McFetrich; *m* 1937, Kathleen M. Proom; four *s. Educ:* Cowan Terrace Sch., Sunderland; Skerry's Coll., Newcastle upon Tyne. Qual. Chartered Accountant, 1933. After varied industrial and professional experience, joined Bartram & Sons Ltd, South Dock, Sunderland, as Sec., 1936; apptd a Dir, 1939; responsible for sales and marketing, 1945-. Mem., Sunderland Town Council, 1942-51 (Chm. Finance Cttee, 1943-44); served on various Nat. Savings Cttees, 1940-63; Chairman: Sunderland Savings Cttee, 1947-63; N Regional Industrial Savings Cttee, 1956-62. Liveryman, Worshipful Co. of Shipwrights; Mem., River Wear Commn. *Recreations:* golf, bowls. *Address:* 8 Belle Vue Drive, Sunderland, Durham. *T:* Sunderland 6502. *Clubs:* City Livery; Sunderland (Sunderland).

**MACFIE, Prof. Alec Lawrence,** MA, LLB, DLitt (Glasgow); Hon. LLD (Glasgow); Professor of Political Economy, University of Glasgow, 1946-58, retired; *b* 29 May 1898; *s* of Rev. W. G. Macfie, Mowbray, Cape Town; unmarried. *Educ:* High School of Glasgow; University of Glasgow. Served European War, 1917-18, The 2nd Bn The Gordon Highlanders. Lecturer in Political Economy, Glasgow Univ., 1930-45. *Publications:* Theories of the Trade Cycle, 1934; An Essay on Economy and Value, 1936; Economic Efficiency and Social Welfare, 1943; The Individual in Society: Papers on Adam Smith, 1967. *Address:* Torbeg, Heathfield Drive, Milngavie, Dunbartonshire. *T:* 041-956 1649. *Club:* Art (Glasgow).

**MACFIE, Maj.-General John Mandeville,** CB 1951; CBE 1946; MC 1917; OStJ 1945; *b* 13 Dec. 1891; *s* of Rev. W. G. Macfie, Mowbray, Cape Town; unmarried. *Educ:* S. African College School; Glasgow High Sch.; Glasgow Univ. MB, ChB (with honours) Glasgow, 1915. FRCP Glasgow, 1964. Lieut, RAMC, 1915: Dep. Assistant Director of Pathology, India, 1926-29; Dep. Assistant Director-General of Army Medical Services, War Office, 1932-36; Dep. DGAMS War Office, 1943-46; DDMS, East Africa Command, 1946-48; DDMS, Scottish Command, 1949; Commandant RAM Coll., 1949-50; KHS 1950; Dep. Director of Medical Services, Western Command, UK, 1950-51; retired pay, Jan. 1952; Colonel Commandant RAMC, 1951-56. Governor, Glasgow School of Art. Commander Order Leopold II of Belgium, 1949. *Recreations:* golf, fishing. *Address:* 10 Heathfield Drive, Milngavie, by Glasgow. *Clubs:* Royal Scottish Automobile; Glasgow Art.

**McGARVEY, Daniel,** CBE 1970; President, Amalgamated Society of Boilermakers, Shipwrights, Blacksmiths and Structural Workers, since 1965; *b* 16 Sept. 1919; British parentage; *m* 1942, Jean Scullion; two *d. Educ:* Our Holy Redeemer's RC Sch., Clydebank; St Patrick's High Sch., Dumbarton. Elected Mem., Exec. Council, Amalgamated Soc. Boilermakers etc., 1951; Exec. Council of Confederation of Shipbuilding and Engineering Unions, 1954; Chm. Boilermakers' Executive Council, 1954; National Executive of the Labour Party, 1958-65; Gen. Sec. Soc. Boilermakers Section of Amalgamated Soc., 1964. Mem., Gen. Council, TUC, 1965-. Member: Shipbuilding Industry Training Bd; Shipbuilding and Shiprepairing Council. *Recreations:* gardening, football, reading. *Address:* (home) 5 Coldstream Road, Newcastle upon Tyne 5. *T:* Newcastle upon Tyne 38619; (office) Lifton House, Eslington Road, Newcastle upon Tyne. *T:* Newcastle upon Tyne 813205.

**McGAW, William Rankin,** CB 1955; *b* 17 Jan. 1900; *er s* of late William McGaw; *m* 1928, Agnes Hannah Scott; no *c. Educ:* Allen Glen's Sch., Glasgow; Glasgow Univ. (BSc). Entered Civil Service, Air Ministry Development staff, 1924. Served Royal Aircraft Establishment, Farnborough, 1924-39. Appointed Dir of Aircraft Equipment Production, 1941, Ministry of Aircraft Production and later Ministry of Supply. Director: of Aircraft Supplies (General), 1946-48; of Production, 1948-52; Dir-Gen. of Aircraft Production, Ministry of Supply, 1952-61. FRAeS 1953. *Recreations:* fly-fishing, gardening. *Address:* Orchard Lodge, Sycamore Road, Farnborough, Hants. *T:* Farnborough, Hants. 41013.

**McGEE, Prof. James Dwyer,** OBE 1952; FRS 1966; MSc Sydney; PhD Cantab; ScD; CEng; FIEE; FInstP; FRAS; Hon. ARCS; Professor of Applied Physics, Imperial College of Science and Technology, London, SW7, since 1954; *b* Canberra, ACT, 17 Dec. 1903; *s* of Francis and Mary McGee; *m* 1944, Hilda Mary, *d* of George Winstone, Takapuna, Auckland, NZ; no *c. Educ:* St Patrick's Coll., Goulburn, NSW; St John's Coll., Sydney Univ. (MSc); Clare Coll., Cambridge (PhD). 1851 Exhibition Scholar from Sydney Univ. to Cambridge. Nuclear physics research, Cavendish Laboratory, Cambridge, 1928-31; Research physicist, Electric and Musical Industries Research Laboratories, Hayes, Middx. Engaged on research on photo-electricity and electronic problems of Television, 1932-39; research on electronic problems in connection with military operations, in particular the use of infra-red light, 1939-45; returned to work on photo-electronic devices for television and other scientific purposes, 1945-54. Awarded Research Fellowship, Carnegie Inst., Washington, 1960; Hon. Research Associate, Carnegie Inst., 1960, 1962, 1966. *Publications:* chap. on Electronic Generation of Television Signals in Electronics (ed B. Lovell), 1947; ed Vols XII, XVI, XXII, XXVIII, Advances in Electronics: Symposia on Photoelectronic Devices, 1960, 1962, 1966, 1969. Technical papers in Engineering, Physical and Technical Jls. *Recreations:* gardening, music. *Address:* 56 Corringway, W5. *T:* 01-997 7160. *Clubs:* Athenæum; Ski Club of Great Britain.

**McGEE, Rt. Rev. Joseph;** *see* Galloway, Bishop of, (RC).

**McGEOCH, Vice-Adm. Sir Ian (Lachlan Mackay),** KCB 1969 (CB 1966); DSO 1943; DSC 1943; Flag Officer, Scotland and Northern Ireland, 1968-70; *b* 26 March 1914; 3rd *s* of L. A. McGeoch of Dalmuir; *m* 1937, Eleanor Somers, *d* of Rev. Hugh Farrie; two *s* two *d*. *Educ:* The Nautical Coll., Pangbourne. Midshipman, 1932; Comdr 1947; Captain 1955; Rear-Adm. 1964; Vice-Adm. 1967. Comd HM Submarine Splendid, 1942-43; Staff Officer (Ops) 4th Cruiser Sqdn, 1944-45; Comd: HMS Fernie, 1946-47; 4th Submarine Squadron, 1949-51; 3rd Submarine Squadron, 1956-57; Dir of Undersurface Warfare, Admiralty, 1959; IDC 1961; Comd HMS Lion 1962-64; Admiral Pres., RNC, Greenwich, 1964-65; Flag Officer Submarines, 1966-67. MBIM. *Publications:* contrib. to Jl of Royal United Service Instn. *Recreations:* sailing, music, literary research. *Address:* Mansefield, Thornhill, Dumfriesshire. *Clubs:* United Service; Royal Naval, Royal Yacht Squadron, Royal Naval Sailing Association.

**McGHEE, George Crews,** Legion of Merit; former diplomat; Director: Mobil Oil Co., since 1969; Procter and Gamble Co., since 1969; American Security & Trust Co., since 1969; *b* Waco, Texas, 10 March 1912; *s* of George Summers McGhee and Magnolia (*née* Spruce); *m* 1938, Cecilia Jeanne DeGolyer; two *s* four *d*. *Educ:* Southern Methodist Univ., Dallas; Univ. of Oklahoma; Oxford Univ. (Rhodes Schol.); Univ. of London. BS (Oklahoma) 1933; DPhil (Oxon) 1937. Served with US Navy, 1943-45 (Asiatic ribbon with three battle stars). Geologist and geophysicist, 1930-40; Oil producer, sole owner, McGhee Production Co., 1940-. Special Asst to Under-Sec of State for Economic Affairs, 1946; Coordinator for Aid to Greece and Turkey, 1947; Asst Sec. of State for Near Eastern, South Asian and African Affairs, 1949; US Ambassador to Turkey, 1951; Consultant, Nat. Security Council, 1958; Mem. President's Cttee to Study Mil. Asst Program, 1958; Counselor of Dept of State and Chm. of State Dept Policy Planning Council, 1961; Under-Sec. of State for Political Affairs, 1961; US Ambassador to the Federal Republic of Germany, 1963-68; Ambassador-at-Large, 1968-69. Chairman: English Speaking Union, 1969-; Business Council for Internat. Understanding, 1969-; Member: Salzburg Seminar, 1969-; Nat. Civil Service League, 1969-; Population Crisis Cttee, 1969-; Population Crisis Foundn of Texas, 1969-. Trustee: Duke Univ.; Cttee for Economic Development, 1957-; Aspen Institute for Humanistic Studies, 1958-. Hon. Fellow, Queen's Coll., Oxford, 1969. Distinguished Service Citation, Univ. of Oklahoma, 1952; Hon. DCL, Southern Methodist Univ., 1953; Hon. LLD: Tulane Univ., 1957; Univ. of Maryland, 1965; Hon. DSc, Univ. of Tampa, 1969. Ouissam Alaouite Cherifien, Govt Morocco, 1950; Hon. Citizen, Ankara, Turkey, 1954. *Publications:* contribs to Foreign Affairs, Gewerkschaftliche Rundschau, Werk und Wir, Europa Archiv, Universitas, Ruperto-Carola Weltraumfahrt-Raketentechnik, Europa. *Recreations:* hunting, tennis, photography. *Address:* 2808 North Street, NW, Washington, DC 20007, USA; Farmers' Delight, Middleburg, Va, USA. *Clubs:* Metropolitan (Washington, DC); Chevy Chase (Maryland); Brook, Century Association (New York); City Tavern Association (Georgetown, DC).

**McGHIE, James Ironside;** Counsellor (Commercial), British Embassy, Stockholm, since 1970; *b* 12 Oct. 1915; *s* of William I. McGhie and Annie E. Ratcliffe; *m* 1946, Ellen-Johanne Gran; two *s* one *d*. *Educ:* King Henry VIII Sch., Coventry. Journalist, 1933-39. Army, 1940-46. Entered Foreign Service, 1946; Stockholm, 1946-49; Helsinki, 1949-52; Foreign Office, 1952-54; Tokyo, 1954-57; Singapore, 1957-58; First Sec., Saigon, 1958-60; Foreign Office, 1960-62; Bucharest, 1962-64 (acted Chargé d'affaires, 1962 and 1963); First Sec., DSAO, 1964-67; Consul-General, Seattle, 1967-70. *Recreations:* walking, languages. *Address:* British Embassy, 115-27 Stockholm, Sweden. *T:* 67-01-40.

**McGHIE, Maj.-Gen. John,** QHP; MD, DPM; Director of Army Psychiatry and Consultant in Psychiatry to the Army, since 1970; *b* Larkhall, Scotland; *s* of Henry and Agnes McGhie; *m* 1940, Hilda Lilian Owen; two *s*. *Educ:* Hamilton Academy; Glasgow University. Medical Officer: Glasgow Western Infirmary, 1936-37; Bellshill Maternity Hosp., 1937; Captain, RAMC, 1938; MO, British Mil. Hosp. Rawalpindi, 1939; Major, 2nd in Comd Field Ambulance, 1939-43; Lt-Col, OC Field Amb., 1943-45; Comd Psychiatrist: Scottish Comd, 1948; Far East, 1949-52; OC, Royal Victoria Hosp., Netley, 1956-61; Dir of Army Psychiatry, 1961-67; DDMS, Malaya and Western Comd, 1967-70. *Recreations:* golf, motoring. *Address:* Mandavara, 9 Ross Road, South Norwood, SE25. *T:* 01-653 7488.

**McGILL, Maj.-Gen. Allan,** CB 1969; CBE 1964 (OBE 1945; MBE 1943); Director of Electrical and Mechanical Engineering (Army), 1966-69; *b* 1914; *s* of William McGill; *m* 1945, Kathleen German. *Educ:* George Heriot's, Edinburgh; Heriot-Watt Coll. (now Heriot-Watt Univ.). Served War of 1939-45 (despatches, 1943). Dir, Electrical and Mechanical Engineering, British Army of the Rhine, 1965-66. Brig., 1961; Maj.-Gen., 1966. Col Comdt, REME, 1969-. MIMechE. *Recreations:* motor rallying, ski-ing. *Address:* c/o Ministry of Defence (Army), Whitehall, SW1; 2a, Plympton Road, NW6.

**McGILL, Air Vice-Marshal Frank Scholes,** CB 1945; RCAF, retired; *b* Montreal, 1894; *m* 1924, Margaret, *d* of Thomas Williamson, Montreal; one *s* two *d*. *Educ:* Montreal High Sch.; McGill Univ., Montreal. Entered service of Dominion Oilcloth and Linoleum Co., 1913; Advertising Manager to this firm, 1924; Dir and Sec., 1930-62, Vice-Pres. (Sales), 1954-62, retired 1962 (still a Dir). Dir, Canadair Ltd. Hon. Pres., Montreal Gen. Hospital; Chm., Donner Canadian Foundation. *Address:* 3150 Trafalgar Avenue, Montreal, Quebec, Canada. *Clubs:* Mount Royal, St James's, University, Montreal Racket, United Services, Canadian, Seigniory, Mount Bruno Country (Montreal); Rideau (Ottawa).

**MacGILL, George Roy Buchanan,** CBE 1965; General Manager, Cumbernauld Development Corporation, 1956-70; *b* 20 Dec. 1905; *s* of George Buchanan MacGill; *m* 1934, Jean Ferguson Anderson; two *d*. *Educ:* Glasgow High Sch. Chartered Accountant, 1928.

FIMTA 1938. Town Chamberlain, Airdrie, 1932; Burgh Chamberlain, Dunfermline, 1947. *Recreation:* golf. *Address:* 6 Collylinn Road, Bearsden, Glasgow.

**McGILL, Maj.-Gen. Nigel Harry Duncan,** CB 1966; Chief of Staff to Commandant-General, Royal Marines, 1967-68, retired, 1968; *b* 15 Oct. 1916; *s* of Lt-Col H. R. McGill; *m* 1944, Margaret Constance Killen; two *s* one *d. Educ:* Victoria Coll., Jersey. Commissioned 2nd Lt RM 1934; Maj.-Gen. 1964; Comdr, Portsmouth Group, RM, 1964-67. *Recreations:* cricket, golf. *Address:* Bryn House, Atlow, Ashbourne, Derbyshire. *Club:* Army and Navy.

**McGILL, Rt. Rev. Stephen;** *see* Paisley, Bishop of, (RC).

**McGILLIGAN, Denis Brian;** in Office of the Legal Adviser, Ministry of Agriculture, Fisheries and Food; *b* 26 June 1921; *s* of Michael McGilligan, SC, and Mary Georgina McGilligan (*née* Musgrave); *m* 1952, Hazel Patricia Pakenham Keady; one *s* two *d. Educ:* St Gerard's, Bray, Co. Wicklow; Trinity Coll., Dublin (BA). Practised at Irish Bar, 1945-52; Crown Counsel, Sarawak, and Dep. Legal Adviser, Brunei, 1952-58; Senior Magistrate, Sarawak, 1958-59; Acting Puisne Judge, Combined Judiciary, 1959-60; Senior Magistrate, Sarawak, 1960-63; Puisne Judge, Combined Judiciary of Sarawak, North Borneo and Brunei, March, 1963; Judge of the High Court in Borneo, Malaysia, 1963-66. Called to the Bar, Gray's Inn, 1966. *Recreations:* any available ball game, in particular hockey; swimming, sailing, reading. *Address:* Greenlands, Rotherfield, Sussex. *T:* Rotherfield 215. *Clubs:* Civil Service; Civil Service Squash; Sarawak (Kuching); Brunei Yacht (Brunei).

**MacGILLIVRAY, Prof. Ian,** MD, FRCOG; Regius Professor of Obstetrics and Gynæcology, University of Aberdeen, since 1965; *b* 25 Oct. 1920; *yr s* of W. and A. MacGillivray; *m* 1950, Edith Mary Margaret Cook; one *s* twin *d. Educ:* Vale of Leven Academy, Alexandria; University of Glasgow. Gardiner Research Schol., 1949-51; Lecturer in Midwifery, 1951-53; University of Glasgow; Senior Lecturer: in obstetrics and Gynæcology Univ. of Bristol, 1953-55; in midwifery and gynæcology, Univ. of Aberdeen, 1955-61; Prof. of Obstetrics and Gynæcology, University of London, at St Mary's Hospital Medical Sch., 1961-65. MB, ChB 1944, FRCOG 1959 (MRCOG 1949), MD 1953, University of Glasgow. *Publications:* Outline of Human Reproduction, 1963. Contrib. to: British Medical Journal, Lancet, Journal of Obstetrics and Gynæcology of the British Empire; Clinical Science. *Address:* Greenway, 279 N Deeside Road, Cults, Aberdeen AB1 9PA. *T:* 48777.

**McGINNETY, Frank Edward,** CBE 1961; *b* 29 March 1907; *s* of William Henry and Margaret McGinnety; *m* 1949, Doris Marie Grigson. *Educ:* Rutherford Coll., Newcastle upon Tyne; Armstrong Coll., University of Durham (MSc). Min. of Supply: Signals Research and Development Establishment, 1929-54; asst Dir, Electronics Research and Development, 1954-55; Dir of Inspectorate of Electrical and Mechanical Equipment, 1955-57; Dep. Dir-Gen. of Inspection, Min. of Supply, 1957-59, Min. of Aviation, 1959-60; Dir-Gen. of Inspection, Min. of Aviation, 1960-66. CEng, FIEE; Mem. and Past Pres., Instn of Engineering Inspection. *Recreations:* sailing, horticulture, painting, photography. *Address:* Broadlands, Malmains Way, Beckenham, Kent. *T:* 01-650 7503.

**McGIRR, Prof. Edward McCombie,** BSc, MD Glasgow; FRCP, FRCPE, FRCPGlas; Muirhead Professor of Medicine, Glasgow University, since Oct. 1961; Physician, Glasgow Royal Infirmary; *b* 15 June 1916; *yr s* of William and Ann McGirr, Hamilton, Lanarkshire; *m* 1949, Diane Curzon, *y c* of Alexander Woods, MBE, TD, DL, and Edith E. C. Woods, Birmingham and London; one *s* three *d. Educ:* Hamilton Academy; Glasgow Univ. BSc 1937; MB, ChB (Hons) Glasgow, 1940; MD (Hons) and Bellahouston Medal, 1960. Served RAMC, 1941-46, in UK, India, Burma, Siam, Indo-China; Medical Specialist; demobilized with hon. rank of Major. External Examiner in Medicine for BDS Edinburgh Univ., 1957-60, MB ChB, Edinburgh Univ. 1962-65, Birmingham Univ., 1966-69, Aberdeen Univ., 1967-69, and Hong Kong Univ., 1968; Examiner for MRCP Edinburgh, Glasgow and London. Visitor, Royal Coll. of Physicians and Surgeons of Glasgow, 1968-. Member: Medical Appeals Tribunals, 1961-; Scottish Health Services Coun. 1965-; National Panel of Specialists; Assoc. of Physicians of Gt Britain and Ireland (mem. of editorial panel, quarterly journal of Medicine, 1968-); Scottish Soc. of Physicians; Scottish Soc. for Experimental Med. (Treas., 1960-66); Soc. of Endocrinology; European Thyroid Assoc.; Corresp. Member: Amer. Thyroid Assoc.; Medical Research Soc. (mem. of council, 1967-69); Royal Medico-Chirurgical Soc. of Glasgow (Pres., 1965-66). *Publications:* chiefly in relation to thyroid gland dysfunction. *Recreations:* family life, medical work, and detective fiction. *Address:* Anchorage House, Bothwell, by Glasgow. *T:* Bothwell 2194; University Department of Medicine, Royal Infirmary, 86 Castle Street, Glasgow, C4. *T:* 041-552 3535, extension 370. *Clubs:* Royal Scottish Automobile, Western (Glasgow).

**McGLASHAN, Rear-Adm. (retd) Sir Alexander Davidson,** KBE, *cr* 1954; CB 1953; DSO 1946; FIMechE; *b* 8 Oct. 1901; *s* of Dugald and Margaret Neilson McGlashan (*née* Davidson); *m* 1926, Irene Margaret Cooke; two *s* one *d. Educ:* Perth Acad. Cadet, RN, 1919; Midshipman, 1921; Sub-Lt, 1922; Lt (E) 1923; Lt-Comdr (E), 1931; Comdr (E), 1935; Capt (E), 1944; Rear-Adm. (E), 1951. Retired, 1955. *Recreations:* gardening, carpentry. *Address:* Rotherway, Potterne Wick, Devizes, Wilts. *T:* Devizes 2950. *Club:* Royal Automobile.

**McGLASHAN, Archibald A.,** RSA 1939 (ARSA 1935); Artist Painter; *b* 16 March 1888; *s* of John Crooks McGlashan and Agnes Thomson; *m* 1922, Teresa Giuliani; one *s* two *d. Educ:* Paisley; Glasgow. Trained at Glasgow Sch. of Art; Travelled extensively on the Continent, visiting chief Art centres. Pictures purchased by:–Scottish Modern Art Assoc.; Glasgow, Belfast, Newcastle, Aberdeen, Paisley, Perth, Dundee, and Edinburgh Corporations; Glasgow Univ., Arts Council of Great Britain. Has exhibited pictures at Royal Scottish Acad., Royal Acad., The Royal Glasgow Institute of the Fine Arts, The Paisley Art Institute, Walker Art Gallery, Liverpool and in America and Canada; is a mem. of the Soc. of Eight. *Address:* Gayfield, Serpentine Road, Rothesay, Bute. *Club:* Art (Glasgow).

**McGONIGAL, Ambrose Joseph,** MC 1943 and bar 1944; **Hon. Mr Justice McGonigal;** Judge of the High Court of Justice, Northern Ireland, since 1968; *b* 22 Nov. 1917; 2nd *s* of late Judge John McGonigal, KC and late Margaret McGonigal; *m* 1941, Patricia, *o d* of Robert

Taylor; two *s* two *d*. *Educ:* Clongowes Wood Coll.; Queen's Univ., Belfast. Served HM Forces, 1939-46; commnd RUR, 1940; 12th Commando, 1943-44; Special Boat Service, 1944-45 (despatches). Called to Bar, N Ireland, 1948; to Inner Bar of N Ireland, 1956; Bencher, The Inn of Court of N Ireland, 1964. Member: Cttee on Public Library Service in N Ire.; Cttee on Adult Education in N Ire.; N Ire. Charities Central Investment Fund Advisory Cttee, 1966-; Senate, QUB, 1969-. Governor: Armagh Observatory, 1968-; St Joseph's Coll. of Education, 1969-. *Recreations:* various. *Address:* 16 Hawthornden Road, Belfast 4. *Club:* Special Forces.

**MacGONIGAL, Maurice,** PRHA; Hon. RA; Hon. RSA; Professor of Painting, Royal Hibernian Academy; Member of Board of Governors, National Gallery of Ireland; Member of Advisory Committees: of Municipal Gallery of Modern Art; for Wolfe Tone Memorial; Coun. of Industrial Design; Coun. of Cultural Relations, Ireland; *b* Dublin, Jan. 1900; *s* of Frank MacGonigal and Caroline Lane; *m*; two *s*. Studied at Dublin Metropolitan Sch. of Art; Taylor Scholarship in Painting, 1924; Interested in Irish Landscape and Genre Painting; exhibited London, America, etc.; is represented by pictures: Municipal Gallery of Modern Art, Dublin, Cork, Belfast and Limerick Galleries; Senate Chambers, Leinster House, Dublin RCP. Silver Medal for Landscape Painting Tailteann Games, Eire, 1928. *Address:* 14 Garville Avenue, Rathgar, Dublin 6. *T:* 974621.

**MACGOUGAN, John;** General Secretary, National Union of Tailors and Garment Workers; *b* 21 Aug. 1913; *m* 1941, Betty Faulkner; three *s* one *d*. *Educ:* various Northern Ireland Schs; Technical Sch.; Correspondence courses. Accountancy profession, 1930-45. Irish Officer, NUTGW, in charge of all Irish affairs, 1945-69. Contested (Irish Labour) N Ireland Parly Elections, Oldpark 1938, Falls Div. 1951; Westminster Parly Election, South Down 1950; Member: Belfast Corporation, 1949-58; Executive, Irish TUC, 1950-69 (Pres. 1957-58 and 1963-64); TUC General Council, 1970-. *Recreations:* proletarian pastimes. *Address:* 16 Ansdell Terrace, W8. *T:* 01-937 4656. *Club:* Irish.

**McGOUGAN, Malcolm;** Barrister-at-law; Recorder of Poole, since 1954; Deputy-Chairman, Surrey Quarter Sessions, since 1956; *b* 19 Aug. 1905; *s* of late Angus McGougan, Nottingham; *m* 1929, Enid Monica, *y d* of late Albert Hopkinson, Cambridge; two *s*. *Educ:* Nottingham High Sch.; Pembroke Coll., Cambridge (MA). Called to the Bar, 1929. Western Circuit and Wilts Sessions. Served RAFVR, Middle East, North Africa and UK, 1940-45 (despatches four times); Wing Comdr. Recorder of Andover, 1948-54. *Recreation:* fishing. *Address:* 1 Paper Buildings, Temple, EC4; Stubbetts, Forest Green, near Dorking, Surrey. *Clubs:* United University; Hampshire.

**McGOVERN, Sir Patrick (Silvesta),** Kt 1959; CBE 1954; Company Director; *b* 4 April 1895; *s* of late John and Elizabeth McGovern; *m* 1922, Henrietta Rose, *d* of late John Laurissen and of Matilda Laurissen; two *d*. *Educ:* State Schs, Vic.; Beechworth Coll. Entered Commonwealth Public Service, 1911; Income Tax Assessor, 1925-30; Chief Investigation Officer, Sales Tax, 1930-39; Dep. Comr of Taxation, Canberra, 1939-42; Second Comr of Taxation, 1942-46; Commissioner of Taxation, Commonwealth of Australia, 1946-61. *Recreation:* golf. *Address:* 4 Barkly Crescent, Forrest, Canberra, ACT. *T:* U1850. *Clubs:* Commonwealth (Canberra); Melbourne (Melbourne); Union (Sydney).

**McGOWAN,** family name of **Baron McGowan.**

**McGOWAN,** 3rd Baron, *cr* 1937; **Harry Duncan Cory McGowan;** *b* 20 July 1938; *e s* of Harry Wilson McGowan, 2nd Baron McGowan, and Carmen, *d* of Sir (James) Herbert Cory, 1st Bt; *S* father, 1966; *m* 1962, Lady Gillian Angela Pepys, *d* of 7th Earl of Cottenham; two *d*. *Educ:* Eton. *Heir:* *b* Hon. Dominic James Wilson McGowan, *b* 26 Nov. 1951. *Address:* House of Lords, Westminster, SW1; 25 St Luke's Street, SW3. *T:* 01-352 2056. *Club:* St James'.

**McGOWAN, Bruce Henry,** MA; FRSA; Headmaster, Solihull School, since 1964; *b* 27 June 1924; *er s* of late Rt Rev. Henry McGowan, sometime Bishop of Wakefield, and Nora Heath McGowan (*née* Godwin); *m* 1947, Beryl McKenzie (*née* Liggitt); one *s* three *d*. *Educ:* King Edward's Sch., Birmingham; Jesus Coll., Cambridge. War service, Royal Artillery, 1943-46. Asst Master, King's Sch., Rochester, 1949-53; Senior History Master, Wallasey Gram. Sch., 1953-57; Headmaster, De Aston Sch., Market Rasen, Lincs, 1957-64. Page Scholar of the English-Speaking Union, 1961. Member: Church Assembly, 1963-70; Public Schools Commn, 1968-70; Chm., Boarding Schools Assoc., 1967-69. *Recreations:* camping, mountain-walking, music, the theatre, rugby refereeing. *Address:* Solihull School, Warwicks. *T:* 021-705 0958. *Club:* English-Speaking Union.

**MACGOWAN, Gault;** Journalist; FJI; Editor and Publisher, European Life, since 1955; *b* England, Feb. 1894; *m* 1923, Wendy (*d* 1961), *y d* of late J. H. Corley Smith, Simla and Transvaal; one *s*. Late Captain Indian Cavalry, R of O; served France, Italy, Mesopotamia; Associated Press Correspondent N W Frontier, India, 1922-23; Editor Times of Mesopotamia, 1924; Sub-Editor, The Times, 1925; Staff Correspondent Daily Express, Paris, 1926-27; Asst Editor and Leader Writer Evening Express, Cardiff, 1927-28; Editor Londoner's Diary, Newspaper Features Ltd, 1928-29; Managing Editor, Trinidad Guardian, 1929-34; joined New York Sun, 1934, European Manager from 1946 until its amalgamation with New York World-Telegram, 1950. Delegate West Indies 4th Imperial Press Conference, 1930; Hon. Sec. on Council Institute of Journalists representing West Indies, 1930-35; Selfridge Prizeman; Company of Newspaper Makers, 1932; Officier de l'Instruction Publique, 1930; Officer of Military Order of Christ, Portugal, 1933; Chevalier de la Légion d'Honneur, 1934; Officer of the Order of Ouissam Alaouite Cherifien, Morocco, 1938; Croix de Guerre, 1943; Médaille de la France Libérée, 1949; Liveryman of the Stationers' Company and Freeman of the City of London since 1937. *Travels:* Notably, Himalayas, discovered new pass into Little Thibet (received thanks Survey of India); first flight over Orinoco delta and across Venezuelan Llanos Trinidad-Maracay; first flight, Trinidad-British Guiana; Special Correspondent, New York Times, with Beebe Bathysphere Expedition to Bermuda, 1934; Special Correspondent The Sun, at the Coronation of King George VI, Spanish Civil War, and with the French Foreign Legion in Algeria and Morocco, 1937; accredited War Correspondent with the British and US Armies, War of 1939-45; Battle of Britain; Battle of the Atlantic and with the

Commandos; African and European Campaigns, 1942-45 (wounded, Purple Heart). Captured by Germans in Allied drive to Paris; escaped and joined French Maquis until liberated, 1944. Potsdam Conference, 1945; UNO, London, 1946, and subsequently with NATO forces. *Publications:* To the End of the World and Beyond; My Desert Dash to Damascus; Heidelberg Confidential!; Switzerland Confidential!; Bavaria Confidential!, 1956; Elizabeth Stuart: Her Story, 1963. *Address:* 15 Schlierbacher Aue, Heidelberg, Germany. *Clubs:* Authors', Press.

**McGRATH, Sir Charles (Gullan),** Kt 1968; OBE 1964; Chairman, Repco Ltd, since 1957; *b* 22 Nov. 1910; *s* of David Charles McGrath and Elizabeth McGrath; *m* 1934, Madge Louise; one *s* four *d. Educ:* Ballarat High Sch. Gen. Man., Replacement Parts Pty Ltd, 1946-53; Repco Ltd: Dir, 1948; Man. Dir, 1953-67, retd; Chm. of Dirs, 1957. Vice-President: Australia-Japan Business Co-operation Cttee; Defence Industrial Cttee; Member: Victorian Pipelines Commn; Consultative Council, Export Payments Insurance Corp.; Adv. Council, CSIRO. *Recreations:* golf, swimming. *Address:* 46 Lansell Road, Toorak, Vic. 3142, Australia. *Clubs:* Athenæum, Commonwealth, Kelvin, West Brighton (all in Australia).

**McGRATH, John Cornelius,** FCA; full-time Board Member and Financial Controller of British Airports Authority since 1966; *s* of Patrick and Johanna McGrath; bachelor. *Educ:* St Ignatius Coll. Schoolmaster, 1925-27; Asst to Public Auditor, 1927-34; Lectr in Accountancy and Finance, 1928-39; appointed Public Auditor by HM Treasury, 1934; qual. as Chartered Accountant, 1938; Dep. Man. of Audit Dept, CWS, 1938-66; Chief Accountant and Financial Adviser to LCS, 1947-66. Bd Mem. for Finance of Post Office, 1968-69. Mem., Worshipful Co. of Inn-holders, 1951; Freeman, City of London. MInstT 1970. *Recreations:* music, motor racing, travel, swimming. *Address:* 8 River Court, Surbiton, Surrey. *T:* 01-546 3833. *Clubs:* Reform, Royal Automobile, Royal Aero.

**McGRATH, Raymond,** BArch (Sydney); FRIBA; FRIAI; RHA; FSIA; Architect; *b* Sydney, NSW, 7 March 1903; *s* of Herbert Edgar McGrath, NZ, and Edith Sorrell, NSW; *m* 1930, Mary Catherine Crozier, Dallas, Texas; one *s* one *d. Educ:* Fort Street Boys Schs; Univ. Sydney (University Medal for English Verse. BArch with first class hons and University Medal, 1926, Wentworth Travelling Fellowship, 1926); Clare Coll., Cambridge (Research Student of Architecture, 1927-29). Australian Medallion of Board of Architects of NSW, 1928; Consultant to the British Broadcasting Corporation, 1930-35; in private practice in London, 1930-39; Principal Architect, Office of Public Works, Dublin, 1948-68. *Architectural works:* Finella, Cambridge, 1928; studios, furniture and equipment for BBC, 1930-34; interiors of Aircraft for Imperial Airways, 1932; various restaurants, showrooms and exhibitions; The Cenotaph, Leinster Lawn, Dublin, 1950. Appointed architect for The Kennedy Memorial Concert Hall, Dublin, 1964. Domestic work: Frognal House, Hampstead, St Ann's Hill, Chertsey; various commercial buildings; offcial works: remodelling of President's House, Dublin; adaptation of Irish Embassies in London and Paris, etc. *Drawings and paintings:* Wood engravings for illustrations; various topographical drawings; paintings in water-colour, gouache and oil. Commissioned as official War Artist, Feb. 1940, to make drawings of Aircraft Production. *Industrial Design:* Furniture, glassware, carpets. *Publications:* Twentieth Century Houses (in Basic English), 1934; Glass in Architecture and Decoration (with A. C. Frost), 1937 (new edn 1961). *Address:* Somerton Lodge, Rochestown Avenue, Co. Dublin. *T:* 804603.

**MACGREGOR, Prof. Alastair Goold,** MD, BSc, FRCP, FRCPE, FRCPGlas; Regius Professor of Materia Medica, Department of Therapeutics and Pharmacology, University of Aberdeen, since 1959; Hon. Physician, Royal Infirmary, Aberdeen; *b* 23 Dec. 1919; *er s* of late Prof. George H. C. Macgregor, DD; *m* 1944, Janet Elizabeth, *e d* of late Andrew McPherson, Sec., Boys' Brigade, Scotland; three *s* one *d. Educ:* Fettes Coll., Edinburgh; University of Glasgow. BSc 1941; MB, ChB 1943; MD (High Commendation) 1951; FRCPGlas 1947; FRCPE 1957; FRCP 1963. Surgeon Lt RNVR, 1944-46. Clinical Asst, Western Infirmary, Glasgow, 1946-48; Lecturer in Therapeutics, University of Sheffield, 1948-52; Senior Lecturer in Therapeutics, University of Edinburgh, 1952-59. Member: National Formulary Cttee, Assoc. of Physicians of Great Britain, Med. Research Soc., British Pharmacological Soc. Chm., Standing Joint Cttee for Classification of Proprietary Preparations, Ministry of Health. *Publications:* Practical Prescribing, 1953; chapters in books on therapeutics, genetics and endocrine disorders; various contributions to medical and pharmacological literature, chiefly on thyroid function and metabolic disease. *Recreations:* gardening, golf, travel and photography. *Address:* Ardruighe, Milltimber, Aberdeenshire. *T:* Aberdeen 47480; Department of Therapeutics and Pharmacology, Foresterhill, Aberdeen. *T:* Aberdeen 23423.

**MacGREGOR, Air Vice-Marshal Andrew,** CB 1949; CBE 1945; DFC 1918; retired; *b* 25 Oct. 1897; *s* of late Andrew MacGregor, Glen Gyle, Crieff; *m* 1939, Isobel Jane, *d* of Gordon Eadie, Crieff; three *d. Educ:* Morrison's Acad., Crieff. Commissioned Argyll and Sutherland Highlanders and attached RFC, 1917. Served in Egypt and Iraq, 1919-27; graduated RAF Staff Coll., 1928; served in Sudan and Palestine, 1932-37; Dep. Directorate Organisation, Air Ministry, 1940; Senior Air Staff Officer, HQ, No. 4 Group, 1940-42; Air Officer Administrative, N Africa, 1942-44; Asst Commandant, Staff Coll., 1944; Air Officer comdg No. 28 Group, 1945-46; Air Officer Administrative, HQ Fighter Command, 1946-49. Comdr Legion of Honour, 1944; Comdr Order of Crown of Belgium, 1948; Officer of Legion of Merit (USA), 1944; Croix de Guerre. *Address:* Glen Gyle, Crieff, Perthshire, Scotland. *T:* Crieff 2583. *Club:* Caledonian United Services (Edinburgh).

**MacGREGOR, Sir Colin (Malcolm),** Kt 1959; Chief Justice of Jamaica, 1957-62, retired; *b* 10 April 1901; *s* of John Malcolm MacGregor, Solicitor, Mandeville, Jamaica, and Ann Katherine (*née* Muirhead); *m* 1926, Dorothy Constance Scarlett; one *s* one *d. Educ:* Munro Coll., Jamaica; Denstone Coll., England. Called to Bar, 1922; Clerk, Resident Magistrates' Court, Jamaica, 1925; Resident Magistrate, Jamaica, 1934; Puisne Judge, Jamaica, 1947; Sen. Puisne Judge, Jamaica, 1954-57. Acted as Chief Justice, Jamaica, May-Nov. 1955. *Publications:* (ed) 5 and 6 Jamaica Law Reports. *Recreations:* golf, bridge, philately. *Address:* Garth, Knockpatrick, Jamaica. *Clubs:* Liguanea (Halfway Tree); Manchester (Mandeville, Jamaica).

**MacGREGOR, Duncan;** Convenor of the Council of Fellows in Dental Surgery, Royal College of Surgeons of Edinburgh, 1965-67; President Odonto-Chirurgical Society of Scotland, 1956-57; President, British Dental Association, 1960-61 (now Vice-President); *b* 17 Feb. 1892; *s* of A. D. MacGregor and Jessie Steel Proudfoot; *m* 1921, Elizabeth Ruth Doig; one *s* one *d. Educ:* George Heriot's Sch.; Royal Coll. of Surgeons and Edinburgh Dental Hospital and Sch. LDS, RCS Edinburgh 1916; Surgeon Probationer, RNVR 1915-17; Surg. Lt (D) RNVR 1917-19; Surg. Lt-Comdr (D) RNVR, retd 1937. Hon. Dental Surg., Edinburgh Dental Hosp. and Sch., 1921-48; Consultant Dental Surg., Edinburgh Dental Hosp., 1948-61; Member: Dental Board of the UK 1946-56; Gen. Dental Council, 1956-66. Fellowship in Dental Surgery, Royal Coll. of Surgeons, Edinburgh, 1951. *Publications:* contributions to dental journals. *Recreations:* angling, gardening. *Address:* 37 Grange Road, Edinburgh 9. *T:* 031-667 5071. *Club:* Caledonian (Edinburgh).

**MacGREGOR, Edward Ian Roy,** CMG 1966; HM Consul-General, Michigan, since 1968; *b* 4 March 1911; *s* of late John MacGregor and late Georgina Agnes MacGregor (*née* Barbor); *m* 1944, Lilianne, *d* of William Swindlehurst, Washington, DC, USA; one *s* one *d. Educ:* Methodist Coll., Belfast; Queen's Univ., Belfast (MSc). Wing Comdr RAF, 1936-47. Asst Civil Air Attaché, Washington, 1948-52; Ministry of Transport and Civil Aviation, 1952-59; Civil Air Attaché, Washington, 1959-65; Asst Sec., BoT, 1965-67; Counsellor, FO, 1967-68. *Address:* Spinneys, Brock Way, Virginia Water, Surrey.

**MACGREGOR, Sir Edwin (Robert),** 7th Bt, *cr* 1882; Plant Manager, Union Carbide Canada Ltd, Metals and Carbon, Welland, Ontario, Canada, since 1967; *b* 4 Dec. 1931; *e s* of Sir Robert McConnell Macgregor, 6th Bt, and of Annie Mary Lane; *S* father, 1963; *m* 1952, (Margaret Alice) Jean Peake; two *s* two *d. Educ:* University of British Columbia. BASc 1955, MASc 1957, Metallurgical Engineering. *Publications:* contribs to Trans Amer. Inst. of Mining, Metallurgical and Petroleum Engrg, Jl Amer. Chem. Soc. *Recreations:* reading; participation in several outdoor sports such as golf, swimming, fishing, etc.; music. *Heir: s* Robert Lionel Frederick Macgregor, *b* 10 May 1953. *Address:* 158 Woodside Drive, St Catharine's, Ontario, Canada. *T:* 684-5725.

**MacGREGOR, Geddes;** *see* MacGregor, J. G.

**McGREGOR, Hon. Sir George Innes,** Kt 1967; **Hon. Mr Justice McGregor;** Judge of the Supreme Court of New Zealand since 1953; *b* 14 May 1899; *s* of Arthur Eldred McGregor, Akaroa, NZ; *m* 1930, Elizabeth Isabella Muriel Young; two *d. Educ:* Waitaki Boys' High Sch.; University of Otago. BA, LLB, 1920; LLM hons (NZ), 1922. Barrister and Solicitor, Palmerston North, NZ, 1922-53; Crown Solicitor, Palmerston North, 1946-53. *Publications:* contribs to New Zealand Law Jl. *Recreation:* golf. *Address:* 3 Gladstone Terrace, Kelburn, Wellington W1, NZ. *Clubs:* Wellington, Hawke's Bay, Manawatu (New Zealand).

**McGREGOR, Prof. Gordon Peter;** Principal, Bishop Otter College, Chichester, since Sept. 1970; **b** Aldershot, Hants, 13 June 1932; 2nd *s* of William A. K. McGregor and Mary A. McGregor (*née* O'Brien); *m* 1957, Jean Olga Lewis; three *d. Educ:* St Brendan's Coll., Bristol; Univ. of Bristol. BA Hons (Bristol) 1953; Dip. (Coll. of Teachers of the Blind), 1958; MEd (E Africa), 1965. Educn Officer, RAF, 1953-56; Asst Master, Worcester Coll. for the Blind, 1956-59; Asst Master, King's Coll., Budo, Uganda, 1959-62; Lecturer in Language Method, Makerere Univ. Coll., Uganda 1963-66; Univ. of Zambia: Sen Lecturer in Educn, 1966; Head of Dept of Education, 1967; Reader and Head of Dept, 1968; Prof. of Educn, 1970. *Publications:* King's College, Budo, The First Sixty Years, 1967; Educating the Handicapped, 1967; English for Education?, 1968; Teaching English as a Second Language, 1970; English in Africa, (UNESCO), 1971. *Recreations:* music, literature, cricket, swimming. *Address:* Bishop Otter College, Chichester, Sussex. *T:* Chichester 83390.

**MacGREGOR of MacGregor, Lt-Col Sir Gregor,** 6th Bt, *cr* 1795; Scots Guards; 23rd Chief of Clan Gregor; *b* 22 Dec. 1925; *o s* of Capt. Sir Malcolm MacGregor of MacGregor, 5th Bt, CB, CMG, and Hon. Gylla Lady MacGregor of MacGregor, *qv*; *S* father 1958; *m* 1958, Fanny, *o d* of C. H. A. Butler, Shortgrove, Newport, Essex; two *s. Educ:* Eton. Commissioned Scots Guards, 1944; served War of 1939-45. Served in Palestine, 1947-48; Malaya, 1950-51; Borneo, 1965. Staff Coll. Course, 1960; Brigade Major, 16th Parachute Bde Gp, 1961-63; Joint Services Staff Coll., 1965; commanding 1st Bn Scots Guards, 1966-69; GSO1 (BLO) Fort Benning, USA, 1969. Mem. of the Royal Company of Archers (Queen's Body Guard for Scotland). *Heir: s* Malcolm Gregor Charles MacGregor of MacGregor, *b* 23 March 1959. *Address:* Edinchip, Lochearnhead, Perthshire. *T:* Lochearnhead 204. *Clubs:* Guards, Pratt's.

**MacGREGOR of MacGregor, Hon. Lady; (Gylla Constance Susan),** OBE 1948; *y d* of late Hon. Eric Norman Rollo; *m* 1925, Capt. Sir Malcolm MacGregor of MacGregor, 5th Bt, CB, CMG (*d* 1958); one *s* (*see* Sir Gregor MacGregor, 6th Bt) one *d. Educ:* privately. Three months' training in theatres at Guy's Hospital; in charge of Plaster Dept, Edmonton Special Military Hospital, 1917-19; private sec. to late Ian Colvin, Morning Post, 1921-24; Chm. National Exhibition of Needlework, Edinburgh, 1934; Mem. of Council of Management Empire Exhibition, Glasgow, 1938; Mem. Executive of Scottish Development Council, 1934-46; Vice-Chm. Scottish Cttee of Council for Art and Industry, 1934; Mem. Scottish Housing Advisory Cttee, 1939-42; Mem. of Council of National Trust for Scotland, 1937-46; Chairman of Women's Land Army Cttee Perth West; Mem. of Scottish Tourist Cttee; Mem. of Executive Cttee of Enterprise Scotland, 1947; Chairman Amenity Cttee: North of Scotland Hydro-Electric Board; S of Scotland Electricity Bd; Member: Scottish Cttee of Council of Industrial Design, 1941-49; Royal Fine Art Commission for Scotland, 1943-63. Order of the Vasa, 1st Cl., 1954. *Address:* Craggan House, Lochearnhead, Perthshire. *T:* Lochearnhead 250.

**McGREGOR, Air Marshal Sir Hector (Douglas),** KCB 1960 (CB 1953); CBE 1945; DSO 1940; *b* 15 Feb. 1910; *m* 1931, Jean Martin; one *s* three *d. Educ:* Napier, New Zealand. Joined RAF, 1928; OC 33 (F) Squadron, 1938-39; OC 213 (F) Squadron, 1940; Special Planning Staff, 1941; OC Tangmere Sector, 1942-43; Dep. Dir Operations, Intelligence and Plans, Mediterranean Allied Air Forces, 1943-44; AOC Levant, 1945-46; idc 1947; Air Ministry, 1948-49; NATO Standing Group Staff, Washington, 1950-51; AOC 2 Group, Germany, 1951-53; Director of Guided Missile Development, at Ministry of Supply, 1953-55; Assistant Controller Aircraft, Ministry of

Supply, 1956; Chief of Staff (Air Defence) SHAPE, Paris, 1957-59; Air Officer Commanding-in-Chief: Fighter Command, RAF, 1959-62; Far East Air Force, 1962-64. Retired from RAF, 1964. US Legion of Merit, 1945. *Recreations:* sailing, fly-fishing, ski-ing, shooting. *Address:* Bull's Cottage, Old Bosham, West Sussex. *Club:* Royal Air Force.

**McGREGOR, James Reid,** CB 1948; CBE 1945; MC 1916; *m* 1933, Dorothy Janet, *d* of Mr and Mrs Comrie, Ayr; one *s* one *d*. *Educ:* Edinburgh Academy, RMC Sandhurst. Served European War, 1914-18, Gordon Highlanders, 1915-19 (despatches, wounded, MC); War of 1939-45, Director of Army contracts, 1940-44; Private Secretary to Sir James Grigg, Secretary of State for War, 1944-45; Director of Finance, War Office, 1945-59. Member, Public Health Laboratory Service Board, 1961-69. *Address:* Torphins, Burntwood Road, Sevenoaks, Kent.

**McGREGOR, Sir James Robert,** KBE 1956; Proprietor J. W. McGregor and Co., and of J. R. McGregor Pty Ltd, wool exporters, Australia; *b* 1889; *s* of James Wigham McGregor; *m* 1921, Freda Bruce Taylor (*d* 1941), Queensland. Formerly Chairman Australian Council of Wool Buyers; Technical Member of Central Wool Cttee during War of 1939-45. *Address:* Neidpath, 2 Carthona Avenue, Darling Point, Sydney, NSW, Australia.

**MacGREGOR, Prof. Rev. Canon (John) Geddes,** DèsL (Sorbonne), DPhil, DD Oxon, BD Edinburgh et Oxon, LLB Edinburgh; Distinguished Professor of Philosophy, University of Southern California, since 1966; Dean of Graduate School of Religion, 1960-66; first holder of Rufus Jones Chair of Philosophy and Religion, Bryn Mawr, USA, 1949-60; Canon Theologian of St Paul's Cathedral, Los Angeles, since 1968; *b* 13 Nov. 1909; *o s* of late Thomas and Blanche Geddes MacGregor, Angus; *m* 1941, Elizabeth, *e d* of late Archibald McAllister, Edinburgh; one *s* one *d*. *Educ:* Universities of Edinburgh, Paris, Heidelberg; The Queen's Coll., Oxford. Senior Assistant to Dean of Chapel Royal in Scotland, at St Giles' Cathedral, Edinburgh, 1939-41; served in Civil Defence, War of 1939-45; Minister, Trinity Church, Glasgow, S1, 1941-49; Assistant to Prof. of Logic and Metaphysics, Edinburgh Univ., 1947-49; Examiner: Swarthmore Coll., USA, 1950, 1953, 1955-57; Hebrew Union Coll., USA, 1959, 1961; Visiting Lectr, Columbia Univ., Amherst Coll., Swarthmore Coll., Princeton Univ., Rutgers Univ., Toronto Univ., Lyola Univ., Villanova Univ.; Visiting Prof., 1958-59, and Graduate Sch. Research Lecturer, 1963, University of Southern California. Visiting Prof.: Univ. of British Columbia, 1963, 1966; Hebrew Union Coll., 1964-65; Univ. of Santa Clara, 1968; Visiting Fellow, Dept of Religious Studies, Yale Univ., 1967-68. Special Preacher: St Paul's Cathedral, London, 1969; Westminster Abbey, 1970. A Governor, American-Scottish Foundation, Inc., NY. FRSL 1948. Gold Medal, Commonwealth Club of California, for best non-fiction work by Californian author in 1963. *Publications:* Aesthetic Experience in Religion, 1947; Christian Doubt, 1951; Les Frontières de la Morale et de la Religion, 1952; From a Christian Ghetto, 1954; The Vatican Revolution, 1957; The Tichborne Impostor, 1957; The Thundering Scot, 1957; Corpus Christi, 1959; Introduction to Religious Philosophy, 1959; The Bible in the Making, 1959; The Coming Reformation, 1960; The Hemlock and the Cross, 1963; God Beyond Doubt, 1966; A Literary History of the Bible, 1968; The Sense of Absence, 1968; So Help Me God, 1970; articles, recordings, reviews. *Recreation:* manual labour. *Address:* 876 Victoria Avenue, Los Angeles, California 90005, USA. *T:* 213-938-4826. *Clubs:* Athenæum, English-Speaking Union, Royal Commonwealth Society; Caledonian (Edinburgh); Union Society (Oxford).

**McGREGOR, Kenneth,** CB 1963; CMG 1951; Member: Performing Right Tribunal; Iron and Steel Consumers' Council; Islington Borough Council; company director; *b* 11 Feb. 1903; *o c* of late James McGregor and Eugénie Lydia Johnson; *m* 1930, Dorothy Laura Roope, *o d* of late Judge R. Roope Reeve, QC; two *s*. *Educ:* Westminster (King's Scholar); New Coll., Oxford (Scholar). 1st class Hons MA. Called to the Bar (Lincoln's Inn). Ministries of Health, Supply and Production; Board of Trade (Under-Secretary); Senior British Trade Commissioner in Canada; retired, 1963. *Publication:* Selling to Canada, 1965. *Address:* 10 Furlong Road, London, N7; Kings Rythe, Emsworth, Hants. *T:* 01-607 4553. *Club:* Oxford and Cambridge University.

**MACGREGOR, Lewis Richard,** CBE 1938; LLB (Glasgow); Certified Public Accountant (Australia); JP; Australian Foreign Service Official; Company Director; *b* 1886; *s* of late Thomas Macgregor, HM Royal Marines, Aberfeldy, Scotland and Portsmouth, England; *m* Mary Hannah, *d* of late Joseph White, Bournemouth, and niece of late H. Brashaw, JP, Mayor of Bunbury, Western Australia; one *s* one *d*. *Educ:* Allan Glens School; Glasgow and West Scotland Technical Coll.; Glasgow Univ. (LLB). Wheat Export Control for Western Australian Government during European War, 1914-18; special mission to United Kingdom on behalf of Western Australia, 1919; Director of Agricultural Organization, Queensland Govt, 1922; Director of Marketing, Queensland Government, 1926; Queensland Government Representative on various Boards and Commissions, 1922-30; Australian Government Commissioner in Canada, 1930-38; negotiated first commercial agreement between Canada and Australia (still in force); Australian Delegation to Imperial Conference, London, 1930, and Ottawa, 1932; Special Trade Missions on behalf of Australia to Newfoundland, 1932, British West Indies, 1933, Far East, 1934, Union of South Africa and Rhodesia, 1937; Australian Government Trade Commissioner in USA, 1938-41; Commissioner General for Australian Government to New York World's Fair, 1939; Director-General, Commonwealth of Australia War Supplies Mission, Washington and Ottawa, 1941-45; HM Australian Minister to Brazil, 1945-49; Member: USAF Contract Review Board, Korean War, 1950-54. *Address:* Casuarina, Sandy Lane, St James, Barbados, West Indies; PO Box Box 371, Millbrook, New York 12545, USA. *Clubs:* Canadian (NY); Bridgetown (Barbados).

**McGREGOR, Prof. Oliver Ross;** Professor of Social Institutions in the University of London, and Head of Department of Sociology, at Bedford College, since 1964; *b* 25 Aug. 1921; *s* of late William McGregor and late Anne Olivia Ross; *m* 1944, Nellie Weate; three *s*. *Educ:* Worksop Coll.; University of Aberdeen; London School of Economics. Temp. civil servant, War Office and Ministry of Agriculture, 1940-44. Asst Lecturer and Lecturer in Economic History, University of Hull, 1945-47; Lecturer, Bedford Coll., 1947-60, Reader in University of London, 1960-64; Simon Senior Research Fellow, University of Manchester, 1959-60; Joint Director,

Rowntree Legal Research Unit, 1966-. Member: Cttee on Enforcement of Judgment Debts, 1965; Cttee on Statutory Maintenance Limits, 1966; Cttee on Land Use (Recreation and Leisure), 1967; National Parks Commission, 1966-68; Independent Television Authority's General Advisory Council, 1967-; Countryside Commission, 1968-; Legal Aid Adv. Cttee, 1969-; Cttee on One-Parent Families, 1969-. *Publications:* Divorce in England, 1957; ed, Lord Ernle, English Farming Past and Present, 6th edn, 1960; Bibliography of the National Association for the Promotion of Social Science, 1969; (jtly) Separated Spouses, 1970; various papers in British Journal of Sociology and other journals. *Address:* Far End, Wyldes Close, NW11. *T:* 01-458 2856. *Club:* Reform.

**MacGREGOR, Robert Barr,** CMG 1946; MB, ChB, FRCPEd; Ship's Surgeon, Royal Fleet Auxiliary, since 1967; *b* 14 July 1896; *s* of Patrick MacGregor; *m* 1921, Helen May Harper (*d* 1964); one *s*. *Educ:* Dunbar Sch.; Edinburgh University. Served in RAMC, 1918-20; joined Straits Settlements Medical Service, 1920; Director, Medical Services, Straits Settlements and Adviser, Medical Services, Malay Straits, 1940; Director, Medical Services, Federation of Malaya, retired 1951; SMO, Malacca Agricultural Medical Board, 1951-58; RMO, Wooley Hosp., 1965-67. CStJ. *Address:* c/o Glyn, Mills & Co., Holt's Branch, Kirkland House, Whitehall, SW1. *Club:* Royal Commonwealth Society.

**MacGREGOR, William Duncan,** CIE 1933; FIEE; *b* 20 Oct. 1878; *s* of Alexander Downie MacGregor and Jessie Steel Proudfoot; *m* 1906, Marie Adelaide Achard (*d* 1942); (*s* killed in action in New Guinea, 1943; *d* decd 1946); *m* 1948, Christine Johanne Aschehoug (*d* 1963), Oslo, Norway. *Educ:* George Heriot's School and Heriot-Watt Coll., Edinburgh; appointed to Indian Posts and Telegraphs Department, 1900; Divisional Engineer, 1910; Deputy Chief Engineer, 1921; Officiating Postmaster-General, Central Provinces, 1922; PMG Burma, 1925; Officiating Chief Engineer Posts and Telegraphs, 1931; PMG Bengal and Assam, 1932; retired, 1933. *Address:* 37 Grange Road, Edinburgh 9.

**McGRIGOR, Captain Sir Charles Edward,** 5th Bt, *cr* 1831; Rifle Brigade, retired; Member Royal Company of Archers (HM Body Guard for Scotland); Exon, Queen's Bodyguard, Yeoman of the Guard, since 1970; *b* 5 Oct. 1922; *s* of Lieut-Colonel Sir Charles McGrigor, 4th Bt, OBE, and of Lady McGrigor; *S* father, 1946; *m* 1948, Mary Bettine, *e d* of Sir Archibald Charles Edmonstone, 6th Bt; two *s* two *d*. *Educ:* Eton. War of 1939-45 (despatches); joined Army, 1941, from Eton; served with Rifle Bde, N. Africa, Italy, Austria. ADC to Duke of Gloucester, 1945-47, in Australia and England. *Recreations:* fishing, shooting, ski-ing, gardening. *Heir: s* James Angus Rhoderick Neil McGrigor, *b* 19 Oct. 1949. *Address:* Upper Sonachan, Dalmally, Argyll; 18 Cranmer Court, SW3. *Club:* Boodle's.

**McGUFFIE, Kenneth Cunningham;** Admiralty Registrar, Royal Courts of Justice, London, since 1957; Registrar of the Shipping Claims Tribunal, since 1958; *b* 30 June 1913; *y s* of late Thomas Chalmers McGuffie and Jenny (*née* Dunlop). *Educ:* Windlesham House Sch.; Harrow; Christchurch, Oxford; Geneva Univ.; Glasgow Univ (BL). Called to Bar, Gray's Inn, 1946; admitted Advocate, Scots Bar, 1946; Councillor (Co.) Walton and Weybridge UDC (St George's Hill Ward), 1947 until resigned, 1948; practised in London, Admiralty and Scots Law, 1946-57; Dep. Admiralty Registrar (during Registrar's illness), 1956. *Publications:* ed 10th edn, Marsden's Law of Collisions at Sea, 1953, 11th edn, 1961 (Vol. 4 of British Shipping Laws), and Supplement, 1965; ed 4th edn, Kennedy's Law of Civil Salvage, 1958; contributor to Encyclopædia Britannica and Halsbury's Laws of England, 3rd edn, shipping law; Joint Asst Gen. Editor, British Shipping Laws, 1961- (new encyclopædic work, to be in 14 vols); author, Notes on Four Admiralty Registry Letter Books, 1795-1810, 1853-54, 1854-55, 1855-56, 1st edn, 1964; joint author, McGuffie, Fugeman and Gray's Admiralty Practice, 1st edn, 1964 (vol. 1 of British Shipping Laws) and Supplements, 1965, 1970; joint Editor (Admiralty practice) The Annual Practice, 1964, 1965, and 1966 and Supplements; The Supreme Court Practice, 1967, 1970 and Supplements. *Address:* Shardeloes, Amersham, Bucks. *T:* Amersham 5426.

**McGUIGAN, His Eminence Cardinal James Charles;** *see* Toronto, Cardinal-Archbishop of.

**McGUINNESS, James Henry,** CB 1964; Assistant Under-Secretary of State, Scottish Office; Chairman, Scottish Economic Planning Board, since 1965; *b* 29 Sept. 1912; *s* of James Henry McGuinness, Scotstoun; *m* 1939, Annie Eveline Fordyce, Ayr; one *s* two *d*. *Educ:* Glasgow Univ.; Trinity Coll., Oxford. Under-Secretary, Dept of Health for Scotland, 1959-62; Scottish Development Department, 1962-64. *Address:* 10 Greenhill Terrace, Edinburgh 10. *Club:* Scottish Arts.

**McGUINNESS, Norah Allison;** Artist; Hon. Member Royal Hibernian Academy (HRHA); *b* Londonderry; *e d* of late Joseph Allison and Jessie McGuinness; *m* 1925, Geoffrey Phibbs, *e s* of Basil Phibbs, Lisheen, Sligo (marr. diss., 1931). *Educ:* Londonderry High Sch. Studied painting at College of Art, Dublin, Chelsea Polytechnical, London, and with André Shotte, Paris; Illustrated: Sentimental Journey; Stories from Red Hanorhan (W. B. Yeats), etc. Designed for the Abbey Theatre, Dublin; held Exhibitions in London, Dublin, New York, Paris, Holland and Canada, and represented Ireland at Biennial Exhibition, Venice, 1950. Pictures in private collections in many countries. President of Irish Exhibition of Living Art. *Recreations:* gardening and bird watching. *Address:* 13 Fitzwilliam Square, Dublin. *Club:* Irish (London).

**McGUIRE, (Dominic) Paul,** CBE 1951; HM Australian Diplomatic Service, retired; *b* 3 April 1903; *s* of James and Mary McGuire; *m* 1927, Frances Margaret Cheadle. *Educ:* Christian Brothers' Coll., Adelaide; University of Adelaide (Tinline Scholar in Australian History). WEA and University Extension Lecturer at University of Adelaide for several years; lectured extensively in USA, 1936-40 and 1946; served with Royal Australian Naval Volunteer Reserve in War of 1939-45. Australian Delegate to United Nations Assembly, 1953; Australian Minister to Italy, 1954-58, Ambassador to Italy, 1958-59; Envoy Extraordinary to Holy See on occasion of Coronation of HH Pope John XXIII, 1958. Commendatore, Order of Merit, Italy, 1967. Knight Grand Cross of St Sylvester, 1959. *Publications:* The Two Men, 1932; The Poetry of Gerard Manley Hopkins, 1935; 7.30 Victoria, 1935; Prologue to the Gallows, 1935; Cry Aloud for Murder, 1936; Born to be Hanged, 1936; Burial Service, 1937; W1, 1937; Restoring All Things (with J. Fitzsimons), 1938; Australian Journey, 1939; Spanish Steps, 1940; Westward the Course, 1942; Price of Admiralty (with F. M.

McGuire), 1945; The Three Corners of the World; Experiment in World Order, 1948; (with B. P. Arnott and F. M. McGuire) The Australian Theatre, 1948; Freedom for the Brave, 1949, etc. *Address:* 136 Mills Terrace, North Adelaide, South Australia 5006, Australia. *Clubs:* Athenæum (London); Naval and Military (Adelaide).

**McGUIRE, Michael Thomas Francis;** MP (Lab) Ince since 1964; *b* 3 May 1926; *m* 1954, Marie T. Murphy; three *s* two *d*. *Educ:* Elementary Schools. Coal mining: Face-worker; Whole-time Union Branch Secretary, 1957. *Recreations:* most out-door sports, especially Rugby League football; traditional music, especially Irish traditional ballads and ceili and pipe band music. *Address:* House of Commons, SW1.

**McGUIRE, Robert Ely,** CMG 1948; OBE 1943; Indian Civil Service (retired); *b* 22 Aug. 1901; *s* of late Major E. C. McGuire, 2nd Bn York and Lancaster Regt; *m* 1930, Barbara, *d* of late Sir Benjamin Heald, ICS, Judge of the High Court of Judicature, Rangoon; one *s* one *d*. *Educ:* High Sch., Dublin; Trinity Coll., Dublin. MA (Hons). Entered ICS, 1926; Warden, Burma Oilfields, 1932 and 1940-42; Dep. Commissioner, 1932-42. Secretary to Government of Burma (temp. in India), 1942-45. Dep. Director of Civil Affairs, with rank of Brigadier, British Military Administration in Burma, 1945. Divisional Comr, Burma, 1946-47; Secretary to Governor of Burma, 1947 to 4 Jan. 1948 (date of Independence of Burma). Secretary Cement Makers Federation, 1949-64. *Address:* Green Meadows, Lindfield, Haywards Heath, Sussex. *Clubs:* East India and Sports; University (Dublin).

**McGUSTY, Victor William Tighe,** CMG 1942; OBE 1937; OStJ; MB; DTM; *b* 20 June 1887; *m* 1912, Annie Bayliss; one *s* one *d*. *Educ:* Coleraine (Ireland) Academical Institution; Trinity Coll., Dublin. Entered Colonial Medical Service, Fiji, 1912; retired, 1945; Director of Medical Services Colony of Fiji; also Director of Civil Defence and Secretary for Indian Affairs; held various other administrative posts as well as medical in the Colony. *Address:* Nantor, 32 Hororata Road, Takapuna N2, New Zealand.
*See also Sir R. H. Garvey.*

**McHARDY, Rev. Archibald,** CB 1950; CBE 1945; MC 1919; DL; *b* 6 April 1890; *y s* of late Archibald McHardy, Edinburgh; unmarried. *Educ:* George Heriot's Sch., Edinburgh; Edinburgh Univ. MA Edinburgh, 1911; DD Edinburgh, 1944. Served European War, RAMC Field Ambulance. Sergeant RAMC, 1914-17; France, 1915-17 (wounded, Ypres, 1917); Army Chaplain, France and Germany, 1917-19; RAF Chaplain, 1919-50; Principal Chaplain (Church of Scotland) RAF, 1928-50; retired, 1950. Served at home, also tours of duty in Egypt, Palestine, Iraq, Far East, etc. Hon. Chaplain to the King, 1942-50. Vice-President of National Council of the YMCA. DL County of City of Edinburgh, 1960. *Recreation:* golf. *Address:* 51 Lauderdale Street, Edinburgh 9. *Clubs:* Royal Air Force, Royal Commonwealth Society.

**McHARDY, William Duff;** Regius Professor of Hebrew, Oxford University, and Student of Christ Church, since 1960; *b* 26 May 1911; *o s* of late W. D. McHardy, Cullen, Banffshire; *m* 1941, Vera, *y d* of late T. Kemp, York; one *d*. *Educ:* Fordyce Academy; Universities of Aberdeen, Edinburgh, and Oxford (St John's College). MA, BD (Aberdeen), MA (Edinburgh), DPhil (Oxford). Research Fellow in Syriac, Selly Oak Colleges, Birmingham, 1942; Lecturer in Aramaic and Syriac, University of Oxford, 1945; Samuel Davidson Professor of Old Testament Studies in the University of London, 1948-60. Examiner, Universities of Aberdeen, Cambridge, Durham, Edinburgh, Leeds, London, Oxford and University Colleges of the Gold Coast/Ghana and Ibadan. Hon. Curator of Mingana Collection of Oriental Manuscripts, 1947. Grinfield Lecturer on the Septuagint, Oxford, 1959-61. Hon. DD Aberdeen, 1958. *Publications:* articles in journals. *Address:* Christ Church, Oxford; 44 Davenant Road, Oxford. *T:* Oxford 55432.

**MACHIN, Arnold,** OBE 1965; RA 1956 (ARA 1947); sculptor, FRBS 1955; Master, Royal Academy School of Sculpture, since 1958; Tutor, Royal College of Art, 1951-58; *b* 1911; *s* of William James Machin, Stoke-on-Trent; *m* 1949, Patricia, *d* of late Lt-Col Henry Newton; one *s*. *Educ:* Stoke School of Art; Derby School of Art; Royal College of Art. Silver Medal and Travelling Scholarship for Sculpture, 1940; two works in terracotta: St John the Baptist and The Annunciation, purchased by Tate Gallery, 1943; Spring terracotta purchased by President and Council of Royal Academy under terms of Chantrey Bequest, 1947; designed new coin effigy, 1964, 1967 (decimal coinage). *Recreation:* music. *Address:* 4 Sydney Close, SW3; Offley Rock, Bishop's Offley, Staffordshire.

**MACHTIG, Sir Eric Gustav,** GCMG, *cr* 1948 (KCMG, *cr* 1939; CMG 1935); KCB, *cr* 1943; OBE 1926 (MBE 1918); *b* 1889; *s* of late F. G. Machtig, Wimbledon; *m* 1941, Norah Marguerite Friend (*d* 1943). *Educ:* St Paul's Sch. (Scholar); Trinity Coll., Cambridge (Scholar). 1st Class 2nd Division Classical Tripos, 1911; entered Colonial Office 1912; transferred to Dominions Office (later Commonwealth Relations Office) as Assistant Secretary, 1930; Assistant Under-Secretary of State, 1936; Dep. Under-Secretary of State, 1939; Permanent Under-Secretary of State for Commonwealth Relations, 1940; seconded for special duties, Dec. 1948; retired from Service, 1949. A Dir, Barclay's Bank (DCO), 1949-69. Chm. Working Cttee, Lord Mayor's Nat. Thanksgiving Fund, 1950; Chm., Sister Trust, 1950-65; a Vice-Chm. Victoria League, 1950-62. *Recreations:* music, travelling. *Address:* 11 Belvedere Drive, SW19. *T:* 01-946 3241.

**McHUGH, Dr Mary Patricia;** Coroner for Southern District of London, since 1965; *b* 5 June 1915; *d* of J. C. McHugh, MB, BS, BAO, Royal Univ., Dublin, and Madeleine Jeffroy Leblan, Brittany, France; *m* 1943, E. G. Murphy, FRCS (marr. diss., 1952); one *s* two *d*. *Educ:* Nymphenburg, Munich, Bavaria; Notre Dame, Clapham; Birmingham Univ. MB, ChB, 1942; Birmingham House Physician and Anæsthetist, St Chad's Hospital, Birmingham, 1942-43; General Practice, London, 1944-65. Called to the Bar, 1959. Chm., Whole Time Coroner's Assoc.; Mem., British Academy of Forensic Sciences, 1963; Founder Mem., RCGP. *Recreations:* cooking, languages. *Address:* 8 Hitherwood Drive, College Road, Dulwich, SE19. *T:* 01-703 3492; Gwennola, Great Brickhill, Bucks. *T:* Great Brickhill 243.

**McILWAIN, Charles Howard,** MA (Oxford), PhD, LHD, LittD, LLD, DCL, Professor (retired); *b* Saltsburg, Pennsylvania, 15 March 1871; *s* of William R. McIlwain and Anne Elizabeth Galbraith; *m* 1st, 1899, Mary B. Irwin (decd); 2nd, 1916, Kathleen Thompson (decd); two *s* two *d*. *Educ:* Princeton Univ.; Harvard Univ. Professor of History, Miami Univ., 1903-05; Preceptor, Princeton Univ.,

1905-10; Thomas Brackett Reed Professor of History and Political Science, Bowdoin Coll., 1910-11; Assistant Professor, 1911-16, Professor of History and Government, 1916-25, Eaton Professor of the Science of Government, 1925-48, in Harvard Univ.; George Eastman Visiting Professor, Oxford, 1944; Visiting Professor, Yale Univ., 1930-31; Lecturer, Princeton Univ., 1947-49; Associate Member of Colonial Society of Massachusetts; Member of Massachusetts Historical Society; Member of American Philosophical Society; Fellow of American Academy of Arts and Sciences; Fellow of Mediæval Academy of America; Corresponding Member of Royal Historical Society; Corresponding Fellow of British Academy; President of American Historical Assoc., 1935-36; Trustee of Princeton Univ., Emeritus. *Publications:* The High Court of Parliament, 1910; Wraxall's Abridgment of the New York Indian Records (Editor), 1915; The Political Works of James I (Editor), 1918; The American Revolution, 1924; The Growth of Political Thought in the West, 1932; Constitutionalism and the Changing World, 1939; Constitutionalism Ancient and Modern, 1939, revised edn, 1947; (with Professor Paul L. Ward) Lambarde's Archeion (Editor). *Recreations:* lawn tennis, music, and the search for old books. *Address:* 84 Hinckley Road, Milton, Mass 02118, USA.

**McILWAIN, Prof. Henry,** DSc, PhD; Professor of Biochemistry in the University of London at Institute of Psychiatry, British Postgraduate Medical Federation, since 1954; Hon. Biochemist, Bethlem Royal Hospital and Maudsley Hospital, since 1948; *b* Newcastle upon Tyne, 20 Dec. 1912; *e s* of John McIlwain, Glasgow, and Louisa (*née* Widdowson), Old Whittington; *m* 1941, Valerie, *d* of K. Durston, Bude, Cornwall; two *d. Educ:* King's Coll., Newcastle upon Tyne (University of Durham); The Queen's Coll., Oxford. Leverhulme Research Fellow and later Mem. of Scientific Staff, Medical Research Council, in Council's Dept of Bacterial Chemistry (Middlesex Hosp., London) and Unit for Research in Cell Metabolism (Univ. of Sheffield), 1937-47; Lectr in Biochemistry, Univ. of Sheffield, 1944-47; Senior Lectr (later Reader) in Biochemistry, Inst. of Psychiatry (British Postgraduate Medical Fedn), Univ. of London, 1948-54; Mem. Editorial Bd, Biochemical Jl, 1947-50; Research Associate, Univ. of Chicago, 1951; Visiting Lectr, Univ. of Otago, New Zealand, 1954. *Publications:* Biochemistry and the Central Nervous System, 1955; Chemotherapy and the Central Nervous System, 1957; (with R. Rodnight) Practical Neurochemistry, 1962; Chemical Exploration of the Brain, 1963; about 200 papers in the Biochemical Journal and other scientific and medical publications. *Address:* 73 Court Lane, SE21. *T:* 01-693 5334.

**MacINNES, Rt. Rev. Angus Campbell,** CMG 1961; Assistant Bishop of Salisbury, and Master of St Nicholas Hospital, Salisbury, since 1968; *b* 18 April 1901; *s* of late Rennie MacInnes, DD, Bishop in Jerusalem, 1914-31, and late Janet Waldegrave Carr, MRCS, LRCP; *m* 1928, Florence Isabella Joy Masterman, MB, BS, *d* of E. W. G. Masterman, MD, FRCS, FRGS; two *s* two *d. Educ:* Harrow; Trinity Coll., Cambridge. BA 1923; MA 1927. Teacher Jerusalem Men's Coll., 1923-25; Westcott House, Cambridge, 1925-26; Deacon, 1926; Curate, St Mary Magdalene, Peckham; Priest, 1927; CMS Missionary, Palestine, 1928; Principal, Bishop Gobat Sch., Jerusalem, 1930-44; Secretary of CMS Palestine Mission, 1940-50; Archdeacon in Palestine and Transjordan and Exam. Chaplain to Bishop in Jerusalem, 1943-51; Vicar of St Michael's, St Alban's, 1951-54; Rural Dean of St Albans, 1953-57; Residentiary Canon, St Alban's Abbey, 1953-57; Bishop Suffragan of Bedford, 1953-57; Archbishop in Jerusalem and Metropolitan, 1957-68. Sub-Prelate and Chaplain, Order of St John of Jerusalem, 1957. Coronation Medal, 1937. DD (Lambeth) 1957. *Address:* St Nicholas Hospital, Salisbury, Wilts. *T:* Salisbury 6874.

**MacINNES, Charles Malcolm,** CBE 1959; Hon. LLD Dalhousie, 1952; Hon. LLD Alta, 1958; Emeritus Professor of Imperial History, University of Bristol; *b* Calgary, Alberta, 21 Dec. 1891; *s* of Malcolm MacInnes, Calgary, and Catherine MacArthur; *m* 1926, Violet Ethel (*d* 1969), *d* of Dr A. W. Peake, South Lodge, Druid Stoke, Bristol; one *s. Educ:* Dalhousie Univ., Halifax, Nova Scotia; Balliol Coll., Oxford. Assistant Lecturer in History, University of Bristol, 1919, Lecturer, 1922, Reader in Imperial History, 1930; Professor of Imperial History, University of Bristol, 1943-57; Dean of Faculty of Arts, 1952-55; Editor of Universities Review, 1924-62; President, Assoc. of University Teachers of UK, 1950-51; Vice-Pres., Historical Assoc.; Vice-Chairman Royal Empire (later Commonwealth) Society, Bristol Branch, 1934-52, Chairman, 1952-; Vice-Pres., Royal Commonwealth Soc., 1969-. Emergency Information Officer for the City of Bristol, 1941-45. Commander of Order of Orange Nassau, 1952; Commandeur de l'Ordre de l'Etoile Noire, 1956. *Publications:* The British Commonwealth and its Unsolved Problems, 1925; The Early English Tobacco Trade, 1926; In the Shadow of the Rockies, 1930; England and Slavery, 1934; An Introduction to the Economic History of the British Empire, 1935; A Gateway of Empire 1939 (2nd edn, 1968); The British Empire and Commonwealth, 1815-1949, 1951; The British Empire and the War, 1941; (Jt Editor) Bristol and its Adjoining Counties (for British Assoc.), 1955; (ed) Principles and Methods of Colonial Administration, 1950; Bristol at War, 1962; contrib. to other books, pamphlets and articles. *Recreations:* riding, rowing. *Address:* 5 Queen's Court, Clifton, Bristol, 8. *Clubs:* Savile, Royal Commonwealth Society; Savages (Bristol).

**MacINNES, Colin;** Author; *b* 1914; *s* of J. Campbell MacInnes and Angela (Novelist, as Angela Thirkell, who *m* 2nd, G. L. Thirkell), *d* of J. W. Mackail, OM. *Educ:* in Australia. Served War of 1939-45: Sergeant, Intelligence Corps. *Publications:* To the Victors the Spoils, 1950; June in Her Spring, 1952; City of Spades, 1957; Absolute Beginners, 1959; Mr Love and Justice, 1960; England, Half English, 1961; All Day Saturday, 1966; Sweet Saturday Night, 1967; Westward to Laughter, 1969; Three Years To Play, 1970. *Address:* c/o MacGibbon & Kee Ltd, 3 Upper James Street, Golden Square, W1R 4BP.

**MacINNES, Helen Clark;** Novelist; *b* 7 Oct. 1907; *d* of Donald McInnes and Jessica Cecilia Sutherland McDiarmid; *m* 1932, Gilbert Highet, *qv*; one *s. Educ:* The Hermitage Sch., Helensburgh; The High School for Girls, Glasgow; Glasgow Univ. (MA); University College, London. *Publications:* Above Suspicion, 1941; Assignment in Brittany, 1942; The Unconquerable, 1944; Horizon, 1945; Friends and Lovers, 1947; Rest and Be Thankful, 1949; Neither Five Nor Three, 1951; I and My True Love, 1953; Pray for a Brave Heart, 1955; North from Rome, 1958; Decision at Delphi, 1961; The Venetian Affair, 1963; Home is the Hunter (play), 1964; The Double Image, 1966; The Salzburg Connection, 1968. *Recreations:* two-piano duets; the American West. *Address:* 15 Jefferys Lane, East Hampton, NY 11937, USA.

**McINNES, James,** MBE 1941; JP 1941; *b* 19 May 1901; *s* of James William McInnes, Engineer, and Jean McKirdy, Restaurateur; *m* 1925, Elizabeth Hislop Cowie (*d* 1963); one *s. Educ:* Glasgow (Lambhill Street Secondary Sch.). Member Glasgow Town Council, 1933-50, Leader Labour Group, 1949; Magistrate, City of Glasgow, 1937; Principal Administrative Officer, Western Region, NFS, 1941; Member of Fire Service Commission, 1941; Member of Scottish Building Costs Commission, 1947; Chairman Scottish Housing and Town Planning Council, 1948. MP (Lab) Glasgow Central, 1950-66, retired. *Recreations:* golf, bowling. *Address:* 94 Bellahouston Drive, Glasgow SW2. *T:* 041-882 2576.

**MacINNES, Robert Ian Aonas,** QC (Scotland), 1946; Sheriff Substitute of Lanarkshire at Hamilton, 1953-55; *b* 23 July 1902; *yr s* of late Rev. Dr Alexander MacInnes, Kirkliston, Edinburgh. *Educ:* privately; Edinburgh Univ. Contested (L) W Stirlingshire, 1923; called to Scottish Bar, 1924; Sheriff Substitute of Ross and Cromarty and Sutherland at Stornoway, 1934-40; of Argyll at Dunoon, 1940-41; of Bute at Rothesay, 1940-41; of Lanarkshire at Glasgow, 1948-53. Contested (Lab) Caithness and Sutherland, 1945. *Recreation:* fishing. *Address:* c/o The Westminster Bank Ltd, 6 Cambridge Crescent, Harrogate, Yorkshire.

**MacINNES, William Alexander,** MC, MA (Glasgow), DèsL (Paris); Officier d'Académie; Professor of French, Hull University, 1932-57; retired; Emeritus Professor since 1958; *b* 11 April 1892; *s* of William and Jemima MacInnes; *m* 1918, Madeleine Elizabeth Bauer; one *d. Educ:* Glasgow High Sch., Univs of Glasgow, Paris, Grenoble, Florence. Private in Artists' Rifles; 2nd Lieut, 4th Bn Highland Light Infantry; Lieut and Captain, 11th Border Regt (MC and Bar, wounded); Head of Modern Language Dept, Senior War Office School of Education, Cambridge and Newmarket, 1919; studied in Paris and Grenoble, 1920-24; Assistant Lecturer in French, The Victoria Univ., Manchester, 1924-29; Assistant Lecturer in French, The University, Glasgow, 1930-32. *Publications:* edited Swinburne's Ballads of the English Border, 1925; L'Œuvre française de Swinburne, 1933; Thomas Gray en France, 1933; contributor to various French literary reviews and periodicals. *Recreations:* walking, writing. *Address:* 201 Victoria Avenue, Hull, East Yorkshire. *T:* Hull Central 42008.

**McINTOSH, Alastair (James),** CMG 1960; OBE 1953; retired as Principal Adviser to the High Commissioner, Aden (1963-July 1964); *b* 5 Aug. 1913; *s* of Alexander McIntosh, Dundee. *Educ:* Merchant Taylors' Sch.; St John's Coll., Oxford; Bonn Univ.; American Univ., Beirut. Asst Lectr, Manchester Univ., 1939-40. Served War of 1939-45, 1940-47. Political Officer, Aden Protectorate, 1947; Dep. British Agent, Eastern Aden Protectorate, 1954; Asst Chief Sec., Aden, 1955; Res. Adviser and British Agent, Eastern Aden Protectorate, 1958; Protectorate Sec., Aden, 1960. Merchant Taylor and Citizen of London. *Recreation:* music. *Address:* Latchets, Barford St Martin, Wilts. *T:* Wilton 2159.

**McINTOSH, Alister Donald,** CMG 1957; *b* Picton, NZ, 29 Nov. 1906; *e s* of Harry Hobson and Caroline McIntosh; *m* 1934, Doris Hutchinson Pow; one *s. Educ:* Marlborough Coll., Blenheim; Victoria University College, Wellington, NZ (MA); University of Michigan, Ann Arbor, USA. Labour Dept, 1925; Parliamentary Library, 1926-34; Carnegie Travelling Fellowship, 1932-33; Prime Minister's Dept, New Zealand, 1935-66; Secretary of War Cabinet, 1943-45; Sec. of External Affairs, NZ, 1943-66; Permanent Head, Prime Minister's Dept, 1945-66; New Zealand Ambassador to Italy, 1966-70. Attended many Commonwealth Prime Ministers' conferences and United Nations Assemblies as adviser or delegate, 1944-. Hon. LLD, Univ. of Canterbury, NZ, 1965. *Publication:* Marlborough Provincial History, 1939. *Recreation:* gardening. *Address:* 11 Wesley Road, Wellington, New Zealand. *Club:* Wellington.

**McINTOSH, Prof. Angus;** Forbes Professor of English Language, University of Edinburgh; *b* 10 Jan. 1914; *s* of late Kenneth McIntosh, and of Mary McIntosh (*née* Thompson), Cleadon, Sunderland, Co. Durham; *m* 1939, Barbara, *d* of late Dr William Seaman Bainbridge, and of Mrs Bainbridge (*née* June Wheeler), New York City; two *s* one *d. Educ:* Ryhope Grammar Sch., Co. Durham; Oriel Coll., Oxford (BA, 1st Class Hons, English Lang., and Lit., 1934); Merton Coll., Oxford (Harmsworth Scholar); (Dip. of Comparative Philology, University of Oxford, 1936); Harvard Univ. (Commonwealth Fund Fellow, AM, 1937). MA (Oxford) 1938. Lecturer, Dept of English, University College, Swansea, 1938-46. Served War of 1939-45, beginning as trooper in Tank Corps, finishing as Major in Intelligence Corps. University Lecturer in Mediæval English, Oxford, 1946-48; Lecturer in English, Christ Church, Oxford, 1946-47; Student of Christ Church, 1947-48; Rockefeller Foundation Fellowship, US, June-Sept. 1949. *Publications:* books, articles and reviews on subject of English language and related topics. *Recreations:* tennis, squash, fishing, gardening, painting. *Address:* 32 Blacket Place, Edinburgh 9. *T:* 031-667 5791. *Club:* Savile.

**MacINTOSH, Prof. Frank Campbell;** FRS 1953; FRSC 1956; J. M. Drake Professor of Physiology, McGill University, Montreal, Canada, since 1949; *b* 24 Dec. 1909; *s* of Rev. C. C. MacIntosh, DD, and Beenie MacIntosh (*née* Matheson); *m* 1938, Mary M. MacKay; two *s* three *d. Educ:* Dalhousie Univ., Halifax, NS (MA); McGill Univ. (PhD). Member of research staff, Medical Research Council of Great Britain, 1938. Member: Scientific Adv. Panel of CIBA Foundn; Nuffield Foundn Canadian Policy Cttee (Chm.); Science Council of Canada (Chm., Basic Biology Review Cttee); Defence Med. Research Adv. Cttee. Editor, Canadian Jl of Physiology and Pharmacology. Hon. LLD (Alberta) 1964, (Queen's) 1965. *Publications:* papers in physiological journals. *Address:* Department of Physiology, McGill University, Montreal 2, PQ, Canada; 145 Wolseley Avenue, Montreal West, PQ, Canada. *T:* 481-7939.

**McINTOSH, Very Rev. Hugh;** Provost of St Mary's Cathedral, Glasgow, since 1966; *b* 5 June 1914; *s* of Hugh Burns McIntosh and Mary (*née* Winter); *m* 1951, Ruth Georgina, *er d* of late Rev. William Skinner Wilson and Enid (*née* Sanders); two *s* one *d. Educ:* Hatfield Coll., Durham (Exhibr); Edinburgh Theological Coll. (Luscombe Schol.). LTh, 1941; BA (dist.), 1942; MA 1945. Deacon and Priest, 1942. Precentor and Senior Chaplain, St Paul's Cathedral, Dundee, 1942-46; Senior Chaplain, St Mary's Cathedral, Edinburgh, 1946-49; Curate, St Salvador's, Edinburgh, 1949-51; Rector, St Adrian's, Gullane, 1951-54; Rector, St John's, Dumfries, 1954; Canon of St Mary's Cathedral, Glasgow, and Synod Clerk of Glasgow and Galloway, 1959. *Recreations:* reading, travel. *Address:* 10

Holyrood Crescent, Glasgow, NW. *T:* 041-339 6691.

**McINTOSH, Ian Donald,** MA; Headmaster of Fettes College, Edinburgh, 1958-July 1971; *b* 4 July 1908; *o s* of late Donald McIntosh, Inverness, and of Lilian Barritt; *m* 1942, Florence Anne, *d* of late Lockhart Boyne, Inverness; one *s* two *d*. *Educ:* Inverness Academy; Aberdeen Univ. 1st Class Mod. Lang., 1930; Open Schol., Trinity Coll., Cambridge, 1932, 1st Class Mod. Lang. Trip. Part 2, 1934. Assistant Master, Bradfield Coll., 1934-37; Assistant Master, Winchester Coll., 1937-53 (Senior Mod. Lang. Master from 1945). Head Master, George Watson's Coll., Edinburgh, 1953-58. Hon. LLD Aberdeen 1962. *Recreations:* cricket, football (Cambridge Univ. Assoc. Football XI, 1933). *Address:* Fettes College, Edinburgh. *Club:* New (Edinburgh).

**McINTOSH, Vice-Admiral Ian Stewart,** CB 1970; DSO 1944; MBE 1941; DSC 1942; Deputy Chief of Defence Staff (Operational Requirements), since 1971; *b* 11 Oct. 1919; *s* of A. J. McIntosh, Melbourne, Australia; *m* 1943, Elizabeth Rosemary Rasmussen; three *s* (one *d* decd). *Educ:* Geelong Grammar Sch. Entered RN, 1938; comd HM Submarine: H44, 1942; Sceptre, 1943-44; Alderney, 1946-48; Aeneas, 1950-51; Exec. Officer, HMS Ark Royal, 1956-58; comd 2nd Submarine Sqn, 1961-63; comd HMS Victorious, 1966-68; Dir-Gen., Weapons (Naval), 1968-70. Captain, 1959; Rear-Adm., 1968; Vice-Adm., 1971. *Recreations:* friends, reading, music. *Address:* 19 The Crescent, Alverstoke, Hants. *T:* Gosport 80510. *Club:* Royal Over-Seas League.

**McINTOSH, Robert,** CSI 1947; MBE 1937; BSc, MIE(Ind); *b* 1894; *s* of D. H. McIntosh; *m* 1925, Isabella Davidson, *d* of A. Butchart; one *d*. *Educ:* Edinburgh and St Andrews Universities. Joined Indian Service of Engineers, 1920; Chief Engineer, Public Works Dept (General and Defence), Madras, 1945; retired. *Address:* 2 Bingham Terrace, Dundee. *T:* Dundee 44555. *Club:* Madras (Madras).

**MACINTOSH, Sir Robert (Reynolds),** Kt 1955; MA, DM, FRCSE, DA; FFARCS; Hon. Fellow: Faculties of Anæsthetists of Australasia, 1950, of Ireland, 1964, of England, 1968; Royal Society of Medicine, 1966; Pembroke College, Oxford, 1965; Nuffield Professor of Anæsthetics, Oxford University, 1937-65; former Hon. Consultant in Anæsthetics, Royal Air Force; *b* Timaru, New Zealand, 17 Oct. 1897; *s* of C. N. Macintosh. *Educ:* Waitaki, New Zealand; Guy's Hospital. Served European War (despatches), Spanish Civil War (Order of Military Merit); War of 1939-45 (Order of Liberty, Norway). Dr hc Univs of Buenos Aires, Aix-Marseilles and Poznan; Hon. DSc Univ. of Wales. *Publications:* Textbooks, Essentials of General Anæsthesia, Physics for the Anæsthetist, Lumbar Puncture and Spinal Analgesia, Local Anæsthesia, Brachial Plexus; various articles on anæsthesia in medical and dental journals. *Recreations:* golf, tennis. *Address:* 326 Woodstock Road, Oxford. *Club:* Bath.

**McINTOSH, Ronald Robert Duncan,** CB 1968; Deputy Under-Secretary of State, Department of Employment and Productivity, since 1970; *b* 26 Sept. 1919; *s* of Thomas Steven McIntosh, MD, FRCP, FRCS, and late Christina Jane McIntosh; *m* 1951, Doreen Frances, *o d* of late Commander Andrew MacGinnity, Frinton-on-Sea. *Educ:* Charterhouse (Scholar); Balliol Coll., Oxford. Served in Merchant Navy, 1939-45; Second Mate, 1944-45. Assistant Principal, Board of Trade, 1947; seconded to Dollar Exports Board as General Manager, 1949-51; Trade Commissioner, New Delhi, 1957-61; attached to Lord President's office for work on problems of North East England, April-Oct. 1963; Under-Secretary: Board of Trade, 1963-64; Dept of Economic Affairs, 1964-66; Dep. Under-Secretary, 1966-68; Dep. Secretary, Cabinet Office, 1968-70. *Recreations:* sailing, travel. *Address:* 24 Ponsonby Terrace, SW1. *T:* 01-828 4265. *Clubs:* Travellers'; Medway Yacht.

**MACINTYRE, Hon. Sir Donald,** Kt 1961; CBE 1947; MP Bulawayo Central, from 1934; *b* Glasgow, 9 Sept. 1891; *s* of Peter Macintyre; *m* 1912, Gertrude Gill, Redruth, Cornwall, England. *Educ:* Dowanhill Sch., Glasgow. Councillor of Bulawayo (Mayor, various periods). Chairman: Osborn's Bakeries Ltd (also Managing Director); Rhodesian Investment Trust Co. Ltd; Founder and Director McIntyre & Son; Director of other companies. Minister of Finance, Federation of Rhodesia amd Nyasaland, 1953-62. JP Southern Rhodesia, 1935; 1st Alderman, City of Bulawayo, 1950; Freedom of City of Bulawayo, 1955. *Address:* 24 King's Avenue, Bulawayo, Rhodesia.

**McINTYRE, F(rederick) Donald (Livingstone),** QC 1955; **His Honour Judge McIntyre;** Judge of County Courts (West London) since 1964 (Bow, 1962-64); *b* 8 July 1905; 2nd *s* of William and Marjorie McIntyre. *Educ:* Cardiff High Sch.; St Olave's; St John's Coll., Cambridge (History Scholar and MacMahon Law Student; BA, LLB). Called to Bar, Gray's Inn, 1928; joined Inner Temple, 1936. Served War, 1941-46; Officer Royal Air Force (POW, Far East, 1942-45). Dep. Chairman Inner London Sessions, 1965; JP Surrey. *Recreations:* cricket and chess. *Address:* 118 Clifford's Inn, EC4. *T:* 01-405 4127. *Clubs:* Royal Automobile; Union Society (Cambridge).

**McINTYRE, Rev. Canon James;** Fellow, University College, Durham, since 1950; working in Trinity College, Toronto, since 1968; *e s* of late Robert and Matilda Anne McIntyre, Auchterarder, Scotland; *m* 1st, 1915, Sybil Mary (*d* 1960), *d* of late Sir H. F. Norbury, KCB, KHS, RN; one *d*; 2nd, 1961, Isolde Brünhilde Rosine Dorothea Meinhardt, *d* of late Gustav Adolf Meinhardt and Marie Dorothea Meinhardt. *Educ:* Merchant Taylors' Sch.; University College, Durham (BA, MLitt); Ely Theological Coll.; S John's Coll., University of Manitoba (BD 1st class); Trinity Coll., University of Toronto (DD). Deacon, 1913; Priest, 1914; Curate of Holy Trinity, Eltham, 1913-15; Incumbent of S Mary, Edmonton, Canada, 1915-16; Minister of S Barnabas, Epsom, 1916-18; Rector of Washford Pyne, 1918-21; Curate in charge of S Paul's, Newton Abbot, 1922-25; Vicar of Bishop's Teignton, 1925-30; Rector of Holy Trinity, Bath, 1930-32; of Lympstone, 1932-46. Chapter Librarian, Gloucester Cathedral, 1946-52; Receiver, 1955-68. Proctor in Convocation (Diocese of Exeter), 1929-31 and 1936-45. Canon Residentiary of Gloucester Cathedral, 1946-68, Canon Emeritus, 1968-. JP for City of Gloucester, 1950-68. Examining Chaplain to Bishop of Worcester, 1953-68; Chaplain to City High Sheriff, Gloucester, 1953. *Recreations:* sea lore and life. *Address:* University College, Durham; Trinity College, Toronto 5, Canada.

**McINTYRE, Cardinal, His Eminence James Francis Aloysius;** Archbishop of Los Angeles, California, 1948-70; *b* New York, 25 June 1886;

*s* of late James F. McIntyre and Mary (*née* Pelley). *Educ:* Public Sch. 70; Cathedral Coll. and St Joseph's Seminary, New York. Began work as runner at New York Curb Exchange, 1899; with H. L. Horton Co., Wall Street, 1902-15, rising to Office Manager; studied at evening schs and left business world, 1915. Graduated from Cathedral Coll., 1916; Priest, 1921; Curate of St Gabriel's Church, 1921-23; Asst Chancellor and Asst Diocesan Sec., New York, 1923; Chancellor, 1934; Papal Chamberlain, 1934; Domestic Prelate, 1936; Mem. Diocesan Board of Consultors, 1939; Titular Bishop of Cyrene and Auxiliary Bishop of New York, 1941; a Vicar-Gen., Diocese of New York, 1945; Coadjutor Archbishop and Titular Archbishop of Paltus, 1946; Cardinal, 1953. Knight Grand Cross of the Holy Sepulchre, 1946. *Address:* 637 South Kingsley Drive, Los Angeles, Calif 90005, USA.

**McINTYRE, James Gordon;** *see* Sorn, Hon. Lord.

**McINTYRE, Rev. Prof. John,** DD, DLitt; Professor of Divinity, University of Edinburgh, since Oct. 1956, and Principal Warden, Pollock Halls of Residence, University of Edinburgh, since May 1960; Principal of New College, and Dean of Faculty of Divinity, since 1968; *b* 20 May 1916; *s* of late John C. McIntyre, Southfield, Bathgate, Scotland, and Annie McIntyre; *m* 1945, Jessie B., *d* of late William Buick, Coupar Angus; two *s* one *d*. *Educ:* Bathgate Academy; University of Edinburgh; MA (1938); BD (1941); DLitt (1953). Ordained, 1941; Locum Tenens, Parish of Glenorchy and Inishall, 1941-43; Minister of Parish of Fenwick, Ayrshire, 1943-45. Hunter Baillie Prof. of Theology, St Andrew's Coll., University of Sydney, 1946-56; Principal of St Andrew's Coll., 1950-56. DD *hc* (university of Glasgow), 1961. *Publications:* St Anselm and His Critics, 1954; The Christian Doctrine of History, 1957; On the Love of God, 1962; The Shape of Christology, 1966. Articles and reviews in various learned jls of Theology. *Address:* Pollock Halls of Residence, Edinburgh 9. *T:* 031-667 6560.

**McINTYRE, Air Commodore Kenneth John,** CB 1958; CBE 1951; JP; RAF retired; *b* 23 July 1908; *s* of late William Seymour McIntyre and Winifred May McIntyre, Clevedon, Somerset; *m* 1936, Betty Aveley, *o d* of late Lt-Col Percie C. Cooper, Dulwich. *Educ:* Blundell's Sch.; RMC Sandhurst. Commissioned Royal Tank Regt, 1928; served UK and India; seconded to RAF 1934; permanent commission RAF, 1945. Served War of 1939-45 in UK, France and Belgium. Dep. Dir of Organisation, Air Ministry, 1945-47; Joint Services Staff Coll., 1947-48; Group Capt. 1947; Group Capt. Operations, HQ MEAF, 1948-50; idc 1951; SHAPE (Paris), 1952-54; Air Commodore, 1955; Dir of Policy (Air Staff), Air Ministry, 1955-58. Mem., Dorset CC, 1967; JP Poole, 1967. *Address:* 9 Mount Grace Drive, Lilliput, Poole, Dorset. *T:* Canford Cliffs 78250.

**McINTYRE, Sir Laurence Rupert,** Kt 1963; CBE 1960 (OBE 1953); Australian Permanent Representative to the United Nations, New York, since 1970; *b* Hobart, Tasmania, 22 June 1912; *s* of late L. T. and Hilda McIntyre; *m* 1938, Judith Mary, *d* of John H. Gould; two *s*. *Educ:* Launceston Grammar Sch.; Tasmania Univ.; Exeter Coll., Oxford (Rhodes Scholar). Served Aust. High Commissioner's Office, London, 1936-40; Dept of External Affairs, Canberra, 1940-42; Aust. Embassy, Washington, 1942-47; Counsellor, Dept of External Affairs, Canberra, 1947-50; Actg Commissioner to Malaya, 1950-51; Asst Sec., Dept of External Affairs, Canberra, 1951-52; Commissioner to Malaya, 1952-54; Sen. External Affairs Officer (Minister), London, 1954-57; Aust. Ambassador to Indonesia, 1957-60, to Japan, 1960-65; Deputy Secretary, Australian Dept of External Affairs, 1965-70. *Publication:* contrib. to Some Australians Take Stock, 1938. *Address:* 1 Beekman Place, New York, USA; Department of External Affairs, Canberra, ACT, Australia. *Clubs:* University (Sydney); Commonwealth (Canberra).

**McINTYRE, Robert Douglas,** MB, ChB (Edinburgh), DPH (Glasgow); JP; Consultant Chest Physician; *b* Dec. 1913; 3rd *s* of Rev. John E. McIntyre and Catherine, *d* of Rev. William Morison, DD; *m* 1954, Letitia, *d* of Alexander Macleod; one *s*. *Educ:* Hamilton Acad.; Daniel Stewart's Coll.; University of Edinburgh. MP (Scottish Nationalist), Motherwell and Wishaw, 1945; Pres., Scottish National Party; Mem., Stirling Town Council (Hon. Treas., 1958-64, Provost, 1967-). JP Co. Stirling. *Publications:* Numerous articles on Scottish, political and medical subjects, including regular contribs to the Scots Independent. *Recreation:* yachting. *Address:* 8 Gladstone Place, Stirling. *T:* Stirling 3456. *Clubs:* Scottish Arts; Royal Northern Yacht.

**McINTYRE, Prof. William Ian Mackay,** PhD; MRCVS; Professor of Veterinary Medicine, University of Glasgow, since Oct. 1961; *b* 7 July 1919; *s* of George John and Jane McIntyre; *m* 1948, Ruth Dick Galbraith; three *s*. *Educ:* Altnaharra Primary and Golspie Secondary Sch., Sutherland; Royal (Dick) Veterinary Coll. (MRCVS); University of Edinburgh (PhD). Clinical Asst, Royal (Dick) Veterinary Coll., 1944-48; Lectr, Vet. Med., Royal (Dick) Vet. Coll., 1948-51; Sen. Lectr, Vet. Med., University of Glasgow, 1951-61. Seconded to University of East Africa, University Coll., Nairobi, as Dean, Faculty of Veterinary Science, and Prof., Clinical Studies, 1963-67. *Publications:* various, on canine nephritis, parasitic diseases and vaccines and clinical communications. *Address:* University of Glasgow Veterinary Faculty, Bearsden Road, Bearsden, Glasgow. *T:* 041-942 2301.

**McINTYRE, Surgeon Rear-Adm. William Percival Edwin,** CB 1961; RN retired; *b* 21 Aug. 1903; *s* of George McIntyre, Rathgar, Dublin; *m* 1964, Mrs Eve Robertson-Rodger, *widow* of P. J. Robertson-Rodger. *Educ:* St Andrews Coll.; Trinity Coll., Dublin. MB, BCh, BAO 1925; MA, MD 1929. Joined RN as Surg. Lt 1925; Surg.-Comdr 1937; Surg.-Captain 1949. Senior Medical Officer (Medical Sect.), RN Hospital, Chatham, 1950-52 and RN Hospital, Plymouth, 1956-58; Fleet Medical Officer, Home Fleet, 1952-54; Surgeon Rear-Adm. 1958; Dep. Medical Dir-Gen., RN, 1958-62. QHP 1958-62. OStJ 1950; CStJ 1960. *Recreations:* golf, tennis. *Address:* 65 Eaton Square, SW1; Chasmoor, 68 Terenure Road West, Dublin 6. *Club:* Naval and Military.

**MacIVER, Alan Squarey,** CBE 1960; MC 1918; *b* 2 Aug. 1894; *y s* of late David MacIver, MP; *m* 1922, Lois Katharine Scott-Moncrieff; two *s* two *d*. *Educ:* Shrewsbury Sch.; Christ Church, Oxford (MA). Served European War, 1914-18; commd Lancashire Fusiliers (wounded). Called to Bar (Inner Temple), 1922. Managing Dir, David MacIver & Co., Ltd, Steamship Owners, 1925-32. Institute of Chartered Accountants in England and Wales: Asst Sec., 1935, Dep. Sec., 1945, Sec., 1950-62. War of 1939-45, Gen. Staff, War Office, 1940-45. Sec. Sixth International Congress on Accounting, London, 1952. *Address:* 3 Ravenscroft Road, Henley-on-Thames, Oxon. *Club:* Leander.

**MacIVER, Prof. Arthur Milne;** Professor of Philosophy, University of Southampton, since 1960; *b* Liverpool, 24 March 1905; *s* of Andrew T. S. MacIver, shipowner, Birkenhead; *m* 1st, 1932, Margaret Willoughby Moon (*d* 1937); one *d*; 2nd, 1944, Miriam Frances Round; one *s* one *d* (and one *s* decd). *Educ:* Winchester Coll.; New Coll., Oxford. BA 1928, MA 1931. Asst in Philosophy, University of Edinburgh, 1931-32; Temp. Lecturer, University of Leeds, Nov.-April 1932-33; Asst Lecturer, University of Birmingham, 1933-34; Lecturer, University of Leeds, 1934-38. Served War of 1939-45, with Political Warfare Exec., 1942-45. Sen. Lecturer, University Coll. (now University of Southampton), Southampton, 1949-60. Pres. Mind Association, 1958; Pres. Aristotelian Soc., 1961-62. *Publications:* articles and reviews in Proc. Aristotelian Soc., Analysis, Philosophy, Mind, etc. *Address:* Oakhill, 126 Highfield Lane, Southampton. *T:* Southampton 54669.

**MACK, Prof. Alan Osborne,** MDS; LDS RCS; Professor of Dental Prosthetics, Institute of Dental Surgery, University of London, since 1967; Consultant Dental Surgeon, Eastman Dental Hospital; *b* 24 July 1918; *s* of Arthur Joseph Mack, Glos, and Florence Emily Mack (*née* Norris); *m* 1943, Marjorie Elizabeth (*née* Westacott); two *s* one *d*. *Educ:* Westbourne Park Sch.; London Univ. LDS RCS 1942; MDS Durham, 1958. House Surgeon, Royal Dental Hosp., Sch. of Dental Surgery, University of London, 1942-43; served in RAF Dental Branch, 1943-47; Demonstrator, Prosthetics Dept Royal Dental Hosp., 1948; successively Asst Dir, Prosthetics Dept, and Senior Lecturer, London Univ., Royal Dental Hosp., 1949-56; Prof. of Dental Prosthetics, Univ. of Newcastle upon Tyne (formerly King's Coll., Univ. of Durham), 1956-67; Examiner in Dental Prosthetics, Royal Coll. of Surgeons of England, 1956; Examiner, University of Manchester, 1959, Leeds, 1961, Glasgow, 1961, Liverpool, 1965, London, 1965; Examination Visitor, GDC. Mem. Board of Faculty, Royal College of Surgeons, 1959. Pres. British Soc. for Study of Prosthetic Dentistry (BSSPD), 1963. Hon. Mem., Amer. Acad. of Implant Dentures, 1966. *Publications:* articles in British Dental Jls. *Recreations:* gardening, horse riding. *Address:* Institute of Dental Surgery, Eastman Dental Hospital, Gray's Inn Road, WC1. *T:* 01-837 7251.

**MACK, Sir Henry;** *see* Mack, Sir W. H. B.

**MACK, Hon. Sir William (George),** KBE 1967; **Hon. Mr Justice Mack;** Chief Justice of the Supreme Court of Queensland, Australia; *b* 2 Nov. 1904; *s* of late A. G. Mack; *m* 1957, Ida, *d* of H. W. Mocatta; one *s* one *d*. *Educ:* Maryborough Gram. Sch., Australia. Called to the Bar, Queensland, 1930; associate to Mr Justice Henchman; served War of 1939-45 (Major), New Guinea and Pacific Islands: Lecturer in Probate, Divorce and Admiralty Law, University of Queensland; Judge of the Supreme Court of Queensland, 1950. Chm., Central Sugar Cane Prices Board, 1957. *Address:* Supreme Court, Brisbane, Queensland, Australia.

**MACK, Sir (William) Henry (Bradshaw),** GBE 1952; KCMG 1947 (CMG 1942); LLD (Dublin) 1948; HM Diplomatic Service, retired; *b* 21 Aug. 1894; 2nd *s* of late Rev. A. W. Bradshaw Mack, Dalkey, Co. Dublin; *m* 1921, Lilian May, *o d* of late F. Lonsdale North, JP, Dublin; one *s*. *Educ:* The High Sch., Dublin; Trinity Coll., Dublin (Scholar, double Sen. Mod. BA). Served European War (RA) in France and Flanders, 1916-19; temporarily employed Treasury, 1920; entered Foreign Office and Diplomatic Service, 1921. Served at Istanbul, Berlin, Foreign Office, Cairo, Prague, Vienna, Rome, and Paris to 1940. Head of French Dept, Foreign Office, 1940. British Civil Liaison Officer to Allied Comdr-in-Chief in North Africa in 1942 and accompanied Gen. Dwight D. Eisenhower to North Africa, Nov. 1942 (Asst Under-Sec. of State in Foreign Office while so employed); returned to Foreign Office, 1943; Dep. Commissioner (Civil) Allied Commission for Austria, 1944; UK Political Representative in Austria and Political Adviser to British High Commissioner and GOC-in-C British Troops in Austria, 1945; HM Minister to Austria, 1947-48; Ambassador to Iraq, 1948-51; Ambassador to the Argentine Republic, 1951-54 retired, 1955. *Address:* Rose Lawn, Ballybrack, County Dublin, Ireland. *Club:* Royal Irish Automobile (Dublin).

**McKAIG, Rear-Adm. John Rae,** CBE 1966; Flag Officer, Plymouth, Commander Central Sub Area, Eastern Atlantic, and Commander Plymouth Sub Area, Channel, since 1970; *b* 24 April 1922; *s* of late Sir John McKaig, KCB, DSO, and Lady (Annie Wright) McKaig (*née* Lee); *m* 1945, Barbara Dawn, *d* of Dr F. K. Marriott, MC, Yoxford, Suffolk; two *s* one *d*. *Educ:* Loretto Sch. Joined RN as Special Entry Cadet, 1939; served in cruisers and destroyers in Home and Mediterranean Waters, 1940-43; in Amphibious Force S at invasion of Normandy, 1944; in coastal forces until 1945; qual. in Communications, 1945; Commander, 1952; Captain, 1959; served as Dep. to Chief Polaris Exec., 1963-66; comd HM Signal Sch., 1966-68; Asst Chief of Naval Staff (Operational Requirements), 1968-70. *Recreations:* offshore sailing, shooting, fishing. *Address:* Hill House, Hambledon, Hants. *Clubs:* United Service, Royal Ocean Racing.

**MACKAIL, Denis George,** FRSL; *b* 3 June 1892; *o s* of late J. W. Mackail, OM; *m* 1917, Diana (*d* 1949), *o c* of Sir Guy Granet, GBE; two *d*. *Educ:* St Paul's Sch.; Balliol Coll., Oxford. *Publications:* What Next?, 1920; Romance to the Rescue, 1921; Bill the Bachelor, 1922; According to Gibson; Summertime, 1923; The *Majestic* Mystery, 1924; Greenery Street, 1925; The Fortunes of Hugo, 1926; The Flower Show, 1927; Tales from Greenery Street, 1928; Another Part of the Wood; How Amusing!, 1929; The Young Livingstones; The Square Circle, 1930; David's Day; Ian and Felicity, 1932; Having Fun, 1933; Chelbury Abbey; Summer Leaves, 1934; The Wedding, 1935; Back Again, 1936; Jacinth, 1937; London Lovers; Morning, Noon and Night, 1938; The Story of J.M.B.: A Biography, 1941; Life with Topsy, 1942; Upside-Down, 1943; Ho!; Tales for a Godchild, 1944; Huddleston House, 1945; Our Hero; We're Here!, 1947; Where Am I?, 1948; By Auction; Her Ladyship, 1949; It Makes the World Go Round, 1950; numerous short stories in various periodicals. *Address:* 10/74 Elm Park Gardens, SW10. *Club:* Athenæum.

**MACKAY,** family name of **Earl of Inchcape** and **Baron Reay.**

**MACKAY, Alastair,** CMG 1966; Under-Secretary, HM Treasury; *b* 27 Sept. 1911; *s* of late Alexander Mackay; *m* 1939, Janetta Brown Ramsay; one *s* one *d*. *Educ:* George Heriot's Sch.; Edinburgh Univ.; Berlin Univ. Entered HM Treasury, 1940. Member UK Treasury and Supply Delegation, Washington, 1951-54; seconded to Foreign Service Inspectorate, 1957-59; Financial Adviser to the British High Commissioner in India, 1963-66. *Recreations:* golf, gardening. *Address:*

Thorncroft, 47 Crescent Road, Caterham, Surrey.

**McKAY, Alick Benson,** CBE 1965; Director, International Publishing Corporation Ltd (formerly Daily Mirror Group), 1963-69; *b* Adelaide, S Australia, 5 Aug. 1909; *s* of George Hugh McKay, Master Mariner; *m* 1935, Muriel Frieda Searcy (decd); one *s* two *d*. *Educ:* Thebarton High Sch.; private tuition. Joined News Ltd, Adelaide, 1933; Manager, News Ltd, Melbourne, 1939; Manager, News Ltd, Sydney, 1941; Dir and Gen. Man., Argus & Australasian Ltd, 1952; joined Daily Mirror Group, London, 1957, Dir, 1958; Dir, George Newnes Ltd, 1961, Chm., 1962-68; Dir, Internat. Publishing Corporation Ltd, since formation in 1963. Chm. in London, Victoria Promotion Cttee, Australia; Chm., British Heart Foundation Appeal; Mem. Council of the Foundation. *Recreations:* charity work, gardening. *Clubs:* Devonshire, Hurlingham, Garrick.

**MACKAY, A(rthur) Stewart,** ROI 1949; formerly Lecturer, Hammersmith College of Art; *b* 25 Feb. 1909; British. *Educ:* Wilson's Grammar Sch.; Regent Street Polytechnic School of Art. Art Master, Regent Street Polytechnic School of Art, 1936, Assistant Lecturer, 1936-60. Served War of 1939-45: enlisted Army, Jan. 1942; released with rank of Captain, 1946. Exhibitor: RA (23 pictures), Paris Salon, ROI, RBA, Leicester Galleries, Imperial War Museum; Royal Scottish Academy; New York. *Publication:* How to Make Lino Cuts, 1935; articles for Artist, 1953, 1963. *Recreations:* tennis and golf. *Address:* 4 Dog Kennel Hill, East Dulwich, SE22.

**McKAY, Sir Charles Holly,** Kt 1963; CBE 1956; State President, Returned Sailors', Soldiers' and Airmen's League of Australia, Victoria, since 1956; Commissioner, Melbourne Harbour Trust; *b* Great Western, Victoria, 19 Aug. 1896; *m* 1934, Frances E., *d* of W. Deans. *Educ:* Church of England Grammar Sch., Ararat, Victoria. Served 12th Infantry Bn. *Address:* St Marnocks, Beaufort, Victoria, Australia. *Club:* Naval and Military (Melbourne).

**MacKAY, Prof. Donald MacCrimmon,** BSc, PhD, FInstP; Granada Research Professor of Communication, University of Keele, since 1960; Joint Editor, Experimental Brain Research; *b* 9 Aug. 1922; *o s* of Dr Henry MacKay; *m* 1955, Valerie Wood; two *s* three *d*. *Educ:* Wick High Sch.; St Andrews Univ. BSc (St Andrews) 1943; PhD (London) 1951. Radar research, Admiralty, 1943-46; Assistant Lecturer in Physics, 1946-48, Lecturer, 1948-59, Reader, 1959-60, King's Coll., London. Rockefeller Fellow in USA, 1951. Eddington Lectr, 1967; Vis. Prof., Univ. of California, 1969. *Publications:* (with M. E. Fisher) Analogue Computing at Ultra-High Speed, 1962; (ed) Christianity in a Mechanistic Universe, 1965; Freedom of Action in a Mechanistic Universe, 1967; Information, Mechanism and Meaning, 1969; Chapters in: Communication Theory, 1953; Information Theory, 1956, 1961; Sensory Communication, 1961; Man and his Future, 1963; Science in its Context, 1964; Information Processing in the Nervous System, 1964; Brain and Conscious Experience, 1966; Structure and Function of Inhibitory Neuronal Mechanisms, 1968; Evoked Brain Potentials, 1969, etc.; scientific papers on electronic computing, information theory, experimental psychology, electro-physiology. *Recreation:* photography. *Address:* The Croft, Keele, Staffs. *T:* Keele Park 300.

**MACKAY, Sir (George Patrick) Gordon,** Kt 1966; CBE 1962; with World Bank since 1965; *b* 12 Nov. 1914; *s* of Rev. Adam Mackay and Katie Forrest (*née* Lawrence); *m* 1954, Margaret Esmé Martin; one *s* two *d*. *Educ:* Gordon Sch., Huntly; Aberdeen Univ. Joined Kenya and Uganda Railways and Harbours (later East African Railways and Harbours), 1938; Chief Asst to Gen. Manager, 1948; Chief Operating Supt, 1954; Dep. General Manager, 1960, General Manager, 1961-64. MInstT 1961. OStJ 1964. *Recreations:* golf and gardening. *Address:* 8226 Lilly Stone Drive, Bethesda, Maryland, USA. *T:* 469-7561. *Club:* Nairobi (Kenya).

**MACKAY, Gillian Helen;** Public Relations Consultant; private pilot; *b* 20 Sept. 1923; *er d* of Stuart Mackay. *Educ:* Hunmanby Hall. WRNS, 1942-46. Dep. Press Officer, Conservative Central Office, 1947-52; BOAC, 1952-56. Executive Secretary, Guild of Air Pilots and Air Navigators, 1956-68 (Freeman; Liveryman, 1968); Press Officer to Liberal Party Leader, 1968-69; Campaign Manager, Health Education Council, 1969-. Vice-Chm., British Women Pilots' Assoc., 1969- (Chm., 1964-69); Member Council, Air League, 1966-. Companion, Royal Aeronautical Society, 1960. Tissandier Diploma, Fédération Aéronautique Internat., 1966. *Recreations:* flying, ski-ing. *Address:* 5 Hay's Mews, W1. *Clubs:* Ski Club of Great Britain, Eagle Ski Club.

**MACKAY, Sir Gordon;** *see* Mackay, Sir G. P. G.

**MACKAY, Ian Keith,** CMG 1963; Broadcasts Supervisor, Papua-New Guinea, since 1968; *b* 19 Oct. 1909; *s* of David and Margaret Mackay; *m* 1960, Lilian Adele Beatty; one *d*. *Educ:* Nelson Coll., New Zealand. New Zealand Broadcasting Service: Announcer, 1935-36; Sports Announcer, 1937; Station Manager, 1938-43; Senior Executive, Commercial Network, 1943-50; Australia: Asst Manager, Station 2GB, 1950-51; Production Manager, Macquarie Network, 1951-61; Director-General, Nigerian Broadcasting Corporation, 1961-64; Advisor on Mass Media to Minister and NBC Board of Governors, 1964-65; PRO, Papua and New Guinea Administration, 1966-68. Member, Royal Society of Literature; Member, Society of Authors. *Publications:* Broadcasting in New Zealand, 1953; Broadcasting in Australia, 1957; Macquarie: The Story of a Network, 1960; Broadcasting in Nigeria, 1964; Presenting Papua and New Guinea, 1967; articles on social and historical aspects of broadcasting and articles on broadcasting in developing countries in numerous jls; also papers for UN agencies. *Recreations:* conchology, philately. *Address:* Department of Information, Konedobu, Papua-New Guinea.

**MACKAY, Sir James (Mackerron),** KBE 1966; CB 1964; Member: Highlands and Islands Development Board, since 1967; Scottish Tourist Board, since 1967; Countryside Commission for Scotland, since 1968; *b* 9 Aug. 1907; *o s* of Alexander and Annie Mackay; *m* 1938, Katherine, *d* of R. C. Hamilton; two *s*. *Educ:* Forres and Hamilton Academies; Glasgow and Oxford Universities. Glasgow Univ.: MA, 1929; Assistant in Greek, 1929-30. Balliol Coll., Oxford, 1930-34; Exhibitioner; Mods. and Greats. Lecturer in Humanity, Glasgow Univ., 1934-40. Entered Secretariat, Admiralty, 1940; Assistant Secretary, 1945; Under-Secretary, 1958; Deputy Secretary, 1961; Deputy Under Sec. of State, Min. of Defence, April 1964; Deputy Sec., Min. of Aviation, 1964-66; Deputy Under-Sec. of State, Home Office, 1966-67. *Recreation:* fly-fishing. *Address:* Cluny, Drumnadrochit,

Inverness. *T:* Drumnadrochit 268. *Clubs:* Highland (Inverness); Scottish Arts (Edinburgh).

**MACKAY, James Peter Hymers,** QC (Scotland) 1965; *b* 2 July 1927; *s* of James Mackay and Janet Hymers; *m* 1958, Elizabeth Gunn Hymers; one *s* two *d*. *Educ:* George Heriot's Sch., Edinburgh. MA Hons Maths and Nat. Philosophy, Edinburgh Univ., 1948; Lectr in Mathematics, Univ. of St Andrews, 1948-50; Major Schol., Trinity Coll., Cambridge, in Mathematics, 1947, taken up 1950; Senior Schol. 1951; BA (Cantab) 1952; LLB Edinburgh (with Distinction) 1955. Admitted to Faculty of Advocates, 1955; Standing Junior Counsel to: Queen's and Lord Treasurer's Remembrancer; Scottish Home and Health Dept; Commissioners of Inland Revenue in Scotland. *Publication:* Armour on Valuation for Rating, 3rd edn (with J. J. Clyde and J. G. Milligan), 1961. *Recreation:* walking. *Address:* 34 Dick Place, Edinburgh. *T:* 031-667 5995. *Club:* New (Edinburgh).

**McKAY, Rt. Hon. James Wilson;** Lord Provost of Edinburgh and Lord Lieutenant of the County of the City of Edinburgh since May 1969; *b* 12 March 1912; *s* of John McKay; *m* 1942, Janette Urquhart; three *d*. *Educ:* Dunfermline High Sch.; Portobello Secondary Sch., Edinburgh. Insurance Broker; Man. Dir, John McKay (Insurance) Ltd, Edinburgh; Dir, George S. Murdoch & Partners Ltd, Aberdeen. Served with RN, 1941-46 (Lieut, RNVR). Order of Cross of St Mark (Greek Orthodox Church), 1970. *Recreations:* walking, gardening, reading. *Address:* T'Windward, 11 Cammo Gardens, Edinburgh 4. *T:* 031-336 3615. *Clubs:* Caledonian (Hon. Mem.); Caledonian (Edinburgh); University (Aberdeen); RNVR (Glasgow); Caledonian (Hon Mem.) (San Francisco).

**MACKAY, John;** Headmaster, Bristol Grammar School, since 1960; *b* 23 June 1914; *s* of William Mackay, Nottingham, and Eliza Mackay; *m* 1952, Margaret Ogilvie; two *s* two *d*. *Educ:* Mundella Grammar Sch., Nottingham; University of Nottingham; Merton Coll., Oxford. BA London (External) 1st Class Hons (English), 1935; Cambridge Teacher's Certificate, 1936. On staff of SCM, 1936-38; English Lecturer, St John's Coll., York, 1938-40. Served War of 1939-45, in Royal Navy, 1940-46. Merton Coll., Oxford, 1946-48; DPhil (Oxon) 1953. English Master, Merchant Taylors' School, Crosby, Liverpool, 1948-54; Second Master, Cheltenham Coll., 1954-60. Chm., HMC, 1970. *Recreations:* literature, gardening, cricket, arguing. *Address:* The Headmaster's House, The Grammar School, Bristol BS8 1SJ. *T:* Bristol 37832. *Club:* Athenæum.

**MACKAY, John Alexander,** MA, LittD, DD, LLD, LHD; President of Princeton Theological Seminary, 1936-59, President Emeritus, 1959; *b* Inverness, Scotland, 17 May 1889; *s* of Duncan Mackay and Isabella Macdonald; *m* 1916, Jane Logan Wells; one *s* three *d*. *Educ:* University of Aberdeen (MA 1912, 1st Cl. Hons in Philosophy); Princeton Theological Seminary (BD 1915). Studied at the University of Madrid, 1915-16, and University of Bonn, 1930. LittD, University of San Marcos, Lima, 1918; DD Princeton Univ., 1937, Aberdeen Univ., 1939, University of Debrecen, Hungary, 1939; LLD Ohio-Wesleyan, 1937, Lincoln Univ., 1953; LHD Boston, 1939; and Hon. Degrees from several colleges; Hon. Fellow, Leland Stanford Univ., 1941. Principal, Anglo-Peruvian Coll., Lima, Peru, 1916-25; Prof. Philosophy, Univ. of San Marcos, Peru, 1925; Writer and Lecturer, South American Fedn YMCA, 1926-32; Pres. Bd Foreign Missions of Presbyterian Church, USA, 1945-51; Pres., World Presbyterian Alliance, 1954-59; Member: Central Cttee World Council of Churches, 1948-54 (Provl Cttee, 1946-48); Council on Theological Education, Presbyterian Church, USA, 1944-46 (Chairman); International Missionary Council, 1948-58 (Chairman); Joint Cttee World Council of Churches and International Missionary Council, 1949- (Chairman, 1949-54); Advisory Council, Dept of Philosophy, Princeton Univ., 1941-62; American Theological Soc.; Hon. For. Mem., British and Foreign Bible Soc.; Trustee of Mackenzie Univ., São Paulo, Brazil (Pres. Bd of Trustees, 1948). Special Lectr at many Univs and Colleges since 1932. Pres., American Assoc. of Theological Schs, 1948; Moderator, General Assembly of the Presbyterian Church in USA, 1953. Comendador, Palmas Magistrales (Peru), 1964. *Publications:* Mas Yo Os Digo, 1927; El Sentido de la Vida, 1931; The Other Spanish Christ, 1932; That Other America, 1935; A Preface to Christian Theology, 1941; Heritage and Destiny, 1943; Christianity on the Frontier, 1950; God's Order, 1953; The Presbyterian Way of Life, 1960; His Life and our Life, 1964; Ecumenics: The Science of the Church Universal, 1964; Christian Reality and Appearance, 1969; Realidad y Idolatria, 1970. Editor, Theology Today, 1944-51 (Chairman Editorial Council, Theology Today, 1951-59). *Recreations:* walking and motoring. *Address:* Meadow Lakes, Apartment 31-02, Hightstown, NJ, USA. *Club:* Cosmos (Washington).

**McKAY, John (Andrew),** CBE 1966; QPM 1968; Chief Inspector of Constabulary for England and Wales, since 1970; *b* 28 Nov. 1912; *s* of late Denis McKay, Blantyre, Lanarkshire; *m* 1947, Gertrude Gillespie Deighan; two *d*. *Educ:* Glasgow Univ. MA Glasgow, 1934. Joined Metropolitan Police, 1935; seconded to Army for service with Military Govt in Italy and Austria, 1943-47 (Lt-Col); Asst Chief Constable, then Deputy Chief Constable, Birmingham, 1953-58; Chief Constable of Manchester, 1959-66; HM Inspector of Constabulary, 1966-70. Hon. MA, Manchester, 1966. *Address:* c/o Home Office, Horseferry House, Dean Ryle Street, SW1. *T:* 01-834 6655. *Clubs:* United Service, Challoner.

**MACKAY, Brigadier Kenneth,** CBE 1955 (OBE 1941); DSO 1942; *b* 26 June 1901; *s* of William Mackay, Herne Bay, Kent; *m* 1923, Eve, *d* of E. Ll. Ingram, Parkstone, Dorset; three *s*. *Educ:* Imperial Service Coll.; Royal Military Academy. Commissioned, Royal Engineers, 1921; Captain, 1932; Major, 1938. Served War of 1939-45 (despatches twice): Greece, Crete, Western Desert, N Africa, NW Europe; CRE 1st Armoured Div. and Chief Engineer, Airborne Corps. Colonel, 1948; Brigadier, 1952; retired, 1954. Chief Administrative Engineer, Eastwoods' Group, 1958-63. Bronze Star Medal (USA), 1944. *Recreations:* painting and gardening. *Address:* The Lawn Cottage, Winterborne Houghton, Blandford Forum, Dorset.

**MACKAY, Maj.-Gen. Kenneth,** CB 1969; MBE 1943; idc, psc; Quartermaster General AHQ since 1968; *b* 17 Feb. 1917. *Educ:* University High Sch., Melbourne; RMC Duntroon. Served War of 1939-45: Artillery, and Liaison Officer HQ 9th Australian Division, Middle East, 1940-41; ME Staff Sch., 1942; Bde Maj. 26 Bde, 1942-44; MO 12, War Office, 1944-45; Joint Sec., JCOSA, 1945-48; CO, 67 Inf. Bn, 1948; CO, 3 Bn Royal Aust. Regt, 1949; AHQ, 1949-52; Chief Instructor, Sch. of Tactics and Admin. 1952-55; Asst Aust. Defence Rep. UK,

1955-57; successively Dir of Maintenance, Personnel Admin., Quartering and Military Training, 1957-61; IDC, 1962; Dir Military Operations and Plans, Army HQ, Canberra, 1962-66; Comdr Aust. Force Vietnam, 1966; Commander 1st Division Australian Army, 1967-68. *Recreations:* fishing, golf. *Address:* Army HQ, Canberra, ACT 2600, Australia. *Club:* Federal Golf.

**McKAY, Mrs Margaret;** Public Relations Consultant; *b* Jan. 1911. *Educ:* Elementary. Joined Labour Party 1932. Chief woman officer, TUC, 1951-62; Member of Co-operative Society, 1928-. Held administrative posts with Civil Service Clerical Association and Transport and General Workers' Union. MP (Lab) Clapham, 1964-70. *Publications:* Generation in Revolt (pen name Margaret McCarthy), 1953; Women in Trade Union History (TUC). *Address:* 8a Dalebury Road, SW17.

**McKAY, Rev. Roy;** Rector of St James, Garlickhythe, EC4, since 1965; Hon. Canon, Chichester Cathedral, since 1957; *b* 4 Nov. 1900; *s* of William McKay and Sarah Evelyn (*née* Littlewood); *m* 1927, Mary Oldham Fraser; one *s* one *d*. *Educ:* Marlborough Coll.; Magdalen Coll., Oxford. Curate, S Paul's, Kingston Hill, 1926; Curate-in-charge and Vicar of St Mark's Londonderry, Smethwick, 1928; Vicar of Mountfield, Sussex, 1932; Chaplain of Christ's Chapel of Alleyn's College of God's Gift, Dulwich, 1937; Vicar of Goring-by-Sea, Sussex, 1943; Chaplain of Canford Sch., 1948; Head of Religious Broadcasting, 1955-63; Preacher to Lincoln's Inn, 1958-59. *Publications:* Tell John (with Bishop G. F. Allen), 1932; The Pillar of Fire, 1933; Take Care of the Sense, 1964. *Address:* 115a Ashley Gardens, SW1.

**MACKAY, Sir William (Calder),** Kt 1968; OBE 1957; MC 1918; JP; Chairman, Farmers' Trading Co. Ltd; Deputy Chairman, South British Insurance Co. Ltd; Director, New Zealand Forest Products Ltd; Chairman of Directors, Calder Mackay Co. Ltd; Director, Guardian Trust & Executors Co. of New Zealand Ltd; *b* 5 Aug. 1896; *s* of William Scoular Mackay and Anne Armstrong Henderson; *m* 1920, Constance May Harris; one *s*. *Educ:* Hillhead High Sch., Glasgow. Served European War, 1914-18, NZEF (Adjt), France; served War of 1939-45 as Hon. YMCA Comr i/c welfare work in military camps, Air Force stations and naval establishments, Auckland Province. Past Member Board, Auckland Provincial Patriotic Fund; Director, Christchurch YMCA, 1929-33; Director, Auckland YMCA, 1934-45; President, YMCA, 1939-45; Chairman, Campaign Cttee for new Auckland YMCA, 1954; Life Member, YMCA, 1966. Past Member: Council, Auckland Chamber of Commerce; Exec. Cttee, Auckland Provincial Retailers' Assoc.; Auckland City Council, 1948-54; Auckland Harbour Bridge Authority; Council, Auckland, War Memorial Museum (Hon. Life Member, 1962). President, Rotary Club of Auckland, 1944-45; District Gov., Rotary, 1948-49; Member Aims and Objects Cttee, Rotary International, 1949-50. Provincial Comr, Boy Scouts, 1958; Organising Comr for Pan-Pacific Boy Scouts Jamboree, 1959 (Medal of Merit). Patron, Crippled Children Soc. (Mem. Exec., 1935-66, past Vice-Pres., and Pres., 1958-66, Auckland Branch); Vice-President: NZ Crippled Children Soc., 1964; St John Amb. Assoc. Auckland Centre Trust Bd, 1970; Area Co-ordinator, Duke of Edinburgh Award for Auckland Province and Mem. NZ Council, 1963. Foundn Mem. Bd, St Andrews Presbyterian Hospital and Hostel for Aged. JP 1940. *Recreations:* fishing, outdoor bowls. *Address:* 11 Victoria Avenue, Remuera, Auckland 5, New Zealand. *T:* 52-495. *Club:* Northern (Auckland).

**MACKAY-TALLACK, Sir Hugh,** Kt 1963; Deputy Chairman and Managing Director, Inchcape & Co. Ltd; Chairman, Assam & African Investments Ltd; Director: Gray Dawes & Co. Ltd; Gray Mackenzie & Co. Ltd; Smith Mackenzie & Co. Ltd; Duncan Macneill & Co. Ltd; Binny & Co. Ltd; *s* of E. H. Tallack and Deborah Lyle Mackay; unmarried. *Educ:* Kelly Coll., Devon; Heidelberg Univ. Served War of 1939-45, with 17th Dogra Regt, in Middle East and Burma; Private Sec. to C-in-C ALFSEA, and Mil. Sec. (Col) to Admiral Mountbatten, Supreme Allied Comdr, SEAC. Formerly: Chm., Macneill & Barry Ltd (Inchcape Gp) Calcutta; Governor of State Bank of India; Director numerous other cos in India; Chm., Indian Tea Assoc., 1954-55; Vice-Chairman, Tea Board of India, 1954-55; Member Government of India Tea Auction Cttee, 1954-55; Chairman, Ross Inst. of India, 1951-64; Pres., Bengal Chamber of Commerce and Industry and Associated Chambers of Commerce of India, 1962-63. Mem., Fedn, Commonwealth Chambers of Commerce. *Recreation:* riding. *Address:* Bicknor Park, near Hollingbourne, Kent; 24 Barrie House, Lancaster Gate, Hyde Park, W2. *T:* 01-262 5877. *Clubs:* Bath, Oriental, City of London; Bengal, Tollygunge, Turf (all in Calcutta).

**McKEAG, Major William;** *b* 1897; *s* of William McKeag, Belmont, Durham; *m* 1922, Marie Elizabeth, *d* of William Corn Crowe, Newcastle upon Tyne; two *s* one *d*. *Educ:* Belmont School and Johnston's School, Durham; privately. Solicitor; Partner in firm of Molineux McKeag and Cooper, Newcastle upon Tyne and Durham; Director of various companies; served European War, 1914-18, various theatres, and in Russia with Denikin and Wrangel (MSM, Russian Orders of St Stanislaus and St Anne). Served War of 1939-45, Deputy Assistant Adjutant General. Contested Durham at General Elections, 1924 and 1929; MP (L) Durham Division, 1931-35; contested Newcastle North, Gen. Election, 1945; Newcastle East, Gen. Election, 1950; Alderman of City of Newcastle upon Tyne; Deputy Lord Mayor of City of Newcastle upon Tyne, Lord Mayor, 1951-52 and 1953-54; President Newcastle upon Tyne Law Students Assoc.; Member of Newcastle upon Tyne Law Society Council; Under Sheriff, Newcastle upon Tyne; Governor of Royal Victoria Infirmary, Newcastle upon Tyne; Governor Newcastle Royal Grammar Sch.; Chairman, Parliamentary Cttee, Newcastle Corporation; Chairman, Progressive Party, Newcastle upon Tyne; Member Tyneside Industrial Development Board; Tyne Improvement Commissioner; President: Tynemouth Liberal Assoc.; Elswick British Legion; Skal Club of NE England; Newcastle Br. United Commercial Travellers' Assoc.; NE Sporting Club; Member, Management Cttee, Matfen Hall, Northumberland Cheshire Home; Chairman, Newcastle United FC. Consul for Iceland; President, Consular Corps of Newcastle; Hon. Freedom, City of Newcastle upon Tyne, 1966; Member Society of Antiquaries. Médaille d'Argent de la Ville de Paris; Commander, Order of the Falcon, Iceland. *Publications:* The Evils of Legislation by Regulation; various articles, Sociology, Foreign Affairs, European Problems, etc. *Recreations:* travel, golf, riding. *Address:* 30 Jesmond Road, Newcastle upon Tyne. *T:* Newcastle 81-1212; 60 Sadler Street, Durham City. *T:* Durham 4011; 19 Windsor Terrace,

Newcastle upon Tyne. *T:* 811948. *Clubs:* National Liberal; Pen and Palette (Newcastle).

**McKEAN, Douglas;** Under-Secretary, HM Treasury, since 1962; *b* 2 April 1917; *s* of late Alexander McKean, Enfield, Mddx; *m* 1942, Anne, *d* of late Roger Clayton, Riding Mill, Northumberland; two *s*. *Educ:* Merchant Taylors' Sch.; St John's Coll., Oxford. War Office, 1940; transferred to HM Treasury, 1949; Asst Secretary, 1956. *Address:* 7 Bazile Road, Grange Park, N21. *T:* 01-360 4498. *Club:* United University.

**McKEARNEY, Philip;** Counsellor and Consul-General, British Embassy, Baghdad, since 1968; *b* 15 Nov. 1926; *s* of Philip McKearney, OBE; *m* 1950, Jean Pamela Walker; two *s*. *Educ:* City of London Sch.; Hertford Coll., Oxford. 4/7th Dragoon Guards, 1946-53; joined HM Diplomatic Service, 1953; 3rd Sec., British Embassy, Damascus, 1955-56; 1st Sec., British Legation, Bucharest, 1959-62; British Political Agent, Qatar, 1962-65. *Address:* c/o Foreign and Commonwealth Office, SW1.

**McKEE, Air Marshal Sir Andrew,** KCB 1957 (CB 1951); CBE 1944; DSO 1942; DFC 1941; AFC 1938; Director, English Electric New Zealand; *b* 1901; *s* of Samuel Hugh McKee, Eyredale, Oxford, Canterbury, NZ; *m* 1949, Cecelia Tarcille, *er d* of Michael Keating, NZ; two *d*. *Educ:* Christchurch Boys' High Sch., NZ. Joined RAF, 1927. AOC No. 205 Group Mediterranean Allied Air Force, 1945-46; Senior Air Staff Officer, MEAF, 1946-47; Comdt OATS, 1947-49; First Comdt, RAF Flying Coll., 1949-51; Air Vice-Marshal, 1952; AOC No. 21 Group, 1952-53; Senior Air Staff Officer, Bomber Command, 1953-54; Air Marshal, 1957; Air Officer Commanding-in-Chief, Transport Command, 1955-59, retired. *Address:* Green Hill, Waikanae, New Zealand. *Club:* Royal Air Force.

**McKEE, Major Sir Cecil;** *see* McKee, Major Sir William Cecil.

**McKEE, Dermot St Oswald; His Honour Judge McKee;** Judge of County Courts, since 1952; *b* 22 Sept. 1904; *o s* of Rev. W. S. McKee, Bradford; *m* 1st, 1928, Violet, *d* of late Eli Dalton, Leeds; no *c*; 2nd, 1970, Mary K. Wallace, *d* of late Eli Dalton. *Educ:* privately; Leeds Univ. (LLB). Called to Bar, Gray's Inn, 1926. Practice, NE Circuit. Served War of 1939-45; Sqdn Leader, RAF, 1940-45. West Riding Quarter Sessions: Deputy Chairman, 1952; Chairman, 1957; Chairman: Cttee Reorganisation of Parishes Measure for Northern Province, 1957; Conscientious Objectors Tribunal, NE Area, 1958; County Court Rules Cttee, 1969- (Mem. 1956-). *Recreations:* fly-fishing and shooting. *Address:* Thatched Cottage, Tockwith, York. *T:* Tockwith 281. *Club:* Leeds.

**McKEE, Major Sir (William) Cecil,** Kt 1959, ERD; JP; Estate Agent; *b* 13 April 1905; *s* of late W. B. McKee and M. G. B. Bulloch; *m* 1932, Florence Ethel Irene Gill; one *d*. *Educ:* Methodist Coll., Belfast; Queen's Univ., Belfast. Alderman, Belfast Corporation, 1934; High Sheriff, Belfast, 1946; Deputy Lord Mayor, 1947, Lord Mayor of Belfast, 1957-59. Served with Royal Artillery in War of 1939-45. CStJ 1969. Hon. LLD Queen's Univ., Belfast, 1960. *Recreation:* golf. *Address:* 250 Malone Road, Belfast. *T:* Belfast 666979. *Clubs:* Ulster Reform (Belfast); Royal County Down Golf.

**McKEEFRY, His Eminence Cardinal Peter T. B.;** *see* Wellington (NZ), Archbishop of, (RC).

**McKEEVER, Ronald Fraser;** Ambassador to Togo and Dahomey, 1967-70; *b* 20 Aug. 1914; *yr s* of late Frederick Leonard McKeever and of late Elizabeth Moore McKeever (*née* Bucher); *m* 1944, Margaret Lilian (*née* Sabine); one *s*. *Educ:* George Watson's Coll., Edinburgh; Edinburgh Univ. Served in Indian Police, 1935-47. Joined Foreign Service, 1948; Vice-Consul: Dakar, 1948; Chicago, 1950; Consul, Kansas City, 1953; British Embassy, Bonn, 1954; Consul, Gdynia, 1957; Brazzaville, 1959 (Chargé d'Affaires, 1960); Foreign Office, 1961; Consul, Tamsui (Formosa), 1962. *Recreations:* tennis, bird-watching. *Address:* c/o Foreign and Commonwealth Office, SW1.

**Mac KEITH, Ronald Charles,** MA, DM, FRCP; Physician Children's Department, since 1948, and Director Newcomen Clinic, since 1964, Guy's Hospital; Hon. Pædiatrician: Tavistock Clinic, since 1948; Cassel Hospital, since 1960; *b* 22 Feb. 1908; 6th *s* of Alexander Arthur Mac Keith, MB, ChM, and of Alice, *d* of H. Gadd; *m* 1943, Elizabeth Mary, *er d* of Clement Osborn Bartrum, BSc, FRAS, and of Kate, *d* of F. F. Shattock; two *s* two *d*. *Educ:* King Edward VI Sch., Southampton; Queen's Coll., Oxford; St Mary's Hospital; Bellevue Hospital, New York. Radcliffe Travelling Fellow, University of Oxford, 1935-36. Temp. acting Surgeon Lieut-Commander, RNVR, 1940-45. Lecturer, WHO Seminar, Sydney, 1953; WHO Study Group, Stockholm, 1954; Secretary, Child Health Sect., BMA, 1956; organised Internat. Study Groups on Child Neurology, Oxford, 1958-70; Member: British Pædiatric Assoc.; Soc. for Psychosomatic Research. Joint Sec., Little Club; FRSocMed (Sec., Section of Pædiatrics 1954; Chm. 1970); Chm. Assoc. Child Psychology and Psychiatry, 1961-62; Jt Sec., European Assoc. Paediatric Neurologists. Editor, Developmental Medicine and Child Neurology; Corresp. Mem., Soc. française de Pédiatrie; Pædiatric Soc., Catalonia; world commn on Cerebral Palsy; Mem. Comité de patronage, Revue de Médicine psychosomatique. *Publications:* Infant Feeding and Feeding Difficulties, 3rd edn (with P. R. Evans), 1958, 4th edn (with C. B. S. Wood), 1970; (with J. Sandler) Psychosomatic Aspects of Pædiatrics, 1961; (with J. Apley) The Child and his Symptoms, 1962, 2nd edn 1969; (with M. C. O. Bax) Minimal Cerebral Dysfunction, 1963; (with M. C. Joseph) New Look at Child Health, 1966; (with Peter Gardiner and Vernon Smith) Aspects of Paediatric Ophthalmology, 1969; (with Dorothy Egan and Ronald Illingworth) Developmental Screening 0 to 5 years, 1969; papers, chapters, articles, films and broadcasts on medical and other subjects. *Recreation:* reading. *Address:* 35 Bloomfield Terrace, SW1. *T:* 01-730 8164. *Club:* Athenæum.

**McKELL, Rt. Hon. Sir William John,** GCMG, *cr* 1951; PC 1948; *b* Pambula, NSW, 26 Sept. 1891; *m* 1920; one *s* two *d*. *Educ:* Public Sch., Surry Hills, Sydney. Served apprenticeship as boiler-maker, Morts' Dock and Engineering Co., Sydney; elected Financial Secretary, Boilermakers' Union; elected Member Legislative Assembly, NSW, at 25 years of age; Member, 1917-47; Minister of Justice (1920-22) at age of 28 years; Minister of Justice and Assistant Colonial Treasurer, 1925-27; visited London and New York on financial mission for State of New South Wales, 1927; Minister for Local Government, 1930; Minister of Justice, 1931-32; Leader of the Opposition, 1939-41; Premier and Colonial Treasurer of New South Wales, 1941-47; official visit to United States and Great Britain, 1945; Governor-General of Australia, 1947-53. Member Malayan Constitutional Commission, 1956-57.

Barrister of Supreme Court of New South Wales, 1925; QC 1945. Chairman of Sydney Cricket Ground Trust, 1938. Hon. LLD, Sydney. *Recreations:* always active in football and boxing circles; played first-grade football and boxed in amateur championships. *Address:* 286 New South Head Road, Edgecliff, NSW 2027, Australia.

**McKELVEY, Air Cdre John Wesley,** CB 1969; MBE 1944; CEng, AFRAeS, MBIM; RAF, retired; *b* 25 June 1914; *s* of late Captain John Wesley McKelvey, Enfield, Mddx; *m* 1938, Eileen Amy Carter, *d* of John Charles Carter, Enfield; two *s*. *Educ:* George Spicer Sch., Enfield. RAF Aircraft Apprentice, 1929; commnd 1941 (Eng Branch); served 1939-45, Egypt, Syria, Iraq and Bomber Comd (despatches, 1943); Group Captain 1960; Dep. Dir Intelligence (Tech.), 1962-64; Dir of Aircraft and Asst Attaché, Defence Research and Development, British Embassy, Washington, 1964-66; Air Officer Wales and CO, RAF St Athan, 1966-69; retd Aug. 1969. *Recreations:* photography, gardening. *Address:* Inchmerle, Manorway, Bush Hill Park, Enfield, Mddx. *T:* 01-360 4054. *Club:* Royal Air Force.

**MACKEN, Frederic Raymond,** CMG 1964; Secretary, New Zealand Law Society; *b* 23 Sept. 1903; *s* of Charles Alfred Macken and Ella (*née* Steadman); *m* 1929, Alma Doris (*née* Keesing); one *d*. *Educ:* Whangarei High Sch.; Auckland Univ., New Zealand. LLM (with Hons), 1927. Retired as Commissioner of Inland Revenue for New Zealand, 1964. *Recreations:* bowls, golf. *Address:* 9 Harley Grove, Lower Hutt, Wellington, New Zealand. *T:* 65-205. *Club:* Civil Service (Wellington, NZ).

**MacKENNA, Hon. Sir Bernard Joseph Maxwell (Hon. Sir Brian MacKenna),** Kt 1961; **Hon. Mr Justice MacKenna;** Judge of the High Court of Justice (Queen's Bench Division), since 1961; QC 1950; *b* 12 Sept. 1905; unmarried. Called to the Bar, Inner Temple, Jan. 1932; Western Circuit; Master of the Bench of the Inner Temple, 1958. *Address:* 2 Paper Buildings, Temple, EC4. *T:* 01-405 7211. *Club:* United University.

**MacKENNA, Sir Brian;** *see* MacKenna, Sir Bernard Joseph Maxwell.

**McKENNA, David,** CBE 1967 (OBE 1946; MBE 1943); Member, British Railways Board, since 1968; *b* 16 Feb. 1911; *s* of late Rt Hon. Reginald McKenna and Pamela Margaret McKenna (*née* Jekyll); *m* 1934, Lady Cecilia Elizabeth Keppel, *d* of 9th Earl of Albemarle, *qv*; three *d*. *Educ:* Eton; Trinity Coll., Cambridge. London Passenger Transport Board, 1934-39, and 1946-55; Asst General Manager, Southern Region of BR, 1955-61; Chief Commercial Officer, HQ, BR, 1962; General Manager, Southern Region of BR, and Chairman Southern Railway Board, 1963-68; Chairman, British Transport Advertising, 1968-. War Service with Transportation Service of Royal Engineers, 1939-45; Iraq, Turkey, India and Burma; Lieut-Colonel. Chairman of Governors, Sadlers Wells, 1962. Hon. Secretary, Royal College of Music; Chairman of Bach Choir. FRCM. *Publications:* various papers on transport subjects. *Recreations:* music, sailing. *Address:* 81 Onslow Square, SW7. *T:* 01-589 6295; Rosteague, Portscatho; Truro, Cornwall. *Clubs:* Brooks's; Royal Cornwall Yacht (Falmouth).

**MacKENNA, Robert Merttins Bird,** MA, MD, FRCP; Hon. Colonel RAMC; Dermatologist, King Edward VII's Hospital for Officers; Hon. Consultant in Dermatology to the British Army, 1946-64; Councillor Royal College of Physicians, 1956-59; President: Dermatological Section, Royal Society of Medicine, 1966-67; British Association of Dermatology, 1966-67; Physician in charge of the Department for Diseases of the Skin, St Bartholomew's Hospital, 1946-68, now Hon. Consultant in Dermatology; *b* 16 Nov. 1903; *s* of late R. W. MacKenna and Harriet A. S. Bird; *m* 1st, 1927, Helen, *e d* of Thomas Todrick; two *d*; 2nd, 1943, Margaret, *d* of Christmas Hopkins; two *s*. *Educ:* RN Colleges, Osborne and Dartmouth; Clare Coll., Cambridge Univ.; St Thomas' Hospital. Resigned from the Navy, 1919; studied at Liverpool Univ., 1920-21; Cambridge, 1921-24; BA (Nat. Sci. Tripos), 1924; MRCS, LRCP, 1926; MA, MB, BCh Cambridge, 1928; MRCP, 1928; MD Cambridge 1931; FRCP, 1941. Junior Asst MO Venereal Diseases Dept, and Clinical Asst, Dermatological Dept, St Thomas' Hosp., 1927-28; Clinical Asst, St John's Hosp., for Diseases of the Skin, 1928; Hon. Asst Dermatologist Liverpool Radium Inst., 1929; Hon. Dermatologist, Liverpool Stanley Hosp., 1929-34; Hon. Dermatologist, Royal Liverpool United Hosp., (Royal Southern Hospital), 1934-46; Dermatologist, Catterick Military Hosp., Oct. 1939; Comd Specialist in Dermatology, Northern Comd, 1940-41; Adviser in Dermatology and Asst Dir, Hygiene (c), War Office, 1941-43; Cons. Dermatologist to British Army, 1943-45. Malcolm Morris Meml Lectr, 1955; Watson Smith Lectr, 1957; Prosser White Orator, 1968. Hon. Fellow, Amer. Med. Assoc. Hon. Member: Dermatological Section, RSM; Dermatological Assoc. of Australia; Soc. for Investigative Dermatology; Canadian Dermatological Assoc.; NY Dermatolog. Soc.; Deutsche Dermatologische Gesellschaft; Sociedad Venezolana de Dermatologia; Alpha Omega Alpha Honor Med. Soc.; Corresp. Member: Amer. Dermatological Assoc.; Nederlandse Vereniging van Dermatologen; Societas Dermatologica Danica; Societas Dermatologica Austriaca; Societas Dermatologica Svecica; La Société Française de Dermatologie et de Syphiligraphie; Israeli Dermatological Soc. OStJ 1954. *Publications:* Aids to Dermatology, 1929, 1939, 1946, 1954, 1956; Diseases of the Skin, 1932, 1937, 1949 and 1952; Dermatology (jointly with E. L. Cohen), 1964. Joint Editor of The Medical History of Liverpool, 1936; Sections on Dermatology in Medical Annual, 1944-63; editor, Modern Trends in Dermatology, Series I, 1948, Series II, 1953, Series III, 1966; Associate Editor for Dermatological subjects British Encyclopædia of Medical Practice, 2nd Edition, 1950; various papers on dermatological subjects in current medical journals. *Address:* 117 Harley Street, W1; 1 Aubrey Road, W8.

**MacKENNA, Robert Ogilvie,** MA, ALA; University Librarian and Keeper of the Hunterian Books and MSS, Glasgow, since 1951; *b* 21 March 1913; *s* of late Dr John G. MacKenna and of Katherine Ogilvie; *m* 1942, Ray, *o d* of late Samuel Mullin, Glasgow. *Educ:* Paisley Grammar Sch.; Glasgow Univ. Assistant Librarian, Glasgow Univ., 1936; Sub-Librarian, Leeds Univ., 1946; Librarian, King's Coll., Newcastle upon Tyne (University of Durham), 1947. Served War as officer, RNVR, 1939-45. Trustee, National Library of Scotland, 1953-. President, Scottish Library Association, 1966; Chairman, Standing Conference of National and University Libraries, 1967-69. President Scottish Cricket Union, 1968. *Recreations:* cricket (played for Scotland, 1935-39 and 1946); hill-walking. *Address:* Glasgow

University Library, Glasgow, W2. *T:* 041-339 8855; 2 Turnberry Avenue, Glasgow, W1. *Clubs:* Authors'; College (Glasgow).

**McKENNA, Siobhán, (Mrs Denis O'Dea);** actress; *b* Belfast, 24 May 1923; *d* of Prof. Owen McKenna and Margaret O'Reilly; *m* 1946, Denis O'Dea; one *s. Educ:* St Louis Convent, Monaghan; Galway Univ. (BA). Semi-professional stage appearances in An Taibhdhearc Theatre, Galway, 1940-43. Joined Abbey Theatre, Dublin, 1944-47. First London appearance in The White Steed, Embassy, 1947. *Films:* Hungry Hill, Daughter of Darkness, The Lost People, The Adventurers, King of Kings, Playboy of the Western World, The Cavern, Dr Zhivago. *Plays:* Fading Mansions, Duchess, 1949; Ghosts, Embassy; Héloise, Duke of York's; Stratford Festival, 1952; Playboy of the Western World, Edinburgh and Paris Festivals; Saint Joan, Arts, 1954, St Martin's, 1955; The Chalk Garden, NY, 1955; Saint Joan, NY, 1956; The Rope-Dancers, NY, 1957; Shakespearian seasons at Stratford, Ontario and Cambridge Drama Festival. (Again in) Playboy of the Western World, Gaiety, Dublin, and Piccadilly, London, 1960; Captain Brassbound's Conversion, Philadelphia, 1961; Saint Joan of the Stockyards, Dublin Festival, 1961, Queen's, London, 1964; Play with a Tiger, London, 1962; Laurette, Dublin Festival, 1964; Juno and the Paycock, Gaiety, Dublin, 1966; Best of Friends, Strand, 1970; Here are Ladies, Criterion, 1970. Also television for BBC, and New York and Los Angeles. *Recreations:* reading poetry and talking. *Address:* c/o Christopher Mann Ltd, 140 Park Lane, W1.

**MACKENZIE,** family name of **Baron Amulree** and **Earl of Cromartie.**

**MACKENZIE;** *see* Montagu-Stuart-Wortley-Mackenzie, family name of Earl of Wharncliffe.

**MACKENZIE of Gairloch;** *see under* Inglis of Glencorse.

**MacKENZIE, Alasdair Francis,** CMG 1961; *b* 11 April 1910; *e s* of Alexander MacKenzie; *m* 1937, Elizabeth Medea Haynes; one *s* one *d. Educ:* Archbishop Tenison's Sch.; Royal College of Science; Downing Coll., Cambridge; Imperial College of Tropical Agriculture. Agricultural Officer, Sierra Leone, 1935; Senior, 1946; Deputy Director, 1951; Director of Agriculture, British Guiana, 1954; Agricultural Adviser, West Indies, 1958; General Adviser on Tropical Agriculture to Govt of Bolivia, 1962-65. *Publications:* various reports on Commissions of Inquiry on Sugar Industry in West Indies. *Recreations:* fishing, shooting, golf. *Address:* The Knoll, London Road, Liphook, Hants. *Clubs:* West Indian, Flyfishers'.

**MACKENZIE, Alasdair Roderick;** *b* 9 Aug. 1903; *m* 1948, Annie Mackay; one *s* one *d. Educ:* Broadford Junior Secondary Sch., Skye. CC Ross and Cromarty, 1935-55; Convener, Council Educn Cttee, 5 years; Mem. Crofters' Commn, 5 years; Mem., Bd of Govs of North of Scotland Coll. of Agriculture, 7 years. Farmer. MP (L) Ross and Cromarty, 1964-70; Liberal Spokesman, House of Commons, for Agriculture and Fisheries. Gaelic Scholar. *Address:* Heathmount Tain, Ross-shire. *T:* Tain 55. *Club:* National Liberal.

**McKENZIE, Sir Alexander,** KBE 1962; Past Dominion President, New Zealand National Party (1951-62); *b* Invercargill, New Zealand, 1896; *m* 1935, Constance Mary Howard; two *s* two *d. Educ:* Isla Bank Primary Sch.; Southland Technical Coll.; Southland Boys' High Sch. Chairman, Ponsonby Electorate, NZ Nat. Party, 1938-41; Chairman, Auckland Division, NZ Nat. Party, 1941-51. Overseas Representative for NZ Forest Products Ltd, 1925-29; engaged in Stock and Share Broking, 1929-; Member Auckland Stock Exchange; Director of 15 companies covering finance, transport merchandising, manufacturing, engineering, etc. Member Anglican Church. *Recreations:* trout fishing, surfing, bowling, gardening. *Address:* 54 Wallace Street, Herne Bay, Auckland, NZ. *Club:* Auckland (Auckland, NZ).

**MACKENZIE, Alexander,** OBE 1964; JP; Lord Provost of Dundee and Lord Lieutenant of the County of the City of Dundee, 1967-70; *b* 12 Dec. 1915; *o s* of Alex. and Elizabeth Mackenzie; *m* 1940, Edna Margaret, *d* of Fred Holder; one *d. Educ:* Morgan Academy, Dundee. Secretary (Dundee Branch), League of Nations, 1935-38; Secretary (Dundee Branch), UNA, 1946-49. Member, Dundee Town Council, 1947-; Chairman, Tay Road Bridge Joint Board, 1967-70; Chairman, Dundee High Sch. Directors, 1967-70; Vice-Chairman: Governors, Dundee Coll. of Art and Technology, 1967-70; Tayside Economic Planning Consultative Group, 1969 (Chm. Publicity Cttee, 1969-70); Member: Univ. Court of Dundee, 1967-70; Dundee Harbour Trust, 1967-70. Pres., Dundee Brotherhood, 1948. Assessor, Dundee Repertory Theatre, 1964-70. JP County of the City of Dundee, 1951. *Recreation:* reading. *Address:* 18 Whitehall Crescent, Dundee. *T:* 25774.

**MACKENZIE, Sir (Alexander George Anthony) Allan,** 4th Bt, of Glen-Muick, *cr* 1890; CD 1957; retired; *b* 4 Jan. 1913; *s* of late Capt. Allan Keith Mackenzie (3rd *s* of 2nd Bt) and Hon. Louvima, *o d* of 1st Viscount Knollys (she *m* 2nd, 1922, Richard Henry Spencer Checkley); *S* uncle, 1944; *m* 1937, Marjorie McGuire, Vancouver, BC; four *d. Educ:* Stowe School. Page of Honour to King George V; Member Royal Canadian Mounted Police, 1932-37; served War of 1939-45, with Seaforth Highlanders of Canada (Captain), in Italy and in NW Europe. Subsequently Black Watch (RHR) of Canada (Regular Army). Canada Centennial Medal, 1967. *Heir: u* Col Eric Dighton Mackenzie, *qv. Address:* RR1, Cobble Hill, Vancouver Island, British Columbia, Canada.

**MACKENZIE, Sir Allan;** *see* Mackenzie, Sir (Alexander George Anthony) Allan.

**MACKENZIE, Archibald Robert Kerr,** CBE 1967; British Ambassador to Tunisia, since 1970; *b* 22 Oct. 1915; *s* of James and Alexandrina Mackenzie; *m* 1963, Virginia Ruth Hutchison. *Educ:* Glasgow, Oxford, Chicago and Harvard Universities. Diplomatic Service, with duty at Washington, 1943-45; United Nations, 1946-49; Foreign Office, 1949-51; Bangkok, 1951-54; Cyprus, 1954; Foreign Office, 1955-57; OEEC, Paris, 1957-61; Commercial Counsellor, HM Embassy, Rangoon, 1961-65; Consul-General, Zagreb 1965-69. *Recreation:* golf. *Address:* c/o Foreign and Commonwealth Office, SW1. *Club:* Oxford and Cambridge University.

**MACKENZIE, Chalmers Jack,** CC (Canada) 1967; CMG 1943; MC 1918; FRS 1946; FRSC; MEIC; Chancellor, Carleton University, 1954-68; Member Atomic Energy Control Board, 1946-61, and President, 1948-61; President, National Research Council of Canada, 1939-52; Member Defence Research Board, 1946-52; President Atomic Energy of Canada, Limited,

1952; Director: Canadian Patents and Development Ltd, since 1947; Chemcell Ltd and Columbia Cellulose Co. since 1954; Member Army Technical Development Board, 1942; Chairman War Technical and Scientific Development Cttee, 1940; Inventions Board, 1940-46; *b* 10 July 1888; *s* of late James Mackenzie, St Stephen, NB; *m* 1st, 1916, Claire Rees (*d* 1922); one *s*; 2nd, 1924, Geraldine Gallon; two *d*. *Educ:* St Stephen, NB; Dalhousie Univ. (BE 1909); Harvard Univ. (MCE 1915). Engineering Firm, Maxwell & Mackenzie, 1912-16; Overseas 54th Canadian Infantry Bn, 1916-18 (MC); Prof. Civil Engineering, 1918-39, Dean of College of Engineering, 1921-39, University of Sask., President, Engineering Institute of Canada, 1941; Chairman Saskatoon City Planning Commission, 1928-39; Chairman Saskatoon City Hospital Board, 1937-39. Dir Canadian Geographical Soc., 1937-60. Hon. LLD: Dalhousie, 1941, Western Ontario, 1943, Queen's, and Algiers, 1944, Saskatchewan, 1945; Carleton, 1969; DEng, Toronto, 1944; Hon. DSc: McGill 1941. Laval and Cambridge, 1946, BC, 1947, Princeton, 1949, Nova Scotia Technical Coll., 1950, McMaster Univ., 1951, Universities of New Brunswick, Montreal, Manitoba, Ottawa, 1958, also RMC; Hon. DCL Bishop's Univ., 1952. US Medal for Merit, 1947; Chevalier de la Légion d'Honneur, 1947; Kelvin Medal, InstMechE, 1954; R. B. Bennett Empire Prize, RSA, 1954; Royal Bank Award, 1968. *Publications:* in scientific and technical press. *Recreations:* golf, curling. *Address:* 210 Buena Vista Road, Rockcliffe Park, Ottawa, Canada. *Clubs:* Rideau, Royal Ottawa Golf (Ottawa).

**MACKENZIE, Colin Hercules,** CMG 1946; *b* 5 Oct. 1898; *o s* of late Maj.-Gen. Sir Colin Mackenzie, KCB, and Ethel, *er d* of Hercules Ross, ICS; *m* 1940, Evelyn Clodagh, 2nd *d* of Charles and Lady Aileen Meade; one *d*. *Educ:* Summerfields; Eton (Schol.); King's Coll., Cambridge (1st Class Hons in Economics. Exhibitioner and Senior Scholar, also Chancellor's Medal for English Verse). Served France with 1st Bn Scots Guards in 1918 (wounded). Served in India and with South-East Asia Command, 1941-45 (CMG, Officier de la Légion d'Honneur). British Economic Mission to Greece, 1946. Chairman: Scottish Council, FBI, 1957-59; Scottish Cttee on Electricity, 1961-62; Scottish Arts Council, 1962-70; Inverness Conservative and Unionist Assoc., 1967-70. Hon. Sheriff Substitute, Inverness-shire. Hon. LLD St Andrews, 1970. *Address:* Kyle House, Kyleakin, Isle of Skye. *T:* Kyleakin 217. *Clubs:* Special Forces; New (Edinburgh); Highland (Inverness).

**MACKENZIE, Sir Compton,** Kt, *cr* 1952; OBE 1919; FRSL; CLit, 1968; Hon. LLD (Glasgow, St Francis Xavier University, Antigonish, NS); Hon. RSA; author; *b* West Hartlepool, 17 Jan. 1883; *e s* of Edward Compton (Mackenzie) and Virginia Bateman; *m* 1st, 1905, Faith (*d* 1960), *y d* of late Rev. E. D. Stone, sometime Master of Eton Coll.; 2nd, 1962, Christina MacSween (*d* 1963), *e d* of late Malcolm MacSween, Tarbert, Harris; 3rd, 1965, Lilian MacSween, *y d* of late Malcolm MacSween, Tarbert, Harris. *Educ:* St Paul's Sch.; Magdalen Coll., Oxford, BA; 2nd Class Modern History, 1904. 2nd Lieut, 1st Herts Regt, 1900-01; Lieut, Royal Marines, 1915; Captain, 1916; served with RND in Dardanelles Expedition, 1915; invalided Sept. 1915; Military Control Officer, Athens, 1916; Director Ægean Intelligence Service, Syra, 1917 (OBE, 1915 Star, Chevalier of the Legion of Honour and of the Redeemer, 4th class of the White Eagle with swords); Captain, Home Guard, 1940-44; President: Wexford Festival, 1951-; Croquet Association, 1954-66; Songwriters' Guild, 1956-; Patron, Poetry Society, 1964- (Pres., 1961-64); Governor-General of the Royal Stuart Society, 1961-; Rector of Glasgow University, 1931-34; Literary critic of the Daily Mail, 1931-35; President: Dickens Fellowship, 1939-46; Guild of Independent Publishers, 1969. Invited by the Indian Government to visit all the battlefields of the Indian Army during War of 1939-45, 1946-47. Kt Comdr, Royal Order of the Phoenix (Greece), 1966. *Publications:* Poems, 1907; The Passionate Elopement, 1911; Carnival, 1912; Kensington Rhymes, 1912; Sinister Street, vol. i, 1913; Sinister Street, vol. ii, 1914; Guy and Pauline, 1915; Sylvia Scarlett, 1918; Sylvia and Michael, 1919; Poor Relations, 1919; The Vanity Girl, 1920; Rich Relatives, 1921; The Altar Steps, 1922; The Seven Ages of Woman, 1922; The Parson's Progress, 1923; Gramophone Nights (with Archibald Marshall), 1923; The Heavenly Ladder, 1924; Santa Claus in Summer, 1924; The Old Men of the Sea (Paradise for Sale, 1963), 1924; Coral, 1925; Fairy Gold, 1926; Rogues and Vagabonds, 1927; Vestal Fire, 1927; Extremes Meet, 1928; Extraordinary Women, 1928; The Three Couriers, 1929; Gallipoli Memories, 1929; April Fools, 1930; Told, 1930; Athenian Memories, 1931; Buttercups and Daisies, 1931; Our Street, 1931; Unconsidered Trifles, 1932; Greek Memories, 1932 (withdrawn, reissued, 1940); Prince Charlie, 1932; Water on the Brain, 1933; Literature in my Time, 1933; Reaped and Bound, 1933; The Darkening Green, 1934; Marathon and Salamis, 1934; Prince Charlie and his Ladies, 1934; Catholicism and Scotland, 1936; The Book of Barra (with J. L. Campbell), 1936; Figure of Eight, 1936; Pericles, 1937; The Four Winds of Love; The East Wind, 1937; The South Wind, 1937; The West Wind, 1940; West to North, 1940; The North Wind, Vol. I, 1944; The North Wind, Vol. II, 1945; The Windsor Tapestry, 1938; A Musical Chair, 1939; Aegean Memories, 1940; The Red Tapeworm, 1941; The Monarch of the Glen, 1941; Calvary, 1942; Wind of Freedom, 1943; Keep the Home Guard Turning, 1943; Mr Roosevelt, 1943; Brockhouse, 1944; Dr Benes, 1946; The Vital Flame, 1946; Whisky Galore, 1947; All Over the Place, 1949; Hunting the Fairies, 1949; Coalport, 1951; Eastern Epic, Vol. I, 1951; I Took a Journey, 1951; The Rival Monster, 1952; The Queen's House, 1953; Echoes, 1953; Realms of Silver, 1953; The Savoy of London, 1953; Ben Nevis Goes East, 1954; My Record of Music, 1955; Thin Ice, 1956; Sublime Tobacco, 1957; Rockets Galore, 1957; The Lunatic Republic, 1959; Cats' Company, 1960; Greece in My Life, 1960; Mezzotint, 1961; Catmint, 1961; On Moral Courage, 1962; Look at Cats, 1964; Little Cat Lost, 1965; The Stolen Soprano, 1965; Paper Lives, 1966; Robert Louis Stevenson, 1968; The Strongest Man on Earth, 1968; The Steps that Kept Going Down, 1968; The Secret Island, 1969; Butterfly Hill, 1970; My Life and Times: Octave One, 1963; Octave Two, 1963; Octave Three, 1964; Octave Four, 1965; Octave Five, 1966; Octave Six, 1967; Octave Seven, 1968; Octave Eight, 1969; Octave Nine, 1970. *Plays:* The Gentleman in Grey, 1906; Carnival, 1912; Columbine, 1920; The Lost Cause, 1931. *Recreations:* gramophone: Editor of The Gramophone, 1923-61; cats: President of the Siamese Cat Club, 1928-. *Address:* 31 Drummond Place, Edinburgh 3. *T:* 031-556 2926; Pradelles, Les Arques, Lot, France. *T:* 4 Les Arques. *Clubs:* Savile, Pratt's, Authors' (President); Scottish Arts (Edinburgh). *See also Fay Compton.*

**MacKENZIE, Brig. David Alexander Laurance,** CBE 1944; DSO 1937 (bar 1945); Brigadier, retired, Indian Army; *b* 2 May 1897; *s* of late David MacKenzie, Killen, Fortrose, Ross-shire; *m* 1st, 1927, Muriel Edith Gertrude McIntyre (*d* 1947); three *s*; 2nd, 1950, Francesca Cristine Boileau-Lessy; two *d* (one *s* decd). *Educ:* Dunblane, Perthshire; RMC, Sandhurst. Served European War in 1st Bn Grenadier Guards, BEF France, 1916-17 (two medals). Commissioned into 12 Frontier Force Regt, IA, 1918; EEF, Palestine, 1919-20. NWF Campaign, Waziristan, 1923-24 (Medal and clasp); psc 1932. Staff (Captain) Quetta Bde, 1935-36; Bde Major, Rawalpindi Bde, 1936-39; NWF Campaigns: 1936-37, 1937-38 (Medal and clasp, DSO). War of 1939-45: GSO1, War Office, 1939-42; Comd 9/12 FF Regt, 1943; Burma Campaign: Bde Comdr, 32 Ind. Infantry Bde, 1943-45 (CBE, Bar to DSO, 5 medals). Brigadier Infantry and Dep. Director Military Training at GHQ, India, 1945 (May)-1946; Comdt Tactical and Admin. School, India, 1947; Director, Military Training, AHQ, India, 1948; Military Adviser to High Commissioner for India in London, 1948-50. Commandant, Surrey Army Cadet Force, 1949-52. Commandant, Home Office Civil Defence Experimental Mobile Column, 1951-54; Commandant, Home Office Civil Defence School, Falfield, Glos, 1955-62. Adviser in Civil Defence to Cento, 1962-66. *Recreations:* motoring, gardening and cricket. *Address:* The White House, Spetisbury, Blandford, Dorset. *T:* Sturminster Marshall 366.

**MACKENZIE, David James Masterton,** CMG 1957; OBE 1947 (MBE 1944); FRCP; Visiting Scientist, Malaria Eradication Program, Communicable Disease Center, Atlanta, Georgia, 1965-69; Director of Medical and Health Services in Hong Kong, 1958-64; Colonial Medical Service, retired; *b* 23 July 1905; *s* of John Henderson Mackenzie and Agnes Masterton; *m* 1934, Patricia Eleanor Margaret Bailey; two *d*. *Educ:* Rutherford College School; Edinburgh Univ. MB, ChB, Edinburgh, 1929; DPH (Edinburgh), 1948; MRCPE 1956, FRCPE 1959. Edinburgh Royal Infirmary, 1930-31. Joined Colonial Medical Service, 1934; DDMS Bechuanaland Protectorate, 1944, DMS 1946; DMS Nyasaland, 1949-55; DMS Northern Nigeria, 1955-57. *Recreations:* golf, fishing. *Address:* c/o Royal Bank of Scotland Ltd, 4 Shandwick Place, Edinburgh EH2 4RW; 1 Saxe Coburg Street, Edinburgh EH3 5BN. *T:* 031-556 5714. *Clubs:* West Indian; Zomba Gymkhana (Malawi).

**MACKENZIE, Col Eric Dighton,** CMG 1935, CVO 1939; DSO 1917; *b* 22 Aug. 1891; *s* of Sir Allan Mackenzie, 2nd Bt of Glenmuick, Aberdeenshire; *m* 1948, Elizabeth, *d* of late Capt. J. W. G. Innes, CB, RN, and late Marchioness of Aberdeen, and has issue. *Educ:* Eton Coll. Joined Scots Guards, 1911; served European War (wounded thrice, DSO, despatches twice); retired, 1926; re-employed, 1939-44; Comptroller of the Household to Gov.-Gen. of Canada, 1931-39; JP (Argyll); OStJ. *Address:* Calgary House, Tobermory, Isle of Mull. *Club:* St James'.

**MacKENZIE, Prof. Fraser;** Professor of French Language and Literature, University of Birmingham, since 1946; *b* Wellington, NZ, 3 Nov. 1905; *s* of late Hugh MacKenzie, Prof. of English Language and Literature, Victoria UC, Wellington, NZ, and late Annie Catherine Watson Stewart. *Educ:* Wellington Coll., NZ; Victoria University Coll., NZ; Sorbonne, Paris. Asst Lecturer in French, University of St Andrews, 1934-39; Sen. Lecturer in French, University of Aberdeen, 1939-46. Exchange Prof. of French, University of Montpellier, France, March 1948, 1950, 1952, 1954; Guest Prof. of Mod. Langs, Victoria University Coll., Wellington, NZ, 1955. Hon. Pres., Birmingham Univ. Mathematical Soc., 1961-62; Hon. Pres., Birmingham Univ. Electrical Engineers Soc., 1962-63. DèsL (Paris), 1946; Doctorate (*hc*): University of Montpellier, 1952; University Laval, Quebec, 1967. Chevalier de la Légion d'honneur, 1954. *Publications:* Les Emprunts réciproques de l'anglais et du français, 2 vols (Paris), 1946. ed Studies in French Language, Literature and History offered to Prof. R. L. Graeme Ritchie, 1950. *Recreations:* swimming, travel. *Address:* c/o Department of French, University of Birmingham, PO Box 363, Birmingham, B15 2TT. *T:* 021-472 1301.

**MacKENZIE, Gregor;** *see* MacKenzie, J. G.

**MACKENZIE, Vice-Adm. Sir Hugh (Stirling),** KCB 1966 (CB 1963); DSO 1942 and Bar 1943; DSC 1945; *b* 3 July 1913; 3rd *s* of Dr and Mrs T. C. Mackenzie, Inverness; *m* 1946, Helen Maureen, *er d* of Major J. E. M. Bradish-Ellames; one *s* two *d*. *Educ:* Cargilfield Sch.; Royal Naval Coll., Dartmouth. Joined Royal Naval Coll., 1927; qualified in Submarines, 1935. Served throughout War of 1939-45 in Submarines, comdg HMS Thrasher, 1941-43; HMS Tantalus, 1943-45; Comdr 1946; Capt. 1951; Rear-Adm. 1961; Flag Officer, Submarines, 1961-63; Chief, Polaris Executive, 1963-68; Vice-Adm. 1964; retired 1968. Chm., Navy League, 1969; Dir, Atlantic Salmon Research Trust Ltd, 1969. Hon. Freeman, Borough of Shoreditch, 1942. *Recreation:* the country. *Address:* Sylvan Lodge, Puttenham, near Guildford, Surrey. *Clubs:* Naval and Military; Naval (Portsmouth).

**MACKENZIE, Ian Clayton,** CBE 1962; HM Diplomatic Service, retired; Ambassador to Korea, 1967-69; *b* 13 Jan. 1909; *m* 1948, Anne Helena Tylor; one *s* one *d*. *Educ:* Bedford Sch.; King's Coll., Cambridge. Student Interpreter, China Consular Service, 1932; a Vice-Consul, China, 1935; Actg Consul, Chungking, 1939-40; Shanghai, 1940; Consul, Brazzaville, 1942, Actg Consul-Gen., 1943; Foreign Office, rank of Consul, 1945; 1st Sec., Commercial, Shanghai, 1946; Santiago, 1949-53; Commercial Counsellor: Oslo, 1953-58; Caracas, 1958-63 (acted as Chargé d'Affaires, 1959, 1960 and 1963); Stockholm, 1963-66. *Address:* Koryo, Armstrong Road, Brockenhurst, Hants.

**MacKENZIE, (James) Gregor,** JP; MP (Lab) Rutherglen since May 1964; *b* 15 Nov. 1927; *o s* of James and Mary MacKenzie; *m* 1958, Joan Swan Provan; one *s* one *d*. *Educ:* Queen's Park Sch.; Royal Technical College; Glasgow Univ. (School of Social Studies). Joined Labour Party, 1944. Contested (Lab): East Aberdeenshire, 1950; Kinross and West Perthshire, 1959. Chm., Scottish Labour League, 1948; Mem. and Magistrate, Glasgow Corporation, 1952-55, 1956-64; Parly Private Sec. to Chancellor of the Exchequer, 1966-67, to Home Secretary, 1967-70. JP Glasgow, 1962. *Address:* 19 Stewarton Drive, Kirkhill, Cambuslang, Lanarkshire. *T:* Cambuslang 3654; 7 Carrick Court, Kennington Park Road, SE11. *T:* 01-735 2957.

**MACKENZIE, James Young;** *b* 13 Jan. 1914; *s* of late J. A. Mackenzie; *m* 1953, Edith, *d* of late Air Commodore F. Beaumont, CB; two *s*. *Educ:* Kelvinside; Christ Church, Oxford. Entered Diplomatic Service, 1938; Montevideo, 1941; Beirut and Damascus,

1942; Chungking, 1945; Nanking, 1946; Foreign Office, 1948; Baghdad, 1953; Athens, 1954; Vienna, 1959; Seville, 1963-67. *Address:* 31 Giselastrasse, Munich, Germany. *Club:* St James'.

**McKENZIE, John,** CMG 1970; PhD; MBE 1947; HM Ambassador to Iceland, since 1970; *b* 30 April 1915; *m* 1943, Sigridur Olafsdóttir; two *s* one *d. Educ:* Archbishop Holgate's Grammar Sch., York; Leeds Univ. Appointed Second Sec. and Vice-Consul, Reykjavik, 1945; joined Foreign Service, 1947; Consul, Helsinki, 1948; First Sec., 1949; Foreign Office, 1950; Sofia, 1953 (Chargé d'Affaires, 1954, 1955, 1956); Baghdad, 1956; Foreign Office, 1958; Counsellor, seconded to Cabinet Office, 1962; Helsinki, 1964 (Chargé d'Affaires, 1965, 1966); Dep. High Comr Calcutta, 1967-70. *Address:* c/o Foreign and Commonwealth Office, SW1.

**MACKENZIE, Brig. John Alexander,** CBE 1955; DSO 1944 and Bar, 1944; MC 1940 and Bar, 1940; ADC to the Queen 1967-70; Commandant and Inspector of Intelligence 1967-70; *b* 9 March 1915; *s* of late Louis Robert Wilson Mackenzie; *m* 1952, Beryl Cathreen Culver; one *s. Educ:* Nautical Coll., Pangbourne; RMC, Sandhurst. 2nd Bn Gloucestershire Regt, 1935-43; Bn Comd, 2nd Bn Lancs Fusiliers, Tunisia, Sicily and Italy Campaigns, 1943-44 (despatches, 1944); Bde Comd: 11 Inf. Bde, Italy, 1944; 10 Inf. Bde, Greece, 1945-46; psc 1947; GSO1 HQ British Troops, Berlin, 1948-49; AAG (Organisation), HQ, BAOR, 1950; jssc 1951; GSO1 HQ Western Comd, 1951-54; Comd: Britcom Sub-area, N Korea, 1955; Inf. Trng Team, HQ Jordan Arab Army, 1956; Jt Concealment Centre, 1957-58; Small Arms Sch., Hythe, 1958-59; idc 1960; Comd: 1 Bde, Nigeria, 1961-63; 3 Bde, Congo, 1962; Actg GOC, Royal Nigerian Army, 1963; BGS Army Trng, MoD, 1964-67. *Recreations:* swimming, sailing, climbing. *Address:* Iffin Farmhouse, Iffin Lane, near Canterbury, Kent. *T:* Canterbury 62776. *Club:* Army and Navy.

**MACKENZIE, John Gurney,** CMG 1955; Colonial Administrative Service, retired; *b* 6 Oct. 1907; *s* of William Cossar Mackenzie DSc, and Mary Ann Mackenzie (*née* Sheppard); *m* 1939, Kathleen Hope Harris; one *s* one *d. Educ:* Fettes Coll. Edinburgh; Magdalene Coll., Cambridge (BA Hons). Colonial Administrative Service, Nigeria, 1929-56. Financial Sec., Eastern Region, 1951; Civil Sec., 1952. Chm. Public Service Commission, Eastern Region, Nigeria, 1954-Dec. 1956. Retired, 1956. Chm., Civil Service Commission, Bahamas, 1961-64. *Address:* Ardloch, Lochearnhead, Perthshire.

**MACKENZIE, John Moncrieff Ord;** Vice-Lieutenant of Peeblesshire; *b* 1911; *s* of Kenneth Mackenzie, Dolphinton; *m* 1936, Delia Alice, *d* of late Wyndham Damer Clark, DL, JP, London, SW3; one *s* four *d. Educ:* Rugby; Corpus Christi Coll., Cambridge. WS, 1936. Captain, Lanarkshire Yeomanry (TA); served War of 1939-45 (despatches, Bronze Star Medal, US): GHQ, Liaison Regt. JP 1947, DL 1953, Vice-Lieutenant, 1956, Peeblesshire. *Address:* Dolphinton House, Dolphinton, Peeblesshire. *T:* Dolphinton 286. *Club:* New (Edinburgh).

**MACKENZIE, Kenneth Edward,** CMG 1970; *b* 28 April 1910; *s* of late A. E. Mackenzie, Dundee, and late K. M. Mackenzie (*née* Foley); *m* 1935, Phyllis Edith Fawkes; one *s. Educ:* schools in India, Australia and in the UK; University Coll., London. Engineering industry, 1926-29; University Coll., London, 1929-32, BSc (Hons) in civil and mechanical engineering. Inst. of Civil Engineers, 1932-34; Dept of Overseas Trade, 1934-36; HM Embassy, Brussels, 1936-40; interned in Germany, 1940-41; HM Embassy, Tehran, 1942-45. Trade Commissioner: in India, 1945-48; in Malaya, 1949-54; Asst Sec., Bd of Trade, 1954-66; Counsellor (Commercial), HM Embassy, Stockholm, and Chargé d'Affaires *ad interim,* 1966-70. *Publications:* Economic Survey of Malaya, 1951. Articles in British and foreign publications on economics and trade. *Recreations:* reading, gardening, walking, riding, swimming, music, metaphysics. *Address:* 24 London Road, Datchet, Slough, Buckinghamshire. *T:* Slough 41852. *Club:* Royal Commonwealth Society.

**MACKENZIE, Kenneth Roderick,** CB 1965; Clerk of Public Bills, House of Commons, since 1959; *b* 19 April 1908; *s* of late Walter Mackenzie; *m* 1935, Mary Howard, *e d* of Lt-Col C. H. Coode, RM; three *s* one *d. Educ:* Dulwich Coll.; New Coll., Oxford (scholar). 1st class Classical Moderations; 2nd class Literæ Humaniores. Asst clerk, House of Commons, 1930; senior clerk, 1943; Clerk of Standing Cttees, 1953. *Publications:* The English Parliament, 1950; Parliament, 1959; editions of Sir Bryan Fell's Guide to the Palace of Westminster, 1944-; verse translations of: Słowacki's In Switzerland, 1953; Mickiewicz's Pan Tadeusz, 1964; Virgil's Georgics, 1969. *Recreations:* riding, gardening. *Address:* Woodnorton, Mayfield, Sussex. *T:* Mayfield 2317. *Club:* Polish Hearth.

**MacKENZIE, Kenneth William Stewart,** CMG 1958; Assistant Secretary, Ministry of Housing and Local Government, since 1970; *b* 30 July 1915; *s* of late W. S. MacKenzie and E. MacKenzie (*née* Johnson); *m* 1939, Kathleen Joyce Ingram; one *s* one *d. Educ:* Whitcliffe Mount Gram. Sch., Cleckheaton; Downing Coll., Cambridge. 1st Cl. Hist. Tripos, Part I, 1935; Class II, Div. I, 1936; 1st Cl. Arch. and Anthrop. Tripos, Section A, 1937. Cadet, Colonial Administrative Service, Basutoland, 1938; Asst Sec., Mauritius, 1944; Administrative Officer, Kenya, 1948; Asst Financial Sec., 1950; HM Treasury, 1951-53; Dep. Sec., 1954 and Permanent Sec., 1955, Treasury, Kenya; Minister for Finance and Development and Financial Sec., Kenya, 1959-62. MLC Kenya, 1955-62. Retired, 1963 to facilitate constitutional change. Re-employed as Principal, Colonial Office, 1963; Principal, HM Treasury, 1966-70. *Publication:* pamphlet, How Basutoland is Governed, 1944. *Recreations:* reading, gardening. *Address:* Beaumont, Greenhurst Lane, Oxted, Surrey. *T:* Oxted 3848. *Clubs:* Royal Over-Seas League; Achilles; Nairobi (Nairobi).

**MACKENZIE, Sir (Lewis) Roderick Kenneth,** 9th Bt of Scatwell, *cr* 1703 (Nova Scotia); and presumably 11th Bt of Tarbat, *cr* 1602 (Scotland); *b* 8 Aug. 1902; *o s* of Sir Kenneth D. Mackenzie, 8th Bt, and Stephanie Corinne (*d* 1921), *y d* of Dr J. Espinet, MD, Trinidad; *S* father, 1930. *Educ:* The School House, Oakham. Formerly with Empire Cotton Growing Corporation, Southern Rhodesia. *Heir: kinsman,* Roderick Campbell Mackenzie, *b* 15 Nov. 1954.

**MACKENZIE, Maxwell Weir,** CMG 1946; Director: Canadian Imperial Bank of Commerce, since 1955; Canron Ltd, since 1961; Imperial Life Assurance Co. of Canada, since 1962; RCA Victor Ltd, since 1963; International Multifoods Corp., since 1964; Member of Economic Council of Canada, since 1963; *b* 30 June 1907; *s* of late Hugh Blair Mackenzie, Gen. Man., Bank of Montreal, Montreal, and Maude Marion Weir; *m* 1931,

Jean Roger Fairbairn; two *s* two *d*. *Educ:* Lakefield Preparatory Sch., Lakefield, Ont.; Trinity Coll. School, Port Hope, Ont.; McGill Univ., Montreal (BCom 1928). Joined McDonald, Currie & Co., Chartered Accountants of Montreal, 1928; Mem. Soc. of Chartered Accountants of the Province of Quebec, 1929; Jr Partner, McDonald, Currie & Co., Montreal, 1935; on loan to Foreign Exchange Control Board, Ottawa, 1939-42; to Wartime Prices and Trade Board, Ottawa, 1942-44 (Dep. Chm. 1943-44); Mem., Royal Commission on Taxation of Annuities and Family Corporation, 1944; Dep. Minister of Trade and Commerce, 1945-51; Dep. Minister of Defence Production, Canada, 1951-52; Pres., Canadian Chemical & Cellulose Company, Ltd, 1954-59 (Exec. Vice-Pres., 1952-54), Chm., Royal Commission on Security, 1966. *Recreation:* ski-ing. *Address:* Como, PQ, Canada. *Clubs:* Rideau (Ottawa); Mount Royal (Montreal).

**MACKENZIE, Melville Douglas,** CMG 1947; MD (London), DTM, DTH (Cambridge), DPH; retired as Principal Medical Officer, Ministry of Health; Chief UK Delegate to first, second, third, fourth, fifth and sixth World Health Assemblies; Chairman of Executive Board, 1953-54; *b* 29 June 1889; *s* of Frederick Lumsden Mackenzie, MD, North House, Lockwood, Huddersfield; *m* 1934, Caroline Faith, *d* of Capt. R. H. R. Mackay, OBE, JP, RN, Petham, Kent; two *s* one *d*. *Educ:* Epsom Coll.; St Bartholomew's Hosp., London. MB, BS (London), 1911; MD (London) 1920; DTM, DTH (Cambridge) 1920; DPH 1921; served European War 1914-18, Capt. RAMC 1917-19 (despatches); Sen. MO to Russian Famine Relief Administration, 1921-23; sometime Special Comr of Council of League of Nations to Governments of Liberia and China, Acting-Dir of League of Nations Epidemiological Bureau, Singapore, and Chm. of European Health Cttee of UNRRA; British Delegate with Plenipotentiary powers to World Health Conference, NY, 1946. *Publications:* various articles in medical journals. *Address:* Petham Lodge, near Canterbury, Kent. *T:* Petham 214.

**MacKENZIE, Norman Archibald MacRae,** CC (Canada) 1969; CMG 1946; MM and Bar, 1918; CD 1968; QC; BA, LLB (Dalhousie); LLM (Harvard); FRSC 1943; Hon. LLD (Mount Allison, New Brunswick, Toronto, Dalhousie, Ottawa, Bristol, Alberta, Glasgow, St Francis Xavier, McGill, Sydney, Rochester, Alaska, California, British Columbia, RMC (Cambridge); DCL (Saskatchewan, Whitman College); DSc Social, Laval; DLitt, Memorial University of Newfoundland; President Emeritus, Hon. Professor of International Law, University of British Columbia, Vancouver, since 1962; President of the University, 1944-62; appointed to The Senate of Canada, 1966, retired 1969; *b* Pugwash, Nova Scotia, Canada, 5 Jan. 1894; *s* of Rev. James A. MacKenzie and Elizabeth MacRae; *m* 1928, Margaret, *d* of A. W. and Helen Thomas; one *s* two *d*. *Educ:* Pictou Acad.; Dalhousie Univ. (BA 1921, LLB 1923); Harvard (LLM 1924); St John's Coll., Cambridge (Postgrad. Dipl., 1925); Grays' Inn, London. Read Law with McInnes, Jenks and Lovitt; called to Bar of Nova Scotia, 1926; KC 1942; Legal Adviser, ILO, Geneva, 1925-27; Assoc. Prof. of Law, 1927-33, Prof. of International and Canadian Constitutional Law, 1933-40, Toronto Univ.; Pres., University of New Brunswick, 1940-44; Pres., Nat. Conf. of Canadian Universities, 1946-48; Pres., Canadian Club of Toronto, 1939-40; Chm., Research Commission, Canadian Inst. of Internat. Affairs, 1929-40; Founding Mem. and Hon. Chm., National Council CIIA; Chm., Wartime Information Board, Canada, 1943-45; Chm., Reconstruction Commn, Province of New Brunswick, 1941-44; Pres., Toronto Branch, League of Nations Soc., 1932-36; Delegate to Institute of Pacific Relations Conferences, Shanghai 1931, Banff 1933, Yosemite 1936, Virginia Beach 1939, Mont Tremblant 1942; Delegate to British Commonwealth Conferences, Toronto, 1933, Sydney, Australia, 1938; Delegate to 7th Congress on Laws of Aviation, Lyons, France, 1925; War Record: Canadian Inf., 1914-19; 6th Canadian Mounted Rifles' 85th Bn, Nova Scotia Highlanders (MM and Bar); Vice-Pres., National Council of Canadian YMCA's; Chm. Victory Loan Executive Cttee, Fredericton and York, New Brunswick, 1941-44; Mem., University Advisory Board, Dept of Labour; Mem., Advisory Cttee on University Training for Veterans, Dept of Veterans Affairs; Hon. Pres. Save the Children Fund, Canada; Mem., Legal Survey Cttee (Survey of Legal Profession of Canada), 1949-57; Chm., Consultative Cttee on Doukhobor Problems; Mem., Royal Commission on National Development in the Arts, Letters and Sciences, 1949-51; Dir, Bank of Nova Scotia, 1960-69; Mem. Vancouver Advisory Board, Canada Permanent Trust Company, 1962-; East African Commission on University Educn, 1962. Trustee: Teachers Insurance and Annuity Association of America, 1948; Carnegie Foundation for the Advancement of Teaching, 1951- (Chm. Bd Trustees, 1959); Pres. Canadian Assoc. for Adult Education, 1957-59; Chm., University Grants Cttee, Prov. of NS, 1963-69; Mem. Royal Commission on Higher Educn, Prov. of PEI; Pres., Canadian Centenary Council; Dir, Centennial Commn (Canada); Dir, Fathers of Confedn Memorial Foundn; Pres., Nat. Assoc. of Canadian Clubs. Hon. Fellow, St John's Coll., Cambridge, 1964. *Publications:* Legal Status of Aliens in Pacific Countries, 1937; Canada and Law of Nations (with L. H. Laing), 1938; Canada in World Affairs (with F. H. Soward, J. F. Parkinson, T. W. L. MacDermot), 1941; The Challenge to Education, 1953; First Principles, 1954; (with Jacob Austin) A Canadian View of Territorial Seas and Fisheries, 1956, etc. Contributor to: Canadian Bar Review, Law Journals, etc. *Recreations:* fishing, hunting, golf, tennis, badminton, ski-ing. *Address:* 4509 West 4th Avenue, Vancouver, BC, Canada. *Clubs:* Vancouver, University, Faculty (Vancouver).

**MACKENZIE, Sir Robert Evelyn,** 12th Bt, *cr* 1673; Member of Lloyd's; *b* 15 Feb. 1906; *s* of 11th Bt and Evelyn Mary Montgomery (*d* 1908), *d* of Major-Gen. Sir Edward W. Ward; *S* father, 1935; *m* 1st, 1940 Mrs Jane Adams-Beck (*d* 1953); 2nd, 1963, Mrs Elizabeth Campbell. *Educ:* Eton; Trinity Coll., Cambridge. Mem. of Lloyd's, 1932. Intelligence Corps, 1939; British Embassy, Paris, 1944; Foreign Office, 1947; Washington, 1948; Foreign Office, 1951. *Heir: kinsman* Rev. Ramsay Malcolm Bolton Mackenzie [*b* Aug. 1893; *m* 1920, Margaret Cecilia (*d* 1965), *o d* of Rev. G. A. S. Metford]. *Address:* 18 Melton Court, Old Brompton Road, SW7. 44 *Club:* St James'.

**MACKENZIE, Sir Robert H. Muir;** *see* Muir Mackenzie.

**McKENZIE, Robert Trelford;** Professor of Sociology (with special reference to Politics), London School of Economics and Political Science, since 1964; *b* 11 Sept. 1917; *s* of William Meldrum McKenzie and Frances (*née* Chapman). *Educ:* King Edward High Sch., Vancouver; University of British Columbia

(BA); University of London (PhD). Taught at University of British Columbia, 1937-42. Served with Canadian Army, 1943-46. Has taught at London Sch. of Economics and Political Science since 1949. Visiting Lectr on Politics at Harvard and Yale Univs, Sept. 1958-Jan. 1959. Hon. LLD Simon Fraser Univ., 1969. *Publications:* British Political Parties: The Distribution of Power within the Conservative and Labour Parties, 1955, 2nd rev. edn, 1964 (translated into Spanish, German and Japanese); (with Allan Silver) Angels in Marble: Working Class Conservatism in Urban England, 1968. *Recreation:* broadcasting. *Address:* London School of Economics and Political Science, Houghton Street, Aldwych WC2. *T:* 01-405 7686.

**MACKENZIE, Sir Roderick;** *see* Mackenzie, Sir L. R. K.

**MacKENZIE, William Forbes,** CMG 1955; CBE 1951 (OBE 1946); *b* 5 June 1907; *e s* of late Dr A. J. MacKenzie, Salisbury, S Rhodesia; *m* 1934, Marion Elizabeth, *d* of late F. H. Glenton, Johannesburg, S Africa; no *c. Educ:* Merchiston Castle Sch.; Caius Coll., Cambridge. Native Affairs Dept, S Rhodesia, 1927-36; District Officer, Bechuanaland Protectorate, 1937-48; Asst Administrative Sec. to High Comr for Basutoland, Bechuanaland Protectorate and Swaziland, 1948-49; Dep. Resident Comr and Govt Sec., Swaziland, 1949-51; Dep. Res. Comr and Govt Sec., Bechuanaland Protectorate, 1951-53. Res. Comr, Bechuanaland Protectorate 1953-56, retired. *Recreations:* fishing, shooting and golf. *Address:* Courtenay Rise, Addington Lane, PO Highlands, Salisbury, Rhodesia. *T:* Salisbury 882063. *Clubs:* Country (Johannesburg); Bulawayo, Salisbury (Rhodesia).

**MACKENZIE, Prof. William James Millar,** CBE 1963; FBA 1968; Edward Caird Professor of Politics, Glasgow University, since 1970; *b* 8 April 1909; *s* of Laurence Millar Mackenzie, WS, Edinburgh; *m* 1943, Pamela Muriel Malyon; one *s* four *d. Educ:* Edinburgh Academy; Balliol Coll., Oxford (MA) (Ireland Schol. 1929); Edinburgh Univ. (LLB); Fellow of Magdalen Coll., Oxford, 1933-48; Temp. Civil Servant, Air Ministry, 1939-44; Official War Historian, SOE (part-time), 1945-48. Faculty Fellow of Nuffield Coll., 1948; Lecturer in Politics, Oxford Univ., 1948; Prof. of Government, Manchester Univ., 1949-66, Glasgow Univ., 1966-70; Special Comr, for Constitutional Development, Tanganyika, 1952; Co-opted Mem., Manchester City Educn Cttee, 1953-64; apptd Mem., British Wool Marketing Board, 1954-66; Mem. Royal Commn on Local Govt in Greater London, 1957; Constitutional Adviser, Kenya, 1959; Vice-Chm., Bridges Cttee on Training in Public Administration for Overseas Countries, 1962; Member: Maud Cttee on Management in Local Govt, 1964-66; Cttee on Remuneration of Ministers and Members of Parliament, 1963-64; North-West Regional Economic Planning Council, 1965-66; Social Science Research Council, 1965-69; Parry Cttee on University Libraries, 1964-67; Adv. Cttee for Scientific and Technical Information, 1966-; Rowntree Working Party on Social Work (Scotland) Act, 1968-69 (Chm.). Hon. LLD: Dundee, 1968; Lancaster, 1970. *Publications:* (In part) British Government since 1918, 1950; (Jtly) Central Administration in Great Britain, 1957; Free Elections, 1958; (ed with Prof. K. Robinson) Five Elections in Africa, 1959; Politics and Social Science, 1967; (jtly) Social Work in Scotland, 1969. *Address:* Department of Politics, Glasgow University.

**MACKENZIE CROOKS, Air Vice-Marshal Lewis,** CBE 1963 (OBE 1950); Consultant Adviser in Orthopaedic Surgery, RAF, 1966-70, retired; *b* 20 Jan. 1909; *s* of David Mackenzie Crooks and Mary (*née* McKechnie); *m* 1936, Mildred, *d* of A. J. Gwyther; two *s* one *d. Educ:* Epworth Coll.; Liverpool Univ. MB, ChB 1931; FRCS 1937; ChM (Liverpool) 1945. House Surgeon: Northern Hosp., Liverpool, 1931-32; Shropshire Orthop. Hosp., Oswestry, 1932-33; Sen. House Surgeon: Selly Oak Hosp., Birmingham, 1933-34; All Saints Hosp., London, 1934-35; commnd RAF, 1935; surgical hosp. appts in RAF, 1936-52; overseas service: Palestine, 1937-39; Iraq, 1939-42; Egypt, 1950-51. Clinical Tutor, Edinburgh Royal Infirmary, 1947; Cons. in Orthop. Surgery, 1952; Sen. Cons. in Orthop. Surgery, 1955. QHS, 1966-70. *Publication:* article on chondromalaca patellae in Jl of Bone and Joint Surgery. *Recreation:* golf. *Address:* Trelwaney, Harlyn Road, St Merryn, Padstow, Cornwall. *Club:* Royal Air Force.

**McKENZIE JOHNSTON, Henry Butler;** HM Consul-General, Munich, from April 1971; *b* 10 July 1921; *er s* of Colin McKenzie Johnston and Bernardine (*née* Fawcett Butler); *m* 1949, Marian Allardyce Middleton, *e d* of late Brig. A. A. Middleton and Winifred (*née* Salvesen); one *s* two *d. Educ:* Rugby. Served with Black Watch (RHR), 1940-46; Adjt 6th Bn, 1944-45; Temp. Major 1945. Staff of HM Embassy, Athens, 1946-47; entered Foreign (subseq. Diplomatic) Service, 1947; Paris, 1948-51; British High Commn, Germany, 1951-54; FO, 1954-56; 1st Sec. (Commercial), Montevideo, 1956-60; FO, 1960-63; Counsellor (Information), Mexico City, 1963-66; Dep. High Comr, Port of Spain, 1966-67; seconded to Min. of Overseas Develt, 1968-70. *Address:* c/o Foreign and Commonwealth Office, SW1; 6 Pembroke Gardens, W8. *Club:* Oxford and Cambridge University.

**MACKENZIE-KENNEDY, Brig. Archibald Gordon,** CBE 1952 (OBE 1949); DSO 1945; Colonel and temporary Brig. late Royal Scots; *b* 1904; *s* of late Maj.-Gen. Sir Edward Charles William Mackenzie-Kennedy, KBE, CB; *m* 1937, Jean Katherine, *d* of H. A. Law, Marble Hill, Ballymore, Co. Donegal. *Educ:* Marlborough; Royal Military College, Sandhurst. 2nd Lt Royal Scots, 1924. Served War of 1939-45: Burma, 1941-45 (DSO); Lt-Col, 1943; Brig., 1947; Comdr Eritrea District, 1950-52. *Address:* Beltany Lodge, Mountjoy, Omagh, Co. Tyrone, Northern Ireland.

**MACKEOWN, John Ainslie,** CIE 1942; Secretary, Arthur Guinness Son & Co. (Dublin) Ltd, 1952-67; retired; *b* 27 Oct. 1902; *s* of late Rev. William Mackeown; *m* 1935, Vivienne, *d* of J. L. Musgrave, Hayfield House, Cork; two *s. Educ:* Radley; Worcester Coll., Oxford. Joined ICS, 1925; left India, 1947, after holding posts, Jt Sec. to Govt of India and Comr, Ambala Div. *Recreations:* golf, music, reading, bridge, sailing. *Address:* 57 Leeson Park, Dublin. *T:* Dublin 67964.

**McKEOWN, Prof. Thomas,** BA British Columbia, PhD McGill, DPhil Oxon, MB, BS London, MD Birmingham, FRCP; Professor of Social Medicine, University of Birmingham, since 1944; *b* 2 Nov. 1912; *s* of William McKeown; *m* 1940, Esmé Joan Bryan Widdowson; one *s* one *d. Educ:* Universities: British Columbia; McGill (National Research Council Schol.); Trinity Coll., Oxford (Rhodes Scholar); London (Guy's Hospital: Poulton

Research Scholar). Demonstrator in biochemistry, McGill; demonstrator in physiology, Guy's Hosp. *Publications:* A Balanced Teaching Hospital (Jointly), 1965; Medicine in Modern Society, 1965; Introduction to Social Medicine (Jt), 1966; Screening in Medical Care (Jointly), 1968; contributions to scientific journals. *Address:* 23 Hintlesham Avenue, Edgbaston, Birmingham. *T:* 021-454 2810.

**MACKEOWN, Thomas Frederick William;** Administrator and Secretary, University College Hospital, London, 1946-63; *b* 3 Jan. 1904; *s* of Rev. William Mackeown, Rushbrooke, Co. Cork; *m* 1936, Lorraine, *d* of Major R. Hayes, Sherburh-in-Elmet, Yorks; one *d*. *Educ:* Felsted; Worcester Coll., Oxford (MA). Qualified as Chartered Accountant, 1927. Hospital Administrator: Liverpool Stanley Hospital, 1934-37; Clayton Hospital, Wakefield, 1937-45; Royal Infirmary, Sunderland, 1945-46; Hill Homes, Highgate (actg), 1966; King Edward VII Memorial Hospital, Bermuda, 1967; Mem. Management Cttee, Harefield and Northwoods Hosps; undertook Hosp. Domestic Staff Survey under aegis of King Edward's Hosp. Fund for London, 1968. *Recreations:* travelling, gardening, golf. *Address:* 93 Hillway, N6. *T:* 01-348 1952. *Club:* Athenæum.

**MACKERRAS, (Alan) Charles;** Musical Director, Sadler's Wells Opera, since 1970; Conductor, Hamburg State Opera, since 1966; *b* 17 Nov. 1925; *s* of Alan Patrick and Catherine Mackerras, Sydney, Australia; *m* 1947, Helena Judith (*née* Wilkins); two *d*. *Educ:* Sydney Grammar Sch. Principal Oboist, Sydney Symphony Orchestra, 1943-46; Staff Conductor, Sadlers Wells Opera, 1949-53; Principal Conductor BBC Concert Orchestra, 1954-56; freelance conductor with most British orchestras, 1957-66; frequent tours of opera and concerts in Scandinavia, Germany, Italy, Czechoslovakia, Hungary, Rumania, USSR, Belgium, Holland, Australia, S Africa, Canada. Frequent broadcasts BBC; TV programmes of opera and ballet; commercial recordings; appearances at many internat. festivals and opera houses. *Publications:* ballet arrangements of Pineapple Poll and of Lady and the Fool; articles in Opera Magazine, Music and Musicians and other musical jls. *Recreations:* languages, yachting. *Address:* 10 Hamilton Terrace, NW8. *T:* 01-286 4047.

**MACKERRAS, Charles;** *see* Mackerras, A. C.

**McKERRON, Robert Gordon;** Emeritus Professor of Law, Rhodes University, South Africa; *b* 20 March 1900; *yr s* of late Prof. R. G. McKerron; *m* 1st, 1928, Nancy (*d* 1937), *o d* of H. A. Green, Johannesburg; one *s*; 2nd, 1939, Elsie, *d* of late J. E. Healey; one *d* (and one *s* decd). *Educ:* Aberdeen Grammar Sch.; Fettes Coll., Edinburgh; Aberdeen Univ. (1st cl. Hons Classics); Oriel Coll., Oxford (1st cl. Hons BA, Hons Sch. of Jurisprudence, 1924; 1st cl. BCL, 1925); Vinerian Law Schol., 1926; Bacon Scholarship, Gray's Inn, 1926; DCL Oxon, 1947. QC (SA), 1955; Advocate, Supreme Ct of SA; Barrister-at-law, Gray's Inn. Prof. of Law and Dean of the Faculty in University of the Witwatersrand, 1926-46; practised Johannesburg Bar, 1947-54; Prof. and Dean of Faculty of Law, Rhodes Univ., 1955-68. For duration of War, Major SA Defence Force (despatches, POW, Italy). *Publication:* Law of Delict, 6th edn, 1965. *Recreations:* formerly playing, now watching, cricket, golf and tennis. *Address:* 401 Ashbourne, Main Road, Kenilworth, Cape Province, S Africa. *Clubs:* Rand (Johannesburg), Kelvin Grove (Cape Town).

**MACKESON, Sir Rupert (Henry),** 2nd Bt *cr* 1954; *b* 16 Nov. 1941; *s* of Brig. Sir Harry Ripley Mackeson, 1st Bt, and Alethea, Lady Mackeson, *d* of late Comdr R. Talbot, RN, Maxpoffle, St Boswells; *S* father, 1964; *m* 1968, Camilla, *d* of Sir Kenneth Keith, *qv*. *Educ:* Harrow; Trinity Coll., Dublin (MA). Capt, Royal Horse Guards, 1967, retd 1969. *Recreations:* racing, coursing. *Heir:* none. *Address:* 5 Pembroke Gardens, W8. *T:* 01-937 1882. *Clubs:* Turf; Kildare Street (Dublin).

**MACKESSACK, Lt-Col Kenneth;** Vice-Lieutenant, Moray, since 1964; *b* 1902; *s* of late George Ross Mackessack; *m* 1st, 1929, Rose Elizabeth (marr. diss., 1947), *d* of late Sir Henry D. Craik, 3rd Bt, GCIE, KCSI; one *s* one *d*; 2nd, 1947, Nora Joyce, *d* of late Maj.-Gen. C. E. Edward-Collins; one *d*. *Educ:* Rugby; RMC, Sandhurst. Commissioned Seaforth Highlanders, 1923; Adjt 1935. NW Frontier Ops, 1931; served in Middle East and N Africa, 1940-43 (wounded, despatches); on Gen. Staff and with 51st Highland and 4th Indian Divs; Military Attaché, Washington, 1943-46; retd 1947. Convenor, Moray County Council, 1958-. Chm. TA Assoc. of Moray, 1954-62. DL Moray, 1954. *Recreations:* shooting, fishing. *Address:* Ardgye, Elgin, Morayshire. *T:* Alves 250. *Club:* MCC.

**MACKEY, Prof. William Arthur,** TD; St Mungo Professor of Surgery, University of Glasgow, since 1953; *b* 1 Oct. 1906; *s* of Arthur Edward Mackey, Schoolmaster, and Elizabeth Annie (*née* Carr); *m* 1939, Joan Margaret Sykes; two *s* two *d*. *Educ:* Ardrossan Academy; Univ. of Glasgow. MB, ChB (hons). Asst to Prof. of Pathology, Univ. of Glasgow, 1928; Asst to Regius Prof. of Surgery, University of Glasgow, 1931. Hon. FACS. *Recreations:* golf, gardening, repenting plans and pottering around Bohemia. *Address:* 6 Sinclair Drive, Helensburgh, Dunbartonshire. *T:* Helensburgh 3659. *Clubs:* Royal Commonwealth Society; Royal Scottish Automobile (Glasgow), Glasgow Golf.

**MACKIE, Edwin Gordon;** Hon. Ophthalmic Surgeon, United Sheffield Hospitals, Ophthalmic Medical Referee, County Court Circuits 13 and 16-18; *b* 1896; *e s* of late David Cable Mackie, FSA (Scotland), and Charlotte Fyffe McDonald; *m* 1st, 1931, Mary Owen (*d* 1968), *y d* of F. P. Stokes, Melbourne, Australia; one *s* two *d*; 2nd, 1970, Peggy Lever Brundell Bovill, *o d* of Basil Pickering, MC, JP, East Markham. Educ: Madras Coll.; St Andrews Univ.; Birmingham. Served European War: MEF, BEF, Lt The Royal Scots. MA 1919; MB, ChB, 1924 (Medal Ophthalmology). Resident Posts: Dundee Royal Infirm.; Birmingham and Midland Eye Hospital; DOMS (England), FRCSGlas. Temp. Tutor, Edinburgh, 1927; Asst Surgeon, Royal Hosp., Sheffield, 1927, Surg. 1935. Formerly: Surg., Beckett Hosp., Barnsley; visiting oculist, State Instn, Rampton, etc; Clin. Lectr in Ophthalmology; Lectr in Applied Anat., University of Sheffield; Ext. Examr Queen's Univ., Belfast, and Examr for Dipl. in Ophthalmology, Examining Bd in England; Mem. Council, Sheffield Univ., 1949-51; Mem. Bd of Govs, United Sheffield Hosps, 1954-57. Served War of 1939-45: RAMC; France, Comd Ophthalmologist UK, Lt-Col OC Hosp. MEF. President: N of England Ophthalmological Soc., 1947; Sheffield Medico Chirurgical Soc., 1957. Member: Oxford Ophthalmological Congress; Ophthal. Soc. of UK; Ophthal. Gp Cttee, BMA, 1945-65; Council, Faculty of Ophthalmologists, 1946-66 (Pres., 1959-61); Court, University of Sheffield, 1963-. Chm., Zachary Merton Charity for Convalescents. Ophthalmic

Lecture Tour, Australia and India, 1955. Middlemore Memorial Lectr, 1955. Is also Mem., Ophthalmic Adv. Panel, Min. of Labour; Convenor, Ophth. Adv. Cttee, Sheffield Region, 1948-63; Referee, Min. of Pensions and National Ins. Visitor, Educational Establishments and Examinations, General Optical Council, UK. *Publications:* articles and papers to: Brit. Jl of Ophthalmology; Trans. Ophthalmolog. Soc. of UK, etc. *Recreations:* antiquities, heraldry, shooting. *Address:* 287 Glossop Road, Sheffield 10. *T:* 24635; 357 Fulwood Road, Sheffield 10. *T:* Sheffield 62206. *Club:* Sheffield (Sheffield).

**MACKIE, George Yull,** DSO 1944; DFC 1944; Chairman: Caithness Glass Ltd, since 1966; Caithness Cheese, since 1969; *b* 10 July 1919; *s* of Maitland Mackie, OBE, LLD; *m* 1944, Lindsay Sharp; three *d*. *Educ:* Aberdeen Grammar Sch.; Aberdeen Univ. Served War of 1939-45, RAF; Bomber Command, (DSO, DFC); Air Staff, 1944. Farming at Ballinshoe, Kirriemuir, from 1945. Contested (L) South Angus, 1959; MP (L) Caithness and Sutherland, 1964-66. Chm. Scottish Liberal Party, 1965-70. Mem. Cttee, Wider Share Ownership Council, 1965-. *Publication:* Policy for Scottish Agriculture, 1963. *Address:* Ballinshoe, Kirriemuir, Angus. *T:* Kirriemuir 2270. *Clubs:* Garrick, Farmers'; Scottish Liberal (Edinburgh).

**MACKIE, James Richard,** CMG 1941; BSc (Agric); *b* 1896; *s* of J. H. Mackie, JP, Castle Cary, Somerset; *m* 1929, Sylvia M. Miller; one *s*. *Educ:* Sexey's Sch., Bruton; University Coll., Reading. Army, 1914-18 (despatches, Belgian Croix de Guerre). Superintendent in Agricultural Dept, Nigeria, 1921; Dept. Asst Dir of Agriculture, 1928; Asst Dir of Agriculture, 1929; Dir of Agriculture, Nigeria, 1936-45. Mem. Executive Council of Nigeria, 1942-45. Member: Colonial Adv. Cttee for Agriculture, Forestry and Animal Health, 1946-49; Scientific Adv. Cttee, Empire Cotton Growing Corp.; Soulbury Commission (investigating sugar industry in West Indies), 1948-49; Governing Body of Imperial Coll. of Tropical Agriculture, Trinidad, 1949-56; SW Regional Hospital Board: Mem., 1954-63, Chm., Mental Health Cttee, 1957-63. *Address:* 3 Bec-en-Hent, Bickwell Valley, Sidmouth, Devon. *T:* Sidmouth 2707.

**MACKIE, John;** MP (Lab) Enfield East since 1959; Farming on own account; *b* 24 Nov. 1909; *s* of Maitland Mackie, OBE, Farmer, and Mary Ann Mackie (*née* Yull); *m* 1934, Jeannie Inglis Milne; three *s* two *d*. *Educ:* Aberdeen Gram. Sch.; North of Scotland Coll. of Agriculture. Farming at: Bent, Laurencekirk, Kincardineshire, 1930-; Glentworth, Gainsborough, Lincolnshire, 1947-; Harold's Park Farm, Nazeing, Waltham Abbey, Essex, 1953-. Jt Parly Sec., Min. of Agriculture, 1964-70. *Publication:* (for Fabian Soc.) Land Nationalisation. *Recreations:* golf and tennis. *Address:* Bent, Laurencekirk, Kincardineshire. *T:* Laurencekirk 309; Harold's Park, Nazeing, Waltham Abbey, Essex. *T:* Nazeing 2202. *Club:* Farmers'.

**McKIE, Rt. Rev. John David;** Assistant Bishop of Coventry since 1960; Vicar of Great and Little Packington since 1966; *b* 14 May 1909; *s* of Rev. W. McKie, Melbourne, Vic; *m* 1952, Mary Lesley, *d* of late Brig. S. T. W. Goodwin, DSO and of Mrs Goodwin, Melbourne, Vic; four *d*. *Educ:* Melbourne Church of England Grammar Sch.; Trinity Coll., Melbourne Univ.; New Coll., Oxford. BA (Trinity Coll., Melbourne Univ.). 1931; MA (New Coll., Oxford), 1945; Deacon, 1932; Priest, 1934; Asst Chap. Melbourne Church of England Grammar Sch., 1932-33; Chap. and lecturer, Trinity Coll., Melbourne, 1936-39; served War of 1939-45 (despatches): AIF, 1939-44; Asst CG; Vicar Christ Church, South Yarra, 1944-46; Coadjutor, Bishop of Melbourne (with title of Bishop of Geelong) and Archdeacon of Melbourne, 1946-60, Chaplain and Sub-Prelate, Order of St John of Jerusalem, 1949. *Address:* Little Packington Rectory, Meriden, Coventry. *Club:* Athenæum.

*See also Sir W. N. McKie.*

**MACKIE, John Duncan,** CBE 1944; MC, MA, Hon. LLD St Andrews and Glasgow; HM Historiographer in Scotland since 1958; Professor of Scottish History and Literature in the University of Glasgow, 1930-57, retired; Dean of Faculties (Deputy-Principal), 1940-45; visiting Canadian and S African Universities on British Council travel grants; Member Scottish Records Advisory Council and Chairman, Scottish National Register of Archives; a Vice-President, of Society of Antiquaries of Scotland, 1949-53; President of Scottish History Society; President of Historical Association of Scotland, 1949-53; Member, Scottish National Portrait Gallery Advisory Committee; President of Glasgow Archæological Society, 1936-39; *b* 1887; *e s* of late John Beveridge Mackie of the Dunfermline Journal and Lilias Agnes, *d* of James Robb; *m* 1917, Cicely Jean, *e d* of Alexander Stephen Paterson, Advocate, Edinburgh; two *s* one *d*. *Educ:* Middlesbrough High Sch.; Jesus Coll., Oxford. 2nd Cl. Classical Mods; 1st Cl. History Finals; Lothian Essay Prize; Hon. LLD (St Andrews), 1950; Hon. LLD (Glasgow). 1959. Lecturer in Modern History, and head of the Dept of Modern History in the University of St Andrews, 1908-26; Prof. of Modern History in the University of London (Bedford Coll.), 1926-30. Served European War, 1914-19, with 14th Battalion Argyll and Sutherland Highlanders, Capt. (Acting Major, twice wounded); Chm. of Glasgow Joint Recruiting Board, 1939-46. Chevalier de la Légion d'Honneur, 1946; KStJ 1955 (CStJ 1948). *Publications:* essays and reviews in the Scottish Historical Review, English Historical Review, History, Encyclopædia Britannica, etc; The Sixteenth Century, in Cassell's History of the British People (1925); Negotiations between James VI and I and Ferdinand I of Tuscany (1927); The Estate of the Burgesses in the Scots Parliament (1923) (with Dr G. S. Pryde); Cavalier and Puritan, 1930; Andrew Lang and House of Stuart, 1935; Thomas Thomson's Memorial on Old Extent (Stair Soc.), 1946; The Earlier Tudors, 1485-1558, 1952; The University of Glasgow, 1451-1951: A Short History, 1954; Scottish History (Readers' Guide), 1956; A History of the Scottish Reformation, 1960; Introd. to Polwarth Papers, V, 1962; A History of Scotland (Pelican), 1964; (ed) Calendar of State Papers relating to Scotland and Mary Queen of Scots, Vol. XIII, 1597-1603, 1969. *Address:* 67 Dowanside Road, Glasgow, W2.

**McKIE, Sir William Neil,** Kt 1953; MVO 1948; MA, Hon. DMus Oxon, Melbourne; FRSCM, FRCM, FRCO, FTCL, Hon. RAM; Hon. Secretary, Royal College of Organists, 1963-67; Hon. Fellow, Worcester College, Oxford, 1954; Organist and Master of the Choristers, Westminster Abbey, 1941-63 (on leave of absence, 1941-45, during war service, RAF, Volunteer Reserve); *b* Melbourne, Australia, 22 May 1901; *s* of Rev. William McKie; *m* 1956, Phyllis Ross, *widow* of Gerald Walker Birks, OBE, and *d* of John Wardrope Ross, Montreal. *Educ:* Melbourne Grammar Sch.; Royal Coll. of Music; Worcester Coll., Oxford. Organist

St Agnes, Kennington Park, 1920-21; organ scholar, Worcester Coll., Oxford, 1921-24; asst music master, Radley Coll., 1923-26; Dir of Music, Clifton Coll., 1926-30; City Organist, Melbourne, 1931-38; Organist and Instructor in Music, Magdalen Coll., Oxford, 1938-41; Organist at Sheldonian Theatre, 1939-41; Organ prof., Royal Acad. of Music, 1946-62; Hon. Associate Dir, Royal School of Church Music, 1947-52; Dir of Music, Coronation Service, 1953; President: Incorporated Association of Organists, 1950-52; Royal College of Organists, 1956-58; London Soc. of Organists, 1958-59; Incorporated Soc. of Musicians, 1959. Hon. Mem., American Guild of Organists; Hon. Fellow: Westminster Choir Coll., Princeton, NJ, 1965; Royal Canadian Coll. of Organists, 1965. Comdr with Star, Order of St Olav, Norway, 1964. *Address:* 10 Driveway, Ottawa 4, Canada. *Club:* Athenæum. *See also Rt Rev. J. D. McKie.*

**McKIE REID, Col Andrew;** *see* Reid.

**MACKILLIGIN, Robert Springett,** CMG 1944; OBE 1919; MC 1916; MIMM; *b* 23 March 1890; *s* of Robert Marquis Mackilligin; *m* 1938, Patricia Margaret Elizabeth, *d* of Lt-Col F. S. Waldegrave, OBE, MC, QO Cameron Highlanders; one *s* one *d*. *Educ:* Cranbrook Sch., Kent; Camborne Sch. of Mines, Cornwall. Mining Engineering in Burma and West Africa, 1910-15; served in France, Capt. RE, 1915-17; N Russia, RE, 1917-19 (despatches twice, MC and bar, OBE); with Anglo-Iranian Oil Co. in Persia and Patagonia, 1920-36; Inspector of Mines and Petroleum Technologist, Trinidad, 1936-46. *Address:* c/o Lloyds Bank Ltd, 6 Pall Mall, SW1.

**McKILLOP, Edgar Ravenswood,** CMG 1952; OBE 1942; Company Director; Commissioner of Works and Permanent Head, Ministry of Works, NZ, 1944-55, retired; *b* 26 July 1895; *s* of Alexander McKillop and Jean Cameron; *m* 1930, Marguerita Anne Mary Dennis. *Educ:* Canterbury Univ. Coll., New Zealand. Civil engineer, New Zealand Government engaged on developmental works; railway construction, irrigation and hydro-electric projects. Served 1914-18 with 1st NZEF overseas (twice wounded). Lt-Col NZ Eng. 2nd NZ Exp. Force, in Pacific, 1939-42; Dep. Comr Def. Constr., 1942-44, in NZ and South Pacific. Past mem. Scientific and Industrial Research Council; FICE and past mem. of Council; FNZ Inst. of Engineers and mem. of Council. *Recreation:* golf. *Address:* PO Box 3009, Raumati South, Paraparaumu, New Zealand.

**McKILLOP, Sybil Laurie;** Headmistress, Westbourne School for Girls (direct grant), Glasgow, W2, since 1965; *b* 9 Sept. 1913; *d* of John McKillop, Solicitor, Kirkcaldy, Scotland. *Educ:* Kirkcaldy High Sch.; University of Edinburgh. MA with 1st Cl Hons in Classics (Edinburgh), 1934; Diploma in Education (Edinburgh), 1935; BD with Hons (London), 1942. Senior Classics Mistress, Blackburn Girls' High Sch., 1936-44; Dep. Head, 1941-44; Classics and Divinity Mistress, Cheltenham Ladies' Coll., 1944-47; Headmistress: Priory Girls' Gram. Sch., Shrewsbury, 1947-62; Clifton High Sch. for Girls, Bristol, 1962-64. *Publication:* Twenty Psalms for Schools, 1962. *Recreations:* books, music, art, country walks. *Address:* 37 Ralston Road, Bearsden, near Glasgow. *T:* 041-942 4670.

**MACKINLAY, Sir George Mason,** Kt 1955; Director: Atlas Assurance since 1957; McLeod Russel and Co. Ltd, since 1957, etc.; *b* 18 Oct. 1906; *s* of late Charles Alexander Mackinlay; *m* 1936, Ellen Margaret Greaves; one *s*. *Educ:* Loretto. Pres. of the Associated Chambers of Commerce and of the Bengal Chamber of Commerce, 1954-55. Lately Chm. and Man. Dir Jardine Henderson Ltd, Calcutta, and Dir of State Bank of India. *Address:* 17 St Helen's Place, EC3. *Club:* Oriental.

**McKINLEY, Air Vice-Marshal David Cecil,** CB 1966; CBE 1957; DFC 1940; AFC 1944, Bar 1945; RAF; *b* 18 Sept. 1913; *s* of David McKinley, Civil Engineer, and May McKinley (*née* Ward); *m* 1940, Brenda Alice (*née* Ridgway); three *s*. *Educ:* Bishop Foy Sch., Waterford; Trinity Coll., Dublin. Radio Engineering, Ferranti Ltd, 1935. Entered (regular) Royal Air Force, 1935; served continuously since that date; AOC Malta and Dep. C-in-C (Air), Allied Forces, Mediterranean, 1963-65; SASO, Transport Command, 1966, Air Support Command, 1967-68. Freeman, The Guild of Air Pilots and Air Navigators, 1959. FIN 1949. *Recreations:* sailing, fishing, water ski-ing, gardening. *Address:* Sundial Cottage, Fawley, Hants. *T:* Fawley 231; Midland Bank, Bushey, Herts. *Clubs:* Junior Army and Navy, Royal Air Force.

**McKINNEY, Mrs J. P.;** *see* Wright, Judith.

**McKINNEY, Sir William,** Kt 1964; CBE 1956; *b* 14 Nov. 1897; *s* of James and Edith McKinney; *m* 1st, 1925, Lisla Chesney, *d* of Robert Clyde; one *s*; 2nd 1936, Mary E., *d* of William T. Unsworth. *Educ:* Belfast Royal Academy. Joined Board of Management of Royal Victoria Hospital, Belfast, 1931; subsequently Hon. Sec. First Vice-Chm., Northern Ireland Hospitals Authority, 1948-50 and 1953-55. Custodian Trustee, Belfast Savings Bank (Chm., 1946 and 1967). Chm., Northern Ireland Hospitals Authority, 1956-65. Hon. Treasurer, Queen's Univ., 1966. Hon. LLD Queen's Univ., 1966. *Address:* 5 Deramore Park South, Belfast BT9 5JY. *T:* Belfast 666396. *Club:* Ulster Reform (Belfast).

**MacKINNON, Prof. Donald MacKenzie,** MA; Norris-Hulse Professor of Divinity, Cambridge University, since 1960; Fellow of Corpus Christi College, Cambridge, since 1960; *b* Oban, 27 Aug. 1913; *o s* of late D. M. MacKinnon, Procurator Fiscal, and late Grace Isabella Rhind; *m* 1939, Lois, *e d* of late Rev. Oliver Dryer; no *c*. *Educ:* Cargilfield Sch., Edinburgh; Winchester Coll. (scholar); New Coll., Oxford (scholar). Asst in Moral Philosophy (to late Prof. A. E. Taylor) at Edinburgh, 1936-37; Fellow and Tutor in Philosophy at Keble Coll., Oxford, 1937-47; Dir of Course for special courses in Philosophy for RN and RAF cadets at Oxford, 1942-45; Lectr in Philosophy at Balliol Coll., 1945-47; Wilde Lectr in Natural and Comparative Religion at Oxford, 1945-47; Regius Prof. of Moral Philosophy at Aberdeen, 1947-60. Lectures: Scott Holland, 1952; Hobhouse, 1953; Stanton, in the Philosophy of Religion, Cambridge, 1956-59; Gifford, Edinburgh, 1965-66; Prideaux, Exeter, 1966; Coffin, London, 1968; Riddell, Newcastle-upon-Tyne, 1970. Hon. DD Aberdeen 1961. Mem. Labour Party. *Publications:* (ed) Christian Faith and Communist Faith, 1953; The Notion of a Philosophy of History, 1954; A Study in Ethical Theory, 1957; (with Prof. G. W. H. Lampe) The Resurrection, 1966; Borderlands of Theology and other papers, 1968; The Stripping of the Altars, 1969; articles, reviews. *Recreations:* walking, cats, the cinema. *Address:* 9 Parker Street, Cambridge; Tigh Grianach, North Connel, Argyll.

**MACKINNON, Duncan;** *b* 18 Sept. 1909; *e s* of late Capt. William Mackinnon, Loup, Clachan, Argyll; *m* 1932, Pamela Rachel, 2nd *d* of late Capt. R. B. Brassey; one *s* one *d*. *Educ:* Eton; Magdalen, Oxford. Served War of 1939-45, Argyll and Sutherland Highlanders. Chm. Smith St Aubyn & Co. Ltd, White Lion Court, Cornhill, EC3; Dep. Chm. Eagle Star Assurance Co. Ltd; Director: The Ashdown Investment Trust Ltd; Hambros Investment Trust Ltd; Chm. London Discount Market Assoc., 1959-61. JP Oxfordshire, 1945-56; High Sheriff of Oxfordshire, 1949-50. *Recreations:* fishing, shooting. *Address:* 23 Hyde Park Place, W2; Swinbrook House, Burford, Oxfordshire. *T:* Burford 2216. *Club:* White's.

**MacKINNON, Georgina Russell Davidson, (Gena MacKinnon),** OBE 1964; Chairman of Drambuie Liqueur Co.; *b* 1885; *d* of John and Margaret Davidson; *m* 1914, Malcolm MacKinnon; one *s* one *d*. *Educ:* James Allen's Girls' Sch., London; Wick Acad., Caithness. Company Chm. and Farmer of pedigree Jersey cattle. *Address:* Williamcraigs, Linlithgow, West Lothian, Scotland. *T:* Linlithgow 2072. *Clubs:* White Elephant, Siegis, 21.

**McKINNON, Hector Brown,** CMG 1944; retired as Chairman, Tariff Board, Canada; *b* Priceville, Grey Co., Ont, 6 Dec. 1890; *s* of Neil McKinnon and Elizabeth Brown; *m* 1929, Phyllis, *d* of Aldham Wilson, Brandon, Man.; two *s*. *Educ:* Jarvis Coll. Inst., Toronto; Coll. Inst., Owen Sound, Ont; Normal Sch., Toronto. Past Commissioner of Tariff; Chm. Wartime Prices and Trade Board, 1940-41; Pres., Commodity Prices Stabilization Corporation, 1941-46; Mem., Economic Advisory Cttee; Dir, Canadian Commercial Corporation. Prior to 1926, was engaged in newspaper work in various capacities on staff of The Globe; served as agric. editor, western corresp., city editor, Parly corresp. and editorial writer; served in European War, 1914-18, as Adjt 110th Inf. Bn. Seconded in Eng. to RFC (despatches). Presbyterian. *Address:* 121 Carleton Road, Rockliffe Park, Ottawa, Ont, Canada.

**McKINNON, Sir James,** Kt 1956; Chief Inspector, Board of Customs and Excise, 1954-59; retired Dec. 1959; *b* 24 Sept. 1894; *m* 1919, Margaret Simpson; two *s* one *d*. *Educ:* Rothesay Academy. Entered Bd of Customs and Excise, 1914; Collector, Customs and Excise, Belfast, 1950-52; Dep. Chief Inspector, Bd of Customs and Excise, 1952-54. *Address:* 3 Gainsborough Terrace, Manor Road, Cheam, Surrey. *T:* 01-642 1659.

**MACKINNON, Col Lachlan,** CBE 1956; DSO 1919; TD; DL; MA, LLB; Advocate in Aberdeen; *b* 9 Sept. 1886; *s* of Lachlan Mackinnon and Theodora Thompson; *m* 1st, 1914, Marjory Gordon (*d* 1940); two *s* one *d*; 2nd, 1950, Ann Paul Scott. *Educ:* Robert Gordon's Coll. and University, Aberdeen; partner, 1909-66, in firm of L. Mackinnon and Son; Hon. Sheriff-Substitute for Aberdeenshire; Lecturer in International Law, University of Aberdeen, 1936-51. Commissioned to 4th Batt. Gordon Highlanders TA. 1905; Lt, 1906; Capt., 1910; served European war in France and Flanders for 35 months, Temp. Lt-Col comdg 14th (S) Batt. Argyll and Sutherland Highrs, 1918 (despatches twice, DSO, TD, Croix de Guerre, 1914-15 star); commanded 4th Gordon Highrs, 1920-23; Brevet Col; Chm. City of Aberdeen TA Assoc., 1934-37; Palmes d'Officer d'Académie, 1939; Médaille d'honneur, 1950; Médaille Civique, 1st class (Belgian), 1954. Chevalier de l'ordre de Léopold, 1956; Chevalier de la Légion d'Honneur, 1956. DL County of the City of Aberdeen, 1959. *Publications:* Leading Cases in the International Private Law of Scotland, 1934; Manual of Company Law and Conveyancing (Joint), 1939. *Recreations:* golf and fishing. *Address:* Woodcote, Torphins, Aberdeenshire. *T:* Torphins 292. *Club:* Royal Northern (Aberdeen).

**McKINNON, Neil Nairn,** QC 1957; **His Honour Judge McKinnon;** Barrister-at-Law, Lincoln's Inn, since 1937; an Additional Judge, Central Criminal Court, since 1968; *b* 19 Aug. 1909; *s* of late Neil Somerville and Christina McKinnon, Melbourne; *m* 1937, Janet, *d* of late Michael Lilley, Osterley; three *s* four *d*. *Educ:* Geelong Coll.; Trinity Hall, Cambridge (MA). Squadron Leader, RAFVR, Feb. 1940-Dec. 1945. Recorder of Maidstone, 1961-68. Bencher, Lincoln's Inn, 1964. *Recreation:* cricket. *Address:* 1 Harcourt Buildings, Temple, EC4. *T:* 01-353 9631; Thornbury, The Rose Walk, Purley, Surrey. *T:* 01-668 1582. *Clubs:* United University; Hawks (Cambridge).

**MacKINNON, Peter Ralph,** DSC 1942; Underwriting Member of Lloyd's; *b* 6 May 1911; *s* of Norman MacKinnon; *m* 1934, Jean Mary, *d* of G. N. Ogilvie; one *s* two *d*. *Educ:* Wellington Coll.; Jesus Coll., Cambridge. Entered Lloyd's, 1931; Underwriting Mem., 1932; Dep. Chm., 1964; Member: Cttee, Lloyd's Underwriters Assoc., 1958, 1964, 1968; Cttee of Lloyd's, 1961; Cttee Lloyd's Register of Shipping, 1958. Served War of 1939-45: RNVR, 1940; Combined Ops, Europe, N Africa, India, Malaya, Pacific (DSC, despatches twice); retd as Comdr RNVR, 1945. *Recreations:* golf, tennis. *Address:* Gorse Heath, Gerrards Cross, Bucks. *T:* Gerrards Cross 83451. *Clubs:* City University; All England Lawn Tennis; Denham Golf.

**McKINNON, Maj.-Gen. Walter Sneddon;** CB 1966; CBE 1961 (OBE 1947); Chairman, New Zealand Broadcasting Corporation, since 1969; *b* 8 July 1910; *s* of Charles McKinnon and Jessie Robertson McKinnon (*née* Sneddon); *m* 1937, Anna Bloomfield Plimmer; four *s* one *d*. *Educ:* Otago Boys High Sch., Dunedin, NZ; Otago Univ. (BSc); various military courses, including Staff Coll., Camberley, England. Entered NZ Government Service; commissioned in NZ Army, 1935. Served War of 1939-45: Pacific, Italy (Lt-Col; despatches), Japan (occupation) (OBE); Brigadier, 1953; subsequent appointments: Comdr, Southern Mil. Dist (NZ), 1953; Head, NZ Joint Mil. Mission, Washington, DC, 1954-57; Comdr, Northern Military District, 1957-58; Adjutant-General, 1958-62; Quartermaster-General, 1963-64, Maj.-General, 1965; Chief of the General Staff, NZ Army, 1965-67; retired, 1967. *Recreations:* golf and gardening. *Address:* 12 Ardal Grove, Melling, Lower Hutt, New Zealand. *T:* 63084. *Clubs:* Wellesley, United Services Officers' (Wellington); Wellington Golf (Heretaunga, NZ).

**MACKINTOSH,** family name of **Viscount Mackintosh of Halifax.**

**MACKINTOSH OF HALIFAX,** 2nd Viscount, *cr* 1957; Baron, *cr* 1948; Bt, *cr* 1935; **John Mackintosh,** BEM 1946; Director, John Mackintosh & Sons Ltd, since 1950; *b* 7 Oct. 1921; *s* of Harold Vincent Mackintosh (1st Viscount, Baron and Bt) and Constance (*née* Stoneham); *S* father, 1964; *m* 1st, 1946 (marr. diss., 1956); two *d*; 2nd, 1956, Gwynneth Charlesworth, *yr d* of Charles H. Gledhill, Halifax, Yorkshire; two *s*. *Educ:* Bedales Sch.;

Trinity Coll., USA. RAOC, 1942-47. Director: Tom Smith & Co. Ltd, 1956; Tudor Auto Services, 1961. President: Confectioners' Benevolent Fund, 1959-60 (Vice-Chm., 1964-67, Chm., 1967-); Leeds Inst. of Marketing, 1966-68; Chairman: Norwich Savings Cttee, 1965-; Inst. of Directors (Norwich Branch), 1968-; Governors, Town Close Preparatory Sch., Norwich; Governor, Earsham Hall Sch., Bungay. Hon. Treas., London Cttee, World Council Christian Education, 1965-. *Recreations:* cricket, tennis. *Heir: s* Hon. (John) Clive Mackintosh, *b* 9 Sept. 1958. *Address:* The Old Hall, Barford, Norwich, Norfolk NOR 38X. *T:* Barnham Broom 271. *Clubs:* Royal Automobile, MCC.

**MACKINTOSH, Hon. Lord; Charles Mackintosh,** MC; Hon. LLD (Edinburgh); Hon. Fellow, Wadham College, Oxford; one of the Senators of the College of Justice in Scotland, 1944-64; *b* 28 May 1888; *s* of Hugh and Henrietta I. Mackintosh; *m* 1921, Mary Lawrie Prosser; four *d. Educ:* Edinburgh Academy; Wadham Coll., Oxford; Edinburgh Univ. Called to Scots Bar, 1914; served European War, Gallipoli, Palestine, France, 1914-19; KC 1935; Sheriff of Argyll, 1937-42; Sheriff of Inverness, Elgin and Nairn, 1942-44. *Recreation:* golf. *Address:* 55 Northumberland Street, Edinburgh. *T:* 031-556 3681. *Club:* New (Edinburgh).

**MacKINTOSH, Angus MacKay,** CMG 1958; DK (Brunei) 1963; British High Commissioner in Ceylon and Ambassador to the Republic of Maldives, since 1969; *b* 23 July 1915; *s* of Angus MacKintosh, JP, Inverness; *m* 1947, Robina Marigold, *d* of J. A. Cochrane, MC; one *s* three *d. Educ:* Fettes Coll., Edinburgh; University College, Oxford (MA, BLitt). Agricultural Economics Research Institute, Oxford, 1938-41; Nuffield Colonial Research, Oxford, 1941-42. Served Army, 1942-46: Adjutant, 2nd Bn Queen's Own Cameron Highlanders; Major; despatches. Entered Colonial Office as Principal, 1946; Principal Private Secretary to Secretary of State, 1950; Assistant Secretary, 1952; seconded to Foreign Service as Dep. Commissioner-General for the UK in SE Asia, 1956-60; seconded to Cabinet Office, 1961-63; HM High Comr for Brunei, 1963-64; Asst Sec., Min. of Defence, 1964-65; Asst Under-Sec. of State, 1965-66; Senior Civilian Instructor, Imperial Defence Coll., 1966-68; Asst Under-Sec. of State, FCO, 1968-69. *Address:* c/o Foreign and Commonwealth Office, SW1; 17 Belsize Lane, NW3. *T:* 01-794 3570; Fenecreich, Gorthleck, Inverness-shire. *Clubs:* Oxford and Cambridge University, Royal Commonwealth Society.

**MACKINTOSH, Charles;** *see* Mackintosh, Hon. Lord.

**MACKINTOSH, (Charles Ernest Whistler) Christopher,** BA; Director: International Publicity and Advertising Ltd; Gillon & Co. Ltd; Five Ocean Film Co. Ltd; *b* 31 Oct. 1903; *e s* of late Charles E. Mackintosh, Chaville, France; *m* 1st, 1927, Lady Jean Douglas-Hamilton (divorced 1946), *e d* of 13th Duke of Hamilton; two *s* two *d*; 2nd, 1946, Irene, *d* of Colonel Mann Thomson, Melton Mowbray; one *s* one *d. Educ:* Eastbourne Coll.; University College, Oxford. Honours School of Mod. Hist.; Public Schools Doubles Tennis Champion, 1921; Oxford Rugby Blue and Athletic Blue; Scottish International Rugby; Olympic Games, 1924; Member of British Bobsleigh Team winning World Championships, 1937; Oxford University Ski Team; British Ski Team. Chairman and Managing Director of Sir Henry Lunn Ltd, and Alpine Sports Ltd, 1931-44. *Recreations:* Rugby football, cricket, athletics, golf, ski-ing, tennis, shooting, fishing. *Address:* Pebbles Court, Holyport, nr Maidenhead, Berks; 18 Half Moon Street, W1. *Clubs:* Bath, Queen's, Royal Automobile.

**MACKINTOSH, Christopher;** *see* Mackintosh, C. E. W. C.

**MACKINTOSH, David Forbes;** Headmaster of Loretto, 1945-60; retired; *b* 7 May 1900; *s* of late Very Rev. Professor H. R. Mackintosh, DD; *m* 1930, Caroline Elisabeth, *o d* of Cyril Meade-King, Clifton, Bristol; three *s* one *d. Educ:* Merchiston; Oriel Coll., Oxford (MA); Princeton Univ., NJ (AM). Assistant Master at Clifton Coll., 1924-45; Housemaster, 1930-45. Conroy Fellow, St Paul's Sch., USA, 1960. Chm., Scottish Assoc. of Boys' Clubs, 1962-69. *Recreation:* golf. *Address:* Dunmore, Hill Road, Gullane, East Lothian. *T:* Gullane 2234. *Clubs:* Public Schools; New (Edinburgh).

**MACKINTOSH, Duncan Robert,** CBE 1969 (OBE 1948); *b* 4 Oct. 1902; *s* of Duncan H. Mackintosh; *m* 1937, Mary Isa Grant; one *s* three *d. Educ:* RN Colleges Osborne and Dartmouth; University Coll., London. Joined Royal Dutch Shell Group of Oil Cos, 1923: served in China, 1924-33; Middle East, 1933-47; Gen. Manager, Cairo, Consolidated Petroleum Co. and Anglo-Egyptian Oilfields, 1945-47; Head of Personnel Admin., Shell Internat. Petroleum, 1952-58. Mem. British Council. Chm. Exec. Cttee, Voluntary Service Overseas, (VSO), 1962-70. *Publications:* (with Alan Ayling): A Collection of Chinese Lyrics, 1965; A Further Collection of Chinese Lyrics, 1969. *Recreations:* bird-watching, gardening. *Address:* Etchilhampton House, Devizes, Wilts. *T:* Devizes 2927. *Club:* Athenæum.

**MACKINTOSH, Eric Donald,** CBE 1949; Chairman: John Mackintosh & Sons Ltd, since 1965; Tom Smith & Co. Ltd, since 1951; Deputy Chairman, Rowntree Mackintosh Ltd; Vice-Chairman, East Anglian Trustee Savings Bank, since 1942; *b* 1906; *s* of late John Mackintosh, JP, Halifax; *m* 1928, Gwendolyn, *d* of H. L. France, Halifax; two *s* one *d. Educ:* Halifax New Sch.; Manchester Univ. Director, Cocoa Chocolate and Confectionery Division, Ministry of Food, 1942-45; President, Cocoa, Chocolate and Confectionery Alliance Ltd, 1946-48 (Vice-Pres., 1949-51; Treas., 1957-). Director: Norwich Union Fire Insurance Soc.; Norwich Union Life Insurance Soc.; Scottish Union & National Insurance Co. Ltd; Maritime Insurance Co. Ltd. JP, Norwich. *Recreations:* music, fishing. *Address:* Brooke House, Brooke, Norwich NOR 37W. *Clubs:* Royal Automobile; Norfolk (Norwich).

**MACKINTOSH, (Hugh) Stewart,** CBE 1956; Chairman, Scottish Sports Council, 1966-68; Chief Education Officer, Glasgow, 1944-68; *b* 1903; *s* of William Mackintosh, Helmsdale, Sutherland; *m* 1933, Mary, *d* of James Wilson. *Educ:* Helmsdale, Sutherland; Glasgow Univ. (MA, BSc, Med); Aberdeen Univ. (PhD). Director of Education: Wigtownshire, 1931-37; Aberdeen, 1937-44; Glasgow, 1944. FEIS 1958; Hon. LLD, Glasgow, 1969. *Address:* 12 Merrylee Road, Glasgow, S3; Bayview, Helmsdale, Sutherland.

**MACKINTOSH, John Pitcairn;** MP (Lab) Berwick and East Lothian since 1966; *b* 24 Aug. 1929; *s* of Colin M. Mackintosh and Mary Victoria (*née* Pitcairn); *m* 1963, Catherine Margaret Una Maclean; one *s. Educ:* Melville Coll., Edinburgh; Edinburgh, Oxford and Princeton Univs. DLitt Edinburgh, 1967. Asst Lectr, Glasgow Univ., 1953-54; Lectr in History, Edinburgh Univ., 1954-61; Sen. Lectr in Government, University of Ibadan, Nigeria, 1961-63; Senior Lecturer in Politics, Glasgow Univ., 1963-65; Professor of Politics, Univ. of Strathclyde, 1965-66. Member, Select Cttees on Agriculture, 1967-69, Scottish Affairs, 1968-70, Procedure, 1966-70; Vice-Chm., British Council GB/East Europe Centre. *Publications:* The British Cabinet, 1962; Nigerian Politics and Government, 1966; The Devolution of Power, 1968. *Recreations:* foreign travel, theatre. *Address:* Nether Liberton House, Gilmerton Road, Edinburgh. *T:* 031-664 3911. *Club:* Edinburgh University.

**MACKINTOSH, Captain Sir Kenneth (Lachlan),** KCVO 1966; Royal Navy (retired); Serjeant at Arms, House of Lords, 1962-70; Yeoman Usher of the Black Rod, 1953-70; Secretary to the Lord Great Chamberlain, 1953-70; *b* 6 July 1902; *s* of Stewart Mackintosh and Alice Ballard; *m* 1st, 1929, Elizabeth (*d* 1960), *d* of Captain Bertram Fawcett; two *s* one *d* (and one *s* decd); 2nd, 1962, Yolande, *d* of Leonard Bickford-Smith. *Educ:* RN Colleges, Osborne and Dartmouth. Directing Staff of RN Staff Coll., 1938; served in: French Fleet, 1939; HMS Duke of York, 1940; HMS Fencer (comd), 1945; HMS Liverpool (comd), and as Chief of Staff to Earl Mountbatten, 1948; Naval Attaché, Paris, 1950; retired, 1953. *Address:* Windalls, Slinfold, Sussex. *T:* Slinfold 242.

**MACKINTOSH, Stewart;** *see* Mackintosh, H. S.

**MACKINTOSH, William Archibald,** CC (Canada), 1967; CMG 1946; *b* 21 May 1895; *s* of William and Agnes Cowie Mackintosh; *m* 1928, Jean Easton; one *d*. *Educ:* Queen's Univ., Kingston (MA 1916); Harvard Univ. (PhD 1922). Department of Political and Economic Science, Queen's Univ., Kingston, Ontario, Canada, 1920-51; Vice-Chancellor and Principal, 1951-61; Vice-Chancellor, 1961-65; Member of National Employment Commission, 1936-38; Research Adviser, Royal Commission on Dominion-Provincial Relations, 1938-39; on leave of absence, 1939-46 to serve in various capacities in Departments of Finance and Reconstruction and Supply, Ottawa. Chairman of Council, Association of Universities of British Commonwealth, 1954. President, Royal Society of Canada, 1956-57. Member, Canada Council, 1957-60. Member Cttee on Organization of Government of Ontario, 1958-59; Member Royal Commission on Banking and Finance, 1962-64; Director, Bank of Canada, 1964-70. Canada Council Medal, 1966; Innis-Gerin Medal, Royal Society of Canada, 1967. *Publications:* Agricultural Cooperation in Western Canada, 1924; Prairie Settlement (Canadian Frontiers of Settlement), 1934; Economic Problems of the Prairie Provinces (Canadian Frontiers of Settlement), 1935; Economic Background of Dominion-Provincial Relations (Appendix 2 of Report of Royal Commission on Dominion-Provincial Relations), 1940. *Address:* Alwington Place, Kingston, Canada.

**McKISACK, Prof. May;** Emeritus Professor of History, University of London, since 1967; *b* 30 March 1900; *o d* of Audley John McKisack, solicitor, Belfast, and Elizabeth (*née* McCullough). *Educ:* Bedford High Sch.; Somerville Coll., Oxford. Mary Somerville Research Fellow, Somerville Coll., Oxford, 1925-28; Lecturer in Mediæval History, University of Liverpool, 1927-35. Fellow and Tutor, Somerville Coll., 1936-55; University Lecturer, 1945-55; Professor of History, University of London (Westfield Coll.), 1955-67; Hon. Fellow, Somerville Coll., 1956; James Bryce Memorial Lecturer, Somerville Coll., 1959; Member of UGC Cttee on Teaching Methods in Universities, 1961. Visiting Professor, Vassar Coll., USA, 1967-68. FRHistS 1928; FSA 1952. *Publications:* The Parliamentary Representation of the English Boroughs in the Middle Ages, 1932; The Fourteenth Century, 1959; articles, reviews in English Historical Review, Review of English Studies, Medium Aevum, etc. *Address:* 36 Chalfont Road, Oxford. *T:* Oxford 58494.

**McKISSOCK, Wylie,** OBE 1946; MS (London), FRCS; Consulting Neurological Surgeon in London, since 1936; Neurological Surgeon, National Hospital for Nervous Diseases, Queen Square and Metropolitan Ear, Nose and Throat Hospital; Neurological Surgeon, Hospital for Sick Children, Great Ormond Street; Neurological Surgeon, St Andrew's Hospital, Northampton; Visiting Neurological Surgeon, Graylingwell Hospital, Chichester, St James's Hospital, Portsmouth, Belmont Hospital, Sutton, and Park Prewett Hospital, Basingstoke; Associate Neurological Surgeon, Royal Marsden Hospital; Director of Institute of Neurology, Queen Square; Surgeon in Charge, Department of Neuro-Surgery, Atkinson Morley Hospital branch of St George's Hospital; Hon. Civil Consultant in Neuro-Surgery to RAF; Hon. Neurological Surgeon, Welsh Regional Hospital Board; Teacher of Surgery, St George's Hospital Medical School (University of London); Member, Panel of Consultants, Royal Navy, British European Airways, British Overseas Airways Corporation; *b* 27 Oct. 1906; *s* of late Alexander Cathie McKissock; *m* 1934, Rachel, *d* of Leonard Marcus Jones, Beckenham, Kent; one *s* two *d*. *Educ:* King's Coll. and St George's Hospital, University of London. Junior University Schol., St George's Hospital, 1928; Laking Memorial Prize, 1932-33 and 1933-34; Rockefeller Schol. in Neuro-Surgery, 1937-38; Casualty Officer, House Surgeon, House Physician, House Surgeon to Ear, Nose, Throat and Eye Depts, Assistant Curator of Museum, Surgical Registrar, Surgical Chief Asst, St George's Hosp.; Surgical Registrar, Maida Vale Hosp. for Nervous Diseases, Hosp. for Sick Children, Great Ormond St, and Victoria Hospital for Children, Tite St. FRSM; Fellow, Society of British Neurological Surgeons (President, 1966); FFR (Hon.) 1962; Corresponding Member, American Association of Neurological Surgeons, 1968. Hon. DSc, Newcastle upon Tyne, 1966. *Publications:* contributions to medical journals. *Recreations:* wine, food, gardening, ornithology, literature and antagonism to Bureaucracy. *Address:* The National Hospital, Queen Square, WC1. *T:* 01-837 2503 (Secretary and Office, 01-946 7711). *Club:* Hanstown.

**MACKLEN, Victor Harry Burton;** Deputy Chief Scientific Adviser (Projects and Nuclear), Ministry of Defence, since 1969; *b* 13 July 1919; *s* of H. Macklen and A. C. Macklen, Brighton, Sussex; *m* 1950, Ursula Irene Fellows; one *d*. *Educ:* Varndean Sch., Brighton; King's Coll., London. Air Defence Experimental Establishment, 1941; Operational Research Group, 1942; served Army, 1943-49; WO Scientific Staff, 1949-51; Head, Operational Research Section, BAOR, 1951-54; MoD Scientific Staff, 1954-60; Head, Technical Secretariat Reactor Group, UKAEA, 1960-64; Dep. Director, Technical Operations Reactor Group, UKAEA, 1966-67; Asst Chief Scientific Adviser (Studies and Nuclear), MoD, 1967-69. *Address:* Stepp House, Hartlip, near Sittingbourne, Kent. *T:* Newington 591; The Thatch, Burton, near Christchurch, Hants. *T:* Christchurch 3424. *Club:* Army and Navy.

**MACKLEY, Garnet Hercules,** CMG 1938; MLC, 1950; *b* Port Chalmers, 9 Dec. 1883; *s* of John Charles Mackley and Esther Styles; *m* 1914, Isabel Robertson; one *s. Educ:* Grammar Sch., Invercargill. Cadet in clerical division, Traffic Branch, NZ. Government Railways Department, 1900; had varied experience in railway work in all parts of Dominion in executive capacity; promoted through various ranks of District Office and Head Office; Chief Clerk, Railways Head Office, Wellington, 1928; Assistant General Manager, 1931; General Manager, 1933-40. MP for Masterton, 1943-46; for Wairarapa, 1946-49; MLC, 1950. *Recreations:* fishing, racing, golf, swimming, field athletics. *Address:* Tamatea, 72 Marine Parade, Paraparaumu Beach, Wellington, NZ. *T:* 1278D.

**MACKLEY, George,** RE 1961 (ARE 1950); *b* 13 May 1900; *m* 1927, Caroline Toller, Hemingford Grey; no *c. Educ:* Judd Sch., Tonbridge. Art master, various schools in Kent and Surrey, 1921-45; Headmaster, Thames Ditton Primary Sch., 1945-53; Headmaster, Sutton East Secondary Sch. and Art Department, 1953-60. Associate Soc. of Wood Engravers, 1946. Mem., 1948; Mem., Art Workers' Guild, 1959. Works in permanent collections: Victoria and Albert Museum; Ashmolean Museum; Fitzwilliam Museum; South London Art Gallery; Nat. Museum of Art, Stockholm; Hunt Botanical Library, Pittsburgh. *Publication:* Wood Engraving, 1948. *Recreations:* lurking by, and drawing, waterways and canal and river craft. *Address:* 7 Higham Lane, Tonbridge, Kent. *T:* Tonbridge 3968.

**MACKLIN, Sir Albert Sortain Romer,** Kt 1946; Indian Civil Service (retired); *b* 4 March 1890; *s* of late Albert Romer Macklin, County Court Judge, and Kate, *d* of Benjamin Warren, of Deal; *m* 1920, Marjorie Vivian, MBE, 1943, *d* of late G. H. Kent; one *d. Educ:* Westminster; Christ Church, Oxford. Entered ICS, 1913; posted to Bombay Presidency; Puisne Judge, High Court, Bombay, 1935-47. Chairman Medical Appeal Tribunal, Liverpool, 1952-62. *Recreations:* fishing, sailing. *Address:* 32b St John's Road, Eastbourne, Sussex. *Club:* Flyfishers'.

**MACKNIGHT, Dame Ella (Annie Noble),** DBE 1969; Hon. Consultant Obstetrician and Gynaecologist, Queen Victoria Hospital, Melbourne, since 1964; *b* 7 Aug. 1904; 4th *d* of Dr Conway Macknight. *Educ:* Toorak Coll., Melbourne; Univ. of Melbourne, resident student, Janet Clarke Hall. MB, BS 1928; MD Melbourne 1931; DCO Melbourne 1936; MRCOG 1951; FRCOG 1958. Hon. Obstetrician and Gynaecologist, Queen Victoria Hosp., Melbourne, 1935-64; Vice-Pres., Queen Victoria Hosp., Melbourne, 1965-; Hon. Sec., 1963-67, Vice-Pres., 1967-70, Pres., 1970-, Australian Council, RCOG. *Recreation:* golf. *Address:* 692 Toorak Road, Malvern, Victoria 3144, Australia. *Clubs:* Lyceum (Melbourne); Royal Melbourne Golf.

**MACKWORTH, Commander Sir David Arthur Geoffrey,** 9th Bt, *cr* 1776; RN retired; *b* 13 July 1912; *o s* of late Vice-Admiral Geoffrey Mackworth, CMG, DSO, and Noel Mabel, *d* of late William I. Langford; *S* uncle, 1952; *m* 1941, Mary Alice, *d* of Thomas Henry Grylls, 26 Great Ormond Street, WC1; one *s. Educ:* Farnborough Sch., Hants; RNC Dartmouth. Joined RN 1926; served HMS Eagle, HMS Suffolk, 1939-45; Commander, 1948; Naval Adviser to Director of Guided Weapon Research and Development, Ministry of Supply, 1945-49; retired, 1956. *Heir: s* Digby John Mackworth, *b* 2 Nov. 1945. *Club:* Royal Naval (Portsmouth).

**MACKWORTH-YOUNG, Robert Christopher;** *see* Young, R. C. M.

**McLACHLAN, Angus Henry;** Director, John Fairfax Ltd, Publishers of Sydney Morning Herald, Australian Financial Review, Sun, Sun-Herald, etc (Managing Director, 1965-69); *b* 29 March 1908; *s* of James H. and Mabel McLachlan; unmarried. *Educ:* Scotch Coll., Melbourne; University of Melbourne. Melbourne Herald, 1928-36; joined Sydney Morning Herald, 1936; News Editor, 1937-49; General Manager, John Fairfax & Sons Ltd, 1949-64. Director: Australian Associated Press Pty Ltd (Chairman, 1958-59, 1964-65); Reuters Ltd, London, 1966-. Amalgamated Television Services Pty Ltd, 1955-; Macquarie Broadcasting Holdings Ltd, 1966-; David Syme & Co. Ltd, Publishers of The Age, 1970-; Federal Capital Press Ltd, Publishers of Canberra Times, 1970-; Mem. Council, Public Library of NSW, 1966-; Member, Sydney University Extension Board, 1960-. *Address:* c/o John Fairfax Ltd, Box 506, GPO, Sydney, NSW 2001, Australia. *T:* 20-944. *Clubs:* London Press; Australian, University, Union (Sydney); Royal Sydney Yacht Squadron.

**McLACHLAN, Donald Harvey,** OBE 1945; author and journalist; *b* 25 Sept. 1908; *s* of David James McLachlan, London; *m* 1934, Katherine, *d* of late N. Bishop Harman, FRCS; three *s* one *d. Educ:* City of London School; Magdalen Coll., Oxford. 1st class PPE, 1930; Laming Fellow, Queen's Coll., Oxford, 1932-33; Editorial staff of The Times, 1933-36; Assistant Master, Winchester Coll., 1936-38; Editor, The Times Educational Supplement, 1938-40. Naval Intelligence, 1940-45; Assistant Editor (Foreign), The Economist, 1947-54; Deputy Editor of the Daily Telegraph, 1954-60; Editor, Sunday Telegraph, 1961-66. Visiting Fellow of Nuffield Coll., Oxford, 1960-68. Member, General Advisory Council, BBC, 1961-65. *Publications:* Room 39: A Study in Naval Intelligence, 1968; In the Chair: Barrington-Ward of The Times, 1970. *Recreations:* music, walking. *Address:* Coneycroft, Selborne, Hants. *T:* Selborne 224, (in London) 01-834 2012. *Club:* Brooks's.

**McLACHLAN, Gordon,** CBE 1967; BCom; FCA; Secretary, Nuffield Provincial Hospitals Trust, since 1956; *b* 12 June 1918; *s* of late Gordon and Mary McLachlan; *m* 1951, Monica Mary Griffin; two *d. Educ:* Leith Academy; Edinburgh Univ. Served with RNVR, 1939-46; Gunnery Specialist, 1943-46. Accountant, Edinburgh Corp., 1946-48; Dep. Treas., NW Met. Regional Hosps Bd, 1948-53; Accountant Nuffield Foundn, Nuffield Provincial Hosps Trust, Nat. Corp. for Care of Old People, 1953-56. Asst Dir, Nuffield Foundn, 1955-56. Henry Cohen Lectr, Univ. of Jerusalem, 1969. Consultant, American Hospitals Assoc. and American Hospitals Research and Educational Trust, 1964-65; Member Council, American Hospitals Research and Educational Trust, 1965-; Consulting Editor, Health Services Research Journal (US), 1966-. *Publications:* (ed) Casualty Services and Their Setting, 1960; (ed) Problems and Progress in Medical Care, 1964, 1966, 1968, 1970; (ed jtly) Computers in Service of Medicine, I and II, 1968; (ed jtly) In the Beginning, 1970; contrib. to Lancet, Practitioner, Times, Twentieth Century, etc. *Recreations:* reading, watching ballet, theatre, Rugby football. *Address:* 95 Ravenscourt Road, W6. *T:* 01-748 8211. *Club:* Caledonian.

**McLACHLAN, Air Vice-Marshal Ian Dougald,** CB 1966; CBE 1954; DFC 1940; Chairman,

Mainline Corporation; Consultant, Northrop Corporation; company director; *b* Melbourne, 23 July 1911; *s* of Dougald McLachlan, author and teacher, and Bertha Frances (*née* Gilliam); *m* 1946, Margaret Helen Chrystal (marr. diss. 1968); one *d*. *Educ:* Melbourne High Sch.; Royal Military Coll., Duntroon. CO 3 Squadron RAAF, Egypt, 1940-41; CO 81 Wing RAAF, Labuan, 1945; SASO, HQ, British Commonwealth Air Forces in Japan, 1945-48; Air Cdre, Operations, RAAF, 1948-51; Imperial Defence Coll., 1954; Dir, Flying Trng, Air Min., London 1955-56; AOC Trng Comd, 1957-59; Dep. Chief of Air Staff, Australia, 1959-61; Australian Defence Adviser, Washington, 1962-63; Air Mem. for Supply and Equipment, Australian Air Bd, 1964-68. *Recreations:* tennis, squash, golf. *Address:* 4 Mitchell Road, Darling Point, NSW 2027, Australia. *T:* 32-7997. *Clubs:* Australian (Sydney); Naval and Military (Melbourne); Royal Wimbledon Golf, Melbourne Cricket, Royal Canberra Golf, Royal Sydney Golf.

**MacLACHLAN, Robert Boyd,** CIE 1935; MInstCE; Superintending Engineer, Indian Service of Engineers (retired); *b* 5 Sept. 1880; *s* of James Boyd and Mary Sinclair MacLachlan; unmarried. *Educ:* Rutland Coll., Dublin; Queen's Coll., Galway. Graduated from the Royal University of Ireland in Degrees of Arts and Engineering in 1902, and 1903; Assistant Engineer in the Indian Public Works Department, 1905; served in the Irrigation Department in the Bombay Presidency and in Sind, 1905-22; Under Secretary to Government in the Public Works Department, 1923; Superintending Engineer in charge of the Western Circle of the Lloyd Barrage and Canal Construction Project, 1923-33; a Member of the Sind Administrative Cttee, 1934. *Recreations:* shooting, fishing, riding. *Address:* Albert Place, Kilkee, Co. Clare. *Clubs:* East India and Sports; Sind (Karachi).

**MACLACHLAN, Thomas Kay,** MA, MB, BCh (Cambridge), FRCPE, FRFP&S; late Area Consultant Physician, Counties of Stirling, Clackmannan and West Perth; Member Associations of: Physicians of Great Britain; British Neurologists; International Society of Internal Medicine; Physician for Diseases of the Nervous System, Victoria Infirmary, Glasgow; Senior Assistant Physician, Glasgow Royal Infirmary; Consulting Neurologist, Glasgow Eye Infirmary; Physician, Glasgow Royal Cancer Hospital; Medical Specialist to Ministry of Pensions; Examiner in Neurology and Psychiatry for Fellowship of Royal Faculty of Physicians and Surgeons; *b* 17 Feb. 1895; *s* of Lachlan Maclachlan, Dainabruaich, Helensburgh; *m* Sarah, *yr d* of John Nelson, Eaglesfield, Dumfriesshire; one *s* one *d*. *Educ:* Merchiston Castle Sch.; Pembroke Coll., Cambridge; London, Strassburg, Paris. Fearnsides Research Scholar in Nervous Diseases, Cambridge Univ.; Foulis Memorial Scholar, Glasgow Univ. Served European War, 1914-17, Argyll and Sutherland Highlanders (wounded). *Publications:* Familial Periodic Paralysis; Disseminated Encephalomyelitis after Spinal Anæsthesia; Narcolepsy; The Liver Treatment of Pernicious Anæmia; Diabetes and its Complications since the Institution of Insulin Therapy. *Recreations:* golf and gardening. *Address:* Leewood House, Dunblane, Perthshire. *T:* Dunblane 2161.

**MACLAGAN, Noel Francis,** DSc, MD, FRCP, FRIC; Professor of Chemical Pathology in University of London at Westminster Medical School; Chemical Pathologist; Westminster Hospital; *b* 1904; *y s* of late Oscar Frederick and Ada Maclagan, Newcastle and London; *m* 1933, Annemarie, *d* of Curt and Marie Herzog, London; one *s* one *d*. *Educ:* University Coll. Sch.; University Coll., London (First Cl. Hons BSc Chemistry, 1925); Middlesex Hosp. Medical School (MSc London in Biochemistry, 1933). DSc London, 1946; MD London, 1935; MRCP, 1933; FRIC 1946; FRCP 1952. Asst in Courtauld Inst. of Biochemistry, Middlesex Hosp., 1926-33; House Physician Middlesex Hosp., 1932; whole-time worker for Medical Research Council, 1933-34; Biochemist, Westminster Hosp., 1935-46; Pathologist, EMS, 1939-45; Chemical Pathologist at Westminster Hosp. Medical Sch., 1946-47. *Publications:* contributions to medical textbooks on various biochemical subjects and articles in scientific journals on thymol turbidity test, thyroid function, lipid metabolism, etc. *Recreations:* music and chess. *Address:* Chelsworth, 6 Fitzalan Road, N3. *T:* 01-346 0921; Westminster Medical School, Page Street Wing, SW1. *T:* 01-828 9811. *Clubs:* Athenæum, Savage.

**MACLAGAN, William Gauld,** MA (Oxford), PhD (Edinburgh); Professor of Moral Philosophy, University of Glasgow, 1946-69; *b* 22 April 1903; 2nd *s* of Rev. P. J. Maclagan, DD, and of Emily Elizabeth Gauld; *m* 1943, Catharine Hannah Mair; one *s* one *d*. *Educ:* City of London Sch.; Exeter Coll., Oxford; Edinburgh Univ. Assistant, Department of Logic and Metaphysics, Edinburgh Univ., 1928-29; Lecturer in Philosophy, Oriel Coll., Oxford, 1930-46; Fellow, 1931-46. Temporary Civil Servant, HM Treasury, 1940-46. Edward Cadbury Lecturer, Birmingham Univ., 1955-56. *Publications:* The Theological Frontier of Ethics, 1961; papers in various philosophical journals. *Address:* Dunrivach, Aberfoyle, Stirling. *T:* Aberfoyle 332.

**McLAREN,** family name of **Baron Aberconway.**

**MacLAREN, Andrew;** *b* 1883; *s* of John MacLaren of Glasgow; two *s*. *Educ:* Technical Coll. and School of Art, Glasgow. MP (Lab) Burslem Div. of Stoke-on-Trent, 1922-23, 1924-31 and 1935-45. *Address:* 5 St Oswald's Studios, Sedlescombe Road, SW6. *T:* 01-385 0877. *Clubs:* Beefsteak, Garrick.

**MacLAREN, Sir Hamish (Duncan),** KBE 1951; CB 1946; DFC; Director of Electrical Engineering, Admiralty, 1945-60; *b* 7 April 1898; *s* of Rev. Peter MacLaren, MA, and Constance Hamilton Simpson; *m* 1927, Lorna Cicely, *d* of late Dr R. P. N. B. Bluett, MC, Harrow; one *s* one *d*. *Educ:* Fordyce Academy, Banffshire; Edinburgh Univ. (BSc 1921). Served European war, 1914-18, in RNVR, RNAS and RAF (DFC and Bar, French Croix de Guerre with Palm). After completing degree at Edinburgh Univ. in 1921 joined British Thomson Houston Co., Rugby, as student apprentice. Awarded Bursary by Commission for Exhibition of 1851 for 1921-23; British Thomson Houston Fellowship to spend one year with the GE Co. of Schenectady, USA, 1923-24; on staff of British Thomson Houston, Rugby, 1924-26; joined Admiralty Service as Asst Electrical Engineer, 1926. In Admiralty Service at HM Dockyards, Chatham, Devonport, at Dir of Dockyards Dept, Admiralty, 1933-37, and in Ceylon, 1931-33; Superintending Electrical Engineer, HM Naval Base, Singapore, 1937-40; Asst Dir, Electrical Engineering Dept, Admiralty, 1940-45. Pres. Instn of Electrical Engineers, 1960-61. Consultant to Yarrows Ltd. Hon. LLD St Andrews, 1954; Hon. DSc Bath, 1970. *Address:* 104 Heath Road, Petersfield, Hants. *T:* Petersfield 4562.

**McLAREN, Prof. Hugh Cameron;** Professor of Obstetrics and Gynæcology, University of Birmingham, since 1951; *b* 25 April 1913; *s* of John and Flora McLaren, Glasgow; *m* 1939, Lois Muirhead, Bridge of Weir, Scotland; one *s* six *d*. *Educ:* High Sch. of Glasgow; Univ. of Glasgow; postgraduate studies Glasgow and Aberdeen. MB, ChB Glasgow 1936; MD (Glasgow). Served RAMC, 1941-46; Surgical Specialist (Lt-Col). Univ. of Birmingham, 1946, Reader, 1949. FRCPGlas; FRCSE; FRCOG. *Publications:* contribs to Journal of Obstetrics and Gynæcology, Lancet, Brit. Med. Jl, etc. *Recreations:* golf, gardening. *Address:* 26 Ampton Road, Birmingham 15. *T:* 021-440 3223.

**McLAREN, John Watt,** MA, FRCP, FFR; Physician in charge of X-Ray Department, St Thomas' Hospital, since 1946; *b* 26 Nov. 1906; *s* of John McLaren and Florence Mary Atkinson. *Educ:* Cheltenham Coll.; Univ. of Cambridge and St Thomas' Hospital, London. MA (Cantab); FRCP; MRCPE; FFR. Junior appointments at St Thomas' Hosp., 1932-35; Chief Asst, X-Ray Dept, 1935-39. Radiologist, Queen Mary's Hosp., East End, 1935-38. Cons. Radiologist, Metropolitan Police, 1946-; Examiner in Radiology, Univs of London and Edinburgh and Faculty of Radiologists; Underwriter at Lloyd's, 1948. *Publications:* (ed) Modern Trends in Diagnostic Radiology, Series 1, 2, 3, 1948, 1953, 1960; various papers in radiological journals. *Recreations:* motoring, travelling, sailing. *Address:* St Thomas' Hospital, SE1. *T:* 01-928 5656; 118 Castelnau, Barnes, SW13. *T:* 01-748 6101. *Club:* Royal Automobile.

**McLAREN, Martin;** MP (C) Bristol North-West, 1959-66 and since 1970; Parliamentary Private Secretary to Secretary of State for Foreign and Commonwealth Affairs, since 1970; *b* 11 Jan. 1914; *s* of late Hon. Francis McLaren and of Lady Freyberg, *qv*; *m* 1943, Nancy Ralston; two *s* (and one *s* decd). *Educ:* Eton Coll. (Scholar); New Coll., Oxford; Harvard Univ. (Henry Fellow). Asst Principal, Home Office, 1938. Served War of 1939-45, Grenadier Guards, Major. Principal, Home Office, 1946-47. Barrister, Middle Temple, 1948. An Asst Govt Whip, 1961-63; a Lord Comr of the Treasury, 1963-64; an Opposition Whip, 1964-66. Director: Scientific & Electronic Industries Trust Ltd; Archway Investment Co. Ltd. *Recreation:* squash rackets (half-blue). *Address:* 30 Smith Square, SW1. *T:* 01-222 6626. *Clubs:* Brooks's, Carlton; Constitutional (Bristol).

**McLAREN, Moray;** Author; *b* 24 March 1901; *s* of John Shaw McLaren, MD, FRCS, and Eva Helen Inglis; *m* 1946, Lennox Milne (OBE 1956). *Educ:* Merchiston Castle; Corpus Christi Coll., Cambridge. Studied in Paris, 1924-25. Asst editor, The London Mercury, under Sir John Squire; joined BBC staff, 1928; first asst editor upon foundation of The Listener, 1929; first Programme Director for Scotland, 1933; Asst Dir talks, then Features and Drama, 1935-40; attached to Foreign Office as Head of Polish Region Political Intelligence Dept, 1940-45; then returned to live in Edinburgh and write. *Publications:* Return to Scotland; A Wayfarer in Poland; The Noblest Prospect (novel); Poland's Progress; Escape and Return (novel); A Dinner with the Dead (Short Stories); Stern and Wild; By Me . . . (A Shakespearean Study); The Unpossesed (novel); The Capital of Scotland; Stevenson and Edinburgh; A Small Stir–Letters on the English (with James Bridie); The Scots (Pelican); A Singing Reel; Scotland in Colour; The Highland Jaunt; Lord Lovat of The '45; Understanding the Scots; The Pursuit (novel); Fishing As We Find It (with Gen. R. N. Stewart); The Wisdom of the Scots; Union Compleat (satire); If Freedom Fail; The Shell Guide to Scotland; Corsica Boswell; Rivers and Lochs of Scotland (with W. B. Currie); Walter Scott, Man and Patriot: A Biographical Study; The Intuitive Prince (biography); plays: One Traveller Returns; Heather on Fire (award Foyle Trust); The Non-Resident; Muckle Ado. Author of many radio plays and feature programmes. Regular literary reviewer, The Glasgow Herald, The Scotsman, and other jls. *Recreations:* trout-fishing, travel and croquet (Founder and first Pres. of Edinburgh Croquet Club). *Address:* Peg de Lone, Station Avenue, Haddington, East Lothian. *Clubs:* Savile; Scottish Arts, Edinburgh Croquet (Edinburgh).

**McLAREN, Ross Scott,** DSO 1940; OBE 1964 (MBE 1945); TD 1944; DL; JP; BSc; retired as Production Director, Northumberland and Durham Division, National Coal Board, 1966; *b* 3 March 1906; *s* of late H. B. McLaren, Lumley Grange, Fence Houses, Co. Durham; *m* 1935, Marjorie Stratton; two *d*. *Educ:* Rossall Sch.; King's Coll., Durham Univ. Mining Engineer (MIME). JP 1950. *Address:* The Dene, Riding Mill, Northumberland.

**McLAUCHLAN, Madeline Margaret Nicholls;** Head Mistress, North London Collegiate School, since 1965; *b* 4 June 1922; *o c* of late Robert and Gertrude McLauchlan, Birmingham. *Educ:* King Edward VI Grammar Sch. for Girls, Camp Hill, Birmingham; Royal Holloway College, University of London. Asst Mistress: Shrewsbury High Sch., GPDST, 1944; Manchester High Sch., 1952. Senior Walter Hines Page Scholar, English-Speaking Union, 1955. Head Mistress, Henrietta Barnett Sch., 1958. Member: Exec. Cttee, Assoc. of Head Mistresses, 1966; Education Cttee, English Speaking Union, 1966; Exec. Cttee, Universities' Central Council on Admissions, 1968; Governor of Imperial Coll., 1968. *Recreations:* music, mountain walking, housekeeping. *Address:* North London Collegiate School, Canons, Edgware, Mddx. *T:* 01-952 0912. *Club:* English-Speaking Union.

**McLAUGHLAN, Rear-Adm. Ian David,** CB 1970; DSC 1941 and Bar, 1953; Admiral Commanding Reserves and Director General, Naval Recruiting, since 1970; *b* 2 May 1919; *s* of Richard John and Margaret McLaughlan; *m* 1942, Charity Pomeroy Simonds; two *d*. *Educ:* St Paul's Sch. Entered Navy, 1937; served in destroyers, 1940-45 (despatches three times); comd HMS: Flint Castle, 1948-50; Concord, 1950-52; jssc 1952; Armed Forces Staff Coll., Norfolk, Va, 1953; HMS Jupiter, 1953-55; comd HMS: Chieftain, 1955; Chevron, 1955-56 (despatches); Staff of C-in-C, Portsmouth, 1957-59; Asst Dir of Plans, Admty, 1959-61; Capt. (F), 2nd Frigate Sqdn, 1961-62; idc 1963; Dir, Naval Ops and Trade, 1964-66; comd HMS Hampshire, 1966-67; Chief of Staff to Comdr Far East Fleet, 1967-70. Comdr 1951; Capt. 1958; Rear-Adm. 1968. Commendador d'Aviz, 1956. *Recreations:* gardening, house husbandry. *Address:* The Five Gables, Mayfield, Sussex. *T:* Mayfield 2218. *Club:* United Service.

**McLAUGHLAN, Roy James Philip,** CMG 1955; CVO 1956; Inspector-General of Police, Nigeria, retired 1956; *b* 25 July 1898; *s* of late Henry Peter Marius McLaughlan and late Elfrida Greenwood; *m* 1931, Catherine Elizabeth Plaisted, *d* of late Lt-Col Thomas Valentine Plaisted McCammon and Charlotte Amelia Garratt. *Educ:* The English Sch., Cyprus; Stonyhurst Coll., Lancs. Gen. Staff Intelligence, Macedonia, Greece and Turkey,

1917-23. Inspector and Surveyor of Roads, Cyprus, 1925; Nigeria: Asst Supt Police, 1927; Supt, 1944; Asst Comr, 1949; Comr, 1951; Inspector-Gen., 1952. Colonial Police Medal, 1942; King's Police Medal, 1950. OStJ 1955. *Recreations:* shooting and bridge. *Address:* 7 Rosemary Park, Belfast, N Ireland. *T:* Belfast 665755.

**McLAUGHLIN, Charles Redmond,** MA, MB, ChB, BChir, FRCSE; Hon. consultant Plastic Surgeon: Queen Victoria Hospital, East Grinstead, since 1948; Kent and Canterbury Hospital, Canterbury, since 1953; St Bartholomew's Hospital, Rochester, since 1962; *b* 1 Oct. 1909; *s* of late W. H. McLaughlin, JP, DL and Emma Margaret Brough (*née* Warren); *m* 1936, Rosemary Macdonald; two *s* one *d*. *Educ:* Rugby Sch.; Emmanuel Coll., Cambridge; University of Edinburgh. House Phys, Royal Infirmary, Edinburgh; House Surg., Royal Hants County Hosp., Winchester, 1935; Hon. Surg. to Out-patients, Royal Surrey County Hosp., Guildford, 1937-38. Served with RAFVR, Medical Br., 1940-45; Wing Comdr i/c surgical div., 1945. EMS Surg., Queen Victoria Hosp., E Grinstead, 1946-48; Cons. Surg. to SE Metrop. Regional Hosp. Bd, 1948-69. Founder Mem. Brit. Assoc. of Plastic Surgeons, 1948 (Hon. Sec., 1957-59; Mem. Coun., 1960-62); Mem. Ed. Bd, Brit. Jl of Plastic Surgery, 1950-69; Chm. of Adv. Cttee on Plastic Surgery to Regional Bd, 1964-69. *Publications:* Plastic Surgery, 1951; chapters in several surgical textbooks; articles in British, American and French jls; editorials in Lancet. *Recreation:* music. *Address:* The Oast, Mayfield, Sussex. *T:* Mayfield 3064.

**McLAUGHLIN, Mrs Patricia;** *b* 23 June 1916; *o d* of late Canon F. B. Aldwell; *m* 1937, Henry, *o s* of late Major W. McLaughlin, of McLaughlin & Harvey Ltd, London, Belfast and Dublin; one *s* two *d*. *Educ:* Ashleigh House, Belfast; Trinity Coll., Dublin. MP (UU) Belfast West, 1955-64; Past Chm., Unionist Soc.; Vice-Chm., Women's National Advisory Cttee of Cons. Party. Has been active in voluntary work for many years; Mem., Inst. of Health Education; Vice-Pres., Royal Society for Prevention of Accidents. *Recreations:* talking and travelling. *Address:* The Grey House, Craigavad, Co. Down. *T:* Holywood 2885; 2 Buckingham Palace Mansions, SW1. *Clubs:* Constitutional, Royal Commonwealth Society.

**MACLAY,** family name of **Baron Maclay** and **Viscount Muirshiel.**

**MACLAY,** 3rd Baron *cr* 1922, of Glasgow; **Joseph Paton Maclay;** Bt 1914; *b* 11 April 1942; *s* of 2nd Baron Maclay, KBE, and of Nancy Margaret, *d* of R. C. Greig, Hall of Caldwell, Uplawmoor, Renfrewshire; *S* father, 1969. *Educ:* Winchester. *Heir: b* Hon. David Milton Maclay, *b* 21 March 1944. *Address:* Duchal, Kilmacolm, Renfrewshire.

**MACLEAN, Alistair;** author; *b* Scotland, 1922; *m* Gisela Maclean; three *s*. An Underwriting Member of Lloyd's. *Educ:* Glasgow Univ. *Publications:* HMS Ulysses, 1955, The Guns of Navarone (filmed 1959), 1957; South by Java Head (filmed 1959), 1958; The Last Frontier (filmed 1960), 1959; (as The Secret Ways, 1961); Night Without End, 1960; Fear Is the Key, 1961; The Golden Rendezvous, 1962; (for children) All About Lawrence of Arabia, 1962; Ice Station Zebra (filmed 1968), 1963; When Eight Bells Toll (filmed 1970), 1966; Where Eagles Dare (filmed 1968), 1967; Force 10 From Navarone, 1968; Puppet on a Chain (filmed 1970), 1969; *as Ian Stuart:* The Dark Crusader, 1961; Snow on the Ben, 1961; The Satan Bug, 1962. *Screen plays:* Where Eagles Dare, Deakin, Caravan to Vaccares. *Address:* c/o Wm Collins Sons & Co. Ltd, 14 St James's Place, SW1.

**McLEAN, Calvin Stowe;** retired as Chairman of General Mining, and as a Director of all Mining and Finance Boards, 1965; *b* 21 July 1888; *s* of Hugh McLean; *m* Olive Aileen, *d* of late William Sealswood; one *s* two *d*. *Educ:* Rothesay Collegiate Sch., New Brunswick; McGill Univ., Montreal (BSc (Mining)). Came to S Africa, 1910. Joined Gen. Mining and Finance Corp. Ltd, 1920; Cons. Engr, 1936-50; Dep. Chm. and Tech. Dir, 1950-63; Chm., 1963-65. Mem., Assoc. of Mine Managers of the Transvaal, 1920- (Vice-Pres. 1935); Mem. Exec. Cttee, Transvaal and OFS Chamber of Mines, 1941-65 (Pres., 1945-46, 1948-49, 1952-53); Mem., SA Atomic Energy Bd, 1955-64; Mem., SA Electricity Supply Commission, 1948-54. Pres., 7th Commonwealth Mining and Metallurgical Congress, SA, 1961. Chm., St Andrew's Sch. for Girls, Johannesburg, SA, 1939-68. Hon. LLD. Witwatersrand, 1961. *Publications:* technical papers. *Recreations:* bowls, motoring. *Address:* 29 Bompas Road, Dunkeld, Johannesburg, SA. *T:* 42-2418 and 836-1121. *Clubs:* Rand, Johannesburg Country, Wanderers' (Pres.), Royal Johannesburg Golf (all in Johannesburg); Durban Country (Durban).

**MacLEAN, Col Charles Allan,** CBE 1941 (MBE 1918); MC; *b* 22 May 1892; *s* of John MacLean, Tobermory, Isle of Mull, Scotland; *m* 1920, Mabel Elsie, *y d* of Alfred Matthews, Sherborne St John, Hants; three *s* one *d*. *Educ:* Tobermory and Kingussie Sch.; Edinburgh Univ. MA 1914; BSc (Agric) 1920; in France with 11th Argyll and Sutherland Highlanders, 1915-19 (MBE, MC, Croix de Guerre, despatches). Joined Indian Agricultural Service, 1920; Cane Commissioner, Bihar, 1939-43; Dir of Agriculture, 1943-46; Commissioner of Agriculture, Baroda, 1946-49; Field Agricultural Officer, Jordan, with UN Relief and Work Agency, 1951-55. Commanded Chota Nagpur Regt AF(I), 1934-38, and Bihar Light Horse AF(I), 1939-41. Mem., Tobermory Town Council, 1958-62; Provost of Tobermory, 1959-62. Pres. Mull and Iona Council of Social Service, 1959-66; President, Mull Highland Games Club. *Address:* Ulva Cottage, Tobermory, Scotland. *T:* Tobermory 2044.

**MACLEAN, Major Sir Charles (Hector Fitzroy),** 11th Bt, *cr* 1631, of Duart and Morvaren, Argyllshire; KT 1969; KBE 1967; 27th Chief of Clan Maclean; Scots Guards, Major, retired; Lord Lieutenant of Argyll since 1954; Chief Scout of the Commonwealth, since 1959; Brigadier, Royal Company of Archers (Queen's Body Guard for Scotland); President, Argyll T & AFA; *b* 5 May 1916; *e surv. s* of late Hector F. Maclean and Winifred Joan, *y d* of late J. H. Wilding; *S* grandfather, 1936; *m* 1941, Elizabeth, *er d* of late Frank Mann, Upper Farm House, Milton Lilbourne, Wilts; one *s* one *d*. *Educ:* Canford Sch., Wimborne. Served War of 1939-45 (despatches). Chief Commissioner for Scotland, Boy Scouts Assoc., 1954-59. Hon. Pres., Mull and Iona Assoc. Fellow: Royal Commonwealth Soc.; Zoological Soc. JP 1955. *Recreation:* travelling. *Heir: s* Lachlan Hector Charles Maclean, Captain Scots Guards [*b* 25 Aug. 1942; *m* 1966, Mary Helen, *e d* of W. G. Gordon; two *d*]. *Address:* Duart Castle, Isle of Mull. *T:* Craignure 309. *Clubs:* Guards, Pratt's; Royal Highland Yacht (Oban).
*See also D. G. Graham-Campbell, Brig. F. W. B. Marsham.*

**MacLEAN, Captain Donald Murdo,** DSC 1944; RD 1940; RNR; Retired from Cunard Line, 1962; Commodore Captain Cunard Fleet and commanding RMS Queen Elizabeth, 1960-62; *b* 9 June, 1899; *s* of William MacLean and Isobel (*née* Graham); *m* 1929, Bernice Isobel Wellington; one *s* one *d*. *Educ:* The Nicholson Sch., Lewis Island. Apprenticed to Cunard Line, 1917-21; served, as Officer, 1921-39. Served War of 1939-45 (despatches): RNR, 1939-46; Trg Comdr RNC, Greenwich, 1941-43; Sen. Officer, 7th Escort Gp, Murmansk and Atlantic and Mediterranean Convoys; Staff Officer C-in-C Mediterranean, 1944-45. Returned to Cunard Line, 1946. ADC to Lord High Comr for Scotland, 1946. *Publication:* Queens' Company, 1965. *Recreations:* golf, fishing, reading and travel. *Address:* Southwinds, Saxholm Way, Southampton. *T:* Southampton 68945. *Club:* Master Mariners (Southampton).

**MACLEAN, Sir Fitzroy Hew,** 1st Bt, *cr* 1957; CBE 1944; MP (C) Bute and North Ayrshire Division of Ayrshire and Bute since Oct. 1959 (Lancaster Division of Lancashire, 1941-Sept. 1959); *b* 11 March 1911; *s* of Major Charles Maclean, DSO; *m* 1946, Hon. Mrs Alan Phipps, 2nd *d* of 16th Baron Lovat, KT; two *s*. *Educ:* Eton; Cambridge. 3rd Sec., Foreign Office, 1933; transferred to Paris, 1934, and to Moscow, 1937; 2nd Sec., 1938; transferred to Foreign Office, 1939; resigned from Diplomatic Service, and enlisted as private in Cameron Highlanders; 2nd Lt Aug. 1941; joined 1st Special Air Service Regt Jan. 1942; Capt. Sept. 1942; Lt-Col 1943; Brig. Comdg British Military Mission to Jugoslav partisans, 1943-45. Lees Knowles Lecturer, Cambridge, 1953. Parliamentary Under-Sec. of State for War and Financial Sec. War Office, Oct. 1954-Jan. 1957. Hon. LLD Glasgow 1969; Hon. DLitt Acadia, 1970. French Croix de Guerre, 1943; Order of Kutusov, 1944; Partisan Star (First Class), 1945. *Publications:* Eastern Approaches, 1949; Disputed Barricade, 1957; A Person from England, 1958; Back to Bokhara, 1959; Jugoslavia, 1969; A Concise History of Scotland, 1970; The Battle of Neretva, 1970. *Heir: s* Charles Maclean, *b* 31 Oct. 1946. *Address:* 42 Lowndes Square, SW1. *T:* 01-235 5812; Strachur House, Argyll. *T:* Strachur 242. *Clubs:* White's, Pratt's; Puffin's (Edinburgh).

**McLEAN, Sir Francis (Charles),** Kt 1967; CBE 1953 (MBE 1945); Technical Director, EVR Partnership; Assistant to President, CBS/Comtec Group; *b* 6 Nov. 1904; *s* of Michael McLean; *m* 1930, Dorothy Mabel Blackstaffe; one *s* one *d*. *Educ:* University of Birmingham (BSc). Chief Engineer, Psychological Warfare Division, SHAEF, 1943-45. Dep. Chief Engineer, BBC, 1952-60; Dep. Dir of Engineering, BBC, 1960-63; Director, Engineering, BBC, 1963-68. Chm., BSI Telecommunications Industry Standards Cttee. FIEE. *Publications:* contrib. Journal of IEE. *Address:* Clent Cottage, Thornford Road, Crookham Common, near Newbury, Berks. *T:* Headley 319.

**MACLEAN, Brig. Gordon Forbes,** CBE 1943; MC; DL; *b* 29 May 1897; *s* of George Buchanan Maclean, Pentreheylin, Maesbrook, Shropshire; *m* 1926, Claire, *d* of John Lehane, Melbourne, Australia; one *s*. *Educ:* Shrewsbury School, Sandhurst, 1914-15; Argyll and Sutherland Highlanders, 1915; Staff Coll., Camberley, 1930-31; Colonel, 1945; retired pay, 1946, with hon. rank of Brigadier. High Sheriff of Shropshire, 1965. DL Shropshire, 1966. *Address:* Pentreheylin, Maesbrook, Salop. *Club:* Army and Navy.

**MacLEAN, Vice-Adm. Sir Hector Charles Donald,** KBE 1962; CB 1960; DSC 1941; JP; *b* 7 Aug. 1908; *s* of late Captain D. C. H. MacLean, DSO, The Royal Scots; *m* 1933, Opre, *d* of late Captain Geoffrey Vyvyan, Royal Welch Fusiliers; one *s* two *d*. *Educ:* Wellington. Special Entry into Navy, 1926; Captain 1948; idc 1951; Comd HMS Saintes and 3rd Destroyer Sqdn, 1952-53; Dir of Plans, Admiralty, 1953-56; Comd HMS Eagle, 1956-57; Chief of Staff, Home Fleet, 1958-59; Chief of Allied Staff, Mediterranean, 1959-62; Vice-Adm. 1960; retired 1962. JP Norfolk, 1963. *Address:* Deepdale Old Rectory, Brancaster Staithe, King's Lynn, Norfolk. *T:* Brancaster 281. *Clubs:* Hunts; Norfolk (Norwich).

**MACLEAN, Hector Ronald;** Sheriff-Substitute Renfrew and Argyll since 1968; *b* 6 Dec. 1931; *s* of Donald Beaton Maclean and Lucy McAlister; *m* 1967, Hilary Elizabeth Jenkins; two *d*. *Educ:* High Sch. of Glasgow; Glasgow Univ. Admitted to Faculty of Advocates, 1959. *Recreations:* golf, shooting. *Address:* West Rowantreehill, Glencairn Road, Kilmacolm, Renfrewshire. *T:* Kilmacolm 2145.

**MACLEAN, Rear-Admiral Iain G.,** CB 1954; OBE 1944; retired; *b* 25 Nov. 1902; *s* of late Norman H. Maclean; *m* 1931, Evelyn Marjorie, *d* of late R. A. Reid, and Mrs Winton Reid; one step *d*. *Educ:* Cargilfield; RN Colleges, Osborne and Dartmouth. Joined RN, 1916; Captain, 1945; Rear-Admiral, 1952; Served War of 1939-45: in Combined Operations, HMS Renown and Admiralty. Imperial Defence Coll., 1951; Dep. Engineer in Chief of the Fleet, 1952-55; retired, Nov. 1955. Director, Marine Development, Brush Group, 1956-60. Research Survey for National Ports Council, 1963-64. *Recreations:* fishing, gardening. *Address:* Pinkney's Folly, Pinkney's Green, Maidenhead, Berks. *T:* Maidenhead 27049. *Clubs:* United Service, Number Ten.

**MACLEAN, Ian Albert Druce;** President, Halifax Building Society; Director, Barclays Bank Ltd (West Yorkshire local board), and other companies; *b* 23 June 1902; *s* of Alec and Nina Maclean; *m* 1937, Diana, *d* of John and Gertrude Marsden-Smedley; twin *s*. *Educ:* Marlborough; Pembroke Coll., Cambridge. Tobacco Industry, 1924; Cotton Industry, 1926; Carpet Industry, 1937; Halifax Building Society, 1953. Former Dir, Carpets International Ltd. *Recreations:* anything in the open air. *Address:* Ashday Hall, Southowram, Halifax, Yorks. *T:* Halifax 54441. *Clubs:* Bath; Royal Windermere Yacht.

**McLEAN, Ian Graeme;** Metropolitan Stipendiary Magistrate since 1970; *b* Edinburgh, 7 Nov. 1928; *s* of Lt-Gen. Sir Kenneth McLean, *qv*; *m* 1957, Eleonore Maria Gmeiner, Bregenz, Austria; two *d*. *Educ:* Aldenham Sch.; Christ's Coll., Cambridge. BA Hons Law 1950; MA 1955. Intell. Corps, 1946-48. Called to Bar, Middle Temple, Nov. 1951; practised London and on Western Circuit, 1951-55; Crown Counsel, Northern Nigeria, 1955-59; Sen. Lectr and Head of Legal Dept of Inst. of Administration, Northern Nigeria, 1959-62; Native Courts Adviser, 1959-62; returned to English Bar, 1962; practised London and South Eastern Circuit, 1962-70; occasional Dep. Chm., Inner, NE, SW and Mddx Areas, London QS, 1968-70; occasional Dep. Recorder, Oxford, 1969-70; Adjudicator under Immigration Acts, 1969-70. *Publications:* Cumulative Index West African Court of Appeal Reports, 1958; (with Abubakar Sadiq) The Maliki Law of Homicide, 1959; (with Sir Lionel Brett) Criminal Law Procedure and Evidence of Lagos, Eastern and Western Nigeria, 1963; (with Cyprian

Okonkwo) Cases on the Criminal Law, Procedure and Evidence of Nigeria, 1966; (with Peter Morrish) A Practical Guide to Appeals in Criminal Courts, 1970. *Recreations:* family, gardening, writing, languages. *Address:* Horseleas, Bradfield, Berks. *T:* Bradfield 220.

**McLEAN, John,** CBE 1947; Member, Council of Foreign Bondholders; a UK Representative on Commonwealth Economic Committee, 1950-62; a General Commissioner of Income Tax for City of London, 1956-68; *b* 19 April 1893; *s* of late Thomas Crawford McLean; *m* 1915, Catherine Kydd Strachan; one *s* two *d. Educ:* Hyndland Sch., Glasgow. Company Director; Chairman George Wills & Sons Ltd, Exporters and Importers, 1949-59, retired. Vice-President, London Chamber of Commerce, 1946 (Chairman, 1944-46); Vice-President, Federation of Commonwealth Chambers of Commerce, 1951 (Chairman, 1948-51); President, Association of British Chambers of Commerce, 1948-50; Member: Export Credits Guarantee Advisory Council, 1952-63; Port of London Authority, 1955-64. *Recreation:* golf. *Address:* Glenesk, Brookmans Avenue, Brookmans Park, Hatfield, Herts. *T:* Potters Bar 53336. *Club:* Devonshire.

**McLEAN, (John David) Ruari (McDowall Hardie),** DSC 1943; Senior Partner, Ruari McLean Associates (Design Consultants) (Founder Partner with Fianach Jardine, 1965); Art Editor, The Connoisseur; *b* 10 June 1917; *s* of late John Thomson McLean and late Isabel Mary McLean (*née* Ireland); *m* 1945, Antonia Maxwell Carlisle; two *s* one *d. Educ:* Dragon Sch., Oxford; Eastbourne Coll. First studied printing under B. H. Newdigate at Shakespeare Head Press, Oxford, 1936. Industrial printing experience in Germany and England, 1936-38; with The Studio, 1938; Percy Lund Humphries, Bradford, 1939. Served Royal Navy, 1940-45. Penguin Books, 1945-46; Book Designer (freelance), 1946-53; Tutor in Typography, Royal College of Art, 1949-53; Typographic Adviser to Hulton Press, 1953; Founder Partner, Rainbird, McLean Ltd, 1951-58; Founder Editor, and Designer, Motif, 1958-67. Typographic Consultant to The Observer, 1960; Hon. Typographic Adviser to HM Stationery Office, 1966. Croix de Guerre (French), 1942. *Publications:* George Cruikshank, 1948; Modern Book Design, 1958; Wood Engravings of Joan Hassall, 1960; Victorian Book Design, 1963; Tschichold's Typographische Gestaltung (Trans.), 1967; The Reminiscences of Edmund Evans (ed), 1967; Magazine Design, 1969. *Recreations:* sailing, reading, collecting books. *Address:* 47 Blackheath Park, SE3. *T:* 01-852 1409. *Clubs:* Arts, Double Crown; RNVR Sailing.

**MACLEAN, Colonel John Francis,** JP; Lord Lieutenant of Herefordshire, since 1960; *b* 1 March 1901; *s* of late Montague Francis and Florence Maclean; *m* 1925, Vivienne A. M. Miesegaes (*d* 1969); two *s. Educ:* Eton Coll. Started in coal trade with Cannop Coal Co. Ltd, Forest of Dean, 1921; became a Director and Commercial Manager, in 1927, after being employed with United Collieries Ltd, Glasgow. Commnd Herefordshire Regt (TA), 1919-23. Coal Supplies Officer for Forest of Dean, 1939-40; commnd in Grenadier Guards, Sept. 1940, reaching rank of Major. Appointed JP, 1946, High Sheriff, 1951, and DL Herefordshire, 1953-60. KStJ, 1960. Hon. Colonel, Herefordshire Light Infantry (TA), 1963-67. *Recreations:* golf, shooting; formerly lawn tennis and cricket (kept wicket for Worcestershire, 1922-24, and occasionally for Gloucestershire, 1929-30; toured Australia and New Zealand with MCC team, 1922-23). *Address:* Bromsash House, Ross-on-Wye, Herefordshire. *T:* Lea 243. *Clubs:* Brooks's, MCC.

**McLEAN, Lieut-General Sir Kenneth Graeme,** KCB, *cr* 1954 (CB 1944); KBE, *cr* 1951; US Legion of Merit, 1945; Officer, Legion of Honour (France); Croix de Guerre (France); *b* 11 Dec. 1896; *s* of late Arthur H. McLean, WS; *m* 1926, Daphne Winifred Ashburner Steele; two *s. Educ:* Edinburgh Academy; RMA Woolwich. Commissioned RE 1918; served, in Ireland, 1919-20, and with KGO Bengal Sappers and Miners in India, 1923-29; Staff Coll., Quetta, 1930-31; on General Staff, AHQ, India, 1932-36; Assistant Secretary Cttee of Imperial Defence, 1938; Student at Imperial Defence Coll., 1939. Served France and Germany, 1944-45; Deputy Adjutant-General, GHQ, Far East, 1945-46; Dep. Adjutant-General, GHQ, Middle East, 1946; Vice-Adjutant-General, War Office, 1947-49; Chief of Staff, CCG, and Deputy Military Governor, British Zone in Germany, 1949; Military Secretary to the Secretary of State for War, 1949-51; Chief Staff Officer, Ministry of Defence, 1951-52; Special Duty, War Office, 1952-54. Retired, 1954. Colonel Comdt RE, 1956-61. *Address:* Greenways, Melrose, Roxburghshire.

*See also I. G. McLean.*

**MacLEAN, Kenneth Smedley,** MD, FRCP; Consultant Physician to Guy's Hospital 1950; *b* 22 Nov. 1914; *s* of Hugh MacLean and Ida Smedley; *m* 1939, Joan Hardaker; two *s* one *d. Educ:* Westminster; Clare Coll., Cambridge. MRCS, LRCP, 1939; House appts at Guy's, 1939; MB, BChir 1939. RNVR, 1939-46, Surg.-Lt and Surg.-Lt-Comdr. MRCP 1946; House Officer and Medical Registrar, Guy's Hosp., 1946-48; MD Cantab 1948; FRCP 1954; elected to Assoc. of Physicians of Great Britain and Ireland, 1956. Assistant Director, Dept of Medicine, Guy's Hospital Medical Sch., 1949, Director, 1961-63. *Publication:* Medical Treatment, 1957. *Recreation:* golf. *Address:* Heathdown, The Ridge, Woldingham, Surrey. *T:* Woldingham 2260.

**McLEAN, Lieut-Colonel Neil Loudon Desmond,** DSO 1943; *b* 28 Nov. 1918; *s* of Neil McLean; *m* 1949, Däska Kennedy (*née* Ivanović-Banac), Dubrovnik, Jugoslavia. *Educ:* Eton; RMC, Sandhurst. Gazetted Royal Scots Greys, 1938; Palestine Campaign, 1939; served War of 1939-45, Middle East and Far East: Ethiopia under 101 Mission, 1941; Head of First Military Mission to Albania, 1942 amd 1943; Lieut-Colonel, 1943; Far East, 1944-45. Contested (C) Preston South, 1950 and 1951; MP (C) Inverness, Dec. 1954-Sept. 1964. Member Highland and Islands Advisory Panel, 1955. Member of Queen's Body Guard for Scotland, Royal Company of Archers. Distinguished Military Medal of Haile Selassie I, 1941. *Publications:* contributions to Chatham House, Royal Central Asian Society Reviews. *Recreations:* travel, riding, shooting, underwater fishing. *Address:* 17 Eaton Square, SW1. *Clubs:* White's, Buck's, Cavalry, Pratt's; Highland (Inverness).

**MACLEAN, Sir Robert (Alexander),** Kt 1955; DL; Chartered Accountant; Chairman of: A. F. Stoddard & Co. Ltd; Scottish Industrial Estates Corporation; Navan Carpets Ltd (Eire); Vice-President, Scottish Council (Development and Industry); Member, National Freight Corporation, since 1969; *b* 11 April 1908; *s* of Andrew Johnston Maclean, JP, Cambuslang, Lanarkshire, and Mary Jane Cameron; *m* 1938, Vivienne Neville Bourke, *d* of Captain Bertram Walter Bourke, JP, Heathfield, Co. Mayo; two *s* two *d. Educ:*

Glasgow High Sch. President: Glasgow Chamber of Commerce, 1956-58; Association British Chambers of Commerce, 1966-68. Chairman: Council of Scottish Chambers of Commerce, 1960-62; Scottish Cttee, Council of Industrial Design, 1949-58; Council of Management, Scottish Industries Exhibns, 1949, 1954 and 1959; Scottish Exports Cttee, 1966-70; Pres., British Industrial Exhibn, Moscow, 1966; Member: Pigs and Bacon Marketing Commn, 1955-56; BNEC, 1966-70; Regional Controller (Scotland): Board of Trade, 1944-46; Factory and Storage Premises, 1941-44. DL Renfrewshire, 1970 OStJ. *Recreations:* golf, fishing. *Address:* Woodend, Houston, Renfrewshire. *T:* Bridge of Weir 2005. *Clubs:* Junior Carlton; Western (Glasgow).

**McLEAN, Robert Colquhoun,** MA, DSc, FLS; Professor of Botany, University College of South Wales and Monmouthshire, Cardiff, 1919-55; retired Dec. 1955; *b* Kilcreggan, Dunbartonshire, 18 July 1890; *s* of Rev. Robert McLean, MA, Kilcreggan, Dunbartonshire; *m* 1914, Freda Marguerite (*d* 1955), *d* of George Washington Kilner, MA; three *s. Educ:* The Leys School, Cambridge; University College, London; St John's Coll., Cambridge. Lecturer in Botany at University Coll., Reading, 1913; has travelled in many parts of the world for botanical purposes and for comparative study of University Systems; General Secretary of International University Conference, founded 1934; President Assoc. of University Teachers, 1940-41; President, International Assoc. of University Professors, 1950; Member: Nature Conservancy, 1949-56; National Parks Commission, 1949-56; Universities Advisory Cttee, British Council, 1953. *Publications:* Plant Science Formulæ, Textbook of Theoretical Botany, Text Book of Practical Botany, and Practical Field Ecology (with W. R. I. Cook); numerous articles in scientific periodicals, etc. *Recreation:* sleep. *Address:* Hickley Lodge, Old Cogan, Penarth, Glam.

**McLEAN, Ruari;** *see* McLean, J. D. R. McD. H.

**MacLEARY, Donald Whyte;** principal male dancer with the Royal Ballet since 1959; *b* Glasgow, 22 Aug. 1937; *s* of Donald Herbert MacLeary, MPS, and Jean Spiers (*née* Leslie). *Educ:* Inverness Royal Academy; The Royal Ballet School. *Classical Ballets:* (full length) Swan Lake, Giselle, 1958; Sleeping Beauty, Cinderella, Sylvia, 1959; Ondine, La Fille Mal Gardée, 1960, (centre male rôle) in Ashton's Symphonic Variations, 1962; Sonnet Pas de Trois, 1964; Romeo and Juliet, 1965; Eugene Onegin, Stuttgart, 1966; Apollo, 1966; Nutcracker, 1968. *Creations:* (1954-69): Solitaire, The Burrow, Danse Concertante, Antigone, Diversions, Le Baiser de la Fée, Jabez and the Devil, Raymonda Pas de Deux (for Frederick Ashton), two episodes in Images of Love; Song of the Earth; Lilac Garden (revival); Jazz Calendar; Raymonda (for Nureyeff). *Recreations:* reading, theatre, records (all types); riding, fox hunting, swimming. *Address:* 41 Kensington Park Gardens, W11. *T:* 01-727 7202; Bunyan Cottage, Wainwood, Preston, Herts. *Club:* Queen's.

**McLEAVY,** family name of **Baron McLeavy.**

**McLEAVY,** Baron (Life Peer), *cr* 1967, of City of Bradford; **Frank McLeavy;** *b* 1 Jan. 1899; *y s* of late John McLeavy, Congleton, Cheshire; *m* 1924; two *s* one *d. Educ:* Elementary Sch. and Evening Institutes. Road Passenger Transport Officer; Mayor of Bebington, 1939-41; formerly: JP Co. of Chester; Alderman Cheshire County Council; Chairman, Bebington ATC Cttee; MP (Lab) Bradford East Div., 1945-66, retired. Mem. of Cheshire Standing Joint Cttee; Chm. of all-party Cttee which organised Parliamentary Presentation to Sir Winston Churchill on his eightieth birthday. Mem. of Cheshire Police Authority. JP Co. Middlesex, 1951-. *Address:* 9 Sheridan Terrace, Whitton Avenue, Northolt, Mddx.

**McLEAY, Hon. Sir John,** KCMG 1962; MM; MP; retired as Speaker of the House of Representatives, Canberra, Australia (1956-66); Federal Member for Boothby, South Australia, 1949; *b* 19 Nov. 1893; *m* 1921, Eileen H., *d* of late H. Elden, Geelong; two *s* one *d.* Stretcher Bearer, 13 Field Ambulance, 1st AIF (awarded Military Medal); Life Member, Hindmarsh Ambulance. Formerly: Mayor of City of Unley; Lord Mayor of Adelaide; Member for Unley, House of Assembly, SA; Member Council of Governors, Adelaide Univ. and Scotch Coll., Adelaide. President or Past President various organisations; Hon. Member Town Planning Institute, SA, etc. *Address:* 188 Cross Road, Malvern, SA 5061, Australia.

**MacLEAY, Oswell Searight,** JP; **His Honour Judge MacLeay;** Deputy-Chairman, Inner Division Greater London Sessions, since 1965; Barrister-at-law; *b* 11 Dec. 1905; *o s* of late Oswell Sullivan MacLeay and Ida Marion MacLeay, 29 Draycott Place, SW1; *m* 1930, Viola Elizabeth Mary French, *o d* of late Frank Austen French, MRCS, LRCP, and Dora Emmeline French, Hollamby House, Herne Bay; two *s. Educ:* RN College, Osborne; RN College, Dartmouth; Charterhouse; Magdalen Coll., Oxford. Called to the Bar, Inner Temple, 1932; South Eastern Circuit. Recorder of Maidstone, 1959-61. Dep. Chairman, West Kent Quarter Sessions, 1954-62; Asst Chairman of County of Middlesex Sessions, 1959-60; Dep. Chairman, 1960-61; Dep. Chairman County of London Sessions, 1961-65; Member Mental Health Review Tribunal, 1960-61. Served War, RNVR, 1939-45; Sub-Lieut, 1939; Lieut, 1939; Lieut-Commander, 1941. JP Kent. Member Kent Standing Joint Cttee and Police Authority, 1956-64; Member Malling Rural District Council, 1949-55 (Chairman, 1951-55); Member Visiting Cttee, Maidstone Prison, 1954-58. President Sevenoaks Conservative and Unionist Assoc., 1959-61. *Recreations:* watching and umpiring cricket; naval and military history; travel (particularly by rail). *Address:* The Old Farm House, Wrotham, Kent. *T:* Borough Green 4138; Sessions House, Newington Causeway, SE1. *T:* 01-407 1306. *Clubs:* Naval and Military, MCC, RNVR; Band of Brothers (Kent); RAF Reserves (Hon. Life Member).

**MACLEHOSE, Crawford Murray,** CMG 1964; MBE 1946; HM Diplomatic Service; Ambassador to Denmark, since 1969; Governor and Commander-in-Chief designate, Hong Kong; *b* 16 Oct. 1917; *s* of Hamish A. Maclehose and Margaret Bruce Black; *m* 1947, Margaret Noël Dunlop; two *d. Educ:* Rugby; Balliol Coll., Oxford. Served War of 1939-45, Lieut, RNVR. Joined Foreign Service, 1947; Acting Consul, 1947, Acting Consul-General, 1948, Hankow; promoted First Secretary, 1949; transferred to Foreign Office, 1950; First Secretary (Commercial), and Consul, Prague, 1951; seconded to Commonwealth Relations Office, for service at Wellington, 1954; returned to Foreign Office and transferred to Paris, 1956; promoted Counsellor, 1959; seconded to Colonial Office and transferred to Hong Kong as Political Adviser; Counsellor, Foreign Office, 1963;

Principal Private Secretary to Secretary of State, 1965-67; Ambassador to Vietnam, 1967-69. *Recreations:* sailing, fishing. *Address:* c/o Foreign and Commonwealth Office, SW1; Beoch, Maybole, Ayrshire. *Clubs:* Royal Commonwealth Society; Royal Northern Yacht; Prestwick Golf.

**MacLEISH, Archibald;** *b* 7 May 1892; *s* of Andrew MacLeish and Martha Hillard; *m* 1916, Ada Hitchcock; two *s* one *d* (and one *s* decd). *Educ:* The Hotchkiss Sch., Lakeville, Connecticut; Yale Univ. (AB); Harvard Univ. (LLB). Hon. MA Tufts, 1932; Hon. LittD, Wesleyan, 1938, Colby, 1938, Yale, 1939, University of Pennsylvania, 1941; University of Illinois, 1947; Hon. LLD, Dartmouth, 1940, Johns Hopkins Univ., 1941, University of California, 1943; Hon. DCL, Union Coll., 1941; Hon. LHD, Williams Coll., 1942; Washington Univ., 1948; LLD, Queens Coll. (Canada), 1948; University of Puerto Rico, 1953; Amherst Coll., 1963; LittD, Rockford Coll., 1952, Columbia, 1954, Harvard Univ., 1955; Princeton Univ., 1965; Univ. of Massachusetts, 1969. Enlisted as private, United States Army, 1917; discharged with rank of Captain, 1919; spent 12 months in American Expeditionary Force, France. An instructor in government at Harvard, 1919-21; practised law in Boston offices of Choate, Hall and Stewart, 1920-23; devoted his time to travel and literature, 1923-30; Editor of Fortune, 1929-38; Librarian of Congress, 1939-44; Director Office of Facts and Figures, 1941-42; Asst Director of Office of War Information, 1942-43; Asst Secretary of State, 1944-45. Chairman, American Delegation to London Conference, UN, to establish a Cultural and Educational Organisation, 1945; American Member Exec. Board of UNESCO, 1946. Boylston Professor, Harvard Univ., 1949-62. Simpson Lecturer, Amherst Coll., 1963, 1964, 1965, 1966. President American Academy of Arts and Letters, 1953-56; Commander, Légion d'Honneur (France); Commander, El Sol del Peru. *Publications:* The Happy Marriage (verse), 1924; The Pot of Earth, 1925; Nobodaddy (verse play), 1925; Streets in the Moon, 1926; The Hamlet of A. MacLeish, 1928; New Found Land, 1930; Conquistador (Pulitzer poetry prize), 1932; Frescoes for Mr Rockefeller's City, 1933; Union Pacific–a Ballet, 1934; Panic (verse play), 1935; Public Speech (verse), 1936; The Fall of the City (verse play for radio), 1937; Land of the Free (verse), 1938; Air Raid (verse play for radio), 1938; America was Promises (verse), 1939; The Irresponsibles (prose), 1940; The American Cause (prose), 1941; A Time to Speak (prose), 1941; American Opinion and the War (Rede Lecture at Cambridge Univ., 1942), 1943; A Time to Act (prose), 1943; The American Story (radio broadcasts), 1944; Actfive and Other Poems, 1948; Poetry and Opinion (prose), 1950; Freedom Is The Right To Choose (prose), 1951; Collected Poems, 1952 (Bollingen Prize, National Book Award, Pulitzer poetry prize); This Music Crept By Me Upon The Waters (verse play), 1953; Songs For Eve (verse), 1954; J.B. (verse play), 1958 (produced NY, Dec. 1958; Pulitzer Prize for Drama, 1959); Poetry and Experience (prose), 1961; The Eleanor Roosevelt Story, 1965 (filmed, 1965, Academy Award, 1966); Herakles (verse play), 1967; A Continuing Journey (prose), 1968; The Wild Old Wicked Men and other poems, 1968. *Address:* Conway, Mass 01341, USA. *Clubs:* Century Association (NY); Tavern, Somerset (Boston).

**McLELLAN, David,** CMG 1957; ED, 1951; Education Consultant, International Bank for Reconstruction and Development, since 1965; *b* 23 Dec. 1904; *e s* of David McLellan; *m* 1934, Winifred (*née* Henderson); three *s*. *Educ:* King Edward VII Sch., Lytham; Queen's Coll., Cambridge. Colonial Education Service: Hong Kong, 1931, Chief Inspector of Schools, 1951; Singapore, Dep. Director of Education, 1953; Director of Education and Permanent Secretary to Min. of Education, 1955; Regional Education Adviser to Comr General for UK in SE Asia, 1959-62; Director, Cultural Relations, SEATO, Bangkok, 1963-65. *Recreations:* cricket, golf, photography. *Address:* Rushmore House, Shepreth, nr Royston, Herts.

**MacLELLAN, Prof. George Douglas Stephen,** MA, PhD (Cantab); CEng; FIMechE, FIEE; Professor and Head of Department of Engineering, University of Leicester, since 1965; *b* Glasgow, 1 Nov. 1922; *e s* of late Alexander Stephen MacLellan. *Educ:* Rugby Sch.; Pembroke Coll., Cambridge; Massachusetts Institute of Technology. Mech. Sci. Tripos, 1942. Dept of Colloid Science, Cambridge, and Callenders Cable and Construction Co. Ltd, 1942-44; Fellow, Pembroke Coll., 1944-59; Vickers-Armstrong Ltd, Elswick Works, Newcastle upon Tyne, 1944-46; Director of Studies in Engineering, 1946-59, Asst Tutor, 1950-59, Pembroke Coll., Cambridge; University Demonstrator and Lecturer in Engineering, Cambridge, 1947-59; Rankine Professor of Mechanical Engineering (Mechanics and Mechanism), University of Glasgow, 1959-65. Commonwealth Fund Fellow, MIT, 1948-49; Visiting Professor, Michigan State University, 1958; MIT, 1962. Pres. of the Soc. of Instrument Technology, 1964-65. Vice-Chm., United Kingdom Automation Council, 1961-64. Governor, Kelvinside Academy, 1963-65. *Publications:* papers in Jl Inst. Metals, Trans Soc. Instr. Technology, Proc. Inst. Mech. Engrg, etc. *Address:* Department of Engineering, The University, Leicester. *T:* Leicester 50000. *Clubs:* Oxford and Cambridge University, Leander.

**McLELLAN, James Kidd,** QPM 1966; Chief Constable, Lanarkshire, since 1967; *b* 16 Oct. 1914; *s* of John Young McLellan, MPS, FBOA, Chemist and Optician, and Robina (*née* Kidd); *m* 1942, Margaret A. G. F. Selby; two *s* one *d*. *Educ:* Lenzie Academy; Glasgow Univ.; Royal Technical Coll. (now Strathclyde Univ.). MA Hons, BSc; ARIC 1948, FRIC 1965. City of Glasgow Police, 1936-65: i/c Police Laboratory, attached to Identification Bureau, 1946-60; Det. Supt (ii) in Ident. Bureau and Scottish Criminal Record Office, 1960; Det. Supt (i) i/c SCRO and IB, 1962; Chief Constable, Motherwell and Wishaw Burgh, 1965. Past Chm. (Scottish Section), Soc. for Analytical Chemistry; Chm. (Glasgow and W of Scotland) Royal Inst. of Chemistry. *Publications:* articles in Police Jl, Fire Service Jl. *Recreation:* youth work. *Address:* 181 Manse Road, Motherwell, Lanarkshire. *T:* Motherwell 62812.

**MacLENNAN, Maj.-Gen. Alastair,** OBE 1945; Curator, Royal Army Medical Corps Historical Museum, Mytchett, Hants, since 1969; *b* 16 Feb. 1912; *s* of Col. Farquhar MacLennan, DSO; *m* 1940, Constance Anne Cook; two *s* one *d*. *Educ:* Aberdeen Grammar Sch.; University of Aberdeen (MB, ChB). Commissioned Lieut, RAMC, 1934; Captain, 1935; Major, 1942; Lieut-Colonel, 1942; Colonel, 1952; Brigadier, 1964; Maj.-General, 1967. Appointments held include regimental, staff and Ministry of Defence in UK, Malta, NW Europe, India, Malaya, Korea, Egypt and Germany; ADGMS (Army), Min. of Defence, 1957-61; DDMS, HQ, BAOR, 1961-64; Inspector Army Medical Services, 1964-66;

DDMS: 1 (Br) Corps, 1966-67; HQ Eastern Command, 1967-68; Dep. Dir-Gen., Army Med. Services, MoD, 1968-69. US Bronze Star Medal, 1952. OStJ, 1966. QHP, 1968-69. *Publications:* papers on history of military firearms and on Highland Regts in North America 1756-1783. *Recreations:* bird-watching, military history, collecting antique military firearms and swords, vintage motor-cars. *Address:* 56 Reigate Road, Ewell, Epsom, Surrey. *T:* 01-393 2132.

**MacLENNAN, Sir Hector,** Kt 1965; MD, FRCPGlas, FRCOG; Chairman, Scottish Tourist Board, since 1969; *b* 1 Nov. 1905; *s* of Robert Jackson MacLennan and Amy Florence Ross; *m* 1933, Isabel Margaret Adam; three *s* one *d. Educ:* Glasgow High Sch.; University of Glasgow. President Glasgow Univ. Union, 1927. Cons. Surgeon, Glasgow Royal Maternity and Women's Hospital, 1934; Senior Cons. Gynæcologist, Victoria Infirmary, Glasgow, 1948; Mem. W Regional Hosp. Bd, 1950-56. Mem. GMC, 1965-69. External Examr in Obst. and Gynæc., Univs of Birmingham, Newcastle, Aberdeen, Edinburgh, Oxford, Dundee and Cambridge. Blair-Bell Lectr, 1944; Lloyd-Roberts Lectr, 1964; Osler Lectr, 1966; Joseph Price Oration, 1966. Past President: RCOG; RSM, 1967-69; Chairman: Medico-Pharmaceutical Forum, 1968-; Scottish Postgraduate Med. Assoc. Hon. FACOG, 1964; Hon. FRCSE, 1967; Hon. Fellow, American Assoc. of Obsts and Gynæcs, 1967. Hon. FCSOG; Hon. Alumnus, Sloane Hosp. for Women, NY. *Publications:* contribs to Combined Textbook of Obstetrics and Gynæcology and British Practice of Obstetrics and Gynæcology (1st edn). *Recreations:* fishing, shooting. *Address:* 91 Dowanhill Street, Glasgow, W2. *T:* 041-339 4979. *Club:* Western (Glasgow). *See also R. A. R. MacLennan.*

**MacLENNAN, Hugh;** CC (Canada) 1967; Professor, English Literature, McGill University, since 1967 (Associate Professor, 1951-67); *b* 20 March 1907; *s* of Dr Samuel John MacLennan and Katherine MacQuarrie; *m* 1st, 1936, Dorothy Duncan (*d* 1957); 2nd, 1959, Frances Aline, *d* of late Frank Earle Walker and Isabella Scott Benson. *Educ:* Dalhousie Univ.; Oriel Coll., Oxford; Graduate Coll., Princeton. Rhodes Schol. (Canada at large), 1928; PhD (Princeton) 1935. Classics Master, Lower Canada Coll., Montreal, 1935-45; writing, 1945-51. FRS Canada, 1953 (Gold Medal, 1951); FRSL, 1959. Governor-General's Award for Fiction, 1945, 1948, 1959; Governor-General's Award for non-fiction, 1949, 1954. Hon. DLitt: Waterloo Lutheran, 1961; Carleton Univ., 1967; Western Ontario, 1953, Manitoba, 1955; Hon. LLD: Dalhousie, 1956, Saskatchewan, 1959; McMaster, 1965; Toronto, 1966; Laurentian, 1966; Sherbrooke, 1967; British Columbia, 1968; St Mary's, 1968; Hon. DCL Bishop's, 1965. *Publications:* Oxyrhynchus: An Economic and Social Study, 1935; Barometer Rising, 1941; Two Solitudes, 1945; The Precipice, 1948; Cross Country (essays), 1949; Each Man's Son, 1951; Thirty and Three (essays), 1954; The Watch That Ends The Night, 1959; Scotchman's Return (essays), 1960; Return of the Sphinx, 1967. *Recreations:* tennis, walking, gardening. *Address:* 1535 Summerhill Avenue, Montreal, PQ, Canada. *T:* We. 2-8566. *Clubs:* Montreal Indoor Tennis, McGill Faculty (Montreal).

**MACLENNAN, Sir Ian (Morrison Ross),** KCMG 1957 (CMG 1951); HM Diplomatic Service, retired; *b* 30 Oct. 1909; *s* of late W. Maclennan, Glasgow; *m* 1936, Margherita Lucas, *d* of late F. Lucas Jarratt, Bedford; one *s* one *d. Educ:* Hymers Coll., Hull; Worcester Coll., Oxford. Appointed Colonial Office, 1933; Dominions Office, 1937; UK High Commissioner's Office, Ottawa, 1938; Pretoria, 1945; UK High Commissioner S Rhodesia, 1951-53; Federation of Rhodesia and Nyasaland, 1953-55; Assistant Under-Secretary of State, CRO, 1955-57; UK High Commissioner in Ghana, 1957-59; Ambassador to the Republic of Ireland, 1960-63; High Commissioner in New Zealand, 1964-69. *Recreations:* squash, golf. *Address:* 26. Ham Street, Richmond, Surrey. *Clubs:* Travellers'; Kildare Street (Dublin).

**McLENNAN, Sir Ian (Munro),** KBE 1963 (CBE 1956); Chairman, The Broken Hill Proprietary Co. Ltd, since 1970 (Managing Director, 1967-70); *b* 30 Nov. 1909; *s* of R. B. and C. O. McLennan; *m* 1937, Dora H., *d* of J. H. Robertson; two *s* two *d. Educ:* Scotch Coll., Melbourne; Melbourne Univ. Broken Hill Pty Co. Ltd: Cadet engineer, 1933; Asst Manager, Newcastle Steelworks of BHP Co. Ltd, 1943; Asst Gen. Man., BHP Co. Ltd, 1947; Gen. Man., 1950; Sen. Gen. Man., 1956; Chief Gen. Man., 1959. Chairman: Defence (Industrial) Cttee; Jt War Production Cttee, 1956-69; Australian Mineral Development Laboratories, 1959-67, remaining as Mem. Council; Dep. Chm., Immigration Planning Council, 1949-67. *Recreations:* golf, tennis, swimming. *Address:* Apt 3, 112-120 Walsh Street, South Yarra, Victoria 3141, Australia. *T:* 80.4398. *Clubs:* Melbourne, Athenæum, Australian (all Melbourne); Union (Sydney); Newcastle (Newcastle); Commonwealth (Canberra); Royal Melbourne Golf; Melbourne Cricket.

**MACLENNAN, Robert Adam Ross;** MP (Lab) Caithness and Sutherland since 1966; Barrister-at-law; *b* 26 June 1936; *e s* of Sir Hector MacLennan, *qv; m* 1968, Mrs Helen Noyes, *d* of Judge Ammi Cutter, Cambridge, Mass, and *widow* of Paul H. Noyes; one *d. Educ:* Glasgow Academy; Balliol Coll., Oxford; Trinity Coll., Cambridge; Columbia Univ., New York City. Called to the Bar, Gray's Inn, 1962. Parliamentary Private Secretary: to Secretary of State for Commonwealth Affairs, 1967-69; to Minister without Portfolio, 1969-; Member: House of Commons Estimates Cttee, 1967-69; House of Commons Select Cttee on Scottish Affairs, 1969-. *Recreations:* theatre, music. *Address:* 74 Abingdon Villas, W8; Birchwood, Rogart, Sutherland.

**MacLENNAN, Sir Robert Laing,** Kt, *cr* 1947; CIE 1943; Chairman of Assam Valley Branch, Indian Tea Association, Assam; retired; *b* 1888; *s* of Donald McLennan, Inverness-shire and Aberdeen; *m* 1st, Anne Williamson (*d* 1929); 2nd, Christina Comniti, *d* of Walter Taylor, Aberdeen. *Address:* Bridgebank, Milltimber, Aberdeenshire, Scotland.

**MacLEOD,** family name of **Baron MacLeod of Fuinary.**

**MacLEOD OF FUINARY,** Baron, *cr* 1967 (Life Peer), of Fuinary in Morven; **Very Rev. George F. MacLeod,** Bt, 1924; MC; BA Oxford; DD (Glasgow); Moderator of the General Assembly of the Church of Scotland, May 1957-May 1958 (designation, Very Rev.); Founder of the Iona Community (Leader, 1938-67); Chairman of Scottish Central After Care Council (for ex-prisoners and Borstal inmates); one of Her Majesty's Chaplains in Scotland; Rector of Glasgow University, since 1968; *b* 17 June 1895; 2nd *s* of Sir John MacLeod, 1st Bt; *S* nephew, 1944; *m* 1948, Lorna Helen Janet, *er d* of late Rev. Donald Macleod, Balvonie of Inshes, Inverness; two *s* one *d. Educ:* Winchester; Oriel Coll., Oxford (Hon. Fellow 1969); Edinburgh Univ. Post

Graduate Fellow, Union Theological Coll., New York, 1921; Missioner, British Columbia Lumber Camps, 1922; Collegiate Minister, St Cuthbert's Parish Church, Edinburgh, 1926-30; Minister of Govan Parish Church, Glasgow, 1930-38; Hon. Chaplain Toc H in Scotland; served European War, 1914-18; Captain Argyll and Sutherland Highlanders (MC and Croix de Guerre); Warrack Lecturer on Preaching at Edinburgh and St Andrews Universities, 1936; Select Preacher, Cambridge Univ., 1943 and 1963; Cunningham Lecturer on Evangelism, 1954; first holder of Fosdick Professorship (Rockefeller Foundation), Union Theological Seminary, New York, 1954-55; Danforth Lecturer, USA Universities, 1960 and 1964. Pres. and Chm. of Council of International Fellowship of Reconciliation, 1963. DLitt Muskingum Univ., USA; Dr of Laws, Iona Coll., New Rochelle, USA. *Publications:* Govan Calling: a book of Broadcast Sermons and Addresses, 1934; contributor to Way to God Series for the BBC; Speaking the Truth in Love: a book on Preaching, 1936; We Shall Rebuild (the principles of the Iona Community), 1944; Only One Way Left, 1956. *Heir* (to Baronetcy only): *s* Hon. John Maxwell Norman MacLeod, *b* 23 Feb. 1952. *Address:* (summer) Iona, by Oban, Argyll; (winter) 23 Learmonth Terrace, Edinburgh 4. *T:* 031-332 3262.

**McLEOD, Sir Alan Cumbrae Rose,** KCVO 1966 (CVO 1955); Surgeon Dentist to The Queen since 1952 (to King George VI, 1946-52); *b* Brisbane, Queensland, 9 Dec. 1904; *yr s* of late Frederick Rose McLeod and of Mrs Ellen McLeod; *m* 1939, Noreen Egremont King; one *s* two *d*. *Educ:* Toowoomba Grammar Sch., Queensland. Matric. University of Queensland; DDS University of Pennsylvania, USA, 1928; BSc (Dent) Univ. of Toronto, Canada, 1929; LDS RCS 1930; FDS RCS 1948; Undergraduate and Postgraduate Teaching, 1932-46. East Grinstead Maxillo-Facial Unit, 1939-45. FACD 1959. *Publications:* contributions to dental literature. *Recreation:* woodwork. *Address:* 66 Wimpole Street, W1. *T:* 01-580 2488.

**MacLEOD, Alexander Cameron,** FRCS; Hon. Consulting Surgeon: Charing Cross Hospital; Hampstead General Hospital; Connaught Hospital, Walthamstow; formerly: Consultant Surgeon, Wanstead Hospital; Surgical Registrar and Assistant, Bland-Sutton Institute of Pathology, Middlesex Hospital; *b* London, 7 Dec. 1899; *e s* of late C. E. Alexander MacLeod, FRCS; *m* 1934, Jean Marjorie, *o d* of late Col Arthur Charles Fergusson, CMG, DSO, RA; one *s* two *d*. *Educ:* Haileybury Coll.; Middlesex Hosp. MB, BS (London). Served with HM Land Forces, 1918-19, temporary 2nd Lieut RH and RFA. Senior Fellow Assoc. of Surgeons of Great Britain and Ireland; Late Mem. Bd of Examiners in Dental Surgery (Surgical Sect.), RCS. Served RAMC, 1940-45, temp. Lt-Col officer i/c Surgical Div., Cambridge Hosp., Aldershot, 1940-42; MEF, 1942-45. *Publications:* The MacLeods of St Kilda (Clann Alasdair Ruaidh), 1968; papers on surgical subjects in medical journals. *Recreations:* fly-fishing, music, gardening, walking. *Address:* 41 Downshire Hill, NW3. *T:* 01-435 1625.

**MacLEOD, Angus,** CBE 1967; Procurator Fiscal of Edinburgh and Midlothian, 1955; *b* 2 April 1906; *s* of late Alexander MacLeod, Glendale, Skye; *m* 1936, Jane Winifred, *d* of late Sir Robert Bryce Walker, CBE, LLD; three *s*. *Educ:* Hutchesons Grammar Sch.; Glasgow Univ. (MA, LLB). Solicitor, 1929; general practice, 1929-34; Depute Procurator Fiscal, Glasgow and Edinburgh, 1934-42; Procurator Fiscal of Dumfriesshire, 1942-52, of Aberdeenshire, 1952-55. *Recreations:* reading, walking, interested in sport. *Address:* 7 Oxford Terrace, Edinburgh 4. *T:* 031-332 5466.

**MacLEOD, Archibald Corrie M.;** *see* Macnab of Macnab, A. C.

**MacLEOD, Aubrey Seymour H.;** *see* Halford-MacLeod.

**MacLEOD, Cameron;** *see* MacLeod, A. C.

**McLEOD, Sir Charles Henry,** 3rd Bt, *cr* 1925; *b* 7 Nov. 1924; *o surv. s* of Sir Murdoch Campbell McLeod, 2nd Bt, and Annette Susan Mary (*d* 1964), *d* of Henry Whitehead, JP, 26 Pelham Crescent, SW7; *S* father 1950; *m* 1957, Gillian, *d* of Henry Bowlby, London; one *s* two *d*. *Educ:* Winchester. *Heir:* *s* James Roderick Charles McLeod, *b* 26 Sept. 1960. *Club:* Brooks's.

**MACLEOD OF MacLeod, Dame Flora,** DBE 1953; JP; 28th Chief of MacLeod; *b* 3 Feb. 1878; *d* of Sir Reginald MacLeod of MacLeod, KCB, 27th Chief, and Lady Agnes Northcote; *m* 1901, Hubert Walter (*d* 1933); two *d*. *Address:* Dunvegan Castle, Isle of Skye. *T:* Dunvegan 206.

*See also A. C. Macnab of Macnab.*

**McLEOD, (James) Walter,** OBE; FRS 1933; FRSE 1957; Hon. ScD (Dublin), 1946; Hon. LLD (Glasgow), 1961; Emeritus Professor, University of Leeds, since 1952; research work (Royal Society grants) Central Microbiological Laboratories, Western General Hospital, Edinburgh, since 1963; *b* 2 Jan. 1887; *s* of John McLeod and Lilias Symington McClymont; *m* 1st, 1914, Jane Christina Garvie, MA (Glasgow) (*d* 1953); one *s* five *d*; 2nd, 1956, Joyce Anita Shannon, MB ChB (St Andrews). *Educ:* George Watson's Coll., Edinburgh; Collège Cantonal, Lausanne; Mill Hill Sch.; Glasgow Univ., Coates Scholar, 1909-10, Carnegie Scholar, 1910-11. Research work in Bacteriology, Glasgow Univ. Assistant Lecturer in Pathology, Charing Cross Hospital, London, 1912-14; Temp. Lieut and Captain, RAMC, 1914-19 (despatches four times, OBE); Leeds University: Lecturer in Bacteriology, 1919, Dean of Medical Faculty, 1948-52, Brotherton Prof. of Bacteriology, 1922-52; research work under Scottish Hospital Endowments Research Trust, in the Dept of Surgery, Edinburgh Univ., 1954-63; President of the Society for General Microbiology, 1949-52. Corresponding member of the Société de Biologie, Paris, 1928; Hon. Mem. Scottish Soc. for Experimental Medicine, 1957; Hon. Mem., Pathological Soc. of Great Britain and Ireland, 1961. *Publications:* papers on Bacteriology, etc, in Journal of Pathology, Biochemical Journal, Journal of Hygiene, and Lancet; chapter on bacterial oxidations and reductions in Newer Knowledge of Bacteriology, 1928; chapters on bacterial oxidations, etc, System of Bacteriology, MRC, 1931; Section on Diphtheria, Encyclopædia Britannica, 1961. *Recreations:* golf, fishing. *Address:* 30 Ravelston Gardens, Edinburgh 4. *T:* 031-337 1524.

*See also Earl of Cromartie.*

**MacLEOD, Sir John,** Kt 1963; TD; *b* 23 Feb. 1913; *y s* of late Duncan MacLeod, CBE, Skeabost, Isle of Skye; *m* 1938, Rosemary Theodora Hamilton, *d* of late Frederick Noel Hamilton Wills, Miserden Park, Stroud, Glos; two *s* three *d*. *Educ:* Fettes Coll., Edinburgh. TA 1935. Served War of 1939-45, 51st Highland Division; France, 1940. MP (Nat. Liberal) Ross and Cromarty Div., 1945-64. *Address:* Turkdean Manor, near Northleach,

Glos. *T:* Northleach 410; 43 Chelsea Towers, SW3. *T:* 01-352 6216. *Clubs:* Army and Navy; Highland (Inverness).

**MACLEOD, Prof. John,** DD; Professor of Christian Dogmatics, University of Aberdeen, 1938-61, now Emeritus; *b* 28 Aug. 1891; *s* of late John and Christina Macleod, Aird Point, Stornoway, Isle of Lewis; unmarried. *Educ:* Nicolson Institute, Stornoway; Glasgow Univ. First Class Hons in Mental Philosophy (Glasgow), Ferguson Open Schol. in Philosophy. Asst in Dept of Logic, Glasgow Univ., 1914-16; entered as First Divinity Bursar, Trinity Coll., Glasgow (Hons Dipl.); Tutor in Greek for one year. Minister of: St Columbia's Church, Stirling, 1920-28; Kilcreggan, Dunbartonshire, 1928-31. Examiner for BD Degree, St Andrews, 1927-31, Glasgow, 1940-43, and Edinburgh, 1946-49. Professor of Systematic Theology, Emmanuel Coll., University of Toronto, 1931; studied at Tübingen, Germany, 1933. Hon. DD Pine Hill Coll., Halifax, Canada, 1936, Glasgow Univ., 1947. *Publications:* articles and reviews in Hibbert Jl, Expository Times, etc. *Recreations:* fishing, golfing. *Address:* Friarbank, Manse Road, Linlithgow. *T:* Linlithgow 2945.

**MACLEOD, Joseph Todd Gordon;** Author and play-producer; *b* 24 April 1903; *o surv s* of late James Gordon Macleod; *m* 1st, 1928, Kate Macgregor (*d* 1953), *d* of late Robert Davis, Uddingston; 2nd, Maria Teresa, *d* of late Ing. Alfredo Foschini, Rome; one *s* one *d. Educ:* Rugby Sch.; Balliol Coll., Oxford. BA 1925; MA 1945; called to Bar, Inner Temple, 1928. Was book-reviewer, private tutor, actor, producer, lecturer on theatre-history. Directed the Festival Theatre, Cambridge, 1933-36; visited theatres in USSR, 1937; Secretary of Huntingdonshire Divisional Labour Party, 1937-38, also Parliamentary Candidate; announcer BBC, 1938-45. Managing Director, Scottish National Film Studios, Glasgow, 1946-47; Convener, Drama, Gœthe Festival Society, 1948-49; produced The Lady from the Sea, Festival of Britain, Aberdeen, 1951; Scottish Episcopal Church chronicle play St Mary's Cathedral, Edinburgh, 1952; toured Holland as guest of Dutch Ministry of Fine Arts, 1946; visited Soviet Union as guest of Moscow and Kiev Cultural Relations Societies, 1947; Silver Medal, Royal Society of Arts for paper on the Theatre in Soviet Culture, 1944. Hon. Member, British Actors' Equity. *Plays performed:* The Suppliants of Aeschylus translated with a verse sequel, 1933; A Woman Turned to Stone, 1934; Overture to Cambridge, 1934; A Miracle for St George, 1935; Leap in September (Arts Council Prize), 1952. *Publications:* Beauty and the Beast, 1927; The Ecliptic (poem), 1930; Foray of Centaurs (poem), 1931; Overture to Cambridge (novel), 1936; The New Soviet Theatre, 1943; Actors Cross the Volga, 1946; A Job at the BBC, 1947; A Soviet Theatre Sketchbook, 1951; The Passage of the Torch (poem), 1951; A Short History of the British Theatre (Italian edn), 1958; Abstractions, 1967; People of Florence, 1968; The Sisters D'Aranyi, 1969; poetry under *non-de-plume* Adam Drinan: The Cove, 1940; The Men of the Rocks, 1942; The Ghosts of the Strath, 1943; Women of the Happy Island, 1944; Script from Norway, 1953; contribution on Theatre history to Chambers's Encyclopædia. *Music:* The Kid from the City, 1941. *Recreations:* painting, music, bird-watching. *Address:* Via delle Ballodole 9/7, Trespiano, Firenze, Italy. *T:* Firenze 417056.

**MacLEOD, Maj.-Gen. Minden Whyte-Melville,** CB 1945; CBE 1943; DSO 1918; Commander, US Legion of Merit, 1946; late Royal Artillery; British Advisory Staff, Polish Resettlement Corps, 1946-49; Colonel Commandant Royal Artillery, 1952-61; *b* 1896; *y s* of late M. N. MacLeod, Behar, India; *m* 1926, Violet, *o d* of late Major J. Elsdale Molson and Mrs Molson, of the Pound House, Angmering, Sussex; two *d. Educ:* Rugby; Woolwich; graduated Staff Coll., Dec. 1932; served European War, 1914-18 (DSO, despatches); Iraq, 1920 (medal and clasp); Waziristan, 1921-24 (medal and clasp); North West Frontier of India, 1930 (clasp); War of 1939-45 (despatches, CBE, CB); retired pay, 1949. *Address:* 12 Lower Sloane Street, SW1. *Club:* Naval and Military.

**MACLEOD, Norman Donald,** MA, LLB; Advocate; Sheriff-Substitute of Lanarkshire at Glasgow since 1967; *b* 6 March 1932; *s* of Rev. John MacLeod, Loch Carron, and late Catherine MacRitchie; *m* 1957, Ursula Jane, *y d* of George H. Bromley, Inveresk; two *s* two *d. Educ:* Mill Hill Sch.; George Watson's Boys' Coll., Edinburgh; Edinburgh Univ.; Hertford Coll., Oxford. Passed Advocate, 1956. Colonial Administrative Service, Tanganyika: Dist. Officer, 1957-59; Crown Counsel, 1959-64; practised at Scots Bar, 1964-67. *Recreations:* playing with water, in it, on it, and around it. *Address:* 27 Cleveden Drive, Glasgow W2. *T:* 339-1607. *Club:* Edinburgh Sports.

**MACLEOD, Robert Duncan;** Founder and Past Editor of the Library Review; *b* Greenock, Renfrewshire; unmarried. Served in public libraries at Greenock and Glasgow; first librarian to Carnegie United Kingdom Trustees; Fellow of the Library Association, with honours in classification and cataloguing; helped to start official library training classes in Glasgow, and promoted other library activities; founder of County Library Circle, and of Strathclyde Librarians' Club; declined Presidency of the Scottish Library Association; past Hon. Secretary, Scottish PEN. *Publications:* Rural Libraries and Rural Education, 1922; County Rural Libraries: Their Policy and Organisation, 1923; The Scottish Publishing Houses, 1953; Morris without Mackail, 1954, new edn, 1957; John Davidson, 1956; Poems and Ballads by John Davidson, 1958; The Anglo-American Library Associations, 1958; editor of various catalogues, including Modern Scottish Literature: a Guide Book, 1933; contributor to British, American, and Indian periodicals. *Clubs:* Savage, Press; Western, Art (Glasgow).

**McLEOD, Gen. Sir Roderick (William),** GBE 1964 (CBE 1945); KCB 1958 (CB 1952); DL; *b* 15 Jan. 1905; *s* of Col Reginald George McQueen McLeod, DSO, late RA, and Cicely Knightley (*née* Boyd); *m* 1st, 1933, Camilla Rachel Hunter (*d* 1942), *d* of late Sir Godfrey Fell, KCIE, CSI, OBE; one *d*; 2nd, 1946 Mary Vavasour Lloyd Thomas, MBE (*née* Driver), *widow* of Major R. J. H. Thomas, MVO, RHA. *Educ:* Wellington Coll., Berks; RMA, Woolwich. Commissioned 1925, operations, NW Frontier, India, 1931-32; Staff Coll., 1938. Comdr SAS Troops, 1944-45; Dir Military Operations, India, 1945-46; idc 1947; Asst Comdt, Staff Coll., 1948-49; CRA 7th Armoured Div., 1950; Dir of Military Operations, War Office, 1951-54; GOC 6th Armoured Div., 1955-56; Chief Army Instructor, Imperial Defence Coll., Jan.-Dec. 1957; Dep. Chief of Defence Staff, 1957-60; Comdr British Forces, Hong Kong, 1960-61; Gen. 1961; GOC-in-C, Eastern Comd, 1962-65; ADC (Gen.) to the Queen, 1963-65. DL Surrey, 1967. Comdr Order of Leopold II,

1946; Chevalier Legion of Honour, 1945; Croix de Guerre avec Palme, 1945. *Recreations:* ski-ing, sailing. *Address:* Fairhill, The Hockering, Woking, Surrey. *T:* Woking 61477. *Clubs:* Army and Navy, Ski Club of Great Britain, Eagle Ski Club.

**MacLEOD, Walter;** *see* MacLeod, J. W.

**MACLEOD-SMITH, Alastair Macleod,** CMG 1956; *b* 30 June 1916; *s* of late R. A. Smith, MIEE, and of Mrs I. Macleod-Smith (*née* Kellner); *m* 1945, Ann (*née* Circuitt); one *s* one *d*. *Educ:* The Wells House, Malvern Wells, Worcs; Ellesmere Coll., Salop; The Queen's Coll., Oxford. BA Oxon 1938. Entered HM Oversea Service as administrative cadet, Nigeria, 1939; Asst Dist Officer, 1942, Dist Officer, Nigeria, 1949; seconded to Windward Islands as Financial and Economic Adviser, 1949-52; Financial Sec., Western Pacific High Commission, 1952-57; Financial Sec., Sierra Leone, 1957-61; since when with Selection Trust Ltd (Dir, 1967). *Recreations:* golf, sailing. *Address:* Roughetts Lodge, Coldharbour Lane, Hildenborough, Kent. *Club:* United University.

**Mac LIAMMOIR, Micheál;** actor, designer, playwright; Director of Dublin Gate Theatre Productions since 1928; *b* Cork, Ireland, 25 Oct. 1899; *s* of Alfred Antony Mac Liammóir and Mary Elizabeth (*née* Lawler Lee). *Educ:* privately. First appearance on stage (as child) at Little Theatre, London, in The Goldfish, 1911; West End parts, 1911-15; studied painting at Slade Sch., 1915-16. Painted and designed for Irish Theatre and Dublin Drama League; lived abroad studying painting till 1927; returned to Ireland and joined Anew McMaster's Shakespearean Co. With Hilton Edwards: opened Galway gaelic Theatre; they also estab. Dublin Gate Theatre, 1928; has since acted in, and designed for, over 300 prodns there; apptd Dir of Govt subsidized Dublin Gaelic Theatre, 1928; with Dublin Gate Theatre Co., London, 1934; toured in Egypt, 1936-38, Balkan States, 1939. With Hilton Edwards and Gate Co. he played in (his own) Ill Met by Moonlight, Vaudeville, London, 1947; season, Embassy, 1947. First appearance on New York Stage as Larry Doyle in John Bull's Other Island, Mansfield, 1948. Iago in film Othello, 1949; in (his own) Home for Christmas, Gate, 1950; Hedda Gabler, Lyric, Hammersmith, 1954; in revue Gateway to Gaiety (setting, costumes, and contrib. material), Gaiety, Dublin, 1956; The Hidden King, Edinburgh Fest., 1957. The Key of the Door, The Heart's a Wonder (setting and costumes), Lyric, Hammersmith, 1958; appeared in The Informer (adaptation and decor), Dublin, 1958; Much Ado About Nothing, NY, 1959. One-man entertainment, The Importance of Being Oscar, Dublin, 1960, London, 1960 (1966), since 1960 in this programme in Europe, USA, S America, Australia, New Zealand, etc.; One-Man programmes: I Must be Talking to my Friends and Talking about Yeats, in Dublin, subseq. London, etc. Various Irish awards for plays, etc. Kronborg Gold Medal, Elsinore, 1952. Hon. LLD, TCD, 1962. *Publications: in Irish:* Oícheanna Sidhe (faery tales), 1922; Oíche Bhealtaine (play), 1933; Lá agus Oíche (short stories), 1934; Diarmuid agus Gráinne (play), 1935; Ceo Meala Lá Seaca (essays), 1952; Aisteoirí faoi dhá Sholas (memoirs), 1956; Bláth agus Taibhse (poems), 1964; *in English:* All for Hecuba (autobiography), 1946; Put Money in thy Purse (diary), 1954; Ill Met by Moonlight (play), 1957; Each Actor on his Ass (memoirs), 1960; Where Stars Walk (play), 1961; The Importance of Being Oscar, 1963; Ireland (a study of the country and its people), 1966; An Oscar of No Importance (autobiography and study of Wilde), 1968. *Recreations:* travel, balletomania. *Address:* 4 Harcourt Terrace, Dublin, Ireland. *T:* Dublin 6.7609. *Club:* Arts (Dublin).

**McLINTOCK, Sir William Traven,** 3rd Bt, *cr* 1934; *b* 4 Jan. 1931; *s* of Sir Thomas McLintock, 2nd Bt and Jean, *d* of R. T. D. Aitken, New Brunswick; *S* father 1953; *m* 1952, André, *d* of Richard Lonsdale-Hands; three *s*. *Educ:* Harrow. *Heir: s* Michael William McLintock, *b* 13 Aug. 1958. *Address:* Tudor Cottage, Marsh Lane, Mill Hill, NW7. *T:* 01-959 1447.

**McLOUGHLIN, Brig. (Air Vice-Marshal) Eduardo Francisco;** Minister of the Interior, Argentina, 1970, resigned; *b* 13 May 1918; *m* 1943, Mónica Murphy. *Educ:* Salesian primary and high sch.; military coll. Asst Air Attaché to Argentine Embassy in London and Mem. Argentine Aeronautical Mission for Europe, 1946; subseq. cont. services in Air Force. Apptd Dir-Gen., Air Min., 1956; Minister Sec. of State for the Air Force, 1957; Air Attaché to Argentine Embassy, Washington, 1958-61; Mem. Argentine Delegn to Inter-American Defense Bd, 1958-61. Promoted Brig. (Air Vice-Marshal), Dec. 1959; retd from active service, Oct. 1961. Apptd Minister Sec. of State for Air, Dec. 1962; Pres. Honour Tribunal for the Armed Forces, 1965; Ambassador to London, 1966-70. Holds foreign decorations. *Address:* c/o Ministry of the Interior, Buenos Aires, Argentina.

**MACLURE, (John) Stuart;** Editor, Times Educational Supplement, since 1969; *b* 8 Aug. 1926; *s* of Hugh and Bertha Maclure, Highgate, N6; *m* 1951, Constance Mary Butler; one *s* two *d*. *Educ:* Highgate Sch.; Christ's Coll., Cambridge. 1st class Hons. History Tripos, 1950, MA. Joined The Times, 1950; The Times Educational Supplement, 1951; Editor, Education, 1954-69. *Publications:* Joint Editor (with T. E. Utley) Documents on Modern Political Thought, 1956; Editor, Educational Documents, 1816-1963, 1965; A Hundred Years of London Education, 1970. *Recreations:* ornithology, cricket. *Address:* 109 College Road, Dulwich, SE21. *Club:* MCC.

**MACLURE, Stuart;** *see* Maclure, J. S.

**MACLURE, Lt-Col Sir John William Spencer,** 3rd Bt, *cr* 1898; OBE 1945; *b* 4 Feb. 1899; *er s* of Col Sir John Maclure, 2nd Bt, and Ruth Ina Muriel (*d* 1951), *e d* of late W. B. McHardy, Comdr, RN, and Chief Constable of Lanarkshire; *S* father, 1938; *m* 1929, Elspeth King, *er d* of late Alexander King Clark, Wykeham Hatch, West Byfleet; two *s* one *d*. *Educ:* Wellington Coll.; Royal Military College, Sandhurst. Joined KRRC 1917; Lt-Col 1939; served in France and Flanders, 1918; North Russia, 1919; India, 1920-22 and 1925-28; Burma, 1936-38; commanded Rifle Depôt, 1939-40 and 1941-44; commanded 37 Reinforcement Holding Unit, BWEF, 1944 (OBE); commanded 113 Transit Camp, BLA; at Osnabruck; Comdr British Troops Holland, and 41 (Hook) Garrison, Holland, 1946; RARO 1949-54. *Heir: s* John Robert Spencer Maclure [*b* 25 March 1934; *m* 1964, Jane Monica, *d* of Rt Rev. T. J. Savage, MA; two *s*]. *Address:* 6 Bereweeke Close, Winchester, Hants. *Clubs:* United Service, MCC, British Automobile Racing.

**McLUSKEY, Rev. J(ames) Fraser,** MC; MA, BD, DD; Minister at St Columba's Church of Scotland, Pont Street, London, SW1, since 1960; *b* 1914; *s* of James Fraser McLuskey and Margaret Keltie; *m* 1st, 1939, Irene (*d* 1959), *d* of Pastor Calaminus, Wuppertal; two *s*; 2nd 1966, Ruth Quartermaine (*née* Hunter), *widow* of Lt-Col Keith Briant. *Educ:* Aberdeen Grammar Sch.; Edinburgh Univ. Ordained Minister of Church of Scotland, 1938; Chaplain to Univ. of Glasgow, 1939-47. Service as Army Chaplain, 1943-46 (1st Special Air Service Regt, 1944-46); Sub Warden Royal Army Chaplains' Training Centre, 1947-50; Minister at Broughty Ferry East, 1950-55; Minister at New Kilpatrick, Bearsden, 1955-60. *Publication:* Parachute Padre, 1951. *Recreations:* walking, music, reading. *Address:* 1a Lennox Gardens, SW1. *T:* 01-589 6781. *Clubs:* Caledonian, Special Forces.

**MacLYSAGHT, Edward,** DLitt, MRIA; Chairman of Irish Manuscripts Commission since 1956; Chief Herald and Genealogical Officer, Office of Arms, Dublin Castle, 1943-54; Keeper of Manuscripts, National Library of Ireland, 1949-55; *b* at sea, 1889 (bapt. Co. Clare); *m* 1st, 1915, Maureen Pattison; one *s* one *d*; 2nd, 1936, Mary Frances Cunneen; three *s*. *Educ:* abroad; Nat. Univ. of Ireland (MA). Engaged in cattle-breeding and forestry since 1911; mem. of Irish Convention, 1917-18, Irish Senate, 1922-25; working in South Africa, 1929-30, 1936-38; inspector Irish Manuscripts Commission, 1939-43. *Publications:* The Gael, 1919; Cùrsaí Thomáis, 1927, new edn 1969; Toil Dé 1933; Short Study of a Transplanted Family, 1935; Irish Life in the Seventeenth Century, 1939, 3rd edn 1969; (ed) The Kenmare Manuscripts, 1942; (ed) Analecta Hibernica (14 and 15), 1944; An Aifric Theas, 1947, East Clare (1916-21), 1954; Irish Families: Their Names, Arms and Origins, 1957, More Irish Families, 1960; Supplement to Irish Families, 1964; Guide to Irish Surnames, 1965; The Surnames of Ireland, 1969; (ed) Forth the Banners Go, reminiscences of William O'Brien, 1969, etc. *Address:* Raheen, Tuamgraney, Co. Clare. *Club:* United Arts (Dublin).

**McMAHON, Christopher William;** Executive Director, Bank of England, since 1970; *b* Melbourne, 10 July 1927; *s* of late Dr John Joseph McMahon and late Margaret Kate (*née* Brown); *m* 1956, Marion Elizabeth, *d* of late A. E. Kelso; two *s*. *Educ:* Melbourne Grammar Sch.; Univ. of Melbourne; Magdalen Coll., Oxford. 1st cl. hons PPE, 1953. Tutor in English Lit., Univ. of Melbourne, 1950; Econ. Asst, HM Treasury, 1953-57; Econ. Adviser, British Embassy, Washington, 1957-60; Fellow and Tutor in Econs, Magdalen Coll., Oxford, 1960-64 (Sen. Tutor, 1961-63); Tutor in Econs, Treasury Centre for Admin. Studies, 1963-64; Mem., Plowden Cttee on Aircraft Industry, 1964-65; entered Bank of England as Adviser to the Governors, 1966-70. *Publications:* Sterling in the Sixties, 1964; (ed) Techniques of Economic Forecasting, 1965. *Recreation:* reading. *Address:* 12 Lyndhurst Road, NW3. *T:* 01-435 1458.

**MacMAHON, Gerald John,** CB 1962; CMG 1955; *b* 26 Sept. 1909; 2nd *s* of late Jeremiah MacMahon and Kathleen MacMahon (*née* Dodd); unmarried. *Educ:* Clongowes Wood Coll., Co. Kildare, Ireland; Emmanuel Coll., Cambridge (BA). Entered Board of Trade, 1933; Asst Sec., 1942. Imperial Defence Coll., 1949. Senior UK Trade Commissioner in India, 1952-58; Under-Sec., Board of Trade 1958-62 and 1964-70; Admiralty, Nov. 1962-64. *Recreation:* golf. *Address:* 19 Lower Park, Putney Hill, SW15. *Club:* Reform.

**McMAHON, Sir Patrick;** *see* McMahon, Sir W. P.

**MACMAHON, Lt-Gen. Peadar;** Secretary, Department of Defence, Ireland, since 1927; *b* 10 Jan. 1893; *m* 1924, Anne Parkinson; three *s* one *d*. Gen. Officer Commanding Curragh Training Camp, 1922-24; Chief of Staff, 1924-27. *Address:* Gracemount, Howth, Co. Dublin. *T:* 322832.

**McMAHON, Rt. Hon. William,** PC 1966; MP for Lowe (NSW); Minister for External Affairs, Commonwealth of Australia, since 1969; *b* 23 Feb. 1908; *s* of William Daniel McMahon; *m* 1965, Sonia R. Hopkins: one *s* one *d*. *Educ:* Sydney Gram. Sch.; St Paul's Coll., Univ. of Sydney (LLB, BEc). Practised as solicitor until 1939. Australian Army, 1940-45, Major. Elected to House of Representatives for Lowe, NSW, in gen. elections, 1949, 1951, 1954, 1955, 1958, 1961, 1963, 1966, 1969. Minister: for Navy, and for Air, 1951-54 (visited Korea and Japan in that capacity, 1952); for Social Services, 1954-56; for Primary Industry, 1956-58; for Labour and National Service, 1958-66; Treasurer, 1966-69; Vice-Pres., Executive Council, 1964-66; Dep. Leader of Liberal Party, 1966-; Acting Minister for Trade, May-Aug. and Oct.-Nov., 1956; Acting Minister in Charge, CSIRO, Oct.-Dec., 1956; Acting Minister for National Development, Oct. 1959; Leader of Aust. Delegation to Commonwealth Parliamentary Conf., New Delhi, Nov. 1957-Jan. 1958; Visiting Minister to ILO Conf., Geneva, June 1960 and June 1964; Pres., ILO Asian Regional Conf., Melbourne, Nov.-Dec., 1962; Acting Attorney Gen., Sept.-Oct., 1960; Acting Minister for Territories, Oct.-Nov., 1962; Treasurer, Commonwealth of Australia, 1966-69. Mem., Bd of Govs, IMF and World Bank, 1966-69. Chm., Bd of Govs, Asian Development Bank, 1968-69. Led Australian delegns to Bangkok, Djakarta, Manila and Saigon, 1970. *Recreations:* golf, squash. *Address:* Commonwealth Parliament Offices, Sydney, NSW, Australia. *Clubs:* Union, Royal Sydney, Elanora, Tattersalls (Sydney); Melbourne (Melbourne); Commonwealth (Canberra).

**McMAHON, Sir (William) Patrick,** 7th Bt, *cr* 1817; in private practice as Land Agent; *b* 24 April 1900; *s* of Lt-Col Sir Eyre McMahon, 6th Bt, and Lydia Mary (*d* 1933), *widow* of Slingsby Cradock and *d* of Major W. P. Hoey, Co. Wicklow; *S* father 1935; *m* 1939, Ruth Stella Hahlo (marriage dissolved, 1960), *yr d* of late P. R. and late Mrs Kenyon Slaney; two *s* *Educ:* Wellington Coll. Fellow of the Land Agents Soc.; Professional Associate of Surveyors Institution. *Heir:* *s* Brian Patrick McMahon, *b* 9 June 1942. *Address:* Les Buttes, St Martin, Jersey, CI. *T:* East 2367. *Club:* Victoria (Jersey).

**MacMANUS, Emily Elvira Primrose,** CBE 1947 (OBE 1930); SRN, SCM, retired; *b* 18 April 1886; *d* of Leonard Strong McManus, MD, of Battersea, London, and Killeaden House, Kiltimagh, Co. Mayo, Eire, and Julia Emily Boyd, Howth, Co. Dublin. *Educ:* Governess and private schs. Gen. Nursing Training, Guy's Hosp., 1908; Midwifery Training, East End Mothers' Home, 1912; Sister, Kasr en Aini Hospital, Cairo, and Private Nursing, Egypt; Sister, King's Lynn; Sister, Guy's Hospital; Sister, QAIMNSR, France, 1915-18 (despatches twice); Asst Matron, Guy's Hosp., 1919; Asst Medical Research Council, Food Experiment, Dr Barnardo's Boys' Garden City, 1922; Matron, Bristol Royal Infirmary, 1923; Matron, Guy's Hosp., 1927-46; Sector Matron, Sector 10, EMS, 1939-46; Principal Matron, TANS, 1923-46; late Mem. Gen. Nursing Council; Chm., Voluntary Advisory Nursing Board for HM Prisons,

1936-46; Mem. Council Queen's Dist Nursing Assoc., Eire; late Mem. Council Queen's Dist Nursing Assoc., and Overseas Nursing Assoc.; Pres. Royal College of Nursing, 1942-44; Nursing Missions: British West Indies, 1946-47; Persia 1948, Turkey, 1949, Holland 1952. Broadcast series, BBC, Mary and her Furry Friends, 1964; Broadcasts, BBC: Silver Lining in series Home this afternoon, 1965; Desert Island Discs, 1966. *Publications:* Hospital Administration for Women, 1934; Nursing in Time of War (Jt), 1939; Matron of Guy's 1956. *Recreations:* fishing, gardening, literature. *Address:* Terry Lodge, Terrybawn, Bofeenaun, Ballina, Co. Mayo, Eire. *Club:* Royal Irish Automobile (Dublin).

**McMANUS, Francis Joseph;** MP (Unity) Fermanagh and South Tyrone since 1970; *b* 16 Aug. 1942; *s* of Patrick and Celia McManus. *Educ:* St Michael's Enniskillen; Queen's University, Belfast. BA 1965; Diploma in Education, 1966. Subsequently a Teacher. *Address:* Chonliff, Macken, Enniskillen, Co. Fermanagh, N Ireland. *T:* Enniskillen 3401.

**MacMANUS, John Leslie Edward,** TD 1945; QC 1970; *b* 7 April 1920; *o s* of E. H. MacManus and H. S. MacManus (*née* Colton); *m* 1942, Gertrude (Trudy) Mary Frances Koppenhagen; two *d. Educ:* Eastbourne College. Served 1939-45 with RA: Middle East, Italy, Crete, Yugoslavia; Captain 1942; Major 1945. Called to Bar, Middle Temple, 1947. Dep. Chm., East Sussex QS, 1964-. *Recreations:* gardening, odd-jobbing, travel. *Address:* The Old Rectory, Twineham, Haywards Heath, Sussex. *T:* Bolney 221; 1 Crown Office Row, Temple, EC4. *T:* 01-353 3372. *Clubs:* Sussex, Sussex Martlets.

**McMANUS, Maurice,** CBE 1966; DL; JP; Lord Provost of Dundee and Lord Lieutenant of the County of the City of Dundee, 1960-67; *b* 17 Jan. 1906; *s* of Patrick and Ann McManus; *m* 1931, Lillian, *d* of James and Isobel Lindsay; three *s* two *d. Educ:* West Calder. Tutor at National Council of Labour Coll., 1945-. Chm. Dundee City Labour Party, 1950-56. Member: Exec. Cttee, Scottish Council for Development and Industry; Scottish Advisory Cttee for Civil Aviation; Court of St Andrews Univ.; Council of Queen's Coll., Dundee; Chairman: Tay Road Bridge Jt Bd; Dundee Coll. of Art and Technology. DL Dundee, 1967-. *Recreation:* gardening. *Address:* 44 Clement Park Road, Dundee. *T:* Dundee 69568.

**McMASTER, Ian,** OBE 1960; *b* 28 Jan. 1898; *s* of Rev. Kenneth McMaster and Gertrude Lucy Strachan; *m* 1924, Jane Harvey, MA, FRHistS (*d* 1958); one *d*; *m* 1963, Mary Isabella Blewitt Neville, Warden, St Luke's Home, Oxford. *Educ:* King's Sch., Canterbury; University Coll. Sch., London; Queen's Coll., Oxford (Scholar); Grenoble Univ. Chief History Master, King Edward VI Sch., Birmingham, 1922-35; History Master, Eton Coll., 1935-40; Consul in Florence and Consul-Gen. to Republic of San Marino, 1952-60; HM Foreign Service, retd 1960. Warden, Sheffield Diocesan Conference House, 1960-64. Mem. Archbishop's Council for Inter-Church Relations; Diocesan Lay Reader. *Recreation:* human problems. *Address:* 8 Garford Road, Oxford. *T:* Oxford 58017.

**McMASTER, Stanley Raymond,** MP (UU) for Belfast East since March 1959; *b* 23 Sept. 1926; *o s* of F. R. McMaster, Nottinghill, Belfast, N Ireland; *m* 1959, Verda Ruth Tynan, SRN, Comber, Co Down, Northern Ireland; two *s* two *d* (and one *d* decd). *Educ:* Campbell Coll., Belfast; Trinity Coll., Dublin (BA (Mod.) and BComm). Called to the Bar, Lincoln's Inn, 1953; Common law practice from 4 Paper Bldgs, Temple, EC4; Lectr in Company Law, Polytechnic, Regent Street, 1954-. Parliamentary and Legal Sec., to Finance and Taxation Cttee, Association of British Chambers of Commerce, 1958-59. *Publications:* various articles in legal and commercial journals. *Recreations:* golf, rowing and shooting. *Address:* Nottinghill, Malone Road, Belfast. *Clubs:* Knock Golf, etc.

**McMEEKAN, Brig. Gilbert Reader,** CB 1955; DSO 1942; OBE 1942; JP, 1956; retired, Regular Army, 1955; *b* 22 June 1900; *s* of late Major F. H. F. R. McMeekan, RA; *m* 1932, Marion Janet, *d* of late Sir John Percival, KBE; one *s* two *d. Educ:* Wellington Coll.; RMA Woolwich. Commissioned RE 1919; BAOR 1922-24; Sudan Defence Force, 1924-31; Aldershot, 1931-37; Malta, 1938-42; o/c Fortress, RE Malta, 1940-42; CRE 10 Armoured Div. (Alamein), 1942-43; Liaison Staff, USA, 1944-45; Chief Superintendent, Military Engineering Experimental Establishment, Christchurch, 1946-50; Comdr, 25 Eng. Group TA, 1950-52; Comdr, RE Ripon, 1952-55. Officer, American Legion of Merit, 1946. *Address:* Greenacres, Painswick, Glos. *T:* Painswick 2395.
*See also Baron Dickinson.*

**McMEEKIN, Maj.-Gen. Terence Douglas Herbert,** OBE 1960; Commandant, Joint Services Staff College, since 1970; *b* 27 Sept. 1918; *s* of late Herbert William Porter McMeekin, Cogry, Co. Antrim, and Mrs J. K. McMeekin; *m* 1947, Averil Anne Spence Longstaff, 7th *d* of late Dr T. G. Longstaff and Mrs D. H. Longstaff, Fritham, Hants; one *s* two *d. Educ:* King William's Coll., IOM; RMA Woolwich. 2nd Lt RA, 1938; served War of 1939-45 (despatches); GSO2 (L) HQ 8th Army, 1943; Staff Coll., Haifa, 1943; GSO2 (Ops), HQ 3 Corps, 1944; Bde Major RA, 1 Airborne Div., 1945; Battery Comdr, 6 Airborne Div., Palestine, 1945-46; Instructor in Gunnery, 1947-48; GSO2 (Tactics), School of Artillery, Manorbier, 1949-50; DAQMG, HQ 1 (British) Corps, 1952-54; jssc 1955; Battery Comdr, 5 RHA, 1955-57; Bt Lt-Col, 1957; AA & QMG, HQ Land Forces, Hong Kong, 1958-60; comd 29 Field Regt, RA, 1960-62; converted Regt to Commando role, 1962; Col 1962; Chief Instructor (Tactics), School of Artillery, Larkhill, 1962-64; comd 28 Commonwealth Inf. Bde Gp, Malaya, 1964-66; Dir of Public Relations (Army), 1967-68; GOC 3rd Div., 1968-70. Pres., Army Cricket Assoc., 1969. *Recreations:* cricket, most field sports. *Address:* The Old Rectory, Beverstone, near Tetbury, Glos. *T:* Tetbury 735. *Clubs:* Army and Navy, Stragglers of Asia.

**McMENEMEY, William Henry,** MA, DM, FRCP, FCPath, DPM; Emeritus Professor of Pathology, Institute of Neurology, University of London, and Hon. Consulting Pathologist, National Hospitals for Nervous Diseases; *b* 16 May 1905; *s* of William Henry McMenemey and Frances Annie (*née* Rankin); *m* Robina Inkster, MD (Aberdeen); one *s* one *d. Educ:* Birkenhead Sch.; Merton Coll., Oxford; St Bartholomew's Hospital. Formerly: House Physician and Junior Demonstrator in Pathology, St Bart's Hosp.; Registrar in Neurology, Maida Vale Hosp.; Pathologist, Napsbury and Shenley Hosps and Asst Pathologist, West End Hosp. for Nervous Diseases, 1934-37; Asst Pathologist, Radcliffe Infirmary, Oxford, 1937-40; Pathologist, Royal Infirmary, Worcester, 1940-49 and EMS Pathologist, Barnsley Hall, All Saints and Ronkswood Hosps; Pathologist, Maida Vale Hosp. for Nervous Diseases, 1949-70; Prof. of

Pathology, Inst of Neurology, 1965-70. Savill Prize, 1932; Charles Hastings Memorial Lectr, 1951; Pres., International Soc. of Clinical Pathology, 1966-69; Sec.-General: Internat. Soc. of Neuropathology, 1967-70; 1st Internat. Congress of Clinical Pathology, 1951; 2nd Internat. Congress of Neuropathology, 1955; President: Assoc. of Clinical Pathologists, 1958 (Sec. 1943-57); Brit. Neuropathological Soc., 1957-60; Sect. of Neurology, 1960-61 and Sect. of History of Medicine, 1962-64, RSM; Hon. Member: Amer. Soc. of Clinical Pathology; Amer. Assoc. of Neuropathologists; Australian Coll. of Pathologists; Soc. Française de Biologie Medicale; Rumanian Soc. of Medical Sciences; John Shaw Billings Hist. of Medicine Soc.; Corresp. Member: Vereinigung Deutsch. Neuropathologen u. Neuroanat.; Soc. Française de Neurologie. *Publications:* History of Worcester Royal Infirmary, 1947; James Parkinson, 1955; Pathology of Dementia and Diseases of Basal Ganglia, in Greenfield's Neuropathology, 1963; The Life and Times of Sir Charles Hastings, 1959; Pathology of Central Nervous System in Systemic Pathology (ed G. Payling Wright & W. St C. Symmers), 1966; various writings on neuropathology, clinical pathology and medical history. *Recreations:* music, gardening. *Address:* Manor House, London Road, Morden, Surrey. *T:* 01-648 3571. *Club:* Athenæum.

**McMICHAEL, Sir John,** Kt 1965; FRS 1957; MD, FRCP, FRCPE; FACP (Hon.); Hon. LLD (Edinburgh); MD (Melbourne); Hon. DSc (Newcastle, Sheffield, Birmingham, Ohio); Hon. ScD (Dublin); Director, British Post-graduate Medical Federation, since Oct. 1966; Emeritus Professor of Medicine, University of London; *b* 25 July 1904; *s* of James McMichael and Margaret Sproat; *m* 1942, Sybil E. Blake (*d* 1965); four *s*; *m* 1965, Sheila M. Howarth. *Educ:* Kirkcudbright Acad.; Edinburgh Univ. Ettles Scholar, 1927; Beit Memorial Fellow, 1930-34; Johnston and Lawrence Fellow., Royal Society, 1937-39; Univ. teaching appointments in Aberdeen, Edinburgh and London. Dir, Dept of Medicine, Post-grad. Med. Sch. of London, 1946-66; Mem. Medical Research Council, 1949-53. A Vice-Pres., Royal Soc., 1968-. Pres., World Congress of Cardiology, 1970. Hon. Member: American Medical Association, 1947; Medical Soc., Copenhagen, 1953; Norwegian Medical Soc., 1954; Assoc. Amer. Physicians, 1959. For. Mem. Finnish Acad. of Science and Letters, 1963. Thayer Lectr, Johns Hopkins Hosp., 1948; Oliver Sharpey Lectr, 1952; Croonian Lectr, 1961, RCP; Watson Smith Lectr RCPEd, 1958. Cullen Prize, RCPEd, 1953. Jacobs Award, Dallas, 1958; Morgan Prof., Nashville, Tenn, 1964. Moxon Medal, RCP, 1960; Gairdner Award, Toronto, 1960; Wihuri Internat. Prize, Finland, 1968. Trustee, Wellcome Trust, 1960. *Publications:* Pharmacology of the Failing Human Heart, 1951. Numerous papers on: Splenic Anaemia, 1931-35; Cardiac Output in Health and Disease, 1938-47; Lung Capacity in Man, 1938-39; Liver Circulation and Liver Disease, 1932-43. *Recreation:* gardening. *Address:* 2 North Square, NW11. *T:* 01-455 8731. *Club:* Athenæum.

**MacMICHAEL, Nicholas Hugh,** FSA; Keeper of the Muniments of Westminster Abbey since 1967; *b* 2 Feb. 1933; *o s* of late Canon Arthur William MacMichael and of Elizabeth Helen Royale, *o d* of late Rev. Arthur William Newboult; unmarried. *Educ:* Eastbourne Coll.; Magdalene Coll.; Cambridge. Asst Librarian and Asst Keeper of the Muniments of Westminster Abbey, 1956-66; Hon. Sec., 1961-64, Hon. Editor, 1964-70, Harleian Soc. FSA 1962; Fellow, Soc. of Genealogists, 1969. *Publications:* articles in learned jls. *Recreations:* genealogical and heraldic research; ecclesiology; watching cricket. *Address:* 2b Little Cloister, Westminster Abbey, SW1. *T:* 01-799 6893. *Club:* Oxford and Cambridge University.

**McMILLAN, Col Donald,** CB 1959; OBE 1945; Chairman, Cable & Wireless Ltd, and associated companies, since Nov. 1967; *b* 22 Dec. 1906; *s* of Neil Munro McMillan and Isabella Jamieson; *m* 1946, Kathleen Ivy Bingham; one *s*. *Educ:* Sloane Sch., Chelsea; Battersea Polytechnic. Post Office Engineering Dept, 1925-54; Director External Telecommunications, Post Office External Telecommunications Executive, 1954-67. BSc Eng (London); FIEE. *Publications:* contribs to Institution Engineers Journal, Post Office Institution Engineers Journal. *Recreations:* golf and gardening. *Address:* 46 Gatehill Road, Northwood, Middx. *T:* Northwood 22682. *Club:* Grim's Dyke Golf.

**McMILLAN, Prof. Duncan;** Professor of French Language and Romance Linguistics, University of Edinburgh, since 1955; *b* London, 1914; *o s* of late Duncan McMillan and Martha (*née* Hastings); *m* 1945, Geneviève, *er d* of late M Robert Busse, Paris, and of Mme Robert Busse, Paris; one *s*. *Educ:* St Dunstan's Coll.; University Coll., London; Sorbonne, Paris. BA, PhD (London); Diplôme de L'Ecole des Hautes Etudes, Paris. Lecteur d'anglais, Univ. of Paris, 1938-40; Lectr in French and Romance Philology, Univ. of Aberdeen, 1946-50, Univ. of Edinburgh, 1950-55. Served in the Army, 1940-46. Chevalier de la Légion d'Honneur, 1958. *Publications:* La Chanson de Guillaume (Société des anciens texte français), 2 vols. 1949-50; (in collaboration with Madame G. McMillan) An Anthology of the Contemporary French Novel, 1950; articles in Romania and other learned journals. *Address:* 4 Clarendon Crescent, Edinburgh. *T:* 031-332 1943.

**McMILLAN, Prof. Edwin Mattison;** Professor of Physics, University of California, since 1946; *b* Redondo Beach, Calif, 18 Sept. 1907; *s* of Edwin Harbaugh McMillan and Anna Marie (*née* Mattison); *m* 1941, Elsie Walford Blumer; two *s* one *d*. *Educ:* Calif Institute of Technology (MS); Princeton Univ. (PhD). Univ. of California: National Research Fellow, 1932-34; Research Assoc., 1934-35; Instructor, 1935-36; Asst Prof., 1936-41; Assoc. Prof., 1941-46. Leave of absence for war research, 1940-45. Mem. of staff of Radiation Laboratory, Univ. of Calif., 1934-; Assoc. Dir, 1954-58; Dir, 1958-; Mem. General Advisory Cttee to Atomic Energy Commission, 1954-58. Member: Commission on High Energy Physics of International Union for Pure and Applied Physics (IUPAP), 1960-66; Scientific Policy Cttee of Stanford Linear Accelerator Center (SLAC), 1962-66; Physics Adv. Cttee, Nat. Accelerator Lab. (NAL), 1967-; Trustee, Univs Research Assoc., 1969-; Chm., Cl. I, Nat. Acad. of Sciences, 1968-71. Fellow Amer. Physical Soc. Member: Nat. Acad. of Sciences (USA); American Philosophical Soc.; Fellow, Amer. Acad. of Arts and Sciences. Research Corp. 1950 Scientific Award, 1951; (jtly) Nobel Prize in Chemistry, 1951; (jtly) Atoms for Peace Award, 1963; Alumni Dist. Service Award, Calif. Inst. of Tech., 1966; Centennial Citation, Univ. of California, Berkeley, 1968. Hon. DSc, Rensselaer Polytechnic Institute; Hon. DSc, Gustavus Adolphus Coll. *Address:* University of California, Berkeley, Calif

94720, USA. *Clubs:* Bohemian (San Francisco); Cosmos (Washington).

**MacMILLAN, Sir Ernest Campbell,** Kt 1935; MusD, LLD, LittD, Hon. RAM, FRCM, FRCO; Dean Faculty of Music, University of Toronto, 1927-52; Principal, Toronto Conservatory of Music, 1926-42; Conductor: Toronto Symphony Orchestra, 1931-56; Toronto Mendelssohn Choir, 1942-57; Past President, Composers, Authors and Publishers Association of Canada; Hon. President, Canadian Music Centre; Member Canada Council, 1957-63; *b* near Toronto, 18 Aug. 1893; *s* of Rev. Alexander MacMillan, DD, and Winnie Ross; *m* 1919, Laura Elsie Keith; two *s. Educ:* Toronto; Edinburgh. At an early age took an interest in music, especially the organ, making many public appearances from the age of nine onwards, passed Associateship Royal College of Organists at age of 13, Fellowship at age of 17 (winning Lafontaine Prize) and graduated as MusB at Oxford the same year; Arts course (Hons in Mod. History) Univ. of Toronto; was in Germany in summer of 1914 and after outbreak of war interned in Ruhleben Camp; while there, wrote a setting (chorus and orchestra) of Swinburne's England, which was accepted for the degree of MusD, Oxford, 1918; after release returned to Canada. Richard Strauss Medal, 1957; Canada Council Medal, 1964. *Publications:* England, an Ode for Chorus and Orchestra; Sketches for String Quartet; Songs; Choral Compositions; Canadian Song Book; various arrangements of French Canadian Songs for Voice and Piano, male voice choir, etc.; Six Bergerettes du Bas Canada (Voices with Oboe, Violin, Cello and Harp). Various educational publications. ed, Music in Canada, 1955. *Recreations:* water sports, travelling, reading. *Address:* 115 Park Road, Toronto, Canada. *T:* Walnut 1-9787. *Clubs:* Arts and Letters (Past Pres.), (Toronto), Faculty (Univ. of Toronto).

**MacMILLAN of MacMillan, Gen. Sir Gordon Holmes Alexander,** of Knap, KCB, 1949 (CB 1945); KCVO, 1954; CBE 1943; DSO 1943; MC (two bars); hereditary Chief of the Clan MacMillan; Colonel The Argyll and Sutherland Highlanders, 1945-58; Hon. Colonel The Argyll and Sutherland Highlanders of Canada; 402 (A. and S. H.) Lt Regt RA (TA), 1956-61; Vice-Lieutenant Co. of Renfrew, since 1955; *b* 7 Jan. 1897; *s* of D. A. MacMillan and L. W. Allardice; *m* 1929, Marian Blakiston-Houston, OBE, CStJ, four *s* one *d. Educ:* St Edmund's Sch., Canterbury. RMC, Sandhurst, 1915; commissioned in Argyll and Sutherland Highdrs, 1915; served European War in 2nd Bn Argyll and Sutherland Highdrs, France, 1916-18 (MC and two bars): Adjutant, 1917-20; Staff Coll., Camberley, 1928-29; Staff Capt., War Office, 1930-32; GSO3, 1932-34; GSO2 RMC, Kingston, Ont., 1935-37; GSO2 WO and Eastern Command, 1937-40; GSO1, 1940-41; commanding Infantry Brigade, 1941; BGS UK and N Africa, 1941-43 (CBE); commanding Infantry Brigade, Sicily, 1943 (DSO); commanding 15th Scottish, 49 (WR) and 51st Highland Divs, 1943-45, UK, Normandy, Holland and Germany (CB); GOC Palestine, 1947-48; DWD War Office, 1945-46; Gen. Officer, C-in-C, Scottish Command, and Gov. of Edinburgh Castle, 1949-52; Gov. and C-in-C of Gibraltar, 1952-55, retd 1955. Chairman: Cumbernauld New Town Corporation, 1956-65; Greenock Harbour Trust, 1955-65; Erskine Hospital, 1955; Firth of Clyde Dry Dock, 1960-67. DL Renfrewshire, 1950, Vice-Lt, 1955. Kt Grand Cross Order of Orange Nassau; KStJ. Mem. of The Queen's Body Guard for Scotland. Hon. LLD (Glasgow), 1964. *Recreation:* shooting. *Address:* Finlaystone, Langbank, Renfrewshire. *Club:* Caledonian.

**MACMILLAN, Rt. Hon. Harold;** *see* Macmillan, Rt Hon. M. H.

**MacMILLAN, Harvey Reginald,** CBE 1943; Company Director; Member: Lloyd's; British Columbia Board, The Canada Trust Co.; *b* 9 Sept. 1885; *s* of John Alfred MacMillan and Joanna Willson; *m* 1911, Edna, *d* of C. Mulloy; two *d. Educ:* Toronto Univ. (BScA); Yale Univ. (MScF). Chief Forester of British Columbia, 1912; Founder and Pres., H. R. MacMillan Export Co. Ltd, 1919; Timber Controller for Canada, 1940; Pres., Wartime Merchant Shipbuilding Ltd for Canada, 1941. Director: MacMillan, Bloedel Ltd; British Columbia Packers Ltd; Mem., Adv. Cttee, International Nickel Co. of Canada Ltd; Gov., Canadian Council, International Chamber of Commerce; Hon. DSc, Univ. of British Columbia, 1950; Hon. LLD: Univ. of Toronto, 1957; Univ. of Guelph, 1966. Hon. Patron of the Vancouver Public Aquarium. *Recreations:* shooting and fishing. *Address:* (home) 3741 Hudson Street, Vancouver, BC, Canada; (office) 1075 West Georgia Street, Vancouver 5, BC, Canada. *Clubs:* University, Terminal City, Vancouver, Faculty, Union (Vancouver, BC); Union (Victoria, BC).

**MacMILLAN, His Honour James;** Judge of County Courts, 1950-65, retired; *b* Schoolhouse, Fisherton, Ayrshire, 18 April 1898; *s* of George Arthur MacMillan, MA, and Catherine, *d* of late Alexander McQuiston; *m* 1931, Marjorie J. Triffitt, DSc (*d* 1957); one *d. Educ:* Troon Sch.; Ayr Acad.; Glasgow Univ. (MA, LLB). Royal Artillery, 1917-19, Lt. Called to Bar, Middle Temple, 1925, Midland Circuit; Legal Adviser, Ministry of Pensions, 1939-44. Mem. Bar Council, 1947-50; Mem. Supreme Court Rule Cttee, 1948-50; Dep. Chm. Beds Quarter Sessions, 1949-50; County Court Judge, Circuit 37, April-June 1950, Circuit 38, 1950-55, Circuit 39, 1955-65. *Recreation:* walking. *Address:* 28 Battlefield Road, St Albans, Herts. *T:* St Albans 56152. *Club:* Reform.

**McMILLAN, James Athole,** CBE 1957 (OBE 1945); BSc (Agric.); Director, National Agricultural Advisory Service, Ministry of Agriculture, Fisheries and Food, 1959-Feb. 1961, retired; *b* 25 Feb. 1896; *m* 1949, Marian R. Watson; three *s* one *d. Educ:* George Watson's Coll., Edinburgh; Edinburgh Univ. BEF France, 1916-18. Asst Agricultural Organiser, Derbys CC, 1919-20; Lecturer in Agriculture, Leeds Univ., 1921-27; Agricultural Organiser, Lindsey CC, 1927-30; Agricultural Organiser, Cambs CC, 1930-39; Executive Officer, Cambs War Agricultural Executive Cttee, 1939-46; Provincial Dir, National Agricultural Advisory Service, 1946-48; Senior Education and Advisory Officer, Nat. Agric. Adv. Service, Min. of Agric., Fisheries and Food, 1948-59. *Recreations:* Rugby and cricket interests. *Address:* 7 Bonaly Drive, Edinburgh 13. *T:* 031-441 3869.

**McMILLAN, John,** CBE 1969; Director of Sport, Independent Television, and representative of ITV companies at European Broadcastkng Union, since 1968; *b* 29 Jan. 1915; *s* of late William McArthur McMillan, Sydney; *m* 1958, Lucy Mary, *d* of late Edward Moore, DSO; three *s* two *d. Educ:* Scots Coll., Sydney. Programme Dir, Internat. Broadcasting Co., 1934-39; joined horsed cavalry as trooper, 1939; commnd S Wales Borderers, 1940; OC No 1 Field Broadcasting Unit, British Forces Network, 1945-46; Asst and later Chief Asst to Controller, BBC Light

Programme, 1946-52; Controller of Programmes, Gen. Man. and Dir, Rediffusion Television Ltd, 1955-68. Dir, Theatre Royal Windsor Co., 1964-. *Recreations:* swimming, gardening, study of 1919-39 European history. *Address:* 6 Park Towers, Brick Street, W1. *T:* 01-493 1891; Residence Moderne, Bormes, Var, France. *T:* 94-71 04 12. *Club:* Naval and Military.

**MacMILLAN, Kenneth;** Resident Choreographer to the Royal Ballet, Covent Garden, and Co-Director since 1970; Director of Ballet, Deutsche Oper, Berlin, since 1966; *b* 11 Dec. 1929. *Educ:* Great Yarmouth Gram. Sch. Started as Dancer, Royal Ballet; became Choreographer, 1953. First professional ballet, Danses Concertantes (Stravinsky-georgiades). Principal ballets: The Burrow; Solitaire; Agon; The Invitation; Romeo and Juliet; Diversions; La Création du Monde; Images of Love; The Song of the Earth; Concerto; Anastasia; Cain and Abel; Olympiad; Solitaire. Has devised ballets for: Ballet Rambert, American Ballet, Royal Ballet Sch., Theatre, Television, Cinema, Musical Shows. *Recreation:* cinema. *Address:* c/o Royal Opera House, Covent Garden, WC2.

**MACMILLAN, Malcolm K.;** journalist; *b* 21 Aug. 1913; *s* of Kenneth Macmillan and Mary Macaulay; is married. *Educ:* Edinburgh Univ. Served as Private, Infantry, 1939-40. MP (Lab) Western Isles, 1935-70; Chm., Scottish Parliamentary Labour Party, 1945-51; Chm., Govt Advisory Panel on Highlands and Islands, 1947-54; Mem. Post Office Advisory Council, 1946-51; Mem. Scottish Advisory Council on Civil Aviation, 1947-53; Mem. Scottish Economic Conf., 1949-. Chm., Parly Cttee for East West Trade, 1965-69. *Address:* 60 Bellshill Road, Uddingston, Lanarkshire.

**MACMILLAN, Rt. Hon. (Maurice) Harold,** PC 1942; FRS 1962; Chancellor, University of Oxford, since 1960; Chairman Macmillan (Holdings), since 1963 (Chairman Macmillan & Co. and Macmillan (Journals), 1963-67). Prime Minister and First Lord of The Treasury, Jan. 1957-Oct. 1963; MP (C) Bromley, Nov. 1945-Sept. 1964; *b* 10 Feb. 1894; *s* of late Maurice Crawford Macmillan; *m* 1920, Lady Dorothy Evelyn Cavendish, GBE 1964 (*d* 1966), *d* of 9th Duke of Devonshire; one *s* two *d* (and one *d* decd). Educ: Eton (Scholar); Balliol Coll., Oxford (Exhibitioner). 1st Class Hon. Moderations, 1919; served during war, 1914-18, in Special Reserve Grenadier Guards (wounded 3 times); ADC to Gov.-Gen. of Canada, 1919-20; retired, 1920; MP (U) Stockton-on-Tees, 1924-29 and 1931-45; contested Stockton-on-Tees, 1923 and 1945; Parliamentary Sec., Ministry of Supply, 1940-42; Parliamentary Under-Sec. of State, Colonies, 1942; Minister Resident at Allied HQ in North-West Africa, 1942-45; Sec. for Air, 1945; Minister of Housing and Local Government, 1951-54; Minister of Defence, Oct. 1954-April 1955; Sec. of State for Foreign Affairs, April-Dec. 1955; Chancellor of the Exchequer, Dec. 1955-Jan. 1957. First Pres., Game Research Assoc., 1960-65. A Vice-Pres., Franco-British Soc., 1955; a Trustee, Historic Churches Preservation Fund, 1957-. Freeman of: City of London (Stationers' and Newspaper Makers' Company, 1957), 1957; Bromley, Kent, 1957; Hon. Freedom of City of London, 1961; Toronto, 1962; Stockton-on-Tees, 1968. Hon. Fellow Balliol Coll., Oxford, 1957. Hon. DCL Oxford, 1958; DCL Oxford (by diploma), 1960; LLD Cambridge, 1961, Sussex, 1963. *Publications:* Industry and the State (jointly), 1927; Reconstruction: A Plea for a National Policy, 1933; Planning for Employment, 1935; The Next Five Years, 1935; The Middle Way, 1938 (re-issued 1966); Economic Aspects of Defence, 1939; Winds of Change (Vol. I of Memoirs), 1966; The Blast of War (Vol. II of Memoirs), 1967; Tides of Fortune (Vol. III of Memoirs), 1969; Riding the Storm, 1956-1959 (Vol. IV of Memoirs), 1971. *Address:* Macmillan & Co. Ltd, 4 Little Essex Street, WC2; Birch Grove House, Chelwood Gate, Haywards Heath, Sussex. *Clubs:* Athenæum, Carlton, Turf, Pratt's, Beefsteak, Buck's.

*See also Rt Hon. Julian Amery, M. V. Macmillan.*

**MACMILLAN, Maurice Victor;** MP (C) Farnham, since 1966; Chief Secretary to the Treasury, since 1970; *b* 27 Jan. 1921; *s* of Rt Hon. Harold Macmillan, *qv*; *m* 1942, Hon. Katharine Margaret Alice Ormsby-Gore, 2nd *d* of 4th Baron Harlech, KG, PC, GCMG; three *s* one *d* (and one *s* decd). *Educ:* Eton; Balliol Coll., Oxford. Served War of 1939-45 with Sussex Yeomanry. Mem. of Kensington Borough Council, 1949-53. Contested (C) Seaham Harbour, 1945, Lincoln, 1951, Wakefield, by-election, 1954; MP (C) Halifax, 1955-64; Economic Sec. to the Treasury, Oct. 1963-64. Chairman: Macmillan & Co. Ltd, 1967-70; Macmillan Journals Ltd, 1967-70; Macmillan & Cleaver Ltd, 1967-70; Dep. Chm., Macmillan (Holdings) Ltd, 1966-70; formerly also Director: Monotype Corporation Ltd; Yorkshire Television Ltd; and Exec. Chm., Wider Share Ownership Council. *Address:* 12 Catherine Place, SW1; Highgrove, Doughton, near Tetbury, Glos. *Clubs:* Turf, Beefsteak, Pratt's, Garrick.

**MACMILLAN, Norman,** OBE 1956; author; Wing Comdr RAFVR (T), retired 1958; first Air Force Member, Cornwall TAAFA, 1947-61, Vice-Chairman (Air), 1953-54 and 1956-57; DL (Cornwall); *b* Glasgow, 9 Aug. 1892; 2nd *s* of John Campbell Macmillan, Carsphairn, Kirkcudbrightshire, and Jeanie Hamilton, Hamilton, Lanarkshire; *m* Gladys Mary Peterkin, *d* of James Alfred Peterkin Mitchell, Dundee. *Educ:* Allan Glen's Sch.; Royal Technical Coll. Served European War, HLI, Belgium and France, 1914-16; RFC and RAF, France and Italy, 1916-19 (MC, AFC, 1914 Star); commanded Special Mobile Flight, RAF, 1921; retains rank of Captain; Royal Aero Club Aviator's Certificate, 1917; Pilot's B Licence, 1919; Air Ministry approved test pilot; Founder Assoc. MIAeE, 1919; consultant test pilot, 1919-23, to various companies; Instructor Spanish naval and military aviation schs, 1922; pilot of first attempt to fly round world, 1922; first flight London-Sweden in one day, 1923; winner speed prize first international light aeroplane competition, 1923; chief test pilot Fairey Aviation Co., 1924-30; AFRAeS, 1928; Founder Mem. and Warden Guild of Air Pilots, 1929, Dep. Master, 1934-35, Upper Freeman, 1956, Liveryman, 1958; Air Navigator's Licence, 1929; Chief Consultant Test Pilot and a principal foreign representative Armstrong Siddeley Development Co., 1931-33; first British pilot to fly over Andes Mountains, 1931; publicly advocated powerful British air rearmament from 1934 onwards, on platform and in Press; Pres. Nat. League of Airmen, 1935-38; FRSA 1936-57; Special Aviation and Air Corres. Daily Mail, 1936-39; served War of 1939-45 with RAFVR(T), (Sqdn Ldr), and as War Correspondent; Founder Mem. Circle of Aviation Writers, 1941; Dist Inspecting Officer, ATC Cornwall, 1945-47 and OC Cornwall Wing, ATC, 1947-58. Flew on operational flights during Malayan emergency, 1958. Special contributor to Aeronautics from its inception in 1939. UK Special

Correspondent, Aircraft, Melbourne, Aust.; Contributor: Wehr und Wirtschaft, Germany; deutscher aerokurier; Grolier Encyclopedia, New York; Shell Aviation News. *Publications:* The Art of Flying, 1928; Into the Blue, 1929, rev. augmented edn with new illustrations, 1969; The Air Tourist's Guide to Europe, 1930; An Hour of Aviation, 1931; The Romance of Flight, 1934; Sefton Brancker, 1935; The Romance of Modern Exploration and Discovery, 1936; Freelance Pilot, 1937; The Chosen Instrument, 1938; How We Fly (edited), 1939; Best Flying Stories (edited), Air Strategy, 1941; How to Pilot An Aeroplane, 1942; The Pilot's Book on Advanced Flying, 1943; Aeroplanes section of Railways, Ships and Aeroplanes, 1944; The Royal Air Force in the World War, Vol. 1, 1942; Vol. 2, 1944; Vol. 3, 1949; Vol. 4, 1950; Great Airmen, 1955; Great Aircraft, 1960; Tales of Two Air Wars, 1963; Great Flights and Air Adventures, 1964; Wings of Fate, Strange True Tales of the Vintage Flying Days, 1967. *Address:* Trecara Lodge, 2 Edward Street, Truro, Cornwall. *T:* Truro 3692.

**MACMILLAN, Prof. Robert Hugh;** Director, The Motor Industry Research Association, since 1964; *b* 27 June 1921; *s* of H. R. M. Macmillan and E. G. Macmillan (*née* Webb); *m* 1950, Anna Christina Roding, Amsterdam; one *s* two *d. Educ:* Felsted Sch.; Emmanuel Coll., Cambridge. Technical Branch, RAFVR, 1941; Dept of Engrg, Cambridge Univ., 1947; Prof. of Mech. Engrg, Swansea, 1956. Assoc. Prof., Warwick Univ., 1965; Industrial Prof., Loughborough Univ., 1968. *Publications:* Theory of Control, 1951; Automation, 1956. *Recreations:* music, philately. *Address:* 11 Lillington Avenue, Leamington Spa, Warwicks. *T:* Leamington Spa 25165. *Club:* Royal Automobile.

**McMILLAN, Thomas McLellan;** MP (Lab) Glasgow Central since 1966; *b* 12 Feb. 1919; *s* of James and Isabella McMillan; *m* 1946, Mary Elizabeth Conway; one *s* one *d. Educ:* secondary sch. Glasgow City Councillor, 1962; Magistrate and Bailie of Burgh, 1964. *Address:* 1 Firpark Terrace, Glasgow E1. *T:* 041-554 1327.

**MACMILLAN, Wallace,** CMG 1956; now with Management Selection Ltd; *b* 16 Oct. 1913; *s* of late David Hutchen Macmillan and late Jean Wallace, Newburgh, Fife; *m* 1947, Betty Bryce, *d* of late G. R. Watson and of Mrs M. Y. Watson; three *s. Educ:* Bell-Baxter Sch.; University of St Andrews; Kiel Univ.; Corpus Christi Coll., Oxford. Administrative Officer, Tanganyika, 1937; District Officer, 1947; Administrator of Grenada, BWI, 1951-57. Acted as Governor, Windward Is, periods 1955. Federal Establishment Sec. (subsequently Permanent Sec., Min. of Estabts and Service Matters), Federation of Nigeria, 1957-61. Mem., Victoria League. *Recreations:* bridge, chess, tennis, golf. *Address:* The Willows, Blueberry Road, Bowdon, Cheshire.

**McMILLAN, William,** CVO 1956; RA 1933 (ARA 1925); RBS 1932 (ARBS 1928); sculptor; *b* Aberdeen, 31 Aug. 1887; *m* 1916, Dorothy Williams (*d* 1964), Carlisle. *Educ:* Gray's School of Art, Aberdeen; Royal College of Art. *Works:* George V Statue, Calcutta; Earl Haig at Clifton Coll., Bristol; Hugh Oldham, Bishop of Exeter, founder of Manchester Grammar Sch.; Beatty Memorial Fountain, Trafalgar Square; Statue of King George VI, Carlton Gardens, London; Statue of Sir Walter Raleigh, Whitehall, SW1; Statue of Lord Trenchard, Victoria Embankment. Great War Medal. Victory Medal, and various other medals, busts, etc. Works in Tate Gallery, etc. *Address:* 65 Glebe Place, Chelsea, SW3. *Club:* Chelsea Arts.

**MACMILLAN, Prof. William Miller,** MA; Hon. DLitt, Oxford, 1957, Natal, 1962; *b* Aberdeen, 1885; *s* of late Rev. John Macmillan, MA, formerly of Madras; *m* 1st, Jean, *d* of late John Sutherland, MA; 2nd, Mona, *e d* of late Admiral Sir Hugh J. Tweedie, KCB; two *s* two *d. Educ:* Stellenbosch, SA; Merton Coll., Oxford. Rhodes Scholar, 1903-06; studied in Aberdeen, Glasgow, and Berlin, 1906-10; Lecturer in History and Economics, Rhodes Univ. Coll., Grahamstown, SA, 1911; Prof. of History, University of the Witwatersrand, Johannesburg, SA, 1917-34; Assoc. Member of All Souls Coll., Oxford, 1926-27 and 1933; Membre de l'Institut Colonial Internat., 1931; African Travel, 1930-33, 1938, 1958-59, 1962, 1964; USA and W Indies, 1934-35; Hon. Life Member Royal African Society, 1935; African Studies Assoc. of UK, 1966; Hon. Vice-President, Anti-Slavery and Aborigines Protection Society, 1965. Heath Clark Lecturer (joint), University of London, 1938-39; Member of Advisory Cttee on Education in the Colonies, 1938-41; Empire Intelligence Section, BBC, 1941-43; Senior Representative of the British Council in West Africa, 1943-46; Colonial Labour Advisory Cttee, 1946-52; Director of Colonial Studies, Univ. of St Andrews, 1947-54. Hoernlé Memorial lecturer, SA, 1949; Mission to Tanganyika for Tanganyika Government, 1950; Observer Mission to Bechuanaland Protectorate, 1951; Central Africa, 1952; acting Prof. of History, Univ. Coll. of the West Indies, Jamaica, 1955. Coronation Medal, 1953; Chevalier, Royal Belgian Order of the Lion, 1953. *Publications:* The South African Agrarian Problem, 1919; The Cape Colour Question: a Historical Survey, 1927, 1969; Bantu, Boer, and Briton: the Making of the SA Native Problem, 1929 (new edn, 1963); Complex South Africa, 1930; Warning from the W Indies, 1936, reissued in Penguin Series, 1938; Africa Emergent, 1938 (Pelican 2nd edn 1948); Europe and West Africa, 1940; Democratize the Empire, 1941; The Road to Self-Rule, A Study in Colonial Evolution, 1959. *Recreation:* walking. *Address:* Yew Tree Cottage, Long Wittenham, Abingdon, Berks. *T:* Clifton Hampden 358. *Clubs:* Royal Commonwealth Society; Royal and Ancient Golf.

**McMORRAN, Helen Isabella,** MA; Life Fellow, Girton College, Cambridge; *b* 26 July 1898; *d* of late Thomas McMorran and late Louise Maud White. *Educ:* Sutton High Sch., GPDST; Girton Coll., Cambridge. Assistant Librarian, Bedford Coll., London, 1921-28; Girton Coll., Cambridge: Librarian, 1930-62; Vice-Mistress, 1946-62; Registrar of the Roll, 1947-69. Member of Council, Girls' Public Day School Trust, 1952-69; Trustee, Homerton Coll., Cambridge, 1954-67. *Publications:* Editor, Girton Review, 1932-62; Joint Editor (with K. T. Butler) of Girton College Register, 1869-1946, 1948. *Address:* 41 Sherlock Close, Cambridge. *T:* Cambridge 51359. *Club:* University Women's.

**MACMORRAN, Kenneth Mead,** QC 1932; *b* 1883; *o s* of late Alexander Macmorran, KC; *m* 1920, Freda Mary, *y d* of late W. F. Knight, of The Mount, Duppas Hill, Croydon; no *c. Educ:* Westminster; King's Coll., Cambridge (MA, LLB). Barrister (Middle Temple), 1907; served European War, 1915-20; Staff Captain to Judge Advocate-General, 1919; mentioned, Secretary of State's list for War Services, 1919; Chancellor: Dioceses of Chichester, 1922-64, St Albans, 1922-62, Ely, 1924-65, Guildford, 1927-68, Lincoln, 1937, and

Newcastle, 1942; JP (Surrey) 1933; Dep. Chairman, Surrey Quarter Sessions, 1941-44, Assistant Chairman, 1944-48; Member of Church Assembly, 1930-37; Bencher, Middle Temple, 1937; Member, Enemy Aliens Tribunal (Germans and Austrians), 1940; Probation Advisory Cttee (Home Office), 1946; a Referee under National Health Insurance, Widows and Orphans (etc.) Pensions and Family Allowances Acts, 1926-50; Master Treasurer of the Middle Temple, 1956. *Publications:* A Handbook for Churchwardens and Parochial Church Councillors; Cripps on Church and Clergy, 8th edn. *Address:* 5 Lion Street, Chichester, Sussex. *T:* Chichester 83733.

**MacMULLAN, Charles W. Kirkpatrick,** CBE 1947; (Writer under the name of C. K. Munro); *b* 17 Feb. 1889; *o s* of Professor S. J. MacMullan, Queen's Coll., Belfast, and Anne Marshall Weir, Cookstown, Co. Tyrone; *m* Mary Sumner (*d* 1956), *d* of H. A. Sumner, Birmingham; one *s*. *Educ:* Harrow; Pembroke Coll., Cambridge. Under Secretary, Ministry of Labour (retired). *Plays:* Wanderers, 1915; At Mrs Beam's, 1922; The Rumour, 1923; Storm, 1924; The Mountain, 1926; Cocks and Hens, 1927; Mr Eno, 1928; Veronica, 1930; Bluestone Quarry, 1931; Ding & Co., 1934. *Broadcast Plays:* The New Vicar, 1963; Jonsen, 1964. *Publications: essays:* The True Woman, 1931; Watching a Play (Shute Lectures), 1933; The Fountains in Trafalgar Square, 1952. *Address:* 2 The Rosery, South Heath, Great Missenden, Bucks.

**McMULLEN, Col Denis,** CBE 1966; consultant; Chief Inspecting Officer of Railways, Ministry of Transport, 1963-68 (Inspecting Officer, 1948); retired; *b* 21 April 1902; *e s* of Norman McMullen and Helen Mary McMullen (*née* Macpherson); *m* 1928, Ida Wilhelmina Taylor; two *s* one *d* (and one *s* decd). *Educ:* Cheltenham Coll.; Royal Military Academy (Woolwich). Commissioned in Royal Engineers, 1921; posted India, 1924; seconded Indian State Railways (NW Railway), 1925-39. Served in France, Iraq and India (despatches), 1940-45. Controller of Railways, Allied Commn, Austria, 1945-46; seconded to Indian State Railways (NW Railway), 1946-47; seconded to Pakistan State Railways (NW Railway) (Chief Operating Superintendent), 1947-48. CEng, FICE; MInstT. Member Instn Railway Signal Engineers, 1949. *Recreations:* fishing, gardening. *Address:* Merlewood, Woodham Road, Woking, Surrey. *T:* Woking 65955. *Club:* United Service.

**McMULLEN, Rear-Admiral Morrice Alexander,** CB 1964; OBE 1944; Flag Officer, Admiralty Interview Board, HMS Sultan, Gosport, 1961-64, retired; Director, Civil Defence for London, 1965-68; *b* Hertford, 16 Feb. 1909; *m* 1946, Pamela (*née* May), *widow* of Lt-Comdr J. Buckley, DSC, RN; two step *s*; (marr. diss., 1967). *Educ:* Oakley Hall, Cirencester; Cheltenham Coll. Entered Royal Navy, as Paymaster Cadet, HMS Erebus; various appointments abroad and in Admiralty. Served War of 1939-45 (despatches, OBE); Atlantic, North Sea, Norwegian waters; served in HMS Prince of Wales (battle with Bismarck, and Atlantic Charter Meeting, working for Sir Winston Churchill, then Prime Minister); HQ, Western Approaches as Secretary to Chief of Staff, 1941-43; Member Allied Anti-Submarine Survey Board, 1943; served Mediterranean, 1944-45 (Anzio Landing, re-entry into Greece, invasion of S. France). Post-war appointments at home; Captain of Fleet to C-in-C Far East Station, Singapore, 1959-61. Chairman Royal Naval Ski Club, 1955-58. *Recreations:* fishing, sailing, ski-ing, shooting. *Address:* 3 The Crescent, Alverstoke, Hants. *T:* Gosport 82974. *Clubs:* Naval and Military, Royal Cruising, Royal Naval Sailing Association.

**McMULLIN, Hon. Sir Alister (Maxwell),** KCMG 1957; President of the Australian Senate since 1953, retiring June 1971; Chancellor, University of Newcastle, NSW; Chairman: Parliamentary Library Committee; Commonwealth Parliamentary Association, 1960 (Chairman, General Council, CPA, 1969-); Deputy Chairman, Council, National Library of Australia; *b* Scone, NSW, Australia, 14 July 1900; *s* of W. G. McMullin, Aberdeen, NSW; *m* 1945, Thelma Louise (*née* Smith); one *d*. *Educ:* Public Sch., Australia. Elected to the Australian Senate, 1951, Senator to New South Wales. Chairman of Scott Memorial Hospital, Scone, NSW, 1934-40. Hon. DLitt Newcastle, NSW, 1966. *Address:* Parliament House, Canberra, ACT 2600, Australia. *T:* Canberra U05.

**MACMURRAY, John,** MC; MA (Glasgow and Oxon); LLD (Glasgow); retired as Professor of Moral Philosophy, University of Edinburgh (1944-58); *b* Maxwellton, Kirkcudbrightshire, 16 Feb. 1891; *s* of James Macmurray, Civil Servant; *m* 1916, Elizabeth Hyde, *d* of George Campbell of Umsinga, Natal, and Banchory, Kincardineshire; no *c*. *Educ:* Grammar Sch. and Robert Gordon's Coll., Aberdeen; Glasgow Univ.; Balliol Coll., Oxford. Graduate of Glasgow Univ., 1913; Snell Exhibitioner and Newlands Scholar of Balliol Coll., 1913; War Service, 1914-19: as private, RAMC 1914; Lieut, QO Cameron Highlanders, 1916 (MC); John Locke Scholar in Mental Philosophy of the University of Oxford, 1919; Lecturer in Philosophy, University of Manchester, 1919; Professor of Philosophy in the University of the Witwatersrand, Johannesburg, S. Africa, 1921; Fellow and Classical Tutor and Jowett Lecturer in Philosophy, Balliol Coll., Oxford, 1922-28; Grote Professor of the Philosophy of Mind and Logic, University of London, 1928-44. *Publications:* Freedom in the Modern World, 1932; Interpreting the Universe, 1933; Philosophy of Communism, 1933; Creative Society, 1935; Reason and Emotion, 1935; Structure of Religious Experience, 1936; The Clue to History, 1938; The Boundaries of Science, 1939; Challenge to the Churches, 1941; Constructive Democracy, 1943; Conditions of Freedom, 1949; The Self as Agent, 1957; Persons in Relation, 1961; Science, Art and Religion, 1961; Search for Reality in Religion, 1965; (with other contributors) Adventure, 1927; Some Makers of the Modern Spirit, 1933; Marxism, 1934; Aspects of Dialectical Materialism, 1934. *Recreation:* gardening. *Address:* 8 Mansionhouse Road, Edinburgh EH9 1TZ. *T:* 031-667 5784.

**McMURTRIE, Group Captain Richard Angus,** DSO 1940; DFC 1940; Royal Air Force, retired; *b* 14 Feb. 1909; *s* of Radburn Angus and Ethel Maud McMurtrie; *m* 1st, 1931, Gwenyth Mary (*d* 1958), 3rd *d* of Rev. (Lt-Col) H. J. Philpott; no *c*; 2nd, 1963, Laura, 4th *d* of Wm H. Gerhardi. *Educ:* Royal Grammar Sch., Newcastle on Tyne. First commissioned in Territorial Army (72nd Brigade, RA), 1927; transferred to Royal Air Force, 1929, as Pilot Officer; served in No. 2 (AC) Squadron, 1931-32, and Fleet Air Arm (442 Flight, and 822 Squadron in HMS Furious), 1932-33; Cranwell, 1934-35; Flt-Lieut, 1935; Calshot and No. 201 (Flying Boat) Squadron, 1935-38; Squadron Leader, 1938, and commanded Recruits Sub-Depot, RAF, Linton-on-Ouse; served War of 1939-45 (despatches thrice, DFC, DSO); No. 269 GR Squadron, 1939-41;

Wing Commander, 1940; HQ No. 18 Group RAF, 1941; Group Captain, commanding RAF Station, Sumburgh (Shetlands), 1942-43; HQ Coastal Command, 1943; RAF Staff Coll., Air Ministry, Whitehall, and HQ Transport Command, 1944; commanded RAF Station, Stoney Cross, Hants, 1945; and formed and commanded No. 61 Group (Reserve Command), 1946; Joint Services Mission, Washington, DC, 1946-49; commanded RAF Station, Cardington, 1949-52; HQ No. 1 Group, RAF, 1952-54; Royal Naval College, Greenwich, 1954; HQ, Supreme Allied Commander, Atlantic (NATO), Norfolk, Virginia, USA, 1954-56; HQ, Coastal Command, RAF, Northwood, Mddx, 1957-59. Chm., Falmouth Branch, Nat. Farmer's Union, 1970-71. *Recreations:* sailing, photography. *Address:* Rose in Vale Farm, Constantine, Falmouth, Cornwall. *TA* and *T:* Constantine 338. *Club:* RAF Yacht (Hon. Life Mem.), Royal Cornwall Yacht.

**MACNAB of Macnab, Archibald Corrie,** CIE 1943; *b* 1 Dec. 1886; 4th *s* of James William Macnabb (*de jure* 19th of Macnab), HEICS, JP, Arthurstone, Binfield, Berks, and Alice Corrie; assumed in addition the name of MacLeod, 1943 (relinquished it and reverted to surname of Macnabb, 1949; recognised as 22nd chief of clan, as A. C. Macnab of Macnab, 1954); his wife assumed the name of Alice Macnabb MacLeod of MacLeod, 1943 (changed to Alice MacLeod Macnabb, 1949, to Alice MacLeod Macnab of Macnab, 1954); *m* 1931, Alice (Kaisar-i-Hind silver and gold medals), *er d* of Hubert Walter and Dame Flora MacLeod of MacLeod, *qv*; no *c. Educ:* Eton Coll.; Balliol Coll., Oxford. Entered ICS 1911. Dep. Comr: Karnal, 1921, Shahpur, 1923, Attock, 1933; Commissioner Rawalpindi, 1934; Administrator, Lahore Municipality, 1937; Commissioner Jullundur, 1940; Financial Commissioner, Punjab, 1945; retired, 1948. *Publications:* Delhi Municipal Manual and History, 1917; Shahpur District Gazetteer, 1929; Brief Story of the Clan Macnab, 1951; various reports. *Recreation:* travel. *Heir: gt nephew* James Charles Macnab, yr of Macnab [*b* 14 April 1926; *m* 1959, Diana Mary, *er d* of Baron Kilmany, *qv*; two *s* two *d*]. *Address:* Kinnell House, Killin, Perthshire. *T:* Killin 212. *Club:* Leander.

**MACNAB, Brigadier Sir Geoffrey (Alex Colin),** KCMG 1962 (CMG 1955); CB 1951; retired; *b* 23 Dec. 1899; *s* of Brig.-General Colin Macnab, CMG; *m* 1930, Norah Cramer-Roberts. *Educ:* Wellington Coll.; RMC Sandhurst. 1st Commission, 1919, Royal Sussex Regt; Captain, Argyll and Sutherland Highlanders, 1931; psc 1931; Military Attaché, Prague and Bucharest, 1938-40; served War of 1939-45, campaigns Western Desert, Greece, Crete; Brigadier, 1944; Military Mission, Hungary, 1945; DMI, Middle East, 1945-47; Military Attaché, Rome, 1947-49; Military Attaché, Paris, 1949-54; retired 1954. Service in Ireland, Germany, Far East, India, Middle East. Secretary, Government Hospitality Fund, 1957-68. *Address:* Stanford House, Stanford, Ashford, Kent. *T:* Sellindge 2118. *Clubs:* Army and Navy, MCC.

**MACNAB, Brigadier John Francis,** CBE 1957 (OBE 1943); DSO 1945; *b* 15 Sept. 1906; *o surv s* of late Colonel Allan James Macnab, CB, CMG, FRCS, IMS, and Nora, *d* of Lieut-General Sir Lewis Dening, KCB, DSO; *m* 1938, Margaret, *d* of C. M. Treadwell; one *s* one *d. Educ:* Wellington Coll., Berks; RMC Sandhurst. Joined Queen's Own Cameron Highlanders, 1926; Lieut, 1929; seconded for service with KAR, 1929-35 and 1937; served with Cameron Highlanders, Catterick, and Regimental Depôt, Inverness, 1935-37; served War of 1939-45, Italian Somaliland, Abyssinia, Madagascar, Burma (despatches twice); Comd 1st Nyasaland Bn, KAR, 1941-43; Commander: 30th E. African Inf. Bde, 1943; 21 (E. African) Inf. Bde. Monsoon Campaign, Burma, 1944. Dep. President Regular Commissions Board, 1946; Comd 2nd Bn The Seaforth Highlanders, 1947; Colonel, Vice-President Sandhurst Selection Board, 1948; Comd: 6th Highland Bde, 2nd Div. BAOR, 1949-51; 153 Highland Bde, Highland Div., 1951-54; GHQ Troops, E. Africa, 1954-57; Dep. Commander East Anglian District, Nov. 1957-Dec. 1959, retired. Late Hon. Colonel, Tanganyika Rifles and late Hon. Colonel, 6th and 2/6th Bn, KAR. Representer of House of Barravorich in Clan Macnab. *Recreations:* fishing and piping. *Address:* c/o Glyn, Mills (Holt's Branch), Kirkland House, Whitehall, SW1; 45/4 Marina Street, Pieta, Malta, GC. *Club:* United Service.

**MACNABB, Archibald Corrie;** *see* Macnab of Macnab, A. C.

**MACNAGHTEN, Sir Antony,** 10th Bt, *cr* 1836; Chairman, London Discount Market Association, 1957-59; Manager, Alexanders Discount Co. Ltd, 1946-60; *b* 15 Nov. 1899; *s* of Rt Hon. Sir Malcolm Martin Macnaghten, KBE (*d* 1955) and Antonia Mary (*d* 1952), *e d* of Rt Hon. Charles Booth, FRS; *S* uncle, Hon. Sir Frederic Fergus Macnaghten, 9th Bt, 1955; *m* 1926, Magdalene, *e d* of late Edmund Fisher; three *s* one *d. Educ:* Eton Coll.; Trinity Coll., Cambridge. *Heir: s* Patrick Alexander Macnaghten [*b* 24 Jan. 1927; *m* 1955, Marianne, *d* of Dr Erich Schaefer, Cambridge; three *s*]. *Address:* Dundarave, Bushmills, Co. Antrim, N Ireland. *T:* 215. *Club:* United University.

**McNAIR,** family name of **Baron McNair.**

**McNAIR,** 1st Baron, *cr* 1955, of Gleniffer; **Arnold Duncan McNair,** Kt, *cr* 1943; CBE 1918; QC; FBA; LLD, Cambridge; Hon. LLD, Glasgow, Liverpool, Birmingham, Salonika, Brussels; Hon. DCL, Oxford; Hon. DLitt, Reading; Fellow of Gonville and Caius College; Bencher of Gray's Inn, Treasurer, 1947; *b* 4 March 1885; *e s* of late John McNair, of Lloyds, and Jeannie Ballantyne, both of Paisley; *m* 1912, Marjorie, *yr d* of late Sir Clement M. Bailhache; one *s* three *d. Educ:* Aldenham; Gonville and Caius Coll., Cambridge. Admitted solicitor, 1906; Law Tripos, 1908, 1909; President of Cambridge Union, 1909; Secretary of Advisory Board of Coal Controller, 1917-19; Secretary of Coal Industry (Sankey) Commission, 1919; Chairman: Cttee on Supply and Training of Teachers, 1942-44; Palestine Jewish Education Commn, 1945; Cttee on Recruitment to the Dental Profession, 1955-56; Burnham Cttee, 1956-58. Reader in International Law in the University of London, 1926-27; Tagore Professor in the University of Calcutta, 1931; Whewell Professor of International Law, University of Cambridge, 1935-37; Vice-Chancellor, Liverpool University, 1937-45; KC 1945. British Member, Permanent Court of Arbitration at The Hague, 1945-65; President of the International Court of Justice, 1952-55 and Judge, 1946-55; President of the European Court of Human Rights, 1959-65. Manley Hudson Gold Medal, American Society of International Law, 1959. *Publications:* Legal Effects of War, 1920, 4th edn (with A. D. Watts), 1966; Law of the Air, 1932, 3rd edn (by M. R. E. Kerr and A. H. M. Evans), 1964; (with W. W. Buckland) Roman Law and Common Law, 1936, 2nd edn 1952; Law of Treaties, 1938 and 1961; Dr Johnson and the Law, 1949; International Law Opinions, 1956; Expansion of International Law, 1962. *Heir: s* Hon. Clement John McNair [*b* 11 Jan. 1915; *m* 1941, Vera, *d* of Theodore James Faithfull; two *s* one *d*]. *Address:* 25 Storey's Way, Cambridge. *T:* Cambridge 53595.

**McNAIR, Brigadier John Kirkland,** CBE 1942; *b* 21 Oct. 1893; *s* of late Rev. H. B. McNair, Vicar of Aylesbury, Bucks; *m* 1st, 1915, Evelyn Dorothy Rastricke, *er d* of late E. R. Hanson, Chulmleigh, N. Devon; one *d*; 2nd, 1944, Nancy Adeleiza, *er d* of late W. A. Della Gana, Little Sunte, Lindfield; one *s* one *d*. *Educ:* Rugby; RMA, Woolwich. First Commission, Royal Regt of Artillery, 1913; Captain, 1917; Bt-Major, 1930; Major, 1931; Bt Lieut-Colonel, 1935; Lieut-Colonel, 1938; Colonel, 1938; Temp. Brigadier, 1940; served European War, 1914-18, in France in RFA (wounded twice); Staff Coll., Quetta, 1923-24; GSO 2 India, 1925-27; DAQMG India, 1927-29; RAF Staff Coll., Andover, 1931; GSO 2 Air Co-operation, 1932-34; GSO 2 War Office, 1934-36; idc, 1938; GSO 1 War Office, 1939-40; Dep. Director Military Operations War Office, 1940-41; Brig., RA Southern Command, 1941-42; Brigadier General Staff (Operations and Plans), Joint Staff Mission, Washington, 1942-44; retired, 1946; late Senior Administrative Officer, Imperial War Graves Commission; Officer Legion of Merit. *Address:* Little Putlands, Fairwarp, Uckfield, Sussex. *T:* Nutley 2676. *Club:* Naval and Military.

**McNAIR, Sir William Lennox,** Kt, *cr* 1946; Judge of the Queen's Bench Division, High Court of Justice, 1950-66; *b* 18 March 1892; *s* of late John McNair of Lloyds; unmarried. *Educ:* Aldenham (Schol.); Gonville and Caius Coll., Cambridge (Classical Schol.). First Class Law Tripos, Part I, 1913; Part II, 1914; LLM, 1919; Whewell Exhibitioner in International Law, 1919. Called to Bar, Gray's Inn, 1917; Bencher, 1938; KC 1944; Treasurer, 1951; Vice-Treasurer, 1952. Served with Royal Warwicks. Regt, 1914-18, Captain (despatches). Legal Adviser, Ministry of War Transport, 1941-45. Hon. Fellow Gonville and Caius College, Cambridge, 1951. *Publications:* Joint Editor of Temperley's Merchant Shipping Acts; Joint Editor of Scrutton on Charterparties and Bills of Lading. *Address:* 130 Court Lane, Dulwich, SE21.

**McNAIR-WILSON, Michael;** *see* McNair-Wilson, R. M. C.

**McNAIR-WILSON, Patrick Michael Ernest David;** MP (C) New Forest, since 1968 (Lewisham West, 1964-66); Company Director and Consultant; *b* 28 May 1929; *s* of Dr Robert McNair-Wilson; *m* 1953, Diana Evelyn Kitty Campbell Methuen-Campbell, *d* of Hon. Laurence Methuen-Campbell; one *s* three *d*. *Educ:* Eton. Regular Commission Coldstream Guards, 1947-51; Exec. in French Shipping Co., 1951-53; various appointments at Conservative Central Office, 1954-58; Staff of Conservative Political Centre, 1958-61; Director, London Municipal Society, 1961-63; Public Relations Executive with The British Iron and Steel Federation, 1963-64. Vice-Chm., Conservative Parly Power Cttee, 1969-70; Opposition Front Bench Spokesman on Fuel and Power; PPS to Minister for Transport Industries, Dept of the Environment, 1970-. Editor of The Londoner, 1961-63. *Recreations:* sailing, photography. *Address:* 5 Kelso Place, W8. *T:* 01-937 3564; Godfreys Farm, Beaulieu, Hampshire. *T:* Beaulieu 300. *Club:* Guards.

*See also R. M. C. McNair-Wilson.*

**McNAIR-WILSON, (Robert) Michael (Conal);** MP (C) Walthamstow East since 1969; *b* 12 Oct. 1930; *y s* of late Dr Robert McNair-Wilson and of Mrs Doris McNair-Wilson. *Educ:* Eton College. During national service, 1948-50, was commissioned in Royal Irish Fusiliers. Farmed in Hampshire, 1950-53. Journalist on various provincial newspapers, and did freelance work for BBC in Northern Ireland, 1953-55. Joined Sidney-Barton Ltd, internat. public relations consultants (Dir 1961-). Contested (C) Lincoln, Gen. Elec., 1964; Mem. Council, Bow Group, 1965-66. *Publications:* Blackshirt, a biography of Mussolini (jointly), 1959; No Tame or Minor Role, (Bow Group pamphlet on the Common Market) (jointly), 1963. *Recreations:* golf, sailing, skiing, riding. *Address:* Flat 30, 5 Elm Park Gardens, SW10. *T:* 01-352 3590. *Club:* Royal Lymington Yacht.

*See also P. M. E. D. McNair-Wilson.*

**McNAIRN, Edward Somerville,** CB 1962; a Commissioner of Inland Revenue, 1958-69; *b* 5 Sept. 1907; *er s* of Edward B. McNairn and Mary Craig Sharp; *m* 1934, Nancy Stevenson; three *d*. *Educ:* Hutchesons' Grammar Sch., Glasgow; Glasgow Univ. Inland Revenue, 1929-69. *Recreations:* gardening; theatre; anything to do with railways. *Address:* Farleigh, Woodcote Avenue, Wallington, Surrey. *T:* Wallington 6229.

**McNAMARA, (Joseph) Kevin;** MP (Lab) Kingston-upon-Hull (North) since Jan. 1966; *b* 5 Sept. 1934; *s* of late Patrick and of Agnes McNamara; *m* 1960, Nora (*née* Jones), Warrington; four *s* one *d*. *Educ:* various primary schools; St Mary's Coll., Crosby; Hull Univ. (LLB). Head of Dept of History, St Mary's Grammar Sch., Hull, 1958-64; Lecturer in Law, Hull Coll. of Commerce, 1964-66. *Recreations:* family and outdoor activities. *Address:* 57 Inglemire Lane, Beverley High Road, Hull. *T:* 853196.

**McNAMARA, Kevin;** *see* McNamara, J. K.

**McNAMARA, Robert Strange;** Medal of Freedom with Distinction; Legion of Merit; Distinguished Service Medals of Army, Navy and Air Force; President, International Bank for Reconstruction and Development, International Development Association, and International Finance Corporation, since 1968; *b* San Francisco, 9 June 1916; *s* of Robert James McNamara and Clara Nell (*née* Strange); *m* 1940, Margaret McKinstry Craig; one *s* two *d*. *Educ:* University of California (AB); Harvard Univ. (Master of Business Administration); Asst Professor of Business Administration, Harvard, 1940-43. Served in USAAF, England, India, China, Pacific, 1943-46 (Legion of Merit); released as Lieut-Colonel. Joined Ford Motor Co., 1946; Executive, 1946-61; Controller, 1949-53; Asst General Manager, Ford Div., 1953-55; Vice-President, and General Manager, Ford Div., 1955-57; Director, and Group Vice-President of Car Divisions, 1957-61, President, 1960-61; Secretary of Defense, United States of America, 1961-68. Trustee: Ford Foundn; Brookings Instn. Holds several hon. doctorates; Phi Beta Kappa. *Publication:* The Essence of Security, 1968. *Address:* 1818 H Street, NW, Washington, DC 20433, USA; 2412 Tracy Place, NW, Washington, DC 20008, USA.

**MACNAMEE,** family name of **Baroness Audley.**

**McNARNEY, Gen. Joseph T.,** Hon. KCB 1946; Director, General Dynamics Corporation; *b* Emporium, Pa, 28 Aug. 1893; *s* of James Pollard McNarney and Helen Taggart; *m* 1917,

Helen Wahrenberger; one *d*. *Educ:* US Military Academy (BS 1915). Graduate Air Corps Tactical Sch., 1921, Command and General Staff Sch., 1926, Army War Coll., 1930. Comd 2nd Lieut, US Army, 1915, through grades to General, 1945; with Aviation Section, Army Signal Corps, 1916; comdg corps observation groups, overseas, 1917-19; Instructor Air Corps Tactical Sch., 1920-25; General Staff, War Dept, 1926-29; comdg March Field, California, 1930-31, 7th Bombardment Group, 1932-33; Instructor Army War Coll., 1933-35; Asst Chief of Staff, GHQ Air Force, 1935-38; comdg 7th Bomber Group, 1939; General Staff, War Dept, 1939-41; Chairman War Dept Reorganization Cttee, Jan. 1942; Dep. Chief of Staff, US Army, March 1942; Dep. Supreme Allied Commander, Mediterranean Theatre of Operations, 1944; Military Governor of Germany and Commanding General, US Forces in Europe, 1945-47; commanding General, US Air Force Materiel command, 1947; Senior US Army Representative on Military Staff Cttee of United Nations, 1947; Chairman Dept of Defense Management Cttee, 1949-52; retired, 1952. President Convair, a Division of General Dynamics Corporation, 1952-58. *Address:* 1225 North Granada Avenue, Apt 12, Alhambra, Calif 91801, USA.

**McNEE, Sir John (William),** Kt dso 1918; MD; DSc, FRCP (London, Edinburgh and Glasgow); FRS(E); Regius Professor of Practice of Medicine, Glasgow University, 1936-53; Professor Emeritus, 1953; Physician to the Queen in Scotland, 1952-54 (and to King George VI, 1937-52); Consulting Physician to Royal Navy, 1935-55; Consulting Physician to University College Hospital, London, and to the Western Infirmary, Glasgow; *b* 17 Dec. 1887; *o s* of late John McNee, Glasgow and Newcastle upon Tyne; *m* 1923, Geraldine Z. L., MSc (London), *o d* of late Cecil H. A. Le Bas, The Charterhouse, London. *Educ:* Royal Grammar Sch., Newcastle upon Tyne; Glasgow, Freiburg, and Johns Hopkins, USA, Universities. MB (Hons), 1909; MD (Hons) and Bellahouston Gold Medal, 1914; DSc 1920. asst Professor of Medicine and Lecturer in Pathology, Glasgow University; Asst Professor of Medicine, and Associate Physician, Johns Hopkins Univ., USA; Consulting Physician UCH, London, and formerly Holme Lecturer in Clinical Medicine, UCH Medical Sch.; Lettsomian Lecturer, Medical Society of London, 1931; Croonian Lecturer, Royal College of Physicians, 1932; Harveian Lecturer, Harveian Society, London, 1952; Vicary Lecturer, Royal College of Surgeons, 1958. Examiner in Medicine, Universities of Cambridge, St Andrews, Sheffield, Glasgow, Aberdeen, Edinburgh, Leeds, National University of Ireland, and Conjoint Board. Visiting Prof., Harvard Univ., USA (Brigham Hospital), 1949. President: Royal Medico-Chirurgical Society of Glasgow, 1950-51; Gastro-Enterological Society of Great Britain, 1950-51; Assoc. of Physicians, Great Britain and Ireland, 1951-52; BMA 1954-55. Editor, Quarterly Journal of Medicine, 1929-48. Master of the Barbers' Company of London, 1957-58; Served European War, Major, RAMC, 1914-19 (despatches, DSO, Comm. Military Order Avis). Served War of 1939-45, Surgeon Rear-Admiral RN, and Consulting Physician to the Navy in Scotland, 1939-45. Hon. MD (NUI); LLD (Glasgow), LLD (Toronto). *Publications:* Diseases of the Liver-Gall-Bladder and Bile-Ducts (3rd edn, 1929, with Sir Humphrey Rolleston); Text-book of Medical Treatment (with Dunlop and Davidson), 6th edn, 1955; numerous medical papers, especially on diseases of liver and spleen and various war diseases (Trench Fever, Gas Gangrene, War Nephritis, Immersion Foot (RN). *Recreations:* country sports. *Address:* Barton Edge, Worthy Road, Winchester, Hants. *T:* Winchester 5444. *Clubs:* Athenæum, Fly-fishers'.

**MacNEECE, W. F.;** *see* Foster, Air Vice-Marshal W. F. MacN.

**McNEICE, Sir Percy;** *see* McNeice, Sir Thomas P. F.

**McNEICE, Sir (Thomas) Percy (Fergus),** CMG 1953; OBE 1947; *b* 16 Aug. 1901; *s* of late Canon W. G. McNeice, MA, and Mary Masterson; *m* 1947, Yuen Peng Loke, *d* of late Dr Loke Yew, CMG, LLD; one *s* one *d*. *Educ:* Bradford Grammar Sch.; Keble Coll., Oxford (MA). Malayan Civil Service, 1925; Captain, Straits Settlements Volunteer Force (Prisoner of War, 1942-45). MLC, Singapore, 1949; MEC 1949; President of the City Council, Singapore, 1949-56, retired. FZS. *Recreations:* bird watching, walking and swimming. *Address:* Cathay Building, Singapore 9. *Club:* Royal Commonwealth Society.

**McNEIL, Anne,** CBE 1950 (OBE 1946); Secretary, Service Women's Club, 52 Lower Sloane Street, London, 1950-64, retired; *d* of Archibald and Elizabeth McNeil, Thorganby, York. *Educ:* privately. Served WRNS, 1940-50; last appointment, Superintendent (training). *Address:* Birkwood, Thorganby, York.

**McNEIL, Sir Hector,** Kt 1969; CBE 1966; Chairman: Babcock & Wilcox Ltd, since 1968 (Managing Director, 1958-68); British Nuclear Design & Construction Ltd; *b* 20 July 1904; *s* of late Angus McNeil, New Zealand, and late Mary McNeil; *m* 1939, Barbara J. Turner, *d* of late P. S. Turner; one *s* one *d*. *Educ:* Christchurch, NZ. University of New Zealand (BE). Public Works Dept, New Zealand, 1927-29; State Electricity Commission of Victoria, Australia, 1929-31; joined Babcock & Wilcox Ltd, 1931; General Manager, 1947; Director, 1950; Dep. Managing Director, 1953; Director of German, French, and Spanish Associated Babcock & Wilcox Companies; Director, National Bank of New Zealand, 1959-. Chm., Export Council for Europe, 1966-69; Mem., Export Guarantees Advisory Council, 1968-. President of Inst. of Fuel, 1957-58; FIEE; FIMechE; CIMarE. *Recreations:* shooting, golf. *Address:* Bramber, St George's Hill, Weybridge, Surrey. *T:* Weybridge 48484. *Club:* Bath.

**MACNEIL of Barra, Prof. Ian Roderick, The Macneil of Barra,** 46th Chief of Clan Macneil and of that Ilk; Professor of Law, Cornell University, Ithaca, New York, USA since 1963 (Associate Prof., 1962; Asst Prof., 1959); *b* 20 June 1929; *s* of Robert Lister Macneil of Barra, 45th Chief, and Kathleen, *d* of Orlando Paul Metcalf, NYC, USA; *m* 1952, Nancy, *e d* of James Tilton Wilson, Ottawa, Canada; two *s* one *d* (and one *s* decd). *Educ:* Univ. of Vermont (BA 1950); Harvard Univ. (JD 1955). Lieut, Infty, Army of US, 1951-53 (US Army Reserve, 1950-69, discharged honorably, rank of Major). Clerk, US Court of Appeals, 1955-

56; Associate, law firm Sulloway Hollis Godfrey & Soden, Concord, NH, USA, 1956-59. Fulbright Vis. Prof. of Law, University Coll., Univ. of East Africa, Dar es Salaam, Tanzania, 1965-67. Mem. Exec. Cttee, Assoc. of American Law Schools, 1970-71. Member, Standing Council of Scottish Chiefs. *Publications:* Contracts: Instruments of Social Co-operation–East Africa, 1968; Bankruptcy Law in East Africa, 1966; (with R. B. Schlesinger, *et al*) Formation of Contracts: A Study of the Common Core of Legal Systems, 1968; (with R. S. Morison) Students and Decision Making, 1970; contrib. US and African law jls. *Recreations:* tennis, gardening. *Heir:* *s* Roderick Wilson Macneil, Younger of Barra, *b* 22 Oct. 1954. *Address:* 110 Northway Road, Ithaca, New York 14850, USA. *T:* 607-272-5307; Kisimul Castle, Isle of Barra, Scotland. *T:* Castlebay 300. *Clubs:* Puffin's (Edinburgh); Statler (Ithaca, New York).

**McNEIL, John Struthers,** CBE 1967; Chief Road Engineer, Scottish Development Department, 1963-69; *b* 4 March 1907; *s* of R. H. McNeil, Troon; *m* 1931, Dorothea Yuille; two *s*. *Educ:* Ayr Academy; Glasgow Univ. BSc Hons, Civil Engineering, 1929; MICE 1955 (FICE 1968). Contracting and local government experience, 1929-35; joined Ministry of Transport as Asst Engineer, 1935; Divisional Road Engineer, NW Div. of England, 1952-55; Asst Chief Engineer, 1955-57; Dep. Chief Engineer, 1957-63. Telford Gold Medal, ICE. *Publications:* contribs. to technical journals. *Recreations:* fishing, gardening. *Address:* 28 Braid Farm Road, Edinburgh 10. *T:* 031-447 7013.

**McNEILE, Robert Arbuthnot,** MBE 1943; Managing Director, Arthur Guinness Son & Co. Ltd, since 1968; *b* 14 March 1913; *s* of A. M. McNeile, Housemaster at Eton College; *m* 1944, Pamela Rachel Paton (*née* Pollock); three *s* one *d*. *Educ:* Eton Coll.; King's Coll., Cambridge. Asst Master, Eton Coll., 1935; joined Arthur Guinness Son & Co. Ltd, 1936. Served War of 1939-45 in Royal Engineers, First Airborne Div., HQ 21st Army Group, Control Commn for Germany; Lt-Col. *Recreations:* archaeology, history, ornithology, Tennis, ski-ing, shooting. *Address:* St John's House, Chiswick Mall, W4. *T:* 01-994 5507; Broad Lane House, Brancaster, Norfolk. *T:* Brancaster 227.

**McNEILL, Maj.-General Alister Argyll Campbell,** CB 1943; MB, ChB; IMS retired; *b* 21 Nov. 1884; *s* of late Alexander McNeill, JP. *Educ:* High Sch., Glasgow; Glasgow Univ. (MB, ChB, 1906); Lieut, IMS, 1908; Captain, 1911; Major, 1920; Lieut-Colonel, 1928; Bt Colonel, 1935; Colonel, 1937; Maj.-General, 1941. Served European War, 1914-19 (despatches twice); KHS 1935-43. *Address:* c/o National and Grindlay's Bank Ltd, 13 St James's Square, SW1. *Club:* Royal and Ancient (St Andrews).

**McNEILL, David Bruce,** QC 1966; Recorder of Blackburn, since 1969; *b* 6 June 1922; *s* of late Ferguson and Elizabeth Bruce McNeill; *m* 1949, Margaret Lewis; one *s* three *d*. *Educ:* Rydal Sch.; Merton Coll., Oxford. BCL, MA Oxon., 1947. Called to Bar, Lincoln's Inn, 1947 (Cassel Schol.); Northern Circuit. Lecturer in Law, Liverpool Univ., 1948-58. Member, Bar Council, 1968-. Commissioned into Reconnaissance Corps, 1943; served In N. Africa, Sicily, Italy; Staff Captain (War Crimes), Hamburg, 1945-46. *Address:* Hill Grove, Eleanor Road, Bidston, Cheshire. *T:* 051-652 1708; 5 Essex Court, Temple, EC4. *T:* 01-353 4365. *Club:* University (Liverpool).

**McNEILL, Florence Marian,** MBE 1962; Author, Journalist, Lecturer and Broadcaster; *b* Orkney, 26 March 1885; *d* of Rev. Daniel McNeill, MD, and Janet McNeill (*née* Dewar). *Educ:* Orkney; Glasgow (MA); Paris; Rhineland. Spent a period as art student. Social work, London, 1913-17. Founded Clan MacNeil Assoc. of Scotland, 1932. Scottish Secretary of State's Advisory Cttee on Rural Housing, 1944-45. *Publications:* Iona: a History of the Island, 1920; The Scots Kitchen: its Traditions and Lore, with Old-Time Recipes, 1929; The Road Home (novel), 1932; Recipes from Scotland, 1946; An Iona Anthology, 1947; The Scots Cellar, 1956; The Silver Bough: a Four-volume Study of the National and Local Festivals of Scotland, 1956-61. (In collaboration with F. J. Wakefield) An Inquiry in Ten Towns in England and Wales into the Protection of Minor Girls, 1916. *Recreations:* clarsach (Celtic harp), ceilidh (Highland social gathering), kitchen. *Address:* 31 St Alban's Road, Edinburgh 9. *T:* 031-667 4160. *Club:* Scottish PEN.

**McNEILL, Maj.-Gen. John Malcolm,** CB 1963; CBE 1959 (MBE 1942); *b* 22 Feb. 1909; *s* of Brig.-General Angus McNeill, CB, CBE, DSO, TD, Seaforth Highlanders, and Lilian, *d* of Maj.-General Sir Harry Barron, KCVO; *m* 1939, Barbara, *d* of Colonel C. H. Marsh, DSO, Spilsby, Lincs; two *d*. *Educ:* Imperial Service Coll., Windsor; RMA, Woolwich. 2nd Lieut, RA, 1929. Served Western Desert, Sicily, Italy, N.W. Europe and Burma, 1939-45; Temp. Lieut-Colonel, 1943; Colonel, 1953; Brigadier, 1957. Commanded 1st Regt RHA, 1948-51; Student Imperial Defence Coll., 1952; Dep. Secretary, Chiefs of Staff Cttee, Ministry of Defence, 1953-55; Comdr RA 2nd Div. 1955-58; Comdt School of Artillery, 1959-60; Commander, British Army Staff, and Military Attaché, Washington, DC, 1960-63; Col Comdt RA, 1964; Principal Staff Officer to Sec. of State for Commonwealth Relations, 1964-69. ADC to the Queen, 1958-60. *Recreations:* riding, sailing, shooting. *Address:* Beales House, Pilton, Shepton Mallet, Som. *T:* Pilton 212. *Clubs:* Army and Navy, English-Speaking Union.

**McNEILL, Peter Grant Brass,** PhD; Sheriff Substitute of Lanarkshire at Glasgow, since 1965; *b* 3 March 1929; *s* of William Arnot McNeill and Lillias Philips Scrimgeour; *m* 1959, Matilda Farquhar Rose, *d* of Mrs Christina Rose; one *s* three *d*. *Educ:* Hillhead High Sch., Glasgow; Morrison's Academy, Crieff; Glasgow Univ. MA (Hist.) 1951; LLB 1954; Carnegie Fellowship, 1955; Faulds Fellowship, 1956-59; Scottish Bar, 1956; PhD, 1961. Hon. Sheriff Substitute of Lanarkshire, and of Stirling, Clackmannan and Dumbarton, 1962; Standing Junior Counsel to Scottish Development Dept (Highways), 1964; Advocate Depute, 1964. *Publications:* (ed) Balfour's *Practicks* (Stair Society), 1962-63; legal and historical articles in Juridical Review, Scots Law Times, Glasgow Herald, etc. *Recreations:* legal history, gardening, bookbinding. *Address:* 185 Nithsdale Road, Glasgow, S1. *T:* 041-423 2499.

**McNICOLL, Vice-Adm. Sir Alan (Wedel Ramsay),** KBE 1966 (CBE 1954); CB 1965; GM 1941; Australian Ambassador to Turkey, since 1968; *b* 3 April 1908; 2nd *s* of late Brig.-Gen. Sir Walter McNicoll and Lady McNicoll; *m* 1st, 1937; two *s* one *d*; 2nd, 1957, Frances, *d* of late J. Chadwick. *Educ:* Scotch Coll., Melbourne; Royal Australian Naval Coll. Joined Navy, 1922; Lieut, 1930; Captain, 1949; Rear-Admiral, 1958; Dep. Chief of Naval Staff, 1951-52; Commanded 10th Destroyer Flotilla, 1950; HMAS Australia, 1953-54; IDC, 1955; 2nd Naval Member, Commonwealth Naval Board, 1960-61; Commanded Australian Fleet, 1962-64; Vice-Admiral, 1965; Chief of Naval Staff, Australia, 1965-68. Comdr of Order of Orange Nassau, 1955. *Recreations:* music, painting, fly-fishing. *Address:* c/o Department of External Affairs, Canberra 2601, Australia.

*See also H. Chadwick, Sir J. E. Chadwick, W. O. Chadwick.*

**MACNIE, William Alexander,** CMG 1949; OBE 1941; *b* 1899. *Educ:* High Sch. and University, Glasgow. Served European War, 1914-18, Lieut, 1917-20. Sub-Inspector, Police, British Guiana, 1921; District Inspector, 1925; seconded as additional Assistant Colonial Secretary, 1931; District Commissioner, 1932; Senior District Commissioner, 1936; Principal Assistant Colonial Secretary, 1945; seconded as Competent Authority and Controller of Supplies and Prices, British Guiana, 1939-45; Colonial Secretary, Leeward Islands, 1945-49. *Address:* The Little House, Cliff Plantation, St John, Barbados, West Indies.

**MACONCHY, Elizabeth, (Mrs W. R. Le Fanu);** Composer of serious music; *b* 19 March 1907; of Irish parentage; *d* of Gerald E. C. Maconchy, Lawyer, and Violet M. Poë; *m* 1930, William Richard Le Fanu (author of Bibliography of Edward Jenner, 1951, Betsy Sheridan's Journal, 1960, etc); two *d. Educ:* privately; Royal College of Music, London. Held Blumenthal Scholarship and won Sullivan Prize, Foli and other exhibitions, at RCM; pupil of Vaughan-Williams; travelled with Octavia Scholarship, 1929-30. First public performance: Piano Concerto with Prague Philharmonic Orchestra, 1930. Sir Henry Wood introduced "The Land", Promenade Concerts, 1930; performances and broadcasts at home and abroad followed. Has had works performed at 3 Festivals of International Society for Contemporary Music (Prague, 1935; Paris, 1937; Copenhagen, 1947). Largest output has been in Chamber Music; String Quartets played as a series in BBC Third Programme, 1955. Chairman, Composers Guild of Great Britain, 1960. *Publications:* Symphony, Suite for Orchestra, The Land; Nocturne, Overture, Proud Thames (LCC Coronation Prize, 1953); Dialogue for Piano and Orchestra; Viola Concerto; Serenata Concertante for Violin and Orchestra, 1963; Symphony for Double String Orchestra; Concertino for: Bassoon and String Orchestra; Clarinet and String Orchestra; Piano and String Orchestra; Concerto for Oboe, Bassoon and String Orchestra; Variazioni Concertanti for Oboe, Clarinet, Bassoon, Horn and Strings, 1965; Variations for String Orchestra; Nine String Quartets (No 5, Edwin Evans Prize; No 9, Radcliffe Award, 1969); Oboe Quintet (Daily Telegraph Prize); Violin Sonata; Viola Sonata; Cello Divertimento; Duo for 2 Violins; Duo for Violin and Cello; Variations for Solo Cello; Reflections, for Oboe, Clarinet, Viola and Harp (Gedok International Prize, 1961); Clarinet Quintet; Carol Cantata, A Christmas Morning; Samson and the Gates of Gaza for Chorus and Orchestra, 1964; 3 settings of Gerard Manley Hopkins for Soprano and Chamber Orchestra; Sonatina for Harpsichord and Notebook for Harpsichord, 1965; Three Donne settings, 1965; Nocturnal for unaccompanied chorus, 1965; Music for Brass and Woodwind, 1966; An Essex Overture, 1966; 6 Miniatures for Solo Violin, 1966; Duo for piano duet, 1967; Extravaganza, The Birds, after Aristophanes, 1968; Three Cloudscapes for Orchestra, 1968; And Death shall have no Dominion for Chorus and Brass, 3 Choirs Festival, 1969; Sonata for Clarinet and Viola, 1969; The Jesse Tree, masque for Dorchester Abbey, 1970. Songs, Piano Pieces, etc. Three One-Act Operas (The Sofa, The Three Strangers, The Departure). *Address:* Shottesbrook, Boreham, Chelmsford, Essex. *T:* Boreham 286.

**MACOUN, Michael John,** CMG 1964; OBE 1961; QPM; Overseas Police Adviser, Foreign and Commonwealth Office, since 1967; *b* 27 Nov. 1914; *o s* of late John Horatio Macoun, Comr of Chinese Maritime Customs; *m* 1940, Geraldine Mabel, *o d* of late Brig.-Gen. G. C. Sladen, CB, CMG, DSO, MC; two *s. Educ:* Stowe Sch., Buckingham; Univ. of Oxford (MA). At Metropolitan Police Coll., 1938; Tanganyika Police, 1939-42, 1945-58; Inspector-Gen. of Police, Uganda, 1959-64; Directing Staff, Police Coll., Bramshill, 1965; Commonwealth Office, 1966. War Service, 1943-44. Colonial Police Medal, 1951; Queen's Police Medal, 1954; OStJ 1959. *Recreations:* tennis, fishing, ski-ing. *Address:* Furzedown, Rowledge, near Farnham, Surrey. *T:* Frensham 3196. *Club:* English-Speaking Union.

**McOWAN, George,** MA, BSc, PhD; retired; *b* Alva, 1894; *m* 1928, Jan D. M., MA, *yr d* of A. Gibson, MB, ChB, FRCSE, FSA (Scotland), JP, Baillieston, Scotland; three *d*; *m* 1958, Graeme Lambert, *yr d* of late A. T. Wilson, Rangoon. *Educ:* St Andrews Univ. Lt 8th Royal Scots Fusiliers, 1914-18; Captain and Officer-Commanding St Andrews Univ. OTC, 1921-27; Lecturer in Chemistry, Univ. of St Andrews, 1923-27; Prof. of Chemistry, Raffles Coll., Singapore, 1927; Principal, Raffles Coll., 1938. *Publications:* contributions to Journal of Chemical Society. *Recreations:* golf, tennis. *Address:* 11 Marchhall Crescent, Edinburgh.

**MacOWAN, Michael Charles Henry;** Principal, London Academy of Music and Dramatic Art, 1954-66; *b* 18 April 1906; *s* of Norman MacOwan and Violet (*née* Stephenson); *m* 1932, Alexis McFarlane (Alexis France); one *d. Educ:* Haileybury Coll. Started as an actor, in 1925; abandoned acting for production; apptd producer Hull Repertory, 1931; Asst Producer and Master of Students, Old Vic, 1933-35; Producer, Westminster Theatre, 1936-39; A Month in the Country, Mourning Becomes Electra, Troilus and Cressida (in modern dress), etc. War service, 1939-45. Apptd Drama Dir Arts Council of Great Britain, 1945; produced Macbeth, Stratford-on-Avon, 1946. London productions include: The Linden Tree, 1947; Cockpit, 1948; A Sleep of Prisoners, 1951; The River Line, 1952; The Applecart, 1953; The Burning Glass, 1954; The Seagull, 1956; The Potting Shed, 1958. Has also undertaken radio and television productions and extensive lecturing and teaching, at home and abroad. *Recreations:* travel and country pursuits. *Address:* 135 Old Church Street, Chelsea, SW3. *T:* 01-352 8542. *Club:* Savile.

**McPETRIE, Sir James (Carnegie),** KCMG 1966 (CMG 1961); OBE 1953; HM Diplomatic Service; Legal Adviser, Foreign and Commonwealth Office, since 1968; *b* 29 June 1911; *er s* of late James Duncan McPetrie and late Elizabeth Mary Carnegie; *m* 1941, Elizabeth, *e d* of late John Howie; one *d. Educ:* Madras Coll., St Andrews; Univ. of St Andrews; Jesus Coll., Oxford (Scholar), MA (St Andrews) 1933; BA (Oxford) 1937; Harmsworth Schol., Middle Temple, 1937; Barrister, Middle Temple, 1938. Served War of 1939-45, Royal Artillery and staff of JAG (India); commissioned, 1940; Major, 1944. Legal Asst, Commonwealth Relations Office and Colonial Office, 1946, Sen. Legal Asst, 1947, Asst Legal Adviser, 1952; Legal Adviser, Colonial Office, 1960, Commonwealth Office, 1966. *Address:* Gladsmuir, 11 Alders Road, Reigate, Surrey. *T:* Reigate 44925. *Club:* Oxford and Cambridge.

**McPETRIE, James Stuart,** CB 1960; *b* 13 June 1902; *s* of John McPetrie and Mary (*née* Simpson); *m* 1931, Helen Noreen McGregor; one *s. Educ:* Robert Gordon's Coll. Aberdeen; Aberdeen Univ. National Physical Laboratory, 1925-43; Radio Physicist, British Supply Mission, Washington, DC, 1943-44; Research Superintendent, Signals Research and Development Establishment, Ministry of Supply, 1944-50; Head of Radio Dept, Royal Aircraft Establishment, 1950-58; Dir-Gen. of Electronics Research and Development at Ministry of Aviation, 1958-62; Consulting Electronic Engineer, 1962-; Dir, Racal Electronics, 1965-69. *Publications:* series of papers on various aspects of radio research to learned societies. *Address:* Middlegrounds Farm, Slapton, Devon. *T:* Torcross 239.

**MACPHERSON,** family name of **Barons Drumalbyn, Macpherson of Drumochter** and **Strathcarron.**

**MACPHERSON OF DRUMOCHTER,** 2nd Baron, *cr* 1951, of Great Warley, Essex; **(James) Gordon Macpherson;** Chairman and Managing Director of Macpherson, Train & Co. Ltd, and Subsidiary and Associated Companies, since 1964; *b* 22 Jan. 1924; *s* of 1st Baron (*d* 1965) and Lucy Lady Macpherson of Drumochter; *S* father, 1965; *m* 1947, Dorothy Ruth Coulter; one *s* two *d. Educ:* Loretto; Wells House, Malvern. Served War of 1939-45, with RAF; 1939-45 Campaign medal, Burma Star, Pacific Star, Defence Medal, Victory Medal. Member: Council, London Chamber of Commerce, 1958-; East European Trade Council, 1969-; Exec. Cttee, W India Cttee, 1959-. Freeman of City of London, 1969; Mem., Butchers' Co., 1969. Governor, Brentwood Sch. JP Essex, 1961. FRES, FZS. *Recreations:* shooting, fishing, golf. *Heir: s* Hon. Thomas Ian Macpherson, *b* 25 July 1948. *Address:* Normans, Great Warley, Brentwood, Essex. *T:* Brentwood 117. *Clubs:* Devonshire; Thorndon Golf, House of Lords Yacht; Royal and Ancient (St Andrews).

**McPHERSON, Brig. Alan Bruce,** CBE 1944; MVO 1933; MC 1915; Indian Army, retired; *b* 6 Jan. 1887; *s* of late Donald William McPherson, Dunvegan, Isle of Skye; *m* 1915, Gladys Lawrie, *d* of late Col W. H. Riddell, Bedfordshire Regt; one *d. Educ:* Bedford Sch.; RMC Sandhurst. 2nd Lt IA 1906; Lt, 1909; Captain 1915; Major, 1921; Brevet Lt-Col, 1930; Substantive Lt-Col, 1931; Col, 1933; Served European war in France, 1914-15; Egypt, 1915; Mesopotamia, 1915-16 (wounded, despatches twice, MC); DAAG (Demobilization) Bombay 1918-19; Staff Coll. 1920-21; GSOII (Intelligence) 1922; DAAG 1922-26 and 1928-30; Officer in Command Indian War Memorial contingent, Neuve Chapelle, France, 1927; Commandant, 2/9th Jat Regt, 1931-34; Officer in charge the King's Indian Orderly Officers, 1933; AAG Northern Command, India, 1935-37; Operations NWF India, 1936-37; Comdr 11th (Ahmednagar) Infantry Brigade, India and Egypt, 1937-40; Dep. Dir of Mobilization, War Office, 1940-46; retired 1947; re-employed War Office 1947-49, 1950-57. *Publications:* Official Historical Monographs (2nd World War), on Mobilization and Discipline. *Recreation:* golf. *Address:* 15 Calonne Road, Wimbledon, SW19. *Club:* Naval and Military.

**MACPHERSON of Pitmain, Lt-Col Alexander Kilgour,** MVO 1928; Senior Chieftain of the Clan Macpherson; *b* 6 March 1888; *er s* of late Dr F. A. Macpherson and Florence, *d* of late Archdeacon W. F. Taylor, DD, Liverpool, and Abergele; *m* 1st, Margaret G. Moore (*d* 1920); 2nd, 1924, Margaret M. Ramsay Crowley (*d* 1965); two *d. Educ:* Liverpool; Royal Military Coll., Sandhurst. Commissioned, 1908; attached 2nd Royal Berks Regt; posted 12th Pioneers, Indian Army, 1909; served France, 1914 (wounded), Waziristan, 1917, and with Marri Field Force, 1918; Captain 1915; Major, 1924; Lt-Col, 1932; commanded 1st Bn Corps of Bombay Pioneers, Indian Army, 1932-34; retired, 1934; called up active service Sept. 1939; commanded Nabha Akal Infantry, Eritrea and Cyprus, Middle East Force; Col (AQMG), GHQ, India; returned to pension establishment, Dec. 1943. DL, Inverness-shire, 1950-53. *Publication:* The Darkening Scene, 1967 (2nd edn 1968). *Recreations:* big-game shooting, riding, mountaineering. *Address:* Newtonmore, Inverness-shire. *Club:* United Service.

**MACPHERSON, Hon. Campbell Leonard,** OBE 1949; Lieutenant-Governor of Newfoundland, 1957-63; *b* 4 July 1907; *s* of late Cluny Macpherson, CMG; *m* 1932, Faith Vilas; two *s* one *d. Educ:* Westminster Sch., London, England. President, The Royal Stores Ltd, and associated companies, 1963. Mem. Bd of Regents: Memorial Univ. of Newfoundland, 1949-57; Mount Allison Univ.; Chm., Children's Hosp. Corp. Pres., Newfoundland Grenfell Assoc.; Dir, Internat. Grenfell Assoc. KJStJ, 1958. Hon. LLD: Mount Allison Univ., 1962; Memorial Univ. of Newfoundland, 1963. *Recreations:* motoring, golf. *Address:* Westerland, St John's, Newfoundland (PO Box 5847). *Clubs:* Naval and Military; Canadian (New York); Bally Haly Golf (St John's); Mount Royal (Montreal).

**MACPHERSON, Rt. Rev. Colin;** *see* Argyll and the Isles, Bishop of, (RC).

**MacPHERSON, Donald,** CIE 1946; *b* 22 March 1894; *s* of D. MacPherson, Edinburgh; *m* 1931, Marie Elizabeth, *d* of John Nicholson, Sydney, NSW; two *d. Educ:* Royal High Sch. and Univ., Edinburgh. Indian Civil Service; District Magistrate, Bengal, 1928; Commissioner of Excise, 1935; Commissioner of Division, 1944. Retired, 1948. *Address:* 11 Melville Place, Edinburgh 3. *T:* 031-225 5716.

**McPHERSON, Donald George;** Assistant Under-Secretary of State, responsible for Health, Welsh Office, since 1969; *b* 5 Jan. 1914; *s* of George and Catherine McPherson; *m* 1943, Sybil Jean Blackley; two *s. Educ:* Newport (Mon) High Sch. Entered Estate Duty Office, 1932; called to Bar, Gray's Inn, 1937. Asst Sec., Board of Inland Revenue, 1950; Mem., Ceylon Taxation Commn, 1954-55; Establishment Officer, UKAEA, 1959-61; Sec., War Damage Commn, 1961-65; UN Adviser on Taxation, Cyprus, 1963; Sec.,

Royal Mint, 1966-67; Asst Sec., Min. of Health, 1967-69; Chm., Welsh Board of Health, 1969 (until Welsh Office take-over). *Recreation:* sport (particularly sailing and tennis) (Life Mem., CS Sports Council, Vice-Pres., CS LTA, Chm. Cardiff Area, CS Sports Council). *Address:* Robin Hill, Twyncyn, Dinas Powis, Glam. *T:* Dinas Powis 2339. *Clubs:* Royal Commonwealth Society, Wig and Pen.

**MACPHERSON, George Philip Stewart,** OBE 1943; TD 1945; Director, Kleinwort Benson Lonsdale, since 1960; *b* 14 Dec. 1903; *s* of late Sir T. Stewart Macpherson, CIE, LLD, ICS, and of Lady (Helen) Macpherson, K.-I.-H. (*née* Cameron); *m* 1939, Elizabeth Margaret Cameron, *d* of late James Cameron Smail, OBE; three *s*. *Educ:* Edinburgh Acad.; Fettes Coll. (Schol.); Oriel Coll., Oxford (Schol.; 1st class Classical Mods, 1st class Lit. Hum.; MA 1944); Yale Univ., USA (Schol.); Edinburgh Univ.; Chartered Accountant (Edinburgh), 1930; partner in Layton-Bennett, Chiene and Tait, CA, 1930-36; Man. Dir, Robert Benson and Co. Ltd, Merchant Bankers, 1936; Chm., Robert Benson Lonsdale & Co. Ltd, 1958-60; Dir, Kleinwort Benson Ltd, 1960-69 (Vice-Chm., 1960-66); Dir Standard Life Assurance Co. Ltd and of several industrial companies and investment trusts. Chm., Issuing Houses Association, 1955, 1956; Mem. Exec. Cttee, Investment Trust Assoc., 1955-68. Governor, Fettes Coll., 1957-. 7/9 Battalion The Royal Scots, 1927-36; 1st Bn London Scottish, 1939, sc; Brig. 1945, Dir Finance Div. (Brit. Element) Allied Control Commn to Austria, 1945-46. *Publications:* contrib. to Accountants' Magazine. *Recreations:* active outdoor occupations and gardening. Formerly Rugby football and athletics (Oxford XV, 1922-24; Edinburgh Univ. Athletic Blue; Rep. Scotland Long Jump and Hurdles, 1929, and Rugby football, 1922-32). *Address:* The Old Rectory, Aston Sandford, near Aylesbury, Bucks. *T:* Haddenham 335. *Clubs:* Caledonian, English-Speaking Union; New (Edinburgh).

**MACPHERSON, James;** Administrative Adviser, Scottish Office, since 1970; *b* 16 Dec. 1911; *s* of late John Campbell Macpherson and Agnes Arkley Mitchell, Auchterarder, Perthshire; *m* 1939, Marion Cooper Cochrane Allison; two *s* one *d*. *Educ:* George Heriot's Sch. Asst Preventive Officer, subseq. Officer, Customs and Excise, 1932-39; Gunner, TA, 1939; 54th Light AA Regt, RA; service in France, Belgium, Italy, Austria, 1939-46; Brig. 1946; Dir Finance Div. (Br Element), Allied Control Commn to Austria; Princ., Min. of Civil Aviation, 1946-48; Treasury, 1949-53; Asst Sec., Treasury, 1953-63; Scottish Home and Health Dept, 1963-66; Scottish Development Dept, 1966-67 Under-Sec., Scottish Develt Dept, 1967-70; retired and re-employed in Scottish Office. *Recreations:* reading, golf. *Address:* 92 Ravelston Dykes, Edinburgh 12. *T:* 031-337 6560. *Clubs:* Royal Commonwealth Society; New (Edinburgh); Hon. Company of Edinburgh Golfers, Royal Burgess Golfing Society.

**MACPHERSON, Sir John (Stuart),** GCMG 1951 (KCMG 1945; CMG 1941); Vice-Chairman, Advisory Committee on Distinction Awards for Consultants, since 1962; *b* 25 Aug. 1898; *er s* of late James P. Macpherson, JP; *m* 1928, Joan, *er d* of late Dr W. E. Fry; one *s*. *Educ:* Watson's Coll., Edinburgh; Edinburgh Univ. (MA 1921). Served European War, 1917-19, France, Commissioned in Argyll and Sutherland Highlanders; Malayan Civil Service, 1921-37 (Seconded Colonial Office, 1933-35); Principal Asst Sec., Nigeria, 1937-39; Chief Sec., Palestine, 1939-43; Head of British Colonies Supply Mission in Washington, and Member of Anglo-American Caribbean Commission, 1943-45; Comptroller for Development and Welfare in the West Indies and British co-Chairman Caribbean Commission, 1945-48; Governor of Nigeria, 1948-54; Gov.-Gen., Federation of Nigeria, 1954-55. Chm., UN Visiting Mission to Trust Territories of the Pacific, 1956; Permanent Under-Sec. of State for the Colonies, 1956-59; Chairman: Cable & Wireless Ltd, 1962-67; Basildon Develt Corp., 1964-67 (Dep. Chm., 1960-64). A Vice-President: Royal Commonwealth Soc.; Royal African Soc.; Mem. Council, Voluntary Service Overseas. Hon. Associate, Univ. Coll., Ibadan, 1950. Hon. LLD Edinburgh, 1957. KStJ 1952. *Address:* 141 Marsham Court, Westminster, SW1. *T:* 01-834 8807. *Club:* Athenæum.

**MacPHERSON, Malcolm,** MBE 1945; MP (Lab), Stirling and Falkirk Burghs, since 1948; Vice-Chairman, Parliamentary Labour Party, 1964-67; *b* 1904; *s* of late John MacPherson and late Mary MacKay; *m* 1929, Janet Elder (*d* 1961), *d* of late William McKay; two *s* two *d*. *Educ:* Trinity Acad., Edinburgh; Univ. of Edinburgh. Taught in George Heriot's Sch., Edinburgh, 1926-28; Univ. of New Brunswick, Canada, 1928-38; University Coll., Exeter, 1938-40; Canadian Army, 1940-45; Labour Candidate, Yeovil Div., Gen. Election, 1945. *Address:* Airlie Mount, Alyth, Perthshire. *T:* Alyth 515.

**MACPHERSON, Roderick Ewen;** Registrary, University of Cambridge, since 1969; *b* 17 July 1916; *s* of Ewen Macpherson, Chief Charity Commissioner, and Dorothy Mildred Hensley; *m* 1941, Sheila Joan Hooper, *d* of H. P. Hooper; two *s* two *d*. *Educ:* Eton College; King's College, Cambridge. Math. Tripos, Part II, Wrangler; Math. Tripos, Part III, Distinction; Smith's Prizeman, 1940. Served RAFVR, 1940-46, Navigator (Radio). Fellow, King's Coll., Cambridge, 1942-; Third Bursar, King's College, 1947-50, Second Bursar, 1950-51, First Bursar, 1951-62; University Treasurer, Univ. of Cambridge, 1962-69; Member: Council of the Senate, 1957-62; Financial Board, 1955-62. *Recreations:* gardening, hill-walking. *Address:* Orion, Coton Road, Grantchester, Cambridge CB3 9NX. *T:* Trumpington 2266.

**MacPHERSON, Stewart Myles;** Radio Commentator; Journalist; Variety Artist; Director of Programs, C-Jay Television, Winnipeg, since 1960; *b* Winnipeg, Canada, 29 Oct. 1908; *m* 1937, Emily Comfort; one *s* one *d*. *Educ:* Canada. Started broadcasting, 1937, on ice hockey; War Correspondent. Commentator on national events and world championships. Question Master, Twenty Questions and Ignorance is Bliss. Compère, Royal Command Variety Performance, 1948. *Publication:* The Mike and I, 1948. *Recreations:* golf, bridge, poker. *Address:* Winnipeg Enterprises Corporation, Winnipeg, Canada; c/o Canadian Broadcasting Corporation, Ottawa, Ontario, Canada.

**MACPHERSON, Very Rev. William Stuart,** MA Cantab; Dean of Lichfield, 1954-69, Dean Emeritus, 1969; Hon. Canon, Ripon Cathedral, 1953-54; *b* 30 Sept. 1901; *s* of late Henry Macpherson, Headingley Hall, Leeds; *m* 1937, Peggy Josephine Wilton; two *s* one *d*. *Educ:* Sedbergh Sch.; Pembroke Coll., Cambridge. BA Cambridge, 1923. Priest, 1932; Curate of Richmond, Yorks, 1932-37; Minor Canon, Ripon Cathedral, 1937-39; Chaplain RNVR, 1939-45; Archdeacon of Richmond, 1951-54, Rector of Richmond, 1945-54. Proctor in Convocation, 1949. *Address:* Yew

Tree Cottage, Hawkchurch, Axminster, Devon. *T:* Hawkchurch 485.

**MACPHERSON-GRANT, Sir Ewan (George),** 6th Bt, *cr* 1838; TD; DL; Member Scottish Faculty of Advocates; Hon. Sheriff Substitute, Counties of Perth and Angus; Director, Scottish Equitable Life Assurance Society; *b* 29 Sept. 1907; *s* of late George Bertram Macpherson-Grant, OBE (2nd *s* of 3rd Bt) and of Dorothy Eleanor Kellie-MacCallum (*d* 1952); *S* cousin, 1951; *m* 1937, Evelyn Nancy Stopford, *yr d* of late Major Edward Spencer Dickin, Spenford House, Loppington, Salop; one *d. Educ:* Winchester; Christ Church, Oxford. DL, Co. Banff, 1952. Mem. of Royal Company of Archers. *Heir:* none. *Address:* Ballindalloch Castle, Ballindalloch, Banffshire. *T:* Ballindalloch 206; Craigo, by Montrose, Angus. *T:* Hillside 205. *Club:* Army and Navy.

**McQUAID, Most Rev. J. C.;** *see* Dublin, Archbishop of, (RC).

**MACQUARRIE, Rev. Prof. John,** TD 1962; Professor of Divinity, University of Oxford, and Canon of Christ Church, since 1970; *b* 27 June, 1919; *s* of John Macquarrie and Robina Macquarrie (*née* McInnes); *m* 1949, Jenny Fallow (*née* Welsh); two *s* one *d. Educ:* Paisley Grammar Sch.; Univ. of Glasgow. MA 1940; BD 1943; PhD 1954; DLitt 1964. Royal Army Chaplains Dept, 1945-48; St Ninian's Church, Brechin, 1948-53; Lecturer, Univ. of Glasgow, 1953-62; Prof. of Systematic Theology, Union Theological Seminary, NY, 1962-70, and Chm., Theological Field, 1968-70. consultant, Lambeth Conf., 1968. Hon. degrees: STD: Univ. of the South, USA, 1967; General Theological Seminary, New York, 1968; DD, Univ. of Glasgow, 1969. *Publications:* An Existentialist Theology, 1955; The Scope of Demythologising, 1960; Twentieth Century Religious Thought, 1963; Studies in Christian Existentialism, 1965; Principles of Christian Theology, 1966; God-Talk, 1967; God and Secularity, 1967; Martin Heidegger, 1968; Three Issues in Ethics, 1970. *Recreation:* numismatics. *Address:* Christ Church, Oxford. *Club:* Glasgow University Club of America (New York).

**MacQUARRIE, Hon. Josiah H.,** Justice of the Supreme Court of Nova Scotia, Canada, since 1947; *b* 12 Nov. 1897; *s* of James T. and Agnes MacWhinnie MacQuarrie; *m* 1921, Mattie, *d* of Ethelbert and Annie Atkinson; one *s* two *d. Educ:* Pictou Academy; Acadia Univ.; Dalhousie Univ. Practised law at Pictou, Nova Scotia, with firm of Macdonald and MacQuarrie, 1921-32; Head of Legal firm New Glasgow, Nova Scotia, of MacQuarrie and MacQuarrie, 1932-40; Mem. Parliament of Nova Scotia, Attorney Gen. and Min. of Lands and Forests of Nova Scotia, 1933-47; Min. of Municipal Affairs, Prov. of Nova Scotia (from beginning of Dept), 1937-47. *Recreations:* golf, swimming. *Address:* Halifax, Nova Scotia. *TA:* Halifax Nova Scotia. *T:* Halifax 2-2087. *Clubs:* Scotia, (New Glasgow); Halifax (Halifax).

**MacQUEEN, Maj.-Gen. John Henry,** CBE 1943; CD; retired; *b* Canada, 19 Sept. 1893; *s* of John T. and Emma Olding MacQueen; *m* 1917, Aimee Olive Miller Roy; no *c. Educ:* New Glasgow High Sch.; Royal Military College of Canada; Military Coll. of Science, England. Commissioned RCOC 1914; European War, 1914-19, Canada and England; District Ordnance Officer, Military District No. 10, Winnipeg, Manitoba, 1929-38; Dir of Ordnance Services, Canada, 1938-39; Senior Ordnance Officer, 1939, and Asst Quartermaster-Gen. (Ordnance Services), 1940, Dep. Quartermaster Gen., Canadian Military Headquarters, London, England, 1941-45; Master Gen. of the Ordnance, 1945. Pres. Canadian Arsenals Ltd, 1947-61. Served War of 1939-45, Canada, England, France, Italy. Legion of Merit, USA, 1948. Coronation Medal, 1937. *Recreations:* shooting, fishing, golf, bridge. *Address:* 33 Loch Isle Road, RR No 2, Bells Corners, Ont, Canada. *Clubs:* Rideau (Ottawa); Royal Ottawa Golf (Hull, PQ).

**MACRAE, Angus;** Vice-President, British Medical Association, since 1960; *b* 1893; *s* of late Rev. Duncan Mackenzie Macrae, Minister at Helmsdale and at Lochearnhead; *m* 1926, Marjorie Isobel, *d* of late G. M. Brotherston; two *s. Educ:* George Watson's Coll. and Univ. of Edinburgh (MA 1919; MB, ChB, 1924). Served European War, 4th Seaforth Highlanders, 1915-19. Investigator, Nat. Institute of Industrial Psychology, 1925. Asst Sec., 1935, Dep. Sec., 1948, BMA; Sec., Central Medical Recruitment Cttee, 1950-58; Hon. Sec., British Commonwealth Medical Conference, 1950-58; Sec., BMA, 1950-58; retd; Information Officer, Nat. Inst. of Indust. Psychol., 1958-63. Hon. MD (NUI), 1952; Hon. LLD, Edinburgh, 1959. *Publications:* Talents and Temperaments, 1932; various articles on psychological subjects. *Address:* 1 Embassy Lodge, Regent's Park Road, Finchley, N3. *T:* 01-346 8923.

**MACRAE, Christopher,** CBE 1956; MA, DPhil; Vice-President, Ashridge Management College, since 1969 (Principal, 1962-69); *b* 6 Jan. 1910; *s* of John Tait Macrae and Mary (*née* Mackenzie), Kintail, Ross-shire; *m* 1939, Mary Margaret Campbell Greig, *er d* of Robert Elliott, Glasgow; two *s* one *d* (*er d* decd in infancy). *Educ:* Dingwall Acad.; Glasgow Univ. (MA); New Coll., Oxford (DPhil). Civil Servant, 1937-46; Chief Exec. Scottish Counc. (Devel. and Industry), 1946-56; Prof. of Industrial Admin., The Royal Coll. of Science and Technology, Glasgow, and Head of Chesters Residential Management Educn Centre, 1956-62. *Publications:* various articles and papers. *Recreations:* reading, walking, climbing, sailing. *Address:* 7 and 8 Water End, Hemel Hempstead, Herts. *T:* Hemel Hempstead 52875.

**MACRAE, Col Robert Andrew Alexander Scarth,** MBE 1953; Vice-Lieutenant for Orkney, since 1967; Farmer; *b* 14 April 1915; *s* of late Robert Scarth Farquhar Macrae, Grindelay House, Orphir, Orkney; *m* 1945, Violet Maud, *d* of late Walter Scott MacLellan; two *s. Educ:* Lancing; RMC Sandhurst. 2nd Lt Seaforth Highlanders, 1935; Captain 1939; Major 1948; Lt-Col 1958; Col 1963; retd 1968. Active Service: NW Europe, 1940-45 (despatches, 1945); Korea, 1952-53; E Africa, 1953-54. DL, Co. of Orkney, 1946. *Recreations:* sailing, fishing. *Address:* Grindelay House, Orkney. *T:* Orphir 228. *Clubs:* Army and Navy, United Hunts; New (Edinburgh).

**MACREADY, Sir Nevil (John Wilfrid),** 3rd Bt *cr* 1923; Director, Mobil Oil Company Ltd, since 1962; *b* 7 Sept. 1921; *s* of Lt-Gen. Sir Gordon (Nevil) Macready, 2nd Bt, KBE, CB, CMG, DSO, MC, and Elisabeth (*d* 1969), *d* of Duc de Noailles; *S* father 1956; *m* 1949, Mary, *d* of late Sir Donald Fergusson, GCB; one *s* three *d. Educ:* Cheltenham; St John's Coll., Oxford. Served in RA (Field), 1942-47 (despatches); Staff Captain, 1945. BBC European Service, 1947-50. *Recreations:* racing, theatre. *Heir: s* Charles Nevil Macready, *b* 19 May 1955. *Address:* Langley House, Pirbright, Surrey. *T:* Brookwood 2172. *Club:* Naval and Military.

**MacRITCHIE, Prof. Farquhar,** CBE 1968; MA, LLB (Aberdeen); Professor of Conveyancing at Aberdeen University, since 1946; *b* 1 Nov. 1902; *s* of Donald MacRitchie, Isle of Lewis; *m* 1941, Isobel, *d* of William Ross, Aberdeen; one *s*. *Educ:* Aberdeen Univ. Asst Lecturer in Law, Aberdeen Univ., 1940-45; Lecturer in Mercantile Law, Aberdeen Univ., 1945-46. Hon. Sheriff Substitute in Aberdeen. Convener, Legal Education Cttee, Law Soc. of Scotland, 1955-; Vice-Pres., Law Soc. of Scotland, 1963. Mem. of firm of Morice & Wilson, Advocates, Aberdeen. Hon. LLD (Edinburgh), 1965. *Recreation:* golf. *Address:* 60 Rubislaw Den North, Aberdeen. *T:* 35458. *Club:* University (Aberdeen).

**McROBERT, Sir George Reid,** Kt 1947; CIE 1942; Col IMS (retired); Consulting Physician, Hospital for Tropical Diseases, University College Hospital, London; *b* 21 Jan. 1895; *s* of late A. T. McRobert, Aberdeen; *m* 1919, Catherine Ellen (*d* 1969), *d* of late G. T. C. Gregory, New Malden, Surrey; two *d*. *Educ:* Gordon's Coll., Aberdeen; Aberdeen Univ. MB 1917; MD 1923; MRCP 1923; FRCP 1935; DTM&H Eng 1924; Hon. FRCPEd 1970. RAMC (SR) 1917-20. France and Mesopotamia; IMS 1920; Waziristan Campaign; entered Civil side of IMS 1925; Prof. of Physiology, Rangoon Univ., 1925-30; Prof. of Medicine and Senior Physician, Madras, 1934-45; Inspector-Gen. of Hospitals, Bihar, 1945-47; Mem. Medical Bd, India Office and Commonwealth Relations Office, 1947-58; Medical Adviser to Sec. of State for Commonwealth Relations, 1958-62; Consulting Physician to Colonial Office and to Officers Convalescent Home, Osborne, 1951-60; Mem. Bd of Governors, University Coll. Hosp., 1955-63; Mem. of Governing Council, Epsom Coll., 1955-67; Physician, Tropical Diseases Hosp., London, 1951-60; Adviser for Colombo Plan Affairs, Dept of Technical Co-operation, 1961-62; Pres., Royal Society of Tropical Medicine and Hygiene, 1961-63. Jubilee and Coronation Medals. *Publications:* numerous in Professional Journals; part author Rogers and Megaw's Tropical Medicine. *Recreation:* writing. *Address:* 45 Higher Green, Ewell, Surrey. *T:* 01-393 3231. *Club:* Athenæum.

**McROBERT, Brig. Leslie Harrison,** CBE 1943 (OBE 1937); TD 1937; DL; Chartered Accountant; Executive Director, 1945-64, Deputy Chairman, 1951-61, Chairman, 1961-64, Cerebos Ltd and associated cos; Member, North Eastern Railway Board, 1956-64; Member, Local Employment Act, 1960, etc, Advisory Committee, Ministry of Technology (formerly Treasury, later Board of Trade), 1945-70; *b* 22 Aug. 1898; *s* of late James William McRobert, West Hartlepool; *m* 1st, 1929, May (*d* 1962), *d* of late W. G. Smith, Alston, Cumberland; two *d*; 2nd, 1963, Mrs Dorothy Ruddy. *Educ:* Royal Gram. Sch., Newcastle on Tyne. European War 1914-18, France and Belgium, RFC and RAF; commanded 55th (Northumbrian) Medium Bde RA and 63rd (Northumbrian) HAA Regt RA and 30, 59 and 28 AA Brigades during 1939-45 War. Chm. TA & AF Assoc., Co. of Durham, 1958-63. Chm. Hartlepools Hosp. Management Cttee, 1950-58. Hon. Colonel: 377 Corps Locating Regt RA (TA), 1955-56; 274 N Field Regt RA (TA), 1956-60; Durham Univ. (now Northumbrian Univs) OTC, 1960-68. DL Durham, 1941; Vice-Lieutenant, 1959-69; High Sheriff of Co. Durham, 1954-55. *Recreations:* fishing, golf, etc. *Address:* Eusemere, Pooley Bridge, Penrith, Cumberland.

**MacROBERT, Norman Murie,** CMG 1952; retired; *b* 30 May 1899; 3rd *s* of George Findlay MacRobert and Mabel Louisa, *d* of late Gen. Nugent; unmarried. *Educ:* Shrewsbury Sch. Lt Rifle Brigade, 1918-20. Colonial Administrative Service, 1927. Served in Royal West African Frontier Force, Sierra Leone, 1940; Major, 1941-42. Provincial Commissioner, 1946; Acting Chief Comr, 1952 and 1953; retired 1954. *Recreations:* gardening, photography. *Address:* 8 Rowans Court, Prince Edwards Road, Lewes, Sussex.

**McSHANE, John J.,** JP; Retired Secondary School Headmaster, Walsall; *b* Wishaw, Lanarkshire, 1 Oct. 1882; *s* of Philip McShane, miner; *m* Annie, *d* of Fred W. Bromwich, Walsall; one *s* two *d*. *Educ:* St Ignatius RC Sch., Wishaw; Glasgow Univ. Training Coll. Left Elementary Sch. at 14 years; went to work at railway wagon works; studied at night sch. and worked during day; ultimately passed to coll.; Headmaster, Armadale RC Sch. (West Lothian), 1909; after six years, went to Walsall; Headmaster, St Mary's RC Sch., Walsall, 1922-29; MP (Lab) Walsall Borough, 1929-31; mem. of NUT; Pres., South Midland Federation Class Teachers, 1920; Pres., Walsall Debating Soc., 1924; Pres., Walsall Labour Party, 1921-22; Chm., Walsall Board of Guardians, 1929. Dir Walsall Co-op Soc. 1933-55; Chm. Midland Section, CWS Representation Cttee, 1944-55. *Recreations:* tennis, golf, reading, and politics. *Address:* 3 Glenelg Mews, Beacon Road, Walsall, Staffs. *T:* 021-360 4445.

**McSHEEHY, Maj.-Gen. Oswald William,** CB 1943; DSO 1915; OBE 1919; MB, BS, London; RAMC, retired; *b* 27 Nov. 1884; *y s* of late Surgeon-Major E. L. McSheehy, MD, FRCSI, JP, Limerick, and Teresa, *d* of Joseph Hirst, JP, Huddersfield; *m* 1911, Caroline, (*d* 1950), *e d* of late Col H. Paterson, Indian Army; two *s* three *d*; *m* 1954, Teresa Delaine. *Educ:* St Edmund's Coll., Ware; St Thomas's Hospital. Entered army, 1909; Capt., 1912; Major, 1921; Bt Lt-Col 1926; Lt-Col 1934; Col 1937; Brig. 1940; Maj.-Gen. 1941; served European War, 1914-18 (despatches twice, DSO, OBE); Dep. Asst Dir-Gen., War Office, 1922-26; Dep Dir-Gen. Army Medical Services, War Office, 1938-41; served S Africa, India and Malaya; Dep. Dir of Medical Services, SE and E Cd at home, 1941-45; Hon. Surgeon to the King, 1941-44; retired pay, 1945; Dep Dir of Health, UNRRA, London, 1945-46; Col Comdt, RAMC, 1946-50, Rep. Comdt, 1948. *Address:* Creagh, Waverley Lane, Farnham, Surrey.

**McSHINE, Hon. Sir Arthur Hugh,** Kt 1969; Chief Justice of Trinidad and Tobago, since 1968; *b* 11 May 1906; *m* Dorothy Mary Vanier; one *s* one *d*. *Educ:* Queen's Royal Coll., Trinidad. Called to Bar, Middle Temple, 1931. Practised at Trinidad Bar for eleven years; Magistrate, 1942; Senior Magistrate, 1950; Puisne Judge, 1953; Justice of Appeal, 1962. Acting Governor-Gen., Trinidad and Tobago, 1970. *Recreations:* music and chess (Pres., Trinidad Chess Assoc.); flying (holder of private pilot's licence). *Address:* Chief Justice's Chambers, Court of Appeal of Trinidad and Tobago, Port-of-Spain, Trinidad. *Clubs:* Trinidad and Tobago Turf, Trinidad and Tobago Yacht.

**MacTAGGART, Sir Andrew (McCormick),** Kt, *cr* 1951; Civil Engineer; Company Director since 1928; *b* 13 July 1888; *s* of Matthew MacTaggart, Waterside House, Fenwick, Ayrshire; *m* 1st, 1919, Marie Louise (marriage dissolved, 1961), *d* of Gaston Petit, France; 2nd, 1961, Irene Countess of Craven. *Educ:* Kilmarnock; Glasgow. Completed a 4-year pupilage with Warren & Stewart, Glasgow, 1904-8; Asst Engineer on Nigerian Railways,

1912-16, promoted to permanent staff, resigned, 1916. Served European War, 1914-18, joined Royal Engineers with commission in France, 1917. Rejoined Balfour, Beatty & Co. Ltd in 1919. Responsible for the design and construction of Grampian Company's hydro-electric development in Scotland; in charge of construction of Lochaber Hydro-Electric Scheme in Scotland; responsible for construction of hydro-electric developments in Italy, India, and E Africa, and construction of large irrigation and railway works in Iraq. Pres., Power Securities Corp.; Pres. Fedn of Civil Engineering Contractors, 1948-49, 1949-50, 1950-51; Mem. of Council, British Employers' Confederation, 1940-62. *Recreations:* shooting and fishing. *Address:* Ockhams, Edenbridge, Kent. *T:* Edenbridge 2173. *Club:* Caledonian.

**MACTAGGART, Sir Ian (Auld),** 3rd Bt *cr* 1938; Managing Director The Western Heritable Investment Company and Director of several Property and other Companies; *b* Glasgow, 19 April 1923; *e s* of Sir John (Jack) Mactaggart, 2nd Bt, Nassau, Bahamas; *S* father 1960; *m* 1946, Rosemary (marr. diss. 1969), *d* of Sir Herbert Williams, 1st Bt, MP; two *s* two *d*. *Educ:* Oundle; Clare Coll., Cambridge. Served with Royal Engineers in India, 1942-45. Contested (U) Gorbals div. of Glasgow, 1945. Mem. (C) London County Council, for Fulham, 1949-51. Chm., Nat. Council for Individual Freedom; Pres., Free Radio Assoc. *Heir: s* John Auld Mactaggart, *b* 21 Jan. 1951. *Address:* 7 Charles Street, W1. *T:* 01-499 5110. *Club:* English-Speaking Union.

**MacTAGGART, Sir William,** Kt 1962; PPRSA; FRSE 1967; Hon. RA 1959; ARA 1968; Hon. RSW; RSA 1948 (ARSA 1937); Hon. FRIAS 1968; Hon. LLD Edinburgh, 1961; President, Royal Scottish Academy, 1959-69; *b* 15 May 1903; *er s* of late Hugh H. McTaggart, Engineer and Managing Dir of MacTaggart, Scott & Co. Ltd, Loanhead, and *g s* of late William McTaggart, RSA; *m* 1937, Fanny Margaretha Basilier, Kt 1st Cl. Order of St Olav, Norway, *er d* of late Gen. Ivar Aavatsmark, Oslo, Norway. *Educ:* privately; Edinburgh Coll. of Art; abroad. Elected professional mem. Soc. of Scottish Artists, 1922 (Pres., 1934-36); Mem. Soc. of Eight. Has held one-man exhibitions at home and abroad. Works purchased by Tate Gallery, Contemporary Art Soc. and the Arts Council; also represented in public galleries in Glasgow, Edinburgh, Aberdeen and Bradford, and in USA and Australia. Chevalier de la Légion d'Honneur, 1968. *Address:* 4 Drummond Place, Edinburgh. *T:* 031-556 1657. *Club:* Scottish Arts (Edinburgh).

**MACTAGGART, William Alexander,** CBE 1964; JP; Chairman, 1960-70, and Managing Director, 1945-68, Pringle of Scotland Ltd, Knitwear Manufacturers, Hawick; *b* 17 Aug. 1906; *o s* of late William Alexander and Margaret Mactaggart, Woodgate, Hawick; *m* 1932, Marjorie Laing Innes; two *s* one *d*. *Educ:* Sedbergh Sch., Yorks. Joined Robert Pringle & Son Ltd (later Pringle of Scotland Ltd), 1925; Dir, 1932; Joint Managing Dir, 1933. Served War of 1939-45: Captain, RASC, Holland, Belgium, France, 1942-45. Elder of Lilliesleaf Parish Church. Pres. of Vertish Hill Sports. *Recreation:* hunting. *Address:* Bewlie House, Lilliesleaf, Melrose, Roxburghshire. *T:* Lilliesleaf 267. *Club:* Bath.

**MacTIER, Sir (Reginald) Stewart,** Kt 1961; CBE 1946; Director: The Ocean Steam Ship Co. Ltd, 1955-67; Glen Line Ltd, London, 1939-67; *b* 9 Dec. 1905; *s* of late Major H. C. MacTier, Newton St Loe, Somerset, and of Mary Fitzroy MacTier, *d* of Sir Charles Hobhouse, 3rd Bt; *m* 1941, Mary, *d* of Brig. C. G. Ling, CB, DSO, MC; two *s* one *d*. *Educ:* Eton; Magdalene Coll., Cambridge. Mansfield & Co. Ltd, Singapore, Shipping Agents, 1928-37; Dep. Dir and subseq. Dir of Port and Transit Control, Min. of War Transport, 1940-45. Chm. Liverpool Steam Ship Owners' Assoc. and Gen. Council of British Shipping, 1960-61; Pres., Inst. Marine Engineers, 1966-67. Comdr Order of Maritime Merit (French); Medal of Victory with silver palm (US). *Recreations:* ski-ing, sailing. *Address:* Tervine, Kilchrenan, By Taynuilt, Argyll. *T:* Kilchrenan 216.

**McTIERNAN, Rt. Hon. Sir Edward (Aloysius),** PC 1963; KBE 1951; Justice of the High Court of Australia since 1930; *b* 16 Feb. 1892; *s* of Patrick and Isabella McTiernan; *m* 1948, Kathleen, *d* of Sidney and Ann Lloyd, Melbourne. *Educ:* Marist Brothers' High Sch., Sydney; Sydney Univ. (BA, LLB, 1st cl. Hons). Admitted to Bar, NSW, 1917; Lecturer in Law, Sydney Univ.; NSW Parliament, 1920-27; Attorney-Gen., 1920-22 and 1925-27; NSW Govt Representative in London, 1926; MHR for Parkes, Commonwealth Parl., 1928, Papal Chamberlain, 1927. *Address:* Breffni, Chilton Parade, Warrawee, Sydney, NSW; High Court of Australia, Darlinghurst, Sydney. *T:* JW 3103, FA 3668. *Clubs:* Australian (Sydney); Athenæum (Melbourne).

**McVEIGH, Rt. Hon. Sir Herbert Andrew,** PC (N Ireland) 1965; Kt 1964; Lord Justice of Appeal, Supreme Court of Judicature, N Ireland, since 1964 (Judge of High Court of Justice, N Ireland, 1956-64, also Judge of the Restrictive Practices Court and Deputy-Chairman Boundaries Commission, N Ireland, 1957-64); *b* 8 Dec. 1908; *s* of late John McVeigh, JP, Londonderry; *m* 1940, Mary Elizabeth Mabel, *e d* of late Adam Reade, Portstewart, Co. Londonderry; two *d*. *Educ:* Foyle Coll., Londonderry; Queen's Univ., Belfast (BA). Pres. Students' Representative Council, 1929-30. Junior Crown Counsel, Co. Antrim; Senior Crown Counsel: Co. Fermanagh; Co. Tyrone; Co. Antrim; Member: Bar Council, 1938-56; Nat. Arbitration Tribunal; Distinction Awards Cttee (NI) relating to Hosp. Authority Consultants; several official cttees on legal questions. Dep. Umpire under Insurance and Employment Acts. Barrister, Inn of Court, NI, 1931, KC (NI) 1948, Bencher, 1954; mem. of Gray's Inn; Chairman: Education Cttee of Benchers; Finance and Libraries Cttee of Benchers; N Ireland Assoc. for Mental Health. President: Queen's Univ. Assoc.; Foyle Coll. Old Boys Assoc.; Belvoir Park Golf Club; Gov., Victoria Coll., Belfast. *Publication:* Law of Valuation, 1935. *Recreations:* swimming, golf. *Address:* 25 Cambourne Park, Belfast BT9 6RL. *T:* 660927. *Club:* Northern Counties (Londonderry).

**McVEY, Sir Daniel,** Kt 1954; CMG 1950; MIE (Australia); President, Dunlop Rubber Australia Ltd; also Director several other cos; *b* 1892; *s* of Daniel McVey, Falkirk, Stirlingshire, and Jeanie, *d* of Robert Cunningham Kay; *m* 1919, Margaret Gardiner, *d* of Thomas Packman, Brisbane; two *s* one *d*. *Educ:* Falkirk High Sch., Scotland. Joined Commonwealth Public Service, 1914; served with AIF, 1915-19; Lt, 45th Battery, AFA; Communications Engineer, 1914-30; Asst Supt of Mails, NSW, 1930-33; Supt of Mails, NSW, 1933-37; Asst Commissioner, Commonwealth Public Service Board, 1937-38; Commissioner, National Insurance Commission, 1938-39; Sec., Dept of Supply and Development, May-Dec. 1939; Dir-Gen. of Posts and Telegraphs, 1939-46; Dir of War

Organisation of Industry, 1941-42; Sec. Dept of Aircraft Production, Dep. Chm., Aircraft Advisory Cttee, 1942-45; Dir-Gen. of Civil Aviation, Australia, 1943-46; Dir-Gen. of Aircraft Production, 1945-46; Chm. Radiophysics Advisory Board and Mem. Radio Research Board until June 1946. Commissioner, Australian National Airlines Commission, Feb.-June 1946. Leader of Australian Air Mission to the USA, Canada, and the UK, Jan.-May 1942; Leader of delegation to British Commonwealth Communications Council, London, April-July 1944; Adviser to Australian Prime Minister on Civil Aviation and Telecommunications at Prime Ministers' Conference, London, May 1944; Delegate to Civil Aviation Conference, Wellington, NZ, Oct. 1944; Delegate to International Civil Aviation Conference, Chicago, USA, Nov.-Dec. 1944; Delegate to British Commonwealth Civil Aviation Conference, Montreal, Dec. 1944; Leader of Australian Delegation at British Commonwealth Air Transport Conference, London, July 1945; Leader of Australian Delegation at British Commonwealth Telecommunications Conference, London, July-Aug. 1945; Delegate to British Commonwealth Civil Aviation Conference, Wellington, NZ, March 1946. Mem. Bd of Trustees, Nat. Museums of Victoria, 1945-46; Chm. and Man. Dir, STC Pty Ltd, 1946-49; Man. Dir Metal Manufactures, Ltd and Austral Bronze Co. Pty Ltd, 1949-62; Chm. Commonwealth-State Consultative Cttee on Electric Power, 1951-52; Chm. Materials Industry Advisory Cttee to Minister of Defence Production, 1953-66; Mem. Australian Atomic Energy Commission Business Advisory Group, 1954-64. Kernot Memorial Medal, Univ. of Melbourne, 1945. Hon. Life Gov., Alfred Hospital, Melbourne. *Recreation:* golf. *Address:* Strathyre, Killeaton St West, St Ives, NSW, Australia. *Clubs:* Melbourne, Australian, Savage (Melbourne); Union, Australian (Sydney).

**MACVICAR, Neil,** QC (Scotland) 1960; MA, LLB; Sheriff Substitute of the Lothians and Peebles, at Edinburgh, since 1968; *b* 16 May 1920; *s* of late Neil Macvicar, WS; *m* 1949, Maria, *d* of Count Spiridon Bulgari, Corfu; one *s* two *d*. *Educ:* Loretto Sch.; Oriel Coll., Oxford; Edinburgh Univ. Served RA, 1940-45. Called to Scottish Bar, 1948. Chancellor, Dio. of Edinburgh, 1961. *Address:* 32 Dick Place, Edinburgh 9. *T:* 031-667 4793. *Club:* New (Edinburgh).

**McVITTIE, Maj.-Gen. Charles Harold,** CB 1962; CBE 1953; *b* 6 Aug. 1908; *s* of Col R. H. McVittie, CB, CMG, CBE; *m* 1939, Margaret Wark, *d* of Dr T. Divine, Huddersfield; two *s*. *Educ:* Haileybury; Brighton Coll.; Sandhurst. 2nd Lt Queen's Own Royal West Kent Regt, 1928; transferred to RAOC, 1935; Served War of 1939-45, ADOS Singapore Fortress, 1941-42; POW, 1942-45; comd Vehicle Organization, 1948-50; DOS, GHQ. Far ELF, 1951-53; comd Technical Stores Organization, 1953-56; comd RAOC Trg Centre, 1956-60; Comdr Stores Organization, RAOC, 1960-63. Hon. Col AER Units RAOC, 1961-64. Col Commandant, RAOC, 1965-69. *Recreation:* fencing (Blue, Sandhurst, 1928). *Address:* Gowans, Pidham Hill, East Meon, near Petersfield, Hants. *T:* East Meon 241.

**McVITTIE, George Cunliffe,** OBE 1946; MA Edinburgh, PhD Cantab; Professor of Astronomy, University of Illinois, since 1952; *b* 5 June 1904; *e s* of Frank S. McVittie; *m* 1934, Mildred Bond, *d* of Prof. John Strong, CBE; no *c*. *Educ:* Edinburgh Univ.; Christ's Coll., Cambridge. Asst Lecturer, Leeds Univ., 1930-34; Lecturer in Applied Mathematics, Liverpool Univ., 1934-36; Reader in Mathematics, King's Coll., London, 1936-48; Prof. of Mathematics, Queen Mary Coll., London, 1948-52. War service with Meteorological Office, Air Ministry, and a Dept of the Foreign Office, 1939-45. FRS (Edinburgh), 1943. Mem. Sub-Cttee of Meteorological Research Cttee, 1948-52. Jt Editor of The Observatory, 1938-48. Jt Exec. Editor of Quarterly Journal of Mechanics and Applied Mathematics, 1947-51; Pres., Commn on Galaxies, Internat. Astronomical Union, 1967-70; Sec., American Astronomical Soc., 1961-69. *Publications:* Cosmological Theory, 1937; General Relativity and Cosmology, 1956, 2nd edn, 1965; Fact and Theory in Cosmology, 1961; (Ed.) Problems of Extra-galactic Research, 1962; papers on Relativity and its astronomical applications, classical mechanics, etc., Proc. Royal Soc. and other journals. *Address:* (during 1971) Electronics Laboratory, University of Kent, Canterbury, Kent; University of Illinois Observatory, Urbana, Ill 61801, USA. *Club:* Athenæum.

**McVITTIE, Wilfrid Wolters,** CMG 1958; *b* 24 May 1906; *s* of Francis McVittie and Emily McVittie (*née* Weber); *m* 1938, Harriett Morna Wilson, *d* of Dr G. Wilson, Toronto; one *s* two *d*. *Educ:* abroad; King's Coll., Univ. of London. Entered Japan Consular Service, 1930; Consul at Yokohama, 1938; 1st Sec. (Commercial), Buenos Aires, 1946; Counsellor (Commercial), British Embassy, Mexico City, 1948; Counsellor (Commercial) and Consul-Gen., British Embassy, Lisbon, 1952; HM Ambassador to the Dominican Republic, 1958-62. Comendador, Military Order of Christ (Portugal), 1957. *Recreations:* travel, shooting, golf. *Address:* White House, Itchenor, Sussex.

**McWATTERS, Stephen John;** Headmaster, Clifton College, since 1963; *b* 24 April 1921; *er s* of late Sir Arthur Cecil McWatters, CIE; *m* 1957, Mary Gillian, *o d* of late D. C. Wilkinson and Mrs G. A. Wilkinson; one *s* two *d*. *Educ:* Eton (Scholar); Trinity Coll., Oxford (Scholar, MA). 1st Cl. Class. Mods, 1941. Served in The King's Royal Rifle Corps, 1941-45. Distinction in Philosophy section of Litterae Humaniores, Oxford, 1946. Asst Master, Eton Coll., 1947-63 (Master in Coll., 1949-57, Housemaster, 1961-63). *Recreations:* music, bird-watching. *Address:* The Headmaster's House, Clifton College, Clifton Down, Bristol 8. *T:* Bristol 35613.

**McWEENY, Prof. Roy;** Professor of Theoretical Chemistry, University of Sheffield, since 1966; *b* 19 May 1924; *o s* of late Maurice and Vera McWeeny; *m* 1947, Patricia M. Healey; one *s* one *d*. *Educ:* Univ. of Leeds; University Coll., Oxford. BSc (Physics) Leeds 1945; DPhil Oxon. 1949. Lectr in Physical Chemistry, King's Coll., Univ. of Durham, 1948-57; Vis. Scientist, Physics Dept, MIT, USA, 1953-54; Lectr in Theoretical Chemistry, Univ. Coll. of N Staffs, 1957-62; Associate Dir, Quantum Chemistry Gp, Uppsala Univ., Sweden, 1960-61; Reader in Quantum Theory, Univ. of Keele, 1962-64; Prof. of Theoretical Chemistry, 1964-66. *Publications:* Symmetry, an Introduction to Group Theory and its Applications, 1963; (with B. T. Sutcliffe) Methods of Molecular Quantum Mechanics, 1969; Spins in Chemistry, 1970; contrib. sections in other books and encyclopædias; many research papers on quantum theory of atomic and molecular structure in Proc. Royal Soc., Proc. Phys. Soc., Phys. Rev., Revs. Mod. Phys., Jl Chem. Phys., etc. *Recreations:* drawing, sculpture, walking, swimming.

*Address:* 10 Dore Road, Sheffield. *T:* Sheffield 360298.

**McWHINNIE, Donald;** Freelance Director, Stage and Television, since 1960; *b* 16 Oct. 1920; *s* of Herbert McWhinnie and Margaret Elizabeth (*née* Holland). *Educ:* Rotherham Gram. Sch.; Gonville and Caius Coll., Cambridge. MA Cantab 1941. Served War of 1939-45: RAF, 1941-46. Joined BBC, 1947; Asst Head of Drama (Sound), 1953-60, resigned. Theatrical productions include: Krapp's Last Tape, Royal Court, 1958; The Caretaker, Arts and Duchess, 1960, Lyceum, NY, 1961; The Duchess of Malfi, Aldwych, 1960; Three, Arts and Criterion, 1961; The Tenth Man, Comedy, 1961; A Passage to India, Ambassador, NY, 1962; Everything in the Garden, Arts and Duke of York's, 1962; Macbeth, Royal Shakespeare, 1962; Rattle of a Simple Man, Garrick, 1962, Booth, NY, 1963; Doctors of Philosophy, Arts, 1962; The Doctor's Dilemma, Haymarket, 1963; Alfie, Mermaid and Duchess, 1963; Out of the Crocodile, Phœnix, 1963; The Fourth of June, St Martin's, 1964; End Game, Aldwych, 1964; The Creeper, St Martin's, 1965; All in Good Time, Royale, NY, 1965; The Cavern, Strand, 1965; This Winter's Hobby, US Tour, 1966; The Astrakhan Coat, Helen Hayes, NY, 1967; Happy Family, St Martin's, 1967; Tinker's Curse, Nottingham Playhouse, 1968; Vacant Possession, Nottingham Playhouse, 1968; Hamlet, Covent Garden, 1969; No Quarter, Hampstead, 1969; There'll be Some Changes Made, Fortune, 1969; The Apple Cart, Mermaid, 1970; also numerous television productions for BBC and ITV. *Publication:* The Art of Radio, 1959. *Address:* 16 Chepstow Place, W2. *T:* 01-229 2120.

**MACWHIRTER, Clara Elizabeth Littlewort,** OBE 1957; Headmistress, Central High School for Girls, Manchester, 1931-59; *d* of Francis Littlewort Macwhirter and Isobel Macwhirter (*née* Stewart). *Educ:* University of Edinburgh; University of Rennes, France. Teacher of French: at Leith Academy, 1919-22; at Holly Lodge High Sch., Liverpool, 1922-31. *Recreations:* languages, travel. *Address:* 150a Barlow Moor Road, West Didsbury, Manchester 20.

**McWHIRTER, Prof. Robert,** CBE 1963; FRCSEd; FRCPEd; FFR; FRSE; Professor of Medical Radiology, Edinburgh University, since 1946; Director of Radiotherapy, Royal Infirmary, Edinburgh, since 1935; President, Medical and Dental Defence Union of Scotland, since 1959; Cons. Adviser in Radiobiology, Scottish Home and Health Department, since 1962; Chairman, Scottish Health Services Council Standing Cancer Commission, Scottish Home and Health Department, since 1963; *b* 8 Nov. 1904; *s* of Robert McWhirter and Janet Ramsay Gairdner; *m* 1937, Dr Susan Muir MacMurray; one *s*. *Educ:* Girvan Academy; Glasgow and Cambridge Universities. MB, ChB (High Commendn), Glasgow, 1927; FRCS Edinburgh 1932; DMRE Cambridge, 1933; FFR 1939. Formerly: Student, Mayo Clinic; British Empire Cancer Campaign Research Student, Holt Radium Institute, Manchester; Chief Assistant, X-Ray Dept, St Bartholomew's Hospital, London. Member, British Institute of Radiology; Fellow Royal Society Med. (President, Sect. of Radiology, 1956); Fellow Faculty of Radiologists (Twining Memorial Medal, 1943; Skinner Memorial Lecturer, 1956; Warden, 1961-66; Knox Memorial Lecturer, 1963, Pres. 1966-69); Mem., Grand Council, British Empire Cancer Campaign; Past Pres., Internat. Radio Therapists Visiting Club; Hon. Member, American Radium Society; Membre Corresp. Etranger, Société Française d'Electro-Radiologie Médicale, 1967; Membro d'onore, Società Italiana della Radiologia Medica e Medicine Nucleare, 1968. Caldwell Memorial Lecturer, American Roentgen Ray Society, 1963; Hon. Fellow: Australasia College of Radiologists, 1954; American College of Radiology, 1965; Faculty of Radiologists, RCSI, 1967. *Publications:* contribs to medical journals. *Recreation:* golf. *Address:* 2 Orchard Brae, Edinburgh 4. *T:* 031-332 5800. *Clubs:* Athenæum; University (Edinburgh).

**McWILLIAM, Frederick Edward,** CBE 1966; Sculptor; *b* 30 April 1909; *yr s* of Dr William Nicholson McWilliam, Banbridge, County Down, Ireland; *m* 1932, Elizabeth Marion Crowther; two *d*. *Educ:* Campbell Coll., Belfast; Slade School of Fine Art; Paris. Served War of 1939-45, RAF, UK and Far East. Member of Staff, Slade Sch. of Fine Art, London Univ., 1947-66. Mem. Art Panel, Arts Council, 1960-68. First one-man exhib., sculpture, London Gall., 1939; subsequently Hanover Gallery, 1949, 1952, 1956; Waddington Galleries, 1961, 1963, 1966, 1968; Felix Landau Gallery, Los Angeles, 1963; Travers Gallery, 1969. Has exhibited in International Open-Air Exhibitions, London, Antwerp, Arnheim, Paris. Work included in British Council touring exhibitions USA, Canada, Germany, South America. Works acquired by: Tate Gallery; Victoria and Albert Museum; Museum Modern Art, New York; National Gallery, S Australia; Art Inst., Chicago; Open-Air Museum, Middleheim, Antwerp; Art Galls, Belfast, Leeds, Coventry, Oldham, New Zealand, Toronto, etc. Hon. DLit Belfast, 1964. *Relevant Publication:* McWilliam, Sculptor, by Roland Penrose, 1964. *Address:* 8A Holland Villas Road, W14. *T:* 01-603 4859.

**McWILLIAM, Sir John,** Kt 1970; HM Lieutenant, County of Fife, since 1965; *b* 3 April 1910; *s* of James McWilliam and Flora Campbell Elgin; *m* 1935, Ann Tyson McPherson; one *s* two *d*. *Educ:* Radnor Park and Clydebank High Schs. convener, County Council of Fife, 1961-70; Vice-Chairman, Forth Road Bridge Board, 1961-70; Vice-Chairman, Tay Road Bridge Board, 1961-70; Member, Glenrothes Development Corp., 1962- (Dep. Chairman, 1964-); Chairman: Countryside Commn for Scotland, 1968-; Forth Ports Authority, 1969-. Member, Police Council of Great Britain, 1960-70; Vice-Chairman, Assoc. of County Councils in Scotland, 1962-70; Member, several Government Cttees of Inquiry relative to Local Government. *Recreations:* reading, public service. *Address:* Kilbowie, Kinghorn, Fife. *T:* Kinghorn 555. *Clubs:* Royal Automobile, Royal Scottish Automobile (Glasgow).

**McWILLIAM, William Nicholson,** CB 1960; *b* 26 Nov. 1897; *er s* of W. N. McWilliam, MD, Banbridge, Co. Down; *m* 1927, V. Maureen, *er d* of H. H. Mussen, Asst Chief Crown Solicitor; one *s* two *d*. *Educ:* Excelsior Academy, Banbridge; Campbell Coll., Belfast; Trinity Coll., Dublin. Served European War, 1916-18, Lieut, RGA, 1916-18. BA, BAI, 1921. Entered NI Civil Service, 1922; Asst Sec. to Cabinet, NI, 1945-57; Dep. Clerk of the Privy Council, NI, 1945-57; Permanent Sec., Min. of Labour and National Insurance, NI, 1957-62 (retired). Member Boundary Commn for NI, 1963-69. *Recreation:* golf. *Address:* Garryard, 34 Massey Avenue, Belfast BT4 2JT. *T:* Belfast 63179.

**MADAN, Sir Janardan Atmaram,** Kt 1942; CSI 1939; CIE 1929; BA (Bombay, Oxon); Chairman, Provincial Co-operative Institute, Bombay; *b* Bombay, 12 Feb. 1885; *s* of late A. H. Madan; *m* Champubai, *d* of H. P. Pitale, JP; two *s* one *d. Educ:* Elphinstone High Sch., Bombay; Bombay Univ.; Oxford; Trinity Coll., Cambridge. Appointed to the Indian Civil Service, 1908; commenced service as Assistant Collector in Bombay, 1909; served as Assistant Settlement Officer; Assistant Registrar of Co-operative Societies, 1919; Collector and Registrar, Co-operative Societies, 1920; Member of the Bombay Legislative Council, 1925; Joint Secretary of the Royal Commission on Agriculture in India, 1926-28; Collector and District Magistrate, Bombay, Presidency, 1928-29; Chairman, Provincial Banking Inquiry Cttee, Bombay, 1929; Director of Labour Intelligence, and Commissioner, Workmen's Compensation, Bombay, 1930; Secretary to Government, Revenue Dept, Bombay; Commissioner, Central Division, Poona; Commissioner, Southern Division, Belgaum; Adviser to Governor of Bombay, 1939; Chairman: Bombay Public Service Commission, 1942-47; Saurashtra Public Service Commn, 1947-50; Chairman, Saurashtra Agrarian Reforms Commission, 1951. *Recreations:* tennis, golf, riding. *Address:* 28 Altamont Road, Bombay, India. *Clubs:* Radio, Orient (Bombay); Poona (Poona); Rajkot (Rajkot).

**MADANG, Archbishop of, (RC),** since 1966; **Most Rev. Adolf Noser;** *b* Belleville, Ill., 4 July 1900. *Educ:* Angelicum Univ., Rome. Ordained Priest, 1925. Seminary Professor, US, 1927-34; Seminary Rector, US, 1934-39; Superior of Accra, Ghana, 1939-47; Bishop of Accra, 1947; transferred to Alexishafen, 1953. Dr of Sacred Theology, 1927. *Publications:* pamphlets and magazine articles. *Address:* Archbishop's Residence, PO Alexishafen, via Madang, Territory of New Guinea. *T:* Madang 2727.

**MADARIAGA, Don Salvador de,** MA; Honorary President, International Liberal Union and Congress for Freedom of Culture; Founder President, College of Europe (Bruges); Hon. Fellow of Exeter College, Oxford; Member: Spanish Academy of Letters and of Moral and Political Sciences; French Academy of Moral and Political Sciences; Academy of History of Caracas and many other Spanish-American Institutions of Learning; *b* Corunna, Spain, 23 July 1886; *s* of Don Jose de Madariaga, Colonel, Spanish Army, and Dona Ascension Rojo de Madariaga; *m* Constance Archibald, MA Hons (Glasgow) (*d* 1970); two *d. Educ:* Instituto del Cardenal Cisneros, Madrid; College Chaptal, Paris; Ecole Polytechnique, Paris; Ecole Nationale Supérieure des Mines, Paris. Technical Adviser to Superintendent of Line, Spanish Northern Railway, 1911-16; Journalist, Publicist and Literary Critic, London, 1916-21; Member of Press Section League of Nations Secretariat, Geneva, 1921-22; Director of Disarmament Section of League of Nations Secretariat, 1922-27; King Alphonso XIII Prof. of Spanish Studies, Oxford, 1928-31; Secretary of the Temporary Mixed Commission for Disarmament, then of the Preparatory Commission for a Disarmament Conference; Secretary of the Third (Disarmament) Commission of the Assembly of the League of Nations, 1922-27; Secretary General of the International Conference for the Supervision of the Trade in Arms, Geneva, April-May 1925; Spanish Ambassador to USA, 1931, to France, 1932-34; Spanish Permanent Delegate to the League of Nations, 1931-36; Visiting Prof. of Spanish, Princeton Univ., 1954. Hans Deutsch European Prize, 1963; Hanseatic Goethe Prize, 1967. MA by Decree of University of Oxford, 1928; Hon. Doctor Universities of Arequipa, Lima, Oxford, Poitiers, Princeton, Liège, Lille; Matricula d'Onore, University of Pavia, 1966; Knight Grand Cross of Orders of the Spanish Republic, Légion d'Honneur (France), Jade-in-Gold of China, White Lion of Tchecoslovakia, Aztec Eagle of Mexico, Boyacá of Colombia, Merit of Chile, Sun of Peru, etc. *Publications:* apart from several publications in Spanish and French, has published: Shelley and Calderon and other Essays on Spanish and English Poetry, 1920; Spanish Folksongs, 1922; The Genius of Spain, 1923; The Sacred Giraffe, 1926; Englishmen, Frenchmen, Spaniards, 1928; Disarmament, 1929; Sir Bob, 1930; I, Americans, 1930; Don Quixote, 1934; Anarchy or Hierarchy, 1937; Theory and Practice in International Relations, 1938; The World's Design, 1938; Christopher Columbus, 1939; Hernán Cortés, 1941; Spain, 1942; The Heart of Jade, 1944, new edn 1956; Victors, Beware, 1946; The Rise of the Spanish American Empire, 1947; The Fall of the Spanish American Empire, 1947; On Hamlet, 1948; Bolivar, 1952; Portrait of Europe, 1952; Essays with a Purpose, 1953; A Bunch of Errors, 1953; War in the Blood, 1957; Democracy versus Liberty?, 1958; Latin-America between the Eagle and the Bear, 1962; Portrait of a Man Standing, 1967; frequent contributions to the English, American, Spanish, and Spanish-American press. *Recreation:* a change of work. *Address:* 3 St Andrew's Road, Oxford. *Clubs:* Reform; Ateneo (Madrid).

*See also Prof. L. B. Schapiro.*

**MADDAN, Martin;** MP (C) Hove, since 1965; Chairman, AGB Research Ltd, since 1962; *b* 1920; *s* of late James Gracie Maddan, CBE; *m* 1958, Susanne, *d* of late R. C. Huband, JP; two *s* two *d. Educ:* Fettes Coll., Edinburgh; Brasenose Coll., Oxford. Served Royal Marines, 1939-46; Major, 1944. Contested (C) North Battersea, 1950. MP (C) Hitchin Division of Herts, 1955-64; Parliamentary Private Secretary to Minister of Health, 1961-63. Joint Hon. Treasurer, British Council, European Movement (earlier Britain in Europe group), 1956-; UK Sponsor, Declaration of Atlantic Unity, 1958-; Council Oxford and Bermondsey Club, 1952-; Fellow, St Michael's Coll., Tenbury, 1964-; Mem., Market Research Society, 1953-. *Publications:* Profitable Export Marketing, 1955. *Address:* House of Commons, SW1.

**MADDEN, (Albert) Frederick (McCulloch),** DPhil; Reader in Commonwealth Government, Oxford, since 1957; Fellow (and Dean) of Nuffield College since 1958; *b* 27 Feb. 1917; *e s* of A. E. and G. McC. Madden; *m* 1941, Margaret, *d* of Dr R. D. Gifford; one *s* one *d. Educ:* privately, by mother; Bishop Vesey's Grammar Sch.; Christ Church, Oxford. Boulter and Gladstone exhibns; BA 1938, BLitt 1939, DPhil 1950. Dep. Sup., Rhodes House Library, 1946-48; Beit Lectr, 1947-57; Sen. Tutor to Overseas Service Courses, 1950-; Dir, Inst. of Commonwealth Studies, 1961-68; Vice-Chm., History Bd, 1968-; Canadian Visiting Fellowship, 1970. FRHistS 1952. *Publications:* (with V. Harlow) British Colonial Developments, 1774-1834, 1953; (with K. Robinson) Essays in Imperial Government, 1963; chapter in Cambridge History of British Empire III, 1959; Imperial Constitutional Documents, 1765-1965, 1966; reviews in English Historical Review, etc. *Recreations:* acting; photographing islands and highlands, hill towns, country houses, churches, and grand-daughter; Renaissance art; writing music and listening. *Address:* The Oaks, Shotover Hill, Oxford. *T:* Oxford 62972.

**MADDEN, Admiral Sir Charles (Edward),** 2nd Bt, *cr* 1919; GCB 1965 (KCB 1961; CB 1955); Vice-Lieutenant of Greater London since 1969; *b* 15 June 1906; *s* of Admiral of the Fleet Sir Charles E. Madden, 1st Bart, GCB, OM, and Constance Winifred (*d* 1964), 3rd *d* of Sir Charles Cayzer, 1st Bart; *S* father, 1935; *m* 1942, Olive, *d* of late G. W. Robins, Caldy, Cheshire; one *d*. *Educ:* Royal Naval Coll., Osborne. ADC to the Queen, 1955. Commander, 1939; Captain, 1946; Rear-Admiral, 1955; Vice-Admiral, 1958; Admiral, 1961. Chief of Naval Staff, NZ, 1953-55; Dep. Chief of Naval Personnel, 1955-57; Flag Officer, Malta, 1957-59; Flag Officer, Flotillas, Home Fleet, 1959-60; C-in-C Plymouth, 1960-62; C-in-C Home Fleet and NATO C-in-C Eastern Atlantic Command, 1963-65; retired, 1965. Dep. Chairman, Royal National Mission to Deep Sea Fishermen, 1966; Vice-Chairman, Sail Training Assoc., 1968-70. Trustee, National Maritime Museum, 1968. DL Greater London, 1969. *Recreation:* painting. *Heir:* *b* Lieut-Colonel John Wilmot Madden, MC, 1944, RA [*b* 1916; *m* 1941, Beatrice Catherine Sievewright; two *s* one *d*]. *Address:* 21 Eldon Road, W8. *Clubs:* Arts; Royal Western Yacht.

**MADDEN, Rear-Admiral Colin Duncan,** CB 1966; CBE 1964; MVO 1954; DSC 1940 and Bar, 1944; Director, The Brewers' Society, since 1969; Gentleman Usher of the Scarlet Rod to the Order of the Bath, since 1968; *b* 19 Aug. 1915; *s* of late Archibald Maclean Madden, CMG, and Cecilia Catherine Moor; *m* 1943, Agnes Margaret, *d* of late H. K. Newcombe, OBE, Canada and London, and Eleanor Clare; two *d*. *Educ:* RN Coll., Dartmouth. During War of 1939-45, took part in blocking Ijmuiden harbour and Dutch evacuation; Navigating Officer of 7th Mine Sweeping Flotilla; HMS Arethusa; Assault Group J1 for invasion of Europe, and HMS Norfolk. Thence HMS Triumph. Commander, 1950; Comd HMS Crossbow, 1952; staff of Flag Officer Royal Yachts, SS Gothic and Comdr (N) HM Yacht Britannia, for Royal Commonwealth Tour, 1953-54; Captain, Naval Attaché, Rome; Captain D 7 in HMS Trafalgar; IDC. Comd HMS Albion, 1962; Rear-Admiral, 1965; Senior Naval Member Directing Staff, Imperial Defence Coll., 1965-67; retired, 1967. Dir, Nat. Trade Develt Assoc., 1967-69. *Recreations:* sailing, gardening, tapestry. *Address:* c/o Coutts & Co., 440 Strand, WC2. *Clubs:* United Service, Royal Ocean Racing.

**MADDEN, Frederick;** *see* Madden, A. F. McC.

**MADDEX, Sir George (Henry),** KBE, *cr* 1948; Government Actuary, 1946-58, retired; *b* 1895; *m* 1921, Emily Macdonald Jeffrey (one *s* killed on active service, 1943). *Educ:* Owen's Sch. Pres., Inst. of Actuaries, 1948-50. Dep. Govt Actuary, 1944-46. Fellow, Society of Actuaries (US), 1949; Hon. Fellow, Faculty of Actuaries in Scotland, 1956. *Address:* Heath House, Colley Manor, Reigate, Surrey. *Clubs:* United Service, St Stephen's.

**MADDISON, Vincent Albert,** CMG 1961; TD 1953; *b* 10 Aug. 1915; *s* of late Vincent Maddison; *m* 1954, Jennifer Christian Bernard; two *s* one *d*. *Educ:* Wellingborough Sch.; Downing Coll., Cambridge (MA). Colonial Administrative Service, 1939. Served War of 1939-45: Ethiopian and Burma Campaigns. District Officer, Kenya, 1947; seconded to Secretariat, 1948; Director, Trade and Supplies, 1953; Secretary, 1954, Perm. Secretary, 1957-63, Min. of Commerce and Industry; retired from Kenya Government, 1963; Director: Tana River Development Co. Ltd (Chairman); The Kenya Power Co. Ltd (Chairman); Nyali Ltd; Kisauni Ltd; East African Trust and Investment Co. Ltd (Chm.). *Recreations:* riding, gardening, sailing. *Address:* PO Box 8454, Nairobi, Kenya. *Clubs:* East India and Sports; Muthaiga Country (Kenya).

**MADDOCK, Rt. Rev. David Rokeby;** *see* Dunwich, Suffragan Bishop of.

**MADDOCK, Ieuan,** CB 1968; OBE 1953; FRS 1967; Controller (Industrial Technology), Ministry of Technology, since 1967; *b* 29 March 1917; British; *m* 1943, Eurfron May Davies; one *s*. *Educ:* Gowerton Grammar Sch., Glamorgan; University of Wales, Swansea. Entered Government service, Explosives Res. and Develt, 1940; Principal Scientific Officer, Armament Res. Dept, Fort Halstead, 1949; Head of Field Experiments Div., Atomic Weapons Research Establishment, 1960; Asst Director, AWRE, 1965-; Dep. Controller B, Min. of Technology, 1965. Hon. DSc Wales, 1970. *Publications:* in various scientific and technical jls. *Address:* 13 Darell Road, Caversham, Reading, Berks. *T:* Reading 74096.

**MADDOCKS, His Honour George;** County Court Judge, retired; *b* 5 April 1896; *s* of William and Sarah Alice Maddocks, Southport; *m* 1928, Harriet Mary Louisa Day; two *s* one *d*. *Educ:* Christ Church Hall, Southport; Manchester Univ. Called to Bar, Middle Temple, 1923. *Address:* Allan Bank, Grasmere, Westmorland. *T:* Grasmere 227.

**MADDOCKS, Sir Kenneth (Phipson),** KCMG 1958 (CMG 1956); KCVO 1963; *b* 8 Feb. 1907; *s* of Arthur P. Maddocks, Haywards Heath, Sussex; *m* 1951, Elnor Radcliffe, CStJ, *d* of late Sir E. John Russell, OBE, FRS; no *c*. *Educ:* Bromsgrove Sch.; Wadham Coll., Oxford. Colonial Administrative Service, Nigeria, 1929; Civil Secretary, Northern Region, Nigeria, 1955-57; Dep. Governor, 1957-58. Acting Governor, Northern Region, Nigeria, 1956 and 1957. Governor and Commander-in-Chief of Fiji, Governor Pitcairn Island and Consul-General for Western Pacific, 1958-63; Dir and Secretary, E Africa and Mauritius Assoc., 1964-69. KStJ. *Recreations:* fishing, walking. *Address:* Abbey House, Sutton Montis, near Yeovil, Som. *T:* Corton Denham 268. *Club:* Athenæum.

**MADDOX, Sir (John) Kempson,** Kt 1964; VRD 1948; Hon. Consulting Physician: Royal Prince Alfred Hospital, Sydney; Royal Hospital for Women, Sydney; *b* Dunedin, NZ, 20 Sept. 1901; *s* of Sidney Harold Maddox and Mabel Kempson; *m* 1940, Madeleine Scott; one *s* one *d*. *Educ:* N Sydney Boys' High Sch.; Univ. of Sydney. MD, ChM (Sydney) 1924; MRCP 1928; FRACP 1935; FRCP 1958. Served War of 1939-45, Surgeon Comdr, RANR. President: BMA (NSW), 1950; Cardiac Soc. of Australia and NZ, 1958; Asian-Pacific Soc. of Cardiology, 1960-64; Vice-President: Internat. Soc. of Cardiology, 1962, Pres., 1966; Nat. Heart Foundn of Australia, 1960-64. President, NSW Division National Heart Foundation of Australia, FACC 1965; corresp. FACP 1968. Hon. AM (Singapore) 1963. Chevalier de l'Ordre de la Santé Publique, France, 1961; Comendador, Orden Hispolito Unanue (Peru), 1968. *Recreations:* golf, fishing, tennis. *Address:* 8 Annandale Street, Darling Point, Sydney, NSW 2027, Australia. *T:* 32-1707. *Clubs:* Australian (Sydney); Royal Sydney Golf.

**MADDOX, John (Royden);** Editor, Nature, since 1966; Managing Director, Macmillan

(Journals) Ltd, since 1970; Director, Macmillan & co. Ltd, since 1968; *b* 27 Nov. 1925; *s* of A. J. and M. E. Maddox, Swansea; *m* 1st, 1949, Nancy Fanning (*d* 1960); one *s* one *d*; 2nd, 1960, Brenda Power Murphy; one *s* one *d*. *Educ:* Gowerton Boys' County Sch.; Christ Church, Oxford; King's Coll., London. Asst Lecturer, then Lecturer, Theoretical Physics, Manchester Univ., 1949-55; Science Correspondent, Guardian, 1955-64; Affiliate, Rockefeller Institute, New York, 1962-63; Asst Director, Nuffield Foundation, and Co-ordinator, Nuffield Foundation Science Teaching Project, 1964-66. Member: Council, Consumers' Assoc.; BBC General Advisory Council. *Publications:* (with Leonard Beaton) The Spread of Nuclear Weapons, 1962; Revolution in Biology, 1964. *Address:* 5 Ponsonby Road, SW15. *T:* 01-788 0548. *Club:* Reform.

**MADEL, William David;** MP (C) South Bedfordshire since 1970; *b* 6 Aug. 1938; *s* of William R. Madel and Eileen Madel (*née* Nicholls). *Educ:* Uppingham Sch.; Keble Coll., Oxford. MA Oxon 1965. Graduate Management Trainee, 1963-64; Advertising Exec., Thomson Organisation, 1964-70. *Recreations:* cricket, hockey, travel, reading. *Address:* 3 Observatory Gardens, W8. *Clubs:* Junior Carlton, Coningsby; Mid-Cheshire Pitt (Chester).

**MADGE, Prof. Charles Henry;** Professor of Sociology, University of Birmingham, 1950-70; *b* 10 Oct. 1912; *s* of Lieut-Colonel C. A. Madge and Barbara (*née* Hylton Foster); *m* 1st, Kathleen Raine (marr. diss.); one *s* one *d*; 2nd, Inez Pearn; one *s* one *d*. *Educ:* Winchester Coll. (Scholar); Magdalene Coll., Cambridge (Scholar). Reporter on Daily Mirror, 1935-36; founded Mass-Observation, 1937; directed survey of working-class saving and spending for National Institute of Economic and Social Research, 1940-42; Research staff of PEP, 1943; Director, Pilot Press, 1944; Social Development Officer, New Town of Stevenage, 1947. Mission to Thailand on UN Technical Assistance, 1953-54. UNESCO Missions to India, 1957-58, to South-East Asia, 1959 and 1960 and Leader of Mission to Ghana for UN Economic Commission for Africa, 1963. *Publications:* The Disappearing Castle (poems), 1937; The Father Found (poems), 1941; part-author of Britain by Mass-Observation, 1938, and other books connected with this organisation; War-time Pattern of Saving and Spending, 1943; (ed) Pilot Papers: Social Essays and Documents, 1945-47; Society in the Mind, 1964; contributions to Economic Journal, Town Planning Review, Human Relations, etc. *Address:* Les Espédrels, La Rivière, Mirandol-Bourgnounac, Tarn, France.

**MADGE, James Richard;** Head of Policy Planning Unit, Ministry of Transport, since 1969; *b* 18 June 1924; *s* of James Henry Madge and Elisabeth May Madge; *m* 1955, Alice June Annette, *d* of late Major Horace Reid, Jamaica; two *d*. *Educ:* Bexhill Co. Sch.; New Coll., Oxford. Pilot in RAFVR, 1942-46. Joined Min. of Civil Aviation, 1947; Principal Private Secretary: to Paymaster-General, 1950-51; to Minister of Transport, 1960-61; Asst Secretary, Min. of Transport, 1961-66; Under-Sec., Road Safety Gp, 1966-69. *Recreations:* lawn tennis, swimming, furniture-making. *Address:* 7 Little Brownings, Sydenham Rise, SE23. *T:* 01-699 4277.

**MADGWICK, Sir Robert Bowden,** Kt 1966; OBE 1962; Chairman, Australian Broadcasting Commission, since 1967; Vice-Chancellor, University of New England, New South Wales, 1954-66; *b* 10 May 1905; *s* of R. C. Madgwick, N Sydney; *m* 1937, Ailsa Margaret (*d* 1967), *d* of H. J. Aspinall, Sydney; three *d*. *Educ:* North Sydney High Sch.; University of Sydney; Balliol Coll., Oxford. MEc (Sydney); DPhil (Oxon). Lecturer in Economics, University of Sydney, 1929-33; Senior Lecturer in Economic History, University of Sydney, 1936-41; Director, Army Education, Australia, 1941-46; Warden, New England Univ. Coll., 1947-54. Hon. DLitt: Univ. of Sydney, 1961; Univ. of Newcastle, 1966; Univ. of New England, 1969; Hon. LLD, Univ. of Queensland, 1961. *Publications:* (with E. R. Walker) An Outline of Australian Economics, 1932; Immigration into Eastern Australia, 1788-1851, 1937. *Recreation:* fishing. *Address:* Broadcast House, 145 Elizabeth Street, Sydney, NSW, Australia. *Clubs:* University (Sydney); Commonwealth (Canberra).

**MADOC, Maj.-Gen. Reginald William,** CB 1959; DSO 1957; OBE 1951; Royal Marines, retired; *b* 15 Aug. 1907; *s* of late Lieut-Colonel H. W. Madoc, CBE, MVO, Garwick, Isle of Man; *m* 1938, Rosemary, *d* of late Dr Cyril Shepherd, Sydney, Australia; one *d*. *Educ:* King William's Coll., Isle of Man. 2nd Lieut, RM, 1926; HMS Rodney, 1929-31; HMS Royal Oak, 1932-34; ADC to Governor of Madras, 1934-38; HMS Furious, 1938-39; RM Mobile Naval Base Defence Org., UK, Egypt, Crete, 1940-41 (despatches twice, POW, 1941-45). Instructor, Officers' Sch., RM, 1946; Staff Coll., Camberley, 1947; Instructor, School of Combined Ops, 1948; HMS Vanguard, 1948-49; CO, 42 Commando, RM, Malaya, 1950-51 (despatches); CO Commando Sch., RM, 1952-53; Chief Instructor, School of Amphibious Warfare, 1953-55; Commanded 3rd Commando Bde, RM, Malta, Cyprus, Port Said, 1955-57; ADC to the Queen, 1955-57; Maj.-Gen., Plymouth Gp, RM, 1957-59; Maj.-Gen., Portsmouth Gp, RM, 1959-61; retired 1961. Col Comdt, RM, 1967-68; Rep. Col Comdt, RM, 1969-70. *Recreation:* hunting. *Address:* The Malthouse, Meonstoke, by Southampton, SO3 1NH. *T:* Droxford 323. *Club:* United Service.

**MADRAS, Bishop in,** since 1965; **Rt. Rev. James Edward Lesslie Newbigin,** DD; *b* 8 Dec. 1909; *s* of Edward Richmond Newbigin, Shipowner, Newcastle, and Annie Ellen Newbigin (*née* Affleck); *m* 1936, Helen Stewart, *d* of Rev. Robert Henderson; one *s* three *d*. *Educ:* Leighton Park Sch.; Queens' Coll., Cambridge; Westminster Coll., Cambridge. Intercollegiate Secretary, Student Christian Movement, Glasgow, 1931-33. Ordained by Presbytery of Edinburgh and appointed to Madras Mission of Church of Scotland, 1936; served as missionary in Chingleput and Kancheepuram, 1936-46; Bishop in Madura and Ramnad, Church of South India, 1947. Chairman, Advisory Cttee on Main Theme for Second Assembly, World Council of Churches, 1954; Vice-Chairman, Commission on Faith and Order, 1956; Chairman, International Missionary Council, 1958. Resigned from See of Madura, 1959. General Secretary, International Missionary Council, 1959; Associate General Secretary, World Council of Churches, 1959-65. Hon. DD: Chicago Theological Seminary, 1954; St Andrews Univ., 1958; Hamburg, 1960; Basel, 1965. *Publications:* Christian Freedom in the Modern World, 1937; The Reunion of the Church, 1948; South India Diary, 1951; The Household of God, 1953; Sin and Salvation, 1956; A Faith for This One World?, 1962; Honest Religion for Secular Man, 1966; The Finality of Christ, 1969. *Recreations:* music, walking. *Address:* Bishop's House, Cathedral, Madras 6, South India.

**MAEGRAITH, Brian Gilmore,** CMG 1968; MA, MB, BSc, DPhil; FRCP, FRCPE; Professor, Tropical Medicine, School of Tropical Medicine, Liverpool University, since 1944; Dean of Liverpool School of Tropical Medicine since 1946; *b* 26 Aug. 1907; *s* of late A. E. R. Maegraith, Adelaide, S Australia; *m* 1934, Lorna Langley, St Peters, Adelaide; one *s. Educ:* St Peter's and St Mark's Colleges, Adelaide University (MB 1930); Magdalen and Exeter Colleges, Oxford (Rhodes Scholar, Rolleston Memorial Prize). Beit Memorial Fellow, 1932-34; Medical Fellow, Exeter Coll., Oxford, 1934-40; Hon. Fellow, St Marks Coll., 1956. University Lecturer and Demonstrator in Pathology, Dean of Faculty of Medicine, Oxford Univ., 1938-44; War of 1939-45, OC Army Malaria Research Unit. Med. Advisory Cttee ODM, 1963-. Tropical Med. Research Board, MRC, 1960-65; 1966-; Cttees on Malaria and Abnormal Haemoglobins, 1960-; Physician: Liverpool Royal Infirmary, Liverpool; Tropical Diseases Centre, Sefton General, Liverpool; Adviser: Council for Health in Socio-economic Developments, Thailand, 1964-; Faculty Tropical Medicine, Bangkok, 1959-; International Centre for Tropical Medicine, SE Asia; Sec.-Gen., Council of Institutes of Tropical Medicine, Europe and USSR, 1969-; Pres., Royal Society Tropical Medicine, 1969- (Vice-Pres., 1949-51 and 1957-59; Chalmers Gold Medal, 1951); Le Prince Award and Medal of American Society of Tropical Medicine, 1954; Membre d'Honneur: de Soc. Belg. de Méd. Tropicale; Soc. de Pathologie Exotique, Paris; Hon. Member American Assoc. Tropical Medicine, 1961; Lichfield Lecturer, Oxford Univ., 1955; Visiting Prof., University of Alexandria, 1956; Bernhard Nocht Medal (Hamburg), 1957; Maurice Block Lectr, Glasgow, 1969. DSc (*hc*), Bangkok. *Publications:* Pathological Processes in Malaria and Blackwater Fever, 1948; (with A. R. D. Adams), Clinical Tropical Diseases, 5th edn, 1970; Tropical Medicine for Nurses, 3rd edn, 1969; (with C. S. Leithead), Clinical Methods in Tropical Medicine, 1962; Exotic Diseases in Practice, 1965; (with H. M. Gilles) Management and Treatment of Diseases in the Tropics, 1970. Papers and articles in technical and scientific journals on various subjects. Co-editor Annals Tropical Medicine and Parasitology. *Address:* School of Tropical Medicine, Pembroke Place, Liverpool. *TA:* Malaria, Liverpool. *T:* 051-709 7611; 23 Eaton Road, Cressington Park, Liverpool 19. *T:* 051-422 1133. *Clubs:* Athenæum, East India and Sports; University, Liver (Liverpool).

**MAELOR,** Baron, *cr* 1966 (Life Peer), of Rhosllanerchrugog; **Thomas William Jones;** MP (Lab) Merioneth, 1951-66; JP (Chairman Ruabon Bench); *b* 1898; *m*; one *s* one *d.* Began working life as a miner; became pupil teacher and went to Bangor Coll. Welfare Officer and Education Officer for Merseyside and North Wales Electricity Board in North Wales. Formerly: Chairman North Wales Labour Federation; Chairman Wrexham Trades Council. *Address:* Brohedd, Clark Street, Wrexham, Denbighshire.

**MAFFEY,** family name of **Baron Rugby.**

**MAGGS, Air Vice-Marshal William Jack,** CB 1967; OBE 1943; Fellow and Domestic Bursar, Keble College, Oxford, since 1969; *b* 2 Feb. 1914; *s* of late Frederick Wilfrid Maggs, Bristol; *m* 1942, Margaret Grace, *d* of Thomas Liddell Hetherington, West Hartlepool; one *s* one *d. Educ:* Bristol Grammar Sch.; St John's Coll., Oxford (MA). Management Trainee, 1936-38. Joined RAF, 1939; Unit and Training duties, 1939-42; Student, Staff Coll., 1942; Planning Staffs, and participated in, Algerian, Sicilian and Italian landings, 1942-44; SESO Desert Air Force, 1944; Jt Admin. Plans Staff, Cabinet Offices, Whitehall, 1945-48; Instructor, RAF Coll., Cranwell, 1948-50; comd No 9 Maintenance Unit, 1950-52; exchange officer at HQ, USAF Washington, 1952-54; Student Jt Services Staff Coll., 1954-55; No 3 Maintenance Unit, 1955-57; Dep. Director of Equipment, Air Ministry, 1958-59; SESO, HQ, NEAF, Cyprus, 1959-61; Student, Imperial Defence Coll., 1962; Director of Mech. Transport and Marine Craft, Air Ministry, 1963-64; Director of Equipment, Ministry of Defence (Air), 1964-67; SASO, RAF Maintenance Comd, 1967-69. Group Captain, 1958; Air Commodore, 1963; Air Vice-Marshal, 1967. *Recreations:* golf, gardening, cabinet-making. *Address:* Hillside, Noke, near Oxford, OX3 9TT. *T:* Kidlington 3139. *Club:* Royal Air Force.

**MAGILL, Air Vice-Marshal Graham Reese,** CB 1966; CBE 1962 (OBE 1945); DFC 1941 and Bar, 1943; retired Jan. 1970; *b* 23 Jan. 1915; *s* of late Robert Wilson Magill and late Frances Elizabeth Magill, Te Aroha, NZ; *m* 1942, Blanche Marie Colson; two *s. Educ:* Te Aroha High Sch.; Hamilton Technical Coll., NZ. Joined Royal Air Force, 1936. Served War of 1939-45, Sudan, Egypt, UK, NW Europe; subsequently, UK, Egypt, France. Director of Operations (Bomber and Reconnaissance), Air Ministry, 1959-62; Commandant, RAF College of Air Warfare, Manby, Lincs, 1963-64; Director-General of Organisation (RAF), Ministry of Defence, 1964-67; AOC, 25 Group, RAF, 1967-68; AOC 22 Group, RAF, 1968-69. Member, BIM. *Recreations:* generally interested in sport, water sports and motoring. *Address:* Apartmentos Gommar 202, Apartado 7, Puerto de Pollensa, Majorca. *Club:* Royal Air Force.

**MAGILL, Sir Ivan Whiteside,** KCVO 1960 (CVO 1946); FRCSEng 1951; FFARCS; MB, BCh, Belfast, 1913; DA 1935; Hon. Consulting Anæsthetist, Westminster, Brompton and St Andrew's, Dollis Hill, Hospitals; *b* Larne, 1888; *s* of Samuel Magill; *m* 1916, Edith, 3rd *d* of Thomas Robinson Banbridge. *Educ:* Larne Grammar Sch.; Queen's Univ., Belfast. Formerly: Consultant Army, Navy, EMS; Senior Anæsthetist, Queen's Hospital, Sidcup; Anæsthetist, Seamens Hospital, Greenwich; Res. MO, Stanley Hospital, Liverpool; Examiner, DA; Robert Campbell Memorial Orator, Belfast, 1939; Bengué Memorial Lecturer, Royal Institute of Public Health, 1950; Hon. Member: Liverpool Medical Institution; American Society of Anæsthesiologists; New York State Society of Anæsthesiologists; British Assoc. of Plastic Surgeons; Canadian Society of Anæsthetists; Hon. Fellow: Royal Society of Medicine, 1956; Faculty of Anæsthetists, Royal College of Surgeons, 1958; Assoc. of Anæsthetists of Great Britain and Ireland, 1958; Hon. FFARCSI, 1961. Henry Hill Hickman Medal, 1938; John Snow Medal, 1958; Canadian Anæsthetists Society Medal, 1963; Medal, American Assoc. of Plastic Surgeons, 1965; Gillies Mem. Lecturer, British Assoc. of Plastic Surgeons, 1965; Ralph M. Waters Prize, Chicago, 1966. Hon. DSc, Belfast, 1945. Frederic Hewitt Lecturer for 1965. *Publications:* contributions and chapters in various medical journals. *Recreation:* trout fishing. *Address:* 149 Harley Street, W1. *T:* 01-935 4444.

**MAGINNIS, John Edward,** JP; MP (UU) Armagh, since Oct. 1959; *b* 7 March 1919; *s* of late Edward Maginnis, Mandeville Hall, Mullahead, Tanderagee; *m* 1944, Dorothy, *d* of late R. J. Rusk, JP, of Cavanaleck, Fivemiletown, Co. Tyrone; one *s* four *d*. *Educ:* Moyallon Sch., Co. Down; Portadown Technical Coll. Served War of 1939-45, Royal Ulster Constabulary. JP, Co. Armagh, 1956. Group Secretary, North Armagh Group, Ulster Farmers' Union, 1956-59; Member, Co. Armagh Agricultural Society. Vice-Pres., Portadown Football Club. Stadtholder, Williamite and Glorious Revolution Soc., QUB. *Recreations:* football, hunting, shooting. *Address:* Mandeville Hall, Mullahead, Tandragee, Portadown, Co. Armagh, N Ireland. *T:* Tandragee 260; Queensway Court Hotel, 36 Queensway, W2. *T:* 01-229 4663.

**MAGNANI, Anna;** Italian stage and film actress; b Rome, Italy, 1918. *Educ:* Academy of Dramatic Art, Rome. First appeared on legitimate stage and worked in repertory companies. First film appearance in Blind Woman of Sorrento, 1934. Films include: Open City, 1946; Before Him All Rome Trembled, 1947; Volcano, 1953; The Gold Coach, 1954; The Rose Tattoo, 1955; Suor Letizia, 1958; The Fugitive Kind, 1960; Nella Cittã l'Inferno, 1961; The Secret of Santa Vittoria, 1970. Returned to the stage in La Lupa, Florence, 1965, London, 1969. Many awards, including Venice Film Festival Award, Italian Ribbon of Silver and Oscar (USA). *Address:* c/o Ercole Graziadei, Via Veneto 96, Rome, Italy.

**MAGNAY, Harold Swindale;** Consultant, OECD, Paris, since 1964; *b* 24 Jan. 1904; *e s* of late Andrew Magnay and late Phœbe Elizabeth Swindale, Newcastle upon Tyne; *m* 1931, Meg, *e d* of late Thomas Wood and Meggie Huntley, Felling-on-Tyne; one *s*. *Educ:* Elswick Road Council Sch. and Royal Grammar Sch., Newcastle upon Tyne; St John's Coll., Cambridge (Exhibitioner in History, Law Schol.). Game Ranger and District Reclamation Officer, Tanganyika, 1925-27; Asst Master, RGS, 1927-30; Asst Director of Education, Newcastle upon Tyne, 1930-34; Director of Education: Barnsley, 1934-40; Leicester, 1940-46; Liverpool, 1946-64. Past President Assoc. of Education Officers; Past Chairman, Assoc. of Art Institutions. Hon. Secretary various educational cttees, etc; National Council Boy Scouts' Assoc.; Past Chairman, BBC Northern Advisory Council; formerly President, Liverpool Sunday School Union; Member: Percy Cttee on Higher Technological Education; Reynolds Cttee on Remand Homes and Approved Schools; Fulton Commn on Education in Sierra Leone. Member University Grants Cttee, 1946-53; Member Advisory Cttee on Education in the Colonies, 1955-58, and of other cttees to date. Hon. FRIBA. Hon. MA Liverpool, 1959. Silver Medal of Honour, City of Amsterdam, 1964. *Recreations:* walking and talking. *Address:* 25 Grange Park, Bishop's Stortford, Herts. *T:* Bishop's Stortford 2588. *Clubs:* United University; University (Liverpool).

**MAGNER, Jeremiah John,** CB 1948; MC 1918; Major-General (late RAMC), retired; Medical Director, National Mass Radiography Association, since 1951; *b* 26 June 1891; 2nd *s* of late David Magner, Carrigville, Cork; *m* 1927, Sarah Gabriel, *d* of John Magner, Clonmel; no *c*. *Educ:* National University of Ireland; London Univ. MB, BCh, BAO (NUI) 1914; DMR (London) 1935. FFR, RCS(I), Founder Fellow. Served European War, 1914-19, France, Belgium, Balkans, Russia (despatches, MC, 1914 Star and two medals); War of 1939-45, 8th Army, Desert Campaign, Italy (despatches twice, CB). KHP 1948-51; DDMS, HQ Northern Command, York, 1948-51; retired pay, 1951. *Recreations:* hunting, golf, fishing. *Address:* 6 Herbert Park, Balls Bridge, Dublin. *T:* 684740.

**MAGNIAC, Rear-Admiral Vernon St Clair Lane,** CB 1961; HM Dockyard, Devonport, 1957-62, retired; *b* 21 Dec. 1908; *s* of late Major Francis Arthur Magniac and of Mrs Beatrice Caroline Magniac (*née* Davison); *m* 1947, Eileen Eleanor (*née* Witney); one *s* one *d*. (and one *d* decd). *Educ:* Clifton Coll. Cadet, RN, 1926; HMS Erebus and RN Engineering Coll. (under training), 1926-31; served in Courageous, 1931-32; Effingham, 1932; Resolution, 1933-35; Diamond, 1935-37; RN Engineering Coll., 1937-39; Renown, 1940-43; Combined Operations, India, 1943-45; HMS Fisgard, 1945-47, HMS Gambia, 1948, HMS Nigeria, 1948-50; Chatham Dockyard, 1950-52; Admiralty Fuel Experimental Station, 1952-55; Malta Dockyard, 1955-57. *Recreations:* golf, tennis, fishing. *Address:* The Dower House, Stockland, Honiton, Devon.

**MAGNUS, Hilary Barrow,** TD; QC 1957; National Insurance Commissioner, since Oct. 1964; *b* 3 March 1909; *yr s* of late Laurie Magnus, 34 Cambridge Square, W2; *b* and *heir-pres.* to Sir Philip Magnus-Allcroft, *qv; m* 1950, Rosemary, *d* of G. H. Masefield and *widow* of Quentin Hurst; one *s* one *d* and one step *s*. *Educ:* Westminster; Christ Church, Oxford. Barrister, Lincoln's Inn, 1933. Bencher, 1963. President, Tribunal of Appeal, London Building Acts. Served War of 1939-45, Rifle Brigade TA (Lieut-Colonel). JP (Kent) 1948. *Recreation:* shooting. *Address:* The Gate House, Leigh, nr Tonbridge, Kent. *T:* Hildenborough 2157; 3 Temple Gardens, EC4. *T:* 01-353 7884. *Clubs:* Garrick, Beefsteak.

**MAGNUS-ALLCROFT, Sir Philip,** 2nd Bt, *cr* 1917; MA; FRSL; JP; author; *b* 8 Feb. 1906; *er s* of late Laurie Magnus and Dora, *e d* of late Sir I. Spielman, CMG; *S* grandfather, 1933; *m* 1943, Jewell Allcroft, Stokesay Court, Onibury, Shropshire, *d* of late Herbert Allcroft and of Mrs John Rotton. Formally assumed surname of Allcroft (in addition to that of Magnus), 1951. *Educ:* Westminster Sch.; Wadham Coll., Oxford. Civil Service, 1928-32 and 1946-50. Served War of 1939-45 in Royal Artillery and Intelligence Corps (Iceland and Italy); Major. CC 1952, CA 1968, Shropshire (Chairman, Planning Cttee); Chairman of Governors, Attingham Coll.; JP Shropshire, 1953-. Trustee, National Portrait Gall., 1970-. *Publications:* (as Philip Magnus): Life of Edmund Burke, 1939; Selected Prose of Edmund Burke (with Introduction), 1948; Sir Walter Raleigh, 1951 (revised edns, 1956, 1968); Gladstone–A Biography, 1954; Kitchener–Portrait of an Imperialist, 1958 (revised edn, 1968); King Edward the Seventh, 1964. *Heir:* *b* Hilary Barrow Magnus, *qv*. *Address:* Stokesay Court, Onibury, Shropshire. *T:* Onibury 202. *Clubs:* Athenæum, Brooks's, Beefsteak; Shropshire (Shrewsbury).

**MAGOR, Major (Edward) Walter (Moyle),** CMG 1960; OBE 1956 (MBE 1947); Assistant Secretary, Board of Trade; *b* 1 June 1911; *e s* of late Edward John Penberthy Magor, JP, Lamellen, St Tudy, Cornwall, and Gilian Sarah Magor, JP; *m* 1939, Daphne Davis, *d* of late Hector Robert Lushington Graham, Summerhill, Thomastown, Co. Kilkenny; two *d*. *Educ:* Marlborough; Magdalen, Oxford; Magdalene, Cambridge. M.A. Indian Army, 1934-47; RARO, 10th Hussars, 1949-61; Indian Political Service, 1937–39 and 1943-47; Colonial, Administrative Service 1947-61; Kenya: Asst Chief Secretary, 1953; Permanent Secretary, Ministry of Defence.

1954; Acting Minister for Defence, 1956; Secretary to the Cabinet, 1958. Principal, Home Civil Service, 1961; Asst Secretary, 1964. Lord of the Manor of Kellygreen. *Recreation:* gardening. *Address:* Lamellen, St Tudy, Cornwall. *T:* St Tudy 207. *Club:* Cavalry.

**MAGOWAN, Joseph Irvine,** CB 1956; DL; Permanent Secretary, Ministry of Agriculture, Northern Ireland, 1953-56, retired; *b* 16 Jan. 1901; *s* of Wm H. Magowan, Mountnorris, and S. A. Magowan; *m* 1933, Mima Hazlett Kennedy; one *s* three *d. Educ:* Mountnorris; privately; Dublin; Edinburgh. Member RCVS, 1924; private practice, 1924-27; Diploma of Veterinary State Medicine, 1928; Min. of Agriculture, NI, 1929, Dep. Chief Veterinary Officer, 1940-47; Asst Secretary, Ministry of Agriculture, Northern Ireland, 1947-53. DL Co. of Armagh. *Recreations:* field sports, pigeon racing, gardening. *Address:* Mountnorris, Armagh, N Ireland. *T:* Glenanne 209. *Club:* City (Armagh).

**MAGUINNESS, Prof. William Stuart;** Professor of Latin Language and Literature, University of London, King's College, since 1946; Head of Department of Classics; General Editor, Methuen's Classical Texts; Vice-President, Classical Association, Orbilian Society, Virgil Society and London Classical Society; *b* 12 Oct. 1903; *s* of George J. Maguinness, Belfast; *m* 1933, Olive D., *d* of George T. Y. Dickinson, Sheffield; one *d. Educ:* Royal Belfast Academical Institution; Trinity Coll., Dublin (Classical Sizarship, Classical Foundation Scholarship; Sen. Moderatorships with Gold Medals in Classics and Modern Literature (French and Italian) and Univ. Studentship in Classics 1926; MA 1929). FKC 1966. Asst Lecturer in Classics, University of Manchester, 1927-30; Lecturer in Classics, University of Sheffield, 1930-46; Visiting Lecturer in various Universities in France, Holland, Italy, Poland and Greece. *Publications:* contributions on Classical subjects to the Oxford Classical Dictionary, Encyclopædia Britannica, Proc. Leeds Philosophical Society, Classical Review, Classical Quarterly, Revue de la Franco-ancienne, Wiener humanistische Blätter, Rivista di Cultura classica e medioevale, Phoenix, Antiquité classique, Estudios Clásicos, Notes and Queries, Vita Latina, various Actes de Congrès and other journals, 1928-70; Edition of Racine's Bérénice, 1929 (2nd edn, 1956); of Virgil's Aeneid, Book XII, 1953 (2nd edn, 1960); 4th (revised) edn of Stobart's Grandeur that was Rome (in collaboration with H. H. Scullard), 1961; Index to the Speeches of Isaeus (in collaboration with the late W. A. Goligher), 1964; English translation of P. Grimal's La Civilisation romaine, 1963, and F. Chamoux' La Civilisation grecque, 1965; Chapter in volume on Lucretius, 1965. *Address:* 25 Hillway, Highgate, N6. *T:* 01-340 3064.

**MAGUIRE, (Albert) Michael,** MC 1945, MM 1943; QC 1967; Recorder of Carlisle, since 1970; *b* 30 Dec. 1922; *s* of Richard Maguire and late Ruth Maguire. *Educ:* Hutton Grammar Sch.; Trinity Hall, Cambridge (BA 1948). Served War of 1939-45, North Irish Horse (Captain), in Africa (MM) and Italy (MC). Inns of Court Regt, 1946. War Crimes Investigation Unit, 1946. Called to the Bar, Middle Temple, 1949 (Harmsworth Scholar). *Address:* Chestnuts, Lower Bank Road, Fulwood, Preston, Lancs. *T:* Preston 79291. *Clubs:* Oxford and Cambridge; Racquet (Liverpool).

**MAGUIRE, Conor A.;** Chief Justice of Eire, 1946-61; *b* 16 Dec. 1889; *s* of C. J. O'L. Maguire, MD, and Florence O'Neill; *m* 1921, Nora Whelan; three *s. Educ:* Clongowes Wood Coll.; Univ. Coll., Dublin. MA, LLB National University of Ireland; Solicitor, 1914; Judge and Land Settlement Commissioner Dail, 1920-22; Called to Bar of Ireland, 1922; Inner Bar, 1932; prominent in the Sinn Fein movement; Member of Dail Eireann for National University of Ireland; Attorney-General, Irish Free State, 1932-36; Judge of the High Court and Judicial Commissioner, 1936; President of the High Court, 1937-46; Chairman Central Council, Irish Red Cross Society, 1940-46; President International Celtic Congress, 1957-61; Irish Representative European Commission of Human Rights, Strasbourg, 1963-65. Commandeur Légion d'Honneur; Order of St Raimon de Penafort (Spain); Grosse Verdienstkreuz (Federal Republic of Germany). LLD (*hc*): NUI; Dublin University. *Recreations:* fishing and shooting. *Address:* St Alban's, Albany Avenue, Monkstown, Co. Dublin.

**MAGUIRE, Air Marshal Sir Harold John,** KCB 1966 (CB 1958); DSO 1946; OBE 1949; Director-General of Intelligence, Ministry of Defence, since 1968; *b* 12 April 1912; *s* of Michael Maguire, Maynooth, Ireland, and Harriett (*née* Warren), Kilkishen, Co. Clare, Ireland; *m* 1940, Mary Elisabeth Wild, Dublin; one *s* one *d. Educ:* Wesley Coll., Dublin; Dublin Univ. Royal Air Force Commn, 1933; service in flying boats, 230 Sqdn, Egypt and Far East, 1935-38; commanded night fighter sqdn, UK, 1939-40 and day fighter sqdn, 1940; OC 266 (Fighter) Wing, Dutch E Indies, 1942; POW, Java, 1942; Staff Coll., 1947; Fighter Command Staff Duties, 1948-50; OC, RAF, Odiham, 1950-52; Senior Air Staff Officer, Malta, 1952-55; staff of CAS, Air Ministry, 1955-58; Senior Air Staff Officer, HQ No 11 Group, RAF, 1958-59; AOC No 13 Group, RAF, 1959-61; AOC No 11 Group, Fighter Command, 1961-62; SASO Far East Air Force, 1962-64; ACAS (Intelligence), 1964-65; Dep. Chief of Defence Staff (Intelligence), 1965-68; retired, 1968. *Address:* Ministry of Defence, Whitehall, SW1. *Club:* Royal Air Force.

**MAGUIRE, Hugh,** FRAM; Leader, Allegri String Quartet, since 1968; *b* 2 Aug. 1927; *m* 1953, Suzanne Lewis, of International Ballet; two *s* three *d. Educ:* Belvedere Coll., SJ, Dublin; Royal Academy of Music, London; Paris (Georges Enesco). Leader: Bournemouth Symphony Orchestra, 1952-56; London Symphony Orchestra, 1956-62; BBC Symphony Orchestra, 1962-67; Cremona String Quartet, 1966-68. Harriet Cohen Internat. Award; Councils Gold Medal (Ireland), 1963. *Address:* 1 Alverstone Road, NW2. *T:* 01-459 4787.

**MAGUIRE, Michael;** *see* Maguire, A. M.

**MAGUIRE, Rt. Rev. Robert Kenneth;** *see* Montreal, Bishop of.

**MAHALANOBIS, Prasanta Chandra,** FRS 1945; Hon. FSS 1954; FNI; BSc Calcutta, MA Cantab; Statistical Adviser to Cabinet, Government of India, since 1949; Member, Planning Commission, Government of India, 1955-67; Hon. President Internat. Statistical Institute, 1957 (Member 1937, Hon. Member 1952); Hon. Professor of Statistics, Calcutta University; Secretary and Director, Indian Statistical Institute, Calcutta, since 1931; Founder Editor, Sankhyā: the Indian Journal of Statistics, since 1933; *b* 29 June 1893; *s* of late Probodh Chandra Mahalanobis and late Nirodbasini Mahalanobis; *m* 1923, Nirmal

Kumari Maitra; no *c*. *Educ:* Brahmo Boys' Sch. and Presidency Coll., Calcutta; King's Coll., Cambridge (Senior Scholar, 1915). BSc (Hons Physics) Calcutta Univ. 1912; Cambridge Mathematical Tripos, Part I, 1914; Nat. Sci. Tripos, Part II (Physics), 1915. Indian Educational Service, 1915-48; Head of Dept of Physics, Presidency Coll., 1922-45; Principal, 1945-48, Prof. Emeritus, 1948-; Lecturer, Calcutta Univ. Postgraduate Dept, 1917-40, Hon. Head of its Postgraduate Dept of Statistics, 1941-45; Meteorologist, Calcutta, in charge of Alipore Observatory (in addition to duties in Presidency Coll.), 1922-26; Lectures and Scientific tours in many countries; also delegate to internat. conferences and representative at meetings and on commns, from 1946. Chm. UN Sub Commns on Statistical Sampling, 1947-51. Foundation Fellow, Nat. Inst. of Sciences of India (Pres. 1957-58); Fellow, Indian Acad. of Sciences, Nat. Acad. of Sciences, India, Royal Statistical Soc., London; Foundation Vice-Pres., International Biometric Soc., 1947; Mem., Int. Population Union. Presided over Anthropology Section, 1925, and Mathematics and Statistics Section, 1942, of Indian Science Congress; Gen. Sec., Indian Science Congress, 1945-48; Treas., 1952-55; Pres. 1950; Mem. UN Statistical Commn, 1946- (Chm. 1954-58); Hon. Gen. Sec., Rabindranath Tagore's Visvabharati from its inception, 1921 to 1931; Past Ed., Visvabharati Quarterly. Awarded Weldon Medal and Prize by Univ. of Oxford, 1944. Deva Prasad Sarbadhikari Gold Medal and Hon. DSc, Calcutta Univ., 1957; Gold Medal, Czechoslovak Acad. of Sciences, 1964; Durga Prasad Khaitan Meml Gold Medal, Asiatic Soc., 1968; For. Mem., USSR Acad. of Sciences, 1958. Hon. Fellow, King's Coll., Cambridge, 1958; Hon. Desikottama, Visvabharati, 1961; Hon. DSc, Sofia State Univ., 1961; Hon. DSc Delhi Univ., 1964. Padma Vibhushan, 1968. *Publications:* Experiments in Statistical Sampling in the Indian Statistical Institute, 1961; Talks on Planning, 1961; An Approach of Operational Research to Planning in India, 1963. About 150 research papers and publications on statistical subjects; literary and philosophical essays and articles in English and Bengali. *Address:* 204 Barrackpore Trunk Road, Calcutta 35. *T:* 56-3223; The Cabinet Secretariat, Government of India, 8 King George Avenue, New Delhi.

**MAHEU, René G.;** Director-General, United Nations Educational Scientific and Cultural Organization (Unesco), since Nov. 1962, re-elected Nov. 1968; *b* Saint-Gaudens, France, 28 March 1905; *s* of Joseph Maheu and Madeleine Roucoule; *m* 1928, Inès Allafort du Verger; one *s*. *Educ:* Lycée de Toulouse, Lycée Louis-le-Grand, Paris; Ecole Normale Supérieure; Sorbonne, Paris. Prof. of philosophy: Lycée de Coutances, France, 1930; Univ. of Cologne (Romanisches Seminar), Germany, 1931-33; Institut Français du Royaume Uni, London, 1933-39; Collège Franco-Musulman Moulay-Idriss, Fès, Morocco, 1940-42; attached to Cabinet Civil of French Resident-Gen., Rabat, Morocco, 1944-46; joined Secretariat of Unesco, Sept. 1946; Head, Div. of Free Flow of Information, 1946-48; Dir, Cabinet of Dir-Gen., 1949-53; Asst Dir-Gen., 1954-59 (Rep. to UN, 1955-58); Dep. Dir-Gen., 1960-61; Acting Dir-Gen., 1961-62. *Publication:* La civilisation de l'universel, 1966. *Address:* 89 Avenue Niel, Paris XVIIe. *Club:* Union Interaliée (Paris).

**MAHLER, Kurt,** FAA 1965; FRS 1948; PhD, DSc; Professor of Mathematics, Ohio State University, USA, since 1968; *b* 1903. *Educ:* Univs of Frankfurt and Göttingen. Research work at Univs of Göttingen, Groningen, and Manchester. Asst Lecturer at Manchester Univ., 1937-39, 1941-44; Lecturer, 1944-47; Senior Lecturer, 1948-49; Reader, 1949-52; Prof. of Mathematical Analysis, 1952-63; Prof. of Mathematics, Institute of Advanced Studies, ANU, 1963-68. *Publications:* Lectures on Diophantine Approximations, 1961; papers on different subjects in pure mathematics (Theory and Geometry of Numbers) in various journals, from 1928. *Recreations:* Chinese, photography. *Address:* Mathematics Department, Ohio State University, Columbus, Ohio 43210, USA.

**MAHON, Denis;** *see* Mahon, J. D.

**MAHON, Sir George Edward John,** 6th Bt, *cr* 1819; *b* 22 June 1911; *s* of 5th Bt and late Hon. Edith Dillon, 2nd *d* of 4th Lord Clonbrock; *S* father, 1926; *m* 1st, 1938, Audrey Evelyn (*d* 1957), *o c* of late Dr Walter Jagger and of Mrs Maxwell Coote; two *s* one *d*; 2nd, 1958, Suzanne, *d* of late Thomas Donnellan, Pirbright, Surrey, and of Mrs Donnellan, Castleknock, Co. Dublin; one *d*. *Heir: s* William Walter Mahon [*b* 4 Dec. 1940; *m* 1968, Rosemary Jane, *yr d* of Lt-Col M. E. Melvill, Symington, Lanarkshire]. *Address:* Castlegar, Ahascragh, Co. Galway; Castleknock Lodge, Castleknock, Co. Dublin.

**MAHON, Sir Gerald MacMahon,** Kt 1962; Chairman, Medical Appeal Tribunals under Industrial Injuries Acts, since 1964; *b* 24 July 1904; *o surv. s* of late Foster MacMahon Mahon, and of Mrs Lilian Frances Mahon, OBE (*née* Moore), Sheringham, Norfolk; *m* 1938, Roma Irene Maxtone Mailer; two *s*. *Educ:* Alleyn Court Preparatory Sch., Dulwich Coll.; Brasenose Coll., Oxford (BA). Called to the Bar (Inner Temple), 1928. Resident Magistrate, Tanganyika, 1936; Judge, HM High Court of Tanganyika Territory, 1949-59; Chief Justice of Zanzibar, 1959-64, retired. *Address:* Moat Cottage, Stratton Audley, Bicester, Oxon. *Clubs:* East India and Sports; Vincent's (Oxford).

**MAHON, Rt. Rev. Gerald Thomas;** Auxiliary Bishop of Westminster (RC) and Titular Bishop of Eanach Duin since 1970; *b* 4 May 1922; *s* of George Elborne Mahon and Mary Elizabeth (*née* Dooley). *Educ:* Cardinal Vaughan Sch., Kensington; Christ's Coll., Cambridge. Priest, 1946. Teaching, St Peter's Coll., Freshfield, 1950-55; missionary work in Dio. of Kisumu, Kenya, 1955-63; Superior General of St Joseph's Missionary Society of Mill Hill, 1963-70. *Address:* Archbishop's House, Westminster, SW1.

**MAHON, (John) Denis,** CBE 1967; MA Oxon; FBA 1964; Art Historian; Trustee of the National Gallery, 1957-64 and since 1966; *b* 8 Nov. 1910; *s* of late John FitzGerald Mahon (4th *s* of Sir W. Mahon, 4th Bt) and Lady Alice Evelyn Browne (*d* 1970), *d* of 5th Marquess of Sligo. *Educ:* Eton; Christ Church, Oxford. Has specialised in the study of 17th-Century painting in Italy and has formed a collection of pictures of the period; is a member of the Cttee of the Biennial Exhibitions at Bologna, Italy; was awarded, 1957, Medal for Benemeriti della Cultura by Pres. of Italy for services to criticism and history of Italian art; Accademico d'Onore, Clementine Acad., Bologna, 1964. Corresp. Fellow: Accad. Raffaello, Urbino, 1968; Deputazione di Storia Patria per le provincie di Romagna, 1969. Hon. DLitt, Newcastle, 1969. *Publications:* Studies in Seicento Art and Theory, 1947; Mostra dei Carracci, Catalogo critico dei Disegni, 1956

(1963); Poussiniana, 1962; Catalogues of the Mostra del Guercino (Dipinti, 1968; Disegni, 1969); contributed to: Actes of Colloque Poussin, 1960; Friedlaender Festschrift, 1965; Problemi Guardeschi, 1967; articles, including a number on Caravaggio and Poussin, in art-historical periodicals, *eg*, The Burlington Magazine, Apollo, The Art Bulletin, Journal of the Warburg and Courtauld Institutes, Bulletin of the Metropolitan Museum of New York, Gazette des Beaux-Arts, Art de France, Paragone, Commentari, Zeitschrift für Kunstwissenschaft; has collaborated in the compilation of catalogues raisonnés of exhibitions, *eg*, Artists in 17th Century Rome (London, 1955), Italian Art and Britain (Royal Academy, 1960), L'Ideale Classico del Seicento in Italia (Bologna, 1962), Omaggio al Guercino (Cento, 1967). *Address:* 33 Cadogan Square, SW1. *T:* 01-235 2530.

**MAHON, Peter;** Alderman, JP; *b* 4 May 1909; *m* 1935, Margaret Mahon (*née* Hannon); three *s* one *d*. *Educ:* St James Elementary Sch.; St Edward's Coll. (Irish Christian Brothers). Local Govt Service, 1933-; Bootle: Council, 1933; Mayor, 1954-55; Chm. or Dep. Chm. numerous cttees; Mem. Nat. Cttee of TGWU. Contested (Lab) Blackburn, 1952-54, Preston, 1962-64; MP (Lab) Preston South, 1964-70. *Recreations:* football and swimming enthusiast; fond of music. *Address:* 2 Radnor Drive, Bootle 20, Lancs. *T:* 051-922 5989.

**MAHON, Simon;** MP (Lab) Bootle, since 1955; *b* 1914. *Educ:* St James Elementary Sch.; St Joseph's Coll. Alderman of Bootle Borough Council; Mayor, 1962. Opposition Whip, 1959-61. Served War of 1939-45; commissioned, Royal Engineers. *Address:* House of Commons, SW1.

**MAHONY, Lt-Col John Keefer,** VC 1944; *b* 30 June 1911; *s* of Joseph Jackson and Louise Mary Mahony; *m* 1950, Bonnie Johnston, Ottawa; two *d*. *Educ:* Duke of Connaught Sch., New Westminster, BC, Canada. On editorial staff of Vancouver Daily Province (newspaper) until outbreak of war of 1939-45; mem. Canadian Militia (equivalent of British Territorials) from 1936 until going on active service in Sept. 1939. Served War of 1939-45 (VC): (Canada, UK, Africa, Italy) Westminster Regt, Canadian Army; Major, 1943. Liaison Officer, US Dept of the Army, Washington, DC, 1954; retd as AA and QMG, Alberta Area, 1963. Now Exec. Dir, Junior Achievement of London, Inc. *Recreations:* swimming, lacrosse, baseball. *Address:* 657 Santa Monica Road, London, Ontario, Canada.

**MAHTAB, Maharajadhiraja Bahadur Sir Uday Chand, of Burdwan,** KCIE, 1945; *b* 1905; *s* of late Maharajadhiraja Bahadur Sir Bijay Chand Mahtab of Burdwan, GCIE, KCSI, IOM; *m* 1929, Radharani Devi, Amritsar, Punjab; three *s* three *d*. *Educ:* Presidency Coll., Calcutta; Calcutta Univ. (BA 1926). Pres. Non-Muslim block of Bengal Partition meeting, June 1947; Mem., Constituent Assembly. MLA Bengal, 1937-52; is a Zemindar; a Mem. of Damodar Canal Enquiry Cttee, 1938, and of Select Cttee on Calcutta Municipal (amendment) Bill, 1940; Chm. of Burdwan District Flood Relief and Bengal Central Flood Relief Cttees, 1943-44, of Indian Red Cross Appeal (Bengal), 1943-46, of Calcutta War Cttee, 1943-46, and of Damodar Flood Control Enquiry Cttee, 1944; a Mem. of Bengal Tanks Improvement Bill Select Cttee, 1944, of Advisory Cttee to examine cases of Terrorist Convicts in Bengal, 1944, of W Bengal Forest Denudation Enquiry Cttee, 1944, and of Select Cttee on Bengal Agricultural Income Tax Bill, 1944; Pres., British Indian Association; Mem., Central Jute Board, 1951-52; Dir of over 30 business firms and Chm. of several Boards. Mem. of Managing Body of several Government Organisations. Silver Jubilee (1935) and Coronation (1937) medals. *Address:* The Palace, Burdwan, India; Bijay Manzil, Alipore, Calcutta. *Clubs:* Calcutta (Calcutta); Aftab (Burdwan); Gymkhana (Darjeeling).

**MAIDMENT, Kenneth John,** MA; *b* 29 Oct. 1910; *s* of Francis George Maidment and Jessie Louisa Taylor; *m* 1937, Isobel Felicity, *d* of Archibald Leitch; one *s* three *d*. *Educ:* Bristol Gram. Sch.; Merton Coll., Oxford. Hertford Scholar, 1929; First Class Classical Hon. Mods, 1930; Craven Scholar, 1930; First Class Litt. Hum., 1932; Junior Research Fellow, Merton Coll., 1932-34; Fellow and Classical Tutor, Jesus Coll. (Oxford), 1934-38; Fellow and Classical Tutor, Merton Coll., 1938-49; Oxford and Bucks Lt Infantry, 1940; seconded War Office, 1941; liaison duties in US, 1942-45, Lt-Col; University Lecturer in Greek Literature, 1947-49; Principal, Auckland Univ. Coll., 1950-57; Vice-Chancellor, Univ. of Auckland, 1957-70. Hon. LLD Auckland. *Publications:* Critical edition and translation of Antiphon and Andocides (Loeb Library), 1940; articles and reviews in classical journals. *Address:* 9 Highfield Avenue, Headington, Oxford.

**MAIDSTONE, Viscount; Daniel James Hatfield Finch Hatton;** *b* 7 Oct. 1967; *s* and *heir* of 16th Earl of Winchilsea, *qv*.

**MAIDSTONE, Suffragan Bishop of,** since 1969; **Rt. Rev. Geoffrey Lewis Tiarks,** MA Cantab; Senior Chaplain to the Archbishop of Canterbury since 1969; *b* 8 Oct. 1909; *s* of Lewis Herman Tiarks, Clerk in Holy Orders, and Edith Margaret Tiarks; *m* 1934, Betty Lyne, *d* of Henry Stock; one *s* (one *d* decd). *Educ:* Marlborough; S John's College, Cambridge. Ordained at Southwark, 1932; Curate of St Saviour's with St Peter, Southwark, 1932-33; Chaplain, RN, 1934-47; Chaplain, Diocesan College, Rondebosch, CP, 1948-50; Rector of S Paul's, Rondebosch, 1950-54; Vicar of Lyme Regis, Dorset, 1954-61; Archdeacon of the Isle of Wight, 1961-65; Archdeacon of Portsmouth, 1965-69. *Address:* Lambeth Palace, SE1. *T:* 01-928 8282.

**MAIDSTONE, Archdeacon of;** *see* Prichard, Ven. T. E.

**MAILER, Norman;** *b* 31 Jan. 1923; *s* of Isaac Barnett Mailer and Fanny Schneider; *m* 1st, 1944, Beatrice Silverman (marr. diss., 1951); one *d*; 2nd, 1954, Adèle Morales (marr. diss., 1962); two *d*; 3rd, 1962, Lady Jeanne Campbell (marr. diss., 1963); one *d*; 4th, 1963, Beverly Bentley; two *s*. *Educ:* Harvard. Infantryman, US Army, 1944-46. Co-founder of Village Voice, 1955; An Editor of Dissent, 1953-63. Democratic Candidate, Mayoral Primaries, New York City, 1969. *Publications:* (American): The Naked and the Dead, 1948; Barbary Shore, 1951; The Deer Park, 1955 (dramatized, 1967); Advertisements for Myself, 1959; Deaths For The Ladies, 1962; The Presidential Papers, 1963; An American Dream, 1964; Cannibals and Christians, 1966; Why Are We In Vietnam?, 1967 (a novel); The Armies of the Night, 1968 (Pulitzer Prize, 1969); Miami and the Siege of Chicago, 1968 (National Book Award, 1969). *Address:* c/o Rembar, 19 W 44th Street, NY 10036, USA.

**MAILLART, Ella (Kini);** Explorer; *b* 20 Feb. 1903; Swiss father and Danish mother; unmarried. *Educ:* Geneva; and also while teaching French at two schools in England.

Took to the seas at 20, cruising with 3 ton Perlette, 10 ton Bonita, 45 ton Atalante–all these manned by girls; then 120 ton Volunteer, 125 ton Insoumise; in Mediterranean, Biscay, Channel; sailed for Switzerland Olympic Games, Paris, 1924 single-handed competition; Hockey for Switzerland as captain in 1931; Ski-ed for Switzerland in the FIS races in 1931-34; went to Russia for 6 months, 1930; travelled in Russian Turkestan for 6 months 1932; went to Manchoukuo for Petit Parisien, 1934; returned overland accompanied by Peter Fleming, via Koko Nor; travelled overland to Iran and Afghanistan in 1937 and 1939, in South India, 1940-45, Nepal, 1951, Everest Base Camp, 1965. Fellow RGS, London; member: Royal Central Asian Soc.; Club des Explorateurs, Paris. Sir Percy Sykes Medal. *Publications:* Parmi la Jeunesse Russe, 1932; Des Monts Célestes aux Sables Rouges, 1934 (in English as Turkestan Solo, 1934); Oasis Interdites, 1937 (in English as Forbidden Journey, 1937); Gipsy Afloat, 1942; Cruises and Caravans, 1942; The Cruel Way, 1947; Ti-Puss, 1952; The Land of the Sherpas, 1955. *Recreations:* ski-ing, gardening. *Address:* c/o David Higham Associates Ltd, 76 Dean Street, W1; 10 Avenue G. Vallette, Geneva, Switzerland. *T:* Geneva 46.46.57; Atchala, Chandolin sur Sierre, Switzerland. *Clubs:* Kandahar; (hon.) Ski Club de Dames Suisse; (hon.) Ski Club of Great Britain; (hon.) Ladies Alpine.

**MAIN, Frank Fiddes,** CB 1965; FRCPEd; Chief Medical Officer, Ministry of Health and Social Services, Northern Ireland, 1954-68, retired; *b* 9 June 1905; *s* of Frank and Mary Main, Edinburgh; *m* 1931, Minnie Roberta Paton; two *s* two *d*. *Educ:* Daniel Stewart's Coll., Edinburgh; Edinburgh Univ. MB, ChB 1927; DPH 1931; MRCPEd 1954; FRCPEd 1956. Medical Officer of Health, Perth, 1937-48; Senior Administrative Medical Officer, Eastern Regional Hosp. Bd (Scotland), 1948-54. Crown Mem., Gen. Med. Council, 1956-69. QHP 1956-59. *Recreation:* golf. *Address:* Bruce's Cottage, Kilconquhar, Elie, Fife. *T:* Colinsburgh 612; 10 Morningside Terrace, Edinburgh 10. *T:* 031-447 5687. *Club:* Royal Scottish Automobile (Glasgow).

**MAIN, Brig. John Walter,** CBE 1943; ED 1944; *b* 30 May 1900; *s* of late Chas F. and Hilda S. Main, Glenelg, Woodville, S Australia; *m* 1st, 1923, Violet Plunket (*d* 1937), Adelaide, S Australia; one *s* (and one *s* decd); 2nd, 1940, Hilda R. Pender, Maitland, New South Wales. *Educ:* High Sch. and Univ., Adelaide. Draughtsman, J. S. Bagshaw & Sons, Engineers, Adelaide, Munitions Supply Board, Melbourne, 1924-25; Chief Draughtsman, Melbourne Tramway Board, Rolling Stock and Wksp Branch, 1925-36; Design Engineer, Broken Hill Pty Steelworks, Newcastle, NSW, 1936-39. Citizen Military Forces, 1921-40; AIF 1940; Middle East: Major and Fd Coy Comd, 1940-41; Lt-Col and CRE Corps, 1941-42; New Guinea, Brig. and Chief Engr, Corps, and Army, 1942-44; R of O, 1945-49; Citizen Military Forces, 1950-55, as Brigade Comdr; R of O 1955; Retired List, 1956. Engineer and Supt, Newcastle Steelworks, from 1945 and Gen. Supt of Transportation from 1953, retd 1965. MInstT; Fellow Aust. Institute of Management. *Recreations:* motoring, caravan, bowls. *Address:* 3 Hillcrest Road, Merewether, NSW 2291, Australia. *Clubs:* Imperial Service (Sydney); Newcastle; United Service; Newcastle Masonic; Legacy (Past Pres.) (Newcastle, NSW).

**MAINE, Rev. Basil Stephen,** MA; Member of the Critics' Circle; Life Member, Royal College of Organists; Hon. Member, Incorporated Society of Musicians; *b* Norwich, 4 March 1894; *e s* of Stephen Frederick Maine and Kate Elizabeth Maine. *Educ:* City of Norwich Sch.; Queens' Coll., Cambridge (Organ Scholar); Winchester Reading Prize, Ryle Reading Prize, and Hughes Essay Prize, History Tripos; studied music under Dr Charles Wood and Sir Charles Stanford; Music and Mathematics Master at Durnford Sch., Langton Matravers; later Asst Organist Durham Cathedral; one of the Music Critics of the Daily Telegraph, 1921-26; later joined the Morning Post Staff; gave Weekly Talks on Music for BBC, 1927-28; Editor of the Music Bulletin, 1925-29; created the rôles of the Young King in Laurence Binyon's The Young King, of Jesus in John Masefield's The Trial of Jesus, and of the Prophet in Masefield's A King's Daughter; performed the rôle of the Soldier in first broadcast performance (here) of Stravinsky's Soldier's Tale (Glasgow, 1927); performed the rôle of the Narrator in Honegger's King David, given at Three Choirs' Festival, Gloucester, 1928; has lectured on British Music throughout this country, in USA, Canada, and at the Conservatoire of Music, Prague; was the Orator in first performance of Arthur Bliss' Morning Heroes, Norwich Fest., 1930; also 1961; also in first London performance of the same work, Queen's Hall, 1931; and first performance in America, 1931; one of English reps at First International Congress of Music at Florence, 1933. Ordained 1939. Gave Bach Commemoration Lecture, Norwich Cathedral, 1950. *Publications:* Receive It So (Essays); Reflected Music (Essays); Rondo (novel), 1930; Plummers Cut (novel), 1932; Life and Works of Elgar, 1933; Life of Chopin, 1933; Study of Paderewski, 1934; Edward VIII, Duke of Windsor, 1937; The Best of Me (Autobiography), 1937; People are Much Alike, 1938; Franklin Roosevelt, 1938; The BBC and its Audience, 1939; New Paths in Music, 1940; Maine on Music, 1946; Music and the BBC, 1948; Twang with our Music, 1957. Songs, Orchestral and Choral Music and Works for Violoncello; Te Deum (first performed at Colchester Festival of Britain, 1951); Shakespearean Speeches recorded for HMV and Decca. *Address:* Beacon Lodge, Overstrand Road, Cromer, Norfolk.

**MAINGOT, Rodney,** FRCS; Surgeon and writer; Consulting Surgeon: Royal Free Hospital and Southend General Hospital; late Regional Consultant in Surgery, Emergency Medical Service; Fellow, Surgical Section, RSM (late President); Fellow, Association of Surgeons of Great Britain and Ireland; Editor-in-Chief, British Journal of Clinical Practice; Chairman, Editorial Board, London Clinic Medical Journal; *b* Trinidad, BWI; *m* Rosalind Smeaton (*d* 1957), Brisbane, Australia; *m* 1965, Evelyn Plesch, London. *Educ:* Ushaw Coll., Durham. House Surg. (twice), Surgical Receiving Officer and Chief Asst to a Surgical Unit, St Bartholomew's Hospital; Surgical Registrar, West London Hospital. Served War of 1914-18 (Captain RAMC) in Egypt and Palestine (despatches twice). Sydney Body Gold Medallist, 1958. *Publications:* Post Graduate Surgery, 1936; Technique of Gastric Operations, 1941; The Surgical Treatment of Gastric and Duodenal Ulcer, 1945; Techniques in British Surgery, 1950; The Management of Abdominal Operations, 2nd edn 1957; Abdominal Operations, 5th edn 1969; contributor to Surgery of the Gallbladder and Bile Ducts, ed Smith and Sherlock, 1964, also in Operative Surgery, 2nd ed Rob and Smith, 1969; Dr Frank H. Lahey Memorial Lecture in Boston, 1963. *Recreations:* painting, writing. *Address:* 149 Harley Street, W1. *T:* 01-935 4444 and 1714; 25 Wimpole Street, W1. *T:* 01-580 3341.

**MAINI, (Sir) Amar (Nath),** Kt 1957; CBE 1953 (OBE 1948); *b* Nairobi, 31 July 1911; *e s* of late Nauhria Ram Maini, Nairobi, Kenya, and Ludhiana, Punjab, India; *m* 1935, Ram Saheli Mehra, Ludhiana; two *s*. *Educ:* Govt Indian Sch., Nairobi; London Sch. of Economics (BCom, Hons 1932). Barrister-at-law, Middle Temple, London, 1933. Advocate of Supreme Court of Kenya, and of High Court of Uganda. Sometime an actg MLC, Kenya, and Mem., Nairobi Municipal Council. From 1939 onwards, in Uganda; associated with family cotton business of Nauhria Ram & Sons (Uganda) Ltd. Formerly: Mem., Kampala Township Authority, Chm., Kampala Municipal Council, 1st Mayor of Kampala (1950-55); Dep. Chm., Uganda Electricity Board; Member: Uganda Development Corporation; Lint Marketing Board; Civil Defence Bd; Asian Manpower Cttee; Transport Bd; Supplies Bd; Immigration Advisory Bd; Advisory Bd of Health; Railway Advisory Council; Advisory Bd of Commerce; Rent Restriction Bd; Makerere Coll. Assembly, etc. Past Pres. Central Council of Indian Assocs in Uganda; Indian Assoc., Kampala; served on Cttees of Cotton Association. Formerly: Mem. Uganda Legislative and Exec. Councils; Development Council, Uganda; EA Legislative Assembly; EA Postal Advisory Bd; EA Transport Adv. Council; EA Air Adv Council, etc. Minister for Corporations and Regional Communications in the Government of Uganda, 1955-58; Minister of Commerce and Industry in Uganda, 1958-61; Speaker, E African Central Legislative Assembly, 1961-67; Mem., E African Common Market Tribunal, 1967-69. Dep. Chm. Kenya Broadcasting Corp., 1961-63. *Recreation:* golf. *Address:* 55 Vicarage Road, East Sheen, SW14. *T:* 01-878 1497; PO Box 372, Kampala, Uganda. *T:* 5287. *Clubs:* Reform; Uganda (Kampala), Nairobi.

**MAINLAND, Prof. William Faulkner,** MA; Professor of German, University of Sheffield, 1953-70; *b* 31 May 1905; *s* of late George Mainland and of Ada (*née* Froggatt); *m* 1930, Clarice Vowles, *d* of late A. E. Brewer; no *c*. *Educ:* George Heriot's Sch.; Univ. of Edinburgh. 1st Class Hons. Vans Dunlop Schol. in German; Postgrad. studies in London under late Prof. J. G. Robertson, and in Germany. Asst for French and German at London Sch. of Economics, 1929-30; thereafter attached to German Depts of Univs of: Manitoba, 1930; Manchester, 1935; London (UC, 1937, King's Coll., 1938, Birkbeck Coll., 1938); Sheffield, 1946; Leeds, 1947. Public Orator, Univ. of Sheffield, 1968-. *Publications:* German for Students of Medicine, 1938; German Lyrics of the Seventeenth Century (with Prof. August Closs), 1941; E. T. A. Hoffman, Der goldene Topf (Editor), 1942, 2nd edn, 1945; Schiller, Uber naive und sentimentalische Dichtung (Editor), 1951; Schiller and the Changing Past, 1957; chapters on Th. Storm, H. Sudermann, Fr. v. Unruh, H. Kasack, in German Men of Letters, 1961, 1963, 1964, 1966; Schiller, Jungfrau v. Orleans (Editor with Prof. E. J. Engel), 1963; Schiller, Wilhelm Tell (Editor), 1968. Reviews and articles on German and Dutch literature. *Recreations:* drawing, painting; Flemish language and folklore. *Address:* 2 Severn Road, Tree Root Walk, Sheffield 10. *Club:* University Staff (Sheffield).

**MAINWARING, Brig. Hugh Salusbury Kynaston,** CB 1945; CBE 1944; DSO 1942; TD; Lord Lieutenant of Flintshire since 1951; *b* 22 Jan. 1906; *s* of late Col Sir W. R. K. Mainwaring, CB, CBE, Hafod-y-Coed, St Asaph; *m* 1935, Diana (*d* 1967), *d* of late Major W. M. Dugdale, CB, DSO; three *s* one *d*. *Educ:* Eton; Christ Church, Oxford. Served 10th Royal Hussars, 1928-35; 5th Bn RWF (TA), 1936 onwards (converted to RA 1939); War of 1939-45, Middle East, Italy, Greece, 1940-45; GSO1 Eighth Army; BGS Allied Armies in Italy; BGS Land Forces, Greece; BGS Southern Command. DL 1945; JP 1945. KStJ 1970. *Address:* Hafod-y-Coed, St Asaph, N Wales. *T:* Trefnant 655. *Club:* Cavalry.

**MAINWARING, Capt. Maurice K. C.;** *see* Cavenagh-Mainwaring.

**MAINWARING, William Henry;** *b* 1884; *s* of William Mainwaring, Swansea. *Educ:* Central Labour Coll., London. Lecturer in Economics and Vice-Principal, Central Labour Coll., 1919; miners' agent for the Rhondda district, 1924. MP (Lab) East Rhondda, 1933-Sept. 1959. *Address:* 38 Harbord Road, Oxford. *T:* 57042.

**MAIR, Prof. Alexander;** Professor of Social and Occupational Medicine (formerly of Public Health and Social Medicine), University of Dundee, since 1954; *m* 1945, Nancy Waddington; two *s* one *d*. *Educ:* Aberdeen Univ. MB, ChB, 1942, DPH, 1948, MD (Hons), 1952 (Aberdeen); DIH (London) 1955; FRCP (Edinburgh) 1966. RAMC 1942-46. Lecturer, Univ. of Aberdeen, 1948-52; Senior Lecturer, Univ. of St Andrews, at Dundee, 1952-54. Medical Dir, Scottish Occupational Health Laboratory Service, Ltd; Mem., Steering Cttee and Founder Mem., Dundee and District Occupational Health Service Ltd; Chm., Scottish Cttee for Welfare of Disabled and Sub-Cttee on Rehabilitation; Regional Med. Adviser, Dept of Employment and Productivity, Scotland; Consultant, Occupational Health, to RN in Scotland. First Chm., British Soc. for Agriculture Labour Science. *Publications:* Student Health Services in Great Britain and Northern Ireland, 1966; (jointly) Custom and Practice in Medical Care, 1968; Sir James Mackenzie, MD, 1971; contrib.: Cerebral Palsy in Childhood and Adolescence, 1961; Further Studies in Hospital and Community, 1962; numerous publications on Researches into Occupational Diseases, especially Silicosis, Byssinosis, etc. *Address:* Tree Tops, Castle Roy, Broughty Ferry, Angus. *T:* 78727.

**MAIR, Prof. Lucy Philip;** Professor of Applied Anthropology, London School of Economics, 1963-68; *b* 28 Jan. 1901; *d* of David Beveridge Mair and Jessy Philip. *Educ:* St Paul's Girls' Sch.; Newnham Coll., Cambridge. London Sch. of Economics: Asst Lectr, 1927; Lectr, 1932; Reader, 1946; Prof., 1963. Australian Land Headquarters Civil Affairs Sch., 1945-46; Lugard Memorial Lectr, Internat. African Inst., 1958; Gildersleeve Visiting Prof. Barnard Coll., Columbia Univ., 1965; Frazer Lecture, Cambridge, 1967. Wellcome Medal, Royal Anthropological Inst., 1936. *Publications:* An African People in the Twentieth Century, 1934; Native Policies in Africa, 1936; Australia in New Guinea, 1948, 2nd edn 1971; Primitive Government, 1962; New Nations, 1963; An Introduction to Social Anthropology, 1966; The New Africa, 1967; Witchcraft, 1969; contribs to Africa, Cahiers d'Etudes Africaines, etc. *Recreations:* music, cooking. *Address:* 19 Hallgate, Blackheath Park, SE3. *T:* 01-852 8531.

**MAIR, Prof. William Austyn,** CBE 1969; Francis Mond Professor of Aeronautical Engineering, University of Cambridge, since 1952 and Fellow of Downing College, Cambridge; *b* 24

Feb. 1917; *s* of William Mair, MD; *m* 1944, Mary Woodhouse Crofts; two *s*. *Educ:* Highgate Sch.; Clare Coll., Cambridge. Aerodynamics Dept, Royal Aircraft Establishment, Farnborough, 1940-46; Dir, Fluid Motion Laboratory, Univ. of Manchester, 1946-52. Mem. various cttees, Aeronautical Research Council. *Publications:* papers on aerodynamics. *Address:* 74 Barton Road, Cambridge. *T:* Cambridge 50137. *Club:* Oxford and Cambridge.

**MAIS,** family name of **Baron Mais.**

**MAIS, Baron,** *cr* 1967 (Life Peer); **Alan Raymond Mais,** OBE 1944; TD 1944; ERD 1958; JP; Colonel; Alderman, City of London, Ward of Walbrook, 1963, Sheriff, 1969-70; Director: Royal Bank of Scotland, since 1969; Slag Reduction Co. Ltd; Elevators & Engineering Group; Sterling Industrial Securities (Chairman); Ronald Lyon Holdings; L. I. & P. C. Ltd (Chairman); William Sindalls Ltd; *b* July 1911; *s* of late Capt. E. Mais, Mornington Court, Kensington; *m* 1936, Lorna Aline, *d* of late Stanley Aspinall Boardman, Addiscombe, Surrey; two *s* one *d*. *Educ:* Banister Court, Hants; Coll. of Estate Management, London Univ. Commissioned Royal West Kent Regt, 1929; transf. RE 1931; Major 1939, Lt-Col 1941, Col 1944; served War of 1939-45; France, BEF 1939-40 (despatches); Special Forces, Egypt, Iraq and Persia, 1941-43 (despatches); Normandy and NW Europe, 1944-46 (OBE, despatches). Worked for Richard Costain and other cos on Civil Engrg. Works at home and abroad, 1931-38; Private Practice, A. R. Mais & Partners, Structural Engineers & Surveyors, 1938-39 and 1946-48. Dir Trollope & Colls Ltd, Bldg and Civil Engrg contractors and subsid. cos, 1948 (Asst Man. Dir, 1953; Man. Dir 1957; Dep.-Chm. 1961; Chm. and Man. Dir 1963; retired, 1968). Dir, Nat. Commercial Bank of Scotland, 1967-69. Past Pres., London Master Builders' Assoc.; Mem., Land Commn, 1967-69. mem., Corp. of City of London Cttees for Police, City of London Schs, Rates Finance, and Billingsgate and Leadenhall Markets. Mem. Ct, Worshipful Company of Paviors; Master, Worshipful Company of Cutlers, 1968-69. CRE 56 Armd Div. (TA), 1947-50; Comd Engr Gp (AER), 1951-54; Member: EDC Cttee for Constructional Industry, 1964-68; BNEC Cttee for Canada; Marshall Aid Commemoration Commn. Governor: Ewell Technical Coll., 1954-66; London Univ. Board of Studies; Royal Alexandra and Albert Sch. (Hon. Treas.); Hurstpierpoint Coll. JP; DL Co. London, 1952; Lieut, City of London, 1963. FICE, FIStructE, MSocCE (France), FIArb. Hon. BSc. Order of Patriotic War (1st class), USSR, 1942. *Publication:* Yerbury Foundation Lecture, RIBA, 1960. *Recreations:* golf, family, Territorial Army. *Address:* Chesham House, Wilderness Road, Chislehurst, Kent. *T:* 01-467 0735. *Clubs:* City Livery, Royal Automobile, Special Forces.

**MAIS, Robert Hugh; His Honour Judge Mais,** JP; Judge of the County Courts, since 1958; *b* 14 Sept. 1907; *s* of late Robert Stanley Oliver Mais, Chobham, Surrey; *m* 1938, Catherine, *d* of J. P. Pattinson; one *s*. *Educ:* Shrewsbury Sch.; Wadham Coll., Oxford (MA). Called to the Bar, Inner Temple, 1930; Mem. of Northern Circuit. Chancellor of the Diocese of: Manchester, 1948; Carlisle, 1950; Sheffield, 1950. Judge of County Courts: Circuit No 37 (West London), 1958-60; Circuit No 42 (Marylebone) from 1960. Dep. Chm., Berkshire QS, 1964-; Commissioner of Assize SE Circuit, 1964, 1967, Oxford Circuit, 1968, 1969. Member: County Court Rules Cttee; Winn Cttee on Personal Injuries Litigation; Lord Chancellor's Legal Aid Adv. Cttee. Served as Wing Comdr, RAF, 1940-44. *Publication:* Joint Ed., County Court Practice. *Recreations:* fishing, golf, lawn tennis. *Address:* Ripton, Streatley-on-Thames, Berks. *T:* Goring 2397. *Clubs:* Oxford and Cambridge; Berkshire (Reading).

**MAIS, Stuart Petre Brodie,** MA; FRSA, broadcaster; televiser; novelist; lecturer on books, travel and the countryside; free-lance journalist; late Professor of English at RAF Cadet College; Examiner and Lecturer to University of London; *b* 4 July 1885; *o c* of late Rev. Brodie Mais, Tansley Rectory, Matlock; *m*; four *d*. *Educ:* Denstone; Christ Church, Oxford. Blue for three-mile race, 1907, 1909; blue for cross-country running, 1906, 1908; hons in Math. Mods, 1907, and in English Literature Finals, 1909; BA 1909; MA 1913; Schoolmaster: Rossall, 1909-13; Sherborne, 1913-17; Tonbridge, 1917-20; Radley, 1941-45; Literary Critic to the Evening News, 1918; Literary Critic to Daily Express, 1921-23; Literary editor of Daily Graphic, 1923-26; leader-writer and book-reviewer to daily Telegraph, 1926-31. *Publications:* several school text-books; April's Lonely Soldier, 1916; Interlude, 1917; Rebellion, 1917; From Shakespeare to O. Henry, 1917; A Schoolmaster's Diary, 1918; Lovers of Silver, 1918; The Education of a Philanderer, 1919; Books and their Writers, 1919; Uncle Lionel, 1920; Colour Blind, 1920; Why we should Read, 1920; Breaking Covert, 1921; Caged Birds, 1922; Quest Sinister, 1922; Oh! To Be in England, 1922; Prunello, 1923; Some Modern Authors, 1923; Perissa, 1924; Eclipse, 1925; Orange Street, 1926; See England First, 1927; Do You Know? 1927; Glorious Devon, 1928; The Cornish Riviera, 1928; First Quarter, 1929; Sussex, 1929; Frolic Lady, 1930; It Isn't Far from London, 1930; England of the Windmills, 1931; Delight in Books (BBC talks), 1931; Southern Rambles, 1931; This Unknown Island (BBC talks), 1932; The Highlands of Britain, 1932; Some Books I Like (BBC talks), 1932; These I have Loved, 1933; SOS Talks on Unemployment (BBC talks), 1933; Week-Ends in England, 1933; A Modern Columbus (BBC talks), 1934; Isles of the Island (BBC talks), 1934; More Books I Like (BBC talks), 1934; Round About England, 1935; England's Pleasance, 1935; The Writing of English (BBC talks, 1935); Walking at Week-Ends, 1935; A Chronicle of English Literature, 1936; England's Character, 1936; All the Days of My Life, 1937; The Three-Coloured Pencil, 1937; Let's Get Out Here, 1937; Light over Lundy, 1938; Old King Coal, 1938; Walking in Somerset, 1938; Britain Calling, 1938; Highways and Byways in the Welsh Marches, 1939; Listen to the Country, 1939; Hills of the South, 1939; Fifty years of the LCC, 1939; Raven among the Rooks, 1939; Men in Blue Glasses, 1940; There'll Always be an England, 1940; A Cluster of Grapes, 1941; Diary of a Citizen in War-Time, 1941; Black Spider, 1941; Youth after the War, 1943; Caper Sauce, 1947; I Return to Scotland, 1947; I Return to Switzerland, 1948; I Return to Ireland, 1948; Who Dies?, 1948; The Story of Oxford, 1949; I Return to Wales, 1949; What to see in Britain, 1949; The English Scene Today, 1949; We Wander through the West, 1949; The Land of the Cinque Ports, 1949; Little England Beyond Wales, 1949; I Loved You Once, 1949; The Best in their Kind, 1949; The Riviera, New Look and Old, 1950; Arden and Avon, 1950; Madeira Holiday, 1951; Britannia 1651-1951, 1951; Norwegian Odyssey, 1951; Come Love, Come Death, 1951; Winter Sports Holiday, 1951; Austrian Holiday, 1952; Buffets and Rewards, 1952; The Channel Islands, 1953; The Happiest Days of My Life, 1953; Italian Holiday, 1954; The Isle of Man, 1954; Spanish Holiday, 1955; Majorcan Holiday, 1956; Our Village Today, 1956; Roman Holiday, 1957; Mediterranean Cruise Holiday, 1958; South American Holiday, 1959; Continental Coach Holiday, 1960; Dutch Holiday, 1960; Round Africa Holiday, 1961; Greek Holiday, 1962; Caribbean Cruise Holiday, 1963; Round Britain Coach Holiday, 1963; Round the World Cruise Holiday, 1965; An English Course for Everybody, 1968; This Delicious Madness, 1968. *Recreations:* cricket, walking, riding, bicycling, flying, travel of any sort anywhere. *Address:* Flat 20, Bliss House, Finches Gardens, Lindfield, Haywards Heath, Sussex. *T:* Lindfield 3529. *Clubs:* Achilles, Sette of Old Volumes; Vincent's.

**MAISKY, Ivan Mikhailovich;** Member of Academy of Sciences of USSR, 1946; *b* Kiriloff, Novgorod Province, 19 Jan. 1884; *m* 1922, Agnes Alexandrovna Skippin; no *c. Educ:* Secondary Sch., Omsk, Siberia; St Petersburg and Munich Univs. Journalist; entered Soviet Diplomatic Service; Chief of Press Dept, Moscow Foreign Office, 1922; Counsellor at Soviet Embassy in London, 1925-27; Counsellor at Soviet Embassy in Tokio, 1927-29; Minister to Finland, 1929-32; Ambassador of USSR in Great Britain, 1932-43; Asst People's Commissar for Foreign Affairs, USSR, 1943-46; negotiated and signed Non-Aggression Treaty with Finland, 1932; Temporary Trade Agreement with Great Britain, 1934; Anglo-Soviet Naval Treaty, 1937; Soviet-Polish Pact of Mutual Assistance, 1941, Soviet-Czechoslovak Pact of Mutual Assistance, 1941, Soviet-Canadian Agreements on the establishment of Diplomatic and Consular Relations, 1942; The Agreement on the establishment of Consular Relations between the USSR and South Africa, 1942; The Canadian-Soviet Credit Agreement, 1942; The Agreements on the establishment of Diplomatic Relations with (*a*) Holland, (*b*) Ethiopia, (*c*), Egypt, 1943. Order of Lenin, 1942; Order of Labour Red Banner, 1944; Order of Labour Red Banner, 1945; Order of Labour Red Banner, 1964. *Publications:* Germany and the War, 1916; Political Germany, 1917; Modern Mongolia, 1921; Foreign Policy of RSFSR, 1922; Before the Storm, 1944; Spain (1808-1917), 1957; So Near and Yet So Far (novel), 1958; Mongolia on the Eve of Revolution, 1959; Reminiscences of Soviet Ambassador in Britain, 1960; Journey into the Past, Reminiscences, 1960; Spanish Notebooks, Reminiscences, 1962; Who helped Hitler, Reminiscences, 1962; Memoirs of a Soviet Ambassador (3 vols), 1964-65; Bernard Shaw and the Others, Reminiscences, 1967. *Address:* Academy of Sciences, Moscow, USSR.

**MAITLAND,** family name of **Earl of Lauderdale.**

**MAITLAND, Viscount; Ian Maitland;** Master of Lauderdale; Lieutenant RNR; Product Marketing Manager, De la Rue Instruments Ltd; *b* 4 Nov. 1937; *s* and *heir* of Earl of Lauderdale, *qv*; *m* 1963, Ann Paule, *d* of Geoffrey Clark; one *s* one *d. Educ:* Radley Coll., Abingdon; Brasenose Coll., Oxford (MA Modern History). Various appointments since 1960; with De La Rue Group, 1968-. Probationary Lay Reader, Church of England. *Recreations:* photography, sailing, dining. *Heir: s* Master of Maitland, *qv. Address:* 10 Ovington Square, SW3. *T:* 01-589 7451.

**MAITLAND, Master of; Hon. John Douglas Maitland;** *b* 29 May 1965; *s* and *heir* of Viscount Maitland, *qv*.

**MAITLAND, Alastair George,** CBE 1966; Director-General, British Trade Development Office, New York, since 1968; *b* 30 Jan. 1916; *s* of Thomas Douglas Maitland, MBE, and Wilhelmina Sarah Dundas; *m* 1943, Betty Hamilton; two *s* one *d. Educ:* George Watson's Coll., Edinburgh; Universities of Edinburgh (MA First Class Hons), Grenoble and Paris. Vice-Consul: New York, 1938; Chicago, 1939; New York, 1939; Los Angeles, 1940; apptd to staff of UK High Commissioner at Ottawa, 1942; apptd to Foreign Office, 1945; Brit. Middle East Office, Cairo, 1948; Foreign Office, 1952; UK Delegation to OEEC, Paris, 1954; Consul-General: at New Orleans, 1958-62; at Jerusalem, 1962-64; at Cleveland, 1964-68. CStJ. *Recreations:* music, golf, gardening, reading. *Address:* 770 Park Avenue, New York, NY, USA. *Club:* Rolls-Royce Owners' Club (US).

**MAITLAND, Donald James Dundas,** CMG 1967; OBE 1960; HM Diplomatic Service; Chief Press Secretary, 10 Downing Street, since 1970; *b* 16 Aug. 1922; *s* of Thomas Douglas Maitland and Wilhelmina Sarah Dundas; *m* 1950, Jean Marie Young, *d* of Gordon Young; one *s* one *d. Educ:* George Watson's Coll.; Edinburgh Univ. Served India, Middle East, and SE Asia, 1941-47 (Royal Scots; Rajputana Rifles). Joined Foreign Service, 1947; Consul, Amara, 1950; British Embassy, Baghdad, 1950-53; Private Sec. to Minister of State, Foreign Office, 1954-56; Director, Middle East Centre for Arab Studies, Lebanon, 1956-60; Foreign Office, 1960-63; Counsellor, British Embassy, Cairo, 1963-65; Head of News Dept, Foreign Office, 1965-67; Principal Private Sec. to Foreign and Commonwealth Secretary, 1967-69; Ambassador to Libya, 1969-70. *Recreations:* golf, photography, hill-walking. *Address:* c/o Foreign and Commonwealth Office, SW1. *Club:* Travellers'.

**MAITLAND, Hugh Bethune,** MD (Toronto); MSc (Manchester); MRCS; LRCP; Professor Emeritus of Bacteriology, University of Manchester; *b* Port Perry, Ont., Canada, 1895; *m* 1926, Mary Logan Cowan, BA, MB (Toronto); one *s* one *d. Educ:* Univ. of Toronto. Temporary Surgeon-Lt RN, 1917-19; Lecturer and Asst Prof. in Bacteriology, Univ. of Toronto, 1919-24; Research work in Germany, 1924-25; Bacteriologist to the Scientific Advisory Cttee on Foot-and-Mouth Disease of the Ministry of Agriculture and Fisheries, working at the Lister Institute of Preventive Medicine, 1925-27; Mem. of the Bacteriological Staff of the Lister Institute, 1927; Prof. of Bacteriology, Univ. of Manchester, 1927-62; Colombo Plan Bacteriologist, Inst. for Med. Res., and Med. Faculty, Univ. of Malaya, Kuala Lumpur, 1962-66. *Address:* 9 Rowbury Drive, Ashby Road, Burton-upon-Trent, Staffs.

**MAITLAND, Comdr Sir John (Francis Whitaker),** Kt 1960; *b* 1903; *o s* of late William Whitaker Maitland, CVO, OBE, Loughton Hall, Essex; *m* 1930, Bridget, *er d* of E. H. M. Denny, Staplefield Place, Sussex; four *s* one *d. Educ:* Osborne, Dartmouth. Royal Navy: retired 1934, rejoined 1939-45; Comdr, 1943. MP (C) Horncastle Div. of Lincolnshire, 1945-66. Pres. Institute of Patentees and Inventors, 1966-. DL Essex, 1934; JP Essex, 1935; DL Lincolnshire, 1957. Dir, Expanded Metal Group. Mem. Lindsey CC, 1967. Chm. Council of St John for Lincolnshire; OStJ. FRSA. *Address:* Harrington Hall, near Spilsby, Lincs. *T:* Spilsby 2281. *Club:* Carlton.
*See also John Bruce-Gardyne.*

**MAITLAND, Col Mark Edward Makgill Crichton,** CVO 1952; DSO 1917; 3rd *s* of late Maj.-Gen. D. M. and Lady Margaret Crichton Maitland; *b* 1882; *m* 1924, Patience Irene Fleetwood, 2nd *d* of late Sir John Fuller and late Mrs H. Forestier-Walker, of Cottles, Melksham, Wilts; two *s* one *d*. *Educ:* Eton; RMC, Sandhurst. 2nd Lieut, Grenadier Guards, 1901; Lieut, 1904; Captain, 1910; Major, 1915; (Temp.) Lieut-Colonel in command 1st Batt. 1916; 2nd Batt. 1919; 3rd Batt. 1923-27; Colonel commanding The Regt, 1939; ADC Governor, New Zealand, 1910 and 1911; served S African War, 1902 (medal and clasp); European War, 1914-18 (wounded, DSO, Croix de Guerre); retired pay, 1928; HM Bodyguard, Hon. Corps of Gentlemen-at-Arms, 1928-52; HM Body Guard for Scotland, Royal Company of Archers, retired Dec. 1960. JP, DL Wiltshire. *Address:* The Island House, Wilton, Salisbury, Wilts. *T:* Wilton 3241. *Club:* MCC.

*See also Sir J. Gerard H. F. fuller.*

**MAITLAND, Air Vice-Marshal Percy Eric,** CB 1945; CBE 1951; MVO 1935; AFC 1918; *b* 26 Oct. 1895; *s* of Surgeon-Captain P. E. Maitland, Royal Navy; *m* 1927, Alison Mary Kettlewell; six *s*. *Educ:* RN Coll., Osborne and Dartmouth. Royal Navy, 1908-18, attached RNAS 1915 for Airships (AFC); transferred to Royal Air Force 1918 as Captain; specialised in Navigation. Served in Egypt and Iraq; Navigator in Far East Flight to Australia, 1928-29; Staff Officer for Royal Review, 1935 (MVO); Singapore, 1937-39, promoted Group Captain; Flying Training Command, 1939-40; Bomber Command, 1940-43; Air Ministry, Director of Operational Training, 1943; AOC No 2 Group, BAOR, 1945; AOC, No 84 Group, BAOR, 1945-47; AOC No 22 Group; Technical Training Command, 1948-50; retired, 1950. JP Somerset, 1952. *Recreation:* fishing. *Address:* 14 Merrick Square, SE1. *T:* 01-407 1646.

**MAITLAND, Sir Richard John,** 9th Bt, *cr* 1818; *b* 24 Nov. 1952; *s* of Sir Alexander Keith Maitland, 8th Bt, and of Lavender Mary Jex, *y d* of late Francis William Jex Jackson, Kirkbuddo, Forfar; *S* father, 1963. *Heir: b* Robert Ramsay Maitland, *b* 14 July 1956. *Address:* Burnside, Forfar, Angus.

**MAITLAND-MAKGILL-CRICHTON;** *see* Crichton.

**MAIZELS, Prof. Montague,** FRS 1961; MD, FRCP; Professor in Clinical Pathology, University of London, 1951-64, now Emeritus; *b* 30 Sept. 1899; *s* of Joseph and Deborah Maizels; *m* 1938, Dulcie Speight; one *d*. *Educ:* Guy's Hospital. Clinical Pathologist, University College Hospital, 1931. *Publications:* in Journal of Physiology, Lancet, etc. *Recreation:* photography. *Address:* 8 Decoy Avenue, NW11; University College, Gower Street, WC1.

**MAJITHIA, Dr Sir Surendra Singh,** Kt 1946; Landlord and Industrialist; *b* 4 March 1895; *s* of late Hon. Sardar Bahadur Dr Sir Sunder Singh Majithia, CIE, DOL; *m* 1921, Lady Balbir Kaur, *d* of General Hazura Singh, of Patiala. *Educ:* Khalsa Collegiate High Sch.; Khalsa Coll., Amritsar. Chairman: Saraya Sugar Mills Private Ltd; Saraya Engineering Works Private Ltd; Co-operative Development Union Ltd, Sardarnagar; Co-operative Development Union Ltd, Hata; Sardarnagar Block Development Block Cttee; Senior Managing Partner: Saraya Distillery; Saraya Oil Works; Saraya Surkhi Mill; Saraya Dairy Farm; Fairweather's, Gorakhpur, UP; Proprietor, Saraya Estate; Director: Punjab & Sindh Bank Ltd, Dehradun; Member: Khalsa College Council, Amritsar; Akal College Council, Gursagar, etc.; Executive Council, University of Gorakhpur; UP Tuberculosis Assoc., Lucknow; UP Fruit Development Board, Lucknow. President, Chairman, etc., of many educational foundations and social activities. Past Member various Advisory and Consultative Cttees. Chairman, Lady Parsan Kaur Charitable Trust. Patron, Wrestling Federation of India; President, UP Badminton Assoc.; Member, Garden Advisory Cttee, Gorakhpur. Hon. DLitt Gorakhpur, 1970. PO Sardarnagar, Dist Gorakhpur, Uttar Pradesh, India. *Clubs:* Gorakhpur, Union, Nipal (all in Gorakhpur).

**MAJOR;** *see* Henniker-Major.

**MAJOR, James Perrins,** CBE 1937; MD; FRACP; Consultant Physician; Hon. Physician to In-Patients and Lecturer in Clinical Medicine, Alfred Hospital, Melbourne; Lecturer in Therapeutics, University of Melbourne; *b* 22 Dec. 1878; *s* of Frank Major, Melbourne; *m* 1933, Beatrice, *d* of John Lloyd Williams; one *s* one *d*. *Educ:* Cumloden; University of Melbourne. Member of Standing Cttee of Convocation, University of Melbourne; Past-President of Victorian Branch of BMA; Lieut-Colonel, AAMC, 2 AIF, is also Director of Australasian Medical Publishing Company; Member, Board of Management of QM Infectious Diseases Hospital. *Address:* 3 Moonga Road, Toorak, Victoria 3142, Australia.

**MAJOR, Kathleen;** Professor (part-time) of History, University of Nottingham, since 1966; Principal of St Hilda's College, Oxford, 1955-65; Hon. Fellow, St Hilda's College, 1965; *b* 10 April 1906; *er d* of late George Major and Gertrude Blow. *Educ:* various private schools; St Hilda's College, Oxford. Honour School of Modern History, 1928; BLitt 1931. Librarian, St Hilda's College, 1931. Archivist to the Bishop of Lincoln, 1936; Lecturer, 1945, subsequently Reader in Diplomatic in the University of Oxford, until July 1955. Hon. Secretary and General Editor, Lincoln Record Society, 1935-. Hon. DLitt Nottingham, 1961. Member Academic Planning Board for the University of Lancaster, 1962, and of Academic Advisory Cttee, 1964-70. Trustee of the Oxford Preservation Trust, 1961-65; a Vice-President, Royal Historical Society, 1967-. *Publications:* (joint editor with late Canon Foster) Registrum Antiquissimum of the Cathedral Church of Lincoln, vol. IV, 1938, (sole editor) VOLs V-IX, 1940-68. *Acta Stephani Langton,* 1950. Articles in English Hist. Review, Journal of Ecclesiastical Hist., etc. *Recreation:* reading. *Address:* 21 Queensway, Lincoln. *Club:* English-Speaking Union.

**MAJURY, Maj.-Gen. James Herbert Samuel,** MBE 1961; GOC West Midland District, Shrewsbury, since 1970; *b* 26 June 1921; *s* of Rev. Dr M. Majury, BA, DD, and Florence (*née* Stuart), Antrim, N Ireland; *m* 1948, Jeanetta Ann (*née* Le Fleming); two *s*. *Educ:* Royal Academical Institution, Belfast; Trinity College, Dublin. Royal Ulster Rifles, 1940; attached 15 Punjab Regt, 1942; seconded South Waziristan Scouts, 1943-47; Korean War, 1949 (Royal Ulster Rifles); Prisoner of War, Korea, 1950-53 (despatches 1954); Parachute Regiment, 1957-61; Comd Royal Irish Fusiliers, 1961-62; Comd 2nd Infantry Bde, 1965-67; idc 1968. *Recreations:* golf, coursing. *Address:* Nine Mile Water House, Nether Wallop, Stockbridge, Hants. *T:* Broughton, Hants, 279. *Club:* United Service, XL.

**MAKARIOS III, Archbishop;** Archbishop and Ethnarch in Cyprus, Oct. 1950; elected President of Cyprus in 1959 and took up official duties when Cyprus became a Republic in 1960; re-elected, 1968; *b* Panayia, Paphos, Cyprus, 13 Aug. 1913; *s* of a farmer. *Educ:* Kykko Monastery; secondary sch., Nicosia; Schools of Theology and Law, Athens Univ.; School of Theology, Boston Univ., USA (awarded schol. by World Council of Churches). Deacon, 1938; Grad. Theology, 1942; Priest, 1946. Bishop of Kitium, 1948 (elected while still student at Boston). Suggested Pancyprian plebiscite in which Greek Cypriot population voted 97 per cent in favour of union with Greece (Enosis), 1950; attended General Assembly of UNO, New York, 1952; press conferences in USA, London and Athens; visited Athens, and persuaded Greek Government to place Cyprus question before UN, 1954; attended 9th Session General Assembly, New York, when Cyprus was discussed, 1954; supported revolutionary armed struggle led by Nat. Organisation of Cypriot Fighters (EOKA), lasting 1955-59. He attended 1st Afro-Asian Conference, Indonesia, 1955; had meetings with the Secretary of State for the Colonies, Mr Lennox-Boyd (now Lord Boyd of Merton), in Cyprus, and with the Governor of Cyprus, Field-Marshal Sir John Harding (now Lord Harding of Petherton), in which they discussed the future of the Island, without agreement, and as a consequence the Archbishop was exiled to the Seychelles Islands, 1956; visited there by delegates of the British Government, who asked him to accept the proposed Radcliffe Constitution, he rejected it; released, on condition that he should not return to Cyprus, he then went to Athens, 1957; continued to attend General Assemblies, UN, where the Cyprus question was discussed; invited to London for talks, 1959; these resulted in signing of London Agreement (continuation of Zürich Agreement) by Great Britain, Greece and Turkey, under which Cyprus would be declared an Independent Republic (Sir Hugh Foot being the last Governor); returned to Cyprus, March 1959; talks on implementation of the agreements followed, at a five-partite conference, on ceding of bases, etc., in London and in Cyprus, 1960; Cyprus was admitted a member of the Commonwealth, and the Archbishop represented the Island at the Commonwealth Prime Ministers' Conference, March 1961, and subsequently. Represented Cyprus, Conference Non-Aligned Countries, Belgrade, 1961. Has made official visits abroad and was awarded several hon. doctorates by universities. Holds foreign decorations and has been awarded gold medals of cities. *Address:* Presidential Palace, Nicosia, Cyprus.

**MAKGILL, Sir (John) Donald (Alexander Arthur),** 12th Bt of Makgill, *cr* 1627, late Lt Coldstream Guards; RARO; *b* 31 Dec. 1899; *e s* of 11th Bart and Frances Elizabeth (*d* 1947), *e d* of Alexander Innes Grant, of Merchiston, Otago, NZ; *m* 1927, Esther Lilian (marr. diss. 1943), *y d* of late Sir Robert Bromley, 6th Bt; one *d*; *m* 1955, Mrs Maureen Gillington, *y d* of late Lt-Colonel A. T. S. Magan, CMG; *S* father, 1926. *Recreation:* fishing. *Heir: nephew* George Hubbard Makgill [*b* 7 Jan. 1934; *m* 1967, Alison Campbell, *d* of late Neils Max Jensen, Randers, Denmark; twin *s*]. *Address:* The Colonel's Flat, Blairquhan, Maybole, Ayrshire. *Clubs:* Guards; New (Edinburgh).

**MAKIN, Hon. Norman John Oswald;** *b* Petersham, NSW, Australia, 31 March 1889; *s* of John Hulme Makin and Elizabeth Makin; *m* 1932, Ruby Florence Jennings; two *s*. *Educ:* Superior Public Sch., Broken Hill. Member Commonwealth Parliament for Hindmarsh, 1919-46; Member Joint Cttee Public Accounts, 1922-26; Member Select Cttee case ex-Gunner Yates; Temp. Chairman of Cttees, 1923-29; Speaker House of Representatives, Commonwealth of Australia, 1929-32; Member Advisory War Council, 1940; Ministry for Navy and Munitions, Australia, 1941-46; Minister for Aircraft Production, 1945-46. Australian Ambassador to United States, 1946-51. MP for Sturt, 1954-Nov. 1955, for Bonython Division, Dec. 1955-Nov. 1963, Commonwealth Parliament; retired. President Labour Party, 1936; Secretary Federal Parliamentary Labour Party, 1931; Member of Delegation to United Kingdom, King George V Jubilee in 1935 and to King George VI Coronation in 1937; 1st President of Security Council, Jan. 1946, and President, 1947; Leader, Australian Delegation to United Nations; Leader, Australian Delegation to ILO Conference, San Francisco. Alternate Governor, International Bank and International Monetary Fund; Member, Far Eastern Commn, 1947-48. Hon. Doctor of Laws, Univ. of Syracuse. *Publications:* A Progressive Democracy; Federal Labour Leaders, 1961. *Address:* Flat 219, 7 Raymond Grove, Glenelg, SA 5045, Australia.

**MAKINS,** family name of **Baron Sherfield.**

**MAKINS, Sir (Alfred) John (Ware),** Kt, *cr* 1950; General Manager Commercial Union Assurance Co. Ltd, 1938-58, retired; Director, 1958-65; *b* 31 Aug. 1894; *e s* of late Alfred William Bayley Makins, and of Lucy Jane (*née* Arnold); *m* 1927, Barbara Lilla, *surv d* of late Charles and Lilla Copland; one *s* one *d*. *Educ:* St Paul's Sch., West Kensington; abroad. Entire career with Commercial Union Group; Germany and France, 1910-13; Foreign Fire Dept at Head Office, 1919-24; Manager in Japan, 1925; Asst Manager in China, 1926; Asst US Manager at New York, 1927-31; Fire Manager at Head Office, 1931-35; Manager, 1935-38. President, Insurance Institute of London, 1944-45; President, Insurance Orphans' Fund, 1951-52; Chairman: British Insurance Assoc., 1947-48, 1948-49; British Aviation Insurance Co. Ltd, 1949-58; Trade Indemnity Co. Ltd, 1951-58; formerly Member, Cttee of Management, Institute of Cardiology, retd 1969. Served European War, 1914-18. RFA (TF), Captain. *Address:* 9 Hampstead Way, NW11. *T:* 01-455 4710. *Clubs:* Oriental, The Pilgrims, Ends of the Earth.

**MAKINS, Sir John;** *see* Makins, Sir (Alfred) J. (W.).

**MAKINS, Sir Paul (Vivian),** 4th Bt *cr* 1903; Company Director since 1962; *b* 12 Nov. 1913; *yr s* of Sir Paul Makins, 2nd Bt, and Gladys Marie (*d* 1919), *d* of William Vivian, Queen's Gate, London; *S* brother, 1969; *m* 1945, Maisie, *d* of Oswald Pedley and widow of Major C. L. J. Bowen, Irish Guards; no *c*. *Educ:* Eton Coll.; Trinity Coll. Cambridge (MA). Commissioned in Welsh Guards, 1935. Served War of 1939-45: France, 1940; Italy, 1944-45. Dir and Sec. Vitalba Co. Ltd (Gibraltar), 1962-; Dir, Compañia Rentistica SA (Tangier), 1967-. Kt of Magistral Grace, SMO Malta, 1955; JP Gibraltar, 1964-70. *Heir:* none. *Address:* 315 Main Street, Gibraltar. *T:* Gibraltar 5952. *Clubs:* Guards, Pratt's.
*See also Rt Rev. M. G. Bowen.*

**MAKINSON, William;** Member and Chief Executive, Department of Engineering, National Research Development Corporation, since 1965; *b* 11 May 1915; *s* of Joshua Makinson and Martha (*née* Cunliffe); *m* 1952,

Helen Elizabeth Parker; one *s* three *d*. *Educ:* Ashton-in-Makerfield Grammar Sch.; Manchester Univ. Asst Lecturer, Electronics, Manchester Univ., 1935-36; Education Officer, RAF Cranwell, 1936-39; RAE Farnborough, 1939-52; Hon. Squadron-Ldr, RAF, 1943-45; Superintendent, Blind Landing Experimental Unit, 1952-55; Defence Research Policy Staff, 1955-56; Managing Director, General Precision Systems, Ltd, 1956-64; Group Jt Managing Director, Pullin, 1964-65. *Publications:* papers to Royal Aeronautical Society. *Recreation:* golf. *Address:* Tiffany, East Drive, Virginia Water, Surrey. *T:* Wentworth 3490. *Club:* Royal Aero.

**MALALASEKERA, Gunapala Piyasena,** OBE 1949; DLitt (London); Chairman, Ceylon National Council for Higher Education, since 1967; *b* 1899; *m* 1933, Lyle Wijewardene; three *s* three *d*. *Educ:* St John's Coll., Ceylon; University of London. Head of Department of Oriental Languages, University Coll., Colombo, 1927-42; Prof. and Head of Dept of Pali and Buddhist Civilisation, Univ. of Ceylon, 1942-57; Ambassador for Ceylon to USSR, 1957-61; High Commissioner to Canada, 1961-63; Permanent Rep. of Ceylon to UN, 1961-63; High Commissioner to Great Britain, 1963-66. President, World Fellowship of Buddhists, 1950-58. General President Indian Philosophical Congress, 1957. Chief Editor, Encyclopædia of Buddhism, 1956-. Hon. DPhil (Moscow). *Publications:* Dictionary of Pali Proper Names (2 vols), 1938; The Pali Literature of Ceylon; The Buddha and his Teaching, 1957, etc. *Recreations:* reading, meeting people of all types. *Address:* 12 Longden Terrace, Colombo 7, Ceylon. *T:* 85808, 86123.

**MALAMUD, Bernard;** Writer; Member, Division of Literature, Bennington College, since 1961; *b* 26 April 1914; *s* of Max and Bertha Malamud; *m* 1945, Ann de Chiara; one *s* one *d*. *Educ:* The City Coll., New York; Columbia Univ. Taught at Oregon State Coll., 1949-61, while writing first four books. Visiting Lecturer, Harvard Univ., 1966-68. Partisan Review Fiction Fellowship, 1956; Ford Foundation Fellowship, Humanities and Arts Program, 1959-60; Member: National Institute of Arts and Letters, 1964; American Academy of Arts and Sciences, 1967. *Publications:* The Natural, 1952; The Assistant, 1957 (Rosenthal Prize, Daroff Memorial Award, 1958); The Magic Barrel (short stories), 1958 (National Book Award, 1959); A New Life, 1961; Idiots First (short stories), 1963; The Fixer, 1966 (National Book Award and Pulitzer Prize for Fiction, 1967); Pictures of Fidelman, 1969. *Recreations:* reading, music, walking. *Address:* Bennington College, Bennington, Vermont 05201, USA.

**MALAWI, Bishop of,** since 1961; **Rt. Rev. Donald Seymour Arden;** *b* 12 April 1916; *s* of Stanley and Winifred Arden; *m* 1962, Jane Grace Riddle; two *s*. *Educ:* St Peter's Coll., Adelaide; University of Leeds (BA); College Resurrection, Mirfield, Deacon, 1939; Priest, 1940. Curate of: St Catherine's, Hatcham, 1939-40; Nettleden with Potten End, 1941-43; Asst Priest, Pretoria African Mission, 1944-51; Director of Usuthu Mission, Swaziland, 1951-61; Bishop of Nyasaland, 1961 (name of diocese changed, when Nyasaland was granted independence, July 1964). *Recreations:* photography, farming. *Address:* Diocese of Malawi, PO Kasupe, Malawi. *T:* Kasupe 0-1820.

**MALCOLM, Angus (Christian Edward),** CMG 1952; Bursar, The American Museum in Britain, Bath; *b* 6 Oct. 1908; 3rd *s* of late Sir Ian Malcolm, KCMG, of Poltalloch; *m* 1947, Jacqueline Marie (marr. diss. 1967), *o d* of late Maj.-Gen. F. H. Theron, CB, CBE; four *d*. *Educ:* Eton; New Coll., Oxford. Entered Foreign Office, 1933; Madrid, 1936; Washington, 1938; Foreign Office, 1942; Rome, 1944; Mexico City, 1947; Prague, 1949; Foreign Office, 1950; Minister, Vienna, 1953; HM Ambassador and Consul-General, Tunis, 1956-60. Retired, 1961. Rootes Ltd, 1961-67. *Recreation:* sightseeing. *Address:* 14 Royal Crescent, Bath, Somerset. *T:* Bath 26493.

**MALCOLM, Lt-Col Arthur William Alexander,** CVO 1954 (MVO 1949); *b* 31 May 1903; *s* of Major Charles Edward Malcolm, London; *m* 1928, Hester Mary, *d* of S. F. Mann, Lawrenny-Caramut, Victoria, Australia; two *s*. *Educ:* Repton. 2nd Lieut, Welsh Guards, 1924; psc 1938; served War of 1939-45 (POW); Lieut-Colonel, 1945; comd 3rd, 2nd and 1st Bn, Welsh Guards, 1945-49. ADC to Governor of Victoria, Australia, 1926-28. Asst Military Attaché, British Embassy, Paris, 1950-52; retired from Army, 1952. Private Secretary to Governor of South Australia, 1953-55; Queen's Foreign Service Messenger, 1955-68. *Recreations:* golf, shooting, fishing. *Address:* Faraway, Sandwich Bay, Kent. *T:* Sandwich 2054. *Clubs:* Royal St George's Golf, Prince's Golf (Sandwich).

**MALCOLM, Dugald,** CMG 1966; CVO 1964; TD 1945; Ambassador to Luxembourg, 1966-70; *b* 22 Dec. 1917; 2nd *s* of late Maj.-Gen. Sir Neill Malcolm, KCB, DSO, and Lady (Angela) Malcolm; *m* 1957, Patricia Anne Gilbert-Lodge, *widow* of Captain Peter Atkinson-Clark; one *d* one *step d*. *Educ:* Eton; New Coll., Oxford. Served Argyll and Sutherland Highlanders, 1939-45; discharged wounded. Appointed Foreign Office, Oct. 1945. Served Lima, Bonn, Seoul. HM Vice-Marshal of the Diplomatic Corps, 1957-65. Member Queen's Body Guard for Scotland (Royal Company of Archers). *Address:* c/o Foreign and Commonwealth Office, SW1. *Club:* Travellers'.

**MALCOLM of Poltalloch, Lieut-Colonel George Ian,** DL, JP; 18th Laird and Hereditary Chief of the Clan; farmer; Breeder of PB Arabs; *b* 26 April 1903; *e s* of Sir Ian Malcolm, KCMG (*d* 1944) and Jeanne Marie (decd), *o c* of Edward Langtry, Jersey, and Emily le Breton, afterwards Lady de Bathe; *m* 1st, 1929, Enid Sybil, *d* of Maj.-Gen. H. S. Gaskell, CB, DSO (marr. diss. 1944); one *s* one *d*; 2nd, 1946, Muriel Hobhouse, BEM, *d* of Ernest Presgrave Hebblethwaite. *Educ:* Eton; RMC Sandhurst. Joined Argyll and Sutherland Highlanders, 1923; ADC (India), 1927-28; Adjutant 8th (Argyllshire) Bn, 1933-37; Lieut-Col, 1943; Comd 8th Bn in Austria, 1945-46 (Bn disbanded); retired, 1947. Service in India, Egypt, Sudan, Palestine (despatches). War of 1939-45: with 1st Bn A and SH, on Staff, and in Combined Operations in Middle East and Central Pacific; Staff Coll., Haifa, 1940. Member Royal Company of Archers (Queen's Body Guard for Scotland), 1935. Producer: Vienna Tattoo, 1946; Kelvin Hall, 1948; Edinburgh Tattoo, 1949-50-51; London District Tattoo, 1950-51; Organizer of Clan Gathering at Festival of Britain, 1951; Producer, Royal Tournament, 1953, Stirling Castle Tattoo, 1953; The Queen's Volunteers, Kelvin Hall, 1958; Cowal Military Display, 1959-61. Chm. Argyll T&AFA, 1957-67; Rep. Chm. Scotland Council of T&AFA, 1961-66; Hon. Colonel Glasgow Univ. OTC, 1962-67. Dir. Royal Highland Agricultural Soc., 1955-66; Mem. Scot. US Museum Adv. Cttee, 1955; Gen. Commr Income Tax, Mid-Argyll Division, 1960; Mem., Exec. Cttee, Nat. Army

Museum, 1966. Lay Reader, Diocese of Argyll; Patron of living of Holy Trinity, Lamorbey. Chm. N Argyll Scout Cttee. FSA Scotland 1942. DL 1948, JP 1949, Vice-Lieutenant 1958, Argyll. *Publications:* History of the Argyll and Sutherland Highlanders, 1794-1949, 1950; Argylls in Korea, 1952; Historical Record of the British Legion, Scotland, 1959; Argyllshire Highlanders, 1860-1960, 1960; articles and verse in Punch, The Field, Blackwood's Magazine, and other periodicals; songs. *Recreations:* shooting, military history. *Heir: s* Robin Neill Lochnell Malcolm, *b* 1934. *Address:* Duntrune Castle, Lochgilphead, Argyll. *T:* Kilmartin 216 and 203; 6 Malta Terrace, Edinburgh. *T:* 031-332 3499. *Clubs:* Naval and Military; New (Edinburgh); Royal Scottish Automobile (Glasgow); Royal Highland Yacht (Oban) (Commodore 1968-70); Western Meeting (Ayr).

**MALCOLM, George (John),** CBE 1965; musician; *b* London, 28 Feb. 1917; *o s* of George Hope Malcolm, Edinburgh, and Johanna Malcolm. *Educ:* Wimbledon Coll.; Balliol Coll., Oxford (Scholar); Royal College of Music (Scholar). MA, BMus (Oxon). Served in RAFVR, 1940-46. Master of the Cathedral Music, Westminster Cathedral, 1947-59, training unique boys' choir for which Benjamin Britten wrote Missa Brevis, Op. 63. Now mainly known as harpsichordist (making frequent concert tours), and as conductor. Cobbett Medal, Worshipful Company of Musicians, 1960; Hon. RAM, 1961; Hon. Fellow, Balliol Coll., Oxford, 1966. Knight of the Order of St Gregory the Great, 1970. *Address:* 38 Cheyne Walk, SW3. *T:* 01-352 5381. *Club:* Athenæum.

**MALCOLM, Prof. John Laurence;** Regius Professor of Physiology, University of Aberdeen, since 1959; *b* 28 Aug. 1913; *s* of late Professor J. Malcolm, Dunedin, New Zealand; *m* 1st, 1940, Sylvia Bramston (*d* 1958), *d* of late Basil B. Hooper, Auckland, New Zealand; one *s* one *d*; 2nd, 1961, Margaret Irvine Simpson (*d* 1967), *d* of late Colonel J. C. Simpson, Skene, Aberdeenshire. *Publications:* contributions to the Proceedings of Royal Society, Journal of Physiology, Journal of Neuro-physiology. *Address:* House of Kinmundy, Kingswells, Aberdeenshire. *Club:* Royal Northern (Aberdeen).

**MALCOLM, Kenneth Robert,** CBE 1964; Assistant Under-Secretary of State, Department of Health and Social Security, since 1969; *b* 17 Dec. 1908; 2nd *s* of Ronald Malcolm, Walton Manor, Walton-on-the Hill, Surrey; *m* 1950, Iris Lilian Knowles; two *s* one *d*. *Educ:* Eton College; New College, Oxford. Indian Civil Service, 1932-47; Home Civil Service (Ministry of National Insurance, subseq. Dept of Health and Social Security), 1947-. *Address:* Ferndale, Dry Arch Road, Sunningdale, Ascot, Berks. *T:* Ascot 22946. *Club:* Travellers'.

**MALCOLM, Sir Michael Albert James,** of Balbedie, Innertiel and Lochore, 10th Bt, *cr* 1665; Director of the Lothian Coal Co. Ltd, until Nationalisation; *b* 9 May 1898; *s* of 9th Bt and Evelyn Alberta (*d* 1947), 3rd *d* of Albert George Sandeman, and *g d* of Viscount de Moncorvo; *S* father, 1927; *m* 1st, 1918, Hon. Geraldine M. Digby (marr. diss. 1946; she *d* 1965), *d* of 10th Baron Digby; one *s* two *d*; 2nd, 1947, Kathleen Melvin, *d* of late G. J. Gawthorne, Commander, RN. *Educ:* Eton. Major, Scots Guards; served European War, 1914-18 (severely wounded); ADC to GOC in C, Scottish Command, 1919-23; ADC to Lord High Commissioner, General Assembly of Church of Scotland, 1924-25; employed War Office in AG Dept, 1940-41; MS Branch, 1941-42 and 1945; PID Foreign Office, 1944. Member of Royal Company of Archers (HM Body Guard for Scotland). Member: Cttees Earl Haig Fund (Scottish Branch); The Economic League, Central Council; Chairman East of Scotland Sub-Area; Standing Council of Baronetage. *Heir: s* David Peter Michael Malcolm, CA, Major, Scots Guards [*b* 7 July 1919; *m* 1959, Hermione, *d* of Sir David Home, Bt, *qv*; one *d*]. *Address:* Milton Lodge, North Berwick, East Lothian. *Clubs:* Guards; New (Edinburgh).

**MALCOLMSON, Kenneth Forbes,** MA, BMus (Oxon), FRCO; Precentor and Director of Music, Eton College, since 1956; *b* 29 April, 1911. Organ Scholar, Exeter Coll., Oxford, 1931-35; Commissioner, Royal School of Church Music, 1935-36; Temporary Organist, St Alban's Cathedral, 1936-37; Organist, Halifax Parish Church, 1937-38; Organist and Master of the Music, Newcastle Cathedral, 1938-55. *Recreations:* tennis, squash, swimming, walking. *Address:* 3 Savile House, Eton College, Windsor. *T:* Windsor 65411.

**MALDEN;** *see* Scott-Malden.

**MALE, Peter John Ellison,** CMG 1967; MC 1945; Minister, British High Commission, New Delhi, since 1970; *b* 22 Aug. 1920; *s* of H. J. G. Male and Mrs E. A. Male; *m* 1947, Patricia Janet Payne; five *s* two *d*. *Educ:* Merchant Taylors' Sch.; Emmanuel Coll., Cambridge. HM Forces, 1940-45. HM Foreign Service (now HM Diplomatic Service), 1946; served in: Damascus, 1947-49; Wahnerheide, 1949-53; London, 1953-55; Guatemala City, 1955-57; Washington, 1957-60; London, 1960-62; Oslo, 1962-66; Bonn, 1966-70. *Recreations:* gadgets, gardening. *Address:* c/o Foreign and Commonwealth Office, SW1; Swinley Edge, South Ascot, Berks. *Club:* Oxford and Cambridge University.

**MALENKOV, Georgi Maximilianovich;** Manager of Ust-Kamenogorsk Hydro-Electric Station, since 1957; *b* Orenburg, 1901; *m* 1st (marr. diss.); 2nd, Elena Khrushcheva. *Educ:* Moscow Higher Technical Coll. Member of the Communist Party, 1920-; Member of Organisation Bureau of Central Cttee of the Communist Party, 1934; Member Cttee for State Defence, 1941; Member Cttee for Economic Rehabilitation of Liberated Districts, 1943; Dep.-Chairman, Council of Ministers, 1946; Dep.-Chairman, Council of Ministers of the Soviet Union, 1955-57 (Dep.-Chairman, 1946, Chairman, 1953-55); Minister of Electric Power Stations, 1955-57. Holds title Hero of Socialist Labour, Hammer and Sickle Gold Medal, Order of Lenin (twice). *Address:* The Hydro-Electric Station, Ust-Kamenogorsk, Kazakh SSR, USSR.

**MALET, Colonel Sir Edward William St Lo,** 8th Bt, *cr* 1791; OBE 1953; 8th King's Royal Irish Hussars; retired; *b* 27 Nov. 1908; *o s* of Sir Harry Charles Malet, DSO, OBE, 7th Bt and Mildred Laura (*d* 1951), *d* of Captain H. S. Swiney, Gensing House, St Leonards; *S* father, 1931; *m* 1935, Baroness Benedicta Maasburg, *e d* of Baron William von Maasburg; one *s* two *d*. *Educ:* Dover Coll.; Christ Church, Oxford. BA. Dep.-Chief Civil Affairs Officer, HQ, British Troops, Egypt, 1953-55. President Bridgwater Division, Conservative Assoc., 1959. High Sheriff of Somerset, 1966. *Heir: s* Harry Douglas St Lo Malet, late Lieut, The Queen's Royal Irish Hussars, now Special Reserve [*b* 26 Oct. 1936; *m* 1967, Julia Harper, Perth, WA. *Educ:* Downside; Trinity Coll., Oxford]. *Address:* Chargot, Washford, Somerset. *Club:* Cavalry.

**MALHERBE, Ernst G.,** MA, PhD; Hon. LLD Universities of: Cambridge, Queen's (Kingston, Ont), Melbourne, McGill, Capetown, Rhodes, Natal, Witwatersrand; Principal and Vice-Chancellor, University of Natal, Pietermaritzburg and Durban, 1946-65; *b* OFS, 8 Nov. 1895; *s* of late Rev. E. G. Malherbe, Villiersdorp, Cape Province, French Huguenot descent; *m* Janie A., *d* of Rev. Paul Nel, Moderator of Dutch Reformed Church, Transvaal; three *s* one *d*. *Educ:* Stellenbosch Univ., Stellenbosch, CP (BA, Hons, MA in Philosophy); Columbia Univ., New York (MA and PhD in Education). Union Government Scholarship for 2 years to study Education overseas; Oxford, The Hague, Amsterdam, Germany, etc.; 3 years in succession H. B. Webb Research Scholar for overseas Research in Educational Administration; Fellow of Teachers Coll., Columbia Univ., 1923-34; Chalmers Memorial Prize for Essay on Educational Administration, 1923; invited as special SA representative to Centenary meeting of British Assoc., London, 1931; teacher at Cape Town Training Coll.; Lecturer in Educational Psychology, University of Stellenbosch; Senior Lecturer in Education, University of Cape Town, 5 years; Chief Investigator Education Section Carnegie Poor White Commission of Research, 1928-32; Member of Government Commission to investigate Native Education in South Africa, 1935; Director, National Bureau of Educational and Social Research for SA, 1929-39; Sec. Government Commission on Medical Training in S Africa, 1938. Director of Census and Statistics for Union of South Africa, 1939-40; (Lieut-Col) Director of Military Intelligence, S African Army and Director Army Education Services, 1940-45. Member of Social and Economic Planning Council, 1946-50; of National Council for Social Research, 1945-50; Chairman National War Histories Cttee, 1945-49; President SA Assoc. for the Advancement of Science, 1950-51; President SA Institute of Race Relations, 1966-67. *Publications:* Education in S Africa, 1652-1922, 1925; Chapters on S Africa in Year-books of Education, 1932-56; Education and the Poor White, 1929; articles in Chambers's Encyclopædia; numerous articles in Educational and Scientific Journals; Carnegie Commmission's Poor White Report on Education, 1932; Education in a Changing Empire, 1932, Educational Adaptations in a Changing Society (Editor), 1937; Entrance Age of University Students in Relation to Success, 1938; Whither Matric?, 1938; Educational and Social Research in SA, 1939; The Bilingual School, 1943; Race Attitudes and Education, 1946; Our Universities and the Advancement of Science, 1951; The Autonomy of our Universities and Apartheid, 1957; Education for Leadership in Africa, 1960; Problems of School Medium in a Bilingual Country, 1962; Into the 70's: Education and the Development of South Africa's Human Resources, 1966; The Need for Dialogue, 1967; The Nemesis of Docility, 1968; Bantu Manpower and Education, 1969. *Recreations:* golf, swimming; Full Blue, Stellenbosch University; Half Blue, Capetown University; captained Hockey Team representing CP at inter-provincial tournament. *Address:* By-die-See, Salt Rock, Umhlali, Natal, South Africa. *Club:* Durban (Durban).

**MALIK, Bidhubhusan;** *b* 11 Jan. 1895; *s* of Raibahadur Chandrasekhar Malik, Chief Judge, Benares State; *m* 1916, Leelabati, *d* of Saratkumar Mitra, Calcutta; two *s*. *Educ:* Central Hindu Coll., Benares (graduated, 1917); Ewing Christian Coll. (MA in Economics, 1919); Allahabad Univ. (LLB 1919); LLD (*hc*), Saugur Univ. Vakil, Allahabad High Court, 1919; started practice in the civil courts in Benares; left for England in Sept. 1922; called to Bar, Lincoln's Inn, 1923; joined Allahabad High Court Bar, 1924; Member of Judicial Cttee of Benares State, 1941; Special Counsel for Income Tax Dept, 1943; Judge, Allahabad High Court, 1944; Chief Justice, High Court, Allahabad, Dec. 1947; thereafter Chief Justice, UP, from 26 July 1948-55, excepting 3 March-1 May 1949, when acted as Governor, Uttar Pradesh. Commissioner for Linguistic Minorities in India, 1957-62. Member: Constitutional Commission for the Federation of Malaya, 1956-57; Air Transport Council of India, 1955-62; National Integration Commission. Constitutional Adviser to Mr Jomo Kenyatta and the Kenya African National Union, Lancaster House Conference, London, 1962; Constitutional Expert for Republic of Congo appointed by UNO, Aug.-Oct. 1962; Constitutional Adviser to Kenya Government, Kenya Independence Conference, Lancaster House, Sept.-Oct. 1963; Adviser, Mauritius Constitutional Conference, London, Sept. 1965. Vice-Chancellor, Calcutta Univ., 1962-68. President: Harijan Ashram, Allahabad, 1968-; Jagat Iaran Girls' Intermediate Coll., Allahabad, 1968. *Recreation:* golf. *Address:* 23 Muir Road, Allahabad, India.

**MALIK, Jacob Alexandrovich;** Order of Lenin, 1944 and 1945; Soviet Deputy Foreign Minister, 1946-53, and since 1960; *b* in Ukraine, 1906; *m*; one *s* one *d* (and one *s* decd). *Educ:* University of Kharkov; Soviet Institute for Foreign Affairs, Moscow; Dep. Chief, Press Dept, Ministry of Foreign Affairs, 1937; Counsellor, 1939, Ambassador, 1942-45, at Tokyo. Political Adviser, Allied Council for Japan, 1946; Permanent Representative of USSR to United Nations, 1948-52; Soviet Ambassador to the Court of St James's, 1953-60. *Address:* The Kremlin, Moscow, USSR.

**MALIK, Sardar Hardit Singh,** CIE 1941; OBE 1938; Indian Diplomat, retired, 1957; *b* 23 Nov. 1894; *s* of Malik Mohan Singh and Lajanwanti; *m* 1919, Prakash; one *s* two *d*. *Educ:* Eastbourne Coll.; Balliol Coll., Oxford, England. BA Hons in Mod. Hist., 1915. Served with French Army on Western Front, 1916. Fighter Pilot in RFC, 1917-18 (wounded in air combat over France, 1917); served in RAF, France, Italy and in home defence of UK. Entered ICS; Asst Commissioner, Punjab, 1922-23; Deputy Commissioner, Punjab, 1924-30; Dep. Trade Commissioner, London and Hamburg, 1931-34; Dep. Secretary Government of India, Commerce Dept, 1934-36; Joint Secretary, Government of India, Commerce Dept, 1937; Indian Government Trade Commissioner, New York, 1938; Delegate to International Cotton Conf., Washington, 1939, International Labour Office Conf., New York, 1940, UN Food Conf., Hotsprings, Virginia, 1943, and UN Relief Conf., Atlantic City, USA, 1943. Prime Minister, Patiala, 1944-47. Leader Indian States Industrial Delegation to UK and USA, 1945-46; represented Government of India at First and Second Sessions of Prep. Cttee of UN Conf. on Trade and Employment in London, Nov. 1946, and Geneva, April 1947, respectively. Leader Indian Delegation to UN Conf. on Trade and Employment, Havana, Nov. 1947; High Commissioner for India in Canada, 1947-49; Indian Ambassador to France, 1949-56, also Indian Minister to Norway, 1950-56. President, 3rd General Assembly of International Civil Aviation Organisation, Montreal, 1949; Leader of Indian Delegation to UN General Assembly,

Paris, 1952. Grand Officier, Légion d'Honneur, 1954. *Recreations:* golf, cricket and tennis. *Address:* 28 Golf Links, New Delhi. *Clubs:* Gulmarg (Kashmir); Imperial Gymkhana (New Delhi); Delhi Golf; Pine Valley Golf (USA).

**MALIM, Rear-Adm. Nigel Hugh,** MVO 1960; FIMechE; Chief Staff Officer Technical to the Commander-in-Chief, Western Fleet, since 1969; *b* 5 April 1919; *s* of late John Malim, Pebmarsh, and Brenda Malim; *m* 1944, Moonyeen, *d* of late William and Winefride Maynard; two *s* one *d*. *Educ:* Weymouth Coll.; RNEC Keyham. Cadet, RN, 1936; HMS Manchester, 1940-41; HMS Nofolk, 1942; RNC Greenwich, 1943-45; HMS Jamaica, 1945-47; Staff of RNEC, 1948-50; Admty, 1951-54; HMS Triumph, 1954-56; Admty, 1956-58; HM Yacht Britannia, 1958-60; District Overseer, Scotland, 1960-62; Asst, and later Dep., Dir Marine Engrg, 1962-65; idc 1966; Captain, RNEC Manadon, 1967-69. *Recreations:* offshore racing and cruising. *Address:* Trinity House, HM Dockyard, Portsmouth. *Clubs:* Royal Ocean Racing, Royal Naval Sailing Association.

**MALIN, Peter;** *see* Conner, Rearden.

**MALIPIERO, G. Francesco;** composer; Professor of History of Music at University of Padua; *b* Venice, 18 March 1882. *Educ:* under Stefan Stocker, Vienna, and Enrico Bossi, Venice. Formerly Director of the Conservatorio Musicale, Venice. Member American Academy Arts and Letters, New York. Member Royal Flemish Academy of Belgium, Brussels. Works for theatre: L'Orfeide, Tre Commedie Goldoniane, Filomelae l'Infatuato, Torneo Notturno, Pirandello's Favola del Figlio Cambiato, Shakespeare's Julius Cæsar and Antony and Cleopatra, Ecuba, La Vita è Sogno, I Capricci di Callot, Allegra Brigata, Mondi celesti e infernali, Vergilii Aeneis, Don Giovanni, as operas, etc. Symphonic works: 3 series of Impressioni dal Vero, Pause del Silenzio, Concerti, 11 Symphonies, Fantasie Concertanti, Dialoghi; 6 piano concertos; 2 violin concertos; Eight Quartets (first one winner of Coolidge Prize, 1920) Sonate a tre, a quattro, a cinque; great deal of piano music and songs; edited and published himself complete works of Claudio Monteverdi and Antonio Vivaldi. Written several books on musical subjects. *Relevant publication:* L'Opera di Gian Francesco Malipiero. *Address:* Asolo, Treviso, Italy.

**MALKIN, H(arold) Jordan,** CBE 1964; Director of Postgraduate Studies, Royal College of Obstetricians and Gynæcologists, since 1967; *b* 27 April 1898; *s* of late Sydney and Edith Jordan Malkin (*née* Stormer); *m* 1932, Theresa Joyce Ferris Bearder, *d* of late Cyril Horner Bearder and of Mrs Dora Christiana Bearder, Abingdon, Berks; two *d*. *Educ:* Epworth Coll.; University Coll. and Hospital, London. Royal Field Artillery, 1916-19. University Coll., University Coll. Hospital, 1916 and 1919-24. Consultant Obstetrician and Gynæcologist, Nottingham, 1928-67. Rockefeller Travelling Fellowship, 1926. MD London, 1926; FRCSEd 1925; FRCOG 1938. *Address:* 19 Cavendish Crescent South, The Park, Nottingham. *T:* Nottingham 47015; Ivy Cottage, Wargrave Road, Henley-on-Thames, Oxon. *T:* Wargrave 2453. *Club:* Oriental.

**MALLABAR, Sir John (Frederick),** Kt 1969; FCA; Senior Partner, J. F. Mallabar & Co., Chartered Accountants, since 1929; Director: David Brown Corporation Ltd; Chubb & Son Ltd, and of other companies; *b* 19 July 1900; *e s* of Herbert John Mallabar and Gertrude Mallabar, *d* of Hugh Jones, Barrow; *m* 1st, 1931, Henrietta, *d* of George Goodwin-Norris; 2nd, 1949, Annie Emily (Pat), *widow* of Richard Howard Ford, Bodweni, Merionethshire; no *c*. *Educ:* Sunbury House Sch.; King's Coll., London. Served European War, 1914-18: Inns of Court Regt and 5th KRRC, 1918-19. Financial Adviser, National Farmers' Union. An Underwriting Member of Lloyds. Chm., Harland and Wolff Ltd, 1966-70. Chm., Cttee on Govt Industrial Establishments, 1968-. *Recreations:* stalking, salmon fishing. *Address:* 39 Arlington House, St James's, SW1; (office) 15 King Street, St James's, SW1. *Clubs:* Royal Thames Yacht, Flyfishers'.

**MALLABY, Sir (Howard) George (Charles),** KCMG 1958 (CMG 1953); OBE 1945; *b* 17 Feb. 1902; *s* of William Calthorpe Mallaby and Katharine Mary Frances Miller; *m* 1955, Elizabeth Greenwood Locker (*née* Brooke), one *step s* two *step d*. *Educ:* Radley Coll.; Merton Coll., Oxford. BA 1923; MA 1935; MA (Cantab) 1965; Asst Master Clifton Coll., 1923-24; Diocesan Coll., Rondebosch, S Africa, 1926; Assistant Master and House Master, S Edward's Sch., Oxford, 1924-26 and 1927-35; Headmaster, St Bees Sch., Cumberland, 1935-38; District Commissioner for the Special Area of West Cumberland, 1938-39; Dep. Regional Transport Commissioner for North Western Region, 1939-40; Captain, Gen. List, 1940; Major, 1941; Lieut-Col, 1943; Colonel, 1945; served in Military Secretariat of War Cabinet, 1942-45; US Legion of Merit (Degree of Officer), 1946. Secretary, National Trust, 1945-46; Asst Secretary, Ministry of Defence, 1946-48; Secretary-General Brussels Treaty Defence Organisation, 1948-50; Under Secretary, Cabinet Office, 1950-54; Secretary, War Council and Council of Ministers, Kenya, 1954; Dep. Secretary, University Grants Cttee, 1955-57; High Commissioner for the United Kingdom in New Zealand, 1957-59; First Civil Service Commissioner, 1959-64, retired. Chairman of Council of Radley Coll., 1952-57. Governor: St Edward's Sch.; Bedford Coll., London Univ.; Chairman, Cttee on the Staffing of Local Government, 1967. Extraordinary Fellow, Churchill Coll., Cambridge, 1964-69. *Publications:* Wordsworth (Extracts from the Prelude with other Poems), 1932; Wordsworth: A Tribute, 1950; From My Level, 1965; (ed) Poems by William Wordsworth, 1970. *Address:* Down The Lane, Chevington, W Suffolk. *T:* Chevington 308. *Club:* Army and Navy.

**MALLALIEU, Edward Lancelot,** QC 1951; MP (Lab) Brigg Division of Lincolnshire since 1948; Barrister-at-law; Governor Royal Agricultural Society of England; *b* 14 March 1905; *s* of County Alderman F. W. Mallalieu, MP, JP; *m* 1934, Betty Margaret Oxley, *d* of Dr Pride, late of Bridlington, *g d* of late J. W. Oxley of Leeds; one *s* two *d*. *Educ:* Dragon Sch., Oxford; Cheltenham Coll.; Trinity Coll., Oxford. MA 1930; called Bar, Inner Temple, 1928; NE Circuit; MP (L) Colne Valley, Yorks, 1931-35; Parliamentary Private Secretary to Rt Hon. Sir Donald Maclean, President Board of Education, 1931-32. Sometime Farmer in Co. Wicklow, and Director of Farming, College of St Columba; Member Exec., Inter-Parliamentary Union (Geneva), Chairman British Group; Secretary-General, World Assoc. of World Federalists, The Hague (Parliamentary Adviser, 1966); Chairman, Franco-British Parliamentary Relations Cttee; Co-Chairman, Channel Tunnel Parliamentary Cttee. Hon. Vice-President, Parliamentary Group for World

Government; Mem., Speaker's Panel of Chairmen, 1964. A Director of the French Hospital, Rochester. Second Church Estates Comr, 1965-70. Chevalier, Legion of Honour, 1957. *Address:* 40 Westminster Gardens, Marsham Street, SW1. *Clubs:* Royal Cruising, Farmers'.

*See also J. P. W. Mallalieu.*

**MALLALIEU, Joseph Percival William;** MP (Lab) Huddersfield, 1945-50, East Division of Huddersfield, since 1950; *b* 18 June 1908; 3rd *s* of late County Alderman F. W. Mallalieu, MP; *m* 1945, Harriet Rita Riddle Tinn; one *s* one *d.* *Educ:* Dragon Sch., Oxford; Cheltenham; Trinity Coll., Oxford; University of Chicago. Oxford Rugger Blue, 1927; President Oxford Union, 1930; Commonwealth Fellow, University of Chicago, 1930-32; worked on London newspapers, 1933-41; served in Royal Navy, 1942-45. pps to Under-Sec. of State for Air, 1945-46, to Minister of Food, 1946-49; Under-Secretary of State for Defence (Royal Navy), 1964-66; Minister: of Defence (Royal Navy), 1966-67; of State, Board of Trade, 1967-68, Min. of Technology, 1968-69. *Publications:* Rats, 1941; Passed to You, Please!, 1942; Very Ordinary Seaman, 1944; Sporting Days, 1955; Extraordinary Seaman, 1957; Very Ordinary Sportsman, 1957. *Recreations:* walking, gardening; watching Huddersfield Town. *Address:* Village Farm, Boarstall, Aylesbury, Bucks. *Club:* Press.

*See also E. L. Mallalieu.*

**MALLAM, Lieut-Colonel Rev. George Leslie,** CSI 1947; CIE 1943; *b* 13 Dec. 1895; *o s* of late George Mallam, Parkstone, Dorset; *m* 1st, 1934, Constance Marie (KIH, silver) (*d* 1944), *d* of late Dr E. J. W. Carruthers; two *s*; 2nd, 1950, Mary Sophronia, *o d* of Canon Cory, St Audrey's, Wilden; one *d.* *Educ:* Malvern. Commissioned IA, 1916; joined Political Dept, 1921; Counsellor British Legation, Kabul, Afghanistan, 1932. Financial Secretary to Government North-West Frontier Province, 1939; then Chief Secretary, Planning and Development Comr and Revenue and Divisional Comr. Called to Bar, Gray's Inn, 1926. Deacon, 1949; Priest, 1950; Vicar of Eckington, near Pershore, Worcs, 1952-65, retired 1965. *Address:* Abbey Place, Defford Road, Pershore, Worcs. *T:* Pershore 2223.

**MALLEN, Sir Leonard (Ross),** Kt 1967; OBE 1958; JP (S Australia); Medical Practitioner; *b* 18 Dec. 1902; *m* 1926, Eunice M. Pitcher; one *d.* *Educ:* St Peter's Coll., Adelaide; University of Adelaide. MB, BS, 1925. Member Fed. Council, BMA in Australia, 1948-62; Member Fed. Council AMA, 1962-67; Chairman Fed. Assembly, AMA, 1962-67; Chairman, Pharmaceutical Benefits Advisory Cttee (Australia), 1957-; President, World Medical Assoc., 1968-69 (Member Council, 1951-61; Chairman Council, 1958-60); Fellow, AMA, 1964; FRACGP, 1963. *Recreations:* golf, tennis. *Address:* 36 Greenwood Grove, Urrbrae Park, SA 5064, Australia. *T:* 79-3700. *Clubs:* Naval, Military and Air Force of S Australia, Adelaide (both Adelaide).

**MALLESON, Lady Constance; (Colette O'Niel);** *b* Castlewellan, County Down, 1895; *y d* of 5th Earl Annesley and his cousin, Priscilla Cecilia Armytage Moore, Arnmore, Co. Cavan; *m* 1915, W. Miles Malleson, (from whom she obtained a divorce, 1923; he *d* 1969). *Educ:* Dresden; Paris; RADA, London. Professional appearances: lead in Le monde ou l'on s'ennui, Queen's; lead in L'Enfant Prodigue, Kingsway; The Quaker Widow in Abraham Lincoln, Lyceum; lead in Orphans of the Storm, Lyceum; Helen, in Euripides' The Trojan Women; lead in Masefield's The Faithful (Stage Society); leading lady at various Repertory theatres and at Scala; lead in Miles Malleson's Young Heaven, Hull and London, 1925; toured S Africa, the Rhodesias, Egypt, Palestine, with Dame Sybil Thorndike and Sir Lewis Casson; leading lady on Sir Frank Benson's Farewell Tour, playing Portia, Olivia, Kate Hardcastle, Lady Teazle, Lydia Languish. Member: Howard League for Penal Reform; Summerhill Society; Private Libraries Assoc.; Anti-Slavery Society; Society for the Preservation of Ancient Buildings; Suffolk Preservation Society; National Trust. Worked for English Mental Hospital Reform, and for British Army Blood Supply Depot (1939); lectured in Sweden, 1936-37, and in Finland, 1941 and 1946; volunteered for service in Finland during Russian Invasion, 1939-40. *Publications:* After Ten Years, 1931; Fear in the Heart, 1936; In the North: Autobiographical Fragments, in Norway, Sweden and Finland, 1936-46, 1947; Queen Margaret of Norway (trans. from Norwegian of Trygve Kielland's Historical play), 1954; (ed) As the Sight is Bent: the Unfinished Autobiography of Mabel M. Annesley, 1964; Contrib. to Bertrand Russell: Philosopher of the Century, 1967. Contrib. to Guardian, The Countryman, Helsingin Sanomat. *Address:* Lavenham, Suffolk.

**MALLESON, Comdr Wilfrid St Aubyn,** VC 1915; RN, retired; *m* 1927, Cecil Mary Collinson. Served Dardanelles, 1914-15 (VC), during landing of Expeditionary Force swam with line from lighter to lighter; retired list, 1941.

**MALLET, Hooper Pelgue;** Commodore P&OSN Company, 1960-61, retired; *b* 4 June 1901; *s* of Wesley John Mallet and Harriet Anley; *m* 1932, Ethel Margaret Stewart, Launceston, Tasmania; no *c.* *Educ:* Oxenford House Sch., Jersey; HMS Worcester. Royal Naval Reserve, 1918-19; joined P&OSN Co., 1919. *Recreations:* chess, bowls. *Address:* 9 Selworthy Avenue, Melbourne, Vic 3167, Australia.

**MALLET, Sir Ivo;** *see* Mallet, Sir W. I.

**MALLET, Sir (William) Ivo,** GBE 1960; KCMG 1951 (CMG 1945); retired as Ambassador to Spain (1954-60); *b* 7 April 1900; *yr s* of late Sir Charles Mallet; *m* 1929, Marie-Angèle, *d* of Joseph Wierusz-Kowalski; two *s* one *d.* *Educ:* Harrow; Balliol Coll., Oxford. Entered Diplomatic Service, 1925. Served in Constantinople, Angora, London, Berlin, Rome; Asst Private Secretary to Secretary of State for Foreign Affairs, 1938-41; Acting Counsellor in FO, 1941; Counsellor, 1943; Consul-General, Tangier, 1946; Asst Under-Secretary, Foreign Office, 1949; HM Ambassador, Belgrade, 1951. *Address:* Chalet La Combe, Rossinière, Vaud, Switzerland.

**MALLETT, Richard;** Film Critic for Punch, since 1938; *b* 3 April 1910; *s* of Alfred Edward Mallett and Bertha Ann Richards. *Educ:* Lowestoft Secondary Sch. Contributor to Punch since 1928; Evening News editorial staff, July 1931-Aug. 1934; Punch editorial staff, 1937-; Acting Assistant Editor during much of War of 1939-45; member of Punch Table, 1945-. *Publications:* Doggerel's Dictionary, 1946; Amos Intolerable, 1948; Literary Upshots, 1951. *Recreation:* sketching. *Address:* 103 Cliffords Inn, EC4. *T:* 01-405 3641. *Clubs:* Press, Savage.

**MALLEY, Cecil Patrick;** Aural Surgeon St Mary's Hospital for Women and Children, Plaistow, Acton Hospital and Hounslow Hospital; Surgeon Metropolitan Ear, Nose and Throat Hospital, Fitzroy Square; *b*

Castlebar, Co. Mayo, 5 April 1902; *s* of Luke Malley and Marrion Kearney; *m*; two *s* one *d*. *Educ:* O'Connell's Schools; University College, Dublin. MB, BCh, BAO, 1925; FRCS 1933; FICS. Late Resident Surgical Officer St Mary's Hospital, Plaistow; House Surgeon All Saints Hosp.; Aural Registrar Charing Cross Hosp.; Registrar Golden Square Hosp.; Senior Clinical Asst Metropolitan Ear, Nose and Throat Hospital; late Clinical Assistant Ear, Nose and Throat Dept, West London Hospital. *Publications:* Acute Mastoiditis, Otalgia Charing Cross Journal, Section on Larynx in Pye's Surgical Handicraft. *Recreations:* golf, yachting. *Address:* 74 Redcliffe Gardens, SW10. *Clubs:* Royal Thames Yacht, National University.

**MALLINSON, Sir Paul;** *see* Mallinson, Sir W. P.

**MALLINSON, Col Sir Stuart Sidney,** Kt 1954; CBE 1938; DSO 1918; MC; DL; Hon. President, William Mallinson & Sons, Ltd, London (Director, 1912-44, Chairman and Managing Director, 1944-62); President, Timber Research and Development Association, since 1963; Director, Eastern Electricity Board, 1954; *b* 1888; *s* of Sir Wm Mallinson, 1st Bt; *m* 1916, Marjorie Gray, CBE 1960 (*d* 1969), *d* of late Rev. Alfred Soothill; two *s* (and one *s* killed in action, 1944, one *d* decd). *Educ:* Ashville Coll., Harrogate; Leys Sch., Cambridge. Entered the firm of Wm Mallinson & Sons, Ltd, 1907; joined HAC Aug. 1914; France, Sept. 1914; commissioned April 1915; MC June 1916; transferred to RE as Captain, Sept. 1916; Major, Dec. 1916; Lt-Col, March 1917; (DSO; despatches three times); Officier du Mérite Agricole, 1918; Hon. Colonel 28th Essex AA, 1937-45; Hon. Colonel 563 Regt (Essex) TA, RA, 1947-55; Hon. Colonel 517 Regt (5th Essex) RA, TA, 1955-57. Governor Leys Sch., 1920; Governor: St Felix Sch., Southwold; Chigwell Sch.; Ashville Coll., Harrogate; President, National Sunday School Union, 1923-24; Vice-Pres., English-Speaking Union of the Commonwealth. JP Essex; DL, Essex, 1937; High Sheriff of Essex, 1939; Chairman, Leyton Employment Exchange, 1931-38, 1951-63; DL Greater London, 1966; Sector Commander HG; Chairman Essex National Fitness Cttee; County War Welfare Officer; Chairman Essex Playing Fields Assoc., 1945; President Essex County Football Assoc., 1954. OStJ 1951. *Recreations:* fishing, travel. *Address:* The White House, Woodford Green, Essex. *T:* 01-504 1234. *Clubs:* British Sportsman's, Royal Commonwealth Society, English-Speaking Union.

**MALLINSON, Sir (William) Paul,** 3rd Bt, *cr* 1935; MA, BM, BCh, FRCP; Hon. Consulting Psychiatrist to St George's Hospital, SW1; Civilian Consultant in Psychiatry to Royal Navy; Chairman, Wm Mallinson & Denny Mott Ltd; *b* 6 July 1909; *s* of Sir William Mallinson, 2nd Bt, and Mabel (*d* 1948), *d* of J. W. Rush, Tunbridge Wells; *S* father, 1944; *m* 1st, 1940, Eila Mary (marr. diss. 1968), *d* of Roland Graeme Guy, Hastings, NZ; one *s* two *d*; 2nd, 1968, Margaret Cooper Gorrill, BA, MB, BS. *Educ:* Westminster; Christ Church, Oxford; St Thomas's Hospital. Late Surgeon Lieut-Commander, RNVR. *Heir:* *s* William John Mallinson [*b* 8 Oct. 1942; *m* 1968, Rosalind Angela, *o d* of Rollo Hoare, Dogmersfield, Hampshire; one *s*]. *Address:* 25 Wimpole Street, W1. *T:* 01-580 7919; Banavie, Bembridge, Isle of Wight. *T:* 2239. *Clubs:* Athenæum; Royal Thames Yacht; MCC.

**MALLOCK, Brig. Arthur Richard Ogilvie,** CIE 1939; Indian Army, retired; *b* 21 Oct. 1885; *m* 1910, Dulce, *y d* of J. T. R. de Havilland. Entered Indian Army, 1905; DAAG India, 1924-28; GSO 1st Grade, India, 1932-36; Brigade Commander 12th (Secunderabad) Inf. Brigade, 1936; retired, 1939. *Address:* 56 Queen's Park, West Drive, Bournemouth, Hants.

**MALLOWAN, Lady;** *see* Christie, Agatha.

**MALLOWAN, Sir Max (Edgar Lucien),** Kt 1968; CBE 1960; MA, DLit, FBA, FSA; Fellow of All Souls College, Oxford, since 1962; Professor of Western Asiatic Archæology, University of London, 1947-62, now Emeritus Professor; *b* London, 1904; *s* of Frederick Mallowan, London; *m* 1930, Agatha Mary Clarissa Miller (Agatha Christie, *qv*). *Educ:* Lancing; New Coll., Oxford. Archæologist. Assistant on staff of British Museum and of Museum of University of Pennsylvania Expedition to Ur of the Chaldees, 1925-30 and on staff of British Museum Expedition to Nineveh, 1931-32. Subsequently directed excavations on behalf of British Museum and British School of Archæology in Iraq, at Arpachiyah, 1933; in Syria, at Chagar Bazar, 1934-36, at Brak and at various sites in the Balikh valley, 1937-38. During War of 1939-45 served in RAFVR with rank of Wing Commander; posted for duty with British Military Administration in Tripolitania 1943-44 and served as Adviser on Arab Affairs and subsequently as GSO 1, Deputy Chief Secretary. Director, British School of Archæology in Iraq, 1947-61 (Chairman, 1966-); President British Institute of Persian Studies, 1961-; Vice-Pres., Egypt Exploration Soc., 1968-. Excavated in Zab valley, 1948, 1955, at Nimrud, 1949-58. FBA, and corresp. Member: Arab Acad., Baghdad, 1954; German Archæological Inst., 1962; Foreign Mem., Académie des Inscriptions et Belles-Lettres, Paris, 1964; Schweich Lectr, British Academy, 1955; Museum of Univ. of Pennsylvania, Lucy Wharton Drexel Gold Medal, 1957; Hon. Fellow Metropolitan Museum of Art, New York, 1958. Lawrence of Arabia Meml Medal, RCAS, 1969. Editor of Near Eastern and Western Asiatic series of Penguin books, 1948-65; Editor of Iraq, 1948-. *Publications:* Prehistoric Assyria; Excavations at Chagar Bazar; Excavations in the Balikh Valley; Excavations at Brak: archæological articles in Iraq, Antiquity, The Times, Illustrated London News, etc; Twenty-five Years of Mesopotamian Discovery, 1932-56; (with Sir Leonard Woolley) Ur Excavations, The Neo-Babylonian and Persian Periods, 1962; Early Mesopotamia and Iran, 1965; Nimrud and its Remains, 2 Vols, 1966; contrib. chapters to Cambridge Ancient History, 1967. *Recreations:* trees, travel. *Address:* Winterbrook House, Wallingford, Berks. *Clubs:* Athenæum, Boodle's.

**MALMESBURY,** 6th Earl of *cr* 1800; **William James Harris;** TD 1944 (2 Clasps); DL; Baron Malmesbury, 1788; Viscount FitzHarris, 1800; Official Verderer of the New Forest, since 1966; served Royal Hampshire Regt, TA; *b* 18 Nov. 1907; *o s* of 5th Earl and Hon. Dorothy Gough-Calthorpe, CBE (Lady of Grace, Order of St John of Jerusalem, Order of Mercy, with bar), *y d* of 6th Lord Calthorpe; *S* father 1950; *m* 1932, Hon. Diana Carleton, *e d* of 6th Baron Dorchester, OBE; one *s* two *d*. *Educ:* Eton; Trinity Coll., Cambridge (BA). Vice-Pres. of the Cambridge Univ. Conservative Association, 1930; Professional Associate of Surveyors Institution, 1937. Personal Liaison Officer to Min. of Agric., SE Region, 1958-64; Mem., Agric. and Forestry Cttee, RICS, 1953-69; Chm., Hants Agric. Exec. Cttee, 1959-67; Cttee which produced White Paper on the Growing Demand for

Water, 1961. Chairman: Hants Br., Country Landowners Assoc., 1954-56; T&AFA, Hants and IoW, 1960-68; Eastern Wessex TA&VRA, 1968-70. Mem. Basingstoke RDC, 1946-52; County Councillor, Hants CC, 1952; Vice-Lt, Co. Southampton, 1960-. Hon. Col 65th (M) Signal Regt, Royal Signals (TA), 1959-66. Master, Worshipful Co. of Skinners, 1952-53. Coronation Medal, 1937, 1953. *Heir:* *s* Viscount FitzHarris, *qv.* *Address:* Greywell Hill, Basingstoke, Hants. *T:* Odiham 2033. *Clubs:* Bath; Royal Yacht Squadron (Cowes).

**MALMESBURY, Suffragan Bishop of,** since 1962; **Rt. Rev. Clifford Leofric Purdy Bishop;** Canon of Bristol since 1962; *b* 1908; *s* of Rev. E. J. Bishop; *m* 1949, Ivy Winifred Adams. *Educ:* St John's, Leatherhead; Christ's Coll., Cambridge (MA); Lincoln Theological Coll. Deacon 1932; Priest, 1933; Curacies, 1932-41; Vicar, St Geo., Camberwell, 1941-49; Rural Dean, 1943-49; Curate-in-charge, All Saints, Newington, 1944-47; Rector of: Blakeney, 1949-53 (Rural Dean of Walsingham, 1951-53); Bishop Wearmouth, 1953-62 (Rural Dean of Wearmouth and Surrogate, 1953-62); Hon. Canon of Durham, 1958-62. *Address:* 15 Henleaze Road, Westbury on Trym, Bristol BS9 4EX. *T:* Bristol 621861.

**MALONE, Denis George Withers,** OBE 1967; retired as Governor, HM Prison, Dartmoor, (1960-66); lately, HM Prison Service; *b* 12 July 1906; *s* of Col William George Malone and Ida Katharine Withers; *m* 1935, Anita Cecilie Sophie Wolfermann. *Educ:* Douai Sch., Woolhampton, Berks. Asst Housemaster, Housemaster, Dep. Gov. (Gov. Cl. IV) and Gov. (Cl. III, II, I) Borstal and Prison Service of England and Wales, 1931-67; Seconded Foreign Office (German Section), Control Officer I and Sen. Control Officer, CCG Legal Div., Penal Branch, 1947-49; Seconded Colonial Office; Asst Commissioner, Prisons Dept, Kenya, 1950-54; Dir of Prisons, Prisons Dept, Cyprus, 1958-60 (despatches). Vice-Pres., Kerikeri and Dist Beautifying Soc.; Mem., Kerikeri Public Library Cttee. *Recreations:* foreign travel and outdoor activities. *Address:* Kerikeri, Bay of Islands, Northland, New Zealand.

**MALOTT, Deane Waldo;** President Cornell University, Ithaca, NY, 1951-63, President Emeritus, 1963; Consultant, Association of American Colleges, 1963-70; *b* 10 July 1898; *s* of Michael Harvey Malott and Edith Gray Johnson; *m* 1925, Eleanor Sisson Thrum; one *s* two *d.* *Educ:* Univ. of Kansas (AB); Harvard Univ. (MBA). Asst Dean, Harvard Business Sch., 1923-29; Assoc. Prof. of Business, 1933-39; Vice-Pres., Hawaiian Pineapple Co., Honolulu, 1929-33; Chancellor, Univ. of Kansas, 1939-51. Educational Advisor, Ops Analysis Div., US Army Air Corps, 1943-45; Mem., Business Council, Washington, DC, 1944-; Trustee: Corning museum of glass, 1952-; Teagle Foundation, 1952-; William Allen White Foundation, 1952-; Kansas Univ. Endowment Assoc., 1962-; Pacific Tropical Botanical Garden, 1964-; Director: General Mills, Inc., 1948-70; Citizens Bank, Abilene, Kans, 1944-; Pitney-Bowes, Inc., 1951-; First Nat. Bank, Ithaca, Ny, 1951-; Owens-Corning Fiberglas Corp., 1951-; Lane Bryant, Inc., 1963-; Servomation Corp., 1963-; Hon. LLD: Washburn Univ., 1941; Bryant Coll., 1951; Hamilton Coll., 1951; Univ. of California 1954; Univ. of Liberia, 1962; Univ. of New Hampshire, 1963; Emory Univ., 1963; Juniata Coll., 1965; DCS, Univ. of Pittsburgh, 1957; Hon. DHL, Long Island Univ., 1967. Holds foreign Orders. *Publications:* Problems in Agricultural Marketing, 1938; (with Philip Cabot) Problems in Public Utility Management, 1927; (with J. C. Baker) Introduction to Corporate Finance, 1936; (with J. C. Baker and W. D. Kennedy) On Going into Business, 1936; (with B. F. Martin) The Agricultural Industries, 1939; Agriculture–the Great Dilemma (an essay in Business and Modern Society), 1951. *Address:* 322 Wait Avenue, Cornell University, Ithaca, NY 14850, USA. *Clubs:* University, Cornell, Harvard (New York); Bohemian (San Francisco).

**MALRAUX, André;** Compagnon de la Libération; Officier de la Légion d'Honneur; Author; Minister of State for Cultural Affairs, Fifth Republic of France, 1960-69; *b* 3 Nov. 1901; *s* of Fernand Malraux and Mme (*née* Lamy); *m* 1st; one *d* (two *s* decd); *m* 2nd, 1948, Madeleine Lioux. *Educ:* Paris. Studied archæology and orientalism; first Asian visit, China and Indo-China, 1923-25. Pres. World Cttee for liberation of Dimitroff; responsible for taking protests to Hitler against trial of Reichstag offenders; served with Spanish Republican Government as organiser and head of foreign aviation, 1936. Served War of 1939-45 (wounded, taken prisoner, escaped 1940); Chef des services de dynamitage in the Corrèze-Dordogne-Lot inter-regional centre; comdr, attack against German div. Das Reich; Col Comdt, Alsace-Lorraine Bde; Minister of Information, 1945-46; Mem., Council of Musées de France: Ministre délégué à la Présidence du Conseil, France, June 1958-Jan. 1959 (was also in charge of Information from 1 June to 7 July). Minister of State, Fifth Republic, 1959-60. Hon. DCL Oxon, 1967. DSO; Commandeur de la République Espagnole. *Publications:* La Tentation de l'Occident; La Voie Royale; Les Conquérants, 1926-27; La Condition Humaine, 1933 (trans. in 18 languages); Le Temps du Mépris, 1935; L'Espoir (novel and film), 1938; Les Noyers de l'Altenburg, 1941 (Eng. trans.: The Walnut Trees of Altenburg, 1952); Goya–Oeuvres Complètes, 1945-46; Psychologie de l'Art, 1950 (Eng. trans.: Psychology of Art, 1949-51); Les Voix du Silence, 1951 (Eng. trans.: The Voices of Silence, 1954); La Métamorphose des Dieux, 1957 (Eng. trans.: The Metamorphosis of the Gods, 1960); Antimémoires, 1967. *Address:* 24 rue Montpensier, Paris 1e.

**MALTA, Archbishop of, (RC),** since 1943; **Most Rev. Michael Gonzi,** KBE, *cr* 1946; DD, ICD, BLit; Assistant at the Pontifical Throne since 1949; *b* Vittoriosa, Malta, 13 May 1885; *s* of Joseph Gonzi and Margaret Tonna. *Educ:* Malta Seminary; Malta Univ.; Beda Coll., Rome. Priest, 1908; Prof. of Holy Scripture and Hebrew at the Malta Univ., 1915; Sec. to the Archbishop of Malta, 1921; Mem. of the Senate of the Maltese Parliament, 1921; Canon Theologian of the Malta Cathedral, 1923; Bailiff Grand Cross of the Order of Malta, St John of Jerusalem, 1949; Coadjutor to Bishop of Malta, 1943. *Address:* Valletta, Malta.

**MALTBY, Antony John,** MA; Headmaster of Trent College since 1968; *b* 15 May 1928; *s* of G. C. Maltby and Mrs Maltby (*née* Kingsnorth); *m* 1959, Jillian Winifred (*née* Burt); four *d.* *Educ:* Clayesmore Sch., Dorset; St John's Coll., Cambridge. BA Hons (History) 1950. Schoolmaster: Dover Coll., 1951-58; Pocklington Sch., 1958-68. *Recreations:* squash, tennis, travel. *Address:* School House, Trent College, Long Eaton, Nottingham, NG10 4AD. *T:* Long Eaton 2737. *Clubs:* Public Schools; Hawks (Cambridge).

**MALTBY, Maj.-Gen. Christopher Michael,** CB 1946; MC; DL; retired pay; *b* 13 Jan. 1891; *er s* of late Christopher James Maltby,

Felmersham, Beds; *m* 1927, Hélène Margaret Napier-Clavering; two *d.* *Educ:* King's Sch., Canterbury; Bedford Sch.; RMA, Woolwich. Commissioned 1910; joined Indian Army, 1911; Capt., 1915; Bt Major, 1919; Major, 1927; Bt Lt-Col 1933; Lt-Col 1935; Col 1938; Brig. 1939; Maj.-Gen. 1941. Passed Staff Coll., Quetta, 1923-24; passed RAF Staff Coll., Andover, 1927-28; GSO2 and DAAG AHQ India; GSO1, Quetta Staff Coll. and Baluchistan Dist; Comdr 3rd Jhelum Bde, Calcutta Bde, 19th Indian Inf. Bde, Deccan Dist and British Troops in China. Served Persian Gulf, 1913-14. European War, 1914-18 (wounded, despatches thrice, MC, Bt Maj.); NWF India, 1923-24, 1937 (despatches); commanded in Hong Kong, 1941. DL Somerset, 1953. *Recreation:* shooting. *Address:* Greenacre, Shoreditch, Taunton, Somerset. *T:* Taunton 3015. *Club:* Naval and Military.
*See also Sir Paul Maltby.*

**MALTBY, Air Vice-Marshal Sir Paul (Copeland),** KCVO 1962; KBE 1946; CB 1941; DSO 1917; AFC; RAF retired; DL; *b* 5 Aug. 1892; 2nd *s* of C. J. Maltby, Felmersham, Beds; *m* 1921, Winifred Russell, *d* of late J. H. Paterson, 6 Moray Place, Edinburgh; one *s* (and *e s* killed in action 1945) one *d.* *Educ:* Bedford Sch. Royal Military College, Sandhurst. Gazetted to Royal Welch Fusiliers, serving in India, 1911-14; France, 1914-15; transferred to RFC, 1915, serving in France and England to end of the European War; with RAF in India, 1919-24; RAF Staff Coll., 1926; Imperial Defence Coll., 1931; Commandant of the Central Flying Sch., 1932-34; AOC RAF in Mediterranean, 1935-38; AOC 24 (Training) Group, 1938-40; 71 (AC) Group, 1940-41; AOC RAF in Java, 1942; retired, 1946; Serjeant-at-Arms, House of Lords, 1946-62. DL Southampton, 1956-. Grand Officer of Order of Orange Nassau (Netherlands). *Address:* Froglanes, Rotherwick, Basingstoke, Hants.
*See also C. M. Maltby.*

**MALTBY, Sir Thomas Karran,** Kt 1949; Commissioner of Public Works, Victoria, Australia, 1955-61; *s* of Thomas Karran and Ada Agnes Maltby; *m* 1913, Margaret McDonald; one *s* two *d.* *Educ:* School of Mines, Bendigo, Victoria, Australia. Served European War, 1914-18 (despatches); commissioned Australian Imperial Forces, 1914; Gen. Staff, 1918. Legislative Assembly, 1929-. Opposition Whip, 1929; Government Whip, 1930; Sec. to Cabinet, 1933-34; Hon. Minister, 1934; Minister for Lands and Forests, 1935; AA & QMG, 1942; Dep. Premier, Chief Sec., Minister in Charge Elec. Undertakings, 1945; Speaker, Legislative Assembly, Victoria, 1947-49. *Address:* 10 Culbin Avenue, Belmont, Geelong, Victoria 3216, Australia. *T:* 433931.

**MALVERN,** 1st Viscount *cr* 1955, of Rhodesia and of Bexley; **Godfrey (Martin) Huggins,** PC 1947; CH 1944; KCMG 1941; DCL (Oxon) 1951; (Rhodes) 1957; LLD (Witwatersrand) 1953, (London) 1955; Prime Minister, Federation of Rhodesia and Nyasaland, 1953-56 (of Southern Rhodesia, 1933-53); Director of: Merchant Bank of Central Africa; Rothman's (of Pall Mall) Rhodesia Ltd; *b* 6 July 1883; *e s* of late Godfrey Huggins and late Emily Blest; *m* 1921, Blanche Elizabeth, *d* of late James Slatter, Pietermaritzburg, South Africa; two *s.* *Educ:* Malvern Coll.; St Thomas's Hosp., MRCS, LRCP, 1906; FRCS 1908. Hon. FRCPE 1959. After 2½ years holding post-grad. appts at St Thomas's Hosp. became House Physician and subsequently Medical Superintendent at the Hospital for Sick Children, Great Ormond Street, London; came to Southern Rhodesia, 1911; general practitioner and surgeon, S Rhodesia, until 1921; since that date only as consultant surgeon; served with RAMC, England, Malta, France, European War, 1914-17; MLA, Southern Rhodesia, representing Salisbury North, 1923-33; Salisbury District, 1934-39, Salisbury North, 1939-53; Salisbury Suburbs (Federal), 1953-58. Minister of Native Affairs, 1933-49; Minister of Defence, 1948-56. KGStJ. *Publications:* Amputation Stumps: Their Care and After-Treatment; technical and other articles in various publications. *Recreation:* horticulture. *Heir:* *er s* Hon. John Godfrey Huggins [*b* 26 Oct. 1922; *m* 1946, Patricia Marjorie, *d* of Frank Renwick-Bower, Durban, S Africa; two *s* one *d.* *Educ:* Winchester. Joined RAF 1940; Flight Lt 1944; retd 1945; re-joined RAF, 1952]. *Address:* Craig Farm, PO Highlands, salisbury, Rhodesia. *Clubs:* Athenæum, No 10; Salisbury, New (Salisbury); Mashonaland Turf; numerous Country (Rhodesia).

**MALVERN, Harry Ladyman,** CBE 1970; Managing Director of Remploy Ltd since 1964; *b* 4 June 1908; *s* of late Harry Arthur Malvern, Wirral, Cheshire; *m* 1935, Doreen, *d* of late John James Peters; one *s* one *d.* *Educ:* Birkenhead Sch., Cheshire. FCA; FInstD. Joint Man. Dir, Spratts Patent Ltd, 1961-64. Pres., Cookham Soc., 1970. *Recreations:* gardening, reading, archaeology. *Address:* The Coppice, Winter Hill, Cookham Dean, Berks. *T:* Marlow 2043.

**MAMO, Sir Anthony Joseph,** Kt 1960; OBE 1955; Chief Justice and President of HM Court of Appeal, Malta, since 1957; President, HM Constitutional Court, Malta, since 1964; *b* 9 Jan. 1909; *s* of late Joseph Mamo and late Carola (*née* Brincat); *m* 1939, Margaret Agius; one *s* two *d.* *Educ:* Royal Univ. of Malta. BA 1931; LLD 1934. Mem. Statute Law Revision Commn, 1936-42; Crown Counsel, 1942-51; Prof., Criminal Law, Malta Univ., 1943-57; Dep. Attorney-Gen., 1952-54, Attorney-Gen., 1955, Malta. QC (Malta) 1957. CStJ 1958. *Publications:* Lectures on Criminal Law and Criminal Procedure delivered at the University of Malta. *Address:* 49 Stella Maris Street, Sliema, Malta. *T:* 30708. *Clubs:* Casino Maltese, United Services Sports (Malta).

**MAMOULIAN, Rouben;** stage and screen director; *b* 8 Oct. 1897; *s* of Zachary Mamoulian and Virginia Kalantarian; *m* Azadia Newman, Washington, DC. *Educ:* Lycée Montaigne, Paris; Gymnasium, Tiflis; Univ., Moscow. First English production, Beating on the Door, at St James's Theatre, London, Nov. 1922; arrived in Rochester, New York, Aug. 1923; from that date to summer of 1926 was Director of Production at the Eastman Theatre, producing Grand Operas, Operettas, Dramas, and stage presentations, among which were the following; Carmen, Faust, Boris Godounoff, Shanewis, Gilbert and Sullivan Operettas, Sister Beatrice, etc; also organised and was Director of the Eastman Theatre Sch.; came to New York at the end of 1926; started there as a Director of the Theatre Guild Sch.; first production of a play on Broadway, 10 Oct. 1927, Porgy, for the Theatre Guild; Porgy was followed by direction of the following plays on Broadway: Marco Millions, Congai, Wings over Europe, These Modern Women, RUR, The Game of Love and Death, A Month in the Country, A Farewell to Arms, and Solid South; also an opera at the Metropolitan Opera House, Hand of Fate, with L. Stokowski and the Philadelphia Orchestra; Opera Porgy and Bess (music by George Gershwin) for Theatre Guild, New York, 1935; in Los Angeles and San Francisco, 1938. Directed following motion pictures: Applause in 1928; City Streets and Dr Jekyll and Mr Hyde, in 1932; Love Me Tonight, in 1933, and Song of Songs, in 1933; Queen Christina in 1933 and We Live Again in 1934; Becky Sharp (Technicolor) in 1935; The Gay Desperado in 1936; High, Wide and Handsome in 1937; Golden Boy in 1939; The Mark of Zorro in 1940; Blood and Sand (Technicolor) in 1941; Rings on Her Fingers in 1942; Summer Holiday (technicolor musical, based on Eugene O'Neill's Ah Wilderness) in 1947; Silk Stockings (musical film, cinemascope, color) 1957. *stage productions:* Oklahoma!, 1943; Sadie Thompson, 1944, and Carousel, 1945, St Louis Woman, 1946, musical dramas in New York; Lost In The Stars (musical tragedy), 1949; Arms And The Girl (musical play), 1950, New York; Oklahoma! (for Berlin Arts Festival), 1951; Adolph Zukor's Golden Jubilee Celebration, Hollywood, 1953; Carousel (New Prod.), Los Angeles and San Francisco, 1953; Oklahoma!, new production for Paris, Rome, Milan, Naples and Venice, 1955. Co-Author (with Maxwell Anderson) of musical play The Devil's Hornpipe (made musical film Never Steal Anything Small), 1959. World Première Perf. of Shakespeare's Hamlet, A New Version, Lexington, Ky, 1966. Tribute to Rouben Mamoulian (showing all films), Gall. of Modern Art, NY, 1967; Festival of Mamoulian Films, Nat. Film Theatre, London, 1968; Retrospective Showings: American Film Inst., Center of Advanced Studies, Beverly Hills, 1970; Nat. Gallery of Art, Washington, DC, 1970; Metropolitan Museum of Art, NY, 1970. *Publications:* Abigayil, 1964; Hamlet Revised and Interpreted, 1965; contrib. Scoundrels and Scalawags, 1968. *Recreations:* swimming, horseback riding, and reading detective stories. *Address:* 1112 Schuyler Road, Beverly Hills, Calif 90210, USA.

**MAN, Maj.-Gen. Christopher Mark Morrice,** CB 1968; OBE 1958; MC 1945; President, Regular Army Commissions Board, 1967-69, retired; *b* 20 April 1914; *s* of late Rev. M. L. Man, MA, and Evelyn Dora Man, Tenterden, Kent; *m* 1940, Georgina, *d* of late James Marr, Edinburgh; no *c*. *Educ:* Eastbourne Coll.; Emmanuel Coll., Cambridge. (MA). Lieut, Middlesex Regt, 1936; 1st Bn, The Middlesex Regt, 1937-45. Commanded Army Air Transport Training and Development Centre, 1953-55; GSO 1, WO, 1955-57; comdg Infantry Junior Leaders Battalion, 1957-59; comdg 125 Infantry Bde (TA), 1959-62; Head of Commonwealth Liaison Mission, UN Command, Korea and British Military Attaché, Seoul, 1962-64; GOC 49th Infantry Div. TA and N Midland District, 1964-67; Colonel, The Middlesex Regt, 1965-66; Dep. Colonel The Queen's Regt, 1967-69, Hon. Colonel, 1970-. *Address:* The Old Schoolhouse, Struan, Calvine, Perthshire. *T:* Calvine 224. *Clubs:* Army and Navy, MCC.

**MAN, Morgan Charles Garnet,** CMG 1961; *b* 6 Aug. 1915; *s* of Henry Morgan Stoe Man and Nora Loeck; *m* 1956, Patricia Mary (*née* Talbot). *Educ:* Cheltenham Coll.; Queen's Coll., Oxford. Joined HM Consular Service, 1937; Vice-Consul, Beirut, 1937-39; Assistant Oriental Secretary, HM Embassy, Bagdad, 1939; 2nd Secretary, HM Embassy, Jedda, 1943; Consul, Atlanta, Ga, USA, 1946; Consul, Kirkuk, 1948; First Secretary, HM Legation, Damascus, 1949; Oriental Secretary, HM Embassy, Bagdad, 1951; Assistant in American Dept, Foreign Office, Sept. 1953; Head of American Dept, 1954; Counsellor at HM Embassy, Oslo, Nov. 1956; Deputy Political Resident, Bahrain, 1959-62; Minister, HM Embassy, Ankara, 1962-64; HM Ambassador to Saudi Arabia, 1964-68; Senior Civilian Instructor, Imperial Defence Coll., 1968-69. *Address:* 272 Earl's Court Road, SW5. *Club:* Junior Carlton.

**MAN, Maj.-Gen. Patrick Holberton,** CB 1966; CBE 1962 (OBE 1946); DSO 1956; MC 1940; Personnel Manager, Manganese Bronze Ltd, Ipswich; *b* 17 March 1913; *s* of Colonel Hubert William Man, CBE, DSO, and Mrs Beryl Man (*née* Holberton); *m* 1938, Barbara Joan Marion Marsh; two *d*. *Educ:* Rugby Sch.; RMC, Sandhurst. Commissioned into The Hampshire Regt, 1933. Served France and Belgium, 1939-40; Staff Coll., Camberley, 1941; served South-East Asia, 1943-45. RAF Staff Coll., 1946-47; served Middle East, 1950-52; Imperial Defence Coll., 1953; served Malaya, 1954-56, and BAOR, 1959-63; GOC Aldershot District, 1963-66; Dir of Personal Services (Army), 1966-68, retd. Colonel Comdt, Military Provost Staff Corps, 1967-. Bronze Star, 1945; Selangor Meritorious Service, 1956. *Recreation:* ski-ing. *Address:* Quill Farm, Campsea Ashe, nr Woodbridge, Suffolk.

**MAN SINGH, Rai Bahadur,** CBE 1932; *b* 3 July 1883; *s* of Anand Sahai and Lakshmi; *m* 1902; three *s* two *d*. *Educ:* Muir Central Coll., Allahabad (BA). Joined the United Provinces Police as Deputy Superintendent of Police, 1906; Rai Bahadur, 1917; King's Police Medal for bravery, 1920; Indian Imperial Police, 1917; retired as Officiating Deputy Inspector-General of Police, 1937; Member, United Provinces Public Service Commission, until 1942; Chairman Improvement Trust, Cawnpore, 1942-45. Member Zonal Advisory Board, Central Zone Life Insurance Corporation of India, 1957. *Recreations:* played cricket, hockey, tennis, golf, and polo, riding and shooting special hobbies. *Address:* Man-Bhawan, Fatehpur, UP, India.

**MANANDHAR, Rama Prasad,** Suprasiddha Pravala Gorkha Dakshina Bahu (Nepal), 1960; GCVO (Hon.), 1960; CBE (Hon.), 1949; *b* 8 Jan. 1914; *s* of Sahu Kool Narayan Manandhar and Srimati Ratna Maya; *m* 1935, Lakshmi Kumari Debi, *d* of Sahu Dan Bahadur of Gwachhemugal; two *s* six *d*. *Educ:* Durbar High Sch.; Tri-Chandra Coll.; Patna Univ., India (MA). Prof. of English Literature, Tri-Chandra Coll., Katmandu, 1936-49; Counsellor of Embassy, Nepalese Embassy, London, 1949-52 (concurrently Counsellor of Nepalese Embassies in Paris and Washington with office in London): Foreign Secretary, 1953-54, Secretary for Education and Health, 1954-55, Government of Nepal; Nepalese Ambassador to the Court of St James's, 1956-61 (concurrently Nepalese Ambassador to France and to the Federal German Republic, and Minister to Switzerland). Rep. Government of Nepal at General Conference of UNESCO, Paris, 1949, in Florence, 1950, and again in Paris, 1951; was in Delegations which presented Ojaswi Rajanya (Nepal's highest decoration) to Queen Elizabeth II (then Princess Elizabeth), also to Queen Juliana of the Netherlands; represented Government of Nepal at World Power Conference, London, 1950, and International Conference on Education, Geneva, 1951; Nepal's Delegate at UN Food and Agriculture Organization, Rome, 1951; King of Nepal's Special Representative at International Buddhist Conference, Sanchi, 1952; Member Pay Commn, Government of Nepal; in Nepalese Delegation Colombo Plan Conference, New Delhi, 1953; Secretary, Nepal Interim Nat. Commn for UNESCO; Alternate Delegate of Government of Nepal with rank of King's Special Envoy at Asian

African Conference, Bandung, 1955. Commander of Order of Orange-Nassau (Netherlands), 1949! Officer of Legion of Honour (France), 1950; Grosskreuz des Verdienstordens der Bundesrepublik Deutschland, 1961. *Recreations:* travel, tennis, riding. *Address:* Peace Grotto, Pyaphal Tole, Katmandu, Nepal.

**MANBY, Mervyn Colet,** CMG 1964; *b* 20 Feb. 1915; *s* of late Harold B. and Mary Manby (*née* Mills), late of Petistree, Suffolk; *m* 1949, Peggy Aronson, Eastern Cape, South Africa; one *s* one *d. Educ:* Bedford Sch., Bedford; Pembroke Coll., Oxford. Colonial Police Service, 1937; Malaya, 1938-47; Basutoland, 1947-54; Kenya, 1954-64. Dep. Inspector General, Kenya Police, 1961-64; retired, 1964. United Nations Technical Assistance Adviser to Government of Iran, 1965. *Recreations:* reading, travel. *Address:* Old Well Cottage, Barham, Canterbury, Kent. *T:* Barham 369.

**MANCE, Henry Stenhouse;** Chairman of Lloyd's, 1969, 1970 (Deputy Chairman, 1967, 1968); *b* 5 Feb. 1913; *e s* of late Brig.-Gen. Sir H. O. Mance, KBE, CB, CMG, DSO; *m* 1940, Joan Erica Robertson Baker; one *s* three *d. Educ:* Charterhouse; St John's Coll., Cambridge (MA). Entered Lloyd's, 1935; Underwriting Member of Lloyd's, 1940; elected to Cttee of Lloyd's, 1966. Chairman, Lloyd's Underwriters' Assoc., 1965 and 1966; Member, Cttee of Lloyd's Register, 1966-. Min. of War Transport, 1941-46. Member CMS Exec. Cttee, 1941- (Chairman, 1954-56); Chairman, Overseas Bookshop Supplies Ltd, 1965-; Trustee of Ridley and Wycliffe Halls. *Recreations:* gardening, carpentry, fishing. *Address:* Gatefield Cottage, Okehurst, Billingshurst, Sussex. *T:* Billingshurst 2155. *Club:* National Liberal.

**MANCHESTER,** 10th Duke of, *cr* 1719; **Alexander George Francis Drogo Montagu,** OBE 1940; Earl of Manchester, 1626; Viscount Mandeville, Baron Montagu of Kimbolton, 1620; Commander, Royal Navy, retired; *b* 2 Oct. 1902; *er s* of 9th Duke of Manchester and Helena (who obtained a divorce, 1931 and *m* 1937, 11th Earl of Kintore), *d* of late Eugene Zimmerman, USA; *S* father, 1947; *m* 1st, 1927, Nell Vere Stead (*d* 1966), Melbourne; two *s*; 2nd, 1969, Mrs Elizabeth Crocker, Pebble Beach, Calif. *Educ:* Osborne; Dartmouth. Retired from Royal Navy, 1930. *Recreations:* shooting, etc. *Heir: s* Viscount Mandeville, *qv. Address:* Kapsirowa, Hoey's Bridge PO, Kenya. *Club:* Junior Naval and Military.

**MANCHESTER, Bishop of,** since 1970; **Rt. Rev. Patrick Campbell Rodger;** *b* 28 Nov. 1920; *s* of Patrick Wylie and Edith Ann Rodger; *m* 1952; two *s. Educ:* Cargilfield; Rugby; Christ Church, Oxford; Theological College, Westcott House, Cambridge, Deacon, 1949; Priest, 1950. Asst Curate, St John's Church, Edinburgh, 1949-51, and Chaplain to Anglican Students in Edinburgh, 1951-54. Study Secretary, SCM of Gt Brit. and Ire., 1955-58; Rector, St Fillan's, Kilmacolm, with St Mary's Bridge of Weir, 1958-61; Exec. Sec. for Faith and Order, World Council of Churches, 1961-66; Vice-Provost, St Mary's Cathedral, Edinburgh, 1966-67; Provost, 1967-70. *Publications:* The Fourth World Conference on Faith and Order, Montreal (ed.), 1964; Contrib., Theological jls in English and French. *Recreations:* music and walking. *Address:* Bishopscourt, Bury New Road, Manchester M7 0LE. *T:* 061-792 2096.

**MANCHESTER, Dean of;** *see* Jowett, Very Rev. Alfred.

**MANCHESTER, Archdeacon of;** *see* Price, Ven. S. H.

**MANCHESTER, William;** author; Purple Heart (US) 1945; Fellow, East College, Wesleyan University, since 1968; Lecturer in English since 1968; *b* 1 April 1922; *s* of William Raymond Manchester and Sallie E. R. (*née* Thompson); *m* 1948, Julia Brown Marshall; one *s* two *d. Educ:* Springfield Classical High School; Univ. of Massachusetts; Dartmouth Coll., NH; Univ. of Missouri. Served US Marine Corps, 1942-45 (Presidential Unit Citation). Reporter, Daily Oklahoman, 1945-46; Reporter, foreign corresp., war corresp., assoc. editor, Baltimore Sun, 1947-55; Man. editor, Wesleyan Univ. Press, 1955-65; Fellow Wesleyan Univ. Center for Advanced Studies, 1959-68. Trustee, Friends of Univ. of Massachusetts Library, 1970-. Guggenheim Fellow, 1959; Dr of Humane Letters, Univ. of Mass, 1965; Dag Hammarskjold Internat. Prize in Literature, 1967; Overseas Press Club (New York) Award for Best Book of the Year on Foreign Affairs, 1968; Univ. of Missouri Gold Medal, 1969. *Publications:* Disturber of the Peace, 1951 (publ. UK as The Sage of Baltimore, 1952); The City of Anger, 1953; Shadow of the Monsoon, 1956; Beard the Lion, 1958; A Rockefeller Family Portrait, 1959; The Long Gainer, 1961; Portrait of a President, 1962; The Death of a President, 1967; The Arms of Krupp, 1968; contrib. to various periodicals. *Recreation:* photography. *Address:* Wesleyan University, Middletown, Conn 06457, USA. *T:* 203-346-4789. *Clubs:* Authors' Guild (New York), Wesleyan Faculty (Middletown).

**MANCROFT,** family name of **Baron Mancroft.**

**MANCROFT,** 2nd Baron, *cr* 1937, of Mancroft in the City of Norwich; Bt, *cr* 1932; **Stormont Mancroft Samuel Mancroft;** KBE 1959 (MBE 1945); TD 1950; MA; *b* 27 July 1914; *s* of 1st Baron and Phœbe (*d* 1969), 2nd *d* of Alfred Chune Fletcher, MRCS; *S* father, 1942; *m* 1951, Mrs Diana Elizabeth Quarry, *o d* of Lieut-Colonel Horace Lloyd; one *s* two *d. Educ:* Winchester; Christ Church, Oxford. Called to Bar, Inner Temple, 1938; Member of Bar Council, 1947-51; Member St Marylebone Borough Council, 1947-53; Chancellor Primrose League, 1952-54; a Lord in Waiting to the Queen, 1952-54; Parliamentary Under-Secretary for Home Dept, Oct. 1954-Jan. 1957; Parliamentary Secretary, Min. of Defence, Jan.-June 1957; Minister without Portfolio, June 1957-Oct. 1958, resigned. Member, Board of Directors, Cunard Steam-ship Co., 1966-; Dep. Chairman, Cunard Line Ltd, 1966-. Member: Board, British Travel Assoc., 1966-; Council of Industrial Design, 1960-63; Chairman, American Cttee, BNEC, 1967-70; President: The Institute of Marketing, 1959-63; St Marylebone Conservative Assoc., 1961-67; London Tourist Board. Served RA (TA), 1939-46; Lieut-Colonel (despatches twice, MBE); commissioned TA, 1938; rejoined TA 1947-55. Hon. Col Comdt, RA, 1970. Croix de Guerre. *Publication:* Booking the Cooks (essays from Punch), 1969. *Heir: s* Hon. Benjamin Lloyd Stormont Mancroft, *b* 16 May 1957. *Address:* 80 Eaton Square, SW1. *T:* 01-235 4684. *Clubs:* Carlton, Pratt's; West Ham Boys.

**MANDELSTAM, Prof. Joel;** Iveagh Professor of Microbiology, University of Oxford, since 1966; *b* S Africa, 13 Nov. 1919; *s* of Leo and Fanny Mandelstam; *m* 1954, Dorothy Hillier; one *s* one *d. Educ:* Jeppe High Sch., Johannesburg; University of Witwatersrand; Queen Elizabeth Coll., London. Lecturer, Medical Sch., Johannesburg, 1947; Scientific

Staff, Nat. Institute for Med. Research, London, 1952-66. Fulbright Fellow, US, 1958-59. Editorial Board, Biochemical Journal, 1960-66. *Publications:* Biochemistry of Bacterial Growth (with K. McQuillen), 1968; articles in journals and books on microbial biochemistry. *Recreation:* walking in mountainous regions. *Address:* Microbiology Unit, Department of Biochemistry, South Parks Road, Oxford. *T:* Oxford 55740.

**MANDELSTAM, Prof. Stanley,** FRS 1962; Professor of Physics, University of California. *Educ:* University of the Witwatersrand, Johannesburg, Transvaal, South Africa (BSc); Trinity Coll., Cambridge (BA). PhD, Birmingham. Formerly Professor of Math. Physics, University of Birmingham. *Publications:* (with W. Yourgrau) Variational Principles in Dynamics and Quantum Theory, 1955 (revised edn, 1956); papers in learned journals. *Address:* Department of Physics, University of California, Berkeley, California 94720, USA.

**MANDER, Sir Charles (Marcus),** 3rd Bt, *cr* 1911; Underwriting Member of Lloyd's; Director, Oxvar Ltd, since 1951; Director Manders (Holdings) Ltd, Mander Brothers Ltd, until 1958; *b* 22 Sept. 1921; *o s* of Sir Charles Arthur Mander, 2nd Bart, and late Monica Claire Cotterill, *d* of G. H. Neame; *S* father, 1951; *m* 1945, Maria Dolores Beatrice, *d* of late Alfred Brodermann, Hamburg; two *s* one *d*. *Educ:* Eton Coll., Windsor; Trinity Coll., Cambridge. Commissioned Coldstream Guards, 1942; served War of 1939-45, Canal Zone, 1943; Italy, 1943, Germany, 1944; War Office (ADC to Lieut-General R. G. Stone, CB), 1945. High Sheriff of Staffordshire, 1962-63. *Recreations:* shooting, music. *Heir:* *s* Charles Nicholas Mander, *b* 23 March 1950. *Address:* Little Barrow, Moreton-in-Marsh, Glos. *T:* Stow-on-the-Wold 265.

**MANDER, Lady (Rosalie); (R. Glynn Grylls),** MA Oxon; Biographer; Lecturer; Cornish ancestry; *m* 1930, Sir Geoffrey Mander (*d* 1962), sometime MP for East Wolverhampton; one *s* one *d*. *Educ:* Queen's Coll., Harley Street, London; Lady Margaret Hall, Oxford. Curator (National Trust), Wightwick Manor. Lectures frequently in USA. *Publications:* Mary Shelley, 1936; Trelawny, 1950; Portrait of Rossetti, 1965. *Address:* Wightwick Manor, Wolverhampton, Staffs; 35 Buckingham Gate, SW1.

**MANDEVILLE, Viscount; Sidney Arthur Robin George Drogo Montagu;** *b* 5 Feb. 1929; *er s* of 10th Duke of Manchester, *qv*; *m* 1955, Adrienne Valerie, *d* of J. K. Christie. *Address:* Ol Goroshe Farm, PO Subukia, Kenya. *Club:* Muthaiga (Nairobi, Kenya).

**MANDI, Lt-Col Raja (Sir) Joginder Sen Bahadur of;** KCSI 1931; *b* 20 Aug. 1904; *s* of late Mian Kishan Singh; *m* 1930, *d* of late Kanwar Prithiraj Sinhji, Rajpipla; two *s* two *d*. *Educ:* Queen Mary's Coll. and Aitchison Coll., Lahore. Ascended Gadi, 1913; full ruler, 1925. Visited various countries. Ambassador of Republic of India to Brazil, 1952-56; Member of Lok Sabha, 1957-62. Hon. Lt-Col 3rd/17th Dogra Regt and Bengal Sappers and Miners. *Address:* Bejai Palace, Mandi, Mandi District, India.

**MANDLEBERG, J. Harold;** *b* 2 Sept. 1885; *e s* of late Sir G. Charles Mandleberg; *m* 1921, Jessie, *d* of late Arthur Entwisle, Bolton; one *d*. *Educ:* Harrow; Trinity Coll., Cambridge. Hons in Natural Science, MA 1910; FRIC; FIRI; FCS. European War, 1914-18, and War of 1939-45, in Army. Chairman, NW Regional Board for Industry, Dec. 1947-April 1949 (apptd by Chancellor of Exchequer); Director: North-Western Industrial Estates Ltd (appointment by President of Board of Trade), 1946-54. Ex-Chairman, NW Regional Council FBI. *Publication:* Physical Chemistry made Plain, 3rd edn, 1966. *Address:* Flat 4A, Harcourt House, 19A Cavendish Square, W1. *Clubs:* White's; Leander (Henley-on-Thames).

**MANDLEBERG, Brig. Lennard Charles,** CBE 1938; DSO 1919; MC and bar; late 8th Battalion Lancashire Fusiliers; *b* 1893; *y s* of late Sir G. Charles Mandleberg; *m* 1919, Marjorie Helen, *y d* of late John Craig; one *s*. *Educ:* Harrow; Trinity Coll., Cambridge. Served European War, 1914-19 (despatches, DSO, MC and bar); Commander 164th (North Lancashire) Infantry Brigade, TA, 1936-39; Commander Infantry Brigade, 1939. *Address:* Oldany Lodge, nr Lochinver, By Lairg, Sutherland. *Club:* White's.

**MANGWAZU, Timon Sam;** High Commissioner in London for the Republic of Malawi and Ambassador to Belgium, Portugal, the Netherlands and the Holy See, 1967-69; *b* 12 Oct. 1933; *s* of Sam Isaac Mangwazu, Farmer; *m* 1958, Nelly Kathewera. *Educ:* Ruskin Coll., Oxford. Teacher at Methodist Sch., Hartley, S Rhodesia, 1955; Clerical Officer, Government Print, Agricultural Dept and Accountant General's Dept, 1956-62; Asst Registrar of Trade Unions, Ministry of Labour, 1962-63; Malawi Ambassador, West Germany, Norway, Sweden, Denmark, Netherlands, Belgium, Switzerland and Austria, 1964-67. *Recreation:* fishing. *Address:* Brasenose College, Oxford. *Club:* Travellers'.

**MANHOOD, Harold Alfred;** Writer; *b* 6 May 1904; *m* 1937. *Educ:* Elementary Schooling. *Publications:* Nightseed, 1928; Apples by Night, 1932; Crack of Whips, 1934; Fierce and Gentle, 1935; Sunday Bugles, 1939; Lunatic Broth, 1944 (collections of short stories); Gay Agony (novel), 1930; Selected Stories, 1947; A Long View of Nothing (short stories), 1953. *Address:* Holmbush, nr Henfield, Sussex.

**MANIFOLD, Hon. Sir Chester;** *see* Manifold, Hon. Sir (T.) Chester.

**MANIFOLD, Hon. Sir (Thomas) Chester,** KBE 1965; Kt 1953; Grazier, Australia; *b* 1897; *s* of Hon. J. Chester and Lilian E. Manifold; *m* 1923, Gwenda, *d* of Maj.-Gen. H. W. and Winifred Grimwade; three *d*. *Educ:* Geelong Grammar Sch., Victoria; Jesus Coll., Cambridge. Served European War, RFA, 1916-19; War of 1939-45: 2nd AIF, 1940-43 (despatches); VDC, 1943-45. Councillor, Shire of Hampden, 1926-41; Member for Hampden, State Parliament, 1929-35; Hon. Minister, Argyle Government, 1932-33. Chairman, Totalizator Agency Bd of Victoria, 1960-68. Chairman, Victoria Racing Club, 1952-62, Vice-Chairman, 1943-52 and 1962. *Recreations:* racing, golf, tennis. *Address:* Talindert, Camperdown, Victoria 3260, Australia. *T:* Camperdown 4. *Clubs:* Melbourne, Athenæum, Naval and Military (Melbourne, Victoria).

**MANKIEWICZ, Joseph Leo;** American writer and film director (independent, no contractual affiliations); *b* 11 Feb. 1909; *s* of Frank Mankiewicz and Johanna (*née* Blumenau); *m* 1939, Rosa Stradner (*d* 1958); two *s* (and one *s* by previous marriage); *m* 1962, Rosemary Matthews; one *d*. *Educ:* Columbia Univ. (AB 1928). Has written, directed and produced for the screen, 1929-. Received Screen Directors' Guild Award, 1949 and 1950; Screen Writers' Guild Award for best American comedy, 1949 and 1950; First Awards for direction and screen play, Motion Picture Academy, 1950, 1951. President, Screen Directors' Guild of America, 1950. Formed own company, Figaro Inc., 1953, dissolved, 1961. Films include: Manhattan Melodrama, Fury, Three Comrades, Philadelphia Story, Woman of the Year, Keys of the Kingdom, A Letter to Three Wives, No Way Out, All About Eve, People Will Talk, Five Fingers, Julius Caesar, The Barefoot Contessa, Guys and Dolls; The Quiet American; Suddenly Last Summer; The Honey Pot; There Was a Crooked Man. Directed La Bohème for Metropolitan Opera, 1952. *Address:* 527 Madison Avenue, New York City, NY 10022, USA.

**MANKOWITZ, Wolf;** author; *b* 7 Nov. 1924; *s* of Solomon and Rebecca Mankowitz; *m* 1944, Ann Margaret Seligmann; four *s*. *Educ:* East Ham Grammar Sch.; Downing Coll., Cambridge (MA, English Tripos). *Publications: novels:* Make Me An Offer, 1952; A Kid for Two Farthings, 1953; Laugh Till You Cry, 1955 (USA); My Old Man's a Dustman, 1956; Cockatrice, 1963; The Biggest Pig in Barbados, 1965; Penguin Wolf Mankowitz, 1967; *short stories:* The Mendelman Fire, 1957; *histories:* Wedgwood, 1953; The Portland Vase, 1953; An Encyclopedia of English Pottery and Porcelain, 1957; *plays:* The Bespoke Overcoat and Other Plays, 1955; Expresso Bongo (musical), 1958-59; Make Me An Offer (musical), 1959; Belle, 1961 (musical); Pickwick, 1963 (musical); Passion Flower Hotel (musical), 1965; *films:* Make Me An Offer, 1954; A Kid for Two Farthings, 1954; The Bespoke Overcoat, 1955; Expresso Bongo, 1960; The Millionairess, 1960; The Long and The Short and The Tall, 1961; The Day the Earth Caught Fire, 1961; The Waltz of the Toreadors, 1962; Where The Spies Are, 1965; Casino Royale, 1967; The Assassination Bureau, 1969; Bloomfield, 1969. *Recreation:* sleeping. *Address:* 2 Dorset Street, W1. *T:* 01-935 1741. *Club:* Savile.

**MANKTELOW, Sir (Arthur) Richard,** KBE 1957; CB 1948; retired as Deputy Secretary, Ministry of Agriculture, Fisheries and Food (1954-60); Chairman, Alexander Duckham & Co., since 1969; *b* 8 April 1899; *s* of late Richard Manktelow, Worthing; *m* 1st, 1926, Edith Helen (*d* 1965), *d* of late Harry Saxby, Grove Park; three *s* one *d*; 2nd, 1967, Mrs Dorothea Taylour. *Educ:* King Charles the Martyr Sch., Tunbridge Wells; London School of Economics. Entered Civil Service as boy clerk, 1914. Served European War, 1917-19, London Irish Rifles and Machine Gun Corps. Asst Secretary, 1937; Principal Asst Secretary, 1945; Under-Secretary, 1946; Principal Finance Officer, 1951-54. Trustee of National Society for Cancer Relief, 1959-; Sponsor, Colostomy Welfare Gp. member, Hops Marketing Board, 1960-70; Director, Agricultural Mortgage Corporation, 1961-; Member, Council, Royal Veterinary College. Chairman: Regional Public Services Survey Commission for West Indies, 1961-62; East Caribbean Civil Service Commission, 1962-63. Knight Order of St Olav of Norway, 1947. *Address:* Little Frolbury, Sutton Abinger, Dorking, Surrey. *T:* Dorking 730656. *Clubs:* Farmers', Royal Commonwealth Society.

**MANLEY, Prof. Gordon;** Emeritus Professor and Research Associate since 1968, University of Lancaster, (Professor of Environmental Sciences, 1964-68); *b* 3 Jan. 1902; *s* of Valentine Manley, Chartered Accountant; *m* 1930, Audrey Fairfax, *d* of late Professor Arthur Robinson, MA, DCL, Master of Hatfield Coll., Durham; no *c*. *Educ:* Queen Elizabeth's, Blackburn; Manchester Univ.; Caius Coll., Cambridge; MA (Cantab), DSc (Manchester); Meteorological Office, 1925; Greenland Expedition, 1926; Assistant Lecturer, Birmingham, 1926; Lecturer and Head of Department, Durham, 1928; University Demonstrator and Lecturer, Cambridge, 1939-48; Professor of Geography, University of London (Bedford Coll.), 1948-64. President, Royal Meteorological Society, 1945-46; Leverhulme Award for work on Pennines, 1937; Buchan Prize (Royal Met. Society), 1943; Symons Lecturer, 1944; Murchison Grant (RGS), 1947. Flt-Lieut, Cambridge University Air Squadron, 1942-45. Correspondent for glaciology, British National Cttee for the International Geophysical Year, 1955-61. Air Ministry, Sub-Cttee for Meteorological Research, 1958-62. Ministry of Technology Visitor, 1964-69. External Examiner, Universities of Bristol, St Andrews, and others. Vis. Prof., Texas A&M Univ., 1969. *Publications:* Climate and the British Scene, (4th imp. 1969); papers, chiefly on British and Polar climatology, also on history of cartography, etc, in scientific journals. *Recreation:* travel among mountains. *Address:* 3 Whitwell Way, Coton, Cambridge.

**MANN, Hon. Sir Alan (Harbury),** Kt 1964; MBE 1946; QC (Australia) 1955; Chief Justice of Supreme Court, Territory of Papua and New Guinea, since 1957; Judge of Court of Appeal for Island of Nauru, 1957-65. President of Trustees, Territory Museum and Art Gallery, since 1958; *b* 14 May 1914; *s* of late Robert Henry Mann, Melbourne, and late Catherine (*née* Ross); *m* 1940, Yvonne, *d* of late William Stanley Stanton and late Florence Isobel (*née* Moss), Melbourne; four *d*. *Educ:* Haileybury Coll., Victoria; Geelong Church of England Grammar Sch.; Melbourne Univ. Called to Victorian Bar, 1938. In practice as Barrister until Oct. 1942. Served as Navigator in RAAF, 1942-46; 10 Squadron RAAF, Mt Batten, Plymouth, 1943-45 (Acting Bombing Leader and Photographic Officer). Resumed practice at Victoria Bar, 1946. Member Victoria Bar Council, 1946-57. Member Executive Cttee, Law Council of Australia, 1948-51. Part-time lecturer in law subjects at School of Accounting, Royal Melbourne Technical Coll., 1946-50. *Publications:* (jointly) Research Lecture on The Divisible Profits of Trading Companies; minor articles and text books for students in Company Law. *Recreations:* oil and water colour painting, applied arts and sciences, especially natural history, Bush walking and collecting, orchids and boating. *Address:* c/o Supreme Court, Port Moresby, New Guinea; 18 Armit Street, Port Moresby. *T:* Port Moresby 2087.

**MANN, Arthur Henry,** CH 1941; Honorary LLD Leeds; *b* Warwick, 1876. Editor of Yorkshire Post, 1919-39; formerly Editor of the Evening Standard; Member of Board of Governors of BBC, 1941-46. *Address:* 180 Sandgate Road, Folkestone, Kent. *Club:* Devonshire.

**MANN, Bruce Leslie Home D.;** *see* Douglas-Mann.

**MANN, Mrs Christopher;** *see* Joyce, Eileen.

**MANN, Sir (Edward) John,** 2nd Bt, *cr* 1905; *b* 26 Jan. 1883; *e s* of Sir Edward Mann, 1st Bt, and Anna Jane (*d* 1928), *d* of Paul Bell, Stiffkey, Norfolk; *S* father 1943; *m* 1951, Clare Helen, *d* of Robert Graham Dryden Alexander, Brentwood, Essex. *Educ:* Marlborough Coll.; Pembroke Coll., Cambridge, BA; High Sheriff of Norfolk, 1939-40. *Heir:* *g n* Rupert Edward Mann, *b* 11 Nov. 1946. *Address:* Thelveton

Hall, Diss, Norfolk. *T:* Dickleburgh 213. *Club:* Norfolk (Norwich).

**MANN, Frederick George,** FRS 1947; ScD (Cantab), DSc (London), FRIC; Reader Emeritus in Organic Chemistry, Cambridge University, 1946; Fellow of Trinity College, Cambridge; *b* 29 June 1897; *s* of William Clarence Herbert and Elizabeth Ann Mann; *m* 1st, 1930, Margaret Reid (*d* 1950), *d* of William Shackleton, FRAS; two *d*; 2nd, 1951, Barbara, *d* of Percy Thornber; one *d*. *Educ:* London Univ. London Univ., 1914-17, 1919; served European War, finally as 2nd Lieut Special Bde, RE, BEF, France, 1917-19; BSc (London), 1919; research student, Downing Coll., Cambridge, 1920-23; PhD (Cantab) 1923; Assistant to Professor of Chemistry (Sir William Pope), 1922; DSc (London), 1929; Lecturer in Chemistry, Cambridge Univ., 1930; FRIC 1929; Fellow and Lecturer, Trinity Coll., Cambridge, 1931, Praelector in Chemistry, 1960; ScD (Cantab) 1932; Member Council of Chemical Society, 1935-38, 1940-43, 1946-49, Vice-President, 1958-61; Tilden Lecturer, 1944; Member Council of Royal Institute of Chemistry, 1942-45, 1948-51; Visiting Senior Prof. of Chemistry, University of Hawaii, 1946-47. *Publications:* Practical Organic Chemistry, 1936; Introduction to Practical Organic Chemistry, 1939 (both with Dr B. C. Saunders). The Heterocyclic Derivatives of Phosphorus, Arsenic, Antimony, Bismuth, and Silicon, 1950 (2nd edn, 1970). Numerous papers in Proceedings of the Royal Society, Journal of the Chemical Society, Journal of Society of Chemical Industry, etc. *Recreations:* walking, golf, ornithology. *Address:* 24 Porson Road, Cambridge; Trinity College, Cambridge. *T:* Cambridge 52704.

**MANN, Rev. George Albert Douglas;** General Secretary, Free Church Federal Council, since 1970; *b* 17 April 1914; *er s* of George and Alice Mann; *m* 1940, Mabel Harwood; no *c*. *Educ:* Clifford Road Sch., Ipswich; Manchester Baptist Coll.; Manchester Univ. Minister, Mount Pleasant Baptist Church, Burnley, 1940-42. Chaplain to HM Forces, 1942-45 (now Hon. CF); Sen. Staff Chaplain, ALFSEA, 1945-46. Minister: Park Tabernacle Baptist Church, Great Yarmouth, 1947-52; Union Baptist Church, High Wycombe, 1952-58. Mem. Baptist Union Council, 1948-; Asst Sec., and Sec. of Hosp. Chaplaincy Bd, Free Church Federal Council, 1958-69. *Recreations:* cricket, football, gardening, philately. *Address:* c/o Free Church Federal Council, 27 Tavistock Square, WC1H 9HH. *T:* 01-387 8413.

**MANN, Ida,** CBE 1950; MA Oxon, DSc London; MB, BS London; FRCS; FRACS; Fellow, College of Physicians of Philadelphia; Cons. Surgeon, Royal London Ophthalmic (Moorfields) Hospital; Member Expert Committee, WHO; late Cons. Ophthalmologist to Government of Western Australia; *b* London, 1893; *d* of F. W. Mann, MBE, and Ellen Packham; *m* 1944, William Ewart Gye, FRS, MD, FRCP (*d* 1952). *Educ:* University of London. Ophthalmic surgeon and research worker; late Research Student, Institute of Pathology, St Mary's Hospital; Henry George Plimmer Fellow of the Imperial College of Science and Technology; Assistant Surgeon, Central London Ophthalmic Hospital; Ophthalmic Surgeon, Royal Free Hospital and Elizabeth Garrett Anderson Hospital; Pathologist, Central London Ophthalmic Hospital; Senior Surgeon Oxford Eye Hospital; Margaret Ogilvie Reader, University of Oxford, 1941, Professor 1945-47; War Service as Head of Research Team for Ministry of Supply. Fellow of St Hugh's College; Gifford Edmonds Prize in Ophthalmology, 1926; Arris and Gale Lecturer, 1928; Doyne Memorial Lecturer, 1929; Montgomery Lecturer, 1935; Nettleship Prize, 1930; Mackenzie Memorial Medal, 1935; Howe Memorial Medal, 1958; Bowman Medal, 1961. Member: Ophthalmological Society of UK and other societies. *Publications:* The Development of the Human Eye; Developmental Abnormalities of the Eye; Culture, Race, Climate and Eye Disease; and numerous papers in medical journals. *Recreation:* travel. *Address:* 56 Hobbs Avenue, Nedlands, Western Australia 6009, Australia.

**MANN, Sir John;** *see* Mann, Sir E. J.

**MANN, Julia de Lacy,** MA; Principal, St Hilda's College, Oxford, 1928-July 1955; *o d* of James Saumarez Mann, MA, sometime Fellow of Trinity College, Oxford; *b* Aug. 1891. *Educ:* Bromley High Sch.; Somerville Coll., Oxford. Classical Hon. Mods. 1912; Lit. Hum. 1914; Secretarial work, Admiralty and Foreign Office, 1915-19; Vice-Principal, St Hilda's Coll., 1923-28. *Publications:* (with A. P. Wadsworth), The Cotton Trade and Industrial Lancashire, 1600-1780, 1931, Ed. Documents illustrating the Wiltshire Textile Trades in the 18th Century (Wilts Arch. Society, Records Branch, Vol. XIX), 1964. *Address:* The Cottage, Bower Hill, Melksham, Wilts. *Club:* University Women's.

**MANN, Keith Cranston,** CBE 1953; *b* 23 Sept. 1903; *s* of Frederick Thomas Mann, Dublin; *m* 1930, Millicent Grace, *d* of late G. Philip Girling, Portadown, Co. Armagh, N Ireland; three *d*. *Educ:* St Stephen's Green Sch., Dublin; Trinity Coll., Dublin Univ. Asst Civil Engineer, Public Works Office, Ireland, 1926-29; entered Air Min. as Asst Civil Engr, Directorate Gen. of Works, 1929; Superintending Engr, 1939-42; Chief Engr, RAF Maintenance Command, 1942-46; Chief Engr, Middle East Air Force, 1946-48; Dep. Dir of Works, Air Min., 1948-50; Dir of Works, Overseas Dept, 1950-58; Dep. Dir Gen. of Works, Air Min., 1958-63; Chief Civil Engr, Min. of Public Building and Works, 1963-64. *Publications:* contributor to Proc. Instn of Civl Engrs on Airfields. *Recreations:* tennis, country pursuits and music. *Address:* Field Cottage, Chedworth, Cheltenham, Glos. *T:* Fossebridge 279.

**MANN, Murray G.;** *see* Gell-Mann.

**MANN, Ronald;** Deputy Chairman, National and Grindlays Bank Ltd, since 1964; *b* 22 April 1908; *s* of Harry Ainsley Mann and Millicent (*née* Copplestone); *m* 1935, Beatrice Elinor Crüwell Wright; one *s* three *d*. *Educ:* Cranleigh Sch., Surrey. The Eastern Produce and Estates Co. Ltd: Asst, Ceylon, 1930-35; Man., Ceylon, 1935-46; Man. Dir, London, 1947-; Chm., Eastern Produce Holdings Ltd, 1957-. *Recreations:* golf, gardening. *Address:* Fernhurst Rise, Fernhurst, near Haslemere, Surrey. *T:* Fernhurst 220. *Club:* Oriental.

**MANN, Thaddeus Robert Rudolph,** CBE 1962; FRS 1951; Biochemist; Professor of the Physiology of Reproduction, University of Cambridge, since 1967 (Reader in Physiology of Animal Reproduction, 1953-67); Director of the Agricultural Research Council Unit of Reproductive Physiology and Biochemistry, Cambridge, since 1954; Fellow of Trinity Hall, Cambridge, since 1961; Member of the Staff of Agricultural Research Council since 1944; *b* 1908; *s* of late William Mann and Emilia (*née* Quest); *m* 1934, Dr Cecilia Lutwak-Mann. *Educ:* Trin. Hall, Cambridge; MD Lwŏw 1935,

PhD Cantab 1937, ScD Cantab 1950; Rockefeller Research Fellow, 1935-37; Beit Mem. Research Fellow, 1937-44. Awarded Amory Prize of Amer. Academy of Arts and Sciences, 1955; Senior Lalor Fellow at Woods Hole, 1960; Vis. Prof. in Biology at Florida State Univ., 1962; Vis. Prof. in Biological Structure and Zoology, Univ. of Washington, 1968. Gregory Pincus Meml Lectr, 1969; Albert Tyler Meml Lectr, 1970. Dr of Veterinary Medicine (*hc*), Ghent. Cavaliere Ufficiale, Order of Merit (Italy), 1966. *Publications:* The Biochemistry of Semen, 1954; The Biochemistry of Semen and of the Male Reproductive Tract, 1964; papers on Carbohydrate Metabolism of Muscle, Yeast and Moulds, on Metaloprotein Enzymes, and on Biochemistry of Reproduction. *Address:* Reproductive Physiology and Biochemistry Unit, University of Cambridge, Downing Street, Cambridge.

**MANN, William Neville,** MD, FRCP; Physician: to the Queen, 1964-70; to Guy's Hospital since 1946; to King Edward VII's Hospital for Officers, since 1965; *b* 4 April 1911; *s* of William Frank Mann and Clara, *d* of John Chadwick; *m* Pamela, *yr d* of late H. E. Chasteney; two *s* four *d*. *Educ:* Alleyn's Sch.; Guy's Hospital. MB, BS (London), 1935; MRCP 1937; MD (London), 1937; FRCP, 1947. House Physician, Demonstrator of Pathology and Medical Registrar, Guy's Hospital, 1935-39. Served, 1940-45, in RAMC in Middle East and Indian Ocean (Temp. Lt-Col). Hon. Visiting Physician to Johns Hopkins Hosp., Baltimore, USA, 1950. Physician to HM Household, 1954-64. Sen. Censor and Sen. Vice-Pres., RCP, 1969-70. *Publications:* Clinical Examination of Patients (jointly), 1950; The Medical Works of Hippocrates (jointly), 1950. Editor, Conybeare's Text-book of Medicine, 15th edn, 1970. *Address:* 16 Upper Wimpole Street, W1. *T:* 01-935 8806. *Club:* Garrick.

**MANN, William Somervell;** Music Critic, The Times, since 1960; Radio Broadcaster on music since 1949; Associate Editor, Opera, since 1954; President, The Critics' Circle, 1963-64; *b* 14 Feb. 1924; *s* of Gerald and Joyce Mann; *m* 1948, Erika Charlotte Emilie Sohler; four *d*. *Educ:* Winchester Coll.; Magdalene Coll., Cambridge (BA, MusB). Music Critic, Cambridge Review, 1946-48; Asst Music Critic, The Times, 1948-60. *Publications:* Introduction to the Music of J. S. Bach, 1950; (contrib. to symposium) Benjamin Britten, 1952; (contrib. to): The Concerto, 1952; The Record Guide, 1955; Chamber Music, 1957; The Analytical Concert Guide (English Editor), 1957; (contrib.) Music and Western Man, 1958; Let's Fake an Opera (with F. Reizenstein), 1958; Richard Strauss's Operas, 1964; Wagner's The Ring, Introduction and Translation, 1964; (contrib. to symposium) Michael Tippett, 1965; Wagner's Tristan, Introduction and Translation, 1968. Contributor: Music and Letters, Music Review, Musical Times, Opera, The Gramophone. *Recreations:* camping, interior decoration, food and drink, foreign languages, darts, making music. *Address:* 14 Belvedere Drive, SW19. *T:* 01-946 0773. *Clubs:* Camping Club of GB and Ireland; Royal Musical Association; The Critics' Circle.

**MANNERING, Rev. Ernest;** *b* 28 Sept. 1882; 2nd *s* of George Willsher and Annie Southey Mannering, of Beckenham, Kent; *m* 1921, Irene, *y d* of late Rt Rev. J. Denton Thompson, Bishop of Sodor and Man. *Educ:* Dulwich Coll.; BNC, Oxford (Scholar); 2nd class Classical Moderations, 3rd class Lit. Hum.; BA 1905, MA 1908; Wycliffe Hall, Oxford, 1906. Deacon, 1906; Priest, 1907; Curate of Holy Trinity, S Marylebone, 1906-11; Christ Church, Woking, 1911-13; Temporary Chaplain to the Forces, 1915-19; Principal of Bishop Wilson Theological Coll., Isle of Man, and Domestic Chaplain to the Bishop of Sodor and Man, 1913-15 and 1919-20; Vice-Principal of St Aidan's Coll., Birkenhead, 1920-21; Vicar of St Mark's, Sheffield, 1921-30; Vicar of St Peter's, Brockley, 1931-35; Vicar of Wadhurst, 1935-46; Rural Dean of Etchingham, 1935-46; Rector of Westonbirt with Lasborough and Chaplain to Westonbirt Sch., 1946-50; Vicar of Hanmer Springs, New Zealand, 1950-52. *Address:* The Firs, West Malvern, Worcs.

**MANNERING, Rev. Canon Leslie George,** MC; MA; Canon Residentiary, Bristol Cathedral, 1932-53, now Canon Emeritus, 1953; Chaplain to the Queen, 1952-69 (to King George VI, 1951-52); *b* 27 Oct. 1883; *s* of George Willsher Mannering and Annie Southey Mannering; *m* 1919, Constance Marguerite Douthwaite; no *c*. *Educ:* Dulwich Coll.; Sidney Sussex Coll., Cambridge (Scholar). 2nd Class Classical Tripos, BA; Ridley Hall, Cambridge; 3rd Class Theological Tripos; MA; Deacon, 1907; Priest, 1908; Curate, Emmanuel, West End, Hampstead, 1907-10; Curate, Holy Trinity, Cambridge, 1910-14; Chaplain, Pembroke Coll., Cambridge, 1912-14; Chaplain to the Forces, 1914-19; Senior Chaplain 17th Div. BEF, 1916-17 (MC); Vicar, St Matthew's, Brixton, SW2, 1920-26; St John the Evangelist, Redhill, Surrey, 1926-32; Rural Dean, Reigate, 1929-32; Commissary to Bishop of Victoria, Hong Kong, 1924-32; Founder of the Bible Reading Fellowship; Select Preacher, Cambridge Univ., 1937; Lecturer in Pastoral Theology, Cambridge Univ., 1939. *Address:* Trevescan, 95 Andrews Road, Malvern, Worcs WR1L 3PU. *T:* Malvern 2303.

**MANNERS,** family name of **Baron Manners,** and **Duke of Rutland.**

**MANNERS,** 4th Baron, *cr* 1807; **Francis Henry Manners,** MC; DL; JP; Hants CC; late Captain Grenadier Guards; Brevet Colonel late 5/7 Battalion Hampshire Regiment, TF; *b* 21 July 1897; *s* of 3rd Baron and Constance (*d* 1920), *d* of Col Henry E. H. Fane, MP, of Clovelly Court, Devon; *S* father, 1927; *m* 1921, Mary Edith, *d* of late Rt Rev. Lord William Cecil, Bishop of Exeter; three *s* one *d*. *Educ:* Eton. Served European War, 1914-19 (wounded MC). *Heir: s* Flight Lt Hon. John Robert Cecil Manners, RAFVR [*b* 13 Feb. 1923; *m* 1949, Jennifer Selena, *d* of Ian Fairbairn, 4 More's Garden, Chelsea, and of Mrs C. Fairbairn; one *s* two *d*]. *Address:* Tyrrell's Ford, Christchurch, Hants. *T:* Bransgore 317.

**MANNERS, Elizabeth Maude,** TD 1962; MA; Headmistress of Felixstowe College, Suffolk, since Sept. 1967; *b* 20 July 1917; *d* of William George Manners and Anne Mary Manners (*née* Sced). *Educ:* Stockton-on-Tees Sec. Sch.; St Hild's Coll., Durham Univ. BA (Dunelm) 1938; MA 1941. Teacher of French at: Marton Grove Sch., Middlesbrough, 1939-40; Ramsey Gram. Sch., IOM, 1940-42; Consett Sec. Sch., Durham, 1942-44; Yarm Gram. Sch., Yorks, 1944-54; Deputy Head, Mexborough Gram. Sch., Yorks, 1954-59; Head Mistress, Central Gram. Sch. for Girls, Manchester, 1959-67. Vice-Pres., Girl Guides Assoc., Co. Manchester, 1959-67. Mem. Education Cttee, Brit. Fedn of Univ. Women, 1966-68. Enlisted ATS (TA), 1947; commissioned, 1949. Coronation Medal, 1953. *Recreations:* foreign travel, theatre, motoring, good food and wine. *Address:* Muirfield, Foxgrove Lane,

Felixstowe, Suffolk. *T:* Felixstowe 3325/4269. *Club:* Public Schools.

**MANNHEIM, Hermann,** OBE 1959; Dr juris; Reader in Criminology, University of London, 1946-55, retired; Hon. Director, Criminological Research Unit, London School of Economics, 1956-61; naturalised British subject, 1940; *b* 26 Oct. 1889; *s* of Wilhelm Mannheim and Clara Marcuse; *m* 1919, Mona Mark. *Educ:* Munich, Freiburg, Strasbourg, Koenigsberg Univs. Judge in Criminal Courts and Court of Appeal (Kammergericht), Berlin, 1923-33 (Promoted by West German Govt to rank of retd Pres. of Div. of Court of Appeal, 1952); Lectr and Prof. in Faculty of Law, Berlin Univ., 1923-33; Lecturer in Criminology, London Sch. of Economics, 1935-46; Visiting Prof., Univs of Oregon and Pennsylvania, 1953. Leon Fellow Univ. of London, 1936-37; Pres. Scientific Cttee, Internat. Soc. of Criminology until 1962; Vice-President: Inst. for Study and Treatment of Delinquency; British Soc. of Criminology; Mem. Joint Cttee on Psychiatry and the Law of BMA and Magistrates' Assoc., resigned 1956; Mem., Colonial Office Advisory Cttee on Treatment of Offenders, until 1961; Chm. Programme Cttee, Third Internat. Congress on Criminology, London, 1955; Jt Dir Fourth Internat. Course in Criminology, London, 1954. Chm. Scientific Group for the Discussion of Delinquency Problems, 1956-58; Lecture tours, Holland, 1949, Norway and USA, 1953, Western Germany, 1956, USA and Canada, 1957. Hon. Dr of Law, Utrecht, 1957; Hon. DSc Econ Wales, 1970. Hon. Fellow, London Sch. of Economics, 1965. Coronation Medal, 1953; Grosses Verdienstkreuz der Bundesrepublik Deutschland, 1965; Golden Beccaria Medal of German Society of Criminology, 1965. *Publications:* Der Masstab der Fahrlässigkeit im Strafrecht, 1912; Die Revision im Strafverfahren, 1925; Pressrecht, 1927; The Dilemma of Penal Reform, 1939; Social Aspects of Crime in England between the Wars, 1940; War and Crime, 1941; Criminal Justice and Social Reconstruction, 1946; Juvenile Delinquency in an English Middletown, 1948; (with A. M. Carr-Saunders and E. C. Rhodes) Young Offenders, 1942; (with L. T. Wilkins) Prediction Methods in relation to Borstal Training, 1955; Group Problems in Crime and Punishment, 1955; (Co-author) The Teaching of Criminology (UNESCO), 1957; Courts for Adolescents, 1959; (Co-author) Law and Opinion in England in the Twentieth Century, 1959; Deutsche Strafrechtsreform in englischer Sicht, 1960. Editor Pioneers in Criminology, 1960; Comparative Criminology (2 vols), 1965. Joint Editor British Journal of Criminology (resigned 1966); Joint Editor Library of Criminology, 1960-66. *Recreations:* music and travelling. *Address:* 16 Heathfielde, Lyttelton Road, N2.

**MANNHEIM, Lucie;** actress; *b* Berlin, 30 April 1905; *d* of late Louis Mannheim and Gertrud Mannheim (*née* Zander); *m* 1941, Marius Goring, *qv. Educ:* Dorothean Schule and Eupel Schule, Berlin. Made first appearance at age of twelve, 1917, as Kaethie in Alt Heidelberg; joined Berlin Volksbuehne, 1919, playing among other parts Cordelia in King Lear, Aman in Tagore's Post Office, Agafia in Gogol's Marriage. Became leading actress at Berlin State Theatre, playing among other parts, 1924-33: Nora in Ibsen's Doll's House, Juliet in Romeo and Juliet, Irina in Chekov's Three Sisters, Kaetchen in Kleist's Kaetchen von Heilbronn. Played concurrently, in many other theatres, musical plays, comedies, farces in Berlin dialect and straight plays such as Verneuil's Monsieur Lamberthier, The Trial of Mary Dugan. Left Germany, 1933. First appearance in London in Nina, Criterion, 1935; Girl Unknown, New, 1936; The Last Straw, Comedy, 1937; in management at Duke of York's Theatre with Marius Goring producing Doll's House, revival of Nina, 1938-39. Worked for BBC German Service, 1940-46. Toured Germany with Monsieur Lamberthier, playing in English and German, 1947. Arts Theatre Festival 1948: playing Rebecca West in Ibsen's Rosmersholm, Sweetie in Shaw's Too True to be Good, Madame Popof in Chekov's Bear, Fyokla in Gogol's Marriage, Germaine in Monsieur Lamberthier (also produced last 3 plays). Daphne Laureola and The Corn is Green, in Berlin, 1949-50; Rose Tattoo, Berlin, 1952; Relative Values, Berlin, 1953; Hauptmann's Ratten, 1954; Tolstoy's Light Shines in Darkness, 1956; Look Homeward Angel, 1958; Biberpelz, 1959; Tonight at 8.30, 1960; La Voix Humaine, 1960; Anouilh's The Grotto, 1962; Ratten, Hamburg, 1965; The Skin of our Teeth, Hamburg, 1966; two Berlin musicals (also prod Hamburg), 1967; Anouilh's Pauvre Antoine, Berlin, 1967. Has done many broadcasts for BBC and made several films in Berlin, Paris and London; has appeared on TV in England and Germany. Awarded Verdienst Kreuz, 1953 and Grand Cross of Merit, 1959, by President of German Federal Republic for services to the theatre. Made Berlin State Actress by Berlin Senate, 1963. *Recreations:* skating, sunbathing. *Address:* Middle Court, The Green, Hampton Court, Surrey. *T:* 01-977 4030.

**MANNIN, Ethel,** author; *e d* of Robert Mannin and Edith Gray; *b* London, 1900; *m* 1920, J. A. Porteous (*d* 1954); one *d*; *m* 1938, Reginald Reynolds (*d* 1958). *Educ:* Local Council Sch. Stenographer in advertising agency at 15; Associate-Editor with Sir Charles Higham of the old sporting and theatrical paper, The Pelican, 1918; joined ILP 1932. *Publications:* Martha, 1923; Hunger of the Sea, 1924; Sounding Brass, 1925; Pilgrims, 1927; Green Willow, 1928; Crescendo, 1929; Children of the Earth, 1930; Confessions and Impressions, 1930; Ragged Banners, 1931; Commonsense and the Child, 1931; Green Figs (stories), 1931; Linda Shawn, 1932; All Experience (travel sketches), 1932; Venetian Blinds, 1933; Dryad (stories), 1933; Men are Unwise, 1934; Forever Wandering (travel sketches), 1934; Cactus, 1935; The Falconer's Voice (stories), 1935; The Pure Flame, 1936; South to Samarkand (travel), 1936; Women also Dream, 1937; Commonsense and the Adolescent, 1938; Women and the Revolution, 1938; Rose and Sylvie, 1938; Darkness my Bride, 1939; Privileged Spectator (sequel to Confessions), 1939; Julie, 1940; Rolling in the Dew, 1940; Christianity or Chaos: a Re-Statement of Religion, 1940; Red Rose: a Novel based on the Life of Emma Goldman, 1941; Commonsense and Morality, 1942; Captain Moonlight, 1942; The Blossoming Bough, 1943; No More Mimosa (stories), 1943; Proud Heaven, 1944; Bread and Roses, A Survey of and a Blue-Print for Utopia, 1944; Lucifer and the Child, 1945; The Dark Forest, 1946; Comrade, O Comrade, 1947; Late Have I Loved Thee, 1948; Connemara Journal (memoirs), 1948; German Journey (travel), 1948; Every Man a Stranger, 1949; Jungle Journey (travel), 1950; Bavarian Story, 1950; At Sundown, the Tiger . . ., 1951; The Fields at Evening, 1952; The Wild Swans (Tales from the Ancient Irish), 1952; This Was a Man (biography), 1952; Moroccan Mosaic (travel), 1953; Lover Under Another Name, 1953; Two Studies in Integrity (biography), 1954; So Tiberius (novella), 1954; Land of the Crested Lion (travel), 1955; The Living Lotus, 1956; Pity the Innocent, 1957; Country of the Sea (travel), 1957; A Scent of Hyacinths, 1958; Ann and Peter in Sweden (Children's book), 1958; Ann and Peter in Japan, 1960; Ann and Peter in Austria, 1961; The Blue-eyed Boy, 1959; Brief Voices (autobiography) 1959; The Flowery Sword (travel), 1960; Sabishisa, 1961; Curfew at Dawn, 1962; With Will Adams through Japan, 1962; A Lance for the Arabs (Travels in the Middle East), 1963; The Road to Beersheba (novel), 1963; Rebels' Ride, the Revolt of the Individual, 1964; Aspects of Egypt, some Travels in the United Arab Republic, 1964; The Burning Bush, 1965; The Lovely Land: the Hashemite Kingdom of Jordan, 1965; The Night and its Homing, 1966; Loneliness, A Study of the Human Condition, 1966; An American Journey, 1967; The Lady and the Mystic, 1967; England for a Change (travel), 1968; Bitter Babylon, 1968; The Saga of Sammy-Cat (children's story), 1969; The Midnight Street (novel), 1969; Practitioners of Love, Some Aspects of the Human Phenomenon, 1969; England at Large (travel), 1970; Free Pass to Nowhere (novel), 1970; Young in the Twenties (autobiography), 1971. *Recreations:* gardening, walking, entertaining friends. *Address:* Oak Cottage, Burghley Road, SW19.

**MANNING, Cecil Aubrey Gwynne;** *b* 1892; *s* of Charles Walter Manning; *m* 1915, *d* of William Twitchett; two *s* two *d*; *m* 1919, *d* of William Green; one *s*. Mem. LCC 1922-32 and 1937 and 1949. Leader of Opposition, 1929-30, Dep. Chm., 1930-31. JP 1927, DL 1931, Co. London. MP (Lab) N Camberwell, 1944-50.

**MANNING, Prof. Charles Anthony Woodward;** Montague Burton (formerly Cassel) Professor of International Relations, London School of Economics, University of London, 1930-62, now emeritus; *b* 18 Nov. 1894; *s* of Dumaresq Williamson Manning and Helena Isabella Bell; *m* 1939, Marion Somerville (Maisie) Johnston. *Educ:* Diocesan Coll (Bishops), Rondebosch; South African Coll., Cape Town; Brasenose Coll., Oxford. Bishops Rhodes Schol., 1914. Enlisted 18th Royal Fusiliers, 1914; commissioned 7th Oxford and Bucks Lt Inf., 1915; active service France and Salonika, 1915-17 (wounded, despatches twice); Instr 11th Officer Cadet Bn (Actg Capt.), 1917-18; BA Oxon Greats (distinction), 1920; BA Oxon Jurisprudence (1st Cl.), 1921; BCL (1st Cl.), 1922; Sen. Hulme Schol., 1921; Barr., Middle Temple, 1922; ILO (Diplomatic Div.), 1922; League of Nations (Personal Asst to Sec.-Gen.), 1922; Fellow, New Coll., and Law Lecturer, New and Pembroke Colls, Oxford, 1923; Laura Spellman Rockefeller Fellow (Harvard), 1925-26; Dep. Prof. of Internat. Law and Diplomacy, Oxford, 1927; Examiner in Roman Law to Council of Legal Education, 1927-32. Tutor, Zimmern Sch. of International Studies, Geneva, 1925 and subs. summers. Sen. Specialist, Wartime Chatham House, 1939-43. Chm., South Africa Soc., 1964-. *Publications:* The Policies of the British Dominions in the League of Nations, 1932; (trans.) Völkerrecht im Grundriss by Hatschek, 1930; (editor) Salmond's Jurisprudence, 8th edn, 1930; (edited and contrib. to) Peaceful Change, 1937; University Teaching of Social Sciences, International Relations (Unesco), 1952; The Nature of International Society, 1962; Empire into Commonwealth (in Promise of Greatness), 1968; Austin To-day (in Modern Theories of Law), 1933, and other articles. *Recreations:* watercolour, gardening, music. *Address:* 34 Newton Road, W2. *T:* 01-229 7088; Gatehouse, Felsted, Essex. *T:* 298.

**MANNING, Dame (Elizabeth) Leah,** DBE 1966; *d* of Charles and Margaret Perrett, Rockford, Ill; *m* 1914, William Henry Manning (decd), The Observatory, Cambridge. *Educ:* St John's Sch., Bridgwater; Homerton Coll., Cambridge. Past Organising Sec. of Nat. Union of Teachers; Past Headmistress of Open Air Sch., Cambridge; Past Pres. of National Union of Teachers; MP (Lab.) East Islington, Feb.-Oct. 1931; Epping Div. of Essex, 1945-50. Company Dir from 1955, now retired. *Publications:* What I Saw in Spain, 1933; A Life for Education (autobiography), 1970. *Recreations:* travelling, swimming, motoring. *Address:* Willow Cottage, Hatfield Broad Oak, Essex. *T:* Hatfield Broad Oak 247.

**MANNING, Frederick Allan,** CVO 1954; JP; Commissioner for Transport, Queensland, since 1967 (Deputy Commissioner, 1960-67); *b* Gladstone, Qld, Australia, 27 Aug. 1904; British parentage; *m* 1934, Phyllis Maud Fullerton; no *c*. *Educ:* Central Boys' State Sch. and Boys' Gram. Sch., Rockhampton, Qld. Entered Qld State Public Service as Clerk in Petty Sessions Office, Rockhampton, 1920; Clerk of Petty Sessions and Mining Registrar, 1923; Stipendiary Magistrate and Mining Warden, 1934; Petty Sessions Office, Brisbane, 1926; Relieving Clerk of Petty Sessions and Mining Registrar, 1931 (all parts of State); seconded to Commonwealth Govt for service in Qld Directorate of Rationing Commission, 1942; Asst Dep. Dir of Rationing, 1943. Dep. Dir, 1944, for Qld; returned to Qld Public Service, 1947; Sec., Dept of Transport, 1947-60; JP, Qld, 1925-. Coronation Medal, 1953; State Dir, Royal Visit to Queensland, 1954 (CVO). Exec. Vice-Chm, Qld Road Safety Coun., and Qld Rep. Aust. Road Safety Coun., 1962. Mem. Royal Historical Soc. of Queensland. *Recreation:* bowls. *Address:* 126 Indooroopilly Road, Taringa, Brisbane, Qld 4068, Australia. *T:* 701936. *Club:* Tattersalls (Brisbane).

**MANNING, Frederick Edwin Alfred,** CBE 1954; MC 1919; TD 1937; BSc (Eng.); Hon. MA London; Hon. DEng Nova Scotia Technical College; CEng; FIMechE; FIEE; FINucE; DPA (London); Adviser on the Athlone Fellowship Scheme, since 1961; *b* 6 April 1897; *s* of late Francis Alfred Manning and late Ellen Lavinia Manning; *m* 1927, Alice Beatrice Wistow, BSc; one *s* one *d* (and one *s* decd.). *Educ:* Christ's Hospital; St Olave's; Univ. of London. Academic Diploma of Mil. Studies, Univ. of London; Certificate in Statistics, Univ. of Vienna. War Service, 1915-20 (Order of St Stanislas, 2nd Class; Order of St Vladimir, 4th Class); RE (TA) 1920-38; Royal Signals (TA), 1938-52. Hon. Col, Univ. of London OTC, 1958-68, retired 1968, retaining rank of Col. Entered GPO 1925; idc 1937; Home Office and Min. of Home Security, 1938-41; GPO, 1941; SHAEF, 1943-45; Asst Sec., Foreign Office (Allied Commission for Austria), 1945-47; GPO, 1947; Dir of the Post Office in Wales and Border Counties, 1950-59, retired; Chm. Boards for the CS Commn, 1961-68; Hon. Sen. Treas., Univ. of London Union, 1928-52, Chm. of Union Court, 1952-69, Chm., Sports Finance Cttee, 1969-; Mem. of Senate, Univ. of London, 1952- (Chm. Military Educ. Cttee, 1952-55); First Chm. of Convocation, The City Univ., 1967-70. Metrop. Special Constabulary (Comdt, GPO Div.), 1931-41. *Recreations:* gardening, Rotary (Pres. Shepperton, 1964-65). *Address:* 1 Range Way, Shepperton, Surrey. *T:* Walton-on-Thames 23400. *Clubs:* Civil Service, Royal Commonwealth Society.

**MANNING, Air Cdre Frederick John,** CB 1954; CBE 1948; retired, 1967; *b* 5 May 1912; *s* of Frederick Manning; *m* 1937, Elizabeth Anwyl, *er d* of late Rev. Æ. C. Ruthven-Murray, BA,

Bishop Burton, Beverley; four *d* (and one *s* decd). Cadet, P&OSN Co., 1928; Midshipman, RNR, 1929; Actg Sub-Lt, RNR, 1933; Pilot Officer, RAF, 1934; Flt Lt, 269 Squadron, 1938; Actg Group Capt., 1942; Dir of Organisation (Establishments), Air Ministry, 1944-45 (actg Air Commodore); commanding RAF Station Shaibah, Abu Sueir Shallufa, 1945-47 (acting Group Capt.); Group Capt., Organisation, HQ, RAF, Mediterranean and Middle east, 1947-48; Senior Air Adviser, and Dep. Head of Mission, British Services Mission, Burma, 1949-52; Senior Officer i/c Administration HQ Transport Command, 1952; Dep. Dir of Work Study, Air Ministry, 1956-59; Dir of Manning (2) Air Ministry, 1960-63; Air Officer Administration: HQ Near East Air Force, 1963-65; RAF Fighter Comd. Headquarters, 1965-67. *Address:* c/o Lloyds Bank, Cox's & King's Branch, 6 Pall Mall, SW1. *Clubs:* Royal Commonwealth Society, Royal Air Force.

**MANNING, Sir George,** Kt 1967; CMG 1960; MA; DipSocSci; Mayor of Christchurch, NZ, 1958-68; *b* 11 Feb. 1887; *s* of Richard Manning; *m* 1923, S. E. Willmore; one *s*. *Educ:* Gowerton Gram. Sch., Wales; Canterbury Univ., NZ. Steelworker, 1906-10; emigrated to NZ, 1910; Secretary: Canterbury WEA, 1921-48; New Zealand WEA, 1923; Dominion Pres., WEA, 1946-49; Adult Education and WEA Lecturer, 1948-58. Councillor, Christchurch City Council, 1927-29 and 1936-58. Member: Christchurch Tramway Board, 1933-50; Lyttelton Harbour Bd, 1939-40, 1946-70; Council, Univ. of Canterbury, 1958-68. *Recreations:* bowls, gardening. *Address:* 7 Bletsoe Avenue, Christchurch, NZ.

**MANNING, Dame Leah;** *see* Manning, Dame E. L.

**MANNING, Olivia, (Mrs R. D. Smith);** author; *o d* of late Oliver Manning, Commander, RN, and Olivia, *e d* of late David Morrow, Down, Ireland; *m* 1939, Reginald Donald Smith, Drama Writer-Producer, BBC. *Publications: novels:* The Wind Changes, 1938; Artist Among the Missing, 1949; School for Love, 1951; A Different Face, 1953; The Doves of Venus, 1955; The Balkan Trilogy (The Great Fortune, 1960; The Spoilt City, 1962; Friends and Heroes, 1965); The Play Room, 1969; *short stories:* Growing Up, 1948; A Romantic Hero, 1966; *history:* The Remarkable Expedition, 1947; *travel:* The Dreaming Shore, 1950; *humour:* My Husband Cartwright, 1956; *general;* Extraordinary Cats, 1967. Contributed to Horizon, Windmill, Spectator, New Statesman, Punch, the Observer, Sunday Times, Times Literary Supplement, Vogue, Harper's, The Queen, Saturday Book, Best Short Stories, Winter's Tales, Transatlantic Review, Encounter, Adam. *Recreation:* cats. *Address:* 36 Abbey Gardens, NW8. *T:* 01-624 1025.

**MANNING, Richard Joseph;** *b* 28 March 1883; *s* of Richard Manning; *m* 1912, Ada Agnes Baird, 2nd *d* of Capt. James Brown; two *s* (and one *s* lost in the War of 1939-45) three *d*; *m* 1939, Margaret Asher, *o d* of John Wilson, Blundellsands. *Educ:* Clongowes Wood Coll.; University Coll., Blackrock. Inspector of Police, British Guiana, 1909-20; Resident Magistrate, Tanganyika, 1920-25; Resident Magistrate, Jamaica, 1925-27; Police Magistrate, Gold Coast, 1927-32; Puisne Judge, Trinidad and Tobago, 1932-36; Senior Puisne Judge, Palestine, 1936-39; Puisne Judge, SS, 1939; seconded as Puisne Judge, Uganda, 1942-46; retired, 1946. Chm. Advisory Cttee on Detainees, Palestine, 1947 and 1948; Additional Judge, British Guiana, 1948-50. Commissioner, Caura Inquiry, Trinidad, 1950. Acting Judge, Windward and Leeward Islands, 1950-54, 1959, 1960; Chm. Public Utilities Bd, Barbados, 1955-58. Jubilee Medal, 1935; Coronation Medals, 1937 and 1953; Palestine Gen. Service Medal, 1939. *Publication:* British Guiana Police Manual. *Address:* 61 Sunset Crest, St James, Barbados.

**MANNING, Thomas Henry;** zoologist; *b* 22 Dec. 1911; *s* of Thomas E. and Dorothy (*née* Randall) Manning, Shrublands, Dallington, Northampton; *m* 1938, Ella Wallace Jackson. *Educ:* Harrow; Cambridge. Winter journey across Lapland, 1932-33; Survey and Zoological work on Southampton Island, 1933-35; Leader, Brit. Canadian-Arctic Exped., 1936-41; Royal Canadian Navy, 1941-45; Geodetic Service of Canada, 1945-47; Leader Geographical Bureau Expedition to Prince Charles I. (Foxe Basin), 1949; Zoological and Geographical work in James Bay, 1950; Leader Defence Research Board Expeditions: Beaufort Sea, 1951; Banks Island, 1952, 1953; Nat. Mus. Canadian Expedition; King William Island, Adelaide Peninsula, 1957, Prince of Wales Island, 1958. FRGS (Patron's Gold Medal, 1948); Bruce Memorial Prize (Royal Society of Edinburgh, RPS, RSGS), 1944. Guggenheim Fellow, 1959. *Publications:* The Birds of North Western Ungava, 1949; Birds of the West James Bay and Southern Hudson Bay Coasts, 1952; Birds of Banks Island, 1956; Mammals of Banks Island, 1958; A Biological Investigation of Prince of Wales Island, 1961; articles in The Auk, Journal Mamm. and Geog. Journal, Canadian Geog. Jl., Canadian Field-Naturalist, Arctic, Nat. Mus. Can. Bull. *Recreations:* shooting, book-binding, cabinet-making, farming. *Address:* RR4, Merrickville, Ont., Canada. *T:* 269-4940.

**MANNINGHAM-BULLER,** family name of **Viscount Dilhorne.**

**MANSAGER, Felix Norman;** President-Chairman, Hoover Co. and Hoover Worldwide Corporation, since 1966; Chairman, Hoover Ltd, since 1966; *b* 30 Jan. 1911; *s* of Hoff Mansager and Alice (*née* Qualseth); *m* Geraldine (*née* Larson); one *s* two *d*. *Educ:* South Dakota High Sch., Colton. Joined Hoover Co. as Service Salesman, 1929; Vice-Pres., Sales, 1959; Exec. Vice-Pres. and Dir, 1961. Dir, Nat. Foreign Trade Coun.; Trustee, Indep. Coll. Funds of America; Member: Vacuum Cleaner Manufacturers Assoc. (USA); Council on Foreign Relations; Newcomen Soc. in N America; Assoc. of Independent Colls and Univs in Ohio; Bd of Regents, Capital Univ.; Assoc. of Ohio Commodores; Rotary International; Masonic Shrine (32nd degree Mason); Hon. Mem., World League of Norsemen. Hon. Dr of Laws, Capital Univ., 1967; Hon. LLD, Strathclyde, 1970. Grand Officer, Dukes of Burgundy; Chevalier, Order of Leopold. *Recreation:* golf. *Address:* 3421 Lindel Court NW, Canton, Ohio 44718, USA. *T:* 492-3828. *Club:* Metropolitan (NYC).

**MANSEL, Rev. James Seymour Denis,** JP; Sub-Dean of HM Chapels Royal, Deputy Clerk of the Closet, Sub-Almoner and Domestic Chaplain to the Queen, since 1965; *b* 18 June 1907; *e s* of Edward Mansel, FRIBA, Leamington, and Muriel Louisa (*née* Denis Browne); *m* 1942, Ann Monica, *e d* of Amyas Waterhouse, MD, Boars Hill, Oxford, and Ruth (*née* Gamlen); one *d*. *Educ:* Brighton Coll. (Scholar); Exeter Coll., Oxford (Exhibitioner) (MA); Westcott House. Asst Master, Dulwich Coll., 1934-39; Asst Master, Chaplain and House Master, Winchester Coll.,

1939-65. Mem., Winchester City Coun., 1950-56. JP, City of Winchester, 1964. *Address:* Marlborough Gate, St James's Palace, SW1. *T:* 01-930 6609; Field House, Pitt, Winchester. *T:* Winchester 4812. *Clubs:* Athenæum, Alpine.

**MANSEL, Sir Philip,** 15th Bt, *cr* 1621; *b* 3 March 1943; *s* of Sir John Mansel, 14th Bt and Hannah, *d* of Ben Rees; *S* father, 1947; *m* 1968, Margaret, *o d* of Arthur Docker. *Heir: u* Regnier Ranulf Dabridgecourt Mansel [*b* 6 July 1919; *m* 1941, Mary Germaine, *d* of Wing Comdr W. St J. Littlewood, OBE; three *s* two *d*]. *Address:* Greenfields, Rockcliffe, Carlisle, Cumberland.

**MANSELL, Lt-Col George William,** CBE 1959; DL; RA, retired; Chairman, Dorset County Council, since 1967; *b* 25 Dec. 1904; *s* of late Lt-Col Sir John H. Mansell, KBE, DL, RA (retd); *m* 1st, 1934, Joan (*d* 1940), *d* of late Spencer Dawson, Stratton Hall, Levington, Ipswich; one *s* one *d*; 2nd, 1941, Mary Elizabeth, *d* of late Major C. L. Blew, Hafod, Trefnant, Denbigh. *Educ:* Wellington Coll., Berks; RMA Woolwich. Commnd into RA, 1924; wounded N Africa, 1942; invalided as a result, 1947. Dorset CC, 1950; Alderman, 1955; Vice-Chm., 1966; Chm., 1967. DL Dorset, 1968. *Recreation:* fishing. *Address:* Kit Robins, Lytchett Matravers, Poole, Dorset. *T:* Morden (Dorset) 240.

**MANSELL, Gerard Evelyn Herbert;** Director of Programmes, Radio, BBC, since 1970; *b* 16 Feb. 1921; 2nd *s* of late Herbert and of Anne Mansell, Paris; *m* 1956, Diana Marion Sherar; two *s*. *Educ:* Lycée Hoche, Versailles; Lycée Buffon, Paris; Ecole des Sciences Politiques, Paris; Chelsea Sch. of Art. Joined HM Forces, 1940; served in Western Desert, Sicily and NW Europe, 1942-45; Brigade IO 151 (Durham) Bde, 1942-44; GSO3 (I) 50th (N) Div., 1944; GSO2 (I) 8th Corps, 1944-45 (despatches); GSO2 (I) MI4 (a) War Office, 1946. Joined BBC European Service, 1951; Asst Head, Overseas Talks and Features Dept, 1958, Head, 1961; Controller, BBC Radio 4 (formerly Home Service), and Music Programme, 1965-69. French Croix de Guerre, 1945. *Publication:* Tragedy in Algeria, 1961. *Recreations:* painting, reading. *Address:* Broadcasting House, W1.

**MANSERGH, Vice-Adm. Sir Aubrey;** *see* Mansergh, Vice-Adm. Sir C. A. L.

**MANSERGH, Vice-Adm. Sir (Cecil) Aubrey (Lawson),** KBE, *cr* 1953; CB 1950; DSC 1915; retired; *b* 7 Oct. 1898; *s* of Ernest Lawson Mansergh and Emma Cecilia Fisher Hogg; *m* 1st, 1928, Helen Raynor Scott (*d* 1967); two *s*; 2nd, 1969, Dora, widow of Comdr L. H. L. Clarke, RN. *Educ:* RN Colleges Osborne and Dartmouth. Served European War, 1914-18; Comdr, 1932; Captain, 1938; Commanded HMNZS Achilles, 1942 and HMNZS Leander, 1943, in Pacific; Commodore 1st Cl., Admiralty, 1944-46; Commanded HMS Implacable, 1946-47; Rear-Adm. 1948; Vice-Controller of Navy and Dir of Naval Equipment, 1948-50; Commanded 2nd Cruiser Squadron, 1950-52; Vice-Adm., 1951. Pres., Royal Naval Coll., Greenwich, 1952-54, retired Dec. 1954. *Address:* Hillside, The Green, Rottingdean, Sussex. *T:* Brighton 32213.

**MANSERGH, Gen. Sir (E. C.) Robert,** GCB 1956 (KCB 1953; CB 1946); KBE 1947 (CBE 1946; OBE 1942); MC 1932; Commander-in-Chief of the United Kingdom Land Forces, 1956-59, retired; Master Gunner, St James's Park, since 1960; *b* 12 May 1900; *s* of C. L. W. Mansergh, CBE, ISO. *Educ:* Rondebosch, South Africa; RMA, Woolwich. Commissioned in 1920 in RFA; served UK and abroad, Regimental and Staff, appointed RHA; Military Mission to Iraq, 1931-35; Adjt RMA, Woolwich; served War of 1939-45: Eritrea, Abyssinia, W Desert, Libya, Middle East, Persia and Iraq Force, Arakan, Assam, Burma, Liberation Singapore; Lt-Col 1941; Col 1945; Actg Maj.-Gen. 1944; Comdg 11 (EA) Div. 1945; 5th Indian Div. 1945; Maj.-Gen. 1946; Actg Lt-Gen. 1946; Comdr 15th Indian Corps; C-in-C Allied Forces, Netherlands East Indies, 1946; Dir Territorial Army and Cadets, 1947; Lt-Gen. 1948; Military Sec. to Sec. of State for War, 1948-49; Comdr, British Forces, Hong Kong, 1949-51; Dep. C-in-C, Allied Forces, Northern Europe, 1951-53, Comdr-in-Chief, 1953-56. Gen. 1953. ADC Gen. to the Queen, 1956-59. Order of Rafidain, 1935. Col Comdt RA 1950-; Col Comdt RHA 1957-. Pres., Westminster Chamber of Commerce, 1962-63. *Recreation:* gardening. *Address:* 18 Douai Grove, Hampton-on-Thames, Mddx. *T:* 01-979 5210. *Club:* Travellers'.

**MANSERGH, Prof. Philip Nicholas Seton,** OBE 1945; MA, DPhil 1936; DLitt Oxon 1960; LittD Cantab 1970; OF St John's College, Cambridge, since 1969 (Fellow, 1955-69); Editor-in-chief, India Office Records on the Transfer of Power, since 1967; *b* 27 June 1910; *yr s* of late Philip St George Mansergh and late Mrs Mansergh, Grenane House, Tipperary; *m* 1939, Diana Mary, *d* of late G. H. Keeton, Headmaster's Lodge, Reading; three *s* two *d*. *Educ:* Abbey Sch., Tipperary; College of St Columba, Dublin; Pembroke Coll., Oxford. Sec. OU Politics Research Cttee and Tutor in Politics, 1937-40; Empire Div., Ministry of Information, 1941-46; Dir, 1944-46; Asst Sec., Dominions Office, 1946-47; Abe Bailey Research Prof. of British Commonwealth Relations, RIIA, 1947-53; Smuts Prof. of History of British Commonwealth, Univ. of Cambridge, 1953-April 1970. Visiting Professor: Nat. Univ. of Australia, 1951; Univ. of Toronto, 1953; Duke Univ., NC, 1957 and 1965 (W. K. Boyd Prof. of History); Indian Sch. of International Studies, New Delhi, 1958 and 1966; Reid Lecturer, Acadia Univ., 1960. Member: Editorial Board, Annual Register, 1947-; Gen. Advisory Council, BBC, 1956-62; Adv. Council on Public Records, 1966-; Councillor, RIIA, 1953-57; Chm. Faculty Board of History, Cambridge Univ. 1960-62. Hon. Fellow, Pembroke Coll., Oxford, 1954. FRSA 1963. *Publications:* The Irish Free State: Its Government and Politics, 1934; The Government of Northern Ireland, 1936; Ireland in the Age of Reform and Revolution, 1940; Advisory Bodies (Jt Editor), 1941; Britain and Ireland, 1942, 2nd edn 1946; The Commonwealth and the Nations, 1948; The Coming of the First World War, 1949; Survey of British Commonwealth Affairs (2 vols), 1931-39, 1952 and 1939-52, 1958; Documents and Speeches on Commonwealth Affairs, 1931-62 (3 vols), 1953-63; The Multi-Racial Commonwealth, 1955; (jointly) Commonwealth Perspectives, 1958; South Africa, 1906-1961, 1962; The Irish Question, 1840-1921, 1965; The Commonwealth Experience, 1969. *Recreation:* lawn tennis. *Address:* The Master's Lodge, St John's College, Cambridge. *T:* Cambridge 55075. *Clubs:* United University; University (Dublin).

**MANSERGH, Gen. Sir Robert;** *see* Mansergh, Gen. Sir E. C. R.

**MANSFIELD,** family name of **Baron Sandhurst.**

**MANSFIELD AND MANSFIELD,** 7th Earl of, *cr* 1776 and 1792, Gt Britain; **Mungo David Malcolm Murray,** MA Oxon; FLS, FZS, FZS

(Scotland), FRHS, MBOU; Lord Lieutenant of Perthshire since 1960; JP Perthshire and Dumfriesshire; Baron Scone, 1605; Viscount Stormont, 1621; Baron Balvaird, 1641; (Earl of Dunbar, Viscount Drumcairn, and Baron Halldykes in the Jacobite Peerage); Hereditary Keeper of Bruce's Castle of Lochmaben; Chairman, Edinburgh Board of Royal Insurance Company; President: Perthshire Agricultural Society; Wildfowlers Association of Great Britain and Ireland; Perth Division Conservative and Unionist Association, 1935; Past President, British Empire Union; Chairman, Perth Division Unionist Association, 1945-60; Mem. of Perth County Council since 1935; Mem. of Executive of West India Committee; DL Perthshire, 1947; Brig. Royal Company of Archers (Queen's Body Guard for Scotland); late Lt 6/7th Black Watch; TA; Major in Home Guard, 1940-43; *b* 9 Aug. 1900; *o s* of 6th Earl and Margaret Helen Mary (*d* 1933), *d* of late Rear-Adm. Sir Malcolm MacGregor of MacGregor, 4th Bt; *S* father, 1935; *m* 1928, Dorothea Helena, *y d* of late Rt Hon. Sir Lancelot Carnegie, GCVO, KCMG; one *s* two *d*. *Educ:* privately; Christ Church, Oxford (BA (Hons) 1922, MA). Mem. of Perthshire Education Authority, 1925-30; MP (U) Perth, 1931-35; contested (U) N Lanark March (bye-election) and again May 1929; Gov. of Edinburgh and East of Scotland Coll. of Agriculture, 1925-30; Founder of Imperial Policy Group, 1934; Chm. of Directors of James Murray's Royal Asylum, Perth, 1935-48; Chm., Perthshire Mental Hosp. Bd, 1948-51; ex-Chm. Royal Scottish Society for Prevention of Cruelty to Children; Hon. Sec., British Group, Interparliamentary Union, 1932-35; First Chm. of British Trust for Ornithology, 1933-39; Hon. Pres., Scottish Chamber of Agriculture, 1936-38; Mem. Perthshire Agricultural Exec. Cttee, 1940-47; Vice-Preses, the Perth Hunt, Preses, 1929 and 1953; Member: Departmental Cttee on Scottish Farm Buildings, 1943-45; Advisory Cttee on Conservation of the Water Supplies of Scotland; has sat on many Scottish Provisional Order Commissions; Mem. Tay Salmon Fisheries Board and Tay Pollution Prevention Board; President: Scottish Association of Salmon Fishing Boards; Scottish Section, Franco-Scottish Soc. Mem. Council, Zoological Soc. of London (Vice-Pres., 1960-1963). Vice-Lieutenant of Perthshire, 1959-60. An Elder of the Church of Scotland; Lord High Commissioner to the Gen. Assembly of Church of Scotland, 1961 and 1962. Ex-Pres. The Cactus Soc. of Great Britain; Vice-Pres. Scottish League for European Freedom; Past Pres., Soc. for Individual Freedom; Member: Coun. of Royal Highland and Agric. Soc. of Scotland (Vice-Pres., 1948-49, 1964-65); Sec. of State for Scotland's Adv. Cttee on Protection of Birds; Adv. Cttee on JPs for Scotland. Chevalier, Legion of Honour; Medal of City of Paris. *Publications:* Articles on Ornithology, Shooting, Wildfowling, Agriculture, Forestry, Politics, and the West Indies, especially Jamaica. *Heir:* *s* Viscount Stormont, *qv*. *Address:* Scone Palace, Perthshire. *Clubs:* Pratt's, Carlton, Lansdowne, MCC; New (Edinburgh); Jamaica (Kingston).

*See also Lord Doune.*

**MANSFIELD, Hon. Sir Alan (James),** KCMG 1958; KCVO 1970; Governor of Queensland since 1966; *b* 30 Sept. 1902; 3rd *s* of Judge Edward Mansfield, Brisbane, Qld; *m* 1933, Beryl Susan, *d* of C. G. Barnes; one *s* one *d*. *Educ:* Sydney Church of England Gram. Sch.; St Paul's Coll., Sydney Univ. (LLB Hons). Admitted to Bars of New South Wales and Queensland, 1924; Lecturer in Law, Univ. of Queensland, 1938-39; Judge of Supreme Court of Queensland, 1940; Chm. Aliens Tribunal, 1942-45; Chm. Land Appeal Court (Qld), 1942-45; Chm. Royal Commns on Sugar Industry, 1942 and 1950; Acting Pres., Industrial Court (Qld), 1945; Mem. Bd of Inquiry into War Atrocities, 1945; Australian Rep., UN War Crimes Commn, London, 1945; Chief Aust. Prosecutor, Internat. Military Tribunal for the Far East, Tokyo, 1946; Senior Puisne Judge, 1947; Actg Chief Justice of Queensland, 1950, Chief Justice, 1956-66. Chm., Central Sugar Cane Prices Bd, 1955-56; Warden of Univ. of Qld, 1956-65; Chancellor of Univ. of Queensland, 1966-. Administrator of Govt of Qld, Jan. 1957-March 1958, 1963, 1965. Hon. Col, 2/14 Queensland Mounted Inf., 1966-; Hon. Air Cdre, 23 Sqdn, CAF, 1966-. KStJ 1966. *Recreation:* fishing. *Address:* Government House, Brisbane, Qld 4001, Australia. *Clubs:* Queensland, Johnsonian (Brisbane).

**MANSFIELD, Rear-Adm. David Parks,** CB 1964; *b* 26 July 1912; *s* of Comdr D. Mansfield, RD, RNR; *m* 1939, Jean Craig Alexander; one *s* one *d*. *Educ:* RN Coll., Dartmouth; RN Engineering Coll., Keyham. Lt (E) 1934; HMS Nelson, 1934-36; Staff of C-in-C Med., 1936-39; HMS Mauritius, 1939-42; Lt-Comdr (E) 1942; HMS Kelvin, 1942-43; Chatham Dockyard, 1943-46; Comdr (E) 1945; Admty (Aircraft Maintenance Dept), 1946-49; Staff of FO Air (Home), 1949-51; HMS Kenya, 1951-53; RN Engrg Coll., 1953-55; Capt 1954; RNAS Anthorn (in command), 1955-57; RN Aircraft Yard, Fleetlands (Supt.), 1957-60; Admty Dir of Fleet Maintenance, 1960-62; Rear-Adm. 1963; Rear-Adm. Aircraft, on Staff of Flag Officer Naval Air Command, 1963-65. *Recreations:* reading, sketching, gardening. *Address:* The Outlook, St Margaret's at Cliffe, near Dover, Kent. *T:* St Margaret's Bay 2237. *Club:* Army and Navy.

**MANSFIELD, Rear-Adm. Edward Gerard Napier;** Flag Officer Sea Training, since 1971; *b* 13 July 1921; *s* of late Vice-Adm. Sir John Mansfield, KCB, DSO, DSC, and of Alice Talbot Mansfield; *m* 1943, Joan Worship Byron, *d* of late Comdr John Byron DSC and late Frances Byron; two *d*. *Educ:* RNC, Dartmouth. Entered Royal Navy, 1935. Served War of 1939-45 in destroyer and Combined Ops (despatches), taking part in landings in N Africa and Sicily. Comdr, 1953; comd HMS Mounts Bay, 1956-58; Captain 1959; SHAPE, 1960-62; Captain (F) 20th Frigate Sqdn, 1963-64; Dir of Defence Plans (Navy), 1965-67; Cdre Amphibious Forces, 1967-68; Senior Naval Member, Directing Staff, IDC, 1969-70. *Address:* White Gate House, Ewshott, Farnham, Surrey. *T:* Crondall 325. *Club:* United Service.

**MANSFIELD, Philip (Robert Aked);** Counsellor, HM Diplomatic Service, since 1969; *b* 9 May 1926; *s* of Philip Theodore Mansfield, *qv*; *m* 1953, Elinor Russell MacHatton; two *s*. *Educ:* Winchester; Pembroke Coll., Cambrdige. Grenadier Guards, 1944-47. Sudan Political Service, 1950-54. Entered HM Diplomatic Service, 1955; served in: Addis Ababa, Singapore, Paris, Buenos Aires; Head of Rhodesia Political Dept. *Recreations:* sailing, tennis, gardening. *Address:* Gill Mill, Stanton Harcourt, Oxford. *T:* Witney 2554. *Club:* Guards.

**MANSFIELD, Philip Theodore,** CSI 1941; CIE 1936; late ICS; *b* 1 Feb. 1892; 2nd *s* of G. J. Mansfield, Blackheath, SE, formerly of Singapore; *m* 1922, Helen Rosamund, *d* of H. E. Aked, Harrogate; three *s* one *d*. *Educ:* Charterhouse; Pembroke Coll., Cambridge (MA). ICS, 1915; 2nd Lt IARO, 1918; Chief

Sec. Orissa Govt, 1936, Bihar Govt, 1944; Retired, 1946. Asst Sec. Ministry of Town and Country Planning, 1946-47. *Address:* Knockronan, Church Road, Wickham Bishops, Witham, Essex. *T:* Wickham Bishops 178. *Clubs:* Royal Over-Seas League, English-Speaking Union.

*See also P. R. A. Mansfield.*

**MANSFIELD COOPER, Prof. Sir William,** Kt 1963; LLM; Professor of Industrial Law, University of Manchester, 1949-70; Vice-Chancellor of the University, 1956-70; *b* Newton Heath, Manchester, 20 Feb. 1903; *s* of William and Georgina C. Cooper; *m* 1936, Edna Mabel, *o c* of Herbert and Elizabeth Baker; one *s*. *Educ:* Elementary Sch.; Ruskin Coll., 1931-33; Manchester Univ., 1933-36 (LLB, Dauntesey Jun. Law Schol., Dauntesey Special Prizeman in International Law). Grad. Res. Schol., 1936-37; Lecturer WEA (LLM 1938). University of Manchester: Asst Lecturer, 1938; Lecturer, 1942; Asst to Vice-Chancellor, 1944; Registrar and Senior Lecturer in Law, 1945; Professor of Industrial and Commercial Law, 1949, continuing as Joint Registrar until 1952; Acting Vice-Chancellor, Nov. 1953-May 1954 and July 1954-Oct. 1954. Called to the Bar (Gray's Inn), 1940. Chairman John Rylands Library, 1956-70; Chairman Cttee of Vice-Chancellors and Principals, 1961-64; President, Council of Europe Cttee on Higher Education and Research, 1966-67; Vice-President, Standing Conference of European Rectors and Vice-Chancellors, 1964-69. Hon. LLD: Manitoba; Liverpool; Manchester; Hon. DLitt Keele, 1967; Hon. DSc Kharkov; Hon. DHL Rochester. *Publications:* Outlines of Industrial Law, 1947, 4th edn, 1962; papers and reviews in learned journals. *Recreations:* gardening, bird-watching. *Address:* Fieldgate Cottage, Meldreth, Royston, Herts. *Club:* Athenæum.

**MANT, Sir Cecil (George),** Kt 1964; CBE 1955; consultant and company director; Controller-General, Directorate-General of Works, Ministry of Public Building and Works, 1963-67; *b* 24 May 1906; *o s* of late George Frederick Mant and Beatrice May Mant; *m* 1940, Hilda Florence (*née* Knowles); three *d*. *Educ:* Trinity County Sch.; Hornsey School of Art; Northern Polytechnic School of Architecture. ARIBA 1929, FRIBA 1944, resigned 1970. Entered HM Office of Works, 1928. Visiting Lecturer in Architecture and Building to Northern Polytechnic, 1930-39; Departmental Liaison Officer to Works and Buildings Priority Cttee, 1939-40. Deputy Director-General of Works, 1950-60; Director-General of Works, 1960-63. Served as member and chairman of various cttees, to British Standards Institution and Codes of Practice; Departmental Working Parties and Investigating Boards, Civil Service Commission Selection Boards, Joint Min. of Works and P.O. Study Group on P.O. Buildings Costs and Procedure, etc. Assessor to Advisory Cttee on Building Research, 1958-67; Member, Architecture Consultative Cttee, at Hammersmith College of Art and Building. Mem., Guild of Freemen of City of London. *Address:* 44 Hamilton Court, Maida Vale, W9. *T:* 01-286 8719. *Club:* Royal Automobile.

**MANTLE, Philip Jaques,** CMG 1952; *b* 7 Aug. 1901; 2nd *s* of late Paul Mantle; *m* 1930, Gwendolen, *d* of late John Webb, CMG, CBE, MC; one *s* one *d*. *Educ:* Bancroft's Sch., Woodford; St John's Coll., Oxford (Scholar, Goldsmiths' exhibitioner, 1st class Mod. Hist. Finals). Entered Inland Revenue Dept, 1923 (Taxes); Secretaries' office, 1928; Asst Secretary Min. of Supply, 1940, Board of Trade, 1942; Deputy Head, Administration of Enemy Property Dept, 1949; Controller-General, 1955-57; Companies Dept, 1957-61; with Charity Commission, 1962; retired 1966. *Address:* 27 Kensington Mansions, Trebovir Road, SW5. *T:* 01-370 3683.

**MANTON,** 3rd Baron, *cr* 1922, of Compton Verney; **Joseph Rupert Eric Robert Watson;** Landowner and Farmer; *b* 22 Jan. 1924; *s* of 2nd Baron Manton and of Alethea, 2nd *d* of late Colonel Philip Langdale, OBE; *S* father, 1968; *m* 1951, Mary Elizabeth, twin *d* of Major T. D. Hallinan, Ashbourne, Glounthaune, Co. Cork; two *s* three *d*. *Educ:* Eton. Joined Army, 1942; commissioned Life Guards, 1943; Captain, 1946; retired, 1947; rejoined 7th (QO) Hussars, 1951-56. *Recreations:* hunting, shooting, racing. *Heir:* *s* Hon. Miles Ronald Marcus Watson, *b* 7 May 1958. *Address:* Houghton Hall, Sancton, York. *T:* Market Weighton 3234. *Clubs:* Cavalry, Jockey.

**MANTON, Prof. Irene,** BA, ScD, PhD; FRS 1961; formerly Professor of Botany, University of Leeds; retired 1969. *Educ:* Girton Coll., Cambridge. BA 1927, PhD 1930, ScD 1940, Cambridge. Has made studies with the light and electron microscope on the ultramicroscopic structure of plants, and studies on the cytology and evolution of ferns. Hon. Member: Danish Acad. of Sciences and Letters, 1953; Deutsche Akad. Leopoldina, 1967; Amer. Acad. of Arts and Sciences, 1969. Hon. DSc: McGill Univ., Canada; Durham Univ., 1966; Hon. Doctorate, Oslo Univ., 1961. *Publications:* Problems of Cytology and Evolution in the Pteridophy Pteridophyta, 1950; papers in scientific journals. *Address:* 15 Harrowby Crescent, West Park, Leeds 6.

**MANTON, Sidnie M.,** FRS 1948; MA, PhD, ScD (Cantab); **(Mrs J. P. Harding);** retired as Research Fellow, Queen Mary College, London, 1967; *b* 4 May 1902; *d* of George S. F. Manton, LDS, RCS, and Milana Manton, London; *m* 1937, J. P. Harding, *qv*; one *s* one *d*. *Educ:* St Paul's Girls' Sch., Hammersmith; Girton Coll., Cambridge. Scholar, 1921-25; Research Student, 1925-28; Fellow, 1928-48; Director of Studies in Natural Sciences, Girton Coll., 1935-42; Demonstrator in Comparative Anatomy, University of Cambridge, 1927-35; Visiting Lecturer, King's Coll., London, 1943-46, Asst Lecturer, 1946-49; Reader in Zoology, University of London, 1949-60. Hon. Dr, Lund, Sweden, 1968. Linnean Gold Medal, 1963. *Publications:* papers in scientific journals on zoological subjects. *Recreation:* cat breeding (new varieties). *Address:* 88 Ennerdale Road, Richmond, Surrey. *T:* 2908.

**MANUEL, Archibald Clark,** JP; *b* 1 March 1901. Joined Labour Party, 1927. Engine driver; member Associated Society of Locomotive Engineers and Firemen. MP (Lab) Central Ayrshire Div. of Ayrshire and Bute, 1950-55, 1959-70. Formerly executive member Scottish Housing and Town Planning Council. Member: Ayr County Council; Ardrossan Town Council; Western Regional Hospital Board; Ayrshire Exec. Council (Health Service). JP 1938. *Address:* Eorna Cottage, Salen, Acharacle, Argyll.

**MANUEL, Joseph Thomas,** CBE 1970; QPM 1967; one of HM's Inspectors of Constabulary, since 1963; *b* 10 June 1909; *s* of George and Lucy Manuel; *m* 1933, Millicent Eveline Baker; one *s*. *Educ:* Dorchester Boys' Sch., Dorchester, Dorset. Joined Metropolitan Police, 1929. Served in Allied Military Government, Italy (rank of Captain and Major), 1943-46. Returned Metropolitan Police and promoted: Superintendent, 1954;

Chief Superintendent, 1957; Dep. Commander, 1958; Commander 1959. *Recreations:* golf, walking, motoring. *Address:* 30 Roehampton Gate, SW15. *T:* 01-876 4010. *Club:* Royal Automobile.

**MANUWA, Chief the Honourable Sir Samuel (Layinka Ayodeji),** Kt 1956; CMG 1953; OBE 1948; MD, ChB; FRCS; FRCP; FACP; LLD; DSc; DLitt; FRS (Edinburgh); The Oloye (Chief) Iyasere of Itebu-Manuwa, The Obadugba of Ondo, and The Olowa Luwagboye of Ijebu Ode; Chief Medical Adviser to the Federal Government of Nigeria (Colonial Medical Service), 1954-59, retired; Pro-Chancellor and Chairman of Council, University of Ibadan; *b* 4 March 1903; *e s* of Rev. Benjamin Ilowo Manuwa (Church Missionary Society), *s* of late Alaiyeluwa Oba Kuehin, Elero (Head Chief) of Itebu-Manuwa, and Matilda Omolara Thomas, Ondo; *m* 1st, Theodora Obafunmilayo (marr. diss.), *y d* of late Rt Rev. Bishop Oluwole, MA, DD; one *d*; 2nd, Isabella Inyang, *y d* of Prince Ibok Eyo Ita, *s* of late Eyo Honesty III, Obong (Head Chief) of Creek Town, Calabar; two *s* one *d*. *Educ:* CMS Grammar Sch. and King's Coll., Lagos; Universities of Edinburgh and Liverpool. MB, ChB (Edinburgh) 1926; LM (Dublin) 1926; DTM (Liverpool) 1926; MD (Edinburgh) 1934; DTH (Liverpool) 1934; FRCS (Edinburgh) 1938; M 1957, FRCP (Edinburgh) 1960; FRS (Edinburgh) 1967. Edinburgh University: Robert Wilson Memorial Prize and Medal (Chemistry), Wellcome Prize and Medal (Medicine); Demonstrator in Human Anatomy, 1925-26. MO, subs. Surgical Specialist and Senior Specialist in Colonial Medical Service, Nigeria, 1927-48; DDMS, 1948-51; DMS, 1951; Inspector-General of Medical Services, 1951-54. Member, W Nigeria House of Assembly, 1948-51; MLC and MEC 1951-52; Member, Governor's Privy Council, 1952-54; PC Federation of Nigeria, 1954-60; Member Federal Advisory Council on the Prerogative of Mercy, 1960-66; President, Assoc. of Surgeons of West Africa, 1960-62; Pres., Assoc. of Physicians of W Africa, 1962-68; Representative of grouped African, Mediterranean and Middle East Branches on Central Council of BMA, 1961-64; First Comr, Federal Public Service Commn. Formerly Examiner in Anat. and Surgery, Yaba Medical School; Hon. Assoc. Univ. Coll. of Ibadan, Nigeria; Member Council, university of Ife, Western Nigeria, 1961-66; Council, Imperial Society of Knights Bachelor, 1957-. FRSA London; Member New York Acad. Sciences; Fellow of the American College of Physicians; Fellow, American Public Health Assoc. Vice-President at 6th International Congresses on Tropical Medicine and Malaria, Lisbon, 1958; Vice-President, 1964-65, President, 1965-66, World Federation for Mental Health. CStJ. Hon. LLD Edinburgh 1953; Hon. DSc: University of Nigeria, 1963; Ibadan, 1965. Hon. DLitt, University of Ife, 1967. John Holt Medal, University of Liverpool, 1959, for services to Tropical Medicine. Director of May and Baker (West Africa) Ltd. *Publications:* various papers in scientific journals dealing with tropical medicine, surgery and mental health. *Recreations:* walking, gardening. *Address:* Federal Public Service Commission, Lagos, Nigeria, (*T:* 24711); 2 Alexander Avenue, Ikoyi (*T:* 53588), Lagos, Nigeria; Pro-Chancellor's Lodge, University of Ibadan, Nigeria (*T:* Ibadan 21051). *Clubs:* Royal Commonwealth Society; Island, Metropolitan (Lagos); University Union (Edinburgh).

**MANVELL, (Arnold) Roger,** PhD (London); writer on film, biographer, broadcaster, scriptwriter and lecturer; Director, British Film Academy, 1947-59; Consultant to the Society of Film and Television Arts and Editor of its Journal; Director: Rationalist Press Association Ltd; Pemberton Publishing Co. Ltd, etc; *b* 10 Oct. 1909; *s* of Canon A. E. W. Manvell; *m* 1956, Louise, *d* of Charles Luson Cribb, London. *Educ:* King's Sch., Peterborough; University College, Leicester. Schoolmaster and Lecturer in adult education, 1931-37; Lecturer in Literature and Drama, Dept Extramural Studies, University of Bristol, 1937-40; Ministry of Information, specialising in film work, 1940-45; Research Officer, British Film Institute, 1945-47. Has lectured on film subjects for British Film Institute, British Council and other authorities in Great Britain, US, Canada, Far East, India, Caribbean, W Africa and most European countries; regular broadcaster for BBC, including BBC's programme The Critics; Visiting Fellow, Sussex Univ.; Governor, London Film School; Member Cttee of Management, Society of Authors, 1954-57, 1965-68; Chairman, Society of Lecturers, 1959-61; Chairman, Radiowriters' Assoc., 1962-64. Commander of the Order of Merit of the Italian Republic, 1970. *Publications:* Film, 1944, revised 1946 and 1950; A Seat at the Cinema, 1951; On the Air (a study of broadcasting in sound and vision), 1953; The Animated Film, 1954; The Film and the Public, 1955; The Dreamers (novel), 1958; The Passion (novel), 1960; The Living Screen (a study of film and TV), 1961; This Age of Communication, 1967; New Cinema in Europe, 1966; New Cinema in the USA, 1968; Ellen Terry, 1968; New Cinema in Britain, 1969; Sarah Siddons, 1970; Shakespeare and the Film, 1971; (ed and contributed) Experiment in the Film, 1949; (contributed) Twenty Years of British Film, 1947; collaborated: with Paul Rotha in revised edn of Movie Parade, 1950; with John Huntley in The Technique of Film Music, 1957; with John Halas in The Technique of Film Animation, 1959, Design in Motion, 1962, and Art in Movement, 1970; with Heinrich Fraenkel in: Dr Goebbels, 1959, Hermann Goering, 1962, The July Plot, 1964, Heinrich Himmler, 1965, The Incomparable Crime, 1967, the Canaris Conspiracy, 1969, History of the German Cinema, 1970. Editor: Three British Screenplays, 1950; Penguin Film Review, 1946-49; The Cinema, 1950-52; The Year's Work in the Film (for British Council), 1949 and 1950. Contributed to journals at home and overseas concerned with history and art of the film and history of the Nazi régime. *Recreation:* travel abroad. *Address:* Hennerton Lodge, Wargrave, Berks RG10 8PD. *T:* Wargrave 2315.

**MANZINI, Raimondo;** Cavaliere di Gran Croce all'Ordine della Repubblica Italiana; GCVO (Hon.) 1969; Italian Ambassador to the Court of St James's, since Dec. 1968; *b* 25 Nov. 1913. *Educ:* Bologna Univ.; Clark Univ., Mass; Univ. of California. Entered Diplomatic Service, 1940; Sec. to Italian Legation, Lisbon, 1941-43; Ministry of Foreign Affairs in Brindisi (1943) and Salerno (1944); Sec. to Italian Embassy, London, 1944-47; Consul General for Congo, Nigeria and Gold Coast, 1947-50; Consul General, Baden Baden, 1951-52; Head of Information Service, CED, Paris, 1952-53; Ministry of Foreign Affairs, 1953-55; Adviser to the Minister of Foreign Trade, 1955-58; Chef de Cabinet of Minister for Foreign Affairs, 1958; Diplomatic Adviser to the Prime Minister, 1958-59; Adviser to the Minister of Industry, 1959-64; Italian Ambassador to OECD in Paris, 1965-68. *Address:* 4 Grosvenor Square, W1. *T:* 01-629 8200.

**MANZONI, Sir Herbert (John Baptista),** Kt 1954; CBE 1941; City Engineer and Surveyor, Birmingham, 1935-63; Consultant W. V. Zinn and Associates, Consulting Engineers; *b* 21 March 1899; *s* of Giovanni Carlo Manzoni, Milan and Birkenhead; *m* 1923, Lilian May, *d* of A. N. Davies of Birkenhead; two *s* (and one *s* decd). *Educ:* Birkenhead; Liverpool Univ. Served European War, 1914-18, 12th Lancer Regt and 7th Middlesex Regt; Chief Engineer, Sewers and Rivers, Public Works Dept, Birmingham, 1927-29; Dep. City Surveyor, Birmingham, 1929-35. President, Institute Civil Engineers, 1960-61; Past President, Institute Municipal Engineers; Member, Town Planning Institute; FRSH; Registered Architect. Chairman: Building Research Board, DSIR 1954-60; Elford Internal Drainage Board, 1944-; President British Standards Institution, 1956-58; Member: West Midland Group on Post-War Reconstruction and Planning; Member of Court, Loughborough Univ. of Technology; Life Governor, Birmingham Univ.; Nat. President, Federation of Master Builders, 1964-70; Chairman: Civil Engineering Research Assoc., 1964-67; Construction Industry Research and Information Assoc., 1967-. Hon. Assoc. University of Aston. Hon. Member Institution of Royal Engineers. Hon. DSc (Birmingham), 1961; Hon. DTech (Loughborough), 1967. *Publications:* papers and communications to professional bodies. *Recreation:* fishing. *Address:* 20 Viceroy Close, Bristol Road, Birmingham 5. *T:* 021-440 2371.

**MANZÙ, Giacomo;** sculptor; *b* 22 Dec. 1908; *s* of Angelo and Maria Manzù; *m* 1934, Antonia Oreni; three *s* decd. *Educ:* Milan. Professor of Sculpture, Brera Accad., Milan, 1941-54; International Summer Acad., Salzburg, 1954-60. Sculpture Prize, Venice Biennale, 1948; Society of Portrait Sculptors' International Award (Jean Masson Davidson Medal), 1965. Works include: Cathedral main door, Salzburg, and re-designing of bronze doors of St Peter's, Rome, 1963 (commission won in open international competition); The Door of Peace and War, St Laurenz Church, Rotterdam, 1968. Exhibition of Paintings and Drawings: Haus der Kunst, Munich, 1959; Tate Gall., 1960 Hanover Gall., London, 1965; Moscow, Leningrad, and Kiev, 1966; Bordeaux, 1969. Established permanent collection of his most important works at Ardea, near Rome, 1969. Hon. Member: American Academy of Arts and Letters; National Academies of Argentina and Belgium; Accademia di Belle Arti Sovietica. Premio Internazionale Lenin per la pace, 1966. *Publication:* La Porta di S Pietro, 1965. *Revelvant publications:* J. Rewald, Giacomo Manzù, 1966; B. Heynold von Graefe, The Doors of Rotterdam, 1969. *Address:* 00040 Ardea, Rome, Italy.

**MAPLES, Rev. Jeffrey Stanley;** Vicar of St James, Milton, Portsmouth, since 1967; Rural Dean of Portsmouth, since 1968; *b* 8 Aug. 1916; *o s* of Arthur Stanley and Henrietta Georgina Maples; *m* 1945, Isobel Eileen Mabel Wren; four *s* (and one *s* decd). *Educ:* Downing Coll., Cambridge; Chichester Theological Coll. Asst Curate St James, Milton, Portsmouth, 1940-46; Asst Curate, Watlington, Diocese of Oxford, 1946-48. Vicar of Swinderby, Dio. Lincoln, and Diocesan Youth Chaplain, 1948-50; Vicar of St Michael-on-the-Mount, Lincoln, and Director of Religious Education: for Lincoln Dio., 1950-56; for Salisbury Dio., 1956-63; Canon of Lincoln, 1954-56; Chancellor of Salisbury Cathedral, 1960-67; Director of the Bible Reading Fellowship, 1963-67; Proctor in Convocation for Salisbury Diocese, 1957-; Canon Emeritus of Salisbury Cathedral, 1967-. *Address:* St James's Vicarage, Milton, Portsmouth PO4 8PG. *T:* Portsmouth 32786. *Club:* Royal Commonwealth Society.

**MAPLES EARLE, Ven. E. E.;** *see* Earle.

**MAPP, Charles;** JP; *b* 1903. *Educ:* elementary and grammar schools. Railway goods agent (retired). Member, Sale Borough Council, 1932-35, 1945-46. Contested: Northwich, 1950; Stretford, 1951; Oldham East, 1955; MP (Lab) Oldham East, Oct. 1959-70, retired. JP 1949-. *Address:* 5 Hazel Close, Marple, Stockport, Cheshire.

**MAPPIN, Sir Frank Crossley,** 6th Bt, *cr* 1886; *b* 15 Aug. 1884; *s* of Sir Samuel Wilson Mappin, 5th Bt, and Laura (*d* 1937), *d* of William Morton; *S* father 1942; *m* 1909, Ruby, *d* of George Lamberton Thomson, Auckland, NZ; three *d*. *Educ:* Felsted; Gonville and Caius Coll., Cambridge. KStJ 1952. *Heir:* none. *Address:* Birchlands, 119 Mountain Road, Auckland, SE1, New Zealand.

**MAPSON, Dr Leslie William,** ScD Cantab 1969; FRS 1969; Deputy Chief Scientific Officer, Agricultural Research Council, since 1967; *b* 17 Nov. 1907; *s* of William John and Elizabeth Mapson; *m* 1949, Dorothy Lillian (*née* Pell); one *d*. *Educ:* Univ. of Cambridge (BA, PhD). Scientific Officer, DSIR, 1938; Principal Scientific Officer, 1950; Sen. Principal Scientific Officer, 1956. *Publications:* contribs to The Vitamins; many scientific papers in Biochemical Jl of New York Acad. of Sciences, and other scientific jls. *Recreations:* tennis, swimming, gardening. *Address:* Food Research Institute, Colney Lane, Norwich. *T:* Norwich 56122 (ext. 57).

**MAR,** 30th Earl of (ante 1404); **James (Clifton) of Mar;** Premier Earl of Scotland; Baron Garioch, 1336; (recognised in the surname "of Mar" by warrant of Court of Lord Lyon, 1959, in lieu of that of Lane); *b* 22 Nov. 1914; *o surv. s* of Charles Macdonald Lane, CSI (*d* 1956); *S* kinsman (Lionel Walter Young Erskine, 29th Earl) 1965; *m* 1st, 1939, Millicent Mary Salton (marr. diss., 1958); two *d* (one *s* decd); 2nd, 1960, Marjorie Aileen Grice, *d* of late J. R. Miller, and *widow* of Major C. W. S. Grice, Central India Horse. *Educ:* Marlborough. KStJ 1965. *Recreations:* gardening, fishing. *Heir: er d* Mistress of Mar, *qv*. *Address:* Fernleigh, Haddington, East Lothian, Scotland.

**MAR, Mistress of; Lady Margaret of Mar;** *b* 19 Sept. 1940; *er d* and *heiress* of 30th Earl of Mar, *qv*; *m* 1959, Edwin Noel Artiss; one *d*; she was recognised in the surname "of Mar" by warrant of Court of Lord Lyon, 1967, when she abandoned her second forename; her husband also took the surname "of Mar". *Address:* Corgarff, 3 The Greenway, Colletts Green, Powick, Worcs.

**MAR,** 13th Earl of, *cr* 1565, **and KELLIE,** 15th Earl of, *cr* 1619; **John Francis Hervey Erskine;** Baron Erskine, 1429; Viscount Fentoun, 1606; Baron Dirleton, 1603; Premier Viscount of Scotland; Hereditary Keeper of Stirling Castle; Representative Peer for Scotland, 1959-63; Major Scots Guards; retired 1954; Major, Argyll and Sutherland Highlanders (TA) retired 1959; Lord Lieutenant, Co. Clackmannan, since 1966; *b* 15 Feb. 1921; *e s* of late Lord Erskine (John Francis Ashley Erskine), GCSI, GCIE; *S* grandfather, 1955; *m* 1948, Pansy Constance (Chairman: Enterprise Youth; Board of Governors, Church of Scotland Youth Leadership Training Centre; Joint Vice-Chairman,

Scottish Standing Conference of Voluntary Youth Organisations; Dep. Chairman, National Assoc. of Youth Clubs; Pres., Scottish Marriage Guidance Council), *y d* of late General Sir Andrew Thorne, KCB; three *s* one *d*. *Educ:* Eton; Trinity Coll., Cambridge. 2nd Lieut, Scots Guards, 1941; served in Egypt, N. Africa, Italy and Germany with 2nd Bn Scots Guards and HQ 201 Guards' Brigade, 1942-45 (wounded, despatches). Staff Coll., Camberley, 1950; DAAG, HQ, 3rd Infantry Div., 1951-52. DL Clackmannanshire, 1954, Vice-Lieutenant, 1957, JP 1962; County Councillor for Clackmannanshire, 1955- (Vice-Convener, 1961-64); Chairman: Forth Conservancy Board, 1957-68; Clackmannanshire T&AFA, 1961-68. An Elder of the Church of Scotland. Member of the Queen's Body Guard for Scotland (Royal Company of Archers). KStJ 1966. *Heir: s* Lord Erskine, *qv*. *Address:* Claremont House, Alloa, Clackmannanshire. *T:* Alloa 2020. *Clubs:* Guards; New (Edinburgh).

**MARA, Ratu Sir Kamisese Kapaiwai Tuimacilai;** KBE 1969 (OBE 1961); Tui Nayau; Tui Lau; Chief Minister of Fiji and Member of Council of Ministers, since Sept. 1967; Hereditary High Chief in the Lau Islands; *b* 13 May 1920; *s* of late Ratu Tevita Uluilakeba, Tui Nayau; *m* 1951, Adi Lady Lala Mara (Roko Tui Dreketi); three *s* five *d*. *Educ:* Fiji; Sacred Heart Coll., NZ; Otago Univ., NZ; Wadham Coll., Oxford (MA); London Sch. of Economics (Dip. Econ. & Social Admin.). Administrative Officer, Colonial Service, Fiji, Oct. 1950; Fijian MLC, 1953-, and MEC, 1959-; Elected MLC and MEC, 1966. Member for Natural Resources and Leader of Govt Business; Alliance Party, 1964 (Founder of Party, 1964). Hon. Dr of Laws, Univ. of Guam, 1969. *Recreations:* athletics, cricket, Rugby football, golf, fishing. *Address:* 11 Battery Road, Suva, Fiji. *T:* 23529. *Clubs:* Oxford and Cambridge University, Achilles (London); Defence (Suva, Fiji).

**MARCEL, Gabriel;** French philosopher and author; Membre de l'Institut; *b* Paris, 7 Dec. 1889; *s* of Henry Marcel and Laure Meyer; *m* 1919, Jacqueline Boegner; one *s*. *Educ:* Lycée Carnot, Sorbonne, Paris (agrégé de philosophie). Several years of teaching; later worked in collaboration with publishers Plon and Grasset; contributed dramatic and literary criticism to numerous periodicals, including Nouvelle Revue Française, Europe Nouvelle, Nouvelles Littéraires, etc. Gifford Lecturer, Aberdeen, 1949-50. Grand Prix de Littérature de L'Académie Française, 1948; Peace Prize, Frankfurt, 1964; Erasmus Prize, 1969. Officer, Legion of Honour. *Publications:* Journal métaphysique, 1927; Etre et avoir, 1934; Du refus à l'invocation, 1940; Homo Viator, 1945; La Métaphysique de Royce, 1945; Le Mystère de l'être (Gifford Lectures), 1951; Les Hommes contre l'humain, etc. *Plays:* Un Homme de Dieu, 1929; Le Chemin de Crête, 1936; Le Fanal, 1936; Le Dard, 1937; La Soif, 1938; L'Horizon, 1945; L'Emissaire–Le Signe de la croix, 1949; Rome n'est plus dans Rome, 1951; Mon Temps n'est pas le vôtre, 1955; Croissez et multipliez, 1955; Fragments philosophiques, 1909-1914, 1963. *Relevant publication:* Gabriel Marcel, by Seymour Cain, 1963. *Address:* 21 rue de Tournon, Paris, France. *T:* Danton 29.28.

**MARCH and KINRARA, Earl of; Charles Henry Gordon-Lennox;** *b* 19 Sept. 1929; *s* of 9th Duke of Richmond and Gordon, *qv*; *m* 1951, Susan Monica, *o d* of Colonel C. E. Grenville-Grey, CBE, Hall Barn, Blewbury, Berks; one *s* two *d*. *Educ:* Eton; William Temple Coll. 2nd Lieut, 60th Rifles, 1949-50. Chartered Accountant, 1956. Member of Church Assembly, 1960-; Church Commissioner, 1963-; Chairman, Missionary and Ecumenical Council of the Church Assembly, 1967-. Mem., Central Cttee, World Council of Churches, 1968-. *Heir: s* Lord Settrington, *qv*. *Address:* Goodwood House, Chichester, Sussex. *T:* (office) Chichester 7107; (home) Chichester 7312.

**MARCH, George Frederick,** CMG 1946; MC 1917; *b* 6 July 1893; *o s* of late Frederick J. March, Ockbrook Grange, Derbyshire; *m* 1935, Myrtle Lloyd, Carmarthen; two *s*. *Educ:* Rugby Sch.; Wye Agricultural Coll. (dip. Agric. 1914). Commissioned in Sherwood Foresters, Aug. 1914; France, 1915-19 (wounded thrice); Egypt (Alexandria), 1919-21; demobilised, 1921; Inspector of Agriculture, Sudan Government, 1921; Senior Inspector of Agriculture, 1928; Asst Director, Agriculture and Forests, 1935; Dep. Director, 1942; Director, 1944-47. Chairman, Rural Water Supplies and Soil Conservation Board. Member Governor-General's Council (Sudan). Agricultural Consultant on mission to Swaziland by Colonial Development Corporation, Jan.-April, 1950; Manager and Secretary, Flishinghurst Farms Ltd, 1950-52; now farming on own (hops, fruit, etc.), in Kent. *Recreations:* fishing, shooting, tennis, golf. *Address:* The Well House, Limes Grove Farm, Hawkhurst, Kent. *TA:* Hawkhurst. *T:* Hawkhurst 2398.

**MARCH, Henry Arthur,** MA (Oxon); *b* 14 March 1905; *s* of late Edward Gerald March, MD, Reading; *m* 1943, Mary (*d* 1968), *d* of late Rev. P. P. W. Gendall, Launceston; two *s* one *d*. *Educ:* Leighton Park Sch.; St John's Coll., Oxford. Asst Master, Merchant Taylors' Sch., 1929-39; Head of Modern Language side, 1940-54, and Housemaster, 1945-54, Charterhouse; Headmaster, Cranleigh Sch., 1954-59; Temp. Asst Master, Marlborough Coll., 1959-61; Asst Master, 1961-65. Acting Headmaster, Charterhouse, 1964. *Address:* Horsna Parc, St Tudy, Bodmin, Cornwall.

**MARCH, Prof. Norman Henry;** Professor of Physics, University of Sheffield, since Oct. 1961; *b* 9 July 1927; *s* of William and Elsie March; *m* 1949, Margaret Joan Hoyle; two *s*. *Educ:* King's Coll., London Univ. University of Sheffield: Lecturer in Physics, 1953-57; Reader in Theoretical Physics, 1957-61. *Publications:* The Many-Body Problem in Quantum Mechanics (with W. H. Young and S. Sampanthar), 1967; Liquid Metals, 1968; many scientific papers on quantum mechanics and statistical mechanics in Proceedings Royal Society, Phil. Magazine, etc. *Recreations:* music, chess, cricket. *Address:* 25 Clarendon Road, Sheffield 10. *T:* Sheffield 302354.

**MARCHAMLEY,** 3rd Baron, *cr* 1908, of Hawkstone; **John William Tattersall Whiteley;** late Lieutenant, Royal Armoured Corps; *b* 24 April 1922; *s* of 2nd Baron and Margaret Clara, *d* of Thomas Scott Johnstone of Glenmark, Waipara, New Zealand; *S* father, 1949; *m* 1967, Sonia Kathleen Pedrick; one *s*. Served War of 1939-45, Captain, 19th King George V Own Lancers. *Heir: s* Hon. William Francis Whiteley, *b* 27 July 1968. *Address:* Whetcombe, North Huish, South Brent, Devon.

**MARCHANT, Edgar Vernon;** Under-Secretary, National Board for Prices and Incomes, since 1968; *b* 7 Dec. 1915; *s* of E. C. Marchant, Sub-rector of Lincoln College, Oxford; *m* 1945, Joyce Allen Storey; one *s* two *d*. *Educ:* Marlborough Coll.; Lincoln Coll., Oxford. Engr, Bahrain Petroleum Co., 1938; various technical and scientific posts in Min. of Aircraft Production, Min. of Supply and RAE, 1940-51; Principal, Min. of Supply, 1951; Principal, BoT, 1955; Asst Sec., BoT, 1959; Asst Registrar of Restrictive Trading Agreements, 1964; Asst Sec., Dept of Economic Affairs, 1966; Asst Sec., Nat. Board for Prices and Incomes, 1967. *Recreations:* gardening, messing about with boats. *Address:* 17 Devonshire Gardens, Chiswick, W4. *Club:* United University.

**MARCHANT, Ernest Cecil,** CIE 1946; *b* 27 Sept. 1902; *s* of E. J. Marchant, Cambridge; *m* 1933, Margaret Glen, *d* of Major George Lamb, IMS; two *d. Educ:* Perse Sch.; St John's Coll., Cambridge (Scholar). Asst Master, Oakham Sch., 1925-28; Asst Master, Geelong Sch., Australia, 1929-30; Asst Master, Marlborough Coll., 1931-38; Principal: The Daly Coll., India, 1939-46. HM Inspector of Schools, 1947-66. *Address:* Airlie, Doctors Commons Road, Berkhamsted, Herts. *T:* Berkhamsted 4574.

**MARCHANT, Sir Herbert (Stanley),** KCMG 1963 (CMG 1957); OBE 1946; MA Cantab; *b* 18 May 1906; *s* of E. J. Marchant; *m* 1937, Diana Selway, *d* of C. J. Selway, CVO, CBE; one *s. Educ:* Perse Sch.; St John's Coll., Cambridge (MA 1929). Asst Master, Harrow Sch., 1928-39; Foreign Office, 1940-46; Consul, Denver, Colorado, USA, 1946-48; First Secretary, British Legation, Bucharest, 1948-49; Counsellor, British Embassy, Paris, 1950-52; Consul-General, Zagreb, 1952-54; Land Commissioner and Consul-General for North Rhine/Westphalia, 1954-55; Consul-General, Düsseldorf, 1954-57; Consul-General, San Francisco, 1957-60; Ambassador to Cuba, 1960-63; Ambassador to Tunisia, 1963-66. Asst Dir, Inst. of Race Relations, 1966-68; UK Representative, UN Cttee for Elimination of Racial Discrimination, 1969-. *Publication:* Scratch a Russian, 1936. *Recreations:* mountains, spear fishing, theatre. *Club:* Travellers'.

**MARCHWOOD,** 2nd Viscount, *cr* 1945, of Penang and of Marchwood, Southampton; Baron, *cr* 1937; **Peter George Penny,** Bt, *cr* 1933; MBE 1944; Executive Director, Geo. Wimpey & Co. (Contractors), since 1960; *b* 7 Nov. 1912; *s* of 1st Viscount Marchwood, KCVO; *S* father, 1955; *m* 1935, Pamela, *o d* of John Staveley Colton-Fox, JP, Todwick Grange, nr Sheffield; two *s* one *d. Educ:* Winchester. Editorial Staff, Sheffield Daily Telegraph and Daily Telegraph and Morning Post, 1929-35; Financial Advertising Staff, Daily Telegraph and Morning Post, 1935-47. Served War of 1939-45, Major, RA. Joined Vine Products Ltd, as General Manager, 1947; Dep. Managing Director, 1951; Chairman and Managing Director, 1955-59. *Recreations:* racing, shooting, tennis. *Heir: s* Hon. David George Staveley Penny [*b* 22 May 1936; *m* 1964, Tessa Jane, *d* of W. F. Norris; three *s*]. *Address:* Manor House, Cholderton, near Salisbury, Wilts. *T:* Cholderton 200. *Club:* White's.

**MARCUSE, Herbert,** PhD; Professor of Philosophy, University of California at San Diego, since 1965; *b* Berlin, 19 July 1898; *m* Sophie (*d* 1951); one *s*; *m* 1955, Inge Werner; two step-*s*; American nationality, 1940. *Educ:* Univs of Berlin and Freiberg. Went to USA, 1934; Inst. of Social Research, Columbia Univ., 1934-40; served with Office of Strategic Services and State Dept, 1941-50; Russian Inst., Columbia and Harvard Univs, 1951-53; Prof. of Politics and Philosophy, Brandeis Univ., 1954-65. *Publications:* Reason and Revolution, 1941; Eros and Civilization, 1954; Soviet Marxism, 1958; One-Dimensional Man, 1965; The Ethics of Revolution, 1966; Negations, 1968. *Address:* University of San Diego, Calif 92038, USA.

**MARDER, Prof. Arthur Jacob;** Professor of History, University of California at Irvine, since 1964; *b* 8 March 1910; *s* of Maxwell J. Marder and Ida (*née* Greenstein); *m* 1955, Jan North; two *s* one *d. Educ:* Harvard Univ. BA 1931; MA 1934; PhD 1936. MA Oxon, 1969. Asst Professor of History, University of Oregon, 1936-38; Research Assoc., Bureau of International Research, Harvard Univ., 1939-41; Research Analyst, Office of Strategic Services, 1941-42; Assoc. Professor, Hamilton Coll., 1943-44; Assoc. Professor, University of Hawaii, 1944-51; Professor, 1951-58; Sen. Professor, 1958-64. Visiting Prof., Harvard Univ., 1949-50; Eastman Prof., Oxford, 1969-70. FRHistS 1966; Fellow: J. S. Guggenheim Foundation, 1939, 1945-46, 1958; American Philosophical Society, 1956, 1958, 1963, 1966; Rockefeller Foundation, 1943; UK Fulbright Fellow Alt., 1954. Corresp. FBA, 1970. Chesney Memorial Gold Medal of RUSI, 1968. *Publications:* The Anatomy of British Sea Power, 1940 (G. L. Beer Prize, American History Assoc., 1941); Portrait of an Admiral, 1952; Fear God and Dread Nought, 3 vols, 1952, 1956, 1959; From the Dreadnought to Scapa Flow, 5 vols, 1961, 1965, 1966, 1969, 1970; contributions to American Hist. Review, Journal of Modern History, etc. *Recreations:* golf, hiking, Chinese cooking. *Address:* 1726 Skylark Lane, Newport Beach, California 92660, USA. *T:* (714) 646-3578.

**MARDON, Lt-Col John Kenric La Touche,** DSO 1945; TD 1943; DL; MA; JP; Chairman, Mardon, Son & Hall, Ltd, Bristol, 1962-69; Director, Bristol & West Building Society; *b* 29 June 1905; *e s* of late Evelyn John Mardon, Halsway Manor, Crowcombe and late Maud Mary (*née* Rothwell); *m* 1933, Dulcie Joan, 3rd *d* of Maj.-General K. M. Body, *qv*; two *s* one *d. Educ:* Clifton; Christ's Coll., Cambridge. Commissioned in Royal Devon Yeomanry, 1925; Major, 1938; Lieut-Colonel, RA, 1942; served War of 1939-45, in N.W. Europe, 1944-45 (despatches). JP Somerset, 1948; High Sheriff of Somerset, 1956-57; DL 1962. Master, Society of Merchant Venturers, Bristol, 1959-60; Governor, Clifton Coll., 1957. Pres., Bristol YMCA. *Recreations:* shooting, lawn tennis, squash rackets (rep. Cambridge v. Oxford, 1925). *Address:* Cameley House, Cameley, Temple Cloud, near Bristol. *T:* Temple Cloud 297.

**MAREK, Kurt W.** (pseudonym **C. W. Ceram**); Writer (free-lance, 1934-45, and since 1952); *b* Berlin, 20 Jan. 1915; *s* of Max Marek and Anna Marek (*née* Mistol); *m* 1952, Hannelore Schipmann; one *s. Educ:* Hohenzollern Upper Secondary Sch.; Lessing High Sch.; Berlin Univ. Began journalistic career, 1932; lit. theatre critic, Berlin Newspapers, 1935; staff Die Welt, 1946-50; editor-in-chief Rowohlt publ. Hamburg, 1946-52; co-owner and co-publ. of Benjamin (weekly for young people), Hamburg, 1946-49. Served from Private to 1st Lieut, Anti-Aircraft Unit, German Army, 1938-45. Wrote and directed 6 documentaries about archæology for international television (German production) 1961-62. Member: Archaeological Inst. of America; Amer. Anthropological Assoc. (With Ernest Hemingway) Roman Bancarella Book Award, 1953. *Publications:* (his books have been translated into 26 languages): Gods, Graves and Scholars, 1951; Narrow Pass, Black Mountain, 1955; A Picture History of Archæology, 1957. (Ed. and Introd.) Diary of an Anonymous Woman: A Woman in Berlin,

1955; Archæology of the Cinema, 1955; Yestermorrow, Notes on Man's Progress, 1965; The World of Archæology, ed. and introd. C. W. Ceram, 1966. Contributions to professional publications. *Recreation:* travelling. *Address:* (home) Woodstock, NY 12498, USA. *T:* Oriole 9-2551. *Club:* PEN (Member in Germany and USA).

**MARENGO, Kimon Evan;** *see* Kem.

**MARETT, Sir Robert (Hugh Kirk),** KCMG 1964 (CMG 1955); OBE 1942; FRAI; Seigneur de Franc Fief, in Jersey; Vice-President, Société Jersiaise; Director, Royal Trust Co. of Canada (CI) Ltd; *b* 20 April 1907; *s* of late Dr Robert Ranulph Marett, one-time Rector of Exeter Coll., Oxford, and Nora Kirk; *m* 1934, Piedad, *d* of late Vicente Sanchez Gavito, Mexico City; one *d. Educ:* Dragon Sch., Oxford; Winchester Coll. Entered business: Norton, Megaw & Co. Ltd, 1926-30; Mexican Railway Co. Ltd, 1931-36; Shell Petroleum Co., 1937-39; Times Correspondent in Mexico, 1932-38; Ministry of Information, London, Mexico, Washington and Ottawa, 1939-46; First Secretary, HM Foreign Service, 1946; New York, 1946-48; Lima, 1948-52; Foreign Office, 1952-55; Secretary, Drogheda Cttee, 1952-53; Counsellor (Head of Information Policy Dept, of FO), 1953-55; HM Consul-General, Boston, 1955-58; Asst Under-Secretary of State, Foreign Office, 1959-63; British Ambassador to Peru, 1963-67. *Publications:* Archæological Tours from Mexico City, 1932; An Eye-Witness of Mexico, 1939; Through the Back Door, An Inside View of Britain's Overseas Information Services, 1968; Peru, 1969. *Address:* Mon Plaisir, St Aubin, Jersey, CI. *Clubs:* Travellers'; Royal Channel Islands Yacht.

**MARGADALE,** 1st Baron, *cr* 1964; **John Granville Morrison,** TD; JP; Lord Lieutenant of Wiltshire, since 1969; Member Royal Company of Archers (Queen's Body Guard for Scotland); Hon. Colonel: The Royal Yeomanry Regiment; The Royal Wiltshire Yeomanry Squadron; *b* 16 Dec. 1906; *s* of late Hugh Morrison; *m* 1928, Hon. Margaret Esther Lucie Smith, 2nd *d* of 2nd Viscount Hambleden; three *s* one *d. Educ:* Eton; Magdalene Coll., Cambridge. Served 1939-45: recruited with Royal Wilts Yeomanry; in MEF, 1939-42. MP (C) Salisbury Division of Wilts, 1942-64; Chairman, Conservative Members' (1922) Cttee, 1955-64. DL 1950, JP 1936, High Sheriff, 1938, Wilts. MFH S and W Wilts Foxhounds, 1932-66. *Heir: s* Major Hon. James Ian Morrison, TD, Royal Wiltshire Yeomanry [*b* 17 July 1930; *m* 1952, Clare, *d* of Anthony Lister Barclay, Broad Oak End, Hertford; two *s* one *d*]. *Address:* Fonthill House, Tisbury, Wilts. *T:* Tisbury 202; Islay House, Bridgend, Argyll. *Clubs:* Carlton, Turf, Buck's, Jockey.

*See also Hon. C. A. Morrison.*

**MARGAI, Sir Albert (Michael),** Kt 1965; Lawyer and Politician, Sierra Leone; *b* 10 Oct. 1910; 6th *s* of late M. E. S. Margai and Ndaneh Margai, Gbangbatoke and Bonthe; *m* 1949, Esther; ten *c. Educ:* St Patrick's Roman Catholic Sch., Bonthe; St Edward's Secondary Sch., Freetown; Middle Temple, London. Male Nurse and Dispenser, 1932-44. Practising Barrister, 1948; Sierra Leone Government: MLC and Minister of Education and Local Government and Welfare, 1950-57; MP 1957; Min. of Natural Resources, 1960; Minister of Finance, 1962; Prime Minister of Sierra Leone and Minister of Defence, 1964-67. Founder Member, People's National Party, 1958-. Knight Grand Cross of St Gregory (Vatican), 1962. *Recreation:* tennis.

**MARGERISON, Thomas Alan;** Chief Executive, London Weekend Television Ltd, since 1969; *b* 13 Nov. 1923; *s* of Ernest Alan Margerison and Isabel McKenzie; *m* 1950, Pamela Alice Tilbrook; two *s. Educ:* Huntingdon Grammar Sch.; Hymers Coll., Hull; King's Sch., Macclesfield; Sheffield University. Research Physicist, 1949; film script writer, Film Producers Guild, 1950; Scientific Editor, Butterworths sci. pubns, Ed. Research, 1951-56; Man. Editor, Heywood Pubns and National Trade Press, 1956. First Scientific Editor, The New Scientist, 1956-61; Science Corresp., Sunday Times, 1961; Dep. Editor, Sunday Times Magazine, 1962; Man. Dir, Thomson Technical Developments Ltd, 1964; Dep. Man. Dir, London Weekend Television Ltd, 1967. Scientific broadcaster and journalist, worked for many years with Tonight team on BBC. Responsible for applying computers to evening newpapers in Reading and Hemel Hempstead. A Dir, Computer Technology Ltd. *Publications:* articles and television scripts, indifferent scientific papers; (ed) popular science books. *Recreation:* sailing. *Address:* London Weekend Television Ltd, 25 Old Burlington Street, W1. *T:* 01-734 9431. *Club:* Savile.

**MARGESSON,** family name of **Viscount Margesson.**

**MARGESSON,** 2nd Viscount *cr* 1942, of Rugby; **Francis Vere Hampden Margesson;** Information Officer, British Consulate-General, New York, since 1964; *b* 17 April 1922; *o s* of 1st Viscount Margesson, PC, MC, and Frances H. Leggett, New York; *S* father, 1965; *m* 1958, Helena, *d* of Heikki Backstrom, Finland; one *s* three *d. Educ:* Eton; Trinity Coll., Oxford. Served War of 1939-45, as Sub-Lt, RNVR. A Director of Thames & Hudson Publications, Inc., New York, 1949-53. ADC to Governor of the Bahamas, 1956. *Heir: s* Hon. Richard Francis David Margesson, *b* 25 Dec. 1960. *Address:* 133 East 64 Street, New York, NY 10021, USA; Stone Ridge, New York, NY 12484, USA. *Clubs:* Travellers'; Coffee House (New York).

**MARGETSON, Major Sir Philip (Reginald),** KCVO 1953 (CVO 1948); MC 1916; Assistant Commissioner of Police of the Metropolis, 1946-57, retired; *b* 2 Jan. 1894; *s* of late William Parker Margetson and late Ellen Maria Snell; *m* 1918, Diana, *er d* of late Sir John Edward Thornycroft, KBE; one *s* (and *er s* killed on active service in N. Africa, 1943). *Educ:* Marlborough; RMC, Sandhurst. Gazetted to RSF, 1915; European War, 1914-18, served 1914-19 (MC); Adjutant 1st Bn 1923; Captain, 1923; Bt Major, 1933; Staff Captain 54th East Anglian Div. (TA) and East Anglian Area, 1928-32; retired and joined Metropolitan Police, 1933; Chief Constable No. 2 District, 1936, No. 1 District, Feb.-Nov. 1938, No. 3 District, Nov. 1938-Feb. 1940; Dep. Asst Commissioner A Dept, New Scotland Yard, Feb.-Aug. 1940; Dep. Asst Commissioner No. 1 District, Aug. 1940-June 1946; Asst Commissioner i/c D Dept, New Scotland Yard, June-Oct. 1946, transferred to A Dept, Oct. 1946. Chairman: Securicor Ltd; British Security Industry Assoc., 1966-; Director, Security Services Ltd. CStJ; Queen's Police Medal for Distinguished Service, 1956; Officer of the Legion of Honour; Officer of Orange Nassau (Netherlands); Commander Order of the Dannebrog (Denmark); Commander Order of St Olaf (Norway). *Recreations:* cricket, shooting and fishing. *Address:* 16 Tufton Court, SW1. *T:* 01-222 5544; Steyne Wood Battery, Bembridge, IoW. *T:* Bembridge 2424. *Clubs:* United Service, MCC; Bembridge Sailing (Bembridge).

**MARGETTS, Frederick Chilton,** CBE 1966 (MBE 1943); Chairman and Managing Director, Transportation Systems and Market Research Ltd, and Consultant to BR Board; Director: Winn International Containers Ltd; Collico Ltd; Consultant, Containerisation; *b* 2 Nov. 1905; *m* 1929, Dorothy Walls; one *d.* *Educ:* Driffield Grammar Sch.; St Martin's Grammar Sch., Scarborough. Asst Operating Supt, LNER Scotland, 1946; BR Scotland, 1949; Chief Operating Supt, BR Scotland, 1955; Chief Traffic Manager, 1958, Asst General Manager, 1959, General Manager, 1961, BR York; Member BR Cttee, 1962; Operating Mem., BR Board, 1962-67. *Recreation:* œnology. *Address:* 45 Chiltern Court, Baker Street, NW1. *T:* 01-486 3147; 9 Riseborough House, York. *T:* York 26207.

**MARION, Dr Leo Edmond,** CC (Canada) 1967; MBE 1946; FRSC 1942; FRS (London), 1961; Dean, Faculty of Pure and Applied Science, University of Ottawa, 1965-69, retired; *b* 22 March 1899; *s* of Joseph Marion and Emma Vezina; *m* 1933, Paule Lefort; no *c.* *Educ:* Queen's (BSc 1926, MSc 1927); McGill (PhD 1929); University of Vienna. Research chemist, National Research Council, 1929-42; Head, Organic Chemistry Section, 1943; Editor in Chief of all Canadian Journals of Research, 1947-65; Vice-President (scientific), National Research Council, Ottawa, 1963-65. Hon. Member Société Chimique de France, 1957; President, Chemical Institute of Canada, 1961. President Royal Society of Canada, 1964. Hon. degrees: DSc: Laval, 1954; Ottawa, 1958; Queen's, 1961; D. de l'U., Montreal, 1961; Paris, 1962; LLD, Toronto, 1962; DSc: British Columbia, 1963; Royal Military Coll., 1965; Carleton, 1965; McGill, 1966; Poznan, 1967; Saskatchewan, 1968; DCL, Bishop's, 1966. Member American Chemical Society; Association Canadienne-Française pour l'Avancement des Sciences Medal, 1948; Chem. Inst. of Canada Medal, 1956; City of Paris Medal, 1957; Professional Institute of Canada Medal, 1959; Chem. Inst. of Canada Montreal Medal, 1969. *Publications:* chapters in: The Alkaloids; 195 papers on chemistry of alkaloids. *Address:* 984 Goren Avenue, Ottawa 8, Canada. *T:* 731-6754.

**MARITAIN, Jacques;** Professor Emeritus of Philosophy, Princeton University; Professor of Philosophy, Princeton University, 1948-52; Docteur en Philosophie; Agrégé de l'Université; *b* 18 Nov. 1882. *Educ:* Université de Paris. Late Professeur de philosophie à l'Institut Catholique de Paris et à l'Institut d'études médiévales de Toronto. Visiting Prof. at Columbia Univ. and at Princeton Univ., 1940-44; French Ambassador to the Holy See, 1945-48. Grand Prix de Littérature, Académie Française, 1961; Grand Prix National des Lettres, 1963. *Publications:* Art et Scolastique, 1920, 3e édn, 1935, trad., en anglais, 1927; Frontières de la Poésie, 1935; La Philosophie bergsonienne, 1914, 1930; Introduction à la philosophie, 1920, trad. anglaise, 1930; Théonas, 1921, trad. anglaise, 1933; Réflexions sur l'Intelligence, 1923, 1930; Trois Réformateurs, 1925, 1931, trad. anglaise, 1928; Réponse à Jean Cocteau, 1926; Quelques pages sur Léon Bley, 1927; Primauté du Spirituel, 1927, trad. anglaise, 1930; Le Docteur Angélique, 1930, trad. anglaise, 1931; Religion et Culture, 1931, trad. anglaise, 1931; Le Songe de Descartes, 1932; Distinguer pour unir ou Les Degrés du Savoir, 1932; Du Régime temporel et de la Liberté, 1933, trad. anglaise, 1935; Sept Leçons sur l'être, 1934 (trad. anglaise: A Preface to Metaphysics, 1940); La Philosophie de la Nature, 1935; Questions de Conscience, 1938; Humanisme Intégral, 1936 (trad. anglaise: True Humanism, 1939); Anti-semitism; The Living Thoughts of St Paul; A travers le Désastre; Redeeming the Time; The Rights of Man and Natural Law; Christianity and Democracy; De Bergson à Thomas d'Aquin; Principes d'une Politique humaniste; Messages; Pour la Justice; Education at the Crossroads, 1939-45; La Personne et le Bien commun; Court Traité de l'Existence et de l'Existant, 1947; Man and the State, 1951; The Range of Reason, 1952; Creative Intuition in Art and Poetry, 1953; On the Philosophy of History, 1957; Reflections on America, 1958; The Responsibility of the Artist, 1960; La Philosophie Morale, 1960; Eng. trans. (Moral Philosophy), 1964; On the Use of Philosophy, 1961; Dieu et la permission du mal, 1963, Eng. trans. 1966; Carnet de Notes, 1965; Le Paysan de la Garonne, 1966, Eng. trans. 1968. With Madame Raïssa Maritain: De la vie d'Oraison, 1925, 1933, Eng. trans., 1928; Situation de la poésie, 1938. *Address:* 26 Linden Lane, Princeton, NJ, USA.

**MARJOLIN, Robert E.;** Officier de la Légion d'Honneur, 1956; Officier du Mérite Agricole, 1958; economist; *b* 27 July 1911; *s* of Ernest Marjolin and Elise Vacher; *m* 1944, Dorothy Smith; one *s* one *d.* *Educ:* Sorbonne and Law Sch., Paris; Yale Univ., New Haven, Conn. Asst to Professor Charles Rist at Institut Scientifique de Recherches Economiques et Sociales, 1934-37; Chief Asst, 1938-39. Joined General de Gaulle in London, 1941; Head of French Supply Mission in USA, 1944; Directeur des Relations Economiques Extérieures, Ministère de L'Economie Nationale, 1945; Commissaire Général Adjoint du Plan de Modernisation et d'Équipement, 1946-48; Secretary General, Organisation for European Economic Co-operation, 1948-55; Professor of Economics, University of Nancy, 1955-58; Vice-President, Commission of European Economic Community (Common Market), 1958-67; Prof. of Economics, Univ. of Paris, 1967-69. Foreign Hon. Member American Academy of Arts and Sciences, 1963. Hon. LLD: Yale, 1965; Harvard, 1967; University of East Anglia, 1967. American Medal of Freedom, 1947; King's Medal, 1947; Grand-Croix de l'Ordre d'Orange-Nassau (Holland), Cavaliere di Gran Croce nell' Ordine Al Merito della Repubblica (Italy). Grand-Croix du Mérite de la République Fédérale d'Allemagne, Grand-Croix de l'Ordre Royal du Phœnix (Greece), 1955, Commandeur de l'Ordre du Drapeau (Yugoslavia), 1956. Grand-Officier de l'Ordre de la Couronne (Belgique); Hon. CBE (Great Britain), 1957; Grand Croix de l'Ordre du Dannebrog (Denmark), 1958; Grand Croix de l'Ordre de Leopold II (Belgique), 1967. *Publications:* L'Evolution du Syndicalisme aux Etats-Unis. de Washington à Roosevelt, 1936; Prix, monnaie, production–Essai sur les mouvements économiques de longue durée, 1945; Europe and the United States in the World Economy, 1953. *Address:* 9 rue de Valois, Paris 1er. *T:* 231.3684.

**MARJORIBANKS, Sir James Alexander Milne,** KCMG 1965 (CMG 1954); Ambassador and Head of the UK Delegation to the European Community, the European Atomic Energy Community and the European Coal and Steel Community, since 1965; *b* 29 May 1911; *y s* of Rev. Thomas Marjoribanks, DD, and Mary Ord, *d* of William Logan, Madras CS; *m* 1936, Sonya Patricia, *d* of David Stanley-Alder, Alderford Grange, Sible Hedingham, Essex, and Sylvia Marie Stanley; one *d.* *Educ:* Merchiston; Edinburgh Academy; Edinburgh Univ. (MA, 1st class hons). Entered Foreign Service, Nov. 1934; HM Embassy, Peking, 1935-38; Consulate-General, Hankow, 1938; Marseilles, 1939-40; Consul, Jacksonville,

1940-42. Vice-Consul, New York, 1942-44; Asst to UK Political Rep., Bucharest, 1944-45; Foreign Office, 1945-49; Dep. to Secretary of State for Foreign Affairs in Austrian Treaty negotiations, 1947-49; Official Secretary, UK High Commn, Canberra, 1950-52; Dep. Head of UK Delegation to High Authority of European Coal and Steel Community, 1952-55; Cabinet Office, 1955-57; HM Minister (Economic), Bonn, 1957-62; Asst Under-Secretary of State, Foreign Office, 1962-65. *Recreations:* mountaineering, tennis, golf. *Address:* 21 Avenue Henri Pirenne, Brussels 18; 13 Regent Terrace, Edinburgh 7. *Club:* Boodle's.

**MARK, James,** MBE 1943; Under-Secretary, Ministry of Overseas Development since 1965; *b* 12 June 1914; *s* of late John Mark and Louisa Mary (*née* Hobson); *m* 1941, Mary Trewent Rowland; three *s* two *d*. *Educ:* William Hulme's Grammar Sch., Manchester; Trinity Coll., Cambridge; Universities of Munich and Münster. MA 1939. PhD 1939, Cambridge. Intelligence Corps, 1940-46. Principal, Control Office for Germany and Austria, 1946-48; HM Treasury, 1948-64; Asst Secretary, 1950; Economic Counsellor, Washington, 1951-53. *Publications:* The Question of Christian Stewardship, 1964; articles and reviews on theological and related subjects. *Recreations:* reading, music, gardening. *Address:* 32 North Cray Road, Bexley, Kent. *T:* Crayford 23084.
*See also Robert Mark.*

**MARK, Robert,** QPM 1965; Deputy Commissioner, Metropolitan Police, since 1968; *b* Manchester, 13 March 1917; *y s* of late John Mark and Louisa Mark (*née* Hobson); *m* 1941, Kathleen Mary, *o d* of Daniel William and Hannah Cecilia Leahy, Broadwaters, Kidderminster; one *s* one *d*. *Educ:* William Hulme's Grammar Sch., Manchester. Constable to Chief Superintendent, Manchester City Police, 1937-42, 1947-56; Chief Constable of Leicester, 1957-67; Assistant Commissioner, Metropolitan Police, 1967-68. Vis. Fellow, Nuffield Coll., Oxford, 1970-. Member: Standing Advisory Council of Penal System, 1966; Adv. Cttee on Police in Northern Ireland, 1969; Assessor to Lord Mountbatten during his Inquiry into Prison Security, 1966. Royal Armoured Corps, 1942-47: Lieut, Phantom (GHQ Liaison Regt), North-West Europe, 1944-45; Major, Control Commission for Germany, 1945-47. Has appeared on TV. Hon. LLM Leicester Univ., 1967. *Publications:* articles on law and police administration in Times, Guardian, New Law Journal, Law Society Gazette, Lawyer, Criminal Law Review, JP and Local Government Review, Police Journal, etc. *Address:* New Scotland Yard, Broadway, SW1. *T:* 01-230 1212.
*See also James Mark.*

**MARK-WARDLAW, Rear-Adm. (retired) Alexander Livingstone Penrose;** Governing Director, Loseberry Enterprises Ltd; UK Representative, 1st Genoa International Nautical and Telecommunications Exhibition, 1963; President of Honour, International Cargo Handling Co-ordination Association (ICHCA), since Sept. 1959 (Co-Founder and President Executive, 1951-59); UK Representative: Barracuda Center KB Sweden; CRM Milan; Autronica Norway; Werkspoor NV; Vredestein-International of The Hague; Rudolf Bauer, Austria; *b* 9 March 1891; *s* of late Colonel W. L. P. MarkWardlaw, North Staffordshire Regt, and late Mrs Florence Emily Mark-Wardlaw; *m* 1916, Irene Marjorie Cochran Carr (*d* 1961); one *s* one *d*. *Educ:* Fosters, Stubbington; RN Colleges, Osborne and Dartmouth. Comd submarines during European War, 1914-18; selected as 1st specialist (E †) from Exec. Branch under Selborne Fisher Scheme, 1918, with permanent retention of Military Command status. Asst Naval Attaché, Washington, 1934-37; served War of 1939-45, with Home Fleet; Combined Operations HQ, as acting Rear-Admiral, 1942-44; ADC to the King, 1943; served on staff of Allied Naval C-in-C X Force and subs. Allied Naval C-in-C Germany, 1944-46; promoted for war services of particular merit to rank of Rear-Admiral, 1946; Control Office for Germany and Austria, 1946; Shipping Adviser Foreign Office, 1949, Military Security Board, Germany, 1950. MRINA, 1937. MIMechE 1948. MIMarE 1951; Assoc. Institute of Transport. Member: Fertilizer Society; Inst. of Navigation; Inst. of Directors. Military Medal for Greece, Order of the Redeemer, Greece, 1931. *Recreation:* gardening. *Address:* Loseberry, Claygate, Surrey. *T:* Esher 62882. *Club:* United Service.

**MARKALL, Most Rev. Francis;** *see* Salisbury (Rhodesia), Archbishop of.

**MARKELIUS, Sven Gottfrid;** Architect; Professor *hc*; *b* Stockholm 25 Oct. 1889; *m* 1938, Ka (*née* Simon); three *s* two *d*. *Educ:* Stockholm Institute of Technology; Dept of Architecture, Royal Academy of Fine Arts. Chief of Planning Section, Royal Board of Building, Stockholm, 1938-44; City Planning Director, Stockholm, 1944-54. Visiting Professor: Yale, 1949; MIT 1962; University of California, Berkeley, 1962. Member, Swedish Royal Academy of Fine Arts, 1942; President Federation of Swedish Architects Societies, 1953-56; Member World Academy of Art and Science; Member Group of Consultants of UN Headquarters in New York, 1947; Member Advisory Cttee of UNESCO Headquarters in Paris, 1952- (Member Art Cttee, 1954-56). Works include: Student's Clubhouse, Stockholm Inst. of Technology, 1929; Hälsingborg Concert Hall, 1932; Cooperative Apartment Hotel, Stockholm, 1935; Office Bldg for Stockholm Builders' Assoc., 1937; Swedish Pavilion, New York World Fair, 1939; Trade Union Centre, Linköping, 1953; Trade Union Centre, Stockholm, 1960; Forest Industries Centre, Stockholm, 1961; Bürgerhaus, Giessen, W Germany, 1965; Park Hotel, Stockholm, 1967; Sweden House, Stockholm, 1968; private and apartment houses. Howland Memorial Prize, Yale Univ., 1949; Medal of St Erik, 1959; Medal of Prince Eugen, 1961; Royal Gold Medal, RIBA, 1962. Dr ing *hc* Techn. Hochschule Aachen, 1966. *Publications:* Acceptera (in collaboration), 1930. Articles in professional journals. *Address:* Kevingestrand 5, Danderyd, Sweden. *T:* 755 4466.

**MARKER, Edwin Henry Simon,** CB 1946; Under-Secretary, Board of Trade, 1946-52; retired from Civil Service, 1952; *b* 22 Jan. 1888; *s* of late Alfred H. Marker, Parkwood, Sevenoaks, Kent; *m* 1931, Christina, *er d* of late G. J. Francis; two *s* two *d*. *Educ:* St Paul's Sch.; Wadham Coll., Oxford. First Class Classical Mods., 1909; First Class Lit. Hum., 1911; entered Board of Trade, 1912; Secretary to Cttee on Shipping and Shipbuilding, 1916; Comptroller, Companies Dept, 1934; Member of Cttee on Compulsory Insurance, 1936; Principal Assistant Secretary, Insurance and Companies Dept, 1941; Member of Cttee on Shares of No Par Value, 1952-53. Visited India as Adviser to Government of India in connection with Indian Company Law amendment, 1953, 1955-56. *Address:* 35

Hazlewell Road, Putney, SW15. *T:* 01-788 6728. *Club:* United University.

**MARKHAM, Rt. Rev. Bernard;** *see* Nassau and The Bahamas, Bishop of.

**MARKHAM, Sir Charles (John);** 3rd Bt, *cr* 1911; *b* 2 July 1924; *s* of Sir Charles Markham, 2nd Bt, and Gwladys, *e d* of late Hon. Rupert Beckett; *S* father 1952; *m* 1949, Valerie, *o d* of Lt-Col E. Barry-Johnston, Makuyu, Kenya; two *s* one *d. Educ:* Eton. Served War of 1939-45, Lieut in 11th Hussars (despatches). *Heir: s* Arthur David Markham, *b* 6 Dec. 1950. *Address:* PO Box 2263, Nairobi, Kenya, East Africa. *Club:* Cavalry.

**MARKHAM, Sir F.;** *see* Markham, Sir S. F.

**MARKHAM, Roy,** FRS 1956; MA, PhD; John Innes Professor of Cell Biology and Director, John Innes Institute, University of East Anglia, Norwich, since 1967; Director, Agricultural Research Council Virus Research Unit, 1960-67 (Hon. Director, 1967-68); *b* 29 Jan. 1916; *m* 1940, Margaret Mullen. *Educ:* St Paul's; Christ's Coll., Cambridge. Fellow of Christ's Coll., Cambridge, 1965-67. Mem. of Council, John Innes Inst., 1964-67. Hon. Mem., Amer. Soc. of Biological Chemists. *Publications:* various. *Address:* John Innes Institute, Colney Lane, Norwich NOR 70F. *T:* Norwich 52571; 10 Daniels Road, Norwich NOR 47D. *T:* Norwich 53429. *Club:* Royal Automobile.

**MARKHAM, Sir (Sydney) Frank,** Kt 1953; DL; Company Director; Major psc on General List (served with 3rd Army Corps in France and with 1st Army in N Africa, 2nd Army in Germany); *b* 19 Oct. 1897; *m* 1928; three *s* two *d. Educ:* Wadham Coll., Oxford. MA, BLitt, Dip. Econ. MP (Lab) Rochester (Chatham Div.), 1929-31; MP (Nat) S Nottingham, 1935-45; MP (C) Buckingham Div. of Bucks, 1951-64. Parliamentary Private Sec. to Prime Minister, 1931-32, to the Lord Pres. of the Council, 1936-37; Pres. Museums Association, 1939-42; Chm. Parliamentary Science Cttee, 1938-41; Mem. Select Cttee on Estimates, 1953-62, Chm., 1962-64; Chm. Parliamentary Delegation to Kenya, 1961, to Malta, 1963 and to Far East, 1964. DL Beds, 1966. *Publications:* Climate and the Energy of Nations, 1942 (American edn, 1944); A History of Stony Stratford. *Address:* Heath Park Road, Leighton Buzzard, Beds. *T:* Heath and Reach 208.

**MARKING, Henry Ernest,** CBE 1969; MC 1944; CompRAeS 1953; MInstT 1955; Chief Executive, British European Airways, since 1964; *b* 11 March 1920; *s* of late Isaac Marking and Mrs Hilda Jane Marking. *Educ:* Saffron Walden Gram. Sch.; University Coll., London; Middle East Centre of Arab Studies. Served War of 1939-45: 2nd Bn The Sherwood Foresters, 1941-45; North Africa, Italy and Middle East; Adjutant, 1944-45. Middle East Centre of Arab Studies, Jerusalem, 1945-46. Admitted solicitor, 1948. Asst Solicitor, Cripps, Harries, Hall & Co., Tunbridge Wells, 1948-49; Asst Solicitor, 1949, Sec., 1950, British European Airways. Trustee, Cheshire Foundn Homes for the Sick, 1962-. *Club:* Reform.

**MARKOVA, Dame Alicia,** DBE 1963 (CBE 1958); **(Dame Lilian Alicia Marks);** Prima Ballerina Assoluta; Distinguished Lecturer on Ballet at College-Conservatory of Music, University of Cincinnati, 1970; *b* London 1910; *d* of Arthur Tristman Marks and Eileen Barry. With Diaghilev's Russian Ballet Co., 1925-29; Rambert Ballet Club, 1931-33; Vic-Wells Ballet Co., 1933-35; Markova-Dolin Ballet Co., 1935-37; Ballet Russe de Monte Carlo, 1938-41; Ballet Theatre, USA, 1941-46. Appeared with Anton Dolin, guest and concert performances, 1948-50. Co-Founder and Prima Ballerina, Festival Ballet, 1950-51; Guest Prima Ballerina, Royal Danish Ballet, 1955; Royal Ballet, 1953 and 1957; Festival Ballet, 1958 and 1959; Guest appearances at Metropolitan Opera House, New York, 1952, 1953-54, 1955, 1957, 1958; Dir, Metropolitan Opera Ballet, 1963-69. concert, television and guest appearances (general), 1952-61. Vice-Pres. Royal Academy of Dancing, 1958-. BBC series, Markova's Ballet Call, 1960. Hon. DMus Leicester, 1966. *Publication:* Giselle and I, 1960. *Address:* c/o Barclays Bank Ltd, 451 Oxford Street, W1.

**MARKS,** family name of **Baron Marks of Broughton.**

**MARKS OF BROUGHTON,** 2nd Baron, *cr* 1961; **Michael Marks;** *b* 27 Aug. 1920; *o s* of 1st Baron and Miriam, *d* of Ephraim Sieff; *S* father 1964; *m*; one *s* two *d. Educ:* St Paul's Sch.; Corpus Christi Coll., Cambridge. *Heir: s* Hon. Simon Richard Marks, *b* 3 May, 1950.

**MARKS, Derek John;** Editor, Daily Express; *b* 15 Jan. 1921; *e s* of late H. J. Marks and Mrs L. Marks; *m* 1942, Jean, *d* of Edward Greenhalgh and late Mrs Emily Greenhalgh, Edgerton, Huddersfield; one *s* two *d. Educ:* Seaford Coll. RAF, 1940-46. Huddersfield Examiner, 1946-48; East African Standard (Nairobi), 1948-49; Yorkshire Post (London), 1950-52; Daily Express, 1952. Various appts within Beaverbrook Newspapers; finally Dep. Editor, Evening Standard until apptd Editor of Daily Express and a Dir of Beaverbrook Newspapers, July 1965. *Address:* 121-128 Fleet Street, EC4. *T:* 01-353 8000. *Clubs:* Chelsea Arts, Press.

**MARKS, John Emile,** CBE 1970; President of DV Group Ltd since 1958; *b* 1 Dec. 1913; *s* of late Hyam and Miriam Marks; *m* 1947, Cassandra Emily (*née* Brierly); two *s* two *d. Educ:* Eton College. Served War of 1939-45 (despatches 1944; 1939-45 Star, France and Germany Star, Defence and Victory Medals). Man. Dir, Moulded Rubber Products, Enfield, 1936-40; Man. Dir, Britannia Rubber, Wembley, 1947-51; emigrated to Canada, 1951; estab. John Marks Ltd, importers and distributors of sporting goods, 1952; Pres., Douglas Engineering Co. Ltd, 1956; estab. Canair Ltd, Windsor, England, 1962 (Chm. and majority shareholder); bought controlling interest in DV Group Ltd, 1963 (inc. Douglas Engrg, Vibro-Acoustics Ltd and EngMark Ltd, all Toronto). *Recreations:* tennis, golf, squash. *Address:* 17 Donwoods Drive, Toronto 319, Ont, Canada. *T:* 483-3094; DV Group Ltd, 16 Lesmill Road, Don Mills, Ont, Canada. *Clubs:* Royal Automobile; Lambton Golf and Country, Toronto Cricket, Skating and Curling, Queen's (Toronto); United Services (Montreal).

**MARKS, Kenneth;** MP (Lab) Gorton since Nov. 1967; *b* 15 June 1920; *s* of Robert P. Marks, Electrician and Edith Collins, Cotton Weaver; *m* 1944, Kathleen Lynch; one *s* one *d. Educ:* Peacock Street Sch., Gorton; Central High Sch., Manchester; Didsbury Coll. of Education. Worked in offices of LNER, 1936-40. Joined ranks, Grenadier Guards, 1940-42; commnd into Cheshire Regt, 1942-46 (Capt.); served in Middle East, Malta, Italy, NW Europe and Germany as Infantry Platoon and Company Comdr. Taught in Manchester schs, 1946-67; Headmaster, Clough Top Sec. Sch. for Boys, 1964-67. Mem., House of Commons

Select Cttee for Educn and Science, 1968-70; PPS to Rt Hon. Anthony Crosland, Nov. 1969. *Address:* 1 Epping Road, Denton, Manchester, *T:* 061-336 4147.

**MARLAR, Edward Alfred Geoffrey,** MBE 1944; MA, LLB Cantab; retired as Headmaster of Whitgift School, Croydon (1946-July 1961); *b* 2 Jan. 1901; *s* of J. F. Marlar; *m* 1924, Winifred Stevens; one *s* one *d. Educ:* Brighton Coll.; Selwyn Coll., Cambridge (Hons History and Law). Senior History Master, Dunstable Gram. Sch., 1922-27; Senior History and VIth Form Master, Worksop Coll., 1927-34; Headmaster, Moulton Gram. Sch., 1934-37; Headmaster, King Edward VI Sch., Lichfield, 1937-46. Served as Major in Home Guard, in War of 1939-45. *Address:* Warren Edge, Salisbury Road, Eastbourne, Sussex.

**MARLBOROUGH,** 10th Duke of, *cr* 1702; **John Albert Edward William Spencer-Churchill;** Baron Spencer, 1603; Earl of Sunderland, 1643; Baron Churchill, 1685; Earl of Marlborough, 1689; Marquis of Blandford, 1702; Prince of the Holy Roman Empire; Prince of Mindelheim in Suabia; Captain, 1st Life Guards, 1916; retired, 1927; Military liaison officer to Regional Commander, Southern Region, 1942; Lt-Col liaison officer, US Forces, 1942-45; *b* 18 Sept. 1897; *e s* of 9th Duke and Consuelo (*d* 1964), *d* of late W. K. Vanderbilt, New York; *S* father, 1934; *m* 1920, Hon. Mary Cadogan (CBE 1953), (*d* 1961), *d* of late Viscount Chelsea, and late Lady Charles Montagu; two *s* three *d. Educ:* Eton. Mayor of Woodstock, 1937-38, 1938-39. *Heir: s* Marquess of Blandford, *qv. Address:* Blenheim Palace, Woodstock, Oxon. Died 1972.

*See also Earl of Sunderland.*

**MARLER, Leslie Sydney,** OBE 1957; TD 1946; Hon. President, Capital & Counties Property Co. Ltd (Chairman, 1950-71); Director (London Board) Norwich Union Insurance Societies; *b* 7 July 1900; *e s* of L. T. Marler, Birdham, Sussex; *m* 1926, Doris Marguerite (JP Bucks, 1946), 3rd *d* of late H. E. Swaffer, Brighton; one *s* one *d* (and one *s* decd). *Educ:* St Paul's Sch. Served European War, 1914-18, with HAC, 1917-19; re-employed, 1939, as Captain RA; Major 1941; retd 1945. Chm. Buckingham Div., Conservative Assoc., 1946-56, Pres., 1956-. Master, Worshipful Co. of Merchant Taylors, 1960. Life Mem., Court of The City University, 1970. High Sheriff, Bucks, 1971-72. *Recreations:* fox-hunting, bloodstock breeding, golf, collecting first editions, travel. *Address:* Bolebec House, Whitchurch, Bucks. *T:* Whitchurch 231. *Clubs:* Carlton, Junior Carlton, Royal Thames Yacht, Farmers'.

**MARLEY,** 2nd Baron *cr* 1930, of Marley in the County of Sussex; **Godfrey Pelham Leigh Aman;** Film Producer; *b* 6 Sept. 1913; *s* of 1st Baron and Octable Turquet (*d* 1969), *d* of late Sir Hugh Gilzean-Reid, DL, LLD, formerly MP for Aston Manor; *S* father 1952; *m* 1956, Catherine Doone Beal. *Educ:* Bedales Sch. Royal Marines, 1939-45. *Heir:* none. *Address:* 104 Ebury Mews, SW1. *T:* 01-730 4844.

**MARLING, Lt-Col Sir John Stanley Vincent,** 4th Bt, *cr* 1882; OBE 1945; *b* 26 July 1910; *s* of Sir Charles Murray Marling, GCMG, CB, and Lucia, CBE (*d* 1927), *o c* of late Maj.-Gen. Sir John Ramsay Slade, KCB; *S* uncle, 1936; *m* 1st, 1939, Georgina Brenda (Betty) (marr. diss., 1957, she *d* 1961), *o d* of late Henry Edward Fitzroy-Somerset; one *s* three *d*; 2nd, 1957, Marjorie Frances Esclairmonde, *widow* of Maj. Gustavus March-Phillipps, and 3rd *d* of late Sir Francis Hugh Stewart, CIE. *Educ:* Winchester Coll.; RMC, Sandhurst. Joined 17th/21st Lancers, 1930; retired 1947. *Heir: s* Charles William Somerset Marling, *b* 2 June 1951. *Address:* Woodcray Manor Farm, Wokingham, Berks.

**MARMION, Prof. Barrie P.;** Professor of Bacteriology, University of Edinburgh, since 1968; *b* 19 May 1920; *s* of J. P. and M. H. Marmion, Alverstoke, Hants; *m* 1953, Diana Ray Newling, *d* of Dr P. Ray Newling, Adelaide, SA; one *d. Educ:* University Coll. and University Coll. Hosp., London. MD London 1947, MCPA 1963, DSc London 1963, FCPath 1962. House Surg., UCH, 1942; Bacteriologist, Public Health Laboratory Service, 1943-62; Rockefeller Trav. Fellow, at Walter and Eliza Hall Inst., Melbourne, 1951-52; Foundation Prof., Microbiology, Monash Univ., Melbourne, Australia, 1962-68. *Publications:* numerous papers on bacteriology and virology. *Recreations:* tennis, squash, music. *Address:* Flat 1 Ravelston Heights' Ravelston House Park, Edinburgh EH4 3LX. *T:* 031-332 8185.

**MARNAN, John Fitzgerald,** MBE 1944; QC 1954; **His Honour Judge John Fitzgerald Maman;** Chairman, North East London Quarter Sessions, since 1968; *b* 23 Jan. 1908; *s* of late T. G. Marnan, Irish Bar; *m* 1st, 1934, Morwenna (marr. diss., 1958), *d* of late Sir Keith Price; one *s* (and one *s* decd); 2nd, 1958, Mrs Diana Back (marr. diss., 1963), *o d* of late Comdr Charles Crawshay, RN (retd), and late Mrs M. L. Greville; 3rd, 1966, Joanna, *o d* of late Maj.-Gen. W. N. Herbert, CB, CMG, DSO. *Educ:* Ampleforth; Trinity Coll., Oxford. Called to Bar, 1931; joined Chester and N Wales Circuit; joined Supplementary Reserve, Irish Guards, 1936; served War of 1939-45 (MBE, despatches); Western Europe with Irish Guards, and on staff of 15th (Scottish) Div.; Major (GSO2), 1944; Capt. (Hon. Major), RARO, 1947, retired from RARO, 1958. A Metropolitan Magistrate, 1956-58, resigned. Crown Counsel in the Ministry of Legal Affairs, Kenya Government, 1958-59; Federal Justice of the Federal Supreme Court, the West Indies, 1959-62; subseq. Justice of Appeal of the British Caribbean Court of Appeal. Sat as Commissioner at Crown Courts, at Manchester, 1962-63, at Liverpool, 1963, and at Central Criminal Court, 1964-66; a Dep. Chm., Greater London Sessions, 1966-68. *Recreations:* field sports and sailing. *Address:* 166 Cranmer Court, SW3. *T:* 01-589 5629. *Clubs:* Guards, Pratt's.

**MARNHAM, Harold,** MBE 1945; QC 1965; Barrister-at-law; Deputy Chairman, Oxfordshire Quarter Sessions, since 1966; Leader of Parliamentary Bar, since 1967; *b* 14 July 1911; *y s* of late Arthur Henry Marnham and late Janet Elizabeth Marnham; *m* 1947, Hilary, *y d* of late Ernest Jukes; two *s. Educ:* Stellenbosch Boys' High Sch.; Stellenbosch Univ.; Jesus Coll., Cambridge. Called to Bar, Gray's Inn, 1935; Bencher, 1969. Served War 1939-45; BEF, 1939-40; BLA, 1944-45 (despatches); 2nd Lt RA (TA); Capt. 1940; Major 1942; Lt-Col 1945. *Address:* 9 Crescent Place, SW3. *T:* 01-584 6703. *Clubs:* Hawks (Cambridge); Leander (Henley-on-Thames).

**MARNHAM, John Ewart,** CMG 1955; MC 1944; TD 1949; HM Diplomatic Service; British Government Representative, West Indian Associate States, since 1970 (resident in Castries, St Lucia); *b* Hampstead, 24 Jan. 1916; *er s* of Col Arthur Ewart Marnham, MC, TD, DL, JP, Foxley Grove, Holyport, Berks, and of late Dorothy Clare Morgan; *m* 1944, Susan, *er d* of Walter Foster (formerly Friedenstein), Vienna and London; two *s. Educ:* Mill Hill; Jesus Coll., Cambridge. Asst Principal,

Colonial Office, 1938. Served War, 1939-45: BEF 1939-40; BLA 1944-45 (despatches); 2nd Lt RA (TA) 1938; Major, 1942; Lt-Col, Commanding 353 (London) Medium Regt RA (TA), 1954-57; Brevet Col, 1958. Principal, Colonial Office, 1946; Asst Sec. 1948; Asst Under-Sec. of State: CO, 1964; Foreign Office, 1966-67; Consul-Gen., Johannesburgh, 1967-70. Imperial Defence Coll., 1961. *Recreations:* reading, gardening, riding. *Address:* c/o Foreign and Commonwealth Office, SW1; Foxley Grove, Holyport, Berks. *T:* Maidenhead 23543. *Club:* United University.

**MARNHAM, Sir Ralph,** KCVO 1957; MChir, FRCS; Serjeant Surgeon to the Queen; Consulting Surgeon to: St George's Hospital; King Edward VII's Hospital for Officers; Fellow: Medical Society of London; Association of Surgeons of Great Britain and Ireland; *b* 7 June 1901; *e s* of Arthur Henry Marnham and late Janet Elizabeth Micklem; *m* 1st, 1927, Muriel, *y d* of Herbert Marnham; one *d*; 2nd, 1942, Helena Mary, *e d* of Patrick Daly; two *s*. *Educ:* Diocesan Coll., Rondebosch, South Africa; Gonville and Caius Coll., Cambridge; St George's Hospital. Allingham Scholarship Surgery; Sir Francis Laking Research Scholarship; Moynihan Fellow Assoc. of Surgeons of Great Britain and Ireland. War of 1939-45: Officer in Charge Surgical Divs of No. 62 and 6 Gen. Hospitals. Cons Surgeon, 9th Army, East Africa and Southern Command (despatches twice). Usual House Appointments St George's Hospital; also Asst Curator of Museum, Surgical Registrar, and Resident Asst Surgeon. *Publications:* various in medical journals. *Recreation:* golf. *Address:* 90a Harley Street, W1. *T:* 01-935 9525. *Clubs:* Buck's, Pratt's.

**MARPLES, Brian John;** Emeritus Professor of Zoology, University of Otago, NZ; *b* 31 March 1907; 2nd *s* of George and Anne Marples; *m* 1931, Mary Joyce Ransford; two *s*. *Educ:* St Bees Sch.; Exeter Coll., Oxford. Lecturer in Zoology, Univ. of Manchester, 1929-35; Lecturer in Zoology, Univ. of Bristol, 1935-37; Prof. of Zoology, Univ. of Otago, NZ, 1937-67. *Publications:* Freshwater Life in New Zealand, 1962; various technical zoological papers. *Address:* 1 Vanbrugh Close, Old Woodstock, Oxon.

**MARPLES, Rt. Hon. Ernest,** PC 1957; MP (C) Wallasey since 1945; *b* 9 Dec. 1907; *s* of late Alfred Ernest Marples and late Mary Marples; *m* 1956, Mrs Ruth Dobson. *Educ:* Stretford Gram. Sch. Chartered Accountant, 1928; joined London Scottish, July 1939; 2nd Lt Royal Artillery, Jan. 1941; Captain, 1941. Parliamentary Sec., Ministry of Housing and Local Government, 1951-54; Joint Parliamentary Sec., Ministry of Pensions and National Insurance, Oct. 1954-Dec. 1955; Postmaster-Gen., 1957-59; Minister of Transport, Oct. 1959-64, and Chm., Nationalized Transport Advisory Council, 1963-64; Shadow Minister of Technology, 1964-66; Sponsor, Conservative Party Public Sector Research Unit, 1967-70. Chairman: Boase, Massimi and Pollitt, 1968-; Minalka UK, 1970-. *Publication:* The Road to Prosperity, 1947. *Recreations:* tennis, mountaineering. *Address:* 33 Eccleston Street, SW1. *Clubs:* Carlton, Queen's.

**MARQUAND, David (Ian);** MP (Lab) Ashfield since 1966; *b* 20 Sept. 1934; *s* of Rt Hon. Hilary Marquand, *qv*; *m* 1959, Judith Mary (*née* Reed); one *s* one *d*. *Educ:* Emanuel Sch.; Magdalen Coll., Oxford; St Antony's Coll., Oxford (Sen. Schol.). 1st cl. hons Mod. Hist., 1957. Teaching Asst, Univ. of Calif., 1958-59; Leader Writer, The Guardian, 1959-62; Research Fellow, St Antony's Coll., Oxford, 1962-64; Lectr in Politics, Univ. of Sussex, 1964-66. Contested (Lab) Barry, 1964; PPS to Minister of Overseas Develt, 1967-68; Member: Select Cttee on Estimates, 1966-68; Select Cttee on Procedure, 1968-70; British Delegn to Council of Europe, 1970. Mem., MRC, 1968-69. *Publications:* articles and reviews in Guardian, New Statesman, Encounter, Commentary, etc. *Recreation:* walking. *Address:* House of Commons, SW1.

**MARQUAND, Rt. Hon. Hilary Adair,** PC 1949; MA, DSc; Deputy Chairman, National Board for Prices and Incomes, 1965-68; *b* 24 Dec. 1901; *s* of Alfred Marquand and Mary Adair; *m* 1929, Rachel Eluned, BA, *d* of D. J. Rees, Glanyronen, Ystalyfera; two *s* one *d*. *Educ:* Cardiff High Sch.; University Coll., Cardiff (State Scholar). BA Wales (1st Cl. Hons History, 1923; 1st Cl. Hons Economics, 1924); Gladstone and Cobden prizeman; MA (with Distinction), 1928; DSc 1938; Laura Spelman Rockefeller Fellow in Social Sciences in the USA, 1925-26; Lecturer in Economics, Univ. of Birmingham, 1926-30; Prof. of Industrial Relations, University Coll., Cardiff, 1930-45, Mem. Council, 1967-; Dir of Industrial Surveys of South Wales, 1931 and 1936; Mem. Cardiff Advisory Cttee UAB; spent a year in the USA in the study of Industrial Relations, 1932-33; Visiting Prof. of Economics, Wisconsin Univ., 1938-39; Acting Principal, Board of Trade, 1940-41, and Dep. Controller, Wales Div., Ministry of Labour, 1941-42; Labour Adviser Ministry of Production, 1943-44; MP (Lab) East Cardiff, 1945-50, East Div. of Middlesbrough, 1950-61; Sec. for Overseas Trade, 1945-57; Paymaster-Gen., 1947-48; Min. of Pensions, 1948-51; Min. of Health, Jan.-Oct. 1951. Hon. Mem. Phi Beta Kappa; Mem. Labour Party since 1920; Lecture Tours for Brit. Council in India, Pakistan and Ceylon, 1952-53, in WI, 1954 and 1959 and in Finland, 1957. Chm. Information Cttee Inter-Parl. Union, London Conf., 1957 and Mem. delegns to Turkey, 1953 and Finland, 1955; Representative at Assemblies of Council of Europe and W European Union, 1957-59. Mem. Commonwealth Parl. Assoc. Conf., 1961; Leader delegn to Gambia and Sierra Leone. Sidney Hillman Lecturer, Univ. of Wisconsin, 1956. Dir, Internat. Inst. for Labour Studies (Geneva), Dec. 1961-April 1965. *Publications:* Dynamics of Industrial Combination, 1931; Industrial Survey of South Wales (part author), 1932; Industrial Relations in the USA 1934; South Wales Needs a Plan, 1936; Second Industrial Survey of South Wales (joint), 1937; Organized Labour in Four Continents (joint), 1939; Articles and Reviews in Political Quarterly, The Times, Manchester Guardian, Economic Journal, Observer, etc. *Recreations:* travel, gardening. *Address:* 9 Grove Court, Drayton Gardens, SW10.

*See also D. I. Marquand.*

**MARQUIS,** family name of **Earl of Woolton.**

**MARR, Allan James,** CBE 1965; Director, Doxford & Sunderland Shipbuilding and Engineering Co. Ltd; *b* 6 May 1907; *s* of William Bell Marr (*heir pres* to Sir Leslie Lynn Marr, 2nd Bt, *qv*) and Hilda May Marr; *m* 1935, Joan de Wolf Ranken; one *s* two *d*. *Educ:* Oundle; Durham Univ. Apprenticeship, Joseph L. Thompson & Sons Ltd, 1926-31; joined Sir James Laing & Sons Ltd, 1932. Dir, Doxford and Sunderland Shipbuilding and Eng. Co. Ltd. Pres. Shipbuilding Conf., 1963-65; Fellow of North-East Coast Inst. of Engineers and Shipbuilders (Pres., 1966-68); Mem., RINA. Chm., Research Council of British Ship Research Assoc., 1965-.

*Recreations:* sailing, fishing, shooting. *Address:* The Hawthorns, Sea View Road, Sunderland. *Clubs:* Royal Thames Yacht, Royal Ocean Racing.

**MARR, Sir Leslie Lynn,** 2nd Bt, *cr* 1919; BA Cambridge; late Flight Lieutenant RAF; *b* 14 Aug. 1922; *o s* of late Col John Lynn Marr, OBE, TD, (and *g s* of 1st Bt,) and Amelia Rachel, *d* of late Robert Thompson, Overdinsdale Hall, Darlington; *S* grandfather 1932; *m* 1948, Dinora Delores Mendelson; one adopted *d. Educ:* Shrewsbury; Pembroke Coll., Cambridge. *Heir: u* William Bell Marr [*b* 4 Oct. 1881; *m* 1906, Hilda, *d* of George Carse, Wilton, Salisbury; three *s*].

**MARRACK, Rear-Adm. Hugh Richard,** CBE 1943; DSC 1918; Rear-Admiral, retired; *b* 5 July 1888; *s* of late John Reed Marrack, Tiverton, N Devon; *m* 1917, Christine (*d* 1969), *widow* of Lt George Pilkington, RN, and *d* of late A. M. Hallett; no *c. Educ:* Blundell's Sch., Tiverton; HMS Britannia. Joined HMS Britannia, 1902; Sub-Lt, Submarine Branch of Navy, 1908; Commanded HM Submarine A10, 1911-12; European War, 1914-18, Commanded HM Submarines C19 and E51 (minelayer), 1912-19; Commanded HM Submarines L71, K8, M3 and HM Australian Submarine Oxley, 1918-28; Commanded Portland Submarine Flotilla, 1929-31; Commanded China Submarine Flotilla, 1931-33; Commanded HMS Carlisle, 1934-37; Commodore i/c and Supt Sheerness, 1939-43; Commodore Supt Gibraltar, 1943-45; Comdr, 1923; Captain, 1931; ADC to the King, 1940; Rear-Adm., 1941; retired, 1941. *Address:* Flat 2, Chessington, Craneswater Park, Southsea, Hants.

**MARRACK, Prof. Emer. John Richardson,** DSO 1917; MC; Emeritus Professor of Chemical Pathology, London University; *b* 26 Nov. 1886; *s* of late John Reid Marrack; *m* 1st, 1913, Bertha Ada Fitzgerald Whiddington; one *s*; 2nd, 1922, Alice May Swaffield Milward; three *s. Educ:* Blundell's Sch., Tiverton; Cambridge Univ. (MA, MD); London Hosp. Late Prof. of Chemical Pathology at London Hosp. Medical Coll. and Univ. Lecturer Chemical Pathology, Cambridge Univ.; late Visiting Prof., University of Texas; John Lucas Walker Student, Cambridge Univ., Beit Memorial Fellow, Fellow St John's Coll., Cambridge. Served European War, 1914-19 (despatches, DSO, MC). *Publications:* The Chemistry of Antigens and Antibodies, MRC Report; (with Dr Panton) Clinical Pathology; Food and Planning, 1942. *Recreation:* walking. *Address:* 9 Woodlark Road, Cambridge.

**MARRE, Sir Alan, (Samuel),** KCB 1970 (CB 1955); Second Permanent Under-Secretary of State, Department of Health and Social Security, since 1968; *b* 25 Feb. 1914; *s* of late Joseph and late Rebecca Marre; *m* 1943, Romola Mary Gilling; one *s* one *d. Educ:* St Olave's and St Saviour's Grammar Sch., Southwark; Trinity Hall, Cambridge (Major open Schol.) John Stewart of Rannoch Schol. and 1st cl. hons Class. Trip. Parts I and II. Ministry of Health: Asst Principal, 1936; Principal, 1941; Asst Sec., 1946; Under-Sec., 1952-63; Under-Sec., Ministry of Labour, 1963-64; Dep. Sec.: Ministry of Health, 1964-66; Min. of Labour (later Dept of Employment and Productivity), 1966-68. *Recreations:* reading, walking. *Address:* 44 The Vale, NW11. *T:* 01-458 1787. *Club:* Athenæum.

**MARRIAN, Guy Frederic,** CBE 1969; FRS 1944; Fellow of University College, London, 1946; Director of Research, Imperial Cancer Research Fund, 1959-68; Professor of Chemistry in Relation to Medicine in the University of Edinburgh, 1939-Sept. 1959; *b* 3 March 1904; *s* of late Frederick York Marrian, AMICE, and of late Mary Eddington Currie; *m* 1928, Phyllis May Lewis; two *d. Educ:* Tollington Sch., London N; University Coll., London. BSc (Hons), 1925; DSc (London), 1930; FRIC 1931; Meldola Medallist, Institute of Chemistry, 1931; William Julius Mickle Fellowship, University of London, 1932; Francis Amory Prize, Amer. Acad. Arts and Sciences, 1948; Beit Memorial Fellowship for Medical Research, 1927-30; Sir Henry Dale Medallist of the Society for Endocrinology, 1966. Lecturer in Dept of Biochemistry, University Coll., London, 1930-33; Assoc. Prof. of Biochemistry, University of Toronto, 1933-36; Prof. of Biochemistry, Univ. of Toronto, 1936-38. *Publications:* papers in Biochemical Journal, Journal of Biological Chemistry, etc, mainly on the chemistry of the sex-hormones. *Address:* School Cottage, Ickham, Canterbury, Kent. *T:* Littlebourne 317. *Club:* Athenæum.

**MARRIC, J. J.;** *see under* Creasey, John.

**MARRIOTT, Cyril Herbert Alfred,** CBE 1949; *b* Chambly, Quebec, 28 Sept. 1897; *s* of Basil Sterling Talbot Marriott and Daisy Cecilia Bareham; *m* 1919, Helen Milne (*d* 1964); one *s* two *d. Educ:* Trent Coll. Entered Royal Navy as Asst Clerk, 1915; served in HMS Africa and as Secretary's Clerk to Admiral Sir John R. Jellicoe in HMS Iron Duke and to Admiral Sir David Beatty in HMS Iron Duke and Queen Elizabeth, and to Rear-Admiral Sir Wm E. Goodenough in HMS Orion, and to Rear-Admiral Maurice Woollcombe in HMS Colossus, and as Sec. to Flag Captain Arthur J. Davies in HMS King George V; left Navy 1919, as Acting Paymaster Sub-Lt to enter Consular Service; Vice-Consul Copenhagen, 1919; Braila, 1921; Acting Consul, Stockholm, 1924; Vice-Consul, New York, 1924; Antwerp, 1927; Panama (Chargé d'Affaires in 1933), 1931; Consul-General, Galatz, and Deputy British Commissioner on European Commission of the Danube, 1934; Consul, Bahia, 1937-41; Consul, Porto Alegre, 1941-44; Consul-General, Counsellor, and Counsellor (Commercial), Copenhagen, 1945-48; Political Adviser to GOC British Forces in Palestine, April-June 1948; Consul-General Haifa, 1948-49. Consul-General, Zürich, 1949-57. Appeals Sec., Crusade of Rescue, 1957-66. *Recreation:* motoring. *Address:* Fircroft, St John's Road, Cove, near Farnborough, Hants. *T:* Farnborough, Hants, 41038. *Clubs:* Royal Automobile, Royal Over-Seas League.

**MARRIOTT, Hugh Leslie,** CBE 1946; MD London; FRCP; formerly: Consulting Physician; Physician Middlesex Hospital; Lecturer in Middlesex Hospital Medical School; Hon. Consulting Physician to the Army; Examiner to the Conjoint Board of the Royal Colleges of Physicians and Surgeons and to Oxford, London and Glasgow Universities; Croonian Lecturer, Royal College of Physicians; Editor Quarterly Journal of Medicine; Member Association of Physicians of Great Britain; Fellow and ex-Member of Council Royal Society of Medicine; Fellow Royal Society of Tropical Medicine and Hygiene; *b* Nov. 1900; *s* of Samuel Augustus Marriott; *m* 1930, Vida Cureton; no *c.* Served RAMC 1939-45; Brig. 1942-45; Mission to Middle East for War Office and Medical Research Council, 1941; Consulting Physician to Army and Hon. Consultant to Royal Air Force, India Command, 1942-44; Consulting Physician to Allied Land Forces and Hon. Consultant to Royal Air Force, South-East Asia Command, 1944-45; Burma campaign

(CBE). *Publications:* various papers in medical journals and articles in medical text-books. *Address:* Shepherd's Down, Ridgeway, Friston, Eastbourne. *T:* East Dean 3123.

**MARRIOTT, Maj.-Gen. Sir John (Charles Oakes),** KCVO, *cr* 1950 (CVO 1937; MVO 1935); CB 1947; DSO 1917; MC; *b* 1895; *s* of late Charles Marriott of Stowmarket, Suffolk; *m* 1920, Maud (*d* 1960), *d* of Otto Kahn, New York; one *s*. *Educ:* Repton. Entered Northants Regt, 1914; served European War, 1915-18 (wounded, despatches, MC, DSO, Croix de Guerre); Military Attaché's Staff, Washington, 1919-20; transferred to Scots Guards, 1920; DAA & QMG London District, 1933-37; commanded 2nd Bn Scots Guards, 1938; served Middle East, 1941-42 (Bar to DSO); commanded 29 Indian Inf. Bde and 201 Guards Bde. Commander Guards Div. 1945-47; GOC London District, 1947-50; retd pay, 1950. *Address:* 7 Pelham Crescent, SW7. *Clubs:* Guards, Turf.

**MARRIOTT, John Hayes,** CB 1965; OBE 1953; *b* 14 June 1909; *s* of late Sir Hayes Marriott, KBE, CMG, and late Alice (*née* Smith), Malayan Civil Service; *m* 1936, Barbara Rosemary (*née* Salmon); two *s* two *d*. *Educ:* Uppingham Sch.; King's Coll., Cambridge (MA). Admitted solicitor, 1934; Partner in Deacon & Co., solicitors, 149 Leadenhall Street, EC3, 1936-45. Royal Artillery (HAC), 1939-40; attached MoD, formerly War Office, 1940-69; retd 1969. Royal Order of the Crown, Yugoslavia, 1945. *Address:* Preachers House, Ewhurst, Robertsbridge, Sussex. *T:* Staplecross 275. *Club:* Rye Golf.
*See also R. D'A. Marriott.*

**MARRIOTT, Marjorie Jane,** OBE 1959; Matron, The Middlesex Hospital, London, W1, 1946-65; *d* of F. C. Marriott, Kingston-on-Thames, Surrey. Guy's Hospital; Nursing Training, 1928-32; Asst Matron, 1939-40; Matron, County Hosp., Orpington, 1940-46. Vice-Pres., The Assoc. of Hosp. Matrons; Mem., NW Met. Reg. Hosp. Bd, etc. Hon. Sec. National Florence Nightingale Memorial Cttee. *Recreations:* music, painting. *Address:* 84 Cranmer Court, SW3.

**MARRIOTT, Patrick Arthur;** retired as Governor, HM Prison, Parkhurst, Isle of Wight (1951-59); *b* 20 July 1899; *s* of late Canon P. A. R. Marriott, St George's Coll., Jerusalem, and late Gertrude E. Marriott; *m* 1929, Honor Chalfont, *d* of late Major W. W. Blackden, Royal Munster Fusiliers, and Mrs Blackden, Byways, Yateley, Hants; two *s*. *Educ:* Christ's Hospital. Sub. Lieut RNAS and Lieut RAF, 1917-21; Lieut British North Borneo Armed Constabulary, 1924-29; joined HM Prison Service as Governor, Class IV, 1929, and has been Governor of Nottingham, Lincoln, Brixton, Pentonville and Parkhurst Prisons. Captain, Hampshire Yeomanry, 1929-35; Major, Royal Artillery, 1939-45. *Address:* Whitewells, Much Birch, Hereford.

**MARRIOTT, Sir Ralph G. C. S.;** *see* Smith-Marriott.

**MARRIOTT, Richard D'Arcy,** CBE 1965; DFC 1944; Assistant Director of Radio (formerly of Sound Broadcasting), BBC, 1957-69; *b* 9 June 1911; *s* of late Sir Hayes Marriott, KBE, CMG, Malayan Civil Service; *m* 1951, Dawn Kingdon; two *d*. *Educ:* Uppingham; Corpus Christi Coll., Cambridge. Joined BBC, 1933; Foreign Liaison Officer, BBC, 1936; started BBC Monitoring Unit, at outbreak of war, 1939; served as navigator in Fighter Command, RAF, 1942-45 (DFC and Bar); attached as Wing Commander to Control Commission for Germany, in charge of German Broadcasting Service in British Zone, 1945-46. Re-joined BBC as Head of European Liaison, 1946; Head of Transcription Service, BBC, 1951-52; Head of Monitoring Service, BBC, 1952-53; Controller, BBC, Northern Ireland, 1953-56. *Address:* 6 Windmill Hill, Hampstead, NW3.
*See also J. H. Marriott.*

**MARRIOTT, Brig. Sir Robert Ecklin,** Kt 1943; VD; FInstCE; BSc; with Sir Owen Williams and Partners, on M1 Construction, 1953-68; retired, 1968; *b* 15 Oct. 1887; *m* 1920, Valerie Hoch; four *d*. *m* 1953, Mary Bauer; no *c*. Joined Indian State Railways, 1910; Indian Sappers and Miners (East Africa), 1915-1920; Chief Engineer, 1937, Gen. Man., EI Rly, 1939; Dir Gen. Rlys Calcutta Area, 1944; Dir General Rlys, Control Commission Germany, 1945; Royal Engineers, 1945-47; Col Commandant, East Indian Rly Regt, Aux. Force, India; ADC to the Viceroy. Bursar, Administrative Staff Coll., Henley-on-Thames, 1948; Air Ministry Works Department, 1951. *Address:* Hartfield, Crick, near Rugby.

**MARRIS, Adam Denzil,** CMG 1944; *b* 11 June 1906; *o s* of late Sir William Marris, KCSI, KCIE; *m* 1934, B. Waterfield; one *s* two *d*. *Educ:* Winchester; Trinity Coll., Oxford. With Lazard Bros & Co. Ltd, 11 Old Broad Street, London, 1929-39; Ministry of Economic Warfare, London, 1939-40; First Sec., HM Embassy, Washington, 1940-41; Counsellor, British Embassy, Washington, 1941; Secretary-General Emergency Economic Cttee for Europe, Aug. 1945-Feb. 1946, with temp. rank of Principal Asst Sec., Foreign Office; Deputy Leader of United Kingdom Delegation to Marshall Plan Conference, July-Sept. 1947, and to Washington Conf. of Cttee for European Economic Co-operation, Nov.-Dec. 1947. Since 1947: Man. Dir Lazard Bros & Co. Ltd; Director: P & O Steam Navigation Co.; New Zealand Shipping Co., Federal Steam Navigation Co.; Commercial Union Assce Co. Ltd; Barclays Bank Ltd; English, Scottish and Australian Bank; William Cory & Son; British Aircraft Corporation; Tobacco Securities Trust Ltd; Australia and New Zealand Banking Group Ltd. *Address:* Hampen House, Andoversford, Glos. *T:* 279; 36 King's Court North, SW3. *T:* 01-352 8656; 01-588 2721. *Clubs:* Brooks's. Boodle's; Melbourne (Vic).
*See also R. L. Wade-Gery.*

**MARRIS, Eric Denyer,** CB 1950; *b* 27 July 1891; 2nd *s* of late George Suffield Marris, Birmingham, and late Mary Twining, *d* of William Denyer George; *m* 1921, Phyllis, *d* of T. H. F. Lapthorn, JP, Portsmouth; two *s* one *d*. *Educ:* Bromsgrove Sch., Worcs; Emmanuel Coll., Cambridge. Mathematical Tripos, 1913. Lieut, Royal Warwicks Regt, 1915-19. Board of Education and Ministry of Education, 1919; Under-Sec., Ministry of Education, 1947-51; seconded to Ministry of Food, 1939-40; retired, 1951. *Address:* 78 Heath Road, Petersfield, Hants.

**MARS-JONES, Hon. Sir William (Lloyd),** Kt 1969; MBE 1945; **Hon. Mr Justice Mars-Jones;** a Judge of the High Court of Justice, Queen's Bench Division, since 1969; *b* 4 Sept. 1915; *s* of Henry and Jane Mars Jones, Llansannan, Denbighshire; *m* 1947, Sheila Mary Felicity Cobon; three *s*. *Educ:* Denbigh County Sch.; UCW, Aberystwyth (LLB Hons); St John's Coll., Cambridge (BA). Entrance Schol., Gray's Inn, 1936; Pres. Students' Rep. Counc. and Central Students' Rep. Counc., UCW, 1936-37; MacMahon Studentship, 1939; Barrister-at-Law, 1941, QC 1957. War of 1939-

45, RNVR (MBE); Lt-Comdr RNVR 1945. Contested W Denbigh Parly Div., 1945. Joined Wales and Chester Circuit, 1947. Recorder of: Birkenhead, 1959-65; Swansea, 1965-68; Cardiff, 1968-69; Dep. Chm., Denbighshire Quarter Sessions, 1962-68. Bencher, Gray's Inn, 1964. Comr of Assize, Denbigh and Mold Summer Assize, 1965. Member: Bar Council, 1962; Home Office Inquiry into allegations against Metropolitan Police Officers, 1964; Home Secretary's Adv. Coun. on Penal System, 1966-68. *Publications:* contrib. Atkins' Encycl. of Court Forms and Precedents. *Address:* 3 Gray's Inn Square, WC1. *T:* 01-405 3632; The White House, Rhosneigr, Anglesey. *T:* Rhosneigr 293. *Club:* Garrick.

**MARSABIT, Bishop of, (RC),** since 1964; **Rt. Rev. Charles Cavallera;** *b* Centallo, Cuneo, Italy, 1909. *Educ:* International Missionary College of the Consolata of Turin; Pontifical Univ. of Propaganda Fide of Rome (degree in Missionology). Sec. to Delegate Apostolic of British Africa, 1936-40; Vice-Rector, then Rector, of Urban Coll. of Propaganda Fide of Rome, 1941-47; formerly Titular Bishop of Sufes; Vicar-Apostolic of Nyeri (Kenya), 1947-53; Bishop of Nyeri, 1953-64. *Address:* PO Box 281, Nanyuki, Kenya. *TA:* Bishop Cavallera, Marsabit (Kenya).

**MARSDEN, Allen Gatenby,** CBE 1945; MInstT; Hon. President of International Transport-Users Commission, Paris; *b* 13 Sept. 1893; *s* of late William Allen Marsden, OBE, and Marianne Turvey; *m* 1st, 1918, Mabel Kathleen Buckley (*decd*); one *s* two *d*; 2nd, 1933, Janet Helen Williamson; one *s*. *Educ:* Wadham House, Hale; Bedford Grammar Sch. Joined staff of London & North-Western Railway as a probationer, 1909; served European War with commission in 8th Bn Manchester Regt, TF, 1914-16, in Egypt, Cyprus and Gallipoli, invalided home with rank of Capt.; under Dir-Gen. of Transportation, France, 1916-17; asst railway transport and storage officer for Liverpool Division, Ministry of Food, 1917; Divisional Railway Transport and Storage Officer at Port of Manchester, 1918; traffic asst, Ministry of Transport, 1920; transport manager of Cadbury Bros Ltd, Bournville, 1921; subsequently transport Supervisor, Cadbury-Fry Joint Transport until 1940; Dir of Transport, Ministry of Food, Aug. 1940-May 1946; Transport Adviser to Bd of Unilever Ltd, 1946-58. *Recreations:* golf, fishing. *Address:* The Whins, Callander, Perthshire. *T:* Callander 256.

**MARSDEN, Arthur Whitcombe,** MSc, DIC, ARCS, FRIC; Education Officer, Meat and Milk Group, FAO, Rome, 1964; *b* Buxton, Derbyshire, 14 June 1911; *o s* of late Hubert Marsden and Margaret Augusta Bidwell; *m* 1940, Ailsa Anderson, *yr d* of late William Anderson McKellar, physician, and Jessie Reed Macfarlane, of Glasgow and Chester-le-Street, Co. Durham; one *s* two *d*. *Educ:* St Paul's; Imperial Coll. (Royal College of Science), London. BSc Special and ARCS, 1933; research in agricultural chemistry at Imperial Coll., 1933-36; research asst, 1936; demonstrator, 1937; asst lecturer, 1939; MSc and DIC, 1940. Temp. Instr Lieut RN, 1942; HMS Diomede, 1943; HMS King Alfred, 1944; RN Coll., Greenwich, and HMS Superb, 1945. Lecturer, Imperial Coll., London, 1946; Dept Head, Seale-Hayne Agricultural Coll., Newton Abbot, 1946-48; dir of research to grain companies in Aberdeen, 1948-49. Dir of Commonwealth Bureau of Dairy Science and Technology, Shinfield, Reading, 1950-57; Organising Secretary: 15th International Dairy Congress, London, 1957-60; 2nd World Congress of Man-made Fibres, 1960-63. Hon. Sec., Agriculture Group, Soc. of Chem. Industry, 1947-52, Chm., 1954-56; Organising Cttee of 2nd International Congress of Crop Protection, London, 1949; delegate on OEEC Technical Assistance Mission in USA and Canada, 1951; toured research centres in Pakistan, India, Australia, NZ and USA, Oct. 1954-Feb. 1955. *Publications:* papers in scientific journals. *Recreations:* travel, music, meeting and talking to people, especially from developing countries. *Address:* Via Giovanni Gemelli Careri 16, 00147 Rome, Italy. *T:* Rome 5123717. *Club:* Royal Naval Volunteer Reserve.

**MARSDEN, Col Sir Ernest,** Kt 1958; CMG 1946; CBE 1935; MC 1918; DSc; FRS 1946; JP; Hon. LLD; MIEE; FRSNZ; *b* 19 Feb. 1889; *s* of Thomas and P. Marsden; *m* 1913, Margaret Sutcliffe; one *s* one *d*; *m* 1958, Joyce W. Chote. *Educ:* Queen Elizabeth Grammar Sch., Blackburn; Victoria Univ. John Harling Fellow, University of Manchester; Lecturer in Physics, University of London; Professor of Physics, Victoria Univ. Coll., Wellington, NZ, 1914-22; Asst Dir of Education, NZ, 1922-27; Sec., Dept of Scientific and Industrial Research, NZ, 1927-47; NZ Scientific Liaison Officer, London, 1947-57. Chm. NZ Defence Science Advisory Council, 1956; Past Pres. RSNZ. Hon. DSc; Oxon; Wellington, NZ; Hon. LLD Manchester. US Medal of Freedom (with palms). Commander, Royal Swedish Order of the North Star, 1966. *Publications:* Proc. Royal Society; Phil. Mag.; Proc. Phys. Soc.; papers on Atomic Physics and Biophysics. *Address:* Cheviot Road, Lowry Bay, Wellington, New Zealand.

**MARSDEN, Sir John Denton,** 2nd Bt, *cr* 1924; *b* 25 Aug. 1913; *s* of Sir John Marsden, 1st Bt, and Agnes Mary (*d* 1951), *d* of Thomas Robert Ronald of Little Danson, Welling, Kent; *S* father, 1944; *m* 1939, Hope, *yr d* of late G. E. Llewelyn; two *s* two *d*. Served European War of 1939-45 (prisoner); Lt RA. JP; High Sheriff of Lincs, 1955-56. *Recreations:* shooting, fishing. *Heir: s* Nigel John Denton Marsden [*b* 26 May 1940; *m* 1961, Diana Jean Dunn, *er d* of Air Marshal Sir Patrick H. Dunn, *qv*; three *d*]. *Address:* White Abbey, Linton-in-Craven, Skipton, Yorks.

**MARSDEN, Leslie Alfred,** CMG 1966; *b* 25 Sept. 1921; *s* of late William Marsden, Stanmore, Middx, and of Kitty Marsden; *m* 1947, Doris Winifred, *d* of late Walter Richard Grant and of Winifred Grant; two *d*. *Educ:* Kingsbury County Sch. Served War: The Queen's Own Royal West Kent Regt, 1940-42; 14th Punjab Regt, Indian Army, 1942-46; serving in India, Burma and Thailand; retd as Hon. Major. Joined Nigeria Police Force, 1946; Commissioner of Police, 1964; Asst Inspector-General, 1966-68. Associate Director, Sierra Leone Selection Trust, 1969; Security Adviser, Standard Telephones and Cables Ltd, 1970. Nigeria Police Medal, 1964; Queen's Police Medal, 1964; Colonial Police Medal, 1958. *Recreations:* golf, swimming, walking, reading. *Address:* Ashbank, 14 Orchard Rise, Groombridge, Sussex. *T:* Groombridge 486. *Club:* Royal Over-Seas League.

**MARSH, Ven. Bazil Roland,** BA; Archdeacon of Northampton, Non-Residentiary Canon of Peterborough, and Rector of St Peter's, Northampton, since 1964; *b* Three Hills, Alta, Canada, 11 Aug. 1921; *s* of late Ven. Wilfred Carter Marsh and late Mary Jean (*née* Stott), Devil's Lake, North Dakota, USA; *m* 1946, Audrey Joan, *d* of Owen George Oyler, farmer, of Brookmans Park, Hatfield, and Alma Lillian

Oyler; three *s* one *d*. *Educ:* State schs in USA and Swindon, Wilts; Leeds Univ.; Coll. of the Resurrection, Mirfield, Yorks. Curate of: St Mary the Virgin, Cheshunt, Herts, 1944-46; St John Baptist, Coventry, 1946-47; St Giles-in-Reading, Berks, 1947-51; Rector of St Peter's, Townsville, Qld, Australia, 1951-56; Vicar of St Mary the Virgin, Far Cotton, Northampton, 1956-64. *Recreations:* gardening, photography. *Address:* 11 The Drive, Northampton NN1 4RZ. *T:* Northampton 34637. *Club:* Royal Commonwealth Society.

**MARSH, Prof. David Charles;** Professor of Applied Social Science, University of Nottingham, since 1954; *b* 9 Jan. 1917; *s* of F. C. Marsh, Aberdare, Glam., S Wales; *m* 1941, Maisie Done; one *s*. *Educ:* University of Birmingham. Research Scholar University of Birmingham, 1938-39. Military Service, 1940-46, Royal Artillery. Lecturer, University Coll. of Swansea, 1947-49; Professor of Social Science, Victoria Univ. Coll., Wellington, NZ, 1949-54. *Publications:* National Insurance and Assistance in Great Britain, 1949; The Changing Social Structure of England and Wales, 1958. The Future of the Welfare State, 1964. *Recreation:* tennis. *Address:* The White House, 239 Chilwell Lane, Bramcote, Notts. *T:* 25-7567.

**MARSH, Rt. Rev. Donald Ben;** *see* Arctic, Bishop of the.

**MARSH, Dame Edith Ngaio;** *see* Marsh, Dame Ngaio.

**MARSH, Maj.-Gen. Edward Bertram,** MC 1918; Retired Army Officer; Chairman, RAMC Charities General Fund, since 1958; *b* 3 March 1890; *s* of late Dr N. Percy Marsh, Liverpool; *m* 1920, Stephanie Maud, *o c* of late Sir Edward A. Gait, KCSI, CIE; two *s*. *Educ:* Liverpool Coll.; Liverpool Univ.; Guy's Hospital. MB, ChB (Hons) Liverpool, 1913; MRCP 1925. Served in 1st W Lancs Field Amb. (TA) as Driver, 1908-12; Lieut RAMC (SR) Sept. 3, 1914; Reg. Commn, 1918. Served European War, 1914-18, BEF (despatches twice). Served Waziristan Field Force, 1919-20 (Medal and two clasps); Lieut-Col 1937; Cons. Phys. Middle East, 1938-39. Served War of 1939-45; Middle East, UK, and as DDMS Gibraltar, 1942-44; Col 1943, Temp. Maj.-Gen. 1946. Comdt, Royal Army Med. Coll., 1946-48; retired 1949 with hon. rank Maj.-Gen. *Recreations:* golf, lawn tennis, gardening. *Address:* 14 Orchard Rise, Kingston Hill, Surrey. *T:* 01-942 8688. *Clubs:* New Zealand Golf, Royal Liverpool Golf.

**MARSH, George Fletcher Riley,** CB 1951; *b* 16 Oct. 1895; *s* of late Richard Howard Heywood Marsh, director of Geo. Fletcher & Co. Ltd, Derby; *m* 1927, Phyllis Henderson, *d* of late Frank Barton, Brasted, Kent; one *s* one *d*. *Educ:* Bedford Sch. Entered Civil Service (Naval Store Dept, Admiralty), 1914; Deputy Dir of Stores, 1942; Dir of Stores, 1949-55; retired, 1955. *Address:* Beverley, Sea Way, Middleton-on-Sea, Sussex. *T:* 2973.

**MARSH, Rt. Rev. Henry Hooper,** MA; *b* 6 Oct. 1898; *s* of Rev. Canon Charles H. Marsh, DD; *m* Margaret D. Heakes; one *s* one *d*. *Educ:* Wycliffe Coll., Toronto. BA 1921, MA 1925; DD Wycliffe Coll., Toronto, 1962. Deacon, 1924; Priest, 1925; Curate of St Anne, Toronto, 1924-25; Curate of St Paul, Toronto, 1925-30; Priest-in-charge of St Timothy's Mission, City and Diocese of Toronto, 1930-36; Rector, Church of St Timothy, 1936-62; Canon of Toronto, 1956-62; Bishop of Yukon, 1962-67. *Recreation:* bird watching. *Address:* Hedgerows, RR3, Cobourg, Ont., Canada.

**MARSH, (Henry) John,** CBE 1967; Director-General (previously Director), British Institute of Management, since 1961; Member, National Coal Board, since 1969; *b* 1913; *s* of late Jasper W. P. Marsh and Gladys M. Carruthers; *m* 1950, Mary Costerton; two *s* two *d*. *Educ:* Chefoo Sch., China; Queen Elizabeth's Grammar Sch., Wimborne. Commerce, China, 1930-32; Shanghai Volunteer Force, 1930-32; engineering apprenticeship and apprentice supervisor, Austin Motor Co., 1932-39. Served War of 1939-45, Royal Army Service Corps TA, 48th and 56th Divisions; Singapore Fortress; BEF France, 1940; Malaya, 1941-42 (despatches twice); Prisoner of War, 1942-45; released with rank of Major, 1946. Personnel Officer, BOAC, 1946-47; Dir of Personnel Advisory Services, Institute of Personnel Management, 1947-49; Dir, Industrial (Welfare) Soc., 1950-61. Hon. Administrator, Duke of Edinburgh's Study Conference, 1954-56; Chm. Brit. Nat. Conference on Social Work, 1957-60; Member: Youth Service Cttee, 1958-59; BBC General Advisory Council, 1959-64; Advisory Cttee on Employment of Prisoners, 1960-63; Council for Technical Educn and Training for Overseas Countries; UK Advisory Council on Education for Management, 1962-66; Russell Cttee on Adult Educn, 1969-; Court and Council, University of Surrey, 1962-69; Food Manufacturing EDC, 1967-69; Adv. Council, Civil Service College, 1970-. British Information Service Lecture Tour, India and Pakistan, 1959 and 1963, Nigeria, 1964, Malaysia, 1965, Australia, 1967. Hon. DSc Bradford, 1968. *Publications:* Ardeshir Dalal Memorial Lecture, India, 1953; The Clarke Hall Lecture, 1957; E. W. Hancock Lecture, 1960; MacLaren Memorial Lecture, 1962; People at Work; Work and Leisure Digest; Partners in Work Relations; Tullis Russell Lecture, 1967; Ethics in Business, 1970. *Recreation:* gardening. *Address:* (home) 13 Frank Dixon Way, Dulwich, SE21; Management House, Parker Street, WC2. *TA:* Brinsman, London. *T:* 01-405 3456. *Club:* Reform.

**MARSH, Prof. the Rev. John,** CBE 1964; MA (Edinburgh et Oxon), DPhil (Oxon); DD (Hon.) Edinburgh; Moderator, Free Church Federal Council, 1970-71; Principal, Mansfield College, Oxford, 1953-70; *b* 5 Nov. 1904; *s* of George Maurice and Florence Elizabeth Ann Marsh, East Grinstead, Sussex; *m* 1934, Gladys Walker, *y d* of George Benson and Mary Walker, Cockermouth, Cumberland; two *s* one *d*. *Educ:* The Skinners Company Sch., Tunbridge Wells; Yorkshire United Coll., Bradford; Edinburgh Univ.; Mansfield Coll. and St Catherine's Soc., Oxford; Marburg Univ. Lecturer, Westhill Training Coll., 1932; Minister, Congregational Church, Otley, Yorks, 1934; Tutor and Chaplain, Mansfield Coll., Oxford, 1938; Prof. of Christian Theology, The University, Nottingham, 1949-53. Gray Lectr, Duke Univ., NC; Reinecke Lectr, Prot. Episc. Semin., Alexandria, Va, 1958. Delegate: First Assembly, World Council of Churches, Amsterdam, 1948; Second Assembly, Evanston, Ill., 1954; Third Assembly, New Delhi, 1961; Fourth Assembly, Uppsala, 1968. Sec. World Conference on Faith and Order's Commn on "Intercommunion"; Chm., Section 2 of British Council of Churches Commn on Broadcasting, 1949; Mem., Working Cttee, Faith and Order Dept, World Council of Churches, 1953; Sec., European Commission on Christ and the Church, World Council of Churches, 1955; Mem. Central

Religious Advisory Cttee to BBC, 1955-60; Mem. Sub-Cttee of CRAC acting as Religious Advisory Panel to ITA, 1955-65; Chm. British Council of Churches Commn of Faith and Order, 1960-62. Mem. Central Cttee, World Council of Churches, 1961-68; Chm. Division of Studies, World Council of Churches, 1961-68; Select Preacher, University of Oxford, 1962; Chm. Congregational Union of England and Wales, 1962-63; Chairman: Inter-Church Relationships Cttee, Congregational Church in England and Wales, 1964-67; Board of Faculty of Theology, Oxford Univ., 1966-; Exec. Cttee, Congregational Church in England and Wales, 1966-; Joint Chm. Joint Cttee for Conversations between Congregationalists and Presbyterians, 1965-; Governor, Westminster Coll., Oxford, 1967-. *Publications:* The Living God, 1942; Congregationalism Today, 1943; (jtly) A Book of Congregational Worship, 1948; (Jt Ed.) Intercommunion, 1952; contrib. Biblical Authority Today, 1951; and Ways of Worship, 1951; The Fulness of Time, 1952; The Significance of Evanston, 1954; trans. Stauffer, Theology of the New Testament, 1955; A Year with the Bible, 1957; contributed to Essays in Christology for Karl Barth, 1957; Amos and Micah, 1959; trans. Bultmann, The History of the Synoptic Tradition, 1963; Pelican Commentary on St John's Gospel, 1968. *Recreations:* fishing, mountain walking, wood turning. *Address:* Rannerdale Close, Buttermere, Cumberland. *T:* Buttermere 232.

**MARSH, John;** *see* Marsh, H. J.

**MARSH, Nevill Francis,** CBE 1969; a Deputy Chairman, Electricity Council, since 1962; *b* 13 Aug. 1907; *m* 1935, Betty (*née* Hide); one *s* one *d*. *Educ:* Oundle Sch., Northants; Clare Coll., Cambridge (MA). Traction Motor Design Staff, Metropolitan-Vickers Electrical Co. Ltd, 1930-32; Mid-Lincolnshire Electric Supply Co. Ltd: Dist Engineer, 1932-38; Engineer and Manager, 1938-48; Chief Commercial Officer, E Midlands Electricity Board, 1948-55; Dep.-Chm., N Eastern Electricity Board, 1955-57; Dep.-Chm., E Midlands Electricity Board, 1957-59; Chm., East Midlands Electricity Board, 1959-61. Also formerly: Dir, Altrincham Electric Supply Ltd, and Public Utilities (Elec.) Ltd, and Supervising Engineer, Campbeltown & Mid-Argyll Elec. Supply Co. Ltd, and Thurso & District Elec. Supply Co. Ltd. FIEE; Pres. of Assoc. of Supervising Electrical Engineers, 1966-68. *Publications:* jt contrib. Jl Inst. Electrical Engineers, 1955. *Address:* Stocksfield, First Avenue, Frinton-on-Sea, Essex. *T:* Frinton 2995.

**MARSH, Dame Ngaio,** DBE 1966 (OBE 1948); FRSA; Novelist and Theatrical Producer, NZ; *b* 23 April 1899; *d* of Henry Edmond and Rose Elizabeth (Seager) Marsh. *Educ:* St Margaret's Coll., NZ; Canterbury Univ. Coll. Sch. of Art, Christchurch, NZ. On stage for two years; to England in 1928; in partnership with Hon. Mrs Tahu Rhodes as house decorator; first novel published in 1934; travelled in Europe, 1937-38; in New Zealand at outbreak of war and joined Red Cross Transport unit. Producer D. D. O'Connor Theatre Management, 1944-; Hon. Lecturer in Drama, Canterbury Univ., 1948. Hon. DLit Canterbury, NZ. *Publications:* A Man Lay Dead, 1934; Enter a Murderer, 1935; Nursing Home Murder (with Henry Jellett), 1936; Death in Ecstasy, 1937; Vintage Murder, 1937; Artists in Crime, 1938; Death in a White Tie, 1938; Overture to Death, 1939; Death at the Bar, 1940; Surfeit of Lampreys, 1941; Death and the Dancing Footman, 1942; Colour Scheme, 1943; Died in the Wool, 1945; Final Curtain, 1947; Swing, Brother, Swing, 1948; Opening Night, 1951; Spinsters in Jeopardy, 1953; Scales of Justice, 1954; Off With His Head, 1957; Singing in the Shrouds, 1959; False Scent, 1960; Hand in Glove, 1962; Dead Water, 1964; Black Beech and Honeydew, 1966; Death at the Dolphin, 1967; Clutch of Constables, 1968; When in Rome, 1970. *Play:* A Unicorn for Christmas, 1962 (Libretto to David Farquhar's Opera from this play). *Recreations:* Theatre production, painting, books, travel, gardening. *Address:* c/o Hughes Massie, 18 Southampton Place, WC1; (Residence) 37 Valley Road, Cashmere, Christchurch, New Zealand. *Club:* PEN.

**MARSH, Norman Stayner,** QC 1967; Law Commissioner, since 1965; *b* 26 July 1913; *o s* of Horace Henry and Lucy Ann Marsh, Bath, Som; *m* 1939, Christiane Christinnecke, 2nd *d* of Professor Johannes and Käthe Christinnecke, Magdeburg, Germany; two *s* two *d*. *Educ:* Monkton Combe Sch.; Pembroke Coll., Oxford. 2nd Class Hons, Final Honour Sch. of Jurisprudence, 1935; 1st Cl. Hons BCL. Vinerian Scholar of Oxford Univ., Harmsworth Scholar of Middle Temple, called to Bar, 1937; practice in London and on Western Circuit, 1937-39; Lieut-Col Intelligence Corps and Control Commission for Germany, 1939-46. Stowell Civil Law Fellow, University Coll., Oxford, 1946-60; University Lecturer in Law, 1947-60; Estates Bursar, University Coll., 1948-56; Secretary-General, International Commission of Jurists, The Hague, Netherlands, 1956-58. Mem. Bureau of Conference of Non-Governmental Organisations with Consultative Status with the United Nations, 1957-58; Mem. Internat. Cttee of Legal Science (Unesco), 1960-63. Dir of British Institute of International and Comparative Law, 1960-65. General editor, International and Comparative Law Quarterly, 1961-65; Mem., Editorial Board, 1965-. *Publications:* The Rule of Law as a supra-national concept, in Oxford Essays in Jurisprudence, 1960; The Rule of Law in a Free Society, 1960; articles on common law and comparative law in English, American, French and German law jls. *Address:* Law Commission, Conquest House, 37/38 John Street, Theobalds Road, WC1. *T:* 01-242 0861; (private) Wren House, 13 North Side, Clapham Common, SW4. *T:* 01-622 2865.

**MARSH, Rt. Hon. Richard William;** PC 1966; MP (Lab) Greenwich, since Oct. 1959; Director: Michael Saunders Management Services, since 1970; National Carbonising Co. Ltd; Concord Rotoflex International Ltd; *b* 14 March 1928; *s* of William Marsh, Belvedere, Kent; *m* 1950, Evelyn Mary, *d* of Frederick Andrews, Southampton; two *s*. *Educ:* Jennings Sch., Swindon; Woolwich Polytechnic; Ruskin Coll., Oxford. Contested Hertford, 1951; Health Services Officer, National Union of Public Employees, 1951-59; Mem., Clerical and Administrative Whitley Council for Health Service, 1953-59; co-opted mem. LCC Children's Cttee, 1959; Promoted Offices Act 1961; Member: Select Cttee Estimates, 1961; Chm. Interdepartmental Cttee to Co-ordinate Govt Policy on Industrial Training, 1964; Parly Sec., Min. of Labour, 1964-65; Joint Parly Sec., Min. of Technology, 1965-66; Minister of Power, 1966-68; Minister of Transport, 1968-69. Pres., Council ECSC, 1968. Member: Council for Management Educn; Executive, PEP.

**MARSH, William Thomas,** OBE 1944; MA; Headmaster, St Albans School, 1931-64, retd; Commander RNVR (Sp); *b* Birmingham, 18 March 1897; *o s* of W. T. Marsh; *m* 1923, Olive Constance Nightingale; three *s*. *Educ:*

Northampton Sch.; Queens' Coll., Cambridge (Open Classical Scholar). RNVR, 1916-19; First-class Hons Classical Tripos, 1922; VIth Form Classical Master, Brighton Coll., 1923-27; Headmaster Hertford Grammar Sch., 1927-31. Blue for Athletics and Cross Country. *Recreations:* archæology, music. *Address:* Priory Close, Bishops Cleeve, Cheltenham, Glos. *T:* Bishops Cleeve 3171. *Clubs:* Achilles, Public Schools.

**MARSH SMITH, Reginald Norman,** CSI 1946; CIE 1942; KPM 1925; *b* 1891; *s* of Capt. S. Marsh Smith, RAVC; *m* 1919; one *s. Educ:* Bromsgrove Sch. Indian Police, 1911; Inspector-General Police, Gwalior State, 1936 and 1946; Deputy Inspector-General Police, UP, 1939; Sec. to Govt United Provinces Rationing Dept; Inspector-General Police; Madhya Bharat, India, 1948; retired, 1949. King's Police Medal, 1925; Indian Police Medal, 1932; Bar to King's Police Medal, 1934. *Address:* The Croft, Nunthorpe, Teesside, Yorks.

**MARSHALL, Arthur C.;** *see* Calder-Marshall.

**MARSHALL, Arthur Hedley,** CBE 1956; MA; BSc (Econ); PhD; City Treasurer, Coventry, 1944-64, retired; Senior Research Fellow in Public Administration, Birmingham University, since Sept. 1964; *b* 6 July 1904; *s* of Rev. Arthur Marshall; *m* 1933, Margaret L. Longhurst; one *s. Educ:* Wolverhampton Grammar Sch.; London Sch. of Economics. Incorporated Accountant (Hons), 1934; Fellow Institute Municipal Treasurers and Accountants and Collins gold medal, 1930 (Pres. 1953-54); DPA (London) 1932. Chm. Royal Institute of Public Administration, 1952-53; Adviser in Local Govt to Sudan Govt, 1948-49; and to Govt of British Guiana, 1955. Chm., Cttee on Highway Maintenance, 1967-70; Member: Colonial Office Local Government Advisory Panel, 1950-; Central Housing Adv. Cttee, 1957-65; Cttee for Training Public Administration in Overseas Countries, 1961-62; Building Research Station: Urban Planning Cttee, 1962-; Arts Council Drama Panel, 1965-; Uganda Commission, 1961; Kenya Commission, 1962; Royal Commission on Local Government in England, 1966-69. *Publications:* Local Authorities: Internal Financial Control, 1936; Consolidated Loans Funds of Local Authorities (with J. M. Drummond), 1936; Report on Local Government in the Sudan, 1949, and on British Guiana, 1955; Financial Administration in Local Government, 1960; Various contribs to learned jls on Local Government and Accountancy. *Recreation:* music. *Address:* 39 Armorial Road, Coventry. *T:* Coventry 67808. *Club:* Reform.

**MARSHALL, Bruce;** novelist; *b* 24 June 1899; *s* of Claude Niven Marshall, Edinburgh; *m* 1928, Phyllis, *d* of late William Glen Clark, Edinburgh; one *d. Educ:* Edinburgh Acad.; Trinity Coll., Glenalmond; St Andrews and Edinburgh Univs. Served in Royal Irish Fusiliers, 1914-18 War and in Royal Army Pay Corps and Intelligence in War of 1939-45; MA Edinburgh, 1924; B Com. Edinburgh, 1925; admitted a mem. of the Soc of Accountants in Edinburgh, 1926. *Publications:* Father Malachy's Miracle, 1931; Prayer for the Living, 1934; The Uncertain Glory, 1935; Yellow Tapers for Paris, 1943; All Glorious Within, 1944; George Brown's Schooldays, 1946; The Red Danube, 1947; Every Man a Penny, 1950; The White Rabbit, 1952; The Fair Bride, 1953; Only Fade Away; Thoughts of my Cats, 1954; Girl in May, 1956; The Bank Audit, 1958; A Thread of Scarlet, 1959; The Divided Lady, 1960; A Girl from Lübeck, 1962; The Month of the Falling Leaves, 1963; Father Hilary's Holiday, 1965; The Bishop, 1970. *Address:* c/o Lloyds Bank, 6 Pall Mall, SW1.

**MARSHALL, Comdr Sir Douglas,** Kt 1963; RNVR; *b* 2 Oct. 1906; *s* of Captain William Worth Marshall, 63rd Punjab LI; *m* 1st, 1929, Joan Annette Sherry (*d* 1952); one *d*; 2nd, 1953, Mrs Peter Symons; one *d. Educ:* Plymouth Coll. Director: Alfred Booth & Co. Ltd; New World and General Investments Ltd; Planned Savings Life Assurance Co. Ltd; Shamrock Unit Fund Managers Ltd; Parcar (Clifton) Ltd; Preferential Investment Trust; Trewsbury Investment Trust; Parcar Ltd; Thames Securities Corp. Ltd; Nexus Securities Ltd; Fortrose Investment Trust Ltd; Preferential Securities Ltd; Friends Provident and Century Insurance, Century Insurance Co. Ltd, Century Insurance Trust, Ltd, Melbourne & General Investment Trust; General Securities & Investment Trust; Unit Construction Co. Ltd; Parcar Utilities Ltd; The National Group of Unit Trusts, Ltd; Domestic Trust Managers Ltd; National Fixed Investment Trust Ltd; Commercial Fixed Trust Ltd; Edendale Properties Ltd; Moorgate Unit Trust Managers Ltd; Proved Securities Ltd; Shield Fund Managers Ltd; Parcar (Reading), Ltd; Parcar (King Street), Ltd; Gas Industry and Power Unit Fund Managers Ltd; Second Re-Investment Trust Managers Ltd; United Kingdom & Overseas Investment Co. Ltd; Hillsedge Ltd. Joined Trade Division, Admiralty, Sept. 1939; Lieut RNVR 1939; Commander, 1944; on Staff of Allied Naval Commander Expeditionary Force, 1944-45; Post-Hostilities Plans War Cabinet Sub-Cttee, 1943. MP (C) Bodmin Div. of Cornwall, 1945-64. Mem. Public Accounts Cttee, 1951-53; Mem. Inter-Parliamentary Delegn to Yugoslavia, 1950, to Turkey, 1959; Hon. Mem., Commonwealth Parly. Assoc. (Mem. Delegn to WI 1953 and Leader 1963 Delegn; also Leader Delegn to Basutoland, Bechuanaland and Swaziland, 1964). Member: RIIA; FZS; RHS; Council of Salmon and Trout Assoc.; Marine Biological Assoc. of UK; Vice-President: The Men of the Trees; European Fedn of Sea Anglers. Licensed Reader of Diocese of Cornwall. Hon. Freeman, Borough of Bodmin, 1965. Coronation Medal, 1953. *Recreations:* fishing, shooting and travel. *Address:* Hatt, near Saltash, Cornwall. *T:* Saltash 2669; Pembroke Cottage, Fowey, Cornwall. *Clubs:* Carlton, Beefsteak, MCC; Hurlingham, Royal Navy Volunteer Reserve; (Hon. Mem.) House of Commons Yacht; Royal Fowey Yacht (Fowey).

**MARSHALL, Frank Shaw;** Solicitor (in private practice); Director: Leeds & Holbeck Building Society (President, 1967-69); Barr & Wallace Arnold Trust Ltd and other companies; North Regional Director, Friends' Provident & Century Group; *b* Wakefield, 26 Sept. 1915; 4th *s* of Charles William and Edith Marshall; *m* 1941, Mary, *e c* of Robert and Edith Barr; two *d. Educ:* Queen Elizabeth's Sch., Wakefield; Downing Coll., Cambridge (Scholar). MA, LLB. Served 1940-46, Captain Royal Tank Regt and Staff Officer JAG's Dept, WO. Leeds CC: Leader, and Chm. Finance Cttee, 1967-; Alderman, 1967-. Chairman: Leeds and Bradford Airport, 1968-69; Assoc. of Municipal Corps of England, Wales and NI, 1968-; Jt Negotiating Cttee for Town Clerks and District Council Clerks; Jt Negotiating Cttee for Chief Officers of Local Authorities; Public Administration Adv. Bd, Sheffield Polytechnic; Leeds Council of Christians and Jews, 1960-; City of Leeds Conservative Assoc., 1967-; Local Govt Information Office of England and Wales; Leeds Grand Theatre and Opera House Ltd. Member: Court and Council, Leeds Univ., 1965-; Court, Bradford Univ., 1967-; BBC North Regional Council; Leeds Radio Council, BBC; Gen. Purposes Cttee of Nat. Exec. of Conservative and Unionist Party; Exec. Council (British Section) of Internat. Union of Local Authorities; European Conference of Local Authorities; Council, Leeds Philosophical and Literary Soc. *Recreations:* theatre, reading, relaxing. *Address:* Wigton Manor, Manor House Lane, Leeds 17. *T:* Leeds 684104. *Clubs:* Leeds, Leeds and County Conservative (Leeds).

**MARSHALL, Sir Geoffrey,** KCVO, *cr* 1951; CBE 1951 (OBE 1917); MD, FRCP (London); Consulting Physician: Guy's Hospital; King Edward VII Hospital, Midhurst, and Brompton Hospital for Diseases of Chest; Hon. Consulting Physician to Ministry of Pensions; Medical Referee to the Civil Service Commission; Chairman Chemotherapy of Tuberculosis Trials Committee of Medical Research Council; Censor and Harveian Orator, Royal College of Physicians; *b* 1887; *s* of Henry Marshall, Bognor, Sussex; *m* 1918, Belle, *d* of George Philip, Dundee; (one *s* died on active service, MEF, 1941). *Educ:* St Paul's Sch. Demonstrator of Physiology and Medical Registrar, Guy's Hospital; Gold Medal, London MD; Major RAMC, SR, served with Brit. Exp. Force (despatches twice, OBE); Med. Officer i/c Tuberculosis Dept, Sub-dean of Medical Sch. (Guy's Hospital); Pres. Royal Society of Medicine, 1958-60 (late Pres., Section of Medicine, RSM); Hon. Mem. (Past Pres.) Thoracic Soc.; Hon. FRCPI; Hon. FRSocMed. *Publications:* Papers on Medical Subjects, *eg* Surgical Shock in Wounded Soldiers; and many on Respiratory Disease; (Editor) Diseases of the Chest, 1952. *Address:* 149 Harley Street, W1. *T:* 01-935 4444. *Club:* Royal Automobile.

**MARSHALL, Hedley Herbert,** CMG 1959; QC (Nigeria) 1955; LLB (London); FRGS; Deputy Director, British Institute of International and Comparative Law, since 1968; Attorney-General, Northern Nigeria, 1954-62, retired; *b* 28 March 1909; *s* of late Herbert Marshall, Sydenham, and Elizabeth, *d* of late Edwin Smith Adams; *m* 1952, Faith, *widow* of Wing-Comdr John Collins Mayhew, RAF; one step-*d*. *Educ:* Dulwich Coll. Prep. Sch.; Dulwich Coll.; London Univ. Admitted Solicitor of Supreme Court, England, 1931; joined Army, 1940; 2nd Lieut 1941; Captain, 1942; Major, 1945; after service at home and overseas, released 1946 and joined Colonial Service; Asst Administrator-Gen., Nigeria, 1946; Magistrate Grade I, 1946; called to Bar, Gray's Inn, 1949; Crown Counsel, Nigeria, 1950; Senior Crown Counsel, 1951; Legal Sec., Northern Region of Nigeria, 1952; Chancellor of Diocese of Northern Nigeria, 1953; Dir of Public Prosecutions, Northern Nigeria, 1959-62; Member: House of Assembly, House of Chiefs and Executive Council, Northern Nigeria, 1951-62; Privy Council, Northern Nigeria, 1954-59; Advisory Cttee on the Prerogative of Mercy, Northern Nigeria, 1959-62. Adviser to Government of Northern Nigeria at Nigerian Constitutional Conferences, 1957 and 1958; Mem. Provisional Council of Ahmadu Bello Univ., 1961. Commissioner for Revision of Laws of Northern Nigeria, 1962-63. Asst Dir (Commonwealth), Brit. Inst. Internat. and Comparative Law, 1963-68. *Publications:* Natural Justice, 1959; rev. edn of The Laws of Northern Nigeria, 1963, in 5 Vols (Vols I to III with F. A. O. Schwarz Jr); contribs to legal and other periodicals. *Recreations:* tennis, swimming, photography. *Address:* The Red House, Bassingbourn, Royston, Herts. *Club:* Royal Commonwealth Society.

**MARSHALL, Herbert Percival James;** film, theatre and TV producer, director, scriptwriter, author and translator; *b* London, 20 Jan. 1906; *s* of Percival Charles Marshall and Anne Marshall (*née* Organ); *m* 1935, Fredda Brilliant, sculptress, actress. *Educ:* Elementary Sch., Ilford; evening classes, LCC; Higher Inst. of Cinematography, Moscow, USSR. Began as Assistant Film Editor, Empire Marketing Bd Film Unit, 1929-30; Asst Dir various Moscow theatres; Drama Dir, Moscow Radio (English), 1933-35; Founder, Dir, Unity Theatre; prod. documentary films, Spanish Civil War; Principal, Unity Theatre Trg Sch.; Lecturer, LCC Evening Insts, 1935-39; Founder and Artistic Dir, Neighbourhood Theatre, S Kensington; Script-writer (with Fredda Brilliant) and Associate Producer (Ealing Studios), 1939-40; apptd Dir, Old Vic (theatre bombed); toured England; Dir for Sadler's Wells Opera Company; Lectr, RADA, 1940-41; i/c of production, Russian, Czech, Polish and Yugoslav films for Europe (8 langs); broadcasts, BBC, in Russian, 1942-45; Lectr on film art, Amer. Univ., Biarritz, 1945-46; Indep. Film Producer: prod. for J. Arthur Rank, Min. of Educn, Nat. Coal Bd, etc; prod., scripted and dir. (with Fredda Brilliant), Tinker (Edinburgh Festival Award), 1946-50; dir. Man and Superman, Arena Theatre (Fest. of Brit.), 1951; prod. official Mahatma Gandhi Biog. Documentary, etc, India, 1951-55; Exec. Producer, TV closed circuit and films for Advision Ltd, London, 1955-56; Film Producer for Govt of India; Principal, Natya Acad. of Dramatic Art, Bombay; Producer, Natya Nat. Theatre Company, 1957-60; Dir, Centre for Soviet and E European Studies, Southern Illinois Univ., apptd Professor, Academic Affairs, 1970. Theatre Architecture Consultant to various projects: Indian National Theatres, 1955-59; Centre 42, London, 1962; Morrison Civic Arts Centre, Lambeth, 1965; Samuel Beckett Theatre, Oxford Univ., 1968-. Lecturer: Royal College of Art, and New York Univ., 1964; University of Illinois, and Oxford Univ., 1968. Distinguished Visiting Prof., Sch. of Communications, Southern Illinois Univ., Carbondale, 1965, 1968. Many well-known actors and actresses have been produced or directed by him. FRSA 1967. *Publications:* Mayakovsky and His Poetry, 1964 (London); Hamlet Through the Ages (jointly), 1953 (London); Ira Aldridge, The Negro Tragedian (with Mildred Stock), 1953 (London, New York); Poetry of Voznesensky (London and New York) and Yevtushenko (London and New York), 1965; (jtly) Collected Works of Eisenstein (London and USA), 1969; Stanislavsky Method of Direction (London and New York) 1969; Anthology of Soviet Poetry, 1970; (ed) Internat. Library of Cinema and Theatre (20 vols). Score: English Text and Lyrics, Ivan the Terrible (Oratorio by S. Prokoviev and S. M. Eisenstein), 1962 (Moscow). *Recreations:* reading and TV. *Address:* 1204 Chautauqua Street, Carbondale, Ill 62901, USA; Southern Illinois University, Carbondale, Ill 62901, USA.

**MARSHALL, Howard Percival;** Director of Personnel and Public Relations, Richard Thomas and Baldwins Ltd; *b* 22 Aug. 1900; *o s* of Percival Marshall. *Educ:* Haileybury Coll.; Oriel Coll., Oxford. Special correspondent Westminster Gazette, Daily Telegraph, Daily Mail, etc; Asst News Editor BBC, 1928; BBC Sports and Special Events Commentator, 1930-; Director of Public Relations, Ministry of Food, 1940-43; Dir of War Reporting and

War Correspondent, BBC, 1943-45 (N Africa and Invasion of Europe). *Publications:* Slum (book on housing); With Scott to the Pole; (with W. W. Wakefield) Rugger; (with H. R. L. Sheppard) Fiery Grains; Under Big Ben; Over to Tunis; Oxford v. Cambridge: the Story of the University Rugby Match; Coronation Day; Men Against Everest; Anthologies of Boxing, Cricket, Rugger; Ed. Dent's Modern Sports Series; Co-Founder, The Angling Times and Trout and Salmon. *Recreation:* fishing. *Address:* Easton Lodge, Easton, near Newbury, Berks. *T:* Boxford 229. *Clubs:* Flyfishers', Savile.

**MARSHALL, Sir Hugo Frank,** KBE, *cr* 1953; CMG 1950; JP; retired; *b* 1905; *s* of late Henry Mieres Marshall and Cecil Mabel Balfour; *m* 1931, Christine Phyllida, *d* of late Major R. Brinckman, OBE; two *s* one *d*. *Educ:* Malvern Coll.; Exeter Coll., Oxford. Colonial Service, Nigeria, 1928; Administrative Officer, Class I, 1946; Staff Grade, 1947; Administrative Sec., Nigeria, 1947-52; Lt-Governor, Western Region, Nigeria, 1952-54; Chief Sec., Federation of Nigeria, 1954-55. JP Wilts 1958. *Recreations:* sailing, ornithology. *Address:* Murhill House, Limpley Stoke, near Bath. *T:* Limpley Stoke 2162.

**MARSHALL, Sir James,** Kt, *cr* 1953; DL; JP; *b* 23 Oct. 1894; *s* of James and Julia Harriet Marshall, Hounslow, Middlesex; *m* 1939, May Florence Kent; two *s* two *d*. *Educ:* Whitgift, Croydon. Croydon Borough: Councillor, 1928; Alderman, 1936-68; Mayor, 1945-46. Chm., Croydon Food Control Cttee, 1939-53; Mem. Crawley Development Corporation, 1945-61; Chm. Whitgift Governors, 1944-69. JP 1937; DL Surrey, 1952; DL Greater London, 1966. *Recreations:* lawn tennis, horticulture, philately. *Address:* 8 Rose Walk, Purley, Surrey. *T:* 01-660 1409. *Club:* Royal Automobile.

**MARSHALL, John,** MA; Headmaster, Robert Gordon's College, Aberdeen, since 1960; *b* 1 July 1915; *s* of Alexander Marshall and Margaret Nimmo Carmichael; *m* 1940, May Robinson Williamson; two *d*. *Educ:* Airdrie Acad.; Glasgow Univ. MA (1st cl. hons Classics), 1935; Medley Memorial Prizeman, History 1934; John Clark Schol., Classics, 1935. Asst Master: Bluevale Sch., 1937-39; Coatbridge Sec. Sch., 1939-41; Principal Teacher of Classics, North Berwick High Sch., 1941-50; Rector, North Berwick High Sch., 1950-60. Mem., Adv. Coun. on Educn for Scotland, 1955-57; Trustee, Scottish Sec. Schools Travel Trust, 1960- (Vice-Chm. 1964- ); Pres., Headmasters' Assoc. of Scotland, 1962-64; Mem. Gen. Teaching Coun. for Scotland, 1966-. JP City of Aberdeen, 1967. *Publications:* numerous articles on educational subjects. *Recreations:* fishing, photography, writing, language studies. *Address:* 110 Hamilton Place, Aberdeen. *T:* Aberdeen 23214.

**MARSHALL, Rt. Hon. John Ross,** PC 1966; BA; LLM; Deputy Prime Minister, Minister of Overseas Trade, New Zealand, since 1960; Labour Minister, Attorney-General and Minister of Immigration, since 1969; Chairman, National Development Council, since 1969; *b* 5 March 1912; *m* 1944, Margaret Livingston; two *s* two *d*. *Educ:* Whangarei, Otago Boys' High Sch.; Victoria Univ. Coll. Barrister and Solicitor, 1936; served War, with 2nd NZEF, Pacific Is. and Italy, 1941-46 (Inf. Major); MP (Nat.) for Mount Victoria, 1946-54, for Karori, 1954-; Lectr in Law, Victoria Univ. Coll., 1948-51; Minister, Asst to Prime Minister, in charge of State Advances Corp., Public Trust Office and Census and Statistics Dept, 1949-54; Minister of Health, 1951-54, and Information and Publicity, 1951-57; Attorney-Gen. and Minister of Justice, 1954-57; Dep. Prime Minister, 1957; Dep. Leader of the Opposition, 1957-60; Minister of Industries and Commerce, 1960-69. NZ Rep. at Colombo Plan Conf., New Delhi, 1953; visited US on Foreign Leader Grant, April 1958; NZ Representative: GATT, 1961, 1963, 1967, and ECAFE, 1962, 1964, 1965, 1966, 1968, 1970; Commonwealth Prime Ministers' Conf., 1962; Trade Ministers' Conf., 1963, 1966; Commonwealth Parly Conf., 1965. *Publication:* The Law of Watercourses, 1957. *Recreations:* fishing, golf. *Address:* Parliament House, Wellington, NZ.

**MARSHALL, Col Kenric Rudolphus,** CMG 1918; DSO 1916; President and Director several Companies; President Canadian & Foreign Securities Co. and other Investment Companies; Retired Chairman and President Canada Steamship Lines Ltd; *b* Toronto; *e s* of Noel G. L. Marshall and Harriette Isabelle, *d* of John Hogg, JP, of York Mills, Canada; *m* Marion Janet, *d* of Angus Kirkland, Toronto; one *s*. *Educ:* private primary schs; Upper Canada Coll. Proceeded overseas with his battalion (48th Highlanders) in the 1st Canadian Contingent, Sept. 1914; Staff Capt. 12th Canadian Infantry Brigade, May 1916; rose to AA and QMG, serving in such capacity for 18 months (DSO, CMG, despatches three times); Commanded 48th Highlanders of Canada and 6th Inf. Bde; Hon. ADC to Governor-Gen. of Canada. *Recreations:* racing, riding, literature. *Address:* 97 Glen Road, Toronto; Lowfields Farm, Pickering, Canada. *Clubs:* United Service (London, England); York, Toronto, Ontario Jockey (Chm.), Toronto Hunt, National, Military (Toronto); Mount Royal, St James's (Montreal).

**MARSHALL, Martin John,** CMG 1967; HM Consul-General, Cleveland, Ohio, since 1968; *b* 21 March 1914; *s* of late Harry Edmund Marshall and late Kate Ann (*née* Bishop); *m* 1938, Olive Emily Alice, *d* of Thomas and Olive King; two *d*. *Educ:* Westminster City Sch.; London Sch. of Economics, University of London. Customs and Excise Officer, 1935-39; Technical Officer, Min. of Aircraft Prod., 1940-46; Principal, Min. of Supply, 1947-50. Called to Bar, Gray's Inn, 1947. Trade Commissioner: Montreal, 1950-52; Atlantic Provinces, 1953; Alberta, 1954-57; Principal Trade Commissioner: Montreal, 1957-60; Calcutta (for Eastern India), 1961-63; Dep. High Comr, Sydney, 1963-67. *Recreations:* ski-ing, golf. *Address:* 1828 The Illuminating Building, Public Square, Cleveland, Ohio, USA; c/o Barclays Bank Ltd, 19 Great Cumberland Place, W1. *Clubs:* St James', Royal Automobile.

**MARSHALL, Norman;** play producer; *b* 16 Nov. 1901; *s* of Lt-Col D. G. Marshall, IMS, and Elizabeth Mackie. *Educ:* Edinburgh Academy; Worcester Coll., Oxford. Producer, Cambridge Festival Theatre, 1926-33; directed Gate Theatre, 1934-40. Produced many plays in West End, including Parnell, 1936, Victoria Regina, 1937, Of Mice and Men, 1939, The Petrified Forest, 1942, Uncle Vanya, 1943, The First Gentleman, 1946, The Indifferent Shepherd, 1948. Later did a series of productions in countries abroad, including France, Germany, Italy, Israel, India and Pakistan. Shute Lecturer on the Art of the Theatre, Liverpool Univ., 1951. Head of Drama for Associated-Rediffusion Television, 1955-59. Chairman: British Council's Adv. Cttee on Drama, 1961-68; Assoc. of British Theatre Technicians; British Drama League;

Joint Chm., National Theatre Building Cttee; Vice-Chm., Theatre's Advisory Council. Extensive lecture tours of Canada and Australia, 1961 and 1962; directed Romeo and Juliet, and Hamlet, South Africa; lectured for Universities of Cape Town and Natal, 1964; directed at Chichester Theatre Festival, 1966. *Publications:* The Other Theatre, 1948; The Producer and the Play, 1957 (new edn 1962). *Address:* 9 Arundel Court, Jubilee Place, SW3. *T:* 01-352 0456. *Club:* Garrick.

**MARSHALL, Norman Bertram,** MA, ScD; FRS 1970; Senior Principal Scientific Officer, British Museum (Natural History), since 1962; *b* 5 Feb. 1915; *s* of Arthur Harold and Ruby Eva Marshall; *m* 1944, Olga Stonehouse; one *s* three *d. Educ:* Cambridgeshire High Sch.; Downing Coll., Cambridge. Plankton Biologist, Dept of Oceanography, UC Hull, 1937-41; Army (mostly involved in Operational Research), 1941-44; Antarctic Expedn (Operation Tabarin), 1944-46; British Museum (Natural History), marine fishes, 1947-. Polar Medal (Silver), 1948. *Publications:* Aspects of Deep Sea Biology, 1954; The Life of Fishes, 1965; Explorations in the Life of Fishes, 1970; Ocean Life, 1971; various papers in learned jls. *Recreations:* fishing, golf. *Address:* 6 Park Lane, Saffron Walden, Essex. *T:* Saffron Walden 2528.

**MARSHALL, Prof. Oshley Roy,** CBE 1968; Vice-Chancellor, University of the West Indies, since 1969; *b* 21 Oct. 1920; *s* of Fitz Roy and Corene Carmelita Marshall; *m* 1945, Eirwen Lloyd; one *s* three *d. Educ:* Harrison Coll., Barbados, WI; Pembroke Coll., Cambridge; University Coll., London. Barbados Scholar, 1938; BA 1945, MA 1948 Cantab; PhD London 1948. Barrister-at-Law, Inner Temple, 1947. University Coll., London: Asst Lecturer, 1946-48; Lecturer, 1948-56; Sub-Dean, Faculty of Law, 1949-56; Prof. of Law and Head of Dept of Law, Univ. of Sheffield, 1956-69, Vis. Prof. in Faculty of Law, 1969-. On secondment to University of Ife, Ibadan, Nigeria, as Prof. of Law and Dean of the Faculty of Law, 1963-65. *Publications:* The Assignment of Choses in Action, 1950; A Casebook on Trusts (with J. A. Nathan), 1967; Theobald on Wills, 12th edn, 1963. *Recreations:* racing and cricket. *Address:* University of the West Indies, Mona, Kingston 7, Jamaica, West Indies.

**MARSHALL, Peter Harold Reginald;** Counsellor and Head of Chancery, British Embassy, Paris, since 1969; *b* 30 July 1924; 3rd *s* of late R. H. Marshall; *m* 1957, Patricia Rendell Stoddart; one *s* one *d. Educ:* Tonbridge; Corpus Christi Coll., Cambrdige. RAFVR, 1943-46. Entered Foreign Service, 1949; FO, 1949-52; 2nd Sec. and Private Sec. to Ambassador, Washington, 1952-56; FO, 1956-60; on staff of Civil Service Selection Board, 1960; 1st Sec. and Head of Chancery, Baghdad, 1961, and Bangkok, 1962-64; Asst Dir of Treasury Centre for Administrative Studies, 1965-66; Counsellor, UK Mission, Geneva, 1966-69. *Recreations:* music, golf. *Address:* 39 rue du Faubourg St Honoré, Paris 8, France. *Club:* Travellers'.

**Marshall, Air Cdre Philippa Frances,** OBE 1956; Director of the Women's Royal Air Force, since 1969; *b* 4 Nov. 1920; *d* of late Horace Plant Marshall, Stoke-on-Trent. *Educ:* St Dominic's High Sch., Stoke-on-Trent. Joined WAAF, 1941; Comd WRAF Admin. Officer, Strike Comd, 1968-69, Air Cdre 1969; ADC, 1969-. *Recreations:* music, cookery. *Address:* c/o Ministry of Defence, Adastral House, Theobald's Road, WC1. *Club:* Royal Air Force.

**MARSHALL, Robert,** MD (with distinction), DPH Queen's University, Belfast; FRCP; FRCPI; FRCPS (Hon.); retired; Hon. Governor and Consulting Physician at the Royal Victoria Hospital and Ulster Hospital, Belfast; *b* 9 Sept. 1889; *s* of late W. J. Marshall, JP, Belfast, and Bertha Shaw; *m* 1916, Evelyn Mary, *d* of William Marshall, Bangor, Co. Down; (one *s* killed on active service, 1945) one *d. Educ:* Methodist Coll. and Queen's Univ., Belfast. MB with Hons and 1st place in medicine, 1912; Resident Medical Officer, National Hosp. for Diseases of Heart, London, 1914; joined RAMC Aug. 1914; served in France with 1st and 3rd Cavalry Divisions; Mem., Royal College of Physicians of Ireland, 1920, Fellow, 1921 and Censor to the Coll., 1930-33; FRCP; formerly: Mem. of Senate and Clinical Lectr in Medicine Queen's Univ. of Belfast; External Examiner in Medicine of University of Glasgow and Trinity Coll., Dublin. Hon. Mem. of the Post-Graduate Medical Assoc. of America; Hon. Fellow of the Royal College of Physicians and Surgeons of Glasgow; Senior Mem., Assoc. of Physicians of Great Britain and Ireland, British Cardiac Soc., and British Paediatric Assoc.; Hon. Fellow, Ulster Medical Soc. (Pres., 1942-43); Fellow, British Medical Assoc. OStJ. Hon. LLD Queen's University, Belfast, 1970. *Publications:* The Book of Belfast, British Medical Association, 1937; The Royal Victoria Hospital, Belfast, 1903-53; and various papers on medical and cardiological subjects. *Recreations:* reading, photography. *Address:* 9 College Gardens, Belfast. *T:* Belfast 665853.

**MARSHALL, Robert Braithwaite,** CB 1968; MBE 1945; Secretary, Department of Trade and Industry, since Oct. 1970; *b* 10 Jan. 1920; *s* of Alexander Halford Marshall and Edith Mary Marshall (*née* Lockyer); *m* 1945, Diana Elizabeth Westlake; one *s* three *d. Educ:* Sherborne Sch.; Corpus Christi Coll., Cambridge. Mod. Langs, Pt I, 1938-39; Economics Pts I and II, 1945-47. BA Cambridge. Foreign Office temp. appointment, 1939-45. Entered Home Civil Service, 1947; Ministry of Works, 1947-50; Cabinet Office, 1950-53; Min. of Works, 1953-62; Min. of Aviation, 1962-66; Min. of Power, 1966-69; Central Economic Gp, 1969-70, Industry Gp, 1970, Min. of Technology. Coronation Medal, 1953. *Recreations:* travel, gardening, music and arts. *Address:* Brooklands, Lower Bourne, Farnham, Surrey. *T:* Frensham 2879.

**MARSHALL, Robert Smith,** CBE 1954; Animal Health Adviser, Department of Technical Co-operation, 1961-63 (to the Secretary of State for the Colonies, 1955-61), retired; *b* 5 April 1902; *s* of late Rev. Thomas Marshall, Dalziel North Manse, Motherwell; *m* 1937, Agnes Inglis Melville; one *d. Educ:* Hamilton Academy; West of Scotland Agricultural Coll.; Glasgow Veterinary Coll. NDA, NDD, 1923; MRCVS 1926; DVSM (Edinburgh) 1927; Academic Diploma of Bacteriology (London) 1929. Asst Veterinary Pathologist, Nigeria, 1929-38; Sen. Veterinary Research Officer, Nigeria, 1938-44; Principal, Veterinary Sch., Nigeria, 1944-48; Dep. Dir Veterinary Services, Nigeria, 1948-51; Inspector-Gen., Animal Health Services, Nigeria, 1951-55. *Publications:* scientific papers in Jl of Bacteriology and Jl of Comparative Pathology. *Recreations:* golf, fishing. *Address:* Hazelrig, Victoria Road, Lundin Links, Fifeshire. *Club:* Royal Over-Seas League.

**MARSHALL, Maj.-Gen. Roy Stuart,** CB 1970; OBE 1960; MC 1945; MM 1940; Deputy Master-General of the Ordnance, 1969-70, retired; *b* 28 Oct. 1917; *s* of Andrew Adamson

Marshall and Bessie Marshall, Whitley Bay, Northumberland; *m* 1946, Phyllis Mary Rawlings; two *s*. *Educ:* Whitley Bay and Monkseaton High Sch. Joined TA 88 (West Lancs) Field Regt, 1939; commd into RA, 1942; War Service in Europe and Middle East, 1939-45; Staff Coll., Camberley, 1947; GSO 2, 2 Inf. Div., 1948-50; DAA & QMG, 6 Inf. Bde, 1950-51; jssc 1952-53; AA & QMG, 1 (BR) Corps, 1958-60; CO 12th Regt RA, 1960-62; Comdr 7th Artillery Bde, 1962-64; Indian Nat. Def. Coll., 1965; Maj.-Gen. RA, BAOR, 1966-69. *Recreations:* fishing, golf, bridge. *Address:* 2 Newhayes, Kilmington, Axminster, Devon. *T:* Axminster 2361. *Club:* Army and Navy.

**MARSHALL, Sheina Macalister,** OBE 1966; FRS 1963; FRSE; DSc (Glasgow); Zoologist at the Marine Station, Millport, 1922-64; *b* 20 April 1896; *d* of John Nairn Marshall, MD, and Jean Colville Binnie. *Educ:* home; Rothesay Academy; St Margaret's Sch., Polmont; Glasgow Univ. Carnegie Fellowship, 1920-22; Zoologist, Millport, 1922. Mem., Great Barrier Reef Expedition, 1928-29. *Publications:* (with Dr A. P. Orr): The Biology of a Marine Copepod, *Calanus finmarchicus*, 1955; Seashores, 1965; The Fertile Sea, 1969; papers in Jl Marine Biological Assoc. of the UK and elsewhere. *Recreations:* walking, embroidery. *Address:* Bellevue, Millport, Isle of Cumbrae. *T:* Millport 406.

**MARSHALL, Sir Sidney,** Kt 1952; DL; JP; Alderman Surrey County Council, since 1941 (Chairman, 1947-50; Chairman Education Committee since 1942); Alderman Sutton and Cheam Boro' Council; Hon. Freeman of Sutton and Cheam, 1948; *b* 17 July 1882; *s* of William Robert Marshall, Mitcham; unmarried. *Educ:* Elementary and Private Schs. In industry in Food, Chemical and Dye Industry. Chm. several companies. JP 1937; Surrey County Councillor, 1931; Chm. Sutton and Cheam UDC, 1932-34; Charter Mayor, 1934; Mayor, 1936-37, Dep. Mayor, 1935 and 1937-38; Chm. Surrey assistance board advisory cttee; Sutton and District juvenile advisory cttee; Member: Surrey agricultural wages cttee; London tribunal for hearing conscientious objectors; Educational Trust for Visual Aids. DL Surrey, 1950. MP (C) for Sutton and Cheam, 1945-54. *Recreations:* mainly own work, plus listening to good music and reading. *Address:* 66 The Crescent, Belmont, Surrey. *T:* 01-642 1417; Headley Grove Farm, Epsom. *T:* Headley 95. *Club:* Constitutional.

**MARSHALL, Stirrat Andrew William J.;** *see* Johnson-Marshall.

**MARSHALL, Thomas Humphrey,** CMG 1947; MA; Professor Emeritus, University of London; *b* London, 19 Dec. 1893; *s* of William C. Marshall, architect, and Margaret, *d* of Archdeacon Lloyd, sometime Archdeacon of Waitemata, New Zealand; *m* 1st, 1925, Marjorie Tomson (*d* 1931); 2nd, 1934, Nadine, *d* of late Mark Hambourg; one *s*. *Educ:* Rugby; Trinity Coll., Cambridge. Civilian prisoner in Germany, 1914-18; Fellow of Trinity Coll., Cambridge, 1919-25; Lecturer LSE, 1925; Reader in Sociology, London, 1930; Research Dept of FO, Head of German Section and Dep. Dir, 1939-44; Head of the Social Science Dept, London Sch. of Economics and Political Science, 1944-50; Mem. of Lord Chancellor's Cttee on Practice and Procedure of Supreme Court, 1947-53; Educational Adviser in the British Zone of Germany, 1949-50; Member: UK Cttee for Unesco; UK Delegation to Unesco General Conference, 1952. Martin White Prof. of Sociology, London Sch. of Economics, London Univ., 1954-56; Dir of the Social Sciences Dept, Unesco, 1956-60; Pres., Internat. Sociological Assoc., 1959-62. Hon. DSc Southampton 1969. *Publications:* James Watt, 1925; Class Conflict and Social Stratification (ed), 1938; The Population Problem (ed), 1938; Citizenship and Social Class, 1950; Sociology at the Crossroads and other Essays, 1963; Social Policy, 1965; numerous articles in Economic Journal, Economic History Review, Sociological Review, etc. *Recreation:* music. *Address:* 6 Drosier Road, Cambridge.

**MARSHALL, Thurgood;** Associate Justice of US Supreme Court, since 1967; *b* 2 July 1908; *s* of William C. and Norma A. Marshall; *m* 1st, 1929, Vivian Burey (*d* 1955); 2nd, 1955, Cecilia A. Suyat; two *s*. *Educ:* Lincoln Univ. (AB 1930); Howard Univ. Law Sch. Admitted Maryland Bar, 1933. Special Counsel, NAACP, 1938-50 (Asst, 1936-38); Dir, NAACP Legal Defense and Educ. Fund, 1940-61. Judge, 2nd Circuit Court of Appeals, 1961-65; Solicitor-Gen. of USA, 1965-67. Holds hon. doctorates at many US Univs. Spingarn Medal, 1946. *Address:* 6233 Lakeview Drive, Falls Church, Va 22041, USA.

**MARSHALL, Dr Walter Charles;** Director, Atomic Energy Research Establishment, Harwell, since 1968; Director, Research Group, UKAEA, since 1969; Member, National Research Development Corporation, since 1969; *b* 5 March 1932; *s* of late Frank Marshall and Amy (*née* Pearson); *m* 1955, Ann Vivienne Sheppard; one *s* one *d*. *Educ:* Birmingham Univ. Scientific Officer, AERE, Harwell, 1954-57; Research Physicist: University of California, 1957-58; Harvard Univ., 1958-59; AERE, Harwell: Group Leader, Solid State Theory, 1959-60; Head of Theoretical Physics Div., 1960-66; Dep. Dir, 1966-68. *Publications:* research papers on magnetism, neutron scattering and solid state theory. *Recreations:* croquet, chess, gardening, origami. *Address:* Bridleway House, Goring-on-Thames, Oxon. *T:* Goring-on-Thames 2890.

**MARSHALL, William;** Assistant Under-Secretary of State, Ministry of Defence (Navy), since 1968; *b* 30 Sept. 1912; *e s* of Allan and Julia Marshall, Whitecraigs, Renfrewshire; *m* 1st, 1940, Jessie Gardner Miller (*d* 1962); one *s*; 2nd, 1963, Doreen Margaret Read. *Educ:* Allan Glen's Sch., Glasgow; Glasgow Univ. MA Glasgow 1932, LLB (*cum laude*) Glasgow 1935. War of 1939-45: Temp. Asst Principal, Air Ministry, 1940; Service with Royal Navy (Ord. Seaman), and Admin. Staff, Admty, 1941. Private Sec. to Permanent Sec. of Admty (Sir J. G. Lang), 1947-48; Principal Private Sec. to successive First Lords of Admty (Lord Hall, Lord Packenham and Rt Hon. J. P. L. Thomas, later Lord Cilcennin), 1951-54; Gold Staff Officer at Coronation, 1953; Asst Sec. in Admty, 1954; on loan to HM Treasury, 1958-61; returned to Admiralty, 1961. *Recreations:* golf, travel, gardening. *Address:* 37 West Drive, Cheam, Surrey. *T:* 01-642 3399. *Clubs:* Golfers'; Kingswood Golf (Tadworth).

**MARSHALL, Prof. William Thomas;** Regius Professor of Civil Engineering, University of Glasgow, since 1952; *b* 14 Oct. 1907; *s* of Thomas and Edith Marshall; *m* 1939, Margaret Ewing Adam; one *s* one *d*. *Educ:* Westminster City Sch.; Imperial Coll. of Science. Reinforced Concrete Designer with British Reinforced Concrete Eng. Co. Ltd, Stafford, 1929-34; Engineering Asst with F. A. Macdonald & Partners (Glasgow) Ltd, 1934-36; Lecturer in Civil Engineering, Imperial Coll. of Science, 1936-45; Technical Officer,

Instn Struct. Engrs, 1945-46; Prof. of Engineering, St Andrews Univ., 1946-52. Visiting Professor: Northwestern Univ., Ill., 1960; University of Western Australia, 1967. *Publications:* Fundamental Principles of Reinforced Concrete Design, 1951; Solutions to Problems in Structures, 1958; (with H. M. Nelson) Structures, 1969; a number of papers on structural engineering. *Recreations:* cricket, youth organisations. *Address:* James Watt Engineering Laboratories, The University, Glasgow, W2.

**MARSHALL-CORNWALL, Gen. Sir James (Handyside),** KCB, *cr* 1940 (CB 1936); CBE 1919; DSO 1917; MC; *b* 27 May 1887; *o s* of late Jas Cornwall, Postmaster-Gen. UP, India; *m* 1921, Marjorie, *d* of late W. Scott Owen, OBE, JP of Cefngwifed, Newtown, Montgomeryshire; one *d* (and one *s* killed on active service, 1944). *Educ:* Cargilfield; Rugby; RMA, Woolwich. Commissioned in Royal Artillery, 1907; served European War in France and Flanders, 1914-18, as Intelligence Officer and Gen. Staff Officer (despatches 5 times, DSO, MC, Bt Major 1916; Bt Lt-Col 1918; Legion of Honour, Belgian Ordre de la Couronne (Croix d'Officier), Belgian Croix de Guerre, American Distinguished Service Medal, Order of the Nile); served on Gen. Staff at War Office, 1918; attended Peace Conference at Paris as mem. of British Delegation, 1919 (CBE); passed Staff Coll., 1919; served in Army of the Black Sea, 1920-23; acted as British Delegate, Thracian Boundary Commission, 1924-25; served in Shanghai Defence Force, 1927; Military Attaché, Berlin, Stockholm, Oslo and Copenhagen, 1928-32; Comdr RA 51st (Highland) Div. TA, 1932-34; Chief of British Military Mission to Egyptian Army, 1937-38; Dir-Gen. Air and Coast Defence, War Office, 1938-39; Special Employment, War Office, 1939-40; III Corps, Comdr, 1940; GOC British Troops in Egypt, 1941; GOC-in-C Western Command, 1941-42 (despatches twice); retd pay, 1943; Amer. Legion of Merit (Comdr), 1946. Editor-in-Chief of Captured German Archives, attached Foreign Office, 1948-51. Pres., Royal Geographical Society, 1954-58. *Publications:* Geographic Disarmament, 1935; Marshal Massena, 1965; Napoleon, 1967; Grant, 1970. *Recreations:* travel, sport, and gardening. *Address:* 36 Cadogan Place, SW1. *T:* 01-235 2237; Keeper's Cottage, Seacox, Hawkhurst, Kent. *Clubs:* Brooks's, Beefsteak, Geographical.

*See also Hon. D. M. G. J. Willoughby.*

**MARSHALL FOSTER, E.;** *see* Foster, E. M.

**MARSHALL-REYNOLDS, Clyde Albert,** QC 1962; retired; *b* 11 March 1898; *o c* of late Leslie Clyde Reynolds and Amy Maud Marshall-Reynolds (*née* Marshall); unmarried. *Educ:* Sydney Grammar Sch., Australia; private tutor in England; Wadham Coll., Oxford. Called to Bar, Middle Temple, 1926; Mem. Middle Temple and Inner Temple. Bencher, Middle Temple, 1958. Special Commissioner in Divorce, 1965, 1966, 1967 and 1968. Freeman, City of London, 1954. *Recreations:* motoring, gardening. *Address:* 28 Brechin Place, SW7; Yews Farm, Blackboys, East Sussex.

**MARSHAM,** family name of **Earl of Romney.**

**MARSHAM, Brig. Francis William Bullock-,** DSO 1918; MC; late 19th Royal Hussars; *b* 1883; *m* 1922, Mrs Cordy-Simpson, *widow,* Hope Court, Crowborough, *o d* of Sir Fitzroy Maclean, 10th Bt. *Educ:* Eton. Served European War, 1914-19 (despatches, DSO, MC); Lt-Col 1927; Bt-Col 1931; Col 1931; commanded 3rd Carabiniers, 1927-31; 5th Cavalry Brigade, 1931-32; Comdr 1st Cavalry Brigade, 1932-36; Aide-de-camp to the King, 1935-38; retired with rank of Brig., 1938. Chief Umpire 1st Armd Div., 1939-40; GSO1 Home Guard, 1940-42; County Cadet Comdt, Berks Cadets, 1942-46. *Address:* Overblow, Shorne, Kent. *T:* Shorne 2254. *Clubs:* Cavalry, Royal Automobile.

**MARSHAM, (Hon. Mrs Sydney), Dame Joan,** DBE, *cr* 1945 (CBE 1937; OBE 1918); Chairman: The Personal Service League; National Women's Auxiliary, YMCA; *d* of William Warry, ISO, Shapwick, Somerset; *m* 1911, Hon. Sydney Marsham (*d* 1952), *y s* of 4th Earl of Romney; one *s*. *Address:* c/o Coutts & Co., 440 Strand, WC2.

**MARSON, Air Vice-Marshal John,** CB 1953; CBE 1950; CEng; RAF (retired); *b* 24 Aug. 1906; *s* of late Wing Comdr T. B. Marson, MBE, and late Mrs E. G. Marson, (*née* Atkins); *m* 1935, Louise Joy Stephen Paterson; two *s*. *Educ:* Oakham Sch. RAF Coll., Cranwell, 1924-26. STSO, HQ, Coastal Command, 1949-50; AOC 42 Group, 1951-54; Pres., Ordnance Board, 1956-57 (Vice-Pres., 1954-56); Dir-Gen. of Technical Services, 1957-58; AOC 24 Group, 1959-61. *Recreations:* sailing, golf. *Address:* Marygold, Aldeburgh, Suffolk. *Clubs:* Royal Air Force; Royal Cruising; Aldeburgh Golf.

**MARTELL, Edward Drewett;** Chairman of The Freedom Group; *b* 2 March 1909; *e s* of E. E. Martell and Ethel Horwood; *m* 1932, Ethel Maud Beverley; one *s*. *Educ:* St George's Sch., Harpenden. In Coal trade, 1926-28, then entered journalism. Past: News Editor, World's Press News; Gen. Manager, The Saturday Review; Managing Editor, Burke's Peerage and Burke Publishing Co.; Sports staff of The Star. Served War of 1939-45, with RAC (Capt.). On demobilisation established own bookselling and publishing company. Mem. LCC, 1946-49; contested (L) Rotherhithe, 1946, and N. Hendon, 1950; East Ham (Ind.), 1957; SE Bristol (Nat. Fellowship C), 1963; Dep. Chm., Liberal Central Assoc., 1950-51; Trustee, Winston Churchill Birthday Trust, 1954-. Founded: Free Press Soc., 1955; People's League for the Defence of Freedom, 1956 (first Chm.); Anti-Socialist Front, 1958; National Fellowship (co-founder), 1962; New Daily (also Editor), 1960. *Publications:* (with R. G. Burnett) The Devil's Camera, 1932; (with R. G. Burnett) The Smith Slayer, 1940; The Menace of Nationalisation, 1952; The Menace of the Trade Unions, 1957; Need the Bell Toll?, 1958; (with Ewan Butler) Murder of the News-Chronicle and the Star, 1960; Wit and Wisdom–Old and New, 1961; A Book of Solutions, 1962. *Recreations:* lawn tennis; Sherlock Holmes and Father Brown. *Address:* 87 George Street, W1.

**MARTELL, Vice-Adm. Sir Hugh (Colenso),** KBE 1966 (CBE 1957); CB 1963; *b* 6 May 1912; *s* of late Engineer Capt. A. A. G. Martell, DSO, RN (Retd) and of Mrs S. Martell; *m* 1941, Marguerite Isabelle, *d* of late Sir Dymoke White, 2nd Bt; five *s* one *d*. *Educ:* Edinburgh Academy: RNC Dartmouth. Royal Navy, 1926-; served War, 1940-45 (despatches): Gunnery Officer in HMS Berwick and HMS Illustrious. Naval Adviser to Dir Air Armament Research and Development, Min. of Supply, 1952-54; Capt. (F) 7 and in Comd HMS Bigbury Bay, 1954-55; Overall Operational Comdr, Nuclear Tests, in Monte Bello Is as Cdre, 1956; IDC, 1957; Capt., HMS Excellent, 1958; Dir of Tactical and Weapons Policy, Admiralty and Naval Mem. Defence Research Policy Staff, Min. of Defence, 1959-

62; Admiral Commanding Reserves and Dir-Gen. of Naval Recruiting, 1962-65; Chief of Allied Staff, Mediterranean, Aegean and Black Sea, 1965-67. Director: Derritron Electronics Ltd; Reslosound Ltd; City and Military Personnel Consultants Ltd; Directors Secretaries Ltd; Chairman: Bury Manor Schools Trust Ltd; Brockhampton Land Co. Ltd. *Recreation:* sailing. *Address:* Long Reach, Bosham, near Chichester, Sussex. *T:* Bosham 3184. *Clubs:* United Service; Itchenor Sailing.

**MARTEN, Francis William,** CMG 1967; MC 1943; Assistant Secretary, Ministry of Overseas Development, since 1967; *b* 8 Nov. 1916; *er s* of late Vice-Adm. Sir Francis Arthur Marten and Lady Marten (*née* Phyllis Raby Morgan); *m* 1940, Hon. Avice Irene Vernon (*d* 1964); one *s* one *d*; 2nd, 1967, Miss Anne Tan. *Educ:* Winchester Coll.; Christ Church, Oxford. Served HM Forces, 1939-46. Entered HM Foreign Service, 1946 (Counsellor, 1960; now Diplomatic Service). Served Foreign Office, 1946-48; Washington, 1948-52; Foreign Office, 1952-54; Teheran, 1954-57; NATO Defence Coll., Paris, 1957-58; Bonn, 1958-62; Leopoldville, 1962-64; Imperial Defence Coll., 1964-65; Dep. High Comr, Eastern Malaysia, 1965-67. *Recreation:* ski-ing. *Address:* c/o Foreign and Commonwealth Office, SW1. *Club:* Boodle's.

**MARTEN, H. N.;** *see* Marten, Neil.

**MARTEN, Neil;** MP (C) Banbury Division of Oxon, since 1959; *b* 3 Dec. 1916; 3rd *s* of F. W. Marten; *m* 1944, Joan Olive, *d* of Vice-Adm. W. J. C. Lake, CBE; one *s* two *d. Educ:* Rossall Sch.; Law Soc. Solicitor, 1939. Served War of 1939-45 (despatches); Army, 1940-45, Northants Yeomanry, Special Forces, French Resistance, Norwegian Resistance. Foreign Office, 1947-57, Egypt, Turkey, Germany. Croix de Guerre; Norwegian War Medal. PPS to Pres. of Board of Trade, 1960-62; Parliamentary Sec., Ministry of Aviation, 1962-64. Chm., Anglo-Norwegian Parly Group; Member: Exec., 1922 Cttee; Estimates Cttee. Vice-President: Disabled Drivers Assoc.; Council, Voluntary Service Overseas. *Recreations:* tennis, ski-ing, mountaineering. *Address:* Swalcliffe House, near Banbury, Oxon. *Clubs:* Carlton, Special Forces.

**MARTIN;** *see* Holland-Martin.

**MARTIN, Sir Alec,** KBE 1959; Kt 1934; LLD 1960; *b* London, 25 Nov. 1884; *s* of Samuel and Rosina Martin; *m* 1909, Ada Mary Fell; three *s* two *d. Educ:* All Saints Church Sch., Knightsbridge. Started at Christies at the age of twelve, and was Managing Dir of the firm, 1940-58; Governor and Guardian of the Nat. Gallery of Ireland, Dublin; Chm. of Trustees of the Wallace Collection; Hon. Sec. Nat. Art-Collections Fund; a Governor of the Foundling Hosp. KStJ 1958. *Recreations:* lots. *Address:* 16 Dover Park Drive, Roehampton, SW15. *T:* 01-788 0376.

*See also Sir Martin Flett.*

**MARTIN, Prof. Andrew,** QC 1965; PhD (London); Professor of International and Comparative Law, University of Southampton, since 1963; Member: Law Commission, 1965-70; Law Reform Committee, since 1970; *b* 21 April 1906; *m* 1932, Anna Szekely; one *s. Educ:* Lutheran Coll., Budapest; Universities of Budapest, Paris, Vienna, Berlin and London. Barrister-at-Law, Middle Temple, 1940. *Publications:* A Commentary on the Charter of the United Nations (with Norman Bentwich), 1950; Collective Security, 1952; The Changing Charter (with J. B. S. Edwards), 1955; Restrictive Trade Practices and Monopolies, 1957; Law Reform Now (jt ed. and part-author), 1963; Legal Aspects of Disarmament, 1963; numerous papers and articles published by learned socs and jls. *Recreations:* chamber music and alpine driving. *Address:* 4 Pump Court, Temple, EC4. *T:* 01-353 9178. *Clubs:* Reform, Garrick.

**MARTIN, Archer John Porter,** CBE 1960; FRS 1950; MA, PhD; Consultant to Wellcome Research Laboratories, 1970; *b* 1 March 1910; *s* of Dr W. A. P. and Mrs L. K. Martin; *m* 1943, Judith Bagenal; two *s* three *d. Educ:* Bedford Sch.; Peterhouse, Cambridge. Nutritional Lab., Cambridge, 1933-38; Chemist, Wool Industries Research Assoc., Leeds, 1938-46; Research Dept, Boots Pure Drug Co., Nottingham, 1946-48; staff, Medical Research Council, 1948-52; Head of Phys. Chem. Div., National Inst. of Medical Research, 1952-56; Chemical Consultant, 1956-59; Director, Abbotsbury Laboratories Ltd, 1959-70. Extraordinary Prof., Technological Univ. of Eindhoven, 1965-. Berzelius Gold Medal, Swedish Medical Soc., 1951; (jointly) Nobel Prize for Chemistry, 1952; John Scott Award 1958; John Price Wetherill Medal, 1959; Franklin Institute Medal, 1959; Leverhulme Medal, Royal Society, 1963; Kolthoff Medal, Acad. of Pharmaceutical Science, 1969. Hon. DSc, Leeds, 1968. *Address:* Abbotsbury, Barnet Lane, Elstree, Herts. *T:* 01-953 1031. *Club:* Chemists' (New York).

**MARTIN, Charles Emanuel;** Professor of International Law and Political Science, University of Washington, Seattle, Washington, 1925-62; Director University of Washington Institute International Affairs, 1935-62; Emeritus Professor of International Law and Political Science since 1962; *b* Corsicana, Texas, 11 Sept. 1891; *s* of Emanuel Cobb Martin and Roxie Annie Moon; *m* 1921, Jewell Boone; no *c. Educ:* University of California, Berkeley (BA 1914, MA 1915); Columbia Univ. (PhD 1918); Hon. LLD University S Cal. 1942; Columbia Univ, Fellow Int. Law, 1916-17; War Trade Bd and Food Adm. US Govt 1917-18; Coast Artillery Corps, US Army, 1918; Carnegie Endowment Fellow Int. Law, 1918-19; Lecturer on Int. Law and Politics and Sec. Bureau Int. Relations, University Calif., Berkeley, 1919-20; Head Dept Pol Science, University Cal. at Los Angeles, 1920-25; Dean Faculty Social Science, University of Washington, 1926-29 and Head Political Science Dept, 1925-52; mem. Carnegie Endowment European Int. Law Conference, 1926; visiting Prof. Int. Relations, University of Hawaii, 1929; Carnegie Endowment Prof. Int. Relations accredited to universities in Orient and Antipodes, 1929-30; Dir Sch. Pacific and Oriental Affairs, University of Hawaii, 1932; Mem. Govt Bd on Immigration and Naturalization Service, US Dept Labor, 1933; Exchange Prof. Int. Law and Adm., American Univ., Washington, DC, 1942-43; Ednl consultant, Nat. Inst. Public Affairs, Washington, DC, 1942-43; Special Expert to Sec. of US Army and Chm. Bd of Consultants of US Cultural and Social Science Mission to Japan, Sept. 1948-Jan. 1949. Deleg. Inst. Pacific Relations Confs, 1929, 1936, 1950, 1954; in Japan, US, and India. University of Washington and Rockefeller Foundation Research professorship, East and SE Asia, 1954-55; Lectr, Inter-Amer. Acad. of Comparative and Internat. Law, Havana, Cuba, Feb. 1957; Prof. of Amer. Studies, University Philippines, 1962-63; Haynes Prof. Internat. Law, Whittier Coll., Calif., 1964. United States-Mexican pre-recognition Conference, Mexico City, 1923; Summer

Sessions at California, Harvard, Texas, Michigan, George Washington, Stanford, Southern California, Hawaii Univs; Special Lecturer at Miss., Emory, La, and NC Univs; lecturer Canadian Inst. Int. Affairs, 1933, 1943, 1951, 1953; Trustee Am. Inst. Pacific Relations; Dir and Ex Comm, Inst. World Affairs; Ex Comm., Council For. Relations (Seattle Comm.); Am. Commission on Org. of Peace; Pres. World Affairs Symposium (Seattle). Late Pres. and Chm. Board Trustees Seattle World Affairs Council; Trustee Seattle Art Museum, 1940-52. Pres., American Soc. of International Law, 1960-61; Mem., Indian and Philippine Internat. Law Societies. *Publications:* Policy of the US as Regards Intervention, 1921; An Introduction to the Study of American Constitution, 1926; American Government and Citizenship (with W. H. George), 1927, Politics of Peace, 1929; Permanent Court of International Justice and Question of American Adherence, 1932; various articles on civic, political, public and international affairs; Report of US Cultural and Social Science Mission to Japan (in collaboration), 1949; South and South-east Asia, 1951; Rebirth of a Nation (Japan), 1953; Universalism and Regionalism in International Law and Organization, 1959. Edited: The Pacific Area, 1929; Pacific Problems, 1932; War and Society, 1941; Problems of the Peace, 1945; San Francisco Conference and the UN Organization, 1946; The World in Crisis, 1948; Prospects for World Stability, 1950; New Weapons for the New Diplomacy, 1953. *Recreations:* foreign travel, teaching assignments abroad; organizing internat. relations institutes as an avocation, summer home at seashore, Bainbridge Island. *Address:* 3828 48th Avenue NE, Seattle, Washington 98105, USA; Dept Political Science, University of Washington, Seattle, Washington 98105. *T:* Lakeview 4-1117, (office) 543-2780; R6, Box 6862, Bainbridge Island, Washington, USA. *T:* Viking 2-2197. *Clubs:* Rainier, Monday, Faculty, China (Seattle); Cosmos (Washington, DC); Army and Navy (Manila, RP).

**MARTIN, Rt. Rev. Clifford Arthur,** MA Cantab; DD Lambeth; LLD Liverpool; *b* 11 Nov. 1895; *s* of Arthur Henry Martin; *m* 1926, Margaret La Trobe, *d* of late Rev. Frederick La Trobe Foster; one *s* three *d*. *Educ:* Fitzwilliam Coll., Cambridge; Ridley Hall, Cambridge. Served as an officer in Royal Sussex Regt 1915-19; ordained 1920, to Christ Church, Croydon; Sec. Young People's Dept, Church Missionary Soc., 1924-27; Vicar Christ Church, Croydon, 1927-33; Vicar Christ Church, Folkestone, 1933-39; Vicar St Andrew, Plymouth, 1939-44; Chaplain to the King, 1941-44; Bishop of Liverpool, 1944-65. Select Preacher Cambridge Univ., 1945. Hon. Fellow, St Peter's Coll., Oxford, 1965. *Address:* School Lane, Middle Littleton, near Evesham, Worcs.

**MARTIN, Brig. Cyril Gordon,** VC 1915; CBE 1938; DSO 1914; *b* 19 Dec. 1891; *s* of late Rev. John Martin, Foochow, China; *m* 1917, Mab, *o d* of late Major E. Hingston, RE; one *s* (and one killed in action 1944) one *d*. *Educ:* Bath Coll.; Clifton Coll. Entered army, 1911; Major, 1928; Lt-Col, 1936; Col, 1939; served European War, 1914-15 (despatches, VC, DSO); EEF Palestine, 1918; NW Frontier of India, 1930-31 (despatches, Bt Lt-Col); Waziristan, 1937 (CBE); Dep. Chief Engineer, Northern Command, India, 1939; Chief Engineer British Troops in Iraq, 1941 (despatches); Chief Engineer NW Army, India; ADC to the King, 1945-47; retired pay, 1947. *Address:* Millaton Lodge, Bridestowe, near Okehampton, Devon. *T:* Bridestowe 303. *Club:* United Service.

**MARTIN, Sir David (Christie),** Kt 1970; CBE 1960; FRSE, FRIC; Executive Secretary, The Royal Society, since 1947; *b* 7 Oct. 1914; 3rd *s* of late David Christie Martin and Helen Linton; *m* 1943, Jean MacGaradh Wilson, *d* of late Thomas Hay Wilson, Edinburgh. *Educ:* Kirkcaldy High Sch.; Edinburgh Univ. BSc (Chemistry) 1937, PhD 1939, Edinburgh. Asst Sec., Royal Society of Arts, 1939-45; seconded to Dept of Research and Develt, Min. of Supply, 1939-45; Gen. Sec., Chemical Soc., 1945-47; Comr for Gen. Purposes of Income Tax, 1950-; Sec., 1950-54 and Recorder, 1955-58 of Chemistry Sect. of Brit. Assoc. for Advancement of Science, and Mem. Coun., 1959-69; Manager, Royal Instn, 1951-52; Mem. Exec. Coun., Ciba Foundn, 1967-; Mem., Inter-Union Commn on Solar-Terrestrial Relationships of Internat. Coun. of Scientific Unions, 1967-; Chm. Ed. Bd, Annals of the International Years of the Quiet Sun, 1967-70; Coun. of Management, Soc. for Protection of Science and Learning, 1967-; Chm., BBC Science Consultative Gp, 1968-; Member: BBC Gen. Adv. Council, 1968-; Chem. Soc.; Soc. of Chem. Industry; RSA. Hon. DSc, Edinburgh, 1968. *Publications:* contrib. to The Royal Society: Its Origins and Founders; papers and articles in scientific jls. *Recreation:* fishing. *Address:* Flat 1, 6 Carlton House Terrace, SW1. *T:* 01-839 5260. *Club:* Athenæum.

**MARTIN, Rt. Rev. Denis Maurice Laidlaw,** OSB; Abbot of Belmont since 1955; *b* 4 April 1911; 3rd *s* of Walter Henry Martin and Clara Martin (*née* Allwood). *Educ:* Salesian Coll., Farnborough, Hants. Accountancy, Rio de Janeiro, 1928-30; Ecclesiastical Studies, Belmont Abbey and Abbaye de Saint Andre, Bruges, 1930-38. Army Chaplain, 1939-43. Parochial Ministry, Hereford, Ormskirk and Whitehaven, 1944-53. Staff of Belmont Abbey, 1953-55. *Address:* Belmont Abbey, Hereford. *T:* Belmont 211.

**MARTIN, Douglas Whitwell;** Chairman, Gill & Duffus Ltd, 1964-70; *b* 17 Feb. 1906; *s* of Rev. T. H. Martin, MA, and Lily Janet Vaughan Martin; *m* 1st, 1931, Jessie Milroy Lawrie (*d* 1965); three *s*; 2nd, 1967, Margaret Helen Simms, FCIS. *Educ:* Rossall Sch.; Lausanne University. Member of staff, Export Dept of Lever Brothers Ltd, 1923-27; joined Gill & Duffus Ltd, 1929. *Recreations:* fishing, reading, theatre. *Address:* 1 Embankment Gardens, SW3; 119 Admirals Walk, Bournemouth, Hants. *Club:* Boodle's.

**MARTIN, Lt-Col Edward C. de R.;** *see* De Renzy-Martin.

**MARTIN, Edward Kenneth;** Consulting Surgeon, University College Hospital; Fellow of University College, London; *s* of Dr Edward Fuller Martin, Weston-super-Mare; *m* 1923, Philippa Parry Pughe (*see* Philippa P. Martin); three *d*. *Educ:* Charterhouse; University Coll., London. MS, FRCS (Mem. of Court of Examiners); BEF, 1914-18; Temp. Major RAMC. *Publications:* various contributions to medical journals. *Recreation:* travelling. *Address:* 97 Dorset House, Gloucester Place, NW1. *T:* 01-935 6322.

**MARTIN, Frank,** Dr *hc*; Composer; *b* Geneva, 1890; *s* of Charles Martin and Pauline Duval; *m* 1940, Maria Boeke; two *s* four *d*. *Educ:* Gymnasium, Geneva. Studied under M. Joseph Lauber. Compositions include: Le Vin herbé; In Terra Pax; Golgotha (oratorio); Der Cornet (mezzo-soprano and small orch.); 6 Monologues from Jedermann; Petite symphonie concertante (harp, harpsichord, piano and double string orch.); 8 Preludes (piano); Concerto (7 wind instrs); Ballades for: 'cello and piano or orch.; flute and piano or orch.; saxophone and orch.; trombone and piano or orch.; piano and orch.; Der Sturm (opera, The Tempest); 4 Etudes (string orch.); Concerto (violin and full orch.); Ouverture en Rondeau (full orch.); Pseaumes (mixed choir and orch.); Concerto (harpsichord and small orch.); Mystère de la Nativité (9 soloists, 2 mixed choirs, orch.; mediaeval text); Monsieur de Pourceaugnac (opera, Molière); Les 4 Eléments, études symphoniques (full orch.); Pilate (oratorio breve, 4 soloists, choirs, orch.); Concerto (cello and small orch.); String Quartet; String Trio; Maria-Triptychon (soprano, violin and orch.); Erasmi Monumentum (full orch. and organ). His music is frequently performed in England. Many years resident in Holland. *Address:* Bollelaan 11, Naarden (NH), Netherlands. *T:* Bussum 12781.

**MARTIN, Frank Vernon,** RE 1961 (ARE 1955); MA; MSIA; Wood Engraver; Etcher; Book Illustrator; Senior Lecturer in Graphic Design, Camberwell School of Art, 1965, Teacher of Etching and Engraving since 1953; *b* 14 Jan. 1921; *er s* of Thomas Martin, *qv*; *m* 1942, Mary Irene Goodwin; three *d. Educ:* Uppingham Sch.; Hertford Coll., Oxford; St Martin's Sch. of Art. History Schol., Hertford Coll., Oxford. Served War of 1939-45, Army, 1941-46. Book illustrations for Folio Society, Hutchinson, Geoffrey Bles, Burns Oates, Vine Press and other publishers. One-man exhibitions of prints and drawings, London, 1956, 1961 and 1968; works represented in: Victoria and Albert Museum; Manchester City Art Gallery; Whitworth Art Gallery, Manchester; Fitzwilliam, Cambridge; other public collections at home and abroad. Sec., Royal Society of Painter-Etchers and Engravers, 1956-57. Hon. Academician, Accademia delle Arti del Disegno, Florence, 1962. *Publications:* articles, book reviews, etc, on Engraving and the Graphic Arts. *Recreation:* photography. *Address:* Studio L, 416 Fulham Road, SW6. *T:* 01-385 1089; 2 Ranelagh Avenue, SW6. *T:* 01-736 8896.

**MARTIN, The Hon. Fred Russell Beauchamp,** MC; Justice of the Supreme Court of Victoria, 1934-57; *b* 28 May 1887; *s* of Frederick Martin and Alice Maud Evelyn Wood; *m* 1915, Ethel Muriel Swinburne; three *s. Educ:* Wesley Coll., Melbourne; Melbourne Univ. (Queen's Coll.). Called to Victoria Bar, 1911; served in 38th Bn AIF 1915-19 (MC). *Recreations:* golf, bowls. *Address:* Berkeley Street, Hawthorn, Victoria 3122, Australia. *Clubs:* Royal Automobile (Victoria); Peninsula Country Golf.

**MARTIN, Frederick George Stephen,** CIE 1941; MC; MIME; *b* 26 Aug. 1890; *s* of Frederick Martin, Newcastle-under-Lyme; *m* 1939, Mrs Herta Portzeba, *d* of Fritz Loose, Berlin; no *c.* Served European War, 1914-18 (despatches, MC, wounded twice); entered Indian State Rlys, 1923; Dep. Chief Mechanical Engineer, EI Rly, 1928; Controller of Stores, EI Rly, 1930; Dep. Dir-Gen., Engineering and Civil Production, Dept of Supply, Govt of India, 1939-42; Addl Dir, Gen. Supply Dept, India, 1942-43; Dir in charge, Tata Aircraft Ltd, 1943-46; Tech. Adviser, Tata Industries and Tata Ltd, 1946-59, retired. *Address:* Golmuri, Cranham, Gloucester. *T:* Painswick 2061.

**MARTIN, Sir George William,** KBE, *cr* 1935; JP; LLD (Leeds), 1951; Chairman of Directors of Wilkinson and Warburton Ltd and David Dixon and Son Ltd; Chairman Edward Dennison Yeadon Ltd; Dir of The North Eastern Trading Estate, Gateshead-on-Tyne, 1935-48; Dir Wallace Arnold Trust Ltd; Underwriting Mem. of Lloyd's; Chairman Leeds Musical Festival, 1942-54; Member National Assistance Board, 1948-56; *b* 24 June 1884; *s* of Edward and Ester Margret Martin; *m* 1913, Doris Dixon Marshall (*d* 1966); no *c.* Chairman of the PAC Cttee of Assoc. of Municipal Corporations, 1931-33 and 1935-44, and of its Health Cttee, 1942-45; Vice-Chm Finance Cttee, City of Leeds, 1929-30; Mem. of National Radium Commission, and Central Cttee for Refugees; Mem. and Chm. of Employers Panel Rushcliffe Cttee on Nurses Salaries, 1941-47; Chm. Nuffield Provincial Hospital Trust Regionalization Cttee, Chm. Yorks Regionalization Cttee; Chm. of Leeds Public Dispensary and Hosp. and Mem. of the Board of the General Infirmary at Leeds, 1929-48, and Leeds Tradesmen's Benevolent Institution; Chm. City of Leeds Health Cttee, 1935-45, 1951-52; Lord Mayor City of Leeds, 1946-47; Chm. United Leeds Hospital Board, 1948-61; Mem. Advisory Cttee of National Fitness Council; Mem. of the Court and Council, Leeds Univ., 1948-58. Pres. Leeds Chamber of Commerce, 1948-52; Vice-Chm., Teaching Hosp. Association; Chm. Wartime Trading Cttee of Chamber of Commerce; Chm. of the Leeds Convalescent Soc.; Master of Court Company of Feltmakers, 1951-52; Trustee of Thomas Wade; Chm. of Governors of East Moor Sch.; Chm. of Governors, Woodhouse Grove Sch.; Mem. of the Council of the Wholesale Textile Assoc., London, 1938-60; Mem. of Departmental Cttee to consider Laws relating to Rag Flock, 1938-39; Treasurer and Chm. Yorks Council British Empire Cancer Campaign. High Sheriff of Yorks, 1954. Pres. Leeds YMCA. Contested (C) West Leeds, 1929. Hon. Freeman, City of Leeds, 1966. *Recreation:* shooting. *Address:* Adel Lodge, Adel, Leeds. *T:* 673216. *Clubs:* Carlton; Leeds, Leeds County Conservative (Leeds); Alwoodley Golf.

**MARTIN, Rt. Rev. Henry David,** DD; Hon. Assistant Bishop, Diocese of British Columbia; *b* London, England, 30 June 1889; *s* of H. W. and M. E. Martin; *m* 1919, Margaret Kathleen Wilson; two *d. Educ:* St Paul's Sch., London; University of Toronto; Wycliffe Coll., Toronto. Deacon 1915, Curate, St Luke's Church, Saint John, NB; Priest 1916, Curate, St James' Cathedral, Toronto; Priest-in-Charge, Holy Trinity Church, Winnipeg, 1917-18; Rector, St George's Church, Winnipeg, 1918-39; Canon of St John's Cathedral, Winnipeg, 1932; Bishop of Saskatchewan, 1939-59. *Recreations:* swimming, golf, walking. *Address:* 2715 Beach Drive, Victoria, BC, Canada.

**MARTIN, Lt-Gen. Henry James,** CBE 1943; DFC; Chief of Defence Staff, South African Defence Force, retired; *b* 10 June 1910; *s* of Stanley Charles Martin and Susan C. Fourie; *m* 1940, Renée Viljoen; one *s* two *d. Educ:* Grey Coll. Sch., Bloemfontein; Grey Univ. Coll., Bloemfontein. Joined S African Air Force, 1936, and played important rôle in British Empire Training Scheme in South Africa; commanded No 12 Sqdn in Western Desert (DFC, Croix Militaire de première classe Belgique); commanded No 3 Wing (a unit of Desert Air Force) and campaigned from El Alamein to Tunis; returned to Union, 1943. *Recreations:* rugger (represented Orange Free State, 1931-34, Transvaal, 1935-37, South Africa, 1937), golf, tennis. *Address:* 10 Crescent Road, Waterkloof Ridge, Pretoria, S Africa. *Clubs:* Rand (Johannesburg); Pretoria (Pretonia).

**MARTIN, Sir James,** Kt 1965; CBE 1957 (OBE 1950); DSc; CEng; FIMechE; FRAeS; Managing Director and Chief Designer,

Martin-Baker Aircraft Co. Ltd, since formation of Company, 1934; *m*; two *s* two *d*. Founder, Martin Aircraft Co., 1929. Designed: Martin patent balloon barrage cable cutter; 12 gun nose for Havoc night fighter; Spitfire jettison hood; flat feed for 20 mm Hispano gun; M-B1, 2, 3, and 5 prototype aeroplanes; started work on aircraft ejector seats, 1945; explosive hood jettison gear; rocket ejection seats. RAeS Wakefield Gold Medal, 1952; Barbour Air Safety Award, 1958; Cumberbatch Air Safety Trophy, 1959; Royal Aero Club Gold Medal. Hon. Fell., Manchester Inst. of Science and Technology, 1968. Pioneer and authority on aircraft seat ejection. *Publications:* numerous papers on air-survival (read by learned socs in UK and USA). *Recreation:* design work. *Address:* Southlands Manor, Denham, Bucks. *T:* Denham 2214. *Club:* Royal Aero.

**MARTIN, James Arthur,** CMG 1970; FASA; company director; *b* 1903; *s* of late Arthur Higgins Martin and Gertrude, *d* of George Tippins; unmarried. *Educ:* Stawell and Essendon High Schools, Victoria. FASA 1924. Joined The Myer Emporium Ltd, Melbourne, 1918; The Myer Emporium (SA) Ltd, Adelaide, 1928, Man. Dir 1936, Chm. and Man. Dir, 1956-68, retd; Dir, Myer (Melbourne) Ltd, department store, 1936-68, retd. *Recreations:* horse riding, tennis. *Address:* 17 Hawkers Road, Medindie, South Australia 5081. *Clubs:* South Australian Cricket, South Australian Jockey, Adelaide Racing, Tattersalls, Commonwealth (Adelaide); Tattersalls (Sydney); Royal Automobile (Melbourne).

**MARTIN, Maj.-Gen. James Mansergh Wentworth,** CB 1953; CBE 1944; late 8th King George V's Own Light Cavalry; *b* 5 Aug. 1902; *er s* of late James Wentworth Martin, Castle Jane, Glanmire, Co. Cork, Ireland, and late Mrs J. Wentworth Martin, Great Meadow, Hambledon, Surrey; *m* 1944, Mrs Jean Lindsay Barnes, *d* of late Sir Henry Cowan, MP. *Educ:* Charterhouse; Royal Military Academy, Woolwich. Joined RFA 1922; with Royal West African Frontier Force, 1925-27; Private Sec. to Governor of Assam, 1928-29; transferred to Indian Army, 1930. During War of 1939-45, Persia and Iraq, Syria, Tunisia, Sicily, Italy and Burma; Brig., Gen. Staff, 1943-44. Comd 1st Indian Armoured Bde, 1945-47; transferred to Royal Scots Greys, Jan. 1948; Chief of Staff, British Forces in Trieste, 1948-49; Comd 9th Armoured Brigade, 1949-51; Dep. Chief of Staff Allied Land Forces Central Europe, Fontainebleau, 1951-53; GOC Salisbury Plain District, 1953-56; retired Sept. 1956. Vice-Pres. Army Ski Assoc.; Hon. Vice-Pres. Army Football Assoc.; Liveryman of the Merchant Taylors' Company. *Address:* Great Meadow, Hambledon, Surrey. *T:* Wormley 2665. *Club:* United Hunts.

**MARTIN, James Purdon,** MA, MD, BCh (Belfast), FRCP; Consulting Physician to the National Hospital for Nervous Diseases, Queen Square, WC1; *b* Jordanstown, County Antrim, 1893; *s* of late Samuel Martin, Garmoyle, Bangor, Co. Down; *m* 1st, Majorie, MB, BS (*d* 1937), *d* of Richard Blandy, Madeira; two *s*; 2nd, Janet Smiles Ferguson, MA. *Educ:* Royal Academical Institution and Queen's Univ., Belfast; (Medical Schs: Belfast, St Bart's, St Mary's) BA (first class hons in Mathematical subjects), 1915; Purser Studentship; MB, BCh, BAO, 1920; MRCP, 1922; FRCP 1930; Neurologist to British Post-Graduate Medical Sch., 1935-57. Mem. of the Senate of Queen's Univ. (representative for Students), 1916-17. Neurologist Eastern Command, Home Forces, 1940-44. Vis. Prof. of Neurology, University of Colorado, 1959. Lumleian Lecturer, RCP, 1947; Arris and Gale Lecturer, RCS, 1963. Hon. Mem., Assoc. of British Neurologists; Hon. Assoc. Mem., Soc. of Brit. Neuropathologists. FRSocMed (Pres. Neurolog. Sect., 1945-46). *Publications:* The Basal Ganglia and Posture, 1967; many papers on neurological subjects in Brain, The Lancet, etc. *Address:* Craignish, Turner Drive, NW11. *T:* 01-455 5856. *Club:* Athenæum.

**MARTIN, Brig. John Douglas K.;** *see* King-Martin.

**MARTIN, Vice-Adm. John Edward Ludgate,** CB 1968; DSC 1943; Deputy Supreme Allied Commander, Atlantic, since 1970; *b* 10 May 1918; *s* of late Surgeon Rear-Admiral W. L. Martin, OBE, FRCS and of Elsie Mary Martin (*née* Catford); *m* 1942, Rosemary Ann Deck; two *s* two *d*. *Educ:* RNC, Dartmouth. Sub Lt and Lt, HMS Pelican, 1938-41; 1st Lt, HMS Antelope, 1942; navigation course, 1942; Navigation Officer, 13th Minesweeping Flotilla, Mediterranean, 1943-44, including invasions N Africa, Sicily, Pantelleria, Salerno; RNAS Yeovilton, 1944; Naval Officer: HMS Manxman and HMS Bermuda, 1944-46; HMS Nelson, 1947; HMS Victorious, 1948; Staff Coll., 1949; Naval Officer, HMS Devonshire, 1950-51; Dirg Staff, Staff Coll., 1952-54; Jt Services Planning Staff, Far East, 1954-55; Exec. Off., HMS Superb, 1956-57; Jt Services Staff Coll., 1958; Dep. Dir Manpower Planning and Complementing Div., Admty, 1959-61; Sen. Naval Off., W Indies, 1961-62; Comdr Brit. Forces Caribbean Area, 1962-63; Capt. Britannia Royal Naval Coll., Dartmouth, 1963-66; Flag Officer, Middle East, 1966-67; Comdr, British Forces Gulf, 1967-68 (despatches); Dir-Gen., Naval Personal Services and Training, 1968-70. Comdr 1951; Capt. 1957; Rear-Adm. 1966. *Recreations:* fishing, shooting, beagling (Jt Master Britannia Beagles, 1963-66), sailing. *Address:* Carr House, Soberton, near Southampton. *T:* Droxford 454. *Clubs:* Army and Navy; Royal Naval Sailing Association.

**MARTIN, John Hanbury;** *b* 4 April 1892; *s* of W. A. H. Martin, DL, JP, and Frances Hanbury-Williams; *m* 1st, 1934, Avice Blaneid (marriage dissolved, 1938), *d* of Herbert Trench; 2nd, 1950, Dorothy Helen, *d* of E. Lloyd-Jones, Plas Mancott, Flints. *Educ:* Wellington; Brasenose Coll., Oxford. Labour candidate for Great Yarmouth, 1931; MP (Lab) Central Southwark, 1939-48. Co-founder and Chm., Southwark Housing Assoc., 1930-. Mem., London Insurance Cttee, 1936-45; Sec. Franco-British Parly Assoc., 1943-48. *Publications:* Corner of England; Peace Adventure; contrib. to New Survey of London Life and Labour; numerous articles and reviews. *Address:* c/o Martin's Bank Ltd, 68 Lombard Street, EC3. *Club:* Brooks's.

**MARTIN, Sir (John) Leslie,** Kt 1957; MA, PhD Manchester; MA Cantab; MA Oxon; Hon. LLD Leicester; Hon. LLD Hull; FRIBA; Professor of Architecture, University of Cambridge, since 1956; Fellow, Jesus College, Cambridge; *b* 17 Aug. 1908; *s* of late Robert Martin, FRIBA; *m* 1934, Sadie Speight, MA (Arch.), ARIBA; one *s* one *d*. *Educ:* Manchester Univ. Sch. of Architecture. Asst Lectr and Master of Design, Manchester Univ., 1930-34; Head of Sch. of Architecture, Hull, 1934-39; Principal Asst Architect, London Midland and Scottish Railway, 1939-48; Dep. Architect, LCC 1948-53; Architect to the LCC, 1953-56; Consultant to Gulbenkian Foundn, Lisbon, 1959-69; Slade Prof. of Fine Art, Oxford, 1965-66; Ferens Prof. of Fine Art, Hull, 1967-68. Buildings include work in

Cambridge and for Univs of Oxford, Leicester and Hull. Mem. Council, RIBA, 1952-58 (Vice-Pres., 1955-57); Mem. Royal Fine Art Commn. Gropius Lectr, Harvard, 1966. Hon. Mem., Assoc. of Finnish Architects. RIBA Recognised Schs Silver Medallist, 1929; Soane Medallist, 1930; London Architecture Bronze Medallist, 1954; RIBA Distinction in Town Planning, 1956; Civic Trust Award, Oxford, 1967. Comdr, Order of Santiago da Espada, Portugal. *Publications:* Jt Editor, Circle, 1937; The Flat Book, 1939 (in collab. with wife); Whitehall: a Plan for a National and Government Centre, 1965; The Framework of Planning, inaugural Lectr, Hull, 1967; contrib. various jls; papers include: An Architect's Approach to Architecture; Education Without Walls; Education Around Architecture. *Address:* The King's Mill, Shelford, Cambridge. *T:* Shelford 2399. *Club:* Athenæum.

**MARTIN, Sir John (Miller),** KCMG, *cr* 1952; CB 1945; CVO 1943; British High Commissioner in Malta, 1965-67; *b* 15 Oct. 1904; *s* of late Rev. John Martin; *m* 1943, Rosalind Julia, 3rd *d* of Sir David Ross, *qv*; one *s*. *Educ:* The Edinburgh Acad.; Corpus Christi Coll., Oxford (Scholar, MA). Entered Civil Service (Dominions Office), 1927; seconded to Malayan Civil Service, 1931-34; Sec. of Palestine Royal Commission, 1936; Private Sec. to the Prime Minister (Rt Hon. Winston Churchill), 1940-45 (Principal Private Sec. from 1941); Asst Under-Sec. of State, 1945-56, Dep. Under-Sec. of State, 1956-65, Colonial Office. KStJ 1966. *Publication:* contrib. to Action This Day–Working with Churchill, 1968. *Address:* The Barn House, Watlington, Oxford. *T:* Watlington 487. *Club:* Athenæum.

**MARTIN, Maj.-Gen. John Simson Stuart,** CSI 1945; MB, MRCP (Edinburgh); VHS 1939; KHS 1942; IMS, retired; *b* 18 June 1888; *s* of Rev. D. J. Martin and Letitia Tennant Stuart; *m* 1924, Caroline Lorna Halkett; two *s* two *d*. *Educ:* Oban High Sch.; Rockhampton Grammar Sch. (Queensland); Edinburgh Univ. MB, ChB 1911; MRCP (Edinburgh) 1928; Lt IMS 1912; Capt. 1915; Major, 1923; Lt-Col 1931; Col 1938; Acting Brig., later Acting Maj.-Gen. 1942; Subst. Maj.-Gen. 1943; retired, 1945. Served European War, 1914-18 (despatches). Owns about 5000 acres. *Address:* Glendale, Isle of Skye. *T:* Glendale 206.
*See also N. A. Mitchison.*

**MARTIN, Leonard Charles James;** Under-Secretary, Ministry of Overseas Development, since 1968; *b* 26 June 1920; *s* of Leonard Howard Martin and Esther Martin (*née* Avis); *m* 1945, Althea Lilian Charles; three *d*. *Educ:* Brighton, Hove and Sussex Grammar Sch.; London Sch. of Economics. Served RAFVR, 1941-45. Min. of Educn, and Dept of Educn and Science, 1946-64. Min. of Overseas Development, 1965-. UK Permanent Delegate to UNESCO, 1965-68. *Address:* 87 Downside, Shoreham-by-Sea, Sussex. *T:* 4674.

**MARTIN, Leonard Cyril,** MA; BLitt; King Alfred Professor of English Literature, University of Liverpool, until Oct. 1951; *b* Leyton, Essex, 21 March 1886; 2nd *s* of Edward John Martin and Ellen Heavens; *m* 1920, Dorothy Mary, *y d* of late John and Martha Green, Peebles. *Educ:* Chigwell Sch., Essex; Keble Coll., Oxford. Lecturer in English, Trinity Coll., University of Toronto, 1909-13; University of Lund, 1913-15; Asst Commercial Attaché, British Legation, Copenhagen, 1915-18; Representative in Denmark of Ministry of Information, 1918-19; Lecturer in English, University Coll., Reading, 1919; Maître de Conférences, Sorbonne, 1920-22; Senior Lecturer in English Literature, University of Liverpool, 1923-29 (in charge of Dept, 1926-29); Foyle Research Fell. Shakespeare Inst., Stratford-on-Avon, 1953-55; Hon. Mem. Modern Language Assoc. of America, 1965. *Publications:* Editor: The Works of Henry Vaughan; The Poems of Richard Crashaw; Milton's Paradise Regained; The Poems of Nathaniel Wanley; The Poems of Marlowe; Cowley, Poetry and Prose; The Poems of Herrick; Religio Medici and other works of Sir Thomas Browne. Contributions to Modern Language Review, etc. *Address:* Glencairn, Peebles. *T:* Peebles 2393.

**MARTIN, Sir Leslie;** *see* Martin, Sir J. L.

**MARTIN, Sir Leslie Harold,** Kt 1957; CBE 1954; FRS 1957; FAA; PhD (Cantab); DSc (Australian National University, Melbourne, Qld, NSW, Adelaide); LLD (WA); DLitt (Sydney); Dean of Military Studies, and Professor of Physics, Royal Military College, Duntroon, Canberra, since 1967; *b* 21 Dec. 1900; *s* of Richard Martin, Melbourne; *m* 1923, Gladys Maude Elaine, *d* of H. J. Bull; one *s* (and one *s* decd). *Educ:* Melbourne High Sch.; Melbourne Univ.; Trinity Coll., Cambridge. Scholar of Exhibn of 1851, 1923; apptd to Natural Philosophy Dept of Melbourne Univ., 1927; Syme Prize, 1934; Associate Professor of Natural Philosophy, University of Melbourne, 1937-45; Professor of Physics, 1945-59; Emeritus Prof., 1960. Defence Scientific Adviser to Aust. Govt, and Chm., Defence Res. and Develt Policy, 1948-67; Comr, Atomic Energy Commn of Aust, 1958-68; Chm., Aust. Univ. Commn, 1959-66. *Recreation:* golf. *Address:* 46 Getting Crescent, Campbell, ACT, Australia. *T:* 480113.

**MARTIN, Louis Claude,** ARCS, DIC, DSc (London); *b* 16 June 1891; *s* of late Alfred Harry Martin and Eleanor Gertrude Martin, Norwich; *m* 1916, Elsie Maud Lock; one *s* one *d*. *Educ:* King Edward VI Middle Sch., Norwich; Royal College of Science. Lecturer, West Ham Municipal Technical Coll., 1913-14; served European War, Royal Naval Divisional Engineers, 1914-16; Lecturer and Asst Prof. in Technical Optics, Imperial College, 1917-43, Professor of Technical Optics, 1943-51. Visiting Prof., University of Rochester, NY, USA, 1936-37; Chm. Lens Research Sub-Cttee, Min. of Aircraft Prod., 1941-45; Manager Royal Institution, 1947-49 and 1951-52; Chm. of Optical Group, Physical Soc., 1947-50; Vice-Pres., International Optic Commission, 1950-53; Hon. Fellow, Royal Microscopical Soc., 1967. Deacons' Sec., Beckenham Congregational Church, 1947-49. Lay Reader: Diocese of Norwich, 1958, 1969; Diocese of Winchester, 1960. Liveryman, Worshipful Company of Spectacle Makers. *Publications:* (with W. Gamble) Colour and Methods of Colour Reproduction, 1923; Optical Measuring Instruments, 1924; Introduction to Applied Optics, 1930; (with B. K. Johnson) Practical Microscopy, 1931; Technical Optics, 1949; Geometrical Optics, 1955 (with W. T. Welford) Technical Optics, 2nd edn, 1966; Theory of the Microscope, 1966. About forty papers mainly on optical subjects, especially the theory of the microscope. *Recreations:* poetry, sketching. *Address:* Meadow Cottage, Hindringham, Fakenham, Norfolk. *T:* Thursford 311.

**MARTIN, Prof. Nicholas Henry,** TD 1947; FRCP, FRIC, FCPath; Professor of Chemical Pathology, University of London, since 1952; Consultant to St George's Hospital since 1947; Member Lister Institute since 1954; Hon. Consultant in Chemical Pathology to the Army since 1963;*b* 26 Oct. 1906; *s* of late

William and Ellen Renfree Martin, Crellow, Cornwall, and Newcastle; *m* 1948, Ursula, 2nd *d* of William Brodie and *widow* of T. H. Worth, Lincs; two *s*. *Educ:* Sedbergh Sch.; Durham, Oxford and Munich Univs. Buckle Travelling Fellow, 1929; Oxford Univ. Scholar, Middlesex Hosp., 1932. Served War of 1939-45: Asst Dir of Pathology, 21st Army Group (despatches twice); Consultant to UNRRA, 1945-46; Fellow, Harvard Univ., 1946-47. Chm., Association of Clinical Pathologists, 1963-68, Pres., 1969-70; Vice-Pres., College of Pathologists, 1966-69. *Publications:* numerous medical and scientific publications in internat. literature. *Recreations:* sailing, gardening, reading. *Address:* Woottons, Woolhampton, Berks. *T:* Woolhampton 3351; St George's Hospital, SW1. *T:* 01-730 7151. *Clubs:* Athenæum, Bath.

**MARTIN, Hon. Sir Norman (Angus),** Kt 1949; Resident Director in Australasia for Thomas Cook and Son; Director several cos; Chairman: Ball & Welch Ltd; Victorian Inland Meat Authority; Australia Day Council; *b* 24 April 1893; *s* of Angus Martin, Portland, Vic.; *m* 1919, Gladys, *d* of Captain Barrett, MC; one *s* one *d*. *Educ:* Werribee. Minister of Agriculture, Victoria. A Vice-Pres. of Land and Works, 1943-; MLA for Gunbower, 1934-. Served European War, AIF, 1914-18. Councillor of Cohuna Shire since inauguration of Shire, Pres. 1930-31 and 1939-40; Agent-General for Victoria in the UK, 1945-50. Pres. Leitchville Branch United Country Party, Vic., for Fifteen years. *Recreations:* golf, tennis, shooting. *Address:* Longleat, 133 Alexandra Avenue, South Yarra, Victoria 3141, Australia; c/o Thomas Cook and Son, 267 Collins Street, Melbourne, Victoria 3000, Australia. *Clubs:* Royal Automobile; Australian, Savage, VRC (Melbourne).

**MARTIN, Olaus Macleod,** CIE 1937; *b* Stornoway, 1 Feb. 1890; *s* of Rev. Donald John Martin; *m* 1919, Helen Frances Steele (Kaisar-i-Hind Gold Medal, 1943); four *s* one *d*. *Educ:* Edinburgh and Oxford Univs. MA (1st Class Hons Classics and Mental Philosophy) 1911; Indian Civil Service, 1913; Magistrate-Collector, 1921; Divisional Commissioner, 1940; Development Commissioner, Bengal, 1945; retired from ICS, 1948. British Administration, Eritrea, 1947-51. *Recreations:* riding, tennis, shooting, fishing. *Address:* Dunard, Tobermory, Isle of Mull.

**MARTIN, Oliver Samuel,** QC 1970; *b* 26 Nov. 1919; *s* of Sidney Edward Martin and Nita Martin; *m* 1954, Marion Eve; two *s*. *Educ:* King's College Sch., Wimbledon; London University. Served RNVR, 1939-46. Called to Bar, Gray's Inn, 1951. *Recreations:* golf, music. *Address:* 3 Temple Gardens, EC4. *T:* 01-353 1244.

**MARTIN, Patrick William,** TD; MA; JP; Headmaster of Warwick School since 1962; *b* 20 June 1916; *e s* of Alan Pattinson Martin, Bowness-on-Windermere, Westmorland; *m* 1939, Gwendoline Elsie Helme, MA, St Hilda's Coll., Oxford; two *d*. *Educ:* Windermere Grammar Sch.; Balliol Coll., Oxford. 2nd cl. hons in Modern History, Balliol Coll., 1937. Asst Master, Abingdon Sch., Berks, 1938-40. Commissioned in TA, 1938; served War of 1939-45, on active service with Royal Artillery, 1940-46; Battery Capt., 1940-42; Comdt Sch. of Artillery, S India; Staff College, Quetta; GSO 2, and 1 HQRA 14th Army in Burma (despatches); British Mil. Mission to Belgium, 1946. Schoolmaster, 1946-49; Asst Dir of Educn, Brighton, 1950-52; Headmaster: Chipping Norton Gram. Sch., 1952-57; Lincoln Sch., 1958-62. Chm. or Mem. of several cttees. *Publications:* articles in educational and other periodicals. *Recreations:* books, music, foreign countries and people; being alone in the countryside. *Address:* Headmaster's House, Warwick School, Warwick. *T:* Warwick 42484.

**MARTIN, Hon. Paul Joseph James,** QC (Canada); Government Leader in the Senate, Canada, since 1968; Secretary of State for External Affairs, 1963-68; President, North Atlantic Council, 1965-66; *b* Ottawa, 23 June 1903; *s* of Philip Ernest Martin and Lumina Marie Chouinard; *m* 1936, Alice Eleanor Adams; one *s* one *d*. *Educ:* Pembroke Separate Schs; St Alexandre Coll.; St Michael's Coll.; University of Toronto (MA); Osgoode Hall Law Sch., Toronto; Harvard Univ. (LLM); Trinity Coll., Cambridge; Geneva Sch. of Internat. Studies. Wilder Fellow, 1928; Alfred Zimmern Schol., 1930; Barrister-at-Law; Partner, Martin, Laird & Cowan, Windsor, Ont, 1934-63; QC 1937. Lectr, Assumption Coll., 1931-34. Can. Govt Deleg., 19th Ass. League of Nations, Geneva, 1938; Parl. Asst to Minister of Labour, 1943; Deleg. to ILO Confs, Phila, 1944, London, 1945. Apptd Sec. of State, 1945. Deleg. to 1st, 4th, 7th, 9th, 10th General Assembly, UN (Chm. Can. Del., 9th, 18th, 19th, 20th, 21st). Deleg. 1st, 3rd, 5th sessions, Economic and Social Council, 1946-47. Minister of National Health and Welfare, Dec. 1946-June 1957. First elected to Canadian House of Commons, Gen. Elec., 1935; Rep. Essex East until 1968; apptd to Senate, 1968. Holds several hon. doctorates. Hon. Life Mem., Canadian Legion. Christian Culture Award, 1956. *Address:* The Senate, Ottawa, and Windsor, Ontario, Canada. *Clubs:* Rideau (Ottawa); Beach Grove Golf and Country (Windsor, Ont.).

**MARTIN, Rev. Canon Philip Montague;** Canon Residentiary and Chancellor of Wells Cathedral, since 1971; Fellow of St Cross College, Oxford (by special election), 1970; *b* 8 Aug. 1913; *o s* of Montague Egerton and Ada Martin; *m* 1940, Mollie Elizabeth, *d* of John Mitchell Ainsworth; one *s* one *d*. *Educ:* Whitgift Sch.; Exeter Coll., Oxford. Hasker Scholar and Squire Scholar, Oxford; BA 1936, MA 1939; Teachers' Diploma (London) 1945. Deacon, 1937; Priest, 1938, Southwark. Curate of Limpsfield, 1937-40; Curate of Minehead, 1940-44; Asst Master, Clifton Coll., 1944; Chaplain and Lecturer, St Luke's Coll., Exeter, 1945-48; Canon Residentiary of Newcastle Cathedral and Diocesan Dir of Religious Education, 1948-61; Vicar of St Mary the Virgin (University Church), Oxford, 1961-71, with St Cross (Holywell), 1966-71; Chaplain, Nuffield Coll., Oxford, 1969-71. Examining Chaplain to Bishop of Newcastle, 1952-; Rural Dean of Oxford, 1965-68. *Publications:* Mastery and Mercy: a study of two religious poems, 1957; None but He and I and other poems, 1966. *Address:* 8 The Liberty, Wells.

**MARTIN, Philippa Parry;** Consulting Surgeon: Western Ophthalmic Hospital; St Mary's Hospital Group; Fellow of University College, London; Hunterian Professor, The Royal College of Surgeons of England; *d* of late Canon T. St J. P. Pughe, Penn, Bucks; *m* 1923, Edward Kenneth Martin, *qv*; three *d*. *Educ:* Switzerland; St Felix Sch., Southwold; University Coll., and University Coll. Hospital, London. MS, FRCS. Formerly Chm. Editorial Cttee, Med. Women's Fedn. *Publications:* articles in medical journals. *Recreation:* travelling. *Address:* 97 Dorset House, NW1. *T:* 01-935 6322; Goose Neck, Chinnor Hill, Oxon. *T:* Kingston Blount 242.

**MARTIN, Most Rev. Pierre;** *see* Noumea, Archbishop of, (RC).

**MARTIN, Col Reginald Victor,** CIE 1938; IMS, retired; MRCS, LRCP, DOMS; *b* 20 March 1889; *s* of B. R. Martin, MB, Killeshandra, Cavan, Ireland; *m* 1913, Katherine (*d* 1968), *d* of Maj.-Gen. R. M. Clifford; two *s* two *d*. *Educ:* St Paul's Sch., Kensington; St Mary's Hospital, Paddington. Entered Indian Medical Service, 1913; war service 1914-18 (despatches); Waziristan, 1923; Inspector-General of Prisons, Province of Bombay, 1936-38; Waziristan, 1940-41; VHS, 1942-43; ADMS, 1941-44 (Brigadier 1942-43); KHP, 1943-44; retired 1944; re-employed, 1944-46. *Recreations:* golf, tennis. *Address:* 35 Manor Orchard, Taunton, Somerset.

**MARTIN, Col Robert Andrew St George,** OBE 1959 (MBE 1949); JP; Lord Lieutenant of Leicestershire since 1965; *b* 23 April 1914; *o s* of late Major W. F. Martin, Leics Yeo., and late Violet Anne Philippa (*née* Wynter); *m* 1950, Margaret Grace (JP Leics 1967), *e d* of J. V. Buchanan, MB, ChB; one *s*. *Educ:* Eton Coll.; RMC Sandhurst. Commissioned Oxon. and Bucks Lt Inf., 1934; ADC to Gov.-Gen. of S Africa, 1938-40; war service 4 Oxon and Bucks, 1940-42; 2/7 R Warwick Regt, 1942-44; 5 DCLI, 1944-45 in NW Europe (despatches); DAMS, HQ ALFSEA, 1946; Mil. Asst to C of S, GHQ, SEALF, 1946-49 (MBE); Chief Instr, School of Mil. Admin., 1949-50; 1 Som. LI, 1950-52; AMS, HQBAOR, 1952-54; 1 Oxon and Bucks, 1954-55; Military Sec. to Gov.-Gen. of Australia, 1955-57; Comd 1 Oxon and Bucks Lt Inf. and 1 Green Jackets, 1957-59; Bde Col Green Jackets Bde, 1959-62; Comd Recruiting and Liaison Staff, HQ Western Command, 1962-65. JP Leics, 1965. KStJ 1966. Order of Orange Nassau, 1950. *Recreations:* hunting, shooting, cricket, gardening. *Address:* The Brand, Woodhouse Eaves, Loughborough, Leics. *T:* Woodhouse Eaves 269. *Clubs:* Army and Navy, MCC.

**MARTIN, Ronald,** MBE 1945; Director of Marketing, Telecommunications Headquarters, GPO, since 1968; *b* 7 Nov. 1919; *o s* of late Albert and Clara Martin; *m* 1943, Bettina, *o d* of late H. E. M. Billing; one *d*. *Educ:* St Olave's Grammar Sch. Asst Traffic Superintendent, GPO, 1939. Served War of 1939-45, Royal Signals, NW Europe. GPO: Asst Princ., 1948; Princ., 1950; Treasury, 1954; Princ. Private Sec. to PMG, 1955; Staff Controller, GPO, London, 1956; Asst Sec., 1957; Dir Establishments and Organisation, GPO, 1966; Dir Telecommunications Personnel, 1967. *Recreations:* music, motoring, amateur mechanics. *Address:* 50 Parkhill Road, Bexley, Kent. *T:* Crayford 23080.

**MARTIN, Rupert Claude,** MA; JP; *b* 2 July 1905; *s* of late Col C. B. Martin, CMG; *m* 1931, Ellen (*d* 1966), *d* of Henry Wood, Guernsey, CI; one *s* two *d*. *Educ:* Shrewsbury Sch.; Queen's Coll., Oxford (Classical Scholar), 2nd Class in Greats, 1927; Asst Master at St Paul's Sch., 1927-37; House Master, 1930-37; Headmaster of King's Sch., Bruton, Som., 1937-46; representative of British Council in Switzerland, 1946-48; Headmaster, St Dunstan's, Burnham-on-Sea, 1948-66. Vice-Chm., Incorporated Assoc. of Preparatory Schs, 1957. *Publications:* (Lands and Peoples Series) Switzerland; Italy; Spain; Morocco. *Recreations:* mountaineering, travel. *Address:* Quantocks, Burnham on Sea, Som. *Clubs:* MCC, I Zingari, Free Foresters, Alpine; Vincent's, Authentics (Oxford).

**MARTIN, Thomas,** MSc; DIC; FInstP; *b* Norwood, 26 July 1893; *er s* of late Thomas Martin; *m* 1918, Dorothy Sylvia, *yr d* of late Frederick Vernon, Dulwich; two *s*. *Educ:* Alleyns Sch.; University Coll., London. Served in Royal Artillery, 1914-19 and 1939, Captain RA. Metallurgical research, Royal School of Mines, 1919-23; Sec., Brit. Empire Exhibition Cttee of Royal Society, 1923-25; Sec., Optical Convention, 1926; Sec., Institute of Physics, 1926-29, and Editor, Journal of Scientific Instruments, 1928-29; General Sec., Royal Institution of Great Britain, 1929-50; Sec., Royal Institution Cttee, Faraday Celebrations, 1931; Asst and later Deputy Dir of Instrument Production, Ministry of Supply, 1939-46; Principal Scientific Officer, Home Office, 1951-64; Consultant, Ministry of Defence, Navy Dept, 1964-65. Chm. Cinematograph Equipment Allocation Cttee, 1941-46; Mem. Anglo-American Mission to European Countries on Instrument Requirements, 1946; Chm. Film Sub-Commn, UNESCO Commn on Technical Needs, Paris, 1947; Pres. British Soc. for the History of Science, 1962-64. *Publications:* Faraday, 1934; ed. Faraday's Diary, 1932-36; The Royal Institution (for British Council), 1942; Faraday's Discovery of Electro-Magnetic Induction, 1949; articles in scientific journals. *Address:* 8 Bramerton Street, Chelsea, SW3. *T:* 01-352 1116. *Clubs:* Athenæum, Savile.
*See also Frank Vernon Martin.*

**MARTIN, Thomas Ballantyne;** stockbroker; *b* 1901; *s* of late Angus Martin, FRCS, Newcastle upon Tyne, and Robina, *d* of Thomas Pringle, Middleton Hall, Northumberland; *m* 1953, Jean Elisabeth, *e d* of Lt-Col O. D. Bennett and Audrey, *d* of Sir Hamilton Grant, 12th Bt of Dalvey; two *d*. BA Cambridge 1923. MP (C) Blaydon Div. of Co. Durham, 1931-35. Political Correspondent of Daily Telegraph, 1937-40. RAFVR; Squadron Leader, Middle East Intelligence Centre, 1940-43; Adviser on Public Relations to UK High Comr in Australia, 1943-45; Sec. of United Europe Movement, 1947-48; Sec. to British all-party delegn to Congress of Europe at The Hague. *Address:* The Mill House, Great Horkesley, Colchester, Essex. *T:* Gt Horkesley 296. *Clubs:* Travellers', Pratt's.

**MARTIN, Victor Cecil;** Deputy British High Commissioner, Madras, since 1968; *b* 12 Oct. 1915; *s* of Cecil Martin and late Isabel Katherine Martin (*née* Hickman). *Educ:* Cheltenham Coll.; Jesus Coll., Cambridge (Scholar; Classical Tripos Parts 1 and 2; MA). Asst Principal, Board of Education, 1939. Served Intelligence Corps, 1940-45; Major 1944, Persia and Iraq Force. Principal, Min. of Education, 1946; transferred to CRO, 1948; British High Commn, New Delhi, 1951-54, 1956-60; Asst Sec., CRO, 1962; Head of West Africa Dept, 1961-64; Head of S Asia Dept, 1964-66; Head of Cultural Relations Dept, 1966-68. *Recreations:* ornithology, travel. *Address:* c/o Foreign and Commonwealth Office, Whitehall, SW1. *Clubs:* United University, Royal Commonwealth Society, English-Speaking Union; Madras (Madras).

**MARTIN, William McChesney, jun.;** Chairman, Board of Governors of the Federal Reserve System, 1951-70; *b* St Louis, Mo, 17 Dec. 1906; *s* of William McChesney Martin and Rebecca (*née* Woods); *m* 1942, Cynthia Davis; one *s* two *d*. *Educ:* Yale Univ. (BA 1928); Benton Coll. of Law, St Louis, 1931. Graduate student (part time), Columbia Univ., 1931-37. (Hon.) Doctor of Laws: Temple Univ., Phila, 1951; Tulane Univ., New Orleans, La, 1953; Amherst Coll., Amherst, Mass, 1954; Marietta Coll., Ohio, 1956; Washington Univ., St Louis,

1956; Trinity Coll. Conn, 1956; University of Pennsylvania, 1957; Yale Univ., 1958; Bowdoin Coll., Brunswick, Me, 1958; Washington and Lee Univ., Lexington, Va, 1960; Hamilton Coll., Clinton, NY, 1960; Harvard, 1962; Tufts Univ., Medford, Mass, 1964; Princeton, 1962; Columbia, 1965; New York Univ., 1965; Rutgers, 1965; Middlebury Coll., Vermont, 1966; Bishop's Univ., Can., 1968. Served in bank examination dept of Federal Reserve Bank of St Louis, 1928-29; Head of statistics dept, A. G. Edwards & Sons, St Louis, 1929-31; partner, May 1931-July 1938. Mem., New York Stock Exch., June 1931-July 1938; Gov., 1935-38; Chm. Cttee on Constitution, 1937-38; Sec. Conway Cttee to reorganize the Exchange, 1937-38; Chm. Bd and Pres. pro. tem. May-June 1938; Pres. July 1938-April 1941. Asst Exec. President's Soviet Protocol Cttee and Munitions Assignments Board, Wash., DC, 1942; appointed Mem. Export-Import Bank, Nov. 1945; Chm. and Pres., 1946-49 (as Chm. of Federal Reserve Board, serves on National Advisory Council on Internat. Monetary and Financial Problems). Asst Sec. of the Treasury, Feb. 1949-April 1951; US Exec. Dir Internat. Bank for Reconstruction and Devel., Dec. 1949-Feb. 1952. Trustee: Berry Schs, Atlanta, Ga; Johns Hopkins Univ., Baltimore; Chapter of Washington Cathedral, DC; Yale Univ.; Nat. Geographic Soc. Drafted, Selective Service Act, private, US Army, 1941, Sergeant, GHQ Army War Coll., 1941; Commnd 1st Lt, Inf., Feb. 1942; Captain Aug. 1942; Major, 1943; Lt-Col 1944; Col 1945. Legion of Merit, 1945. *Recreations:* tennis, squash. *Address:* 2861 Woodland Drive, NW, Washington, DC 20008, USA. *Clubs:* West Side Tennis, Yale; Metropolitan, Jefferson Island, Alibi (Washington); Chevy Chase (Md).

**MARTIN-BATES, James Patrick,** MA; JP; FCIS; FBIM; Principal, Administrative Staff College, Henley-on-Thames, Oxon, since Sept. 1961; *b* 17 April 1912; *er s* of late R. Martin-Bates, JP, Perth, Scotland; *m* 1939, Clare, *d* of late Prof. James Miller, MD, DSc; one *s* two *d*. *Educ:* Perth Academy; Glenalmond; Worcester Coll., Oxford. BA 1933; MA 1944. Lamson Industries, 1933-36; Dorman Long & Co. Ltd, 1936-38; PE Group, 1938-61; Man. Dir Production Engineering Ltd, 1953-59; Vice-Chm. PE Holdings, 1959-61; Hutchinson's Ltd (Dir 1957-); Dir, Averys Ltd, 1970-. Chm. Management Consultants Association, 1960; Member: Council, British Institute of Management, 1961-66; UK Advisory Council on Education for Management, 1961-66; Council, Glenalmond, 1963-; Bd of Visitors, HM Borstal, Huntercombe, 1964-67; The Council for Technical Education and Training for Overseas Countries, 1962-; Council, University Coll., Nairobi, 1965-68; Council Chartered Institute of Secretaries, 1965-; EDC for Rubber Industry, 1965-69. Fellow Internat. Acad. of Management, 1964. FCIS 1961; FBIM 1960. *Publications:* various articles in Management Journals. *Recreations:* golf, fishing. *Address:* Greenlands, Henley-on-Thames, Oxon. *T:* Hambleden (Bucks) 454. *Clubs:* Caledonian; Royal and Ancient (St Andrews).

**MARTIN-LEAKE, Hugh;** *see* Leake.

**MARTINEAU, Rt. Rev. Robert Arnold Schürhoff;** *see* Huntingdon, Bishop Suffragan of.

**MARTONMERE,** 1st Baron, *cr* 1964; **John Roland Robinson,** PC 1962; KCMG 1966; Kt 1954; MA, LLB; Governor and C-in-C of Bermuda since 1964; *b* 22 Feb. 1907; *e s* of Roland Walkden Robinson, Solicitor, Blackpool; *m* 1930, Maysie, *d* of late Clarence Warren Gasque; one *s* one *d*. *Educ:* Trinity Hall, Cambridge. Barrister-at-law, 1929 (Certificate of Honour and Buchanan Prize Lincoln's Inn, 1928); MP (U) Widnes Division of Lancs, 1931-35, Blackpool, 1935-45, S Blackpool, 1945-64. W/Cdr RAFVR, 1940-45. Pres. Royal Lancs Agricultural Society, 1936; Past Pres. Assoc. of Health and Pleasure Resorts; Past Pres. Residential Hotels Assoc. of Great Britain. Past Chm. Conservative Party Commonwealth Affairs Cttee; Chm. Gen. Council, Commonwealth Parliamentary Assoc., 1961-62. Past Dep. Chm. United Kingdom Branch, Commonwealth Parliamentary Association. Officer, Legion of Merit (USA). *Heir: s* Hon. Richard Anthony Gasque Robinson [*b* 11 March 1935; *m* 1959, Wendy Patricia, *d* of James Blagden; two *s* one *d*]. *Address:* Government House, Bermuda. *Clubs:* Carlton, Junior Carlton; Royal Lytham and St Annes Golf (St Annes); Royal Yacht Squadron (Cowes); Royal Bermuda Yacht (Hon. Life Mem.), Mid-Ocean (Bermuda).

**MARTY, Cardinal François,** Chevalier de la Légion d'honneur; Archbishop of Paris since 1968 and Cardinal since 1969; Member of the Secretariat of the Roman Catholic Synod since 1970; *b* Pachins, Aveyron, 18 May 1904; *s* of François Marty, cultivateur, and Zoé (*née* Gineste). *Educ:* Collège de Graves et Villefranche-de-Rouergue; Séminaire de Rodez; Institut Catholique de Toulouse. DenTh. Priest, 1930. Curate: Villefranche-de-Rouergue, 1932; Rodez, 1933; Parish Priest: Bournazel, 1940; Rieupeyroux, 1943; Archpriest, Millau, 1949; Vicar-General, Rodez, 1951; Bishop of Saint Flour, 1952; Coadjutor Archibishop, 1959, and Archbishop of Rheims, 1960. Pres., Episcopal Cttee of Mission de France, 1965, and French Episcopal Conf., 1969. Mem. Bureau, then Vice-Pres., Perm. Council of French Episcopate, 1966; Mem. Rome Commissions: on the Clergy; for Revision of Canon Law; Secretariat for Unbelievers. *Address:* Archevêché de Paris, 32 rue Barbet de Jouy, Paris 7, France.

**MARTYN, Joan,** OBE 1962; Governor Class II, HM Prison Commission; Governor, Bullwood Hall, 1962-64, retired; *b* 9 Aug. 1899; 3rd *d* of George Harold and Eve Martyn. *Educ:* Municipal Coll., Grimsby; Queenwood, Eastbourne; Bedford Physical Training Coll. (diploma). Staff of St Mary's Coll., Lancaster Gate, London, W2, 1919-36; staff of HM Borstal Institution, Aylesbury, 1937 (Governor 1946-59); Governor, HM Borstal, Cardiff, 1959-62. *Address:* 57 Bargate, Grimsby, Lincs.

**MARTYN-HEMPHILL,** family name of **Baron Hemphill.**

**MARWICK, Sir Brian (Allan),** KBE 1963 (CBE 1954; OBE 1946); CMG 1958; Permanent Secretary, Ministry of Education, Nassau, Bahamas, since 1968; *b* 18 June 1908; *s* of James Walter Marwick and Elizabeth Jane Flett; *m* 1934, Riva Lee, *d* of Major H. C. Cooper; two *d*. *Educ:* University of Cape Town; CCC, Cambridge. Administrative Officer: Swaziland, 1925-36; Nigeria, 1937-40; Swaziland, 1941-46; First Asst Sec.: Swaziland, 1947-48; Basutoland, 1949-52; Dep. Resident Comr and Govt Sec., Basutoland, 1952-55; Administrative Sec. to High Comr for Basutoland, the Bechuanaland Protectorate and Swaziland, 1956; Resident Comr, Swaziland, 1957-63; HM Comr, Swaziland, 1963-64; Permanent Sec., Min. of Works and Town Planning Dept, Nassau, Bahamas, 1965-68. *Publication:* The Swazi, 1940. *Recreations:*

polo, tennis, golf. *Address:* Ministry of Education, PO Box 213, Nassau, Bahamas. *Club:* Royal Commonwealth Society.

**MARWOOD, Sidney Lionel,** CIE 1941; *b* 8 April 1891; *s* of John Marwood, Shipbroker, Liverpool; *m* 1924, Agnes (*d* 1952), *e d* of Adam Rolland Rainy, MP; two *s* one *d*; *m* 1953, Mary, *d* of William Logsdail. *Educ:* St Paul's Sch.; Hertford Coll., Oxford, MA. Commissioned in West Lancs Divisional Engineers, RE (TF), in 1914; saw service in India and Mesopotamia, 1914-19; reverted to Indian Civil Service, 1920, posted to Bihar Province. Collector, 1924, Commissioner, 1939, Revenue Commissioner, Orissa, 1943; retired 1947. Kaisar-i-Hind Gold Medal (I Class) in 1934 after Bihar earthquake. *Address:* The Angles, Rustington, Sussex.

**MARX, Enid Crystal Dorothy,** RDI, 1944; Painter and Designer; *b* London, 20 Oct. 1902; *y d* of Robert J. Marx. *Educ:* Roedean Sch.; Central Sch. of Arts and Crafts; Royal College of Art Painting Sch. Designing and printing handblock printed textiles, 1925-39. Exhibited in USA and Europe; various works purchased by Victoria and Albert Museum, Musée des Arts Décoratifs, Boston Museum, Scottish Arts Council, etc. Mem. Society of Wood Engravers. Wood engraving and autolithography for pattern papers, book jackets, book illustration and decorations, trademarks, etc.; designed moquettes and posters for LPTB. Industrial designing for printed and woven furnishing fabrics, wallpapers, ceramics, plastics; FRSA, FSIA; original mem. National Register of Industrial Designers of Central Institute of Art and Design. Mem. of Bd of Trade design panel on utility furniture. Designed ½d.-2d. postage stamps for first issue Elizabeth II. Lectures on textiles and folk art. *Publications:* (jointly) English Popular and Traditional Art, 1947; (with Margaret Lambert), English Popular Art, 1951; articles and broadcasts on aspects of industrial design in various countries; author and illustrator of ten books for children. *Recreations:* study of popular art in different countries; gardening. *Address:* The Studio, 39 Thornhill Road, Barnsbury Square, N1.

**MARY REGIS, Sister;** *see* Morant, Dame Mary Maud.

**MARYON-WILSON, Sir Hubert (Guy Maryon),** 13th Bt *cr* 1661; *b* 27 July 1888; *s* of Rev. George Maryon Wilson (*d* 1906), 5th *s* of 9th Bt, and Albinia Frances Short (*d* 1920); assumed surname of Maryon by deed poll; *S* kinsman 1965; *m* 1923, Janet Mary, *d* of late Rev. Ernest Arthur Moxon, Lincs. *Educ:* Radley. *Heir:* none. *Address:* The Grange, Great Canfield, Dunmow, Essex.

**MASCALL, Rev. Prof. Eric Lionel,** DD Oxon, DD Cantab, BSc London; Professor of Historical Theology, London University, at King's College, since Oct. 1962; Dean, Faculty of Theology, London University, since 1968; *b* 12 Dec. 1905; *s* of John R. S. Mascall and S. Lilian Mascall, *née* Grundy; unmarried. *Educ:* Latymer Upper Sch., Hammersmith; Pembroke Coll., Cambridge (Scholar); Theological Coll., Ely. BSc (London) 1926; BA (Wrangler) 1927, MA 1931, BD 1943, DD 1958 Cantab; DD Oxon, 1948. Sen. Maths Master, Bablake Sch., Coventry, 1928-31; ordained, 1932; Asst Curate, St Andrew's, Stockwell Green, 1932-35; St Matthew's, Westminster, 1935-37; Sub-warden, Scholae Cancellarii, Lincoln, 1937-45; Lecturer in Theology, Christ Ch., Oxford, 1945-46; Student and Tutor of Christ Ch., Oxford, 1946-62, Emeritus Student, 1962-; University Lectr in Philosophy of Religion, 1947-62; Chap. at Oxford to Bishop of Derby, 1947-48; Bampton Lecturer, Oxford, 1956; Bampton Lecturer, Columbia Univ., NY, 1958; Commissary to Archbishop of Cape Town, 1964-; Examng Chaplain to Bishop of Willesden, 1970-. Boyle Lecturer, 1965-66; Charles A. Hart Memorial Lectr, Cath. Univ. of America, Washington, DC, 1968; Gifford Lectr, Univ. of Edinburgh, 1971. Fellow, King's Coll., London, 1968. Hon. DD St Andrews, 1967. *Publications:* Death or Dogma, 1937; A Guide to Mount Carmel, 1939; Man, his Origin and Destiny, 1940; The God-Man, 1940; He Who Is, 1943 (rev. edn 1966); Christ, the Christian and the Church, 1946; Existence and Analogy, 1949; Corpus Christi, 1953 (rev. edn 1965). Christian Theology and Natural Science, 1956; Via Media, 1956; Words and Images, 1957; The Recovery of Unity, 1958; The Importance of Being Human, 1958; Pi in the High, 1959; Grace and Glory, 1961; Theology and History (Inaugural Lecture), 1962; Theology and Images, 1963; Up and Down in Adria, 1963; The Secularisation of Christianity, 1965; The Christian Universe, 1966; Theology and The Future, 1968; (jt author) Growing into Union, 1970; Editor: The Church of God, 1934; The Mother of God, 1949; The Angels of Light and the Powers of Darkness, 1954; The Blessed Virgin Mary, 1963. *Address:* King's College, Strand, WC2. *T:* 01-836 5454; 30 Bourne Street, SW1. *T:* 01-730 2423. *Clubs:* Athenæum, National Liberal.

**MASEFIELD, Peter Gordon,** MA(Eng), Cantab; CEng; FRAeS; MInstT; Hon. FAIAA (USA); CInstMechE; Chairman: British Airports Authority; Director, Beagle Aviation Finance Ltd; Chairman, Royal Aero Club, since 1968; Member Council Business Aircraft Users Association; Vice-Chairman, Board of Trustees, Imperial War Museum; *b* 19 March 1914; *e s* of Dr W. Gordon Masefield, CBE, and Marian A. Masefield, Eastbourne, Sussex; *m* 1936, Patricia Doreen, 3rd *d* of late Percy H. Rooney, Wallington, Surrey; three *s* one *d*. *Educ:* Westminster Sch.; Chillon Coll., Switzerland; Jesus Coll., Cambridge. On Design Staff, The Fairey Aviation Co. Ltd, 1935-37; joined The Aeroplane newspaper, 1937, Technical Editor, 1939-43; Air Correspondent Sunday Times, 1940-43; War Corresp. with US Army Eighth Air Force on active service, 1943; Chm. Editorial Cttee, The Inter-Services Journal on Aircraft Recognition, MAP, 1942-45; Personal Adviser on Civil Aviation to the Lord Privy Seal (Lord Beaverbrook) and Sec. of War Cabinet Cttee on Post War Civil Air Transport, 1943-45; first British Civil Air Attaché, British Embassy, Washington, DC, 1945-46; Dir-Gen. of Long Term Planning and Projects, Ministry of Civil Aviation, 1946-48; Chief Executive and Mem. of Board of BEA, 1949-55; Managing Dir, Bristol Aircraft Ltd, 1956-60; Man. Dir, Beagle Aircraft Ltd, 1960-67, Chm., 1968-70. Member: Cairns Cttee on Aircraft Accident Investigation, 1960; Min. of Aviation Advisory Cttees on Civil Aircraft Control and on Private and Club Flying and Gliding; Aeronautical Research Council, 1958-61; Cambridge Univ. Appointments Bd, 1956-60. Director, Pressed Steel Co. Ltd, 1960-67. RAeS Brit. Commonwealth and Empire Lectr, 1948; Brancker Memorial Lectr, Inst. Transport, 1951, 1967; RAeS/AFITA Bleriot Lectr, 1966; Chm., Nat. Jt Council for Civil Air Transport, 1950-51. Liveryman and Upper Freeman, Guild of Air Pilots and Air Navigators; Pres., Inst. of Transport, 1955-56. Chm. Aviation Cttee, Royal Aero Club, 1960-65; President: RAeS, 1959-60 (Mem. Council); Inst. of Travel Managers, 1967-70.

*Publications:* articles on aeronautical subjects; photographs of battlefields of First World War. *Recreations:* flying, reading, writing, gardening, photography. *Address:* Rosehill, Doods Way, Reigate, Surrey. *T:* Reigate 42396. *Clubs:* Royal Aero, Royal Automobile.

**MASHAM, Lord; David Yarburgh Cunliffe-Lister;** *b* 21 March 1937; *s* of Major Hon. John Yarburgh Cunliffe-Lister (*d* of wounds received in action, 1943) and late Anne Irvine, *yr d* of late Rev. Canon R. S. Medlicott (she *m* 2nd, 1944, Donald Chapple-Gill); *g s* and *heir* of 1st Earl of Swinton, *qv*; *m* 1959, Susan Lilian Primrose Sinclair (*see* Baroness Masham of Ilton); one *s* one *d* (both adopted). *Educ:* Winchester; Royal Agricultural College. *Address:* Dykes Hill House, Masham, Yorks. *T:* Masham 241; c/o Midland Bank Ltd, 1 Sydney Place, Onslow Square, SW7.

**MASHAM OF ILTON,** Baroness *cr* 1970 (Life Peeress); **Susan Lilian Primrose Cunliffe-Lister;** *b* 14 April 1935; *d* of Sir Ronald Sinclair, 8th Bt and of Reba Blair (who *m* 2nd, 1957, Lt-Col H. R. Hildreth, MBE), *d* of Anthony Inglis, MD; *m* 1959, Lord Masham, *qv*; one *s* one *d* (both adopted). *Educ:* Heathfield School, Ascot; London Polytechnic. Has made career in voluntary social work. *Recreations:* breeding highland ponies, swimming, table tennis, fishing. *Address:* Dykes Hill House, Masham, near Ripon, Yorks. *T:* Masham 241.
*See also Sir J. R. N. B. Sinclair, Bt.*

**MASHONALAND, Bishop of,** since 1968; **Rt. Rev. John Paul Burrough,** MBE 1946; MA Oxon; *b* 5 May 1916; *s* of Canon E. G. Burrough; *m* 1962, Elizabeth (Bess), *widow* of Stephen John White; one step-*d*. *Educ:* St Edward's Sch.; St Edmund Hall, Oxford; Ely Theol. College. Coach, Tigre Boat Club, Buenos Aires, 1938-39. Captain, Royal Signals, Malaya Campaign (POW), 1940-45. Asst, Aldershot Parish Church, 1946-51; Mission Priest, Dio. of Korea, 1951-59; Anglican Chaplain to Overseas Peoples in Birmingham, 1959-68; Canon Residentiary of Birmingham, 1967-68. Chaplain and Sub-Prelate, Order of St John of Jerusalem, 1969-. *Publication:* Lodeleigh, 1946. *Recreation;* rowing (Oxford crews, 1937 and 1938). *Address:* Bishop's Mount, Salisbury, Rhodesia. *Clubs:* Leander (Henley); Vincent's (Oxford); Salisbury (Salisbury).

**MASIH, Rt. Rev. Inayat;** *see* Lahore, Bishop of.

**MASON,** family name of **Baron Blackford.**

**MASON, Prof. Basil John,** FRS 1965; DSc (London); Director-General of the Meteorological Office since 1965; *b* 18 Aug. 1923; *s* of late John Robert and Olive Mason, Docking, Norfolk; *m* 1948, Doreen Sheila Jones; two *s*. *Educ:* Fakenham Grammar Sch.; University Coll., Nottingham. Commissioned, Radar Branch RAF, 1944-46. BSc 1st Cl. Hons Physics (London), 1947, MSc 1948; DSc (London) 1956. Shirley Research Fellow, University of Nottingham, 1947; Asst Lecturer in Meteorology, 1948, Lecturer, 1949, Imperial Coll. Warren Research Fellow, Royal Society, 1957; Visiting Prof. of Meteorology, University of Calif., 1959-60; Professor of Cloud Physics, Imperial Coll. of Science and Technology (University of London), 1961-65. Hon. Gen. Sec. British Assoc., 1965-; President: Physics Section, British Assoc., 1965; Royal Meteorolog. Soc., 1968-. Mem. Exec. Cttee, World Meteorological Org., 1966-. Hugh Robert Mill Medal, Royal Meteorolog. Society, 1959; Charles Chree Medal and Prize, Inst. Physics and Phys. Soc., 1965. Hon. DSc Nottingham. *Publications:* The Physics of Clouds, 1957; Clouds, Rain and Rain-Making, 1962; papers in physics and meteorological journals. *Recreations:* foreign travel, music. *Address:* 64 Christchurch Road, East Sheen, SW14. *T:* 01-876 2557. *Club:* Athenæum.

**MASON, Sir Dan (Hurdis),** Kt 1961; OBE 1940; Director, Reckitt & Colman Ltd; *b* 24 July 1911; *e s* of late Charles Mason; *m* 1933, Joyce Louise, *d* of late Horace Young Nutt, Radlett, Herts; three *s* one *d*. *Educ:* Blundell's; Germany. Chm., West London Hospital, 1947-48; Governor, West London Hosp. Med. Sch., 1947-62; Chm., West London Hosp. Med. Trust, 1962-; Chm., Horsham Conservative Assoc., 1951-58; Sussex Conservative Council, 1955-58; Chm., SE Area of Conservative Nat. Union, 1957-62; Chm., Nat. Union of Conservative Assocs, 1966; Mem., Nat. Exec. Cttee of Conservative Party, 1956-; Hon. Treas., Nat. Florence Nightingale Mem. Cttee, 1956-66; Dep. Pres. 1966-. Served War of 1939-45, Royal Engineers (Supplementary Reserve) (OBE). *Recreations:* shooting, do-it-yourself, crosswords. *Address:* Chatley House, Norton St Philip, Bath, Somerset. *T:* Beckington 325. *Club:* Naval and Military.

**MASON, Vice-Adm. Dennis Howard,** CB 1967; *b* 7 Feb. 1916; *s* of Wilfred Howard Mason, Broadwater, Ipswich, and Gladys (Mouse) Mason (*née* Teague), Trevenson, Cornwall; *m* 1940, Patricia D. M. (*née* Hood); three *d*. *Educ:* Royal Naval Coll., Dartmouth. Served War of 1939-45, Coastal Forces, Frigates and Destroyers. Comdr 1951; Captain 1956. Senior Naval Officer, Northern Ireland, 1961-63; Dir RN Tactical Sch., 1964-65; Chief of Staff to Commander, Far East Fleet, 1965-67; Comdt, Jt Services Staff Coll., 1968-70, retired. ADC 1965. *Recreations:* shooting, fishing, gardening. *Club:* Naval and Military.

**MASON, Vice-Adm. Sir Frank (Trowbridge),** KCB 1955 (CB 1953); FIMechE; MIMarE; retired; Director English Electric Diesels Ltd, since 1964; Member of Council for Scientific and Industrial Research, 1958-63 (Vice-Chairman, 1962); *b* 25 April 1900; *s* of late F. J. Mason, MBE, JP; *m* 1924, Dora Margaret Brand; one *s* two *d*. *Educ:* Ipswich Sch. RNC, Keyham, 1918; RN Coll., Greenwich, 1921-22; RN Engineering Coll., Keyham, 1922-23; Fleet Gunnery Engineer Officer, Home Fleet, 1943-44; Chief Gunnery Engineer Officer and Dep. Dir of Naval Ordnance, 1947-48; idc 1949. Deputy Engineer-in-Chief of The Fleet, 1950-52; Staff of C-in-C The Nore, 1952-53; Commander, 1934; Captain, 1943; Rear-Adm., 1950; Vice-Adm., 1953; Engineer-in-Chief of the Fleet, 1953-57, retired. Parsons Memorial Lectr, 1956. Chm. Steering Cttee, Nat. Engineering Laboratory, 1958-69, Chm. Adv. Board, 1969; Mem. Steering Cttee, Nat. Physical Laboratory, 1966-68; Chm., Froude Cttee, 1966. Mem. Council, Institution of Mechanical Engineers, 1953-57, and 1961 (Vice-Pres., 1962, Pres., 1964); Institute of Marine Engineers, 1958 (Chm. of Council, 1962, Vice-Pres. 1963, Pres. 1967); Dep. Chm., Schools Science and Technology Cttee, 1968; Mem. Governing Body: National Council for Technological Awards, 1960-64; Royal Naval Sch., Haslemere, 1953; Ipswich Sch., 1961; Further Education Staff Coll., 1964; Navy League, 1967; Hurstpierpoint Coll., 1967; Brighton Polytechnic, 1969; Mem. Council and Exec. Cttee, City and Guilds of London Inst., 1968. Asst to Court, Worshipful Co. of Shipwrights. Mem. Smeatonian Soc. of Civil Engineers. High Steward of Ipswich, 1967. *Address:* Townfield House, 114 High Street, Hurstpierpoint, Sussex. *T:* 3375. *Club:* United Service.

**MASON, Sir Frederick (Cecil),** KCVO 1968; CMG 1960; Assistant Under-Secretary of State, Foreign and Commonwealth Office, since Oct. 1970; *b* 15 May 1913; *s* of late Ernest Mason and Sophia Charlotte Mason (*née* Dodson); *m* 1941, Karen Rærholm; two *s* one *d* (and two *d* decd). *Educ:* City of London Sch.; St Catharine's Coll., Cambridge. Vice-Consul: Antwerp, 1935-36; Paris, 1936-37; Leopoldville, 1937-39; Elisabethville, 1939-40; Consul at Thorshavn during British occupation of Faroes, 1940-42; Consul, Colon, Panama, 1943-45; First Sec., British Embassy, Santiago, Chile, 1946-48; First Sec. (Information), Oslo, 1948-50; Asst Labour Adviser, FO, 1950-53; First Sec. (Commercial), UK High Commission, Bonn, 1954-55; Counsellor (Commercial), HM Embassy, Athens, 1955-56; Counsellor (Economic), HM Embassy, Tehran, 1957-60; Head of Economic Relations Dept, Foreign Office, 1960-64; Under-Sec., Ministry of Overseas Development, 1965, and CRO, 1966; Ambassador to Chile, 1966-70. Grand Cross, Chilean Order of Merit Bernardo O'Higgins, 1970. *Recreations:* ball games and Sunday painting. *Address:* c/o Foreign and Commonwealth Office, SW1. *Clubs:* Royal Automobile, Canning.

**MASON, (George Frederick) Peter,** QC 1963; **His Honour Judge Mason;** a Deputy Chairman, Inner London Quarter Sessions, since 1970; *b* 11 Dec. 1921; *s* of George Samuel and Florence May Mason, Keighley, Yorks; *m* 1950, Faith Maud Bacon, *e d* of Reginald Kingsley and Janette Maud Bacon, Austwick, near Lancaster; two *s* two *d* (and one *d* decd). *Educ:* Lancaster Royal Grammar Sch.; St Catharine's Coll., Cambridge. Open Exhibnr St Catharine's Coll., 1940. Served with 78th Medium Regt RA (Duke of Lancaster's Own Yeo.) in Middle East and Italy, 1941-45, latterly as Staff Capt. RA, HQ 13 Corps. History Tripos Pt 1, 1st cl. hons with distinction, 1946; called to Bar, Lincoln's Inn, 1947; MA 1948; Cholmeley Schol., 1949. Asst Recorder of Huddersfield, 1961; Dep. Chairman: Agricultural Land Tribunal, W Yorks and Lancs, 1962; West Riding of Yorks, Quarter Sessions, 1965-67; Recorder of York, 1965-67. *Recreations:* fell walking, gardening. *Address:* 11 King's Bench Walk, Temple, EC4. *T:* 01-236 3337; 28 Church Crescent, N10. *Club:* Hawks.

**MASON, Hon. Henry Greathead Rex,** CMG 1967; QC (NZ) 1946; *b* 3 June 1885; *s* of Harry Brooks and Henrietta Emma Mason; *m* 1912, Dulcia Martina Rockell; one *s* two *d* (and one *s* decd). *Educ:* Wellington Coll., New Zealand (Scholar); Victoria University Coll., Wellington (Scholar). BA (NZ) 1906; MA (Hon. Maths and Math. Physics), 1907; LLB 1910; admitted Solicitor, 1909; Barrister, 1923; Practised as Solicitor, Pukekohe, 1911, Auckland, 1923, 1924-42 in partnership with brother, Spencer R. Mason; MP New Zealand, 1926-66 (Eden, 1926-28; Auckland Subs., 1928-46; Waitakere, 1946-63, New Lynn, 1963-66). National President New Zealand Labour Party, 1931; Attorney-General and Minister of Justice, New Zealand, 1935-49; Minister of Education, 1940-47; Native Minister, 1943-46; Attorney-General, Minister of Justice and Minister of Health, 1957-60. Mayor of Pukekohe, 1915-19; Mem. Auckland Transport Board, 1931-39; Chm., 1935-39. Head of New Zealand Delegation to Paris Peace Conference, 1946. Fellow, Royal Numismatical Soc. of NZ (Inc.). Hon. LLD Victoria Univ., Wellington, NZ. *Address:* Flat 12, Newman Court, 16/20 Tinakori Road, Wellington 1, NZ. *T:* 42538.

**MASON, James;** Actor; *b* 15 May 1909; *s* of John Mason and Mabel Gaunt; *m* 1941, Pamela Kellino (marr. diss., 1965); one *s* one *d*. *Educ:* Marlborough Coll.; Peterhouse, Cambridge. Début on professional stage in The Rascal, Hippodrome, Aldershot, 1931; Old Vic, 1933-34; Gate Theatre, Dublin, 1934-35. Début in Films, Late Extra, 1935. *Films include:* I Met a Murderer; Thunder Rock; The Man in Grey; Fanny by Gaslight; A Place of One's Own; They were Sisters; The Seventh Veil; The Wicked Lady; Odd Man Out; The Upturned Glass; Caught; The Reckless Moment; Pandora and the Flying Dutchman; Rommel–Desert Fox; Five Fingers; Julius Caesar; The Man Between; A Star is Born; Bigger than Life; North by North-West; Twenty Thousand Leagues under the Sea; Journey to the Center of the Earth; Touch of Larceny; Lolita; Heroes' Island; Tiara Tahiti; The Fall of the Roman Empire; The Pumpkin Eater; Lord Jim; Les Pianos Mécaniques; The Blue Max; Georgy Girl; The Deadly Affair; Duffy; Mayerling; Age of Consent; The Seagull; Spring and Port Wine. *Publication:* (with Pamela Kellino) The Cats in Our Lives, 1949 (US). *Recreation:* painting. *Address:* c/o Al Parker, Ltd, 50 Mount Street, W1.

**MASON, John Charles Moir;** Director of Trade Development and Deputy Consul-General, New York, since 1968; Counsellor in HM Diplomatic Service; *b* 13 May 1927; *o s* of late Charles Moir Mason, CBE and late Madeline Mason; *m* 1954, Margaret Newton; one *s* one *d*. *Educ:* Manchester Grammar Sch.; Peterhouse, Cambridge. Lieut, XX Lancs Fusiliers, 1946-48; BA 1950, MA 1955, Cantab; Captain, Royal Ulster Rifles, 1950-51 (Korea); HM Foreign Service, 1952; 3rd Sec., FO, 1952-54; 2nd Sec. and Private Sec. to Ambassador, British Embassy, Rome, 1954-56; 2nd Sec., Warsaw, 1956-59; 1st Sec., FO, 1959-61; 1st Sec. (Commercial), Damascus, 1961-65; 1st Sec. and Asst Head of Dept, FO, 1965-68. *Address:* c/o Foreign and Commonwealth Office, SW1. *Club:* Athenæum.

**MASON, Mrs J. R.;** *see* Garland, Ailsa Mary.

**MASON, Lieut-Col Kenneth,** MC; late RE; MA; Professor of Geography, Oxford University, 1932-53; Hon. Fellow of Hertford College, Oxford, 1953; late Superintendent, Survey of India; *b* 10 Sept. 1887; *s* of late Stanley Engledue Mason of Oakhurst, Crofton, Orpington; *m* 1917, Dorothy Helen Robinson; two *s* one *d*. *Educ:* Homefield, Sutton; Cheltenham Coll.; Royal Military Academy, Woolwich. 2nd Lieut Royal Engineers, 1906; Lieut, 1907; Capt., 1914; Brev.-Maj., 1918; Subs.-Maj., 1925; Lieut-Col, 1933; joined Survey of India, 1909; in charge of expedition connecting Indo-Russian Surveys on Pamirs, 1913; in charge Shaksgam Exploration, 1926; awarded Cuthbert Peek Grant by Royal Geographical Society, 1926, and Royal Founders Gold Medal, 1927; Hon. Mem. French Alpine Club, 1930; Councillor Royal Geographical Soc., 1932-45, 1952-54; Vice-Pres., 1937-42; Hon. Fellow, 1965; served European War Western Front, 1914-15 (wounded); Mesopotamia, Persia, etc., 1916-19 (MC, Brevet-Majority, despatches thrice); Attached NID Admlty, 1940-46. Founder and Hon. Editor: The Himalayan Journal, 1928-45. Freeman and Mem. of Court of Drapers' Company, City of London, Master, 1949. Life mem. of Council, Cheltenham Coll.; Pres., Cheltonian Soc., 1958. *Publication:* Abode of Snow, 1955. *Recreations:* mountaineering, travel. *Address:* Appledore, Summerhill Lane, Haywards Heath, Sussex. *Clubs:* Alpine; Himalayan (Calcutta).

**MASON, Rt. Rev. Kenneth Bruce;** *see* Northern Territory, Australia, Bishop of.

**MASON, Ven. Lancelot,** MA; Archdeacon of Chichester since 1946; Canon Residentiary of Chichester Cathedral since 1949; *b* 22 July 1905; *s* of late Canon A. J. Mason, DD; unmarried. *Educ:* RN Colls Osborne and Dartmouth; Trinity Coll., Cambridge. Deacon, 1928; Priest, 1929; Rector of Plumpton, 1938; Chaplain RNVR, 1939-46 (despatches). *Address:* No 2 The Chantry, Canon Lane, Chichester. *T:* Chichester 82902.

**MASON, Michael Henry,** DL 1949; Lieutenant-Commander RNVR, retired; *b* 3 Oct. 1900; *s* of late James Francis and Lady Evelyn Mason, Eynsham Hall, Witney, Oxon.; *m* 1st, 1925, Hon. Annette Sydney Baird (*d* 1950), *e d* of 1st Visc. Stonehaven, PC, GCMG, DSO; no *c*; 2nd, 1951, Dorothy Margaret Sturdee, Thames Ditton, Surrey; two *s* one *d*. *Educ:* Eton; Sandhurst. Has travelled extensively, mostly in wild places, 1939-45, served in the Royal Navy throughout the war; Atlantic, Mediterranean and Far East. High Sheriff of Oxon, 1951. Hon. Director: Royal Agricultural Society of England, 1950-52, and of Oxon Agricultural Soc., 1947-70. CC 1947-61. OStJ 1952. *Publications:* The Arctic Forests, 1924; Deserts Idle, 1928; Trivial Adventures in the Spanish Highlands, 1931; Where Tempests Blow, 1933; Where the River Runs Dry, 1934; The Paradise of Fools, 1936; Spain Untroubled, 1936; The Golden Evening, 1957; The Wild Ass Free, 1959; One Man's War (privately), 1966; In Pursuit of Big Fish, 1969; Willoughby the Immortal, 1969. *Recreations:* wild beasts and birds, sailing. *Address:* Scott's House, Eynsham Park, Witney, Oxon. *T:* Freeland 283. *Clubs:* Beefsteak, White's, Turf, Royal Ocean Racing (Cdre, 1937-47), Special Forces; Royal Yacht Squadron (Cowes); Cruising of America (Hon. Life Mem.); Zerzura; Cabo Blanco Fishing (Peru).

**MASON, Sir Paul,** KCMG 1954 (CMG 1947); KCVO 1958; HM Diplomatic Service, retired; *b* 11 June 1904; *m* 1938, Roberta, *d* of late J. Lorn McDougall, KC, Ottawa; one *s* one *d*. *Educ:* Eton; King's Coll., Cambridge. 1st Cl. Hons Modern History, 1926. Entered Foreign Service, 1928; has served at Brussels, Prague, Ottawa, Lisbon and in Foreign Office; Asst Private Sec. to Sec. of State, 1934-36; Private Sec. to Parliamentary Under Sec. of State, 1936-37; Acting Counsellor, 1945; Minister at Sofia, 1949-51; Asst Under Sec. of State, Foreign Office, 1951-54; Ambassador to The Netherlands, 1954-60; UK Permanent Rep. on N Atlantic Council, 1960-62; Alternate Delegate to Minister of State in Geneva Delegation on Disarmament and Nuclear Tests, 1962-64. High Sheriff of Notts, 1970. Chev. Order of Leopold; Gd Cr., Order of House of Orange, 1958. *Recreations:* various. *Address:* Morton Hall, Retford, Notts. *Club:* Lansdowne.

**MASON, Peter;** *see* Mason, G. F. P.

**MASON, Peter Geoffrey,** MBE 1946; High Master, Manchester Grammar School, since 1962; *b* 22 Feb. 1914; *o s* of Harry Mason, Handsworth, Birmingham; *m* 1939, Mary Evelyn Davison; three *d*. *Educ:* King Edward's Sch., Birmingham; Christ's Coll., Cambridge (Scholar). Goldsmith Exhibitioner, 1935; Porson Scholar, 1936; 1st Class, Classical Tripos, Pts 1 and 2, 1935, 1936. Sixth Form Classical Master, Cheltenham Coll., 1936-40, Rugby Sch., 1946-49; Headmaster, Aldenham Sch., 1949-61. War Service, 1940-46: commissioned into Intelligence Corps, 1940; various staff appointments including HQ 21 Army Group; later attached to a dept of the Foreign Office. Member: Advisory Cttee on Education in the Colonies, 1956; Council, University of Salford; Court of Governors, The University of Manchester Inst. of Science and Technology; Chm., British Volunteer Programme, Council of Educn for World Citizenship; Mem. ITA Educnl Adv. Council, 1964-69. *Publications:* articles and reviews in classical journals. *Recreations:* travel, fly-fishing, squash, tennis. *Address:* 143 Old Hall Lane, Fallowfield, Manchester M14 6HL. *T:* 061-224 3929. *Club:* Athenæum.

**MASON, Philip,** CIE 1946; OBE 1942; writer; Director, Institute of Race Relations, 1958-69; *b* 19 March 1906; *s* of Dr H. A. Mason, Duffield, Derbs; *m* 1935, Eileen Mary, *d* of Courtenay Hayes, Charmouth, Dorset; two *s* two *d*. *Educ:* Sedbergh; Balliol. 1st Cl. Hons Philosophy, Politics and Economics, Oxford, 1927; ICS; Asst Magistrate United Provinces, 1928-33; Under-Sec., Government of India, War Dept, 1933-36; Dep. Commissioner Garhwal, 1936-39; Dep. Sec. Govt of India, Defence Co-ordination and War Depts, 1939-42; Sec. Chiefs of Staff Cttee, India, and Head of Conf. Secretariat, SE Asia Command, 1942-44; represented War Dept in Central Assembly, 1946; Joint Sec. to Government of India, War Dept, 1944-47; Tutor and Governor to the Princes, Hyderabad, 1947; retd from ICS, 1947. Mem. Commn of Enquiry to examine problems of Minorities in Nigeria, 1957. Dir of Studies in Race Relations, Chatham House, 1952-58. Chairman: National Cttee for Commonwealth Immigrants, 1964-65; Exec. Cttee, UK Council for Overseas Student Affairs, 1969. *Publications:* (as Philip Woodruff) Call the Next Witness, 1945; The Wild Sweet Witch, 1947; Whatever Dies, 1948; The Sword of Northumbria, 1948; The Island of Chamba, 1950; Hernshaw Castle, 1950; Colonel of Dragoons, 1951; The Founders, 1953; The Guardians, 1954; (as Philip Mason) Racial Tension, 1954; Christianity and Race, 1956; The Birth of a Dilemma, 1958; Year of Decision, 1960; Common Sense about Race, 1961; Prospero's Magic, 1962; Patterns of Dominance, 1970; Edited: Man, Race and Darwin, 1960; India and Ceylon: Unity and Diversity, 1967; Patterns of Dominance, 1970. *Recreation:* living in the country. *Address:* Hither Daggons, Cripplestyle, Alderholt, near Fordingbridge, Hants. *T:* Cranborne 318. *Club:* Travellers'.

**MASON, Richard;** author; *b* 16 May 1919. *Educ:* Bryanston School. *Publications: novels:* The Wind Cannot Read, 1947; The Shadow and the Peak, 1949; The World of Suzie Wong, 1957; The Fever Tree, 1962. *Address:* c/o A. M. Heath & Co. Ltd, 35 Dover Street, W1.

**MASON, Robert Whyte,** CMG 1956; *b* Glasgow, 1905; *s* of William Whyte Mason and Jane Miller MacKellar Watt; *m* 1952, Monica, *d* of late George H. Powell, Truro. *Educ:* Glasgow Academy; Morrison's Academy, Crieff. Served War of 1939-45, in Army, 1940-45; Lt-Col Gen. Staff, Gen. Headquarters, Middle East; seconded to Ministry of Information as Dir of Policy, Middle East Services, 1943. 1st Sec., British Embassy, Baghdad, 1945; Foreign Office, 1947-48; Political Adviser in Eritrea and Somalia, 1948; 1st Sec. and Consul, British Legation, Amman, 1949; Consul-Gen., Brazzaville, 1951, Chicago, 1954-59; Dir of Research, Librarian and Keeper of the Papers at the Foreign Office, 1960-65. *Publications:* Murder to Measure, 1934; The Slaying Squad, 1934; Courage for Sale, 1939; And the Shouting Dies, 1940; Three Cheers for Treason, 1940; Cairo Communiqué, 1942;

More News from the Middle East, 1943; Arab Agent, 1944; Tandra, 1945; There is a Green Hill, 1946; Tender Leaves, 1950; No Easy Way Out, 1952. *Recreations:* golf, opera; writing thrillers. *Address:* 25 Sussex Square, Brighton 7. *T:* 685093. *Club:* Travellers'.

**MASON, Rt. Hon. Roy,** PC 1968; MP (Lab) Barnsley since March 1953; *b* 18 April 1924; *s* of Joseph and Mary Mason; *m* 1945, Marjorie Sowden; two *d. Educ:* Carlton Junior Sch.; Royston Senior Sch.; London Sch. of Economics (TUC course). National Union of Mineworkers branch official, 1947-53; mem. of Yorks Miners' Council, 1949-53; Minister of State (Shipping), Bd of Trade, 1964-67; Minister of Defence (Equipment), 1967-April 1968; Postmaster-Gen., April-June 1968; Minister of Power, 1968-69; President, Bd of Trade, 1969-70. *Address:* 12 Victoria Avenue, Barnsley, Yorks.

**MASON, Walter W.;** *see* Wynne Mason.

**MASSEREENE and FERRARD,** 13th Viscount, *cr* 1660; **John Clotworthy Talbot Foster Whyte-Melville Skeffington;** Baron of Loughneagh, 1660; Baron Oriel, 1790; Viscount Ferrard, 1797; Baron Oriel (UK), 1821; DL; *b* 23 Oct. 1914; *s* of 12th Viscount (*d* 1956) and Jean Barbara (*d* 1937), *e d* of Sir John Stirling Ainsworth, MP, JP, 1st Bt, of Ardanaiseig, Argyllshire; *S* father 1956; *m* 1939, Annabelle Kathleen, *er d* of late Henry D. Lewis and of Mrs Henry D. Lewis, Combwell Priory, Hawkhurst, Kent; one *s* one *d. Educ:* Eton. Lt, Black Watch SR, 1933-36, re-employed, 1939-40 (invalided); retired; served in Small Vessels Pool, Royal Navy, 1944. Dir of public and private cos; Freeman, City of London, and Mem. Worshipful Company of Shipwrights. Posts in Conservative Constituency organizations. Patron of one Living. One of original pioneers in commercial development of Cape Canaveral, Florida; presented operetta Countess Maritza at Palace Theatre, London. Driver of leading British car, Le Mans Grand Prix, 1937. Jt Master, Ashford Valley Foxhounds, 1953-54. Gold Staff Officer, Coronation, 1953. Mem. of inter-Parliamentary Union Delegation to Spain, 1960; Whip, Conservative Peers Cttee (IUP), House of Lords, 1958-65, Jt Dep. Chm., 1965-; in change: Deer Act, 1963, House of Lords; Riding Establishments Act, 1964, House of Lords; introduced: Export of Animals for Research Bill, 1968; Riding Establishments Act, 1970; moved debates on Overseas Information Services and other matters. Pres. of Charitable and other organisations. Chm. Kent Branch Victoria League. Treasurer Kent Assoc. of Boys' Clubs. Promoted first scheduled air service Glasgow-Oban-Isle of Mull, 1968. DL Antrim, 1957. *Publications:* contributes articles to newspapers, chiefly sporting and natural history. *Recreations:* all field sports; farming; forestry; racing. *Heir: s* Hon. John David Clotworthy Whyte-Melville Skeffington, *b* 3 June 1940. *Address:* Knock, Isle of Mull, Argyll. *T:* Aros 56; (Seat) Chilham Castle, Kent. *T:* Chilham 319. *Clubs:* Carlton, Turf, Pratt's.

**MASSEVITCH, Prof. Alla;** Vice-President of the Astronomical Council of the USSR Academy of Sciences since 1952; Professor of Astrophysics, Moscow University, since 1946; *b* Tbilisi, Georgia, USSR, 9 Oct. 1918; *m* 1942; one *d. Educ:* Moscow Univ. Lectured at the Royal Festival Hall, London, and at the Free Trade Hall, Manchester, etc., on The Conquest of Space, 1960; she is in charge of network of stations for tracking Sputniks, in Russia. Pres. Working Group 1 (Tracking and Telemetring) of COSPAR (Internat. Cttee for Space Research) 1961-66. Pres., Commission 35 (Internal Structure of Stars) of the Internat. Astronom. Union, 1967. Foreign Mem. Royal Astronomical Society, 1963. Internat. Award for Astronautics (Prix Galabert), 1963; Mem. Internat. Acad. Astronautics, 1964. *Publications:* 79 scientific papers on the internal structure of the stars, stellar evolution, and optical tracking of artificial satellites, in Russian and foreign astronomical and geophysical journals. *Address:* 34 Ulitsa Vavilova, Moscow, USSR. *T:* 1355481; 1 Vosstania Ploshad 403, Moscow. *Club:* Club for Scientists (Moscow).

**MASSEY, Anna (Raymond);** Actress; *b* 11 Aug. 1937; *d* of Raymond Massey, *qv*, and of Adrianne Allen; *m* 1958, Jeremy Huggins (marriage dissolved, 1963); one *s. Educ:* London; New York; Switzerland; Paris; Rome. *Plays:* The Reluctant Debutante, 1955; Dear Delinquent, 1957; The Elder Statesman, 1958; Double Yolk, 1959; The Last Joke, 1960; The Miracle Worker, 1961; The School for Scandal, 1962; The Doctor's Dilemma, 1963; The Right Honourable Gentleman, 1964; The Glass Menagerie, 1965; The Prime of Miss Jean Brodie, 1966; The Flip Side, 1967. *Films:* Gideon's Day, 1957; Peeping Tom, 1960; Bunny Lake is Missing, 1965; The Looking Glass War, 1969; David Copperfield, 1969; Hamlet, 1970. *Recreations:* letter writing and crossword puzzles. *Address:* 14 Herbert Crescent, SW1.

**MASSEY, Sir Arthur,** Kt 1956; CBE 1941; Chief Medical Officer, Ministry of Pensions and National Insurance, 1947-59, retired; *b* 1894; *s* of late Albert Massey, Keighley, Yorks; *m* 1924, Dorothy Blanche Ince, *d* of late Rev. H. H. T. Cleife, MA Cantab; one *d. Educ:* University of Leeds, MD, etc; Hon. Fellow, American Public Health Assoc.; Vice-President: Royal Society Health; Vocational Guidance Assoc.; KHP, 1950-52; QHP, 1952-53; Examiner in Public Health, Universities of London and Bristol, 1947-50, and Birmingham, 1952-55; MOH, City of Coventry, 1930-46. Chairman: Chadwick Trust, 1969-; Central Council for Health Educn, 1944-46. Lecturer in USA 1944, Yale Univ. 1954. Served 1915-18 in RFA (Lt), and 1943-45 in HG (Lt-Col, Zone Medical Adviser). *Publications:* Epidemiology and Air Travel, 1933; (ed) Modern Trends in Public Health, 1949; various contributions to the medical literature on hospital policy, public health and social insurance. *Recreations:* bridge, gardening, watching cricket. *Address:* 93 Bedford Gardens, W8. *T:* 01-727 6951. *Club:* Athenæum.

*See also Sir W. J. Rowley, Bt.*

**MASSEY, Sir Harrie Stewart Wilson,** Kt 1960; FRS 1940; BA, MSc Melbourne; PhD Cantab; Hon. DSc: Belfast; Leicester 1964; Hull 1968; LLD Melbourne; Hon. LLD Glasgow 1962; Quain Professor of Physics, University College, London, since 1950; *b* 1908; *s* of Harrie and Eleanor Massey, Melbourne, Australia; *m* Jessica, *d* of Alex and Alice Mary Barton Bruce, Western Australia; one *d. Educ:* University High Sch., Melbourne; Melbourne Univ.; Trinity Coll., Cambridge; Aitchison Travelling Scholar, Melbourne Univ., 1929-31; Research at Cavendish Laboratory, Cambridge, 1929-33; Exhibition of 1851 Senior Research Student, 1931-33; Independent Lecturer in Mathematical Physics, Queen's Univ., Belfast, 1933-38; Goldsmid Prof. of Mathematics, University of London, University Coll., 1938-50. Rutherford Memorial Lectr, 1967. Temp. Senior Experimental Officer, Admiralty Research Laboratory, 1940; Dep. Chief Scientist, 1941-

43, Chief Scientist, 1943, Mine Design Dept, Admiralty; Technical Officer, DSIR Mission to Berkeley, Calif, 1943-45. Vice-President: Atomic Scientists Assoc., 1949-53 (Pres. 1953-57), Royal Astronomical Society, 1950-53; Council Member: Royal Society, 1949-51, 1959-60 (Physical Sec., and Vice-Pres., 1970-); Physical Soc., 1949- (Pres. 1954-56). Mem., Governing Board of National Institute for Research in Nuclear Science, 1957-65. Governor: Rugby Sch., 1955-59; Chelsea Polytechnic, 1956-59; Chm. Brit. Nat. Cttee for Space Research, 1959-; Mem. Bureau of Cttee on Space Research, 1959-; Mem. Advisory Council of the Science Museum, 1959-61; Pres. European Prep. Commn for Space Research, 1960-64; Pres. Council European Space Research Organization, 1964; Chm. Council for Scientific Policy, 1965-69; Mem., Central Advisory Council for Science and Technology, 1967-69. Vice-Provost, University Coll., London, 1969-. Hughes Medal, Royal Society, 1955; Royal Medal, Royal Society, 1958. *Publications:* Theory of Atomic Collisions (with N. F. Mott), 1933, 3rd ed., 1965; Negative Ions, 1938, 2nd edn, 1951; Electronic and Ionic Impact Phenomena (with E. H. S. Burhop), 1952, 2nd edn 1969; Atoms and Energy, 1953; The Upper Atmosphere (with R. L. F. Boyd), 1958; Ancillary Mathematics (with H. Kestelman), 1958; New Age in Physics, 1960; Space Physics, 1964; various publications on atomic physics in Proc. of Royal Society and other scientific jls. *Recreations:* cricket, tennis, billiards and snooker, badminton, travel, study of other sciences. *Address:* Kalamunda, Pelhams Walk, Esher, Surrey. *Club:* Athenæum.

**MASSEY, Raymond;** Actor and Producer; *b* Toronto, Canada, 30 Aug. 1896; *s* of Chester D. Massey and Anna Vincent; *m* 3rd, Dorothy, *d* of Dr Nelson Amos Ludington; two *s* one *d* (*see* Anna Massey) by previous marriages. *Educ:* Appleby Sch., Ontario; Toronto Univ.; Balliol Coll., Oxford. Hon. DLitt Lafayette Univ. 1939; Hon. LLD Queen's Univ., Kingston, Ontario, 1949; Hon. LittD Hobart Coll., NY, 1953; Hon. Dr Fine Arts: Northwestern Univ., 1959, Ripon Coll., 1962, Wooster Coll., 1966; Hon. Dr Hum., American International Coll., 1960. Served European War, 1915-19 as Lt in Canadian Field Artillery; in France, 1916 (wounded), in USA as Instructor in Field Artillery at Yale and Princeton Univs, 1917 and in Siberia, 1918; staff of Adj.-Gen. Canadian Army, rank of Major, 1942-43; naturalized US Citizen, March 1944. First appearance on professional stage at Everyman Theatre, 1922, in In the Zone, Jonty in The Round Table, played Captain La Hire and Canon D'Estivet in Saint Joan, 1924; in 1926 with Allan Wade and George Carr, entered on management of the Everyman Theatre, producing a number of plays and taking a variety of parts; played James Bebb in At Mrs Beam's, the Khan Aghaba in The Transit of Venus, the Rev. MacMillan in An American Tragedy, Robert in Beyond the Horizon, 1926, and Reuben Manassa in the Golden Calf, 1927; Austin Lowe in The Second Man, Joe Cobb in Spread Eagle, and Lewis Dodd in The Constant Nymph, 1928; Randolph Calthorpe in The Black Ace, 1929; Raymond Dabney in The Man in Possession, 1930; Topaze in Topaze, 1930; Randall in Late Night Final, 1931; Hamlet in the Norman Bel Geddes production at Broadhurst Theatre, New York, 1931; Smith in Never Come Back, 1932; Hugh Sebastian in The Rats of Norway; Von Hagen in the Ace, 1933; David Linden in the Shining Hour: At Booth Theatre, New York, 1934, and at St James' Theatre, 1935; Ethan in Ethan Frome, at the National Theatre, New York, 1936; at Apollo Theatre 1938, presented with Henry Sherek, Idiot's Delight, playing the part of Harry Van; Abraham Lincoln in Abe Lincoln in Illinois, Plymouth Theatre, New York, 1938-39; toured the US in this play, 1939-40; in The Doctor's Dilemma, Candida, Pygmalion, Lovers and Friends, The Father, John Brown's Body, The Rivalry, J. B.; I Never Sang for my Father, Duke of York's, 1970. Productions include: The White Chateau, The Crooked Billet, Spread Eagle, The Sacred Flame, The Stag, The Silver Tassie, Symphony in Two Flats, The Man in Possession, Lean Harvest, Late Night Final, Grand Hotel, The Rats of Norway, The Shining Hour, Idiot's Delight and J.B. *Films played-in include:* The Scarlet Pimpernel, The Old Dark House, Things to Come, Fire Over England, Under the Red Robe, The Prisoner of Zenda, The Hurricane, The Drum, Abe Lincoln in Illinois, Santa Fé Trail, Reap the Wild Wind, Arsenic and Old Lace, Invaders (49th Parallel), Action in the North Atlantic, The Woman in the Window, God is my Co-Pilot, Hotel Berlin, A Matter of Life and Death, Possessed, Mourning Becomes Electra, Fountainhead, David and Bathsheba, Come Fill the Cup, East of Eden, The Naked and the Dead, The Queen's Guards. Co-star, as "Dr Gillespie" in Television series Dr Kildare. Author of play, The Hanging Judge, produced New Theatre, London, 1952. *Recreations:* golf, carpentry. *Address:* 913 Beverly Drive, Beverly Hills, California 90210, USA. *Clubs:* Garrick, Century (New York).

**MASSEY, William Edmund Devereux,** CBE 1961; retired from HM Diplomatic Service; *b* 1901; *m* 1942, Ingrid Glad-Block, Oslo; one *d*. Entered Foreign Office, 1922; served in diplomatic and consular posts in Poland, France, Japan, Brazil, Roumania, Sweden, Luxembourg, Germany; Ambassador and Consul-General to Nicaragua, 1959-61. Hon. Consul for Nicaragua in London, 1969-. Freeman of City of London. Representative in Sweden of Order of St John of Jerusalem, 1945-47. Chm., Permanent Cttee on Geographical Names. FRGS. Grand Ducal Commemorative Medal, Luxembourg, 1953. *Address:* 59 Redcliffe Gardens, SW10. *T:* 01-370 2552.

**MASSIAH, Sir (Hallam) Grey,** KBE 1966 (CBE 1956); Kt 1960; President of Legislative Council, Barbados, since 1958; MLC Barbados since 1943; *b* 18 July 1888; *s* of Hon. Hallam Massiah, MD, Barbados, and Florette Massiah; *m* 1915, Enid Leger (decd), Montreal; one *s* one *d*. *Educ:* Lodge Sch., Barbados; Durham Univ.; McGill Univ., Montreal. BA 1910, MA 1932, Durham; MD, CM 1915, McGill. Police Surg., Barbados, 1918-48; Visiting Surg., Gen. Hosp., Barbados, 1919-48. *Recreations:* book collecting, shooting. *Address:* Merton Lodge, Highgate Gardens, Barbados, West Indies. *T:* Barbados 7644. *Clubs:* Royal Commonwealth Society; Savannah, Bridgetown, Royal Barbados Yacht (Barbados).

**MASSIGLI, René,** (Hon.) GCVO 1950; (Hon.) KBE 1938; (Hon.) CH 1954; Grand Cross, Legion of Honour, 1954; French President of Channel Tunnel Study Group since 1958; *b* 22 March 1888; *s* of late Charles Massigli and late Marguerite Michel; *m* 1932, Odette Boissier; one *d*. *Educ:* Ecole normale supérieure. Mem. of the Ecole Française de Rome, 1910-13; Chargé de cours at the University of Lille, 1913-14; Gen. Sec. at the Conference of Ambassadors, 1920; Maître des Requêtes at the Conseil d'Etat, 1924-28; Ministre plénipotentiaire, Head of the League of Nations' Section at the Ministry of Foreign

Affairs, 1928-33; Asst Dir of Political Section at the Ministry of Foreign Affairs, 1933-37, Dir, 1937-38; Ambassador to Turkey, 1939-40; escaped from France, 1943; Commissioner for Foreign Affairs, French Cttee of National Liberation, 1943-44; French Ambassador to Great Britain, Sept. 1944-Jan. 1955; Sec.-Gen. at the Quai d'Orsay, Jan. 1955-June 1956; retired 1956. *Publications:* Quelques Maladies de l'Etat, 1958; La Turquie devant la guerre, 1964. *Address:* 3 Avenue d'Orsay, Paris 7e.

**MASSINE, Leonide;** Choreographer; *b* Moscow, 9 Aug. 1896; *s* of Teodor Affanasievitch and Eugenia Nikolaevna; *m* 1939, Tatiana Vladimirovna Milisnikova; one *s* one *d*. *Educ:* Imperial Ballet Sch., Moscow; pupil of Domashoff, Enrico Cecchetti and Nicolas Legat. Choreographer and principal dancer, Diaghilev Ballet Russe, 1914-20; choreographer, dancer, and artistic dir, Ballet de Monte Carlo, 1932-41; National Ballet Theatre, NY, 1941-44; organized Ballet Russe Highlights, 1945-46; guest artiste and choreographer: Sadler's Wells Ballet, Covent Garden, Royal Opera House, Copenhagen, Teatro Alla Scala, Milan, Opéra-Comique, Paris, 1947-51. Edinburgh Festival 1960; Ballets Européens de Nervi. *Ballets:* Soleil de Nuit, 1915; Las Meninas, 1916; Good Humoured Ladies, Contes Russes, Parade, 1917; La Boutique Fantasque, Le Tricorne, 1919; Le Sacre du Printemps, Le Astuzie Feminili, Pulcinella, Le Rossignol, 1920; Salade, Gigue, Le Beau Danube, Les Facheux, 1924; Les Matelots, Zephire et Flore, 1925; Cimarosiana, 1926; Le Pas d'Acier, Ode, Mercure, 1927; Les Enchantements d'Alcine, Le Roi David, Amphion, 1929-30; Le Beau Danube (2nd version), Belkis, Vecchia Milano, La Belle Hélène, 1932; Les Présages, Les Jeux d'Enfants, The Miracle, 1933; Choreartium, Scuola di Ballo, 1933-34; Le Bal, Union Pacific, Jardin Public, 1935; Symphonie Fantastique, 1936; Gaité Parisienne, Seventh Symphony, St Francis (Nobilissima Visione), 1938; Capriccio Espagnol, Rouge et Noir, Bogatyri, Bacchanal, 1939; Wien 1814, The New Yorker, 1940; Labyrinth, Saratoga, 1941; Aleko, Don Domingo, 1942; Mlle Angot, 1943; Antar, Daphnis et Chloe, Unfortunate Painter, Rêverie Classique, Moonlight Sonata, Mad Tristan, 1944; Bullet in the Ballet, Les Arabesques (revived), Les Matelots (rev.), 1945-46; Boutique Fantasque, Tricorne (rev.), 1946; Mam'selle Angot (2nd version), 1947; Capriccio (de Stravinsky), Episode de la Vie d'un Artiste, Clock Symphony, Sacre du Printemps (rev.), 1948; Quattro Stagioni, Mad Tristan (rev.), Good Humoured Ladies (rev.), Suite Bergamasque, Le Peintre et son Modèle, 1949; La Valse (de Ravel), 1950; Le Bal du Pont du Nord, Symphonie Allégorique (Les Saisons), Donald of the Burthens, Capriccio Espagnol (rev.), 1951; (created) Laudes Evangelli, M'selle Angot (rev.), dances for: Wilhelm Tell, Armida, Didone, Gioconda, 1952; Rezurrezione e Vita, 1954, Arianna, 1954; Commedia Umana, 1960; Le Bal des Voleurs, 1960. *Staged:* for Royal Ballet, 1968: Boutique Fantasque; Mam'selle Angot. *Films:* (prod. dances and appeared) Carnival in Costa Rica, 1945; (comp. and danced his part): Red Shoes, 1948; Tales of Hoffmann, 1951; Carosello Napoletano, 1953. *Publication:* My Life in Ballet, 1968.

**MASSY,** family name of **Baron Massy.**

**MASSY,** 9th Baron *cr* 1776; **Hugh Hamon John Somerset Massy;** *b* 11 June 1921; *o s* of 8th Baron, and of Margaret, 2nd *d* of late Richard Leonard, Meadsbrook, Ashbourne, Co. Limerick, and *widow* of Dr Moran, Tara, Co. Meath; *S* father 1958; *m* 1943, Margaret, *d* of late John Flower, Barry, Co. Meath; four *s* one *d*. *Educ:* Clongowes Wood Coll.; Clayesmore Sch. Served War, 1940-45, Private, RAOC. *Heir: s* Hon. David Hamon Somerset Massy, *b* 4 March 1947. *Address:* 14 Lutterworth Road, Leicester.

**MASSY, Brig. Charles Walter,** CBE 1940; DSO 1918; MC; *b* 2 May 1887; *s* of late Arthur W. Massy, Cuffern, Roch, Pembrokeshire, and Cottesmore, Haverfordwest; *m* 1st, 1920, Muriel Lorna, *d* of J. A. Hallinan, Glandalane, Fermoy; two *s*; 2nd, 1958, Irene Gillbee, *d* of late Richard Gillbee Thorold, and *widow* of Clifford Hackney, MRCS. *Educ:* Cheltenham Coll.; RMA Woolwich. 2nd Lt RFA, 1907; Lt 1910; Captain 1914; Major, 1917; Lt-Col 1935; Col 1938; retired pay, 1942; served in France in RHA and RFA, 1914-18 (DSO, MC, despatches twice). Served in France, 1940. DL Monmouthshire, 1948-55. *Recreation:* fishing. *Address:* Tiddler's Well, Dalditch Lane, Budleigh Salterton, Devon. *Club:* Pembrokeshire County (Haverfordwest).

**MASTER, Alfred,** CIE 1931; DPhil; ICS (retired); Assistant Keeper, India Office Library, 1951-57; *b* 12 Feb. 1883; *s* of George Reginald Master, MRCS, late of Sheringham; *m* 1909, Dorothy Amy (*d* 1952), *d* of Rev. H. A. Thorne; three *d*. *Educ:* Epsom Coll.; BNC, Oxford (MA; DPhil 1962). Entered ICS, 1906; Municipal Commissioner, Ahmadabad, 1917; Military Mission to Turkestan, Persia, 1918; officiating Sec. to Government of Bombay, General Dept, 1925; Collector of Bombay City and Suburbs, 1932-34; Lecturer: in Marathi, 1937-38; in Gujarati, 1938-39, in Indian Philology, 1944-50, at the School of Oriental and African Studies, London Univ.; Member Governing Body, School of Oriental and African Studies, 1952-60. *Publications:* Introduction to Telugu Grammar, 1947; Catalogue of the Gujarati & Rajasthani Manuscripts in the India Office Library by J. F. Blumhardt, revised and enlarged, 1954; A Grammar of Old Marathi, 1964; English edn of L'Indo-Aryen, by Jules Bloch, 1965; articles in journals on Local Government, Linguistics, and Numismatics. *Address:* Woodchurch, Burleigh Road, Ascot, Berks. *T:* 22897. *Club:* Royal Commonwealth Society.

**MASTERMAN, Sir Christopher Hughes,** Kt, *cr* 1947; CSI 1944; CIE 1939; ICS (retired); *b* 7 Oct. 1889; *s* of late Capt. J. Masterman, RN; *m* 1921, Hope Gladys, *d* of late Henry Gearing; two *s*. *Educ:* Winchester; Trinity Coll., Oxford, MA. Entered Indian Civil Service, 1914; Sec. to Govt Education and Public Health Depts, Madras, 1936-39; Collector and District Magistrate, Vizagapatam, 1939-42; Mem. Board of Revenue, Madras, 1943; Chief Sec. and Adviser to the Governor of Madras, 1946; Deputy High Commissioner for UK, Madras, 1947. *Address:* Homefield, North Bovey, Devon.

**MASTERMAN, Sir John (Cecil),** Kt 1959; OBE 1944; Royal Order of Crown of Yugoslavia (3rd cl.), 1945; Provost of Worcester College, Oxford, 1947-61; MA; Hon. LLD Toronto; Hon. DCL University of King's College, Halifax, NS; Hon. DLitt Heriot-Watt University; Hon. Fellow Worcester College, Oxford; Hon. Student of Christ Church, Oxford; Hon. Fellow St Catharine's College, Cambridge; *b* 12 Jan. 1891; *s* of late Captain J. Masterman, Royal Navy, JP. *Educ:* Royal Naval Colleges, Osborne and Dartmouth; Worcester Coll., Oxford (Sch.); Freiburg Univ. Midshipman 1908. First Class Mod. Hist. Sch., Oxford, 1913; Lecturer, Christ Church, 1913; Student of Christ Church, 1919-46; Censor of Christ Church, 1920-26;

Interned in Germany, 1914-18. Lieut Intelligence Corps, 1940; Major (Local) and specially employed, 1941-45. Represented OUAC v. Cambridge, 1912-13; represented England at lawn tennis v. Ireland and Scotland, 1920; represented England at hockey v. Scotland, Ireland, and France, 1925, and v. Scotland, 1927; MCC Canadian Tour, 1937. Governor, Wellington Coll., 1944-65; Fellow of Eton, 1942-64. Mem. Governing Body: Cranleigh Sch., 1935-47; Eastbourne Coll., 1926-57; Atlantic Coll., 1962-68; Governor, St Edward's Sch., 1944-58. Chm. of Cttee on the Political Activities of Civil Servants, 1948; Chm. Army Education Advisory Board, 1952-56; Mem. BBC Gen. Advisory Council, 1952-59. Adviser on personnel matters to Birfield Ltd, 1961-68. Vice-Chancellor, Oxford Univ., 1957-58. Pres. Oxfordshire County Cricket Club, 1956-65. *Publications:* An Oxford Tragedy, 1933; Fate Cannot Harm Me, 1935; Marshal Ney, 1937; To Teach the Senators Wisdom or An Oxford Guide Book, 1952; The Case of the Four Friends, 1957; Bits and Pieces, 1961; The XX System in the War of 1939 to 1945. *Recreations:* cricket and other games. *Address:* 6 Beaumont Street, Oxford OX1 2LR. *Clubs:* United University, MCC; Vincent's (Oxford).

**MASTERS, John,** DSO 1944; OBE 1945; Author; *b* 26 Oct. 1914; *s* of John Masters, 16th Rajputs, and Ada (*née* Coulthard); *m*; one *s* one *d* (one *d* decd). *Educ:* Wellington; RMC, Sandhurst. Commissioned 2nd Lieut, Indian Army, 1934; 2nd Bn, 4th PWO Gurkha Rifles, 1935; Adjutant, 1939; Comdt 3rd Bn, 1944; Bde Major, 114 Ind. Inf. Bde, 1942; 111 Ind. Inf. Bde, 1943; GSO1 19 Ind. Div., 1945; GSO1, MO1, GHQ (I), 1946; GSO2 Staff Coll., Camberley, 1947; retired 1948. Active service: NW Frontier, 1936-37; Iraq, Syria, Persia, 1941; Burma, 1944-45. *Publications:* Nightrunners of Bengal, 1951; The Deceivers, 1952; The Lotus and the Wind, 1953; Bhowani Junction, 1954; Coromandel, 1955; Bugles and a Tiger, 1956; Far, Far the Mountain Peak, 1957; Fandango Rock, 1959; The Venus of Konpara, 1960; The Road Past Mandalay, 1961; To the Coral Strand, 1962; Trial at Monomoy, 1964; Fourteen Eighteen, 1965; The Breaking Strain, 1967; The Rock, 1969. *Recreations:* mountains, railways. *Address:* c/o Viking Press, Inc., 18 E 48th Street, New York City, NY 10017, USA.

**MASTERTON, William,** CA; Finance Director, British Aircraft Corporation (Holdings), since 1960; *b* 20 April 1913; *s* of John Crichton Masterton, Solicitor, and Margaret Bower Masterton (*née* Hunter); *m* 1955, Kathlyn Aimee Milligan. *Educ:* Waid Academy; Edinburgh University. Qualified CA, Edinburgh, 1935; Thomson McLintoch & Co., London, 1935-39; joined Bristol Aeroplane Co., 1939; Sec., 1946; Finance Dir, 1952; Dep. Chm., 1964; Chairman: Bristol Aeroplane Co., 1968-69; Bristol Aerojet, 1967-69; Dep. Chm., British Aircraft Corp., 1965-; Director: Bristol Siddeley Engines, 1959-67; Short Bros & Harland, 1964-69; Rolls Royce Ltd, 1966-69; Rolls Royce Holdings, Canada, 1968-69; Lloyds Bank, Regional Board, 1967-. *Recreations:* golf, gardening. *Address:* Mount Elton, Clevedon, Som. *T:* Clevedon 3238.

**MASTON, Charles James,** CB 1965; CBE 1954; Assistant Under-Secretary of State, Department of Employment and Productivity; *b* 15 May 1912; *s* of James and Amelia Maston; *m* 1940, Eileen Sybil Stopher; no *c*. *Educ:* Yeadon and Guiseley Secondary Sch.; Bradford Gram. Sch.; St John's Coll., Cambridge. Asst Principal, Min. of Labour, 1934; Asst Private Sec. to Minister, 1937-39; Principal, 1939. Served HM Forces, 1942-44. Asst Sec., Min. of Labour (became Dept of Employment and Productivity, 1968), 1944; Industrial Relations Dept, 1953-56; Under Sec. Military Recruitment Dept 1957-60; Employment Dept, 1960-64; Industrial Relations Dept, 1964-65; Safety, Health and Welfare Dept, 1965-68; Employment Services Div., 1968-. *Recreations:* hill walking, philately. *Address:* Flaska, Doggetts Wood Lane, Chalfont St Giles, Bucks. *T:* Little Chalfont 2033. *Club:* Royal Automobile.

**MATCHAN, Leonard Joseph;** Chairman, Cope Allman International Ltd, and other companies; *b* 26 March 1911; *s* of late George Matchan and Elsie Harriet Greenleaf; *m* 1933, Kathleen Artis; one *s* one *d*. *Educ:* Trinity, Croydon. FACCA; JDipMA; Certified Accountant. Vice President and European General Manager, Max Factor, Hollywood, 1936-50. Practice as accountant, 1950-55; Chairman, Cope Allman International Ltd, 1955-. President, Toilet Preparations Assoc., 1940-48. *Recreation:* work. *Address:* Island of Brecqhou, Channel Islands. *T:* Brecqhou 1.

**MATHER, Carol;** *see* Mather, David Carol MacDonell.

**MATHER, (David) Carol (MacDonell),** MC 1944; MP (C) Esher since 1970; *b* 3 Jan. 1919; *s* of Loris Emerson Mather, *qv*; *m* 1951, Hon. Philippa Selina Bewicke-Copley, *o d* of 5th Baron Cromwell, DSO; one *s* three *d*. *Educ:* Harrow; Trinity Coll., Cambridge. War of 1939-45: commissioned Welsh Guards, 1940; served with Commandos, Special Air Service; Western Desert Campaigns, 1941-42; PoW, 1942; escaped, 1943; NW Europe, 1944-45; wounded, 1945; Palestine Campaign, 1946-48. Asst Mil. Attaché, British Embassy, Athens, 1953-56; GSO 1, MI Directorate, War Office, 1957-61; Mil. Sec. to GOC-in-C, Eastern Command, 1961-62; retd as Lt-Col., 1962. Conservative Research Dept, 1962-70. Councillor, Eton Rural Dist., 1965; contested (C) Leicester (NW), 1966. *Address:* Brookfield, Horton, near Slough, Bucks. *Clubs:* Brooks's; St Stephen's.
*See also Sir W. L. Mather.*

**MATHER, Prof. Kenneth,** CBE 1956; FRS 1949; DSc (London), 1940; Vice-Chancellor, the University of Southampton, August 1965-Sept. 1971; *b* 22 June 1911; *e c* and *o s* of R. W. Mather; *m* 1937, Mona Rhodes; one *s*. *Educ:* Nantwich and Acton Grammar Sch.; University of Manchester (BSc 1931). Ministry of Agriculture and Fisheries Research Scholar, 1931-34; Lecturer in Galton Laboratory, University Coll., London, 1934-37; Rockefeller Research Fellow, at California Institute of Technology and Harvard University, 1937-38; Head of Genetics Dept, John Innes Horticultural Institution, 1938-48; Professor of Genetics, University of Birmingham 1948-65. Member: Agricultural Research Council, 1949-54, 1955-60, and 1969-; Science Research Council, 1965-69; Academic Adv. Cttee of Bath Univ. of Technology, 1967-; Ministry of Health Advisory Cttee on the Irradiation of Food, 1967-; Wessex Regional Hosp. Bd, 1968-. *Publications:* The Measurement of Linkage in Heredity, 1938; Statistical Analysis in Biology, 1943; Biometrical Genetics, 1950; Human Diversity, 1964; The Elements of Biometry, 1967. (Jointly): The Elements of Genetics, 1950; Genes, Plants and People, 1950. Many papers on Genetics, Cytology, and Statistics. *Address:* The University, Southampton SO9 5NH. *T:* 56331.

**MATHER, Leonard Charles;** Director and Chief General Manager, Midland Bank Ltd, since 1968; Director: Midland Bank Executor & Trustee Co. Ltd, since 1968; Midland & International Banks Ltd, since 1969; Montagu Trust, since 1969; Vice-President, Institute of Bankers, since 1969; *b* 10 Oct. 1909; *s* of Richard and Elizabeth Mather; *m* 1937, Muriel Armor Morris. *Educ:* Oldershaw Sch., Wallasey. BCom. (London). Entered Midland Bank, Dale Street, Liverpool, 1926; transf. to London, 1937; served in Gen. Managers' Dept at Head Office, 1937-45; Man., Bolton, 1945-48; Princ., Legal Dept, 1948-50; Asst Gen. Man., 1950-56; Gen. Man., Midland Bank Executor & Trustee Co. Ltd, 1956-58; Jt Gen. Man., Midland Bank Ltd, 1958-63; Asst Chief Gen. Man., 1964-66; Dep. Chief Gen. Man., 1966-68. FCIS; FIB (Dep. Chm., 1967-69; Pres., 1969-70); *Publications:* The Lending Banker, 1955; Banker and Customer Relationship and the Accounts of Personal Customers, 1956; The Accounts of Limited Company Customers, 1958; Securities Acceptable to the Lending Banker, 1960. *Recreations:* golf, bridge. *Address:* Rochester House, Parkfield, Seal, Sevenoaks, Kent. *T:* Sevenoaks 61007. *Club:* East India and Sports.

**MATHER, Loris Emerson,** CBE 1945; FIMechE; retired as Chairman Mather & Platt, Ltd, 1960; *b* Manchester 1886; *s* of late Rt Hon. Sir William Mather, LLD, MICE; *m* 1912, Leila, *d* of late John S. Morley; two *s* one *d*. *Educ:* Harrow; Trinity Coll., Cambridge; Germany. Commission in RE (TA), 1909-19 (Captain); Member, Royal Commission of Awards to Inventors, 1953-55. *Address:* Meadow Croft, Parkside, SW19. *T:* 01-946 4672. *Club:* United University.

*See also D. C. M. Mather, Sir W. L. Mather.*

**MATHER, Sir William (Loris),** Kt 1968; OBE 1957; MC 1945; TD and 2 clasps 1949; MA, CEng, FIMechE; DL; Chairman, Mather & Platt Ltd, Manchester, since 1960; *b* 17 Aug. 1913; *s* of Loris Emerson Mather, *qv*; *m* 1937, Eleanor, *d* of Prof. R. H. George, Providence, RI, USA; two *s* two *d*. *Educ:* Oundle; Trinity Coll., Cambridge (MA Engrg and Law, 1939). Commnd Cheshire Yeomanry, 1936; served War of 1939-45: Palestine, Syria, Iraq, Iran, Western Desert, Italy, Belgium, Holland, Germany (wounded twice, MC); Instructor, Staff Coll., Camberley, and GSO1, 1944-45. Chm., Jackson & Bro. Ltd; Director: National Westminster Bank Ltd, North Regional Board; Kelly & Lewis (Pty) Ltd, Australia. Chairman: NW Regional Economic Planning Council; Civic Trust for the NW; Council, BBC Radio Manchester; Manchester Inst. of Dirs; British Pump Manufrs Assoc.; past Pres., Manchester Chamber of Commerce; Vice-Pres., Assoc. of British Chambers of Commerce; Member: Exec. Cttee, Russo-British Chamber of Commerce; BSC/Strip Mills Div.; Council of Industrial Design. Member Court: Manchester Univ.; Salford Univ.; Royal College of Art; Mem. Council, Manchester Business Sch.; Governor: Manchester University Inst. of Science and Technology; Manchester Grammar Sch.; Feoffee, Chetham's Hosp. Sch.; Chm., Manchester YMCA. Comdr, Cheshire Yeomanry, 1954-57; Col and Dep. Comdr, 23 Armoured Bde, TA, 1957-60; ADC to the Queen, 1961-66; Mem., TA&VRA for Lancs and Cheshire. DL City and County of Chester, 1963; High Sheriff of Cheshire, 1969-70. FIMechE 1958. *Recreations:* field sports, ski-ing, swimming. *Address:* Whirley Hall, Macclesfield, Cheshire. *T:* Macclesfield 2077. *Clubs:* Bath; Leander (Henley-on-Thames); St James's (Manchester).

*See also D. C. M. Mather.*

**MATHER-JACKSON, Sir (George) Christopher (Mather),** 5th Bt, *cr* 1869; *b* 12 March 1896; *s* of William Birkenhead Mather Jackson (*d* 1934) (2nd *s* of 2nd Bt) and Georgiana Catherine (*d* 1932), *d* of Rev. Brabazon Hallowes. *S* cousin, Sir Edward Arthur Mather-Jackson, 4th Bt, 1956; assumed additional surname of Mather-, 1957; *m* 1941, Victoria Emily Ford, *d* of Indrick Freyberg, Mitau, Latvia. *Educ:* Wellington Coll. Formerly Managing Dir of coal, iron and engineering companies and Dir of other companies; now retired. Served European War, 1914-18 (despatches). *Recreations:* golf, shooting, motoring. *Heir: b* Anthony Henry Mather Jackson [*b* 9 Nov. 1899; *m* 1923, Evelyn Mary, *d* of Lieut-Col Sir Henry Kenyon Stephenson, 1st Bt, DSO; three *d*]. *Address:* West Court, Crondall, near Farnham, Surrey. *T:* Crondall 448. *Club:* White's.

**MATHESON, Captain Alexander Francis,** RN (retired); Lord Lieutenant of Ross and Cromarty, since 1968; *b* 6 Feb. 1905; *e s* of late Hugh Mackay Matheson; *m* 1937, Frances Mary, *d* of late Col J. P. Heywood Lonsdale, DSO, OBE and Hon. Mrs Heywood Lonsdale; one *s* two *d*. *Educ:* RN Colleges, Osborne and Dartmouth. Entered RN, 1918; served War of 1939-45; Captain, 1946; retired, 1949. Mem., Queen's Body Guard for Scotland (Royal Company of Archers). DL 1956. Convener, 1961-66, Vice-Lieutenant, 1957-68, Ross and Cromarty. *Address:* Brahan, Conon-Bridge, Ross-shire. *T:* Conon-Bridge 284. *Club:* United Service.

**MATHESON, Arthur Alexander,** QC Scotland 1956; MA, LLB; Professor of Scots Law at the University of Dundee (formerly Queen's College in the University of St Andrews), since 1949; *b* 17 June 1919; *o s* of Charles Matheson, MA, FRSGS, and Edith Margaret Matheson, MA; unmarried. *Educ:* Daniel Stewart's Coll., Edinburgh; Balliol Coll., Oxford (Classical Exhibnr); University of Edinburgh (MA, 1st Cl. Hons in Classics; LLB with distinction). Admitted to Faculty of Advocates, 1944. Queen's College, Dundee: Lectr in Public Internat. Law, 1950-60; Dean of Faculty of Law, 1955-58 and 1963-64; Master, 1958-66. Hon. Sheriff-Substitute of Perth and Angus at Dundee, 1950. *Address:* Ardvreck, 516 Perth Road, Dundee. *T:* Dundee 68111. *Club:* New (Edinburgh).

**MATHESON, Donald Macleod,** CBE 1945; Director, John Smedley Ltd, retired, 1967; *b* 20 June 1896; *o s* of Rev. Donald Matheson; *m* 1931, Enid Futvoye, *e d* of John Marsden-Smedley, Lea Green, near Matlock; no *c*. *Educ:* St George's, Harpenden; Balliol Coll., Oxford. RGA, 1915-18; BEF France, Captain (Acting) Major. Trustee Ernest Cook Trust, 1952-65. Treasurer, Peabody Fund, 1952-62. USA 1919-20; Gas Light & Coke Co., 1921-34, Asst Sec., etc. Sec. National Trust, 1934-45, mem. Cttees, 1945-62. Mem., War Works Commn, 1945-64. *Publications:* translations from French published in UK, India, and Pakistan, 1959-69. *Address:* Grimsbury Bank, Hermitage, Berks.

**MATHESON, James Adam Louis,** MBE 1944; Vice-Chancellor, Monash University, Melbourne, since 1960; *b* 11 Feb. 1912; *s* of William and Lily Edith Matheson; *m* 1937, Audrey Elizabeth Wood; three *s*. *Educ:* Bootham Sch., York; Manchester Univ. (MSc 1933); Lecturer, Birmingham Univ., 1938-46 (PhD 1946); Professor of Civil Engineering, University of Melbourne, Australia, 1947-50; Beyer Professor of Engineering, University of Manchester, 1951-59. FICE (Mem. Council, 1965-); MIStructE (Vice-Pres., 1967-);

FIEAust (Mem. Council, 1961-); Fellow, Aust. College of Educn, 1966; Member: Mission on Technical Educn in W Indies, 1957; Royal Commn into failure of King's Bridge, 1963; Ramsay Cttee on Tertiary Educn in Victoria, 1961-63; CSIRO Adv. Council, 1962-67; Exec., Aust. Council for Educational Research, 1964-; Interim Council, University of Papua and New Guinea, 1965-68; Chairman: Council, Inst. of Higher Technical Educn, Papua and New Guinea, 1966-; Aust. Vice-Chancellors' Cttee, 1967-68; Assoc. of Commonwealth Univs, 1967-68. *Publications:* Hyperstatic Structures; various articles on engineering and education. *Recreation:* music. *Address:* Monash University, Clayton, Victoria 3168, Australia. *Club:* Melbourne.

**MATHESON, Maj.-Gen. John Mackenzie,** OBE 1950; TD 1969; Commandant and Director of Studies, Royal Army Medical College, Millbank, SW1, since 1969; *b* Gibraltar, 6 Aug. 1912; *s* of late John Matheson and late Nina Short, Cape Town; *m* 1942, Agnes, *d* of Henderson Purves, Dunfermline; one *d*. *Educ:* George Watson's Coll., Edinburgh; Edinburgh Univ. (Vans Dunlop Schol.). MB, ChB 1936; MRCP 1939; MD 1945; FRCSEd 1946; FRCS 1962. Royal Victoria Hosp. Tuberculosis Trust Research Fellow, 1936-37; Lieut, RAMC (TA), 1936. Served War of 1939-45: Middle East, N Africa and Italy; Regular RAMC Commn, 1944 (despatches). Clinical Tutor, Surgical Professorial Unit, Edinburgh Univ., 1947-48; Med. Liaison Officer to Surgeon-Gen. US Army, Washington, DC, 1948-50; Asst Chief, Section Gen. Surgery, Walter Reed Army Hosp., Washington, DC, 1950-51; Cons. Surgeon: MELF, 1963-64; BAOR, 1967; Far East, 1967-69. Jt Prof. Mil. Surg., RAM Coll. and RCS of Eng., 1964-67; Brig. 1967. QHS 1969-. Alexander Medal, 1961; Simpson-Smith Memorial Lectr, 1967; Gordon-Watson Lectr, RCS of Eng., 1967. Fellow: Assoc. of Surgeons of GB and Ireland; Royal Soc. of Med., Med. Soc. of London. *Publications:* papers (on gun-shot wounds, gas-gangrene and sterilisation) to medical jls. *Recreation:* travel. *Address:* Royal Army Medical College, Millbank, SW1. *T:* 01-834 9060.

**MATHESON, Sir Torquhil (Alexander),** 6th Bt, *cr* 1882; *b* 15 Aug. 1925; *s* of General Sir Torquhil George Matheson, 5th Bt, KCB, CMG; *S* father, 1963; *m* 1954, Serena Mary Francesca, *o d* of Lt-Col Sir Michael Peto, 2nd Bt, *qv*; two *d*. *Educ:* Eton. Served War of 1939-45; joined Coldstream Guards, July 1943; commnd, March 1944; 5th Bn Coldstream Guards, NW Europe, Dec. 1944-May 1945 (wounded). Served with 3rd Bn Coldstream Guards: Palestine, 1945-48 (despatches); Tripoli and Egypt, 1950-53; seconded King's African Rifles, 1961-64. Captain, 1952; Major, 1959; retd 1964. 4th Bn, Wilts Regt, TA, 1965-67; Royal Wilts Territorials (T & AVR III), 1967-69. *Heir: b* Major Fergus John Matheson [*b* 22 Feb. 1927; *m* 1952, Hon. Jean Elizabeth Mary Willoughby, *yr d* of 11th Baron Middleton, *qv*; one *s* two *d*]. *Address:* Standerwick Court, Frome, Som. *Clubs:* Guards; Leander (Henley-on-Thames).

**MATHEW, Rev. Anthony Gervase,** MA; STL; FSA; University Lecturer in Byzantine Studies, Oxford, since 1947; *b* 14 March 1905; 2nd *s* of Francis Mathew and Agnes, *d* of James Tisdall Woodroffe. *Educ:* privately; Balliol Coll., Oxford. Joined the Dominican Order, 1928; ordained, 1934; degree of Lector in Theology, 1936; Lecturer in Greek Patristics and on Byzantine art and archaeology, University of Oxford, 1937; Mem. of History Faculty at Oxford, and Lecturer on Medieval Social Theory, 1938-; Mem. of the English Faculty and Lecturer on 14th century English literature, 1945-. Archæological survey for Government of Tanganyika, 1950, for the Government of British Somaliland Protectorate, 1951, for the Govt of Uganda, 1953, in South Arabia, 1962. Mem. of Sub-Faculty of Anthropology, Oxford, 1956-; Visiting Prof. of History, University of California, 1965. *Publications include:* The Reformation and the Contemplative Life (with David Mathew), 1934; Byzantine Painting, 1950; Byzantine Aesthetics, 1963; The Court of Richard II, 1967; contrib. to Cambridge Mediaeval History, Journal of Roman Studies, Journal of Hellenic Studies, Antiquity, Oriental Art. *Address:* Blackfriars, St Giles, Oxford.

**MATHEW, Most Rev. David,** MA, LittD, FSA; FRSL; Archbishop of Apamea; Assistant at the Pontifical Throne; *b* 15 Jan. 1902; *e s* of late Francis Mathew and Agnes, *d* of James Tisdall Woodroffe, Advocate-General of Bengal. *Educ:* Osborne and Dartmouth (Midshipman RN 1918-19); Balliol Coll., Oxford. Research Student at Balliol, 1923-24; Preston Read Scholar, 1924-25; ordained priest, 1929; assistant priest at St David's Cathedral, Cardiff, 1930-34; Chaplain to the Catholics in University of London, 1934-44; Conventual Chaplain of the Knights of Malta since 1936; mem. of Catholic Education Council; titular Bishop of Aelia and Bishop Auxiliary of Westminster, 1938-46; Apostolic Visitor to Ethiopia, 1945; Apostolic Delegate in Africa, 1946-53; Bishop-in-Ordinary (RC) to HM Forces, 1954-63; Sec., Pontifical Commn on the Missions, 1960; Consultor of the SC de Propaganda Fide; LittD, Trinity Coll., Dublin, 1933; Ford's Lectr in English History, Oxford, 1945-46. Ballard Mathews Lectr in University of Wales, 1952. Hon. LLD Glasgow, 1958. *Publications:* The Celtic Peoples and Renaissance Europe, 1933; The Reformation and the Contemplative Life, 1934 (with Gervase Mathew); Catholicism in England, 1936; The Jacobean Age, 1938; British Seamen, 1943; The Naval Heritage, 1944; Acton, 1945; Ethiopia, 1946; The Social Structure in Caroline England (Ford Lectures), 1947; Sir Tobie Mathew, 1950; The Age of Charles I, 1951; Scotland Under Charles I, 1955; James I, 1967; Lord Acton and His Times, 1968; The Courtiers of Henry VIII, 1970; *novels:* Steam Packet, 1936; In Vallombrosa, trilogy, 1950-53. *Address:* Stonor Park, near Henley-on-Thames, Oxon. *Club:* Athenæum.

**MATHEWS, Rev. Arthur Kenneth,** OBE 1942; DSC 1944; Vicar of Thursley, since 1968; Rural Dean of Godalming, since 1969; *b* 11 May 1906; *s* of late Reverend Canon A. A. and Mrs Mathews; *m* 1936, Elisabeth, *d* of late E. M. Butler and Mrs Butler; no *c*. *Educ:* Monkton Combe Sch.; Balliol Coll., Oxford (Exhibitioner); Cuddesdon Theol. Coll. Deacon 1932, priest 1933, at Wakefield; Asst Curate of Penistone; Padre of the Tanker Fleet of the Anglo-Saxon Petroleum Co. Ltd; licensed to officiate, Diocese of Wakefield, 1935-38; Vicar of Forest Row, 1938-44; Temp. Chaplain, RNVR, 1939-44 (Chaplain HMS Norfolk, 1940-44); on staff of Christian Frontier Council, 1944-46; Vicar of Rogate and Sequestrator of Terwick, 1946-54; Rural Dean of Midhurst, 1950-54; Hon. Chaplain to Bishop of Portsmouth, 1950-55; Commissary to: Bishop of Singapore, 1949-64; Bishop of Wellington, 1962-. Student of Central Coll. of Anglican Communion at St Augustine's Coll., Canterbury, 1954-55; Dean and Rector of St Albans, 1955-63; Rector of St Peter's, Peebles, 1963-68. Hon. Chaplain to Bishop of Norwich, 1969-. Mem. Council of Marlborough Coll.;

Mem. Governing Body, Monkton Combe Sch. *Recreations:* walking and gardening. *Address:* Thursley Vicarage, near Godalming, Surrey. *Club:* Brooks's.
*See also Baroness Brooke of Ystradfellte.*

**MATHEWS, Denis Owen,** CMG 1965; OBE 1959; *b* 21 Feb. 1901; *s* of Albert Edward Mathews and Edith (*née* Benton); *m* Violet Morgan; one *s. Educ:* Latymer Sch., London; Varndean, Brighton. Served with RAF, 1918; Royal Engineers, 1940-43. Uganda Survey Dept, 1921-46; East Africa Tourist Travel Assoc., 1948-65; UN Tourist Expert, 1965; Dir of Tourism, and Information and Broadcasting, Seychelles, 1965-66. *Publications:* technical papers on tourism and wild-life. *Address:* PO Box 9455, Nairobi, Kenya.

**MATHEWS, Henry Mends,** CIE 1944; CEng, FIEE; *b* 16 Feb. 1903; *s* of late Henry Montague Segundo Mathews, CSI, JP, Northam, Devon; *m* 1st, 1928, Dorothy Bertha Gubbins (*d* 1941); one *s*; 2nd, 1943, Christina Adam (*née* Nemchinovich; marr. diss., 1960); one *d. Educ:* The Wells House Sch., Malvern Wells, Worcs; Cheltenham Coll. Asst Engineer, City of Winnipeg Hydro-Electric System, 1924-26; on staff of Merz & McLellan, consulting engineers, 1927-41; Electrical Commissioner to Govt ot India, 1941-48; Chm., Central Technical Power Board, India, 1945-48; joined English Electric Co. Ltd, London, 1948; Dir of Engineering, 1954-68; Dir, Nuclear Design & Construction Ltd, 1966-68; retd, 1968. *Address:* Trotts Hill, Trotts Lane, Westerham, Kent. *Clubs:* Junior Carlton; Bengal, Saturday (Calcutta); Royal Bombay Yacht.

**MATHIAS, Brig. Leonard William Henry,** DSO 1918; late IA; *b* 31 Oct. 1890; *s* of late Col Leonard John Mathias, IA, and *g s* of late Maj.-Gen. Henry Vincent Mathias, B Staff Corps; *m* 1920, Winifrede Violet, *d* of late David Landale Johnston, Esq., ICS, Norfolk, and *g d* of late Rev. Maurice Howard Marsden of Moreton Rectory, Dorset; one *s* one *d. Educ:* private sch.; RMC Sandhurst. Received 1st Commission, 1910; attached Royal Warwickshire Regt, Bombay; appointed 128th Pioneers, 1911; proceeded Mesopotamia, 1915; besieged Kut-el-Amara, 1915-16, attached 22nd Coy. 3rd Sappers and Miners (despatches, DSO); taken prisoner by Turks, 1916, and interned at Yozgad, Asia Minor; released from captivity, Dec. 1918; Deputy Dir of Transport, QMG's Branch, India, 1939; Brig. RIASC, 1940-43; ADC to the King, 1941-43; Area Comdr, 1943-45; Control Commission for Germany (BE), 1945-49; Comdt 5th C/Bn The Gloucestershire Regt, 1949-59. *Recreations:* shooting, sailing. *Address:* Hambutts Orchard, Painswick, Glos. *T:* Painswick 3466. *Club:* United Service.

**MATHIAS, Lionel Armine,** CMG 1953; *b* 23 Jan. 1907; *s* of Hugh Henry Mathias and Amy Duncan Mathias (*née* Mathias); *m* 1935, Rebecca Gordon Rogers; three *d. Educ:* Christs Coll., New Zealand; St Paul's Sch.; Keble Coll., Oxford. Appointed Asst District Commissioner, Uganda, 1929; Labour Commissioner, 1949-53; Mem. of Legislative Council, Uganda, 1949-53; Uganda Students Adviser, 1953-62. *Address:* Copthall, Shoreham, Kent. *T:* Otford 2040.

**MATHIAS, Prof. Peter,** MA; Chichele Professor of Economic History, University of Oxford, and Fellow of All Souls College, Oxford, since 1968; *b* 10 Jan. 1928; *o c* of John Samuel and Marion Helen Mathias; *m* 1958, Elizabeth Ann, *d* of Robert Blackmore, JP, Bath; two *s* one *d. Educ:* Colston's Sch., Bristol; Jesus Coll., Cambridge (Schol.). 1st cl. (dist) Hist. Tripos, 1950, 1951. Research Fellow, Jesus Coll., Cambridge, 1952-55; Asst Lectr and Lectr, Faculty of History, Cambridge, 1955-68; Dir of Studies in History and Fellow, Queen's Coll., Cambridge, 1955-68. Tutor, 1957-68; Senior Proctor, Cambridge Univ., 1965-66. Asst Ed., Econ. History Rev., 1955-57; Treas., Econ. History Soc., 1968-; Sec., Internat. Econ. History Assoc., 1959-62. Vis. Professor: University of Toronto, 1961; School of Economics, Delhi, 1967; University of California, Berkeley, 1967. Governor: Solihull Sch., 1966-; Milton Abbey Sch., 1969-. Chm., Business Archives Council, 1968-. *Publications:* The Brewing Industry in England 1700-1830, 1959; English Trade Tokens, 1962; Retailing Revolution, 1967; The First Industrial Nation, 1969; (Gen. Editor) Debates in Economic History, 1967-. *Recreation:* travel. *Address:* All Souls College, Oxford. *T:* Oxford 49641.

**MATHIAS, Sir Richard Hughes,** 2nd Bt, *cr* 1917; Member London Stock Exchange; *b* 6 April 1905; *s* of Sir Richard Mathias, 1st Bt, and Annie, *y d* of Evan Hughes, Cardiff; *S* father 1942; *m* 1st, 1937, Gladys Cecilia Turton (marr. diss., 1960), *o d* of late Edwin Hart, New Hextalls, Bletchingley, Surrey; two *d*; 2nd, 1960, Mrs Elizabeth Baird Murray, *er d* of late Dr and Mrs Miles of Hendrescythan, Creigiau, Glamorgan. *Educ:* Eton; Balliol Coll., Oxford. RAF 1940-46 (Staff appt Air Ministry, 1942-46). Mem. Council Royal Nat. Mission to Deep Sea Fishermen, 1953-54. Fellow Corp. of S. Mary and S. Nicolas (Woodard Schs), 1965; Mem. Council, Hurstpierpoint Coll., 1965, Chm. 1967. *Address:* 8 Oakwood Court, W14. *T:* 01-602 2635. *Club:* Reform.

**MATHIESON, William Allan Cunningham,** CB 1970; CMG 1955; MBE 1945; Deputy Secretary, Ministry of Overseas Development, since 1968; *b* 22 Feb. 1916; *e s* of Rev. William Miller Mathieson, BD, and Elizabeth Cunningham Mathieson (*née* Reid); *m* 1946, Elizabeth Frances, *y d* of late Henry Marvell Carr, RA; two *s. Educ:* High Sch. of Dundee; Edinburgh and Cambridge Univs. Joined Colonial Office, 1939; served War, 1940-45; Royal Artillery in UK, France and Germany (Major, despatches). Rejoined Colonial Office, 1945; Middle East Dept, 1945-48; Private Sec. to Minister of State, 1948-49; Asst Sec., Colonial Office, 1949; Counsellor (Colonial Affairs) UK Delegn to UN, New York, 1951-54; Head of East African Department, CO, 1955-58; Minister of Education, Labour and Lands, Kenya, 1958-60; Under-Secretary: Dept of Technical Co-operation, 1963-64; ODM, 1964-68. Chm., Executive Council, Commonwealth Agricultural Bureaux, 1963. *Recreations:* photography, travel. *Address:* 22 Scarsdale Villas, W8. *Club:* Travellers'.

**MATHIESON, William Gordon,** CMG 1963; BEc; FASA; *b* 5 July 1902; *s* of James L. Mathieson; *m* 1934, Margery Macdonald; two *d* (and two *d* decd). *Educ:* Fort Street High Sch.; University of Sydney. Permanent Head, NSW State Treasury, 1959-63; Vice-Pres., Sydney Water Board, 1960-63; Mem., Sydney Harbour Transport Board, 1959-63; Chm., Companies Auditors Board, 1963-67; Auditor General of New South Wales, 1963-67. *Address:* 25 Bell Street, Gordon, NSW 2072, Australia. *T:* 49-1444.

**MATHYS, Herbert Reginald,** TD; Deputy Chairman, Courtaulds Ltd, since Nov. 1961 (Director, 1954); *b* 28 March 1908; *s* of Albert William Mathys and Minnie (*née* Bullen); *m*

1939, Marjorie Kay; one *s* one *d. Educ:* Cranleigh Sch.; Birkbeck Coll., London Univ. Chartered Patent Agent in gen. practice, 1926-39. Served War of 1939-45, RE, England (Anti-Aircraft) and India. Joined Courtaulds Ltd as Head of Patent Dept, 1946; Chm., British Cellophane Ltd (part-owned subsid.), 1956-65; Dir, British Nylon Spinners Ltd, 1961-64, Chm. 1964. Vice-Pres., Trade Marks, Patents and Designs Fedn, 1954-; Chm., Standing Adv. Cttee on Patents, 1967; Mem. Coun., FBI, 1959-65; Mem., Brit. Nat. Export Coun., 1964-; Mem. Coun., CBI, 1965-; Chm., EDC for Newspaper, Printing and Publishing Industry, 1966-67; Mem., Nat. Savings Cttee, 1966-70; a Governor: Birkbeck Coll., 1967-; Cranleigh Sch., 1968-. Mem. Livery Founders' Company. *Publications:* articles in journals, primarily on matters relating to Letters Patent for Invention. *Recreation:* sailing small boats. *Address:* Catherine's Cottage, Lymore Valley, Lymore, Lymington, Hants. *T:* Milford-on-Sea 2634. *Clubs:* Royal Thames Yacht, Keyhaven Yacht.

**MATOKA, Hon. Peter Wilfred,** MP; High Commissioner for the Republic of Zambia in London and Ambassador to the Holy See since 1970; MP for Mwinilunga in Parliament of Zambia; *b* 8 April 1930; member of Lunda Royal Family; *m* 1957, Grace Joyce; two *s* one *d. Educ:* Mwinilunga Sch.; Munali Secondary Sch.; Univ. Coll. of Fort Hare (BA Rhodes); AMmerican Univ., Washington (Dipl. Internat. Relations). Minister: of Information and Postal Services, 1964-65; of Health, 1965-66; of Works, 1967; of Power, Transport and Works, 1968; of Luapula Province, 1969. Pres., AA of Zambia, 1969-70 (Vice-Pres. 1970-71). Kt of St Gregory the Great, 1964; Kt, UAR, 1964; Kt, Ethiopia, 1965. *Recreations:* fishing, shooting, discussion, photography. *Address:* Offices of High Commission for Zambia, 7-11 Cavendish Place, W1. *T:* 01-580 0691; (residence) 56 Cumberland Terrace, W1. *Club:* Royal Automobile.

**MATTERS, Sir (Reginald) Francis,** Kt 1961; VRD; MS, MD (Adelaide); FRCS (Edinburgh), FRACS, FRCOG; Hon. Cons. Gynaecologist, Royal Adelaide Hospital; Hon. Cons. Obstetrician, Queen Elizabeth Hospital; Hon. Cons. Obstetrician, Queen Victoria Hospital; *b* 23 July 1895; *s* of late Thomas James Matters, Adelaide; *m* Elbe Cornwall, *d* of late John Mitchell, Sydney; one *s* one *d. Educ:* Prince Alfred Coll., Adelaide; Universities of Sydney and Adelaide. Served European War, AAMC France and Belgium (Captain, wounded twice); War of 1939-45, Surg. Comdr RAN, SW Pacific. Studied in London, Edinburgh and Vienna. Aust. representative: Internat. Gynaecological Congress, London, 1949; Internat. Hosp. Fedn, Edinburgh, 1959; on Govt Commn to enquire into diagnosis and treatment of cancer, 1935; studies of same in UK, USA, Canada and Europe, 1949, 1951 and 1959. Was Mem. two Anthropological expedns to study Australian Aborigines in N Australia. SA Past Fellows rep., Aust. Regional Council of RCOG (Co-opted Councillor, RCOG, London, 1951 and 1959). Past President: Navy League of SA Div.; Royal Society of St George (SA); Camellia Res. Soc. of SA; Past Chm. SA Council of Fairbridge Soc. of London; Past Chm., Royal College of Obstetricians and Gynaecologists SA State Cttee. Mem. Debating Club. Vice-Pres. Council of St John; OStJ. *Publications:* The Cervix Uteri; many papers in Med. and Sci. jls; several papers of original research especially referring to cancer investigation; papers on surgical operative procedure. *Recreations:* walking, golf, shooting, yachting and, until recently, polo, hunting and tennis. *Address:* 8 Carter Street, Thorngate, SA 5082, Australia. *T:* 69934. *Clubs:* Naval, Military and Air Force, Legacy (Past Pres.) (Adelaide); Royal Adelaide Golf; Senior Golfers' Society.

**MATTHEW, Sir Robert (Hogg),** Kt 1962; CBE 1952; FRIBA; MTPI; FRIAS; FRSE; ARSA; MA; *b* 12 Dec. 1906; *s* of late John F. Matthew and Annie B. Matthew (*née* Hogg); *m* 1931, Lorna Louisa Pilcher; one *s* two *d. Educ:* Melville Coll., Edinburgh. Chief Architect and Planning Officer, Dept of Health for Scotland, 1945; Architect to the London County Council, 1946-53. Prof. of Architecture, Edinburgh Univ., 1953-68. Member: Royal Fine Art Commission for Scotland; Historic Buildings Council, Scotland; Pres., International Union of Architects, 1961-65; Mem., BBC General Advisory Council, 1963-. Soane Medallist, 1932, Bossom Gold Medallist, 1936, Distinction in Town Planning, 1949, Royal Gold Medal for Architecture, 1970, RIBA; President: RIBA, 1962-64; Commonwealth Assoc. of Architects, 1965-. Hon. LLD Sheffield, 1963. *Address:* Keith Marischal, Humbie, East Lothian. *T:* Humbie 281; 24 Park Square East, NW1. *T:* 01-486 4222; 31 Regent Terrace, Edinburgh. *T:* 031-556 5621. *Club:* Reform.

**MATTHEWS, Sir Arthur,** Kt 1941; OBE; Retired; *b* 15 June 1886; *s* of late Robert Matthews, Heaton Mersey, near Manchester; *m* 1914, Josephine Mason Hutchinson (*decd*); one *s* one *d*; *m* 1933, Constance Dorothy Morris. *Educ:* The Leys Sch., Cambridge; Jesus Coll., Cambridge. Apprentice rising to Works Manager of Armstrong Whitworth and Co., Ltd, Openshaw, Manchester, 1908-22; Works Manager and Local Dir Thos. Firth and Sons, Sheffield, 1922; General Works Manager and Dir Thos Firth and John Brown, Ltd, Sheffield, 1930, Managing Dir, 1944-51. Past Dir of other companies. *Address:* Spring Bank, 60 Stumperlowe Crescent Road, Sheffield 10. *T:* Sheffield 31058.

**MATTHEWS, Sir Bryan Harold Cabot,** Kt 1952; CBE 1944; FRS 1940; MA, ScD; Professor of Physiology, University of Cambridge, since 1952; Fellow of King's College, since 1929; *b* 14 June 1906; *s* of Harold Evan Matthews and Ruby Sarah Harrison; *m* 1926; one *s* two *d. Educ:* Clifton Coll.; King's Coll., Cambridge. BA. Hons, 1st Class Part II Physiology, 1927; Beit Memorial Fellow for Med. Res., 1928-32; Corresponding Mem. Société Philomatique de Paris; British Mem. of the 1935 International High Altitude Expedition for Physiological Research; Chm. of Flying Personnel Research Cttee, RAF; Consultant to RAF in Applied Physiology; Head of RAF Physiological Research Unit, 1940; Head of RAF Institute of Aviation Medicine, 1944-46. Asst Dir of Physiological Research, Cambridge, 1932-48, Reader, 1948-52. Dir of Studies, King's Coll., 1932-52. Oliver-Sharpey Lecturer, RCP, 1945; Kelvin Lecturer, Instn of Electrical Engineers, 1948. Pres. Section I British Association, 1961; Vice-Pres., Royal Society, 1957 and 1958. *Publications:* Electricity in our Bodies; Essay on Physiological Research in Cambridge University Studies, 1933; Papers on Electrical Instruments and electrical phenomena in the nervous system, etc. in the Journal of Physiology, Proceedings of the Royal Society, etc. *Recreations:* ski-ing, sailing. *Address:* King's College, Cambridge.

**MATTHEWS, David Napier,** OBE 1945; MA, MD, MCh (Cambridge); FRCS; Surgeon and Surgeon in charge of Plastic Department, University College Hospital, since 1946;

Plastic Surgeon: Hospital for Sick Children, since 1946; Royal Masonic Hospital, since 1954; Civilian Consultant in Plastic Surgery to the Royal Navy since 1954; Adviser in Plastic Surgery, Ministry of Health; *b* 7 July 1911; *m* 1940, Betty Eileen Bailey Davies; two *s* one *d*. *Educ:* Leys Sch., Cambridge; Queens' Coll., Cambridge; Charing Cross Hosp. Qualified as doctor, 1935. Surgical Registrar, Westminster Hospital, until 1940; Surgeon Plastic Unit, East Grinstead, 1939-41; Surgical Specialist, RAFVR, 1941-46; Plastic Surgeon, Royal Nat. Orthopædic Hosp., 1947-54. Consulting Practice as Surgeon 1946-; Hunterian Professor, RCS, 1941 and 1944; Pres. British Assoc. of Plastic Surgeons, 1954; Sec., Harveian Soc. of London, 1951, Vice-Pres., 1954, Pres., 1962; Gen. Sec. Internat. Confederation for Plastic Surgery, 1959; Pres., Chelsea Clinical Soc., 1962. *Publications:* Surgery of Repair, 1943, 2nd edn, 1946; (Ed.) Recent Advances in the Surgery of Trauma, 1963; chapters in surgical books; contrib. to Lancet, BMJ and Post Graduate Jl etc. *Recreations:* golf, painting. *Address:* 152 Harley Street, W1. *T:* 01-935 2714; (home) 18 Bell Moor, East Heath Road, Hampstead, NW3. *T:* 01-435 7910. *Clubs:* Royal Automobile, Oriental.

**MATTHEWS, Denis;** Concert Pianist; *b* Coventry, 27 Feb. 1919; *o s* of Arthur and Elsie Randall Matthews; *m* 1941, Mira Howe (marriage dissolved, 1960); one *s* three *d*; *m* 1963, Brenda McDermott. *Educ:* Warwick. Thalberg Scholar, 1935, Blumenthal Composition Scholar, 1937, at RAM; studied with Harold Craxton and William Alwyn; Worshipful Co. of Musicians' Medal, 1938; first public appearances in London at Queen's Hall and National Gallery, 1939; has broadcast frequently, made records, given talks on musical subjects; soloist at Royal Philharmonic Society's concerts, May and Nov. 1945; toured USA and visited Potsdam with Royal Air Force Orchestra, 1944-45; Vienna Bach Festival, 1950; Canada, 1951, 1957, 1963; South Africa, 1953, 1954, 1962; Poland, 1956, 1960; Egypt and Far East, 1963; World Tour, 1964; N Africa, 1966; W and E Africa, 1968; Latin America, 1968. Favourite composers: Bach, Mozart, Beethoven, Wagner. *Publications:* piano pieces, works for violin, 'cello; in Pursuit of Music (autobiog.), 1966. *Recreations:* astronomy, filing-systems, reading aloud. *Address:* 34 Warwick Avenue, W9.

**MATTHEWS, Edwin James Thomas,** TD 1946; Master of the Supreme Court (Taxing Office) since 1965; *b* 2 May 1915; *s* of Edwin Martin Matthews (killed in action, 1917); *m* 1939, Katherine Mary Hirst, BA (Oxon.), Dip. Soc. Sc. (Leeds); two *d*. *Educ:* Sedbergh Sch., Yorks. Admitted as Solicitor of Supreme Court, 1938; practice on own account in Middlesbrough, 1938-39. Served in Royal Artillery, 1939-46, UK, France and Belgium (Dunkirk 1940); released with rank of Major. Partner, Chadwick Son & Nicholson, Solicitors, Dewsbury, Yorks, 1946-50; Area Sec., No. 6 (W Midland) Legal Aid Area Cttee of Law Soc., 1950-56; Sec. of Law Soc. for Contentious Business (including responsibility for administration of Legal Aid and Advice Schemes), 1956-65. Toured Legal Aid Offices in USA for Ford Foundation and visited Toronto to advise Govt of Ontario, 1963. Mem., Council, British Academy of Forensic Sciences, 1965-68. Special consultant to NBPI on Solicitors' Costs, 1967-68. *Publications:* contrib. Halsbury's Laws of England, 1961 and Atkins Encyclopaedia of Forms and Precedents, 1962; (with The Master Graham Greene) Costs in Criminal Cases and Legal Aid, 1965; contribs to journals. *Recreations:* trout fishing, theatre, gardening. *Address:* Romany Cottage, Greenhill Road, Otford, Kent. *T:* Otford 3467.

**MATTHEWS, Prof. Ernest,** DDS, PhD, MSc, ARCS, DIC, FDS, RCS; Director of Prosthetics, University of Manchester, since 1935; *b* 14 Dec. 1904; *s* of James Alfred Matthews, Portsmouth; *m* 1928, Doris Pipe; one *d* (two *s* decd). *Educ:* Imperial Coll., London; Cambridge; Guy's Hospital, London. Demonstrator and Lecturer, Guy's Hospital Medical and Dental Schs, 1926-34; Prosthetic Dental Surgeon, Manchester Royal Infirmary, 1937; Dean and Dir, Turner Dental Sch., 1966-69; Cons. Dental Surgeon, Christie Hosp., 1945; Hon. Adviser in Dental Surgery to Manchester Regional Hospital Board, 1951. *Publications:* 40 papers on scientific and dental subjects. *Recreations:* gardening, apiculture. *Address:* Fir Trees, Park Hill Road, Hale, Cheshire. *T:* 061-980 2204.

**MATTHEWS, Maj.-Gen. Francis Raymond Gage,** CB 1949; DSO 1945; Commandant, Civil Defence Staff College, 1956; Director of Civil Defence for SW Region, 1960-66; *b* 26 Jan. 1903; *s* of late H. F. Matthews, MA, ICS, Nicholas Nymet, North Tawton, Devon, and of late Mrs H. B. Jones (she *m* 2nd, 1914, Col H. B. Jones, CB; he died 1952); *m* 1st, 1936, Jean Frances Graham (*d* 1961), *d* of Gen. Sir David Campbell, GCB; one *s*; 2nd, 1970, Heather Rosalie Shackleton, Dublin. *Educ:* Cheltenham Coll.; RMC, Sandhurst. Commissioned 1923 into York and Lancaster Regt; promoted into The South Wales Borderers, 1935; Staff Coll., 1937-38; GSO2, 1939-40; GSO1 Div., 1940-41; Bn Comd, MEF, 1941; DMT, Middle East, 1943; Bde Comd, Italy and NW Europe, 1943-44; Div. Comd, BAOR, 1945; First Comdt, RMA, Sandhurst, 1946-48; GOC Land Forces, Hong-Kong, 1948-49. Pres., No. 1 Regular Commissions Board, War Office, 1949-50; Commander, 1st Infantry Division, 1950-52; Dir of Infantry, War Office, 1952-55. Col The South Wales Borderers, 1954-61. Joint Master, South and West Wilts Foxhounds, 1966-. *Recreation:* riding. *Address:* Horseshoe Cottage, Crockerton, Warminster, Wilts. *Club:* United Service.

**MATTHEWS, Ven. Frederick Albert John;** Archdeacon of Plymouth since 1962; Vicar of Plympton St Mary, Devon, since 1961; *b* 4 Jan. 1913; *s* of Albert and Elizabeth Anne Matthews; *m* 1941, Edna Stacey; one *d*. *Educ:* Devonport High Sch.; Exeter Coll., Oxford. Curate of Stoke Damerel, Plymouth, 1936-44; Vicar of Pinhoe, Devon, 1944-61; Rural Dean of Aylesbeare, 1957-61. *Recreations:* Association football (spectator), walking, photography. *Address:* St Mary's Vicarage, Plympton, Plymouth. *T:* Plymouth 36157.

**MATTHEWS, Gordon (Richards),** FCA; *m*; one *s* one *d* (and one *d* decd). *Educ:* Repton Sch. Chartered Accountant, 1932. Contested (U) General Election, Deritend, 1945, and Yardley, 1950; MP (C) Meriden Division of Warwicks, 1959-64; PPS to the Postmaster-General, 1960-64. Hon. Treas., Deritend Unionist Assoc., 1937-45; Hon. Sec., Birmingham Unionist Association, 1948-53. Pres. City of Birmingham Friendly Soc., 1957-64; Mem. Board of Management, Linen and Woollen Drapers Institution and Cottage Homes, 1950-65 (Pres. of Appeal, 1954-55); Chm. of Exec. Cttee, Birmingham Area of YMCA, 1951-59; Mem., Nat. Council and Nat. Exec. Cttee, YMCA, 1968-; Chm., Finance Cttee, YWCA, Birmingham Area. Chm., West Midlands Cons. Council, 1970- (Dep. Chm.,

1967-70). *Recreations:* fly-fishing and foreign travel. *Address:* Medford House, Mickleton, Chipping Campden, Glos. *T:* Mickleton 310. *Clubs:* Carlton; Conservative (Birmingham); Midland Fly-fishers'.

**MATTHEWS, Sir (Harold Lancelot) Roy,** Kt 1967; CBE 1943; Chairman, Abbey National Building Society since 1964 (Deputy Chairman, 1963); Director: Lloyds Bank Ltd; Sun Alliance & London Insurance Ltd, and other cos; *b* 24 April 1901; *s* of Harold Hamilton and Jeanie Matthews; *m* 1927, Violet Mary, **d** of T. L. Wilkinson, Solicitor, Liverpool and Dublin; one *s* one *d*. *Educ:* Preparatory Sch., Eastbourne; The Leys, Cambridge. Was abroad, 1919-22; articled to Matthews & Goodman, Chartered Surveyors, 1923; qualified, 1925; Partner Matthews & Goodman, 1927. Emergency R of O, 1938. Served War of 1939-45 (temp. Brigadier) (despatches four times); France (BEF), 1939-40; War Office, 1940-43; N Africa, Middle East, Italy, 1943-44; Normandy, 1944; Belgium, Holland, Germany, 1945. Resumed City activities, 1946-. Legion of Merit (USA) Degree of Officer, 1945; Order of Orange Nassau (Holland) Degree of Commander, 1945. *Recreation:* gardening. *Address:* Marling House, Wadhurst, Sussex. *T:* Wadhurst 2522. *Club:* Carlton.

**MATTHEWS, Horatio Keith,** CMG 1963; MBE 1946; HM Diplomatic Service; British High Commissioner in Ghana, 1968-70; *b* 4 April 1917; *s* of late Horatio Matthews, MD and of Ruth Matthews (*née* McCurry); *m* 1940, Jean Andrée Batten; two *d*. *Educ:* Epsom Coll.; Gonville and Caius Coll., Cambridge. Entered Indian Civil Service, 1940, and served in Madras Presidency until 1947; appointed to Foreign Service, 1948; First Sec., 1949; Lisbon, 1949; Bucharest, 1951; Foreign Office, 1953; Imperial Defence Coll., 1955; Political Office with Middle East Forces, Cyprus, 1956; Counsellor, 1958; Counsellor, UK High Commission, Canberra, 1959; Political Adviser to GOC Berlin, 1961; Corps of Inspectors, Diplomatic Service, 1964; Minister, Moscow, 1966-67. *Address:* Elm House, Bembridge, IoW. *T:* Bembridge 2327. *Club:* Travellers'.

**MATTHEWS, Ven. Hubert John,** MA; Archdeacon Emeritus of Hampstead, since 1962, Archdeacon, 1950-62; Rector of St Andrew Undershaft, 1954-62; Chaplain of the Order of St John of Jerusalem, 1946; Examining Chaplain to the Bishop of London, 1950-62; *b* 18 June 1889; *s* of Henry Arthur and Edith Kate Matthews; *m* 1920, Kathleen Frances, *d* of A. M. Cawthorne; one *s* two *d*. *Educ:* Winchester; St John's Coll., Oxford. Originally intended for legal career; articled to Ellis Peirs & Co., solicitors, 1911; Cuddesdon Theol Coll., 1913; Curate of St Martin-in-the-Fields, 1914-21; Temp. Chaplain RN (HMS Malaya), 1917-19; Vicar of All Hallows, East India Docks, 1921-25; Curate-in-Charge, Christ Church, Kensington, 1925-30; Vicar of St Jude's, South Kensington, 1930-42; Rector of St Marylebone, 1942-54; Chaplain to Grocers' Company, 1944; Rural Dean of St Marylebone, 1946-50; Prebendary of St Paul's Cathedral, 1948-50; clerical sec. of London Diocesan Conf., 1948-50; on HQ Cttee of Emergency Help Scheme of British Red Cross and Order of St John, 1926-62 (vice-chm. 1944-62). *Recreations:* reading, travel. *Address:* Martyn House, Baldric Road, Folkestone, Kent. *Club:* Radnor (Folkestone).

**MATTHEWS, Sir James (Henry John),** Kt 1966; JP; retired as District Secretary, Workers' Educational Association; *b* 25 March 1887; *s* of James Alfred and Mary Matthews; *m* 1919, Clara Collin; one *d*. *Educ:* Higher Grade Sch., Portsmouth. Shipbuilding, Portsmouth Dockyard and Admty, 1901-24; Officer of WEA, 1924-52. Vice-Pres., Nat. Inst. of Adult Educn; Vice-Chm. of Coun., University of Southampton; Chm., Southern Regional Council for Further Educn, 1963-. Mem. Southampton County Council, 1934-67, Alderman, 1945-67. JP Hants, 1942-. Hon. Freeman, City of Southampton, 1958. Hon. MA, Bristol Univ., 1949; Hon. LLD, Southampton Univ., 1962. *Publications:* articles on local government and adult education. *Recreation:* gardening. *Address:* 56 Ethelburt Avenue, Southampton. *T:* Southampton 57334.

**MATTHEWS, Prof. James Robert,** CBE 1956; LLD; MA, FRSE, FLS; Regius Professor of Botany, University of Aberdeen, and Keeper of Cruickshank Botanic Garden, 1934-59; Chm. Macaulay Institute for Soil Research, 1947-59; Chm. Scottish Horticultural Research Inst., 1952-59; Member, Nature Conservancy (Scottish Cttee) (ex-Chm.), 1949-61; Gov., North of Scotland Coll. of Agriculture, 1937-59; Member: Aberdeen Coll. of Education Cttee, 1945-55; Cttee for Brown Trout Research, 1948-59; Governing Body, Rowett Research Institute, 1955-59; Vice-Pres. Royal Society of Edinburgh, 1958-61; *b* 8 March 1889; *yr s* of Robert Matthews, Dunning, Perthshire, and Janet McLean; *m* 1st, 1916, Helen Donaldson, Milnathort (*d* 1926); 2nd, 1928, Christine Young Blackhall, Edinburgh; two *s*. *Educ:* Perth Acad.; Edinburgh Univ. Lecturer in Botany, Birkbeck Coll., London, 1913-16; Temp. Protozoologist at Liverpool Sch. of Tropical Medicine (Western Command), 1916-19; Lecturer in Botany, University of Edinburgh, 1920-29; Prof. of Botany, University of Reading, 1929-34. Veitch Memorial Medal in Horticulture, 1958; Neill Prize and Medal for Natural History, Royal Society Edinburgh, 1964. *Publications:* Origin and Distribution of the British Flora, 1955; various papers on the Taxonomy of British Plants (especially Rosa), on Plant Distribution, and on Plant Morphology; also numerous papers on the Protozoology of Dysentery. *Recreation:* gardening. *Address:* Duncruib, Banchory, Kincardineshire.

**MATTHEWS, Jessie,** OBE 1970; actress; singer; *b* Soho, London, 11 March 1907; *d* of late George Ernest Matthews and late Jane Townshend; *m* 1st, 1926, Lord Alva Lytton (Henry Lytton Jr) (from whom she obt. a div., 1929, and who *d* 1965); 2nd, 1931, John Robert Hale-Monro (Sonnie Hale) (from whom she obt. a div., 1944, and who *d* 1959); one *d* (one *s* decd); 3rd, 1945, Brian Lewis (from whom she obt. a div., 1959); one *s* decd. *Educ:* Pulteney St (LCC) Sch. for Girls, Soho. Trained as a classical ballet dancer under Mme Elise Clare, and Miss Terry of Terry's Juveniles; first London appearance, in Bluebell in Fairyland, Alhambra, 1917. Early successes in: The Music Box Revue, Palace, 1923; Charlot's Revue, Prince of Wales, 1924; The Charlot Show of 1926, Prince of Wales, 1926. Then (C. B. Cochran contract) starred in (London Pavilion): One Damn Thing After Another, 1927; This Year of Grace, 1928; Wake Up and Dream, 1929; Evergreen, Adelphi, 1930 (during these years she originated songs, incl.: Noel Coward's A Room with a View; Cole Porter's Let's Do It; Harry Woods' Over My Shoulder; Richard Rodgers' My Heart Stood Still and Dancing on the Ceiling). London stage (cont.) in: Hold my Hand, Gaiety, 1931; Sally Who?, Strand, 1933; Come Out to Play, Phœnix, 1940; Wild Rose, Princes, 1942; Maid to Measure, Cambridge, 1948; Sweethearts and Wives, Wyndhams, 1949; Sauce Tartare, Cambridge, 1949-50; Five Finger Exercise, Unity, 1960; A Share in the Sun, Cambridge, 1966. First New York appearance, in André Charlot's Revue of 1924, Times Square, 1924; then in Wake Up and Dream, Selwyn, 1929-30; The Lady Comes Across, Shubert, 1941. Films (1923-) include: The Princes in the Tower, The Beloved Vagabond, Straws in the Wind, Out of the Blue, There Goes the Bride, The Man from Toronto, The Midshipmaid, The Good Companions, Friday the Thirteenth, Waltzes from Vienna, Evergreen, First a Girl, It's Love Again, Head Over Heels, Gangway, His Majesty the Baby, Sailing Along, Climbing High, Forever and a Day (in Hollywood), Candles at Nine, Victory Wedding (as director), Making the Grade, Life is Nothing without Music, Tom Thumb. Starred in two seasons of cabaret, Society, London, 1964 and 1966. Recording star, 1927-70, on many labels. Television: many appearances in plays, programmes, etc. Radio: Mrs Dale, in serial, The Dales, 1963-69. *Address:* c/o Vincent Shaw Associates, 39a Welbeck Street, W1M 8DD.

**MATTHEWS, L(eonard) Harrison,** FRS 1954, MA, ScD; Scientific Director, Zoological Society of London, 1951-66; *b* 12 June 1901; *s* of Harold Evan Matthews and Ruby Sarah Matthews (*née* Harrison); *m* 1924, Dorothy Hélène Harris; one *s* one *d*. *Educ:* Bristol Grammar Sch.; King's Coll., Cambridge. BA Hons 1st Class Nat. Sci. Trip., 1922; Vintner Exhibitioner King's Coll., University Frank Smart Prize. Has carried out biological researches in Africa, S America, Arctic and Antarctic, etc. Mem. of scientific staff "Discovery" Expedition, 1924; special lectr in Zoology, Univ. of Bristol, 1935; Radio Officer, Anti-Aircraft Command, 1941; Sen. Scientific Officer, Telecommunications Research Establishment, 1942; Radar liaison duties with RAF, 1943-45; Research Fell. Univ. of Bristol, 1945. Pres. Section D, British Assoc. for the Advancement of Science, 1959; President: British Academy of Forensic Science, 1962; Ray Soc., 1965; Chm., Seals Sub-Cttee, NERC, 1967. Member Council: Marine Biological Assoc. of UK, 1944-51; Zoological Soc. of London, 1943-45, 1946-49; 1950-51 (Vice-Pres., 1944-45, 1947-49, 1950-51); Inst. of Biology, 1954-57; Linnean Soc., of London, 1953-57; Sec., 1947-48, Pres., 1960, Assoc. of British Zoologists; Chm., World List of Scientific Periodicals, 1959-66. Has made numerous sound and TV broadcasts. *Publications:* South Georgia, the Empire's Subantarctic Outpost, 1931; Wandering Albatross, 1951; British Mammals (New Naturalist), 1952; Amphibia and Reptiles, 1952; Sea Elephant, 1952; Animals in Colour, 1959; The Senses of Animals (with Maxwell Knight), 1963; (ed) The Whale, 1968; The Life of Mammals, Vol. I, 1969, Vol. II, 1970; numerous scientific papers on zoological subjects in jls of learned socs, Discovery Reports, Philosophical Transactions, Encyclopædia Britannica, etc. *Address:* The Old Rectory, Stansfield, via Sudbury, Suffolk.

**MATTHEWS, Mrs Pamela Winifred (Mrs Peter Matthews),** BSc (Econ.); Principal, Westfield College (University of London), 1962-65; *b* 4 Dec. 1914; *d* of Lt-Col C. C. Saunders-O'Mahony; *m* 1938, H. P. S. Matthews (*d* 1958); one *s* one *d*. *Educ:* St Paul's Girls' Sch.; London Sch. of Economics. Royal Institute of International Affairs, 1938-39; Foreign Office, 1939-40; The Economist Newspaper, 1940-43; Foreign Office, 1943-45; Reuters, 1945-61; Nat. Inst. for Social Work Trg, 1961-62. Independent Mem., Advertising Standards Authority, 1964-65. Governor, Northwood Coll., Middlesex, 1962-. *Publications:* diplomatic correspondence for Reuters. *Recreations:* travel, theatre. *Address:* 1 Edwardes Place, Kensington High Street, W8. *T:* 01-603 8458.

**MATTHEWS, Paul Taunton,** MA, PhD, FRS 1963; Professor of Theoretical Physics, Imperial College, London, since 1962; *b* 19 Nov. 1919; *s* of Rev. Gordon Matthews and Janet (*née* Viney); *m* 1947, Margit Zohn; two *s* two *d*. *Educ:* Mill Hill Sch.; Clare Coll., Cambridge. Research Fellow, Inst. for Advanced Study, Princeton, USA, 1950-51; ICI Research Fellow, Cambridge, 1951-52; Lectr, Univ. of Birmingham, 1952-57; Visiting Prof., Univ. of Rochester, USA, 1957; Reader in Theoretical Physics, Imperial Coll., London, 1957-62. Mem., SRC, 1970-. *Publications:* Quantum Mechanics, 1963 (USA). Papers on elementary particle physics in Proc. Royal Soc., Phil. Mag., Phys. Review, Nuovo Cimento, Review Mod. Phys., Annals of Physics. *Address:* 40 Digswell Road, Welwyn Garden City, Herts. *T:* Welwyn Garden 23876.

**MATTHEWS, Mrs Peter;** *see* Matthews, Mrs Pamela W.

**MATTHEWS, Peter Alec;** Managing Director, Vickers Ltd, since 1970; *b* 21 Sept. 1922; *s* of Major Alec Bryan Matthews and Elsie Lazarus Barlow; *m* 1946, Sheila Dorothy Bunting; four *s* one *d*. *Educ:* Shawnigan Lake Sch., Vancouver Island; Oundle Sch. Served Royal Engineers (retired as Major), 1940-46. Joined Stewarts and Lloyds Ltd, 1946; Director of Research and Technical Development, 1962; Member for Research and Devclt, BSC, 1968-70. Member, Iron and Steel Inst. Council. *Recreations:* sailing, gardening. *Address:* Oneacre, Warkton, Kettering, Northants. *T:* Kettering 2978. *Club:* Royal Thames Yacht.

**MATTHEWS, Robert Charles Oliver;** FBA 1968; Drummond Professor of Political Economy, Oxford, and Fellow of All Souls College, since 1965; *b* 16 June 1927; *s* of Oliver Harwood Matthews, WS, and Ida Finlay; *m* 1948, Joyce Hilda Lloyds; one *d*. *Educ:* Edinburgh Academy; Corpus Christi Coll., Oxford (schol.). 1st Cl. Hon. Classical Mods, 1945; 1st Cl. PPE 1947. Student, Nuffield Coll., Oxford, 1947-48; Lectr, Merton Coll., Oxford, 1948-49; University Asst Lectr in Economics, Cambridge, 1949-51, and Univ. Lectr, 1951-65. Fellow of St John's Coll., Cambridge, 1950-65. Visiting Prof., University of California, Berkeley, 1961-62. Member: Central Advisory Council for Science and Technology; Social Science Research Council (Chm., Economics Cttee); Council, Royal Economic Society; Exec. Cttee, Nat. Inst. of Economic and Social Research. *Publications:* A Study in Trade Cycle History, 1954; The Trade Cycle, 1958; articles in learned journals. (With M. Lipton and J. M. Rice) Chess Problems: Introduction to an Art, 1963. *Recreation:* chess problems. *Address:* Gowan Lea, Mill End, Kidlington, Oxford.

**MATTHEWS, Sir Roy;** *see* Matthews, Sir (H. L.) R.

**MATTHEWS, Rt. Rev. Seering John,** OBE 1967; *b* 26 March 1900; *s* of Seering Frederick and Sarah Jane Matthews; *m* 1944, Barbara, *d* of Rev. H. G. Browning, Althorne, Essex; three *s* two *d*. *Educ:* St John's Coll., Auckland; Fort Street High Sch., Sydney; Moore Theol Coll., Sydney. ThL 1925. Deacon, 1925; Priest, 1926. Curate, Christ Church, Sydney, 1925-29; permission to officiate Dio. Canterbury, 1930; Priest-in-Charge, St Mary's Fitzroy, Melbourne, 1931-32; Vicar, St James',

Calcutta, 1933-38; Principal, Bp Westcott Sch., Namkum, 1938-42; Chap. RAF (India), 1942-46; Vicar, St Bartholomew's, Ipswich, Suffolk, 1946-51; Chap. Southport Sch., Brisbane, 1951-54; Rector, St Paul's Cathedral, Rockhampton, 1954-60; Archdeacon of Rockhampton, 1954-60; Bishop of Carpentaria, 1960-68. *Recreation:* fishing. *Address:* 117 Esplanade, Point Vernon, Qld 4650, Australia. *Club:* United Service (Brisbane).

**MATTHEWS, Sir Stanley,** Kt 1965; CBE 1957; professional footballer; *b* Hanley, Stoke-on-Trent, 1 Feb. 1915; *s* of late Jack Matthews, Seymour Street, Hanley; *m* 1935, Elizabeth Hall Vallance; one *s* one *d*. *Educ:* Wellington Sch., Hanley. Played in first Football League match, 1931; first played for England, 1934, and fifty-five times subsequently; Blackpool FC, 1947-61 (FA Cup, 1953); Stoke City FC, 1961-65. Freedom of Stoke-on-Trent, 1963. *Publication:* The Stanley Matthews Story, 1960. *Recreations:* golf, tennis. *Address:* The Grange, St Annes Road, Blackpool, Lancs. *T:* 41371. *Club:* National Sporting.

**MATTHEWS, Thomas Stanley;** journalist; *b* 16 Jan. 1901; *s* of late Rt Rev. Paul Matthews, sometime Bishop of New Jersey, and late Elsie Proctor; *m* 1st, 1925, Juliana Stevens Cuyler (*d* 1949); four *s*; 2nd, 1954, Martha Gellhorn; 3rd, 1964, Pamela, *widow of Lt-Col V. Peniakoff. Educ:* Park Hill, Lyndhurst, Hants; Shattuck Sch. (Minn.); St Paul's Sch. (Concord, NH); Princeton Univ.; New Coll., Oxford (MA). Doctor of Humane Letters, Kenyon Coll., Ohio; Doctor of Letters, Rollins Coll., Florida. Editorial staff: The New Republic, 1925-29; Time, 1929; Exec. Editor, Time, 1942; Managing Editor Time, 1943-50, Editor, 1950-53. *Publications:* To the Gallows I Must Go, 1931; The Moon's No Fool, 1934; The Sugar Pill, 1957; Name and Address, 1960; O My America!, 1962; The Worst Unsaid (verse), 1962; Why So Gloomy? (verse), 1966. *Recreation:* lawn tennis. *Address:* Cavendish Hall, Cavendish, Suffolk. *T:* Clare 296. *Clubs:* Athenæum, Buck's, Garrick; Century Association, Coffee House (New York); Reading Room (Newport, RI).

**MATTHEWS, Very Rev. Walter Robert,** KCVO 1935; CH 1962; DD, DLit (London), Hon. DD (Cambridge, St Andrews, Glasgow, Trinity College, Dublin, Trinity College, Toronto), Hon. STD (Columbia University, USA); Hon. STP (St John's College, Winnipeg); Hon. LLD (London), 1969; FRSL 1948; Dean of St Paul's, 1934-67; Dean Emeritus since 1967; Dean of Order of the British Empire, 1957-67; Hon. Bencher, Gray's Inn; *b* 1881; *s* of P. W. Matthews, Chief Inspector, Bankers' Clearing House; *m* 1912, Margaret Bryan, BSc (*d* 1963); one *s* one *d* (and one *s* killed in action, 1940). *Educ:* Wilson's Grammar Sch., Camberwell; King's Coll., London. Curacies St Mary Abbots, Kensington, and St Peter, Regent Square; Asst Chaplain Magdalen Hosp.; Lecturer in Philosophy at King's Coll., 1908-18, also in Dogmatic Theology, 1909-18; Vicar of Christ Church, Crouch End, 1916-18; Dean of King's Coll., London, 1918-32 (now Fellow); Prof. of the Philosophy of Religion, King's Coll., 1918-32; Dean of Exeter, 1931-34; Canon Theologian of Liverpool Cathedral, 1930; Chaplain to Gray's Inn, 1920; Preacher to Gray's Inn, 1929; examining Chaplain to the Bishop of Oxford; Boyle Lecturer, 1920-22; Chaplain to the King, 1923-31; White Lecturer, 1927; Noble Lecturer, 1928; Wilde Lecturer, 1929; Warburton Lecturer, 1938. FRSL 1948; Fellow Westfield Coll., University of London, 1948. Freedom Cross of King Haakon VII (Norway), 1947; Order of White Lion (3rd class) Czechoslovakia, 1947. *Publications:* Studies in Christian Philosophy, 1921; 2nd edition, 1928; an edition of Butler's Ethical Writings in Bohn Library; The Idea of Revelation, 1924; The Psychological Approach to Religion, The Gospel and the Modern Mind, 1925; God and Evolution, 1926; joint editor, Library of Constructive Theology; Editor, Dogma in History and Thought, 1929; God in Christian Thought and Experience, 1930; 7th edn 1942; Seven Words, 1933; The Adventures of Gabriel in his Search for Mr Shaw, 1933; Essays in Construction, 1934; Hope of Immortality; The Purpose of God, 1935; Our Faith in God, 1936; The Christian Faith, 1936; Signposts to God, 1938; Teaching of Christ, 1939; Following Christ; Moral Issues of the War, 1940; The Foundations of Peace, 1942; Strangers and Pilgrims, 1945; St Paul's in War-time, 1946; The Problem of Christ in the 20th Century, 1951; Some Christian Words, 1956; joint editor, A History of St Paul's Cathedral and the Men Associated with it, 1957; The Search for Perfection, 1957; The Lord's Prayer, 1958; The Thirty-Nine Articles, 1961; Memories and Meanings, 1969; The Year Through Christian Eyes, 1970; many papers. *Address:* 29 Buckingham Palace Mansions, SW1. *Club:* Athenæum.

**MATTURI, Sahr Thomas,** CMG 1967; BSc, PhD; Principal, Njala University College, since 1963; Vice-Chancellor, University of Sierra Leone, 1968-70 (Pro-Vice-Chancellor, 1966-68); *b* 22 Oct. 1925; *s* of Sahr and Konneh Matturi; *m* 1956, Anna Adella Stephens; two *s* one *d*. *Educ:* University Coll., Ibadan; Hull Univ. School Teacher, 1944-47, 1954-55; University Lecturer, 1959-63. *Recreations:* cricket, lawn tennis, shooting. *Address:* Njala University College, Private Mail Bag, Freetown, Sierra Leone, West Africa. *T:* 5206.

**MAUCHLINE, Lord; Michael Edward Abney-Hastings;** *b* 22 July 1942; *s* and *heir* of Countess of Loudoun (13th in line), *qv* and *s* of Captain Walter Strickland Lord (whose marriage to the Countess of Loudoun was dissolved, 1945; his son assumed, by deed poll, 1946, the surname of Abney-Hastings in lieu of his patronymic). *Address:* Mayfield, The Croft, Hastings, Sussex.

**MAUCHLINE, Rev. Prof. John,** MA, BD (Glasgow), DD (Edinburgh); Professor of Old Testament Language and Literature, University of Glasgow, since 1935 and Principal of Trinity College, Glasgow, since 1953; *b* 5 July 1902; *m* 1930, Helen Brisbane Paterson, MA; three *s*. *Educ:* Hutchesons' Grammar Sch.; Glasgow Univ. (First Class Hons in Semitic Langs); British Sch. of Archæology, American Sch. of Oriental Research, and l'Ecole St Etienne, Jerusalem. Maclean Scholar, 1926; Faulds Fellow, 1926-29; Minister of South Dalziel Church, Motherwell, 1929-34; Prof. of Old Testament Language and Literature, Trinity Coll., Glasgow, 1934. Principal Pollok Lecturer in Pine Hill Divinity Hall, Halifax, Nova Scotia, 1949. *Publications:* God's People Israel; The Balaam-Balak Songs and Saga, in W. B. Stevenson Anniversary Volume; Hosea in The Interpreter's Bible; 1st and 2nd Kings, in Peake's Commentary on the Bible (new and revised edn); Isaiah 1-39 (Torch Bible Commentary); (Ed.) An Introductory Hebrew Grammar, by A. B. Davidson, 26th edn, 1967; articles in periodicals. *Address:* 31 Manse Road, Bearsden, Glasgow. *T:* 041-942 4993.

**MAUD,** *see* Redcliffe-Maud, family name of Baron Redcliffe-Maud.

**MAUDE,** family name of **Viscount Hawarden.**

**MAUDE, Col Alan Hamer,** CMG 1919; DSO 1917; TD; DL Greater London; *b* Highgate, 18 Aug. 1885; *e s* of Edmund Maude and Claudine Ina, *d* of G. A. Pridmore, JP, Coventry; *m* 1910, Dorothy Maude (*d* 1960), *o d* of Frederic Upton; one *s*. *Educ:* Rugby (scholar); Oriel Coll., Oxford (exhibitioner, MA). Sub-Editor Daily Chronicle, 1912-14; on Editorial Staff of The Times, 1920-50. Joined Army Service Corps (TF), 1909; served in France and Belgium, 1915-19 (despatches twice, CMG, DSO); Commanded 47th (London) Divl Train, 1918-19 and 1924-29, and 59th Divl Train, 1919; Bt-Col 1928; Col (TA), 1929; ADS&T, GHQ, BEF, 1939; AQMG and Controller, Central Purchase Bd, BEF, 1940; CRASC, Bordon District, 1940-43, and Kent District, 1943-45; Hon. Col 56th (London) Armoured Divl Column, RASC, TA, 1947-53. Pres. Old Rugbeian Soc., 1952-53. *Publications:* Edited War History of the 47th Division, 1914-19; Rugby School Register, 1911-46; and many special numbers of The Times. *Recreations:* formerly rifle-shooting (Captain, Rugby and Oxford teams); gardening, photography, genealogy. *Address:* Stone House, Petworth, Sussex. *T:* Petworth 2314.

*See also A. E. U. Maude.*

**MAUDE, Angus Edmund Upton,** TD; MP (C) Stratford-on-Avon Division of Warwickshire, since Aug. 1963; author and journalist; *b* 8 Sept. 1912; *o c* of Col Alan Hamer Maude, *qv*; *m* 1946, Barbara Elizabeth Earnshaw, *o d* of late John Earnshaw Sutcliffe, Bushey; two *s* two *d*. *Educ:* Rugby Sch. (Scholar); Oriel Coll., Oxford (MA). Financial journalist, 1933-39: The Times, 1933-34; Daily Mail, 1935-39. Commissioned in RASC (TA), May 1939; served in RASC 1939-45, at home and in North Africa (PoW, Jan. 1942-May 1945); Major 56th (London) Armd Divl Column RASC (TA), 1947-49; TARO, 1950. Engaged in economic and social research, 1946-48; Dep. Dir of PEP, 1948-50; MP (C) Ealing (South), 1950-57, (Ind. C), 1957-58; Dir, Conservative Political Centre, 1951-55. Editor of the Sydney Morning Herald, 1958-61. Contested S Dorset, by-election, Nov. 1962. *Publications:* (with Roy Lewis) The English Middle Classes, 1949; Professional People, 1952; (with Enoch Powell) Biography of a Nation, 1955; Good Learning, 1964; South Asia, 1966; The Common Problem, 1969. *Recreation:* gardening. *Address:* South Newington House, near Banbury, Oxon. *Club:* Carlton.

**MAUDE, Brig. Christian George,** DSO 1918; OBE 1919; MC; *b* 4 Sept. 1884; *s* of late Lt-Col A. Maude, 8 Pelham Street, SW7; *m* 1st, 1920, Patience (from whom he obtained a divorce, 1930; she *d* 1935), *e d* of 1st Baron Rochdale, CB; one *d* (and one *s* decd); 2nd, 1931, Hester Joan, *y d* of late Charles and Lady Mabelle Egerton; three *d*. *Educ:* Rugby; RMC Sandhurst. Joined 5th Fusiliers, 1904; transferred to Royal Fusiliers, 1908; to Army Educational Corps, 1920; served Mohmand Expedition, NW Frontier, India, 1908; European War, France and Palestine, 1915-19 (despatches, DSO, OBE, MC); Inspector, Army Educational Corps, War Office, 1937, and Controller AEC, 1943-44; retired pay, 1945; employed with CCG, 1946-54. *Recreation:* fishing. *Address:* The Downs, Broad Oak, Heathfield, Sussex. *T:* Heathfield 3681. *Club:* Boodle's.

**MAUDE, Evan Walter,** CB 1968; a Deputy Secretary, Ministry of Agriculture, Fisheries and Food, since 1970; *b* 11 Feb. 1919; *s* of late Sir E. John Maude, KCB, KBE; *m* 1949, Jennifer, *d* of Edward Stanley Gotch Robinson, *qv*, and *widow* of Capt. O. T. Bulmer; three *d*. *Educ:* Rugby; New Coll., Oxford. Served in RNVR (Fleet Air Arm), 1940-45 (despatches). Entered HM Treasury, 1946; Asst Private Sec. to Chancellor of the Exchequer and Economic Sec., 1947-48; Private Sec. to Sec. of State for Co-ordination of Transport, Fuel and Power, 1951-53; Principal Private Sec. to Chancellor of Exchequer, 1956-58; Asst Under-Sec. of State, Dept of Economic Affairs, 1964-66; Dep. Under-Sec. of State, 1966-67; Economic Minister in British Embassy, Washington, 1967-69; Third Sec., Treasury, 1969-70. *Recreations:* sailing, ski-ing, music. *Address:* 5 Downshire Hill, NW3. *Club:* Oxford and Cambridge University.

**MAUDE, John Cyril,** QC 1942; **His Honour Judge Maude;** Additional Judge, Mayor's and City of London Court, 1954; Additional Judge, Central Criminal Court, 1964-68; *b* 3 April 1901; *s* of Cyril Maude and Winifred Emery; *m* 1st, 1927, Rosamond Willing Murray (from whom he obtained a divorce, 1955), *d* of late Dr T. Morris Murray, Boston, Mass, USA; one *d*; *m* 2nd, 1955, Maureen Constance (who *m* 1st, 1930, 4th Marquess of Dufferin and Ava, killed in action, 1945; one *s* two *d*; 2nd, 1948, Major (Harry Alexander) Desmond Buchanan, MC (from whom she obtained a divorce, 1954)), 2nd *d* of late Hon. Arthur Ernest Guinness. *Educ:* Eton; Christ Church, Oxford. Joined Gen. Staff, War Office, temporary civil asst, 1939; Intelligence Corps, actg major, 1940; offices of War Cabinet, 1942. Barrister, Middle Temple, 1925; KC 1943; Bencher, 1951; Mem., Bar Council, 1952. Counsel to PO at Central Criminal Court, 1935-42; Jun. Counsel to Treasury at Central Criminal Court, 1942-43; Recorder of Devizes, 1939-44, of Plymouth, 1944-54; MP (C) Exeter, 1945-51. Chancellor of the Diocese of Bristol, 1948-50. Dir, Old Vic Trust Ltd, 1951-54; Chairman of the British Drama League, 1952-54; Governor, Royal Victoria Hall Foundn, 1953. Chm., Family Service Units, 1954; Mem. Bd, Middlesex Hosp., 1951-62. *Address:* 4 Hans Crescent, SW1. *T:* 01-235 1432; The Owl House, Lamberhurst, Kent. *Clubs:* Beefsteak, Garrick.

*See also Marquess of Dufferin and Ava.*

**MAUDLING, Rt. Hon. Reginald,** PC 1955; MP (C) Barnet Division of Hertfordshire since 1950; Home Secretary, since 1970; Deputy Leader of the Conservative Party; Hon. Fellow Merton College, Oxford, 1958; *b* 7 March 1917; *m* 1939, Beryl Laverick; three *s* one *d*. *Educ:* Merchant Taylors'; Merton Coll., Oxford. 1st Class in Greats. Called to the Bar, Middle Temple, 1940. Contested Borough of Heston and Isleworth, 1945. Parliamentary Sec. to Minister of Civil Aviation, 1952; Economic Sec. to the Treasury, 1953-April 1955; Minister of Supply, April 1955-Jan. 1957; Paymaster-Gen., 1957-59; Pres. of the Board of Trade, 1959-61; Sec. of State for the Colonies, Oct. 1961-July 1962; Chancellor of the Exchequer, July 1962-Oct. 1964. Pres., Nat. Union of Conservative and Unionist Assocs, 1967. *Address:* Bedwell Lodge, Essendon, Herts.

**MAUDSLAY, Major (James) Rennie,** CVO 1967; MBE 1945; Assistant Keeper of HM's Privy Purse since 1958; *b* 13 Aug. 1915; *o s* of late Joseph Maudslay and of Mrs Ruth Maudslay (*née* Partridge), Pinewood Copse, Boundstone, Farnham, Surrey; *m* 1951, (Jane) Ann, *d* of A. V. McCarty, Helena, Arkansas; two *s* one *d*. *Educ:* Harrow Sch. 2nd Lt, KRRC, 1938; served 1938-45 (despatches five times); Hon. Major, 1945. Dep. Chm., Mid-Southern Water Co.; Director: Airkem Inc.; Lyon, Lohr & Sly Ltd; Mem. of Lloyds. Pres.,

Farnham Conservative Assoc., 1954-57; Pres., Maudslay Soc., 1963-65; Hon. Mem., Jun. Instn of Engineers. Employed Lord Chamberlain's Office, 1952-53. Holds Order of: Verdienst (Germany), 1958; Taj (Iran), 1959; Dakshuna Bahu (Nepal), 1960; Legion of Honour (France), 1960; Crown of Thai (Thailand), 1960; Phœnix (Greece), 1963; Al Kawkab (Jordan), 1966; Ordine al Merito della Repubblica (Italy), 1969. *Recreations:* shooting, gardening. *Address:* Frensham Vale, Rowledge, Surrey. *T:* Frensham 2854; 25a St James' Palace, SW1. *T:* 01-930 4110. *Clubs:* White's, MCC.

**MAUFE, Sir Edward,** Kt 1954; RA 1947 (ARA 1938); MA Oxon, FRIBA; architect; Hon. Fellow of St John's College, Oxford; Hon. LLD The Queen's University, Northern Ireland; Hon. Master of the Bench, Gray's Inn; *b* 1883; *s* of Henry Maufe, Red House, Bexley Heath, Kent; *m* Gladys Prudence, *d* of Edward Stutchbury, Geological Survey of India; (one *s* decd). Educ: St John's Coll., Oxford; articled to W. A. Pite, FRIBA. Served Salonica Forces, Capt. RA, ADC to GOC, RA XIIth Corps. Vice-Pres., RIBA, 1939-43. Chief Architect and Artistic Adviser to Commonwealth War Graves Commission, 1943-69; Royal Fine Art Commission, 1946-53; Treasurer of the Royal Academy, 1954-59; Mem. of Lloyd's; Medallist, Paris Exhibition, 1925; Royal Gold Medal for Architecture, 1944. *Works include:* Guildford Cathedral; The Runnymede Memorial; buildings for Trinity and St John's Colls, Cambridge, and St John's and Balliol, Oxford; Morley Coll., London Hosp. Students' Hostel; Kelling Hall, Norfolk; Yaffle Hill, Dorset; BBC Chapel; St Saviour's, Acton; St Thomas's, Hanwell; Festival Theatre, Cambridge; Playhouse, Oxford; The Magna Carta Memorial. Architect for Reconstruction of: Gray's Inn; Middle Temple; St Columba, Pont St. *Address:* Shepherd's Hill, Buxted, Sussex. *Clubs:* Arts, Chelsea Arts.

**MAUGHAM,** family name of **Viscount Maugham.**

**MAUGHAM,** 2nd Viscount, *cr* 1939, of Hartfield; **Robert Cecil Romer Maugham;** author (as Robin Maugham); barrister-at-law; *b* 17 May 1916; *o s* of 1st Viscount Maugham, PC, KC, and Helen Mary (*d* 1950), *d* of Rt Hon. Sir Robert Romer, GCB; *S* father 1958. *Educ:* Eton; Trinity Hall, Cambridge. Served War of 1939-45; Inns of Court Regt, 1939; commissioned Fourth County of London Yeomanry, 1940; Western Desert, 1941-42 (despatches, wounded); Middle East Intelligence Centre, 1943; invalided out, 1944. Called to Bar, Lincoln's Inn, 1945. *Publications:* Come to Dust, 1945; Nomad, 1947; Approach to Palestine, 1947; The Servant, 1948 (dramatised 1963; filmed, 1965); North African Notebook, 1948; Line on Ginger, 1949; Journey to Siwa, 1950; The Rough and the Smooth, 1951; Behind the Mirror, 1955; The Man With Two Shadows, 1958; The Slaves of Timbuktu, 1961; November Reef, 1962; The Joyita Mystery, 1962; Somerset and all the Maughams, 1966; The Green Shade, 1966; The Second Window, 1968; The Link, 1969. *Plays:* The Last Hero; Odd Man In (adaptation); Its in the Bag (adaptation); The Lonesome Road (in collaboration with Philip King); The Claimant, 1964; Enemy!, 1969. *Recreations:* reading and travel. *Address:* Casa Cala Pada, Santa Eulalia del Rio, Ibiza, Baleares, Spain. *Club:* Garrick.

**MAUND, Rt. Rev. John Arthur Arrowsmith;** *see* Lesotho, Bishop of.

**MAUNDER, Prof. Leonard,** BSc; PhD; ScD; CEng; FIMechE; Professor of Mechanical Engineering and Head of Department, University of Newcastle upon Tyne; *b* 10 May 1927; *s* of Thomas G. and Elizabeth A. Maunder; *m* 1958, Moira Anne Hudson; one *s* one *d. Educ:* Bishop Gore Grammar Sch., Swansea; University Coll. of Swansea (BSc); Edinburgh Univ. (PhD); Massachusetts Institute of Technology (ScD). Instructor, 1950-53, and Asst Prof., 1953-54, in Dept of Mechanical Engineering, MIT; Head of Structures Section at Aeronautical Research Lab., Wright Air Development Center, US Air Force, 1954-56; Lecturer in Post-Graduate Sch. of Applied Dynamics, Edinburgh Univ., 1956-61. Mem. Council, IMechE, 1963-66, 1969-70; Vice-Pres. NE Coast Inst. Engineers and Shipbuilders. *Publications:* (with R. N. Arnold) Gyrodynamics and Its Engineering Applications, 1961; scientific papers in the field of applied mechanics. *Recreations:* squash rackets, gardening. *Address:* Stephenson Building, The University, Newcastle upon Tyne 2.

**MAUNDRELL, Captain Arthur Goodall,** CB 1937; CIE 1935; Royal Indian Navy, retired; *b* 1884; *y s* of late Ven. Archdeacon H. Maundrell, Japan and Winchester; *m* 1916, Amy Florence Mary, *o d* of late Capt. George B. Graham, Duke of Wellington's Regt. Joined RIM, 1906; served European War, 1914-19; Port Officer, Akyab, Burma, 1923-26; Chief of Staff, Navy Office, and Capt. Superintendent Dockyard, Bombay, Hon. ADC to Viceroy of India, 1934-38; retired, 1938; recalled to service Sept. 1939 to Sept. 1945 as Commodore of Convoys and RINLO. Admiralty for 2½ and 3½ years respectively. *Address:* St Elmo, Grouville, Jersey, CI. *Club:* United Service.

**MAUNDRELL, Rev. Wolseley David;** Residentiary Canon of Winchester Cathedral, 1961-70 (Treasurer, 1961-70; Vice-Dean, 1966-70); *b* 2 Sept. 1920; *s* of Rev. William Herbert Maundrell, RN, and Evelyn Helen Maundrell; *m* 1950, Barbara Katharine Simmons; one *s* one *d. Educ:* Radley Coll.; New Coll., Oxford. Deacon, 1943; Priest, 1944; Curate of Haslemere, 1943; Resident Chaplain to Bishop of Chichester, 1949; Vicar of Sparsholt and Lainston, Winchester, 1950; Rector of Weeke, Winchester, 1956. Examining Chaplain to the Bishop of Winchester, 1962-70. *Address:* c/o Lloyds Bank Ltd, Canterbury, Kent.

**MAUNSELL, Mark Stuart Ker,** CBE 1952 (OBE 1944); DSO 1943; Inspector-General of Prisons, 1967-70; Director, Gallaher Ltd, since 1963 (Deputy Managing Director, 1965); *b* 24 July 1910; *s* of Ernest Oliver Henry Maunsell, Flamsteadbury, Redbourn; *m* 1939, Ruth Hunter Mason, *d.* of T. A. C. Mason, Headley, Surrey; one *s* one *d. Educ:* Cheltenham; RMA, Woolwich. Commissioned, RA, 1930; RHA Palestine (Clasp, 1934-35). Served War of 1939-45, Burma; Chief of Staff, Control Commn, Saigon, FIC, 1945; Asst Comdt, RMA, Sandhurst, 1946; Chief of Staff, Allied Forces Hong Kong, 1949; Chief of Staff, 1 (Br) Corps, 1954. Dir of Trading, John Lewis Partnership, 1957. Croix de Guerre (France); Commandeur, Légion d'Honneur, 1947. *Recreation:* National Hunt racing. *Address:* Mizbrook Farm, Capel, Surrey. *T:* Capel 2368. *Club:* United Service.

**MAUNSELL, Brig. Raymund John,** CBE 1944 (OBE 1941); late Brigadier General Staff, SHAEF; *b* 25 Nov. 1903; *y s* of Major M. C. Maunsell; *g s* of Gen. Sir Frederick Maunsell, KCB, RE; *m* 1st, 1931, Nora Constance

Richmond (*d* 1956); one *s* one *d*; 2nd, 1960, Mrs Beryl Preston. *Educ:* Beaumont Coll.; RMC, Sandhurst. Commissioned into Royal Tank Corps, 1923; served with Trans-jordan Frontier Force, 1930-31; Gen. Staff, HQ British Troops in Egypt, 1932-37; Major special appointment, 1937-39; at GHQ Middle East and SHAEF: Lt-Col GS 1939-42; Col GS 1942-43, Brig. GS, 1943-46, retd 1946. Company Official, 1948-63. US Legion of Merit, 1946. *Address:* La Maison Haute, Mont de la Rocque, St Aubin, Jersey, Channel Islands. *T:* Central 41802. *Clubs:* Army and Navy; Victoria (Jersey).

**MAURITIUS and SEYCHELLES,** Bishop of, since 1966; **Rt. Rev. Ernest Edwin Curtis;** *b* 24 Dec. 1906; *s* of Ernest John and Zoe Curtis; *m* 1938, Dorothy Anne Hill (*d* 1965); one *s* one *d*; *m* 1970, Evelyn Mary Josling. *Educ:* Sherborne; Foster's Sch.; Royal College of Science, London. BSc (hons Chem.) London, 1927; ARCSc 1927; Dipl. Educn, London, 1928. Asst Master, Lindisfarne Coll., Westcliff, 1928-31; Wells Theol Coll., 1932-33; Asst Curate, Holy Trinity, Waltham Cross, 1933-36; Chaplain i/c parishes Rose Hill and Bambous, and Principal, St Paul's Theol Coll., Mauritius, 1937-44; Missions to Seamen Chaplain, Port Louis, 1944; Priest i/c St Wilfrid, Portsmouth, 1945-47; Vicar, All Saints, Portsmouth, and Chaplain, Royal Portsmouth Hospital, 1947-55; Priest i/c St Agatha, Portsmouth, 1954-55; Vicar, St John Baptist, Locks Heath, 1955-66; Warden of Readers, Dio. Portsmouth, 1956-66; Rural Dean of Alverstoke, 1964-66. Fellow Royal Commonwealth Society, London. *Recreations:* walking, hill-climbing, piano. *Address:* Bishop's House, Phœnix, Mauritius. *T:* Vacoas 58.

**MAVOR, Air Marshal Sir Leslie (Deane),** KCB 1970 (CB 1964); AFC 1942; Air Officer Commanding-in-Chief, RAF Training Command, since 1969; *b* 18 Jan. 1916; *s* of William David Mavor, Edinburgh; *m* 1947, June Lilian Blackburn; four *s*. *Educ:* Aberdeen Grammar Sch. Commissioned RAF, 1937. Served War of 1939-45 in India, Middle East and Burma. Commanded RAF Lindholme, 1959-61; Dir of Air Staff Briefing, Air Ministry, 1961-64; AOC, No. 38 Group, 1964-66; Asst CAS (Policy), 1966-69. *Recreations:* golf, fishing. *Address:* c/o Lloyds Bank Ltd, Cox's & King's Branch, 6 Pall Mall, SW1. *Club:* Royal Air Force.

**MAVROGORDATO, John George,** CMG 1952; *b* 9 May 1905; 2nd *s* of late George Michel and Irene Mavrogordato. *Educ:* Charterhouse; Christ Church, Oxford (BA 1927). Called to Bar, Gray's Inn, 1932; practised at Chancery Bar, 1932-39. Asst Dir, Ministry of Aircraft Production, 1943. Advocate-Gen., Sudan Government, 1946; Legal Adviser to Governor-Gen. of the Sudan, 1953. Senior Legal Counsel, Ministry of Justice, Sudan, 1958-61; retired, 1961. President: British Falconers' Club; Internat. Assoc. of Falconry and Conservation of Birds of Prey. MBOU. *Publications:* A Hawk for the Bush, 1960; A Falcon in the Field, 1966. *Recreations:* falconry, ornithology, photography. *Address:* South Manor, Tilshead, Wilts.

**MAWBY, Colin (John Beverley);** Master of Music, Westminster Cathedral, since 1961; *b* 9 May 1936; *e s* of Bernard Mawby and Enid Mawby (*née* Vaux); unmarried. *Educ:* St Swithun's Primary Sch., Portsmouth; Westminster Cathedral Choir Sch.; Royal Coll. of Music. Organist and Choirmaster of Our Lady's Church, Warwick St, W1, 1953; Choirmaster of Plymouth Cath., 1955; Organist and Choirmaster of St Anne's, Vauxhall, 1957; Asst Master of Music, Westminster Cath., 1959. Musical and Liturgical Adviser (Catholic) Publisher, LJ Cary & Co., 1963; Vice-Pres., Brit. Fedn of *Pueri Cantores*, 1966; Mem. Nat. Cath. Music Commn, 1965; Mem. Governing Body, Nat. Catechetical Centre and Corpus Christi Coll., London, 1966; Mem. Council: Church Music Assoc., 1965; Latin Liturgical Assoc., 1969. Broadcaster and recording artist; occasional free lance journalism. *Publications:* Church music including four Masses, Anthems, Motets and Holy Week music. *Recreations:* politics and psychology. *Address:* 16 Stafford Mansions, Stafford Place, SW1. *T:* 01-828 8124.

**MAWBY, Sir Maurice (Alan Edgar),** Kt 1963; CBE 1959; Chairman: Conzinc Riotinto of Australia Ltd; Hamersley Iron Pty Ltd; Bougainville Copper Pty Ltd; Queensland Alumina Ltd; Interstate Oil Ltd; Director: The Rio Tinto-Zinc Corporation Ltd, London; New Broken Hill Consolidated Ltd, London; *b* 31 Aug. 1904; *s* of Charles Curtis and Alice Maud Mawby (*née* Smith); *m* 1929, Lena White; one *s*. *Educ:* Broken Hill High Sch. and Broken Hill Technical Coll., NSW, Australia. Fellow, Aust. Acad. of Science, 1969. Hon. DSc, NSW University of Technology, Sydney, 1955. *Publications:* technical papers. *Address:* 102 Mont Albert Road, Canterbury, Victoria 3126, Australia. *T:* 83.8888. *Clubs:* Melbourne, Athenæum (Melbourne); Commonwealth (Canberra); Broken Hill (Broken Hill, NSW).

**MAWBY, Raymond L.;** MP (C) Totnes Divison of Devon since 1955; *b* 6 Feb. 1922; *m* 1944; one *d* (one *s* decd). *Educ:* Long Lawford Council Sch., Warwicks. One-time Pres. Rugby branch Electrical Trades Union; one-time mem. of Rugby Borough Council. Asst Postmaster-Gen., 1963-64. *Address:* 29 Applegarth Avenue, Newton Abbot, S Devon.

**MAWSON, Christian;** *see* Barman, Christian.

**MAXSE, Dame Marjorie,** DBE *cr* 1952 (CBE 1941); *b* 1891; *d* of late E. G. B. Maxse, CMG, and Alice, *o d* of T. N. Miller. Administrator, subsequently Chief Organisation Officer, Conservative Central Office, 1921-39; Dir Children's Overseas Reception Board, Vice-Chm. WVS, 1940-44; Vice-Chm. Conservative Party Organisation, 1944-51. *Address:* Court House, Barcombe, Lewes, Sussex. *Club:* University Women's.

**MAXWELL,** family name of **Baroness de Ros** and **Baron Farnham.**

**MAXWELL, Sir Alexander Hyslop,** KCMG, *cr* 1951; Kt, *cr* 1943; *b* 21 April 1896; *s* of late Judge A. Hyslop Maxwell; *m* 1st, 1924, Doris Galbraith (marriage dissolved 1957), *d* of late Henry Pattinson, Liverpool; one *s* one *d*; 2nd, 1958, Phyllis Hargreaves, New Zealand. *Educ:* Moorland House, Heswall; Trinity Coll., Glenalmond; Switzerland. Served European War of 1914-18; in Royal Naval Div.; interned in Holland after fall of Antwerp, Oct. 1914. Joined family business of W. A. & G. Maxwell & Co. Ltd, Tobacco Importers, of Liverpool, 1919; Dir, 1924; Man. Dir Macmillan Maxwell & Co. Ltd, 1931, Chm., 1946-; Chm. British India Tobacco Corporation. Director: Ronson Products, Ltd; Knott Hotels (London) Ltd. Govt Delegate to Greece and Turkey, 1940 and 1946; Tobacco Adviser Board of Trade, 1940; Tobacco Controller, Board of Trade, 1940-45, remaining at Board of Trade as Adviser to Govt and Chm. of Tobacco Advisory Cttees. Chm. British Travel and

Holidays Assoc., 1950-54 (British Tourist and Holidays Bd, 1947-50). Pres. Inst. of Travel Managers, 1959-66; Pres. Hosp. Caterers' Assoc., 1951-66; Governor, Royal Shakespeare Theatre, Stratford upon Avon. Mem. Bd of Govs, University Coll. Hosp., 1945 (Vice-Chm., 1948-51, Chm. 1951-63). Officer Legion of Honour; Comdr Order of Orange Nassau; Comdr Order Ouissam Alaouite (Morocco). *Address:* 61 Cadogan Square, SW1. *T:* 01-235 8422. *Clubs:* American, Pilgrims; Salisbury (Rhodesia).

**MAXWELL, Hon. Allan Victor,** CMG 1967; retired Australian Judge; *b* 12 May 1887; *s* of late Francis Augustus Maxwell; *m* 1919, Margaret Lawless; one *s* three *d*. *Educ:* Birchgrove; Fort Street; University of Sydney (BA, LLB). Called to Bar, 1913; KC 1929. Justice, Supreme Court, NSW, 1934-55; Senior Puisne Judge, 1950. Royal Commissioner (Federal and State). NSW delegate to First Australian Law Convention, 1933. President: Royal Blind Soc. of NSW, 1945-61; Aust. Nat. Council for the Blind, 1959-; NSW Rowing Assoc., 1943-. *Recreation:* golf. *Address:* 452 Edgecliff Square, Edgecliff, Sydney, NSW, Australia. *T:* 32.2724. *Clubs:* Australian (Sydney); Royal Sydney Golf (Rose Bay).

*See also D. C. Miller.*

**MAXWELL, Colonel (Arthur) Terence,** TD; Director: Australia and New Zealand Banking Group Ltd; Australia and New Zealand Bank Ltd; English Scottish & Australian Bank Ltd; Vickers Ltd; Alliance Investment Company Ltd; First National City Trust Co. (Bahamas) Ltd; Governor, Rugby School; British Representative Investments Committee, International Labour Office; *b* 19 Jan. 1905; *s* of late Brig.-Gen. Sir Arthur Maxwell, KCB, CMG, DSO, and late Eva Jones; *m* 1935, Beatrice Diane, *d* of late Rt Hon. Sir J. Austen Chamberlain, KG, PC, MP, and late Ivy Muriel Dundas, GBE; two *s* one *d*. *Educ:* Rugby; Trinity Coll., Oxford, MA. Travelled in Africa as James Whitehead travelling student, 1926-27, and in South America; Barrister-at-Law, 1929; served 7th City of London Regt Post Office Rifles, 1923-35; Captain TA Reserve of Officers, 1935. Capt. KRRC 1940; Staff Coll., 1941; Leader Ministry of Economic Warfare Mission to the Middle East with rank of Counsellor, 1941-42; Col General Staff, AFHQ, 1943-44; Deputy Chief, Military Government Section; attached SHAEF etc. A Managing Dir, Glyn, Mills & Co., bankers, until 1945; Chm., Powers-Samas Accounting Machines Ltd, 1952-70; Dep. Chm., International Computers and Tabulators Ltd, 1959-67, Chm., 1967-68; Chm., International Computers (Holdings) Ltd, 1968, Dep. Chm. 1969; Chm. computer Leasings Ltd, 1963-69; Director: Steel Co. of Wales, 1948-67; English Steel Corp. Ltd, 1954-67. Vice-Chm. Cttee on Rural Bus Services (1959), Ministry of Transport; Vice-Pres. and Treas. City and Guilds of London Institute, 1959-67; Mem. Delegacy of City and Guilds Coll., Imperial Coll., University of London, 1959-64. *Recreations:* forestry, golf, shooting. *Address:* Roveries Hall, Bishop's Castle, Shropshire. *T:* Bishops Castle 402; 52 Onslow Square, SW7. *Clubs:* Carlton; Swinley Forest.

**MAXWELL, Sir Aymer,** 8th Bt of Monreith, *cr* 1681; Hon. Captain Scots Guards; *b* 7 Dec. 1911; *s* of late Leiutenant-Colonel Aymer Maxwell, Royal Naval Div., Captain Grenadier Guards and Lovat Scouts, and Lady Mary Percy, 5th *d* of 7th Duke of Northumberland; *S* grandfather 1937. *Educ:* Eton; Magdalene Coll., Cambridge. BA (Hon.); JP Wigtownshire. *Address:* Monreith, Wigtownshire. *T:* Portwilliam 248; Lansdowne House, W11. *T:* 01-727 6394; Katounia, Limni, Euboea, Greece. *Clubs:* Boodle's; New (Edinburgh).

**MAXWELL, Maj.-Gen. Sir Aymer,** Kt 1957; CBE 1941; MC; JP; Vice-Lieutenant of Stewartry of Kirkcudbright since 1956; *b* 27 Dec. 1891; *s* of Wellwood Maxwell of Kirkennan; *m* 1915, Isobel Frances Hawthorn, *d* of Maj.-Gen. D. G. L. Shaw. *Educ:* Cheltenham; RMA, Woolwich. Commissioned in Royal Artillery, 1911; served European War, France, 1914-18; War of 1939-45, Middle East; retd pay, 1944. Chm. British Legion, Scotland, 1954-58. Mem. of the Queen's Body Guard for Scotland (The Royal Company of Archers); Convener, County Council of Stewartry of Kirkcudbright, 1959-64 (Vice Convener, 1956-59). *Address:* Kirkennan, Dalbeattie, Kircudbrightshire. *T:* Palnackie 211.

**MAXWELL, Bertram Wayburn,** BA, MA, PhD; Adjunct Professor of History and Political Science, Wagner College, Staten Island, New York, and Literary Adviser to Macmillan Publishing Co., New York, USA; *b* 14 Jan. 1891; *s* of Mark Maxwell and Sarah Martha Bender; *m* 1936, Margaret Evelyn Wright. *Educ:* Privately; Hamline Univ.; State Univ. of Iowa. Served in US Army, 1918-19; Mem. of American Political Science Association. *Publications:* Contemporary Municipal Government of Germany, 1928; The Soviet State, 1935; Co-Author of Propaganda and Dictatorship, 1936; Comparative Local Government (joint), 1938; International Relations, 1938; trans. (with Margaret Maxwell) Hombu, Indian Life in the Brazilian Jungle, 1963, etc; contributes to various academic journals. *Address:* 81 Charles Street, New York, NY 10014, USA.

**MAXWELL, Denis Oliver;** General Manager (Special Duties), Barclays Bank, since Dec. 1969; Director, Barclays Bank DCO, since 1968; *b* 27 Feb. 1906; 2nd *s* of William and Sarah Maxwell; *m* 1932, Lilian Hannah Sheppard; two *s*. *Educ:* St Ignatius Coll., London. Entered Martins Bank Ltd, London, 1924; Jt Gen. Manager, 1954; Dep. Chief Gen. Manager, 1961; Director, 1965; Chief Gen. Manager, 1966. Mem. Coun., Inst. of Bankers; Hon. Treas., Merseyside Hospitals Council Inc. *Recreation:* golf. *Address:* Windle Wood, Vyner Road North, Bidston, Birkenhead, Cheshire, L43 7PY. *T:* 051-652 4411. *Club:* Royal Liverpool Golf.

**MAXWELL of Ardwell, Col Frederick Gordon,** CBE 1967; TD; MInstT; DL; *b* 2 May 1905; *s* of late Lt-Col Alexander Gordon Maxwell, OBE, HM Bodyguard; *m* 1st, 1935, Barbara Margaret (from whom he obt. a divorce, 1964), *d* of late Edward Williams Hedley, MBE, MD, Thursley, Surrey; two *s* one *d*; 2nd, 1965, True Hamilton Exley, *d* of Francis George Hamilton, Old Blundells Cottage, Tiverton, Devon. *Educ:* Eton. OC 2nd Bn The London Scottish, 1939-42; GSO1, 52nd (Lowland) Div., 1943-44, in Holland and Germany (despatches); GSO1, Allied Land Forces SE Asia, 1945; OC 1st Bn The London Scottish, 1947-50. Joined London Transport, 1924; Operating Manager (Railways), London Transport, 1947-70. Mem., Co. of London T&AFA, 1947-68; Lt-Col RE (T&AVR, IV), 1956-70; Regimental Col, London Scottish, 1969. DL, Co. of London, 1962; DL, Greater London, 1966. OStJ 1969. *Address:* (business): 55 Broadway, Westminster, SW1. *T:* 01-222 5600; (private) 41 Cheyne Court, Cheyne Place, SW3. *T:* 01-352 9801. *Clubs:* Naval and Military, MCC, Highland Brigade.

**MAXWELL, Rt. Rev. Harold Alexander;** Hon. Canon of Leicester Cathedral; *b* 17 Dec. 1897; *s* of J. Maxwell; *m* 1929, Grace, *d* of Bishop W. W. Cassels, W China; one *s* one *d*. *Educ:* Liverpool Coll.; Liverpool Collegiate Sch.; Liverpool Univ. (BA in Philosophy, Hon. MA 1946); Ridley Hall, Cambridge (Theology). Deacon, 1924; Priest, 1925; joined CMS and sailed for China, 1926; engaged in educational and pastoral work for eleven years; Lecturer at Union Theological Coll., Chengtu, 1940-43; Sec. of Church Missionary Soc., W China, 1940-50; Elected to Exec. Cttee National Christian Council, China, 1942; Vice-Chm. Board of Managers W China Univ., 1949; Asst Bishop of West Szechwan Diocese, China, 1943-50; Vicar of Copt Oak, Leicester, 1950-52; Ab-Kettleby with Wartnaby and Holwell, 1952-59; Rector of Swithland, 1959-65; an Asst Bishop of Leicester, 1950-65; retired 1965. *Publications:* Vital Truths (in Chinese), 1939; Confronted with Christ (Chinese and English), 1944. *Address:* 4 Wessex Avenue, New Milton, Hants.

**MAXWELL, Herbert William;** *b* 24 March 1888; *s* of James Ward Maxwell and Charlotte Eleanor Morris; *m* 1915, Winifred J. Coysh (*d* 1961); one *s* one *d*. *Educ:* Kent Coll., Canterbury. Surveyor and Land Agent, 1906-14; Sergeant 1/25th London Cyclist Battalion, 1908-16; Lieut Royal Engineers, 1916-19; Secretary: British Institute of Industrial Art; Palace of Arts, BEE Wembley; Exhibition of Flemish and Belgian Art; Advisory Cttee, Royal Mint, 1920-27; Curator, Stoke-on-Trent Museums, 1927-30; Dir Bristol Museum and Art Gallery, 1930-45; Fellow, Royal Society of Arts; Mem. of Council, Museum Association, 1930-32; Pres., South-western group of Museums and Art Galleries 1931-32; Hon. Sec., Council for the Preservation of Ancient Bristol; Hon. Gen. Sec. Theatre Royal, Bristol, Preservation Fund, 1938-48. In South America with exhibition of British Contemporary Art for British Council, 1943-44; Mem. Advisory Council, Victoria and Albert Museum, 1945-50, Acting Hon. Sec. Royal West of England Academy, 1946-51; Dir, City Art Gallery, Bristol, 1945-52; Curator, Snowshill Manor, Glos (The National Trust), 1952-62. Elected to Morden Coll., 1967. *Publications:* Exhibition Catalogues, Magazine articles, etc. *Address:* Morden College, Blackheath, SE3.

**MAXWELL, (Ian) Robert;** MC 1945; *b* 10 June 1923; *s* of Michael and Ann Hoch; *m* 1945, Elisabeth (*née* Meynard); three *s* four *d* (and one *s* decd). *Educ:* self-educated. Served War of 1939-45 (MC). In German Sect. of Foreign Office (Head of Press sect., Berlin), 1945-47. Chm., Robert Maxwell & Co. Ltd, 1948-; Publisher and Chm. of Bd, Pergamon Press Inc., New York, 1949-; Founder, Publisher and Chm. of Bd, Pergamon Press, Oxford and London, 1949-69; Chm. and Chief Exec., Internat. Learning Systems Corp. Ltd, 1968-69; Dir, Gauthier-Villars (Publishers), Paris, 1961-. MP (Lab) Buckingham, 1964-70. Chm., Labour Nat. Fund Raising Foundn, 1960-69; Chm., Labour Working Party on Science, Govt and Industry, 1963-64; Mem., Council of Europe (Vice-Chm., Cttee on Science and Technology), 1968. Treas., Centre 42, 1965-. Co-produced films: Mozart's Don Giovanni, Salzburg Festival, 1954; Bolshoi Ballet, 1957; Swan Lake, 1968. *Publications:* (ed) Information USSR, 1963; The Economics of Nuclear Power, 1965; Public Sector Purchasing, 1968 (jt author) Man Alive, 1968. *Recreations:* chess, mountain-climbing. *Address:* 4 Fitzroy Square, W1. *T:* 01-387 4455; Headington Hill Hall, Oxford. *T:* 64881.

**MAXWELL, Surgeon Rear-Adm. Joseph Archibald,** CB 1950; CVO 1939; CBE 1944 (OBE 1938); *b* 1890; *s* of Thomas Henry Maxwell, KC, LLD; *m* 1919, Dorothy Anna, ARRC, *d* of John Arthur Perkin, The Grange, Matfield, Kent; two *s* two *d*. *Educ:* Trinity Coll., Dublin (MB, BCh 1912); FRCS Edinburgh 1926. Surgeon Rear-Adm. 1946; in charge: Hospital Ship Oxfordshire, 1943-44; RN Aux. Hosp. Sydney, 1944-46; RN Aux. Hosp. Sherborne, 1946-48; RN Hosp. Haslar, 1948-49; formerly Surgical Specialist, RN Hosps, Haslar, Malta, Chatham, and Plymouth; retired, 1949; CStJ 1949, KHS 1946-49. Medical Superintendent, St Mary's Hospital, Portsmouth, retired 1955. *Address:* The Old Vicarage, Compton Chamberlayne, Salisbury, Wilts.

**MAXWELL, Patrick;** Solicitor; *b* 12 March 1909; *e s* of late Alderman Patrick Maxwell, Solicitor, Londonderry; *m* 1st, 1935 (wife *d* 1962); two *d*; 2nd, 1969. *Educ:* Convent of Mercy, Artillery Street, Londonderry; Christian Brothers Sch., Brow-of-the-Hill, Londonderry; St Columb's Coll., Londonderry. Solicitor, 1932; entered Londonderry Corporation as Councillor, 1934; resigned as protest against re-destribution scheme, 1937; Leader of Anti-Partition Party in Londonderry Corporation from 1938; did not seek re-election, 1946; first Chairman of Irish Union Association, 1936; Chairman of Derry Catholic Registration Association, 1934-52. MP (Nat) Foyle Division of Londonderry City, Northern Ireland Parliament, 1937-53. Resident Magistrate, Londonderry, 1968-. president: Law Society of Northern Ireland, 1967-68 (Vice-Pres., 1966-67); Londonderry Rotary Club, 1958-59; Chm. Rotary in Ireland, 1963-64; Mem., Council, International Bar Association, 1968. *Address:* 3 Talbot Park, Londonderry. *T:* Brookhall 425.

**MAXWELL, Sir Patrick I. Heron-;** *see* Heron-Maxwell.

**MAXWELL, Mrs Patrick Perceval-;** *see* King-Hall, Magdalen.

**MAXWELL, Peter,** QC (Scotland) 1961; Sheriff of Dumfries and Galloway, since 1970; *b* 21 May 1919; *s* of Comdr and late Mrs Herries Maxwell, Munches, Dalbeattie, Kirkcudbrightshire; *m* 1941, Alison Susan Readman; one *s* two *d* (and one *s* decd). *Educ:* Wellington Coll.; Balliol Coll., Oxford; Edinburgh Univ. Served Argyll and Sutherland Highlanders, and late RA, 1939-46. Called to Scottish Bar, 1951. *Address:* 46 Heriot Row, Edinburgh 3. *T:* 031-225 3040.

**MAXWELL, Robert;** *see* Maxwell, I. R.

**MAXWELL, Sir Robert (Hugh),** KBE 1961 (OBE 1942); *b* 2 Jan. 1906; *s* of William Robert and Nancy Dockett Maxwell; *m* 1935, Mary Courtney Jewell; two *s*. Comdr of Order of George I of Greece, 1961; Order of Merit of Syria. *Address:* 4 Meleagrou, Athens, Greece. *Clubs:* St James'; Athens (Athens).

**MAXWELL, Col Terence;** *see* Maxwell, Col A. T.

**MAXWELL, Rear-Adm. Thomas Heron,** CB 1967; DSC 1942; idc, jssc, psc; Director-General of Naval Training, Ministry of Defence, 1965-67; retired, 1967; *b* 10 April 1912; *s* of late H. G. Maxwell; *m* 1947, Maeve McKinley; two *s* two *d*. *Educ:* Campbell Coll., Belfast; Royal Naval Engineering Coll. Cadet, 1930; Commander, 1946; Captain, 1956; Rear-Adm., 1965. FIMechE. *Recreation:* fishing.

*Address:* Middle Twinhoe, Bath, Somerset. *T:* Combe Down 2242. *Club:* Army and Navy.

**MAXWELL, William Wayland,** MA (Cantab); CEng, FIMechE, FIEE; Operating Manager (Railways), London Transport Executive, since 1970; *b* 10 March 1925; *s* of Somerset Maxwell; *m* 1963, Eugenie Pamela Cavanagh, *d* of F. L. Crump; no *c. Educ:* Bedales Sch.; Trinity Hall, Cambrdige (Mech. Scis Tripos). Entered London Transport, 1947; Development Engr (Victoria Line), 1963; Mechanical Engr: (Development: Railways), 1964; Ltd, (Running: Railways), 1969. Dir, Whelpdale, Maxwell & Codd Ltd, piano and harpsichord makers. Major, Engr and Railway Staff Corps RE (T&AVR). *Publications:* papers in Proc. IMechE and Proc. IEE. *Recreations:* sailing, gardening, theatre. *Address:* 40 Elm Bank Gardens, Barnes, SW13. *T:* 01-876 9575.

**MAXWELL-HYSLOP, Robert John;** MP (C) Tiverton Division of Devon since 1960; *b* 6 June 1931; 2nd *s* of Capt. A. H. Maxwell-Hyslop, AM, RN, and late Mrs Maxwell-Hyslop; *m* 1968, Joanna Margaret, *er d* of Thomas McCosh. *Educ:* Stowe; Christ Church, Oxford (MA). Hons Degree in PPE Oxon., 1954. Joined Rolls-Royce Ltd Aero Engine Div., as graduate apprentice, Sept. 1954; served 2 years as such and then joined Export Sales Dept; apptd PA to Dir and GM (Sales and Service), 1958; left Rolls-Royce Aug. 1960. Contested (C) Derby (North) General Election, 1959. *Recreations:* motoring, swimming, tennis. *Address:* 4 Tiverton Road, Silverton, Exeter, Devon.

**MAY,** family name of **Baron May.**

**MAY,** 3rd Baron, *cr* 1935, of Weybridge; **Michael St John May;** 3rd Bt, *cr* 1931; late Lieut, Royal Corps of Signals; *b* 26 Sept. 1931; *o s* of 2nd Baron May and *d* of George Ricardo Thomas; *S* father 1950; *m* 1st, 1958, Dorothea Catherine Ann (marriage dissolved, 1963), *d* of Charles McCarthy, Boston, USA; 2nd, 1963, Jillian Mary, *d* of Albert Edward Shipton, Wroxton Mill, Wroxton, Oxon.; one *s* one *d. Educ:* Wycliffe Coll., Stonehouse, Glos.; Magdalene Coll., Cambridge. 2nd Lieut, Royal Signals, 1950. *Recreations:* flying, travel. *Heir: s* Hon. Jasper Bertram St John May, *b* 24 Oct. 1965. *Address:* Pool Farmhouse, Wroxton, Oxon.

**MAY, Surgeon Vice-Adm. Sir Cyril;** *see* May, Surgeon Vice-Adm. Sir R. C.

**MAY, Major Frederick;** (Fred May); MBE 1939; TD; CStJ; Artist and Caricaturist; Chevalier Légion d'Honneur; Officier Palmes d'Académie; Médaille au Mérite (Française); *b* 25 Jan. 1891; *s* of late John Morritt May and Annie (*née* Gittins); *m* 1916, Amy Kidger; one *s* one *d. Educ:* Wallasey Coll. of Art; Reading Univ. Major, late The Green Howards; served: European War, 7 Bn France, 1916-17 (wounded); War of 1939-45, The 4th Bn Green Howards, GSO, GHQ 21 Army Gp (MI), HQ Fighter Command and SHAEF G3 Div., France and Germany, 1944-46. Formerly artist on North Eastern Daily Gazette, Middlesbrough, Liverpool Daily Post and Echo, and later The Tatler, Graphic, and Weekly Sketch for 33 years. Rejoined new edn of The Tatler, 1968. Contrib. to several jls, from New Zealand to Vancouver; successful Loan Exhibn of own paintings and sketches, Municipal Libraries, Middlesbrough, Nov. 1930; permanent collections in Sir John Hunt Art Gallery, York, Artists' Club, Liverpool, Bentley Priory, Stanmore, Mddx, and Polo Museum, Midhurst; work chosen by Japanese Govt, as being correct representative of British Caricature and to contribute to permanent Art Collection at Tokyo, 1921; King George VI Coronation Medal; Staff Officer to Gen. Sir Eric S. Girdwood, Chief Gold Stick Officer, Westminster Abbey, 12 May 1937. *Publications:* The 4th Battalion, Green Howards; The York and Lancaster Regiment; City Lights. *Recreations:* walking, swimming. *Address:* Rokeby, Allcroft Road, Reading, Berks. *T:* Reading 81008. *Club:* Artists (Liverpool).

**MAY, Harry Blight,** MD, FRCP; Director of Clinical Laboratories, The London Hospital, since 1946; Consultant Pathologist to Royal Navy since 1950; *b* 12 Nov. 1908; *s* of John and Isobel May, Plymouth, Devon; *m* 1949, Dorothy Quartermaine; no *c. Educ:* Devonport; St John's Coll., Cambridge (Scholar). 1st cl. Natural Science Tripos, 1929. Postgraduate study Harvard Medical Sch., 1936. Dean, Faculty of Medicine, Univ. of London, 1960-64; Dean of Med. and Dental Sch., The London Hosp. Med. Coll., 1953-68; Mem. Senate, Univ. of London; Mem. Governing Body, Royal Veterinary Coll.; Examiner, Royal College of Physicians of London and Univ. of Oxford. *Publications:* Clinical Pathology (6th edn), 1951; papers on Antibacterial Agents and other medical subjects. *Address:* 3 Littlemead, Littleworth Road, Esher, Surrey. *T:* Esher 62394. *Club:* Athenæum.

**MAY, John Douglas,** QC 1965; *b* 28 June 1923; *s* of late E. A. G. May, Shanghai, and of Mrs May, Sprimont Place, SW3; *m* 1958, Mary, *er d* of Sir Owen Morshead, *qv*; two *s* one *d. Educ:* Clifton Coll.; Balliol Coll., Oxford. Lieut (SpSc) RNVR, 1944-46. Barrister-at-Law, Inner Temple, 1947. *Address:* 39 St Leonard's Terrace, SW3. *T:* 01-352 9660. *Clubs:* Hurlingham; Vincent's (Oxford).

**MAY, John Otto,** CBE 1962 (OBE 1949); HM Consul-General, Gothenburg, since 1968; *b* 21 April 1913; *s* of late Otto May, FRCP, MD; *m* 1939, Maureen McNally, one *d. Educ:* Sherborne; St John's Coll., Cambridge. Apptd to Dept of Overseas Trade, 1937. Private Sec. to Comptroller-General, 1939; Asst Commercial Secretary: Copenhagen, 1939; Helsinki, 1940; Ministry of Economic Warfare (Representative in Caracas), 1942-44; First Sec. (Commercial): Rome, 1945, Bucharest, 1948; Foreign Office, 1950-53; First Sec., Helsinki, 1954. Acted as Chargé d'Affaires in 1954, 1955, and 1956; Counsellor (Commercial) and Consul-General, HM Embassy, Athens, 1957-60; Consul-General: Genoa, 1960-65; Rotterdam, 1965-68. *Recreations:* photography, walking, philately. *Address:* Willowdale, Lower Glenageary Road, Dun Laoghaire, Co. Dublin. *T:* Dublin 803.696; c/o National Westminster Bank, 55 High Street, Hampstead, NW3. *T:* 01-435 5222. *Clubs:* Oxford and Cambridge University, Challoner.

**MAY, Paul,** CBE 1970; retired 1970; *b* 12 July 1907; *s* of William Charles May and Katharine Edith May; *m* 1st, 1933, Dorothy Ida Makower (*d* 1961); two *s* one *d*; 2nd, 1969, Frances Maud Douglas (*née* Tarver); two step *s. Educ:* Westminster; Christ Church, Oxford (MA). United Africa Co. Ltd, 1930-32; John Lewis Partnership, 1932-40; Min. of Aircraft Production, 1940-45; John Lewis Partnership, 1945-70 (Dep. Chm., 1955-70). Mem. Exec. Cttee, Land Settlement Assoc. Ltd, 1962-71. *Recreations:* walking, reading, etc. *Address:* Chesterford, Whittingham, Northumberland. *T:* Wittingham 642.

**MAY, Percy;** DSc (London), FRIC; Consulting Chemist and Chartered Patent Agent; *b* London, 1886; 4th *s* of late William and Emma May; *m* 1942, Marjorie Stone, *o d* of late T. R. Maynard; one *s* one *d*. *Educ:* Tollington Park Coll.; University Coll., London; Tuffnell Scholarship, 1908; BSc, 1908 (first-class hons), DSc, 1916; Research Work, 1908; Lecturer and Demonstrator in Chemistry, University of Birmingham, 1911-12; Chemical Research Work in London, 1912-16; at Oxford 1916-21. *Publications:* various papers in Journal of Chemical Society and other scientific journals; Chemistry of Synthetic Drugs, 1st edn 1911, 4th edn 1939, 5th edn 1959. *Recreations:* reading, music, photography. *Address:* 36 Woodstock Road North, St Albans, Herts. *T:* St Albans 51619; 70 Chancery Lane, WC2. *T:* 01-405 4405.

**MAY, Peter Barker Howard;** Lloyd's Insurance Broker since 1953; Underwriting Member of Lloyd's, 1962; *b* 31 Dec. 1929; *m* 1959, Virginia, *er d* of A. H. H. Gilligan, of Franklins, Shamley Green, Surrey; four *d*. *Educ:* Charterhouse; Pembroke Coll., Cambridge (BA). Cambridge cricket and football XIs v. Oxford, 1950, 1951 and 1952; Surrey County Cricket Cap, 1950; played cricket for England v. S Africa 1951, v. India 1952, v. Australia 1953, v. W Indies 1953, v. Pakistan, Australia and New Zealand 1954; captained England v. S Africa, 1955, v. Australia 1956, v. S Africa 1956-57, v. W Indies, 1957, v. New Zealand 1958, v. Australia, 1958-59, v. India, 1959, v. West Indies, 1959-60, v. Australia, 1961. *Publication:* Peter May's Book of Cricket, 1956. *Recreation:* golf. *Address:* Briarfield, Cranleigh, Surrey. *T:* Cranleigh 2498. *Clubs:* MCC, Surrey County Cricket, Forty, National Sporting.

**MAY, Surgeon Vice-Adm. Sir (Robert) Cyril,** KBE 1958 (OBE 1942); CB 1956; MC 1918; FRCS 1957; Medical Director-General of the Navy, 1956-60; *b* 12 June 1897; *yr s* of Robert May, Belgrave Road, London; *m* 1925, Mary, *d* of Patrick James Robertson, Cupar, Fife; one *s*. *Educ:* Westminster Sch.; Guy's Hospital. Served European War, 1916-18; 2nd Lieut RGA 1915; Actg Major 1917; comd 139 Siege Battery. MRCS, LRCP 1925. Surgeon Lieut RN, 1925; Surgeon Comdr, 1937; Asst to Med. Dir.-Gen., 1938-46; Surgeon Capt., 1946; Senior Medical Officer (Surgical Sect) RN Hosp., Chatham, 1946-49 and 1951-53; Fleet Medical Officer, Home Fleet, 1949-50; Surgeon Rear-Adm., 1953; Medical Officer-in-Charge, RN Hosp., Malta, and Medical Adviser to C-in-C, AFMed., 1953-56; QHS, 1953-60; Surg. Vice-Adm., 1956. KStJ 1959. *Recreations:* cricket, lawn tennis, golf. *Address:* 45 Belsize Court, Lyndhurst Gardens, NW3. *T:* 01-435 5233. *Club:* Army and Navy.

**MAYALL, Alexander Lees,** CMG 1964; CVO 1965; HM Vice-Marshal of the Diplomatic Corps since 1965; *b* 14 Sept. 1915; *s* of late Alexander Mayall, Bealings End, Woodbridge, Suffolk, and Isobel, *d* of F. J. R. Hendy; *m* 1st, 1940, Renée Eileen Burn (marr. diss., 1947); one *d*; 2nd, 1947, Hon. Mary Hermione Ormsby Gore, *e d* of 4th Baron Harlech, KG, PC, GCMG; one *s* two *d*. *Educ:* Eton; Trinity Coll., Oxford (MA). Entered HM Diplomatic Service, 1939; served with armed forces, 1940; transferred to HM Legation, Berne, 1940-44; First Secretary: HM Embassy, Cairo, 1947-49, Paris, 1952-54; Counsellor, HM Embassy: Tokyo, 1958-61; Lisbon, 1961-64; Addis Ababa, 1964-65. *Recreations:* travelling, reading. *Address:* Flat H, Alec Court, 47 Catherine Place, SW1. *T:* 01-834 7554; c/o Foreign and Commonwealth Office, SW1; Sturford Mead, Warminster, Wilts. *T:* Chapmanslade 219. *Clubs:* Travellers', Beefsteak.

**MAYCOCK, Rev. Francis Hugh;** Principal of Pusey House, Oxford, 1952-70; *b* 4 Oct. 1903; *s* of Canon H. W. Maycock and Mrs M. M. Maycock; unmarried. *Educ:* Tonbridge Sch.; Christ Church, Oxford; Cuddesdon Theological Coll. Christ Church, Forest Hill, SE 23, 1927-29; Corpus Christi Mission, Camberwell, 1929-31; Chaplain, Sidney Sussex Coll., Cambridge, 1931-36; Diocese of Borneo, 1936-40; Chaplain of Westcott House, Cambridge, 1940-44; Vicar of St Mary's the less, Cambridge, 1944-52. Examining Chaplain to the Bishop of Ripon, 1959. *Publication:* Original Sin (Mirfield Series), 1948. *Address:* S Augustine's College, Canterbury.

**MAYDON, Lt-Comdr Stephen Lynch Conway,** RN retired, DSO 1942 (and Bar 1943); DSC 1945; *b* 15 Dec. 1913; *y s* of J. G. Maydon, one time MLA, and Min. of Railways and Harbours, Natal, S Africa, and Dorothy Isabel Cope; *m* 1938, Joan Mary Doligny Baker, *d* of C. V. Baker, Betchworth, Surrey; three *s*. *Educ:* Twyford Sch., near Winchester; Royal Naval College, Dartmouth. Served in submarines throughout 1939-45 War. Retired from Royal Navy, 1949. Contested (C) Bristol South, 1950; MP (C) Wells Division of Somerset, 1951-70; Jt Parly Sec., Min. of Pensions and Nat. Insce, 1962-64. *Address:* Bruin Wood, Wraxall, near Bristol BS19 1PN. *Club:* Army and Navy.

**MAYER, Col Edward Rudolph,** TD; DL; Member, Consultative Council for Industry, 1961-67; *b* 9 Aug. 1902; *s* of Max Mayer; *m* 1936, Rosemary, *d* of Thomas Craven. *Educ:* Harrow; Trinity Coll., Cambridge (MA, LLB). TA Commission, 1924, Brevet Col, 1950. Served War of 1939-45, E Africa, India and Burma (despatches); Commanded: 304 LAA/A Tank Regt East African Artillery, 1943; 264 (7th London) Field Regt RA (TA), 1947-50; Hon. Col 1953-61; Hon. Col 254 (City of London) Regt RA (TA), 1961-63; Mem. County of London T and AFA, 1947-58. Mem. Board of Trade Advisory Cttees: Revolving Fund for Industry, 1953-58 (Chm. 1958) and Census of Production, 1955-65; Mem., Export Council for Europe, 1963-66. Pres., National Association of British Manufacturers, 1960-63; Mem. Council CBI, 1965-. DL County of London, 1954; Hants CC, 1970-. *Recreation:* shooting. *Address:* The Old House, Rotherwick, near Basingstoke, Hants. *T:* Hook 2167. *Club:* St James'.

**MAYER, Prof. Maria Goeppert;** Professor of Physics, University of California at San Diego, since 1960; *b* Kattowitz, Upper Silesia, 28 June 1906; *o c* of Friedrich Goeppert and Maria (*née* Wolff); became US citizen, 1933; *m* 1930, Joseph Edward Mayer; one *s* one *d*. *Educ:* public and private schs, Göttingen; University of Göttingen (PhD). Volunteer Associate, Johns Hopkins Univ., 1931-39; Lecturer in Chemistry: Columbia Univ., 1939-46; Sarah Lawrence Coll., 1942-45; Physicist, SAM Laboratories, Columbia Univ., 1942-45; Senior Physicist, Argonne National Laboratory, 1946-60; Professor of Physics, University of Chicago, and Enrico Fermi Institute for Nuclear Studies, 1946-60. Member: Nat. Acad. of Sciences; Amer. Physical Soc.; Amer. Philosophical Soc.; Amer. Acad. of Arts and Sciences; Sigma Xi; Corresp. Mem., Akademie der Wissenschaften, Heidelberg. Hon. DSc: Russell Sage Coll., 1960; Mount Holyoke Coll., 1961; Smith Coll., 1961; University of Portland, 1968; Ripon Coll., 1970. Nobel Prize for Physics (jointly),

1963. *Publications:* (with J. E. Mayer) Statistical Mechanics, 1940; (with J. D. Jensen) Elementary Theory of Nuclear Shell Structure, 1955. *Address:* Department of Physics, University of California, San Diego, Calif 92037, USA; 2345 Via Siena, La Jolla, Calif 92037.

**MAYER, René;** Grand Officier de la Légion d'Honneur; Croix de Guerre, 1914-18; Médaille des Evadés; Commandeur du Mérite Maritime; President of the High Authority of European Coal and Steel Community, 1955-57, resigned; *b* Paris, 4 May 1895; *m* 1921 Denise Bloch; one *d* (one *s* killed in War of 1939-45). *Educ:* University of Paris (Licencié en lettres et en droit). Maitre des Requêtes, Conseil d'Etat; Vice-Prés., Chemins de Fer du Nord, 1930; Administrateur and Membre du Comité de Direction, SNCF, 1938; Deputy for Constantine, French National Assembly, 1946-56; Commr for Communications, French Cttee for National Liberation, Algiers, 1943; Minister of Public Works and Transport, 1944; Minister of Finance and Economic Affairs, 1947, 1951; Minister of National Defence, 1948; Keeper of the Seals, Ministry of Justice, 1950; Premier, Jan. 1953. Medal of Freedom with silver palm (USA); Grand Cross: of Orange Nassau (Netherlands); of Order of Pahlevi (Iran); of Order of George I (Greece); of Merit of the Republic of Italy; of Order of Crown of Oak (Luxembourg); of Order of Crown (Belgium). *Publication:* Le Pacte Atlantique, (Paris) 1950. *Address:* 9 Rue Vaneau, Paris 7e, France.

**MAYER, Sir Robert,** Kt 1939; FRCM; FTCL (Hon.); Hon. GSM; Chairman, First British American Corporation; Founder: Robert Mayer Concerts for Children; Transatlantic Foundation Anglo-American Scholarships; Founder and Chairman, Youth and Music; Executive: London Symphony Orchestra; National Music Council; English Chamber Orchestra; Wind Music Society; Council of Christians and Jews; Anglo-Israel Association, Morley College; *b* 1879; *s* of Emil Mayer; *m* 1919, Dorothy Moulton, *d* of George Piper; two *s* one *d*. Hon. LLD Leeds, 1967; Hon. DSc City University, 1968; Hon. Dr of Music, Cleveland, O, 1970. Grand Cross, Order of Merit (Germany), 1967; Ordre de la Couronne (Belgium), 1969. *Publications:* Young People in Trouble; Crescendo. *Recreations:* philanthropy, music. *Address:* 2 Mansfield Street, W1. *TA:* Robmayer. *T:* 01-636 1204. *Club:* Athenæum.

**MAYERS, Norman,** CMG 1952; *b* 22 May 1895; 2nd *s* of late S. A. Mayers, Bolton, and Mary Alice, *e d* of late Charles Ditchfield. *Educ:* King's Coll., London; Caius Coll., Cambridge; abroad. Served in India, 1914-19, Middlesex and Hampshire Regts (Territorials). Entered Levant Consular Service, 1922, and served in Lebanon and Saudi Arabia; Asst Oriental Sec. at the Residency, Cairo, 1927-34; Oriental Sec., Addis Ababa, 1935-37; Consul at Alexandria, 1937; Bucharest, 1938; Shiraz and Isfahan, 1941; Mersin, 1941; served at Foreign Office, 1943-44; Chargé d'Affaires at San José, Costa Rica, 1944-45; Minister to El Salvador, 1945-48; Consul-Gen., São Paulo, 1948-51; Ambassador to Ecuador, 1951-55; retired. Consul (Hon.) Palma de Mallorca, 1957-63. *Recreations:* drawing, painting. *Address:* Calle Virgen de la Bonanova, 13, Genova, Palma de Mallorca, Spain. *Club:* United University.

**MAYFIELD, Ven. Guy;** Archdeacon of Hastings since 1956; *b* 23 June 1905; *yr s* of late Alfred and Beatrice Mayfield, Hull; *m* 1932, Thelma R., *e d* of late Engineer-Captain M. Johnson; three *s*. *Educ:* Lancing Coll.; Magdalene Coll., Cambridge (MA). 2nd Class Hons Law Tripos; ordained, 1930; Curate: St John's, Fitzroy Square; St Saviour's, Walton Street, SW; Hurstpierpoint. Asst Editor, The Guardian, 1936-39; Chaplain, RAFVR, 1939, Duxford, Gibraltar; Sen. Chaplain, Egypt and The Sudan, 1943. Rector: St Paul's, St Leonards-on-Sea, 1946; Little Horsted, 1948; Dir of Religious Education, Chichester Diocese, 1948; Dep. Diocesan Sec., Press Sec., 1950; Prebendary in Chichester Cathedral, 1956. Select Preacher, Cambridge Univ., 1964. *Publications:* The Church of England: its members and its business, 1957; Towards Simplicity in Prayer, 1964; Like Nothing on Earth, 1965. *Recreations:* squash, painting. *Address:* Rush Wind, Ninfield Road, Bexhill, Sussex. *Club:* Royal Commonwealth Society.

**MAYHEW, Christopher Paget;** MP (Lab) Woolwich East since June 1951; *b* 12 June 1915; *e s* of late Sir Basil Mayhew, KBE; *m* 1949, Cicely Elizabeth Ludlam; two *s* two *d*. *Educ:* Haileybury Coll. (Scholar); Christ Church, Oxford (Open Exhibitioner, MA). Junior George Webb-Medley Scholar (Economics), 1937; Pres., Union Soc., 1937. Gunner Surrey Yeomanry RA; BEF Sept. 1939-May 1940; served with BNAF and CMF; BLA 1944 (despatches); Major, 1944. MP (Lab) S Norfolk, 1945-50; Parly Private Sec. to Lord Pres. of the Council, 1945-46; Parly Under-Sec. of State for Foreign Affairs, 1946-50; Minister of Defence (RN), 1964, resigned 1966. Chm. Lab. Middle East Council. Chm., Nat. Assoc. for Mental Health. *Publications:* Planned Investment–The Case for a National Investment Board, 1939; Socialist Economic Policy, 1946; "Those in Favour . . ." (television play), 1951; Dear Viewer . . ., 1953; Men Seeking God, 1955; Commercial Television: What is to be done?, 1959; Coexistence Plus, 1962; Britain's Role Tomorrow, 1967; Party Games, 1969. *Recreations:* music, golf. *Address:* House of Commons, SW1.

**MAYHEW, Capt. George Henry,** CBE 1959; Group Marine Superintendent, British and Commonwealth Shipping Group, 1961-64, retired; Director, Union-Castle Line, 1961-64, retired; Commodore, Union-Castle Line, 1953-60; Commodore Master, RMS Windsor Castle (including maiden voyage) during 1960, retired from Sea Service, 1960; *b* 16 Jan. 1901; *s* of George H. and Winifred Mayhew; *m* 1934, Betty, *er d* of Major H. Cardwell, Bowden, Cheshire; one *s*. *Educ:* Blyth Grammar Sch. Joined Union Castle Line as cadet, 1917. War service, 1917-18 and 1939-45. Commanded: Pretoria Castle, Coronation Spithead Review; Pendennis Castle, maiden voyage, 1959. *Address:* A431 St Martini Gardens, Cape Town, S Africa. *Club:* South African Master Mariners (Capetown).

**MAYNARD, Edwin Francis George;** Counsellor (Commercial), British High Commission, New Delhi since 1968; *b* 23 Feb. 1921; *s* of late Edwin Maynard, MD, FRCS, DPH, and late Nancy Frances Tully; *m* 1945, Patricia Baker; one *s* one *d*; *m* 1963, Anna McGettrick; two *s*. *Educ:* Westminster. Served with Indian Army (4/8th Punjab Regt and General Staff) (Major, GSO II), Middle East and Burma, 1939-46. BBC French Service, 1947; Foreign Office, 1949; Consul and Second Sec., Jedda, 1950; Second, later First, Sec., Benghazi, 1952; FO 1954; Bogota, 1956; Khartoum, 1959; FO, 1960; Baghdad, 1962; Founder Dir, Diplomatic Service Language Centre, 1966; Counsellor, Aden, 1967. *Recreations:* shooting, fishing, languages, gardening. *Address:* c/o Foreign and Commonwealth Office, SW1; 11 Orchard Street, Mosta, Malta.

**MAYNARD, Air Vice-Marshal Forster Herbert Martin,** CB 1941; AFC 1919; Commander Legion of Merit, USA, 1945; Manager to the Conservative Central Board of Finance, 1946-51; *b* 1 May 1893; *s* of late Rev. H. M. Maynard; *m* 1920, Irene, *d* of late Dr J. H. Pim; one *s* (one *s* decd). *Educ:* St John's Sch., Leatherhead; University Coll., London. Sapper and Corporal Royal Naval Division, Aug. 1914-April 1915; Flight Sub-Lieut RNAS, May 1915; served France, and UK during European War, with RNAS and RAF; permanent commission, Flight-Lieut, 1919; Air Commodore, 1940; Air Vice-Marshal, 1941; RAF Staff Coll., 1924-25; Imperial Defence Coll., 1931; commanded 12 (Bomber) Squadron, 1929-30, and University of London Air Squadron, 1935-36; Air Officer Commanding RAF, Malta, 1940-41; Air Officer in charge of Administration, Coastal Command, 1941-44; Air Officer Commanding 19 Group, 1944-45; retired Nov. 1945. *Recreations:* market gardening, croquet, golf. *Address:* Overdale, West View, Colyford, E Devon. *T:* Colyton 487.

*See also Air Vice-Marshal N. M. Maynard.*

**MAYNARD, Brig. Francis Herbert,** CB 1937; DSO 1937; MC 1916; Squadron Leader RAFVR; *b* Ottawa, Canada, 21 Dec. 1881; *s* of M. W. Maynard, Canadian Civil Service, and Ellen, *d* of Senator Hon. R. B. Dickey, Father of Confederation; *m* 1914, Ethel Bates; three *d*. *Educ:* RMC Kingston, Canada. Commissioned to Indian Staff Corps; joined 2nd Battalion Oxon and Bucks in Bombay, 1902, 25th Bombay Rifles, 1903; served in European War with 5/6 Rajputana Rifles, 57th Wildes Rifles, 4th Suffolks, 4th Black Watch, 2/30th Punjabis (despatches twice, MC); 3rd Afghan War; with Wana Column, operations in Waziristan, 1936-37 (CB); Waziristan, 1937 (despatches twice, DSO); operations Waziristan, 1938 (despatches); Commanded 5/6 Rajputana Rifles; held appointment Inspector of PT India; Commander Bannu Brigade, Bannu, NWFP, India, 1934-38; ADC to the King, 1937-38; retired, 1938, awarded good service pension; Hon. Col 5/6 Rajputana Rifles, 1939; Jubilee medal; Coronation medal; served as Flt-Lieut, RAFVR, 1939-40; successively PO, Sqn Ldr and Wing Comdr, RAF, 1940-45. *Recreations:* riding, shooting, and golf. *Address:* Russett's, High Street, Angmering, Sussex.

**MAYNARD, Air Vice-Marshal Nigel Martin,** CBE 1963; DFC 1942; AFC 1946; Commander, Far East Air Force, since 1970; *b* 28 Aug. 1921; *s* of Air Vice-Marshal F. H. M. Maynard, *qv*; *m* 1946, Daphne, *d* of G. R. P. Llewellyn, Baglan Hall, Abergavenny; one *s* one *d*. *Educ:* Aldenham; RAF Coll., Cranwell. Coastal Comd, UK, Mediterranean, W Africa, 1940-43; Flt-Lieut 1942; Sqdn-Ldr 1944; Mediterranean and Middle East, 1944; Transport Comd, 1945-49; comd 242 Sqdn on Berlin Air Lift; Air Staff, Air Min., 1949-51; Wing Comdr 1952; psa 1952; Staff Officer to Inspector Gen., 1953-54; Bomber Comd, 1954-57; jssc 1957; Gp Capt. 1957; SASO 25 Gp, 1958-59; CO, RAF Changi, 1960-62; Gp Capt. Ops, Transport Comd, 1963-64; Air Cdre 1965; Dir of Defence Plans (Air), 1965; Dir of Defence Plans and Chm. Defence Planning Staff, 1966; idc 1967; Commandant, RAF Staff College, Bracknell, 1968-70. *Recreations:* tennis, squash, shooting. *Address:* Manor House, Piddington, Bicester, Oxon. *T:* Brill 270. *Club:* Royal Air Force.

**MAYNE, Mrs Roger;** *see* Jellicoe, P. A.

**MAYNEORD, Prof. William Valentine,** CBE 1957; FRS 1965; Emeritus Professor of Physics as Applied to Medicine, University of London; formerly Director of Physics Department, Institute of Cancer Research, Royal Cancer Hospital; a Trustee, National Gallery, since 1966; *b* 14 Feb. 1902; *s* of late Walter Mayneord; *m* 1963, Audrey Morrell, Kingston-upon-Thames. *Educ:* Prince Henry's Gram. Sch., Evesham; Birmingham Univ. BSc 1921, MSc 1922, DSc 1933. Chairman: Hon. Adv. Scientific Cttee of Nat. Gallery, 1966- (Member, 1952-); Internat. Commn on Radiological Units, 1950-53; Med. Res. Coun. Cttee on Protection against Ionising Radiations, 1951-58; Member: Internat. Commn on Radiological Protection, 1950-58; UK Delegn to UN Scientific Cttee on the Effects of Atomic Radiation, 1956-57; MRC Cttee on Hazards to Man of Nuclear and Allied Radiations, 1955-60; President: British Inst. of Radiology, 1942-43; 1st Internat. Conf. on Medical Physics, 1965; Internat. Org. for Medical Physics, 1965-; Consultant: UKAEA; CEGB; WHO; Mem. Council, and Chm. Scientific Cttee, Imp. Cancer Research Fund. Many awards and hon. memberships of British and foreign learned societies. Gold Medal: Royal Swedish Acad. of Science, 1965; Faculty of Radiologists, 1966. Hon. LLD Aberdeen, 1969. *Publications:* Physics of X-Ray Therapy, 1929; Some Applications of Nuclear Physics to Medicine, 1950; Radiation and Health, 1964; articles on chemical carcinogenesis, and on applications of physics to medicine and radiation hazards. *Address:* 7 Downs Way Close, Tadworth, Surrey. *T:* Tadworth 2297. *Club:* Athenæum.

**MAYO,** 10th Earl of, *cr* 1785; **Terence Patrick Bourke;** Baron Naas, 1766; Viscount Mayo, 1781; Lieut RN (retired); Managing Director, Irish Marble Ltd, Merlin Park, Galway; *b* 26 Aug. 1929; *s* of Hon. Bryan Longley Bourke (*d* 1961) and Violet Wilmot Heathcote Bourke (*d* 1950); *S* uncle, 1962; *m* 1952, Margaret Jane Robinson Harrison; three *s*. *Educ:* St Aubyns, Rottingdean; RNC Dartmouth. Lieut, RN, 1952; Fleet Air Arm, 1952; Suez, 1956; Solo Aerobatic Displays, Farnborough, 1957; invalided, 1959. Mem., Gosport Borough Council, 1961-64; Pres., Gosport Chamber of Trade, 1962; Gov., Gosport Secondary Schs, 1963-64. Mem., Liberal Party, 1963-65; contested (L) Dorset South, 1964. *Recreations:* sailing, riding, shooting, fishing. *Heir: s* Lord Naas, *qv*. *Address:* Doon House, Maam, Co. Galway, Eire. *Clubs:* RNVR; County Galway.

**MAYO, Eileen;** artist, author. *Educ:* Clifton High School; Slade School of Art. Exhibited Royal Academy, London Group, United Society of Artists, Festival of Britain, etc.; works acquired by British Council, British Museum, Victoria and Albert Museum, Contemporary Art Society, and public galleries in UK, USA, Australia and NZ. Designer of Australian mammals series of postage stamps, 1959-62, and Barrier Reef series, 1966; four Cook Bicentenary stamps, NZ, 1969, and other NZ stamps, 1970. *Publications:* The Story of Living Things; Shells and How they Live; Animals on the Farm. *Recreations:* painting, gardening. *Address:* 90 Malcolm Avenue, Christchurch, New Zealand.

**MAYO, Hon. Sir Herbert,** Kt, *cr* 1948; Senior Puisne Justice of Supreme Court of SA, 1942-66; *b* Adelaide, S Australia, 3 June 1885; *s* of George Gibbes Mayo, Adelaide, Civil Engineer; *m* 1st, 1911, Clarice Gwendoline Thomson Melrose (*d* 1957), Aldgate, SA; one *s* (and one lost at sea, HMAS Sydney, 1941) three *d*; 2nd, 1958, Gwen Alister Brookes, *d* of John MacInnes, Naracoorte, SA. *Educ:* St

Peter's Coll., Adelaide; Trinity Coll., Melbourne Univ.; Adelaide Univ. LLB 1909; admitted to SA bar, 1909; KC 1930; Justice Supreme Court, 1942. Actg Chief Justice, May-Dec. 1957. Pres., Phœnix Soc. of S Australia; Pres. British and Foreign Bible Society (SA Auxiliary); Deleg. to London Conf., E-SU, 1951. Formerly: Chancellor of Dioceses of Adelaide and of Willochra (Anglican); Pres. Law Council of Australia, 1933-34, Vice-Pres. 1940-42; Pres. Law Soc. of SA Inc., 1932-33, 1934-35, 1939-40, and 1940-41. Pres. (SA br.), Fellow (Qld br.), Royal Geographical Society of Australasia; Pres. (SA br.), English-Speaking Union; Lectr in Jurisprudence, and in Commercial Law II, University Adelaide; Bd of Govs St Peter's Coll., Adelaide; Jt Ed for SA of Australian Law Jl. *Address:* 90 Northgate Street, Unley Park, Adelaide, South Australia. *Clubs:* Adelaide (Adelaide); Australasian Pioneers (Sydney); Royal SA Yacht Squadron.

**MAYO, Rear-Adm. Robert William,** CB 1965; CBE 1962; *b* 9 Feb. 1909; *s* of late Frank Mayo, Charminster; *m* 1942, Sheila, *d* of late John Colvill, JP, of Cambeltown; one *s. Educ:* Weymouth Coll.; HMS Conway. Royal Naval Reserve and officer with Royal Mail Steam Packet Co., 1926-37; Master's Certificate; transferred to Royal Navy, 1937. Served War, 1939-45; Korea, 1952; Capt., 1953; Rear-Adm., 1964; retired, 1966. *Recreations:* gardening, fishing, yachting. *Address:* Bellgrove, Campbeltown, Argyll. *T:* Campbeltown 2101. *Clubs:* United Service; Royal Scottish Automobile.

**MAZE, Paul Lucien,** DCM, MM, Légion d'Honneur, Croix de Guerre; Painter; *b* Havre, 21 May 1887; *s* of Georges Henry Maze and Catherine Branchard; *m* 1st, 1921, Mrs T. A. Nelson (Margaret Balfour) (marr. diss., 1949; she *d* 1967); one *s* (one *d* decd); 2nd, 1950, Jessie Lawrie. *Educ:* Havre and England. *Publication:* A Frenchman in Khaki, 1934. *Address:* Mill Cottage, Treyford, Midhurst, Sussex. *T:* Harting 464.

**MBANEFO, Sir Louis (Nwachukwu),** Kt 1961; Chief Justice of Eastern Region of Nigeria, since Dec. 1959; *b* 13 May 1911; *s* of Chief Mbanefo, the Odu of Onitsha; *m* 1943, Elizabeth Bona Coker; three *s. Educ:* King's Coll., Lagos; University Coll., London (LLB 1935); King's Coll., Cambridge (BA (Hist. Tripos) 1937). Set up in Legal Practice, Nigeria, 1937; Mem. Eastern Nigeria House of Assembly, 1950-52; Mem. of Nigerian Legislative Council, 1950-51; Judge of Supreme Court of Nigeria, 1952, of E Region, 1956; Judge of Federal Supreme Court of Nigeria, 1958-59. Pro-Chancellor, University of Ibadan, Nigeria, 1965-67. Hon. LLD University of Nigeria, 1963. *Recreations:* tennis and golf. *Address:* The High Court, Enugu, Nigeria.

**MBEKEANI, Nyemba W.;** Ambassador for Malawi to USA, and Permanent Representative for Malawi at the United Nations; *b* 15 June 1929; Malawi parentage; *m* 1950, Lois Mosses (*née* Chikankheni); two *s* three *d. Educ:* Henry Henderson Institute, Blantyre; London Sch. of Economics (Economic and Social Administration, 1963). Local Government Officer, 1945-58; political detention in Malawi and Southern Rhodesia, 1959-60; Business Executive, 1960-61; Local Govt Officer, 1963-64; Foreign Service, 1964-. High Commissioner for Malawi in London, 1964-67. *Recreations:* football, squash and flower gardening. *Address:* Malawi Mission to the United Nations, 777 Third Avenue, 24th Floor, New York, NY 10017, USA.

**MEACHER, Michael Hugh;** MP (Lab) Oldham (West) since 1970; *b* 4 Nov. 1939; *s* of George Hubert and Doris May Meacher; *m* 1962, Molly Christine (*née* Reid); two *s* one *d. Educ:* Berkhamsted Sch., Herts; New College, Oxford. Greats, Class 1. Sec. to Danilo Dolci Trust, 1964; Research Fellow in Social Gerontology, Univ. of Essex, 1965-66; Lecturer in Social Administration: Univ. of York, 1967-69; London Sch. of Economics, 1970. *Publications:* Taken for a Ride: Special Residential Homes for the Elderly Mentally Infirm, a study of segregation in social policy, 1971; Fabian pamphlets: The Care of the Old, 1969; Wealth and Poverty: a National Equities Issue Solution, 1971. *Recreations:* music, sport, reading. *Address:* 61 Heslington Lane, York. *T:* York 77130.

**MEAD, Sir Cecil,** Kt 1967; lately Chairman and Chief Executive, International Computers and Tabulators Ltd (1965-67); *b* 24 Dec. 1900; *s* of James Frederick Mead; *m* 1929, Anne Muriel, *d* of William Tysoe Boyce; three *d.* Joined Guest, Keen & Nettlefolds Ltd, 1916. Served War of 1914-18, RNVR. The British Tabulating Machine Co. Ltd: joined Tech. Service org., 1924; Sales Man., 1939; Dep. Man. Dir, 1949-55; Man. Dir, 1955-59; ICT (formed by merger of Br. Tabulating Machine Co. Ltd and Powers-Samas Accounting Machines Ltd): Man. Dir, 1959-60, 1964; Dep. Chm., 1960-65. Dir, Internat. Tutor Machines, 1962. Chm., BIM, 1963-64, now a Vice-Pres.; Chm., BIM Cttee to reappraise and restate Institute's aims; Gov., Ashridge Management Coll.; Mem. Coun., Foundn for Management Educn. *Address:* 20 Wolsey Road, East Molesey, Surrey.

**MEAD, Dr Margaret;** American Anthropologist; Adjunct Professor of Anthropology, Columbia University; Professor and Chairman of Social Sciences, Fordham University; Curator of Ethnology Emeritus, American Museum of Natural History, New York (Curator, 1964-69); *b* Philadelphia, 16 Dec. 1901; *d* of Edward Sherwood Mead and Emily (*née* Fogg); *m* 1936, Gregory Bateson; one *d. Educ:* Doylestown High Sch. and New Hope Sch. for Girls, Pennsylvania; De Pauw Univ., Greencastle Indiana; Barnard Coll. (BA); Columbia Univ. (MA; PhD 1929). Nat. Research Council Fellow for Study of Adolescent Girls in Samoa, Associate at Bishop Museum, Honolulu, 1925; Asst Curator of Ethnology, Amer. Museum of Nat. History, 1926-42; Social Science Research Council Fellow for Study of Young Children, Admiralty Is., 1928-29, and extensive field work in New Guinea, etc., during subsequent years; Visiting Lectr in Child Study, Vassar Coll., 1939-41; Exec. Sec., Cttee on Food Habits, Nat. Research Council, 1942-45; Associate Curator of Ethnology, American Museum of Natural History, New York, 1942-64. Lectr, Teachers Coll., 1947-51; Dir Columbia Univ. Research in Contemporary Cultures, 1948-50; Adjunct Prof. of Anthropology, Columbia Univ., 1954-; Consultant, 1968, Chm. (and Prof. of Anthropology), 1969-70, Social Sciences Div., Fordham Univ. Liberal Arts Coll., Lincoln Center, NY; Pres. World Federation for Mental Health, 1956-57; Visiting Prof., Dept of Psychiatry, University of Cincinnati, 1957-; Sloan Prof., Meninger Foundation, 1959-63; Pres. Amer. Anthropological Assoc., 1960. TV film, Margaret Mead's New Guinea Journal 1928-68, 1968. Hon. DSc of several univs. *Publications:* An Inquiry into the Question of Cultural Stability in Polynesia, 1928; Coming of Age in Samoa, 1928; Growing Up in New Guinea, 1930; The Changing Culture of an Indian Tribe, 1932; Sex and Temperament in

Three Primitive Societies, 1935; Ed. Cooperation and Competition among Primitive Peoples, 1937; (with Gregory Bateson) Balinese Character: A Photographic Analysis, 1942; And Keep Your Powder Dry, 1942; Male and Female: A Study of the Sexes in a Changing World, 1949; Soviet Attitudes Toward Authority, 1951; (with Frances Macgregor) Growth and Culture: a Photographic Study of Balinese Childhood, 1951; Ed. (with Rhoda Metraux): Study of Culture at a Distance, 1953, also Themes in French Culture, 1954; (with Nicolas Calas) Primitive Heritage, 1953: ed Cultural Patterns and Technical Change, 1953; (with Martha Wolfenstein) Childhood in Contemporary Cultures, 1955; New Lives for Old: Cultural Transformation, Manus, 1928-1953, 1956; An Anthropologist at Work: Writings of Ruth Benedict, 1959; People and Places, 1959; Continuities in Cultural Evolution, 1964; Anthropologists and What They Do, 1965; (With Ken Heyman) Family, 1965 (ed, with Th. Dobzhansky and E. Tobach) Science and the Concept of Race, 1968; (with Paul Byers) The Small Conference: an innovation in communication, 1968; Culture and Commitment, 1969; (with Rhoda Metraux) A Way of Seeing, 1970. *Address:* American Museum of Natural History, Central Park West at 79th Street, New York 10024, USA.

**MEAD, Stella;** Journalist and Authoress; *d* of John Mead. *Educ:* Stewkley C of E School; Toulouse University; Deutsches Institut für Ausländer an der Universität Berlin. After two years at Toulouse, went to Paris, did journalism, and attended lectures at the Sorbonne; spent three years in Berlin, studied folklore, contributed to several German papers (children's sections), taught English, and told English stories in German schools; spent two years, 1933-35, travelling in British India, and also in various Native States; contributed to Statesman (Calcutta), Times of India, Illustrated Weekly of India; did series of broadcasts to Bengali children from Calcutta Broadcasting House in co-operation with late J. C. Bose; occasional contributor to English and American Journals. *Publications:* The Land of Legends and Heroes; The Land of Happy Hours; The Land where Stories Grow; The Land where Tales are Told; The Land where Dreams come true; Princes and Fairies; Great Stories from many Lands; The Land of Never-grow-old; Rama and Sita; The Shining Way; Morning Light; Golden Day; Under the Sun; Traveller's Joy; Magic Journeys. *Recreations:* reading, gardening. *Address:* c/o Westminster Bank, Wembley Park, Mddx.

**MEAD, Brig. Stephen,** DSO 1918; *s* of F. Mead, Metropolitan Magistrate; *b* 1882; *m* 1910, Beatrice Eleanor (*d* 1953), *d* of Commander L. P. Willan, RN; one *s* (and one killed in action). *Educ:* Tonbridge School; RMA Woolwich. Commission, RA 1901; Adjutant of Territorials; Instructor in Gunnery; Adjutant (regular) twice; Served European War, France and Flanders, 1916-19; Brigade Major 22nd Corps Heavy Art. 1917-19 (despatches twice, DSO); Comdr, Royal Artillery, 54th (East Anglian) Div., TA, 1935-39; retired pay, 1939. *Address:* c/o Lloyds Bank Ltd, Cox's and King's Branch, 6 Pall Mall, SW1.

**MEAD, William Howard Lloyd;** *b* 14 April 1905; *yr s* of late F. J. Mead; *m* 1951, Mary Pattinson, *e d* of late L. Borthwick Greig, Kendrew, S Africa. *Educ:* Marlborough; London Univ. BSc (Econ.) Hons. Industrial and Commercial Law, 1925. Chartered Accountant, 1930; RNVR 1938. Served War of 1939-45: in HMS Orion, 1939-41; Flag Lt to Vice-Adm. at Dover, 1942-45. Lt-Comdr (Sp) RNVR, retired, 1950. Clerk to the Vintners' Co., 1947-69. Dir, Royal Insurance Gp (London Bd), 1967-69. *Address:* c/o The National Bank of Malta, Kingsway, Valletta, Malta GC. *Clubs:* Oxford and Cambridge University; MCC; Royal Corinthian Yacht (Burnham-on-Crouch).

**MEAD, Prof. William Richard;** Professor and Head of Department of Geography, University College, London, since 1966; *b* 29 July 1915; *s* of William Mead and Catharine Sarah Stevens; unmarried. *Educ:* Aylesbury Gram. Sch.; London Sch. of Economics. DSc(Econ) London, 1968. Asst Lectr and Lectr, University of Liverpool, 1947-49; Rockefeller Fellowship, held in Finland, 1949-50; Lectr, 1950, Reader, 1953, University Coll., London. Chm., Anglo-Finnish Soc., 1966; Vice-Pres., Inst. of British Geographers, 1969, Pres., 1971; Hon. Sec., Royal Geographical Society, 1967-. Gill Memorial Award, RGS, 1951. Dr *hc,* University of Uppsala, 1966; DPhil *hc,* Univ. of Helsinki, 1969. Chevalier, Swedish Order of Vasa, 1962; Comdr, Order of Lion of Finland, 1963 (Chevalier, 1953). *Publications:* Farming in Finland, 1953; Economic Geography of Scandinavian States and Finland, 1958; (with Helmer Smeds) Winter in Finland, 1967; Finland (Modern Nations of the World Series), 1968; other books on Norway, Canada and USA. *Recreations:* riding, music. *Address:* Flat 2, 1 Hornton Street, W8.

**MEADE,** family name of **Earl of Clanwilliam.**

**MEADE, (Charles Alan) Gerald,** CMG 1951; *b* 9 Aug. 1905; *s* of Charles Austin Meade; *m* 1936, Beatrix Audibert, Paris; one *s* two *d. Educ:* Leighton Park Sch., Reading; St John's Coll., Oxford. Entered Consular Service, 1927; Vice-Consul: Bangkok, 1927; Saigon, 1930; Barcelona, 1932; Chargé d'Affaires, Tegucigulpa, 1935; Consul: Savannah, Ga, 1936; Jacksonville, Florida, 1937; Second Sec., 1941, First Sec., 1943, Lima; First Sec., Buenos Aires, 1946. Counsellor, Washington, 1948; Minister (Economic and Social) to UK Delegation to UN, 1952. Permanent UK Representative to Council of Europe with rank of Minister, and Consul Gen. at Strasbourg, 1955-59; British Ambassador to Ecuador, 1959-62; retired, 1963. *Address:* Casa de d'Alt, Capdepera, Mallorca, Spain. *T:* Capdepera 206.

**MEADE, Sir Geoffrey;** *see* Meade, Sir R. G. A.

**MEADE, Gerald;** *see* Meade, C. A. G.

**MEADE, James Edward,** CB 1947; FBA 1951; MA Oxon, MA Cantab; Hon. Doc. University of Basel; Hon. Doc. University of Hull; Hon. Fellow: London School of Economics; Oriel College, Oxford; Hertford College, Oxford; Nuffield Research Fellow, since 1969, and Fellow of Christ's College, Cambridge, since 1957; *b* 23 June 1907; *s* of Charles Hippisley Meade and Kathleen Cotton-Stapleton; *m* 1933, Elizabeth Margaret, *d* of Alexander Cowan Wilson; one *s* three *d. Educ:* Malvern Coll. (Open Schol. in Classics); Oriel Coll., Oxford (Open Schol. in Classics); Trinity Coll., Cambridge. 1st Class Hon. Mods 1928; 1st Class Philosophy, Politics, and Economics, 1930. Fellow and Lecturer in Economics, 1930-37, and Bursar, 1934-37, Hertford Coll., Oxford; Mem. Economic Section of League of Nations, Geneva, 1938-40. Economic Asst (1940-45), and Dir (1946-47), Economic Section Cabinet Offices. Prof. of Commerce, with special reference to International Trade, London Sch. of Economics, 1947-57; Prof. of Political Economy, Cambridge, 1957-68.

Member: Coun. of Royal Economic Society, 1945-62 (Pres., 1964-66, Vice-Pres., 1966-); Council of Eugenics Soc., 1962-68 (Treasurer 1963-67). Visiting Prof., Australian National Univ., 1956. Pres. Section F, British Assoc. for the Advancement of Science, 1957; Chm. Economic Survey Mission, Mauritius, 1960. Trustee of Urwick, Orr and Partners Ltd, 1958-. Governor: Nat. Inst. of Economic and Social Research, 1947-; LSE, 1960-. Hon. Mem., Amer. Economic Assoc., 1962; For. Hon. Mem. Amer. Acad. of Arts and Sciences, 1966. *Publications:* Public Works in their International Aspect, 1933; The Rate of Interest in a Progressive State, 1933; Economic Analysis and Policy, 1936; Consumers' Credits and Unemployment, 1937; League of Nations' World Economic Surveys for 1937-38 and 1938-39; The Economic Basis of a Durable Peace, 1940; (with Richard Stone) National Income and Expenditure, 1944; Planning and the Price Mechanism, 1948; The Theory of International Economic Policy, Vol. I, 1951, Vol. II, 1955; A Geometry of International Trade, 1952; Problems of Economic Union, 1953; The Theory of Customs Unions, 1955; The Control of Inflation, 1958; A Neo-Classical Theory of Economic Growth, 1960; Three Case Studies in European Economic Union, 1962 (Joint Author); Efficiency, Equality, and the Ownership of Property, 1964; Principles of Political Economy, Vol. 1, the Stationary Economy, 1965, Vol. 2, The Growing Economy, 1968. *Address:* 38 High Street, Little Shelford, Cambridge CB2 5ES. *T:* Shelford 2491. *Club:* Oxford and Cambridge University.

*See also G. M. Wilson, Prof. R. C. Wilson, S. S. Wilson.*

**MEADE, Patrick John,** OBE 1944; Director of Services, Meteorological Office, since 1966; *b* 23 Feb. 1913; *s* of late John Meade, Caterham, Surrey; *m* 1937, Winifred Jessie, *d* of Bertram Kent, Fawley, Hants; two *s* one *d. Educ:* Sir Joseph Williamson's Math. Sch., Rochester; Imperial Coll. of Science and Technology (Royal College of Science). ARCSc, BSc; Lubbock Mem. Prize in Maths, London Univ., 1933. Entered Met. Office, 1936; Southampton, 1937; Flt Lt RAFVR, Fr., 1939-40; Sqdn Leader, Sen. Met. Off., GHQ Home Forces, 1940-42; Wing Comdr (Gp Capt. 1944), Chief Met. Off., MAAF, 1943-45; Chief Met. Off., ACSEA, 1945-46; Head of Met. Office Trng Sch., 1948-52; London Airport, 1952-55; Research, 1955-60; idc 1958; Dep. Dir for Outstations Services, 1960-65. Hon. Sec., Royal Meteorological Society, 1956-61, Vice-Pres., 1961-63. *Publications:* papers in jls on aviation meteorology and on meteorological aspects of air pollution, atmospheric radioactivity and hydrology. *Recreations:* music, gardening. *Address:* Luccombe, Coronation Road, South Ascot, Berks. *T:* Ascot 23206.

**MEADE, Sir (Richard) Geoffrey (Austin),** KBE 1963; CMG 1953; CVO 1961; *b* 8 March 1902; *s* of late Austin Meade, MA; *m* 1929, Elizabeth Ord, MA Oxon, 2nd *d* of late G. J. Scott, JP; three *d. Educ:* Ecole Alsacienne, Paris; Balliol Coll., Oxford. BA 1925. Entered Consular Service, 1925; served at Tangier, 1927, Salonica, 1929, Aleppo, 1930, Athens, 1931, Salonica, 1933, Tangier, 1935, Valencia, 1939, Crete, 1940, FO, 1941, Dakar, 1943, Tetuan, 1943, Cassablanca, 1945; Istanbul, 1947; idc, 1950; Marseilles, 1951; Tangier, 1956; Düsseldorf, 1957; Milan, 1958-62. Retired, 1962. *Address:* Baker's Close, Lower Radley, Abingdon, Berks. *T:* Abingdon 1327.

**MEADE-KING, Charles Martin,** MA; Headmaster, Plymouth College, since Sept. 1955; *b* 17 Aug. 1913; *s* of late G. C. Meade-King, solicitor, Bristol; *m* 1948, Mary (*née* Frazer); one *s* one *d. Educ:* Clifton Coll.; Exeter Coll., Oxford (Stapeldon Scholar). Asst Master, King's Sch., Worcester, 1935-38; Asst Master, Mill Hill Sch., 1938-40. Intelligence Corps, 1940-45. Housemaster, Mill Hill Sch., 1945-55. *Recreations:* history, arts, games. *Address:* Headmaster's House, Plymouth Coll., Plymouth. *T:* Plymouth 63353.

**MEADEN, Rt. Rev. John Alfred,** DD, MA, LTh. *Educ:* Queen's Coll., Newfoundland; University Coll., Durham, England. LTh Durham, 1916, BA 1917, MA 1935. Deacon, 1917, Nova Scotia for Newfoundland; Priest, 1918, Newfoundland. Incumbent of White Bay, 1917-21; Rector of Burin, 1921-29; Pouch Cove, 1929-34; Sec.-treasurer of Executive Cttee of Newfoundland Diocesan Synod, 1934-47; Examining Chaplain to the Bishop of Newfoundland, 1943-47; Canon of St John Baptist's Cathedral, St John's, Newfoundland, 1938-57. Principal of Queen's Coll., St John's, 1947-57. Bishop of Newfoundland, 1956-65. Hon. DCL, Bishop's Univ., Lennoxville, 1957; Hon. DD, Trinity Coll., Toronto, 1959; Hon. LLD, Memorial Univ. of Nfld, 1961.

**MEADOWS, Bernard William;** Sculptor; Professor of Sculpture, Royal College of Art, since 1960; *b* Norwich, 19 Feb. 1915; *s* of W. A. F. and E. M. Meadows; *m* 1939, Marjorie Winifred Payne; two *d. Educ:* City of Norwich Sch. Studied at Norwich Sch. of Art, 1934-36; worked as Asst to Henry Moore, 1936-40; studied at Royal College of Art, 1938-40 and 1946-48. Served with RAF, 1941-46. Commissioned by Arts Council to produce a work for Festival of Britain, 1951. Rep. (Brit. Pavilion) in Exhib. of Recent Sculpture, Venice Biennale, 1952; in Exhib., Kassel, Germany, 1959, etc. Exhibited in International Exhibitions of Sculpture (Open Air): Battersea Park, 1951, 1960; Musée Rodin, Paris, 1956; Holland Park, 1957; in 4th International Biennial, São Paulo, Brazil, 1957; also in Exhibns (Open Air) in Belgium and Holland, 1953-. *One man exhibitions:* Gimpel Fils, London, 1957, 1959, 1963, 1965, 1967; Paul Rosenberg, New York, 1959, 1962, 1967. *Works in Collections:* Tate Gallery; Victoria and Albert Museum; Arts Council; British Council; Museum of Modern Art, New York; also in public collections in N and S America, Israel, Australia, and in Europe. Awarded Italian State Scholarship, 1956. *Publication:* 34 etchings and box (for Molloy by Samuel Beckett), 1967. *Address:* 34 Belsize Grove, NW3. *T:* 01-722 0772.

**MEADOWS, Swithin Pinder,** MD, BSc, FRCP; Consulting Physician: Westminster Hospital; National Hospital, Queen Square; Moorfields Eye Hospital; Neurologist, British European Airways; Civil Consultant, Ministry of Aviation; *b* 18 April 1902; *er s* of late Thomas and late Sophia Florence Meadows; *m* 1934, Doris Steward Noble; two *s* two *d. Educ:* Wigan Grammar Sch.; University of Liverpool; St Thomas' Hosp. Kanthack Medal in Pathology; Owen T. Williams Prize; Samuels Memorial Scholarship; House Physician and House Surgeon, Liverpool Royal Infirmary; House Physician, Royal Liverpool Children's Hospital; Medical Registrar and Tutor, St Thomas' Hosp.; RMO National Hosp., Queen Square; Medical First Asst, London Hosp.; Examiner in Neurology and Medicine, University of London; Hosp. Visitor, King Edward's Hosp. Fund for London; Mem. of Assoc. of Physicians and Assoc. of British

Neurologists; Hon. Mem., Aust. Assoc. of Neurologists; Hunterian Prof., Royal College of Surgeons, 1952; Pres., Section of Neurology, Royal Society of Medicine, 1965-66; Visiting Prof., University of California, San Francisco, 1954; Doyne Meml Lectr, Oxford Ophthalmological Congress, 1969. Hon. Neurologist, Newspaper Press Fund. *Publications:* contributions to medical literature. *Recreations:* walking, music, country life. *Address:* 142 Harley Street, W1. *T:* 01-935 1802. *Club:* Savage.

**MEAGHER, Sir Thomas,** Kt, *cr* 1947; MB, BS; JP; medical practitioner; *b* Menzies, W Australia, 26 March 1902; *s* of Philip Francis and Ann Agnes Meagher, Bendigo, Victoria, Australia; *m* 1927, Marguerite Winifred Hough (*d* 1952); four *s* two *d*; *m* 1953, Doris Ita Walsh. *Educ:* Christian Brothers Coll., Perth; University of Western Australia; Newman Coll.; Melbourne Univ. Graduated 1925; House Surg., Royal Perth Hospital and Children's Hosp., 1925-26; in practice Victoria Park since 1927; Councillor, City of Perth, 1937-38; Lord Mayor, City of Perth, 1939-45; Past-Pres. RAC, W Australia; Past-Pres. Australian Automobile Assoc.; Pres. and Life Mem., Amateur Athletic Assoc., WA; Olympic Fed. Brit. Empire and Commonwealth Games Assoc., Pentathlon Assoc.; Pres. Industrial Fund for Advancement of Science Education in Schools; Pres. King's Park Board; KStJ; Mem. of Chapter, Commandery of St John of Jerusalem and of Ambulance Assoc. of WA; Past Pres. Royal Commonwealth Society; Chm. Museum Bd of WA; Trustee and Past Pres. Coun., Justices' Assoc. of WA; Pres. Nat. Safety Council; Vice-Patron Nat. Rose Soc.; Trustee Police Boys' Clubs; Life Member, Old Aquinians, Ex-Naval-Men's Assoc., Greek Ex-Service Men's Assoc.; Hon. Mem. Rotary Club, Perth. *Recreations:* fishing, gardening, sport. *Address:* Boolah Mia, Albany Highway, East Victoria Park, W Australia; Saranna, The Esplanade, Rockingham, Qld.

**MEANY, George;** President, American Federation of Labor and Congress of Industrial Organizations, since 1955; *b* 16 Aug. 1894; *s* of Michael Meany and Anne Cullen; *m* 1919, Eugenie A. McMahon; three *d*. *Educ:* American public schs. Mem., Journeymen Plumbers Union, 1915; Business Agent, Local 463 of Plumbers Union, 1922; Pres. NY State Federation of Labor, 1934-39; Sec.-Treasurer, American Federation of Labor, 1940-52, Pres., 1952-55. Chm. Mem., or Adviser numerous bds and cttees. Laetare Medallist, University of Notre Dame, Ind., 1955; Hon. Dr of Laws of several American Univs; Rerum Novarum Award, St Peter's Coll., Jersey City, NJ, 1956; Presidential Medal of Freedom, US, 1963. Holds, also, foreign decorations. *Recreations:* golf, painting. *Address:* AFL-CIO Building, 815 Sixteenth Street, NW, Washington, DC 20006, USA. *T:* 293-5213. *Clubs:* Columbia Country, International (Washington, DC).

**MEARS, Lady;** *see* Tempest, Margaret M.

**MEARS, Brig. Gerald Grimwood,** CBE 1945; DSO 1944; MC 1918; *b* 15 Oct. 1896; *o s* of late Sir Grimwood Mears, KCIE; *m* 1925, Margaret (MBE 1946), *y d* of late Maj.-Gen. Sir Gerald Giffard; two *d*. *Educ:* St Paul's Sch. RA temp. commission Sept. 1914, regular Oct. 1915; BEF France, 1915-19 (1914-15 Star, Gen. Service and Victory medals, MC and Bar); India Frontier, 1919; ADC to Viceroy, 1921-22; Razmak Field Force, 1923; Staff Coll., Quetta, 1928-29; GSO 3 Sch. of Army Co-operation, Old Sarum, 1931-33; Staff Officer RA Southern Command, 1933-35; GSO 2 War Office, 1936-39; GSO 2 Allied Military Cttee, 1939-40; GSO 1 War Office and Home Forces, 1940-41; BGS Northern Command, 1942-43; CRA 3rd British Infantry Div., 1943-45 (DSO, CBE); CCRA and Chief of Staff, 1st British Corps, BRA, ALFSEA, 1946; BRA Southern Command, 1947; Commandant, Sch. of Artillery, 1947-49; ADC to the King, 1947-49; retd 1949. *Recreations:* yachting, fly-fishing, shooting. *Address:* Steeple Langford, Salisbury, Wilts. *T:* Stapleford 375.

**MEASHAM, Richard John Rupert,** CMG 1944; OBE 1919; *b* 2 June 1885; *s* of Rev. Richard Measham, MA, RN, and Frances Sarah, *d* of Capt. J. Woon, RMLI; *m* 1914, Beatrice Louisa Baynham; one *d* (and one *d* decd). *Educ:* RN Sch., Eltham; Wadham Coll., Oxford (scholar). 1st Class Classical Mods; 2nd class Lit Hum; Asst Surveyor, Class II, GPO, 1907; Class I, 1919; Surveyor, Eastern Scotland, 1930; Postal Controller Scottish Region, 1935; Regional Dir, Scottish Region, 1939; Dir of Postal Services, 1942-44; Regional Dir, Scottish Region, GPO, 1944-45; served European War with Royal Engineers (Postal Section), 1914-19 (despatches twice, OBE). *Address:* c/o Lloyds Bank, The Strand, Exmouth.

**MEATH,** 14th Earl of, *cr* 1627; **Anthony Windham Normand Brabazon;** Baron Ardee, Ireland, 1616; Baron Chaworth, of Eaton Hall, Co. Hereford, UK, 1831; late Major Grenadier Guards; *b* 3 Nov. 1910; *o s* of 13th Earl of Meath, CB, CBE and Lady Aileen Wyndham-Quin (*d* 1962), *d* of 4th Earl of Dunraven; *S* father 1949; *m* 1940, Elizabeth Mary, *d* of late Capt. Geoffrey Bowlby, Royal Horse Guards, and of Hon. Mrs Geoffrey Bowlby, *qv*; two *s* two *d*. *Educ:* Eton; RMC Sandhurst. Joined Grenadier Guards, 1930. ADC to Governor of Bengal, 1936; Capt., 1938; served War of 1939-45, Grenadier Guards (wounded); Major, 1941; retired, 1946. *Heir:* *s* Lord Ardee, *qv*. *Address:* Kilruddery, Bray, Co. Wicklow, Ireland.

**MEATH, Bishop of,** since 1959; **Most Rev. Robert Bonsall Pike,** MA (Dublin), Hon. DD (Dublin); *b* 19 Oct. 1905; *s* of Rev. Canon William Pike and Harriet Florence (*née* Surridge); *m* 1938, Helen Kathleen Joan Moffat-Wilson; two *s* two *d*. *Educ:* Trinity Coll., Dublin. Deacon, 1929; Priest, 1930; Curate, Drumcree, 1929-35; Curate-in-charge, Aghavilly, 1935-36; Incumbent, Maryborough with Dysart Enos (with Ballyfin, 1950-57), 1936-57; Rural Dean of Aghade, 1942-57; Prebendary of Tullomagimma in Leighlin Cathedral and Aghour in St Canice's Cathedral, Kilkenny, 1951-57; Diocesan Sec., Diocese of Leighlin, 1952-59; Incumbent of Kilkenny-Freshford Group. Dean of Ossory, Canon of Aghold (Leighlin) and Rural Dean of Aghour, 1957-59. Examining Chaplain to Bp of Ossory, 1958. *Address:* Bishop's House, Killucan, Westmeath, Ireland. *T:* Killucan 7344. *Club:* University (Dublin).

**MEATH, Bishop of, (RC),** since 1968; **Most Rev. John McCormack;** *b* 25 March 1921; *s* of Peter McCormack and Bridget Mulvany. *Educ:* St Finian's Coll., Mullingar; Maynooth Coll.; Lateran Univ., Rome. Priest, 1946. Ministered: Multyfarnham, 1950-52; St Loman's Hosp., 1952-58; Mullingar, 1958-68; Diocesan Sec., 1952-68. *Address:* Cathedral House, Mullingar, Co. Westmeath, Ireland. *T:* Mullingar 8338.

**MEDAWAR, Sir Peter (Brian),** Kt 1965; CBE 1958; FRS 1949; MA, DSc (Oxford); Director, National Institute for Medical Research, Mill

Hill, since 1962; *b* 28 Feb. 1915; *s* of Nicholas Medawar and Edith Muriel Dowling; *m* 1937, Jean Shinglewood, *d* of Dr C. H. S. Taylor; two *s* two *d*. *Educ:* Marlborough Coll.; Magdalen Coll., Oxford. Christopher Welch Scholar and Senior Demy of Magdalen Coll., 1935; Fellow of Magdalen Coll., 1938-44, 1946-47; Fellow of St John's Coll., 1944; Mason Prof. of Zoology, Birmingham Univ., 1947-51; Jodrell Prof. of Zoology and Comparative Anatomy, University Coll., London, 1951-62. Croonian Lectr, Royal Society, 1958; Reith Lecturer, 1959; Romanes Lectr, 1968. Pres., Brit. Assoc. for the Advancement of Science, 1968-69; Member: Agricultural Research Council, 1952-62; University Grants Cttee, 1955-59; Royal Commn on Med. Educn, 1965-68; Foreign Member: New York Acad. of Sciences, 1957; Amer. Acad. Arts and Sciences, 1959; Amer. Philosophical Soc., 1961; National Acad. of Sciences, 1965; Indian Acad. of Sciences, 1967. Fellow of St Catherine's Coll., 1960; Hon. Fellow: Magdalen Coll., 1961; American Coll. of Physicians, 1964; Royal College Physicians and Surgeons, Canada, 1966; RCS, 1967, RSE, 1965, RCP Edinburgh, 1966; Prof. at Large, Cornell Univ., 1965; Royal Medal of Royal Society, 1959, Copley Medal, 1969. Nobel Prize for Medicine, 1960. Hon. ScD Cambrdige; Hon. D de l'Univ.: Liège; Brussels; Hon. DSc: Birmingham, Hull, Southampton, Glasgow, Brazil, Alberta, Dundee, Dalhousie, Chicago, Exeter. *Publications:* The Uniqueness of the Individual, 1957; The Future of Man, 1960; The Art of the Soluble, 1967; Induction and Intuition, 1969. *Address:* National Institute for Medical Research, Mill Hill, NW7; Mount Vernon House, Holly Hill, NW3. *T:* 01-435 0822. *Club:* Athenæum.

*See also Sir Ian McAdam.*

**MEDD, Patrick William,** OBE 1962; Recorder of Abingdon since 1964; Deputy Chairman, Court of Quarter Sessions, Shropshire, since 1967; *b* 26 May 1919; *s* of E. N. Medd; *m* 1945, Jeananne Spence Powell; three *d*. *Educ:* Uppingham Sch.; Selwyn Coll., Cambridge. Called to Bar, Middle Temple, 1947, Bencher 1969. *Publication:* Romilly, 1968. *Recreation:* gardening. *Address:* Sheardown House, Malshanger, near Basingstoke, Hants. *T:* Oakley (Hants) 431. *Club:* Carlton.

**MEDLEY, Brig. Edgar J.,** DSO 1940; OBE 1938; MC 1916; *b* 16 Dec. 1893; 2nd *s* of late Prof. D. J. Medley; *m* 1929, Norah Templer; one *s*. *Educ:* Sedbergh; RMA, Woolwich. Commissioned Royal Artillery, 1914; served European War, 1914-18, with 6th and 29th Divs; in India, 1919-27, with 37th Field Battery RA; Staff Coll., Camberley, 1927-28; Staff Officer RA Aldershot, 1929-32; Gen. Staff (GSO 3) War Office, 1932-33; RAF Staff Coll., Andover, 1934; Gen. Staff, Malaya, 1936-38: Comdr 19th SL Militia Depot, June-Oct. 1939; Comdr 53 A/Tk Regt RA (Worcs Yeomanry), Nov. 1939; served in France, Jan.-June 1940; Brig. and Comdr Corps Medium Artillery, July 1940; Comdr Corps RA, Feb. 1941; went to MEF, June 1941; Brig. RA, Sept. 1941; GSO 1 Senior Officers Sch., 1942; Asst Commandant Staff Coll., 1943-44; Dep. Military Sec., War Office, Nov. 1944-46; retired Dec. 1946. *Address:* 1 Thanes House, Shaftesbury, Dorset.

**MEDLEY, Robert;** Painter and Theatrical Designer; *b* 19 Dec. 1905; *s* of late C. D. Medley, and A. G. Owen. *Educ:* Gresham's Sch., Holt. Studied art in London and Paris; Art Dir of the Group Theatre and designed the settings and costumes for plays by T. S. Eliot, W. H. Auden, Christopher Isherwood, Louis Macneice, and Verdi's Othello, Sadler's Wells Theatre, Coppelia, Sadler's Wells Theatre Ballet; exhibited in London and New York World's Fair; pictures bought by: Tate Gallery; V. & A. (collection of drawings); Walker Art Gallery, Liverpool; City Art Gallery, Birmingham, and other provincial galleries; National Gallery of Canada, Ontario; Contemporary Art Society; Arts Council for Festival of Britain, 1951; Official War Artist, 1940. Retrospective Exhibition, Whitechapel Art Gallery, 1963. *Address:* 5 The Grange, SW19.

**MEDLICOTT, Sir Frank,** Kt 1955; CBE 1945; Solicitor; *b* 10 Nov. 1903; *s* of John James and Ethel Laura Medlicott; *m* 1931, Helen Elizabeth, *d* of Rev. Walter T. Penny; two *s*. *Educ:* North Town Elementary Sch., and Huish's Grammar Sch., Taunton. MP (L Nat) E Norfolk, 1939-50, (Nat L and C) Central Div. of Norfolk, 1951-59. Parl. Private Sec., Min. of Health, 1943. Gunner, RA, Sept. 1939; Col South-Eastern Command Staff, 1941; Brig., 21st Army Gp, 1944-45 (despatches); Bronze Star Medal (USA). Director: Temperance Permanent Building Soc.; Wembley Stadium Ltd. Treasurer, Liberal Party, 1969-; *Recreations:* walking, music. *Address:* Carlton House, Lower Regent Street, SW1. *Club:* Royal Commonwealth Society.

**MEDLICOTT, Professor William Norton,** DLit, MA (London), FRHistS; Stevenson Professor of International History, University of London, 1953-67; Professor Emeritus, 1967; Senior Editor of Documents on British Foreign Policy, 1919-39, since 1965; *b* 11 May 1900; *s* of William Norton Medlicott and Margaret Louisa McMillan; *m* 1936, Dr Dorothy Kathleen Coveney. *Educ:* Aske's Haberdashers' Sch., Hatcham; University College, London; Institute of Historical Research. Gladstone Prizeman, Hester Rothschild Prizeman, UCL; Lindley Student, Univ. of London; Lecturer, University Coll., Swansea, 1926-41; visiting Prof., Univ. of Texas, USA, 1931-32; Principal, Board of Trade, 1941-42; official historian, Ministry of Economic Warfare, 1942-58; Prof. of History, University Coll. of the South West, 1945-53; Vice-Principal, 1953. Creighton Lectr, Univ. of London, 1968. Fellow of UCL. Travel and research in US, 1946, 1952, and 1957; Hon. Sec. Historical Association, 1943-46. Pres., 1952-55; Chm. editorial board, International Affairs, 1954-62; Mem. Institute for Advanced Studies, Princeton, 1952, 1957; Chm. British Co-ordinating Cttee for Internat. Studies. Hon. DLitt Wales. *Publications:* The Congress of Berlin and After, 1938, 2nd edn 1963; British Foreign Policy since Versailles, 1940, new edn, 1968; The Economic Blockade, vol. i, 1952, vol. ii, 1959; Bismarck, Gladstone, and the Concert of Europe, 1956; The Coming of War in 1939, 1963; Bismarck and Modern Germany, 1965; Contemporary England, 1914-1964, 1967; Britain and Germany: The Search for Agreement, 1930-1937, 1970; numerous articles and reviews. *Address:* 2 Cartref, Ellesmere Road, Weybridge, Surrey. *T:* Weybridge 43842. *Club:* Athenæum.

**MEDLYCOTT, Sir (James) Christopher,** 8th Bt, *cr* 1808; *b* 17 April 1907; *e s* of Sir Hubert Mervyn Medlycott, 7th Bt, and Nellie Adah (*d* 1964), *e d* of late Hector Edmond Monro, Edmondsham, Dorset; *S* father, 1964. *Educ:* Harrow; Magdalene Coll., Cambridge. BA 1930. *Heir: nephew* Mervyn Tregonwell Medlycott, *b* 20 Feb. 1947. *Address:* The Yard House, Milborne Port, near Sherborne, Dorset. *T:* Milborne Port 312. *Club:* Challoner.

**MEDWAY, Lord; Gathorne Gathorne-Hardy;** *b* 20 June 1933; *er s* of 4th Earl of Cranbrook, *qv*; *m* 1967, Caroline, *o d* of Col Ralph G. E. Jarvis, Doddington Hall, Lincoln; one *s*. *Educ:* Eton; Corpus Christi Coll., Cambridge (MA); University of Birmingham (PhD). Asst, Sarawak Museum, 1956-58; Fellow, Jajasan Siswa Lokantara (Indonesia), 1960-61; Sr Lectr in Zoology, Univ. of Malaya, 1961-70. Skinner and Freeman of the City of London. FLS; FZS; MBOU. OStJ. *Heir:* *s* Hon. John Jason Gathorne-Hardy, *b* 26 Oct. 1968. *Address:* Great Glemham House, Saxmundham, Suffolk IP17 1LP.

**MEDWIN, Robert Joseph G.;** *see* Gardner-Medwin.

**MEE, Mrs Ellen Catherine,** CBE 1956; MA; Consultant, Schools' Broadcasting Council, BBC, since 1963; retired as Chief Inspector, Ministry of Education (1952-58); *d* of William Henry and Rebecca Catherine Oakden; *m* 1945, Frederick George Mee, MC, BA. *Educ:* Birmingham Univ. (MA, Arts Fellowship); Somerville Coll., Oxford (Research). Lecturer in Education, Education Dept, Bristol Univ.; Lecturer in English, Goldsmiths' Coll., London Univ., 1921-29; Exchange Lecturer in English, USA, 1924-25; HM Inspector of Schools, 1929. Staff Inspector (Training of Teachers), 1945. Mem. Advisory Cttee on Educn in the Colonies, Colonial Office, 1938-52. Asst Sec. McNair Cttee on Training of Teachers, 1942-44 (Min. of Education). *Address:* 112 Murray Avenue, Bromley, Kent. *T:* 01-460 0031.

**MEECH, Sir John Valentine,** KCVO 1967 (CVO 1963); JP (NZ); retired Civil Servant, New Zealand Government; *b* 25 Jan. 1907; *s* of Edwin Arthur Wilton Meech and Jane Meech; *m* 1938, Rachel Crease Anderson; no *c*. *Educ:* Island Bay and Eastern Hutt Schs; Hutt Valley High Sch.; Public Service Coll. Sec. for Internal Affairs, Sec. of Civil Defence and Clerk of the Writs, NZ Govt, 1959-67; Mem. various Bds and Cttees, 1959-67; New Zealand Sec. to the Queen, 1962-63; Dir of Royal Visits, Heads of State etc., 1959-67. JP 1949-; Mem. Council of Duke of Edinburgh's Award in New Zealand, 1963-69. Chm. of Bd of Trustees, Nat. Sch. of Ballet, 1969-; Member: Music Advisory Cttee, Queen Elizabeth II Arts Council, 1967-; Electricity Distribution Commn, 1968- (Dep. Chm); Life Mem., NZ Inst. of Town Clerks and Municipal Treasurers. *Recreations:* golf, racing, gardening, reading, arts. *Address:* 205 Barnard Street, Highland Park, Wellington 1, NZ. *T:* 47-280. *Clubs:* Civil Service, Miramar Golf (Wellington).

**MEEK, Charles Innes,** CMG 1961; Chief Executive, White Fish Authority; *b* 27 June 1920; *er s* of late Dr C. K. Meek; *m* 1947, Nona Corry Hurford; two *s* one *d*. *Educ:* King's Sch., Canterbury; Magdalen Coll., Oxford (MA). Demyship, Magdalen Coll., Oxford, 1939. Served in Army, 1940-41; District Officer, Tanganyika, 1941; Principal Asst Sec., Tanganyika, 1958; Permanent Sec., Chief Secretary's Office, 1959; Permanent Sec. to Prime Minister, Sec. to Cabinet, 1960; Government Dir, Williamson Diamonds; Head of the Civil Service, Tanganyika, 1961-62, retd. FRSA 1969. *Publications:* occasional articles in Journal of African Administration, etc. *Address:* Hunter's Lodge, Burwash Weald, Sussex. *T:* Burwash 321.

**MEEK, John Millar,** DEng; FInstP; FIEE; David Jardine Professor of Electrical Engineering, University of Liverpool, since 1946; *b* Wallasey, 21 Dec. 1912; *s* of Alexander Meek and Edith Montgomery; *m* 1942, Marjorie, *d* of Bernard Ingleby; two *d*. *Educ:* Monkton Combe Sch.; University of Liverpool. College Apprentice, Metropolitan-Vickers Electrical Co. Ltd, 1934-36; Research Engineer, Metropolitan-Vickers Electrical Co. Ltd, 1936-38, 1940-46. Commonwealth Fund Research Fellow, Physics Dept, University of California, Berkeley, 1938-40. Mem. of Council, IEE, 1945-48, 1960-63 (Vice-Pres. 1964-68, Pres., 1968-69). Mem. ITA, 1969-. *Publications:* The Mechanism of the Electric Spark (with L. B. Loeb), 1941; Electrical Breakdown of Gases (with J. D. Craggs), 1953; High Voltage Laboratory Technique (with J. D. Craggs), 1954; papers in various scientific journals concerning research on electrical discharges in gases. *Address:* Hendred, 13 Abbey Road, West Kirby, Cheshire. *T:* 051-625 5850. *Clubs:* National Liberal; University (Liverpool).

**MEERE, Sir Frank, (Francis Anthony),** Kt 1960; CBE 1955; FAIM; Comptroller General of Customs, Canberra, 1952-60; *b* 24 July 1895; *s* of Philip Francis and Harriet Charlotte Meere of Daylesford, Vic.; *m* 1920, Helena Agnes, *d* of late Wm G. Doyle; two *s*. *Educ:* Christian Brothers Coll., East St Kilda, Vic. Joined Australian Commonwealth Public Service, 1913; Deputy Dir, Division of Import Procurement, Brisbane, 1942-45; Dir, Division of Import Procurement, Sydney, 1945-47; Asst Comptroller General of Customs, Canberra, 1947-52. *Recreation:* gardening. *Address:* 3 Meehan Gardens, Canberra, ACT 2603, Australia. *Club:* Commonwealth (Canberra).

**MEERES, Norman Victor,** CB 1963; Under-Secretary, Ministry of Technology since 1967; *b* 1 Feb. 1913; *m* 1938, Elizabeth Powys Fowler; two *s* one *d*. *Educ:* Sloane Sch., Chelsea; Magdalene Coll., Cambridge. Asst Principal, Air Ministry, 1935; Principal, 1940, Asst Sec., 1944, Ministry of Aircraft Prod.; Asst Sec., Min. of Supply, 1946; Under Sec., Min. of Supply, 1956; Min. of Aviation, 1959-67; seconded to Dipl. Service in Australia, with title Minister (Defence Research and Civil Aviation), 1965-68. *Recreations:* music, lawn tennis. *Address:* 89 Grove Way, Esher, Surrey. *T:* 01-398 1639.

**MEGARRY, Hon. Sir Robert (Edgar),** Kt 1967; FBA 1970; **Hon. Mr Justice Megarry;** Judge of the High Court of Justice, Chancery Division, since 1967; Reader in Equity in the Inns of Court (Council of Legal Education) since 1951 (Assistant Reader, 1946-51); Chairman of Board of Studies, and Vice-Chairman, Council of Legal Education, since 1969; *b* 1 June 1910; *e s* of late Robert Lindsay Megarry, OBE, MA, LLB, Belfast, and of late Irene, *d* of Maj.-Gen. E. G. Clark; *m* 1936, Iris, *e d* of Elias Davies, Neath, Glam.; three *d*. *Educ:* Lancing Coll.; Trinity Hall, Cambridge. MA, LLD (Cantab); Solicitor, 1935-41; taught for Bar and Solicitors' exams, 1935-39; Mem., Faculty of Law, Cambridge Univ., 1939-40; Certificate of Honour, and called to Bar, Lincoln's Inn, 1944, in practice, 1946-67; QC 1956-67; Bencher, Lincoln's Inn, 1962. Principal, 1940-44, and Asst Sec., 1944-46, Min. of Supply; Book Review Editor and Asst Ed., Law Quarterly Review, 1944-67; Dir of Law Society's Refresher Courses, 1944-47; Sub-Lector, Trinity Coll., Cambridge, 1945-46; Member: Gen. Coun. of the Bar, 1948-52; Lord Chancellor's Law Reform Cttee, 1952-; Senate of the Four Inns of Court, 1966-, and several other legal cttees and councils; consultant to BBC for Law in Action series, 1953-66; Chairman: Notting Hill Housing Trust, 1967-68; Friends of Lancing Chapel,

1969-. Visiting Professor: New York Univ. Sch. of Law, 1960-61; Osgoode Hall Law Sch., Toronto, 1964. Pres. Soc. of Public Teachers of Law, 1965-66. Hon. LLD (Hull), 1963. *Publications:* The Rent Acts, 1939, 10th edn 1967; A Manual of the Law of Real Property, 1946, 4th edn 1969; Lectures on the Town and Country Planning Act, 1947, 1949; Miscellany-at-Law, 1955; (with H. W. R. Wade) The Law of Real Property, 1957, 3rd edn 1966; Lawyer and Litigant in England (Hamlyn Lectures, 1962); Arabinesque-at-Law, 1969; Editor, Snell's Equity, 23rd edn 1947, 26th edn (with P. V. Baker), 1966; contrib. to legal periodicals. *Recreations:* heterogeneous. *Address:* The Royal Courts of Justice, Strand, WC2A 2LL. *T:* 01-405 7641; 3 Fife Road, SW14. *T:* 01-876 7547; 15 Old Square, Lincoln's Inn, WC2. *T:* 01-242 8607.

**MEGAW, Arthur Hubert Stanley,** CBE 1951; MA Cantab; FSA; *b* Dublin, 1910; *s* of late Arthur Stanley Megaw; *m* 1937, Elene Elektra, *d* of late Helias Mangoletsi, Koritsa, Albania; no *c.* *Educ:* Campbell Coll., Belfast; Peterhouse, Cambridge. Walston Student (University of Cambridge), 1931. Macmillan Student, British School of Archæology at Athens, 1932-33, Asst Dir, 1935-36; Dir of Antiquities, Cyprus, 1936-60; Field Dir, Byzantine Institute, Istanbul, 1961-62; Dir, British Sch. of Archæology, Athens, 1962-68. CStJ, 1967. *Publications:* (with A. J. B. Wace) Hermopolis Magna-Ashmunein, Alexandria, 1959; various papers in archæological journals. *Recreation:* travel. *Address:* 27 Perrin's Walk, NW3; 4-6 Anapiron Polemou, Athens 140, Greece.

**MEGAW, Rt. Hon. Sir John,** PC 1969; Kt 1961; CBE 1956; TD 1951; **Rt. Hon. Lord Justice Megaw;** a Lord Justice of Appeal, since 1969; *b* 16 Sept. 1909; 2nd *s* of late Hon. Mr Justice Megaw, Belfast; *m* 1938, Eleanor Grace Chapman; one *s* two *d.* *Educ:* Royal Academical Institution, Belfast; St John's Coll., Cambridge Univ. (open schol. in classics; Hon. Fellow, 1967); Harvard Univ. Law Sch. (Choate Fellowship); Barrister-at-Law, Gray's Inn, 1934 (Certificate of Honour, Bar Final exam.); Bencher, 1958; QC 1953; QC (N Ire.) 1954; Recorder of Middlesbrough, 1957-61; Judge of the High Court of Justice, Queen's Bench Div., 1961-69; Pres., Restrictive Practices Court, 1962-68. Hon. LLD Queen's Univ., Belfast, 1968. *Address:* 14 Upper Cheyne Row, SW3. *Club:* Athenæum.

**MEGRAH, Maurice Henry;** Barrister-at-Law; *b* 5 Feb. 1896; *e s* of Henry Barnard Megrah and Annie, *d* of H. Jepps; *m* 1917, Jessie Halstead; one *d.* *Educ:* London Sch. of Economics. MCom. (London) 1931. Westminster Bank Ltd, 1914. Served European War, 1914-18, London Scottish, 1915; commissioned Royal Field Artillery, 1917. Returned Westminster Bank Ltd, 1919; Secretary, Inst. of Bankers, 1935-59, Hon. Fellow 1959. Called to Bar, Gray's Inn, 1937; Gilbart Lecturer, University of London, 1950, 1951, 1952, 1958, 1959, 1960, 1962, 1963, 1969. *Publications:* Bills of Exchange Act, 1882, 1929; The Banker's Customer, 1932; (Ed.) 7th Edition Paget's Law of Banking, 1966; (Ed.) 22nd Edn Byles on Bills of Exchange, 1965; 4th Edn, Gutteridge and Megrah on Law of Bankers' Commercial Credits, 1968; contributions to Halsbury's Laws of England, and to law and banking periodicals. *Recreation:* riding. *Address:* 5 Paper Buildings, EC4. *T:* 01-353 8494. *Clubs:* Athenæum, Overseas Bankers'.

**MEHTA, Sir Chunilal Bhaichand,** Kt, *cr* 1942; Merchant; *b* Jan. 1888; *s* of Bhaichand Mehta; *m* Tapibai; one *s* two *d.* *Educ:* in Bombay. Started his business career in 1910; Pres., Federation of Indian Chambers of Commerce and Industry, 1941-42; Indian Stock Exchange Ltd; Vice-Pres., Indian Central Cotton Cttee; Dir of several leading commercial concerns; Editor, The Financial News, Bombay; Sheriff of Bombay, 1935-36, during which he had the honour of reading two proclamations of Accession to the Throne of Their Majesties King Edward VIII and King George VI. Has travelled round the world twice. Recently visited United States as Leader of Indian Delegation to International Business Confernece held at Rye, New York, Nov. 1944. *Address:* 52 Ridge Road, Malabar Hill, Bombay. *TA:* Cibimehta, Bombay. *T:* 364783. *Clubs:* Willingdon Sports, Orient; Royal Western India Turf (Bombay).

**MEHTA, Dr Jivraj Narayan,** MD (London), MRCP; *b* 29 Aug. 1887; *m* 1924, Hansa Manubhai Mehta; one *s* one *d.* *Educ:* Amreli High Sch., Gujarat State; Grant Med. Coll., Bombay; London Hosp. Med. Coll., London. Actg Asst Dir, Hale Clinical Lab., London Hosp., 1914-15; Chief MO, Baroda State, 1923-25; Dean, Seth GS Med. Coll. and KEM Hosp., Bombay, 1925-42; Dir-Gen. of Health Services, and Sec. to Govt of India in Min. of Health, 1947-48; Dewan, Baroda State, 1948-49; Elected Pres., Indian Med. Assoc., 1930, 1943, 1945; Mem. Syndicate, University of Bombay, 1928-29; Mem. Academic Coun., University of Bombay, 1934-43; Mem. Syndicate, University of Baroda, 1949-60; Fellow, Shrimati Nathibhai Thackersey Univ. for Women, 1916-60; Pres., Indian Conf. on Social Work, 1950, 1952-54; Mem. Governing Body, Indian Research Fund Assoc., 1931-32, 1937-39, 1946-51; Mem. Scientific Adv. Bd, Indian Coun. of Med. Research, 1946-51, 1953-56; Mem. Bd of Trustees, Kamala Nehru Memorial Hosp., Allahabad, 1940-; Vice-Pres., Bombay Nurses, Midwives and Health Visitors Coun., 1942; Mem. Bd of Scientific and Industrial Research, India, 1944-63; Chm., Pharmaceutical and Drugs Cttee, Coun. of Scientific and Industrial Research, 1954-60; Mem. Atomic Research Cttee, Coun. of Scientific and Industrial Research, 1951-60; Mem. Adv. Cttee, All India Med. Inst., New Delhi, 1955-57; Mem. Governing Body, All India Inst. of Med. Sci., 1957-63; Chm., Children's Aid Soc., Bombay, 1949; Vice-Chm., Gandhi Memorial Leprosy Foundn, 1952-; Chm. Executive Council: Central Drug Research Institute, Lucknow, 1958-63; Central Salt and Marine Chemicals Research Institute at Bhavnagar, 1961-63, 1967-. Vice-Pres., All India Prohibition Council, 1968-. Mem. Medical Council of India, 1938-43, 1947-64 (Chm. Post-Grad. Cttee, 1962-64); Mem. Constituent Assembly, New Delhi, 1948-49; MLA Bombay, 1946-47 and 1949-60; Minister for Public Works, Bombay Govt, 1949-51; Finance Minister, Bombay Govt, 1952-60; Chief Minister, Gujarat State, 1960-63; High Comr for India in UK, 1963-66. Mem. Nat. Cttee Mahatma Gandhi Centenary Celebrations, 1966-70. Imprisoned for participation in Nat. Independence movt, 1932 (for 2 years) and 1942 (for 2 years). *Publications:* articles in Lancet and Jl of Indian Med. Assoc. *Address:* Everest House, 14 Carmichael Road, Bombay 26, India. *T:* 364159. *Club:* National Sports; Willingdon Sports (Bombay).

**MEHTA, Ved Parkash;** Staff Writer on The New Yorker magazine since 1961; *b* Lahore, 21 March 1934; 2nd *s* of Dr Amolak Ram Mehta, MD, retired Dep. Director General of Health Services, Govt of India, and Shanti Mehta (*née* Mehra). *Educ:* Arkansas Sch. for the Blind; Pomona Coll.; Balliol Coll., Oxford; Harvard Univ. BA Pomona, 1956; BA Hons Mod. Hist.

Oxon, 1959; MA Harvard, 1961; MA Oxon, 1962. Phi Beta Kappa, 1955. Watumull Scholar, 1952-54; Hazen Fellow, 1956-59; Harvard Prize Fellow, 1959-60. *Publications:* Face to Face, 1957 (Secondary Educn Annual Book Award, 1958; repr. UK, 1967); Walking the Indian Streets, 1960 (rev. edn 1971); Fly and the Fly-Bottle, 1963; The New Theologian, 1966; Delinquent Chacha (novel), 1967; Portrait of India, 1970; articles and stories in Amer., British and Indian newspapers and magazines from 1957. *Recreations:* listening to Indian and Western music, playing chess. *Address:* c/o The New Yorker Magazine, 25 West 43rd Street, New York, NY 10036, USA. *T:* OX 5-1414. *Clubs:* Savile; Century Association (NY); Gymkhana (New Delhi).

**MEHTA, Zubin;** Music Director of Los Angeles Philharmonic Orchestra, since 1962; Musical Adviser, Israel Philharmonic Orchestra; *b* 29 April 1936; *s* of Mehli Mehta; *m* 1st, 1958, Carmen Lasky (marr. diss. 1964); one *s* one *d*; 2nd, 1969, Nancy Kovack. *Educ:* St Xavier's Coll., Bombay; Musikakademie, Vienna. First Concert, Vienna, 1958; first prize internat. comp., Montreal 1958; US debut, Philadelphia Orch., 1960; debut with Israel and Vienna Philharmonic Orchs, 1961; apptd Music Director, Montreal Symphony Orch., 1961; European tour with this orch., 1962; guest conducting, major European Orchs, 1962. Opera debut, Montreal, Tosca, 1964; debut Metropolitan Opera, Aida, 1965. Australian tour, Israel Philharmonic, 1966; World tour (incl. debut in India) with Los Angeles Philharmonic, 1967. Operas at Metropolitan incl.: Tosca, Turandot, Otello, Carmen, Mourning becomes Elektra (world première), Trovatore, etc. Holds hon. doctorates, and numerous awards; Padma Bhusan (India), 1967, etc. *Address:* 135 North Grand Avenue, Los Angeles, Calif 90012, USA. *T:* MA6-5781.

**MEIGGS, Russell,** MA; FBA 1961; *b* 1902; *s* of William Herrick Meiggs, London; *m* 1941, Pauline Gregg; two *d*. *Educ:* Christ's Hospital; Keble Coll., Oxford. Fellow of Keble Coll., 1930-39; Fellow and Tutor in Ancient History, Balliol Coll., Oxford, Hon. Fellow, 1970; Univ. Lectr in Ancient History, 1939-70; Praefectus of Holywell Manor, 1945-69. Vis. Prof., Swarthmore Coll., 1960, 1970-71; Kipling Fellow, Marlborough Coll., Vermont, 1967. *Publications:* Home Timber Production, 1939-1945, 1949; (ed) Bury's History of Greece, 3rd edn, 1951, 4th edn, 1970; (ed, jtly) Sources for Greek History between the Persian and Peloponnesian Wars, new edn, 1951; Roman Ostia, 1960; (ed, with David Lewis) Selection of Greek Historical Inscriptions to the end of the 5th century BC, 1969; The Athenian Empire, 1971. *Recreations:* gardening, America. *Address:* The Malt House, Garsington, Oxford.

**MEIKLE, Alexander,** CBE 1964; CA; Chairman since 1969 (General Manager 1943-66, Director 1958), Woolwich Equitable Building Society; *b* 22 Oct. 1905; *s* of David and Marion Meikle; *m* 1935, Margaret Alice, *d* of Wilfred G. Wallis; three *s*. *Educ:* Shawlands Academy; Glasgow Univ. CA 1928. Asst Sec., Woolwich Equitable Building Soc., 1929. Vice-Pres. 1970 (Mem. Council, 1947-70, Chm., 1958-60), Building Societies Assoc.; Vice-President: Metropolitan Assoc. of Building Socs; Building Socs Inst.; Vice-Pres. and Mem. Council, Internat. Union of Building Socs; Vice-Pres., Nat. House Builders' Registration Council; Dir, 1966-, and Chm. Metropolitan Board, Legal and General Assurance. Member: Housing Corp.; Nat. Housing Advisory Cttee. *Recreation:* golf. *Address:* Pilgrims, Church Road, Sundridge, near Sevenoaks, Kent. *T:* Westerham 2558. *Club:* Caledonian.

**MEIKLEJOHN, Ven. Robert;** Archdeacon Emeritus; *b* 20 Dec. 1889; *s* of John Robert Meiklejohn and Emma Madeleine Wharton; *m* 1915, Lisa Lockyer (*d* 1953); no *c*. *Educ:* Haberdashers' Aske's Hampstead Sch.; King's Coll., London (LLB, BD, AKC). Ordained, 1914; temp. Chaplain, RN, 1915-19; Vicar of Dorrington, Salop, 1920-25; Chaplain Missions to Seamen, 1926-29; Rector, Felbrigg with Metton, 1930 (and Sustead, 1947) until 1961, Rural Dean of Repps, dio. of Norwich, 1945-54; Hon. Canon of Norwich Cathedral, 1948-54; Archdeacon of Norwich, 1954-61, emeritus, Oct. 1961. *Address:* 3 Metton Hall, Roughton, Norwich. *T:* Hanworth 292.

**MEINERTZHAGEN, Peter,** CMG 1966; Controller, Commonwealth Development Corporation; *b* 24 March 1920; *y s* of late Louis Ernest Meinertzhagen, Theberton House, Leiston, Suffolk; *m* 1949, Dido Pretty; one *s* one *d*. *Educ:* Eton. Served Royal Fusiliers, 1940-46 (Croix de Guerre, France, 1944). Alfred Booth & Co., 1946-57; Commonwealth Development Corporation, 1958-. Mem. Council, London Chamber of Commerce, 1968-69. *Address:* 59 Cleaver Square, SE11. *T:* 01-735 6263. *Club:* Muthaiga Country (Nairobi).

**MEIR, Mrs Golda;** Prime Minister of Israel since 1969; Member of Parliament since 1948; *b* Kiev, SW Russia, 1898; one *s* one *d*. *Educ:* Teachers' Seminary, Milwaukee, Wis. Teacher, and leading mem. Poalei Zion (Zionist Labour Party), Milwaukee. Delegate US section World Jewish Congress until 1921 when immigrated Palestine, joined Merhavia collective farm village; with Solel Boneh, Labour Federation (Histadruth) Contracting and Public Works Enterprise, 1924-26. Apptd Sec. Women's Labour Council of Histadruth, 1928; Mem. Exec. and Secretariat Fedn of Labour, 1929-46; Chm. Board of Directors Workers Sick Fund, also Head Political Department Fedn of Labour. Mapai (Labour Party) delegate Actions Cttee, World Zionist Organization, 1936; Mem. War Economic Advisory Council of Palestine Govt. Leading Mem. Hagana struggle. Head Political Dept Jewish Agency for Palestine, Jerusalem, 1946-48; Israel Minister to Moscow, Aug. 1948-April 1949; Minister of Labour and Social Insurance in Israeli cabinet, 1949-56; Minister for Foreign Affairs, 1956-66; Gen. Sec. of Mapai (Israel Labour Party), 1966-68. Leading figure at numerous Zionist, Internat. Labour and Socialist congresses. *Address:* Office of the Prime Minister, Jerusalem, Israel.

**MEISS, Prof. Millard;** Professor of the History of Art, Institute for Advanced Study, Princeton, NJ, since 1958; *b* 25 March 1904; *s* of Leon Meiss and Clara (*née* Loewenstein); *m* 1928, Margaret Louchheim; one *d* (one *s* decd). *Educ:* Princeton Univ. (BA); New York Univ. (MA, PhD). Lectr, History of Art, New York Univ., 1931-33; Lectr, Asst Prof., Associate Prof., Prof., Fine Arts and Archæol., Columbia Univ., 1934-53; Prof. of Fine Arts, Curator of Paintings, Fogg Museum, Harvard Univ., 1954-58. Hon. Trustee, Met. Museum of Art; Member: Amer. Acad. of Arts and Sciences; Amer. Philosophical Soc.; Medieval Acad. of America, Fellow and Haskins Medal, 1953; Corresp. Member: Accademia Senese degli Intronati; Soc. des Antiquaries de France; Accademia della Arti del Disegno, Florence; Accademia Clementina, Bologna. Morey Award, College Art Assoc., 1969. Stella della Solidarietà (Italy), 1949. Hon. DLitt

Florence, 1968. *Publications:* Painting in Florence and Siena after the Black Death, 1951; Andrea Mantegna as Illuminator, 1957; Giotto and Assisi, 1960; The Painting of the Life of St Francis in Assisi (with Leonetto Tintori), 1962; Giovanni Bellini's St Francis, in the Frick Collection, 1964; French Painting in the Time of Jean de Berry: The Late XIV Century and the Patronage of the Duke, 1967; The Boucicaut Master, 1968; Illuminated Manuscripts of the Divine Comedy (with P. Brieger and C. Singleton), 1969; The Great Age of Fresco, 1970; contributor to Burlington Magazine, Gazette des Beaux-Arts, Art Bulletin, etc. *Address:* Institute for Advanced Study, Princeton, NJ 08540, USA.

**MEKIE, David Eric Cameron,** OBE 1955; FRCSEd; FRSEd; FRCPEd; Conservator, Royal College of Surgeons of Edinburgh since 1955; Director of Studies to Edinburgh Post Graduate Board for Medicine; *b* 8 March 1902; *s* of Dr D. C. T. Mekie and Mary Cameron; *m* 1930, Winifred Knott (*d* 1970); two *s* one *d*. *Educ:* George Watson's Coll., Edinburgh; University of Edinburgh. MB, ChB 1925; FRCSEd 1928; FRSEd 1962; MRCP 1962; FRCPEd, 1966. Tutor, Dept of Clinical Surgery, University of Edinburgh, 1928-33; Ernest Hart Scholar, 1931-33; Professor of Clinical Surgery and Surgery, University of Malaya, 1935-55 (now Prof. Emeritus). Surgeon, Singapore General Hospital and Hon. Surgical Consultant, Far East Command. *Publications:* Handbook of Surgery, 1936; numerous surgical papers. *Recreations:* fishing, gardening. *Address:* 11 Minto Street, Edinburgh; Royal College of Surgeons of Edinburgh, Nicolson Street, Edinburgh EH9 1RG. *T:* 031-667 1203.

*See also Eoin Cameron Mekie.*

**MEKIE, Eoin Cameron,** CBE 1955; BL, CompIEE, MInstT; *b* 3 Nov. 1906; *s* of Dr D. C. T. Mekie and Mary Cameron; *m* 1932, Margaret Blench; two *s* two *d*. *Educ:* George Watson's College, Edinburgh; Edinburgh Univ.; Lincoln's Inn, London. Scottish Solicitor, 1929; Balfour Beatty & Co. (London and Edinburgh), 1930-35; Legal Adviser, Edmundsons Electricity Corp., 1935-39. Served 3rd Bn London Scottish, 1939-41. Sec., Legal Adviser and Joint General Manager to the Edmundsons Electricity Supply Group of Companies, 1941 until Nationalisation in 1948; Chm., Silver City Airways, 1950-62; Dir of increasing number of Cos., 1948; Chairman: Mekie and Co. Ltd; Bunker-Ramo (UK) Ltd; J. B. Holdings Ltd; Mekie Howard & Co. Ltd; Constellation Investments Ltd; Grampian Chemicals Ltd. Contested (U and Nat. L) Leith Div. of Edinburgh, 1950, 1951. Underwriter of Lloyd's; Liveryman of Worshipful Guild of Air Pilots and Navigators of the British Empire. *Publications:* Electricity (Supply) Acts 1882-1935 (with D. H. James), 1935; Town and Country Planning Law (with Harold B. Williams), 1948. Miscellaneous political articles and pamphlets. *Recreations:* fishing and golf. *Address:* 3 Wilton House, 87 Knightsbridge, SW1. *T:* 01-235 7263; 126 Sandy Lane, Cheam, Surrey. *T:* 01-642 7759. *Clubs:* Caledonian, Royal Automobile.

*See also David Eric Cameron Mekie.*

**MELANESIA, Bishop of,** since 1967; **Rt. Rev. John Wallace Chisholm;** *b* 14 Sept. 1922; *y s* of James and Eleanor Chisholm. *Educ:* Trinity Coll., University of Melbourne (Kew Schol.). BA 1942; Dipl. Educn 1943; Bromby Greek Prize, 1944; Leeper Prize, 1945. Curate, St Stephen's, Rochester Row, Westminster, 1947-51; Sub-Dean, Cathedral of St Peter and St Paul, Dogura, Papua and New Guinea, 1953, Canon, 1954; Auxiliary Bishop of New Guinea, 1964-67. *Recreations:* under-water swimming, music. *Address:* Bishop's House, Honiara, British Solomon Islands Protectorate. *Club:* Royal Commonwealth Society.

**MELBOURNE, Archbishop of,** since 1957; **Most Rev. Frank Woods;** *b* 6 April 1907; *s* of late Rt Rev. E. S. Woods, DD, Bishop of Lichfield; *m* 1936, Jean Margaret Sprules; two *s* two *d*. *Educ:* Marlborough; Trinity Coll., Cambridge. Deacon, 1931; priest, 1932; Curate of Portsea Parish Church, 1932-33; Chaplain, Trinity Coll., Cambridge, 1933-36; Vice-principal, Wells Theological Coll., 1936-39; Chaplain to the Forces, 1939-45; Vicar of Huddersfield, 1945-52; Suffragan Bishop of Middleton, 1952-57. Proctor in Convocation, 1946-51; Chaplain to the King, 1951-52; Chaplain, Victoria Order St J, 1962. *Recreation:* walking. *Address:* Bishopscourt, Clarendon Street, Melbourne East, Vic. 3002, Australia.

**MELBOURNE, Archbishop of, (RC),** since 1967; **Most Rev. James Robert Knox,** DD, DCL; *b* 2 March 1914; *s* of John Knox and Emily (*née* Walsh). *Educ:* St Ildephonsus Coll., New Norcia, Australia; Pontifical Urban College de Propaganda Fide, Rome. Priest, 1941; Vice-Rector, Pontifical Urban College de Propaganda Fide, Rome, 1945-48; attached to Secretariat of State of HH Pope Pius XII, 1948-50; Sec. of Apostolic Internunciature in Tokyo, Japan, 1950-53; Apostolic Delegate to British East and West Africa, 1953-57; Titular Archbishop of Melitene and Apostolic Internuncio in India, 1957-67. *Publication:* De Necessitudine Deiparam Inter et Eucharistiam, 1949. *Address:* St Patrick's Cathedral, Melbourne, Vic, 3002, Australia.

**MELBOURNE, Bishops Coadjutor of;** *see* Arnott, Rt Rev. F. R., Dann, Rt Rev. R. W.

**MELCHETT,** 3rd Baron, *cr* 1928, of Landford; **Julian Edward Alfred Mond;** Bt, *cr* 1919; Chairman British Steel Corporation, since 1967; Director: Guardian Assce Co. Ltd; British Field Products Ltd; *b* 9 Jan. 1925; 2nd *s* of 2nd Baron and Amy Gwen Wilson, Klerksdorp, Transvaal; *S* father, 1949; *m* 1947, Sonia Elizabeth, *er d* of Lieut-Col R. H. Graham; one *s* two *d*. *Educ:* Eton Coll. Served War of 1939-45: Air Br., RNVR. Member: NEDC, 1969-; Council, CBI, 1969-. *Heir: s* Hon. Peter Robert Henry Mond, *b* 24 Feb. 1948. *Address:* 16 Tite Street, Chelsea, SW3. *T:* 01-352 7645. *Club:* Brooks's.

*See also Eva Marchioness of Reading.*

**MELCHIOR, Lauritz L. H.;** Singer to the Royal Court of Denmark (Kgl. Kammersanger); Leading Dramatic Tenor, Metropolitan Opera, New York, Covent Garden Opera, London, Grand Opera, Paris, San Francisco, Chicago, Royal Opera, Copenhagen, Metro-Goldwyn-Mayer Pictures, Paramount Pictures; *b* Copenhagen, Denmark, 20 March 1890; *s* of Rector (Skolebestyrer) Jörgen Melchior and Julie Möller; *m* 1925, Maria Hacker (*d* 1963); one *s* one *d*; *m* 1964, Mary Markham (marriage dissolved). *Educ:* Melchiors Sch., Copenhagen; Royal Opera Sch., Copenhagen. Debut as Silvio in Bajazzo at the Royal Opera, Copenhagen, 1913; later Tenor, sang 6 years in the Wagner Festivals in Bayreuth (Sigmund, Siegried-Parsifal–Tannhauser, Tristan); since 1924, Covent Garden Opera, London, 1925, Metropolitan Opera, New York, 1930, Grand Opera Paris; Guest Performances at Buenos Aires, San Francisco, Berlin, Hamburg, Vienna, Copenhagen, Chicago, Barcelona, Bruxelles, etc. Holds several hon. degrees. Pres. Royal Danish Guards, Societies (abroad). Vassar College gold medal for outstanding service to music in America; Distinguished Achievement Grand Lodge Medal, 1944. Commander: Dannebrog (Denmark); White Rose of Finland; El Merito of Chili; Grand Cross, Order of St Brigitte (Catholic); Grand Cross, Alfaro, Panama; Grand Cross of Merit of Federal Republic of Germany, etc.; Knight of Malta. *Recreation:* hunting. *Address:* The Viking, 13671 Mulholland Drive, Beverly Hills, California 90210, USA. *Clubs:* Danish; Bohemian (San Francisco); Liederkranz (New York).

**MELCHIOR-BONNET, Christian;** Author; former Editor-in-chief of Petit Journal and Flambeau; former Literary Director of Fayard editions; Director of the reviews: Oeuvres libres, Historia, A la Page and Journal de la France; co-director of Jardin des Arts; Literary Adviser to Nouvelles Littéraires; Privy Chamberlain to Pope Paul VI; former secretary to M. Pierre de Nolhac; *b* Marseille, 10 April 1904; *m* Bernardine Paul-Dubois-Taine. *Educ:* St Jean de Béthune, Versailles. *Publications:* Scènes et portraits historiques de Chateaubriand; Mémoires du Cardinal de Retz; Mémoires du Comte Alexandre de Tilly, ancien page de la reine Marie-Antoinette; Napoléon par Chateaubriand; Principes d'action de Salazar. *Address:* 17 Boulevard de Beauséjour, Paris XVIe, France.

**MELDRUM, Andrew,** CBE 1962 (OBE 1956); Chief Inspector of Constabulary for Scotland, 1966-69, retired; *b* 22 April 1909; *s* of late Andrew Meldrum, Burntisland, Fife; *m* 1937, Janet H., *d* of late Robert Crooks, Grangemouth; one *s* one *d*. *Educ:* Burntisland, Fife. Joined Stirlingshire Police, 1927; Deputy Chief Constable, Inverness Burgh, 1943, Chief Constable, 1946; Chief Constable, County of Angus, 1949; Chief Constable of Fife, 1955; Inspector of Constabulary for Scotland, 1965-66. King's Police Medal, 1952. *Recreation:* golf. *Address:* 32 Craigleith View, Edinburgh 4. *Clubs:* New Golf (St Andrews); Royal Burgess Golfing Society of Edinburgh.

**MELGUND, Viscount; Gilbert Edward George Lariston Elliot-Murray-Kynynmound;** MBE 1955; JP; late Captain Scots Guards; *b* 19 June 1928; *er s* of 5th Earl of Minto, *qv*; *m* 1st, 1952, Lady Caroline Child-Villiers (from whom he obtained a divorce, 1965), *d* of 9th Earl of Jersey; one *s* one *d*; 2nd, 1965, Mary Elizabeth, *d* of late Peter Ballantine and of Mrs Ballantine, Gladstone, New Jersey, USA. *Educ:* Eton; RMA, Sandhurst. Served Malaya, 1949-51; ADC to C-in-C FARELF, 1951, to CIGS, 1953-55, to HE Governor and C-in-C Cyprus, 1955; transferred to RARO, 1956. Mem. of Royal Company of Archers (Queen's Body Guard for Scotland). JP Roxburghshire, 1961-. *Heir:* *s* Hon. Gilbert Timothy George Lariston Elliot-Murray-Kynynmound, *b* 1 Dec. 1953. *Address:* Minto, Hawick, Scotland. *T:* Denholm 321. *Club:* Puffin's (Edinburgh).

**MELLANBY, Kenneth,** CBE 1954 (OBE 1945); ScD Cantab; FIBiol; Director, Monks Wood Experimental Station, Huntingdon, since Oct. 1961; *b* 26 March 1908; *s* of late Emeritus-Professor A. L. Mellanby; *m* 1933, Helen Neilson Dow, MD (marr. diss.); one *d*; *m* 1948, Jean Copeland, MA, JP; one *s*. *Educ:* Barnard Castle Sch.; King's Coll., Cambridge (Exhibitioner). Research Worker, London Sch. of Hygiene and Trop. Med., 1930-36 and 1953-55; Wandsworth Fellow, 1933; Sorby Research Fellow of Royal Society of London, 1936; Hon. Lecturer, University of Sheffield; CO (Sqdn Ldr RAFVR) Sheffield Univ. Air Sqdn. Dir Sorby Research Institute, 1941; first Principal, University Coll., Ibadan, Nigeria, 1947-53; Major, RAMC (Specialist in Biological Research), overseas service in N Africa, SE Asia, etc.; Dep. Dir, Scrub Typhus Research Laboratory, SEAC; Reader in Medical Entomology, University of London, 1945-47; Head of Dept of Entomology, Rothamsted Experimental Station, Harpenden, Herts, 1955-61. Vice-Pres. and Mem. Council, Royal Entomological Soc. of London; Pres. Assoc. for Study of Animal Behaviour; Member; Inter-university Council for Higher Education Overseas; ARC Research Cttee on Toxic Chemicals; Council, and Chm., Tropical Group, Brit. Ecological Soc.; Vice-Pres. of the Institute of Biology; Hon. Professorial Fellow, University Coll. of S Wales; Hon. Reader in Biology, Univ. of Leicester. Hon. DSC: Ibadan, 1963; Bradford, 1970. *Publications:* Scabies, 1943; Human Guinea Pigs, 1945; The Birth of Nigeria's University, 1958; Pesticides and Pollution, 1967; many scientific papers on insect physiology, ecology, medical and agricultural entomology; ed, Monographs on Biological Subjects; British Editor of Entomologia Experimentalis et Applicata; Editor, Environmental Pollution. *Recreations:* walking, travelling, wine and food, gardening. *Address:* Hill Farm, Wennington, Hunts. *T:* Abbots Ripton 392. *Club:* Athenæum.

**MELLANBY, Lady; May;** MA, ScD Cantab; Hon. DSc Sheffield, 1933; Hon. DSc Liverpool, 1934; Charles Mickle Fellow, Toronto University, 1935-36; Member of the Empire Marketing Board Research Grants Committee until disbanded; Investigator for Medical Research Council; *b* London, 1882; *e d* of late Rosa and George Tweedy, London; *m* 1914, Sir Edward Mellanby, GBE, KCB, FRS, FRCP (*d* 1955). *Educ:* Hampstead and Bromley High Schs; Girton Coll., Cambridge. Natural Science Tripos Parts I. and II.; Research Scholar and Lecturer, London Univ. (Bedford Coll.) 1906-14; Hon. Fellow, Girton Coll., 1958; Hon. Mem. British Dental Assoc.; Hon. Mem. Stomatological Soc. of Greece. *Publications:* many publications of a scientific nature principally dealing with conditions affecting the structure of the teeth and related tissues and their resistance to disease including MRC Special Report Series 140, 153 and 191. *Address:* 5 East Heath Road, Hampstead, NW3. *Club:* English-Speaking Union.

**MELLERS, Prof. Wilfrid Howard,** DMus; Composer; Professor of Music, University of York, since 1964; *b* 26 April 1914; *s* of Percy Wilfrid Mellers and Hilda Maria (*née* Lawrence); *m* 1950, Peggy Pauline (*née* Lewis); two *d*. *Educ:* Leamington Coll.; Downing Coll., Cambridge. BA Cantab 1939; MA Cantab 1945; DMus Birmingham 1962. Supervisor in English and College Lecturer in Music, Downing Coll., Cambridge, 1945-48; Staff Tutor in Music, Extra Mural Dept, University of Birmingham, 1949-60; Visiting Mellon Prof. of Music, University of Pittsburgh, USA, 1960-62. *Publications:* Music and Society, 1946; Studies in Contemporary Music, 1948; François Couperin and the French Classical Tradition, 1950; Music in the Making, 1951; Man and his Music, 1957; Harmonious Meeting, 1964; Music in a New Found Land, 1964; Caliban Reborn: renewal in 20th-century music, 1967 (US), 1968 (GB). Published Compositions include: Canticum Incarnations, 1960; Alba in 9 Metamorphoses, 1962; Rose of May, 1964; Life-Cycle, 1967; Yeibichai, 1968; Canticum Resurrectionis, 1968; Natalis Invicti Solis, 1969; The Word Unborn, 1970; The Ancient Wound, 1970. *Address:* Honeystones, East Lane, Shipton by Beningbrough, York. *T:* Beningbrough 392.

**MELLING, Cecil Thomas,** CBE 1955; MScTech, CEng, FIEE, FIMechE, FInstF, FBIM; *b* Wigan, 12 Dec. 1899; *s* of late William and late Emma Melling; *m* 1929, Ursula Thorburn Thorburn; two *s* one *d* (and one *s* and one *d* decd). *Educ:* Manchester Central High Sch.; College of Technology, University of Manchester. 2nd Lieut RE 1918. Metropolitan Vickers Electrical Co. Ltd, 1920-34; Yorkshire Electric Power Co., 1934-35; Edmundson's Electricity Corporation Ltd, 1935-43. Borough Electrical Engineer, Luton, 1943-48. Mem. of British Electricity Authority, 1952-53, and 1957; Chm., Eastern Electricity Board, 1948-57; Full-Time Mem., Electricity Council, 1957-61. Chm. Utilization Sect., Institution of Electrical Engineers, 1949-50; Vice-Pres., IEE, 1957-62, Pres., 1962-63; Chm. of Council, British Electrical Development Association, 1951-52, Founder-Chm. 1945, and Pres. 1947, Luton Electrical Soc.; Pres. Ipswich & District Electrical Assoc., 1948-57; Chm. of Council, British Electrical and Allied Industries Research Assoc., 1953-55; Pres. Assoc. of Supervising Electrical Engineers, 1957-62; a Dep. Chm. Electricity Council, 1961-65; Chm., British Nat. Cttee for Electro-Heat, 1958-68; Vice-Pres. Internat. Union for Electro-Heat, 1964-68, Pres., 1968-; Chm., British Electrical Approvals Bd for Domestic Appliances, 1964-; Chm., Electricity Supply Industry Trg Bd, 1965-68. *Publications:* contribs to proc. Engineering Instns and Confs. *Address:* 3 Townsend Drive, St Albans, Herts. *T:* St Albans 55119. *Club:* Athenæum.

**MELLISH, Rt. Hon. Robert Joseph,** PC 1967; MP (Lab) for the Rotherhithe Division of Bermondsey, 1946-50, for Bermondsey, since 1950; Opposition Chief Whip, since 1970; Official, Transport and General Workers' Union; *m*; five *s*. Served War of 1939-45, Capt. RE, SEAC. Parliamentary Private Sec. to Minister of Pensions, 1951 (to Minister of Supply, 1950-51); Jt Parliamentary Sec., Min. of Housing, 1964-67; Minister of Public Building and Works, 1967-69; Parly Secretary to the Treasury and Govt Chief Whip, 1969-70. *Address:* c/o House of Commons, SW1.

**MELLON, Paul;** Trustee, National Gallery of Art, Washington, DC, since 1945 (President since 1963); *b* 11 June 1907; *s* of late Andrew William Mellon and of Nora McMullen Mellon; *m* 1st, 1935, Mary Conover (decd); one *s* one *d*; 2nd, 1948, Rachel Lambert. *Educ:* Choate Sch., Wallingford, Conn.; Yale and Cambridge Univs. Trustee, Andrew W. Mellow Foundn (successor to merged Old Dominion and Avalon Foundns), 1969-; Chm., A. W. Mellon Educational and Charitable Trust, Pittsburgh, 1950-; Governor, T. Mellon & Sons, Pittsburgh, 1945-; Dir, Mellon Nat. Bank & Trust Co., Pittsburgh, 1960-; Trustee, Virginia Mus. of Fine Arts, Richmond, Va, 1938-68, 1969-. Hon. Citizen, University of Vienna, 1965. Yale Medal, 1953; Horace Marden Albright Scenic Preservation Medal, 1957; Distinguished Service to Arts Award, Nat. Inst. Arts and Letters, 1962; Benjamin Franklin Medal, Royal Society of Arts, 1965, Benjamin Franklin Fellow, 1969; Alumni Seal Prize Award, Choate Sch., 1966. Hon. DLitt, Oxford Univ., 1961; Hon. LLD, Carnegie Inst. of Tech., 1967; Hon. DHL, Yale, 1967. Order of Homayoun, Iran, 1966. *Recreations:* fox-hunting, thoroughbred breeding and racing, sailing, swimming. *Address:* (office) 1729 H Street NW, Washington, DC 20006, USA; (home) Oak Spring, Upperville, Va 22176. *Clubs:* Buck's; Travellers (Paris); Jockey, Knickerbocker, Links, Racquet and Tennis, River, Yale, Grolier (New York); Metropolitan, 1925 F Street (Washington); Duquesne, Fox Chapel, Golf, University, Rolling Rock (Pittsburgh).

**MELLOR, Brig. James Frederick McLean,** CBE 1964 (OBE 1945); Norfolk County Commandant, Army Cadet Force, since 1969; *b* 6 June 1912; *s* of late Col A. J. Mellor, RM, Kingsland, Hereford; *m* 1942, Margaret Ashley, *d* of Major F. A. Phillips, DSO, Holmer, Hereford; one *s* one *d*. *Educ:* Radley Coll.; Faraday House. C. A. Parsons, 1933; Yorkshire Electric Power, 1935. Commnd in Regular Army as Ordnance Mechanical Engr, 1936; France, Belgium, Dunkirk, 1940; Burma, Malaya, HQ, SEAC, 1944-47 (despatches, 1945); Brig. A/Q Northern Comd, 1961-64; Dir of Technical Trng and Inspector of Boys' Trng (Army), MoD, 1966-69; ADC to the Queen, 1963-69. Various appts in engineering and technical educn. DFH, FIMechE, FIEE. *Recreations:* sailing, shooting. *Address:* Muckleburgh, Kelling, Holt, Norfolk. *T:* Weybourne 227. *Clubs:* Naval and Military, Royal Automobile.

**MELLOR, Sir John (Serocold Paget),** 2nd Bt, *cr* 1924; *b* 6 July 1893; *er s* of 1st Bt and Mabel, *d* of G. E. Serocold Pearce-Serocold, of Cherryhinton, Torquay; *S* father, 1929; *m* 1st, 1922, Rachael Margaret (who obtained a divorce, 1937), *d* of Sir Herbert F. Cook, 3rd Bt, of Doughty House, Richmond; one *s*; 2nd, 1937, Mrs Raie Mendes (*d* 1965). *Educ:* Eton; New Coll., Oxford. Barrister, Inner Temple; formerly Capt. Prince Albert's Somerset LI. Served overseas 1914-18 (1914-15 Star, twice wounded, taken prisoner-of-war by Turks at Kut); rejoined Somerset LI, Sept. 1939; contested (C) Workington Division, 1929; adopted Conservative Candidate for Luton Division, 1931, but withdrew in favour of Liberal National Candidate; MP (C) Tamworth Division of Warwicks., 1935-45, Sutton Coldfield Division of Warwicks., 1945-55. Director: Prudential Assurance Co. Ltd (Chm., 1965-70); City and International Trust Ltd; CLRP Investment Trust Ltd. *Heir: s* John Francis Mellor, *b* 9 March 1925. *Address:* Binley House, near Andover, Hants. *Club:* Carlton.

**MELMOTH, Christopher George Frederick Frampton,** CMG 1959; South Asia Department, International Bank for Reconstruction and Development, since 1962; *b* 25 Sept. 1912; *s* of late George Melmoth and Florence Melmoth; *m* 1946, Maureen Joan (*née* Brennan); three *d*. *Educ:* Sandringham Sch., Forest Gate. Accountant Officer, Co-ordination of Supplies Fund, Malta, 1942-45; Administrative Officer, Hong Kong, 1946-55; Minister of Finance, Uganda, 1956-62. *Recreations:* tennis, golf, walking. *Address:* c/o International Bank for Reconstruction and Development, 1818 H Street, NW Washington, DC 20433, USA; 4120 Aspen Street, Chevy Chase, Md 20015, USA.

**MELONEY, Mrs W. B.;** *see* Franken, Rose.

**MELVILLE,** 8th Viscount *cr* 1802; **Henry Charles Patric Brouncker Dundas;** Baron Dunira, 1802; *b* 5 March 1909; *er s* of 7th Viscount and Agnes Mary Florence (*d* 1954), *e d* of Henry Brouncker, Boveridge Park, Cranbourne; *S* father, 1935. *Educ:* King's Sch., Canterbury. *Heir: n* Robert David Ross Dundas, *b* 28 May 1937. *Address:* Melville Castle, Lasswade, Midlothian.

*See also Sir R. D. Harington.*

**MELVILLE;** *see* Leslie Melville.

**MELVILLE, Alan;** revue writer and author; *b* 9 April 1910. *Educ:* Edinburgh Academy. BBC features and drama producer and scriptwriter, 1936-40. Served War with RAF, 1940-46. *Publications: revues:* Rise Above It (Comedy), 1940; Sky High (Phoenix), 1941; Sweet and Low, Sweeter and Lower, Sweetest and Lowest (Ambassadors), 1943-46; A La Carte (Savoy), 1948; At the Lyric (Lyric, Hammersmith), 1953; Going to Town (St Martin's), 1954; All Square (Vaudeville), 1963; *plays:* Jonathan (Aldwych), 1948; Top Secret (Winter Garden), 1949; Castle in the Air (Adelphi), 1949-50; Dear Charles (New), 1952-53; Simon and Laura, 1954; The Bargain (Ethel Barrymore Theatre, New York), 1953; Mrs Willie, 1955; Change of Tune, (Strand), 1959; Devil May Care, 1963; Fuender Bitte Melden (Stadt Theater, Baden-Baden), 1966; Demandez Vicky (Théatre des Nouveautés, Paris), 1966; *musical plays:* Gay's the Word (Saville), 1951; Bet Your Life (Hippodrome), 1952; Marigold (Savoy), 1959; *Films:* Derby Day, 1952; Hot Ice, 1952; As Long as They're Happy, 1954; All for Mary, 1955; Simon and Laura, 1955; *novels:* Week-end at Thrackley, 1935; Death of Anton, 1936; Quick Curtain, 1937; The Vicar in Hell, 1938; Warning to Critics, 1939; *war autobiography:* First Tide, 1945; *autobiography:* Myself When Young, 1956; *TV series:* A-Z, Merely Melville, Melvillainy, What's My Line?, Parade, Raise Your Glasses, Whitehall Worrier, Before the Fringe, Misleading Cases, The Very Merry Widow; also Titipu, iolanthe. *Recreations:* tennis, swimming. *Address:* c/o Eric Glass Ltd, 28 Berkeley Square, W1.

**MELVILLE, Archibald Ralph,** CMG 1964; Agricultural Adviser, Ministry of Overseas Development, since 1965; *b* 24 May 1912; *e s* of late James Melville, MA, Edinburgh, and Mrs K. E. Melville, Lynton, Devon; *m* 1943, Theresa Kelly, SRN, SCM, QAIMNS; two *d*. *Educ:* George Heriot's Sch., Edinburgh; University of Edinburgh; Royal College of Science, London; Imperial Coll. of Tropical Agriculture, Trinidad. BSc in Agriculture with Hons Zoology, Edinburgh, 1934; AICTA, Trinidad, 1936. Entomologist, Kenya Dept of Agriculture, 1936; Senior Entomologist, 1947; Chief Research Officer, 1956; Dir of Agriculture, 1960-64, Kenya Government Service. Served 1939-44 with Kenya Regt and East African Army Medical Corps (Major). *Publications:* contributions to technical journals. *Recreations:* golf, gardening, natural history. *Address:* Spearpoint Cottage, Kennington, Ashford, Kent. *T:* Ashford 20056. *Club:* Farmers'.

**MELVILLE, Sir Eugene,** KCMG 1965 (CMG 1952); Ambassador; Permanent UK Representative to United Nations and other International Organisations at Geneva since 1966; *b* 15 Dec. 1911; *s* of George E. Melville; *m* 1937, Elizabeth, *d* of Chas M. Strachan, OBE; two *s* one *d*. *Educ:* Queen's Park Sch., Glasgow; St Andrews Univ. (Harkness Residential Scholar; 1st cl. Hons Classics; 1st cl. Hons Economics). Appointed to Colonial Office, 1936; Colonies Supply Mission, Washington, 1941-45; PS to Sec. of State for Colonies, 1945-46; Financial Adviser, Control Commission for Germany, 1949-52; Asst Under-Sec. of State, Colonial Office, 1952; Asst Under-Sec. of State, Foreign Office, 1961; Minister (Economic), Bonn, 1962-65; Permanent UK Delegate to EFTA and GATT, 1965. *Address:* UK Mission, 37-39 rue de Vermont, Geneva; Walford Cottage, Aldeburgh, Suffolk. *Club:* Reform.

**MELVILLE, Sir Harry (Work),** KCB 1958; FRS 1941; FRIC; PhD Edinburgh and Cantab; DSc Edinburgh; MSc Birmingham; Principal, Queen Mary College, University of London, since 1967; *b* 27 April 1908; *s* of Thomas and Esther Burnett Melville; *m* 1942, Janet Marian, *d* of late Hugh Porteous and Sarah Cameron; two *d*. *Educ:* George Heriot's Sch., Edinburgh; Edinburgh Univ. (Carnegie Res. Scholar); Trinity Coll., Cambridge (1851 Exhibitioner). Fellow of Trinity College, Cambridge, 1933-44. Meldola Medal, Institute of Chemistry, 1936; Davy Medal, Royal Society, 1955; Colwyn Medal, Instn of the Rubber Industry. Asst Dir, Colloid Science Laboratory, Cambridge, 1938-40; Professor of Chemistry, University of Aberdeen, 1940-48; Scientific Adviser to Chief Superintendent Chemical Defence, Ministry of Supply, 1940-43; Superintendent, Radar Research Station, 1943-45; Dr Mann lecturer, Royal Society of Arts, 1940; Tilden and Liversidge lecturer, Chemical Society, 1941; Bruce-Preller lecturer, Royal Society of Edinburgh, 1943; Mason Professor of Chemistry, University of Birmingham, 1948-56. Chief Scientific Adviser for Civil Defence, Midlands Region, 1952-56; Bakerian Lecture, Royal Society, 1956. Member: Ministry of Aviation, Scientific Advisory Council, 1949-51, 1953-; Advisory Council, Dept of Scientific and Industrial Research, 1946-51; Research Council, British Electricity Authority, 1949-56; Chemistry Research Bd, Dept of Scientific and Industrial Research, 1946-50, Chm. 1955-56; Fuel Research Bd, 1953-56; Royal Commission on Univ. Education in Dundee, 1951-52; Governing Board of National Institute for Research in Nuclear Science, 1957-65; Research Council, Dept of Scientific and Industrial Research, 1961-65; Chm., Adv. Council on Research and Develt, Min. of Technology, 1970-; Sec. to Cttee of the Privy Council for Scientific and Industrial Research, 1956-65; Chm., Science Research Council, 1965-67. Mem., London Electricity Bd, 1968-. Hon. LLD Aberdeen; Hon. DCL Kent; Hon. DSc: Exeter; Birmingham; Liverpool; Leeds; Heriot-Watt; Hon. DTech Bradford. *Publications:* papers in Proceedings of Royal Society, etc. *Address:* Queen Mary College, Mile End Road, London, E1; Norwood, Dodds Lane, Chalfont St Giles, Bucks. *T:* 2222; 30 The Marlowes, NW8. *Club:* Athenæum.

**MELVILLE, Henry Edward;** Director of National Provident Institution for Mutual Life Assurance, 1941-63 (its Manager and Actuary until end of 1945); *b* 6 Dec. 1883; *e s* of Thomas and Mary E. Melville; *m* 1911, Edith Ann, *d* of late Thomas Bagnall Read; three *s*. *Educ:* City of London Sch. FIA 1908; Assistant Actuary, Star Assurance Society, 1913; Life Manager, Eagle Star and British Dominions Insurance Co., Ltd, 1921; Actuary and Secretary, National Provident Institution, 1931; Chairman, Life Offices' Association, 1935-37; Chairman, Investment Protection Committee, of British Insurance Association, 1940-42; President, Institute of Actuaries, 1942-44. *Address:* Devoncourt Hotel, Exmouth, S Devon.

*See also Sir R. H. Melville.*

**MELVILLE, Dr James,** CMG 1969; Director, Waite Agricultural Research Institute, University of Adelaide, since 1956; *b* 10 July 1908; *s* of Andrew Melville, Lovells' Flat, NZ; *m* 1938, Margaret, *d* of Charles Ogilvie, Christchurch, NZ; one *s* two *d* (and one *d* decd). *Educ:* Otago, London & Yale Univs. MSc (NZ) 1930, PhD (London) 1934. Commonwealth Fund Fellow, Yale Univ., 1934-36; Asst Chemist, Wheat Research Inst., NZ, 1936-38; Dir, Plant Chemistry Laboratory, DSIR, NZ, 1939-50. War Service: S and SW Pacific Areas, 1941-45. Dir, Grasslands Div., DSIR, NZ, 1951-55. Mem.,

CSIRO Exec., 1958-65. Chm., Bushfire Research Cttee, 1959-; Chm., Aust. Wool Industry Conf., 1964-66. FRACI 1958; FAIAS 1968. *Publications:* contrib. scientific jls (agricultural and chemical). *Address:* Urrbrae House, Waite Institute, Glen Osmond, S Australia 5064. *T:* 79-3728.

**MELVILLE, Sir Leslie Galfreid,** KBE 1957 (CBE 1953); Member of the Board of the Reserve Bank, 1959-63, and since 1965; Chairman of Commonwealth Grants Commission, since 1965; Chairman, Tariff Advisory Committee of Territory of Papua and New Guinea, since 1969; *b* 26 March 1902; *s* of Richard Ernest Melville and Lilian Evelyn Thatcher; *m* 1925, Mary Maud Scales; two *s. Educ:* Sydney Church of England Grammar Sch. Bachelor of Economics, University of Sydney, 1925; Fellow of Institute of Actuaries, London, 1928; Public Actuary of South Australia, 1924-28; Prof. of Economics, University of Adelaide, 1929-31; Economic Adviser to Commonwealth Bank of Australia, 1931-49; Asst Gov. (Central Banking) Commonwealth Bank of Australia, 1949-53; Mem. of Commonwealth Bank Bd, 1951-53; Exec. Dir of International Monetary Fund and International Bank for Reconstruction and Development, 1950-53. Mem. of Cttees on Australian Finances and Unemployment, 1931 and 1932; Financial Adviser to Australian Delegates at Imperial Economic Conference, 1932; Financial Adviser to Australian Delegate at World Economic Conference, 1933; Mem. of Financial and Economic Advisory Cttee, 1939; Chm. of Australian Delegation to United Nations Monetary Conf. at Bretton Woods, 1944; Mem. of Advisory Council of Commonwealth Bank, 1945-51; Chm. UN Sub-Commn on Employment and Economic Stability, 1947-50; Member: Immigration Planning Council 1956-61; Develt Adv. Service of Internat. Bank, 1963-65; Chm. of Tariff Bd, Australia, 1960-62. Vice-Chancellor Australian National Univ., Canberra, ACT, 1953-60. Hon. LLD Toronto, 1958. *Address:* 71 Stonehaven Crescent, Canberra, ACT 2600, Australia. *Clubs:* Melbourne (Melbourne); University (Sydney); Commonwealth.

**MELVILLE, Sir Ronald (Henry),** KCB 1964 (CB 1952); Permanent Secretary, Ministry of Aviation Supply, since 1970; *b* 9 March 1912; *e s* of Henry Edward Melville, *qv*; *m* 1940, Enid Dorcas Margaret, *d* of late Harold G. Kenyon, Ware; two *s* one *d. Educ:* Charterhouse; Magdalene Coll., Cambridge. 1st Class Classical Tripos, Pts I and II, Charles Oldham Scholarship. Entered Air Ministry, 1934; Private Sec. to Chief of Air Staff, 1936-40; Principal Private Sec. to Sec. of State, 1940-43; Asst Under-Sec. of State, 1946-58; Dep. Under-Sec., Air Ministry, 1958-60; Dep. Under-Sec., War Office, 1960-63; Second Permanent Under-Sec. of State, Ministry of Defence, 1963-66; Permanent Sec., Ministry of Aviation, 1966-67; Secretary (Aviation), Min. of Technology, 1967-70. *Recreations:* rifle shooting (has represented Cambridge Univ., TA, and Scotland; Vice-Pres., Nat. Rifle Assoc.), painting, bird-watching, gardening. *Address:* Whitacre, Bengeo, Hertford. *T:* Hertford 2929. *Club:* Brooks's.

**MELVIN, Air Cdre James Douglas,** CB 1956; OBE 1947; idc 1956; retired; Property Manager, Coutts & Co.; *b* 20 Feb. 1914; *s* of William Adamson Melvin, The Square, Turriff, Aberdeenshire, and Agnes Fyffe, The Hunghar, Kirriemuir; *m* 1946, Mary Wills; one *d* (one *s* decd). *Educ:* Turriff Secondary Sch. Apprentice, Halton, 1930; Cadet, Cranwell, 1933. Dep. Dir Organization, Air Ministry, 1951-53; Group Capt. Organization, MEAF, 1953-55; Dir of Organization, Air Ministry, 1957-61, retd. *Address:* Kyrenia Cottage, Old Bosham, Sussex. *Club:* Royal Air Force.

**MELVIN, John Turcan,** TD and star; MA Cantab; Headmaster, Kelly College, since 1959; *b* 19 March 1916; *m* 1951, Elizabeth Ann Parry-Jones; one *s* three *d. Educ:* Stowe Sch.; Trinity Coll., Cambridge; Berlin Univ. (Schol.). Asst Master, Sherborne Sch., 1938. Served with Dorset Regt, 1939-46; Bde Major 71 Bde, and 185 Bde, 1945. Housemaster, Sherborne Sch., 1950. *Recreations:* walking, reading, tennis, dramatics. *Address:* School House, Kelly College, Tavistock, Devon. *T:* Tavistock 3005. *Club:* Public Schools.

**MENAUL, Air Vice-Marshal Stewart William Blacker,** CB 1963; CBE 1957; DFC 1941; AFC 1942; Director-General, Royal United Service Institution, Whitehall, since 1968; *b* 17 July 1915; 2nd *s* of late Capt. W. J. Menaul, MC, and Mrs M. Menaul, Co. Armagh, N Ireland; *m* 1943, Hélène Mary, *d* of late F. R. Taylor; one *s* one *d. Educ:* Portadown; RAF Coll., Cranwell. Bomber Command Squadrons, 1936-39; on outbreak of war serving with No. 21 Sqdn until 1940; Flying Instructor, 1940-41; No. 15 Sqdn, 1941-42; Air Staff No. 3 Gp, Bomber Command, 1943; Pathfinder Force, 1943-45; RAF Staff Coll., 1946; Air Ministry, 1947-49; Imperial Defence Coll., 1950-51; Air Ministry, Dep. Dir of Operations, 1951-54; Comd British Atomic Trials Task Forces, Monte Bello and Maralinga (Australia), 1955-56; Commanding Officer, Bombing Sch., Lindholme, 1957-58; Air Officer Administration, Aden, 1959-60; Senior Air Staff Officer, Headquarters Bomber Command, 1961-65; Commandant, Joint Services Staff Coll., 1965-67. *Recreations:* ornithology, painting. *Address:* The Lodge, Frensham Vale, Farnham, Surrey. *Club:* Royal Air Force.

**MENDE, Dr Erich;** Member of the Bundestag, German Federal Republic, since 1949; *b* 28 Oct. 1916; *m* 1948, Margot (*née* Hattje); three *s* one *d. Educ:* Humane Coll., Gross-Strehlitz; Universities of Cologne and Bonn (Dr jur). Military service in Infantry Regt 84, Gleiwitz. Served War of 1939-45, Comdr of a Regt (wounded twice, prisoner of war); Major, 1944. Co-founder of FDP (Free Democratic Party), 1945; Mem. Exec. Cttee, British Zone, FDP, 1947; Dep. Chm. FDP in North Rhine Westphalia, 1953-; Mem. 1949-, Dep. Chm. 1956-, Exec. Cttee of Federal Organisation of FDP; Mem. Exec. Cttee, German Council and Parliamentary Section of European Movement; Parliamentary Group of FDP: Whip, and Mem. Exec. Cttee, 1950-53; Dep. Chm., 1953; Chm., 1957; Chm. of FDP, 1960. Vice-Chancellor and Minister for All-German Affairs, Federal Republic of Germany, 1963-66. Chm., Investors Overseas Services in Germany, 1967-70. *Address:* Bundeshaus, 53 Bonn, Germany. *T:* 16 3255; (home) Am Stadtwald 62, 53 Bonn-Bad Godesberg, Germany.

**MENDELSON, John Jakob;** MP (Lab) for Penistone Division of West Riding of Yorkshire since June 1959; *b* 1917; *s* of late J. C. Mendelson. *Educ:* in London and abroad; University of London (BSc Econ). Lecturer in Economics and Public Administration, Extra Mural Studies, University of Sheffield, 1949-59; formerly: Vice-Pres., Sheffield Trades and Labour Council. Mem. Public Accounts Cttee, 1964-66. *Publications:* (jointly) The History of the Sheffield Trades and Labour Council. Articles in various national weekly papers. *Recreations:* book-collecting, music, Association football, chess. *Address:* House of Commons, Westminster, SW1; 407 Fulwood

Road, Sheffield 10; Flat 15a, Dunrobin Court, 391 Finchley Road, NW3. *T:* 01-794 5472.

**MENDELSSOHN, Kurt Alfred Georg,** FRS 1951; MA Oxon; MA, DPhil Berlin; Reader in Physics, Oxford University, since 1955; Fellow of Wolfson College, since 1966; *b* 7 Jan. 1906; *s* of Ernst Mendelssohn and Eliza Ruprecht, Berlin; *m* 1932, Jutta Lina Charlotte Zarniko, Heiligenbeil; one *s* four *d*. *Educ:* Goethe-Sch., Berlin; Berlin Univ. Research and teaching appointments: Berlin Univ., 1930; Breslau Univ., 1932; Oxford Univ., 1933; Visiting Professor: Rice Institute, Texas, 1952; Purdue Univ., 1956; Tokyo Univ., 1960; Kumasi, Ghana, 1964; Tata Inst., Bombay, 1969. Vice-Pres. Physical Soc., 1957-60; Chm., Internat. Cryogenic Engineering Cttee, 1969-. Editor, Cryogenics, 1960-. Hughes Medal, Royal Society, 1967; Simon Memorial Prize, 1968. *Publications:* What is Atomic Energy?, 1946; Cryophysics, 1960; The Quest for Absolute Zero, 1966; In China Now, 1969; in Proc. Royal Society and other scientific and med. jls, mainly on low temperature research and medical physics. *Recreations:* travel, oriental art. *Address:* 235 Iffley Road, Oxford. *T:* 43747. *Club:* Athenæum.

**MENDÈS-FRANCE, Pierre;** Officer of the Legion of Honour; Lawyer; *b* Paris, 11 Jan. 1907; *m* 1933, Lily Cicurel (*d* 1967); two *s*. Prof., Ecole Nationale d'Administration. Under-Sec. for the Treasury, 1938; tried by Vichy Administration, 1940, escaped to serve with Fighting French Air Force. Finance Minister, French Provisional Govt, 1943-44; Head of French Financial Missions, Washington and Breton Woods, 1944; Minister of National Economy, 1944-45; Governor for France of International Bank for Reconstruction and Development and Monetary Fund, 1946-58, resigned. Prime Minister and Minister of Foreign Affairs, France, June 1954-Feb. 1955; Minister of State without portfolio, France, Jan.-May 1956. Docteur en Droit (*hc*). *Publications:* L'Œuvre financière du gouvernement Poincaré, 1928; La Banque internationale, 1930; Liberté, liberté chérie . . ., 1942 (trans. Eng. as The Pursuit of Freedom, 1956); Gouverner c'est choisir, 1953; Sept Mois, dix-sept jours, 1955; La Science économique et l'action (with Gabriel Ardant), 1954 (trans. Eng. and other langs); (with A. Bevan and P. Nenni) Rencontres, 1959; La Politique et La vérité, 1959; La République Moderne, 1962; trans. Eng. as A Modern French Republic, 1963, new edn, 1965; Pour préparer l'avenir, 1968. *Address:* Les Monts, 27 Louviers, France.

**MENECES, Maj.-Gen. Ambrose Neponucene Trelawny,** CB 1963; CBE 1944; DSO 1945; MD; *b* London, 19 March 1904; *s* of Joseph and Amy Meneces, London; *m* 1934, Elsie Gertrude, *d* of Rev. F. Hunt, Lutterworth, Leics; no *c*. *Educ:* St Benedict's; Univ. Coll. Hosp. MB, BS London 1928; MD London 1946; FRCP 1960; DTM&H London 1948. Commissioned into RAMC 1928; served on North-West Frontier, 1935-36; Burma, 1942-45 (despatches three times); Korea, 1952-54. Prof. of Tropical Medicine, Royal Army Medical College, 1949-52; Chief of Medical Divs, SHAPE, 1956; Dir of Medical Services, Western Command, 1958-61, BAOR, 1961-62; Commandant and Dir of Studies, Royal Army Medical College, 1963-66. Fellow of University Coll., London, 1964-. Chadwick Medal, 1964. OStJ 1954; QHP 1960-66. *Publications:* Heat Stroke and Heat Exhaustion, 1950; First Aid for Nuclear Casualties, 1956; Transport of Casualties by Air, 1949; contribs to British Encyclopædia of Medicine, etc. *Recreation:* fishing. *Address:* Glenmore, 15 Highlands Road, Seaford, Sussex.

**MENEVIA, Bishop of, (RC),** since 1947; **Rt. Rev. John Edward Petit;** *b* 22 June 1895; *s* of Edward John Petit and Mary Bridget O'Dowd. *Educ:* English College and Pontifical University, Valladolid, Spain; S Edmund's Coll., Ware; Christ's Coll. and S Edmund's House, Cambridge. BA 1921, Historical Tripos; ordained Diocese of Brentwood, 1918; Curate, S Anne's, Victoria Docks, London, 1921; Bishop's Sec., 1921; Parish Priest, Maldon, Essex, 1923; Vice-Rector, English Coll., Valladolid, 1924; Parish Priest, N Dagenham, 1930; Parish Priest, Grays, Essex, 1931; Master, S Edmund's House, Cambridge, 1934 (Hon. Fellow, 1968); Rector, S Hugh's Seminary, Tollerton, Notts, 1946. *Address:* Bishop's House, Wrexham, Denbighs. *T:* Wrexham 2054.

**MENEVIA, Auxiliary Bishop of (RC);** *see* Fox, Rt Rev. L. D.

**MENGES, Herbert,** OBE 1963; Conductor and Composer; *b* 27 Aug. 1902; *s* of John George Menges and Katherine Whitcher, both musicians; *m* Evelyn Stiebel (marr. diss.); two *s* one *d*. First public appearance, aged 4, at Hove, as violinist; afterwards studied piano with Mathilde Verne and Arthur de Greef and later composition at the Royal College of Music under Gustav Holst and Vaughan Williams. Appointed Musical Director and Conductor in Chief to the Brighton Philharmonic Society in 1925, and has now completed 45 years in the position. Dir of Music to the Old Vic and to the Old Vic Theatre Company, 1931-50, for which he wrote or arranged music for many plays, notably for the Shakespeare productions. Associate Conductor, Sadler's Wells Opera Co., 1940-44; appointed Dir of Music to Laurence Olivier Productions Ltd, 1950, and to Chichester Festival Theatre, 1962. In the symphonic field he appears as guest conductor with all of the leading British Orchestras and Societies, including the Royal Philharmonic Society, London Philharmonic Orchestra, BBC Symphony Orchestra, New Philharmonia Orchestra, London Symphony Orchestra, Royal Liverpool Philharmonic Society, Hallé Society, etc.; and in America with Columbia Broadcasting System Orchestra. Records for HMV and Mercury Records (USA), etc. *Recreations:* books, gardening. *Address:* 64 Belsize Park Gardens, NW3. *T:* 01-722 1953.
*See also Isolde Menges.*

**MENGES, Isolde;** Hon. FRCM; violinist; Professor of violin, Royal College of Music, since 1931; *b* 1893; *m* 1920, Tod Boyd; one *s*. *Educ:* Under Prof. Leopold Auer. First Orchestral Concert in London, 1913; founded Menges String Quartet, 1931. *Address:* 69 Castlenau, SW13. *T:* 01-748 3787.
*See also Herbert Menges.*

**MENNEER, Stephen Snow,** CB 1967; retired, 1970, as Assistant Under-Secretary of State, Department of Health and Social Security; *b* 6 March 1910; *s* of Sydney Charles Menneer, LLD, and Minnie Elizabeth Menneer; *m* 1935, Margaret Longstaff Smith; one *s* one *d*. *Educ:* Rugby Sch.; Oriel Coll., Oxford. Min. of Information, 1939; Min. of National Insurance, 1948; Under-Sec., Min. of Pensions and Nat. Insurance, then Min. of Social Security, 1961. *Address:* 2 Gordon Mansions, Charles Road, St Leonards-on-Sea, Sussex. *T:* Hastings 30624.

**MENNELL, Peter,** CMG 1970; MBE 1945; Ambassador to Ecuador, since 1970; *b* 29 Aug.

1918; *s* of Dr James B. Mennell, London, and Elizabeth Walton Allen, St Louis, Mo.; *m* 1946, Prudence Helen Vansittart; two *s* two *d*. *Educ:* Oundle Sch.; King's Coll., Cambridge (MA). Served 67th Field Regt, RA, 1939-46 (despatches, MBE). Vice-Consul, New York (commercial), 1946-49; 1st Sec., Foreign Office, 1949-51; 1st Sec., Moscow, 1951-54; Foreign Office, 1954-57; Madrid, 1959-61; HM Consul-Gen., Cleveland, Ohio, 1961-64; Inspector, HM Diplomatic Service, 1964-66; Counsellor, Democratic Republic of the Congo, 1966-70; intermittently Chargé d'Affaires, there and in Burundi, 1966-70. Liveryman of Worshipful Company of Grocers, 1954; Col in Hon. Order of Kentucky Colonels, 1961; Visiting Cttee of Bd of Govs, Western Reserve Univ. for Lang. and Lit., 1964. *Recreations:* usual outdoor sports and choral singing. *Address:* c/o Foreign and Commonwealth Office, SW1. *Clubs:* Oxford and Cambridge University; Pilgrims Society.

**MENON, Vengalil Krishnan K.;** *see* Krishna Menon.

**MENOTTI, Gian Carlo;** Composer; teacher of composition at Curtis Institute of Music, Philadelphia, 1948-55; *b* Cadegliano, Italy, 7 July 1911. *Educ:* The Curtis Institute of Music, Philadelphia, Pa. Has been resident in the United States since 1928. First performances of works include: Amelia Goes to the Ball (opera), 1936; The Old Maid and the Thief (radio opera), 1939 (later staged); Sebastian (ballet), 1944; Piano Concerto in F, 1945; The Medium (opera), 1946 (later filmed); The Telephone (opera), 1947; Amahl and the Night Visitors (television opera), 1949; The Consul (opera), 1950 (Pulitzer Prize); Apocalype (orchestral), 1951; Violin Concerto in A Minor, 1952; The Saint of Bleeker Street (opera), 1954 (Pulitzer Prize); Maria Golovin (television opera), 1957; The Unicorn, The Gorgon, and the Manticore, 1957; The Last Savage (opera), 1963; The Death of the Bishop of Brindisi (oratorio), 1963; Martin's Lie (opera), 1964. Prod. Vanessa (opera, by Samuel Barber), 1958, 1961. *Publications:* his major works have been published, also some minor ones; he is the author of all his libretti, most of which have been written in English. *Address:* Capricorn, Mt Kisco, New York, USA.

**MENSFORTH, Sir Eric,** Kt 1962; CBE 1945; MA Cantab; CEng; FBIM; FIMechE; FRAeS; FIProdE; Deputy Chairman John Brown & Co. Ltd; Vice-Chairman, Westland Aircraft Ltd, (Chairman, 1953-68); *b* 17 May 1906; 2nd *s* of late Sir Holberry Mensforth, KCB, CBE; *m* 1934, Betty, *d* of late Rev. Picton W. Francis; three *d*. *Educ:* Altrincham County High Sch.; University Coll. Sch.; King's Coll., Cambridge (1st class mechanical sciences tripos). Engineering work at Woolwich Arsenal, Mather & Platt Ltd, Bolckow Vaughan Ltd, Kloecknerwerke A. G., Dorman Long Ltd, English Electric Ltd, Markham & Co. Ltd, T. Firth & John Brown Ltd, Chief Production Adviser to Chief Executive, Ministry of Aircraft Production, 1943-45. Master Cutler, Sheffield, 1965-66. Chairman: EDC for Electronics Industry, 1968-70; Cttee on Quality Assurance, 1968-; Council of Engineering Instns; Mem. British Productivity Council, 1964-69; Pres., IProdE, 1967-69; Mem. Council, RGS, 1968-70. hon. DEng, Sheffield; Hon. DSc, Southampton. *Address:* Lees Common, Barlow, Sheffield. *T:* Dronfield 3438. *Clubs:* Royal Aero, Alpine.

**MENTER, James Woodham,** MA, PhD, ScD Cantab; FInstP; FRS 1966; Director of Research and Development, Tube Investments Ltd, since 1965; *b* 22 Aug. 1921; *s* of late Horace Menter and late Jane Anne Lackenby; *m* 1947, Marjorie Jean, *d* of late Thomas Stodart Whyte-Smith, WS; two *s* one *d*. *Educ:* Dover Grammar Sch.; Peterhouse, Cambridge. PhD 1949, ScD 1960. Experimental Officer, Admty, 1942-45; Research, Cambridge Univ., 1946-54 (ICI Fellow, 1951-54; Sir George Beilby Mem. Award, 1954); Tube Investments Research Laboratories, Hinxton Hall, 1954-68; Director: Tube Investments Res. Labs, 1961-68; Round Oak Steelworks Ltd, 1967-. Mem. Science Res. Council, 1967-. Extraordinary Fellow, Churchill Coll., Cambridge, 1966. Pres., Inst. of Physics and the Physical Society, 1970-. *Publications:* scientific papers in Proc. Royal Society, Advances in Physics, Jl Iron and Steel Inst., etc. *Recreation:* fishing. *Address:* Pampisford Lodge, Pampisford, Cambridge. *T:* Sawston 3186.

**MENTETH, Sir James (Wallace) Stuart-,** 6th Bt, *cr* 1838; with Imperial Chemical Industries Ltd, Paints Division; *b* 13 Nov. 1922; *e s* of 5th Bt and Winifred Melville (*d* 1968), *d* of Daniel Francis and *widow* of Capt. Rupert G. Raw, DSO; *S* father, 1952; *m* 1949, Dorothy Patricia, *d* of late Frank Greaves Warburton; two *s*. *Educ:* Fettes; St Andrews Univ.; Trinity Coll., Oxford (MA). Served War of 1939-45, with Scots Guards, 1942-44; on active service in North Africa and Italy (Anzio) (severely wounded). *Recreations:* motoring, swimming, gardening, ornithology. *Heir:* *s* Charles Greaves Stuart-Menteth, *b* 25 Nov. 1950. *Address:* Broomhurst, Deepcut, Camberley, Surrey.

**MENUHIN, Yehudi,** KBE (Hon.) 1965; violinist; *b* New York, 22 April 1916; *s* of Moshe and Marutha Menuhin; *m* 1938, Nola Ruby, *d* of George Nicholas, Melbourne, Australia; one *s* one *d*; *m* 1947, Diana Rosamond, *d* of late G. L. E. Gould and late Lady Harcourt (Evelyn Suart); two *s*. *Educ:* private tutors; studied music under Sigmund Anker and Louis Persinger, in San Francisco; Georges Enesco, Rumania and Paris; Adolph Busch, Switzerland. Made début with orchestra, San Francisco, aged 7, Paris, aged 10, New York, 11, Berlin, 13; since then has played with most of world's orchestras and conductors; has introduced among contemp. works Sonata for Violin alone, by Béla Bartók (composed for Mr Menuhin), as well as works by William Walton, Ben-Haim, Georges Enesco, Pizzetti, Ernest Bloch, etc. During War of 1939-45 devoted larger part of his time to concerts for US and Allied armed forces and benefit concerts for Red Cross, etc (500 concerts). Series of concerts in Moscow (by invitation), 1945; three visits to Israel, 1950-; first tour of Japan, 1951; first tour of India (invitation of Prime Minister), 1952. Largely responsible for cultural exchange programme between US and Russia, 1955, and for bringing Indian music and musicians to West. Initiated his own music festival in Gstaad, Switzerland, 1957, and in Bath, 1959-69; Jt Artistic Dir, Windsor Festival, 1969. Makes world tours every Year. Hon. Fellow, St Catherine's Coll., Cambrdige, 1970; Hon. DMus: Oxford, 1962; Cambrdige, 1970, and 9 other degrees from Brit. Univs. Freedom of the City of Edinburgh, 1965; City of Bath, 1966. *Films:* Stage Door Canteen; Magic Bow. He records for His Master's Voice; appears regularly in American and British Television. Jawaharlal Nehru Award for International Understanding, 1970; Decorations include: Gold Medal, Royal Philharmonic Society, 1962; Legion of Honour, Order of Arts and Letters (France); Order of Leopold (Belgium); Ordre de la Couronne (Belgium); Order of Merit (W

German Republic); Royal Order of the Phœnix (Greece). *Relevant Publication:* Yehudi Menuhin, The Story of the Man and the Musician, by Robert Magidoff, 1956 (USA). *Address:* (agents) Kurt Weinhold, Columbia Artists Management, 165 W 57th Street, New York City; Harold Holt, 122 Wigmore Street, W1, England; (home) Alma, California. *Club:* Athenæum.

**MENZIES, Rt. Hon. Sir Douglas (Ian),** PC 1963; KBE 1958; Justice of the High Court of Australia since 1958; *b* 7 Sept. 1907; *s* of Rev. Frank Menzies; *m* 1936, Helen Jean, *d* of Rev. Dr William Borland; one *s* three *d*. *Educ:* University of Melbourne (Jessie Leggatt Schol., J. B. Nunn Prize, Supreme Court Prize); Fellow of Queen's Coll., Melbourne. Sec., Australian Defence Cttee and Chiefs of Staff Cttee, 1941-45; QC (Australia) 1949; Pres. Medico-Legal Soc., Victoria, 1956; Pres. Law Council of Australia, 1957-58; Chm. Victorian Bar Council, 1958; Vice-Pres. Internat. Bar Assoc., 1958; Pres. National Heart Foundation of Australia, 1964; Chancellor, Monash Univ., 1968. *Publication:* (jointly) Victorian Company Law, 1940. *Recreation:* farming. *Address:* Cambridge, 165 Hotham Street, East Melbourne, Victoria 3002, Australia. *Clubs:* Melbourne, Union (Sydney); Savage (Melbourne).

**MENZIES, Sir Laurence James,** Kt 1962; Deputy Chairman, hall Thermotank Ltd, since 1965; Director: Trade Indemnity Co. Ltd, since 1965; The Commercial Banking Co. of Sydney (London Board), since 1966; The Commercial Export Credit Co. Ltd, since 1966 (Chairman since 1967); *b* 23 Dec. 1906; *yr s* of late James Menzies, Coupar Angus, Perthshire; *m* 1935, Agnes Cameron, *yr d* of John Smart; one *s* one *d*. *Educ:* Wandsworth Sch. Entered Bank of England, 1925; Asst Chief Cashier, 1943; Dep. Chief Cashier, 1952; Adviser to the Govs, 1957-58, 1962-64; Sec. of the Export Credits Guarantee Dept, 1958-61. Pres., Union d'Assureurs des Crédits Internationaux (Berne Union), 1960-61. *Recreation:* golf. *Address:* Timbers, Vincent Close, Esher, Surrey. *T:* Esher 64257. *Clubs:* Overseas Bankers', Bath, MCC.

**MENZIES, Marie Ney;** Actress Producer; *d* of William Fix and Agnes Rohan; *m* 1930, T. H. Menzies (marr. diss., 1949; remarried to T. H. Menzies, 1959, he *d* 1962). *Educ:* St Mary's Convent, Wellington, NZ. stage debut in Melbourne, 1917; played in Australia until 1922, supporting among other visiting stars Marie Tempest; leading lady at the Old Vic 1924-25; parts included Ophelia, Lady Macbeth and Beatrice; visited Cairo 1927 with company invited by the Egyptian Government, parts included Desdemona, Portia and Viola; leading roles in London include Kate Hardcastle in Sir Nigel Playfair's production She Stoops To Conquer, Milady in The Three Musketeers, Miss Janus in John Van Druten's London Wall; leading part in J. B. Priestley's Dangerous Corner; star role in The Lake by Dorothy Massingham and Murray Macdonald; this play was especially written for her; leading role in Touch Wood; played leading role in Mrs Nobby Clark under her own management; Olga, in Anton Tchehov's Three Sisters (Old Vic); lead with Frank Vosper in Love from a Stranger; Mrs Alving in Ghosts; leading part in Sanctity, by Mrs Violet Clifton; leading roles in G. Bernard Shaw's The Millionairess (Dublin and Hull) and Candida (Dutch Tour 1939); Australian Season, Sydney and Melbourne, 1940-41; Ladies in Retirement, No Time for Comedy, Private Lives; Shakespearean Recitals, Australia, Malaya; with South African Broadcasting Corporation, Johannesburg Production, etc., 1942, 1943, 1944; African-Middle-East Tour, Shakespeare's Women, for British Council and ENSA; Italy and Holland, 1945, and performances for Arts Council; Hecuba in Trojan Women for Company of 4, Lyric Theatre; King of Rome, Fish in the Family, Native Son, Bolton's Theatre, SW10, 1947-48; Nurse Braddock in the Gioconda Smile, 1948; Lady Corbel in Rain on the Just, 1948; Sara Cantrey in The Young and Fair, St Martin's, 1949; Mrs Cortelyon in The Second Mrs Tanqueray, Haymarket, 1950; Martha in The Other Heart, Old Vic, 1952; Mary in Fotheringhay, Edinburgh Festival, 1953. Played in films including The Wandering Jew; Brief Ecstasy; Jamaica Inn; Uneasy Terms; Conspirators; Romantic Age; Seven Days to Noon; Lavender Hill Mob; Night was our Friend; Simba. Television: The Little Dry Thorn, The Infernal Machine, Family Reunion, The Lake, The Sacred Flame, Time and the Conways, The Wrong Side of the Park, Do you Remember the Germans. *Recreations:* reading, riding, walking, painting. *Address:* London International-Famous Agency Ltd, 11 Hanover Street, W1. *Club:* Lansdowne.

**MENZIES, Dame Pattie (Maie),** GBE 1954; *b* 2 March 1899; *d* of late Senator J. W. Leckie; *m* 1920, Robert Gordon Menzies (*see* Rt Hon. Sir Robert Menzies); two *s* one *d*. *Educ:* Fintona Girls' Sch., Melbourne; Presbyterian Ladies' Coll., Melbourne. *Address:* 2 Haverbrack Avenue, Malvern, Melbourne, Vic. 3144, Australia. *Club:* Quamby (Melbourne).

**MENZIES, Peter Thomson;** Deputy Chairman, Imperial Chemical Industries Ltd, since 1967 (Director since 1956); Director: National Westminster Bank Ltd since 1968; Commercial Union Assurance Co. Ltd since 1962; Imperial Metal Industries Ltd since 1962 (Chairman, since 1964); Member, Panel on Takeovers and Mergers; Part-time Member, Central Electricity Generating Board, since 1960; *b* 15 April 1912; *s* of late John C. Menzies and late Helen S. Aikman; *m* 1938, Mary McPherson Alexander, *d* of late John T. Menzies and late Agnes Anderson; one *s* one *d*. *Educ:* Musselburgh Grammar Sch.; University of Edinburgh, MA. 1st Class Hons Math. and Natural Philosophy, 1934. Inland Revenue Dept, 1933-39; Treasurer's Dept, Imperial Chemical Industries Ltd, 1939-56 (Asst Treas. 1947, Dep. Treas. 1952). A Vice-Pres., Siol na Meinnrich. FInstP. *Address:* Kit's Corner, Harmer Green, Welwyn, Herts. *Club:* Caledonian.

**MENZIES, Rt. Hon. Sir Robert (Gordon),** KT 1963; PC 1937; CH 1951; QC 1929; FRS 1965; LLM; Chancellor, University of Melbourne, since 1967; MHR for Kooyong, 1934-66; Prime Minister, Australia, 1939-41 and 1949-66 (also Minister for External Affairs, 1960-61; led Mission to Pres. Nasser on Suez Canal, 1956); *b* Jeparit, 20 Dec. 1894; *s* of late James Menzies; *m* 1920, Pattie Maie (*see* Dame P. Menzies); two *s* one *d*. *Educ:* State Schs; Grenville Coll., Ballarat; Wesley Coll., Melbourne; Melbourne Univ. (first class Final Hons). First Australian Hon. LLD Melbourne Univ., also Hon. LLD: QUB, Bristol Univ., Universities of BC Sydney, McGill, Lavel, Montreal, Harvard, Royal University of Malta, Tasmania, Cambridge, Leeds, Adelaide, Edinburgh, Birmingham, Aust. Nat. Univ. Canberra, Sussex; Hon. DCL, Oxford and Univ. of Kent at Canterbury; Hon. DSc, University of NSW. Hon. Fellow, Worcester Coll., Oxford, 1968. Practised as a Barrister at the Victorian Bar; entered Victorian Parliament, 1928; MLC East Yarra, 1928-29;

MLA Nunawading, 1929-34; Hon. Minister, McPherson Government, 1928-29; Attorney-Gen., Minister for Railways and Dep. Premier of Victoria, 1932-34; Attorney-Gen., Commonwealth of Australia, 1934-39; Treasurer, 1939-40; Minister: for Trade and Customs, Feb.-March 1940; for Co-ordination of Defence, 1939-42; for Information and for Munitions, 1940; Prime Minister, 1939-41; Leader of Opposition, 1943-49. Freeman of Cities of Swansea, 1941; Edinburgh, 1948; London, 1952; Oxford, 1953; Athens, 1955; Melbourne, 1966; Hastings, 1966; Sandwich, 1967; Deal, 1969; Hon. Master of Bench, Gray's Inn, 1935; FRSA; Hon. FRACP, 1955; Hon. FRAIA, 1956; Hon. FInstM, 1957; Hon. FAA, 1958; Hon. FRCPEd 1960; Hon. FRCOG 1961; Hon. FRCS 1965; Hon. Freeman: Clothworkers' Co.; Goldsmiths' Co.; Trustee, Melbourne Cricket Ground. Constable of Dover Castle, Lord Warden of the Cinque Ports, 1965-; Pres., Dover Coll., 1966-; Pres., Kent County Cricket Club, 1969. *Publications:* The Rule of Law during War, 1917; To The People of Britain at War from the Prime Minister of Australia, 1941; The Forgotten People, 1943; Speech is of Time, 1958; Afternoon Light (Memoirs), 1967; Central Power in the Australian Commonwealth, 1967; The Measure of the Years, 1970; (jt) Studies in Australian Constitution; contribs to contemporary art and legal jls. *Recreations:* walking and watching first-class cricket. *Address:* 2 Haverbrack Avenue, Malvern, Melbourne, Vic 3144, Australia; (Business) 95 Collins Street, Melbourne, Vic. 3000. *Clubs:* Athenæum, Savage, Pratt's, MCC, (Pres. 1962) Lord's Taverners'; Athenæum, Australian, Savage, (Pres.) Melbourne Scots (all Melbourne).

**MENZIES ANDERSON, Sir Gilmour,** Kt 1962; CBE 1956 (MBE 1943); solicitor; *b* 29 April 1914; *s.* of William Menzies Anderson, DSO, MC, and Jessie Jack Gilmour; *m* 1943, Ivy Beryl Shairp (*née* Chadwick); one *d. Educ:* Glasgow High Sch.; Glasgow Univ. (LLB). Solicitor, 1939. Mem. Glasgow Corporation, 1938-39 and again, 1945-47. Commissioned 6th HLI (TA), 1939; served with "Chindits", India and Burma, 1942-45; in comd 16th Inf. Bde, 1945; demob., 1945, with rank Hon. Brig. Chm., Glasgow Unionist Assoc., 1954-57; Pres., Scottish Unionist Assoc., 1960-61; Chm. Conservative Party in Scotland, 1967- (Dep. Chm. 1965-67). *Recreations:* fishing and shooting. *Address:* Craigievern Cottage, Balfron Station, Stirlingshire. *T:* Drymen 320. *Club:* Conservative (Glasgow) (Chm. 1959-60).

**MERCER, David;** Playwright since 1961; *b* 27 June 1928; has one *d. Educ:* King's Coll., Newcastle upon Tyne. Writers' Guild Award (Best Teleplay): A Suitable Case for Treatment, 1962; In Two Minds, 1967; Let's Murder Vivaldi, 1968; Evening Standard Drama Award (Most Promising Dramatist): Ride a Cock Horse, 1965; British Film Academy Award (Best Screen Play): Morgan, 1965. *Publications:* The Generations, 1964; Three TV Comedies, 1966; Ride a Cock Horse, 1966; The Parachute and Other Plays, 1967; Belcher's Luck, 1967; The Governor's Lady, 1968; On the Eve of Publication and Other Plays, 1970; After Haggerty, 1970; Flint, 1970. *Recreation:* political studies. *Address:* c/o Margaret Ramsay Ltd, 14a Goodwin's Court, WC2.

**MERCER, Rt. Rev. Eric Arthur John;** *see* Birkenhead, Bishop Suffragan of.

**MERCER, Howard,** CBE 1951; MC 1917; DFC 1919; *b* 14 May 1896; 2nd *s* of E. J. Mercer; *m* 1940, Mary Noble; two *s. Educ:* Elstow Sch., Bedford. Served European War, 1914-18, France and Salonika: commissioned to Devonshire Regt, 1916 (despatches); seconded to Royal Air Force, 1918; with RAF in S Russia, 1919; appointed to Administrative Service, Nigeria, 1921; seconded to British Military Administration, Tripolitania, 1942; Chief Sec., 1945-51, with Rank of Col. Dir of Establishments to Government of Tripolitania; retired from Colonial Service, 1951, and from Tripolitania, 1952. Order of St Stanislaus (Russia), 1919; Cross of St George (Russia), 1919. *Recreation:* golf. *Address:* 3a Parkside Road, Parkstone, Dorset.

**MERCER, Sir Walter,** Kt 1956, FRCS, FRS (Edinburgh), FACS (Hon.); FRCS (Hon.); FCSSoAf (Hon.); FRoyMedSoc, Edinburgh (Hon.); MChOrth (Liverpool) (Hon.); FRCSI (Hon.); FRCS (Can.) (Hon.); DL; Emeritus Professor of Orthopædic Surgery, University of Edinburgh; late Director of Orthopædic Services, South-East region of Scotland; Past President, Royal College of Surgeons of Edinburgh; Past Chairman Standing Advisory Committee on Artificial Limbs, Ministry of Health; Chairman, Editorial Board, Journal of Royal College of Surgeons of Edinburgh; *b* 19 March 1890; 2nd *s* of E. B. Mercer, Stow, Midlothian; *m* 1923, Helen Maisie Lunan; one *s. Educ:* George Watson's Coll., Edinburgh; University of Edinburgh, MB, ChB (Edinburgh), 1912; FRCS (Edinburgh), 1921; FRS Edinburgh, 1935; FACS, 1954; Asst Surgeon, Royal Infirmary, Edinburgh, 1925; Surgeon, Chalmers Hosp., Edinburgh, 1931; Consultant Surgeon, Ministry of Pensions, Edinburgh, 1924; Surgeon, South-Eastern Counties of Scotland Sanatorium, 1926; Surgeon, Royal Infirmary, Edinburgh, 1943; Prof. of Orthopædic Surgery, University of Edinburgh, 1948; Fellow Royal Society of Medicine; Fellow Assoc. of Surgeons of Great Britain and Ireland, 1930; Fellow British Orthopædic Assoc., 1925; Mem. International Soc. of Surgery, 1948; Hon. Mem., Société Internationale de Chirurgie Orthopédique et de Traumatologie, 1950; Corres. Mem. American Orthopædic Assoc., 1954; Hon. Fellow: Royal College of Surgeons of England, 1956; Alberta Orthopædic Soc.; Hon. Member: Canadian Orthopædic Assoc., 1959; Société Française d'Orthopédie et de Traumatologie, 1960. Served European War, 1915-20, as Capt. RAMC, in France, Italy and the Mediterranean. DL County of City of Edinburgh, 1960. *Publications:* Textbook, Orthopædic Surgery (6th edn), 1963; contrib. to jls, including: Lancet, BMJ, Br. Jl of Surgery, Edinburgh Medical Jl, The Practitioner, The Prescriber, Journal of Chartered Society of Massage, Journal of Bone and Joint Surgery; contrib. to Maingot's Techniques of British Surgery, Illingworth's Surgical Treatment, Thomson & Miles' Manual of Surgery, McIntosh's War and the Doctor, Handfield-Jones and Porritt's Essentials of Modern Surgery. *Recreations:* golf, curling, shooting, postal history, photography, reading. *Address:* Bidston, 7 Easter Belmont Road, Edinburgh. *T:* 031-337 4923. *Clubs:* Golfers'; New (Edinburgh).

**MERCER NAIRNE PETTY-FITZMAURICE,** family name of **Marquess of Lansdowne.**

**MERCHANT, Livingston Tallmadge;** *b* New York City, 23 Nov. 1903; *s* of Huntington Wolcott Merchant and Mary Floyd Tallmadge; *m* 1927, Elizabeth Stiles; one *s* one *d. Educ:* Hotchkiss Sch.; Princeton Univ. AB cum laude, 1926; Hon. LLD 1960; Hon. LLD: Hofstra Univ., 1959; Queen's Univ., Canada, 1961; Harvard, 1968; Hon. DCL, Bishop's Univ., Quebec, 1962; Associate in firm of

Scudder, Stevens and Clark (Boston), 1926-30; General partner Scudder, Stevens and Clark (New York), 1930-42. Dir of several insurance companies, investment trusts, and a national bank. Joined Dept of State, 1942; Asst Chief, Div. of Defense Materials, 1942-43; Chief, War Areas Economic Div., 1944-45; Economic Counselor with personal rank of Minister, Paris, 1945; Chief Aviation Div., Dept of State, 1946; Foreign Service Officer, Cl. 2, 1947; Class 1, 1950; Career Minister, 1954; Career Ambassador, 1960. Counselor of Embassy, Nanking, 1948-49; Dep. Asst Sec. of State for Far Eastern Affairs, 1949-51; Dep. to US Special Rep. in Europe with Personal Rank of Ambassador, and US Alternate Perm. Rep. on NATO, 1952-53; Asst Sec. of State for European Affairs, 1953-56, 1958-59, United States Ambassador to Canada, 1956-58, 1961-62; Under Sec. of State for Political Affairs, State Dept, Washington, 1959-61. Delegate, or Senior Adviser, Bermuda, Berlin, Geneva, London, Paris and NATO Confs, 1953-56, 1958-60. Director: Glens Falls Insce Co.; Research Analysis Corp.; Nat. Life Assce Co. of Canada. US Director of The World Bank, 1965-68. *Address:* 4101 Cathedral Avenue, NW, Washington, DC 20016, USA. *Clubs:* Princeton, Metropolitan, Alfalfa, The Alibi (Washington); Princeton (New York); Chevy Chase (Chevy Chase, Md); University Cottage (Princeton, NJ).

**MERCHANT, Vivien, (Mrs Harold Pinter);** actress since 1943; *b* 22 July 1929; *d* of William Thomson and Margaret McNaughton; *m* 1956, Harold Pinter, *qv*; one *s*. *Educ:* Bury Convent, Manchester. Major roles include: Sarah in The Lover (stage and TV), 1963; Ruth in The Homecoming (stage, London and NY), 1965-67; Natasha Petrovna in A Month in the Country (TV), 1966; Lily in Alfie (film), 1966; Lady Macbeth in Macbeth (Royal Shakespeare Co.), 1967; Victoria in Flint, Criterion, 1970. *Recreations:* table tennis, listening to jazz, reading. *Address:* 7 Hanover Terrace, NW1. *Clubs:* Ronnie Scott's, Pickwick.

**MERCHANT, Rev. Prof. William Moelwyn;** Professor of English, University of Exeter, since Oct. 1961; *b* 5 June 1913; *s* of late William Selwyn and Elizabeth Ann Merchant, Port Talbot, Glamorgan; *m* 1938, Maria Eluned Hughes, Llanelly; one *s* one *d*. *Educ:* Port Talbot Grammar Sch.; (Exhibnr) University Coll., Cardiff. BA, 1st Cl. English hons 1933; 2nd Cl. 1st div. Hist., 1934; MA 1950; DLitt 1960. Hist. Master, Carmarthen Grammar Sch., 1935; English Master, Newport High Sch., 1936; English Lectr, Caerleon Trg Coll., 1937; University Coll. Cardiff: Lectr in Eng. Lang. and Lit., 1939; Sen. Lectr, 1950; Reader, 1961. Fellow, Folger Shakespeare Library, Washington, DC, and Fulbright Fellow, 1957; Woodward Lectr, Yale Univ., 1957; Dupont Lectr, Sewanee Univ., Tenn, 1963; Willett Prof. of English and Theology, Univ. of Chicago, 1971. Ordained to Anglican Orders, 1940. Welsh Cttee of Arts Council of Gt Brit., 1960; Council, Llandaff Festival, 1958-61. Examining Chaplain to the Bishop of Salisbury; Chancellor and Canon of Salisbury Cathedral, 1967-. *Publications:* Wordsworth's Guide to the Lakes (illus. John Piper), 1952 (US 1953); Reynard Library Wordsworth, 1955 (US 1955); Shakespeare and the Artist, 1959; Creed and Drama, 1965; (ed) Merchant of Venice, 1967; (ed) Marlowe's Edward the Second, 1967; Marlowe's Tamburlaine, 1970. Articles in Times Literary Supplement, Warburg Jl, Shakespeare Survey, Shakespeare Quarterly, Shakespeare Jahrbuch, Encyc. Britannica, etc. *Recreations:* theatre and typography. *Address:* 2 Mount Radford Crescent, Exeter, Devon. *T:* Exeter 56004; 57a The Close, Salisbury, Wilts. *T:* Salisbury 22473.

**MEREDITH, Air Vice-Marshal Sir Charles Warburton,** KBE, *cr* 1947 (CBE 1941); CB 1943; AFC, 1918; RAFVR retd; *b* 1896; *s* of late C. J. Meredith; *m* 1926, Honoria Druce, *d* of J. T. Davidson; one *s* one *d*. *Educ:* Wynberg High Sch. Grad. RAF Staff Coll., Andover, England. Formerly Comdt-Gen. SR Forces. *Club:* Salisbury (Rhodesia).

**MEREDITH, George Patrick,** MSc, MEd (Leeds); PhD (London); FBPsS; Professor of Psychophysics, University of Leeds, 1967-69, now Professor Emeritus; Director of Epistemic Communication Research Unit, retired 1969; *b* 10 May 1904; *s* of Edgar and Helen Meredith; *m* 1942, Gillian Tremaine; one *s*. *Educ:* Wolverley Sch.; University of Leeds; University Coll. and Institute of Education, University of London. Taught science in Switzerland, London and Gloucestershire, 1926-38; Lecturer in Educational Psychology and Visual Education, UC, Exeter, 1938-47; established and directed Visual Education Centre, Exeter; Research Grants: Leon Trust, 1945; DSIR, 1954; Dept of Educ. and Science, 1965. Lecturer in Educational Psychology, University of Leeds, 1947-49; Professor of Psychology, 1949-67. Editor-in-Chief, International Jl of the Educational Sciences. *Publications:* Visual Education and the New Teacher, 1946; Materials for Visual Aids, 1947; The Method of Topic Analysis, 1948; Algebra by Visual Aids (4 vols), 1948; The Modular Calculus, 1958; Semantic Matrices, 1959; Learning, Remembering and Knowing, 1961; Instruments of Communication, 1966. Articles in Forum of Education, Occupational Psychology, New Era, Nature, Times Ed. Supp., Jl of Ed., Brit. Jl of Psychology, 20th Century, Proc. of Aristotelian Soc., BMJ, etc. *Recreations:* astronomy, walking, climbing, dramatics. *Address:* 7 Grosvenor Mount, Leeds 6. *T:* Leeds 55997. *Club:* Athenæum.

**MEREDITH, Leonard Arthur De Lacy,** CMG 1933; OBE 1923; BA; *b* 1888; *s* of late Arthur Meredith, CSI, ICS. *Educ:* Eton; Balliol Coll., Oxford. Solicitor, 1914; Lieut 3rd Glos Regt, 1914; invalided, 1915; entered Department of Overseas Trade, 1918; General Manager, Travel Association of Great Britain and Ireland, 1930-39; Ministry of Supply, 1939; Board of Trade, 1946-52. *Clubs:* Boodle's, MCC.

**MEREDITH, Margaret;** Composer; *d* of late Ralph Elliot and Mrs T. H. Lewin; *m* 1892, W. M. Meredith (*d* 1937), *s* of late George Meredith; one *s*. *Educ:* Cheltenham Coll.; musical studies pupil of Dannreuther and Ernst Pauer. Founder of the Independent Music Club for the protection and advancement of art and artists, also of the Independent Musical World, the monthly journal issued in connection with the IMC. *Compositions*, as follows: The Pilgrim's Way, a musical allegory; Symphonic Tone Poem, Sursum Corda; Recessional, Rudyard Kipling's words; Sacramentum Supremum, words by Sir Henry Newbolt; Requiem on the death of Queen Victoria; Passing of King Edward VII; quintet flute, clarinet, violin, violoncello, piano; oratorio, The Atonement; The Immortelle or The Children's Heritage, A Musical Idyll; violin rhapsody, a symphony, an oratorio, a pageant and many songs, etc. *Recreations:* reading, chamber music, and lawn tennis. *Address:* 13 Pembroke Gardens, W8.

**MERITT, Benjamin Dean;** Professor of Greek Epigraphy, School of Historical Studies at Institute for Advanced Study, Princeton, NJ,

1935-69, Emeritus since 1969; *b* at Durham, North Carolina, 31 March 1899; *s* of Arthur Herbert Meritt and Cornelia Frances Dean; *m* 1st, 1923, Mary Elizabeth Kirkland; two *s*; 2nd, 1964, Lucy T. Shoe. *Educ:* Hamilton Coll. (AB 1920, AM 1923, LLD 1937); American Sch. of Class. Studies at Athens. AM Princeton 1923, PhD 1924, LittD 1947; DLitt Oxford, 1936; LLD Glasgow, 1948; LHD, University of Pennsylvania, 1967; Dr *h c* Sch. of Philosophy, Univ. of Athens, 1970. instr Greek Univ. of Vermont, 1923-24; Brown Univ. 1924-25; asst prof. Greek, Princeton, 1925-26; asst dir Am. Sch. of Class. Studies at Athens, 1926-28; assoc. prof. Greek and Latin, University of Michigan, 1928-29, prof. 1929-33; visiting prof. Am. Sch. Class. Studies at Athens, 1932-33; dir Athens Coll., 1932-33; Francis White prof. of Greek, Johns Hopkins, 1933-35; lecturer at Oxford, 1935; annual prof. Am Sch. of Class. Studies at Athens, 1936, 1954-55; Eastman prof., Oxford Univ., 1945-46; Sather prof., University of California, 1959; Member: American Philosophical Soc.; German Archae. Inst.; Fellow American Academy of Arts and Sciences; Corr. fellow British Academy; hon. councillor, Greek Archæ. Soc.; hon. mem. Michigan Acad. of Sciences, Arts and Letters, Society for the Promotion of Hellenic Studies; Assoc. Mem., Royal Flemish Acad.; Foreign Mem., Acad. of Athens; Pres. Amer. Philological Assoc., 1953. Commander, Order of the Phœnix (Greece). *Publications:* The Athenian Calendar in the Fifth Century, 1928; Supplementum Epigraphicum Graecum, Vol. V (with Allen B. West), 1931; Corinth, Vol. VIII, Part I–Greek Inscriptions, 1931; Athenian Financial Documents, 1932; The Athenian Assesment of 425 BC (with Allen B. West), 1934; Documents on Athenian Tribute, 1937; The Athenian Tribute Lists (with H. T. Wade-Gery and M. F. McGregor), Vol. I, 1939, Vol. II, 1949, Vol. III, 1950, Vol. IV, 1953; Epigraphica Attica, 1940; The Chronology of Hellenistic Athens (with W. K. Pritchett), 1940; The Athenian Year, 1961. *Recreation:* fishing. *Address:* Institute for Advanced Study, Princeton, NJ 08540, USA.

**MERIVALE, Dame Gladys;** *see* Cooper, Dame Gladys.

**MERLE, Robert;** Croix du Combattant, 1945; Officier de l'Instruction publique, 1953; Professor of English Literature: University of Rennes, Brittany, since 1944 (on leave, 1950-51); University of Toulouse since 1957; University of Caen-Rouen, since 1960; University of Algiers, 1962-64; University of Paris, since 1965; *b* 29 Aug. 1908; father an officer; *m* 1st; one *d*; *m* 2nd, 1949; three *s* one *d*; 3rd, 1965; one *s*. *Educ:* Lycée Michelet, Paris; Sorbonne, Paris. Professor, 1934. Mobilised, 1939; Liaison agent with BEF (prisoner, 1940-43). *Publications:* Oscar Wilde, 1948; Week-end à Zuydcoote, 1949 (awarded Prix Goncourt); La Mort est mon métier, 1953; L'Ile, 1962 (awarded Prix de la Fraternité) (translated, as The Island, 1964); *plays:* Flamineo (inspired by Webster's White Devil), 1953; Nouveau Sisyphe; *historical essays:* Moncada, 1965; Ben Bella, 1965; Un Animal doué de raison, 1967; translations, articles. *Recreations:* swimming, tennis, yachting. *Address:* Le Bousquet de la Malonie, Marquay, Dordogne, France.

**MERMAGEN, Air Commodore Herbert Waldemar,** CB 1960; CBE 1945 (OBE 1941); AFC 1940; retired, 1960; Director, Sharps, Pixley & Co. Ltd; *b* 1 Feb. 1912; *s* of late L. W. R. Mermagen, Southsea; *m* 1937, Rosemary, *d* of late Maj. Mainwaring Williams, DSO and late Mrs Tristram Fox, Cheltenham; two *s*. *Educ:* Brighton Coll., Sussex. Joined RAF, 1930; Squadron Leader, 1938; served War of 1939-45 in Fighter Command, UK, Middle East, France and Germany (SHAEF); AOC British Air Command, Berlin, 1945-46; Sen. RAF Liaison Officer, UK Services Liaison Staff, Australia, 1948-50; AOC, RAF Ceylon, 1955-57; Air Officer i/c Administration, Headquarters, RAF Transport Command, 1958-60. Air Commodore, 1955. Comdr Legion of Merit (USA), 1946; Medal for Distinguished Services (USSR), 1945; Chevalier, Légion d'Honneur (France) 1951. *Recreations:* golf, sailing. *Address:* Roseacre, Wargrave, Berks. *T:* Wargrave 2580.

**MERMAGEN, Patrick Hassell Frederick,** TD; MA Cantab; Headmaster, Ipswich School, since 1950; *s* of late L. H. Mermagen, MA, Taunton; *m* 1st, 1934, Neva Sonia (*d* 1953), *d* of late E. Haughton James, Forton House, Chard, Somerset; two *s* one *d* (and one *s* decd); 2nd, 1965, Inge (*née* Schütt), Hamburg; one *s* one *d*. *Educ:* Sherborne Sch.; Pembroke Coll., Cambridge (Open Scholar in Mathematics). Asst master, Loretto Sch., 1933-39, Radley Coll., 1939-50. Served War of 1939-45, Sept. 1940-Feb. 1946, The Royal Berkshire Regt; Staff Coll., Camberley (sc), 1944; held appointments as DAQMG in NW Europe and in SE Asia. *Recreations:* cricket, golf. *Address:* The School House, Ipswich, Suffolk. *T:* Ipswich 52611. *Club:* East India and Sports.

**MERRELLS, Thomas Ernest;** Alderman, City of Cardiff; Lord Mayor of Cardiff, May 1970-71; *b* 5 Aug. 1894; *s* of Thomas Arthur Merrells, OBE, JP, and Kate Merrells, Swansea; *m* 1922, Vera Pughe Charles; one *s* one *d*. *Educ:* Bishop Gore Grammar Sch., Swansea. Served European War, 1914-18, in France; commissioned in Welsh Regt; seconded to HQ Staff, Royal Engineers, 1917; War of 1939-45: Chm., S Wales Area Nat. Dock Labour Bd; Mem., Exec. Cttee, Regional Port Director of Bristol Channel. Dep. Chm., S Wales Fedn of Port Employers, 1926-47, and Chm., Jt Conciliation Cttee for S Wales Ports. Councillor, City of Cardiff, 1951; Alderman, 1966. Chevalier, Order of Mérite Social (France), 1958. *Recreation:* golf. *Address:* 151 Cyncoed Road, Cardiff. *T:* Cardiff 753321. *Clubs:* Cardiff Athletic and Rugby; Cardiff Golf.

**MERRIMAN, James Henry Herbert,** CB 1969; OBE 1961; MSc, AInstP, CEng, FIEE; Member for Technology, Post Office Corporation, since 1969 (Member, Post Office Board, and Senior Director of Development, 1967-69); *b* 1 Jan. 1915; *s* of Thomas P. Merriman, AMINA and A. Margaretta Jenkins; *m* 1942, Joan B. Frost; twin *s* one *d*. *Educ:* King's Coll. Sch., Wimbledon; King's Coll., University of London. BSc (Hons) 1935; MSc (Thesis) 1936. Entered GPO Engrg Dept (Research), 1936; Officer i/c Castleton Radio Stn, 1940; Asst Staff Engr, Radio Br., 1951: Imp. Def. Coll., 1954; Dep. Dir, Organisation and Methods, HM Treasury, 1956; GPO: Dep. Engr-in-Chief, 1965; Sen. Dir Engrg, 1967. Vis. Prof. of Electronic Science and Telecommunications, Strathclyde Univ., 1969. Mem. Council, IEE, 1965 (Chm. Electronics Div. Bd, 1968; Vice-Pres. 1969; Faraday Lectr 1969-70). *Publications:* contribs to scientific and professional jls on tele-communications subjects. *Recreations:* rough walking, organ playing, Gouache, Crusader class leader, church work. *Address:* 5 Melville Avenue, Copse Hill, W Wimbledon, SW20. *T:* 01-946 9870.

**MERRIMAN, Sir Walter Thomas,** Kt 1954; Managing Director, Merryville Pty Ltd, Stud Merino Sheep and Beef Cattle Breeders, Yass,

New South Wales, Australia; *b* Ravensworth, 18 May 1882; *s* of late George Merriman, Ravenswoth, Yass; *m* 1908, Kate, *d* of Samuel Sleeman; two *s* four *d*. *Educ:* Murrumbateman State Sch., New South Wales. Life Mem. Royal Agric. Society of NSW and of Pastoral and Agric. Socs of Yass, Cootamundra and Boorowa; formerly: Councillor Goodradigbee Shire; Pres. Yass and Dist Soldiers' Memorial and Literary Inst.; Chm., Yass Pastures Protection Bd; Pres. Yass Pastoral and Agric. Assoc.; Dir, Yass Dist Hosp.; Master Yass Masonic Lodge of Concord; Dist Grand Inspector. *Address:* Merryville, Yass, New South Wales, Australia.

**MERRISON, Dr Alexander Walter,** FRS 1969; Vice-Chancellor, University of Bristol, since 1969; *b* 20 March 1924; *s* of late Henry Walter and Violet Henrietta Merrison; *m* 1st, 1948, Beryl Glencora Le Marquand (*d* 1968); two *s*; 2nd, 1970, Maureen Michèle Barry. *Educ:* Enfield Gram. Sch.; King's Coll., London. BSc (London) 1944; PhD (Liverpool) 1957. Res. in Radio Wave Propagation, as Experimental Officer, Signals Research and Development Establishment, Christchurch, 1944-46; Research in Reactor and Nuclear Physics, as Sen. Scientific Officer, AERE, Harwell, 1946-51; Research in Elementary Particle Physics, as Leverhulme Fellow and Lecturer, Liverpool Univ., 1951-57; Physicist, European Organisation for Nuclear Research (CERN) Geneva, 1957-60; Prof. of Experimental Physics, Liverpool Univ., 1960-69, and Dir, Daresbury Nuclear Physics Lab., SRC, 1962-69. Charles Vernon Boys Prizeman of Inst. of Physics and the Physical Soc., 1961, and Mem. Council, 1964-66; Mem., Council of Scientific Policy, 1967-. Governor, Bristol Old Vic Trust, 1969-. *Publications:* contrib. to scientific jls on nuclear and elementary particle physics. *Address:* The University, Senate House, Bristol, BS8 1TH. *T:* Bristol 24161, ext. 84.

**MERRIVALE,** 3rd Baron, *cr* 1925, of Walkhampton, Co. Devon; **Jack Henry Edmond Duke;** *b* 27 Jan. 1917; *o s* of 2nd Baron Merrivale, OBE, and Odette, *d* of Edmond Roger, Paris; *S* father 1951; *m* 1939, Colette, *d* of John Douglas Wise, Bordeaux, France; one *s* one *d*. *Educ:* Dulwich; Ecole des Sciences Politiques, Paris. Served War of 1939–45, RAF, 1940; Flight-Lieut, 1944 (despatches). President: Inst. of Traffic Administration, 1953-70; Railway Development Assoc., 1959; Chm., Anglo-Malagasy Soc., 1961. FRSA 1964. Chevalier, Nat. Order of Malagasy, 1968. *Recreations:* sailing, riding, photography. *Heir:* *s* Hon. Derek John Philip Duke, *b* 16 March 1948. *Address:* 16 Brompton Lodge, 9-11 Cromwell Road, SW7. *T:* 01-589 4111.

**MERSEY,** 3rd Viscount, *cr* 1916, of Toxteth; **Edward Clive Bigham;** Baron, *cr* 1910; *b* 5 June 1906; *e s* of 2nd Viscount Mersey, PC, CMG, CBE, and Mary, *d* of late Horace Seymour, CB (nominated, but not invested as KCB); *S* father 1956; *m* 1933, Lady Katherine Fitzmaurice, *er d* of 6th Marquess of Lansdowne (she succeeded Aug. 1944, on the death of her brother, 7th Marquess, to the Barony of Nairne); three *s*. *Educ:* Eton Coll.; Balliol Coll., Oxford (BA). Served Irish Guards, 1940-45. Mem. LCC, 1955-65. *Heir:* *s* Master of Nairne, *qv*. *Address:* Bignor Park, Pulborough, Sussex; Derreen, Lauragh, Killarney, Ireland. *Clubs:* Brooks's, Pratt's, MCC, White's, Beefsteak.

*See also Baron Ponsonby.*

**MERTHYR,** 3rd Baron, of Senghenydd, Co. Glamorgan, *cr* 1911; **William Brereton Couchman Lewis,** PC 1964; KBE 1969; TD; Bt *cr* 1896; Barrister-at-Law, Inner Temple, 1927; *b* Saundersfoot, 7 Jan. 1901; *o s* of 2nd Baron and Elizabeth Anna (*d* 1925), *d* of late Maj.-Gen. R. S. Couchman; *S* father, 1932; *m* 1932, Violet, *y d* of late Brig.-Gen. Sir Frederick Charlton Meyrick, 2nd Bt, and Mary, Lady Meyrick, of Bush, Pembroke; five *s*. *Educ:* Sunningdale Sch.; Eton Coll.; Magdalen Coll., Oxford (MA). JP, Co. Pembroke, 1925; DL 1932; Vice-Lieutenant, 1959; Chairman, Council, dyfed-Powys Police Authority; Pres. National Association of Parish Councils; Vice-President: National Marriage Guidance Council; Family Planning Assoc.; Mem. Pembrokeshire CC, 1928-39; OC 185th Heavy Battery, RA (TA) 1930-40; Mem. Royal Commission on Local Govt on Tyneside, 1936; Mem. Deptl Cttee on Justices' Clerks, 1938; Chm. Deptl Cttee on Rag Flock Acts, 1938; Chm. Narberth RDC, 1939; Mem. Royal Commission on Justices of the Peace, 1948; Pres. Royal Forestry Society of England and Wales, 1948-50; Dep.-Chm. Haverfordwest Quarter Sessions, 1948-51; A National Parks Comr, 1950-53; Chairman: Pembrokeshire Quarter Sessions, 1950-70; Nat. Marriage Guidance Council, 1951-57; Magistrates' Assoc., 1952-70; RSPCA, 1953-57; Hon. Treas. NSPCC, 1952-57; Chm. Deptl Cttee on Hedgerow and Farm Timber, 1953; Chm. Constituency Delineation Commission: Malaya, 1954; Nigeria, 1957-58; Lord Chm. of Cttees and Deputy Speaker, House of Lords, 1957-65. Served War of 1939-45 (prisoner). CStJ. *Recreation:* yacht cruising. *Heir:* *s* Hon. Trevor Oswin Lewis [*b* 29 Nov. 1935; *m* 1964, Susan Jane, *yr d* of A. J. Birt-Llewellin; one *d*]. *Address:* Saundersfoot, Pembrokeshire. *TA:* Saundersfoot. *Clubs:* Lansdowne, Leander, Royal Cruising.

**MERTON, John Ralph,** MBE 1942; Painter; *b* 7 May 1913; *s* of late Sir Thomas Merton, KBE, FRS; *m* 1939, Viola Penelope von Bernd; three *d*. *Educ:* Eton; Balliol Coll., Oxford. Served War of 1939-45 (MBE); Air Photo reconnaissance research, Lieut-Col 1944. Works include: Mrs Daphne Wall, 1948; The Artist's daughter, Sarah, 1949; The Countess of March (silver point); Altar piece, 1952; The Countess of Dalkeith, 1958; A myth of Delos, 1959; Clarissa, 1960; Lady Georgianan Pelham, 1970. Legion of Merit (USA), 1945. *Recreations:* music; making things. *Address:* The Grange, Enford, near Pewsey, Wilts. *T:* Enford 275; Flat E, 57 Princes Gate, SW7. *T:* 01-584 0435.

**MERTON, Air Chief Marshal Sir Walter (Hugh),** GBE 1963 (OBE 1941); KCB 1959 (CB 1953); Inspector General of Civil Defence, 1964-68; *b* 29 Aug. 1905; *s* of late G. R. Merton; *m* 1st, 1930, B. H. B. Kirby (from whom he obtained a divorce, 1932); one *s*; 2nd, 1938, Margaret Ethel Wilson, 2nd *d* of late J. C. Macro Wilson, Cossington Manor, Som. *Educ:* Eastbourne Coll.; RAF Cadet Coll., Cranwell. Commissioned, 1925; Wing Comdr, 1940; served War of 1939-45 (despatches thrice); Middle East, 1940-43: Directing Staff and Asst Comdt, RAF War Staff Coll., 1943-44; Dir of Organization, Air Ministry, 1944-45. Air Attaché, Prague, 1947-48; AOC and Head of RAF Delegation, Greece, 1949-50. AOC No. 63 (Western and Welsh) Group, 1951-52; AOC No. 22 Gp, Tech. Trg Comd, 1952-53; Chief of the Air Staff, Royal NZ Air Force, 1954-56; Air Officer in charge of Administration, Headquarters Bomber Command, RAF High Wycombe, 1956-59; Chief of Staff, Allied Air Forces, Central Europe, 1959-60; Air Mem. for Supply and Organisation, April 1960-Aug. 1963, retd. Air Cdre, 1949; Air Vice-Marshal, 1953; Air Marshal, 1959; Air Chief Marshal, 1961. Air ADC to the Queen, 1962-63. Gold

Cross, Royal Order of George I, with crossed swords (Greece), 1941; Order of the Phœnix, Class I (Greece), 1963. *Address:* Hart House, Martin, Fordingbridge, Hants. *T:* Martin Cross 237. *Club:* Royal Air Force.

**MERVYN DAVIES, David Herbert;** *see* Davies, D. H. M.

**MERZ, Charles;** Editor, The New York Times, 1938-41, Editor Emeritus since 1961; *b* 23 Feb. 1893; *m* 1924, Evelyn Scott. *Educ:* Yale Univ. Associate Editor, New York World, 1924-31; Mem. of the Editorial Staff of the New York Times, 1931-38. LittD: Colgate Univ., 1939; Wooster Coll., 1939; Yale Univ., 1942; Columbia Univ., 1945. *Publications:* The Great American Bandwagon, 1928; The Dry Decade, 1931. *Address:* 10 Gracie Square, New York, NY 10028, USA. *T:* RE 7-4118. *Clubs:* Century, Yale (New York); Elizabethan (New Haven).

**MESSEL, Professor Harry,** PhD (NUI) 1951; Professor and Head of the School of Physics, and Director of Science Foundation for Physics, University of Sydney, Australia, since 1952; Joint Director, Astronomy Centre, Cornell-Sydney University, since 1964; *b* 3 March 1922. *Educ:* Rivers Public High Sch., Rivers, Manitoba. Entered RMC of Canada, 1940, grad. with Governor-General's Silver Medal, 1942. Served War of 1939-45: Canadian Armed Forces, Lieut, Canada and overseas, 1942-45. Queen's Univ., Kingston, Ont., 1945-48; BA 1st Cl. Hons in Mathematics, 1948, BSc Hons in Engineering Physics, 1948; St Andrews Univ., Scotland, 1948-49; Institute for Advanced Studies, Dublin, Eire, 1949-51; Sen. Lectr in Mathematical Physics, University of Adelaide, Australia, 1951-52. *Publications:* Chap. 4, Progress in Cosmic Ray Physics, vol. 2, (North Holland Publishing Company), 1953; numerous papers published in: Proc. Physical Soc., London; Philosophical Magazine, London; Physical Review of America; Co-author and Editor of: A Modern Introduction to Physics (Horwitz-Grahame, Vols I, II, III, 1959, 1960, 1962); Selected Lectures in Modern Physics, 1958; From Nucleus to Universe, 1960; Space and the Atom, 1961; A Journey through Space and the Atom, 1962; The Universe of Time and Space, 1963; Light and Life in the Universe, 1964; Science for High School Students, 1964; Time, 1965; Senior Science for High School Students, 1966; Atoms to Andromeda, 1966; Apollo and the Universe, 1967; Man in Inner and Outer Space, 1968; Nuclear Energy Today and Tommorrow, 1969. *Recreations:* water ski-ing, hunting and fishing. *Address:* University of Sydney, Sydney, NSW 2006, Australia. *T:* 660 0522.

**MESSEL, Oliver Hilary Sambourne,** CBE 1958; *b* 13 Jan. 1904; 2nd *s* of Lieut-Col Leonard Messel, OBE, TD, Homestead, Cuckfield, Sussex, and Maud Frances, *o d* of Edward Linley Sambourne. *Educ:* Eton; Slade School of Art. *Theatrical Productions: plays:* Cochran Revue, 1926, This Year of Grace, 1928, Wake Up and Dream, 1929, Cochran Revues, 1930-31, all at London Pavilion; Helen, Adelphi; The Miracle, Lyceum, 1932; Glamorous Night, Drury Lane, 1935; The Country Wife, Old Vic and New York, 1936; A Midsummer Night's Dream, Old Vic, 1937; The Tempest, Old Vic; The Infernal Machine, Arts, 1940; Big Top, His Majesty's, 1942; The Rivals, Criterion, 1945; Tough at the Top, Adelphi, The Lady's Not for Burning, Globe and New York, 1949; Ring Round the Moon, Globe, and Copenhagen, The Little Hut, Lyric and New York, 1950; Romeo and Juliet, New York, 1951; Under the Sycamore Tree, Aldwych, Letter from Paris, Aldwych, 1952; The Dark is Light Enough, Aldwych and New York, The House of Flowers, New York, 1954; The School for Scandal, Copenhagen, 1958; Rashomon, New York, 1958; *operas:* The Magic Flute, Covent Garden, 1947; Ariadne auf Naxos, Glyndebourne; Queen of Spades, Covent Garden, 1950; Idomeneo, Glyndebourne, 1951; La Cenerentola, Glyndebourne, 1952; Il Barbiere di Siviglia, Le Comte Ory, Glyndebourne, La Cenerentola, Glyndebourne, Berlin, 1954; Zemire et Azore, Bath Festival, Le Nozze di Figaro, 1955; Die Entführung aus dem Serail, Die Zauberflöte, Glyndebourne, 1956; Samson, Covent Garden, 1958; Der Rosenkavalier, Glyndebourne, 1959; Le Nozze di Figaro, Metropolitan, New York, 1959; Ariadne, Metropolitan, New York, 1962; *ballets:* Francesca da Rimini, Covent Garden and New York, 1937; Comus, New Theatre, 1942; Sleeping Beauty, Covent Garden and New York, 1946; Homage to the Queen, Covent Garden and New York, 1953. *Films:* Private Life of Don Juan, 1934; Romeo and Juliet, 1936; Caesar and Cleopatra, 1945; The Queen of Spades, 1949; Suddenly Last Summer, 1959. *Exhibitions:* Masks, Claridge Galls, 1925; Designs and Maquettes, Lefevre Galls, 1933; Leicester Galls, 1936; Portrait Paintings, Leicester Galls, 1938; Paintings and Designs, Carol Carstairs Galls, New York, 1938; Designs for film Queen of Spades, Leicester Galleries, 1949; Paintings and Designs, Redfern Galleries, 1951; Sagittarius Gallery, New York, 1959; O'Hana Gallery, 1962. *Decorations:* for Royal Command Performance, Covent Garden, for President of France, 1950, and Gala Performance for King of Sweden, 1954. Served in HM Forces, Captain, 1940-44. Fellow of University Coll. London, 1956. Hon. Associate, Regional Coll. of Art, Manchester, 1960. *Publications:* Stage Designs and Costumes, 1933; Designs for (Batsford) Romeo and Juliet, 1936; Designs for (Folio Society) A Midsummer Night's Dream, 1957; Designs for (Adrianne Allen and Marjorie Salter) Delightful Food, 1958. *Recreation:* gardening. *Address:* Maddox, St James', Barbados, West Indies.

**MESSENT, Sir Philip (Santo),** Kt, *cr* 1951; Hon. Consulting Surgeon, Royal Adelaide Hospital, since Nov. 1953; Hon. Surgeon, Royal Adelaide Hospital, 1933, retired; *b* 22 Feb. 1895; *s* of late P. S. Messent, ISO, and late A. E. Messent; *m* 1920, Agnes May Rich; one *s* three *d*. *Educ:* Kyre Coll., Unley Park; University of Adelaide. MB, BS 1918, MS 1923, University of Adelaide; FRACS 1927. Hon. Asst Surgeon, 1928, Hon. Surgeon, 1933, Royal Adelaide Hospital; Associate Lecturer in Surgery, University of Adelaide; Dir of Surgical Studies, 1950, retired. Pres. Med. Bd of SA; Governor, Scotch Coll., Adelaide. *Recreations:* tennis, gardening. *Address:* 26 Westall Street, Hyde Park, S Australia. *T:* LA 3917. *Club:* Adelaide.

**MESSER, Sir Frederick,** Kt, *cr* 1953; CBE 1949; JP; Middlesex County Alderman, 1938-52, retired; Vice-President Medical Superintendents' Society; *b* 12 May 1886; father, Poor Law Officer; *m* 1908, Edith B. Chapman; one *s* (and one *d* decd). Mem. of French Polishers Union, 1909-; Mem. of EC of Union, 1915-21; Gen. Treas. of Union, 1917-21; Chm., S Tottenham Labour Party, 1920-29; Middx County Council for Town Hall Ward, 1925; JP 1928; Chm. County Labour Group, 1925-40. MP (Lab.) South Tottenham, 1929-31, and 1935-50, MP (Lab.-Co-op.) Tottenham, 1950-Sept. 1959. Chm. Industrial Orthopædic Soc. Southern Area (Council, 1919-22, Acting General Sec., 1922-24);

formerly Chm. North-West Metropolitan Regional Hospital Board; Chm. Central Health Services Council, 1948-57; Chm. Ministry of Education Advisory Cttee on Handicapped Children, 1944-56; Chm. Croydon Hosp. Management Cttee, 1961-64. Freeman of Borough of Tottenham, 1955. *Address:* 189 Kingsdown Avenue, Croydon, Surrey. *T:* 01-660 4712.

**MESSER, Malcolm,** CBE 1949; *b* 1901; *s* of late Andrew Messer, MB, ChM; *m* 1943, Mary (*d* 1951), *er d* of G. F. Grigs; one *d*. *Educ:* Edinburgh Univ. (MA); Oxford Univ. (BA). Research Asst, Agricultural Economics Research Institute, Oxford, 1927-34; Technical Editor, Farmers' Weekly, 1934-38; Editor, Farmers' Weekly, 1938-66, retired editorship, 1 July 1966. Chm., Farm Journals Ltd, 1966-69. *Address:* Sanham House, Sanham Green, Hungerford, Berks. *Club:* Travellers'.

**MESSERVY, Professor Albert;** Professor of Veterinary Surgery, University of Bristol, since 1953; *b* 18 Feb. 1908; 2nd *s* of late E. P. Messervy, Jersey; *m* May, *d* of late F. E. Luce, Jersey; two *s* one *d*. *Educ:* Victoria Coll., Jersey; Royal Veterinary Coll., London. Private practice, 1929-40; Lecturer. Dept of Veterinary Surgery, Royal Vet. Coll., 1941-45; private practice, 1945-53. Mem. of Council, Royal Coll. of Veterinary Surgeons, 1957-65. Hon. MSc, 1964. *Publications:* clinical veterinary. *Recreation:* fishing. *Address:* Little Orchard, Sandford, Bristol. *T:* Churchill 317.

**MESSERVY, Gen. Sir Frank Walter,** KCSI 1947; KBE 1945; CB 1942; DSO 1941 (and Bar, 1944); late IAS; *b* 9 Dec. 1893; *s* of W. J. Messervy and Myra Naida de Boissiere; *m* 1927, Patricia, *d* of Col E. Waldegrave Courtney, Silksworth, Camberley; one *s* one *d* (and one *s* decd). *Educ:* Eton; Royal Military College, Sandhurst. 2nd Lieut IA 1913; 9th Hodson's Horse, 1914; served European War, France, Palestine, and Syria; Kurdistan, 1919; Staff Coll., Camberley, 1925-26, psc; Bt Major, 1929; Bt Lt-Col 1933; commanded 13th DCO Lancers, 1938-39; GSO1, 5th Indian Division, 1939-40; Col 1939; comd Gazelle Force, Sudan and Eritrea, 1940-41; comd 9 Ind. Inf. Bde at Keren, 1941; comd 4 Ind. Div. Western Desert and Cyrenaica, 1941-42; comd 1 Armd Div. Cyrenaica, 1942; comd 7 Armd Div. Western Desert, 1942; DCGS, GHQ, MEF 1942; comd 43 Ind. Armd Div. 1942-43; DAFV, GHQ India Command, 1943; Maj.-Gen. 1943; commanded 7th Indian Division in Arakan and at Kohima, 1944; commanded 4th Corps, Burma, Tamu to Rangoon, 1944-45; Lieut-Gen. 1945; GOC-in-C Malaya Command; GOC-in-C Northern Command, India, 1946-47; Commander-in-Chief Pakistan Army, 1947; retired, 1948; despatches 4 times. Col 16th Lt Cav., 1946-49; Col The Jat Regt, 1947-55; Deputy Chief Scout, April 1949-50. Berks County Councillor, 1953-56. Legion of Merit, USA, Commander; Order of the Nile 4th Class. *Recreations:* shooting, gardening. *Address:* North End House, Heyshott, Midhurst, Sussex. *T:* Midhurst 2069.

**MESSITER, Air Commodore Herbert Lindsell,** CB 1954; *b* 1902; 2nd *s* of late Col Charles Bayard Messiter, DSO, OBE, Barwick Park, Yeovil, Som, and Alice Lindsell; *m* 1933, Lucy Brenda Short; one *d*. *Educ:* Bedford Sch. Served War of 1939-45 (despatches 4 times): Egypt, N Africa, Belgium, Germany. Command Engineer Officer, Far East Air Force, 1950-52; Senior Technical Staff Officer, Bomber Command, RAF, 1952-56; Senior Technical Staff Officer, Middle East Air Force, 1956-59, retired. *Address:* c/o Lloyds Bank Ltd, 6 Pall Mall, SW1; Roquemont, St Helier, Jersey, CI. *Club:* Roehampton.

**MESTON,** family name of **Baron Meston.**

**MESTON,** 2nd Baron, *cr* 1919, of Agra and Dunottar; **Dougall Meston;** *b* 17 Dec. 1894; *s* of 1st Baron and Jeanie, CBE (*d* 1946), *o d* of James M'Donald; *S* father, 1943; *m* 1947, Diana Mary Came, *o d* of late Capt. O. S. Doll, 16 Upper Cheyne Row, Chelsea; two *s*. *Educ:* Charterhouse; RMA, Woolwich. Served European War, 1914-19; Capt., RA, 1917; N-W Frontier, India (Afghan War, 1919, Waziristan, 1919-20); retired, 1922; Barrister, Lincoln's Inn, 1924; South Eastern Circuit. Hon. Mem. Incorporated Association of Architects and Surveyors. President: British Soc. of Commerce; Assoc. of Cashiers. Contested (L) Southend Bye-Election, 1927, and General Election, 1929. *Publications:* Law of Moneylenders; Law of Nuisances; The Restrictive Trade Practices Act, 1956; The Rent Act, 1957; The Town and Country Planning Act, 1959; The Rating and Valuation Act, 1961; The Betting, Gaming and Lotteries Act, 1963; The Offices, Shops and Railway Premises Act, 1963; Weights and Measures Act, 1963; Rent Act, 1965; Leasehold Reform Act, 1967; The Gaming Act, 1968; Betterment Levy; several works on Gaming, Landlord and Tenant, War Damage, Local Government, Highways, Trade Wastes, Public Health and Housing Acts; Jt Ed. of Mather's Sheriff and Execution Law (3rd edn); Legal Adviser to Business Encyclopædia. *Heir:* *s* Hon. James Meston, *b* 10 Feb. 1950. *Address:* Hurst Place, Cookham Dene, Berks; Queen Elizabeth Building, Temple, EC4. *T:* 01-353 1727, 01-353 3911. *Club:* Reform.

**METCALF, Maurice Rupert,** CMG 1954; OBE 1945; seconded to Central African Office, 1962 (from CRO), retired, 1964; *b* 5 May 1905; *s* of late Henry E. Metcalf; *m* 1928, Dorothy Stuart (*d* 1963), *d* of George S. Ring, New York, USA; two *s*. *Educ:* Oundle Sch.; Sidney Sussex Coll., Cambridge. Horace Plunkett Foundation, 1927-32; National Farmers' Union, 1932-41; Ministry of Food, 1941; Prin. Private Sec. to Minister, 1943; Prin. Private Sec. to Minister of Reconstruction, 1943; Personal Asst to Lord President of the Council, 1945; Ministry of Food, 1945; transf. to Commonwealth Relations Office, 1949; Dep. UK High Commissioner in Ceylon, 1950-53; Establishment Officer, 1954; UK High Commissioner for Federation of Rhodesia and Nyasaland, 1955-61; Asst Under-Sec. of State, CRO, 1961. *Address:* The Old Post Office, Jevington, Polegate, Sussex.

**METCALFE, Maj.-Gen. John Francis,** CB 1960; CBE 1954; *b* 30 June 1908; *s* of late Brigadier-General F. H. Metcalfe, DSO; *m* 1938, Natalia Eleanor, *d* of late Col N. E. Margetts, US Army; one *d*. *Educ:* Radley Coll.; Royal Military Coll., Sandhurst. Commissioned, Queen's Royal Regt, 1928; served in India and Burma, 1939-45; Instructor, Staff Coll., Quetta, 1942-43; OC 2nd Bn Queen's Royal Regt, 1944; Brigadier, Q, HQ ALFSEA, 1945; Col i/c Administration, South Wales District 1946; Instructor, Joint Services Staff Coll., 1947-49; OC 1st Bn East Surrey Regt, 1949-51; Brigadier General Staff, HQ Western Command, 1952-53; Imperial Defence Coll., 1954; Commander 2nd Federation Infantry Brigade, Malaya, 1955-57; Dir of Personnel Administration, War Office, 1958-61; GOC Aldershot District, 1961-63, retd. Col, The Queen's Royal Surrey Regiment, 1959-64. *Recreation:* golf. *Address:* Windlesham, Littlestone, New Romney, Kent. *Club:* Army and Navy.

**METCALFE, Percy,** CVO 1937; RDI 1938; Sculptor and Medallist; *b* 14 Jan. 1895; 2nd *s* of John and Hannah Metcalfe; *m* 1920, Eveline Mabel Smith; two *d*. *Educ:* Royal College of Art (associate). *Address:* 70 Madrid Road, SW13. *T:* 01-748 3786.

**METCALFE, Sir Ralph Ismay,** Kt 1943; Director of Wm Cory & Son Ltd, and Associated Companies until 1961; Director, Petrofina (Great Britain) Ltd, until 1968; *b* 20 May 1896; *s* of George Metcalfe, Maryport, Cumberland, and Southampton; *m* 1st, 1920, Betty, *d* of E. H. Pelling; 2nd, 1947, Dorothea, *d* of C. E. Gibbs. *Educ:* King Edward VI Sch., Southampton. Entered Civil Service (Admty), 1915; resigned, 1920, on joining Wm Cory & Son Ltd; Dir of Tanker Division, Ministry of War Transport, 1939-42, and Dir of Sea Transport, 1942-45; Mem., Port of London Authority, 1949-67. Master, Company of Watermen and Lightermen of the River Thames, 1959-60; Prime Warden, Worshipful Co. of Shipwrights, 1963-64. Served European War, 1914-18, in RFC and RAF. Chevalier Légion d'Honneur (France); US Medal of Freedom with Gold Palm; Comdr Order of Orange-Nassau; Commander Order of St Olav. *Address:* Elmtree House, West Mersea, Essex. *T:* West Mersea 2934. *Clubs:* Athenæum, City of London, Alpine, Travellers'.

**METCALFE, Sir Theophilus (John),** 8th Bt, *cr* 1802; *b* 14 Oct. 1916; *s* of late Lieut-Col Eric Debonnaire Theophilus Metcalfe, OBE, MC, Indian Army, half-brother of 7th Bt, and Winifred Crampton, *d* of E. Neild Shackle, Hayes, Middx; *S* uncle, 1950. *Educ:* Haileybury. *Heir:* none. *Address:* 3 Kensington House, 35 Kensington Court, W8.

**METFORD, Professor John Callan James;** Professor of Spanish, University of Bristol, since 1960; *b* 29 Jan. 1916; *s* of Oliver Metford and Florence Stowe Thomas; *m* 1944, Edith Donald; one *d*. *Educ:* Porth Grammar Sch.; Universities of Liverpool, Yale and California. Commonwealth Fund Fellow, 1939-41; British Council Lecturer in Brazil, 1942-44; Regional Officer, Latin American Department of the British Council, 1944-46; Lecturer in Latin American Studies, University of Glasgow, 1946-55; Head of Department of Spanish, and Portuguese, University of Bristol, 1955-. Vis. Prof., Lehigh Univ., USA, 1968-69. Vice-Chm., Council of Westonbirt Sch. *Publications:* British Contributions to Spanish and Spanish American Studies, 1950; San Martin the Liberator, 1950, 2nd edn 1970; Modern Latin America, 1964; The Golden Age of Spanish Drama, 1969; articles in Bulletin of Spanish Studies, Bulletin of Hispanic Studies, Liverpool Studies in Spanish, International Affairs, etc. *Recreation:* iconography. *Address:* 2 Parry's Close, Bristol BS9 1AW. *T:* 682284. *Clubs:* Royal Commonwealth Society, New Arts (London); Royal Commonwealth Society (Bristol).

**METHUEN,** family name of **Baron Methuen.**

**METHUEN,** 4th Baron, *cr* 1838, **Paul Ayshford Methuen,** MA Oxon; DipAg; RA 1959 (ARA 1951); RWS; FSA; Hon. ARIBA; painter and zoologist; Member Royal Fine Art Commission, 1952-59; Trustee of National Gallery, and of Tate Gallery, 1938-45; Trustee Imperial War Museum, 1950-52; *b* 29 Sept. 1886; *e s* of 3rd Baron and Mary Ethel, CBE (*d* 1941), *d* of late William Ayshford Sanford, Nynehead Court; *S* father, 1932; *m* 1915, Eleanor (Norah) (*d* 1958), *d* of late W. J. Hennessy of Rudgwick, Sussex. *Educ:* Eton; New Coll., Oxford. 2nd Class Hons Nat Sc. 1910; MA 1914; DipAg 1920. Asst Transvaal Museum, Pretoria, 1910-14; Lieut Scots Guards (SR), 1914-19 (seeing active service in France); Ministry of Agriculture as Live Stock, and later as Marketing, Officer, 1925-32. Has held several one-man Exhibitions at the Leicester Galleries, etc., and has had works bought by Tate Gallery, Victoria and Albert Museum, Cont. Art Soc., etc. Staff Capt. HQ London District, 1940-44 and Major as Monuments and Fine Arts Officer, CA 21 Army Group, AEF, 1944-45. Hon. LLD: Bristol, 1963; Bath, 1970. Chevalier, Legion of Honour, France. *Publications:* Normandy Diary, 1952; several scientific articles. *Heir:* *b* Capt. Hon. Anthony Paul Methuen, *qv*. *Address:* Corsham Court, Wilts. *T:* Corsham 2214; 6 Primrose Hill Studios, NW1.

**METHUEN, Hon. Anthony Paul;** Captain; *heir-presumptive* to brother, 4th Baron Methuen, *qv*; *b* 26 June 1891; 2nd *s* of late Field-Marshal Lord Methuen; *m* 1920, Grace, *d* of Sir Richard Holt, 1st Bt; two *s* one *d*. *Educ:* Wellington; New Coll., Oxford. SR Scots Guards, 1914-18; Chartered Architect. *Address:* Ivy House, Corsham, Chippenham, Wilts. *T:* Corsham 2263.

**METSON, Gilbert Harold,** MC 1940; MSc, PhD, DSc; Consulting Engineer; formerly Director of Research, Post Office; *b* 4 July 1907; British; *m* 1932, Una (*née* Pyke); two *d*. *Educ:* Mercers' Sch., Queen Elizabeth's Sch., Barnet. BSc (Eng.) London; MSc, PhD and DSc Queen's Univ. of Belfast. Post Office Engineer. Served War, in Royal Signals, 1939-45; comd 11th L of C Signals in N Africa and Italy; GSO1, War Office. *Publications:* wide range, mainly concerned with thermionic emission from oxide cathodes. *Recreation:* fly-fishing. *Address:* 68 Chandos Avenue, Whetstone, N20. *T:* 01-445 7067.

**MEXBOROUGH,** 7th Earl of, *cr* 1766; **John Raphael Wentworth Savile,** DL; Baron Pollington, 1753; Viscount Pollington, 1766; *b* 11 Oct. 1906; *o s* of 6th Earl and Hon. Marjorie Knatchbull-Hugessen, *d* of 2nd Baron Brabourne; *S* father 1945; *m* 1930, Josephine, *d* of Capt. Fletcher of Saltoun; two *s* one *d*. *Educ:* Downside Sch.; Pembroke Coll., Cambridge (MA). JP North Riding of Yorks; DL, North Riding of Yorks, 1967. Capt., Intelligence Corps, 1942; in India, May 1941-Jan. 1945; ADC to Governor of Bihar, 1944-45. *Heir:* *s* Viscount Pollington, *qv*. *Address:* Arden Hall, Helmsley, Yorks. *T:* Bilsdale 213; Methley Park, Leeds. *Clubs:* St James', Queen's, All England Lawn Tennis.

**MEYER, Professor Alfred;** Professor of Neuropathology in the University of London, Institute of Psychiatry, 1949-56, retired; *b* 3 Feb. 1895; *m* 1949, Nina Cohen. Assoc. Prof. of Neurology at University of Bonn, 1931; Rockefeller Research Fellow in Pathological Laboratory, Maudlsey Hosp., London, 1933; Neuropathologist in the Pathological Laboratory, Maudsley Hospital, 1943. *Publications:* numerous articles on neuroanatomical and neuropathological subjects. *Address:* 38 Wood Lane, N6.

**MEYER, Sir Anthony John Charles,** 3rd Bt, *cr* 1910; MP (C) West Flint since 1970; *b* 27 Oct. 1920; *o s* of Sir Frank Meyer, MP, 2nd Bt, Ayot House, Ayot St Lawrence, Herts; *S* father, 1935; *m* 1941, Barbadee Violet, *o c* of late A. Charles Knight, JP, and of Mrs Charles Knight, Herne Place, Sunningdale; one *s* three *d*. *Educ:* Eton (Capt. of Oppidans); New Coll., Oxford. Served Scots Guards, 1941-45 (wounded); HM Treasury, 1945-46; entered HM Foreign Service, 1946; HM Embassy, Paris, 1951; 1st Sec., 1953; transferred to HM

Embassy, Moscow, 1956; London, 1958. MP (C) Eton and Slough, 1964-66. Cons. Research Dept, 1968. Jt Hon. Sec., British Council, European Movement, 1970-. Trustee of Shakespeare National Memorial Theatre. Founder and Dir of political jl, Solon, 1969. *Publication:* A European Technological Community, 1966. *Heir: s* Anthony Ashley Frank Meyer, *b* 23 Aug. 1944. *Address:* Garden House, Sunningdale, Berks. *T:* Ascot 22549; Rhewl House, Llanasa, Flints. *Clubs:* Carlton, Beefsteak.

**MEYER, Ven. Conrad John Eustace;** Archdeacon of Bodmin since 1969; Hon. Canon of Truro since 1966; *b* 2 July 1922; *s* of William Eustace and Marcia Meyer; *m* 1960, Mary Wiltshire; no *c. Educ:* Clifton Coll.; Pembroke Coll., Cambridge; Westcott House. BA 1946, MA 1948. Served War of 1939-45: Royal Navy (commissioned from lower deck), 1942-46. Lieut (S) RNVR, post war, until apptd Chaplain, RNVR, 1950-54. Deacon, 1948; Priest, 1949; Asst Curate: St Francis, Ashton Gate, Bristol, 1948-51; Kenwyn, Truro, 1951; Falmouth Parish Church, 1954; Vicar of Devoran, Truro, 1956-65; Diocesan Youth Chaplain, 1956; Asst Dir of Religious Educn, 1958; Diocesan Sec. for Educn, 1960-69. Hon. Diocesan Sec., Nat. Soc., 1960-69. Fellow, Woodard Corp. of Schools; Provost, Western Div., Woodard Corp., 1970-. Associate Fellow Inst. of Civil Defence. *Recreations:* swimming, walking, military history, civil defence, archaeology. *Address:* Archdeacon's House, St Catherine's Hill, Launceston, Cornwall PL15 7EJ. *T:* Launceston 2714. *Clubs:* United Service, Royal Commonwealth Society.

**MEYER, Heinerich Carl,** CMG 1956; ISO 1950; MM 1917; BSc; retired as Commissioner, The South Australian Harbors Board (1950-65); *b* 3 March 1896; *s* of late Henry and Lavinia Meyer, Adelaide, South Australia; *m* 1st, 1924, Jessica Chilman (*d* 1936); two *d*; 2nd, 1940, Monica, *d* of late Jas. B. Thompson; one *s*. *Educ:* University of Adelaide. Apptd to staff of S Australian Harbors Bd when just constituted, 1914. Chief Engineer, 1935-50; General Manager, 1942-61. Server European War, 1914-18, AIF in Egypt, Gallipoli (took part in landing, April 1915), and France (wounded); Australian Naval and Mil. Expeditionary Force and Admin. of Mandated Territory of New Guinea, 1920-22. Sent abroad by S Australian Govt to investigate port ops equipment and develt in world ports, 1946-47 and 1959. *Address:* 15 Myrtle Avenue, Myrtle Bank, S Australia 5064. *T:* 79.4753. *Club:* Naval, Military and Air Force of South Australia.

**MEYER, Matt;** Newspaperman, USA; *b* Tilden, Ala, 28 Aug. 1904; *s* of Matthew Meyer and Julia Patterson; *m* 1931, Emily Cluett Dorlon; three *d. Educ:* New York University, USA (BCS). With Scripps-Howard Newspapers, 1932: Advertising Dir, Washington Daily News, 1938-47, Pres. and Business Manager, 1947-59; Asst Gen. Business Manager, Scripps-Howard Newspapers, 1959-62; Vice Pres., Business Manager, New York World-Telegram and Sun, 1962-65, Pres., 1965-66; Pres., 125 Barclay Street Inc., 1966-; Gen. Management, Scripps-Howard Newspapers, 1967-; Director: Bureau of Advertising; Scripps-Howard Investment Co.; New York World Telegram Corp.; Allied Newspapers Inc.; Amer. Newspaper Publishers Assoc. (Mem. Labor Relations Cttee); Advertising Council Inc.; Pres., World-Journal-Tribune Inc., 1966-. Vice-Chm., Newspaper Publishers Premium Fund Cttee; Chm., Publishers Association, New York City, 1963-65. *Recreations:* golf, photography, reading. *Address:* 69 Chase Road, Scarsdale, NY, USA. *Clubs:* Union League (New York); Scarsdale Golf.

**MEYER, Rollo John Oliver,** OBE 1967; Headmaster of Millfield School, 1935-71, Life Warden, from Sept. 1971; *b* 15 March 1905; *s* of Canon Rollo Meyer and Arabella Ward; *m* 1931, Joyce Symons; two *d. Educ:* Haileybury Coll.; Pembroke Coll., Cambridge. MA 1926. Cottonbroker, Gill & Co., Bombay, 1926-29; Private Tutor, Limbdi, Porbandar, Dhrangadhra, 1929-35; founded Millfield Sch., 1935; founded Edgarley Hall Preparatory Sch., Glastonbury, 1945. *Recreations:* ornithology, any game with a ball in it, chess, gardening, writing. *Address:* Millfield School, Street, Som. *T:* Street 2683. *Clubs:* MCC, English-Speaking Union.

**MEYJES, Richard Anthony;** Head of the Business Team in Mr. Heath's Administration, since Aug. 1970; *b* 30 June 1918; *s* of Anthony Charles Dorian Meyjes and Norah Isobel Meyjes; *m* 1939, Margaret Doreen Morris; three *s. Educ:* University College School, Hampstead. Articled Clerk, Messrs Hortin and Nash, Solicitors, London W2, 1935-39. War Service, RASC, Sept. 1939-Jan. 1946 (temp. Captain). Qualified as Solicitor, June 1946; Legal Dept, Anglo-Saxon Petroleum Co., 1946-56; Manager, Thailand and Vietnam Division, Shell International Petroleum Co., 1956-58; Marketing Manager, Shell Co. of Philippines, Ltd, Manila, 1958-61; President, 1961-64; Head of Regional Marketing Div., Shell International Petroleum Co., London, 1964-66; Marketing Coordinator, 1966-70. Seconded to HM Govt as Head of Business Team, Aug. 1970. Officer of Philippine Legion of Honour, 1964. *Recreations:* gardening, walking, golf. *Address:* Longhill House, The Sands, near Farnham, Surrey. *T:* Runfold 2601. *Clubs:* Institute of Directors; Farnham Golf.

**MEYNELL, Dame Alix (Hester Marie); (Lady Meynell),** DBE 1949; *b* 2 Feb. 1903; *d* of late Surgeon Commander L. Kilroy, RN, and late Hester Kilroy; *m* 1946, Sir Francis Meynell, *qv*; no *c. Educ:* Malvern Girls' Coll.; Somerville Coll., Oxford. Joined civil service, Board of Trade, 1925. Seconded to the Monopolies and Restrictive Practices Commission as Sec., 1949-52; Under-Sec., Board of Trade, 1946-55; resigned from the Civil Service, 1955. Called to the Bar, 1956. Chm. Consultative Council, South Eastern Gas Board, 1956-63. Member: Harlow New Town Corpn; Performing Right Tribunal; Cttees of Investigation for England, Scotland and Great Britain under Agricultural Marketing Acts, 1956-65; SE Gas Board, 1963-69; Monopolies Commn, 1965-68. Mem., Cosford RDC, 1970. *Address:* The Grey House, Lavenham, Suffolk. *T:* Lavenham 526. *Club:* Oxford and Cambridge University.

**MEYNELL, Sir Francis,** Kt 1946; RDI; book designer, publisher and poet; Director: Nonesuch Press Ltd; Bodley Head, Ltd; typographic adviser (unpaid) to HM Stationery Office, 1945-66; since 1954: Member Royal Mint Advisory Committee; Hon. Member Art Workers Guild; Society of Typographic Designers (President 1958-62); Member Council, Royal College of Art, 1959-61; Vice-President, Poetry Society, since 1960; *b* 12 May 1891; *y s* of late Wilfrid Meynell, CBE and late Alice Meynell; *m* 1st, 1914, Hilda Saxe; one *d*; 2nd, 1925, Vera Mendel; one *s*; 3rd, 1946, Alix Hester Marie Kilroy (*see* Dame Alix Meynell). *Educ:* Downside; Trinity Coll., Dublin. Dir, Daily Herald, 1918-20; founded Nonesuch Press, 1923; regular contributor to News-Chronicle, 1934; on loan from Mather and Crowther Ltd, of which he was a Dir, to Bd of Trade for wartime duties as Adviser on Consumer Needs, 1940; Royal Designer for Industry, 1945; one-time Member: Coun. of Industrial Design, and of Advisory Council Victoria & Albert Museum. Dir-Gen. Cement and Concrete Association, 1946-58. Hon. DLitt Reading, 1964. *Publications:* The Typography of Newspaper Advertisements, 1929; The Week-End Book, 1923; The Nonesuch Century, 1936; Seventeen Poems, 1945; English Printed Books, 1946; Poems and Pieces, 1961. Designer of all Nonesuch Press Books. *Recreations:* village cricket, family bridge, oceanic table-tennis. *Address:* The Grey House, Lavenham, Suffolk. *Clubs:* Double Crown, Savile.

**MEYNELL, Laurence Walter; (Robert Eton);** Author; *b* Wolverhampton, 1899; *y s* of late Herbert and Agnes Meynell; *m* 1932, Shirley Ruth (*d* 1955), *e d* of late Taylor Darbyshire; one *d*; *m* 1956, Joan Belfrage (*née* Henley). *Educ:* St Edmund's Coll., Old Hall, Ware. After serving in the Honourable Artillery Company became successively schoolmaster, estate agent and finally professional writer; Royal Air Force in War of 1939-45 (despatches). Literary Editor, Time and Tide, 1958-60, Past Pres. Johnson Soc. *Publications:* as *Robert Eton:* The Pattern; The Dividing Air; The Bus Leaves for the Village; Not In Our Stars; The Journey; Palace Pier; The Legacy; The Faithful Years; The Corner of Paradise Place; St Lynn's Advertiser; The Dragon at the Gate; as *Laurence Meynell:* Bluefeather; Paid in Full; The Door in the Wall; The House in the Hills; The Dandy; Third Time Unlucky; His Aunt Came Late; The Creaking Chair; The Dark Square; Strange Landing; The Evil Hour; The Bright Face of Danger; The Echo in the Cave; The Lady on Platform One; Party of Eight; The Man No One Knew; Give me the Knife; Saturday Out; Famous Cricket Grounds; Life of Sir P. Warner; Builder and Dreamer; Smoky Joe; Too Clever by Half; Smoky Joe in Trouble; Rolls, Man of Speed; Young Master Carver; Under the Hollies; Bridge Under the Water; Great Men of Staffordshire; Policeman in the Family; James Brindley; Sonia Back Stage; The Young Architect; District Nurse Carter; The Breaking Point; One Step from Murder; The Abandoned Doll; The House in Marsh Road; The Pit in the Garden; Virgin Luck; Sleep of the Unjust; Airmen on the Run; More Deadly Than the Male; Double Fault; Die by the Book; Week-end in the Scampi Belt; Death of a Philanderer; The Curious Crime of Miss Julia Blossom; as *A. Stephen Tring* (for children); The Old Gang; The Cave By the Sea; Penny Dreadful; Barry's Exciting Year; Penny Triumphant; Penny Penitent; Penny Dramatic; Penny in Italy; Penny Goodbye. *Recreations:* walking, trying to write a play. *Address:* 9 Clifton Terrace, Brighton BN1 3HA. *Clubs:* Authors', Savage.

**MEYNER, Robert Baumle;** Lawyer since 1934; Governor, State of New Jersey, USA, 1954-62; *b* 3 July 1908; *s* of late Gustave H. Meyner and Sophia Baumle Meyner; *m* 1957, Helen Day Stevenson. *Educ:* Lafayette Coll. (AB); Columbia Univ. Law Sch. (LLB). State Senator from Warren County, 1948-52; Senate Minority (Democrat) Leader, 1950; Director: Prudential Insurance Co.; Engelhard Minerals & Chemicals Corp.; Phillipsburg (NJ) National Bank and Trust Co.; First National State Bank, Newark (NJ); US Sav. Bank, Newark (NJ); Delaware and Bound Brook Railroad. Administrator, Cigarette Advertising Code. Hon. degrees: Dr of Laws: Rutgers (The State Univ.) 1954; Lafayette Coll., 1954; Princeton Univ., 1956; Long Island Univ., 1958; Fairleigh Dickinson Univ., 1959; Syracuse Univ., 1960; Lincoln Univ., 1960; Colorado Coll., 1961. *Address:* (business) 24 Commerce Street, Newark, New Jersey 07102, USA; 16 Olden Lane, Princeton, NJ 08540, USA. *Clubs:* Columbia University, River (New York).

**MEYNINK, John Fitzsimmons,** CMG 1958; *b* 4 June 1887; Australian; *s* of late J. E. Meynink, Sydney and Moree, NSW; *m* 1919, Jane Ellen Crothers; two *s*. *Educ:* Maitland High Sch., NSW. Began career as Grazier (Qld). Served 3 years in Field Artillery, 1st Div. AIF, France, 1916-18. Pres. United Graziers Assoc. of Qld, Aust., 1939-41 (now Trustee); Mem. for 10 years of Graziers Federal Council of Aust., and Aust. Wool Council; Mem. for 5 years of State Cttee of Aust. Central Wool Cttee, handling Australia's complete wool clip throughout War of 1939-45; Dir of Qld Trustees, 1938, Dep. Chm., 1953, Chm., 1960 (retired from Board, 1962). Mem. Cttee Qld Turf Club, 1938-. Chm. Licensing Cttee and Trustee, Vice-Chm., 1966-; Mem. Adv. Bd of Aust. Comforts Fund, Qld Div., throughout War of 1939-45; Councillor, 1945-, Trustee and Treasurer, Patriotic Fund of Qld. *Recreation:* racing. *Address:* Unit 1A, Camden, Toorak Road, Hamilton, Qld 4007, Australia. *Clubs:* Queensland, Tattersalls (Brisbane).

**MEYRICK, Lt-Col Sir George David Eliott Tapps-Gervis-,** 6th Bt, *cr* 1791; MC 1943; *b* 15 April 1915; *o s* of Major Sir George Llewelyn Tapps-Gervis-Meyrick, 5th Bt, and Marjorie (*née* Hamlin); *S* father 1960; *m* 1940, Ann, *d* of Clive Miller; one *s* one *d*. *Educ:* Eton; Trinity Coll., Cambridge (BA). 2nd Lieut, 9th Queen's Royal Lancers, 1937. Served War of 1939-45 (wounded, MC): BEF, 1940; Middle East, 1941-43; Italy, 1945; Captain, 1940 Lt-Col, 1947; retired, 1952. Mem. Ringwood and Fordingbridge RDC; Dir, Southampton FC, 1953-. *Recreations:* shooting, travel. *Heir:* *s* George Christopher Cadafael Tapps-Gervis-Meyrick [*b* 10 March 1941; *m* 1968, Jean Louise Montagu Douglas Scott, *d* of late Lt-Col Lord William Scott and of Lady William Scott, Beechwood, Melrose, Scotland; one *s*]. *Address:* Hinton Admiral, Christchurch, Hants. *T:* Highcliffe 2887; Bodorgan, Isle of Anglesey. *T:* Bodorgan 204. *Clubs:* Cavalry; Royal Yacht Squadron.

**MEYRICK, Admiral Sir Sidney Julius,** KCB, *cr* 1938 (CB 1934); *b* 28 March 1879; *e s* of late Julius Meyrick; *m* 1901, Judith (*d* 1963), *e d* of late Admiral Sir John R. T. Fullerton; two *s* (and one killed in action, 1942). *Educ:* HMS Britannia. Entered Navy, 1893; Lieut, 1899; Commander, 1915; Commander, HMS Resolution, Grand Fleet, 1916-18; Captain, 1919; Flag-Captain and Chief Staff Officer, HMS Courageous, Reserve Fleet, 1920-21; Captain (D), Sixth Destroyer Flotilla, 1921-22; Flag-Captain and Chief Staff Officer, HMS Revenge, Atlantic Fleet, 1922-23; Staff of War Coll., Greenwich, 1923-26; Dir of Training and Staff Duties, Admiralty, 1926-27; Flag-Captain and Captain of the Fleet, HMS Nelson, Atlantic Fleet, 1927-29; Captain Royal Naval College, Dartmouth, 1929-32; Naval ADC to the King, 1931-32; Rear-Adm., 1932, Naval Sec. to the First Lord of the Admiralty, 1932-34; Commanding Second Cruiser Squadron, 1934-36; Vice-Adm., 1936; Admiral, 1940; Commander-in-Chief America and West Indies Station, 1937-40; retired list, 1941. *Address:* Norton House, near Chichester, Sussex. *T:* Eastergate 2198.

**MEYRICK, Col Sir Thomas Frederick,** 3rd Bt, *cr* 1880; TD; late 15th/19th Hussars; DL, JP, Pembrokeshire; *b* 28 Nov. 1899; *o s* of

Brigadier-General Sir Frederick Charlton Meyrick, 2nd Bt; *S* father, 1932; *m* 1926, Ivy Frances (*d* 1947), *d* of late Lieut-Col F. C. Pilkington, DSO; three *s* three *d*; *m* 1951, Gladice Joyce, *d* of Bertram W. Allen, Cilrhiw, Narberth, Pembs; one *s*. Capt. 15/19 Hussars, 1927; Equitation Instructor, Weedon, 1922-27, and RMC, 1930-34; retd pay, 1934; Captain 102 (Pembroke and Cardigan), Field Brigade RA (TA), 1937; Major, 1939; Hon. Col 302 Pembroke Yeo. Field Regt, RA (TA), 1955-59. Sheriff of Pembrokeshire, 1938; Master Pembrokeshire Foxhounds, 1934-35, South Pembrokeshire, 1936-39; V. W. H., Lord Bathurst's, 1939, Pembrokeshire, 1946-58; Pres. Royal Welsh Agricultural Soc., 1955; Chm., Pembs Branch, NFU, 1968. *Heir: s* David John Charlton Meyrick [*b* 2 Dec. 1926; *m* 1962, Penelope Anne Marsden-Smedley; three *s*]. *Address:* Gumfreston, Tenby, Pembrokeshire. *Clubs:* United Hunts, English-Speaking Union; Royal Yacht Squadron.

*See also Baron Merthyr.*

**MEYSEY-THOMPSON, Sir (Humphrey) Simon,** 4th Bt *cr* 1874; *b* 31 March 1935; *s* of Guy Herbert Meysey-Thompson (*d* 1961), and of Miriam Beryl Mersey-Thompson; *S* kinsman, Sir Algar de Clifford Charles Meysey-Thompson, 1967. *Address:* 39 Chesham Street, SW1; 10 Church Street, Woodbridge, Suffolk.

**MIALL, (Rowland) Leonard,** OBE 1961; Controller Overseas and Foreign Relations, British Broadcasting Corporation, since 1971; *b* 6 Nov. 1914; *e s* of late Rowland Miall and of S. Grace Miall; *m* 1941, Lorna, *o d* of G. John Rackham; three *s* one *d*. *Educ:* Bootham Sch., York (Scholar); Freiburg Univ.; St John's Coll. Cambridge (Sizar). BA (Cambridge) 1936, MA 1940; Pres. Cambridge Union, 1936; Ed. Cambridge Review, 1936. Lectured in US, 1937; Sec. British-American Associates, 1937-39; joined BBC; inaugurated talks broadcast to Europe, 1939; BBC German Talks and Features Editor, 1940-42. Mem. British Political Warfare Mission to US, 1942-44 (Dir of News, San Francisco, 1943; Head of New York Office, 1944); Personal Asst to Dep. Dir-Gen., Political Warfare Exec., London, 1944; attached to Psychological Warfare Division of SHAEF, Luxembourg, 1945. Rejoined BBC: Special Correspondent, Czechoslovakia, 1945; Actg Diplomatic Corresp., 1945; Chief Corresp. in US, 1945-53; Special Corresp., Bogota, 1948, United Nations, 1950, Canada, 1951; Head of Television Talks, 1954; Asst Controller, Current Affairs and Talks, Television, 1961; Special Asst to Dir of Television, planning start of BBC-2, 1962; Asst Controller, Programme Services, Television, BBC, 1963-66; BBC Rep. in US, 1966-70. Mem. BBC Delegation to USSR, 1956; Mem., The Pilgrims, 1959; Inaugurated BBC Lunchtime Lectures, 1962; Advisor, Cttee on Broadcasting, New Delhi, 1965; Delegate to 8th Commonwealth Broadcasting Conf., Jamaica, 1970. *Publications:* Richard Dimbleby, Broadcaster, 1966; articles on the United States. *Recreations:* bridge, gardening, doing it oneself. *Address:* Maryfield, Taplow, Bucks. *T:* Burnham 4195. *Clubs:* Garrick; Century, Coffee House (NY); Metropolitan (Washington); Union (Cambridge).

**MICHAEL, David Parry Martin,** MA; Headmaster, Newport High School, Mon., since 1960; *b* 21 Dec. 1910; *m* 1937, Mary Horner Hayward; one *s*. *Educ:* University Coll., Cardiff. Major, RAOC, combined ops, 1941-46 (despatches). Asst Master, Bassaleg Gram. Sch., Mon., 1935-41 and 1946-50; Headmaster, Cathays High Sch. for Boys, Cardiff, 1950-60. Member: Coun., University Coll., Cardiff, 1961-; Governing Body, Church in Wales, 1963-. Gov., Nat. Library of Wales, 1967-; Mem., Broadcasting Council for Wales, 1969-. Pres., Incorporated Assoc. of Headmasters, 1968. Ed., Welsh Secondary Schools' Review, 1965-. *Publications:* The Idea of a Staff College, 1967; Guide to the Sixth Form, 1969; Arthur Machen, 1971; articles and reviews in educational and other jls. *Recreations:* collecting Victorian Staffordshire portrait figures; setting and solving crosswords. *Address:* 28 Fields Road, Newport, Mon. *T:* Newport (Mon) 62747.

**MICHAEL, Dr Ian (Lockie);** Vice-Chancellor, University of Malawi, since 1964; *b* 30 Nov. 1915; 4th *c* of late Reginald Warburton Michael and Margaret Campbell Kerr; *m* 1942, Mary Harborne Bayley, *e c* of late Rev. Walter Henry Bayley; one *s* one *d*. *Educ:* St Bees Sch.; private study. BA (London) 1938; PhD (Bristol) 1963. Schoolmaster: St Faith's Sch., Cambridge, 1935-40; Junior Sch., Leighton Park, 1941-45, Headmaster, 1946-49; Lectr in Educn, Bristol Univ., 1950-63; Prof. of Educn, Khartoum Univ., 1963-64. *Publication:* English Grammatical Categories, 1970. *Address:* University of Malawi, PO Box 5097, Limbe, Malawi. *T:* Blantyre 30011.

**MICHAELIS, Sir Archie,** Kt, *cr* 1952; *b* 19 Dec. 1889; *s* of Frederick David and Esther Zillah Michaelis, St Kilda, Australia; *m* 1920, Claire Esther Hart; three *d*. *Educ:* Wesley Coll., Melbourne; Harrow Sch., England. Served European War, 1914-18, with HAC in Egypt and Aden, and afterwards in Salonika with RA (SR). Mem. State Parliament of Vic., Legislative Assembly, 1932-52, as Mem. for St Kilda; Hon. Minister Macfarlan Administration, 1945, Speaker, 1950-52. Mem. Patriotic Funds Council of Vic., Chm. 1947-51, and connected with various Jewish and charitable activities; former Chm., Michaelis, Hallenstein & Co. Pty Ltd, and Associated Leathers Ltd, Melbourne. Vice-President: Kipling Society, London; Alfred Hospital, Melbourne. *Recreation:* reading. *Address:* 281 Williams Road, South Yarra, Vic. 3141, Australia. *T:* 24.3866. *Clubs:* Royal Automobile (Victoria); Naval and Military (Melbourne).

**MICHAELS, Michael I.,** CB 1960; Under-Secretary, Ministry of Technology, since 1964; British Member of Board of Governors, International Atomic Energy Agency, since 1957; *b* 22 Dec. 1908; *m* 1932, Rosina, *e d* of late Joseph Sturges; one *s* one *d*. *Educ:* City of London College; London Sch. of Economics (Social Science Research Scholar, 1931). Asst Sec., New Survey London Life and Labour, 1932-34. Deputy Director, Programmes and Statistics, Ministry of Supply, 1940-45. Asst Sec., Ministry of Health, 1946-54; Under-Sec., Atomic Energy Office, 1955-59; Office of the Minister for Science (Atomic Energy Division), 1959-64. *Recreations:* music, walking and history. *Address:* 23 Holly Park, Finchley, N3. *T:* 01-346 1629; Queens Cottage, Hacheston, Woodbridge, Suffolk. *T:* Wickham Market 273.

**MICHALOPOULOS, André,** CBE 1937 (OBE 1919); FRSA; Professor Emeritus of Classical Literatures and Civilizations, since 1964, Professor 1957-64, Member of University Council, since 1962, Fairleigh-Dickinson University; *b* 1897; one *s* two *d*. *Educ:* St Paul's Sch., London; Oriel Coll., Oxford (Scholar). BA 1st Cl. Hons Litt Hum., 1920; MA 1927; Priv. Sec. to Eleutherios Venizelos, Prime Minister of Greece, 1917 and 1921-24; Mem. Greek Delegation, Lausanne Peace Conference, 1922-23; Civil Governor of

Lemnos, Imbros, Tenedos, and Samothrace, 1918-19; Governor of Corfu and adjacent islands, 1924-25; left Public Service for business, 1925; Managing Dir of Athens-Piraeus Water Coy; Dir of several Banking, Industrial, and Commercial Corpns in Athens; Pres. of the Anglo-Hellenic League, Athens, 1935-45; broadcast nightly English news commentary from Athens during Greco-Italian War, 1940-41; joined Greek forces in Crete, April 1941; Gen. Sec. of Nat. Cttee of Greeks of Egypt for resistance, May 1941; followed Greek Govt to S Africa, Aug. 1941; Mem. Greek Cabinet (Minister of Information in London, Washington and Cairo), Sept. 1941-May 1943. Lectured and broadcast extensively in S Africa, Great Britain, USA, Canada, 1941-43; Minister Plenipotentiary for Greece i/c information in America, 1945-46; Special Adviser on American Affairs to Royal Greek Embassy in Washington, 1950-67; Mem., Supreme Educnl Council of Greek Orthodox Archdiocese in N and S America, 1962-70. Visiting Professor, Kansas City University, 1949. Participated as Chm. or panel-mem., in Invitation to Learning programme, Columbia Broadcasting System, 1947-65; Master of Ceremonies and political and literary commentator on weekly Hellenic Television Hour, New York, 1955-56. Broadcast to Greece on Voice of America programme, 1950-55. Participated in annual American Foreign Policy Conf., Colgate Univ., 1951-61; has lectured and broadcast in the 48 States of USA and in Canada. Archon, Order of St Andrew; Grand Protonotary of Oecumenical Patriarchate of Constantinople, 1967. Commander Order of George I (Greece) with swords, 1941; Commander Order of the Phœnix (Greece), 1936; Chevalier Legion of Honour (France), 1934; Commander Order of Orange Nassau (Netherlands), 1939. FRSA 1936; Mem. Academy of American Poets, 1956; Mem. Poetry Society of America, 1957. Fellow, Ancient Monuments Soc. (London), 1958. Hon. LittD Westminster Coll., Utah. *Publications:* Homer, an interpretative study of the Iliad and Odyssey, 1965; and Greek Fire: a collection of broadcasts, articles and addresses, 1943; two collections of Verse 1923 and 1928; contribs to Encyclopedia Americana and Funk & Wagnall's Reference Encyclopaedia; chapts and articles in Greek, English, Scottish, American, Canadian, Egyptian, French, and South African books, reviews and newspapers; weekly book reviews for King Features Syndicate (USA), 1959-. *Address:* Grasshopper Hill, Irvington-on-Hudson, New York, NY 10533, USA. *T:* 914-591-9140.

**MICHALOWSKI, Jerzy;** Ambassador of Poland to the USA, since 1967; *b* 26 May 1909; *s* of Andrzej and Maria Michalowski; *m* 1947, Mira Krystyna; two *s*. *Educ:* University of Warsaw. Asst In Polish Inst. of Social Affairs, 1933-36; Dir of Polish Workers Housing Organisation, 1936-39; Chief of Housing Dept of Warsaw City Council, 1945; Counsellor of Polish Embassy in London, 1945-46; Deputy Deleg. of Poland to UN, March-Nov. 1946; Ambassador of Republic of Poland to the Court of St James, 1946-53; Head of a department, Ministry of Foreign Affairs, Warsaw, 1953-54; Under Sec. of State for Educ., 1954-55; Deleg. of Poland to the Internat. Commn in Vietnam, 1955-56; Permanent Representative of Poland to UN, 1956-60; Dir-Gen., in Ministry of Foreign Affairs, Warsaw, 1960-67. Pres. of Foreign Affairs, 1960-67. Pres. of ECOSOC, UN, 1962. *Publications:* Unemployment of Polish Peasants, 1934; Housing Problems in Poland (Publ. by League of Nations), 1935. *Recreations:* tennis and winter sports. *Address:* Ministry of Foreign Affairs, Warsaw, Poland.

**MICHELHAM,** 2nd Baron, *cr* 1905, of Hellingly; **Herman Alfred Stern;** Bt, *cr* 1905; a Baron of Portugal; *b* 5 Sept. 1900; *e s* of 1st Baron Michelham; *S* father, 1919; *m* 1919, Berthe Isabella Susanna Flora (*d* 1961), *d* of Arthur Joseph Capel. *Educ:* Malvern Coll. *Heir:* *b* Hon. Jack Herbert Michelham [*b* 23 Dec. 1903; assumed by deed poll, 1923, the surname of Michelham. *Educ:* Harrow; Magdalen Coll., Oxford].

**MICHELIN, Reginald Townend,** CMG 1957; CVO 1953; OBE 1952; Security Manager, Jamaica Tourist Board, since 1964; *b* 31 Dec. 1903; *s* of V. A. Michelin, Planter, Jamaica; *m* 1940, Nina Gladys Faulkner, Iffley, Oxford; one *s* one *d*. *Educ:* Exeter Sch., England. Sub-Inspector, Police, Jamaica, 1924; Inspector, Police, Leeward Islands, 1928; Asst Commissioner of Police, Nigeria, 1930; Comr of Police, Barbados, 1949; Commissioner of Police, Jamaica, 1953-58, retd. *Address:* After All, Runaway Bay, Jamaica, West Indies.

**MICHELL, Alan,** CMG 1966; HM Diplomatic Service; Foreign Office, since 1961; *b* 11 Nov. 1913; *s* of late Pierre William Michell and late Mary Michell; *m* 1941, Glenys Enid Davies (*d* 1965); one *s* two *d*. *Educ:* Barry School; Jesus Coll., Oxford (Stanhope Univ. Prize, 1934). Served Royal Tank Regt, 1940-46. Asst Master, King's Sch., Canterbury, 1937-40; Foreign Office, 1947; Second Sec., Paris, 1952; Nicosia, 1954; Singapore, 1956; First Sec., Saigon, 1959. *Address:* 4 Frank Dixon Close, Dulwich, SE21.

**MICHELL, Francis Victor,** CMG 1955; *b* 17 Jan. 1908; *s* of late Pierre William Michell and late Mary Michell; *m* 1943, Betty Enid Tempest, *d* of late William Tempest Olver, JP, Tamworth; no *c*. *Educ:* Barry Sch.; Jesus Coll., Oxford. Attaché British Embassy, Rio de Janeiro, 1943-46; First Sec., Istanbul, 1947-51; First Sec., Commissioner-General's Office, Singapore, 1951-53; Foreign Office, 1953-65. *Address:* Whitehall Lodge, Ifield, Sussex. *T:* Crawley 24269. *Club:* Travellers'.

**MICHELL, Harry Denis,** DFC 1945; Senior Directing Staff (Civil), Joint Services Staff College, Latimer, since 1969; *b* 29 Oct. 1923; *s* of late Henry Michell and Belle Emslie Ledingham; *m* 1951, Jillian, *d* of A. S. Green; one *s* one *d* (and one *s* decd). *Educ:* Royal Grammar Sch., Colchester; St Edmund Hall, Oxford. RAFVR, 1942-46. Joined Foreign Service (now Diplomatic Service), 1949; Vice-Consul, Alexandria, 1949-50; Asst Political Agent, Kuwait, 1950; Political Officer, Trucial Coast, 1950-51; Asst Political Agent, Kuwait, 1951-52; FO, 1952-53; 2nd, later 1st Sec., Cape Town/Pretoria, 1953-57; Middle East Centre for Arab Studies, Lebanon, 1957-58; Private Sec. to Minister of State, FO, 1959-62; Head of Chancery, Damascus, 1962-63; FO, later DSAO, 1963-65; Counsellor, Prague, 1965-69; Civil Service Fellow Commoner, Downing Coll., Cambrdige, 1969. *Recreations:* music, cookery. *Address:* Bosky Dean, Jordans, Bucks. *T:* Chalfont St Giles 4152. *Clubs:* Pathfinder, Royal Air Force.

**MICHELMORE, Clifford Arthur,** CBE 1969; Television Broadcaster and Producer; *b* 11 Dec. 1919; *s* of late Herbert Michelmore and Ellen Alford; *m* 1950, Jean Metcalfe (Broadcaster); one *s* one *d*. *Educ:* Cowes Senior Sch., Isle of Wight. Entered RAF, 1935; commnd 1940; left RAF 1947. Head, Outside Broadcasts and Variety, BFN, 1948; Dep. Station Dir, BFN, also returned to freelance as Commentator and Producer, 1949. Entered Television, 1950. Has taken part in numerous radio and television programmes in Britain, Europe and the USA. Introduced: "Tonight" series, 1957-65; 24 Hours series, 1965-68; General Election Results programmes, 1964, 1966, 1970; Our World, 1967; With Michelmore (interviews), 1968-; Talkback, 1968-; Apollo Space Programmes, 1960-70; Holiday, 1969-70, etc. Television Society Silver Medal, 1957; Guild of TV Producers Award, Personality of the Year, 1958; TV Review Critics Award, 1959; Variety Club Award, 1961. *Publications:* various articles on television and broadcasting. *Recreations:* golf, cricket and doing nothing. *Address:* White House, Reigate, Surrey; Brookfield, Bembridge, Isle of Wight. *Clubs: Royal Air Force, MCC; Walton Heath Golf.*

**MICHELMORE, Sir Walter Harold Strachan,** Kt 1958; MBE 1945; Company Director; *b* Chudleigh, Devon, 4 April 1908; 2nd *s* of late Harold G. Michelmore; *m* 1933, Dorothy Walrond (*d* 1964), *o c* of late E. W. Bryant; one *d*; *m* 1967, Mrs Dulcie Mary Scott, *d* of late Leonard Haughton. *Educ:* Sherborne Sch.; Balliol Coll., Oxford. Joined Bird & Co., Calcutta, 1929. Served Indian Army (Staff), 1940-46 (MBE). Managing Dir, Bird & Co. (Pvt) Ltd and F. W. Heilgers & Co. (Pvt) Ltd, Calcutta, 1948-63; Dep. Chm., 1955, Chm. 1961; retired 1963. Pres. Bengal Chamber of Commerce and Industry and Associated Chambers of Commerce of India, 1957. Chairman: Metal Traders (Aust.) Pty Ltd; Metramar Minerals Ltd; Fund of Australia Services Ltd; Australian Continental Resources Ltd. *Recreations:* golf, fishing. *Address:* 176 Queen Street, Woollahra, NSW 2025, Australia. *Clubs:* Oriental, Queen's; Bengal (Calcutta); Australian, Union (Sydney).

**MICHELMORE, Maj.-Gen. Sir (William) Godwin,** KBE 1953; CB 1945; DSO 1919; MC, TD; DL, County of Devon; JP (Devon) 1950; Solicitor and Notary Public, Deputy Diocesan Registrar, Bishop's Secretary; *b* 14 March 1894; 3rd *s* of late Henry William Michelmore of Exeter; *m* Margaret Phœbe (*d* 1965), *d* of late Sir F. G. Newbolt, KC; one *s* two *d*. *Educ:* Rugby; LLB (London Univ.). Served European War, 1914-19 (despatches, MC, DSO); Commanded 43rd (Wessex) Div. Signals TA, 1919-29; Dep. Chief Signal Officer, Southern Command, 1929-33; commanded 4th Bn Devonshire Regt, 1936-39; commanded Infantry Brigade, 1939-41, Division Commander, 1941-45; ADC to the King, 1942-45; Mayor of Exeter, 1949-50. Chm. Devon T & AFA, 1948-58; Vice-Chm. Council of T & AFA, 1956-59; Chm. Devon Magistrates Courts Cttee; Chm. Govs, St Luke's Coll., Exeter; Gov., Blundell's Sch.; Mem. Coun., University Exeter. *Address:* 10 St Leonard's Road, Exeter, Devon EX2 46A. *T:* 59585. *Club:* Army and Navy.

**MICHENER, James Albert;** Author; *b* New York City, 3 Feb. 1907; *s* of Edwin Michener and Mabel (*née* Haddock); *m* 1st, 1935, Patti Koon (marr. diss. 1948); 2nd, 1948, Vange Nord (marr. diss., 1955); 3rd, 1955, Mari Yoriko Sabusawa; no *c*. *Educ:* Swarthmore Coll., Pennsylvania; St Andrews Univ., Scotland; Harvard Coll., Mass. Teacher, George Sch., Pa, 1933-36; Prof., Colorado State Coll. of Educn, 1936-41; Visiting Prof., Harvard, 1940-41; Associate Editor, Macmillan Co., 1941-49; Mem. advisory cttee on the arts, US State Dept, 1957. Served with USNR on active duty in South Pacific, 1944-45. Sec., Pennsylvania Constitutional Convention, 1968. Hon. DHL, LLD, and LittD, from numerous univs. *Publications:* Unit in the Social Studies, 1940; Tales of the South Pacific (Pulitzer prize for fiction), 1947; The Fires of Spring, 1949; Return to Paradise, 1951; The Voice of Asia, 1951; The Bridges at Toko-ri, 1953; Sayonara, 1954; Floating World, 1955; The Bridge at Andau, 1957; (with A. Grove Day) Rascals in Paradise, 1957; Selected Writings, 1957; The Hokusai Sketchbook, 1958; Japanese Prints, 1959; Hawaii, 1959; Caravans, 1964; The Source, 1965; Iberia, 1968; Presidential Lottery, 1969; The Quality of Life, 1970; The Drifters, 1971; ed, Future of Social Studies for NEA, 1940. *Recreations:* photography, philately, tennis. *Address:* Pipersville, PA 18947, USA.

**MICHENER, Rt. Hon. Roland,** CC (Canada) 1967; PC (Canada) 1962; CD; QC (Canada); Governor-General and Commander-in-Chief of Canada since 1967; *b* Lacombe, Alta, 19 April 1900; *s* of late Senator Edward Michener and Mary Edith (*née* Roland), Lincoln Co., Ontario; *m* 1927, Norah Evangeline, *d* of Robert Willis, Manitoba; two *d* (and one *d* decd). *Educ:* Universities of Alberta and Oxford. BA (Alta) 1920; Rhodes Scholar for Alta, 1919; BA 1922, BCL 1923, MA 1929, Oxon. Served with RAF, 1918. Called to Bar, Middle Temple, 1923; Barrister, Ontario, 1924; KC (Canada) 1943. Practising lawyer with Lang, Michener & Cranston, Toronto, 1924-57. Mem. Ontario Legislature for St David, Toronto, 1945-48, and Provincial Sec. and Registrar for Ontario, 1946-48; elected to Canadian House of Commons, 1953; re-elected 1957 and 1958; elected Speaker, 1957 and May 1958; Canadian High Commissioner to India, 1964-67. Gen. Sec. for Canada, Rhodes Scholarships, 1936-64. Formerly: Governor, Toronto Western Hosp.; Hon. Counsel, Chm. of Exec. Cttee (now Hon. Vice-Pres.), Canadian Inst. of Internat. Affairs; Hon. Counsel, Red Cross Ont. Div.; Chm. of Exec., Canadian Assoc. for Adult Educn; Officer and Dir of various Canadian mining and financial companies. Chancellor and Principal Companion, Order of Canada, 1967-; KJStJ (Prior for Canada), 1967. Hon. Fellow: Hertford Coll., Oxford, 1961; Acad. of Medicine, Toronto, 1967; Trinity Coll., Toronto, 1968. Hon. FRCP(C) 1968; Hon. FRAIC, 1968. Hon. Mem., Canadian Medical Assoc., 1968; Hon. Bencher, Law Soc. of Upper Canada, 1968. Hon. LLD: Ottawa, 1948; Queen's, 1958; Laval, 1960; Alberta, 1967; St Mary's, Halifax, 1968; Toronto, 1968; RMC Canada, 1969; Mount Allison, 1969; Brock, 1969; Manitoba, 1970; Hon. DCL: Bishop's, 1968; Windsor, 1969; Oxford Univ., 1970. *Address:* Government House, Ottawa, Canada. *Club:* University (Toronto).

**MICHIE, Charles Watt,** CMG 1960; OBE 1943; Secretary: Scottish Universities Entrance Board, since 1967 (Assistant to Secretary, 1963-67); Scottish Universities Council on Entrance, since 1968; *b* 1 Sept. 1907; *s* of late Charles Michie and late Emily (*née* MacGregor); *m* 1935, Janet Leslie Graham Kinloch; two *d*. *Educ:* Aberdeen Gram. Sch.; Aberdeen Univ. Cadet, Colonial Admin. Service, 1930; Cadet, N Region of Nigeria, 1931; Consul for Spanish Territories of Gulf of Guinea and Labour Officer in Nigerian Department of Labour, 1940-42; Labour Officer on Nigerian tin minesfield, 1942; N Regional Secretariat, Kaduna, 1944; Chm. Labour Advisory Bd for Nigerian tin minesfield, 1947; District Administration, 1948; Sen. District Officer, and Asst Sec., Actg Principal, Nigerian Secretariat, 1949; returned to provincial administration and promoted Resident, 1954; Sen. Resident, 1954; Permanent Sec. to N Region Min. of

Agriculture in Nigeria, 1957; retired 1960. Asst Teacher, Mod. Langs, Morgan Academy, Dundee, 1960-63. Defence Medal, 1945; Coronation Medal, 1953. *Recreations:* gardening, photography. *Address:* Nethermiln, Blebo Craigs, Cupar, Fife. *T:* Cupar 2316. *Club:* Royal and Ancient (St Andrews).

**MICKLEM, Rev. Nathaniel,** MA Oxon, Hon. LLD Queen's University, Ontario; Hon. DD Queen's University, Ontario and Glasgow; Principal and Professor of Dogmatic Theology, Mansfield College, Oxford, 1932-53; Wilde Lecturer in Natural and Comparative Religion, 1948-51; President of the Liberal Party, 1957-58; Select Preacher, Oxford University, 1960; President of Liberal International (British Group), since 1959; *b* 10 April 1888; *s* of late Nathaniel Micklem, QC, and Ellen Ruth Curwen; *m* 1916, Agatha Frances (*d* 1961), *d* of Thomas Ball Silcock, JP, Bath; three *s. Educ:* Rugby; New Coll. and Mansfield Coll., Oxford. Professor of Old Testament Literature and Theology at the Selly Oak Colleges, Birmingham, 1921-27; Professor of New Testament Literature and Criticism, Queen's Theological Coll., Kingston, Ont., 1927-31. *Publications:* National Socialism and The Roman Catholic Church; Law and the Laws; The Labyrinth; The Tree of Life; The Abyss of Truth; The Place of Understanding; The Box and the Puppets, 1888-1953; My Cherry Tree; Christian Thinking Today, 1968. *Address:* Monks Staithe, Princes Risborough, Bucks. *T:* Princes Risborough 3571. *Club:* Authors'.

**MICKLEM, Brig. Ralph,** CMG 1918; CBE 1945; late RE; *b* 30 Jan. 1884; *s* of late Leonard Micklem; *m* Eva May, *y d* of late Commander Sir Trevor Dawson, 1st Bt, RN; one *s* (and one *s* killed on active service, 1944). *Educ:* Eton (scholar); RMA, Woolwich. Entered RE, 1902; Captain 1913; Major, 1917; served Egyptian Army, 1907-15; 4th Medjidieh, 1912; 4th Nile, 1917; European War, 1914-18 (wounded, despatches, CMG); retired, 1919; Lieut-Col R of O, 1927; re-employed, 1939-45, War Office; Brig. 1941. *Address:* Heriots, Stanmore, Middx. *Club:* United Service.

**MICKLETHWAIT, Sir Robert (Gore),** Kt 1964; QC 1956; Chief National Insurance Commissioner since 1966 (Deputy Commissioner, 1956; National Insurance Commissioner and Industrial Injuries Commissioner, 1961); *b* 7 Nov. 1902; 2nd *s* of late St J. G. Micklethwait, KC; *m* 1936, Philippa J., 2nd *d* of late Sir Ronald Bosanquet, QC; three *s* one *d. Educ:* Clifton Coll.; Trinity Coll., Oxford (2nd Class Lit Hum., MA). Called to Bar, Middle Temple, 1925, Bencher, 1951; Autumn Reader, 1964! Dep. Treasurer, 1970. Oxford Circuit; Gen. Coun. of the Bar 1939-40, and 1952-56; Supreme Court Rule Cttee, 1952-56. Royal Observer Corps, 1938-40; Civil Asst, WO, 1940-45; Recorder of Worcester, 1946-59. Deputy Chm., Court of Quarter Sessions for County of Stafford, 1956-59. *Address:* Llanthony, 71 Harvest Road, Englefield Green, Surrey. *T:* Egham 2521.

**MICKLETHWAIT, Rear-Adm. St John Aldrich,** CB 1952; DSO 1939, and Bars 1940 and 1942; DL; Royal Navy Retired; *b* 4 March 1901; *e s* of late St J. G. Micklethwait, KC; *m* 1929, Clemence Penelope Olga Welby-Everard; two *s* one *d. Educ:* Osborne; Dartmouth. Midshipman, 1917; Comdr, 1935; Capt., 1940; Rear-Adm., 1950. Served War of 1939-45 (DSO and two Bars, prisoner). Flag Officer, Training Squadron, 1950-51; Flag Officer, Gibraltar, 1952-53; retired Dec. 1953. High Sheriff of Monmouthshire, 1959; DL, 1960. *Address:* Penhein, near Chepstow, Mon. *T:* Penhow 210. *Club:* United Service.
*See also Major Sir Geoffrey Tritton.*

**MIDDLEBROOK, Sir Harold,** 2nd Bt, *cr* 1930; *b* 5th Oct. 1887; *s* of Sir William Middlebrook, 1st Bt, and Alma Jackson; *S* father 1936; *m* 1914, Mabel Vasey. Solicitor, 1911. *Heir:* none. *Address:* 8 Park Road, Harrogate, Yorks.

**MIDDLEDITCH, Edward,** MC 1945; ARA 1968; ARCA 1951; Painter; Visiting Head of Fine Art Department, Norwich School of Art, since 1964; *b* 23 March 1923; *s* of Charles Henry Middleditch and Esme Buckley; *m* 1947, Jean Kathleen Whitehouse; one *d. Educ:* Mundella School, Nottingham; King Edward VI Grammar Sch., Chelmsford; Royal College of Art. Served Army, 1942-47, France, Germany, India, W Africa; commissioned Middx Regt 1944. Nine Exhibitions, London, 1954-69; exhibited: Paris; Rome; Venice Biennale, 1956. Paintings in private and public collections, including: Tate Gall.; Arts Council; V & A Museum; Contemporary Art Soc.; Manchester City Art Gall.; Ferens Art Gall., Hull; Nat. Gall. of Victoria; Nat. Gall. of S Aust.; Nat. Gall. of Canada; Chrysler Art Museum, Mass; Toledo Musuem of Art, Ohio. *Address:* School House, Edwardstone, Boxford, near Colchester, Essex. *T:* Boxford (Suffolk) 240.

**MIDDLEMISS, Prof. John Howard,** CMG 1968; Professor of Radiodiagnosis, University of Bristol, and Director of Radiology, United Bristol Hospitals, since 1949; *b* 14 May 1916; *s* of Thomas Middlemiss, Monkseaton, Northumberland; *m* 1942, Isobel Mary, *d* of Ivan Pirrie, MC, MD, Maldon, Essex; one *s* two *d. Educ:* Repton; Durham Univ. MB, BS 1940; MD 1947; DMRD 1946; FFR 1948; MRCP 1964. Served with RAMC as Temp. Major and Actg Lieut-Col, 1941-46. Asst Radiologist, Royal Victoria Infirmary, Newcastle upon Tyne, 1946-48. Adviser in Radiology to Governments of: Nigeria, 1953, 1959, 1962; Uganda, 1953, 1955, 1960, 1963, 1966, 1969; Tanzania, 1966, 1969; Burma, 1963-68; Pakistan, 1968; Universities of: Ibadan, 1955, 1970; Jamiaca, 1964-70; Ghana, 1966, 1970; Ahmedu Bello, 1970; Mem., Med. Adv. Cttee, Min. of Overseas Development; Cons. to WHO; Mem., Inter-University Council, 1969-. Warden, Faculty of Radiologists, 1966-71; FRSocMed. *Publications:* Radiology in Surgery, 1960; Tropical Radiology, 1961; numerous scientific papers in Clinical Radiology, British Jl of Radiology, etc. *Recreations:* international relations, wine, travel. *Address:* 11 Pembroke Road, Clifton, Bristol 8. *T:* Bristol 38553; White Cottage, Wellington Heath, Ledbury, Herefordshire. *Clubs:* Sesame, English-Speaking Union.

**MIDDLEMORE, Sir William Hawkslow,** 2nd Bt, *cr* 1919; *b* 10 April 1908; *s* of 1st Bt and Mary, *d* of late Rev. Thomas Price, Selly Oak, Birmingham; *S* father, 1924; *m* 1934, Violet Constance, *d* of Andrew Kennagh, Worcester. *Heir:* none. *Address:* St Joseph's, Shurdington Road, Cheltenham, Glos. *T:* Cheltenham 25414.

**MIDDLESBROUGH, Bishop of, (RC),** since 1967; **Rt. Rev. (John) Gerard McClean;** *b* Redcar, Yorks, 24 Sept. 1914; *s* of Robert and Elizabeth McClean. *Educ:* Marist Coll., Middlesbrough; Ushaw Coll., Durham. Ordained, 1942. Titular Bishop of Maxita and Coadjutor of Middlesbrough, Feb. 1967; Bishop of Middlesbrough, June 1967. *Recreation:* golf. *Address:* Bishop's House, 16 Cambridge Road, Middlesbrough, Teesside. *T:* Middlesbrough 88253.

**MIDDLESEX, Archdeacon of;** *see* Eastaugh, Ven. J. R. G.

**MIDDLETON,** 11th Baron, *cr* 1711; **Michael Guy Percival Willoughby,** Bt, *cr* 1677; KG 1957; MC; TD; LLD; Major late 10th Lancers, IA; late Col commanding 5th Battalion The Green Howards (T); also commanded 5th and 30th Battalions, East Yorks Regt; Lord-Lieutenant for East Riding, Yorks, 1936-68; *b* 21 Oct. 1887; *er surv s* of 10th Baron and Ida Eleanora Constance (*d* 1924), *d* of G. W. H. Ross; *S* father, 1924; *m* 1920, Angela Florence Alfreda, *er d* of Charles Hall, Eddlethorpe Hall, Malton, Yorks; two *s* two *d.* Dir, Birdsall Estates Ltd. Owns about 13,000 acres. Chancellor, Univ. of Hull, to 1970. JP ER Yorks, 1925. Hon. Freeman, City of Hull, 1968. KStJ. Hon. LLD: Leeds Univ., 1955; Hull Univ. Silver Wolf, Boy Scouts, 1968. *Heir: s* Hon. (Digby) Michael (Godfrey John) Willoughby, *qv. Address:* Birdsall House, Malton, Yorks. *Clubs:* Cavalry; Yorkshire (York).

*See also Sir T. A. Matheson, Bt.*

**MIDDLETON, Suffragan Bishop of,** since 1959; **Rt. Rev. Edward Ralph Wickham;** *b* 3 Nov. 1911; *s* of Edward Wickham, London; *m* 1944, Dorothy Helen Neville Moss, *d* of Prof. Kenneth Neville Moss, Birmingham; one *s* two *d. Educ:* University of London (BD); St Stephen's House, Oxford. Deacon, 1938; Priest, 1939; Curate, Christ Church, Shieldfield, Newcastle upon Tyne, 1938-41; Chaplain, Royal Ordnance Factory, Swynnerton, 1941-44; Curate-in-charge, Swynnerton, 1943-44; Diocesan Missioner to Industry, Sheffield, 1944-59; Hon. Chaplain to Bishop of Sheffield, 1950-59; Canon Residentiary, Sheffield, 1951-59. Sir H. Stephenson Fellow, Sheffield University, 1955-57. *Publications:* Church and People in an Industrial City, 1957; Encounter with Modern Society, 1964; contributions to: Theology, The Ecumenical Review, Industrial Welfare, etc. *Recreations:* mountaineering, rock-climbing. *Address:* Maitland House, 1 Portland Road, Eccles, Manchester. *T:* 061-789 3144.

**MIDDLETON, Drew,** OBE 1947 (Hon.); Military Correspondent of The New York Times, since 1970; *b* 14 Oct. 1914; *o s* of E. T. and Jean Drew Middleton, New York; *m* 1943, Estelle Mansel-Edwards, Dinas Powis, Glamorgan; one *d. Educ:* Syracuse Univ., Syracuse, New York. Correspondent: for Associated Press in London, 1939; for Associated Press in France, Belgium, London, Iceland, with the British Army and RAF, 1939-42; for The New York Times with US and British Forces in North Africa, Sicily, Britain, Normandy, Belgium and Germany, 1942-45; Chief Correspondent in USSR, 1946-47, in Germany, 1948-53, and in London, 1953-63; Chief Correspondent in Paris, 1963-65; Chief Correspondent, UN, 1965-69; European Affairs Correspondent, 1969-70. Correspondent at four meetings of Council of Foreign Ministers, also Potsdam and Casablanca Conferences. Medal of Freedom (US). English-Speaking Union Better Understanding Award, 1955. Doctor of Letters (*hc*) Syracuse Univ., 1963. *Publications:* Our Share of Night, 1946; The Struggle for Germany, 1949; The Defence of Western Europe, 1952; The British, 1957; The Sky Suspended, 1960; The Supreme Choice: Britain and the European Community, 1963; Crisis in the West, 1965. *Recreations:* tennis, the theatre. *Address:* The New York Times, 229 W 43rd Street, New York, NY 10036, USA. *Clubs:* Beefsteak, Press, Garrick; Travellers' (Paris); The Brook, Players (New York).

**MIDDLETON, Francis;** Advocate; Sheriff Substitute of Lanarkshire at Glasgow, since 1956; *b* 21 Nov. 1913; Scottish; *m* 1942, Edith Muir; two *s* one *d. Educ:* Rutherglen Academy; Glasgow Univ. MA, LLB 1937. Practising as Solicitor, 1937-39; volunteered Sept. 1939; Private, Cameronian Scottish Rifles; commissioned to 6th Battn 11th Sikh Regt, Indian Army, 1940; Capt., 1940; Major 1942, injured; Interpreter 1st Class in Hindustani, 1943; posted to Judge Advocate's Branch, 1944; released Dec. 1945. Admitted Faculty of Advocates in Scotland, 1946. Sheriff Substitute of Inverness, Moray, Nairn and Ross and Cromarty, 1949-52, Fife and Kinross, 1952-56. *Recreations:* reading, gardening, golf. *Address:* 33 Kirklee Road, Glasgow, W.2.

**MIDDLETON, Sir George (Humphrey),** KCMG 1958 (CMG 1950); HM Diplomatic Service, retired; *b* 21 Jan. 1910; *e s* of George Close Middleton and Susan Sophie (*née* Harley, subsequently Elphinstone). *Educ:* St Lawrence Coll., Ramsgate; Magdalen Coll., Oxford. Entered Consular Service, 1933, Vice-Consul, Buenos Aires; transferred to Asuncion, 1934, with local rank of 3rd Sec. in Diplomatic Service; in charge of Legation, 1935; transferred to New York, 1936; to Lemberg (Lwow), 1939; local rank of Consul; in charge of Vice-Consulate at Cluj, 1939-40; appointed to Genoa, 1940, to Madeira, 1940, to Foreign Office, 1943; 2nd Sec. at Washington, 1944; 1st Sec. 1945; transferred to FO, 1947; Counsellor, 1949; Counsellor, British Embassy, Tehran, Jan. 1951; acted as Chargé d'Affaires, 1951 and 1952 (when diplomatic relations severed); Dep. High Comr for UK, in Delhi, 1953-56; British Ambassador at Beirut, 1956-58; Political Resident in the Persian Gulf, 1958-61; British Ambassador to: Argentina, 1961-64; United Arab Republic, 1964-66. Mem. *Ad hoc* Cttee for UN Finances, 1966. Consultant, Industrial Reorganisation Corporation, 1967-68; Chm., Michael Rice (Overseas) Ltd. Chief Executive, British Industry Roads Campaign, 1969-. *Recreations:* fishing, tennis, talking. *Address:* 53 Albert Hall Mansions, SW7. *Clubs:* Travellers', Pratt's, Royal Automobile.

**MIDDLETON, Sir George (P.),** KCVO 1962 (CVO 1951; MVO 1941); MB, ChB (Aberdeen); Medical Practitioner; Surgeon Apothecary to HM Household at Balmoral Castle since 1932; *b* Schoolhouse, Findhorn, Morayshire, 26 Jan. 1905; *s* of late A. Middleton, FEIS, Kincorth, Elgin; *m* 1931, Margaret Wilson (*d* 1964), *er d* of late A. Silver; one *s* one *d. Educ:* Findhorn; Forres Academy; Aberdeen Univ. Entered the Faculty of Medicine, 1921; Graduated, 1926, Bachelor of Medicine and Bachelor of Surgery, Ogston Prize and 1st medallist in Senior Systematic Surgery, 1st Medallist in Operative Surgery, House Surgeon Ward X, and House Physician Ward 4, Aberdeen Royal Infirmary, 1926; went to practice in Sheffield, 1927; Asst to late Sir Alexander Hendry, 1928; into partnership, 1929; partnership dissolved, 1931; taken into partnership, Dr James G. Moir, 1948. *Recreations:* golf, association football, bowling. *Address:* Highland Home, Ballater, Aberdeenshire. *TA:* Highland Home, Ballater. *T:* Ballater 478.

**MIDDLETON, George Walker,** CBE 1952; retired as General Secretary of the Scottish Trades Union Congress (1949-63); Chairman, Herring Industry Board; Vice-Chairman, Economic Planning Council for Scotland; *b* 4 April 1898; *s* of William and Margaret Middleton; *m* 1935, Marjorie Murray. *Educ:* Rockvilla Elementary and Keppochhill Schs.

Mem. of National Union of Shop, Distributive and Allied Workers. *Address:* 58 Castlebay Street, Glasgow, N2.

**MIDDLETON, Kenneth William Bruce;** Sheriff-Substitute of the Lothians and Peebles at Edinburgh since 1950 (of Perth and Angus at Forfar, 1946-50); *b* Strathpeffer, Ross-shire, 1 Oct. 1905; 2nd *s* of W. R. T. Middleton; *m* 1938, Ruth Beverly, *d* of W. H. Mill; one *s* one *d. Educ:* Rossall Sch.; Merton Coll., Oxford; Edinburgh Univ. BA Oxford, LLB Edinburgh; called to Scottish Bar, 1931; Vans Dunlop Scholar in International Law and Constitutional Law and History, Edinburgh Univ.; Richard Brown Research Scholar in Law, Edinburgh Univ.; served War of 1939-45 with Royal Scots and Seaforth Highlanders; attached to Military Dept, Judge Advocate-Gen.'s Office, 1941-45. *Publication:* Britain and Russia, 1947. *Address:* Sheriff Court House, Lawnmarket, Edinburgh.

**MIDDLETON, Lucy Annie;** Vice-President, Trade Union, Labour and Co-operative Deomcratic History Society, since 1969; Director and Foundation Chairman of War on Want, 1958-68; *b* 9 May 1894; 2nd *d* of late Sydney J. Cox, Keynsham, Somerset; *m* 1936, James S. Middleton (*d* 1962), sometime Sec. of Labour Party. *Educ:* Elementary Sch.; Colston's Girls' High Sch., Bristol; Bristol Univ. Held teaching appts under Gloucester and Bristol Authorities until 1924 when she became Organising Sec. in the Peace Movement; political adviser to Hindu Minorities during sittings of Round Table Conferences; joined staff of Labour Party, 1934. Governor of Chelsea Polytechnic, 1936-57. Certificated Advertising Consultant. Attended Inter-Parliamentary Union Confs Brussels, Nice, Rome, Stockholm, presenting Reports on Maternity and Child Welfare, Family Allowances, and Safeguarding of Women in Employment throughout the World; formerly Mem. of House of Commons Estimates Cttee. MP (Labour) Sutton Div. of Plymouth, 1945-50 (re-elected for enlarged Div., 1950-51). *Recreations:* cooking, gardening, golf. *Address:* 7 Princes Road, Wimbledon, SW19. *T:* 01-542 2791.

**MIDDLETON, Ronald George,** DSC 1945; Solicitor: Partner in Coward, Chance & Co., since 1949; *b* 31 July 1913; *o s* of late Sir George Middleton; *m* 1959, Sybil Summerscale; no *c. Educ:* Whitgift Middle Sch.; University Coll., London. Solicitor, 1936. RNVR, 1939-47 (Lt-Comdr); Radar Officer HMS Queen Elizabeth, 1944-45; Fleet Radar Officer, Indian Ocean, 1945. Dir, Morgan Crucible Co. Ltd; Dir, Kearney & Trecker-CVA Ltd. Part-time Mem., NBPI, 1965-68. Governor, Hurstpierpoint Coll. *Recreation:* sailing. *Address:* Lidde Hill, Henfield, Sussex. *T:* Henfield 2910. *Clubs:* Reform, Royal Ocean Racing.

**MIDDLETON, Stanley;** novelist; Head of English Department, High Pavement School, Nottingham, since 1958; *b* Bulwell, Nottingham, 1 Aug. 1919; *y s* of Thomas and Elizabeth Ann Middleton; *m* 1951, Margaret Shirley, *y d* of Herbert and Winifred Vera Welch; two *d. Educ:* High Pavement Sch.; University Coll., Nottingham (later Univ. of Nottingham). Served Army (RA and AEC), 1940-46. *Publications:* novels: A Short Answer, 1958; Harris's Requiem, 1960; A Serious Woman, 1961; The Just Exchange, 1962; Two's Company, 1963; Him They Compelled, 1964; Terms of Reference, 1966; The Golden Evening, 1968; Wages of Virtue, 1969; Apple of the Eye, 1970. *Recreations:* music, walking, listening, argument. *Address:* 42 Caledon Road, Sherwood, Nottingham NG5 2NG. *T:* Nottingham 63085. *Club:* PEN.

**MIDDLETON, Sir Stephen Hugh,** 9th Bt, *cr* 1662; *b* 1909; *s* of Lt Hugh Jeffery Middleton, RN, 3rd *s* of Sir Arthur Middleton, 7th Bt; *S* uncle 1942; *m* 1962, Mary, *d* of late Richard Robinson. *Educ:* Eton; Magdalene Coll., Cambridge. *Heir:* *b* Lawrence Monck Middleton, *b* 1912. *Address:* Belsay Castle, Northumberland.

**MIDGLEY, Eric Atkinson,** CMG 1965; MBE 1945; Ambassador to Switzerland, since 1970; *b* 25 March 1913; *s* of Charles Ewart Midgley, Keighley, Yorks; *m* 1937, Catherine Gaminara; two *d. Educ:* Christ's Hosp.; Merton Coll., Oxford. Indian Civil Service, 1937; Trade Commissioner at Delhi, 1947; Board of Trade, 1957; Commercial Counsellor at The Hague, 1960; Minister (Economic) in India, 1963-67; Minister (Commercial), Washington, 1967-70. *Recreations:* shooting, sailing. *Address:* British Embassy, Berne, Switzerland. *Club:* Travellers'.

**MIDLETON,** 2nd Earl of, *cr* 1920; **George St John Brodrick,** MC; Viscount Midleton, *cr* 1717, of Midleton, Ireland; Viscount Dunsford of Dunsford, Surrey, 1920; Baron Brodrick, Midleton, Ireland, 1715; Baron Brodrick, Peper Harow, 1796; late Capt., Surrey Yeomanry; *b* 21 Feb. 1888; *e s* of 1st Earl of Midleton and Lady Hilda Charteris (*d* 1901), *d* of 9th Earl of Wemyss; *S* father, 1942; *m* 1st, 1917, Margaret (marr. diss. 1925), *d* of J. Rush, Cromer, Norfolk; 2nd, 1925, Guinevere, *widow* of George J. Gould and *d* of Alexander Sinclair, Dublin. *Educ:* Eton; Balliol Coll., Oxford. Served World War I, 1914-17 (despatches, Legion of Honour, Military Cross). Served World War II, 1939-45 (ADC to C-in-C Home Forces). *Heir:* (to Viscountcy of Midleton and Barony of Brodrick only) *cousin,* Trevor Lowther Brodrick [*b* 7 March 1903; *m* 1940, Sheila Campbell, *d* of Charles Campbell Macleod]. *Address:* Thornton Hall, Upper King's Cliff, St Helier, Jersey, Channel Islands. *T:* Central 32558. *Club:* Carlton.

*See also Gen. Sir H. C. Lloyd.*

**MIERS, Rear-Adm. Sir Anthony (Cecil Capel),** VC 1942; KBE 1959; CB 1958; DSO 1941; Royal Navy retired; joined, in 1962, firms of: Mills and Rockleys Ltd; David Allen & Sons Ltd; London and Provincial Poster Group; *b* 11 Nov. 1906; 2nd *s* of late Capt. D. N. C. C. Miers, Queen's Own Cameron Highlanders (killed in France, Sept. 1914); *m* 1945, Patricia Mary, *d* of late D. M. Millar, of the Chartered Bank of India, Australia and China; one *s* one *d. Educ:* Stubbington House; Edinburgh Academy; Wellington Coll. Special entry cadet RN 1924. Joined submarines, 1929; commanded HM Submarine L54, 1936-37 (Coronation medal at HM's review in 1937); HMS Iron Duke, 1937-38; naval staff course, 1938 (psc); on staff of Admiral of the Fleet Sir Charles Forbes, C-in-C Home Fleet, in HM Ships Nelson, Rodney, and Warspite, 1939-40; commanded HM Submarine Torbay, 1940-42 (DSO and Bar, VC); Staff of Fleet Adm. C. W. Nimitz, C-in-C US Pacific Fleet, 1943-44 (US Legion of Merit, degree of Officer, 1945); Comdr S/M 8th Submarine Flotilla in HMS Maidstone, 1944-45; Commanded HMS Vernon II (Ramillies and Malaya), 1946; jssc 1947; Comd HMS Blackcap (RN Air Station, Stretton), 1948-50; Comd HMS Forth and Capt. S/M, 1st Submarine Flotilla, 1950-52. Capt. of the RN Coll., Greenwich, 1952-54 (Coronation medal, 1953); Commanded HMS Theseus, 1954-55; Flag Officer, Middle East, 1956-59. Obtained pilot's certificate ("A" License), 1948. Governor, Star and Garter

Home, Richmond, 1970-; Chm., RN Scholarship Fund, 1968-. Nat. Pres., Submarine Old Comrades Assoc., 1967-. Burgess and Freeman of Burgh of Inverness, 1955; Mem., Royal Highland Soc., 1966. Councillor, Lawn Tennis Assoc., 1954-; Pres. RN Squash Rackets Assoc., 1960-70; Pres. RN Lawn Tennis Assoc., 1962-; FInstD 1960. Freeman of the City of London, 1966; Mem., Court of Assistants, Worshipful Company of Tin Plate Workers, 1969; Hon. Kt, Hon. Soc. of Knights of Round Table, 1967. *Recreation:* tennis. *Address:* 17 Dover Park Drive, Roehampton, SW15. *T:* 01-788 6863. *Clubs:* Army and Navy, National Sporting, Hurlingham, MCC, British Sportsman's; London Scottish Football; Royal Navy 1765 and 1785; Hampshire Hog Cricket; Anchorites (President 1968).

**MIEVILLE, Arthur Leonard,** DSO 1919, MC; Development Engineer, The Cementation Co. Ltd, since 1954; Managing Director of Associated Cos throughout Asia of John Blackwood Hodge Ltd since 1951; *b* 31 Oct. 1879; *s* of Frederick Louis Miéville and Fanny Stokes Richardson; *m* 1915, Emma Plimsoll Vaux, SSStJ; one *s* one *d*. *Educ:* Horton; Bedford County Sch., Elstow; London University. Life Mem. Civil Engineering Inst. of Canada; FIMechE. Formerly: Managing Dir Bailimo Ltd; Vice-Pres. British American Industries Ltd, New York; Dep. Dir opencast coal production, Ministry of Fuel, and representative of the Ministry at Washington; Gen. Man. of General Aircraft Ltd; Adviser to Ministry of Aircraft Production; Senior Technical Officer, Ministry of Labour HQ; Consulting Engineer in Canada; War Service with Canadian Engineers; Gen. Manager Montevideo Tramways; served European War, 1915-19 (DSO, MC, despatches). Inventions: Roller Bearings, Wind Tunnel. *Publication:* Astronomical Navigation without Mathematics, 1945 (New York). *Address:* 17 Allington Court, Allington Street, SW1. *T:* 01-834 2064. *Clubs:* Bengal, Royal Calcutta Golf (Calcutta).

**MIEVILLE, Sir Eric Charles,** GCIE, *cr* 1947 (KCIE, *cr* 1936); KCVO, *cr* 1943; CSI 1933; CMG 1930; *b* 31 Jan. 1896. *Educ:* St Paul's Sch. Student Interpreter in the Far Eastern Consular Service, 1919; Local Vice-Consul, 1921; Private Sec. to successive British Ministers in Peking, 1920-27; Sec. to the Governor-Gen. of Dominion of Canada, 1927-31; Priv. Sec. to the Viceroy of India, 1931-36; Sec. to Executive Council of Governor-Gen. of India, 1935-36; Private Sec. to the Duke of York, 1936; Asst Private Sec. to the King, 1937-45; a senior mem. of staff of Viceroy of India, 1947. *Recreations:* golf, tennis, etc. *Clubs:* White's, Buck's.

**MIGDALE, Hon. Lord; James Frederick Gordon Thomson,** MA; a Lord Commissioner of Justiciary, Scotland, and a Senator of HM College of Justice in Scotland since Nov. 1953; Lord Lieutenant of Sutherland since 1962; *b* 22 June 1897; *s* of late William Thomson, advocate, and Emmeline E. Gordon; *m* 1938, Louise Carnegie (*d* 1947), *d* of Roswell Miller and Mrs Carnegie Miller, of NY and Skibo Castle, Dornoch; one *s* four *d*. *Educ:* Edinburgh Academy and Clayesmore; Edinburgh and Glasgow Univs. Served European War, 1914-19, Royal Scots; War of 1939-45, Lt-Col Home Guard. Mem. Faculty of Advocates, 1924; Advocate-Depute, 1939-40; Standing Counsel to Board of Inland Revenue in Scotland, 1944-45; QC (Scotland) 1945; Sheriff of Ayr and Bute, 1949-52; Home Advocate Depute, 1952-53. Life Trustee, Carnegie UK Trust. DL Sutherlandshire, 1959. *Address:* 26 Heriot Row, Edinburgh EH3 6EN; Ospisdale, Dornoch, Sutherland. *Clubs:* New (Edinburgh); Highland (Inverness); Hon. Company of Edinburgh Golfers.

**MIKARDO, Ian;** MP (Lab) Poplar since 1964; Chairman, National Executive of Labour Party, since 1971 (Member 1950-59, and since 1960); President, Association of Scientific Technical and Managerial Staffs; Member, National Joint Council for Civil Air Transport; Chairman, Select Committee on Nationalized Industries, 1966-70; *b* 1908; *m* 1932, Mary Rosette; two *d*. *Educ:* Portsmouth. MP (Lab) Reading, 1945-50, South Div. of Reading, 1950-55, again Reading, 1955-Sept. 1959. *Publications:* Centralised Control of Industry, 1944; Frontiers in the Air, 1946; (with others) Keep Left, 1947; The Second Five Years, 1948; The Problems of Nationalisation, 1948; (joint) Keeping Left, 1950; The Labour Case, 1950; It's a Mug's Game, 1951; Socialism or Slump, 1959. *Address:* 24 Palace Chambers, Bridge Street, SW1.

**MIKES, George,** LLD (Budapest); Author; *b* Siklós, Hungary, 15 Feb. 1912; *s* of Dr Alfred Mikes and Margit Gál; *m* 1st, 1941, Isobel Gerson (marriage dissolved), one *s*; 2nd, 1948, Lea Hanak; one *d*. *Educ:* Cistercian Gymnasium, Pécs; Budapest Univ. Theatrical critic on Budapest newspapers, 1931-38; London correspondent of Budapest papers, 1938-41; working for Hungarian Service of BBC, 1941-51. *Publications:* How to be an Alien, 1946; How to Scrape Skies, 1948; Wisdom for Others, 1950; Milk and Honey, 1950; Down with Everybody!, 1951; Shakespeare and Myself, 1952; Über Alles, 1953; Eight Humorists, 1954; Little Cabbages, 1955; Italy for Beginners, 1956; The Hungarian Revolution, 1957; East is East, 1958; A Study in Infamy, 1959; How to be Inimitable, 1960; Tango, 1961; Switzerland for Beginners, 1962; Mortal Passion, 1963; Prison (ed), 1963; How to Unite Nations, 1963; Eureka!, 1965; (with the Duke of Bedford) Book of Snobs, 1965; How to be Affluent, 1966; Not by Sun Alone, 1967; Boomerang, 1968; The Prophet Motive, 1969; HumourIn Memoriam, 1970; The Land of the Rising Yen, 1970. *Recreation:* tennis. *Address:* c/o André Deutsch Ltd, 105 Great Russell Street, WC1. *Clubs:* Garrick, Hurlingham, PEN.

**MIKKELSEN, Captain Ejnar;** Knight of Dannebroge; Hon. PhD Copenhagen, 1956; *b* 23 Dec. 1880; *s* of Aksel Mikkelsen, Government Inspector of Danish Slöjd; *m* 1st, 1913, Naja (*d* 1918), *d* of Captain Gustav Holm, RN; 2nd, Ella, *d* of Barrister Holm-Jensen; two *s*. *Educ:* Copenhagen. Went to Sea, 1894; travelled all about the world; Mem. of the Amdrups Expedition to East Coast of Greenland, surveying from Scoresby Sound to Angmasalik, 1900; Mem. of the Baldwin-Ziegler Polar Expedition to Franz Joseph's Land, 1901-02; Chief Officer on the International Hydrographic Expedition to Northern Atlantic, 1903-04; Jt Comdr with Mr Ernest de K. Leffingwell of Expedition to the North of Alaska, 1906-08; Commander of Expedition to North-Eastern Greenland, 1909-12; Commander, Colonizing Expedition to Scoresby Sound, 1924; Commander of experimental fishing cruise to West Greenland, 1925; Commander of Expedition to SE Greenland, 1932; Manager of the Faroe Whaling Co. Ltd; Pres. of the Scoresby Sound Cttee; Expert-Mem. of Government Delegation about Danish sovereignty, East Greenland before Internat. Court in The Hague, 1932; Inspector-Gen. of E Greenland, 1933, retd 1951. Pres. Greenland Soc., 1934-56; attached Danish Legation in Washington as

Adviser in Greenland Matters, 1944; Governor of Arctic Inst. of North America, 1948 (hon. mem. 1956); Chm. Danish Arctic Institute, 1954. Awarded medals from Belgian, Scottish, Danish, and French Geog. Socs; Medal of Merit in silver and gold; Patron's Gold Medal, RGS, 1934; Livingstone Gold Medal, RSGS, 1948. Officer of French Legion of Honour. *Publications:* Conquering the Arctic Ice; Lost in the Arctic; Report on the Alabama Expedition; Frozen Justice; John Dale; Danes in Argentine; Med Grönland til Scoresby Sound; Nachbarn des Nordpols, De ostgrönd landske Eskimoirs Historie; The East Greenlanders–Possibilities of Existence, their Production and Consumption, and different papers to Meddelelser om Gronland. Fra Hündevagt til Hündeslade, 1953; Mirage in the Arctic, 1955; Farlig Tomandsfärd, 1956; Two Against the Ice, 1957; Fra Fribytter til Embedsmand, 1957; Svündne Tider Tider i Ost-Grönland, 1960. *Address:* Vilhelmshaabsvej, Charlottenlund, Denmark. *T:* Ordrup 1414; (summer) Gudhjem, Bornholm.

**MIKOYAN, Anastas Ivanovich;** five Orders of Lenin; Order of the Red Banner; Hero of Socialist Labour; Hammer and Sickle Gold Medal, etc; Member of the Presidium of the Supreme Soviet, USSR, since 1965; Member of the Presidium of the Central Committee of the Communist Party of Soviet Union, 1952-66; Member Supreme Soviet since 1937; *b* Sanain, Armenia, 25 Nov. 1895; *m*; one *s*. *Educ:* Armenian Ecclesiastical Seminary, Tiflis. Joined Communist Party, 1915; fought in Revolution, Baku (imprisoned and escaped thrice), 1917-19; Mem. All-Russian Central Exec. Cttee, 1919-23; Mem. All-Union Central Exec. Cttee, 1923-27; Mem. Central Cttee, Communist Party, 1923-; Peoples' Commissar of Trade, 1926; Mem. Council of Labour and Defence, 1926; Peoples' Commissar of Supply, 1930-34, of the Food Supply Industry, 1934-38; Mem. Political Bureau of the Central Cttee, 1935- (Candidate, 1926-35); Dep. Chm., Council of People's Commissars, 1937-46; People's Commissar of Foreign Trade, 1938-46; Mem. State Defence Cttee, 1942-45; Vice-Chm., Council of Ministers of USSR, 1946 and simultaneously Minister of Foreign Trade, 1946-49; Minister of Trade, 1953; First Vice-Chm., Council of Ministers of the USSR, 1955-64; Chm., Presidium of the USSR Supreme Soviet, 1964-65. *Address:* Presidium of the Supreme Soviet of the USSR, Kremlin, Moscow, USSR.

**MILBANK, Major Sir Mark (Vane),** 4th Bt, *cr* 1882; KCVO 1962; MC 1944; Extra Equerry to the Queen since 1954; Master of HM's Household, 1954-67; *b* 11 Jan. 1907; *e s* of Sir Frederick Milbank, 3rd Bt; *S* father, 1964; *m* 1938, Hon. Verena Aileen (she *m* 1st, 1934, Charles Lambert Crawley who died 1935), *yr d* of 11th Baron Farnham, DSO; two *s*. *Educ:* Eton; RMC, Sandhurst. Coldstream Guards, 1927-36 and 1939-45; ADC to Governor of Bombay, 1933-38; Comptroller to Governor General of Canada, 1946-52; Chm., Securicor North-East, 1967-; Dir, Norwich Union, London Advisory Board, 1964-. *Heir: s* Anthony Frederick Milbank [*b* 16 Aug. 1939; *m* 1970, Belinda Beatrice, *yr d* of Brigadier Adrian Gore, Sellindge, Kent]. *Address:* Barningham Park, Richmond, Yorks. *T:* Barningham 202. *Club:* Turf.

**MILBORNE-SWINNERTON-PILKINGTON, Sir T. H.;** *see* Pilkington.

**MILBURN, Sir John (Nigel),** 4th Bt *cr* 1905; *b* 22 April 1918; *s* of Sir Leonard John Milburn, 3rd Bt, and Joan, 2nd *d* of Henry Anson-Horton, Catton Hall, Derbs; *S* father 1957; *m* 1940, Dorothy Joan, *d* of Leslie Butcher, Dunholme, Lincoln; one *s* decd. *Educ:* Eton; Trinity Coll., Cambridge. Served War of 1939-45 with Northumberland Hussars. *Recreations:* Joint-Master West Percy Foxhounds, 1955-59, 1963-. *Heir: b* Major Rupert Leonard Eversley Milburn, Royal Scots Greys, retd [*b* 8 May 1919; *m* 1944, Anne, *d* of late Major A. Scott Murray and of Mrs Colin Davy, Heckfield Place, Basingstoke, Hants; two *s* two *d*]. *Address:* Brainshaugh, Acklington, Northumberland. *T:* Shilbottle 631. *Club:* Northern Counties (Newcastle upon Tyne).

**MILBURN, Very Rev. Robert Leslie Pollington,** MA; Master of the Temple since 1968; *b* 28 July 1907; *er s* of late George Leslie and Elizabeth Esther Milburn; *m* 1944, Margery Kathleen Mary, *d* of Rev. Francis Graham Harvie; one *d* (one *s* decd). *Educ:* Oundle; Sidney Sussex Coll., Cambridge; New Coll., Oxford. Asst Master, Eton Coll., 1930-32; Select Preacher, University of Oxford, 1942-44; Fellow and Chaplain of Worcester Coll., Oxford, 1934-57, Tutor, 1945-57, Estates Bursar, 1946-57 (Junior Bursar, 1936-46). University Lectr in Church History, 1947-57; Bampton Lectr, 1952. Examining Chaplain to Bishop of St Edmundsbury and Ipswich, 1941-53, to Bishop of Southwark, 1950-57, to Bishop of Oxford, 1952-57; Dean of Worcester, 1957-68, now Emeritus. Mem. of Oxford City Council, 1941-47. A Trustee, Wallace Collection. Grand Chaplain, United Grand Lodge of England, 1969. OStJ. *Publications:* Saints and their Emblems in English Churches, 1949; Early Christian Interpretations of History, 1954; articles in Journal of Theological Studies and Church Quarterly Review. *Recreations:* lawn tennis, squash rackets, ornithology. *Address:* The Master's House, Temple, EC4. *Club:* Athenæum.

**MILES, Prof. Albert Edward William,** LRCP; MRCS; FDS; Professor of Dental Pathology at The London Hospital Medical College since 1950; Hon. Curator, Odontological Collection, Royal College of Surgeons of England since 1955; *b* 15 July 1912; *m* 1939, Sylvia Stuart; one *s* decd. *Educ:* Stationers' Company Sch.; Charing Cross and Royal Dental Hosps. John Tomes Prize, RCS, 1954-56. Charles Tomes Lecturer, RCS, 1957. FRSocMed. *Publications:* contrib. to scientific literature. *Address:* 51 Cardigan Street, Kennington, SE11. *T:* 01-735 5350; Ivy Cottage, Wisborough Green, Sussex. *Club:* Tetrapods.

**MILES, Sir (Arnold) Ashley,** Kt 1966; CBE 1953; FRS 1961; MA, MD, FRCP, FRCPath; Professor of Experimental Pathology, University of London; Director of the Lister Institute of Preventive Medicine, London; *b* 20 March 1904; *s* of Harry Miles, York; *m* 1930, Ellen Marguerite, *d* of Harold Dahl, Cardiff; no *c*. *Educ:* Bootham Sch., York; King's Coll., Cambridge; St Bartholomew's Hosp., London. Demonstrator in Bacteriology, London Sch. of Hygiene and Tropical Medicine, 1929; Demonstrator in Pathol., University of Cambridge, 1931; Reader in Bacteriology, British Postgraduate Medical Sch., London, 1935; Prof. Bacteriology, University of London, 1937-45; Acting Dir Graham Medical Research Laboratories, University Coll. Hosp. Medical Sch., 1943-45; London Sector Pathologist, Emergency Medical Services, 1939-44; Dir, Medical Research Council Wound Infection Unit, Birmingham Accident Hosp., 1942-46; Dep. Dir, 1947-52 and Dir of Dept of Biological Standards, 1946-52, National Institute for Medical Research,

London. Biological Sec. and Vice-Pres., Royal Society, 1963-68. Trustee, Beit Memorial Fellowships, 1970-. Hon. DSc, Newcastle, 1969. *Publications:* (with G. S. Wilson), Topley and Wilson's Principles of Bacteriology and Immunity, 1945, 1955, 1964; various scientific papers. *Recreations:* various. *Address:* Lister Institute, Chelsea Bridge Road, SW1. *T:* 01-730 2181. *Club:* Athenæum.

**MILES, Sir Ashley;** *see* Miles, Sir A. A.

**MILES, Basil Raymond,** CBE 1968; Puisne Judge, Kenya, 1957-67, retired; *b* 10 Oct. 1906; *s* of John Thomas Miles and Winifred Miles, Wrexham, Denbighshire; *m* 1944, Margaret Baldwin Neilson; one *s* one *d*. *Educ:* Harrow; Magdalen Coll., Oxford. Barrister, Inner Temple, 1931; appointed Resident Magistrate, Tanganyika, 1946; Judge of the Supreme Court, The Gambia, 1953-57. *Recreation:* music. *Address:* Mbeya, Chesham Road, Bovingdon, Herts. *T:* 3187.

**MILES, Sir Bernard,** Kt 1969; CBE 1953; Actor; Founder, with his wife, of the Mermaid Theatre, Puddle Dock, EC4, 1959 (first opened in North London, 1950); *b* 27 Sept. 1907; *s* of Edwin James Miles and Barbara Fletcher; *m* 1931, Josephine Wilson; one *s* two *d*. *Educ:* Uxbridge County Sch.; Pembroke Coll., Oxford (Hon. Fellow, 1969). First stage appearance as Second Messenger in Richard III, New Theatre, 1930; appeared in St Joan, His Majesty's, 1931; spent 5 years in repertory as designer, stage-manager, character-actor, etc; frequent appearances on West End Stage from 1938. Entered films, 1937, and has written for, directed, and acted in them. First went on Music-hall stage, London Palladium, etc., 1950. Mermaid Theatre seasons: Royal Exchange, 1953: Macbeth, Dido and Aeneas, As You Like It, Eastward Ho! Formed Mermaid Theatre Trust which built City of London's first theatre for 300 years, the Mermaid, Puddle Dock, EC4. Opened May 1959, with musical play Lock Up Your Daughters. *Address:* Mill Cottage, Little Bardfield, near Dunmow, Essex.

**MILES, Maj.-Gen. Eric Grant,** CB 1943; DSO 1917; MC 1915; *b* 1891; 2nd *s* of late George H. Miles, Homestall, Welwyn, Herts; *m* 1924, Lady Marcia Valda, *y d* of 7th Earl of Roden; one *d*. *Educ:* Harrow; RMC. Joined King's Own Scottish Borderers, 1911; served European War, 1914-19 (wounded, despatches 5 times, DSO, MC); Capt. KOSB, 1916; Brevet Major, 1919; psc 1922; GSO 3 War Office, 1923; Brigade Major Shanghai Defence Force, 1927-28; Major, 1928; General Staff Officer, 2; War Office, 1930-33; Bt Lt-Col 1931; Imperial Defence Coll., 1934; Lt-Col 1936; commanded 1st Bn Royal Berks Regt, 1936-38; Col 1934; Gen. Staff Officer, 1st Grade, Malaya, 1938-39; Brig., 1940; Maj.-Gen., 1940; served in Flanders, 1940 (despatches); North Africa, 1943 (wounded); commanded 126th Inf. Bde 1940, 42nd (East Lancs) Div. 1941, 56th (London) Div. 1941-43; GOC Kent and South-Eastern Districts, 1943-46; Actg Lt-Gen., Sept.-Nov. 1944, as GOC-in-C South-Eastern Command; retired pay, 1946; Col KOSB, 1944-54. A Mem. of the House of Laity, Church Assembly, 1955-60; Dep. Chm. Lichfield Diocesan Board of Finance, 1954-60; Chm. since 1960. *Address:* The Rope Walk, Lyth Hill, Shrewsbury. *T:* Bayston Hill 2053. *Club:* Naval and Military.

**MILES, (Frank) Stephen,** CMG 1964; HM Diplomatic Service; British Consul-General, St Louis, USA, since 1967; *b* 7 Jan. 1920; *s* of Harry and Mary Miles; *m* 1953, Margaret Joy (*née* Theaker); three *d*. *Educ:* John Watson's Sch., Edinburgh; Daniel Stewart's Coll., Edinburgh; St Andrews Univ.; Harvard Univ. (Commonwealth Fellowship). Served with Fleet Air Arm, 1942-46 (Lt (A) RNVR). Scottish Home Dept, 1948; Commonwealth Office (previously CRO), 1948-; served in: New Zealand, 1949-52, Pakistan, 1954-57; Ghana, 1959-62; Uganda, 1962-63; British Dep. High Commissioner, Tanzania, 1963-65 (Acting High Commissioner, 1963-64); Acting High Commissioner in Ghana, March-April 1966. *Recreations:* cricket, tennis. *Address:* c/o Foreign and Commonwealth Office, Downing Street, SW1; Maytrees, Park Road, Limpsfield, Surrey. *Clubs:* Travellers', RNVR, Royal Commonwealth Society.

**MILES, Frederick George,** FRAeS; MSAE; Chairman and Managing Director: F. G. Miles Engineering Ltd; Miles Electronics Ltd; Miles-Hivlot Ltd; Miles Marine and Structural Plastics Ltd; Freeman of the Guild of Air Pilots and Air Navigators; *b* 22 March 1903; *m* 1932, Maxine Forbes-Robertson (*see* M. F. M. Miles); one *s* (and one *d* decd). *Educ:* Brighton. Career: mostly flying. *Address:* Batts, Ashurst, Steyning, Sussex. *Club:* Royal Aero.

**MILES, Adm. Sir Geoffrey John Audley,** KCB, *cr* 1945 (CB 1942); KCSI, *cr* 1947; *b* 2 May 1890; 3rd *s* of Audley Charles Miles and Eveline Cradock-Hartopp; *m* 1918, Alison Mary Cadell; two *s*. *Educ:* Bedford; HMS Britannia. Joined the Royal Navy, served with Submarines and Destroyers during European War, 1914-18; later appointments include: Dep. Dir Staff Coll., Dir Tactical Sch.; Capt. HMS Nelson, 1939-41; Rear-Adm., 1941; Vice-Adm., 1944; Adm., 1948. Head of Mil. Mission in Moscow, 1941-43; Flag Officer Comdg Western Mediterranean, 1944-45; C-in-C, Royal Indian Navy, 1946-47. *Address:* Clunie Rowledge, Farnham, Surrey. *Clubs:* United Service, St James'.

**MILES, Prof. Herbert William,** MSc (Bristol), DSc (Manchester); Professor of Horticulture, University of London, at Wye College, 1947-65; Emeritus, 1965; Hon. Consultant in Horticulture to Royal Agricultural Society of England since 1948; Adviser and Lecturer in Entomology, University of Manchester, 1927-42; Advisory Entomologist, University of Bristol (Long Ashton Research Station), 1942-46; Deputy Provincial Director (West Midland Province), National Agricultural Advisory Service, 1946-47. *Publications:* (with Mary Miles, MSc) Insect Pests of Glasshouse Crops, revised edn 1947; original papers on Economic Entomology in leading scientific journals; original studies on the biology of British sawflies. *Address:* 2 Wood Broughton, Grange-over-Sands, North Lancs.

**MILES, Dame Margaret,** DBE 1970; BA; Headmistress, Mayfield School, Putney, since 1952; *b* 11 July 1911; 2nd *d* of Rev. E. G. Miles and Annie Miles (*née* Jones). *Educ:* Ipswich High Sch., GPDST; Bedford Coll., University of London. Asst Mistress: Westcliff High Sch., 1935-39; Badminton Sch., 1939-44; Lectr, Dept of Educn, University of Bristol, 1944-46; Headmistress, Pate's Gram. Sch., Cheltenham, 1946-51. Governor, Chelsea Coll.; Member of Council: Bedford Coll.; London Inst. of Education; Central Register and Clearing House Ltd; Mem. Exec. Cttee, Assoc. of Headmistresses; Chm., nuffield Resources for Learning Cttee; Educnl Adv. Cttee of Nat. Commn for Unesco; Trustee, Central Bureau, Educnl Visits and Exchanges. *Publications:* And Gladly Teach, 1965; Comprehensive Schooling, Problems and Perspectives, 1968. *Recreations:* theatre, concerts and films, when time; reading, gardening, walking, golf. *Address:* 31 Grosvenor Gardens, Kingston upon Thames, Surrey. *T:* 01-546 9835. *Club:* Aberdovey Golf.

**MILES, Maurice Edward;** Conductor; Professor of Conducting, Royal Academy of Music and Royal Military School of Music; *b* 1908; *s* of T. S. Miles; *m* 1936, Eileen Spencer Wood; one *s* two *d.* *Educ:* Wells Cathedral Gram. Sch.; Royal Academy of Music, London. Employed BBC, 1930-36; Conductor of Buxton Municipal Orchestra and of Bath Municipal Orchestra, 1936-39. Served in RAC, 1940-43. Returned to BBC, 1943; Conductor: Yorks Symphony Orchestra, 1947-54; City of Belfast Orchestra and Belfast Philharmonic Society, 1955-66; Ulster Orchestra, 1966-67. FRAM. *Recreations:* walking, reading. *Address:* Fairwinds, Burrows Lane, Gomshall, near Guildford, Surrey. *T:* Shere 2062.

**MILES, Maxine Frances Mary;** lately Director of F. G. Miles Engineering Ltd, Riverbank Works, Old Shoreham Road, Shoreham, Sussex; *b* 22 Sept. 1901; *d* of late Sir Johnston Forbes-Robertson; *m* 1932, Frederick George Miles, *qv*; one *s* (and one *d* decd). *Address:* Batts, Ashurst, Steyning, Sussex.

**MILES, Richard;** former Director of a number of Companies (chiefly engineering) in UK and abroad and Chairman, Head Wrightson & Co. Ltd, retired 1959; *b* 3 Feb. 1893; *s* of Thomas Vivian and Elizabeth Miles; *m* 1917, Alice Miller; one *s* one *d.* *Educ:* Nottingham High Sch.; Sheffield Univ. (MechEng). Major KOYLI and Machine Gun Corps, 1914-18. Major, Home Guard, 1939-44. Asst Gen. Manager, 1919-28, and Gen. Manager, 1928-32, Newton Chambers & Co. Ltd, Thorncliffe Ironworks, near Sheffield. Past-Pres., Institute of British Foundrymen, 1941-42. MIMechE. Former Dir, North Eastern Trading Estates Ltd; Former Mem. of Council, University of Newcastle upon Tyne, and Mem., National Research Development Corp.; Past Pres. Brit. Cast Iron Research Assoc. *Publications:* contrib. to financial, technical, and similar periodicals. *Recreations:* gardening, music. *Address:* Borth Wen Farm, Llandegfan, Menai Bridge, Anglesey. *T:* Glyn Garth 381. *Club:* Royal Anglesey Yacht.

**MILES, Surgeon Rear-Adm. Stanley,** CB 1968; Dean of Postgraduate Medical Studies, University of Manchester, since 1969; *b* 14 Aug. 1911; *s* of late T. C. Miles, Company Dir, Sheffield; *m* 1939, Frances Mary Rose; one *s* one *d.* *Educ:* King Edward VII Sch.; University of Sheffield. MSc Sheffield, 1934; MB, ChB, 1936; DTM & HEng, 1949; MD, 1955. Joined RN Medical Service, 1936; served in China, W Africa, Pacific and Mediterranean Fleets. Medical Officer-in-Charge, RN Medical Sch. and Dir of Medical Research, 1961; Consultant in Physiology; Med. Officer-in-Charge, Royal Naval Hosp., Plymouth, 1966-69. Surg. Captain 1960; Surg. Rear-Adm. 1966. Gilbert Blane Medal, RCS, 1957. QHP 1966-69. CStJ 1968. *Publication:* Underwater Medicine, 1962. *Recreations:* tennis, golf. *Address:* 1 White Cottage, Morley, Wilmslow, Cheshire SK9 4LX. *Clubs:* Savage, National Liberal.

**MILES, Stephen;** *see* Miles, F. S.

**MILES, Sir William (Napier Maurice),** 6th Bt, *cr* 1859; Chartered Architect; Consultant in firm Miles & Wills, Chartered Architects; *b* 19 Oct. 1913; *s* of Sir Charles William Miles, 5th Bt, OBE; *S* father, 1966; *m* 1946, Pamela, *d* of late Capt. Michael Dillon; one *s* two *d.* *Educ:* Stowe; University of Cambridge (BA). Architectural Assoc. Diploma, 1939. *Recreations:* swimming, sailing. *Heir:* *s* Philip John Miles, *b* 10 Aug. 1953. *Address:* Old Rectory House, Walton-in-Gordano, near Clevedon, Somerset. *T:* Clevedon 3365; Hillcrest House, 1 Sandquay Road, Dartmouth. *T:* Dartmouth 2275. *Clubs:* Clifton (Bristol); Royal Dorset Yacht; Dartmouth Sailing.

**MILFORD,** 2nd Baron *cr* 1939; **Wogan Philipps;** Bt 1919; farmer and painter; *b* 25 Feb. 1902; *e s* of 1st Baron Milford; *S* father, 1962; *m* 1st, 1928, Rosamond Nina Lehmann, *qv*; one *s* (and one *d* decd); 2nd, 1944, Cristina, Countess of Huntingdon (who *d* 1953); 3rd, 1954, Tamara Rust. *Educ:* Eton; Magdalen Coll., Oxford. *Heir:* *s* Hon. Hugo John Laurence Philipps [*b* 27 Aug. 1929; *m* 1st, 1951 (marr. diss., 1958); one *d*; 2nd, 1959, Mary, *e d* of Baron Sherfield, *qv*; three *s* one *d*]. *Address:* Butler's Farm, Colesbourne, Cheltenham, Glos. *T:* Coberley 260. *Club:* St James'.

*See also Hon. J. P. Philipps, Hon. R. H. Philipps.*

**MILFORD, Rev. Canon Campbell Seymour,** MC 1918; Canon Residentiary of Bristol Cathedral, 1962-67; retired, 1967; *b* 20 July 1896; *s* of Robert Theodore and Elspeth Milford; *m* 1926, Edith Mary (*née* Sandys); one *s.* *Educ:* Marlborough; Brasenose, Oxford. Lieut R West Kent Regt, 1915-19. BA 1st Class Lit. Hum., 1921; Lecturer, S Paul's Coll., Calcutta, 1922-25; MA and Diploma in Theology, Oxford, 1926. Deacon 1926, Priest 1927; Curate, Christ Church, Hampstead, 1926-28; Vice-Principal, S Paul's Coll., Calcutta (CMS), 1928-44; Lecturer and Fellow, Calcutta Univ., 1937-44; Canon of Calcutta Cathedral, 1943-44; Sec. for West Asia, CMS, London, 1944-57; Incumbent, Christ Church, Colombo, 1957-62. *Publications:* India Revisited, 1952; Middle East, Bridge or Barrier, 1956. *Recreation:* music. *Address:* 2 Priory Road, Bristol 8. *T:* Bristol 38566.

*See also Rev. Canon T. R. Milford.*

**MILFORD, Maj.-Gen. Edward James,** CB 1947; CBE 1945; DSO 1919; psc; Australian Military Forces: Dir of Artillery, 1938-39; CRA Australian Division AIF, 1940; Master-General of the Ordnance, 1941; Divisional Commander, 1942; Adjutant-General, 1946; retired from Australian Military Forces, 1948. *Address:* Mornington, Victoria, Australia. *Club:* Naval and Military (Melbourne).

**MILFORD, Rev. Canon Theodore Richard;** Master of the Temple, 1958-68; *b* 10 June 1895; *e s* of Robert Theodore Milford, MA, and Elspeth Barter; *m* 1st, 1932, Nancy Dickens Bourchier Hawksley; two *d*; 2nd, 1937, Margaret Nowell Smith; two *d.* *Educ:* Denstone; Fonthill, East Grinstead; Clifton; Magdalen Coll., Oxford; Westcott House, Cambridge. Served European War, 1914-18, 19th Royal Fusiliers, 1914; Oxford & Bucks LI, 1915-19 (Mesopotamia, 1916-18); Magdalen Coll., Oxford, 1919-21; BA (1st Cl. Lit. Hum), 1921; Union Christian Coll., Alwaye, Travancore, 1921-23; St John's Coll., Agra, 1923-24, 1926-30, 1931-34; Sec. Student Christian Movement, 1924-26 and 1935-38; Westcott House, 1930-31; Deacon, 1931; Priest, 1934 (Lucknow); Curate All Hallows, Lombard Street, 1935-37; Vicar of St Mary the Virgin, Oxford (University Church), 1938-47; Canon and Chancellor of Lincoln, 1947-58; Canon of Norton Episcopi, Lincoln Cathedral, 1947-68, Canon Emeritus, 1968. Chm., Oxfam, 1942-47 and 1960-65. Greek Red Cross (Bronze), 1947. *Publications:* Foolishness to the Greeks, 1953; The Valley of Decision, 1961. *Recreations:* music, chess. *Address:* 1 Kingsman Lane, Shaftesbury,

Dorset. *T:* Shaftesbury 2843. *See also Rev. Canon C. S. Milford.*

**MILFORD HAVEN,** 4th Marquess of, *cr* 1917; **George Ivar Louis Mountbatten;** Earl of Medina, 1917; Viscount Alderney, 1917; *b* 6 June 1961; *s* of 3rd Marquess of Milford Haven, OBE, DSC, and of Janet Mercedes, *d* of late Major Francis Bryce, OBE; *S* father, 1970. *Heir: b* Lord Ivar Alexander Michael Mountbatten, *b* 9 March 1963. *Address:* Tindon Manor, Saffron Walden, Essex. *See also Earl Mountbatten of Burma.*

**MILHAUD, Darius;** composer; hon. Professor of Composition, Conservatoire de Musique, Paris, 1947; *b* Aix-en-Provence, 4 Sept. 1892; *m* 1925, Madeleine Milhaud; one *s. Educ:* Paris Conservatory. Attached to French Legation, Brazil, 1917-18. Prof. of Music, Mills Coll., California, 1940-. Grand Officier, Légion d'Honneur, 1965. *Works:* La Brébis Egarée, L'Homme et son Désir; La Création du monde; Le Retour de l'enfant prodigue; Protée; L'Orestie d'Eschyle; Le Bœuf sur le toit; Le Train Bleu; Salade; Les Malheurs d'Orphée; Esther de Carpentras; Le pauvre Matelot; Christophe Colomb; Maximilien; Les Songes, La Sagesse, Bolivar, David, La Mère Coupable, etc. *Address:* 10 Boulevard de Clichy, Paris. *T:* Montmarte 67-66.

**MILINGO, Most Rev. Emanuel;** *see* Lusaka, Archbishop of, (RC).

**MILKINA, Nina; (Mrs A. R. M. Sedgwick);** Concert Pianist; *b* Moscow, 27 Jan. 1919; *d* of Jacques and Sophie Milkine; *m* 1943, Alastair Robert Masson Sedgwick, Dir Gillette Industries Ltd; one *s* one *d. Educ:* privately. Musical studies with the late Leon Conus of the Moscow Conservatoire and at the Paris Conservatoire, also with Profs Harold Craxton and Tobias Matthay, London. First public appearance at age of 11 with Lamoureux Orchestra, Paris; has since been broadcasting, televising, and touring in Great Britain and abroad. At inauguration of Third Programme, was commissioned by BBC to broadcast series of all Mozart's piano sonatas; invited to give Mozart recital for bicentenary celebration of Mozart's birth, Edinburgh Festival, 1956; recorded for Westminster Co. of New York, and Pye Record Co., London. Widely noted for interpretation of Mozart's piano works. *Publications:* works for piano. *Recreations:* reading, chess, fly fishing. *Address:* 20 Paradise Walk, SW3; Vicarage Cottage, Rogate, Petersfield, Hants.

**MILKOMANE, G. A. M.;** *see* Sava, George.

**MILL, Rear-Adm. Ernest,** CB 1960; OBE 1944; Director General, Aircraft, Admiralty, 1959-62; *b* 12 April 1906; *s* of Charles and Rosina Jane Mill; *m* 1939, Isobel Mary Neilson. *Educ:* Merchant Venturers Sch. Fleet Engr Officer on staff of C-in-C, Mediterranean, 1957; Rear-Adm., 1958. *Recreations:* sailing, fishing. *Address:* Oak Royal, Crondall, Hants. *Club:* Army and Navy.

**MILL, Laura Margaret Dorothea,** OBE 1962; MB, ChB, Diploma Psych; Medical Commissioner, Mental Welfare Commission for Scotland, 1962-63, retired; *b* 28 Nov. 1897; *d* of Rev. William Alexander Mill, MA and Isabel Clunas. *Educ:* The Park Sch., Glasgow; Glasgow Univ. House Surg., Samaritan Hosp. for Women, and Royal Maternity Hospital, Glasgow, House Physician, Royal Hospital for Sick Children, and Senior Medical Officer Out-patient Dispensary, Glasgow; Resident Medical Officer, York General Dispensary; Asst Physician, Riccartsbar Mental Hosp., Paisley, and Murray Royal Mental Hosp., Perth; Clinical Medical Officer, Glasgow Public Health Dept. Dep. Medical Commissioner, Gen. Board of Control for Scotland, 1936; Medical Commissioner, Gen. Board of Control for Scotland (later Mental Welfare Commission), 1947, and Senior Medical Officer, Dept of Health for Scotland. *Address:* 7 Montpelier Terrace, Edinburgh EH10 4NE. *T:* 031-229 7982.

**MILL IRVING, David Jarvis,** CBE 1955; Hon. President, Scottish National Party, Haddington Branch; Ambassador to Costa Rica, 1956-61, retired; *b* 11 April 1904; 2nd *s* of late W. Mill Irving, Edinburgh, and Mary Low Jarvis; *m* 1934, Margaret Estella Orchardson Moxon; one *s. Educ:* Daniel Stewart's Coll., Edinburgh; Edinburgh Univ.; Pembroke Coll., Cambridge. MA (Hons) Edinburgh, 1929. Entered HM Foreign Service as Probationer Vice-Consul in former Levant Consular Service, 1927; served in Egypt, 1929-32, and in Morocco, 1932-34; Vice-Consul: at Suez, 1934; at Rabat, 1940; Asst Oriental Sec. at Cairo with rank of 1st Sec., 1941; Consul at Fez, 1945; served as 1st Sec. in Foreign Office, 1945-49. Mem. UK Deleg. to Internat. Conf. for revision of Conventions relating to War Victims, 1949; Special Ambassador for Inauguration of President of Hayti, 1950; Minister to Hayti, 1950-53; Ambassador, 1953-55; Consul-Gen. for Algeria, 1955. Special Ambassador for the Inauguration: of the President of Honduras, 1957; of the President of Costa Rica, 1958. Coronation Medal, 1953. *Recreation:* Scottish historical research. *Address:* Langlaw, Upper Saltoun, East Lothian. *T:* Pencaitland 266. *Club:* Royal Automobile.

**MILLAIS, Sir Ralph (Regnault),** 5th Bt, *cr* 1885; *b* 4 March 1905; *s* of Sir Geoffroy William Millais, 4th Bt, and Madeleine Campbell (*d* 1963), *d* of C. H. Grace; *S* father, 1941; *m* 1st, 1939, Felicity Caroline Mary Ward Robinson (marriage dissolved), *d* of late Brig.-Gen. W. W. Warner, CMG; one *s* one *d*; 2nd, 1947, Irene Jessie, *er d* of E. A. Stone, FSI. *Educ:* Marlborough; Trinity Coll., Cambridge. Business career. Joined RAFVR at outbreak of war, 1939, Wing Comdr. *Recreations:* fishing, travel and the restoration of famous Vintage and Historic cars. *Heir: s* Geoffroy Richard Everett Millais, *b* 27 Dec. 1941. *Address:* Primrose Hill, Hawkhurst, Kent.

**MILLAN, Bruce;** MP (Lab) Craigton Division of Glasgow since 1959; *b* 5 Oct. 1927; *s* of David Millan; *m* 1953, Gwendoline May Fairey; one *s* one *d. Educ:* Harris Academy, Dundee. Chartered Accountant, 1950-59. Chm. Scottish Labour Youth Council, 1949-50. Contested: West Renfrewshire, 1951, Craigton Div. of Glasgow, 1955. Parly Under-Sec. of State for Defence, (RAF), 1964-66, for Scotland, 1966-70. *Address:* 46 Hardy Road, SE3. *T:* 01-858 5634.

**MILLAND, Raymond Alton, (Ray Milland);** film actor and director, US; *b* Wales, 3 Jan. 1907; *s* of Alfred Milland and Elizabeth Truscott; *m* 1932, Muriel Weber; one *s* one *d. Educ:* private schs in Wales and England; Monks Preparatory Sch.; University of Wales. Served with Household Cavalry, 1926-29; became actor in 1930; went to USA, 1930, and became naturalized citizen, 1938. *Films include:* Payment Deferred; Bolero; Four Hours to Kill; The Glass Key; Ebb Tide; Beau Geste; The Lost Weekend; French Without Tears; So Evil My Love; Circle of Danger; A Man Alone; Lisbon; The Safecracker (also directed); Kitty; Golden Earrings; It Happens Every Spring; Alias Nick Beal; Dial M for Murder; 3 Brave

Men; Man Alone. Received Motion Picture Acad. Award for best actor, for part in The Lost Weekend. Has also appeared on stage and television. *Address:* 360 N Camden Drive, Beverly Hills, California, USA.

**MILLAR,** family name of **Baron Inchyra.**

**MILLAR, Dame Elizabeth;** *see* Hoyer-Millar.

**MILLAR, George,** DSO 1944; MC; Farmer and Writer; *b* 19 Sept. 1910; 2nd *s* of Thomas Andrew Millar, architect, and Mary Reid Morton; *m* 1945, Isabel Beatriz, *d* of Montague Paske-Smith, CMG, CBE; no *c*. *Educ:* Loretto; St John's, Cambridge. Architect, 1930-32; journalist, with Daily Telegraph and Daily Express, 1934-39; Paris correspondent Daily Express, 1939; served War of 1939-45, The Rifle Bde; escaped from German POW camp to England, then served as agent in France; Chevalier de la Légion d'Honneur; Croix de Guerre avec Palmes. Tenant farmer, 400 acres, 1962; increased to 1000 acres, 1966. *Publications:* Maquis, 1945; Horned Pigeon, 1946; My Past was an Evil River, 1946; Isabel and the Sea, 1948; Through the Unicorn Gates, 1950; A White Boat from England, 1951; Siesta, 1952; Orellana, 1954; Oyster River, 1963; Horseman, 1970. *Recreation:* sailing. *Address:* Sydling St Nicholas, Dorset. *T:* Cerne Abbas 205.

**MILLAR, Ian Alastair D.;** *see* Duncan Millar.

**MILLAR, Oliver Nicholas,** CVO 1963 (MVO 1953); FBA 1970; Deputy Surveyor of the Queen's Pictures, since 1949; *b* 26 April 1923; *er s* of Gerald Millar, MC and of Ruth Millar; *m* 1954, Delia Mary, 2nd *d* of late Lt-Col Cuthbert Dawnay, MC; one *s* three *d*. *Educ:* Rugby; Courtauld Institute of Art, University of London (Academic Diploma in History of Art). Unable, for medical reasons, to serve in War of 1939-45. Asst Surveyor of the King's Pictures, 1947-49. FSA. *Publications:* Gainsborough, 1949; William Dobson, Tate Gallery Exhibition, 1951; English Art, 1625-1714 (with Dr M. D. Whinney). 1957; Rubens' Whitehall Ceiling, 1958; Abraham van der Doort's Catalogue, 1960; Tudor, Stuart and Early Georgian Pictures in the Collection of HM the Queen, 1963; Zoffany and his Tribuna, 1967; Later Georgian Pictures in the Collection of HM the Queen, 1969; articles in the Burlington Magazine, etc.; numerous catalogues. *Recreations:* drawing, gardening, cricket. *Address:* Yonder Lodge, Penn, Bucks. *T:* Penn 2124. *Club:* Brooks's.

**MILLAR of Orton, Maj.-Gen. Robert Kirkpatrick,** CB 1954; DSO 1944; DL; late Royal Engineers; *b* 29 June 1901; *s* of late Professor John Hepburn Millar and late Margaret Wilhelmina, *e d* of late J. W. Wharton Duff, of Orton, Morayshire; *m* 1934, Frances Rhodes, *yr d* of late Col W. G. Beyts, CBE; two *s* (and one *s* decd). *Educ:* Edinburgh Academy; RMA Woolwich. 2nd Lt Royal Engineers, 1921; served in India and China, 1925-33; served War of 1939-45 (despatches 5 times, 1939-46, DSO); Field Co. 49 (WR) Div. (Norway), 1940; CRE 15 (Scottish) Div. 1942-45 (France and Germany); CE London District, 1949-51; CE Scottish Command, 1951-53; Engineer-in-Chief, Pakistan Army, 1953-57. DL Moray, 1959-. *Recreations:* golf, shooting, fishing. *Address:* Mains of Orton, By Fochabers, Moray. *T:* Orton 284.

**MILLAR, Prof. William Malcolm,** MD; Professor of Mental Health, University of Aberdeen, since 1949; *b* 20 April 1913; *s* of Rev. Gavin Millar, BD, Logiealmond, Perthshire, and Margaret Malcolm, Stanley, Perthshire; *m* 1941, Catherine McAuslin Rankin; two *s* four *d*. *Educ:* George Heriot's Sch., Edinburgh; Edinburgh Univ. MB, ChB (Edinburgh) 1936; MD (Edinburgh) 1939; Dip. Psych. (Edinburgh) 1939; MRCPE 1958; FRCPE 1962. Asst Physician, Royal Edinburgh Hospital for Mental Disorders, 1937-39. Served 1939-46 (Lieut, Captain, Major), Specialist in Psychiatry, RAMC. Senior Lecturer, Dept of Mental Health, Aberdeen Univ., 1946-49. Mem., Medical Research Council, 1960-64; Dean, Faculty of Medicine. FBPsS 1946. *Publications:* contributions to various learned journals. *Recreations:* golf, chess, gardening. *Address:* 16 The Chanonry, Aberdeen. *T:* Aberdeen 43845. *Club:* University (Aberdeen).

**MILLAR-CRAIG, Hamish,** CMG 1960; OBE 1958; Director, East African Staff College, since 1965; *b* 25 Sept. 1918; *yr s* of late Captain David Millar-Craig and late Winifred Margaret Cargill; *m* 1953, Rose Ernestine Boohene. *Educ:* Shrewsbury; Keble Coll., Oxford. Served War of 1939-45, 2nd Lt Royal Scots, 1940; Colonial Civil Service, Gold Coast, 1940-57; Ghana Civil Service, 1957-62; Reader in Public Administration (UN Technical Assistance) Ghana Institute of Public Administration, 1962-65. Economic Development Institute, Washington, 1957-58. *Recreations:* cricket, philately. *Address:* c/o Lloyds Bank Ltd, Taunton, Somerset.

**MILLARD, Guy Elwin,** CMG 1957; CVO 1961; Minister, HM Embassy, Washington, since 1970; *b* 22 Jan. 1917; *s* of Col Baldwin Salter Millard, and Phyllis Mary Tetley; *m* 1st, 1946, Anne (marr. diss., 1963), *d* of late Gordon Mackenzie; one *s* one *d*; 2nd, 1964, Mary Judy, *d* of late James Dugdale and of Pamela, Countess of Aylesford; two *s*. *Educ:* Charterhouse; Pembroke Coll., Cambridge. Entered Foreign Office, 1939. Served Royal Navy, 1940-41. Asst Private Sec., to Foreign Sec., 1941-45; British Embassy, Paris, 1945-49, Ankara, 1949-52; Imperial Defence Coll., 1953; Foreign Office, 1954, Counsellor, 1955; Private Sec. to Prime Minister, 1955-57; British Embassy, Tehran, 1959-62: Foreign Office, 1962-64; Minister, UK Delegation to NATO, 1964-67; Ambassador to Hungary, 1967-70. *Address:* c/o Foreign and Commonwealth Office, SW1; Fyfield Manor, Southrop, Glos. *T:* Southrop 234. *Club:* Boodle's.

**MILLARD, Raymond Spencer,** CMG 1967; PhD; FICE; MIStructE; Deputy Director, Road Research Laboratory, since 1965; *b* 5 June 1920; *s* of Arthur and Ellen Millard, Ashbourne, Derbs; *m* 1945, Irene, *d* of William and Mabel Guy; one *s* one *d*. *Educ:* Ashbourne Gram. Sch.; University Coll., London (BSc (Eng)). Contractor's Engineer, 1941-44. Road Research Laboratory: Bituminous Sect., 1944; Officer i/c Scottish Br., 1949; Head of Bituminous Sect., 1951; Head of Tropical Sect., 1955. *Publications:* scientific and technical papers on road planning and construction. *Recreation:* painting. *Address:* 19 Clarence Drive, Englefield Green, Surrey. *T:* Egham 5579.

**MILLBOURN, Rev. Arthur Russell;** Canon Emeritus; *b* 10 May 1892; 2nd *s* of Arthur and Harriet Lucie Millbourn, London; *m* 1st, 1920, Ethel Mary (*d* 1960), *d* of John and Mary Congreve, Cambridge; 2nd, 1962, Eleanor Mary, *widow* of T. D. Fairgrieve and *d* of late P. B. Halcombe, Bournemouth. *Educ:* Christ's Hospital; Pembroke Coll., Oxford (Classical Scholar). Class. Hon. Mods II, 1913; Lit. Hum. II, 1915; Asst Master, S. John's Sch., Leatherhead, and House Tutor, 1915-22;

Headmaster, Colston's Sch., Stapleton, Bristol, 1923-39; Deacon 1928; Priest 1929; Canon Residentiary of Bristol Cathedral, 1939-61. *Recreations:* music, foreign travel, railway engineering. *Address:* Piper's Court, Penpol, Truro, Cornwall. *T:* Feock 498.

**MILLBOURN, Sir Eric;** *see* Millbourn, Sir P. E.

**MILLBOURN, Sir (Philip) Eric,** Kt 1955; CMG 1950; MIMechE; Adviser on Shipping in Port to Minister of Transport, 1946-63; Chairman Council of Administration, Malta Dockyard, since 1963; *b* 1 June 1902; *s* of late Philip Millbourn, Brunswick Square, Hove, Sussex; *m* 1931, Ethel Marjorie, *d* of late Joseph E. Sennett; one *s* one *d. Educ:* privately; London Univ. Director: National Employers' Mutual General Insurance Association; Tozer, Kemsley and Millbourn (Holdings) Ltd; National Employers' Life Assurance Assoc.; Felixstowe Dock and Railway Co. Chm., The London Airport Development Cttee. *Address:* Conkwell Grange, Limpley Stoke, near Bath. *T:* Limpley Stoke 3102. *Club:* Travellers'.

**MILLER, Alan Cameron;** MA; LLB; MInstT; Advocate; Legal Adviser (Scotland) to The British Railways Board since 1962 (to British Transport Commission, 1952-62); *b* 10 Jan. 1913; *o s* of Arthur Miller, Edinburgh; *m* 1945, Audrey Main; one *s* one *d. Educ:* Fettes Coll.; Edinburgh Univ. MA 1934; LLB 1936; Advocate, 1938; served War of 1939-45, RN; Interim Sheriff-Substitute at Dundee, 1946; Sheriff-Substitute of Inverness, Moray, Nairn, Ross and Cromarty, at Fort William, 1946-52. *Recreations:* golf and music. *Address:* 42 Great King Street, Edinburgh, Scotland. *Clubs:* Royal Naval Volunteer Reserve; New, Arts (Edinburgh).

**MILLER, Alastair Cheape,** MBE 1948; TD; Governor, HM Prison, Pentonville, London N7, since 1970; *b* 13 March 1912 (twin-brother); *s* of John Charles Miller, Banker, Glasgow, and Jessie Amelia Miller; *m* 1943, Elizabeth S. Hubbard (marr. diss. 1967); one *s* one *d. Educ:* Melville Coll., Edinburgh; Bedford Sch., Bedford. Territorial Army, 1930-46; War Service (Gibraltar and Italy); 5th Beds and Herts Regt, 1st Herts Regt and 4th KOYLI, 1948-51. Barclays Bank Ltd; Junior Clerk to Cashier, 1929-45. Housemaster, Approved Sch., April-Nov. 1946. Prison Service: Asst Governor, Wakefield, Dec. 1946-Jan. 1953; Governor: Dover, 1953-59; Winchester, 1959-62; Hindley Borstal, 1962-65; Parkhurst Prison, 1966-70. *Recreations:* golf, sailing. *Address:* The Governor's House, HM Prison, Pentonville, N7. *Clubs:* Civil Service; Seaford Golf (Seaford); Island Sailing (Cowes); Royal Solent Yacht (Yarmouth).

**MILLER, Alexander James Nicol,** CB 1959; Commissioner of Inland Revenue, since 1957; *b* 24 April 1911; *s* of late James John Miller; *m* 1940, Doris Martha Hankins; no *c. Educ:* Queen Mary's Grammar Sch., Walsall; Jesus Coll., Oxford. Entered Inland Revenue Dept, 1934. *Address:* 22 Waverley Lane, Farnham, Surrey.

**MILLER, Alexander Ronald,** CBE 1970; Chairman and Managing Director, Motherwell Bridge (Holdings) Ltd, since 1958; *b* 7 Nov. 1915; *s* of Thomas Ronald Miller and Elise Hay. *Educ:* Craigflower; Malvern Coll.; Royal Coll. of Science and Technology. Royal Engineers and Royal Bombay Sappers and Miners, 1940-46. FRSA; Associate of IMechE; Mem. Instn of Royal Engineers. *Address:* Lairfad, Auldhouse, by East Kilbride, Lanarks. *T:* Auldhouse Cross 275. *Club:* Royal Scottish Automobile (Glasgow).

**MILLER, Archibald Elliot Haswell,** MC, Hon. MA Edinburgh 1951; RSW; Keeper and Deputy Director, National Galleries of Scotland, 1930-52 (retired); Secretary, Royal Fine Art Commission for Scotland, 1930-52 (retired); Secretary (later Director) National Buildings Record, Scottish Council, 1945-53 (retired); *b* Glasgow, 10 June 1887; *s* of William Miller and Elizabeth Haswell; *m* 1916, E. Josephine Cameron (Josephine Haswell Miller, ARSA); one *d. Educ:* Glasgow Academy. Studied Munich, Berlin, Vienna and Paris; Asst Professor in Glasgow Sch. of Art, 1910-14 and 1919-30; war services 1914-19 with 7th Bn Highland Light Infantry (MC), and 1939-45 with Intelligence Corps. Represented by works in Glasgow Art Gallery, National Gallery of New South Wales, and Imperial War Museum (Series of drawings representing all types of dress and equipment of the 1914-18 war period); has made a special study of military uniforms and Highland dress. Mem. of Soc. of Mural Decorators and Painters in Tempera; has carried out mural paintings in Livingstone Memorial Museum, Blantyre. *Publication:* Military Drawings and Paintings in the Royal Collection, vol i, 1966, vol ii, 1970. *Address:* Yew Tree Cottage, Kington Magna, Gillingham, Dorset. *T:* East Stour 326.

**MILLER, Arjay;** Dean, Graduate School of Business, Stanford University, since 1969; Vice-Chairman, Ford Motor Company, 1968-69 (Director, 1962-69, President, 1963-68); *b* 4 March 1916; *s* of Rawley John Miller and Mary Gertrude Schade; *m* 1940, Frances Marion Fearing; one *s* one *d. Educ:* University of California at Los Angeles (BS with highest hons, 1937). Graduate Student and Teaching Asst, University of California at Berkeley, 1938-40; Research Technician, Calif. State Planning Bd, 1941; Economist, Federal Reserve Bank of San Francisco, 1941-43. Captain, US Air Force, 1943-46. Asst Treas, Ford Motor Co., 1947-53; Controller, 1953-57; Vice-Pres. and Controller, 1957-61; Vice-Pres. of Finance, 1961-62; Vice-Pres., Staff Group, 1962-63. Trustee: Urban Inst. (Chm.); Eisenhower Exchange Fellowships; Brookings Instn, Washington; Kent Sch., Conn.; Cttee for Economic Develt; National Industrial Conference Board, 1965; Member: Adv. Cttee, Harvard Univ. Program on Technology and Society; Vis. Cttee, Jt Center for Urban Studies, MIT and Harvard; President's Public Adv. Cttee on Trade Policy; LLD; University of California (LA), 1964; Whitman Coll., 1965; University of Nebraska, 1965. *Address:* Graduate School of Business, Stanford University, Stanford, Calif, USA. *Clubs:* Economic (Detroit, Mich); Detroit (Detroit); Barton Hills Country (Ann Arbor, Mich).

**MILLER, Arthur;** Playwright; *b* 17 Oct. 1915; *s* of Isadore Miller and Augusta Barnett; *m* 1940, Mary Grace Slattery (marriage dissolved); one *s* one *d*; *m* 1956, Marilyn Monroe (marriage dissolved, 1961; she *d* 1962); *m* 1962, Ingeborg Morath; one *d. Educ:* University of Michigan, USA (AB). Pres. of PEN Club, 1965-. *Publications:* Situation Normal (reportage), 1944; Focus (novel), 1945; All My Sons (play) (New York Drama Critics Award, 1948), 1947; Death of A Salesman (play) (New York Drama Critics Award, 1949, Pulitzer Prize, 1949), 1949; The Crucible (play), 1953; A View from the Bridge (play), 1955, filmed, 1962; A Memory of Two Mondays (play), 1955; Collected Plays, 1958; The Misfits (motion picture play), 1960; After the Fall (play), 1963; Incident at Vichy (play), 1964; I Don't Need You Anymore (collected stories), 1967; The Price (play), 1968; (jt author) In Russia, 1969; contrib. stories and essays to Esquire, Colliers, Atlantic Monthly, etc. *Address:* c/o IFA Inc., 1301 Avenue of The Americas, New York City, USA.

**MILLER, Sir Bernard;** *see* Miller, Sir O. B.

**MILLER, Bruce;** *see* Miller, John D. B.

**MILLER, Maj.-Gen. Charles Harvey,** CB 1942; CBE 1941; DSO 1943; Legion of Honour, 1943; Croix de Guerre avec Palmes; Legion of Merit, Degree of Commander, 1945; *b* 11 Sept. 1894; *s* of late Robert Miller, Dummer Grange, Basingstoke; *m* 1923, Hon. Bridget Violet Douglas-Pennant, *d* of 5th Baron Penrhyn; one *d. Educ:* Winchester; RMA, Woolwich. Joined 18th Hussars, 1914; served European War, 1914-19 (wounded twice). Staff Coll., Camberley, 1927-29; Comd Transjordan Frontier Force, 1932-36; Brevet Col, 1936; commanded 13/18 Hussars, 1937-38; commanded 5 Cavalry Brigade, 1940; on the staff HQ BTE (despatches) 8th Army, 1941-42; MGA 18 Army Group and 15 Army Group, 1943, served in Western Desert, Tunis, Sicily, and Italy; MGA Southern Command, 1943-45; Temp. Maj.-Gen. 1943; Maj.-Gen. 1944; retired pay, 1946; Chief of Staff to the Duke of Gloucester, in Australia, 1946-47; Fellow of Royal Commonwealth Society and Royal Geographical Society. DL Suffolk, 1953. *Address:* Old Rectory, Badingham, Suffolk. *T:* Badingham 222. *Club:* Cavalry.

**MILLER, Desmond Campbell,** QC 1961; TD; *b* 17 Dec. 1914; *y s* of late Robert Miller, DD, sometime Bishop of Cashel and Waterford, and of Mary Miller (*née* Potter); *m* Ailsa, *y d* of Hon. Mr Justice (A. V.) Maxwell, *qv*; two *s* one *d. Educ:* Dean Close Sch., Cheltenham; St Columba's Coll., Rathfarnham; Pembroke Coll., Oxford. Called to Bar, Inner Temple, 1939, Gray's Inn (*ad eundem*), 1960; Master of the Bench, Inner Temple, 1968-. Served War of 1939-45 (despatches): Middx Yeo.; Northants Yeo.; 2nd, 6th and 11th Armoured Divs; HQ 1 Corps; HQ, ALFSEA; Staff Coll., Camberley, 1942. Lt-Col TA. Mem. General Council of the Bar, 1964-68 (Chm., Taxation and Retirement Benefits Cttees). *Recreations:* golf, flyfishing. *Address:* 1 Temple Gardens, Temple, EC4. *T:* 01-353 4636; 116 Rivermead Court, SW6. *T:* 01-736 5753. *Clubs:* Brooks's, MCC, Hurlingham; Royal Mid-Surrey Golf.

**MILLER, Donald C.;** *see* Crichton-Miller.

**MILLER, Sir Douglas;** *see* Miller, Sir I. D.

**MILLER, Douglas Sinclair,** CBE 1956 (OBE 1948); Secretary, King George's Jubilee Trust, since 1961; *b* 30 July 1906; British parentage; m 1933, Valerie Madeleine Carter; one *d. Educ:* Westminster Sch.; Merton Coll., Oxford. HM Overseas Colonial Service, 1930-61: Supt of Native Educn, N Rhodesia, 1930-45; Director of Education: Basutoland, 1945-48; Nyasaland, 1948-52; Uganda, 1952-58; Kenya, 1958-59; Dir of Educn and Permanent Sec., Min. of Educn, Kenya, 1959-60; Temp. Minister of Educn, Kenya, 1960-61. *Address:* Flat 3, Avenue House, Belsize Park Gardens, NW3. *T:* 01-794 6952. *Clubs:* Royal Commonwealth Society; Kampala (Uganda).

**MILLER, Prof. Edward;** Professor of Medieval History, University of Sheffield, since 1965; *b* Acklington, Northumberland, 16 July 1915; *e s* of Edward and Mary Lee Miller; *m* 1941, Fanny Zara Salingar; one *s. Educ:* King Edward VI's Gram. Sch., Morpeth; St John's Coll., Cambridge (Exhibnr, Schol.). BA 1937; MA 1945; Strathcona Res. Student, 1937-39 and Fellow, 1939-65, St John's Coll., Cambridge. Nat. Service, 1940-45 in Durham Light Inf., RAC and Control Commn for Germany; Major. Dir of Studies in History, 1946-55 and Tutor, 1951-57, St John's Coll., Cambridge; Asst Lectr in History, 1946-50 and Lectr, 1950-65, University of Cambridge; Warden of Madingley Hall, Cambridge, 1961-65. FRHistS; Mem., Victoria Co. Histories Cttee of Inst. Hist. Research; Mem. Couns of Selden and Lincoln Record Societies. *Publications:* The Abbey and Bishopric of Ely, 1951; Portrait of a College, 1961; (Jt Ed.) Cambridge Economic History of Europe, Vol. iii, 1963; Historical Studies of the English Parliament, 2 vols, 1970; articles in Victoria County Histories of Cambridgeshire and York, English Hist. Rev., Econ. History Rev., Trans Royal Historical Society, Past and Present, etc. *Recreations:* with advancing years watching any form of sport, especially Rugby and cricket. *Address:* 18 Rutland Park, Sheffield, S10 2PB. *T:* Sheffield 60434.

**MILLER, Lt-Gen. (retired) Sir Euan (Alfred Bews),** KCB 1954 (CB 1949); KBE 1951; DSO 1945; MC 1918; DL; Lieutenant of the Tower of London, 1957-60; *b* 5 July 1897; *s* of Dr A. E. Miller; *m* 1926, Margaret (*d* 1969), *d* of late Captain H. C. R. Brocklebank, CBE; one *s* two *d. Educ:* Wellington Coll.; RMC Sandhurst. 2nd Lieut, KRRC, 1915. Served European War, France and Salonika, 1915-18 (despatches, MC). Staff Coll., 1926-27; Bt Lt-Col, 1936; served War of 1939-45, GSO1, GHQ, BEF, 1939; OC2 KRRC, 1940 (despatches, prisoner of war, DSO). Col, 1945; Brig., 1946; Dep. Mil. Sec., 1946; ADC to the King, 1946-48; Comdr Hanover Dist, 1948; Maj.-Gen., 1948; Chief of Staff, Middle East Land Forces, 1949-51; Lieut-Gen. 1951; Military Sec. to the Sec. of State for War, 1951; retired, 1955. Col Comdt, 1 KRRC, 1954-61. Chm. Kent T&AFA, 1956-61. DL Kent, 1958. *Address:* Farningham House Cottage, Farningham, Kent. *T:* Farningham 3243. *Club:* United Service.

*See also J. M. Clay.*

**MILLER, Air Chief Marshal Frank Robert,** CBE 1946; CD; Chief of Defence Staff, Canada, 1964-66; *b* Kamloops, BC, April 1908; *m* Dorothy Virginia Minor, Galveston, Texas. *Educ:* Alberta Univ. (BSc, Civil Engrg). Joined RCAF, 1931. Served War of 1939-45: commanded Air Navigation Schs at Rivers, Man., and Penfield Ridge, NB, and Gen. Reconnaisance Sch., Summerside, PEI; subseq. Dir of Trng Plans and Requirements and Dir of Trng, Air Force HQ; service overseas with Can. Bomber Gp as Station Comdr, later Base Comdr, 1944; Tiger Force, 1945 (despatches); Chief SO (later AOC), Air Material Comd, 1945; US Nat. War Coll., 1948; Air Mem. Ops and Trng, Air Force HQ, 1949; Vice Chief of Air Staff, 1951; Vice Air Deputy, SHAPE HQ, Paris, 1954; Dep. Minister, Dept of Nat. Defence, 1955; Chm., Chiefs of Staff, 1960; first Pres., NATO Mil. Cttee, 1963-64. Air Chief Marshal, 1961. Hon. LLD Alta, 1965. *Recreations:* golf, fishing. *Address:* 2 Seneca, Ottawa, Ontario, Canada.

**MILLER of Glenlee, Sir (Frederick William) Macdonald,** 7th Bt *cr* 1788; Conservative Agent for Lowestoft since 1965; *b* 21 March 1920; *e s* of Sir Alastair George Lionel Joseph Miller of Glenlee, 6th Bt; *S* father, 1964; *m* 1947, Marion Jane Audrey Pettit; one *s* one *d. Educ:* Tonbridge. Conservative Agent for: Whitehaven, 1947-50; Wembley North, 1950-52; North Norfolk, 1952-65. *Recreation:* gardening. *Heir: s* Stephen William Macdonald Miller of Glenlee [*b* 20 June 1953. *Educ:* Rugby]. *Address:* Holton Lodge, Holton St Peter, Halesworth, Suffolk. *T:* Halesworth 2109.

**MILLER, Brigadier George Patrick Rose-,** DSO 1940; MC; retired; *b* 20 July 1897; 3rd *s* of late John Gardner Miller, Mayfield, Perth; *m* 1929, Millicent Rose Lang-Rose; two *s* two *d*. *Educ:* Trinity Coll., Glenalmond; RMC, Sandhurst. Gazetted to Queen's Own Cameron Highlanders, 1915; served in France and Belgium, 1916-17 (MC); served with 1st Bn in India, Burma and Sudan; Commanded 1st Bn in France 1940 (DSO); Raised and Commanded 227 Brigade; Commanded 155 Brigade. *Publications:* Articles on agricultural subjects. *Address:* Rehiran, Cawdor, Nairnshire. *T:* Croy 218. *Club:* Naval and Military.

**MILLER, Gerald Cedar,** MC; MA; Headmaster Forest School, near Snaresbrook, 1936-60; *b* 11 May 1894; *s* of Rev. Ernest George and Emilie Miller; *m* 1st, 1930, Alice Rosemary Taylor (*d* 1957); three *d*; 2nd, 1960, Molly Sherry. *Educ:* University Sch., Victoria, BC; Ardingly Coll., Sussex; Keble Coll., Oxford. Served European War, 1914-19, Commission in Oxon. and Bucks Lt Infty, in France and Salonika; Asst Master Ardingly Coll., 1921-25; Sch. House Master, 1925-28; Second Master and Junior House Master, 1928-35. *Address:* Home Close, Gubblecote, near Tring, Herts. *Club:* Public Schools.

**MILLER, Henry;** Author and Painter; *b* New York City, 26 Dec. 1891; *m*; two *c*. *Educ:* City Coll., New York; Cornell Univ. Worked in the United States until 1930; lived in Paris and was employed on editorial work, 1930-39; Greece, 1939; returned to the United States, 1940. *Publications:* (include): Tropic of Cancer, 1931 (England, 1963); Black Spring, 1936 (autobiographical short stories; England, 1965); Tropic of Capricorn, 1938 (England, 1964); The Cosmological Eye, 1939; The Wisdom of the Heart, 1941; The Colossus of Maroussi, 1941; (with M. Fraenkel) Hamlet: a Philosophic Correspondence, 2 vols, 1939-41; Sunday After the War, 1944; The Air-Conditioned Nightmare (2 vols; vol. 2, Remember to Remember), 1945-47; The Smile at the Foot of the Ladder, 1948; The Books in My Life, 1952; Big Sur and the Oranges of Hieronymus Bosch, 1958; A Letter, 1962; Plexus, (England), 1963; Black Spring, 1963; Greece, 1964; Nexus, (England) 1964; Just Wild about Harry (play), (England) 1964; Selected Prose, Vols 1 and 2 (England), 1965; Sexus (England), 1969. Exhibition of Paintings, Los Angeles, 1966. *Address:* Big Sur, near Monterey, Calif, USA.

**MILLER, Henry George,** MD, FRCP; Vice-Chancellor of University of Newcastle upon Tyne, since 1968 (Dean of Medicine, 1966-68, and Professor of Neurology, 1964-68); *b* 13 Dec. 1913; *s* of John Miller, Stockton-on-Tees, Co. Durham; *m* 1942, Eileen Cathcart Baird, MRCOG; two *s* two *d*. *Educ:* University of Durham. MB 1937, MD 1940, MRCP 1940, DPM 1943, FRCP 1953. Asst Resident Pathologist, Johns Hopkins Hospital, Baltimore, 1938; clinical appts at Hospital for Sick Children, Gt Ormond Street, 1939; Neuropsychiatric Specialist, RAF Med. Service, 1942-46; Hammersmith Hosp. and Nat. Hosp., Queen Square, 1946-47; Asst Physician, Royal Victoria Infirmary, Newcastle upon Tyne, 1947-64. Examiner in Medicine, University of Liverpool; Vis. Prof. of Medicine, University of Queensland, 1963. Dir, Planning Unit, BMA, 1969-. Hon. For. Mem., Soc. Française de Neurologie; American Neurological Assoc.; Sec.-Gen.-Treas., World Fedn of Neurology. *Publications:* Early Diagnosis, 1961; Modern Medical Treatment, 1963; (with R. Daley) Progress in Clinical Medicine, 1947-66; many papers on medical and neurological subjects. *Address:* Vice-Chancellor's Lodge, Adderstone Crescent, Newcastle upon Tyne 2. *T:* Newcastle 813021. *Clubs:* Athenæum, Garrick.

**MILLER, Rear-Adm. (retd) Hugh,** CB 1935; DSO 1918; *b* 1880; *s* of late Joseph Charles Miller, Beckenham, Kent; *m* 1919, Muriel, *d* of late Dr Edward Baines Holwell, Leeds. *Educ:* Whitgift Sch. Legion of Honour and Orders of Sacred Treasure of Japan, Nile of Egypt, and Striped Tiger of China; retired list, 1935. *Address:* Highbury, Tilmore, Petersfield, Hants. *T:* Petersfield 3473. *Club:* Army and Navy.

**MILLER, Mrs Hugh;** *see* Katzin, Olga.

**MILLER, Sir (Ian) Douglas,** Kt 1961; FRCS; Hon. Consulting Neurosurgeon since 1960 (Hon. Neurosurgeon, 1948), St Vincent's Hospital, Sydney, and Repatriation General Hospital; Chairman of Board, St Vincent's Hospital, since 1966; Dean of Clinical School, St Vincent's Hospital, Sydney, 1931-64; *b* Melbourne, 20 July 1900; *m* 1939, Phyllis Laidley Mort; three *s* two *d*. *Educ:* Xavier Coll., Melbourne; University of Sydney. MB, ChM Sydney 1924; FRCS 1928. Hon. Asst Surgeon, St Vincent's Hosp., Sydney, 1929; Lectr in Surgical Anat., University, Sydney, 1930; Hon. Surg., Mater. Hosp. Sydney, 1934; Hon. Surg., St Vincent's Hosp., 1939; Major AIF, Surgical Specialist, 1940; Lt-Col (Surgical CO), 102 AGH, 1942; o/c Neurosurgical Centre, AIF; Mem. Ct of Examrs 1946, Mem. Council, 1947, RACS; President: RACS, 1957-59; Asian Australasian Soc. of Neurological Surgeons, 1964-67. Chairman: Editorial Cttee, ANZ Jl of Surgery; Editorial Bd, Modern Medicine in Australia. *Publications:* contrib. Med. Jl of Aust., 1956, 1960; Earlier Days, 1970. *Recreation:* agriculture. *Address:* 149 Macquarie Street, Sydney, NSW 2000, Australia. *T:* BU 5077, JJ 2431. *Clubs:* Australian, Royal Sydney Golf (Sydney).

**MILLER, Dr Jacques Francis Albert Pierre,** FRS 1970; FAA 1970; Head of Experimental Pathology Unit, Walter and Eliza Hall Institute of Medical Research, since 1966; *b* 2 April 1931; French parents; *m* 1956, Margaret Denise Houen; one *d*. *Educ:* St Aloysius' Coll., Sydney. BSc (Med.) 1953, MB, BS 1955, Sydney; PhD 1960, DSc 1965, London. Sen. Scientist, Chester Beatty Res. Inst., London, 1960-66; Reader, Exper. Pathology, Univ. of London, 1965-66. For. Mem., Académie Royale de Médicine de Belgique, 1969. Langer-Teplitz Cancer Research Award (USA), 1965; Gairdner Foundn Award (Canada), 1966; Encyclopaedia Britannica (Australia) Award, 1966; Scientific Medal of Zoological Soc. of London, 1966. *Publications:* over 100 papers in scientific jls and several chapters in books, mainly dealing with thymus and immunity. *Recreations:* music, photography. *Address:* Walter and Eliza Hall Institute of Medical Research, Royal Melbourne Hospital PO, Parkville, Victoria 3050, Australia. *T:* 347-1511.

**MILLER, Sir James,** GBE 1965; Kt 1953; DL, JP; *b* 16 March 1905; *s* of James Miller, Architect, Edinburgh; *m* 1933, Ella Jane Stewart; two *s* one *d* (and one *s* decd). *Educ:* George Heriot's Sch., Edinburgh. Trained as Architect, thereafter Man. Dir James Miller & Partners Ltd, Building & Civil Engineering Contractors, Edinburgh, London and Wakefield. Edinburgh Town Council, Nov. 1936-54; Lord Provost of the City of Edinburgh, May 1951-54; Sheriff, City of London, 1956; Alderman of Bishopsgate, 1957; Lord Mayor of London, 1964-65. DL

Edinburgh, 1955. Master of the Worshipful Company of Coachmakers and Coach Harness Makers, 1964-. Hon. LLD; Hon. DSc, City Univ., 1966. KStJ. *Recreations:* yachting, golf, etc. *Address:* Belmont, Ellersly Road, Edinburgh. *T:* 031-337 1822; 1 Queen's Gate, Kensington, SW7. *T:* 01-584 6980. *Clubs:* Royal Automobile, City Livery; Scottish Conservative, Royal Forth Yacht (Edinburgh).

**MILLER, James,** RSA 1964; RSW 1934; Artist, Painter; *b* 25 Oct. 1893; *s* of William Miller and Margaret Palmer; *m* 1934, Mary MacNeill, MA; no *c. Educ:* Woodside Sch.; Sch. of Art, Glasgow. Teaching, 1917-47. Commissioned by Artists' Adv. Coun. of Min. of Information to make drawings of buildings damaged by enemy action in Scotland, 1939-41; travelled extensively in Spain looking at buildings and making drawings; made drawings for Pilgrim Trust, 1942. Paintings have been bought by Bradford, Newport, Glasgow, Dundee, Hertford, Paisley, Nat. Gall. of S Australia, Melbourne, Arts Coun., Aberdeen, Dumbarton, Perth and Muirhead Bequest, Edinburgh. Has held several one-man shows in Glasgow. *Recreations:* listening to gramophone records, reading. *Address:* Tigh-na-bruaich, Dunvegan, Isle of Skye. *Club:* Art (Glasgow).

**MILLER, Bt Col Sir James (MacBride),** Kt 1958; MC; TD; DL; *b* 18 June 1896; *s* of Rev. John Miller, Eyemouth, Berwickshire; *m* 1925, Jane Elizabeth Simson Elliot, *d* of Francis Elliot, Middlestots, Duns, Berwickshire. *Educ:* Berwickshire; George Watson's Coll., Edinburgh. Royal Artillery, TA, 1915-36. Convener, Berwickshire County Council, 1949-61; President of the Association of County Councils of Scotland, 1956-58. DL Berwickshire, 1948. Hon. Sheriff Substitute, Duns. *Address:* Duneaton, West Bay Road, North Berwick. *Club:* New (Edinburgh).

**MILLER, John,** RSA 1966 (ARSA 1958); PRSW 1970; (RSW 1952); Lecturer (Drawing and Painting), Glasgow School of Art, since 1944; *b* 21 March 1911; *s* of John Miller; *m* 1954, Barbara Neilson Brodie, BArch (Strathclyde); two *s* one *d. Educ:* Glasgow Sch. of Art (Dipl. and Post-Dipl.); Hospitalfield Art Coll., Arbroath. Exhibited at: Royal Acad.; Royal Scottish Acad.; Soc. of Scottish Artists; Royal Glasgow Inst.; Royal Scottish Society of Painters in Water Colours. Work in Permanent Collections: Glasgow Art Galls; Dundee Art Gall.; Paisley Art Gall.; Newport Art Gall.; Arts Coun.; Corp. of Edinburgh (Watson Bequest). *Recreation:* walking. *Address:* 15 Ardenconnel Way, Rhu, Dunbartonshire. *T:* Rhu 326. *Club:* Art (Glasgow).

**MILLER, Lt-Comdr John Bryan Peter Duppa-,** GC and King's Commendation 1941; *b* 22 May 1903; *er s* of Brian Stothert Miller, JP, Posbury Devon, and Mary (*née* Sadler); *m* 1st, 1926, Barbara, *d* of Stanley Owen, 1st Viscount Buckmaster, GCVO; three *s*; 2nd, 1944, Clare, *d* of Francis Egerton Harding, JP, Old Springs, Market Drayton. *Educ:* Rugby Sch.; Hertford Coll., Oxford. Dep. County Educn Officer, Hants, 1930-35; Asst Sec., Northants Educn Cttee, 1936-39; Torpedo and Mining Dept, Admty, 1940-45; a Dep. Dir-Gen., Trade and Econs Div., Control Commn for Germany, 1945; Inspector-Gen., Min. of Educn, Addis Ababa, 1945-47; Educn Dept, Kenya, 1947-57; Chm. of European Civil Servants' Assoc., and formation Chm. Staff Side, Central Whitley Coun. for Civil Service; Sec. to Kenya Coffee Marketing Bd, 1960-61; Sec. to Tanganyika Coffee Bd, 1961-62; Asst Sec. and Marketing Officer, Min. of Lands and Settlement, Kenya, 1963-65. *Publication:* Saints and Parachutes, 1951. *Recreations:* yachting, economics. *Address:* c/o Standard Bank, Adderley Street, Cape Town, South Africa. *Club:* Reform.

**MILLER, Prof. J(ohn) D(onald) Bruce;** Professor of International Relations, Research School of Pacific Studies, Australian National University, since 1962; *b* 30 Aug. 1922; *s* of Donald and Marion Miller, Sydney, Australia; *m* 1st, Enid Joyce Huthnance; one *s*; 2nd, Margaret Martin (*née* MacLachlan); one *s. Educ:* Sydney High Sch.; University of Sydney. BEc, 1944; MEc 1951. Announcer and Talks Officer, Australian Broadcasting Commission, Sydney and Canberra, 1939-46; Staff Tutor, Department of Tutorial Classes, University of Sydney, 1946-54; Asst Lecturer in Political Science and International Relations, London Sch. of Economics, 1953-55; Lecturer in Politics, University Coll., Leicester, 1955-57; Prof. of Politics, University of Leicester, 1957-62; Dean of Social Sciences, 1960-62; Public Orator, 1961-62. Visiting Professor: Indian Sch. of International Studies, 1959; Columbia Univ., New York, 1962, 1966; Macrossan Lectr, University of Queensland, 1966. Joint Editor, Journal of Commonwealth Political Studies, 1961-62; Editor, Australian Outlook, 1963-69. *Publications:* Australian Government and Politics, 1954; Richard Jebb and the Problem of Empire, 1956; Politicians (inaugural), 1958; The Commonwealth in the World, 1958; The Nature of Politics, 1962; The Shape of Diplomacy (inaugural), 1963; Australia and Foreign Policy (Boyer Lectures), 1963; The Distintegrating Monolith (ed. with T. H. Rigby), 1965; Britain and the Old Dominions, 1966; Australia, 1966; The Politics of the Third World, 1966; (Ed.) India, Japan, Australia: Partners in Asia?, 1968. *Recreations:* books, garden, dachshund. *Address:* 16 Hutt Street, Yarralumla, ACT 2600, Australia. *T:* Canberra 813138. *Club:* Commonwealth (Canberra).

**MILLER, John Duncan,** CMG 1968; Representative in Continental Europe for Baring Brothers & Co. Ltd since 1968; *b* 6 April 1902; *e s* of late Hubert James Miller and Elsa Mary (*née* Collmann), Old Court House, Knutsford; *m* 1926, Leila Madeline, *o d* of late Gen. Sir John Asser, KCB, KCMG, KCVO; one *s. Educ:* Wellington Coll.; Trinity Hall, Cambridge. Served War of 1939-45: War Office, 1940-41; British Army Staff, Washington, 1941-43; HQ 11th Army Gp and Allied Land Forces, SE Asia, 1943-45. Dir, British Information Services, Middle West of USA, 1945-47; Washington Corresp. of The Times and The Economist, 1947-54; Special Representative in Europe of Internat. Bank for Reconstruction and Develt, 1955-68. Order of Legion of Merit (US), 1946. *Publication:* Who's Who in the Wars, 1940. *Recreations:* music, sea and Sardinia. *Address:* 101 rue de la Faisanderie, Paris 16e, France. *T:* Paris 870-9119; Capriccioli, Porto Cervo, Costa Smeralda, Sardinia, Italy. *Club:* Reform.

**MILLER, Sir John Francis C.;** *see* Compton Miller.

**MILLER, Sir John Holmes,** 11th Bt *cr* 1705, of Chichester, Sussex; *b* 1925; *er s* of 10th Bt and of Netta Mahalah Bennett; *S* father 1960; *m* 1950, Jocelyn Robson Edwards, Wairoa, NZ; two *d. Heir: b* Harry Holmes Miller [*b* 1927; *m* 1954, Gwynedd Margaret Sheriff; one *s* two *d*]. *Address:* Te Whare, Kohinui, Pahiatua, NZ.

**MILLER, Lt-Col John Mansel,** CVO 1966; DSO 1944; MC 1944; Crown Equerry since 1961; *b* 4 Feb. 1919; 3rd *s* of Brig.-Gen. Alfred Douglas Miller, CBE, DSO, DL, JP, Royal Scots Greys, and of Ella Geraldine Fletcher, Saltoun, E Lothian. *Educ:* Eton; RMA, Sandhurst. 2nd Lieut Welsh Guards, 1939; Adjt 1942-44; ADC to F-M Lord Wilson, Washington, DC, 1945-47; Regtl Adjt, 1953-56; Brigade Major 1st Guards Brigade, 1956-58; comd 1st Bn Welsh Guards, 1958-61. *Recreations:* hunting, shooting, polo, driving. *Address:* Shotover House, Wheatley, Oxon. *T:* Wheatley 450; The Crown Equerry's House, Buckingham Palace, SW1. *T:* 01-930 4832. *Clubs:* Guards, Pratt's, Buck's, White's.

**MILLER, Dr Jonathan Wolfe;** Research Fellow in the History of Medicine, University College, London, since 1970; *b* 21 July 1934; *s* of late Emanuel Miller, DPM, FRCP; *m* 1956, Helen Rachel Collet; two *s* one *d*. *Educ:* St Paul's Sch.; St John's Coll., Cambridge. MB, BCh 1959. Co-author and appeared in Beyond the Fringe, 1961-64; Ed. BBC Monitor, 1965; directed films for BBC TV (incl. Alice in Wonderland), 1966; stage directing in London and New York, 1965-67; directed: School for Scandal, Nottingham Playhouse, 1968; The Seagull, Nottingham Playhouse, 1969; King Lear, National Theatre, 1970; The Merchant of Venice, Old Vic, 1970; The Tempest, Mermaid, 1970; Hamlet, Arts Theatre, Cambridge, 1970. *Recreation:* deep sleep. *Address:* 63 Gloucester Crescent, NW1. *T:* 01-485 6973.

**MILLER, Karl Fergus Connor;** Editor of the Listener since 1967; *b* 2 Aug. 1931; *s* of William and Marion Miller; *m* 1956, Jane Elisabeth Collet; two *s* one *d*. *Educ:* Royal High School, Edinburgh; Downing Coll., Cambridge. Asst Prin., HM Treasury, 1956-57; BBC TV Producer, 1957-58; Literary Editor, Spectator, 1958-61; Literary Editor, New Statesman, 1961-67. *Publications:* (ed) Poetry from Cambridge, 1952-54, 1955; (ed, with introd.) Writing in England Today: The Last Fifteen Years, 1968; (ed) Memoirs of a Modern Scotland, 1970. *Recreation:* football. *Address:* 26 Limerston Street, SW10. *T:* 01-352 1735.

**MILLER, Dame Mabel,** DBE 1967; LLB; JP; Barrister: Australian Representative to Status of Women Commission, United Nations, since 1967; *b* Broken Hill, NSW; *d* of J. C. Goodhart, Victor Harbour, S Australia; *m* 1930, Alan Miller; one *d*. *Educ:* Girton House, Adelaide; University of Adelaide. Joined WAAAF, 1941; Dep. Dir, WAAAF, 1942-43 (Sqdn Officer); Staff Officer, WAAAF, North Eastern Area, 1944. Alderman, Hobart, 1952- (Dep. Lord Mayor, 1954-56, 1964-66, 1966-68); MHA for Franklin, Tasmania, 1955-64. Foundn Mem., Tasmanian Women's Air Trng Corps (Women's Vol. Auxiliary); Member Committee: Queen Alexandra Hospital Country Women's Assoc.; Red Cross; Girl Guides; Past Pres., Nat. Coun. of Women. *Recreations:* golf, reading. *Address:* 403 Sandy Bay Road, Hobart, Tasmania. *T:* 52084. *Clubs:* Queen Mary, Air Force, Royal Automobile, Business and Professional Women's, (Assoc. Mem.) Naval, Military and Air Force (Hobart); Lyceum (Melbourne).

**MILLER of Glenlee, Sir Macdonald;** *see* Miller of Glenlee, Sir F. W. M.

**MILLER, Maurice Solomon,** MB; MP (Lab) Kelvingrove Division of Glasgow since 1964; *b* 16 Aug. 1920; *s* of David Miller; *m* 1944, Renée, *d* of Joseph Modlin, Glasgow; two *s* two *d*. *Educ:* Shawlands Academy, Glasgow; Glasgow University. MB, ChB 1944. Mem. of Glasgow Corporation since 1950; Bailie of Glasgow, 1954-57; JP Glasgow, 1957. Asst Govt Whip, 1968-69. Medical Adviser in the Port of Glasgow to the British and Commonwealth Shipping Company Ltd. Visited Russia as mem. of medical delegation, 1955. *Publication:* Window on Russia, 1956. *Address:* 82 Springkell Avenue, Glasgow S1.

**MILLER, Rev. Norman,** MA; *s* of late E. Banbury Miller, Bristol; *m* 1942, Annette Daukes, *e d* of late Rt Rev. F. W. Daukes, sometime Bishop of Plymouth; two *s*. *Educ:* Clifton Coll.; Queen's Coll., Cambridge (Schol.); University Stewart of Rannoch Schol. for Classics. Sixth Form Master, Berkhamsted Sch.; ordained, 1914; Asst Master in Haileybury Coll.; House-Master, 1919-26; Headmaster of Kelly Coll., Tavistock, 1926-38; Vicar of St Albans, Bristol, 1939-51; Rector of Swanage, Dorset, 1951-61. *Address:* Barn Cottage, Quenington, Glos.

**MILLER, Sir (Oswald) Bernard,** Kt 1967; Chairman, John Lewis Partnership, since 1955; *b* 25 March 1904; *s* of late Arthur Miller and of Margaret Jane Miller; *m* 1931, Jessica Rose Marie ffoulkes; three *s*. *Educ:* Sloane Sch.; Jesus Coll., Oxford (Hon. Fellow, 1968); Stanhope Prize, 1925; BA 1927; MA 1930. Joined John Lewis Partnership, 1927; Dir, 1935. Chm., Retail Distributors Assoc., 1953; Member: Council of Industrial Design, 1957-66; Monopolies Commission, 1961-69; EDC for Distributive Trades, 1964-. *Publication:* Biography of Robert Harley, Earl of Oxford, 1927. *Recreations:* fishing, gardening, opera and theatre. *Address:* The Field House, Longstock, Stockbridge, Hants. *T:* Stockbridge 627. *Club:* Garrick.

**MILLER, Rev. Peter Watters,** MA, BD, DD (Edinburgh); Professor of Old Testament Language and Literature, Free Church College, Edinburgh, 1936-66, Principal, 1945-66, Principal Emeritus since 1966; *b* 10 May 1890; *s* of Donald Miller and Christina Watters; *m* 1918, Annie Smith (*d* 1961). *Educ:* Castletown Sch., Caithness; Edinburgh Univ.; Free Church Coll., Edinburgh. Ordained in 1915 and settled as Minister of Free Church in Campbeltown, Argyllshire; served abroad during European War for two years as a Chaplain to the Forces in France and Germany; Minister of Partick Congregation of Free Church of Scotland, 1923-36; Lecturer in Religious Instruction in the Teachers' Training Centre at Jordanhill, Glasgow, 1931-36; Moderator of General Assembly of Free Church, 1936. *Address:* 69 Arden Street, Edinburgh EH9 1BT.

**MILLER, Sir Richard Hope,** Kt 1955; Regional Secretary of the Empire Rheumatism Council, for the North West, since 1961; Hon. Secretary, Manchester and District Branch, Institute of Directors, since 1966; *b* 26 July 1904; 2nd *s* of late Hubert James Miller, The Old Court House, Knutsford, Cheshire, and of Elsa Mary Colimann; unmarried. *Educ:* Wellington Coll.; Trinity Hall, Cambridge. BA 1925; MA 1930. Served War of 1939-46: commissioned in 7th Bn (TA) The Manchester Regt; Adjutant 1941; Major 1945; served in Staff appointments (Britain, Ceylon, and Singapore), 1942-46. From 1926 has held offices in Conservative Party, including: Chm. Knutsford Div. Conservative Assoc., 1952-57. *Recreations:* ski-ing and tennis. *Address:* West Court, Knutsford, Cheshire. *T:* Knutsford 3422; Lloyds Bank Ltd, Cox's & King's Branch, 6 Pall Mall, SW1; District Bank Ltd,

Knutsford, Cheshire. *Club:* Oxford and Cambridge.

**MILLER, Robert Sydney;** Puisne Judge, British Guiana, 1959-63, retired; Judge Advocate, Guyana Defence Force; Member: Judicial Service Commission; Income Tax Board of Review; *b* 23 April 1901; *o s* of late Dr Robert Sydney Miller, British Guiana Medical Service, and Alice Matilda Miller (*née* Dodson); *m* 1942, Kathleen Elaine (*née* Fraser); one *s* one *d*. *Educ:* Queen's Coll., British Guiana; Weybridge Grammar Sch.; Skerry's Coll.; Jesus Coll., Oxford University. Called to Bar, Inner Temple. Practised at the Bar, British Guiana; Magistrate, British Guiana, 1944; acted Crown Counsel, 1949-50; acted Registrar of Supreme Court and of Deeds, 1953; Coronation Medal, 1953; Senior Magistrate, 1956; acted Puisne Judge, 1955-59. Chm., Adv. Cttee on Treatment of Offenders; held public inquiry into accidents to Cessna aircraft, 1967; Arbitrator (Guyana Mine Workers Union and Reynolds (Guyana) Mines Ltd), 1968. National Insurance Commissioner. *Recreations:* walking and reading. *Address:* A54, Amakura Place East, Bel Air Park, Georgetown, Guyana. *T:* 62515. *Clubs:* West Indian, Corona; Guyana Defence Force Officers.

**MILLER, Sir Roderick (William),** Kt 1970; CBE 1962; Chairman and Managing Director, R. W. Miller (Holdings) Ltd and associated companies since 1958; *b* 12 Nov. 1911; *s* of R. W. Miller, Queensferry, Scotland; *m* 1957, Elizabeth, *d* of C. E. Barberie; two *s* two *d*. *Educ:* Scots Coll., Sydney. Sales Manager, R. W. Miller & Co., 1931, Director from 1931. Served 1940-45, Gunner 2/1st Aust. AA Regt; Lieut 1942; Captain 1945. *Recreations:* golf, boating, fishing, swimming; formerly prominent in GPS football, rowing, athletics, rep. NSW in Rugby Union. *Address:* 9 Hillside Avenue, Vaucluse, NSW 2030, Australia. *T:* (office) 27-4361. *Clubs:* Royal Automobile of Australia, Tattersalls, Victoria (Melbourne); Royal Motor Yacht; Manly Golf; Sydney Turf; Australian Jockey.

**MILLER, Prof. Ronald,** MA, PhD, FRSE, FRSGS; Professor of Geography, Glasgow University, since 1953; Dean of the Faculty of Science, 1964-67; *b* 21 Aug. 1910; *o c* of John Robert Miller and late Georgina Park; *m* 1940, Constance Mary Phillips, SRN, SCM; one *s* one *d*. *Educ:* North Queensferry; Stromness Acad.; Edinburgh Univ. Silver Medal, Royal Scottish Geographical Soc.; MA 1st cl Hons Geog., 1931; Carnegie Research Fellowship at Marine Laboratory of Scottish Home Dept, Aberdeen, 1931-33; PhD 1933; Asst Lecturer Manchester Univ., 1933-36; Education Officer, Nigeria, 1936-46; Royal West African Frontier Force, 1939-44; Lecturer, Edinburgh Univ., 1947-53; Guest Lecturer: University of Montpellier, 1957; University of Oslo and Handelshøyskole Bergen, 1966; Simon Fraser Univ., 1967. Hon. Editor, Scottish Geographical Magazine; Chm., Glasgow Centre, RSGS. Member: Livingstone Trust; Bd of Governors, Notre Dame Coll. of Education; National Cttee for Geography; Nature Conservancy, Scotland. *Publications:* (with MacNair) Livingstone's Travels; The Travels of Mungo Park; (with Tivy) ed. The Glasgow Region, 1958; (with Watson) Ogilvie Essays, 1959; Africa, 1967; papers on geographical topics in journals. *Address:* 583 Anniesland Road, Glasgow, W3. *T:* 041-959 3424.

**MILLER, Comdr Ronald S.;** *see* Scott-Miller.

**MILLER, Sir Stanley N.;** *see* Norie-Miller.

**MILLER, Stephen James Hamilton,** MD, FRCS; Surgeon-Oculist to HM Household since 1965; Ophthalmic Surgeon: St George's Hospital since 1951; National Hospital, Queen Square, since 1955; King Edward VII Hospital for Officers, since 1965; Surgeon, Moorfields Eye Hospital, since 1954; Recognised Teacher in Ophthalmology, St George's Medical School and Institute of Ophthalmology, University of London; *b* 19 July 1915; *e s* of late Stephen Charles Miller and Isobel Hamilton; *m* 1949, Heather P. Motion; three *s*. *Educ:* Arbroath High Sch.; Aberdeen Univ. House Physician and Surgeon, Royal Infirmary, Hull, 1937-39. Surgeon Lieut-Comdr RNVR, 1939-46 (Naval Ophthalmic Specialist, RN Aux. Hosp., Kilmacolm and RN Hosp., Malta). Resident Surgical Officer, Glasgow Eye Infirmary, 1946; Registrar and Chief Clinical Asst, Moorfields Eye Hosp., 1947-50; Registrar St George's Hosp., 1949-51; Research Associate, Institute of Ophthalmology, 1949-. FRSocMed; Fellow Faculty of Ophthalmology; Member: Editorial Bd, British Journal of Ophthalmology and of Ophthalmic Literature; Ophthalmological Soc. of UK; Oxford Ophthalmological Congress (Master, 1969-70); Examiner in Ophthalmology for Royal Colls and Brit. Orthoptic Bd. CStJ (Deputy Hospitaller). *Publications:* articles in BMJ, Brit. Jl of Ophthalmology, Ophthalmic Literature. *Recreation:* sailing, music, golf. *Address:* 149 Harley Street, W1. *T:* 01-935 4444. *Club:* Garrick.

**MILLER, Prof. Terence George,** TD 1960; Visiting Professor, University of Reading; *b* 16 Jan. 1918; *o s* of late George Frederick Miller, Cambridge, and late Marion Johnston, Port William, Wigtownshire; *m* 1944, Inga Catriona, 3rd *d* of Austin Priestman, MD, Folkestone, Kent; one *s* three *d*. *Educ:* Perse (foundn schol.); Jesus Coll., Cambridge (schol.). Wiltshire Prizeman, 1939. Served War of 1939-45: RA, Special Forces, Glider Pilot Regt. Harkness Scholar, 1948; Research Fellow, Jesus Coll., 1949-54. University Demonstrator, 1948; Lectr in Geology, University of Keele, 1953; Sen. Lectr, 1963. Lt-Col RE (AER), 1964. Prof. of Geography, University of Reading, 1965-67; Principal, University Coll. of Rhodesia, 1967-69. *Publications:* Geology, 1950; Geology and Scenery in Britain, 1953; scientific papers in various jls. *Recreations:* studies in military history and geography; camping, sailing, walking, upsetting establishments. *Address:* 36 Blenheim Gardens, Reading, Berks.

**MILLER, William Christopher;** retired as Director of Equine Research Station of the Animal Health Trust, Newmarket (1946-66); Courtauld Professor of Animal Husbandry, Royal Veterinary College, 1935-46; *b* 19 May 1898; *s* of late William Warden Miller and Annie Riddle Bell; *m* 1926, Margaret Alice Munro; two *s*. *Educ:* Colchester Royal Grammar School; Royal (Dick) Veterinary College, Edinburgh. Mem., Royal College of Veterinary Surgeons, 1919; Lecturer, Zootechny and Animal Management, Royal (Dick) Veterinary College, 1919; Lecturer, Veterinary Hygiene, Edinburgh and East of Scotland Coll. of Agriculture, 1920; University Lecturer and Research Asst, Institute of Animal Genetics, University of Edinburgh, 1928; Fellow Royal Society of Edinburgh, 1929; Pres. Nat. Vet. Med. Assoc., 1944-45; Steele Memorial Gold Medal, 1956; Victory Gold Medal, Central Vet. Soc., 1958; awarded Fellowship of RCVS, by election, 1964. Hon. Mem. RSM, 1967. *Publications:* Parasites of British Sheep; Editor–Black's Veterinary Dictionary (with West); Practical

Animal Husbandry (with Robertson); Care and Management of Horses on Thoroughbred Studs, 1964; Feeding of Ponies, 1966. Articles and papers in Veterinary Record; Veterinary Jl, Jl of Agricultural Science; The British Racehorse; Empire Jl of Experimental Agriculture; Jl of Textile Institute; Proceedings of Royal Society; Proceedings of Royal Society Medicine; Animal Health; Handbuch der Tierzüchtung, etc. *Recreations:* fishing, shooting. *Address:* The Cottage, Whitchurch, Hants. *T:* Whitchurch (Hants) 2468. *Club:* Farmers'.

**MILLER, Comdr William Ronald;** Royal Navy (retired); Clerk to the Worshipful Company of Haberdashers since 1966; *b* 6 Dec. 1918; *y s* of Col Joseph Sidney Miller, DSO and Florence Eva Drabble; *m* 1942, Betty Claelia Otto, Richmond, Natal; one *d. Educ:* Cranleigh Sch., Surrey. Entered RN, 1936. Sec. to Flag Officer (Submarines), 1955-57; Exec. Asst to Dep. Supreme Allied Comdr Atlantic (as Actg Capt.), 1958-60; Sec. to C-in-C Home Fleet (as Actg Capt.), 1960-62; Sec. to C-in-C Portsmouth (as Actg Capt.), 1963-65; retd from RN at own request, 1966. Called to Bar, Lincoln's Inn, 1958. Liveryman, Haberdashers' Co., 1969. *Recreations:* golf, tennis, gardening. *Address:* Dolphin House, Pewley Hill, Guildford, Surrey. *T:* Guildford 60846. *Club:* Naval.

**MILLER JONES, Keith;** Chairman, Board of Governors of the National Hospitals for Nervous Diseases since 1963; Member, Board of Governors of the Hospital for Sick Children; Solicitor; *b* 7 April 1899; *o s* of late Frank W. Jones, Headingley, Leeds; *m* 1950, Hon. Betty Ellen Askwith, *qv, o d* of late Baron Askwith, KCB, KC, LLD. *Educ:* privately; New Coll., Oxford (Hon. Exhibr); Leeds Univ. Admitted Solicitor, 1925; Mem., firm of Braby & Waller, 1925-62. Mem., Paddington Group HMC, 1948-60; Dep. Chm., Georgian Group; Founder Mem., Hansard Soc. for Parly Govt, 1944 (Mem. Coun.); Founder Mem., Wildfowl Trust, 1946 (Mem. Coun., 1946-67). *Recreations:* music, golf. *Address:* 8 Egerton Terrace, SW3. *T:* 01-589 7126. *Clubs:* Brooks's; Richmond Golf.

**MILLER PARKER, Agnes;** *see* Parker, A. M.

**MILLES-LADE,** family name of **Earl Sondes.**

**MILLIGAN, Rt. Hon. Lord; Rt. Hon. William Rankine Milligan,** PC 1955; Senator of College of Justice in Scotland since 1960; *b* 12 Dec. 1898; *er s* of late Very Rev. George Milligan, DD, Glasgow; *m* 1925, Muriel Jean, *er d* of late James MacLehose, LLD; one *s* three *d. Educ:* Sherborne; University Coll., Oxford; University of Glasgow. Served HLI 1917-19; represented Oxford in the Inter-University sports, 1920-23; Pres. OUAC 1923; represented Scotland against England and Ireland 1920; admitted to Faculty of Advocates, 1925; QC Scot. 1945; Solicitor-Gen. for Scotland, 1951-54; Lord Advocate, Dec. 1954-March 1960; MP (C) Edinburgh North, 1955-60. Pres., Scottish Amateur Athletic Assoc., 1936; Mem. Queen's Bodyguard for Scotland (Royal Company of Archers); Chm. of Cttee Edinburgh and East of Scotland Branch of Overseas League, 1938-46; Hon. President: Scottish Amateur Athletic Assoc.; Atalanta Club. *Recreations:* gardening, golf, fishing. *Address:* 38 India Street, Edinburgh. *T:* 031-225 4937. *Clubs:* New (Edinburgh); Western (Glasgow).

*See also A. D. Walder.*

**MILLIGAN, Patrick Ward;** Chairman, Sedgwick Collins (Holdings) Ltd; *b* 27 May 1910; 2nd *s* of James Knowles Milligan, MRCS, LRCP and Arabella Milligan; *m* 1934, Betty Mavis, *yr d* of Frank Rogerson; one *s* one *d. Educ:* Winchester Coll. Joined Lloyd's, 1928; underwriting mem., 1932. Served War of 1939-45, Queen's Royal Regiment; AQMG, BTE, 1945, Lt-Col. Member: Cttee Non Marine Assoc., Lloyd's, 1949-62 (Chm., 1958); Cttee of Lloyd's, 1954-57 and 1959-62; Dep. Chm. of Lloyd's, 1957, 1960, Chm., 1962; Chm., Lloyd's Brokers' Assoc., 1967. Chm. Transport Users Consultative Cttee (SE Area), 1966-. *Recreations:* golf, cricket. *Address:* Orchard Cottage, Crastock, near Woking, Surrey. *T:* Worplesdon 2025. *Club:* Gresham.

**MILLIGAN, Terence Alan;** actor; author; *b* 16 April 1918; *s* of late Leo Alphonso Milligan, IA, and of Florence Winifred Milligan; *m*; one *s* three *d. Educ:* Convent of Jesus and Mary, Poona; Brothers de La Salle, Rangoon; SE London Polytechnic, Lewisham. Appearances (comedy) as Spike Milligan: stage: The Bed-Sitting Room; Son of Oblomov; BBC (Sound) Goon Show; TV: Show called Fred, ITV; World of Beachcomber, BBC; Q5, BBC. TV Writer of the Year Award, 1956. *Publications:* Silly Verse for Kids; Dustbin of Milligan; The Little Pot Boiler; Puckoon; A Book of Bits; The Bed-Sitting Room (play); The Bald Twit Lion. *Recreations:* restoration of antiques, oil painting, water colours, gardening, eating, drinking, talking, wine, jazz. *Address:* 9 Orme Court, W2. *T:* 01-727 1544.

**MILLIGAN, Rt. Hon. William Rankine;** *see* Milligan, Rt. Hon. Lord.

**MILLIGAN, Wyndham Macbeth Moir,** MBE 1945; TD 1947; Principal of Wolsey Hall, Oxford, since 1968; *b* 21 Dec. 1907; *s* of Dr W. Anstruther Milligan, MD, London, W1; *m* 1941, Helen Penelope Eirene Cassavetti, London, W1; three *s* two *d. Educ:* Sherborne; Caius Coll., Cambridge. Asst Master, Eton Coll., 1932-, House Master, Eton Coll., 1946; Warden, Radley Coll., 1954-68. Served 1939-45, with Scots Guards, in NW Europe (Major). Chm., N Berks Area Youth Cttee. Governor: St Mary's, Wantage (Chm.); Reed's Sch., Cobham; Member: Berkshire Deanery Synod; Administrative Council, King George's Jubilee Trust. FRSA 1968. *Recreation:* gardening. *Address:* South Lodge, Pusey, by Faringdon, Berks. *Club:* Bath.

**MILLING, Air Vice-Marshal Denis C.;** *see* Crowley-Milling.

**MILLING, Geoffrey;** Chairman, Bowring Steamship Company, 1965-68; Deputy Chairman, Lloyd's Register of Shipping; *b* 1 Sept. 1901; *s* of Henry Milling, Warrington, Lancs; *m* 1928, Dorothy Gordon Baird, St John's, Newfoundland; one *s* one *d. Educ:* Radley; Merton Coll., Oxford (MA). In USA, 1923, as Sec. to Sir Wilfred Grenfell; joined Lever Brothers, England, 1924; Hudson's Bay Co., 1926 (2 years in Baffin Land, as Manager of trading post, etc.); Bowring Brothers Ltd, St John's, 1935-48, returning to parent firm, London, 1948. Chm., Royal Alfred Merchant Seamen's Soc., 1951-59; Chm., London General Shipowners' Soc., 1959-60; Mem. Port of London Authority, 1959-67. *Recreation:* golf. *Address:* 11a Porchester Terrace, W2. *T:* 01-262 6927. *Clubs:* Leander; Swinley Forest Golf.

**MILLING, Peter Francis,** MB, BChir, FRCS; Surgeon, Ear, Nose and Throat Department, University College Hospital; Surgeon in charge, Throat and Ear Department, Brompton Hospital; Consultant Ear, Nose and Throat Surgeon: Epsom District Hospital; Oxted and Limpsfield Cottage Hospital; Visiting Laryngologist Benenden Chest Hospital. *Educ:* Cambridge University. BA Hons, 1937; MRCS, LRCP, 1940; MA, MB, BChir, 1941; FRCS, 1946. Formerly Chief Assistant, Ear, Nose and Throat Department, St Thomas's Hospital; Chief Clinical Assistant and Registrar, Ear, Nose and Throat Department, Guy's Hosp.; Surgical Registrar, Ear, Nose and Throat Dept, Royal Cancer Hospital. Member British Association of Otolaryngologists. FRSocMed. *Publications:* contributions to medical text-books and journals. *Address:* 84 Harley Street, W1. *T:* 01-580 2506; Oaklands, The Ridge, Woldingham, Surrey. *T:* 2197.

**MILLINGTON, Air Commodore Edward Geoffrey Lyall,** CB 1966; CBE 1946; DFC 1943; Air Commander, Zambia Air Force; *b* 7 Jan. 1914; *s* of late Edward Turner Millington, Ceylon CS; *m* 1st, 1939, Mary Bonynge (marr. diss. 1956), *d* of W. Heaton Smith, FRCS; 2nd, 1956, Anne Elizabeth, *d* of Robert Brennan. *Educ:* Nautical Coll., Pangbourne. Served Cameron Highlanders, Palestine, 1936 (despatches); War of 1939-45, RAF, in N Africa, Sicily, Italy (actg Gp Capt.; despatches); Air Cdre, 1960; Comdr, RAF Persian Gulf, 1964-66. psc; idc; Order Mil. Valour (Poland). *Address:* c/o Glyn Mills & Co., Holt's Branch, 22 Whitehall, SW1. *Club:* Royal Air Force.

**MILLINGTON, Wing Comdr Ernest Rogers,** DFC 1945; Adviser in Secondary Curriculum, London Borough of Newham, since 1967; *b* 15 Feb. 1916; *s* of Edmund Rogers Millington and Emily Craggs; *m* 1937, Gwendolyn Dorothy Pickard; four *d. Educ:* Chigwell Sch., Essex; College of S Mark and S John, Chelsea; Birkbeck Coll., London Univ. Clerk; Accountant; Company Sec.; served War of 1939-45, soldier, gunner officer, pilot RAF, instructor and heavy bomber, CO of a Lancaster Sqdn. MP (Commonwealth) for Chelmsford, 1945-50. Re-joined Royal Air Force, 1954-57. Head of Social Educn, Shoreditch Comprehensive Sch., London, 1965-67. *Recreations:* mainly talking; cultivating grandsons; educational research; social curiosity. *Address:* 9 St Johns Park, Blackheath, SE3. *T:* 01-858 0191.

**MILLINGTON-DRAKE, Sir Eugen (John Henry Vanderstegen),** KCMG 1942 (CMG 1938); Vice-President: Hispanic Council, since 1948; Anglo-Spanish Society, since 1953; Poetry Society, since 1942; Member, Comité d'Honneur, since 1955, and Council, since 1950, Fédération Britannique de l'Alliance Française; *b* 26 Feb. 1889; *o s* of late Henry Millington-Drake; *m* 1920, Lady Effie Mackay, 4th *d* of 1st Earl of Inchcape; two *s* one *d* (and one *d* decd). *Educ:* Eton; Magdalen Coll., Oxford (MA, Hons in Hist.); Berlin Univ. HM Diplomatic Service, 1912; St Petersburg, 1913; Buenos Aires, 1915; Paris (Peace Delegation, 1919, and Embassy, 1920); First Sec. and at times Chargé d'Affaires at Bucharest, 1921-24; at Brussels, 1924-27; at Copenhagen, 1927-28; Counsellor of Embassy, Buenos Aires, 1929-33; Minister to Uruguay, 1934-41. Hon. Pres. Uruguayan Delegation to Olympic Games, 1936; Special Ambassador for inauguration of new President of Uruguayan Republic, 1938; Founding Pres. Friends of Uruguay Soc., 1940; seconded from FO as Chief Representative of British Council in Spanish America, 1942-46. Rep. Oxford, Cambridge and London Univs, at Centenary of University of Santiago de Chile, 1942. Hon. Dr Catholic Univ. of Chile, 1943; Hon. Dr Univ. of Buenos Aires and Hon. Prof. Univ. of Montevideo, 1946. Hon. Citizen of Montevideo. Founder, Hudson Institute, 1947; Chm. Reception Cttee of XIV Olympiad, London, 1948; represented Hispanic Council at San Martin Centenary, Boulogne, 1950; Vice-Pres. Council, Royal India, Pakistan and Ceylon Society for which visited the East on Cultural Missions, 1949-50 and 1960; Lecture tours of Africa, Madagascar, Mauritus and Reunion, representing various cultural and sports institutions, 1952 and 1953. Medal of Société des Poètes Français for services to French culture overseas, 1953. FRSA 1960. Liveryman of Grocers' Company. Donated Macnaghten War Memorial Library to Eton Coll., and instituted French Declamation Prize, 1938; also Latin-American Prizes at Eton and Harrow, 1947; founded Sir John O'Conor Memorial Scholarship for doctors of British Hospital, Buenos Aires, to study in Britain, 1946; Donor with Lady Effie of site of Royal Air Force Memorial on Coopers Hill by Runnymede. Presented: Leclerc Prize for Shooting for NATO Armies, 1950; Canning Prize for general knowledge of Latin America, open to teams of three from all Secondary Schs in the UK; Harwood Prize for Spanish at Dartmouth; Bourne Cup for public schs at Reading Head of River Regatta. *Publications:* Hugh Macnaghten's House Record, 1899-1920, 1932; Joyas de la Poesia Inglesa (Anthology of Spanish-American translations of English Poetry), 1941; Poesias de las Provincias que he conocido (Anthology of Poetry of Argentine Provinces), 1949; Walter Owen: Interpreter of Hispanic Epic Poetry to the English-Speaking World, 1954; A Round the World Goodwill Lecture Tour, 1961-62; The Drama of Graf Spee and the Battle of the Plate, 1964. *Recreations:* rowing, Eton VIII, 1905-08 (winners of Ladies Plate 1905); rowed in Magdalen Coll. crews head of river and winners of the Grand at Henley 1910, winners Oxford University Boat Club Fours, 1909-10, Oxford VIII 1911 (winners in then record time). Vice-Pres. National Amateur Rowing Assoc., 1950-55; Mem. Exec. Cttee Assoc. Internat. de Boxe Amateur, 1946-54; Rep. Uruguay on Fedn Internat. Socs d'Aviron and Internat. Lawn Tennis Assoc. *Address:* Palazzo Taverna, Via di Monte Giordano 36, Rome. *Clubs:* Garrick, Leander, All England Lawn Tennis, Internat. Lawn Tennis, Vincent's (Oxford).

**MILLIS, Charles Howard Goulden,** DSO 1918; OBE 1946; MC; *b* 1894; *e s* of C. T. Millis; *m* 1919, Violet, *o c* of late Herbert J. Gifford; one *s* one *d. Educ:* King's Coll. Sch.; Oxford, MA. Served European War, 1914-18 (despatches, DSO, MC and bar); served War of 1939-45 (OBE). Managing Director, Baring Brothers & Co. Ltd, 1933-55; Vice-Chm., BBC, 1937-45; Mem., Nat. Res. Develt Corp., 1955-65; Rhodes Trustee, 1948-61. *Address:* 22 Belvedere Grove, SW19.

**MILLIS, Leonard William Francis,** CBE 1970 (OBE 1948); JP; Secretary since 1939, subsequently Director, British Waterworks Association; *b* 1 Aug. 1908; *o s* of William John Millis and Jessie Millis, Hackney; *m* 1932, Ethel May, *o c* of John T. W. Willmott, Enfield; two *d* (and one *d* decd). *Educ:* Grocers' Company Sch., Hackney; London Sch. of Economics (BSc Econ). Called to Bar, Inner Temple, 1936; served with Metropolitan Water Board; Asst Sec., British Waterworks Assoc.; Sec.-Gen., Internat. Water Supply Assoc., 1947-; Chm., SW Suburban Water Co., 1956-; Thames Conservator, 1959-; Dir, Sutton District Water Co., 1965-; Sec., Public Works and Municipal Services Congress Council, 1965-; Vice-Pres. and Hon. Treas., Freshwater Biological Assoc.; Vice-Chm. of

Council, Water Research Assoc.; Mem. Court, Plumbers' Co.; Mem., Water Supply Industry Trng Board. Gen. Editor, Water Industry Jl; Editor, British Waterworks Year Book and Directory. Hon. MIWE 1966; Hon. Mem., Amer. Water Works Assoc., 1969. JP Mddx (Barnet Div.). *Publications:* contribs to scientific and technical papers, also other papers about water supply. *Recreations:* reading, gardening, sport. *Address:* Covenden, 17 Beech Hill, Hadley Wood, Barnet, Herts. *T:* 01-449 6164. *Club:* Lansdowne.

**MILLN, Rear-Adm. William Bryan Scott,** CB 1969; *b* 15 March 1915; *e s* of late Surg.-Captain James Duff Scott Milln; *m* 1944, Maureen Alice Gardner; four *d. Educ:* Mount House, Plymouth; RNC Dartmouth. RNEC, 1933-36 and 1942-44; RNC Greenwich, 1937-39; served in HMS: Royal Oak, 1932-33; Apollo, 1936-37; Birmingham, 1939-42; Tumult, 1944-46; Glory, 1952-54; Thunderer, 1954-57; Victorious, 1957-59; Engr-in-Chief's Dept, Admty, 1946-52; Staff of C-in-C Far East, 1959-61; Dep. Dir of Marine Engrg, 1961-64; Captain, HMS Thunderer, 1964-67; Asst Chief of Staff (Logistics), SHAPE, 1967-69, retired. Lt 1937; Lt-Comdr 1944; Comdr 1948; Captain 1959; Rear-Adm. 1967. FIMechE. *Recreations:* practically everything, now reduced to golf. *Address:* Burhill Golf Club, Walton-on-Thames, Surrey. *Club:* Army and Navy.

**MILLNER, Ralph;** QC 1965; *b* 25 Jan. 1912; *o s* of Ralph Millner, Merchant, Manchester; *m* 1st, 1935, Bruna, *d* of Arturo Rosa, Este, Italy (marriage dissolved, 1949); one *d* decd; 2nd, 1949, Monica, *d* of Prof. P. W. Robertson, Wellington, NZ; one *s* two *d. Educ:* William Hulme's Gram. Sch., Manchester; Clare Coll., Cambridge (MA). Called to English Bar, Inner Temple, 1934; Ghana Bar (Gold Coast), 1950; Sierra Leone Bar, 1957; Nigerian Bar, 1959; Guyana Bar (formerly British Guiana), 1961. Mem., Italian Institute. *Address:* 25 St Albans Road, NW5.

**MILLOTT, Prof. Norman;** Professor of Zoology, Bedford College, University of London, 1955; Director of the University Marine Biological Station, Millport, since 1970; *b* 24 Oct. 1912; *s* of Reuben Tomlinson Millott and Mary Millott (*née* Thistlethwaite); *m* 1939, Margaret Newns; three *d. Educ:* The Brunts Sch., Mansfield, Notts; Univs of Sheffield, Manchester, Cambridge. BSc 1935, MSc 1936 (Sheffield); PhD 1944 (Cambridge). Demonstrator in Zoology, Manchester Univ., 1935-36; Rouse Ball Student, Trinity Coll., Cambridge, 1936-38; Lectr in Zoology, Manchester Univ., 1938-40 and 1945-47. Commissioned RAFVR Technical Branch, 1940-45. Prof. of Zoology, University Coll. of the West Indies, 1948-55. Staff Councillor, 1957-60, and Dean of Faculty of Science, Bedford Coll., 1958-60; Chm. of Board of Studies in Zoology, Univ. of London, 1961-65; Chm. Photobiology Group, UK, 1960-62; Chm. Academic Advisory Board, Kingston-upon-Thames Technical Coll., 1960-66; Vice-Pres., International Congress of Photobiology, 1964. DSc (Sheffield), 1961. *Publications:* scientific papers chiefly on invertebrate morphology, histology, physiology, and biochemistry. *Address:* The University Marine Biological Station, Millport, Isle of Cumbrae, Scotland.

**MILLS,** family name of **Baron Hillingdon** and **Viscount Mills.**

**MILLS,** 2nd Viscount, *cr* 1962; **Roger Clinton Mills;** Bt 1953; Baron 1957; Company Executive since 1963; *b* 14 June 1919; *o s* of 1st Viscount Mills, PC, KBE, and Winifred Mary, *d* of George Conaty, Birmingham; *S* father, 1968; *m* 1945, Joan Dorothy, *d* of James Shirreff; one *s* two *d. Educ:* Canford Sch.; Jesus Coll., Cambridge. Served War as Major, RA, 1940-46. Administrative Officer, Colonial Service, Kenya, 1946-63. Barrister, Inner Temple, 1956. *Heir: s* Hon. Christopher Philip Roger Mills, *b* 20 May 1956. *Address:* Banbury Cross, 84 Pannal Ash Road, Harrogate, Yorks. *T:* Harrogate 2385.

**MILLS, Maj.-Gen. Alan Oswald Gawler;** Director-General of Artillery, Ministry of Defence (Army), 1967-69, retired; *b* 11 March 1914; *o s* of John Gawler Mills; *m* 1941, Beata Elizabeth de Courcy Morgan Richards; one *s* one *d. Educ:* Marlborough Coll.; RMA, Woolwich. Commissioned RA, 1934; Hong Kong, 1938-45; Br. Jt Services Mission, USA, 1951-53; Techn SO Grade I, Min. of Supply, 1955-57; Mil. Dir of Studies, RMCS, 1957-61; Sen. Mil. Officer, Royal Armament Research and Develt Estabt, 1961-62; BGS, WO, 1962-65; Dir, Guided Weapons Trials, Min. of Aviation, 1966. CEng, AFRAeS. *Recreations:* sailing, ski-ing. *Address:* 3 Seafield Terrace, Seaview, IoW. *T:* Seaview 3166. *Club:* Seaview Yacht.

**MILLS, Prof. Bernard Yarnton,** FRS 1963; FAA 1959; DSc Eng; Professor of Physics (Astrophysics), University of Sydney, since 1965; *b* 8 Aug. 1920; *s* of Ellice Yarnton Mills and Sylphide Mills; *m* 1942, Lerida Karmalsky (*d* 1969); one *s* two *d. Educ:* King's Sch., New South Wales; University of Sydney. BSc 1940, DSc Eng 1959 (Sydney). Joined the then Council for Scientific and Industrial Research and worked on Develt of mil. radar systems; after working for many years on radioastronomy he joined Sydney Univ. to form a radioastronomy group in Sch. of Physics, 1960; Reader in Physics, 1960-65; has recently put into operation there, a large radio-telescope. Lyle Medal of Australian Academy of Science, 1957. *Publications:* many contrib. sci. jls in Australia, England and America, mainly on subject of radioastronomy. *Address:* 7 Murdoch Street, Turramurra, NSW 2074, Australia. *T:* 44-6117.

**MILLS, (Charles) Ernest;** Member for Economic Planning, Gas Council, since 1968; *b* 9 Dec. 1916; *s* of late Charles and Mary Elizabeth Mills; *m* 1943, Irene Hickman; one *s* one *d. Educ:* Barnsley and District Holgate Grammar Sch.; Manchester Coll. of Technology. Administrative Staff Coll., Henley, 1958. Inspector of Naval Ordnance, 1939-45. Engrg Asst, Rochdale Corp. Gas Dept, 1945-51; East Midlands Gas Board: Asst Divisional Engr, 1951-54; Divisional Engr, 1954-58; Asst Chief Engr and Production Controller, 1958-61; Chief Engr and Production Controller, 1961-64; Dep. Chm., E Midlands Gas Bd, 1964-66, Chm., W Midlands Gas Bd, 1966-68. *Recreations:* travel, sports. *Address:* Long Rafters, Sheethanger Lane, Felden, Boxmoor, Herts. *T:* Hemel Hempstead 55220.

**MILLS, Vice-Adm. Sir Charles (Piercy),** KCB 1968 (CB 1964); CBE 1957; DSC 1953; Lieutenant-Governor and Commander-in-Chief of Guernsey, since 1969; *b* 4 Oct. 1914; *s* of late Capt. Thomas Piercy Mills, Woking, Surrey; *m* 1944, Anne Cumberlege; two *d. Educ:* RN College, Dartmouth. Joined Navy, 1928; Comdr 1947; Capt. 1953; Rear-Adm. 1963; Vice-Adm. 1966. Served War of 1939-45, Home Waters, Mediterranean and Far East; Korea, 1951-52; Flag Officer, Second in Command, Far East Fleet, 1966-67; C-in-C Plymouth, 1967-69. US Legion of Merit, 1955. KStJ 1969. *Recreations:* golf, tennis, sailing.

*Address:* Government House, Guernsey, CI. *Club:* United Service.

**MILLS, Edward (David),** CBE 1959; FRIBA; Architect and Design Consultant in private practice since 1937; *b* 19 March 1915; *s* of Edward Ernest Mills; *m* 1939, Elsie May Bryant; one *s* one *d*. *Educ:* Ensham Sch.; Polytechnic Sch. of Architecture. ARIBA 1937, FRIBA 1946. Mem. of RIBA Council, 1954-62 and 1964-69; Chm. RIBA Bd of Architectural Education, 1960-62 (Vice-Chm., 1958-60); RIBA Alfred Bossom Research Fellow, 1953; Churchill Fellow, 1969; Vice-Pres. Soc. of Christian Artists; MSIA 1959. Mem. Faculty Architecture, British School at Rome. Architect for British Industries Pavilion, Brussels Internat. Exhibn, 1958; works include churches, schools, industrial buildings, research centres, flats and houses in Great Britain and overseas. *Publications:* The Modern Factory, 1951; The New Architecture in Great Britain, 1953; The Modern Church, 1956; Architects Details, Vols 1-6, 1952-61; Factory Building, 1967; contribs to RIBA journal, Architectural Review, etc. *Recreations:* photography, foreign travel. *Address:* Gate House Farm, Newchapel, Lingfield, Surrey. *T:* Lingfield 241.

**MILLS, Eric Robertson;** Registrar of the Privy Council since 1966; *b* 27 July 1918; *s* of late Thomas Piercy Mills, Woking, Surrey; *m* 1950, Shirley Manger; two *d*. *Educ:* Charterhouse; Trinity Coll., Cambridge (BA). Served Royal Artillery, 1939-46; Major 1944. Called to Bar, Inner Temple, 1947; Mem. of Western Circuit. Dep. Judge Advocate, 1955; Chief Clerk, Judicial Cttee of Privy Council, 1963. *Recreations:* gardening, tennis, golf. *Address:* 3 Fairway, Merrow, Guildford, Surrey. *T:* Guildford 4639.

**MILLS, Ernest;** *see* Mills, C. E.

**MILLS, Frank;** Head of Personnel Policy Department, Foreign and Commonwealth Office, since 1969; *b* 3 Dec. 1923; *s* of Joseph Francis Mills and Louisa Mills; *m* 1953, Trilby Foster; one *s* two *d*. *Educ:* King Edward VI Sch., Nuneaton; Emmanuel Coll., Cambrdige. RAFVR, 1942-45. CRO, 1948; 2nd Sec., British High Commn in Pakistan, 1949-51; Private Sec. to Parly Under-Sec. of State, 1952-53; Sec., UK Delegn to Colombo Plan Conf., Ottawa, 1954; 1st Sec., British High Commn in S Africa, 1955-58; Principal Private Sec. to Sec. of State, 1960-62; British High Commn in Malaya, 1962-63; Counsellor, British High Commn in Malaysia (Kuala Lumpur and Singapore), 1963-65; Dep. High Comr in Singapore, 1965-66; Dep. Head of Personnel Operation Dept, DSAO and FCO, 1966-69. *Recreations:* golf, music, history. *Address:* 22 Hitherwood Drive, SE19. *Clubs:* Royal Commonwealth Society; Singapore Island Country.

**MILLS, Air Chief Marshal Sir George (Holroyd),** GCB 1959 (KCB 1954; CB 1945) DFC 1940; Gentleman Usher of the Black Rod, House of Lords, 1963-70; *b* 26 March 1902; *s* of late W. B. S. Mills, The Priory, Swanley, Kent; *m* 1926, Mary, *d* of late S. Austen Smith, The Old Place, Swanley, Kent; two *s* one *d*. *Educ:* Berkhamsted; Royal Air Force Coll., Cranwell. Commissioned, 1921; Iraq, 1922-24; India, 1930-34; RAF Staff Coll., 1935; Air Ministry, 1935-39; Served War of 1939-45 in Bomber Command, Staff Coll., Air Ministry, and as AOC Balkan Air Force, 1945; Egypt, 1945-46; Dir of Plans, Air Ministry, 1946-48; Air Officer Commanding No. 1 Group, 1949-50; Head of United Kingdom Military Delegation to Western Union Military Staff Cttee, 1950-51; AOC, Malaya, 1952; AOC-in-C, Bomber Comd, 1953-55; Comdr, Allied Air Forces, Central Europe, 1956-69; Chm., British Defence Staffs, Washington, DC, and UK Representative on Standing Group of NATO Military Cttee, 1959-62; Air ADC to the Queen, 1956-62; retired, 1962. Trustee, Imperial War Museum, 1963-. *Address:* c/o Lloyds Bank Ltd, 6 Pall Mall, SW1.

**MILLS, Herbert Horatio,** MC 1944; Rector of the Edinburgh Academy since Sept. 1962; *b* Jan. 1919; *s* of Edward Charles and Sarah Mills. *Educ:* Marling Sch.; St Catharine's Coll., Cambridge (PhD). Commonwealth Fellow, University of Pennsylvania, USA, 1950. Asst Master, Sedbergh Sch., 1953-62. *Recreations:* mountaineering; Cambridge Rugby XV, 1947, 1948. *Address:* 50 Inverleith Place, Edinburgh. *Clubs:* Alpine; Scottish Arts (Edinburgh).

**MILLS, Ivor Henry;** Professor of Medicine in the University of Cambridge since 1963; Fellow Churchill College, Cambridge; Hon. Consultant to United Cambridge Hospitals; *b* 13 June 1921; 3rd *s* of late J. H. W. Mills and late Priscilla Mills; *m* 1947, Sydney Elizabeth Puleston (*née* Roberts); one *s* one *d*. *Educ:* Selhurst Grammar Sch., Croydon; Queen Mary Coll., London; Trinity Coll., Cambridge. BSc (London) 1942; PhD (London) 1946; BA (Cantab) 1948; MB, BChir Cantab 1951; MRCP 1953; MD Cantab 1956; MA Cantab 1963; FRCP 1964. Pres. Cambridge Univ. Medical Soc., 1947-48; Sen. Schol., Trinity Coll., Cambridge, 1948; MRC (Eli Lilly) Trav. Fellow, 1956; Vis. Scientist, Nat. Inst. of Health, 1957; Lectr in Medicine and Chem. Path., St Thomas's Hosp. Medical Sch., 1954; Reader in Medicine, St Thomas's Hosp. Medical Sch., London, 1962. Sec., Soc. for Endocrinology, 1963-. *Publications:* Clinical Aspects of Adrenal Function, 1964; contrib. Lancet, Science Jl of Endocr., Clin. Science, etc. *Recreation:* gardening. *Address:* Addenbrooke's Hospital, Cambridge.

**MILLS, Col Sir John (Digby),** Kt 1958; TD, DL, JP; Member of House of Laity, 1944-60; Church Commissioner, 1948-58; 2nd and *o surv s* of late Rev. Cecil Mills, Bisterne, Ringwood, Hants, and Taverham Hall, Norfolk, and Anne H. F., *e d* of late Capt. F. H. G. Nicolls, 4th Dragoon Guards; *b* 1879; *m* 1918, Carola (JP (Hants), 1937); *o d* of late Judge S. P. Tuck, International Court of Appeals, Alexandria, Egypt, and of Maryland, USA; three *s*. *Educ:* Charterhouse; Oriel Coll., Oxford, BA. Joined Warwicks Yeomanry as 2nd Lieut, 1901; Major, 1911-20; served with WY in Egypt, Gallipoli, and France (despatches 3 times); MP (C) New Forest and Christchurch Division (Hants), Feb. 1932-July 1945; Second Church Estates Commissioner, 1943-45; Mem. of Hants County Council, 1907-64; County Alderman, 1925-64; a Verderer of the New Forest, 1922-38 and 1945-55; Chm., New Forest and Christchurch Div. Conservative Assoc., 1925-32; Chm., Winchester Diocesan Bd of Finance, 1948-54. Lt 8th (HD) Bn, Hants Regt, Sept. 1939-May 1940; Group Organiser LDV, 1940; Col and Comdr, New Forest Group, Home Guard, 1941-43, 2 i/c Hants Zone, 1943-45. Hon. Col Home Guard. *Recreations:* formerly shooting and fishing. *Address:* White House, Hangersley, Ringwood, Hants. *T:* Ringwood 3653. *Club:* Cavalry.

**MILLS, John F. F. P.;** *see* Platts-Mills.

**MILLS, John (Lewis Ernest Watts),** CBE 1960; Actor, Producer, Director; *b* 22 Feb. 1908; *m* 1941, Mary Hayley Bell, playwright; one *s* two *d*. *Educ:* Norwich. 1st appearance, stage, 1929. *Plays:* Cavalcade, London Wall, Words and

Music, Five O'clock Girl, Give Me a Ring, Jill Darling, Floodlight, Red Night, We at the Cross Roads, Of Mice and Men, Men in Shadow, Duet for Two Hands, etc.; Old Vic Season, 1938; Top of the Ladder; Figure of Fun, Aldwych; Ross, New York, 1961; Power of Persuasion, Garrick, 1963. *Films:* The Midshipmaid, Britannia of Billingsgate, Brown on Resolution, OHMS, Cottage To Let, The Young Mr Pitt, We Dive at Dawn, In Which We Serve, The Way to the Stars, Great Expectations, So Well Remembered, The October Man, Scott of the Antarctic, The History of Mr Polly, The Rocking Horse Winner, Morning Departure, Mr Denning Drives North, Gentle Gunman, The Long Memory, Hobson's Choice, The Colditz Story, The End of the Affair, Above Us the Waves, Town on Trial, Escapade, Its Great to be Young, The Baby and the Battleship, War and Peace, Around the World in Eighty Days, Dunkirk, Ice Cold in Alex, I Was Monty's Double, Summer of the Seventeenth Doll, Tiger Bay, Swiss Family Robinson, The Singer not the Song, Tunes of Glory, Flame in the Streets, The Valiant, Tiara Tahiti, The Chalk Garden, The Truth about Spring, King Rat, Operation X Bow, Red Waggon, Sky West and Crooked (directed), The Wrong Box, The Family Way, Chuka, Showdown, Oh What a Lovely War, The Return of the Boomerang, Ryan's Daughter, Run Wild, Run Free, Emma Hamilton, Dulcima. RADA Council, 1965-. *Recreations:* ski-ing, golf, painting. *Address:* c/o International Famous Agency, 11 Hanover Street, W1. *Club:* Garrick.

**MILLS, Prof. John Norton,** MA, DM Oxon, MD Cantab; Brackenbury Professor of Physiology, University of Manchester since October 1965; *b* 28 June 1914; *s* of George Percival Mills, Consultant Surgeon, and T. M. Cristabel (*née* Humphreys); *m* 1942, June Rosemary Jill Brenan; one *s* two *d*. *Educ:* Winchester; New Coll., Oxford; Christ Church, Oxford. Lecturer, New Coll., Oxford, 1941-46; Fellow and Lecturer, Jesus Coll., Cambridge, 1946-50; University of Manchester: Lecturer in Human Physiology, 1950; Sen. Lecturer, 1955; Reader in Physiology, 1959. *Publications:* Chapters in Recent Advances in Physiology (ed R. Creese), 1962; Chapter in A Companion to Medical Studies (ed Passmore and Robson), 1968; (with R. T. W. L. Conroy) Human Circadian Rhythms, 1969; papers in Jl Physiol., Clin. Sci., Jl Endocrin., Brit. Med. Bulletin, etc. *Recreations:* rock climbing, walking, field botany. *Address:* 4 Lancaster Road, Didsbury, Manchester M20 8TY. *T:* 061-445 2949.

**MILLS, John Robert;** Director, Signals Research and Development Establishment, Ministry of Technology, since 1967; *b* 12 Nov. 1916; *s* of Robert Edward Mills and Constance H. Mills; *m* 1950, Pauline Phelps; two *s*. *Educ:* Kingston Grammar Sch., Kingston-upon-Thames; King's Coll., London (BSc); AInstP 1941. Air Ministry Research Estab., Dundee, 1939; RAE Farnborough, 1940-42; TRE, later RRE, Malvern, 1942-60; Supt (Offensive), Airborne Radar, RRE, 1954-60; Asst Dir, Electronics R and D (Civil Aviation), Min. of Aviation, 1960-61; Head of Radio Dept, RAE Farnborough, 1961-65; Electronics Div., Min. of Technology, 1965-67. *Publications:* (jointly) Radar article in Encyclopædia Britannica; various papers in journals. *Address:* Little Chewton, Chewton Farm Road, Highcliffe, Christchurch, Hants.

**MILLS, (John) Vivian G.;** *b* 22 Sept. 1887; *s* of late Comdr J. F. Mills, ISO, RN (retd); *m* 1st, 1915, Lilian (*d* 1947), *d* of late A. Brisley; no *c*; 2nd, 1968, Marguerite Mélanie, *d* of late Jean Hoffman. Educ: privately; Merton Coll., Oxford; Classical Mods and Lit Hum; BA. Barrister-at-law, Middle Temple, 1919; Cadet, Malayan Civil Service, 1911; qualified in Chinese, 1914; held various administrative, legal and judicial appointments, 1914-28; Solicitor-Gen., Straits Settlements, 1928-32; acting Attorney-Gen., and Mem. of the Executive and Legislative Councils, 1932; Commissioner of Currency, 1932; Puisne Judge, Straits Settlements, 1933; Judge, Johore, 1934; retired, 1940; Attached to office of Federal Attorney-Gen., Sydney, Australia, 1944-45; Additional Lecturer in Chinese Law, School of Oriental and African Studies, London, 1946-47; Pres. of Malayan Branch, Royal Asiatic Society, 1936; Joint Hon. Sec., Hakluyt Soc., 1950-53. *Publications:* Eredia's Malaca, Meridional India and Cathay, 1930; Malaya in the Wu-pei-chi Charts, 1937, etc.; various official publications. *Recreations:* Oriental research and watching first-class cricket. *Address:* c/o Barclays Bank, 95 Queensway, W2.

**MILLS, John William,** OBE 1945; QC 1962; *b* 24 Oct. 1914; *s* of late John William Mills, OBE and Jessie Mills; *m* 1942, Phyllis Mary, *yr d* of late Arthur Gibson Pears; no *c*. *Educ:* Clifton; Corpus Christi Coll., Cambridge (MA). Called to Bar, Middle Temple, 1938; Bencher, 1968. Lt-Col, Royal Signals, 1944; Comdr, Royal Signals, 46 Div., 1944. Member: Bar Council, 1961-64; Clifton Coll. Council, 1967-. *Publications:* The Building Societies Act, 1960, 1961, Wurtzburg and Mills, Building Society Law, 1964-. *Recreations:* sailing, golf. *Address:* 38 Adam and Eve Mews, W8. *T:* 01-937 1259; 11 Old Square, Lincoln's Inn, WC2. *T:* 01-405 5243; Greenleas, Highleigh, Chichester, Sussex. *T:* Sidlesham 396.

**MILLS, Leonard Sidney,** CB 1970; Deputy Director General (2), Highways, Ministry of Transport, since 1970; *b* 20 Aug. 1914; *s* of late Albert Edward Mills; *m* 1940, Kathleen Joyce Cannicott; two *s*. *Educ:* Devonport High Sch.; London Sch. of Economics; Birkbeck Coll., University of London. Entered Exchequer and Audit Dept, 1933; Private Sec. to Comptroller and Auditor Gen., 1944-46; transferred to Min. of Civil Aviation, as Principal, 1946; Asst Sec., 1950; Min. of Transport: Under-Sec., 1959; Chief of Highway Administration, 1968-70. Commonwealth Fund Fellow, 1953-54. *Recreations:* walking and gardening. *Address:* Coneyhurst, Wray Lane, Reigate, Surrey. *T:* Reigate 46130.

**MILLS, Maj.-Gen. Percy Strickland,** CIE 1938; IMS, retired; *s* of William James Mills, London, and Helen Anne Mills; *m* 1920, Norah Catharine Lake; one *s* one *d*. *Educ:* Dulwich Coll.; Guy's Hosp. Entered Indian Medical Service, 1906; served Mohmand Campaign, 1908, and European War, 1914-20 (despatches twice); Lt-Col, 1925; Col., 1935; Maj.-Gen., 1937; Hon. Physician to the King, 1938-41. Served in India in War of 1939-45; retired, 1941. *Recreations:* golf, bridge. *Address:* c/o Standard Bank of South Africa, George, South Africa.

**MILLS, Sir Peter (Frederick Leighton),** 3rd Bt, *cr* 1921; *b* 9 July 1924; *s* of Major Sir Frederick Leighton Victor Mills, 2nd Bt, MC, RA, MICE, and Doris (*née* Armitage); *S* father 1955; *m* 1954, Pauline Mary, *d* of L. R. Allen, Calverton, Notts; one *s* one adopted *d*. *Educ:* Eastbourne Coll.; Cedara Coll. of Agriculture, University of Natal (BSc Agric.). Served HM Forces, 1943-47. CS, Fedn Rhodesia and Nyasaland, 1953; with Rhodesia Min. of Agric., 1964-. *Heir: s* Michael Victor Leighton Mills, *b* 30 Aug. 1957. *Address:* Henderson

Research Station, P. Bag 222a, Salisbury, Rhodesia.

**MILLS, Peter McLay;** MP (C) Torrington since 1964; Farmer; *b* 22 Sept. 1921; *m* 1948, Joan Weatherley; one *s* one *d*. *Educ:* Epsom; Wye Coll. Farmer since 1943. Mem. House of Laity and Church Assembly; Vice-President: Nat. Assoc. of Parish Councils; Rural District Councils Assoc. *Recreations:* work and staying at home for a short time. *Address:* Yendon Farm, Mount Lane, Ashwater, West Devon.

**MILLS, Air Cdre Stanley Edwin Druce,** CB 1968; CBE 1959; Royal Air Force, retired; Bursar, Roedean School, since 1968; *b* 1913; *s* of Edwin J. Mills; *m* 1938, Joan Mary, *d* of Robert Ralph James; one *s* one *d*. *Educ:* Collegiate Sch., Bournemouth, RAF Staff Coll. Entered RAF 1939; served RAF Middle East and Italy, 1942-45; Station Comdr, RAF Innsworth, 1957-60; Comd Accountant, RAF Germany, 1960-63; Dir of Personnel (Policy) (Air), MoD, 1963-65; Dir of Personal Services (Air), MoD, 1966-68. FCA. *Recreations:* caravanning, gardening. *Address:* Orana, Cuckmere Road, Seaford, Sussex. *Club:* Royal Air Force.

**MILLS, Brig. Stephen Douglas,** CBE 1943; MC; *b* 1892; *s* of late Stephen E. Mills, JP, Longmead, Havant, Hants; *m* 1923, Rosamond, *d* of late W. R. Merk, CSI, CIE, ICS; one *s* one *d*. *Educ:* Bradfield Coll.; RMC, Sandhurst. Late Beds and Herts Regt, European War 1914-19, in France, Belgium, and Palestine (wounded, MC, 1914 Star, two Medals; Palestine, 1936-39 (despatches, Medal with clasp); War of 1939-45 in Middle East (despatches, CBE); retired pay, 1946. *Address:* Glebe Farm, Fifield Bavant, near Salisbury, Wilts. *T:* Broadchalke 243.

**MILLS, Stratton;** *see* Mills, W. S.

**MILLS, Vivian;** *see* Mills, J. V. G.

**MILLS, Maj.-Gen. William Graham Stead,** CBE 1963; GOC West Midland District, 1968-70; *b* 23 June 1917; *s* of William Stead Mills and Margaret Kennedy Mills; *m* 8 July 1941, Joyce Evelyn (*née* Ransom); three *s*. *Educ:* Merchiston Castle Sch., Edinburgh. Regtl duty, Royal Berks Regt, in India, 1938-43; Staff Coll., India, 1944; GSO2 and GSO1, Ops HQ 14th Army, Burma, 1944-45; WO and Washington, USA, 1946-50; Regtl duty with Parachute Regt, comdg 17th Bn, The Parachute Regt, 1958-60; GSO1, 2 Div. BAOR, 1956-58; Regtl Col The Parachute Regt, 1960-62; Comdg TA Brigade, Winchester, 1963-64; Brig. GS, HQ Middle East Comd, Aden, 1965-66. Imperial Defence Coll., Student, 1967. *Recreations:* gardening, photography. *Address:* Wrockwardine Hall, Wellington, Salop. *Club:* Army and Navy.

**MILLS, (William) Stratton;** MP (UU) Belfast North since Oct. 1959; Company Director; Partner in Mills, Selig & Bailie, Solicitors, Belfast; *b* 1 July 1932; *o s* of late Dr J. V. S. Mills, CBE, Resident Magistrate for City of Belfast, and Margaret Florence (*née* Byford); *m* 1959, Merriel E. R. Whitla, *o d* of Mr and Mrs R. J. Whitla, Belfast; two *s*. *Educ:* Campbell Coll., Belfast; Queen's Univ., Belfast (LLB). Vice-Chm., Federation of University Conservative and Unionist Assocs, 1952-53 and 1954-55; admitted a Solicitor, 1958. PPS to Parly Sec., Ministry of Transport, 1961-64; Member: Estimates Cttee, 1964-; Exec. Cttee, 1922 Cttee, 1967-; Hon. Sec. Conservative Broadcasting Cttee, 1963-; Mem., Mr Speaker's Conference on Electoral Law, 1967. *Address:* House of Commons, SW1; (office) 20 Callender Street, Belfast 1. *T:* Belfast 43878; (home) 17 Malone Park, Belfast 9. *T:* Belfast 665210. *Clubs:* Junior Carlton; Ulster (Belfast).

**MILLS-OWENS, Richard Hugh; Hon. Mr Justice Mills-Owens;** Puisne Judge, Hong Kong, since 1967 (also 1961-64); Chief Justice, Fiji, 1964-67; *b* Jan. 1910; *s* of George Edward Owens and Jessie Mary Mills; *m* 1935, Elizabeth Ann Hiles (*d* 1968); two *s*. *Educ:* Rhyl Grammar Sch. Admitted Solicitor, 1932; Clifford's Inn Prizeman; Barrister-at-law, 1956, Middle Temple. Practised in Wales (including service with Carmarthenshire County Council) until 1949 when joined Colonial Legal Service as a Registrar of Titles; Principal Registrar, Kenya; Crown Counsel and Legal Draftsman, 1952; Magistrate, 1956, District Judge, 1958, Hong Kong. *Recreation:* golf. *Address:* Supreme Court, Hong Kong.

**MILLWARD, William,** CB 1969; CBE 1954; with Government Communications Headquarters (Superintending Director, 1958-69); *b* 27 Jan. 1909; *s* of William John and Alice Millward; *m* 1937, Nora Florella Harper; one *s* one *d*. *Educ:* Solihull Sch.; St Catherine's Society, Oxford. Asst Master, Dulwich Coll., 1930-41; RAF, 1941-46; Govt Communications Headquarters, 1946-. *Recreations:* music, reading, walking. *Address:* Three Poplars, Evesham Road, Cheltenham, Glos. *T:* Cheltenham 25732.

**MILMAN, Sir Dermot (Lionel Kennedy),** 8th Bt, *cr* 1800; Liaison Officer for Hostel Development, British Council since 1963; *b* 24 Oct. 1912; *e s* of Brig.-Gen. Sir Lionel Charles Patrick Milman, 7th Bt, CMG, and Marjorie Aletta, *d* of Col A. H. Clark-Kennedy, late Indian Civil Service; *S* father, 1962; *m* 1941, Muriel, *o d* of J. E. S. Taylor, King's Lynn; one *d*. *Educ:* Uppingham; Corpus Christi Coll., Cambridge. BA 1934, MA 1938. Served War of 1939-45, Royal Army Service Corps, in France, Belgium and Burma (despatches), Major. Hon. Major, RCT (formerly RARO, RASC). Assistant Dir, British Council Overseas Service (Bogota, Santiago, Lima, Milan, Peshawar), 1946-63. *Recreations:* Rugby football (Eng., 1937-38), cricket (Beds, Vice-Capt. 1935). *Heir: b* Malcolm Douglas Milman [*b* 18 May 1915; *m* 1940, Sheila Maud (marriage dissolved), *d* of Albert Maurice Dudeney; two *d*]. *Address:* 7 Old Westhall Close, Warlingham, Surrey. *T:* 01-820 4843.

**MILMAN, Lt-Col Octavius Rodney Everard,** DSO 1917, Hon. MA Oxford, 1930; late Royal Artillery; sometime Fellow and Bursar of Keble College, Oxford; *b* 23 April 1882; *y s* of late Lt-Col Everard Stepney Milman, Royal Artillery; *m* 1911, Mary Freya, *d* of late Rev. Canon W. E. Haigh; two *d*. *Educ:* Uppingham; Merchant Taylors'; RMA, Woolwich. Commissioned Royal Artillery, 1900; retired, 1921; served European War, 1914-18, Egypt, Gallipoli, and France; Administrative Staff Army and General Headquarters (despatches, Brevet majority, DSO). *Address:* 84 Greenhill, Prince Arthur Road, NW3.

**MILMO, Hon. Sir Helenus Patrick Joseph,** Kt 1964; DL; **Hon. Mr Justice Milmo;** Judge of High Court of Justice, Queen's Bench Division, since 1964; *b* 24 Aug. 1908; 3rd *s* of late Daniel Milmo, Furbough, Co. Galway, Eire; *m* 1933, Joan Frances, *d* of late Francis Morley, London; two *s* three *d* (and one *d* decd). *Educ:* Downside; Trinity Coll., Cambridge. Barrister, Middle Temple, 1931; Bencher, 1955; QC 1961. Civil Asst, General Staff, War Office, 1940-45. Dep. Chm., West Sussex Quarter Sessions, 1960-64. DL Sussex, 1962. *Recreations:* hunting, fishing, wine.

*Address:* Church Farm, Shipley, near Horsham, Sussex. *T:* Coolham 261. *Club:* United University.

**MILNE,** family name of **Baron Milne.**

**MILNE,** 2nd Baron, *cr* 1933, of Salonika and of Rubislaw, Co. Aberdeen; **George Douglass Milne;** Partner, Arthur Young McClelland Moores Co., Chartered Accountants; *b* 10 Feb. 1909; *s* of 1st Baron Milne, GCB, GCMG, DSO, Field Marshal from 1928, and Claire Marjoribanks, MBE, DGStJ, *d* of Sir John N. Maitland, 5th Bt; *S* father, 1948; *m* 1940, Cicely, 3rd *d* of Ronald Leslie, United University Club; two *s* one *d*. *Educ:* Winchester; New Coll., Oxford. Mem. of the Institute of Chartered Accountants of Scotland. Master of the Grocers' Company, 1961-62. Served War of 1939-45, Major Royal Artillery (TA); prisoner of war, 1941; NWEF and MEF (wounded, despatches). *Recreation:* art: has exhibited RA, ROI, RP. *Heir: s* Hon. George Alexander Milne, *b* 1 April 1941. *Address:* 33 Lonsdale Road, Barnes, SW13. *T:* 01-748 6421; (professional) Arthur Young McClelland Moores Co., Moor House, London Wall, EC2.

**MILNE, Alasdair David Gordon;** Controller, BBC Scotland, since 1968; *b* 8 Oct. 1930; *s* of Charles Gordon Shaw Milne and Edith Reid Clark; *m* 1954, Sheila Kirsten Graucob; two *s* one *d*. *Educ:* Winchester Coll.; New Coll., Oxford. Commnd into 1st Bn Gordon Highlanders, 1949. Hon. Mods Oxon 1952; BA Oxon Mod. Langs, 1954. Joined BBC, 1954; Dep. Editor, 1957-61, Editor, 1961-62, of Tonight Programme; Head of Tonight Productions, 1963-65; Partner, Jay, Baverstock, Milne & Co., 1965-67; rejoined BBC, Oct. 1967. *Recreations:* piping, salmon fishing, golf, tennis. *Address:* Glenmiln House, Campsie Glen, Stirlingshire. *T:* Lennoxtown 501. *Club:* Savile.

**MILNE, Alexander George,** CIE 1945; FICE, FIMechE; *b* Skene, Aberdeenshire, 27 July 1891; *s* of Alexander Milne; *m* 1927, Mary Agnes Murphy, MB, BCh, DTM, *d* of P. J. Murphy, Macroom, Cork; one *d*. *Educ:* Robert Gordon's Coll., Aberdeen. Pupil with late R. Gordon Nicol, OBE, MICE, MIMechE, Harbour Engineer, Aberdeen, 1908-13; in Admiralty Works Dept service HM Dockyard, Rosyth and Cromarty, 1913-18; Resident Engineer and Contractors' Agent various Public Works, England, 1918-23; Senior Asst Engineer and Exec. Engineer, Bombay Port Trust, 1923-27; from 1927 was engaged on opening up and development of Cochin Harbour, S India, as Exec. Engineer and Dep. Chief Engineer; Administrative Officer and Chief Engineer, Cochin Harbour, 1941-48. *Recreation:* golf. *Address:* 11 Gray Street, Aberdeen. *T:* 50967. *Club:* East India and Sports.

**MILNE, Alexander Taylor;** Secretary and Librarian, Institute of Historical Research, University of London, since 1946; *b* 22 Jan. 1906; *s* of late Alexander Milne and Shanny (*née* Taylor); *m* 1960, Joyce Frederica Taylor, Dulwich. *Educ:* Christ's Coll., Finchley; University Coll., London. BA History Hons 1927; Diploma in Education, 1928; MA (London), 1930; FRHistS, 1938; Vice-Pres., Historical Assoc., 1956-; Asst Officer and Librarian, Royal Historical Society, 1935-40; Hon. Librarian, 1965-. Served War of 1939-45, Buffs and Maritime Artillery, 1940-42; Army Bureau of Current Affairs, 1942-44; Research Dept, FO, 1944-46. Director, History Today. *Publications:* History of Broadwindsor, Dorset, 1935; Catalogue of the Manuscripts of Jeremy Bentham in the Library of University College, London, 1937, 2nd edn 1961; Writings on British History, 1934-45: a Bibliography (8 vols), 1937-60; Centenary Guide to Pubns of Royal Historical Society, 1968; (part-author) Historical Study in the West, 1968; (ed) Librarianship and Literature, essays in honour of Jack Pafford, 1970; contribs to Cambridge History of the British Empire, Encyclopædia Britannica and learned journals. *Recreation:* lawn tennis. *Address:* 9 Frank Dixon Close, Dulwich, SE21. *T:* 01-693 6942. *Clubs:* Athenæum, Dulwich.

**MILNE, Sir David,** GCB 1958 (KCB 1947; CB 1942); retired as Permanent Under-Secretary of State for Scotland (1946-59); *b* Edinburgh, 1896; *s* of late Rev. David Munro Milne, BD; *m* 1928, Winifrede, *e d* of late Surgeon-Capt. L. Kilroy, RN; one *s* one *d*. *Educ:* Daniel Stewart's Coll.; Edinburgh Univ. Military Service, 9th Royal Scots, 1915-19. Entered Scottish Office, 1921; Private Sec. to successive Secs of State for Scotland, 1930-35; Asst Sec., 1935; Deputy-Sec., Scottish Home Dept, 1939; Sec., 1942-46. National Governor for Scotland, BBC, 1960-65; Mem. Cttee Inquiry into Security Procedures and Practices, 1961. *Publication:* The Scottish Office, 1958. *Address:* 36 Greenhill Gardens, Edinburgh. *T:* 031-447 3574. *Clubs:* Athenæum, Savile; New (Edinburgh).

**MILNE, Edward James,** MP (Lab) Blyth since Nov. 1960; *b* 18 Oct. 1915; *s* of Edward James Milne and Isabella Stewart; *m* 1939, Emily Constable; three *d*. *Educ:* George Street and Kittybrewster Primary; Sunnybank Intermediate; Robert Gordon's Coll., Aberdeen (Schol.). Lecturer and Organiser, National Council of Labour Colls, 1942-47; Area Organiser, Union of Shop Distributive and Allied Workers, 1952-61. PPS to Sir Frank Soskice, Home Sec., 1964-65; Vice-Chm., Parly Labour Party, 1967-68. Grand Order of Star of Africa (Liberia), 1964. *Recreations:* walking, swimming. *Address:* Strathearn, Alston Grove, Seaton Sluice, Northumberland. *T:* Seaton Sluice 324.

**MILNE, Ian Innes,** CMG 1965; OBE 1946; HM Diplomatic Service, retired; *b* 16 June 1912; *e s* of Kenneth John Milne, CBE, and Maud Innes; *m* 1939, Marie Mange; one *d*. *Educ:* Westminster Sch.; Christ Church, Oxford. Advertising, 1935-40; RE, 1940-46 (Lieut-Col). FO, 1946-. 2nd Sec., Teheran, 1948-51; 1st Sec., Berne, 1955-56; 1st Sec., Tokyo, 1960-63. US Leg. of Merit (Off.), 1946. *Recreations:* cricket, music, gardening. *Address:* c/o Lloyds Bank, 79 Brompton Road, SW3.

**MILNE, James L.;** *see* Lees-Milne.

**MILNE, Kenneth Lancelot;** Agent General and Trade Commissioner for South Australia in the United Kingdom since 1966; *b* 16 Aug. 1915; *s* of F. K. Milne, Adelaide; *m* 1941, Mary, *d* of E. B. Hughes; two *s* one *d*. *Educ:* St Peter's Coll., Adelaide. Entered Public Practice as a Chartered Acct, 1946; Elected to State Council, 1951, Chm. 1958-60, Mem. Gen. Council, 1956-60. Served with RAAF, 1940-45, attaining rank of Flt Lieut. Municipality of Walkerville: Councillor, 1960; Mayor, 1961-63; Municipal Assoc. 1961 (Pres. 1964-65); Pres. SA Br Aust. Inst. of Internat. Affairs, 1958-60; Mem. Faculty of Economics, University of Adelaide, 1963-65. *Publications:* Ostrich Heads, 1937; Forgotten Freedom, 1952; The Accountant in Public Practice, 1959. *Recreations:* rowing, tennis, conchology. *Address:* South Australia House, 50 Strand, WC2. *T:* 01-930 7471; 43 Duchess of Bedford

House, W8. *T:* 01-937 8902. *Clubs:* East India and Sports, Royal Automobile, Thames Rowing; Adelaide, Amateur Sports, Adelaide Rowing, Commerce (all in SA).

**MILNE-THOMSON, Louis Melville,** CBE 1952; MA, DSc; FRSE; Professor of Applied Mathematics, University of Arizona, since 1961; *b* 1891; *e s* of Col A. Milne-Thomson, CMG; *m* Gertrude, *e d* of Dr Karl Frommknecht; three *d. Educ:* Clifton Coll. (Classical Scholar); Corpus Christi Coll., Cambridge (Mathematical Scholar). First Class, Mathematical Tripos Pt I; Wrangler with distinction Mathematical Tripos Pt II; Asst Master, Winchester Coll., 1914-21; Professor of Mathematics, RN Coll., Greenwich, 1921-56; Gresham Professor of Geometry; Visiting Professor of Applied Mathematics, Brown Univ., Rhode Island; Mathematics Research Center, Univ. of Wisconsin; Visiting Professor: Univ. of Rome, 1968; Univ. of Queensland, 1969; Univ. of Calgary, 1970. Mem. of British Assoc. Mathematical Tables Cttee; External Examiner in the University of London; Examiner for the Universities of Bristol and Nottingham, Oxford and Cambridge Joint Board, Civil Service Commission, etc; Fellow of: the Royal Astronomical Soc.; the Cambridge Philosophical Soc.; Inst. of the Aerospace Sciences; Mem. of the London Mathematical Soc., the American Mathematical Soc., and of the Circolo Matematico di Palermo. Hon. ScD, Bucharest, 1969. *Publications:* Standard Table of Square Roots; Standard Four Figure Mathematical Tables; Elliptische Funktionen, 1931; The Calculus of Finite Differences, 1933; Theoretical Hydrodynamics, 1938 (5th edn, 1968); Theoretical Aerodynamics, 1948 (4th edn, 1968); Jacobian Elliptic Function Tables, 1950; Hidrodinámica Teórica, 1951; Plane Elastic Systems, 1960 (2nd edn 1968); Antiplane Elastic Systems, 1962; Russian-English Mathematical Dictionary, 1962; Systèmes élastiques plans, 1968. Papers on Mathematics, in scientific periodicals. *Recreations:* sailing, foreign travel. *Address:* Mathematics Department, University of Arizona, Tucson, Arizona 85721, USA; 2 Bullfinch Lane, Riverhead, Sevenoaks, Kent. *T:* Sevenoaks 53366. *Clubs:* Athenæum, Carlton; Hope (Providence, RI).

**MILNE-WATSON, Sir (David) Ronald,** 2nd Bt, *cr* 1937; *b* 15 July 1904; *s* of Sir David Milne-Watson, 1st Bt, and Olga Cecily (*d* 1952), *d* of Rev. George Herbert; *S* father, 1945. *Educ:* Trinity Coll., Glenalmond; Balliol Coll., Oxford; Capt. IA, 1942-45. *Recreations:* shooting, gardening. *Heir: b* Sir Michael Milne-Watson, *qv. Address:* The Stables, Oakfield, Mortimer, Berks; 38 Hugh Street, SW1. *T:* 01-834 5166. *Club:* Travellers'.

**MILNE-WATSON, Sir Michael,** Kt 1969; CBE 1953; MA; Chairman, The William Press Group of Companies, since Dec. 1969; Director: Commercial Union Assurance Co. Ltd; Industrial and Commercial Finance Corporation Ltd; *b* 16 Feb. 1910; *yr s* of Sir David Milne-Watson, 1st Bt, and Lady Milne-Watson; *heir-pres.* to 2nd Bt; *m* 1940, Mary Lisette, *d* of late H. C. Bagnall, Auckland, New Zealand; one *s. Educ:* Eton; Balliol Coll., Oxford. Served War of 1939-45. RNVR, 1943-45. Joined Gas Light & Coke Co., 1933; Managing Dir, 1945; Governor, 1946-49; Chairman: North Thames Gas Board, 1949-64; Richard Thomas & Baldwins Ltd, 1964-67; a Dep. Chm., BSC, 1967-69 (Mem. Organizing Cttee, 1966-67); Mem., Iron and Steel Adv. Cttee, 1967-69. Mem. Court of Governors, Administrative Staff Coll., Henley-on-Thames. *Address:* 57 Eaton Place, SW1. *T:* 01-235 3467; Oakfield, Mortimer, Berks. *T:* Burghfield Common 2200. *Clubs:* Athenæum, MCC; Leander.

**MILNER,** family name of **Baron Milner of Leeds.**

**MILNER OF LEEDS,** 2nd Baron, *cr* 1951; **Arthur James Michael Milner; Director, Reeves & Sons Ltd; Partner, Milners, Curry & Gaskell, Solicitors, London, WC2;** *b* 12 Sept. 1923; *o s* of 1st Baron Milner of Leeds, PC, MC, TD and of Lois Tinsdale, *d* of Thomas Brown, Leeds; *S* father, 1967; *m* 1951, Sheila Margaret, *d* of Gerald Hartley, Leeds; one *s* two *d. Educ:* Oundle; Trinity Hall, Cambridge (MA). Served: RAFVR, 1942-46, Flt Lt; 609 (W Riding) Sqn, RAuxAF. 1947-52, Flt Lt. Admitted Solicitor, 1951. Member: Clothworkers' Co.; Pilgrims; Hon. Treas, Soc. of Yorkshiremen in London, 1967. *Recreations:* water ski-ing, motor rallying. *Heir: s* Hon. Richard James Milner, *b* 16 May 1959. *Address:* 54 Porchester Terrace, W2. *Club:* Royal Air Force.

**MILNER, Sir (George Edward) Mordaunt,** 9th Bt *cr* 1716; *b* 7 Feb. 1911; *er s* of Brig.-Gen. G. F. Milner, CMG, DSO; *S* cousin (Sir William Frederick Victor Mordaunt Milner, 8th Bt) 1960; *m* 1st, 1935, Barbara Audrey (*d* 1951), *d* of Henry Noel Belsham, Hunstanton, Norfolk; two *s* one *d*; 2nd, 1953, Katherine Moodie Bisset, *d* of D. H. Hoey, Dunfermline. *Educ:* Oundle. Served War of 1939-45, Royal Artillery. Stipendiary Steward, Jockey Club of South Africa, 1954-59; Steward, Cape Turf Club, 1959-. *Publications:* (novels) Inspired Information, 1959; Vaulting Ambition, 1962; The Last Furlong, 1965. *Heir: s* Timothy William Lycett Milner, *b* 11 Oct. 1936. *Address:* Knavesmire, Constantia, Cape, S Africa. *T:* 77-3014. *Clubs:* Rand (Johannesburg); Jockey Club of SA.

**MILNER, John Giddings;** Consulting Surgeon, Moorfields Eye Hospital, since 1956; Consulting Ophthalmic Surgeon: Charing Cross Hospital since 1966; St Andrew's Hospital, Dollis Hill, since 1966; *b* 7 Dec. 1900; 2nd *s* of late T. J. Milner, Blythwood, Radlett, and late Carrie, *d* of John Carpenter; *m* 1928, Monica Thrale, *d* of late Henry Mardall, Harpenden; one *s* two *d. Educ:* Marlborough Coll.; Trinity Coll., Cambridge; St Bartholomew's Hosp. MRCS, LRCP, 1925; MA, MB, BCh Cantab, 1929; FRCS, 1930. Ophthalmic Surgeon, Hertford County Hosp., 1929-46; Surgeon, Moorfields, Westminster and Central Eye Hosp., 1936-56; Wing Comdr RAFVR Medical Branch, 1940-45; Cons. Ophthalmic Surgeon, Hertford County Hosp., 1947; Surgeon Oculist to the late Queen Mary, 1948-53. Coronation Medal, 1953. *Publications:* Modern Treatment in General Practice (contribution), 1949; Brit. Jl Opth., 1934; Brit. Medical Jl, 1941, 1944. *Recreations:* golf, natural history. *Address:* 34 Wimpole Street, W1. *T:* 01-935 2828; Blythwood, Watford Road, Radlett, Herts. *T:* 5750. *Club:* Oxford and Cambridge University.

**MILNER, Joseph;** Queen's Fire Service Medal for Distinguished Service, 1962; Chief Officer of the London Fire Brigade, since 1970; *b* 5 Oct. 1922; *s* of Joseph and Ann Milner; *m* 1943, Bella Grice, *e d* of Frederick George Flinton; one *s* one *d. Educ:* Ladybarn Sch., Manchester. Served King's Regt (Liverpool), 1940-46: India/Burma, 1943-46 (Wingate's Chindits). Nat. Fire Service, 1946-48; North Riding Fire Bde, 1948-50; Manchester Fire Bde, 1950-51; Hong Kong Fire Bde, 1951-60; Dep. Dir, Hong Kong Fire Services, 1961-65; Dir, Hong Kong Fire Services, and Unit Controller, Auxiliary

Fire Service, 1965-70. Mem., Hong Kong Council, Order of St John, 1965-70; JP Hong Kong, 1965-70. Regional Fire Commander (designate), 1970. Mem. Bd, Fire Service College, 1970. Mem., Instn of Fire Engineers; Associate Mem., Inst. of British Engineers. *Recreations:* walking, poetry. *Address:* 8 Albert Embankment, SE1. *Club:* Hong Kong (Hong Kong).

**MILNER, Sir Mordaunt;** *see* Milner, Sir G. E. M.

**MILNER, Ralph;** *see* Millner, Ralph.

**MILNER-BARRY, Philip Stuart,** CB 1962; OBE 1946; Ceremonial Officer, Civil Service Department (formerly Treasury), since 1966; *b* 20 Sept. 1906; *s* of late Prof. E. L. Milner-Barry; *m* 1947, Thelma Tennant Wells; one *s* two *d*. *Educ:* Cheltenham Coll.; Trinity Coll., Cambridge (Major Schol.). 1st Class Hons, Classical Tripos (Pt I), Moral Science Tripos (Pt II). With L. Powell Sons & Co., Stockbrokers, 1929-38; Chess Correspondent, The Times, 1938-45; temporary civil servant, a Dept of the Foreign Office, 1940-45; Principal, HM Treasury, 1945; Asst Sec., 1947; Dir of Organisation and Methods, Treasury, 1954-58; Dir of Establishments and Organisation, Min. of Health, 1958-60; Under-Sec., Treasury, 1954-66. *Recreations:* Chess: British Boy Champion, 1923; British Championship Second, 1953; mem. British Internat. teams, 1937-61; Pres. British Chess Fedn, 1970- (Dep. Pres., 1967-70); walking. *Address:* 43 Blackheath Park, SE3. *T:* 01-852 5808. *Club:* Brooks's.

**MILNES, G. Turquet;** *see* Turquet, Gladys.

**MILNES, Nora,** LLD (Hon.); BSc (London); Reader Emeritus in Social Study, University of Edinburgh (Director, Edinburgh School of Social Study, 1918-28, Department of Social Study, 1928-51); Reader in Social Study, 1946; *b* 1882; 3rd *d* of Alfred Milnes, DLit. *Educ:* North London Collegiate Sch. for Girls; and privately. Worked for London COS, 1911-13. Tutor and Lecturer, Social Science Dept, London Sch. of Economics, 1913-18; Lecturer in Economics, King's Coll. for Women, Household and Social Science Dept, 1915-18; awarded Commonwealth Grant to study Child Guidance in USA, 1929; Visiting Lecturer, Dept of Social Science and Administration, University of Chicago, 1929. Mem. apptd, by Scottish Educ. Dept, to Gen. Nursing Council for Scotland, 1920-23; re-appointed until resigned, 1942; organized for Ministry of Labour, short courses of training to qualify Personnel Managers for wartime industries ("Bevin Babies"), 1940-44; Mem. Selection Cttee for Supplementary Register, Min. of Labour; Mem. Appeals Tribunal for Scotland under Further Education and Training Scheme, Min. of Labour, 1946-52. Hon. LLD Edinburgh 1958. *Publications:* Child Welfare, from the Social Point of View, 1920; Economics of Wages and Labour, 1926; A Study of Industrial Edinburgh, 1923-34, Vol. I, 1936; contributions to various journals. *Recreation:* listening to music. *Address:* 9 Vale Court, Mallord Street, Chelsea, SW3. *T:* 01-352 5664.

**MILNES-COATES, Sir Clive;** *see* Coates.

**MILNES WALKER, Robert;** *see* Walker, R. M.

**MILSOM, Hilda Maud,** CVO 1946; CBE 1935 (OBE 1927); *d* of William Griffith Milsom, Reading. *Educ:* Polam Hall, Darlington. Clerk in His Majesty's Private Secretary's Office, 1915-45; Chief Clerk 1919-45. *Address:* Southcot, Lester Point, Combe Martin, Ilfracombe, N Devon. *T:* Combe Martin 2234.

**MILSOM, Stroud Francis Charles,** FBA 1967; Professor of Legal History, University of London, since 1964; Literary Director, Selden Society, since 1964; *b* Merton, Surrey, 2 May 1923; *yr s* of Harry Lincoln Milsom and Isobel Vida, *d* of late W. E. Collins, Wellington, NZ; *m* 1955, Irène, *d* of late Witold Szereszewski, Wola Krysztoporska, Poland. *Educ:* Charterhouse; Trinity Coll., Cambridge. Admiralty, 1944-45. Called to the Bar, Lincoln's Inn, 1947, Hon. Bencher, 1970; Commonwealth Fund Fellow, University of Pennsylvania, 1947-48; Yorke Prize, University of Cambridge, 1948; Trinity Coll., Cambridge: Prize Fellow, 1948; Fellow and Lectr, 1949-55; University Asst Lectr and Lectr in Law, Cambridge, 1949-55; Asst Lectr, LSE, 1955-56; Fellow and Tutor, New Coll., Oxford, 1956-64; CUF Lectr in Law, Oxford, 1956-64; Lectr, Council of Legal Education, 1962-; Vis. Lectr, New York Univ. Law Sch., 1958, 1961, 1964, 1967, 1970; Vis. Prof., Yale Law Sch., 1968. *Publications:* Novae Narrationes (introd., trans. and notes), 1963; introd. reissue Pollock and Maitland, History of English Law, 1968; Historical Foundations of the Common Law, 1969; articles in learned jls. *Address:* 30 Dartmouth Row, Greenwich, SE10. *T:* 01-692 3132. *Clubs:* Athenæum, Oxford and Cambridge University.

**MILSTEIN, Nathan;** violinist; *b* Odessa, Russia, 31 Dec. 1904; *s* of Miron and Maria Milstein; *m* 1945, Thérèse Weldon; one *d*. *Educ:* St Petersburg Conservatory of Music. Studied under Eugène Isaye, Brussels. Many tours in Russia, 1920-26; left Russia, 1926; annual tours throughout Europe, also in North, Central and South America, from 1920, except for war years. Chevalier, Légion d'Honneur. *Address:* c/o Hurok Concerts Inc., 730 Fifth Avenue, New York, NY, USA.

**MILTHORPE, Prof. Frederick Leon,** DSc London, MScAgr, DIC; FInstBiol; Professor of Biology, Macquarie University, Sydney, New South Wales, since 1967; *b* 24 Sept. 1917; 2nd *s* of S. G. and Annie Milthorpe, Hillston, NSW; *m* 1941, Elma Joan, *o d* of R. K. Hobbs, Sydney; two *s*. *Educ:* McCaughey Memorial High Sch.; Univ. of Sydney; Imperial Coll. of Science, London. Walter and Eliza Hall Agricultural Fellow, 1940-42; Plant Pathologist, NSW Dept of Agriculture, 1942-46; Farrer Memorial Scholar, 1946-48; Leverhulme Research Fellow, 1948-49; Senior Plant Physiologist, Waite Agricultural Research Inst., University of Adelaide, 1949-54; Prof. of Agricultural Botany, University of Nottingham, 1954-67. *Publications:* various papers on plant physiology in scientific journals. *Address:* Macquarie University, North Ryde, NSW 2113, Australia.

**MILTON, Ernest;** Actor; *b* 10 Jan. 1890; *m* 1926, Naomi Royde Smith (*d* 1964). His parts have included Rupert Cadell in Rope, Ferdinand De Levis in Loyalties, Dr Oetternschlag in Grand Hotel, Lord Beaconsfield in Victoria Regina, the name part in Pirandello's Henry IV (The Mock Emperor); the title part in Francis Thompson; the leading character in Night's Candles, an English version of De Musset's Lorenzaccio; Hamlet in entirety version, 23 April 1934; Evan in wife's play, A Balcony; among his Shakespearean parts at the Old Vic have been Hamlet, Shylock, King Lear, Macbeth, Romeo, Orsino, Richard II, Oberon, and Armado; Old Vic Company, playing Sir Andrew Aguecheek and Svengali, and visiting the mining villages of County Durham as Shylock in the Merchant of Venice.

Later parts have been King John, Sir Giles Overreach, Macbeth, Father Zossima in The Brothers Karamazov, Count Mancini in He Who Gets Slapped, Hugo von Gerhardt in The Compelled People, and Malvolio in the Old Vic's Italian tour of Twelfth Night, 1950; Lodovico in Othello, Old Vic, 1951; The Duke in The Comedy of Errors, Royal Court Theatre, 1952; Lorenzo Querini in The Strong are Lonely, Piccadilly Theatre, 1955, also at Haymarket Theatre, 1956; Pope Paul in Malatesta, Lyric, Hammersmith, 1957; The Narrator in the Finsbury Story, Sadler's Wells Theatre, 1960; King Philip II of Spain in Teresa of Avila, Dublin Festival and Vaudeville, 1961; The Lord Cardinal in Women Beware Women, Arts, 1962; Bishop Tihon in The Possesed, Mermaid, 1963; Nicodemus in This is For Now, Westminster Cathedral, 1966. Joseph Piller in The Deadly Game, Savoy, 1967. *Publications:* Christopher Marlowe, a play; To Kiss the Crocodile, a novel; has written and produced his own play, Paganini, and his play Mary of Magdala, in which he played the rôle of Quintus; Two Novelettes by Quite a Gentleman. *Address:* Barclays Bank Ltd, 52 Regent Street, W1.

**MILTON, Sir Frank,** Kt 1970; MA; Chief Metropolitan Magistrate since 1967; *b* 6 Jan. 1906; *s* of late G. Lowenstein, Director of S. Japhet & Co. Ltd of London; *m* 1st, 1940, Barbara McFadyean (marr. diss. 1945); 2nd, 1954, Iris Averil, *e d* of late Sheffield Airey Neave, CMG, OBE; two *s* (adopted). *Educ:* Bembridge Sch.; St John's Coll., Oxford. Called to Bar, Lincoln's Inn, 1930 (Bencher, 1967); on the south-eastern circuit; contested (L) South Islington, 1929. Served War of 1939-45, Royal Artillery, Major. Metropolitan Magistrate, 1952-67; Chm., Epping Group Hosp. Management Cttee, 1958-63; Member: Standing Cttee on Criminal Law Revision, 1959-; Cttee on Immigration Appeals, 1966-67. Dep. Chm., Herts Quarter Sessions, 1965-. *Publications:* In Some Authority, 1959; More Than a Crime, 1962; The English Magistracy, 1967. *Recreations:* watching village cricket, chess. *Address:* 7 Stone Buildings, Lincoln's Inn, WC2. *T:* 01-405 0304; Riverside, Hewish, Crewkerne, Som. *T:* Crewkerne 3465. *Club:* Garrick.

**MILVERTON,** 1st Baron, *cr* 1947, of Lagos and of Clifton; **Arthur Frederick Richards,** GCMG, *cr* 1942 (KCMG, *cr* 1935; CMG 1933); KStJ 1945; Freedom Medal (USA), with silver palm, 1946; 2nd *s* of late W. Richards; *b* 21 Feb. 1885; *m* 1927, Noelle Benda Whitehead; two *s* one *d*. *Educ:* Clifton Coll.; Christ Church, Oxford. Cadet, Malayan Civil Service, 1908; in various district posts in the Federated Malay States, Kelantan and Kedah, 1910-20: 2nd Asst Colonial Sec., Straits Settlements, 1920; Sec. to Select Cttee on Constitution of Legislative Council, 1921; 1st Asst Colonial Sec. SS; and Clerk of Councils, Sec. to Trade Commissions, Straits Settlements and Federated Malay States; General Sec., Straits Settlements Retrenchment Cttee, 1922; Sec. to High Commissioner for Malay States, 1923; Chm., Executive Cttee, British Malaya, British Empire Exhibition, 1924; Sec., Opium Cttee, British Malaya; Sec. Cttee to enquire into organisation of Postal Services, Straits Settlements, Federated Malay States and Unfederated Malay States, 1924; Under-Sec. to Government FMS, 1926; Acting General Adviser to Government of Johore, 1929; Governor of North Borneo, 1930-33; Governor and Commander-in-Chief, Gambia Colony, 1933-36; Governor and Commander-in-Chief of Fiji and High Commissioner for Western Pacific, 1936-38; Capt.-Gen. and Governor-in-Chief of Jamaica, 1938-43; Governor and C-in-C, Nigeria, 1943-47. A part-time Dir, Colonial Development Corp., 1948-51; Chm. of Council, London Sch. of Hygiene and Tropical Medicine, 1948-51; a Vice-Pres. of Royal Empire Society; Mem. of Board of Governors of Clifton Coll. Pres. Assoc. of British Malaya, 1948-50. Chairman: Empire Day Movement, 1948-50; British Empire Leprosy Relief Assoc., 1948-50; Royal African Soc., 1963-65; Director: West Indies Sugar Co. Ltd; Bank of West Africa, 1950-65; Kamuning (Perak) Rubber & Tin Co. Ltd, 1956-65. *Recreations:* golf, sailing. *Heir:* *s* Rev. Hon. Fraser Arthur Richard Richards [*b* 21 July 1930; *m* 1957, Mary Dorothy, *d* of Leslie Fly, Bickley, Kent; two *d*]. *Address:* The Lodge, Cox Green, Maidenhead, Berks. *T:* Maidenhead 20040. *Clubs:* Athenæum, Oxford and Cambridge University, West Indian.

**MILWARD, Sir Anthony (Horace),** Kt 1966; CBE 1960 (OBE 1945); MInstT; Chairman of British European Airways, 1964-70; part-time Member of the Board of British Overseas Airways Corporation 1964-70; *b* 2 March 1905; *s* of Henry T. and Elsie T. Milward, Redditch, Worcs; *m* 1931, Frieda Elizabeth Anne von der Becke; one *s* one *d*. *Educ:* Rugby Sch.; Clare Coll., Cambridge (BA). With Glazebrook, Steel & Co. Ltd, Manchester, 1926-40. Served Fleet Air Arm, RNVR, as Pilot, 1940-45, reaching rank of Lieut-Cdr. With BEA in various capacities, 1946-. Mem., Air Registration Board, 1964-70. *Recreations:* fishing, shooting, walking. *Address:* Tyler End, Penn, Bucks. *T:* Penn 2162. *Club:* Royal Automobile.

**MILWARD, John Frederic;** Stipendiary Magistrate for Birmingham since 1951; *b* 26 June 1908; *s* of late Charles Frederic and Emily Constantia Milward, Alvechurch, Worcs; *m* 1946, Doris Evelyn McMurdo, 2nd *d* of Aston E. McMurdo, Charlottesville, Va; two *s*. *Educ:* Bedales Sch.; Clare Coll., Cambridge. Called to Bar, Middle Temple, 1932. Associate of Oxford Circuit, 1942-51. JP Worcs, 1940-; Chm. of Worcs QS, 1964- (Dep. Chm., 1943-64); a Life Governor of Birmingham Univ., 1952. Liveryman of Needlemakers' Company. *Address:* Stable Door House, Alvechurch, Worcs. *T:* 021-445 1218. *Club:* Union (Birmingham).

**MIMPRISS, Trevor Walter,** MS; FRCS; Surgeon to St Thomas' Hospital since 1946; Surgeon-in-Charge, Urological Division, St Peter's Hospital, Chertsey, Surrey, since 1946; *b* 12 May 1905; *s* of late S. T. Mimpriss, Bromley, Kent; *m* 1938, Eleanor Joan, *d* of Gordon Innes; two *s* one *d*. *Educ:* Brighton Coll.; St Thomas' Hospital, London Univ. FRCS 1932; MS London 1935. Cheselden Medal for Surgery, St Thomas' Hospital, 1932; Louis Jenner Research Scholarship, 1936-37. Hunterian Professor of Royal College of Surgeons, 1938. *Publications:* various papers in medical journals. *Recreations:* shooting, fishing, golf. *Address:* Muskoka, Kingsley Green, Haslemere, Surrey. *Club:* United Service.

**MINIO-PALUELLO, Lorenzo,** FBA 1957; Reader (Senior Lecturer since 1948) in medieval philosophy, University of Oxford, since 1956; Fellow of Oriel College since 1962; *b* 21 Sept. 1907; *s* of Michelangelo Minio and Ersilia (*née* Bisson); *m* 1938, Magda Ungar; one *s* one *d* (and one *d* decd). *Educ:* Ginnasio-Liceo Foscarini, Venice; Univ. of Padua; Sorbonne and Ecole des Hautes Etudes, Paris. Dr of Philosophy (Padua), 1929; Asst Librarian, University of Padua, 1929-32; Fellow of Warburg Inst., Univ. of London, 1947-48; DPhil Oxon, MA Oxon, 1948; Barlow

Lectr, Univ. of London, 1955; Prof. straord, of medieval and humanistic philology, Univ. of Padua, for 1956-57; Dir of Aristoteles Latinus (Union Acad. Internat.), 1959-; Mem., Inst. for Advanced Study, Princeton, 1969-70; Corresp. Fellow, Amer. Mediaeval Acad., 1970. *Publications:* Education in Fascist Italy, 1946; editions of Aristotle's Categoriae and De interpr. (1949, 1957), Plato's Phaedo (medieval Latin trans., 1950), Aristotle's Categ., De interpr., Prior and Post. Anal. Topics (Ancient and Medieval Latin Trans. and paraphrases, 1953, 1954, 1961, 1962, 1965, 1967, 1969), Ps. Arist.'s De Mundo (Apuleius' Rinucio's, Sadoleto's trans., 1965), Porphyry's Isagoge (Boethius' trans., 1966); 'Liber VI Princip.' (1966); co-ed Aristot. Lat. Codices, vol. ii, and Suppl. Alt. (1955, 1961), and Poetics (Latin trans., 1953, 1968); Twelfth Century Logic, vol. i, 1956, vol. ii, 1958; articles in The Classical Quart. Jl of Hellenic Studies, Mediaeval and Renaiss. Studies, Riv. di Filos. Neoscolastica, Studi Medievali, Rev. Philos. de Louvain, Traditio, Encyclopædia Britannica, Dizion. Biograf. degli Ital., Dictionary of Scientific Biography, etc. *Address:* 22 Polstead Road, Oxford. *T:* Oxford 57798.

**MINION, Alderman Stephen,** OBE 1954; JP; Director and General Manager, The Lancashire & Cheshire Rubber Co. Ltd; *b* 2 June 1908; *s* of Stephen and Elizabeth Minion; *m* 1935, Ada, *d* of George and Jane Evans; no *c*. *Educ:* Liverpool Technical and Commercial Colleges. Commenced as Junior Clerk, The Lancashire & Cheshire Rubber Co. Ltd. City Councillor 1940, Alderman 1961, Lord Mayor 1969-70, Liverpool. JP Liverpool, 1954. *Recreations:* outdoor sports, reading, history, theatre and music. *Address:* Glen Cairn, 223 Booker Avenue, Liverpool L18 9TA. *T:* 051-724 2671. *Club:* Racquet (Liverpool).

**MINNEY, Rubeigh James;** Novelist, Biographer, Playwright, Film Producer; *b* 29 Aug. 1895; *s* of late J. R. Minney; *m*; one *s* one *d*. *Educ:* King's Coll., London. Editorial Staff, Pioneer, Allahabad; Englishman, Calcutta; represented The Times in Calcutta; special representative with Duke of Connaught to India, 1920; Daily Express, London; Asst Editor, Sunday News, London; Editor, Everybody's Weekly, 1925-35; Dir Everybody's Publications, Ltd, until 1935; Dir Chapman and Hall, Ltd, 1934-36; Editor, Sunday Referee, 1935-39; Editor, The Era; Editor The War Weekly, 1939-41; Editor The Strand Magazine, 1941-42. In films since 1942. Hon. Pres. London Sch. of Economics Film Soc., 1948-49; Mem. of Executive and General Council, Association of Cine-Technicians, 1953-56; Vice-Chm. ACT Films Ltd, 1951-68, Chm. 1968-. Parly Candidate (Lab) for Southend East, 1950, for Bexley, 1955. Went to Peking to speak at George Bernard Shaw Centenary celebration, July 1956. *Publications: Novels:* Maki, 1921; The Road to Delhi, 1923; Distant Drums, 1935; Governor General, 1935; How Vainly Men . . ., 1940; A Woman of France, 1945; Nothing to Lose, 1946 (filmed as Time Gentlemen Please, 1952); Bring out the Drum, 1950; The Governor's Lady, 1951; (with Margot Duke) The Rising, 1970. *Biographies, etc:* Clive of India, 1931; Shiva, or The Future of India; Midst Himalayan Mists; Excursions in Ink; Across India by Air; The Journalist; Night Life of Calcutta; India Marches Past, 1933; Hollywood by Starlight, 1935; Talking of Films, 1947; Chaplin, The Immortal Tramp, 1954; Viscount Southwood, 1954; Carve Her Name with Pride, 1956 (filmed 1957); Next Stop Peking, 1957; Viscount Addison, Leader of the Lords, 1958; The Private Papers of Hore-Belisha, 1960; Fanny and the Regent of Siam, 1962; No. 10 Downing Street: A House in History, 1963; The Film Maker and his World, 1964; The Edwardian Age, 1964; I Shall Fear No Evil: the story of Dr Alina Brewda, 1966; The Two Pillars of Charing Cross, 1967; The Bogus Image of Bernard Shaw, 1969 (US, Recollections of George Bernard Shaw); The Tower of London, 1970. *Plays:* Clive of India (with W. P. Lipscomb), first prod. by village players of Great Hucklow in Derbyshire, 1933; filmed by Twentieth Century, Hollywood, 1934; They Had His Number (with Lady Rhys-Williams), first produced at Hippodrome, Bolton, 1942; Gentle Caesar (with Sir Osbert Sitwell), first produced Alexandra Theatre, Birmingham, 1943; The Voice of the People, first produced Southend, 1950. *Films:* (as producer): Madonna of the Seven Moons; Osbert Sitwell's A Place of One's Own; The Wicked Lady; The Magic Bow; The Idol of Paris; Terence Rattigan's The Final Test, etc. *Address:* 32 Albion Street, W2; Falconwood House, Groombridge, Sussex. *Club:* Savage.

**MINNIS, Samuel Ellison,** CBE 1941; *b* March 1882; *s* of late Rev. Alexander Minnis, Saltersland, Co. Londonderry; *m* 1906, Mary Rose Davidson, *d* of late James Eakin; three *d*. *Educ:* Rainey Sch., Magherafelt; Queen's Coll., Galway; Royal University of Ireland (Scholar Mod. Lang.). Entered Civil Service, Inland Revenue Dept, 1904; Comptroller of Stamps and Income Tax and Asst Registrar of Joint Stock Companies for Ireland, 1919; Asst Sec., Board of Inland Revenue, 1922. *Address:* 16 Deansway, East Finchley, N2. *T:* 01-883 8166.

*See also Rear-Adm. H. J. B. Grylls.*

**MINNITT, Robert John,** CMG 1955; *b* 2 April 1913; *s* of Charles Frederick Minnitt and Winifred May Minnitt (*née* Buddle); *m* 1943, Peggy Christine Sharp; one *s* two *d*. *Educ:* Marlborough Coll.; Trinity Coll., Cambridge. Appointed to Colonial Administrative Service, Hong Kong, 1935; Chief Sec., Western Pacific High Commission, 1952-58, retired. Furniture designer and craftsman, 1960-66; temp. Civil Servant, CO, 1966; FCO, 1968-69. *Address:* Knigh, Heath End, Petworth, Sussex. *T:* Petworth 2134.

**MINTER, Sir Frederick (Albert)** GCVO 1959 (KCVO 1935; CVO 1931); JP, Surrey, 1935; President F. G. Minter, Ltd, Berkeley Electrical Engineering Co. Ltd, *b* 11 July 1887; *s* of late F. G. Minter; *m* 1912, Greeta Constance West; three *s*. *Educ:* Framlingham Coll. Capt. Royal Marines, 1916-19; Engineer, Otira Gorge Tunnel, New Zealand, 1908; restored The King's Beasts, St George's Chapel, Windsor Castle; Dir Ancient Buildings Trust, Ltd; Fellow of Institute of Builders; FIStructE. Chm. the Royal Alexandra and Albert Sch., 1952-63; Mem. of Governing Body, Framlingham Coll.; Vice-Pres. London Police Court Mission; Mem. of British Commonwealth Relations Conference in Sydney, 1938; Chm. Board of Governors, Queen Charlotte's and Chelsea Hosp. for Women, 1948-54; Mem. Gen. Council, King Edward's Hosp. Fund for London. *Recreation:* fishing. *Address:* Flat 32, 55 Park Lane, W1. *T:* 01-499 3574. *Clubs:* Carlton, Flyfishers', Royal Automobile.

**MINTO,** 5th Earl of, *cr* 1813; **Victor Gilbert Lariston Garnet Elliot (-Murray-Kynynmound);** Baron of Nova Scotia; Bt 1700; Baron of Minto, 1797; Viscount Melgund, 1813; *b* 12 Feb. 1891; *s* of 4th Earl and Mary (author of India: Minto and Morley, 1905-10, 1934; she *d* 1940), *d* of Gen. Hon. Charles Grey; *S* father, 1914; *m* 1921, Marion (OBE 1956), *d* of G. W.

Cook, Montreal; two *s* two *d.* Late Lieut Lothians and Border Horse Yeomanry; Capt. Scots Guards. Owns about 25,000 acres. *Heir: s* Viscount Melgund, *qv. Recreations:* hunting, shooting, fishing. *Address:* Braehead, St Boswells, Roxburghshire, Scotland. *T:* St Boswells 3203. *Clubs:* Bath, Royal Automobile, New (Edinburgh).

*See also Baron Astor of Hever, Earl of Cromer.*

**MINTON, Yvonne Fay;** mezzo-soprano; *b* 4 Dec. 1938; *er d* of R. T. Minton, Sydney; *m* 1965, William Barclay. *Educ:* Sydney Conservatorium of Music. Elsa Stralia Scholar, Sydney, 1957-60; won Canberra Operatic Aria Competition, 1960; won Kathleen Ferrier Prize at s'Hertogenbosch Vocal Competition, 1961. Joined Royal Opera House as a Principal Mezzo-Soprano, 1965. Major roles include: Octavian in Der Rosenkavalier; Dorabella in Cosi Fan Tutte; Marina in Boris Godounov; Helen in King Priam; Cherubino in Marriage of Figaro; Orfeo in Gluck's Orfeo. Recordings include Octavian in Der Rosenkavalier, Mozart Requiem, Elgar's The Kingdom, etc. Guest Artist with Cologne Opera Company, Oct. 1969-. *Recreations:* reading, gardening. *Address:* 57 Park View Road, Ealing, W5. *T:* 01-997 6087.

**MIREPOIX, Duc de L.;** *see* Lévis Mirepoix.

**MIRO, Joan;** artist; *b* Barcelona, 20 April 1893; *s* of Miguel and Dolores Miró; *m* 1929, Pilar. *Educ:* Barcelona Academy of Fine Art. Work includes paintings, ceramics, sculptures, engravings, lithographs. Guggenheim Award for ceramic mural in grounds of Unesco Building, Paris, 1958. *Exhibitions include:* Galerie Pierre, 1925; Goeman's Gallery, 1928; Galerie Maeght, Paris, 1948, 1953, 1956, 1960, 1970; Pierre Matisse Gallery, New York, 1946, 1953, 1956, 1961, 1965, 1967, 1970; Tate Gallery, London, 1964; Marlborough Fine Art Gallery, London, 1966; Tokyo, Kyoto, 1966; Barcelona, 1968; Maeght Foundn, St Paul de Vence, 1968; Munich, 1968; Museum of Modern Art, NY. *Recreation:* walking. *Address:* Pierre Matisse Gallery, 41 East 57th Street, New York, NY 10022, USA; 13 rue de Téhéran, Paris, 8e, France.

**MIRON, Wilfrid Lyonel,** CBE 1969 (OBE 1946; MBE 1945); TD 1950; JP; DL; Regional Chairman (Midlands), National Coal Board, since 1967 and Regional Chairman (South Wales), since Sept. 1969; *b* 27 Jan. 1913; *s* of late Solman Miron and late Minnie Pearl Miron; *m* 1958, Doreen (*née* Hill); no *c. Educ:* Llanelli Gram. Sch. Admitted Solicitor, 1934; private practice and Legal Adviser to Shipley Collieries and associated companies. TA Commn, Sherwood Foresters, 1939; served War of 1939-45: Home Forces, 1939; France and Dunkirk, 1940; Home Forces, IO 139 Inf. Bde and GSO3 Aldershot Dist, 1941-42; Staff Coll., Quetta, 1942 (SC); DAAG 17 Ind. Div., 1943-44, and AA&QMG 17 Ind. Div., 1944-45, Chin Hills, Imphal, Burma (despatches, 1944). E Midlands Div. NCB: Sec. and Legal Adviser, 1946-51; Dep. Chm., 1951-60; Chm., 1960-67. Vice-Chm., Berry Hill Hosp. Man. Cttee; Chm., Midland Dist Miners' Fatal Accident Relief Soc.; Mem., E Mids Regional Planning Council (Chm., Industry and Trade Cttee); Mem. Ct and Law Adv. Cttee, Nottingham Univ.; Mem. Gov. Body, Trent Polytechnic; Trustee, Nottingham Trustee Savings Bank. Freeman (by redemption) City of London, Mem. Pattenmakers' Company. Hon. Lieut-Col; JP Notts, 1964; DL Notts, 1970. frsa 1965. OStJ 1962. *Publications:* Bitter Sweet Seventeen, 1946; articles and papers in mining and other jls. *Recreations:* cricket, Rugby football, music, reading, crosswords. *Address:* 24 Calstock Road, Woodthorpe, Nottingham. *T:* Nottingham 268343. *Clubs:* Army and Navy, MCC; XL; Nottingham and Notts United Services (Nottingham).

**MIRRLEES, Prof. James Alexander;** Professor of Economics, University of Oxford, and Fellow of Nuffield College, since 1968; *b* 5 July 1936; *s* of George B. M. Mirrlees; *m* 1961, Gillian Marjorie Hughes; two *d. Educ:* Douglas-Ewart High Sch., Newton Stewart; Edinburgh Univ.; Trinity Coll., Cambridge. MA Edinburgh maths, 1957; BA Cantab Maths, 1959; PhD Cantab econs, 1963. Adviser, MIT Center for Internat. Studies, New Delhi, 1962-63; Cambridge Univ. Asst Lectr in Econs and Fellow of Trinity Coll., 1963, University Lectr, 1965; Adviser to Govt of Swaziland, 1963; Res. Assoc., Pakistan Inst. of Develt Econs, Karachi, 1966-67. Vis. Prof., MIT, 1968. *Publications:* (joint author) Manual of Industrial Project Analysis in Developing Countries, 1969; articles in economic jls. *Recreations:* reading detective stories and other forms of mathematics, playing the piano, travelling, listening. *Address:* Nuffield College, Oxford; 11 Field House Drive, Oxford OX2 7NT. *T:* Oxford 52436.

**MIRRLEES, Robin Ian Evelyn Stuart de la Lanne-;** ADC to HM the King of Yugoslavia, since 1963; Richmond Herald, 1962-67; *b* Paris, 13 Jan. 1925; Step *s* of late Maj.-Gen. W. H. B. Mirrlees, CB, DSO, MC; godson of 11th Duke of Argyll. *Educ:* Merton Coll., Oxford (MA). Several language diplomas. Served India, 1942-46; Captain RA, 1944; Gen. Staff, New Delhi, 1946; Embassy Attaché, Tokyo, 1947; Rouge Dragon Pursuivant of Arms, 1952-62 (and as such attended Coronation). Co-editor, Annuaire de France, 1966-. Has raised substantial funds for humanitarian organisations; undertook restoration of Inchdrewer Castle, Scotland, and Palazzo Venaria, Sicily; proprietor of Island of Great Bernera, Hebrides, Freeman of City of London, 1960. Various foreign orders of knighthood. *Recreations:* foxhunting, piloting, travelling, painting, collecting objects d'art. *Address:* 25 Holland Park Avenue, W11; 115 Rue de la Pompe, Paris 16me; Inchdrewer Castle, Banff, Scotland; Les Lambins, Le Touquet, France; Schloss Ratzenegg, Carinthia, Austria. *Clubs:* Buck's, Turf, Lansdowne; Travellers' (Paris).

**MISCAMPBELL, Norman Alexander;** MP (C) Blackpool North since 1962; *b* 20 Feb. 1925; *s* of late Alexander and of Eileen Miscampbell; *m* 1961, Margaret Kendall; one *s* two *d. Educ:* St Edward's Sch., Oxford; Trinity Coll., Oxford. Called to Bar, Inner Temple, 1952; N Circuit. Mem., Hoylake UDC, 1955-61. Contested (C) Newton, 1955, 1959. *Address:* 7 Abbey Road, West Kirby, Cheshire.

**MISHCON, Victor,** DL; Solicitor; Senior Partner, Victor Mishcon & Co. and Blatchfords; Member of Greater London Council for Lambeth, 1964-67 (Chairman General Purposes Committee, 1964-67); *b* 14 Aug. 1915; *s* of Rev. Rabbi Arnold and Mrs Queenie Mishcon. *Educ:* City of London Sch. Admitted Solicitor, 1937. Mem. Lambeth Borough Coun., 1945-49 (Chm. Finance Cttee, 1947-49); Mem. London CC for Brixton, 1946-65 (Chairman: Public Control Cttee, 1947-52; Gen. Purposes Cttee, 1952-54; Council, April 1954-55; Supplies Cttee, 1956-57; Fire Brigade Cttee, 1958-65). Member: Inner London Educn Authority, 1964-67; Inner London Educn Cttee, 1964-67. Chm. Governors: Cormont and Loughborough Secondary Schools, 1947-60; Governor:

Stockwell Manor Sch., 1960- (Chm. of Governors, 1960-67, 1970-); JFS Comprehensive Sch., 1970-; Philippa Fawcett Coll. of Educn, 1970-. Member: Standing Joint Cttee, Co. of London Sessions, 1950-65 (Vice-Chm. 1959-61); Nat. Theatre Board, 1965-, and its Finance Sub-Cttee, 1965-67; London Orchestra Bd, 1966-67; Exec. Cttee, London Tourist Board, 1965-67; Government Cttee of Enquiry into London Transport, 1953-54; Departmental Cttee on Homosexual Offences and Prostitution, 1954-57. Vice-Pres., Bd of Deputies of British Jews; Hon. President, Brit. Technion Soc.; Mem. Bd of Governors, Technion, Israel; Vice-Pres. (Past Pres.) Assoc of Jewish Youth; Chm., British Council of the Shaare Zedek Hosp., Jerusalem; Chm. of Deputy Lieutenants' Cttee of Lambeth, 1956-68. Contested (Lab) NW Leeds, 1950, Bath, 1951, Gravesend, 1955, 1959. DL Co. London, 1954. Comdr Royal Swedish Order of North Star, 1954; Star of Ethiopia 3rd Class, 1954. *Address:* 12 Chelwood House, Gloucester Square, W2.

**MISKIN, James William,** QC 1967; *b* 11 March 1925; *s* of Geoffrey Miskin and late Joyce Miskin; *m* 1951, Mollie Joan Milne; two *s* two *d*. *Educ:* Haileybury; Brasenose Coll., Oxford (MA). Sub-Lt, RNVR, 1943-46. Oxford, 1946-49 (Sen. Heath Harrison Exhibnr). Called to Bar, Inner Temple, 1951; Mem. of Bar Council, 1964-67. *Recreations:* golf, gardening. *Address:* 17 Ladbroke Grove, W11. *T:* 01-727 9319. *Clubs:* Garrick; Vincent's (Oxford).

**MISSELBROOK, (Bertram) Desmond;** Chairman, Construction Industry Training Board, since 1970; Senior Research Fellow in Business Studies, Edinburgh University, since 1970 (part-time); *b* 28 May 1913; *s* of late C. J. and E. P. Misselbrook; *m* 1949, Anne, *er d* of late F. O. Goodman; two *s*. *Educ:* Chatham House, Ramsgate; Bristol Univ. Admiralty Psychologist, 1942-45. Lectr in Psychology and Dir, Unit of Applied Psychology, Edinburgh Univ., 1945-49. Personnel Adviser, 1949, Dir. 1955, Dep. Chm. 1963-70, British-American Tobacco Co. Ltd; Chm., Evershed and Vignoles Ltd, 1961-65; Chm., Mardon Packaging International Ltd, 1962-70; Dir. 1963, Dep. Chm. 1966-69, Wiggins Teape Ltd. Chm., Bd of Governors, Oversea Service, 1963-70; Mem. Council, British Inst. of Management, 1967 (a Vice-Chm., 1969); Chm., Economic Development Cttees for Building and Civil Engineering Industries, 1969-; Member: Adv. Council on Social Work (Scotland), 1970-; Economic Consultant, Scottish Office, 1970-. *Recreations:* fishing, gardening, walking. *Address:* Craigrarrich, Strathtay, Perthshire. *T:* Strathtay 235; 22 Belgrave Crescent, Edinburgh 4. *T:* 061-332 6531.

**MISSEN, Leslie Robert,** CMG 1956; MC 1918; Research Consultant; *b* 2 May 1897; *e s* of Robert Symonds Missen, Chesterton, Cambs; *m* 1932, Muriel, *o d* of Robert Alstead, OBE, Gathurst, Lancs, formerly MP for Altrincham; two *s*. *Educ:* Perse Sch. and Christ's Coll., Cambridge. Served European War, Capt., 7th Bn N Stafford Regt, Mesopotamia, Persia and Caucasus, 1915-19. Asst Education Officer, Leeds, 1922-26; Dep. Chief Educ. Officer, Middlesborough, 1926-30; Chief Educ. Officer: Wigan, 1930-36; East Suffolk County Council, 1936-62; Mem., Local Govt Commn for England, 1962-66. Educational Adviser to: Ministry of Education, 1950-57; Ministry of Agriculture, 1944-54; Colonial Sec., 1952-55; Royal Navy, 1958-64; Chairman: Working Party on Educn in Trinidad, BWI, 1954; Trustees of Homerton Coll., Cambridge, 1946-62; President: Assoc. of Education Officers, 1952; Old Persean Soc., 1953-55; Education Section of British Assoc., 1957; County Educn Officers' Soc., 1960; Chm., Ipswich and District War Pensions Cttee, 1942-70. *Publications:* War History of 7th Bn N Stafford Regt, 1920; The Employment of Leisure, 1935; Anecdotes and After Dinner Stories, 1961; Quotable Anecdotes, 1966; Toptable Talk, 1968. *Recreations:* gardening, writing, piano. *Address:* Badger's Hill, Tuddenham Saint Martin, Ipswich. *T:* Witnesham 240.

**MISSENDEN, Sir Eustace James,** Kt, *cr* 1944; OBE 1937; Chairman, Railway Executive, 1947-51; *b* 3 March 1886; *s* of late James Missenden; *m* 1912, Lilian Adeline Gent (*d* 1959); no *c*. *Educ:* Folkestone, Kent. Entered Service SE and C Rly, 1899; SR Docks and Marine Manager, 1933; Traffic Manager, 1936; Gen. Manager, 1939; Col-Comdt, Engineer and Railway Staff Corps, RE (TA), 1949-51. KStJ; Officer of Legion of Honour (France); Chevalier, Order of Leopold (Belgium); American Medal of Freedom with Gold Palm. *Recreations:* golf, gardening. *Address:* Deepdene Warren, Dorking, Surrey. *T:* Dorking 3536.

**MITCHELL, Andrew Park,** CMG 1948; *b* 23 Aug. 1894; *s* of Andrew John Mitchell, Kew, Surrey; *m* 1922, Evangeline (*d* 1957), *d* of William Morris, Edinburgh; (one *s* killed in action, 1944), one *d*. *Educ:* St Paul's Sch.; London Univ. Survey of Egypt, 1919-27; Dir of Lands and Surveys, Transjordan, 1927-40; Dir of Surveys, Palestine, 1940-48; Dir of Surveys, Nigeria, 1948-51, Inspector-Gen., 1951-53. Served European War, 1914-19, in India, Egypt and France: Pilot RFC. mem. of Cttee of enquiry into application of Land Transfer Regulations, 1945; Dir of Surveys, Land Officer and Comr of Mines, Uganda, 1954-57; Mem. Land Admin. Commn, Malaya, 1957; Survey Enquiry, Cyprus, 1958; Land Registration and Survey Enquiry, Seychelles, 1959. 2nd Class Order of Istiqlal, Transjordan. Represented England in athletics, 1914. *Recreations:* golf, bridge. *Address:* 36 Pensford Avenue, Kew Gardens, Richmond, Surrey.

**MITCHELL, Air-Cdre Arthur Dennis,** CVO 1961; DFC 1944, and Bar, 1945; AFC 1943; an Extra Equerry to the Queen since 1962; *b* 26 May 1918; 2nd *s* of Col A. Mitchell, DSO, Carrickfergus, Belfast, N Ireland; *m* 1949, Comtesse Mireille Caroline Cornet de Ways Ruart; one *s*. *Educ:* Nautical Coll., Pangbourne; RAF Coll., Cranwell. Joined RAF, 1936. Served 1939-45, India, Burma, UK and NW Europe. US Air Force, 1951-53. Captain of the Queen's Flight, 1956-59 and 1962-64; ADC to the Queen, 1958-62. Gen. Agent, Spanta, SA; Man. Dir, Brussels Airways SA; Exec. Dir, Unipron, SA. *Recreations:* riding, golf. *Address:* 1 Rue de l'Eveque, Brussels 1. *T:* 12.47.68; Le Clos de Belloy, 9 Rue de Belloy, Rixensart, Brabant, Belgium. *T:* 53.41.92. *Clubs:* Royal Air Force, Royal Aero, Anglo-Belgian.

**MITCHELL, Prof. Basil George;** Nolloth Professor of the Philosophy of the Christian Religion, Oxford University, and Fellow of Oriel College, since 1968; *b* 9 April 1917; *s* of George William Mitchell and Mary Mitchell (*née* Loxston); *m* 1950, Margaret Eleanor Collin; one *s* three *d*. *Educ:* King Edward VI Sch., Southampton; Queen's Coll., Oxford (Southampton Exhibitioner. 1st cl. Lit Hum 1939). Served Royal Navy, 1940-46; Lt RNVR 1942, Instructor Lt RN 1945. Lectr, Christ Church, Oxford, 1946-47; Fellow and Tutor in Philosophy, Keble Coll., Oxford, 1947-67; Sen. Proctor, 1956-57; Hebdomadal Council, 1959-

65. Vis. Prof., Princeton Univ., 1963; Stanton Lectr in Philosophy of Religion, Cambridge Univ., 1959-62; Edward Cadbury Lectr, University of Birmingham, 1966-67. Mem. Council, St David's Coll., Lampeter, 1959-. *Publications:* (Ed.) Faith and Logic, 1957; Law, Morality and Religion in a Secular Society, 1967; Neutrality and Commitment, 1968; articles in philosophical and theological periodicals. *Address:* Bridge House, Wootton, Woodstock, Oxford. *T:* Woodstock 265; 6 Charlbury Road, Oxford. *T:* Oxford 58491.

**MITCHELL, Bertram,** CB 1963; retired as Chief Inspector, Board of Customs and Excise (1960-63); *b* 19 Sept. 1898; *s* of James and Mary A. Mitchell; *m* 1931, Dora M. Alway. *Educ:* Newton Abbot Grammar Sch. Collector, Customs and Excise, Manchester, 1956-58; Dep. Chief Inspector, Board of Customs and Excise, 1958-59. *Address:* 14 Mildenhall, West Cliff Road, Bournemouth, Hants. *T:* Westbourne 65740.

**MITCHELL, Lt-Col Brian Granville Blayney,** DSC 1940; RM (Retired); DL; *b* 14 March 1900; *er s* of William Blayney Mitchell, Drumreaske, Co. Monaghan, Eire; *m* 1937, Violet Gwyndolin, *o d* of late Major Sir Charles Price, DL, Haverfordwest, Pembs; two *d. Educ:* King's Sch., Bruton, Somerset. Joined Royal Marines, 2nd Lt 1917; Lt 1919; HMS Erin, 1919; Emperor of India, Mediterranean, 1921-22; Hood, Atlantic and Round the World Cruise, 1923-24; Instructor, Sigs Portsmouth, 1925-27; HMS Champion, Home, 1928; Capt. 1928; Queen Elizabeth, Mediterranean, 1929-31; St Vincent (Boys' Training Estab.), 1932-33; Hermes, China, 1934-37; Coronation Review, Spithead, 1937; Supt of Sigs, RM, 1938-40; Major 1937; Actg Lt-Col 1940; Hook of Holland, 1940; The RM Div., 1941-42; Commando Group, Chief Signal Officer, 1943-44; Actg Col 1945; CO Molcab IV, 1945; retired, 1945. DL 1956, High Sheriff, 1959, County of Pembroke. Mem. Governing Body, Church in Wales, 1960. Order of Orange Nassau with Crossed Swords (Netherlands), 1940. *Address:* Manor House, Wiston, Pembs. *T:* Clarbeston 258.

**MITCHELL, (Charles) Julian (Humphrey);** writer; *b* 1 May 1935; *s* of William Moncur Mitchell and Christine Mary (*née* Browne). *Educ:* Winchester; Wadham Coll., Oxford. Mem., Literature Panel, Arts Council, 1966-69. John Llewelyn Rhys Prize, 1965; Somerset Maugham Award, 1966. *Publications: novels:* Imaginary Toys, 1961; A Disturbing Influence, 1962; As Far As You Can Go, 1963; The White Father, 1964; A Circle of Friends, 1966; The Undiscovered Country, 1968; *play:* A Heritage and Its History (adapted from I. Compton-Burnett), 1965. *Address:* 68 Christchurch Street, SW3. *T:* 01-352 3169.

**MITCHELL, Lt-Col Colin (Campbell);** MP (C) West Aberdeenshire since 1970; *b* 17 Nov. 1925; *o s* of Colin Mitchell, MC, and Janet Bowie Gilmour; *m* 1956, Jean Hamilton Susan Phillips; two *s* one *d. Educ:* Whitgift Sch. Served War of 1939-45: enlisted British Army, 1943; commissioned Argyll and Sutherland Highlanders, 1944, serving in Italy (wounded); Palestine, 1945-48 (wounded); Korea, 1950-51; Cyprus, 1958-59; Borneo, 1964 (brevet Lt-Col); Aden, 1967 (despatches). Qualified Camberley Staff Coll., 1955; subsequently: GSO2, 51st Highland Div. (TA); Bde Major, King's African Rifles, and GSO1 Staff of Chief of Defence Staff at MoD. Retired at own request, 1968; subseq. became: writer and lecturer on problems of world peace-keeping; Special Correspondent, Vietnam; industrial management trainee. *Publication:* Having Been A Soldier, 1969. *Recreations:* golf, shooting, squash, poetry, antiques, travel. *Address:* Leith Hall, Kennethmont, by Huntly, Aberdeenshire. *T:* Kennethmont 638. *Clubs:* Caledonian, Garrick, Lansdowne, Public Schools.

**MITCHELL, Craig,** CB 1949; Chairman: Building Standards Advisory Committee; *b* Loanhead, Midlothian, 5 Oct. 1896; *m* 1921, Jean Manson McDonald; one *s* one *d* (and one *s* decd). *Educ:* George Heriot's Sch.; University of Edinburgh. Served European War, Argyll and Sutherland Highlanders, 1915-19. Entered Civil Service, 1912; Private Sec. to Parly Under-Sec. of State for Scotland, 1934; Asst Sec., Dept of Health for Scotland, 1939; Dep. Principal Officer, Scotland Civil Defence Region, 1940-43; Principal Asst Sec., Dept of Health for Scotland, 1943-44; Dep. Sec. Dept of Health for Scotland, 1944-59; Member: Gen. Dental Council, 1959-69; Bd of Management, Royal Edinburgh Hosp., 1962-66; Chm., Scottish Water Adv. Cttee, 1962-69. *Address:* 11 Pentland Avenue, Colinton, Edinburgh 13. *T:* 031-441 2630. *Club:* Royal Commonwealth Society.

**MITCHELL, David Bower;** MP (C) Basingstoke since 1964; *b* June 1928; *er s* of James Mitchell, Naval Architect, and Mona Elizabeth, *d* of Sir Alfred Bower, 1st and last Bt; *m* 1954, Pamela Elaine Haward; two *s* one *d. Educ:* Aldenham. An Opposition Whip, 1965-67. Dir of El Vino Ltd. Liveryman of the Vintners' Company. *Recreations:* riding, gardening. *Address:* 46 Eaton Terrace, SW1. *T:* 01-730 4470; Berry Horn Cottage, Odiham, Hants. *T:* 2161.

**MITCHELL, Derek J.,** CB 1967; CVO 1966; Economic Minister and Head of UK Treasury Delegation, Washington, since 1969; also UK Executive Director for the International Monetary Fund and International Bank for Reconstruction and Development; *b* 5 March 1922; *s* of Sidney Mitchell, Schoolmaster, and Gladys Mitchell; *m* 1944, Miriam Jackson; one *s* two *d. Educ:* St Paul's Sch.; Christ Church, Oxford. Served War of 1939-45: Royal Armoured Corps and HQ London District, 1942-45. Asst Principal HM Treasury, 1947; Private Sec. to Economic Sec., 1948-49; Private Sec. to Permanent Sec. and Official Head of Civil Service, 1954-56; Principal Private Sec. to: Chancellor of Exchequer, 1962-63; The Prime Minister (Mr Harold Wilson, previously Sir Alec Douglas-Home), 1964-66; Under-Sec., 1964; Dep. Under-Sec. of State, DEA, 1966-67; Dep. Sec., Min. of Agriculture, Fisheries and Food, 1967-69. *Recreations:* music, theatre, avoiding gardening. *Address:* 76 Kalorama Circle NW, Washington, DC 20008, USA. *T:* 462-6212.

**MITCHELL, Douglas Svärd;** Director of Establishments, Greater London Council, since 1964; *b* 21 Aug. 1918; *er s* of late James Livingstone Mitchell and Hilma Josefine (*née* Svärd); *m* 1943, Winifred Thornton Paterson, *d* of late William and Ellen Paterson; one *s* two *d. Educ:* Morgan Academy, Dundee. Royal Ordnance Factories, 1937-51; Principal, Min. of Supply, 1951-55; Dir of Personnel and Admin., in Industrial, Production and Engineering Groups, UK Atomic Energy Authority, 1955-63; Authority Personnel Officer for UK Atomic Energy Authority, 1963-64. *Address:* Hatton Orchard, Yester Park, Chislehurst, Kent. *T:* 01-467 1393.

**MITCHELL, Air Vice-Marshal Frederick George Stewart,** CB 1956; CBE 1953 (OBE 1942); *b* Simonstown, S Africa, 14 Dec. 1901; *s* of Capt. F. Mitchell; *m* 1932, Beryl Barley; one *s* one *d. Educ:* Brighton Technical Coll.; RAF Coll.,

Cranwell. Pilot Officer, 1921; squadron duties at home and India, 1922-25; Armament and Gunnery Sch., Eastchurch, 1926-29; Armament officer duties at home and in Egypt, 1929-31 and 1935-39; Directorate of Trng, Air Min., 1931-33; No. 4 (AC) Squadron, Farnborough, 1933-35; Air Force Experimental Officer, Chem. Defence Experimental Station, Porton, 1939-42; Directorate of Armament Research and Develt, Min. of Supply, 1942-46; Br. Jt Services Mission (Tech. Services), Washington, 1946-48; Vice-Pres. (Air) Ordnance Bd, 1948-50; Air Cdre, 1949; Director of: Armament, 1950, Tech. Requirements, 1951, Armament Engineering, 1952, all at Air Min.; AOC No. 43 Group, 1952-55; Air Officer i/c Administration, Maintenance Command, 1955-58. Air Vice-Marshal, 1956; retired 1958. Officer, Legion of Merit (US), 1947. *Address:* 10 Amberley Close, Highcliffe, Christchurch, Hants.

**MITCHELL, Rt. Rev. Frederick Julian,** DD; *b* 30 July 1901; *s* of late Rev. R. J. Mitchell, MA, The Rectory, Trillick, Co. Tyrone; *m* Kathleen Louise, *d* of Rev. R. Watson, BD, Castle Archdall, Co. Fermanagh. *Educ:* Campbell Coll.; Trinity Coll., Dublin. Deacon, 1924, St Mary's, Belfast; Priest, 1925; Incumbent of S Polycarp, Finaghy, Belfast, 1928; Dean of Residences, QUB, 1934; Incumbent of Kilconriola and Ballyclug, 1936; Rural Dean of Ballymena, 1945; Canon and Prebendary of Kilroot in Chapter of S Saviour of Connor, and Bishop of Kilmore, Elphin and Ardagh, 1950-55; Bishop of Down and Dromore, 1955-69. *Publication:* A Pageant of the Book of Common Prayer (for Quarter Centenary of 1549 Prayer Book); Pageant of the Holy Bible (in connection with Festival of Britain); Hail Caesar!; It Happened in Nazareth. *Address:* Glen Lodge, Belmont Road, Belfast 4, Northern Ireland.

**MITCHELL, Prof. George Archibald Grant,** OBE 1945; TD 1950; Professor of Anatomy and Director of Anatomical Laboratories, Manchester University, since 1946, late Dean of Medical School and Pro-Vice-Chancellor; Ex-President of the Anatomical Society of Great Britain and Ireland; Ex-President, Manchester Medical Society; *b* 11 Nov. 1906; *s* of George and Agnes Mitchell; *m* 1933, Mary Cumming; one *s* two *d*. *Educ:* Fordyce Academy; Aberdeen Central Sch.; Aberdeen Univ. MB, ChB (1st Cl. Hons), 1929; ChM 1933; MSc (Manchester); DSc (Aberdeen) 1950; FRCS 1968. Hon. Alumnus of University of Louvain. Lecturer in Anatomy, 1930-33, in Surgery, 1933-34, Aberdeen Univ.; Surgical Specialist, Co. Caithness, 1934-37; Sen. Lecturer in Anatomy, Aberdeen Univ., 1937-39. Served War, 1939-45: Surgical Specialist, Officer i/c No. 1 Orthopædic Centre, MEF; Officer i/c Surgical Divs, Adviser in Penicillin and Chemotherapy, 21 Army Gp. Hon. Alumnus, Univ. of Louvain, 1944; Hon. Mem. Société Med. Chir. du Centre. Chevalier First Class Order of the Dannebrog. *Publications:* The Anatomy of the Autonomic Nervous System, 1952; Basic Anatomy (with E. L. Patterson), 1954; Cardiovascular Innervation, 1956; ed Symposium, Penicillin Therapy and Control in 21 Army Group, 1945. Sections in: Penicillin (by Sir A. Fleming), 1946; Medical Disorders of the Locomotor System (by E. Fletcher), 1947; British Surgical Practice (by Sir Rock Carling and Sir J. Patterson Ross), 1951; Peripheral Vascular Disorders (by Martin, Lynn, Dible and Aird), 1956; Essentials of Neuroanatomy, 1966; Editor, Nomina Anatomica, 1966. Numerous articles in Jl Anatomy, British Jl Surg., Jl Bone and Joint Surg., Brit. Jl Radiol., BMJ, Lancet, Acta Anat., Nature, Brit. Jl Urol., Edinburgh Medical Jl, Jl Hist. Med., Aberdeen Univ. Rev., Ann. Méd. Chir. du Centre, etc. *Recreations:* wood carving; studying antiques. *Address:* 596 Wilmslow Road, Manchester, 20. *T:* 061-445 1561.

**MITCHELL, George Hoole,** CBE 1967; FRS 1953; FRSE 1955; formerly Assistant Director (Scotland), Geological Survey of Great Britain; *b* 31 Dec. 1902; *s* of George Richard and Emma Mitchell; *m* 1930, Vera Margaret Richardson; two *s*. *Educ:* Liverpool Coll.; Liverpool Univ. (DSc); Imperial Coll. of Science and Technology. Beit Scientific Research Fellow, 1926. Wollaston Fund, 1936, Bigsby Medal, 1947, Murchison Medal, 1964, Geological Soc. of London; Liverpool Geological Soc. Medal, 1951; Pres., Yorks Geological Soc., 1955-56, Sorby Medal; Pres., Section C, British Assoc., 1957; Pres., Edinburgh Geological Soc., 1961-63 (Clough Medal, 1969-70). Geological Survey of Great Britain, 1929-67. Fellow, Imperial Coll., 1967. *Address:* 57 Ladysmith Road, Edinburgh EH9 3EY.

**MITCHELL, George Irvine,** CB 1970; Legal Secretary to Lord Advocate and First Parliamentary Draftsman for Scotland, since 1969; *b* 18 Feb. 1911; *e s* of late John Irvine Mitchell and Mrs L. J. Mitchell; *m* 1945, Elizabeth, *d* of late Charles Leigh Pemberton; one *s* one *d*. *Educ:* George Watson's Coll.; Edinburgh Univ. MA 1932; LLB 1935; Vans Dunlop Scholarship in Law, 1937. Admitted to Faculty of Advocates, 1937; called to English Bar, Inner Temple, 1945. Served War of 1939-45, Border Regt, War Office. Draftsman in Lord Advocate's Dept, 1946-. *Address:* 14 Rodway Road, Roehampton, SW15. *T:* 01-788 6649.

**MITCHELL, Gladys (Maude Winifred);** Writer; *b* 19 April 1901; *e d* of James Mitchell and Annie Julia Maude Simmonds. *Educ:* The Green Sch., Isleworth; Goldsmiths' and University Colls, University of London. First novel published, 1929; followed by other novels, short stories, BBC short detective plays, BBC excerpts from books, BBC Talks on Home Service. Fellow, Ancient Monuments Soc.; Member: Soc. of Authors; Crime Writers' Assoc.; Detection Club. *Publications:* Speedy Death, 1929; and subsequently numerous other detective novels, including Dead Men's Morris; My Father Sleeps; Rising of the Moon; Dancing Druids; Tom Brown's Body; Groaning Spinney; The Devil's Elbow; The Echoing Strangers; Merlin's Furlong; Faintley Speaking; Watson's Choice; Twelve Horses and the Hangman's Noose; The Twenty-third Man; Spotted Hemlock; The Man Who Grew Tomatoes; Say It With Flowers, 1960; The Nodding Canaries, 1961; My Bones Will Keep, 1962; Adders on the Heath, 1963; Death of a Delft Blue, 1964; Pageant of Murder, 1965; The Croaking Raven, 1966; Skeleton Island, 1967; Three Quick and Five Dead, 1968; Dance to Your Daddy, 1969; Gory Dew, 1970; *books as Malcolm Torrie:* Heavy As Lead, 1966; Late and Cold, 1967; Your Secret Friend, 1968; Churchyard Salad, 1969; Shades of Darkness, 1970; *children's books:* Outlaws of the Border, The Three Fingerprints, Holiday River, 1948; Seven Stones Mystery, 1949; The Malory Secret, 1950; Pam at Storne Castle, 1951; On Your Marks, 1954; Caravan Creek, 1954; The Light-Blue Hills, 1959. *Recreations:* reading, studying architecture, telling ghost stories. *Address:* 1 Cecil Close, Corfe Mullen, Wimborne, Dorset.

**MITCHELL, Sir Godfrey Way,** Kt, *cr* 1948; Chairman of George Wimpey & Co., Ltd since 1930; *b* 31 Oct. 1891; *s* of Christopher Mitchell and Margaret Mitchell (*née* Way); *m* 1929, Doreen Lilian Mitchell (*d* 1953); two *d. Educ:* Aske's Sch., Hatcham. Employed in father's business, Rowe & Mitchell, 1908, until European War, 1914-18; served in France; temp. commission RE; demobilized with rank of Capt. Managing Dir of George Wimpey & Co. Ltd, 1919. Hon. Fellow, ICE, 1968. *Address:* Wilton Place, Ledborough Lane, Beaconsfield, Bucks. *T:* Beaconsfield 3128.

**MITCHELL, Graham Russell,** CB 1957; OBE 1951; attached War Office, 1939-63, retired; *b* 4 Nov. 1905; *s* of late Capt. A. S. Mitchell; *m* 1934, Eleonora Patricia (*née* Robertson); one *s* one *d. Educ:* Winchester; Magdalen Coll., Oxford. *Recreations:* yacht racing, chess. *Address:* Barncote, Chobham, Woking, Surrey. *Clubs:* Royal Thames Yacht; Bembridge Sailing (Bembridge, I of W).

**MITCHELL, Sir Hamilton,** KBE 1969; Barrister and Solicitor, in private practice, New Zealand; *b* 24 Feb. 1910; *s* of Ernest Hamilton Mitchell and Catherine Mitchell; *m* 1938, Marion Frances Norman; two *s* one *d. Educ:* Auckland Grammar Sch.; New Zealand Univ. (LLM). Practice on own account, 1941-. Served 2nd NZEF, 1943-46 (Captain, Egypt and Italy). President: Disabled Servicemen's Re-establishment League, 1959-63; NZ Returned Services Assoc., 1962-; Vice-President: World Veterans' Fedn, 1964-66; British Commonwealth Ex-Services League, 1962-; Judge, Courts Martial Appeal Court, 1962-; Dep. Chm., Winston Churchill Trust, 1966-; Chairman: National Art Gallery Management Cttee, 1967-; Canteen Fund Bd, 1967-; NZ Patriotic Fund, 1970-. *Address:* 78 Orangikaupapa Road, Wellington, New Zealand. *T:* 757224. *Clubs:* Wellesley, United Services (Wellington); Royal New Zealand Yacht Squadron.

**MITCHELL, Harold Charles,** CIE 1947; Indian Police (retired); Commissioner for Superior Services (India) Family Pensions Fund, since 1958; *b* 7 March 1896; *s* of late Daniel Charles Mitchell and Late Helen Mitchell; *m* 1923, Edna Evadne Bion; one *d. Educ:* Fairfield. RNVR, Bristol, 1912-19 (Pay Lt). Joined Indian Police, 1920; served as Dist Supt of Police, Bareilly, Benares, Cawnpore, Meerut and other UP districts; Central Intelligence Officer, UP and Ajmer, Home Dept Govt of India; Special Branch, CID, UP; Dep. Inspector-Gen. of Police, CID, UP; Personal Asst to Inspector-Gen. of Police, UP; Dep. Inspector-Gen. of Police, UP HQ and Railways. *Recreations:* golf, fishing. *Address:* Camber Cottage, Camberley, Surrey. *T:* Camberley 22675. *Clubs:* RNVR; Camberley Heath.

**MITCHELL, Col Sir Harold (Paton),** 1st Bt, *cr* 1945; *b* 21 May 1900; *e s* of late Col. Alexander Mitchell, JP, DL, TD, of Tulliallan; *m* 1947, Mary, *d* of late William Pringle; one *d. Educ:* Eton; RMC, Sandhurst; University Coll., Oxford (MA); University of Geneva (Docteur ès Sciences Politiques). Vice-Chm. of Conservative Party, 1942-45; Contested (C) Clackmannan and East Stirlingshire in 1929; MP (C) Brentford and Chiswick Div. of Middlesex, 1931-45; Parliamentary Private Sec. to Rt Hon. John Colville, MP (Dept of Overseas Trade), 1931-35; Parliamentary Private Sec. to Rt Hon. Ralph Assheton, MP (Ministry of Labour, 1939-41, and Ministry of Supply, 1941); Mem. Departmental Cttee on Education and Training of Overseas Students, 1933-34; Mem. Selection Board for Consular Service, 1934-35; Mem. Company Law Amendment Cttee, 1943-45; Command Welfare Officer, AA Command, 1940-48, and Liaison Officer to Polish Forces (France, Belgium, Holland, 1944). Lectr, Hispanic American Studies, Stanford University 1959-65; Research Prof. of Latin American Studies, Rollins Coll. Hon. Col of 61st (City of Edinburgh) Signal Regt, TA, 1947-65. Pres. Luscar Ltd Group, Edmonton, Alberta; sometime Dir London and North Eastern Railway Co.; Joint Master Lauderdale Foxhounds, 1934-35; Mem. Queen's Body Guard for Scotland. Hon. LLD Alberta, rollins and St Andrews. KStJ; Knight Commander of Polonia Restituta; Polish Cross of Valour. *Publications:* Downhill Ski-Racing, 1930; Into Peace, 1945; In My Stride, 1951; Europe in the Caribbean, 1963; Caribbean Patterns, 1967. *Recreation:* ski-ing, represented Gt Britain, 1929, 1931, and 1933. *Address:* Château de Bourdigny, CH 1242 Geneva, Switzerland; Marshall's Island, Bermuda; Prospect Estate, Ocho Rios, Jamaica. *Clubs:* Carlton; Royal Bermuda Yacht.

**MITCHELL, Harvey Allan;** General Manager, New Philharmonia Orchestra, since 1968; *b* 23 Sept. 1932; *s* of Robert Mutter Mitchell and Margaret Massey Mitchell. *Educ:* Edinburgh Univ. (MA Hons). Freelance Journalist, 1955-56; Press Officer, Rank Organization, 1956-58; Sen. Staff, Voice & Vision, 1958-60; Sen. Staff, Barnet & Reef (NY), 1961; Public Relations Administrator, Merck & Co., New York and Brussels, 1962-65; Asst to Vice-Pres., Massey-Ferguson (Toronto), 1965-67. *Publications:* articles on philosophy and the arts. *Recreations:* tennis, bridge, travel. *Address:* 20 Dorset Square, NW1. *T:* 01-262 6290. *Clubs:* Hamilton, Cumberland.

**MITCHELL, Dr Joan Eileen, (Mrs James Cattermole);** Reader in Economics, University of Nottingham, since 1962; *b* 15 March 1920; *d* of late Albert Henry Mitchell, Paper Merchant, and Eva Mitchell; *m* 1956, James Cattermole; one *s* one *d. Educ:* Southend-on-Sea High Sch.; St Hilda's Coll., Oxford. Economist, Min. of Fuel and Power, 1942; Tutor, St Anne's Coll., Oxford, 1945; Economist, BoT, 1947; Research Officer, Labour Party, 1950; Lectr in Econs, Nottingham Univ., 1952. Mem., NBPI, 1965-68. *Publications:* Britain in Crisis 1951, 1963; Groundwork to Economic Planning, 1966. *Recreations:* gardening, cooking, highbrow music. *Address:* Economics Dept, University of Nottingham; 15 Ranmoor Road, Gedling, Nottingham.

**MITCHELL, John Angus Macbeth,** CVO 1961; MC 1946; Under-Secretary, Social Work Services Group, Scottish Education Department, since 1969; *b* 25 Aug. 1924; *s* of John Fowler Mitchell, *qv*: *m* 1948, Ann Katharine Williamson; two *s* two *d. Educ:* Marlborough Coll.; Brasenose Coll., Oxford (Junior Hulme Scholar). Served Royal Armoured Corps, 1943-46: Lieut, Inns of Court Regt, NW Europe, 1944-45; Captain East African Military Records, 1946. Entered Scottish Education Dept, 1949; Private Sec. to Sec. of State for Scotland, 1958-59; Asst Sec., Scottish Educn Dept, 1959-65; Dept of Agriculture and Fisheries for Scotland, 1965-68; Scottish Development Dept, 1968; Asst Under-Secretary of State, Scottish Office, 1968-69. Chm., Scottish Marriage Guidance Council, 1965-69. Kt, Order of Oranje-Nassau (Netherlands), 1946. *Recreation:* maps. 1968; Asst Under-Secretary of State, Scottish Office, 1968-69. 20 Regent Terrace, Edinburgh EH7 5BS. *T:* 031-556 7671. *Clubs:* Royal Commonwealth Society; New (Edinburgh).

**MITCHELL, Prof. John David Bawden,** PhD; LLB (London); LLD (Edinburgh); Solicitor; Salvesen Professor of European Institutions, University of Edinburgh, since 1968; *b* 28 May 1917; *s* of A. Mitchell, OBE; *m* 1945, Jeanne Rosamund, *d* of late Maj-Gen. W. H. S. Nickerson, VC, CB, CMG; two *d. Educ:* Colfe's Grammar Sch.; London Sch. of Economics and Political Science, Univ. of London (Whittuck Schol.). Served War of 1939-45: commissioned North Staffs Regt, 1939; BEF 1940 (despatches); Staff Officer, 1943; released 1946. Admitted Solicitor, 1947; Lectr in Law, University Coll. of Wales, 1947-48; Lectr, Law Soc.'s Sch., 1948-49; Lectr 1949, Reader in English Law in the Univ. of London, 1952, at LSE; Prof. of Constitutional Law, Univ. of Edinburgh, 1954-68. Docteur de l'Université (*hc*), Lille, 1965. *Publications:* Contracts of Public Authorities, 1954; Constitutional Law, 1964 (2nd edn 1968). Articles in various legal periodicals. *Recreations:* talking and walking. *Address:* 10a Succoth Gardens, Edinburgh EH12 6BS. *T:* 031-337 7672. *Club:* New (Edinburgh).

**MITCHELL, John Fowler,** CIE 1935; Indian Civil Service, retired; *b* 30 Dec. 1886; *s* of William Mitchell and Janet Woodrow; *m* 1920, Sheila Macbeth; one *s* two *d. Educ:* Allan Glen's Sch., Glasgow; Royal College of Science, S Kensington; Glasgow Univ.; Merton Coll., Oxford. Entered Indian Civil Service, 1910; served in the Punjab and at Allahabad, Madras, Nagpur and New Delhi; retired 1937. Military Service, 1940-46; Allied Commission for Austria, 1946-47. *Publications:* (with Sheila Mitchell): Monumental Inscriptions (pre-1855) in Kinross-shire, 1967; Monumental Inscriptions (pre-1855) in Clackmannanshire, 1968; Monumental Inscriptions (pre-1855) in West Lothian, 1969; Monumental Inscriptions in Dunbartonshire, pre-1855, 1969; Monumental Inscriptions in Renfrewshire, pre-1855, 1970. *Address:* 7 Randolph Cliff, Edinburgh EH3 7TZ. *T:* 031-225 6074.

*See also J. A. M. Mitchell.*

**MITCHELL, John Newton;** Attorney-General, United States, since Jan. 1969; *b* Detroit, Michigan, 5 Sept, 1913; *s* of late Joseph Charles and Margaret Agnes McMahon Mitchell; *m* 1957, Martha (*née* Beall), Pine Bluff, Ark; one *d* (and one *s* one *d* of a previous marriage). *Educ:* public schs in New York; Jamaica High Sch., Jamaica, NY; Fordham Univ.; Fordham University Law Sch. (LLB); St John's University Law Sch. (post-grad.) Admitted to State Bar of New York, 1938. Served in US Navy, Comdr of Motor Torpedo Boats, 1943-46. Engaged in private practice of law in NYC, 1938-68: Caldwell & Raymond (associate), 1938-42; Caldwell, Trimble & Mitchell (partner), 1942-66; Nixon, Mudge, Rose, Guthrie, Alexander & Mitchell (partner), 1967-68. Mem., NY State and American Bar Associations. Dir and Trustee of Amer. Council to Improve Our Neighbourhoods (ACTION) which later became part of Urban America, Inc. (org. working on mod. city problems); Dir, Nat. Housing Conf., USA; Past President: Municipal Forum of New York; Municipal Bond Club. *Address:* Department of Justice, Washington, DC 20530, USA.

**MITCHELL, John Wesley,** FRS 1956; MSc, PhD; DSc; William Barton Rogers Professor of Physics, University of Virginia; *b* 3 Dec. 1913; *s* of late John Wesley Mitchell and late Lucy Ruth Mitchell; *m* 1968, Jo Overstreet Long; one *d. Educ:* Canterbury University Coll., Christchurch, NZ; Univ. of Oxford. BSc 1934. MSc 1935, NZ; PhD 1938, DSc 1960, Oxford. Reader in Experimental Physics in the Univ. of Bristol, Sept. 1945-Aug. 1959. Prof. of Physics, Univ. of Virginia, Sept. 1959-Sept. 1963; Dir of the National Chemical Laboratory, Oct. 1963-Aug. 1964. *Publications:* various on photographic sensitivity and on plastic deformation of crystals in scientific journals. *Recreations:* mountaineering, colour photography. *Address:* Department of Physics, University of Virginia, Charlottesville, Virginia 22903, USA. *Clubs:* Athenæum; Cosmos (Washington, DC).

**MITCHELL, Prof. Joseph Stanley,** CBE 1951; FRS, 1952; Regius Professor of Physic in the University of Cambridge since 1957; Director, Radiotherapeutic Centre, Addenbrooke's Hospital, Cambridge, since 1943; Fellow, St John's College, Cambridge, since 1936; Hon. Consultant, Atomic Energy Authority; *b* 22 July 1909; *s* of late Joseph Brown Mitchell and Ethel Maud Mary Arnold, Birmingham; *m* 1934, Dr Lilian Mary Buxton, MA, MB, ChB; one *s* one *d. Educ:* Marlborough Road Council Sch., Birmingham; King Edward's High Sch., Birmingham; University of Birmingham; St John's Coll., Cambridge. Nat. Sciences Tripos Part II, Class I, Physics, 1931; MB, BChir Cantab 1934; House Physician, Gen. Hosp., Birmingham; Beit Memorial Medical Research Fellowship; Colloid Science Laboratory, Cambridge, 1934-37; MA Cantab 1935; PhD Cantab 1937; Resident Radiologist Officer, Christie Hosp., Manchester, 1937-38; Asst in Research in Radiotherapy, Dept of Medicine, University of Cambridge, 1938; Prof. of Radiotherapeutics, University of Cambridge, 1946. Radiotherapist EMS, 1939; DMR (RCS), 1943; in charge of medical investigations, National Research Council Laboratory, Montreal, 1944-45. FFR, 1954; MRCP 1956; MD Cantab 1957; DSc (*hc*) Birmingham 1958; FRCP 1958. Linacre Lecturer, 1970. Pres. British Section, Anglo-German Medical Soc., 1959-68. Hon. Mem., German Roentgen Soc., 1967; Pirogoff Medal, 1967. *Publications:* Studies in Radiotherapeutics, 1960; papers in scientific and medical journals on mechanism of therapeutic action of radiations, and the development of radioactive drugs. *Recreations:* walking, modern languages, mathematics. *Address:* Thorndyke, Huntingdon Road, Girton, Cambridge. *T:* Cambridge 76102. *Club:* Royal Over-Seas League.

**MITCHELL, Julian;** *see* Mitchell, C. J. H.

**MITCHELL, Leslie Herbert,** CBE 1955 (OBE 1949); *b* 28 May 1914; *s* of J. W. and A. J. Mitchell; *m* 1937, Margaret Winifred Pellow; three *s. Educ:* Christ's Hospital. Served War of 1939-45 in HM Forces in NW Europe. 2nd Sec., British Embassy, Copenhagen, 1945-50; 1st Sec., British Embassy, Washington, 1953-56; 1st Sec., Bonn, 1956-57; FO, retd 1968. Order of Dannebrog (Denmark), 1947. *Recreations:* music, railways. *Address:* Flint Cottage, Kintbury, Berks. *Club:* Reform.

**MITCHELL, Sir Mark (Ledingham),** Kt 1957; BSc (Hons, Adelaide), MSc Cantab; FRACI; FACE; First Chancellor, Flinders University of South Australia, since 1966; *b* Adelaide, South Australia, 13 June 1902; *s* of late Sir William Mitchell, KCMG. *Educ:* Queen's Sch., Adelaide, SA; University of Adelaide; Cambridge Univ. Lecturer in Biochemistry, University of Adelaide, 1927-38; Prof., 1938-63; Dep. Vice-Chancellor 1950-65. Editor-in-Chief, Australian Journal of Experimental Biology, 1935-63. *Address:* Fitzroy Terrace, Prospect, South Australia. *Clubs:* Adelaide

(Adelaide); Royal South Australian Yacht Squadron.

**MITCHELL, His Honour Norman Frederick,** CMG 1960; Judge of County Courts and Chairman of General Sessions, State of Victoria, Australia, 1946-70; Chairman, County Court Judges, State of Victoria, 1965-70; *b* 19 Feb. 1900; *s* of Frederick John and Catherine Mabel Mitchell; *m* 1927, Jennie Moffitt Graham; one *d* (one *s* decd). *Educ:* University High Sch.; Melbourne Univ. On Staff of Melbourne C of E Grammar Sch., 1918-25; BA 1921; Diploma of Education, 1922; LLB, 1925; admitted to Victorian Bar, 1926. Served War of 1939-45, Area and Group Law Officer, RAAF, 1941-45. Dep. Chm., Workers Compensation Board, 1946; Mem. of Trotting Control Board, 1946-56, Chm., 1953-56; Dep. Pres., Court of Industrial Appeal, 1963-70. Trustee, 1949, Vice-Pres., 1953, Pres., 1956-64, Royal Agricultural Society of Victoria. *Recreations:* cricket, football. *Address:* Cheriton Farm, Longwarry, Vic., Australia. *T:* Longwarry 145.

**MITCHELL, Richard Charles;** *b* 22 Aug. 1927; *s* of Charles and Elizabeth Mitchell; *m* 1950, Doreen Lilian Gregory; one *s* one *d. Educ:* Taunton's Sch., Southampton; Godalming County Gram. Sch.; Southampton Univ. BSc(Econ) Hons 1951. Bartley County Sec. Sch.: Senior Master and Head of Maths and Science Dept, 1957-65; Dep. Headmaster, 1965-66. MP (Lab) Southampton Test, 1966-70. Chm., Educ. Group, Parly Labour Party. *Recreation:* postal chess (rep. Brit. Correspondence Chess Assoc. against other countries). *Address:* 49 Devonshire Road, Polygon, Southampton. *T:* Southampton 21781.

**MITCHELL, Prof. Ross Galbraith,** MD, FRCPE, DCH; Professor of Child Health, University of Aberdeen, and Pædiatrician, Royal Aberdeen Children's Hospital and Aberdeen Maternity Hospital, since 1963; *b* 18 Nov. 1920; *s* of late Richard Galbraith Mitchell, OBE and Ishobel, *d* of late James Ross, Broadford, Skye; *m* 1950, June Phylis Butcher; one *s* three *d. Educ:* Kelvinside Acad.; University of Edinburgh. MB, ChB Edinburgh, 1944. Surg-Lt, RNVR, 1944-47; Jun. hosp. posts, Liverpool, London, Edinburgh, 1947-52; Rockefeller Res. Fellow, Mayo Clinic, USA, 1952-53; Lectr in Child Health, Univ. of St Andrews, 1952-55; Cons. Pædiatrician, Dundee Teaching Hosps, 1955-63. Chm., Scottish Adv. Council on Child Care, 1966-69. Jt Editor Developmental Medicine and Child Neurology. For. Corresp. Mem., Amer. Acad. of Cerebral Palsy. *Publications:* Disease in Infancy and Childhood, (6th edn) 1968; Child Life and Health (5th edn), 1970; contribs to textbooks of medicine and obstetrics and articles in scientific and medical jls. *Recreations:* Celtic language and literature, fishing. *Address:* Harecraig, Culter House Road, Milltimber, Aberdeen AB1 0EN. *T:* Culter 3298.

**MITCHELL, Sir (Seton) Steuart Crichton,** KBE 1954 (OBE 1941); CB 1951; Chairman, Carrier Engineering Ltd, since 1969; Director, parkinson Cowan Ltd, since 1964; *b* 9 March 1902; *s* of A. Crichton Mitchell, DSc, FRSE; *m* 1929, Elizabeth (*née* Duke); no *c. Educ:* Edinburgh Acad.; RN Colls, Osborne and Dartmouth. Joined Royal Navy as Cadet, 1916; at sea in HMS Hercules, Grand Fleet, 1918, subsequently served in HM Ships Ramillies, Sportive, Tomahawk, Marlborough; qualified as Gunnery Specialist, 1927-29, subsequently Gunnery Officer of HM Ships Comus and Frobisher; Naval Ordnance Inspection Dept and Asst Supt of Design, 1931-39; War of 1939-45, Inspector of Naval Ordnance, New York, in charge of Admiralty Ordnance contracts in USA, 1940-44; Chief Engineer and Supt, in charge of Armament Design Establishment, Min. of Supply, 1945; Controller, Guided Weapons and Electronics, Min. of Supply, 1951-56; Controller, Royal Ordnance Factories, 1956-59; Controller, Guided Weapons and Electronics, Ministry of Aviation, 1959-62; Mem., BTC, Feb.-Nov. 1962; Vice-Chm., British Railways Bd, Nov. 1962-64; Chairman: Machine Tool Industry EDC, 1964-; Shipbuilding Industry Trng Bd, 1964-; Mem., Central Trng Council, 1965-; Adviser (part-time) to Min. of Technology, 1965-; Mem. Scottish Economic Planning Council, 1965-67; Mem. Nat. Economic Devslt Council, 1967. Officer Legion of Merit (USA), 1945. *Recreations:* fishing, gardening, antiques. *Address:* 26 Marsham Court, Marsham Street, SW1. *T:* 01-828 6628; Nethertack, Moniaive, Dumfriesshire. *T:* Moniaive 289. *Club:* United Service.

**MITCHELL, Sir Steuart Crichton;** *see* Mitchell, Sir S. S. C.

**MITCHELL, William Eric Marcus,** MC; MB; BS London; FRCS; FRCSC; MRCP; DPH; Surgeon, genito-urinary specialist, Consulting Surgeon, Royal Jubilee Hospital, Victoria, BC, retired; *b* 29 April 1897; *e s* of Dr J. F. Mitchell, formerly of Bangor, Co. Down; *m* 1922, Catherine, *d* of W. F. Hamilton, of Ashwick, NZ; one *d*; *m* 1958, Margery, *d* of D. O. Thomas, Victoria, BC. *Educ:* Campbell Coll., Belfast; St Bartholomew's Hosp., University of London. Served as a Lt with the 11th Battalion Royal Irish Rifles in France, 1916 (wounded, MC); various prizes during sch. and Univ. career; House Surg., St Bartholomew's Hosp.; Chief Asst to a Surgical Unit, St Bartholomew's Hosp.; Clinical Asst, St Peter's Hosp., London; Pres., Abernethian Soc., St Bartholomew's Hosp. War of 1939-45, Lt-Col RAMC, Officer in Charge Surgical Div. No. 13 Gen. Hosp. MEF. *Publications:* Health, Wealth and Happiness, 1969; numerous papers on surgical subjects published in the Lancet, the Canadian Medical Association Journal, St Bartholomew's Hospital Journal. *Recreations:* fishing, ski-ing, mountaineering. *Address:* 2171 Granite Street, Oak Bay, Victoria, BC, Canada. *TA:* Victoria, BC. *Club:* Alpine Club of Canada.

**MITCHELL, Yvonne;** actress and novelist; *d* of Bertie Joseph and Madge Mitchell; *m* 1952, Derek Monsey; one *d. Educ:* Battle Abbey and St Paul's. First stage appearance as the child Estella in Great Expectations, 1940; Plays include: Ophelia in Hamlet, Old Vic and Elsinore, 1950; Katherine in the Taming of the Shrew and Cordelia in King Lear, Stratford-on-Avon, 1952; The Wall, Billy Rose Theatre, New York, 1960; Anna Petrovna in Ivanov, Phœnix, 1965. *Films include:* The Divided Heart (Brit. Film Acad. Award), 1954; Woman in a Dressing-Gown (Berlin Fest. Award and Variety Club of Gt Britain Award), 1957; Sapphire, 1958; Genghis Khan, 1965; Velvet House, 1968; many appearances on TV. *Publications: plays:* The Same Sky (Produced Duke of York's Theatre, 1951) (Arts Council Award); Actress, 1957; (trans. from the French) Measure of Cruelty, 1964; *novels:* The Bedsitter, 1959; Frame for Julian, 1960; A Year in Time, 1964; The Family, 1967; Martha on Sunday, 1970; *for children:* Cathy Away, 1964; Cathy at Home, 1965. *Address:* Domaine du Plan-Sarain, 06 La Roquette sur Siagne, AM, France.

**MITCHELL COTTS, Sir R. C.;** *see* Cotts.

**MITCHELL-HEGGS, Gordon Barrett,** OBE 1944; TD; MD, BS, FRCP, MRCS; Physician-in-Charge Skin Department, and Dean of the Medical School, 1960-67, St Mary's Hospital, W2; Hon. Physician to St John's Skin Hospital and to St Mary's Hospital Medical School; formerly Hon. Dermatologist to the Royal Masonic Hospital, St Luke's Hostel for Clergy, Hospital of St John and St Elizabeth, etc.; formerly Hon. Consultant in Dermatology to the Army; *b* 10 June 1904; *e s* of late Francis Raymond Mitchell Heggs, MRCS, LSA; took name of Mitchell-Heggs by deed poll, 1939; *m* 1937, Nora, *d* of late Rev. H. C. Finch, Abbotts Langley, Herts; one *s*. *Educ:* Nottingham High Sch.; St Mary's Hosp. Medical Sch. (Public Schs and Lord Kitchener Memorial Scholar); Strasbourg, Vienna, Budapest. Hon. Medallist of University of Louvain. Formerly CO, and subsequently Hon. Col, 17th (London) Gen. Hosp., RAMC, TA, until 1960. Served War of 1939-45, BEF France, Madagascar, Middle East Forces, Sicily, Normandy and Belgium campaigns (despatches). Past-President: Hunterian Soc. of London; St John's Hosp. Dermatological Soc.; Section of Dermatology, Royal Society of Medicine; Council Mem., Royal College of Physicians; Mem., and Past Pres., British Assoc. of Dermatology; Hon. Mem. Dermatological Socs of Austria, Iran, Venezuela and Yugoslavia; Corresp. Mem. Dermatological Socs of Belgium, Denmark, France, Holland, Sweden and USA. Representative for Great Britain on International Cttee of Dermatology. Hon. FRIPHH. *Publications:* Modern Practice in Dermatology, 1950. Chapters in: Penicillin (Fleming, 1946 and 1950), and ACTH and Cortisone (Copeman, 1953). Medical papers and articles on Diseases of the Skin. *Recreations:* gardening, fishing. *Address:* 88 Harley Street, W1. *T:* 01-580 2596. *Clubs:* Athenæum, Garrick.

**MITCHELL-THOMSON,** family name of **Baron Selsdon.**

**MITCHESON, Prof. J(ames) Cecil,** CBE 1961; BSc; Hon. ARSM; Fellow, Imperial College of Science and Technology; Professor Emeritus of Mining, London University, since 1963; *b* 18 May 1898; *s* of late G. A. Mitcheson, Hall End Hall, Tamworth; *m* 1928, Jean Hyndman, *d* of late D. S. Macpherson, JP, Greenock, Renfrew; one *s* one *d*. *Educ:* Bootham Sch.; RMA Woolwich; University of Birmingham. Lecturer in Coal Mining, Birmingham Univ., 1923-24; Agent and later Man. Dir, Morris & Shaw, Ltd, 1934-46; Dir of Production for Min. of Fuel and Power, for Warwicks Coalfield, 1944-45; Divl Mining Development Engineer, W Midlands Div., NCB, 1947; Cons. Mining Engineer, 1947-52; Prof. of Mining, Imperial Coll., Royal School of Mines, London Univ., 1953-63. Mem., Mining Qualifications Board, 1950-69; Chm., Safety in Mines Research (Advisory) Bd. FInstME (Pres. 1953-54); MIMM. chm., Geological Survey Board, 1961-65 (Mem. 1959-); Mem., Natural Environment Research Council, 1965-69. Served European War: Lt RFA, with 33rd Div., France and Flanders, 1918. *Publications:* papers in Proceedings Instn of Mining Engineers and other technical jls. *Address:* The Croft, Knotty Green, Beaconsfield, Bucks.

**MITCHISON, Dr Denis Anthony;** Professor of Bacteriology (Infectious Diseases), Royal Postgraduate Medical School, since 1968; Director, Medical Research Council's Unit for Research on Drug Sensitivity in Tuberculosis, since 1956; *b* 6 Sept. 1919; *e s* of Baron Mitchison, CBE, QC, and of Naomi Margaret Mitchison, *qv*; *m* 1940, Ruth Sylvia, *d* of Hubert Gill; two *s* two *d*. *Educ:* Abbotsholme Sch.; Trinity Coll., Cambridge; University Coll. Hosp., London (MB, ChB). House Physician Addenbrooke's Hosp., Royal Berkshire Hosp.; Asst to Pathologist, Brompton Hosp. FRCP; MCPath. *Publications:* numerous papers on bacteriology and chemotherapy of tuberculosis. *Recreations:* squash, computer programming. *Address:* 14 Marlborough Road, Richmond, Surrey. *T:* 01-940 4751.

*See also J. M. Mitchison, N. A. Mitchison.*

**MITCHISON, Prof. John Murdoch,** ScD; FRSE 1966; Professor of Zoology, University of Edinburgh, since 1963; *b* 11 June 1922; *s* of Lord Mitchison, CBE, QC, and of M. Haldane (*see* Naomi M. Mitchison); *m* 1947, Rosalind Mary Wrong; one *s* three *d*. *Educ:* Winchester Coll.; Trinity Coll., Cambridge. Army Operational Research, 1941-46; Sen. and Research Scholar, Trinity Coll., Cambridge, 1946-50; Fellow, Trinity Coll., Cambridge, 1950-54; Lectr in Zoology, Edinburgh, 1953-59; Reader in Zoology, Edinburgh, 1959-62. Mem. Council, Scottish Marine Biol. Assoc., 1961-67; Mem. Exec. Cttee, Internat. Soc. for Cell Biology, 1964-; FInstBiol 1963. *Publications:* papers in scientific jls. *Address:* 6 Dovecot Road, Edinburgh E12 7LE. 031-334 4317.

*See also D. A. Mitchison, N. A. Mitchison.*

**MITCHISON, Naomi Margaret,** (**Lady Mitchison** since 1964, but she still wishes to be called Naomi Mitchison); *b* Edinburgh, 1 Nov. 1897; *d* of late John Scott Haldane, CH, FRS, and Kathleen Trotter; *m* 1916, G. R. Mitchison (*d* 1970), CBE, QC, Created a Baron (Life Peer), 1964; three *s* two *d*. *Educ:* Dragon Sch., Oxford; home student, Oxford. Officier d'Académie Française, 1924; Labour Candidate for Scottish Universities Constituency, by-election 1935; Highland and Island Advisory Panel, 1947-65; Highlands and Islands Develt Consult. Council, 1966; Tribal Advisor to Bakgatla, Botswana, 1963. *Publications:* The Conquered, 1923; When the Bough Breaks, 1924; Cloud Cuckoo Land, 1925; The Laburnum Branch, 1926; Black Sparta, 1928; Anna Comnena, 1928; Nix-Nought-Nothing, 1928; Barbarian Stories, 1929; The Hostages, 1930; Comments on Birth Control, 1930; The Corn King and the Spring Queen, 1931; The Price of Freedom (with L. E. Gielgud), 1931; Boys and Girls and Gods, 1931; The Powers of Light, edited an Outline for Boys and Girls, 1932; The Delicate Fire, 1933; Vienna Diary, 1934; The Home, 1934; We Have Been Warned, 1935; Beyond this Limit, 1935; The Fourth Pig, 1936; Socrates (with R. H. S. Crossman), 1937; An End and a Beginning, 1937; The Moral Basis of Politics, 1938; The Kingdom of Heaven, 1939; As It was in the Beginning (with L. E. Gielgud), 1939; The Blood of the Martyrs, 1939; edited Re-educating Scotland, 1944; The Bull Calves, 1947; Men and Herring (with D. Macintosh), 1949; The Big House, 1950; Spindrift (*play:* with D. Macintosh), Citizens' Theatre, Glasgow, 1951; Lobsters on the Agenda, 1952; Travel Light, 1952; The Swan's Road, 1954; Graeme and the Dragon, 1954; The Land the Ravens Found, 1955; To the Chapel Perilous, 1955; Little Boxes, 1956; Behold your King, 1957; The Far Harbour, 1957; Five Men and a Swan, 1958; Other People's Worlds, 1958; Judy and Lakshmi, 1959; The Rib of the Green Umbrella, 1960; The Young Alexander, 1960; Karensgaard, 1961; The Young Alfred the Great, 1962; Memoirs of a Space Woman, 1962; ed What the Human Race is Up To, 1962; The Fairy who Couldn't Tell a Lie, 1963; When we Become Men, 1965; Ketse and the Chief, 1965; Return to the Fairy Hill, 1966; Friends

and Enemies, 1966; The Big Surprise, 1967; African Heroes, 1968; Don't Look Back, 1969; The Family at Ditlabeng, 1969; The Africans: a history, 1970; Sun and Moon, 1970. *Recreation:* forwarding mutual enjoyment when possible. *Address:* Carradale House, Carradale, Campbeltown, Scotland.
*See also D. A. Mitchison, J. M. Mitchison, N. A. Mitchison.*

**MITCHISON, Prof. Nicholas Avrion,** FRS 1967; Jodrell Professor of Zoology, University College, London, since 1970; *b* 5 May 1928; 3rd *s* of Baron Mitchison, CBE, QC, and of Naomi Margaret Mitchison, *qv*; *m* 1957, Lorna Margaret, *d* of Maj.-Gen. J. S. S. Martin, *qv*; two *s* three *d. Educ:* Leighton Park Sch.; New Coll., Oxford (MA 1949). Fellow of Magdalen College, 1950-52; Commonwealth Fund Fellow, 1952-54; Lecturer, Edinburgh Univ., 1954-61; Reader, Edinburgh Univ., 1961-62; Head of Dir. of Experimental Biology, Nat. Inst. for Med. Research, 1962-70. *Publications:* articles in scientific journals. *Address:* Rhodes Farm, The Ridgeway, Mill Hill, NW7.
*See also D. A. Mitchison, J. M. Mitchison.*

**MITFORD,** family name of **Baron Redesdale.**

**MITFORD, Nancy, (Hon. Mrs Peter Rodd);** *b* 1904; *d* of 2nd Baron Redesdale; *m* 1933, Hon. Peter Rodd (marr. diss. 1958; he *d* 1968). *Educ:* home. *Publications:* Pursuit of Love, 1945; Love in a Cold Climate, 1949; The Blessing, 1951; Madame de Pompadour, 1953, new edn 1968; Voltaire in Love, 1957; Don't Tell Alfred, 1960; The Water Beetle, 1962; The Sun King, 1966; Frederick the Great, 1970; edited: The Ladies of Alderley, 1967; The Stanleys of Alderley, 1968. *Address:* 4 rue d'Artois, 78 Versailles, France.

**MITFORD, Rupert Leo Scott B.;** *see* Bruce-Mitford.

**MITFORD-BARBERTON, I. G.;** *see* Barberton.

**MITFORD-SLADE, Col Cecil Townley;** Lord-Lieutenant of Somerset, since 1968; *b* 19 April 1903; *s* of late Col William Kenyon Mitford, CMG, CVO; assumed additional name of Slade by deed poll, 1941; *m* 1931, Phyllis, *d* of late E. G. Buxton; two *s* one *d. Educ:* Eton; RMC; joined 60th Rifles, 1923; comd 8th Bn KRRC, 1943-44; 1st Bn KRRC, 1948-50; Comdt, WRAC Staff Coll., 1951; one of HM Bodyguard of Hon. Corps of Gentlemen-at-Arms, 1952-; DL, Somerset, 1955; JP, 1953; CC, 1955; High Sheriff, 1963; Vice-Lieut, 1966-68. County Comr, St John Amb. Bde, 1954-68; Chairman: W Region Assoc. for the Blind, 1966; Taunton Race Course Co.; Taunton Vale Polo Club; Dir, Taunton Cider Co. KStJ; Order of Mercy. *Recreations:* shooting, fishing. *Address:* Montys Court, Taunton, Som. *Club:* Naval and Military.

**MITHA, Hon. Sardar Sir Suleman Cassum.** Kt 1933; CIE 1915; MCS; JP; banker and general merchant; five *s* three *d. Address:* Lands End Road, Malabar Hill, Bombay, 6. *TA:* Minerva. *T:* 25904 and 40756. Clubs: Willingdon Sports, Orient (Bombay).

**MITMAN, Frederick S.,** CBE 1941; *b* 21 April 1900; *s* of late William and Elizabeth Mitman; *m* 1925, Helen McNary; one *s* one *d. Educ:* Lehigh Univ., USA (Deg. of Engineer of Mines, 1923). Dir of Light Alloys and Magnesium (Sheet and Strip) Control, Ministry of Aircraft Production, 1939-41; Coordinator of Aircraft Supplies for Fighter and Naval Aircraft, Ministry of Aircraft Production, 1940-41; Adviser on Light Metals Fabrication, Ministry of Aircraft Production, 1941-42. *Address:* 10 Campden House Close, Kensington, W8. *T:* 01-937 9071.

**MITRANY, David,** PhD, DSc (London); Professor in School of Economics and Politics, Institute for Advanced Study, Princeton, New Jersey, since 1933; also Adviser on International Affairs to Board of Unilever & Lever Bros Ltd, since 1943; *b* Bucharest, Rumania, 1 Jan. 1888; *s* of Moscu and Jeannette Mitrany, Bucharest; *m* 1923, Ena Victoria, *d* of Alfred J. Limebeer, London; no *c. Educ:* London Sch. of Economics and Political Science. Editorial Staff of Manchester Guardian, 1919-22; Asst European Editor of Economic and Social History of the World War (Carnegie Endowment for International Peace), 1922-29; Visiting Professor at Harvard Univ. 1931-33; Dodge Lecturer Yale Univ. 1932; Nielsen Research Professor, Smith Coll., 1951; Mem. British Co-ordinating Cttee for Internat. Studies, 1927-30. *Publications:* The Problem of International Sanctions, 1925; Marx v the Peasant, 1927; The Land and the Peasant in Rumania, 1928; The Progress of International Government (Dodge Lectures), 1934; The Effect of the War in South-Eastern Europe, 1937; American Policy and Opinion (Survey of International Affairs), 1940; A Working Peace System, 1943; American Interpretations, 1946; Marx against the Peasant, 1951 (six foreign edns); A Working Peace System (Essays), 1966. Articles in Encyclopædia Britannica, Encyclopædia of the Social Sciences (USA), The Sociological Review, Political Quarterly, Round Table, International Affairs, Agenda, etc. *Recreations:* walking, gardening. *Address:* Lower Farm, Kingston Blount, Oxford. *T:* 236.

**MITSAKIS, Prof. Kariofilis;** Sotheby and Bywater Professor of Byzantine and Modern Greek Language and Literature, University of Oxford, since 1968; *b* 12 May 1932; *s* of Christos and Crystalli Mitsakis; *m* 1966, Anthoula Chalkia; two *s. Educ:* Univs of Thessaloniki, Oxford and Munich. Scientific Collaborator, Royal Research Foundn of Greece, 1959; Associate Prof. of Byzantine and Modern Greek Literature, Univ. of Maryland, 1966; Chm. of Dept of Comparative Literature, Univ. of Maryland, 1967. *Publications:* Problems concerning the text, the sources and the dating of the Achilleid, 1962 (in Greek); The Greek Sonnet, 1962 (in Greek); The Language of Romanos the Melodist, 1967 (in English); The Byzantine Alexander romance from the cod. Vindob. theol. gr. 244, 1967 (in German), etc; contribs to Byzantinisch-Neugriechische Jahrbücher, Byzantinische Zeitschrift, Comparative Literature Studies, Glotta, Hellenika, Jahrbuch der Oesterreichischen Byzantinischen Gesellschaft, Nea Hestia, etc. *Recreation:* music, sports, travelling. *Address:* Exeter College, Oxford. *T:* 57165.

**MITTON, Rev. Dr Charles Leslie,** BA; MTh; PhD; Principal of Handsworth College, Birmingham, 1955-70 (Tutor, 1951-55); *b* 13 Feb. 1907; *s* of Rev. Charles W. Mitton, Bradford, Yorks; *m* 1937, Margaret J. Ramage; one *s* one *d. Educ:* Kingswood Sch., Bath; Manchester Univ.; Didsbury Coll., Manchester. Asst Tutor at Wesley Coll., Headingley, 1930-33; Minister in Methodist Church at: Dunbar, 1933-36; Keighley, 1936-39; Scunthorpe, 1939-45; Nottingham, 1945-51; Tutor in New Testament Studies at Handsworth Coll., Birmingham, 1951-70. Editor of Expository Times, 1965-. Hon. DD, Aberdeen Univ., 1964. *Publications:* The Epistle to the Ephesians: Authorship, Origin and Purpose, 1951; Pauline Corpus of Letters, 1954; Preachers' Commentary on St Mark's Gospel, 1956; The Good News, 1961; The Epistle of James, 1966. *Recreations:* Rugby football, Association football, cricket, tennis. *Address:* 45 Beverley Court Road, Quinton, Birmingham 32. *T:* 021-422 3475.

**MOATE, Roger Denis;** MP (C) Faversham since 1970; Insurance Broker; Director: Moate, Clarke, Hancock & Partners Ltd; Alexander Howden (Insurance Brokers) Ltd; *b* 12 May 1938; *m* 1960, Hazel Joy Skinner. *Educ:* Latymer Upper Sch., Hammersmith. Joined Young Conservative Movement, in Brentford and Chiswick, 1954: Vice-Chm., Greater London area Young Conservatives, 1964; contested (C) Faversham, Gen. Elec., 1966. *Recreations:* skiing, squash. *Address:* Goldenwood, Highsted, Sittingbourne, Kent; 23 Ponsonby Terrace, SW1. *T:* 01-828 0987. *Club:* St Stephen's.

**MOBERLY, John Campbell;** Counsellor, British Embassy, Washington, since 1969; *b* 27 May 1925; *s* of Sir Walter Moberly, *qv*; *m* 1959, Patience, *d* of Major Sir Richard George Proby, Bt, *qv*; two *s* one *d*. *Educ:* Winchester College; Magdalen College, Oxford. War Service in Royal Navy, 1943-47. Entered HM Foreign (now Diplomatic) Service, 1950; Political Officer, Kuwait, 1954-56; Political Agent, Doha, 1959-62; First Secretary, British Embassy, Athens, 1962-66. *Recreations:* mountain walking and climbing, skiing, swimming. *Address:* c/o Foreign and Commonwealth Office, SW1; The Cedars, Temple Sowerby, Penrith, Cumberland. *T:* Kirkby Thore 437. *Clubs:* Travellers', Royal Automobile; Leander (Henley-on-Thames).

**MOBERLY, Maj.-Gen. Richard James,** CB 1957; OBE 1944; retired, 1960, and became Director, Communications Electronic Equipment, War Office, until 1964; *b* 2 July 1906; *o s* of late J. E. Moberly; *m* 1935, Mary Joyce Shelmerdine (*d* 1964); three *d*. *Educ:* Haileybury; Royal Military Academy, Woolwich. Commissioned Royal Signals, 1926; India, 1928-35; comd 1st Airborne Div. Signal Regt, 1942-43; CSO 1st Airborne Corps, 1943-45; Comdt Indian Signal Trng Centre, 1946-47; Dep. Comdt, Sch. of Signals, 1949-52; Dep. Dir of Signals, WO, 1952-54; CSO, Northern Army Gp, 1954-57; Signal Officer-in-Chief, War Office, 1957-60. Col Comdt, Royal Signals, 1960-66. Comr for Dorset, St John Ambulance Bde, 1968. OStJ 1968. *Recreations:* fishing, shooting, motoring. *Address:* Garston House, Sixpenny Handley, Salisbury, Wilts. *T:* Handley 268. *Club:* Army and Navy.

**MOBERLY, Rt. Rev. Robert Hamilton;** *b* 1884; *s* of Canon R. C. Moberly, DD, and Alice Sidney Moberly; *m* 1917, Rosamund Vere, *d* of late Rev. B. B. Smyth and late Grace Elizabeth Augusta Massy Smyth; one *s* (and one *s* killed in War, 1942). *Educ:* Winchester; Oxford, 1st class in Mods, Greats and Theology; Cuddesdon. Asst curate, St Margaret's-at-Cliffe, near Dover, 1909-14; Benoni, Transvaal, 1914-25; CF 1917-19; Principal, Bishops' Coll., Cheshunt, 1925-36; Bishop Suffragan of Stepney and Rector of St Margarets, Lothbury, 1936-52; Dean of Salisbury, 1952-60. White Lecturer, 1930. *Publication:* The Great Friendship, 1934. *Address:* Wadhurst, Pound Road, West Wittering, Sussex.

**MOBERLY, Sir Walter (Hamilton),** GBE, *cr* 1949; KCB, *cr* 1944; Kt, *cr* 1934; DSO 1917; MA; Hon. LLD (Belfast); Hon. DLitt (Manchester, Nottingham and Keele); Hon. Fellow of Lincoln College, Oxford, 1930; Hon. Fellow of Merton College, 1937; Hon. Fellow of New College, 1942; Fellow of Winchester College, 1942-66; *b* 20 Oct. 1881; *s* of late R. C. Moberly, DD, Canon of Christ Church, Oxford, and Alice Sidney, *d* of Walter Kerr Hamilton, Bishop of Salisbury; *m* 1921, Gwendolen, *d* of late W. M. Gardner; four *s*. *Educ:* Winchester; New Coll., Oxford (Scholar). First Class Lit. Hum., 1903; Fellow of Merton Coll., 1904-7; Lecturer in Political Science, Aberdeen, 1905-6; Fellow of Lincoln Coll., 1906-21; Prof. of Philosophy, Birmingham Univ., 1921-24; Principal of University Coll. of the South-West of England, Exeter, 1925-26; Vice-Chancellor of University of Manchester, 1926-34; Chm. of University Grants Cttee, 1935-49; Principal of St Catherine's, Cumberland Lodge, Windsor, 1949-55. Served European War, Oxford and Bucks Light Infantry, France and Belgium (DSO, despatches, twice). *Publications:* The Crisis in the University, 1949; two essays in Foundations, 1912; Responsibility (Riddell Lecture), 1956; The Ethics of Punishment, 1968. *Address:* 7 Fyfield Road, Oxford.
*See also J. C. Moberly.*

**MOCATTA, Hon. Sir Alan Abraham,** Kt 1961; OBE 1944; **Hon. Mr Justice Mocatta;** Judge of the High Court of Justice (Queen's Bench Division) since Oct. 1961; Member, Restrictive Practices Court, since 1961, President, since 1970; *b* 1907; *s* of Edward L. Mocatta and Flora Gubbay; *m* 1930, Pamela Halford, JP; four *s*. *Educ:* Clifton Coll.; New Coll., Oxford. Called to the Bar, Inner Temple, 1930; Bencher, 1960; Northern circuit; QC 1951. Served War of 1939-45: 2nd Lieut 12 LAA Regt, RA, TA, 1939; Bde Major, 56 AA Bde, 1940-41; GSO (2) AA HQ BTNI, 1941-42; Lt-Col GS, Army Council Secretariat, War Office, 1942-45. Chm., Council of Jews' Coll., 1945-61; Vice-Pres., Board of Elders, Spanish and Portuguese Jews' Congregation, Bevis Marks, 1961-67, pres., 1967-; Chm. Treasury Cttee on Cheque Endorsement, 1955-56. Joint editor, 14th-17th editions of Scrutton on Charter parties. *Address:* 1 The Close, Marlborough Place, NW8. *T:* 01-722 2857; 10 Breakwater Road, Bude, Cornwall. *T:* Bude 2745. *Club:* MCC.

**MOCKETT, Sir Vere,** Kt, *cr* 1943; MBE 1918; *b* 25 July 1885; *y s* of Brooke Mockett and Blanche Marion Walker; *m* 1918, Ethel Nora Gaddum Tomkinson (*d* 1969); one *s* two *d*. *Educ:* Marlborough; Worcester Coll., Oxford. BA 1907; MA 1910; called to Bar, Inner Temple, 1908; North Eastern Circuit, 1908-14; practised at Madras Bar, 1921-32; officiated as Judge, High Court, Madras, 1932; Lecturer at Kings Coll., London, Faculty of Law, 1933-34; Judge, High Court of Judicature at Madras, 1934-45; officiated twice as Chief Justice; served European War, 1914-19, 4th and 5th Buffs; Aden Field Force and Mesopotamia, 1915-19; Staff Capt., 1917-19 (MBE, despatches). *Recreations:* shooting, fishing, reading. *Address:* c/o Lloyds Bank Ltd, 222 Strand, WC2. *Clubs:* United University, MCC; Madras (Madras).
*See also D. J. C. Crawley.*

**MOCKLER-FERRYMAN, Col (Hon. Brig.) Eric Edward,** CB 1945; CBE 1941; MC; FZS; Hon. MA London; **b** 27 June 1896; *s* of late Col A. F. Mockler-Ferryman, 43rd LI; unmarried. *Educ:* Wellington; RMA, Woolwich. Commissioned RA, 1915; France and Flanders, 1915-19 (MC); seconded to AMF, 1937-39; served, 1939-45; Brig., 1940; Control Commission, Hungary, 1945-46; retired pay, 1947; Comdr Legion of Merit (US), Chevalier, Légion d'honneur and Fr. Croix de Guerre; Comdr Order of Leopold II and Belgian Croix de Guerre; Comdr Order of Orange Nassau. *Address:* c/o Lloyds Bank, 6 Pall Mall, SW1. *Club:* Army and Navy.

**MOE, Henry Allen;** Foundation Officer; First Chairman of National Endowment for the Humanities, 1965-66; *b* Minnesota, 2 July 1894; *s* of Christian and Sophia Martha Moe; *m* 1925, Edith Louise (*née* Monroe, BA); one *s*. *Educ:* Hamline Univ., Minnesota (BS); Brasenose Coll., Oxford (BA jurisprudence, 1st cl. Hons, BCL). Called to Bar, Inner Temple, London, 1924. Hulme Lectr in Law for Brasenose and Oriel Colls, Univ. of Oxford, 1923-24; Lectr in Law, Columbia Univ. (NYC), Sch. of Law, 1927-29; John Simon Guggenheim Memorial Foundation: Sec., 1925-60; Sec. Gen., 1937-61; Pres. 1961-63; Pres. Harry Frank Guggenheim Foundation, 1970; retired as Pres. Amer. Phil. Soc., 1970; Vice-Chm., Museum of Modern Art (NYC); also is a Trustee of several US instns; was Trustee of Rockefeller Foundn, 1945-60. Hon. Fellow, Brasenose Coll., Oxford, 1955-. Holds numerous hon. degrees, both in USA and abroad, including DCL, Oxford, 1960. Award of Nat. Inst. of Arts and Letters (NYC), 1955; Public Service Medal, Nat. Academy of Sciences (Washington, DC), 1958. *Publications:* articles in Proc. Amer. Phil. Soc., Science, New York History, Physics Today. *Recreations:* gardening, carpentry, stone masonry. *Address:* (office) 30 Wall Street, New York, NY 10005, USA. *T:* 269-1833; (homes) Sherman, Conn 06784; Riverdale-on-Hudson, New York, NY 10471. *Clubs:* Century, India House (New York City).

**MOERAN, Edward Warner;** *b* 27 Nov. 1903; *s* of E. J. Moeran; *m* 1938, Nadine Marie, Countess de Normanville; two *s* one *d*. *Educ:* Christ's Coll., Finchley; University of London. Solicitor. MP (Lab) South Beds, 1950-51. *Publication:* Practical Conveyancing, 1949. *Recreations:* talking, walking. *Address:* 1 Heath Street, Hampstead, NW3.

**MOFFAT, John;** *b* Jarrow-on-Tyne, 19 Nov. 1891; *o s* of late James Moffat, Morpeth and Jarrow, and late Frances Richley Moffat, Peebles; *m* 1927, Jean Wilson, *e d* of late Charlotte and late John Main, Edinburgh. Served European War, 1914-18 and War of 1939-45; retd, 1947, with rank of Major; served on editorial staffs of Scotsman, Glasgow Herald, Daily Express, Manchester Guardian and Manchester Evening News, Yorkshire Post, Manchester Evening Chronicle. Editor-in-Chief, Yorkshire Herald Newspaper Co., 1930-36; GS Publications Officer, Northern Command, 1940-45. Press Chief, British Sector, Berlin, July 1945-April 1946; started Der Berliner, first British newspaper in Berlin in July 1945 and edited it till its cessation in April 1946; Editor, British Zone Review, May 1946-June 1949. Press Officer, War Office, Aug. 1951-Nov. 1958, retired. *Address:* The Old Vicarage, Keyingham, East Yorkshire. *T:* Keyingham 2343.

**MOFFAT, John,** CBE 1919; *b* 13 May 1879; 2nd *s* of late John Moffat, CE, Ardrossan, and Jessie Fulton Arthur (she *m* 2nd, Charles Edward Hay of Somerby House, Leics), *sister* of 1st Baron Glenarthur; *m* 1926, Fern, *d* of Lloyd Stanley King; one *s* (and one *s* decd). *Educ:* Cheam; Eton; Cambridge. During European War, 1914-18, had charge of actual distribution of propaganda in USA in printed form for Production Dept Information Bureau of Foreign Office; also Mem. Advisory Board British and Canadian Recruiting Mission, and Chm. National Allied Commission in USA. Pres. and Founder, Lafayette Memorial Fund; Pres. of Lafayette Preventorium Inc. for 300 French delicate children. Contested Elgin Burghs. Officier, Légion d'Honneur, Commander Order Leopold II, Commander Order of St Sava, Knight Commander of Crown of Italy. Médaille Académie Française. Chevalier du Tastevin. *Publications:* Ray Farley, and other books. *Recreations:* golf, tennis, yachting, fishing, and travelling. *Address:* Château Lafayette, Chavaniac-Lafayette, Haute Loire, France.

*See also Earl of Dundee.*

**MOFFAT, Sir John Smith,** Kt 1955; OBE 1944; MLC Northern Rhodesia, 1951-64; Member Federal Parliament, Salisbury, 1954-62; *b* N Rhodesia, April 1905; *s* of Rev. Malcolm Moffat; *m* 1930, Margaret Prentice; two *d*. *Educ:* Grey High Sch., Port Elizabeth, South Africa; Glasgow Univ. Cadet Northern Rhodesia Provincial Administration, 1927; District Officer, 1929. Served at Serenje, Fort Jameson, etc. Commissioner for National Development, 1945; retd from CS, 1951. Chm. Federal African Affairs Board, and leader Liberal Party until 1962, when disbanded. Farmer.

**MOFFAT, Rennie John,** CBE 1956 (MBE 1918); Consultant on development plans, Cawood, Wharton and Co., 1958-70, retired; *b* 23 May 1891; *o s* of late John and Susan Moffat; *m* 1918, Lottie May, 4th *d* of late Robert and Edith Mizen; one *s*. *Educ:* Central Foundation Sch., London; King's Coll., London. Entered Civil Service, (Patent Office), 1906; Ministry of Munitions, 1915-16; served European War, Inns of Court OTC, 1916-18. Sec., Road Transport Board, 1918; Coal Mines Dept (later Mines Dept), Bd of Trade, 1919-39 (latterly head of Inland Trade Branch); resigned from Civil Service, 1939. General Manager, Midland Coal Mines Schemes, 1939-46; Dep. Dir-Gen. of Marketing, NCB, 1946-55; Dir-Gen. of Marketing, 1955-58. *Address:* 6 Henley Court, Chase Side, Southgate, N14. *T:* 01-882 1233.

**MOFFETT, John Perry,** CMG 1959; *b* 8 March 1909; *s* of John Moffett and Beatrix Heron; *m* 1933, Phyllis M. Brittain, *d* of John Wesley Brittain; one *s* two *d*. *Educ:* Cork Gram. Sch.; Trinity Coll., Dublin (BA, LLB). Provincial Administration, Colonial Service, Tanganyika, 1932-48; Local Courts Adviser, 1948; Commissioner for Social Development, 1953-58. *Publications:* (ed): Tanganyika: A Review of its Resources and their Development, 1956; Handbook of Tanganyika, 1958; Tanganyika Notes and Records, 1950-56. *Recreations:* golf, bird-watching. *Address:* Hill House, Roundhill Drive, Old Woking Road, Woking, Surrey. *T:* Woking 62812. *Club:* Worplesdon Golf.

**MOGG, Gen. Sir (Herbert) John,** KCB 1966 (CB 1964); CBE 1960; DSO 1944; Bar, 1944; Adjutant-General, Ministry of Defence (Army), since 1970; *b* 17 Feb. 1913; *s* of Capt. H. B. Mogg, MC and Alice Mary (*née* Ballard); *m* 1939, Cecilia Margaret Molesworth; three *s*. *Educ:* Malvern Coll.; RMC Sandhurst. Coldstream Guards, 1933-35; RMC Sandhurst (Sword of Honour) 1935-37; commissioned Oxfordshire and Buckinghamshire Light Infantry, 1937. Served War of 1939-45 (despatches); comd 9 DLI (NW Europe), 1944-45; Instructor, Staff Coll., 1948-50; Commander 10th Parachute Bn, 1950-52; Chief Instructor, School of Infantry, Warminster, 1952-54; Instructor (GSO1), Imperial Defence Coll., 1954-56; Comdr, Commonwealth Brigade Gp, Malaya, 1958-60; Meritorious Medal (Perak, Malaya); Dir of Combat Development, War Office, 1961-62; Comdt, Royal Military Academy, Sandhurst, 1963-66; Comdr 1st (British) Corps, 1966-68;

GOC-in-C Southern Comd, 1968; GOC-in-C Army Strategic Comd, 1968-70. Col Comdt: Army Air Corps, 1963-; 1st Bn The Royal Green Jackets (43rd and 52nd), 1965. President: Army Cricket Assoc.; Army Saddle Club, 1969; Chairman: Army Free Fall Parachute Assoc., 1970; Army Football Assoc., 1960-63. *Recreations:* cricket; most field sports. *Address:* c/o Glyn, Mills, Holt's Branch, Whitehall, SW1; Church Close, Watlington, Oxon. *Clubs:* Army and Navy, Flyfishers', MCC.

**MOGG, Sir John;** *see* Mogg, Sir H. J.

**MOGG, Rev. Canon Joseph William,** LTh; Assistant Curate, Cathedral of St Michael and St George, Grahamstown, 1953-58; Hon. Canon of St Cyprian's Cathedral, Kimberley, Diocese of Kimberley and Kuruman, since 1945; *b* Bloemfontein, 21 Dec. 1882; father from Somerset, England; mother a colonial (European), South Africa; *m. Educ:* St Andrew's Coll., Grahamstown; St Paul's Theological Coll., Grahamstown. Deacon, All Saints Church, Beaconsfield, S Africa, 1914-15; Rector of Kuruman and Dir of Kuruman Mission, 1915-28; Archdeacon of Kimberley, 1928-42; Archdeacon of Bechuanaland and Rector of Mafeking, 1942-45; Rector of Swellendam, 1945-53. *Recreations:* bowls, a naturalist, gardening. *Address:* 2 Worcester Street, Grahamstown, CP, South Africa.

**MOGG, W. R.;** *see* Rees-Mogg.

**MOIR, Sir Ernest Ian Royds,** 3rd Bt, *cr* 1916; *b* 9 June 1925; *o s* of Sir Arrol Moir, 2nd Bt, and Dorothy Blanche, *d* of Admiral Sir Percy Royds, CB, CMG; *S* father, 1957; *m* 1954, Margaret Hanham Carter; three *s. Educ:* Rugby; Cambridge Univ. (BA). Served War of 1939-45 in Royal Engineers. *Heir: s* Christopher Ernest Moir, *b* 22 May 1955. *Address:* Three Gates, 174 Coombe Lane West, Kingston, Surrey. *T:* 01-942 7394. *Club:* Royal Automobile.

**MOIR, Rt. Rev. Francis Oag H.;** *see* Hulme-Moir.

**MOIR, George Guthrie,** MA; Controller of Education and Religious Programmes, Thames TV, since 1968; *b* 30 Oct. 1917; *s* of James William and May Flora Moir; *m* 1951, Sheila Maureen Ryan, SRN; one *s* two *d. Educ:* Berkhamsted; Peterhouse, Cambridge. Officer, 5th Suffolk Regt, 1940-46, POW Singapore, 1942. Chief Officer, ST John Ambulance Bde Cadets, 1947-50; Dir, European Youth Campaign, 1950-52; Chm., later Pres., World Assembly of Youth, 1952-56; Education Adviser, Hollerith Tab. Machine Co., 1957; Asst Controller and Exec. Producer, Rediffusion TV, 1958-68. Mem., House of Laity, Church Assembly, 1956-; Mem. Council, Reading Univ. Contested (L) Aylesbury Div., 1950. CC Bucks, 1949-. Papal Bene Merenti Medal 1970, for services to religious and educational broadcasting. *Publications:* (ed) Why I Believe, 1964; (ed) Life's Work, 1965; (ed) Teaching and Television: ETV Explained, 1967; The Suffolk Regiment, 1969; Into Television, 1969; (ed) Beyond Hatred, 1969; contribs to Times, Times Ed. Supplement, Church Times, Contemporary Review, Frontier, etc. *Recreations:* golf, poetry, churches, mountains. *Address:* The Old Rectory, Aston Clinton, Aylesbury, Bucks. *T:* Aston Clinton 393. *Clubs:* Athenæum, National Liberal, Nikaean.

**MOIR, John Chassar,** CBE 1961; MA, DM, FRCSE, FRCOG; Visiting Professor, Royal Postgraduate Medical School; Nuffield Professor of Obstetrics and Gynæcology, University of Oxford, 1937-67, now Emeritus; Fellow, Oriel College, 1937-67; *b* 1900; *s* of late John and I. Moir (*née* Pirie), Montrose; *m* 1933, Grace Hilda Bailey; two *s* two *d. Educ:* Montrose Academy; Edinburgh University. MB, ChB (Edinburgh), 1922; MD, Gold Medal (Edinburgh), 1930; Asst Surgeon, East Surrey Hospital; 1st Asst Obstetric Unit, University Coll. Hospital, London; Reader in Obstetrics and Gynæcology, University of London (British Postgraduate Medical Sch.); Rockefeller Travelling Fellowship, 1932; Visiting Professor, Queen's Univ., Ontario, 1950; Examiner in Obstetrics and Gynæcology, University of Oxford, etc.; late Pres., section Obstetrics and Gynæcology, Royal Society Medicine; Hon. Fellow, American Association of Obstetricians and Gynecologists; Corresponding Fellow, New York Acad. of Medicine, Hon. LLD Queen's Univ., Ont.; Hon. DSc Edinburgh, 1970; Master of Midwifery, *hc,* Soc. Apothecaries, London. *Publications:* 7th edn, Munro-Kerr's Operative Obstetrics, 1964; 2nd edn The Vesicovaginal Fistula, 1967; contributions to scientific journals, and to textbooks on obstetrics and gynæcology. *Address:* 22 Charlbury Road, Oxford.

**MOIR, Percival John;** retired as Professor of Surgery and Dean of the Faculty of Medicine, University of Leeds, 1952-60; Emeritus Professor since 1960; *b* July 1893; 2nd *s* of late Frederick R. Moir; *m* 1926, Joan Evelyn Lander Whitehead; one *s. Educ:* Kelvinside, Glasgow; Univ. Glasgow; London Hospital. MB, ChB Glasgow Univ., 1914; FRCS, 1923; Capt. RAMC, 1914-18, served in Gallipoli, Egypt, Palestine, and France (despatches, MC). Formerly: Senior Hon. Surgeon, General Infirmary at Leeds; Surgeon Leeds Regional Hospital Board and United Leeds Hospitals Board; Mem. Board of Governors, Leeds United Hospitals; Mem., Leeds Regional Hospital Board; Mem., General Medical Council. Hon. Consulting Surgeon Dewsbury, Pontefract, Mirfield, and Ilkley Hospitals; Cons. Surg. WRCC; Prof. of Surgery, University of Leeds, 1940-46; Mem. Court of Examiners, Royal College of Surgeons of England, 1941-47. Fellow, Association of Surgeons of Great Britain and Ireland. *Publications:* contributed articles to Medical Journals. *Address:* 10 Windermere Avenue, SW19. *T:* 01-540 5505. *Club:* National Liberal.

**MOIR CAREY, D. M.;** *see* Carey.

**MOISEIWITSCH, Tanya, (Mrs Felix Krish);** designer for the theatre; *b* 3 Dec. 1914; *d* of late Benno Moiseiwitsch, CBE, and 1st wife, Daisy Kennedy; *m* 1942, Felix Krish (*decd*). *Educ:* various private schs; Central School of Arts and Crafts, London; Scenic painting student at Old Vic, London. Abbey Theatre, Dublin, 1935-39; Q. Theatre, 1940; 1st West End prod. Golden Cuckoo, Duchess, 1940; Weekly Repertory, Oxford Playhouse, 1941-44. Stage designs include: Bless the Bride, Adelphi, 1947; Peter Grimes, Covent Garden, 1947; Beggar's Opera, English Opera Group, Aldeburgh Festival, 1948; Treasure Hunt, Apollo, 1949; Home at Seven, Wyndham's, 1950; The Holly and the Ivy, Lyric (Hammersmith) and Duchess, 1950; Captain Carvallo, St James's, 1950; Figure of Fun, Aldwych, 1951. Has designed for Old Vic Company since 1944; at Playhouse, Liverpool, 1944-45; at Theatre Royal, Bristol, 1945-46; productions for Old Vic Company include: (at New Theatre): Uncle Vanya, The Critic, Cyrano de Bergerac, 1945-46, The Cherry Orchard, 1948, A Month in the Country, 1949;

(at Old Vic): Midsummer Night's Dream, 1951, Timon of Athens, 1952, Henry VIII, 1953; Two Gentlemen of Verona, 1957. Has designed for Royal Shakespeare Theatre, Stratford upon Avon: Henry VIII, 1950; The History Cycle (assisted by Alix Stone), 1951; Othello, 1954; Measure for Measure, 1956; Much Ado about Nothing, 1958; All's Well that Ends Well, 1959; also for 1st, and subsequent seasons, Shakespearean Festival, Stratford, Ont; for The Matchmaker, Edinburgh Festival, 1954, and New York, 1955; for Cherry Orchard, Piccolo Teatro, Milan, 1955; for Merchant of Venice, Habimah Theatre, Israel, 1959; Tyrone Guthrie Theatre, Minneapolis, USA: 1963; Hamlet, The Miser, Three Sisters; 1964: St Joan, Volpone; 1965: The Way of the World; Cherry Orchard; 1966: As You Like It; Skin of our Teeth (with Carolyn Parker); 1967: The House of Atreus; Peter Grimes (Metropolitan Opera, New York), 1967; Volpone, Nat. Theatre, 1968; Macook's Corner, Ulster Players, Belfast, 1969; Caucasian Chalk Circle, Sheffield Playhouse, 1969; Swift, Abbey Theatre, Dublin, 1969; Uncle Vanya, Minneapolis, 1969; Cymbeline, Stratford, Ont., 1970. Hon. DLitt (Birmingham) 1964. *Address:* c/o National Westminster Bank, 185 Sloane Street, SW1.

**MOKAMA, Moleleki Didwell;** BA, LLM; Barrister-at-Law; Advocate of the Supreme Court of Botswana; Attorney-General of Botswana, since 1969; *b* 2 Feb. 1933; *e s* of Mokama Moleleki and Baipoledi Moleleki, Maunatlala, Botswana; *m* 1962, Kgopodiso Vivien Robi; no *c. Educ:* Moeng; Fort Hare; London Univ.; Inner Temple. Crown Counsel to Botswana Govt, 1963-66; High Comr for Botswana in London, 1966-69; Botswana Ambassador Extraordinary and Plenipotentiary: to France, 1967-69; to Germany, 1967-69; to Sweden, 1968-69; to Denmark, 1968-69. Hon. Mem., American Soc. of International Law, 1965. *Recreations:* swimming, shooting, hunting. *Address:* Attorney-General's Chambers, Private Bag 9, Gaberones, Botswana.

**MOLESWORTH,** family name of **Viscount Molesworth.**

**MOLESWORTH,** 11th Viscount, *cr* 1716 (Ireland); **Richard Gosset Molesworth;** Baron Philipstown, 1716; secretarial work since 1959; *b* 31 Oct. 1907; *s* of 10th Viscount and Elizabeth Gladys Langworthy; *S* father, 1961; *m* 1958, Anne Florence Womersley, MA; two *s. Educ:* Lancing Coll.; private tutors. Farmed for many years. Served War, in RAF, 1941-44 (Middle East, 1941-43). *Recreations:* foreign travel, music. *Heir: s* Hon. Robert Bysse Kelham Molesworth, *b* 4 June 1959. *Address:* Garden Flat, 2 Bishopswood Road, Highgate, N6. *T:* 01-348 1366.

**MOLESWORTH, Hender Delves;** *b* Raptsgate Park, Cirencester, 10 Feb. 1907; *s* of late Lionel Charles M. and Saba Maud, *d* of Sir Henry Delves Broughton, 9th Bt; *m* 1934, Evelyn Carnegy, *d* of late M. W. and Edith Galloway, Shelley Hall, Ongar. *Educ:* Stubbington; Oundle; University Coll., Oxford. Joined staff of Victoria and Albert Museum, 1931; Curator of Institute of Jamaica, 1936-38; Ministry of Information, 1940; Press Attaché British Legation, Addis Ababa, 1942-45. Victoria and Albert Museum: Keeper of Sculpture, 1946; Keeper of Woodwork, 1954; retd 1966. *Publications:* articles on art, European sculpture, etc. *Recreations:* travel, painting. *Address:* The Orangery, Langley Park, Wexham, Bucks. *T:* Slough 28815.

**MOLESWORTH-ST AUBYN, Sir John,** 14th Bt, *cr* 1689; CBE 1968; *b* 12 Jan. 1899; *s* of Sir Hugh Molesworth-St Aubyn, 13th Bt, and Emma Sybil (*d* 1929), *d* of Admiral Charles Wake; *S* father, 1942; *m* 1926, Celia Marjorie (*d* 1965), *e d* of late Lieut-Col Valentine Vivian, CMG, DSO, MVO; one *s* two *d. Educ:* Eton; Christ Church, Oxford. Flight Lieut, RAFVR, 1941. Sheriff of Cornwall, 1948. *Heir: s* John Arscott Molesworth-St Aubyn [*b* 15 Dec. 1926; *m* 1957, Iona, *d* of late Admiral Sir Francis Tottenham, KCB, CBE; two *s*]. *Address:* Pencarrow, Washaway, Bodmin, Cornwall; Tetcott, Holsworthy, N Devon. *Club:* Pratt's.

*See also Earl of Morley.*

**MOLEYNS;** *see* Eveleigh-De-Moleyns.

**MOLINE, Most Rev. Robert William Haines,** MC, DD (Lambeth) 1948; *b* Sudbury, Suffolk, 20 Oct., 1889; *s* of late Canon R. P. Moline and Alice Price; *m* 1929, Mirabel Mathilde, *d* of Thomas Rookley Parker, Townsville. *Educ:* King's Sch., Canterbury; Emmanuel Coll., Cambridge (Scholar). Asst Master, Cranleigh Sch., Surrey, 1912-14; served in Rifle Brigade and Machine Gun Corps, 1914-19; granted rank of Major on demobilisation, 1919; Bishop's Coll., Cheshunt, 1919. Deacon, 1920; Priest, 1921; Asst Curate, St Matthew's, Bethnal Green, 1920-22; joined Brotherhood of St Barnabas, North Qld, 1922; Warden of Brotherhood, 1925-27; Archdeacon of North Qld, 1926-29; Rector of North Cadbury, Som, 1929-34; Rector of Poplar, 1934-40; Vicar of St Paul's, Knightsbridge, 1940-47; Archbishop of Perth (Australia), 1947-62, resigned. *Address:* 70 Hipwood Road, Hamilton, Brisbane, Qld 4007, Australia.

**MOLLAN, Maj.-Gen. Francis Robert Henry,** CB 1950; OBE 1943; MC 1918; *b* 20 June 1893; *s* of late Rev. H. J. G. Mollan; *m* 1st, 1921, Violet Samana Desvoeux (*d* 1930); one *s* (and one *s* killed in action, Italy, 1944); 2nd, 1937, Alison Beatrice Hesmondhalgh; two *s* one *d. Educ:* Corrig Sch.; Royal College of Surgeons of Ireland. Served European War, 1915-18, France and Belgium (despatches twice, 1914-15 Star, British War Medal, Victory Medal, MC). Served North-West Frontier of India (Mohmand), 1933 (despatches, Medal and clasp). War of 1939-45 (despatches thrice, OBE, Africa Star and 8th Army clasp). Comdt and Dir of Studies, Royal Army Medical College, 1950-53; Maj.-Gen., 1951; retired 1953; re-employed as Pres., Standing Medical Boards SW District, 1954-61; Area Medical Officer, Taunton, 1961-68. QHS 1952-53 (KHS 1950-52). *Publications:* Contrib. to Jl of the RAMC. *Recreations:* riding, fishing, shooting. *Address:* 5a Mount Street, Taunton, Som. *T:* 3097.

**MOLLER, Marjorie,** MA; *b* 23 June 1899; *e d* of late C. G. C. Moller. *Educ:* Clapham High Sch.; St Hugh's Coll., Oxford (Honour School of Natural Science). Science mistress City of London Girls' Sch., 1923; Walter Page travelling scholarship, 1930; Head of Science dept, 1928, and House mistress at Wycombe Abbey Sch., 1930; Head Mistress of Headington Sch., Oxford, 1934-59; Warden of Denman Coll. (NFWI), 1959-64. *Address:* 26 Bickerton Road, Headington, Oxford.

**MOLLISON, Prof. Patrick Loudon,** FRS 1968; FRCPath, FRCP, MD; Professor of Hæmatology, St Mary's Hospital Medical School, London University, since 1962; Consultant Hæmatologist, St Mary's Hospital since 1960; Part-time Director, Medical Research Council Experimental Hæmatology Unit, since 1960; *b* 17 March 1914; *s* of William

Mayhew Mollison, Cons. Surgeon (ENT), Guy's Hospital; *m* 1940, Margaret D. Peirce (marr. diss., 1964); three *s*. *Educ:* Rugby Sch.; Clare Coll., Cambridge; St Thomas' Hosp., London. MD Cantab 1944; FRCP 1959; FRCPath 1963. House Phys., Medical Unit, St Thomas' Hosp., 1939; Medical Officer, S London Blood Supply Depot, 1939-43; RAMC, 1943-46; Dir, MRC Blood Transfusion Res. Unit, Hammersmith Hosp., 1946-60; Hon. Lectr, then Sen. Lectr, Dept of Medicine, Post-grad. Medical Sch., 1948; Cons. Hæmatologist, Hammersmith Hosp., 1947-60. *Publications:* Blood Transfusion in Clinical Medicine, 1951 (4th edn, 1967); papers on red cell survival and blood group antibodies. *Recreations:* music, gardening, golf. *Address:* 60 King Henry's Road, NW3.

**MOLLO, Victor;** Bridge Correspondent, The Evening Standard since 1970; Bridge Editor, Faber & Faber Ltd, since 1966; *b* St Petersburg, 17 Sept. 1909; Russian parents; *m* 1952, Jeanne Victoria Forbes. *Educ:* privately in Paris; Cordwalles, Surrey (Prep. Sch.); Brighton Coll.; London School of Economics, London Univ. Free lance journalism, also reading French and Russian texts for publishers, 1927-40; sub editor and editor, European Services (now External) BBC, 1940 till retirement in Oct. 1969. *Publications:* Streamlined Bridge, 1947; Card-Play Technique (in collab. with N. Gardener), 1955; Bridge for Beginners (in collab. with N. Gardener) 1956; Bridge Psychology, 1958; Will You Be My Partner?, 1959; Bridge: Modern Bidding, 1961; Success at Bridge, 1964; Bridge in the Menagerie, 1965; Confessions of an Addict, 1966; The Bridge Immortals, 1967; Victor Mollo's Winning Double, 1968; Bridge: Case for the Defence, 1970; also Pocket Guides: ACOL: Winning Bidding, 1969 and Winning Defence, Winning Conventions. Contributing Editor to the Official Encyclopaedia of Bridge. Regular contributor to Bridge Magazines in USA, France, Denmark and Sweden and to Bridge Magazine in Britain. *Recreations:* gastronomy, conversation, bridge. *Address:* 204 Duncan House, Dolphin Square, SW1. *Clubs:* Royal Automobile, Eccentric, Curzon House.

**MOLLOY, William John,** FRGS; MP (Lab) Ealing North since 1964; *b* 26 Oct. 1918. *Educ:* elementary sch., Swansea; University Coll., Swansea (Political Economy, extra-mural). Served Field Coy, RE, 1939-46. Member: TGWU 1936-46; Civil Service Union, 1946-52; Co-op and USDAW, 1952. Chm., Staff-Side Whitley Council, Germany and Austria Sections, FO, and Staff-Side Lectr, 1946-52. Leader, Fulham Borough Council, 1959-62. Vice-Chm., Parly. Labour Party Gp for Common Market and European Affairs; Parly Adviser, London Trades Council Transport Cttee; Mem., House of Commons Estimates Cttee, 1968-70; PPS to Minister of Posts and Telecom., 1969-70. Mem. Assemblies, Council of Europe and WEU, 1969-. Governor, Holland Park Co-ed. Comp. Sch., 1958-64. *Recreations:* horse-riding, music. *Address:* 2a Uneeda Drive, Greenford, Middx.

**MOLOHAN, Michael John Brew,** CMG 1957; MBE 1936; formerly Member of HM Overseas Civil Service; *b* 30 May 1906; *s* of late George Brew Molohan, New Milton, Hants; *m* 1951, Alice Kathleen Branson Wilkinson; no *c*. *Educ:* Cheltenham Coll.; Trinity Coll., Oxford (BA). Entered Colonial Service (Tanganyika) as Administrative Officer, 1929; Labour Comr, Tanganyika, 1948-53; Senior Prov. Comr, 1953-61. *Recreations:* Rugby football, cricket, golf, squash. *Address:* Hollies, 11 Pewley Hill, Guildford, Surrey. *Club:* Royal Commonwealth Society.

**MOLONY, Sir Hugh (Francis),** 2nd Bt, *cr* 1925; MA, MAI, FICE, FIEI; MConsEI; Chartered Engineer, also a Consulting Engineer; Director, Stewarts & Lloyds of Ireland Ltd and other Companies; *b* 2 Sept. 1900; *e s* of Rt Hon. Sir Thomas Francis Molony, 1st Bt, PC (Ireland), KC, and Pauline Mary (*d* 1951), *o d* of Bernard Rispin, Eccles Street, Dublin; *S* father 1949; *m* 1936, Alexandra Campbell Cooper, *d* of late John Alexander Todd, Glasgow, and *widow* of M. Cooper; one *s*. *Educ:* St Benedict's Sch., Ireland; Trinity Coll., Dublin. University of Dublin; BA 1921; MA 1930; Bachelor of Engineering, 1922, Master, 1945. Associate Mem. of Institution of Civil Engineers, 1926, Mem. 1938, Fellow 1968. Pupil in Civil Engineering of late Sir Basil Mott, Bt. Asst and Resident Engineer for Messrs Mott, Hay & Anderson, MMICE, on bridges and tunnel works in England, 1922-27; Bridge Engineer to the Entre Rios & Argentine NE Railways, 1927-38; Engineer on tunnel construction in London, 1938; Engineering Inspector, Ministry of Health and, subsequently, Ministry of Housing and Local Government for Public Health and Civil Engineering Works, 1938-55, including wartime service as Regional Engineer, Min. of Health, Northwestern Region, 1940-46. *Publications:* professional papers for the Institution of Civil Engineers and articles in technical jls. *Heir: s* Thomas Desmond Molony [*b* 13 March 1937; *m* 1962, Doris, *e d* of late G. E. Foley, Cork; four *d*]. *Address:* 140 Lower Baggot Street, Dublin. *T:* Dublin 66869; Cranleigh, Knocksinna, Foxrock, Co. Dublin. *Clubs:* Stephen's Green, University (Dublin); Royal Irish Yacht (Dun Laoghaire).
*See also Sir Joseph Molony.*

**MOLONY, Sir Joseph (Thomas),** KCVO 1970; Kt 1967; QC 1955; Attorney General to the Duchy of Cornwall, 1960-69; Recorder of Bristol since 1964 (Devizes, 1951-54; Exeter, 1954-60; Southampton, 1960-64); *b* 8 Dec. 1907; 2nd *s* of Rt Hon. Sir T. F. Molony, 1st Bt, PC, Lord Chief Justice of Ireland; *m* 1936, Carmen Dent; two *s* two *d*. *Educ:* Downside; Trinity Coll., Cambridge (Senior Scholar). MA, LLM 1933; Barrister, Inner Temple, 1930 (Cert. of Honour, Barstow Scholar, Yarborough-Anderson Scholar); Master of the Bench, 1961. Leader of the Western Circuit, 1964; Mem. Bar Council, 1954-58, 1962; Commissioner of Assize: Midland and South-Eastern Circuits, 1958; North-Eastern Circuit, 1960; Western Circuit, 1968. Chairman: General Council of the Bar, 1963-64, 1964-65, 1965-66; Board of Trade Departmental Cttee on Consumer Protection, 1959; Code of Practice Cttee, Pharmaceutical Industry, 1967. Served War of 1939-45, Sqdn Leader, RAF, 1940-45. *Address:* 4 Parkside Gardens, Wimbledon Common, SW19. *T:* 01-946 3440. *Clubs:* Garrick; Hampshire (Winchester).
*See also Sir Hugh Molony, Bt.*

**MOLOTOV, Vaycheslav Mikhailovich,** (*pseudonym* of V. M. Skryabin); Soviet diplomat; *b* Kirov district (Vyatka), 9 March 1890; son of a ship assistant; as mem. of students' Marxist circles in Kazan, took part in first Revolution, 1905; joined Bolshevik section of Russian Social Democratic Labour Party and organised students, 1906; arrested and deported to Vologda; organised Vologda railwaymen; graduated, 1909; organised students, Petrograd; contributed to Zvezda; part-founder with Stalin and sec. of Pravda, 1911; exiled from Petrograd for political activity, 1912; continued Party work from suburbs, organising elections and work of Party deputies in Duma, 1913; reorganised Moscow Bolshevik Party; exiled to Irkutsk, Siberia, 1915; escaped, returned to Petrograd and appointed mem. of Russian Bureau of Bolshevik Central Committee, 1916; mem. of executive of Petrograd Soviet and of military revolutionary cttee, 1917; chm. of People's Economy Council, Northern Region, 1918; chm. Nijegorodsky regional executive, 1919; sec. of Donets Regional Party cttee, 1920; elected mem. and sec. of Central Cttee of Communist Party of Soviet Union and candidate mem. of Political Bureau, 1921; mem. of Political Bureau of CPSU; worked against Zinovievists, Leningrad, 1926; elected mem. of Central Executive Cttee of Russian Soviet Socialist Republic, 1927; sec., Moscow cttee of CPSU; worked against Bukharinists in Moscow, 1928; elected mem. of Presidium of Central Executive Cttee of USSR, 1929; chm. of Council, of People's Commissars of USSR, 1930-41; 1st Dep. Chm., Council of People's Commissars, 1941-46; Dep. Chm., State Defence Cttee, 1941-45; took part in Teheran, Crimean, Potsdam and San Francisco Conferences; Leader of Soviet Delegn to Paris Peace Conf., 1946, to UN Gen. Assemblies, 1945-48; People's Commissar for For. Affairs, 1930-46, For. Min., 1946-49, 1953-56; First Dep. Chm. of USSR Council of Ministers, 1953-57; Min. of State Control, 1956-57; Dep. to Supreme Soviet, 1937-57; Soviet Ambassador to Mongolia, 1957-60; Chief Permanent Representative of the Soviet Union (rank Ambassador) to the International Atomic Energy Agency, Vienna, 1960-62. Hon. Mem. USSR Acad. of Sciences, 1946. Hero of Socialist Labour (and Hammer and Sickle Medal), 1943; Order of Lenin (4 awards). *Publications:* In the Struggle for Socialism, 1934; Articles and Speeches, 1935-36, 1937; Problems of Foreign Policy, 1948. *Address:* c/o The Kremlin, Moscow.

**MOLSON,** family name of **Baron Molson.**

**MOLSON,** Baron, *cr* 1961, of High Peak (Life Peer); **(Arthur) Hugh (Elsdale) Molson,** PC 1956; *b* 29 June 1903; *o surv s* of late Major J. E. Molson, MP, Gainsborough, and Mary, *d* of late A. E. Leeson, MD; *m* 1949, Nancy, *d* of late W. H. Astington, Bramhall, Cheshire. *Educ:* Royal Naval Colleges, Osborne and Dartmouth; Lancing; New Coll., Oxford. Pres. of Oxford Union, 1925; 1st Class Hons Jurisprudence. Served 36 Searchlight Regt, 1939-41. Staff Captain 11 AA, Div., 1941-42. Barrister-at-Law, Inner Temple, 1931; Political Sec., Associated Chambers of Commerce of India, 1926-29; Contested Aberdare Div. of Merthyr Tydfil, 1929; MP (U) Doncaster, 1931-35. MP (U) The High Peak Div. of Derbyshire, 1939-61. Parly Sec., Min. of Works, 1951-53; Joint Parly Sec., Min. of Transport and Civil Aviation, Nov. 1953-Jan. 1957; Minister of Works, 1957-Oct. 1959. Mem., Monckton Commission on Rhodesia and Nyasaland, 1960; Chairman: Commission of Privy Counsellors on the dispute between Buganda and Bunyoro, 1962; Council for Protection of Rural England, 1968-. *Publications:* articles in various reviews on political and other subjects. *Recreation:* shooting. *Address:* Cherrytrees, Kelso, Roxburghshire. *T:* Yetholm 204; 14 Wilton Crescent, SW1. *T:* 01-235 3948. *Clubs:* Athenæum, Carlton.

**MOLYNEAUX, James Henry;** JP; MP (UU) South Antrim since 1970; *b* 27 Aug. 1920; *s* of late William Molyneaux, Seacash, Killead, Co. Antrim; unmarried. *Educ:* Aldergrove Sch., Co. Antrim. RAF, 1941-46. Vice-Chm., Eastern Special Care Hosp. Man. Cttee; Chm. Antrim Br., NI Assoc. for Mental Health; Hon. Sec., S Antrim Unionist Assoc., 1964-70; Mem. for S Antrim, Exec. Cttee of Ulster Unionist Council; Chm. Antrim Div., Unionist Assoc. JP Antrim, 1957; CC Antrim, 1964. *Recreations:* gardening, music. *Address:* Aldergrove, Crumlin, Co. Antrim, N Ireland. *T:* Crumlin 545.

**MOLYNEUX,** family name of **Earl of Sefton.**

**MOLYNEUX, John Anthony;** HM Diplomatic Service, since 1964; *b* 1 Aug. 1923; *s* of late E. D. Molyneux and Mrs E. Molyneux; *m* 1958, Patricia Dawson; three *s* one *d*. *Educ:* Lancing; Worcester Coll., Oxford (MA). Royal Navy, 1941-46. Joined Commonwealth Relations Office, 1949; 2nd Sec., New Delhi, 1950-52; 1st Sec., Karachi, 1955-59, Canberra, 1959-62; Special Adviser to Governor of N Rhodesia, 1964; Dep. High Comr, Lusaka, 1964-66; Counsellor (Commercial), Belgrade, 1967-70. *Recreations:* gardening, golf. *Address:* c/o Foreign and Commonwealth Office, SW1; *Clubs:* Travellers'; Delhi Gymkhana; Karachi Yacht.

**MOLYNEUX, Wilfrid,** FCA; Finance Member, British Steel Corporation, since 1967; *b* 26 July 1910; *s* of Charles Molyneux and Mary (*née* Vose); *m* 1937, Kathleen Eleanor Young; one *s* one *d*. *Educ:* Douai Sch. With Cooper Brothers & Co., 1934-67. *Address:* 105 Park Road, Brentwood, Essex.

**MOMIGLIANO, Prof. Arnaldo Dante,** DLitt (Turin); FBA 1954; Professor of Ancient History in the University of London at University College, since 1951; *b* 5 Sept. 1908; *s* of late Riccardo Momigliano and late Ilda Levi; *m* 1932, Gemma Segre; one *d*. *Educ:* privately, and at Univs of Turin and Rome. Professore Incaricato di Storia Greca, Univ. of Rome, 1932-36; Professore Titolare di Storia Romana, 1936-38, Professore Ordinario di Storia Romana in soprannumero, 1945-64, Univ. of Turin, *Id,* 1964-, Scuola Normale Superiore of Pisa. Lecturer in Ancient History, 1947-49, Reader in Ancient History, 1949-51, University of Bristol; research work in Oxford, 1939-47. Alexander White Visiting Prof., Univ. of Chicago, 1959; Sather Prof. in Classics, Univ. of California, 1961-62; J. H. Gray Lectr, Univ. of Cambridge, 1963; Wingate Lectr, Hebrew Univ. of Jerusalem, 1964; Vis. Prof. and Lauro de Bosis Lectr, Harvard Univ., 1964-65; C. N. Jackson Lectr, Harvard Univ., 1968. Socio Nazionale: Accademia dei Lincei, 1961 (corresp. mem., 1947-61); Arcadia, 1967; Accademia delle Scienze di Torino, 1968. Foreign Member: Royal Dutch Academy; Amer. Philosophical Soc.; Corresp. Member: German Archæological Institute, 1935; Istituto di Studi Romani, 1954; Hon. Mem., Amer. Hist. Assoc., 1964. Pres., Soc. for Promotion of Roman Studies, 1965-68. Hon. MA Oxford; Hon. DLitt: Bristol; Edinburgh; Oxford. Premio Feltrinelli for historical res. (Accademia dei Lincei award), 1960. Co-editor of Rivista Storica Italiana, 1948-. *Publications:* La composizione della Storia di Tucidide, 1930; Prime Linee di storia della tradizione maccabaica, 1931 (2nd edn 1968); Claudius, 1934 (2nd edn 1961); Filippo il Macedone, 1934; La storiografia sull' impero romano, 1936; Contributo alla storia degli studi classici, 1955; Secondo Contributo alla storia degli studi classici, 1960; Terzo Contributo alla storia degli studi classici, 1966; Studies in Historiography, 1966; Paganism and Christianity in the Fourth Century, 1963; Quarto contributo alla storia degli studi classici, 1969, etc; contribs to Cambridge Ancient History, Jl of Roman Studies,

Classical Quarterly, Jl of Warburg Inst., Enciclopedia Italiana, Encycl. Britannica, etc. *Recreation:* walking. *Address:* University College, Gower Street, WC1.

**MONAHAN, James Henry Francis,** CBE 1962; Controller, European Services of the BBC, since Dec. 1952; *b* 16 Dec. 1912; *s* of late George John Monahan, Indian Civil Service, and Helen Monahan (*née* Kennedy); *m* 1941, Joan Barker-Mill (*née* Eaden); two *s* three *d*; *m* 1965, Merle Park, *qv* (marr. diss. 1970); one *s*. *Educ:* Stonyhurst Coll.; Christ Church, Oxford. Critic and reporter, The Manchester Guardian, London Office, 1937-39; Government Service and attached to BBC German Service, 1939-42; Army Service: (despatches); Special Forces and No 10 Commando, 1942-45; Captain, 1944. British Broadcasting Corporation: Asst Head, West European Services, 1946; Head, West European Services, 1946-51; Asst Controller, West European Services, 1951-52. *Publications:* Far from the Land (poems), 1944; After Battle (poems), 1947; Fonteyn, 1958. Contributions to The Fortnightly, The Nineteenth Century and After, The Listener, Time and Tide and various anthologies. *Recreations:* lawn tennis, squash rackets and bushmen's cricket. *Club:* Hurlingham.

**MONAHAN, Hon. Sir Robert (Vincent),** Kt 1967; Supreme Court Judge, State of Victoria, Australia, since 1955; *b* 11 April 1898; *s* of Patrick Martin Monahan, Victoria, and Mary Frances Monahan (*née* Nolan); *m* 1929, Lillie Elevia, *d* of Peter Donald Bowman, Adelaide; three *s* one *d*. *Educ:* St Patrick's Coll., Ballarat; Newman Coll., Univ. of Melbourne. Admitted to: Victorian Bar, 1922; New South Wales Bar, 1942; Tasmanian Bar, 1948; KC 1947; practised at Common Law and Criminal Law Bar throughout professional career. *Recreations:* golf, racing, fishing. *Address:* Wyalla, 3 Marne Street, South Yarra, Vic 3141, Australia. *T:* 26-2016. *Clubs:* Australian, Athenæum (Melbourne); Melbourne Cricket; Lawn Tennis Association of Victoria; all Melbourne racing; Victoria Golf.

**MONCEL, Lt-Gen. Robert William,** SM 1968; DSO 1944; OBE 1944; CD 1944; retired 1966; *b* 9 April 1917; *s* of René Moncel and Edith Brady; *m* 1939, Nancy Allison, *d* of Ralph P. Bell; one *d*. *Educ:* Selwyn House Sch.; Bishop's Coll. Sch. Royal Canadian Regt, 1939; Staff Coll., 1940; Bde Major 1st Armd Bde, 1941; comd 18th Manitoba Dragoons, 1942; GSO1, HQ 2 Cdn Corps, 1943; comd 4th Armd Bde, 1944; Dir Canadian Armd Corps, 1946; Nat. War Coll., 1949; Canadian Jt Staff, London, 1949-54; Comdr 3 Inf. Bde, 1957; QMG, 1960; GOC Eastern Comd, 1963; Comptroller Gen., 1964; Vice-Chief of the Defence Staff, Canada, 1965-66. Col, 8th Canadian Hussars. Croix de Guerre, France, 1944; Légion d'Honneur, France, 1944. Hon. LLD Mount Allison Univ., 1968. *Recreations:* fishing, sailing, golf. *Address:* 711 Manor Road, Rockcliffe, Ontario. *T:* 745-5061; Windswept, Murder Point, Nova Scotia. *Clubs:* Country (Ottawa); Royal Ottawa Golf; Royal St Lawrence Yacht.

**MONCK,** family name of **Viscount Monck.**

**MONCK,** 6th Viscount *cr* 1800; **Henry Wyndham Stanley Monck,** OBE 1961; Baron Monck, 1797; Baron Monck (UK), 1866; formerly Lieutenant Coldstream Guards (Army Reserve); Company Director; JP Hampshire; Vice-Chairman, National Association of Boys' Clubs; *b* 11 Dec. 1905; *s* of Hon. Charles H. S. Monck (*d* 1914) and Mary Florence (*d* 1918), *d* of Sir W. Portal, 2nd Bt; *S* grandfather, 1927; *m* 1st, 1937, Eva Maria, Baroness Vreto (marriage dissolved, 1951), 2nd *d* of Prof. Zaunmüller-Freudenthaler, Vienna; 2nd, 1951, Brenda Mildred, *o d* of G. W. Adkins, Bowers Close, Harpenden; three *s*. *Educ:* Eton; RMC, Sandhurst. *Heir:* *s* Charles Stanley Monck, *b* 2 April 1953. *Address:* Hurstbourne Priors House, Whitchurch, Hants. *T:* Whitchurch, Hants, 2277. *Club:* MCC.
*See also Brig. C. H. V. Vaughan.*

**MONCKTON,** family name of **Viscount Monckton of Brenchley** and **Baroness Ruthven of Freeland.**

**MONCKTON OF BRENCHLEY,** 2nd Viscount *cr* 1957; **Maj.-Gen. Gilbert Walter Riversdale Monckton,** CB 1966; OBE 1956; MC 1940; DL; retired, 1967; Director: The Anglo-Portuguese Bank since 1967; Ransome, Hoffmann Pollard Ltd; United & General Trust Ltd; Modern Investments Ltd; *b* 3 Nov. 1915; *o s* of 1st Viscount Monckton of Brenchley, PC, GCVO, KCMG, MC, QC, and Mary A. S. (*d* 1964), *d* of Sir Thomas Colyer-Fergusson, 3rd Bt; *S* father, 1965; *m* 1950, Marianna Laetitia, 3rd *d* of Comdr Robert T. Bower, *qv*; four *s* one *d*. *Educ:* Harrow; Trinity Coll., Cambridge. BA 1939, MA 1942. 2/Lt 5th Royal Inniskilling Dragoon Guards, SR 1938; Reg. 1939; France and Belgium, 1939-40; Staff Coll., 1941; Bde Major Armd Bde, 1942; Comd and Gen. Staff Sch., USA, 1943; Sqdn Ldr, 3rd King's Own Hussars, 1944, Italy and Syria; Sqdn Ldr, 5th Royal Inniskilling Dragoon Gds, 1945. RAF Staff Coll., 1949; GSO2, 7th Armd Div., 1949; Sqdn Ldr and 2 i/c 5th Royal Inniskilling Dragoon Gds, Korea and Egypt, 1951-52; GSO1, Mil. Ops, WO, 1954-56; Mil. Adv., Brit. Delegn, Geneva Confs on Indo-China and Korea, 1954; transf. 12th Royal Lancers and comd, 1956-58; Comdr Royal Armd Corps, 3rd Div., 1958-60; psc, idc 1961; Dep. Dir, Personnel Admin., WO, 1962; Dir of Public Relations, WO (subseq. MoD), 1963-65; Chief of Staff, HQ BAOR, 1965-67; Col 9th/12th Royal Lancers (Prince of Wales's), 1967-. Farms 400 acres in Kent. President: Kent Assoc. of Boys' Clubs, 1965; Inst. of Heraldic and Genealogical Studies, 1965; Kent Archæological Assoc., 1968; Maidstone and District Football League, 1968; Medway Productivity Assoc., 1968; Kent Co. Rifle Assoc., 1970; Chm., Thurnham Parish Council, 1968-70. DL Kent, 1970. Liveryman Broderers' Co.; KStJ; Chm., Council of Order of St John for Kent, 1969; Grand Cross of Honour and Devotion, SMO Malta (Chancellor of the British Assoc., 1963-68, Vice-Pres., 1968-); Comdr, Order of Crown (Belgium), 1965. *Recreations:* hunting, cricket, gardening. *Heir:* *s* Hon. Christopher Walter Monckton, *b* 14 Feb. 1952. *Address:* Bertie House, Bearsted, Maidstone, Kent. *T:* Maidstone 37025. *Clubs:* Brooks's, Cavalry, MCC; Casino Maltese (Valetta).
*See also Sir W. B. Goulding.*

**MONCKTON OF BRENCHLEY,** the Dowager Viscountess; *see* Ruthven of Freeland, Lady.

**MONCKTON, Reginald Francis Percy;** Vice-Lieutenant, County of Stafford, 1962-67; *b* 3 June 1896; *y* and *o surv. s* of late Francis Monckton of Stretton Hall and Somerford Hall, Staffs; *m* 1931, Sheila, *y d* of H. G. Stobart of Thornton Hall, Yorks; one *s* one *d* (and one *s* one *d* decd). *Educ:* Eton. Joined Montgomeryshire Yeomanry, 1914; saw service in Palestine; survived the sinking of HMS Aragon off Alexandria, 1918; Dep. Military Governor of Jericho, 1918-20; ADC and Private Sec. to 1st High Comr for Palestine, 1920-25; transferred to Staffs Yeomanry, 1925; saw service in Middle East, 1940-41, with Public Relations Unit. DL

Staffs; High Sheriff of Staffs, 1937; TD; MFH Albrighton, 1929-35, Goathland, 1936-38; Mem. Church Assembly (House of Laity), 1950; Church Commissioner, 1938-68. *Publication:* The Key of Gold. *Recreations:* hunting, fishing, shooting. *Address:* Stretton Hall, Stafford.

**MONCKTON-ARUNDELL,** family name of **Viscount Galway.**

**MONCREIFF,** family name of **Baron Moncreiff.**

**MONCREIFF,** 5th Baron *cr* 1873; **Harry Robert Wellwood Moncreiff;** Bt, Nova Scotia 1626, UK 1871; Lt-Col (Hon.) RASC, retired; *b* 4 Feb. 1915; *s* of 4th Baron; *S* father, 1942; *m* 1952, Enid Marion Watson, *o d* of Major H. W. Locke, Belmont, Dollar; one *s*. *Educ:* Fettes Coll., Edinburgh. Served War of 1939-45 (despatches). Retired, 1958. *Recreations:* Rugby football, tennis, shooting. *Heir: s* Hon. Rhoderick Harry Wellwood Moncreiff, *b* 22 March 1954. *Address:* Tulliebole Castle, Fossoway, Kinross-shire, *T:* Fossoway 236.

**MONCREIFF, Most Rev. Francis Hamilton;** *see* Glasgow and Galloway, Bishop of.

**MONCREIFFE of that Ilk, Sir Iain;** *see* Moncreiffe of that Ilk, Sir R. I. K.

**MONCREIFFE of that Ilk, Sir (Rupert) Iain (Kay),** 11th Bt, *cr* 1685; DL; author; *b* 9 April 1919; *s* of late Lt-Comdr Gerald Moncreiffe, Royal Navy, and Hinda (*d* 1960), *d* of late Comte de Miremont; *S* cousin (Sir David Moncreiffe of that Ilk, Bt, 23rd Laird of Moncreiffe), 1957; *m* 1st, 1946, Diana (marr. diss. 1964), *d* of 22nd Earl of Erroll (*see* Countess of Erroll); two *s* one *d*; 2nd, 1966, Hermione, *d* of late Lt-Col W. D. Faulkner, MC, Irish Guards and of the Countess of Dundee (*d* of late Lord Herbert Montagu-Douglas-Scott). *Educ:* Stowe; Heidelberg; Christ Church, Oxford (MA); Edinburgh Univ. (LLB, PhD). Capt. late Scots Guards; served 1939-46 (wounded in Italy): ADC to Gen. Sir Andrew Thorne (GOC-in-C Scottish Comd), 1944-45; Military Liaison Officer for Norway to Adm. Sir William Whitworth (C-in-C Rosyth), 1945. Private Sec. to Sir Maurice Peterson (Ambassador to USSR) and attaché at British Embassy in Moscow, 1946. Mem. Queen's Body Guard for Scotland (Royal Company of Archers), 1948-; called to Scottish Bar, 1950; Mem. of Lloyd's, 1952-. Mem. Advisory Cttee Scottish Nat. Portrait Gallery, 1957. Hon. Pres., Duodecimal Soc. of Great Britain, 1966-. Hon. Sheriff-Substitute of Perth and Angus, 1958; Albany Herald, 1961; DL Perth, 1961. FSA 1959. OStJ 1949. *Heir: s* Lord Hay, *qv*. *Publications:* (with D. Pottinger) Simple Heraldry, 1953; Simple Custom, 1954; Blood Royal, 1956; Map of Scotland of Old, 1960; (with David Hicks) The Highland Clans, 1967. *Recreations:* shooting and travel. *Address:* Easter Moncreiffe, Perthshire. *T:* Bridge of Earn 338. *Clubs:* Turf, White's, Pratt's, Beefsteak; Royal and Ancient Golf (St Andrews); (Founder) Puffin's (Edinburgh).

**MONCRIEFF;** *see* Scott-Moncrieff.

**MONCRIEFF, Sir Alan (Aird),** Kt 1964; CBE 1952; MD; FRCP; FRCOG; Emeritus Professor of Child Health, University of London; late Physician, Hospital for Sick Children, Great Ormond Street, 1934-64; Consulting Physician, Children's Department, Middlesex Hospital, London; *b* Bournemouth, 9 Oct. 1901; *e surv. s* of Rev. William Moncrieff; *m* 1928, Honor (*d* 1954), *o d* of Cecil Wedmore, Clevedon, Som.; two *s* one *d*; *m* 1955, Mary Katherine, *er d* of Ralph Wedmore. *Educ:* Caterham Sch.; Univ. of London, Middlesex Hosp. Medical Sch. Qualified as a medical practitioner, 1922; Post-Graduate experience in various resident appointments at this Hosp. and at the Hosp. for Sick Children, Great Ormond Street; studied in Paris while working in the Health Div. of the League of Red Cross Socs, 1923-24; studied in Hamburg and other parts of Germany in 1930-31 while holding a Rockefeller Travelling Medical Fellowship; Goulstonian Lectr, RCP, 1935; Charles West Lectr, RCP, 1952; Newsholme Lecturer, London Sch. of Hygiene, 1953; Harben Lecturer, 1962. James Spence Gold Medallist, 1961. Hon. Fellow, American Academy of Pediatrics; Corr. étrang. Académie Nat. de Médecine, France; Mem. Corr. Soc. de Pédiatrie de Paris and Sociedade Portuguesa de Pediatria; Hon. Mem. American and Canadian Pediatric Socs. Chevalier de la Légion d'Honneur, 1968. *Publications:* contribs to scientific and medical journals on matters relating to diseases of children and respiration. *Recreations:* music, reading, and writing. *Address:* Waterford Lodge, Waterford, Hertford. *T:* Hertford 4391.

**MONCTON, Archbishop of, (RC),** since 1942; **Most Rev. Norbert Robichaud;** *b* Saint Charles, Kent Co., NB, 1 April 1905; *s* of Marcel F. Robichaud and Nathalie Robichaud (*née* Gallant). *Educ:* St Ann's Coll., Church Point, NS; Holy Heart Seminary, Halifax, NS. Pontifical Inst. Angelicum, Rome, 1938; DPh St Joseph's Univ., 1943; Doctorate in Arts, Univ. of Montreal, 1946. *Address:* 1081 Main Street, Moncton, NB, Canada. *T:* 9531.

**MOND,** family name of **Baron Melchett.**

**MONDAY, Horace Reginald,** CBE 1967 (OBE 1958); High Commissioner for The Gambia in the United Kingdom and Northern Ireland since Nov. 1968; *b* 26 Nov. 1907; *s* of late James Thomas Monday, Gambia Civil Servant, and late Rachel Ruth Davis; *m* 1932, Wilhelmina Roberta Juanita, *d* of late William Robertson Job Roberts, a Gambian businessman; one *s*. *Educ:* Methodist Mission Schools, in Bathurst, The Gambia; correspondence course with (the then) London Sch. of Accountancy. Clerk, 1925-48; Asst Acct, Treasury, 1948-52; Acct and Storekeeper, Marine Dept, 1953-54; Acct-Gen., The Gambia Govt, 1954-65; Chm., Gambia Public Service Commn, 1965-68; Dir, Gambia Currency Bd, 1964-68; Governor, Gambia High Sch., 1964-68; Pres., Gambia Red Cross Soc., 1967-68. Comdr, National Order of Republic of Senegal, 1968. *Address:* The Gambia House, 28 Kensington Court, W8. *T:* 01-937 0800.

**MONEY, Ernle (David Drummond);** MP (C) Ipswich since 1970; Barrister-at-Law; *b* 17 Feb. 1931; *s* of late Lt-Col E. F. D. Money, DSO, late 4th Gurkha Rifles, and of Sidney, *o d* of D. E. Anderson, Forfar; *m* 1960, Susan Barbara, *d* of Lt-Col D. S. Lister, MC, The Buffs; two *s* two *d*. *Educ:* Marlborough Coll.; Oriel Coll., Oxford (open scholar). Served in Suffolk Regt, 1949-51, and 4th Bn, Suffolks Regt (TA), 1951-56; MA Hons degree (2nd cl.) in mod. hist., 1954. Tutor and lecturer, Swinton Conservative Coll., 1956. Called to Bar, Lincoln's Inn (Cholmeley Scholar), 1958. Mem., Bar Council, 1962-66. Sec., Parly Cons. arts and amenities cttee, 1970-. Governor, Woolverstone Hall Sch., 1967-. Mem. Council, Hintlesham Festival, and of Cttee of Gainsborough's Birthplace, Sudbury. Fine Arts Correspondent, Contemporary Review, 1968-. *Publications:* (with Peter Johnson) The Nasmyth Family of Painters, 1970; regular contrib. various periodiclas and newspapers on antiques and the arts. *Recreations:* music, pictures and antiques, watching Association football. *Address:* Rundle House, Hatfield Broad Oak, Essex. *T:* Hatfield Broad Oak 303; 5 Paper Buildings, Temple, EC4. *T:* 01-583 3724. *Clubs:* Carlton; Ipswich and Suffolk (Ipswich).

**MONEY, George Gilbert;** Vice-Chairman, Barclays Bank DCO, since 1965; Chairman, New York Board of Barclays Bank DCO; *b* 17 Nov. 1914; 2nd *s* of late Maj.-Gen. Sir A. W. Money, KCB, KBE, CSI and late Lady Money (*née* Drummond). *Educ:* Charterhouse Sch. Clerk, L. Behrens & Soehne, Bankers, Hamburg, 1931-32; Clerk, Barclays Bank Ltd, 1932-35; joined Barclays Bank DCO, London, 1935; served in Egypt, Palestine, Cyprus, Ethiopia, Cyrenaica, E Africa, 1936-52; Local Dir, W Indies, 1952; Director: Barclays Bank DCO, 1955; Barclays Bank of California, 1965-; Bermuda Provident Bank Ltd, 1969-; Mem., E Caribbean, W Caribbean and Bahamas Bds, Barclays Bank DCO; Vice-Chm. and Chm., Caribbean Bd, 1965. FIB. *Recreations:* tennis, water ski-ing, aviation, shooting, fishing, bridge. *Address:* 96 Marsham Court, SW1. *Clubs:* Crockfords, West Indian.

**MONEY, Col Reginald Angel,** CBE 1943; MC 1917; ED; FRCS; FRACS; MB, ChM (Sydney); RAAMC; *b* Sydney, Australia, 3 March 1897; *s* of late Angel Money, MD, FRCP, Harley Street, W1, and of late Mrs Amy Money, 138 Ocean Street, Edgecliff, Sydney; *m* 1937, Dorothy Jean Wilkinson, Strathfield, NSW; two *d*. *Educ:* Sydney Grammar Sch.; Univ. of Sydney. Enlisted in AIF and was abroad with Australian Field Artillery, 1916-19 (Lt, MC); CO 2/6 Australian Gen. Hosp., AIF, 1940-44 (Col, CBE); MB, ChM from Medical Sch. of Univ. of Sydney, 1923; House Surgeon, Registrar, and Medical Supt, Royal Prince Alfred Hosp., Sydney, 1923-28, Hon. Asst Surgeon, 1928; Hon. Neuro-Surgeon, 1937-57. FRCS 1932; FRACS 1931; Tutor in Surgery, Sydney Univ., 1933-37; Lecturer in Head and Spinal Injuries, 1935-57; Vice-Chm., Bd of Directors, Royal Prince Alfred Hospital, Sydney, 1968. Hon. Consulting Neuro-Surgeon, Royal Prince Alfred Hosp., Royal North Shore Hosp., and St George Hosp., Sydney; Visiting Neuro-Surgeon, NSW Masonic Hosp., Sydney. Postgraduate Professional Tours of Great Britain, Europe, USA, Canada, USSR, Mexico, South America, Japan, S Africa, Asia, in 1928, 1932, 1935, 1947, 1953, 1957, 1961, 1963, 1965, 1967, 1969. *Publications:* articles and case reports in med. and surgical jls, etc. *Recreations:* golf, swimming, contract bridge. *Address:* 143 Macquarie Street, Sydney, NSW 2000, Australia. *T:* 27-5916; 28 Bathurst Street, Woollahra, Sydney, NSW 2025. *T:* 38-8165. *Clubs:* Australian, Royal Sydney Golf, Australian Jockey (Sydney).

**MONEY, Maj.-Gen. Robert Cotton,** CB 1943; MC; psc; *b* 21 July 1888; *o c* of late Col R. C. Money, CMG, CBE; *m* 1917, Daphne Dorina (*d* 1968), 2nd *d* of Brig.-Gen. C. W. Gartside Spaight, Derry Castle, Killaloe, Ireland; (one *s* killed in action, 1940) one *d*. *Educ:* Arnold House, Llandulas; Wellington Coll.; RMC, Sandhurst. Joined Cameronians (Scottish Rifles), 1909; served with both battalions, European War and India; commanded 1st Bn 1931-34; commanded Lucknow Bde, 1936-39; Commandant Senior Officers' Sch., 1939; comd 15th (Scottish) Div., 1940-41; District Comdr, India, 1942-44; retired pay, 1944. Ministry of Transport, 1944-52; retired, 1952. *Recreation:* gardening. *Address:* The Old Vicarage, Cholesbury, Tring, Herts. *Club:* Army and Navy.

**MONEY-COUTTS,** family name of **Baron Latymer.**

**MONIER-WILLIAMS, Clarence Faithfull,** CB 1952; MBE 1934; *b* 5 May 1893; 2nd *s* of late Dr M. S. Monier-Williams; *m* 1944, Muriel Leonie, *o d* of late J. A. Edwards; no *c*. *Educ:* Westminster Sch.; Lincoln Coll., Oxford (BA). Entered Army, 1914; seconded from Army for service in the Foreign Office, 1917; transferred to Dept of Overseas Trade, 1919, Board of Trade, 1939; Under-Sec., Board of Trade, 1948-54, retired 1954. *Recreations:* travelling, gardening. *Address:* Broad View, Wonham Way, Gomshall, Surrey. *T:* Shere 2286.

**MONIZ DE ARAGÃO, José Joaquim de Lima e Silva;** *b* Rio de Janeiro, Brasil, 12 May 1887; *m* 1926, Isabel Rodrigues Alves; two *s*. *Educ:* Faculty of Law, Rio de Janeiro. Attached to Ministry of Foreign Affairs, Rio de Janeiro, 1908; 2nd Sec., Washington, 1911; 1st Sec., Monte-Video, Madrid, Rome, 1913; Counsellor, Berlin, 1915-18; Counsellor, Brazilian Delegn Peace Conf., Versailles, 1919; Counsellor, Berlin, 1920-25; Minister, League of Nations, Geneva, 1926; Minister Delegate, Internat. Labour Office, Geneva, 1928-29; Minister, Copenhagen, Caracas, 1929-33; Under-Sec. of State for Foreign Affairs, Rio de Janeiro, 1934; Ambassador to Berlin, 1935-38; Brazilian Ambassador to Court of St James's, 1940-52. Brazilian Delegate to UNO Assembly in London, 1945; Chief Brazilian Delegate to: UNESCO Assembly, London, 1945, Paris, 1946; UNRRA Assembly, London, 1946; Internat. Cttee for Refugees in London, 1944, 1945, Paris, 1946. Mem. Royal Philatelic Society. Knight Grand Cross of the Royal Victorian Order, Gt Brit. (Hon. GCVO); Comdr Order of the British Empire (Hon. CBE). *Address:* Avenida Atlantica 1136, 9th Floor, Rio de Janeiro, Brazil. *Clubs:* Rotary, Jockey, Automovel (Rio de Janeiro).

**MONK, Albert Ernest,** CMG 1966; Permanent President, Australian Council of Trade Unions, 1949-69 (Secretary, 1945-49; President, 1934-43); *b* 1900. clerk, Transport Workers' Union, 1919; Clerk, Asst Sec. and Sec., Trades Hall Council, Melbourne, 1924-39. Chm., Victoria State Relief Cttee, 1934-44, 1954-. Member: Governing Body, ILO; Exec. Council, WFTU, 1945-49; Mem. Exec. Bd, Internat. Confederation, Free Trade Unions, 1949-. *Address:* 17-25 Lygon Street, Carlton, Victoria, Australia.

**MONK BRETTON,** 3rd Baron *cr* 1884; **John Charles Dodson;** *b* 17 July 1924; *o s* of 2nd Baron and Ruth (*d* 1967), 2nd *d* of late Hon. Charles Brand; *S* father, 1933; *m* 1958, Zoë Diana Scott; two *s*. *Educ:* Westminster Sch.; New Coll., Oxford (MA). *Recreations:* hunting, farming. *Heir:* *s* Hon. Christopher Mark Dodson, *b* 2 Aug. 1958. *Address:* Conyboro, Lewes, Sussex. *T:* Barcombe 231. *Club:* Brooks's.

**MONKHOUSE, Prof. Francis John;** Professor of Geography, University of Southampton, 1954-66; *b* 15 May 1914; *s* of late Alderman Joseph Monkhouse and Mrs E. L. Monkhouse, Workington; *m* 1938, Bertha Greensmith; one *s* one *d*. *Educ:* Workington Grammar Sch.; Emmanuel Coll., Cambridge (MA). Teaching, 1936-40. Intelligence Div., Naval Staff, 1941-44; Inter-Services Topographical Div., South-East Asia, 1944-45. Univ. of Liverpool, Depts of Geography and Education, 1946-54. Visiting Professor: Miami Univ., Ohio, 1960-61; Univ. of Southern Illinois, 1965-66; Univ. of Maryland, USA, 1968. Hon. DSc Miami Univ., Oxford, Ohio. *Publications:* The Belgian Kempenland, 1949; (with H. R. Wilkinson)

Maps and Diagrams, 1952; Principles of Physical Geography, 1954; A Study Guide in Physical Geography, 1956; Landscape from the Air, 1958; A Regional Geography of Western Europe, 1959; The English Lake District, 1960; Europe, 1961; A Dictionary of Geography, 1965; The Countries of North-Western Europe, 1965; (with A. V. Hardy) The American Landscape, 1965; (with H. R. Cain) North America, 1970. *Recreation:* mountaineering. *Address:* Crag Farm House, Ennerdale, Cleator, Cumberland. *T:* Lamplugh 214.

**MONKS, Air Vice-Marshal Alfred Thomas,** CB 1957; *b* 15 March 1908; *s* of late William Patrick Monks; *m* 1937, Emily Irene, 2nd *d* of late George S. Overton, Navenby, Lincs; no *c.* *Educ:* Sir Joseph Williamson's Mathematical Sch., Rochester, Kent. Aircraft Apprentice, RAF, 1924-26; flying course, 1931; commissioned, 1932; specialised in signals, 1934-35; Chief Signals Officer: AHQ, E Africa, 1943; AHQ, Eastern Mediterranean, 1943-44 (despatches 1944); Dep. Dir of Telecommunications, Air Ministry, 1944-46; commanded: No. 4 Radio Sch., 1946; No. 1 Radio Sch., 1946-48, and 1952-53; Dep. Dir of Signals, Air Ministry, 1949-51; Chief Signals Officer, Allied Air Forces (NATO), Northern Europe, 1953-55; Controller, RAF Telecommunications, 1955-60; SASO Technical Training Command, 1960-63, retired 1963. CEng, FIEE. *Address:* The Grange, Navenby, Lincoln. *Club:* Royal Air Force.

**MONKS, Constance Mary,** OBE 1962; MP (C) Chorley Division of Lanarkshire since 1970; JP; *b* 20 May 1911; *d* of Ellis Green and Bessie A. Green (*née* Burwell); *m* 1937, Jack Monks; one *s* (decd). *Educ:* Wheelton County Sch.; Chorley Grammar Sch.; City of Leeds Training Coll. Apptd Asst Teacher, 1931. Started retail business as partner with husband, 1945. Councillor (C), Chorley (N Ward) 1947-67, Alderman, 1967; Mayor of Chorley, 1959-60; Mem. Lancs CC, 1961-64. JP Chorley, 1954. *Recreations:* reading, gardening, needlework; formerly games. *Address:* 17 Sandridge Avenue, Chorley, Lancs. *T:* Chorley 3115 (office hours). *Club:* Constitutional.

**MONKSWELL,** Barony of (*cr* 1885); title disclaimed by 4th Baron; *see under* Collier, William Adrian Larry.

**MONMOUTH, Bishop of,** since 1968; **Rt. Rev. Eryl Stephen Thomas;** *b* 20 Oct. 1910; *s* of Edward Stephen and Margaret Susannah Thomas; *m* 1939, Jean Mary Alice Wilson; three *s* one *d.* *Educ:* Rossall Sch.; St John's Coll., Oxford; Wells Theological Coll. BA 2nd Class Hon. Theology, Oxford, 1932; MA 1935. Curate of Colwyn Bay, 1933-38, of Hawarden, 1938-43; Vicar of Risca, Mon, 1943-48; Warden of St Michael's Theological Coll., Llandaff, 1948-54; Dean of Llandaff, 1954-68. Chaplain and Sub-Prelate, Order of St John of Jerusalem, 1969-. *Address:* Bishopstow, Stow Hill, Newport, Mon. *T:* Newport 63510.

**MONMOUTH, Assistant Bishop of;** *see* Gresford Jones, Rt Rev. E. M.

**MONMOUTH, Dean of;** *see* Evans, Very Rev. R. E.

**MONNET, Jean;** European political figure; *b* Cognac, Charente, 9 Nov. 1888; *s* of J. G. Monnet. *Educ:* Cognac Coll. French representative, Allied Exec. Cttees for re-allocation of common resources, European War; Dep. Sec.-Gen., League of Nations, 1918; returned to family business; took part in re-organisation of Chinese Railways, 1932; Chm., Franco-British Economic Co-ordination Cttee, 1939; took part in organisation of common defence programme, 1940; Mem. British Supply Council, Washington, 1940-43; Comr for Armament, Supplies and Reconstruction, French National Liberation Cttee, Algiers, 1943-44; created Plan Monnet, 1946; Gen. Comr, Plan for Modernisation and Equipment of France, 1946; Pres. Preparatory Conf. of Schuman Plan, 1950; Pres. European Coal and Steel Community, 1952-55; Chm., Action Cttee for the United States of Europe, 1956-. Holds hon. doctorates of following universities: Columbia, 1953; Glasgow, 1956; Princeton, 1959; Yale, 1961; Cambridge, 1961; Oxford, 1963. Wateler Peace Prize, 1951; Charlemagne Prize, 1953; Grand Cross of Merit of German Federal Republic, 1958; Freedom Award, 1963; Prize of Foundation Gouverneur Emile Cornez, 1963; US Presidential Medal of Freedom, 1963. Hon. GBE 1947. *Publication:* Les Etats Unis d'Europe ont commencé (collection of extracts from speeches). *Address:* Houjarray, par Montfort l'Amaury (Seine-et-Oise), France.

**MÖNNIG, Hermann Otto,** BA, DrPhil, BVSc, DSc (*hc*); Chairman, Agricura Laboratoria Ltd, 1945-70, now Adviser; formerley Chairman, science Advisory Council; Scientific Adviser to Prime Minister, 1962; National Parks Board, 1952; *b* Cape Town, 27 Jan. 1897; *s* of C. J. O. Mönnig and A. H. Schmidt; *m* 1923, Everdina Maria Koning; two *s.* *Educ:* Gymnasium, Paarl; Univs of Stellenbosch, Amsterdam, Zürich, Neuchâtel, SA. Research Officer at Onderstepoort, S Africa, 1922; Graduated in Veterinary Science, Univ. of South Africa, 1926; Pretoria Univ.: Lectr in Helminthology, 1928; Prof. of Parasitology, 1930; Mem. of Council, 1949-70. *Publications:* various scientific articles on parasitology; Veterinary Helminthology and Entomology, 1934. *Recreation:* wood-carving. *Address:* 246 Hay Street, Pretoria, Transvaal, South Africa. *TA:* Agrilab, Silverton. *T:* Pretoria 74-2674.

**MONNINGTON, Sir Thomas;** *see* Monnington, Sir W. T.

**MONNINGTON, Sir (Walter) Thomas,** Kt 1967; PRA (RA 1938; ARA 1931); painter; President of the Royal Academy since 1966; Fellow of University College, London; *b* 1902; *s* of Walter Monnington, Barrister; *m* 1924, Winifred (*d* 1947), *d* of W. H. Knights; one *s*; *m* 1947, Evelyn Janet, 3rd *d* of Bernard Hunt; one *s.* *Educ:* University Coll., London; Slade Sch. (scholar). Trustee, British Museum, 1963-69. Mem. Exec. Cttee National Art Collections Fund. *Address:* Leyswood, Groombridge, Tunbridge Wells, Kent. *T:* Groombridge 205. *Clubs:* Athenæum, Arts.

**MONOD, Jacques Lucien,** Officier de la Légion d'Honneur, Commandeur de l'Ordre National du Mérite; French molecular biologist; Head of Department of Cellular Biochemistry, Pasteur Institute, Paris, since 1954; Professor of Molecular Biology at the Collège de France, since Oct. 1967; *b* 9 Feb. 1910; *s* of Lucien Monod, painter and Charlotte Todd MacGregor; *m* 1938, Odette Bruhl; two *s.* *Educ:* Cannes Lycée; Univ. of Paris. War service, 1939-45; Croix de Guerre, Chevalier de la Légion d'Honneur, Bronze Star Medal. Zoology Asst, 1931, Head of Laboratory, 1945, Institut Pasteur; Prof., Faculty of Sciences, Univ. of Paris, 1959-67. Rockefeller Foundation Fellow, 1936; non-resident Fellow, Salk Inst. Member: American

Academy of Arts and Sciences; Deutsche Akademie der Naturforscher Leopoldina. For. Member: Royal Society, 1968; Nat. Acad. of Sciences of Washington, 1968. Charles-Leopold Mayer Prize, 1964; Nobel Prize for Medicine and Physiology (jointly), 1965. *Publications:* papers on molecular biology. *Recreations:* music (cello), sailing. *Address:* Institut Pasteur, 28 rue du Dr Roux, Paris 15, France.

**MONOD, Prof. Théodore,** DèsSc; Officier de la Légion d'Honneur, 1958; Professor at National Museum of Natural History, Paris, since 1942 (Assistant 1922); *b* 9 April 1902; *s* of Rev. Wilfred Monod and Dorina Monod; *m* 1930, Olga Pickova; two *s* one *d*. *Educ:* Sorbonne (Paris). Docteur ès-sciences, 1926. Sec.-Gen. (later Dir) of l'Institut Français d'Afrique Noire, 1938; Prof., Univ. of Dakar, 1957-59; Doyen, Science Faculty, Dakar, 1957-58. Mem., Academy of Sciences; Member: Acad. des Sciences d'Outre-Mer; Académie de Marine; Corresp. Mem., Académie des Sciences de Lisbonne and Académie Royale des Sciences d'Outre-Mer. Dr *h c* Köln, 1965, Neuchâtel, 1968. Gold Medallist, Royal Geographical Soc., 1960; Gold Medallist, Amer. Geographical Soc., 1961; Haile Sellassie Award for African Research, 1967. Comdr, Ordre du Christ, 1953; Commandeur, Mérite Saharien, 1962; Officer de l'Ordre des Palmes académiques, 1966. etc. *Publications:* Méharées, Explorations au vrai Sahara, 1937; L'Hippopotame et le philosophe, 1942; Bathyfolages, 1954; many scientific papers in learned jls. *Address:* 14 quai d'Orléans, Paris IVe. *T:* Danton 79.50; Muséum National d'Histoire Naturelle, 57 rue Cuvier, Paris V. *T:* Gobelins 40.10.

**MONRO, Hector Seymour Peter;** MP (C) Dumfries since 1964; a Lord Commissioner of HM Treasury, since 1970; *b* 4 Oct. 1922; *s* of late Capt. Alastair Monro, Cameron Highlanders, and Mrs Monro, Craigeleuch, Langholm, Scotland; *m* 1949, Elizabeth Anne Welch, Longstone Hall, Derbs; two *s*. *Educ:* Canford Sch.; King's Coll., Cambridge. RAF, 1941-46, Flight Lt; RAuxAF, 1946-53 (AEM 1953). Mem. of Queen's Body Guard for Scotland, Royal Company of Archers. Dumfries CC, 1952-67 (Chm. Planning Cttee, and Police Cttee); JP Dumfries. Chm. Dumfriesshire Unionist Assoc., 1958-63; Scottish Cons. Whip, 1967-70. Mem. Dumfries T&AFA, 1959-67; Mem., Area Executive Cttee, Nat. Farmers' Union of Scotland. *Recreations:* Rugby football (Mem. Scottish Rugby Union, 1958-69); golf, flying, vintage sports cars. *Address:* Williamwood, Kirtlebridge, Dumfriesshire. *T:* Kirtlebridge 213. *Clubs:* Caledonian, East India and Sports, MCC; Royal Scottish Automobile (Glasgow).

**MONRO, Hon. Lady,** DBE 1919; **Mary Caroline;** *y d* of 1st Baron O'Hagan; *m* 1912, General Sir Charles Carmichael Monro, 1st Bt, GCB, GCSI, GCMG (*d* 1929); no *c*. *Address:* Flat 7, Belgravia House, 2 Halkin Place, SW1. *T:* 01-235 9474. *Club:* Sesame Pioneer and Lyceum.

**MONROE, Elizabeth; (Mrs Humphrey Neame),** MA Oxon; Fellow of St Antony's College, Oxford, since 1963; Hon. Fellow of St Anne's College; *b* 10 Jan. 1905; *d* of late Canon Horace Monroe, Vicar of Wimbledon; *m* 1938, Humphrey Neame (*d* 1968). *Educ:* Putney High Sch., GPDST; St Anne's Coll., Oxford. Secretariat of League of Nations, Geneva, 1931; staff of Royal Institute of International Affairs, 1933; Rockefeller Travelling Fellowship, held in Middle East and French N Africa, 1936-37; Min. of Information, Dir, Middle East Div., 1940; Diplomatic correspondent, The Observer, 1944. UK rep. on UN Sub-Commn for Prevention of Discrimination and Protection of Minorities, 1947-52; staff of Economist Newspaper, London, 1945-58. Leverhulme Research Fellowship, 1969. *Publications:* (with A. H. M. Jones) A History of Abyssinia, 1935; The Mediterranean in Politics, 1938; Britain's Moment in the Middle East: 1914-1956, 1963; contrib. to: The Middle East, a Political and Economic Survey, Chatham House; St Antony's Papers. *Recreation:* entertaining. *Address:* 4 Fairlawn End, Upper Wolvercote, Oxford. *T:* Oxford 57723.

**MONROE, Hubert Holmes,** QC 1960; *b* 2 July 1920; *s* of James Harvey Monroe, KC, late of Dublin; *m* 1946, June Elsie, *d* of Harold Lawson Murphy, KC, late of London; one *s* two *d*. *Educ:* Rugby; Corpus Christi Coll., Oxford. Called to the Bar, Middle Temple, 1948; Bencher, 1965; Member, Bar Council, 1968-69, Hon. Treasurer, 1969-. *Address:* 40 Cleaver Street, SE11. *T:* 01-735 9009.

**MONSARRAT, Nicholas John Turney,** FRSL; author; *b* Liverpool, 22 March 1910; *s* of late K. W. Monsarrat; *m* 1st, 1939, Eileen Rowland (marr. diss. 1952); one *s*; 2nd 1952, Philippa Crosby (marr. diss. 1961); two *s*; 3rd, 1961, Ann Griffiths. *Educ:* Winchester Coll.; Trinity Coll., Cambridge (BA 1931). Heinemann Foundation Prize for Literature, 1951. Coronation Medal, 1953. War of 1939-45; in RN 1940-46; Lt-Comdr RNVR (despatches). Councillor, Kensington Borough Council, 1946. Dir, UK Information Office, Johannesburg, 1946-53; Ottawa, 1953-56. Chm. Nat. War Memorial Health Foundation (South Africa), 1951-53. Board of Governors, Stratford Shakespeare Fest. of Canada, 1956; Bd of Dirs, Ottawa Philharmonic Orchestra, 1956. *Publications:* Think of Tomorrow, 1934; At First Sight, 1935; The Whipping Boy, 1936; This is the Schoolroom, 1939; Three Corvettes, 1945; Depends What You Mean by Love, 1947; My Brother Denys, 1948; The Cruel Sea, 1951; HMS Marlborough Will Enter Harbour, 1952; The Story of Esther Costello, 1953; Boys' Book of the Sea, 1954; Canada Coast-to-Coast, Castle Garac, 1955; The Tribe that Lost its Head, 1956; Boys' Book of the Commonwealth, 1957; The Ship that Died of Shame, 1959; The Nylon Pirates, 1960; The White Rajah, 1961; The Time Before This, 1962; Smith and Jones, 1963; To Stratford with Love, 1963; A Fair Day's Work, 1964; The Pillow Fight, 1965; Something to Hide, 1965; Richer Than all His Tribe, 1968; *autobiography:* Life is a Four-Letter Word, Vol. I, 1966, Vol. II 1970; *play:* The Visitor (Daly's Theatre, 1936); *films:* The Cruel Sea, 1953; The Ship That Died of Shame, 1955; The Story of Esther Costello, 1957; The Way of a Ship (Narration), 1965. *Recreations:* sailing, music. *Address:* c/o Campbell Thomson & McLaughlin Ltd, Clifford's Inn, EC4. *T:* 01-405 8628. *Clubs:* Naval, Lansdowne; Rideau (Ottawa).

**MONSELL,** 2nd Viscount *cr* 1935, of Evesham; **Henry Bolton Graham Eyres-Monsell;** *b* 21 Nov. 1905; *s* of 1st Viscount Monsell, PC, GBE, and Caroline Mary Sybil, CBE (*d* 1959), *d* of late H. W. Eyres, Dumbleton Hall, Evesham; *S* father, 1969. *Educ:* Eton. Served N Africa and Italy, 1942-43 (despatches); Lt-Col Intelligence Corps. US Medal of Freedom with bronze palm, 1946. *Recreation:* music. *Address:* The Mill House, Dumbleton, Evesham, Worcs. *Club:* Travellers'.

**MONSEY, Mrs Derek;** *see* Mitchell, Yvonne.

**MONSON,** family name of **Baron Monson.**

**MONSON,** 11th Baron *cr* 1728; **John Monson;** Bt *cr* 1611; *b* 3 May 1932; *e s* of 10th Baron and of Bettie Northrup (who *m* 1962, Capt. James Arnold Phillips), *d* of late E. Alexander Powell; *S* father, 1958; *m* 1955, Emma, *o d* of late Anthony Devas, ARA, RP; three *s*. *Educ:* Eton; Trinity Coll., Cambridge (BA). *Heir: s* Hon. Nicholas John Monson, *b* 19 Oct. 1955. *Address:* Manor House, South Carlton, near Lincoln. *T:* Scampton 263.

**MONSON, Sir Leslie;** *see* Monson, Sir W. B. L.

**MONSON, Sir (William Bonnar) Leslie,** KCMG 1965 (CMG 1950); CB 1964; Deputy Under-Secretary of State, Foreign and Commonwealth Office (formerly Commonwealth Office), since 1967; *b* 28 May 1912; *o s* of late J. W. Monson and late Selina L. Monson; *m* 1948, Helen Isobel Browne. *Educ:* Edinburgh Acad.; Hertford Coll., Oxford. Entered Civil Service (Dominions Office) 1935; transferred to Colonial Office, 1939; Asst Sec., 1944; seconded as Chief Sec. to West African Council, 1947-51; Asst Under-Sec. of State, Colonial Office, 1951-64; British High Commissioner in the Republic of Zambia, 1964-66. *Recreations:* reading and travel. *Address:* Golf House, Goffers Road, Blackheath, SE3. *Club:* United University.

**MONTAGU;** *see* Douglas-Scott-Montagu.

**MONTAGU,** family name of **Duke of Manchester, Earldom of Sandwich,** and **Baron Swaythling.**

**MONTAGU OF BEAULIEU,** 3rd Baron *cr* 1885; **Edward John Barrington Douglas-Scott-Montagu;** *b* 20 Oct. 1926; *o s* of 2nd Baron and Pearl (who *m* 2nd, 1936, Captain Hon. Edward Pleydell-Bouverie, RN, MVO, *s* of 6th Earl of Radnor), *d* of late Major E. B. Crake, Rifle Brigade, and Mrs Barrington Crake; *S* father, 1929; *m* 1959, Elizabeth Belinda, *o d* of late Capt. the Hon. John de Bathe Crossley, and late Hon. Mrs Crossley; one *s* one *d*. *Educ:* St Peter's Court, Broadstairs; Ridley Coll., St Catharines, Ont.; Eton Coll.; New Coll., Oxford. Late Lt Grenadier Guards; released Army, 1948. Founded Montagu Motor Car Museum, 1952 and World's first Motor Cycle Museum, 1956. *Publications:* The Motoring Montagus, 1959; Lost Causes of Motoring, 1960; Jaguar, A Biography, 1961; The Gordon Bennett Races, 1963; Rolls of Rolls-Royce, 1966; The Gilt and the Gingerbread, 1967; Lost Causes of Motoring: Europe, vol i, 1969, vol ii, 1971; More Equal than Others, 1970; Editor and Publisher of the Veteran and Vintage Magazine. *Heir: s* Hon. Ralph Douglas-Scott-Montagu, *b* 13 March 1961. *Address:* Palace House, Beaulieu, Hants. *T:* 251; 3 Wyndham Place, W1. *T:* 01-262 2603. *Clubs:* Veteran Car, Vintage Sports Car, Historic Commercial Vehicle (Pres.);
*See also Sir E. john Chichester, Bt, Viscount Garnock.*

**MONTAGU, Ainsley Marshall Rendall,** CIE 1945; FCGI; FICE; MIWE; Consultant, Sir Murdoch MacDonald & Partners, Red Lion Street, WC1, 1954-68, retired; *b* 6 Nov. 1891; *s* of Alfred John Montagu and Hester Vaudrey (*née* Holland); *m* 1st, 1918, Margaret Violet Rumsby; two *s*; 2nd, 1940, Phyllis Henley Marion Moreton; one *d*. *Educ:* St Paul's Sch.; City and Guilds Engineering Coll., London. Joined PWD India, 1914; served European War, 1914-18, with KGO Bengal Sappers and Miners and RFC (despatches). Returned to PWD, 1920; Chief Engr and Sec. to Govt, Punjab PWD (Irrigation Br.), 1943; retd, 1947. Engineering Adviser to UNRWA for Palestine Refugees, 1950-52; Dep. Dir, Public Works Dept, Sudan Government, Khartoum, 1952-54. Fellow of City and Guilds of London Institute (FCGI), 1957. *Publications:* papers on hydraulics and hydraulic engineering for learned societies and journals. *Address:* 39 Church Avenue, Pinner, Middlesex. *T:* 01-866 5908.

**MONTAGU, (Alexander) Victor (Edward Paulet);** *b* 22 May 1906; *S* father, 1962, as 10th Earl of Sandwich, but disclaimed his peerages for life, 24 July 1964; *m* 1st, 1934, Rosemary, *d* of late Major Ralph Harding Peto; two *s* four *d*; 2nd, 1962, Anne, MBE, *y d* of Victor, 9th Duke of Devonshire, KG, PC. *Educ:* Eton; Trinity Coll., Cambridge. MA (Nat. Sciences). Lt 5th (Hunts) Bn The Northamptonshire Regt, TA, 1926; served France, 1940, and afterwards on Gen. Staff, Home Forces. Private Sec. to Rt Hon. Stanley Baldwin, MP, 1932-34; Treasurer, Junior Imperial League, 1934-35; Chm., Tory Reform Cttee, 1943-44. MP (C) South Dorset Div. (C 1941, Ind. C 1957, C 1958-62); contested (C) Accrington Div. Lancs, Gen. Elec., 1964. Pres., Anti-Common Market League, 1962. *Publication:* Essays in Tory Reform, 1944. *Heir:* (*to disclaimed peerages*): *s* John Edward Hollister Montagu, *qv*. *Address:* 17 Great College Street, SW1. *T:* 01-930 4246; Mapperton, Beaminster, Dorset. *Clubs:* Carlton, Brooks's.

**MONTAGU, Ashley;** *see* Montagu, M. F. A.

**MONTAGU, Hon. David Charles Samuel;** Chairman, Samuel Montagu & Co. Ltd, since 1970 (Executive Director since 1954); *b* 6 Aug. 1928; *e s* and *heir* of 3rd Baron Swaythling, *qv*, and Mary Violet, *e d* of Major Levy, DSO; *m* 1951, Christiane Françoise (Ninette), *d* of Edgar Dreyfus, Paris; one *s* two *d*. *Educ:* Eton; Trinity Coll., Cambridge. Director: Trades Union Unit Trust Managers Ltd; British Australian Investment Trust Ltd; Carreras Ltd; Dualvest Ltd (Chm.); Fundinvest Ltd (Chm.); United British Securities Trust Ltd; Second United British Securities Trust Ltd; Derby Trust Ltd (Chm.); Union Commercial Investment Co. Ltd; Triplevest Ltd (Chm.); London Weekend Television Ltd; Capel Court Corporation Ltd. *Recreations:* shooting, racing, theatre. *Address:* 113 Oakwood Court, W14. *T:* 01-602 2293; The Kremlin, Newmarket. *T:* Newmarket 2467. *Clubs:* Turf, St James's, Portland.

**MONTAGU, Hon. Ewen Edward Samuel,** CBE 1950 (OBE 1944); QC 1939; The Judge Advocate of the Fleet since 1945; Bencher of the Middle Temple, 1948 (Treasurer, 1968); Chairman, Court of Quarter Sessions, Middlesex Area of Greater London, 1965-69; Deputy Chairman, Hampshire Quarter Sessions, since 1960 (Deputy Chairman, 1948-51; Chairman, 1951-60); *b* 29 March 1901; 2nd *s* of 2nd Baron Swaythling; *m* 1923, Iris Rachel, *d* of late Solomon J. Solomon, RA; one *s* one *d*. *Educ:* Westminster Sch.; Harvard Univ.; Trinity Coll., Cambridge (MA, LLB). Called to Bar, Middle Temple, 1924; Western Circuit. Recorder of Devizes, 1944-51, of Southampton, 1951-60; Chm. Middlesex QS, 1956-65 (Asst Chm., 1951-54; Dep. Chm., 1954-56); Chm. Central Council of Magistrates' Courts Cttees, 1963- (Vice-Chm., 1954-63). Pres. United Synagogue, 1954-62; Vice-President: Anglo-Jewish Assoc.; Nat. Addiction and Research Inst., 1969; Chm. Gen. Purposes Cttee, RYA, 1960-68. DL County of Southampton, 1953. RNVR, 1939-45. *Publication:* The Man Who Never Was, 1953. *Recreations:* sailing, fly-fishing, shooting, beagling, golf, painting, grandchildren. *Address:* 5 Vicarage Gardens, W8; 3 Pump Court, Temple, EC4. *T:* 01-353

4411; Warren Beach, Beaulieu, Hants. *T:* Bucklers Hard 239. *Clubs:* Royal Ocean Racing, Bar Yacht (Hon. Commodore).
*See also Ivor Montagu.*

**MONTAGU, Ivor;** author; *b* 23 April 1904; 3rd *s* of 2nd Baron Swaythling; *m* 1927, Eileen, *d* of late Francis Anton Hellstern. *Educ:* Westminster Sch.; Royal Coll. of Science, London; King's Coll., Cambrdige. Pres. and/or Chm., (Ping Pong Assoc., then Table Tennis Assoc., then) English Table Tennis Assoc., 1922-33, 1936-66, Life Vice-Pres., 1970; Pres. and Chm., International Table Tennis Fedn, 1926-67, Life Founder Pres. 1967-; Chm., Film Soc., 1925-39; film critic, editor, director, writer, producer from 1925; Hon. Mem., Assoc. of Cine and Television Technicians, 1970; Editorial Staff, Daily Worker, 1932-33 and 1937-47; Mem. Secretariat and Bureau, World Council of Peace, 1948-67, Presidential Cttee 1969-. Order of Liberation, 1st Class (Bulgaria), 1952; Lenin Peace Prize, 1959; Order of Pole Star (Mongolia), 1963; Lenin Centenary Commemoration Medal, 1970. *Publications:* Table Tennis Today, 1924; Table Tennis, 1936; The Traitor Class, 1940; Plot against Peace, 1952; Land of Blue Sky, 1956; Film World, 1964; Germany's New Nazis, 1967; With Eisenstein in Hollywood, 1968; The Youngest Son (Vol. I of memoirs), 1970; numerous scenarios, translations, pamphlets, artciles on current affairs, contribs to Proc. Zool. Soc. London. *Recreations:* washing up, pottering about, sleeping through television. *Address:* Digro, Rousay, Orkney. *Clubs:* MCC; Hampshire County Cricket.
*See also Hon. E. E. S. Montagu, Baron Swaythling.*

**MONTAGU, John Edward Hollister;** (Viscount Hinchingbrooke, but does not use the title); *b* 11 April 1932; *er s* of Victor Montagu, *qv* and *heir* to disclaimed Earldom of Sandwich; *m* 1968, Caroline, *o d* of Rev. P. E. C. Hayman, Rogate, W Sussex; one *s*. *Educ:* Eton; Trinity College, Cambridge. *Address:* 69 Albert Bridge Road, SW11.

**MONTAGU, Prof. (Montague Francis) Ashley;** *b* 28 June 1905; *o c* of Charles and Mary Ehrenberg; *m* 1931, Helen Marjorie Peakes; one *s* two *d*. *Educ:* Central Foundation Sch., London; Univ. of London; Univ. of Florence; Colombia Univ. (PhD 1937). Research Worker, Brit. Mus. (Natural Hist.), 1926; Curator, Physical Anthropology, Wellcome Hist. Mus., London, 1929; Asst-Prof. of Anatomy, NY Univ., 1931-38; Dir, Div. of Child Growth and Develt, NY Univ., 1931-34; Assoc.-Prof. of Anat., Hahnemann Med. Coll. and Hosp., Phila, 1938-49; Prof. and Head of Dept of Anthropology, Rutgers Univ., 1949-55; Dir of Research, NJ Cttee on Growth and Develt, 1951-55. Chm., Anisfield-Wolf Award Cttee on Race Relations, 1950-. Vis. Lectr, Harvard Univ., 1945; Regent's Prof., Univ. of Calif, Santa Barbara, 1961. DSc, Grinnell Coll., Iowa, 1967. *Publications:* Coming Into Being Among the Australian Aborigines, 1937; Man's Most Dangerous Myth: The Fallacy of Race, 1942; Edward Tyson, MD, FRS (1650-1708): And the Rise of Human and Comparative Anatomy in England, 1943; Introduction to Physical Anthropology, 1945; Adolescent Sterility, 1946; On Being Human, 1950; Statement on Race, 1951; On Being Intelligent, 1951; Darwin, Competition, and Cooperation, 1952; The Natural Superiority of Women, 1953; Immortality, 1955; The Direction of Human Development, 1955; The Biosocial Nature of Man, 1956; Education and Human Relations, 1958; Anthropology and Human Nature, 1957; Man: His First Million Years, 1957; The Reproductive Development of the Female, 1957; The Cultured Man, 1958; Human Heredity, 1959; A Handbook of Anthropometry, 1960; Man in Process, 1961; The Humanization of Man, 1962; Prenatal Influences, 1962; Race, Science and Humanity, 1963; The Science of Man, 1964; Life Before Birth, 1964; The Human Revolution, 1965; The Idea of Race, 1965; Up the Ivy, 1966; The American Way of Life, 1967; The Anatomy of Swearing, 1967; Man Observed, 1968; Man: His First Two Million Years, 1969; Sex, Man and Society, 1969; Anatomy and Physiology (with E. B. Steen), 2 vols, 1959; The Prevalence of Nonsense (with E. Darling), 1967; The Dolphin in History (with John Lilly), 1963; Man's Evolution (with C. Loring Brace), 1965; The Ignorance of Certainty (with E. Darling), 1970; Immoratality, Religion and Morals, 1971; Touching: the human significance of the skin, 1971; Textbooks of Human Genetics (with M. Levitan), 1971; Editor: Studies and Essays in the History of Science and Learning; The Meaning of Love, 1953; Toynbee and History, 1956; Genetic Mechanisms in Human Disease, 1961; Atlas of Human Anatomy, 1961; Culture and the Evolution of Man, 1962; International Pictorial Treasury of Knowledge, 6 vols, 1962-63; The Concept of Race, 1964; The Concept of the Primitive, 1967; Culture: Man's Adaptive Dimension, 1968; Man and Agression, 1968; The Human Dialogue (with Floyd Matson), 1967. *Recreations:* book collecting, gardening. *Address:* 321 Cherry Hill Road, Princeton, NJ 08540, USA. *T:* Area Code 609 924-3756.

**MONTAGU, Victor;** *see* Montagu, A. V. E. P.

**MONTAGU-DOUGLAS-SCOTT,** family name of **Duke of Buccleuch.**

**MONTAGU-POLLOCK, Sir G. S.;** *see* Pollock.

**MONTAGU-POLLOCK, Sir William H.,** KCMG 1957 (CMG 1946); *b* 12 July 1903; *s* of Sir M. F. Montagu-Pollock, 3rd Bt; *m* 1st, 1933, Frances Elizabeth Prudence (marriage dissolved, 1945), *d* of late Sir John Fischer Williams, CBE, KC; one *s* one *d*; 2nd, 1948, Barbara, *d* of late P. H. Jowett, CBE, FRCA, RWS; one *s*. *Educ:* Marlborough Coll.; Trinity Coll., Cambridge. Served in Diplomatic Service at Rome, Belgrade, Prague, Vienna, Stockholm, Brussels, and at Foreign Office; British Ambassador, Damascus, 1952-53 (Minister, 1950-52); British Ambassador: to Peru, 1953-58; to Switzerland, 1958-60; to Denmark, 1960-62. Retired from HM Foreign Service, 1962. Governor, European Cultural Foundation; Dir, British Nat. Cttee for Cultural Co-operation in Europe; Hon. Treasurer, Soc. for Promotion of New Music; Governor, British Inst. of Recorded Sound. *Address:* 28 Drayton Gardens, SW10. *T:* 01-373 3685; Playa Blanca, Yaiza, Lanzarote, Canary Islands. *Club:* Athenæum.

**MONTAGU-STUART-WORTLEY-MACKENZIE,** family name of **Earl of Wharncliffe.**

**MONTAGUE,** family name of **Baron Amwell.**

**MONTAGUE, Francis Arnold,** CMG 1956; retired; *b* 14 June 1904; *s* of late Charles Edward Montague, OBE, author and journalist, and of Madeleine Montague (*née* Scott), Manchester; *m* 1939, Fanny Susanne, *d* of late E. S. Scorer and Mrs C. D. Scorer; one *d*. *Educ:* Cargilfield Sch., Edinburgh; Rugby Sch.; Balliol Coll., Oxford. Tanganyika: served in Game Preservation Dept, 1925-28; Cadet, Colonial Administrative Service, 1928; Dist

Officer, 1938; Private Sec. to Governor, 1938-40; Asst Chief Sec., 1948; Administrative Sec., Sierra Leone, 1950-58; retired from Colonial Service, Jan. 1958. Deputy-Chairman: Public Service Commn, Uganda, 1958-63; Public Service Commn, Aden, 1963. Mem., Oxon CC; Witney (Oxon) RDC. *Recreations:* gardening, fishing, etc. *Address:* Dolphin House, Burford, Oxon. *T:* Burford 2147. *Club:* Lansdowne.

**MONTAGUE, Leslie Clarence;** Chairman, Johnson Matthey & Co. Ltd, since 1966; *b* 28 May 1901; *s* of Albert Edward Montague and Clara Amelia Chapman; *m* 1926, Ellen Rose Margaret Keene; no *c*. *Educ:* Bancroft's School, Woodford. 50 years' service with Johnson Matthey & Co. Ltd; appointed Secretary, 1934, and a Director, 1946. *Recreations:* walking, gardening. *Address:* Jasmine Cottage, Piddinghoe, near Newhaven, Sussex.

**MONTAGUE, Michael Jacob,** CBE 1970; Chairman and Managing Director, Valor Company Ltd since 1965 (Managing Director, 1963); *b* 10 March 1932; *s* of David Elias Montague and Eleanor Stagg. *Educ:* Magdalen Coll. Sch., Oxford. Founded Gatehill Beco Ltd, 1958 (sold to Valor Co., 1962). Pres., Young European Management Assoc.; Gov., Nat. Inst. of Hardware; Chairman: Asia Cttee, BNEC; Immigration Cttee, Kent Social Service; Hon. Treas., British Assoc. for World Government. *Address:* Roydon Hall, East Peckham, near Tonbridge, Kent. *T:* Wateringbury 438; 28 South Street, W1.

**MONTAGUE BROWNE, Anthony Arthur Duncan,** CBE 1965 (OBE 1955); DFC 1945; Director: Gerrard and National Discount Co. Ltd, since 1967; Columbia (British) Productions, since 1967; Deputy Chairman, International Life Insurance Co. (UK), since 1970 (Director since 1968); *b* 8 May 1923; *s* of late Lt-Col A. D. Montague Browne, DSO, OBE, Bivia House, Goodrich, Ross-on-Wye, and Violet Evelyn (*née* Downes); *m* 1950, Noel Evelyn Arnold-Wallinger ( marr. diss. 1970); one *d*. *Educ:* Stowe; Magdalen Coll., Oxford; abroad. Pilot RAF, 1941-45. Entered Foreign (now Diplomatic) Service, 1946; Foreign Office, 1946-49; Second Sec., British Embassy, Paris, 1949-52; seconded as Private Sec. to Prime Minister, 1952-55; seconded as Private Sec. to Rt Hon. Sir Winston Churchill, 1955-65; Counsellor, Diplomatic Service, 1964; seconded to HM Household (Lord Chamberlain's Office), 1965-67; Trustee Winston Churchill Memorial Trust. *Address:* c/o R3 Section, Lloyds Bank Ltd, Cox's & King's Branch, 6 Pall Mall, SW1. *Clubs:* Boodle's, Pratt's.

**MONTAGUE-JONES, Brigadier (retd) Ronald,** CBE 1944 (MBE 1941); jssc; psc; *b* 10 Dec. 1909; *yr s* of late Edgar Montague Jones, until 1932 Headmaster of St Albans Sch., Herts, and of late Emmeline Mary Yates; *m* 1937, Denise Marguerite (marriage dissolved), *y d* of late General Sir Hubert Gough, GCB, GCMG, KCVO; one *s*; *m* 1955, Pamela, *d* of late Lieut-Col Hastings Roy Harington, 8th Gurkha Rifles, and of the Hon. Mrs Harington; one *s*. *Educ:* St Albans Sch., Herts; RMA, Woolwich; St John's Coll., Cambridge (BA 1933, MA 1937). 2nd Lieut RE 1930; Temp. Brig. 1943; Brig. 1958. Egypt, 1935; Palestine, 1936-39 (despatches twice); War of 1939-45 (MBE, CBE, US Bronze Star, Africa Star, 1939-45 Star, Italy Star, Burma Star, General Service Medal with Clasps Palestine, SE Asia and Malaya). CC Dorset, for Swanage (E), 1964-; Mem., Dorset and Bournemouth Police Authority, 1968-. *Address:* 10 Battlemead, Swanage, Dorset BH19 1PH. *T:* Swanage 3186. *Club:* Royal Commonwealth Society.

**MONTAGUE-SMITH, Patrick Wykeham;** Editor of Debrett since 1962; *b* 3 Jan. 1920; *o s* of late Major Vernon Milner Montague-Smith and of Sybil Katherine, *d* of late William Wykeham Frederick Bourne. *Educ:* Lynfield, Hunstanton and Mercers' Sch. Served RASC, 8 Corps, 1940-46; in NW Europe, 1944-46. Asst Editor of Debrett, 1946-62. Fellow, Soc. of Genealogists, 1969; Member: Heraldry Soc.; Soc. of Descendants of Knights of the Garter (Windsor). Freeman of the City of London. *Publications:* Royal Line of Succession, 1953; The Prince of Wales, 1958; Princess Margaret, 1961; Debrett's Correct Form, 1970; contribs to Encyclopædia Britannica and various journals and newspapers, principally on genealogy, heraldry, and historical subjects, also lectures, television and broadcasts. *Recreations:* genealogy, British history, visiting country houses and browsing in bookshops. *Address:* Brereton, 197 Park Road, Kingston upon Thames, Surrey. *T:* 01-546 8807; Debrett, Neville House, Eden Street, Kingston upon Thames. *T:* 01-546 7722.

**MONTANARO, Brig. Gerald Charles Stokes,** DSO; MA, CEng, FICE, FIMechE, FIEE, AFRAeS, MBIM, ACIS; company director; *b* 16 Sept. 1916; *s* of late Col C. A. H. Montanaro, OBE; *m* 1965, Judith Mary (*née* Newington). *Educ:* Bedford Sch.; RMA and Cambridge Univ. Commissioned, RE, 1936; BEF, France, 1939-40; Commandos, Special Canoe Troop, 1940-42 (DSO); commissioned Lieut-Comdr, RN, 1942-45, in comd flotilla of submersible craft; Staff Coll., 1947; GSO2 and GSO1 (ops) GHQ, MELF, 1947-48; Tech. Staff Course, 1948-49; Mil. Comdg Officer RAE, 1949-52; OC Sqdn and Regt, Hong Kong and Korea, 1952-54; GSO1 War Office, 1954-57; Comd of Regt and CRE, BAOR, 1957-60; Asst Dir Devel., WO, 1960-61; Brig., Gen. Staff, WO, 1962-63; Brig., IDC, 1963-64; Brigadier A/Q HQ ME, Aden, 1964-65. Man. Dir Reed Develt Services Ltd, and Dep. Chm. Reed Transport Ltd, Reed Paper Gp, 1965-66; Dep. Man. Dir, Norton Villiers Ltd, 1967-68. *Recreations:* deer stalking, shooting, sailing. *Address:* Xini, Bay View Court, Cordina Road, Ghajnsielem, Gozo, Malta GC. *T:* 36584. *Clubs:* Naval and Military; Malta Union (Malta).

**MONTAND, Simone H. C.;** *see* Signoret, Simone.

**MONTEAGLE OF BRANDON,** 6th Baron *cr* 1839; **Gerald Spring Rice;** late Captain, Irish Guards; *b* 5 July 1926; *s* of 5th Baron and Emilie de Kosenko, *d* of Mrs Edward Brooks, Philadelphia, USA; *S* father 1946; *m* 1949, Anne, *d* of late Col G. J. Brownlow, Ballywhite, Portaferry, Co. Down; one *s* three *d* (of whom two are twins). *Educ:* Harrow. *Heir: s* Charles James Spring Rice, *b* 24 Feb. 1953. *Address:* Brick House, Wicken Bonhunt, Newport, Saffron Walden, Essex. *Clubs:* Guards, Pratt's; Kildare Street (Dublin).

**MONTEATH, Robert Campbell,** CBE 1964; County Clerk, Treasurer and Local Taxation Officer, Kirkcudbright, since 1946, and Clerk to the Lieutenancy, since 1966; *b* 15 June 1907; *s* of Gordon Drysdale Monteath, Dumbarton; *m*.1936, Sarah McGregor, *d* of John Fenwick, Dumbarton; two *s* one *d*. *Educ:* Dumbarton Academy; Glasgow Univ. Dep. County Clerk, Dunbartonshire, 1937-46; Dep. Civil Defence Controller, 1939-46; Hon. Sheriff-Substitute, Kirkcudbright, 1966-. *Address:* County Offices, Kirkcudbright; Townhead, Kirkcudbright. *T:* Townhead 201. *Clubs:*

Royal Over-Seas League; Royal Scottish Automobile (Glasgow); Caledonian (Edinburgh).

**MONTEFIORE, Rt. Rev. Hugh William;** *see* Kingston-upon-Thames, Bishop Suffragan of.

**MONTEITH, Rt. Rev. George Rae,** BA; Assistant Bishop of Auckland, New Zealand, since 1965; Vicar-General since 1963; *b* 14 Feb. 1904; *s* of John Hodge Monteith and Ellen (*née* Hall); *m* 1931, Kathleen Methven Mules; two *s* one *d*. *Educ:* St John's Coll., Auckland; Univ. of New Zealand. BA 1927. Deacon, 1928; priest, 1929; Curate: St Matthew's, Auckland, 1928-30; Stoke-on-Trent, 1931-33; Vicar of: Dargaville, NZ, 1934-37; Mt Eden, Auckland, NZ, 1937-49; St Mary's Cathedral Parish, Auckland, 1949-69; Dean of Auckland, 1949-69. *Address:* 7 Cathedral Place, Auckland 1, NZ. *T:* 374.449.

**MONTEITH, Lt-Col Robert Charles Michael,** MC 1943; TD 1945; JP; Vice-Lieutenant of Lanarkshire since 1964; Land-owner and Farmer since 1950; *b* 25 May 1914; *s* of late Major J. B. L. Monteith, CBE, and late Dorothy, *d* of Sir Charles Nicholson, 1st Bt; *m* 1950, Mira Elizabeth, *e d* of late John Fanshawe, Sidmount, Moffat; one *s*. *Educ:* Ampleforth Coll., York. CA (Edinburgh), 1939. Served with Lanarkshire Yeomanry, 1939-45: Paiforce, 1942-43; MEF, 1943-44; BLA, 1944-45. Contested (U) Hamilton Division of Lanarkshire, 1950 and 1951. Mem., Mental Welfare Commn for Scotland, 1962-. DL 1955, JP 1955, CC 1949-64, 1967-, Lanarkshire. Mem. Queen's Body Guard for Scotland, Royal Company of Archers; Mem. SMO of Knights of Malta. *Recreations:* shooting, curling. *Address:* Cranley, Cleghorn, Lanark. *T:* Carstairs 330. *Clubs:* New, Puffins (Edinburgh).

**MONTGOMERIE,** family name of **Earl of Eglinton.**

**MONTGOMERIE, Lord; Hugh Archibald William Montgomerie;** *b* 24 July 1966; *s* and *heir* of 18th Earl of Eglinton and Winton, *qv*.

**MONTGOMERY,** family name of **Viscount Montgomery of Alamein.**

**MONTGOMERY OF ALAMEIN,** 1st Viscount *cr* 1946, of Hindhead; **Field-Marshal Bernard Law Montgomery,** KG 1946; GCB 1945 (KCB 1942; CB 1940); DSO 1914; DL; Colonel Commandant: The Parachute Regiment, 1945-55; Royal Tank Regt, 1946-56; Army Physical Training Corps, 1946-61; Colonel, Royal Warwickshire Regiment, 1946-63; *b* 17 Nov. 1887; *s* of late Rt Rev. H. H. Montgomery, KCMG; *m* 1927, Elizabeth (*d* 1937), *widow* of Capt. O. A. Carver, RE; one *s*. *Educ:* St Paul's. Entered Army, 1908; Lieut-Col 1931; Col 1934; Maj.-Gen. 1938; Lt-Gen. 1942; Gen. 1942; Field-Marshal 1944; served European War, 1914-18 (despatches, DSO, Bt Major, War Medals); comd 1st Bn Royal Warwickshire Regt, 1931-34; GSO1, Staff Coll., Quetta, 1934-37; Comdr, 9th Infantry Bde, Portsmouth, 1937-38; comd 8th Div., 1938-39; War of 1939-45 (War Medals); 3rd Div., 1939-40; 5th Corps, 1940; 12th Corps, 1941; SE Comd, 1942; Comdr Eighth Army from July 1942 during campaigns in N Africa, Sicily and Italy; C-in-C Br. Group of Armies and Allied Armies, N France, 1944; comd 21st Army Group, 1944-45; comd BAOR, 1945-46; CIGS, 1946-48; Chm. of Western Europe Commanders' in Chief Cttee, 1948-51; Deputy-Supreme Allied Comdr, Europe, 1951-58; DL Southampton, 1959. Hon. Freeman City of London and many other cities and towns at home and abroad; Freeman of: Mercers' Co., Co. of Fletchers, and Carpenters' Co., London; Bonnetmakers and Dyers, Glasgow; former Governor of St Paul's Sch., London. Pres. and Vice-Pres., Patron, Vice-Patron and Hon. Patron, and Hon. Mem. of numerous socs. Hon. DCL: Oxford; Edinburgh; Dalhousie, Halifax; Newfoundland; Hon. LLD: Cambridge; Queen's, Belfast; Glasgow; St Andrews; Toronto; McGill; British Columbia; Hon. Dr of Science: Louvain; Liège. Has many foreign orders and decorations. *Publications:* Ten Chapters, 1946; Forward to Victory, 1946; Normandy to the Baltic, 1947; Forward from Victory, 1948; El Alamein to the River Sangro, 1948; Memoirs, 1958; An Approach to Sanity: a Study of East-West Relations, 1959; The Path to Leadership, 1961; Three Continents, 1962; History of Warfare, 1968. *Heir: s* Hon. David Montgomery [*b* 18 Aug. 1928; *m* 1953, Mary (marr. diss. 1966), *d* of Sir Charles Connell, Craigallian, Milngavie, Dunbartonshire; one *s* one *d*; 2nd, 1970, Tessa, *d* of late Lt-Gen. Sir Frederick Browning, GCVO, KBE, CB, DSO, and of Dame Daphne du Maurier, *qv*. *Educ:* Winchester; Trinity Coll., Cambridge]. *Address:* Isington Mill, Alton, Hants. *Clubs:* Athenæum, United Service, Savage, Cavalry, Bath.

**MONTGOMERY, Sir (Basil Henry) David,** 9th Bt, *cr* 1801, of Stanhope; Vice-Lieutenant of the County of Kinross since 1966; landowner; *b* 20 March 1931; *s* of late Lt-Col H. K. Purvis-Montgomery, OBE, and of Mrs C. L. W. Purvis-Russell-Montgomery (*née* Maconochie Welwood); *S* uncle, 1964; *m* 1956, Delia, *o d* of Adm. Sir Peter Reid, *qv*; two *s* two *d*. *Educ:* Eton. National Service, Black Watch, 1949-51. DL Kinross-shire, 1960; JP 1966. *Heir: s* James David Keith Montgomery, *b* 13 June 1957. *Address:* Home Farm, Kinross. *T:* Kinross 2256.

**MONTGOMERY, Sir David;** *see* Montgomery, Sir B. H. D.

**MONTGOMERY, Brig. Ernest John,** CB 1953; CBE 1950 (OBE 1944; MBE 1940) JP; retired; *b* 24 March 1901; *s* of late Herbert Elphinstone Montgomery, AMICE; *m* 1931, Rosemary Elizabeth, *d* of Sir John Noble, 1st Bt, of Ardkinglas; one adopted *d*. *Educ:* Rugby Sch.; RMC, Sandhurst. Commnd HLI, 1920; served in Egypt, Palestine, Turkey and India, 1920-34. Personal Asst to Resident, Mysore, 1927; Private Sec. to Governor of Bihar and Orissa, 1928-31, Adjt 2nd Bn, HLI, 1931-34; DAAG, HQ, Scottish Command, 1937-40 (MBE); Staff Coll., 1940; DAAG 52nd Lowland Div., 1940; Comd 1st Bn HLI, 1940-42; AA&QMG, 45th West Country Div., 1942; AQMG 1st Corps, 1942-43; AA&QMG 3rd Div., 1943; Comdr 101 Beach Sub Area, 1943; served in France and Holland, 1944-46 (despatches, OBE); Dep. Asst Chief-of-Staff Organization, CCG, Berlin, 1946-47; Comdr Scottish Beach Bde (TA), 1947-50 (CBE); Brigadier in Charge of Administration, Singapore Base District, 1951-54 (CB), retired. Mem. Royal Company of Archers (Queen's Body Guard for Scotland). JP Argyll. Hon. Sheriff Substitute, 1960. *Recreations:* gardening, shooting, sailing. *Address:* Kinlochruel, Colintraive, Argyll. *Clubs:* Army and Navy; New (Edinburgh).

**MONTGOMERY, Fergus;** *see* Montgomery, (William) Fergus.

**MONTGOMERY, Sir Frank (Percival),** Kt 1953; MC 1916; retired; Hon. Consulting Radiologist: Royal Victoria Hospital; Belfast City Hospital; Ulster Hospital for Children; Pro-Chancellor, Queen's University, Belfast,

1956-67, and Member of Senate, 1942-67; *b* 10 June 1892; *y s* of late Very Rev. Henry Montgomery, MA, DD, Belfast; *m* 1925, Joan, *er d* of late W. Christopherson, Ipswich, Suffolk; two *s* two *d*. *Educ:* Campbell Coll., Belfast; Queen's Univ., Belfast (MB, ChB). Served European War, Capt., RAMC, 1915-19, French Croix de Guerre, 1917. Divisional Inspector, Dept Public Health Egyptian Govt, Cairo, 1919-23; DMRE Cantab, 1924. Consulting Radiologist, Belfast, 1925-68. Mem. Health Advisory Council, N Ireland, 1944-47; Chm. Northern Ireland Hospitals Authority, 1948-56; Hon. Governor, Ulster Hospital, Dundonald, 1956. FFR (London), 1938; Hon. FFR, RCS(I), 1962. Hon. LLD Queen's Univ., Belfast, 1968. *Recreation:* golf. *Address:* 19 Broomhill Park, Belfast. *T:* Belfast 666984. *Club:* Royal County Down Golf (Captain, 1957).

**MONTGOMERY, Prof. George Lightbody,** CBE 1960; TD 1942; MD, PhD, FRCPE, FRCPGlas, FCPath, FRCSE; FRSE; Professor of Pathology, University of Edinburgh, since 1954; *b* 3 Nov. 1905; *o s* of late John Montgomery and Jeanie Lightbody; *m* 1933, Margaret Sutherland, 3rd *d* of late A. Henry Forbes, Oban; one *s* one *d*. *Educ:* Hillhead High Sch., Glasgow; Glasgow Univ. MB, ChB, 1928; Commendation and RAMC Memorial Prize; PhD (St Andrews), 1937; MD Hons and Bellahouston Gold Medal (Glasgow), 1946. House Physician, House Surgeon, Glasgow Royal Infirmary, 1928-29; Lecturer in Clinical Pathology, Univ. of St Andrews, 1931-37; Lecturer in Pathology of Disease in Infancy and Childhood, Univ. of Glasgow, 1937-48; Asst Pathologist, Glasgow Royal Infirmary, 1929-31; Asst Pathologist, Dundee Royal Infirmary, 1931-37; Pathologist, Royal Hospital for Sick Children, Glasgow, 1937-48; Professor of Pathology (St Mungo-Notman Chair), Univ. of Glasgow, 1948-54. Chm. Scottish Health Services Council, 1954-59. Member: Pathological Soc. Gt Britain and Ireland; BMA. Col (Hon.) Army Medical Service. *Publications:* Textbook of Pathology, 1965; General Pathology for Students of Dentistry, 3rd Edn, 1965; numerous contribs to medical and scientific journals. *Recreation:* music. *Address:* 2 Cumin Place, Edinburgh EH9 2JX. *T:* 031-667 6792. *Clubs:* New (Edinburgh); Royal Scottish Automobile (Glasgow).

**MONTGOMERY, Group Captain George Rodgers,** CBE 1946; RAF (Retired); Secretary, Norfolk Naturalists' Trust, since 1963; Hon. Appeal Secretary, and Member of the Court, University of East Anglia, since Nov. 1966; *b* 31 May 1910; *s* of late John Montgomery, Belfast; *m* 1932, Margaret McHarry Heslip, *d* of late William J. Heslip, Belfast; two *s*. *Educ:* Royal Academy, Belfast. Commnd in RAF, 1928; retd 1958. Served in UK and ME, 1928-38. War of 1939-45: Bomber Comd, NI, Air Min. and ME. Served UK, Japan and W Europe, 1946-58: Comdr RAF Wilmslow, 1946-47; Air Adviser to UK Polit. Rep. in Japan, and Civil Air Attaché, Tokyo, 1948-49; Chief Instr RAF Officers' Advanced Trg Sch., 1950; Comdt RAF Sch. of Admin, Bircham Newton, 1951-52; Comdr RAF Hednesford, 1953-54; DDO (Estabts) Air Min. and Chm. RAF Western European Estabts Cttee, Germany, 1955-57. On retirement, Organising Sec. Friends of Norwich Cathedral, 1959-62; Appeal Sec., Univ. of East Anglia, 1961-66. *Recreations:* sketching, gardening, motoring. *Address:* The Croft, Blofield, Norwich, Norfolk. *T:* Brundall 3214. *Clubs:* Royal Air Force; Prince Albert (Brussels).

**MONTGOMERY, Ian,** CB 1963; Deputy Under-Secretary of State (Army), Ministry of Defence, since 1964 (War Office, 1963-64); *b* 25 March 1913; *o s* of John and Mary Montgomery; *m* 1945, Marguerite Dorothy Bryan; one *d*. *Educ:* Newcastle-under-Lyme High Sch.; Magdalen Coll., Oxford. Entered Administrative Class of Home Civil Service, 1936, assigned to Ministry of Labour; HM Treasury, 1938; Private Secretary: to Second Sec., 1940-41, to Financial Sec., 1941-42; Principal, 1942; Grenadier Guards, 1942-44; Offices of the War Cabinet, 1944-45; Private Sec. to Sec. to the Treasury, 1945-46; MoD, as Asst Sec., 1947; Principal Private Sec. to Minister of Defence, 1950-51; Imperial Defence Coll., 1952; Under-Sec., MoD, 1957-63. *Address:* Burcot, Icklingham Road, Cobham, Surrey. *Club:* Athenæum.

**MONTGOMERY, (William) Fergus;** MP (C) Brierley Hill, since 1967; *b* 25 Nov. 1927; *s* of William Montgomery and late Winifred Montgomery. *Educ:* Jarrow Grammar Sch.; Bede Coll., Durham. Served in Royal Navy, 1946-48; Schoolmaster, 1950-59. Nat. Vice-Chm. Young Conservative Organisation, 1954-57, National Chm., 1957-58; contested (C) Consett Division, 1955; MP (C) Newcastle upon Tyne East, 1959-64. Councillor, Hebburn UDC, 1950-58. Has lectured extensively in the USA. *Recreations:* bridge, reading. *Address:* 30 Laxford House, Cundy Street, SW1. *T:* 01-730 2341.

**MONTGOMERY CAMPBELL, Rt. Rev. and Rt. Hon. Henry Colville,** PC 1956; KCVO 1961; MC; DD; *b* 11 Oct. 1887; *s* of Rev. Sidney Montgomery Campbell; *m* 1915, Joyce Mary (*d* 1928), *er d* of late Archdeacon F. N. Thicknesse; one *s* four *d*. *Educ:* Malvern Coll.; Brasenose Coll., Oxford (MA). Curate of Alverstoke; Vicar of St Saviours, Poplar, 1917-19; Rector, W Hackney, 1919-26; Rector of Hornsey, 1926-33; Rural Dean of Hornsey, 1929-33; Rector of St George, Hanover Square, 1933-40; Suffragan Bishop of Willesden, 1940-42; Suffragan Bishop of Kensington, 1942-49; Rector of St Andrew Undershaft with St Mary Axe, London, EC, 1940-49; Bishop of Guildford, 1949-56; Bishop of London, 1956-61. CF, 1915-17 (MC); Chaplain TA, 1926-38; Sub-Prelate Order of St John of Jerusalem, 1940; Dean of the Chapels Royal, 1956-61; Prelate of Order of British Empire, 1956-61. DD (Lambeth), 1950. FKC 1962. *Address:* 3 Vincent Square, SW1.

**MONTGOMERY-CUNINGHAME, Sir J. C. F.;** *see* Cuninghame.

**MONTGOMERY WATT, Prof. William;** *see* Watt.

**MONTGORGE, Alexis Jean;** *see* Gabin, Jean.

**MONTHERLANT, Henry de;** writer; Member of the French Academy since 1960; *b* Paris, 21 April 1896; *s* of Joseph Millon de Montherlant and Marguerite (*née* Camusat de Riancey). *Educ:* Lycée Janson-de-Sailly; Ecole Ste-Croix de Neuilly. Served European War, 1914-18 (Croix de Guerre, Médaille des Combattants Volontaires). Served War of 1939-45, as War Correspondent. Grand Prix de Littérature of French Academy, 1934. Several plays prod. Comédie Française. *Publications:* La Relève du Matin, 1920; Le Songe, 1922; Les Olympiques, 1924; Les Bestiaires, 1926; Aux Fontaines du Désir, 1927; La Petite Infante de Castille, 1929; Mors et Vita, 1932; Encore un Instant de Bonheur, 1934; Les Célibataires, 1934; Service Inutile, 1935; Les Jeunes Filles (4 vols): Les Jeunes Filles, 1936, Pitié pour les Femmes, 1936, Le Démon du bien, 1937, Les Lépreuses,

1939; l'Equinoxe de Septembre, 1938; La Solstice de Juin, 1941; La Reine Morte, 1942; Fils de Personne, 1944; Malatesta, 1946; Le Maître de Santiago, 1947; Demain il fera Jour, 1949; Celles qu'on prend dans ses bras, 1950; La Ville dont le Prince est un Enfant, 1951; Port-Royal, 1954; Carnets, 1958; Don Juan, 1958; Le Cardinal d'Espagne, 1960; La Guerre Civile, 1965; La Rose de Sable, 1968; Les Garçons, 1969. *Address:* Société des Gens de Lettres, Hôtel Massa, 38 rue du Faubourg-Saint-Jacques, Paris 14e, France.

**MONTMORENCY, Sir Reginald de;** *see* de Montmorency.

**MONTREAL, Archbishop of, (RC),** since 1968; **Most Rev. Paul Grégoire;** *b* Verdun, 24 Oct. 1911. *Educ:* Ecole Supérieure Richard; Séminaire de Ste-Thérèse; Univ. of Montreal. Priest, 1937; became Professor, but continued his studies: PhD, STL, LèsL, MA (Hist.), dip. in pedagogy. Subseq. became Director, Séminaire de Ste-Thérèse; Prof. of Philosophy of Educn at l'Ecole Normale Secondaire and at l'Institut Pédagogique; Chaplain of the Students, Univ. of Montreal, 1950-61; consecrated Bishop, 1961, and became auxiliary to Archbishop of Montreal; Vicar-General and Dir of Office for the Clergy; Apostolic Administrator, Archdiocese of Montreal, Dec. 1967-Apr. 1968. Pres., Episcopal Commn on Ecumenism (French sector), 1965. Has presided over several Diocesan Commns (notably Commn for study of the material situation of the Clergy), 1965-68. Dr *hc*: Univ. of Montreal, 1969; St Michael's Coll., Winooski, Vt, 1970. *Address:* Archbishop's House, 1071 Cathedral Street, Montreal 101, Quebec, Canada.

**MONTREAL, Bishop of,** since 1963; **Rt. Rev. Robert Kenneth Maguire,** MA, DD; *b* 31 March 1923; *s* of late Robert Maguire and late Anne Crozier; unmarried. *Educ:* Trinity Coll., Dublin. BA 1945; Divinity Testimonium, 1947. Deacon, 1947; Priest, 1948. Curate of: St Mark, Armagh, 1947-49; St James the Apostle, Montreal, 1949-52; Dean of Residence, Trinity Coll., Dublin, 1952-60; Curate-in-charge of St Andrew's, Dublin, 1954-57; Minor Canon of St Patrick's Cathedral, Dublin, 1955-58; Dean and Rector of Christ Church Cathedral, Montreal, 1961-62. DD (*jure dig.*): Dublin Univ., 1963; Montreal Diocesan Theolog. Coll., 1963; DCL (*hc*), Bishop's Univ., Lennoxville, Que., 1963. *Address:* Bishopscourt, 3630 Mountain Street, Montreal 109, PQ, Canada.

**MONTROSE,** 7th Duke of, *cr* 1707; **James Angus Graham;** *cr* Baron Graham before 1451; Earl of Montrose, 1505; Bt 1625; Marquis of Montrose, 1645; Duke of Montrose, Marquis of Graham and Buchanan, Earl of Kincardine, Viscount Dundaff, Baron Aberuthven, Mugdock, and Fintrie, 1707; Earl and Baron Graham (Peerage of England), 1722; Hereditary Sheriff of Dunbartonshire; *b* 2 May 1907; *e s* of 6th Duke of Montrose, KT, CB, CVO, VD, and Lady Mary Douglas-Hamilton, OBE (*d* 1957), *d* of 12th Duke of Hamilton; *S* father, 1954; *m* 1st, 1930, Isobel Veronica (marr. diss. 1950), *yr d* of late Lt-Col T. B. Sellar, CMG, DSO; one *s* one *d*; 2nd, 1952, Susan Mary Jocelyn, *widow* of Michael Raleigh Gibbs and *d* of Dr J. M. Semple; two *s* two *d*. *Educ:* Eton; Christ Church, Oxford. Lt-Comdr RNVR. MP for Hartley-Gatooma in Federal Assembly of Federation of Rhodesia and Nyasaland, 1958-62; Minister of Agriculture, Lands, and Natural Resources, S Rhodesia, 1962; Minister of Agric., Rhodesia, 1964; (apptd in Rhodesia) Minister of External Affairs and Defence, 1966-68. *Heir:* *s* Marquis of Graham, *qv*. *Address:* Derry Farm, PB 309B, Salisbury, Rhodesia; (Seat) Auchmar, Drymen, Glasgow.

**MOODY, Arthur Seymour;** Member Amalgamated Society of Woodworkers since 1912; *b* 6 June 1891; *s* of William Henry and Elsey Elizabeth Moody; *m* 1937, Edith Mary Coney; one *s* one *d*. *Educ:* Hull Council Schs; Hull Technical Coll. Mem. of Court of Referees, ten years; on Hull City Council, 1934-37. Mem. National Executive of Labour Party, 1942-46. MP (Lab) for Fairfield Div. of Liverpool, 1945-50, Gateshead East, 1950-64. *Recreations:* Rugby football, swimming. *Address:* 150 Boothferry Road, Hull. *T:* Hull 54324.

**MOODY, Helen Wills;** *see* Roark, H. W.

**MOODY, John Percivale,** OBE 1961; Joint Artistic Director, Welsh National Opera Co.; *b* 6 April 1906; *s* of Percivale Sadleir Moody; *m* 1937, Helen Pomfret Burra; one *s* decd. *Educ:* Bromsgrove; Royal Academy Schools. In publishing in the City, 1924-26; Painting; Academy Schs, 1927-28, various London Exhibitions; taught at Wimbledon Art Sch., 1928-29. Studied opera Webber Douglas Sch. Derby Day under Sir Nigel Playfair, Lyric, Hammersmith, 1931. West End plays include: The Brontës, Royalty, 1932; Hervey House, His Majesty's, 1935; After October, Criterion, 1936; played in Old Vic seasons 1934, 1937; Ascent of F6, Dog Beneath the Skin, Group Theatre, 1935; Dir Old Vic Sch., 1940-42. AFS Clerkenwell, 1940 (wounded and discharged). Producer Old Vic Co., Liverpool, 1942-44; Birmingham Repertory Theatre, 1944-45; Carl Rosa Opera Co., 1945; Sadler's Wells Opera Co., 1945-49; Drama Dir, Arts Council of Great Britain, 1949-54; Dir, Bristol Old Vic Co., 1954-59. First productions in England of Verdi's Simone Boccanegra, 1948, Nabucco, 1952, and The Battle of Legnano, 1960; Rimsky's May Night, 1960; also for Welsh Nat. Opera: Rossini's William Tell, 1961; Macbeth, 1963; Moses, 1965; Carmen, 1967; Boris Godunov, 1968. With wife, new translations of Carmen and Simone Boccanegra, 1970. *Recreations:* swimming, gardening. *Address:* 2 Richmond Park Road, Bristol 8. *T:* Bristol 34436.

**MOODY, Sydney,** CMG 1942; OBE 1932; Colonial Secretary, Mauritius, 1939-48; *b* 1889; *s* of Jonathan Moody; *m* Flora Marion, *e d* of late Rev. William Ewing, MC, DD, Edinburgh; two *d*. *Educ:* Oxford (BA). Served European War, 1914-20. *Address:* The Brae, Alyth, Perthshire.

**MOODY, Theodore William,** MA, PhD, DLit; Fellow of Trinity College, Dublin, and Professor of Modern History in Dublin University, since 1939; *b* 26 Nov. 1907; *o s* of William J. Moody, Belfast, and Ann I. Dippie; *m* 1935, Margaret C. P. Robertson, LLB, Bristol; one *s* four *d*. *Educ:* Royal Academical Institution, Belfast; Queen's Univ., Belfast (BA Mediæval and Modern Hist., 1930); Inst. of Historical Research, Univ. of London, 1930-32 (PhD, 1934). Asst in History, Queen's Univ., Belfast, 1932-35, Lectr in History, 1935-39; Trinity Coll., Dublin: Tutor, 1939-52; Senior Tutor, 1952-58; Senior Lectr, 1958-64; first Dean, Faculty of Arts, 1967-69. FRHistS 1934; MRIA 1940; MA Dublin, 1941; Hon. DLit, Queen's Univ., Belfast, 1959. Member: Irish Manuscripts Commn, 1943-; Advisory Cttee on Cultural Relations, Dept of External Affairs, Ireland, 1949-63; Comhairle Radio Eireann (Irish Broadcasting Council), 1953-60; Irish Broadcasting Authority, 1960-; Govt Commn on Higher Education in Ireland, 1960-

67. Leverhulme Res. Fellow, 1964-66; Mem. of Sch. of Historical Studies, Inst. for Advanced Study, Princeton, 1965. Jt Editor, Irish Historical Studies, 1937-; Editor, Studies in Irish History, 1st series, 1944-56, 2nd series, 1960-; Chm. Bd of Editors, A New History of Ireland, 1968-. *Publications:* Ulster Plantation Papers, 1608-13 (Analecta Hibernica, no. 8, 1938); The Londonderry Plantation, 1609-1641: the City of London and the Plantation in Ulster (1939); The Irish Parliament under Elizabeth and James I: a general survey (Proc. of Royal Irish Academy, vol. xiv, sect. C, no. 6, 1939); The History of Poynings' Law, 1494-1615 (with R. D. Edwards, Irish Hist. Studies, no. 8, 1941); Michael Davitt in penal servitude, 1870-1877 (Studies, nos 120-1, Dec. 1941-March 1942); The Ulster Scots in colonial and revolutionary America (Studies, nos 133-4, March-June 1945); Michael Davitt and the "Pen" letter (Irish Hist. Studies, no. 15, 1945); Thomas Davis, 1814-45 (1945); The "new departure" in Irish politics, 1878-9 (Essays in British and Irish History in honour of J. E. Todd, 1949); Michael Davitt and the British labour movement, 1882-1906 (Trans of Royal Hist. Soc., 1953); ed (with J. C. Beckett) and contrib., Ulster since 1800 (2 series: 1955, 1957); The Irish university question of the nineteenth century (History, June 1958); (with J. C. Beckett) Queen's, Belfast, 1845-1949: the history of a university (1959); An Irish countryman in the British Navy, 1809-1815: the memoirs of Henry Walsh (The Irish Sword, nos 16-21), 1960-62; (ed with F. X. Martin and contrib.) The course of Irish history, 1967; (ed and contrib.) Historical Studies VI, 1968; (ed and contrib.) The Fenian Movement, 1968; (ed with J. G. Simms) The Bishopric of Derry and the Irish Society of London, 1602-70, 1968; various contributions to Irish Historical Studies, etc. *Recreations:* listening to music, walking. *Address:* 40 Trinity College, Dublin.

**MOODY-STUART, Sir Alexander,** Kt 1960; OBE 1945; MC 1918; *b* 28 Jan. 1899; *yr s* of late George Moody-Stuart, CBE; *m* 1925, Judith, *d* of late L. I. Henzell, OBE, Antigua; three *s* three *d. Educ:* Winchester; Christ's Coll., Cambridge (BA); Imperial Coll. of Tropical Agriculture, Trinidad. RFA 1917. Became resident of Antigua, 1924; Mem. of Executive and Legislative Councils of Antigua and Leeward Islands for many years. *Address:* Grey House Cottage, Albrighton, near Wolverhampton.

**MOOKERJEE, Sir Birendra Nath,** Kt 1942; MA Cantab, MIE (India); Partner of Martin & Co. and Burn & Co., Managing Director, Martin Burn Ltd, Engineers, Contractors, Merchants, Shipbuilders, etc; Chairman Steel Corporation of Bengal Ltd; President Calcutta Local Board of Imperial Bank of India; Director Darjeeling Himalayan Railway Co. Ltd and many other companies; *b* 14 Feb. 1899; *s* of late Sir Rajendra Nath Mookerjee, KCIE, KCVO, MIE (India), FASB, DSc (Eng); *m* 1925, Ranu Priti Adhikari, *d* of Phani Bhusan Adhikari, late Professor Benares Hindu Univ.; one *s* two *d. Educ:* Bishop's Collegiate Sch., Hastings House, Calcutta; Bengal Engineering Coll.; Trinity Coll., Cambridge. Mem., Viceroy's Nat. Defence Council; Adviser, Roger Mission; Mem., Munitions Production Adv. Cttee. Fellow Calcutta Univ.; Sheriff of Calcutta 1941. *Address:* 7 Harington Street, Calcutta 16; Martin & Co., 12 Mission Row, Calcutta; T. A. Martin & Co., 71 Queen Street, EC4. *Clubs:* National Liberal; Calcutta, Calcutta Polo, Royal Calcutta Turf, Calcutta South, Cricket Club of India (Calcutta), etc.

**MOON, Maj.-Gen. Alan Neilson,** CB 1966; CBE 1961; Director, Army Dental Service, 1963-66; *b* 10 June 1906; *s* of late E. W. Moon, Weston-super-Mare; *m* 1st, 1933, Joyce Beatrix (marr. diss., 1943), *d* of E. E. Searles, Bristol; one *d*; 2nd, 1961, Dorothy Mary, ARRC, *d* of W. H. Wilson, Blairgowrie. *Educ:* Queen's Coll., Taunton; Univ. of Bristol. LDS 1930; commnd Lieut, The Army Dental Corps, 1931; Captain 1934; Major 1941; Lt-Col 1948; Col 1956; Brig. 1959; Maj.-Gen. 1963. Served: India, 1939-45; Middle East, 1950-53; Dep. Dir Dental Service Western Command, 1956, Southern Command, 1957; Asst Dir, War Office, 1958-63. OStJ 1961. *Address:* Fulwood, Torphins, Aberdeenshire AB3 4JS. *T:* Torphins 384. *Club:* Public Schools.

**MOON, Sir (Edward) Penderel,** Kt 1962; OBE 1941; Fellow and Estates Bursar of All Souls College and Faculty Lecturer, Oxford; *b* 13 Nov. 1905; *s* of Dr R. O. Moon, FRCP; *m* 1966, Pauline Marion, *d* of Rev. W. E. C. Barns. *Educ:* Winchester; New Coll., Oxford (MA). Entered ICS, 1929, resigned, 1944; Sec., Development Board and to Planning Advisory Board, Govt of India; Min. of Revenue and Public Works, Bahawalpur State; Chief Comr, Himachal Pradesh; Chief Comr, Manipur; Adviser, Planning Commission. *Publications:* Strangers in India; The Future of India; Warren Hastings and British India; Divide and Quit; Gandhi and Modern India. *Recreations:* hunting, shooting and singing. *Address:* 19 Northmoor Road, Oxford.

**MOON, Prof. Harold Philip,** MA Cantab; Professor of Zoology, University of Leicester, 1950-70, now Professor Emeritus; *b* 15 Jan. 1910; *er s* of Harold Joseph Moon, LRCP, MRCS, and Beatrice Sarah, *yr d* of George Greenwood; *m* 1939, Ruth Hannah, *er d* of late Capt. E. Rivenhall Goffe, RAOC (Retd); three *s* one *d. Educ:* Bootham Sch., York; King's Coll., Cambridge. Asst Naturalist, Freshwater Biological Assoc., 1933-35; Asst Research Officer, Avon Biological Research, University Coll., Southampton, 1936-39 (on leave of absence, Percy Sladen expedn to Lake Titicaca, S America, 1937); Asst Lecturer, Dept of Zoology, Manchester, 1939; Demonstrator, Bedford Coll. for Women, Univ. of London, 1941; Junior Scientific Officer, Operational Research, MAP, 1942; Insect Infestation Branch, MOF, 1943-45; promoted Sen. Inspector, 1944; Lecturer in Charge, Dept of Zoology, University Coll., Leicester, 1945-50. *Publications:* papers on freshwater biology in scientific journals. *Recreation:* walking. *Address:* The Beeches, 48 Elmfield Avenue, Stoneygate, Leicester LE2 1RO. *T:* Leicester 77625.

**MOON, Sir John (Arthur),** 4th Bt, *cr* 1887; Master (retired) Merchant Navy; *b* 27 Oct. 1905; 3rd *s* of Reginald Blakeney Moon (*d* 1927; *g s* of 1st Bt) and Lucy Annie (*d* 1935), *d* of J. Crowther; *S* brother, Sir Richard Moon, 3rd Bt, 1961; *m* 1939, René Henriette Maria Dolores (*d* 1949), *o d* of late Joseph Amedée Amedet, Le Mans, France; no *c. Heir: b* Robert Blakeney Moon [*b* 3 March 1908; *m* 1st, 1936, Margaret (marr. diss. 1941), *d* of W. H. Law; 2nd, 1945, Helen Everard Collier, *d* of late Col C. H. Wiley, Royal Engineers]. *Address:* Les Oliviers, 80 Avenue de Lattre de Tassigny, 06-Cannes, France.

**MOON, Sir Penderel;** *see* Moon, Sir E. P.

**MOON, Sir Peter Wilfred Giles Graham-,** 5th Bt, *cr* 1855; *b* 24 Oct. 1942; *s* of Sir (Arthur) Wilfred Graham-Moon, 4th Bt, and 2nd wife, Doris Patricia, *yr d* of Thomas Baron Jobson, Dublin; *S* father, 1954; *m* 1967, Sarah Gillian

Chater (formerly *m* Major Antony Chater; marr. diss. 1966), *e d* of late Lt-Col Michael Lyndon Smith, MC, MB, BS, and Mrs Michael Smith; one *s*. *Heir: s* Rupert Francis Wilfred Graham-Moon, *b* 29 April 1968. *Address:* The Lower Farm, Leafield, Oxfordshire. *T:* Asthall Leigh 287. *Clubs:* British Automobile Racing; Royal Cork Yacht.

**MOON, Philip Burton,** FRS 1947; Poynting Professor of Physics in the University of Birmingham, since 1950; Dean of the Faculty of Science and Engineering, since 1969; *b* 17 May 1907; *o s* of late F. D. Moon; *m* 1937, Winifred F. Barber; one *s* one *d*. *Educ:* Leyton County High Sch.; Sidney Sussex Coll., Cambridge. *Publications:* Artificial Radioactivity, 1949; various papers on atomic and nuclear physics. *Address:* Department of Physics, PO Box 363, The University of Birmingham, Birmingham B15 2TT.

**MOON, Lieut (Hon. Captain) Rupert Vance,** VC; Director; Queensland Stations Ltd; Richardson's Exchange Pty Ltd; Dennys Lascelles Ltd (retd as General Manager, Sept. 1960); *b* Bacchus Marsh, 1892; *s* of Arthur Moon, of the Nat. Bank of Australasia, Melbourne; *m* 1931, Susan Alison May, *yr d* of R. T. Vincent, Prospect House, Geelong; one *s* one *d*. *Educ:* Kyneton Grammar Sch. Served European War (VC). Formerly Accountant, National Bank of Australasia Ltd, Geelong. *Address:* Calder Park, Mount Duneed, via Geelong, Vic 3221, Australia. *Clubs:* Melbourne, Naval and Military, Victorian Racing, Moonee Valley Racing (Melbourne); Geelong, Geelong Racing (Geelong); Victoria Amateur Turf (Caulfield).

**MOONEY, George Stuart;** *b* 5 Oct. 1900; *s* of Richard Stuart Mooney and Grace Sowden; *m* 1925, Tessie Tait; three *d*. *Educ:* McGill Univ., Montreal; Sir George Williams Coll., Montreal. Exec. Dir, Canadian Fedn of Mayors and Municipalities, 1936-; Exec. Sec., Montreal YMCA, 1922-35; Dir Planning and Research, Montreal Metropolitan Commission, 1935-38; Dir, Montreal Industrial and Economic Bureau, 1938-58; Consultant War Time Prices Trade Bd, Canada, 1940-42; Mem. of Faculty Sir George Williams Coll., Montreal (Public Finance and Administration), 1937-48; Mem. Federal Govt Cttee on Reconstruction (Canada), 1943-44. Dir Greater Montreal Economic Council, 1942-58. Exec. Sec. Administrative Council UNRRA and Head of Secretariat, 1944-46; Dir of Research, Bd of Research on Traffic and Mass Transportation (Montreal), 1949-52; Dir, St Lawrence Municipal Bureau (Montreal), 1955-58. Chm. Nat. Exec., UN Assoc. in Canada, 1948-50; Vice-Pres., Community Planning Assoc. of Canada, 1948-49; Mem. Associate Cttee Nat. Building Code (Nat. Research Council), 1948; Dir of Research: Commn on Problems, Metropolitan Govt, Greater Montreal, 1953-58; Mem. Bd of Governors, Canadian Welfare Council, 1959-. *Publications:* Co-operatives: To-day and To-morrow, 1937; Our Cities: Their Role in the National Economy, 1940; Municipal Finance in Canada, 1942; Municipalities and Reconstruction, 1943; A Housing Programme for Canada, 1944; Public Finance in Canada (1930-1948), 1950. *Recreations:* golf, fishing. *Address:* 3790 Côte des Neiges Road, Montreal, Canada. *T:* WE 5-8089. *Clubs:* Allies, Royal Automobile; Mount Stephen, Reform, Royal St Lawrence Yacht (Montreal).

**MOONMAN, Eric;** with Miles Roman Computer Group, since 1970; *b* 29 April 1929; *s* of Borach and Leah Moonman; *m* 1962, Jane; one *s* one *d*. *Educ:* Rathbone Sch., Liverpool; Christ Church, Southport; Univs of Liverpool and Manchester. Dipl. in Social Science, Liverpool, 1955; Certif. in Personnel Management, Manchester, 1956. Human Relations Adviser, British Inst. of Management, 1956-62; Sen. Lectr in Industrial Relations and Dir of Management Centre, SW Essex Technical Coll., 1962-65; Sen. Research Fellow in Management Sciences, Univ. of Manchester, 1965-66. MSc Manchester Univ., 1967. MP (Lab) Billericay, 1966-70; PPS to Minister without Portfolio and Sec. of State for Educn, 1967-68. Chairman: All-Party Parly Mental Health Information Unit, 1968-; Science and Technology Cttee, Parly Labour Party. Member: Stepney Council, 1961-65 (Leader, 1964-65); Tower Hamlets Council, 1964-67. Governor, Imperial Coll.; Mem. Court, Brunel Univ.; Council Mem., Toynbee Hall Univ. Settlement. *Publications:* The Manager and the Organization, 1961; Employee Security, 1962; European Science and Technology, 1968; Communication in an Expanding Organization, 1970; articles on management-trade union relation in American and British literature. *Recreations:* football, theatre, cinema. *Address:* 3 Highland Grove, Billericay, Essex.

**MOORE,** family name of **Earl of Drogheda.**

**MOORE, Viscount; Henry Dermot Ponsonby Moore;** *b* 14 Jan. 1937; *o s* and *heir* of 11th Earl of Drogheda, *qv*; *m* 1968, Eliza Lloyd, *d* of Stacy Barcroft Lloyd, Jr, and Mrs Paul Mellon. *Educ:* Eton; Trinity College, Cambridge. *Address:* 27 Place Dauphine, Paris I, France.

**MOORE, Antony Ross,** CMG 1965; Director, Selection Trust (Iran) and Kerman Copper Industries, since 1969; *b* 30 May 1918; *o s* of late Arthur Moore and late Eileen Maillet; *m* 1st, 1941, Philippa Weigall (marr. diss.); two *d*; 2nd, 1963, Mary, *yr d* of Prof. V. H. Galbraith, *qv*; one *s*. *Educ:* Rugby; King's Coll., Cambridge. Served in Friends Ambulance Unit, 1939-40; HM Forces, 1940-46. Apptd Mem. Foreign (subseq. Diplomatic) Service, Nov. 1946; transf. to Rome, 1947; FO, Nov. 1949; 1st Sec., 1950; transf. to Tel Aviv, 1952; acted as Chargé d'Affaires, 1953, 1954; apptd Consul, Sept. 1953; FO, 1955; UK Perm. Delegn to UN, New York, 1957; Counsellor and transf. to IDC, 1961; FO, 1962-64; Internat. Fellow, Center for Internat. Affairs, Harvard Univ., 1964-65; Regional Information Officer, Middle East, British Embassy, Beirut, 1965-67; Head of Eastern Dept, FO, 1967; retd from HM Diplomatic Service, Dec. 1968. *Address:* Touchbridge, Boarstall, Aylesbury, Bucks. *T:* Brill 247; c/o Kerman Copper Industries, 34 Latifi Street, Shiraz Avenue, Teheran, Iran. *T:* Teheran 42130.

**MOORE, Archie Murrell Acheson,** FRCS; Hon. FICS, 1962; FRSH; Senior Surgeon and Associate Director, Surgical Unit, London Hospital; Hon. Consultant Surgeon: Poplar Hospital; King George Hospital, Ilford; Dr Barnardo's Homes; St Luke's Nursing Home for the Clergy; Arthur Stanley Institute for Rheumatism; *b* 14 Aug. 1904; *s* of Archie Moore, Aughnacloy, NI; *m* Marjorie Aitken; one *s* two *d*. *Educ:* Boys' High Sch., Pretoria, SA; London Hosp. (Surgical Scholar; Buxton, Lethby and minor surgical prize); King's Coll. FRCS 1930; MRCS, LRCP 1927. Formerly: Surgeon Southend Gen. Hosp. and Essex CC. Examiner in Surgery: Univs of London and Durham; RCS; GDC. Past Mem. Bd of Examiners for primary FRCS; Vice-Pres. and Fellow and Past Treas., BMA; Past Pres. Metropolitan Counties Br. and Chm.

Marylebone Div. BMA; Past Chm. Conf. of Consultants and Specialists, and Chm. Adv. Cttee, Commonwealth Medical Adv. Bureau; Chm. Library sub-Cttee BMA; Chm. Cttee on Accidents in Home. Pres. Bd of Registration of Medical Auxiliaries; Mem. Statutory Chiropodists' Bd; Mem. Governing Body British Post Graduate Medical Fedn; Mem. Bd of Governors, London Hosp.; Past Pres., British Supporting Gp, World Medical Assoc.; Past Hon. Pres. British Medical Students Assoc. Chairman: Academic Bd, London Hosp. Medical Coll.; Cttee of Management Medical Insurance Agency; British Medical Students Trust. Mem., Academy of Forensic Sciences. Gen. Comr of Income Tax. Past Master, Worshipful Soc. of Apothecaries, 1961-62, and Hon. Treas.; Liveryman Worshipful Co. of Barbers; Freeman City of London. Hon. Mem. Assoc. of Police Surgeons; FRSM; Fellow: Assoc. of Surgeons; Medical Soc. London. FZS. CStJ 1968. *Publications:* contribs to medical jls. *Recreation:* fencing. *Address:* London Hospital, Whitechapel, E1. *T:* 01-247 5454; 42 Crag Path, Aldeburgh, Suffolk. *T:* Aldeburgh 2598. *Clubs:* Athenæum, City Livery.

**MOORE, Arthur Claude,** CBE 1938; retired as Assistant Comptroller-General of Customs, Commonwealth of Australia; *b* Strathbogie, 1 March 1898; *s* of Reuben Moore, Strathbogie, Vic, Australia; *m* 1925, Stella Helena, *d* of John Hogan; one *d*. *Educ:* State Schs. Accompanied Delegn Imperial Economic Conf., Ottawa, 1932; Commercial Adviser to Latham Goodwill Mission to Japan, 1934; Princ. Adviser of Sir Henry Gullett, then Minister in Charge of Trade Treaties, in inaugurating Trade Treaty Policy, 1934-37; adviser to Prime Minister's Delegation to London, 1935. *Recreation:* golf.

**MOORE, Bobby;** *see* Moore, Robert.

**MOORE, Brian;** novelist; *b* 25 Aug. 1921; *s* of James Bernard Moore, FRCS, Northern Ireland, and Eileen McFadden; *m* Jean Denney. Guggenheim Fellowship (USA), 1959; Canada Council Senior Fellowship (Canada), 1960. National Institute of Arts and Letters (USA) Fiction Award 1960; Governor-Gen. of Canada's Award for Fiction, 1960, etc. *Publications: novels:* The Lonely Passion of Judith Hearne, 1955; The Feast of Lupercal, 1956; The Luck of Ginger Coffey, 1960; An Answer from Limbo, 1962; The Emperor of Ice-Cream, 1965; I am Mary Dunne, 1968; Fergus, 1970; *non-fiction:* Canada (with Editors of Life), 1964. *Address:* c/o Collins-Knowlton-Wing, 60 East 56th Street, New York, NY 10022, USA. *T:* Plaza 54200.

**MOORE, Air Vice-Marshal Charles Stuart,** CB 1962; OBE 1945; *b* London, 27 Feb. 1910; *s* of late E. A. Moore and late E. B. Moore (*née* Druce); *m* 1st, 1937, Anne (*d* 1957), *d* of Alfred Rogers; 2nd, 1961, Jean Mary, *d* of John Cameron Wilson; one *d*. *Educ:* Sutton Valence Sch.; RAF Coll., Cranwell. Commissioned in General Duties Branch, Dec. 1930; served in Egypt, 1932-34 and 1936-41; Sqdn Ldr 1938; Sudan, 1941-42; Wing Comdr 1940; 11 Group, 1943-44; Gp Capt. 1943; OC, OTU, 1944-45; Gp Capt. Org., HQFC, 1945-46; Staff Coll., Bracknell, 1946-47; Dep. Dir Plans, Air Ministry, London, 1947-49; Student, US National War Coll., Washington, 1949-50; Staff of USAF Air War Coll., Alabama, 1950-53; Air Commodore, 1953; AOC 66 Group, 1953-55; Dir of Intelligence, Air Ministry, London, 1955-58; AOA, NEAF, 1958-62; Actg Air Vice-Marshal, 1960; retired, 1962. Joined HM Foreign Service, Oct. 1962; posted to British Embassy, Tehran, Iran; left HM Diplomatic Service, March 1969. *Recreations:* music, photography and travelling. *Address:* Ferndene, The Avenue, Crowthorne, Berks. *T:* Crowthorne 2300. *Club:* Royal Air Force.

**MOORE, Maj.-Gen. Denis Grattan,** CB 1960; retired; *b* 15 March 1909; *s* of Col F. G. Moore, CBE and Marian, *d* of Very Rev. W. H. Stone, Dean of Kilmore; *m* 1st, 1932, Alexandra, *d* of W. H. Wann; two *d*; 2nd, 1946, Beatrice Glynn, *d* of W. S. Williamson; one adopted *d*. *Educ:* Wellington Coll.; Royal Military College, Sandhurst. Commissioned 1929, Royal Inniskilling Fusiliers; GSO1, HQ Tenth Army, 1943; Asst Dir of Artillery (Weapons), HQ Eighth Army, 1944; GSO1, War Office, 1946; 2nd in comd 3rd Bn, Parachute Regt, 1948-49; comd 1st Bn Royal Inniskillings, 1950-52; GSO1 (Col) War Office, 1952-54; comd 47 Infantry Bde, TA, 1954-57; Dir of Weapons and Development, War Office, 1958-60; Dir of Equipment Policy, War Office, 1960-61; Chief, Jt Services Liaison Staff, BAOR, 1961-63. Col, The Royal Inniskilling Fusiliers, 1960-66. Chm., Ulster Timber Growers Organisation, 1965-. High Sheriff, Co. Tyrone, 1969. *Recreations:* shooting, fishing. *Address:* Mountfield Lodge, Omagh, Co. Tyrone, N Ireland. *T:* Mountfield 206. *Club:* Naval and Military.

**MOORE, Mrs D(oris) Langley;** Founder (1955) and Adviser, Museum of Costume, Assembly Rooms, Bath; author. Has done varied literary work in connection with films, television, and ballet, and has specialized in promoting the study of costume by means of exhibns and lectures in England and abroad. Designer of clothes for period films. *Publications: fiction:* A Winter's Passion, 1932; The Unknown Eros, 1935; They Knew Her When . . ., 1938 (subseq. re-published as A Game of Snakes and Ladders); Not at Home, 1948; All Done by Kindness, 1951; My Caravaggio Style, 1959; *non-fiction:* Anacreon: 29 Odes, 1926; The Technique of the Love Affair, 1928; Pandora's Letter Box, A Discourse on Fashionable Life, 1929; E. Nesbit, A Biography, 1933 (rev. 1966); The Vulgar Heart, An Enquiry into the Sentimental Tendencies of Public Opinion, 1945; The Woman in Fashion, 1949; The Child in Fashion, 1953; Pleasure, A Discursive Guide Book, 1953; The Late Lord Byron, 1961; Marie and the Duke of H., The Daydream Love Affair of Marie Bashkirtseff, 1966; Fashion through Fashion Plates, 1771-1971, 1971; (with June Langley Moore): Our Loving Duty, 1932; The Pleasure of Your Company, 1933. *Recreation:* Byron research. *Address:* 5 Prince Albert Road, NW1.

**MOORE, Rt. Rev. Edward Francis Butler;** *see* Kilmore and Elphin and Ardagh, Bishop of.

**MOORE, Sir Edward Stanton,** 2nd BT *cr* 1923; OBE 1970; *b* 1910; *s* of Major E. C. H. Moore (killed, Vimy Ridge, 1917) and Kathleen Margaret (*d* 1970), *d* of H. S. Oliver, Sudbury, Suffolk; *S* grandfather, 1923; *m* 1946, Margaret, *er d* of T. J. Scott-Cotterell. *Educ:* Mill Hill Sch. Manager, Spain and Western Mediterranean, BEA, 1965-. Pres., British Chamber of Commerce in Spain, 1969-70. *Heir:* *u* Eric Edward James Moore, DSO [*b* 24 Sept. 1894; *m* 1928, Gertrude, *d* of F. F. Vanderhoef, New York; one *d*]. *Address:* BEA, SAn Bernardo 17, Madrid 8, Spain.

**MOORE, (the Worshipful Chancellor the Rev.) E(velyn) Garth;** barrister-at-law; Chancellor, Vicar-General and Official Principal of Diocese of Durham since 1954, of Diocese of Southwark since 1948 and of Diocese of Gloucester since 1957 (and Official Principal of Archdeaconries of Lewisham, Southwark,

Kingston-on-Thames and Ely); Fellow of Corpus Christi College, Cambridge, since 1947, and Director of Studies and Lecturer in Law; High Bailiff of Ely Cathedral since 1961; Member Governing Body of St Chad's College, Durham, since 1955; President, Churches' Fellowship for Psychical and Spiritual Studies, since 1963; Church Commissioner since 1964; *b* 6 Feb. 1906; *y s* of His Honour the late Judge (Robert Ernest) Moore and late Hilda Mary, *d* of Rev. John Davis Letts; unmarried. *Educ:* The Hall, Belsize Sch.; Durham Sch.; Trinity Coll., Cambridge (MA); Cuddesdon Theol Coll., 1962. Deacon, 1962; Priest, 1962. Called to Bar, Gray's Inn, 1928; SE Circuit. Formerly: Tutor of Gray's Inn; Lector of Trinity Coll., Cambridge; Mem. Gen. Council of Bar and of Professional Conduct Cttee. Commnd 2nd Lt RA, 1940; Major on staff of JAG; served at WO and throughout Great Britain, N Ireland, Paiforce, Middle East (for a time local Lt-Col), Greece, etc. Mem. of Church Assembly (for Dio. Ely), 1955-62. JP and Dep. Chm. of QS, Hunts, 1948-63 and Cambs, 1959-63; Lectr in Criminal Procedure, Council of Legal Educn, 1957-68, Lectr in Evidence, 1952-68. Council, St David's Coll., Lampeter, 1949-65 and Westcott House, 1961-65. Legal Assessor to Disciplinary Cttee, RCVS, 1963-68. Vis. Prof., Khartoum Univ., 1961. Mere's Preacher, Cambridge Univ., 1965. *Publications:* An Introduction to English Canon Law, 1966; 8th Edn (with Suppl.) of Kenny's Cases on Criminal Law; (jt) Ecclesiastical Law, in Halsbury's Laws of England (3rd edn); various contribs mainly to legal and theological jls. *Recreations:* travel, architecture, furniture, etc. *Address:* Corpus Christi College, Cambridge. *T:* 59418; 1 Raymond Buildings, Gray's Inn, WC1. *T:* 01-242 3734. *Club:* Pitt (Cambridge).

**MOORE, Maj.-Gen. Francis Malcolm,** CSI 1947; CIE 1946; IA (retired); *b* 2 Feb. 1897; *s* of late D. F. Moore, LLD, and M. O. Moore; *m* 1927, Helen Marian Dunn; no *c*. *Educ:* St Columba's Coll.; Trinity Coll., Dublin. Commissioned 1915, Royal Irish Rifles (wounded in France); transferred to Indian Army, 1917; served with 52nd Sikhs (Frontier Force) in Mesopotamia for 3 years (despatches); after 23 years' service with 2/12th Frontier Force Regt commanded 2/16th Punjab Regt in Malaya, 1940; raised and commanded 100th Indian Infantry Brigade, 1941; commanded 34th Indian Div. 1942 until April 1943, when transferred to command 14th Indian Div. (4 weeks only) and then to command 39th Indian Div. until March 1945; Dir of Selection of Personnel, 1945-46; Military Adviser-in-Chief Indian States Forces, 1946; retd, 1948. *Publications:* numerous articles on military subjects and short stories under nom-de-plume Fan Tan. *Recreations:* Rugby football; boxing (runner-up in Irish Command Heavyweights, 1915); rowing (open Sculls Champion, India, 1925); golf. *Address:* c/o Royal Bank of Ireland, Foster Place, Dublin; Corofin, Greystones, Co. Wicklow, Ireland.

**MOORE, Maj.-Gen. (retired) Frederick David,** CB 1955; CBE 1954; *b* 27 Nov. 1902; *s* of Sir Frederick W. Moore; *m* 1932, Anna Morrell Hamilton, *d* of Col T. H. M. Clarke, CMG, DSO; one *s*. *Educ:* Wellington Coll.; RMA Woolwich. Commnd in RFA, 1923. Served War of 1939-45: BEF 1940, 5th Regt RHA; BLA, 1944-45, CO 5th Regt RHA and CRA 53rd (W) Div.; GOC 5th AA Group, 1953-55; retd, 1956. DL Beds, 1958, Vice-Lieutenant, 1964-70. Officer Order of Crown (Belgian); Croix de Guerre (Belgian), 1940; with palm, 1945. *Recreations:* country pursuits. *Address:* Abbey Lodge, Clonsilla, Co. Dublin, Eire. *T:* 383344. *Club:* Army and Navy.

**MOORE, Frederick Thomas,** OBE 1943; FRCS, FRCSE; Consulting Plastic Surgeon to King's College Hospital, London, since 1948; Plastic Unit East Grinstead since 1948; *b* 19 Oct. 1913; *s* of Francis Moore and Rose Perry; *m* 1957, Margrethe Johanne Holland (actress, as Greta Gynt); one *d*. *Educ:* St Bartholomew's Hosp. MRCS, LRCP 1936; FRCSE 1939; FRCS 1945. Served War of 1939-45 (OBE): RAF, Plastic Surgeon, 1939-48. Mem. Council, British Assoc. Plastic Surgeons, 1949. Founder Mem., British Hand Club. Legion of Honour, 1948. *Publications:* numerous on surgical problems. *Recreations:* golf, sailing, writing, research (medical). *Address:* Flat 1, 30 Harley Street, W1. *T:* 01-636 0955.

**MOORE, Geoffrey Herbert;** Professor of American Literature and Head of the Department of American Studies, University of Hull, since 1962; *b* 10 June 1920; *e s* of late Herbert Jonathan Moore, Norwich; *m* 1947, Pamela Marguerite (marr. diss. 1962), *d* of Bertram Munn, Twickenham; one *s* one *d*. *Educ:* Mitcham Grammar Sch.; Emmanuel Coll., Cambridge; Univ. of Paris. 1st Cl. English Tripos, Cambridge, 1946; MA 1951. War Service (Air Ministry and RAF), 1939-43. Instr in English, Univ. of Wisconsin, 1947-49; Vis. Prof. of English, Univs of Kansas City and New Mexico, 1948, 1949; Asst Prof. of English, Tulane Univ., 1949-51; Vis. Prof. of English, Univ. of Southern California and Claremont Coll., 1950; Extra Mural Lectr, London and Cambridge Univs, 1951-52 and 1953-54; Editor and Producer, BBC Television Talks, 1952-53; Rose Morgan Prof., Univ. of Kansas, 1954-55; Lectr in Amer. Lit., Manchester Univ., 1955-59; Vis. Lectr, Univs of Mainz, Göttingen and Frankfurt, 1959; Rockefeller Fellow, Harvard Univ., 1959-60; Sen. Lectr in Amer. Lit., Manchester Univ., 1960-62; Dean, Faculty of Arts, Univ. of Hull, 1967-69. Visiting Lecturer: Univs of Montpellier, Aix-en-Provence and Nice, 1967; Univs of Frankfurt, Heidelberg, Mainz, Saarbrücken, Tübingen, 1967, 1968; Vis. Prof. of English, York Univ., Toronto, 1969-70; Vis. Prof., Univ. of Tunis, Spring 1970; Fellow, Sch. of Letters, Indiana Univ., Summer 1970. Mem. Cttee, British Assoc. for Amer. Studies, 1957-60. Sen. Scholar Award, Amer. Coun. of Learned Socs, 1965. Ed. and founder, The Bridge (Cambridge lit. mag.), 1946. *Publications:* Voyage to Chivalry (under pseud.), 1947; Poetry from Cambridge in Wartime, 1947; The Penguin Book of Modern American Verse, 1954; (ed) 58 Short Stories by O. Henry, 1956; Poetry Today, 1958; American Literature and the American Imagination, 1964; American Literature, 1964; articles in TLS, Amer. Mercury, BBC Quarterly, Kenyon Review, Review of English Lit., The Year's Work in English Studies, and other scholarly and literary jls. *Recreations:* swimming, driving. *Address:* The University, Hull, Yorks. *T:* 408960. *Club:* Savile.

**MOORE, Rear-Adm. (retired) George Dunbar,** CBE 1944; *b* 10 Oct. 1893; *s* of Dr John Irwin and Susan Moore; *m* 1923, Doretta Ziele Russell; one *d*. *Educ:* The Southport Sch., Queensland; Brisbane Grammar Sch.; HMS Conway. Sub-Lt RAN 1914; Lt 1916; Comdr 1928; Capt. 1935; Commodore, 1942; Acting Rear-Adm., 1944; commanded: HMS Dunoon, 1932-33; HMAS Penguin, 1934-35; HMAS Yarra, 1936-37; HMAS Stuart, 1937-38; HMS Curaçoa, 1939; HMS Dauntless, 1939-41; HMAS Australia, 1941; HMAS Canberra, 1942. 2nd Naval Mem., Australian Commonwealth Naval Board, 1942-44; Flag

Officer-in-Charge, New South Wales, 1944-50; Minister for Australia in the Philippines, 1950-55, retired. *Address:* Bank of New South Wales, King Street and George Street, Sydney, NSW 2000, Australia. *Club:* Royal Sydney Golf (Sydney).

**MOORE, George Edgar; His Honour Deemster Moore;** HM First Deemster and Clerk of the Rolls Isle of Man, since 1969; *b* 13 July 1907; *er s* of Ramsey Bignall Moore, OBE, formerly HM Attorney-General for Isle of Man, and Agnes Carmall Moore; *m* 1937, Joan Mary Kissack; one *s* one *d*. *Educ:* Rydal School. Served in RAF, 1940-45 (Sqdn Ldr). Admitted to Manx Bar, 1930; Attorney-General for Isle of Man, 1957-63; HM Second Deemster, 1963-69; MLC; Chm., Trustees of Manx Blind Welfare Soc.; Pres., Isle of Man Badminton Assoc.; Chm., Manx War Work Trust; Hon. County Representative of Royal Air Force Benevolent Assoc., 1948-. *Address:* Hillcrest, Alexander Drive, Douglas, Isle of Man. *Clubs:* Royal Automobile; Ellan Vannin (IoM).

**MOORE, George Herbert,** MSc; FPS; FRIC; *b* 1 June 1903; *s* of late R. Herbert Moore and Mabel Moore, Bath; *m* 1931, Dora, *d* of Frederick and Emily Blackmore, Bath; one *d*. *Educ:* King Edward's Sch., Bath; Bath Coll. of Chemistry and Pharmacy. FPS 1928, FRIC 1943; MSc Bristol 1953. Merchant Venturers' Technical Coll., Bristol; Lectr in Pharmaceutical Chemistry, 1929-38; Head of Science Dept, 1938-50; Vice-Principal, Bristol Coll. of Technology, 1950-54; Principal, Bristol Coll. of Science and Technology, 1954-66; Vice-Chancellor, Bath Univ., 1966-69. Vice-Pres. Royal Inst. of Chemistry, 1955-57. Hon. LLD Bath, 1968. *Recreations:* music, photography. *Address:* Hilcot, Horsecombe Vale, Combe Down, Bath, Somerset. *T:* Bath 837417. *Club:* Bristol Savages (Bristol).

**MOORE, Gerald,** CBE 1954; pianoforte accompanist; retired from concert platform, 1967; *b* Watford, Herts, 30 July 1899; *e s* of David Frank Moore, Tiverton, Devon; *m* Enid Kathleen, *d* of Montague Richard, Beckenham, Kent. *Educ:* Watford Grammar Sch.; Toronto Univ. Studied piano in Toronto; toured Canada as a boy pianist; returning to England, devoted himself to accompanying and chamber music. Associated with world's leading singers and instrumentalists. Festivals of Edinburgh, Salzburg, Holland, etc. Retired from concert platform but continues to make records and to lecture annually in USA and gives broadcasts and television talks on music and the art of accompanying; Ensemble Classes in USA, Tokyo, Stockholm, Helsinki, Dartington Hall, Salzburg Mozarteum. Awarded Cobbett Gold Medal, 1951, for services to Chamber Music; Pres. Incorporated Soc. of Musicians, 1962. Hon. RAM 1962. Hon. DLitt Sussex, 1968. *Publications:* The Unashamed Accompanist, 1943 (rev. edn 1957); Careers in Music, 1950; Singer and Accompanist, 1953; Am I Too Loud?, 1962; arrangements of songs and folk songs. *Recreations:* reading, bridge. *Address:* Beechwood Cottage, Penn Bottom, Penn, Bucks. *T:* Penn 2507. *Clubs:* Savile, MCC.

**MOORE, Brig. Guy Newton,** CBE 1941; DFC; ED; Chartered Accountant, Senior Partner, A. Capper Moore & Sons; Treasurer of the Royal Federation of Aero Clubs of Australia; *b* 13 Jan. 1893; *s* of A. Capper and Alice Eleanor Moore; *m* 1922, Marguerite Thompson; three *d*. *Educ:* Wesley Coll., Melbourne. Served with Royal Flying Corps and Royal Air Force (Capt.), 1916-18; Hon. Sqdn Leader, Citizens Air Force (Australia); Chief Paymaster, AIF. Dir of Finance Administration, Australian Commonwealth Forces, 1939-45. *Recreations:* golf, swimming, bowls. *Address:* 34 Queen's Road, Melbourne, Victoria 3004, Australia. *Clubs:* Naval and Military, Emerald Country (Life Member) (Melbourne).

**MOORE, Harold,** CBE 1932; DSc (London); PhD, FRIC, FInstP; *b* 5 Jan. 1878; *m* 1st, 1908, Grace Dora (*d* 1921), *d* of late R. J. Read, Norwich; two *d* (and one *d* decd); 2nd, 1922, Una Katharine, *d* of late A. W. Yeo; one *d* (and one *s* decd). Chemist to Islip Iron Co., Northants, 1899-1901; metallurgist to William Beardmore & Co., Parkhead Steel Works, 1901-04; joined Research Dept, Woolwich, as chief metallurgist, 1904; Dir of Metallurgical Research in that dept, 1919-32; Dir of British Non-Ferrous Metals Research Assoc., 1932-44; Editor, Transactions of the Society of Instrument Technology, 1949-56; Past Pres. Institute of Metals and of Institution of Metallurgists. *Publications:* papers on metallurgical and related subjects in journals of Institute of Metals, Iron and Steel Institute, Faraday Society, and other scientific institutions. *Recreation:* music. *Address:* Riverside House, Shoreham, Sevenoaks, Kent. *T:* Otford 3260. *Club:* Athenæum.

**MOORE, Sir Harold (John de Courcy),** Kt, *cr* 1922; *s* of late Hobart Moore of Bengeo, Herts; *b* 8 June 1877; *m* 1st, 1906, Jeanne Germaine, *d* of late Eugene Gokel; two *s* one *d*; 2nd, 1924, Mary (*d* 1965), *d* of late J. C. Cuthbertson; 3rd, 1965, Winifred, *d* of late Edwin Atkin. Alderman of the City of London (Walbrook Ward), 1921-29; Senior Sheriff of the City of London, 1921-22; Lieut of the City of London; Fellow, Inst. of Chartered Accountants; Fellow, Inst. of Arbitrators. Served European War with Royal Flying Corps and Royal Air Force (rank, Major); sometime a Mem. of Board of Financial Control, Air Ministry. Senior Grand Deacon of English Freemasons, 1927-28. *Address:* Hillcroft, Burley, Hants. *Clubs:* Naval; Rand (Johannesburg).

**MOORE, Harry T(hornton);** Research Professor, Southern Illinois University, since 1957; *b* Oakland, California, 2 Aug. 1908; *s* of Lt-Col H. T. Moore, US Army; *m* 1st, Winifred Sheehan; one *s* one *d*; 2nd, 1946, Beatrice Walker. *Educ:* Univ. of Chicago (PhB); Northwestern Univ. (MA); Boston Univ. (PhD). Instructor: Ill. Inst. of Techn., 1940-41; Inst., Northwestern Univ., 1941-42. Served USAAF, 2nd World War, now Lt-Col USAF Reserve. Dept of Hist. and Lit., Babson Inst., 1947-57; Prof. of English, Southern Illinois Univ., 1957-. Visiting Professor: Univ. of Colorado, 1959 and 1963-64; Columbia Univ. and New York Univ., 1961. Pres. of Coll. English Assoc., 1961. Editor: series: Crosscurrents/Modern Critiques; Crosscurrents: Modern Fiction. FRSL 1952-; Guggenheim Fellowships, 1958, 1960. *Publications:* The Novels of John Steinbeck, 1939; The Life and Works of D. H. Lawrence, 1951; The Intelligent Heart, 1955; Poste Restante, 1956; E. M. Forster, 1965; 20th Century French Literature (2 vols), 1966; The Age of the Modern, 1971; Co-author: D. H. Lawrence and his World: a Pictorial Biography, 1966; 20th Century German Literature, 1967; Co-Editor: The Achievement of D. H. Lawrence, 1953; The Human Prospect (by Lewis Mumford), 1956; Phœnix II: Uncollected, Unpublished and other Prose Works by D. H. Lawrence, 1968; Co-Translator: Tragedy is Not Enough (by Karl Jaspers); Editor: D. H. Lawrence's Letters to Bertrand Russell, 1948; D. H. Lawrence's Essays on Sex, Literature, and Censorship, 1953; A D. H. Lawrence

Miscellany, 1959; Selected Letters of Rainer Maria Rilke, 1960; The World of Lawrence Durrell, 1962; The Collected Letters of D. H. Lawrence, 1962 (2 vols); Contemporary American Novelists, 1964; The Elizabethan Age, 1965; contributed NY Times Book Review; Saturday Review; Kenyon Review; New Republic, etc. *Recreation:* listening to Shakespearean recordings. *Address:* 922 South Division Street, Carterville, Illinois 62918, USA. *T:* 985-2014. *Clubs:* Cliff Dwellers (Chicago); PEN.

**MOORE, Henry,** OM 1963; CH 1955; FBA 1966; Hon. ARIBA; sculptor; a Member Royal Fine Art Commission since 1947; a Trustee of the National Gallery, 1955-63, and since 1964; a Trustee of the Tate Gallery, 1941-48 and 1949-56; Member, National Theatre Board, since 1962; a Member of the Arts Council, 1963-67; *b* Castleford, Yorks, 30 July 1898; *s* of Raymond Spencer Moore and Mary Baker; *m* 1929, Irene Radetzky; one *d*. *Educ:* Castleford Grammar Sch. After serving European War, 1917-19, in Army, studied at Leeds Sch. of Art and Royal College of Art. Official War Artist, 1940-42. Exhibitions of his work held: in London 1928, 1931, 1933, 1935, 1936, 1940, 1946, 1948, 1951, 1953, 1955, 1960, 1963, 1967; in Venice, 1929, Berlin, 1929, Stockholm, 1930, Zürich, 1931, Hamburg, 1932, New York, 1943, Paris, 1945. Retrospective exhibitions: Temple Newsam, Leeds, 1941; Museum of Modern Art, New York, 1946; Art Institute of Chicago, 1947; San Francisco Museum of Art, 1947; State Galleries of Australia, 1947-48; the Venice Biennale, 1948 (of which he was awarded First Prize for Sculpture); Brussels, 1949; Paris, 1949; Amsterdam, 1950; Hamburg, 1950; Düsseldorf, 1950; Bern, 1950; Athens, 1951; Tate Gallery, 1951; Berlin, 1951; Vienna, 1951; Stockholm, 1951; Athens, 1951; Cape Town, 1951; Scandinavian Tour, 1952-53; Rotterdam, 1953; Germany Tour, 1953; São Paulo, Dec. 1953-Feb. 1954 (of which he was awarded 1st Prize in Foreign Sculpture); Germany Tour, 1954; New York, 1954; Basle, 1955; USA Tour, 1955; Yugoslavia Tour, 1955; Mexico City, 1964; London, 1965; Holland and Germany, 1968; Tate Gallery, 1968. Examples of work are in the Tate Gallery, Victoria and Albert Museum, Whitechapel Art Gall., and Battersea Park, London; also in Nat. Museum of Wales; St Matthew's Ch., Northampton; the grounds of Dartington Hall, Devon; public galleries in Leeds, Wakefield, Manchester and other provincial cities; the Museum of Modern Art, New York, the Allbright Art Gallery, Buffalo, and other museums in US, Germany, Italy, Sweden, Palestine and Australia. Foreign Corresp. Mem., Acad. Flamande des Sciences; For. Mem., Acad. Lettres et Beaux Arts de Belgique; For. Mem., Swedish Royal Academy of Fine Arts; For. Hon. Mem., Amer. Acad. of Arts and Sciences; Hon. Fellow, Churchill Coll., Cambridge, 1965. Hon. Degrees: Dr of Lit: Leeds, London, Reading, Oxford, Hull, York; Dr of Arts: Yale, Harvard; Dr of Law: Cambridge, St Andrews, Sheffield, Toronto, Manchester; Dr of Letters: Sussex, Warwick; Dr of Engineering, Berlin; Hon. Dr, RCA, 1967; Hon. Prof. Emeritus of Sculpture, Carrara Acad. of Fine Arts, 1967. Feltrinelli Foundn Internat. Sculpture Prize, 1963; Erasmus Prize, 1968; Einstein Prize, 1968. Grand Cross with Star, Order of Merit of Federal Republic of Germany. *Publications:* Heads, Figures and Ideas, 1958; Henry Moore (with J. Hedgecoe), 1968. *Relevant publications:* Henry Moore, by Will Grohmann, 1960 (Berlin and London); Henry Moore, by John Russell, 1968; principal monographs on his work are those by H. Read, J. J. Sweeney and G. C. Argan. *Address:* Hoglands, Perry Green, Much Hadham, Herts. *T:* Much Hadham 2566. *Club:* Athenæum.

**MOORE, Henry Ian,** CBE 1964; MSc, PhD, NDA, Dipl. Agric. Cantab; Principal of Seale-Hayne Agricultural College, Newton Abbot, Devon, since 1948; *b* 6 Oct. 1905; *s* of William Henry and Annie Ellen Moore; *m* 1931, Gwendolen Robinson. *Educ:* University of Leeds; Univ. of Cambridge. Senior Lecturer in Agriculture and Hon. Reader in Crop Husbandry, Univ. of Leeds, 1930-48. Governor: Plant Breeding Inst., Cambridge, 1954-62; Grassland Research Inst., Hurley, 1960-; Member: Grassland Utilisation Cttee, 1957-58; Adv. Cttee on Agricultural Education, 1964; President: Agricultural Education Assoc., 1963-64; British Grassland Soc., 1953-54. *Publications:* Silos and Silage, 1942; Crops and Cropping, 1943; Grassland Husbandry, 1943; Good Husbandry, 1946; Background to Farming, 1947; Root Crops, 1948; Science and Practice of Grassland Farming, 1949; Science and Practice in Cropping for Meat and Milk Production, 1952; Silage and Haymaking, 1959; Winter Keep on the Farm, 1960; Grass and Grasslands, 1966; (ed) McConnell's Agricultural Notebook, 12th, 13th and 14th editions. *Recreations:* country pursuits, photography. *Address:* Principal's House, Seale-Hayne College, Newton Abbot, Devon. *T:* Newton Abbot 4638.

**MOORE, Henry Roderick;** Director, Hill Samuel Group Ltd; Chairman: Associated Engineering Ltd; Staveley Industries, since 1970; *b* 19 Aug. 1915; *er s* of late Roderick Edward Moore; *m* 1944, Beatrice Margaret, *d* of late Major J. W. Seigne; one *s* one *d*. *Educ:* Malvern Coll.; Pembroke Coll., Cambridge. Qualified as mem. of Institute of Chartered Accountants, 1939. Served War of 1939-45: North Africa, Italy, Europe; 2nd Lt Royal Fusiliers, 1939; Lt-Col, 1944. Chm., Bd of Governors, The London Hospital. High Sheriff of Bucks, 1966. *Address:* Bourton Grounds, Buckingham. *T:* Buckingham 2241; 31 Princes Gate Court, SW7. *T:* 01-589 8676. *Clubs:* White's, Pratt's, City of London; Leander.

**MOORE, Adm. Sir Henry Ruthven,** GCB 1946 (KCB 1942; CB 1939); CVO 1937; DSO 1916; DL; *b* 29 Aug. 1886; *e s* of late Col Henry Moore, JP, late King's Own Royal Regiment; *m* 1908, Katherine Henley Joan (*d* 1945), *d* of late H. J. Gillespie, barrister-at-law, The Gables, Windsor; one *s* one *d*; *m* 1948, Catherine Harlow Wilkinson, *widow* of Vice-Adm. T. S. Wilkinson, USN, and *d* of late Richard Austin Harlow, Hockley, Arlington, Virginia. *Educ:* Sherborne. Entered HMS Britannia as Naval Cadet, 1902; Lt, 1908; Comdr, 1919; Capt., 1926; Rear-Adm., 1938; Vice-Adm., 1941; Adm., 1945; served on staff of Royal Naval Staff Coll., 1919-21; Naval Asst Sec. to the Cttee of Imperial Defence, 1921-24; Asst Sec. to British Delegation to Conference for Limitation of Armament, Washington, 1921-22, and at Geneva, 1927; attended Imperial Defence Coll., 1927; Dep. Dir of Plans Div., Admiralty, 1930-32; Dir, 1932-33; HMS Neptune, 1933-35; Cdre 1st Class and Chief of Staff to C-in-C Home Fleet, 1936-38; ADC to the King, 1937-38; Chief of Staff to Comdr-in-Chief, Portsmouth, 1938-39; Rear-Adm. Commanding 3rd Cruiser Sqdn, 1939-40; Asst Chief of Naval Staff (Trade), 1940-41; Vice-Chief of Naval Staff, 1941-43; Second-in-Command Home Fleet, 1943-44; C-in-C Home Fleet, 1944-45; Head of British Naval Mission, Washington, DC, Dec. 1945-Sept. 1948; Naval Representative of British Chiefs of Staff on Military Staff Cttee of Security Council, UN,

1946-48; Comdr-in-Chief, The Nore, 1948-50; First and Principal Naval ADC to the King, 1948-51; retired list, 1951. Served in Grand Fleet in European War of 1914-18 (despatches, DSO); War of 1939-45 (despatches). DL Kent, 1957; High Sheriff of Kent, 1959-60. OStJ. Chief Comdr, Legion of Merit (USA). *Address:* The Beck, Wateringbury, Kent. *T:* Wateringbury 566. *Club:* United Service.

**MOORE, Rear-Adm. Humfrey John Bradley,** CBE 1951; RI 1955; *b* 16 May 1898; *s* of Harry Farr Bradley and Mabel Clara Adelaide Moore; *m* 1925, Doris May Best; one *s* one *d*. *Educ:* Rugby Sch. Served European War, Grand Fleet, 1916-18. Thereafter various afloat and administrative posts, including Royal Naval Engineering Coll., Devonport staff, Admiralty (Engineer-in-Chief's and Naval Ordnance Depts) and Manager, Engineering Depts at Rosyth and Devonport and Staff of C-in-C, The Nore; retired 1952. *Recreations:* painting, ballet, music. *Address:* Prestons Cottage, Ightham, Kent. *T:* Borough Green 2668. *Club:* Arts.

**MOORE, Gen. Sir (James Newton) Rodney,** GCVO 1966 (KCVO 1959); KCB 1960 (CB 1955); CBE 1948; DSO 1944; PMN 1961; Colonel Commandant, HAC, since 1966; *b* 9 June 1905; *s* of late Maj.-Gen. Sir Newton Moore, KCMG, Perth, WA; *m* 1st, 1927, Olive Marion (marr. diss., 1947), *d* of late Lt-Col Sir Thomas Bilbe Robinson, GBE, KCMG; one *s* two *d*; 2nd, 1947, Patricia Margery Lillian, *d* of late James Catty, New York. *Educ:* Harrow; RMC, Sandhurst. Gazetted to Grenadier Guards, 1925, and served with Regt in England until 1933, then served in Egypt until 1936. Returned to England, 1936, and at outbreak of European War was at staff Coll., Camberley. Served War of 1939-45 (despatches, DSO): at GHQ Home Forces, 1940; Bde Major 30th Guards Bde and 6th Guards Armd Bde, 1940-42; GSO1, Guards Armd Div., 1942-44; Comd 2nd Armd Bn Gren. Guards in campaign NW Europe, 1944-45. Brig. comdg 8th Brit. Inf. Bde, Germany, Egypt and Palestine, 1945-46; Comd 1st Guards Bde, Palestine, 1946-47; Chief of Staff, HQ London Dist, 1948-50; idc 1950; Dep. Adjt Gen. HQ BAOR, 1951-53; Chief of Staff, Allied Forces, Northern Europe, 1953-55; GOC, 1st Infantry Div., MELF, 1955; GOC, 10th Armoured Div., 1955-57; Gen. Officer Commanding, London Dist; Maj.-Gen. Commanding Household Brigade, 1957-59; Chief of the Armed Forces Staff and Dir of Border Operations, Federation of Malaya, 1959-64; Defence Services Sec., Min. of Defence, 1964-66, retd. ADC Gen., 1965-66; Gentleman Usher to the Queen, 1966-. Officer Order of Crown of Belgium and Belgian Croix de Guerre with Palm, 1944. Panglima Mangku Negara, 1961. *Recreations:* hunting, polo, fishing. *Address:* Bodens Ride, Ascot, Berks. *Clubs:* Guards, Buck's, Turf.

**MOORE, Miss Jocelyn A. M., (Mrs David Symon),** FRCS; FRCOG; Professor of Obstetrics and Gynæcology, Ahmadu Bello University Hospital, Zaria, N Nigeria; Hon. Consultant Obstetrician and Gynæcologist, Royal Free Hostpital; Emeritus Consultant, South London Hospital for Women; *b* 29 Aug. 1904; *e d* of Maj.-Gen. Sir John Moore, KCMG, CB, FRCVS; *m* 1941, David Symon (decd); no *c*. *Educ:* Wycombe Abbey Sch., Bucks; Royal Free Hospital School of Medicine. Served RAMC, 1941-45, as Specialist in Gynaecology, in the UK, Belgium and Germany. Mem. BMA; FRSocMed; Mem. Medical Women's Fedn. Associate Mem. The Kennel Club. *Recreations:* walking, field sports; Border Terrier breeder. *Address:* 20 Pilgrim's Lane, NW3.

**MOORE, John Michael,** DSC 1944; Under-Secretary (Principal Establishment and Organisation Officer), Ministry of Transport, since 1966; *b* 2 April 1921; *m* 1st, 1945, Kathleen Pawley (marr. diss. 1960); one *s* one *d*; 2nd, Margaret Ward. *Educ:* Whitgift Middle Sch.; Selwyn Coll., Cambridge. Royal Navy, 1940-46. Royal Humane Society Bronze Medal, 1942. Ministry of Transport, 1946; Joint Principal Private Sec. to Minister (Rt Hon. Harold (later Lord) Watkinson), 1956-59; Asst Sec., 1959. Sec. to Jack Cttee on Rural Bus Services and Geddes Cttee on Carriers' Licensing. *Recreations:* making things, walking hills and mountains. *Address:* High Spinney, Old Coach Road, Wrotham, Kent. *T:* Fairseat 340. *Club:* Royal Automobile.

**MOORE, Kenneth Alfred Edgar,** FCA; Director: National Mutual Life Assurance Society, 1935-70 (Chairman, 1941-69); St Austell Brewery Co. Ltd; Lymington Marina Ltd; *b* 30 Dec. 1894; *er s* of late Edgar Richardson Moore and Rose Salter, Barnet, Herts; *m* 1918, Doris (*d* 1966), *d* of late George Arthur Edell; one *s* three *d*. *Educ:* Highgate Sch. Served European War, HAC and Middlesex Regt. Partner in firm of Edward Moore & Sons, Chartered Accountants, 1921-36; Chm., Trinidad Petroleum Development Co. Ltd, 1937-54; Dep. Chm., Ranks, Hovis-McDougall, 1962-64 (Chm., 1935-57, McDougalls Trust Ltd, merged with Hovis Ltd, 1957; Chm., 1957-64, Hovis-McDougall Ltd). Mem. Council, Inst. of Chartered Accountants, 1951-56. Inventor, Sestrel-Moore Compass, and other navigational equipment. *Publication:* (with Michael Moore, FCA) Company Accounts and Balance Sheets, 1931. *Recreations:* fishing, shooting, sailing. *Address:* West Timber, Bucklers Hard, Beaulieu, Hants. *T:* Bucklers Hard 237. *Clubs:* Brooks's; Royal Yacht Squadron (Cowes); Royal Cruising; Royal Lymington Yacht.

**MOORE, Prof. Leslie Rowsell,** BSc, PhD, DSc, CEng, MIMinE, FGS; Professor of Geology, University of Sheffield, since 1949; Warden of Earnshaw Hall; *b* 23 June 1912; *m* 1946, Margaret Wilson MacRae; one *s*. *Educ:* Midsomer Norton Grammar Sch.; Bristol Univ. Univ. of Bristol, 1930-37; Lecturer and Senior Lecturer, Cardiff, 1939-46; Research Dir, Univ. of Glasgow, 1946-48; Reader in Geology, Univ. of Bristol, 1948-49. *Publications:* contributions to: Quarterly Journal Geol. Soc., London; Geological Magazine; S Wales Inst. Engineers. *Recreations:* soccer, cricket, golf. *Address:* Department of Geology, The University, St George's Square, Sheffield S1 3JD. *T:* 78555.

**MOORE, Marianne Craig;** *b* St Louis, Mo, 15 Nov. 1887; *d* of John Milton Moore and Mary (*née* Warner). *Educ:* Bryn Mawr Coll.; Carlisle Commercial Coll. (Pa). Teacher, Carlisle US Indian Sch., 1911-15; Asst, NY Public Libr., 1921-25; Actg Ed., The Dial, 1925-29. Guggenheim Memorial Foundn Fellowship, 1945; Bollingen Prize in Poetry, 1952; Pulitzer Prize in Verse, 1952; Nat. Medal for Literature, 1968, etc. Holds several hon. doctorates, incl. LittD: Washington Univ., St Louis, 1967; New York Univ., 1967; Harvard, 1969. *Publications:* Poems, 1921; Observations, 1924; Selected Poems, 1935; What Are Years?, 1941; Nevertheless, 1944; Collected Poems, 1951; The Fables of La Fontaine (trans.), 1954; Predilections, 1955; Like a Bulwark, 1956; O to be a Dragon, 1959; A Marianne Reader, 1961; The Arctic Ox, 1965; Tell me, Tell me, 1966; The Complete

Poems of Marianne Moore, 1968; Selected Poems, 1969. *Address:* 7b 35 West 9th Street, New York City, NY 10011, USA.

**MOORE, (Sir) Norman Winfrid** (3rd Bt *cr* 1919; has established his claim but does not use the title); Senior Principal Scientific Officer, Nature Conservancy, since 1965 (Principal Scientific Officer, 1958-65); *b* 24 Feb. 1923; *s* of Sir Alan Hilary Moore, 2nd Bt; *S* father 1959; *m* 1950, Janet, *o d* of late Mrs Phyllis Singer; one *s* two *d*. *Educ:* Eton; Trinity Coll., Cambridge. Served War, 1942-45, Germany and Holland (wounded, POW). *Heir:* *s* Peter Alan Cutlack Moore, *b* 21 Sept. 1951. *Address:* The Farm House, Swavesey, Cambridge.

**MOORE, Patrick,** OBE 1968; free-lance author since 1968; *b* 4 March 1923; *s* of late Capt. Charles Caldwell-Moore, MC, and of Mrs Gertrude Lilian Moore. *Educ:* privately (due to illness). Served with RAF, 1940-45: Navigator, Bomber Command. Concerned in running of a school, 1945-52; free-lance author, 1952-65; Dir of Armagh Planetarium, 1965-68. Vice-Pres., British Astronomical Assoc., 1970. Lorimer Gold Medal, 1962; Goodaese Gold Medal, 1968; Arturo Gold Medal (Italian Astronomical Socs), 1969. *Publications:* 59 books, mainly astronomical, including suns, Myths and Men, 1968; Moon Flight Atlas, 1969; Space, 1970; The Amateur Astronomer, 1970. *Recreations:* cricket, chess, tennis, amateurish playing of piano and xylophone. *Address:* Farthings, 39 West Street, Selsey, Sussex. *Clubs:* Pathfinder, National Book League.

**MOORE, Philip Brian Cecil,** CMG 1966; Assistant Private Secretary to the Queen, since Dec. 1966; *b* 6 April 1921; *s* of late Cecil Moore, Indian Civil Service; *m* 1945, Joan Ursula Greenop; two *d*. *Educ:* Dragon Sch.; Cheltenham Coll.; Oxford Univ. Classical Exhibitioner, Brasenose Coll., Oxford, 1940. RAF Bomber Command, 1940-45. Brasenose Coll., Oxford, 1945-46. Asst Private Sec. to First Lord of Admiralty, 1950-51; Principal Private Sec. to First Lord of Admiralty, 1957-58; Dep. UK Commissioner, Singapore, 1961-63; British Dep. High Comr in Singapore, 1963-65; Chief of Public Relations, MoD, 1965-66. *Recreations:* golf; Rugby football (Oxford Blue, 1945-46; International, England, 1951). *Address:* 5a The Old Barracks, Kensington Palace, W8. *T:* 01-937 2272. *Club:* MCC.

**MOORE, Richard Valentine;** GC 1940; CBE 1963; BSc (Eng); FIMechE; FIEE; Managing Director (Reactor Group), UK Atomic Energy Authority, since 1961; *b* 14 Feb. 1916; *s* of Randall and Ellen Moore; *m* 1944, Ruby Edith Fair; three *s*. *Educ:* Strand Sch., London; London Univ. County of London Electric Supply Co., 1936-39. RNVR, 1939-46; HMS Effingham, 1939-40; HMS President, 1940-41; HMS Dido, 1942-44; British Admiralty Delegn, Washington, DC, 1944-46; Lieut-Comdr 1944. AERE Harwell, 1946-53; Dept of Atomic Energy, Risley, 1953; Design and Construction of Calder Hall, 1953-57; Chief Design Engineer, 1955; UKAEA, 1955; Dir of Reactor Design, 1958-61. Faraday Lectr, 1966. *Publications:* various papers to technical institutions. *Recreations:* golf, gardening. *Address:* Culleen House, Cann Lane, Appleton, Ches. *T:* Warrington 61023. *Club:* Royal Naval Volunteer Reserve.

**MOORE, Robert, (Bobby Moore),** OBE 1967; professional footballer; *b* 12 April 1941; *m* 1962, Christina Elizabeth Dean; one *s* one *d*. Captained: England Youth, at 17 years old (18 caps); England Under 23 (8 caps); England Team, 75 appearances. League debut for West Ham against Manchester United, Sept. 1958; England debut against Peru, 1962; played in World Cup, in Chile, 1962; Captained England for first time, against Czechoslovakia, 1963. Footballer of the Year, 1963-64; Holder of: FA Cup Winners' medal, 1964; European Cup Winners' medal, 1965; named Player of Players in World Cup (England the Winner), 1966. *Address:* 29-31 Redchurch Street, E2. *T:* 01-739 9974.

**MOORE, General Sir Rodney;** *see* Moore, General Sir J. N. R.

**MOORE, Roy,** CBE 1962; *b* 10 Jan. 1908; *s* of Harry Moore and Ellen Harriet Post; *m* 1st, 1934, Muriel Edith (*d* 1959), *d* of late C. E. E. Shill; two *s*; 2nd, 1963, Lydia Elizabeth Newell Park, *widow* of David Park, Berkeley, Calif. *Educ:* Judd Sch., Tonbridge; King's Coll., London. 2nd Cl. Hons English, 1928; AKC 1928; MA 1931; Carter Prize for English Verse. Chief English Master, Mercers' Sch., London, 1931-40. Served War of 1939-45, Squadron Leader RAF Bomber Command, 1941-45. Head Master: Lawrence Sheriff Sch., Rugby, 1945-51; Mill Hill Sch., 1951-67. Fellow King's Coll., London, 1956. *Address:* 138 Santo Tomas Lane, Santa Barbara, Calif. 93103, USA. *Club:* Athenæum.

**MOORE, Thomas,** OBE 1968 (MBE 1951); formerly, Chief Constable of City of Nottingham, and Deputy Chief Constable of Nottinghamshire; *b* 16 March 1903; *s* of Alfred and Fanny Moore; *m* 1932, Norah Carruthers; two *s*. *Educ:* The Hickling Sch., Loughborough. *Recreations:* shooting and fishing. *Address:* Lowcroft, Manvers Grove, Radcliffe-on-Trent, Notts. *T:* Radcliffe 2108. *Club:* United Services (Nottingham).

**MOORE, Lt-Col Sir Thomas (Cecil Russell),** 1st Bt *cr* 1956; Kt 1937; CBE 1920 (OBE 1918); Chairman, Sarakan Products Ltd; *y s* of John Watt Moore, Fintona, Co. Tyrone, and Mary, *d* of late Alexander Kirkpatrick, Closeburn Castle, Dumfriesshire; *m* 1925, Jean (*d* 1945), *yr d* of late William Gemmill, Glasgow, and *widow* of John Hislop Pettigrew, Glasgow; *m* 1950, Penelope, *widow* of R. L. Angus, Ladykirk, Monkton, Ayrshire. *Educ:* Portora Royal Sch.; Trinity Coll., Dublin. Joined Regular Army, 1908; served in France, 1914; on General Headquarters Staff in Ireland, 1916-18; in Russia, 1918-20; in Ireland, 1920-23 (Brevet Major, OBE, Order of White Eagle of Serbia, 4th Class, St Anne of Russia, 2nd Class, St Vladimir of Russia, 4th Class, Hungarian Order of Merit, 2nd class, CBE, despatches twice); retired from Regular Army, 1925; contested (U) Coatbridge Div. of Lanarkshire, 1924; MP (U) Ayr Burgh, 1925-50, Ayr Div. of Ayrshire and Bute, 1950-64. Has sponsored nine Acts of Parliament, including Slaughter of Animals Act and Architects Registration Act. Chm. Home Guard Joint Parly Cttee for both Houses of Parliament during entire period that HG existed during War. Vice-Pres., RSPCA; Trustee, International League for the Protection of Horses; Chm. Anglo-Italian Soc. for the Protection of Animals; Chm. Anglo-Hungarian Fellowship; associated with all leading animal protection socs in this country. Formerly Chm., Eastwoods Ltd and subsids. FRGS; Freeman of City of London; Hon. ARIBA; Past Master Needlemakers' Company. *Recreations:* books, golf. *Address:* 87 Harley House, Regent's Park, NW1. *T:* 01-935 7317; Bogside House, Monkton, Ayrshire. *T:* Prestwick 7417. *Clubs:* St James', Carlton, Garrick; Conservative (Glasgow); County (Ayr).

**MOORE, Sir William Samson,** 2nd Bt, *cr* 1932; *b* 17 April 1891; *s* of Rt Hon. Sir William Moore, 1st Bt, PC, LLD, DL, JP; *S* father, 1944; *m* 1915, Ethel (Grig), *d* of W. L. Wheeler, Lennoxvale, Belfast; one *s* one *d*. *Educ:* RNA, Gosport; Marlborough. Served European War, 1914-18. High Sheriff, Co. Antrim, 1944. DL, JP, Co. Antrim. *Heir: s* William Roger Clotworthy Moore [*b* 17 May 1927; *m* 1954, Gillian, *d* of John Brown, Co. Antrim; one *s* one *d*]. *Address:* Moore Lodge, Ballymoney, NI. *T:* Kilrea 322.

**MOORE-BRABAZON,** family name of **Baron Brabazon of Tara.**

**MOORE-COULSON, Maj.-Gen. Samuel,** CB 1959; ERD 1948; *b* 26 May 1908; *s* of late Samuel Coulson and Laura Elizabeth Moore, Leicestershire; *m* 1936, Joan Hardy, *d* of late J. R. H. Watkiss, London; one *s* two *d*. *Educ:* Wyggeston, Leicester; University Coll., Nottingham. Commnd Royal Leicestershire Regt (SRO), 1930; Asst Master, Queen Elizabeth Gram. Sch., Barnet, 1932-39; served with 2nd Bn Royal Leicestershire Regt, Palestine, 1939-40; Western Desert, 1940-41; Crete, 1941; Syria, 1941; Staff Officer, Lebanon, 1941-43; Canal Zone, 1943-44; War Office (AG1), 1945-46; transferred to RAEC, 1946; War Office (AE7/8), 1946-48; Regular Commn, 1948; SO1 Education, Far East, 1949-52; Dep. Dir of Army Education, 1952-55; Chief Education Officer, Eastern Command, 1955-57; Dir of Army Education, 1957-62; Maj.-Gen., 1957; retired, 1962. Head of Educn and Research Div., FBI, 1962-65; Asst Dir, Educn and Training, CBI, 1965-69; Chief Training and Develt Adviser, Dunlop Co. Ltd, 1969-70. Vice-Chm. Governors, Brit. Soc. for Internat. Understanding, 1964-; Chm., Internat. Youth Science Fortnight, 1963-65, Vice-Pres., 1967-. Hon. Fellow, Corporation of Secretaries, 1966; Mem., adv. Cttee, Duke of Edinburgh Award, 1958-62 and 1968-70. *Recreations:* gardening and photography. *Address:* Broadley Lodge, Mead End, Sway, Lymington, Hants. *T:* Sway 517. *Club:* Army and Navy.

**MOOREHEAD, Alan McCrae,** CBE 1968 (OBE 1946); *b* 22 July 1910; 2nd *s* of Richard Moorehead, Croydon, Vic., Aust.; *m* 1939, Lucy, *yr d* of Dr Vincent Milner, Torquay; two *s* one *d*. *Educ:* Scotch Coll., Melbourne; Melbourne Univ. Editor Melbourne Univ. Magazine, 1929. Worked on various newspapers in Australia and England, mostly as war correspondent, 1930-46, when retired from active journalism to write books. *Publications:* Mediterranean Front, 1941; A Year of Battle, 1943; The End in Africa, 1943; African Trilogy, 1944; Eclipse, 1945; Montgomery, 1946; The Rage of the Vulture, 1948; The Villa Diana, 1951; The Traitors, 1952; Rum Jungle, 1953; A Summer Night, 1954; Gallipoli, 1956 (Sunday Times 1956 Book Prize and Duff Cooper Memorial Award); The Russian Revolution, 1958; No Room in the Ark, 1959; The White Nile, 1960; The Blue Nile, 1962; Cooper's Creek, 1963 (Royal Society of Literature Award); The Fatal Impact, 1966; Darwin and the Beagle, 1969. *Address:* c/o National Bank of Australasia, Australia House, Strand, WC2. *Club:* Garrick.

**MOORER, Admiral Thomas Hinman;** US Navy; DSM 1965, 1967, 1968, 1970; Silver Star 1942; Legion of Merit, 1945; DFC 1942; Purple Heart, 1942; Presidential Unit Citation, 1942; Chairman, Joint Chiefs of Staff, USA, since 1970; *b* Mount Willing, Alabama, 9 Feb. 1912; *s* of Dr R. R. Moorer and Hulda Hill Hinson, Eufaula, Ala; *m* 1935, Carrie Foy Moorer; three *s* one *d*. *Educ:* Naval Aviation Trg Sch.; USN Acad.; Naval War Coll. First ship, 1933. Mining Observer, Cominch in UK, 1943; Strategic Bombing Survey in Japan, 1945; Naval Aide to Asst Sec. of Navy, 1956; CO, USS Salisbury Sound, 1957; Special Asst to CNO, 1959; Comdr, Carrier Div. Six, 1960; Dir, Long Range Objectives Group, CNO, 1962; Comdr Seventh Fleet, 1964; C-in-C: US Pacific Fleet, 1965; Atlantic and US Atlantic Fleet, and Supreme Allied Commander, Atlantic, 1965-67; Chief of Naval Operations, 1967-70. Holds twelve foreign decorations. Hon. Dr of Laws, Auburn; Hon. Dr of Humanities, Stanford. *Recreations:* golfing, fishing, hunting. *Address:* Chairman, Joint Chiefs of Staff, Department of Defense, Washington, DC 20301, USA. *T:* 697-9121. *Clubs:* US Naval Inst. (Annapolis, Md); Army-Navy Country (Arlington, Va); Princess Anne Country (Virginia Beach, Va); Chevy Chase (Chevy Chase, Md).

**MOORMAN, Rt. Rev. John Richard Humpidge;** *see* Ripon, Bishop of.

**MOOS, Sorab Nanabhoy,** CIE 1943; MA Cantab; FRSA; IES (retired); *b* 25 Sept. 1890; *s* of Dr N. A. F. Moos, DSc (Edinburgh), FRSE; *m* 1916, Makee Petit; two *s* one *d*. *Educ:* Elphinstone Coll., Bombay; King's Coll., Cambridge. Professor Mathematics and Physics, Victoria Jubilee Technical Coll., 1915-18; Inspector of Schs, 1918-32; Dep. Dir Public Instruction, 1932-39; Dir, Public Instruction, Bombay Province, 1939-45; Mem. Public Service Commission, Bombay-Sind, 1946-47. *Publications:* various articles and reports on Education. *Recreations:* golf, tennis. *Address:* Emsworth, Pali Hill, Bandra, Bombay, India. *T:* Bombay 534003. *Clubs:* Poona, Turf Club of Western India (Poona); Ripon, Willingdon (Bombay).

**MOOSONEE, Bishop of,** since 1963; **Rt. Rev. James Augustus Watton,** BA, DD; *b* 23 Oct. 1915; *s* of Geo. A. Watton and Ada Wynn; *m* 1941, Irene A. Foster; one *s* two *d*. *Educ:* Univ. of Western Ontario (BA); Huron Coll. (STh); Post graduate Univ. of Michigan. Deacon 1938; Priest 1939. DD (*jure dig.*), 1955. *Address:* Bishopstope, Schumacher, Ont., Canada. *T:* Timmins AM-4-0641.

**MOOTHAM, Sir Orby Howell,** Kt 1962; Chairman, Medical Appeals Tribunal, since 1963; Deputy Chairman: Essex Quarter Sessions since 1964; Kent Quarter Sessions, since 1965; Surrey Quarter Sessions, since 1970; *b* 17 Feb. 1901; *s* of Delmé George Mootham, ARIBA; *m* 1931, Maria Augusta Elizabeth Niemöller; one *s* one *d*. *Educ:* Leinster House Sch., Putney; London Univ. MSc (Econ). Called to Bar, Inner Temple, 1926 (Yarborough-Anderson Schol., 1924; hon. Bencher, 1958). An Advocate of Rangoon High Court, 1927-40; DJAG, Army in Burma, 1940-41, thereafter service in Dept of JAG in India and as Chief Judicial Officer, Brit. Mil. Admin. (despatches). Actg Judge, Rangoon High Court, 1945-46; Judge, Allahabad High Court, 1946-55; Chief Justice, 1955-61. Chm., Allahabad Univ. Enquiry Cttee, 1953-54; Legal Adviser's Dept, CRO, 1961-63; Mem. Governing Body, Froebel Educational Inst. *Publications:* Burmese Buddhist Law, 1939. Articles in Brit. Year Book of Internat. Law and other legal jls. *Recreation:* map collecting. *Address:* 3 Paper Buildings, Temple, EC4. *T:* 01-353 1310. *Club:* Athenæum.

**MORAES, Dom;** Indian poet and author; *b* 1938; *s* of Frank Moraes (Editor of the Indian Express and biographer of Nehru); *m* 1963, Judith St John; one *s*. *Educ:* Jesus Coll.,

Oxford. Read English, 1956-59. Took up residence in England at age of 16, after world-wide travel and a 2-yr stay in Ceylon. *Publications:* A Beginning (poems), 1957 (Hawthornden Prize, 1958); Gone Away (Travel), 1960; Poems, 1960; John Nobody (poems), 1965; The Brass Serpent (trans from Hebrew Poetry), 1964; Poems 1955-65 (collected poems), 1966; My Son's Father (autobiography), 1968. *Recreations:* watching cricket, travel. *Address:* c/o Nova, Tower House, Southampton Street, WC1.

**MORAN,** 1st Baron, *cr* 1943, of Manton; **Charles McMoran Wilson,** Kt 1938; MC; Consulting Physician, St Mary's Hospital; *b* Skipton-in-Craven, Yorks; *s* of John Forsythe Wilson, MD; *m* 1919, Dorothy, MBE, *d* of late Dr S. F. Dufton; two *s.* MD London (Gold Medal), 1913; Formerly: Mem. of Senate and Hon. Sec. Faculty of Medicine, Univ. of London; Examiner in Medicine, Univs of Cambridge and Birmingham; Consultant Adviser, Ministry of Health; Chm. Advisory Cttee on Distinction Awards for Consultants. Mem., Association of Physicians; Fellow of Royal Society of Medicine; Mem., Med. Soc. of London and of Harveian Soc.; Medical Officer attached 1st Batt. Royal Fusiliers, 1914-17; Medical Officer i/c medical side, 7th Stationary Hospital, Boulogne, 1917-18; Major RAMC (MC, Italian Silver Medal for Military Valour, despatches twice); Dean, St Mary's Hospital Medical Sch., 1920-45; Pres., Royal College of Physicians, 1941-50. Chm. Army Med. Advisory Bd. Hon. FRCPE; Hon. FFPSG; Hon. FACP; Hon. FRACP. *Publications:* The Anatomy of Courage, 1945; Winston Churchill, The Struggle for Survival, 1966; Med. papers and articles on Medical Education. *Heir: s* Hon. (Richard) John (McMoran) Wilson, *qv. Address:* 25 Bryanston Square, W1. *T:* 01-723 2005; Marshalls Manor, Maresfield, Uckfield, Sussex. *T:* Nutley 2584. *Club:* Athenæum.

**MORAN, Professor Frances E.;** Regius Professor of Laws, Trinity College, Dublin, 1944-63, retired; Professor of Equity Pleading and Practice, King's Inns, Dublin, 1932-68, retired; Professorial Representative on Board of Trinity College, 1958-62; Senior Counsel; Past President, International Federation of University Women; *b* Dublin, 6 Dec. 1893; 2nd *d* of late Senator James and late Elizabeth Moran, St James', Clontarf, Dublin; unmarried. *Educ:* Dominican Coll. and Trinity Coll., Dublin. Called to Bar, 1924; took silk, 1941; Reid Prof. in Law Sch., Trinity Coll., 1925-30; Lecturer in Law, 1930-34; Prof. of Laws, 1934-44; Hon. Fellow, 1968. Hon. Bencher, King's Inns, 1969. Hon. LLD, Queen's Univ., Belfast, 1957. *Recreations:* walking, reading, and foreign travel. *Address:* St James', Howth Road, Clontarf, Dublin. *T:* 339516.

**MORAN, Thomas,** CBE 1946; ScD; DSc; Scientific Adviser, Home Grown Cereals Authority, 1966-69; Director of Research, Research Association of British Flour Millers, 1939-66; *b* 1899; *s* of late Thomas Moran; *m* 1st, 1924, Elizabeth Ann Flynn (*d* 1952); one *s* two *d*; 2nd, 1959, June Patricia Martin. *Educ:* St Francis Xavier's Coll., Liverpool; Liverpool Univ.; Gonville and Caius Coll., Cambridge. Sir John Willox Schol., 1920, Univ. Scholar, 1920, Liverpool Univ.; served European War, 1914-18, with Liverpool Scottish (KLR), 1917-19; with DSIR at Low Temperature Station, Cambridge, 1922-39. Mem. Advisory Scientific Cttee, Food Defence Plans Dept, 1938-39; Dir of Research and Dep. Scientific Adviser, Min. of Food, 1940-46. Mem. Council, British Nutrition Foundation, 1967. *Publications:* Bread (with Lord Horder and Sir Charles Dodds); papers on different aspects of Food Science in scientific and medical journals, 1922-; reports on applied food research published by HM Stationery Office. *Recreations:* gardening, golf. *Address:* 5 Amhurst Court, Grange Road, Cambridge. *T:* Cambrdige 54548. *Club:* Savage.

**MORAND, Paul;** *b* Paris, 1889; *m* Helen Chrissoveloni. *Educ:* in Paris; Oxford Univ. In Diplomacy, 1912-44 (France); Secretary of Embassy in London, 1913-16; Rome, 1917-18; Madrid, 1918-20; French Chargé d'Affaires in Siam, 1925; French Commissioner on the Danube, 1938; Head of French Mission in England of Economic Warfare, Sept. 1939; Minister Plenipotentiary in London, 1940; Minister at Bucarest, 1943; Ambassador at Berne, 1944; started a literary career in 1920. Mem., Académie Française, 1968. *Publications:* Poems (1919-21); Green Shoots, 1922; Open all Night, 1923; Closed all Night, 1924; Europe at love, 1925; Lewis and Irene, 1926; A Frenchman's London, 1933; Bucarest, 1935; L'Homme pressé, 1941; Life of Maupassant, 1942; Montociel, 1945; Journal d'un attaché d'ambassade, 1948; Proust: Le Visiteur du soir, 1949; The Flagellant of Seville, 1951; Fouquet, 1961; The New London, 1962; The Habsburg, 1963; Tais-toi, 1965; Nouvelles des yeux, Nouvelles du cœur, 1965. *Address:* Château de l'Aile, Vevey, Switzerland. *Club:* Automobile of France.

**MORANT, Dame Mary (Maud),** DBE 1969, (**Sister Mary Regis**) (to be addressed as Sr Mary Regis, DBE); Headmistress, Roman Catholic Schools, 1933-70; retired, 1970, to Convent of Notre Dame, Battersea, to give social service; *b* 21 Dec. 1903; *d* of Stephen Augustus and Mary Morant. *Educ:* Notre Dame High Sch. and Notre Dame Coll. of Educn, Mt Pleasant. Asst, Notre Dame Demonstration Sch., 1924; Asst, St Mary's, Battersea, 1929; Headmistress, St John's, Wigan, 1933; Headmistress, Central Sch., Embakwe Mission, S Rhodesia, 1938; Vice-Pres., Chikuni Trg. Coll., N Rhodesia, 1946; Headmistress: St Peter Claver, Kroonstad, 1948; Lowe House, St Helens, Lancs, 1956; Our Lady's, Eldon St, Liverpool, 1961; Preparatory School, Convent of Notre Dame, Birkdale, 1969-70. Pro Pontifice et Ecclesia Medal, 1969, from HH Pope Paul VI. *Recreations:* drama, music. *Address:* Convent of Notre Dame, 8 Battersea Park Road, SW8.

**MORAVIA, Alberto;** Italian author; *b* 28 Nov. 1907; *s* of Carlo and Teresa de Marsanich; *m* 1941, Elsa Morante. Chevalier de la Légion d'Honneur (France), 1952. *Publications: novels:* Gli indifferenti, 1929 (Eng. trans.: The Time of Indifference, 1953); Le ambizioni sbagliate, 1935; La mascherata, 1941 (Eng. trans.: The Fancy Dress Party, 1948); Agostino, 1944 (Eng. trans.: Agostino, 1947); La Romana, 1947 (Eng. trans.: The Woman of Rome, 1949); La disubbidienza, 1948 (Eng. trans: Disobedience, 1950); L'amore Coniugale, 1949 (Eng. trans.: Conjugal Love, 1951); Il Conformista, 1951 (Eng. Trans.: The Conformist, 1952); La Ciociara, 1957 (Eng. trans.: Two Women, 1958); La Noia, 1961 (Viareggio Prize) (Eng. trans.: The Empty Canvas, 1961); The Fetish, 1965; L'attenzione, 1965 (Eng. trans.: The Lie, 1966); *short stories:* (and selections in Eng.); La bella vita, 1935; L'imbroglio, 1937; I sogni del pigro, 1940; L'amante infelice, 1943; L'epidemia, 1945; Racconti, 1952 (Eng. trans.: Bitter Honeymoon, and the Wayward Wife, 1959); Racconti romani, 1954 (Eng. trans.: Roman Tales, 1956); Nuovi racconti romani, 1959; L'automa, 1964; Una cosa è una cosa,

1966; *essays:* L'uomo come fine e altri saggi, 1964 (Eng. trans.: Man as an End, 1966); *plays:* Beatrice Cenci, 1955; Il mondo è quello che è, 1966; Il dio Kurt; *travel:* La rivoluzione culturale in Cina, 1967 (Eng. trans. The Red Book and The Great Wall, 1968). *Address:* Lungotevere della Vittoria 1, Rome, Italy. *T:* 378836.

**MORAY,** 19th Earl **of,** cr 1561; **Archibald John Morton Stuart;** Lord Abernethy and Strathearn, 1562; Lord Doune, 1581; Baron of St Colme, 1611; Baron Stuart (G. Brit.), 1796; *b* 14 Nov. 1894; 2nd *s* of 17th Earl and Edith Douglas (*d* 1945), *d* of late Rear-Adm. George Palmer; *S* brother 1943; *m* 1922, Mabel Helen Maud Wilson (*d* 1968); three *s* (one *d* decd). *Educ:* RNC Osborne and Dartmouth. Entered RN 1907; Lieut-Comdr (retired) 1923. Lived and farmed in Bechuanaland Protectorate, 1923-43. *Heir: s* Lord Doune, *qv. Address:* Darnaway Castle, Forres, Morayshire. *T:* Forres 120. *Clubs:* White's, Naval and Military; New (Edinburgh); Rand (Johannesburg).

*See also Baron Hillingdon, Viscount Stuart of Findhorn.*

**MORAY, Edward Bruce D.;** *see* Dawson-Moray.

**MORAY, ROSS, and CAITHNESS, Dean of;** *see* Gow, Very Rev. W. C.

**MORAY WILLIAMS, Barbara,** ARE, ARCA; (Frú Barbara Arnason); Artist; *b* Petersfield, Hants, 19 April, 1911; *d* of A. Moray Williams, OBE, MA, and Mabel Lizzie Williams; *m* 1937, Magnús A. Arnason, artist; one *s. Educ:* Privately. *Address:* Kopavogi, Iceland. *T:* Reykjavik 40218.

**MORCOM, Rev. Anthony John;** Vicar of St Mary the Less, Cambridge, since 1966; *b* 24 July 1916; *s* of late Dr Alfred Farr Morcom and Sylvia Millicent Morcom (*née* Birchenough); *m* 1st, 1955, Pamela Cappel Bain (*d* 1963); 2nd, 1965, Richenda, *widow* of Frederick Williams. *Educ:* Repton; Clare Coll., Cambridge; Cuddesdon Coll. Curate: St Mary Magdalene, Paddington, 1939-42; St Mary the Virgin, Pimlico, 1942-47; Domestic Chaplain to the Bishop of London, 1947-55; Archdeacon of Middx, 1953-66; Vicar of St Cyprian's, Clarence Gate, 1955-66. *Recreation:* travel. *Address:* 33 Porson Road, Cambridge. *T:* Cambridge 50602. *Clubs:* United University, MCC.

**MORCOS, Bey, Professor Zaki,** FRCVS, MVSc, DVH; Director, Coptic Hospital Laboratory, Cairo; formerly Professor of Bacteriology and Sub-Dean, Cairo Veterinary College, Egypt, and member of Fuad University Senate; *b* 31 July 1894; *s* of Malaty Morcos; *m* 1927, E. Aslett Clark, Algburth, Liverpool; two *s. Educ:* Cairo; Liverpool; Berlin (Robert Koch Laboratory); London and Paris (Pasteur Lab.). Veterinary Inspector, Luxor Quarantine, Egypt; Lieut AVC, EEF; Senior Asst, Bacteriological Laboratory Veterinary Service. Egyptian Veterinary Assoc. Board Mem.; Mem. Veterinary Council of Egypt. *Publications:* Bacteriology (English); Poultry Diseases (Arabic); Research on Poultry and Animal Diseases published in Vet. Record, Vet. Jl, Jl of Amer. Bacteriologists, Egyptian Med. Jl, Amer. Vet. Assoc. Jl and Amer. Jl of Vet. Medicine, etc; Editor, Egyptian Vet. Jl. *Address:* 5 Mehalla Avenue, Heliopolis, Egypt. *TA:* Morcos, Veterinary School, Egypt. *T:* 96887.

**MORDAUNT, Lt-Col Sir Nigel John,** 13th Bt, *cr* 1611; MBE 1945; RA; Member of London Stock Exchange; *b* 9 May 1907; *e s* of late E. C. Mordaunt and Cicely Marion, 2nd *d* of Henry Tubb; *S* uncle 1939; *m* 1938, Anne, *d* of late Arthur F. Tritton, Denford Mill, Hungerford, Berks; three *s* one *d. Educ:* Wellington Coll.; Christ Church, Oxford. Served War of 1939-45 (MBE). *Heir: s* Richard Nigel Charles Mordaunt [*b* 12 May 1940; *m* 1964, Myriam Atchia; one *s* one *d*]. *Address:* Elsenham Place, Bishops Stortford, Herts. *T:* Stansted 2344. *Clubs:* City of London, Buck's.

**MORDECAI, Sir John Stanley,** Kt 1962; CMG 1956; General Manager, Jamaica Industrial Development Corp., since 1962; *b* 21 Oct. 1903; *s* of Segismund T. and Marie A. Mordecai; *m* 1st, 1929, Pearl K. Redmond (*d* 1947); two *s* four *d*; 2nd, 1951, Phyllis M. Walcott; two *s. Educ:* Wolmer's Boys' High Sch., Jamaica; Syracuse Univ., New York, USA. MSc (Pub. Adm.). Entered public service as clerical asst in Treasury, Jamaica, 1920; Finance officer, 1942; asst treasurer, 1944; asst sec. in charge of local government secretariat, 1946; trade administrator and sec. trade control board, 1949; principal, seconded to Colonial Office, 1950; Executive Sec. Regional Economic Cttee of the West Indies, British Guiana and British Honduras, with headquarters in Barbados, 1952-56; Federal Sec., West Indies Federation, 1956-60 (Special work on preparatory arrangements for Federation, 1955-58); Dep. Gov.-Gen., WI Fedn, 1960-62; Chm., Jamaica Public Services Commn, 1962. *Publication:* The West Indies, 1968. *Recreations:* horse racing, music. *Address:* 1 Beethoven Avenue, Kingston 8, Jamaica.

**MORDELL, Louis Joel,** MA Cantab; MSc Manchester; FRS; Emeritus Professor of Pure Mathematics in the University of Cambridge (Sadleirian Professor of Pure Mathematics, 1945-53); Fellow of St John's College since 1945; *b* Philadelphia, Pa, USA, 28 Jan. 1888; *m*; one *s* one *d. Educ:* Central High Sch., Philadelphia; St John's Coll., Cambridge. Formerly lecturer at Birkbeck Coll., London, and lecturer and reader in Mathematics at Manchester Univ.; Visiting Prof. at Chicago Univ., Summer Term, 1923, and at Univ. of Pennsylvania, Fall Term, 1950; Fielden Prof. of Pure Mathematics in the Univ. of Manchester, 1923-45; Lecturer at Summer Seminar of Canadian Math. Congress, Toronto, 1947; Visiting Prof., Univ. of Toronto, 1953-55; Visiting Lecturer, Italian Internat. summer course, Varenna, Lake Como, 1955; Visiting Prof., Univ. Coll. of Ghana, 1957. Nuffield Visiting Professor: University Coll., Ibadan, 1957, Mount Allison Univ., NB, Canada, 1958-59; Visiting Professor: Colorado Univ., 1959-60; Notre Dame Univ., 1960-61; Univ. of Arizona, from 1961 to Spring Semester, 1964; Univ. of Illinois, 1964-65; Catholic Univ. of America, 2nd Semester 1965-66; Waterloo Univ., Ontario, (2nd Semester), 1966-67; Univ. of Toronto, 1st Semester, 1968-69. In recent years has lectured in maths at 180 Univs and Instns in Europe, India, E and W Africa, Canada and USA; De Morgan Medal, 1941, and Berwick Prize, 1946, London Mathematical Soc. Pres. London Mathematical Soc., 1943-45; Sylvester Medal of the Royal Soc., 1949. Foreign member: Norwegian Academy of Science at Oslo; Academy of Science at Bologna; Acad. of Science at Uppsala. Hon. LLD Glasgow, 1956; Hon. DSc Mount Allison Univ., 1959; Hon. DMath Waterloo Univ., 1970. *Publications:* Three Lectures on Fermat's Last Theorem, 1921; A Chapter on the Theory of Numbers, 1947; Reflections of a Mathematician, 1958; Diophantine Equations, 1969; numerous papers on the Theory of Numbers and allied subjects in many math. jls. *Recreations:* walking, swimming, and bridge. *Address:* St John's College, Cambridge; 1 Bulstrode Gardens, Madingley Road, Cambridge. *T:* Cambridge 54281. *Club:* Athenæum.

**MORE, Jasper,** JP, DL; MP (C) Ludlow since 1960; Vice-Chamberlain, HM Household, since 1970; *b* 31 July 1907; *s* of Thomas Jasper Mytton More and Lady Norah, *d* of 5th Marquess of Sligo; *m* 1944, Clare Mary Hope-Edwardes, Netley, Shropshire, *d* of Capt. Vincent Coldwell, 4th Indian Cavalry; no *c*. *Educ:* Eton (Schol.); King's Coll., Cambridge. Barrister, Lincoln's Inn, 1930, and Middle Temple, 1931; Harmsworth Law Schol., 1932; in practice, 1930-39. Served War of 1939-45: in Min. of Economic Warfare, MAP and Light Metals Control, 1939-42; commissioned as legal officer in Military Govt, 1943; with Allied Commission (Italy), 8th Army and 5th Army, 1943-45; Legal Adviser, Military Govt, Dodecanese, 1946. An Asst Government Whip, Feb.-Oct 1964; Asst Opposition Whip, 1964-70. JP Salop, 1950; DL Salop, 1955; CC Salop, 1958-. *Publications:* The Land of Italy, 1949; The Mediterranean, 1956. *Recreations:* shooting, fishing, riding, building, travel and landscape gardening. *Address:* Linley Hall, Bishop's Castle, Shropshire; D5 Albany, W1. *Clubs:* Travellers', Brooks's.

**MORE, Kenneth (Gilbert),** CBE 1970; Actor; *b* Gerrards Cross, Bucks, 20 Sept. 1914; *s* of Charles Gilbert More and Edith Winifred (*née* Watkins); *m* 1st, 1940, Beryl Johnstone (marr. diss.) (she *d* 1969); one *d*; 2nd, 1952, Mabel Edith Barkby (marr. diss.); one *d*; 3rd, 1968, Angela McDonagh Douglas. *Educ:* Victoria Coll., Jersey. First appeared on stage in a revue sketch, Windmill Theatre, 1936. Served War of 1939-45, Lieut RNVR. Returned to stage and took part of Rev. Arthur Platt in revival of And No Birds Sing, Aldwych, Nov. 1946; Eddie, in Power Without Glory, New Lindsey and Fortune, 1947; George Bourne, in Peace In Our Time, Lyric, 1948; John, in The Way Things Go, Phoenix, 1950; Freddie Page, in The Deep Blue Sea, Duchess, 1952; Peter Pounce, in Out of the Crocodile, Phoenix, 1963; Crichton, in Our Man Crichton, Shaftesbury, 1964; Hugh, in The Secretary Bird, Savoy, 1968; Sir Robert Morton in The Winslow Boy, Haymarket, 1970. First appeared in films, 1948, in Scott of the Antarctic. Films include: Chance of a Lifetime; Genevieve; Doctor in the House (Brit. Film Acad. Award as best actor, 1954); Raising a Riot; The Deep Blue Sea (Venice Volpi Cup, as best actor, 1955); Reach for the Sky (Picturegoer annual award for best male performance, as Douglas Bader, also Belgian Prix Femina), 1956; The Admirable Crichton, 1957; Next to No Time, 1958; A Night to Remember, 1958; The Sheriff of Fractured Jaw, 1958; The Thirty Nine Steps, 1959; North West Frontier, 1959; Sink the Bismarck!, 1960; Man in the Moon, 1960; The Greengage Summer, 1961; The Longest Day, 1962; Some People, 1962 (For the Duke of Edinburgh's Award Scheme); We Joined the Navy, 1962; The Comedy Man, 1963; Dark of the Sun, 1967; Oh! What A Lovely War, 1968; Battle of Britain, 1969; Scrooge, 1970. First Eurovision Production by BBC: Heart to Heart, 1963. Played Young Jolyon in The Forsyte Saga, BBC TV, 1966-67. *Publications:* Happy Go Lucky (autobiography), 1959; Kindly Leave the Stage, 1965. *Recreation:* golf. *Address:* Bute House, 9 Ladbroke Terrace, W11. *Club:* Garrick.

**MOREAU, Jeanne;** actress; *b* 23 Jan. 1928; *d* of Anatole-Désiré Moreau and Kathleen Moreau (*née* Buckley); *m* 1949, Jean-Louis Richard (marr. diss.); one *s*. *Educ:* Collège Edgar-Quinet; Conservatoire national d'art dramatique. Comédie Française, 1948-52; Théâtre National Populaire, 1953. Films include: Les amants, 1958; Les liaisons dangereuses, 1959; Moderato cantabile, 1960; Le dialogue des Carmelites, 1960; Jules et Jim, 1961; La Baie des Anges, 1963; Journal d'une femme de chambre, 1963; Viva Maria, 1965; Mademoiselle, 1966; The Sailor from Gibraltar, 1966; The Immortal Story, 1966; Great Catherine, 1967; The Bride wore Black, 1967. Chevalier des Arts et des Lettres, 1966. *Recreation:* reading. *Address:* 9 rue du Cirque, Paris 8e, France. *T:* Elysées 13-33.

**MOREING, Captain Algernon Henry;** formerly partner in Bewick, Moreing & Co., mining engineers, London; *b* 30 Sept. 1889; *s* of late Charles Algernon Moreing and Helena Marian, *d* of Edward Harcourt Longden, HEICS; *m* 1925, Dorothy Maude, *er d* of late J. Holman, JP, of Roswarne, Camborne. *Educ:* Winchester; Trinity Coll., Cambridge, MA. Captain RA (TA); served in France, 1915-18 (despatches); MP (Coalition L) Buckrose Div. of Yorks, Dec. 1918-22; (NL) Camborne Div. of Cornwall, 1922-23; (Constitutional) Camborne, 1924-29; Parliamentary Private Sec. to Rt Hon. Sir Eric Geddes, Minister of Transport, 1920; recalled for military duty, 1940. Past-Master of the Merchant Taylors' Company. *Address:* Fysh House, Bures, Suffolk. *T:* Bures 324.

**MORELL, Mrs A.;** *see* Greenwood, Joan.

**MORETON,** family name of **Earl of Ducie.**

**MORETON, Lord; David Leslie Moreton;** *b* 20 Sept. 1951; *s* and *heir* of 6th Earl of Ducie, *qv*.

**MORETON, John Oscar,** CMG 1966; MC 1944; HM Diplomatic Service; Ambassador to Vietnam, since 1969; *b* 28 Dec. 1917; *s* of Rev. C. O. Moreton; *m* 1945, Margaret Katherine, *d* of late Sir John Fryer, KBE, FRS; three *d*. *Educ:* St Edward's Sch., Oxford; Trinity Coll., Oxford (MA). War Service with 99th (Royal Bucks Yeomanry) Field Regt RA, 1939-46: France, Belgium, 1940; India, Burma, 1942-45. Colonial Office, 1946; Private Sec. to Perm. Under-Sec. of State, 1949-50; seconded to Govt of Kenya, 1953-55; Private Sec. to Sec. of State for Colonies (Rt Hon. Alan Lennox-Boyd), 1955-59; transf. to CRO, 1960; Counsellor, British High Commn, Lagos, 1961-64; IDC 1965; Asst Under-Sec. of State, CRO, 1965-66, CO 1966-68, FCO 1968-69. *Recreations:* tennis; formerly athletics (Oxford Blue and International, 880 yds, 1939). *Address:* c/o Foreign and Commonwealth Office, King Charles Street, SW1. *Club:* Travellers'.

**MOREY, Rev. Dom Adrian,** MA, DPhil; FRHistS; Superior, Downside House of Studies, Cambridge; *b* 10 April 1904; *s* of late John Morey and Charlotte Helen Morey (*née* Nelson). *Educ:* Latymer Upper Sch.; Christ's Coll., Cambridge (Schol.); Univ. of Munich. 1st cl. hons Hist. Tripos Pts I and II, Cambridge. Housemaster, Downside Sch., 1934; Bursar, Downside Abbey and Sch., 1946-50; Headmaster, Oratory Sch., Reading, 1953-67; Rector, St Wulstan's, Little Malvern, Worcs, 1967-69. *Publications:* Bartholomew of Exeter, 1937; (with Prof. C. N. Brooke) Gilbert Foliot and His Letters, 1965; The Letters and Charters of Gilbert Foliot, 1967; articles in English Hist. Review, Jl Eccles. History, Cambridge Hist. Jl. *Address:* Benet House, Mount Pleasant, Cambridge. *T:* Cambridge 54637.

**MORFEE, Air Vice-Marshal Arthur Laurence,** CB 1946; CBE 1943; retired; *b* 27 May 1897; *s* of George Thomas Morfee; *m* Estelle Lillian, *d* of William Edward Hurd of South Carolina, USA; one *s* one *d*. *Educ:* Finchley County Sch. Canadian Army from 1915; served France and Belgium, 19th Can. Inf. (wounded); joined RAF 1918; Air board (Civil Service), 1921-24; appointed RCAF 1924; psa Andover, Eng., 1933; Air Vice-Marshal, 1945; retd 1949. Dir of Air Cadet League; Governor Corps of Commissionaires. US Legion of Merit (Comdr), 1949. *Address:* Annapolis Royal, NS, Canada.

**MORGAN;** *see* Vaughan-Morgan.

**MORGAN, Alun Michael,** CMG 1957; Assistant Under-Secretary of State, Overseas Division, Department of Employment and Productivity, since 1968; *b* 31 March 1915; *s* of Richard Michael Morgan, Rhayader; *m* 1958, Hilary Jane, *d* of late Eric Wilkinson, OBE, Kelsale, Suffolk. *Educ:* St Paul's Sch.; Magdalen Coll., Oxford. Min. of Labour, 1937; Served with Royal Fusiliers, 1940; with Special Forces, 1942-45 (Lieut-Col); Dep. Chief, Manpower Div., CCG, 1946. Asst Sec., Min. of Labour and Nat. Service, 1947; Manpower Counsellor, OEEC, 1948; Counsellor and Labour Attaché, HM Embassy, Washington, 1957-60; Under-Sec., Min. of Labour, 1964. *Address:* 15 Hasker Street, SW3. *Club:* United University.

**MORGAN, Arthur Eustace,** MA; Hon. LLD; FRSC; Warden, Toynbee Hall, 1954-63; Chairman, Purimachos, Ltd; President, The National Boys' Club, 1963-65; *b* Bristol, 26 July 1886; 5th *s* of John Charles Morgan, of HBM Consular Service, and Elizabeth Reid Livingstone-Learmonth; *m* 1909, Mabel Eugénie, *d* of Thomas Walter Warren Melhuish; four *d*. *Educ:* University Coll., Bristol; Trinity Coll., Dublin. Asst Lectr, Univ. of Bristol, 1909-10; Lectr in English Language and Literature, University Coll., Exeter, 1910-19; Professor, 1919-24; Professor of English Language and Literature, Univ. of Sheffield, 1924-26; Principal of the University Coll., Hull, 1926-35; Principal and Vice-Chancellor of McGill Univ., Montreal, 1935-37; Chief Special Officer for National Service, Ministry of Labour, 1939; District Commissioner for the Special Areas (Durham and Tyneside) 1939; Regional Information Officer, Ministry of Information, Newcastle on Tyne, 1939-41; Asst Sec., Ministry of Labour and National Service, 1941-45; Educational Controller, British Council, 1945-50; RA, 1915-19; Captain, Gunnery Instructor No 2 RFA Cadet Sch. (despatches). Has lectured in many parts of the world. *Publications:* Scott and his Poetry; Tendencies of Modern English Drama; First Part of Henry IV, Arden Edition of Shakespeare (with R. P. Cowl); English Plays, 1660-1820; The Needs of Youth (Report to King George's Jubilee Trust), 1939; Young Citizen, 1943; sundry literary and educational pamphlets, papers and articles. *Address:* 34 Downs Park West, Bristol 6. *T:* 626009.

*See also J. R. James.*

**MORGAN, Instr Rear-Adm. Brinley John;** Director of the Naval Education Service since 1970; *b* 3 April 1916; *s* of Thomas Edward Morgan and Mary Morgan (*née* Parkhouse); *m* 1945, Margaret Mary Whittles; three *s*. *Educ:* Abersychan Grammar Sch.; University Coll., Cardiff. Entered Royal Navy as Instr Lt, 1939. Served War of 1939-45: Cruisers Emerald and Newcastle, 1939-41; Aircraft Carrier Formidable, 1941-43; Naval Weather Service (Admty Forecast Section), 1943-45. Staff of C-in-C Medit., 1945-48; HQ, Naval Weather Service, 1948-50; Staff of Flag Officer Trg Sqdn in HM Ships Vanguard, Indefatigable and Implacable, 1950-52; Instr Comdr, 1951; Lectr, RN Coll., Greenwich, 1952-54; Headmaster, RN Schools, Malta, 1954-59; Instr Captain, 1960; Staff of Dir, Naval Educn Service, 1959-61 and 1963-64; Sen. Officers' War Course, 1961; HMS Ganges, 1961-63; Dean, RN Engineering Coll., Manadon, 1964-69; Instr Rear-Adm., 1970. *Recreations:* tennis, squash. *Address:* 11 Selwyn House, Manor Fields, Putney Hill, SW15. *T:* 01-789 3269. *Club:* United Service.

**MORGAN, Mrs Charles (L.);** *see* Vaughan, Hilda.

**MORGAN, Sir Clifford Naunton,** Kt 1966; MS; FRCS; FRCOG; Hon. FRCSI; Hon. FACS; Commander of the Order of the Star of the North (Sweden); Hon. Consulting Surgeon: St Bartholomew's Hospital; St Mark's Hospital for Diseases of the Rectum and Colon; Hospital for Tropical Diseases; Surgeon, King Edward VII's Hospital for Officers; Consulting Surgeon: RAF; (Colon and Rectum) RN; *b* 20 Dec. 1901; *s* of late Thomas Naunton Morgan, Penygraig; *m* 1930, Ena Muriel Evans; two *s* one *d*. *Educ:* Royal Masonic Sch.; University Coll., Cardiff; Univ. of London (St Bartholomew's Hosp.). MB 1924; FRCS 1926. Surgeon: Metropolitan Hosp., 1930; Royal Masonic Hosp.; St Bartholomew's Hospital: Demonstrator of Anatomy, Med. Coll., 1929; Chief Asst to a Surgical Unit, 1930; Casualty Surgeon, 1936; Asst Dir of Surgery, Professorial Unit, 1937. Lectr and Examr in Surgery, Univ. of London; Examr in Surgery, Univs of Cambridge, Glasgow, and Edinburgh. Officer i/c Surgical Divs, MEF, 1941-43 (despatches); Cons. Surgeon: Persia-Iraq Force, 1943-45; E Africa Comd, 1945; Hon. Col and late Brig., AMS. Twice Pres., Section of Proctology, Royal Soc. of Medicine; Mem. Council, RCS of England, 1953-68 (Vice-Pres., 1963-65); Vice-Chm., Imperial Cancer Research Fund. Sims Commonwealth Travelling Prof., 1963; Bradshaw Lectr, RCS, 1964; Vicary Lectr, 1967. Fellow, Assoc. of Surgeons of Great Britain and Ireland (Pres., 1968); Hon. FRCSI; Hon. Fellow, Amer. Surgical Assoc.; Amer. Protologic Soc.; For. Mem., Académie de Chirurgie; Hon. Member: Pennsylvania Proctologic Soc.; Société Nationale Française de Proctologie; Sociedades Argentina, Brasileira and Chilena de Proctologia; Med. Assoc. of Thessaloniki; Burmese Med. Assoc. *Publications:* various chapters in British Surgical Practice and other surgical Text Books. Contributor St Mark's Hosp. Centenary Vol., 1935. Many articles on Surgery of the Colon and Rectum in Brit. and Amer. Jls. *Recreation:* farming. *Address:* 149 Harley Street, W1. *T:* 01-935 4444; 106 Lord's View, St John's Wood Road, NW8. *T:* 01-289 1414; Rolfe's Farm, Inkpen, Berks. *T:* 259.

**MORGAN, (Dafydd) Elystan;** MP (Lab) Cardiganshire since 1966; *b* 7 Dec. 1932; *s* of Dewi Morgan and late Mrs Olwen Morgan; *m* 1959, Alwen, *d* of William E. Roberts; one *s* one *d*. *Educ:* Ardwyn Grammar Sch., Aberystwyth; UCW, Aberystwyth. LLB Hons Aberystwyth, 1953. Research at Aberystwyth and Solicitor's Articles, 1953-57; admitted a Solicitor, 1957; Partner in N Wales (Wrexham) Firm of Solicitors, 1958-68. Chm., Welsh Parly Party, 1967-68; Parly Under-Secretary of State, Home Office, 1968-70. Pres., Welsh Local Authorities Assoc., 1967-. *Address:* Carreg Afon, Dolau, Bow Street, Cardiganshire.

**MORGAN, Sir David John H.;** *see* Hughes-Morgan.

**MORGAN, David Loftus,** CMG 1952; MBE 1943; *b* 21 Nov. 1904; *s* of late George Morgan, CIE; *m* 1929, Phyllis Douglas Russell; one *d*. *Educ:* Harrow; Trinity Coll., Cambridge. District Officer, Kenya, 1926: Dep. Provincial Commissioner, 1945; Provincial Commissioner, 1947-51; Resident Commissioner, Swaziland, 1951-56, retired. Member: Swaziland Railway Board; Swaziland Public Service Commission, 1963-69. Dir of cos. *Recreation:* golf. *Address:* PO Box 84, Mhlambanyati, Swaziland. *Clubs:* Caledonian; Nairobi (Kenya).

**MORGAN, Rev. Dewi, (David Lewis);** Rector, St Bride's Church, Fleet Street, EC4, since 1962; *b* 5 Feb. 1916; *s* of David and Anne Morgan; *m* 1942, Doris, *d* of Samuel and Ann Povey; two *d*. *Educ:* Lewis Sch., Pengam; University Coll. Cardiff (BA); St Michael's Coll., Llandaff. Curate: St Andrew's, Cardiff, 1939-43; Aberdare, 1943-46; Aberavon, 1946-50. Soc. for the Propagation of the Gospel: Press Officer, 1950-52, Editorial and Press Sec., 1952-62; Editor, St Martin's Review, 1953-55; Associate Editor: Church Illustrated, 1955-67; Anglican World, 1960-67. Freeman of City of London, 1963. *Publications:* Expanding Frontiers, 1957; The Bishops Come to Lambeth, 1957; Lambeth Speaks, 1958; The Undying Fire, 1959; 1662 And All That, 1961; But God Comes First, 1962; Agenda for Anglicans, 1963; Seeds of Peace, 1965; Arising From the Psalms, 1965; God and Sons, 1967. Edited: They Became Anglicans, 1959; They Became Christians, 1966; The Church in Transition, 1970. *Recreation:* sleeping. *Address:* St Bride's Rectory, Fleet Street, EC4. *T:* 01-353 1301. *Clubs:* Athenæum; Press (Hon. Chaplain).

**MORGAN, Rt. Rev. Edmund Robert,** DD; resigned as Bishop of Truro (1951-Oct. 1959); *b* London, 28 July 1888; *s* of Joseph John Morgan, solicitor, and Adelaide Holberton; *m* 1916, Isabel Charlotte (*d* 1964), *y d* of Joseph Jupp of Mowbray House, Malvern; one *s* (and two who died in the war). *Educ:* Winchester; New Coll., Oxford; Liverpool Univ. (Dip. in Educn). Curate, Farnham, 1913-15; Eastleigh, 1915-19; Domestic Chaplain to Bishop Talbot of Winchester, 1919-23; Warden, Coll. of the Ascension, Selly Oak, Birmingham, 1923-36; Rector of Old Alresford, 1936-42; Archdeacon of Winchester, 1936-43; Suffragan Bishop of Southampton, 1943-51; Canon of Winchester Cathedral, 1942-51. DD (Lambeth) 1955. Editor, The East and West Review, 1935-46. *Publications:* Editor: Essays Catholic and Missionary, 1928; The Catholic Revival and Missions, 1933; The Mission of the Church, 1946; (ed) The Mission of the Anglican Communion, 1948; The Undiscovered Country, 1962; Reginald Somerset Ward: A Memoir, 1963; The Ordeal of Wonder, 1964. *Recreations:* music, gardening, carpentry. *Address:* Moor Farm, Whiteparish, Salisbury, Wilts.

**MORGAN, Hon. Sir Edward James Ranembe,** Kt 1952; *b* Warwick, Queensland, 25 March 1900; *s* of Edward Ranembe Morgan, Adelaide, and Jean McMillan, *d* of John Brown, Culver Lodge, Much Hadham, Herts; *m* 1924, Dorothy Millar, *o c* of James Waite, MBE; two *s* one *d*. *Educ:* St Peter's Coll., Adelaide; The University of Adelaide (LLB). Called to South Australian Bar, 1921; Stipendiary Magistrate, Adelaide Police Court, 1934-41; Pres. of Industrial Court (South Australia), 1941-52; Judge of Commonwealth Court of Conciliation and Arbitration, 1952-56; Judge, Commonwealth Industrial Court, 1956-60; Judge, Supreme Court of Australian Capital Territory, 1958-60. Mem., Board of Trustees, Nat. Gallery of S Australia, 1940-44, and 1961-63, Chm., 1944-55, and 1963-70; Pres. Nat. Trust of S Australia, 1960-62; Gov., Anti-Cancer Foundn, Univ. of Adelaide, 1962-. *Publications:* The Adelaide Club, 1863-1963; (with S. H. Gilbert) Victorian Adelaide, 1968; (with S. H. Gilbert) Early Adelaide Architecture, 1969. *Address:* 155 Kermode Street, North Adelaide, SA 5006, Australia. *Clubs:* Adelaide (Adelaide), Melbourne (Melbourne).

**MORGAN, Ellis,** CMG 1961; *b* 26 Dec. 1916; *s* of late Ben Morgan and of Mary Morgan, The Grove, Three Crosses, Gower, S Wales; *m* 1948, Molly, *d* of Joseph Burton and Muriel Darby, Bromley, Kent; three *d*. *Educ:* Swansea Grammar Sch. (Bishop Gore Sch.). Dep. Librarian, County Borough of Swansea, 1937-39. Commissioned Royal Artillery, 1941; served War of 1939-45, in India, Burma, Malaya, 1943-47. Entered Foreign (subseq. Diplomatic) Service, 1948; 3rd Sec., 1948-50, 2nd Sec., 1951-53, subseq. 1st Sec., British Embassy, Rangoon; 1st Sec., British Embassy, Bangkok, 1954-55; 1st Sec., Office of Commissioner-Gen., Singapore, 1957-60; Student at Imperial Defence Coll., 1961; Counsellor, UK High Commission, New Delhi, 1964. *Recreations:* walking and books. *Address:* Arun House, Broadbridge Heath, near Horsham, Sussex. *T:* Horsham 5013. *Club:* East India and Sports.

**MORGAN, Elystan;** *see* Morgan, D. E.

**MORGAN, Col Farrar Robert Horton,** DSO 1940; OBE 1946; late Border Regiment; *b* 12 Sept. 1893; *e s* of late Robert Upton Morgan, MBE; *m* 1st, 1915, Alice Winifred May (*d* 1955), *d* of late Thomas R. Cross; two *s* two *d*; 2nd, 1957, Frances Maud, 4th *d* of late Harold and Ida Blackborow and *widow* of Sidney Turner. *Educ:* University Coll. Sch.; Sch. of Oriental Studies, London Univ. First commissioned, 1914, Border Regt; served in France, 1915-16 (despatches, 1915 Star, British War and Victory Medals); King's African Rifles, E Africa, 1917-24; Somaliland, 1920 (Medal and Clasp); Adjt Glasgow and Aberdeen Univs OTC, 1931-35; Lt-Col 1940; Col, 1941; served in China, 1927; Palestine, 1937-39 (Medal and Clasp); war of 1939-45, France, 1939-40 (despatches, DSO); Comd British Troops in Syria, 1944-46 (OBE); retired pay, 1946. Syrian Order of Merit (1st Class). Principal Control Officer, Germany, 1946-49. *Recreation:* painting. *Address:* High Cottage, Stoke Fleming, S Devon. *T:* Stoke Fleming 328.

**MORGAN, Col Frank Stanley,** CBE 1940; ERD 1954; DL; JP; *b* 10 Jan. 1893; *s* of F. A. Morgan, Commissioner Imperial Chinese Customs; *m* 1918, Gladys Joan (*d* 1953), *d* of Lt-Col H. M. Warde, CBE, DL Kent; no *c*; *m* 1956, Minnie Helen Pine, MBE, TD, Lt-Col WRAC, The Manor House, Great Barrow, Cheshire. *Educ:* Marlborough; Christ Church, Oxford. Served European War, 1914-19; public work in Wales; Territorial and Reserve Service, 1919-39; Air Formation Signals, France, North Africa, Italy, Middle East, 1939-45; DL, Glamorgan, 1946; JP 1951; Hon. Col 50 and 81 AF Signal Regts, 1952-60. *Address:* Herbert's Lodge, Bishopston, Swansea. *T:* Swansea 66376.

**MORGAN, Sir Frank William,** Kt 1948; MC; President, Prudential Assurance Co. Ltd, 1965-70; *b* 23 June 1887; *o s* of Alfred and Mary Anne Morgan; *m* 1926, Beatrice Agnes, *widow* of Frederick Christian Dietrichsen, Barrister; no *c*. *Educ:* Parmiter's Sch. Since 1903 with

Prudential Assurance Co.; Manager for India, Burma and Ceylon, 1928-33; Man. for Near East, 1933-34; Gen. Man., Prudential Assurance Co. Ltd, 1941-50, Dir, 1950-53, Chm., 1953-65. Served European War, 1914-18 with Hon. Artillery Company (A Battery), and Royal Field Artillery–commanded 99th Battery RFA (MC). *Recreations:* gardening and fishing. *Address:* Hyde Heath Farm, near Amersham, Bucks. *T:* Chesham 3028. *Club:* Oriental.

**MORGAN, Graham,** CMG 1954; FICE; Chartered Civil Engineer; *b* 12 July 1903; *m* 1931, Alice Jane Morgan; three *d.* *Educ:* King Henry VIII Grammar Sch., Abergavenny; University Coll., Cardiff. BSc Civil Engineering, Wales, 1923; Asst Engineer: Newport, Mon., 1924; Devon CC, 1924; Federated Malay States, 1926; Sen. Exec. Engineer, Malayan Public Works Service, 1941; State Engineer, Johore, 1948; Dir of Public Works, Tanganyika, 1950-Sept. 1954, retired. FICE (Mem. of Council, 1953-55). *Address:* 36 Sandfield Road, Oxford.

**MORGAN, Guy,** FRIBA; AIStructE; FRSA; BA; Senior Partner, in architectural practice; *b* 14 June 1902; *s* of late Francis Morgan and Miriam Hanley; *m* 1937, Violet Guy; one *d* (one *s* decd). *Educ:* Mill Hill; Cambridge; University Coll., London. Andrew Taylor Prizeman, 1923. Lecturer and Year Master, Architectural Assoc., 1931-36. In practice, 1927-; principal works include: large blocks of flats and offices in London and Provinces; aircraft factories and air bases; town planning schemes and housing in England and abroad; agricultural buildings and country houses; ecclesiastical and hospital works; film studios; racing and sports stadia. Past Joint Master, Cowdray Foxhounds. Past Master of Worshipful Company of Woolmen. *Recreations:* foxhunting, sailing, travel; music. *Address:* Lower House Farm, Fernhurst, Haslemere, Surrey. *T:* Fernhurst 222; 12A Eaton Square, SW1. *T:* 01-235 5101. *Clubs:* Royal Thames Yacht, Bath.

**MORGAN, Gwenda,** RE 1961; Wood Engraver; *b* 1 Feb. 1908; *d* of late William David Morgan, JP, and late Mary Morgan. *Educ:* Brighton and Hove High Sch. Studied Art at Goldsmiths' Coll. Sch. of Art, and at Grosvenor Sch. of Modern Art under Iain Macnab. Women's Land Army, 1939-46. Member: National Soc.; Soc. of Wood Engravers. Exhibited in London, provincial and foreign exhibitions. Work represented in Victoria and Albert Museum and Brighton Art Gallery. *Address:* Ridge House, Petworth, Sussex.

**MORGAN, Gwyn;** *see* Morgan, J. G.

**MORGAN, Prof. Henry Gemmell;** Professor of Pathological Biochemistry, University of Glasgow, since 1965; *b* 25 Dec. 1922; *s* of John McIntosh Morgan, MC, MD, FRCPE, and Florence Ballantyne; *m* 1949, Margaret Duncan, BSc, MB, ChB; one *d.* *Educ:* Dundee High Sch.; Merchiston Castle Sch., Edinburgh; Univ. of St Andrews at Univ. Coll., Dundee. BSc 1943; MB, ChB (distinction), 1946; FRCPE 1962; FRCP Glas. 1968; FRCPath 1970. Hon. Consultant, Royal Infirmary, Glasgow, 1966-. Chm., Scottish Br., Nutrition Soc., 1967-68. Adviser to Scottish Home and Health Dept. *Publications:* chapters; papers in medical jls. *Recreations:* golf, foreign travel, history. *Address:* Royal Infirmary, Glasgow, C4; Firwood House, 8 Eaglesham Road, Newton Mearns, Glasgow. *T:* 041-639 4404.

**MORGAN, His Hon. H(opkin) Trevor;** *see* Morgan, Trevor.

**MORGAN, Capt. Horace Leslie,** CMG 1931; DSO 1920; RN, retired; *b* 1888; *s* of Capt. H. H. Morgan, RMLI; *m* 1933, Kathleen Hilda, *o d* of late M. G. Bellhouse and of Mrs Hunter, wife of Lt-Col C. F. Hunter, DSO; three *s.* Served European War, 1914-19 (despatches, DSO); received thanks New Zealand Government for services during the earthquake at Napier (CMG); retired list, 1934. Served War of 1939-45 as a Sea Transport Officer. *Address:* Century Field, Bay View Road, Northam, N Devon.

**MORGAN, Hugh Travers,** CMG 1966; HM Ambassador to Peru, since 1970; *b* 3 Aug. 1919; *s* of Montagu Travers Morgan, *qv*; *m* 1959, Alexandra Belinoff; two *s* one *d.* *Educ:* Winchester Coll.; Magdalene Coll., Cambridge. RAF, 1939-45, prisoner-of-war in Germany, 1941-45. Entered HM Diplomatic Service, 1945, and served: New York, 1946-48; Moscow, 1948-50; Foreign Office, 1950-53; Canadian National Defence Coll., 1953-54; Mexico City, 1954-57; Foreign Office, 1957-58; UK Delegation to Conference on Nuclear Tests, Geneva, 1958-61; Peking (Counsellor), 1961-63; Political Adviser to the British Commandant, Berlin, 1964-67; FCO, 1967-70. *Address:* c/o Foreign and Commonwealth Office, SW1. *Club:* St James'.

**MORGAN, Irvonwy,** MA, BD Cantab, PhD (London); Secretary, Department of the London Mission of the Methodist Church, since 1951; *b* 11 April 1907; *s* of Rev. Llewelyn Morgan and Alice Anna Davies; *m* 1942, Florence Mary Lewis; one *d* (and one *d* decd). *Educ:* Kingswood Sch.; Wesley House, Cambridge (1st cl. hons Theol., Schofield Univ. Prize). PhD London, 1949; BD Cantab 1957. Asst at Poplar Mission; in charge of Poplar Mission from 1937. Methodist Delegate, World Council of Churches, Evanston, 1954; Guest Preacher, Methodist Church of Australasia, 1959; visited US on behalf of World Coun. of Churches, 1962 and 1966. Pres. of the Methodist Conference, 1967-68. Chm., Bible Lands Soc. *Publications:* The Nonconformity of Richard Baxter, 1949; Twixt the Mount and Multitude, 1955; Prince Charles' Puritan Chaplain, 1957; The Godly Preachers of the Elizabethan Church, 1965. *Recreation:* gardening. *Address:* (Home) 12 Heathdene Road, Wallington, Surrey. *T:* Wallington 9418; (Office) 1 Central Buildings, Westminster, SW1. *T:* 01-930 1453. *Club:* Reform.

**MORGAN, James Conwy,** CMG 1966; HM Diplomatic Service, retired; *b* 16 April 1910; *e s* of late Dr Conwy Llewellyn Morgan, MD, and of Mary Morgan (*née* Cowtan); *m* 1933, Cicely Mary Norman Cobb; one *s* two *d.* *Educ:* Malvern Coll.; Brasenose Coll., Oxford. Cadet, Colonial Service, Tanganyika, 1934; Asst District Officer, 1936 (DO (*in absentia*), 1946). Commissioned SR of O, The Royal Sussex Regiment, 1930; subseq. RARO and KAR, RO; called up Sept. 1939, 2/6 KAR (Tanganyika); subseq. Brit. Mil. Admin., Somalia, 1941; Major and GSO 2, 1942 (despatches); Lt-Col and Sen. Civil Affairs Officer, 1945; demob. 1947; cont. in RARO, Major, until retd as Lt-Col, 1958. Transf. from Colonial to Home CS, 1947. Colonial Office: Principal; Asst Sec., 1955; att. to Monckton Commn, 1960; transf. to CRO, 1962; Chief of Staff to Chm. of Dissolution Cttee A, in Salisbury, SR, 1963; Head of Medit. Dept, CRO, 1964; Asst Under-Sec. of State, 1965; British Dep. High Comr, Canberra, 1966-67; Asst Under-Sec. of State, Dependent Territories Div., CO, 1967-68, FCO, 1968-70, retired 1970. *Recreations:* walking, reading. *Address:* Oak Bank, Ashurst, near Tunbridge

Wells, Kent. *T:* Fordcombe 388. *Club:* Naval and Military.

**MORGAN, John Albert Leigh;** Counsellor, and Head of Far Eastern Department of Foreign and Commonwealth Office since 1970; *b* 21 June 1929; *s* of John Edward Rowland Morgan, Bridge, Kent; *m* 1961, Hon. Fionn Frances Bride O'Neill, *d* of 3rd Baron O'Neill, Shane's Castle, Antrim; one *s* two *d*. *Educ:* London School of Economics. Served in Army, 1947-49; entered Foreign (subseq. Diplomatic) Service, 1951; FO, 1951-53; 3rd Sec., HM Embassy, Moscow, 1953-56; 2nd Sec., Peking, 1956-58; FO, 1958-63; 1st Sec., 1960; Head of Chancery, Rio de Janeiro, 1963-64; FO, 1964-65; Moscow, 1965-67; FO, 1968. *Address:* 182 Ebury Street, SW1. *T:* 01-730 1140. *Club:* Travellers'.

**MORGAN, (John) Gwyn(fryn);** Assistant General Secretary, The British Labour Party, since 1969; *b* 16 Feb. 1934; *s* of Arthur G. Morgan, coal miner, and Mary Walters; *m* 1960, Joan Margaret Taylor; one *d*. *Educ:* Aberdare Boys' Grammar Sch.; UCW Aberystwyth. MA Classics 1957; Dip. Educn 1958. Senior Classics Master, The Regis Sch., Tettenhall, Staffs, 1958-60; Pres., National Union of Students, 1960-62; Sec.-Gen., Internat. Student Conf. (ISC), 1962-65; Head of Overseas Dept, British Labour Party, 1965-69. *Publications:* contribs to numerous British and foreign political jls. *Recreations:* cricket, Rugby football, crosswords, wine-tasting. *Address:* (home) 1 June Close, Coulsdon, Surrey. *T:* 01-668 3316; (office) Transport House, Smith Square, SW1. *T:* 01-834 9434. *Club:* Royal Commonwealth Society.

**MORGAN, Col Kevern Ivor,** CBE 1955 (OBE 1934); Chartered Accountant since 1924; Director of Companies; *b* 22 Sept. 1894; *s* of William Morgan, Wolfs Castle, Pembs; *m* 1954, Claudia Jean, *er d* of late Capt. Charles Trueman, MN, Barry Island, Glamorgan; no *c*. *Educ:* Dynevor Gram. Sch.; Swansea Tech. Coll. Served with RAPC (UK), 1939-47. Hon. Col 108 (Welsh) Field Engineer Regt, 1955-59. Chairman: Whole Body of Swansea Justices; Swansea Licensing Magistrates; Swansea Licensing Planning Cttee; Swansea Coun., Order of St John; Minister's Appointee, Swansea Health Service Exec. Coun. (Chm. Med. Service Cttee and Dental Service Cttee); Mem. Management Cttee, Trustees of Swansea Savings Bank. High Sheriff of Breconshire, 1958; JP Swansea, 1939. CStJ. *Recreations:* fishing, shooting. *Address:* 15 Hawthorne Avenue, Uplands, Swansea. *T:* 56218. *Club:* Ffynone (Swansea).

**MORGAN, Montagu Travers,** CMG 1949; MC; MD; *b* 14 Nov. 1889; *s* of Llewellyn A. Morgan, MD, and Dorothy (*née* Hankin); *m* 1914, Maud Elizabeth Bateman (*d* 1949); two *s*; *m* 1949, Marguerite Juliette Félicie Jolly. *Educ:* Liverpool Coll. and Univ. Resident MO City Fever Hosp., Liverpool; Dep. County MOH and Tuberculosis Officer, Herefordshire; RAMC 1915-18 (despatches, MC); County MOH, Pembs; Medical Officer, Board of Education; Medical Officer, Ministry of Health; MOH, Port of London, 1938-54; formerly Pres., International Health Office, Paris; mem. expert Commissions on Mecca Pilgrimage and quarantine, World Health Organisation. Officier, Légion d'Honneur, 1948. Smith Award, 1949. *Publications:* Numerous contributions, reports, etc, to Government Depts; Ergot Poisoning in Rye Bread (Jl Hyg. 1929); (Jointly) Epidemic Jaundice, Min. of Health Medical Series, 1927. *Recreation:* fishing. *Address:* Brandy Mount House, Alresford, Hants. *T:* Alresford 2189.
*See also Hugh Travers Morgan.*

**MORGAN, Sir Morien Bedford,** Kt 1969; CB 1958; MA, CEng, FRAeS; Director, Royal Aircraft Establishment, since 1969; *b* 20 Dec. 1912; *s* of late John Bedford and Edith Mary Morgan, Bridgend, Glam; *m* 1941, Sylvia Axford; three *d*. *Educ:* Rutlish, Merton; St Catharine's Coll., Cambridge. John Bernard Seely Prize in Aeronautics, 1934; apprenticed to Mather & Platt Ltd, 1934-35; joined Aerodynamics Dept, Royal Aircraft Establishment, 1935, and for some years was engaged on flight research and develt, specialising in problems of aircraft stability and control. Pilot's "A" licence, 1944. Head of Aero. Flight Section, RAE, 1946-48. Head of Guided Weapons Dept, RAE, 1948-53; Dep. Dir, RAE, 1954-59; Scientific Adviser, Air Ministry, 1959-60; Dep. Controller of Aircraft (R&D), Min. of Aviation, 1960-63; Controller of Aircraft, 1963-66; Controller of Guided Weapons and Electronics, Min. of Technology, 1966-69. Pres., Royal Aeronautical Society, 1967-68. Silver Medal of the Royal Aeronautical Society, 1957. *Publications:* Reports and Memoranda of Aeronautical Research Council. Lectures to Royal Aeronautical Society. *Recreation:* music. *Address:* Tudor House, 31 Church Avenue, Farnborough, Hants. *T:* Farnborough (Hants) 41732. *Club:* Athenæum.

**MORGAN, Oswald Gayer,** MA, MCh Cantab; FRCS; Consultant Surgeon Emeritus; Past President, Ophthalmological Society of UK; *b* 1889; *m* 1926, Jessie Campbell (*d* 1938), *yr d* of Colin MacDonald, 38 Abbey Road, NW; two *d*. *Educ:* Epsom Coll.; Clare Coll., Cambridge; Guy's Hosp. Surgeon in charge Duchess of Sutherland's Hosp., France, 1914-18; Ophthalmic House Surg. at Moorfield's Eye Hosp., 1920. Vice-Pres., BMA, 1965. *Publications:* The Wounded in Namur; Some Aspects of the Treatment of Infected War Wounds, British Journal of Surgery, 1916; Ophthalmology in General Practice. *Address:* Primrose Cottage, Walberswick, Suffolk.

**MORGAN, Rear-Adm. Sir Patrick (John),** KCVO 1970; CB 1967; DSC 1942; Flag Officer, Royal Yachts, 1965-70, retired; *b* 26 Jan. 1917; *s* of late Vice-Adm. Sir Charles Morgan, KCB, DSO; *m* 1944, Mary Hermione Fraser-Tytler, *d* of late Col Neil Fraser-Tytler, DSO, Aldourie Castle, Inverness, and of Mrs C. H. Fraser-Tytler, *qv*; three *s* one *d*. *Educ:* RN College, Dartmouth. Served War of 1939-45 (despatches, DSC). Naval Attaché, Ankara, 1957-59; Imperial Defence Coll. 1960; Asst Chief of Staff, Northwood, 1961-62; Commanding Officer, Commando Ship, HMS Bulwark, 1963-64. *Recreations:* sports. *Address:* Conway House, Worplesdon, Surrey. *T:* Worplesdon 2006.

**MORGAN, Paul Robert James,** CIE 1947; retired; *b* 1 Feb. 1898; *s* of late W. A. Morgan of the Stock Exchange, and of late Mrs W. A. Morgan, Nice, France; *m* Beatrice Helen Carteret, *o d* of late Lt-Col Hugh Stewart, CIE, Indian Political Dept, and late Mrs D. M. Stewart, Tunbridge Wells, Kent; two *d* (one *s* decd). *Educ:* Sherborne. Served European War, 1914-20, with RE (TF) 3/8 Gurkha Rifles, Indian Army, attained rank of Capt. Entered Indian Police, 1920, and attached to Punjab. Had various district appointments; posted to Provincial Additional Police, 1929-32 and 1939-47, as Commandant Provincial Additional Police, Punjab. Indian Police Medal, 1934. *Recreations:* shooting, tennis. *Address:* Fairway, Headland Avenue, Seaford, Sussex. *T:* Seaford 3934.

**MORGAN, His Honour Trevor,** QC 1936; MC; DL; JP County of Glamorgan; MA, LLB; County Court Judge, Circuit No 31, 1948-64, retired; Chairman Carmarthenshire QS, 1951-66; retired; Deputy Chairman Glamorgan Quarter Sessions, 1948-59; *b* 19 June 1892; *s* of Hopkin Morgan, JP, and Sarah Morgan, Pontypridd; *m* 1932, Leslie, *d* of Col W. D. Phillips, TD, Llwydcoed, Aberdare; two *s*. *Educ:* Mill Hill Sch.; Gonville and Caius Coll., Cambridge. Called to Bar, Inner Temple, 1920. Chm. of Council, University Coll. of Swansea, 1966-. DL Glamorgan, 1958. *Address:* Pilgrim Cottage, Brynfield Road, Langland, Swansea. *Clubs:* Glamorgan County (Cardiff), Bristol Channel Yacht.

**MORGAN, Walter Thomas James,** CBE 1959; FRS 1949; Emeritus Professor of Biochemistry, University of London (Professor of Biochemistry, 1951-68 and Deputy Director, 1952-68, Lister Institute of Preventive Medicine); *b* London, 5 Oct. 1900; *s* of Walter and Annie E. Morgan; *m* 1930, Dorothy Irene Price; one *s* two *d*. *Educ:* Univ. of London. Grocers' Company Scholar, 1925-27; Beit Memorial Med. Res. Fellow, 1927-28; First Asst and Biochemist, Lister Institute Serum Dept (Elstree), 1928-37; Rockefeller Research Fellow (Eidgenössiche Tech. Hochschule, Zürich), 1937. PhD 1927, DSc 1937, London Univ.; DrSc (Tech.) Zürich, 1938; FRIC 1929. Hon. Secretary: Biochemical Soc., 1940-45; Biological Council, 1944-47. Chm. Bd of Studies, Biochem., Univ. of London, 1954-57; Mem. of Scientific Advisory Council, 1956-60; Mem. of Medical Research Council, 1966-70. Croonian Lecturer of Royal Soc., 1959; Vice-Pres., Royal Soc., 1961-64; Royal Medal, Royal Soc., 1968. MD hc Basel, 1964; DSc hc Michigan, 1969. Conway Evans Prize (Royal College of Physicians, London), 1964. (Jointly) Landsteiner Memorial Award (USA), 1967. (Jointly) Paul Ehrlich and Ludwig Darmstädter Prizes, 1968. *Publications:* papers on biochemistry and pathology, mainly in Biochem. Jl and Brit. Jl of Exp. Pathol. *Address:* 57 Woodbury Drive, Sutton, Surrey. *T:* 01-642 2319. *Club:* Athenæum.

**MORGAN, Gen. Sir William Duthie,** GCB, *cr* 1949 (KCB, *cr* 1945; CB 1944); DSO 1919; MC; Hon. LLD (Edinburgh); *b* Dec. 1891; *s* of late Alexander Morgan, OBE, MA, LLD, DSc, Edinburgh; *m* 1921, Amy, *d* of Cromwell Varley of the Manor House, Chislehurst; one *s* one *d*. Served European War, 1914-19 (despatches, MC, DSO, Belgian Croix de Guerre); Waziristan, 1922-23; Military Attaché, Budapest, 1929-31; Chief Instructor RM Academy, 1934-38; served in France, 1939-40, as Regimental Comdr and GSO 1 1st Div.; BGS 1st Corps, 1940; Comdr 55 Div. 1941; Chief of General Staff, Home Forces, 1942-43; GOC-in-C Southern Command, 1944; Chief of Staff to Supreme Allied Comdr, Mediterranean, 1945; Supreme Allied Comdr, Mediterranean Theatre, 1945-47; Comdr, British Army Staff, Washington, and Army Mem. of Joint Staff Mission, 1947-50; retired 1950. Col Comdt RA, 1947-56. Chairman: Siemens Brothers & Co. Ltd, London, 1953-57; Gloucester Railway Carriage & Wagon Co. Ltd, 1957-62. DL County of London, 1958, Vice-Lieutenant, Co. London 1958, Greater London 1965-70. *Address:* c/o Lloyds Bank Ltd, Cox's and King's Branch, 6 Pall Mall, SW1. *Club:* Carlton.

**MORGAN, William Geraint Oliver;** MP (C) Denbigh Division of Denbighshire since Oct. 1959; *b* Nov. 1920; *m* 1957, J. S. M. Maxwell; two *s* two *d*. *Educ:* University Coll. of Wales, Aberystwyth; Trinity Hall, Cambridge. Served War of 1939-45 with Royal Marines; demobilised with Rank of Major, 1946. Called to the Bar, Gray's Inn, 1947; Squire Law Scholar; Holt Scholar; Northern Circuit. Contested: Merioneth, 1951; Huyton, 1955. *Address:* House of Commons, SW1; 13 Owen Road, Prescot, Lancs L35 0PJ.

**MORGAN, Air Vice-Marshal William Gwyn,** CB 1968; CBE 1960 (OBE 1945); RAF, retired 1969; *b* 13 Aug. 1914; *s* of T. S. Morgan; *m* 1962, Joan Russell. *Educ:* Pagefield Coll., Swansea. Joined Royal Air Force, 1939; Group Capt., 1958; Command Acct, HQ, FEAF, 1962; Air Commodore, 1965; DPS (2), RAF, 1965-66; AOA Technical Training Comd, 1966-68, Training Comd, 1968-69. Air Vice-Marshal, 1967; jssc; psc; FACCA; ACWA. *Recreation:* fell walking. *Address:* c/o Lloyds Bank, 6 Pall Mall, SW1. *Club:* Royal Air Force.

**MORGAN, Rt. Hon. William James,** PC (Northern Ireland) 1961; Minister of Health and Social Services, Northern Ireland, 1965-69; MP (Northern Ireland), Oldpark Division of Belfast, 1949-58, Clifton Division of Belfast, 1959-69; JP; *b* 1914; *m* 1942; two *s* one *d*. Transport contractor. Minister of Health and Local Government, Northern Ireland, 1961-64; Minister of Labour and National Insurance, 1964. *Address:* Ministry of Health and Social Services, Dundonald House, Upper Newtownards Road, Belfast, Northern Ireland; Rhanbuoy, Carrickfergus, Co. Antrim. *T:* Carrickfergus 2236.

**MORGAN, William Stanley,** CMG 1965; Colonial Administrative Service, retired; *b* 29 April 1908; *s* of late J. W. Morgan; *m* 1957, Joan Ruth Dixon Williams; two *s* one *d*. *Educ:* Rendcomb Coll.; (Open Scholar in History) Queens' Coll., Cambridge (MA). Malayan Education Service, 1931-50; Colonial Administrative Service, 1950-57; Malaya, 1931-47; Sec., Commn on Univ. Educn in Malaya, 1947; Principal, Colonial Office, 1947-50; Sierra Leone, Ministerial Sec., 1950-57; Asst Adviser to Qatar Govt, 1957-60; Chm., Public and Police Service Commns, Mauritius, 1960-69. *Publication:* Story of Malaya, 1938. *Recreations:* tennis, travel and music. *Address:* Old Vicarage, Maughold, Isle of Man. *T:* Ramsey 2863.

**MORGAN-GILES, Rear-Adm. Morgan Charles,** DSO 1944; OBE 1943 (MBE 1942); GM 1941; MP (C) for Winchester since May 1964; *b* 19 June 1914; *e s* of late F. C. Morgan-Giles, OBE, MINA, Teignmouth, Devon; *m* 1946, Pamela (*d* 1966), *d* of late Philip Bushell, Sydney, New South Wales; two *s* four *d*; *m* 1968, Marigold, *d* of late Percy Lowe. *Educ:* Clifton Coll. Entered Royal Navy, 1932; served on China Station, and in destroyers. War Service: Atlantic convoys and Mediterranean; Tobruk garrison and Western Desert, 1941; with RAF, 1942; Sen. Naval Officer, Vis. (Dalmatia) and liaison with Commandos and Marshal Tito's Partisan Forces, 1943-44. Captain 1953; Chief of Naval Intelligence, Far East, 1955-56; Captain (D) Dartmouth Training Sqdn, 1957-58; HMS Belfast, in command, 1961-62; Rear-Adm. 1962; Adm. Pres., Royal Naval Coll., Greenwich, 1962-64; retd 1964. Vice-Chm., Conservative Defence Cttee, 1965-. Liveryman, Shipwrights' Company. *Recreations:* sailing, country pursuits. *Address:* Upton Park, Alresford, Hants. *T:* Alresford 2443; 93 West Eaton Place Mews, SW1. *T:* 01-235 8413. *Clubs:* Carlton, United Service, Royal Yacht Squadron; Australian (Sydney).

**MORICE, Prof. Peter Beaumont,** DSc, PhD; FICE, FIStructE; Professor of Civil

Engineering, University of Southampton, since 1958; *b* 15 May 1926; *o s* of Charles and Stephanie Morice; *m* 1952, Margaret Ransom; one *s* two *d*. *Educ:* Barfield Sch.; Farnham Grammar Sch.; University of Bristol; University of London. Surrey County Council, 1947-48; Research Div., Cement and Concrete Assoc., 1948-57. *Publications:* Linear Structural Analysis, 1958; Prestressed Concrete, 1958; papers on structural theory in various learned journals. *Recreations:* sailing, reading, listening to music. *Address:* 65 Shaftesbury Avenue, Highfield, Southampton. *T:* 56624.

**MORINI, Erica;** concert violinist; *b* Vienna, 5 Jan. 1910; *m* 1938, Felice Siracusano; no *c*. *Educ:* at age of 4 years under father, Prof. Oscar Morini, and then under Prof. Ottocar Sevcik, masterclass of Viennese Conservatory, at age of 8. Debut under Arthur Nikisch, at age of 9, in Leipzig Gewandhaus (Beethoven Festival); from there on Concert-tours to: Australia, Asia, Africa, Europe; to USA, 1920. Hon. Mem., Sigma Alpha Beta. Hon. MusD: Smith Coll., Mass, 1955; New England Conservatory of Music, Mass, 1963. *Recreations:* mountain climbing and chamber music. *Address:* 1200 Fifth Avenue, New York, NY 10029, USA.

**MORISON, Alastair Malcolm;** QC (Scotland), 1968; *b* 12 Feb. 1931; 2nd *s* of Sir Ronald Peter Morison, *qv*; *m* 1957, Lindsay Balfour Oatts; one *s* one *d*. *Educ:* Cargilfield; Winchester Coll.; Edinburgh Univ. Admitted to Faculty of Advocates, 1956. *Recreation:* golf. *Address:* 6 Carlton Terrace, Edinburgh 7. *T:* 031-556 6766. *Clubs:* New, Hon. Co. of Edinburgh Golfers (Edinburgh).

**MORISON, Lt-Col John,** CIE 1932; MB, ChB, DPH, FRS Edinburgh; IMS (retired); *b* 6 Nov. 1879; *s* of Donald Morison, MD, EP, Mission, Rajshahi, Bengal; *m* 1907, Annie Macdonald, *d* of late Hugh Maclean, Glasgow. *Educ:* High Sch., Glasgow; George Watson's Coll., Edinburgh; Glasgow Univ. House Surgeon, Western Infirmary, Glasgow; Asst Medical Officer, Lugar Iron Works; Asst Medical Officer, Asylums Board; entered Indian Medical Service, 1906; retired 1934; served European War (despatches); Research Dept of Government of India, 1912; Dir, King Edward VII Memorial Pasteur and Medical Research Institute, Shillong, Assam. *Publications:* papers on Enteric fever, Purification of Water Supplies, Bacteriophage in Cholera and Dysentery. *Recreation:* golf. *Address:* 13 Cluny Drive, Edinburgh, 10. *T:* 031-447 4676.

**MORISON, Air Vice-Marshal Richard Trevor,** CBE 1969 (MBE 1944); President, Ordnance Board since 1971; *s* of Oscar Colin Morison and Margaret Valerie (*née* Cleaver); *m* 1964, Rosemary June Brett; one *s* one *d*. *Educ:* Perse Sch., Cambridge; De Havilland Sch. of Aeronautical Engineering. Commnd in RAF, 1940; RAF Staff Coll., 1952; Sen. Techn. Officer, RAF Gaydon, 1955-57; HQ Bomber Comd, 1958-60; STSO HQ 224 Group, Singapore, 1960-61; Dir of Techn. Services, Royal NZ Air Force, 1961-63; Comd Engrg Officer, HQ Bomber Comd, 1963-65; Air Officer i/c Engrg, HQ Flying Training Comd, 1966-68; Air Officer i/c Engrg, HQ Training Comd RAF, 1968-69; Vice-Pres. (Air) Ordnance Bd, 1969-70. *Recreation:* cabinet making. *Address:* 119 Canopus Way, RAF Northwood, Middx. *T:* Northwood 23787. *Clubs:* Royal Aero, Royal Air Force.

**MORISON, Sir Ronald (Peter),** Kt 1960; QC (Scotland) 1936; MA; LLB; Chairman, Police Arbitration Tribunal; *b* 3 June 1900; *e s* of late Rt Hon. Lord Morison, PC; three *s* one *d* by first marriage; *m* 2nd, Johanna Maria Magdalena, *d* of late Peter Hoorweg, Capt. Netherlands Artillery. *Educ:* Winchester Coll.; Edinburgh Univ. (MA; LLB with distinction). Admitted to Scottish Bar, 1923; to English Bar, 1940; 2nd Lt Scots Guards, Sept. 1940; Major, Deputy Judge Advocate, 1942; resumed civilian work in Aug. 1944; Sheriff of Inverness, Elgin and Nairn, 1944-45; Dean of the Faculty of Advocates, 1944-45. Mem. of Industrial Disputes Tribunal, 1944-54; Independent Chm., Executive Cttee of the British Iron and Steel Federation, 1955-62, Legal Consultant to Federation, 1962-67. Chairman: Departmental Cttee on the Probation Service, 1959-62; Commission of Inquiry into labour difficulties in the copper belt, N Rhodesia, 1962; Railway Staff National Tribunal, 1960; Dep. Chm., Criminal Injuries Compensation Board, 1964. *Recreations:* fishing, golf. *Address:* Old Tudor, Iden, Rye, Sussex. *T:* Iden 202. *Club:* White's.

**MORISON, Samuel Eliot,** FBA; Hon. LittD Oxford 1951; historian; Professor of History, Harvard University, 1925-55; served as Historian of Naval Operations with rank of Rear-Admiral in US Naval Reserve, 1942-51; *b* Boston, Mass, 9 July 1887; *s* of John H. Morison and Emily Eliot; *m* 1st, 1910, Elisabeth S. Greene (*d* 1945); three *d* (one *s* decd); 2nd, 1949, Priscilla Barton. *Educ:* Harvard Univ. (AB 1908, PhD 1912, LittD); Ecole des Sciences Politiques, Paris, France. Harold Vyvyan Harmsworth Prof. of American History, Oxford Univ., 1922-25; Attaché, American Commission to Negotiate Peace, 1919; mem. Baltic Commission of Paris Conference, 1919; Jusserand Medal and Loubat Prize, 1938; Commodore of Harvard Columbus Expedition, 1939-40. Fellow, Amer. Philos. Soc., FSA. Balzan Award, 1963; Presidential Medal of Freedom. *Publications:* Life and Letters of H. G. Otis, 1913; Maritime History of Massachusetts, 1921; Oxford History of the United States, 1927; Tercentennial History of Harvard University; (with H. S. Commager) Growth of the American Republic, 1950 (6th edn 1969); Admiral of the Ocean Sea: a Life of Christopher Columbus, 1942; Christopher Columbus, Mariner, 1956; History of US Naval Operations, World War II, 15 vols, 1947-62. American Contributions to Strategy of World War II, 1958; Paul Jones, a Sailor's Biography, 1960; One Boy's Boston, 1962; (with Mauricio Obregón) The Caribbean as Columbus Saw It, 1964; Vistas of History, 1964; Spring Tides, 1965; Oxford History of the American People, 1965; Old Bruin, the Life of Commodore M. C. Perry, 1967; H. G. Otis, Urbane Federalist, 1969; The European Discovery of America: the Northern Voyages, 1971. *Recreations:* riding, sailing. *Address:* Harvard College Library, Cambridge, Mass 02138, USA. *Club:* Athenæum.

**MORLAND, Captain Henry,** CIE 1929; RIN (retired); *b* 12 Oct. 1876; *s* of late Captain Sir Henry Morland, Indian Navy and RIM; *m* 1906, Lilian Crighton (*d* 1963); one *s*. *Educ:* Clifton Coll.; HMS Conway. Sub-Lt Royal Indian Marine, 1898; Lt 1902; Lt-Comdr, 1910; Comdr, 1910; Comdr, 1918; Capt., 1924; Asst Port Officer, Bombay, 1920; Port Officer of Bombay, 1923; Chief of Staff and Dep. Dir, Royal Indian Marine, 1925; Commanded ships of the RIM; served in Somaliland, 1902 (medal with bar); Persian Gulf, 1910 (medal with bar); Commanded Auxiliary Cruiser, HMS Lhasa, 1917; Naval Transport Officer, Aden, 1918; retired, 1929. *Recreations:* usual games. *Address:* c/o Lloyds Bank, Cox's and King's

Branch, 6 Pall Mall, SW1. *Club:* Royal Bombay Yacht (Bombay).

**MORLAND, Sir Oscar Charles,** GBE 1962; KCMG 1959 (CMG 1949); HM Ambassador to Japan, 1959-63, retired; *b* 23 March 1904; *s* of Harold John Morland, MA, FCA; *m* 1932, Alice, *d* of late Rt Hon. Sir F. O. Lindley, PC, GCMG; four *s*. *Educ:* Leighton Park Sch.; King's Coll., Cambridge. Joined HM Consular Service, 1927. Served in Japan, Manchuria, London. Under Sec., Cabinet Office, 1950-53; Ambassador to Indonesia, 1953-56; Asst Under-Sec., FO, 1956-59. *Address:* The High Hall, Thornton-le-Dale, Pickering, Yorks. *T:* Thornton-le-dale 371. *Club:* Travellers'.

**MORLEY,** 6th Earl of, *cr* 1815; **John St Aubyn Parker;** Lt-Col, Royal Fusiliers; *b* 29 May 1923; *e s* of Hon. John Holford Parker (*y s* of 3rd Earl), Pound House, Yelverton, Devon; *S* uncle, 1962; *m* 1955, Johanna Katherine Molesworth-St Aubyn; one *s* one *d*. *Educ:* Eton. 2nd Lt, KRRC, 1942; served NW Europe, 1944-45; Palestine and Egypt, 1945-48; transferred to Royal Fusiliers, 1947; served Korea, 1952-53; Middle East, 1953-55 and 1956; Staff Coll., Camberley, 1957; Comd, 1st Bn Royal Fusiliers, 1965-67. *Heir: s* Viscount Boringdon, *qv*. *Address:* Pound House, Yelverton, Devon. *T:* Yelverton 3162.

**MORLEY;** *see* Headlam-Morley.

**MORLEY, Sir Alexander (Francis),** KCMG 1959 (CMG 1955); CBE 1948; retired from HM Diplomatic Service; re-employed in Foreign Office; *b* 6 Jan. 1908; *s* of late Arthur S. Morley, FRCS; *m* 1939, Hedy, *e d* of late Prof. Julius von Landesberger-Antburg, Vienna; one *d*. *Educ:* Rugby; Queen's Coll., Oxford. Appointed to India Office, 1930; Private Sec. to Parl. Under-Sec. of State, 1933-36; served in Burma Office, 1938-40 and again 1945-47; seconded to Min. of Aircraft Production, 1940-42; Economic Adviser to Lord Privy Sea, 1947-49; with Commonwealth Relations Office, 1949-65; Dep. High Comr for UK in New Zealand, 1950-52 (Actg High Comr March-Nov. 1951). Asst Under-Sec. of State, 1954; Dep. High Comr for UK, Calcutta, 1956-57; British High Commissioner in Ceylon, 1957-62; British High Commissioner in Jamaica, 1962-65; HM Ambassador to Hungary, 1965-67. *Publication:* The Harrap Opera Guide, 1970. *Address:* 47 Campden Hill Square, W8. *Club:* United University.

**MORLEY, Cecil Denis,** CBE 1967; Secretary General, The Stock Exchange, London, since 1965; *b* 20 May 1911; *s* of Cornelius Cecil Morley and Mildred Irene Hutchinson; *m* 1936, Lily Florence Younge; one s. Educ: Clifton; Trinity Coll., Cambridge. Solicitor. Asst Sec., Share & Loan Dept, Stock Exchange, 1936; Sec. to Coun. of Stock Exchange, 1949. Served War of 1939-45, Major RA (TA). *Recreations:* travel, gardening. *Address:* 17a Eldon Road, W8. *T:* 01-937 8383. *Club:* Junior Carlton.

**MORLEY, Air Vice-Marshal George Henry,** CB 1968; CBE 1961 (OBE 1944); Senior Consultant of the Royal Air Force, since 1966; RAF Senior Consultant in Plastic Surgery since 1950, in Surgery since 1966; *b* 22 Feb. 1907; *s* of late Dr G. F. Morley, Portsmouth, Hants; *m* 1944, Kathleen Joan Elizabeth, *d* of late Robin Green, Felmersham, Beds; one *s* one *d*. *Educ:* St Helen's Coll., Southsea; Middlesex Hosp., W1. MRCS, LRCP 1929; FRCS 1935. Hon. Surg. to the Queen, 1958. Pres., British Assoc. of Plastic Surgeons, 1961; Fellow, Assoc. of Surgeons of Gt Britain and Ireland; Royal Society Medicine; Mem., British Club for Surgery of the Hand. First McIndoe Memorial Lecturer, Royal College of Surgeons of England, 1962; Ruscoe Clarke Memorial Lecturer, Birmingham, 1965. Hon. Member: Institute of Accident Surgery, Birmingham, 1965; Assoc. of Mil Surgeons, USA, 1949; Divisional Pres., Wendover Cadets Div., St John Ambulance Brigade, 1962. CStJ 1960. Lady Cade Medal, RCS, 1967. *Publications:* First Aid and Early Treatment of Burns in the Royal Air Force, 1957; several papers on plastic and general surgery, burns and hand injuries. *Address:* South Coombe, Wendover, Bucks. *T:* Wendover 3178. *Clubs:* Guinea Pig, Royal Air Force; Nuffield United Services Officers' (Portsmouth).

**MORLEY, Godfrey William Rowland,** OBE 1944; TD 1946; solicitor; *b* 15 June 1909; *o s* of late Arthur Morley, OBE, KC, and Dorothy Innes Murray Forrest; *m* 1st, 1934, Phyllis Dyce (*d* 1963), *d* of late Sir Edward Duckworth, 2nd Bt; two *s* two *d*; 2nd, 1967, Sonia Gisèle, *d* of late Thomas Ritchie; one *s*. *Educ:* Westminster; Christ Church, Oxford (MA). Solicitor, 1934; Partner in Allen & Overy, 1936. Joined Territorial Army, 1937; served War of 1939-45, Rifle Bde and on Staff in Middle East and Italy; Lt-Col 1944. Law Society: Mem. Council, 1952-; Vice-Pres., 1969-70; Pres., 1970-71. Member: Lord Chancellor's Law Reform Cttee, 1957-; Cttee of Management, Inst. of Advanced Legal Studies, 1961-. Dir, Bowater Paper Corp. Ltd. Bronze Star Medal (US), 1945. *Address:* Hunter's Lodge, Warren Drive, Kingswood, Surrey. *T:* Mogador 2485. *Clubs:* Boodle's, City of London.

*See also Sir William Lindsay.*

**MORLEY, Gordon H.;** *see* Hope-Morley.

**MORLEY, John,** ChM, FRCS; Captain RAMC (T); awarded Croix de Chevalier Legion of Honour for distinguished services in Gallipoli; Hon. Consulting Surgeon, Ancoats Hospital, Manchester, and Manchester Royal Infirmary; Consulting Surgeon for Children, St Mary's Hospital, Manchester; Professor of Surgery (Emeritus), Manchester University; Fellow, Association of Surgeons; Fellow (Hon. Member section of Surgery) Royal Society of Medicine. Ex-President, Manchester Medico-Legal Manchester Surgical, Manchester Medical and Manchester Pathological Societies; formerly External Expert Adviser in Surgery, London University; External Examiner in Surgery, Cambridge, Edinburgh, Birmingham and Durham Universities, etc; *s* of Rev. J. S. Morley, MA; *m* 1st, Mary O. Simon (decd), Stowmarket; two *s* one *d* (and one *s* decd); 2nd, Margaret Hyde Greg, Norcliffe Hall, Handforth. *Educ:* Bishop's Stortford Coll.; Manchester Univ. Formerly Hon. Surg., Ancoats Hosp. and Royal Manchester Children's Hospital; House Surg. and Surgical Registrar, Manchester Royal Infirmary, Demonstrator of Anatomy, and Lecturer in Clinical Anatomy, Manchester Univ.; Tom Jones Surgical Scholar; Ashby Memorial Scholar for Research in Diseases of Children; University Graduate Scholar; etc.; First Class Hons, Manchester Univ., MB, ChB Examination, 1908. *Publications:* Abdominal Pain, 1931; Abdominal Pain and Acute Abdominal Emergencies, Encyclopædia of Practical Medicine, 1936; Reviser, Surgical and Topographical Section, Morris's Anatomy; Jackson's Pericolic Membrane: Its Nature, Clinical Significance and Relation to Abnormal Mobility of the Proximal Colon, Lancet, 1913; Traumatic Intramuscular Ossification, British Medical Journal, 1913; (with N. Monk-Jones) Bishop's Stortford College, 1868-1968: a centenary chronicle,

1969; numerous other articles. *Recreations:* fishing and shooting. *Address:* Edenview, Langwathby, Penrith, Cumberland. *T:* Langwathby 210. *Club:* St James's (Manchester).

**MORLEY, Robert,** CBE 1957; Actor-Dramatist; *b* Semley, Wilts, 26 May 1908; *s* of Major Robert Morley and Gertrude Emily Fass; *m* 1940, Joan North Buckmaster, *d* of Dame Gladys Cooper, *qv*; two *s* one *d*. *Educ:* Wellington Coll. Originally intended for diplomatic career; studied for stage at RADA. First appearance in Treasure Island, Strand Theatre, 1929; appeared in provinces; established repertory (with Peter Bull) at Perranporth, Cornwall; parts include: Oscar Wilde in play of that name, Gate, 1936, and Fulton (first New York appearance), 1938; Alexandre Dumas in The Great Romancer, Strand, 1937; Higgins in Pygmalion, Old Vic, 1937; Sheridan Whiteside in The Man Who Came to Dinner, Savoy, 1941; Prince Regent in The First Gentleman, New, 1945, and Savoy; Arnold Holt in Edward My Son, His Majesty's and Lyric, 1947, Martin Beck Theatre, New York, 1948; toured Australia, 1949-50; The Little Hut, Lyric, 1950; Hippo Dancing, Lyric, 1954; A Likely Tale, Globe, 1956; Fanny, Drury Lane, 1957; Hook, Line and Sinker, Piccadilly, 1958; A Majority of One, Phœnix, 1960; A Time to Laugh, Piccadilly, 1962; Halfway Up The Tree, Queen's, 1968; How the Other Half Loves, Lyric, 1970. Directed: The Tunnel of Love, Her Majesty's Theatre, 1957; Once More, with Feeling, New Theatre, 1959. Entered films, 1937; *films:* Marie Antoinette; Major Barbara; Young Mr Pitt; Outcast of the Islands; The African Queen; Curtain Up; Mr Gilbert and Mr Sullivan; The Final Test; Beat the Devil; The Rainbow Jacket; Beau Brummell; The Good Die Young; Quentin Durward; Loser Takes All; Law and Disorder; The Journey; The Doctor's Dilemma; Libel; The Battle of the Sexes; Oscar Wilde; Go to Blazes; The Young Ones; The Boys; The Road to Hong Kong; Nine Hours to Rama; The Old Dark House; Murder at the Gallop; Take her, She's Mine; Hot Enough for June; Sold in Egypt; Topkapi; Of Human Bondage; Those Magnificent Men in Their Flying Machines; Ghengis Khan; ABC Murders; The Loved One; Life at the Top; A Study in Terror; Way Way Out; Finders Keepers; Hotel Paradiso; Le Tendre Voyou; Hot Millions; Sinful Davey; Song of Norway; Oliver Cromwell; When Eight Bells Toll; Doctor in Trouble. *Publications:* Short Story, 1935; Goodness How Sad, 1937; Staff Dance, 1944; (with Noel Langley) Edward My Son, 1948; (with Ronald Gow) The Full Treatment, 1953; Hippo Dancing, 1953; (with Dundas Hamilton) Six Months Grace, 1957; (with Sewell Stokes) Responsible Gentleman (autobiography), 1966. *Recreations:* conversation, horse racing. *Address:* Fairmans, Wargrave, Berks. *Clubs:* Buck's, Garrick.

**MORLEY, Rev. Canon William Fenton;** Vicar of Leeds, Rural Dean of Leeds, and Hon. Canon of Ripon, since 1961; *b* 5 May 1912; *s* of Arthur Fenton and Margaret Morley; *m* 1937, Marjorie Rosa, *d* of Joseph Temple Robinson, Frinton; one *s* one *d*. *Educ:* St David's, Lampeter; Oriel Coll., Oxford; Wycliffe Hall, Oxford; University of London. Ordained, 1935; Curate of: Ely, Cardiff, 1935-38; Porthcawl, S Wales, 1938-43; Officiating Chaplain to the Forces, 1941-43; Vicar of Penrhiwceiber, 1943-46; Rector of Haseley, Oxon, 1946-50; Director of Music and Lecturer in Hebrew at Cuddesdon Coll., Oxon, 1946-50; Examiner in Hebrew and New Testament Greek, 1947-59 and External Lecturer in Biblical and Religious Studies, 1950-61, Univ. of London; Chaplain and Lecturer of St Gabriel's Training Coll., 1956-61; Education Sec. to Overseas Council of Church Assembly, 1950-56; Warburton Lectr, Lincoln's Inn, 1963-65; Chm., Church of England Deployment and Payment Commission, 1965-68. Public Preacher to Diocese of Rochester, 1950-56; Canon Residentiary and Precentor of Southwark Cathedral, 1956-61; Ed., East and West Review, 1953-64. Chaplain to HM's Household, 1965-; Church Comr, 1968-. *Publications:* One Church, One Faith, One Lord, 1953; The Church to Which You Belong, 1955; The Call of God, 1959. *Recreations:* music, writing. *Address:* Leeds Vicarage, 81 Clarendon Road, Leeds 2. *T:* Leeds 2-7828. *Clubs:* United University; Leeds.

**MORLING, Col Leonard Francis,** DSO 1940; OBE 1946; TD 1942; Architect; *b* 2 Nov. 1904, British; 2nd *s* of late Ernest Charles Morling and Frances Ruth Baldwin; unmarried. *Educ:* Brighton Hove and Sussex Grammar Sch. Architect, 1927-36; Mem. of firm, C. Morling Ltd, Builders and Contractors, Seaford, 1936-39; social work, in London, 1948-50, Malaya, 1950-55; Personnel and Welfare Work, London, 1956-59, Australia, 1960-63, London, 1964. Comnd, Terrtl Army, 1924; Capt. 1930; Major, 1934; Lt-Col, 1943; Col 1946; served France and Flanders (despatches, DSO); Persia, Iraq and India. *Address:* c/o Lloyds Bank Ltd, Seaford, Sussex.

**MORNINGTON, Earl of; Arthur Charles Valerian Wellesley;** *b* 19 Aug. 1945; *s* and *heir* of Marquess Douro, *qv*. *Educ:* Eton; Christ Church, Oxford. *Address:* Park Corner, Heckfield, Basingstoke, Hants. *T:* Heckfield 267.

**MORPETH, Viscount; George William Beaumont Howard;** *b* 15 Feb. 1949; *s* and *heir* of 12th Earl of Carlisle, *qv*. *Educ:* Balliol Coll., Oxford. 2nd Lt 9/12 Royal Lancers, 1967. *Address:* Naworth Castle, Brampton, Cumberland.

**MORPURGO, Jack Eric;** Professor of American Literature, University of Leeds, since 1969; author; Deputy Chairman, National Book League, since 1969; *b* 26 April 1918; *s* of late Mark Morpurgo, Islington; *m* 1946, Catherine Noel Kippe, *d* of late Prof. Emile Cammaerts; three *s* one *d*. *Educ:* Christ's Hosp.; Univ. of New Brunswick; Coll. of William and Mary, USA (BA). Enlisted RA, 1939; served as regimental and staff officer in India, Middle East, Greece and Italy; GSO 2, Public Relations Directorate, War Office. Editorial Staff, Penguin Books, 1946-49; Editor Penguin Parade; General Editor, Pelican Histories, 1949-61; Asst Dir, Nuffield Foundation, 1950-54; Dir-Gen., Nat. Book League, 1955-69; Prof. of American Studies, Univ. of Geneva, 1968-70 Visiting Prof., Michigan State Univ., 1950, George Washington Univ., 1970; has lectured in USA, Canada, Germany, India, Burma, etc. Dir of Unesco Seminar on Production of Reading Materials, Rangoon, 1957, Madras, 1959. Mem., UK-USA Teacher Exchange Cttee; Donation Governor, Christ's Hospital; Governor, British and Foreign School Soc.; Chm. Working Pty on Medical Libraries; Dir, William and Mary Historical Project, 1970-. Phi Beta Kappa, 1948; Hon. Fellow, Coll. of William and Mary, 1949. Hon. LitD Maine, 1961; Hon. DLitt Elmira, 1966; Hon. DHL William and Mary, 1970. *Publications:* American Excursion, 1949; Charles Lamb and Elia, 1949; The Road to Athens, 1963; contributor to: The Impact of America (with Bertrand Russell and others), 1951. Joint

Author of: History of The United States (with Russel B. Nye), 1955; Venice (with Martin Hürlimann), 1964. Edited: Leigh Hunt: Autobiography, 1949; E. J. Trelawny: Last Days of Shelley and Byron, 1952; Selected Poems of John Keats, 1953; Rugby Football: An Anthology (with Kenneth Pelmear), 1958; Cobbett: a year's residence in USA, 1964; Cooper: The Spy, 1968. *Recreation:* watching Rugby football. *Address:* Oxhey Hall, Hampermill Lane, Near Watford, Herts. *T:* Watford 28466; Cliff Cottage, Cliff Road, Leeds 6. *Clubs:* *Arts, Pilgrims.*

**MORRAH, Dermot Michael Macgregor,** FSA; Arundel Herald Extraordinary, since 1953; *b* 26 April 1896; *er s* of late Herbert Arthur Morrah and late Alice Elise, *d* of Major C. A. Macgregor, RE; *m* 1923, Ruth (*see* Ruth Morrah), *er d* of late Willmott Houselander; two *d. Educ:* Winchester; New Coll., Oxford. Served European War in Royal Engineers, 1915-19. 1st class, Modern History, 1921; MA 1921; Fellow of All Souls Coll., 1921-28; FRHistS, 1922-57; Home Civil Service, 1922-28; Leader-writer, Daily Mail, 1928-31, The Times, 1932-61, The Round Table, 1942-44; The Daily Telegraph, 1961-67; Editor, The Round Table, 1944-65. Represented The Times at Coronation, 1937, 1953; royal tour of South Africa, 1947; Mem. Council Commonwealth Press Union, 1945-; and Chm., Press Freedom Cttee, 1956-; Chm., IEC Wine Soc., 1959-63; Chm., Circle of Wine Writers, 1964-66; Hon. Life Mem., Brit. Red Cross Soc., 1945. Freeman of the City of London, 1960. *Publications:* If It Had Happened Yesterday, 1930; The Mummy Case, 1933; The British Red Cross, 1944; Most Excellent Majesty, 1953 (revised as Crown and People, 1959); History of Industrial Assurance, 1955; The Work of the Queen, 1958; To Be a King, 1968. For King George's Jubilee Trust: The Royal Family in Wartime, 1945; Princess Elizabeth, 1947; The Royal Family in Africa, 1947; The Royal Family, 1950; Princess Elizabeth, Duchess of Edinburgh, 1950. *Plays:* Caesar's Friend (with late Campbell Dixon), 1933; Chorus Angelorum, 1937. *Films:* Royal Heritage, 1953; The Coronation Ceremony, 1953. *Recreations:* chess (for Oxford against Cambridge, 1920), ombre, wine. *Address:* 131a Ashley Gardens, SW1. *T:* 01-828 3187. *Clubs:* Oxford and Cambridge, Saintsbury.

**MORRAH, Ruth (Mrs Dermot Morrah),** JP; Chairman, Metropolitan Juvenile Courts, 1945-64; *b* 21 Aug. 1899; *d* of Willmott Houselander; *m* 1923, Dermot Morrah, *qv*; two *d. Educ:* convent schs; St Anne's Coll., Oxford. JP 1944. Pro Ecclesia et Pontifice, 1964. *Recreations:* travelling, needlework. *Address:* 131a Ashley Gardens, SW1. *T:* 01-828 3187.

**MORRELL, A(rthur) Claude,** CBE 1952; MC 1917; Chairman, John Morrell & Co. Ltd, 1929-69; *b* 3 April 1894; *s* of Alfred Morrell, CBE, Liverpool; *m* 1931, Laura May, *d* of Andrew D. Mearns, Blundellsands, Lancs; no *c. Educ:* Malvern Coll. Served European War, 1914-19 (MC): with the King's (Liverpool) Regt and on General Staff, Fourth Army, Dir, Martins Bank, 1944-68. JP (Cheshire), 1945. *Recreations:* golf, music. *Address:* Thor's Hill, Thurstaston, Wirral, Cheshire. *T:* 051-648 1306. *Clubs:* Athenæum, Royal Liverpool Golf (Liverpool).

**MORRELL, Col (Herbert) William (James),** OBE 1954; MC 1944; TD; DL; JP; *b* 1 Aug. 1915; *er s* of James Herbert Morrell, MA, Headington Hill, Oxford; *m* 1947, Pamela Vivien Eleanor, *d* of Richard Stubbs, Willaston, Cheshire; one *s* two *d. Educ:* Eton; Magdalen Coll., Oxford (MA). 2nd Lt RA, 1936; served War of 1939-45 (France, Madagascar, Burma); retired 1948. DL 1961, JP 1959, High Sheriff 1960, Oxon. *Recreations:* hunting, sailing. *Address:* Caphill, Sandford St Martin, Oxon. *T:* Great Tew 291.

**MORRELL, Rt. Rev. James Herbert Lloyd;** *see* Lewes, Suffragan Bishop of.

**MORRELL, Col William;** *see* Morrell, Col H. W. J.

**MORRELL, William Bowes;** Managing Director, Westminster Press Ltd (formerly Westminster Press Provincial Newspapers Ltd), since 1965; *b* York, 18 Feb. 1913; *s* of J. B. Morrell, LLD, JP and Bertha Morrell (*née* Spence Watson); *m* 1939, Kate Lisa, *d* of Prof. E. and Elisabeth Probist; three *s. Educ:* Bootham Sch., York; St John's Coll., Cambridge (MA). Served War of 1939-45 (2 stars, 2 medals), RA; Capt. 1945. Birmingham Gazette and Despatch Ltd; Dir and Manager, 1948-53; Man. Dir, 1953-57; Westminster Press Provincial Newspapers Ltd; Dir and Gen. Man., 1957-58; Advertisement Dir, 1958-64; Dep. Man. Dir, 1964-65. Chairman: Joseph Rowntree Social Service Trust Ltd; Turret Press (Holdings) Ltd; Pearson Longman Ltd; Press Assoc. Ltd; Director: Merritt & Hatcher Ltd; Southern Publishing Co. Ltd; Birmingham Post & Mail Ltd; Evening Mail Ltd; Droitwich Medical Trust Ltd; Ings Property Co. Ltd. Member: Newspaper Soc. Council; Court of Univ. of York. Liveryman, Co. of Stationers and Newspaper Makers. *Recreations:* swimming, golf, sea fishing. *Address:* 99 South End Road, NW3. *T:* 01-435 0785; Flat 1, Ingram House, 90 Bootham, York. *T:* York 23197. *Club:* Lansdowne.

**MORREN, Sir William Booth Rennie,** Kt 1952; CBE 1943; MVO 1937; Chief Constable of the City of Edinburgh, 1935-55, retired: ARP Controller of City of Edinburgh, 1940-45; *b* Aberdeen, 3 July 1890; *s* of late John Morren, OBE, Rhynie, Aberdeenshire, Chief Constable of Counties of Roxburgh, Berwick, and Selkirk; *m* 1916, Grace Evelyn Thorburn, *o d* of John T. Falconer; two *s* one *d*. Served in European War with Royal Scots (Capt.). Pres. Chief Constables Assoc. of Scotland, 1947. Chm., British Police Athletic Assoc., 1950-54; 1st Pres., European Police Sports Union, 1950-56; Life Pres., 1956-. Joint Chm. St Andrews Ambulance Assoc. SE Scotland and Chm. Scottish Ambulance Cttee for Edinburgh, 1960-65. Appointed Dep. Lord High Constable of Scotland during Royal State Visit to Scotland, 1953. Fellow Ancient Monuments Soc., 1957. King Haakon VII Liberty Cross of Norway, 1947; Swedish Police Sports Assoc. Gold Medal of Hon., 1952; Norwegian Police Sports Assoc. Medal of Hon., 1956. Gold Medal of Hon., European Police Sports Union, 1964. *Address:* 9 Murrayfield Drive, Edinburgh.

**MORRIS,** family name of **Barons Killanin, Morris, Morris of Borth-y-Gest, Morris of Grasmere** and **Morris of Kenwood.**

**MORRIS,** 2nd Baron, *cr* 1918; **Michael Morris,** MA Cantab; Squadron Leader, RAFVR (retired); Solicitor; Senior Partner in Blount Petre & Co.; Director, Building Contracting Associates Ltd; *b* 12 April 1903; *s* of 1st Baron and Isabel Langrishe (*d* 1934), *d* of Rev. William Legallais; *S* father 1935; *m* 1st, 1933; two *s* two *d*; 2nd, 1960, Mary, *yr d* of late Rev. A. R. Langhorne, and of Mrs Langhorne. *Educ:* Downside; Trinity Coll., Cambridge. Called to Bar, Inner Temple, 1925. Served RAFVR 1939-43; Legal Staff Officer to RAF,

Middle East Command, and Military Prosecutor of Palestine, 1940-42. Dir and some time Chm. of Solicitors Benevolent Assoc.; Mem. of Conservative Sub-Cttee on Reforms in the Administration of Justice. Has taken part in the BBC Brains Trust. *Recreation:* racing. *Heir: s* Hon. Michael David Morris, *b* 9 Dec. 1937. *Address:* 8 Carlos Place, Grosvenor Square, W1. *T:* 01-499 2807; Chantry, Ogbourne Saint George, Marlborough, Wilts.

**MORRIS OF BORTH-Y-GEST,** Baron (Life Peer) *cr* 1960; **John William Morris,** PC 1951; Kt 1945; CBE, 1945; MC; a Lord of Appeal in Ordinary since 1960; *b* 11 Sept. 1896; *s* of Daniel and Ellen Morris, Liverpool and Portmadoc. *Educ:* Liverpool Institute, Liverpool; Trinity Hall, Cambridge (MA, LLB, Hon. Fellow, 1951); Harvard Law Sch., Harvard Univ., USA. Served in Royal Welch Fusiliers, 1916-19; two years in France; Capt.; Pres. Cambridge Union Soc., 1919; Joseph Hodges Choate Memorial Fellowship, Harvard Univ., USA, 1920-21; called to Bar, Inner Temple, 1921; Bencher, 1943; Reader, 1966; Treasurer, 1967; Northern Circuit; KC 1935; Judge of Appeal, IOM, 1938-45; a Judge of the High Court, King's Bench Division, 1945-51; a Lord Justice of Appeal, 1951-60. Contested Ilford Div. (L) in 1923, 1924; Hon. Standing Counsel to the Univ. of Wales, 1938-45; HM Commissioner of Assize, Northern Circuit, 1942, and at Birmingham, Dec. 1944; Dep. Chm., Home Office Adv. Cttee, under Defence Regns, 1940-45; prepared Report for Treasury on Requisitioning, 1941; Chm., Home Office Cttee on War Damaged Licensed Houses, 1942-43; Chm., Cttee on the Selling Price of Houses, 1945; Chm., Courts of Inquiry into Engineering and Shipbuilding Wages Disputes, 1954; acted as Referee to decide the wage questions upon Settlement of Railway Strike, 1955; Chm. of National Reference Tribunal under the Coal-Mining Industry Conciliation Scheme, 1955-65; Chm., Home Office Cttee on Jury Service, 1963-64. Pres., London Welsh Assoc., 1951-53; Hon. Mem., Canadian and American Bar Assocs; Member: Pilgrims Soc.; Univ. Grants Cttee, 1955-69; Charing Cross Hosp. Council of Management, 1941-48 and of Board of Governors of Group, 1948-68; Pro-Chancellor of Univ. of Wales, 1956-; Mem., the Gorsedd. Commissary of the Univ. of Cambridge, 1968-. JP 1939, DL 1951, Caernarvonshire; Dep.-Chm., Caernarvonshire QS, 1939-43, and Chm., 1943-69. Hon. LLD (Univ. of Wales, 1946; Univ. of British Columbia, 1952; Univ. of Liverpool, 1966; Univ. of Cambridge, 1967). *Address:* House of Lords, SW1; Bryn Gaualit, Portmadoc, North Wales. *Clubs:* Athenæum, Reform, MCC.

**MORRIS OF GRASMERE,** Baron *cr* 1967 (Life Peer), of Grasmere; **Charles Richard Morris,** KCMG 1963; Kt 1953; MA Oxon; Hon. LLD: Manchester, 1951; Aberdeen, 1963; Leeds, 1964; Malta, 1964; Hull, 1965; Hon. DLitt: Sydney, 1954; Lancaster, 1967; Chairman, Councils for Training of Health Visitors and for Training in Social Work, since 1963; *b* 25 Jan. 1898; *s* of M. C. Morris, Sutton Valence, Kent; *m* 1923, Mary de Selincourt; one *s* one *d.* *Educ:* Tonbridge Sch.; Trinity Coll., Oxford. Lt RGA 1916-19; Fellow and Tutor of Balliol Coll., 1921-43; for one year, 1926-27 (while on leave of absence from Balliol), Prof. of Philosophy, Univ. of Michigan, USA; Senior Proctor, 1937-38; Mem. of Council of Girls Public Day Sch. Trust, 1933-38; Oxford City Councillor, 1939-41; Ministry of Supply, 1939-42; Under-Sec., Min. of Production, 1942-43; Head Master, King Edward's Sch., Birmingham, 1941-48; Chm., Cttee of Vice-Chancellors and Principals, 1952-55; Central Joint Adv. Cttee on Tutorial Classes, 1948-58; Commonwealth Univ. Interchange Cttee and Recruitment Sub-Cttee of British Council, 1951; Sch. Broadcasting Council, 1954-64; Inter-Univ. Council for Higher Education Overseas, 1957-64; Independent Chm., Jt Adv. Cttee for Wool Textile Industry, 1952; Pres., Council of Coll. of Preceptors, 1954-63. Vice-Chancellor of Leeds Univ., 1948-63; Pro-Chancellor, Univ. of Bradford, 1966-. Member: Royal Commn on Local Govt in Greater London, 1957; Cttee of Inquiry on Australian Univs, 1957; Chairman: Adv. Bd Of Univs Quarterly, 1960; Local Govt Training Bd, 1967-; President: Brit. Student Tuberculosis Foundn, 1960; Assoc. of Teachers in Colls and Depts of Educn, 1961-64. *Publications:* A History of Political Ideas (with Mary Morris), 1924; Locke, Berkeley, Hume, 1931; Idealistic Logic, 1933; In Defence of Democracy (with J. S. Fulton), 1936; British Democracy, 1939; various essays and papers to learned societies. *Recreation:* fell walking. *Address:* Ladywood, Grasmere, Westmorland. *T:* 286. *Club:* Athenæum.

**MORRIS OF KENWOOD,** 2nd Baron *cr* 1950, of Kenwood; **Philip Geoffrey Morris;** JP; Company Director; *b* 18 June 1928; *s* of 1st Baron Morris of Kenwood, and Florence, *d* of Henry Isaacs, Leeds; *S* father, 1954; *m* 1958, Ruth, *o d* of Baron Janner, *qv*; one *s* three *d.* *Educ:* Loughborough Coll., Leics. Served RAF Nov. 1946-Feb. 1949; July 1951-Oct. 1955. JP Inner London, 1967. *Recreations:* flying, tennis, golf, ski-ing. *Heir: s* Hon. Jonathan David Morris, *b* 5 Aug. 1968. *Address:* Lawn Cottage, Orchard, Rise, Kingston, Surrey. *T:* 01-942 6321.

**MORRIS, Alfred;** MP (Lab and Co-op) Manchester (Wythenshawe) since 1964; *b* 23 March 1928; *s* of late George Henry Morris and Jessie Morris (*née* Murphy); *m* 1950, Irene (*née* Jones); two *s* two *d.* *Educ:* elem. and evening schs, Manchester; Ruskin Coll., Oxford; St Catherine's, Univ. of Oxford (MA); Univ. of Manchester (Postgrad. certif. in Educn). Employed in office of a Manchester brewing firm from age 14 (HM Forces, 1946-48); Schoolmaster and Adult Educn Lectr, Manchester, 1954-56; Asst Sec., NW & Merseyside and N Wales Dist Jt Adv. Councils for Electricity Supply Industry, 1956-59; Asst Sec., Nat. Jt Adv. Coun. for El. Supply Ind., 1959-61; Asst Labour Relations Officer, The Electricity Coun., London, 1961-64. Nat. Chm., Labour League of Youth, 1950-52; contested Liverpool (Garston), Gen. Elec. 1951; Mem., Bureau and Chm. Control Commn, Internat. Union of Socialist Youth, 1951-54; Observer, Coun. Socialist Internat. and Coun. of Europe, 1952-53; PPS to Minister of Agric., Fisheries and Food, 1964-67, and to Lord President of the Council and Leader of House of Commons, 1968-70. Mem. Exec. Cttee British Group, Inter-Parly Union, 1966-; Sec., Britain and Common Market Group of Labour MPs and Peers, 1967; Mem., Gen. Adv. Council, BBC, 1968-; Representative of Privy Council on Council of RCVS, 1969-. Patron of Disablement Income Group, 1970-; Promoted Chronically Sick and Disabled Persons Act, 1970, and Food and Drugs (Milk) Act, 1970, as a Private Member. *Publications:* Ed. lectures (Human Relations in Industry), 1958; Ed. Jl (Jt Consultation) publ. Nat. Jt Adv. Coun. Elec. Supply Ind., 1959-61. *Recreations:* gardening, walking, snooker, chess. *Address:* 146 Stafford Road, Caterham, Surrey. *T:* Caterham 42482.

**MORRIS, Most Rev. (Alfred) Edwin,** DD; retired as Archbishop of Wales (1957-67) and Bishop of Monmouth (1945-67); *b* 8 May 1894; *s* of Alfred Morris, 42 Stourbridge Road, Lye, Stourbridge; *m* 1925, E. L. Davis (*d* 1968); four *s* one *d*. *Educ:* St David's Coll., Lampeter (Senior Scholar); BA 1922 (1st Class Hons Theol); St John's Coll., Oxford (Exhibitioner); BD Lampeter, 1932; DD (Lambeth) 1950; Junior Septuagint Prize, Oxford, 1923; Junior Greek Testament Prize, Oxford, 1924; 1st Cl. Hons in Theology and BA Oxon, 1924; Prof. of Hebrew and Theology at St David's Coll., Lampeter, 1924-45; MA Oxon, 1928; served in France with RAMC (9th Div.), European War; Examining Chaplain to the Bishop of Bangor, 1925-28; Examining Chaplain to the Bishop of Llandaff, 1931-39; Lloyd Williams Fellow of St David's Coll., Lampeter, 1931-45; Hon. Fellow, St John's Coll., Oxford, 1958. Hon. Canon, St David's Cathedral, 1968. Sub-Prelate, OStJ, 1958. *Publications:* The Church in Wales and Nonconformity, 1949; The Problem of Life and Death, 1950; The Catholicity of the Book of Common Prayer, 1952; The Christian Use of Alcoholic Beverages, 1961. *Recreations:* gardening, oil painting. *Address:* Noyadd, Llanfair Clydogau, Lampeter, Cards. *T:* Llangybi 278; Llyndir, Porth Sele, St David's, Pembs.

**MORRIS, Brig. Arthur De Burgh,** CBE 1949 (OBE 1948); DSO 1944; retired; *b* 11 Dec. 1902; *s* of late Lt-Col G. M. Morris, 8th Gurkha Rifles; *m* 1928, Doreen, *d* of late Sir Henry Miller, Londonderry; one *d*. *Educ:* Wellington Coll.; RMC, Sandhurst. Commissioned 2nd Lt, into 1st Sherwood Foresters, 1922; Adjt, 8th Sherwood Foresters, 1930-34; transferred to 8th Gurkha Rifles, 1936; Bde Major, Thal Bde NWFP, 1941-42; Temp. Lt-Col and Comd 1/8 Gurkha Rifles, 1943; served in Arakan and Burma, 1944 (DSO); Temp. Col and 2nd i/c 37 Inf. Bde (Gurkha), 1945; Temp. Brig. and Comd 49 Indian Inf. Bde, Nov. 1945; served in Java, 1946-47 (OBE); Comd North Malaya Sub. Dist, 1947-48 (CBE); Comdr Kowloon Inf. Bde, 1948; Brigade of Gurkhas, 1948; Comdr 48 Gurkha Inf., Bde, Malaya, 1950-53 (despatches); Perak Meritorious Service Medal (Malaya), 1953; retired, 1953. Now Dir and part owner, Osborne and Patton Ltd (wine and spirit co.), Londonderry. High Sheriff, City of Londonderry, 1964. *Recreations:* hunting and shooting. *Address:* Prospect House, Carrigans, Co. Donegal, Eire. *Club:* Army and Navy.

*See also N. G. Morris.*

**MORRIS, Rt. Rev. Arthur Harold;** DD (Lambeth), 1954; *b* 20 Feb. 1898; *s* of E. H. Morris, Ross-on-Wye, Herefordshire; *m* 1924, Evelyn Ethel Woods (*d* 1953); three *s*. *Educ:* Cambridge and County High Sch. for Boys; Fitzwilliam Hall, Cambridge; Ridley Hall, Cambridge. 2nd Lt, The King's (Liverpool Regt), 1917. Took degrees BA and LLB, Cambridge, 1920 (Law Tripos); MA 1924. Deacon, 1922, Priest, 1923. Vicar of Great Clacton with Little Holland, 1926; Metropolitan Sec., Church Pastoral-Aid Soc., 1930; Vicar of St Mark's, Hamilton Terrace, London, 1933; Rural Dean of St Marylebone, 1940; officiating chaplain RAF, 1940-45; Proctor in Convocation for Diocese of London, 1945; Archdeacon of Halifax and Canon of St Hilda in Wakefield Cathedral, 1946; Proctor in Convocation, Diocese of Wakefield, 1946; Bishop Suffragan and Archdeacon of Pontefract, and Canon of St Chad in Wakefield Cathedral, 1949-54; Bishop of St Edmundsbury and Ipswich, 1954-65. Mem. Leeds Regional Hosp. Bd, 1951; Church Commissioner, 1952; Mem. Bd of Governors, Church Comrs, 1954; Chm., Council for Women's Ministry in the Church (called Central Council for Women's Church Work until 1960), 1955-60: Mem. Admin. Cttee, Church Comrs, 1956-64; Vice-Chm. Pastoral Cttee, 1964-65; Mem. of the House of Lords, 1959-65; Chm., Board of Governors, Felixstowe Coll., 1960. *Recreation:* Rotary (President, St Marylebone Club, 1944). *Address:* 41 Heathside Road, Woking, Surrey.

**MORRIS, Brig. Arthur Henry Musgrave,** CBE 1957; DSO 1945; MC 1940; GM 1940; Royal Engineers, retired; Director-General, British Quarrying and Slag Federation; *b* 22 Oct. 1904; *s* of late Col A. E. Morris, Edenderry, Offaly, Ireland; *m* Marianne Müller, Karlsbad; two *d*. *Educ:* Cheltenham; RMA Woolwich. Commd RE (2nd Lt), 1924; service in: India, Burma, 1926-32; UK, 1932-39; France (BEF), 1940; USA (Joint Staff Mission), 1941; Italy, 1943-45 (despatches twice); Austria, 1945-46; Palestine, 1947; Germany, 1948-51; Korea, 1953-54. Col 1951; Brig. 1955; retd 1957. *Recreations:* painting, writing. *Address:* 15 Fort Road, Guildford, Surrey. *T:* 62998.

**MORRIS, Prof. Benjamin Stephen;** Professor of Education, University of Bristol (Director of Institute of Education, 1956-68); *b* 25 May 1910; *s* of Rev. B. S. Morris, Sherborne, Dorset, and Annie McNicol Duncan, Rothesay, Bute; *m* 1938, Margaret, *d* of Mr and Mrs Lamont, Glasgow; two *s* one *d*. *Educ:* Rothesay Academy; Glasgow Univ. BSc 1933, MEd 1937 (Glasgow). Trained as teacher, Jordanhill Training Coll., Glasgow; teacher, primary and secondary schs, 1936-39; Lecturer: in Psychology, Logic and Ethics, Jordanhill Trng Coll., 1939-40; in Educn, Univ. of Glasgow, 1940-46. Temp. Civil Servant, Min. of Food, 1941; Army Psychologist, 1942-46; Sen. Psychologist (WOSB), 1945-46; Hon. Lt-Col 1946. Student at Inst. of Psychoanalysis, London, 1946-50; Senior staff, Tavistock Institute of Human Relations, 1946-50 (Chm. Management Cttee, 1947-49); Dir Nat. Foundation for Educl Research in England and Wales, 1950-56. *Publications:* Arts and Sciences in Education, 1961; contributed to: The Bearing of Recent Advances in Psychology on Educational Problems; The Year Book of Education, 1955; The Function of Teaching, 1959; How and Why Do We Learn?, 1965; Study of Education, 1966; articles in educational and psychological jls. *Recreation:* living in the country. *Address:* Bracken Hill, Wrington, Som.

**MORRIS, C. J.;** *see* Morris, John.

**MORRIS, Sir Cedric Lockwood,** 9th Bt, *cr* 1806, of Clasemont, Glamorganshire; painter and horticulturist; Principal of The East Anglian School of Painting and Drawing, Hadleigh, Suffolk; President, South Wales Art Society; *b* Sketty, Glamorganshire, 11 Dec. 1889; *s* of Sir George Lockwood Morris, 8th Bt; *S* father, 1947; unmarried. *Educ:* Charterhouse; on the Continent. In early years worked as a farmer in Canada; studied art in Paris, Berlin, and Rome; works in most public galleries; served in the ranks, 1914-15; later with Remounts; International Exhibitor at Venice, Chicago, Brussels, etc; Exhibitions at Rome, 1922; New York, 1923; London (private), 1923; New York, 1924; Paris, 1925; London, 1928; The Hague, 1928; London, 1931, 1934, 1936, 1940, 1944, and 1952. RCA (Wales), 1930. Lectr in Design, RCA (London), 1950-53. Vice-Pres., Contemporary Art Soc. for Wales, 1967. *Publications:* reproductions of works in art and general periodicals; illustrations to books treating of plant and bird life; articles and poems. *Heir:* *c* Robert Byng Morris [*b* 25 Feb. 1913; *m* 1947, Christine Kathleen, *d* of Archibald Field, Toddington, Glos; one *s* three *d*]. *Address:* Benton End, Hadleigh, Suffolk.

**MORRIS, Charles Alfred,** RWS 1949 (ARWS 1943); RBA 1948; retired as Vice-Principal Brighton College of Art (1952-59); Vice-President, RWS, 1957-60; *b* 5 Sept. 1898; *s* of G. W. Morris and Susan (*née* Lee); *m* 1927, Alice Muriel Drummond; one *s* two *d. Educ:* Royal Academy Schs and Brighton Coll. of Art. Served with HAC, 1916-19. Teacher of advanced drawing and painting, Liverpool Coll. of Art, 1926; Senior Asst, County Sch. of Art, Worthing, 1931, Principal, 1942. Pres. Soc. of Sussex Painters, 1962. Examples of work in following public collections: Birkenhead, Blackburn, Brighton, Eastbourne, Hove, Worthing. *Recreation:* gardening. *Address:* Hillside Cottage, Burpham, Arundel, Sussex. *T:* Arundel 3019.

**MORRIS, Charles Richard;** MP (Lab) Openshaw Division of Manchester since Dec. 1963; Parliamentary Private Secretary to Rt. Hon. H. Wilson, MP, since 1970; *b* 14 Dec. 1926; *s* of George Henry Morris, Newton Heath, Manchester; *m* 1950, Pauline, *d* of Albert Dunn, Manchester; two *d. Educ:* Brookdale Park Sch., Manchester. Served with Royal Engineers, 1945-48. Pres., Clayton Labour Party, 1950-52. Mem. of Manchester Corporation, 1954-64: Chm. of Transport Cttee, 1959-62; Dep. Chm. of Establishment Cttee, 1963-64. Mem., Post Office Workers Union (Mem. Nat. Exec. Council, 1959-63). Contested (Lab) Cheadle Div. of Cheshire, 1959. PPS to the Postmaster-General, 1964; Govt Asst Whip, 1966-67; Vice-Chamberlain, HM Household, 1967-69; Treasurer, HM Household (Deputy Chief Whip), 1969-70. *Address:* 16 Parkwood Road, Northenden, Manchester 23. *T:* 061-998 5735.

**MORRIS, Prof. Colin John Owen Rhonabwy,** MSc, PhD; Professor of Experimental Biochemistry, London Hospital Medical College, University of London, since 1954; *b* 3 May 1910; *s* of John Jenkin Morris and Annie Margaret (*née* Thomas); *m* 1946, Peggy (*née* Clark); one *d* (and one *d* decd). *Educ:* Cowbridge Grammar Sch.; University Coll., Cardiff (MSc Wales). Lister Institute, London, 1932-36 (PhD London); Kaiser Wilhelm Institute, Heidelberg, 1936-37; London Hospital and London Hospital Med. Coll., 1937-; Reader in Chemical Pathology, 1947. *Publications:* (with Mrs P. Morris) Separation Methods in Biochemistry, 1964; numerous scientific papers in Journal of Chem. Soc., Biochem. Jl, etc. *Recreation:* sailing. *Address:* 14 Trowlock Avenue, Teddington, Middx. *T:* 01-977 4853.

**MORRIS, David Edward;** Scientific Adviser (Civil Aviation), Board of Trade, since 1969; *b* 23 July 1915; *m* 1950, Heather Anne Court; one *s* two *d. Educ:* University Coll. of North Wales, Bangor; Trinity Coll., Cambridge. Aerodynamics Dept, RAE, 1938-56; Chief Supt, A&AEE, 1956-59; Chief Supt, RAE, Bedford, 1959-61; Dir-General, Development (RAF), Min. of Aviation, 1961-65; Dir-Gen., Civil Aircraft and Gen. Services Research and Develt, 1965-69. FRAeS 1956. *Publications:* various reports and memoranda. *Recreations:* walking, swimming, bridge. *Address:* 38 Days Lane, Biddenham, Bedford. *T:* 66644.

**MORRIS, Denis Edward,** OBE 1958; Member, Public Relations and Promotion Sub-Committee, Test and County Cricket Board, since 1968; Head, and ultimately Controller of Light Programme, BBC, 1960-67; *b* 29 June 1907; *s* of Philip and Edith Morris; *m* 1st, 1931, Angela Moore (marr. diss., 1942); one *s*; 2nd, 1943, Catherine Garrett (*née* Anderton); one *s. Educ:* Tonbridge Sch. BBC Talks Producer, 1936; BBC Midland Public Relations Officer, 1938; BBC Empire Public Relations Officer, 1939; MOI Dir, Midland Region, 1940-42; BBC Midland Regional Programme Dir, 1943-48; Head of Midland Regional Programmes, 1948-60. Leicester City Coucil, 1933-36; Chm., Lord Mayor of Birmingham's War Relief Fund Publicity and Appeals Cttee, 1942-48; Member: Hosp. Management Cttee, St Francis Hosp. and Lady Chichester Hosp., 1966-; Exec. Cttee, Nat. Cricket Assoc., 1969- (Chm., Public Relations Standing Cttee, 1969-); Dep. Chm., Lord's Taverners' Council, 1963-65 (Mem., 1962-67); Public Relations Advisor to MCC and the Counties, 1967-68. *Publications:* Poultry-Keeping for Profit, 1949; The French Vineyards, 1958. *Recreations:* swimming, golf, drinking wine and writing about it (for Daily Telegraph and Field). *Address:* The Ring House, Nepcote Green, Findon, Sussex. *T:* Findon 3256. *Clubs:* MCC; Incogniti Cricket; Sussex Martlets CC; Gentlemen of Leicestershire CC; Blackheath Rugby Football; Sussex Rugby Football.

**MORRIS, Desmond John,** DPhil; privately engaged in writing books on animal and human behaviour since 1968; *b* 24 Jan. 1928; *s* of Capt. Harry Howe Morris and Dorothy Marjorie Fuller Morris (*née* Hunt); *m* 1952, Ramona Baulch; one *s. Educ:* Dauntsey's Sch.; Birmingham Univ. (BSc); Magdalen Coll., Oxford (DPhil). Postdoctoral research in Animal Behaviour, Dept of Zoology, Oxford Univ., 1954-56; Head of Granada TV and Film Unit at Zool. Soc. of London, 1956-59; Curator of Mammals, Zool. Soc. of London, 1959-67; Dir, Inst. of Contemp. Arts, London, 1967-68. Chm. of TV programmes: Zootime (weekly), 1956-67; Life (fortnightly), 1965-68. *Publications:* (Jt Ed.) International Zoo Yearbook, 1959-62; The Biology of Art, 1962; The Mammals: A Guide to the Living Species, 1965; (with Ramona Morris) Men and Snakes, 1965; (with Ramona Morris) Men and Apes, 1966; (with Ramona Morris) Men and Pandas, 1966; The Naked Ape, 1967; (ed) Primate Ethology, 1967; The Human Zoo, 1969; Patterns of Reproductive Behaviour, 1970; numerous papers in zoological jls. *Recreations:* painting, archæology. *Address:* Villa Apap Bologna, Attard, Malta.

**MORRIS, Air Marshal Sir Douglas (Griffith),** KCB 1962 (CB 1954); CBE 1945; DSO 1945; DFC 1941; AOC-in-C, RAF Fighter Command, 1962-66; *b* 3 Dec. 1908; 2nd *s* of D. G. Morris, late of Natal, South Africa; *m* 1936, Audrey Beryl Heard; one *s* one *d. Educ:* St John's Coll., Johannesburg, South Africa. Commissioned RAF, 1930; trained as pilot, 1930-31; No. 40 (B) Sqdn, 1931-32; Fleet Air Arm, 1932-34; qualified as Flying Instructor, Central Flying Sch., 1934; on instructor duties, 1934-40; RAF Staff Coll., 1940; Air Ministry, 1940-41; on night fighting ops, 1941-42; Comdg No. 406 RCAF Sqdn, 1941-42, as Wing Comdr; Comd RAF North Weald, as Group Capt., 1942-43; on staff of Allied Exped. Air HQ, 1943-44; Comd No. 132 (F) Wing, 1944-45, in Normandy, Belgium, Holland; SASO No. 84 Gp HQ, as Air Cdre, Feb.-Nov. 1945; in W Africa, Nov. 1945-46; Jt Planning staff, Min. of Defence, 1946-47; Nat. War Coll., Washington, 1947-48; on staff of Brit. Jt Services Mission, Washington, DC, 1948-50; Sector Comdr, Southern Sector, 1950-52; Sector Comdr, Metropolitan Sector, Fighter Comd, 1952-53; idc 1954; Air Vice-Marshal, 1955, and SASO, 2nd TAF ACAS (Air Defence), 1957-59; Chief of Staff, Allied Air Forces, Central Europe, 1960-62. Comdr Order of St Olav, 1945; Comdr Order of Orange-Nassau, 1947; ADC to King George VI, 1949-52; ADC to the Queen, 1952. Retired, 1966. *Recreations:* golf, ski-ing.

*Address:* Friar's Côte, Northiam, Rye, Sussex. *Club:* Royal Air Force.

**MORRIS, Edward Allan,** CMG 1967; OBE 1961; Crown Agent for Oversea Governments and Administrations since 1968; *b* 8 Sept. 1910; *s* of John Morris, Twickenham; *m* 1957, Phyllis, *d* of late Francis Guise, Twickenham; one *s* one *d*. *Educ:* Hampton Grammar Sch.; Univ. of London (BCom). Entered Crown Agents' Office, 1928. RAFVR, 1942-46; Sqdn Leader (King's Commendation, 1946). Crown Agents' Office: Asst Head of Dept, 1956; Head of Dept, 1958; Asst Crown Agent, 1964; Chm., Millbank Technical Services Ltd, 1967-; Dep. Chm., Sterling Industrial Securities Ltd; Dir, City of London Insurance Co. Ltd and other cos. *Address:* 56 Lebanon Park, Twickenham, Middx. *T:* 01-892 5856.

**MORRIS, Air Commodore Edward James,** CB 1966; CBE 1959; DSO 1942; DFC 1944; RAF, retired 1968; *b* 6 April 1915; *s* of late D. G. Morris, and late Mrs E. Morris, Bulawayo, Southern Rhodesia; *m* 1945, Alison Joan, *d* of Sir Charles Henderson, *qv*; two *s*. *Educ:* Michaelhouse, Natal, S Africa. Commnd, 1937; Fighter Comd, 1938-41; Desert Air Force, 1941-45; Staff Coll., 1945-46; BAFO Germany, 1946-49; Old Sarum, 1949-52; Caledonian Sector, Fighter Command, 1952-53; RAF Flying Coll., 1953-54; Exchange Posting with USAF, Florida, 1954-56; SASO HQ 12 Group, 1956-58; OC Wattisham, 1958-59; HQ Fighter Command, 1959-60; Air Ministry, 1960-64; Chief of Staff, Headquarters Middle East Command, 1964-66; AOC Air Cadets, and Comdt Air Training Corps, 1966-68. American DFC 1945. MBIM. *Recreations:* golf, shooting, fishing, ski-ing. *Address:* 26 Edgecliff Drive, Kloof, Natal, South Africa.

**MORRIS, Most Rev. Edwin;** *see* Morris, Most Rev. A. E.

**MORRIS, Gareth (Charles Walter);** Principal Professor of the Flute, Royal Academy of Music, since 1945; Principal flautist in The Philharmonia Orchestra since 1949; Chairman, New Philharmonia Orchestra, since 1966; *b* Clevedon, Som, 13 May 1920, *e s* of Walter and Enid Morris; *m* 1954, Joy Louise Hazelrigg, Kentucky, USA; one *d*. *Educ:* Bristol Cathedral Sch.; Royal Academy of Music, London. First studied the flute at age of twelve under Robert Murchie and later won a scholarship to RAM. Career since then has been as soloist, chamber music and symphonic player, teacher and lecturer. Has been mem. Arts Council Music Panel, and Warden of Incorporated Soc. of Musicians Soloists Section. Played at Her Majesty's Coronation in Westminster Abbey in 1953. ARAM 1945; FRAM 1950; FRSA 1967. *Recreations:* reading and collecting books; astronomy, antiquarian horology. *Address:* 4 Alwyne Place, Canonbury, N1. *T:* 01-226 4752. *Club:* Royal Automobile.

*See also James Morris.*

**MORRIS, Sir Geoffrey N.;** *see* Newman-Morris.

**MORRIS, Captain George Horace Guy,** CBE 1960; retired; *b* 21 Feb. 1897; *o s* of late H. W. T. Morris of Litherland, County of Lancaster; *m* 1919, Nancy (*d* 1963), *o c* of late Josiah Meir, Tunstall, Staffs; one *s* one *d*. *Educ:* Liverpool. Went to sea as apprentice with W. Lowden & Co., Liverpool, 1912; served as Lt RNR, 1916-20; joined Cunard Line as Junior Officer, 1922; Captain, 1947. Commanded: SS Vasconia, SS Arabia, SS Assyria, RMS Parthia, RMS Media, RMS Scythia, RMS Georgic, RMS Britannic, RMS Caronia, RMS Mauretania. Appointed Relieving Captain Queen Liners, 1956; Captain RMS Queen Mary, 1957; Captain RMS Queen Elizabeth, 1958; Commodore Cunard Line, 1958; retired, 1960. *Recreation:* motoring. *Address:* 6 Archers Court, Arrowe Park, Birkenhead, Cheshire. *T:* 051-677 6723.

**MORRIS, Sir George P.;** *see* Morris, Sir Parker.

**MORRIS, Gwyn Rhyse Francis,** QC 1959; *b* 1910; *s* of late Wm John Morris, Co. Pembroke; *m* 1st, 1933, Margaret, *d* of late Ridley Mackenzie, MD; one *s* one *d* (and one *s* decd); 2nd, 1945, Lady Victoria Audrey Beatrice, *d* of Viscount Ingestre and *sister* of 21st Earl of Shrewsbury, *qv*. *Educ:* New Coll., Oxford. Called to Bar, Middle Temple, 1937. Mem. Gen. Council of the Bar, 1964-67; Master of the Bench, Middle Temple, 1966. *Address:* Penylan Hall, Llechryd, Cardiganshire. *T:* Llechryd 335; Goldsmith Building, Temple, EC4. *T:* 01-353 7881; (residence) Carpmael Building, Temple, EC4. *T:* 01-353 1373. *Club:* Travellers'.

**MORRIS, Harry Frank Grave,** CMG 1958; *b* 11 May 1907; *e s* of late Frank Morris; unmarried. *Educ:* Harrow; Balliol Coll., Oxford. MA Oxon 1928. Solicitor, 1931-41. Joined Foreign Service, 1943, Madrid, Lisbon, Budapest, Rome; retired, Dec. 1962. *Address:* 32 Pont Street, SW1. *T:* 01-584 0883. *Club:* Garrick.

**MORRIS, James (Humphry),** FRSL; writer; *b* 2 Oct. 1926; *y s* of late Walter Morris; *m* 1949, Elizabeth, *d* of late Austin Tuckniss; three *s* one *d* (and one *d* decd). *Educ:* Lancing; Christ Church, Oxford (MA). Commonwealth Fellow, USA, 1953. Editorial staff, The Times, 1951-56; Special Correspondent with the British Mount Everest Expedition, 1953; on first motor crossing of Oman, 1955; Editorial Staff, The Guardian, 1957-62. George Polk Memorial Award for Journalism, US, 1961; Heinemann Award, RSL, 1961. *Publications:* Coast to Coast, 1956; Sultan in Oman, 1957; The Market of Seleukia, 1957; Coronation Everest, 1958; South African Winter, 1958; The Hashemite Kings, 1959; Venice, 1960; The Upstairs Donkey, 1962 (for children); The World Bank, 1963; Cities, 1963; The Presence of Spain, 1964; Oxford, 1965; Pax Britannica, 1968; The Great Port, 1970. *Address:* Trefan, Llanystumdwy, Cricieth, Caernarfonshire, Wales. *T:* Cricieth 2709. *Club:* Travellers'.

*See also Gareth Morris.*

**MORRIS, Rt. Hon. John,** PC 1970; MP (Lab) Aberavon Division of Glamorgan since Oct. 1959; *b* Nov. 1931; *s* of late D. W. Morris, Penywern, Talybont, Cardiganshire; *m* 1959, Margaret M., *d* of late Edward Lewis, OBE, JP, of Llandyssul; three *d*. *Educ:* Ardwyn, Aberystwyth; University Coll. of Wales, Aberystwyth; Gonville and Caius Coll., Cambridge; Academy of International Law, The Hague; Holker Senior Exhibitioner, Gray's Inn. Commissioned Royal Welch Fusiliers and Welch Regt. Called to the Bar, Gray's Inn, 1954; Parly Sec., Min. of Power, 1964-66; Jt Parly Sec., Min. of Transport, 1966-68; Minister of Defence (Equipment), 1968-70. Formerly Dep. Gen. Sec. and Legal Adviser, Farmers' Union of Wales. Mem. UK Delegn Consultative Assembly Council of Europe and Western European Union, 1963-64. Chairman: Nat. Pneumoconiosis Jt Cttee, 1964-66; Joint Review of Finances and Management, British Railways, 1966-67; Nat. Road Safety Advisory Council, 1967; Mem. Courts of University Colls, Aberystwyth, Swansea and Cardiff. *Address:* House of

Commons, SW1; Penwern, 4 Yester Drive, Chislehurst, Kent.

**MORRIS, John, (C. J. Morris),** CBE 1957; *b* 27 Aug. 1895; *e s* of late Frank Morris. *Educ:* King's Coll., Cambridge (MA, MSc, Diploma in Anthropology). Served with Leicestershire Regt and 3rd QAO Gurkha Rifles, 1915-34; served European War: France and Belgium, 1915-17 (wounded), Palestine, 1918; Afghanistan, 1919; Waziristan and NW Frontier of India, 1919-21 and 1921-24; travelled extensively in Central Asia, Tibet, Nepal, Bhutan, Africa, the Far East, etc; mem. of 1922 and 1936 Mount Everest Expeditions; Murchison Memorial of Royal Geographical Society, for explorations in Chinese Turkestan, 1929; William Wyse studentship in Social Anthropology, Univ. of Cambridge, 1934-37. Prof. of English Literature at Keio Univ., Tokyo, and Lecturer at Imperial and Bunrika Univs, Tokyo; concurrently adviser to Japanese Dept of Foreign Affairs, 1938-42; BBC: Head of Far Eastern Service, 1943-52; Controller, Third Programme, 1952-58. *Publications:* The Gurkhas (with Major W. Brook Northey), 1928; Handbooks for the Indian Army: Gurkhas, 1935; Living with Lepchas, 1938; Traveller from Tokyo, 1943; The Phœnix Cup, 1947; From the Third Programme (Edited), 1956; Hired to Kill, 1960; A Winter in Nepal, 1963; Eating the Indian Air, 1968. *Recreations:* travel, reading, music. *Address:* 21 Friday Street, Henley-on-Thames, Oxon. *T:* Henley-on-Thames 4369. *Clubs:* Savile, Alpine; University Alpine (Cambridge); Japan Alpine (Tokyo); Himalayan (Calcutta).

**MORRIS, John David,** CB 1947; OBE 1937; *b* 1895; *yr s* of late James Thomas Morris, Newport, Mon; *m* 1950, Marjorie, *o d* of Capt. S. V. Bowden, Kensington, W14. *Educ:* Newport High Sch. Joined Civil Service, 1913; Admiralty, 1914; commissioned RM and served overseas, 1917-19; mem. of British Delegation to Disarmament Conference, Geneva, 1932-34; Dir of Finance, Admiralty, 1944; Under-Sec., 1946-51; Principal Under-Sec., 1951-56; Deputy Sec., Admiralty, 1956-58, retired. *Recreations:* tennis and walking. *Address:* 57 Holland Park, W11. *T:* 01-727 8132. *Club:* Royal Automobile.

**MORRIS, Maj.-Gen. John Edward Longworth,** CB 1963; CBE 1956; DSO 1945; Director of Recruiting, War Office, 1960-64, retired; Managing Director, Tex Abrasives (Allied Products) Colchester; *b* 1 June 1909; *s* of Col A. E. Morris and M. E. Stanyon; *m* 1939, Pamela Gresley Ball; two *d. Educ:* Cheltenham Coll. Commissioned Regular Army, 1929; served War of 1939-45: India, Middle East and NW Europe, Col Comdt, RA, 1966-. *Recreations:* sailing, climbing, photography, music. *Address:* Marshgate, Tolleshunt D'Arcy, Essex. *Club:* Royal Ocean Racing.

**MORRIS, Dr John Humphrey Carlile,** FBA 1966; DCL; Fellow of Magdalen College, Oxford, since 1936; University Reader in Conflict of Laws, since 1951; *b* 18 Feb. 1910; *e s* of H. W. Morris, Solicitor, and J. M. Morris; *m* 1939, Mercy Jane Kinch; no *c. Educ:* Charterhouse; Christ Church, Oxford. DCL Oxford, 1949. Barrister-at-Law, 1934; Fellow and Tutor in Law, Magdalen Coll., Oxford, 1936; All Souls Lecturer in Private Internat. Law, 1939-51. Lt-Comdr RNVR, 1940-45. Visiting Prof., Harvard Law Sch., 1950-51; Assoc. Mem. Amer. Acad. of Arts and Sciences, 1960. *Publications:* Cases in Private International Law, 4th edn, 1968; (with Prof. W. Barton Leach) The Rule against Perpetuities. 2nd edn, 1962; Editor, 9th, 10th and 11th edns of Theobald on Wills, 1939-54; Gen. Editor: Dicey's Conflict of Laws, 6th, 7th and 8th edns, 1949-67; Chitty on Contracts, 22nd edn, 1961. *Recreation:* yacht cruising. *Address:* Magdalen College, Oxford. *T:* Oxford 41781. *Club:* Royal Cruising.

**MORRIS, Hon. Sir Kenneth (James),** KBE 1968; CMG 1964; Senator, Australian National Parliament, 1963-68, retired; *b* 22 Oct. 1903; *s* of J. R. Morris; *m* 1931, Ettie L., *d* of W. H. Dunlop; three *s* one *d* (and one *s* decd). *Educ:* Brisbane Gram. Sch. Business Company Dir prior to 1939. Enlisted AIF, 1939; served in England with 6th Australian Division, then original mem. of 9th Australian Division; served Tobruk, Alamein, New Guinea; transferred to R of O, Major, 1944. Elected Qld Parliament, 1944, as MLA Enoggera (later Mt Coot-tha); served as Whip, 1944-49; Deputy Leader, 1949-53, Leader, 1953-62. Parliamentary Liberal Party; Deputy Premier, Minister of Labour and Industry, 1957-63. *Recreations:* bowls, fishing. *Address:* Cooktown, North Queensland 4870, Australia. *T:* Endeavour 5. *Clubs:* United Service, Masonic (Brisbane).

**MORRIS, Air Marshal Sir Leslie D.;** *see* Dalton-Morris.

**MORRIS, Malcolm John,** QC 1959; Recorder of Southend since 1966; Deputy Chairman, Berkshire Quarter Sessions, since 1966; *b* 11 Sept. 1913; *s* of late Sir Harold Morris, MBE, QC; *m* 1949, Betty Rene, *d* of E. Russ; one *s* one *d. Educ:* Eton; Magdalen Coll., Oxford. Barrister, Inner Temple, 1937; Master of the Bench, Inner Temple, 1965. Served with Royal Artillery, 1939-46; Hon. Lt-Col. Recorder of Margate, 1952-62; Recorder of Croydon, 1962-65. Mem. of the Criminal Law Revision Cttee, 1965-. *Address:* 53 Drayton Gardens, SW10. *T:* 01-373 1335; Farrar's Building, Temple, EC4. *T:* 01-353 3598. *Clubs:* MCC; Leander.

**MORRIS, Nigel Godfrey,** CMG 1955; MVO 1966; QPM 1954; Assistant Director, UK Operations, Intercontinental/Bahama Realty; *b* 11 Nov. 1908; 2nd *s* of late Lt-Col G. M. Morris, 2/8th Gurkha Rifles and late Mrs Morris; *m* 1941, Mrs G. E. Baughan (*widow*), *e d* of late J. C. Sidebottom; one *d* and one step *d. Educ:* Wellington Coll. Asst Superintendent SS Police, 1928; Chinese language course, Amoy, China, 1929; Asst Supt of Police, Singapore CID 1931; Special Branch, 1935; Asst Supt of Police, Town Penang, 1939; interned by Japanese, 1942; repatriated to UK, 1945; Asst Dir, Malayan Security Service, 1946; Dir, Special Branch, Singapore, 1948; Dep. Commissioner, CID, Singapore, 1950, Comr, 1952; Deputy Inspector-General of Colonial Police, Colonial Office, 1957-63; Commissioner of Police, Bahamas. 1963-68, retired. Colonial Police Medal, 1949. *Recreations:* golf, tennis. *Address:* 190 Cranmer Court, Chelsea, SW3. *Club:* Phyllis Court (Henley-on-Thames).

*See also Brigadier Arthur de Burgh Morris.*

**MORRIS, Prof. Norman Frederick;** Professor of Obstetrics and Gynæcology, University of London, Charing Cross Hospital Medical School; *b* Luton, 26 Feb. 1920; *s* of F. W. Morris, Luton; *m* 1944, Lucia Xenia Rivlin; two *s* two *d. Educ:* Dunstable Sch., Dunstable; St Mary's Hospital Medical Sch. MRCS, LRCP 1943; MRCOG 1949; MB, BS (London) 1943; MD (London) 1949; FRCOG 1959. House appts St Mary's Hosp., Paddington and Amersham, 1944-46; Res. Obstetrician and Surg. Officer, East Ham Memorial Hosp., E6; Surg. Specialist RAF (Sqdn Ldr), 1946-48;

Registrar, St Mary's Hosp., W2, and East End Maternity Hosp., E1, 1948-50; Sen. Registrar (Obst. and Gynæcol.), Hammersmith Hosp., 1950-52; First Asst, Obstetric Unit, Univ. Coll. Hosp., WC1, 1953-56; Reader, Univ. of London in Obst. and Gynæcol., Inst. of Obstetrics and Gynæcology, 1956-58. External Examiner, Univs of Sheffield, Leeds, Dundee and Liverpool. Chairman: Assoc. of University Clinical Academic Staff; 3rd World Congress of Psychosomatic Medicine in Obst. and Gynæcol. *Publications:* The Baby Book, 1957; Non-Toxæmic Hypertension in Pregnancy (jointly), 1958; contrib. Lancet, 1960; various articles in medical jls related to obstetric problems, 1952-. *Recreations:* eating, reading and arguing; travelling at home and abroad; music. *Address:* 16 Provost Road, NW3. *T:* 01-722 4244.

**MORRIS, Owen Humphrey,** CMG 1967; Assistant Under-Secretary of State, Welsh Office; *b* 15 June 1921; *o c* of late David Humphreys Morris, Ton Pentre, Rhondda, Glam., and of Mrs Amy Ann Morris (*née* Jones); unmarried. *Educ:* Public Elem. Schs; King's Coll. Sch., Wimbledon (Schol.); Balliol Coll., Oxford (Schol.; MA). Served War of 1939-45: The Welch Regt and King's African Rifles, 1941-45 (Capt.). Asst Princ., Colonial Office, 1946; seconded Sierra Leone Administration, 1952-53; Asst Sec., 1955; Dept of Techn. Cooperation, 1962; Min. of Overseas Development, 1964; Min. of Housing and Local Govt, 1966; Welsh Office, 1969. *Address:* c/o Welsh Office, Cathays Park, Cardiff.

**MORRIS, His Honour Sir Owen (Temple) Temple-,** Kt 1967; QC 1937; Judge of Cardiff County Court Circuit No. 27, 1968-69; Monmouthshire Quarter Sessions, 1950-69; Chancellor of Diocese of Llandaff since 1935; *s* of late Dr Frederick Temple Morris, Cardiff, and Florence, *e d* of Col Charles Lanyon Owen, CB, Portsmouth; *m* 1927, Vera, *er d* of D. Hamilton Thompson; one *s*. Solicitor for five years in practice; Deputy Magistrate's Clerk, Dinas Powis Div., Glamorgan; called to Bar, Gray's Inn, 1925; Wales and Chester Circuits; Judge of County Court Circuit No. 24, Cardiff, etc, 1955-68 (Circuit No. 31, 1942-48; No. 30, 1948-55). Comr of Assize, Oxford Autumn Assize, 1946; Comr of Assize, Welsh Circuit Summer Assize, 1960, 1961, Autumn Assize, 1963, Winter Assize and Summer Assize, 1965, 1966, 1967, 1968, 1969. Mem. Royal Commn on the Police, 1960-62. Prosecuting Counsel to the Post Office, South Wales Circuit, 1931-37; Recorder of Merthyr Tydfil, 1936-42; Acting Recorder of Swansea, 1940-42; Chm. of Quarter Sessions: Town and Co. Haverfordwest, 1942-48; Co. Carmarthenshire, 1942-50, Brecknockshire, 1948-55; Dep.-Chm. of Quarter Sessions: Glamorgan, 1938-48; Pembrokeshire, 1942-48; formerly Chm., County Court Rule Cttee. MP (Nat C) Cardiff East, 1931-42; contested Caerphilly Division of Glamorgan, General Election, 1929; Vice-Pres. Wales and Mon. Conservative and Unionist Association, 1931-42; Chm. Wales and Mon. Conservative Education Cttee, 1938-42; Mem. Governing Body Association of Conservative Clubs, 1929-42; Chm. Wales and Mon. Conservative Clubs Advisory Cttee, 1929-42; Mem. of Governing Body and Vice-Chm., Representative Body of the Church in Wales; Judge of Provincial Court of Church in Wales; Chm. of Legal Cttee and Pensions Cttee of Representative Body, 1945-55; Hon. Lay Sec. Llandaff Diocesan Conf., 1927-35; Mem. of Cymmrodorion Soc.; Chief Comdt Cardiff Volunteer Special Constabulary, 1938-45; Chm. and Sec. Commandants of Special Constabularies Conf., No. 8 Region, 1942-45. CStJ. *Address:* 11 Raglan House, Westgate Street, Cardiff. *Club:* Cardiff and County (Cardiff).

**MORRIS, Sir Parker,** Kt 1941; Town Clerk of Westminster, 1929-56, retired; *b* 15 Sept. 1891; *s* of David and Annie Kent Morris, Manchester; *m* 1918, Dorothy Aylmer Hale, Manchester; one *s* one *d*. *Educ:* Retford; Manchester Univ. LLB (London). Served in European War, 1914-19, in Manchester Regt and Machine Gun Corps. Admitted Solicitor of Supreme Court, Jan. 1919. Deputy Town Clerk of Salford, 1919-23; Town Clerk of Chesterfield, 1923-29; Hon. Clerk to Metropolitan Boroughs Standing Joint Cttee, 1929-56; Jt Sec. Departmental Cttee on London Cleansing, 1929; Mem. Central Valuation Cttee for England and Wales, 1937-49; Mem. Royal Commn on Location of Industry, 1937-39; Chairman: Nat. Fedn of Housing Socs, 1956-61; Cttee for Old People's Housing Socs, 1961-67; Archway Group Hosp. Management Cttee, 1956-63; Study Group on Building Contracts of Local Authorities, Royal Inst. of Public Administration; Mem. Housing Management Sub-Cttee, 1956-59; Chm. Greater London Citizens' Advice Bureaux Advisory Cttee, 1957-67; Mem. Central London Valuation Panel, 1957-58; Member: Central Housing Advisory Cttee, 1957-62; Chm., Housing Standards Sub-Cttee, 1959 (a Report, Homes for Today and Tomorrow, 1961); Mem. NW Metropolitan Regional Hosp. Bd and Chm. of Establishment Cttee, 1960-63. ARP Controller of Westminster, 1939-45. Hon FRIBA, 1970. Chevalier of: Legion of Honour, France, 1950; Order of Orange-Nassau, Netherlands, 1950; Order of the Dannebrog, Denmark, 1951; Order of the North Star, Sweden, 1954; Order of the Star of Ethiopia, 1954; Military Order of Christ, Portugal, 1955; Order of Al Rafidain, Iraq, 1956. *Recreation:* golf. *Address:* Berwyns, One Tree Hill, Guildford, Surrey. *T:* 3678.

*See also Rt Hon. R. H. Jenkins.*

**MORRIS, Sir Philip (Robert),** KCMG 1960; Kt 1946; CBE 1941; MA Oxon; Hon. LLD: Rhodes, 1950; Bristol, 1951; McGill, 1955; Windsor, 1958; NUI, W Ontario, 1960; London, 1965; Bath, 1966; Hon. ARCVS 1958; FRSA 1961; Hon. FRCS 1966; Vice-Chancellor Bristol University, 1946-66; *b* 6 July 1901; 2nd *s* of late M. C. Morris, HM Inspector, and late J. Morris, Sutton Valence; *m* 1926, Florence Redvers Davis, 2nd *d* of Walford Davis Green, Barrister-at-law, and Annie L. Green; two *s* one *d* (and one *d* decd). *Educ:* Tonbridge Sch.; St Peter's, York; Trinity Coll., Oxford. Modern Greats, 1923; Teachers' Diploma, London Univ., 1924; Lectr in History and Classics, Westminster Trng Coll., 1923-25; Administrative Officer, Kent Education Cttee, Asst Dir, 1932; Dir, 1938-43; Dir-Gen. of Army Education, 1944-46; Educational Adviser, HM Prison, 1938-44; Mem. Board of Education Cttee on Training of Teachers and Youth Leaders, 1942-44. Life Trustee of Carnegie UK Trust; UK Deleg. First Conf. of UNESCO, 1946; Chm., Army Educ. Advisory Bd, 1946-48; Vice-Chm., British Council, 1946-59; Chm., Secondary Sch. Examinations Council, 1948-51 (Actg Chm. 1947-48); Chairman: Nat. Advisory Council on Training and Supply of Teachers, 1946-59; Cttee of Vice-Chancellors and Principals, 1955-58; Miners' Welfare Nat. Scholarship Scheme Selection Cttee, 1948-49; Anglo-Czechoslovak Cultural Commn, 1949; Chm. Conference on African Education, 1952; Theatre Royal, Bristol, Management Cttee, 1946-63; Chm. Bristol Old Vic Trust, 1963-; Chm. Commonwealth Education Conference,

1959; Chm. Commonwealth Education Liaison Cttee, 1959-62; Vice-Chm., United Bristol Hosps Bd of Govs, 1948-66; Member: BBC Gen. Adv. Council, 1947-52; Vice-Chm. of BBC, 1954-60 (a Governor, 1952-60); BBC West Reg. Adv. Council, 1961-68 (Chm. 1947-52); SW Regional Hosp. Bd, 1948-53; Central Adv. Council for Educn (England), 1944-48; Adv. Cttee for Educn in the Colonies, 1945-48 and 1949-52, 1953-56, 1959-62; General Nursing Council, 1954-55; Advisory Cttee on Recruiting, 1958; Cttee on Higher Education, 1961-64. Mem. Council, Boy Scouts' Assoc., 1946-59; Vice-Chm. Assoc. Univs of British Commonwealth, 1951-55; Pres., Library Association, 1955; Mem., Governing Bd of National Institute for Research in Nuclear Science, 1957-58; Hon. Mem., Bristol Medico-Chirurgical Soc., 1963-. Hon. Fellow, Bristol Univ., 1966. *Publications:* Christianity and the World of Today, 1961; articles, published addresses etc, on educational subjects. *Recreations:* music, golf. *Address:* Tanglewood, Townsend, Lower Almondsbury, Bristol BS12 4EQ. *TA* and *T:* Almondsbury 2392. *Clubs:* Athenæum, United University.

**MORRIS, Richard Murchison,** CMG 1958; OBE 1949; *b* 14 Sept. 1898; *s* of Richard Henry Morris, Capetown, S Africa; *m* 1928, Kathleen, *d* of Lt-Col C. H. Divine, DSO; one *d* (and one *s* decd). *Educ:* Diocesan Coll., Rondebosch, Cape; London Hospital, Univ. of London. 2nd Lt (Pilot) RAF, 1918. MRCS, LRCP, 1923; House-Surgeon, Poplar Hosp.; MB, BS, 1924; House Physician, etc, London Hosp.; House Physician, Tropical Diseases Hosp.; MD (Gold Medal), 1926; DTM and H, 1926; S Rhodesian Medical Service, 1926; Sen. Govt MO, 1934; DMS, 1946; Sec. for Health, 1948; Sec. to Ministry of Health, Fedn of Rhodesia and Nyasaland, 1954-58, retired. Councillor, Salisbury City Council, 1961. Surg.-Col British S Africa Police, 1946; Col and ADMS Matabeleland, 1939-45; Consultant Physician, RAF Training Group, S Rhodesia, 1940-45. External Examiner in Medicine, Univ. of Capetown, 1950-51. Vice-Chm. Council, University Coll. of Rhodesia, 1968. KStJ 1963. *Publications:* medical papers in Lancet and Central African Jl of Medicine. *Address:* 2 Denmark Avenue, Salisbury, Rhodesia. *T:* Salisbury 21351. *Clubs:* Bulawayo (Bulawayo); Salisbury (Salisbury).

**MORRIS, Most Rev. Thomas;** *see* Cashel and Emly, Archbishop of, (RC).

**MORRIS, Walter Frederick,** LLB; Counsellor, Foreign and Commonwealth Office, since 1970; *b* 15 Oct. 1914; *s* of late Captain Frederick James Morris and Elsie Eleanor (*née* Williams); *m* 1945, Marjorie Vaughan, *o d* of late Thomas Vaughan Phillips and Eleanor Mirren (*née* Jones); one *s* one *d*. *Educ:* Cardiff High Sch.; University Coll., Cardiff (Law Prizeman). Solicitor; LLB, Associate, Chartered Insurance Inst; Legal practice, 1936-39; Served RA (TA), 1939-45: GHQ Home Forces (Intelligence); WO Sch. of Military Administration; Certificate of Merit, Western Comd; GSO1 (Lt-Col), HQ 21st Army Gp, BLA (later BAOR); commanded Legal Aid Organisation, which provided legal assistance to all British Army and RAF personnel in Europe; legal practice (and Hon. District Army Welfare Officer), 1945-47; entered Administrative Home Civil Service, 1947; Min. of Social Security, 1947-68 (Prin., Dep. Chief Insce Off., Asst Sec.); Admin. Staff Coll., Henley, 1953; on loan to Export Credits Guarantee Dept, 1955-57; Manchester Business Sch., 1968; trans. to HM Diplomatic Service, 1968; HM Consul-Gen., UAR, 1968-70. Director: Anglo-Amer. Hosp., Cairo, 1968; ME Centre for Arab Studies, Shemlan, Lebanon, 1969. Member: Law Soc.; Internat. Bar Assoc.; BIM; Egyptian Soc. of Internat. Law. Liveryman, Worshipful Co. of Solicitors of City of London. *Publications:* articles in English legal jls. *Recreations:* yachting, golf. *Address:* 12 Elmhurst Lodge, Christchurch Park, Sutton, Surrey. *T:* 01-643 3981; Rose Lawn, Pilley, near Lymington, Hants. *T:* Lymington 4354. *Clubs:* United Service. Royal Lymington Yacht.

**MORRIS, William Alexander,** CMG 1956; *b* 15 June 1905; *e s* of late William G. Morris, Cheam, Surrey; *m* 1938, Cecilia Mary, *d* of late James M. Anderson, of Istamboul, and Oxted, Surrey; four *d*. *Educ:* St Paul's Sch.; Univ. of London. BSc (Econ.) Hons 1929. Economic Asst to High Comr for Australia, 1935-39; entered Bd of Trade, 1940; transferred to Colonial Office, 1942; seconded to Foreign Office, 1963; HM Consul-Gen., Rotterdam, 1963-65; Dept of Economic Affairs and Cabinet Office, 1966-70, retired 1970. *Address:* Somerset House, Church Street, Widcombe, Bath. *Club:* Travellers'.

**MORRIS, William Alfred,** MVO (4th Class) 1942; late 12th Royal Lancers; *b* 26 Nov. 1912; *s* of late Alfred William Johnson Morris and Adeline Gonthier; *m* 1st, 1939, Patricia Beryl Robertson; one *s* one *d*; 2nd, 1953, Lesley Dade Spurr. *Educ:* Eton. Served War of 1939-45 (Croix de Guerre 1943); retired, 1948. *Address:* Thorpe Mandeville Court, near Banbury, Oxon. *T:* Sulgrave 323; 21 Ennismore Mews, SW7. *T:* 01-589 1733. *Club:* Cavalry.

**MORRIS, Judge William Gerard;** Recorder of Manchester, and Judge of the Crown Court at Manchester, since 1967; *b* 20 June 1909; *s* of Joseph Thomas and Ellen Morris; *m* 1935, Mollie Broadbent; three *s*. *Educ:* Bolton Sch.; Gonville and Caius Coll., Cambridge. Called to Bar, 1931; practised on Northern Circuit till 1961; County Court Judge, 1961-66. Served in RAFVR, 1940-45, rank Sqdn Leader. Asst Recorder of Salford, 1956-61; Recorder of Liverpool, 1966-67. *Recreation:* golf. *Address:* Kingslea, Chorley New Road, Bolton, Lancs. *T:* Bolton 40900.

**MORRIS, Professor William Ian Clinch;** Professor of Obstetrics and Gynaecology, University of Manchester, since 1949; *b* 10 May 1907; *s* of Dr J. M. Morris, Neath; *m* 1938, Mary Farquharson; one *d*. *Educ:* Royal High Sch., Edinburgh; Edinburgh Univ. Obstetrician to Ayr County Council, 1937-46; Sen. Lectr in Obstetrics and Gynaecology, Univ. of Edinburgh, 1946-49. RAMC (TA) 1935; war service, 1939-43. *Publications:* (jointly) A Combined Text-book of Obstetrics and Gynaecology, 1950; contribs to Jl of Obstetrics and Gynaecology of British Commonwealth, Lancet, Edinburgh Med. Jl, etc. *Recreation:* motoring. *Address:* 4 Depleach Road, Cheadle, Ches. *T:* 061-428 2460.

**MORRIS, Rev. William James,** JP; Minister of Glasgow Cathedral since 1967; a Chaplain to the Queen in Scotland, since 1969; *b* Cardiff, 22 Aug. 1925; *o s* of William John Morris and Eliza Cecilia Cameron Johnson; *m* 1952, Jean Daveena Ogilvy Howie, *o c* of Rev. David Porter Howie and Veena Christie, Kilmarnock; one *s*. *Educ:* Cardiff High Sch.; Univ. of Wales; Edinburgh Univ. BA 1946, BD 1949, Wales; PhD Edinburgh, 1954. Ordained, 1951. Asst, Canongate Kirk, Edinburgh, 1949-51; Minister, Presbyterian Church of Wales,

Cadoxton and Barry Is, 1951-53; Buckhaven (Fife): St David's, 1953-57; Peterhead Old Parish, 1957-67; Chaplain, Peterhead Prison, 1963-67; Moderator, Presbytery of Deer, 1965-66. Pres., Rotary Club of Peterhead, 1965-66; Chm., Club Service Cttee, Dist 101, RIBI, 1964-66; Pres., Peterhead and Dist Professional and Business Club, 1967; Trustee, Iona Cath. Trust, 1967; Chm. of Coun., Soc. of Friends of Glasgow Cath., 1967; Mem., Gen. Convocation, Strathclyde Univ. JP, Co. of Aberdeen, 1963. *Recreations:* walking, fishing, golf, gardening. *Address:* 60 Dalziel Drive, Glasgow S1. *T:* 041-427 2757. *Club:* New (Edinburgh).

**MORRIS, Willie,** CMG 1963; HM Ambassador at Jedda, since 1968; *b* 3 Dec. 1919; *m* 1959, Ghislaine Margaret Trammell; three *s*. *Educ:* Batley Grammar Sch., Yorks; St John's Coll., Oxford. Served in Royal Navy, 1940-45. Joined Foreign Service, 1947; Third Sec., Middle East Centre for Arab Studies, 1947; Second Sec., Cairo, 1948; First Sec., 1951; transferred to Foreign Office, 1952; attended course at Canadian Defence Coll., 1954; transferred to Washington, 1955; Counsellor, Amman (Chargé d'Affaires, 1960, 1961 and 1962), 1960-63; Head of Eastern Dept, FO, 1963-67; Fellow, Center for Internat. Studies, Harvard Univ., 1966-67. *Address:* c/o Foreign and Commonwealth Office, King Charles Street, SW1. *Club:* Travellers'.

**MORRIS, Wyn,** FRAM; Conductor: Huddersfield Choral Society since 1969; Bruckner-Mahler Chorale, since 1970; *b* 14 Feb. 1929; *s* of Haydn Morris and Sarah Eluned Phillips; *m* 1962, Ruth Marie McDowell; one *s* one *d*. *Educ:* Llanelli Grammar Sch.; Royal Academy of Music; Mozarteum, Salzburg. August Mann's Prize, 1950; Apprentice Conductor, Yorkshire Symph. Orch., 1950-51; Musical Dir, 17th Trg Regt, RA Band, 1951-53; Founder and Conductor of Welsh Symph. Orch., 1954-57; Koussevitsky Memorial Prize, Boston Symph. Orch., 1957; (on invitation George Szell) Observer, Cleveland Symph. Orch., 1957-60; Conductor: Ohio Bell Chorus, Cleveland Orpheus Choir and Cleveland Chamber Orch., 1958-60; Choir of Royal National Eisteddfod of Wales, 1960-62; London debut, Royal Festival Hall, with Royal Philharmonic Orch., 1963; Conductor: Royal Choral Society, 1968-70; Ceremony for Investiture of Prince Charles as Prince of Wales, 1969; Royal Choral Soc. tour of USA, 1969. FRAM 1964; Mahler Memorial Medal (of Bruckner and Mahler Soc. of Amer.), 1968. *Recreations:* chess, Rugby football, climbing. *Address:* Orchard Gate, North Drive, Wentworth, Virginia Water, Surrey. *T:* Wentworth 3207.

**MORRIS-JONES, Ifor Henry,** QC 1969; *b* 5 March 1922; *s* of late Rev. Prof. and Mrs D. Morris-Jones; *m* 1950, Anne Diana, *d* of S. E. Ferris, Blundellsands; one *s* two *d*. *Educ:* Taunton Sch.; Sidney Sussex Coll., Cambridge. Called to the Bar, Lincoln's Inn, 1947. Joined Northern Circuit, 1962; Assistant Recorder, Carlisle, 1962; Dep. Chm., Cumberland Sessions, 1969. *Recreation:* golf. *Address:* 5 Essex Court, Temple, EC4. *T:* 01-353 4365, 01-353 8273; Trewarren, Dowhills Road, Blundellsands, Liverpool L23 8SP. *T:* 051-924 4848. *Clubs:* Athenæum (Liverpool); County (Carlisle).

**MORRIS-JONES, Sir (John) Henry,** Kt, *cr* 1937; MC; LRCP and S (Edinburgh); DL Denbigh; JP; Hon. Captain, RAMC; *b* Waenfawr, Caernarvonshire, 2 Nov. 1884; *s* of Capt. Morris Jones and Ann Jones; *m* 1931, Leila Augusta Paget-Marsland, *widow* of J. Illidge Marsland. *Educ:* Menai Bridge Grammar Sch.; St Mungo's Coll., Glasgow. For twenty years practised as a general medical practitioner at Colwyn Bay, and took an active part in its public life and in that of the County of Denbigh; Mem. and ex-Chm., UDC, High Sheriff Designate of the County, 1929-30, and Mem. of County Council; MP (L) Denbigh Div., 1929-31, (L Nat), 1931-50; retd 1950; Chm. Exec. Nat. Lib. Party, 1953-54. Chm., Welsh Parliamentary Party, 1941-42; Asst Govt Whip, 1932-35; Lord Commissioner of the Treasury, 1935-37; served as Chm., Div. BMA and Colwyn Bay Medical Soc.; Hon. Treas. and Joint Hon. Sec. Reception Cttee Royal Visit to North Wales, 1937; Mem. of official Parly Delegn to Australia for Sesquicentenary celebrations, 1938; Mem. of Parly Delegn to Buchenwald Concentration Camp, April 1945; Mem. of Gorsedd under Bardic title of Rhoslanydd; Mem. of Governing Body and Representative Body, Church in Wales, 1950-62. Served in France, with 2nd Bn Worcester Regt, 1914-18 (MC); travelled extensively. Hon. Freedom of Colwyn Bay, 1956. *Publications:* Surgical Experiences at Wimereux, France (with Hugh Lett); Doctor in the Whips' Room, 1955. *Recreation:* walking. *Address:* Bryndyfnog, Llanrhaldr, near Denbigh, North Wales. *T:* Llanynys 236. *Club:* Reform.

**MORRIS-JONES, Professor Wyndraeth Humphreys;** Professor of Commonwealth Affairs and Director, Institute of Commonwealth Studies, University of London, since 1966; *b* 1 Aug. 1918; *s* of late William James Jones, Carmarthen, and Annie Mary Jones (*née* Morris); *m* 1953, Graziella Bianca Genre; one *s* two *d*. *Educ:* University Coll. Sch., Hampstead; London Univ. London Sch. of Economics, BSc(Econ.) First Class, 1938; Leverhulme Research Grant, 1939; Christ's Coll., Cambridge Research Schol., 1940; Indian Army, 1941-46 (Lt-Col, Public Relations Directorate, 1944); Constitutional Adviser to Viceroy of India, 1947; Lecturer in Political Science, London Sch. of Economics, 1946-55; Prof. of Political Theory and Instns, Univ. of Durham, 1955-65. Rockefeller Travel Grants, 1954, 1960 and 1967. Vis. Prof. of Commonwealth Hist. and Instns, Indian Sch. of Internat. Studies, New Delhi, 1960; Visiting Professor: Univ. of Chicago, 1962; Univ. of California, Berkeley, 1964-65. Editor, Jl of Commonwealth Polit. Studies, 1964-. *Publications:* Parliament in India, 1957; Government and Politics of India, 1964; articles in Polit. Studies, Asian Survey, Modern Asian Studies, etc. *Recreations:* motoring, gardening, walking, tennis, music. *Address:* Institute of Commonwealth Studies, 27 Russell Square, WC1. *T:* 01-580 5876.

**MORRISON,** family name of **Viscount Dunrossil** and of **Barons Margadale** and **Morrison.**

**MORRISON,** 2nd Baron *cr* 1945, of Tottenham; **Dennis Morrison;** Manufacturing Executive with The Metal Box Co. Ltd since 1957; *b* 21 June 1914; *e* and *o surv. s* of 1st Baron Morrison, PC, and Grace, *d* of late Thomas Glossop; *S* father 1953; *m* 1940, Florence Alice Helena (marr. diss. 1958), *d* of late Augustus Hennes, Tottenham; *m* 1959, Joan, *d* of late W. R. Meech. *Educ:* Tottenham County Sch. Employed by The Metal Box Co. Ltd on research work, 1937-51; Quality Controller,

1952-57. Lord Lieutenant's Representative for Tottenham, 1955-. FSS 1953-57. Mem. Acton Chamber of Commerce, 1962 (Mem., Exec. Cttee, 1962). Hon. President: Robert Browning Settlement, 1967-; 5th Acton Scout Group, 1969. *Recreations:* gardening, football. *Heir:* none. *Address:* 79 Perryn Road, Acton, W3. *T:* 01-743 1989.

**MORRISON, Maj.-Gen. (retd) Albert Edward,** CB 1956; OBE 1942; *b* 17 March 1901; *s* of late Major A. Morrison; *m* 1926, Esther May Lacey. *Educ:* Dover Coll.; RMA Woolwich. Royal Artillery, 1922-26; Royal Signals, 1926-57. Retired as Chief Signal Officer, AFHQ, March 1957. Col Commandant, Royal Corps of Signals, 1959-. Legion of Merit (US), 1946; Order of Rafidain (Iraq), 1940. *Recreation:* golf. *Address:* 17 Wesley Fairways, Ferndown, Dorset.

**MORRISON, Alexander;** Controller of Services, Greater London Council, since 1970; *b* 25 Jan. 1917; *e s* of late Alexander Morrison and Sarah (*née* Drummond); *m* 1941, Jennie, *o d* of late Henry and Ellen Mason; one *s* one *d. Educ:* Boroughmuir Sch., Edinburgh. Tax Officer, Inland Revenue, Edinburgh, 1934-36; Excise Off., Customs and Excise, Edinburgh, 1936; Royal Ordnance Factories: Jun. Exec. Off., Royal Arsenal, Woolwich, 1937-40; Higher Exec. Off.: Wigan, 1940-41; Poole, 1941-43; Sen. Exec. Off., Fazakerley, 1943-49; Chief Exec. Off., London, 1949-50; Overseas Food Corp., E Africa: Stores Controller, 1950-51; Chief Internal Auditor, 1951-52; Chief Accountant, 1952-54; Nat. Coal Board: Stores Controller, London, 1955-58; Purchasing and Stores Controller: W Mids Div., 1958-59; N Eastern Div., 1959-61; Chief Officer of Supplies, LCC, 1961-64; GLC: Dir of Supplies, 1964-67; Exec. Dir, Highways and Transportation, 1967-69; Traffic Comr and Dir of Develt, 1969-70. Pres., Purchasing Officers' Assoc., 1966-67; Mem., Nat. Council for Quality and Reliability, 1963-. Swinbank Medal, Inst. of Purchasing and supply, 1968. *Publication:* Storage and Control of Stock, 1962. *Recreations:* bowls, painting. *Address:* 70 Park Avenue, Bromley, Kent. *T:* 01-464 1460.

**MORRISON, Alexander John Henderson;** Barrister-at-law; Deputy Chairman, Derbyshire QS, since 1964; a Chairman of Industrial Tribunals, since 1966; *b* 16 Nov. 1927; *yr s* of Dr Alexander Morrison and late Mrs A. Morrison. *Educ:* Derby Sch.; Emmanuel Coll., Cambridge. MA, LLB. Called to the Bar, Gray's Inn, 1951. Mem. of Midland Circuit. *Recreations:* golf, music. *Address:* 1 Fountain Court, Birmingham 4. *T:* 021-236 5721.

**MORRISON, Hon. Charles Andrew;** MP (C) Devizes since May 1964; *b* 25 June 1932; *s* of 1st Baron Margadale, *qv*; *m* 1954, Hon. Sara Long, *d* of 2nd Viscount Long of Wraxall; one *s* one *d. Educ:* Eton. Nat. Service in The Life Guards, 1950-52; Royal Wilts Yeo. (TA), 1952-66. Farms in Wilts. County Councillor (Wilts), 1958-65; Chairman: Wilts Educn Cttee, 1963-64; South West Regional Sports Council, 1966-68. *Recreation:* sport of all kinds. *Address:* 12 Gayfere Street, SW1. *T:* 01-799 1460; Fyfield Manor, Pewsey, Wilts. *T:* Pewsey 3438. *Clubs:* Buck's, White's.

**MORRISON, Air Vice-Marshal Ian Gordon,** CB 1965; CBE 1957 (OBE 1946); RNZAF (retired); Development Director, A. S. Cornish Group; *b* 16 March 1914; *s* of W. G. Morrison; *m* 1938, Dorothy, *d* of W. H. Franks; one *s* two *d. Educ:* Christchurch Boys' High Sch., NZ. RAF 1935; RNZAF 1939; No 75 Sqdn, UK, 1939; Comd RNZAF, Omaka, 1941; Comd RNZAF, Gisborne, 1942; SASO, Islands Gp, 1943; Comd No 3 BR Sqdn Pacific, 1944-45; jssc, UK, 1950; Comd RNZAF, Ohakea, 1952; Air Mem. for Supply, 1954; idc, 1958; AOC, RNZAF, HQ London, 1959-60; Air Mem. for Personnel, 1961-62; Chief of the Air Staff, Royal New Zealand Air Force, 1962-66. *Recreations:* golf and angling. *Address:* St Elmo, Lowry Bay, Wellington, NZ. *T:* 64293. *Clubs:* Wellington, United Services Officers, Wellington Golf (all in NZ).

**MORRISON, Prof. James,** OBE 1963; BSc, NDA; Professor of Crop and Animal Husbandry, The Queen's University of Belfast, 1944-65, also Director, Agricultural Research Institute, Hillsborough, NI, 1934-65; retired; *b* 11 Aug. 1900; *m* 1934, Grace F. Stockdale, Clogher, Co. Tyrone; three *d. Educ:* Fordyce Academy, Banffshire, Scotland; Marischal Coll., Aberdeen Univ. Instructor in Agriculture, Co. Tyrone and Co. Down, 1925 and 1926; Sec. and Agric. Organiser, Co. Armagh, 1927-30; Inspector, Min. of Agric. for N Ireland, 1931-33; Lectr in Crop and Animal Husbandry, QUB, 1934. *Recreation:* gardening. *Address:* Loxwood, Lisburn Road, Hillsborough, Co. Down, N Ireland. *T:* Hillsborough (Co. Down) 208.

**MORRISON, John Lamb Murray,** CBE 1957; DSc; FIMechE; Professor of Mechanical Engineering, University of Bristol; *b* 22 May 1906; *s* of late Latto A. Morrison, Biggar, Lanarkshire; *m* 1936, Olga, *d* of late M. Nierenstein, DSc; two *s. Educ:* Biggar High Sch.; Univ. of Glasgow. Lecturer in Mechanical Engineering; Reader in Mechanical Engineering, Univ. of Bristol. Pres., IMechE, 1970. *Publications:* An Introduction to the Mechanics of Machines, 1964; various papers on strength of materials and design of machines. *Recreations:* gardening, golf. *Address:* Queen's Building, University Walk, Bristol 8. *T:* 24161.

**MORRISON, John Sinclair;** President University College, Cambridge, since 1966; Joint Editor of Classical Review; *b* 15 June 1913; *s* of Sinclair Morrison (and *g s* of William Morrison, NY and Stagbury, Chipstead, Surrey) and Maria Elsie, *d* of William Lamaison, Salmons, Kenley, Surrey; *m* 1942, Elizabeth Helen, *d* of S. W. Sulman, Bexhill, Sussex; three *s* two *d. Educ:* Charterhouse; Trinity Coll., Cambridge. fellow Trinity College, Cambridge, 1937-45; Asst Lecturer Manchester University, 1937-39; Editor of Cambridge Review, 1939-40. Ordinary Seaman (Volunteer), 1940-41. In service of British Council, Cairo, Zagazig, Baghdad, 1941-42; British Council Rep. in Palestine and Transjordan, 1942-45; Pres. Jerusalem Rotary Club, 1945; Prof. of Greek and Head of Dept of Classics and Ancient History at the Durham Colls of Univ. of Durham, 1945-50; Fellow Tutor and Senior Tutor of Trinity Coll., Cambridge, 1950-60; Vice-Master and Sen. Tutor of Churchill Coll., Cambridge, 1960-65, now Hon. Fellow. Leverhulme Fellow, 1965. Mem. of Council: Hellenic Soc., 1948, 1952; Classical Assoc., 1949; Member: Sierra Leone Educn Commission, 1954; Annan Cttee on Teaching of Russian, 1961; Hale Cttee on University Teaching Methods, 1961; Schools Council, 1965-67; Jt Working Party on 6th Form Curriculum and Examinations, 1968-70.

governing Bodies Assoc., 1965; Governor: Bradfield Coll., 1963; Wellington Coll., 1963; Culford Sch., 1969; Charterhouse Sch., 1970. *Publication:* (with R. T. Williams) Greek Oared Ships, 1968. *Address:* University College, Cambridge.

**MORRISON, Nicholas Godfrey,** CB 1967; Deputy Secretary, Civil Service Department, since 1969; *b* 31 March 1918; *y s* of late John Wheatley Morrison and Kathleen King, Shotley Bridge, Co. Durham; *m* 1959, Hannah Mary de Groot (*née* Topping); two step *d. Educ:* Cheltenham Coll.; Clare Coll., Cambridge. Entered War Office, 1939; Asst Private Sec. to Sec. of State for War, 1942-44. Served War of 1939-45, in HM Forces, 1944-46. Private Sec. to Minister of Defence, 1952-53; Asst Sec., War Office, 1955; Asst Under-Sec. of State (Dir of Establishments), War Office, 1960; Asst Under-Sec. of State, Min. of Defence, 1964; Under-Sec., HM Treasury, 1967-68, Civil Service Dept, 1968-69. *Address:* 135 Talgarth Road, W14. *T:* 01-748 8307. *Club:* Athenæum.

**MORRISON, Maj.-Gen. Reginald Joseph Gordon,** CB 1969; CBE 1959; MD, FRCP; Physician, The Royal Hospital, Chelsea; Director of Medicine, Ministry of Defence (Army), and Consulting Physician to the Army, 1965-68; *b* 29 March 1909; *s* of R. Morrison; *m* 1947, Norma Jacqueline Nicholson; two *s. Educ:* Dulwich Coll.; St Joseph's Coll., SE19; St Bartholomew's Hosp. House Phys., St Bart's Hosp., 1934; Res. MO, Hove Gen. Hosp. Commnd RAMC, 1936; served as Med. Specialist, RAMC. Adviser in Medicine, EA Command, 1947-50; OC, Med. Div., QA Mil. Hosp., 1950-56; Cons. Phys., Far East, 1956-59; Prof. of Trop. Med., Royal Army Medical College, 1959-65. QHP 1963-68. *Publications:* (with W. H. Hargreaves) The Practice of Tropical Medicine, 1965; chapter in Exploration Medicine, 1965. Various articles in Lancet, BMJ, Proc. RSM, etc. *Recreations:* rose growing, golf. *Address:* Gordon House, The Royal Hospital, Chelsea, SW3. *Club:* Athenæum.

**MORRISON, Prof. Stuart Love;** Professor of Social Medicine, University of Edinburgh, since 1964; *b* 25 Nov. 1922; *o s* of late William James Morrison, Ironfounder, Glasgow and late Isabella Murdoch, Edinburgh; *m* 1947, Dr Audrey Butler Lornie, *yr d* of late Lt-Col W. S. Lornie, MC, TD, MRCVS, Perth; one *d. Educ:* Glasgow Acad.; Dundee High Sch.; St Andrews and London Univs. MB, ChB (St Andrews) 1951; DPH (London) 1954; MRCP Edinburgh, 1966; FRCP Edinburgh, 1968. Served in RAF, 1939-46; Hosp. and gen. practice, 1951-53; Public Health appts, 1954-56; Mem., Scientific Staff, MRC Social Medicine Research Unit, 1956-62; Vis. Fellow, Epidemiology and Statistics, Univ. of N Carolina, 1961-62; Sen. Lectr in Social Med., Univ. of Edinburgh, 1962-64. FSS; Mem., WHO Expert Adv. Panel on Organisation of Medical Care. *Publications:* contribs to med. jls on epidemiology, organisation of medical care and medical administration. *Recreations:* hill walking, book hunting. *Address:* 2a Abbotsford Park, Edinburgh EH10 5DX. *T:* 031-447 4149.

**MORRISON, Rear-Adm. Thomas Kenneth,** CB 1967; CBE 1962 (OBE 1941); DSC; Royal Australian Navy; Flag Officer-in-Charge, East Australia Area, since 1966; *b* 31 Oct. 1911; *s* of late L. N. Morrison, Sydney, Australia; *m* 1938, Dorothy C., *d* of late W. M. Hole; one *s* three *d. Educ:* Jervis Bay Sch.; Royal Australian Naval College. Served War, 1939-45: Indian Ocean, Red Sea, Pacific (despatches, OBE, DSC). Qualified (Short Staff Course) RNC, Greenwich, 1945. Dir, Training and Staff Requirements, Navy Office, Melbourne, 1946-47; Comdr, Royal Australian Naval Coll., 1948-49; Capt., HMAS Tobruk, on commissioning, 1950-51; Dir of Manning, Navy Office, 1951-52; Dep. Chm., Naval Personnel, 1952-53; Commanding: 1st Frigate Squadron, Royal Australian Navy, 1954-55; HMAS Melbourne, 1959; Royal Australian Naval Air Stn, Nowra, NSW, 1961-62; Dep. Chief of the Naval Staff, Royal Australian Navy, 1962-64; Flag Officer Commanding the Australian Fleet, 1965. *Recreations:* cricket, golf, tennis. *Address:* c/o Department of the Navy, Canberra, ACT, Australia.

**MORRISON-BELL, Sir William (Hollin Dayrell),** 4th Bt *cr* 1905; *b* 21 June 1956; *s* of Sir Charles Reginald Francis Morrison-Bell, 3rd Bt and of Prudence Caroline, *d* of late Lt-Col W. D. Davies, 60th Rifles (she *m* 2nd, Peter Gillbanks); *S* father, 1967. *Heir: b* Julian Francis Tarret Morrison-Bell, *b* 14 Feb. 1959. *Address:* Highgreen, Tarset, Hexham, Northumberland. *T:* Greenhaugh 223.

**MORRISON-LOW, Sir James;** *see* Low.

**MORRISON-SCOTT, Sir Terence Charles Stuart,** Kt 1965; DSC 1944; DSc; Director, British Museum (Natural History), 1960-68 (Director, Science Museum, 1956-60); *b* Paris, 24 Oct. 1908; *o s* of late R. C. S. Morrison-Scott, DSO, and Douairière Jhr. R. Quarles van Ufford; *m* 1935, Rita, 4th *d* of late E. J. Layton. *Educ:* Eton; Christ Church (MA of the House, 1947), Oxford; Royal College of Science (1st Class Hons Zoology, BSc, ARCS 1935, MSc 1939). Asst Master, Eton, 1935; Scientific Staff, Brit. Museum (Natural Hist.) in charge of Mammal Room, 1936-39, 1945-55 and part of 1956. DSc London, 1952. Served War of 1939-45, with Royal Navy (DSC). Lt-Comdr RNVR. Treas., Zoological Soc. of London, 1950-; Treas., XVth Internat. Congress of Zoology, 1958. Trustee, Imp. War Museum, 1956-60. Governor, Imperial Coll. of Science and Technology (Fellow, 1963); Mem. Council, Nat. Trust, 1968-. FLS. *Publications:* Palaearctic and Indian Mammals (with J. R. E.), 1951; Southern African Mammals (with J. R. E. and R. W. H.), 1953; papers in scientific jls on taxonomy of mammals. *Address:* Upperfold House, Fernhurst, Haslemere, Surrey. *Clubs:* Athenæum, Brooks's; Vincent's (Oxford); Leander.

**MORROCCO, Alberto,** RSA 1963 (ARSA 1952); Head of School of Painting, Duncan of Jordanstone College of Art, Dundee, since 1950; *b* 14 Dec. 1917; *m* 1941, Vera Cockburn Mercer; two *s* one *d. Educ:* Gray's Sch. of Art, Aberdeen. Carnegie Schol., 1937; Brough Schol., 1938. In the Army, 1940-46. Guthrie Award, 1943; San Vito Prize, Rome, 1959. Pictures in: Scottish Modern Arts Coll.; Contemporary Arts Soc.; Scottish Arts Council Coll.; Hull, Aberdeen, Glasgow, Perth and Dundee Art Galleries. *Recreations:* travel, swimming, eating. *Club:* Scottish Arts.

**MORROGH, Henton,** CBE 1969; FRS 1964; Director of the British Cast Iron Research Association since 1959; *b* 29 Sept. 1917; *s* of Clifford and Amy Morrogh; *m* 1949, Olive Joyce Ramsay; one *d.* Distinguished for his work on the microstructure and solidification of cast iron and for the development of ductile cast iron. Visiting Prof., Dept of Industrial Engineering and Management Univ. of Technology, Loughborough, 1967-. DSc (*hc*), Univ. of Birmingham, 1965; Iron and Steel Inst. Andrew Carnegie Gold Medal, 1946; E. J. Fox Medal Inst. of Brit. Foundrymen, 1951;

McFadden Gold Medal, Amer. Foundrymen's Soc., 1952; Robert Hadfield Medal, Iron & Steel Inst., 1956; Gold Medal, Amer. Gray Iron Founders' Soc., 1961; Pres. Instn of Metallurgists, 1967-68. *Address:* British Cast Iron Research Assoc., Alvechurch, Birmingham. *T:* Redditch 66414; Cedarwood, Penn Lane, Tanworth-in-Arden, Warwicks. *T:* Tanworth-in-Arden 414.

**MORROGH BERNARD, Rt. Rev. Mgr. Canon Eustace Anthony,** LCL; Vicar-General, 1939-63, of Archdiocese of Westminster; *b* Killarney, 1893; *s* of Eustace Morrogh Bernard, Flesk House, Killarney, Co. Kerry, and Mary Anne, 5th *d* of Samuel Jas Brown, Loftus Hill, Yorks. *Educ:* Ampleforth; St Edmund's Ware; Angelico Univ., Rome (LCL). Ordained Catholic Priest, 1918; Asst Dioc. Chancellor of Westminster, 1919-37; Chancellor, 1937-44; Privy Chamberlain to the Pope, 1933; Domestic Prelate, 1938; Protonotary Apostolic *ad instar,* 1960; Canon of Metropolitan Cathedral of Westminster, 1941. *Address:* Nazareth House, Hammersmith Road, W6.

**MORROW, Sir (Arthur) William,** Kt 1959; DSO 1942; ED 1949; FRCP, FRACP; Hon. Physician, Royal Prince Alfred Hospital, Sydney, since 1951; Lecturer in Therapeutics, University of Sydney, since 1938; *b* 12 July 1903; *s* of Arthur John Morrow and Helonar (*née* Harkin); *m* 1937, Jean Buchanan Brown; three *d. Educ:* Newington Coll., Sydney; Sydney Univ. MB, BS Sydney 1927; FRCP 1949; FRACP 1938; Hon. FACP 1968. First Cl. Hons in Medicine at graduation, 1927; RMO, Royal Prince Alfred Hospital, Sydney, 1927; Dep. Supt 1932; Hon. Asst Phys., 1934. Hon. Cons. Phys., Canterbury District Memorial Hosp., Sydney, 1938; Marrickville Dist Hosp., 1939; Western Suburb Hosp., 1937. Served in AIF, War of 1939-45 (finishing rank Col); final posting, Cons. Phys. Advanced HQ (despatches, DSO). Now RAAMC Reserve. Pres. NSW Branch, BMA, 1958-59. Council, RACP, 1957- (Censor, 1953-, Censor-in-Chief, 1962-66, Pres. 1966-68). *Publications:* numerous medical scientific articles, mainly applied to gastro-enterology. *Recreation:* golf. *Address:* 26 Fairfax Road, Bellevue Hill, Sydney, NSW 2023, Australia. *T:* 36 6312; (professional) 185 Macquarie Street, Sydney, NSW 2023. *T:* 221 1351. *Clubs:* Australian, Royal Sydney Golf (Sydney); Australian Jockey.

**MORROW, Ian Thomas,** CA, FCWA; FBIM; CompIEE (Hon.); Managing Director, UK Optical & Industrial Holdings Ltd and Chairman of subsidiary companies; Joint Managing Director, H. Clarkson & Co. Ltd; Chairman: Associated Fire Alarms Ltd; Rowe Bros & Co. (Holdings) Ltd; Crane Fruehauf Trailers Ltd; a Deputy Chairman, Rolls Royce Ltd; also Director of other companies; *b* 8 June 1912; *er s* of Thomas George Morrow and late Jamesina Hunter, Pilmour Links, St Andrews; *m* 1940, Elizabeth Mary Thackray (marr. diss. 1967); one *s* one *d*; *m* 1967, Sylvia Jane Taylor. *Educ:* Dollar Academy, Dollar. Chartered Accountant 1936; FCWA 1945; Asst Accountant, Brocklehurst-Whiston Amalgamated Ltd, 1937-40; Partner, Robson, Morrow & Co., 1942-51; Financial Dir, 1951-52, Dep. Man. Dir, 1952-56, Joint Man. Dir, 1956-57, The Brush Electrical Engineering Co. Ltd (now The Brush Group Ltd), of which he was Man. Dir, 1957-58. Led Anglo-American Council on Productivity Team on Management Accounting to US, 1950. Council Member: British Electrical & Allied Manufacturers' Assoc., 1957-58; British Internal Combustion Engine Manufacturers Assoc., 1957-58; Member: Grand Council, FBI, 1953-58; Council, Production Engineering Research Assoc., 1955-58; Council, Inst. of Cost and Works Accountants, 1952-70 (Pres., 1956-57; Gold Medallist, 1961); Export Council for Europe, 1965-68. mem. Council, Inst. of Chartered Accountants of Scotland (Vice-Pres., 1970-71). Freeman, City of London; Liveryman, Worshipful Co. of Spectaclemakers. *Publications:* papers and addresses on professional and management subjects. *Recreations:* reading, music, gardening, golf, ski-ing. *Address:* 23 Chester Terrace, Regents Park, NW1. *T:* 01-486 4250. *Clubs:* National Liberal, Royal Automobile; Royal and Ancient (St Andrews).

**MORROW, Sir William;** *see* Morrow, Sir A. W.

**MORSE, Christopher Jeremy;** Executive Director, Bank of England, since 1965; Alternate Governor for United Kingdom of International Monetary Fund, since 1966; *b* 10 Dec. 1928; *s* of Francis John Morse, JP, Croix de Guerre, and Kinbarra, *d* of late Edward Armfield Armfield-Marrow, barrister; *m* 1955, Belinda Marianne, *d* of Lt-Col R. B. Y. Mills; three *s* one *d. Educ:* Winchester; New Coll., Oxford. 1st Class Lit. Hum. 1953. 2nd Lt KRRC, 1948-49. Fellow: All Souls Coll., Oxford, 1953-68; Winchester Coll., 1966. Dir, Legal & General Assurance Society Ltd, 1963-64; Dir, Glyn, Mills & Co., 1964. *Recreations:* family, problems and puzzles, golf. *Address:* 102a Drayton Gardens, SW10. *T:* 01-370 2265. *Clubs:* Oxford and Cambridge University, MCC.

**MORSE, David A.;** Director-General of International Labor Office at Geneva, 1948-70; *b* New York City, 31 May 1907; *m* 1937, Mildred H. Hockstader. *Educ:* Somerville Public Schs, NJ; Rutgers Coll., NJ; Harvard Law Sch. LittB (Rutgers), 1929, LLB (Harvard), 1932. Admitted to New Jersey Bar, 1932; Chief Counsel Petroleum Labor Policy Bd, Dept of Interior, 1934-35. US Dept of Interior; Special Asst to US Attorney-Gen., 1934-35; Regional Attorney, National Labor Relations Bd (Second Region), 1935-38. Impartial Chm., Milk Industry Metropolitan Area of New York, 1940-42, when entered Army. Lectr on Labor Relations, Labor Law, Administrative Law, various colleges and law schools, 1938-47. Gustav Pollak Lectr on Research in Govt, Harvard Univ., 1955-56. Formerly: Perm. US Govt Mem. on Governing Body of Internat. Labor Office; US Govt Deleg. to Internat. Labor Confs; Statutory Mem. Bd of Foreign Service; Dep. Chm. Interdepartmental Cttee on Internat. Social Policy; Mem., Bd of Educn, Somerville, NJ; Mem., Cttee for Conservation of Manpower in War Industry, State of NJ; served in N Africa, Sicily and Italy, 1943-44 (Chief of Labor Div., Allied Mil. Govt); arrived in England, 1944. Major, 1944; Chief of Labor Section, US Group Control Council for Germany and prepared Labor Policy and Program for Germany; also advised and assisted SHAEF in preparation of Labor Policy and Program for France, Belgium, Holland, etc; Lt-col and Dir Labor for Mil. Govt Group, 1945; returned to US; Gen. Counsel, Nat. Labor Relations Bd, 1945-46; Asst Sec. of Labor, 1946-47; Under-Sec. of Labor, 1947-48; Actg Sec. of Labor, June-Aug. 1948. Member: Amer. Bar Assoc.; Council on Foreign Relations; World Rehabilitation Fund; NY Foundation; Nat. Council of UN Assoc. of USA; Amer. Arbitration Assoc.; US Cttee of Dag Hammarskjöld Foundn; American Legion; Impartial Chm., Coat and Suit Ind. of Metropolitan Area of NY, 1970.

Hon. LLD: Rutgers, 1957; Geneva, 1962; Strasbourg, 1968; Hon. DSc, Laval, Quebec, 1969. Rutgers Univ. Alumni Award, 1970; Sidney Hillman Foundn Award, 1969. Three Bronze Battle Stars; Legion of Merit; Officier de l'Etoile Equatoriale (Gabon); Ordre de la valeur (Cameroon); Order of Merit of Labour (Brazil). *Address:* 14 East 75th Street, New York, NY 10021, USA. *Clubs:* Harvard, Century Association (New York).

**MORSE-BOYCOTT, Rev. Desmond;** Co-founder with his wife, in 1932, and Hon. Principal and Director of the Music, of St Mary-of-the-Angels Song School–an Anglican Choir School for boys of all classes; Assistant Curate of St Mary the Virgin, Somers Town, 1919-35; *b* 10 Dec. 1892; *y s* of late Frederic Augustus Morse-Boycott, Sennowe, Norfolk, and Octavia Mary, 5th *d* of Matthew John Anketell, Anketell Grove, JP and DL Co. Monaghan; *m* Marguerite Harriet Sandford (*d* 1959), Chailey, Sussex; one *d. Educ:* privately; Lichfield Theological Coll. At the age of 16 entered the service of the West Sussex County Education Cttee; during this period studied commercial subjects and became an expert shorthand teacher; became asst curate at Mayfield in Sussex; Bognor; then Somers Town; entered journalism, teaching himself the craft; became a contributor to all the leading newspapers; conducted a Test Centre for young aspirants for the ministry. Has supplied boys' choirs for various films as well as for Church and secular occasions of importance. LTh (Durham); FRSA. Hon. Fellow, Tonic Sol-Fa Coll. of Music, 1969. *Publications:* Alleluia; Three Holy Fruits; Seven Words of Love; Simplicitas and His Brethren; The Pilgrim's Way; Holy Communion; Ten Years in a London Slum; God and Everyman; Mystic Glow; Wayside Words; We do see Life; Saith the Preacher; Fields of Yesterday, 1932; Lead, Kindly Light; Credo, etc; The Secret Story of the Oxford Movement, 1933; Is it a Sin?, 1935; Great Crimes of the Bible, 1936; A Tramping Parson's Message, 1936; How can I be Happy?, 1937; Fear Not, 1939; They Shine Like Stars, 1948; A Golden Legend of the Slums, 1951; A Tapestry of Toil (autobiog.), 1970. Edits The Angel. *Recreations:* painting, music, philately. *Address:* Crabtrees, Longbottom Lane, Seer Green, near Beaconsfield, Bucks. *T:* Beaconsfield 5923.

**MORSHEAD, Sir Owen (Frederick),** GCVO 1958; KCB 1953; DSO 1917; MC; Librarian, Windsor Castle, 1926-58, after which date appointed Emeritus Librarian; also formerly Assistant Keeper Royal Archives; Fellow Magdalene College, Cambridge, since 1920; Chairman Dorset Historic Churches Trust; *b* 1893; *y s* of late Reginald Morshead, Hurlditch Court, Tavistock, Devon; *m* 1926, Paquita, *d* of J. G. Hagemeyer, Florence, Italy; one *s* two *d. Educ:* Marlborough; RMA, Woolwich; Magdalene Coll., Cambridge. Served European War, 1914-19 (despatches five times, DSO, Bt Major, MC, Croce di Guerra); Legion of Honour (Officier). Comd 9th Berks Bn Home Guard, 1941-45. DL Berks, 1946-58. *Publications:* Everybody's Pepys, 1926; Windsor Castle, 1951; George IV and Royal Lodge, 1965. *Address:* Lindens, Sturminster Newton, Dorset. *T:* Sturminster Newton 209.

*See also J. D. May.*

**MORSON, A(lbert) Clifford,** OBE, FRCS; Consulting Urologist, St Peter's Hospital for Urinary Diseases, Hampstead General Hospital, Whipps Cross Hospital and NW Metropolitan Regional Hospital Board; *s* of Thomas Pierre and Florence Morson; *m* 1917, Adela Frances Maud, *o d* of late Lincoln Phené and Alice Phené; three *s. Educ:* Haileybury Coll. Qualified as a Medical Practitioner at the Middlesex Hosp., 1906; as a student obtained Lyall Gold Medal and Scholarship for practical surgery; Capt. Rugby Football Club; Original Mem., Royal Naval Volunteer Reserve (London Div.), 1903; Various resident Medical appointments, 1907-12; Middlesex Hosp. and St Peter's Hosp. for Urinary Diseases, Registrar and Research Scholar, Cancer Laboratories, Middlesex Hosp., 1912-14; received temporary commission as Surgeon in HM Navy, August 1914; served in HMS Zealandia, and HMS Centurion of Grand Fleet; Surgeon, Hospital Ships Somali and Karapara throughout Gallipoli campaign (OBE, 1914-15 star, general service and Victory medals); demobilised 1919. Pres., 1933-34, Section of Urology, RSM; Hon. Pres. International Soc. of Urology; Past Pres. British Assoc. of Urological Surgeons; lately Mem. Regional Hosp. Bd NW Metropolitan Area. Hon. Member: Brit. Assoc. of Urological Surgeons, Canadian Urological Assoc., Finnish Urological Soc.; Mem. Cttee of Management, Inst. of Urology (London Univ.). Hon. Fellow RSM. *Publications:* A Guide to Urinary Diseases (with Adolphe Abrahams); Urinary Infections, Pocket Monograph series; numerous articles in medical and scientific journals. *Recreations:* all outdoor sports. *Address:* 66 Northway, NW11. *T:* 01-455 0264.

*See also B. C. Morson.*

**MORSON, Basil Clifford,** VRD 1963; MA, DM Oxon; FRCPath; Consultant Pathologist to St Mark's Hospital since 1956; Director of the Research Department, since 1958; *b* 13 Nov. 1921; *s* of A. Clifford Morson, *qv*; *m* 1950, Pamela Elizabeth Gilbert; one *s* two *d. Educ:* Beaumont Coll.; Wadham Coll., Oxford; Middlesex Hosp. Medical Sch. House Surg., Middlesex Hosp., 1949; House Surg., Central Middlesex Hosp., 1950; Asst Pathologist, Bland-Sutton Institute of Pathology, Middlesex Hosp., 1950. Sub-Lt RNVR, 1943-46; Surgeon-Comdr RNR (London Div.). Visiting Prof. of Pathology, Univ. of Chicago, 1959; Hon. Lectr in Pathology, Royal Postgraduate Medical Sch. of London, 1965. Lettsomian Lectures, Med. Soc., 1970. (Scientific) FZS 1959. *Publications:* chap. Pathology of Alimentary tract in Systemic Pathology, ed G. Payling Wright and W. St C. Symmers, 1966; (ed) Diseases of the Colon, Rectum and Anus, 1969; numerous articles in medical journals. *Recreations:* tennis, squash, ornithology, travel. *Address:* 52 Gordon Place, W8. *T:* 01-937 7101. *Club:* Hurlingham.

**MORSON, Clifford;** *see* Morson, A. C.

**MORT, Rt. Rev. John Ernest Llewelyn,** CBE 1965; Canon Residentiary and Treasurer of Leicester Cathedral, since 1970; *b* 13 April 1915; *s* of Trevor Ll. and Ethel Mary Mort. *Educ:* Malvern Coll.; St Catharine's Coll., Cambridge (MA); Westcott House, Cambridge. Asst Curate, Dudley, 1940-44; Worcester Diocesan Youth Organiser, 1944-48; Vicar of St John in Bedwardine, Worcester, 1948-52; Chaplain to the Bishop of Worcester, 1943-52; Bishop of N Nigeria, 1952-69. *Recreations:* riding, tennis. *Address:* (home) 7 St Martin's East, Leicester.

**MORTIMER, Chapman;** *see* Chapman-Mortimer, W. C.

**MORTIMER, Sir Charles Edward,** Kt, *cr* 1950; CBE 1943; *b* 1 Jan. 1886; *s* of Joseph Mortimer; *m* 1920, Winifred Whitehouse; two *s. Educ:* Hartley Coll., Manchester. Methodist Minister, 1910-16; entered Land Dept, Kenya,

1917, as Clerk; Land Asst, 1920-27; Lands Sec., 1928-38; Commissioner of Lands and Settlement, 1938-39; Commissioner for Local Govt, Lands and Settlement, 1939-46; Mem. for Health and Local Government, Kenya Colony, 1946-50, and 1952-54. KStJ 1965. *Address:* PO Box 6890, Nairobi, Kenya.

**MORTIMER, Clifford Hiley,** FRS 1958; DSc, DrPhil; Director, Center for Great Lakes Studies, University of Wisconsin-Milwaukee, since 1966; *b* Whitchurch, Som, 27 Feb. 1911; *er s* of Walter Herbert and Bessie Russell; *m* 1936, Ingeborg Margarete Closs, Stuttgart, Germany; two *d. Educ:* Sibford and Sidcot Schs; Univ. of Manchester. BSc (Manchester) 1932, DSc (Manchester) 1946; Dr Phil (Berlin) 1935. Served on scientific staff of Freshwater Biological Assoc., 1935-41 and 1946-56. Seconded to Admiralty scientific service, 1941-46. Sec. and Dir, Scottish Marine Biological Assoc., 1956-66. *Publications:* scientific papers on lakes and the physical and chemical conditions which control life in them. *Recreations:* music, travel. *Address:* 2501 E Menlo Boulevard, Shorewood, Wisconsin 53211, USA.

**MORTIMER, James Edward;** Member: London Transport Executive, since 1971; National Board for Prices and Incomes since 1968; *b* 12 Jan. 1921; *m*; two *s* one *d. Educ:* Junior Techn. Sch., Portsmouth; Ruskin Coll., Oxford; London Sch. of Economics. Worked in Shipbuilding and Engrg Industries as Ship Fitter Apprentice, Machinist and Planning Engr; TUC Schol., Oxford, 1945-46; TUC Economic Dept, 1946-48; full-time Trade Union Official, Draughtsmen's and Allied Technicians' Assoc., 1948-68. *Publications:* A History of Association of Engineering and Shipbuilding Draughtsmen, 1960; (with Clive Jenkins) British Trade Unions Today, 1965; (with Clive Jenkins) The Kind of Laws the Unions Ought to Want, 1968; Industrial Relations, 1968. *Recreation:* camping.

**MORTIMER, John (Clifford),** QC 1966; barrister; playwright and author; *b* 21 April 1923; *s* of Clifford Mortimer and Kathleen May (*née* Smith); *m* 1949, Penelope Ruth Fletcher; one *s* one *d. Educ:* Harrow; Brasenose Coll., Oxford. Called to the Bar, 1948. Occasional Critic for Evening Standard, Observer and New Statesman. Won the Italia Prize with short play, The Dock Brief, 1958; another short play What Shall We Tell Caroline, 1958. Full-length plays: The Wrong Side of the Park, 1960; Two Stars for Comfort, 1962; A Flea in Her Ear, 1966; The Judge, 1967; (trans.) Cat Among the Pigeons, 1969; Come as You Are, 1970. Film Script: John and Mary, 1970. Scenario for ballet, Home, 1968. *Publications: novels:* Charade, 1947; Rumming Park, 1948; Answer Yes or No, 1950; Like Men Betrayed, 1953; Three Winters, 1956; *travel:* (in collab. with wife) With Love and Lizards, 1957; *plays:* The Dock Brief and Other Plays, 1959; The Wrong Side of the Park, 1960; Lunch Hour and other Plays, 1960; Two Stars for Comfort, 1962; (trans.) A Flea in Her Ear, 1965; writes TV plays; contribs to periodicals. *Recreations:* working, cooking, going to the theatre. *Address:* 16a Blomfield Road, W9. *Club:* Garrick.

**MORTIMER, Raymond,** CBE 1955; Officier de la Légion d'Honneur; *b* 25 April 1895; *s* of Charles Edward Mortimer and Marion Josephine Cantrell. *Educ:* Malvern; Balliol Coll., Oxford. *Publications:* Channel Packet, 1942; Manet's Bar aux Folies-Bergère, 1944; Duncan Grant, 1944. *Recreation:* travel. *Address:* 5 Canonbury Place, N1. *T:* 01-226 3548; Long Crichel House, Wimborne, Dorset. *T:* Tarrant Hinton 250. *Clubs:* Travellers', Beefsteak.

**MORTIMER, Rt. Rev. Robert Cecil;** *see* Exeter, Bishop of.

**MORTIMER, William Charles C.;** *see* Chapman-Mortimer.

**MORTON,** 21st Earl of, *cr* 1458 (*de facto* 20th Earl, 21st but for the Attainder); **Sholto Charles John Hay Douglas;** Lord Dalkeith and Aberdour, 1458; Flight Lt, late RAFVR; *b* 12 April 1907; *s* of Lord Aberdour (*d* 1911; *e s* of 20th, *de facto* 19th, Earl of Morton) and Brenda (*d* 1954), *d* of Lord John Hay, Fulmer Place, near Slough; *S* grandfather, 1935. *Educ:* Magdalen Coll., Oxford (MA). Fellow of the Linnæan Soc. VMH, RHS, 1967. *Heir: c* John Charles Sholto Douglas [*b* 19 March 1927; *m* 1949, Sheila Mary, *d* of late Rev. Canon John Stanley Gibbs, MC, Didmarton House, Badminton, Glos; two *s* one *d*]. *Address:* The Hatch, Churt, Surrey.

**MORTON OF HENRYTON,** Baron (Life-Peer) *cr* 1947, of Henryton; **Fergus Dunlop Morton,** PC 1944; Kt 1938; *b* 17 Oct. 1887; *y s* of late George Morton of Lochgreen, Troon, Ayrshire; *m* Margaret Greenlees, *er d* of James Begg; one *d. Educ:* Kelvinside; St John's Coll., Cambridge. Hon. Foundation Scholar, classics; First Class Law Tripos; MA, LLB. Called to Bar, 1912; temp. commission as Lt Highland Light Infantry, Sept. 1914; Capt., 1915; active service, 1916-18 (MC); War Office, 1918-19; returned to practice at the Bar, Sept. 1919; KC 1929; Judge of Chancery Div., High Court of Justice, 1938-44; a Lord Justice of Appeal, 1944-47; a Lord of Appeal in Ordinary, 1947-59. Bencher of Lincoln's Inn, 1932; Treas., 1953. Hon. Fellow of St John's Coll., Cambridge, 1940. Chairman: Black List Cttee, Min. of Economic Warfare, 1941-46; Council of Legal Educn, 1949-53; Cttee on the Law of Intestate Succession, 1950; Royal Commn on marriage and divorce, 1951. Dep. High Steward, Cambridge Univ. Hon. Mem., Faculty of Advocates; Hon. Mem. Cdn and Amer. Bar Assocs; Hon. LLD: Cambridge, 1951; Glasgow, 1951; St Andrews, 1956; Sydney, 1957. *Recreations:* playing golf and watching every kind of outdoor ball game. *Address:* 78 Melton Court, SW7. *T:* 01-589 8989; Grey Thatch, Winter Hill, Cookham, Berks. *T:* Bourne End 20 233. *Club:* Athenæum.

**MORTON, Alastair;** *see* Morton, S. A.

**MORTON, Anthony;** *see* Creasey, John.

**MORTON, Air Commodore Crichton Charles,** CBE 1945; Command Electronics Officer, HQ Bomber Command, 1962-66, retired; *b* 26 July 1912; *s* of late Charles Crichton Morton, Ramsey, IOM; *m* 1956, Diana Yvonne, *d* of late Maj.-Gen. R. C. Priest, CB, RMS; no *c. Educ:* King William's Coll., IOM; RAF Coll., Cranwell. Various flying duties, 1932-36; RAF Officers Long Signals Course, Cranwell, 1936-37; signals duties, 1937-39; radar duties at HQ Fighter Comd, No 5 Signals Wing France, HQ 60 Signals Gp, Air HQ Iceland, HQ Air Comd SE Asia, 1939-45; Dir of Radar and Dep. Dir of Signals, Air Min., 1945-49; jssc Latimer, 1949-50; OC No. 3 Radio Sch., RAF Compton Bassett, 1950-52; OC Communications Gp, Allied Air Forces Central Europe, 1952-55; Inspector of Radio Services, 1955-58; Dep. Chief Signals Office, HQ, SHAPE, 1958-60; Chm. of Brit. Jt Communications Electronics Board, Ministry of Defence, 1960-62. AMIEE 1955; AFRAeS 1965; MIERE 1965; CEng

1966. *Address:* Apartamento 102, Torre Tramontana, Apartado 50, Playa de Aro, Gerona, Spain. *Clubs:* Royal Air Force, English-Speaking Union.

**MORTON, Major Sir Desmond John Falkiner,** KCB, *cr* 1945 (CB 1941); CMG 1937; *b* 13 Nov. 1891; *o s* of late Col Charles F. Morton, Royal Dragoons, and Edith, *d* of John Tolerton Leather, of Middleton Hall, Northumberland; unmarried. *Educ:* Eton; Royal Military Academy, Woolwich. 2nd Lt RH and RFA, 1911; fought in European War with regiment and on the Staff; ADC to FM Earl Haig, 1917 (despatches, MC, French Croix de Guerre and Médaille d'honneur, Brevet of Major; seconded under Foreign Office, 1919; Dir of Industrial Intelligence Centre, 1930; Principal Asst Sec., Min. of Economic Warfare, 1939; Personal Asst to Prime Minister, 1940-46; UK delegate to Inter-Allied Reparation Agency; UK Comr for Restitution of Monetary Gold, 1946; Vice-Chm. of UN Economic Survey Mission for the Middle East, 1949; lent by Treasury to Ministry of Civil Aviation, 1950; retired 1953. Governor of St Luke's Hosp., Woodside, 1946-48, Middlesex Hosp., 1947-66; Chm. Hammersmith Post-Graduate Group, 1954-66; Chm. London Post-Graduate Cttee, 1964-66. Officier Légion d'Honneur, 1946; Grand Officer Order of Orange-Nassau, 1947. *Address:* 22 Kew Green, Richmond, Surrey. *T:* 01-940 4168. *Clubs:* United Service, Challoner.

**MORTON, Digby;** *see* Morton, H. D.

**MORTON, Prof. Frank,** OBE 1968; DSc 1952, PhD 1936 (Manchester); MSc Tech; FRIC; MIChemE; Professor of Chemical Engineering, University of Manchester, since 1956; a Pro-Vice-Chancellor, since 1968; *b* Sheffield, 11 Aug. 1906; *s* of late Joseph Morton, Manchester; *m* 1936, Hilda May, *d* of John W. Seaston, Withington, Manchester; one *s*. *Educ:* Manchester Univ. Demonstrator in Chemical Technology, 1931-36; Research Chemist, Trinidad Leaseholds Ltd, 1936-40; Superintendent of Research and Development, Trinidad Leaseholds, Trinidad, 1940-45; Chief Chemist, Trinidad Leaseholds Ltd, UK, 1945-49; Prof. of Chemical Engineering, Univ. of Birmingham, 1949-56. Actg Principal, Manchester Coll. of Science and Technology, 1964-65; Dep. Principal, Univ. of Manchester Inst. of Science and Technology, 1966-. Member: Council, Manchester Business Sch., 1964-; Chemical and Allied Products Training Board, 1968-; European Fedn of Chemical Engineering, 1968-. Pres., IChemE, 1963-64. Society of Chemical Industry: Vice-Pres., 1967-; Jubilee Memorial Lectr, 1967-; Medal, 1969. *Publications:* various papers on petroleum, organic chemistry, chemical engineering and allied subjects. *Recreations:* golf, athletics, squash. *Address:* 18 Sevenoaks Avenue, Heaton Moor, Stockport, Cheshire. *T:* 061-432 4889; Department of Chemical Engineering, University of Manchester Institute of Science and Technology, Manchester 1. *Club:* Savage.

**MORTON, G. F.,** MA, BSc, DèsL; Retired Head Master, Leeds Modern School; *b* 31 Dec. 1882; *s* of J. B. Morton and S. E. Figgins; *m* 1915, J. C. B. Templeton, MA, BSc; two *s* one *d*. *Educ:* Macclesfield Grammar Sch.; Emmanuel Coll., Cambridge; Sch. of Economics, London; Faculté de Rennes. Head Master: Katharine Lady Berkeley's Grammar Sch., Wotton-under-Edge, Glos. *Publications:* Childhood's Fears; Hike and Trek; Hike and Hero; La Psychanalyse et l'Education Morale de l'Enfant; Madhouse for the Million, 1939; Highlands and Backwoods, 1958. *Recreations:* walking and camping. *Address:* Uplands, Shipham, near Winscombe, Somerset. *T:* Winscombe 3234.

**MORTON, Major Harold Trestrail;** Member, Agricultural Land Tribunal, 1948-65; *b* 8 Nov. 1894; *s* of late Thomas Morton, JP, Aston Dene, Stevenage, Herts; *m* 1916, Beatrice Nathalie, *d* of late Capt. James Edward Shaw and Adela C. A. Shaw, CBE, JP; one *s* two *d*. *Educ:* Bradfield Coll. Served European War, 1914-19, with East Riding Yeomanry, Capt. 1917, and Royal Horse Guards; Major, 1940, Home Guard. Master of Whaddon Chase Hounds, 1940-47; JP Bucks 1931; High Sheriff of Bucks, 1943. Chairman: Aylesbury Div. Conservative and Unionist Assoc., 1946-55; Bucks Branch of Country Landowners' Assoc., 1944-47 (Pres., 1947-50). Order of the White Lion, Czechoslovakia, 1946. *Recreations:* hunting, shooting, and fishing. *Address:* The Abbey, Aston Abbotts, Aylesbury, Bucks. *T:* Aston Abbotts 202; 97 Gresham Street, EC2. *T:* 01-638 9991; Glenfiddich Lodge, Dufftown, Banffshire. *T:* Dufftown 327. *Clubs:* Gresham, Kennel.

**MORTON, (Henry) Digby;** consultant designer (independent); *b* 26 Nov. 1906; *e s* of Digby Berkeley Morton, Dublin; *m* 1936, Phyllis May, *d* of James Harwood Panting, London. *Educ:* Dublin. Trained in Art and Architecture, Metropolitan Sch. of Art, Dublin, 1923-29. Opened Couture Establishment in London, 1930; worked in USA, 1953-57; Founder Mem., Incorporated Soc. of London Fashion Designers, 1939 (Vice-Pres. 1955-56). *Recreation:* moving. *Address:* 47 South Street, W1. *T:* 01-629 7596.

**MORTON, Henry Vollam,** FRSL; author and journalist. Entered journalism, Birmingham Gazette and Express, 1910; assistant editor, 1912; edited Empire Magazine, London, 1913; sub-editor, Daily Mail, 1913-14; served in Warwicks Yeomanry during War; joined editorial staff Evening Standard in 1919; Daily Express, 1921; special writer, Daily Herald, 1931-42. Comdr, Order of the Phœnix (Greece), 1937; Cavaliere, Order of Merit (Italy), 1965. *Publications:* The Heart of London, 1925; The London Year, 1926; London, 1926; The Spell of London, 1926; The Nights of London, 1926; In Search of England, 1927; The Call of England, 1928; In Search of Scotland, 1929; In Search of Ireland, 1930; In Search of Wales, 1932; Blue Days at Sea, 1932; In Scotland Again, 1933; In the Steps of The Master, 1934; Our Fellow Men, 1936; In the Steps of St Paul, 1936; Through Lands of the Bible, 1938; Ghosts of London, 1939; Women of the Bible, 1940; H. V. Morton's London, 1940; Middle East, 1941; I, James Blunt, 1942; I Saw Two Englands, 1942; Atlantic Meeting, 1943; In Search of South Africa, 1948; In Search of London, 1951; In the Steps of Jesus, 1953; A Stranger in Spain, 1954; A Traveller in Rome, 1957; This is Rome, 1960; This is the Holy Land, 1961; A Traveller in Italy, 1964; The Waters of Rome, 1966; A Traveller in Southern Italy, 1969. *Address:* Schapenberg, Somerset West, Cape Province, South Africa. *Clubs:* Garrick, Civil Service (Cape Town).

**MORTON, John Cameron Andrieu Bingham Michael; (J. B. Morton),** CBE 1952; journalist; since 1924, beachcomber of the Daily Express; *b* 7 June 1893; *s* of Edward Morton, journalist and dramatist, and Rosamond, *d* of Capt. Devereux Bingham, Wartnaby Hall, Leics; *m* 1927, Dr Mary O'Leary, Cappoquin, Co. Waterford. *Educ:* Park House, Southborough; Harrow; Worcester Coll., Oxford. Enlisted, 1914; fought in France; Commission, 1916; Intelligence, MI7b, 1917; received into Catholic Church, 1922. *Publications:* The

Barber of Putney, 1919; Enchanter's Nightshade, 1920; Penny Royal, 1921; Tally-Ho!, 1922; Old Man's Beard, 1923; The Cow Jumped Over the Moon, 1924; Gorgeous Poetry, 1924; Mr Thake, 1929; Mr Thake Again, 1930; By the Way, 1931; Maladetta, 1932; Drink Up, Gentlemen, 1932; 1933 and Still Going Wrong; Sobieski, King of Poland, 1932; Hag's Harvest, 1933; Morton's Folly, 1933; Who's Who at the Zoo, 1933; The Adventures of Mr Thake, 1934; The Death of the Dragon, and other fairy tales, 1934; Skylighters, 1934; Vagabond, 1935; Stuff and Nonsense, 1935; Mr Thake and the Ladies, 1935; The Bastille Falls (Studies of the French Revolution), 1936; Gallimaufry, 1936; The Dauphin (Louis XVII), 1937; Sideways through Borneo (an Unconventional Journey), 1937; The New Ireland, 1938; A Diet of Thistles, 1938; The Dancing Cabman (Collected Verse), 1938; Pyrenean, 1938; Saint-Just, 1939; A Bonfire of Weeds, 1939; I Do Not Think So, 1940; Fool's Paradise, 1941; Captain Foulenough & Company, 1944; The Gascon, 1946; Brumaire; The Rise of Bonaparte, 1948; Here and Now, 1948; The Misadventures of Dr Strabismus, 1949; The Tibetan Venus, 1951; Camille Desmoulins: and Other Studies of the French Revolution, 1951; St Thérèse of Lisieux: The Making of a Saint, 1954; Hilaire Belloc: A Memoir, 1955; Springtime: Tales of the Cafe Rieu, 1956; Marshal Ney, 1958; Merry-go-Round, 1959; The Best of Beachcomber (Selected by Michael Frayn), 1963. *Address:* Melleray, Sea Lane, Ferring, Sussex. *Club:* St Stephen's Green (Dublin).

**MORTON, John Percival,** CMG 1965; OBE 1946; Indian Police Medal for gallantry, 1935, Bar 1940; Director, Ministry of Defence; *b* 15 May 1911; *e s* of late Henry Percy Dee Morton; *m* 1939, Leonora Margaret Sale, *d* of late Hon. Mr Justice S. L. Sale, ICS; one *s* one *d. Educ:* Bedford Modern Sch. Entered Indian (Imperial) Police, 1930; Punjab Govt, 1930-40; Defence Dept, Govt of India and attached HQ, Br. Tps Egypt, 1940; Govt of India, Home Dept, Lahore and Delhi, 1941-44; Punjab Govt, Lahore, 1944-47; AHQ, RAF Iraq, 1947-49; Office of Commissioner-General SE Asia, Singapore, 1949-52; Govt of Fedn of Malaya, 1952-54; Imperial Defence Coll., 1959; Colonial Office, 1961-65. *Recreations:* golf, gardening. *Address:* Courtlands, Pangbourne, Berks. *T:* Pangbourne 2229. *Club:* East India and Sports.

**MORTON, Kenneth Valentine Freeland,** CIE 1947; Secretary East Anglian Regional Hospital Board since 1947; *b* 13 May 1907; *s* of Kenneth John Morton; *m* 1936, Mary Hadwin Hargreaves; four *s* one *d. Educ:* Edinburgh Academy; University Coll., Oxford. Joined ICS, 1930; Under-Sec. (Political) Punjab Govt, 1934-36; Deputy Commissioner, 1936-39; Colonisation Officer, 1939-43; Deputy Sec., Development Dept, 1943-46; Sec. Electricity and Industries Depts, 1946-47; retired, 1947. *Recreations:* shooting and fishing. *Address:* Mulberry House, Little Wilbraham, Cambs. *T:* Bottisham 355. *Club:* East India and Sports.

**MORTON, Sir Ralph (John),** Kt 1960; CMG 1954; OBE 1947; MC 1918; Judge of High Court of Southern Rhodesia, 1949-59; *b* 2 Aug. 1896; *yr s* of John Morton, Wotton-under-Edge, Glos; *m* 1923, Cato Marie van den Berg; one *d. Educ:* Bishop's Stortford; Cambridge Univ. Served European War, RFA, 1915-19. Southern Rhodesia: Solicitor General, 1934; Attorney General, 1944. *Address:* Grosvenor Square, College Road, Rondebosch, CP, South Africa.

**MORTON, Professor Richard Alan,** FRS 1950; PhD, DSc, FRIC; Johnstone Professor of Biochemistry, University of Liverpool, 1944-66; Emeritus Professor since 1966; *b* 22 Sept. 1899; *m* 1926, Heulwen Roberts; one *d. Educ:* Oulton Sch.; Univ. of Liverpool. Lecturer in Chemistry, 1924; Special Lecturer in Spectroscopy, 1931; Visiting Professor, Ohio State Univ., 1930; Meldola Medallist, 1930. Mem. of Council, The Royal Society, 1959-61, Leverhulme Emeritus Fellow, 1970; Chm. Scientific Publications Board, 1961-62; Mem., Editorial Board: Biochem. Society for 7 years; Nutrition Soc., 1963-67; Chm. Cttee Biochem. Soc., 1959-61 (Hon. Mem., 1966); Mem. Scientific Advisory Cttee, British Egg Marketing Board; Mem. Research Grants (Biology Sub-Cttee), DSIR (SRC), 1962-68, subseq. Biology Cttee of Univ. Science and Techn. Bd. Chm., British Cttee for Chemical Education, 1962-65. Chm. Bd of Governors: Liverpool Institute High Sch. for Boys and Blackburne House High Sch. for Girls, 1960-67; Vice-Chm. Board of Governors, Liverpool Coll. of Technology, 1961-67; Mem. of Council, Royal Inst. of Chemistry, 1958-60, Vice-Pres. and Chm. Education Cttee, 1960-62. Mem. Cttees and Panels concerned with vitamins, bread, flour and nutrition generally; Chm., Cttee on Food Additives, 1963-68; Mem. Oceanography and Fisheries Cttee, Natural Environment Research Council, 1965; Mem. Council, Marine Biological Assoc. of UK, 1967-70; Mem. Anglo-Portuguese Mixed Commn, 1967-, 1969; Hon. Mem., Amer. Inst. of Nutrition, 1969; Scientific Gov., Brit. Nutrition Foundn, 1967. Babcock Lecturer, Univ. of Wisconsin, 1960; Hanau W. Loeb Lectr, St Louis Univ., 1960; Royal Society Leverhulme Vis. Prof., Royal Univ. of Malta, 1969. Hon. DSc: Coimbra, 1964; Wales, 1966; Hon. ScD TCD, 1967. *Publications:* Absorption Spectra of Vitamins and Hormones, 2nd edn, 1942; ed, Biochemistry of Quinones, 1965; ed, Protein Utilization by Poultry; ed, An International Encyclopædia of Food and Nutrition, Vol. 9, Fat-soluble Vitamins, 1969; History of the Biochemical Society, 1969; contributions to chemical and biochemical jls. *Address:* 39 Greenhill Road, Liverpool L18 6JJ. *T:* 051-724 1331.

**MORTON, (Stephen) Alastair,** TD 1949; JP; a Senior Treasury Counsel at the Central Criminal Court, since 1964; Recorder of Devizes, since 1957; Deputy Chairman: Dorset Quarter Sessions, since 1957; Norfolk, since 1969; *b* 28 July 1913; *o s* of Philip Morton, formerly of Dune Gate, Dorchester; *m* 1939, Lily Yarrow Eveline, *o d* of J. S. P. Griffith-Jones, Drews, Beaconsfield, Bucks; one *s* one *d. Educ:* private sch.; Trinity Hall, Cambridge. Commnd Dorset Heavy Bde, RA, TA, 1932; served War of 1939-45, Royal Artillery. Called to the Bar, Middle Temple, 1938; Western Circuit, 1938; Master of the Bench, 1964. Counsel to the Crown at County of London Sessions, 1954-59; First Junior Treasury Counsel at the Central Criminal Court, 1959-64. JP Dorset, 1957. *Recreation:* painting. *Address:* 53 Eaton Terrace, SW1. *T:* 01-730 7730; Cringles, Overy Staithe, near King's Lynn, Norfolk. *T:* Burnham Market 339; 2 Harcourt Buildings, Temple, EC4. *T:* 01-353 2112. *Club:* White's.

**MORTON, William Cuthbert,** CBE 1919; MD; late Captain RAMC; *b* 1875; *s* of Rev. John Morton, DD, missionary of Presbyterian Church in Canada, to East Indians in Trinidad, and Sarah Etter, *d* of William Silver, Halifax, NS. *Educ:* Queen's Royal College, Trinidad, WI; Edinburgh Univ. MA (Classical First) 1896, MD 1910; Univs of Berlin and Freiburg. Retired. *Publications:* Principles of Anatomy:

The Abdomen Proper, 1911; The Language of Anatomy (Edited by Dr Robert Bridges), 1922; The Harmony of Verse, 1968. *Address:* 55 Thornton Hill, Exeter. *T:* Exeter 77720.

**MORTON, Prof. W. E.,** MSc Tech; FTI, Dean of the Faculty of Technology in the University of Manchester, 1964-66; Vice-Principal of the Manchester College of Science and Technology, 1957-65; Professor of Textile Technology in the University of Manchester, 1926-57, and Arkwright Professor, 1957-67, now Professor Emeritus; Pro-Vice-Chancellor, 1963-65; *b* 1902; *s* of J. Morton, LDS Edinburgh, Penrith; *m* 1927, Elsie Maud, *d* of Charles Harlow, Fallowfield, Manchester; two *s* two *d*. *Educ:* St Bees Sch., Cumberland; Manchester Univ.; BScTech, 1922; MScTech 1923; Research Studentship, British Cotton Industry Research Assoc., 1923; Technical Asst to the Dir BCIRA, 1924; Technical Adviser to Dir of Narrow Fabrics, Min. of Supply, 1941-45. Chm., Heightside Housing Assoc. Textile Inst. Medal, 1952; Warner Medal, 1957. *Publications:* An Introduction to the Study of Spinning, 1938; (with J. W. S. Hearle) Physical Properties of Textile Fibres, 1963; papers read before the Textile Institute, and contribs to technical journals. *Recreation:* golf. *Address:* Solway, Delahays Drive, Hale, Cheshire. *T:* 061-980 4520.

**MORTON, Sir (William) Wilfred,** KCB 1966 (CB 1958); Chairman, Board of Customs and Excise, 1965-69; *b* 14 April 1906; *s* of late William Morton; *m* 1939, Jacqueline Harriet, *d* of late H. P. B. Newman, Grenfell, New South Wales. *Educ:* Hutchesons' Grammar Sch.; Glasgow Univ. Entered Inland Revenue, 1927. Consultant to Govt of Bolivia, 1952-54; Comr of Inland Revenue and Dir of Establishments, 1955-58; Third Sec., HM Treasury, 1958-65. *Address:* Brook House, Bagnor, Newbury, Berks. *Club:* United Service.

**MOSDELL, Lionel Patrick; Hon. Mr Justice Mosdell;** Judge of the High Court of Kenya since 1967; retired as Judge of The High Court, Tanganyika (1960-64); *b* 29 Aug. 1912; *s* of late William George Mosdell and late Sarah Ellen Mosdell (*née* Gardiner); *m* 1945, Muriel Jean Sillem; one *s* one *d*. *Educ:* Abingdon Sch.; St Edmund Hall, Oxford. Solicitor, England, 1938. Served War of 1939-45, Egypt, Cyrenaica, Eritrea, Abyssinia, Italy (Capt.). Registrar of Lands and Deeds, N Rhodesia, 1946; Resident Magistrate, 1950; Senior Resident Magistrate, 1956. Barrister, Gray's Inn, 1952. *Recreations:* squash-rackets, swimming. *Address:* The High Court, PO Box 61, Nakuru, Kenya. *Clubs:* Special Forces, Royal Commonwealth Society; Nairobi, Mombasa, Rift Valley Sports (Kenya).

**MOSER, Prof. Claus Adolf,** CBE 1965; FBA 1969; Director, Central Statistical Office, and Head of Government Statistical Service, since 1967; Visiting Professor of Social Statistics, London School of Economics; *b* 24 Nov. 1922; *s* of Dr Ernest Moser and Mrs Lotte Moser; *m* 1949, Mary Oxlin; one *s* two *d*. *Educ:* Frensham Heights Sch.; LSE, Univ. of London. RAF, 1943-46. London Sch. of Economics: Asst Lectr in Statistics, 1946-49; Lectr, 1949-55; Reader in Social Statistics, 1955-61; Prof. of Social Statistics, 1961-. Dir, Higher Educn Research Unit, LSE, 1964-. Statistical Adviser, Cttee on Higher Educn, 1961-64; sometime Member: Cttee on Housing in Greater London; Home Office Cttee on Criminal Statistics, Social Science Res. Coun.; Cttee on Manpower Resources for Science and Technology, etc; Mem. Bd of Dirs, Royal Opera House, Covent Garden, 1965-; Mem. Governing Body, Royal Academy of Music, 1967-. Hon. FRAM, 1970. *Publications:* Measurement of Levels of Living, 1957; Survey Methods in Social Investigation, 1958; (jtly) Social Conditions in England and Wales, 1958; (jtly) British Towns, 1961; papers in statistical jls. *Recreation:* music. *Address:* 3 Linnell Close, NW11. *T:* 01-455 8830. *Club:* Reform.

**MOSES, Sir Charles (Joseph Alfred),** Kt 1961; CBE 1954; Secretary-General, Asian Broadcasting Union, since 1965; General Manager, Australian Broadcasting Commission, 1935-65; Company Director; *b* 21 Jan. 1900; *s* of Joseph Moses and Lily (*née* Henderson); *m* 1922, Kathleen, *d* of Patrick O'Sullivan, Bruree, Co. Limerick; one *s* (one *d* decd). *Educ:* Oswestry Grammar Sch.; RMC Sandhurst. Lt 2nd Border Regt, 1918-22, serving in Germany and Ireland; fruitgrower, Bendigo, Australia, 1922-24; in motor business in Melbourne, 1924-30; in radio, ABC: Announcer/Commentator, 1930-32; Talks and Sporting Editor, Sydney, 1933-34; Federal Talks Controller, 1934-35. War of 1939-45 (despatches): AIF in Malaya and Singapore, Major, 1941-42, in New Guinea, Lt-Col, 1942-43. Leader of Austr. Delegn to UNESCO Annual Gen. Conf., Paris, 1952; Chm. Commonwealth Jubilee Arts Cttee, 1951; Vice-Pres., Royal Agricultural Society of NSW, 1951-; Trustee: Elizabethan Theatre Trust; Remembrance Driveway (NSW). Pres., Save the Children Fund (Australia); Hon. Dir, Postgraduate Med. Foundn (NSW). Member Council: Internat. Broadcasting Inst., Rome; Internat. Inst. for Youth and childrens' TV, Munich. *Recreations:* walking, tree-felling, music. *Address:* 78 Beach Road, Darling Point, NSW 2027, Australia. *T:* 32 4224. *Clubs:* Australian, Tattersall's, Rugby Union (Sydney).

**MOSES, Eric George Rufus;** Solicitor of Inland Revunue, since 1970; *b* 6 April 1914; *s* of Michael and Emily Moses; *m* 1940, Pearl Lipton; one *s*. *Educ:* University Coll. Sch., London; Oriel Coll., Oxford. Called to Bar, Middle Temple, 1938. Served Royal Artillery, 1940-46 (Major). Asst Solicitor, Inland Revenue, 1953-65, Principal Asst Solicitor, 1965-70. *Recreations:* mountains, opera. *Club:* National Liberal.

**MOSLEY,** family name of **Baron Ravensdale.**

**MOSLEY, Brig. Henry Samuel,** DSO 1916; MRCVS; Colonel Commandant RAVC, 1943-48; *b* 1879; *m* 1915, Marcia Constance Emmeline (*d* 1966), *d* of late Rev. Dixon Dixon-Brown, Unthank Hall, Northumberland. Entered Army Veterinary Dept, 1902; Col, 1929; served South African War, 1901-02 (Queen's medal with four clasps); European War, 1914-18 (despatches 4 times, DSO, Orders of St Maurice and St Lazarus of Italy and of Crown of Italy); NW Frontier, 1924; commandant of the Royal Army Veterinary Sch. and Sch. of Farriery at Aldershot, 1928-29; Dir of Veterinary Services, Army, Headquarters, India, 1932-36; retired pay, 1936. *Address:* Park House, Henfield, Sussex. *Club:* Naval and Military.

**MOSLEY, Nicholas;** *see* Ravensdale, 3rd Baron.

**MOSLEY, Sir Oswald Ernald,** 6th Bt, *cr* 1781; late 16th Lancers; *b* 16 Nov. 1896; *e s* of Sir Oswald Mosley, 5th Bt; *S* father, 1928; *m* 1st, 1920, Lady Cynthia Curzon (*d* 1933), 2nd *d* of late Marquess Curzon of Kedleston; two *s* one *d*; 2nd, 1936, Hon. Diana Mitford, 3rd *d* of 2nd Baron Redesdale; two *s*. *Educ:* Winchester; RMC, Sandhurst. Served in France during European War with his regt and also the RFC;

MP (C U) Harrow Division of Middx, Dec. 1918-22; (Ind) 1922-24; (Lab) 1924; Smethwick 1926-31; Chancellor of Duchy of Lancaster, 1929-30. *Publications:* The Greater Britain, 1932; My Answer, 1946; The Alternative, 1947; Europe: Faith and Plan, 1958; 300 Questions Answered, 1961; (autobiography) My Life, 1968. *Heir:* s 3rd Baron Ravensdale, *qv. Address:* 1 Rue des Lacs, Orsay 91, Essonne, France. *T:* Orsay 928 4211. *Club:* White's.

**MOSQUERA-CHAUX, Dr Victor;** Senator of Republic of Colombia, since 1958; *b* 1 Oct. 1919; *m* 1951, Señora Cecilia Paz de Mosquera; two *s* three *d. Educ:* Facultad de Derecho, Universidad del Cauca, Colombia. Princ. Rep. to Departmental Assembly of Cauca, 1942-47; Department of Cauca: Princ. Mem., Liberal Directory, 1942-60; Sec. of Govt, 1944-45; Governor, 1959-60; Head of Liberal Party, 1960-62; Rep. for Cauca to House of Commons, 1947-51; Nat. Directive of Liberal Party: Pres. of Exec. Cttee, 1960-62; Princ. Mem., 1962-67; Colombian Ambassador to London, 1967-70. Deleg. to 19th Conf. of UN. *Address:* c/o Partido Liberal, Bogotá, Colombia. *Clubs:* Curzon, Hurlingham, Belfry, Travellers'; Popayán, Campestre (Popayán Colombia).

**MOSS, Dr Alfred Allinson;** Keeper of Minerals, British Museum (Natural History), since 1968; *b* 30 Dec. 1912; *o s* of Frank Allinson and Alice Moss; *m* 1938, Sheila Mary, *o d* of Charles H. Sendell; two *d. Educ:* Ilfracombe Grammar Sch.; University Coll., Exeter. BSc London; PhD London. Chemist: War Dept, 1936; Govt Laboratory, 1937-39; Asst Keeper, Brit. Mus., 1939-40; Chemist, Chief Chemical Inspectorate, Min. of Supply, 1940-45; Asst Keeper, Brit. Mus., 1945-49; Principal Scientific Officer: Brit. Mus., 1949-53; Brit. Mus. (Nat. Hist.), 1953-59; Dep. Keeper of Minerals, Brit. Mus. (Nat. Hist.), 1959; Keeper, 1968. Treas., Mineralogical Soc., 1966-; FSA. *Publications:* papers on archaeological and mineralogical subjects in various jls. *Recreations:* horology, chess, photography, squash rackets. *Address:* 5 Beaconsfield Road, Blackheath, SE3. *T:* 01-858 3556.

**MOSS, Rev. Canon Basil Stanley;** Chief Secretary, Advisory Council for the Church's Ministry, since 1966; Chaplain to Church House, Westminster, since 1966; Honorary Canon of Bristol Cathedral, since 1966; Examining Chaplain to Bishop of Bristol since 1956; *b* 7 Oct. 1918; *e s* of Canon Harry George Moss and Daisy Violet (*née* Jolly); *m* 1950, Rachel Margaret, *d* of Dr Cyril Bailey and Gemma (*née* Creighton); three *d. Educ:* Canon Slade Grammar Sch., Bolton; The Queen's Coll., Oxford. Asst Curate, Leigh Parish Church, 1943-45; Sub-Warden, Lincoln Theological Coll., 1946-51; Sen. Tutor, St Catharine's Cumberland Lodge, Windsor Gt Pk, 1951-53; Vicar of St Nathanael with St Katharine, Bristol, 1953-60; Dir, Ordination Training, Bristol Dioc., 1956-66; Residentiary Canon of Bristol Cath., 1960-66. *Publications:* Clergy Training Today, 1964; (Edited) Crisis for Baptism, 1966. *Recreations:* walking, music. *Address:* Advisory Council for the Church's Ministry, Church House, Dean's Yard, Westminster, SW1. *T:* 01-222 9011. *Club:* Royal Commonwealth Society.

**MOSS, Col Edward Lawton,** CMG 1919; MC; FRCOG; FRSM; MRCS, LRCP; late RAMC; *b* Portsmouth, 1880; *s* of late E. L. Moss, RN, MD, FRCSI; *m* Eileen, *d* of late Col R. Parker, RE; two *s* one *d. Educ:* Dover Coll.; St Thomas's Hospital. Entered RAMC 1905; served European War, 1914-18; France, Salonika, and N Russia (despatches thrice, 2nd class Order of St Anne with Crossed Swords); ADMS N Russian Syren Force; late Officer in charge of Louise Margaret Hospital for Women, 1920-24; and Examiner to War Office in Obstetrics and Gynæcology; retired from Army, 1925. *Recreation:* fly-fishing. *Address:* Donaghmore, Co. Leix, Eire.

**MOSS, Sir Eric (de Vere),** Kt, *cr* 1952; CIE 1943; late ICS; subsequently posts in Pakistan and lately Northern Rhodesia; *b* 13 April 1896; *s* of F. J. Moss; *m* 1919, Monica Meriton-Reed; one *s* three *d. Educ:* Victoria Coll., Jersey. Various appointments in ICS; District Magistrate and Collector of Gorakhpur, UP, 1940-42; War Production Comr, UP, 1943-46; Commissioner Jhansi Division, UP, 1946; Sec. to Min. of Industries and Commerce, Govt of Pakistan, 1947; Pakistan Refugees Commissioner; Sec. to Ministry of Refugees and Rehabilitation, Govt of Pakistan, 1948-49; Sec. to Ministry of Health and Works, Government of Pakistan, 1950; Road Traffic Commissioner, Government of Northern Rhodesia, 1952-62. *Recreations:* shooting and fishing. *Address:* Meriton, 59 Ashley Drive, South Ashley Heath, Ringwood, Hampshire BH24 2JP. *T:* Ringwood 2934. *Club:* East India and Sports.

**MOSS, James Richard Frederick,** OBE 1955; RCNC; Director of Naval Ship Production, since 1968; *b* 26 March 1916; *s* of late Lt-Cdr J. G. Moss, RN, and late Kathleen Moss (*née* Steinberg); *m* 1941, Celia Florence Lucas; three *d. Educ:* Marlborough College; Trinity Coll., Cambrdige (1st Cl. Hons Mech. Sci. Tripos and Maths Pt I); RCNC, 1941; Asst Constructor, Admiralty Mission, Washington, 1941-44; Constructor Commander, Admiralty Tech. Mission, Ottawa, 1944-46; Admiralty Experimental Works, Haslar, 1946-49; Constructor Comdr to C-in-C, Far East Fleet, 1949-52; Aircraft Carrier design, Admiralty, Bath, 1952-55; Chief Constructor, HM Dockyard, Singapore, 1955-58; Chief Constructor, HM Dockyard, Devonport, 1958-62; Management Techniques, Dockyard HQ, Bath, 1962-63; Asst Director, R&D, Ship Dept, Bath, 1963-65; Supt, Naval Construction Research Estab., Dunfermline, 1965-68. *Recreations:* yachting and dinghies, music. *Address:* 120 Midford Road, Bath BA2 5RY. *T:* Combe Down 2056. *Clubs:* Ski of Great Britain, Royal Naval Sailing Association.

**MOSS, John,** CBE 1946; *b* 12 June 1890; *m* Grace Elizabeth Bullard; two *s. Educ:* Loughborough Grammar Sch. 4th Bn Buffs TA, 1919-31. Called to Bar, Gray's Inn, 1915. Mem. Govt Cttee on Care of Children, 1945-46; Public Assistance Officer for Kent, 1930-48; Chm. of the Nat. Old People's Welfare Council, 1951-67. Lectured in United States, Canada, Australia, New Zealand and South Africa on Brit. Social Services. *Publications:* editor and author of various works on local government law and practice; contributor to periodicals in Great Britain and overseas, Halsbury's Laws of England, Macmillan's Local Government Law and Administration, and Encyclopædia Britannica; Editor, Local Government Law and Legislation. *Address:* 20 Cordova Court, Folkestone, Kent. *T:* Folkestone 54965. *Club:* Reform.

**MOSS, Sir John H. T. E.;** *see* Edwards-Moss.

**MOSS, John Ringer;** Deputy Secretary, Ministry of Agriculture, since 1970; *b* 15 Feb. 1920; 2nd *s* of late James Moss and Louisa Moss; *m* 1946, Edith Bland Wheeler; two *s* one *d. Educ:* Manchester Gram. Sch.; Brasenose Coll., Oxford (MA). War Service, mainly India and Burma, 1940-46; Capt., RE, attached Royal Bombay Sappers and Miners. Entered Civil Service (Min. of Agric., Fisheries and Food) as Asst Princ., 1947; Princ. Private Sec. to Minister of Agric., Fisheries and Food, 1959-61; Asst Sec., 1961; Under-Sec., Gen. Agricultural Policy Gp, Min. of Agric., Fisheries and Food, 1967-70. Mem., Economic Develt Cttee for Agriculture, 1969-70. *Recreations:* music, travel. *Address:* 46 High Street, Great Missenden, Bucks. *T:* Great Missenden 2676.

**MOSS, Norman J.**; *see* Jordan-Moss.

**MOSS, Reginald**; MA (London); *b* 5 Dec. 1913; *s* of J. H. Moss, Audley, Staffs; *m* 1940, Marjorie Clara Knapper; one *s* one *d. Educ:* Birmingham and London Univs. BA 1935, DipEd 1936, Birmingham; MA London 1949. Schoolmaster, 1936-; contested (Lab) Hemel Hempstead, 1950; MP (Lab) Meriden Division of Warwicks, 1955-Sept. 1959.

**MOSS, Hon. Alderman Robert,** JP; Director Manchester Ship Canal Company, retired 1966; Manchester City Council, 1930-66; Lord Mayor of Manchester, 1949-50; late Deputy Mayor of Manchester; Chairman, 1947, and 1949-52, Manchester Corporation Transport Committee. Formerly Chairman: Wythenshawe Estate Committee; Young People's Committee; Town Hall Committee, Manchester Corporation; City of Manchester Development Committee. *Recreations:* outdoor sports. *Address:* 7 Alwen Drive, Rhos-on-Sea, Denbighshire.

**MOSS, Rosalind Louisa Beaufort,** FSA; Editor of Topographical Bibliography of Ancient Egyptian Hieroglyphic Texts, Reliefs, and Paintings, since 1924; *b* 21 Sept. 1890; *d* of Rev. H. W. Moss, Headmaster of Shrewsbury Sch., 1866-1908. *Educ:* Heathfield Sch., Ascot; St Anne's Coll., Oxford. Diploma in Anthropology (distinction), 1917, BSc Oxon 1922. Took up Egyptology, 1917. FSA 1949. Hon. DLitt, Oxon, 1961. Hon. Fellow, St Anne's Coll., Oxford, 1967. *Publications:* Life after Death in Oceania. 1925; Topographical Bibliography, Vols I-VII, 1928-51. 2nd edition, 1960-; articles in Journal of Egyptian Archaeology. *Recreation:* travel. *Address:* 10 Glyn Garth Court, Menai Bridge, Anglesey. *T:* Glyn Garth 455.

**MOSS, Stirling,** OBE 1959; FIE; Racing Motorist, 1947-62, retired; Managing Director, Stirling Moss Ltd; Director: Phœnix Travel Ltd; Motor Racing Stables Ltd; SM Fine Jewels; Designs Unlimited Ltd; SM Design & Interior Decorating Co.; America St Garage Ltd; Lema Laundrettes Ltd; Michael Farr (Design Integration) Ltd; Harris and Maisey Ltd; Stirling Moss International Export; Development Consultant, passenger vehicle evaluation, Chrysler Australia; Motoring Correspondent, The Queen Magazine; *b* 17 Sept. 1929; *m* 1st, 1957, Kathleen Stuart (marriage dissolved, 1963), *y d* of F. Stuart Moison, Montreal, Canada; 2nd, 1964, Elaine (marr. diss. 1968), 2nd *d* of A. Barbarino, New York; one *d. Educ:* Haileybury and Imperial Service Coll. Brit. Nat. Champion, 1950, 1951, 1952, 1954, 1955, 1956, 1957, 1958, 1959, 1961; Tourist Trophy, 1950, 1951, 1955, 1958, 1959, 1960, 1961; Coupe des Alpes, 1952, 1953, 1954; Alpine Gold Cup (three consecutive wins), 1954. Only Englishman to win Italian Mille Miglia, 1955. Competed in 466 races, rallies, sprints, land speed records and endurance runs, and won 194 of these. Successes include Targa Florio, 1955; Brit. Grand Prix, 1955, 1957; Ital. GP, 1956, 1957, 1959; NZ GP, 1956, 1959; Monaco GP, 1956, 1960, 1961; Leguna Seca GP, 1960, 1961; US GP, 1959, 1960; Aust. GP, 1956; Bari GP, 1956; Pescara GP, 1957; Swedish GP, 1957; Dutch GP, 1958; Argentine GP, 1958; Morocco GP, 1958; Buenos Aires GP, 1958; Melbourne GP, 1958; Villareal GP, 1958; Caen GP, 1958; Portuguese GP, 1959; S African GP, 1960; Cuban GP, 1960; Austrian GP, 1960; Cape GP, 1960; Watkins Glen GP, 1960; German GP, 1961; Modena GP, 1961. Twice voted Driver of the Year, 1954 and 1961. Pres., Vice-Pres., or Patron of 27 Clubs. *Publications:* Stirling Moss's Book of Motor Sport, 1955; In the Track of Speed, 1957; Stirling Moss's Second Book of Motor Sport, 1958; Le Mans, 1959; My Favourite Car Stories, 1960; A Turn at the Wheel, 1961; All But My Life, 1963; Design and Behaviour of the Racing Car, 1964; *relevant publication:* Stirling Moss, by Robert Raymond, 1953. *Recreations:* snow-ski-ing, water ski-ing, dancing, spear-fishing, model making, the theatre, and designing. *Address:* (business) Stirling Moss Ltd, 46 Shepherd Street, W1; (residence) 44 Shepherd Street, W1. *Clubs:* British Racing Drivers', British Automobile Racing, British Racing and Sports Car, Road Racing Drivers of America, 200 mph, Lord's Taverners, Royal Automobile; Internationale des Anciens Pilotes; Chm. or Pres. of 27 motoring clubs.

**MÖSSBAUER, Rudolf L.,** PhD; Professor of Experimental Physics, Technische Hochschule, Munich, and Visiting Professor of Physics, California Institute of Technology, since Aug. 1964; *b* Munich, 31 Jan. 1929; *m* 1957, Elisabeth Pritz; one *s* one *d. Educ:* High Sch. and Inst. of Technology, Munich (equiv. Bachelor's and Master's degrees). PhD (Munich) 1958. Research Asst Max Planck Inst., Heidelberg, 1955-57; Research Fellow: Inst. of Techn., Munich, 1958-60, and at Caltech, 1960, Sen. Research Fellow, Caltech, 1961. Research Corporation Award, New York, 1960; Röntgen award, Univ. of Giessen, Germany, 1961; Elliot Cresson Medal, Franklin Inst., Philadelphia, 1961; Nobel Prize for Physics, 1961, etc. Bavarian Order of Merit, 1962. *Publications:* Nobel Lecture, Rückstossfreie Kernresonanzabsorption von Gammastrahlung, 1961 (Stockholm). Papers on Recoilless Nuclear Resonance Absorption in learned jls and proc. societies, etc. *Recreations:* photography, music, archæology. *Address:* Physik Department, Technische Hochschule, Arcisstrasse 21, 8 Munich 2, Germany.

**MOSTYN,** 5th Baron, *cr* 1831; **Roger Edward Lloyd Lloyd-Mostyn,** Bt 1778; MC 1943; *b* 17 April 1920; *e s* of 4th Baron Mostyn; *S* father, 1965; *m* 1943, Yvonne Margaret Stuart (marr. diss., 1957), *y d* of A. Stuart Johnston, Henshall Hall, Congleton, Cheshire; one *s* one *d*; 2nd, 1957, Mrs Sheila Edmondson Shaw, *o c* of Major Reginald Fairweather, Stockwell Manor, Silverton, Devon, and of Mrs Fairweather, Yew Tree Cottage, Fordcombe, Kent. *Educ:* Eton; Royal Military College, Sandhurst. 2nd Lt, 9th Queen's Royal Lancers, 1939. Served War 1939-45, France, North Africa, and Italy (wounded, despatches, MC). Temp. Major, 1946. *Heir: s* Hon. Llewellyn Roger Lloyd Lloyd-Mostyn, *b* 26 Sept. 1948. *Address:* Mostyn Hall, Mostyn, Flintshire, North Wales. *T:* Mostyn 222.

**MOSTYN, Sir Jeremy (John Anthony),** 14th Bt *cr* 1670; *b* 24 Nov. 1933; *s* of Sir Basil Anthony Trevor Mostyn, 13th Bt and Anita Mary, *d* of late Lt-Col Rowland Charles Feilding, DSO; *S* father 1956; *m* 1963, Cristina, *o d* of Marchese

Orengo, Turin; two *d. Educ:* Rhodesia and Downside. Contested: Ealing South (L) General Election, 1959; Cities of London and Westminster, LCC Elections, 1960. Green Staff Officer, Investiture of the Prince of Wales, 1969. *Recreation:* saving and restoring old houses. *Heir: b* Trevor Alexander Richard Mostyn, *b* 23 May 1946. *Address:* Stepup Cottage, Sulham, Berks; Casa Orengo, La Mortola di Ventimiglia, Italy; 29 Aynhoe Road, W14. *Club:* Travellers'.

**MOTHERWELL, Bishop of, (RC),** since 1964; **Rt. Rev. Francis Thomson;** Hon. Canon of St Andrews and Edinburgh, since 1961; *b* 15 May 1917; *s* of late Francis Thomson, MA and late Winifred Mary Clare (*née* Forsyth). *Educ:* George Watson's Coll., Edinburgh; Edinburgh Univ.; Christ's Coll., Cambridge; St Edmund's Coll., Ware; Angelicum Univ., Rome. MA Edinburgh 1938; BA Cambridge 1940; Priest, 1946; STL (Angelicum, Rome) 1949. Asst Priest: St Patrick's, Kilsyth, 1946-48; St James', St Andrews, 1949-52; St Cuthbert's, Edinburgh, 1952-53; Prof. of Dogmatic Theology, St Andrew's Coll. Drygrange, Melrose, 1953-60; Rector of St Mary's Coll., Blairs, Aberdeen, 1960-64. *Address:* Bishop's House, Bothwell, Glasgow. *T:* Bothwell 3115.

**MOTT, Sir John (Harmar),** 3rd Bt, *cr* 1930; Regional Medical Officer, Department of Health and Social Security; *b* 21 July 1922; *s* of 2nd Bt and Mary Katherine, *d* of late Rev. A. H. Stanton; *S* father, 1964; *m* 1950, Elizabeth (*née* Carson); one *s* two *d. Educ:* Radley Coll.; New Coll., Oxford. MA Oxford, 1948; BM, BCh, 1951. Served War of 1939-45: Pilot, Royal Air Force, 1943-46. Middlesex Hospital: House Physician, 1951; House Surgeon, 1952. *Recreations:* sailing, photography. *Heir: s* David Hugh Mott, *b* 1 May 1952. *Address:* Daffodil Lodge, Park Road, Waterloo Park, Liverpool L22 3XG. *T:* 051-928 3112.

**MOTT, Sir Nevill (Francis),** Kt 1962; FRS 1936; MA Cantab; Cavendish Professor of Experimental Physics, 1954-Sept. 1971; *b* 30 Sept. 1905; *s* of C. F. Mott, late Dir of Educn, Liverpool, and Lilian Mary Reynolds; *m* 1930, Ruth Horder; two *d. Educ:* Clifton Coll.; St John's Coll., Cambridge. Lecturer at Manchester Univ., 1929-30; Fellow and Lecturer, Gonville and Caius Coll., Cambridge, 1930-33; Melville Wills Prof. of Theoretical Physics in the Univ. of Bristol, 1933-48; Henry Overton Wills Prof. and Dir of the Henry Herbert Wills Physical Laboratories, Univ. of Bristol, 1948-54. Master of Gonville and Caius Coll., Univ. of Cambridge, 1959-66. Hughes Medal of Royal Society, 1941, Royal Medal, 1953; corr. mem., Amer. Acad. of Arts and Sciences, 1954; Pres., International Union of Physics, 1951-57; Pres., Mod. Languages Assoc., 1955; Pres., Physical Soc., 1956-58; Mem. Governing Board of Nat. Inst. for Research in Nuclear Science, 1957-60; Mem. Central Advisory Council for Education for England, 1956-59; Mem. Academic Planning Cttee and Council of University Coll. of Sussex; Chm. Ministry of Education's Standing Cttee on Supply of Teachers, 1959-62; Mem., Inst. of Strategic Studies; Chairman: Nuffield Foundation's Cttee on Physics Education, 1961; Physics Education Cttee (Royal Society and Inst. of Physics), 1965. Foreign Associate, Nat, Acad. of Sciences of USA, 1957; Hon. Member: Akademie der Naturforscher Leopoldina, 1964; Société Française de Physique, 1970. Hon. DSc (Louvain, Grenoble, Paris, Poitiers, Bristol, Ottawa, Liverpool, Reading, Sheffield, London, Warwick, Lancaster). Grande médaille de la Société Française de Métallurgie, 1970. *Publications:* An Outline of Wave Mechanics, 1930; The Theory of Atomic Collisions (with H. S. W. Massey), 1933; The Theory of the Properties of Metals and Alloys (with H. Jones), 1936; Electronic Processes in Ionic Crystals (with R. W. Gurney), 1940; Wave Mechanics and its Applications (with I. N. Snedden), 1948; Elements of Wave Mechanics, 1952; Atomic Structure and the Strength of Metals, 1956; various contribs to scientific periodicals about Atomic Physics, Metals, Semi-conductors and Photographic Emulsions. *Address:* The Cavendish Laboratory, Cambridge; 31 Sedley Taylor Road, Cambridge. *Club:* Athenæum.

**MOTT, Norman Gilbert,** CMG 1962; retired, 1969; *b* 7 Sept. 1910; *s* of late Albert Norman Mott and late Ada Emily Kilby; *m* 1941, Betty Mary, *d* of late Sidney Hugh Breeze; two *s. Educ:* Christ's Coll., Finchley. Served in HM Forces (Intelligence Corps), 1940-47. Joined HM Diplomatic Service, 1948; served since in Foreign Office and at Trieste. *Recreations:* gardening, photography. *Address:* 58 Greenways, Beckenham, Kent. *T:* 01-650 2715.

**MOTT-RADCLYFFE, Sir Charles (Edward),** Kt 1957; Captain Rifle Brigade, Reserve of Officers; *b* 1911; *o s* of Lt-Col C. E. Radclyffe, DSO, Rifle Brigade (killed in action 1915), Little Park, Wickham, Hants, and Theresa Caroline, *o d* of John Stanley Mott, JP, Barningham Hall, Norfolk; *m* 1940, Diana (*d* 1955), *d* of late Lt-Col W. Gibbs, CVO, 7th Hussars; three *d*; *m* 1956, Stella, *d* of late Lionel Harrisson, Caynham Cottage, Ludlow, Salop. *Educ:* Eton; Balliol Coll., Oxford. Hon. Attaché Diplomatic Service, Athens and Rome, 1936-38; Mem. Military Mission to Greece, 1940-41; served as Liaison Officer in Syria, 1941, and with Rifle Brigade in Middle East and Italy, 1943-44; MP (C) Windsor, 1942-70; Parliamentary Private Sec. to Sec. of State for India (Rt Hon. L. S. Amery), Dec. 1944-May 1945; Junior Lord of the Treasury, May-July 1945; Conservative Whip, Aug. 1945-Feb. 1946; Chm. Conservative Parly Foreign Affairs Cttee, 1951-59. A Governor of Gresham's Sch., Holt; a Vice-Chm. British Council; Mem., Historic Buildings Council for England. Comdr, Order of Phoenix (Greece). *Recreations:* cricket, shooting. *Address:* Barningham Hall, Matlaske, Norfolk. *T:* Matlaske 250; Flat 1, 38 Cadogan Square, SW1. *T:* 01-584 5834. *Clubs:* Turf, Buck's, Pratt's, MCC.

**MOTTERSHEAD, Frank William,** CB 1957; Deputy Under-Secretary of State, Department of Health and Social Security (formerly Ministry of Health), since 1965; *b* 7 Sept. 1911; *o s* of late Thomas Hastings and Adeline Mottershead; unmarried. *Educ:* King Edward's Sch., Birmingham; St John's Coll., Cambridge. Entered Secretary's Dept of Admiralty, 1934; Principal Private Sec. to First Lord, 1944-46; idc 1949; Under Sec., 1950; Transferred to Ministry of Defence, 1956; Deputy Sec., 1958; Deputy Under-Sec. of State, 1964. *Address:* 15 Cleveland Square, W2. *T:* 01-262 5822. *Club:* United University.

**MOTTISTONE,** 4th Baron, *cr* 1933, of Mottistone; **David Peter Seely;** Director, Distributive Industry Training Board, Manchester, since 1969; *b* 16 Dec. 1920; 4th *s* of 1st Baron Mottistone; *S* half brother, 1966; *m* 1944, Anthea, *er d* of T. V. W. McMullan, Bangor, Co. Down, N Ireland; two *s* two *d* (and one *d* decd). *Educ:* RN Coll., Dartmouth. Home Fleet, 1939-40; Convoy escorting, Atlantic and Mediterranean, 1941-44; qualified in Communications, 1944; British Pacific Fleet, 1945; service ashore and afloat, Home and Mediterranean, 1946-55; Comdr 1955; NATO staff, Malta, 1956-58; in comd HMS Cossack, FE Flt, 1958-59; Captain 1960; Dep. Dir Signals, Admiralty, 1961-63; in comd HMS Ajax and 24th Escort Sqdn, FE Flt (offensive ops against Indonesian confrontation) (despatches), 1963-65; Naval Advr to UK High Comr, Ottawa, 1965-66; retired at own request, 1967. Dir of Personnel and Training, Radio Rentals Gp, 1967-69. FIERE; MBIM. *Publications:* Articles on Defence policy in periodicals. *Recreation:* yachting. *Heir: s* Hon. Peter John Philip Seely, *b* 29 Oct. 1949. *Address:* Salterswell House, Tarporley, Cheshire. *Clubs:* Royal Commonwealth Society; Royal Cruising, Island Sailing, Royal Navy Sailing Association.

**MOTTRAM, Ralph Hale,** JP; FRSL; *b* Norwich, 30 Oct. 1883; *m*; two *s* one *d*. *Educ:* Norwich; Lausanne. HM Forces, 1914-19; Home Guard, 1940-44. Hon. Doctorate, East Anglia Univ., 1966. *Publications:* The Spanish Farm; Sixty-Four, Ninety-four; The Crime at Vanderlynden's; The Spanish Farm Trilogy; Our Mr Dormer; The English Miss; Ten Years Ago; The Boroughmonger; A History of Financial Speculation; Europa's Beast, 1930; Miniature Banking Histories; The New Providence, Poems Old and New, 1930; Castle Island, 1931; The Headless Hound, 1931; John Crome of Norwich, 1931; Home for the Holidays, 1932; Dazzle, 1932; Through the Menin Gate; The Lame Dog, 1933; East Anglia, 1933; Bumphrey's, 1934; Strawberry Time and the Banquet, 1934; Early Morning, 1935; Flower Pot End, 1935; Journey to the Western Front, 1936; Portrait of an Unknown Victorian, 1936; Time To Be Going, 1937; Success to the Mayor, 1937; Old England, 1937; Noah; There was a Jolly Miller, 1938; Autobiography with a Difference; You Can't have it Back, 1939; Traders' Dream, 1939; Miss Lavington, 1939; Bowler Hat, 1940; The Ghost and the Maiden, 1941; The World turns Slowly Round, 1942; The Corbells at War, 1943; Visit of the Princess, 1946; Buxton the Liberator, 1946; The Gentleman of Leisure, 1947; Come to the Bower, 1949; One Hundred and Twenty-Eight Witnesses, 1951; The Broads, 1952; The Part that is Missing, If Stones Could Speak, 1953; The Window Seat, 1954; Over the Wall, 1955; Scenes that are Brightest, 1956; For Some We Loved, 1956; Another Window Seat, 1957; No-one Will Ever Know, 1958; Vanities and Verities, 1958; Young Man's Fancies, 1959; Musetta, 1960; Time's Increase, 1961; To Hell, with Crabb Robinson, 1962; Happy Birds, 1963; Maggie Mackenzie, 1965; Speaking Likeness, 1967; Behind the Shutters, 1968; The Twentieth Century: a Personal Record, 1969. *Address:* 4a Queensway, King's Lynn, Norfolk.

**MOTTRAM, Vernon Henry,** MA; late Professor of Physiology in the University of London (Queen Elizabeth, formerly King's, College of Household and Social Science, Kensington, W8); *b* 14 March 1882; *s* of late Rev. Wm Mottram and Elizabeth Fruen; *m* 1921, Elsie Bulley (*d* 1970), *d* of late H. S. King, St Albans; three *s*. *Educ:* Caterham and St Olave's Schs; Trinity Coll., Cambridge (Sizar, Scholar, and Fellow). Research under Carl Voit in Munich; Senior Demonstrator and Lecturer in Chemical Physiology in the Univ. of Liverpool; Lecturer in Physiology in McGill Univ. and in the Univ. of Toronto. *Publications:* Manual of Histology; Food and the Family; Functions of the Body: an Outline of Physiology; Manual of Modern Cookery (with Miss J. Lindsay); Properties of Food (with Miss W. M. Clifford); article on Dietetics in Text Book of Hygiene: Health and Hygiene; Sound Catering (with Mrs Mottram); Food and the Principles of Dietetics (with Dr George Graham), 1956; Food Tables (with Miss Radloff); Healthy Eating, 1940; Human Nutrition, 1948; Physical Basis of Personality, 1944; Cooking for the Sick and Convalescent (with Miss Nell Heaton), 1951; various articles in journals of physiology on the metabolism of fat. *Recreation:* reading. *Address:* Waterhouse, Monkton Combe, near Bath, Somerset. *Club:* Penn.

**MOULD-GRAHAM, Colonel Robert,** OBE 1944; MC 1918; TD 1930; DL; FCA; Consultant, Graham Proom & Smith, Chartered Accountants, Newcastle upon Tyne and Sunderland; Director: British Legion Attendants Co. Ltd; Cold Rolling Mills Ltd; A. M. Forster Ltd; Guardian Assurance Co. Ltd (Local Board), 1930-68; Northern Rock Building Society (Chairman, London Board); W. E. Moffett and Co. Ltd, 1946-69 (Chairman); Part-time Member North Eastern Electricity Board, 1956-65; President Tyneside Chamber of Commerce, 1963-65; *b* 1895; *s* of late Joseph Graham, BSc, Corbridge, Northumberland; *m* 1st, 1922, Beatrice, *d* of late H. S. Vincent; one *d*; 2nd, 1937, Jocelyn Edith Katherine, MBE 1946, *d* of late Comdr F. P. Saunders, RN; one *s* one *d* (and one *d* decd). *Educ:* Rutherford Coll., Newcastle upon Tyne. Served European War, 1914-18, with 72 Field Regt, RA (France and Belgium); War of 1939-45 (despatches twice); with 272 Field Regt, RA (TA) and Staff, France, Belgium, N Africa and Italy. Hon. Col 272 Field Regt, 1949-65. A mem. of House of Laity Church Assembly, 1952-60; Newcastle Diocesan Soc., and Diocesan Bd of Finance, 1948-66; Mem., Salisbury Diocesan Bd of Finance, 1967-. Chm., Buckland Newton Br., Brit. Legion, 1966-; Mem., Dorset County Cttee, 1967-. Alderman of Newcastle upon Tyne, 1949-61; Pres. Newcastle Central Br., Brit. Legion, 1948-65; Tyne Improvement Comr, 1947-58; Sheriff of Newcastle upon Tyne, 1951-52, Lord Mayor 1954-55. JP 1948; DL Northumberland, 1953. *Address:* The Manor House, Alton Pancras, Dorchester, Dorset. *T:* Piddletrenthide 354. *Clubs:* Army and Navy; Northern Counties (Newcastle).

**MOULE, Rev. Professor Charles Francis Digby;** FBA 1966; Lady Margaret's Professor of Divinity in the University of Cambridge, since 1951; Fellow of Clare College, Cambridge, since 1944; Canon Theologian (non-residentiary) of Leicester, since 1955; *b* 3 Dec. 1908; *s* of Rev. Henry William Moule and Laura Clements Pope; unmarried. *Educ:* Weymouth Coll., Dorset; Emmanuel Coll., Cambridge (scholar); Ridley Hall, Cambridge. 1st Cl. Classical Tripos Part I, 1929; BA (1st Cl. Classical Tripos Part II), 1931; Evans Prize, 1931; Jeremie Septuagint Prize, 1932; Crosse Scholarship, 1933; MA 1934. Deacon, 1933, priest, 1934; Curate, St Mark's, Cambridge, and Tutor of Ridley Hall, 1933-34; Curate, St Andrew's, Rugby, 1934-36; Vice-Principal, Ridley Hall, 1936-44, and Curate of St Mary the Great, Cambridge, 1936-40. Dean of Clare Coll., Cambridge, 1944-51; Faculty Asst Lecturer in Divinity in the Univ. of Cambridge, 1944-47; Univ. Lecturer, 1947-51. Burkitt Medal for Biblical Studies, British Acad., 1970. Hon. DD Univ. of St Andrews, 1958. *Publications:* An Idiom Book of New Testament Greek, 1953; The Meaning of Hope, 1953; The Sacrifice of Christ, 1956; Colossians and Philemon (Cambridge Greek Testament Commentary), 1957; Worship in the New Testament, 1961; The Birth of the New Testament, 1962; The Phenomenon of the New Testament, 1967; (Co-editor) Christian History and Interpretation, 1968;

contrib., Encyclopædia Britannica, Interpreter's Dictionary of the Bible, Biblisch-Historisches Handwörterbuch. *Address:* Clare College, Cambridge.

**MOULE-EVANS, David,** DMus Oxon; Composer; Conductor; Professor of Harmony, Counterpoint and Composition, Royal College of Music, since 1945; *b* 21 Nov. 1905; *s* of John Evans, MA Cantab, and Emily Blanche Evans (*née* Cookson); *m* 1935, Monica Warden Evans, *d* of Richardson Evans, ICS; no *c*. *Educ:* The Judd Sch.; Royal College of Music. Mem. of Queen's Coll., Oxford. Open Scholarship in Composition, RCM, 1925 (Senior Composition Scholar); Mendelssohn Scholarship, 1928; DMus Oxford, 1930. Carnegie Publication Award (for Concerto for String Orchestra), 1928. Symphony in G Major awarded £1,000 Prize offered by Australian Govt, 1952. Many public and broadcast performances of orchestral and other works; sometimes conducts own works. *Publications: Published orchestral works include:* Overture: The Spirit of London, 1947; Vienna Rhapsody, 1948; The Haunted Place (for String Orchestra), 1949; Old Tupper's Dance, 1951; chamber works: instrumental pieces and songs. *Recreations:* reading and studying subjects other than music; perambulating the countryside and looking at old churches. *Address:* Merry Down, Harrow Road West, Dorking, Surrey. *T:* Dorking 4080.

**MOULT, Thomas;** Poet, Critic, Editor, Novelist, Lecturer; President Poetry Society, 1952-61; *b* Mellor Hall, Derbyshire. *Educ:* Marple; Manchester. Associated with late Charles E. B. Russell of Heyrod Street Lads' Club, Manchester, in Borstal and convict prison work; associated with Harold Wood of Manchester and C. E. Heald in boys' club work in Manchester and London; Music criticism with Manchester Guardian and Manchester City News; art and drama criticism with The Athenæum, The English Review, etc.; Literary Editor and Advisory Sports Editor, Sunday Referee; founded Voices (Magazine of the Arts), 1919; edited Modern Writers and Playwrights series of Critical Biographies, 1929; Chairman, Editorial Board, The Poetry Review, 1952-62. *Publications:* Snow over Elden (novel), 1920; Down Here the Hawthorn (poems), 1921; Brown Earth (choral poem), 1922 (Carnegie Prize-winner); The Best Poems of 1922 (Anthology), 1923; Forty Years in My Bookshop (edited), 1923; The Comely Lass (novel), 1923; Cenotaph (Anthology), 1923; The Best Poems of 1923 (Anthology), 1924; The Best Poems series continued yearly until 1943; The Man who was Born Again (translation with Prince Mirsky), 1926; Poems from Books (Anthology), 1927; Barrie (criticism), 1928; Derbyshire in Prose and Verse, 1929; Sally Go Round the Moon (children's novel), 1931; Saturday Night (novel), 1931; Playing for England, by Jack Hobbs (edited), 1931; Sport's Great Stories (anthology), 1931; Mary Webb, a biography and a criticism, 1932; W. H. Davies (criticism), 1934; Bat and Ball: a New Book of Cricket, 1935; Willow Pattern (cricket poems), 1936; Robin of Sherwood (radio musical play), 1937; Master Showman (autobiography of a Circus King, edited), 1937; Down North: by Tony Onraet, Canadian Trapper (edited), 1942; (editor) Cricket is my Life, by Len Hutton, 1949; All-Sports Special! (autobiographical fragment); The Great Partnership: Hirst and Rhodes; Bat and Ball (new edn with Foreword by Lord Birkett); I Love England; Wind in the Trees (autobiography). *Recreations:* moorland walks, chess, cricket. *Address:* The Mill House, Finchingfield, Braintree, Essex. *T:* Gt Bardfield 357. *Clubs:* Savage, Paternosters, Cricket Writers, Football Writers, PEN. *See also Prof. O. L. Zangwill.*

**MOULTON, Alexander Eric,** RDI; Chairman and Managing Director, Moulton Developments Ltd, since 1956; Director: Moulton Bicycles Ltd since 1967; Moulton Consultants Ltd since 1967; Bicycle Consultants Ltd since 1967; *b* 9 April 1920; *s* of John Coney Moulton and Beryl Latimer Moulton. *Educ:* Marlborough Coll.; King's Coll., Cambridge (MA). Bristol Aeroplane Co., 1939-44: Engine Research Dept; George Spencer, Moulton & Co. Ltd, 1945-56; became Techn. Dir; estab. Research Dept (originated work on rubber suspensions for vehicles, incl. own design Flexitor); formed Moulton Developments Ltd, 1956 to do develt work on own designs of rubber suspensions for BMC incl. Hydrolastic (Queen's Award to Industry, 1967); formed Moulton Bicycles Ltd to produce own design Moulton Bicycle, 1962 (Design Centre Award, 1964). FRSA, 1968; Hon. Dr, RCA, 1967; RDI 1968. *Publications:* articles in Automobile Engr, Jl IMechE, Jl Inst. of Rubber Industry, FISITA Jl. *Recreations:* canoeing, power boating, cycling, motor cycling. *Address:* The Hall, Bradford-on-Avon, Wilts. *T:* Bradford-on-Avon 2991. *Clubs:* Travellers'; Royal Thames Yacht.

**MOULTON, Maj.-Gen. James Louis,** CB 1956; DSO 1944; OBE 1950; retired; *b* 3 June 1906; *s* of Capt. J. D. Moulton, RN; *m* 1937, Barbara Aline (*née* Coode); one *s* one *d*. *Educ:* Sutton Valence Sch. Joined Royal Marines, 1924; Pilot, Fleet Air Arm, 1930; Staff Coll., Camberley, 1938; served War of 1939-45: GSO3 GHQ, BEF, 1940; GSO1, Force 121 (Madagascar), 1942; Commanding Officer, 48 Commando, NW Europe, 1944-45 (DSO); Comd 4th Commando Bde, NW Europe, 1945; CO Commando Sch., 1947-49; Comd 3rd Commando Bde, Middle East, 1952-54; Maj.-Gen. Royal Marines, Portsmouth, 1954-57; Chief of Amphibious Warfare, 1957-61. Col Comdt RM, 1969-. *Publications:* Haste to the Battle, 1963; Defence in a Changing World, 1964; The Norwegian Campaign of 1940, 1966; British Maritime Strategy in the 1970s, 1969. *Address:* Fairmile, Woodham Road, Woking, Surrey. *T:* Woking 5174. *Clubs:* Royal Automobile, Climbers'.

**MOULTON, Air Vice-Marshal Leslie Howard,** DFC 1941; AOC No 90 (Signals) Group RAF since 1969; *b* 3 Dec. 1915; *s* of Peter Moulton, Nantwich, Cheshire and late Mrs M. E. Moulton; *m* Lesley, *d* of late P. C. Clarke, Ilford; two *s* two *d*. *Educ:* Nantwich and Acton School. Joined RAF, 1932; served War of 1939-45, Pilot; Operations with 14 Sqdn in Africa, 1940-42; CFS, 1942-44; specialised in Signals, 1945; Staff Coll., 1950; USAF, Strategic Air Comd, 1954-56; Dep. Dir Radio, Air Min., 1958-61; Comdt RAF Cosford, 1961-63; CSO Fighter Comd, 1963-65; Min. of Technology, 1965-68. Wing Comdr 1955; Gp Captain 1959; Air Cdre 1964; Air Vice-Marshal 1969. Fellow, Instn of Electronic and Radio Engineers, CEng, 1959. *Recreations:* gardening, golf, hill walking. *Address:* Little Hill, Harpsden, Henley-on-Thames, Oxon. *T:* Henley 4454. *Club:* Royal Air Force.

**MOUNSEY, John Patrick David,** MA, MD, FRCP; Provost, Welsh National School of Medicine, since Oct. 1969; *b* 1 Feb. 1914; *s* of late John Edward Mounsey and late Christine Frances Trail Robertson; *m* 1947, Vera Madeline Sara King; one *s* one *d*. *Educ:* Eton Coll.; King's Coll., Cambrdige; King's Coll. Hosp., London. Sherbrook Res. Fellow, Cardiac Dept, London Hosp., 1951; Royal Postgraduate Medical School: Lectr, 1960;

Sen. Lectr and Sub-Dean, 1962; Cons. Cardiologist, Hammersmith Hosp., 1960; Dep. Dir, British Postgrad. Med. Fedn, 1967; Member: GMC, 1970; Welsh Hosp. Board, 1970; British Cardiac Soc.; Assoc. of Physicians; Soc. of Physicians in Wales. Corresp. Mem., Australasian Cardiac Soc.; late Asst Ed., British Heart Jl. *Publications:* articles on cardiology mainly in British Heart Jl. *Recreations:* gardening, music. *Address:* St Quintins, Llanblethian, Cowbridge, Glamorgan. *T:* Cowbridge 2415. *Clubs:* Athenæum, MCC.

**MOUNT, Air Cdre Christopher John,** CBE 1956; DSO 1943; DFC 1940; retired; *b* 14 Dec. 1913; *s* of Capt. F. Mount; *m* 1947, Audrey Mabel Clarke; two *s*. *Educ:* Eton; Trinity Coll., Oxford. Royal Auxiliary Air Force, 1935; Royal Air Force, 1938. Solicitor with C. R. Thomas & Son, Maidenhead. *Address:* Garden House, Bagshot Road, Sunninghill, Ascot, Berks.

**MOUNT, Sir William (Malcolm),** 2nd Bt, *cr* 1921; Lieutenant-Colonel Reconnaissance Corps; Vice-Lieutenant of Berkshire since 1960; *b* 28 Dec. 1904; *s* of Sir William Mount, 1st Bt, CBE, and Hilda Lucy Adelaide (*d* 1950), OBE, *y d* of late Malcolm Low of Clatto, Fife; *S* father, 1930; *m* 1929, Elizabeth Nance, *o d* of Owen John Llewellyn, Badminton Vicarage, Glos; three *d*. *Educ:* Eton; New Coll., Oxford. High Sheriff of Berks, 1947-48; DL Berks, 1946. *Recreations:* fishing, shooting. *Heir: nephew* William Robert Ferdinand Mount [*b* 2 July 1939; *m* 1968, Julia Margaret, twin *d* of Archibald Julian Lucas]. *Address:* Wasing Place, Aldermaston, Berks.

*See also Sir W. S. Dugdale, Bt.*

**MOUNT CHARLES, Earl of; Frederick William Henry Francis Conyngham;** late Captain Irish Guards; *b* 13 March 1924; *e s* of 6th Marquess Conyngham, *qv*; *m* 1950, Eileen Wren, *o d* of Capt. C. W. Newsam, Ashfield, Beauparc, Co. Meath; three *s*. *Educ:* Eton. *Heir: s* Viscount Slane, *qv*. *Address:* Slane Castle, Co. Meath, Eire; Bifrons, near Canterbury. *Club:* Boodle's.

**MOUNT EDGCUMBE,** 7th Earl of, *cr* 1789; **Edward Piers Edgcumbe;** Viscount Mount Edgcumbe and Valletort, 1781; Baron Edgcumbe of Mount Edgcumbe, Co. Cornwall (UK), 1742; *b* 13 July 1903; *s* of George Valletort Edgcumbe (*d* 1947) and Georgina Mildred (*d* 1941), *d* of T. A. Bell; *S* cousin 1965; *m* 1944, Victoria Effie Warbrick (widow), *y d* of late Robert Campbell, N Ireland and NZ. *Heir: b* George Aubrey Valletort Edgcumbe [*b* 15 Sept. 1907; *m* 1st, 1935, Meta (marr. diss. 1943), *d* of C. R. Lhoyer, Nancy, France; one *s* (and one *s* decd); 2nd, 1944, Una Pamela, *d* of late E. L. George, Perth, WA; two *s*]. *Address:* Mount Edgcumbe, Plymouth.

**MOUNTAIN, Lt-Col Sir Brian (Edward Stanley),** 2nd Bt, *cr* 1922; Chairman: Eagle Star Insurance Co. Ltd; Bernard Sunley Investment Trust Ltd; *b* 22 Aug. 1899; *o s* of Sir Edward Mortimer Mountain, 1st Bt, and Evelyn Ellen (*d* 1950), *d* of A. Siegle; *S* father 1948; *m* 1926, Doris Elsie, *e d* of E. C. E. Lamb, 2 Queen Street, Mayfair, W1; two *s* one *d*. *Educ:* Charterhouse; RMC Sandhurst. Served European War, 1914-19, as Lt 9th Lancers and later 96th Royal Devon Yeo. Field Bde; recalled War of 1939-45, served France. Late Gen. Man. Eagle Star Insce Co. *Recreations:* fishing, shooting, racing. *Heir: s* Denis Mortimer Mountain [*b* 2 June 1929; *m* 1958, Hélène Fleur Mary, *d* of John Kirwan-Taylor, Lower Sandhill, Halland, Sussex, and of Mrs Charles Hill, Grove House, Alveston, Glos.; two *s* one *d*]. *Address:* Dunley Manor, Whitchurch, Hants. *T:* Whitchurch 2475. 75 Eaton Square, SW1. *T:* 01-235 5599. *TA:* Eaglestaco, London, EC2. *Clubs:* Carlton, Boodle's, Royal Automobile.

**MOUNTAIN, Surgeon Rear-Adm. (D) William Leonard,** CB 1966; OBE 1953; LDSRCS 1931; Director of Naval Dental Services, Ministry of Defence, 1964-68; *b* 29 Feb. 1908; *s* of William Mountain, LDS, Cowes, IoW; *m* 1946, Glenda Fleming, *d* of late Cyril Fleming, Groombridge, Sussex; one *d*. *Educ:* Sherborne Sch.; Guy's Hosp. Joined Royal Navy in rank of Surg.-Lt (D), 1933; Surg. Lt-Comdr (D) 1939. Served in HM Ships: Glasgow, Woolwich, Duke of York, Furious and Rodney, 1939-45; Fleet Dental Surg., Home Fleet, 1943-45; Surg. Comdr (D), 1948; Asst Dep. Dir-Gen. Dental Services, 1948-55; Surg. Captain (D), 1955; Command Dental Surg., The Nore, 1955-59; Fleet Dental Surg., Mediterranean, 1960; Command Dental Surg., Portsmouth, 1961-64; Surg. Rear-Adm. (D) 1964. QHDS, 1961-68. *Recreation:* golf. *Address:* 20 Yew Tree Road, Southborough, Tunbridge Wells, Kent. *T:* Tunbridge Wells 28378. *Club:* Royal Ashdown Forest.

**MOUNTBATTEN,** family name of **Marquess of Milford Haven** and **Earl Mountbatten of Burma.**

**MOUNTBATTEN OF BURMA,** 1st Earl, *cr* 1947; Baron Romsey, *cr* 1947; Viscount Mountbatten of Burma, *cr* 1946; **Admiral of the Fleet Louis (Francis Albert Victor Nicholas) Mountbatten,** KG 1946; PC 1947; GCB 1955 (KCB 1945; CB 1943); OM 1965; GCSI 1947; GCIE 1947; GCVO 1937 (KCVO 1922; MVO 1920); DSO 1941; FRS 1966; Hon. DCL (Oxford); Hon. LLD (Cambridge, Leeds, Edinburgh, Southampton, London, Sussex); Hon. DSc (Delhi and Patna); AMIEE 1927; AMRINA 1939; Governor of the Isle of Wight, 1965; Personal ADC to the Queen since 1953 (Personal Naval ADC to King Edward VIII, 1936, and to King George VI, 1937-52); Col of the Life Guards, 1965; Col Commandant of the Royal Marines, 1965; Hon. Lt-Gen. and Air Marshal, 1942, and Hon. Colonel: Calcutta Light Horse, 1947; 292 Airborne Field Regt, 1947-55; 428th The Princess Beatrice IoW Rifles Heavy AA Regt, RA(TA), 1950-55; 289 Parachute Regt, RHA(TA), 1956; 4/5th Bn The Royal Hampshire Regiment (TA), 1964; an Elder Brother of Trinity House; Grand President: Brit. Commonwealth Ex-Services League; Royal Life Saving Society; Royal Over-Seas League; Pres. of Council of SSAFA; King George's Fund for Sailors; Royal Naval Film Corporation, Royal Naval Saddle Club, Sailors Home and Red Ensign Club, Gordon Smith Inst., Liverpool, Training Ship Mercury and Commando Benevolent Fund; Society of Genealogists; Britain-Burma Soc.; Soc. of Film and Television Arts; Mem. and Past Pres., Inst. of Electronic and Radio Engineers; Chm. and Founder, National Electronics Research Council; Commodore Sea Scouts; Mem. and Past Prime Warden Shipwrights' Company; Hon. Mem. Honourable Company of Master Mariners; Mem. Mercers', Vintners' and Grocers' Companies; Royal Swedish Naval Soc.; Inner Magic Circle; Sword of Honour and Freedom of City of London, 1946; High Steward, 1940, and First Freeman, 1946, of Romsey; Freedom of City of Edinburgh, 1954; Freedom of Paimpol, 1961; *b* Frogmore House, Windsor, 25 June 1900; *yr s* of Adm. of the Fleet 1st Marquess of Milford Haven and Princess Victoria, *d* of Louis IV, Grand Duke of Hesse, KG, and of Princess Alice, Queen Victoria's Daughter; was known as Prince Louis Francis of Battenberg until, in 1917, his father relinquished title and assumed surname of Mountbatten; *m* 1922, Hon. Edwina Cynthia Annette Ashley (*d* 1960, in North Borneo, on tour as Superintendent-in-Chief, St John Ambulance Brigade), *d* of Lord Mount Temple, PC (Countess Mountbatten of Burma, CI, GBE, DCVO, LLD); two *d*. *Educ:* Locker's Park; Osborne and Dartmouth; Christ's Coll., Cambridge (Hon. Fellow, 1946). Naval Cadet, 1913; Midshipman, 1916; Sub-Lt, 1918; Lt, 1920; Lt-Comdr, 1928; Comdr, 1932; Capt., 1937; Cdre 1st Cl., 1941; Actg Vice-Adm., 1942; Actg Adm., 1943; Rear-Adm., 1946; Vice-Adm., 1949; Actg Adm., 1952; Adm. 1953; Adm. of the Fleet, 1956. Served in HMS Lion, 1916; HMS Queen Elizabeth, 1917; HM Sub. K6, 1918; HMS P31, 1918; HMS Renown, 1920 (Prince of Wales' Tour, Australia and New Zealand); HMS Repulse, 1921; HMS Renown, 1921 (Prince of Wales' Tour to India, Japan, and the Far East); HMS Revenge, 1923; Signal Sch., Portsmouth, 1924; RN Coll., Greenwich, 1925; Reserve Fleet Wireless and Signal Officer, 1926; Asst Fleet Wireless Officer, Mediterranean Fleet, 1927-28; 2nd Destroyer Flotilla Signal and Wireless Officer, 1928-29; Senior Wireless Instructor, Signal Sch., Portsmouth, 1929-31; Fleet Wireless Officer, Mediterranean Fleet, 1931-33; qualified as interpreter in French and German, 1933; in command of HMS Daring, 1934; and of HMS Wishart, 1935; Admiralty (Naval Air Div.), 1936; in command of HMS Kelly, and of the 5th Destroyer Flotilla, 1939 (despatches twice); in command of HMS Illustrious, 1941; Commodore Combined Ops, 1941-42; Chief of Combined Ops, 1942-43, and mem. of British Chiefs of Staff Cttee, 1942-43; Supreme Allied Comd, SE Asia, 1943-46; Viceroy of India, March-Aug. 1947; Governor-Gen. of India, Aug. 1947-June 1948; Flag Officer, Commanding 1st Cruiser Sqdn, Mediterranean Fleet, 1948-49; Fourth Sea Lord, 1950-52; Comdr-in-Chief, Mediterranean, 1952-54; concurrently C-in-C, Allied Forces, Mediterranean, 1953-54; First Sea Lord, 1955-59; Chief of UK Defence Staff and Chm. of Chiefs of Staff Cttee, 1959-65. Designated by the Home Sec. to examine into and report on prison security, Oct. 1966-. Chm., Council of Atlantic Colls, 1968-. For War Service: Legion of Merit, 1943, DSM, 1945 (US); Greek Mil. Cross (Crete), 1941; Grand Cross of Order of George I (Greece), 1946; Special Grand Cordon of the Cloud and Banner (China), 1945; Grand Cross of the Legion of Honour and Croix de Guerre (France), 1946; Grand Cross of: Star of Nepal, 1946; Order of White Elephant of Siam, 1946; Order of the Lion of the Netherlands, 1947. Not for War Service: KStJ 1943; Grand Cross of: Isabella Catolica (Spain), 1922; Crown of Rumania, 1924; Star of Rumania, 1937; Mil. Order of Avis (Portugal), 1951; The Seraphim (Sweden), 1952; Agga Maha Thiri Thudhamma (Burma), 1956; Grand Cross, Order of Dannebrog (Denmark), 1962; Grand Cross of the Order of the Seal of Solomon of Ethiopia, 1965. *Publications:* Time only to Look Forward (Speeches), 1949; Report to the Combined Chiefs of Staff by the Supreme Allied Commander SE Asia (1947), 1950; Reflections on the Transfer of Power and Jawaharlal Nehru, 1968. *Recreations:* polo, shooting and underwater-fishing. *Heir:* (by special remainder to the Earldom) *d* Lady Patricia Mountbatten [*b* 14 Feb. 1924; *m* 1946, 7th Baron Brabourne, *qv*; five *s* two *d*]. *Address:* 2 Kinnerton Street, SW1. *T:* 01-235 0081; Broadlands, Romsey, Hants. *T:* Romsey 3333; Classiebawn Castle, Cliffoney, County Sligo. *T:* Cliffoney 6. *Clubs:* Royal Automobile (Pres.), Royal Thames Yacht (Admiral of the Cumberland Fleet, Cdre, 1944-69), Royal Motor Yacht (Vice-Adm.), United Service, Naval and Military, Royal Air Force, Devonshire, Savage, United Hunts, MCC, Buck's; Royal Yacht Squadron; Royal Southampton Yacht (Admiral); Royal and Ancient; Hampshire Aeroplane (Pres.); Hawks, Cambridge Union.

*See also Marquess of Milford Haven.*

**MOUNTEVANS,** 2nd Baron, *cr* 1945, of Chelsea; **Richard Andvord Evans;** Director, International Federation of The Periodical Press; *b* 28 Aug. 1918; *er s* of 1st Baron Mountevans, KCB, DSO, LLD, and of his 2nd wife, Elsa, *d* of Richard Andvord, Oslo, Norway; *S* father 1957; *m* 1940, Deirdre Grace, *d* of John O'Connell, Buxton House, Buxton Hill, Cork, Ireland; two *s* one *d*. *Educ:* Cranbrook Sch.; Sydney; Stowe. Served War of 1939-45, Lt (S) RNVR; in Holland during German invasion, also in Bombay on the staff of the Senior RN Officer, 1942-45. Subsequently on staff of ICI Ltd, 1946-61. Chm. Anglo-Swedish Group and Vice-Chm., Anglo-Norwegian Group of Inter-Parl. Union. Kt Comdr, Royal Order of Vasa of Sweden. *Recreations:* music, literature, travel. *Heir: s* Hon. Edward Patrick Broke Evans, *b* 1 Feb. 1943. *Address:* 13 York House, York House Place, W8. *T:* 01-937 9063.

**MOUNTFIELD, Alexander Stuart;** *b* 5 Dec. 1902; *s* of Robert Mountfield and Caroline (*née* Appleyard); *m* 1934, Agnes Elizabeth Gurney; two *s*. *Educ:* Merchant Taylors' Sch., Crosby. Entered service of Mersey Docks and Harbour Board as Apprentice, 1918; served through clerical grades and in various administrative capacities. Gen. Man. and Sec., Mersey Docks and Harbour Bd, 1957-62; retd 1962. Mem. Upper Mersey Navigation Commn. MInstT. *Recreations:* gardening, reading. *Address:* Lanthwaite, Hightown, near Liverpool. *T:* Hightown 2115. *Clubs:* Reform; Athenæum (Liverpool).

**MOUNTFORD, Sir James (Frederick),** Kt 1953; MA Oxon, DLitt Birmingham, Hon. DCL Oxon; Vice-Chancellor, University of Liverpool, 1945-63, retired; *b* 15 Sept. 1897; *s* of Alfred Mountford, West Bromwich, Staffs; *m* 1922, Doris May, *e d* of Harry Edwards, Handsworth, Birmingham; three *d*. *Educ:* West Bromwich Grammar Sch.; Univ. of Birmingham and (as a research student) Oriel College, Oxford; Cromer Greek Prize (British Academy), 1919; Fereday Fellow, St John's Coll., Oxford, 1924-27; Lecturer in Classics, King's Coll., Newcastle, 1918; Lecturer in Latin, Edinburgh Univ., 1919-24; Schiff Lecturer, Cornell Univ., 1924; Prof. of the Classics, Cornell Univ., 1924-27; Prof. of Latin, University Coll. of Wales, Aberystwyth, 1928-32; Prof. of Latin, Univ. of Liverpool, 1932-45, and Dean of Faculty of Arts, 1941-45; sometime External Examiner to Univs of Durham, Leeds, Manchester, St Andrews, and Wales; Chm. Cttee Vice-Chancellors and Principals, 1948-49; Mem. Advisory Cttee, Leverhulme Research Awards, 1948- (Chm., 1958-); Chm. of Governors, Birkenhead Sch., 1944-49; Chm. of Governors, Birkenhead High Sch. for Girls, 1953-60; Chm., Northern Univs. Jt Matric. Board, 1947-49; Vice-Chm. Liverpool Regional Hosp. Board, 1948-; Chm. of Govs, Burton Manor Residential Coll., 1946-66; Chm. of Govs, Malayan Federation Teachers' Training Coll., Kirby, 1951-63; Gov., Shrewsbury Sch., 1951-62; Dir, Liverpool Playhouse, 1952-66; Mem., Governing Bd of National Institute for Research in Nuclear Science, 1957-61. President: Classical Assoc., 1962-63; Virgil Soc., 1966-69. Hon. LittD,

TCD; Hon. DLitt, Hull; Hon. LLD, Alberta, Birmingham, Liverpool, London, Manchester, Wales. *Publications:* Quotations from Classical Authors in Medieval Latin Glossaries, 1925; 'Abavus' Glossarium, 1926; Greek Music in Papyri and inscriptions (in New Chaps in Greek Lit.), 1929; The Scholia Bembina to Terence, 1934 (repr. 1969); British Universities, 1966; edn of Kennedy's Revised Latin Primer, 1930; edn of Arnold's Latin Prose Composition (and Latin Versions), 1938-40; edn of Sidgwick's Greek Prose Composition, 1951; joint author of: Glossarium Ansileubi, 1926; Post-Classical Latin Unseens, 1928; Index to Scholia of Servius and Donatus, 1930 (German reprint, 1962); Outline of Latin Prose Composition, 1942; contributions to learned periodicals and articles on education. *Recreations:* music, the theatre, and photography. *Address:* 29 Aigburth Drive, Liverpool, 17. *T:* 051-727 5817. *Club:* University (Liverpool).

**MOUNTFORT, Guy Reginald,** OBE 1970; retired as Director, Ogilvy & Mather International Inc., New York (1964-66); and as Managing Director, Ogilvy and Mather Ltd, London (1964-66); *b* 4 Dec. 1905; *s* of late Arnold George Mountfort, artist, and late Alice Edith (*née* Hughes); *m* 1931, Joan Hartley (*née* Pink); two *d. Educ:* Grammar Sch. General Motors Corporation (France), 1928-38. War service, 1939-46, 12 Regt HAC and British Army Staff (Washington) Lt-Col; service in N Africa, Italy, Burma, Pacific, Germany. Procter & Gamble Inc., USA, 1946-47; Mather & Crowther Ltd, 1947, Dir, 1949; Vice-Chm., Dollar Exports Bd Advertising Cttee, 1948-49. Trustee, World Wildlife Fund; Scientific FZS (Stamford Raffles Award, 1969); Medal of Société d'Acclimatation, 1936. Hon. Sec. Brit. Ornithologists' Union, 1952-62, Pres. 1970 (Union Medal, 1967); Leader of scientific expedns to Coto Donana, 1952, 1955, 1956; Bulgaria, 1960; Hungary, 1961; Jordan, 1963, 1965; Pakistan, 1966, 1967. *Publications:* A Field Guide to the Birds of Europe (co-author), 1954; The Hawfinch, 1957; Portrait of a Wilderness, 1958; Portrait of a River, 1962; Portrait of a Desert, 1965; The Vanishing Jungle, 1969. Contributor to ornithological and other scientific jls; television and radio broadcasts on ornithology and exploration. *Recreations:* ornithology, gardening, photography, travel. *Address:* Plovers Meadow, Possingworth Park, Blackboys, Sussex. *T:* Heathfield 3416.

**MOUNTGARRET,** 17th Viscount (Ireland) *cr* 1550; Baron (UK) *cr* 1911; **Richard Henry Piers Butler;** *b* 8 Nov. 1936; *s* of 16th Viscount; *S* father, 1966; *m* 1st, 1960, Gillian Margaret (marr. diss. 1970), *o d* of Cyril Francis Stuart Buckley, London, SW3; two *s* one *d*; 2nd, 1970, Mrs Jennifer Susan Nelville Fattorini, *o d* of Captain D. M. Wills, Barley Wood, Wrington, near Bristol. Educ: Eton; RMA, Sandhurst. Commissioned, Irish Guards, 1957; retd rank Capt., 1964. *Recreations:* shooting, stalking, cricket. *Heir:* *s* Piers James Richard Butler, *b* 15 April 1961. *Address:* Stainley House, South Stainley, Harrogate, Yorks. *T:* Ripley 587; Wyvis, Evanton, Ross-shire, Scotland. *Club:* White's.

**MOURANT, Arthur Ernest,** DM, FRCP; FRS 1966; Director, Medical Research Council Serological Population Genetics Laboratory and Hon. Senior Lecturer in Haematology, Medical College, St Bartholomew's Hospital, since 1965; *b* 11 April 1904; *er s* of Ernest Charles Mourant and Emily Gertrude (*née* Bray); unmarried. *Educ:* Victoria Coll., Jersey; Exeter Coll., Oxford; St Bartholomew's Hosp. Medical Sch. London. BA 1925, DPhil (Geol.) 1931, MA 1931, BM, BCh 1943, DM 1948, Oxford; FRCP 1960; FCPath 1963. 1st cl. hons Chem., 1926; Sen. King Charles I Schol., Exeter Coll., Oxford, 1926; Burdett-Coutts Schol., Oxford Univ., 1926. Demonstrator in Geology, Univ. of Leeds, 1928-29; Geol Survey of Gt Brit., 1929-31; teaching posts, 1931-34; Dir, Jersey Pathological Lab., 1935-38; Med. Student, 1939-43; House med. appts, 1943-44; Med. Off., Nat. Blood Transfusion Service, 1944-45; Med. Off., Galton Lab. Serum Unit, Cambridge, 1945-46; Dir, Blood Gp Reference Lab., Min. of Health and MRC, 1946-65 (Internat. Blood Gp Reference Lab., WHO, 1952-65); Hon. Adviser, Nuffield Blood Gp Centre, 1952-65. Vis. Prof., Columbia Univ., 1953. Pres., Section H (Anthropology), Brit. Assoc., 1956; Mem. Hon., Société Jersiaise; Corresp. Mem., Académie des Sciences, Inscriptions et Belles-Lettres, Toulouse; Hon. Mem., Peruvian Pathological Soc. Past or present Mem. Ed. Bd of six British, foreign and internat. scientific jls. Oliver Meml Award, 1953; Huxley Memorial Medal, Royal Anthropological Institute, 1961. *Publications:* The Distribution of the Human Blood Groups, 1954; (jtly) The ABO Blood Groups: Comprehensive Tables and Maps of World Distribution, 1958; (jt ed.) Man and Cattle, 1963; numerous papers in scientific jls on blood groups and other biol subjects, geology and archæology. *Recreations:* photography, geology, archæology, travel, reading in sciences other than own, alpine gardening. *Address:* Serological Population Genetics Laboratory, c/o St Bartholomew's Hospital, West Smithfield, EC1. *T:* 01-253 4296. *Club:* Athenæum.

**MOVERLEY, Rt. Rev. Gerald,** JCD; Titular Bishop of Tinisa in Proconsulari; Domestic Prelate to HH Pope Paul VI since 1965; Bishop Auxiliary of Leeds (RC) since 1968; *b* 9 April 1922; *s* of William Joseph Moverley and Irene Mary Moverley (*née* Dewhirst). *Educ:* St Bede's Grammar Sch., Bradford; Ushaw Coll., Durham; Angelicum Univ., Rome. Priest, 1946; Sec. to Bishop Poskitt, Leeds, 1946-51; Angelicum Univ., 1951-54; Chancellor, Dio. Leeds, 1958-68; elected Bishop, Dec. 1967. *Address:* Quarters, Carsick Hill Way, Sheffield, S10 3LT. *T:* Sheffield 301596.

**MOWAT, John Stuart;** Sheriff-Substitute of Fife and Kinross at Dunfermline since 1960; *b* 30 Jan. 1923; *s* of George Mowat and Annie Barlow; *m* 1956, Anne Cameron Renfrew; two *s* two *d. Educ:* Glasgow High Sch.; Belmont House; Merchiston Castle Sch.; Glasgow Univ. (MA, LLB). Served RAF Transport Comd, 1941-46; Flt-Lt 1944. Journalist, 1947-52; Advocate, 1952; contested (L) Caithness and Sutherland, 1955; Office-bearer, Scottish Liberal Party, 1954-58; Life Trustee, Carnegie Dunfermline Trust, 1967. *Recreations:* golf, watching football. *Address:* Newlands, Thistle Street, Dunfermline, Fife. *T:* Dunfermline 24496. *Club:* Royal and Ancient (St Andrews).

**MOWBRAY** (26th Baron *cr* 1283), **SEGRAVE** (27th Baron *cr* 1283), and **STOURTON,** of Stourton, Co. Wilts. (23rd Baron *cr* 1448); **Charles Edward Stourton;** *b* 11 March 1923; *s* of William Marmaduke Stourton, 25th Baron Mowbray, 26th Baron Segrave and 22nd Baron Stourton, MC, and Sheila, *er d* of Hon. Edward Gully, CB; *S* father, 1965; *m* 1952, Hon. Jane de Yarburgh Bateson, *o c* of 5th Baron Deramore, and of Nina Lady Deramore, *d* of Alastair Macpherson-Grant; two *s. Educ:* Ampleforth; Christ Church, Oxford. Joined Army, 1942; Commissioned Gren. Guards, 1943; served with 2nd Armd Bn Gren. Gds, as Lt, 1943-44 (wounded, France, 1944; loss of eye and invalided, 1945). Mem. of Lloyd's

1952; Mem. Securicor, 1961-64; Dir, Securicor (Scotland) Ltd, 1964-70. Mem., Nidderdale RDC, 1954-58. A Conservative Whip in House of Lords, 1967-70; a Lord in Waiting to HM The Queen, 1970-. Kt of Hon. and Devotion, SMO Malta, 1947; Kt Gr. Cross and Grand Prior of Great Britain, Mil. Order of St Lazarus, 1970. *Recreations:* reading, shooting, gardening. *Heir:* *s* Hon. Edward William Stephen Stourton, *b* 17 April 1953. *Address:* Marcus, by Forfar, Angus. *T:* Finavon 219; 23 Warwick Square, SW1. *Clubs:* Turf, White's, Pratt's; Puffin's (Edinburgh).

*See also F. P. Crowder, Hon. J. J. Stourton.*

**MOWBRAY, Sir John Robert,** 6th Bt *cr* 1880; *b* 1 March 1932; *s* of Sir George Robert Mowbray, 5th Bt, KBE, and of Diana Margaret, *d* of Sir Robert Heywood Hughes, 12th Bt; *S* father, 1969; *m* 1957, Lavina Mary, *d* of late Lt-Col Francis Edgar Hugonin, OBE, Stainton House, Stainton in Cleveland, Yorks; three *d*. *Educ:* Eton; New College, Oxford. *Address:* Hunts Park, Great Thurlow, Suffolk.

**MOWLEM, Rainsford,** FRCS; Emeritus Cons. Plastic Surgeon, Middlesex Hospital; Surgeon i/c Department for Plastic Surgery, Middlesex Hospital, 1939-62, retired; Surgeon i/c North West Regional Centre for Plastic Surgery, Mount Vernon Hospital; Consulting Plastic Surgeon to King Edward VII Hospital, Windsor, Luton and Dunstable Hospital, Birmingham Accident Hospital; *b* 21 Dec. 1902; *s* of Arthur Manwell Mowlem, New Zealand; *m* 1933, Margaret West Harvey; two *d*. *Educ:* Auckland Grammar Sch.; Univ. of New Zealand. MB, ChB, NZ 1924, FRCS 1929. Asst Med. Officer i/c Plastic Surgery Unit, LCC, 1933-37; Asst Plastic Surgeon, St Andrews Hosp., Dollis Hill, 1937-39; Surgeon i/c NW Centre Plastic Surgery, Hill End Hosp., 1939-53. Fellow: Assoc. Surgeons of GB and Ireland; RSM; Brit. Orthopædic Assoc.; Past-Pres. Brit. Assoc. of Plastic Surgeons (1950 and 1959); Pres. Internat. Congress on Plastic Surgery, 1959; Mem. Editorial Cttee, British Assoc. of Plastic Surgeons; Hon. Member: Netherlands Assoc. of Plastic Surgeons, Amer. Soc. of Plastic and Reconstructive Surgery; French Soc. of Plastic and Reconstructive Surgery; Sociedad Española de Cirugia Plastica y Reparadora; Hon. Fellow Amer. Assoc. Plastic Surgeons. Corresp. Mem. Italian Soc. of Plastic Surgery. Hunterian Prof., RCS, 1940. Hon. ScD (Trinity Coll., Hartford). *Publications:* various on scientific subjects. *Address:* La Morena, Mijas, Malaga, Spain.

**MOWRER, Edgar Ansel;** Newspaper Columnist; *b* Bloomington, Illinois, USA, 8 March 1892; *s* of Rufus Mowrer and Nellie Scott; *m* 1916, Lilian Thomson, London, England; one *d*. *Educ:* Univ. of Chicago, Chicago, Ill.; Sorbonne, Paris; Univ. of Michigan (AB). Joined Chicago Daily News outbreak world war, serving French and Italian Fronts; later Rome correspondent, subsequently Berlin correspondent during 10 years; Paris correspondent until June 1940. Pulitzer Prize, 1932. Writer on foreign affairs from Washington, DC; Dep. Dir of the Office of Facts and Figures (later called Office of War Information), 1942-43. Amer. Editor, Western World Magazine, 1957-60; *Publications:* Immortal Italy, 1923; This American World, 1928; The Future of Politics, 1930; Germany Puts the Clock Back, 1932; Mowrer in China, 1938; Global War, 1942; The Nightmare of American Foreign Policy, 1948; Challenge and Decision, 1950; A Good Time to be Alive, 1959; An End to Make-Believe, 1961; Triumph and Turmoil, A Personal History of Our Time, 1968. *Recreations:* walking, canoeing. *Address:* Wonalancet, New Hampshire 03897, USA. *Clubs:* Century (New York); Adventurers (Chicago).

**MOYA, (John) Hidalgo,** CBE 1966; FRIBA 1956; architect; *b* Los Gatos, Calif, 5 May 1920; *s* of Hidalgo Moya; *m* 1947, Janiffer Innes Mary Norton; one *s* two *d*. *Educ:* Oundle Sch.; Royal West of England Coll. of Art; AA Sch. of Architecture; AA Dip., 1943. Qualified, 1944; in practice with Philip Powell, 1946-61; with Philip Powell, Robert Henley and Peter Skinner, 1961-; major works include: Churchill Garden Flats, Westminster, 1948-62; Houses at Chichester, 1950; Toys Hill, 1954; Oxshott, 1954; Mayfield Sch., Putney, 1955; Brasenose Coll., Oxford, extensions, 1961; Christ Church Oxford, Picture Gallery and undergraduate rooms, 1967; St John's Coll., Cambrdige, new buildings, 1967; Chichester Festival Theatre, 1962; Public Swimming Baths, Putney, 1967; Mental Hosp. extensions at Fairmile, 1957, Borocourt, 1964; General Hosps at Swindon, High Wycombe and Wythenshawe. Pimlico Housing Scheme, Winning Design in Open Competition, 1946; Vertical Feature Festival of British Winning Design, 1950; RIBA London Architecture Bronze Medal, 1950; Festival of Britain Award, 1951; Mohlg Good Design in Housing Award, 1954; RIBA Bronze Medal, 1958, 1961 (Bucks, Berks, Oxon); Civic Trust Awards (Class I and II), 1961; Architectural Design Project Award, 1965; RIBA Architectural Award, (London and SE Regions), 1967. *Address:* Powell and Moya, Architects, 90 Tottenham Court Road, W1. *T:* 01-580 2794; Day's Farm, Lippitt's Hill, High Beech, Loughton, Essex. *T:* Loughton 5272.

**MOYERS, Bill D.,** BD; Publisher of Newsday, Long Island, 1967-70; *b* 5 June 1934; *s* of John Henry Moyers and Ruby Moyers (*née* Johnson); *m* 1954, Judith Suzanne Davidson; two *s* one *d*. *Educ:* High Sch., Marshall, Texas; Univ. of Texas; Univ. of Edinburgh; Southwestern Theological Seminary. BJ 1956; BD 1959. Personal Asst to Senator Lyndon B. Johnson, 1959-60; Executive Asst, 1960; US Peace Corps: Associate Dir, 1961-63; Dep. Dir, 1963. Special Asst to President Johnson, 1963-66; Press Sec., 1965-67. *Address:* 550 Stewart Avenue, Garden City, Long Island, New York 11530, USA.

**MOYES, Rt. Rev. John Stoward,** CMG 1962; DD (Trinity College, Toronto); MA (Adelaide), ThD (Australian College of Theology); retired as Bishop of Armidale, (1929-64); Episcopal Canon of St George's Cathedral, Jerusalem, 1962-65; *b* Koolunga, S Australia, 25 July 1884; *s* of John Moyes and Ellen Jane Stoward; *m* 1909, Helen Margaret, *e d* of late Sir Richard Butler, Premier and Treasurer of SA; four *s* two *d*. *Educ:* St Peter's Coll., Adelaide (Dux); Univ. of Adelaide; St Barnabas Theological Coll., Adelaide; 1st Class Honours in ThL of Aust. Coll. of Theology; course in hons Maths, gaining BA, 1905; supplemented this with course in Classics, gaining MA degree, 1907. Asst Curate, Port Pirie, 1907-10; S Mary, Lewisham (Southwark), 1911-13; Rector of S Cuthbert's, Prospect, 1913-19; S Paul's, Port Pirie, 1919-21, S Bartholomew's, Norwood, 1921-29; Archdeacon of Adelaide, 1925-29; Examining Chaplain, Bishop of Adelaide, 1925-29; Chaplain Commonwealth Forces, 1918-20. 1st Freeman of: City of Armidale, 1954; City of Tamworth, 1964. Dep. Chancellor, Univ. of New England, 1960-67. DLitt (*hc*) Univ. of New England, 1961. *Publications:* Marriage and Sex; The Church and The Hour; Australia, the Church and the Future (Moorhouse Lectures), 1941; American Journey, 1944; In Journeyings Often

(Oxford Univ. Press), 1949; The Communist Way of Life and The Christian's Answer, 1951; America Revisited, 1955; Third Time of Asking, 1959; Coventry Campaign, 1959. *Recreation:* music. *Address:* Nell Slade Lodge, Mowll Memorial Village, Castle Hill, NSW 2154, Australia.

**MOYLAN, John David FitzGerald; His Honour Judge Moylan;** Judge of the County Courts, Wandsworth, since 1967; *b* 8 Oct. 1915; *s* of late Sir John FitzGerald Moylan, CB, CBE, and late Lady Moylan (*née* FitzGerald); *m* 1946, Jean, *d* of F. C. Marno-Edwards, Lavenham, Suffolk; one *s* two *d*. *Educ:* Charterhouse; Christ Church, Oxford. Served War of 1939-45, with Royal Marines. Inner Temple, 1946; practised on the Western Circuit. *Recreations:* travel and music. *Address:* 29 Lennox Gardens, SW1. *T:* 01-584 4726.

**MOYLE,** family name of **Baron Moyle.**

**MOYLE,** Baron *cr* 1966 (Life Peer), of Llanidloes; **Arthur Moyle,** CBE 1951; JP; Governor, Birmingham University; *b* 25 Sept., 1894; *s* of David and Mary Moyle; *m* 1st, 1921, Elizabeth Evans; one *s*; 2nd, 1951, Lena Bassett. *Educ:* Elem. Sch., Llanidloes; Fircroft Coll., Bournville. MP (Lab): Stourbridge Div. of Worcs, 1945-50; Oldbury and Halesowen, 1950-64; Parliamentary Private Sec. to Rt Hon. Clement Attlee, May 1946-Dec. 1955. Chm. of Nat. Joint Council for Local Authorities' Non-Trading Services (Manual Workers), 1936 and 1937; Mem. of Nat. Joint Council for Local Authorities' Administrative, Professional, Technical and Clerical; Mem. of Rushcliffe Cttee for Nurses' Salaries from its inception to 1946, and of the following bodies from their inception until 1945: TUC Local Govt Advisory Cttee; Nat. Joint Council for County Council Roadmen; Nat. Joint Council for Staffs of Hospitals and Allied Instns; Nat. Officer, Nat. Union of Public Employees. Former Pres. and Vice-Pres. Poultry Assoc. of Great Britain Ltd. *Address:* Hafod, The Bungalow, Grassy Lane, Sevenoaks, Kent.

*See also R. D. Moyle.*

**MOYLE, Roland (Dunstan);** MP (Lab) Lewisham North since 1966; *b* 12 March 1928; *s* of Baron Moyle, *qv*; *m* 1956, Shelagh Patricia Hogan; one *s* one *d*. *Educ:* Infants' and Jun. Elem. Schs, Bexleyheath, Kent; County Sch., Llanidloes, Mont.; UCW Aberystwyth (LLB); Trinity Hall, Cambridge (BA, LLB); Gray's Inn. Barrister-at-Law. Commnd in Royal Welch Fusiliers, 1949-51. Legal Dept, Wales Gas Bd, 1953-56; Asst Industrial Relations Officer, Wales Gas Board, 1956; Asst Industrial Relations Officer, Gas Coun., 1956-62 (Jt Sec., Nat. Jt Industrial Coun., Gas Industry; Jt Sec., Nat Jt Coun. for Gas Staffs); Conciliation Research Officer, Electricity Coun., 1962-65; Jt Sec., Nat. Coun. for Admin. and Clerical Staff in Electricity Supply, Electricity Coun., 1965-66. PPS to Chief Secretary to the Treasury, 1966-69, to Home Secretary, 1969-70. Mem., Select Cttee on Race Relations and Immigration; Chm., Parly Lab. Party Defence Group. *Recreations:* gardening, motoring, swimming, reading. *Address:* 19 Montpelier Row, Blackheath, SE3. *T:* 01-852 4849.

**MOYNE,** 2nd Baron, *cr* 1932, of Bury St Edmunds; **Bryan Walter Guinness,** MA; FRSL; poet, novelist and playwright; Pro-Chancellor, Trinity College, Dublin; Vice-Chairman of Arthur Guinness, Son and Co.; Chairman, Iveagh (Housing) Trust, Dublin; Barrister-at-Law; *b* 27 Oct. 1905; *e s* of 1st Baron Moyne (3rd *s* of 1st Earl of Iveagh) and Lady Evelyn Erskine (*d* 1939), 3rd *d* of 14th Earl of Buchan; *S* father 1944; *m* 1st, 1929, Diana Freeman-Mitford (marriage dissolved, 1934); two *s*; 2nd, 1936, Elisabeth Nelson; four *s* five *d*. *Educ:* Eton; Christ Church, Oxford. Called to Bar, 1930. Capt., Royal Sussex Regiment, 1943; A Governor National Gallery of Ireland, 1955; a Commissioner of Irish Lights, 1956. Mem., Irish Acad. of Letters. Hon. LLD: TCD, 1958; NUI, 1961. *Publications:* (as Bryan Guinness): 23 Poems, 1931; Singing out of Tune, 1933; Landscape with Figures, 1934; Under the Eyelid, 1935; Johnny and Jemima, 1936; A Week by the Sea, 1936; Lady Crushwell's Companion, 1938; The Children in the Desert, 1947; Reflexions, 1947; The Animals' Breakfast, 1950; Story of a Nutcracker, 1953; Collected Poems, 1956; A Fugue of Cinderellas, 1956; Catriona and the Grasshopper, 1957; Priscilla and the Prawn, 1960; Leo and Rosabelle, 1961; The Giant's Eye, 1964; The Rose in the Tree, 1964; The Girl with the Flower, 1966; The Engagement, 1969; *plays:* The Fragrant Concubine, 1938; A Riverside Charade, 1954. *Recreation:* travelling. *Heir:* *s* Hon. Jonathan Bryan Guinness [*b* 16 March 1930; *m* 1st, 1951, Ingrid Olivia Georgia (marr. diss., 1963), *d* of late Major Richard Wyndham; two *s* one *d*; 2nd, 1964, Suzanne, *d* of H. W. D. Lisney; one *s* one *d*]. Address: Biddesden House, Andover, Hants. *T:* Ludgershall (Wilts) 237; Knockmaroon, Castleknock, Co. Dublin. *Clubs:* Athenæum, Carlton; Kildare Street (Dublin).

**MOYNIHAN,** family name of **Baron Moynihan.**

**MOYNIHAN,** 3rd Baron, *cr* 1929; **Antony Patrick Andrew Cairnes Berkeley Moynihan;** Bt 1922; *b* 2 Feb. 1936; *s* of 2nd Baron Moynihan, OBE, TD, and of Ierne Helen Candy; *S* father 1965; *m* 1st, 1955, Ann Herbert (marr. diss., 1958); 2nd, 1958, Shirin Roshan Berry (marr. diss., 1967); one *d*; 3rd, 1968, Luthgarda Maria Fernandez; one *d*. *Educ:* Stowe. Late 2nd Lt Coldstream Guards. *Recreation:* dog breeding. *Heir:* *half-b* Hon. Colin Berkeley Moynihan, *b* 13 Sept. 1955.

**MOYNIHAN, Most Rev. Denis,** DD; Titular Bishop of Suacia; *b* 16 June 1885. *Educ:* St Brendan's Seminary, Killarney; Irish College, Paris. Served in Archdiocese of Liverpool and in Diocese of Kerry. Was Administrator of the Cathedral, Killarney, for fourteen years before appointment to Diocese of Ross; Bp of Ross (RC) 1941-53; Bishop of Kerry, 1953-69. *Address:* Bon Secours Hospital, Tralee, Co. Kerry, Eire.

**MOYNIHAN, Martin John,** MC; Ambassador to Liberia since 1970; *b* 17 Feb. 1916; *e s* of William John Moynihan and Phoebe Alexander; *m* 1946, Monica Hopwood; one *s* one *d*. *Educ:* Birkenhead Sch.; Magdalen Coll., Oxford (MA). India Office, 1939. War of 1939-45: Indian Army, 1940; QVO Corps of Guides; served with Punjab Frontier Force Regt, N-W Frontier, Assam and Burma (MC); UK High Commission, Delhi, Madras and Bombay, 1946-48; Principal, CRO, 1948-52; Jt Sec., Commonwealth Supply and Production Meeting, 1951; UK High Commission, Karachi, 1952; Dep. High Commissioner: Peshawar, 1954-56; Lahore, 1956-58; Head of Technical Assistance Dept, Commonwealth Relations Office, 1959; Dep. High Commissioner: Kuala Lumpur, 1961-63; Port of Spain, 1964-66; HM Consul-General, Philadelphia, 1966-70. *Publications:* The Strangers, 1946; South of Fort Hertz, 1956. *Recreation:* riding. *Address:* British Embassy, Monrovia, Liberia; The Gatehouse, 5 The

Green, Wimbledon Common, SW19. *T:* 01-946 7964. *Club:* Travellers'.

**MOYNIHAN, Rodrigo,** CBE 1953; RA 1954 (ARA 1944); Artist; lately Professor of Painting at the Royal College of Art; *b* 17 Oct. 1910; *s* of Herbert James Moynihan and Maria de la Puerta; *m* 1931, Elinor Bellingham Smith; one *s*; *m* 1960, Anne, *d* of Sir James Hamet Dunn, 1st Bt; one *s*. *Educ:* UCS, London, and in USA. Slade Sch., 1928-31, Slade Schol.; Mem. of London Group, 1933; one-man shows at Redfern Gall., 1940, 1958, 1961; Leicester Gallery, 1946; Hanover Gallery, 1963. Army Service, 1940-43; Official War Artist, 1943-44. Pictures purchased by Chantrey Bequest, Tate Gallery, Contemporary Art Soc., War Artists' Advisory Cttee. Hon. Dr RCA 1969; Fellow UCL, 1970-. *Address:* 70 Avenue du Léman, Lausanne, Switzerland.

**MUCKLOW, Prof. Graham Fernie,** DSc, FIMechE; Professor of Mechanical Engineering, Birmingham University, 1940-59; *b* 2 Jan. 1894; 3rd *s* of Edward Mucklow, Bury, Lancs; *m* 1936, Antonia Mary (*d* 1962), *d* of Col G. A. Kay, Wall, Staffs; two *s*. *Educ:* Rugby Sch.; McGill Univ.; Manchester Univ. Served European War, Northumberland Fusiliers and Anti-Gas Service, 1915-19. Research Asst, Research Assoc. of British Motor and Allied Manufacturers (now Motor Industries Research Assoc.), 1921-22; Lecturer in Engineering, Manchester Univ., 1922. Chm., Midland Branch, Instn of Mech. Engineers, 1951-53. *Publications:* various papers on problems relating to the internal combustion engine, wave-action in gases, etc, ProcIMechE, etc. *Recreation:* sailing. *Address:* 6 Cherry Hill Avenue, Barnt Green, Worcs. *T:* 021-445 1364.

**MUDALIAR, Diwan Bahadur Sir Arcot Lakshmanaswami,** Kt 1945; BA; MD; LLD; DSc; DCL Oxon; FRCOG; FACS; Vice-Chancellor, University of Madras, since 1942; *b* 14 Oct. 1887; *s* of A. Kuppuswami Mudaliar; *m* 1916, Ratha Bai, *d* of V. Damodara Mudaliar; three *s* one *d*. *Educ:* Madras Christian Coll., Madras; Medical Coll., Madras. Prof. of Obstetrics and Gynæcology, Madras Medical Coll., and Superintendent of Govt Hosp. for Women and Children, 1934-42; Principal, Medical Coll., Madras, 1939-42; Hon. Lt-Col, Madras Univ. OTC; Mem., Indian Medical Council since inception; ex-mem., Univ. Commission, 1948; Chm., Secondary Educ. Commission, 1952-53; Dep. leader, Indian deleg., Unesco, 1950; mem. Exec. Bd, Unesco, 1950-; Chm., Standing Cttee, Inter-Univ. Bd, 1949; mem., Legislative Council, Madras. *Publications:* Ante-natal, Natal, and Neo-natal Mortality of Infants; Clinical Obstetrics; Midwifery Casebook for Midwives. *Address:* Kensington, Poonamallee High Road, Kilpauk, Madras, India. *T:* (Office) 3854, (residence) 3263. *Clubs:* Cosmopolitan (Madras); Kodaikanal Boat.

**MUDALIAR, Diwan Bahadur Sir Arcot Ramaswami,** KCSI 1942; Kt 1937; Hon. DCL: Oxford 1946; Durham, 1953; formerly Vice-Chancellor, University of Travancore; *b* 14 Oct. 1887; *s* of A. Kuppuswami Mudaliar; *m* 1910, Kamammal, *d* of V. Damodara Mudaliar; two *s* two *d*. *Educ:* Madras Christian Coll.; Law Coll., Madras. Advocate, Madras; Mem., Legislative Council, Madras, 1920-26; Parly Sec. to Minister Education, 1920-23; Pres. of Corporation of Madras, 1928-30; Mem., Council of State, 1930; Mem., Indian Legislative Assembly, 1931-34 (Dep. Leader of Opposition); Member: Age of Consent Cttee, 1929; Round Table Conference Federal Structure Cttee, Army Retrenchment Cttee (Chm.), Indian Franchise Cttee, NW Frontier Subject Cttee and Special Textile Tariff Board, 1933; Mem., India Council, 1936-37; Reserve Bank Cttee; Statutory Railway Cttee, 1936; a corresp. mem. of Economic Cttee of League of Nations and a Mem. of Imp. Economic Cttee, 1937; Adviser, Sec. of State for India, 1937-39; Commerce Mem. of Governor-General's Executive Council, 1939-42; a representative of India at War Cabinet and Pacific War Council in London, 1942-43; Mem. of Viceroy's Executive Council without portfolio, 1942-43; Dewan of Mysore, 1946-49; Leader Indian Delegation to British Commonwealth Relations Conference, Toronto, 1933; India Delegate, Nine Power Conference, Brussels, 1937; Leader Indian Deleg. UN Conf., San Francisco, 1945, and 1st Gen. Assembly, 1946; Leader, India Delegation IPR, Mont Tremblant, Dec. 1942; Hon. Editor, Justice, 1927-35; Mem. for Supply, 1943-46, for Planning and Development, 1946, Gov.-Gen's Exec. Council, India; Pres., Economic and Social Council, UN, 1946, re-elected 1947; Leader, Ind. Deleg., UN Maritime Conf., 1948, and Freedom of Information Conf., 1948; Mem., Internat. Civil Service Bd, 1949; Senior Vice-Pres. of the Economic and Social Council, United Nations, 1950, 1951. *Recreation:* golf. *Address:* Kensington, Kilpauk, Madras, S India. *Clubs:* National Liberal, Royal Over-Seas League; Cosmopolitan, Madras, Social (Madras).

**MUDD, (William) David;** MP (C) Falmouth and Camborne since 1970; *b* 2 June 1933; *o s* of Capt. W. N. Mudd and Mrs T. E. Mudd; *m* 1965, Helyn Irvine Smith; one *s* one *d* (and one *sted-d*). *Educ:* Truro Cathedral Sch. Journalist, Broadcaster, TV Commentator; work on BBC and ITV (Westward Television). Became Editor of The Cornish Echo; Staff Reporter, Western Morning News and Tavistock Gazette, 1954-. Mem., Tavistock UDC, 1963-65. *Publication:* Cornishmen and True, 1970. *Recreation:* jig-saw puzzles. *Address:* Field End, South Tehidy, Camborne, Cornwall. *T:* Camborne 2141. *Club:* Brevet Flying.

**MUDIE, Sir (Robert) Francis,** KCSI, *cr* 1945 (CSI 1941); KCIE, *cr* 1944 (CIE 1935); OBE 1919; *b* 24 Aug. 1890; *s* of Patrick Spence Mudie, Dundee, and Margaret Lind Heron; *m* 1st, 1919, Mary Spencer (*d* 1960); one *d*; 2nd, 1960, Mary Elizabeth Abercromby (Kaisar-I-Hind Silver Medal, OStJ, Ghazi-i-Azad Kashmir), *d* of late John Ellison Macqueen. *Educ:* Fettes Coll., Edinburgh; King's Coll., Cambridge. Wrangler, 1911; Asst Master, Clifton, 1911; Eton Coll., 1912-13; entered ICS in 1914 and appointed to Bengal; 2nd Lt 6th City of London Rifles, 1914; Indian Army Reserve of Officers, 1915; Asst Magistrate Jhansi, 1919; Joint Magistrate Benares, 1920; Magistrate and Collector, Agra, Sultanpur, Partabgarh, Fatehgarh, 1922-26; Settlement Officer Agra, 1926-29; Sec. Round Table Conference, 1930-31; Magistrate and Collector, Allahabad, Bulandshahr, Cawnpore, 1931-36; Government of India Secretariat, 1936 and 1937; Collector, Agra, 1937-38; Revenue Sec., UP Govt, 1938-39; Chief Sec. UP Govt, 1939-43; Acting Governor of Bihar, 1943-44; Home Mem., Viceroy's Executive Council, 1944-45; Governor of Sind, 1946-47; Governor of West Punjab, 1947-49; Head of British Economic Mission to Yugoslavia, 1951-54; Chm., Mission of Inquiry into Rubber Industry of Malaya, 1954, of the Commission on the Desert Locust Control Organisation, 1955, and of the British Caribbean Federal Capital Commission, 1956; Mem. of the Commission on the Constitution of the Isle of Man, 1958.

*Publication:* Agricultural Debt in the Agra District; (with Comdr I. M. N. Mudie, RN) The Mudies of Angus; (with D. M. Walker) Mains Castle and the Grahams of Fintry. *Recreations:* formerly riding, motoring, mathematics; now crosswords, patience, local history. *Address:* Easter Cott, Broughty Ferry, Angus. *Club:* Caledonian.

**MUFF,** family name of **Baron Calverley.**

**MUGGERIDGE, Douglas;** Controller, BBC Radio 1 and 2, since 1969; *b* 2 Dec. 1928; *s* of Col Harry Douglas Muggeridge, OBE, and Bertha Ursula Rutland; *m* 1953, Diana Marguerite Hakim; two *d. Educ:* Shrewsbury; London Sch. of Economics. Sub-Editor and Leader-Writer, Liverpool Daily Post, 1953; joined BBC as Talks Producer, 1956; Senior Producer, 1959; Chief Publicity Officer, Overseas, 1961; Chief Asst, Publicity, 1964; Head of Overseas Talks and Features, 1965. *Recreations:* music, fishing, vintage cars. *Address:* Castle Hill Cottage, Rotherfield, Sussex. *T:* Rotherfield 770.

**MUGGERIDGE, Malcolm;** *b* 24 March 1903; *s* of late H. T. Muggeridge; *m* 1927, Katherine, *d* of G. C. Dobbs; two *s* one *d* (and one *s* decd). *Educ:* Selhurst Grammar Sch.; Selwyn Coll., Cambridge. Lecturer at Egyptian Univ., Cairo, 1927-30; Editorial Staff, Manchester Guardian, 1930-32; Manchester Guardian correspondent, Moscow, 1932-33; Asst Editor, Calcutta Statesman, 1934-35; Editorial staff, Evening Standard, 1935-36. Served in War of 1939-45, in East Africa, North Africa, Italy and France, Intelligence Corps, Major (Legion of Hon., Croix de Guerre with Palm, Médaille de la Reconnaissance Française). Daily Telegraph Washington Correspondent, 1946-47; Dep. Editor Daily Telegraph, 1950-52; Editor of Punch, Jan. 1953-Oct. 1957. Rector, Edinburgh Univ., 1967-68. *Publications:* Three Flats, produced by the Stage Society, 1931; Autumnal Face, 1931; Winter in Moscow, 1933; The Earnest Atheist, a life of Samuel Butler, 1936; In A Valley of this Restless Mind, 1938; The Thirties, 1940. Edited English edn Ciano's Diary, 1947. Ciano's Papers, 1948; Affairs of the Heart, 1949; Tread Softly for you Tread on my Jokes, 1966; London à la Mode (with Paul Hogarth), 1966; Muggeridge through the Microphone (Edited by C. Ralling); Jesus Rediscovered, 1969. *Recreation:* walking. *Address:* Park Cottage, Robertsbridge, Sussex. *T:* 596. *Club:* Pratt's.

**MUHAMMAD AHMAD SAID KHAN, Nawab Sir,** of Chhitari, GBE, *cr* 1946 (MBE 1918); KCSI, *cr* 1933; KCIE, *cr* 1928 (CIE 1921); late President Nizam's Executive Council, Hyderabad; Home Member of Governor's Executive Council, United Provinces, 1926; Governor of United Provinces, 1933; Member of council of States. *Address:* Chhitari, Bulandshahr District, United Provinces, India.

**MUIL, Maj.-Gen. David John,** CB 1956; OBE 1945; *b* 18 Oct. 1898; *s* of David Muil, Kirkintilloch, Scotland; *m* 1924, Ruth, *d* of Mark Burgess, Alderley Edge, Cheshire; one *d. Educ:* Aston Grammar Sch.; Birmingham Univ. Served European War, 1917-19, with London Scottish, Royal Warwickshire Regt and RAF (France and Belgium). Joined Royal Army Dental Corps, 1923, and served with them War of 1939-45, in India and Far East; Col, 1949. Dir Army Dental Service, 1955-58. QHDS 1955. *Address:* 4 Courtslands, Court Downs Road, Beckenham, Kent. *T:* 01-650 9060.

**MUIR, Air Commodore Adam,** CB 1967; Medical Officer, Army Careers Office, Glasgow, since 1970; *b* 4 Aug. 1908; *s* of George Muir and Mary Gillies Ferguson; *m* 1938, Isobel Janet Arbuckle Turnbull (*d* 1967); one *s* one *d. Educ:* Greenock Acad.; Glasgow Univ. MA 1929; BSc 1931; MB, ChB (Commend.) 1934; DTM&H (Eng) 1954; MRCPE 1955; FRCPE 1963. Joined RAF Medical Branch, 1937, served War of 1939-45, Iceland and Mediterranean Theatres (despatches twice); Dir of Hygiene and Research, RAF, 1959-63; PMO, RAF Germany, 1963-67; retd, 1967; Officer i/c Reception, BMH Rinteln, 1967-70. CStJ 1966. *Recreations:* reading, travel, golf. *Address:* Clachan, Tighnabruaich, Argyll. *T:* Tighnabruaich 378. *Club:* Royal Air Force.

**MUIR, Alec Andrew,** CBE 1968; DL; Chief Constable of Durham Constabulary since 1967; *b* 21 Aug. 1909; *s* of Dr Robert Douglas Muir, MD, and Edith Muir, The Limes, New Cross, SE14; *m* 1948, Hon. Helen (who *m* 1st, 1935, Wm Farr; marr. diss., 1948), *e d* of 1st and last Baron du Parcq (*d* 1949); one *s* one *d* (and one step *s* one step *d*). *Educ:* Christ's Hosp.; Wadham Coll., Oxford (MA). Receivers' Office, Metropolitan Police, 1933; Metropolitan Police Coll., 1934; Supt, 1948; Chief Constable, Durham Co. Constabulary, 1950. Pres., Forensic Science Soc. Mem., Kennel Club. QMP 1961. DL, Co. Durham, 1964. OStJ 1957. *Recreations:* cricket, bowls, squash, sailing. *Address:* Windywalls, Gatehouse-of-Fleet, Kirkcudbrightshire. *T:* Gatehouse 249. *Clubs:* United University, St John House; County (Durham).

**MUIR, Augustus;** *see* Muir, Charles A.

**MUIR, (Charles) Augustus;** Author and journalist; *b* Carluke, Ontario, Canada; *s* of late Rev. Walter Muir and Elizabeth Carlow; *m* Jean Murray Dow Walker. *Educ:* George Heriot's Sch. and Edinburgh Univ.; contributor to various dailies, weeklies, and monthlies; Asst Editor and subsequently Editor, the World; served 1914-19 in Royal Scots, King's Own Scottish Borderers, and on Staff. *Publications:* The Third Warning; The Blue Bonnet; The Black Pavilion; The Shadow on the Left; The Silent Partner; Birds of the Night; The House of Lies; Beginning the Adventure; Scotland's Road of Romance; The Green Lantern; The Riddle of Garth; Raphael, MD; The Crimson Crescent; Satyr Mask; The Bronze Door; The Red Carnation; The Man Who Stole the Crown Jewels; Castles in the Air; The Sands of Fear; The Intimate Thoughts of John Baxter, Bookseller; Heather-Track and High Road; Joey and the Greenwings; Scottish Portrait; The Story of Jesus for Young People; The History of The Fife Coal Company; The History of the Shotts Iron Company; The History of Michael Nairn and Company; 75 Years–The History of Smith's Stamping Works (Coventry) Ltd and Smith-Clayton Forge Ltd, Lincoln; The History of Blyth, Greene, Jourdain & Co. Ltd, Merchant Bankers; Andersons of Islington–The History of C. F. Anderson & Son Ltd; The History of Churchill & Sim Ltd; The Kenyon Tradition–The History of James Kenyon & Son Ltd; The History of Baker Perkins Ltd; In Blackburne Valley, The History of Bowers Mills; The Shippams of Chichester, Annals of a Family Firm; The Life of the Very Rev. Dr John White, CH; Candlelight in Avalon, A Spiritual Pilgrimage; How to Choose and Enjoy Wine; The First of Foot, The History of The Royal Scots (The Royal Regiment) 1633-1960. Joint-Editor The George Saintsbury Memorial Volume and A Last Vintage. *Recreations:* nearly anything except golf. *Address:* Parkhill, Stansted-Mountfitchet, Essex. *T:* Stansted 2289. *Clubs:*

Savage; Royal Scots, Scottish Arts (Edinburgh).

**MUIR, Sir David (John),** Kt 1961; CMG 1959; FCIS, FASA, FAIM, AAUQ; Director of Industrial Development, Queensland, since 1964; *b* 20 June 1916; *s* of John Arthur and Grace Elizabeth Muir, Brisbane; *m* 1942, Joan Howarth; one *s* one *d*. *Educ:* Kangaroo Point State Sch.; State Commercial High Sch., Brisbane. Entered Qld Public Service, 1932, as Clerk in Dept of Public Lands; transf. to Premier's Dept, 1938. Made special study of problems associated with production and marketing of sugar. Permanent Under Sec., Premier and Chief Secretary's Dept, 1948; also Clerk of Exec. Council of Qld and Mem. of State Stores Bd. Agent General for Qld in London and Australian Govt Rep. on Internat. Sugar Council, 1951 (Chm. 1958); Pres., Chartered Institute of Secretaries, 1964. Chm., Queensland Theatre Co. Bd, 1969. James N. Kirby Medal, InstProdE, Australia, 1969. JP. *Recreations:* gardening and golf. *Address:* Department of Industrial Development, Administration Buildings, Elizabeth Street, Brisbane 4000, Australia.

**MUIR, Sir Edward (Francis),** KCB 1956 (CB 1950); FSA 1959; *b* 29 June 1905; *o s* of late W. E. Muir, JP; *m* 1928, Evelyn Mary Whitfield (*d* 1964); one *s* one *d*. *Educ:* Bradfield Coll.; Corpus Christi Coll., Oxford. BA, 1927, MA 1930; entered HM Office of Works, 1927; Under-Sec., 1946-51; Deputy Sec., Ministry of Materials, 1951-54; Ministry of Works, 1954-56; Permanent Secretary: Ministry of Works, 1956-62; Ministry of Public Building and Works, 1962-65. Chm., Assoc. of First Div. Civil Servants, 1948-49; Liveryman of the Worshipful Company of Fan Makers, 1936; Master, 1958. Governor, Central Foundation Schs of London, 1958-68. Pres., Haslemere Educational Museum, 1964; Mem. Standing Commission on Museums and Galleries, 1965; Chairman: Ancient Monuments Board for England, 1966-; Conf. on Training Architects in Conservation, 1969; A Trustee, Oxford Historic Buildings Fund, 1967; Vice-Chm., Fedn of Sussex Amenity Socs, 1968; Mem., Redundant Churches Fund, 1969. Hon. Fellow Corpus Christi Coll., Oxford, 1965-. *Address:* Muirfield, Haslemere, Surrey. *T:* Haslemere 2931. *Clubs:* Athenæum, United University.

**MUIR, Sir Edward (Grainger),** Kt 1970; Surgeon to The Queen since 1964 (formerly Surgeon to HM Household); Senior Surgeon: King's College Hospital; Queen Victoria Hospital, East Grinstead; King Edward VII Hospital for Officers; *b* 18 Feb. 1906; *s* of Dr D. D. Muir; *m* 1929, Estelle Russell; two *s*. *Educ:* Eltham Coll.; Middlesex Hospital. MRCS, LRCP, 1927; MBBS, 1928; FRCS, 1931; MS(London) Gold Medal, 1932; Hon. FRACS. Served in RAMC, 1940-45. Fellow and Hon. Treas. Royal Society of Medicine; Fellow and late Pres., Med. Soc. London. Mem. Court of Examiners and Mem. of Council, RCS; Examiner in Surgery to Univs of Oxford, Cambridge and London; Mem. Army Medical Advisory Board; Cons. Surgeon to the Army. *Publications:* Carcinoma of the Colon, 1961; articles in various medical journals and textbooks. *Address:* 149 Harley Street, W1. *T:* 01-935 4444. *Club:* Athenæum.

**MUIR, Ernest,** CMG 1948; CIE 1937; MD, FRCSE; LLD (Hong Kong); retired; Hon. Medical Adviser British Leprosy Relief Association, 1947-65 (Medical Section, 1935-47); *b* 17 June 1880; *s* of Rev. G. S. Muir; *m* Sophie Vartan (*d* 1961); one *s* one *d*. *Educ:* George Watson's Coll. and University, Edinburgh. Medical Missionary of UFC Church in Kalna, Bengal, 1905-20; Research Worker in Leprosy, Sch. of Tropical Medicine, Calcutta, 1920-35; Medical Superintendent Leper Settlement, Chacachacare, 1940-45. Hon. Sec. Internat. Leprosy Assoc., 1935-54, 1956-58. Kaisar-i-Hind, 1st Class, 1921, and bar, 1932. *Publications:* Handbook of Kala Azar; Handbook of Leprosy; Kala Azar (with Dr Napier); Leprosy (with Sir L. Rogers) 3rd ed. 1946; Manual of Leprosy, 1948. *Address:* 39 Hersham Road, Walton-on-Thames, Surrey.

**MUIR, Frank;** writer and broadcaster; primarily a manufacturer of wit-substitute; *b* 5 Feb. 1920; *s* of Charles James Muir and Margaret Harding; *m* 1949, Polly McIrvine; one *s* one *d*. *Educ:* Chatham House, Ramsgate; Leyton County High Sch. Served RAF, 1940-46. Wrote radio comedy-series and compered TV progs, 1946. With Denis Norden, 1947-64; collaborated for 17 years writing comedy scripts, including: (for radio): Take it from Here, 1947-58; Bedtime with Braden, 1950-54; (for TV): And so to Bentley, 1956; Whack-O,! 1958-60; The Seven Faces of Jim, 1961, and other series with Jimmy Eddwards; resident in TV and radio panel-games; collaborated in film scripts, television commercials, and revues (Prince of Wales, 1951; Adelphi, 1952); joint Advisors and Consultants to BBC Television Light Entertainment Dept, 1960-64; jointly received Screenwriters Guild Award for Best Contribution to Light Entertainment, 1961; together on panel-games My Word!, 1956-67, and My Music, 1967-. Asst Head of BBC Light Entertainment Gp, 1964-67; Head of Entertainment, London Weekend Television, 1968-69, resigned 1969, and reverted to being self-unemployed. *Recreations:* book collecting, staring silently into space. *Address:* Anners, Thorpe, Egham, Surrey. *T:* Chertsey 2759. *Club:* Savile.

**MUIR, John Cochran,** CMG 1951; OBE 1944; retired; Colonial Agricultural Service; Member for Agriculture and Natural Resources, Tanganyika, 1949; *b* 1902; *m* 1936, Cathey, *d* of Maurice Hincks; one *s* two *d*. *Educ:* Allan Glen's Sch.; West of Scotland Agricultural Coll.; Univ. of Glasgow. BSc (agric.); National Diploma in Agriculture; National Diploma in Dairying. Asst Superintendent, Agriculture, Gold Coast, 1925; Senior Agricultural Officer, Zanzibar, 1935; Dir of Agriculture, 1941; Trinidad, 1944; Tanganyika, 1948. *Address:* Peacock Farm, Wicken, Ely, Cambs.

**MUIR, Sir John (Harling),** 3rd Bt, *cr* 1892; TD; DL; Chairman: James Finlay & Co. Ltd, Glasgow, since 1961 (Director 1946-); Scottish Canadian Oil and Trasportation; Director: London and Lancashire Insurance Co. Ltd; Royal Insurance Co. Ltd; National and Grindlay's Bank; Scottish United Investors Ltd; Forth River Purification Board (Chairman), etc; Member, Queen's Body Guard for Scotland (The Royal Company of Archers); *b* 7 Nov. 1910; *s* of James Finlay Muir (*d* 1948), Braco Castle, Perthshire, and of Charlotte Escudier, *d* of J. Harling Turner, CBE; *S* uncle 1951; *m* 1936, Elizabeth Mary, *e d* of late Frederick James Dundas, Dale Cottage, Cawthorne, near Barnsley; five *s* two *d*. *Educ:* Stowe. With James Finlay & Co. Ltd, in. India, 1932-40. Served War of 1939-45; joined 3rd Carabiniers, Sept. 1940, Lieut; transferred 25th Dragoons, 1941, Capt.; Major, 1942; transferred RAC Depot, Poona, i/c Sqdn, 1942; transferred to Staff, HQ 109 L of C Area, Bangalore; held various Staff appointments terminating as AA and QMG with actg rank of Lt-Col; demobilised, 1946, with rank of Major. DL, Perthshire, 1966. *Recreations:* shooting and fishing. *Heir: s*

Richard James Kay Muir [*b* 25 May 1939; *m* 1965, Susan Elizabeth, *d* of G. A. Gardner, Leamington Spa; two *d*]. *Address:* Blair Drummond, by Stirling, Perthshire. *T:* Doune 207. *Clubs:* Oriental, English-Speaking Union; Western (Glasgow); Tollygunge (Calcutta).
*See also Col Sir J. R. Aird, Bt.*

**MUIR, Professor Kenneth;** FBA 1970; King Alfred Professor of English Literature, University of Liverpool, since 1951; *b* 1907; *s* of Dr R. D. Muir; *m* 1936, Mary Ewen; one *s* one *d*. *Educ:* Epsom Coll.; St Edmund Hall, Oxford. Lecturer in English, St John's Coll., York, 1930-37; Lecturer in English Literature, Leeds Univ., 1937-51; Public Orator, 1961-65; Dean of the Faculty of Arts, 1958-61; Visiting Professor, Univ. of Pittsburgh, 1962-63. Editor, Shakespeare Survey, 1966-. Leeds City Councillor, 1945-47, 1950-51; Chm. of Leeds Fabian Soc., 1941-46; Pres., Leeds Labour Party, 1951; Birkenhead Borough Councillor, 1954-57. Docteur de l'Université de Rouen, 1967. *Publications:* The Nettle and the Flower, 1933; Jonah in the Whale, 1935; (with Sean O'Loughlin) The Voyage to Illyria, 1937; English Poetry, 1938; Collected Poems of Sir Thomas Wyatt, 1949; Arden edn Macbeth, 1951; King Lear, 1952; Elizabethan Lyrics, 1953; (edited) Wilkins' Painful Adventures of Pericles, 1953; John Milton, 1955; The Pelican Book of English Prose I, 1956; Shakespeare's Sources, 1957; (edited with F. P. Wilson) The Life and Death of Jack Straw, 1957; (edited) John Keats, 1958; Shakespeare and the Tragic Pattern, 1959; trans. Five Plays of Jean Racine, 1960; Shakespeare as Collaborator, 1960; editor Unpublished Poems by Sir Thomas Wyatt, 1961; Last Periods, 1961; (ed) U. Ellis-Fermor's Shakespeare the Dramatist, 1961; (ed) Richard II, 1963; Life and Letters of Sir Thomas Wyatt, 1963; Shakespeare: Hamlet, 1963; (ed) Shakespeare: The Comedies, 1965; Introduction to Elizabethan Literature, 1967; (ed) Othello, 1968; (ed) The Winter's Tale, 1968; (ed with Patricia Thomson) Collected Poems of Sir Thomas Wyatt, 1969; The Comedy of Manners, 1970; (ed) Double Falsehood, 1970; contributions to Penguin New Writing, Shakespeare Survey (Editor, 1965-), etc. *Recreations:* acting, producing plays, local government. *Address:* 6 Chetwynd Road, Oxton, Birkenhead, Cheshire. *T:* 051-652 3301.

**MUIR, Percival Horace;** Managing Director, Elkin Mathews Ltd, since 1939, Director since 1930; *b* 17 Dec. 1894; *s* of Charles Henry Muir and Annie Hancock; *m* 1935, Barbara Kenrick Gowing (pen-name Barbara Kay); one *s* one *d*. *Educ:* LCC primary and secondary Schs. After varied career in business and as lecturer, journalist and actor, set up on own account as antiquarian bookseller, 1920; joined Dulau & Co. Ltd, as Dir, 1927; Elkin Mathews Ltd, 1930. Chm., Collector Ltd. President: Antiquarian Booksellers' Assoc., 1945-47; Internat. League of Antiquarian Booksellers, 1948-50, thereafter life Pres. of Honour; Hon. Life Mem. Nat. Book League. *Publications:* Points, being extracts from a bibliographer's scrapbook, 1931, 2nd series 1934; Book Collecting, Vol. I, 1944, Vol. II, 1949; English Children's Books, 1954 (new edn, 1969); Minding My Own Business, 1956. Editor and part-author, Talks on Book Collecting, 1952; Printing and the Mind of Man, 1967; Victorian Book Illustration, 1970. *Recreations:* bibliography, music, gardening. *Address:* Taylors, Takeley, Bishop's Stortford, Herts. *T:* Takeley 312.

**MUIR MACKENZIE, Sir Robert (Henry),** 6th Bt, *cr* 1805; *b* 6 Jan. 1917; *s* of Sir Robert Cecil Muir Mackenzie, MC, 5th Bt and Kate Brenda Blodwen (she *m* 2nd, 1929, Major John Campbell-Holberton, who *d* 1962; she *d* 1958), *d* of late Henry Jones, Cardiff; *S* father, 1918; *m* 1st, 1947, Charmian Cecil de Vere (*d* 1962), *widow* of Brig. W. G. Glencairn-Campbell, OBE, and *o d* of Col and Mrs Cecil Brinton, Yew Tree House, Belbroughton, Worcestershire; one *s* one *d*; 2nd, 1963, Mrs J. G. Turner, 98 Mount Street, W1. *Educ:* Marlborough; New Coll., Oxford. Served War of 1939-45, RA, reaching rank of GSO3 (wounded, despatches). *Heir:* *s* Alexander Alwyne Brinton Muir Mackenzie, *b* 8 Dec. 1955. *Address:* Kingsdene, Hampstead Lane, NW3. *T:* 01-455 9121.

**MUIRHEAD, David Francis,** CMG 1964; CVO 1957; HM Diplomatic Service; HM Ambassador to Portugal since 1970; *b* 30 Dec. 1918; *s* of late David Muirhead, Kippen, Stirlingshire; *m* 1942, Hon. Elspeth Hope-Morley, *d* of 2nd Baron Hollenden, *qv*; two *s* one *d*. *Educ:* Cranbrook Sch. Commissioned Artists Rifles (Rifle Brigade), 1937; passed Officers Exam., RMC Sandhurst; apptd to Bedfs and Herts Regt, 1939; served War of 1939-45 in France, Belgium and SE Asia. Hon. Attaché, Brit. Embassy, Madrid, 1941. Passed Foreign Service Exam., 1946; appointed to Foreign Office, 1947; La Paz, 1948; Buenos Aires, 1950; Brussels, 1950; Foreign Office, 1953; Washington, 1955; Foreign Office, 1959; Head of Personnel Dept, DSAO, 1965; Under-Sec., Special Planning Duties, Foreign Office, 1966-67; Ambassador to Peru, 1967-70. *Recreations:* tennis, badminton, cricket. *Address:* British Embassy, Lisbon, Portugal; 16 Pitt Street, W8. *T:* 01-937 2443. *Club:* Travellers'.

**MUIRHEAD, Sir John (Spencer),** Kt, *cr* 1953; DSO 1918; MC; TD; Vice-Lieutenant of Stirlingshire, 1960-64; Brigadier (retired); solicitor; Hon. President George Outram and Co. Ltd (late Chairman); President, Law Society of Scotland, 1950; Dean Royal Faculty of Procurators in Glasgow, 1952; Member Royal Commission on University Education in Dundee, 1951; Member Royal Commission on Scottish Affairs, 1952; Chairman St Andrews University Statutory Commissioners, 1953; Member of the Queen's Body Guard for Scotland (The Royal Company of Archers); Chairman City of Glasgow T&AFA, 1950; Lecturer in Roman Law, Glasgow University, 1920-54; Secretary Glasgow University Court, 1937-45; *b* 19 April 1889; *s* of James Muirhead and Robina Spencer; *m* 1917, Geraldine, *d* of late Maxwell Hedderwick, Glasgow; two *s* one *d* (and one *s* decd). *Educ:* St Ninians, Moffat; Fettes Coll., Edinburgh; Oriel Coll., Oxford (Classical Scholar); Glasgow Univ. BA Oxon 1912 (1st Class Class. Mods; 1st Class Lit. Hum.), MA Oxon 1952, LLB Glasgow 1919, Hon. LLD: Edinburgh, 1951; St Andrews, 1968; Hon. Fellow, Oriel Coll., Oxford, 1962. 2nd Lt RE, TF, 1912; OC VI Corps Signals, 1915, 51st (Highland) Div. Signals, 1917; served with BEF, 1915-19 (despatches thrice); OC 52nd (Lowland) Division Signals, 1922-29, Dep. CSO, Scottish Comd, 1929-32; OC Glasgow Univ. OTC, 1931-33; OC 74th HAA Regt RA, 1938; Brig. Comdg 2nd, 4th and 1st AA Bdes, in MEF, 1940-42 (despatches twice); BAS, Washington, USA, 1942-44. DL Stirlingshire, 1936. *Address:* 10 Clarendon Place, Stirling. *T:* Stirling 343. *Clubs:* Western (Glasgow); New (Edinburgh).

**MUIRHEAD, (Litellus) Russell,** MA; FSA; FSG; Consulting Editor of the Blue Guides, 1963-65 (Editor, 1930-63); Director Ernest Benn Ltd, 1951-63; *b* 1896; *s* of late Findlay Muirhead, Edinburgh and London, and Mary Clench, St Mary's, Ontario, Canada; *m* 1923, Benedetta, *o d* of Didier Lagneau, Paris; one *s*. *Educ:* University Coll. Sch.; Christ's Coll., Cambridge. Served in Gallipoli, Macedonia, Palestine, France (Royal Irish Fusiliers), 1915-19; Asst Editor of the Blue Guides, 1921; Editor of Discovery, 1934-38; Editor of The Chemical Age, 1939-46; Editor of the Penguin Guides, 1938-49; Broadcast series of talks and television programmes on exploring London, etc., 1938-39 and 1949. Served in London Home Guard, 1940-44; Member Council: British Archæological Assoc., 1950-60, 1962; Soc. of Genealogists, 1955-62, 1963-67; Brit. Record Soc., 1959; London Topographical Soc., 1969. *Publications:* Blue Guides to England, Scotland, Wales, Ireland, France, Italy, Spain, Holland, Switzerland, others of the series with late Findlay Muirhead; articles and book reviews in the Fortnightly, the Times, Sunday Times, etc. *Recreations:* archaeology, travel. *Address:* 87 Addison Road, W14. *T:* 01-603 8150. *Club:* Garrick.

**MUIRSHIEL,** 1st Viscount, *cr* 1964, of Kilmacolm; **John Scott Maclay,** PC 1952; CH 1962; CMG 1944; Lord Lieutenant of Renfrewshire since 1967; *b* 26 Oct. 1905; *s* of 1st Baron Maclay, PC; *m* 1930, Betty L'Estrange Astley. *Educ:* Winchester; Trinity Coll., Cambridge. MP (Nat. L and C) for Montrose Burghs, 1940-50, for Renfrewshire West, 1950-64. Head of Brit. Merchant Shipping Mission, Washington, 1944; Parliamentary Sec., Min. of Production, May-July 1945; Minister of Transport and Civil Aviation, 1951-52; Minister of State for Colonial Affairs, Oct. 1956-Jan. 1957; Sec. of State for Scotland, Jan. 1957-July 1962. Pres., National Liberal Council, 1957-67; Chm., Joint Exchequer Board for Northern Ireland, 1965-. Dir, Clydesdale Bank, 1970-. Hon. LLD: Edinburgh Univ., 1963; Strathclyde, 1966; Glasgow, 1970. *Heir:* none. *Address:*Knapps, Kilmacolm, Renfrewshire. *T:* Kilmacolm 2770. *Clubs:* Boodle's; Western (Glasgow); Royal Yacht Squadron.

**MUKERJEE, Most Rev. Arabinda Nath,** DD; *b* 23 May 1892; Indian; *m* 1919, Pronoy Protima Pyne; five *s* three *d*. *Educ:* Univ. of Calcutta. Headmaster, St Stephen's High Sch., 1919-25; deacon, 1923; priest, 1924; Principal, Delhi United Christian High Sch., 1926-36; Financial Sec., Cambridge Mission to Delhi, 1936-39; Head of Cambridge and SPG Mission, 1939-44; Canon of Lahore Cathedral, 1940-44; Asst Bishop of Lahore and Archdeacon of Delhi, 1944-47; Bishop of Delhi, 1947-50; Bishop of Calcutta and Metropolitan of India, Pakistan, Burma and Ceylon, 1950-62, retired. Episcopal Canon of St George's Cathedral, Jerusalem, 1948. Hon. DD Univ. of Toronto, 1954. DD Lambeth, 1958. *Address:* Hill Crest, Nagpur 1, Maharastra, India.

**MULCAHY, General Richard;** *b* Waterford, 10 May 1886; *m* 1919, Mary Josephine, *d* of John Ryan, Tomcoole, Wexford; three *s* three *d*. *Educ:* Irish Christian Brothers. Civil Service, 1903-16; took part in Irish Rising, 1916; Chief of Staff, Irish Volunteers, 1918-21; Minister for Defence, Ireland, 22 Jan.-2 April 1919; Asst Minister for Defence, 1919-21; Minister for Defence, 1922-24; Commander-in-Chief, National Forces, 1922-23; Minister for Local Government and Public Health, 1927-32; Pres. Fine Gael Party, 1944-60; Minister for Education, 1948-51; Minister for Education, 1954-57, and Minister for Gaeltacht, 1956-57. MP (SF) Clontarf Division of Dublin, 1918-22; Mem. of Dail, North City, Dublin, 1921-37, 1938-43, Co. Tipperary, 1944-61; Chm. of Commission of Enquiry into Irish Speaking Districts, 1925. *Address:* 1 Temple Villas, Palmerston Road, Dublin.

**MULGRAVE, Earl of; Constantine Edmund Walter Phipps;** *b* 24 Feb. 1954; *s* and *heir* of 4th Marquis of Normanby, *qv*.

**MULHALL, John Archibald,** CMG 1953; OBE 1947; retired; *b* 19 July 1899; *s* of late Robert Mulhall, Southampton; *m* 1936, Eleanor Beatrice Olive, *e d* of late Harry Arthur Webb; no *c*. *Educ:* University Coll., London (BSc). Served European War, 1916-18, 8th City of London Regt. Entered Ceylon Civil Service, 1921; Asst Colonial Sec., Ceylon, 1928; Asst Chief Sec., 1931; Actg Dep. Chief Sec., 1943; Sec. to C-in-C, Ceylon, 1943; Sec. to Governor, Ceylon, 1944; Sec. to Governor-General, Ceylon, 1948; Chm., Public Service Commission, Ghana, 1951; retired, 1957; reported on establishment of a Public Service Commission in Cyprus, March 1957. *Publication:* The Public Service Commission in Overseas Territories, 1962. *Recreations:* golf and ski-ing. *Address:* Banister's, Burley, Ringwood, Hants. *Clubs:* East India and Sports, royal Commonwealth Society.

**MULHOLLAND,** family name of **Baron Dunleath.**

**MULHOLLAND, Rt. Hon. Sir Henry George Hill,** PC (NIre) 1930; 1st Bt, *cr* 1945; MP County Down, Northern Ireland, 1921-29, Ards since 1929; HM Lieutenant for Co. Londonderry, 1961-65; *b* 20 Dec. 1888; 2nd *surv. s* of 2nd Baron Dunleath and *heir-pres.* to 4th Baron Dunleath, *qv*; *m* 1914, Sheelah, *d* of Sir Douglas Brooke, 4th Bt of Colebrooke, Co. Fermanagh; one *s* one *d*. *Educ:* Eton; Trinity Coll., Cambridge, BA. Served European War, 1914-19; Lt RAF; Asst Parliamentary Sec. to Ministry of Finance, Northern Ireland, 1926-29; Speaker House of Commons of Northern Ireland, 1929-45; National Governor, BBC, for Northern Ireland, 1952-58, retired. *Recreations:* cricket, golf, shooting. *Heir:* *s* Major Michael Mulholland, Oxford and Bucks Light Infantry [*b* 15 Oct. 1915; *m* 1st, 1942, Rosemary Ker (marriage dissolved, 1948); 2nd, 1949, Elizabeth Hyde; one *s*]. *Address:* Ballyscullion Park, Bellaghy, Co. Derry. *T:* Bellaghy 235.

**MULHOLLAND, Hon. Mrs John, (Olivia Vernon),** CVO 1958; Woman of the Bed Chamber to Queen Elizabeth The Queen Mother since 1950; Chairman Elizabeth Garret Anderson Hospital since 1945; Vice-Chairman Royal Free Hospital Group, 1950-61; Member: North London Group Hospital Management Committee, 1961; King Edward's Hospital Fund Management Committee, 1961; *b* 1902; 2nd *d* of 1st Viscount Harcourt and Mary Ethel, Viscountess Harcourt, GBE, *o d* of Walter Haynes Burns, New York and North Mymms Park, Hatfield; *m* 1923, Hon. (Godfrey) John A. M. L. Mulholland (*d* 1948), *y s* of 2nd Baron Dunleath, Ballywalter Park, Co. Down, N Ireland; one *s* two *d*. *Educ:* Notting Hill High Sch.; Lady Margaret Hall, Oxford. *Address:* Weston Mark, Upton Grey, Basingstoke, Hants. *T:* Long Sutton 429.

**MULHOLLAND, Sir (William) Walter,** Kt 1956; OBE 1946; retired Sept. 1961; Member of New Zealand Meat Producers' Board, 1943-61, and of Wheat Committee, since 1936; Director, Meat Export Development Co., 1960-61; *b* Darfield, 1887; *s* of D. Mulholland; *m* 1915, Daisy Eveline Campbell; two *s* one *d* (and one *s* one *d* decd). *Educ:* Darfield. Managed father's farm until 1913 when started farming own 506-acre farm at Darfield; bought land and built new homestead at Ladybank, Darfield, 1920. Branch Sec., Farmers' Union, 1904; served continuously in various offices in this, and its successor, Federated Farmers of NZ (Life Mem.). Formerly Dir NZ Wheatgrowers Co-operative Assoc. (Chm.); Dir, United Wheatgrowers (NZ) Ltd (past Chm.); Dominion President: NZ Farmers' Union (1936 until dissolution); NZ Federated Farmers (1946) and Mem. Dominion Council from its formation, 1944; Chm. Cttee of Meat Industry Research Inst. of NZ, 1955-62; Foundn Mem. Cttee of Wheat Research Inst. of NZ. *Publications:* articles, letters and reports on farm politics, economics and practice. *Recreations:* fishing, photography. *Address:* 6 Maxwell Street, Darfield, Canterbury, New Zealand. *T:* 272 Darfield.

**MULLALY, Terence Frederick Stanley;** Art Critic of The Daily Telegraph since 1958; *b* 14 Nov. 1927; *s* of Col B. R. Mullaly (4th *s* of Maj.-Gen. Sir Herbert Mullaly, KCMG, CB, CSI) and Eileen Dorothy (*née* Stanley); *m* 1949, Elizabeth Helen (*née* Burkitt). *Educ:* in India, England, Japan and Canada; Downing Coll., Cambridge (MA). Archæological studies in Tripolitania, 1948, and Sicily, 1949; has specialised in study of Italian art, particularly Venetian and Veronese painting of 16th and 17th centuries; lecturer and broadcaster. Pres. Brit. Section, Internat. Assoc. of Art Critics, 1967. FRSA 1969. Cavaliere Ufficiale, Order Al Merito, Italy, 1964. *Publications:* Ruskin a Verona, 1966; The Corridors of Art, 1970; Contribs on history of art, to Burlington Magazine, etc. *Recreations:* collecting and travel. *Address:* 74 Greencroft Gardens, Hampstead, NW6. *T:* 01-624 8531.

**MULLAN, Charles Heron;** MA; VRD 1952; Resident Magistrate; Lieutenant-Commander RNVR; retired, 1951; *b* 17 Feb. 1912; *s* of Frederick Heron Mullan, BA, DL, Solicitor, and Minnie Mullan; *m* 1940, Marcella Elizabeth Sharpe McCullagh; one *s. Educ:* Castle Park, Dalkey; Rossall Sch., Fleetwood; Clare Coll., Cambridge. Hons Degree Law, Cambridge, 1934; MA 1939. Joined Ulster Div. RNVR, 1936; called up for active service with Royal Navy, Aug. 1939; served throughout the war (King Haakon VII War Decoration), HMS Rodney 1939-40; escort vessels, North Sea, North Atlantic, etc, 1940-44 (with Royal Norwegian Navy, 1941-43). MP (UU) Co. Down, 1946-50, Imperial Parl.; contested S Down, 1945, for NI Parl. Mem. Ulster Unionist Council, 1946-60. Solicitor 1948; Resident Magistrate, 1960; JP 1960; Chm., Belfast Juvenile Courts, 1964. Mem., N Ireland Section of British Delegn to 3rd UN Congress on Prevention of Crime and Treatment of Offenders, Stockholm, 1965. *Recreations:* tennis, shooting, walking, boating. *Address:* Cairn Hill, Newry, Co. Down, Northern Ireland. *T:* 2003; Casanbarra, Ballycastle, Co. Antrim, Northern Ireland. *T:* 323.

**MULLENS, Sir Harold (Hill),** Kt 1963; President, Reyrolle Parsons Ltd; Deputy Chairman, The Nuclear Power Plant Co. Ltd; Director: Dorman Long (Africa) Ltd; Northern Regional Board, Lloyds Bank Ltd; *b* 19 Feb. 1900; *s* of Harry Joseph Mullens and Gertrude Charlotte (*née* Hill); *m* 1932, Winifred McConnell; one *s* one *d. Educ:* Merchant Taylors' Sch.; Durham Univ. (BSc). Joined North Eastern Electric Supply Co. Ltd, 1924 and held various appointments from asst engineer to deputy General Manager until nationalisation of electricity supply industry. Chm. of North Eastern Electricity Board, 1948-54, when resigned to become Managing Dir of A. Reyrolle & Co. Ltd; Chairman: A. Reyrolle & Co. Ltd, 1958-68; C. A. Parsons & Co. Ltd, 1960-68; Reyrolle Parsons Ltd, 1968; Anglo Great Lakes Corp. Ltd, 1959-68; Sir Howard Grubb Parsons & Co. Ltd, 1960-66; The Bushing Co. Ltd, 1958-70; Director: Parolle Electrical Plant Co. Ltd, 1959-68; Pyrotenax Ltd, 1959-67; Dorman Long & Co. Ltd, and subsids, 1955-67; Internat. Research & Develt Co., 1963-68; The Nuclear Power Group Ltd, 1965-68. Mem. of British Electricity Authority, 1952-53. Vice-Pres. of British Electrical Development Assoc., 1956-59. Pres., British Electrical and Allied Manufacturers' Association, 1962-63; Pres., British Electrical Power Convention, 1963-64. Chm. Governors, Rutherford Coll., 1959-61. Hon. Col 105 Corps Engineer Regt Royal Engineers (TA), 1955-57. *Publications:* technical papers. *Recreations:* gardening and golf. *Address:* 4 Westfield Grove, Gosforth, Newcastle upon Tyne. *T:* Gosforth 854297. *Clubs:* Devonshire; Union (Newcastle).

**MULLENS, Sir William (John Herbert de Wette),** Kt 1963; DSO 1940 and Bar, 1945; TD 1944; DL; Senior Government Broker, 1950-62; *b* 21 July 1909; *s* of late William Herbert Mullens, DL, JP; *m* 1948, Bridget, *d* of D. W. Berdoe-Wilkinson; one *s* one step *d. Educ:* Harrow. Served War of 1939-45 in Kent Yeomanry (despatches twice, DSO and Bar). Treas., Univ. of Surrey, 1966-; Dep. Chm., General Practice Finance Corporation, 1966-. High Sheriff of Surrey, 1964; DL 1966. Chm., SE TA&VRA. *Recreations:* shooting, golf. *Address:* Whiteways, Guildford, Surrey. *T:* 3752. *Clubs:* Carlton, Boodle's, Turf, Pratt's.

**MULLER, Dr Hilgard;** Minister of Foreign Affairs, South Africa, since 1964; MP for Beaufort West since 1964; *b* 4 May 1914; *s* of C. J. Muller; *m* 1943, Nita Dyason; one *s. Educ:* Pretoria Univ.; Oxford Univ.; DLitt Pretoria, BLitt Oxon., LLB S Africa. Rhodes Scholar, 1937; Univ. Lecturer, Pretoria, 1941-47. Solicitor, 1947-61; Dir of Companies and farmer. Mayor of Pretoria, 1953-55; MP for Pretoria East, 1958-61; High Commissioner for Union of South Africa in the UK, Jan.-May, 1961; South African Ambassador to the Court of St James's, 1961-63. Chancellor of the Univ. of Pretoria, 1965-, formerly Pres. of Convocation. PhD (*hc*) Stellenbosch. *Recreations:* golf, farming. *Address:* Department of Foreign Affairs, Pretoria, South Africa. *Clubs:* various in South Africa.

**MULLETT, Leslie Baden;** Chief Scientific Officer, Ministry of Transport, since 1968; *b* 22 Aug. 1920; *s* of Joseph and Edith Mullett; *m* 1946, Katherine Lear (marr. diss. 1968); no *c. Educ:* Gram. Sch., Hales Owen, Worcs; Birmingham Univ. BSc (Hons Physics) 1941. Telecommunications Research Estab., 1941-46; AEA, 1946-60 (Head of Accelerator Div., 1958); Asst Dir, Rutherford High Energy Lab., SRC, 1960-; on secondment to Res. Gp, Ministry of Technology, 1966-68; Ministry of Transport, 1968-. *Publications:* papers in learned jls on particle accelerators. *Recreations:* fishing, caravanning. *Address:* 22 Wellington Court, Spencers Wood, Reading, Berks. *T:* (business) 01-928 7999.

**MULLEY, Rt. Hon. Frederick William,** PC 1964; MP (Lab) Park Division of Sheffield since 1950; Barrister-at-law and economist; *b* 3 July 1918; *er s* of late William and M. A. Mulley, Leamington Spa; *m* 1948, Joan D., *d* of Alexander and Betty Phillips; two *d. Educ:* Bath Place Church of England Sch.; Warwick Sch. (Schol.); Christ Church, Oxford (Adult Scholar, 1945). 1st Class Hons Philosophy, Politics and Economics, 1947; Research Studentship, Nuffield Coll., Oxford, 1947; Fellowship (Economics), St Catharine's Coll., Cambridge, 1948-50. Called to Bar, Inner Temple, 1954. Son of general labourer; clerk,

National Health Insurance Cttee, Warwicks; joined Labour Party and Nat. Union of Clerks, 1936. Served War of 1939-45, Worcs Regt; Lance-Sgt 1940 (prisoner of war in Germany, 1940-45, meanwhile obtaining BSc (Econ.) and becoming Chartered Sec.). Contested (Lab) Sutton Coldfield Division of Warwicks, 1945. Parliamentary delegation to Germany, 1951, and to Kenya, 1957; Parliamentary Private Sec. to Minister of Works, 1951; National Exec. Cttee, Labour Party, 1957-58, 1960-64, 1965-; Editorial Cttee, Socialist Commentary; Delegate to Council of Europe and WEU, 1958-61, also Vice-Pres. Economic Cttee and Vice-Pres. WEU Assembly, 1960. Deputy Defence Sec. and Minister for the Army, 1964-65; Minister of Aviation, Dec. 1965-Jan. 1967; Jt Minister of State, FCO (formerly FO), 1967-69; Minister for Disarmament, 1967-69; Minister of Transport, 1969-70. *Publications:* The Politics of Western Defence, 1962; articles on economic, defence and socialist subjects. *Address:* 192 Sutherland Avenue, W9.

**MULLIGAN, Col Hugh Waddell,** CMG 1954; MD, DSc; Visiting Lecturer, Department of Biology, University of Salford; *b* 13 Nov. 1901; *s* of late Rev. J. A. W. Mulligan and Jem Anderson; *m* Rita, *d* of late J. E. Armstrong; two *s* one *d*. *Educ:* Robert Gordon's Coll., Aberdeen; Aberdeen Univ. MB, ChB 1923; MD (Hons) Aberdeen 1930; DSc, 1934, IMS, 1923-47. Served War of 1939-45 (active service, 1940-43). Commonwealth Fund Fellow, Univ. Chicago, 1933-35. Dir Pasteur Inst. of Southern India, 1938-40; Dir, Central Research Inst., Kasauli, 1944-47; Dir, West African Inst. for Trypanosomiasis Research (Colonial Research Service), 1947-54; Dir and Head of Biological Division, Wellcome Research Laboratories, Beckenham, Kent, 1954-66. *Publications:* papers on protozoology, immunology, pathology, etc. *Recreations:* fishing, shooting, gardening. *Address:* 5 Thorngrove Road, Wilmslow, Cheshire. *T:* Wilmslow 22579.

**MULLIGAN, Most Rev. Patrick;** *see* Clogher, Bishop of, (RC).

**MULLIKEN, Prof. Robert S.,** PhD; Professor of Physics and Chemistry, University of Chicago; *b* Newburyport, Mass, 7 June 1896; *s* of Samuel Parsons Mulliken, Prof. of Organic Chemistry, and Katherine (*née* Mulliken); *m* 1929, Mary Helen von Noé; two *d*. *Educ:* Massachusetts Inst. of Technology; Univ. of Chicago. BS (MIT), 1917; PhD (Chicago), 1921. Nat. Research Coun. Fellow, Univ. of Chicago, and Harvard Univ., 1921-25; Guggenheim Fellow, Europe, 1930 and 1932-33; Fulbright Scholar, Oxford Univ., 1952-54; Vis. Fellow, St John's Coll., Oxford, 1952-53. Jun. Chem. Engr, Bureau of Mines, US Dept of Interior, Washington, 1917-18; Chemical Warfare Service, US Army, 1918 (Pte First-Class); Asst in Rubber Research, New Jersey Zinc Co., Penn., 1919; Asst Prof. of Physics, Washington Sq. Coll., New York Univ., 1926-28; Univ. of Chicago: Assoc. Prof. of Physics, 1928-31; Prof. of Physics, 1931-61 and Chemistry, 1961; Ernest de Witt Burton Distinguished Service Prof., 1956-61; Distinguished Service Prof. of Physics and Chemistry, 1961-; Distinguished Research Prof. of Chemical Physics, Florida State Univ., (Jan.-March) 1965-. Dir, Editorial Work and Information, Plutonium Project, Univ. of Chicago, 1942-45; Scientific Attaché, US Embassy, London, 1955. Baker Lectr, Cornell Univ., 1960; Silliman Lectr, Yale Univ., 1965; Jan van Geuns Vis. Prof., Amsterdam Univ., 1965. Hon. ScD: Columbia, 1939; Marquette, 1966; Cambridge, 1966; Hon. PhD, Stockholm Univ., 1960. Member: Amer. Acad. of Arts and Sciences; Nat. Acad. of Sciences; Amer. Philosophical Soc.; Amer. Chem. Soc.; Fellow: Amer. Physical Soc.; Amer. Acad. for Advancement of Science; Internat. Acad. of Quantum Molecular Science; Hon. Fellow: Chem. Soc. of Gt Britain; Indian Nat. Acad. of Science; Foreign Mem., Royal Soc.; Hon. Mem., Soc. de Chimie Physique, Paris; Corresp. Mem., Soc. Royale des Sciences de Liège. Nobel Prize for Chemistry, 1966; other medals and awards. *Publications:* (with Willis B. Person) Molecular Complexes; over 200 contributions (1919-; in recent years dealing extensively with structure and spectra of molecular complexes) to various American and foreign journals including: Jl Am. Chem. Soc.; Jl Chem. Phys; Rev. Mod. Phys; Phys Rev.; Chem. Rev.; Nature; also contributions: Proc. Nat. Acad. Sci.; Trans Faraday Soc. *Recreations:* driving a car, Oriental rugs, art. *Address:* (home) 5825 Dorchester Avenue, Chicago, Ill 60637, USA; (office) Department of Physics LMSS, University of Chicago, 1100 E 58th Street, Chicago, Ill 60637; (winter office) Inst. of Molecular Biophysics, The Florida State Univ., Tallahassee, Florida 32306. *Clubs:* Quadrangle (Chicago); Cosmos (Washington).

**MULLINS, Rt. Rev. Daniel Joseph;** Titular Bishop of Stowe, and Auxiliary Bishop in Cardiff, since 1970; *b* 10 July 1929; *s* of Timothy Mullins. *Educ:* Mount Melleray; St Mary's, Aberystwyth; Oscott Coll.; UC of S Wales and Mon, Cardiff. Priest, 1953. Curate at: Barry, 1953-56; Newbridge, 1956; Bargoed, 1956-57; Maesteg, 1957-60; Asst Chaplain to UC Cardiff, 1960-64; Sec. to Archbp of Cardiff, 1964-68; Vicar General of Archdiocese of Cardiff, 1968. *Recreation:* golf. *Address:* St Joseph's Presbytery, Penarth, Glam CF6 1RL. *T:* Penarth 708247.

**MUMFORD, Sir Albert (Henry),** KBE 1963 (OBE 1946); CEng, FIEE; Engineer-in-Chief, GPO, 1960-65, retd; Director, mel equipment Co. Ltd; *b* 16 April, 1903; *s* of late George Mumford; *m* 1927, Eileen Berry; two *s* two *d*. *Educ:* Bancroft's Sch.; Queen Mary Coll., Univ. of London. BSc (Eng) 1st Class Hons (London) 1923. Entered GPO Engineering Dept, 1924; Staff Engineer radio branch, 1938; Imperial Defence Coll., 1948; Asst Engineer-in-Chief, 1951; Dep. Engineer-in-Chief, 1954. Treasurer, Instn of Electrical Engineers, 1969- (Chm. Radio Section, 1945-46; Vice-Pres. 1958-63; Pres. 1963-64); Pres. Assoc. Supervising Electrical Engineers, 1964-66; Treas., Instn of Electrical and Electronic Technician Engineers, 1967-. Fellow, Queen Mary Coll., Dec. 1962; Hon. Mem., City and Guilds of London Inst. *Publications:* many scientific papers. *Address:* 27 Grendon Gardens, Wembley Park, Middx. *T:* 01-904 2360.

**MUMFORD, L(awrence) Quincy;** Librarian of Congress since 1954; *b* 11 Dec. 1903; *s* of Jacob Edward Mumford and Emma Luvenia (*née* Stocks); *m* 1930, Permelia Catharine Stevens (*d* 1961); one *d*; *m* 1969, Betsy Perrin Fox. *Educ:* Duke Univ. (AB *magna cum laude;* AM); Columbia Univ. (BS). Mem. staff, Duke Univ. Library, 1922-28; Head of Circulation Dept, 1926; Chief of Reference and Circulation, 1927-28; Student Asst, Columbia Univ. Library, 1928-29; Mem. staff, New York Public Library, 1929-45; General Asst in charge of Director's Office, 1932-35; Executive Asst and Chief of Preparation Div., 1936-43; Exec. Asst and Coordinator Gen. Services Divs, 1943-45; on leave from New York Public Library to serve as dir Processing Dept, Libary of Congress, 1940-41; Asst Dir, Cleveland Public Library, 1945-50, Dir, 1950-

54. Hon. degrees: LittD: Bethany Coll. (WVa), 1954; Rutgers Univ. (NJ), 1956; Duke Univ. (NC), 1957; Belmont Abbey Coll. (NC), 1963; LLD: Union Coll. (NY), 1955, Bucknell Univ. (Pa), 1956; Univ. of Notre Dame (Ind.), 1964; Univ. of Pittsburgh (Pa), 1964. President: Ohio Library Assoc., 1947-48; Amer. Library Assoc., 1954-55; Manuscript Soc., 1968-69. Chairman: Federal Library Cttee; Bd of Visitors, Duke Univ. Library. Member: Lincoln Sesquicentennial Commn, 1958-60; Sponsors Cttee, Papers of Woodrow Wilson; Board of Advisors, Dumbarton Oaks Research Library and Collection; US Nat. Book Cttee. Corresponding Mem. for the US of Unesco's Internat. Advisory Cttee on Bibliography, Documentation and Terminology. Benjamin Franklin Fellow, Royal Soc. for Encouragement of Arts, Manufactures and Commerce (London). Chm. or Mem. ex officio of various cttees, bds, etc. *Publications:* contributions to library periodicals. *Address:* (home) 3721 49th Street NW, Washington DC 20016, USA; (office) Library of Congress, Washington, DC 20540. *T:* Sterling 3-0400. *Clubs:* Cosmos, International (Washington).

**MUMFORD, Lewis;** Writer; *b* 19 Oct. 1895; *s* of Lewis Mumford and Elvina Conradina Baron; *m* 1921, Sophia Wittenberg; (one *s* killed in action 1944) one *d*. *Educ:* Coll. of the City of New York, Columbia Univ. Radio operator (USN) 1918; Associate editor Fortnightly Dial, 1919; Acting Editor Sociological Review (London), 1920; Co-editor American Caravan, 1927-36. Member: National Inst. of Arts and Letters 1930-; Amer. Academy of Arts and Letters, 1956- (Pres., 1962-65); Amer. Philosophical Soc., Amer. Academy of Arts and Sciences; Vice-Pres., la Societé Européenne de Culture; Bd of Higher Educn, City of New York, 1935-37; Commn on Teacher Educn, Amer. Council on Educn, 1938-44; Prof. of Humanities, Stanford Univ., 1942-44. Hon. LLD Edinburgh 1965; Hon. Dr Arch., Rome, 1967. Hon. Phi Beta Kappa, 1957; Hon. Fellow, Stanford Univ., 1941. Hon. ARIBA 1942; Hon. Member: Town Planning Inst., 1946; Amer. Inst. of Architects, 1951; Town Planning Inst. of Canada, 1960; Amer. Inst. of Planners, 1955; Colegio del Arquitectas del Peru; Prof. of City Planning, Univ. of Pennsylvania, 1951-56; Vis. Prof., MIT, 1957-60; Ford Prof., Univ. of Pennsylvania, 1959-60; Univ. of Calif., 1961; Fellow, Wesleyan Univ. Center for Advanced Studies, 1963. Co-chairman Wenner-Gren Foundation Conf. on Man's Use of the Earth, 1955. Made six documentary films on City for National Film Board, Canada, 1964. Townsend Harris Medal, 1939; Ebenezer Howard Memorial Medal, 1946; Medal of Honour, Fairmount Park Art Assoc., 1953; Town Planning Inst. Gold Medal, 1957; RIBA Royal Gold Medal for Architecture, 1961; Presidential Medal of Freedom, 1964; Emerson-Thoreau Medal, Amer. Acad. of Arts and Sciences, 1965; Gold Medal, Belles Lettres, Nat. Inst. of Arts and Letters. *Publications:* The Story of Utopias, 1922; Sticks and Stones, 1924; The Golden Day, 1926; Herman Melville, 1929; The Brown Decades, 1931; Technics and Civilization, 1934; The Culture of Cities, 1938; Whither Honolulu?, 1938; Men Must Act, 1939; Faith for Living, 1940; The South in Architecture, 1941; The Condition of Man, 1944; City Development, 1945; Values for Survival, 1946 (Programme for Survivial (Eng.), 1946); Green Memories: The Story of Geddes Mumford, 1947; The Conduct of Life, 1951; Art and Technics, 1952; In the Name of Sanity, 1954; The Human Prospect, 1955; From the Ground Up, 1956; The Transformations of Man, 1956; The City in History, 1961; Highway and City, 1962; Herman Melville (rev. edn), 1963; The Myth of the Machine, 1967; The Urban Prospect, 1968; The Van Wyck Brooks-Lewis Mumford Letters, 1970; The Pentagon of Power, 1971. Editor, Roots of Contemporary Architecture, 1952. *Recreations:* gardening and sketching. *Address:* Amenia, New York 12501, USA.

**MUMMERY, H. E. L.;** *see* Lockhart-Mummery.

**MUNBY, Alan Noel Latimer,** TD 1945; LittD 1962; Fellow of King's College, Cambridge since 1948; *b* 25 Dec. 1913; *s* of Alan Edward Munby and Ethel Annie (*née* Greenhill); *m* 1st, 1939, Joan Edelsten (*d* 1945); 2nd, 1945, Sheila Rachel Crowther-Smith; one *s*. *Educ:* Clifton Coll.; King's Coll., Cambridge. In antiquarian book-trade with Bernard Quaritch Ltd, 1935-37; Sotheby & Co., 1937-39, 1945-47. Queen Victoria's Rifles, KRRC, 1936-45 (Capt., despatches, POW). Librarian, King's Coll. Cambridge, 1947-; J. P. R. Lyell Reader in Bibliography, Univ. of Oxford, 1962-63; Arundell Esdaile Lecturer, English and Library Associations, 1964; David Murray Lectr, Univ. of Glasgow, 1965; Visiting Fellow, All Souls Coll., Oxford, 1968; Sandars Reader in Bibliography, Univ. of Cambridge, 1969-70. Trustee, British Museum, 1969-. Hon. Fellow, Pierpont Morgan Library, New York. *Publications:* Letters to Leigh Hunt (edited), 1934; English Poetical Autographs (with Desmond Flower), 1938; The Alabaster Hand and other Ghost Stories, 1949; Phillipps Studies, 5 vol., 1951-60; Cambridge Coll. Libraries, 1959; The Cult of the Autograph Letter in England, 1962; The Libraries of English Men of Letters, 1964; Macaulay's Library, 1966; Sir Thomas Phillipps, Portrait of an Obsession (with N. Barker), 1967. Jt-Editor, Trans. Cambridge Bibliograph. Soc., 1949-63. *Recreations:* book collecting, shooting. *Address:* 24 Millington Road, Cambridge. *T:* 57632. *Clubs:* United University, Roxburghe.

**MUNCASTER, Claude,** RBA 1946; RWS 1936 (ARWS 1931); ROI 1948; SMA 1939, PSMA 1958; landscape and marine painter; author and lecturer; *b* 4 July 1903; *s* of late Oliver Hall; adopted name of Claude Grahame Muncaster by deed poll, Nov. 1945; *m* 1933, Primrose Keighley, *y d* of 1st Baron Riverdale, GBE, LLD, JP; two *s*. *Educ:* Queen Elizabeth's Sch., Cranbrook. First exhibited at RA, 1919; first one-man exhibition at Fine Arts Soc., Bond Street, 1926; subsequent one-man exhibitions most years in London, the Provinces and overseas; Public Purchases: Tate Gallery, Birmingham, Glasgow, Sheffield, Brighton, Worthing, Eastbourne, Plymouth, Hull, Newcastle, Bradford, Sunderland, Cape Town, New Zealand, Australia Art Galleries. Oil Painting, Shipyard at Palma in Majorca, purchased by Royal Academy under Edward Stott Fund, 1946; series of watercolours of Windsor, Sandringham and Balmoral commissioned by the Queen, 1946-47; One Man Exhibition; Association of Arts, Cape Town, 1948. Lt-Comdr RNVR 1940-44. Acted as adviser on camouflage of ships at sea to Division at Admiralty responsible for Naval Camouflage. Pres. RWS Art Club, 1951-60; Art Adviser to Worthing Corp., 1954-59; Pres. St Ives Soc. of Artists, 1955-63; Pres. Royal Soc. of Marine Artists, 1957. Hon. Mem., Royal Glasgow Inst. of Fine Arts. Awarded de Lazio Medal, 1957. *Publications:* Rolling Round the Horn, 1933; Students' Book of Watercolour Painting, 1938; Landscape and Marine Painting, 1958. *Recreation:* nature study. *Address:* Whitelocks, Sutton, near Pulborough, Sussex. *T:* Sutton, Sussex 216. *Clubs:* Lansdowne; Conway, Royal Naval

Volunteer Reserve (Hon. Member). *See also Baron Riverdale.*

**MUNDY, John Cloudesley,** CMG 1947; Director: International Aeradio (East Africa) Ltd; Kenya Power Co. Ltd; Tana River Development Co. Ltd; Tanganyika Electric Supply Co. Ltd; Deputy Chairman (Past Chairman) East African Power and Lighting Co. Ltd; Local Chairman, South African Mutual Life Assurance Society, since 1957; Chairman: International Computers (East Africa) Ltd; Fisons (EA) Ltd; Robbialac Paints (Kenya) Ltd; Robbialac Paints (Uganda) Ltd; Robbialac Paints (Tanzania) Ltd; *b* 9 Sept. 1900; *s* of late William Peckham and Amelia Beatrice Mundy, Brighton, Sussex; *m* Annie (decd), *o d* of late Arthur Holden, Skipton, Yorks, and Mary Holden; no *c. Educ:* Varndean, Brighton. Served European War, 1914-18, in RAF, 1918; joined Inland Revenue Dept in UK as Asst Inspector of Taxes; seconded to Kenya as Commissioner of Income Tax, 1937; Mem. for Finance, East Africa High Commission, 1948-57; Mem. of East Africa Central Legislative Assembly, 1948-57. *Recreations:* golf. *Address:* PO Box 763, Nairobi, Kenya. *T:* Nairobi 65360. *Clubs:* East India and Sports; Nairobi (Nairobi).

**MUNN, Rear-Adm. William James,** CB 1962; DSO 1941; OBE 1946; *b* 15 July 1911; *s* of late Col R. G. Munn, CMG, FRGS, and late Mrs R. G. Munn; *m* 1940, Susan Astle Sperling, Teviot Bank, Hawick, Scotland; two *s. Educ:* Britannia Royal Naval College, Dartmouth. Cadet and Midshipman in HMS Nelson, 1929-31. Flag Lt (Battle Cruiser Sqdn during Spanish Civil War); served War of 1939-45 (despatches, DSO): First Lt Destroyer HMS Mohawk; Comd Destroyer HMS Hereward (Battle of Matapan, evacuation of Crete), 1941. POW in Italy and Germany, 1941-45. Comd HMS Venus (Mediterranean during Palestine trouble, OBE), 1945-47; Comdr 1946; psc 1949; Exec. Officer, Cruiser HMS Kenya (Far East Station, Korean War, despatches), 1949-51; Capt., 1951; Capt. of the Britannia Royal Naval College, Dartmouth, 1956-58; Capt. of HMS Gambia, Nov. 1958-Dec. 1960; Rear-Adm. 1960; Chief of Staff to the Comdr-in-Chief, Home Fleet, 1961-63, retd. *Recreations:* golf, sailing. *Address:* The Old Rectory, Langham, near Bury St Edmunds, Suffolk. *T:* Walsham-le-Willows 234. *Club:* Royal Naval (Portsmouth).

**MUNRO, Alison (Mrs),** CBE 1964; High Mistress, St Paul's Girls' School, Hammersmith, since 1964; Member (part-time) Board of BEA, since 1966; *b* 12 Feb. 1914; *d* of late John Donald, MD; *m* 1939, Alan Lamont Munro (killed on active service, 1941); one *s. Educ:* Queen's Coll., Harley Street; Wynberg Girls' High Sch., South Africa; St Paul's Girls' Sch.; St Hilda's Coll., Oxford (MA). Ministry of Aircraft Production, 1942-45; Principal, Ministry of Civil Aviation, 1945; Asst Sec., 1949; Under-Sec., Ministry of Transport and Civil Aviation, 1958; Under-Sec., Ministry of Aviation, 1960. Governor, Charing Cross Group of Hospitals, 1967. *Recreations:* gardening, tennis, sailing. *Address:* 48 Rowan Road, Hammersmith, W6. *T:* 01-603 3166.

**MUNRO, Sir Arthur (Herman),** 14th Bt, *cr* 1634; retired; *b* 10 Sept. 1893; *o s* of Sir Arthur Talbot Munro, 13th Bt, and Frances Emily Emmeline, *d* of William March; *S* father 1953; *m* 1919, Violet Beatrice, *d* of Henry Powles, Nunhead, SE15; two *d* (and one *s* Royal Navy, died on active service, 1945; one *d* decd). *Educ:* Wilson's Grammar Sch., Camberwell, SE. Served European War, 1914-18, with 47th Div. (France and Germany). *Recreation:* golf. *Heir: cousin* Ian Talbot Munro, *b* 28 Dec. 1929. *Address:* 276 Wokingham Road, Reading, Berks. *T:* Reading 61365.

**MUNRO, C(harles) K.;** *see* MacMullan, C. W. K.

**MUNRO, Charles Rowcliffe;** Senior Partner, Romanes & Munro, Chartered Accountants, 25 Abercromby Place, Edinburgh; Partner since 1932; *b* 6 Nov. 1902; *s* of Charles John Munro, CA, Edinburgh, Hon. Sheriff Substitute, County of Selkirk, and of Edith Rowcliffe; *m* 1942, Moira Rennie Ainslie, *d* of Dr Alexander Cruickshank Ainslie; two *s. Educ:* Merchiston Castle Sch., Edinburgh. Chairman: Scottish Life Assurance Co.; Scottish Life Hume Properties Ltd, and other companies. Hon. Treasurer W Edinburgh Unionist Assoc., 1945-61, Hon. Treas. Scottish Nat. Cttee English-Speaking Union of the Commonwealth 1952-64; Pres. Edinburgh Union of Boys' Clubs, 1957-66. *Recreation:* fishing. *Address:* 17 Succoth Place, Edinburgh. *T:* 031-337 2139. *Club:* New (Edinburgh).

**MUNRO, Lt-Col David Campbell Duncan,** DSO 1918; MC; DCM; late Gordon Highlanders; *b* Cairnie, Aberdeenshire, 13 Dec. 1885; *m* 1917, Grace, *e d* of C. T. Studd and *widow* of Martin J. Sutton, Wargrave Manor, Berks; one *s. Educ:* Ruthven Public Sch.; Edinburgh. Entered Army, 1903; served in the ranks, Gordon Highlanders; served in India, and commanded Hood Battalion and Liverpool Scottish; European War in France and Belgium (DSO, MC, DCM, medal of St George of Russia, 1st Class, 1914-15 Star, War and Victory medals, despatches twice); Adjutant, 1st Gordon Highlanders, 1916; retired rank, Lt-Col, 1920; Southern Rhodesia Defence Force, 1922-28; Mem. S Rhodesia Legislative Assembly, 1924-28. Served War of 1939-45 (Defence and War Medals). *Recreations:* golf, tennis. *Address:* Alpi Glen, Haytor, Newton Abbot, Devon. *T:* Haytor 330. *Clubs:* United Service; Salisbury (Rhodesia).

**MUNRO, John Bennet Lorimer,** CB 1959; CMG 1953; *b* 20 May 1905; *s* of late Rev. J. L. Munro; *m* 1st, 1929, Gladys Maie Forbes Simmons (*d* 1965); three *s*; 2nd, 1965, Margaret Deacy Ozanne, Blackfort House, Foxford, County Mayo. *Educ:* Edinburgh Academy; Edinburgh University; Corpus Christi Coll., Oxford. ICS: entered, 1928; Under-Sec. Public Dept, Fort St George, 1934; HM Treasury, 1939; Min. of Supply, 1943; idc, 1949; Div. of Atomic Energy Production, 1950; Chief Administrative Officer, UK High Commission for Germany, 1951; Under-Sec.: Min. of Supply, 1953; Bd of Trade, 1955-62; Export Credits Guarantee Dept, 1962-65; Consultant, Export Council for Europe, 1966-67. *Address:* 8 Napier Road, Kensington, W14. *T:* 01-603 4939.

**MUNRO, Sir Leslie (Knox),** KCMG 1955; KCVO 1957; MP (National) for Hamilton West, New Zealand, since 1969 (for Waipa, 1963-69); *b* 26 Feb. 1901; *s* of Colin Robert and Marie Caroline Munro; *m* 1st, 1927, Christine Mary Priestley (*d* 1929); one *d*; 2nd, 1931, Muriel Olga Sturt; one *d. Educ:* Auckland Grammar Sch.; Auckland Univ. Coll. (LLM 1923; Senior Schol.). Auckland Univ. College: Lecturer in Constitutional Law and Roman Law, 1925-38, Dean of Faculty of Law, 1938. Pres. Auckland District Law Soc., 1936-38; Mem. Council, NZ Law Soc., 1936-39; Associate Editor, New Zealand Herald, 1941, Editor, 1942-51; New Zealand Ambassador to the United States, 1952-58; New Zealand Permanent Representative to the United

Nations, 1952-58. Pres., Trusteeship Council, 1953-54; NZ Delegate to Security Council, 1954-55; Chm., First Political Cttee, UN, 1957; Pres. of the United Nations, 1957-58; UN Rep. on Implementation of Hungarian Resolutions, 1958-62. Sec.-Gen., International Commission of Jurists, 1961-63. Hon. LLD: Harvard, Bradley, Colgate, Michigan, Brooklyn, Hobart, Syracuse, Fairleigh Dickinson, Far Eastern (Manila), Birmingham, and Auckland Univs. *Publications:* United Nations: Hope for a Divided World, 1960; articles in Foreign Affairs and in NZ Law Journal. *Recreations:* golf and tennis. *Address:* 24 Pollock Drive, Hamilton, New Zealand. *Clubs:* Northern, Auckland (Auckland); Metropolitan (Washington, DC).

**MUNRO of Foulis, Captain Patrick,** TD 1958; DL 1949; 30th Chief of Clan Munro; landowner and farmer; Vice-Lieutenant of Ross and Cromarty, since 1968; *b* 30 Aug. 1912; *e s* of late Col C. H. O. Gascoigne, DSO, Seaforth Highlanders, and Eva Marion, *d* of Sir Hector Munro of Foulis, 11th Bt; assumed arms and designation of Munro of Foulis on death of his grandfather; *m* 1947, Eleanor Mary, *d* of Capt. Hon. William French, French Park, Co. Roscommon, Eire; three *s* one *d*. *Educ:* Imperial Service Coll., Windsor; RMC Sandhurst. 2nd Lt Seaforth Highlanders, 1933; Capt. 1939. Served War of 1939-45, France (POW). Mem. Ross and Cromarty T&AFA, 1938. *Address:* Foulis Castle, Evanton, Ross-shire. *T:* Evanton 212; Ardullie, Dingwall, Ross-shire. *Club:* MCC.

**MUNRO, Robert Wilson,** CMG 1967; Deputy High Commissioner, Nairobi, since 1969; *b* 21 Jan. 1915; *yr s* of late J. S. Munro and late Mrs E. G. Munro, Dunedin, NZ; *m* 1946, Annette Kilroy; two *s*. *Educ:* Otago Boys' High Sch., Univ. of Otago, New Zealand, MSc 1936, and Univ. of London, BSc(Econ), 1950. Research Chemist, NZ Dept of Agriculture, 1938-40. Served with 2 NZEF and UK Forces, 1941-45. Sudan Civil Service, 1945-52; HM Diplomatic Service, 1952-; served in London, Warsaw, Paris, Baghdad and Khartoum; Inspector, Diplomatic Service, 1967-69. Order of Nilein, 1965. *Recreations:* camping, shooting. *Address:* c/o Foreign and Commonwealth Office, King Charles Street, SW1. *Clubs:* Travellers'; Muthaiga, Nairobi (Nairobi).

**MUNRO, Sir (Thomas) Torquil (Alfonso),** 5th Bt, *cr* 1825; JP Angus; *b* 7 Feb. 1901; *e s* of 4th Bt and Selina Dorothea (*d* 1902), *d* of Major-General T. E. Byrne; *S* father, 1919; *m* 1st, 1925, Beatrice (who obtained a divorce, 1932), *d* of late Robert Sanderson Whitaker; one *s*; 2nd, 1934, Averil Moira Katharine, *d* of Kenneth Owen Hunter; one *s* one *d*. *Educ:* Winchester. *Heir: s* Alasdair Thomas Ian Munro [*b* 6 July 1927; *m* 1954, Marguerite Lillian, *d* of late Franklin R. Loy, Dayton, Ohio, USA; one *s* one *d*]. *Address:* Lindertis, Kirriemuir, Angus. *TA:* Munro, Lindertis, Kirriemuir, Angus. *T:* Craigton 209.
*See also Baron Colyton.*

**MUNRO, Sir Torquil;** *see* Munro, Sir Thomas Torquil Alfonso.

**MUNRO, William,** QC (Scotland) 1959; *b* 19 April 1900; *s* of William Munro, JP, Kilmarnock, and Janet Thomson Munro; *m* 1950, Christine Frances, *d* of W. B. Robertson, MC, DL, Colton, Dunfermline; three *d*. *Educ:* Glasgow High Sch.; Glasgow Univ. (MA, LLB). Called to Scottish Bar, 1925; called to Bar of Straits Settlements, 1927; Johore, 1927. Practised in Singapore and Malaya, 1927-57; Partner, Allen & Gledhill, Singapore. 1933-57 (Prisoner of war, Feb. 1942-Aug. 1945). Resumed practice Scottish Bar, 1958. *Recreations:* golf, gardening. *Address:* Dundarach, Craiglockhart Park, Edinburgh. *T:* 031-443 2620. *Clubs:* Caledonian; New (Edinburgh), Hon. Company of Edinburgh Golfers.

**MUNRO-LUCAS-TOOTH of Teananich, Sir Hugh (Vere Huntly Duff),** 1st Bt, *cr* 1920; Lieutenant-Colonel Queen's Own Cameron Highlanders; *b* 13 Jan. 1903; *er s* of Major Hugh Munro Warrand of Bught and Beatrice Maud Lucas, *e c* of late Sir Robert Lucas Lucas-Tooth, Bt, of Holme Lacy, Co. Hereford, and *co-heiress* with her sisters in the lordship of the Manor of Holme Lacy; *m* 1925, Laetitia Florence, OBE 1958, *er d* of Sir John R. Findlay, 1st Bt; one *s* two *d*. *Educ:* Eton; Balliol Coll., Oxford. Called to Bar, Lincoln's Inn, 1933; MP (C) Isle of Ely, 1924-29, Hendon South, 1945-70; Parliamentary Under-Sec. of State, Home Office, 1952-55. Sir Robert Lucas-Tooth, 1st Bt, having died, and all his three sons having lost their lives in France during the European War, HM the King was graciously pleased to grant a re-creation of the baronetcy in favour of Sir Robert's eldest grandson, H. V. H. D. Warrand, who assumed the name and arms of Lucas-Tooth in place of Warrand by Royal Letters Patent; changed name by Deed Poll from Lucas-Tooth to Munro-Lucas-Tooth of Teananich, 1965. *Heir: s* Hugh John Lucas-Tooth [*b* 20 Aug. 1932; *m* 1955, Caroline, *e d* of 1st Baron Poole, *qv*; three *d*]. *Address:* Burgate Court, Fordingbridge, Hants.
*See also Sir Michael Oppenheimer.*

**MUNROW, William Davis,** CBE 1963; Chief Inspector of Audit, Ministry of Housing and Local Government, 1965-68; *b* 28 April 1903; 2nd *s* of Alexander Gordon Davis and Charlotte Munrow; *m* 1927, Constance Caroline Moorcroft; one *s*. *Educ:* Council Schs; Birkbeck Coll.; and London Sch. of Economics (BSc(Econ)). District Auditor for London, 1954; Dep. Chief Inspector of Audit, 1958. *Recreation:* golf. *Address:* 60 Withyham Road, Cooden, Bexhill-on-Sea, Sussex. *T:* Cooden 2543.

**MUNSTER,** 5th Earl of, *cr* 1831; **Geoffrey William Richard Hugh FitzClarence,** PC 1954; KBE 1957; Viscount FitzClarence, Baron Tewkesbury, 1831; HM Lieutenant, Surrey, since 1957; *b* 17 Feb. 1906; *o s* of late Major the Hon. Harold E. FitzClarence, 7th *s* of 2nd Earl; *S* uncle, 1928; *m* 1928, Hilary, *o d* of Kenneth Wilson of Cannizaro, Wimbledon. *Educ:* Charterhouse. A Lord-in-Waiting, 1932-38; Mem. LCC for North Paddington, 1931-37; Paymaster-Gen., 1938-39; Parliamentary Under-Sec. of State for War, Feb.-Sept. 1939; Parliamentary Under-Sec. of State for India and for Burma, 1943-44; Parliamentary Under-Sec. of State, Home Office, 1944-45; Parliamentary Under-Sec. of State, Colonial Office, 1951-54; Minister without Portfolio, 1954-57. Chairman, Uganda Relationships Commission, 1960-61. ADC and Military Asst to Gen. Viscount Gort, VC, 1939-41; GSO 2 Malta, 1942; Capt. Grenadier Guards. Chm. Assoc. of Conservative Clubs, 1949-61. Dep. Chm., UK Branch, Commonwealth Parliamentary Assoc., 1955-62. *Heir: cousin,* Edward Charles FitzClarence [late Irish Guards, *b* 3 Oct. 1899]. *Address:* Sandhills, Bletchingley, Surrey. *T:* Bletchingley 204. *Club:* Turf.

**MUNTASSER, Omar Mahmud;** Libyan Ambassador to the Court of St James's, 1964-69; *b* 28 July 1930; *m*; one *s*. *Educ:* Univs of Florence and Oxford. Mem., Libyan Delegn to

UN, 1957; Minister in: Washington, 1960-61; London, 1961-62; Minister of Justice, 1962-63; Minister of Foreign Affairs, 1963-64; Envoy and Minister, The Netherlands, 1964-; Mem., Libyan Delegn to 19th Session of UN; Ambassador to Malta, 1966-. *Recreations:* tennis, squash, swimming. *Address:* c/o Ministry of External Affairs, Tripoli, Libya. *Clubs:* Queen's, Hurlingham, Travellers', Royal Automobile.

**MUNTZ, (Frederick) Alan (Irving),** AFRAeS, MIMechE, MInstPet, MIEx; MIMarE; Consultant; *b* 7 June 1899; *s* of Major Irving Muntz and Jessie Challoner; *m* 1st, 1923, Mary Lee (marr diss., 1934), 3rd *d* of Canon W. L. Harnett; one *s* two *d*; 2nd, 1934, Lady Margaret Frances Anne (marr. diss., 1939), 2nd *d* of 7th Marquess of Londonderry; 3rd, 1948, Marjorie Mary Helena, 2nd *d* of Edward Strickland, Ceylon; one *d*. *Educ:* Winchester; Trinity Coll., Cambridge. (BA Mech. Sciences). Served in France; 2nd Lt 432nd Field Co. RE, 1918; British Petroleum Co., Ltd, 1922-28; Anglo-Iranian Oil Co., Ltd, 1926-28; with Sir Nigel Norman founded Airwork Ltd, and Heston Airport, 1928; with Talaat Harb Pasha, Banque Misr, Cairo, founded Misr Airwork SAE, 1932; with R. E. Grant Govan, Delhi, helped found Indian National Airways Ltd, 1933; founded Alan Muntz & Co. Ltd, to develop Pescara free piston engine system and other inventions, 1937. *Recreations:* golf, fishing, travelling. *Address:* 49 Hornton Street, W8. *T:* 01-937 8230; La Bastide de la Rouvière, Seillans, Var, France. *Clubs:* Bath, Hurlingham.

**MUNTZ, (Isabelle) Hope,** FSA; mediaevalist; *b* Toronto, Canada, 8 July 1907; *er d* of late Rupert Gustavus Muntz and 2nd 1935-45 also Spare-time writing and research; G. F. Muntz, Umberslade, Warwicks; unmarried. *Educ:* private schs, Bournemouth and Eastbourne. Commercial Art, aircraft engineering, secretarial work and free-lance journalism, 1931-39, and research for, and work on, book; ARP and work for precision engineers, 1935-45. Spare-time writing and research, 1931-45, full-time since 1945. FAMS 1968; FSA 1969. *Publications:* The Golden Warrior, England and Commonwealth, 1948, USA, 1949, Sweden, 1950, Norway, 1951, Germany, 1952, Denmark 1954 (also published in Braille and Talking Books); Battles for the Crown, 1966; (with Catherine E. Morton) Carmen de Hastingae Proelio, 1971. Script for The Norman Conquest in the Bayeux Tapestry (film), 1966. Articles, sketches, etc. to journals; contributions to Graya (magazine for members of Gray's Inn). *Recreations:* travel, driving, riding, reading, music, drama. *Address:* c/o Chatto & Windus Ltd, 40/42 William IV Street, WC2. *Clubs:* Sesame, Pioneer, Lyceum.

**MUNTZ, Thomas Godric Aylett,** CMG 1951; OBE 1948; retired; *b* 31 May 1906; *s* of R. A. Muntz, Tansor Manor, Peterborough; *m* 1st, 1932, Marjorie (*d* 1968), *d* of Sir Charles Statham; two *s*; 2nd, 1969, June Robertson. *Educ:* Lancing; Pembroke Coll., Oxford. Appointed to Dept of Overseas Trade, 1929; served at office of HM Trade Commissioner, New Zealand, 1931-38; Embassy, Warsaw, 1938-39; Board of Trade, 1939-40; Montreal, 1940-42; Embassy, Rio de Janeiro, 1942-43; Lisbon, 1944-47; Ankara, 1947-50; Head of Economic Relations Dept, Foreign Office, 1950-51; Tangier, 1952-55; Antwerp, 1957-59. *Address:* Barns, King's Cliffe, near Peterborough.

**MURCHISON, Very Rev. Thomas Moffat,** DD; Minister of St Columba Summertown Church, Glasgow, since 1937; *b* 27 July 1907; *s* of Malcolm Murchison and Ann Moffat; *m* 1940, Mary Black Morton Philp; one *s* two *d*. *Educ:* Portree High Sch.; University and Trinity Coll., Glasgow. DD Glasgow, 1964. Minister of Glenelg, Inverness-shire, 1932-37. Member: BBC National Broadcasting Council for Scotland, 1952-57; Scottish National Parks Cttee, 1946-47; Panel of Religious Advisers, ITA, 1966-; Pres., Highland Development League; Convener, Church of Scotland Home Board, 1959-64; Convener, Church of Scotland Adv. Board, 1967-; Moderator of Gen. Assembly of Church of Scotland, 1969-70. internat. Pres., Celtic Congress, 1966-. Crowned Bard of the National Mod, 1958; Chief of Gaelic Society of Inverness, 1961; Bard of the Gorseth of the Bards of Cornwall, 1969. *Publications:* The Plight of the Smallholders, 1935; (Jt Editor) Alba: A Miscellany, 1948; (ed) The Golden Key, 1950; Gaelic Prose writings of Donald Lamont, 1960; Editor, The Gael, 1946-57; Editor, Gaelic Supplement, Life and Work, 1951-. *Recreations:* Galeic literature, highland history. *Address:* 14 Kinross Avenue, Glasgow SW2. *T:* 041-882 2844.

**MURDOCH, Air Marshal Sir Alister Murray,** KBE 1966 (CBE 1946); CB 1960; Chief of the Air Staff, RAAF since 1965; *b* 9 Dec. 1912; *s* of Brig. T. Murdoch, DSO, Melbourne; *m* 1937, Florence Eilene, *d* of Charles Herbert Miller, Sydney; one *d*. *Educ:* Caulfield Grammar Sch.; RMC Duntroon, Canberra. Attached to Directorate of Operations and Intelligence, 1938-39. Served War of 1939-45 (CBE). Senior Air Staff Officer, RAAF HQ, 1944; Dir, Air Staff Plans and Policy, 1949-52; AOC RAAF Pt Cook, and Comdt RAAF Coll., Pt Cook, 1952-53; AOC Training Command, 1954-58; Dep. Chief of the Air Staff, 1958-59; RAAF Representative in London, 1959-62; AOC, HQ Operational Command, 1962-65; idc. *Recreations:* golf and tennis. *Address:* Department of Air, Canberra, ACT, Australia.

**MURDOCH, Charles,** CBE 1950; JP; DL; Staff Relations Adviser, Edinburgh Headquarters, Scottish Gas Board, since 1958; *b* 30 Aug. 1902. Mem., Scottish Council (Development and Industry); Mem., Scottish Air Advisory Council; Dir, Scottish Industrial Estates. Formerly: Mem. of the Scottish Gas Board; Chm. of the Regional Board for Industry, Scotland. DL City and County of Glasgow. *Address:* 8 Kingsacre Road, Kings Park, Glasgow S4.

**MURDOCH, Dame Elisabeth (Joy),** DBE 1963 (CBE 1961); *b* 1909; *d* of Rupert Greene and Marie (*née* de Lancey Forth); Forth); *m* 1928, Sir Keith (Arthur) Murdoch (*d* 1952); one *s* three *d*. *Educ:* Clyde Sch., Woodend, Victoria. Pres., Royal Children's Hospital, Melbourne, Victoria, Australia, 1953-65. *Recreation:* gardening. *Address:* Cruden Farm, Langwarrin, Victoria 3910, Australia. *Clubs:* Alexandra, Lyceum (Melbourne).
*See also K. R. Murdoch.*

**MURDOCH, Iris;** *see* Murdoch, J. I.

**MURDOCH, (Jean) Iris; (Mrs J. O. Bayley);** novelist and lecturer; Fellow of St Anne's College, Oxford, since 1948, Hon. Fellow, 1963; Lecturer at Royal College of Art, 1963-67; *b* Dublin, 15 July 1919; *d* of Wills John Hughes Murdoch and Irene Alice Richardson; *m* 1956, John Oliver Bayley. *Educ:* Froebel Educational Inst., London; Badminton Sch., Bristol; Somerville Coll., Oxford. Read Classical Mods and Greats, Somerville Coll., Oxford, 1938-42. Asst Principal, Treasury, 1942-44; Administrative Officer with

UNRRA, working in London, Belgium, Austria, 1944-46; Sarah Smithson studentship in philosophy, Newnham Coll., Cambridge, 1947-48. *Publications:* Sartre, Romantic Rationalist, 1953; Under the Net, 1954; The Flight from the Enchanter, 1955; The Sandcastle, 1957; The Bell, 1958; A Severed Head, 1961 (play, Criterion, 1963); An Unofficial Rose, 1962; The Unicorn, 1963; The Italian Girl, 1964 (play, Criterion, 1967); The Red and the Green, 1965; The Time of The Angels, 1966; The Nice and The Good, 1968; Bruno's Dream, 1969; A Fairly Honourable Defeat, 1970; The Sovereignty of Good, 1970; *Play:* The Servants and the Snow (Greenwich), 1970; papers in Proc. Aristotelian Soc., etc. *Address:* Cedar Lodge, Steeple Aston, Oxford.

**MURDOCH, (Keith) Rupert;** Publisher; Chairman: News Ltd, Australia; News of the World Organisation Ltd, UK; *b* 11 March 1931; *s* of late Sir Keith Murdoch and of Dame Elisabeth (Joy) Murdoch, *qv*; *m* 1967, Anna Torv; two *d*. *Address:* 30 Bouverie Street, EC4.

**MURDOCH, Richard Bernard;** Actor (stage, films, broadcasting, television); *b* Keston, Kent; *s* of late Bernard Murdoch and late Amy Florence Scott, both of Tunbridge Wells; *m* 1932, Peggy Rawlings; one *s* two *d*. *Educ:* Charterhouse; Pembroke Coll., Cambridge. Commenced theatrical career in chorus of musical comedies, after which played dancing, light comedy and juvenile rôles in musical comedy and revue. Productions include: The Blue Train; Oh, Kay; That's a Good Girl; Oh, Letty; The Five O'Clock Girl; C. B. Cochran's 1930 Revue; Stand Up and Sing; Ballyhoo; various Charlot revues; Charabang; Stop–Go; a Charlot pantomime, What a Witch; Charlot's The Town Talks; Over She Goes. The advent of broadcasting brought firstly several appearances as an early television star and then the famous partnership with Arthur Askey. At outbreak of War, 1939, was playing in Band Waggon at London Palladium and also making films; these include; The Terror; Over She Goes; Band Waggon; Charlie's Big-Hearted Aunt; The Ghost Train; I Thank You. In Jan. 1941 joined RAF as Pilot-Officer in Admin. and Special Duties Branch; one year at Bomber Command HQ (Intelligence Br.) and subs. Intelligence Officer at various stations all over the country; towards end of War became Sqdn Ldr under Wing-Comdr Kenneth Horne in Directorate of Administrative Plans, Air Ministry. In off-duty hours at Air Ministry during this period Much-Binding-in-the-Marsh was evolved with Kenneth Horne. Also on the air in Puzzle Corner (Monday Night at Eight) and many other broadcasts. Released from RAF Oct. 1945; went on tour with George Black's revue, Strike a New Note. Dame in Emile Littler's Pantomime, Little Miss Muffet, London Casino, Dec. 1949. 20 weeks in Australia for ABC recordings, 1954. Other films include: Three Men and a Girl, Strictly Confidential, Not a Hope in Hell. *Publications:* series of short stories for Strand Magazine. *Recreations:* sailing, golf. *Address:* Thend Cottage, Walton-on-the Hill, Tadworth, Surrey. *Clubs:* Royal Automobile; Walton Heath Golf.

**MURDOCH, Rupert;** *see* Murdoch, K. R.

**MURDOCK, Kenneth Ballard;** Francis Lee Higginson Professor of English Literature, Emeritus, Harvard University, USA and Master Emeritus of Leverett House, since 1964; *b* 22 June 1895; *s* of Harold Murdock and Mary Lawson; *m* 1922, Laurette Eustis Potts; two *d*; *m* 1942, Eleanor Eckhart McLaughlin. *Educ:* Harvard Univ., AB, AM, PhD. Asst in English, Harvard, 1916-17, 1919-20; Asst Dean, Harvard, 1919-24; Instr. in English, Harvard, 1923-26; Asst Prof. English, 1926-30; Associate Prof., 1930-32; Prof., 1932-64; Master of Leverett House, 1931-41; Dean of Faculty of Arts and Sciences, 1931-36; Dir Harvard Centre for Renaissance Culture, 1961-64; Editor of New England Quarterly, 1928-38 and 1939-61, of American Literature, 1929-38 and 1939-49; Editor of Publications of Colonial Soc. of Massachusetts, 1925-30. A trustee of the American-Scandinavian Foundation, USA. Honorary degrees: LittD Middlebury Coll., 1930; LHD Trinity Coll., 1932; LLD Bucknell Univ., 1933; LHD Univ. of Vermont, 1938; FilD Univ. of Uppsala, Sweden, 1950; LittD, Harvard Univ., 1960. Knight of Order of the North Star (Sweden). *Publications:* Portraits of Increase Mather, 1924; Increase Mather, the Foremost American Puritan, 1925; Selections from Cotton Mather (ed), 1926; Handkerchiefs from Paul (ed), 1927; A Leaf of Grass from Shady Hill (ed), 1928; The Day of Doom (ed), 1929; C. Mather, Manuductio ad Ministerium (ed), 1938; The Sun at Noon, 1939; The Notebooks of Henry James (ed), with F. O. Matthiessen), 1947; Literature and Theology in Colonial New England, 1949; Pt I of The Literature of the American People (ed A. H. Quinn), 1951. *Address:* 416 Widener Library, Cambridge 38, Massachusetts, USA. *Clubs:* Harvard, Odd Volumes, Somerset, Tavern (Boston); Harvard, Century (NY).

**MURE, Geoffrey Reginald Gilchrist,** Hon. LLD (St Andrews); Warden of Merton College, Oxford, 1947-63; Hon. Fellow, Merton College, since 1963; Fellow of Wye College; *b* 8 April 1893; *s* of Reginald James Mure and Anna Charlotte Neave; *m* 1927, Kathleen Mary Seton (marriage dissolved, 1963), *d* of Seton de Winton; one *d* decd; *m* 1964, Mrs Josephine Browne. *Educ:* Eton Coll.; Merton Coll., Oxford. 1st Cl. Hon. Mods, 1913; Warwicks RHA (T), 1914-19; served France and Belgium, 1915-18 (MC, despatches, Chevalier Ordre de la Couronne, Croix de Guerre); Fellow and Tutor of Merton Coll., 1922; University Lecturer in Philosophy, 1929-37. Served on Gen. Staff War Office, 21 Army Group, SHAEF in connexion with propaganda, 1939-45; Pro-Vice-Chancellor, Univ. of Oxford, 1957. *Publications:* Translation of Aristotle, Posterior Analytics, 1925; Aristotle, 1932; Josephine, a Fairy Thriller, 1937; The Boots and Josephine, 1939; Introduction to Hegel, 1940; A Study of Hegel's Logic, 1950; Retreat from Truth, 1958; The Philosophy of Hegel, 1965. Articles. *Recreations:* formerly rowing, fox-hunting and miscellaneous ball games, now sketching. *Address:* 105 Bryanston Court, W1. *T:* 01-262 5724. *Clubs:* Savile, Leander.

**MURE, William,** CBE 1945; *b* 9 Aug. 1898; *s* of Col William Mure, Caldwell, Ayrshire, and Georgina, *e d* of 15th Earl of Eglinton and Winton; *m* 1921, Nancy Margaret (*d* 1944), *d* of Col Garton Unwin; one *s* one *d*; 2nd, 1946, Mrs Cecily Vian, *née* Gordon Cumming (*d* 1970). *Educ:* Wellington; RMA, Woolwich. Served European War, RFA and RHA. Retired as Managing Dir British Metal Corpn Ltd, Dec. 1963 (Dep. Chm. 1964-), Joint Controller of Non-Ferrous Metals, 1940-45. *Recreation:* racing. *Address:* 16 Selwood Place, SW7. *T:* 01-370 1560.

**MURGATROYD, Prof. Walter;** Professor of Thermal Power, Imperial College of Science and Technology, since 1968; Member, Anglo-Greek Mixed Commission, since 1963; Member, Anglo-Belgian Mixed Commission, since 1964; *b* 15 Aug. 1921; *s* of Harry G. Murgatroyd and Martha W. Strachan; *m* 1952,

Denise Geneviève, *d* of Robert Adolphe Schlumberger, Paris and Bénouville; two *s* one *d*. *Educ:* St Catharine's Coll., Cambridge. Hawker Aircraft Ltd, 1942-44; Rolls Royce Ltd, 1944-46; Univ. of Cambridge (Liquid Metal and Reactor heat transfer research), 1947-54; UK Atomic Energy Authority, Harwell, 1954-56; Head of Dept of Nuclear Engineering, Queen Mary Coll., Univ. of London, 1956-67, and Dean of Engineering, 1966-67. *Publications:* contrib. to various scientific and technical journals. *Recreation:* music. *Address:* 90 Princes' Way, SW19. *T:* 01-788 7516.

**MURISON, Maj.-Gen. Charles Alexander Phipps,** CB 1944; CBE 1940; MC; *b* Grenfell, Sask., Canada, 7 Oct. 1894; *s* of late W. J. H. Murison, Montreal and Vancouver, and Alice Lepel, *d* of late Major C. E. Phipps; *m* 1920, Mary Pope Shirley, *d* of late Hon. Mr Justice W. H. P. Clement, of Supreme Court of British Columbia; one *d*. *Educ:* Vancouver High Sch.; Trinity Coll. Sch., Ont.; McGill Univ. 2nd Lt Royal Field Artillery, 1914; Brevet Major, 1932; Major, 1934; Brevet Lt-Col and Lt-Col 1939; Col, 1940; Brig., 1940; Temp. Maj.-Gen. 1943; Maj.-Gen. 1945; pac; psc; various Staff Appointments; served European War, 1914-18 (wounded, despatches, MC); War of 1939-45, France (CBE, CB); retired, 1949. *Publications:* sundry articles in military journals. *Recreations:* riding, shooting, fishing, golf, etc. *Address:* 5918 Jaynes Road, Duncan, BC, Canada.

**MURLESS, (Charles Francis) Noel;** Trainer of racehorses, Newmarket; Leading Trainer on the flat for eighth year at end of British flat racing season, 1970 (former years being 1948, 1957, 1959, 1960, 1961, 1967, 1968); The Queen's trainer since flat racing season of 1969; *b* 1910; *m* Gwen Carlow. He made a new record in earnings (£256,899) for his patrons, 1967. Has trained the Derby winning horse twice: 1960 (St Paddy); 1967 (Royal Palace); many successes in other classic races. *Address:* Warren Place, Newmarket, Suffolk. *T:* (house) Newmarket 2387, (office) Newmarket 2024.

**MURNAGHAN, Francis Dominic;** Mathematical Consultant; *b* Omagh, Co. Tyrone, Ireland, 4 Aug. 1893; *s* of George Murnaghan and Angela Mooney; *m* 1919, Ada May Kimbell; one *s* one *d*. *Educ:* Christian Bros Sch., Omagh; Univ. Coll., Dublin. BA, MA, DSc (hon.) National Univ. of Ireland; Travelling Student in Mathematical Physics, 1914-16; PhD The Johns Hopkins Univ., Baltimore. Instructor in Mathematics, The Rice Institute, 1916-18; Associate The Johns Hopkins Univ., 1918-21; Associate Prof., 1921-28; Prof. 1928-48; Dir Mathematics Institute, Rutgers, 1926; Visiting Prof. Univ. of Chicago, 1928 and 1930; Prof., Centro Técnico de Aeronáutica, Brazil, 1948-60; MRIA; MNAS. *Publications:* Vector Analysis and the Theory of Relativity, 1922; Theoretical Mechanics (with J. S. Ames), 1929; Hydrodynamics (with H. L. Dryden and H. Bateman), 1932; Theory of Group Representations, 1938; Analytic Geometry, 1946; Differential and Integral Calculus, 1947; Applied Mathematics, 1948; Finite Deformation of an Elastic Solid, 1951; Algebra elementar e trigonometria, 1954; Cálculo avancado, 1954; Equações diferenciais, 1955; The orthogonal and symplectic groups, 1957; The Laplace Transformation, 1962; The calculus of variations, 1962; The unitary and rotation groups, 1962. *Address:* Montrose Avenue, Baltimore, Md 21212, USA.

**MURNAGHAN, Hon. James Augustine,** MA, LLD; retired, as Judge of Supreme Court (formerly Judge of High Court) Irish Free State; *b* 1881; 2nd *s* of late George Murnaghan, Lisanelly House, Omagh; *m* 1919, Alice, *d* of Thomas Davy, Beaumont, Terenure. Barrister-at-Law (Irish Bar), 1903; Northern and Midland Circuits; on Board of Governors, National Gallery of Ireland, 1925-; Chm., 1962; Prof. of Jurisprudence, Roman Law and International Law, National Univ. of Ireland, 1910-24. *Address:* 25 Upper Fitzwilliam Street, Dublin.

**MURPHY, Sir Alexander (Paterson),** Kt 1954; MC 1918; Medical Consultant; *b* 25 Oct. 1892; *s* of George Sylvester Murphy and Jessie Watson Murphy; *m* 1921, Esme Park Hobson; three *d* (one *s* decd). *Educ:* Brisbane Grammar Sch.; St Andrew's Coll., Sydney Univ. MB, ChM 1916. MD 1947. FRCP, FRACP. Served War of 1917-19, France and Belgium, with AMC, AIF; practice, Brisbane, 1920; First Head, Dept of Medicine, and First Prof. of Medicine, University of Queensland, 1937-50. President: Queensland Branch of BMA, 1933; 7th Session, Australasian Medical Congress, 1950; Mem. Council and Board of Censors of RACP, 1939-52 (Pres., 1952-54). Patron, Aust. Post-Grad. Fedn in Medicine. Bancroft Orator (Brisbane), 1954; Listerian Orator (Adelaide), 1955; Syme Orator, Sydney, 1959. Hon. DSc, Univ. of Tasmania, 1958; Hon. MD, Univ. of Queensland, 1967. *Publications:* contribs to med. jls. *Recreations:* golf, fishing. *Address:* Forres, Whyenbah Road, Hamilton, Brisbane, Qld 4007, Australia. *Clubs:* Queensland (Brisbane); Union (Sydney).

**MURPHY, Prof. Alfred John,** CBE 1964; MSc, FIM, FRAeS; Vice-Chancellor, Cranfield Institute of Technology, 1969-70, retired; *b* 26 Feb. 1901; *s* of late William and Martha Murphy; *m* 1927, Helen Eulalie Blanche, *d* of late Rev. Herbert Findlay Millar, Jamaica, British West Indies; two *s*. *Educ:* Altrincham High Sch.; Univ. of Manchester. 1st Cl. Hons Chemistry, Manchester, 1920. Metallurgical Research, Univ. Coll., Swansea, 1920-23 and National Physical Laboratory, 1923-31; Chief Metallurgist, J. Stone & Co. Ltd, London, 1931-49; Dir, J. Stone & Co. Ltd, Light-Metal Forgings Ltd, Chm. Stone-Fry Magnesium Ltd, 1946-49; Prof. of Industrial Metallurgy, Univ. of Birmingham, 1950-55, and Dir of the Depts of Metallurgy, 1953-55; Principal, Coll. of Aeronautics, Cranfield, Bedford, 1955-69. Past Pres. Instn of Metallurgists; Past Pres. Inst. of Metals; Pres., Brit. Cast Iron Res. Assoc., 1968-; Vice-Chm., British Non-Ferrous Metals Research Assoc.; Member Council: Inter-Service Metallurgical Research Council, 1949-55 (Chm.), 1962-65; Aeronautical Research Council, 1961-64 (Materials Sub-Cttee, 1968-). *Publications:* Non-Ferrous Foundry Metallurgy, 1954; numerous papers on metallurgical subjects. *Recreations:* music, walking. *Address:* 4 Riverside Towers, St Mary's Street, Bedford. *T:* Bedford 59938. *Clubs:* Athenæum, Savage.

**MURPHY, Sir Dermod (Art Pelly),** Kt 1969; CMG 1960; OBE 1955; Governor and Commander-in-Chief, St Helena, since 1968; *b* 10 Aug. 1914; *s* of John J. L. Murphy, Solicitor, Dublin, and Anne Murphy (*née* Pelly), Dublin. *Educ:* Trinity Coll., Dublin (LLB, MA); Oriel Coll., Oxford. Colonial Service, 1938; Western Nigeria: Resident (Provincial Comr), Ibadan Prov., 1954; Perm. Sec., Min. of Local Govt, 1957; Actg Dep. Gov., 1958-60; Actg Gov., 1960; Commissioner for Special Duties, Western Nigeria, 1958-60; Colonial Office, 1960-63. *Recreations:* tennis, travel, photography. *Address:* 7 Radnor Mews, W2; Plantation House, Island of St Helena, South Atlantic

Ocean. *Club:* East India and Sports. *See also J. P. Murphy.*

**MURPHY, Sir Ellis;** *see* Murphy, Sir O. E. J.

**MURPHY, Lt-Col Gerald Patrick,** CIE 1943; IA and Indian Political Service (retired); *b* 8 May 1888; *y s* of Lt-Col Patrick Murphy, IMS, and Helen, *d* of Surgeon James McCraith, FRCS, RN; *m* 1926, Charlotte, *d* of Charles Nelson, Gloucester, Mass, USA; one *s. Educ:* Brighton Coll.; RMC, Sandhurst. 2nd Lt IA 1908; Political Service, 1913; reverted to military employ for European War, 1914-19; served NW Frontier 1915 and in Mesopotamia, 1916-18; held various appointments as Asst Political Agent and Asst Resident till 1926; HBM Consul, Muscat, 1926-30; Political Agent, West India States and Orissa States, 1930-37; Resident Kolhapur and the Deccan States, 1937-38; for the Madras States, 1939-43; retired. *Address:* 13 Millais Park, St Helier, Jersey, CI; c/o National and Grindlay's Bank Ltd, 13 St James's Square, SW1.

**MURPHY, Most Rev. Henry;** *see* Limerick, Bishop of, (RC).

**MURPHY, Most Rev. John A.;** *see* Cardiff, Archbishop of, (RC).

**MURPHY, (John) Pelly;** Resident Judge of HM Court of The Sovereign Base Areas of Akrotiri and Dhekelia, Cyprus, since 1969; *b* 19 March 1909; *s* of late J. J. L. and late Anne Murphy. *Educ:* Mount St Mary's Coll.; Trinity Coll., Dublin. Asst Crown Solicitor, Hong Kong, 1936; Attorney-General: Gambia, 1947; Zanzibar, 1950; Puisne Judge, Supreme Court, Kenya, 1956-64; Asst Legal Adviser, FO, 1966-69. *Recreation:* idling. *Address:* c/o Provincial Bank of Ireland, 8 Throgmorton Avenue, EC2. *Clubs:* Junior Carlton, Travellers'; Royal Irish Yacht (Dun Laoghaire).
*See also Sir Dermod Murphy.*

**MURPHY, Neville Richard,** MA; Principal, Hertford College, Oxford, 1939-59; *b* 3 March 1890. *Educ:* Christ's Hosp.; Brasenose Coll., Oxford. Capt. (SR) Royal Irish Fusiliers and Tank Corps, 1914-18; Fellow of Hertford Coll., Oxford, 1919, Hon. Fellow, 1959; Hon. Fellow of Brasenose Coll., Oxford, 1960. *Publications:* The Interpretation of Plato's Republic, 1951; articles on Plato in Classical Quarterly. *Address:* 22 Walden Way, Hornchurch, Essex.

**MURPHY, Sir (Oswald) Ellis (Joseph),** Kt 1963; ChM, FRCP, FRACP; Chairman: Queensland Cardiac Board; Work Assessment Committee, Australian National Heart Foundation, Brisbane; Blood Transfusion Committee, Australian Red Cross, Brisbane (Deputy Chairman, Queensland Division); *b* 2 April 1895; *s* of Miles Murphy, Sydney; *m* 1924, May Beirne; one *s* two *d* (and one *s* decd). *Educ:* Christian Brothers High Sch., Lewisham, and Univ. of Sydney, Australia. Grad. in Med., First Cl. Hons and Univ. Medal, 1919; Hon. Phys. to Out-patients, Mater Misericordiæ Hosp., Brisbane, 1923-28; London Hosp., 1928, MRCP, Sen. Phys., MM Hosp., 1928-38; Phys., Brisbane Gen. Hosp., 1939-50; Acting Prof. of Medicine, Univ. of Qld, 1950-54. (Foundation) FRACP 1938; Mem. Council, RACP 1958-64; Mem., Qld State Cttee, CSIRO; Trustee, Qld Art Gallery. Hon. Col RAAMC. *Publications:* contributed to Australian Journal of Medicine. *Recreation:* yachting. *Address:* Camden, Toorak Road, Hamilton, Brisbane, Queensland 4007, Australia. *Clubs:* Queensland, United Service, Royal Queensland Yacht Squadron (Brisbane).

**MURPHY, Maj.-Gen. Richard,** CB 1954; CBE 1950; MB, BCh; *b* 1896; *s* of late Richard Paul Murphy, Killarney, County Kerry; *m* 1938, Florence Helen, *d* of late Joseph Patrick Tyndall, Stillorgan, County Dublin; one *s*. *Educ:* Clongowes Wood Coll.; Trinity Coll., Dublin. Lt RAMC 1920; DADGAMS, War Office, 1937-40; served War of 1939-45 (despatches); DDMS, MELF, 1943-46; Comdt Depot, RAMC, 1948-51; DDMS, Scottish Command, 1952. Lt-Col 1944; Col 1948; Brig. 1952; Maj.-Gen. 1953; QHS 1953-56; Dep. Dir Medical Services, Southern Command, 1953-56, retired. CStJ. *Address:* 95 Shirley Drive, Hove, Sussex BN3 6UE.

**MURPHY, Richard Holmes;** retired as Judge, High Court, Tanganyika (1960-64); Senior Lecturer in Law, Holborn College, since 1965; *b* 9 July 1915; *o s* of Harold Lawson Murphy, KC, and Elsie, 4th *d* of Rt Hon. Lord Justice Holmes; *m* 1967, Irene Sybil, *e d* of Reginald and Elizabeth Swift. *Educ:* Charterhouse; Emmanuel Coll., Cambridge (BA, LLB). Called to Bar, Inner Temple, 1939. Enlisted Inns of Court Regt, 1939; Commissioned 3rd Company of London Yeomanry, 1940; served Middle East and Italy, 1941-45; Judge Advocate-Gen.'s Dept, WO, 1945-46; released, rank of Major. Resident Magistrate, Tanganyika, 1948; Chief Registrar, Gold Coast Supreme Ct and Registrar of W African Ct of Appeal, 1951: Sen. Magistrate, Gold Coast, 1955; Puisne Judge, Ghana, 1957-60. *Address:* c/o National Bank Ltd, 180 Strand, WC2. *Club:* Royal Automobile.

**MURPHY, Robert Daniel;** Statesman; *b* Milwaukee, Wisconsin, 28 Oct. 1894; *s* of Francis Patrick Murphy and Catherine Louise Schmitz; *m* 1921, Mildred Claire Taylor; three *d. Educ:* Marquette Academy and Univ.; George Washington Univ., LLB 1920; LLM 1928; clerk Post Office Dept, 1916-17; clerk American Legation, Bern, 1917-19; Asst Chief Treas. Dept, 1919-20; vice-consul, Zürich, 1921; Munich, 1921-25; Consul, Seville, 1925; Dept of State, 1926-30; Consul, Paris, 1930-36; First Sec. Paris, 1936-39; Counsellor, Paris, 1940; Chargé d'Affaires, Vichy, July 1940; detailed Nov. 1940 by President Roosevelt to investigate conditions in French N Africa; concluded economic accord with General Maxime Weygand, Feb. 1941; effected preparations for Allied landings in N Africa, Nov. 1942; conducted negotiations for entry of French W Africa into war, Dec. 1942; appointed President's Personal Rep. with rank of Minister to French N Africa; chief civil affairs officer on staff of Supreme Commander Allied Forces HQ, 1942; DSM (American), 1942; participated in negotiations for Italian armistice, July-Aug. 1943; mem. Mediterranean Advisory Commission with rank of Ambassador, Sept. 1943; US Polit. Adviser with rank of Ambassador, Allied Forces HQ 1943; US Polit. Adviser for Germany with rank of Ambassador, SHAEF, 1944; Political Adviser to the Office of Military Government for Germany (US), 1945-49; Dir, Office of German and Austrian Affairs, US, 1949; US Ambassador in Brussels, 1949-52; US Ambassador in Tokyo, 1952-53; Asst Sec. of State for UN Affairs, 1953; Deputy Under Sec. of State, US, 1954-59; Under Sec. of State for Political Affairs, 1959. Chm., Corning Glass International, 1967. *Publication:* Diplomat among Warriors, 1964. *Recreations:* golf, etc. *Clubs:* Metropolitan (Washington); University (New York); Chevy Chase (Maryland).

**MURPHY, William Parry,** AD, MD; Lecturer on Medicine, Harvard Medical School, 1948-58, Lecturer Emeritus, 1958; Senior Associate in Medicine, Peter Bent Brigham Hospital, 1935-58, Senior Associate Emeritus in Medicine and Consultant in Hematology since 1958; Consultant Hematologist: Melrose Hospital, Melrose, Mass; Quincy City Hospital, Quincy, Mass; Emerson Hospital, Concord, Mass; Consultant in Internal Medicine, Delaware State Hospital, Farnhurst, Delaware; *b* 6 Feb. 1892; *s* of Thomas Francis Murphy and Rose Anna Parry; *m* 1919, Pearl Harriett Adams; one *s* (one *d* decd). *Educ:* Univ. of Oregon (AB); Harvard Med. Sch. (MD). Army, enlisted Medical Reserve, 1917-18; acted as House Officer at the Rhode Island Hosp., 1920-22; as Asst Resident Physician, 1922-23; Junior Associate in Medicine, 1923-28; Associate in Medicine, 1928-35 at Peter Bent Brigham Hospital; Asst in Medicine, 1923-28; Instructor in Medicine, 1928-35; Associate in Medicine, Harvard Medical Sch., 1935-48; has been engaged in the practice of Medicine since 1923, and carried on research at the Peter Bent Brigham Hospital in Boston; Diplomate in Internal Medicine, 1937. Mem. many American and foreign medical and scientific socs; co-discoverer of the liver treatment for pernicious anemia; was awarded the Cameron Prize in Medicine by the Univ. of Edinburgh Medical Faculty in 1930, the Bronze Medal of the American Medical Association in 1934, and the Nobel Prize in Physiology and Medicine in 1934. Hon. Dr of Science, Gustavus Adolphus Coll., 1963; Hon. Member: Univ. of Oregon Med. Alumni Assoc., 1964; Internat. Soc. for Research on Civilisation Diseases and Vital Substances, 1969. Mem. Bd of Dirs of Cordis Corp., 1960-70. Commander of the first rank, Order of the White Rose, Finland, 1934; gold medal, Mass Humane Soc., 1935; National Order of Merit, Carlos J. Finlay, Official, Havana, Cuba, 1952; Dist. Achievement Award, City of Boston, 1965. *Publications:* Anemia in Practice: Pernicious Anemia, 1939; about 75 papers published in medical journals, especially on diseases of the blood. *Recreation:* collector of rare old firearms. *Address:* 1101 Beacon Street, Brookline, Mass 02146, USA. *T:* Longwood 6-4445. *Clubs:* Sigma xi (Harvard); Harvard (Boston); Rotary (Brookline, Mass).

**MURRANT, Sir Ernest Henry,** KCMG 1945; MBE; retired as Chairman of Furness Withy & Co. Ltd and other Cos; *b* 1889; *o s* of Henry John Murrant; *m* 1914, May, *y d* of John Archer, Belfast; one *s*. Min. of War Transport Rep. in Middle East, 1941-44; Pres. (1947) Council of Chamber of Shipping; Chm. General Council of British Shipping, 1947-48. Retired as: Dir of Barclays Bank Ltd, 1960; Chm. Bd of Management, Seamen's Hosp., 1967; Hon. Treas. Royal Alfred Merchant Seamen's Soc., 1969; Prime Warden Shipwrights' Co., 1957; Hon. Member: Hon. Co. of Master Mariners; Assoc. of Old Worcesters. *Recreation:* golf. *Address:* Browning's Manor, Blackboys, Sussex. *T:* Framfield 207. *Club:* Royal Eastbourne (Eastbourne).

**MURRAY**; *see* Erskine-Murray.

**MURRAY,** family name of **Duke of Atholl,** of **Earl of Dunmore,** of **Earl of Mansfield and Mansfield** and of **Baron Murray of Newhaven.**

**MURRAY OF NEWHAVEN,** Baron *cr* 1964 (Life Peer); **Keith Anderson Hope Murray,** KCB 1963; Kt 1955; Chancellor, Southampton University, since 1964; Visitor, Loughborough University of Technology, since 1968; Director, Leverhulme Trust Fund since 1965; *b* 28 July 1903; 2nd *surviving s* of late Rt Hon. Lord Murray, PC, CMG, LLD. *Educ:* Edinburgh Academy; Edinburgh Univ. (BSc); Ministry of Agriculture, 1925-26; Commonwealth Fund Fellowship, 1926-29, at Cornell Univ., New York (PhD); Oriel Coll. and Agricultural Economics Research Institute, 1929-32, University of Oxford (BLitt and MA); Research Officer, 1932-39; Fellow and Bursar, Lincoln Coll., 1937-53, and Rector, 1944-53; Univ. Grants Cttee, 1953-63. Oxford City Council, 1938-40; Min. of Food, 1939-40; RAFVR 1941-42; Dir of Food and Agriculture, Middle East Supply Centre, GHQ, MEF, 1942-45; Oxfordshire Education Cttee, 1946-49; JP, City of Oxford, 1950-53; Chm., Vice-Chancellor's Commission of Enquiry on Halls of Residence, 1947; Mem. of Commission of Enquiry into Disturbances in the Gold Coast, 1948; Development Commissioner, 1948-53; Chairman: Advisory Cttee on Colonial Colleges of Arts, Science and Technology, 1949-53, RAF Education Advisory Cttee, 1947-53; National Council of Social Service, 1947-53. Advisory Cttees on Agricultural Colls, 1954-60, Harkness Fellowship Cttee of Award, 1957-63, Cttee on Provincial Agricultural Economics Service, 1949-57, Cttee on Australian Univs, 1957; World Univ. Service, 1957-62; Dartmouth Review Cttee, 1958; Pres. Agric. Economics Soc., 1959-60; Pres. Agricultural History Soc., 1959-62; Chairman: Colonial Univ. Grants Cttee, 1964-66; London Conf. on Overseas Students, 1963-67; Academic Adv. Cttee for Stirling Univ., 1967-. Vice-Pres., Wellington Coll., 1966-69; Governor, The Charterhouse, 1957-69. Mem. Bd, Wellcome Trustees, 1965-; Hon. Pres., Nat. Union of Students, 1967-70. Chairman: Cttee of Enquiry into Governance of London Univ., 1970-; Royal Commn for Exhibition of 1851, 1962-. Director: Bristol Aeroplane Co., 1963-67; Metal Box Co., 1964-68. Hon. Fellow: Downing Coll., Cambridge; Oriel Coll., Oxford; Lincoln Coll., Oxford. Hon. LLD: Univs of Western Australia and of Bristol, 1963; of Cambridge, Hull, Edinburgh, Southampton, Liverpool and Leicester, 1964; of Calif., 1966; Hon. DCL Oxford, 1964; Hon. DLitt, Keele, 1966; Hon. DUStirling, 1968; Hon. FDSRCS, 1964; Hon. FUMIST, 1965. *Address:* The Leverhulme Trust, 21-23 New Fetter Lane, EC4. *Clubs:* Athenæum, English-Speaking Union. Oxford and Cambridge University.

**MURRAY, Sir Alan John Digby,** 14th Bt, *cr* 1628, **of Blackbarony,** and Hereditary Secretary for Scotland; engaged in livestock-raising and agriculture in Argentina; *b* 22 June 1909; *s* of late Alan Digby Murray and late Eileen Muriel Shaw; *S* cousin, Sir Kenelm Bold Murray, 13th Bt, 1959; *m* 1943, Mabel Elisabeth, *d* of Arthur Bernard Schiele, Arias, Argentina; four *s*. *Educ:* Brighton Coll., Sussex. *Recreations:* golf, tennis, riding. *Heir: s* Nigel Andrew Digby Murray, *b* 15 Aug. 1944. *Address:* (Residences): Estancia La Linda Mora, Arias, Argentina; Four Winds, Los Cocos, Sierras de Cordoba, Argentina. *Clubs:* English (Cordoba); Venado Tuerto Polo; Tigre Boat, Dorado Fishing (Buenos Aires).

**MURRAY, Albert James;** *b* 9 Jan. 1930; *s* of Frederick Clifton Murray and Catherine Murray; *m* 1960, Margaret Anne (*née* Wakeford); one *s* one *d*. *Educ:* Elementary. LCC Southwark Borough Council, 1953-62; LCC 1958-65 (Chm., LCC Schs Planning

Cttee, 1961-65). MP (Lab) Gravesend, 1964-70; Mem., Estimates Cttee, 1966-; PPS to: Minister of Defence (Navy), 1965-66; Minister of State, Board of Trade, 1966-68; Minister of State, Min. of Technology, 1968-69; Parly Sec., Min. of Transport, Oct. 1969-June 1970. *Recreations:* reading, fishing, watching Association football. *Address:* 233 Upper Wrotham Road, Gravesend, Kent. *T:* Gravesend 5958.

**MURRAY, (Alice) Rosemary,** MA, DPhil; JP; President, New Hall, Cambridge, since 1964 (Tutor in Charge, 1954-64); *b* 28 July 1913; *d* of late Adm. A. J. L. Murray and Ellen Maxwell Spooner. *Educ:* Downe House, Newbury; Lady Margaret Hall, Oxford (Hon. Fellow, 1968). MA (Oxon and Cantab); BSc, DPhil (Oxon). Lecturer in chemistry, Royal Holloway Coll., 1938-41. Served War of 1939-45, Experimental Officer, Admiralty Signals Establishment, 1941; WRNS, 1942-46, successively Wren, 3rd, 2nd, 1st and Chief Officer. Lecturer in Chemistry, Univ. of Sheffield, 1941-42; Lecturer in Chemistry, Girton Coll., Cambridge, 1946-54. Fellow, 1949, Tutor, 1951; Demonstrator in Chemistry, Univ. of Cambridge, 1947-52. Member: Federation of Univ. Women; Chemical Soc.; Wages Councils, 1968-. JP City of Cambridge, 1953. *Recreations:* sailing, foreign travel, gardening. *Address:* New Hall, Cambridge. *T:* 51721. *Clubs:* Service Women's, Women's University.

**MURRAY, Sir Alistair;** *see* Murray, Sir Robert Alistair.

**MURRAY, Sir Andrew (Hunter Arbuthnot),** Kt, *cr* 1949; OBE 1945; DL, JP; *b* Edinburgh, 19 Dec. 1903; *s* of late Alfred Alexander Arbuthnot Murray, MA, LLB, WS, JP, FRSE and Mary Moir; unmarried. *Educ:* Daniel Stewart's Coll.; George Heriot's Sch. Councillor of Edinburgh, 1929; (Hon.) City Treasurer, 1943-46; Lord Provost of Edinburgh, 1947-51. Hon. LLD (Edinburgh); DL County of City of Edinburgh. Outstanding interest is Social Services, mainly among Youth and Aged. Former President of Liberal Party Organisation, 1961-65; KStJ 1954, Chancellor of the Priory of Scotland. *Address:* 1 Randolph Place, Edinburgh 3. *T:* 031-225 5698.

**MURRAY, Cecil James Boyd,** MS; FRCS; Surgeon, Middlesex Hospital, since 1946; Surgeon, Royal Masonic Hospital, London, since 1958; *b* 8 Jan. 1910; *s* of Richard Murray, MIEE; *m* 1940, Bona, *o d* of Rev. William Askwith, MA, Ripon; two *s. Educ:* Warriston Sch., Moffat; King's Sch., Canterbury; Middlesex Hospital Medical Sch. MB, BS, 1935; MS 1936; MRCS, LRCP, 1933, FRCS 1936. Formerly: Surgeon, King Edward Memorial Hospital, Ealing; Lecturer in Operative Surgery, Middlesex Hospital Medical Sch. Served War of 1939-45 (despatches), temp. Lt-Col RAMC. Mem., Court of Examiners, Royal College of Surgeons of England; Fellow, Assoc. of Surgeons of Great Britain; FR Soc. Med. *Publications:* papers in medical journals. *Recreation:* fly-fishing. *Address:* 149 Harley Street, W1. *T:* 01-935 4444; 17 Sheldon Avenue, N6. *T:* 01-340 8105. *Clubs:* Flyfishers', MCC.

**MURRAY, Charles de Bois;** Sheriff-Substitute of Roxburghshire at Jedburgh and of Berwickshire at Duns, 1947-63; of Ross and Cromarty at Stornoway, 1945-47; *b* 1891, *e s* of late C. R. Murray, Merchant, Glasgow; *m* 1929, Hope (*d* 1963), 3rd *d* of late James Cruickshank Smith, CBE, LLD; one *d* (one *s* decd). *Educ:* Glasgow Acad.; Glasgow Univ. (MA with 1st class hons in classics, 1912; LLB 1919). During European War, 1914-18, served in France and Belgium with the infantry, and from 1916 with tank corps; demobilised, 1919. with rank of Capt.; called to Scottish Bar, 1919, and to English Bar (Inner Temple), 1922. Contested (L) Tradeston, Glasgow, 1922, and North Midlothian, 1923. Acted as interim Sheriff-Substitute in Edinburgh 1935, in Greenock, 1940, in Ayr, 1942-43. Mem. Internat. Law Assoc., 1926-64; Scottish Mem. Exec. Council, 1955-64. *Publications:* Forbes of Culloden, 1936; How Scotland is Governed, 1938 (second ed. revised, 1947); Rebuilding Europe, 1944; The Law of Wills in Scotland, 1945; The Future of Scots Law, 1961; also many articles to legal and literary journals and reviews. *Address:* 6 Moray Place, Edinburgh. *T:* 031-225 1103.

**MURRAY, Colin Robert Baillie,** CIE 1946; *b* 1892; *s* of late A. A. Murray, Kilcoy, Killearnan, Ross-shire; *m* 1917, Margaret, *d* of E. G. Drake-Brockman, ICS; one *s* one *d. Educ:* Clifton Coll. Entered Indian Police, 1911; served European War, 8th Cavalry, Indian Army, 1915-19. Deputy Dir of Intelligence, Govt of India, 1938; Inspector-General of Police, Orissa, India, 1944-46; retired, 1947. *Recreations:* gardening, bridge. *Address:* Beech Cottage, Seaton Avenue, Hythe, Kent. *T:* Hythe 67714. *Club:* Radnor (Folkestone).

**MURRAY, Donald Frederick;** Counsellor, HM Embassy, Tehran, since 1969; *b* 14 June 1924; *s* of A. T. Murray and F. M. Murray (*née* Byfield); *m* 1949, Marjorie Culverwell; three *s* one *d. Educ:* King's Sch., Canterbury; Worcester Coll., Oxford. Royal Marines, 1943-46. Entered Foreign Office, 1948; served in Warsaw, Vienna, Cyprus, Stockholm and Saigon; Counsellor, Foreign and Commonwealth Office, 1966-69. *Recreations:* gentle sports, gardening, small boats. *Address:* 27K Bramham Gardens, SW5. *Club:* Travellers'.

**MURRAY, Sir (Francis) Ralph (Hay),** KCMG 1962 (CMG 1950); CB 1957; a Governor of the BBC since 1967; Chairman, CGE Internationale (UK) Ltd; Director: Cadmium Nickel Batteries Ltd; Parway Land & Investments Ltd; *b* 3 March 1908; *s* of Rev. Charles Hay Murray and Mabel Umfreville; *m* 1935, Mauricette, *d* of Count Bernhard Kuenburg; three *s* one *d. Educ:* Brentwood Sch.; St Edmund Hall, Oxford. BBC, 1934-39; Foreign Office, 1939-45; Allied Commission for Austria, 1945-46; Special Commissioner's Staff, SE Asia, 1946-47; Foreign Office, 1947-51; Counsellor, HM Embassy, Madrid, 1951-54; Minister, HM Embassy, Cairo, 1954-56; Asst Under-Sec. of State, FO, 1957-61; Dep. Under-Sec. of State, FO, 1961-62; Ambassador to Greece, 1962-67. *Address:* The Old Rectory, Stoke Hammond, Bletchley, Bucks. *T:* Soulbury 247. *Club:* Travellers'.

**MURRAY, George Raymond B.;** *see* Beasley-Murray.

**MURRAY, Gen. Sir Horatius,** GCB 1962 (CB 1945); KBE 1956; DSO 1943; Colonel of The Cameronians (Scottish Rifles), 1958-64, now retired; *b* 18 April 1903; *s* of late Charles

Murray; *m* 1953, Beatrice, *y d* of Frederick Cuthbert. *Educ:* Peter Symonds Sch., Winchester; RMC, Sandhurst. Gazetted to Cameronians, 1923; transferred to Camerons, 1935. Served War of 1939-45, North Africa, Sicily, Italy, France (DSO, CB); GOC 6 Armoured Division, 1944-45; Dir of Personal Services, War Office, 1946-47; GOC 1st Infantry Division, 1947-50; GOC Northumbrian District, 1951-53; Commander, Commonwealth Division in Korea, 1953-54; GOC-in-C, Scottish Command and Governor of Edinburgh Castle, 1955-58; Commander-in-Chief, Allied Forces, Northern Europe, 1958-61, retired. Commander Legion of Merit (US); Knight Commander, Order of the Sword (Sweden). *Recreations:* golf, cricket. *Club:* Royal Commonwealth Society.

**MURRAY, Ian,** MD, FRCP (Glasgow); FRCP (Edinburgh); Consulting Physician; late Visiting Physician and Physician in charge of Department for Metabolic Diseases, Victoria Infirmary, Glasgow; Hon. Lt-Col RAMC; Professor of Physiology, Anderson College, Glasgow; *b* 26 April 1899; *s* of late John and Elizabeth Murray; *m* 1924, Annabel M. T. Tully, MA, PhD; one *s* one *d*. *Educ:* Glasgow Academy; Glasgow Univ. (Carnegie Research Scholar in physiology). Retired from Victoria Infirmary, Glasgow, Oct. 1964. Vice-Pres., Brit. Diabetic Assoc.; Hon. Associate, Brit. Dietetic Assoc. *Publications:* Good Health with Diabetes, 4th edn 1963; The Victoria Infirmary of Glasgow, 1890-1948, 1967; papers in medical jls on nutritional and metabolic subjects. *Address:* Bluerisk, Strathblane, near Glasgow. *T:* Blanefield 214. *Clubs:* Art, Royal Scottish Automobile (Glasgow).

**MURRAY, Jack Keith,** OBE 1959; ED; BA, BScAgr, NDD, DipMilSc; retired as Administrator, Territory of Papua and New Guinea, (1949-52), and President Executive Council, also of Legislative Council of Papua and New Guinea; Member Board of Governors, Women's and Cromwell Colleges, University of Queensland; Hon. Life Member, RSSAILA; *b* Brighton, Vic., 8 Feb. 1889; *s* of late John Murray, Coburg, Melbourne; *m* 1924, Evelyn, BSc Agr., *d* of late Ernest Andrews. *Educ:* Univ. of Sydney; Dairy Sch. for Scotland. Formerly Lecturer in Bacteriology and Dairy Technology, Hawkesbury Agric. Coll., NSW; Principal Qld Agric. Coll., 1923-45; Prof. of Agric., Univ. of Queensland, 1927-45; Mem. Federal Diary Investigation Cttee, 1930; Fellow Aust. Nat. Research Council; Fellow, Aust. and NZ Assoc. for Advancement of Science (Pres. Section "K" Melbourne meeting, 1935); Pres. Royal Society of Queensland, 1936. Served with 1st and 2nd AIF; Lt-Col, CO 25th (Darling Downs) Bn, AMF, 1940; Lt-Col, GSO2 (Training) Northern Command, 1940; Col comdg AIF Training Depots, Northern Comd, 1941-42; Col Comdg 5th Aust. Training Bde, 1943; Research Officer, Directorate of Research, HQ, Allied Land Forces, 1944; Chief Instructor, Allied Land Forces Sch. of Civil Affairs, Duntroon, 1945. Hon. Col, retired list, 1951. Administrator, Provisional Administration of Papua-New Guinea, 1945-49. Macrossan Memorial Lecturer, Univ. of Queensland, 1946. Mem. Australian Delegation to South Seas Conference (South Pacific Commn), 1947. Adviser, under Colombo Plan, in Agricultural Education to Ceylon Dept of Agriculture, 1956-57; Actg Warden, Internat. House, Univ. of Melbourne, 1959; Mem. of Senate, Univ. of Queensland, 1953-68; Mem. Nat. Council, Australian Boy Scouts Assoc., 1959-70. Hon. Life Member: Royal Society Queensland; Queensland Univ. Union. FAIAS Hon. DSc Queensland. *Recreation:* walking. *Address:* 49 Dell Road, St Lucia, Brisbane, SW6, Australia. *Clubs:* United Services (Brisbane); Public Service, Konedobu (both at Port Moresby, Papua).

**MURRAY, James,** CMG 1966; HM Diplomatic Service; Consul-General, San Francisco, since 1970; *b* 3 Aug. 1919; *er s* of late James Hamilton Murray, King's Cross, Isle of Arran, and Hester Macneill Buie. *Educ:* Bellahouston Acad.; Glasgow Univ. Royal Regt of Artillery, 1939; Served India and Burma, 1943-45; Staff Coll., Quetta, 1945; Bde Major (RA) 19 Ind. Div.; GSO II (RA) ALFSEA; GSO II War Office. HM Foreign (subseq. Diplomatic) Service, 1947; Foreign Office, 1947-49; First Sec. (Information), HM Embassy, Cairo, 1949-54; Foreign Office, 1954-56; attached National Defence Coll. of Can., 1956-57; First Sec., HM Embassy, Paris, 1957-61; HM Consul in Ruanda-Urundi, 1961-62; Special Ambassador for Independence celebrations in Ruanda, July 1962, and in Burundi, Sept. 1962; Ambassador to Rwanda and Burundi, 1962-63; Deputy Head of UK Delegation to European Community, Luxembourg, 1963-65; Counsellor, Djakarta, 1965-68; Far Eastern Dept, FCO, 1968-70. *Recreations:* horses, lawn tennis. *Address:* c/o Foreign and Commonwealth Office, SW1. *Clubs:* St James', Queen's.

**MURRAY, James Dalton,** CMG 1957; HM Diplomatic Service, retired; British High Commissioner in Jamaica, 1965-70; Ambassador to Haiti (non-resident), 1966-70; *b* Edinburgh, 6 March 1911; *s* of late Dr James Murray, Edinburgh, and late Eleanor (*née* Mortimer); *m* 1st, 1949, Dora Maud (Denny) Carter (*d* 1958); one *s* two *d*; 2nd, 1959, Merriall Rose, 2nd *d* of Sir Timothy Eden, 8th Bart; two *s*. *Educ:* Stowe; Magdalene Coll., Cambridge (Exhibitioner). Entered HM Consular Service, 1933; Vice-Consul: San Francisco, 1933, Mexico City, 1936; 2nd Sec., Embassy, Washington, 1939; 1st Sec. and Consul, La Paz, 1943; 1st Sec., Prague, 1945; Foreign Office, 1945; Office of Comr-Gen. for SE Asia, Singapore, 1948; Counsellor, HM Foreign Service, and apptd to FO, 1950; seconded to CRO, 1952; Dep. High Comr for UK, Karachi, 1952; returned FO, 1955; Counsellor, British Embassy, Lisbon, 1959-61; Minister, 1961-63, Ambassador, 1963-65, Rumania. *Recreations:* golf; relaxing. *Address:* c/o Foreign and Commonwealth Office, SW1. *Club:* Travellers'.

**MURRAY, Prof. James Greig;** Professor of Surgery, University of London, since 1964; Hon. Consultant Surgeon, King's College Hospital, London; *b* 1 April 1919; *s* of J. A. F. Murray and Christina (*née* Davidson); *m* 1946, Cecilia (*née* Mitchell Park); one *s* one *d*. *Educ:* Peterhead Acad.; Aberdeen Univ. MB, ChB 1942; FRCS Edinburgh 1950; ChM (Aberdeen) 1961; FRCS 1964. Surg.-Lt, RNVR, 1943-46. Lectr in Anatomy Dept, Univ. Coll., London, 1950-54; Clinical Research Fellow, MRC, RCS of England, 1954-56; Sen. Lectr in Surgery, Univ. of Aberdeen, 1958-59. *Publications:* Scientific Basis of Surgery, 1965; Gastric Secretion: Mechanism and Control, 1965; After Vagotomy; articles in scientific and clinical jls on composition of vagus nerves, regeneration of nerves, physiology of gastric secretion and treatment of peptic ulceration, etc. *Recreations:* fishing, golf. *Address:* Six Pillars,

Crescent Wood Road, Sydenham Hill, SE26. *T:* 01-693 3160.

**MURRAY, James Patrick,** CMG 1958; *b* 1906; *m* 1934, Margaret Ruth Buchanan; three *s.* *Educ:* St Edward's Sch., Oxford; Christ Church, Oxford. Cadet, Northern Rhodesia, 1929; District Officer, Northern Rhodesia, 1931; Provincial Commissioner, Northern Rhodesia, 1950; Senior Provincial Commissioner, Northern Rhodesia, 1955; Commissioner for Northern Rhodesia in London, 1961-64 (Country became Independent, as Zambia, 1964). *Address:* Trewen, Shaftesbury Road, Woking, Surrey. *T:* Woking 61988. *Clubs:* East India and Sports, Royal Commonwealth Society.

**MURRAY, John (Arnaud Robin Grey),** MBE 1945; Senior Director of Publishing House of John Murray since 1968; *b* 22 Sept. 1909; *o s* of late Thomas Robinson Grey and Dorothy Evelyn Murray; *m* 1939, Diana Mary, 3rd *d* of late Col Bernard Ramsden James and Hon. Angela Kay-Shuttleworth; two *s* two *d.* *Educ:* Eton; Magdalen Coll., Oxford (BA Hist). Joined publishing firm of John Murray, 1930; Asst Editor, Cornhill Magazine, 1931; Asst Editor, Quarterly Review, 1933. Served with Royal Artillery and Army-Air Support, War Office, 1940-45. Relaunched Cornhill Magazine with Peter Quennell, 1945. Mem. Coun., Publishers' Association. *Publication:* (editor, with Peter Quennell) Byron: A Self-Portrait, 1950. *Recreations:* Byron, archives, forestry. *Address:* (office) 50 Albemarle Street, W1. *T:* 01-493 4361; (home) Cannon Lodge, 12 Cannon Place, NW3. *T:* 01-435 6537. *Clubs:* Pratt's, Beefsteak.

*See also Master of Nairne.*

**MURRAY, Hon. Sir John Murray,** Kt 1958; QC; *b* 9 March 1888; *s* of Charles Murray and Marian Dale; *m* 1916, Izobel Booysen; three *s* one *d.* *Educ:* Victoria Coll., Stellenbosch, S Africa; Worcester Coll., Oxford. Union of S Africa Civil Service, 1911; Advocate of Supreme Court, S Africa, 1914; Judge of Supreme Court of S Africa (Transvaal Provincial Division), 1937; Chief Justice, High Court of Southern Rhodesia, 1955-61. *Address:* PO Box 114, plettenberg Bay, South Africa. *Clubs:* Pretoria (S Africa); Salisbury (Rhodesia).

**MURRAY, Sir (John) Stanley,** Kt 1957; BA; Pastoralist; Past Chairman, The News Ltd, Adelaide; retired 1964; Chairman and Director of companies; *b* 27 March 1884; *s* of late John Murray, Wirrabara, SA; *m* 1910, Winifred Olive, *d* of late Dr A. E. Wigg; two *d.* *Educ:* Trinity Coll., Glenalmond; Collegiate Sch. of St Peter, Adelaide; Trinity Coll., Cambridge. Called to Bar, Inner Temple, 1909. Was Chm., Adelaide Electric Supply Co. Ltd, for ten years prior to its acquisition by the Electricity Trust of SA. *Recreations:* golf, racing. *Address:* Rosebank, Mt Pleasant, South Australia. *T:* Mt Pleasant 2. *Clubs:* Adelaide (Adelaide); Australian (Melbourne).

**MURRAY, Katherine Maud Elisabeth,** MA, BLitt, FSA, FRHistSoc; Principal, Bishop Otter College, Chichester, 1948-70; *b* 3 Dec. 1909; *d* of Harold J. R. Murray (former HMI of Schools) and Kate M. Crosthwaite. *Educ:* Colchester County High Sch.; Somerville Coll., Oxford. Tutor and Librarian, Ashburne Hall, Manchester, 1935-37; Mary Somerville Research Fellow, Somerville Coll., Oxford, 1937-38; Asst Tutor and Registrar, 1938-44, Domestic Bursar, 1942-44, and Junior Bursar, 1944-48, Girton Coll., Cambridge. Chairman of Council, Sussex Archæological Soc., 1964-. *Publications:* The Constitutional History of the Cinque Ports, 1935; Register of Daniel Rough, Kent Record Soc., 1945; articles in Sussex Notes and Queries, Transactions of the Royal Historical Society, Archæologia Cantiana, English Historical Review. *Recreations:* walking, archæology. *Address:* Upper Cranmore, Heyshott, Midhurst, Sussex. *T:* Midhurst 2325.

**MURRAY, Keith (Day Pearce),** MC 1917; RDI 1936; FRIBA; *b* 5 July 1892; *s* of Charles Murray, Auckland, NZ; *m* 1948, Mary Beatrice de Cartaret Hayes, *d* of Lt-Col R. Malet; one *d.* *Educ:* King's Coll., Auckland, NZ; Mill Hill Sch., London. Served RFC and RAF in France, 1915-19 (MC, Croix de Guerre Belge, despatches 5 times); OC No. 10 Sqdn, 1917-19; Major. Served in RAF, 1939-41. Studied at Architectural Association School. Commenced practice as partner with C. S. White, 1936. Designed pottery, glass and silver during the thirties; Master of the Faculty of Royal Designers for Industry, 1945-47. Gold Medal, 5th Triennale of Milan, 1933. Principal works: Wedgwood Factory at Barlaston; Hong Kong Air Terminal; BEA Engineering Base at London Airport; various industrial and office buildings. *Recreation:* trout fishing. *Address:* Tarrant Gunville, Dorset. *T:* Tarrant Hinton 339.

**MURRAY, Sir Kenneth,** Kt 1958; JP, DL (Ross and Cromarty); *b* 23 Aug. 1891; *o s* of T. M. Murray, Geanies, Fearn, Ross-shire; *m* 1919, Edith Maud, *y d* of W. J. Tustin; one *s* three *d.* *Educ:* Winchester; New College, Oxford (BA). Served European War, 1914-18, with Lovat Scouts; discharged early 1918 with rank of Captain on account of ill-health caused by wounds. Mem. of HM's Body Guard for Scotland (Royal Company of Archers). Chm. of the Court, Royal Bank of Scotland, 1946-55 (Dir, 1935-57); Chm. and Dir of various other institutions and companies, 1930-67. Succeeded, in 1936, to the property of Geanies, Fearn, Ross-shire. *Recreations:* shooting, golf, gardening. *Address:* Geanies, Fearn, Ross-shire. *T:* Portmahomack 247. *Clubs:* Travellers'; New (Edinburgh); Highland (Inverness).

**MURRAY, Rear-Adm. Leonard Warren,** CB 1944; CBE 1943; RCN (retired); Barrister at Law, Middle Temple; *b* 22 June 1896; 2nd *s* of Simon Murray; *m* 1st, 1921, Jean Chaplin Scott (*d* 1962); two *s*; 2nd, 1963, Mrs Nina Sergeievna Shtetinin Seaford Warwick, Buxton. Entered RCN, 1911; Lt 1917; served European War, 1914-18, in Atlantic Convoys and Grand Fleet; Commander, 1929; Capt. 1938; Rear-Adm. 1941; commanded HMC Ships Naden, Saguenay, Stadacona and Assiniboine; Senior Naval Officer, Esquimalt, 1929-31; Dir Naval Ops (Can.), 1931-32; Senior Naval Officer Halifax, 1934-36; Deputy Chief of Naval Staff (Can.), 1939-40 and a founding mem. of Canada-US Permanent Joint Defence Board; Command of Canadian Naval Forces Overseas, 1941; Flag Officer, Newfoundland, 1941-42; Comdg Officer Atlantic Coast (Can.), 1942; C-in-C Canadian Northwest Atlantic, 1943-45; retired, 1946. Admitted Middle Temple, 1947; Pres., Inns of Court Students' Union, 1948-49. Called to the Bar, 1949. Commander Legion of Honour, and Croix de Guerre (with palms), 1946; Commander, Legion of Merit (USA), 1946; Cross of Liberation (Norway), 1948. *Recreations:* sailing, ski-ing. *Address:* 6 The Square, Buxton, Derbyshire. *Clubs:* United Service; Bar Yacht.

**MURRAY, Lionel,** OBE 1966; Assistant General Secretary of the TUC since 1969; *b* 2 Aug. 1922; *m* 1945, Heather Woolf; two *s* two *d.* *Educ:* Wellington (Salop) Gram. Sch.; Univ. of

London, 1940-41; New Coll., Oxford, 1945-47. Economic Dept, TUC, 1947, Head of Dept, 1954-69. Member: Social Science Research Coun., 1965-70; Central Adv. Council on Science and Technology, 1970-; Advertising Standards Authority; Governor: Nat. Inst. of Economic and Social Research, 1968; LSE, 1970. *Publication:* Contrib. to Economics and Technical Change. *Address:* 29 The Crescent, Loughton, Essex. *T:* 01-508 4425.

**MURRAY, (Malcolm) Patrick,** CB 1954; *b* 10 July 1905; *s* of late Sir Oswyn Murray, GCB, and Lady Mildred Octavia Murray; *m* 1st, 1934, Betty (*d* 1955), *er d* of A. M. Black, Richmond, Surrey; one *s* one *d* (and one *s* decd); 2nd, 1956, Richilda (Maisie Nora), *d* of Walter Hemingway, Wakefield, Yorks. *Educ:* Uppingham; Exeter Coll., Oxford (Open History Scholar). MA Honour Schools of Modern History and of Jurisprudence. Entered Home Civil Service as Asst Principal, Air Ministry, 1929; Private Sec. to Permanent Sec., 1931-37; graduated Imperial Defence Coll., 1938; Asst Sec., 1939; seconded for special duty, 1943; transferred to Ministry of Fuel and Power, 1946; Under-Sec., Electricity Division, Ministry of Fuel and Power, 1947-59; Dir of Establishments, Ministry of Power, 1959-61; a Deputy Sec., Ministry of Power, 1961-65, retd. *Address:* c/o Barclays Bank Ltd, 171 High Street, Guildford, Surrey. *Club:* Special Forces.

**MURRAY, Margaret Mary Alberta,** DSc (London); Professor Emeritus in the University of London since 1959; Professor of Physiology, Bedford College, University of London, 1947-59. *Address:* 42 Wilton Crescent, Wimbledon, SW19.

**MURRAY, Patrick;** *see* Murray, M. P.

**MURRAY, Peter,** CMG 1959; Ambassador to the Ivory Coast and Upper Volta, since 1970; *b* 18 July 1915; *s* of Rear-Admiral H. P. W. G. Murray, DSO and Mabel C. Avens; *m* 1960, E. M. Batchelor. *Educ:* Portsmouth Gram. Sch.; Merton Coll., Oxford. Burma Commission, 1937-49, including service in Burma RNVR and Military Administration of North Arakan; Foreign Service, July 1947; Rangoon, 1949-51 and 1956-59; Sofia, 1951-53; UK Delegation to NATO, 1959-61; HM Ambassador to Cambodia, 1961-64; HM Consul-General, Marseilles, 1964-67; Inspector, FCO, 1967-70. *Address:* British Embassy, BP 2581, Abidjan, Ivory Coast.

**MURRAY, Peter (John),** PhD (London), FSA; Professor of the History of Art, at Birkbeck College, University of London, since 1967; *b* 23 April 1920; *er s* of John Knowles Murray and Dorothy Catton; *m* 1947, Linda Bramley. *Educ:* King Edward VI Sch., Birmingham; Robert Gordon's Coll., Aberdeen; Gray's Sch. of Art, Aberdeen; Slade Sch. and Courtauld Inst., Univ. of London. Sen. Research Fellow, Warburg Inst., 1961; Chm., Soc. for Renaissance Studies, 1967-70; Pres., Soc. of Architectural Historians of GB, 1969-. Rhind Lecturer, Edinburgh, 1967. *Publications:* Watteau, 1948; Index of Attributions . . . before Vasari, 1959; Dictionary of Art and Artists (with Linda Murray), 1959 (enlarged edition 1965); History of English Architecture (with P. Kidson), 1962 (with P. Kidson and P. Thomson), 1965; The Art of the Renaissance (with L. Murray), 1963; The Architecture of the Italian Renaissance, 1963; contribs to New Cambridge Mod. Hist., Encycl. Britannica, etc.; translations; articles in Warburg and Courtauld Jl, Burlington Mag., Apollo, foreign jls. *Recreation:* driving fast cars. *Address:* 24 Dulwich Wood Avenue, SE19. *T:* 01-670 4808. *Club:* Savile.

**MURRAY, Sir Ralph;** *see* Murray, Sir F. R. H.

**MURRAY, Sir (Robert) Alistair,** Kt 1961; OBE 1957; retired as Manager of three Investment Trust Companies; *b* 3 July 1896; *s* of late Robert Alexander Murray, CA, Pirniehall, Drymen Station, Stirlingshire; *m* 1924, Ottilie Grahame, *d* of late Tom Anderson, 4 Cleveden Cres., Glasgow, C2; one *s* two *d*. *Educ:* Cargilfield Sch. and Fettes Coll., Edinburgh. Served European War, 1914-18, 2nd Lt, 4th Bn Argyll and Sutherland Highldrs, 1915; Salonika, 1915; posted to 1st Bn Argyll and Sutherland Highldrs, 1916, Salonika and Constantinople; regular commission with effect from March 1915; returned to UK, 1919 (despatches); retired from Army, 1919; War of 1939-45, with two searchlight Regts one of which was converted to LAA, also with 11th Argyll and Sutherland Highlanders; demobilised, 1945 (Major). After training, became active in assisting to manage a group of Investment Trust Cos (Man. 1935-61); Dir, various other companies. *Recreations:* golf; race-horse owner. *Address:* 42 Kelvin Court, Glasgow, W2. *Clubs:* Caledonian; Western (Glasgow); Prestwick Golf (Ayrshire); Royal and Ancient (St Andrews); Hon. Company of Edinburgh Golfers, New (Edinburgh).

**MURRAY, Rear-Adm. Ronald Gordon,** CB 1950; CBE 1946; Royal Navy (retired); *b* 24 March 1898; *s* of late Charles Murray, Consulting Engineer and Naval Architect; *m* 1926, Marjorie Coldicott; one *s*. *Educ:* Whitgift, Croydon; HMS Conway; RN Coll., Dartmouth; Emmanuel Coll., Cambridge. Went to sea, 1 Aug. 1914; commanded RN Lewis Gun Detachment, E Africa, 1916-17; Submarine Service for 8 years; Rear-Adm., 1947; Dir, Aircraft Maintenance and Repair, Admiralty, 1947-49; Manager, Engineering Dept, HM Dockyard, Chatham, Dec. 1949-51; retired 1951. *Address:* Little Barns, Emsworth, Hants.

**MURRAY, Ronald King,** QC (Scotland) 1967; MP (Lab) Leith Division of Edinburgh since 1970; *b* 15 June 1922; *s* of James King Murray, MIEE, and Muriel (*née* Aitken), Glasgow; *m* 1950, Sheila Winifred Gamlin; one *s* one *d*. *Educ:* George Watson's Coll., Edinburgh; Univ. of Edinburgh; Jesus Coll., Oxford. MA (1st cl. hons Phil) Edinburgh, 1948; LLB Edinburgh, 1952. Served Army, 1942-46; commnd in REME, 1942; India and SEAC, 1943-46. Asst in Moral Philosophy, Edinburgh Univ., 1949; Lectr, 1955. Standing Jun. Counsel to BoT (Scotland), 1961-64; Hon. Sheriff-Substitute, Lanarkshire, 1961-64; Senior Advocate-Depute, 1967-70. Contested (Lab): Caithness and Sutherland, 1959; North Edinburgh, 1960; Roxburgh, Selkirk and Peebles, 1964 and 1965; Chm., Edinburgh City Labour Party, 1968. *Publications:* articles in various jls. *Recreation:* boating. *Address:* 38 Primrose Bank Road, Edinburgh 5; (Chambers) 12 Moray Place, Edinburgh 3. *T:* 031-552 5602. *Clubs:* Royal Forth Yacht, Forth Corinthian Yacht.

**MURRAY, Rosemary;** *see* Murray, A. R.

**MURRAY, Sir Rowland William Patrick,** 14th Bt *cr* 1630; public relations officer, Arlington Cemetery, Atlanta, USA; *b* 26 Oct. 1910; *s* of late Rowland William Murray, 2nd *s* of 12th Bt, and Gertrude Frances McCabe; *S* uncle 1958; *m*; four *s* two *d*. Served in US Army during War of 1939-45. Captain. *Heir: s* Rowland William Murray, *b* 22 Sept. 1947.

*Address:* 179 Lake View Avenue, NE, Atlanta 5, Ga, USA.

**MURRAY, Sir Stanley;** *see* Murray, Sir J. S.

**MURRAY, Sir William (Patrick Keith),** 11th Bt *cr* 1673; *b* 7 sept. 1939; *s* of Sir Patrick (Ian Keith) Murray, 10th Bt, and Liska, *d* of A. T. Creet, Ghusick, Kalipahari, India; *S* father, 1962; *m* 1963, Susan Elizabeth, *d* of Stacey Jones, Penyrwrlodd, Hay-on-Wye, Herefordshire; one *s*. *Heir: s* Patrick Ian Keith Murray, *b* 22 March 1965. *Address:* Ochtertyre, Crieff, Perthshire (Seat).

**MURRAY-BROWN, Gilbert Alexander,** CIE 1942; OBE 1918; BSc; FICE; *b* 24 Jan. 1893; *m* 1928, Norah Frances, *e d* of late F. H. Burkitt, CIE; two *s*. *Educ:* Glasgow Univ. Joined RE (TF) 1914; served European War, 1914-19; Capt. 1916; Major, AIRO 1928. Joined Indian Service of Engineers, 1919; Chief Engr and Sec. to Govt, PWD, NWFP, India, 1940-46. Pres., Central Bd of Irrigation, India, 1943. *Recreations:* golf, fishing, shooting. *Address:* Kinnelhook, Lockerbie, Dumfriesshire. *T:* Lochmaben 211.

**MURRELL, William Lee,** CIE 1947; OBE 1941; BCE (Melb.); FICE; retired from Indian Service of Engineers; *b* 26 Feb. 1893; *s* of Charles Murrell and Mary Fowler; *m* 1919, Sibyl Hall; two *s*. *Educ:* Caulfield Grammar School, Melbourne; University of Melbourne. BCE 1915; served European War, 1914-18, with AIF 3 years; Lieut 2nd Aust. Pioneer Bn Indian Service of Engineers, 1919-48. On foreign service as State Engineer. Mayurbhanj State, 1923-26; service was with Govt of Bihar. Superintending Engineer, 1935. Addtl Chief Engr, Mil. Works, and Dep. Sec. Bihar Govt, 1943-45; Chief Engr and Sec. to Govt of Bihar, 1947-48. Member: Nat. Trust of Aust. (Vict); Royal Victorian Historical Society. *Address:* 1 Dalgetty Road, Beaumaris, Victoria 3193, Australia. *T:* 99-2886. *Clubs:* Beaumaris Yacht, Beaumaris Bowling.

**MURRIE, Sir William (Stuart),** GCB 1964 (CB 1946); KBE 1952; Permanent Under-Secretary of State for Scotland, 1959-64, retired; *b* Dundee, 19 Dec. 1903; *s* of Thomas Murrie and Catherine Burgh; *m* 1932, Eleanore Boswell (*d* 1966). *Educ:* S America; Harris Acad., Dundee; Edinburgh Univ.; Balliol Coll., Oxford. Entered Scottish Office, 1927; transferred to Dept of Health for Scotland, 1935; Under-Sec., Offices of War Cabinet, 1944; Deputy Sec. (Civil), Cabinet Office, 1947; Deputy Under-Sec. of State, Home Office, 1948-52; Sec. to the Scottish Education Dept, 1952-57; Sec., Scottish Home Dept, 1957-59. Member: Board of Trustees for Nat. Galls of Scotland; Council on Tribunals; General Practice Finance Corporation, 1966-; Adv. Cttee on Rhodesian Travel Restrictions, 1968. General Council Assessor, Edinburgh Univ. Court, 1967. Hon. LLD, Dundee Univ., 1968. *Address:* 7 Cumin Place, Edinburgh EH9 2JX. 9. *T:* 031-667 2612.

**MURSELL, Sir Peter,** Kt 1969; MBE 1941; DL; Chairman, West Sussex County Council, since 1969 (and 1962-67); *b* 20 Jan. 1913; *m* 1938, Cicely, *d* of late Mr and Mrs M. F. North; two *s* two *d*. *Educ:* Bedales Sch.; Downing Coll. Cambridge. Fruit growing, 1934. War Service: Air Transport Auxiliary, 1940-44, Sen. Comdr. Mem., West Sussex CC, 1947-; Cttee on Management in Local Govt, 1965-66; Royal Commn on Local Govt in England, 1966-69. DL Co. Sussex, 1962. *Recreations:* sailing, mountain walking, skiing, squash. *Address:* Dounhurst Farm, Wisborough Green, Billingshurst, Sussex. *T:* Kirdford 209. *Club:* Farmers'.

**MURTAGH, Miss Marion;** Chairman: University Computing Co. (Great Britain) Ltd; Computer Bureau (Shannon) Ltd; Director, Stats (MR) Ltd. Senior Vice-President, UCC International Inc. *Educ:* Waverley Gram. Sch., Birmingham. Qualified as: Certified Accountant, 1947; Chartered Secretary, 1948. Proprietor, The Calculating Bureau, 1938-51. Joint Owner, 1951-61. Mem., Anglo-Thai Soc. (Hon. Sec. Midlands Branch); Mem. West Midlands Bridge Club (Pres.). *Recreation:* bridge. *Address:* 116 Chessetts Wood Road, Hockley Heath, Solihull, Warwicks. *T:* Lapworth 2089.

**MURTON, Lt-Col Henry Oscar,** OBE 1946; TD 1947 (Clasp 1951); MP (C) Poole since 1964; *b* 8 May 1914; *o s* of late H. E. C. Murton, and of E. M. Murton (*née* Renton), Hexham, Northumberland; *m* 1939, Constance F. Murton (*née* Connell), *e d* of late F. O'L. Connell, Low Fell, Co. Durham; one *s* one *d*. *Educ:* Uppingham Sch. Commissioned, TA, 1934; Staff Coll., Camberley, 1939; active service, Royal Northumberland Fusiliers, 1939-46; GSO1, HQ Salisbury Plain Dist, 1942-44; GSO1, SD1, War Office, 1944-46, Managing Dir, Henry A. Murton Ltd, Departmental Stores, Newcastle-upon-Tyne and Sunderland, 1949-57. Dep. Sec. Northern Div. Nat. Coal Board, 1947-49. Mem., Wessex Provincial Area Exec. Cttee of Conservative Party, 1964, etc.; Sec., Cons. Parly Cttee for Housing, Local Government and Land, 1964-67, Vice-Chm., 1967-; Chm., Cons. Parly Cttee for Public Building and Works, 1970; introduced Highways (Amendment) Act, 1965; Mem. Exec. Cttee, Inter-Parliamentary Union British Group, 1970-. A Vice-Pres., Assoc. of Municipal Corporations; Mem. Herrison Hospital (Dorchester) Group Management Cttee, 1963. JP, Poole, 1963. *Recreation:* sailing. *Address:* Old Church House, Church Street, Poole, Dorset. *T:* 5956; 24 Draycott Avenue, Chelsea, SW3. *T:* 01-589 1822. *Clubs:* Royal Motor Yacht, Parkstone Yacht, Poole Yacht (Poole).

**MUSCHAMP, Rt. Rev. Cecil Emerson Barron,** MA, ThL; Dean of Brisbane since 1967; *b* Wing, Bucks, England, 16 June 1902; *s* of late Canon E. G. Muschamp, Launceston, Tasmania; *m* 1931, Margaret Warren Crane; two *s* two *d*. *Educ:* Church Grammar Sch., Launceston, Tasmania; Univ. of Tasmania; Univ. of Oxford; St Stephen's House, Oxford. BA Univ. of Tasmania, 1924, Oxon, 1927; ThL Australian Coll. of Theology, 1925; MA Oxon, 1934; Deacon, 1927; Priest, 1928. Curate of St Luke, Bournemouth, 1927-30; in charge of St Albans and St Aidan's, Aldershot, 1930-32; Curate, Withycombe Raleigh (in charge of All Saints, Exmouth), 1932-37; Vicar of St Michael, City and Diocese of Christchurch, 1937-50; Bishop of Kalgoorlie, 1950-67. Served War of 1939-45: Chaplain in Royal New Zealand Air Force, 1942-45. Asst Bishop of Perth, 1950-55. *Recreation:* golf. *Address:* The Deanery, Ann Street, Brisbane, Qld 4000, Australia. *Club:* Queensland (Brisbane).

**MUSGRAVE, Sir Christopher (Patrick Charles),** 15th Bt *cr* 1611; *b* 14 April 1949; *s* of Sir Charles Musgrave, 14th Bt and of Olive Louise Avril, *o d* of Patrick Cringle, Norfolk; *S* father, 1970. *Heir: b* Julian Nigel Chardin Musgrave, *b* 8 Dec. 1951. *Address:* c/o Mrs Nelson, Tans End, Church Street, Wells-on-Sea, Norfolk.

**MUSGRAVE, Clifford,** OBE 1958; Director Brighton Public Libraries, Art Gallery,

Museums and the Royal Pavilion, 1939-68; *b* 26 July 1904; *s* of William Francis Musgrave, bookseller; *m* 1928, Margaret Esther, *d* of Walter Meakin, journalist; two *s*. Director: Birkenhead Public Libraries and Williamson Art Gallery, 1937-39. Member Council of Museum Association, 1951-54; Pres. South-East Federation of Museums and Art Galleries, 1947-48-49; Mem. Cttee for 18th Century English Taste Exhibition, Royal Academy, 1955-56; Mem. Cttee for Le Siècle de l'Elegance Exhibition, Paris, 1959; Hon. Mem., Georgian Group; Mem. Advisory Council of Victoria and Albert Museum, 1957-69; Fellow Library Assoc.; Fellow Museums Assoc. Hon. DLitt Sussex, 1969. *Publications:* articles and reviews in various journals; Royal Pavilion: an episode in the romantic, 1959; The Story of Brighton, 1959; Late Georgian Architecture, 1760-1810, 1956; Sussex, 1957; Regency Architecture 1810-1830, 1958; Regency Furniture, 1961; Adam and Hepplewhite Furniture, 1965; Life in Brighton, 1969. *Recreations:* music, travel, architectural photography. *Address:* 46 Long Hill Road, Ovingdean, Brighton. *T:* Brighton 32561.

**MUSGRAVE, Sir (Frank) Cyril,** KCB, 1955 (CB 1946); Chairman, The Iron and Steel Board, 1959-67; Member (part-time), British Steel Corporation, 1967-70; Director: Marine and General Mutual Life; Samuel Properties Ltd; Staveley Industries Ltd; Hawthorn Leslie and Co. Ltd; Trustee, British Migraine Trust; *b* 21 June 1900; *s* of late Frank Musgrave; *m* 1st, Elsie Mary, *d* of late Christopher Williams; one *s* one *d*; 2nd, Jean Elsie, *d* of late John Soulsby; two *s*. *Educ:* St George's Coll., London. Entered Civil Service, 1919; served Inland Revenue, 1920-37; Air Ministry, 1937-40; Ministry of Aircraft Production, 1940-46; Under-Sec. (Air), Ministry of Supply, 1946-51; Deputy Sec., 1951-53; Second Permanent Sec., 1953-56; Permanent Sec., 1956-59. *Recreations:* music, gardening. *Address:* Willows House, Walsham-le-Willows, Bury St Edmunds, Suffolk. *T:* Walsham-le-Willows 486.

**MUSGRAVE, Noel Henry;** Editor, Journal of the Royal Institute of British Architects, 1956-64, retired; *b* 15 Jan. 1903; *s* of Harry Musgrave and Mabel Flinn; *m* 1929, Jennie Elizabeth Sharp; no *c*. *Educ:* St Paul's Sch.; Architectural Association Sch. of Architecture. Editor of The Architect and Building News, 1946-56. *Recreations:* painting, sailing, bird watching. *Address:* The Black Cabin, South Wootton, King's Lynn, Norfolk.

**MUSGRAVE, Sir Richard James,** 7th Bt, *cr* 1782; *b* 10 Feb. 1922; *s* of Sir Christopher Norman Musgrave, 6th Bt, OBE, and Kathleen (*d* 1967), 3rd *d* of late Robert Chapman, Co. Tyrone; *S* father 1956; *m* 1958, Maria, *d* of late Col M. Cambanis, and of Mrs Cambanis, Athens, Greece; two *s* four *d*. *Educ:* Stowe. Capt., The Poona Horse (17th Queen Victoria's Own Cavalry), 1940-45. *Recreation:* shooting. *Heir:* *s* Christopher John Shane Musgrave, *b* 23 Oct. 1959. *Address:* Riverstown, Tara, Co. Meath. *T:* Balrath 21. *Club:* Kildare Street (Dublin).

**MUSGRAVE, Thea;** Composer; *b* 1928; *d* of James P. Musgrave and Joan Musgrave (*née* Hacking). *Educ:* Moreton Hall, Oswestry; Edinburgh Univ.; Paris Conservatoire; privately with Nadia Boulanger. *Works include:* Cantata for a summer's day, 1954; The Abbot of Drimock (Chamber opera), 1955; Triptych for Tenor and orch., 1959; Colloquy for violin and piano, 1960; The Phoenix and the Turtle for chorus and orch., 1962; The Five Ages of Man for chorus and orch., 1963; The Decision (opera), 1964-65; Nocturnes and arias for orch., 1966; Chamber Concerto No. 2, in homage to Charles Ives, 1966; Chamber Concerto No. 3 (Octet), 1966; Concerto for orchestra, 1967; Music for Horn and Piano, 1967; Clarinet Concerto, 1968; Beauty and the Beast (ballet), 1968. Performances and broadcasts: UK, France, Germany, Switzerland, Scandinavia, USA, USSR, etc., Edinburgh, Cheltenham, Aldeburgh, Zagreb, Venice and Warsaw Festivals. *Address:* c/o J. & W. Chester Ltd, Eagle Court, EC1.

**MUSGRAVE, Prof. William Kenneth Rodgerson,** PhD, DSc (Birmingham); Professor of Organic Chemistry, since 1960, Head of Department of Chemistry, since 1968, Second Pro-Vice-Chancellor, since 1970, University of Durham; *b* 16 Sept. 1918; *s* of late Charles Musgrave and late Sarah Alice Musgrave; *m* 1944, Joyce Cadman; two *s*. *Educ:* Stanley Grammar Sch., Co. Durham; Univ. of Birmingham. British-Canadian Atomic Energy Project, 1944-45; Univ. of Durham; Lecturer in Chemistry, 1945-56, Senior Lecturer, 1956-60. Personal Readership in Organic Chemistry, 1960. *Publications:* (joint) Advances in Fluorine Chemistry, Vol. I, edited by Stacey, Tatlow and Sharpe, 1960; Rodd's Chemistry of Carbon Compounds, Vol. Ia, edited by Coffey; scientific papers in chemical journals. *Recreations:* gardening, carpentry. *Address:* The Orchard, Potter's Bank, Durham City. *T:* Durham 3196.

**MUSHIN, Prof. William W(oolf),** MA Oxon, 1946; MB, BS (Hons) London, 1933; FRCS 1966; FFARCS 1948, Professor and Director of Anaesthetics, Welsh National School of Medicine, University of Wales, since 1947; *b* London, Sept. 1910; *y s* of Moses Mushin and Jesse (*née* Kalmenson); *m* 1939, Betty Hannah Goldberg; one *s* three *d*. *Educ:* Davenant Sch.; London Hosp. Med. Sch. Buxton Prize in Anatomy, Anderson Prize in Clinical Medicine). Various resident hosp. posts; formerly: Anaesthetist, Royal Dental Hosp.; first Asst, Nuffield Dept of Anaesthetists, Univ. of Oxford. Lectures: Clover, RCS, 1955; Kellogg, George Washington Univ., 1950; Guedel, Univ. of Calif, 1957; John Snow, 1964; Baxter Travenol, Internat. Anaesth. Research Soc., 1970. Visiting Professor or Consultant to univs, academic and other bodies in USA, Argentine, Uruguay, Brazil, Denmark, NZ, Australia, India, Germany, Ghana, S Africa, and Holland. Examiner: Univ. of Oxford for MD and PhD; FFARCS, 1953-; FRCSI, 1962-67. Welsh Regional Hospital Board: Cons. Adviser in Anaesthetics, 1948-; Mem., 1961-. Member: Central Health Services Council, 1962-; Safety of Drugs Cttee, Dept of Health and Social Security, 1964-; Assoc. of Anaesthetists, 1936- (Mem. Council, 1946-59 and 1961-; Vice-Pres., 1953-56); Anaesthetists Group Cttee, BMA, 1950-69; Bd of Governors, United Cardiff Hosps, 1956-65; Court, Univ. of Wales, 1957-58; Commonwealth Scholarships Commn, 1969-. Welsh National School of Medicine: Mem. Senate, 1947-; Mem. Council, 1957-58; Vice-Provost, 1958-60. Royal College of Surgeons: Mem. Bd, Faculty of Anaesthetists, 1954-; Mem. Council, 1961-64; Dean, Faculty of Anaesthetists, 1961-64. Mem. Bd of Management and Consulting Editor, British Jl of Anaesthesia, 1947-; Consulting Editor, Survey of Anaesthesiology, 1956-. Hon. Mem., various societies of anaesthetists. Hon. FFARACS 1959; Hon. FFA(SA) 1962; Hon. FFARCSI 1962. *Publications:* Anaesthesia of the Poor Risk, 1948; (with Sir R. Macintosh) Local Analgesia: Brachial Plexus, 1954, 4th edn 1967; Physics for the Anaesthetist, 1946,

3rd edn 1964; Automatic Ventilation of Lungs, 1959, 2nd edn 1969; (ed) Thoracic Anaesthesia, 1963. Numerous papers on anaesthesia and allied subjects in British and foreign jls. *Address:* Department of Anaesthetics, Welsh National School of Medicine, Heath Park, Cardiff CF2 1YE. *T:* Cardiff 755944. *Club:* Oxford and Cambridge University.

**MUSKER, Sir John,** Kt 1952; Banker; Chairman, Cater, Ryder & Co., Ltd, Bankers; Hon. Treasurer London Municipal Society, since 1936; *b* 25 Jan. 1906; *o s* of late Capt. Harold Musker, JP, Snarehill Hall, Thetford, Norfolk; *m* 1932, Elizabeth, *d* of Capt. Loeffler, 51 Grosvenor Square, W1; two *d*; *m* 1955, Mrs Rosemary Pugh, *d* of late Maj.-Gen. Merton Beckwith-Smith. *Educ:* privately; St John's Coll., Cambridge (BA). Mem. LCC for City of London, 1944-49. Lt, RNVR, 1940. *Address:* Shadwell Park, Thetford, Norfolk. *T:* Thetford 3257; Suffolk House, 117 Park Lane, W1. *Clubs:* White's; Royal Yacht Squadron; Jockey Club Rooms (Newmarket).

**MUSKERRY,** 8th Baron (Ireland), *cr* 1781; **Hastings Fitzmaurice Tilson Deane;** 13th Bt (Ireland), *cr* 1710; Radiologist to Regional Health Authority, Limerick, since 1961; *b* 12 March 1907; 3rd and *o surv. s* of 7th Baron Muskerry and Mabel Kathleen Vivienne (*d* 1954), *d* of Charles Henry Robinson, MD, FRCSI; *S* father, 1966; *m* 1944, Betty Fairbridge, *e d* of George Wilfred Reckless Palmer, South Africa; one *s* one *d*. *Educ:* Sandford Park Sch., Dublin; Trinity Coll., Dublin; MA, MB, BCh, BAO; DMR London. Served War of 1939-45, S African Army (Western Desert; seconded RAMC, Italy, Greece). Specialised in Radiology, London Univ., 1946-48; Consultant Radiologist to Transvaal Administration, 1949-57. *Heir: s* Hon. Robert Fitzmaurice Deane [*b* 26 March 1948. *Educ:* Sandford Park Sch., Dublin; Trinity Coll. Dublin]. *Address:* Springfield Castle, Drumcollogher, Co. Limerick. *T:* Drumcollogher 5.

**MUSKETT, Prof. Arthur Edmund,** OBE 1957; DSc London, ARCS, MRIA; FIBiol; Professor of Plant Pathology and Head of Department of Mycology and Plant Pathology, The Queen's University, Belfast, 1945-65; Professor Emeritus, since 1966; Head of Plant Pathology Division, Ministry of Agriculture, N Ireland, 1938-65; *b* 15 April 1900; *s* of late Arthur Muskett, Wood Farm, Ashwellthorpe, Norwich, Norfolk; *m* 1926, Hilda Elizabeth, *d* of late Henry Smith, Manor Farm, Fundenhall, Norwich; three *s* one *d*. *Educ:* City of Norwich Sch., Norwich; Imperial Coll. of Science, London. BSc, ARCS (Botany); MSc (London) 1931; MRIA 1933; DSc (London) 1938. RAF Flight Cadet A, 1918-19. Asst in Plant Pathology, Min. of Agr., NI and QUB, 1923-26, Junior Lectr QUB 1926; Dep. Head Plant Pathology Div., Min. of Agric. NI and Lectr QUB, 1931; Dean of Faculty of Agriculture, Queen's Univ., Belfast, 1950-57. Pres. British Mycological Soc., 1948; Vice-Pres., Assoc. Applied Biologists, 1954-55. Hon. Sec. and consultant to NI Hort. Development Assoc., 1931; Chairman: Central Gardens Assoc. for Northern Ireland; Ulster Countryside Cttee. *Publications:* Diseases of the Flax Plant, 1947; A. A. McGuckian: A Memorial Volume, 1956; Autonomous Dispersal: Plant Pathology (An Advanced Treatise), Vol. III, 1960. Numerous papers in Annals of Applied Biology, Annals of Botany, Trans Brit. Mycological Soc., etc. *Recreations:* horticulture; extra work. *Address:* The Cottage, Ballynahinch Road, Carryduff, Belfast. *T:* Carryduff 2350.

**MUSPRATT, Gen. Sir Sydney Frederick,** KCB *cr* 1937 (CB 1930); CSI 1922; CIE 1921; DSO; Indian Army, retired; *b* 1878; *s* of late H. Muspratt, ICS; *m* 1925, Rosamonde, *y d* of late Sir Edward Barry, 2nd Bt; two *s*. *Educ:* US Coll.; Sandhurst. Served NW Frontier Expedition, 1908; European War in France, 1914-18 (DSO, Brevet Lt-Col, Legion of Honour); Commanded 4th Indian Infantry Brigade, Nowshera, 1925-27; Dir of Military Operations, AHQ, India, 1927-29; Maj.-Gen., 1929; Dep. Chief of the Gen. Staff, AHQ, India, 1929-31; Sec. Military Dept, India Office, 1931-33 and 1937-41; Comdr Peshawar District, 1933-36; Lt-Gen., 1936; Gen. 1938; ADC Gen. to the King, 1940-41; retired, 1941. *Address:* 56 The Close, Salisbury, Wilts. *Club:* United Service.

**MUSSEN, Surgeon Rear-Adm. Robert Walsh,** CB 1954; CBE 1949; MD; FRCP; retired; *b* 13 May 1900; *s* of Hugh Harper Mussen, JP, Belfast, late Crown Solicitor, N Ireland; *m* 1932, Mary Katherine Anne, *d* of late Surgeon Rear-Adm. H. E. R. Stephens; two *s* two *d*. *Educ:* Campbell Coll., Belfast; Queen's Univ., Belfast; Charing Cross Hosp., London. Entered Royal Navy, 1922. Served in ships and Naval hosps at home and abroad; specialized in Clin. Pathology and Internal Medicine. MD (Belfast); MRCP 1935; FRCP 1949. Sqdn MO, 1st Battle Sqdn, 1938; Brit. Naval Med. Liaison Officer with US Navy, 1943-45; Surgeon Capt., 1944; MO i/c and Dir Med. Studies, RN Medical Sch., 1945-48. Surgeon Rear-Adm., 1952; QHP 1952-55; Medical Officer in Charge, RN Hosp., Chatham, and Command MO on staff of Comdr-in-Chief, the Nore, 1952-55; Min. of Health, 1955-65. Vice-Chm., Chailey RDC. Comdr Order of St John, 1954. *Publications:* various papers on medical subjects and on naval medical history. *Recreations:* golf, walking, reading and writing. *Address:* Cleves, Ditchling, Sussex. *T:* Hassocks 2920. *Clubs:* Army and Navy; Royal Naval (Portsmouth); Ulster (Belfast).

**MUSSON, Maj.-Gen. Alfred Henry,** CB 1958; CBE 1956; pac; late RA; President, Ordnance Board, 1957-58, retired (Vice-President, 1955-57); *b* 14 Aug. 1900; *s* of Dr A. W. Musson, Clitheroe, Lancs; *m* 1932, Joan Wright Taylor; three *s*. *Educ:* Tonbridge Sch.; RMA Woolwich. Served War of 1939-45. *Address:* Lyndon, The Ridgeway, Tonbridge, Kent. *T:* 2766.

**MUSSON, Gen. Sir Geoffrey (Randolph Dixon),** GCB 1970 (KCB 1965; CB 1959); CBE 1945; DSO 1944; BA; Vice-Chairman, National Savings Committee, since 1970; Chairman, HM Forces Savings Committee, since 1970; *b* 9 June 1910; *s* of late Robert Dixon Musson, Yockleton, Shrewsbury; *m* 1939, Hon. Elspeth L. Bailey, *d* of late Hon. Herbert Crawshay Bailey; one *s* one *d*. *Educ:* Shrewsbury; Trinity Hall, Cambridge (BA Hons). 2nd Lt KSLI, 1930. Served War of 1939-45, North Africa and Italy; Comdr 2nd Bn DCLI, 1943-44; Comdr 36th Infantry Bde, 1944-46. Comdr Commonwealth Forces in Korea, 1954-55; Comdt Sch. of Infantry, 1956-58, Comdr 7th Armoured Div., BAOR, 1958; Maj.-Gen. 1958; Comdr of the 5th Div., 1958-59. Chief of Staff, GHQ, Near East Land Forces, 1959-62; Vice-Adjutant-Gen., War Office, subseq. Min. of Defence, 1963-64; GOC-in-C, N Command, 1964-67; Adjutant-General, 1967-70, retired. Colonel: King's Shropshire Light Infantry, 1963-68; The Light Infantry, 1968-. *Address:* (home) Provost Hill, Hurstbourne Tarrant, Hants. *T:* Hurstbourne Tarrant 323. *Club:* United Service.

**MUSSON, Samuel Dixon,** CB 1963; MBE 1943; Chief Registrar of Friendly Societies and Industrial Assurance Commissioner since 1963; *b* 1 April 1908; *e s* of late R. Dixon Musson, Yockleton, Salop; *m* 1949, Joan I. S., 2nd *d* of late Col D. Davies-Evans, DSO, Penylan, Carmarthenshire. *Educ:* Shrewsbury Sch.; Trinity Hall, Cambridge. Called to Bar (Inner Temple), 1930; practised as Barrister, 1930-46; commnd, Pilot Officer, RAFVR, 1941; served Egypt, N Africa, Italy, 1942-45 (despatches). Ministry of Health: Senior Legal Asst, 1946; Asst Solicitor, 1952; Principal Asst Solicitor, 1957. *Recreations:* golf, country pursuits. *Address:* Prospect Hill Farm, Headley, Bordon, Hants. *T:* Headley Down 3183. *Club:* Savile.

**MUSTILL, Michael John,** QC 1968; *b* 10 May 1931; *o s* of Clement William and Marion Mustill; *m* 1960, Beryl Reid Davies. *Educ:* Oundle Sch.; St John's Coll., Cambridge. Royal Artillery, 1949-51 (commissioned, 1950). Called to Bar, Gray's Inn, 1955. *Recreation:* cricket. *Address:* 8 Prior Bolton Street, N1. *T:* 01-226 3032.

**MUSTO, Sir Arnold (Albert),** Kt 1932; CIE 1923; MInstCE; *b* 4 Oct. 1883; *s* of late J. J. Musto, Alderman of London; *m* 1922, Margaret (*d* 1965), 2nd *d* of W. J. McCausland of Magherafelt, Co. Derry, N Ireland; four *d* (one *s* decd). *Educ:* Birkbeck Coll., Univ. of London. Rotherhithe Tunnel Construction, 1905-06; Asst Engineer, Public Works Dept Indian Service of Engineers), Government of Bombay, 1907; Indus River Commission, 1907-09; Mechanical and Agricultural Engineer to the Govt of Bombay, 1909-12; reverted to PWD and designed Lloyd Dam, Poona District; Fuleli Canal District, 1913-14; Executive Engineer, Nasrat Canals District, 1914-15; Indus River Commission, 1915-16; served European War, in Mesopotamia, IARO, 1916-18; Controller of Munitions, Karachi (declined remuneration), 1918; in addition was Executive Engineer, Sukkur Barrage Project District, 1918-20, when he designed and submitted the Complete Project for the Sukkur Barrage and its allied Canal Systems; deputation in England on Barrage Project, 1921; Executive Engineer, Sukkur Barrage Project Div., 1921-23; a Nominated Mem. of the Bombay Legislative Council, 1923; Superintending Engineer, Lloyd Barrage Circle, to construct the Barrage and the Headworks of the Seven Canal Systems, 1923-32; Chm., Planning and Housing Commission, Trinidad, 1939; Regional Transport Commissioner for Midland Region, 1940-46, for Western Area, 1946-53. *Publications:* The Future of Sind; The Sukkur Barrage and Sind Canals. *Address:* Danny, Hurstpierpoint, Hassocks, Sussex. *T:* Hurstpierpoint 2299. *Clubs:* Royal Commonwealth Society; Royal Bombay Yacht; Sind (Karachi).

**MUSTOE, Nelson Edwin,** QC 1952; *s* of Edwin and Edith Mustoe, Wynberg, Cape, SA; *m* 1st, 1929, Edith Lake Patra (*d* 1955), *d* of Carroll Ethelbert Hamby, Sherrill, Missouri, USA; three *s*; 2nd, 1960, Anne, *d* of H. W. Revill, Lenton, Nottingham. *Educ:* High Sch. Wynberg; Trinity Coll., Dublin (MA, LLB, University Prizeman in Economics). Served European War, 1915-18, in South African Field Artillery and RAF, in East Africa and Egypt; formerly on unattached list, TA. Entered Inland Revenue Solicitor's Dept, 1925, leaving in 1939 for private practice. Advocate, Supreme Court of South Africa, 1936. Chm. S Africa Settlement Assoc. (1820 Assoc.), 1954-65; Vice-Chm., Royal African Society, 1966-69; Member: Exec. Cttee, Anglo-Ethiopian Soc., 1956-70 (Chm., 1956-62); Chm., Britain and South Africa Forum; Master, Worshipful Co. of Glaziers. *Publications:* Income Tax on Landed Property; Close Companies; Agricultural Law and Tenant Right; Gen. Ed., Simon's Income Tax, 2nd and 3rd edns; Cons. Ed., British Tax Encyclopædia. *Recreations:* walking, foreign travel. *Address:* 5 Paper Buildings, Temple, EC4. *T:* 01-353 4763; 31 Circus Lodge, NW8. *T:* Cunningham 5023. *Clubs:* United Wards, City Livery.

**MUTCH, Air Cdre James Richard,** CB 1946; Dir of Technical Training at the Air Ministry, 1956-59, retired; *b* 21 July 1905, Scottish; *m* 1938, Beatrice Alexandra Caroline Rae-Smith (*d* 1956); one *s* one *d*. *m* 1960, Dorothy Mona Sadler (*widow*), *née* Longbottom. *Educ:* Aboyne Sch., Aberdeenshire; Royal Air Force Apprentice Sch., Cranwell; Royal Air Force College, Cranwell. RAF apprentice training, 1921-24; RAF cadet training, 1925-26; Pilot Officer, 1926; Flying Officer, 1928; Flight Lt 1932; Sqdn Leader, 1937; Wing Comdr 1940; Group Capt. 1942; Air Commodore (Acting), 1944-46 and 1951-54; Air Cdre (Subs.), 1954; Senior Technical Staff Officer, Headquarters Flying Training Command, 1953-56. Qualified as Engineer Specialist Officer at RAF Sch. of Aeronautical Engineering, 1931-33; psa 1938. *Recreations:* gardening, shooting. *Address:* c/o Lloyds Bank, Cox & King's Branch, 6 Pall Mall, SW1.

**MUTCH, Nathan,** MA, MD Cantab, FRCP (London); Consulting Physician, Guy's Hospital; formerly Staff Examiner in Applied Pharmacology, London University; Examiner in Therapeutics, Cambridge University; Lecturer in Pharmacology, London University; Director of Department of Pharmacology, Guy's Hospital; Member of the first Editorial Board, British Journal of Pharmacology and Chemotherapy; Sector Adviser in Medicine, Emergency Medical Service; Consulting Physician to American Red Cross Society in Europe; *b* 22 May 1886; *s* of Nathan Mutch, Rochdale, and Helen Hollinshead; *m* 1913, Eileen Caroline Arbuthnot, 3rd *d* of Sir W. Arbuthnot Lane, 1st Bt, CB; one *d* (one *s* decd). *Educ:* Manchester Grammar Sch. (The King's prize for Chemistry); Emmanuel Coll., Cambridge (Senior Scholar and Research Student); 1st class Parts I and II, Nat. Science Tripos, 1906-07; Guy's Hosp. Medical Sch., (Univ. Scholar). Mem. of Physiological Soc.; founder Mem. of British Pharmacological Soc.; FRSM. *Publications:* articles on pathology and treatment of intestinal disorders, in scientific journals; also on magnesium trisilicate, other medicinal silicates, alumina and clays. *Address:* Pitt-White, Uplyme, Devon. *T:* Lyme Regis 2094.

**MWENDWA, Hon. Chief Justice Maluki Kitili;** Chief Justice of Kenya, since 1968; *b* 24 Dec. 1929; *s* of Senior Chief M. Kitabi Mwendwa and Mrs Kathuka Mwendwa; *m* 1964, Winifred Nyiva Mangole; one *s* three *d*. *Educ:* Alliance High Sch., Kenya; Makerere University Coll.; London Univ.; Exeter Univ.; St Catherine's Coll., Oxford. DipEd 1950; LLB 1955 (Sir Archibald Bodkin Prize for Criminal Law, 1953); DPA 1956; BA 1959, MA 1963. President: Cosmos Soc., 1959; Jowett Soc., 1959; St Catherine's Debating Soc., 1959, Oxford. Called to the Bar, Lincoln's Inn, 1961. Lectr Kagumo Teacher Training Coll., 1951. Asst Sec., Min. of Commerce and Industry, 1962, Min. of Works and Communications, 1962; Sen. Asst Sec., Min. of Tourism, Forests and Wild Life, 1962-63; Perm. Sec., Min. of Social Services, 1963, and Min. of Home Affairs, 1963-64; Solicitor Gen., 1964-68.

Leader, Kenya Delegn: Commonwealth and Empire Law Conf., Sydney, 1965; World Peace through Law Conf., Washington, 1965; Conf. on Intellectual Property, Stockholm, 1967 (Vice-Pres. of Conf.); UN Special Cttee on Friendly Relations, Geneva, 1967; Conf. on Law of Treaties, Vienna, 1968; Kenya Rep. on 6th Cttee, 21st Session, and on 2nd and 6th Cttees (Vice-Chm. of 6th Cttee), 22nd Session, UN Gen. Assembly; Ambassador to 22nd Session, UN Gen. Assembly, 1967 (Vice-Chm., Kenya Delegn to April/May 1967 Special Session); Chm. UN Assoc., Kenya; Mem., UN Internat. Trade Law Commn. Mem., Executive Council: African Inst. of Internat. Law, Lagos; Donovan Maule Theatre, Nairobi; Agricultural Soc. of Kenya, Nairobi; E African Automobile Assoc., Nairobi. Chm., Bd of Governors, Parklands and Ngara Schools, Nairobi. *Publication:* Constitutional Contrasts in the East African Territories, 1965. *Recreations:* hunting, swimming, cycling, walking. *Address:* Justice House, Upper Hill Road, PO Box 30041, Nairobi, Kenya. *T:* Nairobi 21221. *Clubs:* Executive (Nairobi), Mount Kenya Safari (Nanyuki).

**MYDDELTON, Lt-Col Ririd,** MVO 1945; JP; landowner; Extra Equerry to The Queen since 1952; Vice-Lieutenant of Denbighshire, since 1968; *b* 25 Feb. 1902; *e s* of late Col Robert Edward Myddelton, TD, DL, JP, Chirk Castle, and late Lady Violet, *d* of 1st Marquess of Abergavenny; *m* 1931, Margaret Elizabeth Mercer Nairne (now Lady Margaret Elizabeth Myddelton; granted rank as *d* of a Marquess, 1946), *d* of late Lord Charles Mercer Nairne; two *s* one *d. Educ:* Eton; RMC Sandhurst. 2nd Lt Coldstream Guards, 1923; Adjutant, 3rd Bn, 1928-31; Staff Capt., London District, 1934-37; seconded as Dep. Master of the Household to King George VI, 1937-39; DAAG London District, 1939-40; Staff Coll., Camberley, War Course, 1942; Commanded: 1st (Armd) Bn, Coldstream Guards, 1942-44 (Normandy); retired, 1946. JP 1948, DL 1949, High Sheriff, 1951-52, Denbigh. KStJ 1961. *Recreations:* hunting, shooting. *Address:* Chirk Castle, North Wales. *T:* Chirk 2460. *Club:* Turf.

**MYER, Dame (Margery) Merlyn Baillieu,** DBE 1960 (OBE 1948); *b* Queenscliff, Vic., 8 Jan. 1900; *d* of George Francis Baillieu and Agnes Sheehan; *m* 1920, Sidney Myer (*d* 1934); two *s* two *d. Educ:* Cromarty Girls' Sch., Victoria; Melbourne Univ. Interest in The Myer Emporium Ltd enterprises throughout Australia and abroad (founded by her late husband, Sidney Myer). Member: Cttee of Management of Royal Melbourne Hospital for 25 years; Victorian Council and Nat. Council of Australian Red Cross Soc. for 10 years; Sidney Myer Music Bowl Trust, which administers Sidney Myer Music Bowl. Collector of Jade, Porcelain and Objects d'Art. *Recreations:* garden lover, agricultural and musical interests, travel. *Address:* Cranlana, 62 Clendon Road, Toorak, Victoria 3142, Australia. *T:* BJ4966.

**MYERS, Brig. (Retired) Edmund Charles Wolf,** CBE 1944; DSO 1943; BA Cantab; MICE; Secretary, British Field Sports Society, Northern Region; *b* 12 Oct. 1906; *er s* of late Dr C. S. Myers, CBE, FRS; *m* 1943, Louisa, *er d* of late Aldred Bickham Sweet-Escott; one *d. Educ:* Haileybury; Royal Military Academy, Woolwich; Caius Coll., Cambridge. Commissioned into Royal Engineers, 1926. Served Palestine, 1936 (despatches); War of 1939-45; Middle East, including Balkans, until 1944 (African Star, Italy Star, DSO, CBE); North-West Europe, 1944-45 (France and Germany Star, Dutch Bronze Lion, Norwegian Liberty Medal); Far East, 1945; Korea, 1951-52 (despatches, American Legion of Merit). Chief Engineer, British Troops in Egypt, 1955-56; Dep. Dir, Personnel Administration in the War Office, 1956-59; retired 1959. Chief Civil Engineer Cleveland Bridge & Engineering Co. Ltd, 1959-64. Construction Manager, Power Gas Corp. Ltd, Davy-Ashmore Group, 1964-67. *Publication:* Greek Entanglement, 1955. *Recreations:* horse training and riding, sailing, flying (1st Sec. RE Flying Club, 1934-35), fishing. *Address:* Hartforth Cottage, Richmond, Yorks. *T:* Richmond (Yorks) 2723. *Clubs:* United Service, Special Forces.

**MYERS, Harry Eric,** QC 1967; *b* 10 Jan. 1914; *s* of Harry Moss Myers and Muriel Serjeant; *m* 1951, Lorna Babette Kitson (*née* Blackburn); no *c. Educ:* Bedford Sch. Admitted Solicitor of Supreme Court, 1936; called to Bar, Middle Temple, 1945. Prosecuting Counsel to Bd of Inland Revenue on SE Circuit, 1965. *Address:* 3 Hare Court, Temple, EC4. *T:* 01-353 7742.

**MYERS, Prof. Rupert Horace;** Vice-Chancellor, The University of New South Wales, since 1969, and Foundation Professor of Metallurgy since 1952; *b* 21 Feb. 1921; *s* of Horace Alexander Myers and Dorothy (*née* Harris); *m* 1944, Io Edwina King; one *s* three *d. Educ:* Melbourne High Sch.; Univ. of Melbourne. BSc 1942; MSc 1943; PhD 1947. Commonwealth Res. Fellow, Univ. of Melbourne, 1942-47; Principal Res. Officer, CSIRO, AERE Harwell, 1947-52; Univ. of New South Wales: Dean, Faculty of Applied Science, 1956-61; Pro-Vice-Chancellor, 1961-69. *Publications:* numerous on metallurgy and atomic energy (also patents). *Recreations:* golf, tennis, music. *Address:* University of New South Wales, PO Box 1, Kensington, NSW 2033, Australia. *T:* 663-0351. *Clubs:* Graduates (Univ. NSW), University Union (NSW); Roseville Golf.

**MYERSON, Aubrey Selwyn,** QC 1967; *b* Johannesburg, S Africa, 10 Dec. 1926; *o s* of Michael Colman Myerson, MRCSI, LRCPI, and late Lee Myerson; *m* 1955, Helen Margaret, *d* of Hedley Lavis, Adelaide, S Austr.; one *s* one *d. Educ:* Cardiff High Sch.; University Coll. of S Wales and Mon. Called to Bar, Lincoln's Inn, 1950. *Recreations:* squash, fencing. *Address:* 8 Sloane Court East, Chelsea, SW3. *T:* 01-730 4707; 12 Windsor Court, Penarth, Glam. *T:* 702557. *Clubs:* Reform; Bristol Channel Yacht.

**MYINT, Prof. Hla;** Professor of Economics, London School of Economics, since 1966; *b* Bassein, Burma, 20 March 1920; *m* 1944, Joan (*née* Morris); no *c. Educ:* Rangoon Univ.; London Sch. of Economics. Prof. of Econs, Rangoon Univ., and Econ. Adviser to Govt of Burma, 1946-49; Univ. Lectr in Econs of Underdeveloped Countries, Oxford Univ., 1950-65; Rector of Rangoon Univ., 1958-61. Vis. Prof., Univs of Yale, Cornell and Wisconsin; has served on UN Expert Cttees; Hon. DLitt, Rangoon, 1961. Order of Sithu (Burma), 1961. *Publications:* Theories of Welfare Economics, 1948; The Economics of the Developing Countries, 1964; Economic Theory and the Underdeveloped Countries, 1970; many papers in learned jls. *Recreations:* walking, garden watching. *Address:* 12 Willow Drive, Barnet, Herts. *T:* 01-449 3028.

**MYLES, Capt. Edgar Kinghorne,** VC 1916; DSO 1917; late The King's Regiment and Worcestershire Regiment; *b* 23 July 1894; married. Served European War, Egypt,

Gallipoli 1915; Mesopotamia, 1916-18 (VC, DSO).

**MYNETT, George Kenneth,** QC 1960; JP; Recorder of Stoke-on-Trent since 1961; Deputy Chairman, Oxfordshire Quarter Sessions, since 1969; Member, Court of Governors, University of Keele; *b* 16 Nov. 1913; *s* of E. Mynett, Wellington, Salop; *m* 1940, Margaret Verna Bass-Hammonds; two *s*. *Educ:* Adams Grammar Sch., Newport, Salop; London Univ. Admitted solicitor of Supreme Court, 1937; LLB Hons (London) 1938. Served War of 1939-45, RAF, 1940-46; Dep. Judge Advocate Staff, Dept of JAG, 1945, 1946. Barrister, Middle Temple, 1942, 1st Cl. Hons, Certificate of Hon.; after demobilisation practised on Oxford Circuit. Master of the Bench, Middle Temple, 1967. Member: Council for the Training of Magistrates, 1967; Gen. Council of the Bar, 1968. *Recreations:* landscape painting, golf, travel. *Address:* Tanglewood House, Boar's Hill, Oxford. *T:* Oxford 35156; 12 King's Bench Walk, Temple, EC4. *T:* 01-353 7008. *Clubs:* Lansdowne; Union (Birmingham).

**MYNORS, Sir Humphrey (Charles Baskerville),** 1st Bt, *cr* 1964; Chairman, Finance Corporation for Industry, Ltd; Director: General Electric & English Electric Cos Ltd; Imperial Tobacco Group Ltd; Legal and General Assurance Soc. Ltd; Pilkington Bros Ltd; *b* 28 July 1903; 2nd *s* of Rev. A. B. Mynors, rector of Langley Burrell, Wilts; *m* 1939, Lydia Marian, *d* of late Sir Ellis Minns, LittD, FSA, FBA; one *s* four *d*. *Educ:* Marlborough; Corpus Christi Coll., Cambridge. Fellow of Corpus Christi Coll., Cambridge, 1926-33; Hon. Fellow, 1953. Entered the service of the Bank of England, 1933; a Dir, 1949-54; Dep. Governor, 1954-64. Chm., Panel on Take-overs and Mergers, 1968-69; Dep. Chm., 1969-70. Hon. DCL Durham. *Heir: s* Richard Baskerville Mynors [*b* 5 May 1947; *m* 1970, Fiona Bridget, *d* of Rt Rev. G. E. Reindorp, *qv*]. *Address:* Treago, St Weonards, Herefordshire. *T:* St Weonards 208.

**MYNORS, Sir Roger (Aubrey Baskerville),** Kt 1963; FBA 1944; *b* 28 July 1903; *s* of Rev. A. B. Mynors, Rector of Langley Burrell, Wilts; *m* 1945, Lavinia Sybil, *d* of late Very Rev. C. A. Alington, DD. *Educ:* Eton; Balliol College, Oxford. Fellow and Classical Tutor of Balliol, 1926-44 (Hon. Fellow 1963); Kennedy Prof. of Latin in the Univ. of Cambridge and Fellow of Pembroke Coll., 1944-53 (Hon. Fellow, 1965); Corpus Christi Prof. of Latin Language and Literature, Oxford, 1953-70. Visiting Lecturer, Harvard, 1938; Temp. Principal, HM Treasury, 1940. Pres., Classical Assoc., 1966. Hon. DLitt: Edinburgh; Durham; Hon. LittD Cambridge. Hon. Mem., Amer. Acad. of Arts and Sciences. *Publications:* Cassiodori Senatoris Institutiones, 1937; Durham Cathedral MSS before 1200, 1939; Catulli Carmina, 1958; Catalogue of Balliol MSS; Plinii Epistulae, 1963; Panegyrici Latini, 1964; Vergilii Opera, 1969. *Address:* Treago, St Weonards, Herefordshire. *T:* Weonards 208.

**MYRDAL, Alva;** Swedish Cabinet Minister, diplomatist, sociologist and authoress; Ambassador at large since 1961; Member of Swedish Parliament since 1962; Minister without Portfolio (in charge of disarmament and Church affairs) in Swedish Government, since 1967; *b* 31 Jan. 1902; *d* of Albert and Lova Reimer; *m* 1924, Dr Gunnar Myrdal; one *s* two *d*. *Educ:* Stockholm Univ. (AB); Uppsala Univ. (AM); USA; Geneva Univ. Founder 1936, and Dir, 1936-48, Training Coll. for Pre-Sch. Teachers, Stockholm; Principal Dir, UN Dept of Social Affairs, 1949-50; Dir, Unesco Dept of Social Sciences, 1951-55; Minister to India, Burma, Ceylon and Nepal, 1955-56, Ambassador, 1956-61. Delegate to: ILO Conf., Paris, 1945, Geneva, 1947; Unesco Conf., Paris, 1946, New Delhi, 1956; UN General Assemblies, 1962, 1963, 1965-69. Chief Swedish Delegate to UN Disarmament Cttee, Geneva, 1962-. Chairman: Internat. Inst. for Peace and Conflict Research, Stockholm, 1965-66; UN Expert Group on South Africa, 1964; Swedish Govt Cttee on an International Peace Research Inst., 1964. World Council on Pre-School Educn, 1947-49; Member: World Fedn of UN Assocs; Internat. Fedn of Univ. Women; Swedish Organisation for Cultural Relief in Europe; Swedish Fedn of Business and Professional Women (Chm. 1935-38, 1940-42). Hon. LLD: Mount Holyoke Coll., USA, 1950; Edinburgh Univ., 1964; Dr Humane Letters, Columbia Univ., 1965; Temple Univ., 1968; Hon. PhD, Leeds Univ., England, 1962. West German Peace Prize (with G. Myrdal), 1970. *Publications:* (with G. Myrdal) Crisis in the Population Problem, 1934; City Children, 1935; Nation and Family, 1941; Postwar Planning, 1944; Are We Too Many?, 1950; (with V. Klein) Women's Two Roles, 1956, etc.; numerous contribs to newspapers, periodicals, books and reports. *Recreations:* travel, theatre and reading. *Address:* Foreign Office, Stockholm, Sweden; Vaesterlaanggatan 31, Stockholm.

**MYRES, John Nowell Linton,** LLD, DLitt, DLit, MA, FBA, FSA; President, Society of Antiquaries, since 1966 (Vice-President, 1959-63; Director, 1966-70); Bodley's Librarian, University of Oxford, 1948-65; Student of Christ Church and Fellow of Winchester College; *b* 27 Dec. 1902; *yr s* of late Emeritus Prof. Sir John Linton Myres, OBE; *m* 1929, Joan Mary Lovell, *o d* of late G. L. Stevens, Jersey; two *s*. *Educ:* Winchester Coll. (Scholar); New Coll., Oxford (Scholar). 1st Class Lit Hum., 1924; 1st Class Modern History, 1926; BA 1924; MA 1928; Lecturer, 1926, Student and Tutor, 1928-48, Librarian, 1938-48, of Christ Church; Univ. Lectr in Early English History, 1935-47; served in Min. of Food, 1940-45 (Head of Fruit and Veg. Products Div., 1943-45); mem. of Council of St Hilda's Coll., Oxford, 1937-52; Pres. Oxford Architectural and Historical Soc., 1946-49; Hon. LLD Toronto, 1954; Hon. DLitt Reading, 1964; Hon. DLit Belfast, 1965; Mem. Institute for Advanced Study, Princeton, 1956; Pres. Council for British Archæology, 1959-61; Member: Ancient Monuments Board (England), from 1959; Royal Commn on Historical Monuments (England), 1969-; Chm. Standing Conference of National and Univ. Libraries, 1959-61. Pres: Library Assoc., 1963; Soc. for Medieval Archæology, 1963-66; Soc. of Antiquaries, 1970-. Lectures: Ford's, in English History, 1958-59; O'Donnell, Edinburgh Univ., 1961; Oxford 1966-67; Rhind, Edinburgh, 1964-65; Raleigh, British Acad., 1970. Hon. Mem., Deutsches Archäologisches Institut. Has supervised excavations at Caerleon Amphitheatre, 1926, St Catharine's Hill, Winchester, 1925-28, Colchester, 1930, Butley Priory, 1931-33, Aldborough, 1934-35 and elsewhere. Hon. Foreign Corresp. mem. Grolier Club, New York. *Publications:* part-author: St Catharine's Hill, Winchester, 1930; Roman Britain and the English Settlements, 1936; Anglo-Saxon Pottery and the Settlement of England, 1969; articles and reviews in learned periodicals. *Recreations:* growing of vegetables and fruit; Bibliophily, study of antiquities. *Address:* Manor House, Kennington, Oxford. *T:* Oxford 35353.

**MYSORE, HH the Maharaja Sri Jaya Chamarajendra Wadiyar Bahadur,** GCB 1946; GCSI 1945; Hon. LLD Benares Hindu University, 1942; DLitt Annamalai University, 1955; Governor of Mysore; Chancellor of Mysore University; Chancellor of Karnatak University; *b* 18 July 1919; *o s* of late Sri Kanteerava Narasimharaja Wadiyar, Yuvaraja of Mysore. *Educ:* privately; Univ. of Mysore; BA 1938. The area of the State is over 70,000 square miles and it has a population of over 19 millions. *Recreations:* music, riding, tennis, racquets, big game shooting, golf. *Address:* The Palace, Mysore.

# N

**NAAS, Lord, Charles Diarmuidh John Bourke;** *b* 11 June 1953; *e s* and *heir* of 10th Earl of Mayo, *qv. Educ:* St Aubyn's, Rottingdean.

**NABARRO, Sir Gerald (David Nunes),** Kt 1963; MP (C) South Worcs, since 1966; director of companies; broadcaster, televiser, journalist, and author; *b* 29 June 1913; *e surv s* of S. N. Nabarro, London; *m* 1943, Joan Maud Violet im Thurn, *e d* of late Col B. B. von B. im Thurn, DSO, MC, Dawn House, Winchester, Hants; two *s* two *d. Educ:* LCC Sch. until age of 14. Regular Army, 1930-37; Territorial Army, 1937-43; TARO, 1943-63. Worked in all grades in industry, mostly engineering and sawmilling, from labourer to Managing Dir. Contested (C) West Bromwich Div. of Staffs, 1945; MP (C) Kidderminster Div. of Worcs, 1950-64. Chm. West Midlands Fedn (56 Constituencies) of Young Conservatives, 1946-48 (Pres., 1948-50); Author of Parliamentary legislation for: Clean Air, 1955; Coroners' Act, 1953; Thermal Insulation (Industrial Buildings) Act, 1957; Oil Burners (Standards) Act, 1960. Governor: Univ. of Birmingham; Univ. of Aston. President: Inst. of Marketing (London Branch) 1968-70; British Direct Mail Advertising Assoc.; Chm., Nat. Consultative Cttee for Independent Education; MInstF; FRSA; Member: Soc. of Authors; Inst. of Dirs; Amer. Fedn of Television and Radio Artists (AFTRA). Trustee of birthplace of late Sir Edward Elgar. Pres., numerous sporting, cultural, and welfare organisations in Worcs. Motto, Audax et Fidelis. *Publications:* NAB 1–Portrait of a Politician, 1969; numerous contributions on economics, finance, and industry. *Recreations:* travel, book collecting, trains, walking. *Address:* The Orchard House, Broadway, Worcs; House of Commons, SW1. *T:* 01-930 6240. *Clubs:* Carlton, Army and Navy.

**NABOKOV, Vladimir;** American author and lepidopterist; *b* St Petersburg (now Leningrad), Russia, 23 April 1899; *s* of Vladimir Nabokov and Hélène Rukavishnikov; *m* 1925, Véra Slonim; one *s. Educ:* St Petersburg; Trinity Coll., Cambridge (BA). He then rejoined his family (in exile from Russia) in Berlin, 1922; there, he trans. some English literary works into Russian, including Alice in Wonderland (publ. 1923), and between 1923 and 1940 he wrote in Russian (in Berlin and Paris) novels, poetry, short stories and plays; much of this work has now been published in England and USA (trans. by him, sometimes jointly with his son, Dmitri, and with Michael Scammell). In 1940 he settled in USA (becoming a US Citizen, 1945). Lecturer, Wellesley Coll., 1941-48; Research Fellow in Lepidoptera, Harvard Univ. Museum of Comparative Zoology, 1942-48; Prof. of Russian Literature, Cornell Univ., 1948-59. Grant in Literature, Amer. Acad. Arts and Letters, 1951; Guggenheim Fellow, 1943 and 1953; Brandeis Univ. Medal, 1964; Gold Medal, Amer. Acad. of Arts, 1969. *Publications: novels:* The Real Life of Sebastian Knight (USA, 1941, 1959; Eng., 1945, 1960); Bend Sinister (USA, 1947; Eng., 1960); Pnin (USA and Eng., 1957); Lolita (USA, 1958; Eng., 1959; filmed, 1962); Pale Fire (USA and Eng., 1962); Ada (USA and Eng., 1969); *novels trans. from his Russian:* Camera Obscura (Eng., 1936; USA, as Laughter in the Dark, 1938; Eng., thus, 1961; filmed 1969); Despair (Eng., 1937; USA, 1966); Invitation to a Beheading (USA, 1959; Eng., 1960); The Gift (USA and Eng., 1963); The Defense (USA, 1964; Eng., as The Defence, 1964); The Eye (USA, 1965; Eng., 1966); King, Queen, Knave (USA and Eng., 1968); Mary (USA and Eng., 1970); *poetry:* Poems (USA, 1959; Eng., 1961); Poems and Problems (USA 1971); *biography:* Nikolai Gogol (USA, 1944; Eng., 1947); *short stories:* Nine Stories (USA, 1947); Nabokov's Dozen (13 stories, some from his Russian or French, USA, 1958; Eng., 1959); Nabokov's Quartet (USA, 1966; Eng., 1967); Nabokov's Congeries (USA, 1968); *plays:* several, written from 1923 to 1938, inc. The Waltz Invention (publ. USA, 1966, produced USA and Oxford); *memoirs:* Conclusive Evidence (USA and Eng., 1951; rev. edn, as Speak, Memory, USA and Eng., 1967); *translations from other writers include:* Three Russian Poets (USA, 1945; Eng., 1947); (with D. Nabokov): A Hero of Our Time (by M. Lermontov) (USA, 1958); Song of Igor's Campaign (12th century epic) (USA and Eng., 1960); Eugene Onegin (by A. Pushkin) 4 vol. project, begun by him in 1949: vol. 1, introd. and text; vols 2-4, commentaries, appendix, index (USA, 1964; Eng., 1964); *lepidopterology:* The Nearctic Members of the Genus Lycaeides Hübner (Harvard, 1949) and others. *Recreation:* butterfly hunting. *Address:* c/o McGraw-Hill Book Co., Trade Division, 330, W 42 Street, New York, NY, USA.

**NADESAN, Pararajasingam,** CMG 1955; OBE 1954; Director: The Galle Face Hotel; Cargills (Ceylon) Ltd; Chairman, The Nuwara Eliya Hotels Co. Ltd; Past Chairman, Low Country Products Association; Member: Central Bd of Agriculture; Tea & Coconut Research Institutes; Ceylon Tea Propoganda Bd; *b* 20 Dec. 1917; *s* of Sir Sangarapillai Parajasingam, *qv*; *m* 1st, 1941, Gauri Nair (decd); one *s* one *d*; 2nd, 1953, Kamala Nair; three *d. Educ:* Royal College., and Ceylon Univ. Coll.; Univ. of London (BA Hons). Tutor, Ceylon Univ. Coll., 1940; entered Ceylon Civil Service, 1941; held various appts in sphere of provincial administration, 1941-47; Asst Permanent Sec., Min. of Transport and Works, 1948-53; Dir of Civil Aviation in addition to duties as Asst Sec. Min. of Transport and Works, 1949-54; Sec. to the Prime Minister and Information Officer, Ceylon, 1954-56; Member: Ceylon Delegation to the Bandung Conf.; Commonwealth Prime Minister's Conf.; ICAO Gen. Assembly; ILO Cttee on Plantations. MInstT (London). Officer Order of Merit (Italy), 1954; Knight Comdr Order of the Crown, Thailand, 1955; Comdr Order of Orange Nassau, Netherlands, 1955; Defence Medal, 1947; Coronation Medal, 1953; Ceylon Armed Services Inauguration Medal, 1956. *Recreations:* golf, tennis, gardening, collecting antiques. *Address:* Six 28th Lane A, Inner Flower Road, Colombo 3, Ceylon. *T:* 78202 (Residence), 5695 (Office). *Clubs:* Colombo, Orient, Rotary (Colombo); Colombo Rowing, Gymkhana.

**NAGEON de LESTANG, Sir (Marie Charles Emmanuel) Clement,** Kt 1960; *b* 20 Oct. 1910; *e s* of late M. F. C. Nageon de Lestang, Solicitor and Simone Savy; *m* 1933, Danielle Sauvage; one *s* three *d* (and one *s* decd). *Educ:* St Louis' Coll., Seychelles; King's Coll., London. LLB (Hons) London, 1931. Called to the Bar, Middle Temple, 1931. Private practice, Seychelles, 1932-35; Legal Adviser and Crown Prosecutor to Govt of Seychelles, 1936-39; Actg Chief Justice, Seychelles, 1939-44; Resident Magistrate, Kenya, 1944-47; Puisne Judge, Kenya, 1947-56; Federal Justice, Federal Supreme Court of Nigeria, 1956-58; Chief Justice of the High Court of Lagos, 1958-64, and of the Southern Cameroons, 1958-60; Justice of Appeal, Court of Appeal for Eastern Africa, 1964, Vice-Pres., 1966-69. Chm., Industrial Tribunals. *Recreations:* yachting, fishing, tennis. *Address:* Pennies, Court Drive, Shillingford, Oxon. *Club:* Nairobi (Nairobi, Kenya).

**NAGOGO, Alhaji Hon. Sir Usuman;** Emir of Katsina, KBE 1962 (CBE 1948); CMG 1953; President, Council of Chiefs, North-Central State (formerly Minister without Portfolio, Northern Region of Nigeria, and Member, House of Assembly). *Address:* Katsina, Northern Nigeria.

**NAIPAUL, Vidiadhar Surajprasad;** author; *b* 17 Aug. 1932; *m* 1955, Patricia Ann Hale. *Educ:* Queen's Royal Coll., Trinidad; University Coll., Oxford. *Publications:* The Mystic Masseur, 1957 (John Llewelyn Rhys Memorial Prize, 1958); The Suffrage of Elvira, 1958; Miguel Street, 1959 (Somerset Maugham Award, 1961); A House for Mr Biswas, 1961; The Middle Passage, 1962; Mr Stone and the Knights Companion, 1963 (Hawthornden Prize, 1964); An Area of Darkness, 1964; The Mimic Men, 1967 (W. H. Smith Award, 1968); A Flag on the Island, 1967; The Loss of El Dorado, 1969; In a Free State, 1971. *Address:* c/o André Deutsch Ltd, 105 Great Russell Street, WC1.

**NAIR, Rt. Hon. Sir C. Madhavan,** PC 1941; Kt, *cr* 1939; BA; Barrister-at-law; *b* 24 Jan. 1879; *s* of U. Raman Menon (landlord, Malabar); *m* 1907, *e d* of Sir Sankaran Nair, CIE; two *s* one *d.* *Educ:* Madras Christian Coll.; University Coll., London; Middle Temple. Enrolled as Advocate, Madras High Court, 1904; officiated as Vice-Principal, Madras Law Coll., 1909; Law Reporter, High Court, 1915-16; Prof., Law Coll., 1916-20; for some time, Examiner in Law and Chm. of the Law Examination Board, Univ. of Madras, and Pres. the Law Coll. Council; officiating Principal, Law Coll., 1920; Sec. Students Advisory Cttee; Government Pleader, High Court, Madras, 1920-23; Advocate-General, 1923-24; Judge, High Court, Madras, 1924-39; Pres. Railways Rates Advisory Board, 1940; Mem. Judicial Cttee of Privy Council, 1941-50. *Address:* Lynwood, 52 Kodembakkam High Road, Madras 34, India. *Clubs:* Athenæum, National Liberal; Cosmopolitan (Madras).

**NAIRAC, Hon. Sir André (Lawrence),** Kt 1963; CBE 1953; QC (Mauritius); *b* 1905. *Educ:* Oxford Univ. Formerly Minister of Industry, Commerce and External Communications. Mem. of Legislative Council and Mem. of Executive Council, Mauritius. *Address:* c/o Judicial Dept, Port Louis, Mauritius.

**NAIRN, Bryce James Miller,** CBE 1960 (OBE 1944); Consul-General, Tangier, 1957-63, retired; *b* 9 July 1903; *s* of Cuthbert and Mary Nairn; *m* 1928, Margaret Mary, *d* of T. R. White, Orkney; one *d* (and one *d* decd). *Educ:* Pollokshields Academy, Glasgow. After taking MRCVS, farmed in French Morocco, 1926-32; joined Foreign Service, 1933; served Marrakesh and Tangier, 1933-40; Brazzaville, 1941-43; Marrakesh and Casablanca, 1943-44; Consul: Bordeaux, 1944-48, Madeira, 1948-50, St Paul-Minneapolis, 1950-53; Consul-General, Lourenço-Marques, 1953-57. *Recreations:* riding, shooting, fruit farming, golf. *Address:* BP511, Marrakesh, Morocco. *T:* Dar Tounsi 109.

**NAIRN, Sir Douglas (Leslie) Spencer-,** 2nd Bt *cr* 1933; TD; *b* 24 Dec. 1906; *e s* of Sir Robert Spencer-Nairn, 1st Bt, TD; *S* father, 1960; *m* 1st, 1931, Elizabeth Livingston (marr. diss., 1946), *d* of late Arnold J. Henderson; two *s* one *d*; 2nd, 1947, E. Louise, *d* of late Frederick Vester; one *s* one *d.* *Educ:* Trinity Hall, Cambridge (MA). Mem. of firm of Nairn-Williamson Ltd, Dir, Oct. 1960-68. Served War of 1939-45, Black Watch, ending with rank of Lt-Col. Farmed in Southern Rhodesia, 1947-54. MP (C) Central Ayrshire, 1955-Sept. 1959. *Heir: s* Robert Arnold Spencer-Nairn [*b* 11 Oct. 1933; *m* 1963, Joanna Elizabeth, *d* of late Lt-Comdr G. S. Salt, RN, and Mrs W. J. Lamb; two *s* one *d. Educ:* Eton; Trinity Hall, Cambridge. Late Lt, Scots Guards]. *Address:* Rankeilour, Cupar, Fife; Culligran, Struy, Inverness-shire; 4 Stanhope Mews East, SW7; Villa Franca, Glendale, Rhodesia. *Clubs:* Carlton, Caledonian; New (Salisbury, Rhodesia).

**NAIRN, Sir George;** *see* Nairn, Sir M. G.

**NAIRN, George Alexander Stokes,** MBE 1918; FRSA 1950; *b* 27 Aug. 1889; *s* of George McKie Nairn; *m* 1925, Doreen Mann Watson; one *s* one *d.* *Educ:* Liverpool Coll. Commissioned (TA), 1913; served European War, 1914-18, 9th Battalion, The King's Liverpool Regt, rank of Major. Joined Lever Brothers, 1919; Dir, William Gossage & Sons, Widnes, 1919-32, Chm., 1932-34; Lever Brothers & Unilever Ltd. Continental Liaison Cttee, London and Rotterdam, 1934-40; Pres. Lever Brothers, Canada, 1940-44; Unilever UK Food Executive, 1945-46; Chm., Lever Brothers, Port Sunlight, Ltd, 1947-54; Dir, North-Western Industrial Estates Ltd, 1949-59. Mem. Mersey Docks and Harbour Board, 1949-55; Mem. Merseyside and North Wales Electricity Board, 1949-56. Chm. Liverpool Collegiate Sch. Bd of Governors; Governor, Liverpool Coll.; Council, Manchester Coll. of Sci. and Tech.; Member: Exec. and Finance Cttee, Liverpool Cathedral; Central Board of Finance, Church of England, 1955-65. Former Member: NW Regional Academic Bd for Advanced Technology, also NW Regional Advisory Coun. on Educ. for Industry and Commerce, 1948-57. Central Electricity Authority, 1956-57; Pt-time Mem. of the Central Electricity Generating Bd, 1957-60. *Recreations:* gardening and photography. *Address:* Highlawn, Mill Road, Bromborough, Cheshire. *T:* 051-334 2244.

**NAIRN, Air Vice-Marshal Kenneth Gordon,** CB 1945; Director, Hill Thomson & Co., Edinburgh; Chartered Accountant; *b* 9 Nov. 1898; *m* 1920, Mary Fleming Martin; two *s* one *d.* *Educ:* George Watson's Coll., Edinburgh; Univ. of Manitoba. Lived in Edinburgh till 1911; proceeded to Canada; service in Strathcona Horse and transferred to RFC 1916-19; Pilot, rank Lt; moved to Vancouver from Winnipeg, 1921; in private business and practice. Hon. Wing Commander of 111 Aux. Squadron RCAF 1933; Active Service, 1939-45; on Air Council as Air Mem. Accounts and Finance till Oct. 1944, then Special Adviser to Minister for Air on Finance. Hon. ADC for Province of BC to the Governor-General,

Viscount Alexander, 1947-. Norwegian Cross of Liberation, 1948. *Recreations:* golf, fishing, yachting. *Address:* 1611 Drummond Drive, Vancouver, BC. *TA:* Nairn, Vancouver. *T:* Fairmont 8600. *Clubs:* Royal Air Force; Racquet and Tennis (New York); Rideau (Ottawa); Vancouver, Capitano, Royal Vancouver Yacht (Vancouver).

**NAIRN, Sir (Michael) George,** 3rd Bt, *cr* 1904; TD 1948; *b* 30 Jan. 1911; *s* of Sir Michael Nairn, 2nd Bt, and Mildred Margaret, *e d* of G. W. Neish; *S* father 1952; *m* 1936, Helen Louise, *yr d* of late Major E. J. W. Bruce, Melbourne, Aust., and late Mrs L. Warre Graham-Clarke; two *s. Educ:* Trinity Coll., Glenalmond. Dir, Nairn and Williamson (Holdings) Ltd; Chm. Kirkcaldy and Dist Trustee Savings Bank, 1952. Served War of 1939-45, with The Black Watch (wounded); Major, 1939. Mem. of the Queen's Body Guard for Scotland (Royal Company of Archers). *Heir: s* Michael Nairn, *b* 1 July 1938. *Address:* Pitcarmick, Blairgowrie, Perthshire. *T:* Strath Ardle 214. *Clubs:* Caledonian; New (Edinburgh).
*See also Sir W. G. N. Walker.*

**NAIRNE,** 12th Baroness, *cr* 1681; **Katherine Evelyn Constance Bigham;** *b* 22 June 1912; *d* of 6th Marquess of Lansdowne and Elizabeth (she *m* 2nd, Lord Colum Crichton-Stuart, who *d* 1957; she *d* 1964); *S* to brother's Barony of Nairne, 1944; *m* 1933, Hon. Edward Bigham (now Viscount Mersey, *qv*); three *s. Heir: s* Master of Nairne, *qv. Address:* Derreen, Lauragh, Killarney, Eire; Bignor Park, Pulborough, Sussex. *T:* Sutton Sussex 214.

**NAIRNE, Master of; Hon. Richard Maurice Clive Bigham; film director;** *b* 8 July 1934; *e s* of 3rd Viscount Mersey, *qv*, and of 12th Baroness Nairne, *qv*; *m* 1961, Joanna, *d* of John A. R. G. Murray, *qv*; one *s. Educ:* Eton and Balliol. Irish Guards, 1952-54 (final rank Lt). Films: The Name of the Cloud is Ignorance, 1965 (Plague, Lion of St Mark, and Premio San Giorgio, Venice; Main Award, Salerno); The Threat in the Water, 1968 (Golden Rocket and Dip. of Honour, Rome; Gold Award, BISFA; Brit. Film Acad. award for best specialist film); Cast Us Not Out, 1969 (Silver Award, BISFA). *Address:* 1 Rosmead Road, W11. *T:* 01-727 5057. *Clubs:* Brooks's, Pratt's.

**NAIRNE, Patrick Dalmahoy,** MC 1943; Deputy Under-Secretary of State, Ministry of Defence, since 1970; *b* 15 Aug. 1921; *s* of Lt-Col C. S. and Mrs E. D. Nairne; *m* 1948, Penelope Chauncy Bridges, *d* of Lt-Col R. F. and Mrs L. C. Bridges; three *s* three *d. Educ:* Radley Coll.; University Coll., Oxford (Exhibr). Seaforth Highlanders, 1941-45 (Capt.). 1st cl. hons Mod. Hist. (Oxon), 1947. Entered Civil Service and joined Admty, Dec. 1947; Private Sec. to First Lord of Admty, 1958-60; Asst Sec., 1960; Private Sec. to Sec. of State for Defence, 1965-67; Assistant Under-Sec. of State (Logistics), MoD, 1967-70. *Recreations:* watercolour painting, calligraphy. *Address:* South Lodge, Knipp Hill, Cobham, Surrey. *T:* Cobham 2401. *Club:* Oxford and Cambridge University.

**NAISBY, John Vickers,** MC 1918; TD 1935; QC 1947; *m* 1954, Dorothy Helen, *d* of late J. H. Fellows. *Educ:* Rossall; Emmanuel Coll., Cambridge. Called to Bar, Inner Temple, 1922. Lt-Col and Brevet Col. *Address:* 3 Westmorland Place, SW1. *T:* 01-828 8917.

**NAISH, Lieut-Commander George Prideaux Brabant,** VRD 1965; RNR; Keeper, National Maritime Museum, Greenwich, since 1969; *b* 6 April 1909; *s* of Rev. Francis Clement Prideaux Naish and Irene Stainforth Brabant; *m* 1937, Elizabeth Joan, *o c* of Henry Mills Goldsmith; two *s. Educ:* St Edward's School, Oxford; University College, Southampton. Joined Staff of newly constituted National Maritime Museum, 1935. Served in RNVR during War of 1939-45; transferred to permanent RNVR and RNR shortly after demobilization. Chairman, Cttee for Nautical Archæology. *Publications:* Nelson's Letters to his Wife (ed for Navy Records Soc.), 1958; Spanish Armada Documents (ed for Navy Records Soc.), 1952; Ships and Shipbuilding, chapters in A History of Technology, ed Singer, vol. 3, 1957 and vol. 4, 1958, etc. *Recreation:* yacht cruising. *Address:* 5 Hardy Road, Blackheath, SE3. *T:* 01-858 1333. *Club:* Royal Cruising.

**NALDER, Maj.-Gen. Reginald Francis Heaton,** CB 1944; OBE 1941; BSc; retired; *b* 2 Feb. 1895; *s* of late Francis Henry Nalder; *m* 1916, Kathleen, *d* of late William Heaton Jacob; one *s* one *d. Educ:* Dulwich Coll.; London University. Commissioned Loyal North Lancashire Regt, 1914; E Surrey Regt, 1915; served European War, France, Belgium and Italy, 1916-18; transferred to Royal Signals, 1922; North-West Frontier of India, 1930-31; at War Office, 1935-39; served War of 1939-45: in France and Belgium, 1939-40; Chief Signal Officer, Allied Armies in Italy, 1943-45, and AFHQ, 1945 (despatches, OBE, CB, Commander Legion of Merit, Officer Legion of Honour, French Croix de Guerre). Signal Officer-in-Chief, India, 1946-47; retired, 1947; Colonel Commandant Royal Signals, 1955-60. Princess Mary Medal (Royal Signals Institution), 1966. *Publications:* British Army Signals in the Second World War, 1953; The Royal Corps of Signals, 1958. *Address:* 23 Alexandra Road, Epsom. *T:* Epsom 22041. *Clubs:* United Service, Royal Automobile.

**NALL, Sir Michael (Joseph),** 2nd Bt *cr* 1954; DL; *b* 6 Oct. 1921; *er s* of Colonel Sir Joseph Nall, 1st Bt, DSO, TD, DL; *S* father, 1958; *m* 1951, Angela Loveday Hanbury, *e d* of Air Chief Marshal Sir Alec Coryton, *qv*; two *s. Educ:* Wellington College, Berks. Joined Royal Navy, 1939. Served War of 1939-45 (at sea); psm 1949; Lt-Comdr, 1950-61, retired. General Manager, Guide Dogs for the Blind Association, 1961-64. DL Notts, 1970-. *Recreations:* field sports, farming, finance. *Heir: s* Edward William Joseph Nall, *b* 24 Oct. 1952. *Address:* Hoveringham Hall, Notts. *T:* Lowdham 3634. *Clubs:* Carlton, Royal Commonwealth Society; Nottinghamshire.

**NALL-CAIN,** family name of **Baron Brocket.**

**NAN KIVELL, Rex de Charembac,** CMG 1966; Director of the Redfern Gallery, London, since 1925; *b* 9 April 1899; *s* of George Henry and Mary Louise Nan Kivell. *Educ:* New Brighton School and Canterbury College, New Zealand; Royal College of Science, London. New Zealand Army, 1915-18. Judge's Marshal to the High Court Judges, London, 1920-35. Publisher, books and art publications. Archæologist, working chiefly on Romano-British sites in Wiltshire. Formed the extensive Australasian Collection of early manuscripts, books, paintings, drawings, prints, maps, log-books, etc. now housed in the National Library, Canberra, Australia. Order of Dannebrog, 1935. *Publications:* The La Tene occupation of Britain; Portraits of the Famous and Infamous, 1970; archæological researches; books on English artists; articles for Wiltshire archæological magazines. *Recreations:* studying architecture, gardening, collecting modern paintings. *Address:* 20 Cork Street, Burlington Gardens, W1. *T:* 01-734 1732.

**NANCE, Francis James,** LLM; **His Honour Judge Nance;** a Judge of County Courts and Commissioner, Liverpool and Manchester Crown Courts, since 1966; *b* 5 Sept. 1915; *s* of late Herbert James Nance, South Africa, and of Margaret Ann Nance, New Brighton; *m* 1943, Margaret Gertrude Roe; two *s*. *Educ:* St Francis Xavier's College, Liverpool; University of Liverpool (LLM 1938). Called to the Bar, Gray's Inn, 1936. Served War of 1939-45, Royal Corps of Signals (Captain): Normandy invasion, NW Europe (despatches). Practised on Northern Circuit, 1936-66. Deputy Chairman, Lancashire Quarter Sessions, 1963-. *Recreation:* chess. *Address:* 37 Warren Drive, New Brighton, Wallasey, Cheshire L45 0JW. *T:* 051-639 2915. *Club:* Athenæum (Liverpool).

**NAPIER,** family name of **Barons Napier and Ettrick** and **Napier of Magdala.**

**NAPIER,** 14th Lord of Merchistoun, *cr* 1627 (Scotland), **and ETTRICK,** 5th Baron, *cr* 1872 (UK); **Francis Nigel Napier;** a Bt of Nova Scotia, 1666, 11th Bt of Thirlestane; Capt. Scots Guards (Reserve of Officers); *b* 5 Dec. 1930; *e s* of 13th Baron Napier and 4th Ettrick, TD, and Muir, *e d* of Sir Percy Newson, Bt; *S* father 1954; *m* 1958, Delia Mary, *yr d* of A. D. B. Pearson; one *s* two *d*. *Educ:* Eton; RMA, Sandhurst. Commissioned, 1950; served Malaya, 1950-51; Adjt 1st Bn Scots Guards, 1955-57. Equerry to HRH The Duke of Gloucester, 1958-60, retd, 1960; City, 1960-62. Deputy Ceremonial and Protocol Secretary, Commonwealth Relations Office, 1962-66. Accompanied British Trade Mission from Boston to Houston, USA, in Flying Scotsman, 1969. A Cons. Whip, House of Lords, April-June, 1970. Mem. Roy. Co. of Archers (Queen's Body Guard for Scotland). Freeman, City of London; Liveryman, Worshipful Company of Grocers. Mem. Exec. Cttee, British Council for Rehabilitation of Disabled. Hon. Citizen, State of Texas. *Heir: s* Master of Napier, *qv*. *Address:* (seats) Laidlawstiel, Clovenfords, Selkirkshire. *T:* Clovenfords 216; Thirlestane, Ettrick Selkirk (Mansion House demolished, 1966); (residence) The Manor House, Normandy, near Guildford, Surrey. *T:* Normandy 3304. *Clubs:* Pratt's, Brooks's.

**NAPIER OF MAGDALA,** 5th Baron (UK), *cr* 1868; **Robert John Napier,** OBE 1944; MICE; late Royal Engineers; Brigadier, Chief Engineer, HQ, Scottish Command, retd; *b* 16 June 1904; *o s* of 4th Baron and Florence Martha (*d* 1946), *d* of Gen. John Maxwell Perceval, CB; *S* father, 1948; *m* 1939, Elizabeth Marian, *y d* of E. H. Hunt, FRCS; three *s* two *d*. *Educ:* Wellington. Served Waziristan, 1936-37 (despatches); War of 1939-45, Sicily (OBE). *Heir: s* Hon. Robert Alan Napier [*b* 6 Sept. 1940; *m* 1964, Frances Clare, *er d* of A. F. Skinner, Monks Close, Woolpit, Suffolk; one *s* one *d*]. *Address:* 8 Mortonhall Road, Edinburgh 9. *Club:* New (Edinburgh).

**NAPIER, Master of; Hon. Francis David Charles Napier;** *b* 3 Nov. 1962; *s* and *heir* of 14th Baron Napier (and 5th Baron Ettrick), *qv*.

**NAPIER, Hon. Sir Albert (Edward Alexander),** KCB, *cr* 1945 (CB 1922); KCVO, *cr* 1954; QC 1947; *b* 4 Sept. 1881; *y s* of F. M. 1st Lord Napier of Magdala and late Mary Cecilia, CI, *d* of Major-Gen. E. W. S. Scott; *m* 1917, Amy Gladys Stuart, *d* of late F. M. Sir George Stuart White; one *d* (*o s* killed on active service, 1942). *Educ:* Temple Grove; Eton (King's Scholar); New College, Oxford (Exhibitioner); 1st Class Lit. Hum. 1904. Eldon Law Scholar, 1906; called to the Bar, Inner Temple, 1909; Private Secretary to the Lord Chancellor, 1915-19; Deputy Serjeant-at-Arms in the House of Lords, 1916-19; Assistant Secretary in the Lord Chancellor's office and Deputy Clerk of the Crown, 1919-44; Clerk of the Crown in Chancery and Permanent Secretary to the Lord Chancellor, 1944-54. Bencher of the Inner Temple, 1949. *Address:* 12 Carlyle Mansions, Cheyne Walk, Chelsea, SW3. *T:* 01-352 8378. *Club:* Travellers'.

**NAPIER, Barbara Langmuir,** JP; Senior Tutor to Women Students in the University of Glasgow since 1964; Member, the Industrial Court, since 1963; *b* 21 Feb. 1914; *y c* of late James Langmuir Napier, Consultant Engineer, and late Siblie Agnes Mowat. *Educ:* Hillhead High Sch., Glasgow; Univ. of Glasgow (MA); Glasgow and West of Scotland Coll. of Domestic Science. Org. Sec. Redlands Hosp., Glasgow, 1937-41; Univ. of Glasgow: Warden, Queen Margaret Hall, 1941-44; Gen. Adv. to Women Students, 1942-64; Appts Officer (Women), 1942-65. Founder Mem. Assoc. of Principals, Wardens and Advisers to Univ. Women Students, 1942 (Pres. 1965-68); Local Rep. and later Mem. Coun., Women's Migration and Overseas Appts Soc., 1946-64; Winifred Cullis Lecture Fellowship (midwest USA) of Brit. Amer. Associates, 1950; Governor: Westbourne Sch., Glasg., 1951- (Chm. 1969-); Notre Dame Coll. of Educn, Glasg., 1959-64. Member, Tribunal under National Insurance Acts, 1954-60; President, Standing Conference of Women's Organisations (Glasgow), 1955-57; Member: Scottish Committee, ITA, 1957-64; Executive Cttee, Women's Employment Fedn, 1963-68; Indep. Member: Flax and Hemp Wages Council (GB), 1962-70 (Dep. Chm. 1964-70); Hat, Cap and Millinery Wages Council (GB), 1963-70; Laundry Wages Council (GB), 1968-70. JP Glasg., 1955-. *Publications:* (with S. Nisbet) Promise and Progress, 1970;contrib. University Women's Review, etc. *Recreations:* reading, walking, ballroom dancing, travel, gardening, painting, being with cats. *Address:* Benview, Gartmore, Stirling. *T:* Aberfoyle 206. *Clubs:* Royal Over-Seas; College (Glasgow).

**NAPIER, Charles (Goddard),** RSW; Artist; *b* 1 Aug. 1889; 2nd *s* of late Andrew Nelson Napier, herbalist, Edinburgh; *m* 1934, Hazel May Eadie (*d* 1960), *d* of late Arthur William Ballance, Herringswell. *Educ:* George Watson's Coll., Edinburgh. Studied Edinburgh College of Art; works mostly in water-colours; attracted by architectural subjects; did a series of black and white drawings of prominent Edinburgh buildings; painted in Holland, France and Italy; exhibited RSA, Glasgow Institute, USA, Canada, and New Zealand; first London exhibition of water-colours, Brook Street Art Gallery, Feb. 1934; exhibition of water colours, British Council, Oxford, 1949; second exhibition of Water Colours, Phantasy and Dream, British Council, 1952. Marlborough in Wiltshire purchased 1937, and In Wells Harbour, Norfolk, 1940, for Scottish Modern Arts, Edinburgh. *Address:* 6 St Margaret's Road, Edinburgh 9. *T:* 031-447 1252.

**NAPIER, Ian Patrick Robert,** MC; *b* 24 July 1895; *yr s* of Henry Melvill Napier, Milton House, Bowling, Dunbartonshire; *m* 1st, 1927, Frieda, *o d* of 1st Baron Essendon; two *s*; 2nd, 1942, Nora, *d* of John R. Moore; one *s*. *Educ:* Eton College. Served European War, 1914-18: Argyll and Sutherland Highlanders, Capt. 1916; seconded to RFC, 1916; attached 1st French Army, 1917. Shipbuilding (in family firm) and Shipowning. Member Scottish Transport Council, 1951-63. Mem. Royal Company of Archers (HM Body Guard for Scotland), OStJ Legion of Honour; Croix de Guerre (France). *Recreations:* shooting, fishing. *Address:* 169 Queen's Gate, SW7. *T:* 01-589 3544. *Club:* Brooks's.

**NAPIER, Hon. Sir (John) Mellis,** KCMG 1945; Kt 1943; KStJ; Chief Justice of South Australia, 1942-67; Lieutenant-Governor of South Australia since 1942; Chancellor of the University of Adelaide, 1948-61; *b* Dunbar, Scotland, 24 Oct. 1882; *s* of late Alexander Disney Leith Napier, MD, MRCP, FRSE; *m* 1908, Dorothy Bell (*d* 1959), *d* of Edward Kay, Adelaide; two *s* (and one missing, presumed died, on active service). *Educ:* City of London School; Adelaide University; LLB 1902; LLD (*hc*) Melbourne 1956; LLD (*aeg*) 1959. Called SA Bar, 1903; KC 1922; Puisne Judge of Supreme Court of S Australia, 1924-42; Chairman of Royal Commission on Monetary and Banking Systems of Australia, 1936-37. *Address:* Glenwood, Stirling East, South Australia.

**NAPIER, Sir Joseph William Lennox,** 4th Bt, *cr* 1867; OBE 1944; *b* 1 Aug. 1895; *s* of 3rd Bt and Mabel Edith Geraldine (*d* 1955), *d* of late Rev. C. T. Forster, Vicar of Hinxton, Cambridgeshire; *S* father, 1915; *m* 1931, Isabelle Muriel, *yr d* of late Maj. H. Siward B. Surtees, DL, JP; two *s*. *Educ:* Rugby; Jesus College, Cambridge. Served European War in South Wales Borderers, 1914-18; re-employed 1939, Lt-Col HQ Staff, Eastern Command and Italy. Member of Lloyd's since 1921. Director of Public Companies. *Heir: s* Robert Surtees Napier, *b* 5 March 1932. *Address:* 17 Cheyne Gardens, Chelsea, SW3; Berystede Cottage, Ascot, Berks; Torre la Fuente, San Pedro de Alcantara, Nr Marbella, Spain. *Clubs:* Alpine, City of London.

*See also Brigadier V. J. L. Napier.*

**NAPIER, Brigadier Vivian John Lennox,** MC 1918; late S Wales Borderers; Vice-Lieutenant, Brecknock, since 1964; *b* 13 July 1898; 3rd *s* of Sir William Lennox Napier, 3rd Bt; *m* 1958, Marion Avis, OBE, *d* of late Sir John and Lady Lloyd; no *c*. *Educ:* Uppingham; RMC. Served European War, 1914-18: France and Belgium (wounded, MC); served War of 1939-45: HQ Cairo Bde and 1 Bn Welch Regt, North Africa (despatches, prisoner). Brig. Comdg Mombasa Area, 1948-49; Dep. Comdr S-W District, UK, 1949-51; retd, 1952. Commissioner, St John Ambulance, Breconshire, 1957-62. DL Brecknock, 1958. Order of Leopold (Belgium), 1925; OStJ 1959. *Recreation:* fishing. *Address:* Ty Nant, Groesffordd, Brecon.

*See also Sir Joseph Napier, Bt.*

**NAPIER, Sir William Archibald,** 13th Bt, of Merchiston, *cr* 1627; *b* 19 July 1915; *s* of Sir Robert Archibald Napier, 12th Bt and Violet Payn; *S* father 1965; *m* 1942, Kathleen Mabel, *d* of late Reginald Greaves, Tafelberg, CP; one *s*. *Educ:* Cheam School; Stowe. Captain S African Engineers, Middle East, 1939-45. Mechanical Engineer. AM Inst. of (SA) Mech. Engineers; AM Inst. of Cert. Engineers (Works); Fellow, Inst. of Matériel Handling. *Recreations:* shooting, golf, squash. *Heir: s* John Archibald Lennox Napier, *b* 6 Dec. 1946. *Address:* Merchiston Croft, PO Sandown, Johannesburg, S Africa. *T:* 704-3174. *Clubs:* Junior Carlton; Rand, Johannesburg Country, Wanderers' (Johannesburg).

**NAPOLITAN, Leonard,** CB 1970; Director of Economics and Statistics, Ministry of Agriculture, Fisheries and Food, since 1965; *b* 9 April 1919; *s* of Domenic and Rose G. Napolitan; *m* 1945, Dorothy Laycock; two *d*. *Educ:* Highbury Co. Sch.; Univ. of London (BSc Econ. 1944); LSE (MSc Econ. 1946). Clerk, Import Duties Adv. Cttee, 1936-39; Dept of Customs and Excise, 1939-46; Asst Agric. Economist, Univ. of Bristol, 1947-48; joined Min. of Agric. and Fisheries as Agric. Economist, 1948; Chief Agric. Economist, 1958. Chm., Conf. of Provincial Agric. Economists, 1956-68; Chm., Nat. Food Survey Cttee, 1965-. *Publications:* occasional articles in Jl Agric. Economics, etc. *Address:* Northor, 22 North Road, Berkhamsted, Herts. *T:* 2096. *Club:* Farmers'.

**NAPPER, Professor Jack Hollingworth,** CBE 1968; Professor of Architecture and Head of the School of Architecture in the University of Newcastle upon Tyne since 1963 (held a personal Chair of Architecture in University of Durham, King's College, Newcastle upon Tyne, 1959-60); Head of School of Architecture, University of Durham, King's College, Newcastle upon Tyne, 1960-63; *b* 23 Dec. 1904; *s* of Frederick George Napper, Headmaster, and Edna Napper; *m* 1935, Mary Whitehead; two *s* one *d*. *Educ:* Oldham High Sch.; Univ. of Manchester. Clerk in cotton industry 1918-31; Architectural Assistant (Oldham, Bolton, London), 1935; Lecturer in Architecture, Hull, 1935-38; Lecturer in Architecture, Newcastle upon Tyne (University of Durham), 1938-59. President, Northern Architectural Association, 1958-59. *Publications:* (with Prof. W. Fisher Cassie) Structure in Building, 1952; reviews in Jl of RIBA. *Address:* 15 Brandling Park, Newcastle upon Tyne 2. *T:* 81.0724. *Club:* Arts.

**NAPPER, John,** Painter; *b* 17 Sept. 1916. One-man exhibitions: Leicester Galleries, London, 1949, 1961, 1962; The Adams Gallery, London, 1957 and 1959; The Walker Art Gallery, Liverpool, 1959; La Maison de la Pensée Française, Paris, 1960; Galerie Lahumière, Paris, 1963; Galleries Hervé and Lahumière, Paris, 1965; Larcada Gallery, New York, 1968, 1970. Vis. Prof. of Fine Arts, Southern Illinois Univ., USA, 1968-69. Awarded prize at International Exhibition of Fine Arts, Moscow, 1957. Awarded International Assoc. of Art Critics Prize, 1961. *Address:* c/o The Midland Bank Ltd, 145 Sloane Street, SW1.

**NARAIN, Sase,** CMG 1969; JP (Guyana); solicitor; Deputy Chairman, Public Service Commission, Guyana, since 1966; Member, Police Service Commission, since 1969; *b* 27 Jan. 1925; *s* of Oudit and Sookdai Naraine; *m* 1952, Shamshun Narain (*née* Rayman); four *s*. *Educ:* Modern Educational Inst.; Gibson and Weldon Law Tutors. Solicitor, admitted in England and Guyana, 1957. Town Councillor, City of Georgetown, 1962-; Member: History and Arts Council, 1969-; Republic Cttee of Guyana, 1969; Pres., Guyana Sanatan Dharma Maha Sabha, 1963-. Comr for Oaths to Affidavits, 1961; Notary Public, 1968. JP 1962. *Recreations:* golf, cricket, swimming. *Address:* 217 South Street, Lacytown, Georgetown, Demerara, Guyana. *T:* 61611. *Clubs:* Lusignan Golf, Guyana Indian Cricket (both in Guyana).

**NARASIMHAN, Chakravarthi Vijayaraghava;** Chef de Cabinet of the Secretary-General since Aug. 1961, United Nations, New York; concurrently Deputy Administrator of UN Development Programme, since 1969; *b* 21 May 1915; *s* of Chakravarthi V. and Janaki Vijayaraghavachari; *m* 1938, Janaki, *d* of Dr M. T. Chari; two *d*. *Educ:* University of Madras (BA); Oxford (MA). Indian Civil Service, 1936; Dep. Sec., Development Dept, Government of

Madras, 1945-48; Min. of Agriculture, Govt of India, 1950-53; Joint Sec., Economic Affairs Dept, Ministry of Finance, 1953-56; Executive Sec., UN Economic Commission for Asia and Far East, 1956-59; Under-Sec. for Special Political Affairs, UN, 1959-62; Under-Sec., 1962-67, Under-Sec.-Gen. 1967-69, for Gen. Assembly Affairs, UN. Hon. Doctor of Laws, Williams Coll. Williamstown, Mass, 1960; Hon. Dr of Humane Letters, Colgate Univ., 1966. *Recreations:* Sanskrit literature, South Indian classical music, tennis. *Address:* 300 East 33rd Street, New York, NY 10016, USA. *T:* (212)-686-2398.

**NARAYAN, R. K.;** Author; *b* Madras, India, 1907. *Educ:* Maharaja's College, Mysore, India. Padma Bushan award for distinguished services to literature. Hon. LittD Leeds, 1967. *Publications: novels:* (several published in England); Swami and Friends, 1935; (followed by): The Bachelor of Arts; The Dark Room; The English Teacher; Mr Sampath; The Financial Expert; Waiting for the Mahatma; The Guide, 1958; The Man-Eater of Malgudi, 1961; Gods, Demons and Others, 1964; The Sweet Vendor, 1967; *short stories:* An Astrologer's Day; The Lawley Road; A Horse and Two Goats, 1970, etc; *essays:* Next Sunday, 1955 (India); My Dateless Diary, 1960 (India). *Address:* c/o David Higham Associates, Ltd, 76 Dean Street, London, W1, England; Yadavagiri, Mysore 2, India.

**NASH, (Denis Frederic) Ellison,** FRCS; Consultant Surgeon, St Bartholomew's Hospital, since 1947; *b* 10 Feb. 1913; *m* 1938, Joan Mary Andrew; two *s* two *d*. *Educ:* Dulwich College; St Bartholomew's Medical College. MRCS, LRCP, 1935; FRCS 1938. Served war of 1939-45, RAFVR, Wing-Comdr (Air Efficiency Award, 1943). Hunterian Professor, 1949 and 1956. Arris and Gale Lecturer, 1950. Dean, St Bartholomew's Hospital Medical College, 1957-62. Member: Court of Examiners, RCS; British Assoc. of Urological Surgeons. Fellow, British Orthopædic Assoc. *Publications:* The Principles and Practice of Surgical Nursing, 1955; scientific papers in medical journals particularly concerned with surgery of childhood. *Recreation:* photography. *Address:* 10 Kingswood Drive, SE19. *T:* 01-670 2281.

**NASH, Ellison;** *see* Nash, D. F. E.

**NASH, Gilbert John,** CB 1951; Under-Secretary, Ministry of Labour, 1948-66; *b* 2 Dec. 1905; *s* of Ebenezer Thorp and Alice Nash; *m* 1940, Marguerite Lilian Braisher; one *d*. *Educ:* Royal Grammar Sch., Henley-on-Thames; St Catharine's College, Cambridge (Wrangler, 1927). Asst master, King's Sch., Peterborough, 1928. Entered Ministry of Labour as asst principal, 1928; Principal, 1934; Asst Sec. 1940; Under-Secretary, 1948-66. *Recreations:* painting in oils, pottery, gardening. *Address:* 3 St Margaret's Close, Penn, High Wycombe, Bucks. *T:* Penn 2612.

**NASH, John Northcote,** CBE 1964; RA 1951 (ARA 1940); Artist; *b* London, 11 April 1893; 2nd *s* of late W. H. Nash; *m* Dorothy Christine, *o d* of Mr Kühlenthal, Gerrard's Cross, Bucks. *Educ:* Wellington College. Joined Artists' Rifles, September 1916; France, 1916-18, when he was commssioned to paint war pictures for the Imperial War Museum; was 2nd Lt in this connection; Hon. Commission in Royal Marines, 1940, as one of official War Artists to the Admiralty; Capt. RM 1941; Acting Temp. Major, 1943; reverted to rank of Temp. Capt. on discharge in Nov. 1944. Hon. Member of Society of Wood Engravers; Assistant Teacher of Design, Royal College of Art, 1934-57; Fellow RCA. Hon. DUniv, Essex, 1967. Paintings purchased for public galleries: The Tate Gallery, Manchester, Bath, Leeds, Dublin, Victoria and Albert Museum, South Kensington, Sheffield, also Walker Art Gallery, Liverpool and Bristol. Retrospective exhn, Royal Academy, 1967. *Address:* Bottengoms Farm, Wormingford, nr Colchester, Essex. *T:* Great Horkesley 308.

**NASH, Kenneth Twigg;** Assistant Secretary General, NATO, since 1969; *b* Rotherham, 15 Sept. 1918; *s* of Albert Nash, AIC, AMIChemE, chemical engineer, and Marjorie Nora Twigg; *m* 1960, Patricia Mary Kate Batchelor; two *s*. *Educ:* Rotherham Grammar Sch.; Gonville and Caius Coll., Cambridge. War of 1939-45: joined Army in Sept. 1939; 67th (York and Lancs) Regt as a Gunner; 62nd (1st/3rd East Riding) Regt, when commissioned. Admiralty, 1948; Private Sec. to Sir John Lang; Prin. Private Sec. to three First Lords (Cilcennin, Hailsham, Selkirk); service in civil establishments, finance and as a Head of Military Branch of Admiralty. Called to Bar, Inner Temple, 1955. IDC, 1964; Head of Defence Secretariat and Defence Supply Counsellor at British Embassy, Washington, 1965; Asst Under-Sec. (Policy), MoD, 1968. *Address:* 5 Highbury Terrace, Islington, N5. *T:* 01-226 9750.

**NASH, Ogden;** author; *b* 19 Aug. 1902; *s* of Edmund Strudwick Nash and Mattie Chenault; *m* 1931, Frances Rider Leonard; two *c*. *Educ:* St George's School, Newport, RI; Harvard University. *Publications:* Hard Lines (poems), 1931; Free Wheeling, 1931; Happy Days, 1933; The Primrose Path (poems), 1935; The Bad Parents' Garden of Verse, 1936; I'm a Stranger Here Myself, 1938; The Face is Familiar, 1941; Good Intentions, 1942; Many Long Years Ago (poems), 1945; Versus, 1949; Family Reunion, 1951; The Private Dining Room, 1953; You Can't Get There From Here, 1957; The Christmas That Almost Wasn't, 1957; Collected Verses from 1929 on, 1961; Everyone But Thee and Me, 1963; The Untold Adventures of Santa Claus, 1965; An Ogden Nash Omnibook, 1967; Santa, Go Home, 1968. (Jt) One Touch of Venus (mus. comedy), 1943. Verses to magazines. *Address:* c/o Curtis Brown Ltd, 60 East 56th Street, New York, NY 10022, USA.

**NASH, Thomas Arthur Manly,** CMG 1959; OBE 1944; Dr (Science); Director, Tsetse Research Laboratory, University of Bristol, Veterinary Field Station, Langford, since 1962; *b* 18 June 1905; *s* of late Col L. T. Nash, CMG, RAMC; *m* 1930, Marjorie Wenda Wayte; (one *s* decd). *Educ:* Wellington Coll.; Royal Coll. of Science. Entomologist, Dept Tsetse Research and Reclamation, Tanganyika Territory, 1927; Entomologist, Sleeping Sickness Service, Med. Dept, Nigeria, 1933. Doctorate of Science, 1933. In charge Anchau Rural Development Scheme, 1937-44; seconded as Chief Entomologist, W African Institute for Trypanosomiasis Research, 1948; Deputy Director, WAITR, 1953; Director, 1954; retired 1959. *Publications:* Tsetse Flies in British West Africa, 1948; Africa's Bane, The Tsetse Fly, 1969; numerous scientific publications on tsetse and trypanosomiasis. *Recreations:* fishing and shooting. *Address:* Spring Head Farm, Upper Langford, near Bristol. *T:* Churchill 321.

**NASMITH, David Arthur D.;** *see* Dunbar-Nasmith.

**NASON, Rev. George Stephen,** MA; *b* 30 March 1901; *s* of Edward Noel Nason, MD, Nuneaton, Warwickshire; *m* 1930, Edna

Hartley; one *d*. *Educ:* Shrewsbury; Pembroke Coll., Cambridge. Metropolitan Vickers, Manchester, 1922-25; Humphreys & Glasgow, London, 1925-26; Ely Theological College, 1926-27; St Luke's, Battersea (Curate), 1927-29; Richmond Parish Church (Curate), 1929-33; Rector of Bamford-in-the-Peak, 1933-45; Chaplain RNVR, 1939-45; Dean of Gibraltar, 1945-50; Vicar of St Alfege, Greenwich, 1950-58; Rural Dean of Greenwich and Deptford, 1954-58; Vicar of St Peter and St Paul, Hambledon, Hants, 1958-64; Curate of St John's Meads, Eastbourne, 1964-69. *Address:* 16 The Village, Meads, Eastbourne, Sussex. *Clubs:* Leander, Achilles.

**NASSAU AND THE BAHAMAS, Bishop of,** since 1962; **Rt. Rev. Bernard Markham;** *b* 26 Feb. 1907. *Educ:* Bingley Grammar School; Leeds University; College of the Resurrection (BA Hons History), 1928. Deacon, 1930; Priest, 1931. Curate of: Lidget Green, 1930-35; S Francis, N Kensington, 1935-37; Stoke-on-Trent, 1937-39; Vicar of Bierley, 1939-46; Rector of St Benedict, Ardwick, 1946-59; Vicar of St Margaret's, Liverpool, 1959-62. *Address:* Addington House, PO Box 107, Nassau, Bahamas.

**NASSAU AND THE BAHAMAS, Assistant Bishop of;** *see* Knowles, Rt Rev. D. R.

**NATAL, Bishop of,** since 1951; **Rt. Rev. Thomas George Vernon Inman;** *b* 1904; *s* of late Capt. William James Inman, RE, Durban; *m* 1935, Alma Coker, *d* of late Advocate Duncan Stuart Campbell, Bulawayo, S Rhodesia; three *s one d*. *Educ:* Selwyn Coll., Cambridge; St Augustine's Coll., Canterbury. MA 1932. Deacon, 1930; priest, 1931; Asst Missioner, Wellington Coll. Mission, Walworth, 1930-33; Curate of Estcourt, Natal, 1933; Curate of St Paul, Durban, 1933-37, Vicar, 1937-41; Canon of Natal, 1944-51; Archdeacon of Durban, 1950-51; Dean, Province of S Africa, 1966. Chaplain and Sub-prelate, Order of St John of Jerusalem, 1953. Hon. DD Univ. of the South, Tenn., USA, 1958. *Address:* PO Box 726, Durban, Natal, South Africa. *T:* 316652.

**NATHAN,** 2nd Baron, *cr* 1940; **Roger Carol Michael Nathan;** *b* 5 Dec. 1922; *s* of 1st Baron and of Eleanor, Lady Nathan, *qv*; *S* father, 1963; *m* 1950, Philippa Gertrude, *d* of Major J. B. Solomon, MC; one *s* two *d*. *Educ:* Stowe Sch.; New Coll., Oxford (MA). Served War of 1939-45: Capt., 17/21 Lancers (despatches, wounded twice). Admitted Solicitor (Hons), 1950. Associate Mem., Bar Assoc. of City of New York 1957-; FSA; FRSA; FRGS. Director: J. W. French & Co. Ltd, 1961-; Kleeman Industrial Holdings Ltd; Chm. Pharmitalia (UK) Ltd. Pres., Jewish Welfare Board, 1967-. Treasurer, Central British Fund for Jewish Relief and Rehabilitation, 1959-; Chm. Exec. Cttee, British Empire Cancer Campaign; a Vice-Pres., The Jewish Museum; Chm., City Festival of Flowers, 1964; Master, Worshipful Company of Gardeners, 1963-64. *Heir: s* Hon. Rupert Harry Bernard Nathan, *b* 26 May 1957. *Address:* 20 Copthall Avenue, EC2. *T:* 01-628 9611. *TA:* Client, London; Collyers Farm, Lickfold, Petworth, Sussex. *T:* Lodsworth 284. *TA:* Ronath, Lodsworth. *Clubs:* Athenæum, Cavalry, Gresham.

**NATHAN, (Rt. Hon.) Eleanor Lady; Eleanor Joan Clara Nathan;** *b* 28 Oct. 1892; *d* of late C. Stettauer, LCC; *m* 1919, Major H. L. Nathan (later 1st Baron Nathan, PC, TD, FBA, DL, JP; *d* 1963); one *s* (*see* 2nd Baron Nathan) one *d*. *Educ:* Queen's Coll., London; Girton Coll., Cambridge (MA Cantab). Chairman of Governors: Avery Hill Coll. of Education; Warnham Court Sch.; Coombe Hall Sch.; Governor: Bedford Coll.; JFS Sch.; King Edward's Sch., Witley. Vice-President Royal Geographical Society. JP County of London 1928 (Juvenile Court Panel, 1937-52); President: Women's Farm and Garden Assoc., 1950-70; E London Nursing Assoc.; Central Council for District Nursing in London, 1950-66. Mem. of LCC (NE Bethnal Green, 1928-34) (C Wandsworth, 1937-49); Chm. of LCC, 1947-48; Alderman of LCC, 1951-65; Mem., LCC and ILEA Educn Cttees, 1937-67. FRSA. Pres. Union of Jewish Women, 1945-55. First Chm. of Governors, Holland Park Sch., 1958-67; Former Governor: Girton Coll., Cambridge; Royal Holloway Coll., Univ. of London; former Member, Cambridge University Women's Appointments Board. First Woman Member of Metropolitan Water Board, 1937-46; Member of Home Office Committee of Enquiry into Closing Hours of Shops (Gowers Committee), 1946-49. *Address:* 80 Portman Towers, George Street, Montagu Square, W1. *T:* 01-935 7699.
*See also Sir Bernard Waley-Cohen.*

**NATHAN, Sir Maurice (Arnold),** KBE 1963 (CBE 1957); Lord Mayor of Melbourne, 1961-63; Chairman and Managing Director, Paterson's (Australia) Ltd and associated cos.; Chairman, Courage Breweries Ltd; *b* Kew, Vic, 17 July 1914; *s* of late Harold B. Nathan, Melbourne; *m* 1942, Margaret Frances, *d* of David McKay; one *s*. *Educ:* Geelong C of E Gram. Sch. Served War of 1939-45, Capt. AIF, Pres., Victorian Industries Confederation, Furnishers Soc. of Victoria and Aust. Retail Furnishers Assoc., 1951-53; Mem. Melbourne City Council, 1952- (Chm. General Purposes Cttee; Mem. Finance Cttee); Founder and Chm., Victoria Promotion Cttee; Chm., Olympic Park Cttee of Management; Founder and Chairman, Australian World Exposition Project. *Recreations:* gardening, racing, squash, football, tennis, golf. *Address:* c/o Patersons Pty Ltd, 152 Burke Street, Melbourne 3000, Australia. *T:* 66.6025; 20 St George's Road, Toorak, Vic 3142. *T:* 24.2282. *Clubs:* Victoria Amateur Turf, Victoria Racing, Moonee Valley Racing, Melbourne Cricket, Lawn Tennis Assoc. of Vic, Kelvin, Green Room.

**NATTA, Prof. Giulio;** Director, Institute of Industrial Chemistry, Polytechnic of Milan, since 1938; *b* 26 Feb. 1903; *m* 1936, Rosita Beati; one *s* one *d*. *Educ:* Polytechnic Institute of Milan. Degree in Chemical Engineering, 1924; Professor in General Chemistry, 1927. Assistant Prof. in Analytical Chemistry, Polytechnic of Milan, 1925-32; Full Prof. and Director, Inst. of General Chemistry, Univ. of Pavia, 1933; Chm. of Physical Chemistry, Univ. of Rome, 1935-37; Prof. of Industrial Chemistry, Polytechnic of Turin, 1937-38. Doctor *hc* in Chemistry, Univ. of Turin, 1962; also holds honorary doctorates from foreign universities, etc; 16 gold medals from Italian and foreign Chemical Societies, among them Nobel Prize for Chemistry (jtly), 1963. *Publications:* about 450 articles mainly published in: Die Makromol. Chemie; Jl of Polymer Science; Chimica e Industria; Jl of Amer. Chem. Soc.; Tetrahedron; Rend. Accademia Nazionale Lincei. *Address:* Via Mario Pagano 54, Milan, Italy. *T:* 486.308. *Club:* Rotary (Milan).

**NATTRASS, Frederick John,** MD Durham, FRCP; Emeritus Professor of Medicine, Universities of Durham and Newcastle upon Tyne; Hon. Consulting Physician, Royal Victoria Infirmary, Newcastle upon Tyne; Chairman, Muscular Dystrophy Group of Great Britain; President, Association of Physicians of Newcastle Region; *b* 6 August

1891; *s* of Rev. J. Conder Nattrass, BA, BD; *m* 1st, 1915, Gladys (*d* 1951), *d* of Benjamin Vickers, Lincoln; two *d* (one *s* decd); 2nd, 1963, Helen Byrne Bryce, Burford, Oxford. *Educ:* King Edward's Sch., Birmingham; Univ. of Durham, MB, BS (1st Class Honours) Durham, 1914; MD (gold medal), 1920; Capt., RAMC, 1915-20 (BEF, France; POW). Prof. of Medicine, Univ. of Lagos, Nigeria, 1962-63. Pres., Assoc. of British Neurologists, 1957-59; formerly Examiner in Medicine, University of Bristol, Trinity College, Dublin, Univs. of Manchester, Queen's Belfast, St Andrews, Nat. Univ. of Ireland. Censor Royal College of Physicians, 1950-52; Senior Censor, 1955-56; Lumleian Lecturer, RCP, 1948; Pres., Newcastle and Northern Counties Med. Soc., 1948-49. Pres. Assoc. of Physicians of Gt Britain and Ireland, 1953-54; President Section of Neurology, Royal Society of Medicine, 1954-55. *Publications:* The Commoner Nervous Diseases, 1931; section on nervous diseases in Chamberlain's Textbook of Medicine, 1951; papers and addresses chiefly on disorders of the nervous and muscular systems. *Recreations:* ornithology, music. *Address:* Little Cocklands, Burford, Oxford. *T:* Burford 2110. *Club:* Reform.

**NAUNTON MORGAN, Sir Clifford;** *see* Morgan, Sir C. N.

**NAYLOR, Arthur Holden,** MSc; MInstCE; MIMechE; *b* 1897; *er s* of Rev. John and Eunice Naylor; *m* 1925, Edith Riley; one *s* one *d.* RE, 1916-19 and 1940-43; Aeroplane Research under DSIR 1919; engaged on construction of Johore Causeway and Prai Power Station, Malaya, 1921-24; Sir Lawrence Guillemard Service Reservoir, Penang, 1925-29; Severn Barrage Investigation, 1930-31; Lochaber Water Power Scheme, 1931-34; Kenya and Uganda Hydro-Electric Investigations, 1934-35; Research Officer, Institution of Civil Engineers, 1935-38; Professor of Civil Engineering, Queen's University, Belfast, 1938-63; Professor of Civil Engineering, Ahmadu Bello University, Nigeria, 1963-66; Visiting Lecturer, 1966-67, Senior Research Fellow, School of Engineering, 1967-70, University College of Swansea. *Publication:* Siphon Spillways, 1935. *Address:* 2 Hael Lane, Southgate, near Swansea.

**NAYLOR, Rev. Canon Charles Basil;** Chancellor and Canon Residentiary of Liverpool Cathedral since 1956; *b* 29 Oct. 1911; *s* of Charles Henry Naylor and Eva Garforth. *Educ:* Rugby School; Keble College, Oxford. BA 2nd class Lit. Hum., 1934; MA 1939. Deacon, 1939, priest, 1940, Liverpool; Asst Master, Llandovery Coll., 1935-39; Asst Master, Chaplain and Housemaster, Liverpool College, 1939-43; Chaplain RNVR, 1943-46, East Indies Station and Fleet. Curate, St Peter le Bailey Oxford, 1946-56; Chaplain of St Peter's Coll., 1946-56, Dean, 1946-52, Fellow, 1950-56; Tutor in Theology, 1952-56. Examining Chaplain: to Bishop of Blackburn, 1951-; and to Bishop of Liverpool, 1954-; Senior Proctor of Univ. of Oxford, 1952-53. Exchanged duties with Dean of Christchurch, New Zealand, Dec. 1960-April 1961. Dir of Ordination Candidates and Dir of Post-Ordination Training, Liverpool Dio., 1956-. Mem., Liturgical Commn, 1962-66. *Publication:* Why Prayer Book Revision at all, 1964; contrib. Theological Collections: The Eucharist Then and Now, 1968; Ground for Hope, 1968. *Recreations:* music, walking. *Address:* Liverpool Cathedral, Liverpool 1. *T:* 051-645 6271. *Clubs:* National Liberal; Athenæum (Liverpool).

**NAYLOR, Margot, (Margaret Ailsa);** free-lance financial journalist; regular contributor to Daily Mail and The Director since 1967; *b* 28 Sept. 1907; *e d* of late Thomas Lodge, CB and Isobel (*née* Scott); *m* 1st, 1927, M. F. Wigham Richardson; 2nd, 1937, Guy Naylor; one *d.* *Educ:* Hornsey High Sch., London; Godolphin Sch., Salisbury; Lycée Molière, Paris; Ecole Vinet, Lausanne; Berlin Univ.; Girton Coll., Cambrdige; London Sch. of Economics. Min. of Information, 1940-42; Cabinet Offices, 1942-45; Investors Chronicle, 1954-61; Investment Editor, The Statist, 1961-63; Financial Editor, The Observer, 1963-67. *Publications:* (with Ralph Harris and Arthur Seldon) Hire Purchase in a Free Society, 1958; Your Money, 1966; How to Reduce Your Tax Bill, 1968, 2nd edn, 1969; (ed) Financial Times Yearbook of Business Information, 1969; How to Get the Most out of Life Assurance, 1971. *Recreation:* cooking. *Address:* 107 New Kings Road, SW6. *T:* 01-736 4875. *Club:* Temple Bar.

**NAYLOR, Maj.-Gen. Robert Francis Brydges,** CB 1942; CBE 1941; DSO 1919; psc 1922; *b* 6 Oct. 1889; 2nd *s* of C. T. Naylor, Barton End House, Nailsworth, Glos; *m* 1927, Lady Mary Byng, *yr d* of 6th Earl of Strafford; two *s* one *d.* *Educ:* Charterhouse; Sandhurst. Entered Army, 1909; joined 1st Battalion South Stafford Regiment, 1909; seconded to Royal Engineers (Signal Service), 1912; transferred Royal Signals, 1920; Brevet Major, 1918; Major, 1924; Lt-Col, 1931; Col, 1935; Temp. Maj.-Gen., 1940; Maj.-Gen., 1941; served European War, 1914-18, France and Flanders (despatches seven times, DSO, MC, Bt Major; Chevalier Légion d'Honneur); Brigade Major Signal Training Centre, 1923-25; General Staff Officer, Malta, 1925-27. Instructor, School of Signals, 1927-28; employed with Royal West African Frontier Force, 1928-31; commanded 3rd Divisional Signals, Bulford, 1931-35; GSO1 Scottish Command, 1935-38; Brigadier in charge of Administration, Western Command, 1938-39; Served War of 1939-45 (despatches, CB, CBE); Maj.-Gen. in charge of Administration, 1939-41; Deputy Quartermaster-General, 1941-43; Vice-Quartermaster-General, 1943; Commander L of C 21 Army Group, 1944; Commander Northumbrian District, 1945-46; retired pay, 1946. Col Comdt Royal Corps of Signals, 1944-53. Pres., Royal National Rose Society, 1963-64 and 1967-68. *Address:* Dancers Hill House, Barnet, Herts. *Club:* Army and Navy.

**NAYLOR-LEYLAND, Sir Vivyan (Edward),** 3rd Bt, *cr* 1895; *b* 5 March 1924; *e s* of Sir Edward Naylor-Leyland, 2nd Bt, and Marguerite Helene (*d* 1945), 2nd *d* of late Baron de Belabre; *S* father 1952; *m* 1st, 1952, Elizabeth Anne (marr. diss. 1960), *yr d* of 2nd Viscount FitzAlan of Derwent, OBE; one *s*; 2nd, 1967, Starr Anker-Simmons, one *d.* *Educ:* Eton; Christ Church, Oxford; Royal Agricultural Coll., Cirencester. Grenadier Guards, 1942-47. *Heir:* *s* Philip Vyvyan Naylor-Leyland, *b* 9 August 1953. *Address:* 6 Harbour Mews, Nassau, Bahamas. *T:* Nassau 77523. *Club:* White's (overseas mem.).

**NEAGLE, Dame Anna, (Dame Marjorie Wilcox),** DBE 1969 (CBE 1952); Hon. Ensign FANY Corps, 1950; Actress, Producer; Member: Executive Council, King George VI Memorial Foundation; Council Edith Cavell Homes of Rest for Nurses; Council, King George's Pension Fund for Actors and Actresses; *b* Forest Gate, Essex, 1908; *d* of late Captain Herbert William Robertson, RNR, and Florence Neagle Robertson; *m* 1943, Herbert Wilcox, *qv.* *Educ:* High School, St Albans, Herts; Wordsworth's Physical Training College. Theatre Royal, Drury Lane, Charlot and Cochran revues, London and New York, 1926-30; Stand up and Sing, with Jack Buchanan, 1931; Open Air Theatre–Rosalind and Olivia, 1934; Peter Pan, 1937; Jane Austen's Emma, 1944-45; *later plays include:* The Glorious Days, Palace Theatre, 1952-53; The More the Merrier, Strand, 1960; Person Unknown, 1964; Charlie Girl, Adelphi, 1965-. Has appeared in plays on television. *Films:* Good Night, Vienna, 1931; Bitter Sweet, 1933; Nell Gwyn, 1934; Peg of Old Drury, 1935; Victoria The Great, 1937; Sixty Glorious Years, 1938; Hollywood: Edith Cavell, 1939; Irene, No, No, Nanette, Sunny, 1939-40; England: They Flew Alone, 1941; Yellow Canary, 1943; I Live in Grosvenor Square, 1944; Piccadilly Incident, 1946; The Courtneys of Curzon Street, 1947; Spring in Park Lane, Elizabeth of Ladymead, 1948; Maytime in Mayfair, 1949; Odette, 1950; The Lady With The Lamp, 1951; Derby Day, 1951; Lilacs in the Spring, 1954; King's Rhapsody, 1955; My Teenage Daughter, 1956; No Time for Tears, 1957; The Man Who Wouldn't Talk, 1957; The Lady is a Square, 1958. *Produced:* These Dangerous Years, 1957; Wonderful Things, 1958; Heart of a Man, 1959. Has received numerous awards both international and national. *Recreations:* walking, travel, reading. *Address:* 117b Hamilton Terrace, NW8. *Club:* FANY Regimental.

**NEAL, Prof. Bernard George,** MA, PhD, ScD; Professor of Applied Science (with special reference to Engineering), Imperial College of Science and Technology, since 1961; Dean of the City and Guilds College 1964-67; *b* 29 March 1922; *s* of Horace Bernard Neal, Wembley, and late Hilda Annie Webb; *m* 1948, Elizabeth Ann, *d* of William George Toller, Woodbridge, and of late Bertha Catharine Toller; one *s* one *d*. *Educ:* Merchant Taylors'; Trinity College, Cambridge (Schol.). MA Cantab, 1947; PhD Cantab 1948; ScD Cantab 1965; FInstCE 1960; FIMechE 1961; FIStructE 1966. Temp. Experimental Officer, Admiralty, 1942-45; Research Student, Univ. of Cambridge, 1945-48; Research Associate, Brown University, USA, 1948-49; Demonstrator, 1949-51, Lecturer, 1951-54, Univ. of Cambridge; Research Fellow, 1947-50, Staff Fellow, 1950-54, Trinity Hall, Cambridge; Prof. of Civil Engineering, University Coll. of Swansea, 1954-61; Visiting Prof., Brown Univ., USA, 1959-60. Telford Premium, 1951, Manby Premium, 1952, Instn Civil Engineers. *Publications:* The Plastic Methods of Structural Analysis, 1956; Structural Theorems and their Applications, 1964; technical papers on theory of structures, strength of materials; contrib. to Proc. Roy. Soc., Proc. Instn of Civil Engineers, The Structural Engineer, Jl of Mechanical Engineering Science, etc. *Recreations:* lawn tennis, croquet. *Address:* Imperial College of Science and Technology, South Kensington, SW7. *T:* 01-589 5111.

**NEAL, Harold;** *b* 23 July 1897; two *s* one *d*. *Educ:* Church of England School, Langley Mill. Began work in a coal mine at age of 13. Studied mining at Nottingham University Coll.; Mem. of Heanor UDC, 1930-44, Chm., 1939-40; MP (Lab) for Clay Cross, 1944-50, for Bolsover, 1950-70; travelled extensively in Europe and the Middle East; Mem. Imperial War Graves Commn, 1947-51; Parly Sec., Min. of Fuel and Power, 1951. Active in Co-operative Movement for many years; Dir of Langley Mill Co-op. Soc. First miner MP to represent Clay Cross; formerly Vice-Pres. Derbyshire Miners Association; Chairman: East Midland Group of Labour MPs; Steel and Power Cttee, Parly Labour Party. *Recreations:* gardening and reading. *Address:* Riseholme, Aldreds Lane, Langley, Heanor, Derbyshire. *T:* Langley Mill 3366.

**NEAL, Leonard Francis;** Member of British Railways Board since 1967; (part-time) Professor of Industrial Relations, University of Manchester Institute of Science and Technology, since 1970; *b* 27 Aug. 1913; *s* of Arthur Henry Neal and Mary Neal; *m* 1939, Mary Lilian Puttock; one *s* one *d*. *Educ:* London School of Economics; Trinity College, Cambridge (MA). Labour Manager, Esso, 1956; Employee Relations Manager, Fawley Refinery, 1961; Labour Relations Adviser, Esso Europe Inc. Vis. Fellow, Univ. of Lancaster Sch. of Business and Organisational Studies, 1970-. MInstT, 1969. *Publication:* (with A. Robertson) The Managers Guide to Industrial Relations. *Recreations:* gardening, motoring. *Address:* Stonecroft, Brightling, Sussex. *T:* Brightling 284. *Club:* Savile.

**NEALE, Alan Derrett,** CB 1968; MBE 1945; Third Secretary, Treasury, since 1968; *b* 24 Oct. 1918; *o s* of late W. A. Neale and Florence Emily (*née* Derrett); *m* 1956, Joan, *o d* of Harry and Hilda Frost, Wisbech; one *s*. *Educ:* Highgate School; St John's College, Oxford. War Service, Intelligence Corps, 1940-45. Board of Trade, 1946; Principal Private Secretary, 1957; Assistant Sec., 1958; Under-Sec., 1963; Second Sec., 1967. Commonwealth Fund Fellowship, USA, 1952-53; Fellow of Center for Internat. Affairs, Harvard Univ., 1960-61. *Publications:* The Anti-Trust Laws of the USA, 1960; The Flow of Resources from Rich to Poor, 1961. *Recreations:* music, bridge. *Address:* 37 Stormont Road, N6. *T:* 01-340 5236. *Club:* Reform.

**NEALE, Folliott Sandford;** *b* 11 Nov. 1901; *y s* of Rev. John Neale, Hardingstone Grange, Northants, and of Ada Rossall, *d* of late Humphrey Sandford, Isle of Rossall, Salop; *m* 1929, Gwendolyn (*d* 1970), *o surv. c* of W. W. G. Phillipps, Berwick House, Salop; one *s* one *d*. *Educ:* Marlborough; Loughborough Engineering Coll. Mem. Co. Probation Cttee and Hospital Boards. JP Salop, 1937 (Chm., Mid-Shropshire Bench, 1956-); High Sheriff of Shropshire, 1948-49; Chm., County Licensing and Compensation Cttee. chm. Welsh and Shropshire Jersey Breeders Assoc., 1956-; Pres. Shropshire and West Midland Agricultural Soc., 1961. Chm., Shropshire Antiques Soc., 1968-; *Recreations:* breeder of pedigree Jersey cattle (Berwick Herd); gardening; forestry. *Address:* Berwick House, near Shrewsbury. *T:* Shrewsbury 2941. *Club:* Shropshire (Shrewsbury).

**NEALE, Sir John (Ernest),** Kt 1955; MA; DLitt (Wales, 1948, Birmingham 1954, Leeds 1960, Cambridge 1960); Hon. LittD (Liverpool 1956); Hon. DLit (London 1960); Hon. LHD (Amherst 1958); FBA; Astor Professor of English History, University of London, 1927-56; retired; Professor Emeritus, 1956; Fellow of University College, London; *b* Liverpool, 7 Dec. 1890; *m* 1932, Elfreda, *d* of William Skelton, Harrogate; one *d*. *Educ:* Liverpool University; University College, London. Asst in the Department of History, University College, London, 1919-25; Prof. of Modern History, Univ. of Manchester, 1925-27; Member Treasury Cttee on House of Commons Records, 1929; Lectures: Lady Ardilaun, Alexandra College, Dublin, 1938; Ford's, in English History, Oxford Univ., 1941-42; Ballard Mathews, University Coll. of N Wales, 1942; Raleigh, British Academy, 1948; Creighton, Univ. of London, 1950. Trustee, London Museum, 1945-70. Foreign Hon. Member: American Acad. of Arts and Sciences, 1950; American Historical Assoc.,

1968; Member, Editorial Bd of History of Parliament. *Publications:* various papers on Tudor History in the English Historical Review, History, Transactions of the Royal Historical Society, and Tudor Studies (ed. R. W. Seton-Watson, 1924); Queen Elizabeth, 1934 (awarded James Tait Black Memorial Prize); The Age of Catherine de Medici, 1943; The Elizabethan House of Commons, 1949; Elizabeth I and Her Parliaments, 1559-1581, 1953; Elizabeth I and Her Parliaments, 1584-1601, 1957; Essays in Elizabethan History, 1958. *Address:* Adare, 57 Penn Road, Beaconsfield, Bucks. *T:* Beaconsfield 4466.

**NEALE, Kenneth James,** OBE 1959; Director of Industries and Supply, Home Office, since 1970; *b* 9 June 1922; *s* of late James Edward and Elsie Neale; *m* 1943, Dorothy Willett; three *s* one *d*. *Educ:* Hackney Downs (Grocers') Sch., London. Entered Civil Service as Clerical Officer, Tithe Redemption Commn, 1939. Lieut, RNVR, 1941-46. Exec. Officer, Min. of Nat. Insce, 1947-51; Asst Princ., 1951-55, Principal, 1955-62, Colonial Office; Sec. for Interior and Local Govt, Cyprus, 1957; Dep. Admin Sec., Cyprus, 1958-59; Central African Office, 1962-64; Asst Sec., Commonwealth Office, 1964-67; Asst Sec., Home Office, 1967-70. *Publications:* Discovering Essex in London, 1970; various articles and papers on local history. *Recreations:* reading, local history, travel. *Address:* The Hollies, 17 Gordon Road, Chingford, Essex. *T:* 01-529 8465.

**NEAME, Captain Douglas Mortimer Lewes,** DSO 1940, Bar 1942; RN retired; *b* Oct. 1901; *s* of late Douglas John Neame; *m* 1937, Elizabeth Ogilvy Carnegy; one *s* two *d*. *Educ:* RN Colleges, Osborne and Dartmouth. Served European War, 1917-19; Fleet Air Arm, 1927-31; Commander, 1936; Capt. 1940. Commanded HM Ships Carlisle and Vengeance in War of 1939-45; Commodore 2nd Class, 1947-50; retd 1950. *Recreations:* athletics (member of Olympic Team, Amsterdam, 1928, British Empire Games, Canada, 1930. Vice-Patron AAA; Vice-Pres. LAC). *Address:* 54 St Ann Street, Salisbury, Wiltshire. *T:* Salisbury 3800. *Clubs:* Naval; Milocarian, London Athletic.

**NEAME, Mrs Humphrey;** *see* Monroe, E.

**NEAME, Lt-Gen. Sir Philip,** VC 1914; KBE, *cr* 1946; CB 1939; DSO 1916; psc; idc; DL; Hon. Colonel 131 Airborne Regiment RE (T), 1948-58; Hon. Colonel Kent ACF Regiment RE, 1952-58; President of the Institution of Royal Engineers, 1954-57; *b* 12 December 1888; *y s* of late F. Neame, JP, of Luton, Selling, Faversham; *m* 1934, H. Alberta Drew; three *s* one *d*. *Educ:* Cheltenham Coll. Entered Army, 1908; Capt. 1914; Bt Major 1917; Bt Lt-Col 1922; Major, 1925; Col 1926; Maj.-Gen. 1937; Temp. Lt-Gen., 1940; Lt-Gen., 1947; served European War, 1914-18, Adjutant 15th Field Coy, RE; Brig.-Maj. Inf. Bde, Gen. Staff of Division, Corps and Army (despatches five times, VC, DSO, Chevalier of the Legion of Honour, French Croix de Guerre, Belgian Croix de Guerre); on the Directing Staff, Staff College, Camberley, 1919-23; served in India with KGO Bengal Sappers and Miners, 1925-29; Imperial Defence College, 1930; General Staff Officer, 1st Grade, Waziristan District, India, 1932-33; Brigadier, General Staff, Eastern Command, India, 1934-38; went to Lhasa, Tibet, with political-military mission, 1936; Commandant Royal Military Academy, Woolwich, 1938-39; Deputy Chief of the General Staff, BEF France, 1939-40; Commander 4th Indian Division, Western Desert, 1940; GOC (Lt-Gen.) Palestine, Transjordan, Cyprus, 1940; GOC-in-C and Military Governor, Cyrenaica, 1941 (despatches twice); Commanded British, Australian, and Indian Forces against Rommel's first attack in Cyrenaica, Mar.-Apr. 1941; prisoner of war, 1941, escaped from Italy 1943; retired pay, 1947. Lieutenant-Governor and Commander-in-Chief of Guernsey and its dependences, Channel Islands, 1945-53; Col Comdt RE, 1945. Member, Governing Body of Gordon Boys School; Vice-Pres., Nat. Rifle Assoc.; Pres. North London Rifle Club. DL Kent, 1955. FRGS. KStJ; Knight of Order of White Lion, Czechoslovakia. *Publications:* German Strategy in the Great War, 1923; Autobiography, Playing with Strife, 1946; also various articles on big-game shooting, Tibet, North West Frontier, etc. *Recreations:* gardening and fruit growing, polo, hunting, point to point racing, big and small game shooting, rifle and revolver shooting (in British Olympic Sporting Rifle Team, Gold and Bronze Medals, France, 1924; in Army Revolver VIII and Army Rifle Twenty). *Address:* The Kintle, Selling Court, Faversham, Kent.

**NEAME, Ronald;** Film Producer and Director; *b* 23 Apr. 1911; *s* of Elwin Neame and Ivy Close; *m* 1933, Beryl Yolanda Heanly; one *s*. *Educ:* University College School; Hurstpierpoint College. Entered film industry, 1928; became Chief Cameraman, 1934. In charge of production on: In Which We Serve, This Happy Breed, Blithe Spirit, Brief Encounter, 1942-45; produced: Great Expectations, Oliver Twist, The Magic Box; directed: Take My Life, The Card, 1945-51; The Million Pound Note, 1953; The Man Who Never Was, 1954; Windom's Way, 1957; The Horse's Mouth, 1958; Tunes of Glory, 1960; I Could Go On Singing, 1962; The Chalk Garden, 1963; Mr Moses, 1964; Gambit, 1966; The Prime of Miss Jean Brodie, 1968, Scrooge, 1970. *Address:* Casa Iolanda, La Mortola, Imperia, Italy. *Club:* Savile.

**NEAME, Sir Thomas,** Kt 1960; MBE 1918; FSA; VMH; Farmer and Fruit-grower; *b* 23 Dec. 1885; *s* of late Frederick Neame, Luton, Selling, Faversham; *m* 1920, Gwendolyn Mary, *d* of George Thomson, Torquay (*see* Astra Desmond); two *s* (and one *s* decd). *Educ:* Cheltenham Coll.; Gonville and Caius Coll., Camb. Studied in Germany; at Stewarts & Lloyds Tube Works till 1914. Served European War, 9th Bn Worcestershire Regt, Gallipoli. Joined family farming business, 1919, growing hops and fruit on a large scale; won many prizes at Imperial Fruit Show and in Dairy Herd competitions. Chm., East Malling Research Station, 1945-60; Member of Governing Body of Wye Coll. A Trustee Royal Agricultural Soc. of England; Master of the Farmers' Co., 1958-59; Pres., Kent Archaeological Soc., 1959-66. High Sheriff of Kent, 1948-49. *Recreation:* horticulture. *Address:* Preston Lea, Faversham, Kent. *T:* Faversham 2012. *Club:* Athenæum.

**NEAME, Lady (Thomas)** *see* Desmond, Astra.

**NEAVE, Airey Middleton Sheffield,** DSO 1945; OBE 1947; MC 1942; TD (with 1st clasp) 1945; MP (C) Abingdon Division of Berkshire since July 1953; Director, John Thompson Group, since October 1959; Barrister-at-Law; *b* 23 January 1916; *e s* of late Sheffield Neave, CMG, OBE, DSc; *m* 1942, Diana Josceline Barbara, *d* of Thomas A. W. Giffard, MBE, JP, of Chillington Hall, Wolverhampton; two *s* one *d*. *Educ:* Eton; Merton Coll., Oxford. BA (Hons) Jurisprudence, 1938, MA 1955. Called to the Bar, Middle Temple, 1943. Served War of 1939-45 (despatches, MC, DSO); with RA (TA) in France, 1940; wounded and prisoner,

1940; escaped, 1942; GSO(2) (I), 21 Army Group, 1944-45. Lieut-Col AAG, British War Crimes Executive, 1945-46; served indictments on Goering and major Nazi War Criminals, 1945; Comr for Criminal Organizations. Internat. Mil. Tribunal, Nuremburg, 1946. Lt-Col RA (TA), 1949-51. Contested Thurrock (C), 1950, Ealing North (C) 1951; PPS to Minister of Transport and Civil Aviation, 1954; PPS to Secretary of State for Colonies, 1954-56; Joint Parly Sec., Min. of Transport and Civil Aviation, 1957-59; Parly Under-Sec. of State for Air, 1959. Formerly Vice-Pres., Parly and Scientific Cttee; Mem. Select Cttee of House of Commons on Science and Technology, 1967-70. Hon. Sec., Assoc. of British Chambers of Commerce, 1960-62; a Governor, Imperial College of Science and Technology, 1963. Pres., Cttee for Commonwealth Citizens in China, 1970-. French Croix de Guerre, American Bronze Star and Officer Order Orange Nassau, Holland, 1945. *Publications:* They Have Their Exits, 1953; Little Cyclone, 1954; Saturday at MI9, 1969. *Address:* 32 Westminster Gdns, SW1. *T:* 01-834 4827; The Old Vicarage, Ashbury, Swindon, Wilts. *T:* Ashbury 223; c/o John Thompson Ltd, Tavistock House East, Woburn Walk, Tavistock Square, WC1. *T:* 01-387 9393.

**NEAVE, Sir Arundell Thomas Clifton,** 6th Bt, *cr* 1795; JP; late Major Welsh Guards; *b* 31 May 1916; *e s* of Col Sir Thomas Lewis Hughes Neave, 5th Bt, and Dorina (*d* 1955) (author of 26 years on the Bosphorus, Remembering Kut, 1937, Romance of the Bosphorus, 1950), *d* of late George H. Clifton; *S* father, 1940; *m* 1946, Richenda Alice Ione, *o c* of Sir Robert J. Paul, 5th Bt; two *s* two *d*. *Educ:* Eton. Was at Dunkirk, 1940. JP for Anglesey, 1950. *Heir: s* Paul Arundell Neave, *b* 13 December 1948. *Address:* Pelham Place, Alton, Hants. *T:* Tisted 212. *Clubs:* Carlton, Guards, Pratt's, Kildare St (Dublin).

*See also Sir Richard Williams-Bulkeley.*

**NEDEN, Sir Wilfred (John),** Kt, *cr* 1955; CB 1949; CBE 1946; retired as Chief Industrial Commissioner, Minister of Labour and National Service, (1954-58); Deputy Chairman, BOAC, 1960-63; *b* 24 August 1893; *s* of John Thomas and Margaret Neden; *m* 1st, 1925, Jean Lundie (*d* 1965); one *s* one *d*; 2nd, 1967, Mrs L. Violet Ryan, Hove, Sussex. *Educ:* St Olave's Gram. Sch. Army, 1914-22, Lieut RFA (Regular Commission); served European War, 1914-18. Entered Ministry of Labour, 1922; Under Secretary, 1946; Director of Organisation and Establishments, 1948-54. *Address:* Halfway, Blakeney, Norfolk.

**NEEDHAM,** family name of **Earl of Kilmorey.**

**NEEDHAM, Dorothy Mary Moyle,** FRS 1948; ScD Cantab; Research Worker, Biochemical Laboratory, Cambridge, 1920-63; *b* London, 22 Sept. 1896; *d* of John Moyle and Ellen Davies; *m* 1924, Joseph Needham, *qv*; no *c*. *Educ:* Claremont Coll., Stockport; Girton Coll., Cambridge. Research for DSIR, 1920-24; Gamble Prize, 1924; Beit Meml Research Fellow, 1925-28. Specialised in biochemistry of muscle, carbohydrate metabolism and phosphorylations; carried out research and teaching at Cambridge and in laboratories in USA, France, Germany, Belgium, etc., 1928-40; Research Worker for Ministry of Supply (Chemical Defence), 1940-43; Chemical Adviser and Acting Director, Sino-British Science Cooperation Office, Chungking, China, 1944-45; Research Worker for MRC 1946-52; Research grant from Broodbank Fund, Univ. of Cambridge, 1952-55; Research Worker for ARC, 1955-62; Foulerton Gift Donation, Royal Society, 1961-62; Leverhulme Award, 1963. *Publications:* Biochemistry of Muscle, 1932; Science Outpost (ed jtly), 1948; Machina Carnis: the biochemistry of muscle contraction in its historical development, 1970; numerous original papers in biochemical journals and Proc. Royal Soc. *Address:* Master's Lodge, Caius College, Cambridge. *T:* Cambridge 52183.

**NEEDHAM, Prof. John,** MA (Sheffield); FRIBA, DipArch (Leeds); Professor of Architecture, The University, Sheffield, since 1957; *b* 2 April 1909; British; *s* of P. Needham; *m* 1934, Bessie Grange; three *d*. *Educ:* Belle Vue Grammar School, Bradford; Leeds School of Architecture. Diploma in Architecture, Leeds, 1931; ARIBA 1931, FRIBA 1948; RIBA; Alfred Bossom Silver Medal, 1937; Alfred Bossom Gold Medal, 1938; Soane Medal, 1938; Athens Bursar, 1949. Head, Dundee School of Architecture, 1938-57. 1st Premium in Open Architectural Competition for new County Buildings, Cupar, Fife, 1947. Mem. Amenity Cttee set up by Sec. of State for Scotland under Hydro Electric (Scotland) Development Acts. Hon. Editor, Quarterly Jl of Royal Incorporation of Architects in Scotland, 1946-50. *Address:* Department of Architecture, University of Sheffield. *T:* Sheffield, 78555. Ext. 710.

**NEEDHAM, Joseph,** MA, PhD, ScD (Cantab); FRS; Master of Gonville and Caius College, since 1966; Hon. Counsellor, UNESCO; *b* 1900; *s* of late Joseph Needham, MD, of Harley Street and Clapham Park, and Alicia A. Needham; *m* 1924, Dorothy Mary (*see* D. M. M. Needham), *d* of John Moyle, Babbacombe, Devon. *Educ:* Oundle School. Fellow Gonville and Caius Coll., 1924-66 (Librarian, 1959-60, Pres., 1959-66); Univ. Demonstrator in Biochem., 1928-33; Sir William Dunn Reader in Biochemistry, 1933-66, now Emeritus; Vis. Prof. of Biochem. at Stanford Univ., California, USA, 1929; Hitchcock Prof., Univ. of California, 1950; Vis. Prof., Univ. of Lyon, 1951. Lectures: Terry and Carmalt, Yale Univ.; Goldwin-Smith, Cornell Univ.; Mead-Swing, Oberlin College, Ohio, USA, 1935; Oliver Sharpey, RCP, 1935-36; Herbert Spencer, Oxford, 1936-37; for Polskie Towarzystwo Biologicznej in the Universities of Warsaw, Lwów, Kraków and Wilno, 1937; Comte Memorial, London, 1940; Conway Memorial, London, 1947; Boyle, Oxford, 1948; Noguchi, Johns Hopkins Univ., 1950; Hobhouse, London Univ., 1950; Dickinson, Newcomen Soc., 1956; Colombo, Singapore, Peking and Jaipur Universities, 1958; Wilkins, Royal Society, 1958; Wilde, Manchester, 1959; Earl Grey, Newcastle upon Tyne, 1960-61; Henry Myers, Royal Anthropological Institute, 1964; Harveian London, 1970. Head of the British Scientific Mission in China and Counsellor, British Embassy, Chungking, and Adviser to the Chinese National Resources Commission, Chinese Army Medical Administration and Chinese Air Force Research Bureau, 1942-46; Director of the Dept of Natural Sciences, UNESCO, 1946-48. Chm. Ceylon Government University Policy Commission, 1958. Foreign Member National Academy of China (Academia Sinica); Mem. Internat. Academies of Hist. of Science and of Med.; Hon. Member Yale Chapter of Sigma Xi. Hon. DSc, Brussels and Norwich. Sir William Jones Medallist, Asiatic Society of Bengal, 1963; George Sarton Medallist, Soc. for History of Science, 1968; Leonardo da Vinci Medallist, Soc. for History of Technology, 1968. Order of the Brilliant Star (China). *Publications:* Science, Religion, and Reality (ed), 1925; Man a Machine, 1927; The Sceptical

Biologist, 1929; Chemical Embryology (3 vols), 1931; The Great Amphibium, 1932; A History of Embryology, 1934; Order and Life, 1935; Christianity and the Social Revolution (ed), 1935; Adventures before Birth (tr.), 1936; Perspectives in Biochemistry (Hopkins Presentation Volume; ed), 1937; Background to Modern Science (ed), 1938; Biochemistry and Morphogenesis, 1942; The Teacher of Nations, addresses and essays in commemoration of John Amos Comenius (ed), 1942; Time, the Refreshing River, 1943; History is on Our Side, 1945; Chinese Science, 1946; Science Outpost, 1948; Hopkins and Biochemistry (ed), 1949; Science and Civilisation in China (7 vols), 1954-; The Development of Iron and Steel Technology in China, 1958; Heavenly Clockwork, 1960; Within the Four Seas, 1969; The Grand Titration, 1969; Clerks and Craftsmen in China and the West, 1969; (ed) The Chemistry of Life, 1969. Chart to illustrate the History of Physiology and Biochemistry, 1926; original papers in scientific, philosophical and sinological journals. *Address:* Master's Lodge, Caius College, Cambridge. *T:* Cambridge 52183. *Club:* Oxford and Cambridge.

**NEEDHAM, N. J. T. M.;** *see* Needham, Joseph.

**NEEDHAM, Richard Francis;** (Viscount Newry and Morne, but does not use the title); *b* 29 Jan. 1942; *e s* and *heir* of 5th Earl of Kilmorey, *qv*; *m* 1965, Sigrid Juliana Thiessen-Gairdner, *o d* of late Ernst Thiessen and of Mrs John Gairdner, Hamburg; two *s*. *Educ:* Eton College. Director: R. G. M. Packaging Ltd; R. G. M. Print Ltd; Tuff & Co. Ltd; Site Signs & Co. Ltd. CC Somerset, 1967. *Heir: s* Hon. Robert Francis John Needham, *b* 30 May 1966. *Address:* Little Aldon, Yeovil, Somerset; Flat 41, Belgravia Court, Ebury Street, SW1. *T:* 21496. *Club:* Buck's.

**NEEL, Dr Louis Boyd,** CBE 1953; MA; Hon. RAM; MRCS, LRCP; Musical Director; Founder and Conductor, Boyd Neel Orchestra; Dean Royal Conservatory of Music of Toronto, Canada, since 1953; radio speaker on musical subjects; *b* 19 July 1905; *s* of Louis Anthoine Neel and Ruby le Couteur; unmarried. *Educ:* RNC, Dartmouth; Caius Coll., Cambridge. Originally destined for Navy, but took up a medical career on leaving Dartmouth; qualified as a doctor, 1930; House Surgeon and Physician, St George's Hospital, London. Founded Boyd Neel Orchestra, 1932, and owing to success of this, forsook medicine for music; conducted the orchestra all over Europe; appeared at Salzburg Festival with it, 1937; has also conducted other famous English orchestras on many occasions; conducted first performance at Glyndebourne, 1934, soon after the theatre was built. On outbreak of war in 1939 returned to medical work, and was engaged in the fitting of artificial limbs. Later in the war, undertook a lecture tour of the Mediterranean area at the request of the Admiralty. Conductor Sadler's Wells Opera Co., 1944-45, and two London seasons D'Oyly Carte Opera Co., 1948-49. In 1947 took his orchestra to Paris, then to Australia and New Zealand under auspices of British Council; entire orchestra, instruments and music transported by air across Atlantic and Pacific, thus making history. In 1948-49 his orchestra toured Holland, Germany and Portugal (2nd time) and gave ten concerts at Edinburgh Festival; in 1950, visited France, Denmark, Norway, Sweden and Finland. In 1951 toured Italy, gave concerts in Berlin, and again appeared at Edinburgh Festival. In 1952, gave two concerts at Aix-en-Provence Festival, and took orchestra on tour in Canada and USA. In 1953 toured France and Switzerland and gave concerts at Strasbourg Festival. Founded Hart House Orchestra of Toronto, 1955; toured with it Canada and USA; brought it to Europe, 1958, 1966 (Aldeburgh and Bergen Festivals). Orchestra has made numerous recordings. *Publication:* The Story of an Orchestra. *Address:* c/o Faculty of Music, University of Toronto, Canada.

**NEELANDS, Abram Rupert,** MC, BA, ME, DLS, CEng, MIMM, MIME, MIStructE, FRSA; President, The Cementation Co. Ltd; *b* Winnipeg, Canada; *s* of James Adam Neelands and Jane Oliphant Butchart; *m* Kathleen Agnew (*d* 1941); one *s* two *d*. *Educ:* Wheatland Public School; Brandon Collegiate; Manitoba Univ. (BA); Toronto Univ. (Mining Engineer). Engrg work with Canadian Pacific Rly, British Columbia Copper Company; Private Practice in Engineering and Contracting; Topographical Surveys Dominion Government, Mexican Corporation, Persian Mining Syndicate; served European War with 1st Field Company Canadian Engineers (MC, despatches); rank of Major. *Address:* 66 Chelsea Square, SW3. *T:* 01-352 0602. *Clubs:* Carlton, Constitutional, Mining and Metallurgical, Royal Over-Seas League, Anglo-Spanish.

**NEELY, Air Vice-Marshal John Conrad,** CB 1957; CBE 1952; DM; FRCS; retired; Senior Consultant, 1955, and Consultant in Ophthalmology, RAF Central Medical Establishment, 1950-59; *b* 29 Mar. 1901; *s* of late William Neely; *m* 1st, 1938, Marjorie Monica (*d* 1964), *d* of Dr Ernest Bramley, Eastbourne; 2nd, 1966, Roma, *widow* of Group Capt. Neil McKechnie, GC. *Educ:* Stonyhurst; Oxford Univ.; Guy's Hosp. MRCS, LRCP, 1927; MA, MB, BCh, 1928, DO (Oxon) 1935, DM 1945, Oxford; DOMS London, 1933. Joined RAF 1928; served War of 1939-45; Middle East (despatches); RAF Hosp., Halton. KHS 1951. Wing Comdr, 1940; Air Cdre, 1950; Air Vice-Marshal, 1955; retired, 1959. FRCS 1958. CStJ 1955. *Address:* 27 Vicarage Drive, Eastbourne.

**NEEP, Edward John Cecil,** QC; *b* 13 Oct. 1900; *e s* of late Rev. Edward Neep, Rector of St George's, Southwark, and Florence Emma Neep; *m* 1926, Evelyn, *e d* of late Sir Harry Pritchard. *Educ:* Westminster School (King's Scholar). Works chemist, 1917-20; tutor and journalist, 1920-23; called to Bar, Middle Temple, 1923; practised for twenty-nine years at the Bar and at the Patent and Parliamentary Bars for twenty years. Contested (Lab) Woodbridge 1922 and 1923, Central Leeds 1924, Lowestoft 1931; KC 1946; QC 1952. Deputy Speaker and Chairman of Committees, Kenya Legislative Council, 1952. *Publications:* Seditious Offences; (part author of): A Handbook of Church Law; Pons Asinorum, or the Future of Nonsense; Horatio Nelson; Gladstone: a spectrum. *Address:* 31 Rua de Santo Antonio ā Estrela, Lisbon, Portugal; Quinta Monte de Cruz, Cintra, Portugal. *Club:* Royal British (Lisbon).

**NEGUS, Sir Victor (Ewings),** Kt 1956; Hon. DSc Manchester; MS (University Medal), FRCS, Hon. FRCS, Edinburgh and Ireland; Consulting Surgeon to Ear, Nose, and Throat Department, King's College Hospital, London; *b* London, 1887; *s* of William Negus, DL, JP; *m* 1929, Gladys Rennie; two *s*. *Educ:* King's Coll. School; King's Coll., London; King's Coll. Hospital. House Surgeon and House Physician, King's College Hospital; Fellow of King's College, London; Arris and Gale Lectr, Hunterian Professor, Hunterian Prizeman and Medallist and Lister Medallist,

Royal Coll. of Surgeons of England; Semon Lecturer; Trustee of the Hunterian Collection; Hon. Gold Medal, RCS, 1969. Served European War, RAMC, 1914-19 (Mons Star, despatches); EMS, 1939-46. Late Co-opted Member Council and Member Court of Examiners, RCS; Hon. Fellow American Laryngological, Rhinological and Otological Soc. and Swedish Med. Soc.; Hon. Fellow, Amer. Laryngological Assoc.; Hon. Mem. Amer. Broncho-Esophagological Assoc. and Canadian Otolaryngological Soc. Corresp. Mem. Danish Society of Oto-Laryngology; Hon. Mem. Italian Society of Laryngology, Otology and Rhinology; scientific section of Hungarian Oto-rhino-laryngologists; Austrian Oto-laryngological Society; Turkish Oto-rhino-laryngological Society; and of Laryng. Soc. of New York; Corresp. Mem. Laryngo-Rhinological Soc. of Vienna and of Soc. of Laryngology of the Hosps of Paris; Hon. Mem.: Scottish Otol. Soc., Manchester Med. Soc. and Harveian Soc.; Life Member Anat. Soc.; President International Congress Otolaryngology, London, 1949; Pres. Thoracic Soc., 1949-50; Past Pres. Sect. of Laryngol., RSM; Hon. Fellow, RSM; lately Hon. Treas. Collegium Oto-rhino-laryngologicum; Past Pres. British Assoc. of Otolaryngologists and Asst-Sec. of Aux. RAMC Funds. *Publications:* The Mechanism of the Larynx, 1929; Diseases of the Nose and Throat (with Sir St Clair Thomson), 1937, 6th Edn 1955; Comparative Anatomy and Physiology of the Larynx, 1949; A Hitherto Undescribed Function of the Vocal Cords, Journal of Laryngology and Otology, 1924; Observations on the Evolution of Man from the Evidence of the Larynx, Acta Oto-laryngologica, 1928; Comparative Anatomy and Physiology of the Nose, 1958; The Biology of Respiration, 1965; The History of the Trustees of the Hunterian Collection, 1965; Artistic Possessions at the Royal College of Surgeons of England, 1967. *Recreation:* gardening. *Address:* Hill Farm Lodge, Camelsdale, Haslemere, W Sussex.

**NEIDPATH, Lord; Hon. James Donald Charteris, Lord Douglas of Neidpath;** *b* 22 June 1948; *s* and *heir* of 12th Earl of Wemyss and March, *qv.* *Educ:* Eton; University College, Oxford. *Address:* Gosford House, Longniddry, East Lothian. *Clubs:* Turf; Puffin's (Edinburgh).

**NEIL, Prof. Eric;** John Astor Professor of Physiology in the University of London, at the Middlesex Hospital Medical School, since 1956; *b* 15 Feb. 1918; *s* of George Neil, MC, and Florence Neil; *m* 1946, Anne Baron, *d* of late T. J. M. B. Parker and of Evelyn Maud Parker; two *d.* *Educ:* Heath Grammar School; University of Leeds. BSc Hons (Physiology) (Leeds), 1939; MB, ChB, 1942; MD (Dist.), 1944 and DSc, 1953 (Leeds). Demonstrator and Lecturer in Physiology, Univ. of Leeds, 1942-50; Sen. Lecturer and later Reader in Physiology, Middx Hosp. Med. School., 1950-56. Hon. Treas., Physiological Soc.; Chm., European Editorial Bd of Physiological Reviews; Mem., Brit. Nat. Cttee of Physiological Sciences. Examiner in Physiology, Univs of London, Aberdeen, Leeds, Manchester and Cambridge. *Publications:* (with Prof. C. Heymans) Reflexogenic Areas in the Cardiovascular System, 1958; (with Prof. C. A. Keele) 11th edn of Wright's Applied Physiology, 1964; papers on physiological topics in British and foreign med. scientific jls. *Recreations:* pianoforte, golf. *Address:* 53 Talbot Road, Highgate, N6. *T:* 01-340 0543.

**NEIL, Thomas,** CMG 1962; TD 1951; Director, Thomson Foundation since 1963; *b* 23 December 1913; *s* of W. R. Neil; *m* 1939, Phyllis Selina Gertrude Sargeant; one *d.* *Educ:* King's College, University of Durham (now University of Newcastle upon Tyne) (BSc, NDA). Lectr in Agriculture, Devon County Council, 1936-39; Chief Technical Officer, 1946. Colonial Service: District Officer, 1947; Assistant Chief Secretary, 1957; Permanent Secretary, 1957; Permanent Secretary, Ministry of State, Kenya, 1959-63. Director, Kenya Famine Relief, 1961-63. Served War of 1939-45 with Devonshire Regiment (TA), Lieutenant-Colonel, in UK, E Africa, Middle East. *Recreation:* country life. *Address:* c/o Thomson House, 200 Gray's Inn Road, WC1; Summerhill, Bourne End, Bucks. *T:* Bourne End 20403.

**NEIL, Rev. William,** MA, BD, PhD, DD; Warden of Hugh Stewart Hall since 1953, and Reader in Biblical Studies since 1965, in the University of Nottingham; *b* 13 June 1909; *s* of William Maclaren Neil and Jean Chalmers Hutchison; *m* 1936, Effie Lindsay Park; two *s.* *Educ:* Glasgow Acad.; Univs of Glasgow and Heidelberg. Black Fellow, 1932-33, Faulds Fellow, 1934-37, Univ. of Glasgow. Minister at Bridge of Allan, 1937-46. Chaplain to 4/5 Royal Scots, 1940-43, and 5 Survey Regt RA, CMF 1943-45 (despatches, Italy). Head of Dept of Biblical Study, Univ. of Aberdeen, 1946-53. Croall Lecturer, Univ. of Edinburgh, 1967. Hon. DD Glasgow, 1961. *Publications:* St Paul's Epistles to the Thessalonians (Moffat Commentaries), 1950; The Rediscovery of the Bible, 1954; The Epistle to the Hebrews, 1955; The Plain Man Looks at the Bible, 1956; I and II Thessalonians (Torch Commentaries), 1957; One Volume Bible Commentary, 1962; Jeremiah and Ezekiel (Bible Guides), 1964; The Life and Teaching of Jesus, 1965; Apostle Extraordinary: The Life and Letters of St Paul, 1966; The Christian Faith in Art (with Eric Newton), 1966; Galatians (Cambridge Bible Commentaries), 1967; The Truth About Jesus, 1968; The Truth about the Early Church, 1970; The Bible Story, 1970. Translations: The Bible as History, 1956; Jesus Lived Here, 1958. Editor, The Bible Companion, 1959; General Editor, Knowing Christianity, 1964. Contributor to: Interpreter's Dictionary of the Bible, Peake's Commentary on the Bible, Cambridge History of the Bible, etc. *Address:* The Warden's House, Hugh Stewart Hall, The University, Nottingham. *T:* 254452.

**NEILD, Robert Ralph;** Director, International Institute for Peace and Conflict Research, Stockholm, since 1967; Professor of Economics, University of Cambridge, from Oct. 1971; *b* 10 Sept. 1924; *o s* of Ralph and Josephine Neild, Letchmore Heath, Hertfordshire; *m* 1960, Elizabeth Walton Griffiths; one *s* two *d.* *Educ:* Charterhouse; Trinity Coll., Cambridge. Royal Air Force, 1943-44; Operational Research, 1944-45. Secretariat of United Nations Economic Commission for Europe, Geneva, 1947-51; Economic Section, Cabinet Office and Treasury, 1951-56; Lecturer in Economics, and Fellow, Trinity College, Cambridge, 1956-58; National Institute of Economic and Social Research: at first as Editor of its Quarterly Economic Review; then as Deputy Director of the Institute, 1958-64; MIT Center for International Studies, India Project, New Delhi, 1962-63; Economic Adviser to HM Treasury, 1964-67. *Publications:* Pricing and Employment in the Trade Cycle, 1964; various articles. *Address:* Sandvik-D, 161.32 Bromma, Sweden. *T:* Stockholm 25.76.14.

**NEILL, Alexander Sutherland,** MA; MEd (Newcastle); author and child psychologist; *b*

17 Oct. 1883; *s* of late George Neill and Mary Sinclair Sutherland Neill, Forfar; *m* 1st, Ada Lilian Lindesay-Neustatter (*d* 1944); 2nd, 1945, Ena May Wood; one *d*. *Educ:* father's village school (Kingsmuir); Edinburgh University. Office boy, then draper, teacher, journalist, educator; joint-founder of International School, Hellerau, Dresden, 1921. Hon. LLD Exeter, 1968. *Publications:* A Dominie's Log, 1915; A Dominie Dismissed, 1916; The Booming of Bunkie, 1919; A Dominie in Doubt, 1920; Carroty Broon, 1921; A Dominie Abroad, 1922; A Dominie's Five, or Free School, 1924; The Problem Child, 1926; The Problem Parent, 1932; Is Scotland Educated, 1936; That Dreadful School, 1937; The Last Man Alive, 1938; The Problem Teacher, 1939; Hearts, not Heads, 1945; The Problem Family, 1948; The Free Child, 1953; Summerhill (a compilation), 1962; Talking of Summerhill (in USA, Freedom, not Licence), 1967. *Address:* Summerhill School, Leiston, Suffolk. *T:* Leiston 540.

**NEILL, Brian Thomas,** QC 1968; *b* 2 Aug. 1923; *s* of late Sir Thomas Neill and of Lady (Annie) Neill (*née* Bishop); *m* 1956, Sally Margaret, *d* of late Sydney Eric Backus and of Mrs Marguerite Backus; three *s*. *Educ:* Highgate Sch.; Corpus Christi Coll., Oxford. Rifle Brigade, 1942-46 (Capt.). MA Oxford. Called to the Bar, Inner Temple, 1949. Governor, Highgate Sch., 1969. *Address:* 48 Ham Street, Ham, Richmond, Surrey. *T:* 01-940 9309. *Clubs:* MCC, Hurlingham.

*See also F. P. Neill.*

**NEILL, Francis Patrick,** QC 1966; *b* 8 Aug. 1926; *s* of late Sir Thomas Neill, JP, and of Lady (Annie) Strachan Neill (*née* Bishop); *m* 1954, Caroline Susan, *d* of late Sir Piers Debenham, 2nd Bt, and Lady (Angela) Debenham; four *s* two *d*. *Educ:* Highgate School; Magdalen College, Oxford. Gibbs Law Scholar, 1949; Eldon Law Scholar, 1950. BA 1950; BCL 1951. Fellow of All Souls, 1950-. Called to the Bar, Gray's Inn, 1951; Member, Bar Council, 1967- . *Recreation:* music. *Address:* 8 Milborne Grove, SW10. *T:* 01-373 6775; Blackdown House, Briantspuddle, Dorset. *T:* Bere Regis 231.

*See also B. T. Neill.*

**NEILL, Major Rt. Hon. Ivan;** PC (N Ireland) 1950; DL; MP Ballynafeigh Division of Belfast, Parliament of Northern Ireland, since 1949; Speaker of the House of Commons, Parliament of Northern Ireland, since 1969; *b* Belfast 1 July 1906; *m* 1928, Margaret Helena Allen. *Educ:* Ravenscroft Nat. Sch., Belfast; Shaftesbury House Tutorial Coll., Belfast; Queen's Univ., Belfast (BSc Econ). Served War of 1939-45: RE in UK and FE, 1939-46; Major. Sen Dir, Ivan Neill and Co., Building and Engineering Contractors, 1928-. Government of Northern Ireland: Minister of Labour and National Insurance, 1950-62; Minister of Home Affairs, Aug.-Oct. 1952; Minister of Education, 1962-64; Minister of Finance, 1964-65; Leader of House of Commons, Oct. 1964; resigned from Govt, April 1965; Minister of Develt, Dec. 1968-March 1969. Represented N Ireland at Internat. Labour Confs, 1950-61. Councillor and Alderman in Belfast Corp., 1946-50 (specialised in educn, housing and youth welfare). DL Belfast, 1966. *Address:* Speaker's House, Stormont, Belfast BT4 3TA; The Wood House, Rostrevor, Co. Down, Northern Ireland.

**NEILL, Very Rev. Ivan Delacherois,** CB 1963; OBE 1958; QHC 1960; Provost of Sheffield and Vicar of the Cathedral Church of St Peter and St Paul since 1966; Chaplain to the Queen, 1962-66; *b* 10 July 1912; *s* of Rev. Robert Richard Neill and Bessie Montrose (*née* Purdon); *m* 1938, Enid Eyre Godson (*née* Bartholomew); one *s* one *d*. *Educ:* St Dunstan's College; Jesus College, Cambridge (MA); London College of Divinity. Curate: St Mary, West Kensington, 1936-38; Christ Church, Crouch End, 1938-39. CF 4th Cl., Chatham; served BEF and UK with 3rd Div., Orkneys, Sandhurst, 1941-43; Sen. Chaplain, N Aldershot, 1943; 43rd (Wessex) Div., 1943-45 (despatches); DACG, 1st British Corps, 1945-46; Sen. Chaplain, Guards Depot, Caterham, 1947-50; DACG, N Canal, Egypt, 1950-53; Catterick, 1953; Warden, Royal Army Chaplains Dept Trg Centre Depot, 1954-57; Sen. Chaplain, SHAPE 1957-58; Asst Chaplain-Gen., Middle East Land Forces, 1958-60; Chaplain General to HM Forces, 1960-66. Knight Officer, Order of Orange Nassau (with Swords) 1946. *Address:* Cathedral Vicarage, Cherry Tree Road, Sheffield S11 9AA; Churchtown, Broadway, Co. Wexford, Republic of Ireland. *Clubs:* National, United Service; Sheffield.

**NEILL, Patrick;** *see* Neill, F. P.

**NEILL, Rt. Rev. Stephen Charles,** FBA 1969; Professor of Philosophy and Religious Studies, University of Nairobi, since 1969; *b* 31 Dec. 1900; *s* of Rev. Charles Neill, MB, and of Margaret, *d* of late James Monro, CB. *Educ:* Dean Close School; Trinity College, Cambridge (MA 1926). Fellow of Trinity College, Cambridge, 1924-28; Missionary in dioceses of Tinnevelly and Travancore, 1924-30; Warden, Bishop's Theological College, Tirumaraiyur, Nazareth, S India, 1930-38; Bishop of Tinnevelly, 1939-45; Chaplain of Trinity Coll., Cambridge; Univ. Lecturer in Divinity, 1945-47; Co-Director Study Dept of World Council of Churches, 1947-48; Asst Bishop to Archbishop of Canterbury, 1947-50; Associate Gen. Sec. of World Council of Churches, 1948-51; General Editor, World Christian Books, 1952-62, Director, 1962-70; Prof. of Missions and Ecumenical Theology, Univ. of Hamburg, 1962-67. Hulsean Lecturer, Cambridge, 1946-47; Birkbeck Lecturer, Trinity Coll., Cambridge, 1949-50; Godfrey Day Lecturer in Missions, TCD, 1950; Earle Lecturer, Pacific School of Religions, Berkeley, California, 1950; Cody Memorial Lecturer, Toronto, 1956; Visiting Professor of Missions, University of Hamburg, 1956-57 and 1961; Carnahan Lecturer, Faculty of Theology, Buenos Aires, 1958; Duff Lecturer in Missions, Edinburgh and Glasgow, 1958-59; Moorhouse Lecturer, Melbourne, 1960; Visiting Professor of Theology: Colgate-Rochester Divinity School, 1961-62; Wycliffe College, Toronto, 1962; Firth Lecturer, Nottingham, 1962; Bampton Lecturer, Oxford, 1964; Ziskind Lectr, Dartmouth Coll., NH, 1966; Vis. Prof., Drew Univ., NJ, 1967; Vis. Prof. of Religion, Univ. Coll., Nairobi, 1968. Hon. DD: Trinity Coll., Toronto, 1950; Culver-Stockton, 1953; Glasgow, 1961; Hon. ThD: Hamburg, 1957; Uppsala, 1965; Hon. LittD St Paul's Univ., Tokyo, 1960. *Publications:* Out of Bondage, 1928; Builders of the Indian Church, 1933; Beliefs, 1940; Foundation Beliefs, 1942; The Challenge of Jesus Christ, 1944; Christ, His Church and His World, 1948; The Cross over Asia, 1948; On the Ministry, 1952; The Christian Society, 1952; Christian Partnership, 1952; Towards Church Union, 1937-1952, 1952; Under Three Flags, 1954; The Christian's God, 1954; Christian Faith To-day, 1955; The Christian Character, 1955; Who is Jesus Christ?, 1956; The Unfinished Task, 1957; Anglicanism, 1958; A Genuinely Human Existence, 1959; Creative Tension,

1959; Christian Holiness, 1960; Men of Unity, 1960; Christian Faith and other Faiths, 1961; The Eternal Dimension, 1963; The Interpretation of the New Testament, 1964; A History of Christian Missions, 1964; Colonialism and Christian Missions, 1966; The Church and Christian Union, 1968; Christianity in India and Pakistan, 1970; Bible Words and Christian Meanings, 1970; What do you know of Jesus?, 1970. (Editor) Twentieth Century Christianity, 1961; (ed jtly) A History of the Ecumenical Movement, 1517-1948, 1951-54; (ed jtly) The Layman in Christian History, 1963; (ed jtly) The Concise Dictionary of Christian Missions, 1970; contrib. to: Encyclopædia Britannica; Chambers's Encyclopædia; Die Religion in Geschichte und Gegenwart; Evangelisches Kirchenlexikon; Weltkirchenlexicon. *Address:* 2 Eaton Gate, SW1; University College, PO Box 30197, Nairobi, Kenya.

**NEILSON, Drevor Frederick Acton,** FRCS; Consultant Surgeon, Ear, Nose and Throat Department, St Thomas' Hosp. BA Cambridge. Formerly Surgeon, ENT, Royal Masonic Hosp. Past Pres. Section of Otology, Royal Soc. Med. RAMC (Captain), 1915-19. *Address:* Lilliput, Little River, Jamaica.

**NEILSON, Ian (Godfrey),** DFC 1944; TD 1951; Brigade Secretary, The Boys' Brigade, since 1966; *b* 4 Dec. 1918; *er s* of James Wilson Neilson, solicitor, Glasgow; *M* 1945; D. Alison St Clair Aytoun, Ashintully; one *s* one *d*. *Educ:* Glasgow Acad.; Glasgow Univ. (BL). Legal Trng, Glasgow, 1937; Territorial Army, 1938; War Service, 1939-45: Field Artillery; Air Observation Post, 1941; RA Staff, 1944; comdg War Crimes Investigation Unit, Germany, 1945-46. Enrolled Solicitor, 1946. Royal Institution of Chartered Surveyors; Scottish Sec., Edinburgh, 1946-53; Asst Sec., London, 1953-61; Under-Sec., 1961-65. Hon. Treasurer, Thames Youth Venture Adv. Council, 1968. *Recreations:* golf, music, gardening, sailing. *Address:* 103 Longdown Lane South, Epsom Downs, Epsom, Surrey. *T:* Epsom 20670. *Club:* United Service.

**NEILSON JONES, W.;** *see* Jones.

**NEILSON-TERRY, Phyllis,** FRAM; Actress; *b* 15 Oct. 1892; *d* of late Fred Terry and late Julia Neilson; *m* 1958, Heron Carvic. *Educ:* Waterside, Westgate-on-Sea; Paris; Royal Academy of Music. Played with her father and mother in 1909; Viola in Twelfth Night with Sir Herbert Tree, 1910; Rosalind and Juliet in her father's productions at the New Theatre; Trilby, Portia, Desdemona with Sir Herbert; later was with Charles Frohman, and Sir George Alexander; toured America, 1914-19; went into management on return to England, produced J. B. Fagan's The Wheel, and Temple Thurston's A Roof and Four Walls, at the Apollo, London; toured S Africa, 1927; Candida with Sir Barry Jackson, Malvern Festival; has played at the Open Air Theatre, The Memorial Theatre, Stratford, Queen Katherine and Lady Macbeth. Has broadcast Macbeth, Trilby, Candida, The Scarlet Pimpernel and many other plays. In management with Heron Carvic in his plays The Widow of 40 and The Beggars' Union. Played Mrs Railton-Bell in Separate Tables, St James's, and Music Box Theatre, New York. *Recreation:* reading. *Address:* Upton, Appledore, Kent. *T:* Appledore 355.

**NELIGAN, Desmond West Edmund,** OBE 1961; Commissioner for National Insurance; *b* 20 June 1906; *s* of late Rt Rev. M. R. Neligan, DD (one time Bishop of Auckland, NZ), and Mary, *d* of Edmund Macrory, QC; *m* 1st, 1936, Penelope Ann, *d* of Henry Mason (marr. diss., 1946); two *s*; 2nd, 1947, Margaret Elizabeth, *d* of late Captain Snook, RN; one step *d*. *Educ:* Bradfield Coll.; Jesus Coll., Cambridge. BA Cantab, 1929; Barrister, Middle Temple, 1940. Practising Barrister until 1961. Appointed Umpire under National Service Acts, Nov. 1955. Dep. Comr for National Insurance, 1961-66. Served War of 1939-45, in 2 NZ Division, in Greece, Crete and Western Desert. *Publications:* (ed) 6th, 7th and 8th Editions Dumsday's Parish Councils Handbook; (with Sir A. Safford, QC) Town and Country Planning Act, 1944, and *ibid*, 1947. *Recreations:* formerly: hockey, cricket (Assoc. Mem. MCC), tennis and hunting. *Address:* 54 Longridge Road, SW5. *T:* 01-370 2268.

**NELSON,** family name of **Earl Nelson** and **Baron Nelson of Stafford.**

**NELSON,** 7th Earl, *cr* 1805, of Trafalgar and of Merton; **Henry Edward Joseph Horatio Nelson;** Baron Nelson of the Nile and of Hilborough, Norfolk, 1801; Viscount Merton of Trafalgar and of Merton, 1805; formerly tea planter, Ceylon and India; *b* 22 April 1894; second *s* of 5th Earl Nelson and Geraldine (*d* 1936), *d* of late Henry H. Cave, Northampton; *S* brother 1957; unmarried. *Educ:* Maredsous, Belgium; HMS Conway. Served European War, 1914-18, with Australian Imperial Force; War of 1939-45 with Merchant Navy and as Major, Indian Army. *Recreations:* formerly yachting and boxing. *Heir: b* Hon. George Joseph Horatio Nelson [*b* 20 April 1905; *m* 1945, Mary Winifred, *d* of G. Bevan, Swansea; one *d*]. *Address:* Richmond House, 27 Rabling Road, Swanage, Dorset BH19 1ED. *T:* 2832.

**NELSON OF STAFFORD,** 2nd Baron, *cr* 1960; **Henry George Nelson,** Bt 1955; MA, CEng, FInstCE, FIEE, FRAeS; Chairman, The General Electric and English Electric Companies Ltd, since 1968, Director: Bank of England; The English Electric, Babcock & Wilcox and Taylor Woodrow Atomic Power Construction Co. Ltd (Joint Chairman); British Aircraft Corporation (Joint Deputy Chairman); Marconi International Marine Co. Ltd; National Bank of Australasia Ltd (London Board of Advice); International Computers (Holdings) Ltd; International Nickel Company of Canada; Chancellor of Aston University; *b* Manchester, 2 Jan. 1917; *s* of 1st Baron Nelson of Stafford and late Florence Mabel, *o d* of late Henry Howe, JP; *S* father, 1962; *m* 1940, Pamela Roy Bird, *yr d* of late Ernest Roy Bird, formerly MP for Skipton, Yorks; two *s* two *d*. *Educ:* Oundle; King's Coll., Cambridge. Exhibnr 1935; Mechanical Sciences Tripos, 1937. Practical experience in England, France and Switzerland, 1937-39. Joined the English Electric Co. Ltd, 1939; Supt, Preston Works, 1939-40; Asst Works Man., Preston, 1940-41; Dep. Works Man., Preston, 1941-42; Man. Dir, D. Napier & Son Ltd, 1942-49; Exec. Dir, The Marconi Co. Ltd, 1946-58; Dep. Man. Dir, 1949-56, Man. Dir, 1956-62, Chm. and Chief Exec., 1962-68, The English Electric Co. Ltd. Outside Lectr, Univ. of Cambridge (Mech. Sciences Tripos course on Industrial Management), 1947-49. Member: Govt. Adv. Council on Scientific Policy, 1955-58; Adv. Council on Middle East Trade, 1958-63 (Industrial Leader and Vice-Chm., 1959-63); Civil Service Commn (Part time Mem. Final Selection and Interview Bds), 1956-; Engrg Adv. Council, 1958-; Engrg Employers' Fedn, 1956- (Vice-Pres., 1963, Gen. Council, 1956-. and Management Bd, 1956-); Council, Inst. Electrical Engineers, 1959-62 (Vice-Pres. 1957-62 and 1965-70); Internat. Electrical

Assoc., 1953-57 (Chm. 1955) and 1959-; Middle East Assoc. (Vice-Pres., 1962-); Gen. Bd of NPL, 1959-66; Council, SBAC, 1943-64 (Pres. 1961-62); Council Foundn on Automation and Employment Ltd, 1963-68; Council, BEAMA, 1964- (Pres., 1966); Adv. Council on Technology, 1964-70. World Power Conference: Mem., British Nat. Cttee, 1954-; Mem., Executive Cttee of Brit. Nat. Commn, 1957-; Brit. Nuclear Energy Soc., 1962-. A Rep. of Conf. of Electronics Industry on Nat. Electronic Res. Council, 1963-; Pres. Locomotive and Allied Manufacturers Assoc., 1964-66; Pres., British Electrical Power Convention, 1965-67. Pres., Orgalime (Organisme de Liaison des Industries Métalliques Européennes), 1968-70. Liveryman, Worshipful Co. of Coachmakers and Coach Harness Makers of London, 1944, Asst to Court, 1959-62; Liveryman, Worshipful Co. of Goldsmiths, 1961. Lord High Steward of Borough of Stafford, 1966-. Hon. DSc: Aston; Keele; Hon. FIMechE. Benjamin Franklin Medal, RSA, 1959. *Recreations:* shooting, tennis, ski-ing, riding. *Heir:* *s* Hon. Henry Roy George Nelson [*b* 26 Oct. 1943; *m* 1968, Dorothy, *yr d* of Leslie Caley, Tibthorpe Manor, Driffield, Yorks]. *Address:* 19 Acacia Road, St John's Wood, NW8. *T:* 01-722 4324. *Clubs:* Carlton, Hurlingham.

**NELSON, NZ, Bishop of,** since 1965; **Rt. Rev. Peter (Eves) Sutton;** *m* 1956, Pamela Cherrington, *e d* of R. A. Dalley, Patin House, Kidderminster; one *s* one *d.* *Educ:* Wellesley Coll.; Nelson Coll.; University of New Zealand. BA 1945; MA 1947; LTh 1948. Deacon, 1947; Priest, 1948 (Wellington); Curate of Wanganui, New Zealand, 1947-50; St John the Evangelist, Bethnal Green, 1950-51; Bishops Hatfield, Diocese of St Albans (England), 1951-52; Vicar of St Cuthberts, Berhampore (NZ), 1952-58; Whangarei, Diocese of Auckland, New Zealand, 1958-64; Archdeacon of Waimate, 1962-64; Dean of Dunedin and Vicar of St Paul's Cathedral, Dunedin, 1964-65. *Recreations:* golf (Canterbury Univ. Blue), tennis. *Address:* Bishopdale, Nelson, New Zealand.

**NELSON, NZ, Dean of;** *see* Bretton, Very Rev. William Frederick.

**NELSON, Bertram,** CBE 1956; JP (Liverpool); Partner, Lithgow, Nelson & Co., Chartered Accountants, Liverpool, London, Southport and Wigan; *b* 1905; *s* of W. E. Nelson, Liverpool; *m* 1954, Eleanor Kinsey; one *s* one *d.* *Educ:* The Leys School, Cambridge. Hon. Sec. Merseyside Civic Soc. 1938-53. Chm. Liverpool Chamber of Commerce, 1951-53, Treas., 1953-60; a Vice-Pres. of Assoc. of British Chambers of Commerce, 1956. Pres. Soc. of Incorporated Accountants, 1954-56; Mem. Council of Inst. of Chartered Accountants, 1957- (Chairman of Education Committee, 1961-66). BBC North Regional Council, 1947, 1948, 1955, 1956 and 1957. Mem. Board of Trade Consultative Cttee on Companies, 1954-, and of Bd of Trade Treas. Cttee on Export Credit Guarantees Dept., 1958; Part-time Mem., Merseyside and N Wales Electricity Bd 1967-. Treas. of Liverpool Univ., 1948-57, Vice-Pres., 1957-63, Pres. and Pro-Chancellor, 1963-67, Senior Pro-Chancellor, 1967-; Chm., Univ. Develt Cttee, 1961-68; Governor: The Leys Sch., Cambridge; Staff Coll. for Further Education; Mem. Mersey Docks and Harbour Bd, 1951-65; Chm. Liverpool Youth Welfare Advisory Cttee, 1952-65; Dir, the Playhouse, Liverpool, 1949-63; Chm. of Appeals Cttee on Gradings and Salaries in Colls of Advanced Technology, 1964-65. Trustee, Civic Trust for NW. *Publication:* Tables of Procedure, 1933. *Address:* Derby Square, Liverpool L2 7LY. *T:* 051-236 3602; Imperial House, 15 Kingsway, WC2. *T:* 01-836 9496. *Clubs:* Reform, Athenæum (Pres. 1962), University; University Staff House (Liverpool).

**NELSON, Air Cdre Eric Douglas Mackinlay,** CB 1952; DL; retired, Sept. 1963; Deputy Secretary, East Midland TA&VRA; *b* 2 Jan. 1912; *e s* of late Rear-Adm. R. D. Nelson, CBE, and the late Ethel Nelson (*née* MacKinlay); *m* 1939, Margaret Yvonne Taylor; one *s* one *d.* *Educ:* Dover Coll.; RAF Coll., Cranwell. Commissioned RAF, 1932; served War of 1939-45 (despatches). Group Capt., 1944; ADC to the Queen, 1953-57; Air Commodore, 1956; Commandant, RAF, Halton, 1956-58; Commandant, Royal Air Force Staff College, Andover, 1958-60; AOA Transport Command, 1960-61; Air Officer Commanding and Commandant, Royal Air Force College, Cranwell, 1961-63. DL Lincs, 1966. *Recreations:* boxed for RAF, 1933-39; sailing, hunting. *Address:* (permanent) Jasmine Cottage, Carlton-le-Moorland, Lincoln. *T:* Bassingham 309. *Club:* Royal Air Force.

**NELSON, Maj.-Gen. Sir (Eustace) John (Blois),** KCVO 1966 (MVO 1953); CB 1965; DSO 1944; OBE 1948; MC 1943; General Secretary, National Playing Fields Association, since 1969; *b* 15 June 1912; *s* of late Roland Hugh Nelson and late Hylda Letitia Blois; *m* 1936, the Lady Jane FitzRoy (granted rank and precedence of *d* of a duke, 1931), *er d* of (William Henry Alfred FitzRoy) Viscount Ipswich; two *d.* *Educ:* Eton; Trinity College, Cambridge. BA (Hons) History. Commissioned Grenadier Guards, Sept. 1933; served 1939-45 with 3rd and 5th Bns, Belgium, N Africa, Italy (wounded three times, despatches); comd 3rd Bn Grenadier Guards, 1944-45, Italy. Contested (C) Whitechapel, 1945. Comd 1st Guards Parachute Bn, 1946-48, Palestine; comd 1st Bn Gren. Gds, 1950-52, Tripoli, N Africa. Planning Staff Standing Group, Washington, DC, 1954-56, Imperial Defence College, 1958; comd 4th Guards Bde, 1959-61, Germany; GOC London District, and Maj.-Gen. comdg Household Brigade 1962-65; GOC Berlin (British Sector), 1966-68. Silver Star (USA), 1944. *Recreations:* the countryside, sailing. *Address:* Burpham Lodge, Arundel, Sussex. *T:* Arundel 2225. *Clubs:* White's; Royal Yacht Squadron.

**NELSON, Henry Ince,** QC 1945; BA, LLB; Commissioner of National Insurance, 1968-69 (Deputy Commissioner, 1959-68); retired; *b* 29 May 1897; *s* of late Henry Nelson, OBE, and of late Ada Bell Nelson; *m* 1933, Mary Howard Cooper; three *s* one *d.* *Educ:* Aldenham School; Pembroke Coll., Cambridge. RFA 1915-19, rank Lt (twice wounded); served on Western Front with VI Divisional Artillery. Called to Bar, Inner Temple, 1922; Bencher 1952. Judge of Salford Hundred Court of Record, 1947-48; Judge of Liverpool Court of Passage, 1948-50; Recorder of Liverpool, 1950-54. *Recreations:* gardening and golf. *Address:* Brackendene, Hockering Road, Woking, Surrey. *T:* Woking 61210. *Club:* Golf (Woking).

**NELSON, Air Marshal Sir Richard;** *see* Nelson, Air Marshal Sir S. R. C.

**NELSON, St Elmo Dudley,** CMG 1964; Permanent Secretary, Military Governor's Office, Northern Nigeria, since 1968; *b* 18 March 1919; *s* of Dudley Nelson and Dorothy Maida (*née* Browne), Highton, Victoria, Australia; *m* 1958, Lynette Margaret, *o d* of Philip Anthony Browne, Yarram and Frankston, Victoria, Australia. *Educ:*

privately; Geelong School; Oxford University; Sorbonne. Served War of 1939-45 (despatches): 2/7 Australian Infantry Bn (Major); campaigns N Africa, Greece, Crete, New Guinea; Instructor Staff Coll., Cabalah, 1944. Joined HM Colonial Administrative Service. Nigeria: Cadet 1947; Administrative Officer (Class II), 1957; Resident, Plateau Province, 1961; Resident and Provincial Sec., Kabba Province, 1962; Provincial Sec., Kano Province, 1963-67, Sokoto, 1967-68. *Recreations:* fishing, polo, squash. *Address:* c/o Australia & New Zealand Bank, 71 Cornhill, EC3; Lovely Banks, Victoria, Australia; Military Governor's Office, Kano, Nigeria.

**NELSON, Air Marshal Sir (Sidney) Richard (Carlyle),** KCB 1963 (CB 1962); OBE 1949; Director-General, Royal Air Force Medical Services, 1962-67; Director of Research and Medical Services, Aspro-Nicholas Ltd; *b* Ponoka, Alberta, Canada, 14 Nov. 1907; *s* of M. O. Nelson, BA; *m* 1939, Christina Elizabeth Powell; two *s. Educ:* University of Alberta (MD). Commissioned in RAF, 1935; served: England 1935-36; Egypt and Western Desert, 1936-42; Fighter Command, 1943; UK Delegation (Canada), 1943-44; British Jt Services Mission (Washington), 1945-48; RAF Staff Coll., 1949; Air Ministry, 1949-52; Comd RAF Hosp., Nocton Hall, 1953-55; SMO British Forces, Arabian Peninsula, 1956-57; PMO Technical Training Comd, 1957-59; Bomber Comd, 1959-62, QHP 1961-67. *Recreations:* fishing, golf. *Address:* Caffyn's Copse, Shappen Hill Lane, Burley, Hants. *T:* Burley 3308. *Clubs:* Royal Air Force; Royal London Yacht.

**NELSON, Sir William Vernon Hope,** 3rd Bt, *cr* 1912; OBE 1952; Major (retired) late 8th Hussars; *b* 25 May 1914; *s* of late William Hope Nelson (2nd *s* of 1st Bt); *S* uncle, Sir James Hope Nelson, 2nd Bt, 1960; *m* 1945, Elizabeth Ann Bevil, *er d* of Viscount Falkland, *qv*; three *s* two *d. Educ:* Beaumont; Royal Military College, Sandhurst. Commissioned 2nd Lt, 8th Hussars, 1934. Served in Palestine, 1936-39 (despatches, medal with clasp). Served War of 1939-45; served Korea, 1950-51 (OBE). *Heir: s* Jamie Charles Vernon Hope Nelson, *b* 23 Oct. 1949. *Club:* United Hunts.

**NEMON, Oscar;** Sculptor; *b* 13 March 1906; *s* of Mavro and Eugenia Nemon, Yugoslavia; *m* 1939, Patricia Villiers-Stuart; one *s* two *d. Educ:* Osijek; Brussels; Paris. Exhibitions held in principal capitals of Europe. Examples of his work are in: House of Commons; Windsor Castle; The Guildhall, London; The Union, Oxford. His sitters include: HM The Queen, Rt Hon. Sir Winston Churchill, Rt Hon. Harold Macmillan, Lord Beaverbrook, Sigmund Freud, Sir Max Beerbohm, Lord Montgomery, President Eisenhower. *Recreation:* searching for lost opportunities. *Address:* Pleasant Land, Boars Hill, Oxford. *T:* Oxford 35583.

*See also Sir George Young, Bt.*

**NEPEAN, Lt-Col Sir Evan Yorke,** 6th Bt, *cr* 1802; late Royal Signals; *b* 23 Nov. 1909; *s* of Sir Charles Evan Molyneux Yorke Nepean, 5th Bt, and Mary Winifred, *o d* of Rev. William John Swayne, formerly Vicar of Heytesbury, Wilts, and Custos of St John's Hospital, Heytesbury; *S* father 1953; *m* 1940, (Georgiana) Cicely, *o d* of late Major Noel Edward Grey Willoughby, Middlesex Regiment, of Chancel End House, Heytesbury, Wilts; three *d. Educ:* Winchester; Downing College, Cambridge. BA 1931, MA 1946. North West Frontier of India (Mohmand), 1935. Served War of 1939-45: GSO3, War Office, 1939-40; with Royal Signals (Lt-Col 1943), UK, and Middle East, Major 1946; on Staff Southern Command, 1947; GSO1 Royal Signals, Ministry of Defence, 1950-53; Lt-Col 1952; Cmdg 11 Air Formation Signal Regt, BAOR 1955-56, retired. Civil Servant, 1957-59; joined CSO's branch at HQ Southern Command (Retired Officers' Staff appt), 1959. MIEE. *Recreations:* cricket, sailing. *Heir:* none. *Address:* Goldens, Teffont, Salisbury, Wilts. *T:* Teffont 275.

**NERINA, Nadia;** (*née* **Nadine Judd**); Ballerina, The Royal Ballet, 1952-69; Hon. consultant on ballet to Ohio University, since 1967; *b* Cape Town, S Africa, Oct. 1927; *m* 1955, Charles Gordon. Joined Sadler's Wells School, 1946; after two months joined Sadler's Wells Theatre Ballet; with Sadler's Wells Ballet (now The Royal Ballet) from 1947, as soloist; *creations:* Circus Dancer in Mardi Gras; Fairy Spring in Cinderella; Queen of the Earth in Homage to the Queen; Faded Ballerina in Noctambules; Lise in La Fille mal gardée; Elektra. Has toured Europe and America with Royal Ballet; recital tours (with Alexis Rassine), England and South Africa, 1952 and 1954. Danced (by invitation) at Bolshoi Theatre, Moscow, Autumn, 1960. *Address:* Royal Opera House, Covent Garden, WC2.

**NERVI, Pier Luigi;** Structural engineer, Italy; Partner of and consultant adviser to Nervi & Bartoli, Engineers, since 1932; *b* 21 June 1891; *s* of late Antonio and Luisa Bartoli; *m* 1924, Irene Calosi; four *s. Educ:* Univ. of Bologna (Degree in Civil Engineering). Engineer, Società per Costruzione Cementizie, Bologna, 1913-15, and 1918-23; Officer, Engineering Corps, 1915-18; Partner, Nervi & Nebbiosi, Engineers, 1923-32. Prof. of Technology and Technique of Construction, Faculty of Architecture, Rome, 1947-61; Charles E. Norton Prof., Harvard, 1961-62. Life Mem., Internat. Inst. Arts and Letters, Zürich, 1961; Hon. Member: Amer. Acad.-Inst. of Arts and Letters, 1957; Amer. Acad. Arts and Sciences, 1960; Foreign Mem., Royal Acad. of Fine Arts, Stockholm, 1957; Corresponding Member: Academia Nacionale de Ciencias Exactas Fisicas y Naturales, Buenos Aires, 1959; Bayrische Akademie der Schönen Künste, 1960; Accademico Nazionale, and Accad. di San Luca, Roma, 1960; Special Mem., Architectural Section, Academy of Arts of Berlin, 1964. Holds Hon. Degrees at Universities of Buenos Aires, 1950, Edinburgh, 1960, Warsaw, 1961, Harvard, 1962, at Technische Hochschule, München, 1960, and at Dartmouth Coll., 1962, Univ. of London, 1969. Hon. FAIA 1956; Hon. RA (London), 1967. Alfred Lindau Award, Amer. Concrete Inst., 1963; E. Mörsch Award, Deutsche Beton Verein, 1963; Feltrinelli Award, Rome, 1968. Frank P. Brown Medal, 1957; Royal Gold Medal for Architecture, 1960; Gold Medal: AIA, 1964; IStructE, 1968. Cavaliere di Gran Croce al Merito della Repubblica Italiana; Cavaliere al Merito del Lavoro, Rome, 1962. *Publications:* Arte o scienza del costruire, 1945; El linguaje arquitectonico (Buenos Aires), 1952; Costruire correttamente, 1954; Aesthetics and Technology in Building, 1965; various articles on architecture in Italian, French, English and American technical journals. *Recreation:* sailing. *Address:* Lungo Tevere Arnaldo da Brescia 9, Rome, Italy. *T:* 350292. *Club:* Rotary (Rome).

**NESBITT, Cathleen;** Actress; *b* 24 Nov. 1890; *d* of Captain T. Nesbitt, RN, and Mary Catherine Parry; *m* 1922, Captain C. B. Ramage, *qv*; one *s* one *d. Educ:* Belfast; Lisieux; Paris. 1st London appearance as Perdita in

Granville Barker's production of The Winter's Tale, 1913; subsequently played lead in Quality Street, Justice, Hassan, Spring Cleaning, The Case of the Frightened Lady, Children in Uniform, Our Betters, Message for Margaret, Medea, The Uninvited Guest, and Goneril in Granville Barker's all star production of Lear, 1940. Later appearances in: The Cocktail Party; Gigi (New York); Sabrina Fair (New York and London); My Fair Lady (New York); The Claimant, etc. *Films:* A Fair to Remember, So Long At The Fair, Three Coins in the Fountain, Separate Tables, etc. TV series in Hollywood. *Address:* c/o Ashley-Steiner, 555 Madison Avenue, New York City, NY, USA.

**NESBITT, Maj.-Gen. Frederick G. B.;** *see* Beaumont-Nesbitt.

**NETHERTHORPE,** 1st Baron, *cr* 1959; **James Turner;** Kt 1949; Chairman of Fisons Ltd since Nov. 1962; Deputy Chairman, Richard Costain Ltd; Director: Lloyds Bank Ltd; Abbey National Building Society; Steetley Co. Ltd; Film Development and Research Ltd; *b* 6 Jan. 1908; *s* of late Albert Edward Mann Turner, Anston, Sheffield, and Lucy, *d* of Henry Helliwell; *m* 1935, Margaret Lucy, *d* of James Arthur Mattock; three *s* (and one *s* decd). *Educ:* Knaresborough; Leeds University. BSc Leeds, 1928. Chairman of Notts County Branch, NFU, 1937; Notts Council Deleg., NFU, 1943; Vice-Pres., NFU, 1944; Pres., NFU, 1945-60. Pres. Internat. Fedn of Agricultural Producers, 1946-48; Member: Brit. Productivity Council (Chm., 1963); Animal Health Trust; Council, Royal Assoc. of British Dairy Farmers (Pres. 1964); Council Royal Agricultural Society of England (Pres. 1965); Liveryman of Painter-Stainers Co. and of Farmers Co. LLD (Hon.), Leeds, 1952; LLD (Hon.) Birmingham, 1959. *Recreations:* shooting and golf. *Heir: s* Hon. James Andrew Turner [*b* 23 July 1936; *m* 1960, Belinda, *o d* of F. Hedley Nicholson; one *s* two *d*]. *Address:* Hadley Hurst, Hadley Common, Barnet, Herts. *Clubs:* Boodle's, City Livery, Farmers'.

**NEUBERGER, Albert,** CBE 1964; FRS 1951; PhD (London), MD (Würzburg); FRIC; Professor of Chemical Pathology, St Mary's Hospital, University of London, since Oct. 1955; Physician-in-Chief (*Pro Tem.*), at Peter Bent Brigham Hospital, Boston, and Visiting Lecturer on Biological Chemistry, Harvard Univ., 1964; *b* 15 April 1908; *s* of late Max Neuberger and of Bertha Neuberger; *m* 1943, Lilian Ida, *d* of late Edmond Dreyfus and of Marguerite Dreyfus, London; four *s* one *d*. *Educ:* Gymnasium, Würzburg; Univs of Würzburg and London. Beit Memorial Research Fellow, 1936-40; Research at the Biochemistry Department, Cambridge, 1939-42; Mem. of Scientific Staff, Medical Research Council, 1943; Adviser to GHQ, Delhi (Medical Directorate), 1945; Head of Biochemistry Dept, Nat. Inst. for Medical Research, 1950-55; Principal of the Wright Fleming Institute of Microbiology, 1958-62. Visiting Lectr on Medicine, Harvard Univ. 1960. Mem. of Editorial Bd Biochemical Jl, 1947-55, Chm., 1952-55; Member: Medical Research Council, 1962-66; Governing Body of Lister Inst., 1968; Council of Scientific Policy, 1968-69; Agricultural Research Council, 1970-. Chairman: Advisory Board, Beit Memorial Fellowships, 1967-; Biochemical Soc., 1967-69. FCPath 1964; FRCP 1966. William Julius Mickle Fellowship of Univ. of London, 1946-47; Heberden Medal, 1959; Frederick Gowland Hopkins Medal, 1960. Hon. LLD, Aberdeen, 1967; Hon. PhD, Jerusalem, 1968. *Publications:* papers in Biochemical Jl, Proceedings of Royal Society and other learned journals. *Recreation:* sailing. *Address:* 22 West Heath Avenue, NW11. *T:* 01-455 2217; Department of Chemical Pathology, St Mary's Hospital Medical School, W2. *Club:* Athenæum.

**NEUMANN, Prof. Bernhard Hermann,** FAA 1964; FRS 1959; Professor and Head of Department of Mathematics, Institute of Advanced Studies, Australian National University, Canberra, since 1962; *b* Berlin-Charlottenburg, 15 Oct. 1909; *s* of late Richard Neumann and late Else (*née* Aronstein); *m* 1938, Hanna Neumann, DPhil., DSc, FAA (*née* von Caemmerer) (Prof. and Head of Dept of Pure Mathematics, Sch. of Gen. Studies, ANU), three *s* two *d*. *Educ:* Herderschule, Berlin; Univs of Freiburg, Berlin, Cambridge. Dr phil Berlin, 1932; PhD Cambridge 1935; DSc Manchester 1954. Asst Lectr, University Coll, Cardiff, 1937-40. Army Service, 1940-45. Lectr, University Coll., Hull, 1946-48; Lectr, Senior Lectr, Reader, Univ. of Manchester, 1948-61; Visiting Lecturer: Australian Univs, 1959; Univ. of Cambridge, 1970; Visiting Professor: Tata Inst. of Fundamental Research, Bombay, 1959; New York Univ., 1961-62; Univ. of Wisconsin, 1966-67; Vanderbilt Univ., 1969-70; Vis. Fellow, Fitzwilliam Coll., Cambridge, 1970. Adams Prize, Univ. of Cambridge, 1952-62. Member Council: London Math. Society, 1954-61 (Vice-Pres., 1957-59); Aust. Math. Society, 1963- (Vice-Pres., 1963-64, 1966-68; Pres., 1964-66); Aust. Acad. of Science, 1968- (a Vice-Pres., 1969-70). Mem. Aust. Nat. Cttee for Mathematics, 1963- (Chm., 1966-); (Foundation) Pres., Aust. Assoc. Math. Teachers, 1966-68, Vice-Pres., 1968-69. Hon. Editor, Proc. London Math. Soc., 1959-61; Assoc. Editor, Pacific Jl Math., 1964-; (Foundation) Editor, Bulletin of Aust. Math. Soc., 1969-. *Publications:* Appendix to German and Hungarian translations of A. G. Kuroš: Teoriya Grupp, 1953, 1955: Topics in the Theory of Infinite Groups, Bombay, 1961; Special Topics in Algebra, Vol. I: Universal Algebra, Vol. II: Order Techniques, New York, 1962; papers, mainly on theory of groups, in various mathematical journals. *Recreations:* chess, cycling, music. *Address:* Institute of Advanced Studies, Australian National University, Box 4, PO, Canberra, ACT 2600, Australia.

**NEVADA, Mignon;** British soprano; teacher of singing and operatic technique; *b* Paris; *d* of late Emma Nevada and late Dr R. S. Palmer; made professional *début* at the Costanzi Theatre, Rome, as Rosina in Il Barbiere di Siviglia; appeared at Covent Garden, 1910; since then has appeared in nearly all the leading Opera houses of Europe, many times at Covent Garden; and at the Paris Grand Opera. Was in Government Service through whole of War of 1939-45. *Address:* 7 Augustus Road, Wimbledon, SW19. *T:* 01-788 5291.

**NEVEN-SPENCE, Col Sir Basil Hamilton Hebden,** Kt, *cr* 1945; Landowner (Udaller); FRGS; *b* 12 June 1888; *e s* of late T. W. L. Spence, CB, JP, Uyea, Shetland, and Henrietta Fanny, *d* of R. J. Hebden, DL, JP, Eday, Orkney; *m* 1st, 1917, Margaret Alice (*d* 1961), *d* of G. H. Mackenzie, MD, Edinburgh; one *d* (and one *s* one *d* decd); 2nd, 1963, Constance Eila, *widow* of Maj.-Gen. Sir Hubert Jervoise Huddleston, GCMG, GBE, CB, DSO, MC (she *d* 1967), *d* of late F. H. M. Corbet. *Educ:* Edinburgh Acad.; Univ. of Edinburgh. MB, ChB, 1911; MD, 1924; MRCPEd, 1924; FRCPEd, 1927; Lieutenant RAMC, 1911; seconded to Egyptian Army and Sudan Government, 1914; served Darfur and

Palestine (despatches twice, British and Sudan General Service Medals, Victory Medal, Order of the Nile, Fourth Class); Magistrate; Organiser of sleeping sickness campaign, Bahr El Ghazal; Govt Bacteriologist; Reverted to British Army, 1924; Specialist Physician, Aldershot Command; retired 1927. Vice-Convener of Shetland, 1934-35. MP (U) Orkney and Shetland, 1935-50. Hon. Col 430 Coast Regt RA (Orkney and Shetland) TA, 1950-56. Granted Hon. rank of Colonel 1956. Col comdg A1 Sector Home Guard, 1952-56. Hon. Col 861 (Indep.) LAA Battery, RA (Orkney and Zetland) TA 1957-58. Mem. Scottish Cttee The Nature Conservancy 1948-62 and of The Nature Conservancy, 1955-62, Chairman of the Scottish Cttee, 1955-62. Lord Lieutenant for the County of Zetland, 1952-63. *Address:* Busta House, Brae, Shetland. *T:* Brae 209. *Club:* Caledonian.

**NEVILL,** family name of **Marquess of Abergavenny.**

**NEVILL, Air Vice-Marshal Sir Arthur de Terrotte,** KBE 1950 (CBE 1941); CB 1946; CEng; FRAeS; Director of Civil Aviation, New Zealand, 1956-64, retired; Royal New Zealand Air Force; *b* 29 April 1899; *s* of late H. G. Nevill; *m* 1927, Mary Seton, *d* of E. T. Norris; two *d. Educ:* Auckland Grammar School; Royal Military College, Duntroon. BSc 1921; MSc 1952. Chief of Air Staff, NZ, 1946-51; Member Air Licensing Authority, 1952; Deputy Director of Civil Aviation, New Zealand, Nov. 1952-56. President NZ Div., RAeS, 1949-52. Member: NZ Univ. Grants Cttee, 1955-68 (Dep.-Chm., 1961-68); Research and Scholarships Cttee, UGC; US Educational Foundation in NZ, 1958; NZ Architects Educn and Registration Board, 1964-; Pres. Air Force Association, 1967. Hon. DUniv. Waikato, 1969. Legion of Merit (USA). *Address:* 29 Moana Road, Kelburn, Wellington 5, New Zealand. *Clubs:* United Service; Wellington (Wellington).

**NEVILL, Col Charles William,** OBE 1943; TD and Clasps, 1943; JP; Lord Lieutenant for Carmarthenshire since 1967; *b* 16 Aug. 1907; *o s* of late Col R. A. Nevill, DSO, TD, JP, DL; *m* 1947, Philippa (JP 1968), *o d* of late Capt. H. P. Farrel, sometime Principal of Sinde Univ. Karachi; two *s. Educ:* Clifton College. Chm. and Man. Dir, Nevill, Druce & Co. Ltd; Man. Dir, Nevill's Dock & Railway Co. Ltd; Gen. Comr of Income Tax for Kidwelly Div., 1961; Mem., T&AFA (Carms), 1945 (Chm., 1960-66); Trustee, SW Wales Savings Bank; Patron: Carms Co. Br., British Legion; Carms Red Cross Soc.; Carms Young Farmers Club. President: Carms County Scout Council; Forces Help Soc. and Lord Roberts Workshops for Carms; Sailors', Soldiers' and Airmen's Society for Carms; NSPCC for Carms; St John Council for Carms; Carms Community Council. Sec. and Treasurer, Ferryside Lifeboat Stn RNLI, 1949-60 (when closed). JP 1950, DL 1956, Vice-Lieut 1967, Carmarthenshire. 2nd Lt 4th (Carms) Bn The Welch Regt TA, 1926; Capt. 1931; psc Camberley, 1939; Maj. 1940; Lt-Col 1942. Served War of 1939-45: Norway, 1940; Middle East, Persia and Iraq, N Africa, Corsica, Italy, 1940-45; AQMG British Troops in Egypt, 1942, AFHQ 1943. Hon. Col, 4th (Carms) Welch Cadet Force, 1963-69. CStJ 1968. *Address:* Brondeg, Ferryside, Carmarthenshire. *T:* Ferryside 238.

**NEVILL, Maj.-Gen. (Retired) Cosmo Alexander Richard,** CB 1958; CBE 1954; DSO 1944; War Office, 1958-60; Colonel, Royal Fusiliers, 1959-63; *b* 14 July 1907; *s* of late Maj. Cosmo Charles Richard Nevill, DSO, OBE, Eccleston, Leamington Spa; *m* 1934, Grania, *d* of late Maj. G. V. Goodliffe, MC, Birdstown, co. Donegal; one *s* one *d. Educ:* Harrow; Royal Military College. Commissioned as Second Lieutenant, Royal Fusiliers, 1927; served War of 1939-45 (DSO, OBE): on staff, India; commanded 2nd battalion Devonshire Regiment, Normandy; Lieutenant-Colonel, 1944. A General Staff Officer, Military Staff Committee, United Nations, New York, 1946-48; commanded 1st battalion Royal Fusiliers, 1950-51; temporary Brigadier, 1951; a Brigade Commander, 1951-54; Commandant School of Infantry, 1954-56; Major-General 1957; GOC 2nd Infantry Division, 1956-58. CC West Suffolk, 1962. *Address:* Holt, Edwardstone, Boxford, Suffolk. *T:* Boxford 428. *Clubs:* Army and Navy, MCC; Suffolk County (Bury St Edmunds).

**NEVILL, Lord Rupert Charles Montacute;** JP; DL; Member of London Stock Exchange; Treasurer to the Duke of Edinburgh since 1970; *b* 29 Jan. 1923; 2nd *s* of 4th Marquess and *b* and *heir-pres* of 5th Marquess of Abergavenny, *qv*; *m* 1944, Lady Anne Camilla Eveline Wallop, *e d* of 9th Earl of Portsmouth, *qv*; two *s* two *d. Educ:* Eton. JP 1953, DL 1960, Sussex; High Sheriff of Sussex, 1952-53. Captain, Life Guards, ADC to Lt-Gen. Sir Brian Horrocks, 1945-47. Director: Sun Life Assurance Society; Owners of Middlesbrough Estates Co.; Travel Credit Ltd; National Group of Unit Trusts; West Cumberland Silk Mills; Australian Estates; Household and General Insurance Co. Ltd. President: S Eastern Area Building Socs, 1960; S Eastern Area Trustee Savings Bank, 1964; Vice-Pres., Building Societies Assoc., 1960. Pres. Metropolitan Union of YMCAs, 1956; Mem., World Council of YMCAs, 1956; Vice-Chm., National YMCA, 1963, Pres., 1966. Vice-Chm., Nat. Playing Fields Assoc., 1963-; Chairman: British Olympic Assoc., 1966-; Invalid Children's Aid Assoc., 1969-; Sussex Army Cadets, 1951-68; Greater London and SE Regional Sports Council, 1969-; Vice-Pres., Sussex Boy Scouts, 1950; Vice-Pres., Sussex Boys' Clubs; Pres., Sussex St John Ambulance Cadets, 1952-61; Commander, Sussex St John Ambulance Bde, 1969- (Pres. 1961-69); Mem., Sussex St John's Council, 1952, Chm., 1966-. Member: E Sussex CC, 1954-67; Uckfield RDC, 1949-67. CStJ 1968. *Address:* Horsted Place, Uckfield, Sussex. *T:* Isfield 315; 20A Stanhope Gdns, SW7. *T:* 01-370 1800. *Clubs:* White's, Bucks, Beefsteak.

**NEVILL, Rev. Thomas Seymour,** FRSA; Master of Charterhouse since 1962; Speaker's Chaplain, since 1969; *b* 30 Oct. 1901; *s* of late T. G. Nevill, FSA and late Mrs Nevill; *m* 1966, Muriel Pite (*née* Tasker), *widow* of A. G. Pite. *Educ:* Dover Coll.; Jesus Coll., Cambridge. Westcott House, Cambridge, 1956. BA, 1923; MA, 1926; 2nd Class Honours Mod. and Med. Languages Tripos and Historical Tripos; Asst Masterships at Llandovery Coll., Dover Coll. and Weymouth Coll.; Assoc. Member of Headmasters' Conference; Welsh Hockey XI, 1927, 1929 and 1930; Schools' Secretary of Student Christian Movement, 1934-37; Headmaster of Wellingborough School, 1940-56; a Governor of several schools. Ordained Deacon, 1956; Priest, 1957. Curate at Fareham Parish Church, 1956-58; Charterhouse Missioner in Southwark, 1958-62. Pres., Sion College, 1967-68. *Recreations:* rock-climbing and photography. *Address:* The Master's Lodge, Charterhouse, EC1. *T:* 01-253 0272. *Club:* Hawks (Cambridge).

**NEVILLE,** family name of **Baron Braybrooke.**

**NEVILLE, Prof. Adam Matthew,** MC 1944; TD 1963; Head of Department of Civil Engineering, University of Leeds, since 1968; *b* 5 Feb. 1923; *m* 1952, Mary Hallam Cousins; one *s* one *d*. BSc 1st cl. Hons, MSc, PhD, DSc (Eng) London; FICE, FIStructE. Lectr, Southampton Univ., 1950-51; Engr, Min. of Works, NZ, 1951-54; Lectr, Manchester Univ., 1955-60; Prof. of Civil Engrg, Nigerian Coll. of Technology, 1960-62; Dean of Engrg, Calgary Univ., 1963-67, also Dean of Graduate Studies, 1965-66; Vis. Prof., Swiss Federal Inst. of Technology, 1967-68. Mem. Council, Concrete Soc., 1968- (Chm. Educ. Cttee, 1969-); British Delegate to Concrete Commn of RILEM (Internat. Union of Testing and Research Laboratories for Materials and Structures); Mem. Editorial Boards: Magazine of Concrete Research; Internat. Jl Mechanical Sciences; Jl Cement and Concrete Research; Chm., Editorial Cttee of Univ. of Leeds Review. Queen Mary Coll. Prize, 1950; Univ. of London Postgraduate Scholarship, 1950; NZ Instn of Engineers Prize, 1952; IStructE Research Award, 1960; Reinforced Concrete Assoc. Medal, 1961; Senior Research Fellowship, Nat. Research Council of Cananda, 1967. Stanton Walker Award (US) 1968; IStructE (Yorkshire) Prize, 1970. *Publications:* Properties of Concrete, 1963; (with J. B. Kennedy) Basic Statistical Methods, 1964; (ed) Symposium on Creep of Concrete, 1964; (ed) Bibliography on Creep of Concrete, 1967; Creep of Concrete: plain, reinforced and prestressed, 1970; (with A. Ghali) Structural Analysis: a unified classical and matrix approach, 1971; Hardened Concrete: physical and mechanical aspects, 1971; numerous research papers on concrete and concrete structures. *Recreations:* ski-ing, ski patrol service. *Address:* Charles Morris Hall, Mount Preston, Leeds 2; Creep Cottage, Spring Hill, Tile Lane, Adel, West Yorkshire.

**NEVILLE, Bertie Aylmer Crampton,** CIE 1941; *b* 7 Oct. 1882; *s* of Col W. B. Neville, Inniskilling Fus., Moyfin, Co. West Meath; *m* 1911, Mabel Jess (*d* 1957), *d* of J. O'B. Sceales, Bankura, Bengal; two *s*. *Educ:* Corrig School, Kingstown; Royal College of Surgeons, Ireland. Five years with Bank of Ireland; joined Bank of Bengal, 1906; and Imperial Bank of India, 1921, on amalgamation of Presidency Banks; Sec. and Treas., Calcutta, and a Director of the Bank, 1933-41. *Recreations:* golf, photography, fishing. *Address:* C'an Neville, Atalaya Estate, Paguera, Majorca. *Clubs:* East India and Sports; Bengal (Calcutta).

**NEVILLE, Sir Edmund;** *see* Neville, Sir J. E. H.

**NEVILLE, Lt-Col Sir (James) Edmund (Henderson),** 2nd Bt, *cr* 1927; MC 1918; *b* 5 July 1897; *er s* of Sir Reginald James Neville Neville, 1st Bt and Ida (*d* 1913), 4th *d* of Lt-Col Sir Edmund Y. W. Henderson, KCB, RE; *S* father 1950; *m* 1932, Marie Louise *o d* of C. E. Pierson, Flesk, Burnham, Somerset; two *d*. *Educ:* Eton; RMC Sandhurst. Served European War, 1914-19 (wounded, MC); joined 52nd Light Infantry, 1916; with 43rd Light Infantry to North Russia, 1919 (wounded); captain and adjutant, 1923; Regular Reserve of Officers, 1925; served in 12th London Regt (Rangers), 1931-36; Major; Master Worshipful Company of Bowyers, 1936-38; War of 1939-45, recalled, Aug. 1939; in command Light Infantry Training Centre, 1941-44; trooping, 1945-46; retd as Lt-Col, July 1946. Prime Warden, Fishmongers' Co., 1958; Governor of Gresham's School. Mem. Council, Small Industries in Rural Areas. *Publication:* History of 43rd Light Infantry, 1914-19. *Heir: half-b* Richard Lionel John Baines Neville [*b* July 1921. *Educ:* Eton; Trinity College, Cambridge (MA). Served Burma, 1943-45, as Captain Oxford and Bucks LI, and West African Frontier Force]. *Address:* Sloley Old Hall, Norwich, NOR 14Z. *T:* Swanton Abbot 232. *Clubs:* Army and Navy, Greenjackets, Light Infantry.

*See also R. M. Vick.*

**NEVILLE, John,** OBE 1965; actor, stage and film; Director, Howard & Wyndham Ltd, since 1968; Hon. Professor in Drama, Nottingham University, since 1967; *b* Willesden, 2 May 1925; *s* of Reginald Daniel Neville and Mabel Lillian (*née* Fry); *m* 1949, Caroline Hooper; five *c*. *Educ:* Willesden and Chiswick County Schools; Royal Academy of Dramatic Art. Worked as a stores clerk before studying at RADA. First appearance on stage, walking-on part in Richard II; subseq. parts at Open Air Theatre, in repertory at Lowestoft, and with Birmingham Repertory Co.; Bristol Old Vic Co., 1950-53; Old Vic Co., London, 1953-61; Nottingham Playhouse, 1961-63; Theatre Director, Nottingham Playhouse, 1963-68; Dir, Park Theatre Co., Fortune, 1969. Parts with Old Vic include: Ferdinand in The Tempest, Macduff, Richard II, Orlando in As You Like It, Henry Percy in Henry IV, Part I, Mark Antony; during Old Vic tour of Europe, 1958, Hamlet, Sir Andrew Aguecheek. Played lead in Irma La Douce, Lyric, 1959-60; produced Henry V, Old Vic, 1960; The Lady From the Sea, Queen's, 1961; The School for Scandal, Haymarket, 1962; Alfie, Mermaid and Duchess, 1963. Acted in: The Chichester Festival Theatre, 1962; Beware of the Dog, St Martin's, 1967; Iago in Othello, Nottingham Playhouse, 1967; Mr and Mrs, Palace, 1968; The Apple Cart, Mermaid, 1970. Tour W Africa (Jt Dir and acting), 1963. *Films:* Oscar Wilde; Topaze; Billy Budd; A Study in Terror. Has appeared on television, incl. The First Churchills, series for BBC 2. *Address:* c/o Peter Crouch Ltd, 12 Orange Street, WC2.

**NEVILLE, Captain Philip Lloyd,** CVO 1954; *b* 7 Oct. 1888; 2nd *s* of late Admiral Sir George Neville, KCB, CVO; *m* 1942, Eleanor Fellowes, Toronto, Canada; two *s*. *Educ:* HMS Britannia. Served European War, 1914-18, and War of 1939-45. Gentleman Usher to King George VI, 1937, to The Queen, 1953-66; Extra Gentleman Usher, 1967-. Order of the Nile, Egypt, 4th Class. *Recreations:* shooting, country life. *Address:* Henstridge, Templecombe, Somerset. *T:* Stalbridge 253. *Club:* United Service.

**NEVILLE, Maj.-Gen. Sir Robert Arthur Ross,** KCMG 1952; CBE 1948; late RM; *b* 17 Dec. 1896; *s* of late Col William Neville, DSO, Cheshire Regt; *m* 1943, Doris Marie, *y d* of late Capt. Philip Collen, 14th Sikh Regiment; one *s* one *d*. *Educ:* Cheltenham College. Joined Royal Marines, 1914, served European War, 1914-18, Grand Fleet and France (despatches); Lt-Col, 1940; served War of 1939-45, Admlty, as Asst Dir of Naval Intelligence, Combined Ops, and in Mediterranean; Colonel, 1945; ADC to the King, 1946-48; Maj.-Gen., 1948. Governor and C-in-C, Bahamas, 1950-Dec. 1953. Dir, consortium Property Holdings, and other Cos. President, Palmerston Friendly Soc. *Address:* Oak Hanger, Reeds Lane, Liss, Hants. *T:* Liss 3325. *Club:* White's.

**NEVIN, Robert Wallace,** TD 1948; FRCS; Surgeon St Thomas' Hospital; Consulting Surgeon, Treloar's Hospital, Alton, Hants; Chief Surgeon to the Metropolitan Police since 1957; *b* Burton-on-Trent, Nov. 1907; *s* of Robert Nevin, medical practitioner, and Florence, *d* of Joseph Chamberlain, Burton-on-Trent; *m* 1947, Rosalind Audrey Leeson, *d* of late Rt Rev. Spencer Leeson, DD, Bishop of Peterborough, 1949-56; one *s* two *d*. *Educ:* Clifton; Emmanuel College, Cambridge. BA Cantab, 1929; MB, BChir Cantab, 1932; MRCS, LRCP 1932; FRCS 1933; MA Cantab 1933. Teacher of Surgery in Univ. of London, 1949; Dean, St Thomas's Hosp. Med. Sch., 1957-68; Mem. Bd of Governors, St Thomas' Hosp., 1955-70. Examiner in Surgery, Universities of Cambridge, London, Glasgow; Hunterian Professor Royal College of Surgeons, 1947; Col RAMC (TA), 1947. *Publications:* numerous papers in medical and surgical jls. *Recreations:* gardening, fishing. *Address:* 53 Harley Street, W1. *T:* 01-580 1077; The Old Forge, Greywell, Basingstoke, Hants. *T:* Odiham 2217. *Club:* Athenæum.

**NEVIN, Samuel,** FRCP; retired as Physician, Maida Vale Hospital, and neurologist, King's College Hospital; *s* of Samuel Nevin, District Inspector, Royal Ulster Constabulary; *m* 1950, Margaret Esch; one *s* one *d*. *Educ:* Methodist College, Belfast, Queen's Univ., Belfast. BSc (1st Cl. Hons) 1929; MB, BCh, BAO (1st Cl. Hons) Belfast 1927; MD (Gold Medal) 1930; MRCP 1934; FRCP 1941. Formerly: House Physician, National Hospital, Queen Square; Director Research Laboratory, Inst. Psych., Maudsley Hosp.; Prof. Mental Pathology, Univ. of London. Hon. Lt-Col RAMC. *Publications:* contributions to medical journals. *Address:* 17 Malmains Way, Beckenham, Kent.

**NEVIN, Thomas Richard,** TD 1949 (and Bar), LLB; JP; **His Honour Judge Nevin;** Judge of County Courts (Circuit 16) since 1967; Deputy Chairman of Quarter Sessions: West Riding, since 1965, East Riding, since 1968, Yorkshire; *b* 9 Dec. 1916; *e s* of late Thomas Nevin, JP, and Phyllis (*née* Strickland), Ebchester Hall and Mirfield; *m* 1955, Brenda Micaela, *e d* of Dr B. C. Andrade-Thompson, MC, Scarborough; one *s* (and one *s* decd). *Educ:* Bilton Grange; Shrewsbury School; Leeds University. LLB 1939. Commnd W Yorks Regt (Leeds Rifles) TA, 1935. Served London Bombardment, India and Burma, 1939-46; Indian Artillery, Lt-Col 1944 (despatches); DJAG, XII Army, 1945. Major, TARO, 1951. WR Special Constab., 1938-66 (Queen's Medal). Articled Clerk to Sir A. M. Ramsden, Solicitor, 1935. Called to Bar, Inner Temple, 1948; NE Circuit; Law Lectr, Leeds Coll. of Commerce, 1949-51; Asst Recorder of Leeds, 1961-64; Recorder of Doncaster, 1964-67; Chm., Northern Agricultural Land Tribunal, 1963-67 (Dep. Chm. 1961-63). Director, Bowishott Estates Ltd; Member: Leeds Gp Hospital Management Cttee, 1965-67; Thoresby Soc.; Yorks Archæological Soc.; President, Yorks Numismatic Soc., 1968; Life Member: Guild of Freemen of London; British Numismatic Soc.; Vice-Pres. Leeds Univ. Law Graduates; Associate OStB Nashdom Abbey. FRNS; FRSA; FRGS; Fellow, Inst. of Arbitrators. Freeman of City of London. *Publications:* Hon. Editor, Yorkshire Numismatic Soc.; and various articles. *Recreations:* coinage, our past, gardening, and rest therefrom. *Address:* Rawdon Hall, Rawdon, Yorks; Wooley Park, Allendale; Coomboots, Scalby, Yorks; 11 King's Bench Walk, Temple, EC4. *T:* 01-236 3337.

**NEVINS, Prof. Allan;** author and teacher, USA; formerly Distinguished Senior Research Associate, Huntington Library, San Marino, California; *b* 20 May 1890; *s* of Joseph A. Nevins and Emma Stahl; *m* 1916, Mary Fleming Richardson; two *d*. *Educ:* University of Illinois; Columbia University. Instructor in English Literature, Univ. of Illinois, 1912-13; editorial staff NY Nation, 1913-18; editorial staff, NY Evening Post, 1913-23; Literary Editor NY Sun, 1923-25; editorial staff NY World, 1925-27; professor of history, Cornell Univ., 1927-28; associate in history at Columbia Univ. and asst editor NY World, 1928-31; holder of Sir George Watson Chair in British universities, 1934-35; visiting professor California Institute of Technology, 1937; Harmsworth professor of American history at Oxford, 1940-41, 1964-65; De Witt Clinton Professor of American History, Columbia University, 1931-58; staff Huntington Library, 1958-69; Pres. Amer. Acad. of Arts and Letters, 1965-68; special representative Office of War Information in Australia and NZ, 1943-44; Chief Public Affairs Officer Amer. Embassy, London (summers), 1946-47; visiting prof., Univ. of Jerusalem, 1951-52; Prof., Claremont Colls, 1968-69. Founder: Oral Hist. Research Office, Columbia Univ., 1948; Nevins Chair in Economic History, Columbia Univ., 1965. Chm., US Civil War Centennial Commn, 1961-66; Editor-in-Chief, 15 vol Impact Series for Civil War Centennial Commn; Life Mem., Bd of Dirs of Woodrow Wilson Internat. Center for Scholars, 1969. Hon. DLitt Oxford, 1965. Alexander Hamilton Award, Columbia Univ., 1968. *Publications:* Life of Robert Rogers, 1914; History of the University of Illinois, 1918; American Social History Recorded by British Travellers, 1923; The American States During and After the Revolution, 1925; The Evening Post: A Century of Journalism, 1925; The Emergence of Modern America, 1927; Henry S. White: Thirty Years of American Diplomacy, 1930; Grover Cleveland: A Study in Courage, 1932 (Pulitzer Prize for best biography of the year); Abram S. Hewitt, With Some Account of Peter Cooper, 1935; Life of Hamilton Fish, 1936 (Pulitzer prize for best biography of year); The Gateway to History, 1938; Frémont, Pathmaker of the West, 1939; John D. Rockefeller: The Heroic Age of American Business, 1940; American Foreign Policy in the Light of its Recent History, 1941; A Brief History of the United States, 1941; This is England To-Day, 1941; (with J. B. Brebner) The Making of Modern Britain, 1943; (with H. S. Commager) America, The Story of a Free People, 1944; The Ordeal of the Union (awarded Scribner Centenary Prize and Bancroft Prize, 1947); America Through British Eyes, 1948; The Emergence of Lincoln, (with Frank E. Hill) Ford: the Times, the Man, the Company, 1953; Study in Power: John D. Rockefeller, Industrialist and Philanthropist, 1953; Ford: Expansion and Challenge, 1957; The War for the Union: The Improvised War, 1861-1862, 1959; The War for the Union: War Becomes Revolution, 1862-1863, 1960; The State Universities and Democracy, 1962; Ford: Decline and Rebirth, 1962; Herbert H. Lehman and His Era, 1962; (with Ralph Hidy and Frank E. Hill) Timber and Men–The Weyerhaeuser Story, 1963; James Truslow Adams: Historian of the American Dream, 1968; also Editor: Polk, The Diary of a President, 1845-1849, 1929; The Diaries of Philip Hone, 1936; Letters and Journal of Brand Whitlock, 1936; (with J. Mirsky) The World of Eli Whitney, 1952; Diary of the Civil War, 1860-1865: George Templeton Strong, 1952; Statesmanship of the Civil War, 1953; John C. Frémont, Narratives of Exploration and Adventure, 1956; A Portion of that Field: The Centennial of the Burial of Lincoln, Commemorative Papers by Various Authors, 1957; A Diary of Battle: The Personal Journals of Col Charles S. Wainwright, 1861-1865, 1966; Leatherstocking Saga: James Fenimore Cooper, 1966; The Burden and the Glory: Speeches of John F. Kennedy, 1964; Frémont's Geographical Memoir, 1964. *Recreations:* golf, fishing. *Address:* 1820 White

Oak Drive, Menlo Park, California, USA. *Clubs:* Athenæum; Century, Lotos, Columbia Faculty (New York); National Press (Washington).

**NEW GUINEA, Bishop of,** since 1963; **Rt. Rev. Geoffrey David Hand;** *b* 11 May 1918; *s* of Rev. W. T. Hand. *Educ:* Oriel College, Oxford; Cuddesdon Theological College. BA 1941, MA 1946. Deacon, 1942; Priest, 1943. Curate of Heckmondwike, 1942-46; Missioner, Diocese of New Guinea, 1946-50; Priest in charge: Sefoa, 1947-48; Sangara, 1948-50; Archdeacon, North New Guinea, 1950-65; Bishop Coadjutor of New Guinea, 1950-63. *Address:* PO Box 806, Port Moresby, Papua and New Guinea.

**NEW GUINEA, Assistant Bishop of;** *see* Ambo, Rt Rev. G. S.

**NEW WESTMINSTER, Archbishop of,** since 1968; **Most Rev. Godfrey Philip Gower,** DD; Metropolitan of British Columbia; *b* 5 Dec. 1899; *s* of William and Sarah Ann Gower; *m* 1932, Margaret Ethel Tanton; two *s* one *d*. *Educ:* Imperial College, University of London; St John's College, Winnipeg, University of Manitoba. Served RAF, 1918-19. Deacon 1930; Priest 1931; Rector and Rural Dean of Camrose, Alta, 1932-35; Rector of Christ Church, Edmonton, Alta, 1935-41; Exam. Chaplain to Bishop of Edmonton, 1938-41; Canon of All Saints' Cathedral, 1940-44. Chaplain, RCAF, 1941-44. Rector of St Paul's, Vancouver, 1944-51; Bishop of New Westminster, 1951. Holds Hon. doctorates in Divinity. *Address:* 610 West 49th Avenue, Vancouver 13, BC, Canada. *T:* 327-4045.

**NEW WESTMINSTER, Coadjutor Bishop of;** *see* Somerville, Rt Rev. T. D.

**NEW YORK, Bishop of,** since 1950; **Rt. Rev. Horace W(illiam) B(aden) Donegan,** DD; *b* Matlock, Derbyshire, England, 17 May 1900; *s* of Horace George Donegan and Pembroke Capes Hand. *Educ:* St Stephen's, Annandale, NY; Oxford University, England; Harvard Divinity School; Episcopal Theological Seminary. Rector, Christ Church, Baltimore, 1929-33; Rector, St James' Church, NYC, 1933-47; Suffragan Bishop of New York, 1947-49; Bishop Coadjutor of New York, 1949-50; President, Province of New York and New Jersey, 1962-68. Vice-Pres., Pilgrims, USA; President: School for Deaconesses; St Hilda's and St Hugh's Sch., NY; Galludet Home, Poughkeepsie; Bell Home, NY; Gen. Theol Seminary, NY; Episcopal Mission Soc., NY; Soc. for Religion and Learning, NY; Estate and Property, Diocese of NY; Cathedral Chapter, St John the Divine, NY; Widows and Orphans, NY; Convention of Diocese of NY; Episcopal Visitor: Holy Cross Monastery; Community of St Mary; Sisters of St Helena; Community of the Holy Spirit; Trustee: St Luke's Hosp., NY; Seminary of Puerto Rico; Band Coll., Annandale, NY; Chm., House of Bishops Overseas Mission; Mem., Mayor of NY Commn on Race and Religion; Award, Conf. of Christians and Jews; Hon. President: Seamen's Church Inst.; Youth Consultation Service, NY, Churchill Fellow, Westminster Coll., Fulton, Mo. Hon. degrees: DD New York Univ., 1940; STD Hobart, 1948; STD General Theological Seminary, 1949; DD Univ. of South, 1949; DD Trinity, 1950; DCL Nashotah, 1956; DD Bard, 1957; DD King's Univ., Halifax, 1958; STD Columbia Univ., 1960; Sub Prelate OStJ, 1956; Grand Cross St Joanikije, 1956; Legion of Honour, France, 1957; CBE (Hon.) 1957; Silver Medal of Red Cross of Japan, 1959; Holy Panakie from Armenian Church, 1960; Grand Kt, Order of St Denys of Zante (Greece), 1959. *Publications:* articles in religious publications. *Recreations:* golf, swimming, painting. *Address:* The Bishop's House, Cathedral Heights, New York 25, NY, USA. *T:* Riverside 9-1100. *Clubs:* Athenæum, National (London); Union, Union League, Pilgrims, Century Association, Columbia Faculty, British Schools and Universities, Oxford and Cambridge, St George's Society, Tuxedo Park (all of New York).

**NEW ZEALAND, Primate and Archbishop of,** since 1961; Bishop of Waiapu since 1947; **Most Rev. Norman Alfred Lesser;** MA Cantab; ThD 1962; DD Lambeth 1963; *b* 16 March 1902; *s* of Albert Lesser, Liverpool; *m* 1930, Beatrice Barnes, Southport; one *d*. *Educ:* Liverpool Collegiate Sch.; Fitzwilliam Hall and Ridley Hall, Cambridge. Curate St Simon and St Jude, Anfield, Liverpool, 1925-26; Curate Holy Trinity, Formby, Lancs, 1926-29; Liverpool Cathedral, 1929-31; Vicar St John, Barrow-in-Furness, 1931-39; Rector and Sub-Dean, Nairobi Cathedral, 1939; Provost of Nairobi, 1942. *Recreation:* model-making. *Address:* Bishopscourt, Napier, New Zealand. *TA:* Bishopscourt, Napier. *T:* Napier 7846.

**NEWALL,** family name of **Baron Newall.**

**NEWALL,** 2nd Baron, *cr* 1946; **Francis Storer Eaton Newall;** *b* 23 June 1930; *o s* of 1st Baron (Marshal of the RAF Lord) Newall, GCB, OM, GCMG, CBE, AM; *S* father, 1963; *m* 1956, Pamela Elizabeth, *e d* of E. H. L. Rowcliffe, Pinkney Park, Malmesbury, Wilts; two *s* one *d*. *Educ:* Eton College; RMA Sandhurst. Commissioned into 11th Hussars (Prince Albert's Own), 1950; served in: Germany, 1950-53; Malaya, 1953-55; on staff of GHQ FarELF, Singapore, 1955-56; Adjt Royal Gloucestershire Hussars, 1956-58; retired 1961. *Recreations:* shooting, travel, meeting people. *Heir: s* Hon. Richard Hugh Eaton Newall, *b* 19 Feb. 1961. *Address:* The Old Manor, Farmingville Road, Ridgefield, Conn 06877, USA; c/o Glyn, Mills & Co., 67 Lombard Street, EC3. *Clubs:* Cavalry, United Hunts.

**NEWARK, Archdeacon of;** *see* Woodhams, Ven. Brian Watson.

**NEWARK, Prof. Francis Headon,** CBE 1960; BCL, MA; of Lincoln's Inn, Barrister-at-Law; Professor of Civil Law, Queen's University, Belfast, since 1963; Member, Commission on the Constitution, since 1969; *b* 25 Sept. 1907; *yr s* of late Herbert Hardwick Newark, Leamington Spa; *m* 1934, Kathleen Mary Bainbridge; two *s* one *d*. *Educ:* Warwick School; Exeter College, Oxford. 1st Class Hons School of Jurisprudence, 1928; 1st Class BCL, 1929; Barrister-at-Law, Lincoln's Inn; Lecturer in Law, Queen's University, Belfast, 1937, Professor of Jurisprudence, 1946; Sec. to Academic Council, 1947; Pro-Vice-Chancellor, 1949; Chairman Belfast Hospitals Management Committee, 1950-62; Chm. Northern Ireland Poisons Board, 1956; Mem. Pilkington Cttee on Broadcasting, 1961-62. *Publications:* Editor Northern Ireland Law Reports, 1947-; papers in various legal journals. *Address:* Forest Winds, Ballycoan, Northern Ireland. *T:* Belfast 644102.

**NEWBIGIN, Rt. Rev. James Edward Lesslie;** *see* Madras, Bishop in.

**NEWBOLD, Sir Charles Demorée,** KBE 1970; Kt 1966; CMG 1957; QC (Jamaica) 1947; President, Court of Appeal for East Africa, 1966-70; *b* 11 June 1909; *s* of late Charles Etches and Laura May Newbold; *m* 1936,

Ruth, *d* of Arthur L. Vaughan; two *d. Educ:* The Lodge Sch., Barbados; Keble Coll., Oxford (BA). Called to Bar, Gray's Inn, 1931. Private practice at the Bar, Trinidad, 1931-35; joined Colonial Legal Service, 1936, as Principal Officer, Supreme Court Registry, Trinidad; Magistrate, Trinidad, 1937; Legal Draftsman, Jamaica, 1941; Solicitor-General Jamaica, 1943; Member of Commission of Enquiry into Land Taxation, Jamaica, 1942-43; represented Jamaica at Quarantine Conf. in Trinidad, 1943; at US Bases Conf. in Trinidad, 1944; at Washington, USA, for labour contracts, 1945; Actg Attorney-Gen., 1946; Legal Secretary, East Africa High Commn, 1948-61. Mem. of East Africa Central Legislative Assembly, 1948-61 (Chm. of Committee of Supply, 1948-61); Commissioner for Revision of High Commn Laws, 1951; Vice-Chm. Governing Council of Royal Technical Coll., 1954-59; Justice of Appeal, Court of Appeal for Eastern Africa, 1961-65; Vice-Pres., 1965-66. Star of Africa (Liberia). *Publications:* Joint Editor of Trinidad Law Reports, 1928-33; Editor of East African Tax Cases Reports, 1948-61. *Recreations:* cricket, tennis, croquet, reading. *Address:* Woodvale, Harpsden, Henley-on-Thames, Oxon. *Club:* East India and Sports.

**NEWBOROUGH,** 7th Baron, *cr* 1776; **Robert Charles Michael Vaughan Wynn,** Bt 1742; DSC 1942; *b* 24 April 1917; *er s* of 6th Baron Newborough, OBE, JP, DL, and Ruby Irene (*d* 1960), 3rd *d* of Edmund Wigley Severne, of Thenford, Northamptonshire and Wallop, Shropshire; *S* father, 1965; *m* 1945, Rosamund Lavington Barbour; one *s* two *d. Educ:* Oundle. Served as 2nd Lt, SR, 1935-39, with 9th Lancers, 5th Inniskilling Dragoon Guards, then as Lt with 16th/5th Lancers after 6 months attachment with Royal Dragoon Guards; invalided out of Army, 1940. Took command of vessel attached to Fleet Air Arm, 1940, as civilian, and took part in Dunkirk evacuation; then joined RNVR as Sub Lieut; later had command of MTB 74 and took part in St Nazaire raid, 1942 (wounded, despatches, DSC, POW, escaped 1944). High Sheriff of Merionethshire, 1963. *Recreation:* yachting. *Heir: s* Hon. Robert Vaughan Wynn, *b* 11 Aug. 1949. *Address:* Rhug, Corwen, North Wales. *T:* Corwen 2153; Belan Fort, Llandwrog, near Caernarvon, North Wales. *T:* Llanwnda 220. *Clubs:* Goat, Naval and Military; Bembridge Sailing.

*See also Hon. R. T. B. Wynn.*

**NEWBURGH,** Countess of (10th in line, *cr* 1660); **Donna Maria Sofia Giuseppina Giustiniani Bandini;** Viscountess Kynnaird, Baroness Levingston, 1660; *b* 4 May 1889; *d* of 9th Earl and Donna Maria, *d* of Prince di Trabia e di Butera, Palermo; *S* father, 1941; *m* 1922, Count Manfredi Gravina (*d* 1932). *Heir: cousin* Prince Giulio Cesare Taddeo Cosimo Rospigliosi [ *b* 26 Oct. 1907; *m* 1940, Donna Giulia Visconti di Modrone; two *s*]. *Address:* 5 Via Virginio Orsini, Rome.

*See also Baron Howard of Penrith, Lt-Col Hon. Henry A. C. Howard.*

**NEWBY, Percy Howard;** novelist; Controller, BBC Radio Three; *b* 25 June 1918; *o s* of Percy Newby and Isabel Clutsam (*née* Bryant); *m* 1945, Joan Thompson; two *d. Educ:* Hanley Castle Grammar Sch., Worcester; St Paul's Coll., Cheltenham. Served War of 1939-45, RAMC, 1939-42; BEF, France, 1939-40; MEF, 1941-42; seconded as Lecturer in English Literature, Fouad 1st University, Cairo, 1942-46. Joined BBC, 1949. Atlantic Award, 1946; Somerset Maugham Prize, 1948; Yorkshire Post Fiction Award, 1968; Booker Prize, 1969 (first recipient). *Publications:* A Journey to the Interior, 1945; Agents and Witnesses, 1947; The Spirit of Jem, 1947; Mariner Dances, 1948; The Snow Pasture, 1949; The Loot Runners, 1949; Maria Edgeworth, 1950; The Young May Moon, 1950; The Novel, 1945-50, 1951; A Season in England, 1951; A Step to Silence, 1952; The Retreat, 1953; The Picnic at Sakkara, 1955; Revolution and Roses, 1957; Ten Miles from Anywhere, 1958; A Guest and his Going, 1959; The Barbary Light, 1962; One of the Founders, 1965; Something to Answer For, 1968. *Address:* Upton House, Cokes Lane, Chalfont St Giles, Buckinghamshire. *T:* Little Chalfont 2079.

**NEWCASTLE,** 9th Duke of, *cr* 1756; **Henry Edward Hugh Pelham-Clinton-Hope,** OBE 1945; Earl of Lincoln, 1572; Wing Comdr, retd; *b* 8 April 1907; *o s* of 8th Duke and Olive Muriel (*d* 1912), *d* of George Horatio Thompson, banker, Melbourne, formerly wife of Richard Owen; *S* father 1941; *m* 1st, 1931, Jean (from whom he obtained a divorce 1940), *d* of D. Banks, Park Avenue, New York; 2nd, 1946, Lady Mary Diana Montagu-Stuart-Wortley (marr. diss., 1959), 2nd *d* of 3rd Earl of Wharncliffe; two *d*; 3rd, 1959, Mrs Sally Ann Wemyss Hope (Jamal), *d* of Brig. John Henry Anstice, DSO. *Educ:* Eton; Cambridge. Sqdn Ldr Comdg No. 616 Sqdn, 1938-39; served War of 1939-45 in RAF at home and overseas. *Heir: cousin* Edward Charles Pelham-Clinton, *b* 18 Aug. 1920. *Address:* Shockerwick House, Bath.

**NEWCASTLE, Bishop of,** since 1957; **Rt. Rev. Hugh Edward Ashdown,** MA, DD; *b* 5 July 1904; *s* of William Edward and Sarah Annie Constance Ashdown; *m* 1937, Georgina Sylvia (*née* Battye); one *s* two *d. Educ:* St John's, Leatherhead; Keble College, Oxford; Lincoln Theological College. Deacon, 1929; priest, 1930; curate of St Mary, Portsea, 1929-34; chaplain and lecturer, Lincoln Theol Coll., 1934-37; exam. chaplain to Bishop of Ripon, 1935-46; perpetual curate of St Aidan's, West Hartlepool, 1937-43; Rector of Houghton-le-Spring, 1943-48; Rector of St Saviour with St Peter, Southwark, and Provost of Southwark, 1948-57. *Address:* The Bishop's House, Moor Road South, Gosforth, Newcastle upon Tyne NE3 1PA. *T:* Gosforth 852220.

**NEWCASTLE, Assistant Bishop of;** *see* Ramsbotham, Rt Rev. John Alexander.

**NEWCASTLE, Provost of;** *see* Wolters, Very Rev. C. C.

**NEWCASTLE, NSW, Bishop of,** since 1958; **Rt. Rev. James Alan George Housden;** BA; *b* Birmingham, England, 16 Sept. 1904; *s* of William James and Jane Housden; *m* 1935, Elfreda Moira Hennessey; two *s* one *d. Educ:* Essendon High School; University of Queensland; St Francis College. BA 1st Class, Mental and Moral Philosophy, 1928; ThL 1st Class, 1929. Deacon, 1928; Priest, 1929. Curate St Paul's Ipswich, Qld, 1928-30; Chaplain, Mitchell River Mission, 1930-32; Curate All Souls' Cathedral, Thursday Island, 1932-33; Rector of Darwin, NT, 1933-37; Vicar of Coolangatta, Qld, 1936-40; Rector and Rural Dean, Warwick, 1940-46; Vicar of Christ Church, S Yarra, Melbourne, 1946-47; Bishop of Rockhampton, 1947-58. *Recreation:* bowls. *Address:* Bishop's Court, Newcastle, NSW 2300, Australia. *Club:* Newcastle (Newcastle NSW).

**NEWCASTLE, NSW, Dean of;** *see* Falkingham, Very Rev. J. N.

**NEWCOMB, Wilfrid Davison;** Professor of Morbid Anatomy, University of London, 1937-54; Emeritus Professor, 1954; Morbid Anatomist, St Mary's Hospital, Paddington, 1924-54; *b* 8 June 1889; *s* of Alfred J. Newcomb, Chatham; *m* 1920, Ann G. Nash (*d* 1963); no *c*. *Educ:* King's School, Rochester (King's Scholar); Liverpool Coll.; Trinity Coll., Cambridge (Open Exhibitioner); London Hosp. Med. Coll. First Class Nat. Sci. Tripos, 1910; Price Entrance Schol. London Hosp. Med. Coll., 1912; Surgeon First British Field Hosp., Serbia, 1915; Surgical Specialist Deccan British War Hosp., Poona, 1916; Asst in Inst. of Pathology, London Hosp., 1919; Asst Pathologist, St Mary's Hosp., 1920. Erasmus Wilson Lecturer, RCS, 1928; Examiner in Pathology, Univ. of Cambridge, 1929; Raymond Horton Smith Prize, 1931; Examiner in Pathology, Univ. of London, 1932; Pathologist in EMS, 1939; Chm. Board of Studies in Pathology, Univ. of London, 1947. *Publications:* papers in medical press, chiefly on cancer. *Recreation:* gardening. *Address:* The Hive, Wellesley Road, Andover, Hants. *T:* Andover 3328.

**NEWELL, Arthur (Franklin),** MA; John G. Winant Lecturer, British-American Associates; *b* 19 Dec. 1885; *s* of Elmer Ellsworth Newell, Boston, USA, and Emma A. Newell; *m* 1st, Lena Freeman, Boston, USA; 2nd, Desiree Ames, Frome, Somerset; two *s* three *d*. *Educ:* Boston English High School; Colby Academy; Brown University; Harvard Graduate School. General Secretary, Brown Union, Brown University; Educational Director, War Prisoners' Aid; Executive Secretary, European Division, International YMCA; Professor of International Relations, Robert College, Istanbul, Turkey; Senior Lecturer, British-American Associates; Founder and President, American Outpost in Great Britain; President, Books-Across-The-Sea; Joint Chairman, London International Assembly; President, The Kinsmen; American Rep. Liberal International Council; American Rep. Council of Atlantic Treaty Assoc.; Member Executive Committee David Davies Institute of International Affairs; Vice-Pres., Council for Education in World Citizenship; Sette of Odd Volumes (Pres. 1967-68). *Publications:* articles in various jls in Britain and USA. *Recreations:* music, backgammon and the cruder topiary arts. *Address:* 37 Charles Street, W1. *T:* 01-629 9579; The Green, Jordans, Bucks. *T:* Chalfont St Giles 3159.

**NEWELL, Rev. John Philip Peter;** Headmaster, The King's School, Canterbury, since 1962; *b* 4 Dec. 1911; *s* of late Joseph Newell and Edith Newell; *m* 1955, Mary, *d* of William and Alice Forbes; one *s*. *Educ:* Shrewsbury School; Magdalen Coll., Oxford. Classical Upper Sixth Form Master, Repton School, 1935-36; Assistant Priest, Ashbourne Parish Church, and Organizing Secretary, Derby Diocesan Youth Council, 1936-39; Assistant Master and Chaplain, Diocesan College, Rondebosch, Cape Town, 1939-43; Classical Upper Sixth Form Master and Chaplain, Sedbergh School, 1943-53; Headmaster, Bradford Grammar School, 1953-62. Select Preacher, University of Oxford, 1956, 1960. Hon. Canon, Canterbury Cathedral, 1963. *Recreations:* hills and rivers and village churches. *Address:* Precincts 14, Canterbury, Kent. *Clubs:* United University, Public Schools.

**NEWELL, Philip Staniforth,** CB 1961; Mathematics Master, Pierrepont School, Surrey, since 1969; *b* 1903; *m* 1927, Sylvia May Webb; two *s* one *d*. *Educ:* Uppingham; Emmanuel College, Cambridge (Scholar). First Class Part I, Mathematical Tripos, First Class Mechanical Sciences Tripos; Assistant Master at Uppingham; Chief Mathematical Master, Repton; Headmaster of Gresham's School, Holt, 1935-44; Admiralty, 1944-64; Imperial Defence College, 1955; Under-Secretary, 1956; Principal Finance Officer, 1961-65. Director, Greenwich Hosp., 1964-69. *Address:* Dawson's, Tilford, Surrey. *T:* Frensham 2787. *Club:* Athenæum.

**NEWENS, (Arthur) Stanley;** *b* 4 Feb. 1930; *s* of Arthur Ernest and Celia Jennie Newens, Bethnal Green; *m* 1st, 1954, Ann (*d* 1962), *d* of J. B. Sherratt, Stoke-on-Trent; two *d*; 2nd, 1966, Sandra Christina, *d* of J. A. Frith, Chingford; two *d*. *Educ:* Buckhurst Hill County High Sch.; University Coll., London (BA Hons History); Westminster Training Coll. (Post-Graduate Certificate of Education). Coal face worker in N Staffs mines, 1952-55. Secondary Sch. Teacher (LCC), 1956-65. MP (Lab) Epping, 1964-70. Active Member: Labour Party, holding numerous offices, 1949-; NUM, 1952-55; NUT, 1956-. Chm., Movement for Colonial Freedom, 1967-. *Recreations:* local historical research, family, reading. *Address:* The Leys, 18 Park Hill, Harlow, Essex. *T:* Harlow 20108.

**NEWENS, Stanley;** *see* Newens, A. S.

**NEWEY, John Henry Richard,** QC 1970; *b* 20 Oct. 1923; *s* of Lt-Col T. H. Newey; *m* 1953, Mollie Patricia (*née* Chalk); three *s* two *d*. *Educ:* Ellesmere Coll.; Queens' Coll., Cambrdige. Served Central India Horse, Indian Army, 1942-47 in India, Middle East, Italy and Greece (Captain, last British Adjt). Foundn Schol., Queens' Coll., Cambrdige, 1941-42 and 1947-49 (MA, LLB). Called to Bar, 1948. Prosecuting Counsel to Post Office, South Eastern Circuit, 1964-65; Standing Counsel to Post Office at Common Law, 1965-70; Personal Injuries Junior to Treasury, 1968-70; Dep. Chm., Kent County QS, 1970-. Contested (C) Cannock Div. of Staffs, 1955. Alternate Chm., Burnham and other Teachers' Remuneration Cttees, 1969-. Bronze Star (US), 1944. *Recreation:* excursions with family. *Address:* St David's, The Drive, Sevenoaks, Kent. *T:* Sevenoaks 54597.

**NEWFOUNDLAND, Bishop of,** since 1965; **Rt. Rev. Robert Lowder Seaborn;** *b* 9 July 1911; *s* of Rev. Richard Seaborn and Muriel Kathleen Reid; *m* 1938, Mary Elizabeth Gilchrist; four *s* one *d*. *Educ:* Univ. of Toronto Schs; Trinity Coll., Univ. of Toronto (MA); Oxford Univ. Deacon, 1934; Priest, 1935; Asst Curate, St Simon's, Toronto, 1934-36; Asst Curate, St James's Cathedral, Toronto, 1937-41; Rector, St Peter's, Cobourg, Ont., 1941-48; Chaplain, Canadian Army, 1942-45 (Padre Canadian Scottish Regt); Dean of Quebec and Rector of Parish of Quebec, 1948-57; Rector, St Mary's, Kerrisdale, Vancouver, BC, 1957-58; Asst Bishop of Newfoundland, 1958-65, Coadjutor, June-Dec. 1965. Croix de Guerre avec étoile de vermeil (French), 1945. DD, (*jure dignitatis*), Trinity Coll., 1948; DCL (*hc*), Bishop's Univ., 1962. *Publication:* Faith in our Time, 1963. *Recreations:* camping, golf. *Address:* Bishop's Court, 22 King's Bridge Road, St John's, Newfoundland, Canada.

**NEWHOUSE, Ven. Robert John Darrell;** Archdeacon of Totnes and Canon Residentiary of Exeter Cathedral since 1966; Treasurer of Exeter Cathedral, since 1970; *b* 11 May 1911; *s* of Rev. R. L. C. Newhouse; *m* 1938, Winifred (*née* Elton); two *s*. *Educ:* St Edward's Sch.; Worcester Coll., Oxford; Cuddesdon College. Ordained, 1936. Curate of: St John's, Peterborough, 1936-40; St Giles,

Cambridge, 1940-41; Chaplain, RNVR, 1941-46; Rector of Ashwater, Devon, 1946-56; Rural Dean of Holsworthy, 1954-56; Vicar of Littleham-cum-Exmouth, 1956-66; Rural Dean of Aylesbeare, 1965-66. *Recreation:* gardening. *Address:* 15 The Close, Exeter EX1 1EZ. *T:* 58947.

**NEWIS, Kenneth,** CB 1967; CVO 1970 (MVO 1958); Under-Secretary, Scottish Development Department, since 1970; *b* 9 Nov. 1916; *o s* of late H. T. and G. Newis, Manchester; *m* 1943, Kathleen, *o d* of John Barrow, Davenport, Cheshire; two *d. Educ:* Manchester Grammar Sch.; St John's Coll., Cambridge (Scholar). BA 1938, MA 1942. Entered HM Office of Works, 1938; Private Sec. to Minister of Works (Rt Hon. C. W. Key), 1948-49; Asst Sec., 1949; Under-Sec., 1959; Dir of Management Services, MPBW, 1969-70. Conservator of Wimbledon and Putney Commons, 1963-70. Crown Estate Paving Comr. Governor: Farrington's School; Richmond College, 1964-70. Chm., Merton Family Housing Trust. *Recreation:* music. *Address:* St Andrew's House, Edinburgh 1.

**NEWITT, Dudley Maurice,** MC 1918; FRS 1942; DSc, PhD; Professor Emeritus of Chemical Engineering in the University of London; *b* 1894. *Address:* Imperial College of Science, South Kensington, SW7. *Club:* Athenæum.

**NEWLEY, Edward Frank,** CBE 1960; Director, Atomic Weapons Research Establishment, Aldermaston, since 1965; *b* 9 June 1913; *s* of Frederick Percy Newley; *m* 1946, Sybil Madge Alvis; two *s* one *d. Educ:* King's Coll., London. 1st class hons BSc; MSc. GPO Engineering Dept, Radio Research Branch, 1937-44; GPO Factories Dept, 1944-49; Royal Naval Scientific Service, 1949-55; joined UKAEA, 1955; Dep. Director, AWRE, 1959. *Publications:* sundry scientific and technical papers. *Recreation:* landscape gardening. *Address:* Reades, Heads Hill, Newbury, Berks. *T:* Headley 371.

**NEWLEY, (George) Anthony;** Actor since 1946; Author, Composer; *b* 24 Sept. 1931; *m* 1956, Ann Lynn; *m* 1963, Joan Collins; one *s* one *d. Educ:* Mandeville Street Sch., Clapton, E5. Appeared on West End stage in: Cranks, 1955; Stop the World, I Want to Get Off (co-author and co-composer, with Leslie Bricusse), 1961-62; subseq. starred in New York production, 1962-63; The Roar of the Greasepaint–the Smell of the Crowd (co-author and composer, with Leslie Bricusse, star and director), New York, 1965. Has acted in over 40 films in last 17 years. Films include: Adventures of Dusty Bates; Oliver Twist; Up To His Neck; Cockleshell Heroes; High Flight; Idle on Parade; Jazz Boat; The Small World of Sammy Lee; Dr Doolittle; Sweet November; (wrote, produced and acted) Can Heironymus Merkin ever forget Mercy Humppe and find True Happiness?; (directed) Summertree, 1970. Television appearances include: Anthony Newley Shows; The Strange World of Gurney Slade, 1960-61; Johnny Darling Show, 1962; Lucky in London, 1966; appears on TV in USA. He is also a successful recording star. *Recreations:* photography, painting, fishing. *Address:* c/o Michael Oliver, Berger & Oliver Co., 40 Piccadilly, W1V 0ET.

**NEWMAN, Lieut-Colonel (Augustus) Charles,** VC 1945; OBE 1957; TD; MICE; Civil Engineering and Public Works Contractor; Chairman of the Federation of Civil Engineering Contractors, 1957-58; *b* 19 Aug. 1904; *s* of A. B. and Margaret Newman, Buckhurst Hill, Essex; *m* 1929, Audrey Hickman; one *s* five *d. Educ:* Bancroft's Sch., Essex. Joined firm of W. & C. French Ltd, Civil Engineering and Public Works Contractors, in 1922; retd as Chm., 1969. Commissioned 4th Battalion Essex Regt, 1925; War of 1939-45 (despatches; VC, St Nazaire). DL Essex, 1946-48. Légion d'Honneur, Croix de Guerre (France), 1947. *Address:* Bay House, Sandwich Bay, Kent. *T:* Sandwich 3000. *Club:* East India and Sports.

**NEWMAN, Charles;** *see* Newman, A. C.

**NEWMAN, Charles,** CBE 1965; MD (Cantab); FRCP; retired; Emeritus Dean, Postgraduate Medical School (now Royal Postgraduate Medical School); Harveian Librarian, since 1962, Royal College of Physicians; *b* 16 March 1900; *s* of Charles Arnold Newman and Kate Beck. *Educ:* Shrewsbury Sch.; Magdalene Coll., Cambridge (Scholar); King's College Hospital (Scholar). Murchison Scholar RCP, 1926; FRCP 1932; Volunteer Asst to Prof. Aschoff, Univ. of Freiburg i B. 1930; Hon. Treas., RSocMed, 1946-50; Fellow Medical Society of London (Orator, 1961); Hon. Member Assoc. of Physicians, 1965. Hon. Secretary, 1942-47. Hon. Treasurer, 1948-58; Mem., British Gastro-enterological Soc. (Pres., 1964); Gov. and Chm. of School Management Cttee, St Clement Dane's Sch.; Mem. Cttee of Management of Con-joint Board in England, 1958-68 (Chm., 1965-68). Goulstonian Lectr, 1933; FitzPatrick Lectr, 1954, 1955 and 1968; Linacre Fellow, 1966; Assistant Registrar, RCP, 1933-38; Sub-Editor, EMS, Official Medical History of the War, 1942-47; late Physician, Medical Tutor and Vice-Dean, King's College Hospital and Asst Physician, Belgrave Hospital for Children. *Publications:* Medical Emergencies, 1932, 3rd Edn 1946 and 1948; Evolution of Medical Education in the Nineteenth Century, 1957; articles in medical text-books and encyclopædias; papers on diseases of the liver and gall-bladder, medical history and education. *Address:* Basset, South Road, Oundle, Peterborough, Northants. *T:* Oundle 3310. *Club:* Athenæum.

**NEWMAN, Sir Geoffrey (Robert),** 6th Bt, *cr* 1836; *b* 2 June 1947; *s* of Sir Ralph Alured Newman, 5th Bt, and Ann Rosemary Hope, *d* of late Hon. Claude Hope-Morley; *S* father, 1968. *Educ:* Heatherdown, Ascot; Kelly Coll., Tavistock. Joined 1st Bn, Grenadier Guards, 1967. *Recreations:* shooting, sailing, all sports. *Heir: b* Richard Claude Newman, *b* 2 May 1951. *Address:* Blackpool House, Dartmouth, Devon. *T:* Stoke Fleming 261. *Club:* Guards.

**NEWMAN, Sir Gerard (Robert Henry Sigismund),** 3rd Bt, *cr* 1912; Director, The Rom River Co. Ltd, and other Companies; *b* 19 July 1927; *s* of Sir Cecil Gustavus Jacques Newman, 2nd Bt, and Joan Florence Mary, CBE (*d* 1969), *e d* of late Rev. Canon Hon. Robert Grimston; *S* father, 1955; *m* 1955; Caroline Philippa, *d* of late Brig. Alfred Geoffrey Neville, CBE, MC; three *s* one *d. Educ:* Eton; Jesus Coll., Oxford. *Recreation:* shooting. *Heir: s* Francis Hugh Cecil Newman, *b* 12 June 1963. *Address:* Burloes, Royston, Herts; 27 Bloomfield Terrace, SW1. *T:* 01-730 7540. *Clubs:* Carlton, Boodle's, MCC.

**NEWMAN, Maxwell Herman Alexander,** MA, FRS 1939; Professor Emeritus, University of Manchester; *b* 7 Feb. 1897; *m* 1934, Lyn, *d* of Rev. J. A. Irvine; two *s. Educ:* City of London School; St John's College, Cambridge; Vienna Univ., 1922-23. MA 1924; Fellow of St John's College, Cambridge, 1923-45; Rockefeller Research Fellow at Princeton, 1928-29; University Lecturer in Mathematics, Cambridge University, 1927-45; Fielden

Professor of Mathematics, Manchester Univ., 1945-64; Visiting Professor in Australian National Univ., 1964-65 and 1967; in Univ. of Wisconsin and Rice Univ., 1965-66. Roy. Soc. Coun., 1946-47; Pres., London Mathematical Soc., 1950-51; Pres. Mathematical Assoc., 1959. Hon. DSc Hull, 1968. Sylvester Medal of Royal Society, 1959; De Morgan Medal, 1962. *Publications:* Topology of Plane Sets of Points, 1939, 2nd Edn 1951; papers on mathematics in various journals. *Address:* Cross Farm, Comberton, Cambridge.

**NEWMAN, Philip Harker,** DSO 1940; MC; FRCS; Orthopædic Surgeon, Middlesex Hospital, Royal National Orthopædic Hospital, King Edward VII's Hospital for Officers, W1; *b* 22 June 1911; *s* of John Harker Newman, Mannofield, Ingatestone, Essex; *m* 1943, Elizabeth Anne, *er d* of Rev. G. H. Basset, Turners, Belchamp St Paul, Suffolk; two *s* one *d*. *Educ:* Cranleigh; Middlesex Hospital Medical School (Senior Broderip Scholar and 2nd Year Exhibitioner), MRCS, LRCP, 1934; FRCS, 1938; Hunterian Prof., RCS, 1954; late Lt-Col RAMC; Served War of 1939-45 (DSO, MC); FRSM (formerly Pres., Section of Orthopaedics); Fellow Brit. Orthopædic Assoc. (Vice-Pres., 1969-70); Mem. Council, British Jl of Bone and Joint Surgery; Member British Medical Association. *Publications:* The Prisoner of War Mentality, 1944; Early Treatment of Wounds of the Knee Joint, 1945; Sacroiliac Arthrodesis, 1946; The Etiology of Spondylolisthesis, 1962; The Spine, the Wood and the Trees, 1968; Spinal Fusion, Operative Surgery, 1969; Orthopædic Surgery, Medical Encyclopædia, 1956. *Address:* 107 Harley Street, W1. *T:* 01-935 2776; Hilltop, Watford Road, Radlett, Herts.

**NEWMAN, Prof. Sidney Thomas Mayow,** CBE 1962; MA Oxon; Hon. DMus Dunelm; FRSE; Hon. RAM 1962; FRCO; FTCL; Reid Professor of Music, University of Edinburgh, 1941-70; *b* 4 March 1906; 2nd *s* of late Julian B. Newman and Mary Clissold, Nailsworth, Glos.; *m* 1st, 1940, Joy (*d* 1943), *er d* of late J. G. Pickering, Newcastle on Tyne; one *s*; 2nd, 1946, Elizabeth, *e d* of late Dr J. D. H. Dickson, Edinburgh; three *s*. *Educ:* Clifton Coll.; Christ Church, Oxford; Royal Coll. of Music, London. Organ Scholar, 1924-28, Senior Scholar, 1928-30, Christ Church, Oxford; Wesley Exhibitioner, RCM, 1929. Lecturer in Music, Armstrong College (later King's College), Newcastle on Tyne, in the Univ. of Durham, 1930-41; Conductor Newcastle Bach Choir, 1930-41; Conductor Reid Orchestra, 1941-70; Cramb Lecturer, Glasgow, 1956; Choral and Orchestral Conductor various societies in Newcastle and Edinburgh; Pianoforte Recitalist. Member: Council, Edinburgh Festival Soc., 1946-68; Bd of Directors, Scottish Opera, 1962-70. *Publications:* articles in Music Review, Royal Mus. Assoc., etc. *Recreations:* chamber music; walking; collection and history of British road books and travelling maps. *Address:* Newmarket House, Nailsworth, Glos. *T:* Nailsworth 2715.

**NEWMAN, Sydney Cecil;** film and television producer and executive; Film Commissioner, Canadian Government and Chairman, National Film Board of Canada, since 1970; *b* Toronto, 1 April 1917; *m* 1944, Margaret Elizabeth, *d* of Rev. Duncan McRae, DD; three *d*. *Educ:* Ogden Public School and Central Technical School, Toronto. Painter, stage, industrial and interior designer; still and cinema photographer, 1935-41. Joined National Film Board of Canada under John Grierson as splicer-boy, 1941. Editor and Director of Armed Forces training films and war information shorts, 1942. Producer of Canada Carries On, 1945. Exec. Producer in charge of all films for cinemas, including short films, newsreels, films for children and travel, 1947-52. Over 300 documentaries, including: Suffer Little Children (UN), It's Fun to Sing (Venice Award), Ski Skill, After Prison What? (Canada Award). For Canadian Govt to NBC in New York to report on American television techniques, 1949-50. Joined Canadian Broadcasting Corporation as Television Director of Features and Outside Broadcasts, 1953. Superviser of Drama and Producer of General Motors Theatre, On Camera, Ford Theatre, Graphic, 1954. Produced first plays by Arthur Hailey, inc. Flight Into Danger, Course for Collision. Ohio State Award for Religious Drama; Liberty Award, Best Drama Series. Superviser of Drama and Producer Armchair Theatre, ABC Television, England, 1958-62; Head of Drama Group, TV, BBC, 1963-67; Producer, Associated British Productions Ltd, Elstree, 1968-69; Special Advisor to Chm. and Dir, Broadcast Programmes Branch, Canadian Radio and Television Commn, 1970. Producer: Stephen D, 1963; The Rise and Fall of the City of Mahagonny, 1965; The Tea Party, 1965. Commissioned and prod. first on-air plays of Alun Owen, Harold Pinter, Angus Wilson, Robert Muller, Peter Luke; also plays by Clive Exton and David Perry. FRSA; Fellow Soc. of Film and Television Arts. Desmond Davis Award, 1967, Soc. of Film and Television Arts; President's Award, 1969, and Zeta Award, 1970, Writers Guild of Great Britain. Kt of Mark Twain, USA. *Address:* National Film Board of Canada, 150 Kent Street, Ottawa, Ontario, Canada.

**NEWMAN-MORRIS, Sir Geoffrey,** Kt 1969; ED 1946; Chairman, Australian Red Cross Society, since 1958; *b* 14 May 1909; *s* of John and Eleanor Annie Newman-Morris; *m* 1945, Sheila, *d* of Martin Brown; two *s* one *d*. *Educ:* Melbourne Church of England Grammar Sch.; Trinity Coll., Univ. of Melbourne. MBBS Melbourne 1932, MS Melbourne 1936, FRCS 1937, FRACS 1938. Lt-Col, RAAMC (Ret.); served 1939-45, Mid. East and New Guinea (despatches 1944). Hon. Cons. Surg. Prince Henry's Hosp., Melbourne; Chm. Federal Assembly of Aust. Med. Assoc., 1967; Chief Surg., SJAB in Australia, 1969. Mem., Standing Commn, Internat. Red Cross, 1965-; Vice-Chm., League of Red Cross Socs, 1969-. KStJ 1964. *Publications:* contrib. med jls. *Recreations:* golf, bowls, fishing. *Address:* Flat 1, 111 Kooyong Koot Road, Hawthorn, Vic 3122, Australia. *T:* 81-4769. *Clubs:* Melbourne, Royal Melbourne Golf, Melbourne Cricket (Australia).

**NEWNHAM, Captain Ian Frederick Montague,** CBE 1955; RN Retired; *b* 20 Feb. 1911; *s* of late John Montague Newnham, OBE, DL, JP, and Hilda Newnham; *m* 1947, Marjorie Warden; no *c*. *Educ:* RN College, Dartmouth. Served War of 1939-45 (despatches). Captain, 1952; retd 1961. Lent to Indian Navy as Chief of Material, 1952-55; Chief of Staff to Admiral, British Joint Service Mission, and Naval Attaché, Washington, 1959-61. Gen. Manager, Precision Engineering Div., Short Brothers and Harland, Belfast, 1961-68. *Recreations:* golf, fishing. *Address:* Elsted Green, near Midhurst, Sussex. *Club:* United Service.

**NEWNS, Sir (Alfred) Foley (Francis Polden),** KCMG 1963 (CMG 1957); CVO 1961; MA Cantab; Secretary to the Cabinet, Government of the Bahamas, since December 1963; *b* 30 Jan. 1909; *s* of late Rev. Alfred Newns, AKC; *m* 1936, Jean, *d* of late A. H.

Bateman, MB, BS; one *s* one *d*. *Educ:* Christ's Hospital; St Catharine's College, Cambridge. Colonial Administrative Service, Nigeria, 1932; Sen. District Officer, 1951; Resident, 1951; Secretary to Council of Ministers, 1951; Secretary to Governor-General and the Council of Ministers, Federation of Nigeria, 1955-59; Dep. Governor, Sierra Leone, 1960-61; Acting Gov. during 1960; Adviser to the Government of Sierra Leone after Independence, 1961-63. FRSA 1969. *Recreations:* astronomy, swimming, photography. *Address:* Cabinet Office, PO Box 147, Nassau, Bahamas.

*See also J. Ounsted.*

**NEWNS, Sir Foley;** *see* Newns, Sir A. F. F. P.

**NEWNS, George Henry,** MD, FRCP; Physician, The Hospital for Sick Children, Great Ormond Street, WC1, since 1946; Dean, Institute of Child Health, University of London, since 1949; Pædiatrician to Barnet General Hospital, 1946-67; Civilian Pædiatric Consultant to the Admiralty, since 1962; Hon. Consultant in Pædiatrics to the Army since 1966; *b* 27 July 1908; *s* of late George Newns, Dartford, Kent; *m* 1936, Deirdre, *d* of Lawrence Kenny, Prior Park, Clonmel, Tipperary, Eire; one *s* one *d*. *Educ:* Whitgift School; King's Coll., and King's Coll. Hosp., London. MB, BS (London) 1931; MRCP 1932; MD (London), 1933; FRCP 1951. Registrar: Roy. Northern Hosp., 1933-34; to Children's Dept, King's Coll. Hosp., 1934-35; Med. Registrar and Pathologist, Hosp. for Sick Children, Gt Ormond St, 1935-38; Physician: Bolingbroke Hosp., London, 1938-45; Queen Elizabeth Hosp. for Children, 1939-46. Mem., British Pædiatric Assoc., 1945-; Pres., Pædiatric Section, RSM, 1966-67. *Publications:* contributor to Medical Annual, 1953-61; (with Dr Donald Paterson) Modern Methods of Feeding in Infancy and Childhood, 10th edn, 1955; contrib. to Pædiatric Urology (ed D. I. Williams), 1968. Numerous contributions to med. journals. *Recreations:* reading and looking at paintings. *Address:* 12 Milborne Grove, SW10. *T:* 01-373 2011; (professional) 40 Devonshire Place, W1. *T:* 01-935 8686.

**NEWPORT, Viscount; Richard Thomas Orlando Bridgeman;** *b* 3 Oct. 1947; *s* and *heir* of 6th Earl of Bradford, *qv*. *Educ:* Harrow; Trinity College, Cambridge. *Address:* 61d Eaton Square, SW1. *T:* 01-235 4942; Weston Park, Shifnal, Salop. *T:* Weston-under-Lizard 218.

**NEWRY and MORNE, Viscount;** *see* Needham, R. F.

**NEWSAM, Richard William,** CVO 1961; HM Diplomatic Service; *b* 23 June 1918; *s* of W. O. Newsam, ICS; *m* 1952, Joan Rostgard; one *s*. *Educ:* St Paul's; Trinity Coll., Oxford. Commnd RASC; served War of 1939-45: with East African Forces, Kenya, Abyssinia, Ceylon and Burma. Temporary Administrative Assistant, Colonial Office, 1946; Assistant Principal, Colonial Office, 1947; Principal, 1948; Nigeria secondment, 1952-53; joined Commonwealth Relations Office, 1957; served in: Ceylon, 1958; Pakistan, 1960; Dept of Technical Co-operation, 1963; Ministry of Overseas Development, 1964; Deputy High Commissioner, Dar es Salaam, 1965; Accra, 1967. *Recreations:* golf, sailing. *Address:* 43A Underhill Road, SE22. *Club:* Oxford and Cambridge University.

**NEWSOM, George Harold,** QC 1956; Chancellor, Diocese of St Albans since 1958; Deputy Chairman, Wiltshire Quarter Sessions, since 1964; *b* 29 Dec. 1909; *e s* of late Rev. G. E. Newsom, Master of Selwyn Coll., Cambridge; *m* 1939, Margaret Amy, *d* of L. A. Allen, OBE; two *s* one *d*. *Educ:* Marlborough; Merton College, Oxford. 2nd Class Lit Hum, 1931; 1st Class Jurisprudence, 1932; Harmsworth Senior Scholar; Merton College, 1932; Cholmeley Student, 1933, called to Bar, 1934, Lincoln's Inn; Bencher, 1962. Min. of Economic Warfare, 1939-40; Trading with the Enemy Dept, Treasury and Bd of Trade, 1940-45; Junior Counsel to Charity Comrs, 1947-56; Conveyancing Counsel to PO, 1947-56. Member Gen. Council of the Bar, 1952-56. *Publications:* Restrictive Covenants affecting freehold land, 1st edn (with late C. H. S. Preston), 1940, 2nd edn 1955, 3rd edn 1960, 4th edn 1967; Limitation of Actions, 1st edn (with late C. H. S. Preston), 1939, 2nd edn 1943, 3rd edn (with L. Abel-Smith), 1953; The Discharge and Modification of Restrictive Covenants, 1957. *Recreations:* lawn tennis, golf. *Address:* The Old Vicarage, Bishop's Cannings, Devizes, Wilts. *T:* Cannings 660. *Club:* Athenæum.

**NEWSOM, Rear-Adm. John Bertram,** CB 1957; Senior Technical Adviser to Commander-in-Chief, The Nore, 1955-58, retd; *b* 22 Sept. 1902; *yr s* of J. A. Newsom, Epsom; *m* 1934, Edna Margaret Bowden, Plymouth; three *s*. *Educ:* Epsom Coll. Entered RN, 1920; completed specialist Engineering course at RN Engineering College, 1925. Served in: HMS Eagle, Curacoa, Vimiera, Duchess, Capetown, Frobisher; served War of 1939-45 in HMS Tartar, at Admiralty and in HMS Illustrious. Subsequent service: HM Dockyard, Malta; on staff of Flag Officer, Scotland and N Ireland; HM Dockyards, Sheerness and Malta. *Recreations:* all games; cricket for RN, 1933. *Address:* Blue Haze, Downderry, Cornwall.

**NEWSOM, Sir John (Hubert),** Kt 1964; CBE 1954; Hon. FRIBA; Director, Longman Holdings Ltd and Longman Group Ltd; *b* 8 June 1910; *e s* of late H. N. Newsom; *m* 1931, Barbara Day; one *s* one *d*. *Educ:* Imperial Service Coll.; The Queen's College, Oxford (Scholar; Hon. Fellow, 1969). Varied experience in education, social work and licensed victualling (inc. Director, Community Service Council for Co. Durham), 1931-40; County Education Officer, Hertfordshire, 1940-57. Life Governor: Haileybury and ISC; St Edmund's Ware; Chairman: Central Advisory Council for Education (England), 1961-63 (Vice-Chm., 1963-66) (Council produced report Half our Future and Report on Primary Educn); Public Schools Commn, 1966-68; Harlow Development Corporation, 1966-; Educational Advisory Council of ITA, 1964-70; SRO, 1928-45; Mem. Indep. Schools Tribunal, 1960-; between 1945 and 1960 served on: Arts Council; Nathan Cttee on Charitable Trusts; Executive of Nat. Youth Orchestra; Deptl Cttee on Public Libraries, Colonial Educn, etc. Hon. LLD, University Pennsylvania. Officer, Legion of Honour. *Publications:* On the Other Side, 1930; Out of the Pit, 1936; Willingly to School, 1944; Education of Girls, 1948; Child at School, 1950; Galloway Gamble, 1951; Rogues Yarn, 1953; (as Marius Rose) The Intelligent Teacher's Guide to Preferment, 1954; AD History News Sheets, 1955. *Recreations:* cookery and conversation. *Address:* Corner House, Fair Green, Sawbridgeworth, Herts. *Club:* Athenæum.

**NEWSOME, David Hay,** MA Cantab; Headmaster of Christ's Hospital since 1970; *b* 15 June 1929; *s* of Captain C. T. Newsome, OBE; *m* 1955, Joan Florence, *d* of Lt-Col L. H. Trist, DSO, MC; four *d*. *Educ:* Rossall Sch., Fleetwood; Emmanuel Coll., Cambridge (Scholar). First Cl. in Hist. Tripos Parts I and

II, 1952, 1953. Asst Master, Wellington Coll., 1954-59 (Head of History Dept, 1956-59); Fellow of Emmanuel Coll., Cambridge, 1959-70; Asst Lectr in Ecclesiastical History, Univ. of Cambridge, 1961-66; Univ. Lectr, 1966-70; Sen. Tutor, Emmanuel Coll., Cambridge, 1965-70. Gore Memorial Lecture, Westminster Abbey, 1965; Bishop Westcott Memorial Lecture, Cambridge, 1968. Council of: Ardingly Coll., 1965-69; Eastbourne Coll., 1966-70; Epsom Coll., 1966-70. FRHistS, 1970. *Publications:* A History of Wellington College, 1859-1959, 1959; Godliness and Good Learning, Four Studies in a Victorian Ideal, 1961; The Parting of Friends, a study of the Wilberforces and Henry Manning, 1966; Bishop Westcott and the Platonic Tradition, 1969; articles in Jl of Theological Studies, Jl of Ecclesiastical History, Theology, History Today, Historical Jl. *Recreations:* music, fell-walking. *Address:* Christ's Hospital, Horsham, Sussex. *T:* Horsham 63248. *Club:* Oxford and Cambridge.

**NEWSON-SMITH, Sir Frank (Edwin),** 1st Bt, *cr* 1944; Kt, *cr* 1941; MA (Hon.); DCL (Hon.); Stockbroker; *b* 1879; *s* of Henry Newson-Smith, DL, CA, London; *m* 1904, Lilian Dorothy (*d* 1955), *d* of late Sir Henry Tozer; one *s two d* (and one *s* killed in action, 1944). *Educ:* University College Sch.; Paris. Mem. of London Stock Exchange since 1900; Member of Honourable Artillery Company since 1896; elected to Court of Common Council, 1911; Deputy for Ward of Broad Street, 1928, Chief Commoner, 1930; Member HM Court of Lieutenancy, City of London, 1929; Master Worshipful Company of Turners, 1933; Worshipful Company of Spectacle Makers, 1947 and 1948; Alderman of Farringdon Within Ward, 1938, removed to Bridge Without, 1954-68; Sheriff of City of London, 1939; Lord Mayor of London, 1943-44; Governor: of London House; of Sutton's Hospital in Charterhouse. Chairman Government Committee on Business Training, 1945; Pres. London Chamber of Commerce, 1946, 1947 and 1948. *Heir: s* John Kenneth Newson-Smith [*b* 9 Jan. 1911; *m* 1945, Vera Margaret Greenhouse, *d* of Dr W. G. Allt, CBE; one *s* two *d*]. *Address:* 31 Gresham Street, EC2. *T:* 01-606 7711.

**NEWTH, Brig. Arthur Leslie Walter,** CBE 1938; DSO 1919; MC; TD; DL; JP; *b* 1897; *s* of late Arthur Edward Newth, Westbury-on-Trym, Bristol; *m* 1926, Ruth Buchanan, *d* of P. Steadman, JP; two *s* one *d*. *Educ:* Bristol Grammar School. 2nd Lieut, 4th Gloucestershire Regt, 1914; proceeded to France, March 1915; served there until transferred to Italian Expeditionary Force, Nov. 1917; returned to France, April 1918; after holding various Staff appointments, commanded 6th Bn Cheshire Regiment and 2/23rd Bn The London Regiment (DSO, MC, despatches four times); Adjutant 4th Gloucestershire Regiment, 1924-28; Captain, 1915; Major, 1917; Lieut-Colonel, 1929; Bt Colonel, 1933; Colonel, 1934; Brigadier, 1937; commanded 4th (City of Bristol) Bn Gloucestershire Regt, 1929-34; Commander 144th (Glos and Worcs) Infantry Brigade TA, 1934-38; Commander 135 Infantry Brigade, 1939-42; 1942-43 North African Campaign (despatches, Legion of Merit, Degree of Officer); Served at Allied Force HQ, 1943-45, N Africa and Italy (despatches). DL Glos, 1950; JP 1952-64. Chairman South Western Regional Board for Industry, 1956-65. Governor Bristol Gram. Sch.; Fell. Royal Commonwealth Society. Hon. Colonel 5th Bn The Gloucestershire Regiment, 1961-67. *Recreation:* golf. *Address:* Shepton House, Shepton Montague, Wincanton, Som. *T:* Bruton 2258. *Club:* Naval and Military.

**NEWTH, Prof. David Richmond;** Regius Professor of Zoology, University of Glasgow, since 1965; *b* 10 Oct. 1921; *s* of Herbert Greenway Newth and Annie Munroe (*née* Fraser); *m* 1946, Jean Winifred (*née* Haddon); two *s* one *d*. *Educ:* King Edward VI High Sch., Birmingham. Entered University Coll., London, 1939; graduated in Zoology, 1942. Served War of 1939-45, REME, commnd 1943. Asst Lectr in Zoology at University Coll., London, 1947; Lectr, 1949; Prof. of Biology as Applied to Medicine in the Univ. of London, at the Middlesex Hospital Medical Sch., 1960-65. FRSE 1966. Editor, Journal of Embryology and Experimental Morphology, 1960-69; Jt Editor, Oxford Paperbacks University Series (OPUS). *Publications:* original articles in scientific journals, translations, and contrib. (popular) scientific works. *Recreation:* resting. *Address:* Department of Zoology, The University, Glasgow W2. *Club:* Art (Glasgow).

**NEWTON,** 4th Baron, *cr* 1892; **Peter Richard Legh;** *b* 6 April 1915; *er s* of 3rd Baron Newton, TD, DL, JP, and Hon. Helen Meysey-Thompson (*d* 1958); *S* father 1960; *m* 1948, Priscilla, *yr d* of late Capt. John Egerton-Warburton and *widow* of William Matthew Palmer, Visc. Wolmer; two *s*. *Educ:* Eton; Christ Church, Oxford (MA). 2nd Lt, Grenadier Guards (SR), 1937; Captain, 1941; Major, 1945. JP 1951; CC Hampshire, 1949-52 and 1954-55. Chairman East Hampshire Young Conservatives, 1949-50. MP (C) Petersfield Division of Hants, Oct. 1951-June 1960; PPS to Fin. Sec. to Treasury, 1952-53; Asst Govt Whip, 1953-55; a Lord Comr of Treasury, 1955-57; Vice-Chamberlain of the Household, 1957-59; Treasurer of the Household, 1959-60; Capt. Yeomen of the Guard and Govt Asst Chief Whip, 1960-62; (Joint) Parly Sec., Min. of Health, 1962-64; Min. of State for Education and Science, April-Oct. 1964. *Recreations:* photography, clock repairing, making gadgets. *Heir: s* Hon. Richard Thomas Legh, *b* 11 Jan. 1950. *Address:* Vernon Hill House, Bishop's Waltham, Hampshire. *T:* Bishop's Waltham 2301. *Clubs:* Carlton, Constitutional, Pratt's; Hampshire (Winchester).

*See also Major Hon. Sir F. M. Legh, Viscount Wolmer.*

**NEWTON, Bernard St John,** CIE 1945; retired; *b* 13 April 1890; *s* of late Rev. H. Newton; *m* 1920, Eelin Madeleine, *d* of late Percy Douglas Kirkham (Indian Police); one *d*. *Educ:* Haileybury; London University. ACGI, BSc (London) 1913. Appointed: to Irrigation Branch of PWD, Central Provinces and Berar (India), 1913; Inspector of Munitions, Calcutta, 1916; Asst Controller of Munitions, Calcutta, 1917; returned to PWD, 1919. Chief Engineer, PWD, CP & Berar, 1943-46; retd, 1946. *Address:* 4 Gloucester Mews West, W2. *T:* 01-262 9858.

**NEWTON, Sir Charles (Henry),** Kt, *cr* 1943; *b* 6 June 1882; *s* of late Henry Newton; *m* 1917, Hilda Blanche Smith (*d* 1964); (one *s* killed in action in Western Europe April, 1945). Entered GW Rly Service 1897; Asst to Comptroller Great Eastern Rly 1916; Chief Accountant, Great Eastern Rly, 1922; Chief Accountant, L and NE Rly 1928; Divisional General Manager (Southern Area) 1936; Chief General Manager London and North Eastern Railway, 1939-47, Director 1947; Holder of Brunel Medal London School of Economics, University of London; CStJ; USA Medal of Freedom with gold palm. *Publication:* Railway

Accounts, 1930. *Address:* Furzefield, East Grinstead, Sussex. *T:* 25353.

**NEWTON, Sir Edgar Henry,** 2nd Bt, *cr* 1924; Solicitor (admitted 1919); Consultant with legal firm of Duffield Bruty & Co., of 9 Devereux Court, Temple, WC2, and Waltham Cross and Hoddesdon, Herts; Commissioner for Oaths; *b* 6 May 1893; *er s* of Sir Louis Arthur Newton, 1st Bt of Beckenham, Kent; *S* father, 1945; *m* 1st, 1917 Gladys Maud (*d* 1966), *d* of late Sir James Garnar; one *s* one *d*; 2nd, 1968, Mrs Alice Mary Rosser, *d* of late Henry Barber. *Educ:* Merchant Taylors' Sch. Formerly Mem. of Court of Common Council of City of London; Past Master of Feltmakers Company of London; Governor: Royal Alexandra and Albert Sch.; Royal Hosp. and Home for Incurables, Putney (Mem. Bd of Management); late comdg 1st Anti-Aircraft, RASC, TA; formerly 56th Divisional RASC. Served European War, 1914-18 (despatches), also 1939-42. *Heir: s* Lt-Col Kenneth Garnar Newton, OBE, TD [*b* 4 June 1918; *m* 1944, Margaret Isabel Blair; two *s*. *Educ:* Wellington Coll.]. *Address:* Larkshill, Harpsden Way, Henley-on-Thames, Oxon. *T:* Henley 2677. *Clubs:* Royal Automobile; Phyllis Court (Henley-on-Thames).

**NEWTON, Giles Fendall,** MBE 1918; BA; President, Cape Asbestos Co. Ltd; *b* 27 May 1891; *o s* of William Latham and Violet Newton, Goldington, Bedford; *m* 1921, Mary Cicely, *e d* of Brig.-General Sir Frederick Meyrick, 2nd Bt, Bush, Pembroke; one *s* one *d*. *Educ:* Magdalen Coll. School and Lincoln College, Oxford. Open Exhib. (Hist.) Lincoln Coll., Oxford, 1910; Stillingfleet Prizewinner, 1910; BA 1914; served European War, 1914-18, Queen's Royal West Surrey Regt; commissioned, 1914; RA Adjt 29th Bde, RFA, BEF (MBE); seconded to Ministry of Munitions, 1917; Controller of Inspection (A) Ministry of Supply, 1943; Dep. Chm. London Chamber of Commerce, 1945, Chm. 1946, 1947; Dep. Chm. London Court of Arbitration, 1946, Chm., 1948; High Sheriff of Sussex, 1946-47; member of Lord Chancellor's Committee on Practice and Procedure of High Court, 1947. *Recreations:* golf, racing. *Address:* 100 Eaton Square, SW1. *T:* 01-235 2557; 18 Courtenay Gate, Hove 3, Sussex. *T:* Brighton 71023. *Club:* Bath.

**NEWTON, Sir Gordon;** *see* Newton, Sir L. G.

**NEWTON, Sir (Harry) Michael (Rex),** 3rd Bt, *cr* 1900; Director Thos Parsons & Sons Ltd; *b* 7 Feb. 1923; 2nd and *e surv s* of Sir Harry K. Newton, 2nd Bt, OBE, DL, and Myrtle Irene, *e d* of W. W. Grantham, Balneath Manor, Lewes; *S* father, 1951; *m* 1958, Pauline Jane, *o d* of R. J. F. Howgill, *qv*; one *s*; three adopted *d*. *Educ:* Eastbourne College. Served War of 1939-45, with KRRC, in 8th Army and Middle East, 1941-46 (wounded). Liveryman Girdlers' Company; Freeman of City of London. *Recreations:* shooting, sailing (winner of 1953 Fastnet Race), ski-ing, fencing. *Heir: s* George Peter Howgill Newton, *b* 26 March 1962. *Address:* Weycroft Hall, near Axminster, Devon. *T:* 3232. *Clubs:* Bath, Royal Ocean Racing.

**NEWTON, Major Henry Leigh,** DSO 1916; *b* 1889; *s* of Henry Newton, Tutbury; *m* 1st, 1914, Ellen Marian, *d* of William Ollis, Burton-on-Trent; one *d*; 2nd, 1951, Ellen Margaret Wynne. *Educ:* Uppingham. High Sheriff of Derbyshire, 1949-50. *Recreations:* hunting and yachting. *Address:* Barford Court, Churt, Surrey. *Clubs:* Royal Yacht Squadron, Royal Ocean Racing.

**NEWTON, Sir Hubert,** Kt 1968; Chairman, Leek and Westbourne Building Society, since 1966, and Managing Director, 1966-69; *b* 2 Sept. 1904; *s* of Joe Newton and Gertrude Elizabeth Newton; *m* 1931, Elsie (*née* Wilson); one *d*. *Educ:* Burnley Gram. School. Burnley Building Soc., 1918-23; Mortgage Dept Controller, Northampton Town Building Soc., 1923-26; Controller of Investment Dept, Leeds Perm. Building Soc., 1926-30; Asst Sec., Bristol & West Building Soc., 1930-33; Leek and Moorlands Building Soc.: Sec., 1933-40; Gen. Man., 1940-63; Chm. and Man. Dir, 1963-66, when Leek and Moorlands amalgamated with Westbourne Park Building Soc. to form Leek and Westbourne Building Soc. Mem. Coun., Building Socs Assoc. of Gt Britain (Chm., 1952-54); Mem. Coun. and Exec. Cttee, Internat. Union of Building Socs and Savings Assocs (Dep. Pres., Washington Congress, 1962; Pres., London Congress, 1965); Pres., N Staffs Chamber of Commerce, 1964-65; Vice-President: Building Socs Inst., 1962; Building Socs Assoc. of Jamaica Ltd, 1967; Midland Assoc. of Building Socs, 1969. Mem., Skelmersdale Develt Corp. Past Mem., Central Housing Adv. Cttee; Mem. Coun., Nat. House-Builders Registration Coun.; Liveryman, Gold and Silver Wyre Drawers' Company. Coronation Medal, 1953. *Publications:* contribs to Building Socs Gazette. *Recreations:* golf, travel. *Address:* Birchall, Leek, Staffs ST13 5RA. *T:* Leek 2397. *Clubs:* National Liberal; Union (Buxton).

**NEWTON, Ivor;** FRCM; Pianoforte Accompanist; *b* London; *s* of William and Gertrude Newton. Studied the piano with Arthur Barclay (Dir of Music, Brompton Oratory), York Bowen, and Isidore Snook (Amsterdam); studied Art of Accompanying and Repertoire with Raimund von zur Muhlen and Coenraad Bos (Berlin). Associated as accompanist with Kirsten Flagstad, Melba, Clara Butt, Tetrazzini, Conchita Supervia, Lily Pons, Lotte Lehmann, Elisabeth Schumann, Victoria de los Angeles, Joan Hammond, Kathleen Ferrier, Chaliapine, Gigli, Tito Schipa, John McCormack, Jussi Björling, Tito Gobbi, Ysaye, Yehudi Menuhin, Milstein, Casals, Piatigorsky, Suggia, di Stefano. Toured extensively in Europe, United States, Canada, Africa, Australia, New Zealand and the Orient. Salzburg, Edinburgh and Aldeburgh Festivals. Organised first concert in aid of British War Relief in United States at British Embassy, Washington, 1940; toured Egypt, Irak, and the Persian Gulf giving concerts to forces, 1943; concerts to Royal Navy and Soviet Fleet in Scapa Flow, 1944; toured Germany and Austria with Grace Moore on invitation of American C-in-C, 1946; British Council Tours, Scandinavia with Henry Holst, 1946; France with Maggie Teyte, 1947, Persia, Turkey and Austria with Leon Goossens, 1955. Adviser on music for HM Prisons. *Publication:* At the Piano–Ivor Newton (autobiog.), 1966. *Address:* Kirsten House, Kinnerton Street, Belgrave Square, SW1. *T:* 01-235 2882. *Club:* Garrick.

**NEWTON, John Mordaunt,** CB 1964; Director, Management Development, Post Office, since 1967; *b* 24 April 1913; *o s* of late Wallis and Mabel Newton; *m* 1939, Pamela Frances, *e d* of late Sir E. John Maude, KCB, KBE; five *d*. *Educ:* Manchester Gram. Sch.; CCC, Cambridge (Scholar). BA 1st Cl. History Tripos, 1935. Assistant Principal, Post Office, 1936; Principal: Ministry of Home Security, 1941; Home Office, 1943; Treasury, 1945-47; Assistant Secretary, Post Office, 1949; Under Secretary, 1957; Director of Personnel, GPO, 1957-67. Hon. Secretary, Abbeyfield Chiswick

Soc.; Chm., Abbeyfield West and North-West London Area. *Address:* Thames Bank, Chiswick Mall, W4. *T:* 01-994 1803.

**NEWTON, Sir (Leslie) Gordon,** Kt 1966; Editor of The Financial Times since 1950 (Director, since 1967); Director: Industrial and Trade Fairs Holdings and subsidiaries since 1968; Throgmorton Publications since 1968; Financial Times Business Publications; *b* 1907; *s* of John and Edith Newton; *m* 1935, Peggy Ellen Warren; one *s*. *Educ:* Blundell's School; Sidney Sussex College, Cambridge. Hannen Swaffer Award for Journalist of the Year, 1966. *Address:* 10 Princes Gate Mews, SW7. *T:* 01-589 9470. *Club:* Garrick.

**NEWTON, Prof. Lily;** Professor of Botany, University College of Wales, Aberystwyth, 1930-58, Prof. Emeritus since 1959; Vice-Principal, 1951-52; Acting Principal, May 1952-Sept. 1953; *b* 26 Jan. 1893; *d* of George Batten and Melinda Batten (*née* Casling); *m* 1925, William Charles Frank Newton (*d* 1927). *Educ:* Colston's Girls' School, Bristol; University of Bristol. Assistant Lecturer in Botany, University of Bristol, 1919-1920; Lecturer in Botany, Birkbeck Coll., Univ. of London, 1920-23; research worker, Imperial College of Science and British Museum, Natural History, 1923-25; Lecturer in Botany, University College of Wales, Aberystwyth, 1928-30. President: Section K, British Association, 1949; British Phycological Soc., 1955-57; UK Fedn for Educn in Home Economics, 1957-63. *Publications:* Handbook of British Seaweeds, 1931; Plant distribution in the Aberystwyth district, 1935; (jointly) A Study of certain British Seaweeds and their utilisation in the preparation of agar, 1949; Utilisation of Seaweeds, 1951. Papers in Jl of Linnean Soc., Jl of Ecology, Annals of Applied Biology, Vistas in Botany and others. *Recreations:* cookery, needlework, gardening. *Address:* Banc-y-Rhos, Cae Melyn, Aberystwyth. *T:* Aberystwyth 3490.

**NEWTON, Margaret;** Headmistress, Westonbirt School, since 1965; *b* 20 Dec. 1927; 2nd *d* of F. L. Newton, KStJ, MB, ChB, and Mrs A. C. Newton, MBE, BA. *Educ:* Sherborne School for Girls; St Andrews Univ.; Oxford University. MA Hons St Andrews, 1950; Educn Dip. Oxon 1951. Asst Mistress, King Edward VI Grammar School, Handsworth, Birmingham, 1951-54; Classics Mistress, Queen Margaret's Sch., York, 1954-60 (House Mistress, 1957); House Mistress, Malvern Girls' College, 1960-64 (Head of Classics Dept, 1962). *Address:* Westonbirt School, Tetbury, Gloucestershire; 2 West Court, Westfield Road, Budleigh Salterton, Devon.

**NEWTON, Sir Michael;** *see* Newton, Sir H. M. R.

**NEWTON, Robert,** CMG 1953; retired as Colonial Secretary, Mauritius, 1961; *b* Newcastle upon Tyne, 12 Oct. 1908; *m* 1933, Muriel Winifred, *d* of late R. P. Chinneck and Mrs Chinneck; one *s* two *d*. *Educ:* Aysgarth School; Malvern College; Pembroke College, Cambridge. Joined Colonial Administrative Service as Administrative Officer (Cadet), Nigeria, 1931; served there as an Assistant District Officer until 1937; served Palestine until 1946; idc 1947; seconded for duty in Colonial Office, 1948; Financial Secretary, Jamaica, 1949. Member, British Ornithologists Union. PhD (Exon) 1966. *Publications:* Tarnished Brocade, 1937; Swords of Bronze, 1939; Victorian Exeter, 1968. *Recreations:* ornithology, walking. *Address:* 14 Howell Road, Exeter, Devon.

**NEWTON, Maj.-Gen. Thomas Cochrane,** CB 1940; DSO 1918; OBE 1919; JP Bedfordshire (supplementary list); *b* 1 Jan. 1885; *o surv s* of late G. O. Newton and late Lady Alice Newton, of Croxton Park, St Neots; *m* 1924, Helen, *d* of late Augustus Thorne, DL, JP; one *s* one *d*. *Educ:* Wellington College; RM Academy, Woolwich. Served in Royal Artillery in England and India; France and Belgium, 1914-18 (despatches, DSO, OBE); Commandant, School of Anti-Aircraft Defence, 1935-39; Major-General, General Staff, 1939; retired pay, 1942. High Sheriff of Bedfordshire, 1945-46. *Address:* The Downs, Croxton, Huntingdon. *Club:* Army and Navy.

**NEY, Marie;** *see* Menzies, M. N.

**NGAIZA, Christopher Pastor;** Tanzania's first High Commissioner to Zambia, since 1969; *b* 29 March 1930; parents decd; *m* 1952, Thereza; three *s* two *d* (and one *s* decd). *Educ:* Makerere University Coll.; Loughborough Co-operative College. Local Courts Magistrate, 1952-53; Secretary/Manager, Bahaya Co-operative Consumer Stores, 1955-57; Loughborough Co-operative Coll., 1957-59; Auctioneer and Representative of Bukoba Native Co-operative Union, Mombasa, 1959-61; Foreign Service, 1961-; Counsellor, Mission to UN, 1961-62; Counsellor, Tanganyika High Commn, London, 1962-63; High Commissioner for United Republic of Tanganyika and Zanzibar in London, 1964-65; Tanzanian Ambassador to Netherlands, 1965-67; Mem., E African Common Market Tribunal, 1968-69. *Recreations:* music, tennis. *Address:* Tanzania High Commission, PO Box 1219, Lusaka, Zambia.

**NIAGARA, Bishop of,** since 1949; **Rt. Rev. Walter Edward Bagnall,** DD; *b* 1903. *Educ:* Masonic School, Dublin, Ireland; University of Western Ontario; Huron College, London, Ont. BA, Univ. of Western Ontario, 1927; Licentiate in Theology, Huron Coll., 1927. Deacon, 1927; Priest, 1928; Curate of All Saints, Windsor, Ont, 1927-28; Incumbent of St Mark's, London, Ont, 1928-30; Rector of St John's, Preston, Ont, Canada, 1930-36; Rural Dean of Waterloo, Ont, 1932-36; Rector of All Saints, Hamilton, Ont, 1936-40; Rector of St George's, St Catharine's, Ont, 1940-47; Canon of Niagara, 1944-47; Dean of Niagara and Rector of Ch. Ch. Cathedral, Hamilton, 1947-49. Hon. degrees: DD Univ. of Western Ontario, 1949; DD Trinity Coll., Toronto, 1953; DCL Bishops Univ., Lennoxville, 1956; LLD McMaster Univ., 1959. *Address:* Niagara Church House, 67 Victoria Avenue, South Hamilton, Ont, Canada; (home) 3 St James Place, Hamilton, Ont, Canada.

**NIAGARA, Assistant Bishop of;** *see* Wilkinson, Rt Rev. C. R. H.

**NIARCHOS, Stavros Spyros;** Grand Cross of Order of the Phœnix (Greece), 1957; Commander of Order of George I of Greece, 1954; Commander of Order of St George and St Constantine (Greece), 1964; Head of Niarchos Group of Shipping Companies which controls over 42 million tons of shipping; *b* 3 July 1909; *s* of late Spyros Niarchos and of Eugenie Niarchos; *m* 1st, 1939, Melpomene Capparis (marr. diss., 1947); no *c*; 2nd, 1947, Eugenie Livanos (marr. diss., 1965, she *d* 1970); three *s* one *d*; 3rd, 1965, Charlotte Ford (marr. diss., 1967); one *d*. *Educ:* Univ. of Athens (Dr of Laws). On leaving Univ. joined family grain and shipping business; started independent shipping concern, 1939. Joined Royal Hellenic Navy Volunteer Reserve, 1941; served on destroyer engaged in North Atlantic convoy work (despatches). Demobilised, 1945, with rank of Lieut-Comdr. Returned to Shipping business. Pioneered super-tankers. *Recreations:* yachting, ski-ing. *Address:* c/o Niarchos (London) Ltd, 41/43 Park Street, W1. *T:* 01-629 8400. *Clubs:* Athenian, Royal Yacht Club of Greece (both in Athens).

**NIBLETT, Prof. William Roy,** CBE 1970; BA, BLitt; Professor of Higher Education, University of London, since 1967; *b* 25 July 1906; *m* 1938, Sheila Margaret, *d* of A. C. Taylor, Peterborough; one *s* one *d*. *Educ:* University of Bristol; BA 1st class Hons English; St Edmund Hall, Oxford; BLitt. Senior English Master, Doncaster Grammar Sch., 1930-34; Lectr in Educn, King's Coll., Newcastle, 1934-45 (Registrar of Univ. Durham, 1940-44); Prof. of Educn, University Coll., Hull, 1945-47; Prof. of Education, and Dir, Inst. of Education, Univ. of Leeds, 1947-59. Dean, Univ. of London Inst. of Education, 1960-68; Mem., UGC, 1949-59; Joseph Payne Lectr, 1958; Hibbert Lectr, 1965; Kellogg International Fellow, 1954; Visiting Professor, Univ. of California, 1960; Nuffield Fellow, Univ. of Melbourne, 1960; Wm Evans Prof., Univ. of Otago, 1962; Japan Govt Prof., Univs of Japan, 1967. Member: Nat. Advisory Coun. on Trng and Supply of Teachers, 1950-61; Army Education Advisory Board, 1959-; Council, Royal Holloway College, 1963-; Council, Cheltenham Ladies' College, 1967-. Chairman: UGC Sub-Cttee on Halls of Residence, 1956 (Report, 1957); World Univ. Service, UK, 1960-63; Educn Dept, Brit. Coun. of Churches, 1965-; Council of Europe conf. on Research in Higher Educn, 1969, 1970. *Publications:* Essential Education; Education and the Modern Mind; Christian Education in a Secular Society; (ed) The Expanding University; (ed) Moral Education in a Changing Society; (ed) Higher Education: Demand and Response. Contrib. to: Science and Freedom, World Year Book of Education, Melbourne Studies in Education, etc. *Address:* 33 Tavistock Square, WC1; Pinfarthings, Amberley, Stroud, Glos GL5 5JJ. *Club:* Athenæum.

**NIBLOCK, Henry;** HM Consul-General, Strasbourg, since 1968; *b* 25 Nov. 1911; *s* of Joseph and Isabella Niblock, Belfast; *m* 1940, Barbara Mary Davies, *d* of late Captain R. W. Davies, Air Ministry; two *s*. Vice-Consul: Bremen, 1947-50; Bordeaux, 1951; Second Sec. (Commercial), Copenhagen, 1951-53; Consul, Frankfort-on-Main, 1954-57; First Sec. and Consul, Monrovia, 1957-58; Consul, Houston, 1959-62; Chargé d'Affaires, Port-au-Prince, 1962-63; First Sec. and Consul, Brussels, 1964; Consul (Commercial), Cape Town, 1964-67. *Recreations:* walking, photography. *Address:* c/o Foreign and Commonwealth Office, SW1. *Club:* Royal Over-Seas League.

**NICHOL, Mrs Muriel Edith;** JP Herts; *e d* of late R. C. Wallhead, MP Merthyr Tydfil, 1922-34; *m* James Nichol, MA; one *s*. Onetime Chm., Welwyn Garden City UDC (1937-45); formerly: Dep. Chm., Welwyn Magistrates' Court; Governor, Welwyn Garden City High School. MP (Lab) North Bradford, 1945-50; Mem. Parly Delegation to India, Jan.-Feb. 1946; Mem. "Curtis" Cttee (Home Office) on Care of Children, 1945-46. *Recreations:* local government, social welfare, education. *Address:* 8 Elmwood, Welwyn Garden City, Herts. *T:* Welwyn Garden 22277.

**NICHOLAS, Sir Alfred James,** Kt 1967; CBE 1960 (OBE 1954); Chairman, Aberdare Holdings Ltd 1963-70, Hon. President since 1970; *b* 1900; *s* of George and Harriet Nicholas; *m* 1927, Ethel, *d* of Thomas Platt; one *s*. *Educ:* Bishop's Castle Sch.; Wellington Sch., Salop; Manchester Coll. of Technology. With Metropolitan Vickers Ltd, and Ferguson-Pailin Ltd until 1941. Chm. and Man. Director: Aberdare Cables Ltd; Aberdare Engineering Ltd; Erskine Heap & Co. Ltd; South Wales Group (Pty) Ltd South Africa; South Wales Electric (Pvt) Ltd Rhodesia; South Wales Electric Australia (Pty) Ltd; South Wales Electric Zambia Ltd; Director: Harlech Television Ltd; Electric Switchgear Co. Montreal. Chm., Develt Corp. for Wales; a Vice-Chm., Welsh Council Assoc. Mem. Manchester Coll. of Technology; FIEE; MIEEE (USA); FBIM. Freeman of the City of London; Liveryman, Worshipful Co. of Tin Plate Workers. Hon. LLD Wales. CStJ. *Recreations:* photography, gardening. *Address:* c/o Aberdare Holdings Ltd, Blackwood, Mon; Bovil House, Machen, Mon. *Club:* Reform.

**NICHOLAS, Sir Harry;** *see* Nicholas, Sir Herbert Richard.

**NICHOLAS, Prof. Herbert George,** FBA 1969; Rhodes Professor of American History and Institutions, Oxford University, since 1969; Fellow of New College, Oxford, since 1951; *b* 8 June 1911; *s* of late Rev. W. D. Nicholas. *Educ:* Mill Hill Sch.; New Coll., Oxford (1st cl. Lit. Hum., 1934). Jessie Teresa Rowden Schol., New Coll., 1934. Commonwealth Fund Fellow in Modern History, Yale, 1935-37; MA Oxon, 1938; Exeter College, Oxford: Lectr, 1938, Fellow, 1946-51; Amer. Div., Min. of Information, and HM Embassy, Washington, 1941-46; Faculty Fellow, Nuffield Coll., Oxford, 1948-57; Nuffield Reader in the Comparative Study of Institutions at Oxford Univ., 1956-69. Vis. Prof., Brookings Instn, Washington, 1960; Albert Shaw Lectr in Diplomatic History, Johns Hopkins, 1961; Vis. Fellow, Inst. of Advanced Studies, Princeton, 1964; Vis. Faculty Fellow, Inst. of Politics, Harvard, 1968. Hon. DCL Pittsburgh, 1968. *Publications:* The American Union, 1948; The British General Election of 1950, 1951; To the Hustings, 1956; The United Nations as a Political Institution, 1959, 4th edn 1971; Britain and the United States, 1963; Editor, Tocqueville's de la Démocratie en Amérique, 1961. *Recreation:* gardening. *Address:* 3 William Orchard Close, Old Headington, Oxford. *T:* Oxford 63165. *Clubs:* Athenæum; Lotos (New York).

**NICHOLAS, Sir Herbert Richard, (Sir Harry Nicholas),** Kt 1970; OBE 1949; General Secretary of the Labour Party since 1968; *b* 13 March 1905; *s* of Richard Henry and Rosina Nicholas; *m* 1932, Rosina Grace Brown. *Educ:* Elementary sch., Avonmouth, Bristol; Evening Classes; Correspondence Courses. Clerk, Port of Bristol Authority, 1919-36. Transport and Gen. Workers Union: District Officer, Gloucester, 1936-38; Regional Officer, Bristol, 1938-40; National Officer, London: Commercial Road Transport Group, 1940-42; Chemical Section, 1942-44; Metal and Engineering Group, 1944-56; Asst Gen. Sec., 1956-68 (Acting Gen. Sec., Oct. 1964-July 66). Mem., TUC General Council, 1964-67. Mem., Aneurin Bevan Memorial Fund Trustees. *Publications:* occasional articles in press on Industrial Relations subjects. *Recreations:* Rugby football, fishing, reading, gardening. *Address:* 33 Madeira Road, Streatham, SW16. *T:* 01-769 7989.

**NICHOLAS, John William;** Deputy High Commissioner and Counsellor (Commercial), Ceylon, since 1970; *b* 13 Dec. 1924; *s* of Harry and Gladys Nicholas; *m* 1947, Rita (*née* Jones); two *s*. *Educ:* Holly Lodge Grammar Sch., Birimingham; Birmingham Univ. (BA Hons History). Served 7th Rajput Regt, Indian

Army, 1944-47; joined Home Civil Service, 1949; War Office, 1949-57; transf. to CRO 1957; First Sec., Brit. High Commn, Kuala Lumpur, 1957-61; Economic Div., CRO, 1961-63; Dep. High Comr in Malawi, 1964-66; Diplomatic Service Inspector, 1967-69. *Recreations:* cricket, tennis, squash. *Address:* c/o Foreign and Commonwealth Office, SW1. *Club:* Royal Commonwealth Society.

**NICHOLAS, Reginald Owen Mercer,** CB 1956; retired as Commissioner of Inland Revenue and Secretary, Board of Inland Revenue (1954-65); *b* 20 June 1903; *e s* of Reginald John Nicholas, mining engineer, Gold Coast, and Margaret Mary (*née* Trice); *m* 1929, Joan Estelle, *d* of E. S. Friend, Uplyme, Devon; two *s* one *d. Educ:* Royal Masonic Sch.; Gonville and Caius Coll., Cambridge (Scholar). Entered Inland Revenue Dept, 1925. Mem. War Damage Commn, 1962-64. *Address:* Thornton Cottage, Higher Metcombe, Ottery-St-Mary, Devon.

**NICHOLETTS, Air Marshal Sir Gilbert (Edward),** KBE 1956; CB 1949; AFC 1931 and Bar, 1933; retired; *b* 9 Nov. 1902; *s* of Edward Cornewall Nicholetts and Ellen Fanny Hollond; *m* 1956, Nora Beswick, *d* of Francis John Butt, MB, Chester. *Educ:* RN Colleges, Osborne and Dartmouth. Cranwell Cadet Coll., 1921-22; Calshot, Lee-on-Solent, 1922-24; HMS Eagle (Med. Fleet), 1924-26; Far East Flight and 205 Sqdn, 1927-30; 209 Sqdn, 1931-32; long distance flight (World Record, 5309 miles non-stop), 1933; Air Staff, 23 Group HQ, 1934; Staff Coll., 1935; Air Staff, AHQ Iraq, 1936-38; Air Ministry organization, 1938-39; War of 1939-45, OC 228 Sqdn, 1939-41; Haifa, Shallufa, 1941; POW Far East, 1942-45; AOC Central Photographic Establishment, 1946-48; Dir of Organization, Air Ministry, 1948-51; SASO Coastal Command, 1951; AOC No. 21 Group, Flying Training Command, 1953; SASO Flying Training Command, March-Dec. 1955; AOC Malta, and Dep. C-in-C (Air), Allied Forces, Mediterranean, Jan. 1956-Dec. 1957; Inspector-Gen., Royal Air Force, Jan. 1958-June, 1959; retired, 1959. *Address:* Stoborough Croft, Wareham, Dorset. *T:* Wareham 2992. *Club:* Royal Air Force.

**NICHOLL, Rear-Adm. Angus Dacres,** CB 1950; CBE 1942; DSO 1942; *b* 17 Nov. 1896; 6th *s* of late William Nicholl, FRAM; *m* 1922, Winifred Rose Edkins; one *s* one *d* (and one *d* decd). *Educ:* Brighton Coll. Joined Navy as Special Entry Cadet, 1914; Asst Chief of Naval Staff and Dir of Naval Intelligence, RAN, 1932-34; Naval Asst Sec. Cttee of Imperial Defence, 1936-39; Capt. 1939; Naval Asst Sec. War Cabinet, 1939-41; commanded HMS Penelope in Mediterranean, 1941-42 (despatches, DSO, CBE); Dir of Operations Div. (Foreign), Admiralty, 1942-44; commanded HMS Duke of York, 1944-46; Commodore RN Barracks, Portsmouth, 1947-48; Rear-Adm. 1948; Brussels Treaty Military Cttee, 1948-49; NATO Planning Group, 1949-51; retired list, 1951. Defence Correspondent, BBC External services, 1951-66. *Address:* 4 Spice Island House, Old Portsmouth, Hants. *T:* Portsmouth 811018.

**NICHOLLS, Arthur,** CBE 1941; Royal Corps of Naval Constructors (retired); *b* 16 Jan. 1880; *s* of John Nicholls and Susannah Forster; *m* 1927, Rhoda Brooker (*d* 1958); one *s* three *d* (and one *s* one *d* decd). *Educ:* RNC, Greenwich. Joined Royal Corps of Naval Constructors, 1905; Constructor Comdr, Inter-Allied Commn, Berlin, 1920-21; Chief Constructor, Hong Kong, 1931-34; Manager Constructive Dept, Devonport Dockyard, 1936-41. *Address:* 14 Rokeby Drive, Gosforth, Newcastle upon Tyne, 3.

**NICHOLLS, Bertram,** Hon. RBA; landscape painter; *b* Didsbury, Lancs, 26 Sept. 1883; *s* of W. A. Nicholls and Mary Allen; *m* Mary Laura Eva (*d* 1968), *d* of late James Phillips, Malvern; one *s. Educ:* Manchester Gram. Sch. Studied at the Slade Sch. President: Royal Society of British Artists (1931, 1947), Society of Sussex Painters, Manchester Academy of Fine Arts, 1924-34. Represented at: National Gallery, Millbank, National Gallery of Canada, City of London Guildhall Gallery, Metropolitan Museum, New York; Montreal and principal municipal collections. *Publication:* Painting in Oils. *Recreation:* gardening. *Address:* Hardham House, steyning, Sussex. *T:* Steyning 3298.

**NICHOLLS, Rear-Adm. Francis Brian Price B.;** *see* Brayne-Nicholls.

**NICHOLLS, Sir Harmar,** 1st Bt, *cr* 1960; JP; MP (C) Peterborough Division of Northamptonshire since 1950; *b* 1 Nov. 1912; 3rd *s* of Charles E. C. Nicholls and Sarah Anne Nicholls, Walsall; *m* 1940, Dorothy Elsie, *e d* of James Edwards, Tipton; two *d. Educ:* Dorsett Road Sch., Darlaston; Queen Mary's Gram. Sch., Walsall. Mem. Middle Temple Inn of Court. Partner Nicholls and Jordan, Walsall, Wolverhampton and Stafford, 1934-; Chairman: Nicholls and Hennessy (Hotels) Ltd; Midland and East Anglia Investment Trust Ltd; Malvern Festival Theatre Trust Ltd; Pleasurama, 1970-; Director: J. & H. Nicholls & Co., Paints, etc, 1945-; Winkfields Estates Ltd; Radio Luxemburg (London) Ltd; Internat. Life Insurance Co. (UK); Mem. of Syndicate at Lloyd's. Mem. Darlaston UDC at age of 26 (Chm., 1949-50); County Magistrate, 1946. Vice-Chm. W Midland Fedn, Junior Imperial League, 1937; contested (C) Nelson and Colne, 1945. Preston bye-election, 1946; PPS to Asst Postmaster-Gen., 1951-April 1955; Parliamentary Sec., Ministry of Agriculture, Fisheries and Food, April 1955-Jan. 1957; Parliamentary Sec., Min. of Works, 1957-60; Mem. Conservative Housing Cttee; Sec. of Parliamentary Road Safety Cttee (Conservative); Jt Sec. All party Parliamentary Group Empire Migration. Mem. Govt Overseas Settlement Board on migration to Commonwealth. War of 1939-45: volunteered as sapper, commnd Royal Engineers; served India and Burma. *Recreations:* gardening, reading, walking, theatre. *Address:* Abbeylands, Weston, Stafford. *T:* Weston 252. *Clubs:* St Stephen's, Constitutional; (Pres.) Unionist, City and Counties (Peterborough); Conservative (Darlaston); Unionist (Walsall).

**NICHOLLS, Harry,** VC 1940; Head Messenger, 1947; *b* 21 April 1915; *s* of Florence Leech and John Nicholls; *m* 1937, Constance Carroll; one *d. Educ:* Bosworth Road Sch., Nottingham. Joined Army, Grenadier Guards, 1936; served War of 1939-45 (VC, prisoner). *Recreations:* most sports, boxing (won ISBA heavyweight championship of 1938 and other trophies, Army *v* Denmark, 1937); football, cricket, tennis, rugby, swimming. *Address:* Westwood, 35 Surrey Road, Cliftonville, Margate, Kent.

**NICHOLLS, Maj.-Gen. Sir Leslie,** KCMG 1954; CB 1945; CBE 1943 (OBE 1940); CEng; FIEE; Part-time Member, Central Electricity Generating Bd, 1957-64 (Central Electricity Authority, 1956-57); Chairman: English Telephones Ltd, 1959-69; Cable and Wireless, 1951-56 (Managing Director, 1950-51, Director, 1947-50); Shipton (Automation) Ltd, 1961-67; *b* 3 Sept. 1895; 2nd *s* of late Walter James Nicholls, Burnham, Essex; *m*

1st, 1925, Doris (marr. diss. 1948, she died 1962), *d* of late Ernest Fresson; one *s*; 2nd, 1948, Violet Ethel (marr. diss., 1955; she died 1960); 3rd, 1955, Joan Lady Douglas of Kirtleside. *Educ:* Cheltenham Coll.; University Coll., Univ. of London. Fellow of University Coll., 1948. European War, 1914-19, served with RASC and flying duties RFC and RAF in France and Belgium (twice wounded); transferred to Royal Signals 1925; Shanghai Defence Force, 1927-28; NW Frontier of India, 1936-37 (despatches, medal with clasp); War of 1939-45 in France, Persia, Middle East, N Africa, Italy, France and Germany (despatches, OBE, CBE, CB, US Legion of Merit, Degree of Commander, Legion of Honour (Officer), Croix de Guerre with palm); retired pay, 1946. Freeman of the City of London, 1954; Liveryman of the Worshipful Company of Carmen. *Recreations:* gardening and music. *Address:* 19 Richmond Court, 200 Sloane Street, SW1. *Clubs:* Royal Thames Yacht, Royal Corinthian Yacht.

**NICHOLLS, Philip;** a Forestry Commissioner (Finance and Administration), since 1970; *b* 30 Aug. 1914; *yr s* of late W. H. Nicholls, Radlett; *m* 1955, Sue, *yr d* of late W. E. Shipton; two *s*. *Educ:* Malvern; Pembroke Coll., Cambridge. Asst Master, Malvern, 1936; Sen. Classical Master, 1939; resigned, 1947. Served in Army, 1940-46: 8th Bn, The Worcestershire Regt; HQ, East Africa Command; Allied Commn for Austria. Foreign Office (German Section), 1947; HM Treasury, 1949. Mem. Council, Malvern Coll. (Vice-Chm., 1965). *Address:* 24 Rivermead Court, SW6. *T:* 01-736 1919. *Clubs:* Athenæum, Hurlingham.

**NICHOLLS, Ven. Vernon Sampson;** Archdeacon of Birmingham since Sept. 1967; Diocesan Planning Officer, and Co-ordinating Officer for Christian Stewardship, since 1967; *b* 3 Sept. 1917; *s* of Ernest C. Nicholls, Truro, Cornwall; *m* 1943, Phyllis, *d* of Edwin Potter, Stratford-on-Avon; one *s* one *d*. *Educ:* Truro Sch.; Univ. of Durham and Clifton Theological Coll., Bristol (LTh). Curate: St Oswald, Bedminster Down, Bristol, 1941-42; Liskeard, Cornwall, 1942-43. CF, 1944-46 (Hon. CF 1946). Vicar of Meopham, 1946-56; Rural Dean of Cobham, 1953-56; Vicar and Rural Dean of Walsall, 1956-67; Preb. of Curborough, Lichfield Cath., 1964-67. *Recreations:* meeting people, gardening, motoring. *Address:* Glengarriff, 59 Salisbury Road, Moseley, Birmingham 13. *T:* 021-449 1642. *Club:* Royal Commonwealth Society.

**NICHOLS, Beverley;** author and composer; *y s* of late John Nichols, Solicitor, of Bristol; unmarried. *Educ:* Marlborough Coll.; Balliol Coll., Oxford (Pres. of the Union, Editor of the Isis, Founder and Editor of the Oxford Outlook). *Publications:* Prelude (a public school novel), 1920; Patchwork, 1921; Self, 1922; Twenty-Five (an autobiography), 1926; Crazy Pavements, 1927; Are They the Same at Home?, 1927; The Star Spangled Manner, 1928; Women and Children Last, 1931; Evensong, 1932; Down the Garden Path, 1932; For Adults Only, 1932; Failures, 1933; Cry Havoc, 1933; A Thatched Roof, 1933; A Village in a Valley, 1934; The Fool Hath Said, 1936; No Place Like Home, 1936; News of England, 1938; Revue, 1939; Green Grows the City, 1939; Men do not Weep, 1941; Verdict on India, 1944; The Tree that Sat Down, 1945; The Stream that Stood Still, 1948; All I Could Never Be, 1949; Uncle Samson, 1950; The Mountain of Magic, 1950; Merry Hall, 1951; A Pilgrim's Progress, 1952; Laughter on the Stairs, 1953; No Man's Street, 1954; The Moonflower, 1955; Death to Slow Music, 1956; Sunlight on the Lawn, 1956; The Rich Die Hard, 1957; The Sweet and Twenties, 1958; Murder by Request, 1960; Beverley Nichols' Cats ABC, 1960; Beverley Nichols' Cats XYZ, 1961; Garden Open Today, 1963; Forty Favourite Flowers, 1964; Powers That Be, 1966; A Case of Human Bondage, 1966; The Art of Flower Arrangement, 1967; Garden Open Tomorrow, 1968; The Sun in My Eyes, 1969; *plays:* (Musical and otherwise): The Stag, 1929; Cochran's 1930 Revue, 1930; Avalanche, 1931; Evensong, 1932; When The Crash Comes, 1933; Dr Mesmer, 1934; Floodlight, 1937; Song on the Wind (Operette), 1948; Shadow of the Vine, 1949; Lady's Guide, 1950.

**NICHOLS, Clement Roy,** CMG 1970; OBE 1956; Chairman, Alpha Spinning Mills Pty Ltd and associated companies; *b* 4 Jan. 1909; *s* of C. J. Nichols, Melbourne; *m* 1933, Margareta, *d* of A. C. Pearse, Melbourne; one *s* one *d*. *Educ:* Scotch Coll., Melbourne. Lifetime in wool worsted manufacturing. Past Pres., Wool Textile Mfrs of Australia; Vice-Pres., Internat. Wool Textile Organisation; Mem., Australian Wool Testing Authority; Pres., Victorian Chamber of Mfrs, 1970; Vice-Pres., Associated Chambers of Mfrs of Australia. Mem., Boy Scouts' World Cttee, 1967-; Chm., Far East Scout Region, 1962-64; Chief Comr, Aust. Boy Scouts, 1963-66; Chief Comr, Victorian Br., 1952-58. *Recreation:* photography. *Address:* 12 Finhaven Court, Kew, Victoria 3101, Australia. *Clubs:* Australian, Royal Automobile of Victoria (Melbourne).

**NICHOLS, Edward Henry,** TD; Town Clerk of City of London, since 1954; *b* 27 Sept. 1911; *o s* of Henry James and Agnes Annie Nichols, Notts; *m* 1941, Gwendoline Hetty, *d* of late Robert Elgar, Leeds; one *s*. *Educ:* Queen Elizabeth's Gram. Sch., Mansfield; Selwyn Coll., Cambridge (BA, LLB). Articled Town Clerk, Mansfield, 1933; Asst Solicitor, Derby, 1936-40. Served War of 1939-45, Hon. Lt-Col RA. Dep. Town Clerk, Derby, 1940-48, Leicester, 1948-49; Town Clerk and Clerk of the Peace, Derby, 1949-53. Chevalier, Order of N Star of Sweden; holds other foreign orders. *Address:* 3 Broom Park, Teddington, Mddx. *T:* 01-977 7898.

**NICHOLS, John Winfrith de Lisle,** BSc (Eng); CEng; FIEE; Chief Scientific Officer, Systems and Automation Division, Ministry of Technology; *b* 7 June 1919; *er s* of late John F. Nichols, MC, PhD, FRHistS, FSA, Godalming; *m* 1942, Catherine, *er d* of Capt. A. V. Grantham, RNR, Essex; two *s* two *d*. *Educ:* Sir Walter St John's Sch., Battersea; London University. Royal Navy, 1940-46; GPO, Dollis Hill, 1946-47; RN Scientific Service, 1947-55; Chief Research Officer, Corp. of Trinity House, 1955-59; UKAEA, 1959-65; Min. of Technology, 1965-. *Recreations:* gardening, sailing, caravanning. *Address:* West House, Leybourne, Wormley, Godalming, Surrey. *T:* Wormley 3252.

**NICHOLS, Prof. Roy Franklin;** Emeritus Professor of History, University of Pennsylvania, since 1968 (Professor of History, 1930-68; Dean of Graduate School, 1948-66; Vice-Provost, 1953-66); *b* 3 March 1896; *s* of Franklin Coriell and Anna Cairns Nichols; *m* 1920, Jeannette Paddock; no *c*. *Educ:* Rutgers Univ. (AM); Columbia Univ (PhD). Fellow and Instructor in History, 1920-25; Visiting Professor, 1944-45, Columbia Univ. Asst Professor of History, University of Pennsylvania, 1925-30. Visiting Professor of American History and Institutions, 1948-49, Cambridge Univ. Visiting Prof., Stanford Univ., 1952. Pres.,

Pennsylvania Historical Assoc., 1936-39; Member: Pennsylvania Historical Commn, 1940-43; Philadelphia Historical Commn, 1961-69 (Chm. 1966-69); Bd of Dirs, Amer. Acad. Political and Social Science, 1958-69; Pres., Genealogical Soc. of Pa, 1946-57; Vice-President: Historical Soc. of Pa, 1953-; American Historical Assoc., 1965 (Pres., 1967); Board of Directors Social Science Research Council, 1934-56; Board of Trustees Rutgers Univ., 1944-47, 1950-69; Board of Governors, 1957-69; American Philosophical Soc., 1945 (Vice-Pres., 1962-65); United States Educn Commn in Great Britain, 1948-49. Fellow of Trinity Coll., Cambridge, 1948-49 (MA). Pulitzer Prizewinner in History, 1949. Phi Beta Kappa (Senator, 1961-69). Hon. Doctorates: LittD Franklin and Marshall, 1937, Muhlenberg Coll., 1956, Univ. of Chattanooga, 1966; LHD Rutgers, 1941; LLD Moravian, 1953; Lincoln Univ., 1959; Knox Coll., 1960. DSSc, Lebanon Valley, 1961; DPed, Susquehannah, 1964; DCL, Univ. of Pennsylvania, 1966. *Publications:* Democratic Machine, 1850-1854, 1923; Franklin Pierce, a Biography, 1931 (new edns, 1958, 1969); Disruption of American Democracy, 1948; Advance Agents of American Destiny, 1956; Religion and American Democracy, 1959; The Stakes of Power, 1845-1877, 1961; Blueprints for Leviathan: American Style, 1963; Invention of the American Political Parties, 1967; A Historian's Progress, 1968; (with Jeannette P. Nichols): Republic of the United States, 1941-43, Growth of American Democracy, 1939. *Recreations:* travelling, theatre, music. *Address:* Fairfax Apartments, 43rd and Locust Streets, Philadelphia, Pa 19104, USA. *T:* 386-6630. *Clubs:* Authors'; Rittenhouse (Philadelphia); Cosmos (Washington); Century (New York).

**NICHOLS, William Reginald,** TD, MA; Clerk of the Worshipful Company of Salters since 1946; *b* 23 July 1912; *s* of late Reginald H. Nichols, JP, FSA, Barrister-at-Law; *m* 1946, Imogen, *d* of late Rev. Percy Dearmer, DD, Canon of Westminster, and of Nancy (who *m* 1946, Sir John Sykes, KCB; he died, 1952); one *s* one *d*. *Educ:* Harrow; Gonville and Caius Coll., Cambridge (Sayer Classical Scholar). MA 1938. Called to the Bar, Gray's Inn, 1937. Served War of 1939-45 with Hertfordshire Regt (despatches) and on staff 21st Army Group. Governor of Christ's Hospital; Governor of Grey Coat Hospital Foundation. *Address:* 36 Portland Place, W1. *Clubs:* Athenæum, MCC.

**NICHOLSON, Air Commodore Angus Archibald Norman,** CBE 1961; *b* 8 March 1919; *s* of Major Norman Nicholson and Alice Frances Nicholson (*née* Salvidge), Hoylake, Cheshire; *m* 1943, Joan Mary, *d* of Ernest Beaumont, MRCVS, DVSM; one *s* one *d*. *Educ:* Eton; King's Coll., Cambridge. Cambridge Univ. Air Sqn, 1938-39; commissioned, 1939. Served War 1939-45: flying duties in Bomber Command and Middle East. Air Cdre, 1966; Dir of Defence Plans (Air), Min. of Defence, 1966-67; Defence Adviser to British High Comr in Canada and Head of British Defence Liaison Staff, 1968-70. *Recreations:* sailing, golf, fishing. *Address:* 12 Captain's Row, Lymington, Hants. *Clubs:* Royal Automobile; Leander (Henley); Royal Lymington Yacht.

**NICHOLSON, Sir Arthur (William),** Kt 1968; OBE 1962; Mayor of City of Ballarat, 1952-53, 1960-61, and 1967-68; Chairman of Ballarat Water Commissioners and Ballarat Sewerage Authority, since 1956; *b* 1 June, 1903; *s* of A. H. Nicholson; *m* 1932, Jessie Beryl, *d* of H. A. Campbell; one *s*. *Educ:* Humffray Street State School; Ballarat High School and School of Mines. Master Builderfamily business. Hon. Life Mem. Master Builders' Assoc. (twice Pres.); Mem., Western Moorabool Water Board; Chm., Provincial Sewerage Authorities Assoc. of Victoria, 1959-68; Chm., Waterworks Trusts Assoc. of Victoria. Councillor, City of Ballarat, 1946-; Chm., Clarendon Presbyterian Ladies' Coll., Ballarat; Past Pres., Queen Elizabeth Home, Ballarat; Pres., National Board YMCAs, Australia; Mem., National Board, YMCA; Mem. Council, Ballarat School of Mines and Industries; Chm., Victorian Rural University Assoc.; Mem., Library Council of Victoria (Chm., Library Service Div.); Dir of Ballarat Television Station. Past Pres., Assoc. of Victorian Homes and Hospitals for the Aged and Infirm; twice Pres., Ballarat Caledonian Soc. Mem. Ebenezer Presbyterian Church, Ballarat. *Recreations:* bowls, photography and farming. *Address:* 103 Wendouree Parade, Ballarat, Victoria 3350, Australia. *T:* 55504 Ballarat. *Club:* Old Colonists (Ballarat).

**NICHOLSON, Ben,** OM 1968; painter; *b* 10 April 1894; *s* of late Sir William and Mabel Nicholson; *m* 1st, Winifred Roberts, painter and writer (marr. diss.); two *s* one *d*; 2nd, Barbara Hepworth (*see* Dame Barbara Hepworth) (marr. diss.); one *s* two *d*; 3rd, Dr Felicitas Vogler. *Educ:* Heddon Court, Cockfosters; Gresham Sch. (one term); Slade School of Art (one term); Tours; Milan. Awarded 1st prize Carnegie International, Pittsburgh, 1952; Ulissi prize, Venice Biennale, 1954; Governor of Tokyo prize at 3rd International Exhibition, Japan, 1955; Grand Prix at 4th Lugano International, 1956; 1st Guggenheim Foundation Award, 1957. 1st Internat. Prize, 4th S Paulo Biennial, 1957. Works included in following public collections: Tate Gallery; British Council; Arts Council; Contemporary Art Society; Victoria and Albert Museum, London; City Art Galleries: Leeds; Manchester; Birmingham; Bristol; Glasgow; Nottingham City Museum; Bedford Museum; Museum of Modern Art, New York; Guggenheim Museum, New York; Carnegie Institute, Pittsburgh; Walker Art Centre, Minneapolis; Allbright Museum, Buffalo; San Francisco Art Museum; Philadelphia Museum; Phillips Gallery and American University, Washington; Kunstmuseum, Zürich; Kunstmuseum, Berne; Wintherthur, Kunstmuseum; Kunsthalle, Hamburg; Musée des Beaux Arts, Antwerp; Museum of Fine Arts, Rotterdam; Palais des Beaux Arts, Brussels; Australian National Gallery; Canadian National Gallery; Museum of Fine Arts, Tel-Aviv, Israel; Museo de Arte Moderno, Rio de Janeiro; Museo Nacional de Buenos Aires; Centre National d'Art Moderne; Ohara Museum, Japan, etc. Retrospective one-man exhibitions include: Venice Biennale, 1954; Stedilijk Museum, Amsterdam, 1954; Musée Nationale d'Art Moderne, Paris, 1955; Palais des Beaux Arts, Brussels, 1955; Kunsthalle, Zürich, 1955; Tate Gallery, London, 1955, 1956, 1970; in German Cities, 1959; Kunsthalle, Bern, 1961; Marlborough New London Gallery, 1967; Crane Kalman Gall., 1968; Galerie Beyeler, Basle, 1968; Tate Gallery, 1969. *Publications:* (co-editor) Circle international survey of constructive art, 1937; monographs: Ben Nicholson (introduction Sir John Summerson), Penguin, 1948; Notes on Abstract Art (by Ben Nicholson), included in Ben Nicholson (introduction Sir Herbert Read), Lund Humphries, vol. 1, 1911-, 1948, vol. 2, Work from 1948-1955; Ben Nicholson, The Meaning of His Art (introd. Dr J. P. Hodin), 1957; Ben Nicholson (introd. Sir Herbert Read), 1962; Ben Nicholson (introd. D. Baxandall), 1962; Ben Nicholson (introd.

Ronald Alley), 1962; Ben Nicholson: Drawings, Paintings and Reliefs, 1911-1968 (introd. John Russell), 1969; Ben Nicholson (ed Maurice de Sausmarez), 1969. *Recreations:* painting, tennis, golf, table tennis, etc. *Address:* c/o Banca della Svizzera, Locarno, Ticino, Switzerland.

**NICHOLSON, General Sir Cameron Gordon Graham,** GCB 1954 (KCB 1953, CB 1945); KBE 1950 (CBE 1943); DSO 1940; MC 1918; Governor of the Royal Hospital, Chelsea, 1956-61; Master Gunner, St James's Park, 1956-60; Colonel Commandant, Royal Artillery, 1950-60; Colonel Commandant Royal Horse Artillery, 1956-60; *b* 30 June 1898; *s* of late Brig.-General G. H. W. Nicholson, CB, CMG; *m* 1926, Evelyn Odell Westropp; one *s* two *d*. *Educ:* Northaw Place; Wellington; RMA, Woolwich. 2nd Lieut, RA, 1915; European War, 1915-18 (MC and Bar); RHA, 1917-27 (France, India, Iraq, Palestine, Egypt); Instructor, RMA, Woolwich, 1927-30; Staff Coll., Camberley, 1930-32; Bde Major, RA 2nd Div., 1934-36; MO War Office, 1936-37; Instructor, Staff Coll., Camberley, 1938-39; served War of 1939-45 (DSO and Bar, CBE, CB); GSO1, 45 Div., 1940; GSO1, Sickleforce, Norway, 1940; GSO1, 18 Div., 1940; DCGS Home Forces, 1941; Comd Support Group, 42 Armoured Div., 1941-42; Second-in-Command 6 Armoured Div., 1942; BGS First Army 1943; Commander 44 Indian Armoured Div., 1943-44; Commander 2 British Div., 1945-46; Director of Artillery, War Office, 1946; General Officer Commanding-in-Chief, West Africa Command, 1948-51; General Officer Commanding-in-Chief, Western Command, 1951-53; C-in-C Middle East Land Forces, 1953; Adjutant-General to the Forces, 1953-56; ADC General to the Queen, 1954-56; retired 1956. Hon. Colonel Travel Control Security Group (TA), 1955-60. Governor, Wellington Coll., 1956-68; Governor, Welbeck Coll., 1956-61. Received Order of Legion Merit and Silver Star, USA, in North Africa. *Recreations:* shooting, fishing, golf. *Address:* c/o Lloyds Bank Ltd, 6 Pall Mall, SW1.

**NICHOLSON, Charles Gordon Brown;** Sheriff Substitute of Dumfries and Galloway since 1970; *b* 11 Sept. 1935; *s* of William Addison Nicholson, former Director, Scottish Tourist Board, and late Jean Brown; *m* 1963, Hazel Mary Nixon; two *s*. *Educ:* George Watson's Coll., Edinburgh; Edinburgh Univ. MA Hons (English Lit.) 1956, LLB 1958. 2nd Lieut Queen's Own Cameron Highlanders, 1958-60. Admitted Faculty of Advocates, Edinburgh, 1961; in practice at Bar; Standing Junior Counsel, Registrar of Restrictive Trading Agreements, 1968; Advocate-Depute, 1968-70. *Recreation:* golf. *Address:* Townhead of Glencairn, Moniaive, Dumfriesshire. *T:* Moniaive, 214. *Club:* Bruntsfield Links Golfing Society.

**NICHOLSON, (Edward) Max,** CB 1948; Director-General of the Nature Conservancy 1952-66; Convener, Conservation Section International Biological Programme since 1963; Chairman, Land Use Consultants, since 1966; *b* 1904; *m* 1st, 1932, Eleanor Mary Crawford (marr. diss., 1964); two *s*; 2nd, Marie Antoinette Mauerhofer; one *s*. *Educ:* Sedbergh; Hertford Coll., Oxford. Head of Allocation of Tonnage Division, Ministry of War Transport, 1942-45; Secretary of Office of The Lord President of the Council, 1945-52. Member Advisory Council on Scientific Policy, 1948-64; Secretary, Duke of Edinburgh's Study Conference on the Countryside in 1970, 1963, and Joint Secretary Second Study Conference, Nov. 1965; Albright Lecturer, Univ. of California, 1964; Dep. Leader British Jordan Expedition, 1963. Vice-President: PEP; Wildfowlers' Assoc. of Great Britain and Ireland; Trustee: Fair Isle Bird Observatory; Simon Population Trust. Scientific Fellow Zoological Society of London; Corr. Fellow, American Ornithologists' Union, Hon. Mem., Town Planning Inst., 1970. John C. Phillips medallist International Union for Conservation of Nature and Natural Resources, 1963. Hon. LLD Aberdeen, 1964; Hon. Dr, RCA, 1970. *Publications:* Birds in England, 1926; How Birds Live, 1927; Birds and Men, 1951; Britain's Nature Reserves, 1958; The System, 1967; The Environmental Revolution, 1970; and other books, scientific papers and articles. *Address:* 13 Upper Cheyne Row, SW3. *Club:* Athenæum.

**NICHOLSON, Frank Douglas,** TD; MA Cantab; DL; JP; *b* 30 July 1905; *o s* of late Sir Frank Nicholson, CBE; *m* 1937, Pauline, *y d* of late Sir Thomas Lawson Tancred, 9th Bt, Borobridge; five *s*. *Educ:* Harrow; Clare Coll., Cambridge. Scottish Horse (TA), 1928. Chm., Vaux Breweries and Others. Vice-Chm., Brewers: Soc., 1969. Contested (C) Spennymoor, at 1945 Election. High Sheriff Durham County, 1948-49; DL 1948; JP 1949. *Recreations:* farming, etc. *Address:* Southill Hall, Plawsworth, near Chester-le-Street, Co. Durham. *T:* Chester-le-Street 2286. *Club:* Cavalry.

**NICHOLSON, Major Geoffrey,** CBE 1944; MC 1917; *b* 1894; *s* of late Brig. General George Harvey Nicholson, CB, CMG; *m* 1st, 1920, Jeana Winifred Mary (*d* 1962), *d* of late Major St Andrew Bruce Warde, Chief Constable of Hants; three *d*; 2nd, Dorothy Florence, *d* of A. E. Sedgwick, Hove, Sussex. Educ: HMS Conway; Imperial Service Coll.; RMC, Sandhurst. Joined 1 Bn Hampshire Regt, 1913; served in European War, 1914-19 (despatches thrice), in France and Salonika; Brigade Major, 1918; retired with rank of Bt Major, 1922; Assistant Chief Constable of Hampshire, 1922-30; Chief Constable of Surrey, 1930-46; Royal Humane Society's Bronze Medal for saving life at sea, 1912; serving brother Order of St John of Jerusalem, 1945; Officer of Star of Roumania with swords, 1919. *Recreations:* field sports and yachting. *Address:* Little Durford, Durford Wood, Petersfield, Hants. *T:* Liss 3241.

**NICHOLSON, Sir Godfrey,** 1st Bt, *cr* 1958; Distiller; *b* 9 Dec. 1901; *s* of late Richard Francis Nicholson of Woodcott, Hants, and late Helen Violet Portal; *m* 1936, Lady Katharine Constance Lindsay, 5th *d* of 27th Earl of Crawford; four *d*. *Educ:* Winchester; Christ Church, Oxford. MP (Nat. C) Morpeth, 1931-35; Royal Fusiliers, 1939-42; MP (C) Farnham Division of Surrey, 1937-66; retired. Chairman, Estimates Cttee, 1961-64. FSA. *Address:* Bussock Hill House, Newbury, Berks. *T:* Chieveley 260. *Clubs:* Pratt's, Carlton.

*See also Sir J. C. F. M. Cuninghame.*

**NICHOLSON, Admiral Sir Gresham;** *see* Nicholson, Admiral Sir R. S. G.

**NICHOLSON, Howard;** Physician, University College Hospital, since 1948; Physician, Brompton Hospital, since 1952; Fellow of University College, London, since 1959; *b* 1 Feb. 1912; *s* of Frederick and Sara Nicholson; *m* 1941, Winifred Madeline Piercy. *Educ:* University Coll., London, and University Coll. Hospital. MB, BS, London, 1935; MD London 1938; MRCP 1938, FRCP 1949. House appointments and Registrarship, UCH,

1935-38; House Physician at Brompton Hosp., 1938. Served War, 1940-45, RAMC; Physician to Chest Surgical Team and Officer i/c Medical Div. (Lt-Col). Registrar, Brompton Hosp., and Chief Asst, Inst. of Diseases of Chest, 1945-48. Goulstonian Lecturer, RCP, 1950. *Publications:* sections on Diseases of Chest in The Practice of Medicine (ed J. S. Richardson), 1961, and in Progress in Clinical Medicine, 1961; articles in Thorax, Lancet, etc. *Recreations:* reading, going to the opera. *Address:* 69 Harley Street, W1. *T:* 01-486 2012; 62 Townshend Road, St John's Wood, NW8. *T:* 01-722 4946.

**NICHOLSON, Sir John (Charles),** 3rd Bt, *cr* 1859; TD 1954; FRCS 1934; BM, BCh; Consulting Surgeon; Senior Surgeon, Bethnal Green, St Leonard's and St Matthew's Hospitals, London, retired 1969; *b* 10 Jan. 1904; *s* of Sir Charles Nicholson, 2nd Bt, and Evelyn Louise (*d* 1927), *d* of Rev. H. Oliver; *S* father, 1949; *m* 1928, Caroline Elizabeth, *d* of late Rt Rev. John Frederick McNeice, Bishop of Down; no *c*. *Educ:* Brighton Coll.; New Coll., Oxford; St Bartholomew's Hospital. Major, RAMC, TA (commissioned 1932); Temp. Lieut-Colonel, RAMC, 1942; Hon. Lieut-Colonel 1945. Late Surgical Registrar, Royal National Orthopædic Hospital, etc.; Clinical Fellow in Surgery, Harvard Univ., 1947-48. Qualified 1929; BM, BCh, Oxford, 1929. *Publications:* various on professional subjects in British Medical Journal and other periodicals. *Recreations:* yachting and shooting. *Heir:* none. *Address:* Thames Cottage, Thames Street, Sunbury-on-Thames. *T:* Sunbury 2148.

**NICHOLSON, Brigadier John Gerald,** CMG 1961; CBE 1945; retired; *b* 17 Jan. 1906; *er s* of late Lieut-Colonel Walter Adams Nicholson, RA (killed in action, 1917); *m* 1940, Emmeline Mary, *d* of late Henry Barrington Tristram; two *s* one *d* (and one *s* decd). *Educ:* Wellington Coll.; RMC, Sandhurst. Commnd into The Buffs, 1925; Adjt, 1930; Staff Coll., 1934. Served War of 1939-45 (wounded, despatches, CBE). DAAG, AHQ, India, 1939; DAAG 52 Div., 1940; AA and QMG, 15 Div., 1941; Comd 2nd Bn The Buffs, Western Desert, 1942; GSO1, Cyrenaica Dist., 1943; GSO1, GHQ, MEF, 1943; Brig. GS, Plans, AFHQ, CMF, 1944; DDI, SACSEA, 1945; seconded to Foreign Office, 1946. Retired from Army and entered Foreign Service, 1948; appointed to Political Office, MEF, 1948-51, when transferred to FO; retired, 1966. Dep. Colonel, The Buffs, 1956-58; DL Kent, 1958. Officer of the Legion of Merit (USA), 1944; Comdr Royal Danish Order of the Dannebrog, 1956. *Recreation:* horticulture. *Address:* Stone Cross House, Crowborough, Sussex. *T:* Crowborough 61401. *Club:* United Service.

**NICHOLSON, John Henry;** CBE 1954; MM; Hon. LLD (Leeds) 1955; Hon. LLD (Hull) 1957; *b* 21 Sept. 1889; *s* of late John Richard Nicholson; unmarried. *Educ:* Scarborough Coll.; Christ Church, Oxford. Tutorial Class Tutor, Liverpool Univ., 1913-15; served in HM Forces, RAMC and RGA, 1915-18; Tutor, Ordination Test School, Knutsford, 1919-20; Lecturer in Education, Bristol Univ., 1920-33; Director of Extra-Mural Studies, Bristol Univ., 1925-33; Professor of Education, Armstrong Coll., Newcastle upon Tyne (University of Durham), 1933-35; Principal, Hull University Coll., 1935-54; Vice-Chancellor, Hull Univ., 1954-56. Albert Khan Fellow, 1922-23. *Publications:* The Remaking of the Nations, 1925; School Care Committees, 1925; Education and Modern Needs, 1936; Help for the Handicapped, 1958; New Communities in Britain, 1961. *Recreation:* walking. *Address:* 30 Clifton, York. *Club:* Yorkshire (York).

**NICHOLSON, (John) Leonard;** Chief Economic Adviser to Department of Health and Social Security, since 1968; *b* 18 Feb. 1916; *er s* of late Percy Merwyn Nicholson and late Jane Winifred Nicholson (*née* Morris). *Educ:* Stowe; Institute of Actuaries; London School of Economics. MSc(Econ). Oxford University Inst. of Statistics, 1940-47; Statistician with Ministry of Home Security, 1943-44; Statistician, 1947-52, Chief Statistician, 1952-68, Central Statistical Office. Simon Research Fellow, Manchester Univ., 1962-63. Member: Council, Royal Statistical Society, 1961-66; Editorial Board, Journal of Royal Statistical Society, 1959-. *Publications:* (jointly) The Beveridge Plan for Social Security, 1943; Variations in Working Class Family Expenditure, 1949; The Interim Index of Industrial Production, 1949; Redistribution of Income in the United Kingdom in 1959, 1957 and 1953, 1965; various papers mainly concerned with national income and economic welfare in academic journals. *Recreations:* listening to music, pre-eminently Mozart but all composers before and after Wagner; looking at paintings; real and lawn tennis, skiing and other (but not underwater) sports. *Address:* 53 Frognal, NW3. *T:* 01-435 8015. *Clubs:* Queen's, Reform, Arts Theatre.

**NICHOLSON, Rev. John Malcolm;** Rector of Brightwalton, since 1970; *b* 26 May 1908; 2nd *s* of John and Madeleine Nicholson; *m* 1939, Dorothy Lisle Preston; one *s* two *d*. *Educ:* Whitgift Sch.; King's Coll., Cambridge; Cuddesdon Theological Coll. Asst Curate, St John's, Newcastle upon Tyne, 1932-36; Vicar, St Mary's, Monkseaton, 1936-38; Vicar, Sugley, 1938-46; Vicar, St George's, Cullercoats, 1946-55; Archdeacon of Doncaster, 1955-59; Vicar of High Melton, 1955-59; Headmaster, The King's School, Tynemouth, 1959-70. Examining Chaplain: to Bishop of Newcastle, 1944-55; to Bishop of Sheffield, 1955-59; Select Preacher, Cambridge Univ., 1959. *Address:* Brightwalton Rectory, Newbury, Berks. *T:* Chaddleworth 275.

**NICHOLSON, Sir John (Norris),** 2nd Bt, *cr* 1912; CIE 1946; JP; Chairman, Ocean Steam Ship Co. Ltd; President, Chamber of Shipping of the UK; Director: Barclays Bank Ltd; Royal Insurance Co. Ltd; Lead Industries Group; *b* 19 Feb. 1911; *o c* of late Captain George Crosfield Norris Nicholson, RFC, and Hon. Evelyn Izme Murray, *y d* of 10th Baron and 1st Viscount Elibank (she *m* 2nd 1st Baron Mottistone, PC); *S* grandfather, 1918; *m* 1938, Vittoria Vivien, *y d* of late Percy Trewhella, Villa Sant' Andrea, Taormina; two *s* two *d*. *Educ:* Winchester Coll., Trinity Coll., Cambridge. Captain 4th Cheshires (TA), 1939-41. BEF Flanders 1940 (despatches). Min. of War Transport, India and SE Asia, 1942-46. Chairman: Liverpool Port Employers Assoc., 1957-61; Martins Bank Ltd, 1962-64 (Dep. Chm., 1959-62); Management Cttee, HMS Conway, 1958-65; British Liner Cttee, 1963-67; Cttee, European Nat. Shipowners' Assoc., 1965-69; Mem., Shipping Advisory Panel, 1962-64. *Heir:* *s* Charles Christian Nicholson, *b* 15 Dec. 1941. *Address:* Brooke House, Parkgate, Cheshire. *T:* Neston 1494; Mottistone Manor, Isle of Wight. *Clubs:* Brooks's; Royal Yacht Squadron.

**NICHOLSON, Lewis Frederick,** CB 1963; Deputy Controller of Aircraft (Research and Development), Ministry of Technology, since 1969; *b* 1 May 1918; *s* of Harold and May Nicholson; *m* 1947, Diana Rosalind Fear; one *s* two *d. Educ:* Taunton Sch.; King's Coll., Cambridge. Research Laboratories of GEC, 1939; Royal Aircraft Establishment, 1939-59; Head of Aerodynamics Dept, RAE, 1953-59; Imperial Defence Coll., 1956; Director-General of Scientific Research (Air), Ministry of Aviation, 1959-63; Dep. Director (Air) Royal Aircraft Establishment, 1963-66; Chief Scientist, RAF, 1966-69. *Publications:* (Joint) Compressible Airflow-Tables; Compressible Airflow-Graphs; papers on aerodynamic subjects. *Address:* Abbotsleigh, Church Road East, Farnborough, Hants. *T:* Farnborough, Hants, 41779.

**NICHOLSON, Max;** *see* Nicholson, E. M.

**NICHOLSON, Norman Cornthwaite;** poet and critic; *b* Millom, Cumberland, 8 Jan. 1914; *s* of Joseph and Edith Nicholson; *m* 1956, Yvonne Edith Gardner. *Educ:* local schools. Literary criticism in weekly press. FRSL 1945; MA (Hon.) Manchester Univ., 1959. Cholmondley Award for Poetry, 1967; Grant from Northern Arts Assoc., 1969. *Publications: poetry:* Five Rivers, 1944 (Heinemann Prize, 1945); Rock Face, 1948; The Pot Geranium, 1954; Selected Poems, 1966; *verse drama:* The Old Man of the Mountains (produced Mercury Theatre), 1946; A Match for the Devil, 1955; Birth by Drowning, 1960; *criticism:* Man and Literature, 1943; William Cowper, 1951; *topography:* Cumberland and Westmorland, 1949; The Lakers, 1955; Provincial Pleasures, 1959; Portrait of the Lakes, 1963; Greater Lakeland, 1969. Editor, The Pelican Anthology of Modern Religious Verse. *Address:* 14 St George's Terrace, Millom, Cumberland.

**NICHOLSON, Otho William,** TD 1942; DL; *b* 1891; *e s* of late Colonel Rt Hon. William Graham Nicholson, PC; *m* 1927, Elisabeth (who obtained a divorce, 1932), *er d* of late Frederick C. Bramwell, Clerk of the Journals, House of Commons; two *d. Educ:* Harrow; Magdalene Coll., Cambridge. served World War, 1914-19, in France with the Rifle Brigade and in the Wireless Intelligence, Royal Engineers; late Hon. Colonel 1st Anti-Aircraft Divisional Signals, Royal Corps of Signals (TA); Brigadier Comdg 40th and 51st Anti-Aircraft Brigade; Asst Comdt, School of AA Artillery, Shrivenham. LCC, 1922-25; Mayor of Finsbury, 1923-24; MP (C) Westminster (Abbey Division), March 1924-32; Chm., Finsbury Cons. Assoc. CStJ. *Recreations:* cricket, shooting. *Address:* The Old Vicarage, Burley, Ringwood, Hants. *Club:* Carlton.

**NICHOLSON, Admiral Sir (Randolph Stewart) Gresham,** KBE, *cr* 1950; CB 1946; DSO 1940; DSC 1918; Lieutenant-Governor and Commander-in-Chief of Jersey, 1953-58; *b* 16 Dec. 1892; *s* of W. Gresham Nicholson; *m* Cicely Georgina, CStJ, *d* of the late Rev. Sub-Dean H. Mackworth Drake; one *s* one *d. Educ:* Royal Naval Colleges, Osborne and Dartmouth. Served European War, Harwich Force 1914-18 (DSC, despatches); took part in ZeebruggeOstend operation; Staff RN Coll., Dartmouth, 1919-21; first and principal ADC to Sir Laurence Guillemard, Governor Malaya and SS, 1921-23; Commander, 1929; Commander RNC, Dartmouth, 1929-31; and HMS Revenge, 1932-34; Captain, 1934; Captain D Tribal Destroyer Flotilla, 1938-40 (despatches, DSO); Commodore, RN Barracks, Chatham, 1940-43; Rear-Admiral, 1943; Dep. C-in-C, Eastern Fleet, and Flag Officer, Ceylon, 1943-45; Admiral Superintendent, HM Dockyard, Devonport, 1945-50; Vice-Admiral, 1948; retired list, 1950; Admiral (retired) 1951. KStJ. Greek Cross of Grand Officer of the Royal Order of Phœnix with Swords, 1947. *Address:* The Toll House, Bucks Green, Horsham, Sussex. *T:* Rudgwick 314. *Club:* United Service.

**NICHOLSON, Robert,** FSIA; Designer; *b* Sydney, Australia, 8 April 1920; *m* 1951, Kathleen Poulter, ARCA; one *s* one *d. Educ:* Medway School of Art. Designed The Design Centre (Council of Industrial Design), Haymarket, 1956. Now publishing and writing guide books, including Nicholson's London Guide. Benjamin Franklin Medal, 1960. *Address:* (home) Garden House, Gordon Road, Sevenoaks, Kent; (office) 3 Goodwins Court, St Martin's Lane, WC2. *T:* 01-240 1072.

**NICHOLSON, William Ewart,** CBE 1941; BA, FRAI; *b* 29 Dec. 1890; *s* of Robert Francis Nicholson, Leeds; *m* 1920, Alice Elgie, *d* of W. E. Cork; one *d. Educ:* Leeds Grammar Sch.; Jesus Coll., Oxford. Education Dept, N Nigeria, 1914; Lieut, Nigeria Regt, 1917; Principal, Katsina Coll., 1934; Director of Education, Sierra Leone, 1935-45; Member Fourah Bay College Commission, 1938; Member of Exec. Council, JP, Sierra Leone; Educational Adviser to Government of The Gambia, 1944-45; Secretary Commission of Enquiry into the system of Education of the Jewish Community in Palestine, 1945-46; Director of Training, Ministry of Food, 1946-48. *Address:* 10 West Hill Avenue, Leeds 7.

**NICHOLSON-LAILEY, John Raymond,** FRCS; Consultant Surgeon and Gynæcologist to Taunton and Somerset Hospital since 1930; Vice-President, British Medical Association, 1968 (Chairman Council, 1962-66); *b* 11 April 1900; *s* of Henry George and Ann Blanche Nicholson-Lailey; *m* 1932, Penelope Alice Peach, MB, BS; one *s* two *d. Educ:* Trowbridge High Sch.; Bristol Univ. Served with Artists Rifles, April-Aug. 1918; Royal Artillery, Aug. 1918-Jan. 1919; commissioned 2nd Lieut, RA, on demob. MRCS, LRCP, 1923; MB, ChB, Bristol 1924; FRCS 1925. Res. Surgical Officer: Royal Devon and Exeter Hospital, 1926; Salford Royal Hospital, 1927; Gloucester Royal Infirmary, 1929. Hon. Surgeon, Taunton and Somerset Hospital, 1930. Past President, Bath, Bristol and Somerset Branch, BMA; Fellow, BMA. President, South-West Obstetric Society, 1960; Vice-Chairman Council, World Medical Assoc., 1964. Hon. LLD (Manchester) 1964. FRCOG 1965. Officer, Order of Merit, Grand Duchy of Luxembourg, 1964. *Address:* Orchard Rise, Trull, Taunton, Somerset. *T:* Taunton 7270.

**NICKALLS, Guy Oliver;** Chairman, Amateur Rowing Association, 1952-68 (Hon. Secretary, 1946-52); Member, Committee of Management, Henley Royal Regatta, since 1945 (Steward of Regatta, 1935-); Committee Member, Dogs' Home, Battersea; Past President of Leander Club; *b* 4 April 1899; *er s* of late Guy Nickalls and of Ellen Gilbey, *d* of Henry Gold; *m* 1929, Violet Rachel Pearce, *o d* of late Colonel Serocold, CMG; no *c. Educ:* Eton; Magdalen Coll., Oxford. Active service, Salonika, 2nd Lieut, Rifle Bde, 1918. Served in Foreign Office, 1919-20; Dip. Econ. 1921; Hons Degree Hist. 1923, MA 1964. Joined advertising firm of Alfred Pemberton Ltd, 1926 (Vice-Chairman, 1945-62). *Publications:* (with Dr P. C. Mallam) Rowing, 1939. Edited and contributed to: Life's a Pudding (autobiography of late Guy Nickalls), 1938; With the Skin of Their Teeth, 1946. *Recreations:* rowed for Oxford *v* Cambridge, 1921, 1922, 1923 (President 1923); Henley: (in winning crews) Grand Challenge Cup of 1920, 1921, 1922, 1924, 1925, 1926 and 1928;

Stewards' Four, 1928; Silver Goblets with R. S. C. Lucas, 1920 and 1921; in eight oar which rep. UK in Olympics of 1920 and 1928 (silver medal twice); fishing, shooting, gardening, painting (has exhibited at RA Summer Exhibition). *Address:* 30 Astell Street, Chelsea, SW3. *T:* 01-352 0693. *Clubs:* Garrick, MCC; London Rowing, Thames Rowing (Putney); Leander, Remenham.

**NICKERSON, Albert Lindsay;** Chairman, 1961-69, and Chief Executive Officer, 1958-69, Mobil Oil Corporation; *b* 17 Jan. 1911; *s* of Albert Lindsay Nickerson and Christine (*née* Atkinson); *m* 1936, Elizabeth Perkins; one *s* three *d. Educ:* Noble and Greenough Sch., Mass; Harvard. Joined Socony-Vacuum Oil Co. Inc. as Service Stn Attendant, 1933; Dist. Man., 1940; Div. Manager, 1941; Asst General Manager, Eastern Marketing Div., 1944; Director, 1946; name of company changed to Socony Mobil Oil Co. Inc., 1955; President, 1955-61; Chairman Exec. Cttee, 1958; name of company changed to Mobil Oil Corporation, 1966. Chairman, Vacuum Oil Co. Ltd, London (later Mobil Oil Co. Ltd), 1946. Director, Placement Bureau War Manpower Commission, Washington, 1943. Chm., Federal Reserve Bank of NY, and Federal Reserve Agent, 1969; Mem., The Business Council (Chm. 1967-69). Director: American Management Assoc., NY, 1948-51, 1953-56, 1958-61; Federal Reserve Board of NY, 1964-67; Metrop. Life Insurance Co.; Mobil Oil Corp.; Transportation Assoc. of America, 1969; Trustee: International House, NY City, 1952-62; Cttee for Economic Development, NY, 1961-65; Rockefeller Univ.; American Museum of Natural History, 1958-62, 1964-69; former director and Treas., American Petroleum Institute; Member: Council on Foreign Relations; National Petroleum Council; Harvard Corp., 1965; Fellow, Harvard Coll.; Overseer Harvard Coll., 1959-65. Hon. LLD Hofstra Univ., 1964. Comdr, Order of Vasa (Sweden), 1963. *Recreations:* golfing, fishing, sailing, camping, bird-hunting. *Address:* (office) 150 East 42nd Street, New York, NY 10017, USA. *T:* 212 883-5225; (home) 444 East 57th Street, New York, NY 10022, USA. *T:* (914) Woodbine 7-0394. *Clubs:* Thames Rowing; Harvard Varsity (Cambridge, Mass); Blind Brook (Port Chester, NY); Racquet and Tennis (NY City).

**NICKLIN, Hon. Sir (George) Francis (Reuben),** KCMG 1968; MM 1918; retired; Premier of Queensland, 1957-68; *b* 6 Aug. 1895; *s* of George Francis Nicklin and Edith Catherine Nicklin, *née* Bond; *m* 1922, Georgina (decd), *d* of R. Fleming. *Educ:* Murwillumbah State Sch.; Highfield Coll., Turramurra, NSW. Engaged in tropical fruit culture since leaving school; took leading part in organisation of Queensland fruit industry. MLA for Murrumba, Queensland, 1932-50, for Landsborough, Queensland, 1950-68; Secretary, Parliamentary Country Party, 1935-41; Leader of the Opposition, 1941-57; Premier and Minister for State Development, Queensland, 1957-68. Hon. LLD Queensland, 1961. *Recreations:* cricket, bowls, gardening, Surf Life Saving movement. *Address:* 13 Upper Gay Terrace, Caloundra, Queensland 4551, Australia. *T:* Caloundra 75. *Clubs:* Queensland Cricketers', Queensland Masonic.

**NICKLIN, Robert Shenstone; His Honour Judge Nicklin,** MA; County Court Judge (circuit No. 21, Birmingham) since Nov. 1957 (lately No. 18); *b* 1901; *s* of late P. H. S. Nicklin, Blundellsands, Liverpool; *m* 1935, Mervyn Halley, MB, ChB, *d* of late Matthew Clark, Blundellsands; three *d. Educ:* Uppingham; University Coll., Oxford. Pte Intelligence Corps; Major JAG's department; barrister, Lincoln's Inn, 1925. JP and Dep. Chairman, Cumberland Quarter Sessions, 1953-56; JP Nottingham, 1956, also Dep. Chairman Quarter Sessions; JP Warwick, 1959. *Address:* Hercules Farm, Claverdon, Warwickshire. *T:* Claverdon 2388.

**NICOBAR ISLANDS, Bishop of,** since 1950; **Rt. Rev. John Richardson;** Assistant Bishop and Commissary to the Bishop and Metropolitan of Calcutta, since 1950; nominated Member of House of Parliament, New Delhi, India, by the President, 1952; *b* 6 June 1894; of Car Nicobarese parentage; *m* 1st, 1913; one *s* two *d* (and two *s* one *d* decd); 2nd, 1942; one *s* two *d* (and one *d* decd). *Educ:* SPG Mission Sch., Mandalay, Upper Burma. Leader of the Nicobarese; teacher and catechist, Car Nicobar, 1912; acted as hon. third class Magistrate, Conservator of Port, 1920-33. Hon. DD, Serampore Coll., 1965. Padma Shri Madel, India, 1965. *Recreations:* walking, cycling and fishing. *Address:* Car Nicobar, Andaman and Nicobar Islands.

**NICOL, Rev. Anderson,** DD (Glasgow) 1967; MA (Glasgow); Chaplain to the Queen in Scotland, since 1964 (Extra Chaplain, 1963); Minister, Dundurn Parish Church, St Fillans, Perthshire, since 1967; *b* Stevenston, Ayrshire, 17 June 1906; *s* of George Nicol and Johanna Jessiman; *m* 1932, Jane Brown Williamson, Stevenston; one *s* two *d* (and one *s* decd). *Educ:* Stevenston; High School of Glasgow; University of Glasgow MA 1927. Asst, St Michael's Parish Church, Crieff, 1931-32; Minister: Dunbarney Parish Church, 1932; Braid Church, Edinburgh, 1941. Chaplain, RN, 1943-46 (Naval General Service Medal, 1946); Minister, West Church of St Nicholas (City Church), Aberdeen, 1948-67. Governor, Robert Gordon's Colleges, 1949-67. Presbyterian preacher to USA (under British Council of Churches Interchange of Preachers), 1957 and 1969; Member Broadcasting Council for Scotland, 1958-62; Patron, Seven Incorporated Trades, 1963-. Scouting: various appointments to Asst Commissioner. *Publication:* The Story of the West Church of St Nicholas, Aberdeen, 1961. *Recreations:* reading, photography, touring. *Address:* The Manse, St Fillans, Perthshire. *T:* St Fillans 267.

**NICOL, Claude Scott,** TD; Physician in charge of Venereal Diseases Department, St Thomas' Hospital and St Bartholomew's Hospital, London; Colonel, RAMC (TARO); Hon. Consultant Venereologist to the Army; Adviser in VD to Department of Health and Social Security; *b* 1914; *s* of late Dr C. G. Nicol, barrister-at-law (Lincoln's Inn); *m* 1939, Janet Wickham Bosworth Smith; one *s* two *d. Educ:* Harrow Sch.; St Mary's Hospital; St John's Coll., Oxford. MRCS, LRCP, 1936; MB, BS, 1938; MD 1946; MRCP, 1946; FRCP, 1962. Formerly: Physician, Whitechapel Clinic, London Hospital; Fellow in Medicine, Johns Hopkins Hospital, Baltimore; House Physician, St Mary's Hosp., London. Asst Dist Surgeon, St John Amb. Assoc. and Brigade. Ex-Pres., Medical Soc. for Study of Venereal Diseases; FRSM. QHP 1967-69. *Publications:* contributions to medical textbooks and journals. *Recreations:* squash racquets, tennis. *Address:* 40 Ferncroft Avenue, NW3. *T:* 01-435 1310; 15 Upper Wimpole Street, W1. *T:* 01-486 3329. *Club:* Army and Navy.

**NICOL, Davidson Sylvester Hector Willoughby,** CMG 1964; MA, MD, PhD (Cantab); Permanent Representative and Ambassador for Sierra Leone to the United Nations, since

1969 (Security Council, 1970); Chairman, Committee of 24 (Decolonisation), UN; Hon. Consultant Pathologist, Sierra Leone Government; *b* of African parentage; *m* 1950, Marjorie Esme Johnston, MB, ChB; two *s* one *d*. *Educ:* Schools in Nigeria and Sierra Leone; Cambridge and London Univs. Science Master, Prince of Wales Sch., Sierra Leone, 1941-43. Cambridge: Foundation Schol., Prizeman, 1943-47, Fellow and Supervisor in Nat. Sciences and Med., 1957-59, Christ's Coll.; BA 1946; 1st Cl. Hons (Nat. Sciences), 1947; Beit Mem. Fellow for Medical Research, 1954; Benn Levy Univ. Studentship, Cambridge, 1956; Univ. Schol., House Physician (Medical Unit and Clinical Pathology) Receiving Room Officer, and Research Asst (Physiology), London Hosp., 1947-52; Univ. Lectr, Medical School. Ibadan, Nigeria, 1952; Visiting Lecturer: Univs of Toronto, California (Berkeley), Mayo Clinic, 1958; Aggrey-Fraser-Guggisberg Mem. Lectr, Univ. of Ghana, 1963; Danforth Fellowship Lectr in African Affairs, Assoc. of Amer. Colls, USA, 1968. Sen. Pathologist, Sierra Leone, 1958-60; Principal, Fourah Bay Coll., Sierra Leone, 1960-68, and Vice-Chancellor, Univ. of Sierra Leone, 1966-68. Margaret Wrong Prize and Medal for Literature in Africa, 1952; Chm., Sierra Leone Nat. Library Bd, 1959-65; Member: Governing Body, Kumasi Univ., Ghana; Public Service Commn, Sierra Leone, 1960-68. W African Council for Medical Research, 1959-62; Exec. Council, Assoc. of Univs of British Commonwealth, 1960 and 1966; Commn for proposed Univ. of Ghana, 1960; Chm., Univ. of E Africa Visiting Cttee, 1962. Director: Central Bank of Sierra Leone; Sierra Leone Selection Trust Ltd; Consolidated African Selection Trust Ltd (London). President W African Science Assoc., 1964-66; Vice-Pres. CMS London, 1961; President: SCM, Western Nigeria, 1952-54, Sierra Leone, 1959; Sierra Leone Red Cross Soc., 1962-66; Chm., W African Exams Council, 1964-69; Conference Delegate to: WHO Assembly, 1959, 1960; UNESCO Higher Educn Conf., Tananarive, 1963; Commonwealth Prime Ministers' Conf., London, 1965 and 1969. FRCPath. Hon. LLD, Leeds; Hon. DSc, Newcastle upon Tyne. Independence Medal, Sierra Leone, 1961. Hon. Fellow, Ghana Acad. of Sciences. *Publications:* Africa, A Subjective View, 1964; contribs to: Malnutrition in African Mothers and Children, 1954; HRH the Duke of Edinburgh's Study Conference, Vol. 2, 1958; The Mechanism of Action of Insulin, 1960; The Structure of Human Insulin, 1960; Africans Horton, Black Nationalism 1867, 1969; also to Jl Trop. Med., Biochem. Jl, Nature, Jl of Royal African Soc., etc. *Recreations:* numismatics, creative writing, old maps. *Address:* Suite 608, 30 East 42nd Street, New York, NY 10017, USA. *T:* YU 6-8717. *Clubs:* Oxford and Cambridge University, Royal Commonwealth Society; Senior Dinner (Freetown); Harvard (New York).

**NICOL, James Lauder,** CMG 1954; OBE 1945; retired from HM Colonial Civil Service, 1954; *b* 1889; *s* of James Nicol, Balbardie House, West Lothian; *m* 1912; *o s* killed in action, 1941. *Educ:* New Coll., Edinburgh; Universities of Edinburgh and London (hons Arts and distinction Law). Served European War, 1914-18: in France as Captain, Royal Scots Regt; Reparations Commn, Vienna, 1919-20; Educational Research, 1920-22; HM Colonial Service (Malaya), 1922-36; HMI Min. of Education, and Lectr on Education, University of Cambridge, 1936-39; seconded as Chief Regional Officer, Ministry of Information, 1939-45; Chairman Regional Industrial Publicity Cttee, 1939-45; HM Divisional Inspector, NW Division, Ministry of Education, 1946-49; Educational Adviser to Comptroller, Development and Welfare in West Indies, 1949-54; Chm., Education Commn, British Guiana, 1952. *Recreations:* travel and music. *Address:* Pré Sec, Route Orange, St Brelade, Jersey, CI.

**NICOL, Dr Joseph Arthur Colin,** FRS 1967; Professor of Zoology, University of Texas Institute of Marine Science, since 1967; *b* 5 Dec. 1915; *s* of George Nicol and Noele Petrie; *m* 1941, Helen Wilhelmina Cameron; one *d*. *Educ:* Universities of McGill, Western Ontario and Oxford. BSc (hons Zool.) 1938, McGill; MA 1940, Western Ontario; DPhil 1947, DSc 1961, Oxford. Canadian Army, RCCS, 1941-45. Asst Professor in Zoology, University of British Columbia, 1947-49; Experimental Zoologist, Marine Biological Assoc., UK, 1949 (research on marine amimals, comparative physiology, luminescence, vision, at Plymouth Laboratory, 1949-66). Guggenheim Fellow, Scripps Inst. Oceanography, 1953-54. Vis. Prof., Univ. of Texas, 1966-67. *Publications:* Biology of Marine Animals, 1960; papers on comparative physiology and anatomy in Jl Marine Biol. Assoc. UK, Proc. Royal Soc, Jl Exp. Biol., Biol. Review, etc. *Recreation:* English literature. *Address:* Port Aransas, Texas 78373, USA.

**NICOL, Prof. Thomas,** MD, DSc (Glasgow and London); FRCS; FRCSE; FRSE; FKC; Emeritus Professor of Anatomy, University of London; Professor of Anatomy and Head of Anatomical Department, King's College, University of London, 1936-67 (Senior Professor in all Faculties, 1966-67); Lecturer in Anatomy, Institute of Laryngology and Otology, Brook Hosp., Woolwich; Whittington Hosp.; Member: New York Academy of Sciences; Anatomical Society of Great Britain and Ireland; American Assoc. of Anatomists; International Reticulo-Endothelial Society; Society of Endocrinology; *b* 4 Aug. 1900; *s* of Wm. Nicol and Mary Wilson Gilmour; *m* 1927, Evelyn Bertha (*d* 1966), *d* of Thomas Keeling, MICE, Engineer-in-Chief late Glasgow and South Western Railway; one *s* one *d*. *Educ:* University of Glasgow. Honours and Bellahouston Gold Medal for MD Thesis, University of Glasgow, 1935; Struthers Gold Medal and Prize, University of Glasgow, 1935. Sen. House Surgeon to Sir William Macewen, FRS (the discoverer of asepsis), Western Infirmary, Glasgow, 1921; Demonstrator of Anatomy, 1922-27, Senior Lecturer in Anatomy, 1927-35, University of Glasgow. Lately: Dean of Faculty of Medicine, King's Coll., Univ. of London; Chm., Board of Studies in Human Anatomy and Morphology, Univ. of London; Examiner, Univs of London, Birmingham, Durham, Glasgow, and St Andrews, RCS England, Edinburgh and Ireland, and RCP; John Hunter Lectr in Applied Anatomy, St George's Hosp. Med. Sch.; Malcolm McHardy Lectr, Royal Eye Hosp. Lord of the Manor of Heveningham, Suffolk. *Publications:* research articles on raising body defence against infection and cancer, in British Journal of Surgery, Journal of Obstetrics and Gynaec. of British Empire, Journal of Anatomy, Trans. and Proc. Royal Society of Edinburgh, BMJ, Nature, Journal of Endocrinology. *Recreations:* music, golf, swimming. *Address:* 18 Penn House, Moor Park, Northwood, Middlesex. *T:* Northwood 25081.

**NICOLAREISIS, Demetrios J.;** Knight Commander, Order of the Phœnix; Commander, Order of George I; Member, Royal Order of the Saviour; Military Medals;

Greek Ambassador to the Court of St James's, 1964-67; *b* Samos (Greece), 1908; *m* 1953, Yola; two *d. Educ:* Florence (studied history of Art); University of Athens (grad. Law, Political Science and Economics). Admitted Diplomatic Service, 1936; Vice-Consul and Political Counsellor to Military Government of Northern Epirus at Argyrocastro, 1940; served Crete, 1941, later London, Cairo; Rome, 1944-46; Head of first Political Sect. Min. for Foreign Affairs, 1946-47; Greek Consul, Hamburg and Chargé d'Affaires, Bonn, 1948-52; Head of NATO Dept, Min. for Foreign Affairs, 1952-53; Assistant delegate for Greece at NATO, Paris, 1953-56. Chargé d'Affaires and Counsellor, Royal Greek Embassy, London, 1956-58; Asst Chairman Greco-Yugoslav Commission, 1959, Minister Plenipotentiary, 1959; Greek Ambassador to Yugoslavia, 1960-64. Holds foreign decorations as well as those of Greece. *Publications:* Collected Critical Essays. *Address:* Royal Ministry of Foreign Affairs, 2 Zalokosta Street, Athens, Greece.

**NICOLL, Allardyce;** *see* Nicoll J. R. A.

**NICOLL, Sir John (Fearns),** KCMG, *cr* 1953 (CMG 1946); *b* 26 April 1899; *s* of late John Nicoll; *m* 1939, Irene, *d* of Major J. D. Lenagan, MBE; one *s. Educ:* Carlisle Grammar Sch.; Pembroke Coll., Oxford. S Lancs Regt, 1918-19; Administrative Officer, British N Borneo, 1921-25; Administrative Officer, Tanganyika Territory, 1925-37; Dep. Colonial Sec., Trinidad, 1937-44; Colonial Sec., Fiji, 1944-49; Colonial Sec., Hong-Kong, 1949-52; Governor and Comdr-in-Chief, Singapore, 1952-55, retired. KStJ. *Club:* East India and Sports.

**NICOLL, John Ramsay Allardyce,** MA; Professor Emeritus of English Language and Literature in the University of Birmingham; Andrew Mellon Visiting Professor of English, University of Pittsburg, USA, 1963-64, 1965, 1967, 1969; *b* 28 June 1894; *s* of David Binny Nicoll and Elsie Nicoll (*née* Allardyce); *m* Josephine Calina (*d* 1962); *m* Maria Dubno. *Educ:* Stirling High Sch.; Glasgow Univ. G. A. Clark Scholar in English; Lectr in English, Loughborough Coll.; Lecturer in English, King's Coll., Univ. of London; Prof. of English Lang. and Lit. in Univ. of London; Prof. of the History of Drama and Dramatic Criticism, Chm. Dept of Drama, Yale Univ.; Prof. of English, Univ. of Birmingham, 1945-61 and Dir of Shakespeare Institute, Stratford-upon-Avon, 1951-61. Attached to HM Embassy, Washington, 1942-45. Life Trustee, Shakespeare Birthplace Trust, Stratford-upon-Avon; Editor, Shakespeare Survey, 1948-65; Hon. Member: Mod. Lang. Assoc. of America; Accademia Ligure di Scienze e Lettere; Pres., Soc. for Theatre Research. Hon. DèsL: Toulouse; Montpellier. Hon. DLitt: Durham and Glasgow; Hon. DHL, Brandeis Univ. *Publications:* William Blake, 1922; Dryden as an Adapter of Shakespeare, 1922; An Introduction to Dramatic Theory, 1923; John Dryden, 1923; A History of Restoration Drama, 1923; A History of Early Eighteenth Century Drama, 1925; British Drama, 1925; Sharpham's Cupid's Whirligig, Carlell's Osmond the Great Turk and The Fool Would Be a Favourite (editor) 1926; A History of Late Eighteenth Century Drama, 1927; The Development of the Theatre, 1927; Studies in Shakespeare, 1927; The English Stage, 1928; Readings from British Drama, 1928; Eighteenth Century Comedies (editor) 1928; A History of Early Nineteenth Century Drama, 1930; The Works of Cyril Tourneur (editor) 1930; Masks, Mimes and Miracles, 1931; The Theory of Drama, 1931; Film and Theatre, 1936; The English Theatre, 1936; Stuart Masques and the Renaissance Stage, 1937: A History of Late Nineteenth Century Drama, 1946; World Drama, 1949; A History of English Drama, 1660-1900, 6 volumes, 1952-59; The Elizabethans, 1956; Chapman's Homer (editor) 2 volumes, 1957; The World of Harlequin, A Study of the Commedia dell'Arte, 1963; Theatre and Dramatic Theory, 1963; English Drama: A Modern Viewpoint, 1968; various contributions to Year's Work in English Studies, Modern Language Review, Review of English Studies, Times Literary Supplement, etc. *Address:* Wind's Acre, Colwall, Malvern. *T:* Colwall 310. *Club:* Century, New York.

**NICOLL, William;** Assistant Secretary, Board of Trade; *b* 28 June 1927; *s* of Ralph Nicoll and Christina Mowbray Nicoll (*née* Melville); *m* 1954, Helen Morison Martin; two *d. Educ:* Morgan Acad., Dundee; St Andrews Univ. Entered BoT, 1949; British Trade Comr: Calcutta, 1955-56; New Delhi, 1957-59; Private Sec. to Pres. of BoT, 1964-67; Commercial Inspector, HM Diplomatic Service, 1967-69; BoT Overseas Div. Review, 1969. *Address:* 95 Beechwood Road, South Croydon, Surrey. *T:* 01-657 7030.

**NICOLSON,** family name of **Baron Carnock.**

**NICOLSON, Benedict,** *see* Nicolson, L. B.

**NICOLSON, David Lancaster;** Chairman: Associated British Maltsters Ltd since 1965; BTR Leyland Industries Ltd since 1969 (Deputy Chairman, 1965-69); Shipton Automation Ltd; Director: Charterhouse Group Ltd; Walter Runciman & Co. Ltd; Newton Chambers & Co. Ltd; Delta Metal Co. Ltd; Black & Decker Ltd; Spear & Jackson Ltd; Lines Bros; Bank of Montreal; Richard Costain Ltd; Member, Greater London Regional Board of Lloyds Bank; *b* 20 Sept. 1922; *s* of Charles Tupper Nicolson, consulting engineer, and Margaret Lancaster Nicolson; *m* 1945, Joan Eileen, *d* of Major W. H. Griffiths, RA; one *s* two *d. Educ:* Haileybury; Imperial Coll., London Univ. FCGI; BSc, CEng, FIMechE, FIProdE; FBIM; FRSA. Constructor Lt, Royal Corps Naval Constructors, 1942-45; served Normandy, 1944 (despatches). Management Consultant, Production-Engineering Ltd, 1946-50; Production Manager, Bucyrus Erie Co., Milwaukee, 1951-52; Manager, later Dir, Production-Engineering Ltd, 1953-62; Chm., P-E Consulting Gp, 1963-68. Chm. NEDC Cttee for Hosiery and Knitwear 1966-68; Mem. Council: Brit. Inst. of Management, 1964-69; Inst. of Production Engrs 1966-68; City and Guilds of London Inst. 1968-; Member: Science Research Council, 1970-; SRC Engineering Bd, 1969; Governor of Imperial Coll., London Univ., 1966-; Chm. Management Consultants Assoc., 1964; Mem. Brit. Shipbuilding Mission to India, 1957; Vice-Chm., BNEC Cttee for Canada, 1967, Chm., 1970. *Publications:* contribs to technical jls; lectures and broadcasts on management subjects in UK, USA, Australia, etc. *Recreations:* sailing, golf. *Address:* 5 Southwick Place, W2. *T:* 01-262 0020. *Clubs:* Carlton; Royal Thames Yacht, Hurlingham.

**NICOLSON, Lionel Benedict,** MVO 1947; Editor of The Burlington Magazine since 1947; *b* 6 Aug. 1914; *s* of late Hon. Sir Harold Nicolson, KCVO, CMG and Hon. V. Sackville-West, CH; *m* 1955, Luisa Vertova, Florence (marriage dissolved, 1962); one *d. Educ:* Eton Coll.; Balliol Coll., Oxford. Dep. Surveyor of the King's Pictures, 1939, resigned, 1947. Served War of 1939-45; Commn, 1942, in

Intelligence Corps; Interpreter in Italian POW Camps, 1943; Middle East (Egypt, Palestine, Syria), 1943-44, Italy, 1944-45, Instr in Photo-Intelligence; Capt. 1944. *Publications:* The Painters of Ferrara, 1950; Hendrick Terbrugghen, 1958; Wright of Derby: Painter of Light, 1968. *Recreations:* reading, travel. *Address:* 45b Holland Park, W11. *T:* 01-229 2799. *Clubs:* Brooks's, Beefsteak.

*See also N. Nicolson.*

**NICOLSON, Nigel,** MBE 1945; FSA; Director of Weidenfeld and Nicolson Ltd since 1947; *b* 19 Jan. 1917; 2nd *s* of late Hon. Sir Harold Nicolson, KCVO, CMG and Hon. V. Sackville-West, CH; *m* 1953, Philippa Janet (marr. diss. 1970), *d* of Sir Gervais Tennyson d'Eyncourt, Bt, *qv*; one *s* two *d. Educ:* Eton Coll.; Balliol Coll., Oxford. Capt. Grenadier Guards. Served War of 1939-45 in Tunisian and Italian Campaigns (MBE). Contested (C) NW Leicester, 1950, and Falmouth and Camborne, 1951; MP (C) Bournemouth East and Christchurch, Feb. 1952-Sept. 1959. Chm. Exec. Cttee, UNA, 1961-66. *Publications:* The Grenadier Guards, 1939-45, 1949 (official history); People and Parliament, 1958; Lord of the Isles, 1960; Great Houses of Britain, 1965; (editor) Harold Nicolson: Diaries and Letters, 1930-39, 1966; 1939-45, 1967; 1945-62, 1968; Great Houses, 1968. *Recreation:* archæology. *Address:* Sissinghurst Castle, Kent. *T:* Sissinghurst 250. *Club:* Travellers'.

*See also L. B. Nicolson.*

**NIEBUHR, Rev. Prof. Reinhold,** DD; Graduate Professor Emeritus of Ethics and Theology, Union Theological Seminary, New York City, since 1928; Editor, Bi-Weekly, Christianity and Crisis; *b* 21 June 1892; *s* of Gustave Niebuhr and Lydia Hosto; *m* 1931, Ursula Mary, *y d* of Dr Keppel-Compton, Woodhall Spa; one *s* one *d. Educ:* Elmhurst Coll.; Yale Univ. Minister, Bethel Evangelical Church, Detroit, 1915-18; Contrib. Editor of bi-weekly, Christianity and Crisis. Hon. DD: Grinnell Coll. 1932, Eden Theological Seminary (St Louis), 1933, Wesleyan Univ., 1935, Univ. of Pennsylvania, 1939, Amherst Coll., 1941, Yale Univ., 1942, Oxford Univ., 1943, Harvard Univ., 1944, Princeton Univ., 1946, Glasgow Univ., 1947, NY Univ., 1948, Hobart Coll., 1948, Dartmouth Coll., 1951, Univ. of Manchester, 1954; LLD Occidental Coll., 1945; STD Columbia Univ., 1954; LittD: New Sch. for Social Research, 1951; Hebrew Univ., Jerusalem, 1967. Presidential Medal of Freedom, 1964. *Publications:* Does Civilization Need Religion, 1927; Leaves from the Notebook of a Tamed Cynic, 1930; Moral Men and Immoral Society, 1932; Reflections on the End of an Era, 1934; Interpretation of Christian Ethics, 1935; Beyond Tragedy, 1937; Christianity and Power Politics, 1940; Nature and Destiny of Man, Vol. I, 1941, Vol. II, 1943 (Gifford Lectures); The Children of Light and the Children of Darkness, 1944; Discerning the Signs of the Times, 1946; Faith and History, 1949; The Irony of American History, 1952; Christian Realism, 1953; The Self in Its Dialogues and Dramas, 1955; The Godly and the Ungodly (Essays), 1959; The Structure of Nations and Empires, 1959: A Nation so Conceived, 1963; Man's Nature and His Communities, 1965; Faith and Politics, 1968; (with Paul E. Sigmund) The Democratic Experience, 1969. *Address:* Yale Hill, Stockbridge, Mass 01262, USA.

**NIELD, Hon. Sir Basil Edward,** KT 1957; CBE 1956 (MBE 1945); DL; **Hon. Mr Justice Nield;** Judge of High Court of Justice, Queen's Bench Division, since 1960; *b* 7 May 1903; *yr s* of late Charles Edwin Nield, JP, and Mrs F. E. L. Nield, MBE, LLA, Upton-by-Chester. *Educ:* Harrow Sch.; Magdalen Coll., Oxford (MA). Officers Emergency Reserve, 1938; served War of 1939-45: commnd Captain, 1940; 1941; GHQ MEF (Major), HQs E Africa Force, Abyssinia, Palestine and Syria; Pres., Palestine Military Courts in Jerusalem; 1942; HQs Eritrea and 8th Army; 1943: HQ Persia and Iraq; Asst Dep. Judge Advocate-Gen., ME (Lt-Col; despatches); Home Estab.; 1944: 21 Army Gp; HQ Lines of Communication, BLA, Normandy; HQ 2nd Army, France, Belgium, Holland and Germany (MBE); Home Estab., 1945; RARO until 1948. Called to Bar, Inner Temple, 1925; Northern Circuit, Chambers in Liverpool; KC 1945; Recorder of Salford, 1948-56; Recorder and first permanent Judge of Crown Court at Manchester, 1956-60. MP (U) City of Chester, 1940-56; sponsored as Private Member's Bill the Adoption of Children Act, 1949; Hon. Parly Chm., Dock and Harbour Authorities Assoc., 1944-50; Mem., Special Cttee under Reorganisation Areas Measure for Province of York, 1944. Mem., Gen. Council of Bar, 1951; Master of Bench of Inner Temple, 1952-. Member: Magistrates' Rules Cttee, 1952-56; Legal Bd, Church Assembly, 1952-56; Home Secretary's Adv. Cttee on Treatment of Offenders, 1957. Chancellor, Diocese of Liverpool, 1948-56. Vice-President: Nat. Chamber of Trade, 1948-56; Graduate Teachers Assoc., 1950-56; Corp. of Secretaries, 1950; Assoc. of Managers of Approved Schools, 1956; Cheshire Soc. in London; Spastics Soc., Manchester. Chm., Chester Conservative Assoc., 1930-40. Member: Court, Liverpool Univ., 1948-56; Adv. Council, E-SU, 1951; Oxford Soc.; Imperial Soc. of Knights Bachelor; Life Mem., Royal Soc. of St George. Governor. Harrow Sch. FAMS. JP Co. Lancaster, 1956; DL County Palatine of Chester, 1962-. Freeman, City of London, 1963. *Address:* 7 King's Bench Walk, Temple, EC4. *T:* 01-353 3868. The Stable House, Christleton, near Chester. *T:* Chester 35607. *Clubs:* Carlton, Junior Carlton; City, Grosvenor (Chester).

**NIELD, Sir William (Alan),** KCB 1968 (CB 1966); Permanent Secretary, Cabinet Office, since 1969; *b* 21 Sept. 1913; *s* of William Herbert Nield, Stockport, Cheshire, and Ada Nield; *m* 1937, Gwyneth Marion Davies; two *s* two *d. Educ:* Stockport Gram. Sch.; St Edmund Hall, Oxford. Research and Policy Dept of Labour Party, 1937-39; K-H News Letter Service, 1939. Served Royal Air Force and Royal Canadian Air Force, 1939-46 (despatches, 1944); demobilised as Wing Comdr, 1946. Min. of Food, 1946-47; HM Treasury, 1947-49; Min. of Food and Min. of Agric., Fisheries and Food, 1949-64 (Under-Sec., 1959-64); Dept of Economic Affairs: Under-Sec., 1964-65; Dep. Under-Sec. of State, 1965-66; a Dep. Sec., Cabinet Office, 1966-68; Permanent Under-Sec. of State, DEA, 1968-69. *Address:* South Nevay, Stubbs Wood, Chesham Bois, Bucks. *T:* Amersham 3869. *Club:* Farmers'.

**NIEMEYER, Oscar;** architect; *b* Rio de Janeiro, 15 Dec. 1907; *s* of Oscar Niemeyer Soares; *m* Anita Niemeyer; one *d. Educ:* Escola Nacional de Beles Artes, Univ. of Brazil. Joined office of Lũcio Costa, 1935; worked on Min. of Education and Health Building, Rio de Janeiro, Brazilian Pavilion, NY World Fair, etc., 1936-41. Major projects include: Pamphulha, Belo Horizonte, 1941-43; also Quintandinha, Petrõpolis; Exhibition Hall, São Paulo, 1953; Brasilia (Dir of Architecture), 1957-. Brazilian Rep., UN Bd of Design Consultants, 1947. Lenin Peace Prize, 1963; Prix Internat. de l'Architecture Aujourd'hui, 1966. *Address:* Rua Carvalho Azevedo 96, Rio de Janeiro, Brazil.

**NIEMEYER, Sir Otto (Ernst),** GBE 1927; KCB 1924 (CB 1921); Past Director: Bank of England, 1938-52; Bank for International Settlements, 1931-65 (Chairman of the Board, 1937-40; Vice-Chairman, 1941-64); Member of Council of Foreign Bondholders, since 1935 (Vice-President 1950-55; President, 1956-65); Member Advisory Committee, International Nickel Co. of Canada Ltd (Past Director); *b* 1883; *m* 1910, Sophia Benedicte, *d* of Theodor Niemeyer; two *s* one *d* (and one *s* killed on active service). *Educ:* St Paul's Sch.; Balliol Coll., Oxford. HM Treasury, 1906-27; Controller of Finance, 1922-27; Mem. of Financial Cttee of League of Nations, 1922-37 (Chm., 1927); Dir Banque des Pays de l'Europe (Paris), 1928-57; Financial Mission to Australia and NZ, 1930; Brazil, 1931; Argentine, 1933; India, 1935; China, 1941; Fellow, London Sch. of Economics (Chm. of Govs, 1941-57; Gov., 1958-65); Gov. of St Paul's Sch.; Gov. of Marlborough Coll.; Chm., Provisional National Council for Mental Health, 1943-46; Vice-Pres., National Association for Mental Health (Hon. Treas., 1947-64). High Sheriff, County of London, 1945; a Lt of the City of London. *Address:* Nash House, Lindfield, Sussex. *T:* Lindfield 3209. *Club:* Reform.

**NIEMÖLLER, Rev. D. (Friedrich Gustav Emil) Martin;** a President of the World Council of Churches, 1961-68; Church President of Evangelical Church in Hesse and Nassau, Germany, 1947-64, retired; *b* Lippstadt, Westphalia, 14 Jan. 1892; *s* of Pastor Heinrich Niemoeller; *m* 1919, Else (*née* Bremer) (*d* 1961); three *s* two *d* (and one *s* one *d* decd). *Educ:* Gymnasium, Elberfeld. Midshipman in German Navy, 1910; retd 1919, as Kapitänleutnant; studied Theology, Münster, Westfalen; Pastor, 1924; Pastor of Berlin-Dahlem, 1931; creator of Pastors' Union and Confessing Church; prisoner in concentration camps at Sachsenhausen and Dachau, 1937-45; Pres. Office of Foreign Affairs of Evangelical Church in Germany, 1945-56. Holds Hon. DD of Univ. of Göttingen (Germany), and several foreign hon. doctorates. *Publications:* Vom U-Boot zu Kanzel (Berlin), 1934; . . . Dass wir an Ihm bleiben: Sechzehn Dahlemer Predigten (Berlin), 1935; Alles und in allem Christus; Fünfzehn Dahlemer Predigten (Berlin), 1935; Fran U-Bat till Predikstol (trans.) (Stockholm), 1936; Dennoch getrost: Die letzten 28 Predigten (Switzerland), 1939; Ach Gott vom Himmel sieh darein: Sechs Predigten (Munich), 1946; . . . Zu verkündigen ein Gnädiges: Jahr des Herrn: Sechs Dachauer Predigten (1944-45), (Munich), 1946; Herr ist Jesus Christus: Die letzten 28 Predigten (Gütersloh), 1946; Herr, wohin sollen wir gehen? Ausgewählte Predigten (Munich), 1956; some hundred articles about theological, cultural and political themes. *Address:* Brentanostrasse 3, Wiesbaden, Germany. *T:* 85097.

**NIGHTINGALE, Edward Humphrey,** CMG 1955; Farmer (Kenya) since 1954; *b* 19 Aug. 1904; *s* of Rev. Edward Charles Nightingale and Ada Mary Nightingale; *m* 1944, Evelyn Mary Ray; three *s* one *d*. *Educ:* Rugby Sch.; Emmanuel Coll., Cambridge. Joined Sudan Political Service, 1926; Dep. Civil Sec., Sudan Government, 1951-52; Gov., Equatoria Province, Sudan, 1952-54. Order of the Nile, 4th Class, 1940. *Recreations:* polo, ski-ing, photography. *Address:* Nunjoro Farm, Naivasha, Kenya. *Club:* Rift Valley Sports (Nakuru).

**NIGHTINGALE, Sir Geoffrey Slingsby,** 15th Bt, *cr* 1628; MRCS and LRCP 1929; DPM (England) 1934; Physician Superintendent Warley Hospital, Brentwood, 1946-69; formerly Consultant Psychiatrist Oldchurch Hospital, Romford, and Ilford and Barking Hospitals; *b* 24 Nov. 1904; *s* of late Thomas Slingsby Nightingale, CMG, CBE, and Doris Elizabeth, *d* of Charles Stoughton Collison, East Bilney, Norfolk; *S* cousin, 1953; *m* 1936, Madeleine, *d* of late Richard Doyle, Tramore, Co. Waterford; one adopted *s*. *Educ:* Marlborough; London Hospital. Served 1940-45, as Lt-Col RAMC, Command Psychiatrist, South Eastern and Western Commands and OC Div. 32nd Gen. Hospital, BLA. Formerly Asst Medical Officer, Surrey County Mental Hospital, Netherne; House Physician Skin and Light Depts, London Hospital. Member: Inst. Advanced Motorists. Gold Award, High Performance Club. *Publications:* The First Hundred Years: a History of Warley Hospital, 1953; Dinghy Ownership, 1956, 3rd enlarged edn, 1964; Dinghy Sailing for Boys, 1957 (2nd edn 1959); (jointly) Eagle Book of Ships and Boats, 1959; chapters in The Dinghy Year Book, 1958, 1959, 1960, etc.; contributions to medical journals and yachting press. *Recreations:* fast cars, fishing, small boat sailing, sneezing. *Heir: cousin* Charles Athelstan Nightingale [*b* 23 July 1902; *m* 1932, Nadine, *d* of late Charles Arthur Diggens; one *s* two *d*]. *Address:* Gents Farm, Pilgrims Hatch, Brentwood, Essex. *T:* Coxtie Green 300. *Clubs:* BSC Master Drivers', High Performance Club of British School of Motoring.

**NIGHTINGALE, John Cyprian,** CBE 1970; BEM 1941; QPM 1965; Chief Constable, Essex and Southend-on-Sea Joint Constabulary, since 1969; *b* 16 Sept. 1913; *s* of Herbert Paul Nightingale, Sydenham, London; *m* 1947, Patricia Mary, *d* of Norman Maclaren, Glasgow University. *Educ:* Cardinal Vaughan Sch., Kensington; University Coll., London. Joined Metropolitan Police, 1935; Asst Chief Constable, Essex, 1958; Chief Constable of Essex, 1962. Served with RNVR, 1943-45. *Publications:* various police. *Address:* Springfield Court, Chelmsford, Essex.

**NIGHTINGALE, Michael David,** OBE 1960; BSc; BLitt; FSA; Merchant Banker; Esquire Bedell, University of London, since 1953; *b* 6 Dec. 1927; *s* of late Victor Russell John Nightingale, Wormshill, Kent; *m* 1956, Hilary Marion Olwen, *d* of late John Eric Jones, Swansea; two *s* three *d*. *Educ:* Winchester; Wye Coll.; Magdalen Coll., Oxford. Organised Exhibition from Kent Village Churches, Canterbury, 1951; Asst to Investment Manager, Anglo-Iranian Oil Co., 1951-53; Asst to Principal, Univ. of London, 1953-54; Investment Adviser, Univ. of London, 1954-66; Secretary: Museums Assoc. (and Editor of Museums Jl), 1954-60; Museum Cttee, Carnegie UK Trust, 1954-60; Member: Advisory Council on Export of Works of Art, 1954-60; British Cttee of International Council of Museums, 1956-60; Canterbury Diocesan Advisory Cttee, 1964-; Dep. Steward of Royal Manor of Wye and Hon. Archivist to Wye Coll., 1954-. *Publications:* articles on agrarian and museum subjects. *Address:* Wormshill Court, Sittingbourne, Kent. *T:* Wormshill 235; Perceval House, 21 Dartmouth Row, Greenwich, SE10. *T:* 01-692 6033; Cromarty House, Ross and Cromarty. *T:* Cromarty 265. *Club:* Athenæum.

**NIGHTINGALE, Percy Herbert,** CMG 1957; Lay Assistant to the Bishop of Salisbury since 1964; *b* 22 Dec. 1907; *s* of late Rev. S. J. Nightingale and late Mrs Nightingale; *m* 1935, Doris Aileen Butcher; one *s* one *d*. *Educ:* St Michael's, Limpsfield, Surrey; Monkton Combe Sch., near Bath; Christ's Coll.,

Cambridge. BA Cantab, 1928. Colonial Administrative Service, Fiji, 1930-52; District Commissioner, 1940; Asst Colonial Sec., 1947; Financial Sec., Zanzibar, 1952-60. Appeal Organiser, Monkton Combe Sch., 1960-64. Coronation Medal, 1953; Order of Brilliant Star, Zanzibar (2nd Class), 1960. *Recreation:* gardening. *Address:* Little Bower, Campbell Road, Salisbury, Wilts. *T:* Salisbury 6501.

**NIHILL, Sir (John Harry) Barclay,** KBE 1951; Kt 1948; *b* 1892; *o s* of Rev. H. B. Nihill, Hastings; *m* Nuala, *e d* of late Joseph O'Carroll, MD, Past Pres. Royal Coll. Physicians, Ireland; one *s* (and one killed in action Malta Convoy, 12 Aug. 1942). *Educ:* Felsted; Emmanuel Coll., Cambridge (scholar MA). Pres. of the Union, Cambridge, 1914; served European War, 1914-18, Capt., Royal Munster Fusiliers (MC). Barrister-at-Law, Inner Temple, 1919; Sec., Joint Industrial Councils, Ministry of Labour, 1919; Colonial Civil Service, Hong Kong, 1921; Legal Sec. to High Commission, Baghdad, 1927-33; Solicitor-Gen., Uganda, 1934; KC 1936; Attorney-Gen., British Guiana, 1936; Puisne Judge, Ceylon, 1938; Legal Sec. to Govt of Ceylon, 1942-46; Chief Justice, Kenya, 1947-50 (appointed, 1946); Pres., Court of Appeal for Eastern Africa, 1950-55, retired; Speaker of the Legislative Council, Tanganyika, 1958; Chm., Admiralty Requirements Cttee, 1956; Chm., Tanganyika Sisal Industry Central Joint Consultative Council, 1959-62. Legal Mem. SW Metropolitan Mental Health Tribunal, 1962-65. *Address:* 226 Ashley Gardens, SW1. *T:* 01-828 8621. *Clubs:* United University; Muthaiga (Kenya).

**NIKLASSON, Frau Bertil;** *see* Nilsson, Birgit.

**NIKLAUS, Prof. Robert,** BA, PhD London; LèsL Lille; DrUniv Rennes, *hon. causa,* 1963; FIAL; Professor of French, University of Exeter, since 1952; *b* 18 July 1910; *s* of late Jean Rodolphe and Elizabeth Niklaus; *m* 1935, Thelma (*née* Jones) (*d* 1970); two *s* one *d. Educ:* Lycée Français de Londres; University Coll., London; Univ. of Lille. Sen. Tutor, Toynbee Hall, London, 1931-32; Asst and Asst Lecturer at University Coll., 1932-38; Asst Lecturer, Lecturer, Univ. of Manchester, 1938-52. Dean of the Faculty of Arts, Exeter, 1959-62. Visiting Prof., Univ. of Calif., Berkeley, 1963-64; Dep. Vice-Chancellor, 1965-67. Pres., Assoc. of Univ. Teachers, 1954-55, mem. Executive Cttee, 1947-62; Pres. Internat. Assoc. of Univ. Profs and Lecturers 1960-64 (Vice-Pres., 1958-60); Member: Cttee of Modern Humanities Research Association, 1956-; Cttee, Soc. for French Studies, 1965- (Vice-Pres., 1967-68, Pres., 1968-70); Post-graduate Awards Cttee of Min. of Education, 1956-61; Management Cttee, British Inst., Paris, 1965-67. Gen. Editor, Textes Français Classiques et Modernes, Univ. of London Press. *Publications:* Jean Moréas, Poète Lyrique, 1936; The Nineteenth Century (Post-Romantic) and After (in The Year's Work in Modern Language Studies, VII-XIII), 1937-52; Diderot and Drama, 1942; Beaumarchais, Le Barbier de Séville, 1968; critical editions of: J.-J. Rousseau, Les Rêveries du Promeneur Solitaire, 1942; Denis Diderot, Pensées Philosophiques, 1950; Denis Diderot, Lettre sur les Aveugles, 1951; Marivaux, Arlequin poli par l'Amour, 1959 (in collab. with Thelma Niklaus); Literary History of France, The Eighteenth Century, 1970; articles in Encyclopaedïæ and learned journals; textbooks for schools and universities. *Recreations:* aviculture, the theatre, the cinema. *Address:* The University, Exeter; 17 Elm Grove Road, Topsham, Devon. *T:* Topsham 3627.

**NIKOLAYEVA-TERESHKOVA, Valentina Vladimirovna;** Hero of the Soviet Union; Order of Lenin; Gold Star Medal; Joliot-Curie Peace Medal; Soviet cosmonaut; *b* Maslennikovo, 6 March 1937; *d* of late Vladimir and of Elena Fyodorovna Tereshkova; *m* 1963, Andrian Nikolayev; one *d.* Formerly textile worker, Krasny Perekop mill, Yaroslavl; served on cttees; Sec. of local branch, Young Communist league, 1960; joined Yaroslavl Air Sports Club, 1959, and started parachute jumping; Mem., Communist Party of Soviet Union, 1962; joined Cosmonaut Training Unit, 1962. Became first woman in the world to enter space when she made 48 orbital flights of the earth in spaceship Vostok VI, 16-19 June 1963. Holds honours and citations from other countries. *Address:* Scientific Research Institute of Aviation Medicine, Petrovsky Park, Moscow, USSR.

**NILES, Emory Hamilton;** retired as Chief Judge, Supreme Bench of Baltimore, Maryland, 1962; *b* Baltimore, Md, 15 Oct. 1892; *s* of Judge Alfred S. Niles and Mary Hamilton (Waters); *m* 1922, Anne Whitridge Williams; one *s* two *d. Educ:* Johns Hopkins Univ. (AB, Rhodes Scholar); Oxford Univ. (BA, MA, BCL). Univ. of Maryland (LLB, JD). Ambulance Américaine, France, 1916; served with US Army, 313th Field Artillery, AEF, France, 1917-18 (Lt and Capt.). Amer. Commn for Relief in Near East, Turkey, 1919. Practice of Law, Baltimore, 1920-38; Assoc. Judge, 1938-54; Chief Judge, 1954-62. Lecturer: Univ. of Maryland Law Sch., 1923-59; Johns Hopkins Medical Sch., 1951-68. Chm., War Price and Rationing Boards, Baltimore, 1942-46; Maryland State Fuel Coordinator, 1948; Pres., Assoc. of American Rhodes Scholars, 1970- (Vice-Pres., 1956-70); Chm., Judicial Administration Section, Amer. Bar. Assoc., 1959; Governor, Amer. Bar Assoc., 1966-69; Mem. US Commn on Internat. Rules of Judicial Procedure, 1960; Pres., Maryland State Bar Assoc., 1962; Pres., Inst. of Judicial Administration, New York, 1963-66; Chm., Maryland Judicial Selection Council Inc., 1963. Editor: American Maritime Cases, 1923-; US Aviation Reports, 1928-60. Hon. Fellow, Hertford Coll., Oxford, 1961; Hon. LLD: Univ. of Maryland, 1964; Goucher Coll., 1967. *Publications:* miscellaneous legal articles. *Recreations:* travel, woodworking. *Address:* 5600 Waycrest Lane, Baltimore, Md 21210, USA. *T:* 301-323-3260. *Clubs:* Hamilton Street, Gibson Island, Century (NY).

**NILSSON, Birgit, (Frau Bertil Niklasson);** Swedish operatic soprano; *b* Karup, Kristianstadslaen, 1922. *Educ:* Stockholm Royal Academy of Music. Debut as singer, 1946; with Stockholm Opera, 1947-51. Has sung at Glyndebourne, 1951; Bayreuth, 1953, 1954, 1957-; Munich, 1954-58; Hollywood Bowl, Buenos Aires, Florence, 1956; La Scala, Milan, 1958-; Covent Garden, 1957, 1960, 1962 and 1963; Edinburgh, 1959; Metropolitan, New York, 1959-; Moscow, 1964; also in most leading opera houses and festivals of the world. Particularly well-known for her Wagnerian rôles. Swedish Royal Acad. of Music's Medal for Promotion of Art of Music, 1968. Comdr of the Vasa Order, Sweden, 1968.

**NIMMO, Sir Robert,** Kt 1944; JP; *b* 11 June 1894; *s* of Robert Nimmo, Brewer, Perth; *m* 1922, Dorothy Wordsworth, *d* of Walter Gillies; two *s* one *d. Address:* Hurstridge, Tullylumb Terrace, Perth. *T:* Perth 26905.

**NIMPTSCH, Uli,** RA 1967; (ARA 1958); Sculptor; *b* Berlin, 22 May 1897; of British nationality; *m* 1925, Ruth (*née* Steinthal); one *s. Educ:* studied in Berlin, Rome and Paris. Works are represented in the following galleries and museums: Tate Gallery, London; British Museum; Arts Council; Museum of Leeds; Museum of Liverpool; Museum of Manchester. Statue of Lloyd George, Houses of Parliament. *Address:* 409 Fulham Road, SW10. *T:* 01-352 8679.

**NINEHAM, Rev. Dennis Eric,** MA, BD; Warden of Keble College, Oxford, since 1969; *b* 27 Sept. 1921; *o c* of Stanley Martin and Bessie Edith Nineham, Shirley, Southampton; *m* 1946, Ruth Corfield, *d* of Rev. A. P. Miller; two *s* two *d. Educ:* King Edward VI Sch., Southampton; Queen's Coll., Oxford. Asst Chaplain of Queen's Coll., 1944; Chaplain, 1945; Fellow and Praelector, 1946; Tutor, 1949; Prof. of Biblical and Historical Theology, Univ. of London (King's Coll.), 1954-58; Prof. of Divinity, Univ. of London, 1958-64; Regius Prof. of Divinity, Cambridge Univ., and Fellow, Emmanuel Coll., 1964-69. Fellow, King's Coll., London, 1963-. Examining Chaplain to Archbishop of York and to Bishops of Ripon and Norwich, and (1947-54) to Bishop of Sheffield. Select Preacher to Univ. of Oxford, 1954-56, and to Univ. of Cambridge, 1959; Proctor in Convocation of Canterbury: for London Univ., 1955-64; for Cambridge Univ., 1965-69. Governor of Haileybury, 1966-. Hon. DD (USA). *Publications:* The Study of Divinity, 1960; A New Way of Looking at the Gospels, 1962; Commentary on St Mark's Gospel, 1963; (Editor) Studies in the Gospels: Essays in Honour of R. H. Lightfoot, 1955; The Church's Use of the Bible, 1963; The New English Bible Reviewed, 1965. Contrib. to: Studies in Ephesians (editor F. L. Cross), 1956; On the Authority of the Bible, 1960; Religious Education, 1944-1984, 1966; Theologians of Our Time, 1966; Christian History and Interpretaion, 1967; Christ for us To-day, 1968, etc. *Recreation:* reading. *Address:* Keble College, Oxford. *T:* Oxford 59201.

**NINNES, Bernard,** ROI 1934; RBA 1933; Painter in oils; *b* 5 July 1899; *s* of Richard and Ellen Mary Heather Ninnes; *m* 1930, Edyth Mary Day (*d* 1963), Streatham Park. *Educ:* Slade Sch.; Univ. of London. War Service at Bristol Aeroplane Co., 1940. Painter of Architectural and Figure Compositions, Sea, and Landscape; studied art under Prof. Tonks and Wilson Steer; Mem. of St Ives art colony; represented in Stoke-on-Trent permanent collection, In for Repairs, purchased in 1932; Hereford permanent collection, The Café Born, Palma, purchased 1936; permanent collection at Royal Leamington Spa Municipal Art Gallery, The Boatbuilders' Shop, St Ives, purchased, 1937; Russell-Cotes Art Gallery, Bournemouth permanent collection, Street in Spain, purchased, 1939; Beds CC Education Cttee Purchase, Ludlow Castle, 1950; Festival of Britain 1951, prize for painting, A Cornish Village (St Ives' Permanent Collection); Picture, Drama comes to our Village, exhibited with Outstanding Pictures of the Jubilee Year, 1935; A Break in the Clouds (Albuquerque Gall., New Mexico, USA), 1957. Exhibitor at Royal Academy, Paris Salon, Royal Institute of Oil Painters, Royal Society of British Artists, New English Art Club, Royal West of England Acad., and many provincial towns; Pictures reproduced in The Times, The Artist, Illustrated Sporting and Dramatic News, Bystander, The Sketch, Oil Painting of To-day, Britain's Art Colony by the Sea, etc. Reproductions by Medici Soc., E. S. & A. Robinson, J. Salmon, Ltd, E. T. W. Dennis & Sons, Balding and Mansell, Ltd, Photochrom Co. Ltd, Mardon Son & Hall Ltd, Vivian Mansell & Solomon & Whitehead Ltd, John Arthur Dixon & Co. *Recreations:* music, garden. *Address:* Hayeswood, St Ives, Cornwall. *T:* St Ives 6499.

**NIRENBERG, Dr Marshall Warren;** Research Biochemist, Chief, Laboratory of Biochemical Genetics, National Heart Institute, National Institutes of Health, Bethesda, Md, since 1966; *b* New York, 10 April 1927; *m* 1961, Perola Zaltzman; no *c. Educ:* Univs of Florida (BS, MS) and Michigan (PhD). Univ. of Florida: Teaching Asst, Zoology Dept, 1945-50; Res. Associate, Nutrition Lab., 1950-52; Univ. of Michigan: Teaching and Res. Fellow, Biol Chemistry Dept, 1952-57; Nat. Insts of Health, Bethesda: Postdoctoral Fellow of Amer. Cancer Soc., Nat. Inst. Arthritis and Metabolic Diseases, 1957-59, and of Public Health Service, Section of Metabolic Enzymes, 1959-60; Research Biochemist, Section of Metabolic Enzymes, 1960-62 and Section of Biochem. Genetics, 1962-66. Member: Amer. Soc. Biol Chemists; Amer. Chm. Soc.; Amer. Acad. Arts and Sciences; Biophys. Soc.; Nat. Acad. Sciences; Washington Acad. Sciences; Sigma Xi; Soc. for Study of Development and Growth; (Hon.) Harvey Soc.; Leopoldina Deutsche Akademie der Naturforscher; Neurosciences Research Program, MIT; NY Acad. Sciences. Robbins Lectr, Pomona Coll., 1967; Remsden Mem. Lectr, Johns Hopkins Univ., 1967. Numerous awards and prizes, including Nobel Prize in Medicine or Physiology (jtly), 1968. Hon. Dr Science: Michigan, Yale, and Chicago, 1965; Windsor, 1966; Harvard Med. Sch., 1968. *Publications:* numerous contribs to learned jls and chapters in symposia. *Address:* 7723 Old Chester Road, Bethesda, Maryland 20034, USA. *T:* 301-652-5278.

**NISBET, James Wilkie,** MA, LLB; Professor of Political Economy, University of St Andrews, since 1947; *b* 11 Dec. 1903; *s* of James Nisbet and Helen Bruce Wilkie; *m* 1927, Jean Wheatley; two *s* one *d. Educ:* Hutchesons' Gram. Sch., Glasgow; Univ. of Glasgow. MA, 1st Class Hons Econ. Science, 1925; 1st Class Hons Mental Philosophy, 1926; LLB (with distinction), 1926; Reid Stewart Fellowship and Gladstone Memorial Prize in Econ. Science, 1925; Clark Schol. and Caird Medal in Mental Philosophy, 1926; Robertson Schol. in Law, 1926; Faulds Fellowship in Fac. of Arts, 1926-29; Asst to Adam Smith Prof. of Political Econ., Univ. of Glasgow, 1926-31; Lectr in Political Econ., Univ. of Glasgow, 1935-39; Lectr in Political Econ., St Andrews Univ., 1935-39, Reader, 1939-46; Examiner in Political Economy, Universities of: Glasgow, 1946-48; Bristol, 1947-50; Aberdeen, 1953-55. Canada Council Fellow, 1958. Chm. of Scottish Consumers' Council, 1954-. *Publications:* A Case for Laissez Faire, 1929; Banks and the Finance of Industry, 1934; Post-War Britain and Standard of Life, 1937; Britain's Economic Resources, 1941; Scottish Agriculture and Industry, 1942; The Beveridge Plan, 1943; The Triumvirate of Political Economists in St Andrews, 1947; Thomas Chalmers and Political Economy, 1964. *Recreations:* golf and gardening. *Address:* Balmyle, Buchanan Gardens, St Andrews, Fife. *T:* St Andrews 631. *Club:* Royal and Ancient (St Andrews).

**NISBET, Robin George Murdoch,** FBA 1967; Corpus Christi Professor of Latin, Oxford, since 1970; *b* 21 May 1925; *s* of R. G. Nisbet, Univ. Lecturer, and A. T. Husband; *m* 1969, Anne, *d* of Dr J. A. Wood. *Educ:* Glasgow Academy; Glasgow Univ.; Balliol Coll., Oxford (Snell Exhibitioner). Fellow and Tutor in Classics, Corpus Christi College, Oxford,

1952-70. *Publications:* Commentary on Cicero, *in Pisonem*, 1961; (with M. Hubbard) on Horace, *Odes I*, 1970; articles and reviews on Latin subjects. *Recreation:* 20th century history. *Address:* 1 Appleton Road, Cumnor, Oxford. *T:* Cumnor 3181.

**NISBET, Prof. Stanley Donald;** Professor of Education, University of Glasgow, since 1951; *b* 26 July 1912; *s* of Dr J. L. and Isabella Nisbet; *m* 1942, Helen Alison Smith; one *s* one *d*. *Educ:* Dunfermline High Sch., Edinburgh Univ. MA (1st Cl. Hons Classics), 1934; Diploma in Education, 1935; BEd (with distinction in Education and Psychology), 1940. Taught in Moray House Demonstration Sch., Edinburgh, 1935-39. Served War in RAF, 1940-46; research officer at Air Ministry, 1944-46. Lecturer in Education, Univ. of Manchester, Feb.-Sept. 1946; Prof. of Education, Queen's Univ. of Belfast, 1946-51. FRSE, 1955. *Publications:* Purpose in the Curriculum, 1957; (with B. L. Napier) Promise and Progress, 1970; articles in psychological and educational journals. *Recreations:* walking and climbing. *Address:* Department of Education, The University, Glasgow.

**NISSAN, Alfred Heskel,** PhD, DSc (Chem. Eng, Birmingham), MIMechE, MIChemE, MAIChE, MASME; MACS; Member Sigma XI; Vice-President since 1967, and Corporate Director of Research, since 1962, WESTVACO (formerly West Virginia Pulp and Paper), New York; *b* 14 Feb. 1914; *s* of Heskel and Farha Nissan, Baghdad, Iraq; *m* 1940, Zena Gladys Phyllis, *o d* of late Phillip and Lillian Frances Pursehouse-Ahmed, Birmingham; one *d*. *Educ:* The American Sch. for Boys, Baghdad, Iraq; Univ. of Birmingham. Instn of Petroleum Scholarship, 1936; first cl. Hons BSc 1937; Sir John Cadman Medal, 1937; Instn of Petroleum Medal and Prize and Burgess Prize, 1937; Research Fellow, 1937, Lectr, 1940, Univ. of Birmingham; Head of Central Research Laboratories, Bowater Paper Corporation Ltd, 1947; Technical Director in charge of Research, Bowaters Development and Research Ltd, 1950; Research Prof. of Wool Textile Engineering, the Univ. of Leeds, 1953; Prof. of Chemical Engineering, Rensselaer Polytechnic Inst., Troy, NY, USA, 1957. Schwarz Memorial Lectr, Amer. Soc. of Mech. Engrs, 1967. *Publications:* Edited, Textile Engineering Processes, 1959; papers on physical chemistry and chemical engineering problems of petroleum, paper and textile technology in scientific jls. *Address:* WESTVACO, Westvaco Building, 299 Park Avenue, New York, NY 10017, USA. *Club:* University (New York).

**NISSEN, Karl Iversen,** MD, FRCS; retired Surgeon, Royal National Orthopædic Hospital, W1, 1946-71; Orthopædic Surgeon: Harrow Hospital 1946-71; Peace Memorial Hospital, Watford, 1948-71; *b* 4 April 1906; *s* of Christian and Caroline Nissen; *m* 1936, Margaret Mary Honor Schofield; one *s* one *d*. *Educ:* Otago Boys' High Sch., Dunedin, NZ; Univ. of Otago, NZ. BSc (NZ) 1927; MB, ChB (NZ) 1932; MD (NZ) 1936; FRCS 1936. Served as Orthopædic Specialist, RNVR, 1943-46. Corresp. mem. Belgian, French, Swiss and German Socs of Orthopædics; Vice-Pres., Société Internationale de Chirurgie Orthopédique et de Traumatologie, 1966-. *Recreation:* foreign travel. *Address:* Prospect House, The Avenue, Sherborne, Dorset. *Club:* Naval.

**NIVEN, Sir (Cecil) Rex,** Kt 1960; CMG 1953; MC 1918; *b* 20 Nov. 1898; *o s* of late Rev. Dr G. C. and Jeanne Niven, Torquay, Devon; *m* 1925, Dorothy Marshall, *e d* of late D. M. Mason, formerly MP (Coventry and E Edinburgh); one *d* (and one *d* decd.) *Educ:* Blundell's Sch., Tiverton; Balliol Coll. Oxford (MA Hons). Served RFA 1917-19, France and Italy. Colonial Service Nigeria, 1921-54; served Secretariats, and Provinces; PRO, Nigeria, 1943-45; Senior Resident; twice admin. Northern Govt; Mem. Northern House of Assembly, 1947-59 (Pres. 1952-58; Speaker, 1958-59); Mem., Northern Executive Co., 1951-54; Commissioner for Special Duties in Northern Nigeria, 1959-62; Dep. Sec., Southwark Diocesan Board of Finance, 1962-68, retired. Life Mem., BRCS; Member: Council, RSA, 1963-69; Council, Northern Euboea Foundation; Council, Imp. Soc. of Knights Bachelor, 1969; St Charles's (formerly Paddington) Group Hosp. Management Cttee, 1963-. FRGS. *Publications:* A Short History of Nigeria, 1937; Nigeria's Story, 1939; Nigeria: the Outline of a Colony, 1946; How Nigeria is Governed, 1950; West Africa, 1958; Short History of the Yoruba, 1958; You and Your Government, 1958; Nine Great Africans, 1964; Nigeria (in Benn's Nations of the Modern World), 1967; (collab.) My Life, by late Sardauna of Sokoto, 1962; The War of Nigerian Unity (for Fed. Govt of Nigeria), 1970. *Recreations:* walking, architecture. *Address:* The Old Cottage, Hope Road, Deal, Kent. *T:* Deal 5104. *Club:* English-Speaking Union.

**NIVEN, (James) David (Graham);** Actor-producer (international); *b* 1 March 1910; *s* of late William Graham Niven and late Lady Comyn-Platt, Carswell Manor, Abingdon, Berks; *m* 1st, Primula (*d* 1946), *d* of Hon. William and Lady Kathleen Rollo; two *s*; 2nd, Hjördis Tersmeden, Stockholm; two *d*. *Educ:* Stowe; RMC Sandhurst. Commissioned HLI, 1929, Malta and Home Service; resigned commission, 1932; roamed Canada, USA, West Indies and Cuba till 1935. Journalist; Whisky Salesman; indoor pony-racing promoter; delivery of laundry; etc. Arrived California; became "extra" in films in Hollywood, 1935 ("English Type No. 2008"); played bits and small parts; first starring rôle, Bachelor Mother, 1938, with Ginger Rogers. Returned to England at outbreak of War of 1939-45; rejoined Army; commissioned Rifle Brigade, later to Phantom Reconnaissance Regt; served Normandy, Belgium, Holland, Germany (usual campaign decorations, American Legion of Merit). Subsequent important films: Wuthering Heights, Dawn Patrol, Raffles, The First of the Few, The Way Ahead, A Matter of Life and Death, The Bishop's Wife, Bonnie Prince Charlie, The Elusive Pimpernel, Enchantment, Soldiers Three, Happy Go Lovely, The Moon is Blue, The Love Lottery, Happy Ever After, Carrington VC, Around the World in 80 Days, The Birds and the Bees, Silken Affair, The Little Hut, Oh, Men, Oh, Women, Bonjour Tristesse, My Man Godfrey, Separate Tables, Ask Any Girl, Please don't eat the Daisies, The Guns of Navarone, The Best of Enemies, Guns of Darkness, 55 Days at Peking, The Pink Panther, The King of the Mountain, Bedtime Story, Lady L., Where the Spies Are, Eye of the Devil, Casino Royale; Extraordinary Seaman; Prudence and the Pill; The Impossible Years; Before Winter Comes; The Brain; The Statue. Formed Four Star Television, 1952, which has since produced over 2000 films for TV. Winner Academy Award, 1959; New York Critics' Award, 1960. *Publication:* Round the Rugged Rocks, 1951. *Recreations:* ski-ing, skin diving, oil painting, photography. *Address:* c/o Coutts & Co., 440 Strand, WC2. *Club:* White's.

**NIVEN, Margaret Graeme,** ROI 1936; Landscape and Portrait Painter; *b* Marlow, 1906; *yr d* of William Niven, FSA, ARE, JP, Marlow Place, Marlow, Bucks, and Eliza Mary Niven. *Educ:* Prior's Field, Godalming. Studied at Winchester Sch. of Art, Heatherley Sch. of Fine Art, and under Bernard Adams, RP, ROI; Mem. of National Soc. Painters, Sculptors, and Engravers, 1932. Exhibitor at Royal Academy and Royal Soc. of Portrait Painters. Works purchased by Bradford Art Gallery, The Ministry of Works, Homerton Coll., Cambridge, and Bedford Coll., London. Served with WRNS, 1940-45. *Address:* Broomhill, Sandhills, Wormley, near Godalming, Surrey.

**NIVEN, Sir Rex;** *see* Niven, Sir C. R.

**NIVEN, Col Thomas Murray,** CB 1964; TD 1941; DL; FICE; FIMechE; *b* 20 Aug. 1900; *s* of Thomas Ogilvie Niven, Civil Engineer, Glasgow. *Educ:* Glasgow Academy; Glasgow Univ. Served War of 1939-45 with Royal Signals: comdg 52 (Lowland) Div. Signals, 1938-40; comdg Royal Signals Mobilisation Centre, 1941-43; Dep. Chief Signal Officer, Northern Command, 1944. Comdg 6 Glasgow Home Guard Bn, 1952-56; Hon. Col 52 (Lowland) Signal Regt (TA), 1950-66; Chm., Glasgow T & AFA, 1959-62. Formerly Dir of Mechans Ltd, Engineers, Scotstoun Iron Works, Glasgow. DL Glasgow, 1949. *Recreation:* walking. *Address:* c/o Western Club, Glasgow. *Clubs:* United Service; Western (Glasgow).

**NIVISON,** family name of **Baron Glendyne.**

**NIXON, Sir (Charles) Norman,** Kt, *cr* 1946; Governor of the National Bank of Egypt until 1946; *b* 8 June 1891; *m* Catherine Marwood Ranson (*d* 1954); two *s.* Served European War, 1914-18, Indian Army (despatches). *Address:* 1 The Garden, Lady Street, Dulverton, Som.

**NIXON, Major Sir Christopher John Louis Joseph,** 3rd Bt, *cr* 1906; MC; Royal Ulster Rifles; *b* 21 March 1918; *s* of Major Sir Christopher Nixon, 2nd Bt, DSO, and Louise, *y d* of Robert Clery, JP, The Glebe, Athlacca, Limerick; *S* father, 1945; *m* 1949, Joan Lucille Mary, *d* of R. F. M. Brown, London; three *d.* Served War of 1939-45, Burma. Gurkha Bde (despatches, MC); Palestine, Egypt, 1945-48; UK, attached London Irish Rifles, 1948-50; Korea (despatches). 1950-51. *Heir: b* Rev. Kenneth Michael John Basil Nixon, SJ. [*b* 22 Feb. 1919; in Holy Orders of Church of Rome]. *Address:* c/o Lloyds Bank Ltd, Cox's & King's Branch, 6 Pall Mall, SW1. *Club:* United Service.

**NIXON, Edwin Ronald;** Managing Director since 1965: IBM United Kingdom Holdings Ltd; IBM United Kingdom Ltd; IBM United Kingdom Rentals Ltd; Chairman of IBM World Trade Laboratories Ltd, since 1965; Director, IBM Information Services Ltd, since 1967; *b* 21 June 1925; *s* of William Archdale Nixon and Ethel (*née* Corrigan); *m* 1952, Joan Lilian (*née* Hill); one *s* one *d. Educ:* Alderman Newton's Sch., Leicester; Selwyn Coll., Cambridge (BA Hons). Dexion Ltd, 1950-55; IBM United Kingdom Ltd, 1955-. Mem. Council, Westfield Coll., London, 1969. *Recreations:* music, tennis, squash, sailing, skiing. *Address:* Court's Edge, The Warren, Harpenden, Herts. *T:* Harpenden 2744.

**NIXON, Sir Norman;** *see* Nixon, Sir C. N.

**NIXON, Richard (Milhous);** President of the United States of America since 1969; *b* 9 Jan. 1913; *s* of Francis A. and Hannah Milhous Nixon; *m* 1940, Patricia Ryan; two *d. Educ:* Whittier Coll., Whittier, California (AB); Duke University Law Sch., Durham, North Carolina (LLB). Lawyer, Whittier, California, 1937-42; Office of Price Administration, 1942; Active duty, US Navy, 1942-46. Member 80th, 81st Congresses, 1947-51; US Senator from California, 1951-53. Vice-President of the USA, 1953-61; Republican candidate for the Presidency of the USA, 1960. Lawyer, Los Angeles, 1961-63, NY, 1963-68. Republican Candidate for Governor of California, 1962. Member: Board of Trustees, Whittier Coll., 1939-68; Society of Friends; Order of Coif. *Publication:* Six Crises, 1962. *Address:* The White House, Washington, DC, USA.

**NKRUMAH, Dr Kwame;** *b* 21 Sept. 1909; *m* 1957, Madame Fathia Ritz, Egypt; one *s* two *d. Educ:* Roman Catholic Elementary Sch., Half Assini; Government Teachers' Training Coll., Accra and Achimota; Lincoln Univ., Pennsylvania (BA, STB); Univ. of Pennsylvania (BD, MAPhil, MScEd); London Univ. Schoolmaster, 1931-34; Instructor in History and Philosophy, Univ. of Pennsylvania, 1944; Gen. Sec., W African Nat. Secretariat; Jt Sec. Pan African Congress, London and Manchester; Editor of New African, London, 1945-47; Former Member and first General Secretary, United Gold Coast Convention (UGCC); arrested and detained, Feb. 1948; resigned from UGCC, demanded "Self-Government Now" and formed Convention People's Party (CPP), 1949; his party staged Positive Action, 1950; imprisoned for inciting illegal strikes, 1950; elected to Legislative Assembly under new Constitution, Feb. 1950; released from prison on being elected first Municipal Member for Accra; Leader of Government Business in the Assembly, Feb. 1951; Prime Minister of Gold Coast, 1952-57, of Ghana, 1957-60; Minister of External Affairs, 1957-58, of the Interior, 1958-59; First President of the Republic of Ghana, 1960-66; Head of State and Supreme Commander of the Armed Forces, 1960-66. Attended Commonwealth Prime Ministers' Conference, June 1957, the first African Prime Minister to do so. Convened Conference of eight Independent African States (Chairman), April 1958, and did tour of these, May-June 1958; paid Official Visits to United States and Canada, July 1958. Addressed UN Assembly, 1960, 1961. Has since visited many countries and attended or convened conferences with regard to Africa. Past Chancellor: Univ. of Ghana; Kwame Nkrumah University of Science and Technology. Resident in the Republic of Guinea, 1966-. PC (Great Britain) 1959 (entitling him to prefix "Rt Hon."); Lenin Peace Prize, 1962. Has many hon. doctorates from universities. Holds several foreign Orders. *Publications:* Towards Colonial Freedom, 1946; What I Mean by Positive Action, 1950; Ghana (autobiography), 1957; I Speak of Freedom, 1961; Africa Must Unite, 1963; Consciencism, 1964; Neo-colonialism: the Last Stage of Imperialism, 1965; Challenge of the Congo, 1966; Axioms of Kwame Nkrumah, 1966; Dark Days in Ghana, 1968; Handbook of Revolutionary Warfare: A Guide to the Armed Phase of the African Revolution, 1968; Class Struggle in Africa, 1970. *Recreations:* tennis, swimming, collection of animals. *Address:* Conakry, Guinea.

**NOAD, Sir Kenneth (Beeson),** Kt 1970; Consulting Physician since 1931; President, Australian Postgraduate Federation in Medicine; *b* 25 March 1900; *s* of james Beeson and Mary Jane Noad; *m* 1935, Eileen Mary Ryan; no *c. Educ:* Maitland, NSW; Sydney University. MB, ChM 1924, MD 1953,

Sydney; MRCP 1929; FRCP 1948; Foundn FRACP 1938. Hon FACP 1964; Hon. FRCPE 1968. Served War of 1939-45, Palestine, Egypt, Greece, Crete, New Guinea; Lt-Col Comdr Medical Div. of an Australian General Hospital. *Publications:* papers in Brain, Med. Jl of Australia. *Recreations:* golf, gardening. *Address:* 65 Cranbrook Lane, Bellevue Hill, NSW 2023, Australia. *T:* 36-3244. *Clubs:* Australian (Sydney); Royal Sydney Golf.

**NOAKES, Michael,** VPROI, RP; portrait painter; *b* 28 Oct. 1933; *s* of late Basil and of Mary Noakes; *m* 1960, Vivien Langley, writer; two *s* one *d*. *Educ:* Downside; Royal Academy Schs, London. Nat. Dipl. in Design, 1954; Certificate of Royal Academy Schools, 1960. Commnd, National Service, 1954-56. Has broadcast and televised on art subjects in UK and USA; Art Correspondent, BBC TV programme Town and Around, 1964-68. Vice-Pres. and Mem. Council, ROI; Council Member: RP; NS; Mem. Cttee Contemp. Portrait Soc. FRSA. *Exhibited:* Royal Acad.; Royal Inst. Oil Painters; Royal Soc. Portrait Painters; Contemp. Portrait Soc.; Nat. Society; Young Contemporaries, Grosvenor Galleries, etc.; Art Exhibitions Bureau, touring widely in Britain, USA and Canada. *Portraits include:* Lord Boothby; Lady Boothby; Michael Bonallack; Viscount Boyd of Merton; Lord Chuter-Ede; Lord Fisher of Lambeth; Gilbert Harding, Malcolm Muggeridge; Robert Morley; Cliff Michelmore; Sir Gerald Nabarro; Valerie Profumo; J. B. Priestley; Sir Ralph Richardson; Dame Margaret Rutherford; Dennis Wheatley; Sir Donald Wolfit; Sir Mortimer Wheeler. *Represented in collections:* various Oxford and Cambridge colleges; County Hall, Westminster; Shakespeare Memorial Theatre Picture Gallery. *Publications:* A Professional Approach to Oil Painting, 1968; contributions to various art journals. *Recreation:* idling. *Address:* The Studio, 121 Cambridge Street, SW1. *T:* 01-834 8706; The Studio, Doods Park Road, Reigate, Surrey. *T:* Reigate 46056.

**NOAKES, Philip Reuben,** OBE 1962; HM Diplomatic Service; Counsellor (Information), Ottawa, since 1967; *b* 12 Aug. 1915; *y s* of late Charles William and Elizabeth Farey Noakes; *m* 1940, Moragh Jean Dickson; two *s*. *Educ:* Wyggeston Grammar Sch.; Wycliffe Coll.; Queens' Coll., Cambridge (Open Schol.). Mod. Langs Tripos Part I, Hist. Tripos Part II; BA 1937; MA 1945; Pres., Cambridge Union Soc., 1937. Served War, 1940-46; Capt.-Adjt 2nd Fife and Forfar Yeomanry, RAC (despatches). Public Relations Officer, Royal Over-Seas League, 1947-48; Sen. Information Officer, Colonial Office, 1948; Prin. Information Officer, CO, 1953; Information Adviser to Governor of Malta, 1960-61; Chief Information Officer, CO, 1963-66; Commonwealth Office, 1967. *Recreations:* bird-watching, fishing. *Address:* c/o Foreign and Commonwealth Office, SW1. *Clubs:* Royal Over-Seas League; Rideau (Ottawa).

**NOAKES, Sidney Henry; His Honour Judge Noakes;** County Court Judge, Circuit 56 (Croydon), since 1968; *b* 6 Jan. 1905; *s* of Thomas Frederick Noakes (Civil Servant) and Ada Noakes. *Educ:* Merchant Taylors' Sch.; St John's Coll., Oxford (MA). Called to Bar, Lincoln's Inn, 1928; SE Circuit; Bencher, 1963. War Service, Lt-Col., Intelligence Corps, England and NW Europe. Dep. Chairman, Surrey QS, 1963; Dep. Chairman, Herts QS, 1964; Recorder of Margate, 1965-68. *Publication:* Fire Insurance, 1947. *Recreations:* regretfully now only golf and walking. *Address:* 1 Paper Buildings, Temple, EC4. *T:* 01-353 0165.

**NOBLE, Comdr Rt. Hon. Sir Allan (Herbert Percy),** PC 1956; KCMG 1959; DSO 1943; DSC 1941; Chairman, Tollemache & Cobbold Breweries Ltd; Director, Colonial Mutual Life Assurance Society Ltd (UK Branch); *b* 2 May 1908; *s* of late Admiral Sir Percy Noble, GBE, KCB, CVO, and late Diamantina Campbell; *m* 1938, Barbara Janet Margaret, *o d* of late Brigadier Kenneth Gabbett. *Educ:* Radley College. Entered Royal Navy, 1926; ADC to Viceroy of India (Lord Linlithgow), 1936-38; commanded HM Destroyers Newport, Fernie and Quentin, 1940-42; Commander, 1943. Attended Quebec and Yalta Conferences. Served War of 1939-45 (despatches, DSC, DSO); retired list, 1945. MP (C) for Chelsea, 1945-59; Government Observer, Bikini Atomic Bomb Tests, 1946. PPS to Mr Anthony Eden, 1947-51; Parly and Financial Sec., Admiralty, 1951-55; Parly Under-Sec. of State for Commonwealth Relations, Dec. 1955-Nov. 1956; Minister of State for Foreign Affairs, Nov. 1956-Jan. 1959; Special Ambassador, Ivory Coast, 1961. Member Cttee of Management, Inst. of Cancer Research, Royal Cancer Hosp., 1959-67. Mem., Advisory Cttee on Service Parly Candidates, 1963-. President: Chelsea Cons. Assoc., 1962-66; Cambridgeshire Cons., Assoc., 1967-; a Mem. of Radley Coll. Council, 1947-63; Chm., National Trainers' Assoc., 1963-66. Hon. Freeman: Chelsea, 1963; Royal Borough of Kensington and Chelsea, 1965. Inter Services Athletics (Hurdles), 1931. *Address:* Burrough Green Hall, Newmarket, Suffolk. *T:* Stetchworth 203; 3 Culford Gardens, SW3. *T:* 01-589 0649. *Club:* White's.

**NOBLE, Sir Andrew Napier,** 2nd Bt, *cr* 1923; KCMG 1954 (CMG 1947); *b* 16 Sept. 1904; *s* of Sir John Henry Brunel Noble, 1st Bt, and Amie, *d* of S. A. Walker Waters; *S* father, 1938; *m* 1934, Sigrid, 2nd *d* of M. Michelet, of Royal Norwegian Diplomatic Service; two *s* one *d*. *Educ:* Eton; Balliol Coll., Oxford. Counsellor of the British Embassy, Buenos Aires, 1945-47; Assistant Under-Secretary of State, Foreign Office, 1949; HM Minister at Helsinki, 1951-54; HM Ambassador: Warsaw, 1954-56; Mexico, 1956-60; Netherlands, 1960-64, retired. Mem., Exec. Cttee, Oxford Society. *Publication:* (jt author) Centenary History, OURFC, 1969. *Heir:* *s* Ian Andrew Noble, *b* 1935. *Address:* 41 Gloucester Square, W2. *Club:* Boodle's.

*See also Rt Hon. M. A. C. Noble.*

**NOBLE, Col Arthur,** CB 1965; DSO 1943; TD; Deputy Chairman, W. & C. French Ltd, 1966-68 (Director, 1953-68); Chairman, Harlow and District Sports Trust since 1957; *b* 13 Sept. 1908; *s* of F. M. Noble, Chipping Ongar, Essex; *m* 1935, Irene Susan, OBE 1970, JP, *d* of J. D. Taylor, Wimbledon; three *s* two *d*. *Educ:* Felsted School. Chartered Quantity Surveyor, 1934; joined W. & C. French Ltd, 1945. Essex Regt (Territorial Army), 1927; Served Middle East and Italy, 1939-45; Commanded 4th Essex, 1941-44 and 1947-51; Chief Instructor, Sch. of Infantry, 1944-45. Hon. Col, TA and T&AVR Bn, The Essex Regt, 1955-. Chm. Essex County Playing Fields Assoc., 1956-61; Chm., County of Essex T & AF Assoc., 1958-66; Vice-Chm., Council of TA & VRA, 1966. Mem. of Council, Federation of Civil Engineering Contractors, 1963-68, Mem., Eastern Sports Council, 1966-; Hon. Officer, Nat. Playing Fields Assoc., 1968. DL (Essex) 1946. *Recreations:* many. *Address:* Marchings, Chigwell, Essex. *T:* Hainault 5302. *Clubs:* United Service, Royal Commonwealth Society.

**NOBLE, Fraser;** *see* Noble, T. A. F.

**NOBLE, Kenneth Albert;** Member of Monopolies Commission since 1969; Vice-Chairman, Co-operative Wholesale Society Ltd since 1966; *b* 7 May 1912; *s* of Percival Noble and Hester Noble (*née* Oliver); *m* 1935, Mary Jane Noble (*née* Geraghty); one *s* one *d*. Chief Exec. Officer of various retail co-operative socs. 1935-54. Served War, 1940-46 despatches: Major RASC, France/Germany Campaign. Director, Co-operative Wholesale Society Ltd and other associated organisations, 1954-. Member: Council of Industrial Design, 1957-65; Post Office Users Council, 1965-; Adv. Panel to Min. of Overseas Development, 1968-. *Publications:* contrib., on management and financial subjects, to co-operative and specialist jls. *Recreations:* gardening, reading, travel. *Address:* 23 St Augustine's Avenue, Thorpe Bay, Southend-on-Sea, Essex. *T:* Southend 87026.

**NOBLE, Major Sir Marc (Brunel),** 5th Bt, *cr* 1902; *b* 8 Jan. 1927; *er s* of Sir Humphrey Brunel Noble, 4th Bt, MBE, MC, and Celia, *d* of late Captain Stewart Weigall, RN; *S* father, 1968; *m* 1956, Jennifer Lorna, *yr d* of late John Mein-Austin, Flint Hill, West Haddon, Northants; two *s* one *d* (and one *d* decd). *Educ:* Eton. Commissioned into King's Dragoon Guards as 2nd Lieut, 1947; on amalgamation, transferred Royal Dragoons, 1958. Training Major and Adjutant, Kent and County of London Yeomanry (Sharpshooters), 1963-64; retired, rank of Major, RARO, 1966. *Heir: er s* David Brunel Noble, *b* 25 Dec. 1961. *Address:* Deerleap House, Knockholt, Sevenoaks, Kent. *T:* Knockholt 3222. *Club:* Cavalry.

**NOBLE, Rt. Hon. Michael Antony Cristobal,** PC 1962; MP (C) for Argyllshire since June 1958; Minister for Trade, Department of Trade and Industry, since Oct. 1970; *b* 19 March 1913; 3rd *s* of Sir John Henry Brunel Noble, 1st Bt, of Ardkinglas; *m* 1940, Anne, *d* of Sir Neville Pearson, 2nd Bt, *qv*; four *d*. *Educ:* Eton Coll.; Magdalen Coll., Oxford. Served RAFVR, 1941-45. Argyll County Council, 1949-51. PPS to Sec. of State for Scotland, 1959; Asst Govt Whip (unpaid), 1960 (Scottish Whip, Nov. 1960); A Lord Comr of the Treasury, 1961-62; Sec. of State for Scotland, 1962-63; President of the Board of Trade, June-Oct. 1970. Chm., Unionist Party in Scotland, 1962-63. Chairman: Associated Fisheries, 1966-70; Glendevon Farms (Winchburgh), 1969-70. *Recreations:* gardening, fishing, shooting. *Address:* Strone, Cairndow, Argyll. *T:* Cairndow 204. *Clubs:* Boodle's; New (Edinburgh); Royal Scottish Automobile (Glasgow).

**NOBLE, Sir Peter (Scott),** Kt 1967; Principal of King's College, University of London, 1952-July 1968; *b* 17 Oct. 1899; *s* of Andrew Noble and Margaret Trail; *m* 1928, Mary Stephen; two *s* one *d*. *Educ:* Aberdeen Univ.; St John's Coll., Cambridge. First Bursar at Aberdeen Univ., 1916, MA, with 1st Class Honours in Classics 1921, Simpson Prize and Robbie Gold Medal in Greek, Seafield Medal and Dr Black prize in Latin, Jenkyns Prize in Comparative Philology, Liddell Prize in Greek Verse, Fullerton Scholarship in Classics, 1921, Croom Robertson Fellow (1923-26); Scholar of St John's Coll., Cambridge; 1st class Classical Tripos Part I (1922) Part II (1923), 1st Class Oriental Langs Tripos Part I (1924) Part II (1925), Bendall Sanskrit Exhibition (1924), (1925), Hutchison Student (1925); Lecturer in Latin at Liverpool Univ., 1926-30; Professor of Latin Language and Literature in the University of Leeds, 1930-37; Fellow of St John's Coll., Cambridge, 1928-31; Regius Professor of Humanity, University of Aberdeen, 1938-52; Member of University Grants Cttee, 1943-53; Vice-Chancellor, University of London, 1961-64; Member of General Dental Council, 1955; Member of Educational Trust, English-Speaking Union, 1958; Governor of St Thomas' Hospital, 1960. Hon. LLD Aberdeen, 1955. *Publications:* Joint editor of Kharosthi Inscriptions Vol. III; Reviews, etc. in classical journals. *Address:* Grange Corner, The Avenue, Bushey, Herts.

**NOBLE, (Thomas Alexander) Fraser,** MBE 1947; Vice-Chancellor, University of Leicester, since 1962; *b* 29 April 1918; *s* of late Simon Noble, Grantown-on-Spey and Jeanie Graham, Largs, Ayrshire; *m* 1945, Barbara A. M. Sinclair, Nairn; one *s* one *d*. *Educ:* Nairn Acad; Univ. of Aberdeen. After military service with Black Watch (RHR), entered Indian Civil Service, 1940. Served in NW Frontier Province, 1941-47, successively as Asst Comr, Hazara; Asst Polit. Agent, N Waziristan; Controller of Rationing, Peshawar; Under-Sec., Food Dept and Develt Dept; Sec., Home Dept; Joint Dep. Comr, Peshawar; Civil Adviser to Referendum Comr. Lectr in Political Economy, Univ. of Aberdeen, 1948-57; Sec. and Treas., Carnegie Trust for Univs of Scotland, 1957-62. Mem. and Vice-Chm., Bd of Management, Aberdeen Mental Hosp. Group, 1953-57. Sec., Scottish Economic Soc., 1954-58; Vice-Pres., 1962-. Chm., Scottish Standing Conf. of Voluntary Youth Organisations, 1958-62; Vice-Chm., Standing Consultative Council on Youth Service in Scotland, 1959-62. Mem., Departmental Cttee on Probation Service, 1959-62; Chairman: Probation Advisory and Training Board, 1962-65; Television Research Cttee, 1963-69; Advisory Council on Probation and After-Care, 1965-70; Univs Council for Adult Education, 1965-69; Min. of Defence Cttee for Univ. Assistance to Adult Educn in HM Forces, 1965-70; Advisory Board, Overseas Students' Special Fund, 1967-, Fees Awards Scheme, 1968-; Cttee of Vice-Chancellors and Principals of Univs. of UK, 1970-71. Member: Academic Advisory Cttee, Univs of St Andrews and Dundee, 1964-66; E Midlands Economic Planning Council, 1965-68; Academic Adv. Council for Royal Defence Acad., 1969-. Hon. LLD Aberdeen, 1968. *Publications:* articles in economic journals. *Recreation:* golf. *Address:* Knighton Hall, Leicester LE2 3WG. *T:* Leicester 706677.

**NOCK, Sir Norman (Lindfield),** Kt 1939; Chairman of Directors, Nock & Kirby Ltd, Sydney; Member Australian Council of Retailers; *s* of Thomas Nock, Stanhope Road, Killara, Sydney; *m* 1927, Ethel Evelina Bradford; one *s*. *Educ:* Sydney Church of England Grammar Sch. Alderman for Gipps Ward, City of Sydney, 1933-41; Lord Mayor of Sydney, 1938-39; Chairman, Federal Australian Comforts Fund, 1939-43; Chairman, Australian Comforts Fund, NSW Division, 1939-45; President of the National Roads and Motorists Association, 1954-69; Chairman Royal North Shore Hospital of Sydney, 1940-69; Member National Health and Medical Research Council. JP for New South Wales. *Recreations:* golf, sailing and motoring. *Address:* Box 4250, GPO Sydney, NSW 2001, Australia. *Club:* Royal Sydney Golf (Sydney).

**NOCKELLS HORLICK, Lieut-Colonel Sir James;** *see* Horlick.

**NOCKOLDS, Stephen Robert,** FRS 1959; PhD; Reader in Geochemistry in the University of Cambridge, since 1957; *b* 10 May 1909; *s* of Stephen Nockolds; *m* 1932, Hilda Jackson. *Educ:* Felsted; University of Manchester

(BSc); University of Cambridge (PhD). Fellow of Trinity Coll. and formerly Lectr in Petrology, Univ. of Cambridge. *Publications:* various papers in mineralogical and geological journals. *Recreations:* gardening, motoring. *Address:* Department of Mineralogy and Petrology, Downing Place, Cambridge; Trinity College, Cambridge; The Old Manor House, Linton, Cambridgeshire CB1 6JZ.

**NOEL,** family name of **Earl of Gainsborough.**

**NOEL, Rear-Adm. Gambier John Byng,** CB 1969; Chief Staff Officer (Technical) to Commander-in-Chief, Western Fleet, 1967-69, retired; *b* 16 July 1914; *s* of late G. B. E. Noel; *m* 1936, Miss Joan Stevens; four *d. Educ:* Royal Naval Coll., Dartmouth. Joined Royal Navy, 1931; Served in War of 1939-45, HMS Aurora and HMS Norfolk (despatches twice). Captain 1959; Imperial Defence Coll., 1962; Staff of Commander Far East Fleet, 1964-67; Rear-Admiral 1967. *Recreations:* gardening, golf. *Address:* Olivers, High Street, Haslemere, Surrey. *T:* Haslemere 3824. *Club:* Anglo-Belgian.

**NOEL-BAKER, Francis Edward;** *b* 7 Jan. 1920; *s* of Rt Hon. Philip John Noel-Baker, *qv; m* 1957, Barbara Christina, *yr d* of late Joseph Sonander, Sweden; four *s* one *d. Educ:* Westminster Sch.; King's Coll., Cambridge (Exhibitioner). Left Cambridge to join Army, summer 1940, as Trooper, Royal Tank Regt; Commissioned in Intelligence Corps and served in UK, Middle East (despatches); returned to fight Brentford and Chiswick Div.; MP (Lab) Brentford and Chiswick Div. of Mddx, 1945-50; PPS Admiralty, 1949-50; MP (Lab) Swindon, 1955-69; Sec., 1955-64, Chm., 1964-68, UN Parly Cttee. Chm., Advertising Inquiry Council, 1951-68. Chm., North Euboean Foundation Ltd; Hon. Pres., Union of Forest Owners of Greece, 1968-. Member: Freedom from Hunger Campaign (UK Cttee Exec. Cttee Projects Group), 1961. *Publications:* Greece, the Whole Story, 1946; Spanish Summary, 1948; The Spy Web, 1954; Land and People of Greece, 1957; Nansen, 1958; Looking at Greece, 1967. *Address:* Achmetaga Estate, Prokopion, Euboea, Greece. *TA:* Noelbaker, Mantoudion, Greece. *T:* Prokopion 4. *Club:* Travellers'.

**NOEL-BAKER, Rt. Hon. Philip J.,** PC 1945; b Nov. 1889; *s* of late J. Allen Baker, MP; *m* 1915, Irene (*d* 1956), *o d* of Frank Noel, British landowner, of Achmetaga, Greece; one *s. Educ:* Bootham School, York; Haverford Coll., Pa; King's Coll., Cambridge, MA. Historical Tripos, Part I, Class II, 1910; Economics Tripos, Part II, Class I, 1912; University Whewell Scholar, 1911 (continued, 1913); President CUAC, 1910-12; President Cambridge Union Society, 1912; Vice-Principal, Ruskin Coll., Oxford, 1914; First Commandant Friend's Ambulance Unit, Aug. 1914-July 1915; Officer First British Ambulance Unit for Italy, 1915-18; Mons Star; Silver Medal for Military Valour (Italy), 1917; Croce di Guerra, 1918; League of Nations Section of British Delegation during Peace Conference, 1919; League of Nations Secretariat till 1922; contested (Lab) Handsworth Division of Birmingham, 1924; MP (Lab), for Coventry, 1929-31, for Derby, 1936-50, for Derby South, 1950-70; PPS to the Sec. of State for Foreign Affairs, 1929-31; Parly Sec. to Min. of War Transport, 1942-45; Minister of State, FO, 1945-46; Sec. of State for Air, 1946-47; Sec. of State for Commonwealth Relations, 1947-50; Minister of Fuel and Power, 1950-51. Chairman, Foreign Affairs Group, Parly Labour Party, 1964-70. Late Fellow, King's Coll., Cambridge; Hon. Fellow, since 1961; Sir Ernest Cassel Prof. of International Relations in the Univ. of London, 1924-29; Member of British Delegation to the 10th Assembly of the League of Nations, 1929 and 1930; Principal Asst to the Pres. of the Disarmament Conference at Geneva, 1932-33; British Delegate to UN Preparaotry Commn, 1945; Mem., British Delegn to Gen. Assembly of UN, 1946-47; Delegate to Colombo Conf. on Economic Aid, 1950. Dodge lecturer, Yale Univ., 1934; President, International Council on Sport and Physical Recreation, UNESCO, 1960-; Howland Prize for distinguished work in the sphere of Government, Yale Univ., 1934; Nobel Peace Prize, 1959; Albert Schweitzer Book Prize, 1960. *Hon. Degrees:* Birmingham Univ.; Nottingham Univ.; Manchester Univ.; Univ. of Colombo; Queen's Univ., Ontario; Haverford Coll., USA; Brandeis Univ., USA. *Publications:* The Geneva Protocol, 1925; Disarmament, 1926; The League of Nations at Work, 1926; Disarmament and the Coolidge Conference, 1927; J. Allen Baker, MP, a Memoir (with E. B. Baker); The Juridical Status of the British Dominions in International Law, 1929; The Private Manufacture of Armaments, Vol. I, 1936; The Arms Race: A Programme for World Disarmament, 1958; pamphlets and articles. *Address:* 16 South Eaton Place, SW1. *T:* 01-730 5377.

*See also Francis Noel-Baker.*

**NOEL-BUXTON,** 2nd Baron, *cr* 1930, of Aylsham; **Rufus Alexander Buxton;** writer and painter; *b* 13 Jan. 1917; *s* of 1st Baron Noel-Buxton and Lucy Edith (MP (Lab) North Norfolk, 1930-31, Norwich, 1945-50; *d* 1960), *e d* of late Major Henry Pelham Burn; *S* father, 1948; *m* 1st, 1939, Nancy (marr. diss. 1947; she *d* 1949), *yr d* of late Col K. H. M. Connal, CB, OBE; two *s*; 2nd, 1948, Margaret Elizabeth, *er d* of Stephanus Abraham Cloete, Pretoria, SA; one *s* one *d*. Assumed names of Rufus Alexander Buxton in lieu of those of Noel Alexander Noel-Buxton, 1944. *Educ:* Harrow; Balliol Coll., Oxford (BA). Invalided from 163 OCTU (the Artists Rifles), 1940; Research Asst, Agricultural Economics Research Inst., Oxford, 1941-43; Lecturer to Forces, 1943-45; Producer, BBC North American Service, 1946-48; editorial staff of The Farmer's Weekly, 1950-52. *Publications:* The Ford, 1955; Westminster Wader, 1957. *Heir: s* Hon. Martin Connal Noel-Buxton (assumed by deed poll, 1964, original surname of Noel-Buxton) [*b* 8 Dec. 1940; *m* 1964, Miranda Mary (marr. diss. 1968), *er d* of H. A. Chisenhale-Marsh, Gaynes Park, Epping, and Lady Buxton, Woodredon, Waltham Abbey]. *Address:* The Old Vicarage, Loddiswell, Kingsbridge, Devon.

**NOEL-PATON,** family name of **Baron Ferrier.**

**NOKES, Gerald Dacre;** Professor Emeritus, University of London; Fellow of King's College, London; *b* 26 Aug. 1899; *s* of Walter Frederick and Emma Nokes. *Educ:* Stationers' Sch.; King's Coll., London. 2nd Lieut, RFC and RAF, 1918-19. LLB 1921, LLD 1927 (London); Barrister, Middle Temple, 1922. In practice, England, 1922-33; Judge, High Court, Travancore, S India, 1933-47; on deputation as Public Service Comr, Travancore, 1935-40; Senior Lecturer, 1947, Reader in English Law, 1948, Professor of Law, 1955-66, King's Coll., London; Dean of Faculty of Laws, University of London, 1958-62. *Publications:* Law relating to Mortgages and Receiverships, 2nd edn, 1931; Law relating to Sales by Auction, 1925; History of the Crime of Blasphemy, 1928; Travancore Service Recruitment Manual, 1937; Introduction to

Evidence, 1952, 4th edn, 1967. *Address:* 14 Wetherby Gardens, SW5. *T:* 01-373 9123. *Club:* Royal Commonwealth Society.

**NOLAN, Michael Patrick,** QC 1968; *b* 10 Sept. 1928; *yr s* of James Thomas Nolan and Jane (*née* Walsh); *m* 1953, Margaret, *yr d* of Alfred Noyes, CBE, and Mary (*née* Mayne); one *s* four *d. Educ:* Ampleforth; Wadham Coll., Oxford. Served RA, 1947-49; TA, 1949-55. Called to Bar, Middle Temple, 1953. *Recreation:* fishing. *Address:* Tanners, Brasted, Westerham, Kent. *T:* Westerham 3758.

**NOLAN, Sidney Robert,** CBE 1963; artist; *b* Melbourne, 22 April 1917; *s* of late Sidney Henry Nolan; *m* 1948, Cynthia Hansen. *Educ:* State and technical schools, Melbourne; National Art Gallery Sch., Victoria. Italian Government Scholar, 1956; Commonwealth Fund Fellow, to USA, 1958; Fellow, ANU, 1965 (Hon. LLD, 1968). Exhibited: New Delhi, 1953; Pittsburgh International, 1953, 1954, 1955, 1964, 1967; Venice Biennale, 1954; Pacific Loan Exhibition, 1956; Brussels International Exhibition, 1958; Documenta II, Kassel, 1959; Retrospective Art Gallery of New South Wales, Sydney, 1967; Marlborough New London Gallery, 1968. Ballet Designs for Icare, Sydney, 1941; Rite of Spring, Covent Garden, 1962; The Display, Adelaide Festival, 1964. Works in Tate Gallery, Museum of Modern Art, New York, Australian national galleries, Contemporary Art Society and Arts Council of Great Britain, etc. *Relevant publications:* (Kenneth Clark, Colin MacInnes, Bryan Robertson), Nolan, 1961; (Robert Melville), Ned Kelly, 1964; (Elwyn Lynn), Sidney Nolan: Myth and Imagery, 1967; (Cynthia Nolan) Open Negative 1967; Sight of China, 1969. *Address:* c/o Bank of New South Wales, 9 Sackville Street, W1.

**NONWEILER, Prof. Terence Reginald Forbes,** BSc; PhD; CEng; FRAeS; Mechan Professor of Aeronautics and Fluid Mechanics, Glasgow University, since 1961; *b* 8 Feb. 1925; *s* of Ernest James Nonweiler and Lilian Violet Amalie Nonweiler (*née* Holfert); *m* 1949, Patricia Hilda Frances (*née* Neame); four *s* one *d. Educ:* Bethany Sch., Goudhurst, Kent; University of Manchester, BSc 1944, PhD 1960. Scientific Officer, Royal Aircraft Establishment, Farnborough, Hants, 1944-50; Scientific Officer, Scientific Advisor's Dept, Air Ministry, 1950-51; Senior Lecturer in Aerodynamics, College of Aeronautics, Cranfield, Beds, 1951-57; Senior Lecturer in Aeronautical Engineering, The Queen's Univ. of Belfast, 1957-61. Consultant: to Admiralty, 1951; to Ministry of Aviation, 1959; to Ministry of Agriculture, 1966. Member, International Academy of Astronautics. *Publications:* Jets and Rockets, 1959. Numerous technical papers on aeronautics, space flight, and submarine motion. *Recreations:* acting and stage production. *Address:* 9 The University, Glasgow, W2. *T:* 041-334 1353.

**NOON, Firoz Khan,** (KCSI, 1941; KCIE, 1937; Kt, 1933); MA (Oxon); Leader of the Republican Party, Pakistan, from 1958; MP, Pakistan Parliament, from 1955; lawyer; *b* 7 May 1893; *s* of late Hon. Nawab Sir Malik Mohammed Hayat Khan Noon, Kt, CSI; *m* 1942, Elizabeth Rikh. *Educ:* Aitchison Chiefs' Coll., Lahore; Wadham Coll., Oxford. Called to the Bar, Inner Temple, London. Advocate Lahore High Court, 1917-26; Member of the Punjab Legislature, 1920-36; Minister for Local Self-Government, Punjab Government, 1927-30; Minister for Education and Medical and Public Health, Punjab, 1931-36; High Commissioner for India in United Kingdom, 1936-41; Labour Member of Viceroy's Executive Council, India, 1941-42, Defence Member, 1942-45; Indian rep., British War Cabinet, 1944-45; Member Punjab Provincial Legislature and All Pakistan Constituent Assembly and Legislature, 1947-50; Governor of East Pakistan, 1950-53; Leader (elected) Punjab Moslem League, 1953; Chief Minister of West Punjab, 1953-55; Foreign Minister, Pakistan, 1956-57; Prime Minister, Minister for Foreign Affairs and Commonwealth Relations, and Minister of Interior, Pakistan, 1957-Oct. 1958; Member: Governing Body of ILO, Geneva; Permanent Cttee Internat. Institute of Agriculture, Rome; Internat. Rubber Regulation Cttee; Internat. Tea Cttee; Imperial Economic Cttee; Internat. Sugar Council, London; Imperial Communication Advisory Council; Imperial Shipping Cttee. Hon. Fellow of Wadham Coll., Oxford; Hon. LLD Toronto, Canada, 1938. *Publications:* Canada and India, 1939; Wisdom from Fools, 1940; Illustrated "India", 1940; Scented Dust, 1941; From Memory: an autobiography, 1966. *Address:* Al Viqar, Noon Avenue, Lahore, Pakistan.

**NOOR, Khan Bahadur Khaja Sir Mohamad,** Kt, *cr* 1937; CBE 1929; *b* 28 Sept. 1878; *s* of late Khwaja Wahid Jan; *m* 1908, Fakhrunnissa; three *s. Educ:* Government Sch., Gaya; Patna Coll.; Doveton Coll.; St Xavier's Coll. and Ripon Coll., Calcutta. Graduated in Arts and Law, Calcutta Univ.; practised at the Gaya Bar, 1904-22; Vice-Chairman of the Gaya Municipality and District Board; Member of the Legislative Council since 1913; Fellow of the Patna University since 1917; Vice-Chancellor, Patna University, 1933-36; President, Legislative Council, Bihar and Orissa, India, 1922-30; Judge High Court, Patna, India, 1930-39; Chairman Joint Public Service Commission for Bihar, Central Provinces, and Berar and Orissa, 1940-41. Representative of the Province of Bihar and Orissa in the War Conference convened by the Viceroy in 1918; Khan Bahadur, 1914; Certificate of Honour, Coronation Durbar, 1911. *Recreation:* agriculture. *Address:* Gaya, Bihar, India. *Club:* New Patna.

**NORBURY,** 6th Earl of, *cr* 1827; **Noel Terence Graham-Toler;** Baron Norwood, 1797; Baron Norbury, 1800; Viscount Glandine, 1827; *b* 1 Jan. 1939; *s* of 5th Earl and Margaret Greenhalgh; *S* father 1955; *m* 1965, Anne Mathew; one *s* one *d. Heir: s* Viscount Glandine, *qv. Address:* Stock Exchange, EC2.

**NORDEN, Denis;** scriptwriter and broadcaster; *b* 6 Feb. 1922; *s* of George Norden and Jenny Lubell; *m* 1943, Avril Rosen; one *s* one *d. Educ:* Craven Park Sch., London; City of London Sch. Theatre Manager, 1939-42; served RAF, 1942-45; staff-writer in Variety Agency, 1945-47. With Frank Muir, 1947-64: collaborated for 17 years writing comedy scripts, including: (for radio): Take it from Here, 1947-58; Bedtime with Braden, 1950-54; (for TV): And so to Bentley, 1956; Whack-O!, 1958-60; The Seven Faces of Jim, 1961, and other series with Jimmy Edwards; resident in TV and radio panel-games; collaborated in film scripts, television commercials, and Revues; joint Advisors and Consultants to BBC Television Light Entertainment Dept, 1960-64; jointly received Screenwriters Guild Award for Best Contribution to Light Entertainment, 1961; together on panel-games My Word!, 1956-, and My Music, 1967-. Since 1964, solo writer for television and films. Film Credits include: The Bliss of Mrs Blossom; Buona Sera, Mrs Campbell; The Best House in London; Every Home Should Have One; Twelve Plus one; The Statue. *Recreations:* tennis, reading, loitering.

*Address:* 201 Regent Street, W1. *T:* 01-734 7811. *Club:* Queen's.

**NORDMEYER, Hon. Arnold Henry,** CMG 1970; JP; Leader of the Opposition (Labour), New Zealand, 1963-65; *b* Dunedin, New Zealand, 7 Feb. 1901; *s* of Arnold and Martha Nordmeyer; *m* 1931, Frances Maria Kernahan; one *s* one *d*. *Educ:* Waitaki Boys' High Sch.; Otago Univ. (BA, Dip. Soc. Sci.). Presbyterian Minister for 10 years. Entered New Zealand Parliament, 1935; MP for Oamaru, 1935-49, for Brooklyn, 1951-54, for Island Bay, 1954-69; Minister of: Health, 1941-47; Industries and Commerce, 1947-49; Finance, 1957-60. JP 1970. Hon. LLD Otago, 1970. Recreations: shooting, fishing. *Address:* 53 Milne Terrace, Wellington, New Zealand.

**NORFOLK,** 16th Duke of, *cr* 1483; **Bernard Marmaduke Fitzalan-Howard,** KG 1937; PC 1936; GCVO 1946; GBE 1968; TD 1969; Royal Victoria Chain, 1953; Earl of Arundel, 1139; Baron Maltravers, 1330; Earl of Surrey, 1483; Baron Herries, 1490; Baron FitzAlan, Clun, and Oswaldestre, 1627; Earl of Norfolk, 1644; Earl Marshal and Hereditary Marshal and Chief Butler of England; Premier Duke and Earl; Lord Lieutenant of Sussex since 1949; Reserve of Officers; late 2nd Lieut Royal Horse Guards; Major Royal Sussex Regt; HM Representative at Ascot; President: Council for the Protection of Rural England, since 1945; T&AVR Association, since 1970 (Chairman of Council, 1956-69); Animal Health Trust; Elder Brother, Trinity House, since 1965; *b* 30 May 1908, *s* of 15th Duke and Hon. Gwendolen Constable-Maxwell, 12th Baroness Herries; *S* father, 1917; *m* 1937, Hon. Lavinia Mary Strutt, *o d* of 3rd Baron Belper; four *d*. Mayor of Arundel, 1935-36; Jt Parly Sec. to Min. of Agriculture, 1941-45. Pres., MCC, 1957-58; Manager, MCC team to Australia and New Zealand, 1962-63. Past Steward of the Jockey Club; Vice-Chm., Turf Bd, 1965-68. A Vice-Pres. of St Dunstan's, 1970-. *Heir:* (*to Dukedom*); *c* Baron Howard of Glossop, *qv*; (*to Herries Barony*): *d* Lady Anne Elizabeth Fitzalan-Howard, *b* 12 June 1938. *Address:* Arundel Park, Arundel, Sussex; (Seat) Arundel Castle. *Club:* Turf.
*See also Lady Rachel Pepys.*

**NORFOLK, Archdeacon of;** *see under* Thetford, Suffragan Bishop of.

**NORFOLK, Leslie William,** OBE 1944; TD 1946; Chief Executive, Royal Dockyards, Ministry of Defence, since 1969; *b* 8 April 1911; *e s* of late Robert and Edith Norfolk, Nottingham; *m* 1944, A. I. E. W. (Nancy) Watson (then WRNS), *d* of late Sir Hugh Watson, IFS (retd); two *s* one *d*. *Educ:* Southwell Minster Grammar Sch., Notts; University Coll., Nottingham. Assistant and later Partner, E. G. Phillips, Son & Norfolk, consulting engineers, Nottingham, 1932-36. Served with RE, France, Gibraltar, Home Forces, 1936-45, Lt-Col. Engineer, Dyestuffs Div., ICI Ltd, 1945-53; Resident Engineer, ICI of Canada, Kingston, Ont., 1953-55; Asst Chief Engr, Metals Div., ICI Ltd, 1955-57; Engineering Manager, Severnside Works, ICI Ltd, 1957-59; Engineering Director, Industrias Quimicas Argentinas Duperial SAIC, Buenos Aires, 1959-65; Director, Heavy Organic Chemicals Div., ICI Ltd, 1965-68; retired from ICI, 1968. *Recreations:* golf, sailing, caravanning. *Address:* Beechwoods, Beechwood Road, Combe Down, Bath, Som. *T:* Combe Down 2104.

**NORIE-MILLER, Sir Stanley,** 2nd Bt, *cr* 1936; MC 1918; DL; JP; MA; Governor (late Chairman and Managing Director), General Accident Fire and Life Assurance Corporation Ltd; *b* 4 Aug. 1888; *s* of Sir Francis Norie-Miller, 1st Bt, and Grace Harvey Day; *S* father, 1947; *m* 1921, Grace Janet Euphrosyne Berrangé, *d* of late J. B. Eagar, Somerset East, S Africa; no *c*. *Educ:* Rugby; Hertford Coll., Oxford, Hon. Fellow, 1968. Called to Bar, 1912. Served European War, 1914-18, in The Black Watch (RH), Captain, 1915 (despatches, MC). Freeman, City of Perth; DL, Hon. Sheriff Substitute, and JP for County of Perth. *Heir:* none. *Address:* Murrayshall, nr Perth, Scotland. *T:* Scone 51254. *Club:* Bath.

**NÖRLUND, Niels Erik,** PhD (Copenhagen), Hon. DSc (London), Hon. DEng (Darmstadt); Hon. PhD (Lund); Hon. DSc (Dijon); Hon. PhD (Oslo); Hon. DASc (Copenhagen); Formerly Professor of Mathematics in University of Copenhagen; Director Danish Geodetic Institute; Editor Acta Mathematica; *b* Slagelse, Denmark, 26 Oct. 1885; *m* 1912, Agnete Weaver (*d* 1959); two *d*. *Educ:* University of Copenhagen, Paris and Cambridge. Formerly Pres., International Council of Scientific Unions; Formerly Pres. Rask-Örsted Foundation; lately Pres., Royal Danish Academy of Science; formerly Pres. Baltic Geodetic Commission; formerly Rector of Univ. of Copenhagen; Foreign Mem. Royal Soc., Royal Astronomical Soc., Acad. Science Paris, Rome, Stockholm, Oslo, Helsingfors, Uppsala and Naples; Hon. Member Royal Institution, London. *Publications:* Vorlesungen über Differenzenrechnung (Berlin), 1924; Leçons sur les séries d'interpolation (Paris), 1926; Sur la somme d'une fonction (Paris), 1927; Leçons sur les équations aux différences finies (Paris), 1929; The map of Iceland (Copenhagen), 1944. *Address:* Copenhagen, Malmögade 6, Denmark. *TA:* Copenhagen. *T:* Obro 3046.

**NORMAN, Baroness (Priscilla),** CBE 1963; JP; *b* 1899; *o d* of late Major Robert Reyntiens and late Lady Alice Bertie; *m* 1st, 1921, Alexander Koch de Gooreynd (marr. diss. 1929); two *s*; 2nd, 1933, 1st Baron Norman, PC, DSO (*d* 1950). Member: London County Council, 1925-33; Chelsea Borough Council, 1928-31; Bethlem Royal and the Maudsley Hospital Board, 1951-; South-East Metropolitan Regional Board, 1951-; Exec. Board World Federation for Mental Health, 1952-57. Vice-Chairman, Women's Voluntary Services for Civil Defence, 1938-41; Vice-President, National Association for Mental Health; Vice-President, Royal College of Nursing. JP 1944. *Address:* Aubrey Lodge, Aubrey Road, W8.

**NORMAN, Vice-Admiral Alfred Headley,** CMG 1919; retired; *b* 27 Aug. 1881; *s* of Alfred Reynolds Norman; *m* 1906, Beatrix Mabel Godfrey (*d* 1970); four *s*. *Educ:* King's Sch., Rochester; Dover Coll. Joined Royal Navy, 1896; Lieut, 1903; Commander, 1914; Captain, 1919; Rear-Adm. and retired list, 1931; ADC to King George VI, 1931; Vice-Adm., retired, 1936; served European War (despatches, Battle of Jutland, CMG); awarded Gold Medal of the Royal United Services Institution, 1923. *Address:* White House Nursing Home, Church Crookham, Fleet, Hants.

**NORMAN, Archibald Percy,** MBE 1945; FRCP; MD; Physician, Hospital for Sick Children, since 1950; Paediatrician, Queen Charlotte's Maternity Hospital, since 1951; *b* 19 July 1912; *s* of Dr George Percy Norman and Mary Margaret MacCallum; *m* 1950, Aleida Elisabeth M. M. R. Bisschop; five *s*. *Educ:* Charterhouse; Emmanuel Coll., Cambridge. Served War of 1939-45, in Army, 1940-45. *Publications:* (joint) Fibrocystic Disease of the Pancreas, 1952; (ed) Congenital

Abnormalities, 1962; (ed) Moncreiff's Nursing and Diseases of Sick Children, 1966; contributions to medical journals. *Recreations:* fishing and family. *Address:* White Lodge, Heather Close, Kingswood, Surrey. *T:* Mogador 2626.

**NORMAN, Sir Arthur (Gordon),** KBE 1969 (CBE 1966); DFC 1943; and Bar 1944; Chairman of The De La Rue Company; *b* 18 Feb. 1917; *m* 1944, Margaret Doreen Harrington; three *s* two *d. Educ:* Blundell's Sch. Joined Thomas De La Rue & Co., 1934. Served War of 1939-45 (DFC and Bar); joined RAF, as pilot, 1941; Wing-Comdr, 1943; demobilised, 1946. Rejoined Thomas De La Rue & Co., and appointed Asst General Manager; Director, 1951; Managing Director, 1953; Chairman, 1964. Director: BOAC; Sun Life Assurance Society; Skefco Ball Bearing Co. Ltd, 1970-, Chm., Business and Industry Adv. Cttee to OECD, 1970-; Mem., NEDC, 1968-. Chm., FBI South Eastern Regional Council, 1960-62; Pres., CBI, 1968-70, Vice-Pres., 1970-. Governor, Henley Staff Coll. Trustee: Royal Air Force Museum; World Wildlife Fund (British Nat. Appeal). *Recreations:* tennis, golf, country life. *Address:* De La Rue House, 84/86 Regent Street, W1R 6AB. *T:* 01-734 8020. *Club:* Travellers'.

**NORMAN, Sir Charles,** Kt 1964; CBE 1951; Director of Joseph Rank Ltd, 1952-65; *b* 22 July 1892; *e s* of late Harry Norman, JP, City of Worcester; *m* 1918, Dorothy Mary, 2nd *d* of Thomas Hayes, Worcester; two *s* one *d.* Chm., CIF Buyers (London) Ltd, and Chm., COMPRO Ltd, 1939-45; Chm., Working Party on Millable Wheat and Feeding Barley, 1954-65; Dep. Chm., Home Grown Cereals Authority, 1965. Pres., Corn Exchange Benevolent Company, 1953; Pres., National Assoc. of Compound Manufacturers, 1955-56. Liveryman of The Worshipful Company of Farmers. *Address:* Kingsthorpe, 57 Oakington Avenue, Wembley Park, Middlesex. *T:* 01-904 2853. *Club:* Farmers'.

**NORMAN, Major-General Charles Wake,** CBE 1943; DL; *b* 13 Feb. 1891; *e s* of late Archibald Norman, The Rookery, Bromley Common, Kent; *m* 1925, Nora, *d* of Lieut-Colonel William Beadon, 51st Sikhs; two *s* two *d. Educ:* Eton; Trinity Coll., Cambridge (MA). Joined 9th Lancers, 1913; served France, 1914 (despatches, wounded and prisoner); commanded 9th Lancers, 1936-38; Colonel, 1938; commanded 1st Armoured Reconnaissance Brigade, France, 1940 (despatches); Temp. Maj.-General, 1941; retired, May 1946. Colonel, 9th Lancers, 1940-50. High Sheriff of Kent, 1950-51; Member Kent County Council, 1949-55; DL Kent. *Address:* West Farleigh Hall, Maidstone, Kent. *Club:* Cavalry.

**NORMAN, Duncan Thomas,** MC; MA, LLD; JP Liverpool; Hon. President, Owen Owen Ltd, and associated Companies (retired as Chairman and Managing Director, 1964; 40 years service); *b* 27 June 1889; *s* of A. R. Norman, Runcorn, Cheshire, and Agnes, *d* of Duncan McKechnie, St Helens, Lancs; *m* 1918, Dilys, *d* of Owen Owen, Liverpool and Machynlleth; one *s* three *d* (*er s* killed in action, 1942). *Educ:* Shrewsbury; Emmanuel Coll., Cambridge (MA). Served European War, 1914-18 with 55th Division British Expeditionary Force, Captain, RE (TF) (MC, Chevalier Order of Leopold, Croix de Guerre). Member Council, 1942-63 (retiring as Senior Pro-Chancellor). University of Liverpool; Governor, Shrewsbury Sch., 1943-60 (Chairman, 1956-60). High Sheriff of Cheshire, 1943-44. Hon. LLD: McMaster Univ., Hamilton, Ontario, 1958; Liverpool, 1964. *Address:* Greysfield, Great Barrow, Chester. *T:* Tarvin 219; Cwmrhaiadr, Machynlleth, Montgomeryshire. *Clubs:* Palatine, University (Liverpool); Hamilton (Ontario).

**NORMAN, Sir Edward (James),** Kt 1958; Chief Inspector of Taxes, 1956-64, retired; *b* Bridport, Dorset, 8 Jan. 1900; *s* of Edward Robert Norman; *m* 1923, Lilian May Sly; three *d. Educ:* Weymouth Grammar Sch. Entered Inland Revenue Department, 1917; Assistant Inspector of Taxes, 1920; Principal Inspector, Somerset House, 1947; Assistant Secretary, Board of Inland Revenue, 1948; Dep. Chief Inspector of Taxes, 1950-55. Member, and later Dep. Chm., Housing Corporation, 1964-69. *Address:* Bourn Cottage, West Humble, Dorking, Surrey.

**NORMAN, Vice-Admiral Sir Geoffrey;** *see* Norman, Vice-Admiral Sir H. G.

**NORMAN, Vice-Admiral (retired) Sir (Horace) Geoffrey,** KCVO 1963; CB 1949; CBE 1943; retired, 1950; *b* 25 May 1896; *m* 1924, Noreen Frances, *o d* of late Brig.-General S. Geoghegan; one *s* one *d. Educ:* Trent Coll.; RN Coll., Keyham. HMS Queen Elizabeth and destroyers, 1914-18; Long Gunnery Course, 1929; passed RN Staff Coll., 1929; Commander, 1932; Captain, 1938; idc 1939; Rear-Admiral, 1947; Chief of Staff to C-in-C, Mediterranean Station, 1948-50; Admiralty, 1950; Vice-Admiral (retired), 1950. *Recreations:* fishing and outdoor sports. *Address:* Chantry Cottage, Wickham, Hants; 17 Queen's Gate Terrace, SW7. *Clubs:* United Service, Flyfishers'.

**NORMAN, Brig. Hugh Ronald,** CBE 1970; DSO 1944; *b* 17 Oct. 1905; *e s* of late R. C. Norman; *m* 1937, Margaret, *d* of late Scott Griffin, Toronto; three *s* one *d. Educ:* Eton; RMC, Sandhurst. Joined Coldstream Guards, 1925; served in China, 1927, Palestine, 1936; Adjutant, 3rd Bn, 1934-37; War of 1939-45, on staff of AA Command, 1939; 128 Inf. Bde, 1940; GHQ Home Forces, 1941; HQ London District, 1942; Comd 2nd Bn Coldstream Guards, Africa, 1943, and Italy, 1944 (wounded); Comd 201 Guards Bde (UK), 1945-46, and Victory Parade Camps; retired (from disability), 1947. Kent County Cadet Comdt, 1948-52; Chairman: Territorial Assoc., 1962-68; South East TA&VR Assoc., 1968-69. Member Kent Agricultural Exec. Cttee, 1952-58 (Vice-Chm., 1957); Chm., Kent Branch Country Landowners Assoc. (CLA), 1958-62, Pres., 1967-. JP 1949; DL 1952; High Sheriff of Kent, 1957. *Recreations:* ski-ing, shooting. *Address:* St Clere, Kemsing, Sevenoaks, Kent. *T:* Sevenoaks 61462. *Clubs:* Guards, White's, Pratt's, MCC.

**NORMAN, Sir Mark (Annesley),** 3rd Bt, *cr* 1915; Managing Director, Britten-Norman Sales Ltd; *b* 8 Feb. 1927; *s* of Sir Nigel Norman, 2nd Bt, CBE, and Patricia Moyra (who *m* 2nd, 1944, Sir Robert Perkins, *qv*), *e d* of late Lieut-Colonel J. H. A. Annesley, CMG, DSO; *S* father, 1943; *m* Joanna Camilla, *d* of Lieut-Colonel I. J. Kilgour, Bampton, Oxon; two *s* one *d. Educ:* Winchester Coll. Late Lieut, Coldstream Guards. Flying Officer, 601 (County of London) Squadron Royal Auxiliary Air Force, 1953-56. *Recreations:* flying, shooting, skiing. *Heir: s* Nigel James Norman, *b* 5 Feb. 1956. *Address:* The Grange, Ramsden, Oxfordshire. *T:* Ramsden 367. *Clubs:* Guards, MCC; St Moritz Tobogganing.

*See also W. R. Norman.*

**NORMAN, Mark Richard,** OBE 1945; Managing Director of Lazard Brothers & Co. Ltd; Chairman, Gallaher Ltd; Director of other public companies; *b* 3 April 1910; *s* of late Ronald C. Norman; *m* 1933, Helen, *d* of late Thomas Pinckney Bryan, Richmond, Virginia; two *s* three *d*. *Educ:* Eton; Magdalen Coll., Oxford. With Gallaher Ltd, 1930-32; Lazard Brothers & Co. Ltd, 1932-39. Served War of 1939-45: Hertfordshire Yeomanry; wounded Greece, 1941; an Asst Military Secretary, War Cabinet Offices, 1942-45 (Lieut-Colonel). Partner Edward de Stein & Co., 1946-60. *Address:* Moor Place, Much Hadham, Herts. *T:* Much Hadham 2504; 26 Roebuck House, Palace Street, SW1. *T:* 01-828 0349. *Club:* Brooks's.

**NORMAN, Sir Robert (Wentworth),** Kt 1970; JP; General Manager, Bank of New South Wales, since 1964; *b* 10 April 1912; *s* of William Henry Norman and Minnie Esther Brown; *m* 1942, Grace Hebden, *d* of Sidney Percy Hebden; one *s* one *d*. *Educ:* Sydney Grammar Sch. Served Army 1940-46: Captain, AIF. Joined Bank of New South Wales, 1928; Manager, Head Office, 1961; Dep. Gen. Manager, 1962. Director: Private Investment Company for Asia (PICA); Partnership Pacific Ltd; Australian Resources Development Bank Ltd; Newaim Pty Ltd; Australian Banks' Export Refinance Corp.; Gove Alumina Ltd. Vice-Pres., Australian-American Assoc.; Mem., Exec. Cttee, Australian-Japan Business Co-operation Cttee; Councillor: Australian Administrative Staff Coll.; Bankers' Inst. of Australasia; Mem., Science and Industry Forum, Australian Acad. of Science; Chm., Science Foundn for Physics within Univ. of Sydney; Member: Council of New Guinea Affairs; Immigration Planning Council; Councillor, Inst. of Public Affairs; Senator and Life Mem., Junior Chamber Internat.; Trustee, Sydney Opera House. FAIM (Vice-Pres.). JP NSW, 1956. *Recreations:* bowls, reading. *Address:* 432 Edgecliff Road, Edgecliff, NSW 2027, Australia. *T:* 32 1900. *Clubs:* Imperial Service, Union, Australian, Tattersalls, Royal Sydney Golf, Australian Jockey (Sydney).

**NORMAN, Willoughby Rollo;** Chairman Boots Pure Drug Co. Ltd, and associated companies since 1961; Deputy Chairman, English China Clays Ltd; *b* 12 Oct. 1909; 2nd *s* of Major Rt Hon. Sir Henry Norman, 1st Bt; *m* 1934, Hon. Barbara Jacqueline Boot, *er d* of 2nd and last Baron Trent, KBE; one *s* two *d*. *Educ:* Eton; Magdalen Coll., Oxford. Served War of 1939-45, Major, Grenadier Guards. Chairman, Eastern Region, National Westminster Bank; Director: Guardian Royal Exchange Assurance; Sheepbridge Engineering Ltd. Under-writing member of Lloyd's. Vice-Chairman Boots Pure Drug Co. Ltd, 1954-61. High Sheriff of Leicestershire, 1960. *Recreations:* hunting, shooting and farming. *Address:* Pickwell Manor, Melton Mowbray, Leics. *T:* Somerby 215; 31 Milner Street, SW3. *T:* 01-589 0467. *Club:* White's.

*See also Sir Mark Norman, Bt.*

**NORMAN-WALKER, Sir Hugh (Selby),** KCMG 1966 (CMG 1964); OBE 1961; Colonial Secretary, Hong Kong, since 1969; *b* 17 Dec. 1916; *s* of late Colonel J. N. Norman-Walker, CIE; *m* 1948, Janet Baldock; no *c*. *Educ:* Sherborne; Corpus Christi Coll., Cambridge. Indian Civil Service, 1938-48; Colonial Administrative Service, 1949; Development Secretary, Nyasaland, 1954; Secretary to the Treasury, Nyasaland, 1960-64, Malawi, 1964-65; HM Commissioner, Bechuanaland, 1965-66; Governor and C-in-C, Seychelles, and Comr, British Indian Ocean Territory, 1967-69. KStJ 1967. *Recreations:* sailing, shooting, bridge. *Address:* Victoria House, Hong Kong; Houndwood, Farley, Wilts. *Clubs:* East India and Sports; Island Sailing (Cowes), etc.

**NORMANBY,** 4th Marquis of, *cr* 1838, **Oswald Constantine John Phipps,** MBE 1943; Baron Mulgrave (Ireland), 1767; Baron Mulgrave (Great Britain), 1794; Earl of Mulgrave and Viscount Normanby, 1812; Hon. Colonel, The Green Howards, Territorials (T&AVR); Lord Lieutenant, North Riding of Yorkshire, since 1965; *b* 29 July 1912; *o s* of Rev. the 3rd Marquess and Gertrude Stansfeld, OBE, DGStJ (*d* 1948), *d* of Johnston J. Foster of Moor Park, Ludlow; *S* father, 1932; *m* 1951, Hon. Grania Maeve Rosaura Guinness, *d* of 1st Baron Moyne; two *s* five *d*. *Educ:* Eton; Christ Church, Oxford. Served War of 1939-45, The Green Howards (wounded, prisoner, repatriated). Parliamentary Private Secretary to Secretary of State for Dominion Affairs, 1944-45, to Lord President of the Council, 1945; a Lord-in-Waiting to the King, 1945. Chairman: King's College Hospital; National Library for the Blind; Council of St John for N Riding Yorkshire. KStJ. Hon. DCL Durham Univ. *Heir: s* Earl of Mulgrave, *qv*. *Address:* Mulgrave Castle, Whitby; Argyll House, 211 King's Road, SW3. *T:* 01-352 5154. *Club:* Yorkshire (York).

**NORMAND, Sir Charles William Blyth,** Kt 1945; CIE 1938; MA, DSc; *b* 10 Sept. 1889; *m* 1920, Alison MacLennan (*d* 1953); one *s* (and one *s* decd). *Educ:* Royal High School and University, Edinburgh. Research Scholar at Edinburgh, 1911-13; Imperial Meteorologist, Simla, India, 1913-15 and 1919-27; joined IARO and served in Mesopotamia, 1916-19; Director-General of Observatories in India, 1927-44; on special duty with Govt of India, 1944-45; Symons Gold Medal, Royal Met. Soc., 1944; President, Royal Met. Society, 1951-53; Member, Met. Research Cttee, Air Ministry, 1945-58, Chairman, 1955-58; Secretary International Ozone Commn, 1948-59. *Publications:* articles, mainly on meteorological subjects, in scientific journals. *Address:* 56 Holywell Street, Oxford. *T:* 42922.

**NORMANTON,** 6th Earl of, *cr* 1806; **Shaun James Christian Welbore Ellis Agar;** Baron Somerton, 1795; Viscount Somerton, 1800; Baron Somerton (UK), 1873; Royal Horse Guards, 1965; Blues and Royals, 1969; *b* 21 Aug. 1945; *er s* of 5th Earl of Normanton; *S* father, 1967; *m* 1970, Victoria Susan, *o d* of J. H. C. Beard, Guernsey. *Educ:* Eton. *Recreations:* shooting, power boat racing. *Heir: brother,* Hon. Mark Sydney Andrew Agar, *b* 2 Sept. 1948. *Address:* Somerley, Ringwood, Hants. *T:* Ringwood 3253. *Clubs:* Cavalry, Turf.

**NORMANTON, Tom,** TD; MP (C) Cheadle since 1970; Joint Managing Director of a group of companies; *b* 12 March 1917; *m* 1942, Annabel Bettine (*née* Yates); two *s* one *d*. *Educ:* Manchester Grammar Sch.; Manchester Univ. (BA(Com)). Joined family group of textile cos, 1938. Served War of 1939-45: Army (TA Officer) Europe and N Africa; GS appts, GHQ BEF, HQ First and Eighth Armies; HQ 21 Army Gp (wounded, Calais, 1940; despatches, 1944); demob., rank Major, 1946. Chm., Rochdale YC, 1948; Mem. Rochdale CB Council, 1950-53; contested (C) Rochdale, 1959 and 1964. Manager, Lancashire Fusiliers Compassionate Fund, 1964; Trustee, Cotton Industry War Memorial Fund, 1965; apptd Employer panel, Nat. Bd for Prices and Incomes, 1966; Mem. Council, CBI, 1964; Mem. Exec., UK Automation Council, 1966; Vice-Chm. Manchester Br. of Inst. of Dirs,

1969; Pres., British Textile Employers Assoc., 1970. *Recreations:* sailing, walking, gardening. *Address:* Greenhithe, Weston Road, Wilmslow, Cheshire. *T:* Wilmslow 24930. *Club:* St James's (Manchester).

**NORREYS, Lord; Henry Mark Willoughby Bertie;** *b* 6 June 1958; *s* and *heir* of Earl of Lindsey (14th) and Abingdon (9th), *qv*.

**NORRIE,** family name of **Baron Norrie.**

**NORRIE,** 1st Baron, *cr* 1957, of Wellington, New Zealand, and of Upton, Glos; **Lt-Gen. (Charles) Willoughby (Moke) Norrie,** GCMG 1952 (KCMG 1944); GCVO 1954; CB 1942; DSO 1919; MC 1915; Chancellor, Order of St Michael and St George, 1960-68; Governor General and Commander-in-Chief of New Zealand, 1952-57; *b* 26 Sept. 1893; *s* of late Major G. E. M. Norrie; *m* 1st, 1921, Jocelyn Helen (*d* 1938), *d* of late R. H. Gosling; one *s* one *d*; 2nd, 1938, Patricia Merryweather (DStJ), *d* of late Emerson Bainbridge, MP; one *s* two *d*. *Educ:* Eton; Sandhurst. Joined 11th Hussars, 1913; Captain, 1918; Major, 1924; Lt-Col, 1931; Col, 1935; served European War, 1914-19, Staff Captain 73rd Inf. Brigade, GSO3 XVIII Army Corps, Bde Major 90th Inf. Bde, Bde Major 2nd Tank Bde, GSO2 Tank Corps HQ (wounded four times, despatches twice, MC and bar, DSO); psc; Bde Major, 1st Cavalry Bde, Aldershot, 1926-30; commanded 10th Royal Hussars, 1931-35; Comdr 1st Cavalry Bde, 1936-38; Comdr 1st Armoured Bde, 1938-40; Inspector RAC, 1940; GOC 1st Armoured Div., 1940-41; GOC 30 Corps (Middle East), 1941-42; Comdr RAC, 1943; Colonel, 10th Royal Hussars (PWO), 1945-49; Governor of the State of South Australia, 1944-52. Hon. Colonel, 10th Inf. Bn (The Adelaide Rifles), 1949-57. FRSA 1948. Member: National Hunt Cttee, 1935-68; Jockey Club, 1969. Pres., Combined Cavalry Old Comrades, 1959-68. Prior of the Venerable Order of St John in New Zealand, 1952-57. KStJ. *Heir: s* Hon. George Willoughby Moke Norrie, Major, 11th Hussars (Prince Albert's Own) [*b* 27 April 1936; *m* 1964, Celia Marguerite, *d* of John Mann, Brimpton House, Reading, Berks; two *d*. *Educ:* Eton; Royal Military Academy, Sandhurst]. *Address:* The Ham, Wantage, Berkshire. *T:* Wantage 2110. *Club:* Cavalry.

**NORRINGTON, Sir Arthur (Lionel Pugh),** Kt 1968; MA; JP; President of Trinity College, Oxford, 1954-Aug. 1970; Vice-Chancellor, Oxford University, 1960-62; Warden of Winchester College, since 1970; *b* 27 Oct. 1899; *o s* of late Arthur James Norrington; *m* 1st, 1928, Edith Joyce (*d* 1964), *d* of William Moberly Carver; two *s* two *d*; 2nd, 1969, Mrs Ruth Margaret Waterlow, *widow* of Rupert Waterlow, and *y d* of Edmund Cude. *Educ:* Winchester; Trinity Coll., Oxford (Scholar). Served in RFA, 1918. Joined Oxford University Press, 1923. Secretary to Delegates of Oxford University Press, 1948-54. JP City of Oxford. Hon. Fellow, St Cross and Wolfson Colleges. Officier de la Légion d'Honneur, 1962. *Publication:* (with H. F. Lowry and F. L. Mulhauser), The Poems of A. H. Clough, 1951. *Recreations:* music, gardening. *Address:* Grenville Manor, Haddenham, Bucks. *Club:* United University.

**NORRIS, Alan Hedley;** Chairman, North Eastern Electricity Board, since 1969 (Deputy Chairman, 1968-69); *b* 15 July 1913; *s* of Hedley Faithfull Norris, Solicitor; *m* 1941, Rachel Mary Earle; one *s* two *d*. *Educ:* Bradfield; Clare Coll., Cambridge. Served with RAF, 1940-45. HM Inspector of Factories, 1937-46; Min. of Power: Asst Principal, 1946-48; Principal, 1948-52; Asst Secretary, 1952-65; Under Secretary, 1965-68. *Recreation:* fishing. *Address:* Southwood, Riding Mill, Northumberland. *T:* Riding Mill 466. *Clubs:* Flyfishers', RAF Reserves.

**NORRIS, Sir Alfred (Henry),** KBE 1961; *b* 27 April 1894; *s* of late Alfred James Norris, Hornchurch, Essex, and Charlotte Norris; *m* 1925, Betty K. R. Davidson (decd); *m* 1936, Winifred Gladys, *d* of late Archibald Henry Butler; three *s*. *Educ:* Cranbrook Sch., Kent. Served War of 1914-18, King's Own Royal (Lancaster) Regt. Retired Company Director and Chartered Accountant; formerly of Brazil. *Recreations:* social work, gardening. *Address:* Rua Dr Antonio Martins 20, Estoril, Portugal. *Clubs:* Canning (London); Royal British (Lisbon).

**NORRIS, Vice-Adm. Sir Charles (Fred Wivell),** KBE 1956; CB 1952; DSO 1944; *b* 16 Dec. 1900; *m* 1924, Violet Cremer; one *s*. *Educ:* RNC Osborne and Dartmouth. Comdr, 1934; RN Staff Course, 1935; commanded HMS Aberdeen, 1936-39; Captain, 1941; commanded HMS Bellona, 1943-45; commanded HMS Dryad (Navigation and Direction School), 1945-46; Imperial Defence Coll., 1947; Captain of the Fleet, Home Fleet, 1948-50; Rear-Admiral, 1950; Director of Naval Training, and Deputy Chief of Naval Personnel, 1950-52; Vice-Admiral, 1953; Flag Officer (Flotilla), Mediterranean, 1953-54. Commander-in-Chief, East Indies Station, 1954-56, retired, 1956. Director of the British Productivity Council, 1957-65. *Address:* Clouds, 56 Shepherd's Way, Liphook, Hants. *T:* Liphook 2456. *Club:* United Service.

**NORRIS, Air Marshal Sir Christopher Neil F.;** *see* Foxley-Norris.

**NORRIS, Sir Eric (George),** KCMG 1969 (CMG 1963); British High Commissioner in Kenya, since 1968; *b* 14 March 1918; *s* of late H. F. Norris, Bengeo, Hertford; *m* 1941, Pamela Crane; three *d*. *Educ:* Hertford Grammar Sch.; St Catharine's Coll., Cambridge. Served Royal Corps of Signals, 1940-46 (Major). Entered Dominions Office, 1946. Served in British Embassy, Dublin, 1948-50; UK High Commission in Pakistan, 1952-55; UK High Commission in Delhi, 1956-57; Dep. High Commissioner for the UK, Bombay, 1957-60; IDC 1961; British Dep. High Comr, Calcutta, 1962-65; Commonwealth Office, 1966-68. *Address:* PO Box 30465, Nairobi, Kenya. *Clubs:* East India and Sports; Nairobi, Muthaiga.

**NORRIS, Maj.-Gen. Sir (Frank) Kingsley,** KBE 1957 (CBE 1943); CB 1953; DSO; ED; MD; QHP; Hon. Consultant Pædiatrician, Alfred Hospital, Melbourne, since 1948; *b* 25 June 1893; *s* of Dr W. Perrin Norris; *m* 1920, Dorothy Leonard Stevenson; two *d*. *Educ:* Melbourne Church of England Grammar Sch.; Trinity Coll., Melbourne Univ. Served Australian Imperial Forces, ME, 1914-16; CO 1 CCS, AIF, 1939; ADMS 7 Australian Div. AIF, 1940-43; DDMS 1 Australian Corps AIF, 1943; Service in Middle East, Libya, 1940; Palestine 1941; Syria, 1941; Java, 1942; New Guinea, 1942-44; Korea, 1951-53. DGMS Commonwealth Military Forces, 1948-55; President: Royal Empire Soc., Vic. Br., 1948-54; BMA, Vic. Br., 1947; Good Neighbour Council, Vic., 1958-63; Alcoholic Foundn of Vic., 1961-68. Comr St John's Ambulance Bde, 1956; Chief Comr, Priory of St John Ambulance in Australia. Medical Adviser, Civil Defence, Australia, 1956-61. KStJ 1961 (CStJ 1959). KHP 1948; QPH 1953-55. *Publications:* The Syrian Campaign, 1944; The New Guinea Campaign, 1946; Major-General

Sir Neville Howse, VC, 1965; No Memory for Pain (autobiography), 1970; various papers to medical journals. *Recreations:* bridge, chess, golf, model-ship building, cooking. *Address:* 19 Currajong Avenue, Camberwell, Victoria 3124, Australia. *Clubs:* MCC; Beefsteak, Melbourne, Naval and Military (Melbourne).

**NORRIS, Herbert Walter;** Regional Director, South East Region, National Westminster Bank Ltd; Director, the Diners Club Ltd; Deputy Chief General Manager, Westminster Bank Ltd, 1962-65; *b* 9 Dec. 1904; *s* of Walter Norris, Farnworth, Widnes, Lancs; *m* 1935, Laura Phyllis Tardif, *d* of A. Tardif, St Martin's, Guernsey; no *c*. *Educ:* Liverpool Collegiate School. Joined Westminster Bank, Liverpool Office, 1921; Joint General Manager, Westminster Bank Ltd, 1949. Member Council, Institute of Bankers, 1952-65; (Dep. Chairman, 1959-61); Member of Coopers' Company. *Recreations:* gardening, fishing, music. *Address:* 5 Shepherds Walk, Pembury Road, Tunbridge Wells, Kent. *T:* Tunbridge Wells 31601. *Clubs:* City Livery, Royal Automobile.

**NORRIS, Maj.-General Sir Kingsley;** *see* Norris, Maj.-General Sir F. K.

**NORRIS, Oswald Thomas,** CBE 1957; *b* 1 July 1883; *s* of Arthur James and Dora Norris; *m* 1911, Evelyn Mary Seth-Smith (*d* 1969); two *d*. *Educ:* Charterhouse. Ex-Chairman of Council, National Federation of Young Farmers' Clubs. A Governor of Charterhouse, London, 1951, and member of the Governing Body of Charterhouse School, 1957. *Address:* Tilgate Forest Lodge, Crawley, Sussex. *T:* Handcross 391. *Club:* Bath.

**NORRIS, Rev. Canon Walter Edward,** Chaplain to the Queen since 1962; Vicar and Rural Dean of Romsey, 1952-April 1971; Chairman, Diocesan Advisory Committee for the Care of Churches, since 1968; *b* 8 Dec. 1905; 3rd *s* of late Hugh Littleton Norris and Mabel Grace Norris. *Educ:* Durnford Sch., Langton Matravers; Winchester Coll.; Trinity Coll., Oxford; Cuddesdon Theological Coll. Assistant Curate: Hemsworth, 1930-34; Dewsbury, 1934-36; Vicar: St John's, Huddersfield, 1936-44; St Luke's, Bournemouth, 1944-52; Hon. Canon of Winchester Cathedral, 1955; Proctor in Convocation, 1957; Sub Chaplain, Order of St John of Jerusalem, 1957. Secretary 1946-62, Vice-Chm. 1962-68, Diocesan Adv. Cttee for the Care of Churches. *Recreations:* travel, archæology. *Address:* 32 Cheriton Road, Winchester, Hampshire.

**NORRISH, Ronald George Wreyford,** FRS 1936; ScD, PhD (Cantab); FRIC; Professor Emeritus of Physical Chemistry; Director of Department of Physical Chemistry, Cambridge University, 1937-65; Fellow of Emmanuel College, Cambridge; *b* 9 Nov. 1897; *e s* of Herbert Norrish; *m* 1926, Annie, *e d* of Albert E. Smith, Heaton Mersey, near Manchester; two *d*. *Educ:* Perse Sch.; Emmanuel Coll., Cambridge (Foundation Scholar, 1915); 1st Class Hons Natural Sciences Tripos, I and II, 1920, 1921. Served European War, 1916-19 (POW 1918). Research Fellow of Emmanuel Coll., 1925-31; Humphrey Owen Jones Lecturer in Physical Chemistry, Cambridge Univ.; Meldola Medal of Institute of Chemistry, 1926; Leverhulme Research Fellow, 1935; Council of Chem. Soc. and of Faraday Soc., 1933-36; Council of Senate, Univ. of Cambridge, 1938-41; Scientific Adv. Council of the Min. of Supply, 1942-45; Pres., Faraday Soc., 1953-55; Vice-Pres., Royal Inst. of Chemistry, 1957-59; Liversidge Lecture and Medal, Chem. Soc., 1958; Davy Medal, Royal Soc., 1958; Lewis Medal of Combustion Inst., 1964; Faraday Memorial Lecture and Medal, Chem. Soc., 1965, Longstaff Medal, 1969; Bakerian Lecture, Royal Soc., 1966. Nobel Laureate (Jt) for Chemistry, 1967. Pres. British Assoc., Section B (Chemistry), 1960-61. Liveryman, Worshipful Company of Gunmakers, 1961. Hon. Ddel'U Sorbonne (Paris), 1958; Hon. Member Polish Chemical Soc., 1959; Corr. Mem. Acad. of Sciences, Göttingen, 1960; Corr. Mem., Royal Soc. of Sciences, Liège, 1960; Foreign Mem. Polish Acad., of Sciences, 1962; Hon. Mem. Royal Soc. of Sciences, Uppsala, Sweden, 1964; Hon. Member: Faraday Soc., 1966; NY Acad. of Sciences, 1968; Bulgarian Acad. of Sciences, 1970. Hon. DSc: Leeds Univ., Sheffield Univ., 1965; Liverpool Univ., Lancaster Univ., 1968, Univ. of British Columbia, 1969. *Publications:* Scientific papers in Proceedings of Royal Society, Journal of Chemical Soc., Transactions of Faraday Soc., etc. *Recreations:* recollections of tennis and golf. *Address:* Emmanuel College, Cambridge. *T:* Cambridge 58356; Department of Physical Chemistry, Lensfield Road, Cambridge. *T:* Cambridge 56491; 7 Park Terrace, Cambridge. *T:* 55147. *Club:* Savage.

**NORSTAD, Gen. Lauris,** DSM (US) with Oak Leaf Cluster and Silver Star; Legion of Merit (US) with Cluster; Air Medal; United States Air Forces, retired; Chairman and Chief Executive Officer, Owens-Corning Fibreglass Corporation (President, Owens-Corning Fiberglas International, January-December 1963); Director: United Air Lines; English-Speaking Union; Trustee Rand Corporation; Continental Oil Co.; Abitibi Paper Co.; *b* Minneapolis, USA, 24 March 1907; *s* of Martin Norstad; *m* 1935, Isabelle Helen Jenkins; one *d*. *Educ:* US Military Academy (BS). 2nd Lieut, Cavalry, 1930; graduated, Air Corps Sch., 1931. Served in various branches of Air Force; duty at GHQ Air Force, Langley Field, Va., 1940; Assistant Chief of Staff for Operations, 12th Air Force, 1942, served with 12th Air Force, England and Algiers; Director of Operations, Allied Air Forces, Mediterranean, Dec. 1943; Chief of Staff, 20th Air Force, Washington, 1944; Asst Chief of Staff for Plans, Army Air Force HQ, 1945; Director of Plans and Operations Div., War Dept, Washington, 1946; Dep. Chief of Staff for Operations, USAF, 1947; Acting Vice Chief of Staff, Air Force, May 1950; C-in-C US Air Forces in Europe and C-in-C Allied Air Forces Central Europe, 1951; Deputy (Air) to Supreme Allied Commander, Europe, 1953; C-in-C, US European Comd, 1956-62, and Supreme Allied Commander, Europe, 1956-62; retired, 1963. Has several hon. degrees. Hon. CBE (GB). Holds other foreign orders. *Address:* (business) Fiberglas Tower, Toledo, Ohio 43601, USA.

**NORTH,** family name of **Earl of Guilford.**

**NORTH, Rt. Hon. Sir Alfred Kingsley,** PC 1966; KBE 1964; Kt 1959; **Rt. Hon. Mr Justice North;** Judge of the Court of Appeal, New Zealand, since 1957 (President of the Court, since 1963); *b* 17 Dec. 1900; *s* of late Rev. J. J. North, DD; *m* 1924, Thelma Grace Dawson; two *s* one *d*. *Educ:* Canterbury Coll., Christchurch, New Zealand (LLM). Was, for many years, in the legal firm of Earl Kent and Co., Auckland, New Zealand. One of HM Counsel (KC 1947); Judge of the Supreme Court of New Zealand, 1951-57. Past President Auckland Rotary Club; Past Chairman Auckland Branch of Crippled Children's Society, etc. *Recreation:* trout-fishing. *Address:* 19 Lower Watt Street,

Wadeston, Wellington, New Zealand. *Clubs:* Wellington (Wellington, NZ); Northern (Auckland, NZ).

**NORTH, Rev. Christopher Richard,** DLit (London), Hon. DD (Aberdeen); Methodist Minister; Emeritus Professor of Hebrew at University College of North Wales, Bangor; *b* 1888; *e s* of Richard and Gertrude North; *m* 1st, Dorothy May Atkinson (*d* 1931); one *s* three *d*; 2nd, Helen Ramsay Winter; one *s*. *Educ:* Reed's Sch.; Didsbury Coll.; School of Oriental Studies. Minister in Bangor, Burnley, Worthing, Egham, Leeds, Malvern; short term as missionary in North India; Victoria Chair of Old Testament Languages and Literature, Handsworth Coll., Birmingham, 1925-40; Visiting Professor at Drew Univ., Madison, NJ, 1931; Joint Hon. Secretary Society for Old Testament Study, 1928-48; President, 1949; Treasurer, 1952-57; Examiner to Universities of London, Birmingham, Bristol, Wales; Fernley-Hartley Lecturer, 1946. Dean of Faculty of Theology, University College of North Wales, Bangor, 1948-53; Select Preacher, Cambridge Univ., 1952-53; Acting Head of Dept of OT Literature and Theology, New Coll., Edinburgh, 1962. Member, OT Panel for New English Bible, 1948-62. *Publications:* The Old Testament Interpretation of History, 1946; The Suffering Servant in Deutero-Isaiah, 1948; Isaiah 40-55: Introduction and Commentary, 1952; The Second Isaiah, 1964; articles on Old Testament Subjects in British and foreign journals. *Recreations:* philately, travel. *Address:* Ger Mõn, Bangor, Caernarvonshire. *T:* Bangor 3668.

**NORTH, Brig. Francis Roger,** CB 1942; MC and Bar, 1918; ED 1937; Solicitor, Member of firm of Roberts Leu & North, Solicitors, Townsville, N Queensland; *b* 13 April 1894; *s* of Robert Dundas North, Brisbane; *m* 1929, Margaret May, *d* of Robert Lawrence Craddock; two *d*. *Educ:* The Southport School. Served War of 1914-18 (wounded twice, despatches twice); commissioned 1914, served 9th, 15th and 47th Inf., AIF, Egypt, Gallipoli, France and Flanders; Captain, 1916, Major, 1927, 31st Bn, Lt-Col, 1927; comd 31st Bn, 1924-29 and 1933-40. War of 1939-45; comd 11th Inf. Bde, 1940-42 (temp. Brig.); comd 1st Australian L of C Sub Area, 1942-45; Col R of O 1945; Brig., retired. Chancellor to Bishop of North Queensland, 1928-70; Chancellor to Bishop of Carpentaria, 1930-70; Pres., N Qld br., RSSAILA, 1932-39; Alderman of Townsville City Council, 1936-39. Pres., N Qld Golf Assoc., 1928-38; Trustee Scartwater Trust; Vice-Consul for Sweden. Knight of the Royal Order of Vasa (Sweden), 1953. *Address:* Cleveland Terrace, Melton Hill, Townsville, North Queensland 4810, Australia. *Clubs:* North Queensland, RSSAILA (Townsville); United Services (Brisbane).

**NORTH, Sir George (Cecil),** Kt 1956; CB 1949; MC 1917; Hon. LLD (Dublin) 1945; *b* 23 March 1895; *e s* of Matthew North and Harriet Evelyn Mitchell, Blackrock, Co. Dublin; *m* 1928, Winifred Margaret (*née* McKillop), *widow* of Captain Paget l'Estrange Clayton; one *s* one *d* and one step *d*. *Educ:* St Andrews Coll. and Trinity Coll., Dublin (First Scholar, Senior Moderator and Gold Medallist, LLD). Called to Bar (Lincoln's Inn). Home Civil Service, 1921; Private Secretary to Sir Edward Forber and to Susan Lawrence, MP; Sec. or Mem. of various Commns, Cttees, etc., including National Radium Trust and first Governing Body of British Postgrad. Medical Sch.; Chairman, Central Dental War Cttee, 1939-40; Asst Secretary, Ministry of Health, 1937; Director of Public Relations, 1938-40; Head of Water, etc., Division, 1940-45. Registrar General, 1945-58. A Parliamentary Boundary Commissioner for England and for Wales, 1947-57. Member Court of Governors London School of Economics and Political Science, 1947-64. Chairman, standing Interdepartmental Cttee on Social and Economic Research, 1947-62; a Governor, Nat. Inst. for Economic and Social Research; Alternate or Adviser, Sessions Economic and Social Council of UN, 1946-48; Deleg. to First World Health Assembly, 1948. Donnellan Lectr, Univ. of Dublin, 1951. Hon. MInstWE; Hon. Fellow Soc. Med. Officers of Health. Served RA France, Belgium, Germany, 1916-19 (MC, Major). *Recreations:* travel, languages, Commonwealth relations. *Address:* 2 Corner Green, Ringmer, Lewes, Sussex. *Clubs:* Athenæum; University (Dublin).

**NORTH, Major John,** BA, LLB; Author and Barrister-at-Law; *b* 30 Sept. 1894; *s* of late C. A. North, Leeds; *m* 1923, Freda, *d* of late Ernest H. Lawrence, Librarian of Hertford; one *d*. *Educ:* early youth devoted to musical training; Downing Coll., Cambridge (Historical Scholar, Honours in History and Law), 1913. Lieut, 4th Batt., Northampton Regt; served in France and Belgium with the Northamptonshire and Suffolk Regiments; returned to Cambridge from the Army of Occupation in Germany, 1919; founded and edited a University weekly, The Old Cambridge, 1920; called to Bar, Gray's inn, 1921; joined London Press Exchange, 1922; Director, 1937; General Staff, War Office, 1939; Allied Force HQ, North Africa, 1943; War Office, 1944; missions to Belgium, Holland, Germany, Greece, and Italy, 1944-45; appointed by War Office to write NW Europe volume in HMSO series of short military histories of Second World War. *Publications:* Girl or Boy: A Satire and a Diversion, 1925; A Comedy of Women, 1926; A Daughter of Twenty, 1926; Patricia Lacked a Lover, 1927; Unmarried Life, 1928; St Peter and the Profile, 1930; A Shade Byronic, 1933; Gallipoli: The Fading Vision, 1936 (repr. 1967); North-West Europe, 1944-45; The Achievement of 21st Army Group, 1953; (ed) Men Fighting: Battle Stories, 1958; (ed) The Alexander Memoirs, 1940-45, 1962. *Recreations:* cricket, lubricating the car, visiting the Gallipoli Peninsula. *Address:* Four Winds, Beaconsfield, Bucks. *T:* Beaconsfield 3276; 01-836 2424. *Clubs:* Army and Navy, United and Cecil, Arts Theatre.

**NORTH, Sir Jonathan;** *see* North, Sir W. J. F.

**NORTH, Roger,** JP; Deputy Chairman, Norfolk Quarter Sessions (Chairman QS, King's Lynn, 1942; appointed Deputy Chairman QS, Norfolk, by Royal Warrant, 1962); Chairman West Norfolk Valuation Panel, since 1949; *b* 10 Dec. 1901; *s* of F. K. North, Rougham Hall, King's Lynn, and Grace, *d* of Gen. Sir Percy Feilding; *m* 1934, Pamela Susan, *d* of Rev. H. W. L. O'Rorke, North Litchfield, Hants; one *s* three *d*. *Educ:* Eton; Trinity Coll., Cambridge. Called to the Bar, 1925. Began farming at Rougham, Norfolk, 1932. Late Chairman Tractor Users' Assoc. and Oxford Farming Conference Cttee; Council Member, Instn of Agricultural Engineers, 1954-58. JP Norfolk, 1941. *Publication:* The Art of Algebra, 1965. *Recreations:* veteran motor cars and mathematics. *Address:* Rougham Hall, Rougham, King's Lynn, Norfolk. *T:* Weasenham St Peter 230. *Clubs:* Royal Institution; Norfolk.

**NORTH, Sir (William) Jonathan (Frederick),** 2nd Bt, *cr* 1920; *b* 6 Feb. 1931; *s* of Muriel Norton (2nd *d* of 1st Bt) and Hon. John Montagu

William North (*heir-pres.* to 9th Earl of Guilford, *qv*; he *m* 2nd, 1939, Marion Dyer Chase, Boston, Mass); *g s* of Sir William Hicking, 1st Bt; *S* grandfather, 1947 (under special remainder); *m* 1956, Sara Virginia, *d* of Air Chief Marshal Sir Donald Hardman, *qv*; one *s* two *d*. *Educ:* Marlborough Coll. *Heir: s* Jeremy William Francis North, *b* 5 May 1960. *Address:* Frogmore, Weston-under-Penyard, Herefordshire.

**NORTHAMPTON,** 6th Marquess of, *cr* 1812; **William Bingham Compton;** DSO 1919; Earl of Northampton, 1618; Earl Compton, Baron Wilmington, 1812; *e surv. s* of 5th Marquess and Hon. Mary Florence Baring (*d* 1902), *o d* of 2nd Lord Ashburton; *b* 6 Aug. 1885; *S* father, 1913; *m* 1st, 1921, Lady Emma Thynne, OBE 1943 (marr. diss., 1942), 2nd *d* of 5th Marquess of Bath, KG, PC, CB; 2nd, 1942, Virginia (marr. diss., 1958), *d* of Lt-Col David Heaton, DSO, two *s* two *d*; 3rd, 1958, Elspeth, Lady Teynham. *Educ:* Eton; Balliol Coll., Oxford. Northamptonshire Yeomanry, 1903-06; 2nd Lieut, Royal Horse Guards, 1907; Captain and Adjutant, 1913; served European War, 1914-19 (DSO, wounded, despatches twice); commanded Warwickshire Yeomanry, 1933. JP Northants; DL Northants and Ross-shire; late Chairman Northants CC; resigned, 1955. Owns about 10,000 acres. *Heir: s* Earl Compton, *qv*. *Address:* Compton Wynyates, Tysoe, Warwick; Castle Ashby, Northampton; 5 Pelham Place, SW7. *Clubs:* Turf; Royal Yacht Squadron (Cowes).
*See also Baron Loch.*

**NORTHAMPTON, Bishop of, (RC),** since 1967; **Rt. Rev. Charles Alexander Grant,** MA; LCL; *b* 25 Oct. 1906; *s* of Frank and Sibylla Christina Grant. *Educ:* Perse Sch., Cambridge; St Edmund's, Ware; Christ's Coll., Cambridge; Oscott Coll., Birmingham; Gregorian Univ., Rome. Curate, Cambridge, 1938; Parish Priest: Ely, 1943; Kettering, 1945. Bishop-Auxiliary of Northampton, 1961-67. *Address:* Bishop's House, Northampton. *T:* Northampton 39348.

**NORTHAMPTON, Auxiliary Bishop of, (RC);** *see* Clark, Rt Rev. A. C.

**NORTHAMPTON, Archdeacon of;** *see* Marsh, Ven. Bazil Roland.

**NORTHBOURNE,** 4th Baron, *cr* 1884; **Walter Ernest Christopher James,** Bt, 1791; *b* 1896; *o surv s* of 3rd Baron and Laura Gwenllian (who *m* 2nd, 1935, William Curtis Green, RA; he *d* 1960), *d* of late Admiral Sir Ernest Rice, KCB; *S* father, 1932; *m* 1925, Katherine Nickerson, *d* of Hon. Lady Hood, and late George A. Nickerson, Boston, Mass; one *s* four *d*. *Educ:* Eton; Magdalen Coll., Oxford. Chairman, Kent Agricultural Executive Cttee, 1946-57. Fellow, Wye Coll., 1967. *Publications:* Look to the Land, 1940; Religion in The Modern World, 1963. *Heir: s* Hon. Christopher George Walter James [*b* 18 Feb. 1926; *m* 1959, Marie Sygne, *e d* of M and Mme Henri Claudel; three *s*]. *Address:* Northbourne Court, Deal, Kent. *T:* Deal 4617. *Clubs:* Leander, Farmers'.
*See also T. J. Hemsley.*

**NORTHBROOK,** 5th Baron, *cr* 1866; **Francis John Baring,** Bt 1793; *b* 31 May 1915; *s* of 4th Baron Northbrook and Evelyn Gladys Isabel (*d* 1919), *d* of J. G. Charles; *S* father 1947; *m* 1951, Rowena Margaret, 2nd *d* of late Brig-General Sir William Manning, and of Lady Manning, Hampton Court Palace; one *s* three *d*. *Educ:* Winchester; Trinity Coll., Oxford. JP 1955. *Heir: s* Hon. Francis Thomas Baring, *b* 21 Feb. 1954. *Address:* Shawlands Farm, Hursley, Hants.

**NORTHCHURCH, Baroness (Life Peeress);** *see under* Davidson, Viscountess.

**NORTHCOTE,** family name of **Earl of Iddesleigh.**

**NORTHCOTE, Dr Donald Henry,** FRS 1968; Reader in Plant Biochemistry, University of Cambridge, since 1965; Fellow, St John's College, Cambridge, since 1960; *b* 27 Dec. 1921; *m* Eva Marjorie Mayo; two *d*. *Educ:* Sir George Monoux Grammar Sch., London; London Univ.; Cambridge Univ. *Recreations:* sitting and chatting; strolling about. *Address:* 29 High Street, Chesterton, Cambridge. *T:* Cambridge 54667.

**NORTHCOTE-GREEN, Roger James,** MC 1944; TD 1950; JP; Headmaster, Worksop College, Notts, 1952-70; *b* 25 July 1912; *s* of Rev. Edward Joseph Northcote-Green and Mary Louisa Catt; *m* 1947, Joan, *d* of Ernest Greswell and Grace Lillian (*née* Egerton); three *s* one *d*. *Educ:* St Edward's Sch. and The Queen's Coll., Oxford (MA). Assistant Master, Orwell Park Sch., Ipswich, 1935-36; St Edward's Sch., 1936-39. Served with Oxford and Bucks Light Infantry, 1939-44, in India and Burma; Staff Coll., Quetta, 1944-45; Bde Major, 53rd Ind. Inf. Bde, Malaya, 1945. Assistant Master, St Edward's Sch., 1946-52; Housemaster, 1947. Representative OURFC on RU Cttee, 1946-52. JP Nottinghamshire, 1964. *Recreations:* shooting, fishing. *Address:* Manor Cottage, Woolston, Williton, Som. *T:* Williton 445. *Clubs:* Public Schools, MCC; Vincent's (Oxford).

**NORTHCOTT, Rev. Cecil;** *see* Northcott, Rev. (William) C.

**NORTHCOTT, Prof. Douglas Geoffrey,** FRS 1961; MA, PhD, Cambridge; Town Trust Professor of Mathematics, University of Sheffield, since 1952; *b* London, 1916; *m* 1949, Rose Hilda Austin, Twickenham, Middlesex; two *d*. *Educ:* St John's Coll., Cambridge. *Address:* Department of Pure Mathematics, The University, Sheffield; 25 Parkhead Road, Ecclesall, Sheffield 11.

**NORTHCOTT, Captain Ralph William Frank,** CBE 1960; DSO 1942; RN, retired; *b* 1 July 1907; *s* of late Major F. L. Northcott, Royal Norfolk Regt and of late E. E. Northcott (*née* Badnall); *m* 1934, Molly, *d* of Brig.-General C. H. P. Carter, CB, CMG, CBE; one *s*. *Educ:* Osborne; Dartmouth. Joined Navy, 1821; served mainly in small ships; War of 1939-45, commanded HMS Acheron, Lance and Bicester; served with Army in Tunisian campaign, Sicily, Salerno and Normandy landings. Joint Services Staff Coll. and NATO Defence Coll.; Chief of Staff, Amphibious Warfare, 1955-58; Commodore, Naval Drafting, 1958-60; ADC to the Queen, 1960-61; Asst Gen. Manager (Staff) Rediffusion Television, 1961-69. *Address:* Border Cottage, Rowledge, Farnham, Surrey. *T:* Frensham 2946.

**NORTHCOTT, Rev. (William) Cecil,** MA; PhD; Editorial Secretary United Society for Christian Literature and Editor, Lutterworth Press, since 1952; Editor-at-large, Christian Century of USA, 1945-70; Churches Correspondent of The Daily Telegraph, since 1967; *b* Buckfast, Devon, 5 April 1902; *s* of William Ashplant Northcott and Mary Nance; *m* 1930, Jessie Morton, MA, 2nd *d* of J. L. Morton, MD, Hampstead and Colyford, Devon; one *s* one *d*. *Educ:* Hele's Sch., Exeter; Fitzwilliam Coll., and Cheshunt Coll., Cambridge. 2nd Class Hons Historical and Theological Triposes; BA 1927; MA 1930; PhD

London Univ. (School of Oriental and African Studies), 1961. Three years social work East End of London; Member Cambridge delegation to League of Nations, Geneva, 1926; Joint Proprietor and Editor The Granta, 1927-28; Asst Minister Ormskirk Street Congregational Church, St Helens, 1929-32; Minister Duckworth Street Congregational Church, Darwen, Lancs, 1932-35; Home Secretary and Literary Superintendent London Missionary Society, 1935-50; General Secretary and Editor United Council for Missionary Education (Edinburgh House Press), 1950-52; Chairman London Missionary Society, 1954-55; Delegate World Conferences, Amsterdam, 1948, Willingen, 1952, Evanston, 1954, New Delhi, 1961, Uppsala, 1968. Member, World Council of Churches Information Cttee, 1954-61; Member, British Council of Churches Christian Aid Cttee, 1946-64. Select Preacher, Cambridge, 1958; Danforth Foundation Lecturer, USA, 1961; Visiting Lecturer, Garrett Theological Seminary, USA, 1965, 1967, 1969. British Information Services, USA, 1944; editor, Congregational Monthly, 1953-58. Leverhulme Research Award, 1958. *Publications:* Time to Spare (Collab. BBC Talks); Southward Ho!; Guinea Gold; Who Claims the World?; John Williams Sails On; Change Here for Britain; Glorious Company; Whose Dominion?; Religious Liberty; Venturers of Faith; Voice Out of Africa; Robert Moffat: Pioneer in Africa; Christianity in Africa; ed Encyclopedia of the Bible for Children; People of the Bible. *Recreation:* walking. *Address:* 4 Bouverie Street, EC4. *T:* 01-353 3853; 34 Millington Road, Cambridge. *T:* Cambridge 62905. *Clubs:* National Liberal, Royal Commonwealth Society; Union (Cambridge).

**NORTHCOTT, William Robert;** Chairman, Ready Mixed Concrete Ltd, since 1966 (Director 1962); *b* 26 Aug. 1916; *s* of William George Northcott; *m* 1940, Elizabeth Honor Adams; one *s* two *d*. *Educ:* Crediton Grammar School. Dir, English China Clays Ltd, 1960; Regional Dir, National Westminster Bank Ltd, 1969. Underwriting Member of Lloyd's, 1958. *Recreation:* yachting. *Address:* Newton, Salcombe, South Devon. *T:* Salcombe 2458; Roebuck House, Palace Street, SW1. *T:* 01-828 0343. *Clubs:* Royal Western Yacht, Royal Torbay Yacht.

**NORTHCROFT, Ernest George Drennan,** CBE 1949; *b* 27 Jan. 1896; *s* of late G. A. Northcroft, Jersey, CI; *m* 1st, 1946, Phyllis Kathleen (*d* 1963), *d* of late H. F. Parsons, Portskewett, Mon; 2nd, 1970, Marcia Elizabeth, *d* of late A. W. Gatrall, Southampton. *Educ:* Sherborne Sch.; University Coll., Oxford. Served European War, 1914-18; Bedfordshire Regt, 1917-19; with BEF, 1917 (despatches); with Salonika Force, 1918-19. With Messrs Anglo-Iranian Oil Co. in Iran, 1919-51; Chief Representative Tehran, Anglo-Iranian Oil Co. Ltd, 1945-51. Chm., New Forest Conservative Assoc., 1958-61. Pres., 1962-65; Chm., New Forest RDC, 1964-65 (Chm. Finance and Gen. Purposes Cttee, 1960-63; Chm. Housing Cttee, 1965-70); Mem. Hampshire CC, 1962-. Mem. Southern Gas Consultative Council, 1959-66. *Recreations:* gardening, travelling. *Address:* The Splash, Minstead, Lyndhurst, Hants. *T:* Cadnam 3173. *Clubs:* East India and Sports, Royal Commonwealth Society.

**NORTHERN TERRITORY, AUSTRALIA, Bishop of,** since 1968; **Rt. Rev. Kenneth Bruce Mason;** *b* 4 Sept. 1928; *s* of Eric Leslie Mason and Gertrude Irene (*née* Pearce); unmarried. *Educ:* Bathurst High Sch.; Sydney Teachers' Coll.; St John's Theological Coll., Morpeth; Univ. of Queensland. Deacon, 1953; Priest, 1954. Primary Teacher, 1948-51; St John's Theological Coll., Morpeth, 1952-53 (ThL); Member, Brotherhood of the Good Shepherd, 1954; Parish of: Gilgandra, NSW, 1954-58; Darwin, NT, 1959-61; Alice Springs, NT, 1962; University of Queensland, 1963-64 (BA, Dip Div); resigned from Brotherhood, 1965; Trinity Coll., Melbourne Univ.: Asst Chaplain, 1965; Dean, 1966-67. *Recreations:* squash, listening to sixteenth, seventeenth and eighteenth century music, railways. *Address:* Christ Church Cathedral, PO Box 2267, Darwin, NT 5794, Australia.

**NORTHESK,** 12th Earl of, *cr* 1647; **John Douglas Carnegie;** Baron Rosehill and Inglismaldie, 1639; *b* 16 Feb. 1895; *o surv s* of late Lieut-Colonel Hon. Douglas George Carnegie, 2nd *s* of 9th Earl; *S* cousin, 1963; *m* 1920, Dorothy Mary (*d* 1967), *er d* of late Colonel Sir William Robert Campion, KCMG, DSO, DL, Hassocks, Sussex; one *s* two *d* (and one *s* decd). *Educ:* Gresham's Sch., Holt; King's Coll., Cambridge (BA). Served European War, 1914-18 (despatches); Captain (temp. Major) 95th (Hants Yeomanry) Brigade, Royal Field Artillery (TA). *Heir: s* Lord Rosehill, *qv*. *Address:* Fair Oak, Rogate (Co. Sussex), Petersfield, Hants. *T:* Rogate 8.

**NORTHFIELD, Douglas William Claridge,** MS; FRCS; FRCP; Fellow Royal Society of Medicine, MRCS, LRCP 1925; FRCS 1928; MB, BS (Gold Medal) 1930; MS London, 1931; FRCP 1966. Formerly: Surgeon in charge of Neuro-Surgical Department, London Hospital; Neurological Surgeon, Queen Elizabeth Hospital for Children, Hackney Road; Hunterian Professor, RCS; Surgical Registrar and Demonstrator of Anatomy, Guy's Hospital; Past President: Neurology Section, RSM; Electro Encephalographic Society; British Section, International League against Epilepsy; Past President and Past Secretary, Society of British Neurological Surgeons; Past Secretary, International Congress, Neurological Surgery. *Publications:* contrib. medical journals. *Address:* London Hospital, Whitechapel, E1.

**NORTHROP, Filmer S(tuart) C(uckow),** PhD, LittD, LLD; Sterling Professor of Philosophy and Law Emeritus, the Law School and the School of Graduate Studies, Yale University, USA, since 1962; *b* 27 Nov. 1893; *s* of Marshall Ellsworth Northrop and Ruth Cuckow; *m* 1919, Christine Johnston; two *s*. *Educ:* Beloit Coll. (BA 1915, LittD 1946); Yale (MA 1919); Harvard (MA 1922, PhD 1924); Imperial Coll. of Science and Technology, London; Trinity Coll., Cambridge. Instr. at Yale, 1923-26; Asst Prof., Yale, 1926-29; Associate Prof., Yale, 1929-32, Prof., 1932-47; Master of Silliman Coll., 1940-47; Sterling Prof. of Philosophy and Law, Yale, 1947-62; Visiting Prof., summer session, Univ. of Iowa, 1926; Univ. of Michigan, 1932; Univ. of Virginia, 1931-32; Visiting Prof. and Mem. of East-West Conf. on Philosophy at Univ. of Hawaii, 1939; Prof. Extraordinario, La Universidad Nacional Autonoma de Mexico, 1949; Fellow: American Acad. of Arts and Sciences, 1951; American Acad. of Political and Social Science, 1957; Pres., American Philosophical Assoc. (Eastern Div.), 1952. Hon. LLD: Univ. of Hawaii, 1949, Rollins Coll., 1955; Hon. LittD: Beloit Coll., 1946; Pratt Inst., 1961. Order of the Aztec Eagle (Mexican), 1946. *Publications:* Science and First Principles, 1931; The Meeting of East and West, 1946; The Logic of the Sciences and the Humanities, 1947; The Taming of the Nations, A Study of the Cultural Bases of International Policy, 1952 (Wilkie Memorial Building Award, 1953); European Union and

United States Foreign Policy, 1954; The Complexity of Legal and Ethical Experience, 1959; Philosophical Anthropology and Practical Politics, 1960; Co-Editor, Cross-cultural Understanding: Epistemology in Anthropology, 1964; chapter in Contemporary American Philosophy, second series, 1970; ed, Ideological Differences and World Order, 1949. *Recreations:* travel, baseball. *Address:* 16 Coult Lane, Old Lyme, Conn 06371, USA. *T:* 434-7011. *Clubs:* Century (New York); Beaumont, Berzilius, Elizabethan, Graduates, Mory's (New Haven); American Academy of Arts and Sciences (Philosophy Section) (Boston).

**NORTHROP, John Howard;** Member Rockefeller University (formerly Institute), 1924, Emeritus 1962; Visiting Professor of Bacteriology, University of California, 1949, Emeritus, 1959; Professor Biophysics, 1958, Emeritus 1959; Research Biophysicist, Donner Laboratory, 1958; *b* Yonkers, NY, 5 July 1891; *s* of Dr John I. Northrop, of Department of Zoology, Columbia Univ., and Alice Rich Northrop, of Dept of Botany, Hunter Coll., NY City; *m* 1917, Louise Walker, NY City; one *s one d. Educ:* Columbia Univ. BS 1912; AM 1913; PhD 1915; W. B. Cutting Travelling Fellow, Columbia Univ. (year in Jacques Loeb's laboratory at Rockefeller Inst.), 1915; on staff of Rockefeller Inst. 1916; Member, 1924; Stevens prize, Coll. of Physicians and Surgeons, Columbia Univ., 1931; Captain, Chemical Warfare Service, 1917-18; discovered and worked on fermentation process for manufacturing acetone; ScD Harvard 1936, Columbia 1937, Yale 1937, Princeton 1940, Rutgers 1941; LLD, University of California, 1939; Chandler Medal, Columbia Univ., 1937; DeLamar Lectr, Sch. of Hygiene and Public Health, Johns Hopkins, 1937; Jesup Lectr, Columbia Univ., 1938; Hitchcock Lectr, Univ. of California, 1939; Thayer Lectr, Johns Hopkins, 1940; Daniel Giraud Elliot Medal for 1939 of National Acad. of Science, 1944; Consultant, OSRD, 1941-45. Shared Nobel Prize in Chemistry, 1946. Certificate of Merit, USA, 1948. Alex. Hamilton Medal, Columbia Univ., 1961. Member: Sons of the American Revolution; Delta Kappa Epsilon fraternity, Sigma Xi, Phi Lambda Upsilon; American Society of Biological Chemists; National Acad. of Sciences, Halle Akademie der Naturforscher; Société Philomathique (Paris); American Philosophical Society; Society of General Physiologists; Chemical Society (Hon. Fellow); Fellow World Academy; Benjamin Franklin Fellow, RSA. *Publications:* Crystalline Enzymes, 1939; numerous papers on physical chemistry of proteins, agglutination of bacteria, kinetics of enzyme reactions, and isolation and chemical nature of enzymes; editorial board of Journal of General Physiology, Experimental Biology Monographs. *Recreations:* field shooting, salmon fishing. *Address:* PO Box 1387, Wickenburg, Arizona 85358, USA. *Club:* Century Association (New York).

**NORTHUMBERLAND,** 10th Duke of, *cr* 1766, **Hugh Algernon Percy;** KG 1959; TD 1961; FRS 1970; JP; Earl of Northumberland, Baron Warkworth, 1749; Earl Percy, 1776; Earl of Beverly, 1790; Lord Lovaine, Baron of Alnwick, 1784; Bt, *cr* 1660; Baron Percy (by writ), 1722; Lord Lieutenant and Custos Rotulorum of Northumberland since 1956; Chancellor of University of Newcastle since 1964; Chairman, Medical Research Council, since 1969; *b* 6 April 1914; 2nd *s* of 8th Duke of Northumberland, KG, CBE, MVO (*d* 1930), and Lady Helen Gordon-Lennox (Helen, Dowager Duchess of Northumberland, who *d* 1965), *y d* of 7th Duke of Richmond and Gordon; *S* brother (killed in action), 1940; *m* 1946, Lady Elizabeth Diana Montagu-Douglas-Scott, *er d* of 8th Duke of Buccleuch, *qv*; three *s* three *d. Educ:* Eton; Oxford. Lieut, Northumberland Hussars, 1936; RA, 1940; Captain, 1941; Captain, Northumberland Hussars, 1947; TARO, 1949-64; Chm., T&AFA, 1950-56; Pres., Northumberland T&AFA, 1956-68; Pres., TA&VR Assoc. for North of England, 1968-. A Lord in Waiting, May-July 1945. President: Northern Area, British Legion; Northumberland Boy Scouts' Assoc., 1946-; Northumb. Assoc. of Boys' Clubs, 1942-; British Horse Soc., 1950; North of England Shipowners' Assoc., 1952-; Hunters Improvement and Light Horse Breeding Soc., 1954; Royal Agricultural Soc. of England, 1956, 1962; British Show JUmping Assoc., 1959; The Wildfowl Trust, 1968-. Chairman: Departmental Cttee on Slaughter of Horses, 1952; Court of Durham Univ., 1956-64; Border Forest Park Cttee, 1956-; Agricultural Research Council, 1958-68; Departmental Cttee for Recruitment of Veterinary Surgeons, 1964; Cttee of Enquiry on Foot-and-Mouth Disease, 1968-69. Member: Agricultural Improvement Council, 1953-62; National Forestry Cttee for England and Wales, 1954-60; Hill Farming Advisory Cttee for England and Wales, 1946-60; County Agricultural Exec. Cttee, 1948-59. Hon. Treasurer, Royal National Life Boat Institution; Hon. Associate, RCVS, 1967. Hon. DCL Durham, 1958. Master of Percy Foxhounds, 1940-. KStJ 1957. *Heir: s* Earl Percy, *qv. Address:* Alnwick Castle, Northumberland. *T:* Alnwick 2456; Syon House, Brentford. *T:* Isleworth 2353; Albury Park, Guildford. *T:* Shere 2516. *Clubs:* Boodle's, Northern Counties, Turf.

*See also Duke of Hamilton and Brandon, Sir Aymer Maxwell, Bt, Lord Richard Percy, Duke of Sutherland.*

**NORTHUMBERLAND, Archdeacon of;** *see* Unwin, Ven. C. P.

**NORTON,** family name of **Barons Grantley** and **Rathcreedan.**

**NORTON,** 7th Baron, *cr* 1878; **John Arden Adderley,** OBE 1964; *b* 24 Nov. 1915; *s* of 6th Baron Norton; *S* father, 1961; *m* 1946, Betty Margaret, *o d* of late James Mckee Hannah; two *s. Educ:* Radley; Magdalen Coll., Oxford (BA). Oxford University Greenland Expedition, 1938; Assistant Master, Oundle School, 1938-39. Served War, 1940-45 (despatches); RE (N Africa, Europe). Major, 1944. Asst Secretary, Country Landowners Assoc., 1947-59. *Recreations:* mountaineering, shooting, heraldry and genealogy. *Heir: s* Hon. James Nigel Arden Adderley, *b* 2 June 1947. *Address:* Fillongley Hall, Coventry, Warwickshire. *T:* Fillongley 303.

**NORTON, Sir Charles;** *see* Norton, Sir W. C.

**NORTON, Sir Clifford John,** KCMG 1946 (CMG 1933); CVO 1937; *b* 17 July 1891; *o surv s* of late Rev. George Norton and Clara, *d* of late John Dewey; *m* 1927, Noel Evelyn, *d* of late Sir Walter Charleton Hughes, CIE, MInstCE; no *c. Educ:* Rugby Sch.; Queen's Coll., Oxford, MA 1915. Suffolk Regt, 1914, Gallipoli, Palestine; Captain, General Staff EEF, 1917; Political Officer, Damascus, Deraa, Haifa, 1919-20; entered Diplomatic Service, 1921; Private Secretary to the Permanent Under-Secretary of State for Foreign Affairs, 1930-37; First Secretary, 1933; Counsellor British Embassy, Warsaw, 1937-39; Foreign Office, 1939-42; Minister, Berne, 1942-46; HM Ambassador in Athens, 1946-51; retired, 1951;

Hon. Citizen of Athens, 1951. UK Delegate (alternate) to United Nations Assembly, 1952 and 1953. Past President, Anglo-Swiss Society. Hon. Fellow, Queen's Coll., Oxford, 1963. *Address:* 21a Carlyle Square, SW3; Bothamstead Farm, Hampstead Norris, Berks.

**NORTON, Maj.-General Cyril Henry,** CB 1952; CBE 1945; DSO 1943; Colonel Commandant RA, 1958-63; *b* 4 Nov. 1898; *s* of late F. H. Norton, Tilehurst, Caterham, Surrey; *m* 1934, Ethel, *d* of Kapten R. E. G. Lindberg, Stockholm, Sweden; one *s* one *d. Educ:* Rugby Sch.; RMA, Woolwich. 2nd Lieut, RFA, 1916; Captain, 1929; Major, 1938; Lieut-Colonel, 1945; Colonel, 1946. Brig., 1950; Maj.-Gen., 1951; GOC 5th Anti-Aircraft Group, 1950-53; retired Nov. 1953. Served European War, 1914-19 (Salonika); Palestine, 1937-39 (despatches); War of 1939-45: in Middle East, Sicily and NW Europe. *Address:* Dunn House, Long Melford, Sudbury, Suffolk. *Club:* Army and Navy.

*See also Viscount Davidson.*

**NORTON, Captain Gerard Ross,** VC 1944; MM; 1/4th Hampshire Regiment; *b* S Africa, 7 Sept. 1915; *m* 1942, Lilia Morris, East London, S Africa; one *d. Educ:* Selborne Coll., East London, S Africa. Bank clerk. *Recreations:* Rugger–provincial, tennis, cricket. *Address:* Minnehaha, PO Raffingora, Rhodesia.

**NORTON, Admiral Sir Peter John H.;** *see* Hill-Norton.

**NORTON, Roger Edward,** CMG 1948; OBE 1943; *b* 15 June 1897; *s* of late Henry Turton Norton; *m* 1924, Priscilla Anne Mary, *d* of late J. R. C. Deverell; one *s* two *d. Educ:* Eton College. Served European War, 1914-18, with BRCS (despatches, OStJ, Cav. Order of Crown of Italy, Italian Croce di Guerra). Started farming in E Africa, 1919. Joined Kenya Govt Service, 1938, as Sec. Standing Board of Economic Development; Chm. E African War Supplies Board, 1942; Dir Produce Disposal, 1943; Dep. Chm. EA Production and Supply Council, 1944; East African Comr in London, 1945-51; Regional Controller, East Africa, Colonial Development Corporation, 1951-59, retired. *Address:* 23 Ashley Gardens, SW1. *T:* 01-834 6731. *Clubs:* MCC, Royal Automobile.

**NORTON, Sir (Walter) Charles,** Kt 1956; MBE 1944; MC 1916; *b* 24 May 1896; *s* of late Walter Percy Norton and Louisa May Norton (*née* Kershaw); *m* 1948, Olive Penelope Wood (*née* Murray). *Educ:* Winchester. Served European War in Army, 1914-19; Captain, 9th Bn Royal Sussex Regt; Staff Captain, 1918-19. Admitted Solicitor, 1921. Consultant with Norton, Rose, Botterell & Roche (formerly Senior Partner); Chm., Electronic Rentals & General Holdings Ltd; Director: Currie Line Ltd, Leith; Legal & General Assurance Society Ltd, Gresham Life Assurance Society Ltd, and Gresham Fire & Accident Society Ltd; Walter R. Runciman & Co. Ltd. President, Law Society, 1955-56. Mayor of the City of Westminster, 1957-58; first Lord Mayor of new City of Westminster, 1965-66. Master, City of London Solicitors' Co., 1963-64. *Address:* 56 Rivermead Court, Hurlingham, SW6. *T:* 01-736 2794. *Clubs:* Garrick, Hurlingham (President).

**NORTON, Wilfrid,** ARCA; Pottery Sculptor, Lecturer in Design, and Architecture, Camberwell School of Arts and Crafts; *b* Shropshire; *s* of Edwin and Mary Norton; *m* 1915, Lily Holden Harley. *Educ:* Royal College of Art; abroad. Studentship in Training Scholarship, Royal College of Art; Exhibitor, Royal Academy, Arts and Crafts Society, International exhibitions in Paris, Leipzig and America, and various shows in Bond Street. *Recreations:* Philosophy and walking in unfrequented places. *Address:* Kerama Studio, 13 Chalcot Gardens, NW3. *T:* 01-722 0729.

**NORTON-GRIFFITHS, Sir Peter,** 2nd Bt, *cr* 1922; Barrister-at-Law, Inner Temple, 1931; *b* 3 May 1905; *e s* of late Sir John Norton-Griffiths, 1st Bt, KCB, DSO, and Gwladys Mills Wood, 99 Cadogan Gardens, London, SW3; *S* father, 1930; *m* 1935, Kathryn, *e d* of late George F. Schrafft, Boston, Massachusetts, USA; two *s* one *d. Educ:* Eton; Magdalen Coll., Oxford. Asst to President, Shell Union Oil Corporation, NY, 1936-39; enlisted Intelligence Corps, 1940; Asst Military Attaché, British Embassy, Madrid (GSO2) 1941-42; Instructor School of Military Intelligence, GSO3, 1943-44; GSO3, Intelligence Staff, SHAEF, 1944-45. Asst to General Manager, Deutsche Shell AG, 1948-50; General Manager, Shell Co. of Portugal Ltd, 1950-53; Managing Director, Belgian Shell Co., SA, 1953-60; retired from business. Officier de l'Ordre de la Couronne (Belgium); Officier de l'Ordre de la Couronne de Chêne (Luxembourg). *Recreations:* shooting, music, sight-seeing. *Heir: s* John Norton-Griffiths [*b* 4 Oct. 1938; *m* 1964, Marilyn Margaret, *er d* of Norman Grimley]. *Address:* Quinta do Torneiro, Paço d'Arcos, Portugal. *Clubs:* Boodle's; Eça de Queiroz (Lisbon).

**NORWICH,** 2nd Viscount, *cr* 1952, of Aldwick; **John Julius Cooper;** writer and broadcaster; *b* 15 Sept. 1929; *s* of 1st Viscount Norwich, PC, GCMG, DSO, and of Lady Diana Cooper, *qv, d* of 8th Duke of Rutland; *S* father, 1954; *m* 1952, Anne (Frances May), *e d* of late Hon. Sir Bede Clifford, GCMG, CB, MVO; one *s* one *d. Educ:* Upper Canada Coll., Toronto, Canada; Eton; University of Strasbourg; New Coll., Oxford. Served 1947-49 as Writer, Royal Navy. Entered Foreign Office, 1952; Third Secretary, British Embassy, Belgrade, 1955-57; Second Secretary, British Embassy, Beirut, 1957-60; worked in Foreign Office (First Secretary from 1961) and in British Delegation to Disarmament Conference, Geneva, from 1960 until resignation from Foreign Service 1964. Chm., British Theatre Museum. Makes historical documentary films for BBC TV. *Publications:* Mount Athos (with Reresby Sitwell), 1966; The Normans in the South (as The Other Conquest, US), 1967; Sahara, 1968; The Kingdom in The Sun, 1970. *Recreations:* travel, music, opera, theatre. *Heir: s* Hon. Jason Charles Duff Bede Cooper, *b* 27 Oct. 1959. *Address:* 24 Blomfield Road, W9. *T:* 01-286 5050. *Clubs:* Buck's, Beefsteak, Royal Automobile, White's.

**NORWICH, Diana, Viscountess;** *see* Cooper, Lady Diana.

**NORWICH, Bishop of** (and titular Abbot of St Benet's), since 1959; **Rt. Rev. William Launcelot Scott Fleming,** DD (Lambeth); MA (Cambridge), MS (Yale); *b* 7 Aug. 1906; *y s* of late Robert Alexander Fleming, MD, LLD; *m* 1965, Jane, *widow* of Anthony Agutter. *Educ:* Rugby Sch.; Trinity Hall and Westcott House, Cambridge; Yale Univ. Commonwealth Fund Fellow, Yale Univ., 1929-31; deacon, 1933; priest, 1934; Expeditions to Iceland and Spitzbergen, 1932 and 1933; Chaplain and Geologist, British Graham Land Expedition to the Antarctic, 1934-37; Examining Chaplain to Bishop of Southwark, 1937-49, to Bishop of St Albans, 1940-43, to Bishop of Hereford, 1942-49; Fellow and Chaplain, Trinity Hall, Cambridge, 1933-49. Dean, 1937-49; Director of Scott Polar Research Institute, Cambridge, 1947-49; Bishop of Portsmouth, 1949-59. Chaplain RNVR, HMS King Alfred, 1940; HMS Queen Elizabeth, 1940-43; HMS Ganges, 1943-44; Director of Service Ordination Candidates, 1944-46. Chairman: Church of England Youth Council, 1950-61; Archbishops' Advisers for Needs and Resources, 1963. Vice-Chm., Parly Gp for World Govt, 1970-. Mem., Royal Commn on Environmental Pollution, 1970-. Hon. Chaplain, RNR (RNVR 1950). Hon. Fellow, Trinity Hall, Cambridge, 1956; Hon. Vice-President, Royal Geographical Society, 1961. *Address:* Bishop's House, Norwich, Norfolk NOR 10A.

**NORWICH, Dean of;** *see* Webster, Very Rev. A. B.

**NORWICH, Archdeacon of;** *see* Aitken, Ven. W. A.

**NORWOOD, Christopher Bonnewell Burton;** *b* 17 Dec. 1932; *s* of Harold Norwood and Grace (*née* Bonnewell); *m* 1955, Beryl Goldwyn; one *s*. *Educ:* Hawes Down Elementary Sch., W Wickham, Kent; Whitgift Sch., S Croydon; Gonville and Caius Coll., Cambridge. BA 1953, MA 1957. Trainee with Evans Medical Supplies, Liverpool, 1954-55. Admin. Asst, National Coal Board, 1955-58; then in Marketing Dept (worked underground in Lancs, certificate of competence at coal-face); Asst Economist, Central Electricity Generating Board, 1960-64. Contested: Sutton Coldfield, 1955, Bromsgrove, 1959; MP (Lab) Norwich South, 1964-70. *Recreations:* reading, swimming, squash. *Address:* 115 Great Portland Street, W1.

**NOSER, Most Rev. Adolf;** *see* Madang, Archbishop of, (RC).

**NOSWORTHY, Lt-Gen. Sir Francis Poitiers,** KCB 1944 (CB 1938); DSO 1918; MC; Colonel Commandant RE, 1940-50; Colonel Comdt RIE, 1946; *b* 21 Sept. 1887; 2nd *s* of late Richard Nosworthy, CMG, and Beatrice (*née* Michelin), Constant Spring, Jamaica; *m* 1925, Audrey, 2nd *d* of T. R. Davey, JP, Wraxall Court, Somerset; one *s* one *d*. *Educ:* Exeter School. Entered Army, 1907, Captain, Royal Engineers, 1914; Bt Major, 1916; Bt Lieut-Colonel, 1921; local Colonel, 1926; Lieut-Colonel and Colonel, 1932; Maj.-General, 1937; Lieut-General, 1940; Mishmi Abor Expedition, 1912-13; European War (France), 1914-18, 3rd Afghan War, 1919 (DSO, with bar, MC with bar, Croix de Guerre avec palme, despatches six times); Instructor, Staff College, 1919-22. War Office, General Staff, 1922-26; Chief Staff Officer and Second-in-Command, Sudan Defence Force, 1926-30; Imperial Defence Coll., 1931; General Staff Officer, 1st Grade, the British Troops in China, 1932-35; Commander, 5th Infantry Brigade, 1935-38; Deputy Chief of General Staff, Army Headquarters, India, 1938-40; a Corps Commander, 1940; Commander-in-Chief, West Africa, 1943. *Address:* 70 Wellsway, Bath, Somerset. *T:* Bath 64591. *Clubs:* Lansdowne; Bath and County (Bath).

**NOSWORTHY, Harold George,** CMG 1965; *b* 15 March 1908; *m* 1941, Marjorie Anjelique; two *d*. *Educ:* Kingston Technical High Sch.; private tuition. Entered Jamaica Civil Service, 1929; 2nd class Clerk, 1938; Examiner of Accounts, 1943; Asst Commissioner, Income Tax, 1947; Asst Trade Administrator, 1950; Trade Administrator and Chairman Trade Control Board, 1953; Principal Asst Secretary, Ministry of Finance, 1955; Auditor-General, 1957-66; Dir, Internal Audit Service, UN, 1966-68. Queen's Coronation Medal, 1953; Jamaica Independence Medal, 1962. *Recreations:* reading, billiards, bridge, swimming. *Address:* 18 Hyperion Avenue, Kingston 6, Jamaica.

**NOTT, Charles Robert Harley,** CMG 1959; OBE 1952; retired, New Zealand; *b* 24 Oct. 1904; *e s* of late John Harley Nott, JP, Leominster, Herefordshire and late Mrs Nott, formerly of Bodenham Hall, Herefordshire; *m* 1935, Marion (*née* Macfarlane), Auckland, NZ; one *s* one *d*. *Educ:* Marlborough; Christ's Coll., Cambridge (MA). Colonial Administrative Service: Fiji, 1926; Administrative Officer (Grade II), 1938, (Grade I), 1945. Member of the Legislative Council, Fiji, 1950; HBM's Agent and Consul, Tonga, 1954-57; Sec. for Fijian Affairs, 1957-59; MLC, MEC, retired, 1960. *Recreations:* fishing, golf. *Address:* Matakana, Havelock North, New Zealand.

**NOTT, Commander Sir James Grenvile P.;** *see* Pyke-Nott.

**NOTT, John William Frederic;** MP (C) St Ives Division of Cornwall since 1966; *b* 1 Feb. 1932; *s* of Richard William Kandahar Nott, Bideford, Devon, and Phyllis (*née* Francis); *m* 1959, Miloska Sekol, Maribor, Yugoslavia; two *s* one *d*. *Educ:* King's Mead, Seaford; Bradfield Coll.; Trinity Coll., Cambridge. Lieut, 2nd Gurkha Rifles (regular officer), Malayan emergency, 1952-56; Trinity Coll., Cambridge, 1957-59 (BA Hons Law and Econs); Pres., Cambridge Union, 1959; called to the Bar, Inner Temple, 1959; Gen. Manager, S. G. Warburg & Co. Ltd, Merchant Bankers, 1963-66; Chm., Imperial Eastman (UK) Ltd; Director: Clarkson International Ltd; Les Flexibles Gerland, Flexoger SA, Lyon; Imperial RIV SrL, Turin, 1968. Sec., Cons. Parly Finance Cttee, 1969-70. Alderman, Islington Borough Council, 1968. *Recreation:* fishing. *Address:* 5 John Spencer Square, Canonbury, N1. *T:* 01-226 9705; Trewinnard Manor, St Erth, Cornwall. *T:* Cockwells 444.

**NOTT, Ven. Michael John,** BD; AKC; Archdeacon of Canterbury since 1967; Canon Residentiary of Canterbury Cathedral, since 1965; *b* 9 Nov. 1916; *s* of Frank and Ann Nott; *m* 1942, Elisabeth Margaret Edwards; one *s* one *d*. *Educ:* St Paul's; King's Coll., London; Lincoln Theological Coll. Curate of: Abington, Northampton, 1939-45; St Mary, Reading, 1945-46; Vicar of St Andrew, Kettering, 1946-54; Rural Dean of Kettering, 1952-54; Warden and Chaplain, Heritage Craft Sch. and Hospital, Chailey; Vicar of Seaford, 1957-64; Rural Dean of Seaford, 1961-64; Senior Chaplain to Archbishop of Canterbury, 1964-65; Archdeacon of Maidstone, 1965-67. *Recreations:* reading, walking, tennis, photography, travel. *Address:* 29 The Precincts, Canterbury. *T:* Canterbury 63036. *Club:* Travellers'.

**NOTT-BOWER, Sir John (Reginald Hornby),** Kt 1950; KCVO 1953 (CVO 1937); Commissioner Metropolitan Police, 1953-58, retired; *b* 1892; 2nd *s* of late Sir William Nott-Bower, KCVO; *m* 1928, Kathleen Manners Beresford, *d* of late Major Buck, DLI; two *s* one *d*. *Educ:* Cheltenham; Tonbridge. Indian Police, 1911-33; Chief Constable, Metropolitan Police, 1933; Assistant Commissioner, 1940; Deputy Commissioner, 1946-53; Inspector-General Public Safety, Austria (Allied Commission), 1945-46. King's Police Medal, 1931. *Recreations:* fishing, golf. *Address:* Shady Cottage, Trinity, Jersey, CI.

**NOTT-BOWER, Sir (William) Guy,** KBE, *cr* 1946 (CBE 1937); CB 1942; *b* 9 Oct. 1890; *e s* of late Sir John William Nott-Bower, KCVO; *m* 1914, Frances Winifred (*d* 1966), *d* of late William Macdonald Matthews, Broadwater Downs, Tunbridge Wells; one *s* two *d*. *Educ:* Cheltenham Coll. (Class. Scholar); Brasenose Coll., Oxford (Scholar). BA 1913 (Litt Hum); MA 1962; entered Ceylon Civil Service, 1914; transferred to Inland Reveue Dept, 1916; to Home Office, 1919; to Ministry of Labour, 1919; to Mines Dept, 1920; to Air Ministry, 1939; Deputy Under-Secretary for Mines, 1941-42; Under-Secretary for Mines, 1942; Deputy Secretary, Ministry of Fuel and Power, 1942-48; Director of Public Relations, National Coal Board, 1948-54. Officer of the Order of St John of Jerusalem. *Address:* 44 Arnison Road, East Molesey, Surrey. *T:* 01-979 5061.

**NOTTAGE, Raymond Frederick Tritton,** CMG 1964; Director, Royal Institute of Public Administration, since 1949; *b* 1 Aug. 1916; *s* of Frederick and Frances Nottage; *m* 1941, Joyce Evelyn, *d* of Sidney and Edith Philpot; three *d*. *Educ:* Hackney Downs Secondary Sch. Civil servant, Post Office Headquarters, 1936-49; Editor of Civil Service Opinion, and Member Exec. Cttee, Soc. of Civil Servants, 1944-49; Mem. Hornsey Borough Council, 1945-47; Mem. Cttee on Training in Public Admin. for Overseas Countries, 1961-63; Vice-Pres. Internat. Inst. of Admin. Sciences, 1962-68; Mem. Governing Body, Inst. of Development Studies, Univ. of Sussex, 1966-; travelled abroad as Consultant and Lectr for UN, Unesco, FO, CRO, and overseas univs and institutes. *Publications:* articles in Public Administration and similar jls. *Recreations:* nothing unusual. *Address:* 36e Arkwright Road, NW3. *T:* 01-794 7129. *Club:* Reform.

**NOTTINGHAM, Bishop of, (RC),** since 1944; **Rt. Rev. Edward Ellis;** *b* 1899; *s* of A. Ellis. *Educ:* Ratcliffe Coll.; Ven. English Coll., Rome; Gregorian Univ., DD and PhD. Formerly Administrator at St Barnabas's Cathedral, Nottingham. *Address:* Bishop's House, The Park, Nottingham. *T:* 44786.

**NOTTINGHAM, Archdeacon of;** *see* Brown, Ven. Michael René Warneford.

**NOUMEA, Archbishop of, (RC),** since 1966; **Most Rev. Pierre Martin,** Officer, Legion of Honour, 1967; *b* 22 Feb. 1910. *Educ:* Univ. de Lyon; Lyon Séminaire and in Belgium. Priest, 1939. POW, Buchenwald and Dachau Camps, until 1945. Séminaire de Missions d'Océanie, Lyon: Professor, 1945-47; Supérieure, 1947-53; Provincial, Sté de Marie, Paris, 1953-56; Bishop of New Caledonia, 1956. *Address:* Archbishop's House, BP3, New Caledonia. *T:* 31-49.

**NOURSE, Martin Charles,** QC 1970; *b* 3 April 1932; *yr s* of Henry Edward Nourse, MD, MRCP, Cambridge, and late Ethel Millicent, *d* of Rt Hon. Sir Charles Henry Sargant, Lord Justice of Appeal. *Educ:* Winchester; Corpus Christi Coll., Cambridge. National Service as 2nd Lieut, Rifle Bde, 1951-52; Lieut, London Rifle Bde Rangers (TA), 1952-55. Called to Bar, Lincoln's Inn, 1956; Mem., General Council of the Bar, 1964-68; a Junior Counsel to BoT in Chancery matters, 1967-70. *Address:* North End House, Grantchester, Cambridge; 31 Cadogan Square, SW1; 2 New Square, Lincoln's Inn, WC2. *Clubs:* United University; Cambridge County (Cambridge).
*See also Sir Edmund Sargant.*

**NOVA SCOTIA, Bishop of,** since 1963; **Rt. Rev. William Wallace Davis;** *b* 10 Dec. 1908; *s* of Isaac Davis and Margaret Dixon; *m* 1933, Kathleen Aubrey Acheson (*d* 1966); two *s* two *d*; *m* 1968, Helen Mary Lynton. *Educ:* Bishop's Univ., Lennoxville, PQ. BA 1931, BD 1934; Deacon, 1932; Priest, 1932; Curate, St Matthew's, Ottawa, 1932-36; Rector, Coaticook, PQ, 1936-38; Rector, St Matthew's, Quebec, 1938-52; Archdeacon of Quebec, 1947-52; Dean of Nova Scotia, and Rector of the Cathedral Church of All Saints, Halifax, NS, 1952-58; Bishop Coadjutor of Nova Scotia, 1958-63. DD University of King's Coll., Halifax, 1959; DCL, Bishop's Univ., Lennoxville, PQ, 1960. *Address:* Bishop's Lodge, 1360 Tower Road, Halifax, NS, Canada. *T:* 423-5073.

**NOWELL, Ralph Machattie,** CB 1947; retired; *b* 3 June 1903; *e s* of late Walter Salmon Nowell and Anita Mary Machattie; *m* 1927, Mary McGregor; one *s* one *d*. *Educ:* Marlborough; Brasenose Coll., Oxford. George Webb Medley Junior Scholar, 1924; BA 1926. Retired as Under-Secretary and Tariff Adviser, Board of Trade, 1963. *Address:* 77 Albert Drive, Wimbledon Park, SW19. *T:* 01-788 4951. *Club:* Oxford and Cambridge University.

**NOWELL-SMITH, Prof. Patrick Horace,** AM (Harvard); MA (Oxon); Professor of Philosophy, York University, Toronto, since 1969; *b* 17 Aug. 1914; *s* of Nowell Charles Smith; *m* 1946, Perilla Thyme (marr. diss. 1968), *d* of Sir Richard Vynne Southwell; three *s* one *d*; *m* 1968, Felicity Margret, *d* of Dr Richard Leonard Ward; one *d*. *Educ:* Winchester Coll.; New College, Oxford. Commonwealth Fellow, Harvard Univ., 1937-39. Served War of 1939-45, in Army, 1939-45. Fellow and Lecturer, Trinity Coll., Oxford, 1946-57, Estates Bursar, 1951-57. Professor of Philosophy: University of Leicester, 1957-64; University of Kent, 1964-69. *Publications:* Ethics, 1954; articles in Mind, Proc. Aristotelian Soc., Theoria, etc. *Address:* Department of Philosophy, York University, Downsview, Ont, Canada.
*See also S. H. Nowell-Smith.*

**NOWELL-SMITH, Simon Harcourt,** FSA; *b* 5 Jan. 1909; *s* of late Nowell Charles Smith, sometime Headmaster of Sherborne; *m* 1938, Marion Sinclair, *d* of late W. S. Crichton, Liverpool; two *s* one *d*. *Educ:* Sherborne; New Coll., Oxford (MA). Editorial Staff of The Times, 1932-44; Assistant Editor, Times Literary Supplement, 1937-39; attached to Intelligence Division, Naval Staff, 1940-45; Secretary and Librarian, The London Library, 1950-56; Secretary, Hospital Library Services Survey, 1958-59; President, Bibliographical Society, 1962-64; Lyell Reader in Bibliography, Oxford Univ., 1965-66. OStJ. *Publications:* Mark Rutherford, a bibliography, 1930; The Legend of the Master (Henry James), 1947; The House of Cassell, 1958; (ed) Edwardian England, 1964; Letters to Macmillan, 1967; International Copyright Law and the Publisher, 1968. *Address:* Quarry Manor, Headington, Oxford. *Club:* Athenæum.
*See also Prof. P. H. Nowell-Smith.*

**NTIWANE, Nkomeni Douglas;** High Commissioner, in London, for Swaziland, since Sept. 1968; *b* 16 Feb. 1933; *s* of Isaiah Myotha and Jane Dlamini; *m* 1960, Sophia Pulane Kali; three *s*. *Educ:* DOT Coll., Middelburg, Transvaal, SA; Columbia Univ. (1967-68; Carnegie Fellow in Dipl.). Teacher, East Transvaal, 1955-61; Headmaster (Swaziland): Mponono Sch., 1961-62; Mbekelweni Sch., 1962-63; Mhlume Central Sch., 1964-66; Lozitha Central Sch., Jan.-Sept.

1967. Ambassador: Federal Republic of Germany, March 1969; Republic of France, April 1969. *Address:* Swaziland High Commission, 58 Pont Street, SW1. *T:* 01-589 5447/8.

**NUGENT,** family name of **Earl of Westmeath, Baron Nugent** and **Baron Nugent of Guildford.**

**NUGENT,** 1st Baron, *cr* 1960, of West Harling; **Terence Edmund Gascoigne Nugent,** GCVO 1952 (KCVO 1945; CVO 1937; MVO 1927); MC; late Irish Guards; *b* 11 Aug. 1895; 2nd *s* of late Brig.-General G. C. Nugent, MVO; *m* 1935, Rosalie, *o d* of late Brig.-General Hon. Charles Willoughby, CB, CMG. *Educ:* Eton; Sandhurst. Joined Irish Guards, 11 Nov. 1914; served European War, France (MC); Adjutant, 1st Bn Irish Guards; employed as GSO3, War Office, 1924-26, as Personal Assistant to the Chief of the Imperial General Staff; accompanied the Duke and Duchess of York on their Australian and New Zealand Tour, 1927; retired pay, 1936, Lt-Col. Comptroller, Lord Chamberlain's Dept, 1936-60; Extra Equerry to King George VI, 1937-52, to the Queen, 1952-; a Lord-in-Waiting to the Queen, 1960-70. President MCC, 1962-63. *Heir: none. Address:* 21 Chelsea Square, SW3. *Clubs:* Guards, White's, Turf.

**NUGENT OF GUILDFORD,** Baron, *cr* 1966 (Life Peer), of Dunsfold; **George Richard Hodges Nugent;** Bt, *cr* 1960; PC 1962; *b* 6 June 1907; *s* of late Colonel George H. Nugent, RA; *m* 1937, Ruth, *d* of late Hugh G. Stafford, Tilford, Surrey. *Educ:* Imperial Service Coll., Windsor; RMA, Woolwich. Commissioned RA, 1926-29. MP (C) Guildford Division of Surrey, 1950-66. Parliamentary Secretary: Ministry of Agriculture, Fisheries and Food, 1951-57; Min. of Transport, 1957-Oct. 1959. JP Surrey, CC, 1944-51. Chairman: Thames Conservancy Board, 1960-; House of Commons Select Cttee for Nationalised Industries, 1961-64; Agricultural Market Development Cttee, 1962-68; Animal Virus Research Institute, 1964-; President, Assoc. of River Authorities, 1965-. FRSA 1962. Hon. DUniv, Surrey, 1968. *Address:* Blacknest Farm, Dunsfold, Surrey. *Clubs:* Junior Carlton, Royal Automobile.

**NUGENT of Clonlost, David James Douglas** (7th Baron Nugent, Austrian title *cr* 1859, confirmed by Royal Warrant of Edward VII, 1908); Company director; *b* 24 Nov. 1917; 2nd *s* of Albert Beauchamp Cecil Nugent (5th Baron) and Frances Every Douglas, niece of 3rd Lord Blythswood, KCB, CVO; *S* brother, 1944; *m* 1968, Mary Louise, *er d* of William Henry Wroth, Bigbury Court, Devon. *Educ:* Lancing Coll. *Recreations:* golf, tennis. *Address:* Forde Park, Chagford, Devon; 88 St James's Street, SW1.

**NUGENT, Sir Hugh Charles,** 6th Bt, *cr* 1795; Count of the Holy Roman Empire; *b* 26 May 1904; *s* of late Charles Hugh Nugent, *o s* of 5th Bt and Anna Maria (she *m* 2nd, Edwin John King, Danemore Park, Speldhurst), *d* of Edwin Adams; *S* grandfather, 1927; *m* 1931, Margaret Mary Lavallin, *er d* of late Rev. H. L. Puxley, The White House, Chaddleworth, Newbury, Berks; two *s*. *Educ:* Stonyhurst Coll. Knight of Malta. *Heir: s* John Edwin Lavallin Nugent [*b* 16 March 1933; *m* 1959, Penelope Ann, *d* of Brig. R. N. Hanbury, of Braughing, Hertfordshire; one *s* one *d*]. *Address:* Ballinlough Castle, Clonmellon, Co. Westmeath, Ireland. *T:* Trim 33135.

**NUGENT, Major-General John Fagan Henslowe,** CB 1942; DSO 1916; *b* 1 July 1889; *e s* of late John Nugent, ICS, of Grenan, Thomastown, Co. Kilkenny, and Florence Henslowe; *m* 1st, 1919, Violet Gwendolen, *o d* of Lionel Cox, Colombo, Ceylon; 2nd, 1939, Helena Norah, *er d* of Captain J. V. and the Hon. Mrs Saunderson, Honeybottom, Newbury, Berks. *Educ:* Downside Sch., near Bath; Sandhurst. Joined Indian Army, 28th Punjabis; Major, 1925; Bt Lieut-Colonel 1931; Colonel, 1935; Maj.-General, 1941; ADC to Governor of Ceylon, 1914-15; served European War in Mesopotamia, 1915 (wounded, despatches, DSO); Afghanistan, 1919; Commandant 2nd Bn 2/7th Rajput Regt, 1934-35; AA and QMG Lahore District, 1935-38; Commander of a Brigade in India, 1938-40; ADC to the King, 1940-41; Maj.-General, i/c Administration HQ, North Western Army, India, 1941; retired, 1944. *Address:* La Hougue, St Peter, Jersey, CI. *T:* Western 555. *Club:* United Service.

**NUGENT, Sir Peter Walter James,** 5th Bt, *cr* 1831; *b* 26 Jan. 1920; *s* of Sir Walter Richard Nugent, 4th Bt and of Aileen Gladys, *y d* of late Middleton Moore O'Malley, JP, Ross, Westport, Co. Mayo; *S* father, 1955; *m* 1947, Anne Judith, *o d* of Major Robert Smyth, Gaybrook, Mullingar, Co. Westmeath; two *s* two *d*. *Educ:* Downside. Served War of 1939-45; 2nd Lieut, Hampshire Regt, 1941; Major, 1945. *Heir: s* Walter Richard Middleton Nugent, *b* 15 Nov. 1947. *Address:* Donore, Multyfarnham, Co. Westmeath, Eire.

**NUGENT, Sir Robin (George Colborne),** 5th Bt *cr* 1806; *b* 11 July 1925; *s* of Sir Guy Nugent, 4th Bt and of Maisie, Lady Nugent, *d* of J. A. Bigsby; *S* father, 1970; *m* 1st, 1947, Ursula Mary (marr. diss. 1967), *d* of late Lt-Gen. Sir Herbert Fothergill Cooke, KCB, KBE, CSI, DSO; two *s* one *d*; 2nd, 1967, Victoria Anna Irmgard, *d* of late Dr Peter Cartellieri. *Educ:* Eton; RWA School of Architecture. Lt Grenadier Guards, 1943-48; served Italy, 1944-45. ARIBA 1959. *Recreations:* golf, skiing, travel. *Heir: s* Christopher George Ridley Nugent, *b* 5 Oct. 1949. *Address:* Staneway, Tyrrells Wood, Leatherhead, Surrey. *T:* Leatherhead 3243. *Club:* Guards.

**NUNBURNHOLME,** 3rd Baron, *cr* 1906; **Charles John Wilson;** Hon. Captain, QO York Dragoons; *b* 25 April 1904; *s* of 2nd Baron and Lady Marjorie Wynn-Carrington (*d* 1968), *d* of 1st Marquess of Lincolnshire; *S* father, 1924, *m* 1st 1927, Lady Mary Thynne (from whom he obtained a divorce, 1947; she *m* 2nd, 1947, Rt Hon. Sir Ulick Alexander, *qv*) *y d* of 5th Marquess of Bath, KG, PC, CB; two *s* one *d;* 2nd, 1953, Alex, *o d* of Captain D. Hockly, Kent; one *s*. *Educ:* Eton. Served War of 1939-45 (wounded El Alamein); discharged 1943. *Heir: s* Captain Hon. Ben Charles Wilson, RHG [*b* 16 July 1928; *m* 1958, Ines Dolores Jeanne Walravens; four *d* (including twin *d*]. *Address:* Priory Lands, Appledore, Kent. *T:* Appledore 228.

*See also Viscount Chaplin.*

**NUNN, Jean Josephine,** CBE 1966; Deputy Secretary, Cabinet Office, 1966-70; *b* 21 July 1916; *d* of late Major John Henry Nunn, RHA, and Mrs Doris Josephine Nunn (*née* Gregory); unmarried. *Educ:* The Royal School for Daughters of Officers of the Army, Bath; Girton Coll., Cambridge. Entered Home Office, 1938; Secretary, Royal Commission on the Press, 1947-49; Private Secretary to the Secretary of State, 1949-51; Assistant Secretary, 1952; Assistant Under-Secretary of State, 1961-63; Under-Secretary, Cabinet Office, 1963-66. *Recreations:* gardening, bird-watching, reading. *Address:* 806 Nelson House, Dolphin Square, SW1. *T:* 01-828 6902. *Club:* Royal Commonwealth Society.

**NUNN, Prof. John Francis,** PhD; MD; FFA, RCS; Director, Division of Anaesthesia, Medical Research Council Clinical Research Centre, since 1968; *b* 7 Nov. 1925; *s* of Francis Nunn, Colwyn Bay; *m* 1949, Sheila, *d* of late E. C. Doubleday; one *s* two *d*. *Educ:* Wrekin Coll.; Birmingham Univ. MO, Birmingham Univ. Spitzbergen Expedition, 1948; Colonial Med. Service, Malaya, 1949-53; University Research Fellow, Birmingham, 1955-56; Leverhulme Research Fellow, RCS, 1957-64; Part-time Lectr, Postgrad. Med. Sch., Univ. of London, 1959-64; Consultant Anæsth., Hammersmith Hosp., 1959-64; Prof. of Anaesthesia, Univ. of Leeds, 1964-68. Member Board, Faculty of Anaesthetists, RCS; Hunterian Professor, RCS, 1960; Visiting Professor to various American Universities, 1960-70; British Council Lecturer: Switzerland, 1962; USSR, 1963; Czechoslovakia, 1969. Joseph Clover Lectr, RCS, 1968. Mem., Cambrian Archaeological Soc. *Publications:* Applied Respiratory Physiology, 1969; several chapters in medical text-books, and publications in Journal appl. Physiol., Lancet, Nature, British Journal Anæsth., etc. *Recreations:* archaeology and ski-ing. *Address:* MRC Clinical Research Centre, Northwick Park, Harrow, Middx; 3 Russell Road, Moor Park, Northwood, Middx. *T:* Northwood 26363.

**NUNN, William,** FRHistS; *b* 1879; *m* 1905, Mary (*decd*), *d* of John Fowler, Aberdeen; one *s*. *Educ:* King's Coll., London. Entered Civil Service, 1899; Adviser on Customs and Excise, Siamese Government, 1909-24; MP (C) Whitehaven Division of Cumberland, 1931-35; MP (C) Newcastle West Division, 1940-45. *Address:* Gillgrass, Gosforth, Cumberland. *T:* Gosforth 237. *Club:* Junior Carlton.

**NUNNELEY, John Hewlett;** MInstT; Managing Director, British Transport Advertising Ltd, since 1969; Director: Skyways Coach Air Ltd; Central Outdoor Advertising Sales Ltd; *B* 26 Nov. 1922; *o s* of Lt-Col Wilfrid Alexander Nunneley, Crow's Nest, Sydney, NSW, Aust., and Audrey Mary Nunneley (*née* Tebbitt); *m* 1945, Lucia, *e d* of Enrico Ceruti, Milan, Italy; one *s* one *d*. *Educ:* Lawrence Sheriff Sch., Rugby. Served War of 1939-45: Somerset LI, seconded KAR; Abyssinia, Brit. Somaliland, 1942; Burma campaign, 1944 (wounded, despatches); Captain and Adjt. Various management posts in aircraft, shipping, printing and publishing industries, 1946-55. Exec., Beaverbrook Newspapers, 1955-62; joined BTC, 1962: Chief Publicity Officer, 1962-63; Chief Development Officer (Passenger) BR Bd, 1963-64; Chief Passenger Manager, 1964-69; Pres. and Chm., BR-Internat. Inc., New York, USA, 1966-69; Member: Paddington Borough Council, 1951-53; Inst. of Travel Agents, 1964; Passenger Co-ordination Cttee for London, 1964-69; Outdoor Advertising Council, 1969-. *Publications:* numerous articles on transport and advertising subjects. *Recreation:* walking. *Address:* 11 Riverview Gardens, Barnes, SW13. *Club:* East India and Sports.

**NUREYEV, Rudolf;** ballet dancer and choreographer; *b* Ufa, E. Siberia, 1939, of a farming family. Joined Kirov Ballet School and at age 17 appeared with the Company in 1959; when on tour, in Paris, sought political asylum, May 1961. Joined Le Grand Ballet du Marquis de Cuevas Company and has made frequent appearances abroad; London debut at Royal Academy of Dancing Gala Matinée, organised by Dame Margot Fonteyn, Dec. 1961; debut at Covent Garden in Giselle with Margaret Fonteyn, Feb. 1962; did choreography for, and danced in Nutcracker, Covent Garden, 1968; guest artist in England and America in wide variety of rôles, mostly with Dame Margot Fonteyn. Has danced in many countries of the world. Gold Star, Paris, 1963. *Publication:* Nureyev, 1962. *Recreations:* listening to and playing music. *Address:* c/o Royal Opera House, Covent Garden, WC2.

**NURSE, Ven. Charles Euston,** MA; Archdeacon of Carlisle, 1958-70; *b* 12 June 1909; *s* of Rev. Canon Euston John Nurse, MA, and Mrs Edith Jane Robins Nurse, Windermere Rectory. *Educ:* Windermere Grammar Sch.; Gonville and Caius Coll., Cambridge. Assistant Curate, Holy Trinity, Carlisle, 1932; Vicar of St Nicholas, Whitehaven, 1937; Vicar of St George, Barrow-in-Furness, 1948; Rural Dean of Dalton, 1949; Hon. Canon of Carlisle Cathedral, 1950-. Examining Chaplain to the Bishop of Carlisle, 1959-. *Recreations:* fell-walking, fishing, tennis, entomology. *Address:* 4 The Abbey, Carlisle. *T:* Carlisle 24991.

**NUSSEY, Sir Thomas Moore,** 2nd Bt, *cr* 1909; JP for N. Riding of Yorkshire; *b* 19 July 1898; *s* of Sir William Nussey, 1st Bt, and Edith (*d* 1934), *d* of E. M. Daniel, MD, Fleetwood, and Mrs Daniel, Saxfield, Scarborough; *S* father, 1947; *m* 1941, Viva Frances, *yr d* of late Benjamin Talbot. *Educ:* Eton; RMC, Sandhurst; King's Coll., Cambridge (BA). Lieut, 17th Lancers. Served European War, 1914-18, 1917-22. *Heir:* none. *Address:* Rushwood, East Tanfield, Ripon. *Clubs:* Brooks's, Leander.

**NUTMAN, Dr Philip Sadler,** FRS 1968; Head of Department of Soil Microbiology, Rothamsted Experimental Station, Harpenden, since 1957; *b* 10 Oct. 1914; *s* of John William Nutman and Elizabeth Hester Nutman (*née* Hughes); *m* 1940, Mary Meta Stanbury; two *s* one *d*. *Educ:* Teignmouth Grammar Sch.; Imperial Coll., London Univ. Research Asst, Rothamsted Experimental Station, 1940; Senior Research Fellow, Canberra, Australia, 1953-56; Rothamsted, 1956-. Huxley Medal, 1959. *Publications:* research papers in plant physiological, genetical and microbiological journals. *Recreations:* music, woodworking. *Address:* 2 Lyndhurst Drive, Harpenden, Herts. *T:* Harpenden 4249.

**NUTT, Albert Boswell,** FRCS; Ophthalmic Surgeon, United Sheffield Hospitals, 1948-63; *b* 7 July 1898; *s* of late Ernest Smith Nutt; *m* Olive Margaret Robson; two *s* one *d*. *Educ:* King Edward VII Sch., Sheffield; University of Sheffield; University of London. MSc Sheffield, 1922; MB, ChB Sheffield (Clinical Gold Medal in Medicine and Surgery), 1923; MB, BS London, 1923; FRCS 1949. Formerly Ophthalmic Registrar, House Surgeon and Senior Ophthalmic House Surgeon, Sheffield Royal Infirmary; Hon. Ophthalmic Surgeon, 1927-48; Hon. Ophthalmic Surgeon to Children's Hospital, Sheffield, 1938-48; Hunterian Professor, RCS, 1954; Member: Council, RCS, 1953-58 (Rep. of Ophthalmology); Standing Ophth. Advisory Cttee to Min. of Health; Council of Faculty of Ophthalmology, 1947-68 (Pres. 1963-65, Vice-Pres. 1951-53, Treasurer 1949-51); of Ophthalmic Soc. of UK, 1941-44 (Vice-Pres. 1950-53); Member Court of Examiners, RCS, 1957-63; External Examiner to University of Belfast, 1960-63; Chairman, British Orthoptic Board, 1958-70; Vice-Chm., British Orthoptists' Bd, 1966-70. Hon. Lecturer in Ophthalmology, Univ. of Sheffield, 1960-61; Pres., Faculty of Ophthalmology, 1963-64; Master of Oxford Ophthalmol. Congress, 1961-62; Mem. Council, Court, and Convocation Univ. of Sheffield (Chm. of Convocation, 1964-67); Mem. Court, Univ. of

Bradford. Mem. Sheffield Town Trust. Fellow: Royal Society of Medicine; Hunterian Society; Mem. Soc. Franc. d'Ophthalmologie; Hon. Mem., Australian Coll. of Ophthalmology (Guest Lecturer, 1954, 1963). Past Pres., Sheffield Medico and Chirurgical Soc. Liveryman, Soc. of Apothecaries of London; Freeman, City of London. OStJ. *Publications:* contributions to medical journals, including BMJ, Trans. Ophth. Soc. of UK, Trans. Ophth. Soc. of Australia, British Orthoptic. Journal, The Practitioner, etc. *Recreations:* masonry, golf, gardening. *Address:* 344 Glossop Road, Sheffield S10 2HW. *T:* Sheffield 24876; Thornsett, Dore Road, Sheffield. *T:* 360752. *Clubs:* Sheffield (Sheffield); Lindrick Golf; Royal and Ancient (St Andrews).

**NUTT, A. E. W.**; *see* Woodward-Nutt.

**NUTTALL, Sir Nicholas Keith Lillington,** 3rd Bt, *cr* 1922; *b* 21 Sept. 1933; *s* of Lieut-Colonel Sir E. Keith Nuttall, 2nd Bt, RE (who died on active service, Aug. 1941), and Gytha Primrose Harrison (*d* 1967), *e d* of Sidney H. Burgess, of Heathfield, Bowdon, Cheshire; *S* father, 1941; *m* 1960, Rosemary Caroline, *e d* of Christopher York, *qv*; one *s* one *d*. *Educ:* Eton; Royal Military Academy, Sandhurst. Commissioned Royal Horse Guards, 1953; Captain, 1959; Major 1966; retd 1968. Chm., Edmund Nuttall, Sons & Co. (London) Ltd, 1967-. *Heir:* *s* Harry Nuttall, *b* 2 Jan. 1963. *Address:* Lowesby Hall, Leicester LE7 9DD. *T:* Hungarton 239/225; 12 Lowndes Close, SW1. *T:* 01-235 4918. *Clubs:* Buck's, White's.

**NUTTALL, Major William F. Dixon-**; *see* Dixon-Nuttall.

**NUTTING, Rt. Hon. Anthony**; *see* Nutting, Rt Hon. H. A.

**NUTTING, Rt. Hon. (Harold) Anthony,** PC 1954; *b* 11 Jan. 1920; 3rd and *y* (now *o surv*) *s* of Sir Harold Nutting, 2nd Bt, *qv*; *m* 1st, 1941, Gillian Leonora (marr. diss., 1959), *d* of Edward J. Strutt, Hatfield Peverel, Essex; two *s* one *d*; 2nd, 1961, Anne Gunning Parker. *Educ:* Eton; Trinity College, Cambridge. Leics. Yeo., 1939; invalided, 1940. In HM Foreign Service, 1940-45; MP (C) Melton Division of Leics, 1945-56, resigned. Chairman: Young Conservative and Unionist Movement, 1946; National Union of Conservative and Unionist Associations, 1950; Conservative National Executive Cttee, 1951. Parliamentary Under-Secretary of State for Foreign Affairs, 1951-54; Minister of State for Foreign Affairs, 1954-56, resigned. Leader, UK Delegn to UN General Assembly and to UN Disarmament Commn, 1954-56. *Publications:* I Saw for Myself, 1958; Disarmament, 1959; Europe Will Not Wait, 1960; Lawrence of Arabia, 1961; The Arabs, 1964; Gordon, Martyr and Misfit, 1966; No End of a Lesson, 1967. *Recreation:* fishing. *Address:* 47 Addison Road, W14. *Club:* Boodle's.

**NUTTING, Sir Harold Stansmore,** 2nd Bt, *cr* 1902; DL; Lt-Col Commanding Leics Bn Home Guard; late Captain 17th Lancers; *b* 14 Aug. 1882; *s* of 1st Bt and Mary Stansmore, *d* of Restel R. Bevis, Manor Hill, Claughton, Cheshire; *m* 1913, Enid Hester Nina (*d* 1961), *d* of late F. B. Homan-Mulock, Bellair, King's County; one *s* (two killed on active service); *S* father, 1918. Late ADC to Governor-General, Australia; served in France during European War, 1914-18; Master North Shropshire Hounds, 1919-20; Master of Meynell Hounds, 1920-29; Master of Quorn Hounds, 1930-40. *Heir:* *s* Rt Hon. Harold Anthony Nutting, *qv*. *Address:* Quenby Hall, Leicester. *T:* Hungerton 234; Achentoul Lodge, Kinbrace, Sutherland. *Clubs:* Turf, Cavalry, Bath, Royal Automobile.

**NUTTING, Prof. Jack,** MA, ScD, PhD; Professor of Metallurgy and Chairman, Houldsworth School of Applied Science, University of Leeds, since 1960; *b* 8 June 1924; *o s* of Edgar and Ethel Nutting, Mirfield, Yorks; *m* 1950, Thelma Kippax, *y d* of Tom and Florence Kippax, Morecambe, Lancs; one *s* two *d*. *Educ:* Mirfield Grammar School, Yorks; Univ. of Leeds. BSc Leeds, 1945; PhD Leeds, 1948; MA Cantab, 1952; ScD Cantab, 1967. Research at Cavendish Laboratory, Cambridge, 1948-49; University Demonstrator, 1949-54, University Lecturer, 1954-60, Department of Metallurgy, Cambridge University. Awarded Beilby medal and prize, 1961; Hadfield medal and prize, 1964. Hon. DSc, Acad. of Mining and Metallurgy, Cracow, 1969. *Publications:* numerous papers in Journal of Iron and Steel Institute and Institute of Metals. *Recreations:* foreign travel, mountain walking. *Address:* St Mary's, 57 Westwood Lane, Headingley, Leeds LS1 5NP. *T:* Leeds 51400.

**NYE, Sir Geoffrey (Walter),** KCMG 1960 (CMG 1953); OBE 1944; Chairman, Cotton Research Corporation; *b* 5 September 1902; *e s* of Stanley Nye and Gertrude Maude Kate Nye (*née* Baker); *m* 1929, Jean Etheline Stone; one *s* two *d*. *Educ:* Forest School; Wye College (BSc); Imperial Coll. of Science and Technology; Cambridge Univ.; Imperial Coll. of Tropical Agriculture, Trinidad. Dept of Agriculture, Uganda: Cotton Botanist, 1924; Senior Botanist, 1932; Deputy Director of Agriculture, 1940. Director of Agriculture, Nyasaland, 1945; Asst Agricultural Adviser, Colonial Office, 1947; Dep. Agric. Adviser, 1948-56; Agric. Adviser to: Sec. of State for the Colonies, 1956-61; Dept of Tech. Co-op., 1961-64; Min. of Overseas Develt, 1964-66. Director, Overseas Service Unit, Reading Univ., 1966-67. Awarded Silver Acorn by Chief Scout, 1944. Hon. Fellow of Wye College, 1960. *Recreations:* gardening, philately. *Address:* Barnabas, Brittenden Lane, Waldron, Heathfield, Sussex. *T:* Heathfield 2843.

**NYERERE, Julius Kambarage;** President, United Republic of Tanzania (formerly Tanganyika and Zanzibar), since 1964; Minister of Foreign Affairs since 1965; President Tanganyika African National Union, since 1954; First Chancellor, University of East Africa, since 1963; *b* 1922; *m* 1953, Maria Magige; five *s* two *d*. *Educ:* Tabora Secondary School; Makerere University College; Edinburgh University (MA). Began as Teacher; became President African Association, Dar es Salaam, 1953; formed Tanganyika African National Union, left teaching and campaigned for Nationalist Movement, 1954; addressed Trusteeship Council, 1955, and Cttee of UN Gen. Assembly, 1956. MLC Tanganyika, July-Dec. 1957, resigned in protest; elected Mem. for E Prov. in first elections, 1958, for Dar es Salaam, 1960; Chief Minister, 1960; Prime Minister of Tanganyika, 1961-62; President, Tanganyika Republic, 1962-64. Holds hon. degrees. *Publications:* Freedom and Unity–Uhuru Na Umoja, 1966; Freedom and Socialism–Uhuru na Ujamaa, 1969; Essays on Socialism, 1969; Swahili trans of Julius Caesar and The Merchant of Venice, 1969. *Address:* State House, Dar es Salaam, United Republic of Tanzania.

**NYHOLM, Prof. Sir Ronald (Sydney),** Kt 1967; FRS 1958; DSc; PhD; FRIC; Head of the

Department of Chemistry, University College, London, since 1963, Professor of Chemistry since 1955; Fellow of University College, London, since 1959; *b* Broken Hill, NSW, 29 Jan. 1917; *s* of Eric Edward Nyholm, formerly of Goodwood, S Aust., and Gertrude Mary Nyholm (*née* Woods), Marryatville, SA; *m* 1948, Maureen Richardson, Sydney; one *s* two *d*. *Educ:* Broken Hill High School; Sydney and London Universities. BSc (1st Cl. Hons), Sydney, 1938, MSc 1942. Lecturer in Chemistry, Sydney Technical College, 1940; ICI Fellowship, London Univ., 1947; PhD (Lond.), 1950; DSc (Lond.) 1953; Assoc. Prof. of Inorganic Chemistry, NSW Univ. of Technology, 1952; Pres. Roy. Soc. of NSW, 1954. Corr. Member Finnish Chemical Soc., 1959. Fellow Royal Australian Chemical Institute (Russell-Grimwade Lectr, 1969); Peter C. Reilly Lecturer, Univ. of Notre Dame, USA, 1957; F. P. Dwyer Medallist and Lectr, 1960; Archer D. Little Lectr, MIT, 1969. Pres., Chem. Soc. of London, 1968-70 (Tilden Lectr 1960, Liversidge Lectr, 1968, of the Soc.); Mem. Science Research Council, 1967-68; President: Assoc. for Science Educn, 1967-; XII Internat. Conf. on Coordination Chemistry. Trustee, British Museum, 1968-. Hon. ScD East Anglia, 1968, City Univ., 1968; Univ. of NSW, 1969. Corday-Morgan Medal and Prize, Chem. Soc. London, 1950; H. G. Smith Meml Medal, Royal Aust. Chem. Inst., 1955; Roy. Medal, Roy. Soc. of NSW, 1963; Gold Medal of Italian Chem. Soc., 1968; Sigillum Magnum, Univ. of Podogna, 1969. *Publications:* approx. 250 research papers dealing mainly with chemistry of complex compounds in Jl Chem. Soc. of Lond., Proc. Roy. Soc. of NSW, Inorganic Chemistry, etc. Recent Progress in Stereochemistry (part author), Vols I and II, 1954, 1958. *Recreations:* cricket, tennis, and walking. *Address:* Chemistry Department, University College, WC1; 21 Manor Road South, Hinchley Wood, Esher, Surrey. *T:* 01-398 5338.

# O

**OAKELEY, Sir (Edward) Atholl,** 7th Bt *cr* 1790; retired; *b* 31 May 1900; *s* of late Major E. F. Oakeley, South Lancashire Regiment, and late Everilde A. Oakeley, *d* of Henry Beaumont; *S* cousin (Sir Charles Richard Andrew Oakeley, 6th Bt), 1959; *m* 1st, 1922, Ethyl Felice O'Coffey (marr. diss.); 2nd, (Patricia) Mabel Mary (*née* Birtchnell) (marr. diss.); one *s*; 3rd, Doreen (*née* Wells) (marr. diss.); 4th, 1960, Shirley Church; one *d*. *Educ:* Clifton and Sandhurst. Lieutenant, Oxfordshire and Buckinghamshire Light Infantry, 1919-23; then Chief Contact to late Sir Charles Higham in Advertising; Captain, Amateur International Wrestling Team, 1928-29; Heavyweight wrestling Champion of Europe, 1932; Heavyweight Wrestling Champion of Gt Britain, 1930-35; Manager to World Heavyweight Wrestling Champion, Jack Sherry, 1935-39; Promoter of Championship Wrestling, Harringay Arena, 1949-54. *Recreations:* cricket; hunting; athletics; sailing; wrestling; boxing; weight-lifting. *Heir: s* John Digby Atholl Oakeley [*b* 27 Nov. 1932; *m* 1958, Maureen, *d* of John and Helen Cox, Hamble, Hants; one *s* one *d*]. *Address:* Glen Doone, Oare, Brendon, N Devon. *Club:* Hamble River Sailing.

*See also M. Oakeley.*

**OAKELEY, Mary,** MA Oxon.; Headmistress, St Felix School, Southwold, since 1958; *b* 2 Apr. 1913; *d* of Maj. Edward Francis Oakeley, S Lancs Regt, and Everilde Anne (*née* Beaumont). *Educ:* St John's Bexhill-on-Sea; St Hilda's Coll., Oxford. MA Hons History. Asst Mistress: St James's, West Malvern, 1935-38; St George's, Ascot, 1938-39; Headmistress, Craighead Diocesan Sch., Timaru, NZ, 1940-55; Head of American Section, La Châtelainie, St Blaise, Switz., 1956-58. *Recreations:* ski-ing, gardening, embroidery. *Address:* Cherwell Lodge, Eynsham, Oxon. *T:* Eynsham 305. *Club:* Royal Over-Seas League.

*See also Sir Atholl Oakeley, Bt.*

**OAKES, Sir Christopher,** 3rd Bt, *cr* 1939; *b* 10 July 1949; *s* of Sir Sydney Oakes and Greta, *yr d* of Gunnar Victor Hartmann, Copenhagen, Denmark; *S* father, 1966. *Educ:* Bredon, Tewkesbury; Georgia Mil. Acad., USA. *Heir: uncle* Harry Philip Oakes [*b* 30 Aug. 1932; *m* 1958, Christiane, *o d* of Rudolf Botsch, Hamburg; three *s* one *d*]. *Address:* PO Box 1002, Nassau, Bahamas.

**OAKES, Gordon James;** Solicitor; *b* 22 June 1931; *o s* of James Oakes and Florence (*née* Hewitt), Widnes, Lancs; *m* 1952, Esther O'Neill, *e d* of Councillor Joseph O'Neill; three *s*. *Educ:* Wade Deacon Gram. Sch., Widnes; Univ. of Liverpool. BA (Hon.) English, 1952; Admitted Solicitor, 1956. Entered Widnes Borough Council, 1952 (Mayor, 1964-65). Chm. Widnes Constituency Labour Party, 1953-58; contested (Lab): Bebington, 1959; Moss Side (Manchester) by-election, 1961; MP (Lab) Bolton West, 1964-70; PPS, Home Office, 1966-67, Dept of Education and Science, 1967-70. British Deleg., NATO Parliamentarians, 1967-; Mem., Select Cttee on Race Relations, 1969-. *Publications:* various articles. *Recreations:* conversation, motoring with the family, caravanning. *Address:* Somersby, 9 Birchfield Rd, Widnes, Lancs. *T:* Widnes 4405.

**OAKESHOTT, Keith Robertson,** CMG 1967; Assistant Under-Secretary of State, Foreign and Commonwealth Office, seconded to Civil Service Commission, since 1970; *b* 9 Feb. 1920; *s* of Harold Alan and Cecil Robertson Oakeshott, JP; *m* 1946, Eva Jill Clutterbuck; one *s* four *d*. *Educ:* Royal Grammar School, High Wycombe; Corpus Christi Coll., Oxford (MA). Served in RAF, 1940-46. Joined Foreign (now Diplomatic) Service, 1946; 3rd Sec., FO, 1946; Vice-Consul, Shanghai, 1947; 2nd Sec., FO, 1949; 1st Sec., 1951; 1st Sec. and Head of Chancery, Rangoon, 1953; FO, 1956; 1st Sec. and Head of Chancery, Moscow, 1959; Counsellor, Havana, 1962; HM Consul-General, Hamburg, 1962-67; Home Inspector, 1967-70. *Recreations:* gardening, weekend farming. *Address:* Little Coltstaple Farm, near Horsham, Sussex. *T:* Southwater 385. *Club:* Royal Commonwealth Society.

**OAKESHOTT, Michael Joseph,** FBA 1966; MA; Professor Emeritus, University of London, 1969; *b* 11 Dec. 1901; *s* of Joseph Francis Oakeshott and Frances Maude Hellicar. *Educ:* St George's School, Harpenden; Gonville and Caius College, Cambridge. Fellow: Gonville and Caius College, 1925-; Nuffield College, Oxford, 1949-50 University Prof. of Political Science at LSE, Univ. of London, 1951-69. Served in British Army, 1940-45. Muirhead Lecturer, Univ. of Birmingham, 1953. *Publications:* Experience and its Modes, 1933: A Guide to the Classics (with G. T. Griffith), 1936, 1947; Social and Political Doctrines of Contemporary Europe, 1939; Hobbes's Leviathan, 1946; The Voice of Poetry in the Conversation of Mankind, 1959; Rationalism in Politics and other Essays, 1962. *Address:* 16 New Row, WC2.

**OAKESHOTT, Walter Fraser,** MA, FSA; Hon. LLD (St Andrews); Rector of Lincoln College, Oxford, since April 1954; a Trustee of the Pilgrim Trust since 1949; *b* 11 Nov. 1903; *s* of Walter Field Oakeshott, MD, and Kathleen Fraser; *m* 1928, Noël Rose, *d* of R. O. Moon, MD, FRCP; twin *s* two *d*. *Educ:* Tonbridge; Balliol Coll., Oxford. Class. Mods 1924; Lit. Hum. 1926; Assistant Master, Bec School, SW17, 1926-27; Assistant Master Merchant Taylors', 1927-30; Kent Education Office, 1930-31; Assistant Master Winchester College, 1931-38; released for 15 months (1936-37) for membership of Pilgrim Trust Unemployment Enquiry; High Master of St Paul's School, 1939-46; Headmaster of Winchester College, 1946-54. Vice-Chancellor, Oxford University, 1962-64; Pro-Vice-Chancellor, 1964-66. President, Bibliographical Society, 1966-68. Rhind Lecturer, Edinburgh Univ., 1956. Master, Skinners' Co., 1960-61. *Publications:* Men Without Work (joint), 1938; The Artists of the Winchester Bible, 1945; The Mosaics of Rome, Fourth to Fourteenth Centuries, 1967; various semi-popular books on literature and medieval art. *Recreations:* pictures, books. *Address:* Lincoln College, Oxford. *Club:* Roxburghe.

**OAKHAM, Archdeacon of;** *see* Towndrow, Ven. F. N.

**OAKLEY, Rev. Austin;** Vicar of St John's, Ladbroke Grove, London, W11, 1944-62; Secretary, Anglican and Eastern Orthodox Churches Association, 1945-53, Chairman of Committee, 1953-69, Hon. President, since 1969; *b* India, 1890; *e s* of Rev. E. S. Oakley, MA, KHM, Almora, United Provinces, India; *m* 1928, Mary Alice, MB, BS, DPH (*d* 1963), *o d* of Charles Fraser van Ingen, Indian Telegraphs. *Educ:* School for the Sons of Missionaries, Blackheath; King's College School, Wimbledon; King's College, London; House of the Sacred Mission, Kelham, Newark-on-Trent. Ordained 1915; went out to South Africa, 1920; Director of St Barnabas, Masite, Basutoland, and Principal of Masite Training School, 1922; in charge of Ingwavuma Mission, Zululand, 1925; Priest-in-charge of St Mark's, Limon, Costa Rica, and Archdeacon in Central America, in the diocese of British Honduras, 1928-34; Chaplain to HBM Embassy in Turkey and Crimean Memorial Church, Istanbul, 1934-43. Order of Patriarchal Cross of St Andrew, 1965. *Publications:* The Orthodox Liturgy; articles on Orthodoxy and the Near East. *Recreations:* gardening, painting. *Address:* Breakspear Cottage, Knighton, Shrivenham, Swindon, Wilts. *Club:* Reform.

**OAKLEY, Prof. Cyril Leslie,** CBE 1970; MD; FRS 1957; Brotherton Professor of Bacteriology, University of Leeds, since 1953; *b* 20 June 1907; *er c* of George and Ellen Oakley; *m* 1933, Emily Meadows; two *d*. *Educ:* St Mary's Rd School, Portsmouth; Westminster City School; Chelsea Polytechnic; University College, London; University College Hospital. MRCS, LRCP 1930; MB, BS (London), 1930; BSc (London) 1st Cl. Hons Zoology, 1930. Graham Scholar in Pathology, University Coll. Hosp. Med. Sch., 1930-33; MD (London), 1933; DSc (London), 1953. Experimental Pathologist, Wellcome Research Laboratories, 1934-47; Head, Immunology and Experimental Pathology Dept, Wellcome Research Laboratories, 1947-53. Fellow University Coll. London, 1950. President Association of Scientific Workers, 1956-59. Member of Council, College of Pathologists, 1963-64, 1965-68; First Cameron Lecturer, 1965; Hon. Archivist, 1963-. Mem. Agricultural Research Council, 1963-. Editor: Jl of Pathology and Bacteriology, 1956- (Asst Editor, 1950-55); Jl of Medical Microbiology, 1968-; Jl of Pathology, 1969-. *Recreations:* parasitic copepods, spiders; mediæval churches. *Address:* 14 Cardigan Road, Headingley, Leeds 6. *T:* Leeds 53990.

**OAKLEY, Kenneth Page,** DSc; FBA; Deputy Keeper (Anthropology) British Museum (Natural History), 1959-69; *b* 7 April 1911; *s* of Tom Page Oakley, BSc, LCP, Amersham; *m* 1941, Edith Margaret Martin; two *s*. *Educ:* Amersham Grammar School; University College School, Hampstead; University College, London. BSc in geology and anthropology, 1933; PhD 1938, DSc 1955. Geologist in Geological Survey, GB, 1934-35; Asst Keeper Dept of Geology (Palæontology), Brit. Mus. (Nat. Hist.), 1935 (seconded to Geological Survey for war-time service); Principal Scientific Officer, 1947-55; Senior Principal, 1955-69; head of Anthropology Sub-Dept, 1959-69. Rosa Morison Memorial Medal, University Coll., London, 1933; Wollaston Fund, 1941; Prestwich Medal, Geological Soc. of London, 1963; Henry Stopes Memorial Medal, Geologists' Assoc., 1952. Sec. Geol. Soc. Lond., 1946-49. Pres., Anthropological Section, British Assoc. for Advancement of Science, 1961. Collecting and research expeditions to East Africa, 1947, and South Africa, 1953. Viking Fund (Wenner-Gren Foundn) Lectures, New York, 1950, 1952; Royal Institution Discourse, 1953; Visiting Professor in Anthropology, University of Chicago, 1956. Corresponding Member, Istituto Italiano di Paleontologia Umana, 1955; FSA 1953; FBA 1957; Fellow of University Coll., London, 1958. *Publications:* Man the Tool-maker, Brit. Mus. Nat. Hist., 1949 (5th edn 1961) (reprinted in Phœnix Books, Chicago, 1957); The Fluorine-dating Method (in Year-book of Physical Anthropology for 1949), 1951; (part-author) The Solution of the Piltdown Problem (Bull. Brit. Mus. Nat. Hist.), 1953; Frameworks for Dating Fossil Man, 1964 (3rd edn 1969); The Problem of Man's Antiquity (Brit. Mus. Nat. Hist.), 1964; (Co-ed) Catalogue of Fossil Hominids (Brit. Mus. Nat. Hist.), part 1, Africa, 1967, part 2, Europe, 1971. *Recreations:* listening to music, art, pursuit of the unusual, folklore. *Address:* 2 Islip Place, Summertown, Oxford OX2 7SR. *T:* Oxford 56524; 2 Chestnut Close, Amersham, Bucks.

**OAKLEY, Wilfrid George,** MD, FRCP; Physician, King's College Hospital, since 1946; Hon. Physician, St Andrew's Hospital, Dollis Hill, since 1948; *b* 23 Aug. 1905; *s* of late Rev. Canon G. D. Oakley and Mrs Oakley; *m* 1931, Hermione Violet Wingate-Saul; one *s*. *Educ:* Durham School; Gonville and Caius College, Cambridge; St Bartholomew's Hospital. Tancred studentship in Physic, Gonville and Caius Coll., 1923; Bentley Prize and Baly Research Schol., St Bart's Hosp., 1933. Asst to Med. Prof. Unit, and Casualty Phys., St Bart.'s Hosp.; Exam. Conjoint Bd, 1946-50. MD (Hon. Mention) Cantab 1934; FRCP 1942. FRSocMed; Mem. Assoc. of Physicians of Great Britain. *Publications:* scientific articles and chapters in various text-books on diabetes and other metabolic disorders. *Recreation:* golf. *Address:* 149 Harley Street, W1. *T:* 01-935 4444.

**OAKSEY, Lord;** *see under* Trevethin and Oaksey.

**OAKSHOTT,** family name of **Baron Oakshott.**

**OAKSHOTT,** Baron, *cr* 1964, of Bebington (Life Peer); **Hendrie Dudley Oakshott,** Bt *cr* 1959; MBE 1942; *b* 8 Nov. 1904; *s* of Arthur John Oakshott, JP, Bidston, Cheshire, and Elizabeth Strathearn, *d* of Matthew Leggat, Hamilton, Ont.; *m* 1928, Joan, *d* of Marsden Withington, London and Buenos Aires; two *s*. *Educ:* Rugby; Trinity Coll., Cambridge. Served in Middle East and Italy, 1940-44 (despatches); retired, 1945, Lieutenant-Colonel. MP (C) Bebington, 1950-64. An Assistant Whip (unpaid), 1951-52; a Lord Commissioner of the Treasury, 1952-55; Comptroller of HM Household, 1955-57; Treasurer of HM Household, 1957-59. Parl. Private Sec.: to Foreign Secretary, 1959-60; to Chancellor of the Exchequer, 1960-62. Member, Totalisator Board, 1964-. *Recreation:* racing. *Heir:* (*to Baronetcy*): *s* Hon. Anthony Hendrie Oakshott [*b* 10 Oct. 1929; *m* 1965, Mrs Valerie de Pret-Roose, *d* of Jack Vlasto, Hans Place, SW1]. *Address:* The Mount, Broxton, Cheshire. *T:* 215; 42 Eaton Square, SW1. *T:* 01-235 2107. *Clubs:* Turf, Pratt's, Boodle's.

**OATEN, Edward Farley,** MA, LLB; *b* 24 Feb. 1884; *e s* of Samuel Oaten, Tunbridge Wells; *m* 1st, 1914; one *s* one *d*; 2nd, 1931, Kathleen Mary, *step-d.* of late T. Mullett Ellis, Shepperton; one *d*. *Educ:* Skinners' School, Tunbridge Wells; Tonbridge School; Sidney Sussex College, Cambridge (Scholar); twice Le Bas Cambridge University Prizeman. Appointed to Indian Educational Service as Professor of History, Presidency College, Calcutta, 1909; Calcutta Light Horse to 1916; thence to 1919 in IARO attached 11th KEO Lancers on North-West Frontier and in Punjab, including Waziristan Campaign, 1917; Lt 1917; Acting Captain, 1919; Officiating Assistant Director, Muhammadan Education, Bengal, 1919; Assistant Director of Public Instruction, Bengal, 1921; Officiating Deputy Secretary to Government of Bengal, 1924-25; Director of Public Instruction, Bengal, 1924; retired 1930; nominated Member, Bengal Legislative Council; Fellow, Calcutta Univ.; Major, Auxiliary Force, India, and Commandant, 2nd (Calcutta) Battalion, University Training Corps, 1927; called to Bar (Middle Temple), 1932. *Publications:* A Sketch of Anglo-Indian Literature; European Travellers in India; Glimpses of India's History; Song of Aton and other verses; contributed to Cambridge History of English Literature. *Recreation:* genealogy. *Address:* 9 Beech Close, Walton-on-Thames, Surrey. *T:* Walton-on-Thames 24477.

**OATES, Thomas,** CMG 1962; OBE 1958 (MBE 1946); Permanent Secretary, Gibraltar, since 1968; *b* 5 November 1917; *er s* of Thomas Oates, Wadebridge, Cornwall; unmarried. *Educ:* Callington Grammar School, Cornwall; Trinity College, Cambridge (MA). Mathematical Tripos (Wrangler). Admiralty Scientific Staff, 1940-46; HMS Vernon, Minesweeping Section, 1940-42; British Admiralty Delegn, Washington, DC, 1942-46; Temp. Lieut, RNVR Colonial Administrative Service, Nigeria, 1948-55; seconded to HM Treasury, 1953-55; Adviser to UK Delegn to UN Gen. Assembly, 1954. Financial Sec. to Govt of: British Honduras, 1955-59, Aden, 1959-63; Dep. High Comr, Aden, 1963-67. *Recreations:* photography, walking, ski-ing. *Address:* Permanent Secretary's Office, Gibraltar. *Clubs:* East India and Sports, Royal Commonwealth Society, RNVR.

**OATLEY, Charles William,** OBE 1956; MA; FRS 1969, FIEE, FIEEE; Professor of Electrical Engineering, University of Cambridge, since 1960; Fellow of Trinity College, Cambridge, since 1945; *b* 14 Feb. 1904; *s* of William Oatley and Ada Mary Dorrington; *m* 1930, Dorothy Enid West; two *s*. *Educ:* Bedford Modern Sch.; St John's Coll., Cambridge. Demonstrator, later lecturer, Dept of Physics, KCL, 1927-39. Min. of Supply, Radar Research and Development Establishment, 1939-45. Actg Superintendent in charge of scientific work, 1944-45. Lecturer, later Reader, Dept of Engineering, Cambridge Univ., 1945-60. Member of Council, Inst. of Electrical Engineers, 1954-56, 1961-64 (Chm. of Radio Section, 1954-55); Director, English Electric Valve Company, 1966. Duddell Medal, Inst. of Physics and Physical Soc., 1969; Royal Medal, Royal Soc., 1969; Faraday Medal, Inst. of Electrical Engineers, 1970. *Publications:* Wireless Receivers, 1932; papers in scientific and technical journals. *Recreation:* gardening. *Address:* 16 Porson Road, Cambridge. *T:* Cambridge 56194. *Club:* Athenæum.

**OBAN, Provost of** (St John's Cathedral); *see* Copland, Very Rev. CMcA.

**O'BEIRNE, Cornelius Banahan,** CBE 1964; QC; Attorney-General, Gibraltar, since 1966; *b* 9 September 1915; *e s* of late Captain C. B. O'Beirne, OBE; *m* 1949, Ivanka, *d* of Miloc Tupanjanin, Belgrade; one *s* one *d*. *Educ:* Stonyhurst Coll. Solicitor (Eng.), 1940. Served War, 1940-46; Maj. RA, Eur., Mid. E; Polit. Adviser's Office, Brit. Emb., Athens, 1945-46. Colonial Office, 1947-48. Called to Bar, Lincoln's Inn, 1952. Crown Counsel: Nigeria, 1949-53; High Commn Territories, SA, 1953-59; Solicitor-Gen., 1959; Attorney-General, High Commission Territories, South Africa, 1961-64; Counsellor (Legal), British Embassy, SA, 1964-65; Lord Chancellor's Dept, 1966. QC: Basutoland, Bechuanaland and Swaziland, 1962; Gibraltar, 1967. *Recreations:* photography, modern languages. *Address:* Attorney-General's Chambers, Gibraltar.

**OBERG, Olof David August,** CMG 1953; Deputy Chairman, Commonwealth Immigration Advisory Council, since 1945; President, Area Council Boy Scots' Association of New South Wales; Chairman: Timber Mutual Assurance Ltd; Timber Trade Mutual Assurance Ltd; Timber Tallying Association Ltd; Lumber Operators Pty Ltd; *b* 24 September 1893; *s* of Joseph Nathaniel Oberg, Gevie, Sweden, and Jane Hannah, Ballarat, Australia; *m* 1917, Dulcie Sutton Druce; two *s* two *d* (and one *s* decd). *Educ:* Sydney High School. Early life spent in timber industry, ultimately becoming Gen. Man. Davies & Fehon Ltd, 1921; JP 1924. Formed own Company, Thatcher & Oberg Pty Ltd, 1930; Chairman, retd, 1963. Mem. Council, Sydney Chamber of Commerce, 1928-40; Mem. Unemployment Relief Council of NSW, 1931-34; Pres. Sydney and Suburban Timber Merchants' assoc., 1936-40; Foundaation Pres. (1938-48) of Timber Devel. Assoc. of Austr.; Foundation Pres., Building Industry Congress, 1938-40; Pres. Employers' Federation of New South Wales, 1940-43; Pres. Australian Council of Employers' Fedns, 1943-48. Member Austr. Deleg. to S Francisco World Conf., 1945; led Austr. Employers' Deleg. to Internat. Labour Organisation Conf., Paris, 1945, and Asian Regional Conf., Tokio, 1953. Member Commonwealth Immigration Advisory Cttee, 1945; Member Rotary International Cttees, 1948-56; Dir, Rotary International, 1954 (first Vice-Pres., 1955-56); Vice-Pres. YMCA Jubilee Medal, 1935; Coronation Medal, 1937. Coronation Medal, 1953. *Recreations:* motoring, Gardening, fishing. *Address:* Gardeners Road, Mascot, NSW, Australia. *Clubs:* Royal Sydney

Yacht Squadron, New South Wales, Savage, Rotary (Sydney).

**OBERON, Merle, (Estelle Merle O'Brien Thompson);** Film Actress; *b* Tasmania, 19 Feb. 1917; British; *m* 1st 1939, Sir Alexander Korda (*d* 1956) (marriage dissolved); 2nd, 1945, Lucien Ballard (marriage dissolved, 1949); *m* 1958, Bruno Pagliai, Company President and (founding) Mem. Jockey Club Mexicano. *Educ:* La Martinere College, Calcutta; France. Films include: Henry VIII, Wuthering Heights, Night in Paradise, Temptation, Night Song, Berlin Express, Dark Angel, Song to Remember, Of Love and Desire, Hotel. *Recreations:* riding, swimming, fishing, and reading. *Address:* Selby House, 244 Ladera Drive, Beverly Hills, California, USA; Paseo de Lomas Altas 164, Mexico City.

**OBERT de THIEUSIES, Vicomte Alain;** Grand Officer de la Couronne; Grande Croix de l'Ordre de Léopold II; Grand Cordon de la Couronne de Chêne, etc.; Comdr de la Légion d'Honneur; *b* 10 March 1888; *s* of Vicomte Obert de Thieusies and Vicomtesse Obert de Thieusies (*née* Comtesse de Ribaucourt); *m* 1927, Yolanda, *d* of Baron Romano-Avezzana; three *s. Educ:* Maredsous Abbey; Stoneyhurst College (Doctor of Law). Entered diplomatic service, 1911, as Attaché de Légation; Secrétaire de Légation, Madrid, 1912; Chargé d'Affaires, ad interim, Belgrade, 1913, Sofia, 1913; Secrétaire de Légation (1st Cl.), 1915, Rio de Janiero, 1919; Counsellor, Paris, 1921; Minister Plenipotentiary, 1930; Consul General, Tangiers, 1930; Minister, Prague, 1932, Belgrade, 1938-41; Directeur Général du Commerce Extérieur in London, 1941; Chairman of Liquidation Cttee of Belgian Govt Service in London, 1944; Head of Belgian Economic Mission, 1945; Belgian Ambassador to the Court of St James's, 1946-53. *Recreations:* golf, shooting. *Heir: s* Martel, *b* 30 Apr. 1928. *Address:* Château de Thoricourt, Hainaut, Belgium.

**OBEY, André;** Licencié ès-lettres, Licencié en droit; Playwright; administrateur de la Comédie française, 1945-46; officier de la Légion d'Honneur; *b* 8 May 1892; *s* of Oscar Obey and Elisabeth Hisette; *m*; one *d*; *m* Josie Grégoire. *Educ:* Lycée de Douai. Won a first prize for piano, at the Conservatoire of Douai, his native town; when European war of 1914 was declared was going through the period of his military service; wounded twice very seriously; after the war, came to Paris; for several years belonged to the staff of divers newspapers, as reporter for sporting news, and musical and theatrical critic; his last novel awarded Prix Théophraste Renaudot, 1928; since then he has written exclusively for the stage. *Publications: novels:* Le Gardien de la Ville; L'Enfant inquiet; Savreux Vainqueur; Le Joueur de Triangle; *essays:* L'Orgue du Stade; l'Apprenti Sorcier; *plays:* Noé; Le Viol de Lucrèce; Bataille de la Marne; Vénus et Adonis; Loire; Richard III; Don Juan; Henri IV; Revenu de l'Etoile; Ultimatum; Maria; La nuit des temps, l'Homme de Cendres; Lazare; Une fille pour du vent; Orestie; Les Trois Coups de Minuit. *Recreations:* motoring, angling. *Address:* L'Hirondelle, 49 Montsoreau, France.

**OBOLENSKY, Prof. Dimitri,** MA, PhD; FSA; FRHistS; Professor of Russian and Balkan History in the University of Oxford since 1961, and Student of Christ Church since 1950; *b* Petrograd, 1 April 1918; *s* of late Prince Dimitri Obolensky and Countess Mary Shuvaloy; *m* 1947, Elisabeth Lopukhin. *Educ:* Lycée Pasteur, Paris; Trinity College, Cambridge. Cambridge: 1st Class Modern and Medieval Langs Tripos Parts I and II; Amy Mary Preston Read and Allen Schol.; Fellow of Trinity Coll., 1942-48; Faculty Asst Lecturer, 1944; Lecturer, Trinity Coll., 1945; Univ. Lecturer in Slavonic Studies, 1946. Reader in Russian and Balkan Medieval History in Univ. of Oxford, 1949-61; Vis. Schol., Dumbarton Oaks Center for Byzantine Studies, Harvard Univ., 1952 and 1964; Vis. Prof. of Russian History, Yale Univ., 1957; Birkbeck Lecturer in Ecclesiastical History, Trinity Coll., Cambridge, 1961; Gen. Sec. Thirteenth Internat. Congress of Byzantine Studies, Oxford, 1966. *Publications:* The Bogomils, A Study in Balkan Neo-Manichaeism, 1948; (ed) The Penguin Book of Russian Verse, 1962; (jointly) A Commentary on the 'De Administrando Imperio' of Constantine Porphyrogenitus, 1962; (jointly The Christian Centuries, vol. 2: The Middle Ages, 1969; articles in Oxford Slavonic Papers, Dumbarton Oaks Papers, Slavonic and East European Review, etc.; contrib. to Encyc. Brit. and Chambers's Encyc. *Recreations:* lawn tennis, motoring. *Address:* 29 Harbord Road, Oxford; Christ Church, Oxford. *T:* 58989. *Club:* Athenæum.

**OBOTE, Hon. (Apolo) Milton;** President of Uganda since April 1966; *b* 1924; *m* three *s.* Migrated to Kenya, 1950; worked as clerk, salesman, etc. Founder Member, Kenya Africa Union; joined Uganda National Congress on visit home, 1952; returned to Lango, Uganda, 1955; Member Legislative Council, Uganda, 1957; formed Uganda People's Congress, 1960; Leader of the Opposition, 1961-62; Prime Minister, 1962-66. *Address:* State House, Entebbe, Uganda.

**Ó BRIAIN, Barra; Hon. Mr Justice Ó Briain,** MSM; President of the Circuit Court and, *ex officio,* Judge of High Court in Ireland since 1959 (seconded as President of the High Court of Justice, Cyprus, 1960-62); appointed a Member of Committee of Inquiry into the operation of the Courts in Ireland, 1962; *b* 19 September 1901; *s* of Dr Christopher Michael and Mary Theresa Ó Briain, Merrion Square, Dublin; *m* 1928, Anna Flood, Terenure, Dublin (*d* 1968); three *s* eight *d. Educ:* Belvedere College; University Coll., Dublin; Paris University. Served in IRA in Irish War of Independence, 1920-21; National Army, 1922-27; Mil. Sec. to Chief of Staff, 1926-27. Called to Irish Bar, 1926; is a Bencher of King's Inns. Sen. Counsel, 1940; Circuit Judge, 1943 (S Western Circuit). *Publication:* The Irish Constitution (1927). *Recreations:* fishing, gardening, walking. *Address:* Gūgān Barra, Enniskerry, Co. Wicklow. *T:* 867493; Srahnamanragh Lodge, Ballycroy, Co. Mayo.

**O'BRIEN,** family name of **Baron Inchiquin.**

**O'BRIEN, Brian;** Solicitor and Legal Adviser to Ministry of Health, to Ministry of Housing and Local Government, and to Registrar-General, 1952-57, retired; *s* of late Hon. W. J. O'Brien, OBE, JP, PhD and late Mrs O'Brien, Dunkerrin, Pietermaritzburg, Natal, SA; *m* 1918, Adelaide Money Johnson (*d* 1948), Woldingham, Surrey; one *d. Educ:* Pietermaritzburg College; Natal University; Trinity College, Cambridge; MA, LLB Cantab 1914 (1st Class Honours. Part II Law Tripos). Called to Bar, Inner Temple, 1915; read in chambers, Hon. Sir Malcolm Macnaghten, 1914-15; Ministry of Munitions, 1915-20; Established Civil Servant. Treasury Solicitor's Dept, 1920; transferred Ministry of Health, 1929; seconded to Ministry of Food, as Asst Sec., 1940-45; Assistant Solicitor, 1945, Principal Assistant Solicitor, 1951, Ministry of Health. Chm. and Hon. Sec. Frank Merrick

Society. Order of Orange Nassau (Holland), 1952. *Recreations:* gardening (FRHS); devotee of music (Fellow Royal Philharmonic Soc.) and the arts, letters. *Address:* 29 Gordon Place, Kensington, W8. *T:* 01-937 4258. *Club:* Oxford and Cambridge University.

**O'BRIEN, Bryan Justin,** CMG 1950; *b* 21 Jan. 1902; *s* of late Rev. G. E. O'Brien, Bosley Vicarage, Cheshire; *m* 1937, Maro, *d* of late Cleanthis Constantinides, Famagusta, Cyprus; one *s. Educ:* Uppingham; Queen's College, Oxford. First class honour Mods, second class literæ humaniores; Laming Fellow. Assistant Secretary, Colonial Secretary's Office, Cyprus, 1927; Commissioner, 1936; Assistant Colonial Secretary, Mauritius, 1939; Principal Assistant Colonial Secretary, 1943; Under-Secretary, Trinidad, 1943-47; Colonial Secretary, Gibraltar, 1947-53; Chief Secretary, North Borneo, 1953-56; retired. Mem. Commn on Salaries and Wages, Ghana, 1956-57. Jt Editor, Handbook of Cyprus, 1930 edn. *Club:* Travellers'.

**O'BRIEN, Conor Cruise;** TD (Lab) Dublin North-East, since 1969; *b* 3 November 1917; *s* of Francis Cruise O'Brien and Katherine Sheehy; *m* 1st, 1939, Christine Foster (marr. diss. 1962); one *s* two *d*; 2nd, 1962, Maire Mac Entee; one adopted *s. Educ:* Sandford Park School, Dublin; Trinity College, Dublin (BA, PhD). Entered Department of External Affairs of Ireland, 1944; Counsellor, Paris, 1955-56; Head of UN section and Member of Irish Delegation to UN, 1956-60; Asst Sec., Dept of External Affairs, 1960; Rep. of Sec.-Gen. of UN in Katanga, May-Dec. 1961; resigned from UN and Irish service, Dec. 1961. Vice-Chancellor, Univ. of Ghana, 1962-65; Albert Schweitzer Prof. of Humanities, New York Univ., 1965-69. *Publications:* Maria Cross (under pseud. Donat O'Donnell), 1952 (reprinted under own name, 1963); Parnell and his Party, 1957; (ed) The Shaping of Modern Ireland, 1959; To Katanga and Back, 1962; Writers and Politics, 1965; The United Nations: Sacred Drama, 1967 (with drawings by Felix Topolski); Murderous Angels, 1968; (ed) Power and Consciousness, 1969; Conor Cruise O'Brien Introduces Ireland, 1969; (ed) Edmund Burke, Reflections on the Revolution in France, 1969; Camus, 1969. *Recreation:* travelling. *Address:* Whitewater, Howth Summit, Dublin, Ireland. *T:* Dublin 322474.

**O'BRIEN, Sir David (Edmond),** 6th Bt *cr* 1849; *b* 19 Feb. 1902; *s* of Edmond Lyons O'Brien (*y b* of 3rd Bt) and Audrey Townshend, *d* of late David Crawford, New York; *S* brother, 1969; *m* 1927, Mary Alice, *y d* of Sir Henry Foley Grey, 7th Bt; two *s* one *d. Educ:* Oratory School. *Recreations:* fishing, gardening. *Heir: er s* John David O'Brien [*b* 9 June 1928; *m* 1957, Sheila Winifred, *o d* of Sir Charles Arland Maitland Freake, 4th Bt; two *s* two *d*]. *Address:* Salisbury, Clonmel, Co. Tipperary. *T:* Clonmel 110. *Club:* Kildare Street (Dublin).

**O'BRIEN, Sir (Frederick) Lucius,** Kt 1949; first Chairman (Government appointment) Northern Ireland Housing Trust, 1945-60, Member of Trust, 1960-67; *b* 1896; *s* of Louis Frederick O'Brien; unmarried. *Educ:* Friends' School, Lisburn; Bootham School, York. Honorary Secretary, Belfast Charitable Society, 1935-62, President 1962-; Chairman, Belfast Savings Bank, 1939 and 1951; Custodian Trustee; NI Rep. Exec. on Trustee Savings Bank Assoc., 1952-62, Vice-Pres. 1962-; Chief Welfare Officer 1941 and Member (Govt App.) of Belfast Civil Defence Auth., 1941-45; Member: NI Govt Commn on Charities, 1956; Exec. Belfast Council of Social Welfare; NI Council of Social Service, etc. Mem. of Senate, The Queen's Univ. of Belfast. Mem. Independent Television Authority, 1960-65. *Recreations:* travel and reading. *Address:* 14 Myrtlefield Park, Belfast BT9 6NE, Northern Ireland. *T:* 666726. *Club:* Ulster (Belfast).

**O'BRIEN, Frederick William Fitzgerald,** QC (Scotland) 1960; Sheriff of Caithness, Sutherland, Orkney, and Shetland, since 1965; *b* 19 July 1917; *s* of Dr Charles Henry Fitzgerald O'Brien and Helen Jane; *m* 1950, Audrey Muriel Owen; two *s* one *d. Educ:* Royal High Sch.; Univ. of Edinburgh; MA 1938; LLB 1940. Admitted Faculty of Advocates, 1947. Member of Legal Aid Central Cttee, 1961-64; Comr, Mental Welfare Commission of Scotland, 1962-65; Home Advocate Depute, 1964-65; Hon. Sheriff-substitute, Lothians and Peebles. *Recreations:* golf, music. *Address:* Muskoka, Boswall Road, Edinburgh 5. *T:* 031-552 3147. *Clubs:* Bruntsfield Golf, Scottish Arts.

**O'BRIEN, George,** DLitt (NUI), Hon. LittD (Dublin); Professor of Economics, University College, Dublin, 1926-61; Representative of National University of Ireland in Seanad Eireann, 1948-65; Director: The Economist Intelligence Unit of Ireland Ltd; Ashtown Tin Box (Ireland) Ltd; Ryan's Tourist Holdings Ltd; Phœnix Estates Ltd; *b* Dublin, 1892. *Educ:* St George's Coll., Weybridge; Univ. Coll., Dublin. Called to Irish Bar, 1913; member of Agricultural Commission, 1922, of Fiscal Inquiry Committee, 1923, of Economic Committee, 1928, of Derating Commission, 1930, of Banking Commission, 1934; and of Commission on Agriculture, 1939. President of Statistical and Social Inquiry Society of Ireland, 1942-46; Vice-President of Royal Irish Academy, 1944; Trustee of National Library of Ireland; Vice-Pres., Royal Dublin Society; mem. Pontifica Accademia Degli Arcadi; Chairman Board, Economic and Social Research Institute of Ireland; editorial consultant, The Irish Banking Review. *Publications:* The Economic History of Ireland (3 vols); An Essay on Mediæval Economic Teaching; The Economic Effects of the Reformation; Labour Organisation; Agricultural Economics; Notes on Theory of Profit; The Four Green Fields; The Phantom of Plenty; (ed.) The Bank of Ireland 1783-1946 (by F. G. Hall); contrib. Encyc. Britannica, Encyc. of Social Sciences, Economic Journal, Eng. Historical Review, Economica, Camb. Jl, etc. *Address:* 3 Burlington Road, Dublin. *Clubs:* Kildare St, Dublin University (Dublin); Royal Irish Yacht.

**O'BRIEN, Kate;** Playwright, Novelist; *b* 3 Dec. 1897; *d* of Thomas O'Brien and Catherine Thornhill, Boru House, Limerick, Ireland. *Educ:* Laurel Hill Convent, Limerick; University College, Dublin. *Plays:* Distinguished Villa, at Aldwych Theatre, 1926, afterwards, 1926, at Little Theatre; The Bridge, at Arts Theatre Club, 1927; The Ante-Room (dramatised from novel, with W. A. Carot and Geoffrey Gomer), Queen's Theatre, 1936; The Schoolroom Window, produced by Manuscript Theatre Club, 1937; The Last of Summer (dramatised from novel, with John Perry), Phoenix Theatre, 1944; That Lady (dramatised from novel), USA, 1949. *Publications: novels:* Without My Cloak, 1931 (Hawthornden Prize 1931 and James Tait Black Memorial Prize); The Ante-Room, 1934; Mary Lavelle, 1936; Pray for the Wanderer, 1938; The Land of Spices, 1941; The Last of Summer, 1943; That Lady, 1946; The Flower of May, 1953; As Music and Splendour, 1958;

Presentation Parlour, 1943; *travel:* Farewell Spain, 1937; English Diaries and Journals, 1943; My Ireland, 1962. *Address:* 177 The Street, Boughton, Faversham, Kent.

**O'BRIEN, Rt. Hon. Sir Leslie (Kenneth),** PC 1970; GBE 1967; Governor, Bank of England since 1966; *b* 8 Feb. 1908; *e s* of late Charles John Grimes O'Brien; *m* Isabelle Gertrude Pickett; one *s. Educ:* Wandsworth School. Entered Bank of England, 1927; Deputy Chief Cashier, 1951; Chief Cashier, 1955; Executive Director, 1962-64; Deputy Governor, 1964-66; Director, Commonwealth Develt Finance Co. Ltd, 1962-64. Fellow and Vice-President, Inst. of Bankers, 1964. One of HM Lieutenants for City of London; Freeman, City of London in Co. of Mercers. Hon. DSc City Univ., 1969. *Address:* Bank of England, EC2. *T:* 01-601 4444. *Clubs:* Boodle's, MCC, All England Lawn Tennis.

**O'BRIEN, Sir Lucius;** *see* O'Brien, Sir (F). L.

**O'BRIEN, Rt. Rev. Mgr. Michael Joseph;** Principal Chaplain (RC), Royal Air Force, since 1967; *b* 13 April 1913; *s* of John O'Brien and Anastasia (*née* Corbett). *Educ:* De La Salle, Waterford; Rockwell Coll., Cashel; St John's Coll., Waterford. Ordained, 1936; Curate: Corpus Christi, Weston-super-Mare, 1936-40; St John the Evangelist, Bath, 1940-41; joined RAF Chaplain's Branch, 1941. *Recreation:* golf. *Address:* 54 Ennismore Gardens, SW7. *T:* 01-584 3041, 01-589 1273. *Club:* Royal Air Force.

**O'BRIEN, Terence John,** MC 1945; Ambassador to Nepal, since 1970; *b* 13 Oct. 1921; *s* of Joseph O'Brien; *m* 1950, Phyllis Mitchell (*d* 1952); *m* 1953, Rita Emily Drake Reynolds; one *s* two *d. Educ:* Gresham's Sch., Holt; Merton Coll., Oxford. Ayrshire Yeo., 1942-45. Dominions Office, 1947; CRO, 1947-49; British High Comr's Office, Ceylon, 1950-52; Princ., Treasury, 1953-56; 1st Sec. (Financial), Canberra, 1956-58; Planning Officer, CRO, 1958-60; 1st Sec., Kuala Lumpur, 1960-62; Sec. to Inter-Governmental Cttee, Jesselton, 1962-63; Head of Chancery, New Delhi, 1963-66; Imp. Def. Coll., 1967; Counsellor, FCO (formerly FO), 1968-70. *Recreation:* fishing. *Address:* c/o Foreign and Commonwealth Office, SW1. *Club:* Reform.

**O'BRIEN, Turlough Aubrey,** CBE 1959; Public Relations Manager, Bank of London and South America, since 1968; *b* 30 Sept. 1907; *er s* of late Lieut-Colonel A. J. O'Brien, CIE, CBE; *m* 1945, Phyllis Mary, twin *d* of late E. G. Tew; two *s* one *d. Educ:* Charterhouse; Christ Church, Oxford. Assistant to Director of Public Relations, Board of Trade, 1946-49; Public Relations Officer: Home Office, 1949-53; Post Office, 1953-64; Chief Public Relations Officer, 1964-66; Director, Public Relations, 1966-68. President, Institute of Public Relations, 1965. *Recreation:* fishing. *Address:* Clare Place, Goose Rye Road, Worplesdon, Guildford, Surrey. *T:* Worplesdon 3151. *Club:* United University.

**O'BRIEN, Adm. Sir William (Donough),** KCB 1969 (CB 1966); DSC 1942; Commander-in-Chief, Western Fleet, since Feb. 1970; *b* 13 Nov. 1916; *s* of late Major W. D. O'Brien, Connaught Rangers and I. R. Caroe (*née* Parnis); *m* 1943, Rita Micallef, Sliema, Malta; one *s* two *d. Educ:* Royal Naval Coll., Dartmouth. Served War of 1939-45: HM Ships Garland, Wolsey, Witherington, Offa, 1939-42; Cottesmore i/c, 1943-44; Arakan Coast, 1945. HMS Venus i/c, 1948-49; Commander 1949; HMS Ceylon, 1952; Admiralty, 1953-55; Captain, 1955; Captain (D) 8th DS in HMS Cheviot, 1958-59; HMS Hermes i/c, 1961-64; Rear-Admiral 1964; Naval Secretary, 1964-66; Flag Officer, Aircraft Carriers, 1966-67; Comdr, Far East Fleet, 1967-69; Admiral 1969. *Address:* Drew's Mill, Potterne Road, Devizes, Wilts. *T:* Devizes 3243. *Club:* United Service.

**O'BRIEN TWOHIG, Brig. Joseph Patrick,** CBE 1945; DSO 1943, Bar 1944; *b* 30 May 1905; 4th *s* of J. O'Brien Twohig, Dunowen House, Clonakilty, Co. Cork; *m* 1st, 1933, Barbara, *e d* of W. E. Tower; one *s*; 2nd, 1944, Mary, *e d* of J. P. Blake; two *d. Educ:* privately and Trinity Coll., Dublin (BA). Called to Irish Bar, 1926. 2nd Lieut, KOYLI, 1926; Adjutant, 2nd Gold Coast Regt, 1933; Captain, Royal Inniskilling Fusiliers, 1937; Lieut-Colonel, 1946; CO 2nd Inniskillings, 1943-44. Brigade Commander: Adriatic, 1944-45; 2nd Parachute Bde, 1946; 28 Inf. Bde, 1949; retired, 1951. Dep. Inspector-General Malayan Home Guard, 1952-54. Chairman and Managing Director, London and Kano Trading Co., 1955-60; Dir, Hooker Craigmyle Ltd, 1968. *Address:* Brontë House, St James Street, Ryde, Isle of Wight.

**O'BRIEN-TWOHIG, Colonel Michael Joseph,** OBE 1957; *b* 6 Aug. 1893; *e s* of late John Patrick O'Brien-Twohig, Mawgan Porth, Cornwall, and Dunowen House, Clonakilty, Co. Cork, and Ellen O'Brien, Tullaneasky, Co. Cork; *m* 1st, 1919, Eileen (*d* 1958), *d* of late John Lawlor, DL, JP, Irishtown House, Clondalkin, Co. Dublin; one *d*; 2nd, 1958, Margaret Elizabeth, *o d* of late George Agnew Main, Mansfield, Wemyss Bay, Renfrewshire. *Educ:* Trinity Coll., Cambridge; King's Inns, Dublin. Barrister-at-Law. 2nd Lieut Royal Munster Fusiliers, 1913; served European War, 1914-18, Gallipoli and France; Staff Captain and DAQMG; Captain, 1916; Temp. Major, 1918. ADC, Kenya, 1921-24; Transferred KSLI, 1922. Commanding Gold Coast Defence Force, 1931-34; Staff, GHQ, BEF, 1939; Mil. Comdt "Queen Elizabeth" and "Queen Mary", 1942-44; Acting King's Messenger, 1944; appointed a King's Foreign Service Messenger, 1948; Senior King's Foreign Service Messenger, 1951; Superintending Queen's Foreign Service Messenger, 1952-57, retired. French and Belgian Croix de Guerre. *Publications:* Diplomatic Courier, 1960; contrib. to Encyclopædia Britannica. *Recreations:* yachting, painting. *Address:* Four Chimneys, High Ham, near Langport, Somerset. *T:* Langport 367. *Clubs:* Pratt's, Royal Automobile, Naval; Royal Irish Yacht, Royal Alfred Yacht (Dun Laoghaire).

**O'CALLAGHAN, Most Rev. Eugene,** DD; Titular Bishop of Britonia since 1969; *b* Lisseraw, Camlough, Co. Armagh, 6 Jan. 1888. *Educ:* Drumilly NS; St Colman's Coll., Newry; St Patrick's Coll., Armagh; St Patrick's Coll., Maynooth; Post-Graduate Course in Dunboyne House, Maynooth, STL, BCL, BA.

Ordained, 1913; Diocesan Inspector of Schools, Diocese of Armagh, 1913-21; Curate in Armagh, 1921-32; Administrator of Armagh, 1932-38; PP of St Peter's, Drogheda, 1938-43, and also Vicar-Gen. of the Diocese, 1938-43; Bishop of Clogher, 1943-69. *Address:* c/o Bishop's House, Monaghan.

**OCHOA, Professor Severo;** Professor of Biochemistry, and Chairman of the Department of Biochemistry, New York University School of Medicine, since 1954; President, International Union of Biochemistry, 1961-67; *b* Luarca, Spain, 24 Sept. 1905; *s* of Severo Ochoa and Carmen (*née* Albornoz); *m* 1931, Carmen G. Coblan. *Educ:* Malaga Coll.; University of Madrid. AB, Malaga, 1921; MD, Madrid, 1929. Lecturer in Physiology, University of Madrid Medical School, 1931-35; Head of Physiology Div., Institute for Medical Research, 1935-36; Guest Research Asst, Kaiser Wilhelm Inst., Heidelberg, 1936-37; Marine Biological Lab., Plymouth, July-Dec. 1937; Demonstrator and Nuffield Research Assistant in Biochemistry, University of Oxford Medical School, 1938-41; Instructor and Research Assoc. in Pharmacology, Washington Univ. School of Medicine, St Louis, 1941-42; Research Assoc. in Medicine, New York Univ. School of Medicine, 1942-45; Asst Professor of Biochemistry, 1945-46; Professor of Pharmacology, and Chairman of Dept of Pharmacology, 1946-54. Member: US National Academy of Sciences; American Academy of Arts and Sciences; American Philosophical Society; Deutsche Akademie der Naturforscher (Leopoldina), etc. Nobel Prize (joint) in Physiology and Medicine, 1959. Hon. DSc: Washington Univ., St Louis, Mo, 1957; Universities of: Brazil, 1957; Oxford, 1961; Salamanca, 1961; Wesleyan Univ., 1961, and Pennsylvania, 1964; Gustavus Adolphus Coll., St Peter, Minn, 1963; Brandeis Univ., 1965; DHL Yeshiva Univ., 1965; Hon. LLD Glasgow, 1959; Hon. DMedSci, Univ. of Santo Tomas, Manila, 1963. Foreign Member: Royal Society, 1965; USSR Academy of Science, 1966; Polish Acad. of Science. *Publications:* papers on biochemistry and molecular biology. *Recreations:* colour photography and swimming. *Address:* 530 East 72nd Street, New York, NY 10021, USA. *T:* Trafalgar 9-1480.

**O'COLLINS, Most Rev. James Patrick;** *see* Ballarat, Bishop of, (RC).

**O'CONNELL, Captain Donal Bernard,** CBE 1943; Royal Navy, retired; *b* 3 June 1893; 2nd *s* of Sir Morgan Ross O'Connell, 4th Bt, Lakeview, Killarney, Eire, and Mary Pauline, *e d* of Col J. F. Hickie, Slevoyre, Borrisokane, Eire; unmarried. *Educ:* St Anthony's, Eastbourne; Royal Naval Colleges. European War, Destroyer Service, as Sub-Lieut and Lieut, RN; commanded HMSS Teal (Yangtse, 1926-28) and Gannet (Yangtse, 1932-34); Commander, 1929; retired, 1936; Captain, retired, 1938; Served War of 1939-45. Founded Kerry Archæological Survey, 1936. Fellow Royal Society Antiquaries of Ireland, 1937; MRIA, 1938; Irish National Monuments Commission, 1938. Chevalier de Malte, 1938; VP Cork Hist. and Archæological Society, 1938. *Publication:* Kerry Archæological Survey Publication No. 1. *Recreations:* Local Archæology, Ambulance work (Order of Malta). *Address:* Maulagh, Killarney, Co. Kerry, Eire. *TA:* Beaufort-Kerry Eire. *Club:* Hibernian, United Service (Dublin). *See also Sir Morgan O'Connell, Bt.*

**O'CONNELL, John Eugene Anthony,** MS (London), FRCS; Surgeon in charge of Department of Neurological Surgery at St Bartholomew's Hospital, since 1946; Civilian Consultant in Neurological Surgery to Royal Navy; *b* 16 Sept. 1906; *s* of Thomas Henry and Catherine Mary O'Connell. *Educ:* Clongowes Wood and Wimbledon Colleges; St Bartholomew's Hospital. Held posts of House Surgeon, Senior Demonstrator of Anatomy, and Surgical Chief Assistant, St Bartholomew's Hospital, 1931-39; Studied at Universities of Michigan and Chicago on Rockefeller Foundation Travelling Fellowship, 1935-36; Surgeon in charge of an EMS Neurosurgical Unit, 1939-45. Hunterian Professor, Royal College of Surgeons, 1942 and 1950. *Publications:* papers in neurological, surgical and other journals. *Recreations:* fly-fishing, bird watching and cricket. *Address:* 149 Harley Street, W1. *T:* 01-935 4444; 31 Avenue Close, Avenue Road, NW8. *T:* 01-722 8614.

**O'CONNELL, Sir Morgan (Donal Conail),** 6th Bt, *cr* 1869; *b* 29 Jan. 1923; *o s* of Captain Sir Maurice James Arthur O'Connell, 5th Bt, KM, MC, and Margaret Mary, *d* of late Matthew J. Purcell, Burton Park, Buttevant; *S* father, 1949; *m* 1953, Elizabeth, *o d* of late Major and Mrs John MacCarthy-O'Leary, Lavenders, West Malling, Kent; two *s* four *d*. *Educ:* The Abbey School, Fort Augustus, Scotland. Served War of 1939-45, in Royal Corps of Signals, 1943-46; BLA, 1944-46. *Recreations:* fishing and shooting. *Heir:* *s* Maurice James Donagh MacCarthy O'Connell, *b* 10 June 1958. *Address:* Lakeview, Killarney, Co. Kerry. *T:* 5.

**O'CONNOR, Professor Daniel John;** Professor of Philosophy, University of Exeter, since 1957; *b* 2 April 1914. *Educ:* Birkbeck Coll., University of London. Entered Civil Service, 1933; Commonwealth Fund Fellow in Philosophy, University of Chicago, 1946-47; Professor of Philosophy, University of Natal, SA, 1949-51; Professor of Philosophy, University of the Witwatersrand, Johannesburg, 1951-52; Lecturer in Philosophy, Univ. Coll. of North Staffordshire, 1952-54; Professor of Philosophy, University of Liverpool, 1954-57; Visiting Professor, University of Pennsylvania, 1961-62. *Publications:* John Locke, 1952; Introduction to Symbolic Logic (with A. H. Basson), 1953; Introduction to the Philosophy of Education, 1957; A Critical History of Western Philosophy (ed), 1964; Aquinas and Natural Law, 1968. Various papers in philosophical journals. *Address:* The University, Exeter.

**O'CONNOR, Lieut-General Sir Denis (Stuart Scott),** KBE 1963 (CBE 1949; OBE 1946); CB 1959; DL; *b* Simla, 2 July 1907; *s* of Lieut-Colonel Malcolm Scott O'Connor and Edith Annie (*née* Rees); *m* 1936, Martha Neill Algie (*née* Johnston), Donaghadee, Co. Down; two *s* one *d*. *Educ:* Glengorse, Eastbourne; Harrow School; RMA Woolwich. Commnd 2nd Lieut, Royal Artillery, 1927; India, 1929-35; France, 1939, Captain; Student Staff Coll., 1940; Major Instructor, Staff Coll., 1941, Lieut-

Colonel GSO 1, 11th Armoured Division, 1942-44; N.W. Europe, CO Artillery Regt, 1944 (despatches); Colonel, 14th Army, 1945; Brigadier, Director of Plans, Supreme Allied Commander, South East Asia, 1945-46; Middle East, BGS, 1946-49; Student, IDC 1950; School of Artillery, 1951-52; CRA, 11th Armoured Division, BAOR, 1953-54; Director of Plans, War Office, 1955-56; Maj.-General, Commander, 6th Armoured Division, BAOR, 1957-58; Chief Army Instructor, Imperial Defence Coll., London, 1958-60; GOC, Aldershot District, 1960-62; Vice Chief of Defence Staff, Ministry of Defence, 1962-64; Commander British Forces, Hong Kong, 1964-66, retired. Colonel Commandant, RA, 1963-. Member of Administrative Board of Governors, Corps of Commissionaires. DL Surrey, 1968. *Recreations:* shooting, fishing, golf. *Address:* Springfield Lodge, Camberley, Surrey. *Club:* Army and Navy.

**O'CONNOR, James Malachy;** Professor of Physiology, University College, Dublin, 1920-56; *b* 9 Feb. 1886; *s* of Dr M. R. O'Connor, Limerick; *m* 1919, Genevieve McGilligan; three *s* (and one *s* decd). *Educ:* Crescent Coll., Limerick; University Coll., Dublin. MB 1909, MD 1913. Assistant at Pharmacological Institute, Heidelberg, 1911-12; Assistant to Professor of Physiology, University College, Dublin, 1912-20; Irish Representative on General Medical Council, 1945-60. *Publications:* contributions to Physiology. *Address:* 7 Palmerston Villas, Dublin 6, Eire.

**O'CONNOR, Sir Kenneth Kennedy,** KBE 1961; Kt 1952; MC 1918; QC (Kenya) 1950; *b* 21 Dec. 1896; *s* of Rev. William O'Connor and Emma Louisa O'Connor; *m* 1928, Margaret Helen (*née* Wise); two *s*. *Educ:* Abbey Sch., Beckenham; St Columba's Coll., near Dublin. Indian Army, 14th (KGO) Sikhs, 1915-18 (despatches, MC). Pol. Dept, Mesopotamia, 1919. Foreign and Pol. Dept, Government of India, 1920-22; resigned, 1922. Called to Bar, Gray's Inn, 1924; practised at Bar, London and Singapore, 1924-41. President, Straits Settlements Assoc., 1938, 1939, 1940. Colonial Legal Service, 1943; Acting Attorney-General, Nyasaland, 1944; Colonel, 1945; Attorney-General, Malaya, 1946-48; Attorney-General, Kenya, 1948-51; Chief Justice, Jamaica, 1951-54; Chief Justice of Kenya, 1954; President, Court of Appeal for Eastern Africa, 1957-62, retired. *Publications:* Index Guide to the Law of Property Act, 1925, 1926. Editor Straits Settlements Law Reports. Contributions to legal journals. *Recreations:* cricket, lawn tennis, golf. *Address:* Buckland Court, Betchworth, Surrey. *Clubs:* East India and Sports; Nairobi (Kenya), etc.

**O'CONNOR, Air Commodore Patrick Joseph,** OBE 1943; MD; FRCPE; Consultant Adviser in Neurology and Psychiatry, to the RAF, since 1964; *b* 21 Aug. 1914; *s* of Charles O'Connor, Straffan, Co. Kildare, Eire, farmer; *m* 1946, Elsie, *o d* of David Craven, Leeds, Yorks; one *s* three *d*. *Educ:* Roscrea Coll.; University of Dublin. MB, BCh 1938. Joined RAF, 1940. MD 1950; MRCPE 1950; DPM 1953; FRCPE 1960; MRCP 1960. QHP 1967. Member: Med. Council to Migraine Trust; Med. Council on Alcoholism; Associate Fellow, Aerospace Med. Assoc; FRSM. *Publications:* contrib.: Journal Neurology, Psychiatry and Neurosurgery; British Journal Psychiatry; BMJ. *Recreations:* gardening, shooting. *Address:* Kelvin House, Cleveland Street, WC1. *T:* 01-636 4651; St Benedicts, Bacombe Lane, Wendover, Bucks. *T:* Wendover 3329. *Club:* Royal Air Force.

**O'CONNOR, Hon. Sir Patrick McCarthy,** Kt 1966; **Hon. Mr Justice O'Connor;** Judge of the High Court of Justice, Queen's Bench Division, since 1966; *b* 28 Dec. 1914; *s* of late William Patrick O'Connor; *m* 1938, Mary Garland, *d* of William Martin Griffin, KC, of Vancouver, BC; two *s* two *d*. *Educ:* Downside; Merton Coll., Oxford. Called to the Bar, Inner Temple, 1940; Master of the Bench, 1966. Junior Counsel to the Post Office, 1954-60; QC 1960; Recorder: of King's Lynn, 1959-61; of Southend, 1961-66; Dep. Chairman, IoW QS, 1957-. A Governor of Guy's Hospital, 1956-60. *Recreation:* yachting. *Address:* Royal Courts of Justice, Strand, WC2; 17 Eldon Road, Kensington, W8. *T:* 01-937 9198. *Clubs:* Royal Solent Yacht; Royal London Yacht.

**O'CONNOR, General Sir Richard Nugent,** GCB 1947 (KCB 1941; CB 1940); (Scottish Rifles) DSO 1917; MC; *b* 1889; *s* of Major Maurice Nugent O'Connor, Royal Irish Fusiliers; *m* 1st, 1935, Jean (*d* 1959), *d* of Sir Walter Ross, KBE, of Cromarty; 2nd, 1963, Dorothy, *widow* of Brigadier Hugh Russell, DSO. *Educ:* Wellington Coll.; Royal Military Coll., Sandhurst. Served European War, 1914-18 (despatches 9 times, DSO, bar, MC, Italian Silver medal for valour); GSO 2nd Grade, War Office, 1932-34; Imperial Defence College Course, 1935; Commander Peshawar Brigade, India, 1936-38; Military Governor of Jerusalem, 1938-39; served War of 1939-45; commanded Western Desert Corps in successful Libyan campaign, 1940-41 (prisoner, escaped Dec. 1943); a Corps Commander in France, 1944 (despatches, 1939-45 Star, France and Germany Star, Legion of Honour, Commander, Croix de Guerre with palm); GOC-in-C Eastern Command, India, Jan. 1945; GOC-in-C N. Western Army, India, 1945-46; General, 1945; Adjutant-General to the Forces, 1946-47; ADC General to the King, 1946; retired, 1948. Commandant Army Cadet Force, Scotland, 1948-59; Colonel, The Cameronians (Scottish Rifles), 1951-54. Lord Lieutenant County of Ross and Cromarty, 1955-64. Lord High Commissioner, Church of Scotland General Assembly, 1964. JP Ross and Cromarty, 1952. *Address:* c/o National Westminster Bank, Brompton Square Branch, SW3.

**O'DEA, Mrs Denis;** *see* McKenna, Siobhan.

**O'DEA, William Thomas,** FIEE; FMA; Senior Scientific Consultant, formerly Director-General, Ontario Centennial Centre for Science and Technology; *b* 27 Jan. 1905; *s* of late William O'Dea, MBE; *m* 1933, Kathleen Alice Busby; no *c*. *Educ:* Manchester University (BSc). Entered Science Museum from industry, 1930, as Assistant Keeper; transferred 1939, to Air Ministry (later MAP); Asst Director, Engine Accessories Production, 1940; Acting Director, Propeller Production, 1941; Dep. Regional Controller, London and S.E. England, Ministry of Production, 1942-44; Dep. Controller of Storage, Board of Trade, 1944-46. Keeper, Dept of Aeronautics, and Sailing Ships, Science Museum, SW7, 1948-66. Unesco adviser to Governments of Ceylon and India on establishment of Science Museums, 1956-60; Adviser to Government of UAR, 1962. Chairman, Cttee for Museum of Science and Technology, International Council of

Museums, 1966-71. Hon. Citizen, Quincy, Mass, 1965. *Publications:* The Meaning of Engineering, 1961; The Social History of Lighting, 1958; Science Museum Handbooks on Electric Power, 1933, Radio Communication, 1934, Illumination, 1936, 1948 and 1959; papers in Journals of IEE and IMechE; contributor, Festival Lectures, Royal Society Arts, 1951, and to various societies on history of engineering and illumination. *Address:* Pippins, Lower Farm Road, Effingham, Surrey. *Clubs:* Chelsea Arts; Arts and Letters (Toronto).

**ODELL, John William,** OBE; Joint Managing Director, Lesney Products & Co. Ltd, Diecasting Engineers, London E9. *Address:* Lesney Products & Co. Ltd, Lee Conservancy Road, Hackney Wick, E9. *T:* 01-985 5533/0664.

**ODEY, George William,** CBE 1945; Chairman, Barrow, Hepburn & Gale Ltd, Tanners and Leather Merchants, since 1937; *b* 21 April 1900; *s* of late George William Odey; *m* 1926, Dorothy Christian, *d* of late James Moir; one *s*. *Educ:* Faversham Grammar Sch.; University College, London. President Union Society, UCL, 1921-22. University of London Union Society, 1922. Fellow, UCL 1953; Assistant Secretary, University of London Appointments Board, 1922-25. Joined firm of Barrow, Hepburn & Gale, Ltd, 1925; transferred to Subsidiary Company of Richard Hodgson & Sons Ltd, Tanners, Beverley, 1926; Board of Barrow, Hepburn & Gale, Ltd, 1929, Managing Director, 1933. Representative Ministry of Supply in Washington for negotiations in connection with joint purchase of hides between UK and USA, 1941; Member joint UK and USA Mission on Hides and Leather to S. America, 1943; Chairman: Board of Governors, National Leathersellers Coll., 1951-; United Tanners' Federation, 1951. MP (C) Howdenshire Division of E Yorks, Nov. 1947-Feb. 1950, Beverley Division of the East Riding of Yorkshire, 1950-55; CC East Riding, Yorkshire, 1964-. Leathersellers' Company Livery, 1939. Hon. Air Commodore (RAuxAF), retired. Commodore House of Commons Yacht Club, 1954. President: International Tanners' Council, 1954-67; British Leather Manufacturers Research Assoc., 1964; British Leather Federation, 1965; Federation of Gelatine and Glue Manufacturers, 1955-57; British Gelatine and Glue Research Assoc., 1950-. Member: Western Hemisphere Export Council, 1960-64; Cttee for Exports to the US, 1964; Member of Lloyd's. *Recreations:* farming, yachting, tennis. *Address:* Keldgate Manor, Beverley, E Yorks. *T:* Beverley 882418. *Clubs:* Carlton, Royal Automobile; Royal Yorkshire Yacht; Lloyds Yacht; Scarborough Yacht; House of Commons Yacht.

**ODGERS, Lindsey Noel Blake,** MC 1916; *b* 21 Dec. 1892; *s* of late William Blake Odgers, KC, LLD, and Frances (*née* Hudson); *m* 1923, Constance Attneave (*d* 1969). *Educ:* Rugby; St John's Coll., Cambridge. Served European War in Middlesex Regt, 1914-18, and Royal Engineers, 1918-19. Entered Home Office, 1919; seconded to Chief Secretary's Office, 1920-22; Principal, Home Office, 1926; Assistant Secretary, 1937; Assistant Under Secretary of State, Home Office, 1949-54. *Recreation:* gardening. *Address:* Woodbourne, Groombridge, Tunbridge Wells, Kent. *T:* Groombridge 269.

**ODGERS, Paul Randell,** CB 1970; MBE 1945; TD 1949; Assistant Under-Secretary of State, Office of the Secretary of State for Social Services, since 1968; *b* 30 July 1915; *e s* of late Dr P. N. B. Odgers and Mrs M. A. Odgers (*née* Higgins); *m* 1944, Diana, *d* of late R. E. F. Fawkes, CBE; one *s* one *d*. *Educ:* Rugby; New Coll., Oxford. Assistant Principal, Board of Education, 1937. Army Service, 1939-45 (despatches three times). Asst Secretary: Min. of Educn, 1948; Cabinet Office, 1956; Under-Sec., Min. of Educn, 1958; Asst Under-Sec. of State, Office of First Secretary of State, 1967; Under-Sec., Office of Lord President of the Council, 1968. *Address:* Dudswell House, Northchurch, Berkhamsted, Herts. *T:* Berkhamsted 5070. *Club:* United University.

**ODLING, Maj.-Gen. William,** CB 1963; OBE 1951; MC; Regional Organiser, English Speaking Union, since 1965; *b* 8 June 1909; *s* of late Major W. A. Odling, Middlesex Regt, and of Mrs W. A. Odling, Paxford, Campden, Gloucestershire; *m* 1939, Margaret Marshall (*née* Gardner); one *s* two *d*. *Educ:* Temple Grove; Wellington Coll.; RMA, Woolwich. Commissioned Royal Artillery, 1929; Subaltern RHA and RA, chiefly in India until 1938; Captain, 1938; Major, 1946; Lieut-Colonel, 1951; Colonel, 1953; Brigadier 1957; Maj.-General, 1961; Adjutant, TA, 1939; CRA, Madagascar Force, 1942 (MC); GSO 1, RA, COSSAC, Planning Staff for Operation Overlord, 1943; N.W. Europe Campaign (despatches), 1944; GSO 1, War Office, 1945; GSO 1, Training, GHQMELF, 1948; AQMG, MELF, 1950; AAG Colonel, War Office, Nov. 1953; CRA, E. Anglian Div., 1957; Brigadier, AQ Headquarters, Eastern Command, 1959; Maj.-General in charge of Administration, General Headquarters, Far East Land Forces, 1961-62; Chief of Staff, General Headquarters, Far East Land Forces, 1962-64. *Publication:* Soldier's Bedside Book, 1945. *Recreations:* various offices in the Church of England, beagling, sailing, print collecting. *Address:* Gun House, Fingringhoe, Essex. *T:* Peldon 320. *Club:* Army and Navy.

**ODLUM, Dr Doris Maude;** Hon. Consultant, since 1955, formerly Senior Physician for Psychological Medicine, Elizabeth Garrett Anderson (Royal Free) Hospital, London; Consultant Emeritus, Marylebone Hospital for Psychiatry and Child Guidance, London; Consultant Emeritus, Bournemouth and East Dorset Hospital Group; Fellow, British Medical Association, 1959; *b* 26 June 1890; *d* of Walter Edward and Maude Gough Odlum. *Educ:* Talbot Heath, Bournemouth; St Hilda's Coll., Oxford; St Mary's Hospital and London School of Medicine for Women. MA Oxon; BA London; MRCS; LRCP; DPM; Hon. Consultant Phys., Lady Chichester Hospital for Nervous Diseases, Hove, 1928-48; Hon. Phys. for Psychiatry, Royal Victoria and W. Hants Hospital, Bournemouth, 1928-48; President, British Med. Women's Federation, 1950-53; President, European League for Mental Hygiene, 1953-56; Vice-President, International Med. Women's Assoc., 1950-54; Vice-President, National Assoc. for Mental Health, 1946-; Member Exec. World Federation for Mental Health, 1948-51; Corresponding Member Swiss Psychiatric Assoc., 1946-; Member Home Office Cttee on Adoption, 1954. *Publications:* You and Your Children, 1948; Psychology, the Nurse and the Patient (3rd edn 1959, US edn 1960); Journey Through Adolescence, 1957 (2nd edn, 1965); The Mind of Your Child, 1959; L'Età Difficile, 1962 (2nd edn 1968); Puber Puberteit, 1965. Articles in British Medical Journal, Lancet, Practitioner, etc. *Recreations:* painting, golf, swimming, travel. *Address:* (Residence) Ardmor, 11 Cliff Drive, Canford Cliffs, Poole, Dorset. *T:* Canford Cliffs 77915; 56 Wimpole Street, W1.

**ODLUM, Maj.-Gen. Victor Wentworth,** CB 1918; CMG 1917; DSO 1915 and Bar 1916; VD; LLD; former Canadian Ambassador to China and Turkey; *b* Cobourg, Ontario, 21 Oct. 1880; *s* of Prof. E. Odlum, MA, BSc, and Mary Powell; *m* 1904, Sada Eugenie Tressa, *d* of Isaac and Margaret Rogerson; three *s*. *Educ:* Toronto Univ. Served South African War with 1st Canadian Contingent (2nd RCR), and afterwards in 3rd Canadian Mounted Rifles (medal 3 clasps); Colonial long service medal; served European War, 1914-18 (wounded thrice, despatches 7 times, DSO and bar, CMG, CB); originally commanded 7th Canadian Infantry Batt. (1st British Columbia) CEF, afterwards GOC 11th Canadian Inf. Bde, 1916-19; Order of Danilo, 3rd Class, 1917; Liberal Member for Vancouver City in Provincial Legislature, 1924-28; Governor and Vice-Chairman, Canadian Broadcasting Corporation, 1932-40; Governor University of British Columbia, 1936-40; Publisher of Vancouver Daily Star, 1924-32; commanded 2nd Division Canadian Active Service Force, 1940-41; Canadian High Commissioner to Australia, 1941-42; Canadian Ambassador to China, 1942-46, to Turkey, 1947-52. *Address:* 1509-935 Marine, West Vancouver, BC, Canada. *Clubs:* Vancouver (Vancouver), West Vancouver Yacht, Vancouver Arts.

**O'DOHERTY, Most Rev. Eugene;** *see* Dromore, Bishop of, (RC).

**O'DONNELL, Most Rev. Patrick;** *see* Brisbane, Archbishop of, (RC).

**O'DONNELL, Peadar;** Member Irish Academy of Letters. *Educ:* St Patrick's, Dublin. *Publications:* Storm; Islanders, 1925; Adrigoole, 1928; The Knife, 1930; The Gates Flew Open; On The Edge of the Stream, 1934; Salud; An Irishman in Spain, 1937; The Big Windows, 1955. *Address:* 176 Upper Drumcondra Road, Whitehall, Dublin.

**O'DONOGHUE, Geoffrey Charles Patrick Randal (The O'Donoghue of the Glens);** *b* 8 Oct. 1896; *e s* of late Geoffrey Charles Patrick O'Donoghue and Annie Matilda Deighton (*d* 1921), *y d* of W. Charlton of Clonmancnoise, King's County; two *s* one *d*. *Educ:* Blackrock Coll., Dublin; Stonyhurst. Served European War 1914-19, as Lieut, The Connaught Rangers. *Address:* Ballinahown Court, Athlone, Co. Westmeath.

**O'DONOGHUE, John Kingston,** CBE 1956 (OBE 1947; MBE 1932); *b* 6 October 1894; *s* of Thomas and Elizabeth O'Donoghue; *m* 1925, Mary Carmela Burrell (*d* 1965); two *s* one *d*. *Educ:* St Vincent's College, Castleknock, Dublin. Appointed to Foreign Office, 1915; served European War with 18th London Regt, 1917-19; returned to Foreign Office, 1919; attached to British Delegation to Disarmament Conference, Washington, 1921-22; Archivist to HM Embassy, Berlin, 1924; Foreign Office, 1939; Allied Commission, Germany, 1944-46; Actg Consul-General, Rio de Janeiro, March 1947; Consul, New York, Oct. 1947; Assistant in Personnel Department, Foreign Office, 1950; Consul-General for the States of Pennsylvania, Delaware, etc., 1953-56; retired, 1956. Life member Philadelphia Chamber of Commerce, 1956. *Recreations:* golf, walking. *Address:* Heatherdene, The Paddock, Merrow, Guildford, Surrey. *T:* Guildford 70367.

**O'DONOGHUE, Richard John Langford,** DSO 1918; MA (TCD); MB, BS (London University); MRCP London; DMRE (Cambridge); *b* 22 August 1889; *s* of Cooper Charles O'Donoghue and M. H. Matthews. *Educ:* Campbell Coll., Belfast; Trinity College, Dublin; Guy's Hospital. Served France 1914-18 (DSO, despatches); late Egyptian Civil Service; Private Secretary to the Financial Adviser to the Egyptian Government; Assistant to Controller-General Central Administration Ministry of Finance, Cairo, and Controller of Pensions (Order of the Nile, 4th class). *Recreations:* walking, swimming, music. *Address:* 55 Rotherwick Road, NW11. *T:* 01-455 7150.

**O'FAOLAIN, Sean;** writer. *Publications:* Midsummer Night Madness, 1932; A Nest of Simple Folk, 1933; Constance Markievicz: a biography, 1934; Bird Alone, 1936; A Purse of Coppers, 1937; King of the Beggars: a biography, 1938; She Had to Do Something (play), 1938; An Irish Journey, 1940; Come Back to Erin, 1940; The Great O'Neill: a biography, 1942; Teresa, 1946; The Short Story, 1948; Summer in Italy, 1949; Newman's Way, 1952; South to Sicily, 1953; The Vanishing Hero, 1956; The Stories of Sean O'Faolain, 1958; I Remember! I Remember!, 1962; Vive Moi!, 1965; The Heat of the Sun, 1966; The Talking Trees, 1970. *Address:* Knockaderry, Killiney, Co. Dublin.

**O'FERRALL, Rt. Rev. Ronald Stanhope More,** MA, DD; *b* 1890; *s* of late J. E. O'Ferrall; *m* 1934, Ann Molesworth, *o c* of late J. M. Kindersley; one *s* one *d*. *Educ:* Charterhouse; Trinity Coll., Cambridge; Ely Theological Coll. BA 1913; MA 1916; DD (Lambeth), 1926. Deacon, 1914; Priest, 1915; Curate at Chesterfield Parish Church, 1914-18; With EEF, 1918-19; Asst Priest at St George's Cathedral and House Master at St George's School, Jerusalem, 1919-23; UMCA, Mission Priest in N Rhodesia, 1923-26; Bishop in Madagascar, 1926-40; Rector of Walton on Trent, 1940-44; Vicar of Repton and Foremark, 1944-47; Divinity Master Repton School, 1944-47; Assistant Bishop of Derby and Hon. Canon of Derby Cathedral, 1941-53; Provost of Derby and Proctor in Convocation, 1947-53. Examining Chaplain to Bishop of Derby, 1948-53; Rector of Cranham, Glos, 1953-56; Assistant Bishop of Gloucester, 1955-56; Vicar of Hyde, Fordingbridge, 1956-58, retd. Commissary for the Bishops in Madagascar. *Recreations:* archæology, gardening. *Address:* Broadview, Andover Road, Winchester, Hampshire. *T:* Winchester 3008.

**OFFALY, Earl of; Maurice FitzGerald;** *b* 7 April 1948; *s* and *heir* of Marquess of Kildare, *qv*. *Educ:* Millfield School. *Address:* Langston House, Chadlington, Oxford.

**OFFICER, Maj.-Gen. William James,** CB 1962; CBE 1959 (OBE 1945); MB, ChB; late RAMC; *b* 24 August 1903; *s* of John Liddell Officer, OBE, WS, Edinburgh; *m* 1934, Doris, *d* of William Charles Mattinson, Keswick, Cumberland; three *d*. *Educ:* Edinburgh Acad.; Durham School; Edinburgh University. MB, ChB, Edin., 1927. Joined RAMC, 1929; Major, 1939; Commanding Officer British Military Hosp., Deolali, and Officer-in-Charge RAMC Records, India and Burma, 1939-41; Served War of 1939-45 (despatches twice); in Burma, 1941-45; ADMS, 17th Indian Division and 2nd British Division; DDMS, Chindits Special Force and 33rd Indian Corps. Lt-Col, 1946; Asst Commandant, RAMC Depot and Training Establishment; Commanding Officer, British Military Hospital, Fayid (T/Col), 1949; Col 1951; ADMS, Hannover Dist, 1952; ADMS, N Midland Dist, 1954; DDMS (Actg Brig.), 2 (Br) Corps (Suez), 1956; Brig., 1957; DMS (temp. Maj.-Gen.),

MELF, 1957-60; Maj.-Gen., 1960; Dir of Medical Services, Far East Land Forces, 1960-63; QHS 1961-63, retired 1963. *Recreations:* golf, tennis, swimming. *Address:* c/o Glyn Mills & Co., Kirkland House, SW1. *Club:* Naval and Military.

**OFFICER BROWN, Sir (Charles) James;** *see* Brown, Sir C. J. O.

**OFFLER, Prof. Hilary Seton,** MA; Professor of Medieval History in the University of Durham, since Oct. 1956; Chairman, Board of Studies in Modern History, 1965-68; *b* 3 Feb. 1913; *s* of Horace Offler and late Jenny Whebby; *m* 1951, Betty Elfreda, *d* of late Archibald Jackson, Sawbridgeworth; two *s*. *Educ:* Hereford High School; Emmanuel College, Cambridge. 1st Cl. Historical Tripos Pt I, 1932, Part II, 1933, Theological Tripos Pt II, 1934; Lightfoot Schol., Cambridge, 1934; Research Fellow, Emmanuel Coll., 1936-40. Served with RA in N Africa, Sicily and NW Europe, 1940-46, commissioned 1942. Lecturer, Univ. of Bristol, 1946; Reader in Medieval History, Univ. of Durham, 1947. Sec., Surtees Society, 1950-66. *Publications:* (jointly) ed. Ockham, *Opera politica,* vol. i, 1940, vol. ii, 1963; (with E. Bonjour and G. R. Potter) A Short History of Switzerland, 1952; Ed. Ockham, *Opera politica,* vol. iii, 1956; Medieval Historians of Durham, 1958; Durham Episcopal Charters 1071-1152, 1968; articles in English and foreign hist. jls. *Address:* 28 Old Elvet, Durham.

**OFFORD, Albert Cyril,** FRS 1952; DSc London; PhD Cantab; FRSE; Professor of Mathematics, London School of Economics and Political Science, since 1966, Fellow, University College since 1969, University of London; *b* 9 June 1906; *s* of Albert Edwin and Hester Louise Offord; *m* 1945, Marguerite Yvonne Pickard; one *d*. *Educ:* Hackney Downs School, London; University College, London; St John's College, Cambridge. Fellow of St John's College, Cambridge, 1937-40; Lecturer University College of North Wales, Bangor, 1940-41; Lecturer King's College, Newcastle on Tyne, 1941-45; Professor: King's College, Newcastle on Tyne, 1945-48; Birkbeck Coll., University of London, 1948-66. *Publications:* papers in various mathematical journals. *Address:* 70 Elms Road, Harrow, Mddx HA3 6BS.

**O'FLAHERTY, Liam;** novelist; *b* Aran Islands, Co. Galway. *Educ:* Rockwell College; Blackrock College; University College, Dublin. *Publications:* Thy Neighbour's Wife, a novel; The Black Soul, a novel; Spring Sowing, short stories; The Informer, a novel; The Tent, and other stories, 1926; Mr Gilhooley, 1926; The Life of Tim Healy, 1927; The Assassin, 1928; The Mountain Tavern, and other stories, 1929; A Tourist's Guide to Ireland, 1929; The House of Gold, 1929; Two Years, 1930; I went to Russia, 1931; The Puritan, 1932; Skerrett, 1932; Shame the Devil, 1934; Hollywood Cemetery, 1935; Famine, 1937; Short Stories of Liam O'Flaherty, 1937; Land, 1946; Two Lovely Beasts, short stories, 1948; Insurrection, 1950; The Short Stories of Liam O'Flaherty, 1956. *Address:* c/o A. D. Peters, 10 Buckingham Street, Adelphi, WC2.

**O'FLYNN, Brigadier (Retd) Dennis John Edwin,** CBE 1960 (MBE 1937); DSO 1945; Army Officer retired; *b* 2 Aug. 1907; *s* of late Patrick Horace George O'Flynn and of Katie Alice (*née* Pye); *m* 1936, Winifred Madge Cairn Hogbin; (one *s* and one *d* decd). *Educ:* St Paul's School; RMC Sandhurst. Commissioned 2nd Lieut, Royal Tank Corps, 1928; served in Trans-Jordan Frontier Force, 1932-36; commanded: Westminster Dragoons (2nd Co. Lond. Yeo.), 1947-48; 3rd Royal Tank Regiment, 1948-50. Brigade Commander, 1953-60; retired 1960. Area Comr, St John Ambulance Brigade, 1966-69. OStJ 1967. *Recreations:* golf, gardening, photography. *Address:* High Copse, Pinemount Road, Camberley, Surrey. *T:* Camberley 63736. *Club:* Army and Navy.

**O'FLYNN, Surgeon Rear-Adm. Joseph Aloysius,** CB 1948; MD, DTM & H; retired; *b* 7 Jan. 1889; *s* of late Edmond O'Flynn, JP and late Mary O'Callaghan, Cork, Ireland; *m* 1929, Linda Avis Leonard; two *s*. *Educ:* Clongowes Wood College, Kildare; Queen's College, Cork. Joined RN, 1912; Surg. Lt-Comdr, 1918; Surg. Comdr, 1924; Surg. Capt., 1936; Surg. Rear-Adm., 1944. Employed on initial anti-malarial work at RN Base, Singapore, 1925-26; Work on Active Immunisation against Diphtheria, 1932-33 (Medical Research Council Special Report Series No. 195). Late Medical Officer in Charge, RN Hospital, Haslar, Gosport, Formerly KHP. *Recreation:* golf. *Address:* 30 Bahama Court, 8 Deeban Walk, Cronulla, NSW 2230, Australia. *T:* 523 5619.

**of MAR;** family name of **Earl of Mar.**

**OGDEN, Sir Alwyne (George Neville),** KBE, *cr* 1948 (OBE 1927); CMG 1946; retired; *b* Simla, India, 29 June 1889; *s* of William Ogden, Indian Government Railways, and Emily Mary Stowell; *m* 1922, Jessie Vera (*d* 1969), *d* of Albert Bridge, Adviser to Chinese Government; one *s* one *d*. *Educ:* Dulwich College; Corpus Christi College, Cambridge (Scholar, BA (Hons) in Classics and History). Student-Interpreter in China Consular Service, 1912; special service (War Office) with Chinese Labour Corps, 1917-18, and on Tibetan Frontier, 1922; Actg Consul-General at Chengtu 1922-23, and Tientsin, 1929-30; Consul (Grade II) 1929, (Grade I), 1934. Served at Peking, Tientsin, Tsinanfu, Chengtu, Hankow, Changsha, Kiukiang, Chefoo, Wei-Hai-Wei, Nanking, Shanghai; Consul-General at Tientsin, 1941, Kunming, 1942-45, Shanghai, 1945-48; retired from Foreign Service, 1948. Acting Judge of HBM Supreme Court for China, 1942-43. FRSA 1952. *Address:* Kingsbury, 51 Ridgway Road, Farnham, Surrey. *T:* Farnham 5461. *Clubs:* Junior Carlton, Royal Automobile.

**OGDEN, (Edward) Michael,** QC 1968; Barrister-at-law since 1950; *b* 9 Apr. 1926; *er s* of late Edward Cannon Ogden and Daisy (*née* Paris); *m* 1951, Joan Kathleen, *er d* of late Pius Charles Brodrick and Kathleen (*née* Moran); two *s* two *d*. *Educ:* Downside Sch.; Jesus Coll., Cambridge (MA). Served in RAC (Royal Glos Hussars and 16th/5th Lancers), 1944-47 (Capt.); Inns of Court Regt (TA) 1950-56. Jesus Coll., Cambridge, 1948-49; called to Bar, Lincoln's Inn, 1950. Mem., Criminal Injuries Compensation Bd, 1968-. Contested (C): West Walthamstow, 1964; Epping, 1966. *Address:* 2 Crown Office Row, Temple, EC4. *T:* 01-353 9337; 22 Stanford Road, W8. *T:* 01-937 6275.

**OGDEN, Eric;** MP (Lab) West Derby Division of Liverpool since 1964; *b* 23 Aug. 1923; *s* of Robert and Jane Lillian Ogden, Rhodes, Co. Lancaster; *m* 1945, Mary M. Patricia (*née* Aitken); one *s*. *Educ:* Queen Elizabeth's Grammar School, Middleton, Lancs. Merchant Service, 1942-46. Textiles, 1946-52; NCB, 1952-64. Mem., Nat. Union of Mineworkers. Councillor, Borough of Middleton, 1958-65. NUM sponsored candidate, West Derby, Liverpool, 1962.

*Recreations:* swimming, motoring, gardening, reading. *Address:* House of Commons, SW1. *T:* 01-930 6240.

**OGDEN, Frank Collinge,** CBE 1956; FRGS; *b* 30 Mar. 1907; *s* of Paul and Nora Ogden; *m* 1944, Margaret, *o d* of Fred and Elizabeth Greenwood; one *s* two *d* (and one *d* decd). *Educ:* Manchester Grammar School; King's College, Cambridge. Entered Levant Consular Service, 1930; served in Cairo, Alexandria, Bagdad and Damascus; served War, 1941-42; Min. of Information, 1942; Tabriz, 1942; 1st Sec., Bogotá, 1944, Chargé d'Affaires, 1945; Consul, Shiraz, 1947; transferred to Seattle, 1949; Consul-General, Seattle, 1952; Basra, 1953; Gothenburg, 1955; Couns., Brit. Emb. in Libya, 1958; Chargé d'Affaires, 1958, 1959; Counsellor and Consul-General, Brit. Emb., Buenos Aires, 1960-65; retired. *Recreations:* tennis, swimming, motoring. *Address:* Yellow Sands, Thorney Drive, Selsey, Chichester, Sussex. *Club:* Royal Automobile.

**OGDEN, George Chester,** CBE 1966; Town Clerk, Manchester, since 1966; *b* 7 June 1913; *s* of Harry and Florence A. Ogden, Burnley, Lancs; *m* 1942, Nina Marion (*née* Lewis); one *s* two *d*. *Educ:* Burnley Gram. Sch.; Giggleswick Sch.; Corpus Christi Coll., Oxford (MA). Asst Solicitor, Middlesbrough Corp., 1940. Served in Royal Marines, Middle East, Sicily and NW Europe, 1941-45 (Major). Dep. Town Clerk: Middlesbrough, 1947-53; Leicester, 1953-54; Town Clerk, Leicester, 1955-66. *Recreations:* golf, fell walking. *Address:* Crossways, 42 Arthog Road, Hale, Cheshire. *Clubs:* National Liberal; St James's (Manchester).

**OGDEN, Michael;** *see* Ogden, E. M.

**OGDON, John (Andrew Howard);** Pianist, Composer; *b* 27 Jan. 1937; *s* of late John Andrew Howard Ogdon, School-master, and Dorothy Louise (*née* Mutton); *m* 1960, Brenda Mary Lucas; one *s* one *d*. *Educ:* Manchester Gram. Sch.; Royal Manchester Coll. of Music. Concert Appearances include: Michelangeli Festival, Brescia, 1966; Festivals of Spoleto, Edinburgh, Prague Spring, Zagreb Biennale, Cheltenham. Founded Cardiff Festival (with Alun Hoddinott), 1967, Jt Artistic Dir. Two-piano recitals with Brenda Lucas. Awards: Liverpool, 1959; Liszt Prize, 1961; Tschaikovsky Prize (*ex aequo* with Vladimir Ashkenazy), Moscow, 1962; Harriet Cohen International Award. *Compositions:* large and small, mainly for piano. *Recreations:* history, literature, P. G. Wodehouse, reading Peter Simple. *Address:* 13 Chester Terrace, Regent's Park, NW1. *Clubs:* Savage (Bristol); Scottish Arts (Edinburgh).

**OGG, Sir William Gammie,** Kt, *cr* 1949; Director of Rothamsted Experimental Station, 1943-58, retired; *b* 2 Nov. 1891; *s* of late James Ogg, Cults, Aberdeenshire, farmer; *m* 1922, Helen, *y d* of late Henry Hilbert, Halifax; one *s* one *d*. *Educ:* Robert Gordon's College; Aberdeen University; Christ's College, Cambridge. MA, BSc, BSc (Agr.), Aberdeen Univ., PhD Cantab, LLD Aberdeen, FRSE. Res. Fellow, Bd of Agr. for Scotland, studying in Canada and USA, 1919-20; Researcher, Christ's College, Cambridge, 1920-24; Advisory Officer in Soils, Edinburgh, and East of Scotland College of Agriculture, 1924-30; Director of the Macaulay Institute for Soil Research, Craigiebuckler, Aberdeen, 1930-43, and research lecturer in Soil Science in the University of Aberdeen; Pres. Soc. of Chem. Industry, 1953-55. Hon. Fellow of the Royal Agric. Soc. of England; For. Corresp. of French Acad. of Agriculture; For. Member of Roy. Acad. of Agriculture of Sweden; Foreign Member of All-Union Academy of Agric. Sciences of the USSR. Hon. Coun. Consejo Superior de Investigaciones Cientificas, Spain. Raffaele Piria medal of Societa Chimica Italiana, 1958. *Publications:* Publications on soil chemistry, soil surveys, land reclamation and peat. *Address:* Arnhall, by Edzell, Angus. *T:* Edzell 400.

**OGILVIE, Sir Alec (Drummond),** Kt 1965; Chairman, Powell Duffryn Ltd, since 1969 (Deputy Chairman, 1967-69); *b* 17 May 1913; *s* of late Sir George Drummond Ogilvie, KCIE, CSI; *m* 1945, Lesley Constance, *d* of E. B. Woollan; two *s*. *Educ:* Cheltenham College. Joined Andrew Yule & Co. Ltd, Calcutta, 1935, Man. Dir, 1956, and Chm., 1962-65. Director, Westinghouse Brake & Signal Co. Ltd, 1966-; Pres., Bengal Chamber of Commerce and Industry, 1964-65; Pres., Associated Chambers of Commerce and Industry of India, 1964-65. *Recreations:* golf, walking. *Address:* Brakelands, Warninglid, near Haywards Heath, Sussex. *T:* Warninglid 270. *Clubs:* Oriental, MCC; Bengal (Calcutta).

**OGILVIE, Lady, (Mary Helen);** Principal of St Anne's College, Oxford, 1953-66; *b* 22 March 1900; *e d* of late Rev. Professor A. B. Macaulay, DD, of Glasgow; *m* 1922, (Sir) Frederick Wolff Ogilvie, LLD (*d* 1949), Principal of Jesus College, Oxford, 1945-49; two *s* (and one *s* decd). *Educ:* St George's, Edinburgh; Somerville College, Oxford. BA Hon. Sch. of Mod. Hist., Oxford, 1922, MA 1937. Member Royal Commission on Population, 1944-49; Tutor of Women Students, University of Leeds, 1949-53. Member of Arts Council of Great Britain, 1953-58; on Governing Board of Cheltenham Ladies' College, 1951-; Governing Board of Clifton College, 1960-. Hon. LLD: Wilson College, Pa, 1956, QUB 1960; Leeds Univ., 1962. Hon. Fellow, St Anne's College, Oxford, 1966. *Recreation:* travel. *Address:* Flat 5, Fairlawn, First Turn, Wolvercote, Oxford. *T:* 58137. *Club:* University Women's.

**OGILVIE, Robert Maxwell,** MA DLitt; Headmaster, Tonbridge School, since Sept. 1970; *b* 5 June 1932; *y s* of late Sir Frederick Ogilvie and of Lady Ogilvie, *qv*; *m* 1959, Jennifer Margaret, *d* of D. W. Roberts, Lymington; two *s* one *d*. *Educ:* Rugby; Balliol College, Oxford. First class Hon. Mods, 1952; first class, Lit. Hum., 1954; Harmsworth Sen. Schol. Merton Coll., 1954-55; Fellow and Dir of Studies in Classics, Clare Coll., Cambridge, 1955-57; Fellow of Balliol, 1957-70; Sen. Tutor, 1966-70; Mem., Gen. Board of the Faculties, 1967-70; Mem., Hart Cttee on Relations with Junior Members, 1968. Visiting Special Lecturer, University Coll., Toronto, 1965-66; Vis. Prof., Yale Univ., 1969; Hofmeyr Vis. Fellow, Wits Univ., 1969. DLitt Oxon, 1967; FSA 1968. *Publications:* Latin and Greek: a history of the influence of the classics on English life, 1964; A Commentary on Livy, 1-5, 1965; Tacitus, *Agricola* (with Sir Ian Richmond), 1967; The Ancient World (Oxford Children's Reference Library), 1969; The Romans and Their Gods, 1970. *Recreations:* music, climbing, golf. *Address:* School House, Tonbridge, Kent: Errachd, By Fort William, Inverness-shire. *Clubs:* Athenæum; Gridiron (Oxford).

**OGILVIE, Sir (William) Heneage,** KBE 1946; Consulting Surgeon, Guy's Hospital; Editor of the Practitioner since 1946; formerly Examiner in Surgery, Universities of Oxford and Cambridge; *b* Chile, 1887; *e s* of William Ogilvie, Valparaiso and Harrow Weald; *m* 1915, Vere Magdalen, *e d* of Harry Quilter; one *s* two *d*. *Educ:* Clifton Coll.; New Coll.,

Oxford; Guy's Hospital. First Class Honours Oxford, 1910; MRCS, LRCP, 1913; MB, BCh Oxon, 1913; FRCS Eng., MCh Oxon, 1920; MD Oxon, 1924; FACS (Hon.) 1938; FRCSC (Hon.) 1943; MS Fouad I (Hon.), 1944; FRACS (Hon.) 1947; FRSM (Hon.) 1957; LLD Witwatersrand (Hon.), 1943; Hunterian Prof. RCS, 1924; Surgeon Urgency Cases Hosp., France, 1915-17; RAMC, 1917-20; Surgical Registrar, Guy's Hospital, 1920; Senior Demonstrator of Anatomy, 1922; Assistant Surgeon, 1925; Temp. Gen., Army Medical Service; Consulting Surgeon Expeditionary Force, 1940-45; Fellow Royal Society of Medicine; member Association of Surgeons. Upper Warden, Feltmakers' Co., 1957; Master, 1958. *Publications:* Recent Advances in Surgery; Treatment of Fractures; Forward Surgery in Modern War, 1944; Surgery, Orthodox and Heterodox, 1949; No Miracles among Friends, 1959; Hernia, 1959; Fifty, 1962; The Tired Business Man, 1963; chapters in The Operations of Surgery, and Postgraduate Surgery; contributions to professional periodicals. *Recreation:* sailing. *Address:* 18 Clifton Road, SW19. *TA:* (Monomark) BM/OPRS. *Clubs:* Athenæum; Royal Corinthian; Imperial Poona Yacht.

**OGILVIE-GRANT-STUDLEY-HERBERT;** family name of **Countess of Seafield.**

**OGILVY,** family name of **Earl of Airlie.**

**OGILVY, Lord; David John Ogilvy;** *b* 9 March 1958; *s* and *heir* of 13th Earl of Airlie, *qv.*

**OGILVY, Hon. Angus James Bruce;** Company Director; *b* 14 Sept. 1928; *s* of 12th (*de facto* 9th) Earl of Airlie, KT, GCVO, MC; *m* 1963, HRH Princess Alexandra of Kent; one *s* one *d. Educ:* Eton Coll.; Trinity Coll., Oxford. Captain, Scots Guards, 1946-48. President: Scottish Wildlife Trust; Imperial Cancer Research Fund, 1964-; Chairman, National Association of Youth Clubs, 1964-; Chairman, The Friends of the Poor and Gentlefolk's Help, 1963-; Pres., British Rheumatism and Arthritis Assoc., 1963-; Vice-Patron, Toc H, 1963-; Patron, Livingston Youth Trust. *Address:* Thatched House Lodge, Richmond Park, Surrey. *T:* Kingston 8833. *Club:* White's.
*See also under Royal Family.*

**OGILVY, Sir David (John Wilfrid),** 13th Bt, *cr* 1626; JP; farmer and landowner; *b* 3 February 1914; *e s* of Gilbert Francis Molyneux Ogilvy (*d* 1953) (4th *s* of 10th Bt) and Marjory Katharine, *d* of late M. B. Clive, Whitfield, Herefordshire; *S* uncle, Sir Herbert Kinnaird Ogilvy, 12th Bt, 1956; *m* 1966, Penelope Mary Ursula, *d* of Arthur Lafone Frank Hills, White Court, Kent; one *s. Educ:* Eton; Trinity College, Oxford. Served in the RNVR in War of 1939-45. JP 1957. *Heir: s* Francis Gilbert Arthur Ogilvy, *b* 22 April 1969. *Address:* Winton House, Pencaitland, East Lothian. *T:* Pencaitland 222. *Club:* New (Edinburgh).

**OGILVY, David Mackenzie,** CBE 1967; Chairman, Ogilvy and Mather, International, since 1965; Founder 1948, subsequently President, Ogilvy, Benson & Mather Inc., Advertising Agency, New York; *b* 23 June 1911; *s* of Francis John Longley Ogilvy and Dorothy Fairfield; *m* 1st, 1939, Melinda Street (marriage dissolved, 1957); one *s*; 2nd, 1957, Anne Cabot. *Educ:* Fettes College, Edinburgh; Christ Church, Oxford (Scholar). British Security Coordination, 1942; Second Secretary, British Embassy, Washington, 1944. Trustee, Colby Coll., Maine, 1962. *Publication:* Confessions of an Advertising Man, 1964. *Recreation:* farming. *Address:* 521 East 84th St, NYC 10028, USA. *Club:* Brook (NY).

**OGILVY-WEDDERBURN, Comdr Sir (John) Peter,** 12th and 6th Bt, *cr* 1704 and 1803; RN (retired 1961); *b* 29 Sept. 1917; *o s* of Sir John Andrew Ogilvy-Wedderburn, 11th and 5th Bt, and Aileen Meta Odette (*née* Grogan); *S* father 1956; *m* 1946, Elizabeth Katharine, *e d* of late John A. Cox, Drumkilbo; one *s* three *d. Educ:* The Nautical College, Pangbourne. Entered RN as cadet, 1935; Midshipman, 1936-38; Sub-Lt, 1938-40; Lt, 1940-48; Lt-Comdr, 1948-55; Comdr, 1955; psc 1956; Exec. Officer, Woolwich, 1956; Boom Defence and Marine Salvage Officer, Clyde, 1958. *Recreations:* shooting, forestry, Loch Ness monster hunting. *Heir: s* Andrew John Alexander Ogilvy-Wedderburn, *b* 4 August 1952. *Address:* Silvie, Alyth, Perthshire. *T:* Alyth 362.
*See also F. W. A. Fairfax-Cholmeley.*

**OGLE-SKAN, Peter Henry,** TD 1948; Under-Secretary, Scottish Headquarters, Ministry of Public Building and Works, since 1966; *b* 4 July 1915; 2nd *s* of Dr H. W. Ogle-Skan, Hendon; *m* 1941, Pamela Moira Heslop; one *s* one *d. Educ:* Merchant Taylors' Sch., London. Clerk with Arbuthnot-Latham & Co. Ltd, London, 1933-39. Commnd into Royal Engineers (TA), 1936; War Service, 1939-46; England, 1939-42; India, 1942-45. Temp. Princ., Min. of Works, 1946; Principal, 1948; Asst Sec., 1955. *Recreations:* golf, walking, photography. *Address:* 44 Ravelston Garden, Edinburgh EH4 3LF. *T:* 031-337 6834. *Club:* Scottish Liberal (Edinburgh).

**OGMORE,** 1st Baron, *cr* 1950, of Bridgend; **Lt-Col David Rees Rees-Williams,** PC 1951; TD; *b* 22 November 1903; *o c* of late Wm Rees Williams, FRCVS, and late Jennet Williams, Bridgend, Glamorgan; *m* 1930, Constance Wills (JP), *er d* of W. R. Wills, Lord Mayor of Cardiff, 1945-46; two *s* one *d. Educ:* Mill Hill School; University of Wales. Honoursman Law Society, 1929; practised in Straits Settlements, where he was admitted to Straits Settlements Bar; MP (Lab.) Croydon, South, 1945-50; Parliamentary Under-Secretary of State: Colonial Office, 1947-50; Commonwealth Relations Office, 1950-51; Minister of Civil Aviation, June-Oct. 1951. On active service Aug. 1939-Oct. 1945, Lt-Col RA; Presided over first Gen. Military Court held in Berlin; Staff Officer, 1st Grade. Patron Bridgend Rugby Football Club; Member Government Mission to Sarawak, 1946; Chairman Burma Frontier Areas Committee of Enquiry, 1947; Pres. Bridgend YMCA; UK Deleg. to UN Gen. Assembly in NY, 1950; Leader of UK Deleg. and Chm. of African Defence Facilities Conf., Nairobi, 1951. Director: Property Owners' Building Soc.; Leo Laboratories Ltd; Pres., Welsh Liberal Party; Member: Standing Group of Privy Counsellors on Offical Histories; Nigerian Bar; Investiture Cttee and carried the Coronet, Investiture of HRH The Prince of Wales, 1969. Order Agga Maha Thray Sithu, Union of Burma, 1956. Panglima Mangku Negara (Hon.) in Order Pangkuan Negara (Fedn of Malaya), 1959. *Heir: s* Hon. Gwilym Rees Rees-Williams [*b* 5 May 1931; *m* 1967, Gillian Mavis, *d* of M. K. Slack, Hindley, Lancs; two *d*]. *Address:* 47 Abingdon Court, Kensington, W8. *T:* 01-937 4963.

**O'GORMAN, Rev. Brian Stapleton;** Chairman of the Wolverhampton and Shrewsbury District of the Methodist Church, since 1957; President of the Methodist Conference, 1969-70; *b* 4 March 1910; *s* of William Thomas and Annie Maria O'Gorman; *m* 1939, Margaret, *d* of William and Margaret Huggon, Carlisle;

two *d. Educ:* Bowdon College, Cheshire; Handsworth Theological College, Birmingham. Porlock, 1931-32; Handsworth College, 1932-35; Manchester Mission, 1935-40; Islington Mission, London, 1940-43; Longton Mission, Stoke on Trent, 1943-50; Sheffield Mission, 1950-57. *Address:* 53 York Avenue, Wolverhampton, Staffs. *T:* Wolverhampton 24430.

**OGSTON, Alexander George,** FRS 1955; DPhil, MA; President of Trinity College, Oxford, since 1970; Fellow, 1937, and Bedford Lecturer, 1950, Balliol College; *b* 30 January 1911; *s* of late Walter Henry Ogston and late Josephine Elizabeth Ogston (*née* Carter); *m* 1934, Elizabeth Wicksteed; one *s* three *d. Educ:* Eton College (King's Scholar); Balliol College, Oxford. DPhil 1936, MA 1937. Demonstrator, Balliol College, 1933; Freedom Research Fellow, London Hospital, 1935; Departmental Demonstrator (Biochemistry), 1938. University Demonstrator, 1944. Oxford; Reader in Biochemistry, University of Oxford, 1955-59; Prof. of Physical Biochemistry, John Curtin School of Medical Research, ANU, 1959-70. Chairman, Editorial Bd, Biochemical Journal, 1955-59 (Member of Board, 1951-55). Fellow, Australian Acad. of Science, 1962; Hon. Fellow, Balliol Coll., Oxford, 1969; Hon. Mem. American Soc. of Biological Chemists, 1965. *Publications:* scientific papers on physical chemistry and biochemistry. *Address:* The President's Lodging, Trinity College, Oxford OX1 3BH.

**OGUNDIPE, Brig. Babafemi Olatunde;** River Benue Star (Nigeria), 1965; High Commissioner for Nigeria in the UK, 1966-70; *b* 6 Sept. 1924; *s* of S. O. Ogundipe; *m* Elizabeth Omowunmi, *d* of T. R. P. Phelan, Lagos; three *s* four *d. Educ:* elem. and sec. schs, E. Nigeria. Enlisted Pte. Soldier, 1943; served in India and Burma, 1944-46; commnd, 1953; Comdr 5th Bn, 1961; Comdr, 3rd Bde, 1962; Chief of Staff, UN Forces, Congo, 1963; Comdr 2nd Bde, 1964; Imp. Def. Coll., 1965; Mil. Adviser to Nigerian High Comr in UK, Jan.-Feb. 1966; Chief of Staff, Supreme Mil. HQ, Nigeria, Feb.-July 1966. *Recreations:* swimming, hockey. *Address:* c/o Ministry of External Affairs, Lagos, Nigeria. *Club:* Beacon Golf.

**O'HAGAN,** 4th Baron, *cr* 1870; **Charles Towneley Strachey;** *b* 6 Sept. 1945; *s* of Hon. Thomas Anthony Edward Towneley Strachey (*d* 1955; having assumed by deed poll, 1938, the additional Christian name of Towneley, and his mother's maiden name of Strachey, in lieu of his patronymic) and of Lady Mary Strachey, *d* of 3rd Earl of Selborne, *qv*; *S* grandfather, 1961; *m* 1967, Princess Tamara Imeretinsky; one *d. Educ:* Eton; (Exhibitioner) New College, Oxford. Page to HM the Queen, 1959-62. *Recreation:* writing. *Heir:* *b* Hon. Richard Towneley Strachey, *b* 29 Dec. 1950. *Address:* 15 Ryecroft Street, SW6. *T:* 01-736 0612.

**O'HAGAN, Desmond,** CMG 1957; *b* 4 Mar. 1909; *s* of Captain Claud O'Hagan, Nyeri, Kenya and Eva O'Hagan (*née* Napier Magill); *m* 1942, Pamela, *d* of Major A. H. Symes-Thompson, DSO, Kiambu, Kenya; one *s* two *d. Educ:* Wellington Coll.; Clare Coll., Cambridge. Entered Colonial Administrative Service, Kenya, 1931. Called to Bar, Inner Temple, 1935. Private Secretary to British Resident, Zanzibar, 1937; served with E African Forces in N Province, Kenya, 1940-42; Native Courts Adviser, 1948-51; Provincial Commissioner, Coast Province, Kenya, 1952-59; Chairman, Transport Licensing Authority, Tanganyika, 1959-63. Now coffee farming in Kiambu, Kenya. *Recreations:* tennis, golf. *Address:* Kianjibbi, Kiambu, Kenya. *Clubs:* East India and Sports; Muthaiga (Nairobi).

**O'HALLORAN, Michael Joseph;** MP (Lab) Islington North since Oct. 1969; *b* 20 Aug. 1929; British; *m* 1956, Stella Beatrice McDonald; three *d* (one *s* decd). *Educ:* Clohanes National School, Eire. Railway worker, 1948-63; building worker, 1963-69. *Recreations:* boxing, football, fishing. *Address:* 40 Tytherton Road, N19. *T:* 01-272 0350. *Club:* Finsbury Park Railwaymen's.

**O'HARA, Frank;** Director-General Civil Aircraft, Ministry of Technology, since 1970; *b* 1 Oct. 1917; *s* of Francis O'Hara and Lily Mary O'Hara (*née* Slaven); *m* 1943, Mhuire Wheldon Hattle; one *s* three *d. Educ:* Alloa Academy; Edinburgh Univ.; Christ's Coll., Cambridge. MA Hons Maths and Nat. Phil., Edinburgh, 1938; BA Hons Maths 1940, MA 1944, Cantab. Marine Aircraft Experimental Estab., 1940; Airborne Forces Exper. Estab., 1942; Aircraft and Armament Exper. Estab., 1950; RAE Bedford, 1954; Head, 3' Supersonic Tunnel, 1956; Head, Aero Flight, 1959; Chief Supt and Head Flight Group, 1966. Member: several ARC Cttees; Flight Mech. Panel of Adv. Gp for Aero R&D of NATO. FRAeS 1966. *Publications:* papers in Reports and Memoranda of ARC, and various jls. *Recreations:* literature and the arts, philosophy, golf. *Address:* 27 Cody Road, Clapham, Bedford. *T:* Bedford 67030.

**OHLSON, Sir Eric James,** 2nd Bt, *cr* 1920; *b* 16 March 1911; *s* of Sir Erik Ohlson, 1st Bt, and Jennie (*d* 1952), *d* of J. Blakeley; *S* father 1934; *m* 1935, Marjorie Joan, *d* of late C. H. Roosmale-Cocq, Dorking, Surrey; two *s* one *d. Heir:* *s* Brian Eric Christopher Ohlson, *b* 27 July 1936. *Address:* Belvedere, Scarborough.

**OISTRAKH, David (Fyodorovich);** Russian concert violinist and teacher of violin; conductor; *b* Odessa, 1908; father amateur violinist, mother sang in Odessa Opera; *m* Tamara Ivanovna; one *s. Educ:* Odessa Musical-Dramatic Inst. under Stoliarsky. Played with orchestras throughout the USSR from 1926; made debut with orchestras in Moscow and Leningrad, 1928; 1st place in Ukrainian violin competition, Kharkov, USSR, 1930; Lecturer at the Moscow Conservatory, 1934; won prizes in International Wieniawski Violin Concours, Warsaw, 1935, etc.; travelled to Turkey; made debut in Brussels and Paris, 1937; Professor at the Moscow Conservatory, 1939; awarded Stalin Prize, 1942; there followed numerous appearances in Europe, including Florence Music Festival, 1951, and Palais de Chaillot, Paris, 1953; in Japan and Germany, 1955; toured USA, 1955-56, 1959-69; latest appearances in London, 1954, 1956 (first performances in Western Europe of Shostakovich's new violin concerto which is dedicated to him), 1958 and 1961 (with his son Igor Oistrakh). Hon. RAM London, 1959; Hon. Mem. other foreign academies, 1961-. Lenin Prize, 1960. Hon. MusD Cambridge, 1969. Holds Order of Lenin and other orders and medals. *Address:* c/o State Conservatoire, Herzen Street, Moscow, USSR.

**OISTRAKH, Igor Davidovich;** Russian Violinist; *b* Odessa, 1931; *s* of David Oistrakh, *qv*. *Educ:* Music Sch. and State Conservatoire, Moscow. Many foreign tours (USSR, Europe, South America, Japan); many gramophone records; several concerts with father. 1st prize, Violin Competition, Budapest, 1952, Wieniawki Competition, Poznan, 1952; Honoured Artist of RSFSR. *Address:* State Conservatoire, 13 Ulitsa Herzen, Moscow, USSR.

**OKEDEN, Richard Godfrey Christian;** *see* Parry-Okeden.

**O'KEEFFE, Georgia;** artist; *b* Sun Prairie, Wisconsin, USA, 15 Nov. 1887; *d* of Francis O'Keeffe and Ida Totto; *m* 1924, Alfred Stieglitz. *Educ:* Sacred Heart Acad., Madison, Wis.; Chatham (Va) Episcopal Inst.; Art Inst., Chicago; Art Students' League, NY; Univ. of Va; Columbia Univ. Head of Art Dept, West Texas State Normal Coll., Canyon, 1916-18. Painting, only, 1918-; annual one-man shows, 1923-46, in Stieglitz galls. Retrospective exhibitions: Brooklyn Museum, 1927; Art Inst. of Chicago, 1943; Museum of Modern Art (New York), 1946; Worcester Art Museum, USA, 1960. Paintings in permanent collections of many museums and galleries in USA. Holds several hon. degrees. Member National Institute of Arts and Letters. *Publication:* Georgia O'Keeffe (portfolio of 12 reproductions with text), 1937. *Address:* Abiquiu, Rio Arriba County, New Mexico, USA.

**OKEOVER, Col Sir Ian P. A. M. W.;** *see* Walker-Okeover.

**OKORO, Godfrey;** *see* Benin, Oba of.

**OLAGBEGI II, The Olowo of Owo, (Sir Olateru),** Kt 1960; Oba Alaiyeluwa, Olagbegi II, Olowo of Owo, since 1941; Minister of State, Western Region (now Western Provinces) of Nigeria, 1952; President of the House of Chiefs, Western Region (now Western Provinces), 1965; *b* 1910; *s* of Oba Alaiyeluwa, Olagbegi I, Olowo of Owo; married; many *s* and *d* (some decd). *Educ:* Owo Government School. A Teacher in 1934; Treasury Clerk in Owo Native Administration, 1935-41. Queen's Medal, 1957. *Recreations:* lawn tennis, squash racquets. *Address:* PO Box 1, Afin Oba Olowo, Owo, Western Provinces of Nigeria. *T:* Owo 1.

**OLANG, Most Rev. Festo Habbakkuk;** *see* Kenya, Archbishop of.

**OLDENBOURG-IDALOVICI, Zoë;** writer (as Zoë Oldenbourg); *b* 31 March 1916; *d* of Sergius Oldenbourgh, writer and historicist, and of Ada (*née* Starynkevitch); *m* 1948, Heinric Idalovici; one *s* one *d*. *Educ:* Lycée Molière and Sorbonne, Paris. *Publications:* Argile et cendres, 1946 (Paris) (in English: The World is Not Enough, 1949); La Pierre angulaire, 1953 (Paris) (in English: The Cornerstone, 1954); The Awakened (trans. by Edward Hyams), 1957; The Chains of Love, 1959; Destiny of Fire (trans. by Peter Green), 1961; Massacre at Montségur, 1962; Cities of the Flesh, 1963; Catherine the Great, 1965; The Crusades (trans. by Anne Carter), 1966. *Recreation:* painting. *Address:* c/o Victor Gollancz Ltd, 14 Henrietta St, WC2.

**OLDFIELD, John Richard Anthony;** *b* July 1900; *m* 1953, Jonnet Elizabeth *d* of late Maj. H. M. Richards, DL, JP. *Educ:* Eton; Trinity College, Cambridge; Served in: Coldstream Guards, 1918-20; RN, 1939-45. MP (Lab) South-East Essex, 1929-31; Parliamentary Private Secretary to Sec. of State for Air, 1929-30. Mem. LCC, 1931-58 (Vice-Chairman, 1953). CC Kent, 1965. *Address:* Doddington Place, near Sittingbourne, Kent. *Club:* Guards.

**OLDFIELD, Maurice,** CMG 1964; CBE 1956 (MBE 1946); Counsellor, Foreign Office since 1965; *b* 16 Nov. 1915; *e s* of late Joseph and Ada Annie Oldfield, Over Haddon. *Educ:* Lady Manners School, Bakewell; Manchester Univ. 1st Cl. Hons History; MA 1938. Served War of 1939-45, Intelligence Corps, Middle East, 1941-46 (Lt-Col; MBE). Jones Fellow in History and Tutor, Hulme Hall, Manchester, 1938-39. Attached to Foreign Office, 1947-49; Office of Commissioner-General for UK in South East Asia, Singapore, 1950-52; Foreign Office 1953-55; First Secretary, Singapore, 1956-58; Foreign Office, 1958-59; Counsellor, Washington, 1960-64. *Recreation:* farming. *Address:* 18 Chandos Court, Caxton Street, SW1. *T:* 01-222 2164; Over Haddon, Bakewell, Derbyshire. *T:* Bakewell 2696. *Clubs:* Athenæum; Metropolitan (Washington, DC).

**OLDFIELD, Prof. Richard Charles;** Director, Medical Research Council Speech and Communication Research Unit, Edinburgh University, since 1966; Hon. Professor, Edinburgh University, since 1967; *b* 26 Sept. 1909; *o s* of late Sir Francis du Pré Oldfield, ICS, and of Frances Sophia Henrietta (*née* Cayley); *m* 1933, Lady Kathleen Constance Blanche, 5th *d* of 2nd Earl of Balfour, PC; two *d*. *Educ:* Marlborough; Peterhouse, Cambridge. 2nd Class Nat. Sci. Tripos Pt I, 1930, BA 1931, MA 1935, Cambridge; MA Oxon, 1946. Exhibitioner in Moral Sciences, Peterhouse, 1931; Arnold Gerstenberg Student in Philosophy, Cambridge Univ., 1934; Leverhulme Research Student in Industrial Psychology, 1936; Rockefeller Research Fellow in Psychology, 1938; Univ. Lectr in Gen. Psychology, Univ. of Oxford, 1946, in Experimental Psychology, 1948; Prof. of Psychology, Reading Univ., 1950-56; Fellow of Magdalen College, Professor of Psychology and Director of the Institute of Experimental Psychology, Oxford University, 1956-66; Hon. Director, Medical Research Council, Psycholinguistics Research Unit, 1963-66; Founder-member Experimental Psychology Group, 1947, Pres. 1956-57; Mem., Experimental Psychology Soc., 1959; Sir Frederic Bartlett Lecturer, 1966. Pres. Section J. British Assoc., 1960; Mem. Roy. Soc. of Medicine; Corr. Mem. Sociedad Española de Psicologia; Assoc. Mem., Société de Psychologie Française. Ed. Quarterly Jl of Exptl Psych., 1947-49, Assoc. Ed. 1949-63. Served RAFVR (Radar Br.), 1941-46 (despatches). *Publications:* The Psychology of the Interview, 1941. Papers in scientific jls. *Recreations:* gardening, flowers, fishing. *Address:* MRC Speech and Communication Research Unit, Edinburgh University; Woodhall Cottage, Pencaitland, East Lothian. *Club:* Royal Automobile.

**OLDFIELD-DAVIES, Alun Bennett,** CBE 1955; MA; Controller, Wales, British Broadcasting Corporation, 1945-April 1967; *b* 1905; *s* of Rev. J. Oldfield-Davies, Wallasey, Cheshire; *m* 1931, Lilian M. Lewis, BA. *Educ:* Porth County Sch., Rhondda; University College, Aberystwyth. Schoolmaster and Lecturer to University Extension Classes in Ammanford, Carmarthenshire, and Cardiff, 1926-37. British Broadcasting Corporation: Schools Asst, 1937-40; Welsh Executive, 1940-44; Overseas Services Establishment Officer, 1944-45. Member: Court and Council of University of Wales; Arts Council; Welsh Arts Council; Chairman, Council of Social Service for Wales. Vice-President, National Museum of Wales; President: Welsh Council for Education in World Citizenship; Drama Association of Wales. Formerly Warden, University of Wales Guild of Graduates. Hon. LLD, Univ. of Wales, 1967. *Address:* Ty Gwyn, Llantrisant Road, Llandaff, Cardiff. *T:* 565920. *Club:* National Liberal.

**OLDHAM, Alan Trevor;** CBE 1959; retired from Foreign Service, 1960 (HBM Consul-General, Dakar, 1956-59); *b* 20 June 1904; *s* of A. E. and H. Oldham; *m* 1944, Megan, *d* of Rev. James

Evans. *Educ:* Bolton Sch.; Emmanuel Coll., Cambridge (Chancellor's Medal for English Verse, 1926). Entered HM Consular Service in Siam, 1927, later assimilated in HM Foreign Service; Consul, 1935; acting Consul-Gen., 1932, 1933, 1934, 1937, and 1943; Consul-General, 1949. Served at: Bangkok, Batavia, Saigon, Chiengmai, Nakawn Lampang, Songkhla, Basra, Port Said, Maymyo, Rangoon, Osaka/Kobe, Dakar, with Portuguese Guinea and Togo. Coronation Medal, 1953. *Address:* c/o Foreign and Commonwealth Office, SW1.

**OLDHAM, Rev. Canon Arthur Charles Godolphin,** Canon Residentiary of Guildford Cathedral since 1961; *b* 5 Apr. 1905; *s* of late Sidney Godolphin and Lilian Emma Oldham; *m* 1934, Ursula Finch Wigham Richardson, *d* of late George and Isabel Richardson, Newcastle upon Tyne; one *s* two *d*. *Educ:* King's College School; King's College, London. Business, music and journalism to 1930. Ordained, to Witley, Surrey, 1933; Vicar of Brockham Green, 1936; Rector of Merrow, 1943; Rural Dean of Guildford, 1949; Vicar of Godalming, 1950; Rural Dean of Godalming, 1957; Director of Ordination Training, and Bishop's Examining Chaplain, 1958; Hon. Canon of Guildford, 1959. *Recreations:* music, sketching. *Address:* 4 Cathedral Close, Guildford, Surrey. *T:* Guildford 75140.

**OLDHAM, James Bagot,** CBE 1964; VRD 1942; FRCS; retired as Consulting Surgeon, Liverpool United Hospitals, and Lecturer in Clinical Surgery, University of Liverpool (1925-65), and Consulting Surgeon to the Royal Navy (1944-65); QHS 1952-55; *b* 7 Nov. 1899; *s* of Samuel Charles Oldham; *m* 1931, Kathleen Longton Hicks. *Educ:* Birkenhead Sch.; Liverpool Univ. MB, ChB, 1921; MRCS, LRCP 1924, FRCS 1925. Surgeon Captain, RNVR, retired, 1955. Member Court of Examiners, Royal College of Surg. England, 1943-49; Member Council of RCS, 1947-55; Hunterian Prof., RCS, 1944 and 1951; Past President: Liverpool Medical Institution, 1954; Association of Surgeons of Great Britain and Ireland, 1963. *Publications:* chapters in various text books and papers on surgical subjects in medical journals. *Recreation:* gardening. *Address:* Cyfnant Ganol, Llanarmon-yn-Ial, near Mold, Flintshire CH7 4QD. *T:* Llanarmon-yn-Ial 233.

**O'LEARY, Patrick;** *see* Guerisse, A. M. E.

**OLIPHANT, Air Vice-Marshal David Nigel Kington B.;** *see* Blair-Oliphant.

**OLIPHANT, Sir Mark (Marcus Laurence Elwin),** KBE 1959; FRS 1937; Research School of Physical Sciences, Australian National University, Canberra (Director, 1950-63); President, Australian Academy of Sciences, 1954-57; *b* Adelaide, 8 Oct. 1901; *e s* of H. G. Oliphant; *m* 1925, Rosa Wilbraham, Adelaide, S. Australia; one *s* one *d*. *Educ:* Unley and Adelaide High Schools; University of Adelaide; Trinity Coll., Cambridge (1851 Exhibitioner, Overseas 1927, Senior 1929). Messel Research Fellow of Royal Society, 1931; Fellow and Lecturer St John's Coll., 1934. Hon. Fellow, 1952; Assistant Director of Research, Cavendish Laboratory, Cambridge, 1935, Poynting Professor of Physics, University of Birmingham, 1937-50. Hon. DSc (Toronto, Belfast, Melbourne, Birmingham, New South Wales, ANU, Adelaide); Hon. LLD (St Andrews). *Publications:* Various papers on electricity in gases, surface properties and nuclear physics. *Address:* Australian National University, Box 4, PO Canberra, ACT 2600, Australia. *Club:* Athenæum.

**OLIPHANT, Morton Duff,** MBE 1946; TD 1950; Director: Tate & Lyle; Barclays Bank (London Board); *b* 1912; *m* 1940, Audrey Pilkington; one *s*. *Educ:* Edinburgh Academy; Grenoble University; Trinity Coll., Oxford. President: Dock and Harbour Authorities Assoc., 1967-69; National Union of Manufacturers, 1958-60; Chm., Mersey Docks and Harbour Board, 1964-69 (Mem., 1958-69); Member: Cotton Board and Textile Council, 1964-68; NW Regional Board for Industry, 1955-65; NW Economic Planning Council, 1965-68; Rossall School Council; Liverpool Corporation Arts Cttee, 1951-69.

**OLIPHANT, Patrick James,** TD 1945; Deputy Keeper of Her Majesty's Signet, since 1964; *b* 19 March 1914; 2nd *s* of Kenneth M. Oliphant, MC, WS, and Florence Agnes, *d* of late Abram Lyle; *m* 1938, Margaret Kemp, *er d* of late James Brown, Ironfounder, Stirling; no *c*. *Educ:* Edinburgh Academy; Trinity Coll., Oxford (BA); Edinburgh Univ. (LLB). Admitted WS, 1939. Served RA, 1939-45 (US Bronze Star, 1945). Commanded 278 (City of Edinburgh) Regt RATA, 1948-51; Hon. Colonel, 1961-64. Director: Royal Bank of Scotland Ltd; Norwich Union Fire Insurance Society Ltd; Scottish American Investment Co. Ltd. *Recreations:* shooting, fishing, golf. *Address:* Strathaird, Easter Belmont Road, Edinburgh 12. *T:* 031-337 3971. *Club:* Caledonian; New (Edinburgh).

**OLIVER, Dame Beryl,** GBE 1948 (DBE 1920; CBE 1919); RRC 1916; *b* 20 Aug. 1882; *o d* of Francis Edward Carnegy and Mrs Carnegy of Lour, Angus; *m* 1914, Rear-Admiral Henry Francis Oliver, later Admiral of the Fleet Sir Henry Oliver, GCB, KCMG, MVO (*d* 1965). *Educ:* privately, in England and France. St John Ambulance Brigade, 1910; 2nd in Command Joint Women's VAD Dept, BRCS and Order of St John, 1916-18 (RRC, despatches). DStJ 1916. Head of VAD Dept, BRCS, 1919; Director of Education, BRCS, 1946; Archivist, BRCS, 1956. Order of Mercy, 1908; Coronation Medals, 1911 and 1937; Jubilee Medal, 1935. War Medal, 1914-18; Voluntary Medical Service Medal (7 clasps); Civil Defence Medal, 1939-45; Médaille d'Argent de la Croix Rouge Française, 1945. *Publications:* The British Red Cross in Action; The Church of St Mary the Virgin, Aldermanbury. *Address:* 20 South Eaton Place, SW1. *T:* 01-730 7370. *Club:* VAD Ladies'.

*See also Lt-Col U. E. C. Carnegy of Lour.*

**OLIVER, Sir Ernest;** *see* Oliver, Sir F. E.

**OLIVER, Sir (Frederick) Ernest,** Kt 1962; CBE 1955; TD 1942; DL; Chairman and Joint Managing Director, George Oliver (Footwear) Ltd, since 1950; *b* 31 Oct. 1900; *s* of late Colonel Sir Frederick Oliver and late Lady Oliver, CBE; *m* 1928, Mary Margaret, *d* of late H. Simpson, two *d* (one *s* decd). *Educ:* Rugby School. Member Leicester City Council, 1933-, Lord Mayor, 1950. Officer, Territorial Army, 1922-48. Served UK and Burma, 1939-45. President, Leicester YMCA; President Leicester Conservative Assoc., 1952-66. DL Leicester, 1950. *Recreation:* shooting. *Address:* 6 Westminster Road, Leicester. *T:* 705310. *Club:* Leicestershire (Leicester).

**OLIVER, Admiral (retired) Sir Geoffrey (Nigel),** GBE 1955; KCB 1951 (CB 1944); DSO 1941; *b* 22 Jan. 1898; *er s* of late Prof. F. W. Oliver; *m* 1933, Barbara, *o d* of late Sir Francis Jones, KBE, CB; one *s* (and one *s* one *d* decd). *Educ:* Rugby. Cadet, 1915; Mid. and Sub-Lieut, HMS Dreadnought, 1916; HMS Renown, 1917-20; specialised in Gunnery, 1923; HMS Carlisle, China Station, 1925-27; HMS

Rodney, 1930-32; Commander, 1932; commanded HMS Diana and HMS Veteran, 1st Destroyer Flotilla, Mediterranean, 1934-36; Captain, 1937; served War of 1939-45 (DSO and two Bars, CB); commanded HMS Hermione, 1940-42, Western Mediterranean, Malta, Madagascar, Eastern Mediterranean; Commodore, 2nd class, 1942; Senior Officer Inshore Squadron, North Africa, 1942-43; British Assault Force Commander, Salerno, 1943; Commodore, 1st class, 1944; Commander, Force J, Assault Force, Normandy, 1944; 21st Aircraft Carrier Squadron, 1944-45; Rear-Admiral, 1945; Admiral (Air), 1946; a Lord Comr of the Admiralty and Asst Chief of Naval Staff, 1947-48; Vice-Admiral, 1949; President, RN Coll., Greenwich, 1948-50; Commander-in-Chief, East Indies Station, 1950-52; Admiral, 1952; Commander-in-Chief, the Nore, 1953-55; retired, Dec. 1955. *Address:* Batts, Henfield, Sussex.

**OLIVER, George Harold,** QC 1949; *b* 24 Nov. 1888; *m* 1910, Christina Bennett; one *s.* Barrister, Middle Temple, 1927. MP (Lab) Ilkeston Division of Derbys., 1922-31 and 1935-64; Parliamentary Under-Secretary of State, Home Office, 1945-47. *Address:* Crimbles Court, Scalby, Scarborough, Yorks. *T:* Scarborough 62014.

**OLIVER, Henry John Callard,** BSc; Headmaster, Northampton Grammar Sch., since 1965; *b* 28 April 1915; *s* of late H. J. Oliver, Master Mariner, Wallington, Surrey; *m* 1939, Megan Eluned, *d* of late D. J. Edwards; two *s* one *d. Educ:* Sutton County School; King's Coll., London. 1st class Hons Physics, 1936. Physics Master, St Paul's Sch., 1936; Scientific Officer, MAP, 1940; Senior Science Master, Warwick Sch., 1951; Headmaster, Maidenhead Grammar Sch., 1954. Headmaster Wallasey Grammar Sch., 1960. *Recreation:* dinghy sailing. *Address:* The School House, Billing Road, Northampton. *T:* Northampton 33510.

**OLIVER, Brig. James Alexander,** CB 1957; CBE 1945; DSO 1942 (and Bar to DSO 1943); TD; DL; Vice-Lieutenant, County of Angus, since 1967; *b* 19 March 1906; *s* of Adam Oliver, Arbroath, Angus; *m* 1932, Margaret Whytock Scott; no *c. Educ:* Trinity Coll., Glenalmond. 2nd Lieut, Black Watch (TA), 1926; commanded: 7th Black Watch, 1942; 152 Infantry Bde (Highland Div.), 1943; 154 Infantry Bde (Highland Div.), 1944; served War of 1939-45 in N. Africa, Sicily and N.W. Europe (despatches). DL (Angus) 1948; ADC to the Queen, 1953-63; Hon. Colonel, 6/7th Black Watch, 1960-67; Hon. Colonel, 51st Highland Volunteers, 1967-. Member, Angus and Dundee T&AFA, 1938- (Chairman, 1945-59). Hon. LLD Dundee, 1967. *Address:* West Newton, Arbroath, Angus, Scotland. *T:* Arbroath 2579. *Club:* Naval and Military.

**OLIVER, John Andrew,** CB 1968; Second Secretary, Ministry of Development, Northern Ireland, since 1964; *b* 25 Oct. 1913; *s* of Robert John Oliver, Limavady, Co. Londonderry and Martha Sherrard, Magilligan, Co. Londonderry; *m* 1943, Stella Ritson; five *s. Educ:* Royal Belfast Academical Institution; Queen's Univ., Belfast; Bonn Univ.; Königsberg Univ.; Zimmern School of International Studies, Geneva; Imperial Defence Coll., London. BA 1936; DrPhil, 1951; IDC, 1954. Hon. MTPI, 1964; Hon. Member, Assoc. for Housing and Town Planning, W. Germany, 1966. *Recreations:* walking, maps, languages. *Address:* 107 Circular Road, Belfast 4, N Ireland. *T:* Belfast 68101. *Club:* Royal Over-Seas League.

**OLIVER, John Laurence;** Journalist; *b* 14 Sept. 1910; *s* of late Harold Oliver and of Mrs Teresa Oliver; *m* 1946, Renée Mary Webb; two *s. Educ:* Haberdashers' Aske's Hampstead School. Publicity Manager, The Book Society, 1934; Art Editor, The Bystander, 1935-39. War of 1939-45: served in the Field Security Corps, commissioned 1941. The Suffolk Regt (transferred The Cambridgeshire Regt). Joined staff of The Sphere, 1946; Art Editor, 1947; Assistant Editor, 1956; Editor, 1960-64; Editor, The Tatler, 1961-65. *Publications:* Saint John's Wood Church (with Rev. Peter Bradshaw), 1955; occasional short stories and articles. *Recreations:* reading, theatre going, watching cricket. *Address:* 10 Wellington Place, NW8. *T:* 01-286 5891. *Clubs:* Garrick, MCC.

**OLIVER, Group Captain John Oliver William,** CB 1950; DSO 1940; DFC 1940; RAF retired; *b* 1911; *e s* of William Oliver; *m* 1935 (marr. diss., 1951); one *s* two *d; m* 1962, Anne Fraser Porteous; one *s* two *d* (of whom *s* and *yr d* are twins). *Educ:* Christ's Hospital; Cranwell. Commissioned from Cranwell, GD Pilot Branch p., 1931; served 43 (F) Squadron and 55 (B) Squadron, Iraq; qualified CFS. Served War of 1939-45 (despatches thrice); commanded 85 (F) Squadron, 1940; Fighter Command and Tactical Air Force; Wing Commander, 1940; Group Captain, 1942. Assistant Commandant, RAF Coll., Cranwell, 1948-50; ACOS Ops, Allied Forces Northern Europe, 1958-60; retired, 1961. Personnel Officer, ENV (Engineering) Ltd, 1961; Staff Institute Personnel Management, 1962; Personnel Manager, Humber Ltd, 1963; Manager, Training and Administrative Service, Rootes, Coventry, 1965; Senior Training Officer, Engineering Industry Training Board, 1968. *Address:* 19 Trefusis Walk, Watford, Herts. *Club:* British Ski.

**OLIVER, Leslie Claremont,** FRCS; FACS; Consultant Neurosurgeon: Charing Cross Hospital; Westminster Hospital; West London Hospital; Royal Northern Hospital; Founder and Surgeon i/c Neurosurgical Centre, Oldchurch Hospital, Romford; Hon. Neurological Surgeon, French Hospital, London. *Educ:* Latymer Sch.; Guy's Hospital. LRCP, MRCS, 1933; MB, BS, London, 1953; FRCS England, 1935; FACS 1957. Formerly: 1st Assistant and Registrar, Dept of Neurosurgery, London Hospital; Resident Asst Surgeon, W London Hospital; Surgical Registrar and Teacher in Surgery, Bristol General Hospital. Member Society British Neurological Surgeons; Corr. Member Soc. de Neurochirurgie de Langue Française. Chm. Court of Examiners, RCS. *Publications:* Essentials of Neurosurgery, 1952; Parkinson's Disease and its Surgical Treatment, 1953; (ed and contrib.) Basic Surgery, 1958; Parkinson's Disease, 1967; Removable Intracranial Tumours, 1969. *Recreation:* travel. *Address:* 94 Harley Street, W1. *T:* 01-935 5896. *Clubs:* Royal Society of Medicine, Hurlingham.

**OLIVER, Martin Hugh,** PhD, CEng; Director, Services Electronics Research Laboratory, Ministry of Defence, Baldock, Herts, since 1968; *b* 9 July 1916; *s* of late Thomas Frederick Oliver and of Jessie Oliver (*née* Gibson), Peterborough; *m* 1963, Barbara Rivcah, *d* of Richard Burgis Blakeley, Worcester; one *d. Educ:* King's Sch., Peterborough; Imperial Coll. (City and Guilds Coll.), Univ. of London. BSc (Eng) 1937, PhD (Eng) 1939; ACGI, DIC, MIEE. Metropolitan Vickers Electrical Co. Ltd, Manchester, 1938-41; National Physical Laboratory, Teddington, 1941-43; RRE, Malvern, 1943-65; Head of Radio Dept, RAE,

Farnborough, 1965-68. *Address:* Longthorpe, Sutton, Sandy, Beds. *T:* Potton 648.

**OLIVER, Peter Raymond,** QC 1965; *b* 7 March 1921; *s* of David Thomas Oliver, Fellow of Trinity Hall, Cambridge, and Alice Maud Oliver; *m* 1945, Mary Chichester Rideal, *d* of Sir Eric Keightley Rideal, *qv*; one *s* one *d*. *Educ:* The Leys, Cambridge; Trinity Hall, Cambridge. Military Service, 1941-45, 12th Bn RTR, demobilised as Acting/Captain. Called to Bar, Lincoln's Inn, 1948. *Recreations:* gardening, music. *Address:* 24 Westbourne Park Road, W2. *T:* 01-229 1058.

**OLIVER, Peter Richard,** CMG 1965; Deputy High Commissioner, Lahore, since 1969; *b* 3 June 1917; *yr s* of William Henry Oliver and Muriel Daisy Elisabeth Oliver (*née* Widdicombe); *m* 1940, Freda Evelyn Gwyther; two *s* two *d*. *Educ:* Felsted Sch.; Hanover; Berlin; Trinity Hall, Cambridge. Indian Civil Service, 1939-47; served in Punjab and Bahawalpur State. Transferred to HM Foreign (subsequently Diplomatic) Service, 1947; served in Karachi, 1947-49; Foreign Office, 1949-52; The Hague, 1952-56; Havana, 1956-59; Foreign Office, 1959-61; Djakarta, 1961-64; Bonn, 1965-69. *Recreations:* tennis, golf, sailing. *Address:* (permanent) c/o National & Grindlays Bank, 13 St James's Square, SW1. *Clubs:* Oxford and Cambridge; Hawks (Cambridge); Union (Cambridge).

**OLIVER, Prof. Richard Alexander Cavaye;** Professor of Education and Director of the Department of Education in the University of Manchester, 1938-70; Dean of Faculty of Education, 1938-48, 1962-65; Dean of Faculty of Music, 1952-62, 1966-70; *b* 9 Jan. 1904; *s* of Charles Oliver and Elizabeth Oliver (*née* Smith); *m* 1929, Annabella Margaret White; one *s* one *d*. *Educ:* George Heriot's Sch.; University of Edinburgh; Stanford Univ., California, USA. Held Commonwealth Fund Fellowship at Stanford Univ., 1927-29; research educational psychologist in Kenya, 1929-32; Asst Master Abbotsholme Sch. and on staff of Edinburgh Education Cttee, 1933-34; University Extension Lecturer, 1933-34; Asst Director of Education, Wilts Education Cttee, 1934-36; Dep. Secretary, Devon Education Cttee, 1936-38. Director, University of Manchester School of Education, 1947-51; Pro Vice-Chancellor, 1953-57 and 1960-61; Presenter of Hon. Graduands, 1959-64, 1966. Member National Advisory Council on Training and Supply of Teachers, 1949-59; Chairman, Northern Universities Joint Matriculation Board, 1952-55; Member Secondary School Examinations Council, 1958-64. FBPSS. Hon. Research Fellow, Princeton Univ., 1961. *Publications:* General Intelligence Test for Africans, 1932; (with others) The Educational Guidance of the School Child, 1936; The Training of Teachers in Universities, 1943; Research in Education, 1946; Joint Matriculation Board Occasional Publications; contrib. to Africa, British Journal of Psychology, Yearbook of Education, Universities Quarterly, Research in Education, etc. *Recreation:* gardening. *Address:* Wain Gap, Crook, Kendal, Westmorland. *T:* Staveley 277.

*See also H. A. Hetherington.*

**OLIVER, Vice-Admiral Robert Don,** CB 1948; CBE 1942; DSC 1918; DL; *b* 17 March 1895; *s* of Colonel William James Oliver, CBE, and Margaret Christie Don; *m* 1928, Torfrida Lois Acantha Huddart (*d* 1961); no *c*; *m* 1965, Mrs M. J. Glendinning van der Velde. *Educ:* Osborne and Dartmouth Naval Colleges. Commander, 1930; Captain, 1936; Commanded: HMS Iron Duke, 1939; HMS Devonshire, 1940-42; HMS Excellent, 1943; HMS Swiftsure, 1944; Rear-Admiral, 1945; Asst Chief of Naval Staff (Weapons), 1945-46; Dep. Chief of Naval Staff, 1946-47; Flag Officer Commanding 5th Cruiser Squadron, 1947-48; Vice-Admiral, retired list, 1948. DL Roxburghshire, 1962. *Address:* Lochside House, Kelso, Roxburghshire. *T:* Yetholm 275. *Club:* Royal Over-Seas League.

**OLIVER, Prof. Roland Anthony,** MA, PhD (Cantab); Professor of the History of Africa, London University, since 1963; *b* Srinagar, Kashmir, 30 March 1923; *s* of late Major D. G. Oliver and of Lorimer Janet (*née* Donaldson); *m* 1947, Caroline Florence, *d* of late Judge John Linehan, KC; one *d*. *Educ:* Stowe; King's Coll., Cambridge. Attached to Foreign Office, 1942-45; R. J. Smith Research Studentship, King's Coll., Cambridge, 1946-48; Lecturer, School of Oriental and African Studies, 1948-58; Reader in African History, University of London, 1958-63; Francqui Prof., University of Brussels, 1961; Visiting Professor: Northwestern Univ., Illinois, 1962; Harvard Univ., 1967; travelled in Africa, 1949-50 and 1957-58; org. international Conferences on African History and Archæology, 1953-61; Member Council: Institute of Race Relations; Royal African Society; Corresp. Member, Académie Royale des Sciences d'Outremer, Brussels. Haile Sellassie Prize Trust Award, 1966. *Publications:* The Missionary Factor in East Africa, 1952; Sir Harry Johnston and the Scramble for Africa, 1957; The Dawn of African History (editor), 1961; A Short History of Africa (with J. D. Fage), 1962; A History of East Africa (ed. with Gervase Mathew), 1963; Africa since 1800 (with A. E. Atmore), 1967; (Ed.) The Middle Age of African History, 1967; Ed. (with J. D. Fage) The Journal of African History, 1960. *Address:* 38 Newton Road, W2. *T:* 01-229 4873; Frilsham Woodhouse, Hermitage, Berks. *T:* Yattendon 407. *Club:* Athenæum.

**OLIVER, Lt-Gen. Sir William (Pasfield),** GBE 1965 (OBE 1945); KCB 1956 (CB 1947); KCMG 1962; DL; late Infantry; *b* 8 Sept. 1901; *e s* of late Captain P. V. Oliver, Royal Navy; *m* 1938, Elizabeth Margaret, *o d* of late General Sir J. E. S. Brind, KCB, KBE, CMG, DSO; one *s* one *d*. *Educ:* Radley Coll.; RMC, Sandhurst. Chief of General Staff, GHQ, ME (Maj.-Gen.), 1945-46; Maj.-Gen., 1949; Chief Army Instructor, Imperial Defence Coll., 1949-50; Chief of Staff, Eastern Command, Jan. 1951-Dec. 1952; Principal Staff Officer to High Commissioner, Federation of Malaya, 1953-54; General Officer Commanding Berlin (British Sector), 1954-55; Vice-Chief of Imperial General Staff, 1955-57, retired; Principal Staff Officer to Secretary of State for Commonwealth Relations, 1957-59; British High Commissioner in the Commonwealth of Australia, 1959-65; UK Commissioner General for 1967 Exhibition, Montreal, Canada, 1965-67. Dir, Viyella International Ltd, 1968-69. Colonel, The Queen's Own Royal W. Kent Regt, 1949-59. DL Kent. Governor, Corps of Commissionaires. Hon. DCL, Bishop's Univ., Quebec Province. Commander Legion of Merit (USA), 1946; Knight Grand Cross Royal Order Phoenix (Greece) 1949. *Address:* Little Crofts, Sweethaws, Crowborough, Sussex. *Clubs:* Travellers', Army and Navy.

**OLIVIER, George B.;** *see* Borg Olivier.

**OLIVIER, Henry,** CMG 1954; MScEng, PhD London, DEng; FICE, FASCE, Beit Fellow; a Partner in the firm of Gibb Hawkins and Partners, Johannesburg, since 1963; Chairman, LTA Ltd, and LTA Engineering

Ltd, since 1969; *b* 25 Jan. 1914; *s* of J. Olivier, Umtali, S Rhodesia; *m* 1940, Lorna Renée, *d* of Robert and F. M. Collier, Haywards Heath, Sussex; one *d* (one *s* decd). *Educ:* Umtali High Sch.; Cape Town Univ.; University College, London. BSc (Cape), 1936. MSc (Cape), 1947; PhD (London), 1953. Beit Engineering Schol., 1932-38; Beit Fellow for two Rhodesias, 1939. Engineering post-grad. training with F. E. Kanthack & Partners, Consulting Engineers, Johannesburg, 1937; Sir Alex. Gibb & Partners, Cons. Engineers, London: training 1938, Asst Engineer, 1939. Experience covers design and construction of steam-electric power-stations, hydro-electric, floating harbour, irrigation, and water resources development schemes in UK, Africa, Middle East, and USA; Chief Engineer in charge civil engineering contracts, Owen Falls Hydro-Electric Scheme, Uganda, 1950-54; Partner in firm of Sir Alexander Gibb and Partners (Africa), 1954-55; Resident Director and Chief Engineer (Rhodesia), in firm of Gibb, Coyne & Sogel (Kariba), 1955-60; Consultant (mainly in connection with Indus Basin Project in Pakistan) to Sir Alexander Gibb abd Partners, London, 1960-69 (Sen. Consultant, 1967). Hon. DSc, Cape, 1968. *Publications:* Irrigation and Climate; Papers to Institution Civil Engineering Journal; Int. Commn on Irrigation and Drainage; Water for Peace Conference, Washington, DC. *Recreation:* tennis. *Address:* LTA Ltd, PO Box 312, Johannesburg, South Africa. *Clubs:* St Stephen's; Salisbury (Salisbury, Rhodesia).

**OLIVIER, Lady, (Joan)**; *see* Plowright, Joan.

**OLIVIER, Sir Laurence Kerr,** Kt, 1947; Actor; Director, National Theatre, since 1962; Member, South Bank Theatre Board, since 1967 (South Bank Theatre and Opera House Board, 1962-67); *b* 22 May 1907; *s* of late Rev. G. K. Olivier and Agnes Louise Crookenden; *m* 1st, 1930, Jill Esmond (marr. diss., 1940); one *s*; 2nd, 1940, Vivien Leigh (marr. diss., 1961; she *d* 1967); 3rd, 1961, Joan Plowright, *qv*; one *s* two *d*. *Educ:* St Edward's Sch., Oxford. MA Hon. Tufts, Mass, 1946; Hon. DLitt, Oxon, 1957; Hon. LLD Edinburgh, 1964; Commander, Order Dannebrog, 1949; Officier Legion d'Honneur, 1953; Grande Ufficiale dell' Ordino al Merito della Repubblica (Italian), 1953. First appeared in 1922 at Shakespeare Festival, Stratford-on-Avon special boys' performance, as Katherine in Taming of the Shrew; played in Byron, King Henry IV, toured in sketch Unfailing Instinct, with Ruby Miller, Season with Lena Ashwell, King Henry VIII, 1924-25; Played with Birmingham Repertory Company till 1928; Stanhope in Journey's End, for Stage Society; Beau Geste; Circle of Chalk, Paris Bound, The Stranger Within; went to America, 1929; returned 1930 and played in The Last Enemy, After All and in Private Lives; New York, 1931, played Private Lives, 1933; Rats of Norway, London; Green Bay Tree, New York; returned London, 1934, Biography, Queen of Scots, Theatre Royal; Ringmaster under his own management, Golden Arrow, Romeo and Juliet, 1935; Bees on the Boat Deck and Hamlet at Old Vic, 1936,; Sir Toby Belch in Twelfth Night and Henry V, Hamlet at Kronborg, Elsinore, Denmark, 1937; Macbeth, 1937; Iago in Othello, King of Nowhere, and Coriolanus, 1938; No Time for Comedy, New York, 1939; under his own management produced and played Romeo and Juliet with Vivien Leigh. Lieut (A) RNVR until released from Fleet Air Arm, 1944, to co-direct The Old Vic Theatre Company with Joan Burrell and Ralph Richardson, at New Theatre; played in Old Vic, 1944-45 Season; Peer Gynt, Arms and the Man, Richard III, Uncle Vanya; toured Continent in May 1945 with Peer Gynt, Arms and the Man, Richard III; Old Vic Season, 1945-46; Henry IV, Parts I and II, Oedipus, The Critic, Uncle Vanya, Arms and the Man; six weeks' season in New York with Henry IV, Parts I and II, Oedipus, The Critic, and Uncle Vanya; Old Vic, 1946-47 Season, produced and played King Lear. Made a tour of Australia and New Zealand, 1948, with Old Vic Company, in Richard III, School for Scandal, Skin of our Teeth, Old Vic, 1949 Season, Richard III, The School for Scandal, Antigone. Directed A Street Car Named Desire, Aldwych, 1949; St James's, 1950-51; produced and acted in Venus Observed, under own management, produced Captain Carvallo, 1950, Antony in Antony and Cleopatra, Caesar in Caesar and Cleopatra, 1951; also in US, 1951-52; The Sleeping Prince, Phoenix, 1953; Stratford Season, 1955; Macbeth, Malvolio in Twelfth Night, Titus in Titus Andronicus; Archie Rice in The Entertainer, Royal Court Theatre, 1957; presented The Summer of the Seventeenth Doll, 1957; toured Europe in Titus Andronicus, 1957; Titus in Titus Andronicus, Stoll, 1957; Archie Rice in The Entertainer (revival), Palace Theatre, 1957, and New York, 1958; Coriolanus in Coriolanus, Stratford, 1959; directed The Tumbler, New York; Berenger in Rhinoceros, Royal Court Theatre and Strand Theatre, 1960; Becket in Becket, New York, 1960; Henry II in Becket, US Tour and New York, 1961; Fred Midway in Semi-Detached, Saville Theatre, 1962. Apptd Dir of National Theatre (first, as Old Vic): 1963: (produced) Hamlet; 1963-64; acted in Uncle Vanya and in the Recruiting Officer, 1964; acted in Othello and in The Master Builder, 1964-65. Chichester Festival: first Director, also acted, 1962 (Uncle Vanya; The Broken Heart; also Director, The Chances), 1963 (Uncle Vanya, also Director); National Theatre: (produced) The Crucible; in Love for Love, Moscow and London, 1965; Othello, Moscow and London, 1965; Othello, Love for Love, (dir.) Juno and the Paycock, 1966; Edgar in The Dance of Death, Othello, Love for Love (dir.) Three Sisters, National Theatre, 1967; A Flea in Her Ear, 1968; Home and Beauty, Three Sisters (directed and played Chebutikin), 1968-69, Shylock in Merchant of Venice, 1970, etc. *Films:* Potiphar's Wife, The Yellow Passport, Perfect Understanding, No Funny Business, Moscow Nights, Fire Over England, As You Like It, The First and the Last, Divorce of Lady X, Wuthering Heights, Rebecca, Pride and Prejudice, Lady Hamilton, 49th Parallel, Demi-Paradise; produced, directed, played Henry V; produced, directed, played Hamlet (International Grand Prix, 1948, Oscar award, 1949); Carrie (Hollywood), 1950; Macheath in film The Beggar's Opera, 1953; produced, directed, played Richard III (British Film Academy's Award), 1956; produced, directed and played in The Prince and the Showgirl, 1957; General Burgoyne in The Devil's Disciple, 1959; The Entertainer; Spartacus; Term of Trial; Bunny Lake is Missing; Othello; Khartoum; The Power and The Glory, 1961, (TV) USA; Dance of Death; Shoes of the Fisherman; Oh! What a Lovely War; Battle of Britain;. David Copperfield; directed and played Chebutikin in Three Sisters. Has appeared on Television both in Great Britain and in America. Sonning Prize, Denmark, 1966; Gold Medallion, Swedish Acad. of Literature, 1968. *Recreations:* tennis, swimming, motoring, flying, gardening. *Address:* 8 Norfolk Street, WC2. *Clubs:* Garrick. Green Room. MCC.

*Created a Baron (Life Peer). 1970. Title unknown at time of going to press.*

**OLLERENSHAW, Dr Kathleen Mary,** MA, DPhil, FIMA; Member, Manchester City Council, since 1956, Alderman, since 1970; Chairman: Education Committee, Association of Municipal Corporations, since 1968; Manchester Polytechnic, since 1969; Northern College of Music, Manchester, since 1968; *b* 1 Oct. 1912; *d* of late Charles Timpson, JP, and late Mary Elizabeth Timpson (*née* Stops); *m* 1939; Robert Ollerenshaw; one *s* one *d*. *Educ:* Ladybarn House Sch., Manchester; St Leonards Sch., St Andrews; (open schol. in maths) Somerville Coll., Oxford. BA (Hons) 1934, MA 1943, DPhil 1945; Foundation Fellow, Institute of Mathematics and its Applications (FIMA), 1964. Research Assistant, Shirley Institute, Didsbury, 1937-40; Chairman: Assoc. of Governing Bodies of Girls' Public Schs, 1963-69; Manchester College of Commerce, 1964-69; Manchester Educn Cttee, 1967-70 (Co-opted Mem., 1954-56); Member: Central Advisory Council on Education in England, 1960-63; National Exec., British Assoc. for Commercial and Industrial Education, 1962- (Mem. Delegn to USSR, 1963); Exec., Assoc. of Education Cttees, 1967-; National Advisory Council on Education for Industry and Commerce, 1963-70; Council for National Academic Awards, 1964-; Education Policy Cttee, City and Guilds of London Institute, 1966-; General Advisory Council of BBC, 1966-; Schools Council, 1968-; Management Panel, Burnham Cttee, 1968-; Nat. Foundn of Educational Research, 1968-; Management Cttee of Hallé Concerts Soc., 1967-68; Co-opted Member: Council of Univ. of Salford, 1967-; Court, Univ. of Manchester, 1964-. Rep. governor: Union of Lancashire and Cheshire Institutes, 1967-; Manchester and District Advisory Council for Further Education, 1967-; Associated Local Education Authorities of Lancashire, 1967-70; NW Reg. Council for Further Education, 1959-63, 1967-; Univ. of Manchester Sch. of Education Delegacy for the Training of Teachers, 1967-70; Royal Coll. of Advanced Technology, Salford, 1959-67; Governor: St Leonards Sch., St Andrews, 1950-; Manchester High Sch. for Girls, 1959-69; Ladies Coll., Cheltenham, 1966-68; Chethams Hosp. Sch., Manchester, 1967-; Further Educn Staff Coll., Blagdon, 1960-. Winifred Cullis Lecture Fellow to USA, 1965. *Publications:* Education for Girls, 1958, 1961; The Girls' Schools, 1967; papers in mathematical journals on Geometry of Numbers, 1945-54; articles on education and local govt in national and educational press. *Address:* 2 Pine Road, Manchester M20 0UY. *T:* 061-445 2948. *Club:* English-Speaking Union.

**OLLIS, Prof. William David,** BSc, PhD; Professor of Organic Chemistry, University of Sheffield, since 1963; *b* 22 Dec. 1924; *s* of Albert George and Beatrice Charlotte Ollis; *m* 1951, Sonia Dorothy Mary Weekes; two *d*. *Educ:* Cotham Grammar Sch., Bristol; University of Bristol. Assistant Lecturer in Organic Chemistry, University of Bristol, 1946-49, Lecturer, 1949-62, Reader, 1962-63. Visiting Research Fellow, Harvard, 1952-53; Visiting Professor: University of California, Los Angeles, 1962; University of Texas, 1966; Hon. Prof., Universidade Federal Rural do Rio de Janeiro, Brasil, 1969. Acharya Prafulla Chandra Ray Centenary Lecture, 1961; Robert Gnehm Lecture, 1965; Chemical Soc. Tilden Lectr, 1969. *Publications:* Recent Developments in the Chemistry of Natural Phenolic Compounds, 1961; scientific papers mainly in Journal of Chemical Society. *Address:* 640 Fulwood Road, Fulwood, Sheffield S10 3QL. *T:* 302685.

**O'LOGHLEN, Sir Colman (Michael),** 6th Bt, *cr* 1838; Magistrate; *b* 6 April 1916; *s* of Henry Ross O'Loghlen (*d* 1944; 6th *s* of 3rd Bt) and of Doris Irene, *d* of late Major Percival Horne, RA; *S* Uncle 1951; *m* 1939, Margaret, *d* of Francis O'Halloran, Melbourne, Victoria; six *s* two *d*. *Educ:* Xavier Coll., Melbourne; Melbourne Univ. (LLB). Formerly Captain AIF. Acting Judge, Supreme Court of Territory of Papua and New Guinea, May-Aug. 1957; Stipendiary Magistrate, Lae, Territory of New Guinea. *Heir:* *s* Michael O'Loghlen, *b* 21 May 1945.

**OLORENSHAW, Leslie;** Deputy Chairman, Taylor Woodrow Ltd, since 1967; Chairman: Westview Investment Corporation Ltd, Canada; Octavius Atkinson & Sons Ltd; Taylor Woodrow Homes Ltd; *b* 16 Feb. 1912; *m* 1939, Gladys Beatrice Dean; one *s*. Director: Taylor Woodrow International Ltd; Taylor Woodrow of Canada Ltd; Monarch Investments Ltd, Canada. Formerly Deputy Chairman, BNEC Africa Cttee. *Address:* 27 Linksway, Northwood, Middlesex. *T:* Northwood 24643.

**OLUWASANMI, Hezekiah Adedunmola,** MA, PhD Harvard; Vice-Chancellor, University of Ife, Nigeria, since 1966; *b* 12 Nov. 1919; *s* of John Oluwasanmi and Jane Ola Oluwasanmi; *m* 1959, Edwina Marie Clarke; one *s* two *d*. *Educ:* Morehouse Coll.; Harvard University. Secondary School Teacher, 1940-41; Meteorological Observer, 1941-44; Clerk, Shell Oil Co., 1944-47; Student, 1948-55; Lectr, Sen. Lectr, and Prof. of Agricultural Economics, Univ. of Ibadan, 1963-66. *Publications:* Agriculture and Nigerian Economic Development, 1966; (jt author) Uboma, a socio-economic and nutritional survey of a rural community in Eastern Nigeria, 1966; various reports, contribs to symposia and papers in learned jls. *Recreations:* reading, walking, listening to music. *Address:* University of Ife, Ife-Ife, Nigeria. *T:* Ife 2291.

**OLVER, Stephen John Linley,** CMG 1965; MBE 1947; British High Commissioner, Freetown, since 1969; *b* 16 June 1916; *s* of late Rev. S. E. L. Olver and of Mrs Madeleine Olver (*née* Stratton), Trent, Sherborne, Dorset; *m* 1953, Maria Morena, Gubbio, Italy; one *s*. *Educ:* Stowe. Indian Police, 1935-44; Indian Political Service, Delhi, Quetta, Sikkim and Bahrain, 1944-47; Pakistan Foreign Service, Aug.-Oct. 1947; Foreign Service, Karachi, 1947-50; Foreign Office, 1950-53; Berlin, 1953-56; Bangkok, 1956-58; Foreign Office, 1958-61; Washington, 1961-64; Foreign Office, 1964-66; The Hague, 1967-69. *Recreations:* cricket, photography, painting. *Address:* c/o Foreign and Commonwealth Office, Downing Street, SW1. *Clubs:* Travellers', MCC.

**O'MALLEY, Brian Kevin;** MP (Lab) Rotherham since March 1963; *b* 22 Jan. 1930; *s* of Frank and Eva O'Malley, Mexborough, Yorks; *m* 1959, Kathleen Sylvia Curtiss; one *d*. *Educ:* Mexborough Grammar Sch.; University of Manchester. BA (Hons) History, 1952; Teaching Diploma, 1953. Assistant Government Whip, 1964-66; Dep. Chief Govt Whip and a Lord Comr of the Treasury, 1967-69; Parly Under-Sec. of State, Dept of Health and Social Security, 1969-70; *Recreations:* walking, music. *Address:* 29 Hall Avenue, Mexborough, Yorks. *T:* Mexborough 3535.

**O'MALLEY, Sir Owen St Clair,** KCMG, *cr* 1943 (CMG 1927); *b* 4 May 1887; *s* of late Sir Edward O'Malley; *m* Mary Dolling (*see* Ann Bridge), *d* of James Harris Sanders; one *s* two *d*. *Educ:* Hillbrow, Rugby; Radley; Magdalen Coll., Oxford (MA). Entered Foreign Office,

1911; Counsellor HBM Legation, Peking, 1925; Counsellor, Foreign Office, 1933-37; Envoy Extraordinary and Minister Plenipotentiary to the United States of Mexico, 1937-38; in charge of British Embassy to Spain at St Jean de Luz, 1938-39; British Minister to Hungary, 1939-41; British Ambassador to Poland, 1942-45; British Ambassador to Portugal, 1945-47; retired from Foreign Service, 1947. *Publications:* The Phantom Caravan, 1954. Historical articles in Journal of Galway Archæological and Historical Society, 1950, 1951, 1952. *Address:* 27 Charlbury Road, Oxford.

**OMAN, Carola Mary Anima, (Lady Lenanton),** CBE 1957; FSA; FRSL; FRHistS; Writer; *b* 11 May 1897; *d* of late Sir Charles Oman, KBE; *m* 1922, Sir Gerald Lenanton (*d* 1952). *Educ:* Wychwood Sch., Oxford. Served BRCS, 1916-19 and 1938-58 (Co. President, Hertfordshire Branch, 1947-58). *Publications:* The Menin Road (poetry); Britain Against Napoleon (history); Ayot Rectory; *historical novels:* The Road Royal; Princess Amelia; Crouchback; The Empress; King Heart; Major Grant; The Best of His Family; Over the Water; Miss Barrett's Elopement; *children's books:* Ferry the Fearless; Robin Hood; Johel; Alfred, King of the English; Baltic Spy; *historical biographies:* Prince Charles Edward; Henrietta Maria; Elizabeth of Bohemia; Nelson (awarded Sunday Times annual prize for English literature, 1948); Sir John Moore (James Tait Black Memorial Prize for biography, 1953); David Garrick, 1958; Mary of Modena, 1962; Napoleon's Viceroy; Eugène de Beauharnais, 1966; The Gascoyne Heiress, Diaries of 2nd Marchioness of Salisbury, 1968. *Address:* Bride Hall, Welwyn, Hertfordshire. *T:* Wheathampstead 3160. *Club:* VAD Ladies.

**OMAN, Charles Chichele;** *b* 5 June 1901; *s* of late Sir Charles Oman, KBE; *m* 1929, Joan Trevelyan; one *s* one *d*. *Educ:* Winchester; New Coll., Oxford; British School at Rome. Entered Victoria and Albert Museum, 1924; lent to Ministry of War Transport, 1939-44; Keeper of Department of Metalwork, Victoria and Albert Museum, 1945-66. Liveryman of Company of Goldsmiths, 1946. *Publications:* English Domestic Silver, 1934; English Church Plate, 1957; English Silver in the Kremlin, 1961; Golden Age of Hispanic Silver, 1968; Caroline Silver, 1625-1688, 1970. *Address:* 13 Woodborough Road, Putney, SW15. *T:* 01-788 2744.

*See also Julia Trevelyan Oman.*

**OMAN, Julia Trevelyan;** designer; Director, Oman Productions Ltd; *b* 11 July 1930; *d* of Charles Chichele Oman, *qv*. *Educ:* Royal College of Art, London. Royal Scholar, 1955 and Silver Medal, 1955, RCA. Designer: BBC Television, 1955-67; Alice in Wonderland, BBC TV Film, 1966; Brief Lives, London and New York, 1967; Country Dance, London and Edinburgh, 1967; Art Director (England), The Charge of the Light Brigade, 1967; Art Director, Laughter in the Dark, 1968; Designer: The Enigma Variations (for the Royal Ballet), 1968; 40 Years On, 1968; (Production) Julius Caesar, 1969; The Merchant of Venice, National Theatre, 1970. Des RCA (1st class), 1955; MSIA. Designer of the Year Award for Alice in Wonderland, 1967. *Publications:* Street Children (photographs by Julia Trevelyan Oman; text by B. S. Johnson), 1964; contrib. Architectural Review (photographs). *Address:* 13 Woodborough Road, SW15. *T:* 01-788 2744.

**OMMANNEY, Francis Downes;** *b* 22 April 1903; *s* of Francis Frederick Ommanney and Olive Caroline Owen; unmarried. *Educ:* Aldenham Sch.; Royal College of Science. ARCS, PhD (London); FLS; FRSL. Polar Medal (Bronze), 1942. Lecturer in Zoology, Queen Mary Coll., 1926-29; Scientific Staff of Discovery Cttee, 1929-39; RNVR, 1940-46; British Council, 1946-47; Mauritius-Seychelles Fisheries Survey, 1947-49; Colonial Research Service, 1951-57; Reader in Marine Biology in the Univ. of Hong Kong, 1957-60. *Publications: scientific:* Discovery Reports, 1932, 1933, 1936; Colonial Office Fishery Publications, Vol. I, Nos 3, and 18; *non-scientific:* South Latitude, 1938; North Cape, 1939; The House in the Park, 1944; The Ocean, 1949; The Shoals of Capricorn, 1952; Isle of Cloves, 1955; Eastern Windows, 1960; Fragrant Harbour, 1962; A Draught of Fishes, 1965; The River Bank (autobiog.), 1966; Collecting Sea Shells, 1968. *Club:* Travellers'.

**ONASSIS, Aristotle Socrates;** shipowner; company director; pioneer in super-tanker construction; *b* Smyrna, Ionia, 1906, an Argentine subject of Greek origin; *s* of Socrates and Penelope Onassis; *m* 1946, Athina (Tina) Livanos (marr. diss., 1961; she *m* 1961, Marquess of Blandford); one *s* one *d*; *m* 1968, Mrs Jacqueline Lee Kennedy, *widow* of John F. Kennedy. *Educ:* Evangeliki Scholi, Smyrna. Aged 16 left Smyrna for Greece as refugee; emigrated to Buenos Aires, 1923; revived family tobacco business; later, became Greek Consul in Buenos Aires. Negotiated purchase of his first ships in Canada, 1932-33; ordered his first tanker in Sweden, 1936; has built numerous super-tankers in USA, France, Germany and Japan since 1945; also bulk carriers in Japan; and now has under construction several other ships. Whaling fleet sold to Japanese, 1956; among other businesses, founded Olympic Airways, a Greek company, 1957. Dag Hammarskjoeld Gold Medal for Industrial Merit, 1969. *Recreations:* nautical sports (owner yacht Christina). *Address:* 1668 Alvear Avenue, Buenos Aires; c/o Olympic Maritime, SA, 17 Avenue d'Ostende, Monaco.

**O'NEIL, Most Rev. Alexander Henry;** *see* Fredericton, Archbishop of.

**O'NEILL,** family name of **Barons O'Neill, O'Neill of the Maine,** and **Rathcavan.**

**O'NEILL,** 4th Baron *cr* 1868; **Raymond Arthur Clanaboy O'Neill,** DL; *b* 1 Sept. 1933; *s* of 3rd Baron and Anne Geraldine (she *m* 2nd, 1945, 2nd Viscount Rothermere, *qv*, and 3rd, 1952, late Ian Fleming), *e d* of Hon. Guy Charteris; *S* father, 1944; *m* 1963, Georgina Mary, *er d* of Lord George Montagu Douglas Scott; three *s*. *Educ:* Eton; Royal Agricultural Coll. 2nd Lieut, 11th Hussars, Prince Albert's Own; Major, North Irish Horse, AVR. DL Co. Antrim. *Recreations:* vintage motoring and power boating. *Heir: s* Hon. Shane Sebastian O'Neill, *b* 25 July 1965. *Address:* Shane's Castle, Antrim, Ireland. *T:* Antrim 3264. *Clubs:* Turf, Ulster.

*See also J. A. L. Morgan.*

**O'NEILL OF THE MAINE,** *Baron cr* 1970 (Life Peer), of Ahoghill, Co. Antrim; **Terence Marne O'Neill,** PC (N Ireland) 1956; DL; *b* 10 Sept. 1914; *s* of Capt. Hon. Arthur O'Neill, MP (killed in action, 1914; *s* of 2nd Baron O'Neill, Shane's Castle Antrim) and of late Lady Annabel Crewe-Milnes, *e d* of 1st and last Marquis of Crewe, KG; *m* 1944, Katherine Jean, *y d* of late W. I. Whitaker, Pylewell Park, Lymington, Hants; one *s* one *d*. *Educ:* Eton. Served, 1939-45, Irish Guards. MP (Unionist) Bannside, Parlt of N Ireland, 1946-70; Parl. Sec., Min. of Health, 1948; Deputy Speaker and Chairman of Ways and Means, 1953; Joint

Parl. Sec., Home Affairs and Health, 1955; Minister: Home Affairs, 1956; Finance, 1956; Prime Minister of N Ireland, 1963-69. Director: S. G. Warburg & Co.; International Holdings Ltd; Phoenix Assurance, 1969-. DL Co. Antrim, 1948; High Sheriff County Antrim, 1953. Hon. LLD, Queen's Univ., Belfast, 1967. *Publication:* Ulster at the Crossroads, 1969. *Address:* Glebe House, Ahoghill, Co. Antrim, N Ireland. *T:* Ahoghill 246. *Clubs:* St James'; Ulster (Belfast).

**O'NEILL, Hon. Sir Con (Douglas Walter);** KCMG 1962 (CMG 1953); Deputy Under-Secretary of State, Foreign and Commonwealth Office, since 1969; *b* 3 June 1912; 2nd *s* of 1st Baron Rathcavan, *qv*; *m* 1st, 1940, Rosemary (marriage dissolved 1954), *d* of late H. Pritchard, MD; one *s* one *d*; 2nd, 1954, Baroness Mady Marschall von Bieberstein (*d* 1960), *d* of late Baron von Holzing-Berstett; 3rd, 1961, Mrs Anne-Marie Lindberg, Helsinki. *Educ:* Eton College; Balliol Coll., Oxford (History Scholar). BA 1934 (1st Class, English), MA 1937; Fellow, All Souls College, Oxford, 1935-46; called to Bar, Inner Temple, 1936; entered Diplomatic Service, 1936; Third Secretary, Berlin, 1938; resigned from Service, 1939. Served War of 1939-45 in Army (Intelligence Corps), 1940-Nov. 1943; temp. employed in Foreign Office, 1943-46; Leader-writer on staff of Times, 1946-47; returned to Foreign Office, 1947; re-established in Foreign Service, 1948; served in Frankfurt and Bonn, 1948-53; Counsellor, HM Foreign Service, 1951; Imperial Defence College, 1953; Head of News Department, Foreign Office, 1954-55; Chargé d'Affaires, Peking, 1955-57; Asst Under-Sec., FO, 1957-60; Ambassador to Finland, 1961-63; Ambassador to the European Communities in Brussels, 1963-65; Dep. Under-Sec. of State, FO, 1965-68; Dir, Hill, Samuel & Co. Ltd, 1968-69. *Recreations:* shooting, fishing. *Address:* 37 Flood Street, SW3. *Club:* Travellers'.

**O'NEILL, Denis,** CB 1957; formerly Under-Secretary, Ministry of Transport, retired 1968; *b* 26 Feb. 1908; *e surv. s* of late Very Rev. F. W. S. O'Neill, DD and Mrs O'Neill, Belfast and Manchuria; *m* 1st, 1930, Pamela (marr. diss. 1936), *d* of John Walter; one *s*; 2nd, 1944, Barbara, *d* of Mrs W. E. Norton; one adopted *d*. *Educ:* Royal Academical Institution, Belfast; Oriel Coll., Oxford (scholar). Entered Ministry of Transport, Oct. 1931; successively Private Secretary to following Ministers of Transport: Rt Hon. Leslie (later Lord ) Hore-Belisha, MP 1935-37; Leslie Burgin, MP, 1937-39; Euan Wallace, MP, 1939-40; Sir John (now Lord) Reith, MP, 1940; Lt-Col J. T. C. Moore-Brabazon, MP (later Lord Brabazon of Tara), 1940-41, and (with F. H. Keenlyside) Lord Leathers (Minister of War Transport), Asst Sec., 1943; Under-Sec., Min. of Transport, 1951. *Recreations:* reading, gardening, walking. *Address:* 11 San Anton Court, Birkirkara, Malta. *Clubs:* Savile; Union (Malta).

**O'NEILL, Michael;** *b* 7 Oct. 1909; *s* of Michael and Sarah O'Neill; *m* 1936, Kathleen O'Connor, Ballinasloe, Co. Galway; three *s* three *d*. *Educ:* Dromore NS; Bellisle Academy. Draper's Asst, 1923-29; Haulage Contractor, 1929-31; Tillage Contractor, 1931-45; Farmer, 1945-52. Mem. Exec. Ulster Farmers' Union, 1945-48; Exec. Irish Anti-Partition League, 1946-57; Omagh RDC, 1945-57; Tyrone CC, 1950-57; Tyrone Co. Educ. Cttee, 1950-52; Tyrone Co. Health Cttee, 1950-52; Tyrone Co. Welfare Cttee, 1950-52. MP (Irish Republican) Mid-Ulster, 1951-55. *Recreations:* amateur dramatics, Gaelic football. *Address:* 24 Centenary Park, Omagh, Co. Tyrone, N Ireland.

**O'NEILL, Most Rev. Michael Cornelius;** *see* Regina, Archbishop of, (RC).

**O'NEILL, Prof. Patrick Geoffrey,** BA, PhD; Professor of Japanese, University of London, since 1968; *b* 9 Aug. 1924; *m* 1951, Diana Howard; one *d*. *Educ:* Rutlish Sch., Merton; Sch. of Oriental and African Studies, Univ. of London. Lectr in Japanese, Sch. of Oriental and African Studies, Univ. of London, 1949. *Publications:* A Guide to Nō, 1954; Early Nō Drama, 1958; (with S. Yanada) Introduction to Written Japanese, 1963; A Programmed Course on Respect Language in Modern Japanese, 1966; Japanese Kana Workbook 1967; A Programmed Introduction to Literary-style Japanese, 1968; Japanese Names, 1970. *Recreations:* tennis, photography. *Address:* School of Oriental and African Studies, University of London, WC1.

**O'NEILL, Hon. Phelim Robert Hugh;** Major, late RA; MP (Unionist) North Antrim, Parliament of Northern Ireland; Minister of Agriculture, since 1969; *b* 2 Nov. 1909; *s* and *heir* of 1st Baron Rathcavan, *qv*; *m* 1st, 1934, Clare Désirée (from whom he obtained a divorce, 1944), *d* of late Detmar Blow; one *s* one *d*; 2nd, 1953, Mrs B. D. Edwards-Moss, *d* of late Major Hon. Richard Coke; four *d* (and one *d* decd). *Educ:* Eton. MP (UU) for North Antrim (UK Parliament), 1952-59; Minister of Educn, 1969. *Address:* Lizard Manor, Aghadowey, Londonderry, N Ireland.

**ONIANS, Richard Broxton,** MA (Liverpool), PhD (Cantab); Hildred Carlile Professor of Latin in University of London, 1936-66; now Emeritus; *b* 11 January 1899; *s* of late Richard Henry Onians, Liverpool; *m* 1937, Rosalind, *d* of late Lt-Col Ernest Browning Lathbury, OBE, MD, RAMC, Chipperfield, Herts; two *s* four *d*. *Educ:* Liverpool Inst.; Liverpool Univ. (1st Class Hons Classics); Trinity Coll. Cambridge (Senior Scholarship Examination, Open Research Studentship, Hooper English Oration Prize); Craven Grant for archæological research in Greece, and Hare Prize (Univ. of Cambridge). Member Council Assoc. of Univ. Teachers, 1945-53; Exec. Cttee 1946-51; Chm. London Consultative Cttee (AUT), 1946-48; Chm., Nat. Campaign Cttee for Expansion of Higher Educ., 1947-Feb. 1948 and June 1948-53; Chm. Joint Standing Cttee and Conf. on Library Cooperation, 1948-60; Mem. Exec. Cttee and Finance Committee of National Central Library, 1947-53. Formerly 4th South Lancs and RAF (1917-18); Lecturer in Latin, Univ. of Liverpool, 1925-33; Professor of Classics, Univ. of Wales (Swansea), 1933-35. *Publications:* The Origins of European Thought about the Body, the Mind, the Soul, the World, Time, and Fate: New interpretations of Greek, Roman, and kindred evidence, also of some basic Jewish and Christian beliefs, 1951 (further enl. edn 1971); articles and reviews in Classical Journals. *Recreation:* walking. *Address:* 21 Luard Road, Cambridge. *T:* Cambridge 44250.

**O'NIEL, Colette;** *see* Malleson, Lady Constance.

**ONION, Francis Leo,** CMG 1968; JP; Chairman of Directors, NZ Co-operative Dairy Co. Ltd, since 1961; Chairman, NZ Dairy Board, since 1968 (Deputy Chairman, 1964-68); *b* 10 July 1903; *s* of Edwin Joseph Onion, Blenheim, NZ; *m* 1931, *d* of D. Ross, Otorohanga, NZ; two *s* one *d*. *Educ:* Hamilton High School. Farmer and Company Director; Chairman: Waipa County Council, NZ, 1947-61; New Zealand Counties Ward, 1947-61; Central Waikato

Electric Power Board, 1947-61; Maramurua Coalfields Ltd, 1961-; Auckland Farm Products Ltd, 1967-; New Zealand Dairy Exporter Newspaper, 1963-. JP Hamilton, 1961. Coronation Medal, 1953. *Recreations:* shooting and bowls. *Address:* Te-Kowhai Road, Frankton, New Zealand. *T:* HOT 832 NZ. *Club:* National (Hamilton, NZ).

**ONIONS, Mrs Oliver;** *see* Ruck, Berta.

**ONSAGER, Prof. Lars;** Professor of Theoretical Chemistry, Yale University, USA; *b* Oslo, Norway, 27 Nov. 1903; *s* of Erling Onsager and Ingrid Onsager (*née* Kirkeby); *m* 1933, Margarete Arledter; three *s* one *d. Educ:* Norges Tekniske Högskole, Trondheim, Norway; Eidgenössische Technische Hochschule, Zürich, Switzerland; Yale Univ. (PhD). Went to USA, 1928 (naturalised, 1945). Associate in Chemistry, Johns Hopkins Univ., 1928; Instr in Chem., Brown Univ., 1928-33; Sterling and Gibbs Fellow, Yale Univ., 1933-34; Asst Prof. of Chem., Yale, 1934-40; Associate Prof., 1940-45; J. Willard Gibbs Prof. of Theoretical Chem., 1945-. Fulbright Scholar, Cambridge, England, 1951. Visiting Prof. in US and abroad. In 1931, he showed that past-future symmetry of the laws which govern molecular motion implies a set of reciprocal relations for coupled irreversible processes; the reasoning as much as the results proved helpful in the subsequent development of kinetic theories. Among other consequences, he clarified the status of Kelvin's theory (1851) for thermoelectric phenomena and Rayleigh's "principle of the least dissipation of energy", and he showed just how far these could be generalized. Rumford Medal, 1953; Lorentz Medal, 1958; G. N. Lewis Medal 1962; John G. Kirkwood Medal, 1962; Willard Gibbs Medal, 1962; T. W. Richards Medal, 1964; Debye Award, 1965; Belfer Award, 1966; Nat. Science Medal, 1968. Nobel Chemistry Prize for 1968. FAAAS; Fellow: Amer. Phys. Soc.; Amer. Philos. Soc.; Mem., Amer. Chem. Soc.; Mem., Nat. Acad. of Sciences, and of many other institutions in the USA and abroad. Holds hon. doctorates in science and technology. *Publications:* contrib. articles to learned jls on: electrical properties of ice, crystal statistics, electrolytes, dipole moments in liquids, reciprocal relations in irreversible processes, etc. *Address:* Sterling Chemistry Laboratory, Yale University, New Haven, Conn 06520, USA; (home) 841 Whitney Avenue, New Haven, Conn 06511, USA.

**ONSLOW,** family name of **Earl of Onslow.**

**ONSLOW,** 6th Earl of, *cr* 1801; **William Arthur Bampfylde Onslow,** KBE 1960; MC; TD 1949; Bt 1660; Baron Onslow, 1716; Baron Cranley, 1776; Viscount Cranley, 1801; Colonel RAC (Yeomanry); late Lt Life Guards; Captain of HM Bodyguard of the Yeomen of the Guard, 1951-60; Asst Chief Conservative Whip in House of Lords, 1951-60; High Steward of Guildford; *b* 11 June 1913; *e s* of 5th Earl of Onslow, PC, GBE; *S* father 1945; *m* 1st, 1936, Hon. Pamela Dillon (marriage dissolved, 1962), *o d* of 19th Viscount Dillon, CMG, DSO; one *s* one *d*; 2nd, 1962, Nina Sturdee, MBE, *y d* of Thomas P. Sturdee. *Educ:* Winchester; Royal Military College. Served Middle East, 1941-43 (MC); Italy, 1943; Normandy, 1944 (prisoner). Member: LCC, 1940-49; Surrey CC, 1949-52; Chm., Surrey Agricultural Exec. Cttee, 1956-58. CStJ. *Publication:* Men and Sand, 1961. *Heir: s* Viscount Cranley, *qv. Address:* Temple Court, Clandon Park, Guildford. *Clubs:* Beefsteak, Brooks's, Royal Yacht Squadron.
*See also Dowager Countess of Halifax.*

**ONSLOW, Cranley Gordon Douglas;** MP (C) Woking since 1964; *b* 8 June 1926; *s* of late F. R. D. Onslow and Mrs M. Onslow, Effingham House, Bexhill; *m* 1955, Lady June Hay, *yr d* of 13th Earl of Kinnoull; one *s* three *d. Educ:* Harrow; Oriel Coll., Oxford; Geneva Univ. Served in RAC, Lieut 7th QO Hussars, 1944-48, and 3rd/4th Co. of London Yeo. (Sharpshooters) (TA) as Capt., 1948-52. Joined HM Foreign Service, 1951; Third Sec. Br. Embassy, Rangoon, 1953-55; Consul at Maymyo, N Burma, 1955-56; resigned, 1960. Served on Dartford RDC, 1960-62, and Kent CC, 1961-64. Council Member: Nat. Rifle Assoc.; Air League. *Publication:* Asian Economic Development (ed), 1965. *Recreations:* fishing, shooting, cricket. *Address:* Chobham Park House, Chobham, Woking, Surrey. *Clubs:* MCC, English-Speaking Union.

**ONSLOW, Maj.-Gen. Sir Denzil M.;** *see* Macarthur-Onslow.

**ONSLOW, Sir Geoffrey Henry H.;** *see* Hughes-Onslow.

**ONSLOW, Sir John (Roger Wilmot),** 8th Bt, *cr* 1797; Managing Director, Norwest Hovercraft Ltd; Director: Denny Hovercraft Ltd; Clayton Campbell Engineering Ltd; *b* 21 July 1932; *o s* of Sir Richard Wilmot Onslow, 7th Bt, TD, and Constance (*d* 1960), *o d* of Albert Parker; *S* father, 1963; *m* 1955, Catherine Zoia, *d* of Henry Atherton Greenway, The Manor, Compton Abdale, near Cheltenham, Gloucestershire; one *s* one *d. Educ:* Cheltenham College. *Heir: s* Richard Paul Atherton Onslow, *b* 16 Sept. 1958. *Address:* c/o Barclays Bank Ltd, Fowey, Cornwall.

**ONSLOW, Adm. Sir Richard (George),** KCB 1958 (CB 1954); DSO 1942 (1st and 2nd Bars, 1942, 3rd Bar, 1944); DL; *b* 15 April 1904; *e s* of Major G. A. Onslow, and the late Mrs Onslow; *m* 1932, Kathleen Meriel Taylor, *er d* of late E. C. Taylor, JP; two *s. Educ:* RN Colleges Osborne and Dartmouth. Entered RN, 1918. Served in destroyers almost continuously from 1926 until end of War of 1939-45. Staff College, 1935. Commander, 1938; Plans Division, Admiralty, 1939; HMS Ashanti, 1941; Capt. 1942; HMS Osprey, 1943; Capt. (D) Fourth Dest. Flot. in HMS Quilliam, 1944; idc 1946; Senior Naval Officer, Northern Ireland, 1947; Dir Tactical Div. Naval Staff, 1948; HMS Devonshire, 1951; Rear-Adm., 1952; Naval Secretary to First Lord of the Admiralty, 1952-54; Vice-Adm., 1955; Flag Officer (Flotillas), Home Fleet, 1955-56; Flag Officer Comdg, Reserve Fleet, 1956-57; Admiral, 1958; Commander-in-Chief, Plymouth, Feb. 1958-Nov. 1960. DL Salop, 1962. *Recreations:* country pursuits. *Address:* Ryton Grove, Dorrington, Shrewsbury. *Club:* United Service.

**ONSLOW, William George,** CB 1970; Chairman Yorkshire and Humberside Economic Planning Board, since 1965; *b* 12 June 1908; *s* of Albert Edward and Ann Onslow; *m* Joyce Elizabeth Robson; two *s* one *d. Educ:* Medway Technical College; London University. Board of Trade: Patent Examiner, 1930-39; Principal, 1942-46; Assistant Secretary, 1946-65; Under Secretary, Department of Economic Affairs, 1965, Min. of Housing and Local Govt, 1969. *Recreation:* golf. *Address:* 9 Elmete Avenue, Leeds, Yorkshire. *T:* Leeds 659706.

**ONTARIO, Archbishop and Metropolitan of;** *see under* Algoma, Archbishop of.

**OPENSHAW, William Harrison,** DL; **His Honour Judge Openshaw;** Recorder of Preston and Judge and Assessor of the Borough Court of Pleas since 1958; Chairman Lancashire Quarter Sessions since 1958; *b* 11 Dec. 1912; *s* of late Sir James Openshaw, OBE, JP, DL; *m* 1945, Joyce Lawford; two *s* one *d*. *Educ:* Harrow; St Catharine's, Cambridge. Called to Bar, Inner Temple, 1936; practised on Northern Circuit. DL Lancs, 1968. *Address:* Park House, Broughton, Lancs.

**OPHER, William David,** CBE 1963; CEng, MIMechE; Joint Managing Director, Vickers Limited, 1967-68, retired; *b* 30 May 1903; *s* of William Thomas Opher, London, and Margaret Mary Carson, Belfast; *m* 1930, Marie Dorothy, 3rd *d* of William Fane; one *s*. *Educ:* Borough Polytechnic, London. Apprenticed Arnold Goodwin & Son, Bankside; joined Vickers, 1928; Director: Vickers Ltd, Shipbuilding Group, 1955; Vickers Ltd, 1959; Rolls-Royce & Associates Ltd, 1959; Vickers & Bookers Ltd, 1959; British Hovercraft Corporation, 1966; Chairman Vickers, Ltd, Engineering Group, 1962-67. Mem. Council, Lancaster Univ., 1968; Governor, Borough Polytechnic, 1969. Serving Brother, Order of St John, 1962. *Recreations:* golfing, fishing. *Address:* The Garth, Grange-over-Sands, Lancashire. *T:* (Home) Grange-over-Sands 3151. *Clubs:* East India and Sports; Bexleyheath Golf.

**OPIE, Evelyn Arnold;** Matron, King's College Hospital, SE5, 1947-60; *b* 21 Aug. 1905; *d* of George and Annie Opie. *Educ:* Wentworth School for Girls, Bournemouth. Westminster Sick Children's Hosp., 1924-26 (sick children's trng); Guy's Hosp., SE1, 1926-29; SRN Oct. 1929. Midwifery Trng SCM, 1930, Sister, 1930-32, Guy's Hosp.; private nursing, Bournemouth, 1932-33; Sister (Radium Dept and Children's Ward), 1933-39, Administrative Sister, Asst Matron, Dep. Matron, 1939-47, Guy's Hosp. Diploma in Nursing of London Univ., 1935. *Recreations:* music, gardening. *Address:* Hillside, Dibden, Southampton SO4 5TE. *T:* Hythe (Hants) 2232.

**OPIE, Redvers,** CMG 1944; MA (Oxon and Harvard); PhD (Harvard); President and Director, High Speed Brick Building (US) Inc. (Washington, DC); Director: Business International (New York), since 1954; North American Contracting Corp. (Washington DC); *b* 20 January 1900; *s* of late James Reid and Bessie Hockaday Opie; naturalised US citizen, 1948; *m* 1929, Catharine Crombie Taussig (marr. diss., 1948), Cambridge, Mass; one *s* one *d*. *Educ:* Rutherford Coll.; Univ. of Durham. Lectr in Economics, Univ. of Durham, 1919-23, Wellesley Coll. (USA), 1923-24, Harvard Univ. 1924-30; Fellow of Magdalen College, Oxford, 1931-45, Home Bursar, 1935-40 (on leave of absence for National Service from Sept. 1939); University Lecturer in Economic Science, 1936-39; Counsellor and Economic Adviser to British Embassy, Washington, DC (resigned 1946). Adviser, UK Delegation, International Food Conference, 1943; UK Delegate, International Monetary and Financial Conference, 1944; Member US Govt Mission, on Private Foreign Investment, to Turkey, 1953; Senior Staff Mem., Brookings Institution, Washington, DC, 1947-53. President, American Ligurian Company Inc., New York, 1947-54. Economic Counsellor to American Chamber of Commerce of Mexico; Visiting Professor, Univ. of the Americas, Mexico City. *Publications:* (joint) Major Problems of US Foreign Policy, annually, 1947-52; Anglo-American Economic Relations, 1950; Current Issues in Foreign Economic Assistance, 1951; The Search For Peace Settlements, 1951; American Foreign Assistance, 1953; Selected papers on the Mexican and International Economies, 1966-68, 1968. *Recreations:* tennis and music. *Address:* 1526 Connecticut Avenue NW, Washington, DC 20036. *T:* 265-2060; Paseo de la Reforma 368-503, Mexico 6, DF. *T:* 28-88-45. *Clubs:* Harvard (New York); Metropolitan (Washington, DC); Chevy Chase (Maryland); Churubusco, American (Mexico).

**OPIE, Roger Gilbert;** Member, Monopolies Commission, since 1968; Economic Correspondent, New Statesman, since 1967; Fellow and Lecturer in Economics, New College, Oxford since 1961; *b* 23 Feb. 1927; *o s* of late Frank Gilbert Opie and late Fanny Irene Grace Opie (*née* Tregoning); *m* 1955, Norma Mary, *o d* of Norman and Mary Canter; two *s* one *d*. *Educ:* Prince Alfred Coll. and Adelaide Univ., SA; Christ Church and Nuffield Coll., Oxford. BA 1st Cl. Hons 1948, MA Adelaide 1950; SA Rhodes Schol., 1950; Boulter Exhibnr, 1952; George Webb Medley Jun. Schol., 1952, Sen. Schol., 1953; PPE 1st Cl. 1953; Nuffield Coll. Studentship, 1954; BPhil 1954. Asst Lectr and Lectr, LSE, 1954-61; Econ. Adviser, Econ. Section, HM Treasury, 1958-60; Editor, The Bankers' Magazine, 1960-64; Asst Dir, HM Treasury Centre for Administrative Studies, 1964; Asst Dir, Planning Div., Dept of Economic Affairs, 1964-66; Economic Adviser to Chm., NBPI, 1967-70. *Publications:* co-author: Causes of Crime, 1956; Banking in Western Europe 1962; Sanctions against South Africa, 1964; Economic Growth in Britain, 1966; Crisis in the Civil Service, 1968; Unfashionable Economics, 1970. *Recreations:* sailing, reading, photography. *Address:* 62 Park Town, Oxford. *T:* Oxford 57957. *Clubs:* Reform; Lilliput Sailing (Dorset).

**OPIE, Air Vice-Marshal William Alfred,** CB 1955; CBE 1951; retired; *b* 4 Dec. 1901; *s* of late William Opie, Redruth, Cornwall; *m* 1950, Phyllis Constance Chalk, *d* of late Frederick George Crampton, Sissinghurst, Kent. *Educ:* RAF College, Cranwell. Flying Duties and Engineer Staff Duties, 1923-36; RAF Staff College, 1937; Comdg No. 2 Sqdn, 1938; Comdg No. 18 Sqdn, 1939; Engineer Staff Duties, HQ Bomber Comd, 1940; Dep. Dir Repair & Maintenance (Aircraft), Min. of Aircraft Prod., 1941; Dir Servicing and Maintenance, Air Min., 1944; Comdg RAF Station, St Athan, 1947; STSO, Far East Air Force, 1948; Base Comdr, RAF Maintenance Base, Far East Air Force, Seletar, Singapore, 1951-52; Assistant Controller of Aircraft, Ministry of Supply, 1953-56; AOC No. 41 Gp, RAF, 1956-59. *Address:* Santa Eulalia Del Rio, Ibiza, Baleares. *Club:* Royal Air Force.

**OPPENHEIM, Tan Sri Sir Alexander,** Kt 1961; OBE 1955; FRSE; MA, DSc (Oxon); PhD (Chicago); Visiting Professor, University of Ghana, 1968; Vice-Chancellor, University of Malaya, 1957-65 (Acting Vice-Chancellor, 1955); *b* 4 Feb. 1903; *o s* of late Rev. H. J. and Mrs F. Oppenheim; *m* 1930, Beatrice Templer, *y d* of Dr Otis B. Nesbit, Indiana, USA; one *d*. *Educ:* Manchester Grammar Sch.; Balliol Coll., Oxford (Scholar). Sen. Mathematical Schol., Oxf., 1926; Commonwealth Fund Fell., Chicago, 1927-30; Lectr, Edinburgh, 1930-31; Prof. of Mathematics, 1931-42, 1945-49; Dep. Principal, 1947, 1949, Raffles Coll., Singapore; Prof. of Mathematics, 1949-57; Dean, Faculty of Arts, 1949, 1951, 1953. Hon. degrees: DSc (Hong Kong) 1961; LLD: (Singapore) 1962; (Leeds) 1966; DLitt (Malaya) 1965. L/Bdr, SRA(V), POW (Singapore, Siam), 1942-45; Dean POW University, 1942; Pres. Malayan Mathematical Soc., 1951-55, 1957. Pres.

Singapore Chess Club, 1956-60; Pres., Amer. Univs. Club, 1956. Chm. Bd of Management, Tropical Fish Culture Research Institute (Malacca), 1962; Mem., Unesco-International Assoc. of Universities Study of Higher Education in Development of Countries of SE Asia, 1962. Vis. Prof., Univ. of Reading, in Dept of Mathematics, 1965-68. Panglima Mangku Negara (Fedn of Malaya), 1962; FWA, 1963. *Publications:* papers on mathematics in various periodicals. *Recreations:* chess, bridge, walking, swimming. *Address:* 664 Finchley Road, NW11. *Clubs:* Royal Over-Seas League; Selangor (Kuala Lumpur).

**OPPENHEIM, Sir Duncan (Morris),** Kt 1960; President of British-American Tobacco Co. Ltd since 1966 (Chairman 1953-66); Chairman, Tobacco Securities Trust Co. Ltd, since 1969; Deputy Chairman, Commonwealth Development Finance Co., since 1968; *b* 6 Aug. 1904; *s* of Watkin Oppenheim, BA; TD; and Helen, 3rd *d* of Duncan McKechnie; *m* 1st, 1932, Joyce Mary (*d* 1933), *d* of Stanley Mitcheson; no *c*; 2nd, 1936, Susan May (*d* 1964), *e d* of Brig.-Gen. E. B. Macnaghten, CMG, DSO; one *s* one *d*. *Educ:* Repton Sch. Admitted Solicitor of the Supreme Court, 1929; Messrs Linklaters & Paines, London, Assistant Solicitor, 1929-34; joined British-American Tobacco Ltd group as a Solicitor, 1934; Director: British-American Tobacco Co. Ltd, 1943; Lloyds Bank Ltd, 1956, Equity and Law Life Assurance Society. Chairman: Council, Royal College of Art, 1956; Council of Industrial Design, 1960 (Mem. 1959); British Nat. Cttee of Internat. Chamber of Commerce, 1963; Court of Govs of Administrative Staff Coll., 1963 (Mem. 1957); Overseas Investment Cttee CBI, 1964; Mem., Governing Body of Repton School, 1959. Senior Fellow Royal College of Art. Bicentenary Medal, RSA, 1969. *Recreations:* painting, sailing. *Address:* 43 Edwardes Square, Kensington, W8. *T:* 01-603 7431. *Clubs:* Athenæum; Royal Yacht Squadron, Royal Thames Yacht.

**OPPENHEIM, Mrs Henry M.;** *see* Oppenheim, Sally.

**OPPENHEIM, Sally; (Mrs Henry M. Oppenheim);** MP (C) Gloucester since 1970; *b* 26 July 1930; *d* of Marks and Jeanette Viner; *m* 1949, Henry M. Oppenheim; one *s* two *d*. *Educ:* Sheffield High Sch.; Lowther Coll., N Wales. Exec. Dir, Industrial & Investment Services Ltd; Trustee, Clergy Rest House Trust; Mem. Cttee, Nat. Council for the Single Woman and her Elderly Dependents. *Recreations:* tennis, bridge. *Address:* Ardmore Close, Gloucester. *Clubs:* (Pres.) Conservative (Gloucester).

**OPPENHEIMER, Harry Frederick;** Chairman: Anglo-American Corporation of SA Ltd, and other companies in Anglo-American Group; Zambian Anglo-American Ltd, and other companies in Zambian Anglo Group; Zambia Broken Hill Development Co. Ltd; Anglo-American Rhodesian Development Corporation, Ltd; De Beers Consolidated Mines, Ltd, and other producing, marketing and investment companies in the De Beers Group; African Explosives and Chemical Industries, Ltd; Union Acceptances Ltd; Williamson Diamonds Ltd; Director: Barclays Bank DCO; Banque de Paris et des Pays-Bas; Canadian Imperial Bank of Commerce; General Mining and Finance Corp. Ltd; The Discount House of SA, Ltd and other investment, mining, colliery and development companies; *b* Kimberley S Africa, 28 Oct. 1908; *s* of late Sir Ernest Oppenheimer, DCL; LLD; *m* 1943, Bridget, *d* of late Foster McCall; one *s* one *d*. *Educ:* Charterhouse; Christ Church, Oxford (MA). MP (SA) Kimberley City, 1948-58. Served 4th SA Armoured Car Regt 1940-45. Chancellor, Univ. of Cape Town; Hon. DEcon, Univ. of Natal; Hon. DLaws, Univs of Leeds, Rhodes and Witwatersrand. Instn MM Gold Medal, 1965. *Recreations:* racing, golf, riding. *Address:* Brenthurst, Parktown, Johannesburg, South Africa. *Clubs:* Brooks's; Rand, Inanda (Johannesburg), Kimberley (SA).

**OPPENHEIMER, Sir Michael (Bernard Grenville),** 3rd Bt, *cr* 1921; BLitt, MA; *b* 27 May 1924; *s* of Sir Michael Oppenheimer, 2nd Bt, and Caroline Magdalen (who *m* 2nd, 1935, late Sir Ernest Oppenheimer), *d* of Sir Robert G. Harvey, 2nd Bt; *S* father, 1933; *m* 1947, Laetitia Helen, BPhil, MA, *er d* of Sir Hugh Munro-Lucas-Tooth of Teananich, *qv*; three *d*. *Educ:* Charterhouse; Christ Church, Oxford. Served with South African Artillery, 1942-45. Lecturer in Politics: Lincoln Coll., Oxford, 1955-68; Magdalen Coll., Oxford, 1966-68. *Heir:* none. *Address:* L'Aiguillon, Grouville, Jersey; Via Cherubini 6, Milano, Italy. *Clubs:* Victoria (Jersey); Kimberley (Kimberley).

**OPPENHEIMER, Sir Philip (Jack),** Kt 1970; Managing Director, The Diamond Trading Co. Ltd, since 1950; *b* 29 Oct. 1911; *s* of Otto and Beatrice Oppenheimer; *m* 1935, Pamela Fenn Stirling; one *s* one *d*. *Educ:* Harrow; Jesus Coll., Cambridge. Bronze Cross of Holland, 1943. *Recreations:* golf, horse-racing and breeding. *Address:* Park Place, Englefield Green, Surrey. *T:* Egham 4263. *Clubs:* Portland, White's.

**OPPENHEIMER, Raymond Harry,** CBE 1959; Company Director; *b* 13 Nov. 1905; *s* of Louis Oppenheimer and Charlotte Emily Pollak. *Educ:* Harrow; Christ Church, Oxford. Served in RAFVR, 1940-45 (Fighter Controller). *Recreations:* golf, dog breeding (bull terriers). *Address:* White Waltham Place, Berkshire. *T:* Maidenhead 103. *Clubs:* Royal and Ancient; Royal Lytham, etc.

**OPPERMAN, Hon. Sir Hubert (Ferdinand),** Kt 1968; OBE 1952; Australian High Commissioner in Malta, since 1967; *b* 29 May 1904; Australian; *m* 1928, Mavys Paterson Craig; one *s* (one *d* decd). *Educ:* Armadale, Vic.; Bailieston, Vic. Served RAAF 1940-45; commissioned 1942. Commonwealth Public Service: PMG's Dept, 1918-20; Navigation Dept, Trade and Customs, 1920-22. Cyclist: Australian Road Champion, 1924, 1926, 1927, 1929; Winner French Bol d'Or, 1928, and Paris-Brest-Paris, 1931; holder, numerous world's track and road unpaced and motor paced cycling records. Director, Allied Bruce Small Pty Ltd, 1936-60. MHR for Corio, Vic., 1949-67; Convenor: Commonwealth Jubilee Sporting Sub-Cttee, 1951; Mem. Australian Delegn to CPA Conf., Nairobi, 1954; Chief Govt, Whip, 1955-60; Minister for Shipping and Transport, 1960-63; Minister for Immigration, 1963-66. *Recreations:* cycling, swimming. *Address:* Australian High Commission, Airways House, Sliema, Malta, GC. *T:* 30051. *Clubs:* Royal Automobile (Victoria), Union (Malta), Casino Maltese.

**ORAM, Albert Edward;** MP (Lab and Co-op) East Ham South, since 1955; *b* 13 Aug. 1913; *s* of Henry and Ada Edith Oram; *m* Frances Joan, *d* of Charles and Dorothy Barber, Lewes; two *s*. *Educ:* Burgess Hill Element. Sch.; Brighton Grammar Sch.; University of London (London School of Economics and Institute of Education). Formerly a teacher. Served War 1942-45; Royal Artillery, Normandy and Belgium. Research Officer, Co-operative Party, 1946-55. Parly Secretary, ODM, 1964-69. *Recreations:* country walking, cricket, chess. *Address:* 19 Ridgeside Avenue, Patcham, Brighton BN1 8WD. *T:* Brighton 505333.

**ORAM, Samuel,** MD (London); FRCP; Senior Physician, and Physician-in-charge, Cardiac Department, King's College Hospital; Medical Adviser, Rio Tinto Zinc Corporation Ltd; Consulting Medical Officer, Sun Life Assurance Co. of Canada; *b* 11 July 1913; *s* of Samuel Henry Nathan Oram, London; *m* 1940, Ivy, *d* of Raffaele Amato; two *d. Educ:* King's College, London; King's College Hospital, London. Senior Scholar, KCH, London; Sambrooke Medical Registrar, KCH. Served War of 1939-45, as Lt-Col, RAMC. Examiner in Medicine for Royal Coll. of Phys and Univ. of London; Examiner: in Pharmacology and Materia Medica, The Conjoint Bd; in Medicine, The Worshipful Soc. of Apothecaries. Member: Assoc. of Physicians; Br. Cardiac Society; American Heart Assoc.; Canada Club; Corresp. Member Australasian Cardiac Soc. *Publications:* various cardiological and medical articles in Quart. Jl Med., British Heart Jl, BMJ, Brit. Encyclopaedia of Medical Practice, The Practitioner, etc. *Recreation:* golf (execrable). *Address:* 73 Harley Street, W1. *T:* 01-935 9942. *Club:* Athenæum.

**ORANMORE and BROWNE,** 4th Baron (Ireland), *cr* 1836; Baron Mereworth of Mereworth Castle (UK), *cr* 1926; **Dominick Geoffrey Edward Browne;** *b* 21 Oct. 1901; *e s* of 3rd Baron and Lady Olwen Verena Ponsonby (*d* 1927), *e d* of 8th Earl of Bessborough; *S* father, 1927; *m* 1st, 1925, Mildred Helen (who obtained a divorce, 1936), *e d* of Hon. Thomas Egerton; two *s* two *d*; 2nd, 1936, Oonagh (marr. diss., 1950), *d* of late Hon. Ernest Guinness; one *s* (and two *s* decd); 3rd, 1953, Sally Gray, 5b Mount Street, London, W. *Educ:* Eton; Christ Church, Oxford. *Heir: s* Hon. Dominick Geoffrey Thomas Browne [*b* 1 July 1929; *m* 1957, Sara Margaret, *d* of late Dr Herbert Wright, 59 Merrion Square, Dublin, and of Mrs C. A. West, Cross-in-Hand, Sussex]. *Address:* 52 Eaton Place, SW1. *Club:* Kildare Street (Dublin).

*See also Hon. M. A. R. Cayzer.*

**ORBACH, Maurice;** MP (Lab) Stockport South since 1964; General Secretary Trades Advisory Council since 1940; *b* 13 July 1902; *s* of late Hiam M. and Millicent Orbach, Cardiff and New York; *m* 1935, Ruth Beatrice Huebsch; one *s* one *d. Educ:* Cardiff; New York City. Engineer. Member St Pancras Board of Guardians, 1924; Member, South West St Pancras, LLC, 1937-46; MP (Lab) Willesden East, 1945-Sept. 1959. Governor, Central Foundation Schools; Mem. London Town Planning Committee; Governor, St Paul's, St Peter's, St Barts and St Philip's Hospitals; Chm., British Emigrants Families Assoc.; Mem. World Executive, World Jewish Congress, 1967-. Lecturer on Industry and Commerce and the American Scene. *Publication:* Mission to Madrid, Austria, 1946. *Address:* 76 Eton Hall, Eton College Road, NW3. *T:* 01-722 4696, 01-405 3188.

**ORCHARD, Edward Eric,** CBE 1966 (OBE 1959); Director of Research, Foreign and Commonwealth Office, since 1970; *b* 12 Nov. 1920; British. *Educ:* King's Sch., Grantham; Jesus Coll., Oxford (MA). War Service, 1941-46; FO, and HM Embassy, Moscow, 1948-51; Lectr in Russian, Oxford, 1951-52; FO, 1953-. *Publications:* various articles. *Recreations:* swimming, skating, chess, gardening. *Address:* Sturt Meadow House, Haslemere, Surrey. *T:* Haslemere 3034.

**ORCHIN, Frederick Joseph,** CB 1948; OBE 1941; MInstT; *b* 28 May 1885. Late Under Secretary Ministry of Transport; Chief Financial Officer, Road Haulage Exec., BTC, 1948-50; Deputy Chairman, Road Haulage Disposal Board, 1953-56. *Address:* 2 Raith Avenue, N14. *T:* 01-886 2366.

**ORD JOHNSTONE, Morris Mackintosh,** CB 1960; Chairman: Tobacco Advisory Committee, since 1967; Timber Trade Federation of the United Kingdom, since 1969; *b* 10 Oct. 1907; *s* of late James Ord Johnstone and Emily Morrison; *m* 1935, Violet Springett; one *d. Educ:* Uppingham; Wadham Coll., Oxford. With W. S. Crawford Ltd, Advertising Agents, 1930-41; Board of Trade, 1941-67; Under-Secretary, 1955-67. *Address:* 35 Hall Lane, Shenfield, Brentwood, Essex. *T:* Brentwood 7965.

**ORDE, Alan C. C.;** *see* Campbell Orde.

**ORDE, Sir Charles William,** KCMG *cr* 1940 (CMG 1931); *b* 25 Oct. 1884; *e s* of late William Orde, DL, of Nunnykirk. Morpeth, Northumberland; *m* 1914, Frances Fortune (*d* 1949), *o d* of James Davidson, Dunedin, New Zealand; two *s* two *d. Educ:* Eton; King's College, Cambridge. Minister to Baltic States, 1938-40; Ambassador to Chile, 1940-45. *Recreations:* fishing, music. *Address:* Nunnykirk, Morpeth, Northumberland. *T:* Hartburn 250.

**ORDE, Sir John (Alexander) Campbell-,** 6th Bt *cr* 1790, of Morpeth; *b* 11 May 1943; *s* of Sir Simon Arthur Campbell-Orde, 5th Bt, TD, and of Eleanor, *e d* of Col. Humphrey Watts, OBE, TD, Haslington Hall, Cheshire; *S* father, 1969. *Educ:* Gordonstoun. *Heir: b* Peter Humphrey Campbell-Orde, *b* 18 June 1946. *Address:* 31 The Little Boltons, SW10. *T:* 01-373 9369. *Club:* Caledonian.

**ORDE, Sir Percy Lancelot,** Kt, *cr* 1941; CIE 1927; retired; formerly Inspector-General of Police, Punjab; *b* 19 Jan. 1888; *s* of Col W. Orde, Nunnykirk, Northumberland; *m* 1st, Noëlle, *d* of Lt-Col A. C. Elliott; 2nd Eileen, *d* of Edward Probst; one *s* two *d. Educ:* Malvern. *Recreations:* fishing, racing. *Address:* Aldings, Wherwell, Andover, Hants. *T:* Chilbolton 315.

**ORDE, Brig. Reginald John,** CBE 1945; QC (Dominion); Commander Order of Orange-Nassau (Netherlands); Judge Advocate-General, Department of National Defence, Canada, since 1920; *b* 15 May, 1893; *s* of late Hon. Mr Justice J. F. Orde and Edith C. M. Orde; *m* 1919, Dorothy Cook; no *c. Educ:* Ashbury College; Univ. of Toronto, Osgoode Hall Law School. Royal Artillery and Royal Canadian Artillery, European War; Service in France, Mesopotamia, India, Canada; Assistant Judge Advocate-General, 1918; attended Imperial Defence College, London, 1931. KC (Dominion), 1950. CD (with 2 clasps), 1950; retired from Cdn Army, 1951. KStJ; Legal Adviser, Priory of Canada. *Recreations:* golf, fishing. *Address:* 425 Daly Avenue, Ottawa, Canada. *Clubs:* Rideau (Ottawa); University (Toronto).

**ORDE-POWLETT,** family name of **Baron Bolton.**

**ORENSTEIN, Maj.-Gen. Alexander Jeremiah,** CB 1943; CMG 1919; CBE 1941; LLD (Hon.); DSc; MD; MRCS, FRCP; FRSH; late Director of Pneumoconiosis Research, South African Council of Scientific and Industrial

Research; Hon. Fellow: Royal Society of Tropical Medicine and Hygiene; Institute of Water Pollution Control; RSocMed; Emeritus Fellow, American College of Chest Physicians; Fellow, American Public Health Association; Hon. Member, South African Institute of Mechanical Engineers, 1967; Chevalier Ordre de la Couronne, Belgium; Medical Consultant, Rand Mines Ltd; Gold Medallist, Medical Association of South Africa (BMA); Gold Medal: Institute of Mining and Metallurgy; Mine Medical Officers, 1968; Bernard Nocht Medal (for services to tropical medicine) 1965; *b* 26 September 1879; *m* 1916, Kate Bradbury; one *d*. Acting Director of Medical Services, Col, S African Medical Corps, 1917-19. Panama Canal Medical Services, 1905-12; Special Work in East Africa, 1913-14; Belgian Congo and S West Africa Mandated Territory; Director of Medical Services, East Africa, 1940-41 (CBE); Director of Medical Services UDF in Middle East (despatches, CB), 1941; Director-General of Medical Services, Union of S Africa Defence Force, 1939, and again 1943-Sept. 1945; Delegate to International Labour Conference, Geneva, 1925 and 1928; late President, Federal Council Medical Association of South Africa (BMA); Vice-Pres. and Fellow British Medical Assoc.; Union Leprosy Advisory Council; several other Govt Councils and Cttees; Committee on Industrial Hygiene, International Labour Office; late President Associated Scientific and Technical Societies of South Africa; late President South African Red Cross Society. *Publications:* Numerous professional. *Address:* PO Box 1032, Johannesburg, SA. *Clubs:* Rand, Transvaal Automobile, Scientific and Technical (Johannesburg).

**ORGANE, Sir Geoffrey (Stephen William),** Kt 1968; MD, FFARCS; FRCS; Civilian Consultant in Anæsthetics to Royal Navy; Professor of Anæsthetics, University of London, Westminster Medical School; Consultant Adviser in Anæsthetics, Ministry of Health; *b* Madras, 25 Dec. 1908; *er s* of Rev. William Edward Hartland Organe, K-i-H, and Alice (*née* Williams); *m* 1935, Margaret Mary Bailey, *e d* of Rev. David Bailey Davies, MC; one *s* two *d*. *Educ:* Taunton Sch.; Christ's Coll., Cambridge; Westminster Med. Sch. MRCS, LRCP, 1933; DA, RCP&S, 1937; MA, MD Cantab 1941; FFARCS 1948; FRCS 1965. Various resident appointments and first Anæsthetic Registrar (1938-39), Westminster Hospital; two years in general practice. Hon. Secretary, Medical Research Council's Anæsthetics Sub-Committee of Committee on Traumatic Shock, 1941-47; formerly Hon. Sec. Anæsthetics Cttee, Cttee on Analgesia in Midwifery; Vice-Pres., BMA Sect. Anæsthetics, Harrogate, 1949, Toronto, 1955; Pres., World Fedn of Socs. of Anæsthesiologists, 1964-68 (Sec.-Treas., 1955-64); Mem. Coun., RCS, 1958-61; Mem. Coun., Royal Soc. Med. (Hon. Sec. 1953-58; Pres. Sect. of Anæsthetics, 1949-50); Assoc. of Anæsthetists of Gt Brit. and Ire.: Hon. Sec. 1949-53; Vice-Pres. 1953-54; Mem. Council, 1957-59; Pres. 1954-57; Mem. Cttee of Anæsthetists' Group of BMA (Chm. 1955-58); Pres. SW Metropolitan Soc. of Anæsthetists, 1957-59; Dean, Faculty of Anæsthetists, 1958-61; Examr in Anæsthetics, Conjoint Bd; Examiner for FFARCS. Visited Italy, Turkey, Greece, Syria, Lebanon for Brit. Council; Denmark, Norway for WHO; also Portugal, France, Switzerland, Spain, Belgium, Netherlands, Germany, Finland, USA, Canada, Argentina, Australia, Venezuela, Mexico, Uganda, Peru, Japan, Hong Kong, Philippines, Brazil, Ceylon, Egypt, India, Iran, Israel, Malaysia, Uruguay, Austria, Sweden, Poland, USSR, Bulgaria, Czechoslovakia. Hon. or Corr. Mem., Danish, Argentine, Australian, Austrian, Brazilian, Canadian, Greek, Portuguese, French, German, Italian, Philippine, Spanish, Venezuelan Societies of Anæsthetists; Hon. FFARACS 1957; Hon. FFARCSI 1960. *Publications:* various articles and chapters in medical journals and textbooks. *Recreations:* travel, gardening, photography, competitive sports; Pres. (formerly Vice-Pres., Hon. Treas., Capt. 1933) United Hospitals Athletic Club. *Address:* Department of Anæsthetics, Westminster Hospital, SW1. *T:* 01-828 9811; 9 Fairmile Park Copse, Cobham, Surrey. *T:* Cobham 2800.

**ORGEL, Leslie Eleazer,** DPhil Oxon, MA; FRS 1962; Senior Fellow, Salk Institute, La Jolla, California, USA, and Professor, University of California, San Diego, Calif, since 1964; *b* 12 Jan. 1927; *s* of Simon Orgel; *m* 1950, Hassia Alice Levinson; two *s* one *d*. *Educ:* Dame Alice Owen's Sch., London. Reader, University Chemical Laboratory, Cambridge, 1963-64, and Fellow of Peterhouse, 1957-64. *Publication:* An Introduction to Transition-Metal Chemistry, Ligand-Field Theory, 1960. *Address:* Salk Institute, PO Box 1809, San Diego, Calif 92112, USA.

**ORGILL, Tyrrell Churton,** CIE 1937; MA; Flight Lieutenant, late RAFVR; late Indian Educational Service; *b* 7 June 1884; *s* of Bernard Churton Orgill; *m* 1910, Josephine, *d* of W. T. Scruby, Cambridge; one *s* one *d* (and one *s* decd). *Educ:* Dulwich College; Trinity College, Cambridge. Entered Indian Educational Service, 1913; served European War, 1915-21, NWFP of India, German East Africa, and as political officer in Mesopotamia; Provincial Commissioner Scouts Association, NWFP, 1931; Director of Public Instruction, NW Frontier Province, India, 1931-39; retired, 1939. *Recreations:* gardening and sailing. *Address:* The Anchorage, Summercove, Kinsale, Co. Cork, Eire.

**ORIGO, Marchesa Iris;** FRSL; author; *b* Birdlip, Glos, 15 August 1902; *o d* of W. Bayard Cutting, Westbrook, Long Island, USA, and of Lady Sybil Cuffe; *m* 1924, Marchese Antonio Origo; two *d*. *Educ:* privately, mostly in Florence. Holds honorary doctorates from Smith College and Wheaton College, USA; Isabella d'Este medal for essays and historical studies, Mantua, Italy, 1966. *Publications:* Leopardi, a biography, 1935 (revised 1953); Allegra, 1935; Tribune of Rome, 1938; War in Val d'Orcia, 1947; Giovanna and Jane, 1948; The Last Attachment, 1949; The Merchant of Prato, 1957; A Measure of Love, 1957; The World of San Bernardino, 1963; Images and Shadows, Part of a Life, 1970. *Recreations:* travel, gardening. *Address:* La Foce, Chianciano (Siena), Italy.

**ORKNEY,** 8th Earl of, *cr* 1696; **Cecil O'Bryen Fitz-Maurice;** Viscount of Kirkwall and Baron of Dechmont, 1696; *b* 3 July 1919; *s* of Douglas Frederick Harold FitzMaurice (*d* 1937; *g g s* of 5th Earl) and Dorothy Janette (who *m* 2nd, 1939, Commander E. T. Wiggins, DSC, RN), *d* of late Capt. Robert Dickie, RN; *S* kinsman 1951; *m* 1953, Rose Katharine Durk, *yr d* of late J. W. D. Silley, Brixham. Joined RASC, 1939; served in North Africa, Italy, France and Germany, 1939-46, and in Korea, 1950-51. *Heir: kinsman* Frederick Oliver St John, DSO, MC [*b* 13 Oct. 1886; *m* 1st, 1923, Dotie (marr. diss. 1929), *d* of S. B. Burney, CBE; 2nd, 1931, Elizabeth, *d* of E. H. Pierce, Peachland, BC; one *s*]. *Address:* The Round Top, Berry Head, Brixham, South Devon. *T:* Brixham 2334. *Clubs:* Quent's, Annabel's, Curzon House; Brixham yacht.

**ORMANDY, Eugene,** MusD; Conductor and Music Director of Philadelphia Orchestra since 1936; *b* 18 Nov. 1899; Hungarian; *s* of Benjamin and Rosalie Ormandy; *m* 1st, 1922, Steffy Goldner, harpist, NY Philharmonic Orchestra (divorced, 1947); no *c*; 2nd, 1950, Margaret Frances Hitsch. *Educ:* Royal Conservatory, Budapest. BA, Royal State Acad. of Music, 1914; state diploma for art of violin playing, 1916, and as prof., 1917; Grad. Gymnasium; student Univ. of Budapest, 1917-20. Hon. MusD: Hamline Univ., St Paul, 1934; Univ. of Pennsylvania, 1937; Philadelphia Academy of Music, 1939; Curtis Inst. of Music, 1946; Temple Univ., 1949; Univ. of Michigan, 1952; Lehigh Univ., 1953; Villanova Univ., 1968; Rensselaer Polytechnic Inst., 1968; Peabody Inst., 1968; Univ. of Illinois, 1969; Doctor of Letters: Clark Univ., 1956, Miami Univ., 1959, Rutgers Univ., 1960, Long Island Univ., 1965; Lafayette Coll., 1966; holds many other hon. degrees. Toured Hungary as child prodigy; Head of master classes, State Conservatorium of Music, Budapest, at age of 20; arrived in United States, 1921, naturalised 1927; substituted for Toscanini as Conductor Philadelphia Orchestra; Conductor Minneapolis Symphony Orch., 1931-36; toured Australia, 1944, S America, 1946, Europe, 1950, 1951, 1952, 1953, 1954, 1955, 1957, 1958. Appeared Edinburgh Festival, 1955, 1957. Caballero, Order of Merit of Juan Pablo Duarte, Dominican Republic, 1945; Commandeur, French Legion of Honour, 1958; Knight, Order of Dannebrog, 1st cl., 1952; Knight 1st cl., Order of the White Rose, Finland, 1955; Comdr, Order of Lion of Finland, 1966; Honor Cross for Arts and Sciences, Austria, 1967; Golden Medallion, Vienna Philharmonic Orch., 1967; Freedom Medal, USA, 1970. *Address:* 230 South 15th Street, Philadelphia 2, Pa, USA.

**ORMATHWAITE,** 6th Baron, *cr* 1868; **John Arthur Charles Walsh,** Bt 1804; Farming since 1950; *b* 25 December 1912; *s* of 5th Baron Ormathwaite and Lady Margaret Jane Douglas-Home (*d* 1955), 3rd *d* of 12th Earl of Home; *S* father, 1944; unmarried. *Educ:* Eton College; Trinity College, Cambridge. *Heir:* none. *Address:* Pen-y-Bont Hall, Llandrindod Wells. *T:* Pen-y-Bont 228.

**ORME, John Samuel,** CB 1963; OBE 1945; Assistant Under-Secretary of State, Department of Health and Social Security, since 1970; *b* 7 May 1916; *s* of late Sidney Wilkinson Orme, Solicitor, and late Evelyn Orme; *m* 1940, Jean, *d* of G. H. Harris; three *s* one *d*. *Educ:* The High School, Newcastle under Lyme; St John's College, Oxford (Scholar); Ecole des Sciences Politiques, Paris. BA 1937, 1st Cl. Hons, Sch. of Mod. Hist.; MA 1957. Air Ministry, 1938; served RAF, 1941-45; Wing Comdr, 1944 (despatches, OBE); Air Ministry, 1945; Private Sec. to Secretary of State, 1946-48; Asst Sec. 1949; Deputy to Asst Secretary-General, NATO, Paris, 1954-57; Assistant Under Secretary of State, Air Ministry, 1957-58, and again 1960-64; Under-Secretary; Cabinet Office, 1958-60; Min. of Transport, 1964-66; Asst Under-Sec. of State, Welsh Office, 1966-70. *Address:* Broom House, Seer Green, Bucks. *T:* Beaconsfield 5920. *Club:* Reform.

**ORME, Stanley;** MP (Lab) Salford West since 1964; *b* 5 April 1923; *s* of Sherwood Orme, Sale, Cheshire; *m* 1951, Irene Mary, *d* of Vernon Fletcher Harris, Worsley, Lancashire. *Educ:* elementary and technical schools; National Council of Labour Colleges and Workers' Educational Association classes. Warrant Officer, Air-Bomber Navigator, Royal Air Force Bomber Command, 1942-47. Joined the Labour party, 1944; contested (Lab) Stockport South, 1959. Member of Sale Borough Council, 1958-; Member: Amalgamated Engineering Union; District Committee, Manchester; shop steward. *Address:* House of Commons, SW1; 47 Hope Road, Sale, Cheshire.

**ORMEROD, Rt. Hon. Sir Benjamin,** PC 1957; Kt 1948; *b* 7 Sept. 1890; *er s* of John Aspden Ormerod, JP, North Bank, Blackburn; *m* 1916, Kathleen May Carter (*d* 1968); one *s* two *d*. *Educ:* Queen Elizabeth's Grammar Sch., Blackburn; Manchester Univ. Hon. LLD Manchester Univ., 1949. Solicitor, 1913. Called to bar, Lincoln's Inn, 1924; Northern Circuit: Judge of County Courts, Circuit No. 14 jointly with His Hon. Judge Stewart, 1944-46; Circuit No. 5, 1946-48; Bencher of Lincoln's Inn, 1948; Judge of High Court of Justice, Probate, Divorce and Admiralty Division, 1948, King's Bench Division, 1950-57; Lord Justice of Appeal, 1957-63. Vice-President and Hon. Fellow, Royal Academy of Music. Served 4th Batt. East Lancs Regt, Sept. 1914-Jan. 1919, Captain. *Address:* 16 Old Buildings, Lincoln's Inn, WC2. *T:* 01-405 1325.

*See also J. A. Leavey.*

**ORMEROD, Major Sir (Cyril) Berkeley,** KBE 1960 (CBE 1954, OBE 1946); Director, Public Relations, British Information Services, New York, 1945-62 (Financial Adviser, British Press Service, 1940-45), retired; Chairman, Jersey External Trust Ltd; Dep. Chairman, Bank of Nova Scotia Trust Co. (Bahamas) Ltd, (Jamaica), (West Indies), (Barbados), (Caymans) Ltd; Director: Sceptre Trust (Eagle Star); Imperial Insurance (Bahamas) Ltd; *b* London, 3 Oct. 1897; *s* of late Ernest Berkeley Ormerod, Ashton-under-Lyne, Lancs, and late Alice Heys; *m* 1962, Beatrice, *widow* of Frederick Sigrist, Nassau, Bahamas. *Educ:* Colet Court; St Paul's Sch.; Royal Military Academy. Royal Regt of Artillery, 1916-26; European War, active service in France and Belgium, 1917-18. London Stock Exchange (Foster and Braithwaite), 1929-39. Regular contributor to Financial Times, Investor's Chronicle, Barron's (New York), 1934-39. Member UK Delegation, UN organizational Conference, San Francisco, 1945; Public Relations Adviser to Secretary of State (late Ernest Bevin) Foreign Ministers' Conference, New York, 1946. Specially attached to the Ambassador's Staff as Press Adviser to the Royal Party during American visit of the Queen and the Duke of Edinburgh, Oct. 1957; Press Advisor to the Governor of the Bahamas during Nassau talks between Prime Minister Macmillan and late President Kennedy, Dec. 1962. Member of The Pilgrims; RIIA (Chatham House); FIPR. *Publications:* Dow Theory Applied to the London Stock Exchange, 1937. *Recreations:* cricket (Oxfordshire, The Army, The RA, MCC, I Zingari, Free Foresters, etc), golf (won Army Championship, 1924), bridge. *Address:* PO Box 969, Nassau, Bahamas. *Clubs:* Cavalry, Boodle's, MCC; Royal and Ancient (St Andrews); Berkshire Golf; Knickerbocker, Lotos, Dutch Treat (New York); Travellers' (Paris); Lyford Cay, Coral Harbour Golf (Nassau).

**ORMEROD, Richard Caton;** HM Consul-General, Marseilles, since 1967; *b* 22 Jan. 1915; *s* of late Prof. Henry Arderne Ormerod and Mildred Robina Ormerod (*née* Caton); *m* 1947, Elizabeth Muriel, *yr d* of Sheriff J. W. More, St Andrews; two *s* two *d*. *Educ:* Winchester Coll.; New Coll., Oxford (BA). India Office, 1938. War Service, 1941-45: Indian Army, 7th Light

Cavalry; active service in Imphal and Burma (wounded). Asst Private Secretary to Secretary of State for India and Burma, 1945-46; Principal, Burma Office, 1946; CRO, 1948; First Secretary, British High Commn: Bombay, 1951-53; Wellington, 1956-59; Asst Secretary, 1960; Counsellor, British High Commn, Calcutta, 1962-65; Ministry of Overseas Development, 1965. *Publication:* Ferns in the Waste, 1943. *Recreations:* music, gardening. *Address:* c/o Foreign and Commonwealth Office, SW1; Hatchgate, Epsom Road, Ashtead, Surrey; Chequers, Marden, near Devizes, Wilts. *Club:* East India and Sports.

**ORMOND, Maj.-General Daniel Mowat,** CMG 1919; DSO 1917; Canadian Infantry; Barrister-at-Law; Permanent Force Reserve, Ottawa, Canada; *b* Pembroke, Ontario, 1885; *s* of Daniel Ormond and Frances Hudson; *m* 1910, Ann Laura, *d* of J. O. Cadham; one *s* four *d.* Served European War, 1915-18 (wounded, despatches three times, CMG, DSO and bar, Russian Order of St Stanislas with swords, Croix de Guerre). *Address:* 80 Rideau Terrace, Apartment 55, Ottawa 2, Ontario. *Clubs:* Larimac (Quebec), etc.

**ORMOND, Sir John (Davies Wilder),** Kt 1964; BEM 1940; JP; Chairman, New Zealand Meat Producers Board; Chairman, Exports and Shipping Council; *b* 8 Sept. 1905; *s* of J. D. Ormond and Gladys Wilder; *m* 1939, Judith Wall; four *s* one *d. Educ:* Christ's Coll., Christchurch, New Zealand. Chairman, Waipukurau Farmers Union, 1929; President, Waipukurau Jockey Club, 1950; Member, New Zealand Meat Producers Board, 1934. Active Service Overseas (Middle East), 1940. JP, NZ, 1945. *Recreations:* tennis, polo, Rugby Union football. *Address:* Wallingford, Waipukurau, New Zealand. *T:* Waipukurau 542M. *Club:* Hawke's Bay (New Zealand).

**ORMONDE,** 6th Marquess of, *cr* 1825; **James Arthur Norman Butler,** CVO 1960; MC 1918; Lieut-Colonel, retired; Earl of Ormonde *cr* 1328; Earl of Ossory, 1526; Viscount Thurles, 1537; Baron Ormonde (UK), 1821; 30th Hereditary Chief Butler of Ireland; High Steward of Wokingham, 1956; *b* 25 April 1893; *yr s* of 4th Marquess and Ellen (*d* 1951), *d* of General Anson Stager, US Army; *S* brother, 1949; *m* 1924, Jessie, (*d* 1969), *y d* of late Charles Carlos Clarke, of Welton, Sunninghill; two *d. Educ:* Harrow; RMC, Sandhurst. Commanded 17th/21st Lancers, 1931-35; served European War, 1914-19; re-employed, 1940-45. HM Hon. Corps of Gentlemen-at-Arms, 1936-63, Lieut, 1957-63. DL Kent, 1952-56. *Heir: cousin,* James Hubert Theobald Charles Butler, MBE [*b* 19 April 1899; *m* 1935, Nan, *d* of Garth Gilpin; two *d*]. *Address:* Cantley, Wokingham, Berks. *T:* Wokingham 107. *Clubs:* Cavalry, St James'; Kildare Street (Dublin).

*See also A. C. G. Ponsonby.*

**ORMROD, Hon. Sir Roger (Fray Greenwood),** Kt 1961; **Hon. Mr Justice Ormrod;** a Judge of the High Court of Justice, Probate, Divorce and Admiralty Division, since 1961; *b* 20 Oct. 1911; *s* of Oliver Fray Ormrod and Edith Muriel (*née* Pim); *m* 1938, Anne, *d* of Charles Lush; no *c. Educ:* Shrewsbury Sch.; The Queen's Coll., Oxford. BA Oxon (Jurisprudence) 1935. Called to Bar, Inner Temple, 1936; QC 1958. Hon. Fellow, Queen's Coll., Oxford, 1966. BM, BCh Oxon, 1941; FRCP 1969. House Physician, Radcliffe Infirmary, Oxford, 1941-42. Served in RAMC, 1942-45, with rank of Major. DADMS 8 Corps. Lecturer in Forensic Medicine, Oxford Medical Sch., 1950-59. Governor, St Bartholomew's Hosp., Bethlem Royal Hosp. and Maudsley Hosp. Chairman: The London Marriage Guidance Council; Lord Chancellor's Cttee on Legal Education, 1968; Notting Hill Housing Trust, 1968. Member Cttee Institute of Psychiatry. *Publications:* Ed. (with E. H. Pearce) Dunstan's Law of Hire-Purchase, 1938; (with Harris Walker) National Health Service Act 1946, 1949. *Address:* 4 Aubrey Road, W8. *T:* 01-727 7876. *Club:* Garrick.

**ORMSBY GORE,** family name of **Baron Harlech.**

**O'RORKE, E. Brian,** RA 1956 (ARA 1947); MA (Cantab); FRIBA; RDI 1939 (Master of the Faculty, 1961-63); Architect; *b* New Zealand, 14 June 1901; *s* of E. Dennis and Amy O'Rorke; *m* 1929, Juliet Wigan; one *s* three *d. Educ:* Wellington Coll., Berks; Jesus Coll., Cambridge; Architectural Association School of Architecture. Dawnay Scholar and Bronze Medallist, RIBA, 1926. Work includes interiors of passenger liners, aircraft and trains; Orient Line Building, Sydney, Australia (RIBA Bronze Medal, 1947); Port Line Building, Sydney, Australia; Agriculture Building, Festival of Britain; New Royal Observatory Buildings, Hurstmonceux; Office Building, Three Quays, Tower Hill (Civic Trust Award for City of London, 1961); new Berkeley Hotel, Knightsbridge; University buildings, factories, houses, etc. *Address:* Rock House, River Common, Petworth, Sussex. *TA* and *T:* Lodsworth 243. *Clubs:* Athenæum, Arts, Leander.

**O'RORKE, Lieut-Colonel Frederick Charles,** CMG 1916; resigned appointment in Gibraltar, 1941, owing to War conditions; *m* Dorothy Violet (*d* 1963), 2nd *d* of late J. Whitaker, Rainworth Lodge, Notts; one *s. Educ:* Nottingham High Sch.; Royal Veterinary Coll., London. Gazetted Royal Army Veterinary Corps, 1904; in India, 1905-10; Remount duty at Arborfield Cross Remount Depôt, near Reading, 1911-14; Executive Veterinary Officer at the Base at beginning of European War; joined HQ 3rd Army Corps, Oct. 1914 (despatches); Dep. Assistant Director of Veterinary Services at Headquarters, Inspector-General of Communications, 1915 (despatches twice, CMG); Assistant Director of Veterinary Services, Headquarters, Guards Division, BEF, 1915; Acting Lieut-Colonel, 1918; commanding No. 8 Veterinary Hospital, British Army of Rhine, 1919; Principal, Army Veterinary Sch., Ambala, India, 1920; Dep. Assistant Director of Veterinary Services, AH, India, 1921; Principal, Army Veterinary Sch., Poona, 1922-25; Aldershot Command, 1926; Lieut-Colonel, 1931; ADVS Northern Command 1931-34; retired pay, 1934; re-employed as VO in charge RHA Newport (Mon.), 1937; Government Veterinary Officer, Gibraltar, 1937-41. *Address:* Oatlands Park Hotel, Weybridge, Surrey.

**OROWAN, Egon,** DrIng; FRS 1947; Professor of Mechanical Engineering, Massachusetts Institute of Technology, Cambridge, Massachusetts, USA, 1950-67, now Emeritus (and Senior Lecturer); *b* Budapest, 2 Aug. 1902; *s* of Berthold Orowan and Josephine Ságvári; *m* 1941, Yolande Schonfeld; one *d. Educ:* University of Vienna; Technical Univ., Berlin-Charlottenburg. Demonstrator Technical Univ., Berlin-Charlottenburg, 1928; i/c Krypton Works, United Incandescent Lamp and Electrical Co. Ltd, Ujpest, Hungary, 1936; Research in Physics of Metals, Physics Dept, University of Birmingham, 1937, and Cavendish Laboratory, Cambridge, 1939; Reader in the Physics of Metals,

University of Cambridge. Mem., Nat. Acad. of Sciences; Corresp. Mem., Akademie der Wissenschaften, Göttingen. Thomas Hawksley Gold Medal, MechE, 1944; Bingham Medal, Society of Rheology, 1959; Carl Friedrich Gauss Medal, Braunschweigische Wissenschaftliche Gesellschaft, 1968. DrIng (*hc*) Technische Universität, Berlin, 1965. *Publications:* Papers in scientific and engineering journals. *Address:* Department of Mechanical Engineering, Massachusetts Institute of Technology, Cambridge, Mass 02139, USA.

**ORR,** family name of **Baron Boyd Orr.**

**ORR, Hon. Sir Alan (Stewart),** Kt 1965; OBE 1944; **Hon. Mr Justice Orr;** Judge of High Court of Justice, Probate, Divorce and Admiralty Division, since 1965; Presiding Judge, North-Eastern Circuit, since 1970; *b* 21 Feb. 1911; *s* of late William Orr and Doris Kemsley, Great Wakering, Essex; *m* 1933, Mariana Frances Lilian, *d* of late Captain J. C. Lang, KOSB; four *s*. *Educ:* Fettes; Edinburgh Univ.; Balliol Coll., Oxford. 1st Class Hons Jurisprudence, Univ. of Oxford. Barrister Middle Temple, 1936; Barstow Law Scholar; Harmsworth Scholar. Served with Royal Air Force, 1940-45 (despatches, OBE), Wing Comdr. Member of General Council of the Bar, 1953-57; Junior Counsel (Common Law) to Commissioners of Inland Revenue, 1957-63; QC 1963; Recorder of: New Windsor, 1958-65; Oxford, Jan.-Aug. 1965; Dep. Chairman, Oxford Quarter Sessions, 1964-; Master of the Bench, Middle Temple, 1965. Chancellor's Law Reform Cttee, 1966-. *Recreation:* golf. *Address:* Highfield, Harmer Green, Welwyn, Herts. *T:* Welwyn 4250; Royal Courts of Justice, Strand, WC2. *Club:* Oxford and Cambridge University.

**ORR, David Alexander,** MC 1945; LLB; Vice-Chairman, Unilever Ltd, since 1970 (Director since 1967); *b* 10 May 1922; *s* of late Canon Adrian William Fielder Orr and Grace (*née* Robinson); *m* 1949, Phoebe Rosaleen Davis; three *d*. *Educ:* High Sch., Dublin; Trinity Coll., Dublin. Served Royal Engineers attached QVO Madras Sappers and Miners, 1941-46. With various Unilever companies from 1948: Hindustan Lever, 1955-60; Mem. Overseas Cttee, Unilever, 1960-63; Lever Bros Co., New York, 1963, Pres. 1965-67. *Recreations:* golf, Rugby, travel. *Address:* 81 Lyall Mews West, SW1; Oakhill, Enton Green, Godalming, Surrey. *T:* Godalming 7032. *Clubs:* Lansdowne; Blind Brook (New York).

**ORR, James Bernard Vivian,** CVO 1968 (MVO 1962); Secretary, Medical Commission on Accident Prevention, since 1970; *b* 19 Nov. 1917; *s* of Dr Vivian Bernard Orr and Gladys Constance Orr (*née* Power); unmarried. *Educ:* Harrow; Gordonstoun; RMC, Sandhurst. British South Africa Police, Southern Rhodesia, 1939-46. Attached occupied Enemy Territory Administration in Ethiopia and Eritrea Police Forces, 1941-49; Kenya Police, 1954-57. Private Secretary to HRH The Duke of Edinburgh, 1957-70, an Extra Equerry, 1970-. *Recreations:* horse racing, shooting, tennis, golf. *Address:* 29 Richmond Court, Sloane Street, SW1.

**ORR, Professor John Washington;** Professor of Pathology and Director of Cancer Research, University of Birmingham, and Hon. Pathologist, United Birmingham Hospitals, 1948-66; Professor Emeritus, 1967; *b* 5 Aug. 1901; *er s* of Frederick William and Elizabeth Orr, Belfast; *m* 1932, Nora Margaret (*d* 1965), 2nd *d* of David James and Margaret Carmichael; one *s* one *d*. *Educ:* Royal Academical Institution, Belfast; Queen's University of Belfast. MB, BCh, BAO, Belfast, 1923; BSc (1st class Hons) Belfast, 1924, DPH 1924; MD (Gold Medal) Belfast, 1926; MRCP London, 1940; MD Birmingham, 1948; FRCP London, 1950. Hon. MD Perugia, 1961. Riddell Demonstrator of Pathology, Belfast, 1924; Musgrave student in Pathology, Belfast, 1925; First Assistant Pathologist and Asst Curator of the Museum, St Mary's Hospital, W2, 1926; Lecturer in Exp. Pathology and Asst Director of Cancer Research, University of Leeds, 1932; Reader in Exp. Pathology, 1937; President of Leeds Pathological Club, 1946-47. Senior Research Pathologist, Detroit Institute of Cancer Research, 1966-67; Research Pathologist, Royal Victoria Hosp., Bournemouth, 1967-69. Served War of 1939-45 as Pathologist in EMS and Battalion MO, Home Guard. *Publications:* articles on medical subjects in Journal of Pathology and Bacteriology, British Journal of Exp. Pathology, British Journal of Cancer, Lancet, American Journal of Cancer, etc, especially papers on experimental cancer research. *Recreations:* music, golf, bridge. *Address:* c/o Lloyds Bank, 359 Bristol Road, Birmingham 5.

**ORR, Captain Lawrence Percy Story;** MP (UU) South Down since 1950; *b* 16 Sept. 1918; *s* of late Very Rev. W. R. M. Orr, MA, LLD, sometime Dean of Dromore; *m* 1939, Jean Mary, *d* of late Frederick Cairns Hughes, Donaghadee; four *s* one *d*. *Educ:* Campbell Coll., Belfast; Trinity Coll., Dublin. Served with East Lancashire Regt, Royal Armoured Corps, and Life Guards, 1939-46. Organiser Iveagh Unionist Association, 1947-49; Secretary County Down Unionist Association, 1949; Vice-Chairman, Conservative Broadcasting Cttee, 1959-62; Chairman, Ulster Unionist Parliamentary Party; Joint Chairman, Parliamentary Films Cttee. *Recreations:* fishing and painting. *Address:* House of Commons, SW1.

**ORR, Robin, (Robert Kemsley Orr),** MA, MusD (Cantab); FRCM; Hon. RAM; Composer; Professor of Music, Cambridge University, and Fellow of St John's College, since 1965; *b* Brechin, Scotland, 2 June 1909; *s* of Robert Workman Orr and Florence Mary Kemsley; *m* 1937, Margaret, *er d* of A. C. Mace; one *s* two *d*. *Educ:* Loretto Sch.; Royal Coll. of Music; Pembroke Coll., Cambridge (Organ Scholar); Accademia Musicale Chigiana, Siena. Studied privately with Casella and Nadia Boulanger. Dir of Music, Sidcot Sch., Somerset, 1933-36; Asst Lecturer in Music, Univ. of Leeds, 1936-38. Served War of 1939-45, RAFVR, Photographic Intelligence (Flight Lieut). Organist and Dir of Studies in Music, St John's Coll., 1938-51, and Fellow, 1948-56, Univ. Lecturer in Music, 1947-56, Cambridge; Prof. of Theory and Composition, RCM, 1950-56; Gardiner Prof. of Music, Univ. of Glasgow, 1956-65. Vice-Chm. Carl Rosa Trust, 1958; Chm., Scottish Opera, 1962-. Compositions include: Sonatina for violin and piano, 1941; Three Chinese Songs, 1943; Sonata for viola and piano, 1947; Winter's Tale (Incidental Music), BBC, 1947; Overture, The Prospect of Whitby, 1948; Oedipus at Colonus (Cambridge Univ. Greek Play), 1950; Four Romantic Songs (for Peter Pears), 1950; Festival Te Deum, 1950; Three Pastorals for soprano, flute, viola and piano, 1951; Deirdre of the Sorrows (Incidental Music), BBC, 1951; Italian Overture, 1952; Te Deum and Jubilate in C, 1953; Motet, I was glad, 1955; Spring Cantata, 1955; Sonata for violin and clavier, 1956; Rhapsody for string orchestra; Antigone (Bradfield College Greek Play), 1961; Symphony in one movement, 1963; Full Circle

(Opera), 1967; ed. The Kelvin Series of Scots Songs. *Address:* University Music School, Downing Place, Cambridge; Glenshian, Lochwinnoch, Renfrewshire. *T:* Lochwinnoch 413. *Club:* United University.

**ORR-EWING, Sir (Charles) Ian,** 1st Bt *cr* 1963; OBE 1945; Consultant and Director various companies; *b* 10 Feb. 1912; *s* of Archibald Ian Orr Ewing and Gertrude (*née* Runge); *m* 1939, Joan McMinnies; four *s*. *Educ:* Harrow; Trinity Coll., Oxford. MA (Physics). Apprenticeship to radio firm, 1934, 1937 (EMI Hayes); BBC Television Service, 1938-39, 1946-49. Served RAFVR, 1939-46, N Africa, Italy, France and Germany, Wing Comdr, 1941; Chief Radar Officer, Air Staff, SHAEF, 1945 (despatches twice); BBC Television Outside Broadcasts Manager, 1946-48. Adopted prospective Conservative Candidate N Hendon, 1946; MP (C) North Hendon, 1950-70; Secretary, Conservative Air Cttee in House of Commons, 1950; Joint Secretary, Parliamentary Scientific Cttee, 1950; Vice-Chm., Civil Air Cttee, 1955-57; Vice-Pres., Parliamentary and Scientific Cttee, 1965-; Vice-Chm., 1922 Cttee, 1966-70 (Secretary, 1957); Vice-Chairman, Defence Cttee, 1966-. Parliamentary Private Secretary to Sir Walter Monckton, Minister of Labour and National Service, Nov. 1951-May 1955. Parliamentary Under-Secretary of State, for Air, Air Ministry, 1957-59; Parliamentary and Financial Secretary to Admiralty, 1959; Civil Lord of the Admiralty, 1959-63. Pres. and Chm. of Council, Electronic Engineering Assoc., 1969-70 (Vice-Chm., 1968-69). MIEE. *Recreations:* tennis, light-hearted cricket and ski-ing. *Heir: s* Alistair Simon Orr-Ewing [*b* 10 June 1940; *m* 1968, Victoria, *er d* of Keith Cameron, Fifield House, Milton-under-Wychwood, Oxon; one *s*]. *Address:* The Old Manor, Little Berkhamsted, near Hertford, Herts. *T:* Essendon 262. *Clubs:* Carlton, MCC; Vincents' (Oxford).

**ORR EWING, Major Sir Ronald Archibald,** 5th Bt, *cr* 1886; Major (retired) Scots Guards; *b* 14 May 1912; *e s* of Sir Norman Orr Ewing, 4th Bt, CB, DSO, and Lady Orr Ewing (*née* Robarts), Tile House, Buckingham; *S* father, 1960; *m* 1938, Marion Hester, *yr d* of late Colonel Sir Donald Walter Cameron of Lochiel, KT, CMG, and of Lady Hermione Cameron of Lochiel, *d* of 5th Duke of Montrose, KT; two *s* two *d*. *Educ:* Eton; RMC, Sandhurst. Scots Guards, 1932-53, Major. Served War of 1939-45, Middle East (POW 1942). JP Perthshire, 1956; DL Perthshire, 1963. *Recreation:* shooting. *Heir: s* Archibald Donald Orr Ewing [*b* 20 Dec. 1938; *m* 1965, Venetia Elizabeth, *y d* of Major and Mrs Richard Turner, Co. Dublin]. *Address:* Cardross, Port of Menteith, Stirling. *T:* Port of Menteith 220. *Clubs:* Army and Navy; New (Edinburgh).

**ORR-LEWIS, Sir (John) Duncan,** 2nd Bt, *cr* 1920; Major RASC; *s* of 1st Bt and Maud Helen, *o d* of William Booth, London, Ontario, Canada; *b* 21 Feb. 1898; *S* father, 1921; *m* 1st, 1921; one *d*; 2nd, 1929; 3rd, 1940; 4th, 1950; 5th, 1965. *Educ:* Eton; Cambridge. Military Service: 10th Army, Persia MEF, 1942-43; 2nd Army, France, Germany, Aug. 1944-45. *Heir:* none. *Address:* Le Grand Courtoiseau, Triguères (Loiret), France; Ir-Razzett, Malta. *Clubs:* White's; Travellers' (Paris); Mount Royal (Montreal).

**ORTCHESON, Sir John,** Kt 1967; CBE 1954; Legal Adviser, West Pakistan Water and Power Development Authority, since 1966; Judge of the High Court of Judicature, Lahore, Pakistan, 1954-65; *b* 6 Dec. 1905; *s* of Robert Inches Ortcheson; *m* 1933, Norah Eileen, *d* of late Frank A. Connor; two *d*. *Educ:* Perth Academy; Edinburgh University (MA 1928); Cambridge Univ.; Sorbonne, Paris. Fellow, Royal Commonwealth Society. Coronation Medal, 1953. *Recreation:* golf. *Address:* 4 Club Road, Lahore, Pakistan. *T:* Lahore 4903. *Club:* Punjab (Lahore).

**ORTON, Professor Harold;** Emeritus Professor of English Language and Medieval English Literature, University of Leeds (Professor, 1946-64); *b* 1898; *y s* of Thomas Orton and Emily Blair, Byers Green, Co. Durham; *m* 1925, *y d* of Rev. R. Burnham, Trimley St Mary's Rectory, Suffolk; one *d*. *Educ:* King James I Grammar Sch., Bishop Auckland; Hatfield Coll., University of Durham; Merton Coll., Oxford; Royal University of Uppsala, Sweden. BA 1921, University Research Schol. in English Philology, 1922, BLitt 1923, MA 1924, Oxford. Lektor in English, University of Uppsala, 1924-28; Lecturer in English, King's Coll., Newcastle upon Tyne in the University of Durham, 1928-39, and Senior Research Fellow, 1938-39; Lecturer in charge of Dept of English Language, University of Sheffield, 1939-46; Dep. Education Director, British Council, 1942-44 and Acting Education Director, 1944-45; Dean of Faculty of Arts, Leeds, 1947-49; Chairman, Board of Faculties of Arts, Economics and Commerce and Law, Leeds Univ., 1954-56. Visiting Lecturer, Summer Session, College of Literature, Science and the Arts, University of Michigan, 1954; Visiting Professor: Kansas and Michigan Universities, 1965; Iowa Univ., 1966, 1969; Kansas Univ., 1967, 1968; Tennessee Univ., 1970. Lieut, The DLI (TF), 1917-19 (severely wounded 1918, invalided 1919). Re-commissioned General List (TA), 1940; Acting Captain and Comdg Officer, Sheffield Univ. Sen. Training Corps, 1945-46. Consultant Member, BBC's Advisory Cttee on Spoken English, 1934-40; Member British Council's Advisory Cttee on English Overseas, 1940-44; President, Yorkshire Society for Celtic Studies, 1951-53; Hon. Member: Linguistic Society of America, 1964; Linguistic Soc. of Canada, 1965. Fil. Dr hc Univ. of Uppsala, 1969. Joint Editor, Trans of Yorkshire Dialect Soc., 1947-61 (Hon. Vice-Pres., 1963-; Hon. Life Mem., 1968-); Joint Editor, Leeds Studies in English and Kindred Languages, 1952-64. *Publications:* The Phonology of a South Durham Dialect, 1933; (with W. L. Renwick, *qv*) The Beginnings of English Literature to Skelton, 1939; (with late Prof. E. Dieth, Zürich) A Questionnaire for a Linguistic Atlas of England, 1952; (with late Prof. E. Dieth, Zürich) Survey of English Dialects, 1962-; (with Dr W. J. Halliday) The Basic Material of the Six Northern Counties and the Isle of Man, Vol. I, Part 1, 1962, Parts 2 and 3, 1963; (with M. Wakelin) The Basic Material of the Southern Counties, Vol. IV, Parts 1 and 2, 1967, Part 3, 1968; (with M. V. Barry) The Basic Material of the West Midland Counties, Vol. 2, Part 1, 1969, Part 2, 1970; (with P. M. Tilling) The Basic Material of the East Midland Counties and East Anglia, Vol. 3, Part 1, 1969, Part 2, 1970; various articles on English Language and especially its dialects, in scientific journals. *Recreation:* gardening. *Address:* 11 Harrowby Crescent, Leeds LS16 5HP. *T:* 55451.

**OSBORN, Sir Danvers (Lionel Rouse),** 8th Bt, *cr* 1662; *b* 31 Jan. 1916; *s* of Sir Algernon K. B. Osborn, 7th Bt, JP and Beatrice Elliot Kennard, *d* of William Bunce Greenfield, JP, DL; *S* father, 1948; *m* 1943, Constance Violette, JP, SSStJ, *d* of late Major Leonard Frank Rooke, KOSB; one *s* one *d* (one *s* and one *d* decd). *Educ:* Eton; Magdalene Coll., Cambridge. Employed as Civil Assistant in

Intelligence Dept of War Office, 1940-45. Joined Spicers Ltd, 1955. Director of two Picture Galleries. *Recreations:* golf, tennis, bridge. *Heir: s* Richard Henry Danvers Osborn, *b* 12 Aug. 1958. *Address:* The Dower House, Moor Park, Farnham, Surrey. *T:* Runfold 2658. *Clubs:* St James', MCC.

**OSBORN, Sir Frederic (James),** Kt 1956; Hon. MTPI; Hon. Member: American Institute of Planners; Community Planning Association of Canada; President, Town and Country Planning Association; Vice-President, International Federation for Housing and Planning; Corresponding Member, Akademie für Raumforschung und Landesplanung, Hannover; *b* 26 May 1885; *e s* of T. F. Osborn; *m* 1916, Margaret Paterson Robb, Glasgow (*d* 1970); one *s* one *d. Educ:* London private and Council Schools. Estate Manager, Welwyn Garden City, 1919-36; Hon. Sec. and Chm., Town and Country Planning Assoc., 1936-61; Director, Murphy Radio Ltd, 1936-60; Member New Towns Cttee, 1946. Hon. Editor, Town and Country Planning, 1949-65; Chairman, Welwyn Drama Festival, 1929-65. Silver Medal, American Society of Planning Officials, 1960; Gold Medal, Town Planning Institute, 1963; Ebenezer Howard Memorial Medal, 1968. *Publications:* New Towns after the War, 1918, 1942; Green-Belt Cities, 1946, 1969; Can Man Plan? and Other Verses, 1959; New Towns: The Answer to Megalopolis (with A. Whittick), 1963, 1969, etc. *Recreations:* literature, drama, music, gardening, travel. *Address:* 16 Guessens Road, Welwyn Garden City, Herts. *T:* Welwyn Garden 22317. *Club:* Reform.

**OSBORN, John Holbrook;** MP (C) (NL and U, 1959-64), Hallam Division of Sheffield, since 1964; Steel Company Director; *b* 14 Dec. 1922; *s* of Samuel Eric Osborn and Aileen Decima, *d* of Colonel Sir Arthur Holbrook, KBE, MP; *m* 1952, Molly Suzanne (*née* Marten); two *d. Educ:* Rugby; Trinity Hall, Cambridge. MA Cantab; Part 2 Tripos in Metallurgy; Diploma in Foundry Technology, National Foundry Coll., 1949. Served in Royal Corps of Signals, West Africa, 1943-47 (Captain); served in RA (TA) Sheffield, 1948-55, Major. Director of Samuel Osborn & Co. Ltd, and associated companies, 1951-. Chairman, Hillsborough Divisional Young Conservatives and Liberal Association, 1948-53. PPS to the Secretary of State for Commonwealth Relations and for the Colonies, 1963-64. Searcher, Co. of Cutlers in Hallamshire. Fellow, Institute of British Foundrymen (Member Council, Sheffield Branch, 1954-64); FInstD; Member Council: Sheffield Chamber of Commerce, 1956-; Assocs British Chambers of Commerce Council, 1960-62 (Hon. Secretary, 1962-64); Industrial Society; British Iron and Steel Res. Association, 1965-68; CBI and Yorks and WR Br., CBI; Member: Iron and Steel Institute; Institute of Metals; Sheffield Diocesan Trust and Board of Finance; Court and committees of Sheffield University; Trustee: Zachary Merton Charity for Convalescents; Sheffield Young Children's Trust; Talbot Trust. *Recreations:* golf, tennis, squash, sailing, ski-ing, gardening. *Address:* Folds Head Close, Calver, Sheffield. *T:* Grindleford 253. *Clubs:* Carlton; Sheffield.

**OSBORN, Margaret,** MA; High Mistress of St Paul's Girls' School, Hammersmith, 1948-63, retired; *b* 23 April 1906; *d* of Rev. G. S. Osborn, late Rector of Milton, Cambridge. *Educ:* St Leonard's Sch., St Andrews, Fife; St Hugh's Coll., Oxford. Graduated 1929; MA Hons Lit Hum Oxon. Pelham Student at British School at Rome, 1931; Headmistress of St George's School for Girls, Edinburgh, 1943-48. *Publication:* A Latin Epithet, article in Mnemosyne (Leyden Journal), 1932. *Recreations:* music and walking. *Address:* Roseglen Cottage, Chipping Campden, Glos.

**OSBORN, Theodore George Bentley,** MA, DSc; Professor Emeritus, Oxford and Adelaide Universities; *b* 2 Oct. 1887; *o surv c* of John Ashton Osborn; *m* 1st, 1912, Edith May Kershaw (*d* 1958), Uppermill, Yorks; two *s* (one *s* killed in action); 2nd, 1960, Marjorie Hope Sabine, Adelaide. *Educ:* Burnley Grammar Sch.; University of Manchester. Lecturer in Economic Botany, Manchester Univ., 1908-12; Professor of Botany, Adelaide Univ., and Consulting Botanist to the S Australian Government, 1912-27; Professor of Botany, Sydney Univ., 1928-37; Sherardian Professor of Botany, Oxford Univ., and Fellow of Magdalen Coll., Oxford, 1937-53, Emeritus Fellow, 1970. Member Agricultural Research Council, 1945-49. *Publications:* various scientific, chiefly on fungi and ecology. *Address:* 15a Ayr Avenue, Terrens Park, South Australia 5062, Australia.

**OSBORNE, Sir Basil,** Kt 1967; CBE 1962; Lord Mayor of Hobart, Tasmania, 1959-70, Alderman since 1952; Administrative Staff, Charles Davis Ltd; *b* 19 April 1907; *s* of late Alderman W. W. Osborne, MBE; *m* 1934, Esma, *d* of late T. Green; one *s. Educ:* Metropolitan Business Coll. Chairman: Board of Management, Royal Hobart Hospital, 1968- (Vice-Chairman, 1952-68); Ambulance Commn, Tasmania, 1960. President: Friendly Societies of Tasmania; Tasmanian Branch, Royal Life Saving Society; St John's Ambulance Association; Hobart Orpheus Club. *Recreation:* music. *Address:* 9 Audley Street, Hobart, Tasmania 7015, Australia. *Club:* Royal Autocar (Tasmania).

**OSBORNE, Maj.-General the Rev. Coles Alexander,** CIE 1945; Indian Army, retired; Hon. Assistant Minister St Mark's Church, Darling Point, NSW, Australia, since 1953; *b* 29 July 1896; *s* of late W. E. Osborne, formerly of Dover, Kent; *m* 1930, Joyce, *o d* of late R. H. Meares of Forbes and Sydney, NSW, Australia; two *d. Educ:* Dover County Sch. European War, 1914-18 served with HAC, Royal West Kent Regt, and RFC (wounded); transferred to 15th Sikhs, 1918; served in Afghan War 1919 and in NW Frontier Operations 1920-22 and 1939; Palestine 1938; Middle East 1940. Tactics Instructor at Royal Military Coll., Duntroon, Australia, 1928-30; Bt Major 1933; General Staff (Operations), War Office, 1934-38; Bt Lieut-Col 1936; Comd 1 Bombay Grenadiers, 1940; Deputy Director Military Training, India, 1940; Colonel, 1940; Commandant, Staff Coll., Quetta, 1941-42; Brigadier, 1941; Director Military Operations, GHQ, India and Burma, 1942-43; Temp. Maj.-Gen. 1942; Comd Kohat District, 1943-45; retired 1946. Student at Moore Theological Coll., Sydney, 1947; ordained, 1947; Assistant Minister (Hon.) St Andrew's Cathedral, Sydney, Australia, 1947-53; Personal Chaplain to Anglican Archbishop of Sydney, 1959-66. Director, Television Corp., 1956. Fellow of St Paul's Coll., Sydney Univ., 1953-69. *Address:* 126 Hopetown Avenue, Vaucluse, Sydney, Australia. *T:* 337-2969. 2969. *Clubs:* United Service; Australian (Sydney).

**OSBORNE, Professor John,** (First) Professor of Dental Prosthetics, University of Birmingham, since 1948; Director of Dental Studies, University of Birmingham, 1965-69; Deputy Director, 1953-65; *b* 6 April 1911; *s* of John W. and Gertrude Osborne; *m* 1937, Virginia Preston, *d* of W. H. Fruish; one *s* one *d. Educ:* Bishop Vesey Grammar Sch.;

Birmingham Univ. LDS Birmingham, 1933; PhD Sheffield, 1945; MDS 1948; FDS, RCS, 1948; FFD, RCSI, 1964; House Surgeon and junior staff appointments at Birmingham Dental Hospital, 1933-37; also private practice during same period; Lecturer in Dental Prosthetics, University of Sheffield, 1937; Lecturer in Dental Prosthetics, University of Birmingham, 1946. Visiting Professor NW University, Chicago, 1956-57. Guest lecturer, Australian Dental Assoc., 1962. External Examiner to Universities of Malaya, Liverpool, Durham, London, Manchester, Glasgow, Dundee, Bristol, Edinburgh, Sheffield, Belfast, Lagos, and to Royal College of Surgeons of England and of Ireland. President: British Dental Students Assoc., 1956-58; Central Counties Branch, British Dental Assoc., 1958-59, Hospitals Group, 1968-69. *Publications:* Dental Mechanics for Students, 1939, 6th edn 1970; Acrylic Resins in Dentistry, 1942, 3rd edn 1948; Partial Dentures (with Dr G. A. Lammie), 1954, 3rd edn, 1968; scientific papers in leading dental journals. *Recreations:* philately, gardening, sailing. *Address:* 4 Farquhar Road East, Edgbaston, Birmingham 15. *Clubs:* University Staff, Warwick County Cricket (Birmingham); Island Sailing (Cowes).

**OSBORNE, John (James);** dramatist and actor; Director of Woodfall Films; *b* 12 Dec. 1929; *s* of Thomas Godfrey Osborne and Nellie Beatrice Grove; *m* 1st, 1951, Pamela Elizabeth Lane (marr. diss. 1957); 2nd, 1957, Mary Ure, *qv* (marr. diss. 1963); 3rd, 1963, Penelope Gilliatt (marr. diss. 1968); 4th, 1968, Jill Bennett, *qv*. *Educ:* Belmont Coll., Devon. First stage appearance at Lyceum, Sheffield, in No Room at the Inn, 1948; toured and in seasons at: Ilfracombe, Bridgwater, Camberwell, Kidderminster, Derby, etc; English Stage Company season at Royal Court: appeared in Death of Satan, Cards of Identity, Good Woman of Setzuan, The Making of Moo, A Cuckoo in the Nest; Directed Meals on Wheels, 1965; appeared in: The Parachute (BBC TV), 1967; First Night of Pygmalion (TV), 1969; First Love (film, as Maidanov), 1970; Carter (film), 1971. First play produced, 1949, at Theatre Royal, Huddersfield; other plays include: Personal Enemy, Opera House, Harrogate, 1955; The Blood of the Bambergs, 1962; Under Plain Cover, 1962; The Right Prospectus (TV), 1969. *Plays filmed:* Look Back in Anger, 1958; The Entertainer, 1959. *Publications:* Look Back in Anger (play), 1957 (produced 1956); The Entertainer (play), 1957 (also produced); Epitaph for George Dillon (with A. Creighton), 1958 (produced 1957); The World of Paul Slickey (comedy of manners with music), 1959 (produced 1959); Luther (play), 1960 (produced 1961, New York, 1964); A Subject of Scandal and Concern (TV play), 1960; Plays for England, 1963; Inadmissible Evidence (play), 1964 (produced 1965); A Patriot for Me (play), 1964 (produced 1965); A Bond Honoured, 1966 (produced 1966); The Hotel in Amsterdam, 1967 (produced 1968); Time Present, 1967 (produced 1968); Coriolanus, 1967; The Right Prospectus and Very Like a Whale (TV plays), 1970; contrib. to Declaration (a symposium), 1957; various newspapers, journals. *Film:* Tom Jones, 1964 (Oscar for best screenplay). Hon. Dr RCA, 1970. *Address:* 11a Curzon Street, W1. *Clubs:* Savile, Garrick.

**OSBORNE, Surgeon Rear-Admiral (D) Leslie Bartlet,** CB 1956; *b* 16 Sept. 1900; *s* of late Rev. Joseph Osborne, MA, and of Miriam Duke James; *m* 1929; two *s* one *d*; *m* 1955, Joan Mary Williams (*née* Parnell). *Educ:* Caterham Sch.; Guy's Hospital. LDS, RCS England 1923; FDS, RCS (Edinburgh) 1955. Dental House Surgeon, Guy's Hospital, 1923. Entered Royal Navy, Surgeon Lieutenant (D), 1923; Surgeon Commander (D), 1936; Surgeon Captain (D), 1948; Surgeon Rear-Admiral (D), 1954; Deputy Director-General for Dental Services in the Royal Navy, 1954-57, retired. Served War of 1939-45. KHDS 1951; QHDS 1953-58. *Recreations:* Rugby Football (rep. RN, Sussex and Devonport Services; Hon. Manager British Isles Rugby Union Team to New Zealand and Australia, 1950; Chairman Rugby Football Union Selection Cttee, 1949-51; President, Rugby Football Union, 1956); gardening. *Address:* 4 Westbourne Court, Cooden Drive, Cooden Beach, Bexhill-on-Sea, Sussex. *T:* Cooden 4431.

**OSBORNE, Lithgow;** President and Publisher, Auburn (NY) Citizen-Advertiser; *b* 2 April 1892; *s* of Thos Mott Osborne and Agnes Devens; *m* 1918; three *s*. *Educ:* Harvard Class of 1915. US Diplomatic Service, 1915-19 (Berlin, Copenhagen, Paris Peace Conference); Assistant Secretary, General Conference on Disarmament, 1921-22; Editor Auburn (NY) Citizen-Advertiser, 1922-33; Conservation Commissioner, State of New York, 1933-42; Delegate-at-large, NY State Constitutional Convention, 1938; Office of Foreign Relief and Rehabilitation, Washington, 1942-43; Deputy Director-General, Dept of Services and Areas, UNRRA European Regional Office, 1943-44; American Ambassador to Norway, 1944-46. *Recreations:* golf, fishing, shooting. *Address:* 25 Dill Street, Auburn, NY 13021, USA. *Clubs:* Harvard, Century (NY).

**OSBORNE, Sir Peter (George),** 17th Bt, *cr* 1629; *b* 29 June 1943; *s* of Lt-Col Sir George Osborne, 16th Bt, MC, and Mary (Grace), *d* of C. Horn; *S* father, 1960; *m* 1968, Felicity, *d* of Grantley Loxton-Peacock. *Educ:* Wellington Coll., Berks; Christ Church Coll., Oxford. *Recreations:* theatre, archæology. *Heir:* *b* James Francis Osborne, *b* 18 Feb. 1946. *Address:* 25 Bridstow Place, W2. *T:* 01-727 2894. *Club:* St James'.

**O'SHEA, Alexander Paterson,** CMG 1962; North American Director, New Zealand Meat Producers' Board, USA, 1964-68, retired, 1968; *b* 29 Dec. 1902; *s* of John O'Shea; *m* 1935; one *d*. *Educ:* Otago Boys' High Sch.; Victoria University College (now Victoria Univ. of Wellington). (BCom). Farming, 1919-27. Wellington City Corporation, 1928-35; Secretary, Farmers' Union, 1935-46 (later Federated Farmers of NZ Inc.); General Secretary, Federated Farmers of New Zealand Inc., Wellington, NZ, 1946-64. Fellow (Chartered Accountant) New Zealand Society of Accountants. *Publication:* The Public Be Damned, 1946. *Recreation:* onlooker, Rugby football. *Address:* 26 Sefton Street, Wadestown, Wellington, NZ. *T:* 40.650. *Clubs:* Civil Service, Wellesley (Wellington, NZ).

**O'SHIEL, Kevin Roantree;** Irish barrister; *b* 23 Sept. 1891; *e s* of Francis O'Sheil, solicitor, Highfield, Omagh, Co. Tyrone, and Elizabeth Columba Roantree; *m* 1st, 1922, Louise Frances (*d* 1925), 3rd *d* of late John Conry, FRCSI, and Mrs Conry, Highland Lodge, Kilkelly, Swinford, Co. Mayo; 2nd, 1929, Cecil, 2nd *d* of late Professor T. A. Smiddy; two *d*. *Educ:* Mount St Mary's Coll., Chesterfield; St George's Coll., Weybridge. Called to Bar, King's Inns, Dublin, 1913; called to Inner Bar, 1947. Legal Sec. to Irish Provisional Govt, 1922; Asst Legal Adviser to Irish Free State Executive Council, 1922-23; Member of the Constitution Cttee appointed to draft Constitution of the Irish Free State;

an Irish Free State Delegate to the League of Nations, Sept 1923; formerly a Member of the Standing Committee of Sinn Fein; Legal Commissioner for pacification of Agrarian Outbreak, and Judicial Commissioner, Dail Land Courts, 1920; Land Law Commissioner, Irish Land Commission, from 1923 until September 1963. *Publications:* The Making of a Republic (American War of Independence), 1920; several newspaper and magazine articles on historical, economic and constitutional matters. *Recreation:* ornithology. *Address:* 28 Kenilworth Road, Rathgar, Dublin 6. *Club:* Milltown Golf (Co. Dublin).

**OSMAN, Abdool Raman Mahomed,** CBE 1963; retired as Senior Puisne Judge, Supreme Court, Mauritius, 1960 (Puisne Judge, 1950-59); *b* 29 Aug. 1902, of Mauritian parents; unmarried. *Educ:* Royal College, Mauritius; Inns of Court, London. District Magistrate, Mauritius, 1930-38; Additional Substitute Procureur and Advocate General, 1938-50; Actg Procureur and Advocate-General, 1950-51; Actg Chief Justice, Apr-Nov. 1958. *Address:* Tombeau Bay, Mauritius.

**OSMAN, Louis,** BA (Arch.); FRIBA; architect, artist, and goldsmith; *b* 30 January 1914; *s* of Charles Osman, Exeter; *m* 1940, Dilys Roberts, *d* of Richard Roberts, Rotherfield, Sussex; one *d. Educ:* Hele's School, Exeter; London University. Open exhibn at Bartlett School of Architecture, University Coll. London, 1931, and at Slade School; Donaldson Medallist of RIBA, 1935. With British Museum and British School of Archæology Expeditions to Syria, 1936, 1937; designed private and public buildings, 1937-39. Served War of 1939-45, Major in Intelligence Corps: Combined Ops HQ and Special Air Service as specialist in Air Photography, Beach Reconnaissance Cttee, prior to invasion of Europe. Resumed practice in London, 1945, designed buildings, furniture, tapestries, glass, etc; work in Westminster Abbey, Lincoln, Ely and Exeter Cathedrals; Staunton Harold for National Trust; Bridge, Cavendish Street, with Jacob Epstein; Newnham Coll., Cambridge; factory buildings for Cambridge Instrument Co., aluminium Big Top for Billy Smart's Circus, two villages on Dartmoor, etc; consultant architect to British Aluminium Co.; executed commissions as goldsmith and jeweller, 1956-; commissioned by De Beers for 1st Internat. Jewellery Exhibn, 1961; designed and made Prince of Wales' crown for investiture, 1969; work in precious metals exhibited GB, Denmark, Holland, Germany, America, S Africa, Australia, Japan, etc. Mem. Exec. Cttee The Georgian Group, 1952-56. *Publications:* reviews on artistic subjects and many contributions to learned jls. *Recreations:* music, riding. *Address:* Canons Ashby, Northants, *via* Rugby. *T:* Blakesley 275.

**OSMOND, Mervyn Victor;** Secretary, Council for the Protection of Rural England, since 1966 (Assistant Secretary, 1946; Deputy Secretary 1963); *b* 2 July 1912; *s* of Albion Victor Osmond and Florence Isabel (*née* Edwards), Bristol; *m* 1940, Aimée Margaret Moir; one *d. Educ:* Clifton Coll. (Schol.); Exeter Coll., Oxford (Schol.). 1st cl. Hon. Class. Mods.; 2nd cl. Lit. Hum.; 2nd cl. Jurisprudence; Poland Prizeman (Criminal Law), 1937; called to Bar (Inner Temple), 1938; MA 1939. Practising Barrister, Western Circuit, 1938-40. Joined Gloucestershire Regt, TA, 1931; served war of 1939-45; Royal Fusiliers; DAAG (Major) 352 L of C Sub-Area and 303 L of C Area (Calcutta). *Recreations:* reading, enjoying rural England. *Address:* 39 Stonehill Road, East Sheen, SW14. *T:* 01-876 7138.

**OSMOND, Paul;** *see* Osmond, S. P.

**OSMOND, (Stanley) Paul,** CB 1966; Deputy Secretary, Office of the Lord Chancellor, since 1970; *b* 13 May 1917; *o s* of late Stanley C. and Susan Osmond; *m* 1942, Olivia Sybil, *yr d* of late Ernest E. Wells, Kegworth, Leicestershire; two *s. Educ:* Bristol Grammar School; Jesus College, Oxford. 2nd Cl. Final Hons School of Modern History, Oxford, 1939. Entered Home Civil Service (Board of Education), 1939. Served War of 1939-45, in Army (Gloucestershire Regiment and staff), 1940-46. Ministry of Education, 1946-48; Private Secretary to Prime Minister, 1948-51; Admiralty, 1951, Asst Secretary, 1954; Under-Secretary, 1959; HM Treasury, 1962, Third Secretary, 1965; Dep. Secretary, Civil Service Dept, 1968-70. A Manager of the Royal Institution, 1966-69, 1970-. *Recreations:* theatre, unavoidable gardening. *Address:* 20 Beckenham Grove, Bromley, Kent BR2 0JU. *T:* 01-460 2026. *Club:* Athenæum.

**OSMOND, Thomas Edward,** BA (hons), MB Cantab; MRCS, LRCP; late Hon. Consulting Venereologist to the British Army; *b* Thorpe-le-Soken, 7 Oct. 1884; *s* of Edward Osmond, JP; *m* 1920, Daisy Stewart Mathews (*d* 1963); one *s* one *d. Educ:* King's Sch., Rochester; Emmanuel Coll., Cambridge; St Bart.'s Hospital. MB Cantab 1912; joined RAMC; service in India and Mesopotamia, 1914-18 (despatches); transferred to RARO 1920 and appointed Pathologist VD Dept St Thomas's Hospital; recalled to Army 1 Sept. 1939; served in France; late Brig. RAMC; adviser in venereology to the Army, 1939, Consultant 1943-45; late MO i/c Male VD Dept and Marlborough Path. Lab. Royal Free Hospital, London; late Pres. Med. Society for the Study of Venereal Diseases; Fellow Med. Society of London; President Middlesex Partial County Committee and Ashford (Middlesex) Branch British Legion. *Publications:* Article, Venereal Disease, Encyclopædia Britannica, Book of the Year, 1939; Aids to the diagnosis and treatment of Venereal Diseases, 1946; articles, Venereal Disease and Social Implications of Venereal Disease, Chambers's Encyclopædia, 1947; Venereal Disease in Peace and War, British Journal of Venereal Diseases, 1949; contributions to British Medical Journal, The Practitioner, etc. *Recreations:* gardening, bridge. *Address:* Compton, 34 The Avenue, Clevedon, Somerset. *T:* 3697.

**OSMOND-CLARKE, Sir Henry,** KCVO 1969; CBE 1947; FRCS; Consulting Orthopædic Surgeon: London Hospital, E1 (Orthopædic Surgeon, 1946-70); Robert Jones and Agnes Hunt Orthopædic Hospital, Oswestry (Senior Visiting Surgeon, 1930-70); Hon. Civilian Consultant in Orthopædics, RAF, since 1946; Orthopædic Surgeon to the Queen since 1965; *b* 8 Feb. 1905; *e s* of W. J. Clarke, Brookeborough, Co. Fermanagh, NI; *m* Freda, *e d* of Richard Hutchinson, Bury, Lancs; two *d. Educ:* Clones High School; Trinity College, Dublin University; Vienna, Bologna, New York, Boston, London. BA 1925; MB, BCh (stip. cond.) 1926; FRCSIre 1930; FRCS 1932; Surgical Travelling Prize, TCD 1930. Consultant Orthopædic Surgeon, Oldchurch, Black Notley, Tilbury and East Grinstead Hosps; Orthopædic Surgeon, King Edward VII Hosp. for Officers, London; Cons. King Edward VII Convalescent Home for Officers, Osborne; Hunterian Prof. RCS, 1936. Service Cons. in Orthop. Surg., Air Cdre, RAF, 1941-46; Mayo Clinic Foundation Lecturer, 1948; Orthop. Mem. WHO Mission to Israel, 1951, to India, 1953, to Persia, 1957. Past President, British Orthop. Assoc. (former Editorial Sec. and Acting Sec.);

FRSocMed and several Brit. Med. Socs. Formerly: Clinical Tutor in Orthop. Surg., Manchester Roy. Infirmary and Lecturer in Surg. Pathology (Orthop.), Univ. of Manchester; Orthop. Surg., Crumpsall Hosp., Manchester, and Biddulph Grange Orthop. Hosp., Stoke-on-Trent; Sen. Ho. Surg. and Orthop. Ho. Surg. Ancoats Hosp., Manchester, and Royal Nat. Orthop. Hospital, London. Mem. Council, RCS, 1959-60, Vice-Pres. 1970-. chm. Accident Services Review Cttee of Great Britain and Ireland, 1960. Hon. Mem. American Orthop. Assoc.; American Acad. of Orthopædic Surgery; Australian, New Zealand and Canadian Orthopædic Assocs; Corresp. Mem., French Orthopædic Society and Surg. Soc. of Lyon; Mem. International Soc. of Orthopædics and Traumatology. *Publications:* papers on surgical and orthopædic subjects in leading surgical text-books and med. jls, including Half a Century of Orthopædic Progress in Great Britain, 1951. *Recreations:* travel, reading, fishing. *Address:* 46 Harley House, Upper Harley Street, NW1. *T:* 01-486 9975; Arunbrook, Wormley, near Godalming, Surrey. *T:* Wormley 2876. *Club:* Royal Air Force.

**OSSIANNILSSON, Karl Gustav,** Plaquette of the Swedish Flag; Stipendiate of the Swedish State since 1908; Stipendiate of the Swedish Academy and of the Bonnier and the Kraemer Societies; Grand Prix of the Kraemer Society, 1933; Swedish State Artist Reward, since 1966; *b* Lund, Sweden, 1875; *s* of Rasmus Nilsson, manager of a church organ manufactory, and Elise Timelin; *m* Naemi Arnman (*d* 1961); three *s* (two *s* decd); *m* Vivi Eklund. *Educ:* University of Lund. Teacher, 1897-1900; first book, 1900 since then independent writer (playwright, lyrist, novelist, romances, critic, politician, translator); journeys in Europe and US, 1901-; wrote 1917-18 against the German Propaganda in Sweden, and pleaded vigorously the cause of Swedish independence and friendship with England; member of the Association of Swedish Authors; Hon. FRSL (Great Britain), in 1919; Médaille du Roi Albert (Belgium). *Publications:* Barbarskogen, 1908, 1909, 1919, 1927, 1937, and four score of other novels and historical romances; several of these or other works translated into English, French, German, Russian, Finnish, Dutch, Danish, and Norwegian; Jörgen Kock, Tigerhuden (performed), Thomas Thorild (performed) and other plays; fifteen volumes of lyric, two of criticism, some of short stories, three political pamphlets; Collected Poems, four vols, 1920; Selected Poems, 1934 and 1954; two volumes of Memoirs, 1945 and 1946; Modern Swedish Poetry, part II (translated by C. D. Locock), 1936; translations from Browning, Swinburne, Bennett, Pepys, Addison, Steele, Corneille, Verhaeren; Reviewer, Swedish papers and Mercure de France. *Recreation:* gardening. *Address:* Linghem, Sweden. *T:* Linköping 70027.

**OSSORY, FERNS and LEIGHLIN, Bishop of,** since 1962; **Rt. Rev. Henry Robert McAdoo,** PhD, STD, DD; *b* 1916; *s* of James Arthur and Susan McAdoo; *m* 1940, Lesley Dalziel Weir; one *s* two *d*. *Educ:* Cork Grammar School; Mountjoy School, Dublin; Trinity College, Dublin. Deacon 1939; Priest, 1940; Curate of Holy Trinity Cathedral, Waterford, 1939-43; Incumbent of Castleventry with Ardfield, 1943-48 (with Kilmeen, 1947-48); Rector of Kilmocomogue, Diocese of Cork, 1948-52; Rural Dean of Glansalney West and Bere, 1948-52; Canon of Kilbrittain in Cork Cathedral, and Canon of Donoughmore in Cloyne Cathedral, 1949-52; Dean of Cork, 1952-62. Canon of St Patrick's Cathedral, Dublin, 1960-62. Member, Anglican-Roman Catholic Preparatory Commission, 1967-68; Jt Chm., Jt Permanent Commn of the Roman Catholic Church and the Anglican Communion, 1969-. *Publications:* The Structure of Caroline Moral Theology, 1949; John Bramhall and Anglicanism, 1964; The Spirit of Anglicanism, 1965. *Address:* The Palace, Kilkenny, Eire. *Club:* University (Dublin).

**OSSULSTON, Lord; Charles Augustus Grey Bennet;** Flight Lieutenant RAFVR; *b* 28 July 1921; *er s* of 8th Earl of Tankerville, *qv*; *m* 1943, Virginia Diether (from whom he obtained a divorce, 1950), Vancouver; one *d*; 1954, Georgiana Lilian Maude, *d* of late Gilbert Wilson, DD, of Vancouver, Canada; one *s* two *d* (of which one *s* one *d* are twins). Joined RAF 1941; Flight Lieut 1943. *Address:* 139 Olympia Way, San Francisco, Calif, USA.

**OSTLERE, Dr Gordon;** *see* Gordon, Richard.

**OSTRER, Isidore;** Poet, Economist; Chairman Lothbury Investment Corporation Ltd; Chairman Premier Productions Ltd. Late Senior Partner Ostrer Brothers, Merchant Bankers. Was President and Chairman of Gaumont-British Picture Corporation Ltd for many years. *Publications:* Poems, 1957; Conquest of Gold: Ostrer's Law of Interest; Ostrer's Commodity Gold Standard; Modern Money and Unemployment; has written extensively on economics and general subjects. *Address:* 8/9 Buckingham Place, SW1.

**O'SULLIVAN, Bernard John;** journalist; Editor, The British Racehorse, 1959-67; *b* 22 Sept. 1915; *s* of late P. J. O'Sullivan, Valentia Island, Co. Kerry, and late Teresa McGough, Carlisle. *Educ:* Xaverian College. Joined staff of Raceform, 1936; Editor, 1940-46; Joint-founder and Editor, The Racehorse, 1944-46; Editor and Chief Contributor, The Bloodstock Breeders' Review, 1947-52. *Publications:* (Ed.) The International Family Tables of Racehorses, 1953; contrib. on Thoroughbred breeding and racing to various jls in England and overseas. *Recreations:* cricket, bridge. *Address:* 2 Burcote Road, SW18. *T:* 01-874 8276.

**O'SULLIVAN, (Carrol Austin) John (Naish),** LLB (London); Assistant Public Trustee since 1966; *b* 24 Jan. 1915; *s* of late Dr Carrol Naish O'Sullivan and late Stephanie O'Sullivan (*née* Manning); *m* 1939, Lillian Mary, *y d* of Walter Frank Yate Molineux, Ulverston; one *s* one *d*. *Educ:* Mayfield College. Admitted Solicitor, 1936. Served War of 1939-45, Gordon Highlanders and HQ Special Force SEAC (Captain). Joined Public Trustee Office, 1945; Chief Administrative Officer, 1963-66. Pres., Holborn Law Soc., 1965-66. Chm. of Governors of St Thomas More High Sch. for Boys, Westcliff-on-Sea, 1964-66. *Publications:* articles in legal jls; short stories. *Recreations:* golf, music, photography. *Address:* c/o Public Trustee Office, Kingsway, WC2. *T:* 01-405 4300.

**O'SULLIVAN, Dennis Neil;** Stipendiary Magistrate, Kingston-upon-Hull, since 1952; *b* 20 July 1899; *s* of Dennis O'Sullivan, Barrister-at-Law, late District Judge, Burma, and Laura O'Sullivan; *m* 1926, Eva Stewart, MA, MB, ChB, *d* of A. K. Stewart, Edinburgh; two *s* one *d*. *Educ:* India; Dulwich College. Barrister, Gray's Inn, 1920; practised at Bar in Prov. of Sind, India, 1921-43. Member Indian Legislative Assembly (Bombay European Non-official), 1932-33; Public Prosecutor and Govt Advocate for Sind, 1937-43; Judge of Chief Court of Sind, 1943-48; Judge, and later

Chief Judge, of Control Commission Supreme Court (latterly called Allied High Commission Supreme Court) British Zone, Germany, 1949-52. Served European War, Artists' Rifles, 1917-18 (France); Indian Army, 1940-41; DAAG 10 Ind. Div., 1941. *Address:* The Law Courts, Guildhall, Hull. *Club:* Reform.

**O'SULLIVAN, Rt. Rev. Mgr. James,** MBE 1963; Principal RC Chaplain (Army) since 1969; *b* 2 Aug. 1917; *s* of Richard O'Sullivan and Ellen (*née* Ahern). *Educ:* St Finnbarr's Coll., Cork; All Hallows Coll., Dublin. Ordained, 1941; joined Royal Army Chaplain's Dept, 1942; 49 Infantry Div., Normandy, 1944; Senior RC Chaplain, Malaya, 1952-54 (despatches 1953); Chaplain Irish Guards, 1954-56; Senior RC Chaplain, Berlin, 1956-59; Staff Chaplain (RC), War Office, 1959-64; Senior RC Chaplain, BAOR, 1965-69. *Recreation:* golf. *Address:* 54 Ennismore Gardens, SW7. *T:* 01-589 1273.

**O'SULLIVAN, John;** *see* O'Sullivan, C. A. J. N.

**O'SULLIVAN, Most Rev. Joseph Anthony,** DD, LLD; Titular Archbishop of Maraguia; Archbishop of Kingston, Ontario, (RC), 1944-66; retired; *b* Hamilton, Ontario, 29 Nov. 1886. *Educ:* St Jerome's College, Kitchener, Ontario; Grand Seminary, Montreal, PQ. Ordained priest, Hamilton, 1911; consecrated Bishop of Charlottetown, PEI, Hamilton, 1931. Assistant at Pontifical Throne, 1956. *Address:* c/o Archbishop's House, Kingston, Ontario, Canada.

**OSWALD, Maj.-Gen. Marshall St John,** CB 1965; CBE 1961; DSO 1945; MC 1943; retired as Director of Management and Support Intelligence, Ministry of Defence, 1966; *b* 13 Sept. 1911; *s* of William Whitehead Oswald and Katharine Ray Oswald; *m* 1938, Mary Georgina Baker; one *s* two *d. Educ:* Rugby Sch.; RMA, Woolwich. Commissioned RA, 1931; served in RHA and Field Artillery, UK and India, 1931-39. Served War of 1939-45 (despatches, MC, DSO): Battery Comdr 4 RHA and Staff Officer in Egypt and Western Desert, 1939-42; GSO1, Tactical HQ, 8th Army, 1942-43; 2nd in Comd Field Regt, Italy, 1943-44; CO South Notts Hussars, Western Europe, 1944-45; Col on staff of HQ 21 Army Group, 1945. Mil. Govt Comdr (Col) of Cologne Area, 1946-47; Staff Officer, War Office (Lt-Col) 1948-49; Instructor (Col) Staff Coll., Camberley 1950-52; CO 19 Field Regt, Germany/Korea, 1953-55; GHQ, MELF (Col), 1955-56 (despatches 1957); IDC 1958; CCRA and Chief of Staff (Brig.) 1st Corps in Germany, 1959-62; DMI, War Office, 1962-64, Min. of Defence (Army), 1964-65. Council Mem. and Chalk Stream area organiser, Salmon and Trout Assoc.; Mem. Bd of Directors, Test and Itchen Fishing Assoc. *Recreations:* fishing, shooting, ski-ing. *Address:* Eastfield House, Longparish, near Andover, Hants. *T:* Longparish 228. *Club:* Army and Navy.

**OSWALD, Dr Neville Christopher,** TD 1946; MD Cantab 1946, FRCP 1947; Consultant Physician: St Bartholomew's Hospital; Brompton Hospital; King Edward VII's Hospital for Officers, London; King Edward VII's Hospital, Midhurst; *b* 1 Aug. 1910; *s* of late Col Christopher Percy Oswald, CMG; *m* 1st, 1941, Patricia Rosemary Joyce Cooke (*d* 1947); one *s* one *d*; 2nd, 1948, Marjorie Mary Sinclair; one *d. Educ:* Clifton Coll.; Queens' Coll., Cambridge. Research Fellow, USA, 1938-39. Royal Army Medical Corps, 1939-45. Hon. Physician to the Queen, 1956-58. Hon. Col, 17th (London) General Hospital RAMC (TA), 1963-67, 217 (Eastern) General Hospital RAMC (V), 1967-. *Publications:* Recent Trends in Chronic Bronchitis, 1958; Diseases of the Respiratory System, 1962; many articles upon respiratory diseases. *Recreations:* travel, golf. *Address:* 70 Harley St, W1. *T:* 01-580 3383; 7 Strangways Terrace, W14. *T:* 01-937 7449.

**OSWALD, Thomas;** MP (Lab) Edinburgh, Central Division, since 1951; *b* 1 May 1904; *s* of John Oswald and Agnes Love, Leith; *m* 1933, Colina MacAskill, *d* of Archibald MacAlpine and Margaret MacAskill, Ballachulish, Argyllshire; three *s* one *d. Educ:* Yardheads and Bonnington Elementary Schools. Shipyard worker, transport worker. Official of Transport and General Workers' Union; Scottish Regional Trade Group Secretary, 1941-69. Contested (Lab) West Aberdeenshire, 1950. PPS to Secretary of State for Scotland, 1967-70. Sec. Treasurer, Scottish Parly Lab. Group, 1953-64; Sec., Members' Parly Cttee, 1956-66. *Recreations:* student economic and industrial history; swimming, camping, etc. *Address:* 28 Seaview Terrace, Joppa, Edinburgh 15. *T:* 031-669 5569.

**O'TOOLE, Peter;** actor; *b* 1934; *s* of Patrick Joseph O'Toole; *m* Sian Phillips; two *d. Educ:* Royal Academy of Dramatic Art. With Bristol Old Vic Company, 1955-58; first appearance on London stage as Peter Shirley in Major Barbara, Old Vic, 1956. *Plays include:* Oh, My Papa!, Garrick, 1957; The Long and the Short and the Tall, Royal Court and New, 1959; season with Shakespeare Memorial Theatre Company, Stratford-on-Avon, 1960; Baal, Phœnix, 1963; Hamlet, National Theatre, 1963; Ride a Cock Horse, Piccadilly, 1965; Juno and the Paycock, Gaiety, Dublin, 1966. *Films include:* Kidnapped, 1959; The Day They Robbed the Bank of England, 1959; The Savage Innocents, 1960; Lawrence of Arabia, 1962; Becket, 1963; Lord Jim, 1964; What's New, Pussycat, 1965; How to Steal a Million, 1966; The Bible ... in the Beginning, 1966; The Night of the Generals, 1967; Great Catherine, 1968; The Lion in Winter, 1968; Goodbye Mr Chips, 1969; Brotherly Love, 1970; Country Dance, 1970. *Address:* c/o Keep Films, 5 Eaton Place, SW1. *T:* 01-235 6552. *Club:* Garrick.

**OTTAWA, Archbishop of, (RC),** since 1967; **Most Rev. Joseph Aurèle Plourde;** *b* 12 Jan. 1915; *s* of Antoine Plourde and Suzanne Albert. *Educ:* Bathurst Coll.; Bourget Coll.; Rigaud; Major Seminary of Halifax; Inst. Catholique, Paris, Gregorian Univ., Rome. Auxiliary Bishop of Alexandria, Ont., 1964. Hon. DEducn, Moncton Univ., 1969. *Address:* Archbishop's Residence, 145 Saint Patrick's, Ottawa, Canada. *T:* 237-4540.

**OTTAWA, Dean of;** *see* Gartrell, Very Rev. Frederick Roy.

**OTTAWAY, Prof. Christopher Wyndham,** PhD, FRCVS; Professor of Veterinary Anatomy, University of Bristol, since 1949; Chairman, Board of Veterinary Studies, 1955-59, 1965-67; *b* 6 June 1910; 3rd *s* of W. H. Ottaway; *m* 1938, Grace, *d* of E. Luckin, JP; two *s* one *d. Educ:* Owen's Sch.; Roy. Vet. Coll., London; King's College, Cambridge (Senior Wellcome Scholar). Veterinary Practitioner, 1931-34; Department of Anatomy, Royal Veterinary College, London: Demonstrator, 1934-38; Lecturer, 1938-41; Reader, 1941-45. Wellcome Scholar, 1945-48; Lecturer in Zoology, Cambridge University, 1949. *Publications:* Ed. Stubbs Anatomy of the Horse (1938 edn); Locomotion, in Phys. Farm Animals (Ed. Hammond), 1955. Scientific papers. *Recreations:* music, walking. *Address:* Mount

House, Bucklands Batch, Nailsea, nr Bristol. *T:* Nailsea 2085.

**OTTER, Rt. Rev. Anthony,** MA; an Assistant Bishop, Diocese of Lincoln, since 1965; *b* 8 Sept. 1896; *s* of Robert Charles and Marianne Eva Otter; *m* 1929, Dorothy Margaret Ramsbotham; no *c*. *Educ:* Repton; Trinity College, Cambridge. Served European War, 1914-18, in RNVR, 1914-19. BA (2nd cl. History Tripos), 1920; MA 1925. Cambridge Mission to Delhi, 1921-24; Westcott House, Cambridge, 1924-25; Deacon, 1925; Priest, 1926; Curate of Holy Trinity, St Marylebone, 1925-31; London Secretary of SCM, 1926-31; Vicar of Lowdham with Gunthorpe, Dio. of Southwell, 1931-49; Chaplain of Lowdham Grange Borstal Institution, 1931-45; Ed. of Southwell Diocesan Magazine, 1941-46; Hon. Canon of Southwell Cathedral, 1942-49; Rural Dean of Gedling, 1946-49; Bishop Suffragan of Grantham, 1949-65; Dean of Stamford, 1949. *Publication:* William Temple and the Universal Church, 1949. *Recreations:* country, birds; maintenance of domestic machinery. *Address:* The Old Rectory, Belton, Grantham, Lincs. *T:* Grantham 2061.

**OTTER, Air Vice-Marshal Victor Charles,** CBE 1967 (OBE 1945); Air Officer Engineering, Air Support Command Royal Air Force, 1966-69, retired; *b* 9 February 1914; *s* of Robert and Ada Annie Otter; *m* 1943, Iris Louise Dykes; no *c*. *Educ:* Weymouth Gram. School. RAF Aircraft Apprentice, 1929-32; flying duties, 1935-37; commissioned Engr. Br., 1940; SO (Techn) Controller Research and Development (MAP), 1942-47; Asst Air Attaché, Budapest, 1947-48; Officer Comdg Central Servicing Develt Establt, 1953-55; Chief Engrg Officer, Bomber Comd, 1956-59; OC No 32 Maintenance Unit, 1959-61; STSO Flying Trng Comd, 1961-63; Project Dir, P1154/P1127, 1963-66. CEng, FRAeS, FIMechE, MBIM, psc. *Recreation:* gliding. *Address:* Harpenden, 21 Keats Avenue, Littleover, Derby. *T:* Derby 52048. *Club:* Royal Air Force.

**OTTER-BARRY, Rt. Rev. Hugh Van Lynden,** CBE 1951; Assistant Bishop to the Bishop of Peterborough since 1960; Vicar of Norton and Rector of Whilton since 1960; *b* 7 March 1887; 5th *s* of Robert Melvil Barry Otter-Barry, Horkesley Hall, Colchester. *Educ:* Marlborough; Trinity College, Cambridge; Wells Theological Coll. BA 1908 (2nd class Classical Tripos); MA 1912; ordained, 1910; curate of St Luke, Chelsea, 1910-15; Charleville Bush Brotherhood (Queensland), 1915-19; Vicar of Brill with Boarstall, Bucks, 1920-26; Archdeacon of Mauritius, 1926-31; Bishop of Mauritius, 1931-59. *Address:* Dee House, Hawkhurst, Kent. *Club:* Royal Commonwealth Society.

**OTTER-BARRY, William Whitmore,** BA, JP Essex; late General Manager Sun Insurance Office Ltd; late Director Sun Insurance Office Ltd; Sun Life Assurance Society; Planet Assurance Co. Ltd; *b* 6 Mar. 1878; *e surv s* of late Robert Melvil Barry Otter-Barry of Horkesley Hall, Essex, BA and Isabel Louisa, *d* of Rev. Francis Henry Wolryche-Whitmore of Dudmaston, Salop, JP; *m* 1905, Edith Wrey (*d* 1959), *d* of late Frederick Jaques Myers, of Charlton, Northants, JP; one *s* one *d* (and one *s* decd). *Educ:* Marlborough; Trinity College, Cambridge. Called to Bar, 1901; practised in London and Northern Circuit until 1912; became Assistant Secretary to Fire Offices Committee; Sub-Manager and Assistant Secretary Sun Insurance Office, Ltd, 1919; General Manager, 1923; Pres. Insurance Institute of London, 1926; Chairman London Salvage Corps, 1927-28; Chairman Insurance Clerks' Orphanage, 1930; President Chartered Insurance Institute, 1932; Chairman British Insurance Association, 1936; Member of the Board of Trade Committee on Compulsory Insurance, 1936; High Sheriff of Essex, 1946. *Publication:* Law relating to Fire Insurance, 1911, 3rd edition. *Recreations:* shooting, fishing. *Address:* Horkesley Hall, Colchester, Essex. *T:* Great Horkesley 259. *Club:* United University.

*See also Maj.-Gen. P. H. de Havilland.*

**OTTLEY, Agnes May;** retired as Principal, S Katharine's College, Tottenham, N17, Dec. 1959; *b* 29 June 1899; *d* of late Rev. Canon Robert Lawrence Ottley, Professor of Moral and Pastoral Theology, Oxford. *Educ:* privately; Society of Oxford Home Students. Final Honours School of Modern History, Oxford, 1921; MA Oxon; Assistant Mistress at S Felix School, Southwold, 1925; Lecturer in History, Avery Hill Training College, 1927. *Address:* 48 Wilbury Road, Hove, Sussex. *T:* Brighton 733958.

**OTTLEY, Warner Herbert Taylor,** CB 1945; retired; *b* 1889; *m* 1921, Hilda Mary Edwards; two *s*. *Educ:* Malvern; St John's College, Cambridge. Higher Division Clerk, War Office, 1913; Director of Finance, War Office, 1942; retired, 1949. *Address:* 15 Priory Close, Hastings, Sussex.

**OUDENDYK, Dame Margaret,** DBE, *cr* 1949 (Hon. DBE, *cr* 1918); *b* 29 Sept. 1876; *d* of Edmond Fuller; *m* 1911, Willem Oudendyk (*d* 1953) (William J. Oudendyk, Hon. KCMG). Order of the Sun 2nd Class (Persia), 1913. *Address:* Pound Hall, Long Melford, Suffolk. *T:* Long Melford 285. *Club:* Sesame Imperial and Pioneer.

**OULD, Ernest; His Honour Judge Ould;** Judge of County Courts, Sheffield, Rotherham, Barnsley and Pontefract since Nov. 1955; *b* 9 Dec. 1901; *s* of Percy and Emily Ould, Leeds; *m* 1931, Sarah Ackroyd, Leeds; two *s*. *Educ:* City of Leeds School; Leeds University. Called to the Bar, Gray's Inn, 1937; practised Leeds and North Eastern Circuit. *Recreation:* golf. *Address:* Hollin House, Leeds 16. *T:* Leeds 52043.

**OULSNAM, Sir (Samuel) Harrison (Yardley),** Kt, *cr* 1947; CSI 1946; CIE 1937; MC; late ICS; *b* 17 Jan. 1898; *Educ:* Newcastle-under-Lyme; St John's College, Cambridge, BA. Joined Indian Civil Service, 1921; held appts of Deputy Commissioner, Under Sec. to Central Provs Govt, Reforms Officer to C. P. Govt; Sec. to Eastern Group Supply Conf., 1940; Joint Sec. to Govt of India; Sec. to Govt of India, Dept of Health, 1945-47; retired, on transfer of power, 1947. *Address:* c/o Lloyds Bank, 39 Threadneedle St, EC2.

**OULTON, Air Vice-Marshal Wilfrid Ewart,** CB 1958; CBE 1953; DSO 1943; DFC 1943; FInst Nav; CEng; FIERE; Director: Electrical and Musical Industries (Electronics) Ltd; Emihus Ltd; *b* 27 July 1911; *s* of Llewellin Oulton, Monks Coppenhall, Cheshire; *m* 1935, Sarah, *d* of Rev. E. Davies, Pitsea, Essex; three *s*. *Educ:* University Coll., Cardiff; Cranwell. Commissioned, 1931; Director, Joint Anti-Submarine School, 1946-48; Joint Services Staff College, 1948-50; Air Attaché, Buenos Aires, Montevideo, Asuncion, 1950-53; idc 1954; Director of Operations, Air Ministry, 1954-56; commanded Joint Task Force "Grapple" for first British megaton weapon tests in the Pacific, 1956-58; Senior Air Staff Officer, RAF Coastal Command, HQ, 1958-60; retd. *Recreations:* music, squash, golf, travel. *Address:* Denefield Overstream,

Rickmansworth, Herts. *T:* Rickmansworth 74258. *Club:* United Service.

**OUNSTED, John,** MA Cantab; HM Inspector of Schools, since 1971; *b* London, 24 May 1919; *e s* of Rev. Laurence J. Ounsted, Dorchester Abbey, Oxon (ordained 1965; formerly with Sun Life Assurance); *m* 1940, Irene, 3rd *d* of late Rev. Alfred Newns; one *s* four *d*. *Educ:* Winchester (Scholar); Trinity College, Cambridge (Major Scholar). Math. Tripos Part I, 1st Class; Moral Science Tripos Part II, 1st Class; Senior Scholarship, Trinity College. Assistant Master, King Edward's School, Birmingham, 1940-48; Headmaster, Leighton Park School, 1948-70. First layman ever to be Select Preacher, Oxford Univ., 1964. Page Scholarship to visit USA, 1965. Liveryman, Worshipful Company of Mercers. *Publications:* verses from various languages in the 2 vols of Translation, 1945 and 1947; contributions to Watsonia, The Proceedings of the Botanical Society of the British Isles, and various other educational and botanical periodicals. *Recreations:* botany, camping, being overtaken when motoring. *Address:* Dumney Lane Cottage, Great Leighs, Chelmsford. *T:* Great Leighs 445.
*See also Sir A. Foley Newns.*

**OUTERBRIDGE, Col Hon. Sir Leonard Cecil,** CC (Canada) 1967; Kt 1946; CBE 1926; DSO 1919; CD 1954; Director, Harvey & Co., Ltd, and other Cos, St John's, Newfoundland; *b* 1888; *s* of late Sir Joseph Outerbridge; *m* 1915, Dorothy Winifred, *d* of late John Alexander Strathy, Barrie, Ontario. *Educ:* Marlborough; Toronto Univ. (BA, LLB; Hon. LLD, 1950); Hon. LLD: Laval Univ., 1952; Memorial University of Newfoundland. Solicitor and Barrister, Ontario, 1914; President, Newfoundland Board of Trade, 1923-24; Chairman, Newfoundland Committee arranging Exhibits at British Empire Exhibition (1924 and 1925) (CBE); served European War, 1914-19 (despatches twice, DSO). Hon. Private Sec. to the Governor of Newfoundland, 1931-44; Director of Civil Defence, 1942-45; Lieutenant-Governor of Newfoundland, 1949-57. Hon. Col, Royal Newfoundland Regt, 1950. KStJ 1951. *Address:* Littlefield, Pringle Place, St John's, Newfoundland.

**OUTERIÑO, Felix C.;** *see* Candela Outerino.

**OUTRAM, Sir Alan James,** 5th Bt, *cr* 1858; MA; Schoolmaster, at Harrow School; *b* 15 May 1937; *s* of late James Ian Outram and Evelyn Mary Littlehales; *S* great-uncle, 1945. *Educ:* Spyway, Langton Matravers, Swanage; Marlborough College, Wilts; St Edmund Hall, Oxford. Captain, Royal Engineers (RARO). *Heir: kinsman* Rev. Francis Henry Outram [*b* 2 Aug. 1907; *m* 1946 Eileen Grace, *d* of late Rev. L. A. McC. Newbery; one *s* one *d*]. *Address:* Flat 5, Sandhurst Lodge, Crowthorne, Berks; Harrow School, Harrow-on-the-Hill, Middlesex.

**OVENDEN, Harry,** CBE 1945 (OBE 1941); Fellow of Chartered Surveyors' Institution; *b* 14 Feb. 1876; *s* of Charles Ovenden; *m* 1911, Gladys Winifred Searle (*d* 1948); one *d*. *Educ:* Albemarle College. District Valuer Inland Revenue, 1910-23; Superintending Valuer to 1941; Chief Technical Adviser War Damage Commission, 1941-49. *Recreation:* golf. *Address:* Hollybank House, Ninfield, Sussex. *T:* 466.

**OVERALL, Sir John (Wallace),** Kt 1968; CBE 1962; MC and Bar; Commissioner, National Capital Development Commission, since 1958; Chairman, National Capital Planning Committee, since 1958; *b* 15 July 1913; *s* of late W. Overall, Sydney; *m* 1943, Margaret J., *d* of C. W. Goodman; four *s*. *Educ:* Sydney Techn. College. AIF, 1940-45: CO, 1 Aust. Para. Bn (Lt-Col). Chief Architect, S Australian Housing Trust, 1946-48; private practice, Architect and Town Planner, 1949-52; Dir of Architecture, Commonwealth Dept of Works, 1952-57; Chm. of Olympic Fine Arts Architecture and Sculpture Exhibn, Melb., 1956. FRAIA, FRIBA, FAPI, MTPI. *Publication:* Observations on Redevelopment Western Side of Sydney Cove, 1967. *Recreations:* squash, tennis. *Address:* 44 Mugga Way, Red Hill, Canberra, ACT 2603, Australia. *T:* Canberra 93939. *Clubs:* Australian (Sydney); Naval and Military (Melbourne); Commonwealth (Canberra).

**OVEREND, Douglas,** CB 1965; Assistant Under-Secretary of State, Department of Health and Social Security, since 1968; *b* 22 Nov. 1914; *s* of Simeon and Frances Overend, Rodley, Leeds. *Educ:* Leeds Grammar School; Queen's College (Hastings Scholar, Taberdar), Oxford. 1st cl. Classical Mods. 1936; Greats 1938. Army Service, 1939-46. Entered Min. of Nat. Insce as Principal, 1946; Asst Sec., 1953; Under-Sec., 1959; Min. of Pensions and Nat. Insce, 1959-66; Min. of Social Security, 1966-68. *Recreation:* golf. *Address:* Alexander Fleming House, Elephant and Castle, SE1. *Club:* Oxford and Cambridge University.

**OVEREND, Prof. William George;** Professor of Chemistry in the University of London and Head of Department of Chemistry in Birkbeck College, since 1957; *b* 16 Nov. 1921; *e s* of Harold George Overend, Shrewsbury, Shropshire; *m* 1949, Gina Olava, *y d* of Horace Bertie Cadman, Birmingham; two *s* one *d*. *Educ:* Priory School, Shrewsbury; Univ. of Birmingham. BSc (Hons) 1943, PhD 1946, DSc 1954, Birmingham; FRIC, 1955. Asst Lecturer, Univ. Coll., Nottingham, 1946-47; Research Chemist with Dunlop Rubber Co. Ltd and subsequently British Rubber Producers' Assoc., 1947-49; Hon. Research Fellow, 1947-49, Lecturer in Chemistry, 1949-55, Univ. of Birmingham; Vis. Assoc. Prof., Pennsylvania. State Univ., 1951-52; Reader in Organic Chemistry, Univ. of London, 1955-57. Univ. of London: Mem., Academic Council, 1963-67; Mem., University Entrance and Schools Examination Council, 1966-67. Examiner for Royal Institute of Chemistry, 1958-62; Assessor for Royal Institute of Chemistry, 1959-; Member: Council, 1955-65, Finance Committee, 1956-65, Publications Cttee, 1955-65 (Hon. Sec. for publications and Chairman of Publications Committee, 1958-65), Soc. of Chemical Industry; Brit. Nat. Cttee for Chemistry, 1961-66; Chemical Council, 1960-63 and 1964-69 (Vice-Chm. 1964-69); Publications Board, Chemical Society, 1967- (Council, 1967-70); European Cttee of Carbohydrate Chemists, 1970- (Chm.). Jubilee Memorial Lecturer, Society of Chemical Industry, 1959-60; Lampitt Medallist, Society of Chemical Industry, 1965; Member: Pharmacopœia Commission, 1963-; Home Office Poisons Board. Governor, Polytechnic of the South Bank, 1970-. *Publications:* The Use of Tracer Elements in Biology, 1951; papers in Nature, and Jl of Chemical Soc. *Recreation:* gardening. *Address:* Department of Chemistry, Birkbeck College, Malet Street, WC1. *T:* 01-580 6622. *Club:* Athenæum.

**OVERTON, Sir Arnold (Edersheim),** KCB 1943; KCMG 1939 (CMG 1932); MC; *b* 8 Jan. 1893; *s* of late Canon F. A. Overton and Ella Edersheim; *m* 1920, Bronwen Cecilie, *d* of late Sir Hugh Vincent; three *s* one *d*. *Educ:*

Winchester; New College, Oxford. Served European War in France, Macedonia and Palestine; entered Board of Trade, 1919; private secretary to successive Presidents, 1921-25; on secretariat of Ottawa Conference, 1932; Delegate of United Kingdom Government to negotiate Anglo-American Trade Agreement, in Washington, 1937-38; Permanent Secretary Board of Trade, 1941-45; Head of British Middle East Office, Cairo, 1945-47; Permanent Secretary, Ministry of Civil Aviation, 1947-53; Member Board of BEA, 1953-63. *Address:* 41 Upper Addison Gardens, W14. *Club:* United University. *See also H. T. A. Overton.*

**OVERTON, Hugh Thomas Arnold;** Counsellor (Economic), British Embassy, Bonn, since 1967; *b* 2 April 1923; *e s* of Sir Arnold Overton, qv; *m* 1948, Claire-Marie Binet; one *s* two *d.* *Educ:* Dragon Sch., Oxford; Winchester; Clare Coll., Cambridge. Royal Signals, 1942-45. HM Diplomatic Service, 1947-; served: Budapest; UK Delegn to UN, New York; Cairo; Beirut; Disarmament Delegn, Geneva; Warsaw. *Recreations:* reading, walking, sailing. *Address:* c/o Barclays Bank, 276 Kensington High Street, W8. *Club:* Royal Automobile.

**OVERY, Sir Thomas (Stuart),** Kt 1954; late Senior Partner Allen & Overy, Solicitors; *b* 13 June 1893; *s* of Henry James Overy, Mascalls Court, Brenchley; *m* 1923, Frances Hilda, (*d* 1970), *d* of W. F. Richardson; three *s* one *d.* *Educ:* Kent Coll., Canterbury. Served European War, 1914-18; enlisted Royal Fusiliers, Aug. 1914; 2nd Lieut, The Buffs, 1915; went to France, 8th Bn The Buffs 24th Div., Oct. 1915; Capt. The Buffs, 1918 (despatches); Staff Capt. 92nd Bde, 31st Div. 1918; Staff Capt. QMG, GHQ, 1918-19. Admitted a Solicitor, 1921. *Address:* Warwick Grange Hotel, Warwick Park, Tunbridge Wells, Kent.

**OWEN, Sir Alfred George Beech,** Kt 1961; CBE 1954 (OBE 1946); DL; Chairman and Joint Managing Director, Owen Organisation, Darlaston, since 1930; Pro-Chancellor, University of Keele, since 1962; *b* 8 April 1908; *e s* of Alfred Ernest Owen and Florence Lucy Beech; *m* 1932, Eileen Kathleen Genevieve McMullan; three *s* two *d.* *Educ:* Oundle; Emmanuel College, Cambridge University. Took over Rubery, Owen & Co., Ltd, on the death of his father, 1930. Chairman or Director of over eighty other companies. Chairman of Council of Dr Barnardo's; formerly: President of National Sunday School Union; Former Chm., Staffordshire County Council; Former Mayor of Sutton Coldfield. Mem. Governing Body, Univ. of Birmingham. A Vice-Chm.: Nat. Savings Movement; Nat. Road Safety Advisory Council (Chairman 1965-67). Freeman of Borough of Sutton Coldfield. DL, County of Warwick, 1967. Ferodo Gold Trophy, 1962. Gold Medal of Brit. Automobile Racing Club, 1963. Hon. DSc, Keele, 1965. OStJ. *Address:* New Hall, Walmley, Sutton Coldfield, Warwicks. *T:* Sutton 021-354 2020. *Clubs:* National, Royal Automobile; Union (Birmingham).

**OWEN, Alun (Davies);** writer since 1957; *b* 24 Nov. 1926; *s* of Sidney Owen and Ruth (*née* Davies); *m* 1942, Theodora Mary O'Keefe; two *s.* *Educ:* Cardigan County School, Wales; Oulton High School, Liverpool. Actor in theatre, TV and films, 1942-59. First wrote for radio; *plays:* Two Sons, 1957; Progress to the Park, 1958 (also at Royal Court, 1959, Theatre Workshop, 1960, and Saville, 1961); The Rough and Ready Lot, 1958 (also at Lyric, Hammersmith, 1959); A Little Winter Love, 1963; The Game (Dublin Festival), 1965; The Goose (Dublin), 1967; There'll Be Some Changes Made, 1969; *television plays:* No Trams to Lime St, 1959; After the Funeral, 1960; Lena, Oh My Lena, 1960; The Ruffians, 1960; The Ways of Love, 1961; The Rose Affair, 1961; Dare to be a Daniel, 1962; The Hard Knock, 1962; The Stag, 1963; The Strain, 1963; A Local Boy, 1963; The Making of Jericho, 1966; The Other Fella, 1966; The Winner, 1967; The Loser, 1967; The Fantasist, 1967; The Wake, 1967; Shelter, 1967; George's Room, 1967; Charlie, 1967, Male of the Species, 1969, and other TV plays; *films:* The Criminal, 1960; A Hard Day's Night, 1964. *Publications:* The Rough and Ready Lot, 1960; Three TV Plays, 1961; Progress to the Park (Penguin), 1962; The Rose Affair (included in Anatomy of a Television Play), 1962; A Little Winter Love, 1964. Maggie May (book), Adelphi, 1964. *Recreations:* languages and history. *Address:* c/o Felix de Wolfe & Associates, 61 Berkeley House, 15 Hay Hill, W1.

**OWEN, Sir (Arthur) Douglas,** KBE 1958; CB 1952; Commissioner, HM Customs and Excise, 1949-65; Deputy Chairman Board of Customs and Excise, 1952-65; Chairman, Customs Co-operation Council, Brussels, 1955, re-elected 1956, Président d'Honneur, 1957; Mem., Civil Service Selection Bd, 1965-68; *b* 24 Nov. 1904; *s* of late William Owen and Mrs B. J. Owen, Swansea; *m* 1934, Janet Mabel Morton, MB, ChB, DPH; one *s.* *Educ:* Swansea Grammar School; Wrekin College, Salop; Downing College, Cambridge (Exhibitioner). First Class Historical Tripos; MA. Administrative Class, Home Civil Service, 1928; HM Customs and Excise (Private Sec. to Chm., Sir Edward Forber), Principal, 1933; Assistant Secretary, 1942. *Address:* 30 Foxes Dale, Blackheath Park, SE3.

**OWEN, Dr David Anthony Llewellyn;** MP (Lab) Sutton Division of Plymouth since 1966; *b* Plympton, South Devon, 2 July 1938; *s* of Dr John William Morris Owen and Mary Llewellyn; *m* 1968, Deborah Schabert; one *s.* *Educ:* Bradfield College; Sidney Sussex College, Cambridge; St Thomas' Hospital. BA 1959; MB, BChir 1962; MA 1963. St Thomas' Hospital: house appts, 1962-64; Neurological and Psychiatric Registrar, 1964-66; Research Fellow, Medical Unit, 1966-68. Contested (Lab) Torrington, 1964. PPS to Minister of Defence, Administration, 1967; Parly Under-Sec. of State for Defence, for RN, 1968-70. Governor of Charing Cross Hospital, 1966-68; Patron, Disablement Income Group, 1968-. Chairman of SW Regional Sports Council, 1967-. Fellow Roy. Soc. Med. *Publications:* (ed) A Unified Health Service, 1968; articles in Lancet, Neurology, and Clinical Science. *Recreation:* sailing. *Address:* 78 Narrow Street, Limehouse, E14. *T:* 01-987 5441; Castlehayes, Plympton, Plymouth, Devon. *T:* Plymouth 36130.

**OWEN, Maj.-Gen. David Lanyon Ll.;** *see* Lloyd Owen.

**OWEN, Sir Douglas;** *see* Owen, Sir Arthur D.

**OWEN, Sir Dudley H. C.;** *see* Cunliffe-Owen.

**OWEN, Edwin Augustine,** MA, ScD (Cantab), DSc (London), MSc (Wales), FInstP; Professor of Physics, University College of North Wales, Bangor, 1926-54, Professor Emeritus since 1954; Member of Grand Council British Empire Cancer Campaign; Member of Scientific Advisory Committee National Gallery; Chairman, Board of Governors, Bangor Grammar Schools; Member, Board of Governors, Rydal School;

Fellow: Physical Society; Cambridge Philosophical Society; Hon. Member: Institute of Quarrying; Association of Hospital Physicists; Member: Institute of Metals; British Institute of Radiology; *b* 5 Aug. 1887; *s* of late John and Ellen Owen, Blaenau Festiniog; *m* 1915, Julia May, *o d* of late Robert Vallance, Bangor; one *s. Educ:* Festiniog County School; University College, Bangor; Trinity Coll., Cambridge; University College, London. Open Scholarship (UCNW), 1905; BSc Wales (Honours in Mathematics and in Physics) 1909; 1851 Exhibition Scholar, 1910-12; Research Student at Cavendish Laboratory, Cambridge, 1910-12; Assistant in Metrology Dept, National Physical Laboratory, 1912-15; engaged on Standardisation of Instruments for Ministry of Munitions, 1915-19; Head of Radiology Division, National Physical Laboratory, 1919-26; Hon. Secretary, Röntgen Society, 1920-24; Hon. Secretary British Institute Radiology, 1924-25; Röntgen Award, 1927; Vice-President, Physical Society of London, 1926-28; Hon. Secretary, International Cttee for Radiological Units, 1925-37; Vice-President, British Institute of Radiology, 1939-42; Silvanus Thompson Medallist, 1945; Chairman North Wales District WEA, 1946-56; Member of Welsh Regional Hospital Board and Chairman Hospital Planning Cttee, 1948-62; Vice-President, Institute of Physics, 1957-59. *Publications:* original papers in Proceedings of the Royal Society, Proceedings of the Physical Society, Philosophical Magazine, Mineralogical Magazine, Journals of the Röntgen Society, the British Institute of Radiology, the Iron and Steel Institute and the Institute of Metals, Zeitschrift für Krist, American Chemical Society, on radiology, X-rays and crystal structure of metals and alloys. *Recreations:* golf, angling. *Address:* Penbre, College Road, Bangor, N Wales. *T:* Bangor 3773.

**OWEN, Eric Hamilton;** Deputy Chairman, National and Grindlays Bank Ltd, since 1967; *b* 4 Aug. 1903; *s* of Harold Edwin Owen and Hilda Guernsey; *m* 1937, Margaret Jeannie Slipper. Served Artists' Rifles, 1921-39; RASC, 8th Army, 1940-45; 21st SAS Regt (Artists), 1946-48 (despatches). Director: Charterhouse Investment Trust Ltd (Chairman, 1968-); Daniel Doncaster & Sons Ltd; Exporters' Refinance Corporation Ltd; Gabbitas-Thring Educational Trust Ltd; and subsidiary companies. Member Board of Trade Mission to Ghana, 1959. Member Finance Cttee, BIM. *Recreations:* photography, travel. *Address:* Tawny House, Copsem Lane, Esher, Surrey. *Club:* Army and Navy.

**OWEN, Frank,** (H. F. Owen), OBE; Journalist, Author, Broadcaster and Public Relations Consultant; *b* 1905; *s* of Thomas and Cicely Owen, Hereford; *m* 1939, Grace Stewart McGillivray (*d* 1968), Boston, USA. *Educ:* Monmouth Sch.; Sidney Sussex Coll., Cambridge (Schol.); 1st class hons, History Tripos. South Wales Argus, 1928-29; MP (L) Hereford Division, 1929-31; Daily Express, 1931-37; Editor, Evening Standard, 1938-41; served Royal Armoured Corps, 1942-43; South-East Asia Command, 1944-46; Lieut-Colonel (OBE); Editor, Daily Mail, 1947-50. Freeman of the City of London. *Publications:* (with Cemlyn Jones) Red Rainbow, 1931, novel; (with R. J. Thompson) His was the Kingdom, An Account of the Abdication, 1937; The Three Dictators, 1940; The Campaign in Burma, 1946; Tempestuous Journey: Lloyd George, His Life and Times, 1954; The Eddie Chapman Story, 1956; Peron: His Rise and Fall, 1957; The Fall of Singapore, 1960. *Clubs:* Savage, Press.

**OWEN, George Sherard,** CB 1946; *b* 20 June 1892; *s* of late Rev. E. C. E. Owen (late Master at Harrow School) and Rose Dora Ashington; *m* 1920, Doris Winifred Lyall Haynes, Barbados, BWI. *Educ:* Orley Farm Sch., Harrow; Rossall Sch. (Scholar); University College, Oxford (Lodge Exhibitioner). European War, 1914-16, despatch-rider RE Signals; commissioned RE Signals, 1916-19 (Mons Star, despatches). Ministry of Labour (1928-29 Imperial Defence Coll.), 1919-34; Unemployment Assistance Board, 1934-40; Board of Trade, 1940-42; Ministry of Production, 1942-45; Under-Secretary, Board of Trade, 1945-52; retired, 1952. *Recreations:* gardening, "Times" crossword. *Address:* Flat 5, 36 Belsize Park, NW3. *T:* 01-794 4518. *Club:* United University.

**OWEN, Gerald Victor,** QC 1969; *b* London, 29 Nov. 1922; *s* of Samuel and Ziporah Owen; *m* 1946, Phyllis (*née* Ladsky); one *s* one *d. Educ:* Kilburn Grammar Sch.; St Catharine's Coll., Cambridge. Exhibr, St Catharine's Coll., Cambridge, 1940; Drapers' Company Science Schol., Queen Mary Coll., London, 1940. 1st cl. Maths Tripos I, 1941; Senior Optimes Tripos II, 1942; BA 1943, MA 1946, Cantab; Royal Statistical Soc. Certif., 1947; LLB London (Hons) 1949. Research Ballistics, Min. of Supply, 1942-45; Statistical Officer, LCC, 1945-49. Called to Bar, Gray's Inn, 1949; *ad eundem* Inner Temple, 1969. *Recreations:* tennis, walking, theatre, music, ballet. *Address:* 47 Cranbourne Gardens, NW11. *T:* 01-455 6655; 3 Paper Buildings, Temple, EC4. *T:* 01-353 1182. *Club:* Maccabaeans.

**OWEN, Gwilym Ellis Lane,** FBA 1969; Victor S. Thomas Professor of Philosophy and the Classics, Harvard University, since 1966; *b* 18 May 1922; *o s* of Ellis William Owen, Portsmouth; *m* 1947, Sally Lila Ann Clothier; two *s. Educ:* Portsmouth Grammar Sch.; Corpus Christi Coll., Oxford. MA (Oxon) 1949; BPhil 1950. Res. Fellow in Arts, University of Durham, 1950; University Lecturer in Ancient Philosophy, University of Oxford, 1953; Reader in Ancient Philosophy, 1957; Fellow of Corpus Christi Coll., 1958; Professor of Ancient Philosophy, 1963. Visiting Professor of Philosophy: University of Pennsylvania, 1956; Harvard, 1959; University of California, 1964. *Publications:* (ed, with I. Düring) Aristotle and Plato in the Mid-Fourth Century, 1960; articles in various collections and in Classical Quarterly, Proc. Aristotelian Society, etc. *Address:* The Beeches, Lower Heyford, Oxford. *T:* Steeple Aston 467.

**OWEN, Harrison;** Dramatic author and journalist; *b* Geelong, Australia, 24 June 1890; *s* of late Albert Thomas Owen and Elizabeth Ann Harrison Swindells; *m* Esther (*d* 1964), *d* of George Arthur Dyson, Melbourne, Australia. *Educ:* Private schools. Dramatic critic and special writer for various Australian newspapers; came to London, 1920; leader-writer, Daily Sketch, 1921-32; returned to Australia, 1940. Leader-writer Melbourne Sun, 1940-55. *Publications:* The Mount Marunga Mystery, 1919; Tommyrot Rhymes, 1920; The Playwright's Craft, 1940; Plays: The Gentleman-in-Waiting, 1925; The Happy Husband, 1927; Doctor Pygmalion, 1932; Edge of the Night, 1959. *Recreations:* reading, play-going, golf. *Address:* 1/54 Hotham Street, East St Kilda, Melbourne, Australia.

**OWEN, Maj.-Gen. Harry;** Director of Army Legal Services since 1969; *b* 17 July 1911; *m*

1952, Maureen (*née* Summers); one *s* one *d*. *Educ:* University Coll., Bangor. BA Hons Philosophy, 1934. Solicitor of Supreme Court, 1939. Commissioned in Queen's Own Cameron Highlanders, 1940-43; joined Mil. Dept of Office of Judge Advocate General, 1943: served in: W Africa, 1945-46; Middle East, 1947-50; Austria, 1952-53; Dep. Dir of Army Legal Services: Far East, 1960-62; HQ, BAOR, 1962-67; Brig. Legal Staff, 1968-69. *Recreations:* philosophy, archaeology, history of art, walking, gardening. *Address:* Hedge End, 56 Valley Road, Rickmansworth, Herts. *T:* Rickmansworth 72385.

**OWEN, Captain Hilary Dorsett,** CMG 1944; RN, retired; *b* 25 Aug. 1894; *s* of late J. D. Owen, JP, Plas-yn-Grove, Ellesmere, Shropshire; *m* 1924, Eileen Amy Hamilton (*d* 1952), *e d* of W. B. Dunlop, Seton Castle, Longniddry; one *s*. *Educ:* Belvedere, Brighton; RN Colleges, Osborne and Dartmouth. Midshipman, 1912; served at sea, War of 1914-18; Commander, 1930; Naval Attaché, Lisbon, 1938-44; SHAEF 1944-45; retired list, 1944.

**OWEN, H. F.;** *see* Owen, Frank.

**OWEN, Idris Wyn;** MP (C) Stockport North since 1970; is a director of a company in the construction industry; *b* 1912. *Educ:* Stockport Sch. and Coll. of Technology; Manchester Sch. of Commerce. Contested (C): Manchester Exchange, 1951; Stalybridge and Hyde, 1955; Stockport North 1966. Member, Stockport Borough Council, 1946; Mayor, 1962-63. Vice-Pres., Nat. Fedn of Building Trades Employers, 1965. FIOB. *Address:* House of Commons, SW1.

**OWEN, Sir John Arthur,** 4th Bt, *cr* 1813; *b* 5 Feb. 1892; *s* of 3rd Bt and Martha Roberts Lewis; *S* father, 1909; *m* 1914, Lucy Fletcher, *e d* of Dr Pilkington, Kencot House, nr Lechlade, Glos; two *s*. *Educ:* Llandovery Coll.; St John's Coll., Oxford. *Recreations:* football, cricket, hockey; ex-Captain, Somerset Light Infantry. *Heir: s* Hugh Bernard Pilkington Owen [*b* 1915. *Educ:* Chillon Coll., Switzerland]. *Address:* Cross House, Fishguard, Pembs.

**OWEN, John Arthur Dalziel,** QC 1970; Deputy Chairman of Warwickshire Quarter Sessions since 1967; *b* 22 Nov. 1925; *s* of late R. J. Owen and Mrs V. B. Owen; *m* 1952, Valerie, *d* of W. Ethell; one *s* one *d*. *Educ:* Solihull Sch.; Brasenose Coll., Oxford. MA, BCL 1949. Called to Bar, Gray's Inn, 1951. Mem., General Synod of Church of England, Dio. Coventry, 1970-. *Address:* Lansdowne House, Shipston-on-Stour, Warwicks. *T:* Shipston-on-Stour 521.

**OWEN, John Benjamin Brynmor,** DSc (Oxon), MSc (Wales); FRAeS; MICE; John William Hughes Professor of Civil Engineering, University of Liverpool, since 1950; *b* 2 Sept. 1910; *s* of David Owen (Degwyl) and Mary Alice Owen; *m* 1938, Beatrice Pearn (*née* Clark); two *d*. *Educ:* Universities of Oxford and Wales. Drapers Company Scholar, Page Prize and Medal, University College, Cardiff, 1928-31; Meyricke Scholar, Jesus Coll., Oxford, 1931-32; British Cotton Industry Research Association, 1933-35; Messrs A. V. Roe, Manchester, 1935-36; Royal Aircraft Establishment, Farnborough, 1936-48; Naval Construction Research Establishment, 1948-50. *Publications:* Light Structures, 1965; many contributions to learned journals on design of structures, on helicopters and on investigation of aircraft accidents. *Address:* Department of Civil Engineering, The University of Liverpool, PO Box 147, Brownlow Street, Liverpool L69 3BX. *T:* 051-709 6022.

**OWEN, John Glendwr;** Under-Secretary, HM Treasury, since 1959; *b* 12 May 1914; *s* of George Cecil Owen; *m* 1943, Caroline Gweneth, 2nd *d* of Major Edward Bough; no *c*. *Educ:* Bedford Sch.; Balliol Coll., Oxford. Entered War Office, 1937; transferred to Treasury, 1938; Private Secretary to Financial Secretary, 1940-41, and to Permanent Secretary, 1947-48. Served in Grenadier Guards, 1942-45. Assistant Secretary, Treasury, 1948. *Address:* c/o HM Treasury, Great George Street, SW1.

**OWEN, Sir Leonard;** *see* Owen, Sir W. L.

**OWEN, Professor Paul Robert;** Zaharoff Professor of Aviation, London University, at Imperial College of Science and Technology, since 1963; *b* 24 Jan. 1920; *s* of Joseph and Deborah Owen; *m* 1958, Margaret Ann, *d* of Herbert and Dr Lily Baron; two *s* two *d*. *Educ:* Queen Mary Coll., London Univ. BSc (London) 1940, MSc (Manchester), FRAeS, AFIAeS, FRMetS. Aerodynamics Dept, RAE, Farnborough, 1941-53; Reader and Director of Fluid Motion Laboratory, Manchester Univ., 1953-56; Professor of the Mechanics of Fluids and Director of the Laboratory, Manchester Univ., 1956-62. Member of Cttees of Aeronautical Research Council, and Ministry of Power. Fellow, Queen Mary Coll., 1967. *Publications:* papers on Aerodynamics in R & M series of Aeronautical Research Council, Journal of Fluid Mechanics, etc. *Recreations:* music, theatre, carpentry. *Address:* 1 Horbury Crescent, W11. *T:* 01-229 5111. *Club:* Athenæum.

**OWEN, Peter Granville,** CMG 1965; United Nations Police Adviser, Government of the Somali Republic, since 1968; *b* 28 Oct. 1918; *s* of Walter Lincoln Owen, Highgate, and Ethel Belton, London, N6; *m* 1943, Mercia Louvaine Palmer; one *s* one *d*. *Educ:* Grove House Sch., Highgate; City of Norwich Sch. Great Yarmouth Borough Police, 1938-42; RAF, F/O, 1942-46; Public Prosecutor, Somalia Gendarmerie, 1946; Resident Magistrate, Mogadishu, Somalia, 1948; District Commissioner: Somalia, 1949-50; Eritrea, 1950; Tanganyika Police: Cadet, Asst Superintendent and Dep. Superintendent of Police, 1950; Somaliland Police: Superintendent and Senior Superintendent of Police, 1956; Commissioner of Police: Gibraltar, 1960; British Guiana, 1962; Aden, 1965. OStJ 1960; Queen's Police Medal, 1964; Colonial Police Medal, 1960. *Recreations:* cricket, swimming, walking. *Address:* United Nations, PO Box 24, Mogadicio, Somali Republic. *Clubs:* Royal Commonwealth Society, MCC.

**OWEN, Philip Loscombe Wintringham,** TD 1950; QC 1963; *b* 10 Jan. 1920; *er s* of Rt Hon. Sir Wintringham Stable, *qv*; assumed surname of Owen in lieu of Stable by deed poll, 1942; *m* 1949, Elizabeth Jane, *d* of late Lewis Trelawny Widdicombe, Effingham, Surrey; three *s* two *d*. *Educ:* Winchester; Christ Church, Oxford (MA). Served War of 1939-45, Royal Welch Fusiliers: W Africa, India, Ceylon, Burma, 1939-47; Major TARO. Received into Roman Catholic Church, 1944. Called to Bar, Middle Temple, 1949; Bencher, 1969. Contested (C) Montgomeryshire, 1945. A Deputy Chairman of Quarter Sessions: Montgomeryshire, 1959-; Cheshire, 1961-. Legal Assessor to: Gen. Med. Council, 1970-; Gen. Dental Council, 1970-; RICS, 1970-. JP Montgomeryshire, 1959; JP Cheshire, 1961. President, Montgomeryshire Cons. and Unionist Assoc. *Recreations:* shooting, fishing, forestry, music. *Address:* 1 Brick Court, Temple, EC4. *T:* 01-353 0777; 51 Hartington Road, Chiswick, W4. *T:* 01-994

0415; Plas Llwyn Owen, Llanbrynmair, Montgomeryshire. *T:* 229. *Clubs:* Carlton; Hurlingham; Cardiff and County; Welshpool and District Conservative; Bristol Channel Yacht (Mumbles).
*See also R. O. C. Stable.*

**OWEN, Rear-Adm. Richard Arthur James,** CB 1963; *b* 26 Aug. 1910; *s* of late Captain Leonard E. Owen, OBE, JP; *m* 1941, Jean Sophia (*née* Bluett); one *s* two *d. Educ:* Sevenoaks Sch. Joined RN, 1927; Commander (S) 1945; Captain, 1954; Rear-Admiral, 1961; Director-General, Personal Services, Admiralty, 1962-64; retired. *Address:* 3/25 De Vere Gardens, W8. *T:* 01-937 0694; High Bank, Martin, near Fordingbridge, Hants. *T:* Martin Cross 295. *Club:* United Service.

**OWEN, Robert Davies,** CBE 1962; FRCS; FRCSE; Senior Ear and Throat Surgeon, Cardiff Royal Infirmary, 1928-64, retired; Lecturer in Oto-Laryngology, Welsh National School of Medicine, 1929-64, retired; *b* 8 May 1898; 2nd *s* of late Capt. Griffith Owen and late Mrs Jane Owen; *m* 1928, Janet Miles, Llantrisant; two *d. Educ:* Towyn Grammar Sch. Cadet, Harrison Line, Liverpool, 1916-18; University College, Cardiff, 1918-21; Guy's Hospital, London, 1921-27. BSc (Wales) 1921. MRCS, LRCP 1923; FRCS 1930; FRCSEd 1926. *Publications:* contrib. BMJ, Lancet, Proc. Royal Society of Medicine. *Recreations:* shooting, fishing. *Address:* 24 Park Place, Cardiff. *T:* 23956. *Club:* Cardiff and County.

**OWEN, Robert Penrhyn;** Secretary, Chief Administrative Officer and Solicitor to The Thames Conservancy, since 1969; *b* 17 Dec. 1918; *s* of late Captain Richard Owen; *m* 1949, Suzanne, *d* of late L. H. West; one *s* one *d. Educ:* Friar's School. War service in Army (Infantry), 1939-46, in Madagascar, India, The Arakan and North and Central Burma. Admitted Solicitor, 1947. Asst Solicitor: Berks CC, 1948-50; Leics CC, 1950-54; Chief Asst Solicitor, Lancs CC, 1954-60; 2nd Dep. Clerk and 2nd Dep. Clerk of the Peace, Lancs CC, 1960-63; Gen. Manager, Telford Develt Corp. (New Town), 1963-69. *Recreations:* all sport, reading. *Address:* Pilgrims Wood, Fawley Green, Henley-on-Thames, Oxon. *T:* Henley-on-Thames 2994. *Club:* MCC.

**OWEN, Ronald Hugh,** FIA; Chief General Manager, Prudential Assurance Co. Ltd, since 1969 (General Manager, 1968); *b* 2 June 1910; *er s* of late Owen Hugh Owen and late Jane Tegwedd Owen; *m* 1939, Claire May Tully; one *s. Educ:* King's College Sch., Wimbledon. FIA 1936. Served War of 1939-45: 52 Field Regt, RA (Major); Bde Major RA, 8 Ind. Division, Middle East and Italy. Joined Prudential, 1929: India, 1936-39; Dep. General Manager, 1959-67. Member, Governing Body and Chairman of Finance Cttee, King's College Sch., Wimbledon. *Recreation:* golf. *Address:* 110 Rivermead Court, Hurlingham, SW6. *T:* 01-736 4842. *Clubs:* Hurlingham; Royal Wimbledon Golf.

**OWEN, Rowland Hubert,** CMG 1948; Deputy Controller, HM Stationery Office, 1959-64, retired; *b* 3 June 1903; *s* of William R. and Jessie M. Owen, Armagh, NI; *m* 1st, 1930, Kathleen Margaret Evaline Scott (*d* 1965); no *c*; 2nd, 1966, Shelagh Myrle Nicholson. *Educ:* Royal Sch., Armagh; Trinity Coll., Dublin (BA, LLB). Entered Dept of Overseas Trade, 1926; Private Secretary to Comptroller-General, 1930; Secretary Gorell Cttee on Art and Industry, 1931; idc, 1934; Commercial Secretary, Residency, Cairo, 1935; Ministry of Economic Warfare, 1939; Rep. of Ministry in Middle East, 1942; Director of Combined (Anglo-American) Economic Warfare Agencies, AFHQ, Mediterranean, 1943; transferred to Board of Trade and appointed Senior UK Trade Commissioner in India, Burma and Ceylon, 1944; Economic Adviser to UK High Commissioner in India, 1946; Adviser to UK Delegation at International Trade Conf., Geneva, 1947. Comptroller-General, Export Credits Guarantee Dept, 1953-58; Member Managing Cttee, Union d'Assureurs des Crédits Internationaux, 1954-58. Vice-President, Tilford Bach Society, 1962-69; Organist, St Mary's, Bramshott, 1964-70, St John the Evangelist, Farncombe, 1970-. Staff of National Playing Fields Assoc., 1964-68. US Medal of Freedom. *Publications:* Economic Surveys of India, 1949 and 1952; Insurance Aspects of Children's Playground Management, 1966; Children's Recreation: Statutes and Constitutions, 1967. *Recreations:* music, theatre, gardening. *Address:* Oak Tree Cottage, Holdfast Lane, Haslemere, Surrey.

**OWEN, Samuel Griffith,** MD, FRCP; Second Secretary, Medical Research Council, since 1968; *b* 3 Sept. 1925; *e s* of late Rev. Evan Lewis Owen and of Marjorie Lawton; *m* 1954, Ruth, *e d* of Merle W. Tate, Philadelphia, Pa, USA; two *s* two *d. Educ:* Dame Allen's Sch.; Durham Univ. MB, BS Dunelm 1948; MRCP 1951; MD Dunelm 1954; FRCP 1965; clinical and research appts at Royal Victoria Infirmary, Newcastle upon Tyne, 1948-49 and 1950-53; RAMC, SMO, HM Troopships, 1949-50; Med. Registrar, Nat. Heart Hosp., 1953-54; Instr in Pharmacology, Univ. of Pennsylvania Sch. of Med., 1954-56; Reader in Med., Univ. of Newcastle upon Tyne, 1964-68 (First Asst, 1956, Lectr, 1960, Sen. Lectr, 1961); Hon. Cons. Physician, Royal Victoria Infirmary, Newcastle upon Tyne, 1960-68; Clin. Sub-Dean of Med. Sch., Univ. of Newcastle upon Tyne, 1966-68 (Academic Sub-Dean, 1964-66); Examr in Med., Univ. of Liverpool, 1966-68; Examr in Membership, RCP, 1967-68; Member: Research Cttee, RCP, 1968-; Assoc. of Physicians of GB, 1965-; Brit. Cardiac Soc., 1962-; Consultant to WHO, SE Asia, 1966 and 1967-68; Commonwealth Fund Fellow, Univ. of Illinois, 1966. *Publications:* Essentials of Cardiology, 1961 (2nd edn, 1968); Electrocardiography, 1966. Numerous contribs to med. jls on heart disease, cerebral circulation, thyroid disease, med. educn, etc. *Recreations:* squash rackets, gastronomy. *Address:* 20 Park Crescent, W1; 60 Bath Road, Chiswick, W4. *T:* 01-636 5422. *Clubs:* Athenæum, Royal Societies.

**OWEN, Thomas Joseph,** DL; Town Clerk, Nottingham, 1951-66; *b* 3 Nov. 1903; *s* of late Richard Owen, Sarn, Caernarvonshire; *m* 1935, Marjorie Ethel Tilbury. Articled to late Sir Hugh Vincent, 1921-26; admitted a Solicitor, 1926; Asst Solicitor with Town Clerk, Stoke-on-Trent, 1926-27; Asst Solicitor, Leeds, 1927-30; Asst Solicitor, Brighton, 1930-36; Deputy Town Clerk, Nottingham, 1936-50. President: Nottinghamshire Law Society, 1957-58; E Midlands Scandinavian Society. Trustee: Nottingham Roosevelt Travelling Scholarship Fund; Holbrook Trust (Painting and Sculpture). DL Notts, 1966. *Recreations:* watching Rugby football and cricket; travel abroad, reading. *Address:* Woodlands, Sherwood, Nottingham. *T:* Nottingham 61767. *Clubs:* Royal Aero; Nottinghamshire, Borough (Nottingham).

**OWEN, Commodore Trevor Lewis,** OBE 1942; RD 1938; RNR, retired; *b* 21 Dec. 1895; 4th *s* of D. H. Owen, Wainhams, Shrewsbury; *m* 1920, Freda, 4th *d* of Rev. Prof. John Ramsey,

Ballymoney, Co. Antrim; three *d. Educ:* Arnold House Sch., Chester. Joined Merchant Service, Oct. 1911; Sub-Lieut, RNR, 1918; Master's Certificate, 1919. Commander RNR, 1937; Captain, RNR, 1942; Commodore RNR (Acting), 1942 and served in Atlantic Convoys until 1943. Elder Brother of Trinity House, 1943-62 (Nether Warden 1958); retired as an Active Elder Brother, Aug. 1962. Vice-President, Marine Society, 1961 (Chairman 1960). *Recreations:* gardening, sailing. *Address:* Sevenstones, Stoke Gabriel, Totnes, Devon. *T:* Stoke Gabriel 350. *Club:* Royal Dart Yacht (Dartmouth).

**OWEN, Professor Walter Shepherd,** PhD; Dean, Institute of Technology, Northwestern University, since 1970; *b* 13 March 1920; *s* of Walter Lloyd and Dorothea Elizabeth Owen; *m* 1953, Carol Ann Wood; one *d. Educ:* Alsop High Sch.; University of Liverpool. Metallurgist, D. Napier and Sons and English Electric Co., 1940-46; Asst Lecturer and Lecturer in Metallurgy, 1946-54, Commonwealth Fund Fellow, Metallurgy Dept, Massachusetts Inst. of Technology, USA, 1951-52, on research staff, 1954-57; Henry Bell Wortley Professor of Metallurgy, University of Liverpool, 1957-66. Thomas R. Briggs Prof. of Engineering and Dir of Materials Science and Engineering, Cornell Univ., 1966-70. *Publications:* papers in British and American journals on aspects of physical metallurgy. *Address:* Institute of Technology, Northwestern University, Evanston, Ill 60201, USA. *Clubs:* University (Liverpool); Cornell (NYC), University (Evanton).

**OWEN, Rt. Hon. Sir William Francis Langer,** PC 1963; KBE 1957; Justice of High Court of Australia since 1961; Justice of the Supreme Court of New South Wales, 1936-61; *b* 21 Nov. 1899; *s* of Sir Langer Owen and May Dames Longworth; *m* 1923, Joan Rolin; one *d. Educ:* Sydney Church of England Grammar Sch., Sydney, NSW. Served European War with AIF, 1915-19; admitted to Bar, 1923; KC 1935; Chairman of Commonwealth of Australia Central Wool Cttee, 1942-45. *Recreations:* fishing, golf. *Address:* High Court of Australia, Sydney, NSW. *Clubs:* Union, Royal Sydney Golf (Sydney); Melbourne (Melbourne).

**OWEN, William James;** *b* 18 Feb. 1901; *m* 1930, Ann Smith; one *s* one *d. Educ:* Elementary Sch., Blaina, Mon; Central Labour Coll. Miner, 1914-20; College Student, 1921-22; Tutor-Organiser, National Council Labour Colleges, 1923-30; Urban District Councillor, Blaina, Mon, 1927-30; ILP Secretary, Leicester, 1930-35; City Councillor, Leicester, 1933-38; Education Secretary: Co-operative Society, Burslem, Staffs, 1937-40; London Co-op. Society, 1940-44; Bristol Co-op. Society, 1944-48; Community Welfare Officer, National Coal Board, 1948-51; contested (Lab and Co-op) Dover, 1950 and 1951; MP (Lab and Co-op) Morpeth Div. of Northumberland, 1954-70, resigned. Gen. Secretary, Assoc. of Clothing Contractors, 1960. *Recreations:* walking, gardening, writing, painting. *Address:* 18a Woodstock Road, Carshalton, Surrey.

**OWEN, Sir (William) Leonard,** Kt 1957; CBE 1950; MEng; FICE; FIMechE; MIChemE; Hon. DSc Manchester, 1962; former Chairman: Scottish Aviation Ltd; Cammell Laird & Co. (Shipbuilders and Engineers); Cammell Laird (Anglesey) Ltd; former Director, cammell Laird & Co.; Consultant, United Gas Industries (lately Director); *b* 3 May 1897; *s* of Thomas John and Levina Owen; *m* 1923, Phyllis Condliff; two *s. Educ:* Liverpool Collegiate Sch.; Liverpool Univ. (MEng, 1924). Served European War, 6th King's Liverpool Regt, 1915-18. Brunner, Mond & Company, later ICI (Alkali) Ltd, designing new Chemical Plants and additions to existing Chemical Plant, 1922; loaned to Ministry of Supply as Engineering Director of Royal Filling Factories, 1940-45; Director of Engineering, Ministry of Supply, Dept of Atomic Energy Production, 1946; Asst Controller, Dept of Atomic Energy Production, 1947; Director of Engineering and Dep. Managing Director, Industrial Group, UK Atomic Energy Authority, 1954; Managing Director, United Kingdom Atomic Energy Authority, Industrial Group, Risley, 1957; Member for Production, UKAEA, 1959 and for Engineering also, 1961, ceasing to be full-time June 1962; Member (part-time), 1962-64. *Recreations:* yachting and gardening. *Address:* Eyarth, Rosemary Lane, Beaumaris, Anglesey. *T:* Beaumaris 396. *Clubs:* Royal Automobile; Royal Anglesey Yacht (Beaumaris).

**OWENS, Richard Hugh M.;** *see* Mills-Owens.

**OWLES, Captain Garth Henry Fyson,** DSO 1941; DSC 1940; RN (retired); *b* 25 Aug. 1896; *s* of Henry Beaumont Owles and Emma Harriet Fyson; *m* 1923, Catherine Noel Banham (*d* 1969); one *s* one *d. Educ:* Felsted. Passed into Royal Navy through special entry, 1914; trained at RN Coll., Keyham; served in HMS Princess Royal, 1915-17; Battle of Jutland, 1916; HMS Raglan, 1917-18, sunk by Goeben, Jan. 1918 (despatches); in destroyers till Sept. 1918; joined Submarines Sept. 1918; Trinity Coll., Cambridge, 1919; in Submarines 1918-33, having first command in 1924; this period broken by 3 months in command special service vessel in Pearl and West Rivers, China, during anti-foreign trouble, 1925; also in Caledon, Ramillies and Malaya, 1927-29; Erebus, 1934-37; Staff of Tactical Sch., Portsmouth, 1937; Hawkins and Effingham (Reserve Fleet Flagships), 1937-40; took part in blocking of Zeebrugge harbour, commanding Atlantic Guide, and Dunkirk harbour, commanding Pacifico in May and June 1940 (DSC); Senior Officer Channel Mobile Balloon Barrage, 1940-43 (despatches, DSO); Senior Officer 9th LST Flotilla, 1943-44, Italy, India (despatches), Invasion of Normandy (despatches); Senior Officer LST SE Asia, 1944-46; retired Sept. 1946. Encyclopædia Britannica Ltd, 1946-56. *Address:* Anglesea Cottage, Auckland Road West, Southsea. *T:* Portsmouth 23074.

**OWO, The Olowo of;** *see* Olagbegi II.

**OXBORROW, Brigadier Claud Catton,** CMG 1954; CBE 1945; MC 1917, and Bar 1918; retired; *b* 24 July 1898; *o s* of Arthur J. Oxborrow; *m* 1928, Joy Meredith McDougall (*d* 1965); one *s. Educ:* Portsmouth; Sandhurst. Served European War (MC and Bar): commissioned Royal Hampshire Regt, 1916, France and Italy, Adjutant, 1922-25; ADC to GOC-in-C, Middle East, 1926-28; retired, 1928. War of 1939-45 (CBE): rejoined from RARO, 1939; Lieut-Colonel 1941, Brigadier 1943, France, Normandy, Germany. Temp. Asst Secretary, Foreign Office, 1946-53. US Legion of Merit, 1944. *Recreations:* cricket, shooting. *Address:* Mill Street, Polstead, Suffolk. *T:* Nayland 306.

**OXBURY, Harold Frederick,** CMG 1961; Deputy Director-General, British Council, 1962-66 (Assistant Director-General, 1959); *b*

11 Nov. 1903; *s* of Fredric Thomas Oxbury; *m* 1st, 1928, Violet Bennets (*d* 1954); one *s* one *d*; 2nd, 1954, Helen Shipley, *d* of Amos Perry, FLS, VMH. *Educ:* Norwich Sch.; Trinity Coll., Cambridge. Entered Indian Civil Service, 1928; Chief Collector of Customs, Burma, 1940; Government of Burma Representative, Burma Office, 1942-44; Dep. Controller Finance (Colonel), Military Administration, Burma, 1945; Finance Secretary, Government of Burma, 1946; British Council: Director, Colonies Dept, 1947; Controller Finance, 1956. *Recreations:* walking and gardening. *Address:* Heath Farm, West Runton, Norfolk.

**OXFORD, Bishop of,** since 1971; **Rt Rev. Kenneth John Woollcombe;** *b* 2 Jan. 1924; *s* of Rev. E. P. Woollcombe, OBE, and Elsie Ockenden Woollcombe; *m* 1950, Gwendoline Rhona Vyvien Hodges; three *d. Educ:* Haileybury Coll., Hertford; St John's Coll., Oxford; Westcott House, Cambridge. Sub-Lieut (E) RNVR, 1945. Curate, St James, Grimsby, 1951; Fellow, Chaplain and Tutor, St John's Coll., Oxford, 1953; Professor of Dogmatic Theology, General Theological Seminary, New York, 1960; Principal of Episcopal Theological Coll., Edinburgh, 1963. STD Univ. of the South, Sewanee, USA, 1963. *Publications:* (contrib.) The Historic Episcopate, 1954; (jointly) Essays on Typology, 1957. *Address:* Bishop's House, Cuddesdon, Oxford.

**OXFORD, CHRIST CHURCH, Dean of;** *see* Chadwick, Very Rev. Henry.

**OXFORD, Archdeacon of;** *see* Witton-Davies, Ven. Carlyle.

**OXFORD AND ASQUITH,** 2nd Earl of, *cr* 1925; **Julian Edward George Asquith,** KCMG 1964 (CMG 1961); Viscount Asquith, *cr* 1925; Governor and Commander-in-Chief, Seychelles, 1962-67; Commissioner, British Indian Ocean Territory, 1965-67; *b* 22 April 1916; *o s* of late Raymond Asquith and Katharine Frances, *d* of late Sir John Horner, KCVO; *S* grandfather, 1928; *m* 1947, Anne Mary Celestine, CStJ, *d* of late Sir Michael Palairet, KCMG; two *s* three *d. Educ:* Ampleforth; Balliol Coll., Oxford (Scholar). 1st Class Lit. Hum., 1938. Lieut, RE, 1941; Assistant District Commissioner, Palestine, 1942-48; Dep. Chief Secretary, British Administration, Tripolitania, 1949; Director of the Interior, Government of Tripolitania, 1951; Adviser to Prime Minister of Libya, 1952; Administrative Secretary, Zanzibar, 1955; Administrator of St Lucia, WI, 1958. KStJ. *Heir: s* Viscount Asquith, *qv. Address:* The Manor House, Mells, Frome, Somerset. *T:* Mells 324. *Clubs:* Bath, Brooks's. *See also Baron Hylton.*

**OXLEY, D. G. R.;** *see* Rice-Oxley.

**OXLEY, Humphrey Leslie Malcolm,** CMG 1966; OBE 1956; *b* 9 Oct. 1909; *s* of W. H. F. Oxley, MRCS, LRCP, FRCOG, and Lily Malcolm; *m* 1945, Frances Olga, *d* of George Bowden, San Jose, Costa Rica; twin *s. Educ:* Epsom Coll. Admitted Solicitor, 1933; Junior Legal Assistant, India Office, 1933; Commissioner for Oaths, 1934; Assistant Solicitor, 1944; Commonwealth Relations Office, 1947; Assistant Legal Adviser, 1961; Legal Counsellor, Commonwealth Office, 1965-67; HM Diplomatic Service, 1967; Dep. Legal Adviser, FCO, 1967-69. *Recreations:* sailing, gardening. *Address:* Sandpipers, Crooked Lane, Birdham, Chichester. *Club:* Civil Service.

**OXLEY, Maj.-General Walter Hayes,** CB 1947; CBE 1941; MC 1916; *b* 2 Jan. 1891; *s* of late Edward Hayes Oxley and Bessie Eleanor Paton; *d* of late J. P. Hindley; *m* 1921, Margaret, *d* of late W. James Smith, JP, Gibraltar and Villa Viega, Algeciras; one *d. Educ:* Eastbourne Coll.; RMA, Woolwich. 2nd Lieut, RE, 1911; served European War, 1914-18, in Egypt, Palestine and Macedonia (despatches, MC, Bt Major); Egyptian Army, 1918-19; psc; Military Attaché HM Legations, Belgrade and Prague; Bt Lieut-Colonel, 1931; AQMG British Military Mission to Egyptian Army; Order of Nile, 3rd Class; Brigadier, i/c Admin., Malta; War of 1939-45, commanded 2nd Inf. Bde, Malta, then 7th Inf. Bde 3rd Division in UK; GOC Malta, 1943-44; Commissioner British Military Mission, Bulgaria, 1944-47. Acting Maj.-General, 1943; Temp. Maj.-General, 1944; ADC to the King, 1943-48; retired pay, 1948. *Recreations:* shooting, fishing and golf. *Address:* Charminster House, Dorchester, Dorset. *T:* Dorchester 238. *Club:* Naval and Military.

**OXMANTOWN, Lord; William Brendan Parsons;** Assistant Resident Representative of UN Development Programme in Iran, since 1970; *b* 21 Oct. 1936; *s* and *heir* of 6th Earl of Rosse, *qv; m* 1966, Alison Margaret, *er d* of Major J. D. Cooke-Hurle, Startforth Hall, Barnard Castle, Co. Durham; one *s. Educ:* Eton; Grenoble Univ.; Christ Church, Oxford. BA 1961, MA 1964. 2nd Lieut, Irish Guards, 1955-57. UN Official appointed successively: Admin. Officer, UNTAB, Ghana, 1963-65; Asst Resident Rep., UNDP, Dahomey, 1965-68; Area Officer for Mid-West Africa, 1968-70. *Heir: s* Hon. Laurence Patrick Parsons, *b* 31 March 1969. *Address:* (Home) Birr Castle, Co. Offaly, Ireland. *T:* Birr 23.

# P

**PACE, George Gaze,** FRIBA; Architect in Private Practice since 1949; *b* 31 Dec. 1915; *s* of George Henry and Alice Barbara Pace, Croydon; *m* 1941, Ina Catherine, *d* of Harvey Sheridan Jones; three *s* two *d. Educ:* privately; articled James Ransome, FRIBA, London; School of Architecture, Polytechnic, London. Lecturer, School of Architecture, Polytechnic, London, 1939-41. Queen's Royal Regt, RE, 1941-42; Superintending Valuer, WO (Major, Gen. List), 1942-49. Surveyor to Dio. of Sheffield, 1949-56; Cons. Architect to Cathedrals of: Lichfield, 1949; Llandaff, 1949; Sheffield, 1953-61; Durham, 1954; Peterborough, 1956; Chester, 1961; Liverpool (Anglican), 1962; St Alban's, 1962; Newcastle, 1966; Surveyor, St George's Chapel, Windsor Castle, 1969. Cons. Architect to Dioceses of: Wakefield, 1948, Bradford, 1949, Sheffield, 1956, York, 1957, Llandaff, 1967, and Monmouth, 1969; Hon. Cons. Architect: Historic Churches Preservation Trust; Yorks Architectural and York Archæological Society; Member, York Diocesan Advisory Cttee; Vice-President, New Churches Research Group. RIBA Pugin Student, 1936; Robert Mitchell Gold Medallist, 1936; RIBA Ashpitel Prizeman, 1938; MA Lambeth, 1961. FRIBA 1949; FSA 1950. *Work includes:* rebuilding Llandaff Cathedral, 1949-63; Chapel of the Resurrection, University of Ibadan, 1951-62;

completion schemes, Sheffield Cathedral, 1955-61; Holy Trinity, Newport, Mon, 1958; All Saints', Doncaster, 1958; Scargill Religious Centre, 1958; The Chapel, St Michael's Theological Coll., Llandaff, 1959; New Cathedral, Ibadan, 1960-; St Mark's, Sheffield, 1963; St Mark's, Chadderton, 1963; Caer Eirthin Church, Swansea, 1963; Chapel Complex, Keele Univ., 1965; William Temple Memorial Church, Wythenshawe, 1965; St John's Coll., York Chapel, 1966; Durham Univ. Library, 1966; St Andrew's, Rushmere, 1968; (in association with Paul Paget) King George VI Memorial Chapel and Tomb, Windsor Castle, 1969; Woolston Church, 1970; St Martin, Thornaby, 1970; *restorations include:* Castle Howard; Bramham Park; parish churches of: Boston; Louth; St Mary's, Beverley; Selby Abbey; Doncaster; Branston; *alterations etc to churches include:* Armagh Cathedral; Great St Mary's, Cambridge; Luton; Pershore Abbey; Wycliffe Hall, Oxford; St Martin's, Birmingham; Bramhall; St Aidan's Theological Coll. Chapel; St Michael's, Cambridge; St Martin le Grand, York, 1968. S Mary's Church, Luton, 1969; Organcase, New Coll., Oxford, 1969. *Publications:* contributions to: Chambers's Encyclopædia, 1948 and 1963; Collins' Guide to English Parish Churches, 1958, 1968; The Church and the Arts, 1960; Making the Building Fit the Liturgy, 1962; The York Aesthetic, 1962; The Modern Architectural Setting of the Liturgy, 1964; contributions to technical, archæological and ecclesiological journals. *Recreations:* walking, looking at old buildings. *Address:* 18 Clifton Green, York. *T:* York 55029. *Clubs:* Athenæum, Art Workers' Guild.

**PÄCHT, Otto Ernst,** MA, DPhil; FBA 1956; Professor in the History of Art, and Director of the Kunsthistorisches Institut, Vienna University, since 1963; *b* Vienna, 7 Sept. 1902; *s* of David and Josephine Pächt; *m* 1940, Jeanne Michalopulo; one *s*. *Educ:* Vienna and Berlin Universities. Lecturer in History of Art: Heidelberg Univ., 1933; Oriel Coll., Oxford, 1945. Senior Lecturer in Medieval Art, 1952, Reader, 1962, Oxford Univ. Membre de la Société Archéologique française. Wirkl. Mitgl. Oesterr. Akad. Wissenschaft, 1967. *Publications:* Oesterreichische Tafelmalerei der Gotik, 1929; Master of Mary of Burgundy, 1948; The St Albans Psalter, 1960; The Rise of Pictorial Narrative in Twelfth-century England, 1962; Vita Sancti Simperti, 1964; contrib. to Kritische Berichte, Kunstwissenschaftliche Forschungen, Burlington Magazine, Journal of the Warburg Institute, Revue des Arts. *Address:* Pötzleinsdorferstrasse 66, 1180 Vienna, Austria.

**PACK, Prof. Donald Cecil,** OBE 1969; MA, DSc, FRSE; Professor of Mathematics, University of Strathclyde, Glasgow, since 1953, Vice-Principal, since 1968; *b* 14 April 1920; *s* of John Cecil and late Minnie Pack; *m* 1947, Constance Mary Gillam; two *s* one *d*. *Educ:* Wellingborough School; New Coll., Oxford. Lecturer in Mathematics, University College, Dundee, University of St Andrews, 1947-52; Visiting Research Associate, University of Maryland, 1951-52; Lecturer in Mathematics, University of Manchester, 1952-53. Chm., Scottish Certificate of Educn Examn Bd; Mem. of Various Govt Scientific Cttees, 1952-; Mem., General Teaching Council for Scotland. Fellow and Hon. Treasurer of Institute of Mathematics and its Applications. *Publications:* Papers on fluid dynamics. *Recreations:* music, gardening. *Address:* 3 Horseshoe Road, Bearsden, Glasgow. *T:* 041-942 5764.

**PACK, Captain Stanley Walter Croucher,** CBE 1957; RN, retired; Author since 1927; *b* 14 Dec. 1904; *s* of Walter Edward Pack and Beatrice Eleanor (*née* Croucher); *m* 1934, Dorothea Edna Mary (*née* Rowe); one *s* one *d*. *Educ:* St John's, Malta; Imperial College of Science. Whitworth Scholar, 1924; John Samuel Scholar, 1925; 1st class hons BSc (Engineering) 1926; ACGI 1926; MSc 1927; DIC 1927. Served War of 1939-45: HMS Formidable, 1940-41; British Commonwealth Secretary, Combined Meteorological Cttee, Washington, 1941-43; Chief Naval Met. Officer to SACSEA, 1945. Dep. Director, Naval Weather Service, Admiralty, 1951-54; Dep. Director, Naval Education Service, Admiralty, 1956-58; ADC to the Queen, 1957-60; retired RN, 1960. Member Society of Authors; Member Navy Records Society; Member Cttee, Old Centralians Assoc.; MIEE 1946; FRMetS 1950. Boyle Somerville Memorial Prize for Meteorology, 1938. Officer, Legion of Merit, USA, 1948. *Publications:* Anson's Voyage, 1947; Weather Forecasting, 1948; Admiral Lord Anson, 1960; Battle of Matapan, 1961; Windward of the Caribbean, 1964; The Wager Mutiny, 1965; Britannia at Dartmouth, 1966; History of Sea Power in the Mediterranean, 1971; contributions to Blackwood's Magazine, 1937- and to Daily Telegraph, Sunday Times, The Field, The Navy, etc. *Recreations:* music, sketching. *Address:* Blossom's Pasture, Strete, Dartmouth, Devon. *T:* Stoke Fleming 254. *Club:* Royal Ocean Racing.

**PACKARD, Lt-Gen. Sir (Charles) Douglas,** KBE 1957 (CBE 1945; OBE 1942); CB 1949; DSO 1943; retired as GOC-in-C Northern Ireland Command, 1958-61; *b* 17 May 1903; *s* of late Capt. C. T. Packard, MC, Copdock, near Ipswich; *m* 1937, Marion Lochhead; one *s* two *d*. *Educ:* Winchester; Royal Military Academy, Woolwich. 2nd Lieut, RA, 1923; served War of 1939-45, in Middle East and Italy (despatches, OBE, DSO, CBE); Dep.-Chief of Staff, 15th Army Group, 1944-45; Temp. Maj.-Gen. and Chief of Staff, Allied Commission for Austria (British Element), 1945-46; Director of Military Intelligence, WO, 1948-49; Commander British Military Mission in Greece, 1949-51; Chief of Staff, GHQ, MELF, 1951-53; Vice-Quarter-Master-General War Office, 1953-56; Military Adviser to the West African Governments, 1956-58. Lt-Gen. 1957. Col Comdt, RA, 1957-62. Officer Legion of Merit (USA). *Recreations:* shooting, sailing. *Address:* Limes Farm House, Eyke, nr Woodbridge, Suffolk. *T:* Eyke 298. *Club:* Army and Navy.

**PACKARD, Vance (Oakley);** Author; *b* 22 May 1914; *s* of Philip and Mabel Packard; *m* 1938, Mamie Virginia Mathews; two *s* one *d*. *Educ:* Pennsylvania State Univ.; Columbia Univ. Reporter, The Boston Record, 1938; Feature Editor, The Associated Press, 1939-42; Editor and Staff Writer, The American Magazine, 1942-56; Staff writer, Colliers, 1956; Distinguished Alumni Award, Pennsylvania State University, 1961; Outstanding Alumni Award, Columbia University Graduate School of Journalism, 1963. *Publications:* (books on social criticism): The Hidden Persuaders, 1957; The Status Seekers, 1959; The Waste Makers, 1960; The Pyramid Climbers, 1962; The Naked Society, 1964; The Sexual Wilderness, 1968; numerous articles for The Atlantic Monthly. *Recreations:* reading, boating. *Address:* Mill Road, New Canaan, Conn. 06840, USA. *T:* WO 6-1707.

**PACKER, Sir (Douglas) Frank (Hewson),** Kt 1959; CBE 1951; Managing Director, Australian Consolidated Press Ltd, since 1936;

*b* 3 Dec. 1906; *s* of Robert Clyde and Ethel Maud Packer; *m* 1934, Gretel Joyce (*d* 1960), *d* of Dr H. H. Bullmore; two *s*; *m* 1964, Florence A., *d* of Edmond Porges, OBE, Paris, France. *Educ:* Sydney Church of England Grammar Sch., New South Wales. Cadet Reporter, Daily Guardian, 1923; Asst Business Manager, 1926; Director and Gen. Advertising Manager, Daily Guardian, and Smith's Weekly, 1927. One of founders of Australian Women's Weekly, 1933; President, Australian Newspapers Conf., 1939-40; AIF, 1941-42; Director of Personnel, Allied Works Council, 1942-44; returned to AIF, 1944-45; President, Australian Associated Press Pty Ltd, 1951; Director, Reuters Ltd, 1954-56 and 1962-; Chairman TV Corp. Ltd, 1955; Chairman General TV Corp. Pty Ltd, Melbourne, 1960. *Publications:* Daily Telegraph, 1936; Sunday Telegraph, 1939; Australian Women's Weekly, 1933; Bulletin, 1960. *Recreations:* polo, golf, yachting. *Address:* (home) 76/8 Victoria Road, Bellevue Hill, NSW 2023, Australia. *T:* Sydney 36-5685; (business) Australian Consolidated Press Ltd, Box 4088, GPO, Sydney, NSW 2001, Australia. *T:* Sydney 20-666. *Clubs:* Devonshire, Savage (London); New South Wales, University, Australian Golf, Royal Sydney Yacht Squadron (Sydney); New York Yacht.

**PACKER, Joy, (Lady Packer);** Author; *b* S Africa, 11 Feb. 1905; *d* of late Dr and Mrs Julius Petersen, Cape Town; *m* 1925, Lieut-Commander Herbert Packer, RN (Admiral Sir Herbert Packer, *d* 1962); one *s*. *Educ:* St Cyprian's Sch., Cape Town; University of Cape Town. Free-lance journalist Cape Town, 1924; News Reporter, Daily Express (London), 1931-32; Hongkong Radio Women's Features, 1932-35; in Balkans, 1936-39, contributing articles to various British publications; in London, 1939-43, writing for various War organisations and broadcasting to S Africa for the BBC, London. Lent to Ministry of Information (Egypt), 1943; Psychological Warfare Branch of Allied HQ, Italy, 1944-45. *Publications:* Quintette (travel autobiographies): Pack and Follow, 1945; Grey Mistress, 1949; Apes and Ivory, 1953; Home from Sea, 1963; The World is a Proud Place, 1966; *fiction:* Valley of the Vines, 1955; Nor the Moon by Night, 1957; The High Roof, 1959; The Glass Barrier, 1961; The Man in the Mews, 1964; The Blind Spot, 1967; Leopard in the Fold, 1969; Veronica, 1970. *Recreations:* travel and the study of wild life. *Address:* 101 Grosvenor Square, Rondebosch, Cape Peninsula, S Africa. *Club:* Western Province Sports.

**PADLEY, Walter Ernest;** MP (Lab) Ogmore Division of Glamorganshire since 1950; Member National Exec. Cttee of Labour Party, since 1956 (Chairman, Labour Party, 1965-66; Overseas Cttee, 1963-); represents Labour Party on Bureau of Socialist International and on Action Committee for United States of Europe; *b* 24 July 1916; *s* of Ernest and Mildred Padley; *m* 1942, Sylvia Elsie Wilson; one *s* one *d*. *Educ:* Chipping Norton Grammar Sch.; Ruskin Coll., Oxford. Active in distributive workers' trade union, 1933-; President, Union of Shop, Distributive and Allied Workers, 1948-64. Member of National Council of Independent Labour Party, 1940-46. Minister of State for Foreign Affairs, 1964-67. *Publications:* The Economic Problem of the Peace, 1944; Am I My Brother's Keeper?, 1945; Britain: Pawn or Power?, 1947; USSR Empire or Free Union?, 1948. *Address:* 73 Priory Gardens, Highgate, N6. *T:* 01-340 2969.

**PADMORE, Sir Thomas,** GCB 1965 (KCB 1953; CB 1947); MA; MInstT; Director, Cammell, Laird & Co. Ltd; Member, Metrication Board; *b* 23 April 1909; *e s* of Thomas William Padmore, Sheffield; *m* 1st, 1934, Alice (*d* 1963), *d* of Robert Alcock, Ormskirk; two *d* (one *s* decd); 2nd, 1964, Rosalind Culhane, *qv*. *Educ:* Central Sch., Sheffield; Queens' Coll., Cambridge (Foundation Scholar; Hon. Fellow, 1961). Secretaries' Office, Board of Inland Revenue, 1931-34; transferred to Treasury, 1934; Principal Private Secretary to Chancellor of Exchequer, 1943-45; Second Secretary, 1952-62; Permanent Sec., Min. of Transport, 1962-68. *Address:* 39 Cholmeley Crescent, Highgate, N6. *T:* 01-340 6587. *Club:* Reform.

**PADMORE, Lady (Thomas);** *see* Culhane, Rosalind.

**PADWICK, Surgeon-Captain Harold Boultbee,** DSO 1917; RN, retired; MA, MB, BCh, DMRE (Cambridge), LMSSA (London); retired radiologist; late Hon. Radiologist, Bedford County Hospital; Radiologist, St Peter's Hospital, Bedford; Consulting Radiologist, Kettering General Hospital; Member of British Institute of Radiology; *b* 1889; *o s* of late F. H. Padwick, CBE, of Thorney Manor and West Ashling, Sussex; *m* 1921, Edith Gwendolen Carr; one *s* two *d*. *Educ:* Sherborne; Emmanuel Coll., Cambridge; London Hospital. Served European War, 1914-19 (despatches, DSO); retired as Surgeon Captain RN, 1932; Gilbert Blane medal, 1924. *Recreation:* fly-fishing. *Address:* Swallowfield Park, Swallowfield, nr Reading.

**PAFFARD, Rear-Admiral (retired) Ronald Wilson,** CB 1960; CBE 1943; *b* Ludlow, 14 Feb. 1904; 4th *s* of Murray Paffard and Fanny (*née* Wilson); *m* 1933, Nancy Brenda Malim; one *s* one *d*. *Educ:* Maidstone Grammar Sch. Paymaster Cadetship in RN, 1922; Paymaster Commander, 1940; Captain (S), 1951; Rear-Admiral, 1957. Secretary to Adm. of the Fleet Lord Tovey in all his Flag appointments, including those throughout the War of 1939-45; Supply Officer of HMS Vengeance, 1946-48; Portsmouth Division, Reserve Fleet, 1948-50; HMS Eagle, 1950-51; Asst Director-General, Supply and Secretarial Branch, 1952-54; Commanding Officer, HMS Ceres, 1954-56; Chief Staff Officer (Administration) on staff of Commander-in-Chief, Portsmouth, 1957-60, retired. *Recreations:* painting, golf. *Address:* 2 Little Green Orchard, Alverstoke, Hants.

**PAFFORD, John Henry Pyle,** MA, DLit (London); FSA; FLA; Goldsmiths' Librarian of the University of London, 1945-67; *b* 6 March 1900; *s* of John Pafford and Bessie Pyle; *m* 1941, Elizabeth Ford, *d* of R. Charles Ford and Margaret Harvey; one *d* (and one *d* decd). *Educ:* Trowbridge High Sch.; University Coll., London (Fellow, 1956). Library Asst, University College, London, 1923-25; Librarian, and Tutor, Selly Oak Colleges, 1925-31; Sub-Librarian, National Central Library, 1931-45; Lecturer at University of London School of Librarianship, 1937-61. War Office book supply and libraries for army education, 1944-45. Editor, Year's Work in Librarianship, 1935-38 (jointly), and 1939-46; Library Adviser, Inter-Univ. Council for Higher Education Overseas, 1960-68. *Publications:* Bale's King Johan, 1931, and The Sodder'd Citizen, 1936 (Malone Society); Library co-operation in Europe, 1935; Accounts of Parliamentary Garrisons of Great Chalfield and Malmesbury, 1645-46, 1940; Books and Army Education, 1946; American and Canadian libraries, 1949; W. P. Ker, a bibliography, 1950; Mundy's Chrusothriambos, 1962; The Winter's Tale (Arden Shakespeare), 1963. *Address:* Hillside, Allington Park, Bridport, Dorset. *T:* Bridport 2829.

**PAGAN, Brig. John Ernest,** CMG 1969; MBE 1943; ED; Chairman and Managing Director, P. Rowe Industries Pty Ltd and subsidiary companies, since 1958; *b* 13 May 1914; *s* of late D. C. Pagan, Hay, NSW; *m* 1948, Marjorie Hoskins; one *s* two *d*. *Educ:* St Peter's Coll., Adelaide. Served RAA, AIF, Middle East, Papua/New Guinea, 1939-45; Citizen Military Forces, 1948-62. Chm., P. Rowe International Pty Ltd, 1962-; Director: Northern Life Assurance Co. of Australia Ltd, 1959-68; Adv. Board, Northern Life Assurance Co. of Australia Ltd, 1963-; NSW Permanent Building Society Ltd and subsidiaries, 1963-. Hon. ADC to Governor of NSW, 1950-55; District Comr Boy Scouts' Assoc., 1952-58, Pres., E Metropolitan Area, 1962-; Mem. Board, NSW Soc. for Crippled Children, 1967-; Chm. Council, Big Brother Movement, 1947-; Mem. Board, Church of England Retirement Villages, 1961-; Mem., Commonwealth Immigration Adv. Council, 1959-; Governor, Frensham Sch.; Councillor, Nat. Heart Foundn. Liberal Party of Australia: State Pres., NSW, 1963-66; Federal Pres., 1966-70. *Address:* 93 Wolseley Road, Point Piper, NSW 2021, Australia. *T:* 36 4685. Clubs: Imperial Service, Union, Australasian Pioneers, Royal Sydney Golf (Sydney); Melbourne (Melbourne); Commonwealth (Canberra).

**PAGE, Ven. Alfred Charles;** Archdeacon of Leeds since 1969; Vicar of Arthington, Yorks, since 1969; Hon. Canon of Ripon since 1966; *b* 24 Dec. 1912; *s* of late Henry Page, Homersfield, Suffolk; *m* 1944, Margaret Stevenson, *d* of late Surtees Foster Dodd, Sunderland, Co. Durham. *Educ:* Bungay Grammar Sch.; Corpus Christi Coll., Cambridge (MA); Wycliffe Hall, Oxford. Curate: Wortley-de-Leeds, 1936; Leeds Parish Church, 1940 (Sen. Curate and Priest-in-charge of S Mary, Quarry Hill, 1941); Vicar: St Mark, Woodhouse, Leeds, 1944; Rothwell, Yorks, 1955. Rural Dean of: Whitkirk, 1961; Surrogate, 1963. *Recreation:* photography. *Address:* Arthington Vicarage, Otley, Yorks LS21 1PL. *T:* Arthington 2368.

**PAGE, Col Alfred John,** CB 1964; TD 1945; DL; Chairman, TA&VR Association for Greater London, since 1968 (Chairman, County of London T&AFA, 1957-68); *b* 3 January 1912; *s* of Harry Gould Page, Surbiton, Surrey; *m* 1941, Sheila Margaret Aileen (marr. diss. 1966), *d* of Charles Skinner Wilson, Ugley, Essex; one *s* two *d*; *m* 1969, Margaret Mary Juliet Driver, *widow* of Arnold Driver. Educ: Westminster School. 2nd Lt 19th London Regt (TA), 1931. Served 1939-45 with RA in AA Comd. Brevet Colonel 1952; ADC (TA) to the Queen, 1961-66; Hon. Col, Greater London Regt RA (Territorials), 1967. DL Co. of London, 1951; DL Greater London, 1965. *Address:* 66 Iverna Court, W8. *T:* 01-937 2590. *Clubs:* Army and Navy, Hurlingham.

**PAGE, Annette, (Mrs Ronald Hynd);** Ballerina of the Royal Ballet, 1959-67, retired; *b* 18 Dec. 1932; *d* of James Lees and Margaret Page; *m* 1957, Ronald Hynd, principal dancer and partner in Royal Ballet; one *d*. *Educ:* Royal Ballet School. Audition and award of scholarship to Roy. Ballet Sch., 1944. Entry into touring company of Royal Ballet (then Sadler's Wells Theatre Ballet), 1950; promotion to major Royal Ballet Co. (Sadler's Wells Ballet), 1955. *Roles include:* The Firebird, Dec. 1958; Princess Aurora, May 1959; Odette-Odile, June 1959; Giselle, March 1960; Lise in La Fille Mal Gardée, 1963; Romeo and Juliet, 1965; Cinderella, 1966. *Recreations:* music, books.

**PAGE, (Arthur) John;** MP (C) Harrow West since March 1960; *b* 16 Sept. 1919; *s* of Sir Arthur Page, QC (late Chief Justice of Burma), and Lady Page, KiH; *m* 1950, Anne, *d* of Charles Micklem, DSO, JP, DL, Longcross House, Surrey; four *s*. *Educ:* Harrow, Magdalene College, Cambridge. Joined RA as Gunner, 1939, commissioned, 1940; served War of 1939-45, Western Desert (wounded), France, Germany; demobilised as Major, comdg 258 Battery Norfolk Yeomanry, 1945; various positions in industry and commerce, 1946-63. Chm. Bethnal Green and E London Housing Assoc., 1957-; contested (C) Eton and Slough, Gen. Election, 1959. PPS to Parly Under-Sec. of State, Home Office, 1961-63; Conservative Parly Labour Affairs Cttee: Sec., 1960-61, 1964-, Vice-Chm. 1966, Chm. 1970. Pres., Cons. Trade Unionists Nat. Adv. Council, 1967-69; Mem. Exec., IPU, British Gp, 1970; Vice-Pres., Independent Schools Assoc., 1970. *Recreations:* painting and politics. *Address:* Hitcham Lodge, Taplow, Bucks. *T:* Burnham 5056. *Clubs:* Brooks's, MCC.

**PAGE, Bertram Samuel;** University Librarian and Keeper of the Brotherton Collection, University of Leeds, 1947-69, Emeritus Librarian, since 1969; *b* 1 Sept. 1904; *s* of Samuel and Catherine Page; *m* 1933, Olga Ethel, *d* of E. W. Mason. *Educ:* King Charles I School Kidderminster; University of Birmingham. BA 1924, MA 1926. Asst Librarian (later Sub-Librarian), Univ. of Birmingham, 1931-36; Librarian, King's College, Newcastle upon Tyne, 1936-47. Pres. Library Assoc., 1960 (Hon. Fellow, 1961); Chairman: Standing Conf. of Nat. and Univ. Libraries, 1961-63; Exec. Cttee, Nat. Central Library, 1962- (Trustee, 1963-); Librarianship Bd, Council for Nat. Academic Awards, 1966-. mem. Court of Univ. of Birmingham, 1954-69. Hon. DUniv. York, 1968. *Publications:* contrib. to Stephen MacKenna's trans. of Plotinus, vol. 5, 1930 (revised whole trans. for 2nd, 3rd, 4th edns, 1958, 1962, 1969); A Manual of University and College Library Practice (jt ed.), 1940; articles and reviews in classical and library jls. *Address:* 24 St Anne's Road, Headington, Oxford. *T:* Oxford 65981.

**PAGE, Ven. Dennis Fountain;** Archdeacon of Huntingdon and Vicar of Yaxley, Huntingdonshire, since 1965; *b* 1 Dec. 1919; *s* of Prebendary Martin Fountain Page and Lilla Fountain Page; *m* 1946, Margaret Bettine Clayton; two *s* one *d*. *Educ:* Shrewsbury Sch.; Gonville and Caius Coll., Cambridge (MA); Lincoln Theological Coll. Curate, Rugby Parish Church, 1943; Priest-in-Charge, St George's Church, Hillmorton, Rugby, 1945; Rector of Hockwold, Vicar of Wilton and Rector of Weeting, Norfolk, 1949; Hon. Canon of Ely Cathedral, 1968. *Recreations:* music, carpentry, gardening. *Address:* Yaxley Vicarage, Peterborough. *T:* Yaxley 339.

**PAGE, Prof. Denys Lionel,** LittD 1960; FBA 1952; Master of Jesus College, Cambridge, since 1959; Regius Professor of Greek, Cambridge University, since 1950; Hon. Student of Christ Church, Oxford; Hon. Fellow of Trinity Coll., Cambridge; *b* 1908; *s* of F. H. D. Page, OBE, and Elsie Page, MBE; *m* 1938, Katharine Elizabeth, *d* of late Joseph Michael and Edith Hall Dohan, Philadelphia, Pa, USA; four *d*. *Educ:* Newbury; Christ Church, Oxford (Schol.). 1st Cl. Hons Class. Mods, Chancellor's Prize for Latin Verse,

Gaisford Prize for Greek Verse, de Paravicini Schol., Craven Schol., 1928; 1st Cl. Lit. Hum., Derby, Univ. and Goldsmiths' Company's senior Schols, 1930. Vienna Univ., 1930-31; Lecturer of Ch. Ch., 1931-32; Student and Tutor, 1932-50; Senior Proctor, 1948-49. Dean West Lecturer at Princeton Univ., US, 1939; Flexner Lecturer at Bryn Mawr, 1954; Sather Lecturer, Univ. of California, 1957-58. Dept of Foreign Office, 1939-46. Head of Command Unit, Intelligence Division, HQ South-East Asia, 1945-46. Foreign Mem., Amer. Philosophical Soc.; Hon. Fellow: Archæological Soc. of Athens; Hellenic Soc. of Humanities. Kenyon Medal, British Academy. Hon. LittD: Trinity Coll., Dublin; Newcastle Univ.; Hull Univ. *Publications:* Actors' Interpolations in Greek Tragedy, 1934; Euripides' Medea, 1938; Greek Literary Papyri, 1941; Alcman, 1951; Corinna, 1953; Sappho and Alcaeus, 1955; The Homeric Odyssey, 1955; (co-editor), Poetarum Lesbiorum Fragmenta, 1955; (co-editor), Aeschylus, Agamemnon, 1957; History and Master's Homeric Iliad, 1959; Poetae Melici Graeci, 1962; The Oxyrhynchus Papyri, vol. xxix, 1964; (co-editor), The Greek Anthology: Hellenistic Epigrams, 1965; The Garland of Philip, 1968; Melica Graeca Selecta, 1968; The Santorini Volcano and the Destruction of Minoan Crete, 1971. *Address:* The Master's Lodge, Jesus College, Cambridge. *T:* 53310.

**PAGE, Derek;** *see* Page, J. D.

**PAGE, Brig. (Edwin) Kenneth,** CBE 1951 (OBE 1946); DSO 1945; MC 1918; *b* 23 Jan. 1898; *s* of G. E. Page, Baldock, Herts; *m* 1921, Kate Mildred, *d* of G. H. Arthur, Yorkshire, Barbados, BWI; two *s*. *Educ:* Haileybury College; RMA, Woolwich. 2nd Lt, RFA, 1916; BEF, France, 1916-18. Adjt TA, 1924-27; Staff College, Camberley, 1928-29; Staff Captain, India, 1931-35; GSO2, War Office, 1936-39; Lt-Col, 1939; served War of 1939-45: BEF, France, 1940; Col, 1945; Brig., 1946; Dep. Director, WO, 1946-48; Commander, Caribbean Area, 1948-51; employed War Office, 1951; retired pay, 1952. CC 1961, CA 1968, Dorset. *Address:* 12 De Maulley Road, Canford Cliffs, Poole, Dorset. *T:* Canford Cliffs 77181. *Club:* Army and Navy. *See also Prof. J. K. Page.*

**PAGE, Graham;** *see* Page, R. G.

**PAGE, Harold James,** CMG 1951; OBE 1947 (MBE 1919); BSc, FRIC; Fellow of University College, London; *b* 29 May 1890; *s* of James William Page and Alice (*née* Jones); *m* 1915, Gladys Isabel (*d* 1969); *d* of E. E. Shepperd, Chelsfield, Kent; one *s* one *d* (and one *s* killed on active service). *Educ:* Southend High School; University College, London (Andrews Scholar and University Exhibitioner; Tuffnell Scholar, 1851 Science Research Scholar); Berlin; Paris; Bsc 1910. Lecturer in Biochemistry, University College, London, 1910-12; served Royal Artillery, France, 1914-16, Royal Arsenal, Woolwich, 1917-19 (despatches thrice, Captain); Head of Chemistry Department, Royal Horticultural Society's Laboratories, Wisley, 1919-20; Chief Chemist and Head of Chemistry Department, Rothamsted Experimental Station, 1920-27; Head of ICI Agricultural Research Station, Jealotts Hill, 1927-32; Controller of Agricultural Research of Imperial Chemical Industries, Ltd, 1932-36; Director Rubber Research Institute of Malaya, Kuala Lumpur, Malaya, 1936-46; interned in Sumatra Camp, Mar. 1942 to Aug. 1945; Principal, Imperial College of Tropical Agriculture, Trinidad, 1947-52; on staff of Food and Agriculture Organization of the United Nations, 1952-55; Editor, Empire Journal of Experimental Agriculture, 1955-64. Member of various scientific societies. *Publications:* papers and articles in scientific journals on the results of research in chemistry, soil science, and agriculture. *Recreations:* photography, gardening. *Address:* 19 South Pallant, Chichester, Sussex. *Club:* Farmers'.

**PAGE, Sir Harry (Robertson),** Kt 1968; City Treasurer, Manchester, since 1957; *b* 14 Apr. 1911; *s* of late Henry Page and Dora (*née* Robertson); *m* 1937, Elsie Dixon; two *s*. *Educ:* Manchester Grammar Sch.; Manchester University. BA (Admin) 1932; MA (Admin) 1934. FIMTA 1957 (Associate, 1938; Pres., 1968). Appointed City Treasurer's Dept, Manchester, 1927, Dep. Treas., 1952. Sen. Hon. Financial Adviser to Assoc. of Municipal Corps, 1962-. Haldane Medal (RIPA), 1933. *Publications:* Co-ordination and Planning in the Local Authority, 1936; Councillor's Handbook, 1945; Local Government up-to-date, 1946; contrib. to symposium of papers given to British Assoc., Leeds, 1968; contribs to Local Govt Finance, Bank Reviews, financial jls, etc. *Recreation:* collecting Victorian and other nineteenth century ephemera. *Address:* 205 Old Hall Lane, Fallowfield, Manchester M14 6HJ. *T:* 061-224 2891. *Clubs:* National Liberal; Manchester (formerly Reform, Manchester).

**PAGE, John Brangwyn;** Chief Cashier of the Bank of England since 1970; *b* 23 Aug. 1923; *s* of Sidney John Page, *qv*; *m* 1948, Gloria Vail; one *s* one *d*. *Educ:* Highgate Sch. (Foundation Schol.); King's Coll., Cambrdige (BA). RAF, 1942-46; Cambridge, 1946-48; Bank of England, 1948; seconded to IMF, 1953; worked in various depts of Bank; Asst Chief Cashier, 1966; Deputy Chief Cashier, 1967; 1st Deputy Chief Cashier, 1968. *Recreations:* gardening, music, travel. *Address:* 74 Moor Lane, Rickmansworth, Herts. *T:* Rickmansworth 74531.

**PAGE, (John) Derek;** *b* 14 Aug. 1927; *s* of John Page and Clare Page (*née* Maher); *m* 1948, Catherine Audrey Halls; one *s* one *d*. *Educ:* St Bede's College, Manchester; London University. External BSc (Soc). MP (Lab) King's Lynn, 1964-70. Director: Cambridge Chemical Co. Ltd; Phoenix Aircraft Ltd; King's Lynn Engineering and Fabrication Ltd; Buckmaster and Page Ltd. *Recreation:* private pilot. *Address:* The Vicarage, Whaddon, Royston, Herts. *T:* Arrington 209. *Club:* Reform.

**PAGE, Prof. John Kenneth;** Professor of Building Science, University of Sheffield, since 1960; *b* 3 Nov. 1924; *s* of Brig. E. K. Page, *qv*; *m* 1954, Anita Bell Lovell; two *s* two *d*. *Educ:* Haileybury College; Pembroke College, Cambridge. Served War of 1939-45, Royal Artillery, 1943-47. Asst Industrial Officer, Council of Industrial Design, 1950-51; taught Westminster School, 1952-53; Sen. Scientific Officer, Tropical Liaison Section, Building Research Station, 1953-56; Chief Research Officer, Nuffield Div. for Architectural Studies, 1956-57; Lecturer, Dept. of Building Science, Univ. of Liverpool, 1957-60. Member: Econ. Planning Council, Yorks and Humberside Region; Construction Research Adv. Council. *Publications:* papers on Environmental Design and Planning and on Building Climatology. *Address:* c/o Department of Building Science, University of Sheffield. *T:* Sheffield 78555.

**PAGE, Kenneth;** *see* Page, Edwin Kenneth.

**PAGE, R(odney) Graham,** MBE 1944; LLB (London); MP (C) Crosby since November 1953; Minister for Local Government and Development, Department of the Environment, since Oct. 1970; Solicitor (admitted 1934); Privy Council Appeal Agent; *b* 30 June 1911; *s* of Lt-Col Frank Page, DSO and bar, and Margaret Payne Farley; *m* 1934, Hilda Agatha Dixon; one *s* one *d*. *Educ:* Magdalen College School, Oxford; London University (External). Served War of 1939-45: Flt-Lt, RAFVR. Formerly: A Governor of St Thomas' Hosp., London; Treas., Pedestrians' Assoc. for Road Safety; Vice-Pres., Southwark Chamber of Commerce; Vice-Pres., National Chamber of Trade; Sec., Parly All-Party Solicitors' Group; Dir, Property Owners' Building Soc., United Real Property Trust Ltd, and South of England Housing Soc. Promoter, as Private Member's Bills, of Cheques Act, 1957, Wages Bill, 1958, Pawnbrokers Act, 1960; Road Safety Bills 1960, 1964, 1965; Stock Transfer Act, 1963; National Sweepstakes Bill, 1966. Chm., Select Cttee on Statutory Instruments, 1964-70; an Opposition Front Bench spokesman on Housing and Land, 1965-70; Minister of State, Min. of Housing and Local Govt, June-Oct. 1970. Hon. FCIS; Hon. FIPA; Hon. FIWSP. *Publications:* Law Relating to Flats, 1934; Road Traffic Courts, 1938; Rent Acts, 1966. Contributions to legal journals. *Address:* 92 Highgate Hill, N6. *T:* 01-340 3579; 49/55 Victoria Street, SW1. *T:* 01-799 3074; Myrtle Bank, Crosby Road North, Liverpool 22.

**PAGE, Sidney John,** CB 1949; MC 1917; retired as Adviser (on Transport Charges) Ministry of Transport and Civil Aviation (1951-59, retaining rank of Under-Sec. until 1952); *b* 12 January 1892; *s* of late George Arthur and late E. Page, Douglas, IoM; *m* 1919, Doris Mary (*d* 1968), *d* of late Arthur Binns, CBE; one *s* (*see* J. B. Page). *Educ:* Douglas High School; London University (LLB). 1st Class Clerk, Estate Duty Office, Inland Revenue, 1911; London Univ. OTC, 1914; commissioned Manchester Regt, 1915; transferred to Machine Gun Corps, 1917; served European War, France, 1916-18. Asst Inspector of Taxes, 1919; Sec., Railway Rates Tribunal, 1921-36. Min. of Transport: Asst Princ., 1919; Asst Sec. 1937; Principal Asst Sec., 1941; Under-Sec., 1946-52. *Recreations:* golf, motoring, travel. *Address:* 16 The Glen, Green Lane, Northwood, Middlesex. *T:* Northwood 25879.

**PAGE, William Frank,** CMG 1946; *b* 26 June 1894; *s* of late W. T. Page, civil engineer, Worcester; *m* 1932, Kathleen Margaret, *d* of late Rev. C. A. Stooke, Combe Down, Bath. *Educ:* Clifton. South Wales Borderers, 1914-19, Gallipoli and France, temp. commission, Capt.; farming (War Settlement) Southern Rhodesia, 1919-21; Provincial Administration, Tanganyika Territory, 1922-47; Provincial Commissioner, 1944; Director of Man Power, 1942-46; retired, 1947. *Address:* Le Douit, Sous l'Eglise, St Saviour's, Guernsey, CI. *T:* Guernsey 63995.

*See also Sir George Stooke.*

**PAGE-JONES, Frederick Herbert,** CMG 1955; Executive Officer, International Egg Commission, since 1965; Administrative Director, Export Research Group, since 1968; *b* 29 Dec. 1903; *s* of late Frederick Thomas Page-Jones and Louise Mary Young; *m* 1933, Joan, *d* of late Francis John Edward Bagshawe, CMG, MBE; one *s* two *d*. *Educ:* Manchester Grammar School; Brasenose Coll., Oxford (BA). Colonial Administrative Service, Tanganyika Territory, 1925; Provincial Comr, Tanganyika Territory, 1948; Senior Provincial Comr, 1950; Mem. for Local Govt, 1953; Minister for Local Govt, and Admin., 1957; retired, 1958; Chairman, Tanganyika Broadcasting Corporation, 1958-61. Trustee and Man. Director Tanganyika National Newspapers Co., 1958-61; Manager, latterly Managing Director, Market Research (Tanganyika) Ltd, 1961-63; London representative, Marco Surveys (Marketing Research) Group, Kenya, Tanganyika (now Tanzania), Nigeria, 1963-66. *Address:* Ashton, 35 Redstone Hill, Redhill, Surrey. *T:* Redhill 62477. *Club:* Royal Commonwealth Society.

**PAGE WOOD, Sir Anthony John,** 8th Bt, *cr* 1837; *b* 6 Feb. 1951; *s* of Sir David (John Hatherley) Page Wood, 7th Bt and Evelyn Hazel Rosemary, *d* of late Capt. George Ernest Bellville; *S* father 1955. *Heir: uncle,* Matthew Page Wood [*b* 13 Aug. 1924; *m* 1947; two *d*].

**PAGET,** family name of **Marquess of Anglesey.**

**PAGET, Most Rev. Edward Francis,** CBE 1950; DD (Lambeth); an Assistant Bishop of Natal since 1961; *b* July 1886; *s* of Right Rev. Francis Paget, sometime Bishop of Oxford; *cousin* and *heir-pres* of Capt. Sir James Paget, *qv*; *m* 1932, Rosemary, *d* of Auriol and Rose Sealy Allin. *Educ:* Summerfields, Oxford; Shrewsbury; Christ Church, Oxford; Cuddesdon, MA (Oxford), 1911; DD (Lambeth), 1950. Ordained, 1911; Curate at the Christ Church (Oxford) Mission (St Frideswide's, Poplar); went to Transvaal, 1914 as Vicar of Benoni; served as Chaplain in East Africa during European War (MC); Chaplain-General to SR Forces, 1925-56 (resigned); Bishop of Southern Rhodesia, 1925-52; Bishop of Mashonaland, 1952-57; Archbishop of Central Africa, 1955-57; retired, 1957. Chaplain, Order of St John of Jerusalem, 1952. Comdr of Royal Order of the Phœnix (Greek), 1950. *Address:* Auriol, Everton Road, PO Box 3 Gillitts, Natal, South Africa. *T:* Durban 77802. *Club:* Royal Commonwealth Society.

**PAGET, Capt. Sir James (Francis),** 3rd Bt, *cr* 1871; RN retired; *b* 25 Sept. 1890; *e s* of Sir John Rahere Paget, 2nd Bt, and Julia Norrie (*d* 1926), *d* of George Moke, New York; *S* father, 1938; *m* 1943, Frances Alexandra Hamilton (who *m* 1932, Frederick David Stewart Sandeman, *d* 1938), *d* of late Sir Hugh Fraser, Stromeferry, Ross-shire. Joined RN 1906; served European War, 1914-19; Comdr, 1925; Capt. ret., 1937; rejoined RN 1940 (despatches thrice); served 1940-45. *Heir: cousin,* Most Rev. Edward Francis Paget, *qv*. *Address:* Balgonie, Ballater, Aberdeenshire. *Club:* Naval and Military.

**PAGET, Sir John (Starr),** 3rd Bt *cr* 1886; FIMechE; FIPE; Director: Rank Precision Industries Ltd; Thermal Syndicate Ltd, Wallsend; *b* 24 Nov. 1914; *s* of Sir Richard Paget, 2nd Bt and of Lady Muriel Paget, CBE; *S* father 1955; *m* 1944, Nancy Mary Parish, JP, *d* of late Lieutenant-Colonel Francis Parish, DSO, MC; two *s* five *d*. *Educ:* Oundle; Chateau D'Oex; Trinity College, Cambridge (MA). Joined English Electric Co. Ltd, 1936; Asst Works Supt, English Electric, Preston, 1941; Joined D. napier & Son Ltd, 1943; Assistant Manager, D. Napier & Son Ltd, Liverpool, 1945; Manager, D. Napier & Son Ltd, London Group, 1946; Works Director, Napier Aero Engines, 1961-62 (Dir and Gen. Man. D. Napier & Son Ltd, 1959-61). Dir., Glacier Metal Group, 1963-65. Mem. Council, Brunel Univ. Mem. various cttees concerned with Technical Education. Silver Medal, Institution Production Engineers, 1950. *Recreations:* shooting, fishing, cooking, gardening. *Heir: s*

Richard Herbert Paget, *b* 17 February 1957. *Address:* Haygrass House, Taunton, Somerset. *T:* Taunton 81779; 20 Marloes Road, W8. *T:* 01-373 9760. *Clubs:* Athenæum; Island Sailing (Cowes).

**PAGET, Paul Edward,** FSA, FRIBA; Master, Art Workers Guild, 1971; Member, Redundant Churches Fund, since 1969; Surveyor to the Fabric of St Paul's Cathedral, 1963-69; Senior Partner in Firm of Seely & Paget, Chartered Architects, 1963-69 (from death of late Lord Mottistone, OBE, FSA, FRIBA, in Jan. 1963); Architect to St George's Chapel, Windsor, and Portsmouth Cathedral, 1950-69; *b* 24 Jan. 1901; 2nd and *o surv s* of Bishop Henry Luke Paget and Elma Katie (*née* Hoare); unmarried. *Educ:* Winchester; Trinity Coll., Cambridge. Asst Private Sec. to 1st Viscount Templewood, PC, GCSI, GBE, CMG, 1924-26. Flight Lieutenant, RAuxAF, 1939-44. Asst Director, Emergency Works, 1941-44; Common Councilman, Corporation of London, 1949-55. CStJ 1962. *Principal Works:* Restorations: Eltham Palace; Lambeth Palace; Upper Sch., Eton Coll.; London Charterhouse, Deanery and Little Cloister, Westminster Abbey; Churches; Lee-on-Solent, Six Mile Bottom, All Hallows-by-the-Tower, City Temple, Stevenage New Town; Colleges of Education: Oxford, Norwich, Bristol, Culham. *Address:* 41 Cloth Fair, EC1. *T:* 01-600 8511; Templewood, Northrepps, Norfolk. *T:* Overstrand 243; The Shack, Mottistone Manor, Isle of Wight. *T:* Brighstone 336. *Clubs:* Athenæum; Chelsea Arts; Island Sailing (Cowes); Norfolk (Norwich).

**PAGET, Reginald Thomas;** Lt RNVR; QC 1947; MP (Lab) Northampton since 1945; *b* 2 Sept. 1908; *m* 1931. *Educ:* Eton; Trinity College, Cambridge. Barrister, 1934. Lt RNVR, 1940-43 (invalided). Contested Northampton, 1935. Hon. Sec., UK Council of European Movement, 1954. *Publications:* (with late S. S. Silverman MP) Hanged–and Innocent?; Manstein–Campaigns and Trial. *Address:* 9 Grosvenor Cottages, SW1. *T:* 01-730 4034. *Club:* Hayling Island Sailing.

**PAGLIAI, Mrs Bruno;** *see* Oberon, Merle.

**PAGNOL, Marcel;** Member, French Academy, since 1946; Author and Film Producer; *b* 1895. Films produced include: Topaze, Marius, Fanny, César, La Femme du boulanger, La Fille du puisatier, La Belle Meunière, Manon des sources. Comdr French Legion of Honour. *Publications include:* La Petite Fille aux yeux sombres; Pirouettes; Le Premier Amour; La gloire de mon Père, Le Château de ma Mère (trans. by Rita Barisse, The Days Were Too Short); Le Temps de Secrets (trans. by Rita Barisse, The Time of Secrets). Plays: Jazz; Topaze; Translations: Bucoliques de Virgile; Hamlet; Midsummer Night's Dream. *Address:* Villa La Lestra, Monte Carlo.

**PAICE, Karlo Bruce;** Assistant Under-Secretary of State, Home Office, 1955-66; *b* 18 August 1906; *s* of H. B. Paice, Horsham, Sussex; *m* 1st, 1935, Islay (*d* 1965), *d* of late Paymaster Comdr Duncan Cook; four *s*; 2nd, 1966, Mrs Gwen Morris (*née* Kenyon). *Educ:* Collyer's School, Horsham; Jesus Coll., Cambridge (MA). Second Clerk, Metropolitan Police Courts, 1928; Assistant Principal, Home Office, 1929; Asst Sec. to the Poisons Bd, 1933-35; Private Sec. to successive Parliamentary Under-Secretaries of State for Home Affairs, 1935-39. Principal, 1936; Assistant Secretary, 1941, serving in London Civil Defence Region, Fire Service Department, and Aliens Department. Secretary to the Prison Commission and a Prison Commissioner, 1949-55. *Recreations:* walking, history, music. *Address:* Flat 5, 2 King's Gardens, Hove, Sussex. *T:* Brighton 733194. *Club:* United University.

**PAIGE, Rear-Adm. Richard Collings,** CB 1967; *b* 4 October 1911; *s* of Herbert Collings Paige and Harriet Pering Paige; *m* 1937, Sheila Brambles Ward, *d* of late Dr Ernest Ward, Paignton; two *s*. *Educ:* Blundell's School, Tiverton; RNE College, Keyham. Joined Navy, 1929. Served in HMS Neptune, Curaçao, Maori, King George V, Superb, Eagle (despatches twice); Captain, 1957; Commanding Officer, RNE College, 1960-62; Commodore Supt, HM Naval Base, Singapore, 1963-65; Admiral Supt HM Dockyard, Portsmouth, 1966-68. Rear-Adm. 1965. *Recreations:* golf, tennis. *Address:* Court, Churchstow, Kingsbridge, Devon.

**PAIN, Arthur Bernard,** TD 1946; ChM; FRCS; Senior Clinical Lecturer in Orthopædic Surgery, University of Leeds, 1944-Sept. 1969; Consultant Surgeon in charge Orthopædic Department, United Leeds Hospitals, 1955-July 1969; Dean of Faculty of Medicine, University of Leeds, 1960-Sept. 1969; *b* 13 July 1904; *e s* of late Reverend A. T. Pain; *m* 1933, Irene Allison, *o d* of late William Webb, Harrogate; one *s*. *Educ:* Central High School, Leeds; University of Leeds; St Bartholomew's Hospital, London. MB, ChB (Leeds) Hons, 1927; FRCS 1931; ChM (Leeds), 1932. Resident posts in hospital, 1927-34; Hon. Asst Orthopædic Surgeon, General Infirmary at Leeds, 1934; Consultant Orthopædic Surgeon, United Leeds Hosps, 1948. Lt-Col RAMC (TA) retd. Fellow, British Orthopædic Assoc.; FRSocMed; Member: Soc. Internationale de Chirugie Orthopédique et Traumatique; Bd of Governors, United Leeds Hosps, 1955-69; Leeds Regional Hospital Board, 1962-69; General Medical Council, 1960-69. *Publications:* articles in medical journals and in medical text book. *Recreations:* enjoyment of wine and food and of first-class cricket. *Address:* Rowley Cottage, Scarcroft, Thorner, Leeds. *T:* Thorner 305; 32 Park Square, Leeds LS1 2PF. *T:* Leeds 23385.

**PAIN, Maj.-Gen. Horace Rollo Squarey,** MC 1945; ADC; late 4th/7th Royal Dragoon Guards; General Officer Commanding 2nd Division since 1970; *b* 11 May 1921; *s* of late Horace Davy Pain, Levenside, Haverthwaite, Ulverston, and Audrey Pain (*née* Hampson); *m* 1950, Denys Sophia (*née* Chaine-Nickson); one *s* two *d*. Commissioned into Reconnaissance Corps during War of 1939-45: served NW Europe (MC). After War, served for two years in E Africa and Brit. Somaliland before joining 4th/7th Royal Dragoon Gds in Palestine, 1947; attended Staff Coll., Camberley, 1951; subseq. served in Mil. Ops Directorate, in War Office; served with his Regt in BAOR, 1955-56; Mem. Directing Staff, Staff Coll., Camberley, 1957; GSO1, Brit. Army Staff, Washington, DC, 1960; commanded his Regt in BAOR, 1962; commanded one of the three divs, Staff Coll., Camberley, 1964; commanded 5 Inf. Bde in Borneo, 1965; IDC, 1968; ADC to the Queen, 1969; BGS, HQ, BAOR, 1969-70. *Recreation:* hunting. *Address:* Eddlethorpe Hall, Malton, Yorkshire. *T:* Burythorpe 218. *Clubs:* Cavalry, United Hunts.

**PAIN, Peter (Richard),** QC 1965; *b* 1913; *s* of Arthur Richard Pain and Elizabeth Irene Pain (*née* Benn); *m* 1941, Barbara Florence Maude Riggs; two *s*. *Educ:* Westminster; Christ Church, Oxford. Called to the Bar, 1936; Chm., Race Relations Board Conciliation

Cttee for Greater London, 1968-. *Publications:* Manual of Fire Service Law, 1951; The Law Relating to the Motor Trade (with K. C. Johnson-Davies), 1955. *Recreations:* forestry, cricket. *Address:* Loen, Frimley, Surrey. *T:* Deepcut 5639.

**PAINE, George,** DFC 1944; Director of Statistics and Intelligence, Board of Inland Revenue since Oct. 1957; *b* 14 Apr. 1918; 3rd *s* of late Jack Paine, East Sutton, and Helen Margaret Hadow; unmarried. *Educ:* Bradfield Coll.; Peterhouse, Cambridge. External Ballistics Dept, Ordnance Bd, 1941; RAF, 1942-46; Min. of Agriculture, 1948; Inland Revenue, 1949; Central Statistical Office, 1954; Board of Trade, 1957. *Recreations:* beekeeping, hopdrying. *Address:* 25/2 Catherine Place, SW1. *T:* 01-828 0688.

**PAINE, Sir (Herbert) Kingsley,** Kt 1953; CMG 1944; *b* 26 Jan. 1883; *s* of Herbert Paine, Gawler, South Australia; *m* 1912, Amy Muriel, *d* of James Ford Pearson, Malvern, South Australia; one *s* one *d* (and one *s* and one *d* decd). *Educ:* St Peter's Collegiate Sch., S Aust. LLB, Adelaide University, 1904; admitted to South Australian Bar, 1905; Stipendiary Magistrate, 1922; Judge in Insolvency and Local Court Judge, Adelaide, South Australia, 1926; retired from Local Court Judgeship, 1948; Acting Puisne Judge, Supreme Court, 1949-50, 1951-52. *Address:* 35 Seventh Avenue, St Peter's, South Australia 5069. *T:* 61.1334. *Club:* Adelaide (Adelaide).

**PAINE, Dr Thomas Otten;** Vice-President, General Electric Company, since 1970; *b* 9 Nov. 1921; *s* of George Thomas Paine, Cdre, USN retd and Ada Louise Otten; *m* 1946, Barbara Helen Taunton Pearse; two *s* two *d*. *Educ:* Maury High, Norfolk, Va; Brown Univ.; Stanford Univ. Served War of 1939-45 (US Navy Commendation Ribbon 1944; Submarine Combat Award with two stars, 1943-45). Research Associate: Stanford Univ., 1947-49; GE Res. Lab., Schenectady, 1949-50; Manager: GE Meter & Instruments Lab., Lynn, 1951-58; Technical Analysis, GE R&D Center, Schenectady, 1959-62; TEMPO, GE Center for Advanced Studies, Santa Barbara, 1963-67; Dep. Administrator, US Nat. Aeronautics and Space Admin., Washington, 1968, Administrator 1969-70. MInstMet; Member: Newcomen Soc.; Acad. of Sciences, NY; Sigma Xi. Outstanding Contribution to Industrial Science Award, AAS, 1956. Hon. Dr of Science: Brown, 1969; Clarkson Coll. of Tech., 1969; Nebraska Wesleyan, 1970; New Brunswick, 1970; Hon. Dr Engrg, Worcester Polytechnic Inst., 1970. *Publications:* various technical papers in Physical Review, Jl Applied Physics, Electrical Engrg, Powder Metallurgy, etc; general papers in National Geographic, Air Force and Space Digest, Public Administration Review, Ordnance, etc. *Recreations:* sailing, beachcombing, skin diving, photography, book collecting, oil painting. *Address:* 570 Lexington Avenue, New York, NY 10022, USA. *Clubs:* Lotos, Explorers (New York); Army and Navy, Cosmos (Washington).

**PAINTER, George Duncan;** Biographer and Incunabulist; Assistant Keeper in charge of fifteenth-century printed books, British Museum, since 1954; *b* Birmingham, 5 June 1914; *s* of George Charles Painter and Minnie Rosendale (*née* Taylor); *m* 1942, Isabel Joan, *d* of Samuel Morley Britton, Bristol; two *d*. *Educ:* King Edward's Sch., Birmingham; Trinity Coll., Cambridge (Schol.). Bell Exhibr; John Stewart of Rannoch Schol.; Porson Schol.; Waddington Schol.; 1st cl. hons Class. Tripos pts I and II; Craven Student; 2nd Chancellor's Class. Medallist, 1936; MA Cantab 1945. Asst Lectr in Latin, Univ. of Liverpool, 1937; joined staff of Dept of Printed Books, BM, 1938. FRSL 1965. *Publications:* André Gide, A Critical Biography, 1951, rev. edn 1968; The Road to Sinodun, Poems, 1951; André Gide, Marshlands and Prometheus Misbound (trans.), 1953; Marcel Proust, Letters to his Mother (trans.), 1956; Marcel Proust, A Biography, vol. 1, 1959, vol. 2, 1965 (Duff Cooper Memorial Prize); The Vinland Map and the Tartar Relation (with R. A. Skelton and T. E. Marston), 1965; André Maurois, The Chelsea Way (trans.), 1966; articles on fifteenth-century printing in The Library, Book Collector, Gutenberg-Jahrbuch. *Recreations:* family life, walking, gardening, travel, music. *Address:* 10 Mansfield Road, Hove, Sussex. *T:* Brighton 46008.

**PAISH, Frank Walter,** MC 1918; MA; Professor Emeritus, University of London; *b* 15 January 1898; *e s* of late Sir George Paish; *m* 1927, Beatrice Marie, *d* of late G. C. Eckhard; two *s* one *d*. *Educ:* Winchester College; Trinity College, Cambridge. Served European War (RFA), 1916-19. Employed by Standard Bank of South Africa, Ltd in London and South Africa, 1921-32. Lecturer, London School of Economics, 1932-38; Reader, 1938-49; Professor of Economics (with special reference to Business Finance), 1949-65. Secretary, London and Cambridge Economic Service, 1932-41 and 1945-49; Editor, 1947-49. Deputy-Director of Programmes, Ministry of Aircraft Production, 1941-45. Consultant on Economic Affairs, Lloyds Bank Ltd, 1965-70. *Publications:* (with G. L. Schwartz) Insurance Funds and their Investment, 1934; The Post-War Financial Problem and Other Essays, 1950; Business Finance, 1953; Studies in an Inflationary Economy, 1962; Long-term and Short-term Interest Rates in the United Kingdom, 1966; (ed) Benham's Economics, 8th edn, 1967; How the Economy Works, 1970. Articles in The Economic Journal, Economica, London and Cambridge Bulletin, etc. *Recreation:* golf. *Address:* Shoreys, Ewhurst, Cranleigh, Surrey. *T:* Ewhurst 520. *Club:* Reform.

**PAISLEY, Bishop of, (RC),** since 1968; **Rt. Rev. Stephen McGill;** *b* Glasgow, 4 Jan. 1912; *s* of Peter McGill and Charlotte Connolly. *Educ:* St Aloysius', Glasgow; Blairs College, Aberdeen; Coutances, France; Institut Catholique, Paris. Ordained Priest of St Sulpice, 1936. STL Paris. St Mary's College, Blairs, Aberdeen: Spiritual Director, 1940-51; Rector, 1951-60. Bishop of Argyll and the Isles, 1960-68. *Address:* Bishop's House, Porterfield Road, Kilmacolm, Renfrewshire.

**PAISLEY, Rev. Ian Richard Kyle;** MP (Prot U) North Antrim since 1970; MP (Prot U) Bannside, Co. Antrim, Parliament of Northern Ireland, since April 1970; Minister, Martyrs Memorial Free Presbyterian Church, Belfast, since 1946; *b* 6 April 1926; 2nd *s* of Rev. J. Kyle Paisley and Mrs Isabella Paisley; *m* 1956, Eileen Emily Cassells; two *s* three *d* (incl. twin *s*). *Educ:* Ballymena Model Sch.; Ballymena Techn. High Sch.; S Wales Bible Coll.; Reformed Presbyterian Theol. Coll., Belfast. Ordained, 1946. Moderator, Free Presbyterian Church of Ulster, 1951. Commenced publishing The Protestant Telegraph, 1966. Contested (Prot U) Bannside, NI Parlt, 1969. Hon. DD, Bob Jones Univ., SC. FRGS. *Publications:* History of the 1859 Revival, 1959; Ravenhill Pulpit, Vol. 1, 1966, vol. 2, 1967; Exposition of the Epistle to Romans, 1968; Billy Graham and the Church of Rome, 1970. *Address:* Beechwood, 423

Beersbridge Road, Belfast, N Ireland. *T:* 57106.

**PAISLEY, John Lawrence,** CB 1970; MBE 1946; Consultant with L. G. Mouchel & Partners, Consulting Engineers, since 1971; *b* Manchester, 4 Sept. 1909; *e s* of J. R. and Mrs E. W. Paisley; *m* 1937, Angela Dorothy Catliff; three *d. Educ:* King George V Sch., Southport; Univ. of Liverpool. BEng 1930, MEng 1935. Asst Engineer: Siemens Bros & Co. Ltd, North Delta Transmission Lines, Egypt, 1930-34; Howard Humphreys & Sons, Cons. Engrs, Tunnels and Viaduct on A55, in N Wales, 1934-35; W Sussex CC, 1935-37; Asst Engr in Scotland, Min. of Transport, 1937-39. War Service with Royal Engineers, 1939-46: took part in Dunkirk evacuation and finally as Major, RE (now Hon. Major), commanded 804 Road Construction Co. in UK, France and Germany (MBE). Ministry of Transport: Engr in Scotland, 1946-52; Senr Engr in HQ, London, 1952-60; Divl Rd Engr, NW Div. at Manchester, 1960-64; Dep. Chief Engr, HQ, London, 1964-66; Chief Highway Engr, Min. of Transport, 1966-70. Mem. Council, Instn of Civil Engrs; FICE; MInstHE. *Publications:* contribs Proc. Instn of Civil Engrs. *Recreations:* fell walking, some desultory golf. *Address:* Weybrook, Warren Road, Guildford, Surrey. *T:* Guildford 62798. *Clubs:* Royal Automobile, Civil Service, Victory; Rucksack (Manchester).

**PAKENHAM,** family name of **Earl of Longford.**

**PAKENHAM, Elizabeth;** *see* Longford, Countess of.

**PAKENHAM, Henry Desmond Verner,** CBE 1964; Deputy High Commissioner, Sydney, since 1968; *b* 5 Nov. 1911; *s* of Hamilton Richard Pakenham and Emilie Willis Stringer; *m* 1st, 1946, Crystal Elizabeth Brooksbank (marr. diss., 1960); one *s* one *d* (and one *s* decd); 2nd, 1963, Venetia Maude; one *s* one *d. Educ:* Monkton Combe; St John Baptist College, Oxford. Taught modern languages at Sevenoaks School, 1933-40. Served in HM Forces, 1940-45. Entered Foreign Service, 1946; served in Madrid, Djakarta, Havana, Singapore, Tel Aviv and Buenos Aires. *Recreations:* music and wild life. *Address:* 8 Fisher Avenue, Vaucluse, NSW 2030, Australia. *Club:* Travellers'.

**PAKES, Ernest John,** CBE 1954; Under-writing Member of Lloyd's, since 1956; *b* 28 Jan. 1899; *s* of Ernest William Pakes; *m* 1928, Emilie Pickering; one *s. Educ:* Hampton Gram. Sch. Served with London Scottish, 1917-19 (wounded). Admiralty, 1915-16; Gray Dawes & Co., 1916-21; Mackinnon Mackenzie & Co., India, 1921-40, Ceylon, 1940-44, India, 1945-54 (Chairman, 1951-54). Dep. Rep., Min. of War Transport, Karachi, 1945-46; Chairman: Karachi Chamber of Commerce, 1946-47; Allahabad Bank Ltd, India, 1951-54. Pres. Bengal Chamber of Commerce and Assocd Chambers of Commerce of India, 1953-54; Chm., Outward and Homeward UK and Continental/India and Pakistan Confs, 1956-58. Member of Council, Chamber of Shipping, 1956-62; Chairman, British India Steam Navigation Co. Ltd, 1960-62 (a Managing Director, 1954-62; Deputy Chairman, 1957-60); Director, Chartered Bank, London, 1958-62. Liveryman, Worshipful Co. of Shipwrights. *Recreations:* tennis, golf, photography. *Address:* The Manor, Givons Grove, Leatherhead, Surrey. *T:* Leatherhead 2187. *Clubs:* Oriental; Walton Heath.

**PAKINGTON,** family name of **Baron Hampton.**

**PALETHORPE-TODD, Richard Andrew;** *see* Todd, Richard.

**PALEY, Maj.-Gen. Sir (Alexander George), Victor,** KBE 1960 (CBE 1951; OBE 1940); CB 1958; DSO 1945; DL; *b* 30 April 1903; *s* of late Major George Paley, Rifle Brigade, Freckenham, Suffolk; *m* 1936, Susan, *d* of late Lt-Col Albert Ingraham Paine, CMG, DSO, 60th Rifles, Bledington, Kingham, Oxon; two *d. Educ:* Cheam School; Eton College; RMC, Sandhurst. 2nd Lt, Rifle Bde, 1923; Adjt London Rifle Bde, 1929-31; at Staff College, 1932-33; Brigade Major 2 London Infantry Brigade, 1935-37; Bde Major 8 Inf. Bde, 1937-39; GSO2, HQ British Troops, Egypt, 1939-41; OC 3 Libyan Arabs Battalion, Senussi, 1941-42; British Military Mission, Iraq, 1942-43; OC 1st Battalion Rifle Brigade, 1943-45; Brig. "A", HQ 8 Corps District, Germany, 1945-46; Head Army Branch Combined Services Division, CCG, 1946-48; Brigadier A/Q AA Comd, 1948-51; Commander 47 London Inf. Bde, Dec. 1951-54. ADC to the Queen, 1954-57, Comdr Gold Coast Dist, 1954; GOC, Ghana Army, 1956, and Chief of Defence Staff, Ghana, 1958. Retired, June 1960. Hon. Col: London Rifle Brigade Rangers (Prince Consort's Own), TA, 1960-67; 5th Territorial Bn Royal Greenjackets, 1967-69; London Cadre Royal Greenjackets, 1969-70. High Sheriff of Suffolk, 1967; DL Suffolk, 1968. Governor, Milton Abbey Sch., 1961-. *Address:* Great Barton, Bury St Edmunds, Suffolk. *Clubs:* Army and Navy, Royal Automobile; West Suffolk County.

**PALFREY, William John Henry,** CBE 1970 (OBE 1966); QPM 1960; Chief Constable of Lancashire since 1969; *b* 1 March 1906; *s* of late W. H. Palfrey, Exminster, Devon; *m* 1927, Dorothy, *d* of Henry Cowell, Kenton, Devon; one *s. Educ:* Hele's Sch., Exeter. Portsmouth City Police, 1926; Chief Constable, Accrington, 1940; seconded to Army, 1943-47; served with 1st American Army, Chief Public Safety Officer, Cherbourg, later Paris; Lt-Col i/c Central Register of War Criminals, 1945; War Crime Investigation, Germany, 1946-47; Asst Chief Constable (Operations), Lancs Constabulary, 1951; seconded to Thai Govt to carry out survey of Thai Police, 1955; Dep. Chief Constable, Lancs, 1962. Dep. Sec.-Gen., Internat. Fedn of Senior Police Officers, 1966-. Lectured at Internat. Traffic Confs throughout Europe. Bronze Star (US) and Certif. of Merit (US Army), 1944. *Publications:* contribs to police jls throughout Europe. *Recreations:* motor sport, cinephotography, travel. *Address:* The Laund, Saunders Lane, New Longton, Preston, Lancs. *T:* Preston 54811.

**PALING, Rt. Hon. Wilfred,** PC 1944; *b* Marehay, near Ripley, Derbyshire, 1883. A colliery checkweighman at Bulcroft Colliery; MP (Lab): Doncaster Division of West Riding Yorks, 1922-31; Wentworth Division of Yorks, 1933-50; Dearne Valley Division, W Riding Yorks, 1950-59. A Junior Lord of the Treasury, 1929-31; Lord Commissioner of the Treasury, 1940-41; Parliamentary Secretary, Ministry of Pensions, 1941-45; Minister of Pensions, 1945-47; Postmaster-General, 1947-50. Member of West Riding County Council, 1919-23 (resigned); Member of Bentley with Arksey UDC, 1919 (resigned); formerly Trustee of Yorkshire Mineworkers' Assoc. *Address:* Scawthorpe, Doncaster, Yorks. *T:* Doncaster 3892.

**PALING, William Thomas;** *b* 28 Oct. 1892; *s* of George Thomas Paling, Sutton-in-Ashfield, Notts; *m* 1919, Gladys Nellie, MBE, *d* of William Frith, James Street, Nuncar Gate,

Nottinghamshire; one *s* one *d*. MP (Lab) Dewsbury, 1945-59, retired. *Address:* 3 Lancaster Close, Tickhill, near Doncaster, Yorks.

**PALITANA, Maharaja Shree Sir Bahadursinhji, Thakore Saheb of;** KCSI 1939; KCIE 1930; Ruler of Palitana; *b* 3 April 1900; *s* of late Thakore Saheb Shri Sir Mansinhji, KCSI; *m*; one *s*. *Educ:* The Rajkumar College, Rajkot; Shrewsbury School. *Address:* Palitana, India.

**PALLISER, Arthur Michael,** CMG 1966; Minister, British Embassy, Paris, since 1969; *b* 9 Apr. 1922; *s* of late Admiral Sir Arthur Palliser, KCB, DSC, and of Lady Palliser (*née* Margaret Eva King-Salter); *m* 1948, Marie Marguerite, *d* of Paul-Henri Spaak, *qv*; three *s*. *Educ:* Wellington Coll.; Merton Coll., Oxford. Served with Coldstream Guards, 1942-47; Capt. 1944. Entered HM Diplomatic Service, 1947; SE Asia Dept, Foreign Office, 1947-49; Athens, 1949-51; Second Sec., 1950; Foreign Office: German Finance Dept, 1951-52; Central Dept, 1952-54; Private Sec. to Perm. Under-Sec., 1954-56; First Sec., 1955; Paris, 1956-60; Head of Chancery, Dakar, 1960-62 (Chargé d'Affaires in 1960, 1961 and 1962); Counsellor, and seconded to Imperial Defence College, 1963; Head of Planning Staff, Foreign Office, 1964; a Private Sec. to PM, 1966. Chevalier, Order of Orange Nassau, 1944; Chevalier, Légion d'Honneur, 1957. *Address:* 7 rue François Ier, Paris 8e, France. *Club:* Guards.

**PALLOT, Arthur Keith,** CMG 1966; Director of Finance and Establishments, Commonwealth War Graves Commission, since 1956; *b* 25 Sept. 1918; *s* of Harold Pallot, La Tourelle, Jersey; *m* 1945, Marjorie, *d* of J. T. Smith, Rugby; two *d*. *Educ:* Newton College. Royal Navy, 1936; retired as Lieut-Commander, 1947. Commonwealth War Graves Commission, 1947. Awarded the Queen's Commendation for brave conduct, 1958. *Recreations:* cricket, sailing. *Address:* Carraig, 9 Castle Drive, Maidenhead, Berks. *T:* Maidenhead 26642.

**PALMAR, Derek James;** Director: Hill Samuel Group Ltd; Hill, Samuel & Co. Ltd; Hill Samuel Insurance & Shipping Holdings Ltd; Lambert Brothers Ltd; Noble Lowndes Annuities Ltd; Lowndes Lambert Ltd; Hall-Thermotank Ltd; Rotary Hoes Ltd; Member, British Railways Board; *b* 25 July 1919; *o s* of Lt-Col F. J. Palmar; *m* 1946, Edith Brewster; one *s* one *d*. *Educ:* Dover College. Served Royal Artillery and Staff, 1941-46; psc; Gunner, 1941; Lt-Col 1945; Peat, Marwick, Mitchell & Co., 1937-57; ACA 1947; FCA 1957; Industrial Adviser to Dept of Economic Affairs 1965-67. Chm., Working Party on Wear Shipyards, 1967-68; Mem., Dover Harbour Board, 1965-70. *Address:* The Old Forge, near Bore Place, Chiddingstone, Kent. *T:* Weald 242. *Club:* Boodle's.

**PALMER,** family name of **Earl of Selborne** and **Barons Palmer** and **Rusholme** and **Baroness Lucas of Crudwell.**

**PALMER,** 3rd Baron, *cr* 1933, of Reading; **Raymond Cecil Palmer,** OBE 1968; Bt *cr* 1916; Director, Associated Biscuit Manufacturers Ltd; Chairman: Huntley & Palmers Ltd, since 1969; Huntley Boorne & Stevens Ltd, Reading, since 1956 (Deputy Chairman, 1948); National Savings Southern Region Industrial Advisory Council; President, Thames Valley Trustee Savings Bank, since 1967; Part-time Member, Southern Electricity Board, since 1965; *b* 24 June 1916; *er s* of 2nd Baron Palmer and Marguerite (*d* 1959), *d* of William McKinley Osborne, USA, Consul-General to Great Britain; *S* father 1950; *m* 1941, Victoria Ellen, *o c* of late Captain J. A. R. Weston-Stevens, Maidenhead; two *d* (and one *d* decd). *Educ:* Harrow; University Coll., Oxford. Joined Huntley & Palmers Ltd, 1938, Dep. Chm., 1966-69, Man. Dir, 1967-69. Served War of 1939-45 in Grenadier Guards as Lieut, in UK and North Africa, 1940-43 (invalided). *Recreations:* cricket, rackets, music and gardening; shooting. *Heir:* *b* Col Hon. Gordon William Nottage Palmer, *qv*. *Address:* Farley Hill House, Farley Hill, Reading, Berkshire. *T:* Eversley 2260. *Club:* Guards.

**PALMER, Arthur Montague Frank,** CEng, MIEE, MInstF; MP (Lab and Co-op) Bristol Central since 1964; *b* 4 Aug. 1912; *s* of late Frank Palmer, Northam, Devon; *m* 1939, Marion Ethel Frances Woollaston, BSc, MRCS, LRCP; DPM; two *d*. *Educ:* Ashford Gram. Sch.; Brunel Technical College. Is a Chartered Engineer and a Chartered Fuel Technologist. Studied electrical supply engineering, 1932-35, in London; Member technical staff of London Power Co., 1936-45; now Editor Electrical Power Engineer; Mem. Industrial Training Board for Electricity Supply Industry; Member Brentford and Chiswick Town Council, 1937-45. MP (Lab) for Wimbledon, 1945-50; MP (Lab and Co-op) for Cleveland Div. of Yorks, Oct. 1952-Sept. 1959; Chairman: Parly and Scientific Cttee, 1965-68; House of Commons Select Cttee on Science and Technology. *Publications:* The Future of Electricity Supply, 1943; Modern Norway, 1950; Law and the Power Engineer, 1959; articles on political, industrial, and economic subjects. *Recreations:* walking, motoring, reading novels, history and politics. *Address:* 14 Lavington Court, Putney, SW15. *T:* 01-789 1967; Hill Cottage, Charlcutt, near Calne, Wilts. *T:* Kellaways 653; (office) Station House, Fox Lane North, Chertsey, Surrey. *T:* Chertsey 4131. *Club:* Royal Automobile.

**PALMER, Bernard Harold Michael,** MA; Editor of the Church Times since 1968; *b* 8 Sept. 1929; *e s* of late Christopher Harold Palmer; *m* 1954, Jane Margaret, *d* of late E. L. Skinner; one *s* one *d*. *Educ:* St Edmund's School, Hindhead; Eton (King's Scholar); King's College, Cambridge. BA 1952; MA 1956. Member of editorial staff, Church Times, 1952-; Managing Director, 1957-; Editor-in-Chief, 1960-68; Chm., 1962. *Recreations:* cycling, penmanship. *Address:* 143 Bradbourne Vale Road, Sevenoaks, Kent. *T:* Sevenoaks 53327. *Club:* Royal Commonwealth Society.

**PALMER, Charles Alan Salier,** CBE 1969; DSO 1945; Chairman, Associated Biscuit Manufacturers Ltd, since 1969 (Vice-Chm., 1963); *b* 23 Oct. 1913; *s* of late Sir (Charles) Eric Palmer, Shinfield Grange, near Reading; *m* 1939, Auriol Mary, *d* of late Brig.-Gen. Cyril R. Harbord, CB, CMG, DSO. *Educ:* Harrow; Exeter Coll., Oxford. Joined Huntley & Palmer's, 1934 (Bd, 1938; Dep.-Chm. 1955; Chm., Huntley & Palmer's, 1963). Served War of 1939-45: with Berks Yeo., Adjt, 1939-41; GSO3, HQ 61 Div., 1941-42; GSO2, HQ III Corps, 1942-43; Lt-Col; commanded SOE mission, Albania, 1943-45 (despatches). Pres., Reading Conservative Assoc., 1946-; Chm., Cake & Biscuit Alliance, 1967-70; Mem. Council, CBI 1967-70; Mem. British Productivity Council, 1970-. *Recreations:* shooting, fishing, tropical agriculture. *Address:* Forest Edge, Farley Hill, Reading, Berks. *T:* Arborfield Cross 223.

**PALMER, Sir Charles Mark,** 5th Bt, *cr* 1886; *b* 21 Nov. 1941; *s* of Sir Anthony Frederick Mark

Palmer, 4th Bt, and Henriette, *d* of Comdr Francis Cadogan; *S* father 1941. *Heir: kinsman,* Charles Lionel Palmer [*b* 7 Feb. 1909; *s* of late Capt. Lionel Hugo Palmer (6th *s* of 1st Bt) and 2nd wife, Blanche, *o d* of Walter Balmford, York; *m* 1937, Karoline, *d* of late Major Carl Gach, Vienna; two *d*]. *Address:* Houndsell Place, Mark Cross, Crowborough, Sussex.

*See also Sir Alexander Abel Smith.*

**PALMER, Edward Hurry;** Comptroller of Defence Lands and Claims, Ministry of Defence, since 1968; *b* 23 Sept. 1912; *s* of Harold G. Palmer and late Ada S. Palmer; *m* 1940, Phyllis Eagle; no *c*. *Educ:* Haileybury. Dep. Chief Surveyor of Lands, Admty, 1942; Chief Surveyor of Lands, Admty, 1950; Chief Surveyor of Defence Lands, Min. of Defence, 1964. *Recreations:* gardening, walking, golf and other sports. *Address:* 49 Paines Lane, Pinner, Middlesex. *T:* 01-866 5961. *Club:* Farmers'.

**PALMER, Sir Geoffrey (Christopher John),** 12th Bt, *cr* 1660; *b* 30 June 1936; *er s* of Lieutenant-Colonel Sir Geoffrey Frederick Neill Palmer, 11th Bt, and Cicely Katherine (who *m* 1952, Robert W. B. Newton), *o d* of late Arthur Radmall, Clifton, nr Watford; *S* father 1951; *m* 1957, Clarissa Mary, *er d* of Stephen Villiers-Smith, Knockholt, Kent; four *d*. *Educ:* Eton. *Recreations:* squash, racquets, cricket, shooting. *Heir: b* Jeremy Charles Palmer, *b* 16 May 1939. *Address:* Carlton Curlieu Hall, Leicestershire. *T:* Great Glen 2656. *Clubs:* Boodle's; MCC, I Zingari, Free Foresters, Eton Ramblers, Butterflies, Gentlemen of Leicestershire.

**PALMER, Maj.-Gen. George Erroll P.;** *see* Prior-Palmer.

**PALMER, Gerald Eustace Howell,** Hon. DLitt Reading, 1957; *b* 9 June 1904; *s* of late Eustace Exall Palmer, Chairman of Huntley and Palmers Ltd, and Madeline Mary Howell. *Educ:* Winchester; New College, Oxford (Scholar). MP (Nat. C) for Winchester Division of Hampshire, 1935-45. Served RA, Capt (despatches). President of the Council, Univ. of Reading, 1966-69; A Verderer of the New Forest, 1957-66; Chm., Forestry Commission Regional Adv. Cttee for South-East England, 1954-63; A Forestry Commissioner, 1963-65; Chm., Forestry Commn Nat. Cttee for England, 1964-65. Is also interested in farming. *Publications:* following translations (in collab. with E. Kadloubovsky): Writings from the Philokalia, 1951; Unseen Warfare, 1952; Early Fathers, from the Philokalia, 1954; The Meaning of Icons, by Lossky and Ouspensky. *Address:* Bussock Mayne, Newbury, Berks. *T:* Chieveley 265. *Club:* Brooks's.

**PALMER, Col Hon. Gordon William Nottage,** OBE 1957 (MBE 1944); TD 1950; Sales Marketing Director, Associated Biscuit Manufacturers Ltd since 1965; Managing Dir, Huntley & Palmers Ltd, 1959-65; *b* 18 July 1918; *yr s* of 2nd Baron Palmer and Marguerite Osborne, USA; *heir-pres.* to 3rd Baron Palmer, *qv*; *m* 1950, Lorna Eveline Hope, *d* of Major C. W. H. Bailie; two *s*. *Educ:* Eton Coll.; Christ Church, Oxford. Served War of 1939-45, with Berks Yeo., 1939-41; staff Capt. RA, HQ 61 Div., 1941; DAQMG, Malta, 1942; GSO2, Ops, GHQ Middle East, 1943-44; GSO2, HQ 5 Div., 1944-45; Lt-Col, Instructor Staff College, Camberley, 1945; Comd Berkshire Yeo., TA, 1954-56. Hon. Col Berkshire and Westminster Dragoons, 1966-67; Hon. Col HQ Squadron, Royal Yeomanry Regt, 1967. Dir, Huntley, Boorne & Stevens Ltd, 1948-69; Chm. Cake and Biscuit Alliance, 1957-59. Mem., British National Export Council, 1966-69. Vice-President of Council: Reading Univ., 1966- (Mem. 1954-, Treas., 1955-59); Royal Coll. of Music, 1956-; FRCM 1965; Bradfield College; DL Berks, 1960; JP 1956; High Sheriff, 1965; Chairman, Berkshire T&AFA, 1961-68. *Recreations:* shooting, and gardening. *Address:* Foudry House, Mortimer, Berkshire. *T:* Mortimer 317; Edrom Newton, Duns, Berwickshire. *T:* Chirnside 292. *Club:* Cavalry.

**PALMER, Sir John (Edward Somerset),** 8th Bt, *cr* 1791; Consultant; *b* 27 Oct. 1926; *e s* of Sir John A. Palmer, 7th Bt; *S* father, 1963; *m* 1956, Dione Catharine Skinner; one *s* one *d*. *Educ:* Canford School; Cambridge and Durham Universities. MA (Cantab); MSc (Dunelm). Colonial Service, Northern Nigeria, 1952-61. Senior Executive, R. A. Lister & Co. Ltd, Dursley, Glos, 1962-63; Min. Overseas Develt, 1964-68. Mem. Amer. Soc. of Agric. Engrs; AMIAgrE. *Heir: s* Robert John Hudson Palmer, *b* 20 Dec. 1960. *Address:* The Grange, Wavendon, Nr Bletchley, Bucks. *T:* Woburn Sands 3248. *Club:* Royal Over-Seas League.

**PALMER, Prof. Leonard Robert;** Professor of Comparative Philology, University of Oxford, and Fellow of Worcester College, since 1952; *b* 5 June 1906; *m*; one *d*. *Educ:* High School, Canton, Cardiff; University College of South Wales and Monmouthshire; Trinity College, Cambridge; University of Vienna. BA Wales 1927; PhD Vienna 1931; PhD Cambridge 1936; MA Oxford 1952. Assistant Lecturer in Classics, 1931-35, Lecturer in Classics, 1935-41, Victoria University of Manchester; temp. Civil Servant in Foreign Office, 1941-45; Professor of Greek and Head of Dept of Classics at King's Coll., London, 1945-52. Hon. Secretary Philological Society, 1947-51, President, 1957-. Corresponding Member Deutsches Archäologisches Institut, 1958. *Publications:* Translation of E. Zeller: Outlines of the History of Greek Philosophy, 14th edn, 1931; Introduction to Modern Linguistics, 1936; A Grammar of the Post-Ptolemaic Papyri, Vol. 1 (Publications of the Philological Society), 1945; The Latin Language, 1954; Mycenaeans and Minoans, 1961; The Language of Homer (in A Companion to Homer), 1962; The Interpretation of Mycenaean Greek Texts, 1963; The Find Places 1961, 2nd edn 1965; THE Knossos Tablets, 1963; A New Guide to the Palace of Knossos, 1969; The Penultimate Palace at Knossos, 1969; various articles in English and foreign learned journals. *Address:* Worcester College, Oxford; 60-73 Sistrans, Tyrol, Austria. *T:* Innsbruck 70702.

**PALMER, Leslie Robert,** CBE 1964; Director-General, Defence Accounts, Ministry of Defence, since 1969 *b* 21 Aug. 1910; *s* of Robert Palmer; *m* 1937, Mary Crick; two *s* one *d*. *Educ:* Battersea Grammar School; London University. Entered Admiralty Service, 1929; Assistant Dir of Victualling, 1941; Dep. Dir of Victualling, 1954; Dir of Victualling, Admiralty, 1959-61; Principal Dir of Accounts, Admiralty, 1961-64; Principal Dir of Accounts (Navy) MoD, 1964-68. *Recreation:* music. *Address:* High Meadow, Upper Limpley Stoke, Nr Bath. *T:* Limpley Stoke 3308. *Clubs:* Royal Automobile; Union (Malta).

**PALMER, Hon. Lewis;** *see* Palmer, Hon. W. J. L.

**PALMER, Brig. Sir Otho Leslie P.;** *see* Prior-Palmer.

**PALMER, Maj.-Gen. Peter Garwood,** MBE 1944; FIMechE; MBIM; Commandant, Technical Group REME, Woolwich, 1968-71; *b* 2 March 1914; *s* of H. G. Palmer, Great Yarmouth,

Norfolk; *m* 1945, Isabel Mary Kinsley Boucher; one *s. Educ:* Haileybury College, Herts; Sheffield University (BEng). Petters Ltd, Yeovil, Som.: Graduate Apprentice, 1933-35; Development Engineer, 1935-38. Regular Army Officer: RAOC, 1938-42; REME, 1942- (MBE); Dep. Dir of Electrical and Mechanical Engineering (Army), MoD, 1965-68. MIMechE, 1964. *Recreations:* gardening, photography, sport. *Address:* c/o Glyn Mills & Co., Holt's Branch, Kirkland House, Whitehall, SW1.

**PALMER, Maj.-Gen. (Retd) Philip Francis,** CB 1957; OBE 1945; Major-General late Royal Army Medical Corps; *b* 8 Aug. 1903. MB, BCh, BAO, Dublin, 1926; DPH 1936. Served North West Frontier of India, 1930-31 (medal and clasp). Adjutant Territorial Army, 1932-36. War of 1939-45 (OBE). Director of Medical Services, Middle East Land Forces, Dec. 1955; QHS, 1956-60, retired. Col Comdt, RAMC, 1963-67. *Address:* c/o Glyn Mills and Co., Whitehall, SW1.

**PALMER, Lt-Col Roderick G. F.;** *see* Fenwick-Palmer.

**PALMER, Sidney John,** OBE 1953; Head of Royal Corps of Naval Constructors since 1968; *b* 28 Nov. 1913; *m* 1941, Mavis Beatrice Blennerhassett Hallett; four *s. Educ:* RNC Greenwich. WhSch 1937. Admty Experiment Works, Haslar, 1938; Portsmouth Dockyard, 1942; Chief Constructor, Sydney, 1945; Constructor Comdr, Hong Kong, 1946; Chief Constructor Aircraft Carriers, 1948; Prof. of Naval Architecture, RNC Greenwich, 1952; Asst Dir Dreadnought Project, 1959; Dep. Dir Polaris Programme, 1963; Dir Naval Ship Production, 1966; Dep. Dir General Ships, 1968. Mem. Council, RINA, 1960; Liveryman, Shipwrights' Co., 1968; Hon. Research Fellow, UCL, 1968. *Recreations:* tennis, badminton, bridge. *Address:* Bloomfield Avenue, Bath, Somerset. *T:* Bath 5592.

**PALMER, Hon. (William Jocelyn) Lewis,** FLS; Treasurer, the Royal Horticultural Society, 1953-65; *b* 15 Sept. 1894; 3rd *s* of 2nd Earl of Selborne; *m* 1922, Hon. Dorothy Loder, *d* of 1st Baron Wakehurst; one *s* one *d. Educ:* Winchester; Christ Church, Oxford. MA (Oxon) 1919. Served European War, 1914-19, with Roy. Hampshire Regt. Employed first in shipping, then in industry, 1919-48; Manager and Vice-Chm. Forestal Land Timber and Railways Co., 1942-48; retired, 1948. JP Hants 1941, CC 1945. CA 1957. Master of The Mercers' Company, 1950-51 and 1956-57; Member of Council of Roy. Horticultural Soc. 1937, Vice-Chm. 1952. Victoria Medal of Honour, 1954. *Recreation:* gardening. *Address:* St Michel, Rue à l'Or, St Saviour's, Guernsey, CI. *Club:* Brooks's.

**PALMER, William John; Judge Palmer;** Judge of Her Majesty's Chief Court for the Persian Gulf, since May 1967; *b* 25 April 1909; *o s* of late William Palmer and late Mary Louisa Palmer (*née* Dibb), Suffolk House, Cheltenham; *m* 1st, 1935, Zenaida Nicolaevna (*d* 1944), *d* of late Nicolai Maropoulo, Yalta, Russia; 2nd, 1949, Vanda Ianthe Millicent, *d* of late William Matthew Cowton, Kelvin Grove, Queensland; one *s* two *d. Educ:* Pate's Grammar School, Cheltenham; Christ's College, Cambridge (Lady Margaret Scholar). Barrister, Gray's Inn. Joined Indian Civil Service, 1932; Deputy Commissioner, Jalpaiguri, 1943, Chief Presidency Magistrate, Calcutta, 1945; retired from ICS, 1949. Joined Colonial Legal Service as Magistrate, Nigeria, 1950; Chief Registrar, High Court, Eastern Region, 1956; Judge, 1958; Acting Chief Justice of Eastern Nigeria, Oct.-Dec. 1963 and Aug.-Nov. 1965. Judge of HM's Court for Bahrain and Assistant Judge of the Chief Court for the Persian Gulf, 1965-67. *Recreations:* swimming, travel, history. *Address:* Guys Farm, Icomb, Glos. *T:* Stow-on-the-Wold 30219; Her Majesty's Court, PO Box 114, Bahrain. *Clubs:* Oxford and Cambridge University; Union (Sydney, NSW).

**PALUELLO, L. M.;** *see* Minio-Paluello.

**PANABOKKE, Sir Tikiri Banda,** Kt 1944; First Adigar of Ceylon since 1940; Special Representative of Government of Ceylon in India, New Delhi, since Feb. 1945; JP and unoffical Magistrate; *b* 28 March 1883; *s* of T. B. Panabokke; *m* 1906; four *s* four *d. Educ:* Trinity College and Royal College, Colombo. Proctor Supreme Court, 1906; MLC Ceylon, 1921-24; Member State Council, 1931-36; Minister of Health, 1931-36. Director: Kandy Hotels Co. Ltd, Vidyartha Soc. Ltd; Chm. Board of Directors and Gen. Manager Vidyartha Soc. Schools. Man. Dir Kandy Printers Ltd. *Publication:* Kandyan Law Commissions Report, 1934. *Recreation:* riding. *Address:* Elpitiya Walauwe, Gampola, Ceylon. *T:* Gampola 268. *Club:* Orient (Colombo).

**PANCKRIDGE, Surg. Vice-Adm. Sir (William) Robert (Silvester),** KBE 1962; CB 1960; Medical Director-General of the Navy, 1960-63, retired; *b* 11 Sept. 1901; *s* of W. P. Panckridge, OBE, MB, MRCS, LRCP, and Mrs Panckridge; *m* 1932, Edith Muriel, *d* of Sir John and Lady Crosbie, St John, Newfoundland; one *d. Educ:* Tonbridge School; Middlesex Hospital. FRSM 1955; QHP 1958. PMO, RN Coll., Dartmouth, 1948; Medical Officer-in-Charge; RN Hosp., Hong Kong, 1952; RN Hosp., Chatham, 1958; Surgeon Captain, 1952; Surgeon Rear-Admiral, 1958; Surgeon Vice-Admiral, 1960. QHP, 1958-63. CStJ 1959. *Recreations:* shooting, fishing, gardening. *Address:* Waterfall Lodge, Oughterard, Co. Galway. *T:* Oughterard 68.

**PANDIT, Vijaya Lakshmi, (Mrs Ranjit S. Pandit);** Member of Congress, Uttar Pradesh-Phulpur, India, since November 1964; *b* 18 August 1900; *d* of Motilal Nehru and Sarup Rani Nehru; *m* 1921, Ranjit S. Pandit; three *d. Educ:* privately. Member Municipal Board, Allahabad, and Chm. Education Cttee, 1935; MLA, UP, and Minister of Local Govt and Health in Congress Cabinet of UP, 1937-39, and 1946-47. Leader India delegation to UN General Assembly, 1946, 1947, 1948; Ambassador to Moscow, 1947-49; Ambassador of India to the USA and Mexico, 1949-51; Member of Indian Parliament, 1952-54; High Commissioner for India in London, and Indian Ambassador to Ireland, 1954-61, concurrently Indian Ambassador to Spain, 1958-61; Governor of Maharashtra, 1962-64. Imprisoned three times for participation in national movement, 1932, 1941, 1942. President of the United Nations Assembly, 1953-54. Hon. DCL, Oxford, 1964. *Publication:* The Evolution of India (Whidden Lectures), 1958. *Address:* E-8, Mafatlal Park, B. Desai Road, Bombay 26, India.

**PANET, Brig. Henri de Lotbinière,** CBE 1943 (OBE 1941); *b* 21 Apr. 1896; *s* of late Brig.-Gen. A. E. Panet, CB, CMG, DSO; *m* 1931, Truda Buchanan Hope; one *d. Educ:* Loyola Coll., Montreal; Royal Military Coll., Canada. Served European War, 1915-18. Royal Engineers, France and Salonica (wounded, despatches); Indian State Railways, 1920-34; served Egypt and Palestine, 1935-36 (despatches); Hong Kong, 1938-41 (OBE); Iraq and Persia, 1941-43 (CBE); BLA, 1944-45 (despatches); Director of Fortifications and Works, War Office, 1947-49; retired, 1949. *Recreation:* fishing. *Address:* 161 Wilton Road, Salisbury, Wilts. *T:* Salisbury 3615.

**PANKHURST, Albert Stanley,** CBE 1952; *b* 27 September 1897; 2nd *s* of William Pankhurst, Eltham; *m* 1920, Nellie, *d* of late Captain Walter Palmer, MC, KRRC; two *s* one *d*. *Educ:* Simon Langton School, Canterbury. Entered Ministry of Agriculture (Boy Clerk), 1913; Min. of Labour (Finance Dept and Unemployment Insurance Dept), 1920-34; seconded for service with Commissioner for Special Areas (England and Wales), Dec. 1934-Mar. 1937; International Board for non-Intervention in Spain (successively Chief Clerk, Dir of Accounts, Dep. Sec.), 1937-39; returned to Home Civil Service (Home Office, then Min. of Home Security, Chief Exec. Officer); Asst Chief Admin. Officer, London Civil Defence Region, 1940-42; Asst Sec., 1941; Min. of Production (Establishment Officer, then Dep. Head of Regional Div.), 1942-45; Board of Trade Regional Div., 1945-47. Principal Asst Sec., 1943; Under-Secretary, HM Treasury, 1947-52; Mission to India, 1952; UN Public Administration Adviser: to Govt of Hashemite Kingdom of Jordan, 1953-56; to Govt of Union of Burma, 1956-58; to Govt of Chile, 1959-60. Served European War (first in ranks, then commissioned), 1915-19, RA and RASC. Order of Star of Jordan, Second Class, 1956. *Recreations:* gardening, chess. *Address:* 14 Hartfield Road, Cooden, Bexhill-on-Sea, Sussex. *T:* Cooden 3268. *Club:* East India and Sports.

**PANKHURST, Air Vice-Marshal (Retd) Leonard Thomas,** CB 1955; CBE 1944; Senior partner, Pankhurst & Partners, Management Consultants (formed in August 1961); *b* 26 August 1902; *s* of late Thomas William Pankhurst, Teddington, Middlesex; *m* 1939, Ruth, *d* of late Alexander Phillips, Cromer, Norfolk; one *s* two *d*. *Educ:* Hampton Grammar School. Joined Royal Air Force, 1925; Group Captain, 1942; Air Commodore, 1947; Actg Air Vice-Marshal, 1954. Served War of 1939-45 (despatches, CBE); Directorate of War Organisation, Air Ministry, 1938-41; Coastal Command, 1941-42; Mediterranean Air Forces, 1942-45. Air Officer Commanding 44 Group Transport Command, 1945-46; Asst Comdt RAF Staff Coll., 1946; idc, 1947; Dir Staff Trg, Air Ministry, 1948-50; Air Officer Commanding RAF E Africa, 1950-52; Dir of Postings, Air Ministry, 1953-54; Director-General of Personnel (I), Air Ministry, 1954-57. *Address:* Earl's Eye House, Sandy Lane, Chester. *T:* Chester 20993; (business) 9 Stanley Place, Chester. *T:* Chester 26895. *Club:* United Service.

**PANNA, Maharaja Mahendra of; Lt-Col H.H. Sir Mahendra Maharaja Yadvendra Singh Bahadur,** KCSI 1932; KCIE 1922; *b* 1893; *S cousin* on his deposition, 1902; *m* 1st, 1912, Princess Shri Manhar Kunvarba (*d* 1927), *o d* of late Maharajah of Bhavnagar; 2nd, 1928, Princess Shri Gopal Kumari of Isarda, Rajputana, *e sis* of Maharaja of Jaipur. *Heir: s* Prince Narendra Singh Ju Dev, *b* 1915. The state has an area of 2596 square miles, and a population of about 200,000. *Address:* Panna State, Bundelkhand, Central India.

**PANNA LALL,** CSI 1942; CIE 1939; late ICS; Member, Special recruitment board for all-India services, Government of India, 1950; *b* 23 Nov. 1883; 3rd *s* of M. Hazari Lall; *m* Lakshmi Bai, *d* of M. Kandhaiya Lal Gumashta, Malguzar, Jubbulpur; one *s* three *d*. *Educ:* Agra College, Allahabad Univ. BA (1st Cl. Hons) 1900; BSc (1st Cl. Hons) 1900; LLB (1st in 1st Cl.; Lumsden Gold Medalist) 1903; Calcutta Univ. MA 1900; St John's College, Cambridge (Foundation Scholar and Prizeman) BA 1906; LLB (Double 1st Cl. Hons Nat. Sci. Tripos 1906, and Law Tripos 1907); Cama Prizeman, 1907; MA, 1937. Hon. DLitt Agra, 1939; Barrister-at-Law, 1907 (Gray's Inn). Enrolled Vakil, Allahabad High Court, 1903; entered Government Service, Judicial Department, 1903; entered ICS, 1907; Under Sec. to Government, 1917; Magistrate and Collector 1920; appointed to investigate customary Law in Kumaon, 1919; Sec. UP Excise Committee, 1921; Deputy Sec. to Govt UP, 1927; Sec. to Govt, Education, Industries and Agriculture Depts, 1927; Chief Sec. to Govt, 1938-39; Member, UP Legislative Council, 1927-28; Commissioner of a Division, 1931; Political Agent to Maharaja of Benares, 1931-37; Life Member Court, Allahabad Univ.; Member Academic Council, Allahabad Univ., 1934; Mem. Court and Exec. Council, Benares Hindu Univ. 1938; Examiner, Allahabad and Benares Univs; Mem. of Court, Aligarh Muslim Univ.; Mem. Exec. Council, Agra Univ.; Pres. Numismatic Society of India, 1934 and 1940; Ex-Mem., Indian Hist. Records Commn; Pres., UP Hist. Soc., 1939-45, now Hon. Life Mem.; Mem. Manag. Cttee Provincial Museum, UP and of UP Coin Cttee. Adviser to Governor, UP, 1939-44; mem., Linguistic Provinces Commission, India, 1948. *Publications:* The dates of Skandagupta and his successors, 1918; Some problems in Gupta Chronology; Kumaon Local Customs, 1920; Joint translator of Bhasa's Svapnavasavdatta; Hindu Customary Law, 1942; Ma Anandamayi, 1947; Forest Settlement Reports; articles in journals. *Address:* 19 Thornhill Road, Allahabad.

**PANNELL, Rt. Hon. Charles;** *see* Pannell, Rt Hon. T. C.

**PANNELL, Norman Alfred;** *b* 17 April 1901; 4th *s* of Arthur Harry Pannell and Minnie (*née* Bradberry); *m* 1932, Isabel Morris; two *s* (one *d* decd). *Educ:* Sir George Monoux Grammar Sch., London. Various commercial posts, London and Paris, 1917-30; John Holt & Co. (Liverpool) Ltd; West Africa, 1930-45; Member Nigerian Legislative Council, 1944-45; Finance Manager, Liverpool, 1945-50. Member Liverpool City Council, 1952-57, 1967-70; Chairman, Liverpool Education Cttee, 1967-70; Member, Cheshire County Council, 1970-. Governor, Liverpool Bluecoat Sch., 1953-. MP (C) Kirkdale Division of Liverpool, 1955-64. FCIS 1937. *Publication:* (with Lord Brockway) Immigration–What is the Answer?, 1965. *Address:* Thaxted, Mill Lane, Heswall, Cheshire. *T:* Heswall 1309. *Clubs:* Constitutional; Athenæum (Liverpool).

**PANNELL, Rt. Hon. (Thomas) Charles,** PC 1964; MP (Lab) West Leeds since 1949; *b* 10 Sept. 1902; *s* of James William and Mary Jane Pannell; *m* 1929, Lilian Maud Frailing; one *d*. Hon. Secretary, Trade Union Group Parliamentary Labour Party, 1953-64; Member AEU, 1918-; Branch official; District Cttee and Div. Cttee deleg. and shop steward for many years; Member Walthamstow Borough Council, 1929-36, Chief Whip of Labour Group; Chairman: Rating and Valuation Cttee; Municipal Entertainments Cttee; Erith Borough Council, 1938-55. Leader of Council and Chairman of Finance and General Purposes Cttee, until 1949; responsible Chairman during whole of War of 1939-45, for post-blitz services; Mayor, 1945-46, Alderman, 1944-55. Chairman of NW Kent

Divisional Exec. for Education, 1944-55; Member and Dep. Leader, Kent County Council Labour Group, 1946-49. Member Labour Party, 1918-; Past Chairman Dartford Divisional Labour Party. Parliamentary Delegations, Inter-Parliamentary Union: Berne, 1951; Belgium, 1952; NATO Conference of Parliamentarians, 1955-56-57; Poland, 1958; W Germany, 1960; Singapore, 1966 (Leader); Deleg. Atlantic Congress, 1959. Member Select Cttee on: Accommodation, 1953-54; Procedure, 1958; Law of Privilege, 1967; Member Joint Select Cttee, Lords and Commons, on House of Lords Reform, 1962; Minister of Public Building and Works, 1964-66; British Delegate, CPA Conference, Ottawa, 1966; Member, Cttee of Privileges, 1968-. Vice-Pres., Assoc. of Municipal Corporations. *Address:* 159 Glenview, Abbey Wood, SE2. *T:* Erith 33775.

**PANNETT, Juliet Kathleen, (Mrs M. R. D. Pannett),** FRSA, SGA; Free Lance Artist to The Times, Daily Telegraph, Radio Times, etc; Special Artist to Illustrated London News, 1958-65; *b* 15 July 1911; 2nd *d* of Charles Somers and May Brice, Hove, Sussex; *m* 1938, Major M. R. D. Pannett; one *s* one *d*. *Educ:* Wistons Sch., Brighton; Brighton College of Art. *One Man Exhibitions:* (1957-58) Royal Festival Hall; Qantas Gallery, 1959; New York, 1960; Cleveland, Ohio, 1960; Cooling Gallery, 1961; Coventry Cathedral Festival, 1962; Gloucester Three Choirs Festival, 1962; Brighton Corporation Gallery, Rottingdean, 1967; Arun Art Centre, 1967, 1969; Fine Art Gall., 1969; Migron Gall., Bath, 1970. Exhibitor: Royal Academy; Royal Society of Portrait Painters; Royal Inst. of Painters in Watercolours, etc. Official Artist on Qantas Inaugural Jet Flight, London to Sydney, 1959, 1964. Freeman of Painter Stainers' Company. *Work in Permanent Collections:* portraits in: National Portrait Gallery; Brighton Art Gallery; Cambridge Colleges; Maudsley Hospital; Army Phys. Training Sch., Aldershot; Painter Stainers' Hall, London; Hove Art Gallery; Portrait of HRH Princess Marina, Duchess of Kent, for Devon and Dorset Regt Mess, 1968, etc; Commemorative Stained Glass Window, Garrison church, Münster, 1967. *Publications:* Illustr. articles in The Artist; Illustr. for article in The Lancet; portraits in: S. J. Goldsmith's 20 Twentieth Century Jews; A. Frank's Svetlana Beriosova; action studies, Ballet Annual, 1956, 1957, 1958, 1959, 1960; cover portraits: Gerald Pawle's The War and Colonel Warden; Law Guardian; frontispieces, etc. *Recreations:* travel, music. *Address:* Pound House, Angmering Village, Sussex. *T:* Rustington 4446. *Clubs:* Women's Press; New Arts Theatre.

**PANT, Apasaheb Balasaheb;** Padma Shri 1954; Indian High Commissioner in London since 1969; *b* 11 Sept. 1912; *s* of Pratinidhis of Aundh; *m* 1942, Nalini Pant, MB, BS, FRCS; two *s* one *d*. *Educ:* Univ. of Bombay (BA); Univ. of Oxford (MA). Barrister-at-Law, Lincoln's Inn. Educn Minister, Aundh State; Prime Minister, 1944-48 (when State was merged into Bombay State). Member, AICC, 1948; an alternate Deleg., of India, at UN, 1951 and 1952; Comr for Govt of India in Brit. E Africa, 1948-54; apptd Consul-Gen. for Belgian Congo and Ruanda-Urundi, Nov. 1950, and Comr for Central Africa and Nyasaland, Dec. 1950; Officer on Special Duty, Min. of Ext. Affairs, 1954-55; Polit. Officer in Sikkim and Bhutan with control over Indian Missions in Tibet, 1955-61; Ambassador of India: to Indonesia, Oct. 1961-June 1964; to Norway, 1964-66; to UAR, 1966-69. *Publications:* Tensions and Tolerance, 1965; Aggression and Violence: Gandhian experiments to fight them, 1968; Yoga, 1968; Surya Namaskar, 1969; Mahatma Gandhi. *Recreations:* photography, yoga, tennis, skiing, gliding. *Address:* India House, WC2; (permanent) 893/5, Bhandarkar Institute Road, Deccan Gymkhana, Poona 4, India.

**PANTER-DOWNES, Mollie Patricia; (Mrs Clare Robinson);** London Correspondent The New Yorker, since 1939; *b* 25 Aug. 1906; *o c* of late Major Edward Panter-Downes, Royal Irish Regt; *m* 1927, Clare, 3rd *s* of late Aubrey Robinson; two *d*. *Educ:* mostly private. Wrote novel, The Shoreless Sea, at age of 16 (published John Murray, 1924); wrote in various English and American publications. *Publications:* Letter from England (Atlantic Monthly Press), 1940; Watling Green (children's book) (Scribners), 1943; One Fine Day, 1947; Ooty Preserved, 1967; contributed to The New Yorker Book of War Pieces, 1947. *Address:* Roppelegh's, nr Haslemere, Surrey. *Club:* Lansdowne.

**PANTIN, Most Rev. Anthony;** *see* Port of Spain, Archbishop of.

**PANTIN, William Abel,** MA; FBA 1948; Keeper of the University Archives, 1946-69; Fellow and Lecturer in History, Oriel College, Oxford, 1933-69, now Emeritus Fellow; University Lecturer in Mediæval Archæology and History, 1937-69; *b* Blackheath, 1 May 1902; *s* of Herbert Pantin and Emilie, *d* of late Charles D. Abel, Blackheath. *Educ:* Westminster; Christ Church, Oxford. 1st Class hons, Modern History, 1923; Bryce Research Student, 1924-25; Alexander Prize Essay, 1927; Asst Lecturer in History and Bishop Fraser Lecturer in Ecclesiastical History in the University of Manchester, 1926-33; Birkbeck Lecturer in Ecclesiastical History, Trinity Coll., Cambridge, 1948. *Publications:* Documents illustrating the activities of the General and Provincial Chapters of the English Black Monks, 1215-1540 (Camden Series, 1931-37); Canterbury College, Oxford (Oxford Historical Society), 1947; Durham Cathedral, 1948; The English Church in the Fourteenth Century, 1955; articles and reviews contributed to the English Historical Review, History, Trans. of Royal Historical Society, Bulletin of John Rylands Library, Oxoniensia. *Recreations:* travel, archæology, architectural history. *Address:* Oriel College, Oxford. *Club:* Athenæum.

**PANTON, Air Cdre Alastair Dyson,** CB 1969; OBE 1950; DFC 1939; Provost Marshal and Director of RAF Security since 1968; *b* 2 Nov. 1916; third *s* of William Dickson Panton, Aberdeen, and Mary Ethel Langley, Bedford; *m* 1939, Eileen Isabel Lumley, Bedford; three *s* (and one *s* decd). *Educ:* Bedford School; RAF Coll., Cranwell. Pilot Officer, No 53 Sqdn RAF, 1937; POW 1940-45; OC, Nos 58 and 540 Sqdns, 1946-47; Air Staff, Hong Kong, 1948-50; Wing Comdr Flying, RAF Coningsby, 1951-53; Staff Coll., 1953-54; Air Ministry, 1954-57; Station Comdr, RAF Cranwell, 1957-60, RAF Bircham Newton, 1961-62, RAF Tern Hill, 1963-64; HQ Far East Air Force, 1965-67. *Recreations:* tennis, gardening, poetry, Tchaikovsky. *Address:* 45 Chestnut Avenue, RAF Henlow, Beds. *T:* Henlow Camp 404. *Club:* Royal Air Force.

**PANTON, Dr Francis Harry,** MBE 1948; Assistant Chief Scientific Adviser (Nuclear), Ministry of Defence, since 1969; *b* 25 May 1923; 3rd *s* of George Emerson Panton and Annie Panton; *m* 1952, Audrey Mary (*née* Lane); two *s*. *Educ:* City Sch., Lincoln; University College and Univ. of Nottingham.

PhD Nottingham 1952. Served War of 1939-45: commissioned, Bomb Disposal, Royal Eng., 1943-47. Pres., Univ. of Nottingham Union, 1950-51; Vice-Pres., Nat. Union of Students, 1952-54; Technical Officer, ICI, Billingham, 1952-53; Permanent Under-Secretary's Dept, FO, 1953-55; Office of Political Adviser, Berlin, 1955-57; Dep. Head, Technical Research Unit, MoD, 1957-58; Attaché, British Embassy, Washington, DC, 1958-59; Technical Adviser, UK Delegn to Conf. on Discontinuance of Nuclear Tests, Geneva, 1959-61; Permanent Under-Secretary's Dept, FO, 1961-63; Counsellor (Defence), British Embassy, Washington, DC, 1963-66; Head of Defence Science 6, MoD, 1966-68. FRIC 1961. *Recreations:* bridge, golf, but not seriously; reading local history. *Address:* Traverse Cottage, Bredgar, near Sittingbourne, Kent. *T:* Wormshill 280. *Club:* Reform.

**PANUFNIK, Andrzej;** composer and conductor; *b* 24 Sept. 1914; 2nd *s* of Tomasz Panufnik and Mathilda Thonnes Panufnik; *m* 1963, Camilla Ruth, *yr d* of Commander R. F. Jessel, DSO, OBE, DSC, RN (retired); one *s* one *d*. *Educ:* Warsaw State Conservatoire; Vienna State Acad. for Music (under Professor Felix von Weingartner). Diploma with distinction, Warsaw Conservatoire, 1936. Conductor of the Cracow Philharmonic, 1945-46; Director and Conductor of the Warsaw Philharmonic Orchestra, 1946-47. Conducting leading European orchestras such as L'Orchestre National, Paris, Berliner Philharmonisches Orchester, L'Orchestre de la Suisse Romande, Geneva, and all principal British orchestras, 1947-. Polish decorations: Standard of Labor 1st class (1949), twice State Laureate (1951, 1952). Left Poland and settled in England, 1954; naturalized British subject, 1961. Vice-Chairman of International Music Council of UNESCO, Paris, 1950-53; Musical Director and Conductor, City of Birmingham Symphony Orchestra, 1957-59. Hon. Member of International Mark Twain Society (USA), 1954; Knight of Mark Twain, 1966. The Sibelius Centenary Medal, 1965. *Publications:* Piano Trio, 1934; Five Polish Peasant Songs, 1940; Tragic Overture, 1942; Twelve Miniature Studies for piano, 1947; Nocturne for orchestra, 1947; Lullaby for 29 stringed instruments and 2 harps, 1947; Sinfonia Rustica, 1948; Hommage à Chopin–Five vocalises for soprano and piano, 1949; Old Polish Suite for strings, 1950; Concerto in modo antico, 1951; Heroic Overture, 1952; Rhapsody for orchestra, 1956; Sinfonia Elegiaca, 1957; Polonia-Suite for Orchestra, 1959; Piano Concerto, 1961; Autumn Music, 1962; Landscape, 1962; Two Lyric Pieces, 1963; Sinfonia Sacra, 1963 (first prize, Prix de Composition Musicale Prince Rainier III de Monaco, 1963); Song to the Virgin Mary, 1964; Katyn Epitaph, 1966; Jagiellonian Triptych, 1966; Reflections for piano, 1967; The Universal Prayer, 1967-68; The Thames Pageant, 1969. *Address:* Riverside House, Twickenham, Middlesex.

**PAOLOZZI, Eduardo Luigi,** CBE 1968; Sculptor; *b* 7 March 1924; *s* of Rudolpho Antonio Paolozzi and Carmella (*née* Rossi), both Italian; *m* 1951, Freda Elliott; three *d*. *Educ:* Edinburgh School of Art; Slade Sch. Worked in Paris, 1947-50; Instructor, Central School of Arts and Crafts, London, 1950-55; Lecturer, St Martin's School of Art, 1955-56. First one-man exhibition in London, Mayor Gallery, 1947; first one-man exhibition in New York, Betty Parsons Gallery, 1960; also one-man exhibition there, 1962. Work in permanent collections: Tate Gallery; Contemporary Art Society; Museum of Modern Art, New York, etc. Work exhibited in: British Pavilion, Venice Biennale, 1952; Documenta 2, Kassel, 1959; New Images of Man, New York, 1959; British Pavilion, 30th Venice Biennale; International Exhibition of Sculpture, Boymans Museum, Rotterdam; Open Air Sculpture, Battersea Park, London; Critics Choice, Tooths Gallery, London; City Art Gallery, Manchester, Oct. 1960; British Sculpture in the Sixties, Tate Gallery, March 1965; Chelsea School of Art, 1965; Hanover Gallery, 1967. *Recreation:* music. *Address:* 107 Dovehouse Street, SW3; Landermere, Thorpe-le-Soken, Essex. *T:* Thorpe-le-Soken 210.

**PAPE, Hon. Sir George (Augustus),** Kt 1968; Judge of Supreme Court of Victoria since 1957; *b* 29 Jan. 1903; *s* of George Frederick Pape and Minnie Maud Pape (*née* Bryan); *m* 1952, Mabel, *d* of Alfred Lloyd; no *c*. *Educ:* All Saints Grammar Sch., St Kilda; University of Melbourne (LLB). QC 1955. RAAF, 1940-46. *Recreations:* tennis, golf. *Address:* 146 Kooyong Road, Toorak, Victoria 3142, Australia. *T:* 20-6158. *Club:* Australian (Melbourne).

**PAPE, Jonathan Hector Carruthers;** General Manager and Secretary, National Dock Labour Board, since Aug. 1970; *b* 8 March 1918; *er s* of Jonathan Pape, MA and Florence Muriel Myrtle; *m* 1944, Mary Sullins (*née* Jeffries); one *s*. *Educ:* Merchant Taylors' Sch., Crosby. Mercantile Marine, 1934-46; Master Mariner (FG), 1944 (Liverpool Qualif.). Manager, Master Stevedoring Co., Liverpool, 1947-51; National Dock Labour Board: Dep. Port Manager, London, 1952-57; Asst Gen. Manager, Bd HQ, 1957-69; Dep. Gen. Manager and Secretary, Bd HQ, 1969. Mem., Honourable Co. of Master Mariners, 1965. *Recreations:* swimming, gardening, and riding at anchor in what spare time is left. *Address:* 4 Knole Way, Sevenoaks, Kent. *T:* Sevenoaks 52820.

**PARARAJASINGAM, Sir Sangarapillai,** Kt 1955; Senator, Ceylon, 1954-59; Chairman: Board of Directors, Colonial Motors Ltd; Member, Board of Trustees, Ceylon Social Service League; *b* 25 June 1896; *s* of late W. Sangarapillai, social worker and philanthropist; *m* 1916, Padmavati, *d* of Sir Ponnambalam Arunachalam; one *s* one *d*. *Educ:* St Thomas' Coll., Mt Lavinia. Past President, Board of Directors, Manipay Hindu Coll., Manager, 1929-61; Past President Ceylon Poultry Club; Member National Savings Cttee; Past Chairman, Board Governors, Ceylon Inst. of Scientific and Industrial Research. Formerly Chairman: Board of Directors, Agricultural and Industrial Credit Corporation of Ceylon; Education Cttee, Ceylon Social Service League; Low Country Products Assoc., 1943-44 and 1944-45; Ceylon Coconut Board; Coconut Commn; Past Member: Textile Tribunal; Land Advisory Cttee; Ceylon Tea Propaganda Board; Coconut Research Scheme; Radio Advisory Board; Excise Advisory Cttee; Central Board of Agriculture; Income Tax Board of Review; Rice Advisory Board; Services Standing Wages Board; Board for Approval of Credit Agencies; Commn on Broadcasting; Past President Vivekananda Society; Rotary Club of Colombo; formerly Trustee and Hon. Treasurer, Ceylon Society of Arts; formerly Manager, all Schools managed by Ceylon Social Service League. JP Ceylon 1923. Travelled widely in the UK, Europe, USA, India, Far East. Coronation Medals, 1937 and 1953. *Recreations:* gardening, agriculture and farming. *Address:* No 50, Pathmalaya, Flower Road, Colombo 7, Ceylon. *T:* 23159.

*See also P. Nadesan.*

**PARBURY, George Mark;** Registrar of the High Court of Justice in Bankruptcy, since 1965; *b* 27 April 1908; *s* of Norman Cecil Parbury (living in Queensland) and late Ellen Parbury; *m* 1942, Roma Constance, *d* of late James Robert Raw, JP, New Zealand, and Clare Raw. *Educ:* Geelong, Australia; Jesus Coll., Cambridge. Called to Bar, Lincoln's Inn, 1934. Practised at Chancery Bar, 1934-39. Served War of 1939-45, 1940-45, Temp. Lt-Col., 1944; AAG, AG3e War Office, Mil. Govt 21 Army Group. Again practised at Chancery Bar, 1946-65; Mem. Bar Council, 1961-62. *Recreations:* walking on the Downs; gardening. *Address:* The Orchard, Paine's Twitten, Lewes, Sussex. *T:* Lewes 3529. *Clubs:* Army and Navy; Seaford Golf (Seaford).

**PARC-LOCMARIA, Marquis du, (Alain);** Hon. CVO; Belgian Diplomat, retired; Commander, Ordre de Léopold (glaives); Grand Officier, Ordre de la Couronne (glaives); Grand Officier, Ordre de Léopold II (glaives et palme); Croix du Feu; Croix de Guerre (Belgian) (2 palmes), etc; *b* Brussels, 27 Oct. 1892; *m* Comtesse Elisabeth de Grunne; one *s* one *d*. *Educ:* Oratory Sch., Edgbaston; Louvain University (Doctor of Laws). Served War of 1914-18, Belgian Army (seriously wounded). Entered Diplomatic Service, 1920; Second, then First Secretary, Belgian Embassy, Paris, 1922-28; Dept of Foreign Affairs, Brussels, 1928-39; Couns., 1930; Minister, 1937; Minister to Rumania, 1939; Minister and Commerc. Couns., Belgian Embassy, US, 1942; President, etc; Belgian delegations, including those to FAO, UNRRA, and International Conferences, 1943-45; Minister to Sweden, 1946-48; Ambassador to Canada, 1949-53; Ambassador to Court of St James's, 1953-57, retired. Grand Cordon, Polar Star (Sweden); Officier de la Légion d'Honneur, Medaille Militaire, and Croix de Guerre (France), etc. *Recreation:* shooting. *Heir: s* Comte du Parc Locmaria. *Address:* Château de Thieusies, Hainaut, Belgium. *Club:* Beefsteak.

**PARDOE, John Wentworth;** MP (L) Cornwall North since 1966; *b* 27 July 1934; *s* of Cuthbert B. Pardoe and Marjorie E. W. (*née* Taylor); *m* 1958, Joyce R. Peerman; two *s* one *d*. *Educ:* Sherborne; Corpus Christi Coll., Cambridge (MA). Television Audience Measurement Ltd, 1958-60; Osborne Peacock Co. Ltd, 1960-61; Liberal News, 1961-66. Treasurer of the Liberal Party, 1968-69. Consultant to Nat. Assoc. of Schoolmasters, 1967-. Dir, William Schlackman Ltd, 1968-. *Recreations:* cricket, tennis, singing. *Address:* Rose Cottage, St Mawgan, Newquay, Cornwall.

**PARE, Rev. Canon Clive Frederick,** MA Cantab; Canon Residentiary since 1963 and Precentor since 1966, of Gloucester Cathedral; *b* 27 April 1908; *s* of Frederick William Pare, Nottingham, and Florence May Pare (*née* Hodson), Loughborough; *m* 1954, Hilda Clare, *d* of Thomas Dewsbury Parson, Cape Town; two *s*. *Educ:* Nottingham High Sch.; King's Coll., Cambridge (Choral Scholar); Cuddesdon Theological Coll. Housemaster, Bishop Cotton Sch., Simla, India, 1931. Deacon, 1933; Priest, 1935; Asst Curate, Gillingham with Milton, Dorset, 1934-36; Senior Curate, St John, E Dulwich, 1936-37; Asst Master and Minor Canon, Canterbury, 1937-38; Headmaster, Canterbury Cathedral Choir Sch., 1938-63. Hon. Secretary, Canterbury Dio. Advisory Cttee for the Care of Churches, and Member Central Council for Care of Churches, 1947-63. Private Chaplain to Archbishop of Canterbury (Lord Fisher) for tour of Australia and New Zealand, 1950. Member Canterbury City Council, 1954; Sheriff of Canterbury, 1961-62; Mayor of Canterbury (JP), 1962-63. *Recreations:* music, gardening, walking, camping, local government. *Address:* 7 Miller's Green, Gloucester. *T:* 23695.

**PARE, Very Rev. Philip Norris,** Provost and Vicar of the Cathedral Church of All Saints, Wakefield, since 1962; a Church Commissioner, since 1968; *b* 13 May 1910; *s* of Frederick William and Florence May Pare; *m* 1943, Nancy Eileen, *d* of late Canon C. Patteson; two *s* two *d*. *Educ:* Nottingham High Sch.; King's Coll., Cambridge; Cuddesdon Theological Coll. Curate, All Saints, W Dulwich, 1934-37; Chaplain and Vice-Principal, Bishops Coll., Cheshunt, 1937-39; Curate, St Mary the Less, Cambridge, 1939-40. Chaplain RNVR, 1940-46. Vicar of Cheshunt, Herts, 1946-57; Rural Dean of Ware, 1949-56; Examining Chaplain to Bishop of St Albans, 1952-56; Missioner Canon Stipendiary, Diocese of Wakefield, 1957-62; Diocesan Adviser for Christian Stewardship, 1959-63; Member Board of Ecclesiastical Insurance Office, 1966-. *Publications:* (with Donald Harris) Eric Milner-White, A Memoir, 1965; Re-Thinking Our Worship, 1967; articles in Theology, The Reader, etc. *Recreations:* modern stained glass and architecture; railways, motor cars; church music. *Address:* The Cathedral Vicarage, Margaret Street, Wakefield. *T:* 72402.

**PARENT, Most Rev. Charles Eugène,** ThD; Titular Archbishop of Vassinassa since 1967; *b* Les Trois-Pistoles, Qué, 22 April 1902; *s* of Louis Parent and Marie Lavoie. *Educ:* Rimouski Seminary; Laval University of Quebec; Institutum Angelicum, Rome. ThD 1929. Professor of Theology at Rimouski Seminary and Chaplain at St Joseph's Hospital of Rimouski, 1931-41; Rector of Saint Germain's Cathedral, 1941-45; Auxiliary Bishop at Rimouski, 1944-50; Capitulaire Vicaire, 1950-51; Archbishop of Rimouski, 1951-67. *Publication:* Mandements et circulaires au clergé et au peuple de l'archidiocèse de Rimouski, 3 vols, 1951-67. *Address:* c/o Archevêché de Rimouski, Quebec, Canada.

**PARES, Peter;** *b* 6 Sept. 1908; 2nd *s* of late Sir Bernard Pares, KBE, DCL, and late Margaret Pares (*née* Dixon); unmarried. *Educ:* Lancing Coll.; Jesus Coll., Cambridge (Scholar). Entered Consular Service, 1930; served in Philadelphia, 1930; Havana, 1932; Consul, Liberec and Bratislava, Czechslovakia, 1936-39; Budapest, 1939; Cluj, Rumania, 1940; New York, 1941; Washington, as First Secretary, 1944; Control Commission for Germany, 1946; Foreign Office, 1949; Casablanca, 1952; Strasbourg, 1956; Deputy Consul-General, Frankfurt, 1957; Consul-General, Asmara, Eritrea, 1957-59; Head of Education and Cultural Relations Dept, CRO, 1960-63. *Address:* 17 Beechwood Crescent, Eastbourne, Sussex.

**PARFITT, Rt. Rev. Thomas Richards;** Assistant Bishop of Derby since 1962; Rector of Matlock with Tansley since 1962; *b* 24 May 1911; *s* of Charles Henry John and Maud Sarah Parfitt. *Educ:* S John Baptist Coll., Oxford. BA Oxon 1933 (2nd class Lit. Hum., 1933; 2nd class Theology, 1934); MA 1936. Cuddesdon Coll., 1934-35. Deacon, 1935; Priest, 1936; Asst Curate of New Mills, 1935-39; Curate of Rugby (in charge of Holy Trinity), 1939-43; Chaplain RNVR, 1943-46; Vicar of S Andrew, Derby, 1946-52; Rural Dean of Derby, 1951-52; Bishop in Madagascar, 1952-61. *Address:* Matlock Rectory, Derbyshire, DE4 3BZ. *T:* Matlock 2199.

**PARGETER, Edith;** *b* 28 Sept. 1913; 3rd *c* of Edmund Valentine Pargeter and Edith Hordley; unmarried. *Educ:* Dawley C of E Elementary Sch.; County High School for Girls, Coalbrookdale. Worked as a chemist's assistant, and at twenty succeeded in finding a publisher for first–and unsuccessful–book. WRNS Aug. 1940, teleprinter operator (BEM 1944); dispersed from the Service, Aug. 1945. FIIAL 1962. Gold Medal and Ribbon, Czechoslovak Society for International Relations, 1965. *Publications:* Hortensius, Friend of Nero and Iron-Bound; The City Lies Foursquare, 1939; Ordinary People, 1941; She Goes to War, 1943; The Eighth Champion of Christendom, 1945; Reluctant Odyssey, 1946; Warfare Accomplished, 1947; By Firelight, 1948; The Fair Young Phoenix, 1948; The Coast of Bohemia, 1949; Lost Children, 1950; Fallen Into the Pit, 1951; Holiday with Violence, 1952; This Rough Magic, 1953; Most Loving Mere Folly, 1953; The Soldier at the Door, 1954; A Means of Grace, 1956; Tales of the Little Quarter (trans. from the Czech of Jan Neruda), 1957; Don Juan (trans. from the Czech of Josef Toman), 1958; Assize of the Dying, 1958; The Heaven Tree, 1960; The Green Branch, 1962; The Scarlet Seed, 1963; The Terezín Requiem (trans. from the Czech of Josef Bor), 1963; The Lily Hand and other stories, 1965; Close Watch on the Trains (trans. from the Czech of Bohumil Hrabal), 1968; Report on my Husband (trans. from the Czech of Josefa Slánská), 1969. *Recreations:* walking, preferably with canine as well as human companions; collecting gramophone records, particularly of voice; reading anything and everything; theatre. *Address:* Parkville, Park Lane, Madeley, Telford, Shropshire. *T:* Ironbridge 3335.

**PARGITER,** family name of **Baron Pargiter.**

**PARGITER,** Baron, *cr* 1966 (Life Peer) of Southall; **George Albert Pargiter,** CBE 1961; DL; *b* 16 March 1897; *s* of William Pargiter, Greens Norton; *m* 1919, Dorothy Woods; two *s* one *d*. *Educ:* Towcester Grammar Sch. Engineer by profession. Served 1914-16 Army, at Gallipoli. MP (Lab) Spelthorne Division of Middlesex, 1945-50, Southall, 1950-66; Member Middlesex County Council, 1934-65, County Alderman, 1946 (Chairman, 1959-60). Member several public bodies. Mayor of Southall, 1938-40 (three years); DL Middlesex 1953; DL County of London, 1965. *Address:* 190 Whyteleafe Road, Caterham, Surrey. *T:* Caterham 45588.

**PARGITER, Maj.-Gen. Robert Beverley,** CB 1942; CBE 1945; *b* 11 July 1889; *s* of late F. E. Pargiter, ICS; *m* 1917, Muriel Huxley; one *s* two *d*. *Educ:* Rugby; RMA, Woolwich. Commissioned RA 1909; served with RA, European War, 1914-18, on NWF, India, France, and Belgium (severely wounded, despatches); Military Mission to Baltic States, 1919-21 (Brevet of Major); psc Camberley, 1924; Instructor Staff Coll., Quetta, 1930-33; idc 1934; GSO 1 Operations, WO, 1936-38; War Service, 1939-45; Commander 1st AA Brigade; 4th, 7th and 5th AA Divisions; 3rd AA Group; Maj.-Gen. Anti-Aircraft, Allied Force HQ, N. Africa and Central Mediterranean Forces (despatches, CBE, Commander of Legion of Merit); retired, 1945; Commissioner, British Red Cross and St John's War Organisation, Middle East, 1945, Malaya, 1946. Colonel Comdt RA, 1951-54. *Publication:* (with late Colonel H. Eady) The Army and Sea Power, 1927. *Recreations:* fishing, gardening, braille. *Address:* Nym, Moretonhampstead, Devon.

**PARHAM, Adm. Sir Frederick Robertson,** GBE 1959 (CBE 1949); KCB 1955 (CB 1951); DSO 1944; *b* 9 Jan. 1901; *s* of late Frederick James Parham, Bath, and late Jessie Esther Brooks Parham (*née* Robertson), Cheltenham; *m* 1926, Kathleen Dobrée, *d* of Eugene Edward Carey, Guernsey; one *s*. *Educ:* RN Colleges, Osborne and Dartmouth. Joined HMS Malaya as Midshipman, 1917; specialised in gunnery, 1925; Commander, 1934. Commanded HMS Shikari, 1937, HMS Gurkha, 1938-40. Captain, 1939. Commanded HMS Belfast, 1942-44 (despatches), HMS Vanguard, 1947-49; Dep. Chief, Naval Personnel, 1949-51; Rear-Admiral, 1949; Vice-Admiral, 1952; Flag Officer (Flotillas) and 2nd in command, Mediterranean, 1951-52; a Lord Commissioner of the Admiralty, Fourth Sea Lord and Chief of Supplies and Transport, 1954-55; Commander-in-Chief, The Nore, 1955-58; retired list, 1959. Member British Waterways Board, Jan. 1963-1967, Vice-Chairman (part-time) Aug. 1963-1967. Naval ADC to the King, 1949. Grand Cross of Military Order of Avis (Portugal), 1955; Order of Al Rafidain (Class II, Mil., conferred by the King of Iraq), 1956; Ordine al merito della Repubblica, Grande Ufficiale (Italy) 1958. *Address:* The High House, Elsted, Midhurst, Sussex. *T:* Harting 296. *Club:* United Service.

**PARHAM, Hedley John,** CBE 1955; MA, LLB (Cantab); JP; *b* 29 Oct. 1892; *s* of late Leonard Parham, JP, Gosport, Hants; *m* 1921, Irene, *d* of late H. E. Phillips, JP, Kintbury, Berks; two *s*. *Educ:* Leys Sch., Cambridge; Trinity Hall, Cambridge. Served European War (RE), 1914-19 (despatches). Called to the Bar (Inner Temple), 1919. Joined Department of Director of Public Prosecutions, 1920; Asst Director of Public Prosecutions, 1949-56; retired. JP Glos, 1957. *Address:* Tanners, South Cerney, Cirencester, Glos. GL7 5UP. *T:* South Cerney 258.

**PARHAM, Maj.-Gen. Hetman Jack,** CB 1949; CBE 1943; DSO 1940, and Bar 1943; late Royal Artillery; *b* 27 July 1895. 2nd Lieut, Royal Artillery, 1914; served European War, 1915-19, in France, Belgium, and the Balkans (despatches twice, 1914-15 star, two medals); Major, 1934; served War of 1939-45, in North Africa and North-West Europe (despatches, DSO and Bar, CBE); Brigadier, 1942; Colonel, 1944; Maj.-Gen., 1945. ADC to the King, 1946-47; commanding No 3 Anti-Aircraft Group, 1946-49; retired pay, 1949. Officer of Legion of Merit (USA). *Address:* Hyntle Place, Hintlesham, Ipswich, Suffolk.

**PARIKIAN, Manoug;** violinist; Professor of Violin, Royal Academy of Music, since 1959; *b* Mersin, Turkey, 15 Sept. 1920, of Armenian parentage; *s* of late Stepan Parikian and Vanouhi (*née* Bedelian); *m* 1957, Diana Margaret (*née* Carbutt); two *s*. *Educ:* Trinity College of Music, London (Fellow). Leader: Liverpool Philharmonic Orchestra, 1947-48; Philharmonia Orchestra, London, 1949, until resignation, 1957; has appeared in all European countries as solo violinist, and at following festivals: Aldeburgh, 1949-51, 1968; Edinburgh, 1950-64; Holland, 1951; Aix-en-Provence, 1954; Baalbek, 1957; Three Choirs, 1958; Cheltenham, 1959-60, 1962, 1963, 1965; Lisbon (Gulbenkian), 1960; Llandaff, 1961; Coventry, 1962; Oxford, 1963; York, 1966; Leeds Triennial, 1967. Introduced Shostakovitch Violin Concerto to Scandinavia (Stockholm), 1956; first public performance of works by Iain Hamilton, Rawsthorne, Musgrave, Alexander Goehr, Elizabeth Maconchy, and Gordon Crosse. Toured USSR, April-May 1961, and Nov. 1965. Member Jury, Tchaikovsky violin competition, Moscow, 1970. Hon. RAM, 1963. *Recreations:* collecting early printed books in Armenian; backgammon. *Address:* The Old Rectory, Waterstock, Oxford. *T:* Ickford 603.

**PARIS, Sir Edward (Talbot),** Kt 1954; CB 1947; DSc (London), FInstP; *b* 23 Jan. 1889; *s* of late Edward and Eliza Paris; *m* 1925, Eveline Amy (*d* 1968), *d* of late J. W. Shortt, MD; three *d*. *Educ:* Dean Close Sch., Cheltenham; Imperial College of Science; University College, London. Fellow University College, London, 1921; served European War, 1914-18, RA, 1915-18; seconded to Ministry of Munitions, 1918; Signals Experimental Establishment, War Dept, 1919; Experimental Officer in Air Defence Experimental Establishment, 1923; Dep. Director of Scientific Research, WO, 1938; transferred Ministry of Supply, 1939; Controller of Physical Research, 1941; Controller of Physical Research and Signals Development, 1942; Principal Director of Scientific Research (Defence), Ministry of Supply, 1946; Chief Scientific Adviser, Home Office, 1948-54. US Medal of Freedom with Bronze Palm, 1947. *Publications:* various papers in scientific journals. *Address:* Lavender Cottage, Crazy Lane, Sedlescombe, Sussex. *T:* Sedlescombe 261.

**PARIS, John;** Director, National Army Museum, 1967-69; *b* Hove, 2 May 1912; *s* of Herbert Henry Paris, Comptroller of Telegraphs and Postmaster, Durban, during Boer War; *m* 1940, Beryl Maria Thomson; no *c*. *Educ:* Brighton Coll.; Brighton College of Art; Worcester Coll., Oxford. BA (English) 1936; MA 1938; BLitt 1938. Commissioned into RA, 1940; SO Fixed Defences Scottish Command, 1942; Major. Dep. Director, Walker Art Gallery, Liverpool, 1938-49; Director, National Gallery of S Africa, Cape Town, 1949-62. Hon. Life Vice-President, Friends of Italy; Past President, S African Musuems Assoc.; Kolbe Memorial Lecturer, University of Cape Town, 1961. Has made broadcasts. *Publications:* English Water-Colour Painters, 1945; William Gilpin and the Cult of the Picturesque; introductions, catalogues and articles in learned journals; occasional poems, etc. *Address:* Brook House, Ardingly, Sussex. *T:* Ardingly 274.

**PARISH, David (Elmer) Woodbine,** CBE 1964; Chairman, City and Guilds of London Institute since 1967; *b* 29 June 1911; *o s* of late Walter Woodbine Parish and Audrey Makins; *m* 1939, Mona Blair McGarel, *o d* of late Charles McGarel Johnston, Glynn, Co. Antrim; two *d*. *Educ:* Eton; Lausanne, Switzerland. Chairman and Managing Director, Holliday and Greenwood Ltd, 1953-59; Managing Director, Bovis Holdings Ltd, 1960-66. President London Master Builders Association, 1952; President, National Federation of Building Trades Employers, 1960; Member: Regional Adv. Council for Technological Educn, London and Home Counties, 1952-69; Architects Registration Council, 1952-; National Advisory Council for Education in Industry and Commerce, 1953-; British Institute of Management Council, 1953-62, Board of Fellows, 1966-; National Council for Technological Awards, 1955-61; Board of Building Education, 1955-66; Building Research Board, 1957-60; Industrial Training Council, 1958-64; Council, British Employers' Confedn, 1959-65; Council Foundn for Management Education, 1959-65; British Productivity Council, 1961-70; Human Sciences Cttee (SRC), 1963-66; Construction Industry Training Board, 1964-70. Chairman: UK National Cttee, International Apprentice Competition, 1962-; MPBW Working Party on Research and Information, 1963; Nat. Examinations Bd for Supervisory Studies, 1964-; Nat. Jt Consult. Cttee of Architects, Quantity Surveyors and Builders, 1966-68; Dept of Health and Social Security Cttee of Inquiry on Hosp. Building Maintenance and Minor Capital Works, 1968-70; Member Court: Russia Co., 1937-; City Univ., 1967-; Mem. Board of Governors, Polytechnic, Regent Street, 1967-70; Mem. Court, Polytechnic of Central London, 1970-. Vice-President International Fedn of European Contractors of Building and Public Works, 1967-. Vice-Chm., Bd of Governors, St Thomas' Hosp., 1968-; Chm. Council, St Thomas's Hosp. Med. Sch., 1970. Warden, Clothworkers' Company, 1962-64. FIOB 1940; FRSA 1953; FBIM 1957. *Recreations:* travel and music. *Address:* 5 Lurgan Mansions, Sloane Square, SW1. *T:* 01-730 6512; The Glebe Barn, Pulborough, Sussex. *T:* Pulborough 2613. *Club:* Boodle's.

**PARK, Alexander Dallas,** CMG 1932; JP; FIANZ; FRANZ; Company Director; *b* Waitaki, Otago, New Zealand, 1882; *s* of George Park, Merchant; *m* Ada Emily, *d* of J. C. Mercer, Nelson; one *s*. *Educ:* Waitaki; Waimate. Joined Public Works Dept, 1900; served South African War, 1902; Senior Accountant, Dept of Agriculture, 1918; Inspector for Public Service Commissioner and Treasury, 1919; Secretary for Marine, 1922; Asst Public Service Commissioner, 1924; Asst Secretary to Treasury, 1926; Secretary to Treasury, 1930-35; Chairman, Local Government Loans Board, 1930-35; Deputy Chairman, Stores Control Board, 1930-35; Financial Adviser to Government, 1931-35; Foundation Member Reserve Bank of New Zealand Board, 1934-35; Chairman: Soldiers' Financial Assistance Board, 1940-46; State Advances Corporation of New Zealand, 1936-49. *Recreations:* golf, fishing. *Address:* 14 Park Avenue, Titahi Bay, Wellington, NZ. *T:* Titahi Bay 7414. *Club:* Wellington (Wellington).

**PARK, Daphne Margaret Sybil Désirée,** OBE 1960; HM Consul-General, Hanoi, since 1969; *b* England, 1 Sept. 1921; British parents; unmarried. *Educ:* Rosa Barrett Sch.; Somerville Coll., Oxford. WTS (FANY), 1943-47 (Allied Commn for Austria, 1946-48). FO, 1948; UK Delegn to NATO, 1952; 2nd Sec., Moscow, 1954; FO, 1956; Consul and 1st Sec., Leopoldville, 1959; FO, 1961; Lusaka, 1964; FO, 1967. *Recreations:* good talk, politics, and difficult places. *Address:* c/o Foreign and Commonwealth Office, King Charles Street, SW1; c/o Westminster Bank, 121 High Street, Oxford. *Club:* Royal Commonwealth Society.

**PARK, Hon. Sir Hugh (Eames),** Kt 1965; **Hon. Mr Justice Park;** Judge of the High Court of Justice, Probate, Divorce and Admiralty Division, since 1965; Presiding Judge, Western Circuit, since 1970; *b* 24 April 1910; *er s* of late William Robert and late Helen Beatrice Park; *m* 1938, Beryl Josephine, *d* of late Joseph and Margery Coombe; three *d*. *Educ:* Blundell's; Sidney Sussex Coll., Cambridge (Hon. Fellow, 1968). Called to the Bar, Middle Temple, 1936; QC 1960; Bencher, 1965. Member Western Circuit. Served War, 1940-45; Sqdn Leader, 1945. Recorder of Penzance, 1959-60; of Exeter, 1960-64; of Southampton, 1964-65. Member, Court of Exeter Univ., 1961; Member, Board of Governors, Blundell's Sch., 1961. Commn of Assize, North East Circuit, 1963; Judge of the Courts of Appeal, Channel Islands, 1964-65; Chairman, County of Devon Quarter Sessions, 1964-; Deputy Chairman, Cornwall County Quarter Sessions, 1959-. *Recreation:* fishing. *Address:* Royal Courts of Justice, Strand, WC2; 31 Ferncroft Avenue,

Hampstead, NW3. *T:* 01-435 8909; Gorran Haven, Cornwall. *T:* Mevagissey 2333. *Clubs:* Athenæum; Exeter and County (Exeter).

**PARK, Air Chief Marshal Sir Keith Rodney,** GCB 1946 (KCB 1945; CB 1940); KBE 1942; MC; DFC; DCL, MA (Oxon); *b* 1892; *s* of late Professor J. Park; *m* 1918, Dorothy Margarita, *d* of Lieut-Col Woodbine Parish, CMG, CBE; one *s* (and one *s* killed on active service, 1951). *Educ:* King's Coll., Auckland, NZ; Otago Boys' High Sch., Dunedin. Commanded No 11 Fighter Group during Battle of Britain; commanded RAF Egypt; AOC, RAF, Malta, 1942-43; AOC-in-C Middle East, 1944; Allied Air C-in-C South-East Asia, 1945-46. *Recreation:* sailing. *Address:* Blue Waters, Lucerne Road, Remuera, Auckland, NZ.

**PARK, Merle Florence;** Principal, Royal Ballet; *b* Salisbury, S Rhodesia, 8 Oct. 1937; *d* of P. J. Park, Eastlea, Salisbury, S Rhodesia, C Africa; *m* 1965, James Monahan, *qv* (marr. diss. 1970); one *s*. *Educ:* Elmhurst Ballet Sch. Joined Sadler's Wells Ballet, 1955; Performed solos, 1956; principal soloist, 1959. First danced: Blue Bird (Act III, Sleeping Beauty), 1956; Swanhilda (Coppelia), 1958; Mamzelle Angot (Mamzelle Angot), 1958; Lise (Fille Mal Gardée), 1960; Juliet (Romeo and Juliet), 1965; Giselle, 1967; Clara (Nutcracker), 1968; Celestial (Shadow Play), 1967; Aurora (Sleeping Beauty), 1968. First rôle, a Mouse (Sleeping Beauty prologue); First solo, Milkmaid (Façade), 1955. *Recreations:* tennis, housewifery. *Address:* Flat 1, 69 Holland Park, W11.

**PARK, Trevor;** *b* 12 Dec. 1927; *s* of Stephen Clifford Park and Annie Park (*née* Jackson); *m* 1953, Barbara Black; no *c*. *Educ:* Bury Grammar Sch.; Manchester Univ. (MA). History Master, Bacup and Rawtenstall Grammar Sch., 1949-56; WEA, Tutor and Organiser (NW District), 1956-60; Lecturer, Extramural Dept, University of Sheffield (politics and international relations), 1960-64. Parliamentary Labour Candidate: Altrincham and Sale, General Election, 1955; Darwen, General Election, 1959; MP (Lab) South East Derbyshire, 1964-70. Member, TGWU; Member Select Cttees on Nationalised Industries (1966-68), and on Education and Science. *Recreation:* walking.

**PARK, William,** OBE 1967; Keeper of Manuscripts, National Library of Scotland, since 1946; *b* 14 April 1909; *s* of John Park and Isabella Stephenson Berridge; *m* 1935, Mary Allan, *d* of Robert Wilson; two *d*. *Educ:* Hawick High Sch.; Edinburgh Univ. (MA); School of Librarianship, University College, London. Assistant, National Library of Scotland, 1932-46; seconded to Scottish Home Department, 1940-46. *Address:* 24 Liberton Drive, Edinburgh 9. *T:* 031-664 3695.

**PARKE, Herbert William,** MA (Oxon); LittD (Dublin); Fellow of Trinity College, Dublin, since 1929; Professor of Ancient History since 1934, Vice-Provost since 1952, Curator since 1965, Librarian 1949-65; *b* Moneymore, Co. Londonderry, 7 Sept. 1903; *o s* of William and Bertha Blair Parke; *m* 1930, Nancy Bankart, *y d* of Arthur R. Gurney, Cracoe, Yorks; one *d*. *Educ:* Coleraine Academical Institution; Bradford Grammar Sch.; Wadham Coll., Oxford (Scholar). 1st Class Hon. Mods, 1924; 1st Class Lit. Hum. 1926; A. M. P. Read Scholar, 1927; Craven Fellow, 1928; Cromer Essay Prize, 1928; Member of Royal Irish Academy, 1933; L. C. Purser Lect. in Archæology, 1934; Temp. Principal, Board of Trade, 1942-44; FRNS, 1947. Member Institute for Advanced Study, Princeton, USA, 1960. *Publications:* Greek Mercenary Soldiers, 1933; Delphic Oracle, 1939 (2nd edition with Professor D. E. W. Wormell, 1956); Oracles of Zeus, 1967; Greek Oracles, 1967. Contributor to Journal of Hellenic Studies, Hermathena, etc, articles on Greek History and Mythology in Chambers's Encyclopædia, Encyclopædia Britannica, and Oxford Classical Dictionary. *Address:* Heather Hill, Baily, Dublin. *T:* Dublin 322934. *Club:* University.

**PARKER,** family name of **Earls of Macclesfield** and **Morley,** and of **Baron Parker of Waddington.**

**PARKER, Viscount; George Roger Alexander Thomas Parker;** Lieut RNVR; DL; *b* 6 May 1914; *e s* of 7th Earl of Macclesfield, *qv*; *m* 1938, Hon. Valerie Mansfield, *o d* of 4th Baron Sandhurst, OBE; two *s*. DL Oxfordshire, 1965. *Address:* The Model Farm, Shirburn, Watlington, Oxon.

**PARKER OF WADDINGTON,** Baron (Life Peer), *cr* 1958, of Lincoln's Inn; **Hubert Lister Parker,** PC 1954; Kt 1950; Lord Chief Justice of England since 1958; *b* 28 May 1900; 3rd *s* of Lord Parker of Waddington, PC (*d* 1918), a Lord of Appeal in Ordinary; *m* 1924, Loryn, *d* of O. Tilton Bowser, Kentucky, USA. *Educ:* Rugby Sch.; Trinity Coll., Cambridge (Senior Scholar). Called to Bar, 1924. Junior Counsel in Common Law: to Admiralty, 1934; to the Treasury, 1945-50; Judge of High Court of Justice, King's Bench Division, 1950-54; a Lord Justice of Appeal, 1954-58. *Address:* Royal Courts of Justice, Strand, WC2; Pile Oak Lodge, Donhead St Andrew, Shaftesbury, Dorset.

**PARKER, A(gnes) Miller,** RE; Artist and Wood-engraver; *b* Irvine, Ayrshire, 25 March 1895; *d* of William McCall and Agnes Mitchell Parker; *m* 1918, William McCance, Artist (marr. diss. 1963, and she legally assumed maiden name); no *c*. *Educ:* Glasgow School of Art (Diploma, Haldane Scholar). Instructress, Glasgow School of Art, 1918-20; Art Mistress, Maltmans Green School, Gerrards Cross, 1920-28; Art Mistress, Clapham High School and Training Coll., 1928-30; Walter Brewster Prize, 1st International Exhibition of Engraving and Lithography, Chicago, 1929; Wood-engraver to Gregynog Press, Newtown, Montgomeryshire, 1930-33. *Publications:* Chief Illustrated Editions; Esopes Fables–Caxton (Gregynog Press); Forest Giant–translated from the French by J. H. Ross (Colonel T. E. Lawrence); Through the Woods by H. E. Bates; Down the River by H. E. Bates; Gray's Elegy in a Country Churchyard (Limited Edition Club of New York); Richard II–Shakespeare (Limited Edition Club of New York); A Shropshire Lad–Housman; The Return of the Native–Hardy (Limited Edition Club of New York); Essays in Russet (Herbert Furst); Spring of the Year (Richard Jefferies); The Life of the Fields, Field and Hedgerow, The Open Air, The Old House at Coate (Richard Jefferies); Under the Rainbow (Aloysius Roche); The Faerie Queene by Edmund Spenser, (New York); Tess of the D'Urbervilles, and Far From the Madding Crowd, by Thomas Hardy (New York); The Tragedies of Shakespeare (New York); The Mayor of Casterbridge (Limited Editions Club of New York); Poems of Shakespeare (Limited Editions Club of New York); Jude The Obscure, by Thomas Hardy (Limited Editions Club of New York). *Recreations:* fishing and cats. *Address:* Kings Cross, Arran, Scotland.

**PARKER, Albert,** CBE 1946; DSc; FRIC; MIChemE; FInstGasE; FInstFuel; Consulting Chemical Engineer; *s* of late John Albert and Alice Parker, Manchester; *m* 1922, Lilian Maud, *d* of late Albert Edward Midgley, Birmingham; one *d* (and one *d* decd). *Educ:* Manchester Grammar Sch.; Manchester Univ. First Class Hons Chemistry, Manchester, 1912; Grad. Schol. and Beyer Research Fellow, Manchester, 1912-14; DSc Birmingham, 1916. Lecturer in Phys. Chem. and Thermodynamics, Birmingham Univ., and Chemist Inspector on manufacture of high explosives for Midland area, 1914-19. Research Chem. to University of Leeds and Instn of Gas Engineers, 1919-28. Asst Director Water Pollution Research, DSIR, 1928-39, Director, 1939-43; Director of Fuel Research, DSIR, 1943-56. Officer in charge of team of British and American experts investigating synthetic oil, etc in Germany, March-April 1945. Osborne Reynolds Medal, Instn of Chemical Engineers, 1941; Melchett Medal, Inst. of Fuel, 1955; Telford Premium, 1942, and Chadwick Medal, 1955, Instn of Civil Engineers; Mitchell Gold Medal, Stoke-on-Trent Assoc. of Engineers, 1956; Thomas Hawksley Lecturer, Institution of Mechanical Engineers, 1949; Cantor Lectures, Royal Society Arts, 1960. President, Fuel Luncheon Club, 1953-55; Hon. Secretary, British National Cttee, World Power Conference, 1951-64, and Chm., Consultative Panel on Survey of Energy Resources, 1958-68; Chairman Council, Royal Society of Health, 1955-56; Chairman Expert Cttee on Air Pollution, WHO; President National Society for Clean Air, 1963-65. *Publications:* contrib. various scientific and technical journals and books. *Recreation:* music. *Address:* Stanway, Wellesley Avenue, Northwood, Middlesex. *T:* Northwood 26435. *Club:* Athenæum.

**PARKER, Prof. Alexander Augustine,** MA, LittD; Professor of Spanish Literature, University of Texas, since 1970; *b* Montevideo, 1908; *er s* of Arthur Parker and Laura Bustamante; *m* 1941, Frances Ludwig; two *s* two *d*. *Educ:* Hawkesyard School (later Blackfriars School, Laxton); Gonville and Caius Coll., Cambridge (Exhibn. and scholar). First Class Mod. and Medieval Langs Tripos, Part I 1928, Part II 1930; Gibson Schol., 1931. Fellow of Gonville and Caius Coll., 1933-39. Lecturer and Head of Dept of Spanish, University of Aberdeen, 1939-49; Reader in Spanish, University of Aberdeen, 1949-53; Cervantes Professor of Spanish, University of London (King's Coll.), 1953-63; Prof. of Hispanic Studies, Univ. of Edinburgh, 1963-69. Seconded to University College of the West Indies as Prof. of Modern Languages, 1960-61; Andrew Mellon Visiting Prof., University of Pittsburgh, 1964, 1968, 1969-70. Hon. Councillor of Consejo Superior de Investigaciones Cientificas, 1953. Corr. Member Royal Acad. of Letters of Seville, 1958; Corr. Member Hispanic Society of America, 1960; Corr. Member Spanish Academy, 1964. Commander of the Order of Isabel la Católica, 1956. *Publications:* The Allegorical Drama of Calderón, An Introduction to the Autos Sacramentales, 1943; No hay más Fortuna que Dios, by Calderón, ed. with Introd. and notes, 1949; Literature and the Delinquent: the Picaresque Novel in Spain and Europe (1599-1753), 1967. Papers and articles in The Mod. Lang. Review, Bulletin of Spanish Studies, Revista de Filología Espanola, etc. *Recreations:* opera, horticulture and lepidoptera. *Address:* Department of Spanish and Portuguese, University of Texas, Austin, Texas 78712, USA; 9 West Castle Road, Edinburgh 10. *T:* 031-229 1632.

**PARKER, Arthur D. D.;** *see* Dodds-Parker.

**PARKER, Cecil;** actor, stage and films; *b* Hastings, 3 Sept. 1897; *m* 1927, Muriel Ann Randall Brown; one *d*. *Educ:* St François Xavier Coll.; Bruges, Belgium. Served European War, 1914-18. First stage appearance as Lorenzo in Merchant of Venice, Eastbourne; continued in Charles Doran's company until 1924; leading parts at Liverpool Repertory, 1924-26; first London appearance, Everyman Theatre, 1925; London stage appearances include: The Constant Nymph, Wonder Bar, Mademoiselle, Reunion in Vienna, The Rats of Norway, Little Ladyship, Bonnet over the Windmill, Blithe Spirit (Charles Condamine, 1941-44), Skin of our Teeth. Entered films, 1933; *films include:* Ships with Wings, Cæsar and Cleopatra, The Magic Bow, Hungry Hill, Captain Boycott, The First Gentleman, Quartet, The Weaker Sex, The Chiltern Hundreds, I Believe in You, Isn't Life Wonderful?, Dear Mr Prohack, The Man in the White Suit, Father Brown, For Better for Worse, The Constant Husband, The Court Jester, The Lady Killers, It's Great to be Young, Twenty-three Paces to Baker Street, True as a Turtle, A Tale of Two Cities, Happy is the Bride, Indiscreet, I Was Monty's Double, A French Mistress, The Pure Hell of St Trinian's, A Study in Terror. *Address:* Chalfont End, North Park, Gerrards Cross, Bucks.

**PARKER, Christopher William Oxley,** MA; JP; *b* 28 May 1920; *s* of Lieut-Col John Oxley Parker, *qv*; *m* 1947, Jocelyn Frances Adeline, *d* of Colonel C. G. Arkwright, Southern Rhodesia; one *s* two *d*. *Educ:* Eton; Trinity Coll., Oxford. Local Director, Barclays Bank, Chelmsford Local Board; Director: Strutt and Parker (Farms) Ltd; Lord Rayleighs Farms Inc. Served War of 1939-45, with 147th Field Regt (Essex Yeomanry) Royal Artillery, 1939-42. JP Essex, 1952; High Sheriff of Essex, 1961. *Recreations:* shooting, tennis, golf; estate management. *Address:* Faulkbourne Hall, Witham, Essex. *T:* Witham 3385. *Clubs:* Boodle's, Lansdowne, MCC.

**PARKER, Rt. Rev. Clement George St M.;** *see* Bradford, Bishop of.

**PARKER, Clifford Frederick,** MA, LLB Cantab; JP; Bracton Professor of Law at the University of Exeter since 1957 (Deputy Vice-Chancellor, 1963-65); *b* 6 March 1920; *yr s* of late Frederick James Parker and Bertha Isabella (*née* Kemp), Cardiff; *m* 1945, Christine Alice (*née* Knowles); two *d*. *Educ:* Cardiff High Sch.; Gonville and Caius Coll., Cambridge. Royal Air Force, 1940-43. Solicitor of Supreme Court, 1947. Lecturer in Common Law, University of Birmingham, 1951-57; Senior Tutor and Asst Director of Legal Studies, Faculty of Law, University of Birmingham, 1956-57. JP Devon, 1969. *Publications:* contrib. to legal periodicals. *Recreation:* touring. *Address:* Lynwood, Exton, nr Exeter. *T:* Topsham 4051.

**PARKER, Sir Douglas William Leigh,** Kt 1966; OBE 1954; retired as Director of Orthopædic Services, Tasmanian Government Health Dept, 1966. *Educ:* University of Sydney; University of Liverpool. MB, ChM (Sydney), 1923; FRCSEd 1925; MChOrth (Liverpool), 1930; FRACS, 1935. War of 1939-45: Surgeon, 2/9 AGH, 1940-42, 111 AGH, 1942-46. Senior Orthopædic Surgeon, Royal Hobart Hospital. Comr St John Ambulance Bde, Tasmania. Member Legacy, Hobart. OStJ. *Address:* 30 Fisher Avenue, Lower Sandy Bay, Hobart, Tasmania, Australia. *Clubs:* Tasmanian, Naval and Military and Air Force (Hobart).

**PARKER, Geoffrey,** CB 1966; Under-Secretary, Board of Trade, since 1961 (Principal Establishment and Organisation Officer, 1965); *b* 17 Jan. 1917; *m* 1942, Janet Crawford Chidley; two *s* one *d*. *Educ:* Hulme Grammar Sch., Oldham; New Coll., Oxford; Queen's Coll., Oxford; Universities of Berlin and Berne, MA, DPhil (Oxon). Entered Board of Trade as temp. Assistant Principal, May 1940; established as Principal, 1946. Counsellor (Commercial), HM Embassy, Washington, DC, 1952-55. *Recreations:* reading, languages. *Address:* 20 Malcolm Road, Wimbledon, SW19. *T:* 01-946 2748.

**PARKER, Geoffrey Edward,** DSO 1945; MA, MD, FRCS; late Senior Surgeon to French Hospital in London and Woolwich Group of Hospitals; Surgeon to the Italian Hospital in London and to St Nicholas' Hospital (Woolwich) since 1962; *b* 24 June 1902; *s* of late Geoffrey Leslie Parker and of Gertrude Clara Pook; *m* 1st, 1930, Kathleen Hewlett Johnson (marr. diss.); two *s* one *d*; 2nd, 1968, Lois Margaret Wilsdon. *Educ:* Marlborough; Trinity Hall, Cambridge. Resident and non-resident appointments at St Thomas's Hosp. (Grainger Prize, 1928), W London Hosp., St Peter's Hosp., St Mark's Hosp., Woolwich Memorial Hosp. Mem. Roy. Soc. Med. and Assoc. of Surgeons of Gt Brit. First Chm., 1948-51, Med. Advisory Cttee Woolwich Gp of Hosps; Chm. Med. Cttee, French Hosp. Corr. Member: French Assoc. of Surgeons; French Assoc. of Urol. Surgeons; Mem. Brit. Cttee of Internat. Soc. of Surgery; Hon. Mem., Faculty of Surgery, Univ. of Lyon. Liveryman of Worshipful Soc. of Apothecaries; Freeman, City of London. Commandeur de la Légion d'Honneur, 1968; Croix de Guerre with Palm, and Croix de Guerre with Silver Star (France), 1945; Officier de l'Ordre de Leopold (Belgium), 1956; Commendatore Al Merito della Repubblica Italiana. *Publications:* Surgery of Abdominal Trauma, 1944; The Black Scalpel, 1968; Surgical Cosmopolis, 1969; contrib. on surgery and surgical practice to Br. and continental surgical jls. *Recreations:* painting, writing, swimming; formerly boxing (welter-weight, Cambridge Blue, 1924). *Address:* 36 Hanover House, St John's Wood, NW8. *T:* 01-722 3141; 82 Harley Street, W1. *T:* 01-580 4357. *Clubs:* Savile, Hurlingham.

**PARKER, Sir Harold,** KCB 1949 (CB 1943); KBE 1946; MC 1918; *b* 27 May 1895; *s* of W. G. Parker; *m* 1926, Kathleen Maud Gibbs; two *s*. *Educ:* Haberdashers' School. Exchequer and Audit Department, 1914; Treasury, 1919; Principal Assistant Secretary, 1938; Deputy Secretary, Ministry of Pensions, 1941-45; Secretary, Ministry of Pensions, 1946-48; Permanent Secretary to the Ministry of Defence, 1948-56, retired; Chairman: Corp. of Insurance Brokers Society of Pension Consultants, 1958-70; Member, United Nations Civil Service Advisory Board, 1957-70. President Amateur Swimming Association, 1958. Served European War, 1914-18, Temporary Captain RFA. *Recreations:* golf, swimming. *Address:* 90 Rivermead Court, SW6. *T:* 01-736 6945; Fairlight, Upper Third Avenue, Frinton, Essex. *T:* Frinton 4783. *Clubs:* United Service, Hurlingham.

**PARKER, Henry Michael Denne,** CB 1954; CBE 1950; *b* 31 Dec. 1894; *s* of Henry Parker; unmarried. *Educ:* Edinburgh Academy; Hertford College, Oxford (open scholar). Served 7th Battalion The King's (Liverpool) Regiment, Lieutenant, 1915-18. BA and MA, 1921; Tutor and Dean of Keble Coll., Oxford, 1921-26; Fellow and Tutor 1926-45, Senior Dean of Arts, 1928-33, Vice-Pres., 1938-40, Magdalen College, Oxford; Emeritus Fellow, 1970. Univ. Lecturer in Roman History, 1928-33; Junior Proctor, Oxford Univ., 1927-28; Member of Hebdomadal Council, 1928-41. Temp. Principal and Asst Sec., 1941-45, Established Asst Sec., 1945, Min. of Labour and National Service; Under-Secretary, Ministry of Labour and National Service, 1950-56. *Publications:* The Roman Legions, 1928; History of the Roman World, AD 138-337, 1935 (2nd edn, 1958); articles in Oxford Classical Dictionary, 1949. Volume on Manpower, in Civil History of the War, 1957. *Recreations:* gardening and walking. *Address:* Thistle House, St Catherine's, Argyll. *T:* St Catherine's 209.

**PARKER, Herbert John Harvey;** *see* Parker, John.

**PARKER, Hugh;** Managing Director, McKinsey & Co. (UK); *b* 12 June 1919; *s* of Ross Parker and Ruth Baker Parker; *m* 1957, Elsa del Carmen Mijares Osorio; one *s* one *d*. *Educ:* Tabor Academy; Trinity Hall, Cambridge; Massachusetts Inst. of Technology. North Carolina Shipbuilding Co., 1941-43; General Electric Co., 1945-46; Ludlow Manufacturing Co., 1947-50; McKinsey & Co. Inc., 1951-. *Recreations:* reading, sculling, cooking. *Address:* 11 Chester Street, SW1. *T:* 01-235 8904. *Clubs:* American, Oxford and Cambridge University; Leander (Henley-on-Thames); Racquet and Tennis (New York); Eastern Yacht (Mass).

**PARKER, John,** CBE 1965; MP (Lab) Dagenham since 1945; Hon. Secretary Fabian Society (Chairman, 1950-53, Vice-Chairman, 1946-50); Hon. Secretary Webb Trustees; Member Council, Essex University; Governor, London School of Economics, since 1949; *b* 15 July 1906; *s* of Capt. H. A. M. Parker, retired schoolmaster, and N. P. Parker; *m* 1943, Zena Mimardiere; one *s*. *Educ:* Marlborough; St John's College, Oxford. Chairman Oxford University Labour Club, 1928; Asst to Director, Social Survey of Merseyside (Liverpool University), 1929-32; General Secretary, New Fabian Research Bureau, 1933-39; Gen. Sec. Fabian Society, 1939-45; MP (Lab) Romford, Essex, 1935-45; Parliamentary Private Secretary to Miss Ellen Wilkinson, Min. of Home Security, 1940-42; Parliamentary Under-Secretary of State, Dominions Office, 1945-46; Member: Speaker's Conferences, 1944, 1965-67; Procedure Committee, 1966-70; Parly Delegation to USSR, 1945; National Executive Labour Party, 1943-44; Executive London Labour Party, 1942-47; Select Cttee Parliamentary Disqualifications, 1956; Parly Delegation to Ethiopia, 1964; Leader, Delegation to Windward Islands, 1965; contested (Lab) Holland-with-Boston, Lincolnshire, 1931. *Publications:* The Independent Worker and Small Family Business, 1931; Public Enterprise (Forestry Commission), 1937; Democratic Sweden (Political Parties); Modern Turkey, 1940; 42 Days in the Soviet Union, 1946; Labour Marches On, 1947; Newfoundland, 1950; (Ed.) Modern Yugoslav Novels (English edn), 1958-64; (comp. and ed.) biographies, inc. Harold Wilson, 1964. *Recreations:* architecture and gardening. *Address:* 4 Essex Court, Temple, EC4. *T:* 01-353 8521. *Club:* Arts Theatre.

**PARKER, Sir John;** *see* Parker, Sir W. J.

**PARKER, Comdr (John) Michael (Avison),** CVO 1957 (MVO 1953); RN (retired); Private Secretary to The Duke of Edinburgh, 1947-57; *b* 23 June 1920; *s* of late Capt. C. A. Parker, CBE, Royal Australian Navy, Melbourne; *m*

1st, 1943, Eileen Margaret Anne (*née* Allan) (marr. diss. 1958); one *s* one *d*; 2nd, 1962, Carol, *d* of Sir Ivo Thomson, 2nd Bt, and Mrs Brian Whitmee; one *s* one *d*. *Educ:* Xavier College, Melbourne, Australia. Royal Navy, 1938-47. Equerry-in-Waiting to Princess Elizabeth and the Duke of Edinburgh, 1947-52. *Recreations:* cricket, sailing, tennis, squash. *Address:* 15 Harcourt Street, Hawthorn, Victoria 3123, Australia.

**PARKER, Lt-Col John Oxley,** TD; JP, DL; MA; *b* 28 June 1886; *e s* of Christopher William Parker and Helen Cecilia, *d* of Sir William J. Farrer, Faulkbourne Hall, Essex; *m* 1916, Mary Monica (*d* 1958), *d* of Arnold F. Hills, Hammerfield, Penshurst; one *s* two *d*. *Educ:* Eton; Oriel Coll., Oxford. Local Director (retired) Barclays Bank; President Essex Agricultural Society, 1959. Served European War, 1914-18, Essex Yeo., Major, France (Croix de Guerre Belge); HG, 1940-45 (Lt-Col). High Sheriff of Essex, 1948-49. *Publication:* The Parker Papers, 1964. *Recreations:* shooting, estate management, gardening and forestry. *Address:* The Old Rectory, Faulkbourne, Witham, Essex. *T:* Witham 3221. *Club:* Oxford and Cambridge.
*See also C. W. O. Parker, A. A. S. Stark.*

**PARKER, Sir Karl T.,** Kt 1960; CBE 1954; MA, PhD; FBA 1950; Hon. Antiquary to the Royal Academy, 1963; Keeper of the Ashmolean Museum, Oxford, 1945-62 (retired); Keeper of the Department of Fine Art, Ashmolean Museum, and of the Hope Collection of Engraved Portraits, 1934-62; Trustee, National Gallery, 1962-69; late Assistant Keeper, Department of Prints and Drawings, British Museum; *s* of late R. W. Parker, FRCS, and Marie Luling; *m* Audrey, *d* of late Henry Ashworth James, of Hurstmonceux Place; two *d*. *Educ:* Bedford; Paris; Zürich. Studied art at most continental centres and at the British Museum; edited Old Master Drawings, a Quarterly Magazine for Students and Collectors, since its inception, 1926. Hon. Fellow Oriel College, Oxford. *Publications:* North Italian Drawings of the Quattrocento; Drawings of the Early German Schools; Alsatian Drawings of the XV and XVI Centuries; Drawings of Antoine Watteau; Catalogue of Drawings in the Ashmolean Museum, Vol. I, 1938, Vol. II, 1956; Catalogue of Holbein's Drawings at Windsor Castle, 1945; The Drawings of Antonio Canaletto at Windsor Castle, 1948; Antoine Watteau: Catalogue Complet de son œuvre Dessiné, Vol. I (with J. Mathey), 1957, Vol. II, 1958; and articles, mostly on Old Master drawings, in various English and continental periodicals. *Address:* 4 Saffrons Court, Eastbourne. *Club:* Athenæum.

**PARKER, Kenneth Alfred Lamport;** CB 1959; Receiver for the Metropolitan Police District since 1967; *b* 1 April 1912; *e s* of A. E. A. and Ada Mary Parker; *m* 1938, Freda Silcock; one *s* one *d*. *Educ:* Tottenham Grammar Sch.; St John's College, Cambridge. Home Office, 1934; London Civil Defence Region, 1938-45; (Assistant Secretary, 1942, Deputy Chief Administrative Officer, 1943); Assistant Under-Secretary of State, Home Office, 1955-67. Imperial Defence College, 1947. *Address:* 18 Lichfield Rd, Kew, Surrey. *T:* Richmond 4595. *Club:* Oxford and Cambridge University.

**PARKER, Margaret Annette McCrie Johnston; (Margaret Johnston);** actress; *d* of James and Emily Dalrymple Johnston; *m* 1946, Albert E. W. Parker. *Educ:* North Sydney and Neutral Bay High School; Sydney University, Australia. Student, RADA; studied with Dr Stefan Hock; in repertory and acted as understudies. *Plays:* Murder without Crime, 1943; Fifth Column, 1944; Last of Summer, 1944; Time of Your Life, 1946; Shouting Dies, 1946; Barretts of Wimpole Street, 1947; Always Afternoon, 1949; Summer and Smoke, 1950; Second Threshold, 1951; The Dark is Light Enough, 1954; Sugar in the Morning, 1959; The Ring of Truth, 1959; Masterpiece, 1961. Stratford Memorial Theatre, 1956 season: Othello, The Merchant of Venice, Measure for Measure; Chichester Festival Theatre, 1966 Season: Lady Macbeth. *Films:* Rake's Progress, 1945; Man About the House, 1946; Portrait of Clare, 1949; Magic Box, 1951; Knave of Hearts, 1953; Touch and Go, 1955; Nose on her Face; Life at the Top, 1965; Psychopath; Sebastian. Television plays. *Address:* 50 Mount St, W1. *T:* 01-499 4232, 01-499 3080.

**PARKER, Comdr Michael;** *see* Parker, Comdr (J.) M. (A.).

**PARKER, Peter,** MVO 1957; Chairman, London University Computing Services Ltd; Dillon's University Bookshop Ltd; Director, Associated British Maltsters Ltd; *b* 30 Aug. 1924; *s* of Tom and late Dorothy S. Parker; *m* 1951, Gillian Rowe-Dutton, *d* of late Sir Ernest Rowe-Dutton, KCMG, CB, and of Lady Rowe-Dutton; three *s* one *d*. *Educ:* Bedford Sch.; London Univ.; Lincoln Coll., Oxford. Major, Intelligence Corps, 1943-47. Commonwealth Fund Fellowship to Cornell and Harvard, 1950-51. Contested (Lab) Bedford, 1951. Phillips Electrical, 1951-53; Head of Overseas Dept, Industrial Soc. 1953-54; Sec., Duke of Edinburgh's Study Conf. on Human Problems of Industry, 1954-56; joined Booker McConnell Ltd, 1956; Dir, Booker Bros McConnell & Co. Ltd, 1960-70; Chm., Bookers Engineering & Industrial Holdings Ltd, 1966-70. Part-time Mem., BSC, 1967-70. Vice-Pres., British Mech. Engrg Confedn; Member: Ct of London Univ. (Dep. Chm. 1970-); Political and Econ. Planning Exec.; BBC General Advisory Council; Chairman, Westfield Coll., Univ. of London. Mem. Council, British Institute of Management; Founder Mem., Coun. of Foundn for Management Educn; Trustee, Concordia (Youth Service Volunteers) Ltd; Vice-Pres., Bedford Sch. Holborn Boys' and Girls' Club; Governor, Bedford Coll., London. *Recreations:* Rugby (played for Bedford and E Mids); swimming, browsing. *Address:* 21 Upper Brook Street, W1; 35 Brunswick Gardens, W8. *T:* 01-229 7547. *Club:* Savile.

**PARKER, Rev. Reginald Boden;** Rector of Bentham, Diocese of Bradford, since 1964; *b* Wallasey, Cheshire, 4 June 1901; *s* of Joseph William and Ada Parker. *Educ:* Wallasey Grammar School; St Catherine's College, Oxford University; Ripon Hall, Oxford. BSc (London), 1923; MA (Oxon), 1938. Assistant Master, Ashton Gram. Sch., Lancs, 1925-30; Asst Master, Newton Gram. Sch., Lancs, 1930-32; Curate, Childwall, Liverpool, 1935-37; Curate, St Margaret's, Westminster, 1937-39; Asst Master and Chaplain, Oundle School, 1940-48; Headmaster, Igbobi College, Lagos, 1948-58; Bishop's Chaplain in Liverpool University, 1958-61; Residentiary Canon, Liverpool Cathedral, 1958-61; Precentor, Liverpool Cathedral, 1959-61. Hon. Lecturer in Hellenistic Greek, Liverpool University, 1959; Select Preacher, Oxford University, 1960; Asst Master, Wellington College, 1961-64. Member of Headmasters' Conference, 1950. *Publications:* (with J. P. Hodges): The Master and the Disciple, 1938 (SPCK); The King and the Kingdom, 1939 (SPCK); The Holy Spirit and The Kingdom, 1941 (SPCK).

*Address:* The Rectory, Low Bentham, via Lancaster. *T:* Bentham 422.

**PARKER, Richard Eric,** PhD (London), FRIC; Secretary and Registrar, Royal Institute of Chemistry, since 1962 (Member Council, 1959-62); *b* 6 May 1925; *e s* of late Leonard Parker and of Louisa Mary Parker (*née* Frearson); *m* 1969, Elizabeth Howgego; two step *d. Educ:* Wyggeston Sch., Leicester; University Coll., Leicester. Tutorial Student, King's Coll., London, 1946; Asst Lectr, 1947, and Lectr in Organic Chemistry, 1950-62, Univ. of Southampton. Hon. Treas., Parly and Scientific Cttee, 1966-69; Jt Hon. Sec., Fedn of European Chemical Socs, 1970-. FRSA 1970. *Publications:* papers and articles on physical organic chemistry, mainly in Jl Chem. Soc. *Recreations:* bridge, travel, swimming, Rugby football. *Address:* Royal Institute of Chemistry, 30 Russell Square, WC1B 5DT. *T:* 01-580 3482; 14 The Elms, Vine Road, Barnes, SW13. *T:* 01-876 8428. *Club:* Savage.

**PARKER, Sir Richard (William) Hyde,** 12th Bt, *cr* 1681; *b* 5 April 1937; *o s* of Sir William Stephen Hyde Parker, 11th Bt, and Ulla Ditlef, *o d* of C. Ditlef Nielsen, Dr of Philosophy, Copenhagen; *S* father 1951. *Educ:* Millfield, Street, Somerset; Royal Agricultural College, Cirencester. *Heir: uncle* Harry Hyde Parker [*b* 17 Feb. 1905; *m* 1935, Elizabeth Alice, *d* of late Captain C. C. Trevor-Roper]. *Address:* Melford Hall, Long Melford, Suffolk.

**PARKER, Rear-Adm. Robert William,** CBE 1954; JP; *b* 1902; *s* of Colonel W. F. Parker, Delamore, Cornwood, Devon; *m* 1935, Noemi Vyvian, *d* of C. V. Espeut; no *c. Educ:* Royal Naval Colleges Osborne and Dartmouth. Midshipman, 1918; served in Grand Fleet; specialised Engineering, 1922-24; served as Engineer Officer: HMS Rodney, 1942-44; HMS Indomitable (British Pacific Fleet), 1944-46; comd HMS Caledonia, RN Apprentices Training Establishment, Rosyth, 1949-52; Rear-Adm. (E), 1952, on staff of C-in-C, Plymouth; Deputy Engineer-in-Chief of the Fleet, 1953-55; retired 1955. JP Somerset, 1961. *Recreation:* model engineering. *Address:* The Hermitage, Freshford, near Bath, Som. *T:* Limpley Stoke 3220.

**PARKER, Roger Henry,** CBE 1960; MC; Past Director, Head Office, Barclays Bank Ltd; Local Director, Local Head Office, Cambridge; *b* 1889; *s* of Edmund Henry Parker, MA, LLD, DL, JP, of Thorneycreek, Cambridge; *m* 1922, Helen Mary Finch Foster; three *s* one *d. Educ:* Eton; Trinity Coll., Cambridge (MA). Served European War, 1914-19, Captain SR 5 Dragoon Guards, 1917; Captain, TAR of O, 1931; Lt-Col, 4th Cambridgeshire Bn Home Guard, 1941-45. High Sheriff of Cambridgeshire, 1942; Alderman of Cambridgeshire CC till 1965, of Cambridgeshire and Isle of Ely CC, 1964-67. Vice-Chm., Cambs CC, 1949-52, Chm., 1952-55. Vice-Chm., Bd of Govs, United Cambridge Hosps, 1948-55; Chm., 1955-63; DL Cambridgeshire, 1932-58, Lord Lieutenant, 1958-65. *Recreation:* Joint Master Cambridgeshire Foxhounds, 1935-53, Master 1953-57, Joint Master 1957-60. *Address:* Lyndewode, Grantchester, Cambridge. *T:* Trumpington 2212. *Club:* Oxford and Cambridge University.

**PARKER, Roger Jocelyn,** QC 1961; *b* 25 Feb. 1923; *s* of Captain Hon. T. T. Parker, DSC, RN (Retired) and Marie Louise Leonie (*née* Kleinwort); *m* 1948, Ann Elizabeth Frederika (*née* White); one *s* three *d. Educ:* Eton; King's Coll., Cambridge. Served Rifle Bde, 1941-46. Called to Bar, Lincoln's Inn, 1948, Bencher, 1969. Member, Bar Council, 1968-69, Vice-Chm., 1970-. Dep. Chm., Herts QS, 1969-. *Address:* The Old Rectory, Widford, nr Ware, Herts. *T:* Much Hadham 2593. *Clubs:* Lansdowne; Leander.

**PARKER, Ronald William,** CBE 1959; Chairman, Scottish Gas Board, since 1968; *b* 21 Aug. 1909; *s* of late Ernest Edward Parker, MBE, Accountant of Court, and Margaret Parker (*née* Henderson); *m* 1937, Phyllis Mary (*née* Sherren); two *s. Educ:* Royal High School, Edinburgh. Chartered Accountant, 1933. Secretary, later Director, Weston Group of Companies, 1935; Assistant Director of Finance, Ministry of Fuel and Power, 1942; Partner, J. Aikman, Smith & Wells, CA, 1946. National Coal Board: Finance Director, Scottish Division, 1947; Deputy Chairman, North Western Division, 1954; Chairman, Scottish Division, 1955-67; Regional Chairman, Scottish Region, 1967-68. *Recreations:* golf, gardening. *Address:* Hartfell, 10 Spylaw Park, Colinton, Edinburgh 13. *T:* 031-441 3886. *Clubs:* Caledonian; Scottish Conservative (Edinburgh).

**PARKER, Rt. Rev. T. Leo;** Titular Bishop of Magarmel since 1967; *b* 21 Dec. 1887; *s* of George Parker, Birmingham. *Educ:* St Bede's, Manchester; Ushaw; University, Durham. Ordained, 1915; Secretary to Bishops of Salford, 1915-36; Parish Priest of Higher Broughton, Salford, 1936-40; Bishop of Northampton, 1941-67, retired Jan. 1968. *Address:* Fox Den, Dorney Wood Road, Burnham, Bucks. *T:* Burnham 5057.

**PARKER, Rev. Thomas Maynard,** DD; Fellow and Praelector in Theology and Modern History, University College, Oxford, since 1952; University Lecturer in Theology, Oxford, since 1950; *b* 7 March 1906; *s* of late Thomas Maynard and Emily Mary Parker; unmarried. *Educ:* King Edward VI School, Stratford-on-Avon; Exeter College, Oxford, (Scholar). 1st Class Hon. School of Modern History, 1927; BA 1927; 1st Cl. Hon. Sch. of Theology, 1929; Liddon Student, 1928-30; MA 1931; BD, DD 1956. St Stephen's House, Oxford, 1927-29. Liveryman of Butchers' Company, 1927 (Mem. Ct of Assistants, 1955-57, 1963-65; Warden, 1957-61; Providitor, 1960-61; Renter Asst, 1961-62; Master, 1962-63; Past Master, 1963-); Freeman of City of London, 1927. Deacon, 1930; Priest, 1931; Librarian and Tutor, Chichester Theological College, 1930-32; Curate of St Mary's, Somers Town, London, NW1, 1932-35; Librarian of Pusey House, Oxford, 1935-52; Custodian of the Pusey Memorial Library, 1946-52; Member Faculties of Modern History and Theology, Oxford Univ.; Bampton Lecturer, Univ. of Oxford, 1950; Acting Chaplain and Lecturer in Medieval History and Political Science, Pembroke College, Oxford, 1951-52; Assistant Chaplain, Exeter College, Oxford, 1946-52; Chaplain, University Coll., Oxford, 1952-70; Select Preacher, University of Cambridge, 1955; Lecturer in Theology, Pembroke Coll., Oxford, 1952-61; Chairman: Faculty of Theology, 1963-65; Board of Faculty of Theology, 1964-65; Examiner in: Honour School of Theology, 1963-65; Honour School of Mod. Hist., Oxford, 1953-55; Select Preacher, Oxford Univ., 1960-61. Examining Chaplain to Bishop of Bradford, 1943-55; Birkbeck Lecturer, Trinity College, Cambridge, 1956-57. External Examr, QUB, 1964-66; External Examr in Church History for BD, St David's Coll., Lampeter, 1968-. Member Central Advisory Council for Training of Ministry, 1948-55; Member Faith and Order Department of Brit. Council of

Churches, 1949-55. FRHistS, 1956 (Mem. Council 1964-); FSA, 1962. *Publications:* The Re-Creation of Man, 1940; The English Reformation to 1558, 1950 (2nd edn 1966); Christianity and the State in the Light of History (Bampton Lectures), 1955. Contributor to: Union of Christendom, 1938; The Apostolic Ministry, 1946; Ideas and Beliefs of the Victorians (Broadcast Talks), 1949, new edn 1966; Augustinus Magister, 1955; Oxford Dictionary of the Christian Church, 1957; Miscellanea Historiæ Ecclesiasticæ, Congrès de Stockholm, 1960; Studies in Church History, vol. I, 1964; Trends in Mediæval Political Thought, 1965; Essays in Modern English Church History in Memory of Norman Sykes, 1966; Anglican Initiatives in Christian Unity, 1967; The Rediscovery of Newman, 1967; The New Cambridge Modern History, Vol. III, 1968; Encyclopædia Britannica, Chambers's Encycl., Journal Theol. Studies, English Historical Review, Journal of Eccles. Hist., Speculum, Medium Aevum, Church Quarterly Review, Time and Tide, Oxford Magazine. *Recreation:* study of railways. *Address:* University College, Oxford OX1 4BH. *T:* Oxford 41661. *Club:* Athenæum.

**PARKER, Walter Edmund,** CBE 1946; Partner in Price Waterhouse & Co., Chartered Accountants, since 1944; *b* 24 June 1908; *er s* of late Col Frederic James Parker, CB, and Emily Margaret Joan Parker (*née* Bullock); *m* 1934, Elizabeth Mary Butterfield; one *s*. *Educ:* Winchester. Joined Price Waterhouse & Co., 1926; admitted Mem. Inst. of Chartered Accountants in Eng. and Wales, 1931. 2nd Lieut 1/5 Essex Regt (TA), 1939. Bd of Trade: Chief Accountant, 1940; Asst Sec., 1941-45. Various Govt Cttees, 1946-50; Mem. Council, Inst. of Chartered Accountants, 1957-69 (President, 1967); Chairman, Cinematograph Films Council, 1964-66. Auditor, Duchy of Cornwall, 1956-. *Recreations:* garden and countryside. *Address:* Cleeve Hall, Manuden, near Bishop's Stortford. *T:* Stansted (Essex) 2273.

**PARKER, Vice-Adm. Sir (Wilfred) John,** KBE 1969 (OBE 1953); CB 1965; DSC 1943; Director, Incorporated Society of British Advertisers, since 1969; *b* 12 Oct. 1915; *s* of Henry Edmond Parker and Ida Mary (*née* Cole); *m* 1943, Marjorie Stuart Jones, Halifax, NS, Canada; two *d*. *Educ:* RN College, Dartmouth. Joined Royal Navy, 1929; Joint Services Staff Course, 1947; Imperial Defence College, 1957; Commodore West Indies, 1958-60; Admiralty, Director Signal Division, 1960-61; Captain RNC Dartmouth, 1961-63; Asst Chief of Defence Staff (Operational Requirements), Min. of Defence, 1963-66; Flag Officer, Medway, and Adm. Supt HM Dockyard, Chatham, 1966-69, retd 1969. Commander 1949; Captain 1954; Acting Rear-Adm., Oct. 1963; Rear-Adm., 1964; Vice-Adm., 1967. *Recreations:* tennis, ski-ing, sailing. *Address:* Nyewood Oaks, Rogate, Petersfield, Hants. *Club:* United Service.

**PARKER, Rt. Rev. William Alonzo;** *b* 31 Jan. 1897; *s* of late W. H. Parker, Alkrington, Lancs; *m* 1930, Ellen, *d* of Rev. Robert Hodgson, Hooton Roberts, Yorks; one *s*. *Educ:* Manchester University (MA). Royal Tank Corps, 1916-29; served European War (despatches); Ordained, 1929; Curate of Sheffield Cathedral; Chaplain of St George's Cathedral, Jerusalem, 1931-37; Vicar of St Matthew, Gosport, 1937-42; Vicar of St Chad, Shrewsbury, 1942-45; Rector of Stafford, 1945-55; Archdeacon of Stafford, 1945-59; Bishop Suffragan of Shrewsbury, 1959-69; Prebendary of Tachbrook, 1947-55; Canon Residentiary, Treasurer, and Prebendary of Offley in Lichfield Cathedral, 1955-59, Hon. Canon, 1968-. Prebendary of Freeford, 1959-68; Provost of Denstone, 1960-67. SCF, 1939-40. Sub-Prelate OStJ. *Recreation:* fishing. *Address:* Ashbrook House, Church Stretton, Salop SY6 6JB.

**PARKER, Sir William Lorenzo,** 3rd Bt, *cr* 1844; OBE 1919; DL; late Captain 1/9 Hants Regiment; *b* 9 Jan. 1889; *s* of 2nd Bt and Kathleen Mary, *e d* of L. K. Hall of Holly Bush, Staffs; *S* father 1902; *m* 1915, Ruth Margaret Sillery, *d* of A. B. Hanbury-Sparrow, Hillside, Church Stretton; two *s* one *d*. *Educ:* Eton; New College, Oxford. DL (1948), Vice-Lieutenant, County of Brecknock, 1957; Lord Lieutenant, 1959-64; DL 1965. *Heir: s* William Alan Parker [*b* 20 March 1916; *m* 1946, Sheelagh Mary, *o d* of Dr Sinclair Stevenson; one *s* one *d*]. *Address:* Llangattock Court, Crickhowell, Breconshire. *T:* 240.

**PARKER BOWLES, Mrs Ann;** Chief Commissioner, Girl Guides, since 1966; *b* 14 July 1918; *d* of Sir Humphrey de Trafford, *qv*; *m* 1939, Derek Henry Parker Bowles; three *s* one *d*. County Comr, Girl Guides (Berkshire), 1959-64; Dep. Chief Comr, Girl Guides, 1962-66. *Recreation:* horse racing. *Address:* 24a St Petersburgh Place, W2.

**PARKES, Sir Alan (Sterling),** Kt 1968; CBE 1956; FRS; MA, PhD, DSc, ScD; Fellow of Christ's College, Cambridge, 1961-69, Hon. Fellow 1970; Fellow of University College, London; *b* 1900; *y s* of E. T. Parkes, Purley; *m* 1933, Ruth, *d* of Edward Deanesly, FRCS, Cheltenham; one *s* two *d*. *Educ:* Willaston School; Christ's College, Cambridge; BA Cantab, 1921; PhD Manchester, 1923; Sharpey Scholar, University College, London, 1923-24; Beit Memorial Research Fellow, 1924-30; MA Cantab 1925; Schäfer Prize in Physiology, 1926; DSc London 1927; Julius Mickle Fellowship, University of London, 1929; Hon. Lecturer, University College, London, 1929-31; Member of the Staff of the National Institute for Medical Research, London, 1932-61; Mary Marshall Prof. of the Physiology of Reproduction, Univ. of Cambridge, 1961-67, Professor Emeritus 1968. Foulerton Student of the Royal Society, 1930-34; Sidney Ringer Lecturer, University College Hospital, 1934; ScD Cantab 1931; FRS 1933; Ingleby Lecturer, Univ. of Birmingham, 1940; Galton Lecturer, Eugenics Society, 1950; Addison Lecturer, Guy's Hospital, 1957; Darwin Lecturer, Inst. of Biology. Cameron Prize, 1962. President: Section of Endocrinology, Roy. Soc. Med., 1949-50, Section of Comparative Medicine, 1962-63; Section D Brit. Assoc. for the Advancement of Science, 1958; Inst. of Biology, 1959-61; Assoc. of Scientific Workers, 1960-62. Chairman: Soc. for Endocrinology, 1944-51; Soc. for Study of Fertility, 1950-52, 1963-66; Nuffield Unit of Tropical Animal Ecology, 1966-69. Pres., Eugenics Soc., 1968-70. Ayerst Lectr, American Fertility Soc., 1965; Dale Lectr, Soc. for Endocrinology, 1965; Dick Lectr, Univ. of Edinburgh, 1969; Cosgrove Lectr, Amer. Coll of Obstetricians and Gynaecologists, 1970. Mem. Adv. Cttee on Med. Research of the WHO, 1968-. Executive Editor, Jl Biosocial Science. John Scott Award (jtly with Dr A. U. Smith and Dr C. Polge), City of Philadelphia, 1969. *Publications:* The Internal Secretions of the Ovary, 1929; Sex, Science and Society, 1968; papers on the Physiology of Reproduction, on Endocrinology and on the behaviour of living cells at low temperatures in Jl of Physiology, Proc. Royal Society, and other scientific jls. Ed. Marshall's Physiology of Reproduction, 3rd edn, 1952. *Address:* The

Galton Foundation, 69 Eccleston Square, SW1. *Club:* Athenæum.

**PARKES, Prof. Edward Walter,** MA, PhD (Cantab); FIMechE, MICE; Professor of Mechanics, Cambridge, since 1965; *b* 19 May 1926; *o s* of Walter Frederick Parkes; *m* 1950, Margaret, *d* of John Parr; one *s* one *d*. *Educ:* King Edward's, Birmingham; St John's College, Cambridge. At Roy. Aircraft Establishment and in the aircraft industry, 1945-48; research student and subsequently Univ. Lecturer, Cambridge, 1948-59; Fellow and Tutor of Gonville and Caius College. Visiting Professor, Stanford Univ., California, 1959-60; Head of the Department of Engineering, University of Leicester, 1960-65. *Publications:* Braced Frameworks, 1965; various papers in fields of elasticity, dynamic plasticity or thermal effects on structures. *Address:* 7 Bulstrode Gardens, Cambridge. *T:* 57287. *Club:* Royal Commonwealth Society.

**PARKES, Geoffrey,** CMG 1947; FTI 1942; Deputy Chairman, National Westminster Bank Ltd, North Region, since 1969; *b* 24 April 1902; *er s* of late Harry Clement Parkes, JP, and late Edith Newton; *m* 1925, Marjorie Syddall; no *c*. *Educ:* Clifton College; and L'Institut Technique, Roubaix. Director: Small & Parkes Ltd, 1927-64; Geigy (UK) Ltd, 1943-66; Director of Narrow Fabrics, Ministry of Supply, and Hon. Adviser to Board of Trade, 1939-44; Director-General Textiles & Light Industries Branch, CCG, 1944-46; Dep. Chief (Exec.) Trade and industry Div., CCG, 1946. Director: District Bank Ltd, 1949-69; National Provincial Bank Ltd, 1963-69. Mem. Court, Manchester Univ., 1949-69. MA (*hc*) Manchester Univ., 1966. FRSA 1952. JP Manchester, 1949-65. *Recreations:* gardening, fishing. *Address:* Berth-y-Coed, Colwyn Bay, North Wales. *T:* Colwyn Bay 30377.

**PARKES, Rev. James William,** MA, DPhil; Hon. DHL; Hon. DLitt; *b* 22 Dec. 1896; *s* of late Henry Parkes, and Annie Katharine Bell; *m* 1942, Dorothy E., *d* of F. Iden Wickings, Hildenborough. *Educ:* Elizabeth College, Guernsey; Hertford Coll., Oxford, Open Classical Scholar. Private, Artists Rifles, 1916; 2nd Lieut, Queen's Royal West Surrey Regt, 1917; Captain and Adj., 19th Queen's 1918; BA (Aegrotat) Theology, 1923; MA 1926; Post-Graduate Schol. Exeter College, 1930; DPhil 1934; Internat. Study Sec. Student Christian Movement, 1923-26; Warden, Student Movement House, London, 1926-28; Study Sec. Internat. Student Service, Geneva, 1928-34; Chairman Nat. Com. Commonwealth, 1942-43, Vice-Pres. 1943; Charles William Eliot lecturer, Jewish Inst. of Religion, NY, 1946-47; Pres. Jewish Historical Soc. of England, 1949-51; Director, The Parkes Library, 1956-64; Deacon, 1925; Priest, 1926. Hon. Fellow, Hebrew Univ. of Jerusalem, 1970. *Publications:* The Jew and His Neighbour, 1930, 2nd and revised edn 1938; International Conferences, 1933; The Conflict of the Church and the Synagogue, 1934; Jesus, Paul and the Jews, 1936; The Jew in the Medieval Community, 1938; The Jewish Problem in the Modern World, 1939, 2nd (American) edn 1946, 3rd (German) edn 1948, 4th (Italian) edn, 1953; Oxford Pamphlets on World Affairs; Palestine, 1940; The Jewish Question, 1941; An Enemy of the People: Antisemitism, 1945, 2nd (German) edn 1948; The Emergence of the Jewish Problem, 1878-1939, 1946; Judaism and Christianity, 1948; A History of Palestine from 135 AD to Modern Times, 1949; The Story of Jerusalem, 1949; God at work, 1952; End of an Exile, 1954; The Foundations of Judaism and Christianity, 1960; A History of the Jewish People, 1962 (German, Dutch, Italian and Spanish trans.); Anti-semitism, 1963 (German and Spanish trans.); Prelude to Dialogue, 1969; Voyage of Discoveries: an autobiography, 1969; Whose Land? The Peoples of Palestine, 1970; (as John Hadham) Good God, 1940 (US edn 1965, rev. edn 1966); God in a World at War, 1940; Between God and Man, 1942; God and Human Progress, 1944; Common Sense About Religion, 1961. *Recreations:* architecture and gardening. *Address:* Netherton, Iwerne Minster, Blandford, Dorset. *T:* Fontmell Magna 367.

**PARKES, Sir Roderick Wallis,** KCMG 1960 (CMG 1956); OBE 1945; Ambassador to Jordan, 1962-66; retired; *b* 2 Apr. 1909; *o s* of late Llywelyn Childs Parkes; *m* 1939, Eileen Mary Ernestine, *o c* of late Major Nevile Gardner; two *s*. *Educ:* St Paul's School; Magdalen Coll., Oxford. Entered ICS, 1932; served in Punjab until 1935; Indian Political Service, 1935-47; Asst Political Agent, South Waziristan, 1935; Sec. and later Counsellor, British legation, Kabul, 1936-39; Political Agent, Eastern Kathiawar, 1941-42; served in Rajputana and Baroda, 1943; Kolhapur, 1944; Punjab States, 1945; attached to Food Dept, Govt of India, as Liaison Commissioner (States), 1946-47; retired from Indian Political Service and entered Foreign Service, 1948; Counsellor (Information) British Embassy, Cairo, 1949; Head of Information Div., Brit. Middle East Office, Beirut, 1952; Head of Information Services Dept, FO, 1953; Counsellor, Brit. Embassy, Djakarta, 1954, Chargé d'Affaires, 1954; Ambassador: to Saudi Arabia, 1955-56; to Viet Nam, 1957-60; to Sudan, 1961; seconded to Civil Service Commn as Group Chm. Civil Service Selection Bd, Jan. 1962. Dir, National & Grindlays Bank, 1967; Chm., Aquamarine International (Fisheries & Ocean Development) Ltd. *Address:* The Old House, Castletown, Isle of Man. *T:* Castletown 2384. *Club:* Athenæum.

**PARKHURST, Raymond Thurston,** BSc(Agr), MSc, PhD; Director of South Central Poultry Research Laboratory, State College, Mississippi, 1960-68, retired; *b* Everett, Massachusetts, USA, 24 April 1898; *o s* of Fred Lincoln and Celeste Elizabeth Parkhurst; *m* 1922, Norma F. Langroise; one *s* one *d*. *Educ:* Fitchburg (Massachusetts) High School; Universities of Massachusetts, Idaho and Edinburgh. Extension Poultryman, Iowa State College, 1919-21; Professor of Poultry Husbandry, Experiment Station Poultry Husbandman, and Head, Dept of Poultry Husbandry, University of Idaho, 1921-27; Director, Brit. Nat. Institute of Poultry Husbandry, 1927-32; Head, Department Agricultural Research, National Oil Products Co., 1932-38; Head, Dept of Poultry Husbandry, University of Massachusetts, Amherst, 1938-44; Director, Nutrition and Research, Flory Milling Co., 1944-49; Director of Nutrition and Research, Lindsey-Robinson and Company, Roanoke, Va, USA, 1949-60; Member numerous Poultry, Livestock and Scientific Assocs, etc.; First President of British Poultry Education Association. *Publications:* Vitamin E in relation to Poultry; The Comparative Value of various Protein Feeds for Laying Hens; Factors Affecting Egg Size; Mixed Protein Foods for Layers; The Influence of Anterior Pituitary Sex Hormone Substances on Laying Fowls; Rickets and Perosis in Growing Chickens; Rexing the Rabbit; Corn Distillers By-Products in Poultry Rations; Calcium and Manganese in Poultry Nutrition; Crabmeal and Fishmeal in Poultry Nutrition; Farm Poultry Management; Commercial Broiler Raising; Gumboro Disease, etc.; papers dealing with rearing and nutrition of poultry, farm animals, and pets. *Recreations:* swimming, bridge, stamps, coins. *Address:* 120 Sassafras Drive, Starkville, Miss 39759, USA. *Club:* Kiwanis International.

**PARKIN, Sir Ian (Stanley Colston),** Kt 1953; CBE 1946; *b* 12 Sept. 1896; *e s* of George Treble Parkin, Ashford, Devon; *m* 1920, Gertrude Watkins; three *s* one *d*. *Educ:* Bristol. Secretary Port of Bristol Employers' Association, 1919-40; Technical Adviser on Dock Problems to Minister of Labour, 1940-41; Gen. Man., Nat. Dock Labour Corp., Ltd, 1941-47. Member: Nat. Council of Port Employers, 1920-40; Nat. Jt Council for Dock Labour, 1927-40; Standing Advisory Cttee on Registration and Decasualisation, 1931-40; Nat. Jt Conciliation Bd for Road Motor Transport Industry (Goods), 1934-38; General Manager and Secretary, National Dock Labour Board, 1947-55, retired. *Address:* Anchorage, 15 Carlyon Road, Playing Place, Truro, Cornwall. *T:* Feock 720.

**PARKINSON, Cecil Edward;** MP (C) Enfield West, since Nov. 1970; Partner in West, Wake, Price & Co., Chartered Accountants, Broad Street Place, London EC2, since 1961; *b* 1 Sept. 1931; *s* of Sidney Parkinson, Carnforth, Lancs; *m* 1957, Ann Mary, *d* of F. A. Jarvis, Harpenden, Herts; three *d*. *Educ:* Royal Lancaster Grammar Sch., Lancaster; Emmanuel Coll., Cambridge. BA 1955, MA 1961. Joined Metal Box Company as a Management Trainee; joined West, Wake, Price, Chartered Accountants, 1956; qualified 1959; Partner, 1961; founded Parkinson Hart Securities Ltd, 1967; Director of several medium-sized cos, specialising in financial advisory work, 1965-. Mem., Hemel Hempstead Conservative Assoc.; Branch Treasurer, 1961-64; Constituency CPC Chm., 1965-66; Constituency Chm. and ex-officio Mem. of all cttees, 1966-69; Chm., Herts 100 Club, 1968-69; Contested (C) Northampton, 1970. *Recreations:* golf, skiing; ran for Oxford and Cambridge, 1954 and 1955; ran for Cambridge against Oxford, 1954 and 1955. *Address:* Westfield House, River Hill, Flamstead, near St Albans, Herts. *T:* Markyate 202. *Clubs:* Carlton; Hawks (Cambridge); Northampton and County (Northampton).

**PARKINSON, Cyril Northcote,** MA, PhD, FRHistS; Author, historian and journalist; Seigneur of Anneville, Mauxmarquis and Beauvoir; *b* 30 July 1909; *yr s* of late W. Edward Parkinson, ARCA and late Rose Emily Mary Curnow; *m* 1st, 1943, Ethelwyn Edith Graves (marr. diss.); one *s* one *d*; 2nd, 1952, Elizabeth Ann Fry; two *s* one *d*. *Educ:* St Peter's School, York; Emmanuel College, Cambridge; King's College, London. Fellow of Emmanuel Coll., Cambridge, 1935; Sen. History Master, Blundell's Sch., Tiverton, 1938; Master, RNC, Dartmouth, 1939. Commissioned as Captain, Queen's Roy. Regt, 1940; Instructor in 166 OCTU; attached RAF, 1942-43; Major, 1943; trans. as GSO2 to War Office (General Staff), 1944; demobilised, 1945; Lectr in History, Univ. of Liverpool, 1946; Raffles Professor of History, University of Malaya, Singapore, 1950-58. Visiting Professor: Univ. of Harvard, 1958; Univs of Illinois and California, 1959-60. Mem. French Académie de Marine and US Naval Inst.; Mem. Archives Commission of Govt of India. *Plays:* Helier Bonamy, Guernsey, 1967; The Royalist, Guernsey, 1969. *Publications:* many books including: Edward Pellew Viscount Exmouth, 1934; Trade in the Eastern Seas, 1937; (ed.) The Trade Winds, 1948; The Rise of the Port of Liverpool, 1952; War in the Eastern Seas, 1954; Britain in the Far East, 1955; Parkinson's Law, the Pursuit of Progress, 1958; The Evolution of Political Thought, 1958; British Intervention in Malaya, 1867-1877, 1960; The Law and the Profits, 1960; In-laws and Outlaws, 1962; East and West, 1963; Ponies Plot, 1965; A Law unto Themselves, 1966; Left Luggage, 1967; Mrs Parkinson's Law, 1968; The Law of Delay, 1970; The Life and Times of Horatio Hornblower, 1970. Contributions to Encyclopædia Britannica, Economist, Guardian, New York Times, Fortune and Saturday Evening Post. *Recreations:* painting, travel, sailing, badminton. *Address:* Les Câches House, St Martin's, Guernsey, CI. *Clubs:* Royal Commonwealth Society; Royal Channel Islands Yacht.

**PARKINSON, Maj.-Gen. (Retd) Graham Beresford,** CBE 1945; DSO and Bar; *b* 5 Nov. 1896; *s* of Henry Ainslie Parkinson, MA, and Ethel Constance Young, Hobart, Tasmania; *m* 1925, Barbara Waiohine Howe. *Educ:* Wellington College, NZ, Royal Military College of Australia, Duntroon (graduated 1915). Proceeded overseas and served in France until the Armistice, proceeding to Germany. Internal security expedition to Fiji in 1920; various staff appts until attended Gunnery Staff Course, Woolwich, 1924; various staff appts until appointed Director of Artillery Army HQ, Wellington, 1936; proceeded overseas with 2 NZ Div. on outbreak of war and continued to serve until conclusion of hostilities with Germany; appointments included: Comdr 4th Field Regt; Comdr 6 Inf. Bde; Comdr RA 2 NZ Div.; GOC 2 NZ Div. for a period under NZ Corps; Quartermaster-General, Army HQ, NZ, 1946; NZ Jt Liaison Staff (London), Dec. 1946-Sept. 1949. Legion of Merit Degree of Officer (USA). *Recreation:* horticulture. *Address:* 27 Clifford Avenue, Fendalton, Christchurch, New Zealand.

**PARKINSON, Sir Harold,** KBE, *cr* 1955 (OBE 1942); Kt, *cr* 1946; JP; Vice-President National Savings Committee; *b* 2 July 1894; *m* 1921, Evelyn Green; no *c*. Chairman, Shirley Institute, 1945-49; Chairman NW Housing Production Board, 1952-54; President, Royal Lancs. Ag. Society, 1948; High Sheriff of Lancs, 1950-51. *Address:* Old Vicarage, Hornby, nr Lancaster. *T:* Hornby 297. *Clubs:* National, Lansdowne.

**PARKINSON, Dr James Christopher,** MBE 1963; TD 1962; Associate Director, Brighton Polytechnic, since 1970; *b* 15 Aug. 1920; *s* of late Charles Myers Parkinson, Pharmacist, Blackburn, Lancs.; *m* 1950, Gwyneth Margot, *d* of Rev. John Raymond Harrison, Macclesfield, Ches.; three *s*. *Educ:* Queen Elizabeth's Gram. Sch., Blackburn; Univ. Coll., Nottingham. BPharm, PhD (London), FRIC, FPS, AMBIM. Served in Mediterranean area, Parachute Regt, 1943-46; Parachute Regt TA: 16 AB Div. and 44 Parachute Bde, 1949-63 (Major). Lectr, Sch. of Pharmacy, Univ. of London, 1948-54; Head of Sch. of Pharmacy, Brighton Coll. of Technology, 1954-64; Dep. Sec., Pharmaceutical Soc. of Gt Britain, 1964-67; Principal, Brighton Coll. of Technology, 1967-70. Mem. various pharmaceutical cttees of British Pharmacopœia, British Pharmaceutical Codex and British Veterinary Codex, 1956-64; Examr, Pharmaceutical Soc. of Gt Britain, 1954-64; Mem. Research Cttee and Bds of Studies in Pharmacy and Librarianship, CNAA, 1965-. Member, Gen. Synod of Church of England, 1970-. *Publications:* research papers on applied microbiology in Jl Appl. Bact. and Jl Pharm. (London) and on pharmaceutical education in Pharm. Jl. *Recreation:* do-it-yourself. *Address:* 92 Wickham Hill, Hassocks, Sussex. *T:* Hurstpierpoint 3369. *Club:* Little Ship.

**PARKINSON, Sir John,** Kt 1948; MD London; FRCP; Hon. LLD Glasgow 1951; Hon. DSc NUI 1952; Hon. FRCPE 1953; Hon FACP 1951; Hon. FRCPS Glasgow 1959; Hon. FRCPI 1962; Hon. FRSM 1966; Consultant Physician to Cardiac Department of London Hospital; Consulting Physician to the National Heart Hospital; Consulting Cardiologist to the Royal Air Force, 1931-56; hon. corresponding member French Society of Cardiology; foreign correspondent French Academy of Medicine; Hon. Member International Society of Cardiology; Hon. President European Society of Cardiology; ex-President Association of Physicians of Great Britain and Ireland (1950); President British Cardiac Society, 1951-55; *b* 10 Feb. 1885; *s* of John Parkinson, JP, of Thornton-le-Fylde, Lancs.; *m* 1917, Clara Elvina, *d* of late Alfred Le Brocq, St Heliers; four *d* (one *s* decd). *Educ:* Univ. Coll., London; the London Hosp.; the Univ. of Freiburg. Medical Registrar to the London Hospital, 1911-12; Chief Assistant to Sir James Mackenzie in the Cardiac Department of the London Hospital, 1913-14; served European War, 1914-19; Medical Officer, Casualty Clearing Station, BEF, France, 1914-16; Divisional Officer, Military Hospital for Research on Heart Cases, Hampstead, 1916; Major, RAMC, in charge of Military Heart Centre, Rouen, 1917-19. Fothergill Gold Medal, Medical Soc. of London, 1947; Moxon Medal, RCP, 1957; Gold Stethoscope Award, Internat. Cardiology Foundn, 1966. *Publications:* Harveian Oration, Royal College of Physicians, London, 1945; Lumleian Lecture, RCP, 1936; St Cyres Lecture, 1938; Address in Medicine, Canadian Medical Association, Ottawa, 1924; Address to Czechoslovak Cardiological Soc., Prague, 1935, and California Heart Association, 1946; Convocation Address, American College of Physicians, 1951; Laubry Lecture, International Congress of Cardiology, Washington, 1954; Articles on Diseases of the Heart and Vessels in the Index of Treatment, 1948; various papers on medical and cardiological subjects in the Quarterly Journal of Medicine, Heart, the Lancet, and the British Heart Journal. *Recreation:* gardening. *Address:* 4f, Portman Mansions, Chiltern Street, W1M 1LF. *T:* 01-486 2246.

**PARKINSON, Sir Kenneth Wade,** Kt 1957; DL; MA; *b* 1908; *e s* of late Bertram Parkinson, JP, Creskeld Hall, Arthington; *m* 1937, Hon. Dorothy Lane-Fox, OBE, *d* of 1st and last Baron Bingley, PC; one *d* (and one *d* decd). *Educ:* Uppingham; Clare College, Cambridge. Director: B. Parkinson and Co. Ltd; A. & S. Henry and Co. Ltd; National Westminster Bank Ltd, Eastern Region; Yorkshire Post Newspapers Ltd; United Newspapers Ltd. High Sheriff of Yorkshire, 1963; DL, West Riding, Yorks, 1967. *Address:* (business) 268 Thornton Road, Bradford; (home) Aketon Close, Follifoot, West Riding, Yorks. *T:* Spofforth 222.

**PARKINSON, Dame Nancy,** DCMG 1965; CBE 1946 (OBE 1938); Leverhulme Research Fellow, since 1968. *Educ:* The College, Harrogate; Bedford Coll., Univ. of London. BSc Hons. Hospitality Secretary, National Union of Students, to 1939; Controller, Home Div., British Council, 1939-68. Member: Court, Univ. of Manchester, 1967-; Council, Inst. of Study of Internat. Organisation, Sussex Univ., 1968-. Governor, Bedford Coll., University of London; Chm., Student Cooperative Dwellings, 1968-. Hon. LLD Manchester, 1968. *Recreations:* walking, reading, golf. *Address:* 6 Hanover Terrace, Regent's Park, NW1.

**PARKINSON, Thomas Harry,** DL; Town Clerk, Birmingham, since 1960; *b* Bilston, 25 June 1907; *y s* of G. R. J. Parkinson; *m* 1936, Joan Catherine, *d* of C. J. Douglas-Osborn; two *s* one *d*. *Educ:* Bromsgrove; Birmingham University. LLB Hons 1929. Admitted Solicitor, 1930. RAF, 1939-45. Asst Solicitor, Birmingham Corp., 1936-49; Dep. Town Clerk, Birmingham, 1949-60. Pres., Birmingham Law Soc., 1969-70. Hon. Member: Birmingham Assoc. of Mech. Engrs; Inst. of Housing. DL Warwickshire, 1970. *Recreations:* walking, sailing, caravanning, gardening. *Address:* Stuart House, Middlefield Lane, Hagley, Worcs. *T:* Hagley 2422. *Club:* Union (Birmingham).

**PARKYN, Brian (Stewart);** Director, Scott Bader & Co. Ltd, Chemical Manufacturers, since 1953; *b* 28 April 1923; *o s* of Leslie and Gwen Parkyn, Whetstone, N20; *m* 1951, Janet Anne, *o d* of Charles and Jessie Stormer, Eastbourne; one *s* one *d*. *Educ:* King Edward VI Sch., Chelmsford; technical colleges. Joined Scott Bader & Co. Ltd as Plastics Chemist, 1947; appointed Director, 1953. British Plastics Federation: Chm., Reinforced Plastics Gp, 1961-63; Mem. Council, 1959-. Has travelled widely and lectured on polyester resins and reinforced plastics in N and S America, Africa, Australasia, India, Japan, USSR and China, etc.; Plastics Lectr, Worshipful Co. of Horners, 1967. Contested (Lab) Bedford, 1964; MP (Lab) Bedford, 1966-70; Mem., Select Cttee on Science and Technology, 1967-70; Chm., Sub-Cttee on Carbon Fibres, 1969. FRSA; FPI. *Publications:* many on polyester resins and reinforced plastics throughout world. *Recreations:* writing; interested in industrial democracy. *Address:* Mwnwg, Harrold, Bedford. *T:* Harrold 295.

**PARLBY, Joshua,** CIE 1942; OBE; late Military Accountant-General in India; *b* 3 March 1889; *s* of Joshua Parlby, Hanley, Staffs; *m* 1926, Elizabeth Scott, *d* of Donald Fyfe Stuart; one *s* one *d*. *Educ:* Manchester Grammar School; Victoria University, Machester; Trinity College, Cambridge. Military Accounts Dept (India), 1913; Mesopotamia Expeditionary Force, 1917-21; Civil Administration of Iraq, 1921-25; Comptroller and Auditor-General in Iraq, 1925-35. Order of Rafidain (Iraq), 1935. *Recreations:* walking, shooting, and fishing. *Address:* Richmond Lodge, West Hill Rd, Paignton, Devon. *T:* Paignton 57017.

**PARMOOR,** 2nd Baron, *cr* 1914, of Frieth, **Alfred Henry Seddon Cripps;** *b* 27 Aug. 1882; *e s* of 1st Baron and Theresa (*d* 1893), *d* of Richard Potter; *S* father, 1941; unmarried. *Educ:* Winchester; New Coll., Oxford. Called to Bar, Middle Temple, 1907; contested (U) Wycombe Division, 1906; Bursar, Queen's Coll., Oxford, 1928-45; Fellow, 1929-. Captain Lincolnshire Yeomanry during war. *Heir: b* Hon. Frederick Heyworth Cripps, *qv*. *Address:* 27 Oakwood Court, W14. *Club:* Brooks's.

**PARNALL, Robert Boyd Cochrane;** Recorder of Hereford since Dec. 1956; Deputy Chairman, Monmouthshire Quarter Sessions, since Dec. 1956; *b* 26 Oct. 1912; *s* of R. H. B. Parnall, Glanmor, Newport, Mon; *m* 1937, Wilma Brooks; no *c*. *Educ:* Marlborough; Oriel Coll., Oxford. Called to Bar, Middle Temple, 1936; joined Oxford Circuit, 1936. Served in South Wales Borderers, 1940-43; in Judge Advocate-

General's dept, 1943-46. Elected to Bar Council, 1956. *Address:* 83 Bickenhall Mansions, W1; 2 Harcourt Buildings, Temple, EC4. *T:* 01-353 8549. *Clubs:* Monmouthshire (Newport); Gloucester (Gloucester).

**PARNELL,** family name of **Baron Congleton.**

**PARNELL, Valentine Charles;** *b* 14 Feb. 1894; *s* of Thomas Frederick Parnell, OBE (Fred Russell) and Elizabeth White; *m* 1966, Aileen Cochrane; one adopted *s. Educ:* Godwin Coll., Cliftonville. Began career as office boy with late Sir Walter de Frece, 1907; later, Booking Manager to Variety Theatre Controlling Co. and retained this position with General Theatre Corporation Ltd from 1928 until this Company amalgamated with Moss' Empires Ltd, 1931, when appointed General Manager; Director, Moss' Empires Ltd, 1941-60 (Managing Director, 1945-58); Director of Associated Television Ltd, 1955-66 (Managing Director, 1957-62); retired. *Address:* Le Semiramis, 06 Cannes, France.

**PARR, Martin Willoughby,** CBE 1944 (OBE 1929); Executive Committee, Gordon Boys' School, Woking; *b* 22 Nov. 1892; *s* of Rev. Willoughby Chase Parr and Laura, *d* of Colonel Francklyn, Speen Hill Lodge, Newbury; unmarried. *Educ:* Winchester (Scholar); BNC Oxford (Scholar). Commissioned HLI (SR), 1914; served France 1914-15, Palestine 1917-18, France 1918 (wounded); Sudan Political Service, 1919; Private Secretary to Governor-General, 1927-33; Deputy Civil Secretary, 1933-34; Governor Upper Nile, 1934-36; Governor Equatoria, 1936-42; retired, 1942. Member: NABC Council, 1944; Exec. Cttee of NABC and CMS; Vice-President B&FBS and CMS; Alderman, LCC, 1954-61. *Recreations:* rifle-shooting; played Rugby football for Oxford 1913-14, half-blue rifle shooting, 1913-14. Shot for Sudan and for England in Elcho Shield at Bisley on several occasions. *Address:* 11 Edith Road, W14. *Clubs:* Royal Commonwealth Society; Vincent's (Oxford).

**PARR, Sir Robert,** KBE 1950 (OBE 1927); CMG 1943; DèsL (*hc*) University of Lyons, 1956; *b* 15 May 1894; *e s* of late Rev. Robert Edmund Parr, Medomsley, Co. Durham, and of Harriet, *d* of Alfred William Nicholson; *m* Cicely Emily (*d* 1964), *d* of Henry David Shaw, Hadnall, Salop; one *d* (one *s* Robert Philip, Lieut, Grenadier Guards, killed in action at Minturno, 1944; and one *d* decd). *Educ:* Durham; Magdalen Coll., Oxford. Entered Levant Consular Service, 1919; Vice-Consul, 1926; Consul, 1933; Consul-General, 1940; retired, 1956. Chevalier Serbian Order of White Eagle (Mil.); Serbian Gold Medal for Valour and Alexander I Medal; Freedom of City of Lyons, 1945, of Villefranche-en-Beaujolais, 1949, of Tournus, 1951, of City of Dijon, 1952, of Vienne, 1954, of Grézieu-la-Varenne, 1955, and of La Mulatière, 1958; Médaille d'Honneur of City of Dijon, 1950, Médaille Bimillénaire of City of Lyons, 1958; Associate Member Acad. of Lyons, 1950, Acad. of Mâcon, 1955; Mem. various other learned societies in France; Hon. Dean of Consular Body of City of Lyons; Hon. President: Lyons Fédération des Amicales Régimentaires et d'Anciens Combattants; Union des Jouteurs et Sauveteurs de La Mulatière; Association des Rescapés de Montluc; The Lyons English Club. *Address:* Dudleston, Salop. *Clubs:* Brooks's, Royal Automobile; Shropshire (Shrewsbury); Rotary of Chalon-sur-Saône (Hon.)

**PARRINGTON, Francis Rex,** ScD; FRS 1962; Reader in Vertebrate Zoology, Cambridge, 1963-70; Director, University Museum of Zoology, 1938-70; *b* 20 Feb. 1905; 2nd *s* of late Frank Harding Parrington and Bessie May Parrington (*née* Harding); *m* 1946, Margaret Aileen Knox Johnson (marr. diss., 1963); one *s* one *d. Educ:* Liverpool Coll.; Sidney Sussex Coll., Cambridge. BA 1927; ScD 1958. Asst Director, Museum of Zoology, 1927; Strickland Curator, 1928; Balfour Student, 1933; Demonstrator in Zoology, 1935; Lecturer in Zoology, 1938-63. Palæontological expeditions, East Africa, 1930, 1933. Served Royal Artillery, 1939-45, Major. Deputy Chairman, John Joule & Sons, Stone, Staffs, 1962-64 (Director, 1945-64). *Publications:* various on comparative anatomy and palæontology, Proc. Zoological Society, London, etc. *Recreation:* fly-fishing. *Address:* Kaim Hill, Lochwinnoch, Renfrewshire.

**PARROTT, Sir Cecil (Cuthbert),** KCMG 1964 (CMG 1953); OBE 1947; MA; Professor of Slavic Studies, University of Lancaster, since 1966; Director, Comenius Centre, University of Lancaster, since 1968; *b* 29 Jan. 1909; *s* of Engineer Captain Jasper W. A. Parrott, RN, and Grace Edith West; *m* 1935, Ellen Julie, *d* of Hermann and Marie Matzow, Trondhjem, Norway; three *s. Educ:* Berkhamsted Sch.; Peterhouse, Cambridge. Asst Master at Christ's Hospital and at Edinburgh Acad., 1931-34. Tutor to King Peter of Yugoslavia, at Belgrade, 1934-39; HM Legation, Oslo, 1939-40; Stockholm, 1940-45; HM Embassy, Prague, 1945-48; Foreign Office, 1948-50; Head of UN Political Dept, 1950-52; Principal Political Adviser to UK Delegation to the United Nations, 1951-52; Counsellor, HM Embassy, Brussels, 1952-54; HM Minister, Moscow, 1954-57; Director of Research, Librarian and Keeper of the Papers, at the Foreign Office, 1957-60; Ambassador to Czechoslovakia, 1960-66. Hon. FIL, 1968. *Publications:* various articles on Slavonic History and Literature. *Recreations:* music, theatre, literature, languages. *Address:* University of Lancaster, Bailrigg, Lancaster. *Club:* St James'.

**PARRY;** *see* Gambier-Parry.

**PARRY, Rear-Adm. Cecil Ramsden Langworthy,** CB 1952; DSO 1944; retired 1953; *b* 3 Sept. 1901; *s* of late Colonel P. E. Langworthy Parry, DSO, OBE; *m* 1931, Alison Fielding Blandford; one *s* one *d. Educ:* RNC, Osborne and Dartmouth. Midshipman, HMS Tiger, 1917; qualified as Torpedo Officer; Commander, 1935; on staff of Rear-Admiral (Destroyers), Mediterranean, 1935-37; Tactical School, 1939, in command HMS Vivacious, subsequently HMS Montrose; assistant Naval Attaché and Liaison Officer with US Pacific Fleet, Hawaiian Waters, 1941-42; Captain 1941; Captain (D), 21st Destroyer Flotilla (DSO); Admiralty, 1944-46; Captain of Dockyard, Portsmouth, 1947-48; Captain, HMS Duke of York, 1949; in command HMS Euryalus, Mediterranean, 1949-50; Rear-Admiral, 1951; Flag Officer Ground Training, Lee-on-Solent, 1951-53; retired Sept. 1953. Secretary, Commonwealth Trans-Antarctic Expedition, 1955-59. Secretary, British National Appeal, World Wildlife Fund, 1961-64. *Address:* Coachmans, Westbourne, Emsworth, Hants. *Clubs:* United Service, Royal Automobile.

**PARRY, Claude Frederick,** CIE 1947; OBE 1943; Indian Police (retired); Secretary, The Athenæum, 1951-62; *b* 9 March 1896; *s* of late F. W. Parry; *m* 1930, Sylvia Nancy Irene Kingsley; two *s* one *d. Educ:* St Bees Sch. Served European War, 1914-19 (Mons Star). Joined Indian Police, 1919; Principal, Police

Coll., Saugor, CP, 1933-36; Inspector General of Police, Central Provinces, 1946; retired, 1947. Indian Police Medal, 1943; King's Police Medal, 1945. *Address:* Gambrel West, East Street, Coggeshall, Essex. *Club:* Athenæum.

**PARRY, Prof. Clive,** LLD (Cantab); Professor of International Law, University of Cambridge, since 1969; Fellow of Downing College; *b* 13 July 1917; 2nd *s* of Frank Parry, LRCPI, and Katharine Haughton Billington; *m* 1945, Luba Poole; one *s* one *d.* Barrister, Gray's Inn. Associé de l'Institut de Droit International; Pres. Grotian Soc.; Member, Carlyle Club. *Publications:* Nationality and Citizenship Laws of the Commonwealth and of the Republic of Ireland, vol. 1 1957, vol. 2 1960; The Sources and Evidences of International Law, 1965; (ed) British Digest of International Law, 1965-; (ed) British International Law Cases, 1964-; (ed) Consolidated Treaty Series, 1969-. *Address:* Downing College, Cambridge; 15 Cranmer Road, Cambridge. *T:* Cambridge 56187; 13 Old Square, Lincoln's Inn, WC2. *T:* 01-405 5441. *Club:* Oxford and Cambridge University.

**PARRY, Captain Cuthbert Morris,** CVO 1952; OBE 1947; Captain, RN (retired); *b* 24 April 1907; *s* of late Major and Mrs M. V. Parry; *m* 1943, Joan Stanton Iles; three *s.* *Educ:* RN Colleges, Osborne and Dartmouth. *Recreations:* various. *Address:* Gardener's Cottage, Titchfield Lane, Wickham, Hants. *T:* Wickham 2224. *Club:* Army and Navy.

**PARRY, Sir David Hughes,** Kt 1951; QC 1955; BA (Wales); MA, LLM (Cantab); Professor Emeritus in the University of London since 1959; Professor of English Law, University of London, 1930-59; Director of University of London Institute of Advanced Legal Studies, 1947-59; President, University College, Aberystwyth, 1954-64; *b* Llanaelhaiarn, Caerns, 3 Jan. 1893; *e s* of late John Hughes Parry, JP, and Anne Hughes Parry, Penllwyn, Pwllheli, North Wales; *m* 1923, Haf (*d* 1965), *o d* of late Sir Owen Edwards. *Educ:* Pwllheli County Sch.; UCW, Aberystwyth (1st Class Hons Economics); Peterhouse Cambridge (Class I, Law Tripos Part II; College Prizeman); called to Bar (Certificate of Honour), Inner Temple, 1922; in practice at Lincoln's Inn, 1924-46; War Service in RWF, 1915-19 (France, 1917-18); demobilised with rank of Lieut, 1919; Lecturer in Law, Aberystwyth, 1920-24; Lecturer in Law, London School of Economics, 1924-28; Editor Solicitors' Journal, 1925-28; Reader in English Law, University of London, 1928-30; Examiner, Universities of Cambridge, London, Manchester, Liverpool, Bristol and Wales; Senator of University of London, 1930-70; Member of Court of University of London, 1938-70 (Deputy Chairman, 1958-62; Chm., 1962-70); Chairman of Academic Council of University of London, 1939-45; Deputy Vice-Chancellor, 1940-45; Vice-Chancellor, 1945-48; Member of Council of Hon. Society of Cymmrodorion since 1934; Chairman of Standing Conference of National Voluntary Youth Organisations, 1944-45; Chairman 18-30 Conference, 1947-49; Dep. Chairman National Council of Social Service, 1948-62; Member Colonial Universities Grants Cttee, 1948-53; Chairman Colonial Social Science Research Council, 1951-55; Chairman Cttee of Vice-Chancellors and Principals, 1947-48; Member of University Grants Cttee, 1948-54 (Vice-Chairman, 1951-54); President of Society of Public Teachers of Law, 1948-49; a Vice-President of the Selden Society, 1956-59; Member of Advisory Council on Post-War Reconstruction in Wales; Member War Works Commission, 1944-64; Member Royal Commission on Remuneration of Doctors and Dentists, 1957-60; Member Inter-Departmental Cttee on Business of Criminal Courts, 1958-60; Chairman Cttee of Enquiry on New Zealand University, 1959; Dep. Chairman Caernarvonshire Quarter Sessions, 1950-66; Vice-President National Council of Social Service, 1962-; Chairman, Inter-Departmental Cttee on Legal Status of Welsh Language, 1963-65; Moderator, Presbyterian Church of Wales, 1964-65. Lionel Cohen Lecturer, at Hebrew University of Jerusalem, 1956; Hamlyn Lecturer, 1958; Bencher, Inner Temple, 1952; Hon. Fellow: Peterhouse, Cambridge Univ., 1956; LSE, 1961. Hon. LLD Wales, 1947; Hon. DCL McGill, 1949; Hon. LLD West Ont., 1948, British Columbia, 1949, New Brunswick, 1950, Birmingham, 1952, Cambridge, 1953, Hull, 1955, Exeter, 1960, London 1963. Cymmrodorion Medal, 1958. *Publications:* Law of Succession 1937 (5th edn 1966); 11th edn of Wolstenholme and Cherry's Conveyancing Statutes, 1927 (with late Sir Benjamin L. Cherry and late John Chadwick); 12th edn of Williams on Executors, 1930 (with John Cherry); 12th edn of Wolstenholme and Cherry's Conveyancing Statutes, 1932 (with late Sir Benjamin L. Cherry and J. R. P. Maxwell); 13th edn Williams on Executors, 1953; Changing Conception of Contracts in English Law; Sanctity of Contracts in English Law (Hamlyn Lectures), 1958; contributions to the Law Quarterly Review, Journal of the Society of Public Teachers of Law, Modern Law Review, Annual Survey of English Law, Solicitors' Journal, Toronto Law Journal, Canadian Bar Review, Journal of Legal Education; Cambridge Law Jl; Times Educational Supplement, etc. *Recreation:* gardening. *Address:* Neuadd Wen, Llanuwchllyn, Bala, Merioneth. *T:* Llanuwchllyn 255. *Club:* Athenæum.

**PARRY, Admiral Sir Edward;** *see* Parry, Admiral Sir (William) E.

**PARRY, Ernest J.;** *see* Jones-Parry.

**PARRY, Sir Hugh (Nigel),** Kt 1963; CBE 1954; Acting Head, Middle East Development Division, Beirut, since 1969; *b* 26 Aug. 1911; *s* of Charles Frank Parry and Lilian Maud Parry (*née* Powell); *m* 1945, Ann Maureen Forshaw; two *d.* *Educ:* Cheltenham Coll.; Balliol Coll., Oxford. Entered Colonial Administrative Service, 1939. Chief Secretary, Central African Council, Salisbury, S Rhodesia, 1951-53; Secretary, Office of Prime Minister and External Affairs, Federal Government of Rhodesia and Nyasaland, 1953-63; Ministry of Overseas Development, 1965-. *Recreations:* sailing, motoring. *Address:* Middle East Development Division, British Embassy, Beirut, Lebanon. *Club:* Public Schools.

**PARRY, John Horace,** CMG 1960; MBE 1942; Professor of Oceanic History and Affairs, Harvard University, since Oct. 1965; *b* 26 April 1914; *s* of Walter Austin Parry and Ethel Parry; *m* 1939, Joyce, *d* of Rev. H. C. and Mabel Carter; one *s* three *d.* *Educ:* King Edward's Sch., Birmingham; Clare Coll., Cambridge; Harvard University. Fellow of Clare Coll., Cambridge, 1938; served in RN, 1940-45. Asst Tutor, Clare Coll., Cambridge, and University Lecturer in History, 1945-49; Prof. of Modern History in University College of the West Indies, 1949-56; Principal of University College, Ibadan, Nigeria, 1956-60; Principal of University College, Swansea, 1960-65; Vice-Chancellor, University of Wales, 1963-65. *Publications:* The Spanish Theory of Empire, 1940; The Audiencia of New Galicia, 1948; Europe and a Wider World,

1949; The Sale of Public Office in the Spanish Indies, 1953; A Short History of the West Indies, 1956; The Age of Reconnaissance, 1963; The Spanish Seaborne Empire, 1966; Ed., The European Reconnaissance, 1968. Contributor to historical journals. *Recreations:* sailing, fishing, mountain walking, ornithology. *Address:* Widener 45, Cambridge, Mass 02138, USA. *Clubs:* Athenæum, United University; Harvard (New York).

**PARRY, Robert;** MP (Lab) Liverpool Exchange since 1970; *b* 8 Jan. 1933. *Educ:* Bishop Goss RC School, Liverpool. Became a building trade worker. Former full-time organizer for National Union of Public Employees; now Member of Transport and General Workers' Union. Member of Co-operative Party; specially interested in industrial law and industrial relations, housing, the aged and handicapped persons. Member, Liverpool City Council, 1963-. *Address:* House of Commons, SW1.

**PARRY, Robert Hughes,** MD (London), BS, FRCP, MRCS, DPH; Retired; formerly Principal Medical Officer to the Bristol City Council; formerly Professor of Preventive Medicine, University of Bristol; Past President Society of Medical Officers of Health; President Preventive Medicine Section, BMA (1949); Hon. FAPHA; *b* 3 Nov. 1895; *s* of J. Hughes-Parry, JP, Penllwyn, Pwllheli, and Anne Hughes, Cwmcoryn, Caernarvonshire; *m* Elsie Joan Williams, LRCP, MRCS, two *s* two *d*. *Educ:* Pwllheli (Chairman Scholar); University College of Wales, Aberystwyth; University of London, The Middlesex Hospital (Lyell Scholar and Gold Medallist, Junior Broderip Scholar). Lieut, RAF. MS; Asst to Professor of Experimental Pathology at the Middlesex Cancer Hospital, London, 1922-24; Medical Officer of Health of Bristol, 1930-56; Visiting Prof., Yale Univ., USA, 1956; formerly KHP to King George VI and QHP to the Queen. Medical Consultant, WHO, 1959. Member, Local Government Commission for England, 1959-63. High Sheriff of Caernarvonshire, 1958-59. *Publications:* Under the Cherry Tree (autobiography), 1969; various publications on cancer, health centres and various public health problems. *Recreation:* gardening. *Address:* Cefniwrch, Criccieth, N Wales.

**PARRY, Thomas,** MA, DLitt (Wales); FBA 1959; President, National Library of Wales, since 1969; Principal of the University College of Wales, Aberystwyth, 1958-69; *b* 14 Aug. 1904; *e s* of Richard and Jane Parry, Carmel, Caernarvonshire; *m* 1936, Enid, *o d* of Picton Davies, Cardiff. *Educ:* Pen-y-groes Grammar Sch.; University College of North Wales, Bangor. Assistant Lecturer in Welsh and Latin, University College, Cardiff, 1926-29; Lecturer in Welsh, University College, Bangor, 1929-47; Prof. of Welsh, 1947-53; Librarian of National Library of Wales, Aberystwyth, 1953-58; Vice-Chancellor, University of Wales, 1961-63, 1967-69; Chairman, UGC Cttee on Libraries, 1963-67. Hon. DLitt Celt. NUI; Hon. LLD Wales. *Publications:* Peniarth 49, 1929; Theater du Mond, 1930; Awdl "Mam", 1932; Saint Greal, 1933; Baledi'r Ddeunawfed Ganrif, 1935; Mynegai i Weithiau Ifor Williams, 1939; Hanes Llenyddiaeth Gymraeg, 1945; Llenyddiaeth Gymraeg, 1900-45, 1945; Hanes ein Llen, 1946; Lladd wrth yr Allor (translation of T. S. Eliot's Murder in the Cathedral), 1949; Gwaith Dafydd ap Gwilym, 1952; Llywelyn Fawr (a play), 1954; (ed.) Oxford Book of Welsh Verse, 1962; articles in Bulletin of Board of Celtic Studies, Trans. Hon. Society of Cymmrodorion, Y Traethodydd, Yr Athro, Yorkshire Celtic Studies. *Address:* Gwyndy, 2 Victoria Avenue, Bangor, Caerns. *T:* Bangor 4460. *Club:* Athenæum.

**PARRY, Adm. Sir (William) Edward,** KCB 1950 (CB 1939); *b* 8 April 1893; *s* of late Sir Sydney Parry, KBE, CB; *m* 1922, Maude Mary Phillips; one *s* one *d* (twins). *Educ:* RNC Osborne and Dartmouth. Joined RN 1905; Lieut, 1914; served afloat throughout War of 1914-18; Captain, 1934; commanded Anti-Submarine Establishment (HMS Osprey), 1936-37; Imperial Defence Course, 1938; lent to New Zealand Division, in Command of HMS Achilles, 1939; commanded HMS Achilles in Battle of River Plate, 13 Dec. 1939 (CB); First Naval Member of NZ Naval Board, 1940-42; Command of HMS Renown, 1943; Rear-Admiral, 1944; Naval Commander Force "L" in Invasion of France, 1944; Deputy Head of Naval Division, Control Commission for Germany, Berlin, 1945-46; Director of Naval Intelligence, 1946-48; Vice-Admiral, 1948; Commander-in-Chief, Indian Navy, 1948-51; Admiral, 1951. retired list, 1952. *Address:* Stocks Mill, Wittersham, Tenterden, Kent. *T:* Wittersham 200.

**PARRY BROWN, Arthur Ivor;** *see* Brown, A. I. P.

**PARRY-OKEDEN, Richard Godfrey Christian,** CMG 1964; CBE 1961; JP; Director, John Lysaght (Australia) Ltd, 1936-70 (Chairman, 1946-67, Managing Director, 1946-65); *b* Blandford, Dorset, 25 Dec. 1900; *s* of Lt-Col U. E. Parry Okeden and Carolina Susan Hambro; *m* 1930, Florence, *d* of E. E. Brown, Pymble, Sydney, NSW; one *s* two *d*. *Educ:* Eton College. President: Chamber of Manufactures of NSW, 1951-53; Associated Chambers of Manufactures of Australia, 1952-53. JP New South Wales, 1934. Hon. DSc Sydney, 1957. FAIM; FInstD. *Recreations:* motoring, fishing. *Address:* 1985 Pittwater Road, Bayview, NSW 2104, Australia. *T:* Sydney 99.2863. *Club:* Union (Sydney).

**PARRY-WILLIAMS, Sir Thomas (Herbert),** Kt 1958; MA, DLitt (Wales), DLitt (Oxon), PhD (Freiburg), Hon. LLD Wales; Professor Emeritus; Professor of Welsh Language and Literature, University College of Wales, Aberystwyth, 1920-52; *b* 21 Sept. 1887; *s* of late Henry and Ann Parry-Williams, Schoolhouse, Rhyd-ddu, Caerns; *m* 1942, Amy Thomas. *Educ:* Portmadoc County Intermediate Sch.; University College of Wales, Aberystwyth; Jesus Coll., Oxford; Univ. of Freiburg; Sorbonne, Univ. of Paris. Fellow, University of Wales, 1911-14; Hon. Fellow, Jesus Coll., Oxford, 1968; Member of Staff, University College of Wales, Aberystwyth, 1914-19; Member of University of Wales Press Board, Board of Celtic Studies and Court; President: Hon. Society of Cymmrodorion, 1961-69; National Library of Wales, 1966-69; Court of National Eisteddfod, 1955-67; National Eisteddfod Chair and Crown, both in 1912 and 1915; Medal of the Hon. Society of Cymmrodorion, 1951; Fellow of National Eisteddfod, 1968. Warden of University of Wales Guild of Graduates, 1953-56; Chairman of Advisory Council (BBC, Wales), 1947-52; Member Editorial Board Geiriadur Prifysgol Cymru (A Dictionary of the Welsh Language); O'Donnell Lecturer (Oxford), 1957. *Publications:* Welsh and Breton, 1913; Ystoriau Bohemia, 1921; The English Element in Welsh, 1923; Ysgrifau, 1928; Cerddi, 1931; Llawysgrif Rd Morris o Gerddi, 1931; Carolau Rd White, 1931; Sonnets, 1932; Canu Rhydd Cynnar, 1932; Llawysgrif Hendregadredd (joint), 1933;

Elfennau Barddoniaeth, 1935; Olion, 1935; Pedair Cainc y Mabinogi, 1937; Synfyfyrion, 1937; Ystoriau Heddiw, 1938; Hen Benillion, 1940; Lloffion, 1942; O'r Pedwar Gwynt, 1944; Libretto Cymraeg Faust (Gounod), 1945; Welsh Poetic Tradition (The Sir John Rhys Memorial Lecture, British Academy), 1947; Y Bardd yn ei Weithdy, 1948; Islwyn, 1948; (Ed.) Caniadau Isgarn, 1949; Ugain o Gerddi, 1949; Libretto Cymraeg Elijah (Mendelssohn), 1950; Libretto Cymraeg Samson (Handel), 1951; ed. Awdlau Cadeiriol Detholedig, 1926-50, 1953; ed. Rhyddiaith Gymraeg, 1954; Sir John Rhys, 1954; ed. National Eisteddfod Transactions, 1954; co-ed. Newydd a Hen, 1954; Myfyrdodau, 1957; Ymhēl â Phrydyddu (Annual Radio Lecture, BBC Wales), 1958; Y Ddinas (privately), 1962; Sant Pedr (trans. of libretto, Daniel Jones's Oratorio, Saint Peter), 1965; Y Goresgynwyr (trans. of D. Fraser's The Invaders), 1966; Pensynnu, 1966. *Address:* Wern, North Road, Aberystwyth.

**PARS, Dr Leopold Alexander,** MA, ScD Cantab; Fellow, formerly President, of Jesus College, Cambridge; *b* 2 Jan. 1896; *o s* of late Albertus Maclean Pars and Emma Laura Pars (*née* Unwin). *Educ:* Latymer Upper School; Jesus Coll., Cambridge. Smith's Prizeman, 1921; Fellow of Jesus Coll., 1921-. University Lectr in Mathematics, Cambridge, 1926-61. Visiting Professor: Univ. of California, Berkeley, 1949; Florida Atlantic Univ., 1964; Univ. of Sydney, 1965. *Publications:* Introduction to Dynamics, 1953; Calculus of Variations, 1962; A Treatise on Analytical Dynamics, 1965. Papers on Mathematics in scientific jls. *Recreations:* rock climbing, travel, theatre. *Address:* Jesus College, Cambridge. *T:* Cambridge 54930. *Club:* Athenæum.

**PARSELLE, Air Vice-Marshal Thomas Alford Boyd,** CB 1962; CBE 1950; psa; *b* 15 July 1911; *s* of late John Parselle, Salisbury, S Rhodesia; *m* 1936, Daphne (*d* 1970), *d* of late Lt-Col H. G. Lewis-Hall; two *s* one *d. Educ:* Cheltenham Coll.; RAF Coll., Cranwell. Served Egypt, 208 Squadron, 1932-34; 601 Squadron, RAuxAF, 1935-36 and Japan, 1937-39. Middle East and E. Africa, 1940-42; Bomber Command, 1943 (POW). Staff Coll., 1946-47; Comd RAF Scampton, Hemswell, 1948-50; Air Ministry, 1951-53; Comd RAAF Staff Coll., Point Cook, Australia, 1954-56 (exchange posting); Commandant Royal Air Force College and Air Officer Commanding RAF Cranwell, Lincolnshire, 1956-58; Commander, Task Force "Grapple", 1958-59; Senior Air Staff Officer, Bomber Command, 1959-61; Deputy Air Secretary, Air Ministry, 1961-64. Air Commodore, 1956; Air Vice-Marshal, 1958; retired, 1964. *Address:* Keeper's Cottage, Crowsley Park, Henley-on-Thames, Oxon. *T:* Henley 3698. *Club:* Royal Air Force.

**PARSEY, Edward Moreland,** CBE 1953; Vice-President, London Rent Assessment Panel, since 1966; Chairman, Paddington, St Marylebone and Westminster Rent Tribunals, since 1964; *b* 12 Jan. 1900; *o s* of late Edward William Parsey, MA, MB, BCh Cantab, and Sarah Janet Parsey; *m* 1927, Margaret, 2nd *d* of late Erle Victor Shakespeare, King's Norton; one *s* one *d. Educ:* King Edward's Sch.; privately; Peterhouse, Cambridge. Served European War, 1914-18, with RMA. BA 1921, MA 1925, Cambridge; Barrister, Inner Temple, 1924. Asst Solicitor, Bd of Trade, 1945-63. Chm., Civil Service Legal Soc., 1949-50; Mem. Bar Council, 1950-54; Chm., Peterhouse Soc., 1963-66. *Recreations:* travelling, gardening. *Address:* Gay Hill, Wieland Road, Northwood, Middlesex. *T:* Northwood 25673. *Clubs:* United University; Union (Cambridge).

**PARSHALL, Horace Field,** TD 1947; Receiver-General, Venerable Order of St John of Jerusalem, since 1968 (Chancellor, 1961-66); *b* 16 June 1903; *o s* of late Horace Field Parshall, DSc, and Annie Matilda Rogers; *m* 1st, 1929, Hon. Ursula Mary Bathurst (marr. diss., 1942), *o d* of 1st Viscount Bledisloe; one *s*; 2nd, 1953, Margaret Savage, MB, BS, DPH (*d* 1961), *d* of late Captain Philip Alcock, DL, JP, Wilton Castle, Enniscorthy, and Overton Lodge, Ludlow; one *s* two *d*; 3rd, 1965, Lady (Phyllis Gabrielle) Gore, *o d* of M. von den Porten, New York. *Educ:* Eton Coll.; New Coll., Oxford (MA). Barrister-at-Law, Inner Temple. Served War of 1939-45, with Oxford and Bucks Light Inf.; Hon. Major, TARO. Dep. Commissioner-in-Chief, St John Ambulance Brigade, 1950; Director-General, St John Ambulance Assoc., 1951-60; Vice-Chancellor, Order of St John, 1960. Member Court of Assistants, Merchant Taylors' Company (Master, 1958-59); Director, Pyrene Co. Ltd, 1947-68 (Dep.-Chairman, 1962-68). GCStJ 1960. *Recreations:* gardening, reading and travel. *Address:* Flat 8, 51 Onslow Square, SW7. *T:* 01-589 3371; Rignell Hall, Barford St Michael, Oxford. *T:* Bloxham 410. *Clubs:* Oxford and Cambridge University, Garrick; Shropshire (Shrewsbury).

**PARSLOE, Charles Guy,** MA; Secretary, Institute of Welding, 1943-67, Hon. Fellow, 1968; Vice-President, International Institute of Welding, 1966-69 (Secretary-General, 1948-66); *b* London, 5 Nov. 1900; *o surv s* of Henry Edward Parsloe; *m* 1929, Mary Zirphie Munro, *e d* of J. G. Faiers, Putney; two *s* one *d. Educ:* Stationers' Company's School and University College, London. First Class hons. History, 1921; Franks student in Archæology, 1922; Secretary and Librarian, Institute of Historical Research, 1927-43; Assistant in History, University Coll., 1925-27. Secretary OEEC Welding Mission to USA, 1953; organised Commonwealth Welding Conferences, 1957, 1965; President, Junior Institution of Engineers, 1967. Hon. Freeman, Founders' Company, 1964. Wheatley Medal, Library Association, 1965. *Publications:* The English Country Town, 1932; The Minute Book of the Corporation of Bedford, 1647-64, 1949; some 400 bibliographies in the Cambridge Bibliography of English Literature, 1940; Wimbledon Village Club and Lecture Hall, 1858-1958; Wardens' Accounts of the Worshipful Company of Founders of the City of London, 1497-1681, 1964; papers on historical and bibliographical subjects. *Recreation:* historical research. *Address:* 1 Leopold Avenue, SW19. *T:* 01-946 0764. *Club:* Athenæum.

**PARSONS,** family name of **Earl of Rosse.**

**PARSONS, Anthony Derrick,** CMG 1969; MVO 1965; MC 1945; Counsellor, UK Mission to the United Nations, New York, since 1969; *b* 9 Sept. 1922; *s* of late Col H. A. J. Parsons, MC; *m* 1948, Sheila Emily Baird; two *s* two *d. Educ:* King's Sch., Canterbury; Balliol Coll., Oxford. HM Forces, 1940-54; Asst Mil. Attaché, Baghdad, 1952-54; Foreign Office, 1954-55; HM Embassy: Ankara, 1955-59; Amman, 1959-60; Cairo, 1960-61; FO, 1961-64; HM Embassy, Khartoum, 1964-65; Political Agent, Bahrain, 1965-69. Order of the Two Niles (Sudan), 1965. *Recreations:* modern poetry, ornithology, tennis. *Address:* c/o Foreign and Commonwealth Office, Whitehall, SW1. *Clubs:* MCC, English-Speaking Union.

**PARSONS, Ian Macnaghten,** OBE 1944; Chairman, Chatto & Windus Ltd, and The Hogarth Press Ltd; Joint Chairman, Chatto & Jonathan Cape Ltd; Director: Hunter & Foulis

Ltd; Duralin Bookbinding Products Ltd; Sprint Productions Ltd; Scottish Academic Press Ltd; *b* 21 May 1906; *s* of late Edward Percival and Mabel Margaret Parsons, Pont Street, SW; *m* 1934, Marjorie Tulip Ritchie; no *c*. *Educ:* Winchester Coll.; Trinity Coll., Cambridge. Senior Scholar; 1st Class Eng. Lit. Joined Chatto & Windus, 1928, Partner, 1930-53; Director of Chatto & Windus Ltd, 1953, Chairman, 1954. President, The Publishers Association, 1957-59. *Publications:* Shades of Albany, 1928. Editor: The Progress of Poetry, 1936; Poetry for Pleasure, 1956; Men Who March Away, 1965. *Recreations:* sailing, reading. *Address:* 24 Victoria Square, SW1. *T:* 01-828 4024; Juggs Corner, Kingston by Lewes, Sussex. *T:* Lewes 4707. *Clubs:* Garrick, Beefsteak, MCC, Royal Automobile.

**PARSONS, Sir (John) Michael,** Kt 1970; Chairman, Macdonald Hamilton & Co. Pty Ltd, Australia, since 1970; *b* 29 Oct. 1915; *s* of late Rt Rev. Richard Godfrey Parsons, DD, Bishop of Hereford; *m* 1st, 1946, Hilda Mary Frewen (marr. diss. 1964); one *s* two *d*; 2nd, 1964, Caroline Inagh Margaret Frewen. *Educ:* Rossall Sch.; University Coll., Oxford. Barry & Co., Calcutta, 1937. Served in Royal Garhwal Rifles (Indian Army), 1939-45: Bde Major, 1942; POW, Singapore, 1942. Macneill & Barry Ltd, Calcutta, 1946-70; Chm. & Managing Dir., 1964-70. Vice-Chm., Indian Jute Mills Assoc., 1960-61; Pres., Bengal Chamber of Commerce, 1968-69; Pres., Associated Chambers of Commerce of India, 1969; Mem., Advisory Council on Trade, Bd of Trade, India, 1968-69. *Recreation:* golf. *Address:* c/o Inchcape & Co. Ltd, 40 St Mary Axe, EC3. *T:* 01-283 4680. *Clubs:* Oriental; Bengal, Tollygunge (Calcutta); Union (Sydney).

**PARSONS, Kenneth Charles,** CMG 1970; OBE 1962; Counsellor, Foreign and Commonwealth Office; *b* 9 Jan. 1921; *m* 1949, Monica (*née* Howell); two *d*. *Educ:* Haverfordwest Grammar Sch.; Exeter Coll., Oxford. 2nd class, Lit. Hum., 1941. Served War of 1939-45: with Oxfordshire and Buckinghamshire LI, 1941-46. 1st Class Hons, Mod. Langs (at Oxford), 1948. Joined Diplomatic Service, 1949. *Recreations:* rowing, swimming, walking. *Address:* Grove End, Lower Park Road, Chipstead, Surrey. *T:* Downland 53907.

**PARSONS, Rev. Canon Laurence Edmund;** Hon. Canon of St George's Cathedral, Capetown, 1937, Hon. Provincial Canon since 1946; *b* 22 July 1883; *s* of late Hon. Richard Clere Parsons and Agnes Elizabeth, *d* of late J. F. la Trobe-Bateman, FRS; *g s* of 3rd Earl of Rosse; *m* 1911, Lydia Dorothy (*d* 1964), *yr d* of late Frederic Foster la Trobe-Bateman, and *g d* of late J. F. la Trobe-Bateman, FRS, of Moor Park, Surrey; one *d*. *Educ:* Winchester; Christ Church, Oxford; Cuddesdon Theological College. Curate of St Bartholomew's, Leeds, 1908-11; chaplain to Bishop Burge of Southwark, 1911-14; missionary in Shantung, N China, 1914; Curate of Wimbledon, 1915-16; Vicar of Chippenham, Wilts, 1916-25; Dean of Cape Town, 1925-28; Vicar of Coleman's Hatch, 1931-32; Director of South African Church Institute, 1932-45; General Secretary of SPCK, 1945-54. *Recreations:* travel, photography, gardening. *Address:* 21 Cheyne Walk, SW3. *T:* 01-352 1707.

**PARSONS, Sir Maurice (Henry),** KCMG 1970; Kt 1966; Chairman, Bank of London and South America, since 1970; Director, John Brown & Co., since 1970; *b* 19 May 1910; *s* of late G. H. C. Parsons; *m* 1937, Daphne I. Warner; one *s* one *d*. *Educ:* University College School. Entered Bank of England, 1928; Private Secretary to Governor (Montagu Norman), 1939-43; Alternate Exec. Director for UK on International Monetary Fund, 1946-47; International Bank, 1947; Director of Operations International Monetary Fund, 1947-50; Dep. Chief Cashier, Bank of England, 1950; Asst to Governors, 1955; Executive Director, 1957; Alternate Governor for UK of International Monetary Fund, 1957-66; Dep. Governor, Bank of England, 1966-70. *Address:* Clifford House, Shalford, Surrey. *T:* Guildford 61523. *Clubs:* St James', National, MCC.

**PARSONS, Sir Michael;** *see* Parsons, Sir J. M.

**PARSONS, Rev. Canon Richard Edward;** Governor, Moor Park College for Christian Adult Education, Farnham, Surrey, since 1961 (Founder Warden, 1949-61); *b* 16 Feb. 1888; 5th *s* of late Hon. Richard Clere Parsons and Agnes Elizabeth, *d* of late J. F. La Trobe-Bateman, FRS; *m* 1917, Hester Katherine (*d* 1954), *y d* of late Major John Drummond, Scots Guards; one *s* four *d*. *Educ:* Wellington College; Trinity Coll., Cambridge (Mechanical Sciences Tripos (Hons. 3rd Class), 1910, BA 1910, MA 1923). Great Northern Railway (Engineer's Dept), 1910-14; served European War, 1914-18. Lt-Col RE; Personal Assistant, Chief Engineer GNR, 1918-21; King's Coll., London (Theological), 1921-23, AKC, 1923; Ely Theological College, 1923; Curate of St Paul's, Bedford, 1923-27; Vicar of Oxhey, Watford, 1927-36; Director of Religious Education, Central Council of C. of E. for Religious Education, 1936-41; Hon. Secretary, Joint Conference Anglicans and Free Churchmen, 1937-41; Secretary Churches' Cttee for Religious Education among Men in HM Forces, 1941-48; Rector of Wotton, Surrey, 1943-49. Member, The Adult Education Cttee, British Council of Churches, 1950; Canon, York Minster, 1941, Canon Emeritus, 1968. Select Preacher, University of Cambridge, 1943. *Publications:* Re-educating Adults; The Spirit of the Christian Cell. *Address:* Adam's Row, South Audley Street, W1. *T:* 01-668 4401. *Club:* Athenæum.

**PARSONS-SMITH, Basil Gerald,** OBE 1945; MA, MD, FRCP; Physician, and Physician in Charge, Department of Neurology, Charing Cross and West London Hospitals, 1950; Physician, West End Hospital for Neurology; Hon. Consulting Physician, St Mary's Hospital Group; Teacher in Medicine, London University; *b* 19 Nov. 1911; *s* of late Dr Basil Parsons-Smith, FRCP, and Marguerite, *d* of Sir David Burnett, 1st Bt; *m* 1939, Aurea Mary, *d* of late William Stewart Johnston, Sunningdale; two *s* one *d*. *Educ:* Harrow; Trinity Coll., Cambridge. St George's Hospital; Entrance Exhib., 1933; Brackenbury Prize in Medicine, 1936; House Surgeon, House Physician, Med. Registrar. Physician, Western Ophthalmic Hospital (St Mary's), 1938-60; Physician, Electro Encephalograph Dept, Middlesex Hospital Medical Sch., 1950-55. MRCP 1939. Served War of 1939-45, as medical specialist i/c medical divisions in RAF Hospitals in ME; Sqdn Leader RAFVR (despatches, OBE). MD (Cantab) 1949, Prox. Acc. Raymond Horton-Smith Prize; FRCP 1955. Examiner, RCP. Member: Association of British Neurologists; Ophthalmic Society of UK; Hunterian Society. Liveryman, Society of Apothecaries. *Publications:* Electro Encephalographic Studies, 1949; contributed to scientific journals mostly in connection with diseases of the brain, the nervous system and the eye *Recreations:* gardens and horses. *Address:* 23 Harley Street, W1. *T:* 01-580 2440;

01-224 3929; Roughets House, Bletchingley, Surrey. *Clubs:* Bath, Army and Navy.

**PART, Sir Antony (Alexander),** KCB 1966 (CB 1959); MBE 1943; Permanent Secretary, Department of Trade and Industry, since Oct. 1970 (Board of Trade, 1968-70); *b* 28 June 1916; *s* of late Alexander Francis Part and late Una Margaret Reynolds (*née* Snowdon); *m* 1940, Isabella Bennett; no *c*. *Educ:* Wellesley House, Broadstairs; Harrow; Trinity Coll., Cambridge. First Class Hons Modern and Mediæval Langs Tripos. Entered Board of Education, 1937; Asst Private Secretary to successive Ministers of Supply, 1939-40. Served War of 1939-45 (despatches); Army Service, 1940-44; Lt-Col GS(1), 21st Army Group, 1944. Principal Private Secretary to successive Ministers of Education, 1945-46; Home Civil Service Commonwealth Fellow to USA, 1950-51; Under-Secretary, Ministry of Education, 1954-60; Deputy Secretary, Ministry of: Education, 1960-63; Public Building and Works, 1963-65; Permanent Secretary, MPBW, 1965-68. Chairman, Construction Research Advisory Council, 1967-68; Governor, Administrative Staff Coll., 1968; Governor, LSE, 1968-. Hon. DTech Brunel, 1966. *Recreation:* travel. *Address:* Flat 6, 43 Lowndes Square, SW1. *T:* 01-235 1310. *Clubs:* MCC, Oxford and Cambridge University.

**PARTON, Prof. John Edwin;** Professor of Electrical Engineering, University of Nottingham, since 1954; at University of Tennessee, Knoxville, USA, as Senior Visiting Scientist, National Science Foundation, 1965-66; *b* Kingswinford, Staffordshire, 26 Dec. 1912; *s* of Edwin and Elizabeth Parton; *m* 1940, Gertrude Brown; one *s* one *d*. *Educ:* Huntington Church of England Sch.; Cannock Chase Mining Coll.; University of Birmingham. BSc (1st Class Hons), 1936, PhD, 1938, Birmingham. Training: Littleton Collieries, 1934; Electrical Construction Co., 1935; Asst Engineer, PO Engineering Dept, Dollis Hill Research Station, 1938-39; Part-time Lecturer: Cannock Chase Mining Coll., 1931-38; Northampton Polytechnic, 1938-39. Served RNVR Electrical Branch, Sub-Lt, 1939, to Lt-Comdr, 1943-45. Sen. Sci. Officer, British Iron and Steel Research Assoc., 1946; Lecturer, 1946-54. Senior Lecturer, 1954, University of Glasgow. Chairman, East Midland Centre Institution of Electrical Engineers, 1961-62. FIEE 1966; MIES 1951; FIMechE 1967. 1964. *Publications:* papers in Proc. IEE, Beama Journal, Trans. IES, Instrument Practice, International Journal of Electrical Engineering Education, etc. *Recreation:* golf. *Address:* 87 Wollaton Vale, Nottingham NG8 2PD. *T:* Nottingham 256709. *Club:* Royal Naval Volunteer Reserve.

**PARTRIDGE, Eric Honeywood;** Author; *b* Waimata Valley, Gisborne, New Zealand, 1894; *s* of John and Ethel Partridge; *m* 1925, Agnes Vye-Parminter; one *d*. *Educ:* TGS; Queensland and Oxford Universities. School-teacher, 1910-13; served as private in Australian Infantry, 1915-18; Queensland Travelling Fellow at Oxford, 1921-23 (BLitt in Anglo-French Literature); lecturer Manchester and London Universities, 1925-27; founder and managing director of the Scholartis Press, 1927-31; since 1932 author, since 1963 mainly revision; Army 1940-41; RAF Dec. 1942-Aug. 1945. *Publications:* The French Romantics' Knowledge of English Literature; Eighteenth Century English Romantic Poetry; English Prose; Three Personal Records of the War (with R. H. Mottram and John Easton); Songs and Slang of the British Soldier (with John Brophy); Slang To-day and Yesterday: a History and a Study; A Dictionary of Slang and Unconventional English, revised edn, 1969; The World of Words; A Dictionary of Clichés; Usage and Abusage; A Guide to Good English; A Dictionary of Abbreviations, 1943; Journey to the Edge of Morning, 1946; Shakespeare's Bawdy (a study and a glossary), 1947; (with Wilfred Granville and Frank Roberts) Forces' Slang (1939-45), 1948; English for Human Beings, 1949; A Dictionary of the Underworld, British and American, 1950; Here, There and Everywhere: essays on language, 1950; (with Prof. John W. Clark, University of Minnesota) A History of English in the 20th Century, 1951; From Sanskrit to Brazil, 1952; You Have a Point There (punctuation), 1953; The Concise Usage and Abusage, 1954; English Gone Wrong, 1957; Origins: An Etymological Dictionary of English, 1958 (4th edn 1966); Name This Child (Christian Names), 1959; A Charm of Words (essays), 1960; Adventuring among Words, 1961; Comic Alphabets, 1961; The Gentle Art of Lexicography, 1963. *Recreations:* cricket, reading, persons. *Address:* 15 The Woodlands, Southgate, N14. *Clubs:* Savile; Surrey County Cricket.

**PARTRIDGE, Ernest,** CBE 1954; *b* 10 Aug. 1895; *s* of William Thomas Partridge, DrMed; *m* 1927, Sarah Millicent, *d* of Sinclair Orr Langtry, Co. Armagh. *Educ:* Wilson's Grammar Sch., Camberwell. Private, University and Public Schools. Brigade, Royal Fusiliers, 1914-15; Captain, Durham Light Inf., 1915-16; Captain, Argyll and Sutherland Highlanders (HG), 1942-44. MP (C) Battersea South, 1951-64. PPS to Parliamentary Secretary, Ministry of Transport, 1959-64; PPS to Parliamentary Under-Secretary of State for Defence for Royal Navy, 1964. *Recreations:* shooting, fishing, cricket. *Address:* Mill Cottage, Morecombelake, Bridport, Dorset. *T:* Chideock 455. *Clubs:* St Stephen's, Battersea Conservative.

**PARTRIDGE, (Ernest) John;** Chairman, Imperial Tobacco Group Ltd, since 1964; President, Confederation of British Industry, since 1970 (Deputy President, 1969-70); *b* 18 July 1908; *s* of William Henry and Alice Mary Partridge; *m* 1st, 1934, Madeline Fabian (*d* 1944); one *s* one *d*; 2nd, 1949, Joan Johnson; one *s* one *d*. *Educ:* Queen Elizabeth's Hospital, Bristol. Joined Imperial Tobacco Co., 1923; Asst Secretary, 1944; Secretary, 1946; Dep. Chairman, 1960. Director: British-American Tobacco Co. Ltd, 1963; Tobacco Securities Trust Ltd, 1964; National Westminster Bank, 1968-; Member: Tobacco Advisory Cttee, 1945-58; Cheque Endorsement Cttee, 1955-56; National Economic Development Council, 1967-; British National Export Council, 1968-; Chairman: Tobacco Manufacturers' Standing Cttee (now Tobacco Research Council), 1960-62; Industrial Management Research Assoc., 1964-67; Council of Industry for Management Education, 1967-. Vice-President, Industrial Co-Partnership Assoc., 1966-. Governor: Queen Elizabeth's Hospital; Clifton Coll.; Badminton Sch.; Ashridge Management Coll., 1963-; Member Governing Body, London Graduate School of Business Studies, 1967-; Fellow, British Institute of Management, 1963-. *Recreations:* gardening, mountain and fell walking. *Address:* Wildwood, Haslemere, Surrey. *T:* Haslemere 51002; Flat 5, 5 Grosvenor Square, W1. *T:* 01-499 8839. *Club:* Athenæum.

**PARTRIDGE, John;** *see* Partridge, Ernest John.

**PARTRIDGE, Prof. Maurice William,** BPharm, BSc, PhD (London) 1940; FPS; Lord Trent Professor of Pharmaceutical Chemistry,

University of Nottingham, since 1960 and Head of the Department of Pharmacy since 1967; Vice-Dean, Faculty of Pure Science, since 1968; *b* 15 June 1913; *s* of William Harold Gray and Mary Ann Agnes Partridge; *m* 1940, Monica Agnes (*née* McMain), Professor of Russian Language and Literature, University of Nottingham; no *c*. *Educ:* Magnus Sch., Newark; University College, Nottingham. University College, Nottingham: Leverhulme Scholar, 1934; Demonstrator, 1936-38. Home Office Research Scholar, 1938-39; Research Asst to British Pharmocopœia Commn, 1939-44; Research Chemist, Boots Pure Drug Co. Ltd, 1944-47; Lecturer in Pharmaceutical Chemistry, University College (later University of) Nottingham, 1947-55; Lord Trent Reader in Pharmaceutical Chemistry, Univ. of Nottingham, 1955-60; Examiner: Univ. of Manchester, 1956-59, 1963-66, 1969-; Univ. of Wales, 1956-59; Univ. of Glasgow, 1962-64; Univ. of Strathclyde, 1964-66, 1969-; National University of Ireland, 1967-. *Publications:* Scientific papers, mainly in Journal Chem. Society and British Journal Cancer. *Recreation:* painting (paintings exhibited in London, 1959-). *Address:* The University, Nottingham. *T:* Nottingham 56101.

**PARTRIDGE, Dr Miles;** *see* Partridge, Dr S. M.

**PARTRIDGE, Dr (Stanley) Miles,** FRS 1970; Deputy Director since 1970 and Head of Department of Biochemistry and Physiology since 1968, ARC Meat Research Institute, Langford, Bristol; *b* Whangarei, NZ, 2 Aug. 1913; *s* of Ernest Joseph Partridge and Eve Partridge (now Eve McCarthy); *m* 1940, Ruth Dowling; four *d*. *Educ:* Harrow County Sch.; Battersea Coll. of Technology. PhD Chemistry 1937; MA 1946, ScD 1964, Cantab. Beit Memorial Fellow, Lister Inst. of Preventive Medicine, 1940; Techn. Adviser, Govt of India, 1944; returned to Low Temperature Stn, Cambridge, 1946; Principal Scientific Officer 1952; Dep. Chief Scientific Officer, ARC, 1964. Member: Biochemical Soc. Cttee, 1957-61; Nuffield Foundn Rheumatism Cttee, 1965. Fourth Tanner Lectr and Award, Inst. of Food Technologists, Chicago, 1964. *Publications:* scientific papers, mainly in Biochemical Jl. *Recreation:* gardening. *Address:* Millstream House, St Andrew's Road, Cheddar, Somerset. *T:* Cheddar 130.

**PARTRIDGE, Rt. Rev. William Arthur;** Assistant Bishop of Hereford, since 1963; *b* 12 Feb. 1912; *s* of Alfred and Sarah Partridge; *m* 1945, Annie Eliza Joan Strangwood; one *s*. *Educ:* Alcester Grammar Sch.; Birmingham Univ.; Scholæ Cancellarii, Lincoln. Curate of Lye, Worcs, 1935; SPG Studentship at Birmingham Univ. Education Dept, 1938-39; Educational Missionary, Dio. Madras, 1939-43; Chaplain, RAFVR, 1943-46; Lecturer Meston Training Coll., Madras, 1947-51; Metropolitan's Commissary and Vicar-General in Nandyal, 1951; Asst Bishop of Calcutta (Bishop in Nandyal), 1953-63; Vicar of Ludford, 1963-69. *Publication:* The Way in India, 1962. *Recreation:* the organ. *Address:* Carver House, Overton Road, Ludlow, Salop. *T:* Ludlow 2798.

**PASCAL, Roy,** MA, LittD; FBA 1970; Professor of German, Birmingham University, 1939-69; *b* 28 Feb. 1904; *s* of C. S. Pascal and Mary Edmonds, Birmingham; *m* 1931, Feiga Polianovska; two *d*. *Educ:* King Edward's Sch., Birmingham; Pembroke Coll., Cambridge (Scholar). Studied at Berlin and Munich; Fellow of Pembroke Coll., Cambridge, 1929-34 and 1936-39; Director of Modern Language Studies at Pembroke College, 1936-39; Lecturer in German in the University of Cambridge, 1934-39; President, Assoc. of University Teachers, 1944-45; Chm. Conference of Univ. Teachers of German, 1960-61. Goethe Medal, 1965; Shakespeare Prize, Hamburg, 1969. *Publications:* Martin Luther, The Social Basis of the German Reformation, 1933; The Nazi Dictatorship, 1934; Shakespeare in Germany 1740-1815, 1937; Ed. of the German Ideology by Marx and Engels, 1938; contributor to The German Mind and Outlook, 1944-45; Growth of Modern Germany, 1946; The German Revolution 1848, 1948; Goethe's Faust, in Essays on Goethe, 1949; The German Sturm und Drang, 1952; Moeller van den Bruck (in The Third Reich, ed Vermeil), 1955; The German Novel, 1956; The Art of Autobiography (in Stil und Formprobleme in der Literatur, ed Böckmann), 1959; Design and Truth in Autobiography, 1960; Realism (in Spätzeiten, ed Kohlschmidt), 1962; German Literature 1500-1700, 1967; contributions to: Presentation Vols to R. L. G. Ritchie, 1949; L. A. Willoughby, 1952; H. A. Korff, 1957; J. Boyd, 1959; W. H. Bruford, 1962; K. Hoppe, 1962; P. Böckmann, 1964; Fr Martini, 1969; Introduction to Nietzsche's Thus Spake Zarathustra, Everyman edition, 1958; articles in Modern Language Review, Goethe Society Publications, German Life and Letters. *Recreations:* angling, carpentry. *Address:* 17 Rotton Park Road, Birmingham 16.

**PASHLEY, Dr Donald William,** FRS 1968; Laboratory Director, Tube Investments Research Laboratories; *b* 21 Apr. 1927; *s* of late Harold William Pashley and Louise Pashley (*née* Clarke); *m* 1954, Glenys Margaret Ball; one *s* one *d*. *Educ:* Henry Thornton Sch., London; Imperial Coll., London (BSc). 1st cl. hons Physics, 1947; PhD 1950. Research Fellow, Imp. Coll., 1950-55; TI Res. Labs., Hinxton Hall: Res. Scientist, 1956-61; Gp Leader and Div. Head, 1962-67; Asst Dir, 1967-68; Dir, 1968-. Rosenhain Medal, Inst. of Metals, 1968. *Publications:* (jtly) Electron Microscopy of Thin Crystals, 1965; numerous papers on electron microscopy and diffraction, thin films and epitaxy in Phil. Mag., Proc. Roy. Soc., etc. *Address:* 32 Beeches Close, Saffron Walden, Essex. *T:* Saffron Walden 3509; Tube Investments Research Laboratories, Hinxton Hall, near Saffron Walden, Essex. *T:* Sawston 2381.

**PASKIN, Sir (Jesse) John,** KCMG 1954 (CMG 1944); MC; retired Civil Servant; *b* 15 Nov. 1892; *m* 1st, 1920, Doris Blanche North; one *s*; 2nd, 1947, Alice Marjorie, MBE 1961, *d* of late H. J. Ruston. *Educ:* King Edward's Sch., Stourbridge; St John's Coll., Cambridge (BA). Served European War, 1914-19, with 8th Bn Worcestershire Regt and Machine Gun Corps, France, Belgium, and Germany, Major 1918 (MC, French Croix de Guerre). Assistant Principal, Ministry of Transport, 1920; transferred to Colonial Office, 1921. Successively Private Secretary to Sir C. Davis, Lord Lovat, and Sir S. Wilson, and Assistant Private Sec. to Sec. of State for the Colonies (Mr L. S. Amery and Lord Passfield), 1927-29; Principal, 1929; Asst Secretary, 1939; Principal Private Sec. to Sec. of State for the Colonies (Mr Malcolm Macdonald and Lord Lloyd), 1939-40; Assistant Under-Secretary of State, 1948; retired, 1954. *Recreation:* fly-fishing. *Address:* Wishford, near Salisbury, Wiltshire. *Clubs:* Athenæum, United University; Fly-fishers'.

**PASLEY, Maj.-Gen. Joseph Montagu Sabine,** CB 1952; CBE 1944; MVO 1936; late RA; *b* 5 Sept. 1898; *s* of Montagu Wynyard Sabine and Grace

Lillian Pasley; *m* 1st, 1926; one *d*; 2nd, 1950, Mrs D. B. Parsons; one *s*. *Educ:* Christ's Hospital; RMA. Commissioned RA, 1916; served European War, France, 1918; War of 1939-45 (CBE); Maj.-Gen., 1949. Comdr, 1st Anti-Aircraft Group, 1949-52. Formerly Commissioner for Surrey, St John Ambulance Brigade. OStJ. *Address:* 1 Ryefield Close, Eastbourne, Sussex. *T:* Eastbourne 51478. *Club:* Cavalry.

**PASLEY, Sir Rodney (Marshall Sabine),** 4th Bt, *cr* 1794; retired as Headmaster, Central Grammar School, Birmingham (1943-59); *b* 22 Feb. 1899; *s* of late Captain Malcolm Sabine Pasley, RN, and late Nona Marion Paine; *S* uncle, 1947; *m* 1922, Aldyth Werge Hamber; one *s* one *d*. *Educ:* Sherborne School; University Coll., Oxford. Served European War, 1914-18, 2nd Lt RFA. BA 1921, MA 1925; Asst Master, Alleyn's School, 1921-25; Vice-Principal, Rajkumar Coll., Rajkot, India, 1926-28; Asst Master, Alleyn's School, 1931-36; Headmaster, Barnstaple Grammar School, 1936-43. *Publication:* Private Sea Journals, 1778-1782, kept by Admiral Sir Thomas Pasley, 1931. *Heir: s* John Malcolm Sabine Pasley, Magdalen Coll., Oxford, [*b* 5 April 1926; *m* 1965, Virginia Killigrew Wait; two *s*]. *Address:* Hazel Cottage, Peaslake, Surrey.

**PASMORE, (Edwin John) Victor,** CBE 1959; MA; Artist; *b* Chelsham, Surrey, 3 Dec. 1908; *s* of late E. S. Pasmore, MD; *m* 1940, Wendy Blood; one *s* one *d*. *Educ:* Harrow School; attended evening classes, LCC Central School of Arts & Crafts. Local government service, LCC County Hall, 1927-37; joined the London Artists' Assoc., 1932-34, and the London Group, 1932-52. Associated with the formation of the Euston Road School, 1937-39, and the first post-war exhibitions of abstract art, 1948-53; joined the Penwith Society, St Ives, 1951-53. Visiting teacher, LCC Camberwell School of Art, 1945-49; Central School of Arts and Crafts, 1949-53. Master of Painting, Durham University, 1954-61; consultant architectural designer, South West Area, Peterlee New Town, since 1955. *Retrospective Exhibitions at:* Venice Biennale, 1960; Musée des Arts Décoratifs, Paris, 1961; Stedelijk Museum, Amsterdam, 1961; Palais des Beaux Arts, Brussels, 1961; Louisiana Museum, Copenhagen, 1962; Kestner-Gesellschaft, Hanover, 1962; Kunsthalle, Berne, 1963; Tate Gallery, 1965; São Paolo Biennale, 1965; Marlborough New London Gallery, 1966, 1969. Carnegie Prize for painting, 1964. Works represented in: Tate Gallery, Arts Council and other public collections in Gt Britain, Canada, Australia, Holland, Italy, Austria and the USA. Member of the Institute of Contemporary Art. Trustee, Tate Gall., 1963-66. *Address:* 12 St Germans Place, Blackheath, SE3. *T:* 01-858 0369.

**PASMORE, Victor;** *see* Pasmore, E. J. V.

**PASSEY, Richard Douglas,** MC 1917; Emeritus Professor of Experimental Pathology, University of Leeds; *b* 28 Aug. 1888; *s* of John Passey, The Hollies, Kington, Herefordshire, and Maria Ann Jenkins; *m* 1924, Agnes Pattullo Struth, East Park, Cupar, Fife; three *s* one *d* (and one *s* decd). *Educ:* Lady Hawkins Grammar School, Kington, Herefordshire; Queen's College, Taunton; Guy's Hospital, London. MBBS, 1912 (London); MD, DPH (London) 1919; House Appointments, Guy's Hospital, 1912; Junior Asst Bacteriologist, Guy's Hospital, 1912; temp. commission, RAMC, 1914-15, Gordon Highlanders, 1915-17; Captain RAMC, 1917-19; war service, 1914-19 (MC); Senior Demonstrator and Gull Student in Pathology, Guy's Hospital, 1919; Griffith's Demonstrator of Pathology, 1921-26; Lecturer in Pathology, Welsh Nat. School of Medicine, 1926; Director of Cancer Research, Univ. of Leeds, 1926-53. Lt-Col OC 12th West Riding Bn, Home Guard, 1940-44. *Publications:* medical articles in Jl of Pathology and Bacteriology, BMJ, etc. *Recreations:* painting, fishing, shooting, golf, farming, bridge. *Address:* Chester Beatty Research Institute, Fulham Road, SW3.

**PASSMORE, Rt. Rev. Nicholas Wilfrid;** Abbot of Downside Abbey since 1966; *b* 22 Nov. 1907; *s* of Nicholas Kelly Passmore, Bangkok, Siam, and Amy Mary Touche, Edinburgh. *Educ:* Ladycross; Downside; Christ's Coll., Cambridge. Law Society Schol., 1926; entered Novitiate at Downside Abbey, 1928; Scholar of Christ's College, Cambridge, 1934, First Class Historical Tripos; studied Canon Law at University of Sant Anselmo, Rome, and Louvain University, 1935-38; Priest, 1936; Superior of Downside House of Studies at Cambridge, 1938; Prior of Worth, 1939; Bursar of Downside Abbey, 1939-46; Headmaster of Downside School, 1946-62; Prior of Downside Abbey, 1962-66. *Publications:* contributions to Downside Review, etc. *Address:* Downside Abbey, Stratton-on-the-Fosse, near Bath, Somerset. *T:* Stratton-on-the-Fosse 226.

**PASTON-BEDINGFELD, Sir Edmund George Felix,** 9th Bt, *cr* 1661; Major late Welsh Guards; Managing Director, Handley Walker (Europe) Ltd, since 1969; *b* 2 June 1915; *s* of 8th Bt and Sybil, *e d* of late H. Lyne Stephens of Grove House, Roehampton; *S* father, 1941; *m* 1st, 1942, Joan Lynette (*née* Rees) (*d* 1965); one *s* one *d*; 2nd, 1957, Agnes Kathleen, *d* of late Miklos Gluck, Budapest. *Educ:* Oratory School; New College, Oxford. Under-Sec., Head of Agricultural Div., RICS, 1966-69. *Heir: s* Henry Edgar Paston-Bedingfeld [*b* 7 Dec. 1943; *m* 1968, Mary, *er d* of Brigadier R. D. Ambrose, *qv*; one *d*]. *Address:* Oxburgh Hall, King's Lynn, Norfolk; 15 Highgate Close, N6. *T:* 01-348 3247. *Club:* Guards.

**PASTON BROWN, Dame Beryl,** DBE 1967; Principal of Homerton College of Education, Cambridge, since 1961; *b* 7 March 1909; *d* of Paston Charles Brown and Florence May (*née* Henson). *Educ:* Streatham Hill High School; Newnham Coll., Cambridge (MA); London Day Training College. Lecturer: Portsmouth Training Coll., 1933-37; Goldsmiths' Coll., Univ. of London, 1937-44 and 1946-51. Temp. Asst Lecturer, Newnham Coll., 1944-46. Principal of City of Leicester Training Coll., 1952-61. Chairman, Assoc. of Teachers in Colleges and Depts of Educn, 1965-66. *Address:* Principal's House, Homerton College, Cambridge. *T:* Cambridge 48031.

**PASTOR, Antonio Ricardo,** PhD, BLitt; Fellow of King's College, University of London; of the Consejo Superior de Investigaciones Cientificas, Madrid; a Director of Banco Pastor, FENOSA, GENOSA, and President of PALMESA, etc, Spain, and largely interested in hydro-electric industry in that country; founder and a trustee of Pastor Foundation for Classical Studies (Madrid); Trustee of The Museum and Hon. Citizen of Pontevedra; *b* 14 Sept. 1894; *e s* of late Don Ricardo R. Pastor, a director of the Bank of Spain; *m* 1927, Gabriela Marjorie Ground, painter; one *s* one *d*. *Educ:* privately in La Coruña; Lauenburgische Gelehrtenschule, Ratzeburg (Germany); Univ. of Munich; University of Madrid; Oxford University (Spanish Government Scholar); Senior Student at Balliol College, 1917-20; did research work on Plotinus and his contemporaries; a Taylorian Lecturer in Spanish and attached to Balliol College; appointed Cervantes Reader and Head of the Department of Spanish Studies in the University of London in 1921; Cervantes Professor of Spanish Language and Literature in the University of London, King's College, 1930-45; has acted as Inspector of Spanish Teaching in the Evening Institutes maintained by the London County Council and as Adviser to the Council, 1922-36; has lectured widely in England, Spain, France and the Scandinavian countries and broadcast on Hispanic subjects; assisted the Duke of Windsor, when Prince of Wales, in preparation of South American tour, 1931. Corresponding Member of Royal Academy of History, Madrid, and of Hispanic Society of America. Officier de la Légion d'Honneur, 1934; Knight Comdr of Isabella the Catholic, 1945; Knight Comdr of Order of the Phœnix (Greece), 1957; Grand Cross Alfonso X, 1965. *Publications:* Un Embajador de España en la Escena Inglesa (Count Gondomar), 1925; Letter of the Marquis of Santillana to Don Peter, Constable of Portugal (with Professor Edgar Prestage), 1927; Contemporary Spanish Literature, Spanish Chivalry, 1928; The Idea of Robinson Crusoe, 1929; Spanish Language (with Miss J. Perry) in 14th edn of Encyclopædia Britannica; Aspects of the Spanish Renaissance, 1932; Spanish Spain, 1937; Breve Historia del Hispanismo Ingles, 1948; Presentación de Arnold Toynbee, 1952; Cicerón perseguido, 1961; El Retorno De Odiseus, 1965; many articles. *Recreation:* yachting. *Address:* Maceda 2, Pontevedra, Spain; Serrano 107, Madrid. *Clubs:* Athenæum; Royal Corinthian; Nuevo, Puerta de Hierro (Madrid).

**PATCH, Sir Edmund L. H.;** *see* Hall-Patch.

**PATCH, Air Chief Marshal Sir Hubert (Leonard),** KCB 1957 (CB 1952); CBE 1942; *b* 16 Dec. 1904; *s* of late Captain Leonard W. Patch, RN (retd), St Margarets-on-Thames; *m* 1960, Claude Renée, *d* of Major Jean-Marie Botéculet (Légion d'Honneur, Croix de Guerre, Médaille Militaire, MC (British), killed in action in Morocco, 1925). *Educ:* Stonyhurst; RAF Coll., Cranwell, Lincs. Joined RAF, 1925; Group Captain, 1946; Air Cdre, 1947; Air Vice-Marshal, 1951. Served 1939-44 (despatches, CBE). Senior Air Staff Officer, HQ Far East Air Force, 1952-53; AOC No. 11 Gp, Fighter Comd, Nov. 1953-Jan. 1956; Air Officer Commanding-in-Chief (Temp.), Fighter Command, Jan.-Aug. 1956; Commander-in-Chief, Middle East Air Force, 1956-58; Air Member for Personnel April-Sept. 1959; Commander-in-Chief, British Forces, Arabian Peninsula, October 1959-May 1960; Acting Air Marshal, 1956; Air Marshal, 1957; Air Chief Marshal, 1959. Retired from Royal Air Force, 1961. Representative of British Aircraft Corporation to the NATO countries, 1961-63. *Address:* Loma de Rio Verde, Marbella, Spain; c/o Barclays Bank, Colchester, Essex. *Clubs:* Bath, Royal Air Force.

**PATEL, Ambalal Bhailalbhai,** CMG 1949; *b* 1 May 1898; *e s* of late Bhailalbhai Dharamdas Patel, Changa, Bombay; *m* Gangalaxmi Patel (decd); four *s* one *d. Educ:* Petlad High School; Baroda Coll. (BA); Bombay University (LLB). Barrister-at-Law, Lincoln's Inn, 1923. Advocate, Supreme Court of Kenya, 1924; as Kenya Indian Deleg. gave evidence before Joint Parl. Committee on Closer Union, London, 1931. Pres. E African Indian National Congress, 1938-42, and 1945-46; Pres. Kenya Indian Conf., 1942; Mem. standing and exec. Cttees of EAIN Congress, 1924-56; Chm. Indian Elected Members Organization, 1941-48; Hon. Sec. Coast Elected Members Organization, 1949-56; Mem. Makerere Coll. Assembly, 1938-48. Chm. Central Indian Advisory Man-Power Cttee and Indian E Dist Man-Power Cttee during War of 1939-45. Chm. Indian and Arab Land Settlement Bd, 1946-54; attended African Conf. in London, 1948; Mem. E African Central Legislative Assembly, 1948-52; Minister without Portfolio, Govt of Kenya, 1954-56, retired. MLC 1938-56, MEC Kenya, 1941-56. Mem. Royal Technical College Council, Nairobi, and Makerere University Coll. Council, 1954-56. Gen. Sec. and Treasurer, World Union, 1964-. Pres. or trustee various political, social and cultural institutions at different times. Jt Ed., World Union, 1968-. Coronation Medal, 1953. *Address:* c/o Sri Aurobindo Ashram, Pondicherry (via Madras), India.

**PATEL, Rao Bahadur Ranchhodehai Bhaibabhai,** CIE 1941; Ex-Senior Claims Commissioner under the Bombay Explosion (Compensation) Ordinance, 1944; Retired Prothonotary and Senior Master, High Court, Bombay, India; *b* 18 Dec. 1880; *s* of Bhaibabhai Amthabhai Patel and Hetaba Bhaibabhai Patel; *m* 1892, Jiba, *d* of Bhulabhai Lāxmidas Patel, Komrol; three *d. Educ:* Baroda; St John's College, Cambridge, MA, LLB. Called to Bar, Inner Temple; joined High Court, Bombay, as Deputy Registrar in 1905; after holding various appointments was confirmed as Prothonotary and Senior Master in 1928; Past Pres., Sassoon Reading Room and Library; Grand Superintendent of Grand Chapter of United Scottish Royal Arch Freemasonry in India and Pakistan, including Ceylon, and Hon. 2nd Grand Principal, Scotland; Past Grand Master Depute, ASFI, and Hon. Senior Grand Deacon, Scotland; Asst Grand Master, Grand Lodge of India; Chairman of the Harjivan Vasanji Charitable Trust; President, the Tulsidas Gopalji Charitable and Dhakleshwar Temple Trust; Trustee, Chanda Ramji High School. *Recreations:* reading and walking. *Address:* 3 Babulnath Road, Bombay 7, India. *T:* 75747. *Clubs:* Orient, Willingdon Sports (Bombay).

**PATEMAN, Jack Edward,** CBE 1970; Deputy Chairman, and Joint Managing Director, Elliott Flight Automation, since 1962; *b* 29 Nov. 1921; *s* of William Edward Pateman and Lucy Varley (*née* Jetten); *m* 1949, Cicely Hope Turner; one *s* one *d. Educ:* Gt Yarmouth Grammar Sch. Served War of 1939-45, RAF, 1940-46. Research Engineer: Belling & Lee, 1946-48; Elliott Bros (London) Ltd, 1948-51. Formed Aviation Div. of EBL at Borehamwood, 1951-62. *Recreation:* sailing. *Address:* 40 Lyndhurst Drive, Sevenoaks, Kent. *T:* Sevenoaks 54390.

**PATER, John Edward,** CB 1953; Assistant Under Secretary of State, Local Authority Division, Department of Health and Social Security (formerly Ministry of Health), since 1965; *b* 15 March 1911; *s* of Edward Rhodes and Lilian Pater; *m* 1938, Margaret Anderson, *yr d* of M. C. Furtado; two *s* one *d. Educ:* King Edward VI School, Retford; Queens' College, Cambridge. Foundation Scholar, Queens' College; BA 1933, MA 1935. Assistant Principal, Ministry of Health, 1933; Principal, 1938; Assistant Secretary, 1943; Principal Assistant Secretary, 1945; Under-Secretary, 1947; Director of Establishments and Organisation, 1960-65. Treasurer: Methodist Church Dept of Connexional Funds, 1959-; Finance Bd, 1959-68; Central Finance Bd, 1968-. *Recreations:* reading, archæology, walking (preferably on hills). *Address:* 22 Manor Way, South Croydon CR2 7BR. *T:* 01-688 0349. *Club:* Athenæum.
*See also R. A. Furtado.*

**PATERSON, Dr Alexander Brown;** Director, Veterinary Laboratories and Veterinary Investigation Services, since 1969; *b* 19 Jan. 1917; *s* of Robert Paterson and Catherine Muir; *m* 1945, Margaret Birnie Paterson; one *s* two *d*. *Educ:* Woodside Sch.; Glasgow Veterinary College. ARC Research Fellow, 1942-45; Res. Officer, Biochemistry Dept, MAFF Weybridge, 1945-59; Head, Virology Dept, 1959-65; Dep. Dir, MAFF Lab., 1965-69. FRSocMed. *Publications:* papers in scientific jls. *Recreations:* tennis, geology. *Address:* Royston, 39 London Road, Guildford, Surrey. *T:* Guildford 73147.

**PATERSON, Sir (Alexander) Swinton,** KBE, *cr* 1951 (OBE 1943); CMG, 1947; *b* 12 March 1893; *s* of late William Brockie Paterson, FFA, and Ethel M. Lamplough; *m* 1930, Iseult, *d* of late Theodore Charles Barclay; no *c*. *Educ:* Norwich School. Served European War, North Staffordshire Regt; entered Consular Service, 1920; Vice-Consul at Monrovia, 1921-24; Antwerp, 1924-27; Beira, 1927-29; New York, 1930-35; HM Minister Resident and Consul, Santo Domingo, Dominican Republic, 1935-43; Inspector-Gen. of Consular Establishments, Foreign Office, 1945-50; Senior Inspector, HM Foreign Service Establishments, 1950-54; retd 1954. *Recreations:* tennis, riding. *Address:* 17 Boscombe Overcliff Drive, Bournemouth, Hants. *Clubs:* Royal Automobile; Royal Motor Yacht (Sandbanks).

**PATERSON, A(rthur) Spencer,** MA (Oxon); MD; FRCPE, MRCP; Dipl. Psych.; Consultant Psychiatrist; Physician in Charge, Department of Psychiatry, and Director Psychiatric Laboratory, West London Hospital, 1946-66; *b* 22 Feb. 1900; 4th *s* of late Professor W. P. Paterson, Edinburgh Univ., and late Jane Sanderson; *m* 1933, Antoinette, *d* of late Chas Baxter, WS; two *s* one *d*. *Educ:* Edinburgh Academy; Fettes (Scholar); 2nd Lt RHA 1919. Oriel, Oxford (Hon. Mods and Lit. Hum.; BA 1923); Edinburgh Univ. (MB, ChB 1928). Ho. Phys to Prof. of Medicine, Roy. Infirmary, Edinburgh, 1928-29; Asst Phys., Glasgow Royal Mental Hospital, 1929-30; Rockefeller Fellow, 1930-31; Pinsent-Darwin Research Student in Mental Pathology, Cambridge University, 1931-33; held research posts at: Johns Hopkins Univ., Baltimore, Md, USA, Research Inst. of Psychiatry, Munich; Maudsley Hosp., London. Asst Phys., Cassel Hosp., Penshurst, 1933-36; First Asst, Dept of Psychiatry, Middlesex Hosp., 1936-45, Psychiatrist, Sector V. EMS Metrop. Area, 1939-45. Honeyman-Gillespie Lectr, Edin. Univ., 1948. Membre d'honneur Soc. Méd. Ment. Belge, 1969; Membre Etranger, Soc. Méd.-Psychol., Paris, 1969; Corr. Member: American Psychiat. Association; American Pavlovian Soc. Treasurer, Internat. Soc. for Experimental and Clin. Hypnosis. Hermann Goldman Lectr, NY Coll., Med., 1964. FBPsS. *Publications:* Electrical and Drug Treatments in Psychiatry, 1963; Control of the Autonomic Nervous System by Conditioning and Hypnosis (jointly), 1969; and numerous articles on psychiatric and allied subjects in British and foreign scientific periodicals. *Recreations:* travel, golf, chess. *Address:* 2 Devonshire Place, W1. *T:* 01-935 4560 and 01-935 4600; Ely Hill House, Capel St Andrew, Woodbridge, Suffolk. *T:* Orford 355. *Clubs:* Athenæum; Woodbridge Golf.

**PATERSON, Aylmer John Noel,** CBE 1963; Registrar of the Privy Council, 1954-63; retired May 1963; *b* 16 April 1902; *s* of late Rev. Canon H. D. Noel Paterson, MA; *m* 1935, Kathleen Mary, *er d* of late Sir Noel Goldie, QC. *Educ:* Rugby; Clare Coll., Cambridge (Scholar, BA, LLB). Called to Bar, Middle Temple, 1926; joined Oxford Circuit. Private Secretary to the Lord Chancellor and Deputy Serjeant-at-Arms in House of Lords, 1930-34; Legal Assistant, Lord Chancellor's Office, 1934-39; Chief Clerk, Judicial Committee of the Privy Council, 1939-54. *Recreation:* lawn tennis (rep. Cambridge against Oxford, 1925). *Address:* 8 Metropole Court, Folkestone, Kent. *T:* Folkestone 54601. *Clubs:* Athenæum; Hawks (Cambrdige).

**PATERSON, Frank David; His Honour Judge Paterson;** County Court Judge (Circuit 10, Cheshire and Lancashire), since 1968; *b* 10 July 1918; *yr s* of late David Paterson and Dora Paterson, Liverpool; *m* 1953, Barbara Mary, 2nd *d* of late Oswald Ward Gillow and of Alice Gillow, Formby; one *s* two *d*. *Educ:* Calderstones Preparatory Sch. and Quarry Bank High Sch., Liverpool; Univ. of Liverpool (LLB). Called to Bar, Gray's Inn, 1941; Warden, Unity Boys' Club, Liverpool, 1941; Asst Warden, Florence Inst. for Boys, Liverpool, 1943. Practised on Northern Circuit. Chairman: Min. of Pensions and Nat. Insce Tribunal, Liverpool, 1957; Mental Health Review Tribunal for SW Lancashire and Cheshire, 1963. Asst Dep. Coroner, City of Liverpool, 1960. *Address:* Vailima, 2 West Lane, Formby, Liverpool L37 7BA. *T:* Formby 74345. *Clubs:* National Liberal; University (Liverpool).

**PATERSON, Sir George (Mutlow),** Kt 1959; OBE 1946; QC (Sierra Leone) 1950; Chairman, Industrial Tribunals, 1965; *b* 3 Dec. 1906; *e s* of late Dr G. W. Paterson; *m* 1935, Audrey Anita, *d* of late Major C. C. B. Morris, CBE, MC; one *s* two *d*. *Educ:* Grenada Boys' School; St John's College, Cambridge. Appointed to Nigerian Administrative Service, 1929. Called to the Bar, Inner Temple, 1933. Magistrate, Nigeria, 1936; Crown Counsel, Tanganyika, 1938. War of 1939-45: served with the King's African Rifles, 1939 (wounded 1940); Occupied Enemy Territories Admin., 1941; Lieutenant-Colonel 1945. Solicitor-General, Tanganyika, 1946; Attorney-General, Sierra Leone, 1949, Ghana, 1954-57; Chief Justice of Northern Rhodesia, 1957-61, retired 1961; appointed to hold an inquiry into proposed amendments to the Potato Marketing Scheme, 1962; appointed legal chairman (part-time), Pensions Appeal Tribunals, 1962; appointed chairman Industrial Tribunals, South Western Region, 1965. *Recreations:* shooting and gardening. *Address:* Buckshaw House, Sherborne, Dorset. *T:* Bishop's Caundle 318. *Club:* East India and Sports.

**PATERSON, Maj.-Gen. Herbert MacGregor,** CB 1956; CBE 1954; retired; *b* 29 Nov. 1898; *s* of James Paterson, RSA; PRSW; *m* 1929, Kathleen Mary Tennent; one *d*. *Educ:* Fettes; RMA, Woolwich; Magdalene Coll., Cambridge. 2nd Lt, RA, 1918; Egypt and Palestine, 1918-20. Cambridge University, 1920-23; BA 1923; MA 1935. India, 1923-27; Military College of Science, 1927-34; War Office and Ministry of Supply, 1938-45; Comdt Military Coll. of Science, Bury, 1946-47; Director of Artillery, 1952; Director-General of Artillery, Ministry of Supply, 1953-56. Col 1946; Brig. 1952; Maj.-Gen. 1953; retired 1957. USA Medal of Freedom (Bronze Palm). *Recreation:* music. *Address:* Swan Cottage, Shillingford, Oxford.

**PATERSON, Sqdn-Ldr Ian Veitch,** CBE 1969; DL; JP; County Clerk of Lanarkshire; *b* 17 Aug. 1911; *s* of Andrew Wilson Paterson; *m* 1940, Anne Weir, *d* of Thomas Brown; two *s* one *d*. *Educ:* Lanark Grammar School; Glasgow University. Served RAF, 1940-45.

DL Lanarkshire 1963; JP Lanarkshire. *Address:* 35 Stewarton Drive, Cambuslang, Glasgow.

**PATERSON, (James Edmund) Neil,** MA; Author; *b* 31 Dec. 1915; *s* of late James Donaldson Paterson, MA, BL; *m* 1939, Rosabelle, MA, 3rd *d* of late David MacKenzie, MC, MA; two *s* one *d*. *Educ:* Banff Academy; Edinburgh Univ. Served in minesweepers, War of 1939-45, Lieut RNVR, 1940-46. Director Grampian Television; Member, Films of Scotland Committee, 1954-; Member, Scottish Arts Council; Governor: Nat. Film Sch.; Pitlochry Festival Theatre; British Film Institute, 1958-60; Atlantic Award in Literature, 1946; Award of American Academy of Motion Picture Arts and Sciences, 1960. *Publications:* The China Run, 1948; Behold Thy Daughter, 1950; And Delilah, 1951; Man on the Tight Rope, 1953. Film Stories and screen plays. *Recreations:* golf, fishing. *Address:* St Ronans, Crieff, Perthshire. *T:* 615. *Clubs:* Naval; Scottish Arts (Edinburgh); Royal and Ancient (St Andrews).

**PATERSON, Prof. James Ralston Kennedy,** CBE 1949; MC 1917; MD (Edinburgh); FRCSEd; FRCS; FFR; Professor Emeritus of Radiotherapeutics, University of Manchester, since 1960; Director of Radiotherapy, Christie Hospital and Holt Radium Institute, 1931-62; *b* 21 May 1897; *s* of Rev. David Paterson; *m* 1930, Edith Isabel Myfanwy Irvine-Jones; two *s* one *d*. *Educ:* George Heriot's School, Edinburgh; Edinburgh University. Fellow in Radiology, Mayo Clinic, America, 1926. Acting Director, Radiological Department, Edinburgh, 1930. *Publication:* Treatment of Malignant Disease by Radium and X-rays, 1962. *Recreations:* various. *Address:* Stenrieshill, Moffat, Scotland. *T:* Johnstone Bridge 221. *Club:* Athenæum.

**PATERSON, James Veitch;** Sheriff Substitute of Roxburgh, Berwick and Selkirk at Jedburgh, Duns and Hawick since 1963; *b* 16 April 1928; *s* of John Robert Paterson, ophthalmic surgeon, and Jeanie Gouinlock; *m* 1956, Ailie, *o d* of Lt-Comdr Sir (George) Ian Clark Hutchison, *qv*; one *s* one *d*. *Educ:* Peebles High School; Edinburgh Academy; Lincoln College, Oxford; Edinburgh University. Admitted to Faculty of Advocates, 1953. *Recreations:* fishing, shooting, gardening. *Address:* Sunnyside, Melrose, Roxburghshire. *T:* Melrose 2502. *Club:* New (Edinburgh).

**PATERSON, John Allan;** Agent-General in London and Deputy Minister Abroad for Province of New Brunswick, since 1968; *b* Montreal, 20 May 1909; *s* of William A. and M. Ethel Paterson; *m* 1935, Elizabeth Stewart Messenger; four *s*. *Educ:* Westmount, Quebec; Mount Allison Univ. (BSc 1932); Queen's Univ. Prudential Insurance Co. of America, 1934-46; RCAF 1941-45 (Sqdn Ldr); New Brunswick Dept of Industry, 1946-68 (Deputy Minister, 1956); Provincial Co-ordinator of Civil Defence, 1950-55; Bd of Comrs, Oromocto, 1956-63; Chm., Provincial Govts of Canada Trade and Industry Council, 1956-57, 1961-62 1964-65 and 1966-67.Mem. Bd of Regents, Mount Allison Univ., 1959-63; Pres. Oromocto Develt Corp., 1963-68. *Publication:* (co-author) The New Brunswick Economy, Past Present and Future, 1955. *Recreations:* golf, motoring, fishing. *Address:* 60 Trafalgar Square, WC2.

**PATERSON, Sir John (Valentine) J.;** *see* Jardine Paterson.

**PATERSON, Neil;** *see* Paterson, James Edmund N.

**PATERSON, Noel Kennedy,** CIE 1947; OBE 1943; lately United Kingdom Trade Commissioner, Dublin; *b* 25 Dec. 1905; *s* of Rev. David Paterson, BD, Edinburgh; *m* 1934, Margaret Winifred Schreiber; two *s* two *d*. *Educ:* George Heriot's School, Edinburgh; Edinburgh University; St John's College, Cambridge. Entered Indian Civil Service, 1929; Asst Comr, 1929-34; Under Sec. to Govt of Central Provinces, 1934-36; Deputy Comr, 1936-37 and 1939-45; Under Sec. to Govt of India, 1937-38; Chief Comr, Andaman and Nicobar Islands, 1945-47. *Recreation:* travel. *Address:* Gabriel's Farm, Park Lane, Twyford, Hants. *T:* Twyford 3116.

**PATERSON, Captain Quentin Hunter,** DSC; FIMechE; RN, retired; *b* 25 Aug. 1888; 2nd *s* of late James Paterson, RSA; *m* 1917, Dorothy Scobell, *o d* of late CAptain F. H. Peyton, RN; one *s* one *d* (and one *d* decd). *Educ:* Cheltenham Coll.; HMS Britannia. DSC May 1915 (despatches, May 1918); Naval Ordnance Dept, Admiralty, 1921-38; Armaments Manuf. Beardmores, Glasgow, till 1958. *Recreation:* use of own golf gun for study of ballistics of golf ball. *Address:* No. 1, Penton Hook Farm, Staines, Middlesex. *T:* Staines 53024. *Clubs:* United Service; Royal and Ancient (St Andrews).

**PATERSON, Sir Swinton;** *see* Paterson, Sir A. S.

**PATERSON, William James Macdonald,** CMG 1958; Secretary, Government Hospitality Fund, since 1968; *b* 13 April 1911; *s* of late Robert Duff Paterson and Isobel Findlater; *m* 1946, Eleonōra Māria, *d* of General A. P. Vattay; one *s* one *d*. *Educ:* High School of Glasgow; Glasgow University (MA, LLB). Admitted a Solicitor in Scotland, 1936. Served with HM Forces, 1939-46 (Major, Royal Artillery). Second Secretary, Foreign Office, 1946; First Secretary: Beirut, 1947-50; Damascus, 1950; Santiago, 1951-53; Foreign Office, 1953-55; Counsellor (Commercial), Baghdad, 1955-59; Counsellor, Oslo, 1959-61; British Deputy High Commissioner, Madras, 1961-65; British Consul-General at São Paulo, 1965-68. *Recreations:* golf, reading, wine. *Address:* 135 Marsham Court, Marsham Street, SW1. *Club:* Travellers'.

**PATEY, David Howard,** MS London 1927; FRCS 1924; Consultant Surgeon Emeritus, Middlesex Hospital, W1, since 1964; Director Surgical Studies, Middlesex Hospital Medical School, 1952-64; *b* Oct. 1899; *s* of F. W. Patey and Mrs Patey (*née* Davies); *m* 1927, Gladys Joyce, *d* of Gilbert Summers, Hounslow; two *s* one *d*. *Educ:* Llandovery; London University. Surgical Asst posts at Middlesex Hosp., Hampstead Gen. Hosp., St Mark's Hosp., St Peter's Hosp., Acton Hosp., 1922-32; Surgeon, Middlesex Hospital, 1930-64. Gold Medallist, London MB, 1923; Assoc. of Surgeons Schol., 1927; Jacksonian Prize, RCS, 1930; Streatfield Schol., RCP, 1930; Hunterian Prof., RCS, 1931, 1964. Pres. Section of Surgery, Roy. Soc. Med., 1951-52; Pres., Surgical Research Society, 1958-60. Hon. Fell., American Surgical Assoc., 1964. Colles Lecturer, RCSI, 1957. *Publications:* articles on surgery and surgical pathology. *Recreation:* bowls. *Address:* 65 Montagu Mansions, W1. *T:* 01-935 8037. *Club:* Garrick.

**PATEY, Very Rev. Edward Henry;** Dean of Liverpool since 1964; *b* 12 Aug. 1915; *s* of Walter Patey, MD, and Dorothy Patey; *m* 1942, Margaret Ruth Olivia Abbott; one *s* three *d*. *Educ:* Marlborough College; Hertford College, Oxford; Westcott House, Cambridge. Assistant Curate, St Mary-at-the-Walls, Colchester, 1939; MA (Oxon) 1941; Assistant

Curate Bishopwearmouth Parish Church, Sunderland, 1942; Youth Chaplain to the Bishop of Durham, 1946; Vicar of Oldland, with Longwell Green, Bristol, 1950; Secretary, Youth Department, The British Council of Churches, 1952; Assistant Gen. Secretary, The British Council of Churches, 1955; Canon Residentiary of Coventry Cathedral, 1958. *Publications:* Religion in the Club, 1956; Boys and Girls Growing Up, 1957; Worship in the Club, 1961; A Doctor's Life of Jesus, 1962; Young People Now, 1964; Enquire Within, 1966; Look out for the Church, 1969. *Recreations:* reading, listening to music. *Address:* The Cathedral, Liverpool LI 7A2.

**PATIALA, Lt-Gen. HH the Maharajadhiraj Yadavindra Singh Mahendra Bahadur of,** GCIE 1946; GBE 1942; LLD; *b* 1913; *s* of late HH Maharajadhiraj Sir Bhupindra Singh of Patiala, GCSI, GCIE, GCVO, GBE; *m* 1938, Maharani Mohinder Kaur, *d* of a Noble of Patiala State; two *s* two *d*. *Educ:* Aitchison College, Lahore. Was Rajpramukh of Patiala and East Punjab States Union, 1948-56. Founder and Hon. Life Pres., Asian Games Fedn; Pres., Indian Olympic Assoc., 1938-60. Chm., All India Council of Sports, 1960-65. Patron and President of many other organizations. Was Chancellor of the Chamber of Princes. Served War of 1939-45 in Malaya, Western Desert, Italy, Burma. Delegate of India to XIth Session of United Nations, New York, 1956-57; UNESCO Conference in Paris, 1958, and Leader of Indian Delegation to Food and Agriculture Organization Conference in Rome, 1959, 1961-62, 1963, 1967, 1969; Ambassador to Italy, 1965-66. Mem., Punjab Legislative Assembly, 1967-68. Chm., Horticulture Develt Council, 1970. Hon. LLD: Benares Hindu Univ. 1939, Punjab Univ., 1949. *Recreations:* mountaineering, sports, agriculture and horticulture. *Address:* Motibagh Palace, Patiala, Punjab, India.

**PATNA, HH Maharaja of; Maharaja Sir Rajendra Narayan Singh Deo,** KCIE 1946; *b* 31 March 1912; *S* to Gaddi 1924; *m* 1932, Kailash Kumari Devi, *d* of His late Highness Maharajadhiraj Bhupinder Singh Bahadur of Patiala; two *s* four *d*. *Educ:* Mayo College, Ajmer; St Columba's College, Hazaribagh (Inter-Mediate Arts Exam., 1931). Patron of All India Cattle Show Society, MP (India), 1952-56; MLA and Leader of Opposition, Orissa, 1957-59; Finance Minister, Orissa, 1959-61; MLA and Leader of Opposition, Orissa, 1961-. Chairman, Orissa Public Accounts Committee, 1957-59 and 1961-; Chief Minister, Orissa, 1967-. *Recreation:* walking. *Heir:* Yuvaraj Raj Raj Singh Deo. *Address:* PO Balangir, Orissa, India. *TA:* Patnesh, Balangir. *T:* Balangir 5; Bhubaneswar 234; Lucknow 23213. *Clubs:* Ranchi (Ranchi); International, National Sports (New Delhi).

**PATON;** *see* Noel-Paton, family name of **Baron Ferrier.**

**PATON, Major Adrian Gerard Nigel H.;** *see* Hadden-Paton.

**PATON, Alan (Stewart);** writer; was National President of the South African Liberal Party until it was made an illegal organisation in 1968; living at Botha's Hill, Natal; *b* Pietermaritzburg, 11 Jan. 1903; *s* of James Paton; *m* 1st, 1928, Doris Olive (*d* 1967), *d* of George Francis; two *s*; 2nd, 1969, Anne Hopkins. *Educ:* Natal Univ. (BSc, BEd). Formerly Principal Diepkloof Reformatory; Hon. LHD, Yale, 1954; Hon. DLitt: Kenyon Coll., 1962; Univ. of Natal, 1968. Freedom House Award (USA), 1960. *Publications:* Cry, the Beloved Country, 1948; Too Late the Phalarope, 1953; Land and People of South Africa, 1955; South Africa in Transition (with Dan Weiner), 1956; Debbie Go Home (short stories), 1961; Hofmeyr (biography), 1965; Instrument of Thy Peace, 1968; The Long View, 1969; Kontakion For You Departed, 1969. *Address:* PO Box 278, Hillcrest, Natal, South Africa.

**PATON, Col Alexander,** DSO 1937; MC; RA, retired; *b* 13 Jan. 1897; *s* of Alexander Paton, Glasgow; *m* 1923, Sybil, *er d* of late Sir Grimwood Mears, KCIE; two *s*. *Educ:* Marlborough Coll.; RMA, Woolwich. Commissioned, 1915; served European War, France, 1916-19; Staff Captain, 1918; 15th Corps (despatches twice, MC and bar, General Service and Victory Medals); India, 1919-25; Staff Captain RA, Afghan War, 1919 (1908, General Service Medal, India, and clasp, 1919); Staff Officer RA, Simla, 1921-22; Chitral, NWF India, 1922-24; Home Service, 1925-36; Terr. Adj. 13th (Highland) Brigade, TA, Argyllshire, 1926-30; Company Officer at Royal Military Academy, Woolwich, 1932-34; Adjutant, 3rd Medium Brigade RA, Shoeburyness, 1934-36; India, NWF, 1937 (wounded, despatches, DSO, Medal and clasp); Burma, 1938-40; Comd 21 Mtn Regt NWF, 1940; Comdt MATC Ambala, Punjab, 1941-42; Comdt FATC Muttra, UP, 1942-44; Col 1943-44; Recruiting Staff, Rawalpindi, Punjab, 1944-45. Defence Medal, 1939-45, and War Medal (1939-45). Retd pay, 1947. *Recreation:* philately. *Address:* Willow Cottage, 33 Crofton Lane, Hillhead, Fareham, Hants. *T:* Stubbington 2116; c/o Lloyds Bank, 6 Pall Mall, SW1. *Club:* Royal Over-Seas League.

**PATON, Brig. Charles Morgan,** CVO 1944; CBE 1949; DL; psc; *b* 5 Feb. 1896; *s* of late A. H. Paton; *m* 1920, Mabel Anne, *d* of J. M. Bathgate, JP; one *s*. *Educ:* Berkhamsted; Royal Military College, Sandhurst. Joined Essex Regiment 1914; Captain 1917; Staff College, 1927-28; Bt Major, 1934; Major, 1935; Lt-Col 1941; Col 1944. Served European War, 1914-18, France and Belgium; GSO for Weapon Training, W Comd, 1930-32; DAA & QMG W Comd, 1932-34; DAA & QMG S Comd, 1937-38; DAAG War Office, 1939-40; AAG Mid. East, 1941-42; DA and QMG, Palestine, 1943; DAG Allied Armies in Italy, 1944; retired, 1949. Colonel, The Essex Regiment, 1950-58; Associate Colonel, 3rd East Anglian Regiment (16/44 Foot), 1958-62; Dep. Col The Royal Anglian Regt, 1965-70. DL Essex, 1954. OStJ 1956. *Address:* c/o Lloyds Bank Ltd, 6 Pall Mall, SW1. *Club:* Army and Navy.

**PATON, Douglas Shaw F.;** *see* Forrester-Paton.

**PATON, Florence Beatrice,** JP; *d* of George Walker and Sarah Louise Widdowson, Wolverhampton; *m* 1930, John Paton, *qv*. *Educ:* elementary; secondary; privately. Contested Cheltenham (By-Election), 1928, Rushcliffe 1929 and 1931; MP (Lab) Rushcliffe Div. of Notts, 1945-50. First woman MP Chairman of Standing Cttees, 1947; Delegate, UN Assembly, 1947; first woman MP to preside over the whole House in Committee, 1948. Member Royal Commission on Common Land, 1955-58. *Recreations:* reading, walking, cycling. *Address:* 40 Guessens Court, Welwyn Garden City, Herts. *T:* Welwyn Garden 22901.

**PATON, George Campbell Henderson,** QC (Scotland) 1967; LLD Edin 1969; Reader in Scots Law, Edinburgh University, since 1967; *b* 6 Aug. 1905; *s* of George Grieve Paton, MA, LLB, Solicitor, Glasgow and Mary Campbell Sclanders; *m* 1950, Eva French, *d* of David

French Cranston, Edinburgh; two *d*. *Educ:* Glasgow Academy; Glasgow University. MA 1927; LLB (Distinction) 1930. Solicitor 1931; Advocate 1951. Served Admiralty, 1942-46. Faulds Fellow in Law, Glasgow Univ., 1931-34; Asst to Professor of Law, Glasgow, 1934-46. Lectr in History of Scots Law, Glasgow, 1951-59; Senior Lectr, Dept of Scots Law, Edinburgh, 1959-67. Literary Dir, Stair Soc., 1954-60. *Publications:* Ed., Baron Hume's Lectures (Stair Soc.), 1939-57; Ed. and Contrib., Introductory History of Scots Law (Stair Soc.), 1958; Asst Ed., A Source Book and History of Administrative Law in Scotland, 1956; (with J. G. S. Cameron) Law of Landlord and Tenant in Scotland, 1967; articles in various legal periodicals. *Recreations:* golf, tennis, walking. *Address:* 163 Colinton Road, Edinburgh 11. *T:* 031-443 1660. *Club:* Royal Automobile.

**PATON, George Pearson,** CMG 1942; CBE 1924; *b* 1882; *s* of late George Paton of Baldovan, Angus; *m* 1911, Katharine, *d* of W. B. Scranton, MD; two *s*. *Educ:* Dundee High Sch.; St Andrews Univ.; privately. Apptd Student Interpreter in Japan, 1906; various posts: Japan, China, Korea, Formosa; attached to British High Commission in Siberia, 1918-19; Vladivostok, 1921-28; Consul at Tamsui, Formosa, 1928-30; Commercial Counsellor at Moscow, 1930-37; Consul-General, Istanbul, 1937-42; retired, 1942; Director Intelligence Div., Far Eastern Bureau, British Min. of Information, New Delhi, 1943-46. Légion d'Honneur, 1928. *Address:* c/o Hongkong and Shanghai Banking Corporation, Gracechurch Street, EC3.

**PATON, Sir George Whitecross,** Kt 1957; Vice-Chancellor, University of Melbourne, 1951-68; *b* 16 August 1902; *s* of Rev. Frank H. L. Paton; *m* 1931, Alice Watson; one *s* three *d*. *Educ:* Scotch Coll., Melbourne; University of Melbourne; Magdalen College, University of Oxford. MA (Melb.), 1926; BA (Oxon.), 1928; BCL (Oxon.), 1929. Barrister-at-Law, Gray's Inn, 1929. Asst Lecturer, LSE, 1930; Professor of Jurisprudence, Univ. of Melbourne, 1931-51; Dean of Faculty of Law, 1946-51. Chairman Royal Commission on Television (Australia, 1953-54). LLD (Hons): University of Glasgow, 1953; University of Sydney, 1955; Univ. of Queensland, 1960; Univ. of Tasmania, 1963; Univ. of London, 1963; Monash Univ., 1968; DCL (Hon.), Univ. of Western Ontario, 1958. *Publications:* A Text Book of Jurisprudence, 1946, 3rd edn 1964; Bailment in the Common Law, 1952; (with Barry and Sawer), Criminal Law in Australia, 1948. *Recreations:* tennis, walking, gardening. *Address:* 7 Dunraven Avenue, Toorak, Victoria 3142, Australia. *T:* 24 1034. *Club:* Melbourne (Victoria, Aust.).

**PATON, Harold William,** DSC 1943; **His Honour Judge Paton;** Judge of County Courts, Circuit No. 54 (Bristol, etc) since 1950; Chairman, Somerset Quarter Sessions, since 1965; *b* 6 Oct. 1900; *s* of late Clifford James Paton; *m* 1947, Joan Orby, *d* of late Lt-Col Cecil Gascoigne, DSO, Seaforth Hlrs; one *d*. *Educ:* Winchester College; Christ Church, Oxford. Called to the Bar (Inner Temple), 1923 and practised at Common Law Bar. Served War of 1939-45 in RNVR (Coastal Forces); Lt-Comdr, 1944. *Recreations:* fishing, gardening. *Address:* Sand Hall, Wedmore, Somerset. *Club:* Royal Automobile.

**PATON, John;** late General Secretary Independent Labour Party and editor of New Leader and Penal Reformer; *b* Aberdeen, 1886; working-class parents; *m* 1930, Florence (Beatrice) Paton, *qv*. *Educ:* Elementary School until 12 years of age. Active in Labour Movement, 1902-; Member WEA, etc. MP (Lab), Norwich, 1945-50, North Division of Norwich, 1950-64. *Publications:* Autobiography: Proletarian Pilgrimage, 1935; Left Turn!, 1936. *Address:* 40 Guessens Court, Welwyn Garden City, Herts. *T:* Welwyn Garden 22901.

**PATON, Sir Leonard (Cecil),** Kt 1946; CBE 1944; MC 1915; MA; Director, Harrisons & Crosfield Ltd (Chairman, 1957-62); *b* 7 May 1892; 4th *s* of John Paton, Dunfermline, Fife, Headmaster; *m* 1917, Muriel, *yr d* of William Searles, Maidstone; one *s* one *d*. *Educ:* George Watson's Coll.; Edinburgh University (MA, 1st Class Hons Classics, 1914); Christ Church, Oxford (Exhibitioner). European War, 1914-18, Captain Cameronians (MC, despatches). *Recreations:* fishing, golf. *Address:* 7 Court Royal Mansions, Brighton, Sussex. *Club:* Caledonian.

**PATON, Robert Young,** FRCS; Consulting Orthopædic Surgeon (retired); *b* 18 Jan. 1894; 2nd *s* of Dr Edward Ley Paton, Perth, Scotland; *m* 1st, 1923, Daphne, *y d* of Benjamin Colet Pulleyne, Headingley, Yorks (marr. diss., 1951); 2nd, 1954, Elizabeth Law Milne, *y d* of Rt Hon. Sir John Milne Barbour, 1st and last Bt, of Conway, Dunmurry, Co. Antrim. *Educ:* Perth Academy; St Andrews Univ.; Trinity Coll., Cambridge; St Mary's and St Bartholomew's Hospitals, London. MA (1st Class Hons in Mathematics and Natural Philosophy, Guthrie and Berry Schols., Tullis Medals), St Andrews Univ., 1915. Surgeon-Probationer, RNVR, 1917-18. MRCS, LRCP, 1920. BA 1918, MB, BCh, 1920, Cambridge. FRCS 1920. Casualty House Surgeon, 1921, Surg. Registrar, 1921-23, Med. Superintendent, St Mary's Hospital, Paddington; Registrar, Royal National Orthopædic Hospital, 1924-27; now Cons. Surgeon; Cons. Surgeon, Princess Louise, Kensington, Hospital for Children; Cons. Orthopædic Surgeon: LCC; Nelson Hospital, Wimbledon; Wood Green and Southgate Hospital; Hon. Cons. Surgeon to Royal Scottish Corporation. Late President: London Perthshire Assoc.; London St Andrews University Club. *Publications:* chapters on Fractures and Surgery of Nerves in Essentials of Modern Surgery; many papers and contribs to medical journals. *Recreations:* golf, gardening, foreign travel. *Address:* Gorse Hill Manor, Virginia Water, Surrey. *T:* Wentworth 2101; 9 Astell Street, Chelsea, SW3. *T:* 01-352 2611. *Club:* Wentworth (Virginia Water).

**PATON, Sir Stuart (Henry),** KCVO 1965; CBE 1945; Captain RN, retired; *b* 9 July 1900; *s* of William Henry Paton and Winifred Powell, Norwood; *m* 1925, Dorothy Morgan, Shrewsbury; two *s* two *d*. *Educ:* Hillside, Godalming; RN Colleges, Osborne and Dartmouth. Served European War: Midshipman, HMS Marlborough, Grand Fleet, 1916; Sub-Lt, HMS Orcadia, English Channel, 1918. Specialised as Torpedo Officer; posts Lieut to Commander: Mediterranean and Home Fleets, Admiralty Plans Division, and New Zealand. War of 1939-45: HMS Vernon, Captain, 1940; Admiralty, Joint Intelligence Staff, 1941; Comd HMS Curacoa, E. Coast Convoys, 1942; Comd HMS Nigeria, Home Fleet and Eastern Fleet, 1942-44 (despatches Malta Convoy); Admiralty and served as a Dep.-Director, Admin. Planning, 1945-46; student, IDC, 1947; Comd HMS Newcastle, Mediterranean Fleet, 1948-49; Appointed ADC to King George VI, 1949; retired, 1950; General Secretary to King George's Fund for Sailors, 1950-65. *Recreations:* gardening, photography, golf.

*Address:* West Stroud, Grayswood, Haslemere, Surrey. *T:* Haslemere 3973. *Club:* United Service.

**PATON, Thomas Angus Lyall,** CMG 1960; FRS 1969; Senior Partner, Sir Alexander Gibb & Partners, since 1955; *b* 10 May 1905; *s* of Thomas Lyall Paton and Janet (*née* Gibb); *m* 1932, Eleanor Joan Delmé-Murray (*d* 1964); two *s* two *d*. *Educ:* Cheltenham Coll.; University College, London. Fellow of University College. Joined Sir Alexander Gibb & Partners as pupil, 1925; after experience in UK, Canada, Burma and Turkey on harbour works, hydro-electric projects and industrial development schemes, was taken into partnership, 1938. Responsible for design and supervision of construction of many large industrial factories and for major hydro-electric and irrigation projects, including Owen Falls and Kariba Schemes, and for overall supervision of Indus Basin Project in W. Pakistan; also for economic surveys in Middle East and Africa on behalf of Dominion and Foreign Governments. Member UK Trade Mission to: Arab States, 1953; Egypt, Sudan and Ethiopia, 1955. Mem. NERC, 1969-. Past Chairman Assoc. of Consulting Engineers. FICE, FIStructE, Fellow Amer. Soc. of Civil Engineers, Past Pres., British Section, Soc. of Civil Engineers (France); FRSA. *Publications:* Power from Water, 1960; technical articles on engineering subjects. *Address:* 15 Hillbrow, Richmond Hill, Richmond-on-Thames, Surrey. *T:* 01-940 1907. *Club:* Athenæum.

**PATON, William Calder,** CIE 1945; MC; Major-General IMS (retired); *b* 27 Jan. 1886; *s* of William and Isabella Paton; *m* 1st, 1915, Marian Bruce Williamson (*d* 1948); one *s* two *d*; 2nd, 1950, Isobel, *d* of R. Dean, JP, Beauly. *Educ:* Glasgow Academy; Edinburgh Univ. MB, ChB, Edinburgh, 1910; entered IMS, 1912; FRCS (Ed.), 1920; served European War, 1914-18 (MC and Brevet Major); various appointments on civil side of IMS, including Professor of Midwifery, Medical Coll., Madras, and Civil Surgeon, Delhi; Inspector-General of Civil Hospitals, N-WFP, 1939-41; Surgeon-General, Bengal, 1941-45; KHP; retired from IMS, 1945; Medical Superintendent, Royal Northern Infirmary, 1945-48; Medical Superintendent, Inverness Hospitals, 1948-54. *Publications:* articles in medical journals. *Recreations:* formerly riding, hunting; now walking, golf. *Address:* Ladiesyde, High Cross Avenue, Melrose, Roxburghshire. *T:* Melrose 2510.

**PATON, Prof. William Drummond Macdonald,** CBE 1968; MA, DM; FRS 1956; FRCP 1969; JP; Professor of Pharmacology in the University of Oxford, since Oct. 1959; *b* 5 May 1917; 3rd *s* of late Rev. William Paton, DD, and Grace Mackenzie Paton; *m* 1942, Phoebe Margaret Rooke; no *c*. *Educ:* Winchester House Sch., Brackley; Repton Sch.; New Coll., Oxford (Scholar); University College Hospital Medical Sch. BA (Oxon) Natural Sciences, Physiology, 1st class hons, 1938; Scholarships: Theodore Williams (Physiology), 1938; Christopher Welch, 1939; Jesse Theresa Rowden, 1939; Demonstrator in Physiology, Oxford, 1938-39; Goldsmid Exhibition, UCH Medical Sch., 1939; Ed. UCH Magazine, 1941; Fellowes Gold Medal in Clinical Med., 1941; BM, BCh Oxon, 1942; House physician, UCH Med. Unit, 1942. Pathologist King Edward VII Sanatorium, 1943-44; Member scientific staff, National Institute for Medical Research, 1944-52; MA 1948. Reader in Pharmacology, University College and UCH Med. Sch., 1952-54; DM 1953; Professor of Pharmacology, RCS, 1954-59. Delegate, Clarendon Press, 1967; Rhodes Trustee, 1968. Member: Pharmacological Soc. (Chm. Edtl Bd); Physiological Soc. (Hon. Sec. 1951-57); Med. Research Soc.; MRC, 1963-67; Council, Royal Society, 1967-69; Council, Inst. Study of Drug Dependence, 1969; Central Adv. Council for Science and Technology, 1970-. Hon. Mem. Soc. Franç. d'Allergie; Corresp. Mem., German Pharmacological Soc.; Hon. Lectr, St Mary's Hosp. Med. Sch., 1950; Visiting Lecturer, Swedish Univs, 1953; Brussels, 1956. Robert Campbell Oration, 1957; Clover Lecture, 1958; Bertram Louis Abrahams Lecturer, RCP, 1962. Bengue Meml Prize, 1952; Cameron Prize, 1956; Gairdner Foundn Award, 1959. JP St Albans, 1956. *Publications:* (with J. P. Payne) Pharmacological Principles and Practice, 1968; papers on diving, caisson disease, histamine, synaptic transmission, and drug action in physiological and pharmacological journals. *Recreations:* music, old books. *Address:* 13 Staverton Road, Oxford. *Club:* Athenæum.
*See also Bishop of Kingston-upon-Thames.*

**PATRICK, Graham McIntosh,** CMG 1968; DSC 1943; Assistant Secretary, Ministry of Public Building and Works, since 1963; *b* 17 Oct. 1921; *m* 1945, Barbara Worboys; two *s*. *Educ:* Dundee High Sch.; St Andrews Univ. RNVR (Air Branch), 1940-46. Entered Ministry of Works, 1946; Asst Secretary, 1963; Regional Director, Middle East Region, 1965-67. *Address:* c/o Ministry of Public Building and Works, Lambeth Bridge House, SE1. *Club:* Royal Naval Volunteer Reserve.

**PATRICK, (James) McIntosh,** ROI 1949; ARE; RSA 1957 (ARSA, 1949); Painter and Etcher; *b* 1907; *s* of Andrew G. Patrick and Helen Anderson; *m* 1933, Janet, *d* of W. Arnot Watterston; one *s* one *d*. *Educ:* Morgan Academy, Dundee; Glasgow School of Art. Awarded Guthrie Award RSA, 1935; Painting Winter in Angus purchased under the terms of the Chantrey Bequest, 1935; paintings purchased for National Gallery, Millbank; National Gallery of South Africa, Cape Town; National Gallery of South Australia; Scottish Contemp. Art Assoc. ; and Municipal collections Manchester, Aberdeen, Hull, Dundee, Liverpool, Glasgow, Greenock, Perth, Southport, Newport (Mon.), Arbroath, also for Lady Leverhulme Art Gallery, etc.; etchings in British Museum and other print collections. Served War of 1939-46, North Africa and Italy; Captain (General List). *Recreations:* gardening, music. *Address:* c/o Fine Art Society, New Bond Street, W1; The Shrubbery, Magdalen Yard Road, Dundee. *T:* Dundee 68561. *Club:* Scottish Arts (Edinburgh).

**PATRICK, Brig. John,** MC; *b* 10 June 1898; *s* of Lt-Col John Patrick, DL, and Florence Annie Rutherfoord; *m* (dissolved); two *s*. *Educ:* Harrow-on-the-Hill; RMA, Woolwich. 2nd Lieut, RFA, 1916; Chestnut Troop, RHA, 1919-28; Captain, 15/19th The King's Royal Hussars, 1928-38; psc 1934; retired, 1938; Lt-Col RA (SR), 1939; Brigadier, 1940-45; MP for Mid Antrim in Northern Ireland House of Commons, 1938-45. *Address:* Preston House, Preston, Hitchin, Herts. *T:* 2776.

**PATRICK, John Bowman;** Sheriff-Substitute of Inverness, Moray, Nairn, Ross and Cromarty at Fort William and Portree (Skye), since Oct. 1961; Sheriff Substitute of Renfrew and Argyll at Greenock, since Oct. 1968; *b* 29 Feb. 1916; *s* of late John Bowman Patrick, Boot and Shoe maker, Greenock, and late Barbara Patrick (*née* James); *m* 1945, Sheina Struthers McCrea; one *d*. *Educ:* Greenock Academy; Edinburgh Univ.; Glasgow Univ. MA Edinburgh, 1937. Served War in Royal Navy,

Dec. 1940-Dec. 1945; conscripted as Ordinary Seaman, finally Lieut RNVR. LLB Glasgow 1946. Admitted as a Solicitor in Scotland, June 1947; admitted to Faculty of Advocates, July 1956. *Recreation:* cricket. *Address:* 77 Union Street, Greenock, Renfrewshire. *T:* 20712.

**PATRICK, Nigel Dennis Wemyss;** Actor; *b* 2 May 1913; *s* of Charles Wemyss (Actor) and Dorothy Turner (Actress); *m* 1951, Beatrice Josephine Campbell; one *s* one *d*. *Educ:* privately. Started career as actor, Jan. 1932; first appeared West End stage, Oct. 1934, at Whitehall Theatre; played many parts in West End including appearance in George and Margaret, Wyndham's, until 1939. Joined KRRC as Rifleman, 1939; discharged HM Forces, 1946, with rank of Lt-Col. Resumed career as actor, March 1946 at Lyric Hammersmith, in Tomorrow's Child; subsequently, among many plays, has appeared in: Noose, Saville, 1947; Who Goes There, Vaudeville, 1951; Escapade, St James's, 1953; The Remarkable Mr Pennypacker, New, 1955; The Egg, Saville, 1958. Directed: Not in the Book, Criterion, 1958; Directed and played in The Pleasure of His Company, Haymarket, 1959; Settled Out of Court, Strand, 1960; The Schoolmistress, Savoy, 1964; Present Laughter, Queen's, 1965; Directed: Relatively Speaking, Duke of Yorks, 1967; The Others, Strand, 1967; Avanti, Booth Theatre, New York, 1968; Out of the Question, St Martin's, 1968; directed and played in Best of Friends, Strand, 1970; produced Blithe Spirit, Globe, 1970. Has also appeared in many films, including Morning Departure, Trio, The Browning Version, Pandora and the Flying Dutchman, Sound Barrier, Pickwick Papers, Raintree County, Sapphire, League of Gentlemen, The Trials of Oscar Wilde, Johnny Nobody, The Informers; The Battle of Britain; The Virgin Soldiers; The Executioner. *Recreations:* working, reading and travelling. *Address:* 54 Ovington Street, Chelsea, SW3. *T:* 01-589 4385. *Club:* Garrick.

**PATRICK, Sir Paul Joseph,** KCIE 1946; CSI 1934; *b* 6 Oct. 1888; *s* of late Rev. John Arthur Patrick and Ellen Maria, *d* of Joseph Freeman. *Educ:* Rugby Sch.; Corpus Christi Coll., Oxford. Junior Clerk, Secretary's Office, Post Office, 1913; transferred to India Office, 1913; Lieut, Indian Army, Reserve of Officers, 1916-19, served in NW Frontier and Palestine. Assistant Under-Secretary of State, India Office, 1941, and CRO, 1947; retired, 1949. CStJ 1963. *Address:* 10 Stonehill Road, SW14. *T:* 01-876 6105. *Club:* Travellers'.

**PATRON, Sir Joseph,** Kt 1961; OBE 1945; MC 1917; JP; Speaker of the Legislative Council, Gibraltar, 1958-64; *b* 19 Jan. 1896; *s* of late Joseph Armand Patron, CMG, OBE; *m* 1924, Emily Isham, *d* of John Maxwell Vaughan. *Educ:* Harrow. Served European War, 1914-18, Major; Yeomanry and Machine-Gun Corps (wounded, MC). Managing Director, Saccone and Speed, 1927-45; Company Director and Trustee, John Mackintosh Charitable Trust, Gibraltar; Member, Interdepartmental Cttee to Look After Evacuees, 1940-44. MEC Gibraltar, 1944-47; MLC 1950-58. JP Gibraltar, 1948. *Recreations:* golf, bridge, gardening. *Address:* St Bernard's Road, Gibraltar; San Roque, Spain. *Clubs:* Boodle's; Royal Gibraltar Yacht.

**PATTERSON, Arthur,** CMG 1951; Assistant Secretary, Ministry of Pensions and National Insurance, since 1945; *b* 24 June 1906; 2nd *s* of late Alexander Patterson; *m* 1942, Mary Ann Stocks, *er d* of late J. L. Stocks; two *s* one *d*. *Educ:* Methodist Coll., Belfast; Queen's Univ., Belfast; St John's Coll., Cambridge. Entered Ministry of Labour, 1929; Assistant Secretary, 1941; transferred to Ministry of National Insurance, 1945; lent to Cyprus, 1953; Malta, 1956; Jamaica, 1963. *Address:* 42 Campden Hill Square, W8. *T:* 01-229 3894.

**PATTERSON, Maj.-Gen. Arthur Gordon,** CB 1969; DSO 1964; OBE 1961; MC 1945; Director of Army Training, since 1969; *b* 24 July 1917; *s* of late Arthur Abbey Patterson, Indian Civil Service; *m* 1949, Jean Mary Grant; two *s* one *d*. *Educ:* Tonbridge Sch.; RMC Sandhurst. Commnd, 1938; India and Burma, 1939-45; Staff Coll., Camberley, 1949; jssc 1955; CO 2nd 6th Queen Elizabeth's Own Gurkha Rifles, 1959-61; Comdr 99 Gurkha Inf. Brigade, 1962-64; idc 1965; GOC 17 Div. and Maj.-Gen., Bde of Gurkhas, 1965-69. Col, 6th Queen's Own Gurkha Rifles, 1969-. *Address:* Teston House, Teston, near Maidstone, Kent. *Club:* Naval and Military.

**PATTERSON, Rt. Rev. Cecil John,** CMG 1958; CBE 1954; DD (Lambeth), 1963; DD (University of Nigeria, Nsukka), 1963; Commander of the Federal Republic (CFR) (Nigeria), 1965; Assistant Bishop, Diocese of London, since 1970; Representative for the Archbishops of Canterbury and York for Community Relations; *b* 9 Jan. 1908. *Educ:* St Paul's School; St Catharine's Coll., Cambridge; Bishop's Coll., Cheshunt. London Curacy, 1931-34; Missionary in S Nigeria, 1934-41; Asst Bishop on the Niger, 1942-45; Bishop on the Niger, 1945-69; Archbishop of West Africa, 1961-69. Hon. Fellow, St Catharine's Coll., Cambridge, 1963. *Address:* 6 High Park Road, Kew, Surrey. *T:* 01-876 4354.

**PATTERSON, Eric James;** Political Education Officer, Western Area, 1947; Member of YMCA Central Education Committee for HM Forces; Special Lecturer to Allied and British Forces; *b* 9 May 1891; *s* of late George Patterson, JP, Ballasalla, Isle of Man, and Euphemia Patterson; *m* 1936, Ethel Simkins; one *s*. *Educ:* King William's Coll., Isle of Man; Peterhouse, Cambridge (Graduate); University of Freiburg, Germany. Late University Extension Lecturer and Tutorial Class Tutor, University of Liverpool; University Extension Lecturer, University of London, 1920-21; Head of Department of Extra-Mural Studies, University College, Exeter, 1921-38, and Head of Department of International Politics till 1938; Principal of Bonar Law Coll., Ashridge, Berkhamsted, Herts, 1938-40; Member of Advisory Council for Adult Education in HM Forces, 1940-42; served on Cttee of World Association for Adult Education, on the Vice-Chancellors of Oxford and Cambridge Cttee on University Extension Regulations; held scholarships for the investigation of Adult Education in Germany and for the problem of Education among National Minorities; Visiting Lecturer: in Germany, CCG, 1947; Internationale Akademische Ferienkurse, Zürich, 1950; HM Navy, 1951-53; European Youth Campaign Conference Special Lecturer, 1952; Special Lecturer to RAF, 1954; Saar Plebiscite Commission Delegate, 1955; Western European Union Commission in Saar, 1955-56. Genootschap Nederland-England Lecturer, Holland, 1957; Bursary for lecturing and research, Poznan, 1970. Silver Academic Laurel, Polish Acad. of Literature. *Publications:* Survey of Adult Education in Germany, 1926; Poland, 1934; Pilsudski, Marshal of Poland, 1935; Yugoslavia, 1936; Pilsudski through English Eyes, 1936 (Warsaw); The International Mind, 1937 (USA); The Saar Referendum of 1955; European Year Book, 1958. Contributions to Empire Review and St Martins Review, 1939-

40; Free Europe. Central European Observer, International Affairs (Chatham House). *Recreations:* foreign travel, swimming. *Address:* Stonehedge, Alphington Cross, Exeter. *T:* Exeter 54479. *Club:* Special Forces.

**PATTERSON, Sir John Robert,** KBE, *cr* 1945; CMG 1939; *b* 1892; *s* of G. T. Patterson; *m* 1919, Esther Margaret Sheldon (*d* 1962); two *s*. *Educ:* Cambridge Univ., BA. Asst District Officer, Nigeria, 1915; Secretary, Northern Provinces, 1935; acting Chief Commissioner, Northern Provinces, 1938-39; Acting Chief Commissioner, 1941; Chief Commissioner, Northern Provinces, Nigeria, 1943-48. *Address:* Park Holme, Eamont Bridge, Westmorland. *T:* Penrith 2515.

**PATTERSON, Rear-Adm. Julian Francis Chichester,** OBE 1919; *b* 6 May 1884; *s* of Rev. J. E. C. Patterson; *m* 1st, 1911, Helen Frances (*d* 1950), *d* of Major C. P. Dean; one *d* (and one *d* decd); 2nd, 1952, Sina Victoria, widow of Commander John Howard, RN. *Educ:* Bedford Sch. HMS Britannia, 1899; Lieut, 1904; Commander, 1915; Captain, 1921; Rear-Admiral, 1933; served as Gunnery Officer in HMS Orion, 1914-17, present at Battle of Jutland, 1916 (OBE); retired, 1933, and joined English Steel Corporation Ltd, Vickers Works, Sheffield, retired, 1949. *Address:* 20 Sion Hill, Bath. *Club:* United Service.
*See also Rear-Adm. G. H. Carew Hunt, Maj.-Gen. R. E. Lloyd.*

**PATTERSON, Thomas Redden,** CBE 1954; DL; JP; Chairman, The Scottish Mutual Assurance Society; Chairman, Arthur Fraser Investment Co. Ltd, Glasgow; *b* 7 May 1898; *s* of late James Patterson, Glasgow; *m* 1921, Margaret, *d* of late John Malcolm Forrester, Glasgow; one *s*. *Educ:* Whitehill Sch., Glasgow. Member: Corporation of Glasgow, 1942-59; East Kilbride Development Corp., 1951-56; Cumbernauld Development Corp., 1956-65. Chairman and Man. Director, Nicol & Andrew Ltd. DL and JP for County of City of Glasgow. OStJ 1951. *Address:* 2 Deramore Avenue, Whitecraigs, Renfrewshire. *T:* Newton Mearns 1805. *Clubs:* Conservative, Royal Scottish Automobile (Glasgow).

**PATTINSON, Hon. Sir Baden,** KBE 1962; LLB. Member of the House of Assembly, South Australia, for Glenelg, 1947-65; Minister for Education, Government of South Australia, 1953-65. *Address:* 12 Maturin Road, Glenelg, Adelaide, South Australia 5045.

**PATTINSON, John Mellor,** CBE 1943; MA; Director: Erdölchemie GmbH (Member, Supervisory Board); Chartered Bank; *b* 1889; *s* of late J. P. Pattinson, JP, Mobberley, Cheshire; *m* 1927, Wilhelmina, *d* of late W. J. Newth, Cheltenham; two *s*. *Educ:* Rugby Sch.; RMA; Cambridge Univ. RFA with BEF, 1918-19. Anglo-Iranian Oil Co., South Iran, 1922-45, General Manager, 1937-45. Director until 1969, british Petroleum Co. of Canada Ltd; Triad Oil Co. Ltd; BP Germany AG; Dep. Chm. 1960-65, and Man. Dir 1952-65, British Petroleum Co. Ltd. *Recreations:* gardening, travel. *Address:* Oakhurst, West Byfleet, Surrey. *Club:* East India and Sports.

**PATTISON, Prof. Bruce;** Professor of Education in the University of London since 1948; *b* 13 Nov. 1908; *s* of Matthew and Catherine Pattison; *m* 1937, Dorothy Graham. *Educ:* Gateshead Grammar Sch.; King's Coll., Newcastle upon Tyne; Fitzwilliam House, Cambridge. Henry Mellish Sch., Nottingham, 1933-35; Hymers Coll., Hull, 1935-36; Lecturer in English, University College, London, 1936-48 (Reader, 1948). Board of Trade, 1941-43; Ministry of Supply, 1943-45. *Publications:* Music and Poetry of the English Renaissance, 1948, 2nd edn 1970. *Address:* Coombe Bank, Church Road, Kenley, Surrey CR2 5DU. *T:* 01-660 2991. *Clubs:* National Liberal, National Book League.

**PATTRICK, (William) Michael (Thomas),** FRIBA; AADipl; Principal, Central School of Art and Design, since 1961; *b* 25 Oct. 1913; *s* of late Arthur Devereux Pattrick and of Mrs Gilson Pattrick; *m* 1943, Joan Margaret Leech. *Educ:* Oundle School. Architectural Association School of Architecture, 1931-35; RIBA Howard Colls Scholarship; 1932. AA Studentship, 1934; Lecturer, Cambridge Univ., 1937; Architectural Assoc. Staff, 1945-. Principal, The Architectural Association School of Architecture, 1951-61. *Recreation:* sailing. *Address:* 6 Little Chester Street, SW1. *T:* 01-235 7941.

**PATTULLO, William Ogilvy,** Advocate; Sheriff Substitute of Lanarkshire at Glasgow since 1962; *b* 27 Feb. 1924; *s* of late Henry Pattullo, farmer, and Jean Robbie Ogilvy; *m* 1959, Etty Hoekstra, *d* of De Heer Tijs Hoekstra, Enschede, Holland; one *s* one *d*. *Educ:* Strathallan Sch.; Aberdeen Grammar Sch.; Aberdeen Univ. MA 1948; LLB (Aberdeen), 1948. Navigator, Royal Air Force Vol. Res., 1942-45. Solicitor, 1948-50; called to Scottish Bar, 1951; practised at Scottish Bar, 1951-59 and 1961-62; Senior Lecturer in Mercantile Law, Aberdeen, 1959-61; Professor of Mercantile Law, Khartoum, 1961. Member, Parole Board for Scotland, 1967-. *Recreations:* ski-ing, hill-walking, golf. *Address:* Burncroft, Thorntonhall, Lanarkshire. *T:* 041-644 1887. *Clubs:* University (Aberdeen); Art (Glasgow).

**PAUL VI, His Holiness Pope (Giovanni Battista Montini);** *b* Concesio, Brescia, 26 Sept. 1897; *s* of Giorgio Montini and Giuditta (*née* Alghisi). *Educ:* Istituto Arici, Brescia; Lombard Seminary, Pontifical Ecclesiastical Academy and Gregorian University, Rome. Ordained Priest, Roman Catholic Church, 1920; Attaché, Apostolic Nunciature in Warsaw, 1923; called to service of Secretariat of State, Vatican City, Oct. 1924; National Ecclesiastical Assistant to Italian Federation of Catholic University Students, 1925; Professor of History of Pontifical Diplomacy, 1931-37. Named substitute of the Secretariat of State of His Holiness, 1937; accompanied the Papal Legate, Cardinal Pacelli, to International Eucharistic Congress in Budapest, 1938. Appointed Pro-Secretary of State by Pope Pius XII, 1952; Archbishop of Milan, 1954-63. Created Cardinal, 1958. Elected Pope, 21 June 1963; solemn Coronation, 30 June 1963. *Address:* Apostolic Vatican Palace, Vatican City.

**PAUL, Sir Brian Kenneth,** 6th Bt *re-cr* 1821, of Rodborough; *b* 18 May 1904; *s* of Sir Aubrey Edward Henry Dean Paul, 5th Bt *re-cr* 1821, and Irene Regine (Mme Poldowski) (*d* 1932), *d* of late Henry Wieniawski, Warsaw; *S* father 1961; *m* 1937, Muriel Frances, *d* of late John Lillie, Ontario, Canada, and *widow* of Arthur Edward Pearse Brome Weigall. *Educ:* Downside. Subsequently mural painter and designer. *Heir:* none. *Address:* Glover & Co., 115 Park Street, W1.

**PAUL, Cedar;** Singer, Author, and Translator; retired; *b* Hampstead, *née* Gertrude Mary, *d* of late F. W. Davenport, composer, and *g d* of late G. A. Macfarren, composer, principal RAM, etc. *Educ:* Paris, Genoa, and London. Independent worker since the age of fifteen, maintaining herself by tuition in Germany, Poland, and England; trained for grand opera in Dresden and Stuttgart: Cherubino, Siebel, Marguerite, Elsa, Elizabeth, etc.; Musical career interrupted by war; collaborated with late Eden Paul, in original writings and translations, among their many joint translations being: Romain Rolland's The Forerunners, 1920; Baudouin's Suggestion and Autosuggestion, 1920; Pierre Janet's Psychological Healing, 1925; Plekhanoff's Fundamental Problems of Marxism, 1929; Yugoff's Economic Trends in Soviet Russia, 1930; Treitschke's History of Germany in the Nineteenth Century, 7 vols, 1915-19; Masaryk's The Spirit of Russia, 2 vols, 1919; many works by Stefan Zweig, Emil Ludwig, and Sudermann; Frank's Trenck, 1928; Marx's Capital, 1928; Alfred Neumann's The New Cæsar, 1934; Man of December, 1937; Novikov-Priboy's Tsushima, 1936; Prawdin's Mongolian Empire, 1940; Lermontoff's Hero of Our Own Time; Nattage's Escape to Danger, 1942; Le Verrier's France in Torment, 1942; Sergei Borodin's Dmitri Donskoi, 1945; A. Chapygun's Stepan Razin, 1946; Balzac's Fatal Skin, 1948-49; after the war of 1914-18 resumed musical career, specialising in unaccompanied folk-song, and giving recitals in London and the provinces, Paris, Brussels, and the German capitals. *Address:* 5 Hillside, Tilford Road, Hindhead, Surrey.

**PAUL, Air Cdre (retired) Gerard John Christopher,** CB 1956; DFC 1944; MA; CEng; FRAeS; *b* 31 Oct. 1907; *s* of E. W. Paul, FRCS; *m* 1937, Rosemary, *d* of Rear-Admiral H. G. E. Lane, CB; two *s* one *d*. *Educ:* Cheltenham Coll.; St John's Coll., Cambridge. Entered Royal Air Force, 1929; Fleet Air Arm, 1931-36; served War of 1939-45 in England and N.W. Europe; Commandant, Central Flying School, 1954-56; retired, 1959. Secretary-General of the Air League, 1958-. Life Vice-Pres., RAF Gliding and Soaring Assoc.; Pres., Popular Flying Assoc. Croix de Guerre avec Palme (Belgium), 1944; Military Cross (Czechoslovakia), 1945. *Recreation:* flying. *Club:* Royal Air Force.

**PAUL, Hugh Glencairn B.;** *see* Balfour Paul.

**PAUL, Sir John (Warburton),** GCMG 1965 (KCMG 1962); OBE 1959; MC 1940; Governor and Commander-in-Chief of British Honduras since 1966; *b* 29 March 1916; 2nd *s* of Walter George Paul and Phoebe (*née* Bull), Weymouth; *m* 1946, Kathleen Audrey, CStJ 1962, *d* of Dr A. D. Weeden, Weymouth; three *d*. *Educ:* Weymouth Coll., Dorset; Selwyn Coll., Cambridge (MA). Secretary, Maddermarket Theatre, Norwich, 1936. Commissioned Royal Tank Regt (Suppl. Res.), 1937; regular commission, RTR, 1938; BEF 1940 (despatches, prisoner-of-war); ADC and Private Secretary to Governor of Sierra Leone, 1945 (seconded). Called to the Bar, Inner Temple, 1947. Colonial Administrative Service, Sierra Leone, 1947; District Commissioner, 1952; Permanent Secretary, 1956; Provincial Commissioner, 1959; Secretary to the Cabinet, 1960; Governor and C-in-C, The Gambia, 1962-65; Governor-General of The Gambia, 1965-66. Member Board, West African Airways Corporation, 1954-56. KStJ 1962. *Recreations:* painting, cricket, sea fishing, sailing, shooting. *Address:* Government House, Belize City, British Honduras; Sherrens Mead, Sherfield-on-Loddon, Hampshire. *T:* Turgis Green 331. *Clubs:* Athenæum, Royal Commonwealth Society; Royal Dorset Yacht (Weymouth).

**PAUL, Leslie (Allen);** MA, FRSL; author; *b* Dublin, 1905. *Educ:* at a London Central School. Entered Fleet Street at age of 17; founded a youth organisation when 20; first Book (poems) when 21. Headed a delegation, on co-operation, to USSR, 1931; Editor, Plan, 1934-39; worked on Continent (refugees and underground movement); Tutor, WEA and LCC, 1933-40; called up, infantry, 1941; Middle East (AEC); Staff Tutor, Mount Carmel Coll. (MEF). Atlantic Award in Literature, 1946. Asst Director of Studies, Ashridge College of Citizenship, 1947-48; Director of Studies, at Brasted Place, Brasted, 1953-57. Leverhulme Research Fellow, 1957-59. Member Departmental Cttee on the Youth Service, 1958-60; Research Fellow, King George's Jubilee Trust and Industrial Welfare Society, 1960-61; Research Director, Central Advisory Council for the Ministry, for Church Assembly Enquiry into Deployment and Payment of the Clergy, 1962-64. Resident Fellow, Kenyon Coll., Ohio, 1964; Selwyn Lectr, St John's Coll., NZ, 1969; Lectr in Ethics and Social Studies, Queen's Coll., Birmingham, 1965-70. Scholar-in-Residence, Eastern Baptist Coll., Pa, USA, 1970. *Publications:* (chief books, 1944-): Annihilation of Man, 1944; The Living Hedge, 1946; The Meaning of Human Existence, 1949; Angry Young Man, 1951; The English Philosophers, 1953; Sir Thomas More, 1953; The Boy Down Kitchener Street, 1957; Nature into History, 1957; Persons and Perception, 1961; Son of Man, 1961; The Transition from School to Work, 1962; Traveller on Sacred Ground, 1963; The Deployment and Payment of the Clergy, 1964; Alternatives to Christian Belief, 1967; The Death and Resurrection of the Church, 1968; Coming to Terms with Sex, 1969; Eros Rediscovered, 1970. *Recreations:* bird-watching, photography. *Address:* 6 Church Croft, Madley, Herefore. *T:* Madley 598. *Club:* Royal Commonwealth Society.

**PAUL, Noël Strange;** Secretary, The Press Council, since 1968; *b* 1914; *y s* of late S. Evan Paul, SSC, and Susan, *d* of Dr Henry Habgood; *m* 1950, Mary, *yr d* of Philip J. Bone, FRSA, MRST, Luton. *Educ:* Kingston Grammar School. Journalist, Press Assoc., 1932; served War of 1939-45, Iran and Italy, Major seconded RAF (despatches). Home Counties Newspapers, 1949; Liverpool Daily Post, 1958; Asst Sec., Press Council, 1964. *Recreations:* sailing, photography. *Address:* Plummers, Fordham, Colchester, Essex. *T:* Fordham 388.

**PAUL-BONCOUR, Joseph;** Sénateur du Loir-et-Cher; barrister; *b* Saint-Aignan, 4 Aug. 1873. Docteur en droit; private secretary to Waldeck-Rousseau, 1899-1902, and Viviani, 1906-09; Republican Socialist deputy, 1909; Minister of Labour, 1911; resigned Socialist Party, 1931; War Minister, 1932; Prime Minister, Dec. 1932-Jan. 1933; Foreign Minister, Dec. 1932-Feb. 1934 and March-April 1938; Minister for League of Nations affairs, Jan.-June 1936; formerly President of Foreign Affairs Cttee of the Chamber; Permanent Delegate to the League of Nations. *Publications:* Estienne de la Boëtie et les origines des libertés modernes; Le Fédéralisme économique; Un Débat sur la République et la décentralisation (with Ch. Maurras); Les Syndicats de fonctionnaires; Art et démocratie; Trois plaidoiries. *Address:* 17 rue de Téhéran, Paris VIII; Saint-Aignan, Loir-et-Cher. *T:* Laborde 19-84.

**PAULET,** family name of **Marquess of Winchester.**

**PAULING, Linus (Carl);** Professor of Chemistry, Stanford University, since 1969; Professor of Chemistry, California Institute of Technology, 1931-63; Research Professor, Center for the Study of Democratic Institutions, Santa Barbara, California;

Director of Gates and Crellin Laboratories of Chemistry, and Chairman of Division of Chemistry and Chemical Engineering, California Institute of Technology, 1936-58; *b* 28 Feb. 1901; *s* of Herman William Pauling and Lucy Isabelle Darling; *m* 1923, Ava Helen Miller; three *s* one *d*. *Educ:* Oregon State Coll.; California Institute of Technology. BS Oregon State Coll., 1922; PhD California Inst. of Technology, 1925; Hon. DSc, Oregon State Coll., 1933; University of Chicago, 1941, Princeton Univ., 1946, Yale, 1947, Cambridge, 1947, London, 1947, Oxford, 1948, Brooklyn Polytechnic Inst., 1955; Humboldt Univ. (Berlin), 1959; LLD Reed Coll., 1959; LHD Tampa, 1949; Dr hc Paris, 1948, Toulouse, 1949, Liège, 1955; Montpellier, 1958; UJD, NB, 1950; DFA, Chouinard Art Inst., 1958. Asst in Chemistry and in Mechanics and Materials, Oregon State Coll., 1919-22; Graduate Assistant, California Inst. Technology, 1922-23; Teaching Fellow, 1923-25; Research Associate, 1925-26; National Research Fellow in Chemistry, 1925-26; Fellow of John Simon Guggenheim Memorial Foundation, 1926-27 (Universities of Munich, Zürich, Copenhagen); Asst Professor, California Inst. of Technology, 1927-29; Assoc. Prof., 1929-31; George Fisher Baker Lecturer in Chemistry, Cornell Univ., Sept. 1937-Feb. 1938; George Eastman Prof., Oxford Univ., Jan.-June 1948, etc. American Chemical Society Award in Pure Chemistry, 1931; William H. Nichols Medal, 1941; J. Willard Gibbs Medal, 1946; Theodore William Richards Medal, 1947; Davy Medal of Royal Society, 1947; Presidential Medal for Merit, 1948; Gilbert Newton Lewis Medal, 1951; Thomas Addis Medal, 1955; Amedeo Avogadro Medal, 1956; Pierre Fermat Medal, Paul Sabatier Medal, 1957; International Grotius Medal, 1957; Nobel Prize for Chemistry, 1954; Nobel Peace Prize for 1962, 1963; Linus Pauling Medal, 1966. Member: National Academy of Sciences; American Phil. Society; American Academy of Arts and Sciences, etc.; Hon. Fellow: Chemical Society (London), Royal Institution, etc.; For. Member: Royal Society, Akademia Nauk, USSR, etc.; Associé étranger, Acad. des Sciences, 1966. War of 1939-45, Official Investigator for projects of National Defense Research Cttee on Medical Research, and Office of Scientific Research and Development. Grand Officer, Order of Merit, Italian Republic. *Publications:* The Structure of Line Spectra (with S. Goudsmit), 1930; Introduction to Quantum Mechanics (with E. B. Wilson, Jun), 1935; The Nature of the Chemical Bond, 1939 (3rd ed., 1960); General Chemistry, 1947 (2nd ed., 1953); College Chemistry, 1950 (3rd ed., 1964); No More War!, 1958 (revised edn, 1962); The Architecture of Molecules (with Roger Hayward), 1964; The Chemical Bond, 1967; also numerous scientific articles in the fields of chemistry, physics, and biology including the structure of crystals, quantum mechanics, nature of the chemical bond, structure of gas molecules, structure of antibodies and nature of serological reactions, etc. *Address:* Stanford University, Stanford, California 94305, USA.

**PAULL, Hon. Sir Gilbert James,** Kt 1957; **Hon. Mr Justice Paull;** Judge of High Court of Justice, Queen's Bench Division, since 1957; *b* 18 April 1896; *s* of Alan Paull, FSI, JP; *m* 1922, Maud Winifred, *d* of Charles Harris, Streatham; one *s* one *d*. *Educ:* St Paul's Sch.; Trinity Coll., Cambridge. Called to Bar, Inner Temple, 1920; QC, 1939; Bencher of Inner Temple 1946, Reader 1969, Treasurer 1970; Member of the Council of Legal Education, 1947-65; Recorder of Leicester, 1944-57. *Address:* Flat 6b, Bedford Towers, Brighton. *Club:* Athenæum.

**PAULSON, Godfrey Martin Ellis,** CB 1966; CMG 1959; OBE 1945; HM Diplomatic Service, retired 1970; *b* 6 July 1908; *s* of late Lt-Col P. Z. Paulson, OBE, Manchester Regt and Royal Signals, and Mrs M. G. Paulson, *d* of late W. H. Ellis, Shipley Hall, Bradford, Yorkshire; *m* 1936, Patricia Emma, *d* of late Sir Hugh Murray, KCIE, CBE, and late Lady Murray, Englefield Green House, Surrey; one *s* one *d*. *Educ:* Westminster and Peterhouse, Cambridge. BA (Hons), 1930, MA 1940. Colonial Service; Assistant District Commissioner, Gold Coast Colony, 1930-32. Admitted Solicitor, 1936; practised in City of London until outbreak of war, 1939. Served 1939-45, Manchester Regt and on General Staff in Africa, UK, and North West Europe, including Military Mission to Free French; Lt-Col, 1945 (OBE 1945). Control Commn for Germany, 1945, for Austria, 1947-48. Joined Foreign Service, 1948, and has served since in Venice, Stockholm, Far East (Singapore), Beirut, Rome, Nice and Foreign Office. *Address:* c/o Westminster Bank, Park Row, Leeds. *Clubs:* Oxford and Cambridge University, Bath, Garrick, MCC.

**PAUNCEFORT-DUNCOMBE, Sir Everard;** *see* Duncombe.

**PAVIÈRE, Sydney Herbert,** FSA, FMA, FRSA, FAMS, ARDS; Art Adviser, Bury Corporation; Hon. Curator, Rufford Old Hall Folk Museum, 1959-61; Art Director and Curator, Harris Museum and Art Gallery, Preston, 1926-59; *b* 25 October 1891; *s* of Frederick Leslie Pavière and Edith Mary Hughes; *m* 1915, Gladys Ruth Mary Cronk. *Educ:* Oxford. Assistant to Secretary, Oxford University Museum, 1905-12; Assistant Curator, Maidstone Museum and Art Gallery, 1912-16; Fine Art Valuer, with Hurcomb and Wm Whiteley Ltd, 1921; Assistant Curator, Lady Lever Art Gallery, Port Sunlight, 1922-23; Art Sec. and Curator of Private Collections to 1st Visc. Leverhulme; Pres. North-West Federation of Museums and Art Galls, 1944-45; Leverhulme Research Grant, 1937; Exhibitor (water colours and etchings) Royal Hibernian Academy, Royal Cambrian Academy, etc.; works reproduced in Colour Magazine, The Studio, etc. *Publications:* Monograph on the Devis Family of Painters, Walpole Society Volume, 1937; The Devis Family of Painters, 1950: Dictionary of Flower, Fruit and Still Life Painters, Vol. 1, 1961, Vols 2 and 3, 1963; Vol. 4, 1964; Floral Art, 1964; Dictionary of British Sporting Artists, 1965; Jean Baptiste Monnoyer, 1966; Dictionary of Victorian Landscape Painters, 1968; articles on History of Cotton Printing in Texture Quarterly, 1957. *Address:* 91 Lawrence Avenue, New Malden, Surrey. *T:* 01-337 7039.

**PAVITT, Laurence Anstice;** MP (Lab and Co-op) Willesden West since Oct. 1959; *b* 1 Feb. 1914; *s* of George Anstice Pavitt and May (*née* Brooshooft); *m* 1937, Rosina (*née* Walton); one *s* one *d*. *Educ:* Elementary and Central Sch., West Ham. National Organising Secretary, British Fedn of Young Co-operators, 1942-46; Gen. Secretary, Anglo Chinese Development Soc., 1946-52; Regional Education Officer, Co-operative Union, 1947-52; UN Technical Assistance Programme, Asian Co-operative Field Mission, 1952-55; National Organiser, Medical Practitioners' Union, 1956-59. PPS to: Secretary for Education and Science, 1964-65; Secretary of State for Foreign Affairs, 1965-66; Secretary of State for Economic Affairs, 1966-67.

Member: MRC; Hearing Aid Council; Select Cttee on Overseas Aid. *Recreations:* reading, camping, walking, squash rackets. *Address:* 48 Westminster Mansions, 1 Little Smith Street, SW1. *T:* 01-930 6240.

**PAVLIDES, Sir Paul (George),** Kt, *cr* 1955; CBE 1949; Financier; Company Director; *b* 24 Jan. 1897; *m* 1923; two *d. Educ:* Commercial studies in Lausanne and London. Honorary posts with Cyprus Government; Member Advisory Council, 1933-36 and 1940-42; Member Executive Council, Cyprus, 1946-55. *Address:* 30 Avenue de Grande Bretagne, Monte Carlo, Monaco.

**PAVLIDES, Stelios,** CMG 1951; QC (Cyprus); Legal Practitioner; *b* 26 Sept. 1892; *m* 1923, Maria (*née* Theodotou). *Educ:* Cyprus; Athens; France; England. Called to Bar, Gray's Inn, 1916; Member of Legislative Council, Cyprus, 1925-27; Crown Counsel, 1927-40; Solicitor-General, 1940-44; KC 1942; Attorney-General of Cyprus, 1944-52; retired. *Publications:* contributions to Journal of Comparative Legislation. *Recreations:* sports; fond of animals, particularly dogs; reading; gardening. *Address:* 17 Evagoras Avenue, Nicosia, Cyprus. *T:* 4525. *Clubs:* Curzon House; Nicosia, Hellenic (Cyprus).

**PAWLE, Brig. Hanbury,** CBE 1939 (OBE 1919); TD; DL Herts; Director McMullen and Sons Ltd, Hertford; *b* 7 June 1886; 3rd *s* of late G. S. Pawle, DL, of Widford, Ware, Herts; *m* 1915, Mary Cecil, *d* of N. J. Hughes-Hallett, OBE, DL, of the Knoll, Derby; one *s* two *d. Educ:* Haileybury College; Caius College, Cambridge. Member of Stock Exchange, 1912-14; France, 1914-18, Hertfordshire Regt till 1916, transferred Royal Berkshire Regt; Foreign Service, Mesopotamia, Persia and India till 1924; left Royal Berkshire Regt to command the Hertfordshire Regt 1930. Commanded 161st Infantry Bde TA, 1938; 202 Inf. Bde, 1940. *Publications:* The Sacred Trust, 1930; Tactical Exercises, 1939; The Seven Locks, 1944; In Our Own Hands, 1946; Before Dawn, 1955; The Lost Path, 1962. *Address:* Home Field House, Widford, Ware, Herts. *T:* Much Hadham 2667. *Club:* Army and Navy.

**PAWLEY, Rev. Canon Bernard Clinton;** Canon Residentiary and Chancellor of St Paul's Cathedral, since 1970; *b* 24 Jan. 1911; *s* of Lt-Comdr S. G. Pawley, RN; *m* 1958, Margaret Grozier, *d* of J. J. W. Herbertson, *qv*; one *s* one *d. Educ:* Portsmouth Grammar School; Wadham College, Oxford; Wells Theological College. MA (Oxon), 1933. Deacon 1934, Priest 1936; Curate: Stoke on Trent Parish Church, 1934; Leeds Parish Church, 1937. CF (Emergency Commn), 1940-45 (despatches, 1945). Rector of Elland (dio. Wakefield), 1945-55; Diocesan Sec., Ely, 1955-59; Canon Residentiary, Vice-Dean and Treasurer, Ely, 1959-70. Proctor in Convocation, York, 1949-55, Canterbury, 1955-; Member Church Assembly; Archbishops' Liaison with Vatican Secretariat for Unity, 1960-65; Vice-Chairman, Archbishops' Commission for RC Relations, 1966. Church Commissioner, 1963. Mem., British Council of Churches, 1966-; Delegate, World Council of Churches, 1968. *Publications:* Looking at the Vatican Council, 1962; Anglican-Roman Relations, 1964; (ed) The Second Vatican Council, 1967. *Recreations:* music, foreign languages. *Address:* 1 Amen Court, EC4. *T:* 01-248 4518.

**PAWSEY, Sir Charles Ridley,** Kt 1947; CSI 1945; CIE 1943; MC 1915, and bar 1917; *b* 14 July 1894; *m* 1953, Rita, widow of Hugh Ingle Halliday. *Educ:* Berkhamsted School; Wadham College, Oxford (BA). Entered ICS, 1919; served European War, 1914-18; Burma Campaigns, 1942-44 (CIE, CSI); retired. *Address:* The Priory, Badingham, Woodbridge, Suffolk.

**PAWSON, Albert Guy,** CMG 1935; retired as Secretary General, International Rubber Study Group, 1960; *b* 30 May 1888; *s* of Albert Henry and Alice Sarah Pawson; *m* 1917, Helen Humphrey Lawson; two *s. Educ:* Winchester College; Christ Church, Oxford. 2nd Class Honours School of History; joined Sudan Political Service, 1911; Governor, White Nile Province, 1927-31; Governor, Upper Nile Province, 1931-34. *Recreations:* fishing, cricket, tennis, Oxford Cricket Blue, 1908, 1909, 1910 and 1911, Captain 1910. *Address:* Flat 5, Greathed Manor, Lingfield, Surrey.

**PAWSON, Prof. Henry Cecil,** MBE 1946; FRSE 1949; Emeritus Professor, Universities of Durham and Newcastle upon Tyne, since 1957; *b* 17 May 1897; *s* of late Rev. D. Ledger Pawson; *m* 1927, Edith Jean Sinclair; one *s* two *d. Educ:* Lady Manners Grammar School, Bakewell, Derbyshire; King's College, Newcastle. DSc King's College, 1959. University of Newcastle upon Tyne: Lecturer in Agriculture, 1917, Senior Tutor, 1945; Prof. of Agriculture, 1948-57. Methodist Local Preacher, 1917; Vice-President Methodist Conference of Great Britain, 1951-52. *Publications:* The Study of Agriculture, 1921; Robert Bakewell, Pioneer Livestock Breeder, 1957; Cockle Park Farm, 1960; Agriculture of Northumberland, 1961; Personal Evangelism, 1968; Words of Comfort, 1968; articles and papers on agricultural and religious subjects. *Recreations:* golf and gardening. *Address:* 56 Dunholme Road, Newcastle upon Tyne 4. *T:* 33269. *Clubs:* University Union, YMCA (Newcastle upon Tyne).

**PAXTON, John,** PhD; Editor, The Statesman's Year-Book, since 1969; Director: A. E. Walsh and Partners Ltd; Linolite Ltd; Linolite Special Products Ltd; *b* 23 Aug. 1923; *m* 1950, Joan Thorne; one *s* one *d*. Head of Economics department, Millfield, 1952-63. Asst Editor, 1964-68, and Dep. Editor, 1968, of The Statesman's Year-Book. *Publications:* Trade in the Common Market Countries (with A. E. Walsh), 1965; The Structure and Development of the Common Market (with A. E. Walsh), 1968 (US edn 1969); Trade and Industrial Resources of the Common Market and Efta Countries (with A. E. Walsh), 1970; Smuggling (with John Wroughton), 1971; contrib. to Keesing's Contemporary Archives. *Address:* Smalldown, Evercreech, Shepton Mallet, Somerset BA4 6EL. *T:* Evercreech 310. *Club:* National.

**PAYNE, Dr Arthur Robert;** Director, Shoe and Allied Trades Research Association, since 1968; *b* 2 Nov. 1926; *s* of late Arthur Payne and Helen (*née* Gunn); *m* 1954, Greta (*née* Shaw); one *s* two *d. Educ:* Archbishop Tenison's Grammar Sch., Kennington; Durham University. BSc Hons Physics 1952, MSc and DSc 1966, Durham; FInstP 1963; FIRI 1964; CEng, MIMechE 1966; MBIM 1969. Royal Air Force, 1946-49. Rubber and Plastics Res. Assoc., 1952-62; Principal Physical Group Leader of Engrg Group, Natural Rubber Producers' Res. Assoc., 1962-67. Chm. Council, Instn of Rubber Industry, 1970-; Governor, Leathersellers' Coll.; Mem. Court, Univ. of Leicester. *Publications:* Engineering Design with Rubber, 1964; Rubber in Engineering Practice, 1966; Uses of Rubber in Engineering, 1967; Poromerics in Shoe Industry, 1970; numerous technical and scientific papers on polymers, engrg, vibration and shoe technology; contribs to Faraday Soc.,

Jl of Polymer Science, Jp of Applied Polymer Sci., Rubber Chem. and Technol. *Recreations:* gardening, music. *Address:* 37 Howard Lane, Boughton, Northampton NN2 8RS. *T:* Chapel Brampton 3560.

**PAYNE, Ben Iden;** Professor of Drama, State University of Texas; *b* 5 Sept. 1881; *s* of Rev. Alfred Payne; *m* 1st, Mona Limerick (marr. diss.); 2nd, Barbara Rankin Chiaroni. *Educ:* Privately; Manchester Grammar School. Began his stage career with Sir Frank (then Mr F. R.) Benson's Company, 1899; organised Miss A. E. F. Horniman's Company at Gaiety Theatre, Manchester, and produced for her, 1907-11; organised the first repertory seasons in several provincial cities and toured his own companies until 1913; produced plays in New York, Chicago and Philadelphia, until 1917; was General Stage Director for Charles Frohman Inc. at Empire Theatre, New York, 1917-22; Visiting Professor of Drama and subsequently Head of the Drama Department, Carnegie Institute of Technology, Pittsburgh, also producing plays in New York for various managements, until 1928; produced and acted at the Goodman Theatre, Chicago, 1928-30; Visiting Professor of Drama at Univ. of Iowa and Univ. of Washington, 1930-34; Director of Stratford-on-Avon Shakespeare Memorial Theatre, 1935-42; Visiting Prof. of Drama, State Univs of: Iowa, 1943; Washington, 1943; Missouri, 1947; Colorado, 1953; Michigan, 1954; Dir Shakespeare Summer Festival, San Diego, Calif., 1949-52, 1955, 1957, 1964; Dir at Oregon Shakespearean Festival, Summer, 1956 and 1961; Visiting Prof. of Drama, Banff School of Fine Arts, Alberta, Canada, summer sessions 1957-64. Fifth Annual Award of Amer. Nat. Shakespeare Festival and Acad. for distinguished service to the theatre, 1959; Shakespeare productions, Sch. of Fine Arts, Univ. of Alberta, Canada, 1958-60, 1962; Rodgers and Hammerstein Award for distinguished services to the theatre, 1962; Medal of Honor, Theta Alpha Phi, 1969; Consular Law Soc.'s Award of Merit, 1968. Hon. LLD Univ. of Alberta, Canada, 1963. *Address:* 16 Gramercy Park, New York 3, USA. *Clubs:* Savage; Players (New York).

**PAYNE, Rev. Ernest Alexander,** CH 1968; BA, BD (London), MA, BLitt (Oxon); Hon. DD St Andrews; Hon. LLD McMaster; President, World Council of Churches, since 1968; General Secretary of the Baptist Union of Great Britain and Ireland, 1951-September 1967; *b* 19 Feb. 1902; *er s* of late Alexander William Payne; *m* 1930, Winifred Mary Davies; one *d. Educ:* Hackney Downs Secondary Sch.; King's Coll., London; Regent's Park Coll.; St Catherine's and Mansfield College, Oxford; Marburg University. Bugbrooke Baptist Church, 1928-32; Headquarters Staff, Baptist Missionary Society, 1932-40; Senior Tutor, Regent's Park College, 1940-51; Lecturer in Comparative Religion and the History of Modern Missions, Oxford Univ., 1946-51; Editor, The Baptist Quarterly, 1944-50. Pres., Baptist Historical Soc.; Vice-Chm., Central Cttee World Council of Churches, 1954-68, Pres. 1968-; Moderator Free Church Federal Council, 1958-59; Vice-Pres., 1960-62, Chm., Executive Cttee, 1962-, British Council of Churches; Vice-Pres. Baptist World Alliance, 1965-. Examiner in the Univs of Oxford, Wales, Edinburgh and Bristol. *Publications:* The Saktas, 1933; The Church Awakes, 1942; The Free Church Tradition in the Life of England, 1944; The Fellowship of Believers, 1944; Henry Wheeler Robinson, 1946; The Anabaptists of the 16th Century (Dr Williams's Lecture), 1949; The Baptists of Berkshire, 1952; James Henry Rushbrooke, 1954. The Anabaptists (in New Cambridge Modern History, Vol. II), 1958; The Baptist Union: A short history, 1959; Veteran Warrior (a Memoir of B. Grey Griffith), 1962; Free Churchmen Unrepentant and Repentant, 1965; Contrib. to Twentieth Century Christianity, 1961; From Uniformity to Unity, 1962; The Churches and Christian Unity, 1963 and Journal of Theological Studies, Internat. Review of Missions, Congregational Quarterly, etc. *Recreations:* reading, writing and travel. *Address:* Elm Cottage, Pitsford, Northampton. *T:* Northampton 18519. *Club:* Athenæum.

**PAYNE, Maj.-Gen. George Lefevre,** CB 1966; CBE 1963; Director of Ordnance Services, Ministry of Defence, 1964-68; retired, 1968; *b* 23 June 1911; *s* of Dr E. L. Payne, MRCS, LRCP, Brunswick House, Kew, Surrey; *m* 1938, Betty Maud, *d* of Surgeon Captain H. A. Kellond-Knight, RN, Eastbourne, Sussex; three *s. Educ:* The King's Sch., Canterbury; Roy. Mil. Coll., Sandhurst. Royal Leicestershire Regiment: England, Northern Ireland, 1931-33; India, 1933-37; Royal Army Ordnance Corps: England, 1938-39; France, 1939-40; England, 1941-. Deputy Director Ordnance Services: HQ, BAOR, 1952-54; War Office, 1955-57; Commandant, Central Ordnance Depot, Chilwell, 1957-59; Deputy Director Ordnance Services, War Office, 1959-63; Commander, Stores Organization, RAOC, 1963-64; Col Comdt, RAOC, 1968-. *Recreations:* shooting, gardening. *Address:* Weavers Hill House, Ashmore Green, Newbury, Berks. *T:* Newbury 4232. *Clubs:* Naval and Military, Royal Commonwealth Society.

**PAYNE, Rev. James Richmond,** ThL; JP; Commonwealth Secretary, Bible Society in Australia, since 1968; *b* 1 June 1921; *s* of late R. A. Payne, Sydney, New South Wales; *m* 1943, Joan, *d* of late C. S. Elliott; three *s. Educ:* Drummoyne High School; Metropolitan Business College, Moore Theological College, Sydney. Served War of 1939-45: AIF, 1941-44. Catechist, St Michael's, Surry Hills, NSW, 1944-47; Curate, St Andrew's, Lismore, NSW, 1947-50; Rector, St Mark's, Nimbin, NSW, 1950-52; Chaplain, RAAF, Malta and Amberley, Qld, 1952-57; Rector, St Stephen's, Coorparoo, Qld, 1957-62; Dean of Perth, Western Australia, 1962-68. JP, Queensland, 1960; JP, ACT, 1969. *Publication:* Around the World in Seventy Days, 1965. *Recreations:* sport, walking, reading, family. *Address:* Memorial Bible House, Canberra, ACT 2601, Australia. *T:* 485188. *Club:* Weld (Perth).

**PAYNE, John Anson,** OBE 1945; Director: FMC (Meat); C. & T. Harris (Calne); Marsh and Baxter, and other cos; *b* 19 May 1917; *yr s* of late Major R. L. Payne, DSO and of Mrs L. M. Payne (*née* Duncan); *m* 1949, Deirdre Kelly; one *s* one *d. Educ:* St Lawrence Coll., Ramsgate; Trinity Hall, Cambridge (MA). Entered Civil Service as Assistant Principal, 1939. Served War of 1939-45 (despatches twice, OBE): RAFVR, 1940-45; Wing Commander, 1943. Principal Private Secretary to Minister of Agriculture and Fisheries, 1947-51; Asst Secretary, 1951; seconded to Treasury, 1953-54. Under-Secretary, Min. of Agriculture, 1960-68. *Address:* 47 Bramber Road, N12. *T:* 01-445 2527.

**PAYNE, Keith,** VC 1969; Warrant Officer Instructor, Royal Military College, Duntroon, Australia; *b* 30 Aug. 1933; *s* of Henry Thomas Payne and Remilda Payne (*née* Hussey); *m* 1954, Florence Catherine Payne (*née* Plaw); five *s. Educ:* State School, Ingham, North Queensland. Soldier, Department of Army, Aug. 1951-. Member: VC and GC

Assoc.; Returned Services League; Korea and South East Asia Forces Assoc. (Pres., State Br.). Freeman City of Brisbane and of Shire of Hinchinbrook. Vietnamese Cross of Gallantry, with bronze star, 1969. *Recreations:* football, fishing, hunting. *Address:* 3 Pratt Road, Duntroon, Canberra, ACT. *T:* Canberra 732385.

**PAYNE, Peter Charles John,** PhD; MScAgrEng; Principal, National College of Agricultural Engineering, Silsoe, Beds, since 1962; *b* 8 Feb. 1928; *s* of late C. J. Payne, China Clay Merchant, and of Mrs F. M. Payne; *m* 1961, Margaret Grover; two *s* one *d. Educ:* Plymouth Coll.; Teignmouth Grammar School; Reading University. BSc Reading 1948; Min. of Agriculture Scholar, Durham Univ., MSc (Agr. Eng.) 1950; Scientific Officer, Nat. Institute of Agricultural Engineering, 1950-55; PhD Reading 1954; Lecturer in Farm Mechanisation, Wye College, London Univ., 1955-60; Council of Instn of Agricultural Engineers, 1956-60; Lecturer in Agricultural Engineering, Durham Univ., 1960-61; Vis. Prof., Univ. of Reading, 1969-. FIAgrE (Vice President, 1970), MASAE. *Publications:* various papers in agricultural and engineering journals. *Recreations:* sailing, gardening. *Address:* Principal's Lodge, National College of Agricultural Engineering, Silsoe, Bedford, Beds. *T:* Silsoe 282. *Club:* Farmers'.

**PAYNE, Hon. Sir Reginald Withers,** Kt 1962; **Hon. Mr Justice Payne;** Judge of the Probate, Divorce and Admiralty Division, High Court of Justice, since 1962; *b* 27 Sept. 1904; 2nd *s* of late John Herbert Payne, Solicitor, Hallgate House, Cottingham, E Yorks; *m* 1940, Alice, 3rd *d* of late Ernest Armstrong, Hankham Place, Pevensey; two *s. Educ:* Hymers Coll., Hull. LLB (London), 1927; admitted Solicitor, 1927; called to the Bar, Inner Temple, 1937 (North Eastern Circuit). Bencher, Inner Temple, 1962. Served, 1940-45, in RAFVR (Provost Marshal's Branch for Provost and Security Duties); Deputy Assistant Provost Marshal Yorkshire, Assistant Provost Marshal: Midlands; Karachi Area; Deputy Provost Marshal, Bengal and Assam; Squadron Leader, 1943; Wing Commander, 1945. Recorder of Pontefract, 1955-57; Recorder of Huddersfield, 1957-59; Judge of the County Courts (Circuit 14), Oct. 1959-May 1960; (Circuit 12), 1960-62. Chm., Lord Chancellor's Cttee on Enforcement of Judgments, 1965. *Recreations:* golf, shooting, gardening. *Address:* Royal Courts of Justice, Strand, WC2; 12 King's Bench Walk, Temple, EC4. *T:* 01-353 3114. *Clubs:* Reform, Garrick. *See also C. T. Evans.*

**PAYNE, Sir Robert (Frederick),** Kt 1970; President, The Law Society, 1969-70; Principal in Payne & Payne, Solicitors, Hull, and in Thornton Berger & Lewis, Lincoln's Inn; *b* 22 Jan. 1908; *s* of late Frederick Charles Payne and of Edith Constance Payne (*née* Carlton); *m* 1st, 1937, Alice Marguerite, *d* of William Sydney Cussons, one *s* one *d*; 2nd, 1951, Maureen Ruth, *d* of William Charles Walsh; one *s. Educ:* Hymers Coll., Hull. Solicitor, 1931. Served in RAF (Fighter Command), 1940-44, Sqdn Ldr, 2nd TAF. Pres., Hull Incorporated Law Soc., 1954-55; Founder Mem., British Acad. of Forensic Sciences, 1959. Sheriff of Kingston-upon-Hull, 1957. *Recreations:* golf, music. *Address:* Fairholme, Brough, Yorkshire. *T:* Brough 667188. *Club:* East India and Sports.

**PAYNE, Dr Sylvia May,** CBE 1918; retired Psychiatrist; *b* 6 Nov. 1880; *d* of late Rev. E. W. Moore, Wimbledon and Stoke Doyle, Northants; *m* 1908, John Ernest Payne, FRCS, *s* of late John Payne, Park Grange, Sevenoaks; three *s. Educ:* Wimbledon High School; Westfield College (London University); London (Royal Free Hospital) School of Medicine for Women. MBBS, London, 1906; House Surgeon and Assistant Anæsthetist Royal Free Hospital, 1907-08; Commandant and Medical Officer in charge of Torquay Red Cross Hospitals, 1914-18; Psychiatrist to London Clinic of Psycho-Analysis, 1926; Hon. Sec. to Institute of Psycho-Analysis, 1929, Hon. Training Sec. 1939, Chairman of Directors, 1944-47; Fellow of the Royal Society of Medicine, Vice-President of Psychiatric Section; Pres. British Psycho-Analytical Society; Member of International Psycho-Analytical Society; Fellow British Psychological Society (Medical Section; Chairman, 1936); Hon. Member British Psycho-Analytical Society, 1962. *Publications:* Observations on The Formation and Function of the Super-Ego in Normal and Abnormal Psychological States, The British Journal of Medical Psychology, Vol. vii, Part I, 1927; The Myth of the Barnacle Goose, The International Journal of Psycho-Analysis, Vol. x, Parts 2 and 3, 1929; A Conception of Femininity, The British Journal of Medical Psychology, Vol. xv, Part 1, 1935; Post-war Activities and the Advance of Psychotherapy, The British Journal of Medical Psychology, Vol. xvi, Part I, 1936. *Address:* 49 Chancellor House, Mount Ephraim, Tunbridge Wells, Kent. *Club:* University Women's.

**PAYNE-GALLWEY, Sir Philip Frankland;** *see* Gallwey.

**PAYNTER, Air Cdre Noel Stephen,** CB 1946; DL; retired; *b* 26 Dec. 1898; *s* of late Canon F. S. Paynter, sometime Rector of Springfield, Essex; *m* 1925, Barbara Grace Haagensen; one *s* one *d. Educ:* Haileybury; RMC, Sandhurst. Flying Brevet, 1917; France and Russia, 1918-19 (St Anne 3rd Class); North-West Frontier, 1919-21; North-West Frontier, 1925-30; Malta, 1934; Directorate of Intelligence, Air Ministry, 1936-39; Chief Intelligence Officer, Middle East, 1939-42 (despatches); Chief Intelligence Officer, Bomber Command, 1942-45 (CB); Directorate of Intelligence, Air Ministry, 1946. Chm. Buckinghamshire Playing Fields Assoc., 1958-65; Chm. Bucks Army Cadet Force (TA), 1962-65. High Sheriff, Bucks, 1965. DL Buckinghamshire, 1963. *Address:* Lawn House, Edgcott, near Aylesbury, Bucks. *T:* Grendon Underwood 238.

**PAYNTER, (Thomas) William;** Secretary, National Union of Mineworkers, 1959-68; Member, Commission on Industrial Relations, since 1969; *b* 6 Dec. 1903; *s* of a Miner; *m* 1st, 1937; two *s* (twins); 2nd, 1943; five *s* (one set of twins). *Educ:* Whitchurch (Cardiff) and Porth Elementary Schools. Left school at age of 13 to work on a farm, 1917; commenced work in Rhondda Pits; elected Checkweigher at Cymmer Colliery, Porth, 1929; removed by Court injunction, 1931. Took part in hunger marches, 1931, 1932, 1936. Elected to Executive Committee, South Wales Miners' Federation for Rhondda, 1936; joined Internatonal Brigade, 1937; Miners' agent for Rhymney Area, 1939; President South Wales Miners, 1951. *Publication:* British Trade Unions and the Problem of Change, 1970. *Recreations:* reading and gardening. *Address:* 32 Broadfields Avenue, Edgware, Mddx.

**PAYTON, Stanley Walden,** CMG 1965; Deputy Chief, Overseas Department, Bank of England, since 1965; *b* 29 May 1921; *s* of late Archibald Walden Payton and late Ethel May

Payton (*née* Kirtland); *m* 1941, Joan (*née* Starmer); one *s* one *d*. *Educ:* Monoux School, Essex. Fleet Air Arm, 1940-46: Lieut, HMS Indomitable, HMS Illustrious. Entered Bank of England, 1946; various missions Commonwealth and Middle East for the Bank, 1949-53; assisted Lord Salter to prepare new plan for Iraq in Baghdad, 1953-54; UK Alternate on Managing Board of European Payments Union, Paris, 1957-59; Adviser in Bank of England, 1959-60; First Governor of Bank of Jamaica, 1960-64; Dep. Chief, Overseas Dept, Bank of England, 1965. *Publication:* (with Lord Salter) The Development of Iraq, 1954. *Recreations:* sailing, swimming, music, painting. *Address:* Pollards Park House, Chalfont St Giles, Bucks. *T:* Little Chalfont 2558. *Clubs:* Naval, Overseas Bankers.

**PAYTON, Rev. Wilfred Ernest Granville,** CB 1965; Vicar of Abingdon, since 1969; *b* 27 Dec. 1913; *s* of Wilfred Richard Daniel Payton and Alice Payton (*née* Lewin); *m* 1946, Nita Mary Barber; one *s* one *d*. *Educ:* Nottingham High School; Emmanuel College, Cambridge (MA); Ridley Hall, Cambridge. Ordained, 1938; Chaplain, RAF, 1941; Asst Chaplain-in-Chief, 1959; Chaplain-in-Chief, 1965-69; Archdeacon, Prebendary and Canon of St Botolph, Lincoln Cathedral, 1965-69. Hon. Chaplain to the Queen, 1965-69. *Recreations:* cricket (Cambridge Univ. 1937), hockey (Notts., 1938-39), tennis. *Address:* The Vicarage, Thames Street, Abingdon, Berks. *T:* Abingdon 144. *Clubs:* MCC, Royal Air Force, Hawks (Cambridge).

**PEACEY, Rev. J. R.,** MC, MA; Residentiary Canon, Bristol, 1945-66, now Canon Emeritus; Canon Missioner, diocese of Bristol, 1956-66; Rural Dean of Hurst, since 1969; *b* 16 July 1896; *s* of Reverend Prebendary T. Peacey, Vicar of Hove, and Ellen C. Leeper; *m* 1925, M. E. Hancock; one *d*. *Educ:* Mowden Preparatory School; S Edmund's School, Canterbury; Selwyn College, Cambridge. Lt Sussex RGA, B Battery AA, France, 1915-18; Theological Tripos, Pt I.; Master at Wellington College, 1922-23; Fellow and Dean of Selwyn College, Cambridge, 1923-27; Head Master, Bishop Cotton School, Simla, 1927-35; Principal, Bishop's College, Calcutta, 1935-45. *Recreation:* gardening. *Address:* Speedwell, 88 College Lane, Hurstpierpoint, Sussex. *T:* 2378.

**PEACH, Capt. C. L.;** *see* Keighly-Peach.

**PEACH, Lawrence du Garde,** MA, PhD; Author and Dramatist; *b* 14 Jan. 1890; *s* of Rev. Charles Peach; *m* 1915, Marianne Leeming; no *c*. *Educ:* Manchester Grammar School; Manchester University; Göttingen University; Sheffield University. Lecturer in English Language and Literature, Göttingen University, 1912-14; Manchester Regiment and Staff Intelligence, 1914-19, Captain, 1917; Major, Home Guard, 1941; Lecturer in English, University College of the South West, 1922-26; began writing for Punch and other papers, 1920; Author of 400 radio plays broadcast by BBC and of many film scenarios; Contested Derby (L) 1929; Lecturer and Political speaker. Founder and Director, Great Hucklow Village Players, 1927-. Hon. LittD, Sheffield, 1964. *Publications:* Angela and I–Punch sketches; Unknown Devon; Radio Plays; Five Country Plays; The Path of Glory; Practical Plays for Stage and Classroom; The Castles of England; Famous Men of Britain; Famous Women of Britain; Plays for Young Players; Five Plays for Boys; A Dramatic History of England; Knights of the Round Table; The Story of Sigurd; Plays of the Family Goodman; Story Tellers of Britain; Napoleon couldn't do it, 1941; According to Plan, 1942; You Never Know!, 1943; Legacy at Loon, 1943; Mystery of the Mary Celeste, 1945; The White Sheep of the Family (with Ian Hay), 1948; Mate in Three, 1949; The Town that would have a Pageant, 1951; Women are like that, 1952; A Horse A Horse!, 1953; Love One Another, 1954; Speed the Plough, 1955; Collected Plays, IV Vols, 1955; Any Old Iron, 1956; Bless the Well, 1958; Christmas Comes, 1959; The Village that would have a Dragon, 1960; Heirs and Graces, 1962; Summat Akin, 1963; The Lopotkin Inheritance, 1963; Henry Came to Tideswell, 1964; Friday's Dream, 1965; Beautiful Garden, 1966; A Knife in her Stocking, 1967; Things just so strange, 1967; The Beacon, 1968; Where Witches do Inhabit, 1969; To the Manor Born, 1970; and a long series of Plays for Youth Groups; and many short plays, including many on Biblical subjects, various pageant scripts, including Centenary pageants for: Sheffield, Warrington, Wolverhampton, The Isle of Man, Sheffield Youth and National Co-operative Soc. and Transport and Gen. Workers Union. *Recreations:* Village Drama, painting. *Address:* Foolow, Eyam, via Sheffield. *T:* Tideswell 258. *Club:* Savage.

**PEACOCK, Prof. Alan Turner,** DSC 1945; MA; Professor of Economics, University of York, since October 1962; *b* 26 June 1922; *s* of Professor A. D. Peacock, *qv*; *m* 1944, Margaret Martha Astell Burt; two *s* one *d*. *Educ:* Dundee High School; University of St Andrews (1939-42, 1945-47). Royal Navy, 1942-45 (Lieut RNVR). Lecturer in Economics: Univ. of St Andrews, 1947-48; London Sch. of Economics, 1948-51; Reader in Public Finance, Univ. of London, 1951-56; Prof. of Economic Science, Univ. of Edinburgh, 1957-62. Visiting Prof. of Economics, Johns Hopkins Univ., 1958. Joint Editor, International Economic Papers, 1951-; Member: Commission of Enquiry into land and population problems of Fiji, 1959; Departmental Committee on Electricity in Scotland, 1961; Economists Adv. Gp, 1966; Council, REconS, 1961-; Cttee of Enquiry on impact of rates, 1964; Pres., Internat. Inst. of Public Finance, 1966-69; Chm., Arts Council Enquiry on Orchestral Resources, 1969-70. *Publications:* Economics of National Insurance, 1952; Income Redistribution and Social Policy (Ed.), 1954; National Income and Social Accounting (with H. C. Edey), 1954, 3rd imp. 1967; The National Income of Tanganyika (1952-54) (with D. G. M. Dosser), 1958; The Growth of Public Expenditure in the UK, 1890-1955 (with J. Wiseman), 1961; Government Finance and Economic Development (Ed. and contrib.) 1965; Economic Theory of Fiscal Policy (with G. K. Shaw), 1970; articles on applied economics in Economic Jl, Economica and other journals. *Recreation:* music. *Address:* The Department of Economics, The University, Heslington, York; 5 Rawcliffe Grove, York. *T:* York 55927. *Club:* Reform.

**PEACOCK, Alexander David,** DSc (Durham); LLD (St Andrews); FRSE; Emeritus Professor of Natural History, Queen's College (University of St Andrews), Dundee (Professor 1926-56); *e s* of James and Jane Peacock; *m* 1917, Clara Mary, *d* of William and Ellen Turner; one *s* one *d*. *Educ:* Armstrong College (University of Durham), Newcastle upon Tyne. Graduated in Science, 1908; Prize Demonstrator in Zoology, University of Durham, 1909-11; Government Entomologist, Southern Nigeria, 1911-13; Lecturer in Zoology, University of Durham, 1913-26; on military service, 1914-19; with Field Ambulance and special services, rank of

Captain, RAMC (TF), 1918; principally engaged on problems of medical entomology alone or as member of War Office Trench Fever Commission working party and American Red Cross Trench Fever Commission. *Publications:* Entomological Pests and Problems of Southern Nigeria; The Louse Problem at the Western Front, and several reports on this to the War Office; Report of the American Red Cross Trench Fever Commission (part author); papers on Parthenogenesis and Pharaoh's Ant. *Recreation:* painting. *Address:* 17 St Peter's Grove, York YO3 6AQ. *T:* 55127.

**PEACOCK, David Henry,** MA (Cantab); FRIC; DSc (London), IES (retired); *b* Dec. 1889; *s* of C. G. and Catherine Peacock; *m* 1915, Catherine Tait; no *c. Educ:* Central Foundation School, London; Trinity Coll., Cambridge (Scholar); Gordon Wigan prize for research in Chemistry. Nobel's Explosives Factory Research Department, 1913-16; British Dyes Research Department, 1916-22; Chief Assistant Technical Department, Huddersfield, 1920-22; Professor of Chemistry, University of Rangoon, 1922-40; Special Chemical Adviser to the Government of Burma, 1938-40; Chemical Adviser, Bomber and Maintenance Commands, RAF, 1942-45; Chemical Consultant in Ministry of Supply, 1945-47; Lecturer in Organic Chemistry, University of Sheffield, 1947-55, also Tutor at Stephenson Hall. *Publications:* Life of Joseph Priestley; various papers in Journal of the Chemical Society, Journal of Physical Chemistry, Journal of the Society of Dyers and Colourists, Encyclopædia Britannica. *Address:* Greenways, 70 London Road, Harston, Cambridgeshire.

**PEACOCK, Geoffrey Arden,** MA; Remembrancer, City of London, since 1968; *b* 7 Feb. 1920; *s* of Warren Turner Peacock and Elsie (*née* Naylor); *m* 1949, Mary Gillian Drew, *d* of Dr Harold Drew Lander, Rock, Cornwall; two *d. Educ:* Wellington Coll.; Jesus Coll., Cambridge. Served in War, 1939-46; RA and Roy. Lincs. Regt; Lt-Col 1945; Pres. of War Crimes Court, Singapore. Called to the Bar, Inner Temple. Legal Asst, Treasury Solicitor's Dept, 1949; Princ., HM Treasury, 1954; Sen. Legal Asst, Treasury Solicitor's Dept, 1958. Member: Court of Assistants, Worshipful Co. of Pewterers; Co. of Watermen and Lightermen. Chm., Brighton and Storrington Beagles. Various foreign decorations. *Recreations:* beagling, sailing, rowing. *Address:* Cowfold Lodge, Cowfold, Sussex. *T:* Cowfold 237. *Clubs:* Cruising Association, London Rowing, Leander.

**PEACOCK, (Ian) Michael;** Managing Director, London Weekend Television Ltd, 1967-69; *b* 14 Sept. 1929; *e s* of Norman Henry and Sara Barbara Peacock; *m* 1956, Daphne Lee; two *s* one *d. Educ:* Kimball Union Academy, USA; Welwyn Garden City Grammar School; London School of Economics (BSc Econ.). BBC Television: Producer, 1952-56; Producer Panorama, 1956-58; Asst Head of Television Outside Broadcasts, 1958-59; Editor, Panorama, 1959-61; Editor, BBC Television News, 1961-63; Chief of Programmes, BBC-2, 1963-65; Controller, BBC-1, BBC Television Service, 1965-67. *Recreations:* theatre, cinema, concerts, gardening, sailing. *Address:* 21 Woodlands Road, Barnes, SW13. *T:* 01-876 2025. *Club:* Savile.

**PEACOCK, John Atkins,** CMG 1949; Director, Nurdin & Peacock Ltd, Raynes Park, SW20; Director of Eggs, Ministry of Food, 1940-54; *b* 8 Sept. 1898; *s* of Thomas Peacock; *m* 1925, Phyllis Evelyn Jones; two *s* one *d. Address:* Bushey Road, Raynes Park, SW20; Astra, Vicarage Lane, Send, Surrey. *Club:* Royal Automobile.

**PEACOCK, Michael;** *see* Peacock, I. M.

**PEACOCK, Ronald,** MA, LittD (Leeds), MA (Manchester), DrPhil (Marburg); Professor of German, Bedford College, University of London, since 1962; *b* 22 Nov. 1907; *s* of Arthur Lorenzo and Elizabeth Peacock; *m* 1933, Ilse Gertrud Eva, *d* of Geheimer Oberregierungsrat Paul Freiwald; no *c. Educ:* Leeds Modern Sch.; Universities of Leeds, Berlin, Innsbruck, Marburg. Assistant Lecturer in German, University of Leeds, 1931-38; Lecturer, 1938-39; Professor, 1939-45; Henry Simon Professor of German Language and Literature, University of Manchester, 1945-62; Dean of the Faculty of Arts, 1954-56; Pro-Vice-Chancellor, 1958-62; Visiting Professor of German Literature, Cornell Univ. (USA), 1949; Visiting Professor of German Literature and Comparative Literature, University of Heidelberg, 1960-61; Professor of Modern German Literature, University of Freiburg, 1965, 1967-68. *Publications:* The Great War in German Lyrical Poetry, 1934; Das Leitmotiv bei Thomas Mann, 1934; Hölderlin, 1938; The Poet in the Theatre, 1946 (reprinted with additional essays, 1960); The Art of Drama, 1957; Goethe's Major Plays, 1959; various articles on literature contributed to reviews and periodicals. *Recreations:* music, theatre, travel. *Address:* Bedford College, Regent's Park, NW1.

**PEACOCK, Roydon;** Hon. Consultant Surgeon, Ear, Nose and Throat Department, St George's Hospital, SW1; *s* of late Ralph Peacock; *m* Olive Joan, *d* of late Sir Arthur Blake, KBE. *Educ:* Westminster Sch.; Trinity Coll., Cambridge; St George's Hospital, University Entrance Schol.; Brackenbury Prize, Allingham Scholar. FRCS; BCh Cantab; MRCS, LRCP; 1st Class Hons Natural Sciences Tripos, Cambridge; late Hon. Asst Surgeon Throat, Nose and Ear Hospital, Golden Square, W1; late Hon. Surgeon in charge of Ear, Nose and Throat Dept, Metropolitan Hospital, Kingsland Road; late Hon. Aural Surgeon to Maida Vale Hospital for nervous diseases; late Hon. Laryngologist, King Edward's Memorial Hospital, Ealing; late Hon. Surgeon Royal National Throat, Nose and Ear Hospital; late Surgeon to Ear, Nose and Throat Dept, Canadian Red Cross Memorial Hospital, Taplow, Bucks; late Surgeon, Ear, Nose and Throat Dept, St George's Hospital, SW1; late recog. teacher in Otolaryngology, University of London. *Publications:* Alcoholic Labyrinthine Injection through the oval window in the treatment of aural vertigo, Lancet, Feb. 1938; Meniere's Syndrome, an observation, Lancet, Dec. 1938. *Recreation:* golf. *Address:* Windrush, Bicknoller, Taunton, Somerset. *T:* Stogumber 265.

**PEACOCKE, Rt. Rev. Cuthbert Irvine;** *see* Derry and Raphoe, Bishop of.

**PEAKE,** family name of **Viscount Ingleby.**

**PEAKE, Air Cdre (retired) Dame Felicity (Hyde),** DBE 1949 (MBE 1941); JP; *b* 1 May 1913; *d* of late Colonel Humphrey Watts, OBE, TD, and Mrs Simon Orde; *m* 1st, 1935, John Charles Mackenzie Hanbury (killed on active service, 1939); no *c*; 2nd, 1952, Harald Peake, *qv*; one *s. Educ:* St Winifreds, Eastbourne; Les Grands Huguenots, Vaucresson, Seine et Oise, France. Joined ATS Company of the RAF, April 1939; commissioned in the WAAF, Aug. 1939;

served at home and in the Middle East; Director, Women's Auxiliary Air Force, 1946-49; Director Women's Royal Air Force, from its inception, 1949, until her retirement, 1950. Member Advisory Cttee, Recruitment for the Forces, 1958. Trustee, Imperial War Museum, 1963-. Hon. ADC to King George VI, 1949-50. *Address:* 2 Shepherd's Close, Shepherd's Place, Upper Brook Street, W1. *T:* 01-629 1264; Court Farm, Tackley, Oxfordshire. *T:* Tackley 221.

**PEAKE, Sir Francis,** Kt, *cr* 1951; *b* 31 Jan. 1889; *s* of late John Henry Hill Peake, Chingford, Essex; *m* 1914, Winifred Marie, *d* of late Thomas McKinnon Clark, Wood Green; two *d. Educ:* Tottenham Grammar Sch. Entered Civil Service, 1907. Called to Bar, Lincoln's Inn, 1915. Controller of Death Duties, Aug. 1948-31 July 1951. *Address:* 13 Brockswood Lane, Welwyn Garden City, Herts. *T:* Welwyn Garden 20456.

**PEAKE, Harald,** MA; Director: Lloyds Bank Ltd (Chairman, 1961-69, Deputy Chairman, 1961, Vice-Chairman, 1947-61); Lloyds Bank Europe Ltd; Yorkshire Bank Ltd; National Bank of New Zealand; Lloyds and Scottish; Lloyds Bank Unit Trust Managers Ltd; *b* 28 Oct. 1899; 2nd *surv. s* of late G. H. Peake; *m* 1st, 1933, Countess Resy, OBE 1946 (marr. diss., 1944), *o d* of Count de Baillet Latour, Brussels; one *s*; 2nd, 1952, Dame Felicity Hanbury (*see* Dame Felicity Peake); one *s. Educ:* Eton; Trinity Coll., Cambridge. Served in Coldstream Guards during European War, and subsequently Yorkshire Dragoons Yeomanry; raised and commanded No. 609 (West Riding) Squadron, Royal Aux. Air Force, 1936; Director of the Auxiliary Air Force, Air Ministry, 1938; Director of Public Relations, Air Ministry, 1940-42; Director of Air Force Welfare, 1942-43; Special Duty List, Air Ministry, 1943-45; retired with rank of Air Commodore. Chairman, Steel Co. of Wales, 1955-62. Member, Nye Cttee on War Office Organisation, 1963. Chairman, RAF Benevolent Fund. Pres., Soc. for Health Educn, 1965-. Prime Warden, Goldsmiths' Company, 1958-59. *Recreations:* rowed for Eton, Cambridge and England; Master of Rufford Hounds, 1931-32; Agriculture. *Address:* 2 Shepherd's Close, Shepherd's Place, Upper Brook Street, W1. *T:* 01-629 1264; Court Farm, Tackley, Oxfordshire. *T:* Tackley 221. *Club:* Brooks's.

**PEAKER, Alfred Pearson,** MC; MA; DL; Stipendiary Magistrate, Middlesbrough, 1939-68, Teesside, 1968-69, retired; *b* 22 June 1896; *s* of late Frederick Peaker, Past President, Institute of Journalists, and Eveline Peaker, JP; *m* 1957, Audrey Beare Hall. *Educ:* Dulwich Coll.; Worcester Coll., Oxford (Senior Classical Exhibnr). Served European War in 60th Rifles, 1915-19; Captain, 1917 (MC, wounded); Honour School of Jurisprudence, Oxford, 1920; BA 1920; MA 1922. Called to Bar, Middle Temple, 1921, and practised on North Eastern Circuit; Founder Member and Chairman, Society of Stipendiary Magistrates; Captain 66th (Leeds Rifles) Anti-Aircraft Regt, RA, TA, 1936-39; Lieut-Colonel, commanding 4th Cleveland Cadet Bn, The Green Howards, 1943-48; Hon. Colonel, 1949-64; Member North Riding T&AF Assoc.; Chairman Cadet Force Cttee, 1951-58; formerly Governor, Guisborough Grammar Sch. (Chairman, 1951-62). DL, North Riding of Yorkshire, 1964. *Recreations:* golf, gentle gardening, friendship. *Address:* Priory Cottage, Guisborough, Yorks. *T:* Guisborough 2944. *Clubs:* National Liberal; Cleveland (Teesside).

**PEAR, Professor Tom Hatherley,** MA, BSc; Emeritus Professor of Psychology, University of Manchester, since 1951; *b* Walpole, Norfolk, 1886; *o s* of Alfred John and Mary Ann Pear; *m* Catherine, *y d* of Samuel Henry Robinson, of Whalley Range, Manchester; one *s* (and one *s* decd) two *d. Educ:* Wisbech Grammar Sch.; King's Coll., London; Universities of Würzburg and Giessen. BSc London; MA (Manchester); Fellow of King's Coll., London; Hon. Fellow British Psychological Society. President of British Psychological Society, 1943; Buchanan-Riddell Lecturer, University of Durham, 1936. Formerly Lecturer in Experimental Psychology, Manchester, and on staff of Maghull Military Hospital; President of Psychology Section, British Association, 1928; Member Council, Rossall School. *Publications:* Remembering and Forgetting; Skill in Work and Play; Fitness for Work; The Art of Study; Voice and Personality; The Psychology of Effective Speaking; Religion and Contemporary Psychology; The Maturing Mind, The Psychology of Conversation; English Social Differences; Personality, Appearance and Speech; The Moulding of Modern Man; (ed.) Psychological Factors of Peace and War; Shell Shock and its Lessons (with Professor Sir Grafton Elliot Smith); (joint) The Study of Society; Current Trends in British Psychology; The Nature of Conflict; has contributed to British Journal of Psychology and to various journals devoted to psychology, education, broadcasting and industry. *Address:* Shirkoak House, Woodchurch, Ashford, Kent. *T:* Woodchurch 368. *Club:* English-Speaking Union.

**PEARCE,** family name of **Baron Pearce.**

**PEARCE,** Baron (Life Peer) *cr* 1962, of Sweethaws; **Edward Holroyd Pearce,** PC 1957; Kt 1948; RBA 1940; Chairman of the Press Council, since 1969; Chairman, Appeals Committee, Take-over Panel; *b* 9 Feb. 1901; *s* of late John W. E. Pearce and Irene, *d* of Holroyd Chaplin; *m* 1927, Erica, *d* of late Bertram Priestman, RA; two *s. Educ:* Charterhouse; Corpus Christi Coll., Oxford. Hon. Fellow, Corpus Christi Coll., 1950. Called to Bar, 1925; QC 1945; Bencher, Hon. Society of Lincoln's Inn, 1948; Treasurer, 1966. Deputy Chairman, East Sussex Quarter Sessions, 1947-48; Judge of High Court of Justice, Probate, Divorce and Admiralty Division, 1948-54, Queen's Bench Division, 1954-57; a Lord Justice of Appeal, 1957-62; a Lord of Appeal in Ordinary, 1962-69. Chairman: Cttee on Shipbuilding Costs, 1947-49; Royal Commission on Marriage and Divorce, 1951; Governing Body, Charterhouse Sch., 1943-64; Governor of Tonbridge Sch.; and Governor of Sutton's Hospital in Charterhouse. Past Master and Member of Court of Company of Skinners; President, Imperial Arts League; Trustee, Chantrey Bequest; Hon. FRBS. *Recreations:* painting and pictures. *Address:* House of Lords, SW1; 5 Stone Buildings, Lincoln's Inn, WC2. *T:* 01-242 2233; Sweethaws, Crowborough. *T:* 6150. *Club:* Athenæum.

*See also Hon. R. B. H. Pearce.*

**PEARCE, Austin William,** PhD; Managing Director, Esso Petroleum Company Ltd, since 1968; *b* 1st Sept. 1921; *s* of William Thomas and Florence Annie Pearce; *m* 1947, Maglona Winifred Twinn; three *d. Educ:* Devonport High Sch. for Boys; Univ. of Birmingham. BSc (Hons) 1943, PhD 1945; Cadman Medallist. Joined Agwi Petroleum Corp., 1945 (later Esso Petroleum Co., Ltd): Asst Refinery Manager, 1954-56; Gen. Manager Refining, 1956-62; Dir, 1963; Man. Dir, 1968; Chairman,

Irish Refining Co. Ltd, 1965-; Pres., Inst. of Petroleum, 1968-. *Recreations:* golf, woodwork. *Address:* 32 Shirley Avenue, Cheam, Surrey. *T:* 01-642 0073. *Club:* Royal Wimbledon Golf.

**PEARCE, Clifford James;** Under Secretary, Ministry of Housing and Local Government, since 1968; *b* 14 Aug. 1916; *s* of late Samuel Lightfoot Pearce and Maude Evelyn Neville; *m* 1946, Elaine Hilda (*née* Baggley); one *s* one *d*. *Educ:* Strand Sch.; King's Coll., London; London Sch. of Economics. Entered Inland Revenue, 1935; served in RN, 1941-46 (Lieut, RNVR); entered Min. of Health, 1946; Asst Sec., Min. of Housing and Local Govt, 1957; Under Sec. 1968. *Address:* 156 Burbage Road, Dulwich, SE21; 7 The Forstal, Eridge Green, Tunbridge Wells, Kent.

**PEARCE, Air Commodore Frederick Laurence,** CBE 1945; DSO 1940; DFC; RAF, retired; *b* 9 Aug. 1898; *s* of Reuben Frederick Pearce, 14 Adrian Square, Westgate-on-Sea, Kent; *m* 1st, 1926; one *s* (and one *s* decd); 2nd, 1953, Marie Gwendoline, *d* of Dr G. W. Paterson, Grenada. *Educ:* Godwin Coll.; Aylesbury. HAC 1916; RFC 1917; War of 1939-45 (DSO, despatches, DFC for action over Norway, CBE); Air Officer Commanding, Air Headquarters, Ceylon, 1949-52; retired, 1952. *Address:* Casa Verena, El Planet, Altea, Alicante, Spain. *Club:* Royal Over-Seas League.

**PEARCE, Most Rev. George;** *see* Suva, Archbishop of, (RC).

**PEARCE, Sir George (Alfred),** Kt 1947; OBE 1938; KPM 1946; Indian Police; *b* 28 Oct. 1894; 3rd *s* of Harry Walter and Edith Ellen Pearce; *m* 1st, 1920, Muriel Florence Durrell (*d* 1962); one *s* one *d*; 2nd, 1964, Muriel Sorby (*née* Wright), *widow* of Lt-Col W. J. W. Sorby. *Educ:* City of Norwich Sch.; St John's Coll., Battersea. Served European War, 1914-20, Middlesex Regt and Indian Army; entered Indian Police, 1920, as Asst Superintendent of Police; posted to UP, Superintendent of Police, 1923; Supt of Police, Special Dacoity Police UP, 1926-30; Supt of Police, Aligarh, Cawnpore, Naini Tal, 1931-40; Comdt UP Military Police and Police Training School, 1940; Dep. Inspector-General of Police, 1944; on Special Duty for Police Reorganisation, 1945; Inspector-General of Police, UP, 1946; retired, 1949. Government Communications Headquarters (Foreign Office), 1949-64. *Recreation:* reading. *Address:* Copper Beech House, Malvern Place, Cheltenham, Glos. *Club:* East India and Sports.

**PEARCE, John Dalziel Wyndham,** MA, MD, FRCP, FRCPEd, DPM, FBPsS; Consulting Psychiatrist: St Mary's Hospital; Queen Elizabeth Hospital for Children; Consultant Psychiatrist, Royal Masonic Hospital; Examiner in Medicine, Royal College of Physicians, and University of London; *b* 21 Feb. 1904; *s* of John Alfred Wyndham Pearce and Mary Logan Dalziel; *m* 1929, Grace Fowler (marr. diss., 1964), no *c*; *m* 1964, Ellinor Elizabeth Nancy Draper. *Educ:* George Watson's Coll.; Edinburgh Univ. Member: Home Secretary's Advisory Council on Treatment of Offenders; Advisory Cttee on delinquent and maladjusted children (Chairman), International Union for Child Welfare; Army Psychiatry Advisory Cttee. Formerly: Physician-in-charge, Depts of Psychiatry, St Mary's Hosp. and Queen Elizabeth Hosp. for Children; Hon. physician, Tavistock Clinic and West End Hospital for Nervous Diseases; Medical co-director Portman Clinic, Institute for Study and Treatment of Delinquency (ISTD); medico-psychologist, LCC remand homes; Mem. Academic Boards, Inst. of Child Health, and St Mary's Hosp. Med. Sch. (Univ. of London). lt-Col, RAMC; adviser in psychiatry, Allied Force HQ, CMF (despatches). Formerly Mem. Council, National Assoc. for Mental Health. *Publications:* Juvenile Delinquency, 1952; technical papers in scientific journals. *Recreations:* golf, fishing, painting, breadmaking. *Address:* 96 Harley Street, W1. *T:* 01-580 4180. *Club:* Caledonian.

**PEARCE, John Trevor Archdall,** CMG 1964; Registrar, Papua and New Guinea Institute of Technology, since 1969; *b* 7 May 1916; *s* of late Rev. W. T. L. A. Pearce, Seven Hills, NSW, Australia, and late N. B. Pearce, Prahran, Victoria, Australia; *m* 1948, Isabel Bundey Rankine, Hindmarsh Island, S Australia; no *c*. *Educ:* The King's Sch., Parramatta, Australia; Keble Coll., Oxford, Eng. MA. District Officer, Tanganyika, 1939. War Service: Kenya, Abyssinia, Ceylon, India, Burma, 1940-46, Major RE. Tanganyika: District Commissioner, 1950; Provincial Commissioner, 1959; Permanent Secretary (Admin.), Office of the Vice-President, 1961; Chairman, Public Service Commn, Basutoland, 1963, Swaziland, 1965. *Recreations:* cricket, hill-walking, travel, the Law. *Address:* Institute of Technology, PO Box 793, Lae, New Guinea. *T:* (office) Lae 3222, (home) Lae 3425.

**PEARCE, Kenneth Leslie;** Chairman, East Midlands Gas Board, since 1968; *b* 2 May 1910; *s* of late George Benjamin Pearce and Eliza Jane Pearce; *m* 1940, Evlyn Sarah Preedy (*d* 1957); two *s*. *Educ:* Dudley Grammar Sch.; Birmingham Central Techn. Coll. Engr and Man., Bilston Gas Light & Coke Co., 1939-48; Engr and Man., City of Leicester Gas Dept, 1948-49; East Midlands Gas Board: Divisional Gen. Man., Leicester and Northants, 1949-50; Divisional Gen. Man., Notts and Derby, 1950-62; Chief Distribution Engr, 1962-67; Dep. Chairman, 1967-68. *Recreations:* fishing, gardening. *Address:* East Midlands Gas Board, De Montfort Street, Leicester. *T:* Leicester 50022.

**PEARCE, Malcolm Arthur Fraser,** CVO 1954; CBE 1946; AASA; *b* 19 April 1898; *s* of J. S. Pearce, Kapunda; *m* 1st, 1922, Gladys M. (*d* 1958), *d* of J. Green, Wayville, SA; one *s* one *d* (and one *d* decd); 2nd, 1959, Ivy, *widow* of Rev. F. V. Duffy, Kaniva, Victoria. *Educ:* Kapunda High Sch., SA. Entered Attorney-General's Dept, 1914; Private Secretary and later Official Secretary to Premiers of SA, 1926-54; Under-Secretary, State of SA, Secretary to Minister of Health, Clerk of Exec. Council, 1954-61; Chairman, State Bank Board, 1948-61; Chairman, SA Symphony Orch. Cttee, until 1961; Member, SA Public Debt Commn, 1954-61; Agent-General and Trade Commissioner for South Australia in the UK, 1961-66. Visited England for Jubilee Celebrations, 1935; for Coronation Celebrations, 1953; South Australian State Director for Royal Visits, 1954 (CVO) and 1958. Member Executive, SA Red Cross Soc.; Vice-Pres., meals on Wheels Organisation. *Recreations:* golf, bowls. *Address:* 1 Vauxhall Street, Erindale, Adelaide, South Australia 5066, Australia. *T:* 36371. *Clubs:* Royal Automobile; Commercial Travellers' (Adelaide).

**PEARCE, Hon. Richard Bruce Holroyd,** QC 1969; *b* 12 May 1930; *s* of Lord Pearce, *qv*; *m* 1958, Dornie Smith-Pert; one *s* one *d*. *Educ:* Charterhouse; Corpus Christi Coll., Oxford (MA). Called to Bar, Lincoln's Inn, 1955. *Address:* 9 Stone Buildings, Lincoln's Inn, WC2. *T:* 01-242 6660; Sweethaws,

Crowborough, Sussex. *T:* Crowborough 3888. *Club:* Athenæum.

**PEARCE-HIGGINS, Rev. Canon John Denis;** Hon. Chaplain to the Forces; Residentiary Canon and Vice-Provost of Southwark since 1963; *b* 1 June 1905; 2nd *s* of late Prof. Alexander Pearce Higgins and Mina MacLennan; *m* 1938, Margaret Edna, 2nd *d* of Harry and Marguerite Hodge, Kettering; two *s* three *d. Educ:* St Faith's Sch., Cambridge; Rugby Sch. (scholar); Gonville and Caius Coll., Cambridge (schol. and prizeman). Charles Winter Warr Research Schol. in Ancient Philosophy, 1928; 1st class hons Parts I and II Class. Tripos; Research at Vienna Univ., 1928-29; Ripon Hall Theological Coll., 1934-37. Priest, 1937; Curate: St Agnes, Cotteridge; Priory Church, Malvern, 1940. Chaplain in RAChD, Oct. 1940-Nov. 1945 (invalided; Overseas, Africa Star, Italy, Defence and Victory medals). Vicar of Hanley Castle, Worcs, 1945-53; OCF; Chaplain and Sen. Divinity Lecturer, City of Worcester Training Coll., 1946-53; Vicar of Putney, St Mary with St John and All Saints, Surrogate, 1953-63. Chairman, Modern Churchmen's Union, 1958-68. Vice-Chairman, Churches' Fellowship for Psychical and Spiritual Studies, 1961-. Member Society Psychical Research. *Publications:* Resurrection, 1959. Articles in: Modern Churchman, Journal of SPR. *Recreations:* music, painting. *Address:* 122 Kennington Road, SE11. *T:* 01-735 8322.

**PEARD, Rear-Admiral Sir Kenyon (Harry Terrell),** KBE 1958 (CBE 1951); retired; *b* 1902; *s* of Henry T. Peard; *m* 1935, Mercy Leila Bone; one *s* one *d. Educ:* RN Colleges, Osborne and Dartmouth. Went to sea, 1919; Torpedo Specialist, 1929; transferred to Electrical Branch, 1946, Director, Naval Electrical Dept, Admiralty, 1955-58; retired 1958. *Address:* Finstead, Shorefield Crescent, Milford-on-Sea, Hants.

**PEARKES, Maj.-Gen. Hon. George Randolph,** VC 1918; CC (Canada) 1967; PC (Canada) 1957; CB 1943; DSO 1919; MC; Legion of Merit (US); Lieutenant-Governor, British Columbia, 1960-67, retired; *b* Watford, Herts, 26 Feb. 1888; *m* Constance Blytha, *o d* of W. F. U. Copeman, Sidney, BC; one *s. Educ:* Berkhamsted Sch. Went to Canada; farmed for three years; joined Royal N-W Mounted Police, 1909; enlisted in Canadian Expeditionary Force, 1914; arrived in France, Sept. 1915; Bombing Sgt, Dec. 1915; Lieut on the field, March 1916; Battalion Bombing Officer; Brigade Bombing Officer; Captain, Oct. 1916; Major, Nov. 1917; took command of Battalion, Dec. 1917 (VC, MC, despatches, wounded several times); passed Staff Coll., Camberley, 1919; served on the General Staff of Permanent Force of Canada as GSO at Calgary, Winnipeg, Esquimalt and Kingston; DMT and SD; at Imperial Defence Coll., 1937; DOC, MD 13, Calgary, 1938-40; GOC First Canadian Division, 1940; GOC-in-C Pacific Command, Canada, 1942-45; retired April, 1945. Minister of National Defence, 1957-60. Hon. LLD, University of British Columbia. *Address:* 1268 Tattersall Drive, Victoria, BC, Canada. *Club:* Union (Victoria).

**PEARMAN, Mrs Philip Westrope;** *see* Browne, Coral E.

**PEARS, David Francis,** FBA 1970; Student of Christ Church, Oxford, since 1960; *b* 8 Aug. 1921; *s* of Robert and Gladys Pears; *m* 1963, Anne Drew; one *s* one *d. Educ:* Westminster Sch.; Balliol Coll., Oxford. Research Lecturer, Christ Church, 1948; Fellow of Corpus Christi, Oxford, 1950. *Publications:* Bertrand Russell and the British Tradition in Philosophy, 1966; Ludwig Wittgenstein, 1970. *Address:* The Orchard, The Ridings, Shotover, Oxford. *T:* Oxford 61023.

**PEARS, Harold Snowden;** Recorder of Doncaster since 1968; Deputy Chairman, West Riding County Quarter Sessions, since 1967; Legal Member, Mental Health Review Tribunal, since 1964; *b* 21 April 1926; *s* of late Harold Pears and Florence Elizabeth (*née* Snowden); *m* 1960, Inge Haumann, *d* of Heinrich and Agnes Elvensø, Denmark; no *c. Educ:* Dauntsey's Sch.; Emmanuel Coll., Cambridge (MA). Called to the Bar, Inner Temple, 1948; North Eastern Circuit, 1948-. *Recreations:* gardening, travel. *Address:* 35 Whirlow Park Road, Sheffield. *T:* Sheffield 366244. *Club:* Sheffield (Sheffield).

**PEARS, Peter,** CBE 1957; Tenor; *b* 22 June 1910; *s* of Arthur and Jessie Pears. *Educ:* Lancing; Oxford; Royal College of Music. BBC Singers, 1934-37; New English Singers, 1936-38; American and European tours with Benjamin Britten since 1939, with Julian Bream since 1956. Sadler's Wells Opera, 1943-46; Peter Grimes in Peter Grimes 1945 and 1960; English Opera Group, 1947; Covent Garden Opera, 1948; Co-Founder of Aldeburgh Festival, 1948. First performed many new works by Britten, Tippett, Berkeley, etc. Cramb Lectr, Univ. of Glasgow, 1961. Hon. RAM; Hon. DUniv York, 1969. *Publications:* (with Benjamin Britten) Purcell Edition, 1948-. *Recreation:* none. *Address:* c/o Phipps, 8 Halliford Street, N1.

**PEARS, Sidney John,** FCA; Senior Partner, Cooper Brothers & Co., 1946-70; *b* 5 Aug. 1900; *s* of Sidney Pears and Alice Ella Grossmith; *m* 1927, Molly Kathleen Wallers; three *d. Educ:* Rugby. Member Inst. of Chartered Accountants in England and Wales; ACA 1924; FCA 1931; Member Council, 1946-67. (Chairman Parliamentary and Law Cttee, 1958-59; Vice-President, 1959-60; President, 1960-61; Chairman Investigation Cttee, 1962-65; Chairman General Purposes Cttee, 1965-66; Chairman Overseas Relations Cttee, 1966-67). Member Assembly of Delegates on Union Européenne des Experts Comptables Economiques et Financiers (UEC), 1963-66; Member Exec. Cttee of UEC, 1966-67. Ministry of Supply: Director of Contracts, 1941; Principal Controller of Costs, 1942-45; Vice-Chairman Advisory Cttee on ROF accounting, 1946-50. Ministry of Works: Member Cttee on Enquiry into Cement Industry, 1946; Member Building Working Party, 1948. Board of Trade: Dep. Chairman Wool Working Party, 1946; Director, National Film Finance Corp., 1948-52, and Festival Gardens Ltd, 1952-53; Advisory Cttee, Revolving Fund for Industry, 1953-56; Export Credits Guarantee Dept Cttee, 1955. Treasury: Investigation into Building Material prices; Board of Referees (Board of Inland Revenue), 1956-57; Accountant Adviser, 1955-60, Part-time director, 1960-, UK Atomic Energy Authority. Ministry of Agriculture, Fisheries and Food Cttee on Milk Distributors' Remuneration, 1959-61. Member, Economic Development Cttee for the Electrical Engineering Industry, 1964-. Director and Governor, Cable & Wireless (Holding) Ltd; Chairman: Cables Investment Trust Ltd; Globe Investment Trust Ltd; Electra Finance Co. Ltd; Electra House Ltd; Electra Investments Ltd; Director: Electra Investments (South Africa) Ltd; Electra Investments (Canada) Ltd; Electra Investments (Rhodesia) Ltd; Electra Investments (Zambia) Ltd; Thomas Tilling Ltd. *Recreations:* tennis, golf. *Address:* (office)

Abacus House, 33 Gutter Lane, Cheapside, EC2; Rest Harrow, Ashurstwood, near East Grinstead, Sussex. *T:* Forest Row 2206; Arundel House, Arundel Street, WC2. *T:* 01-836 1068. *Clubs:* Queen's Tennis; Royal Ashdown Forest Golf.

**PEARS, Rear-Admiral Steuart Arnold,** CBE 1950; DL; retired 1956; *b* 24 Feb. 1894; *e s* of S. D. Pears, President Municipality, Madras; *m* 1916, Anne Biggins; one *s* two *d. Educ:* RN Colleges, Osborne and Dartmouth. Sub-Lieut, 1914; Lieut, 1916; Lieut-Commander, 1924; Commander, 1934; Captain, 1947; Rear-Admiral, 1953. Served HMS Hercules, 1911; King George V, 1913; Falmouth, 1914; Oak, 1916; Excellent, 1919; Campbell, 1922; Reserve Fleet, 1924. Executive Officer Visit of Prince of Wales to S. America, 1925; lost right leg, 1926; transf. Inspection Research Design and Experimental Duties, 1927; Research Dept, 1928; Naval Ordnance Inspection Officer, Plymouth, 1932, Mediterranean, 1936; Supt. Experimental Establishment, Pendine, 1940; Chief Inspector, 1947; Vice-President Ordnance Board, 1953; President, 1955; Master, Lord Leycester Hospital, Warwick, 1958-66. DL Warwickshire, 1959. *Recreation:* anything out-of-doors. *Address:* Pythouse, Tisbury, Wilts. *Club:* Royal Navy.

**PEARSE, Prof. Anthony Guy Everson,** MA, MD (Cantab); FRCP, FRCPath; DCP (London); Professor of Histochemistry, University of London, Royal Postgraduate Medical School, since 1965; *b* 9 Aug. 1916; *o s* of Captain R. G. Pearse, DSO, MC, Modbury, Devon, and Constance Evelyn Steels, Pocklington, Yorks; *m* 1947, Elizabeth Himmelhoch, MB, BS (Sydney), DCP (London); one *s* three *d. Educ:* Sherborne Sch.; Trinity Coll., Cambridge. Kitchener Scholar, Raymond Horton-Smith prizeman, 1949-50. Posts, St Bart's Hospital, 1940-41; Surg.-Lt, RNVR, 1941-45. Registrar, Edgware General Hospital, 1946; Asst Lecturer in Pathol., PG Med. School, London, 1947-51, Lecturer, 1951-57; Cons. Pathol., Hammersmith Hospital, 1951; Fulbright Fellow and Visiting Prof. of Path., University of Alabama, 1953-54; Guest Instructor in Histochemistry, University of Kansas, 1957, 1958; Vanderbilt Univ., 1967; Reader in Histochemistry, University of London, 1957-65. Member: Path. Society (GB), 1949; Biochem. Society (GB), 1957; European Gastro Club, 1969; Hon. Member or Member various foreign societies, etc.; Hon. Fellow, Royal Microscop. Society, 1964. MD (Basel) *hc* 1960. Member Editorial Board: Histochemie, 1958; Jl Histochem. Cytochem., 1959-68; Enzymol. biol. clin., 1961-67; Brain Research, 1968-; Cardiovascular Research, 1968-; Virchow's Archiv 'B', 1968-; Histochemical Jl, 1968-; Jl of Royal Microscopical Soc., 1967-69; Jl Microscopy, 1969-; Jl of Neuro-visceral Relations, 1969-; Jl of Molecular and Cellular Cardiology, 1970-. *Publications:* Histochemistry Theoretical and Applied, 2nd edn, 1960, 3rd edn, vol. I, 1968. Numerous papers on theoretical and applied histochemistry, esp. endocrinology. *Recreations:* horticulture (plant hybridization, Liliaceae); foreign touring (motoring, camping). *Address:* The Fortress, Letchmore Heath, Hertfordshire. *T:* Radlett 6466; Hollow Bottom Cottage, Blackford, Yeovil, Somerset. *Club: Naval.*

**PEARSE, Thomas L. S.;** *see* Smith-Pearse.

**PEARSON,** family name of **Viscount Cowdray** and of **Baron Pearson.**

**PEARSON,** Baron (Life Peer), *cr* 1965; **Colin Hargreaves Pearson,** PC 1961; Kt 1951; CBE 1946; a Lord of Appeal in Ordinary, since 1965; *b* 28 July 1899; 2nd *s* of Ernest William and Jessie Borland Pearson, Minnedosa, Manitoba, Canada; *m* 1931, Sophie Grace, *e d* of Arthur Hermann Thomas, LLD, DLitt, FSA, Worthing; one *s* one *d. Educ:* St Paul's Sch.; Balliol Coll., Oxford (Classical Scholar and Jenkyns Exhibitioner); Military service, Feb.-Dec. 1918; called to Bar, 1924; Yarborough Anderson Exhibition, Inner Temple, 1925; Junior Common Law Counsel to Ministry of Works, 1930-49; 1965; Division, 1951-61; Judge of Restrictive Practices Court, 1957-61 (President, 1960-61); a Lord Justice of Appeal, 1961-65. Temporary member of Treasury Solicitor's Department, 1939-45. Member: Legal Cttee on Medical Partnerships, 1948; Supreme Court Rule Cttee, 1957-65; Exec. Council of the Inns of Court, 1962-65; Senate of Inns of Court, 1966-69. Chairman: Cttee on Funds in Court, 1958; Law Reform Cttee, 1963-. Chairman, Courts of Inquiry: into a dispute in the Electricity Supply Industry, 1964; into a dispute in the Shipping Industry, 1966-67; into a dispute in Civil Air Transport Industry, 1967-68; into a dispute in Steel Industry, 1968; the Dock Strike, 1970. Visitor, Balliol Coll., Oxford, 1965-; President, Old Pauline Club, 1960-63; Chairman, St Paul's School Building Appeal, 1966-; Member Council, Bedford Coll., University of London (Vice-Chairman, 1959-62, Chairman, 1962-63), 1958-66. President, Inc. Assoc. of Preparatory Schools, 1965-70. *Address:* 2 Crown Office Row, Temple, EC4. *T:* 01-583 8678. *Clubs:* Garrick, Roehampton.

**PEARSON, Brig. Alastair Stevenson,** CB 1958; DSO; OBE 1953; MC; TD; DL; Farmer; *b* 1 June 1915; *m* 1944, Mrs Joan Morgan Weld-Smith; three *d. Educ:* Kelvinside Acad.; Sedbergh. Coy. Director, 1936-39; served War of 1939-45 (MC, DSO, and three Bars); embodied 6th Bn Highland LI, TA, 1939; transferred to Parachute Regt, 1941; Lt-Col 1942. Commanding Officer 15th (Scottish) Bn The Parachute Regt (TA), 1947-53; Dep. Comd 46 Parachute Bde (TA), 1953-59. Comd Scotland Army Cadet Force, Brigadier, 1967-. ADC to the Queen, 1956-61. Hon. Colonel, 15th (Scottish) Bn The Parachute Regt (TA), 1963-. DL Glasgow, 1951. *Address:* Tullochan, Gartocharn, By Alexandria, Dunbartonshire. *T:* Gartocharn 205.

**PEARSON, Andrew R.;** *see* Pearson, Drew.

**PEARSON, Arthur,** CBE 1949; JP; *b* 31 Jan. 1897; *s* of William Pearson, Pontypridd, Glamorgan. MP (Lab) Pontypridd, 1938-70; Labour Whip, 1939-45; Comptroller of HM Household, 1945-46; Treasurer of HM Household, 1946-51; an Opposition Whip, 1951-64. JP 1939, CC 1928-46, Glamorgan. *Address:* 24 The Avenue, Pontypridd, Glamorgan.

**PEARSON, Bertram Lamb,** CB 1947; DSO 1917; MC; *b* 1893; *y s* of late William Pearson of Wakefield, Yorkshire, and late Mary Ann Pearson; *m* 1920, Gladys Mary, *er d* of John Stewart of Yapham Hall, Pocklington, East Yorkshire. *Educ:* Bedford Grammar Sch.; Wakefield Grammar Sch.; The Queen's Coll., Oxford; 1st Hastings Exhibitioner and Honorary Scholar; 1st Class Honour (Classical) Moderations, 1913; 1st Class Literæ Humaniores, 1919. Served European War, 1914-19, as Captain (wounded twice, despatches, MC, DSO); tutor, The Queen's Coll., Oxford, 1919-20; Private Secretary to Permanent Secretary, Board of Education, 1924-28; Principal Private Secretary to the President of the Board of Education, 1937; Accountant-General to Ministry of

Education, 1944-55; Under-Secretary, 1946-55. Member, Council, Central Council of Physical Recreation, 1956-; Member Council Girls' Public Day School Trust, 1958-69. *Recreations:* cricket, bowls, reading. *Address:* Mountfield, Crowborough, Sussex.

**PEARSON, Prof. Claude Edmund,** MMet; Director, Durham Chemicals Group Ltd, since 1956; *b* 13 May 1903; *s* of Thomas George and Annetta Mary Pearson; *m* 1928, Olga Mary Hunt (*d* 1959); *m* 1961, Catherine Annie Benson. *Educ:* Sir William Turner's Sch., Coatham; Sheffield University. Lecturer in Metallurgy, University of Durham, 1924; Reader, 1943; Professor of Metallurgy, King's Coll., University of Durham, 1945-48. *Publications:* The Extrusion of Metals, 1944; papers to: Institute of Metals, Iron and Steel Institute, Institute of Welding. *Recreation:* angling. *Address:* Middle Drive, Woolsington, Newcastle upon Tyne.

**PEARSON, Colin Bateman;** retired as Puisne Judge; *b* 1 Aug. 1889; *s* of Samuel Pearson, MA, Independent Minister; *m* 1942, Dulcibel Hirst Corner (*née* Hillier); no *c*. *Educ:* Tynemouth Sch., Northumberland; Peterhouse, Cambridge. Durham Light Infantry, 1915-19; Captain, RARO; called to Bar, Middle Temple, 1924; Police Magistrate, Tonga, 1928; Police Magistrate, Gold Coast, 1932; Asst Judge, Nigeria, 1938; Puisne Judge, Uganda, 1942-53 (acted as Chief Justice on occasions, 1946-52); retired, 1953. *Address:* Eastons, Dalwood, Axminster, Devon. *Club:* Oxford and Cambridge University.

**PEARSON, David Morris,** OBE 1969 (MBE 1945); HM Consul-General, Casablanca, since 1969; *b* 21 July 1915; *s* of late Isaac Bedlington Pearson and Margaret Elizabeth Williams; *m* 1945, Camille Henriette Etey; no *c*. *Educ:* Kelvinside Academy, Glasgow; Sedbergh Sch.; Glasgow University. HM Forces, 1939-46 (Intell. Corps, then SOE in France, leading Pedagogue Mission). Personnel Manager, Gold Coast Main Reef Ltd, 1946-50; Sierra Leone Administrative Service, 1950-59; seconded to Foreign Service, in Consulate-General, Dakar, Senegal, 1954-59; entered Foreign Service, 1959; FO, 1960-62; Head of Chancery, Brazzaville, 1962-65; Rio de Janeiro, 1965-67; Kinshasa, 1967-69. French Croix de Guerre (with star), 1945. *Recreations:* music, reading, foreign travel. *Address:* c/o Royal Bank of Scotland, 162 Hyndland Road, Glasgow, W2. *Clubs:* Special Forces; Atlanta (Glasgow).

**PEARSON, Sir Denning;** *see* Pearson, Sir J. D.

**PEARSON, Egon Sharpe,** CBE 1946; FRS 1966; MA, DSc; Professor Emeritus, University of London; *b* 11 Aug. 1895; *s* of late Karl Pearson, FRS; *m* 1st, 1934, Eileen (*d* 1949), *yr d* of Russell Jolly; two *d*; 2nd, 1967, Margaret Turner (*née* Scott), *widow* of L. B. Turner, ScD, MIEE. *Educ:* Dragon Sch., Oxford; Winchester Coll.; Trinity Coll., Cambridge. Lecturer in Statistics at University College, London, 1921-33; Reader, 1933-35, Professor, 1935-60. Editor of Auxiliary Publications of Biometrika; Associate Member, Ordnance Board, Ministry of Supply. President, Royal Statistical Society, 1955-57; Guy Medal in Gold of the Royal Statistical Society, 1955. Hon. Member Institute of Actuaries, 1956. *Publications:* Papers on the mathematical theory of statistics and its applications, in Biometrika and other journals; pamphlet for the British Standards Institution on the application of statistical method in problems of standardisation and quality control, 1935. *Address:* University College, Gower Street, WC1.

**PEARSON, Sir Francis Fenwick,** 1st Bt, *cr* 1964; MBE 1945; JP; farmer and landowner; *b* 13 June 1911; *s* of Frank Pearson, solicitor, Kirby Lonsdale, and Susan Mary Pearson; *m* 1938, Katharine Mary Fraser; one *s* one *d*. *Educ:* Uppingham; Trinity Hall, Cambridge. 1st Gurkha Rifles, 1932; ADC to Viceroy of India, 1934-36; Indian Political Service, 1936; Under-Secretary, Political Dept, 1942-45; Chief Minister, Manipur State, 1945-47; retired, 1947. MP (C) Clitheroe, Oct. 1959-1970; Assistant Whip (unpaid), 1960-62; a Lord Commissioner of the Treasury, 1962-63; PPS to Prime Minister, Nov. 1963-Oct. 1964. JP Lancs, 1952. *Recreation:* fishing. *Heir:* *s* Francis Nicholas Fraser Pearson, *b* 28 Aug. 1943. *Address:* Gressingham Hall, Hornby, Lancs. *T:* Hornby 288. *Club:* Carlton.

**PEARSON, Hon. Sir Glen (Gardner),** Kt 1970; JP; *b* 19 Feb. 1907; *s* of Thomas and Julia Pearson; *m* 1932, Mavis Doreen Croxton; two *s* one *d* (and one *d* decd in infancy). *Educ:* State Schs; Prince Alfred Coll., Adelaide. Sen. Public Certif., 1922. Farming: Yorke's Peninsula, 1923-35; Eyre Peninsula, 1935-. Executive, SA Wheatgrowers Assoc., 1938-51; Mem., Aust. Barley Bd, 1948-56. MHA for Flinders, SA House of Assembly, 1951-70, retd; Minister: of Agriculture and of Forests, 1956-58; of Works and of Marine, 1958-65, also of Aboriginal Affairs, 1962-65, and Dep. Leader, House of Assembly, 1960-65; Dep. Leader of Opposition, 1965-68; Treasurer and Minister of Housing (with prefix Hon.) also Dep. Leader, House of Assembly, SA, 1968-March 1970, and retd from public life, May 1970; served on many local bodies and as Pres. and Sec. of sporting bodies, also sub branch of RS League (Mem.). JP, Cockaleechie, 1948. *Recreations:* cricket, football, tennis; latterly bowls. *Address:* Cockaleechie, SA 5610, Australia. *T:* Cockaleechie 54. *Clubs:* Royal Commonwealth Society; Masonic (SA).

**PEARSON, Air Commodore Herbert Macdonald,** CBE 1944; RAF retired; *b* Buenos Aires, Argentina, 17 Nov. 1908; *s* of John Charles Pearson; *m* 1939, Jane Leslie; one *s* two *d*. *Educ:* Cheltenham Coll.; Cranwell. Left Cranwell, 1928; Malta, 1929-31; Central Flying Sch., 1932; Instructor, Cranwell, 1933-34; attached to Peruvian Government, 1935-36; Asst Air Attaché in Spain, 1936-38; comd No. 54 Sqdn, 1938-39. War of 1939-45, in Fighter Command; then France, Belgium and Germany; Air Attaché, Lima, Peru, 1946; Deputy Director Air Foreign Liaison, Air Ministry, 1949; Commanding Royal Air Force, Kai Tak, Hong Kong, 1951-53; Assistant Chief of Staff Intelligence, Headquarters of Allied Air Forces, Central Europe, 1953-55. Air Commodore, 1953; retired, 1955. *Address:* Mapleridge Barn, Horton, S Glos. *Club:* Canning.

**PEARSON, Sir (James) Denning,** Kt 1963; JP; Chairman and Chief Executive, Rolls-Royce Ltd, since 1969; *b* 8 Aug. 1908; *s* of James Pearson and Elizabeth Henderson; *m* 1932, Eluned Henry; two *d*. *Educ:* Canton Secondary Sch., Cardiff; Cardiff Technical Coll. Senior Wh. Scholarship; BSc Eng. Joined Rolls-Royce Ltd, 1932; Technical Production Engineer, Glasgow Factory, 1941; Chief Quality and Service Engineer (resident in Canada for one year), 1941-45; Gen. Man. Sales and Service, 1946-49; Director, 1949; Director and Gen. Man., Aero Engine Division, 1950; Managing Director (Aero Engine Div.), 1954-65; Chief Exec. and Dep. Chm., 1957-68. President, SBAC, 1963; Member, NEDC, 1964-67. CEng;

FRAeS, 1957-64, Hon. FRAeS, 1964; Hon. FIMechE; FBIM; MIProdE; DrIngEh Brunswick Univ., 1962. Member: Council, Manchester Business Sch.; Governing Body, London Graduate Sch. of Business Studies; Governing Body, Admin. Staff Coll., Henley; Council, Voluntary Service Overseas. Fellow, Imperial Coll. of Science and Technology, 1968-; Hon. Fellow, Manchester Univ. Inst. of Science and Technology, 1969; Hon. DSc: Nottingham, 1966; Wales, 1968; Cranfield Inst. of Technology, 1970; Hon. DTech: Loughborough, 1968; CNAA, 1969. Gold Medal, Royal Aero Club, 1969; Benjamin Franklin Medal, RSA, 1970. FRSA, 1970. *Recreations:* reading, golf, tennis, sailing. *Address:* Holbrook, Derbyshire. *T:* Derby 881137.

**PEARSON, Sir (James) Reginald,** Kt 1959; OBE 1950; DL; retired in Nov. 1962 as Deputy Chairman (1958) and Executive Assistant to Managing Director (1953), Vauxhall Motors Ltd, Luton, Beds; *b* 17 Nov. 1897; *s* of George Henry Pearson and Annie Pearson (*née* Stringer); *m* 1925, Nellie Rose Vittery; one *d*. *Educ:* Dudley, Worcestershire. Apprenticed at Bullers Ltd, Tipton; National Projectile Factory, Dudley; Vauxhall Motors Ltd (1919); Craftsman, Journeyman, Foreman, Area Manager, Production Manager, Factory Manager, Director (1946). Chairman, Dawley Development Corporation, 1962-68. Fellow of Inst. of Directors; Vice-President, Royal Society for the Prevention of Accidents; Member, Board of Governors of Luton Coll. of Technology. President, Industrial Orthopædic Society. High Sheriff of Bedfordshire, 1964; DL Herts, 1968. FIMechE; MIProdE. *Recreations:* golf, gardening; interested in all forms of sport; Hon. Life President, Vauxhall Motors Recreation Club. *Address:* 45 Bloomfield Road, Harpenden, Herts. *T:* Harpenden 3052. *Club:* Royal Automobile.

**PEARSON, Joseph,** DSc (Manchester, Liverpool, Tasmania); FRSE, FLS; *b* 19 April 1881; *s* of Daniel Pearson and Cecilia Parr; *m* 1st, Lilla (*d* 1941), *o d* of Thomas McConnell, Dunboyne, Larne; (two *s* died on active service, War of 1939-45); 2nd, Mavis (*d* 1961), *d* of Frank Meadowcroft, Wellington, New Zealand. *Educ:* Liverpool Coll.; University College, Liverpool; Victoria Univ. 1st class Hons, BSc, Victoria University Scholarship, 1902; MSc, Liverpool, 1905; DSc Liverpool, 1908; MSc Manchester, 1921; DSc Manchester, 1922; DSc Tasmania, 1935; Naturalist to Ulster Fisheries and Biology Assoc., 1903; Asst Lecturer in Zoology, University College, Cardiff, 1904; Lecturer in Zoology, University of Liverpool, 1905-10; Director Colombo Museum, 1910-34; Marine Biologist to Ceylon Government, 1910-34; Inspector of Pearl Banks, 1925-34; Lecturer in Biology in Ceylon Medical Coll., 1910-20; Lecturer in Zoology, University College, Colombo, 1920-24; Acting Archæological Commissioner, 1929-31; Chairman of Commission of Enquiry into the Industries of Ceylon; Director Tasmanian Museum and Art Gallery, 1934-52; Emeritus Director, Tasmanian Museum and Art Gallery, 1952; Member, Australian National Research Council; Fellow Inst. of Biology; President, Section D (Zoology) of Australian and New Zealand Assoc. for the Advancement of Science, 1946; Hon. Member, Royal Society of Tasmania; Comr of International Commission on Zoological Nomenclature, 1946-54; Lieut, RGA, European War, 1914-18; served in Ceylon and France, 1915-19. *Publications:* editor of The Ceylon Journal of Science and Spolia Zeylanica, 1910-34; Editor of Proceedings of Royal Society of Tasmania, 1934-52; has written numerous scientific papers on Marine Biology, Zoology, Comparative Anatomy of the Marsupialia, and Ecology; articles on Archæology and Dutch Colonial furniture. *Address:* c/o Mrs Amy Derksen, Brantholme, Low Langstaffe, Sedbergh, Yorks.

**PEARSON, Rt. Hon. Lester Bowles,** CC (Canada), 1968; PC 1963; PC (Canada), 1948; OBE 1935; MA Oxon; BA Oxon and Toronto; Chairman, Commission on International Development, 1968-69; *b* Toronto, Ont, 23 April 1897; *s* of Rev. Edwin Arthur Pearson and Annie Sarah (Bowles) Pearson; *m* 1925, Maryon Elspeth Moody, Winnipeg; one *s* one *d*. *Educ:* Collegiate Inst. Peterborough and Hamilton, Ont; University of Toronto; St John's Coll., Oxford. Lecturer in Modern History, University of Toronto, 1926-28, Asst Professor, 1926-28; 1st Secretary Dept of External Affairs, 1928; special missions to Washington, London, The Hague, Geneva and throughout Canada; 1st Secretary London Office of High Commr for Canada, 1935-39; appointed Secretary with rank of Counsellor, 1939; Assistant Under-Secretary of State for External Affairs, Ottawa, 1941; Minister-Counsellor, Canadian Embassy, Washington, 1942-45; Ambassador to Washington, 1945-46; Under-Secretary of State for External Affairs, Ottawa, 1946-48; MP (L) Algoma East Ont, Oct. 1948-68; Sec. of State for External Affairs, 1948-57; Leader of the Opposition in Parlt, 1958-63; Leader, Liberal Party of Canada, 1963-68; Prime Minister, 1963-68. One of senior advisers at San Francisco Conference, April-June 1945, that drew up UN Charter and Leader of Canadian delegations to subsequent meetings of UN General Assembly; President General Assembly of UN, 1952-53. Represented Canadian Prime Minister at meeting of Commonwealth Prime Ministers, London, 1949; Chairman, Canadian delegns: Commonwealth Meeting on Foreign Affairs, Colombo, 1950; Japanese Peace Treaty Conf., San Francisco, 1951; 9-Power Conf. on German Rearmament, London, Sept. 1954; Geneva Conference, 1954. Represented Canada at signing of North Atlantic Treaty in Washington and has headed Canadian delegations to subs. North Atlantic Council Meetings (Chairman Council, 1951-52). President: North Atlantic Treaty Assoc., 1957; Inst. for Strategic Studies, 1968-. Chancellor: Victoria Univ., Toronto, 1951-58; Carleton Univ., Ottawa, 1968-. Awarded the Nobel Peace Prize for 1957. Reith Lecturer, 1968. Holds hon. degrees of 49 universities; Hon. Fellow: St John's Coll., Oxford; Weizmann Inst. of Science, 1968. Hon. DCL, Oxford; Hon. Fellow, RAIC; Hon. Freeman, City of London, 1967. *Publications:* Democracy in World Politics (Stafford Little Lectures: publ. Canada, 1955, Great Britain, 1956); Diplomacy in the Nuclear Age, 1959; Peace in the Family of Man, 1968 (Reith Lectures); The Crisis of Development, 1970 (Leffingwell Lectures). *Address:* (home) 541 Montagu Place, Rockcliffe Park, Ottawa, Ont, Canada; (office) Suite 907, 75 Albert Street, Ottawa 4, Ont, Canada. *Clubs:* Athenæum; Rideau (Ottawa).

**PEARSON, Sir Neville,** 2nd Bt *cr* 1916; *b* 13 Feb. 1898; *s* of 1st Bt, and Ethel Lady Pearson, DBE; *S* father, 1921; *m* 1st, 1922, Mary Angela (marriage dissolved, 1928, she *m* 1928, C. Willoughby Hordern and *d* 1937), 2nd *d* of 1st Baron Melchett; one *s* one *d*; 2nd, 1928, Gladys Cooper (*see* Dame Gladys Cooper), (marriage dissolved 1937; she *m* 1937, Philip Merivale); one *d*; 3rd, 1943, Mrs Anne Davis Elebash,

New York. *Educ:* Eton. RFA, European War, 1917-18; subsequently entered firm of C. Arthur Pearson, Ltd; publishers; retired from all directorships, 1968. President St Dunstan's; President Fresh Air Fund. AA Artillery, War of 1939-45. *Recreation:* gardening. *Heir: s* Nigel Arthur Pearson [*b* 30 Aug. 1925; *m* 1956, Frances Elizabeth Ann Hay, *y d* of 11th Marquess of Tweeddale]. *Address:* 7 Cheyne Walk, SW3. *T:* 01-352 6116. *Clubs:* Garrick, Bath.
*See also Rt Hon. M. A. C. Noble.*

**PEARSON, Norman Charles,** OBE 1944; TD 1944; Lay Member, Restrictive Practices Court, since 1968; Director: United Kingdom Provident Institution since 1965; Swift & Co. Ltd, Ashfield, NSW, since 1969; *b* 12 Aug. 1909; *s* of late Max Pearson and Kate Pearson; *m* 1951, Olive May, *d* of late Kenneth Harper, Granston Manor, Co. Leix; one *s* one *d. Educ:* Harrow Sch. (Scholar); Gonville and Caius Coll., Cambridge (Sayer Scholar). Boots Pure Drug Co. Ltd, 1931-37; Borax (Holdings) Ltd, 1937-69; Director, 1951. Commnd Royal Signals (TA), 1932; Middx Yeomanry; served War of 1939-45, N Africa (despatches), Italy, Greece; Lt-Col 1942; comd 6th Armd Div. Signals, 1944; 10 Corps Signals; Mil. Comd Athens Signals; 4th Div. Signals, 1945; subseq. re-formed 56 Div. Signals Regt (TA). *Recreation:* gardening. *Address:* 61 Albert Hall Mansions, SW7. *T:* 01-589 7585; Copt Heath, Cold Ash, Newbury, Berks. *Club:* Junior Carlton.

**PEARSON, Mrs R. O'Neill;** *see* Robins, Mrs Denise.

**PEARSON, Sir Reginald;** *see* Pearson, Sir J. R.

**PEARSON, Rupert Samuel Bruce,** DM Oxon; FRCP; Senior Physician, Queen Elizabeth Hospital, Bridgetown, Barbados; retired as Physician King's College Hospital and Woolwich Group of Hospitals; Examiner in Medicine: Royal College of Physicians; London University; *b* 8 Sept. 1904; *s* of late Dr Bruce Pearson, Buckingham; *m* 1939, Mary Katherine Elizabeth Aldworth (*d* 1958); one *s* one *d*; *m* 1962, Joyce Mary Barmby (*née* Strange). *Educ:* Charterhouse; Trinity Coll., Oxford; Guy's Hospital, Treasurer's Gold Medal, 1929; House Physician, Guy's Hospital, 1929; Med. Registrar, Guy's Hosp., 1930-33; Out-Patient Medical Registrar, Hosp. for Sick Children, Great Ormond St, 1933-35; Asst Clinical Research Unit, Guy's Hosp., 1935 and 1936; Asst Physician, Hampstead General Hospital, 1937. Councillor, RCP, 1962-65. Examiner in Medicine, Oxford Univ., 1959-65. Member: Assoc. of Physicians of Gt Brit.; Brit. Soc. of Gastro-enterology; British Allergy Soc. *Publications:* contribs to Arch. Dis. Child, Quarterly Jl of Med., Proc. Roy. Soc. Med., BMJ, Lancet. *Recreations:* gardening, golf, croquet. *Address:* The Spinney, Hurtmore, Godalming, Surrey. *T:* Godalming 21349.

**PEARSON, Rt. Rev. Thomas Bernard;** Titular Bishop of Sinda, since 1949; Bishop Auxiliary in the Diocese of Lancaster, 1952-62, and since 1965; Episcopal Vicar for Cumberland, Westmorland and Furness, since 1967; *b* Preston, lancs, 18 January 1907; *s* of Joseph Pearson and Alice (*née* Cartmell). *Educ:* Upholland College; Ven. English College, Rome. Pontifical Gregorian University, Rome; PhD 1930; Bachelor of Canon Law, Licent. Sacred Theology, 1933. Priest, 1933; Assistant Priest, 1934-44; Parish Priest, St Cuthbert's, Blackpool, 1944-67. *Recreation:* mountaineering. *Address:* St Herbert's, Windermere, Westmorland. *T:* Windermere 3402. *Clubs:* Alpine, Fell and Rock, English Lake District; Achille Ratti Climbing (Founder President).

**PEARSON, Lt-Gen. Sir Thomas (Cecil Hook),** KCB 1967 (CB 1964); CBE 1959 (OBE 1953); DSO 1940, and Bar, 1943; Military Secretary, Ministry of Defence, since 1968; *b* 1 July 1914; *s* of late Vice-Admiral J. L. Pearson, CMG; *m* 1947, Aud, *d* of late Alf Skjelkvale, Oslo; two *s. Educ:* Charterhouse; Sandhurst. 2nd Lieutenant Rifle Bde, 1934. Served War of 1939-45, M East and Europe; CO 2nd Bn The Rifle Bde, 1942; Dep. Comdr 2nd Independent Parachute Bde Gp 1944; Dep. Comdr 1st Air-landing Bde 1945; GSO1 1st Airborne Div. 1945; CO 1st Bn The Parachute Regt 1946; CO 7th Bn The Parachute Regt 1947; GSO1 (Land Air Warfare), WO, 1948; JSSC, GSO1, HQ Malaya, 1950; GSO1 (Plans), FARELF, 1951; Directing Staff, JSSC, 1953; Comdr 45 Parachute Bde TA 1955; Nat. Defence Coll., Canada, 1956; Comdr 16 Indep. Parachute Bde 1957; Chief of Staff to Dir of Ops Cyprus, 1960; Head of Brit. Mil. Mission to Soviet Zone of Germany, 1960; Major-General Commanding 1st Division, BAOR, 1961-63; Chief of Staff, Northern Army Group, 1963-67; Comdr, FARELF, 1967-68; psc 1942; jssc 1950; ndc Canada 1957. Haakon VII Liberty Cross, 1948. *Recreations:* field sports, yachting. *Address:* c/o Lloyds Bank Ltd, 6 Pall Mall, SW1. *Clubs:* Naval and Military; Island Sailing.

**PEARSON, William,** MD, MCh, FRCSI; lately Professor of Surgery, University of Dublin; *b* Cork, 7 May 1882; *er s* of late Professor Charles Yelverton Pearson; *m* 1927, Esther Margaret, *yr d* of late Arthur H. Hurford, Dublin and Belfast; one *s. Educ:* Cork Grammar School; Trinity College Dublin; USA; Berlin. First place in all Arts Examinations, with First Respondency at BA Degree; first place in all examinations in the School of Physic, Trinity College, Dublin; Trinity College Scholarship in Anatomy and Institutes of Medicine; Fitzpatrick Scholarship; Surgical Travelling Prize and Bennett Medal: Haughton Clinical Medal and Prize for Surgery, Sir P. Dun's Hosp.; Consulting Surgeon, Sir P. Dun's Hospital; Consulting Surgeon, Adelaide Hospital, Dublin; Past President, Royal Coll. of Surgeons in Ireland; sometime Surgeon to Meath Hospital and County Dublin Infirmary; Temporary Major, Surgical Specialist and District Consulting Surgeon RAMC; Visiting and Operating Surgeon, British Ministry of Pensions Special Surgical Hospital, Co. Dublin; holds several Honorary Surgical appts. *Publications:* Numerous contributions to Surgical Journals, especially in connection with the Surgery of Bone and the Thyroid Gland. *Recreations:* yachting, fishing, (salmon and trout). *Address:* 24 Lakelands Park, Terenure, Dublin. *T:* Dublin 900066. *Clubs:* Kildare Street (Dublin); Royal St George Yacht (Kingstown).

**PEART, Donald Richard,** MA, BMus Oxon, FRCM; composer, conductor, violinist; Professor of Music, University of Sydney, New South Wales, since 1948; founder and President of Pro Musica Society, Sydney University; *b* Fovant, Wilts, 9 Jan. 1909; *s* of Herbert and Dorothy Peart, Welling Hill, Haslemere, Surrey; *m* Ellen Lilian, *d* of W. H. Germon; one *s* one *d. Educ:* Cheltenham College (Scholar); Queen's College, Oxford (Bible Clerk). Osgood Memorial Prizeman, University of Oxford, 1932; studied at Royal College of Music, 1932-35; Librarian, 1935-39. War service, 1939-46; commissioned into The Gloucestershire Regt, 1940; served in W

Africa, Burma, and India, 1942-46. Mem., Australian UNESCO Cttee for Music; Pres., Internat. Soc. for Contemp. Music (Australian Section) and of Musicological Society of Australia. Works include: two symphonies; cantata Red Night; string quartets, etc. *Recreations:* travelling, mountain climbing, etc. *Address:* The University of Sydney, Sydney, NSW 2006, Australia. *T:* 6600522.

**PEART, Rt. Hon. Frederick;** *see* Peart, Rt Hon. T. F.

**PEART, Rt. Hon. (Thomas) Frederick,** PC 1964; MP (Lab) Workington Division of Cumberland since 1945; *b* 30 Apr. 1914; *m* 1945, Sarah Elizabeth Lewis; one *s. Educ:* Crook Council; Wolsingham Grammar; Henry Smith Secondary, Hartlepool; Bede Coll., Durham Univ. (BSc); Inner Temple, Inns of Court. Pres. Durham University Union Soc. Councillor Easington RDC, 1937-40. Became a Schoolmaster. Served War of 1939-45, commissioned Royal Artillery, served in North Africa and Italy. PPS to Minister of Agriculture, 1945-51; Minister of Agriculture, Fisheries and Food, 1964-68; Leader of the House of Commons, 1968-70; Lord Privy Seal, April-Oct. 1968; Lord President of the Council, Oct. 1968-1970. Formerly British Delegate to Council of Europe, and Rep. Agriculture Cttee and Cttee for Culture and Science (Vice-Pres.). Privy Council Rep. on Council of RCVS. *Address:* House of Commons, SW1.

**PEART, Prof. William Stanley,** MD; FRS 1969; Professor of Medicine, University of London, at St Mary's Hospital Medical School since 1956; *b* 31 March 1922; *s* of J. G. and M. Peart; *m* 1947, Peggy Parkes; one *s* one *d. Educ:* King's College School, Wimbledon; Medical School, St Mary's Hospital. MB, BS (Hons), 1945; FRCP, 1959; MD (London), 1949. Lecturer in Medicine, St Mary's Hospital, 1950-56. Mem., MRC. Goulstonian Lectr, RCP, 1959. Chm., Medical Research Soc.; President: Section of Experimental Medicine and Therapeutics, RSM; Renal Assoc. Stouffer Prize, 1968. *Publications:* chapters in: Cecil-Loeb, Textbook of Medicine; Renal Disease; Biochemical Disorders in Human Disease; articles in Biochemical Journal, Journal of Physiology, Lancet. *Recreations:* reading, tennis. *Address:* 5 Fordington Road, N6. *T:* 01-883 9346.

**PEASE,** family name of **Barons Daryngton, Gainford,** and **Wardington.**

**PEASE, Sir (Alfred) Vincent,** 4th Bt *cr* 1882; *b* 2 April 1926; *s* of Sir Alfred (Edward) Pease, 2nd Bt (*d* 1939), and of his 3rd wife, Emily Elizabeth (Dowager Lady Pease, JP); *S* half-brother, 1963; unmarried. *Educ:* Bootham School, York. *Heir: b* Joseph Gurney Pease [*b* 16 Nov. 1927; *m* 1953, Shelagh Munro, *d* of C. G. Bulman; one *s* one *d*]. *Address:* Baysdale Cottage, Pinchinthorpe, Guisborough, Yorkshire. *T:* Guisborough 2578.

**PEASE, Dr Rendel Sebastian;** Director, Culham Laboratory, UKAEA, since 1968; *b* 1922; *s* of Michael Stewart Pease and Helen Bowen (*née* Wedgwood); *m* 1952, Susan Spickernell; two *s* three *d. Educ:* Bedales Sch.; Trinity Coll., Cambridge (MA, ScD). Scientific Officer, Min. of Aircraft Prodn at ORS Unit, HQ, RAF Bomber Comd, 1942-46; research at AERE, Harwell, 1947-61; Div. Head, Culham Lab. for Plasma Physics and Nuclear Fusion, UKAEA, 1961-67; Vis. Scientist, Princeton Univ., 1964-65; Asst Dir, UKAEA Research Gp, 1967. Member: Fabian Soc.; Inst. of Physics and Physical Soc.; Amer. Inst. of Physics. *Publications:* articles in physics jls. *Recreation:* music. *Address:* The Poplars, West Ilsley, Newbury, Berks.

**PEASE, Sir Richard (Thorn),** 3rd Bt *cr* 1920; Vice-Chairman, Barclays Bank Ltd, since 1970; *b* 20 May 1922; *s* of Sir Richard Arthur Pease, 2nd Bt, and Jeannette Thorn (*d* 1957), *d* of late Gustav Edward Kissel, New York; *S* father, 1969; *m* 1956, Anne, *d* of late Lt-Col Reginald Francis Heyworth; one *s* two *d. Educ:* Eton. Served with 60th Rifles, Middle East, Italy and Greece, 1941-46. *Heir: s* Richard Peter Pease, *b* 4 Sept. 1958. *Address:* Hindley House, Stocksfield-on-Tyne, Northumberland.

**PEASE, Sir Vincent;** *see* Pease, Sir A. V.

**PEAT, Charles Urie,** MC; MA, FCA; *b* 1892; *s* of late Sir Wm Barclay Peat, CVO; *m* 1914, Ruth Martha, *d* of Rev. Henry John Pulley; two *s* four *d. Educ:* Sedbergh; Oxford. Served European War, 1914-19; MP (U) Darlington, 1931-45; Parliamentary Private Secretary to Mr Oliver Lyttelton, President of Board of Trade, 1941; Joint Parliamentary Secretary, Ministry of Supply, 1942-45; Parliamentary Secretary, Ministry of National Insurance, April 1945. Pres. Inst. of Chartered Accountants in England and Wales, 1959-60. *Address:* 11 Ironmonger Lane, EC2. *T:* 01-606 8888; Wycliffe Hall, Barnard Castle. *T:* Whorlton 241. *Club:* Carlton.

**PEATE, Dr Iorwerth Cyfeiliog,** FSA; Curator, Welsh Folk Museum, 1948-71; *b* 1901; *y s* of George Howard Peate and Elizabeth Peate, Llanbryn-Mair, Mont.; *m* 1929, Nansi, *d* of David and Rachel Davies, Eglwys-fach, Card.; one *s. Educ:* Llanbryn-Mair Sch.; Machynlleth Intermed. Sch.; Univ. Coll. of Wales, Aberystwyth. MA 1924; DSc 1941. Staff Tutor, Univ. Coll. of Wales, Aberystwyth, 1924-27; Nat. Mus. of Wales, Cardiff: Asst Keeper, Dept of Archæology, 1927-32; Asst Keeper i/c Dept of Folk Culture and Industries, 1932-36; Keeper, Dept of Folk Life, 1936-48. Ellis Gruffydd Prizeman, Univ. Wales, 1943; G. T. Clark Prizeman, Cambrian Archæol. Assoc., 1946; Pres., Sect. H (Anthrop.), Brit. Assoc. for Advancement of Science, 1958; Mem. Coun., British Assoc., 1961-66; Ed. of Gwerin, Internat. Jl of Folk Life, 1956-62; Pres., Soc. of Folk-Life Studies, 1961-66; a Vice-Pres., Hon. Soc. of Cymmrodorion; Pres., Cymrodoriaeth Powys. FRAI. Hon. DLitt Celt., Nat. Univ. of Ireland, 1960; Hon. Dlitt Wales, 1970. *Publications:* Y Cawg Aur, 1928; Welsh Bygones, 1929; Cymru a'i Phobl, 1931; Y Crefftwr yng Nghymru, 1933; Plu'r Gweunydd, 1933; Welsh Folk Crafts and Industries, 1935; Sylfeini, 1938; The Welsh House, 1940; Diwylliant Gwerin Cymru, 1942; Clock and Watch Makers in Wales, 1945; Y Deyrnas Goll, 1947; Ym Mhob Pen, 1948; Folk Museums, 1948; Canu Chwarter Canrif, 1957; Syniadau, 1969; *edited:* Studies in Regional Consciousness and Environment, 1930; Hen Gapel Llanbryn-Mair, 1939; Ysgrifau John Breese Davies, 1949; Cilhaul ac Ysgrifau eraill gan Samuel Roberts, 1961. *Address:* Maes-y-coed, St Nicholas, Glam. *T:* Peterston-super-Ely 574.

**PECHELL, Lt-Col Sir Paul,** 8th Bt, *cr* 1797; MC; late Essex Regt and Royal Pioneer Corps; *b* 10 Dec. 1889; *s* of Sir Augustus Brooke-Pechell, 7th Bt; *S* father, 1937; *m* 1920, Helen Gertrude (*d* 1959), 2nd *d* of Rev. J. D. Todd, Newton, Lincs. *Educ:* Malvern; RMC, Sandhurst. Served European War, 1914-19 (wounded, MC, Bt Major) and War of 1939-45; Pres. Hampshire, I of W and Channel Isles Golf

Union, 1951-63. *Recreations:* golf, gardening. *Heir presumptive:* kinsman Ronald Horace Pechell [*b* 4 June 1918; *m* 1949, Dora, *d* of John Crampthorne]. *Address:* Flat 1, 35 Talbot Avenue, Winton, Bournemouth, Hants. *T:* Bournemouth 55553. *Club:* Golfers'. *See also Lt-Col B. Dobrée.*

**PECK, Antony Dilwyn,** CB 1965; MBE 1945; Second Secretary, Board of Trade, since 1968; *b* 10 April 1914; *s* of late Sir James Peck, CB, and late Lady Peck; *m* 1st, 1939, Joan de Burgh Whyte (*d* 1955); one *s* one *d*; 2nd, 1956, Sylvia Glenister; one *s* two *d*. *Educ:* Eton; Trinity College, Oxford. Fellow of Trinity College, 1938-46. Served War of 1939-45, Army, 1940-46 (Major). Joined Treasury as Principal, 1946; Asst Secretary, 1950; Under-Secretary, 1959; Dep. Under-Sec. of State, MoD, 1963-68. *Recreations:* tennis, bridge. *Address:* 45 Argyll Road, W8. *T:* 01-937 2869. *Clubs:* Reform, Hurlingham.

**PECK, Arthur Leslie,** MA, PhD; Fellow of Christ's College, Cambridge, since 1926, and Librarian; Vice-Master, 1957-61; University Lecturer; Public Orator, University of Cambridge, 1965-66; Member Institute for Advanced Study, Princeton, NJ, 1963-64; Governor of Perse School since 1929 (Chairman since 1967); Member Committee, GBA, 1966; Vice-President Hymn Society of Great Britain and Ireland; President Morris Ring (Federation of Morris Men's Clubs), 1947-50; Member Executive Committee English Folk Dance and Song Society, 1947-51; *b* 1902. *Educ:* Perse School; Christ's College, Cambridge (scholar). Craven Univ. Scholar, 1923; Chancellor's Classical Medal, 1924; Prendergast University Student, 1924; temp. appt with Ministry of Food, 1942-45. *Publications:* Papers, etc., in classical periodicals and in journals of the English Folk Dance and Song Soc.; Aristotle, De partibus animalium, revised text and trans. (Loeb Library), 1937, revised edns 1945, 1957; Aristotle, De generatione animalium, revised text and translation (Loeb Library), 1943, revised edn, 1953; Aristotle, Historia animalium, vol. i, revised text and translation (Loeb Library), 1965, vol. ii, revised text and translation, 1970; The Church in Barnwell (a centenary memorial), 1939; This Church of Christ, 1955; Anglicanism and Episcopacy, 1958; The Book of Hours (Eng. verse trans. of R. M. Rilke's Stundenbuch), 1961. *Address:* Christ's College, Cambridge. *T:* Cambridge 59601.

**PECK, David (Edward); His Honour Judge Peck;** Judge of County Courts since Oct. 1969; *b* 6 April 1917; *m* 1950, Rosina Seton Glover Marshall; one *s* three *d*. *Educ:* Charterhouse School; Balliol College, Oxford. Served Army (Cheshire Regiment), 1939-46. Called to Bar, Middle Temple, 1949. *Address:* Odintune Place, Plumpton, Sussex.

**PECK, Sir Edward (Heywood),** KCMG 1966 (CMG 1957); Permanent British Representative to North Atlantic Council, since 1970; *b* 5 Oct. 1915; *s* of Lt-Col Edward Surman Peck, IMS, and Doris Louise Heywood; *m* 1948, Alison Mary MacInnes; one *s* two *d*. *Educ:* Clifton College; The Queen's College, Oxford. 1st Cl. Hons (Mod. Langs), 1937; Laming Travelling Fellow, 1937-38. Entered Consular Service, 1938; served in Barcelona, 1938-39; Foreign Office, 1939-40; Sofia, 1940; Ankara, 1940-44; Adana, 1944; Iskenderun, 1945; Salonica, 1945-47; with UK Deleg. to UN Special Commn on the Balkans, 1947; Foreign Office, 1947-50; seconded to UK High Commissioner's Office, Delhi, 1950-52; Counsellor, Foreign Office, 1952-55; Dep. Comdt, Brit. Sector, Berlin, 1955-58; on staff of UK Commissioner-General for S-E Asia, 1959-60; Assistant Under-Secretary of State, Foreign Office, 1961-66; British High Commissioner in Kenya, 1966-68; Dep. Under-Secretary of State, FCO, 1968-70. *Recreations:* mountaineering and ski-ing. *Address:* 19 The Rise, Sevenoaks, Kent. *Club:* Alpine.

**PECK, Gregory;** Film Actor, US, since 1943; *b* 5 April 1916; *s* of Gregory P. Peck and Bernice Ayres; *m* 1st, 1942, Greta Konen Rice (marr. diss. 1954); three *s*; 2nd, 1955, Veronique Passani; one *s* one *d*. *Educ:* Calif Public Schools; Univ. of Calif (BA). Broadway stage, 1941-43. *Films:* Days of Glory, 1943; Keys of the Kingdom, Valley of Decision, 1944; Spellbound, 1945; Duel in the Sun, The Yearling, 1946; The Macomber Affair, Gentlemen's Agreement, 1947; The Paradine Case, 1948; Yellow Sky, The Great Sinner, Twelve O'Clock High, 1949; The Gun Fighter, 1950; Only the Valiant, Captain Horatio Hornblower, David and Bathsheba, 1951; The World in his Arms, 1952; The Snows of Kilimanjaro, 1952; Roman Holiday, 1953; The Million Pound Note, 1953; Night People, 1954; The Purple Plain, 1954; The Man in the Grey Flannel Suit, 1956; Moby Dick, 1956; Designing Woman, 1957; The Bravados, 1958; The Big Country (co-producer), 1958; Pork Chop Hill, 1959; On the Beach, 1959; Guns of Navarone, 1960; Cape Fear, 1961; To Kill a Mocking Bird, 1962; Captain Newman, MD, 1963; Behold a Pale Horse, 1964; Mirage, 1965; Arabesque, 1965; Mackenna's Gold, 1967; The Chairman, 1968; The Stalking Moon, 1968; The Most Dangerous Man in the World, 1969; Marooned, 1970. Nat. Chm., Amer. Cancer Soc., 1966. Mem., Nat. Council on Arts, 1965-67, 1968-; Pres., Acad. Motion Pictures Arts and Sciences, 1967-70; Chm., Board of Trustees, Amer. Film Inst., 1967-69. Medal of Freedom Award, 1969; Jean Hersholt Humanitarian Award, Acad. of Motion Picture Arts and Sciences, 1968. *Recreations:* riding, swimming, baseball. *Address:* 1041 North Formosa Avenue, Los Angeles, Calif 90046, USA. *Club:* Players (New York).

**PECK, Jasper Augustine,** CMG 1965; *b* 14 July 1905; *s* of late John Herbert Peck, Lt-Col Indian Army, and late Margaret Jane Ada Batt; *m* 1939, Olwen, *d* of late Eliot Crawshay-Williams; no *c*. *Educ:* Westminster (King's Scholar); Univ. Coll., Oxford (Scholar). Called to Bar, Inner Temple, 1930; practised, 1930-39. War Service, Gunner, 86th (HAC) HAA Regt, RA, TA, Major (DAAG), Mil. Dept., Judge Advocate-General's Office, 1939-45. Entered Colonial Office, Sept. 1945; Asst Legal Adviser, Colonial Office, 1950-65, retd. *Recreations:* ornithology, music. *Address:* 50 Saxmundham Road, Aldeburgh, Suffolk. *T:* Aldeburgh 2429. *Club:* Garrick.

**PECK, John Howard,** CMG 1956; HM Diplomatic Service; Ambassador to the Republic of Ireland, since 1970; *b* Kuala Lumpur, 16 Feb. 1913; *o s* of late Howard and Dorothea Peck; *m* 1939, Mariska Caroline, *e d* of Josef Somlo; two *s*. *Educ:* Wellington College; CCC, Oxford. Assistant Private Secretary to First Lord of Admiralty, 1937-39; to Minister for Coordination of Defence, 1939-40; to the Prime Minister, 1940-46; transferred to Foreign Service, 1946; served in United Nations Dept, 1946-47; in The Hague, 1947-50; Counsellor and Head of Information Research Dept, 1951-54; Counsellor (Defence Liaison) and Head of Political Division, British Middle East Office, 1954-56; Director-General of British Information Services, New York, 1956-59; UK Permanent Representative to the Council of Europe, and Consul-General,

Strasbourg, 1959-62; Ambassador to Senegal, 1962-66, and Mauritania, 1962-65; Asst Under-Sec. of State, FO, then FCO, 1966-70. *Publications:* various essays and light verse. *Recreations:* tennis, photography, landscape gardening. *Address:* British Embassy, Dublin, Ireland. *Clubs:* Travellers'; St Stephen's Green (Dublin).

**PECK, Stanley Edwards,** BEM 1954; DL; HM Inspector of Constabulary since October 1964; *b* 1916; *er s* of late Harold Edwards Peck, Edgbaston and Shanghai; *m* 1939, Yvonne Sydney Edwards, *er d* of late John Edwards Jessop, LDS; two *s* two *d. Educ:* Solihull School; Birmingham University. Served with RAF, 1941-45 (Flt-Lt). Joined Metropolitan Police, 1935; Chief Inspector and Supt, New Scotland Yard, 1950-54; Asst Chief Constable, Staffs, 1954-61; Chief Constable, Staffs, 1961-64. DL Staffs, 1962. Pres., Royal Life Saving Soc., UK. OStJ; Queen's Police Medal, 1964. *Recreations:* shooting and sailing. *Address:* Radcliffe Lodge, Radcliffe-on-Trent, Nottinghamshire. *Club:* RAF Reserves.

**PEDDER, Vice-Adm. Sir Arthur (Reid),** KBE 1959; CB 1956; retired as Commander, Allied Naval Forces, Northern Europe (1957-59); *b* 6 July 1904; *s* of late Sir John Pedder, KBE, CB; *m* 1934, Dulcie, *d* of O. L. Bickford; two *s*. *Educ:* Osborne and Dartmouth. Served in various ships, 1921-; qualified as Naval Observer, 1930; promoted Commander and appointed Admiralty, 1937-40; Executive Officer, HMS Mauritius, 1940-42; Admiralty Asst, Dir of Plans (Air), 1942-45; Capt. 1944; comd HM Ships Khedive and Phoebe, 1945-47; idc 1948; Admiralty (Dep. Dir of Plans), 1949-50; Fourth Naval Member of Australian Commonwealth Naval Board, 1950-52; Rear-Adm. 1953; Asst Chief of Naval Staff (Warfare), Admiralty, 1953-54; Flag Officer, Aircraft Carriers, December 1954-May 1956; Vice-Adm. 1956. *Recreations:* everything outdoors; produces 30 tons of beef a year off 80 acres. *Address:* Langhurst, Hascombe, Godalming, Surrey. *T:* Hascombe 294. *Club:* United Service.

**PEDDIE,** Baron *cr* 1961, of City and County of Kingston upon Hull (Life Peer); **James Mortimer Peddie,** MBE 1944; JP; Chairman, National Board for Prices and Incomes, 1970-71 (Member, 1965-71, Deputy Chairman, 1968-70); Chairman, Agrément Board since 1967; Director, TU Unit Trust, since 1965; *b* 4 April 1906; *s* of Crofton and Ethel Peddie; *m* 1931, Hilda Mary Alice Bull; one *s* one *d* (and one *d* decd). *Educ:* St Paul's Church Sch.; Hull Technical Coll.; London Sch. of Economics. Lecturer in Economics and Industrial Admin., Coll. of Commerce, 1928-39; Dir and Publicity Manager, Hull Co-operative Soc. Ltd; Min. of Information, 1940-45. Director (1945-65): CWS Ltd and Co-op. Insurance Soc. Ltd.; Co-op. Permanent Building Soc.; West Norfolk Fertiliser Co.; British Luma Lamp Co.; Travco Hotels Ltd; Governor, British Film Institute, 1948-54; Member, Colonial Office Advis. Cttee, 1950-62; Member Exec. Cttee, Co-op. Union, 1957-65; Chairman, Brit. Co-op. Political Party, 1958-65; Pres., Brit. Co-op. Congress, 1958; Mem., Nat. Coun. of Labour, 1958-65; Vice-Chm., Reith Commn on Advertising, 1965. Trustee and Exec. Mem., Civic Trust for Manchester and the North West, 1961-; Gov., Manchester Coll. of Commerce, 1962-; Industrial Arbitrator, Film Industry, 1964; Chairman: Adv. Cttee, Dept of Technical Co-operation, 1962-65; Adv. Cttee, Min. of Overseas Development, 1965; Post Office Users Nat. Council, 1969-; Mem., Consumer Council, 1963-68. Led Jt Parly delegations: Sweden, 1965; Finland, 1968. JP Cheshire, 1959-. LLD Manchester University, 1966. Hon. Citizen, Forth Worth, Texas, 1963. *Publications:* frequent contributor to jls on Economics and Political subjects. *Recreation:* golf, as an excuse for walking. *Address:* 20 The Ridings, Downs Road, Epsom, Surrey. *Clubs:* Royal Automobile; (Vice-Pres.) Springhead Park Golf (Hull).

**PEDDIE, Maj.-Gen. Graham,** CB 1959; DSO 1945; MBE 1941; *b* 15 Oct. 1905; *s* of late Graham Peddie and of Mrs Peddie; *m* 1937, Dorothy Mary Humfress (decd); one *s* one *d*; *m* 1959, Alexandra Mavrojani. *Educ:* Sherborne School, Royal Military Academy, Woolwich. Commissioned into RA, 1926; served in UK, 1926-30, in Egypt and Sudan, 1930-36; Instructor, RMA, Woolwich, 1937-39. War of 1939-45, in UK and NW Europe; 1st AA Group (Dep. Comd), 1948-50; idc, 1950-51. BAOR 1953-56; Director of Manpower Planning, War Office, 1957-60; retired, 1960. *Address:* Sundridge, Stratton, Cirencester, Glos. *Club:* Army and Navy.

**PEDDIE, John Ronald,** CBE 1937 (MBE 1918); MA 1909; DLitt 1927; FRSE 1942; FEIS 1947; Hon. LLD Glasgow, 1958; lately Secretary and Treasurer of the Carnegie Trust for the Universities of Scotland; retired December 1957; *b* 5 January 1887; *e s* of late Richard Dawes Peddie, Grangemouth; *m* 1914, Euphemia Scott Houston. *Educ:* Grangemouth High School; Glasgow University. Lecturer in English, Glasgow Univ., 1911-19; Official Adviser of Studies, Glasgow Univ. 1919-25; Executive Officer, National Committee for the Training of Teachers in Scotland, 1925-41; OC Glasgow University Contingent, Officers Training Corps, 1916-19; Examiner in English since 1911; a Gov. of Heriot-Watt Univ., Edinburgh, 1957-68; Hon. Treas. Roy. Soc. of Edinburgh, 1957-67; a Gov. of Merchiston Castle School; Trustee of the Cross Trust. Trustee of National Library of Scotland; Vice-President and Trustee of Society of Scottish Artists; Trustee of the Sir J. Donald Pollock Trusts; Chairman, Edinburgh Assoc. for the Provisions of Halls of Residence for Women Students. *Publications:* The Carnegie Trust; The First Fifty Years (1901-1951); Papers on literary and educational subjects. Editor, Glasgow University Roll of Honour. *Recreation:* gardening. *Address:* 7 Bruntsfield Terrace, Edinburgh 10. *T:* 031-229 6055. *Clubs:* New (Edinburgh); Mortonhall Golf.

**PEDLER, Sir Frederick (Johnson),** Kt 1969; Director, William Baird Ltd, 1968; Chairman, Council for Technical Education and Training for Overseas Countries since 1962; Member, Inter-University Council, 1968; *b* 10 July 1908; *s* of Charles Henry Pedler and Lucy Marian (*née* Johnson); *m* 1935, Esther Ruth Carling; two *s* one *d. Educ:* Watford Grammar School; Caius College, Cambridge (MA). Colonial Office, 1930; seconded to Tanganyika, 1934; Secretary to Commission on Higher Educn in E Africa and Sudan, 1937; Sec. to Lord Privy Seal, 1938; Sec. to Lord Hailey in Africa, 1939, Congo, 1940; Chief Brit. Econ. Representative, Dakar, 1942; Finance Dept, Colonial Office, 1944. Joined United Africa Co., 1947, Director, 1951, Deputy Chairman, 1965-68. Director, Unilever Ltd and NV, 1956-68. Chm., E Africa and Mauritius Assoc., 1966-68. Treasurer, London Sch. of Oriental and African Studies, 1969. *Publications:* West Africa, 1951 (2nd edn 1959); Economic Geography of W Africa, 1955. *Recreations:* languages, history, ski-ing, tennis. *Address:* 36 Russell Road, Moor Park, Northwood, Mddx.

**PEDLEY, John Edward,** CSI 1946; CIE 1939; MC; *b* 4 Dec. 1891; *s* of Dr T. F. Pedley; *m* 1928, Effie, *d* of Dr James Craig. *Educ:* Repton; Trinity College, Oxford. Served European War, 1914-19 (MC). Entered Indian Civil Service, 1920. Retired as Member Board of Revenue, UP, 1947. Regional Food Officer, Eastern Region, 1950-51. *Address:* Walden, Ballasalla, Isle of Man.

**PEDLEY, Richard Rodman;** Headmaster, St Dunstan's College, since 1967; *b* 23 Sept. 1912; *s* of F. W. and B. M. Pedley; *m* 1938, Jeanie M. M. Evans; one *s* one *d*. *Educ:* Foster's Sch., Sherborne; Downing Coll., Cambridge (Schol.; MA 1937). RA, 1940-46 (Major). Asst Master: City of Leicester Boys' Sch., 1934-40, 1946; St Olave's Sch., 1946-50; Headmaster: City of Leicester Boys' Sch., 1950-54; Chislehurst and Sidcup Gram. Sch., 1954-67. Pres., Headmasters' Assoc., 1963; Chm., Jt Four Secondary Assocs., 1966-67. *Publications:* (ed) Paradise Lost Bks I and II, 1956; contribs to The Fight for Education (Black Papers). *Recreations:* literature, polemics, watching cricket. *Address:* Headmaster's House, St Dunstan's College, Catford, SE6. *T:* 01-690 0159.

**PEEBLES, Allan Charles Chiappini,** CVO 1956; Secretary of The Athenæum, since 1962; *b* 18 Nov. 1907; *s* of late Lt-Colonel Arthur Stansfeld Peebles; *m* 1930, Jean Ilvira Naish. *Educ:* Charterhouse; Royal Military College, Sandhurst. 2nd Lt Suffolk Regiment, 1927-30; Nigeria Police, 1931-56; Queen's Own Nigeria Regt, 1940-44, Major. Commissioner of Police, Northern Region, Nigeria, 1953-56. Ministry of Aviation, 1958-62. Queen's Police Medal, 1953; Colonial Police Medal, 1951. *Address:* The Athenæum, Pall Mall, SW1. *T:* 01-930 4843; 507 Hawkins House, Dolphin Square, SW1. *T:* 01-834 3800, Ext. Hawkins 507. *Club:* MCC.

**PEECH, Alan James;** Chairman, The United Steel Cos Ltd since 1962; *b* 24 August 1905; *s* of late Albert Orlando Peech; *m* 1948, Betty Leese; no *c*. *Educ:* Wellington College; Magdalen College, Oxford (BA). Governor, Wellington College. Independent Chm., Cement Makers' Fedn, 1970; Dep. Chm., Steetley Co. Ltd; Dir, Tinsley Wire Industries Ltd; Pres., British Iron and Steel Fedn, Jan.-June 1967; Jt Man. Dir, United Steel Cos Ltd, 1962-67; a Dep. Chm., BSC, 1967-70; Man. Dir, Midland Gp BSC, 1967-70. Hon. LLD Sheffield, 1966. *Recreations:* fishing and shooting. *Address:* High House, Blyth, Worksop, Notts. *T:* Blyth 255. *Clubs:* Carlton, MCC.

**PEECH, Neil Malcolm;** Chairman, The Steetley Co. Ltd, since 1935 (Managing Director, 1935-68); *b* 27 Jan. 1908; *s* of Albert Orlando Peech; *m* 1932, Margaret Josephine, *d* of late R. C. Smallwood, CBE, Worplesdon, Surrey; one *s* one *d*. *Educ:* Wellington College; Magdalen College, Oxford. Developed the production of magnesia from seawater and dolomite, 1939. Vice Consul for Sweden, 1949-; Underwriting member of Lloyd's, 1950-69; Director, Sheepbridge Engineering Ltd, 1949-, and Albright & Wilson Ltd 1958-. Chairman, Ministry of Power Solid Smokeless Fuel Committee, 1959. High Sheriff of Yorkshire, 1959. *Recreations:* fishing and shooting. *Address:* Park House, Firbeck, Worksop. *T:* North Carlton 338. *Clubs:* Carlton, MCC.

**PEEK, Sir Francis (Henry Grenville),** 4th Bt, *cr* 1874; *b* 16 Sept. 1915; *o s* of 3rd Bt and Edwine Warner (*d* 1959), *d* of late W. H. Thornburgh, St Louis, USA; *S* father, 1927; *m* 1st, 1942, Ann (marr. diss., 1949), *d* of late Captain Gordon Duff and *widow* of Sir Charles Mappin, Bt (she *m* 1951, Sir William Rootes, later 1st Baron Rootes); 2nd, Marilyn (marr. diss., 1967; she *m* 1967, Peter Quennell), *d* of Dr Norman Kerr, London and Bahamas; one *s*; 3rd, Mrs Caroline Kirkwood, *d* of Sir Robert Kirkwood, *qv*. *Educ:* Eton; Trinity College, Cambridge. ADC to Governor of Bahamas, 1938-39; served Irish Guards, 1939-46. *Heir:* *s* Charles Edward Francis Peek, *b* 5 May 1956. *Address:* 19 St James's Place, SW1. *T:* 01-629 8701; 60 Grosvenor Close, Nassau, Bahamas. *Club:* White's.

**PEEL,** family name of **Earl Peel.**

**PEEL,** 3rd Earl *cr* 1929; **William James Robert Peel;** Bt 1800; Viscount Peel, 1895; Viscount Clanfield, 1929; *b* 3 Oct. 1947; *s* of 2nd Earl Peel and Kathleen, *d* of Michael McGrath; *S* father, 1969. *Educ:* Ampleforth. *Heir:* *b* Hon. Robert Michael Arthur Peel, *b* 5 Feb. 1950. *Address:* Hyning Hall, Carnforth, Lancs; 6 Harley Gardens, SW10.

**PEEL, Lady; (Beatrice);** *see* Lillie, Beatrice.

**PEEL, The Lady Delia (Adelaide Margaret),** DCVO 1950 (CVO 1947); *b* 1889; *d* of 6th Earl Spencer, KG; *m* 1914, Col Hon. Sir Sidney Cornwallis Peel, 1st and last Bt, CB, DSO, TD (*d* 1938). A Woman of the Bedchamber, 1939-50; an Extra Woman of the Bedchamber, 1950, to the Queen; to Queen Elizabeth the Queen Mother, 1952. *Address:* Barton Turf, Norwich, NOR 36Z.

**PEEL, Prof. Edwin Arthur,** DLit; Professor of Education, University of Birmingham, since 1950, and Chairman of School of Education; *b* 11 March 1911; *s* of late Arthur Peel and Mary Ann Miller; *m* 1939, Nora Kathleen Yeadon; two *s* two *d*. *Educ:* Prince Henry's Grammar School, Otley, Yorks; Leeds University; London University. Teaching in various London Schools, 1933-38; LCC School of Building, 1938-41; MA London, 1938; Ministry of Supply, 1941-45; PhD London 1945; Part-time Lecturer London Univ. Institute of Education, 1945; Lecturer in Education, King's College, Newcastle, 1946; Reader in Psychology, Durham University, 1946-48; Professor of Educational Psychology, University of Durham, 1948-50. President British Psychological Society 1961-62. DLit, London, 1961. *Publications:* The Psychological Basis of Education, 1956; The Pupil's Thinking, 1960; various in leading British and Foreign Journals of Psychology. Editor, Educational Review. *Recreation:* painting. *Address:* 47 Innage Road, Birmingham 31. *T:* 021-475 2820.

**PEEL, Capt. Sir (Francis Richard) Jonathan,** Kt 1959; CBE 1943; MC; DL; *b* 10 December 1897; *s* of late Walter Peel, CBE, JP; *m* 1932, Daphne Margaret Holwell, *d* of Commander A. McC. Pakenham, Bath; one *s* one *d*. *Educ:* Malvern College; Pembroke College, Cambridge. RFA, European War, 1915-19; Liverpool City Police, 1920-31; Chief Constable of Bath, 1931-33; Chief Constable of Essex, 1933-62, retired. DL County of Essex, 1959. King's Police Medal, 1952. CStJ 1959. *Address:* Cedarholme, 9 Lexden Road, Colchester, Essex.

**PEEL, John;** *see* Peel, W. J.

**PEEL, Sir John (Harold),** KCVO 1960; FRCS 1933; FRCOG 1944; Surgeon-Gynæcologist to the Queen, since 1961; Consulting Obstetric and Gynæcological Surgeon, King's College Hospital, since 1969; Examiner, University of Cambridge; Emeritus Consulting

Gynæcologist, Princess Beatrice Hospital, since 1965; *b* 10 December 1904; *s* of Rev. J. E. Peel; *m* 1947, Freda Margaret Mellish; one *d*. *Educ:* Manchester Grammar Sch.; Queen's Coll., Oxford. MA, BM, BCh Oxon 1932. King's College Hospital Med. Sch., qualified 1930; Obstetric and Gynæcological Surgeon: King's Coll. Hosp., 1936-69; Princess Beatrice Hosp., 1937; Queen Victoria Hosp., East Grinstead, 1941-69; Surgeon EMS, 1939-45. Director of Clinical Studies, King's College Hospital Medical School, 1948-67. Litchfield Lecturer, Oxford University, 1961 and 1969; Sir Kadar Nath Das Lecturer, Bengal O and G Soc., 1962; Sir A. Mudaliar Lecturer, Madras Univ., 1962; Vis. Prof., Cape Town Univ., 1963; Travelling Prof., S. African Council, RCOG, 1968. Past Examiner, Universities of Oxford, Cambridge, London, Liverpool, Bristol, Glasgow, Newcastle, Nat. Univ. of Ireland, Birmingham, Conjoint Board, RCOG and CMB. Nuffield visitor to Colonies, 1950 and 1953. President, RCOG, 1966-69 (Hon. Treasurer, 1959-66, Councillor, 1955-); Vice-Pres., Internat. Fedn of Obstetrics and Gynæcology; Pres. Chelsea Clinical Society, 1960; Hon. Fellow American Association of Obstetricians and Gynæcologists, 1962 (Joseph Price Oration, 1961); Hon. Member: Canadian Assoc. of O and G, 1955; Italian Assoc O and G, 1960; Hon. FRCS (Canada), 1967; Hon. FCOG (SA), 1968. *Publications:* Textbook of Gynæcology, 1943; numerous contributions to Medical Journals. *Recreations:* fishing, golf. *Address:* 86 Harley Street, W1. *T:* 01-580 2976. Warren Court Farm, West Tytherley, Salisbury, Wilts. *Clubs:* Bath, Boodle's; Royal Automobile; Leckford and Longstock.

**PEEL, Capt. Sir Jonathan;** *see* Peel, Capt. Sir F. R. J.

**PEEL, Prof. Ronald Francis Edward Waite,** MBE 1945; MA (Cambridge) 1937; Professor of Geography, University of Bristol, since 1957; Dean of Science, 1968-70; *b* 22 Aug. 1912; *s* of late Albert Edward Peel, Bridgnorth, Shropshire, and Matilda Mary Peel (*née* Anderson), Helensburgh, Dunbartonshire; *m* 1938, Mary Annette Preston, MA Cantab, *o d* of H. Preston, Northampton; one *d*. *Educ:* Northampton Gram. Sch.; St Catharine's Coll., Cambridge (scholar). Lecturer in Geography, King's College, University of Durham, 1935-39; accompanied Brig. R. A. Bagnold, OBE, FRS, on exploring expedition in Libyan Desert, 1938. Served War of 1939-45, with RE; France, 1939-40; UK (staff appts), 1940-44; N Africa and Italy, 1944-45; UK, 1945. King's College, Newcastle, 1945-46; Department of Geography, Cambridge University, 1946, Lecturer in Geography, 1949; Prof. of Geography, University of Leeds, 1951-57, Head of Dept, 1953-57. Fell. of St Catharine's Coll., Camb., 1949. Cuthbert Peake Award of RGS, 1950; expeditions to Ruwenzori Mountains, 1952; W and C Sahara, 1961. President: Inst. British Geographers, 1965; Section E, British Assoc., 1967. FRGS, FRMetSoc. *Publications:* Physical Geography, 1951; articles on geographical subjects to technical jls, British and foreign. *Recreation:* travel. *Address:* Department of Geography, The University, Bristol 8. *Club:* Hawks (Cambridge).

**PEEL, (William) John;** MP (C) Southeast Division of Leicester since 1957; *b* 16 June 1912; *s* of late Sir William Peel, KCMG, KBE, and Violet Mary Drake, *er d* of W. D. Laing; *m* 1936, Rosemary Mia Minka, *er d* of Robert Readhead; one *s* three *d*. *Educ:* Wellington College; Queens' College, Cambridge. Colonial Administrative Service, 1933-51; on active service, 1941-45; British Resident, Brunei, 1946-48; Res. Comr, Gilbert and Ellice Is Colony, 1949-51. Rugby Portland Cement Co. Ltd, 1952-54. Contested (C) Meriden Division of Warwickshire, 1955; Parliamentary Private Secretary to Economic Secretary to the Treasury, 1958-59; to Minister of State, Board of Trade, 1959-60; Asst Govt Whip (unpaid), 1960-61; a Lord Comr of the Treasury, Nov. 1961-Oct. 1964. Parly Delegate to Assemblies of Council of Europe, WEU, and N Atlantic, 1959-; Vice-Pres., WEU, 1967. *Recreation:* golf. *Address:* 51 Cambridge Street, SW1. *T:* 01-834 8762; 51 Stoneygate Court, London Road, Leicester. *T:* Leicester 707118. *Clubs:* Carlton; Hawks (Cambridge); Leicestershire.

**PEEL YATES, Lt-Gen. Sir David,** KCB 1966 (CB 1963); CVO 1965; DSO 1943, and Bar, 1944; OBE 1943; DL; *b* 10 July 1911; *er s* of late Lt-Col Hubert Peel Yates, DSO, late South Wales Borderers, and Gertrude Loetitia Molyneux (*née* Sarel); *m* 1947, Christine Hilary, *er d* of late Horatio Stanley-Williams, DSO, Irthlingborough, Northants; one *s* one *d*. *Educ:* Haileybury College; RMC Sandhurst. Commissioned S Wales Borderers, 1931; Waziristan operations, 1937; active service in N Africa, Italy and Greece as GSO1 ops First Army, Comdg 6 Bn Lincolnshire Regt, GSO1 4th Div. and BGS (Ops) AFHQ, 1942-45. Commanded 1st Bn S Wales Borderers, 1953-55; Comdr 27 Infantry Bde, Hong Kong, 1955-57; Asst Commandant, Staff College, 1957-60; Chief of Staff, Eastern Command, 1960-62; GOC, Berlin (British Sector), 1962-66; GOC-in-C: Eastern Command, 1966-68; Southern Comd, 1968-69; retd 1969. Colonel: The South Wales Borderers, 1962-69; Royal Regt of Wales (24th/41st Foot), 1969-. Breconshire CC, 1970. DL Breconshire, 1970. Legion of Merit, USA, 1946. *Recreations:* shooting, fishing, ski-ing. *Address:* Glyn Pedr, Llanbedr, Crickhowell, Breconshire. *T:* Crickhowell 333. *Club:* Army and Navy.

**PEERS, Robert,** CBE 1955 (OBE 1946); MC; Hon. DLitt (Nottingham); JP; Professor Emeritus, Nottingham University; Professor of Adult Education, 1922-53; Professorial Research Fellow, 1954-55; Deputy Vice-Chancellor, 1948-53; *b* Liverpool, 1888; *m* 1st, 1916, Gladys, *d* of C. H. Cundy; one *d* (one *d* decd); 2nd, 1945, Eileen Marjorie, *d* of A. Clayton. *Educ:* University of Liverpool; University of Heidelberg. Henry Warren Meade King Scholar, 1911, BA First Class Hons Economics, 1913, University Post-graduate Scholar; Stanley Jevons Research Scholar, 1914; MA, 1919; served in King's Liverpool Regiment and Army Signal Service, 1915-19 (Captain, MC); Lecturer in Economics, University College, Exeter, 1919-20; Director of Extramural Studies, University College, Nottingham, 1920; Albert Kahn Fellow, 1928-29; Asst Regional Controller, Ministry of Labour and National Service, 1941-43; Labour Adviser to the Minister Resident, Middle East, 1943-44; Vice-Principal, University College Nottingham, 1946-47; Acting Principal, 1947-48; Lecture tours, West Indies, 1949, Australia, 1950, East Africa, 1955 and several in Germany; Smith-Mundt award for advanced research, Columbia Univ., 1953. Chm. Central Cttee for Adult Educ. in HM Forces, 1949-57; Chm. Transport Users' Consultative Cttee for the East Midlands, 1951-65; JP Nottingham. *Publications:* many contributions in Journals and Transactions on the theory and practice of Adult Education; Section on Adult Education in The Schools of England (Ed. J. Dover Wilson); Adult Education in Practice (edited with introductory and other chapters), 1934;

Consumers' Co-operation in Great Britain (Joint), 1938; Labour and Employment in the Middle East (Report to the Minister), 1945; Adult Education: A Comparative Study, 1958, with German translation in part, 1963; Fact and Possibility in English Education, 1963. *Recreation:* gardening. *Address:* 21 Cator Lane, Chilwell, Beeston, Nottingham. *T:* Nottingham 255457. *Club:* University (Nottingham).

*See also D. E. Lloyd Jones.*

**PEGG, Arthur John,** OBE 1951 (MBE 1946); AFRAeS 1953; Chief Test Pilot, Bristol Aeroplane Co., 1947-56, General Service Manager of Weston Works since 1957; *b* 5 June 1906; *s* of Major S. Pegg, RAOC; *m* 1933, Eileen Mary Page; one *s* one *d. Educ:* Skinners, Tunbridge Wells. Joined Royal Air Force, 1921; learned to fly, 1925; granted permanent commission, 1930, and appointed test pilot at aeroplane and armament experimental establishments; resigned commission and appointed Asst Chief Test Pilot, Bristol Aeroplane Co., 1935. *Publication:* Sent Flying (autobiography), 1959. *Recreations:* squash and sailing. *Address:* Craigfoot No. 1, 55 South Rd, Weston-super-Mare, Somerset. *T:* Weston-super-Mare 3884. *Club:* Royal Aero.

**PEGLER, James Basil Holmes,** TD; FIA, FSS, FIS; Managing Director, Clerical Medical and General Life Assurance Society, since 1970 (General Manager and Actuary, 1950-69); *b* 6 Aug. 1912; *s* of late Harold Holmes Pegler and late Dorothy Cecil (*née* Francis); *m* 1937, Enid Margaret Dell; one *s* three *d. Educ:* Charterhouse. Joined Clerical, Medical and Gen. Life Assce Soc., 1931. War service, Queen's Royal Regt and RA, 1939-45 (Major). Inst. of Actuaries: Fellow, 1939; Hon. Sec., 1955-57; Pres., 1968-70. Chm., Life Offices' Assoc., 1959-61; Chm., Life Gp of Comité Européen des Assurances, 1964-. *Publications:* contribs to Jl Inst. Actuaries. *Recreations:* mathematics, music, languages, squash rackets. *Address:* 75 Croham Road, South Croydon, Surrey CR2 7HG. *T:* 01-688 6270. *Clubs:* Army and Navy, Royal Automobile.

**PEIERLS, Sir Rudolf (Ernst),** Kt 1968; CBE 1946; FRS 1945; MA Cantab; DSc Manchester, DPhil Leipzig; Wykeham Professor of Physics, University of Oxford, since 1963; Fellow of New College, Oxford, since 1963; *b* Berlin, 5 June 1907; *s* of H. Peierls; *m* 1931, Eugenia, *d* of late N. Kannegiesser; one *s* three *d. Educ:* Humboldt School, Oberschöneweide, Berlin; Universities of Berlin, Munich, Leipzig. Assistant, Federal Institute of Technology, Zürich, 1929-32; Rockefeller Fellow, 1932-33; Honorary Research Fellow, Manchester University, 1933-35; Assistant-in-Research, Royal Society Mond Laboratory, 1935-37; Worked on Atomic Energy Project in Birmingham, 1940-43, in USA, 1943-46. Professor of Mathematical Physics (formerly Applied Mathematics), University of Birmingham, 1937-63. Member Governing Board of National Institute for Research in Nuclear Science, 1957-62. Awarded Royal Medal of Royal Society, 1959; Lorentz Medal of Royal Netherlands Academy of Sciences, 1962; Max Planck Medal, Association of German Physical Societies, 1963; Guthrie Medal, IPPS, 1968. Hon. DSc: Liverpool, 1960; Birmingham, 1967; Edinburgh, 1969. Foreign Hon. Member, American Academy of Arts and Sciences, 1962; Hon. Associate, College of Advanced Technology, Birmingham, 1963; Foreign Associate, Nat. Acad. of Sciences, USA, 1970. *Publications:* Quantum Theory of Solids, 1955; The Laws of Nature, 1955; Papers on Quantum Theory. *Address:* Department of Theoretical Physics, 12 Parks Road, Oxford OX1 3PQ. *Club:* Athenæum.

**PEILE, Vice-Admiral Sir Lancelot Arthur Babington,** KBE 1960; CB 1957; DSO 1941; MVO 1947; DL; retired; *b* 22 Jan. 1905; *s* of late Basil Wilson Peile and Katharine Rosamond (*née* Taylor); *m* 1928, Gertrude Margaret (*née* Tolcher); two *s. Educ:* RN Colleges, Osborne and Dartmouth. Commander (E) 1939; Captain (E), 1947; Rear-Admiral, 1955; Vice-Admiral, 1958. Asst Engineer-in-Chief, 1948; Command of RN Engineering College, 1951; idc 1954. Asst Director of Dockyards, 1955-57; Admiral Superintendent, Devonport Dockyard, 1957-60; retired, 1960. DL Devon, 1969. *Address:* Strawberry How, Thurlestone, Kingsbridge, Devon. *T:* Thurlestone 209. *Club:* Naval and Military.

**PEIRCE, Lt-Col Harold Ernest,** CBE 1960 (OBE 1950); JP; Director of Public Companies, since 1929; *b* 7 Nov. 1892; *s* of Harry and Elizabeth Peirce. *Educ:* Croydon, Surrey. Joined Hall & Co. Ltd, 1907; Director, 1929; Managing Director, 1944. Director, Hall & Ham River Ltd, Holding Board, 1962; Local Director, Lombard Banking Ltd, Croydon, and Lombank Ltd, 1964; Chm., GSPR Ltd. Served European War, 1915-19 (Surrey Yeomanry, Queen's Royal W. Surrey Regt). Founder Member, Ballast, Sand and Allied Trades Assoc. (now called Sand and Gravel Assoc. of Great Britain), 1930 (Chairman, 1943, now Pres.); Founder Member, National Council of Building Material Producers (Vice-President, 1955; Chairman Council, 1956; President, 1965); Member Indust. Development Mission to WI, 1952; Member Board of Trade Bankruptcy Acts Amendment Cttee, 1955. Appointed Member, Dollar Export Delegation to Canada, 1957. Member, Building Centre Council and Governor, The Building Centre Trust, 1964. Comdr Bn of Home Guard, War of 1939-45, and also when later reformed. Chairman, Croydon Playing Fields Assoc. JP, Croydon, 1941-. *Recreations:* cricket and squash. Captain of Addiscombe Cricket Club for 26 years, now President of the Club. *Address:* Selsdon Park, Sanderstead, Surrey. *T:* 01-657 8811. *Clubs:* Devonshire, RAC, MCC; Surrey CCC (member of Committee).

**PEIRIS, Dr Mahapitage Velin Peter,** OBE 1956; *b* 28 July 1898; *s* of M. A. Peiris and H. D. Selestina, Panadura, Ceylon; *m* 1945, Edith Doreen Idona Carey, Negombo, Ceylon; three *s* one *d. Educ:* St John's Coll., Panadura; St Joseph's Coll., Colombo; Ceylon Medical Coll., Colombo. LMS Ceylon, 1926; MB, BS London, 1936; FRCS 1930; FICS 1957; FACS 1959. Served in Ceylon Army Med. Corps, 1930-45: Surg. to Mil. Hosps, Ceylon, 1940-45. Vis. Surgeon: Gen. Hosp., 1936-60; Children's Hosp., Colombo, 1951-60; Surg. to Orthop. Clinic, 1950-60; Cons. Orthop. Surg., Gen. Hosp., Colombo; Medico-Legal Adviser to Crown; Prof. of Surgery, Univ. of Ceylon, 1952-60. Senator, Ceylon Parlt, 1954-68: Minister of Health, 1960; Leader of Senate, and Minister of Commerce and Trade, 1965-68. Ambassador of Ceylon to USSR, 1968-69; High Comr for Ceylon in the UK, 1969-70. Mem. Coun., Univ. of Ceylon, 1960; President: Ceylon Med. Assoc., 1954; University Teachers' Assoc.; UNA of Ceylon, 1966-68. *Publications:* contribs to Indian and Ceylon medical jls. *Recreations:* swimming, photography. *Address:* 165 Dharmapala Mawata, Colombo 7, Ceylon. *T:* 96192. *Club:* Sinhalese Sports (Colombo).

**PEIRSE, Sir Henry C. de la P. B.;** *see* Beresford-Peirse.

**PEIRSON, David Edward Herbert,** CBE 1965; Secretary, UK Atomic Energy Authority, since 1955; *b* 18 May 1915; *s* of Herbert Sidney and Edith Peirson; *m* 1940, Norah Ellen Corney; one *s* two *d*. *Educ:* Wallasey Grammar Sch.; King's Coll., London. LLB 1937; LLM 1938; Passed 5th in Civil Service 1st Division Examination, 1939. Asst Principal, Board of Trade, 1939; Private Secretary to Lord Beaverbrook, MAP, 1941-42; Principal, Ministry of Supply, 1942; Asst Secretary, Ministry of Supply, 1946; idc 1951. *Recreation:* music. *Address:* 15 Aylmer Road, N2. *T:* 01-340 3654. *Club:* Athenæum.

**PELHAM,** family name of **Earls of Chichester** and **Yarborough.**

**PELHAM, Sir (George) Clinton,** KBE 1957; CMG 1949; FRGS; HM Ambassador to Czechoslovakia, 1955-57, retired; *b* 20 May 1898; *s* of George Pelham; *m* 1930, Jeanie Adelina Morton; two *d*. *Educ:* privately. Served European War, 1915-18. Foreign Office, 1920; China Consular Service, 1923; HM Trade Commissioner and Commercial Secretary for South China, 1933; Acting Consul-General, Madagascar, 1943; First Secretary (Commercial), Bagdad, 1945; Counsellor (Commercial), Bagdad, 1946; Counsellor (Commercial), Madrid, 1948-51; HM Ambassador to Saudi Arabia, 1951-55. County Councillor, West Sussex, 1963-70. *Recreations:* music, painting, travel. *Address:* Crespin, Craigweil, Bognor Regis, Sussex. *Club:* Junior Carlton.

**PELHAM-CLINTON-HOPE,** family name of **Duke of Newcastle.**

**PELLETIER, Hector Rooney;** retired; formerly General Manager, BBC Radio Enterprises; *b* 18 Oct. 1911; *s* of Achille Joseph Pelletier and Helen Louise Rooney. *Educ:* University of Ottawa; Queen's Univ., Kingston, Ont. Teaching, followed by journalism with Le Droit (Ottawa) and The Canadian Press (Toronto and Montreal). Freelance writing included poetry and art criticism. Announcer and Head of Quebec programmes for Canadian Broadcasting Corporation; Commentator, Royal Tour of Canada, 1939; War reporter and European Representative, CBC, 1941. BBC posts since 1938 include: Features and Drama producer; Asst Editor, Radio Newsreel; Head of N. American Service; Asst Head, Television Talks; Chief Instructor, Staff Training School; Asst Controller and Controller, Light Programme; Controller Programme Planning (Sound); Chief of Presentation (Sound). *Recreations:* painting; collecting Victorian ephemeral publications. *Address:* Little Dingleden, Benenden, Kent. *T:* Benenden 645. *Club:* Reform.

**PELLETIER, Wilfrid,** CC (Canada) 1967; CMG 1946; DM; *b* 20 June 1896; *m* 1936, Rose Bampton; two *s*. *Educ:* Montreal; Paris (France). Prix d'Europe, 1914; Assistant-conductor with Pierre Monteaux, Albert Wolff and Louis Hasselmans at Metropolitan Opera House, New York City, 1916-19, Conductor, French and Italian Opera, to 1950; Ministère des Affaires Culturelles de la Province de Québec, 1942-70; Director Founder, Conservatoire de la Province de Québec, 1942-61. *Recreations:* farm, collecting music manuscripts, autographs. *Address:* 322 East 57th Street, New York City, NY 10022, USA. *Cable:* Tierpelle Newyork. *Club:* Dutch Treat (New York City).

**PELLEW,** family name of **Viscount Exmouth.**

**PELLEW, Lancelot Vivian,** CMG 1964; President of the Industrial Court of South Australia, Oct. 1952-Dec. 1964, retired; *b* 15 Dec. 1899; *s* of Joseph Henry Pellew and Laura Lee; *m* 1924, Ray Lilian Smith; one *d*. *Educ:* Queen's School, North Adelaide; St Peters Coll., Adelaide. Admitted to Bar, SA Supreme Court, 1923. In practice Adelaide, 1926-42; Acting Dep. Master, Supreme Court, Adelaide, 1942-45; Special Magistrate, Dec. 1945-48. Dep. President, Industrial Court, 1948-52. *Recreations:* golf, bowls. *Address:* 3 Bedford Street, Kensington Park, Adelaide, South Australia. *T:* Adelaide 3-5079. *Clubs:* Adelaide, Royal Adelaide Golf, SA Lawn Tennis Assoc., Adelaide Oval Bowls, SA Cricket Assoc. (Adelaide); Mt Lofty Golf.

**PELLING, Henry Mathison;** Assistant Director of Research (History), Cambridge University, and Fellow of St John's College, since 1966; *b* 27 Aug. 1920; *s* of late D. L. Pelling, Prenton, Cheshire, and of Mrs M. M. Pelling; unmarried. *Educ:* Birkenhead School; St John's Coll., Cambridge. Class. Tripos Part I, 1941; History Tripos Part II, 1947. Army service, 1941-45; Commnd RE, 1942; served NW Europe campaign, 1944-45. Fellow, Queen's Coll., Oxford, 1949-65; Tutor, 1950-65; Dean, 1963-64. Smith-Mundt Schol., University of Wisconsin, USA, 1953-54. *Publications:* Origins of the Labour Party, 1954; Challenge of Socialism, 1954; America and the British Left, 1956; British Communist Party, 1958; (with Frank Bealey) Labour and Politics, 1958; American Labor, 1960; Modern Britain, 1885-1955, 1960; Short History of the Labour Party, 1961; History of British Trade Unionism, 1963; Social Geography of British Elections, 1967; Popular Politics and Society in Late Victorian Britain, 1968; Britain and the Second World War, 1970; articles and reviews in learned journals. *Recreations:* tennis, films. *Address:* St John's College, Cambridge CB2 1TP. *T:* Cambridge 61621. *Clubs:* National Liberal, Oxford and Cambridge University.

**PELLIZZI, Camillo,** DrJ (Pisa), DLit (London); Professor of Sociology, University of Florence, since 1949; *b* Collegno, Italy, 24 Aug. 1896; *s* of G. Battista Pellizzi and Giovanna Ferrari; *m* 1933, Raffaella Biozzi; two *s* one *d*. *Educ:* Pisa. Asst Lecturer, Reader then Professor of Italian at University College, University of London, 1920-40; Head of Division, then Councillor, on Training and Applied Social Sciences, OEEC, 1954-57. *Publications:* Problemi e realtà del Fascismo, 1924; Gli spiriti della vigilia, 1925; Le lettere italiane del nostro secolo, 1929; Il teatro inglese, 1934; Italy, 1939; Una rivoluzione mancata, 1948; Italian Sociology in our Century, 1957; Lineamenti di sistematica sociologica, 1964; Rito e linguaggio, 1964, etc. Ed. (Quarterly) Rassegna Italiana di Sociologia, 1960-. *Address:* Facoltà di Scienze Politiche "C Alfieri", Via Laura 48, Firenze, Italy.

**PELLOE, Rev. Canon John Parker;** a Chaplain to the Queen, 1964; Hon. Canon of Ely Cathedral, 1952-53, and since 1965; *b* 31 May 1905; *e s* of late Rev. E. P. Pelloe; *m* 1945, Kathleen, *d* of late Arthur Bland. *Educ:* Charterhouse; Queen's Coll., Oxford (MA); Cuddesdon Theological Coll. In business, 1922-32. Ordained 1936; Curate: St Columba, Sunderland, 1936-39; St Cuthbert, Kensington, 1939-42; Domestic Chaplain to Bishop of Ely, 1942-46; Vicar of Wisbech, 1946-60 (Rural Dean, 1946-53); Vicar of Stuntney, 1960-68; Archdeacon of Wisbech, 1953-64. *Recreation:* walking. *Address:* 14 Lynn Road, Ely, Cambs. *T:* Ely 2232.

**PELLY, Sir Alwyne;** *see* Pelly, Sir H. A.

**PELLY, Air Chief Marshal Sir Claude (Bernard Raymond),** GBE 1959 (CBE 1943); KCB 1954 (CB 1950); MC 1932; *b* 19 Aug. 1902; *e s* of late Rev. D. R. Pelly, DSO; *m* 1930, Margaret Ogilvie Spencer; two *s* one *d*. *Educ:* Rugby; RAF Coll., Cranwell. Directing Staff, Imperial Defence Coll., 1952-53; C-in-C, MEAF, 1953-56; Controller of Aircraft, Ministry of Supply, 1956-59, ADC (Air) to the Queen, 1957-59; retired 1959. Member for Weapons, Research and Development, UK, AEA, 1959-64. Gold Cross, Order of King George I of Hellenes. *Address:* Green Lane House, Orford, Suffolk. *Club:* Army and Navy.

**PELLY, Cornelius James,** CMG 1952; OBE 1944; *b* 8 April 1908; *e s* of Hyacinth Albert and Charity Mary Pelly, Benmore, Rushbrooke, Co. Cork, Eire; *m* 1949, Una O'Shea, *y d* of Patrick Seaborn O'Shea, Lismore, Co. Waterford; one *s* one *d*. *Educ:* Clongowes Wood Coll., Co. Kildare; Trinity Coll., Dublin. Entered Indian Civil Service by competitive examination, 1930; appointed to Punjab, 1931; Under-Secretary Punjab Government, 1935-36; transferred to Indian Political Service, 1936; Colonization Officer, Bahawalpur State, 1936-39; Political Agent and HM's Consul, Muscat, 1941-44; Consul, Bushire, 1946-47; Political Agent, Bahrain, 1947-51; Political Agent, Kuwait, 1951-55; Acting Political Resident, Persian Gulf, 1950 and 1952; Secretary for Financial Affairs, Sultanate of Muscat and Oman, 1968-. *Recreations:* shooting, tennis, sailing. *Address:* Upper Shalbourne, Church Hill, Camberley, Surrey. *T:* Camberley 3089. *Clubs:* Travellers'; Royal Irish Yacht (Dun Laoghaire).

**PELLY, Major Sir (Harold) Alwyne,** 5th Bt, *cr* 1840; MC 1918; 7th Hussars, retired; *b* 27 Aug. 1893; *e s* of Sir Harold Pelly, 4th Bt, and Anna (*d* 1939), *d* of Robert Poore, Old Lodge, Salisbury; *S* father, 1950; *m* 1917, Carol, *d* of late R. Heywood-Jones of Badsworth Hall, Yorkshire; three *s* one *d* (and one *s* decd). *Educ:* Wellington Coll.; Merton Coll., Oxford. Served European War, France and Mesopotamia (MC); Instructor Cavalry Sch., Netheravon, and Equitation Sch., Weedon, 1920-24; Adjutant, Leicestershire Yeomanry, 1927-31; retired, 1935. *Heir:* *s* Major John Alwyne Pelly, Coldstream Guards [*b* 11 Sept. 1918; *m* 1950, Elsie May, *d* of late L. Thomas Dechow, Rhodesia; one *d*. Served War of 1939-45 (prisoner of war)]. *Address:* Preshaw House, Upham, Southampton SO3 1HP. *T:* Bishops Waltham 2531. *Club:* Cavalry.

*See also Earl of Crawford, Sir Thomas Lees, Bt.*

**PELLY, Sir Kenneth (Raymond),** Kt 1961; MC 1918; Director, Wm France Fenwick & Co. Ltd since 1919 (Chairman, 1941-66); *b* 9 Nov. 1893; *m* 1919, Elspeth Norna Grant; one *s* one *d*. *Educ:* Charterhouse. Served European War, 1914-18, Captain, RASC. Joined Wm France Fenwick & Co. Ltd, 1912; Director, 1918-; Managing Director, 1926-57. Member of the Port of London Authority, 1952-61; President of the Chamber of Shipping of the United Kingdom, 1956-57; Chairman General Council of British Shipping, 1956-57; Chairman (Member 1938) General Cttee, Lloyd's Register of Shipping, 1957-63. *Recreations:* farming, shooting, fishing. *Address:* Newstead Ghyll, Colgate, Horsham, Sussex. *T:* Faygate 233. *Club:* Lansdowne.

**PELLY, Rear-Adm. Peter Douglas Herbert Raymond,** CB 1958; DSO 1942; *b* 24 Sept. 1904; *s* of Rev. Douglas R. Pelly, DSO, and Verena Noellie (*née* Herbert); *m* 1932, Gwenllian Violet Edwardes; three *d*. *Educ:* RNC Osborne and Dartmouth. Joined Navy, 1918; normal peace-time services, except for appointment to Royal Yacht, 1939; served War of 1939-45; Commander, 1940; Comd Destroyer Windsor until 1940; 15th Cruiser Squadron, 1940-43; Plans Divison, Admiralty, 1943-45; Comd: Aircraft Carrier Ameer, 1945; HMS Raleigh, 1945-47; Captain, 1947; Admiralty, 1947-49; Reserve Fleet, Harwich, 1950; Captain (D) in Battleaxe, 1951-52; Chief Staff Officer, Gibraltar, 1952-54; Director of Ops Division, Admiralty, 1954-56; Rear-Admiral, 1956, Admiral Superintendent, HM Dockyard, Rosyth, Sept. 1956-Nov. 1957; Director-General of the Department of Dockyards and Maintenance, Admiralty, 1958-59; retired 1960. Sec., Assoc. of Consulting Engineers, 1960-69. Hon. Member, Smeatonian Society of Civil Engineers, 1965-70. Officer, Order of Orange Nassau (Holland), 1940. *Recreations:* normal. *Address:* Lowmersland, Les Rochers, Alderney, Channel Islands. *Club:* United Service.

**PELLY, Rev. Canon Richard Lawrence;** Canon of Salisbury, 1952, Canon Emeritus, since 1966; *b* 18 July 1886; *s* of Canon R. A. Pelly; *m* 1927, Dr Salome Wordsworth; two *s* four *d*. *Educ:* Marlborough; Clare Coll., Cambridge. Lecturer, Ridley Hall, Cambridge, 1913-15; ACF 1915-18; Vice-Principal, Bishop's College, Calcutta, 1918-26; Rector, St Paul's Sch., Darjeeling, 1928-33; Vicar of Shoreditch, 1934-37; Canon of Newcastle Cathedral, 1937-45; Rector of Trowbridge, Wilts, 1945-54; Vicar of Farley and Pitton, 1954-57; Master of St Nicholas's Hospital, Salisbury, 1957, retd. *Publications:* St Paul to the Romans; Katha Upanishad; Aspects of Holy Communion; Makers of the New Testament. *Address:* 20 Middle Street, Salisbury, Wilts. *T:* 22967.

**PELLY MURPHY, John;** *see* Murphy, J. P.

**PEMBERTON, Francis Wingate William,** CBE 1970; FRICS; Senior Partner, Bidwells, Chartered Surveyors; Director, Agricultural Mortgage Corp. Ltd, since 1969; *b* 1 Oct. 1916; *s* of Dr William Warburton Wingate (assumed Arms of Pemberton, by Royal Licence, 1921) and Viola Patience Campbell Pemberton; *m* 1941, Diana Patricia, *e d* of Reginald Salisbury Woods, *qv*; two *s*. *Educ:* Eton; Trinity Coll., Cambridge (MA). Joined Bidwells, 1939. Mem. Council, Royal Agricultural Soc. of England, 1951; Hon. Director: Royal Show, 1963-68; National Agricultural Centre, 1967-68 (Chm. Exec. Board, 1969); Member: Water Resources Board, 1964-; Winston Churchill Mem. Trust, 1965-; Economic Planning Council for East Anglia, 1965-. High Sheriff, Cambridgeshire and Isle of Ely, 1965-66. *Recreation:* shooting. *Address:* Trumpington Hall, Cambridge. *T:* Trumpington 3157. *Club:* Farmers'.

**PEMBERTON, Prof. John,** MD London; FRCP; DPH Leeds; Professor of Social and Preventive Medicine, The Queen's University, Belfast, since Sept. 1958; *b* 18 Nov. 1912; British; *m* 1937, Winifred Ethel Gray; three *s*. *Educ:* Christ's Hospital; University College and UCH, London. House Physician and House Surgeon, University College Hospital, 1936-37; Rowett Research Institute under Sir John Boyd Orr (now Lord Boyd Orr), 1937-39; Rockefeller Travelling Fellow in Medicine, Harvard, Mass., USA, 1954-55; Director of Medical Research Council Group for research on Respiratory Disease and Air Pollution, and Reader in Social Medicine, University of Sheffield, 1955-58. Member, Health Visitors Training Council. Chm., Internat. Epidemiological Assoc. Mem. Bd, Arts

Council of NI. *Publications:* (with W. Hobson) The Health of the Elderly at Home, 1954; Ed. Recent Studies in Epidemiology, 1958; Ed. Epidemiology: Reports on Research and Teaching, 1963. Articles in Lancet, BMJ, etc. *Recreations:* visual arts and sailing-dinghy racing. *Address:* The Department of Social and Preventive Medicine, The Queen's University, Belfast.

**PEMBERTON, John Leigh;** *see* Leigh-Pemberton.

**PEMBERTON-PIGOTT, Alan Desmond Frederick,** CMG 1965; Deputy Permanent UK Representative to NATO, since 1969; *b* 3 May 1916; *s* of late Maj.-General A. J. K. Pigott, CB, CBE; *m* 1940, M. C. Tallents; one *s* three *d. Educ:* Shrewsbury Sch.; Queen's Coll., Oxford. Served Armed Forces, 1939-46. HM Diplomatic Service, 1946-. HM Consul-General, Hargeisa, Somali Republic, 1960-61; Foreign Office, 1961-64; Minister, HM Embassy, Ankara, 1964-68. *Address:* UK Delegation to NATO, Brussels; 17 Moore Street, SW3. *T:* 01-584 1832. *Clubs:* Travellers', Royal Thames Yacht; Kiwi.

**PEMBROKE,** 17th Earl of, *cr* 1551, and **MONTGOMERY,** 14 Earl of, *cr* 1605; **Henry George Charles Alexander Herbert;** Baron Herbert of Caerdiff, 1551; Baron Herbert of Shurland, 1605; Baron Herbert of Lea (UK), 1861; Hereditary Grand Visitor of Jesus College, Oxford; *b* 19 May 1939; *s* of 16th Earl of Pembroke and Montgomery, CVO, and of Mary Countess of Pembroke, *qv*; *S* father, 1969; *m* 1966, Claire Rose, *o d* of Douglas Pelly, Swaynes Hall, Widdington, Essex; three *d. Educ:* Eton Coll.; Oxford Univ. Royal Horse Guards, 1958-60 (National Service); Oxford University, 1960-63. *Recreations:* shooting, fishing, racing, bird-watching. *Heir: uncle* Hon. David Alexander Reginald Herbert, *b* 3 Oct. 1908. *Address:* Bulbridge House, Wilton, Salisbury, Wilts. *T:* Wilton 3249. *Club:* Turf.

**PEMBROKE, Mary Countess of; Mary Dorothea Herbert,** CVO 1947; Extra Lady-in-Waiting to Princess Marina, Duchess of Kent, 1950-68 (Lady-in-Waiting, 1934-50); *o d* of 1st Marquess of Linlithgow; *m* 1936, Lord Herbert (later 16th Earl of Pembroke and Montgomery, who *d* 1969); one *s* one *d. Address:* The Old Rectory, Wilton, near Salisbury, Wilts. *T:* Wilton 3157.

**PENDER,** 3rd Baron, *cr* 1937; **John Willoughby Denison-Pender;** *b* 6 May 1933; *s* of 2nd Baron and Camilla Lethbridge, *o d* of late Willoughby Arthur Pemberton; *S* father, 1965; *m* 1962, Julia, *yr d* of Richard Nevill Cannon; one *s* two *d. Educ:* Eton. Formerly Lieut, 10th Royal Hussars and Captain, City of London Yeomanry (TA). *Heir: s* Hon. Henry John Richard Denison-Pender, *b* 19 March 1968. *Address:* 10 Albert Place, W8. *Clubs:* White's, Pratt's.

**PENDRED, Air Marshal Sir Lawrence Fleming,** KBE 1954 (MBE 1933); CB 1947; DFC; DL; *b* 5 May 1899; *s* of Dr B. F. and Eleanor Pendred; *m* 1923, Nina Chour; two *s. Educ:* Epsom Coll. Served European War, 1914-18, with RNAS and RAF in France, 1918; Permanent Commission RAF, 1920; served in Egypt and Turkey (208 Squadron), 1920-23; Flying Instructor, including 4 years at Central Flying School, 1924-30; Staff Officer Intelligence, Transjordan and Palestine, 1930-34; psa Andover, 1935; Sqdn Leader, 1935; Chief Flying Instructor, Montrose, 1936-37; Air Ministry, 1937-40; Wing Comdr, 1938; Bomber Station Commander, 1940-41, Group Captain; Chief Intelligence Officer, Bomber Command, 1942; Director of Intelligence, Air Ministry, 1943; Air Commodore, Chief Intelligence Officer, AEAF, 1944; Asst Comdt RAF, Staff Coll., 1944-45; AOC 227 Group, India, 1945; Director of Intelligence to Supreme Commander, South East Asia, 1946; acting Air Vice-Marshal, Dec. 1945; Air Vice-Marshal, 1948; Assistant Chief of Air Staff (Intelligence), 1947-49; Commandant, School of Land-Air Warfare, 1950-52; Air Officer Commanding-in-Chief, Flying Training Command, 1952-55; retired, 1955. Regional Director Civil Defence (Midland), 1955-63. DL Warwickshire, 1959. Grand Officer Polonia Restituta; Commander, Legion of Merit. *Address:* 13 Lansdowne Circus, Leamington Spa, Warwicks. *T:* Leamington Spa 23559. *Club:* Royal Air Force.

**PENDRY, Thomas;** MP (Lab) Stalybridge and Hyde since 1970; *b* 10 June 1934; *m* 1966, Moira Anne Smith. *Educ:* St Augustine's, Ramsgate; Oxford Univ. Mem., Paddington Borough Council, 1962-65; Chm., Derby Labour Party, 1966. *Recreation:* boxing (sometime Middleweight Champion, Hong Kong; boxed for Oxford Univ.). *Address:* Stonehill House, St Chad's Road, Derby. *T:* Derby 47264.

**PENFIELD, Wilder Graves,** CC (Canada) 1967; OM 1953; CMG 1943; FRS 1943; FRSC; MA, MD, DSc; FRCS(C); Hon. FRCS; Hon. FRCP; Hon. FRCSE; Hon. FRCPE; Hon. Fellow, Merton College, Oxford; Hon. Consultant, Montreal Neurological Institute and Hospital, since 1960; President, Vanier Institute of the Family, 1965-68; *b* Spokane, Washington, USA, 26 Jan. 1891; *s* of Dr Charles Samuel Penfield and Jean Jefferson; Naturalised Canadian Citizen in 1934; *m* 1917, Helen Katherine Kermott; two *s* two *d. Educ:* Princeton Univ. (LittB, DSc); Oxford (BA, MA, BSc, DSc); Johns Hopkins Univ. (MD). Rhodes Scholar, Oxford, 1914 and 1918-20; Beit Memorial Res. Fellow, 1920. Served in Hosp. Militaire VR 76, Ris Orangis, France, 1915, and at No. 2 American Red Cross Hospital, Paris, 1917. Junior attending surgeon, Presbyterian Hospital, New York City, 1921-28; Asst Prof. of Surgery, Columbia Univ., 1924-28. Founded Laboratory of Neurocytology, Presbyterian Hospital, 1924; Study of neurohistology, Madrid, 1924, of neurosurgery, Germany, 1928; Neurosurgeon to Royal Victoria and Montreal General Hospitals, Montreal, 1928-60; Professor of Neurology and Neurosurgery, McGill Univ., 1934-54; Director of Montreal Neurological Institute, 1934-60; retired, 1960. President, Royal College of Physicians and Surgeons of Canada, 1939-41; Chairman of Sub-Cttee on Surgery, National Research Council, Canada, 1941-45. Hon. Fellow Association Surg. of Great Britain and Ireland; FRSocMed (London). Visiting Lecture Series, 1947-67. Chevalier Légion d'Honneur, 1950. Hon. DCL (Oxford), 1953; Hon. LLD Wales, 1953; Hon. DSc: Leeds, 1954; RMC Canada, 1970; Hon. LLD: Edinburgh, 1959; Johns Hopkins, 1970; several other hon. doctorates from Canada, USA and Europe. Lister Medal, RCS England, 1961, and other awards. *Publications:* Cytology and Cellular Pathology of the Nervous System, 1932; Epilepsy and Cerebral Localisation (with T. C. Erickson), 1941; Manual of Military Neurosurgery, 1941; (with T. B. Rasmussen) The Cerebral Cortex of Man, 1950; (with K. Kristiansen) Epileptic Seizure Patterns, 1950; (with H. H. Jasper) Epilepsy and the Functional Anatomy of the Human Brain, 1954; No Other Gods, 1954; The Excitable Cortex in Conscious Man, 1958; (with L. Roberts) Speech and Brain-Mechanisms; The Torch, 1960; The Second Career, 1963; The Difficult Art of Giving,

1967; Man and His Family, 1967; Second Thoughts: science, the arts and the spirit, 1970; contributions to medical journals. *Recreations:* farming, sailing, ski-ing, travel. *Address:* c/o Montreal Neurological Institute, 3801 University Street, Montreal. *T:* 842-1251; 4302 Montrose Avenue, Montreal. *T:* We. 5-1889. *Clubs:* Athenæum; University, Mount Royal, Mount Stephen (Montreal); Princeton (New York).

**PENFOLD, Maj.-Gen. Robert Bernard,** CB 1969; MVO 1957; General Officer Commanding, South East District, since 1969; *b* 19 Dec. 1916; *s* of late Bernard Hugh Penfold, Selsey, and Ethel Ives Arnold; *m* 1940, Ursula, *d* of Lt-Col E. H. Gray; two *d. Educ:* Wellington; RMC, Sandhurst. Commnd into 11th Sikh Regt, Indian Army, 1936; served in NWFP and during War of 1939-45 in Middle East, Central Mediterranean Forces; Instructor, Staff Coll., Quetta, 1946-47; transf. to British Army, RA, 1947; RN Staff Coll., 1953; Secretary, British Joint Services Mission, Washington, 1957-59; comdg 6 King's African Rifles, Tanganyika, 1959-61; Comdr 127 Inf. Bde (TA), 1962-64; Security Ops Adviser to High Commissioner, Aden, 1964-65; Imperial Defence Coll., 1966; Chief of Defence Staff, Kenya, 1966-69. *Recreations:* shooting, golf, gardening. *Address:* Wellesley House, Aldershot, Hants. *Club:* Army and Navy.

**PENGELLY, William Lister;** Master of Supreme Court of Judicature, Chancery Division, 1950-64; *b* 21 Dec. 1892; *s* of Frederick Charles Goldsworthy Pengelly; *m* 1919, Gwendolyn Emélie; two *d. Educ:* Varndean, Brighton; Culham Coll., Culham, Oxfordshire. Lady Aubrey Fletcher Exhib. for violin, Brighton School of Music, 1908. Solicitor, 1921; Senior Partner in Pengelly & Co., 8 New Court, Lincoln's Inn, WC2, solicitors, until 1950. Served European War, 1914-18; 2nd Lieut, 2/5 Devon Regt, 1914; Lieut, 1915; in Egypt, 1915-16; in Mesopotamia, 1916 and 1917 with 4th Devon Regt (wounded); Asst Adjutant with 4th (R) Devon Regt, 1918-19; Captain, 1919. War of 1939-45, Major and Supervising Military Liaison Officer (Z Sector), Home Guard. Chairman of The Comedy Club, 1932-59; Captain London Solicitors Golfing Society, 1950-51; Founder Royal Courts of Justice Music Club, 1953. Member Worshipful Company of Musicians; Freeman of the City of London. *Recreations:* music and golf. *Address:* 41 The Avenue, Cheam, Surrey. *T:* 01-642 6454. *Club:* Walton Heath Golf.

**PENLEY, William Henry,** CB 1967; CBE 1961; PhD; Chief Scientist (Army), Ministry of Defence, since 1970; *b* 22 March 1917; *s* of late William Edward Penley and late Clara (*née* Dodgson), Wallasey, Cheshire; *m* 1943, Raymonde Evelyn, *d* of Frederick Richard Gough, Swanage, Dorset; two *s* one *d. Educ:* Wallasey Grammar Sch.; Liverpool Univ.; BEng, 1937; PhD, 1940. FIEE (MIEE 1964); FRAeS, 1967. Head of Guided Weapons Department, Royal Radar Establishment, 1953-61; Director, Royal Radar Establishment, 1961-62; Director-General of Electronics Research and Development, Ministry of Aviation, 1962-64; Deputy Controller of Electronics, Ministry of Aviation, then Ministry of Technology, 1964-67; Dir, Royal Armament R&D Establishment, 1967-70. *Address:* Beechwood, 13 Garth Road, Sevenoaks, Kent. *T:* Sevenoaks 54794.

**PENMAN, Gerard Giles,** MA, MD (Cantab), FRCS; Hon. Consulting Ophthalmic Surgeon, St Thomas' Hospital; Hon. Consulting Surgeon, Moorfields Eye Hospital; Consulting Ophthalmic Surgeon, Royal Hospital for Incurables, Putney; Fellow, Royal Society of Medicine and Hunterian Society; Member Ophthalmological Society of the UK and Oxford Ophthalmological Congress; Vice-Chairman, West Regional Association for the Blind; Member, Executive Council, Royal National Institute for the Blind; *b* Port Elizabeth, 7 March 1899; *s* of late J. C. Penman, Salisbury, Rhodesia; *m* 1928, Janet, *d* of late Dr J. Walter Carr, CBE; three *s. Educ:* Sherborne Sch.; Pembroke Coll., Cambridge; St Thomas' Hospital. Royal Field Artillery, 1917-19; Ophthalmic Surgeon, Royal Northern Hospital, 1926-31; Ophthalmic Surgeon, Hospital for Sick Children, Great Ormond Street, 1931-36; Examiner in Ophthalmology, Royal College of Physicians, 1962-65. *Publications:* The Projection of the Retina in the Lateral Geniculate Body (with W. E. le Gros Clark) (Proceedings of the Royal Society, 1934); The Position occupied by the Peripheral Retinal Fibres at the Nerve Head (with E. Wolff) (Internat. Ophthalmological Congress, 1950), etc. *Recreations:* archaeology, horticulture, philately. *Address:* Silversmiths, Newland, Sherborne, Dorset. *Club:* Public Schools.

**PENMAN, Dr Howard Latimer,** OBE 1962; FRS 1962; Head of Physics Department, Rothamsted Experimental Station, since 1955. Doctorate, Durham Univ., 1937. Has made physical studies of agricultural and botanical problems, particularly on transpiration and the irrigation of crops. *Publications:* Humidity (Monographs for Students, Inst. of Physics), 1955; Vegetation and Hydrology (Comm. Agric. Bur.), 1963. *Recreations:* music, golf. *Address:* Rothamsted Experimental Station, Harpenden, Herts.

**PENMAN, John,** FRCP; Neurologist to: The Royal Marsden Hospital since 1954; St Andrew's Hospital, Dollis Hill, NW2; The County Hospital, Hertford, and Haymeads Hospital, Bishop's Stortford; *b* 10 Feb. 1913; *er s* of late William Penman, FIA; *m* 1938, Joan *d* of late Claude Johnson; one *s* two *d. Educ:* Tonbridge Sch.; University College, Oxford (Senior Classical Scholar); Queen Mary Coll., E1; The London Hospital. MB, BS (London) 1944; MRCP 1948, FRCP 1969. Member of Association of British Neurologists. *Publications:* contributions to medical journals, mainly on tic douloureux and brain tumours; section on trigeminal injection, in Operative Surgery, 1957. *Recreations:* poetry; etymology; looking at Norman cathedrals. *Address:* Granard House, The Royal Marsden Hospital, Fulham Road, SW3; 117 Copse Hill, SW20. *Club:* Royal Automobile.

**PENN, Lt-Col Eric,** CVO 1965; OBE 1960; MC 1944; Comptroller, Lord Chamberlain's Office, since 1964; Extra Equerry to the Queen since 1963; *b* 9 Feb. 1916; *o s* of Capt. Eric F. Penn (killed in action 1915), Grenadier Guards, and late Gladys Ebden; *m* 1947, Prudence Stewart-Wilson, *d* of late Aubyn Wilson and Muriel Stewart-Stevens, Balnakeilly, Pitlochry, Perthshire; two *s* one *d. Educ:* Eton; Magdalene Coll., Cambridge. Grenadier Guards, 1938-60. Assistant Comptroller, Lord Chamberlain's Office, 1960-64. *Address:* Sternfield House, Saxmundham, Suffolk. *T:* Saxmundham 2456; St James's Palace, SW1; *T:* 01-839 3936. *Clubs:* Turf, White's.

**PENNANT;** *see* Douglas-Pennant.

**PENNANT, David Edward Thornton; His Honour Judge Pennant;** County Court Judge since 1961, Circuit 55 (formerly Circuit 28); *b* 2 Aug.

1912; *s* of David Falconer Pennant, DL, JP, Barrister-at-law, late of Nantlys, St Asaph, N. Wales, and late Lilla Agnes Pennant; *m* 1938, Alice Catherine Stainer; three *s* one *d*. *Educ:* Charterhouse; Trinity Coll., Cambridge. Called to Bar, Inner Temple, 1935. Served, 1939-45, with Royal Signals (TA); OC, Signals Officers' Training Sch., Mhow, India, 1944-45. Chancellor, Dio. Monmouth, 1949-. Governing, and Representative Bodies, Church in Wales, 1946-. Dep. Chairman, Brecknockshire QS, 1956-64; Joint Chairman, Medical Appeals Tribunal for Wales, 1957-61; Chairman, Radnorshire QS, 1962-64; Dep. Chairman, Flintshire QS, 1962-. Mem., County Court Rule Cttee, 1970-. *Recreations:* fishing, shooting, mountaineering. *Address:* Parkbury, Balcombe Road, Branksome Park, Poole, Dorset. *T:* Bournemouth 65614. *Club:* National.

**PENNELL, Rev. Canon (James Henry) Leslie,** TD and Bar, 1949; Rector of Foxearth and Pentlow (Diocese of Chelmsford) since 1965, and of Borley and Lyston (Diocese of Chelmsford), since 1969; Hon. Canon, Inverness Cathedral, since 1965 (Provost, 1949-65); *b* 9 Feb. 1906; *s* of late J. H. L. Pennell and late Elizabeth Esmē Gordon Steel; *m* 1939, Ursula Mary, *d* of Rev. A. E. Gledhill; twin *s* and *d*. *Educ:* Edinburgh Academy; Edinburgh University (BL); Edinburgh Theological College. Precentor, Inverness Cathedral, 1929-32; Rector, St Mary's, Dunblane, and Offic. Chaplain to Queen Victoria School, 1932-49; Officiating Chaplain, Cameron Barracks, 1949-64. TA, 1934; BEF, 1940; SCF, 1943; DACG, 34th Ind. Corps, 1945; SCF Corps Troops, Scottish Comd, 1946-50. *Recreations:* reading and travel. *Address:* Foxearth Rectory, Sudbury, Suffolk. *T:* Long Melford 497.

**PENNELL, Rev. Canon Leslie;** *see* Pennell, J. H. L.

**PENNELL, Vernon Charles,** FRCS; Senior and Life Fellow, Pembroke College, Cambridge, since 1914; Consulting Surgeon and Director of Cancer Bureau, Addenbrooke's Hospital, since 1954; *b* 30 Sept. 1889; *s* of C. W. Pennell, Lincoln; *m* 1st, 1915, Alberta Sanders (*d* 1960); one *s*; 2nd, 1960, Catherine Margaret Nesbitt. *Educ:* Harrow School; Pembroke Coll., Cambridge. Exhib. and Schol., Pembroke Coll., Cambridge, 1908; 1st Class Nat. Sci. Tripos, 1911; Fellow, 1914; MA (Cantab), 1915; MB, BChir (Cantab) 1916; FRCS 1920; Univ. Schol., St Thomas' Hosp., 1912. Lecturer and Director of Med. Studies, Pembroke Coll., Cambridge, 1920-54; Supervisor in Surgery to Cambridge University, 1946-61; Hon. Surgeon and later Cons. Surgeon, Addenbrooke's Hospital, 1927-54. Member, Court of Examiners, RCS England, 1945; Examiner in Surgery to Cambridge Univ., 1934; Member Moynihan Chirurgical Club; Fellow Assoc. of Surgeons of Great Britain; Member British Assoc. of Urological Surgeons. *Publications:* numerous medical. *Recreation:* cricket. *Address:* 10 Gurney Way, Cambridge. *T:* 50544. *Club:* County (Cambridge).

**PENNEY,** family name of **Baron Penney.**

**PENNEY,** Baron, *cr* 1967, of East Hendred (Life Peer); **William George Penney,** OM 1969; KBE 1952 (OBE 1946); FRS 1946; MA; PhD; DSc; Rector of the Imperial College of Science and Technology since 1967; *b* 24 June 1909; *s* of W. A. Penney, Sheerness, Kent; *m* 1st, 1935, Adele Minnie Elms (decd); 2nd, 1945, Eleanor Joan Quennell; two *s*. *Educ:* Tech. School, Sheerness; Royal College of Science, London Univ. (BSc, PhD). Commonwealth Fund Fellowship. University of Wisconsin (MA), 1931-33; Senior Student of 1851 Exhibition, Trinity Coll., Cambridge, 1933-36; PhD (Cambridge), DSc (London), 1935; Stokes Student of Pembroke Coll., 1936; Assistant Professor of Mathematics at Imperial College of Science, London, 1936-45; on loan for scientific work to Ministry of Home Security and Admiralty, 1940-44; Principal Scientific Officer, DSIR, at Los Alamos Laboratory, New Mexico, 1944-45; Chief Superintendent, Armament Research, Ministry of Supply, 1946-52; Director Atomic Weapons Research Establishment, Aldermaston, 1953-59; Member for Weapons Research and Development, UK Atomic Energy Authority, 1954-59; Member for Research, UK Atomic Energy Authority, 1959-61; Deputy Chairman, 1961-64; Chairman, 1964-67. Director, Tube Investments, 1968-. Member South Eastern Electricity Board, 1970-. Treasurer, Royal Society, 1956-60 (Vice-President, 1957-60); Fellow, Imperial Coll.; Fellow, Winchester Coll., 1959; Supernumerary Fellow, St Catherine's Coll., Oxford, 1960; Hon. Fellow, Manchester College of Science and Technology, 1962; Hon. Fellow, Pembroke Coll., Cambridge, 1970; For. Assoc., National Academy of Sciences, USA, 1962. Hon. DSc: Durham, 1957; Oxford, 1959; Bath University of Technology, 1966; Hon. LLD Melbourne, 1956. Rumford Medal, Royal Society, 1966; Glazebrook Medal and Prize, 1969. *Publications:* articles in scientific journals on theory of molecular structure. *Recreations:* golf, cricket. *Address:* Imperial College, South Kensington, SW7; Orchard House, East Hendred, Wantage, Berks. *Club:* Athenæum.

**PENNEY, José Campbell,** CMG 1944; OBE 1942; MC 1917; *b* 1893; *e s* of late J. Campbell Penney, Accountant of Court for Scotland; *m* 1920, Joan (*d* 1970), *d* of Kenneth Mackinnon Douglas, MD; one *s* one *d*. *Educ:* Fettes College, Edinburgh; Oriel Coll., Oxford (Classical Scholar; BA 1918). Served European War, 1914-18 with 51st Division (7th Black Watch), France and Flanders; Egyptian Civil Service, 1919-25; Sudan Government Service, 1925-46; Director of Public Security, 1930; Commissioner Police and Prisons, 1940; Political Assistant to Civil Secretary, 1944-46; Political Adviser to British Administrations in ex-Italian colonies in Africa, 1946-50; UK representative on United Nations Council for Libya, 1950-51; British Member of Electoral Commission on Anglo-Egyptian Sudan, 1953; Supervisor of Elections, Zanzibar, 1956-57. War of 1939-45, Lieut-Colonel, 'I' Branch HQ Troops Sudan and Eritrea, 1940-41 (despatches). Order of the Nile (Officer) 1935, Commander, 1944. *Recreations:* fishing, golf. *Address:* Briar Cottage, Dodsley, Midhurst, W Sussex.

**PENNEY, Reginald John;** Assistant Under-Secretary of State, Ministry of Defence, since 1964; *b* 22 May 1919; *s* of Herbert Penney and Charlotte Penney (*née* Affleck); *m* 1941, Eileen Gardiner; one *s* two *d*. *Educ:* Westminster School. War Service, Royal West Kent Regt, 1939-46. Civil Servant, Air Ministry, until 1964, including service with Far East Air Force, Singapore, 1960-63. *Recreation:* golf. *Address:* Rumbow Cottage, How Green, Chipstead, Surrey.

**PENNINGTON-RAMSDEN, Major Sir (Geoffrey) William,** 7th Bt, *cr* 1689; Major, Life Guards, retired; *b* 28 Aug. 1904; *yr* (but *o* surv. *s* of Sir John Frecheville Ramsden, 6th Bt and Joan, *d* of late G. F. Buxton, CB, Hoveton Hall; *S* father 1958; assumed by deed poll,

1925, surname of Pennington in lieu of Ramsden; resumed surname of Ramsden after that of Pennington by deed poll, 1958; *m* 1927, Veronica Prudence Betty, *o d* of F. W. Morley, formerly of Biddestone Manor, Chippenham, Wilts; three *d*. *Educ:* Ludgrove; Eton; Jesus Coll., Cambridge (BA). Joined 11th Hussars, 1925; transferred Life Guards, 1927-38; served War of 1939-45; seconded to Provost Branch; APM 9th Armd Div. and APM 14th Army; Major, 1942. High Sheriff, Cumberland, 1962-63. *Heir: kinsman* Caryl Oliver Imbert Ramsden, *qv*. *Address:* Versions Farm, Brackley, Northants. *T:* Brackley 2412; Ardverikie, Newtonmore, Scotland; (seat) Muncaster Castle, Ravenglass, Cumberland. *T:* Ravenglass 203. *Club:* English-Speaking Union.

**PENNISON, Clifford Francis;** Assistant Director-General, Administration and Finance, Food and Agriculture Organisation of the UN, since 1967; *b* 28 June 1913; *s* of Henry and Alice Pennison; *m* 1940, Joan Margaret Hopkins; three *d*. *Educ:* Taunton Sch.; Bristol Univ. (BA, 1st Cl. Hons, Hist.). Barrister-at-Law, Inner Temple, 1951. Appointed senior management trainee, Unilever Ltd, 1938. Field Security Officer, Army, 1940-46 (Captain). Principal, Home Civil Service, 1946; Assistant Secretary, and Director of Organisation and Methods, Ministry of Food, 1949; Ministry of Agriculture: Director of Statistics Div., 1953; Director of Public Relations Div., 1958; Director of External Relations Div., 1961; FAO: Permanent UK representative, 1963-66; Director, Economic Analysis Div., 1966-67. *Recreations:* travel, reading, foreign languages, tennis. *Address:* 16 Via Parco Pepoli, Rome, Italy. *T:* Rome 57.78.722. *Clubs:* Royal Automobile; Roma (Rome).

**PENNY,** family name of **Viscount Marchwood.**

**PENNY, Francis David,** FRSE; Managing Director, Y. Ard Ltd, since 1969; Director, Yarrow & Co. Ltd; Visiting Professor of Mechanical Engineering, University of Strathclyde; *b* 20 May 1918; *s* of David Penny and late Esther Colley; *m* 1949, Betty E. Smith, *d* of late Oswald C. Smith. *Educ:* Bromsgrove County High School; University Coll., London (BSc). Engineering Apprenticeship, Cadbury Bros Ltd, 1934-39; Armament Design Establishment, Ministry of Supply, 1939-53; Chief Development Engineer, Fuel Research Station, 1954-58; Dep. Dir, Nat. Engineering Laboratory, 1959-66, Dir, 1967-69. FIMechE; Member Council, IMechE, 1964-. *Publications:* various technical papers. *Recreations:* gardening, cricket, walking. *Address:* Forefaulds, East Kilbride, Glasgow. *T:* East Kilbride 20102. *Clubs:* United Service; Royal Scottish Automobile (Glasgow).

**PENNY, Sir James Downing,** KCIE, *cr* 1943 (CIE 1937); CSI 1939; *b* 25 May 1886; *s* of late Edward Penny, MD, Medical Officer, Marlborough Coll.; *m* 1917, Margaret Mary Wilson (*d* 1962); one *d*. *Educ:* Marlborough Coll.; Magdalen Coll., Oxford (Classical Demy); 1st Class Classical Mods, 1907; 1st Class Lit. Hum. 1909; ICS 1910; Captain, IA Reserve of Officers, 1918; Deputy Secretary Government of India Finance Dept, 1926; Finance Secretary, Punjab Government, 1927-30; Officiating Commissioner, Multan Div., 1934, Lahore, 1935, Rawalpindi Div., 1936; Chief Secretary, 1937-41; Financial Commissioner, Development Dept and Secretary to Government of Punjab, 1941; retired, 1945. *Address:* 19 Five Mile Drive, Oxford. *Club:* English-Speaking Union (Oxford).

**PENNYBACKER, Joseph Buford,** CBE 1967; Director, Department of Neurological Surgery, Radcliffe Infirmary, Oxford, since 1954; *b* 23 Aug. 1907; *s* of Claude Martin Pennybacker and Katherine Miller Mershon; *m* 1941, Winifrid Dean; one *s*. *Educ:* Universities of Tennessee and Edinburgh. BA (Tennessee) 1926; MB, ChB (Edinburgh) 1930; FRCS 1935; MA (Oxon) 1938; MD (Edinburgh) 1941. Resident appointments: Royal Infirmary, Edinburgh; Grimsby District Hospital; National Hospital, Queen Square; First Asst, Neurosurgical Dept, London Hospital; First Asst to Nuffield Prof. of Surgery, University of Oxford. Cross of Royal Order of George I, Greece, 1966. *Publications:* papers in neurological and surgical journals. *Recreations:* history, horticulture. *Address:* Poyle Court, Hampton Poyle, Oxon. *T:* Kidlington 3278. *Club:* Athenæum.

**PENNYCUICK, Hon. Sir John,** Kt 1960; Judge of High Court of Justice, Chancery Division, since 1960, Vice-Chancellor, since 1970; *b* 6 Nov. 1899; *s* of late Colonel John Pennycuick, CSI, and Georgiana Grace Pennycuick; *m* 1930, Lucy Johnstone; one *s* one *d*. *Educ:* Winchester; New Coll., Oxford. 2nd Lieut, Coldstream Guards, 1919; BA Oxford, 1922; Barrister, Inner Temple, 1925; KC 1947; Bencher, 1954. *Address:* Old Manor House, Maids Moreton, Buckingham. *T:* Buckingham 2249. *Clubs:* Garrick; All England Lawn Tennis (Wimbledon).

**PENRHYN,** 6th Baron *cr* 1866; **Malcolm Frank Douglas-Pennant,** DSO 1945; MBE 1943; *b* 11 July 1908; 2nd *s* of 5th Baron Penrhyn and Alice Nellie (*d* 1965), *o d* of Sir William Charles Cooper, 3rd Bt; *S* father 1967; *m* 1954, Elizabeth Rosemary, *d* of late Brig. Sir Percy Laurie, KCVO, CBE, DSO, JP; two *d*. *Educ:* Eton; RMC, Sandhurst. Colonel (retd), KRRC. *Heir: b* Hon. Nigel Douglas-Pennant [*b* 22 Dec. 1909; *m* 1st, 1935, Margaret Dorothy (*d* 1938), *d* of T. G. Kirkham; one *s*; 2nd, 1940, Eleanor Stewart, *d* of late Very Rev. H. N. Craig; one *s* one *d*]. *Address:* Dean Farm, Bishops Waltham, Southampton. *T:* 2598. *Clubs:* Naval and Military, MCC.
*See also Maj.-Gen. C. H. Miller.*

**PENRITH, Bishop Suffragan of,** since 1970; **Rt. Rev. William Edward Augustus Pugh,** MA, LRAM (Singing); *b* 22 July 1909; *s* of William Arthur Augustus and Margaret Caroline Pugh; *m* 1937, Freda Mary, *er d* of Charles Frederick and Susannah Merishaw; no *c*. *Educ:* Leeds Univ.; College of the Resurrection, Mirfield. Assistant Curate: Staveley, Derbys, 1934-37; Edwinstowe, Notts, 1937-38; Rector of Bestwood Park, Notts, 1938-44; Vicar of Sutton-in-Ashfield, Notts, 1944-55; Hon. Canon of Southwell, 1954; Vicar of East Retford, Notts, 1955-59; Rector of Harrington, 1959-62; Vicar of Cockermouth, 1962-70, and Archdeacon of West Cumberland, 1959-70. *Recreations:* fishing, music. *Address:* Bishop's House, Brathay, Ambleside, Westmorland. *T:* Ambleside 3158.

**PENROSE, Maj.-Gen. John Hubert,** OBE 1956; MC 1944; Defence Adviser to British High Commissioner in New Delhi since Nov. 1968; *b* 24 Oct. 1916; *e s* of late Brig. John Penrose, MC and Mrs M. C. Penrose (*née* Hendrick-Aylmer); *m* 1941, Pamela Elizabeth, *d* of H. P. Lloyd, Neath, Glam.; four *d*. *Educ:* Winchester Coll.; RMA Woolwich. 2nd Lt, RA, 1936; war service in European Theatre, BEF, 1939-40, and BLA, 1944; subseq. service in India, Germany, Malaya and UK; idc 1964. *Address:*

c/o Lloyds Bank Ltd, 6 Pall Mall, SW1. *Club:* United Service.

**PENROSE, Lionel Sharples,** FRS 1953; MA, MD; FRCP 1962; Director, Kennedy-Galton Centre, Harperbury Hospital, St Albans, since 1965; *b* 11 June 1898; *m* 1928, Margaret Leathes; three *s* one *d. Educ:* Leighton Park School, Reading; St John's College, Cambridge. Res. Dir Royal Eastern Counties Institution, Colchester, 1930; Director of Psychiatric Research, Ontario, Canada, 1939; Galton Professor of Eugenics, University College, London, 1945-65, Emeritus Professor, 1965. Hon. DSc: McGill, 1958; Newcastle, 1968, Edinburgh, 1970; Hon. MD Gothenburg, 1966. *Publications:* The Influence of Heredity on Disease, 1934; The Biology of Mental Defect, 1949 (3rd edn 1963); The Objective Study of Crowd Behaviour, 1951. *Recreation:* chess. *Address:* 1 Rodborough Road, Golders Green, NW11. *T:* 01-455 1457.

**PENROSE, Sir Roland (Algernon),** Kt 1966; CBE 1961; Chairman, Institute of Contemporary Arts, since 1947, President, since 1969; *b* 14 Oct. 1900; *s* of James Doyle Penrose and Hon. Elizabeth Josephine Peckover; *m* 1st, 1925, Valentine Andrée Boué; 2nd, 1947, Lee Miller; one *s. Educ:* Leighton Park School, Reading; Queens' College, Cambridge. BA Cantab 1922; lived in France, studied and painted, 1922-34; returned to London, organised Internat. Surrealist Exhibition, 1936; painted and exhibited in London and Paris with Surrealist Group, 1936-39. served War, 1940-45, WO Lecturer to Home Guard, 1940-42; commissioned Army, Gen. List, Capt. 1943-45. Founder, Inst. of Contemporary Arts; Fine Arts Officer, British Council, Paris, 1956-59; Member Fine Arts Panel: Brit. Coun., 1955-; Arts Coun., 1959-67; Trustee, Tate Gall., 1959-66; organised Picasso Exhibition at Tate Gallery, for Arts Council, 1960. *Publications:* The Road is Wider than Long, 1939; In the Service of the People, 1945; Picasso his Life and Work, 1958; Miró, 1970. *Recreation:* gardening. *Address:* Farley Farm, Chiddingly, nr Lewes, Sussex. *T:* Chiddingly 308. *Club:* Garrick.

**PENSON, John Hubert,** CB 1953; CMG 1942; MC; *b* 21 Jan. 1893; *s* of late Arthur A. Penson, formerly of Cirencester, Glos; *m* 1929, Marjorie Doreen, *d* of late Col F. H. Crawford, Belfast; one *s* two *d.* Served European War, 1914-19 (Lieut 1918) RE (despatches, MC and bar). Barrister, Lincoln's Inn, 1919. Commissioner for Finance, Commission of Government, Newfoundland, 1937-41. Secretary General, British Supply Mission in Washington, USA, 1944-45, Attaché British Embassy, Washington, 1947-53, Executive Secretary, International Materials Conference, Washington, 1953. *Address:* 15 Bladon Drive, Belfast, N Ireland. *T:* Belfast 660715.

**PENSTON, Norah Lillian,** DPhil; FLS; Principal of Bedford College, University of London, 1951-64, retired; *b* 20 Aug. 1903; 2nd *d* of late Andrew Joseph and Louise Mary Penston; unmarried. *Educ:* The Bolton School; St Anne's College, Oxford. BA, 1927; DPhil Oxon 1930. University Demonstrator in Botany, Oxford, 1928-29; Demonstrator in Botany, 1929-33, Assistant Lecturer, 1933-36, Lecturer, 1936-45, Actg Head of the Botany Dept 1940-44, University of London, King's College; Vice-Principal of Wye College, University of London, 1945-51 and Head of Dept of Biological Sciences, 1947-51. Member Academic Sub-Cttee of British Federation of University Women, 1944-, Mem. Exec. Cttee, 1953-55; Council Member, Women's Farm and Garden Assoc., 1947-51; Member Senate of University of London, 1951-64; Member Committee of Management of Sister Trust, 1952-; Gov., Thomas Wall Trust, 1952-; Exhibition Trustee of Hilda Martindale Educational Trust, 1953-70; Mem. Cttee for Award of International Fellowships of Internat. Fed. of Univ. Women, 1953-58, and 1959-64; Univ. of London Rep. on Council of Roedean School, 1953-64, on Council of Dartford College of Physical Education, 1953-64; Chm., Collegiate Council, Univ. of London, 1957-59; Mem. Marshall Aid Commemoration Commn, 1957-60; Governor, Dominion Students' Hall Trust, 1965-. Hon. Fellow, Wye Coll., Univ. of London. *Publications:* contribs to scientific jls. *Address:* 29 Byron Court, Mecklenburgh Square, WC1. *T:* 01-837 8147. *Club:* Oxford and Cambridge University (Ladies' Annexe).

**PENTLAND,** 2nd Baron, *cr* 1909, of Lyth, Caithness; **Henry John Sinclair,** BA; Member American IEE, MICE, MIEE; Director and Vice-President of the American British Electric Corporation (New York), and of Hunting Surveys Inc. (New York), etc.; *b* 1907; *o s* of 1st Baron and Lady Marjorie Gordon, DBE, JP (d 1970), *o d* of 1st Marquis of Aberdeen and *sister* of 2nd Marquis; *S* father, 1925; *m* 1941, Lucy Elisabeth, 3rd *d* of late Sir Henry Babington Smith, GBE, KCB, CH; one *d. Educ:* Cargilfield; Wellington; Trinity College, Cambridge; President, Cambridge Union Society, 1920; Asst Secretary Ministry of Production, and CPRB, Washington, 1944-45. *Recreation:* sailing. *Address:* c/o Lloyds Bank, Cox's and King's Branch, 6 Pall Mall, SW1. *Club:* Riverdale Yacht (New York).

**PENTLAND, Norman;** MP (Lab) Chester-le-Street Division of County Durham since Sept. 1956; *b* 9 Sept. 1912; *s* of William Henry Pentland, Fatfield, County Durham; *m* 1937, Ethel Maude, *d* of Charles Coates, Chester-le-Street, County Durham; two *s. Educ:* Fatfield School. Checkweighman, Harraton Miners' Lodge; Member Durham Miners' Executive Committee, 1952-53; Member Chester-le-Street Rural District Council, 1946-56 (Chairman, 1952-53). Jt Parly Sec., Min. of Pensions and Nat. Insce, 1964-66, Min. of Social Security, 1966-68; Jt Parly Under-Sec. of State (Social Security), Dept of Health and Social Security, 1968-69; Parly Sec., Min. of Posts and Telecommunications, 1969-70. *Address:* House of Commons, SW1; Great Lumley, Chester-le-Street, County Durham.

**PENTNEY, Richard George;** Director, Attlee House, Toynbee Hall, since 1971; *b* 17 Aug. 1922; *s* of late Rev. A. F. Pentney, MC; *m* 1953, Elisabeth, *d* of Sir Eric Berthoud, *qv*; four *d. Educ:* Kingswood School, Bath; St John's Coll., Cambridge. RNVR (Lieut), 1942-46. Asst Master, Sedbergh School, 1947-58; Headmaster, St Andrew's Coll., Minaki, Tanzania, 1958-64; Asst Master, Oundle School, 1964-65; Headmaster, King's Coll., Taunton, 1965-69; Sec. for Appeals, St Christopher's Fellowship, 1969-71. *Recreations:* walking, water-colour painting. *Address:* Attlee House, Toynbee Hall, Commercial Street, E1.

**PENTREATH, Rev. Canon Arthur Godolphin Guy Carleton,** MA (Cambridge); Residentiary Canon, Rochester Cathedral, 1959-65, Emeritus, 1965; Headmaster of Cheltenham College, 1952-59, retired; *b* 30 March 1902; *s* of late Reverend Dr A. G. Pentreath, Royal Army Chaplains' Department, and Helen Guy Carleton, County Cork; *m* 1927, Margaret Lesley Cadman; two *s* one *d. Educ:* Haileybury

College; Magdalene College, Cambridge. (Classical Scholar), 1st class Hon. with distinction in Classical Archæology, Class. Tripos Part II. Westcott House, Cambridge, 1925-26. Master at Oundle School, 1927; Deacon, 1928; Priest, 1929; Chaplain and Master at Michaelhouse School, Natal, 1928-30; Master of the King's Scholars, Westminster School, 1930-34; Headmaster St Peter's College, Adelaide, S Australia, 1934-43; Headmaster of Wrekin College, 1944-51. Hon. Sec. Hellenic Travellers' Club. *Publication:* Hellenic Traveller, 1964. *Recreation:* sailing. *Address:* Wooden Walls, Dock Lane, Beaulieu, Hants. *T:* Beaulieu 348.

**PEPLOE, Denis (Frederic Neil),** RSA 1966 (ARSA 1956); Teacher of drawing and painting at Edinburgh College of Art; *b* 25 March 1914; *s* of late Samuel John Peploe, RSA, and late Margaret Peploe (*née* Mackay); *m* 1957, Elizabeth Marion (*née* Barr); one *s* one *d*. *Educ:* Edinburgh Academy. Studied at Edinburgh College of Art and Académie André Lhote, 1931-37. Served War of 1939-45: Royal Artillery and Intelligence Corps. Appointed Lecturer at Edinburgh College of Art, 1954. *Recreations:* mah-jong, mycology, backgammon. *Address:* 5 McLaren Road, Edinburgh. *T:* 031-667 6219.

**PEPLOE, Mrs J. R.;** *see* Stevenson, D. E.

**PEPPER, Claude Denson;** Member of Congress, former United States Senator (Democrat); *b* Dudleyville, Alabama, USA, 8 Sept. 1900; *s* of Joseph Wheeler Pepper and Lena (*née* Talbot); *m* 1936, Irene Mildred Webster, St Petersburg, Fla; no *c*. *Educ:* University of Alabama (AB); Harvard Law School (LLB). Instr in Law, Univ. of Arkansas, 1924-25. Admitted to Alabama Bar, 1924; Florida Bar, 1925; began practice of law at Perry, Fla; House Mem. Fla State Legislature, 1929; began practice of law, Tallahassee, Fla, 1930; Mem. State Bd of: Public Welfare, 1931-32; Law Examiners, 1933-34; US Senator from Fla, 1936-51; Mem., various cttees; Chm., Middle East Sub-Cttee of Senate Foreign Relations Cttee (12 yrs) etc.; Chm. Fla Delegation to Dem. Nat. Convention, 1940-44; subseq. alternate Delegate, 1948, 1952, 1956, 1960, 1964, Delegate, 1968. Elected to: 88th Congress, Nov. 1962; 89th Congress, Nov. 1964; 90th Congress, Nov. 1966 (without opposition); 91st Congress, Nov. 1968; Member: (88th Congress) House Cttee on Banking and Currency, and sub cttees on Domestic Finance, Internat. Trade, and Internat. Finance; (89th, 90th and 91st Congress) House Rules Cttee; Chm. (91st Congress) House Select Cttee on Crime, Cttee on Internal Security. Member: Board of Directors, Washington Federal Savings & Loan Assoc.; American Bar Assoc.; International Bar Association, etc. Albert Lasker Public Service Award, 1967. Holds hon. degrees. Member, American Legion; Baptist; Mason; Shriner; Elk; Moose, Kiwanian. *Publications:* contributor to periodicals. *Recreations:* fishing, hunting, golf, horseback riding, swimming. *Address:* (home) 2121 North Bayshore Drive, Miami, Florida, USA; 1661 Crescent Place, NW, Washington 9, DC, USA; (offices) 1701 Meridian Avenue, Miami Beach, Fla; Room 432, Common House Office Building, Washington, DC. *Clubs:* Harvard, Jefferson Island, Army-Navy Country, etc (Washington); various country (Florida).

**PEPPER, Brig. Ernest Cecil,** CMG 1967; CBE 1943 (OBE 1940); DSO 1944; DL County of London; *b* 3 Oct. 1899; *s* of W. E. Pepper, The Manor House, Nocton, Lincs; *m* 1929, Margaret, *d* of A. W. Allan, MD, Seacroft, Lincs; two *s*. *Educ:* Royal Military College, Sandhurst. Worcestershire Regt, Aug. 1918; India, 1925; ADC to Governor of UP, 1925-26; China, 1928; promoted Bedfordshire Regt, 1930; Adj. 1931; Staff College, 1935-36; Bde Major, Chatham, 1937-39; GSO2, France, 1939-40; GSO1, War Office, 1940-41; Bn Comdr, 1941-42; BGS Africa, 1942-43; BGS Washington, 1943-44; Brigade-Commander, Normandy, 1944-45; Comdt, School of Infantry, 1945; retd pay at own request, 1946. Warden, Dominion Students Hall Trust, 1945-70. Bd of Governors: Oversea Service College, 1966-; Church of England Children's Society (Waifs and Strays); Royal Over-Seas League. *Recreations:* cricket, golf. *Address:* Nocton, Grove Road, Hindhead. *T:* Hindhead 455. *Club:* Army and Navy.

**PEPPER, Kenneth Bruce,** CB 1965; Commissioner of HM Customs and Excise since 1957; *b* 11 March 1913; *s* of late E. E. Pepper; *m* 1945, Irene Evelyn Watts; two *s*. *Educ:* County High Sch., Ilford; London Sch. of Economics. Joined HM Customs and Excise, 1932; Asst Sec., 1949; Commissioner, 1957. Lieutenant, Intelligence Corps, 1944. *Address:* Kings Beam House, Mark Lane, EC3. *T:* 01-626 1515.

**PEPPERCORN, Trevor Edward;** Chairman: Triplex Holdings Ltd, since 1966; Overseas Development Institute since 1967; *b* 4 June 1904; *s* of late William and Kate Peppercorn; *m* 1935, Sheila, *d* of F. W. Ayre, St John's Newfoundland; one *s*. *Educ:* Beaumont College; Balliol College, Oxford. BA (Hons). Dunlop Rubber Co., Ltd, 1928; Dunlop Rubber Co. (India) Ltd, 1929; Dunlop South Africa Ltd, 1940 (Managing Director, 1943-52); Director, Dunlop Rubber Co. Ltd, 1957-67. *Recreations:* gardening, shooting. *Address:* The Manor House, Yattendon, near Newbury, Berks. *Club:* Boodle's.

**PEPPERELL, Elizabeth Maud, (E. M. Brewin),** OBE 1966; Assistant Director, The Industrial Society, since 1952; *b* 21 June 1914; *d* of late Edward John Pepperell and Mary Anne Pepperell; *m* 1951, Paul Kingsley Brewin, *s* of Rev. G. H. Brewin and Mabel Brewin; two *s* and one step *s*. *Educ:* Thomas Street Central School; Toynbee Hall; London School of Economics. Awarded Mary Macarthur Scholarship, 1938; Dip. Soc. Science, 1940. With Bryant and May Ltd, 1930-38; Chief Personnel Officer, Carreras Ltd, 1940-51. Member: King Edward Hospital Fund, Domestic Staff Cttee, 1946-; Newsom Cttee, Central Adv. Council, Min. of Education; Nat. Youth Employment Council, 1963-; CBI Working Party on Women in Employment; Min. of Labour's Nat. Jt Adv. Cttee Working Party on Part VI of the Factories Act; Bd, Nat. Inst. for Housecraft (Employment and Training) Ltd; Hon. Sec., Mary Macarthur Scholarship Fund; Trustee, Mary Macarthur Educational Trust. USA Lecture Tours, 1949 and 1964, on Human Relationships at Work. FIPM 1949. *Publications:* Office Staff: Selection and Training, 1959; School to Work: Guide to Supervisors, 1960; What They Expect from Work, 1960; Using Secretarial Services, 1962; You and Your Secretary, 1969; articles on general management subjects; broadcasts. *Recreations:* country life, youth work, home entertaining. *Address:* Carisbrooke, 17 Aldersbrook Road, Wanstead, E12. *T:* 01-989 4314; Avishays, Shaftesbury, Dorset.

**PEPPIATT, Sir Kenneth Oswald,** KBE 1941; MC; Hon. Treasurer of Army Benevolent Fund, 1949-64; *b* 25 March 1893; *s* of late W. R. Peppiatt; *m* 1929, Pamela, *d* of late Captain E.

W. Carter, MC; two *s* one *d*. *Educ:* Bancrofts. Entered service of Bank of England, 1911; Chief Cashier, 1939-49; Exec. Dir, 1949-57. Dir, Coutts and Co., 1958-69. Served European War 1914-18, retd rank Major (despatches, MC and Bar, twice wounded). *Recreations:* shooting, fishing. *Address:* Longdens, Knotty Green, Beaconsfield, Bucks. *T:* Beaconsfield 3158. *Club:* Boodle's.

**PEPYS,** family name of **Earl of Cottenham.**

**PEPYS, Rt. Rev. George Christopher Cutts;** *see* Buckingham, Suffragan Bishop of.

**PEPYS, Lady (Mary) Rachel,** DCVO 1968 (CVO 1954); Lady-in-Waiting to Princess Marina, Duchess of Kent, 1943-68; *b* 27 June 1905; *e d* of 15th Duke of Norfolk, KG, PC, CVO (*d* 1917); *m* 1st, 1939, as Lady Rachel Fitz-Alan Howard, Lieutenant-Colonel Colin Keppel Davidson, CIE, OBE, RA (killed in action, 1943), *s* of Col Leslie Davidson, CB, RHA, and Lady Theodora, *d* of 7th Earl of Albemarle; one *s* one *d*; 2nd, 1961, Brigadier Anthony Hilton Pepys, DSO (*d* 1967). *Address:* Highfield House, Crossbush, Arundel, Sussex. *T:* Arundel 3158.

**PERCEVAL,** family name of **Earl of Egmont.**

**PERCEVAL, Viscount; Thomas Frederick Gerald Perceval;** *b* 17 Aug. 1934; *e s* of 11th Earl of Egmont, *qv*.

**PERCEVAL, Robert Westby,** TD 1968; Clerk Assistant, House of Lords, since 1964; *b* 28 Aug. 1914; *m* 1948, Hon. J. I. L. Littleton, *er d* of 5th Baron Hatherton; two *s* two *d*. *Educ:* Ampleforth; Balliol College, Oxford. Joined Parliament Office, House of Lords, 1938. Royal Artillery, 1939-44; General Staff, War Office, 1944-45. *Address:* Sandlea Court, Datchet, Bucks. *Club:* Beefsteak.

**PERCEVAL-MAXWELL, Mrs P.;** *see* King-Hall, Magdalen.

**PERCIVAL, Allen Dain;** Principal, Guildhall School of Music and Drama, since 1965; *b* 23 April 1925; *s* of Charles and Gertrude Percival, Bradford; *m Guildhall Rachel Hay*. *Educ:* Bradford Grammar Sch.; Magdalene Coll., Cambridge. MusB Cantab 1948. Served War of 1939-45, RNVR. Music Officer of British Council in France, 1948-50; Music Master, Haileybury and Imp. Service Coll., 1950-51; Dir of Music, Homerton Coll., Cambridge, 1951-62; Conductor, Cambridge Univ. Musical Soc., 1954-58; Dir of Music Studies, GSM, 1962-65. Also professional continuo playing, broadcasting and conducting. Hon. GSM 1965; Hon. RAM 1966; Hon. FTCL 1967. *Publications:* The Orchestra, 1956; The Teach Yourself History of Music, 1961; contribs to musical and educnl jls. *Recreation:* travel. *Address:* 7 Park Parade, Cambridge. *T:* 53953. *Club:* Naval.

**PERCIVAL, Sir Anthony (Edward),** Kt 1966; CB 1954; Secretary, Export Credits Guarantee Department, since 1962; *b* 23 Sept. 1910; *m* 1935, Doris Cuff; one *d*. *Educ:* Manchester Gram. Sch.; Cambridge. Entered Board of Trade, 1933; Assistant Secretary, 1942; Commercial Counsellor, Washington, on secondment, 1946-49; Under-Secretary, Board of Trade, 1949-58. President: Berne Union of Export Credit Insurance Organisations, 1966-68; Export Credit Gp, OECD, Paris, 1967-70. *Address:* 16 Hayes Way, Beckenham, Kent. *T:* 01-650 2648.

**PERCIVAL, Edgar Wikner,** FRAeS, CEng, FIMechE, MSAE, MIAeE, MIMarE, AFIAeS, FRSA; engaged on Research and Design for national purposes; Founder, Chairman, Managing Director and Chief Designer, Percival Aircraft Ltd, Aircraft Manufacturers; Director: Associated British Engineering Ltd; The Bergius Co. Ltd; H. Widdop & Co. Ltd; Valbank Ltd; Valco Ltd; Percival Power Units Ltd; Edgar Percival & Co.; *b* Albury, New South Wales; *s* of late William and Hilda Percival, Clarendon Park, Richmond, NSW; unmarried. *Educ:* Sydney Tech. Coll.; Sydney Univ. Served 7th Australian Light Horse, 60 Sqdn RFC and founder member 111 Sqdn RFC, RAF, 1914-18. Built and flew gliders, 1912. Air Ministry approved test pilot on flying boats, seaplanes and land planes. Designer of Percival "Gull", EP9, and of all other Percival aeroplanes; is the first to have produced low-wing monoplanes in British Commonwealth; winner of numerous Air races and trophies, both national and international; has flown fastest time in King's Cup Air Races for 6 years; holds record for fastest time ever flown in King's Cup; designed and built: King's Cup Air Race winners for the 3 consecutive years prior to world war II, and winners for 3 years since War; first civil aircraft in British Commonwealth to have a speed of over 200 m.p.h., the Percival Mew Gull, 1933; a group of lakes discovered in Australia in 1934 was named Percival Lakes in his honour; is the first person to have flown to Africa and back in a day (1935); winner of Johnstone Memorial Trophy and of Oswald Watt Memorial Gold Medal; three times winner of International Speed Trophy; designed and built the first aeroplane in the British Empire to carry 1000 pounds load for 1000 miles range. Founder Mem., Guild of Air Pilots and Air Navigators; Mem., Institute of Directors. Mem., Lloyd's of London, 1944-. *Recreations:* flying, horse riding and hunting, swimming, squash, shooting, ski-ing. *Address:* 72 Chesterfield House, Chesterfield Gardens, Curzon Street, W1. *T:* 01-499 2895. *Clubs:* Royal Air Force, Royal Automobile, Royal Aero.

**PERCIVAL, George Hector,** MD, PhD, FRCPE, DPH; Professor Emeritus of Dermatology, University of Edinburgh (Grant Professor, 1946); *b* 1901; *s* of late E. J. Percival, Kirkcaldy; *m* 1937, Kathleen, *d* of late John Dawson, MD, Buckhaven; one *s* one *d*. *Educ:* George Watson's Coll., Edinburgh; Univs of Edinburgh and Paris. Physician to the Skin Dept, Edinburgh Royal Infirmary, 1936. *Publications:* An Introduction to Dermatology; The Histopathology of the Skin. scientific articles in British Med. Journ., Lancet, etc., Encyclopædia of Med., System of Bacteriology (Med. Res. Council). *Recreations:* golf, fishing. *Address:* Woodcroft, Barnton Avenue, Edinburgh 4. *T:* 031-336 2438.

**PERCIVAL, Ian,** QC 1963; MP (C) Southport since Oct. 1959; Barrister-at-Law; *b* 11 May 1921; *s* of Eldon and Chrystine Percival; *m* 1942, Madeline Buckingham Cooke; one *s* one *d*. *Educ:* Latymer Upper School; St Catharine's College, Cambridge (MA). Served HM Forces, 1940-46: 2nd Bn the Buffs, N Africa and Burma; Major. Called to the Bar, 1948; Bencher, Inner Temple, 1970. Sec., Cons. Parly Legal Cttee, 1964-68, Vice-Chm. 1968-70, Chm. 1970-. Mem., Royal Economic Soc. *Recreations:* golf and tennis. *Address:* 4 Paper Buildings, Temple, EC4. *T:* 01-583 4041. *Clubs:* Junior Carlton; Rye Golf.

**PERCIVAL, Robert Clarendon,** FRCS, FRCOG; Obstetric Surgeon, The London Hospital, since 1947, Director, Obstetric Unit, since 1968; *b* 16 Sept. 1908; British; *m* 1944, Beryl

Mary Ind (*d* 1967); one *d*. *Educ:* Barker College, NSW; Sydney University; The London Hospital, Qualified, 1933. Resident appointments: Poplar Hospital; Hosp. for Sick Children, Gt Ormond St; The London Hosp.; Southend Gen. Hosp. Obstetric and Gynæcological 1st Asst, The London Hosp., 1937. Surgeon-Lt-Comdr, RNVR, 1941-45 (Surgical Specialist). *Publications:* (joint) British Obstetric Practice, 1956; Ten Teachers' Midwifery, 1959; Ten Teachers' Diseases of Women (jointly), 1965; (ed) Holland and Brew, Obstetrics, 1969; contrib. to Lancet. *Recreations:* cricket, tennis, golf, ski-ing, fishing. *Address:* 139 Harley Street, W1. *T:* 01-935 4385; Briarwood, The Drive, Snaresbrook, E18. *T:* 01-989 4924. *Club:* Royal Automobile.

**PERCIVAL, (Walter) Ian;** *see* Percival, Ian.

**PERCY,** family name of **Duke of Northumberland.**

**PERCY, Earl; Henry Alan Walter Richard Percy;** *b* 1 July 1953; *s* and *heir* of 10th Duke of Northumberland, *qv*.

**PERCY, Lord Richard Charles;** Lecturer, Department of Zoology, in the University of Newcastle upon Tyne; *b* 11 February 1921; *s* of 8th Duke of Northumberland and Lady Helen Gordon-Lennox (who *d* 1965, as Dowager Duchess of Northumberland, GCVO, CBE); *m* 1966, Sarah Jane Elizabeth Norton, *o d* of Mr and Mrs Petre Norton, The Manor House, Whalton, Northumberland; one *s*. *Educ:* Eton; Christ Church, Oxford; Durham University. BSc. Lieut-Colonel Comdg Northumberland Hussars, TA, 1959-61; late Capt. Gren. Guards. Served War, 1941-45. DL Northumberland, 1968. *Address:* The University of Newcastle upon Tyne; Lesbury House, Alnwick, Northumberland. *T:* Alnmouth 330; 3 Buckley House, 96 Addison Road, W14. *T:* 01-603 2220. *Clubs:* Turf; Northern Counties (Newcastle upon Tyne).

**PERDUE, Rt. Rev. Richard Gordon;** *see* Cork, Cloyne, and Ross, Bishop of.

**PEREIRA, Arthur Leonard,** FRCS; Ear, Nose and Throat Surgeon to St George's Hospital, London; *b* 10 March 1906; British. *Educ:* Merchant Taylors' School. MRCS, LRCP 1929; MB, BS London 1931; FRCS 1936. Otologist to the Metropolitan Hospital, E8, 1941-47; Otologist to St George's Hospital, 1946-. *Address:* 37 Devonshire Place, W1. *T:* 01-935 4224; Leat Cottage, Old Bosham, Sussex. *Clubs:* Bath; Royal Southern Yacht, Birdham Yacht, Bosham Sailing.

**PEREIRA, Herbert Charles,** DSc; FRS 1969; Director, East Malling Research Station, since 1969; *b* 12 May 1913; *s* of H. J. Pereira and Maud Edith (*née* Machin), both of London; *m* 1941, Irene Beatrice, *d* of David Sloan, Belfast; three *s* one *d*. *Educ:* Prince Albert Coll., Saskatchewan; St Albans Sch.; London Univ. Attached Rothamsted Expl Stn for Agric., research at Ottershaw Coll.; PhD 1941. Royal Engineers, 1941-46 (despatches). Colonial Agric. Service, Coffee Research Stn, Kenya, 1947-52; Colonial Research Service, established Physics Div. at East African Agriculture and Forestry Research Org., Kenya, 1952-61; DSc London 1961; Dir, ARC of Rhodesia and Nyasaland, 1961-63; Dir, ARC of Central Africa (Rhodesia, Zambia and Malawi), 1963-67; Chm., ARC of Malawi. Haile Selassie Prize for Research in Africa, 1966. *Publications:* (jtly) Hydrological Effects of Land Use Changes in East Africa, 1962; Land Use and Water Resources, temperate and Tropical, 1971; papers in research jls; Founding Editor, Rhodesian Jl Agric. Research. *Recreations:* fencing, rock-climbing, sailing. *Address:* East Malling Research Station, Maidstone, Kent. *T:* West Malling 3033. *Club:* Salisbury (Rhodesia).

**PEREIRA, Pedro T.;** *see* Theotonio Pereira.

**PEREN, Sir Geoffrey Sylvester,** KBE 1959 (CBE 1953); BSA (Tor.); Brigadier (retired); Emeritus Professor of Agriculture; *b* England; *m* 1923, Violet Essex, *d* of R. J. Surman, Worcester; one *s* one *d*. *Educ:* Toronto University. Four years Ontario Agric. Coll., Guelph; seven years mixed farming in Ontario and British Columbia; served European War with Canadian Field Artillery and RFA (despatches, Croix de Guerre); subsequently on staff of E Malling Agricultural Research Station, Kent; Inspector under Ministry of Agriculture; later at Agricultural and Horticultural Research Station, Long Ashton, Bristol; Prof. of Agriculture, Victoria Univ. Coll., Wellington, NZ, 1924-28; Principal, Massey Agricultural Coll., Univ. of NZ, 1928-59. During war of 1939-45 commanded 2nd Infantry Bde Group and later 4th NZ Division with rank of Brig. Colonel Comdt, 2 Armoured Regt, NZ Forces, 1954-56. Comr for Civil Defence, Central Region NZ, 1960-65. Hon. Life Member: Royal Agric. Soc. of NZ; Cheviot Sheep Soc. of NZ; Galloway Cattle Soc. of NZ. Silver Jubilee Medal, 1935; Coronation Medals, 1937, 1953. *Address:* 14 Collingwood Street, Palmerston North, NZ.

**PERFECT, Rev. Ronald,** MA; Priest-in-charge, Nettlebed, since 1969; Canon Emeritus of Canterbury Cathedral; *b* Bhagalpur, Bihar, India, 7th Feb. 1908; 2nd *s* of late Canon H. Perfect; *m* 1933, F. E. Martin; two *s* two *d*. *Educ:* St Lawrence College, Ramsgate; Emmanuel College, Cambridge. Honours Tripos in Classics, Aeg, and 3rd Cl. in Part II 1930; Schoolmaster at Worthing (private School) and at Seaford College, 1930-34; at Wycliffe Hall, in training for C of E Holy Orders, 1934-45; Curate at All Saints', Crowborough, 1935-36; Master of Junior School, St Lawrence College, Ramsgate, 1936-37, Headmaster, 1938-69. *Recreations:* Hockey (Cambridge XI, 1927-30; England XI, 1932-34) and cricket (Cambridge Crusaders). *Address:* The Vicarage, Nettlebed, Oxfordshire.

**PERHAM, Dame Margery,** DCMG 1965; CBE 1948; FBA 1961; DLitt Oxon; Hon. Fellow of Nuffield College since 1963; *b* 1895. *Educ:* St Stephens Coll., Windsor; St Anne's Sch., Abbots Bromley; St Hugh's College, Oxford, Modern History. Assistant Lecturer in History, Sheffield University; in Somaliland, 1922-23; Fellow and Tutor in Modern History and Modern Greats, St Hugh's College, Oxford, 1924-29; Rhodes Travelling Fellowship for travel and study of administration of coloured races in N America, Polynesia, Australia, Africa, 1929-31; and in West Africa, 1931-32; Research Fellow St Hugh's College, Oxford, 1930-39; Official Fellow, Nuffield College, 1939-63; Reader in Colonial Administration in the University of Oxford, 1939-48; Director of Oxford Univ. Institute of Colonial Studies, 1945-48. Rockefeller Travelling Fellowship of Int. Inst. of African Languages and Culture for travel and study in E Africa and Sudan, 1932; Research Lecturer in Colonial Administration, Oxford, 1935-39; Vice-Chairman, Oxford University Summer School of Colonial Administration, 1937-38; Member: Advisory Committee on Education in the Colonies, 1939-45; Higher Education Commission and West Indies Higher

Education Cttee, 1944; Exec. Cttee of Inter-University Council on Higher Education Overseas, 1946-67; Colonial Social Science Research Council, 1947-61. Editor, Colonial and Comparative Studies, 1946-. Work on the Oxford University Colonial Records Project, 1963-. Reith Lecturer, BBC 1961; President, Universities' Mission to Central Africa, 1963-64. Mem., Amer. Acad. of Arts and Sciences, 1969. Hon. Fellow: St Hugh's College, Oxford, 1962; Makerere College, Uganda, 1963; School of Oriental and African Studies, 1964; Hon. LLD St Andrews Univ., 1952; Hon. DLitt: Southampton University, 1962; London University, 1964; Birmingham, 1969; Hon. LittD, Cambridge, 1966. Gold Wellcome Medal (Royal Africa Soc.). *Publications:* Major Dane's Garden, 1924; Josie Vine, 1925, new edn 1970; The Protectorates of South Africa (with Lionel Curtis), 1935; Ten Africans (ed), 1936; Native Administration in Nigeria, 1937; Africans and British Rule, 1941; African Discovery (with J. Simmons), 1943; Race and Politics in Kenya (with E. Huxley), 1944; The Government of Ethiopia, 1948, rev. edn 1969; Lugard–The Years of Adventure, 1956; The Diaries of Lord Lugard, 1889-1892 (ed with Mary Bull), 1959; Lugard–The Years of Authority, 1960; The Colonial Reckoning, The Reith Lectures for 1961, 1962; Colonial Sequence, Vol. I, 1967, Vol. II, 1970; also articles in the Times, Africa, etc. *Relevant publication:* Essays in Imperial Government presented to Margery Perham, 1963. *Address:* 5 Rawlinson Road, Oxford.

**PERKIN, (Edwin) Graham;** Editor, The Age, Melbourne, since 1966; Deputy Editor-in-Chief, David Syme & Co. Ltd, since 1969; *b* 16 Dec. 1929; *e s* of Herbert E. Perkin and Iris L. Perkin; *m* 1952, Peggy Lorraine Corrie; one *s* one *d*. *Educ:* Warracknabeal High Sch.; Univ. of Melbourne. Joined The Age as cadet, 1949; Kemsley Scholarship in journalism, 1955-56; subseq. London Office of The Age; Canberra Office, 1957-59; Walkley Nat. Award for Journalism, 1959; Dep. News Ed., 1959; News Ed., 1963; Asst Ed., 1964. Lectr in Journalism, Univ. of Melbourne, 1961-63; Mem., Advanced Session, Australian Admin. Staff Coll., 1963. *Recreations:* reading, golf, cricket, tennis, swimming. *Address:* 35 Alicia Street, Hampton, Victoria 3188, Australia. *T:* (home) 983165, (office) 600421 *Clubs:* Royal Auto (Victoria); Savage (Melbourne); Melbourne Cricket; Victoria Golf.

**PERKINS, Alan Hubert Banbury,** MVO 1953; MBE 1936; retired as HM Consul General, Salonika, Greece (1957-59); *b* 9 Aug. 1898; *s* of late Lewis Banbury Perkins and Mary Therèse Lawrence; *m* 1946, Gertrude Ellen Munton. *Educ:* British Schools in Argentina; Hurstpierpoint Coll., Sussex. Served with RAF, 1918-19. Has also held Consular Appointments at Buenos Aires, 1919-47; Barranquilla, 1947-49; Bahia, 1949, Valparaiso, 1949-51; Leopoldville, 1951-52; Colon, 1953-56; Athens, 1956-57. *Recreations:* tennis and golf. *Address:* Carretera del Reventón 15, Monte Coello, Las Palmas, Canary Islands. *T:* Tafira Alta 603.

**PERKINS, Rev. Benson;** *see* Perkins, Rev. E. B.

**PERKINS, Surg. Vice-Adm. Sir Derek Duncombe S.;** *see* Steele-Perkins.

**PERKINS, Dexter;** Professor Emeritus, University of Rochester, USA, also of Cornell University; President, Salzburg Seminar in American Studies, 1950-62; Prof. of History from 1922 and Chairman, Department of History, 1925-54, University of Rochester; John L. Senior Prof. of American Civilization, Cornell University, 1954-59; City Historian of City of Rochester, 1936-48; *b* 20 June 1889; *s* of Herbert William Perkins and Cora Farmer, Boston, Mass.; *m* 1918, Wilma Lois Lord, Rochester, NY; two *s*. *Educ:* Boston Latin School and Sanford School, Redding Ridge, Conn; Harvard University (AB 1909, PhD 1914). Instructor in history, Univ. of Cincinnati, 1914-15; instructor and asst prof. history, Univ. of Rochester, 1915-22; lecturer on Commonwealth Fund at University College, London, 1937; secretary of American Historical Assoc., 1928-39. Served as 1st lieut, later captain, inf. USA, 1918; attached to historical section, GHQ, Chaumont, France, Oct. 1918-Feb. 1919; work connected with the Peace Conf., Feb.-June 1919; gave Albert Shaw Lectures on Diplomatic History at Johns Hopkins Univ., 1932 and 1937; Professor of American History and Institutions, Cambridge Univ., 1945-46, MA Camb., 1946. Official historian for Overseas Branch of Office of War Information for San Francisco Conf. Lectures, Nat. War College, US, 1946-; Lectures, British Universities and RIIA, 1948 and 1952; Visiting Professor, University of Uppsala 1949; Chm. Council, Harvard Foundation for Advanced Study and Research, Harvard Univ., 1951-56. LLD, Union Coll., 1951, LittD, Harvard, 1953. Moderator of Unitarian Churches of US and Canada, 1952-54; Pres., Amer. Hist. Assoc., 1955-56. Pres., Salzburg Seminar in Amer. Studies, 1950-62. Member of Phi Beta Kappa. *Publications:* John Quincy Adams as Secretary of State; The Monroe Doctrine, 1823-26, 1927; The Monroe Doctrine, 1826-67, 1933; The Monroe Doctrine, 1867-1907, 1938; Hands Off! A History of the Monroe Doctrine, 1823-1940, 1941; America and Two Wars, 1944; The United States and the Caribbean, 1947; The Evolution of American Foreign Policy, 1948; The American Approach to Foreign Policy, 1952; The History of The Monroe Doctrine (revised edn, 1955); Charles Evans-Hughes and American Democratic Statesmanship, 1956; Short Biography of Charles Evans Hughes; The New Age of Franklin Roosevelt, 1957; The American Way, 1957; The American Quest for Peace, 1960; The United States and Latin America, 1960; The United States of America: A History (with G. G. Van Deusen), 1962. *Recreations:* bridge and scrabble. *Address:* 316 Oxford Street, Rochester 7, NY, USA; (Summer) Harvard, Mass.

**PERKINS, Prof. Donald Hill,** FRS 1966; Professor of Elementary Particle Physics, Oxford University, since October 1965; *b* 15 Oct. 1925; *s* of George W. and Gertrude Perkins; *m* 1955, Dorothy Mary (*née* Maloney); two *d*. *Educ:* Malet Lambert High School, Hull. BSc London 1945; PhD London 1948; 1851 Senior Scholar, 1948-51. G. A. Wills Research Associate in Physics, Univ. of Bristol, 1951-55; Lawrence Radiation Lab., Univ. of California, 1955-56; Lectr in Physics, 1956-60, Reader in Physics, 1960-65, Univ. of Bristol. *Publications:* The Study of Elementary Particles by the Photographic Method (with C. F. Powell and P. H. Fowler), 1959. About 50 Papers and Review Articles in Nature, Physical Review, Philosophical Magazine, Physics Letters, Proc. Royal Soc., Nuovo Cimento, etc. *Recreations:* squash, tennis. *Address:* c/o Dept of Nuclear Physics, Keble Road, Oxford.

**PERKINS, Dudley;** *see* Perkins, G. D. G.

**PERKINS, Rev. E(rnest) Benson,** MA (Manchester); Hon. LLD; FSS; Hon. CF; Associate Secretary, World Methodist Council, since 1961; Hon. Secretary Department for Chapel Affairs, Methodist

Church; Director, Methodist Insurance Co.; *b* 14 July 1881; *s* of George Perkins, Leicester; *m* 1910, Alice Elsie (*d* 1964) *d* of Arthur J. Bull, Leicester; one *d*. *Educ:* Alderman Newton's School, Leicester; Handsworth Theological Coll., Birmingham. Asst Sec., Christian Citizenship Dept of Methodist Church, 1920-25; Supt Minister, Birmingham Central Mission, 1925-35; Supt Minister, Sheffield Mission and Chm. Sheffield Dist, 1935-39; General Secretary Department for Chapel Affairs of the Methodist Church, 1939-52; Chm. Manchester Dist, 1941-49; Gen. Sec. World Methodist Council, 1951-61; Pres. Methodist Conference, 1948-49. Guest Preacher, Metropolitan Church, Toronto, 1932. Member: Stockholm Conf. on Life and Work, 1925; World Council of Churches, Amsterdam, 1948, Fraternal Delegate, General Council, United Church of Canada, 1950, and Quadrennial Conference, Methodist Church of America, San Francisco, 1952, Vice-President British Council of Churches, 1952-54; Moderator, National Free Church Federal Council, 1954-55; Fraternal Delegate, World Council of Churches, Evanston, Illinois, USA, 1954. Hon. LLD (Centenary, LA, USA), 1956. *Publications:* The Problem of Gambling, 1917; Betting Facts, 1924; Gambling and Youth, 1932; With Christ in the Bull Ring, 1935; (jointly) The Methodist Church Builds Again, 1946; Serving the Church, 1948; Gambling in English Life (Beckly Lecture), 1950 (revised, 1958, 1962); Methodist Preaching Houses and the Law (Wesley Hist. Soc. Lecture), 1952; So Appointed: an autobiography, 1963; Discipline, 1966. *Recreations:* travel, music, photography; special interests: sociology, church architecture, church law. *Address:* 38 Belle Walk, Moseley, Birmingham 13. *T:* 021-449 1919. *Clubs:* National Liberal; Reform (Manchester).

**PERKINS, Rev. Canon Frederick Howard,** MA; Canon Residentiary and Treasurer of Liverpool Cathedral, 1955-63, Canon Emeritus since 1964; Vicar of St Matthew and St James, 1936-63. *Educ:* St Catharine's College, Cambridge (MA); Ridley Hall, Cambridge. Ordained deacon, 1922; priest, 1923. Curate: St John, Ladywood, Birmingham, 1922-26, St Martin, Birmingham, 1926-28; Vicar: St Christopher, Springfield, Worcs, 1928-36; Canon of Liverpool, 1951. Rural Dean of Childwall, 1947-63; Proctor in convocation, Liverpool, 1948-59; Chaplain, Ministry of Pensions Hosp., Mossley Hill, 1936-63; Bishop's Chaplain, Univ. of Liverpool, 1945-55; Examining Chaplain to Bishop of St Edmundsbury and Ipswich, 1960-65. *Address:* Castleford, 25 Tongdean Lane, Brighton BN1 5JD. *T:* Brighton 503220.

**PERKINS, Prof. George,** MC; MCh; FRCS; Consultant Surgeon, Rowley Bristow Hospital, Pyrford. BA (1st cl. Hons), 1914; MA Oxon, 1921; MB, BCh 1916; MCh 1921; FRCS 1921. Formerly Professor of Surgery, St Thomas's Hospital Medical School, University of London; Consultant Orthopædic Surgeon, St Thomas' Hospital. Ex-president British Orthopædic Association. *Publications:* The Foundations of Surgery, 1954; Fractures and Dislocations, 1958; Orthopaedics, 1961. *Address:* Thorpe Lee, Denne Park, Horsham, Sussex.

**PERKINS, (George) Dudley (Gwynne),** MA; Director-General of the Port of London Authority, since 1964; *b* 19 March 1911; *s* of Gwynne Oliver Perkins and Sarah Perkins; *m* 1st, 1939, Enid Prys-Jones (*d* 1943); one *d*; 2nd, 1946, Pamela Marigo Blake; one *d*. *Educ:* Clifton College (Scholar); King's College, Cambridge (Choral Scholar; 1st cl. hons Eng. Lit.). Solicitor, 1937; Asst Legal Adviser, BBC, 1945-48; Asst Legal Adviser, National Coal Board, 1948-51; Chief Solicitor, PLA, 1955-62; Jt Dep. General Manager, PLA, 1962-64. Member: Council of Law Society, 1954-62; Central Transport Consultative Cttee, 1962-69; SE Economic Planning Council, 1966-; MInstT. A Governor of Morley Coll., 1951-; Governor, Clifton Coll., 1969-. Regular broadcaster in Can I Help You and other broadcasts on law and current affairs, 1950-62. *Publications:* Can I Help You, 1959; Family Lawyer, 1962. *Recreations:* music, walking. *Address:* 63 Netherhall Gardens, Hampstead, NW3. *T:* 01-435 0609. *Clubs:* Athenæum, Garrick.

**PERKINS, Col George Forder,** CBE 1941; DSO 1918; late The Royal Hampshire Regiment; Aide-de-Camp to the King, 1934-36; *b* 1884; *s* of late Sir Edwin K. Perkins, CBE, DL; *m* Nora Christine, *d* of late Allen Shuttleworth, Indian Navy; one *s* one *d*. *Educ:* Cheltenham College. Served European War, 1914-18 (despatches, DSO, Brevets Major and Lieut-Col); retired pay, 1936. *Address:* 19 Kingsbury Square, Wilton, Salisbury, Wilts.

**PERKINS, James Alfred,** MA, PhD; President, Cornell University, USA, since 1963; *b* 11 Oct. 1911; *s* of H. Norman Perkins and Emily (*née* Taylor); *m* 1938, Jean Bredin; two *s* three *d*. *Educ:* Swarthmore Coll., Pa (AB); Princeton Univ., NJ (MA, PhD). Instructor Polit. Sci., Princeton Univ., 1937-39; Asst Prof. and Asst Dir, Sch. of Public and Internat. Affairs, Princeton, 1939-41; Dir, Pulp and Paper Div., Office of Price Admin., 1941-43; Asst to Administrator, For. Econ. Admin., 1943-45; Vice-Pres. Swarthmore Coll., 1945-50; Exec. Associate, Carnegie Corp. of NY, 1950-51; Dep. Chm. (on leave) Res. and Develt Bd, Dept of Defense, 1951-52; Vice-Pres., Carnegie Corp. of NY, 1951-63. Carnegie Foundn for the Advancement of Teaching: Sec. 1954-55; Vice-Pres., 1955-63. Chm., Pres. Johnson's Gen. Adv. Cttee on Foreign Assistance Prog., 1965-68; Trustee: Rand Corp., 1961-; United Negro Coll. Fund (Chm. of Bd), 1965-; Educl Testing Service, 1964-68; Council on Foreign Relations; Mem. Gen. Adv. Cttee of US Arms Control and Disarmament Agency, 1963-; Chm. NY Regents Adv. Cttee on Educational Leadership, 1963-67. Mem., Bd of Directors: Chase Manhattan Bank, 1967-. Cornell Aeronautical Lab., 1963-; Stevenson Memorial Fund, 1966-. Mem. Society of Friends, Swarthmore, Pa. Hon. degrees: LLD: Centre Coll., 1958; Univ. of Akron, 1961; Brown Univ., Rutgers Univ., Swarthmore Coll., 1963; Princeton Univ., Lehigh Univ., Northwestern Univ., Syracuse Univ., 1964; Univ. of Rochester, 1965; Notre Dame, 1968; Yale, 1968; Yeshiva Univ., 1968; Univ. of Sydney, 1968; LHD: Case Inst. of Tech., 1961; Ohio Univ., 1962. *Publications:* The University in Transition, 1966; contrib. to: Public Admin. Review, Amer. Polit. Sci. Review, Educational Record, etc. *Address:* Cornell University, USA. *Clubs:* Century Association, Coffee House (NYC); Cosmos (Washington, DC).

**PERKINS, John B. W.;** *see* Ward-Perkins.

**PERKINS, Air Vice-Marshal Maxwell Edmund Massy,** CB 1962; CBE 1957; Director of Engineering, Aviation Division, Smiths Industries Ltd; *b* Portsmouth, Hants, 22 Aug. 1907; *s* of late Donald Maxwell Perkins; *m* 1934, Helena Joan Penelope, *d* of Herbert John Newberry, Hitchin; one *s* two *d*. *Educ:* Portsmouth College; London University (BA). Entered RAF, 1929; India, 1934-38.

Served War of 1939-45, Bomber Command and Burma; America, 1952-54; STSO Fighter Command, 1954-56; Commandant, St Athan, 1956-58; Senior Technical Staff Officer, Bomber Command, 1958-61; Dir-Gen. of Engineering, Air Min., 1961-64, retired. Air Cdre, 1957; Air Vice-Marshal, 1961. CEng 1966, FIMechE (MIMechE 1957); FRAeS 1960. *Recreation:* sailing. *Address:* Keith Lodge, Oldfield Rd, Maidenhead, Berks. *T:* Maidenhead 20624. *Clubs:* Royal Air Force; Royal Dart Yacht (Kingswear).

**PERKINS, Norman Stuart,** OBE 1962; JP; Landowner and Farmer; Member: Pigs Cttee, Meat and Livestock Commission; Agricultural Land Tribunal; Director: NFU Mutual Insurance Society Ltd; Avon Insurance Co. Ltd; *b* 16 May 1904; *s* of David Perkins; *m* 1926, Helen Irene, *d* of Capt. R. E. James, Trinity Service; two *s*. *Educ:* Clifton Coll. Member: Pig Marketing Bd, 1937-57 (Chm. 1956 and 1957); Bacon Development Bd, 1939-57; Founder Mem., Pig Industry Develt Authority, 1957-68; Chm. Pemb. Branch NFU, 1940; Mem. Pemb. CC; Council Royal Welsh Agricultural Soc.; Vice-Chm. Pembs Conservative Assoc.; Chm. Pembs Red Cross Agric. Fund; Mem., Pembs War Agric. Exec. Cttee (Chm. Dist Cttee and Chm. Animal Husbandry Cttee); Chm. Welsh Regional Cttee, Wool Marketing Scheme. 2nd in Comd Bn HG. Mem. Council Central Landowners' Assoc. and Mem. Exec. Cttee; Mem. Min. of Agriculture Livestock Improvement Cttee. JP 1951 (Chm. Bench, 1960-); High Sheriff of Pembrokeshire, 1956. Fellow, Royal Agricultural Soc., 1970. *Address:* St Lawrence, Fishguard, Pembs. *T:* Fishguard 2858. *Clubs:* Farmers'; Pembrokeshire County (Haverfordwest).

**PERKINS, Sir Robert Dempster,** Kt, *cr* 1954; *b* 1903; *s* of late W. Frank Perkins; *m* 1944, Lady Norman, *widow* of Sir Nigel Norman, 2nd Bt. *Educ:* Eton; Trinity Coll., Cambridge, MA. Mechanical Engineer. MP (C) Stroud (by-election May), 1931-45; MP (C) Stroud and Thornbury Division of Gloucestershire, 1950-55; Parliamentary Secretary, Ministry of Civil Aviation, 1945. *Recreations:* aviation and fishing. *Address:* The Manor House, Downton, Wilts. *Club:* Carlton.

**PERKINS, Sir W. R. D.;** *see* Perkins, Sir R. D.

**PERKS, John Clifford,** MC 1944; TD; **His Honour Judge Perks;** County Court Judge since 1970; *b* 20 March 1915; *s* of John Hyde Haslewood Perks and Frances Mary Perks; *m* 1940, Ruth Dyke Perks (*née* Appleby); two *s* (one *s* two *d* decd). *Educ:* Blundell's; Balliol Coll., Oxford. Called to Bar, Inner Temple, 1938; joined Western Circuit; Chancellor, diocese of Bristol, 1950; Deputy Chairman, Devon QS, 1965. *Recreation:* castles. *Address:* 15 Mortimer Road, Bristol BS8 4EY. *T:* Bristol 36947. *Club:* Constitutional (Bristol).

**PERKS, Sir (Robert) Malcolm Mewburn-,** 2nd Bt, *cr* 1908; retired Public Works Contractor, one time Chairman of Sir John Jackson Ltd, and Ford & Walton Ltd; *b* 29 July 1892; *s* of Sir Robert Wm Perks, 1st Bt, and Edith (*d* 1943), *y d* of late Wm Mewburn, DL; *S* father 1934; *m* 1917, Neysa Gilbert, *o c* of late Rev. Dr Cheney, New Rochelle, USA; two *d*. *Educ:* Leys Sch., Cambridge. Served European War, Lieut RNVR, Captain RAF. Director of Building Construction, Ministry of Supply, 1941-43. *Heir:* none. *Address:* Clifford's Inn, EC4.

**PEROWNE, Maj.-Gen. Lancelot Edgar Connop Mervyn,** CB 1953; CBE 1945; Royal Engineers, retired; Company Director; *b* 11 June 1902; 2nd and *e surv s* of late Colonel Woolrych Perowne; *m* 1927, Gertrude Johanna Jenny Stein, Cologne, Germany; one *d*. *Educ:* Wellington Coll.; Royal Military Academy, Woolwich. 2nd Lieut, Royal Engineers, 1923; Temp. Brigadier, 1942; Colonel 1945; Brigadier, 1951; Maj.-General, 1952. Served France, 1940 (despatches); Anti-aircraft Comd, 1940-43, commanded 69 and 37 AA Bdes; India and Burma, 1943-45, commanded 23 Inf. Bde (despatches, CBE); SE Asia, 1945-46, commanded Penang Sub-Area and 72 Indian Inf. Bde (despatches); Comdt School of Combined Operations, 1947-48; Comd 151 Northumberland and Durham Inf. Bde, TA, 1949-51; Commander British Miltary Mission to Greece, 1951-52; Commanded South Malaya District, 1952-55; GOC 17th Gurkha Division, 1952-55 (despatches); Maj.-General, The Brigade of Gurkhas, 1952-55, retired 1955. Colonel, The Gurkha Engineers, 1957-66. CEng; MIEE; KJStJ 1945; Star of Nepal (2nd Class), 1954. *Address:* Benfleet Hall, Green Lane, Cobham, Surrey.

**PEROWNE, Stewart Henry,** OBE 1944; FSA; Orientalist and Historian; Colonial Administrative Service (retired); *b* 17 June 1901; 3rd *s* of late Arthur William Thomson Perowne, DD, Bishop of Worcester, and late Helena Frances Oldnall-Russell; *m* 1947, Freya Madeline Stark, *qv*. *Educ:* Haileybury Coll. (champion sprinter); Corpus Christi Coll., Cambridge; Harvard Univ., USA. BA 1923, MA 1931, Cambridge. Joined Palestine Government Education Service, 1927; Administrative Service, 1930 (Press Officer 1931); Asst District Commissioner, Galilee, 1934; Asst Secretary Malta, 1934; Political Officer, Aden Prot., 1937; recovered inscriptions and sculpture from Imadia and Beihan; Arabic Programme Organiser, BBC, 1938; Information Officer, Aden, 1939; Public Relations Attaché, British Embassy, Baghdad, 1941; Oriental Counsellor, 1944; Colonial Secretary, Barbados, 1947-51; seconded as Principal Adviser (Interior), Cyrenaica, 1950-51; retired 1951. Discovered ancient city of Aziris, 1951. Adviser, UK delegation to UN Assempbly, Paris, Nov. 1951. Helped design stamps for Malta, 1936, Aden, 1938, Barbados, 1949, Libya, 1951; currency notes for W. Indies Federation, 1949, and Libya, 1951; Assistant to the Bishop in Jerusalem for Refugee work, 1952; designer and supervisor of Refugee model villages. FSA 1957. KStJ 1954. Coronation Medal, 1937; Iraq Coronation Medal, 1953; Metropolitan Police Mounted Officers certificate. Member, C. of E. Foreign Relations Council. *Publications:* The One Remains, 1954; Herod the Great, 1956; The Later Herods, 1958; Hadrian, 1960; Cæsars and Saints, 1962; The Pilgrim's Companion in Jerusalem and Bethlehem, 1964; The Pilgrim's Companion in Roman Rome, 1964; The Pilgrim's Companion in Athens, 1964; Jerusalem, 1965; The End of the Roman World, 1966; The Death of the Roman Republic: from 146 BC to the birth of the Roman Empire, 1969; Roman Mythology, 1969; (contrib.) Ancient Cities of the Middle East, 1970; The Siege within the Walls: Malta 1940-43, 1970; articles in Encyclopædia Britannica, The Times, etc. *Recreations:* horses, the arts, archæology. *Address:* 44 Arminger Road, W12. *T:* 01-743 8363. *Clubs:* Travellers'; Casino Maltese; Savannah (Bridgetown); Phoenix-SK (Harvard).

**PERREN, Edward Arthur,** CB 1962; PhD; FRIC; *b* 13 June 1900; *s* of late Arthur Perren, London; *m* 1925, Muriel Davidge, Palmers Green; one *s* one *d* (and one *s* decd). *Educ:* Stationers' Sch., Hornsey; Imperial Coll.,

University of London. BSc Hons (London) 1919; PhD (London) 1922. Joined scientific staff of War Dept, 1922. Chief Superintendent, Suffield Experimental Station, Canada, 1949-51; Superintendent Research Division, CDEE, Porton, 1951-55; Director, CDEE, Porton (Chief Scientific Officer), 1955-61. *Publications:* various papers on Organic Chemistry. *Address:* Larchfield, Appleshaw, Andover, Hants. *T:* Weyhill 434.

**PERRETT, John; His Honour Judge Perrett;** a Judge of County Courts, since 1969; Deputy Chairman, Warwickshire Quarter Sessions, since 1970; *b* 22 Oct. 1906; *er s* of late Joseph and Alice Perrett, Birmingham; *m* 1933, Elizabeth Mary, *y d* of late William Seymour, Nenagh, Co. Tipperary; two *s* two *d. Educ:* St Anne's RC and Stratford Road Schools, Birmingham; King's Coll., Strand, WC2. Entered office of Philip Baker & Co., Solicitors, Birmingham, 1922; joined late Alfred W. Fryzer, Solicitor, Arundel St, WC2, 1925; joined Herbert Baron & Co., Solicitors, Queen Victoria St, EC4, 1934. Served War of 1939-45: RAPC, 1939-45; RASC, 1945. Called to Bar, Gray's Inn, 1946; practised in London and on Midland Circuit. *Address:* 9 The Close, Lichfield, Staffs. *T:* Lichfield 52320; Farrar's Building, Temple, EC4. *T:* 01-583 9241.

**PERRIN, John Henry;** Under Secretary, Ministry of Agriculture, Fisheries and Food, since 1968; *b* 14 Jan. 1916; *s* of Walter William Perrin, Faringdon and Sonning, Berks, and Amelia (*née* Honey), Oxford; *m* 1940, Doris Winifred Barrington-Brider; two *s. Educ:* Minchenden Sch.; London Univ. Royal Navy, 1939-46. Chemist, Harley Street and Crosse & Blackwells Ltd, 1935-36; HM Customs and Excise, 1936-48; Min. of Agriculture, subseq. Min. of Agriculture, Fisheries and Food, 1948-: Principal Private Sec. to Minister (Mr Heathcoat Amory, now Lord Amory), 1955-57; Regional Controller, Eastern Region, 1957-68. Member of Board and Council, Royal Agricultural Soc. of England. *Recreations:* painting and Chinese porcelaine, soccer, motors. *Address:* Beeson End, Harpenden, Herts. *T:* Harpenden 61357. *Clubs:* Naval, Civil Service, Caravan, Jensen.

**PERRIN, Sir Michael (Willcox),** Kt 1967; CBE 1952 (OBE 1946); FRIC; Chairman, The Wellcome Foundation Ltd, 1953-70; *b* 13 Sept. 1905; *s* of late Bishop W. W. Perrin; *m* 1934, Nancy May, *d* of late Bishop C. E. Curzon; one *s* one *d. Educ:* Winchester; New Coll., Oxford (BA, BSc). Post-graduate research, Toronto Univ. (MA), 1928-29; Amsterdam Univ., 1929-33; ICI (Alkali) Research Dept, Northwich, 1933-38; Asst Director, Tube Alloys (Atomic Energy), DSIR, 1941-46; Dep. Controller, Atomic Energy (Technical Policy), Ministry of Supply, 1946-51; Research Adviser, ICI, 1951-52. Chm. (Treasurer) Bd of Governors, St Bartholomew's Hosp. and Pres., Med. Coll. of St Bartholomew's Hosp., 1960-69; Chm. Council, Royal Veterinary Coll., London Univ., 1967-; Member: Council, Sch. of Pharmacy, London Univ., 1963-; Central Adv. Council for Science and Technology, 1969-. Hon. DSc Univ. of British Columbia, 1969. *Publications:* papers in scientific and technical journals. *Address:* 14 Christchurch Hill, Hampstead, NW3. *T:* 01-794 3064; 36 Fair Mile, Henley-on-Thames, Oxon. *T:* Henley 2945. *Clubs:* Athenæum, Junior Carlton.

**PERRING, Sir Ralph (Edgar),** 1st Bt *cr* 1963; Kt 1960; Chairman, Perring Furnishings Ltd; *b* 23 March 1905; *yr s* of late Colonel Sir John Perring, DL, JP; *m* 1928, Ethel Mary, OStJ, *o d* of late Henry T. Johnson, Putney; three *s. Educ:* University College Sch., London. Lieut, RA (TA) 1938-40, invalided. Member Court of Common Council (Ward of Cripplegate), 1948-51; Alderman of City of London (Langbourn Ward), 1951-, one of HM Lieutenants of the City of London, and Sheriff, 1958-59. Lord Mayor of London, 1962-63. Chairman, Spitalfields Market Cttee, 1951-52; JP County of London, 1943-; Member: LCC for Cities of London and Westminster, 1952-55; County of London Licensing Planning Cttee; New Guildford Cathedral Council; Consumer Advisory Council, BSI, 1955-59. Governor: St Bartholomew's Hospital, 1964-69; Imperial College of Science and Technology, 1964-67; Christ's Hospital; Vice-Chairman, BNEC Cttee for Exports to Canada, 1964-67, Chairman, 1968-70; Dir, Confederation Life Assoc. of Canada, 1969-. Vice-President, Royal Bridewell Hospital (King Edward's Sch., Witley, 1964-); Master Worshipful Company of Tin Plate Workers, 1944-45; Court, Worshipful Company of Painters-Stainers, and Farmers; President Langbourn Ward Club, 1951-. KStJ. Grand Cross of Merit (Republic of Germany), 1959; Order of Homayoun (Iran), 1959; Grand Officer, Order of Leopold (Belgium), 1963; Knight Commander, Royal Order of George I (Greece), 1963; Commander de la Valeur Camerounaise, 1963. *Heir: s* John Raymond Perring [*b* 7 July 1931; *m* 1961, Ella, *d* of late A. G. Pelham, Dorking, Surrey; two *s* two *d*]. *Address:* 15 Burghley House, Somerset Road, Wimbledon, SW19. *T:* 01-946 3433. *Clubs:* Constitutional, Royal Automobile, City Livery (President, 1951-52).

**PERRINS, Wesley,** MBE 1952; County Alderman; an official of Municipal and General Workers' Union, Birmingham District Secretary; Member: Worcestershire County Council; West Midlands Economic Planning Council; *b* 21 Sept. 1905; *s* of Councillor Amos Perrins, Stourbridge; *m* 1932, Mary, *d* of Charles Evans; one *s* one *d. Educ:* Wollescote Council Sch.; Upper Standard Sch., Lye. MP (Lab) Yardley Division of Birmingham, 1945-50. Member of: Lye & Wollescote UDC, 1928-31; Stourbridge Borough Council, 1931-46. *Address:* Cromlech Cottage, 19 Walker Avenue, Wollescote, Stourbridge, Worcs. *T:* Stourbridge 4640.

**PERROTT, Sir Donald (Cyril Vincent),** KBE 1949; Chairman and Director of industrial companies; Member, Finance and Administration, Atomic Energy Authority, 1954-60; *b* 12 April 1902; *s* of late Frederick John Perrott and of Alice Perrott, Southampton; *m* 1st, 1925, Marjorie May (*d* 1969), *d* of late William Holway, Taunton; one *s*; 2nd, 1969, Mrs L. L. Byre. *Educ:* Tauntons' Sch., Southampton; University College, Southampton. Inland Revenue Dept, 1920; Ministry of Aircraft Production, 1941; Ministry of Supply, 1942; Dep. Secretary Ministry of Food, 1947-49; Deputy Chairman, Overseas Food Corporation, 1949-51; Chairman: Queensland British Food Corporation, 1950-53; British Ministry of Supply, European Purchasing Commission, 1951-52; Interdepartmental Cttee, Woolwich Arsenal, 1953; Secretary, Department of Atomic Energy and Member for Finance and Administration of Atomic Energy Authority, 1954-60; Member, Governing Board of National Institute for Research in Nuclear Science, 1957-60. *Recreations:* golf and bridge. *Address:* 14 Kingfisher House, Melbury Road, W14. *Club:* Royal Automobile.

**PERRY, Alan Cecil,** MS, FRCS; retired as Senior Surgeon, London Hospital and Poplar Hospital; *b* 26 Nov. 1892; *s* of Major H. Perry,

Ware, Herts; *m* 1922, May Alice, *d* of late Captain C. H. Palmer, RN; no *c*. *Educ:* London Univ. Price Entrance Scholar, Medical Scholarship, Andrew Clark Prize, Anatomy and Biology Scholarship, Anatomy and Physiology Scholarship, Letheby Prize, London Hospital; Begley Studentship, Royal College of Surgeons; Gold Medal, MB, BS (London) 1922 with distinction in Surgery, Medicine, Anatomy, Physiology, Pharmacology, and Organic Chemistry. *Publications:* Practice of Surgery, and House Surgeons Vade Mecum (with Russell Howard); General Nursing (with D. Harvey). *Address:* Dorney, Manor Gardens, Beaminster, Dorset. *T:* Beaminster 234.

**PERRY, Charles Bruce;** Professor of Medicine, University of Bristol, 1935-69, Emeritus since 1969; *b* 1903; *s* of Charles E. and Sarah Duthie Perry; *m* 1929, Mildred Bernice Harvey; three *d*. *Educ:* Bristol Grammar Sch.; University of Bristol, MB, ChB 1926; FRCP, 1936; MD Bristol, 1928; Physician, Bristol Royal Hospital for Sick Children and Women, 1928; Physician, Winford Orthopædic Hospital, 1930; Buckston Browne Prize, Harveian Society of London, 1929; Markham Skeritt Memorial Prize, 1931; Asst Physician, Bristol General Hospital, 1933. Lectures: Long Fox Memorial, 1943; Bradshaw, RCP, 1944; Lumleian, RCP, 1969; Carey Coombs, Univ. of Bristol, 1969. Pro-Vice-Chancellor, University of Bristol, 1958-61; President Assoc. of Physicians of Great Britain and Ireland, 1961-62; Chairman, British Cardiac Society, 1961-62; Censor, RCP, 1962-64. *Publications:* Bacterial Endocarditis, 1936; various papers in the Medical Press dealing with research in Diseases of the Heart. *Address:* Beechfield, 54 Grove Road, Coombe Dingle, Bristol BS9 2RR. *T:* Bristol 682713.

**PERRY, Edward William,** CSI 1946; CIE 1930; *b* 12 June 1891; *s* of Sir William Payne Perry, CB, and Constance Gower Perry; *m* 1930, Mary Thrift, *d* of G. Reavell, Ewhurst, Sussex; three *s* two *d*. *Educ:* St Paul's Sch.; Caius Coll., Cambridge. Entered ICS, 1915; Indian Army Reserve of Officers, 1917-19, served in Palestine; Collector, Bombay suburban district, 1925-26; Bombay, 1926-27; Private Secretary to Governor, 1927; Assistant Secretary, Indian Statutory Commission, 1927-30; Collector, Poona, 1930-31; Secretary, Bombay Reorganisation Cttee; Secretary to Government, 1935-39; Commissioner, 1939-47; Colonial Office, 1948-50. *Address:* The Clock House, Ewhurst, Robertsbridge, Sussex. *T:* Staplecross 324.

**PERRY, Ernest George;** MP (Lab) Battersea South, since 1964; Alderman, London Borough of Wandsworth, since 1964; *b* 25 April 1908; British; *m* 1950, Edna Joyce Perks-Mankelow; one *s*. *Educ:* LCC secondary school. Textiles, 1923-33; Insurance, 1933-64. Member Battersea Borough Council, 1934-65; Mayor of Battersea, 1955-56. Asst Govt Whip, 1968-69; Lord Commissioner, HM Treasury, 1969-70; an Opposition Whip, 1970-. Served with Royal Artillery, 1939-46: Indian Army and Indian Artillery (Troop Sgt); Far East, 1942-45. *Recreations:* Local Government, sport, reading. *Address:* House of Commons, SW1.

**PERRY, George Henry;** b 24 Aug. 1920; *s* of Arthur and Elizabeth Perry; *m* 1944, Ida Garner; two *d*. *Educ:* elementary sch. and technical college. Engineering Apprentice, 1934-41. Naval Artificer, 1941-46 (Atlantic and Italy Stars; 1939-45 Star). Railway Fitter, 1946-66. Derby Town Councillor, 1955-66. Chairman: Derby Water Cttee, 1957-61; S Derbys Water Board, 1961-66; Derby Labour Party, 1961-62; Secretary, Derby Trades Council, 1961-66. Contested (Lab) Harborough, 1964; MP (Lab) Nottingham South, 1966-70. *Recreation:* walking. *Address:* 123 Hawthorn Street, Derby. *T:* Derby 44687.

**PERRY, Kenneth Murray Allan,** MA, MD (Cantab), FRCP; Physician to The London Hospital, since 1946; Physician to the Royal Masonic Hospital, since 1949; Medical Advisor to Central Advisory Council for Training for the Ministry of the Church of England, since 1958; *b* 1 Feb. 1909; *s* of Major H. Perry, Ware, Herts; *m* 1938, Winifred, *d* of F. P. Grassi; no *c*. *Educ:* Christ's Hospital; Queens' Coll., Cambridge. Kitchener Scholar, 1927; Price University Entrance Scholarship, 1930; Medical Registrar, London Hospital, 1935-38; Dorothy Temple Cross Fellowship, Mass. General Hospital, Boston, 1938-39; Research Fellow, Harvard, 1939. Member of Scientific Staff, Medical Research Council, 1942-46. Ernestine Henry Lecturer, Royal College of Physicians, 1955. Visiting Physician, Papworth Village Settlement, 1946-; Consulting Physician, Brentwood District and Warley Hospitals, 1947-. Examiner in Medicine, Universities of Cambridge, London, Liverpool and Hong Kong; Royal College of Physicians, London; Society of Apothecaries of London. UK representative, International Society of Internal Medicine. Member: Assoc. of Physicians of Great Britain and Ireland, 1946; Thoracic Society, 1946. Miembro Correspondiente Extranjeo de Academia Nacional de Medicina de Buenos Aires. *Publications:* (with Sir Geoffrey Marshall) Diseases of the Chest, 1952; Pulmonary Œdema, in British Encyclopædia of Medical Practice, 1948; Industrial Medicine in Chambers's Encyclopædia, 1948; (with Sir Thomas Holmes Sellors) Chest Diseases, 1963. *Recreations:* travel, photography. *Address:* 126 Bickenhall Mansions, W1. *T:* 01-935 3040. *Clubs:* Royal Automobile; Royal Naval (Portsmouth).

**PERRY, Ven. Michael Charles,** MA; Archdeacon of Durham and Canon Residentiary of Durham Cathedral since 1970; Examining Chaplain to the Bishop of Lichfield, since 1965; *b* 5 June 1933; *o s* of Charlie and Kathleen Perry; *m* 1963, Margaret, *o d* of late John Middleton Adshead; two *s*. *Educ:* Ashby-de-la-Zouch Boys' Grammar Sch.; Trinity Coll., Cambridge (Sen. Schol.); Westcott House, Cambridge. Asst Curate of Berkswich, Stafford, 1958-60; Chaplain, Ripon Hall, Oxford, 1961-63; Chief Assistant for Home Publishing, Society for Promoting Christian Knowledge, 1963-70. Sec., Archbishops' Commission on Christian Doctrine, 1967-70. Editor of the Church Quarterly, 1968-71. *Publications:* The Easter Enigma, 1959; The Pattern of Matins and Evensong, 1961; (co-author) The Churchman's Companion, 1963; Meet the Prayer Book, 1963; (contrib.) The Miracles and the Resurrection, 1964; (ed) Crisis for Confirmation, 1967; (co-author) Declaring The Faith: The Printed Word, 1969. *Recreations:* reading, writing, singing. *Address:* The Grove, Quarry Heads Lane, Durham. *T:* Durham 61891.

**PERRY, Lt-Col Robert Stanley Grosvenor,** DSO 1943; DL; *b* 1909; *s* of late Robert Grosvenor Perry, CBE, Barton House, Moreton-in-Marsh, Glos; *m* 1937, Margaret Louisa Elphinstone, *o c* of Horace Czarnikow; one *s*. *Educ:* Harrow; RMC, Sandhurst. 2nd Lieut, 9th Lancers, 1929, Major, 1941; Adjutant, Cheshire Yeomanry, 1938-40; Commanding: 2nd Lothians and Border Yeomanry, 1943; 9th Lancers, 1944-45; served War of 1939-45,

Palestine, Western Desert, N Africa, Italy (despatches, wounded twice); Commandant, RACOCTU, 1945-48. One of HM Bodyguard of Hon. Corps of Gentlemen at Arms from 1959. High Sheriff of Dorset, 1961. DL Dorset, 1962. Member British Olympic Yachting Team, Helsinki, 1952, Melbourne (Silver Medal), 1956; Winner: Cup of Italy with Vision (5.5 Metre), 1956; One Ton Cup with Royal Thames (6 Metre), 1958. *Recreations:* yacht racing, foxhunting, shooting. *Address:* Crendle Court, Purse Caundle, Sherborne, Dorset. *T:* Milborne Port 364. *Clubs:* Cavalry, Royal Yacht Squadron.

**PERRY, Professor Samuel Victor,** BSc (Liverpool), PhD, ScD (Cantab); Professor of Biochemistry, University of Birmingham, since Sept. 1959; *b* 16 July 1918; *s* of late Samuel and Margaret Perry; *m* 1948, Maureen Tregent Shaw; one *s* two *d*. *Educ:* King George V Sch., Southport; Liverpool Univ.; Trinity Coll., Cambridge. Served in War of 1939-45, home and N. Africa; Royal Artillery, 1940-46, Captain; POW 1942-45. Research Fellow, Trinity Coll., Cambridge, 1947-51; Commonwealth Fund Fellow, University of Rochester, USA, 1948-49; University Lecturer, Dept of Biochemistry, Cambridge, 1950-59. *Publications:* scientific papers in Biochemical Journal, Nature, Biochemica Biophysica Acta, etc. *Recreations:* gardening, pottery, Rugby football (Cambridge, 1946, 1947, England, 1947, 1948). *Address:* 64 Meadow Hill Road, King's Norton, Birmingham 30. *T:* 021-458 1511.

**PERRY, Thomas Wilfred,** CMG 1966; Managing Director, Thomas Perry & Sons Ltd, since 1916; *b* 3 March 1899; *s* of Thomas and Florence Perry; *m* 1st, 1922, Winifred Newey Lucas (*d* 1960); four *s*; 2nd, 1962, Ada May Lucas. *Educ:* Technical Coll., Christchurch, NZ. Entered family business, 1916. Director and Chairman of many public companies, 1930-60. *Recreations:* farming, fishing. *Address:* 5 Coldstream Court, Fendalton, Christchurch, New Zealand. *T:* 517-817. *Clubs:* Canterbury (Christchurch); Wellington (Wellington); Northern (Auckland).

**PERRY, Walter Laing MacDonald,** FRSE; OBE 1957; Vice-Chancellor, The Open University, since 1969; *b* 16 June 1921; *s* of Fletcher S. Perry and Flora M. MacDonald; *m* 1946, Anne Elizabeth Grant; three *s*. *Educ:* Ayr Acad.; Dundee High Sch. MB, ChB 1943, MD 1948, DSc, 1958 (University of St Andrews), MRCP (Edinburgh), 1963; FRCP (Edinburgh), 1967. Medical Officer, Colonial Medical Service (Nigeria), 1944-46; Medical Officer, RAF, 1946-47; Member of Staff, Medical Research Council, 1947-52; Director, Department of Biological Standards, National Institute for Medical Research, 1952-58. Prof. of Pharmacology, University of Edinburgh, 1958-68, Vice-Principal, 1967-68. Member, British Pharmacopœia Commission, 1952-68; Secretary, British Pharmacological Society, 1957-61. *Publications:* papers in Journal of Physiology, British Journal of Pharmacology and Chemo-therapy, etc. *Recreations:* making music and playing games. *Address:* The Open University, Walton Hall, Milton Keynes, Bucks. *T:* Bletchley 4066. *Clubs:* Athenæum, Savage; Scottish Arts.

**PERRY-KEENE, Air Vice-Marshal Allan Lancelot Addison,** CB 1947; OBE 1940; RAF (retired); *b* 10 Nov. 1898; *s* of late L. H. A. and M. Perry-Keene; *m* 1923, K. L., *d* of late C. A. S. Silberrad, ICS; two *d*. *Educ:* Wolverley; King Edward's, Birmingham. Served European War, 1914-18; joined RFC, 1917; France, 1918-19; transferred RAF, 1918; Iraq, 1927-29; India, 1935-41; Burma and India, 1942; Director of Ground Training and Training Plans, Air Ministry, 1943-45; AOC 227 Group, India, and 3 (Indian) Group, 1946; Air Officer i/c Administration, Air HQ, India, 1946; Air Commander, Royal Pakistan Air Force, 1947-49. *Recreations:* sailing and photography. *Address:* Wayfarers Cottage, St Mary Bourne, Andover, Hants. *T:* 210.

**PERSE, St John;** *see* Léger, M.-R. A. St-L.

**PERT, Maj.-General Claude Ernest,** CB 1947; DSO 1945; retired; *b* 26 Sept. 1898; *s* of F. J. Pert, late ICS; *m* 1922, Lilian Katherine Nicolls. *Educ:* Royal Naval Coll., Osborne; Clifton Coll. Commissioned into Indian Army, 1917, and joined 15th Lancers; Comd Probyn's Horse, 1940-42; Comd 255 Indian Tank Bde in 14th Army, Burma; Comd 1st Indian Armoured Div., 1945-48; retired 1948. *Recreations:* polo and fishing. *Address:* Polo Manager, Household Brigade Polo Club, Royal Mews, Windsor Castle. *T:* Windsor 62374. *Clubs:* Cavalry, Buck's.

**PERTH,** 17th Earl of, *cr* 1605; **STRATHALLAN,** 13th Viscount, *cr* 1686; **John David Drummond,** PC 1957; Baron Drummond of Cargill, 1488; Baron Maderty, 1609; Baron Drummond, 1686; Lord Drummond of Gilston, 1685; Lord Drummond of Rickertoun and Castlemaine, 1686; Hereditary Thane of Lennox, and Hereditary Steward of Menteith and Strathearn; Representative Peer for Scotland, 1952-63; First Crown Estate Commissioner, since 1962; Chairman, Ditchley Foundation, 1963-66; *b* 13 May 1907; *o s* of 16th Earl of Perth, PC, GCMG, CB, and Hon. Angela Constable-Maxwell (*d* 1965), *y d* of 11th Baron Herries; *S* father 1951; *m* 1934, Nancy Seymour, *d* of Reginald Fincke, New York City; two *s*. *Educ:* Downside; Cambridge Univ. Lieut, Intelligence Corps, 1940; seconded to War Cabinet Offices, 1942-43, Ministry of Production, 1944-45; Minister of State for Colonial Affairs, 1957-62 (resigned). Director: Royal Bank of Scotland; Schroders Ltd; Tate & Lyle Ltd; Dominion-Lincoln Assurance Co. Ltd. *Heir: s* Viscount Strathallan, *qv*. *Address:* 2 Hyde Park Gardens, W2. *T:* 01-262 4667; Stobhall, by Perth.

**PERTH** (Australia), **Archbishop of,** and Metropolitan of Western Australia, since 1969; **Most Rev. Geoffrey Tremayne Sambell;** *b* 28 Oct. 1914; *s* of E. Sambell, Violet Town, Vic.; single. *Educ:* Melbourne High Sch.; Melbourne University. Deacon 1940; Priest, 1941. Army Chaplain, 1942-46 and 1949-58; Dir., Melbourne Diocesan Centre, 1947-62; Archdeacon of Essendon, 1955-61; Bishop Coadjutor, Diocese of Melbourne, 1962-69; Archdeacon of Melbourne, 1961-69. Pres., Victorian Coun. of Social Services, 1956-58. Fellow, Australian Coll. of Theology (Th.Soc.), 1962. *Recreation:* golf. *Address:* Bishop's House, Mounts Bay Road, Perth, WA 6000, Australia. *Clubs:* Melbourne, Royal Automobile of Victoria, Metropolitan Golf (all Melbourne); West Australia, Lake Karrinyup (both Perth).

**PERTH** (Australia), **Archbishop of, (RC),** since 1968; **Most Rev. Launcelot Goody,** PhD, DD; *b* 5 June 1908; *s* of late Ernest John Goody and of Agnes Goody. *Educ:* Christian Brothers' College, Perth, WA; Urban University, Rome. PhD 1927, DD 1931. Ordained priest at Rome, 1930; Asst Parish Priest, Perth Cathedral, 1932-35, Kalgoorlie, 1935-37; P. P. Toodyay, 1937; Director of Seminary, Guilford, 1940-47; P. P. Bedford Park, 1947-51; Auxiliary Bishop of Perth, 1951; first RC Bishop of Bunbury,

1954-68. Domestic Prelate to the Pope, 1947. *Address:* St Mary's Cathedral, Perth, Western Australia. *T:* 232141.

**PERTH** (Australia), **Coadjutor Bishop of;** *see* Macdonald, Rt Rev. Thomas Brian.

**PERTINAX;** *see* Géraud, C. J. A.

**PERTWEE, Captain Herbert Guy,** CBE 1949; DSO 1919; RN, retired; *b* 28 July 1893; *s* of H. A. Pertwee, Great Yarmouth; *m* 1921, Carmen (*d* 1959), 2nd *d* of late T. Waddon-Martyn, Stoke, Devonport; two *s* one *d. Educ:* Gresham's Sch., Holt. Joined Royal Navy, 1911; Falkland Islands action in HMS Carnarvon, 1914; joined staff of Commodore Tyrwhitt in HMS Arethusa, 1915; subsequent flagships of the Harwich Force for 3 years (clasps); secretary to Commodore, Persian Gulf and Mesopotamia Division, and later the Caspian Naval Force, 1918-19 (clasps, DSO, Russian Order of St Anne, 3rd class, Russian Order of Stanislaus, 2nd class, with swords); naval secretary of Naval and Military Commission to Persia, 1920-21 (Naval GS medal and clasp); Staff of C-in-C, The Nore, 1921-24; Naval Staff, Admiralty, 1924-26; secretary to Rear-Admiral, First Battle Squadron, 1926-27; Staffs of Cs-in-C, Portsmouth, Atlantic Fleet, and Mediterranean Fleet, 1928-31; secretary to Vice-Admiral, Commanding Battle Cruiser Squadron, 1932-34, to Deputy Chief of Naval Staff, 1935-38, and to C-in-C, Portsmouth, 1939-42; Staff Supply Officer, West Africa, 1943-44; ADC to the King, 1948; retired list, 1949. Chief Supplies Officer to the Groundnuts Scheme, 1949-51; Comdt, Government Hostel, Dar es Saalam, and Hon. ADC to the Governor, 1951-54; Divisional Comdt, Devon Special Constabulary, 1956-68. *Recreations:* gardening, local government. *Address:* Bickington, near Barnstaple, N Devon. *T:* Barnstaple 4360.

**PERUTZ, Max Ferdinand,** CBE 1963; FRS 1954; PhD; Chairman of the Medical Research Council Laboratory of Molecular Biology. Chairman, European Molecular Biology Organization, 1963-69. PhD 1940. (Jointly) Nobel Prize for Chemistry, 1962. Hon. Fellow, Peterhouse, Cambridge, 1962. Hon. Member American Academy of Arts and Sciences, 1963; Corresp. Member, Austrian Acad. of Sciences, 1963; For. Member, American Philosophical Society, 1968; For. Associate, Nat. Acad. of Sciences, USA, 1970. *Publication:* Proteins and Nucleic Acids, Structure and Function, 1962. *Address:* 42 Sedley Taylor Road, Cambridge; Laboratory of Molecular Biology, Hills Road, Cambridge.

**PERY,** family name of **Earl of Limerick.**

**PESHALL, Samuel Frederick,** CBE 1951; MC 1916; Director, N. Corah and Sons, Leicester, since 1922; *b* 18 Nov. 1882; *s* of Rev. S. Peshall, Oldberrow, Warwickshire; *m* 1919, Mabel Eleanor Whitehurst (*d* 1966), Beaudesert Park, Henley in Arden; no *c. Educ:* Rossall; Caius Coll., Cambridge (MA). Served European War, 1914-18, KRRC. President National Federation of Hosiery Manufacturers, 1943; President, Leicester Chamber of Commerce, 1945; High Sheriff of Leicestershire, 1945; Chairman Regional Board for Industry in North Midlands, 1945-63; Companion, Textile Institute, 1956; Vice-President, Clothing Institute, 1957. *Address:* Quorn Grange, Loughborough, Leics. *T:* Quorn 2167. *Clubs:* Leicestershire (Leicester); Notts County (Nottingham).

**PESKETT, Stanley Victor,** MA; Principal, Royal Belfast Academical Institution, since 1959; Chairman, Northern Ireland Branch, School Library Association; *b* 9 May 1918; *o s* of the late Sydney Timber and of Mary Harvard Peskett; *m* 1948, Prudence Eileen, *o d* of late C. R. A. Goatly, Calcutta; two *s* two *d. Educ:* Whitgift Sch.; St Edmund Hall, Oxford. Served War, 1939-46 (despatches) in Royal Marines, Norway, Shetland, Normandy, India and Java; Lt-Col, 1944; two Admiralty awards for inventions. Senior English Master, 1946-59, Housemaster 1954-59, The Leys School. Chm., Northern Ireland Cttee, Voluntary Service Overseas; Chm., Ulster Branch, Irish Schools Swimming Assoc. *Address:* Fairy Hill, 6 Osborne Gardens, Belfast BT9 6LE; Old Crom Schoolhouse, Aghalane, Co. Fermanagh. *Club:* Royal Commonwealth Society.

**PESTELL;** *see* Wells-Pestell.

**PESTELL, Sir John Richard,** KCVO 1969; an Adjudicator, Immigration Appeals, Harmondsworth, since 1970; *b* 21 Nov. 1916; *s* of late Lt-Comdr Frank Lionel Pestell, RN, and Winifred Alice Pestell; *m* 1951, Betty Pestell (*née* Parish); three *d. Educ:* Portsmouth Northern Secondary Sch. Joined British South Africa Police, Southern Rhodesia, 1939; retired, 1965, with rank of Asst Commissioner. Served, 1944-47, Gen. List, MELF, in Cyrenaica Defence Force. Secretary/Controller to Governor of S Rhodesia, Rt Hon. Sir H. V. Gibbs, 1965-69. *Recreations:* walking, golf. *Address:* (temp.) 74 Cedar Drive, Chichester, Sussex.

**PETCH, Sir Louis,** KCB 1968 (CB 1964); Chairman, Board of Customs and Excise, since 1969; *b* 16 Aug. 1913; *s* of William and Rhoda Petch, Preston, Lancs; *m* 1939, Gwendoline Bolton; one *s* one *d. Educ:* Preston Grammar Sch.; Peterhouse, Cambridge. Entered Administrative Class of Home Civil Service, 1937; Secretaries' Office, Customs and Excise, 1937-40; Home Defence Executive, 1940-45; Treasury, 1945-68; Private Secretary to successive Chancellors of the Exchequer, 1953-56; Third Secretary and Treasury Officer of Accounts, 1962-66; Second Secretary, 1966-68; Second Permanent Sec., Civil Service Dept, 1968-69. *Address:* 15 Cole Park Road, Twickenham, Middlesex. *T:* 01-892 2089. *Club:* United University.

**PETCH, Prof. Norman James;** Cochrane Professor of Metallurgy, University of Newcastle upon Tyne, since 1959, a Pro-Vice-Chancellor, since 1968; *b* 13 Feb. 1917; 3rd *s* of George and Jane Petch, Bearsden, Dunbartonshire; *m* 1949, Eileen Allen; two *d. Educ:* Queen Mary Coll., London; Sheffield Univ. Research at Cavendish Lab., Cambridge, 1939-42; Royal Aircraft Establishment, 1942-46; Cavendish Laboratory, 1946-48; British Iron and Steel Research Assoc., Sheffield, 1948-49; Reader in Metallurgy, Leeds Univ., 1949-56; First Professor of Metallurgy, Leeds Univ., 1956-59. *Address:* 10 Deyncourt, Darras Hall, Ponteland, Northumberland. *T:* Ponteland 3406.

**PETER, Bernard Hartley,** CBE 1943; MIEE; Royal Engineers (retired); *b* 6 June 1885; 2nd *s* of Claude Hurst Peter, Town Clerk, Launceston, Cornwall; *m* Eileen Mary, *d* of Francis Plunkett, Dublin. *Educ:* Blundell's Sch., Tiverton; City and Guilds Coll., London. Central London Railway, 1902-03; District Railway & London Underground Railways, 1903-11; McKenzie Holland & Westinghouse

Power Signal Co. Ltd, and Westinghouse Brake Co., 1911-47.

**PETERBOROUGH, Bishop of,** since 1961; **Rt. Rev. Cyril Eastaugh,** MC 1917; MA (Oxon); *b* 22 Dec. 1897; *y s* of late Robert Wilgress Eastaugh; *m* 1948, Lady Laura Mary Palmer, *d* of 3rd Earl of Selborne, *qv*; one *s* two *d. Educ:* Christ Church, Oxford; Cuddesdon College. Served European War, 1914-18, S. Staffs Regt. Chaplain, Cuddesdon Coll., 1930-34; Vice-Principal, 1934-35; Vicar of St John the Divine, Kennington, 1935-49; Suffragan Bishop of Kensington, 1949-61. Hon. Canon of Southwark, 1945; Proctor in Convocation, 1943; Chaplain and Sub-Prelate of the Order of St John of Jerusalem, 1961-. *Address:* The Palace, Peterborough. *T:* Peterborough 62492. *Club:* Athenæum.

**PETERBOROUGH, Assistant Bishops of;** *see* Graham-Campbell, Rt Rev. A. A., Otter-Barry, Rt Rev. H. V. L., Townley, Rt Rev. G. F.

**PETERBOROUGH, Dean of;** *see* Digby, Very Rev. R. S. Wingfield.

**PETERKIN, Ishbel Allan;** *b* 2 March 1903; *d* of late J. Ramsay MacDonald and late Margaret Ethel Gladstone; *m* 1st, 1938, Norman Ridgley (*d* 1950); 2nd, 1953, James Peterkin (*d* 1956). *Educ:* North London Collegiate. Member of London County Council, 1928-34. Licensee at Plough Inn, Speen, 1936-53. *Address:* 49 MacDuff Street, Lossiemouth, Moray. *T:* Lossiemouth 3201.

**PETERS, Adm. Sir Arthur M.,** KCB 1946 (CB 1943); DSC; *b* 1 June 1888; *o* surv. *s* of Maj.-Gen. W. H. B. Peters and of Hon. Mrs Peters, *d* of 24th Baron Dunboyne; *m* 1912, Agnes Vivien (*d* 1965), *d* of Colonel A. V. Payne, CMG; one *d; m* 1966, Mrs Sophie Maude Magnay, *widow* of Brigadier A. D. Magnay. *Educ:* Stubbington House, Fareham, Hants; HMS Britannia. Went to sea 1904, served in North Sea throughout European War in HMS Southampton and Orion, present at Battle of Heligoland Bight, Dogger Bank, and Jutland (DSC, despatches); Captain, 1930; commanded HMS Southampton, 1936-38; Commodore in Charge of Naval Establishments, Hong Kong, 1939-40; Rear-Admiral, 1940; Naval Secretary to First Lord of the Admiralty, 1941-42; Mediterranean, 1943; Vice-Admiral, 1943; Flag Officer Commanding West Africa, 1943-45; retired, 1945; Admiral (retired), 1946. *Address:* Somerton Lodge, Sidmouth, Devon EX10 8UH. *T:* Sidmouth 3927. *Club:* United Service.

**PETERS, Augustus Dudley,** MA; Literary agent; *b* 1892; *m* 1st, Helen MacGregor; (only son killed on active service, Feb. 1945) one *d*; 2nd, Margaret Lucy Mayne; one *d*; 3rd, Margot Grahame. *Educ:* private; St John's Coll., Cambridge. Served European War, France, 1916-18; Editor of the World, 1920; dramatic critic of Daily Chronicle; established own literary and dramatic agency, 1924; began to produce plays, 1930, and continued to be active in theatrical production at The Duchess and other London theatres. War of 1939-45: Head of Public Relations Division, Ministry of Food, and later Deputy Controller, Factory and Storage, Board of Trade. *Films:* Last Holiday, 1952; An Inspector Calls, 1953; Series of television films, 1955, 1956. *Recreations:* golf, bridge. *Address:* 10 Buckingham Street, WC2. *TA: Literistic Rand Lond. T:* 01-839 2556. *Clubs:* Savile, MCC.

**PETERS, Professor Raymond Harry;** Professor of Polymer and Fibre Science, University of Manchester, since 1955; *b* 19 Feb. 1918. *Educ:* County High Sch., Ilford; King's Coll., London Univ.; Manchester Univ. BSc (London) 1939, PhD (London), 1942, in Chemistry; BSc (Manchester), 1949, BSc (London), 1949, in Mathematics; DSc (London), 1968. Scientist at ICI Ltd, 1941-46 and 1949-55. President, Society of Dyers and Colourists, 1967-68. *Publications:* Textile Chemistry: Vol. I The Chemistry of Fibres, 1963; Vol. II, Impurities of Fibres: Purification of Fibres, 1967; contributions to Journals of Chemical Society, Society of Dyers and Colourists, Textile Institute, British Journal of Applied Physics, etc. *Recreations:* gardening, golf. *Address:* University of Manchester Institute of Science and Technology, Manchester. *T:* 061-236 3311.

**PETERS, Prof. Richard Stanley,** BA (Oxon), BA (London), PhD (London); Professor of the Philosophy of Education, University of London Institute of Education, Malet Street, WC1, since 1962; *b* 31 Oct. 1919; *s* of Charles Robert and Mabel Georgina Peters; *m* 1943, Margaret Lee Duncan; one *s* two *d. Educ:* Clifton Coll., Bristol; Queen's Coll., Oxford; Birkbeck Coll., University of London. War service with Friends' Ambulance Unit and Friends' Relief Service in E. London, 1940-44. Classics Master, Sidcot School, Somerset, 1944-46; Birkbeck Coll., University of London: Studentship and part-time Lecturer in Philos. and Psychol., 1946-49; full-time Lecturer in Philos. and Psychol., 1949-58; Reader in Philosophy, 1958-62. Visiting Prof. of Education, Grad. School of Education, Harvard Univ., 1961; Visiting Fellow, Australian National Univ., 1969. Part-time lectureships, Bedford Coll., LSE; Tutor for University of London Tutorial Classes Cttee and Extension Cttee. Member, American National Academy of Education, 1966. *Publications:* (revised) Brett's History of Psychology, 1953; Hobbes, 1956; The Concept of Motivation, 1958; (with S. I. Benn) Social Principles and the Democratic State, 1959; Authority, Responsibility and Education, 1960; Ethics and Education, 1966; (ed.) The Concept of Education, 1967; (ed) Perspectives on Plowden, 1969; (with P. H. Hirst) The Logic of Education, 1970. *Recreation:* golf. *Address:* Bridge End Orchard, Saffron Walden, Essex. *T:* 2001.

**PETERS, Sir Rudolph (Albert),** Kt, *cr* 1952; MC 1917 (Bar); FRS 1935; FRCP 1952; *s* of Albert Edward Peters, MRCS, LRCP, and Agnes Malvina Watts; *m* 1917, Frances W. Vérel; two *s. Educ:* Warden House, Deal; Wellington Coll., Berks; King's Coll., London; Gonville and Caius Coll., Cambridge. MA Cantab, 1914; MD 1919, St Bartholomew's Hospital; MA Oxon (by decree), 1923; Hon. MD (Liège), 1950; Doctor *hc* (Paris), 1952; Hon. DSc (Cincinnati), 1953; Hon. MD (Amsterdam), 1954; Hon. DSc: London, 1954; Leeds, 1959; Australian National University, 1961; Hon. LLD (Glasgow), 1963; Hon. FRSE, 1957; late Drosier Fellow and Tutor Gonville and Caius Coll., Cambridge; Hon. Fellow Gonville and Caius Coll., Cambridge, 1951; Hon. Fellow Trinity Coll., Oxford, 1958; Thruston Medal, 1918; Royal Medal of Royal Society, 1949; Cameron Prize, Edinburgh, 1949; Hopkins Memorial Medal, 1959; Benn W. Levy Student Biochemistry, Cambridge, 1912-13; formerly, Dunn Lecturer and Senior Demonstrator Biochemistry, Cambridge; Whitley Professor of Biochemistry, University of Oxford, 1923-54; Fellow Trinity Coll., Oxford, 1925-54; Scientific Staff, Agricultural Research Council, 1954-59. Member: Biochemical and Physiological Societies, BMA, Société Philomathique de Paris. Assoc. Sci. Nat.,

Acad. Roy. Belg. For. Member Royal Nether. Acad. Sci. and Letters and Accademia Nazionale dei Lincei, Rome; For. Hon. Member American Academy of Arts and Sciences; Hon. Member: Finnish Biochem. Society; Assoc. Clin. Biochemists; Assoc. of Physicians; Biochemical Society; Celer et Audax Club; Nutrition Society; American Institute of Nutrition; Hon. Fellow: Royal Society of Medicine; American Society Biological Chemists; Physiological Society; Croonian Lecturer, Royal Society; Dixon Memorial Lecturer, RSM, 1948; Louis Abrahams Lecturer, RCP, 1952. Dunham Lecturer, Harvard Univ., 1946-47; Herman Leo Loeb Lecturer, St Louis Univ., 1947; Christian Herter Lecturer, New York Univ., 1947; Dohme Lecturer, Johns Hopkins Univ., 1954; Linacre Lecturer, Cambridge, 1962. Visiting Professor, Canadian MRC, Dalhousie Univ., Halifax, Nova Scotia, 1963; Member Medical Research Council, 1946-50; Military College of Science Advisory Council, 1947-50; Member Sci. Adv. Council, Ministry of Supply, 1950-53. President, International Council of Scientific Unions, 1958-61. President, Cambridge Philosophical Society, 1965-67. RAMC (SR) 1915-18 (MC and bar, Brevet-Major, despatches). Hon. FCPath, 1967. Medal of Freedom with silver palm (USA), 1947. *Publications:* Biochemical Lesions and Lethal Synthesis, 1963; contributions to scientific journals. *Address:* University Department of Biochemistry, Tennis Court Road, Cambridge. *T:* Cambridge 56288; 3 Newnham Walk, Cambridge. *T:* Cambridge 50819. *Club:* Athenæum.

**PETERS, Sidney John;** *b* Cambridge, 2 Dec. 1885; *s* of late Herbert Peters, Cambridge, and Annie M. Wright; *m* 1912, Essie, *d* of late Ald. F. W. Mills, Cambridge; one *s* one *d*. *Educ:* Cambridge County High Sch.; Cambridge and Dublin Universities. MA, LLB, Cambridge, MA, LLD, Dublin. Secretary and Legal Adviser to Central Council Forage Department for Civil Supplies during European War, 1914-18, and Executive Officer, Controlling Department, for same under Board of Trade; formerly Member of Ecclesiastical Cttee; MP (L) Huntingdonshire, 1929-31, (L Nat) 1931-45; formerly Parly Private Secretary to Minister of Mines, and Parliamentary Private Secretary to Minister of Labour to 1940. Retired from practice as a Solicitor. *Address:* Hilton House, Hilton, Hunts. *T:* Papworth St Agnes 289.

**PETERS, Theophilus,** CMG 1967; Director, Diplomatic Service Language Centre, since 1968, and Head of Training Department, Foreign and Commonwealth Office, since 1969; *b* 7 Aug. 1921; *er s* of late Mark Peters and Dorothy Knapman; *m* 1953, Lucy Bailey Summers, *d* of Lionel Morgan Summers, Winter Park, Fla.; two *s* three *d*. *Educ:* Exeter Sch., Exeter; St John's Coll., Cambridge (MA). Served War of 1939-45: 2nd Lieut, Intelligence Corps, 1942; Captain, 8 Corps HQ, 1944; Normandy, 1944; Holland, 1944-45 (despatches); Germany; Major. Entered HM Foreign (subseq. Diplomatic) Service; Vice-Consul/2nd Secretary, Peking, 1948; FO, 1951-52; Tripoli and Benghazi (Libya), 1953; FO, 1956; Dep. Secretary-General, Cento, 1960; Head of Chancery, Manila, 1962; Counsellor (Commercial), Peking, 1965. *Address:* 7 Westcombe Park Road, SE3. *T:* 01-858 6219.

**PETERS, William,** MVO 1961; MBE 1959; Director, International Affairs Division, Commonwealth Secretariat, since 1969; *b* 28 Sept. 1923; *o s* of John William Peters and Louise (*née* Woodhouse), Morpeth, Northumberland; *m* 1944, Catherine B. Bailey; no *c*. *Educ:* King Edward VI Grammar Sch., Morpeth; Balliol Coll., Oxford. MA Lit. Hum. 1948. War Service, Queen's Royal Rifles, KOSB, and 9th Gurkha Rifles, 1942-46. Joined HMOCS as Asst District Comr, Gold Coast, 1950; served in Cape Coast, Bawku and Tamale; Dep. Sec., Regional Comr, Northern Region, 1958-59; joined CRO as Asst Prin., 1959; Prin., 1959; 1st Sec., Dacca, 1960-63; 1st Sec., Cyprus, 1963-67; Head of Zambia and Malawi Dept, CRO, 1967-68; Head of Central African Dept, Foreign and Commonwealth Office, 1968-69. *Publications:* contribs to Jl of African Administration. *Recreations:* music, gardening, carpentry. *Address:* 12 The Hamlet, Champion Hill, SE5. *T:* 01-274 4376. *Clubs:* United University, Royal Commonwealth Society, Royal Over-Seas League.

**PETERSEN, Jeffrey Charles,** CMG 1968; Minister (Commercial), HM Embassy, Rio de Janeiro, since 1968; *b* 20 July 1920; *s* of Charles Petersen and Ruby Petersen (*née* Waple); *m* 1962, Karin Kristina Hayward; two *s* three *d*. *Educ:* Westcliff High Sch.; London School of Economics. Served RN (Lieut, RNVR), 1939-46. Joined Foreign Office, 1948; 2nd Secretary, Madrid, 1949-50; 2nd Secretary, Ankara, 1951-52; 1st Secretary, Brussels, 1953-56; NATO Defence College, 1956-57; FO, 1957-62; 1st Secretary, Djakarta, 1962-64; Counsellor, Athens, 1964-68. *Recreations:* painting, entomology, sailing. *Address:* 32 Longmoore Street, SW1. *T:* 01-834 8262; British Embassy, Rio de Janeiro, Brazil.

**PETERSHAM, Viscount;** *b* 20 July 1945; *s* and *heir* of 11th Earl of Harrington, *qv*; *m* 1966, Virginia Alleyne Freeman Jackson, Mallow; one *s* one *d*. *Educ:* Eton. *Address:* c/o Greenmount, Patrickswell, Co. Limerick, Ireland.

**PETERSON, Alexander Duncan Campbell,** OBE 1946; Director of Department of Education, Oxford University, since 1958; *b* 13 Sept. 1908; 2nd *s* of late J. C. K. Petersen, CIE; *m* 1946, Corinna May, *d* of late Sir Arthur Cochrane, KCVO; two *s* one *d*. *Educ:* Radley; Balliol Coll., Oxford. Assistant master, Shrewsbury Sch., 1932-40; commissioned in MOI (SP), 1940; Deputy Director of Psychological Warfare, SEAC, 1944-46; Headmaster, Adams' Grammar Sch., 1946-52; Director-General of Information Services, Federation of Malaya, 1952-54; Headmaster, Dover College., 1954-57. Contested (L) Oxford City, 1966. Director, International Baccalaureate Office; Chairman Farmington Trust. *Publications:* The Far East, 1948; 100 Years of Education, 1952; Educating our Rulers, 1957; The Techniques of Teaching (ed), 1965; The Future of Education, 1968. *Address:* 33 St Andrews Road, Old Headington, Oxford. *T:* Oxford 61034. *Club:* Special Forces.

**PETERSON, Arthur William,** CB 1963; MVO 1953; Director-General and Clerk to the Greater London Council, since 1968; *b* 22 May 1916; *s* of J. C. K. Peterson and F. Campbell; *m* 1940, Mary Isabel Maples; one *s* two *d*. *Educ:* Shrewsbury; Merton College, Oxford. Asst Principal, Home Office, 1938; Principal Private Secretary to Home Secretary, 1946-49; Secretary, Royal Commission on Betting and Lotteries, 1949-51; Asst Secretary, Home Office, 1951-56; Personal Assistant to Lord Privy Seal, 1957; Dep. Chm., Prison Commission, 1957-60, Chm., 1960-63; Asst Under-Sec. of State, Prison Dept, Home Office, 1963-64; Dep. Sec., DEA, 1964-68. Mem. Bd of Governors, London Business Sch.; Hon. Fellow, Inst. of Local Government Studies, Birmingham Univ. *Address:* 7 Lincoln

House, Basil Street, SW3. *T:* 01-589 2237. *Club:* Travellers'.

**PETERSON, John Magnus,** MA (Oxon); *b* 18 Feb. 1902; *yr s* of late Rev. M. F. Peterson; *m* 1938, Rosemary (*d* 1944), *yr d* of late A. M. McNeile; two *s* one *d*. *Educ:* Shrewsbury Sch.; Oriel Coll., Oxford. Scholar of Shrewsbury School, 1915, and Oriel College, 1921; 1st Cl. Classical Mods, 1923; 1st Cl. Lit. Hum., 1925. Oxford Univ. Assoc. Football XI, 1924 and 1925 (Capt.); OU Authentics. Asst Master, Eton College, 1925-50, House Master, 1938-50; Headmaster of Shrewsbury School, 1950-63. *Recreations:* golf, fishing. *Address:* Lower Farm, Easton Royal, Pewsey, Wilts. *T:* Burbage 343. *Club:* Vincent's (Oxford).

**PETFIELD, Sir Arthur (Henry),** Kt 1968; Managing Director since 1951, and Chairman of Directors since 1958, United Packages Ltd; *b* 10 Sept. 1912; *s* of Arthur Petfield and Florence Jane Petfield (*née* Mott); *m* 1937, Elsie Emily Mylchreest; three *s* one *d*. *Educ:* Milton State School, Brisbane; State Commercial High School, Brisbane. Joined Queensland Can Company Ltd (now United Packages Ltd), 1929; Secretary, 1934; Director and General Manager, 1948. Chm., Overseas Telecom. Commn. Director: Queensland Insurance Co. Ltd; National Mutual Life Assoc. of A/asia Ltd; Barkers Bookstore Holdings Ltd; Member: Manufacturing Industries Adv. Council; Industries Assistance Bd; Greater Brisbane Town Planning Adv. Cttee; Queensland Chamber of Manufactures (Pres., 1955-57); Canmakers Inst. (Pres., 1953-57); Queensland Spastic Welfare League; Nat. Heart Foundn (Chm., Finance Cttee); Nat. Safety Council (Old Div.). *Recreations:* boating, fishing, surfing. *Address:* 15 Feez Street, Yeronga, Queensland 4104, Australia. *T:* 48.1514. *Clubs:* Queensland, Masonic, Brisbane (Brisbane); Rotary of S Brisbane (Pres., 1956-57).

**PETHERICK, Maurice,** MA; *b* 5 Oct. 1894; *s* of George Tallack and Edith Petherick. *Educ:* St Peter's Court, Broadstairs; Marlborough College; Trinity College, Cambridge. 2nd Lieutenant Royal 1st Devon Yeomanry 1914; invalided out, 1915; served in Foreign Office, 1916-17; recommissioned Royal Scots Greys, 1917; served in France, 1918; recommissioned General List Army, Oct. 1939, Capt., Temp. Major, contested (C) Penryn and Falmouth Division, 1929 and 1945; MP (C) Penryn and Falmouth, 1931-45; Financial Secretary, War Office, May-July, 1945; High Sheriff of Cornwall, 1957. Director, Prudential Assurance Co. Ltd. *Publications:* Captain Culverin, 1932; Victoire, 1943; Restoration Rogues, 1950. *Recreations:* shooting, racing, gardening. *Address:* Porthpean House, St Austell, Cornwall. *Clubs:* United University, Carlton.

**PETHICK, Brig. Geoffrey Loveston,** CBE 1960; DSO 1944; Director, British Paper Makers' Association, since 1960; *b* 25 Nov. 1907; *s* of late Captain E. E. Pethick, RN and May (*née* Brook); *m* 1939, Nancy Veronica Ferrand; one *d*. *Educ:* Newton College. Commissioned, Royal Artillery, 1927; RHA 1934; served War of 1939-45; CO, Field Regt, 1942; Far East, 1945. Comdr 3 Army Group, RA, 1951. Chief Instructor, 1949; idc, 1950. Commander, RA 3 Div. 1953; War Office, 1957; retired, 1960. *Recreations:* golf, sailing. *Address:* Little Croft, Fireball Hill, Sunningdale, Ascot, Berks. *T:* Ascot 22018. *Club:* Army and Navy.

**PETIT, Sir Dinshaw Manockjee,** 3rd Bt, *cr* 1890; *b* 24 June 1901; *s* of Sir Dinshaw Manockjee Petit, 2nd Bt, and Dinbai, *d* of Sir J. Jeejeebhoy, 3rd Bt; *S* father, 1933; *m* 1928, Sylla (*d* 1963), *d* of late R. D. Tata; one *s* one *d*. *Educ:* St Xavier's, Bombay; Trinity Hall, Cambridge. Called to Bar, Inner Temple, 1925. President: SPCA, Bombay; Petit Boys Sch., Poona; Petit Girls' Sch., Pali Hill, Bombay; Petit Sanatorium, Cumballa Hill, Bombay; Trustee: V.J.T. Technical Inst., Bombay; Parsee Gen. Hosp., Bombay. Pres., Northbrook Soc., London; Life Gov., Royal Hosp. for Incurables; Hon. Life Mem., RSPCA. Vice-Pres., British Assoc. of Riviera. Citizen of Honour of France. *Heir: s* Nasserwanjee Dinshaw Petit [*b* 13 Aug. 1934 *m* 1964, Nirmala Nanavatty; two *s*]. *Address:* Petit Hall, Malabar Hill, Bombay, India; Savaric, 06 Eze-Village, France; 8 Mount Row, W1.

**PETIT, Rt. Rev. John Edward;** *see* Menevia, Bishop of, (RC).

**PETIT, Roland;** French choreographer and dancer; *b* 1924; *m* 1954, Renée Jeanmaire. *Educ:* Ecole de Ballet de l'Opéra de Paris, studying under Ricaux and Lifar. Premier danseur, l'Opéra de Paris, 1940-44; founded Les Vendredis de la Danse, 1944, Les Ballets des Champs-Elysées, 1945, Les Ballets de Paris de Roland Petit, 1948. Choreographic works include: Les Forains, Le Jeune Homme et la Mort, Les Demoiselles de la nuit, Carmen, Deuil en 24 heures, Le Loup, L'éloge de la Folie, Les Chants de Maldoror, Notre Dame de Paris, Paradise Lost, etc.; choreographer and dancer: La Belle au Bois Dormant; Cyrano de Bergerac. Appeared in films Hans Christian Andersen; Un, Deux, Trois, Quartre (arr. ballets, for film, and danced in 3); 4 ballets, Black Tights. *Address:* 12 rue de la Paix, Paris 2e.

**PETO, Brig. Christopher Henry Maxwell,** DSO 1945; DL; *b* 19 Feb. 1897; 2nd *s* of Sir Basil Peto, 1st Bt, and *heir-pres.* to Sir Michael Peto, *qv*; *m* 1935, Barbara, *d* of E. T. Close, Camberley, Surrey; two *s* one *d*. *Educ:* Harrow. Joined 9th Lancers, 1915 (wounded, despatches); commanded 9th Lancers, 1938; War of 1939-45 (wounded, despatches thrice, DSO); Brig. 1941; Chief Liaison Officer 21 Army Group, 1944; retd pay, 1946. Col, 9th Lancers, 1950-60. MP (C) for Barnstaple Div. of Devon, 1945-50. North Div. of Devonshire, 1950-55. Chm., Wilts TA and AFA, 1957-61. Pres. Conservative Association of Devizes Division of Wilts, 1958-66. Legion of Honour, Croix de Guerre, Orders of Leopold I, Belgian Croix de Guerre, Polonia Restituta, White Lion of Czechoslovakia, Czech War Cross. DL Devon, 1950-55; DL Wilts, 1956; High Sheriff of Wiltshire, 1966. *Recreations:* shooting, fishing. *Address:* Lockeridge House, Nr Marlborough, Wilts. *TA* and *T:* Lockeridge 259. *Club:* Cavalry.

**PETO, Dorothy Olivia Georgiana,** OBE 1920; *b* 15 Dec. 1886; *d* of Morton Kelsall Peto and Olivia Georgiana Elizabeth Maude; unmarried. *Educ:* privately at home. Hon. Sec., New Forest North Div. St John Ambulance Bde, 1912-14; Dep. Director (Director from 1916) Bristol Training School for Women Patrols and Police, 1915-20; Detective Inquiry Officer, Birmingham City Police, 1920-24; Organiser, British Social Hygiene Council, 1925-27; Director, Liverpool Women Police Patrols, 1927-30; Supt Women Police, Metropolitan Force, 1930-46; King's Police Medal, 1945. Member Executive Cttee, Josephine Butler Society, 1947. *Publications:* A Pilgrimage of Truth, 1907; various articles, etc dealing with women police. *Recreation:* gardening. *Address:* The Lawn, Holybourne, Alton, Hants.

**PETO, Comdr Sir Francis;** *see* Peto, Comdr Sir (Henry) F. M.

**PETO, Gladys Emma;** Black and White and Poster Artist; *b* Cannon Court, Maidenhead, Berkshire, 19 June 1890; *o d* of William Peto and Mary J. Reeves; *m* 1922, Colonel C. L. Emmerson, RAMC, *o s* of Dr J. B. Emmerson of Biggleswade, Beds. *Educ:* Harvington College, Ealing. Commenced to study art at the Maidenhead Art School in 1908 and at the London School of Art, Kensington, in 1911; illustrated Simple Simon, by A. Neil Lyons, 1913; the works of Louisa Alcott, 1914; humorous drawings appeared weekly in the Sketch, 1915-26, also numerous illustrations in various periodicals and advertisement drawings and posters; has designed fabrics, pottery, costumes, and scenery; exhibitions of water colour drawings: (Cyprus), Abbey Galleries, London, 1929; (India and Ireland), Magee Gallery, Belfast, 1939; lived abroad in Malta, Egypt and Cyprus, 1924-28 and in India, 1933-38. *Publications:* Gladys Peto's Children's Annual; Gladys Peto's Children's Book; The China Cow, 1928; Malta and Cyprus, 1928; Egypt of the Sojourner, 1928; Gladys Peto's Bedtime Stories, 1931; Gladys Peto's Twilight Stories, 1932; Gladys Peto's Girls' Own Stories, 1933; Gladys Peto's Sunshine Tales, 1935; The Four-Leaved Clover, 1938. *Recreations:* books and gardening. *Address:* Leeke, Limavady, Co. Derry, N Ireland.

**PETO, Comdr Sir (Henry) Francis (Morton),** 3rd Bt, *cr* 1855; RN, retired; *b* 18 Nov. 1889; *s* of late Morton Kelsall Peto and Olive Georgiana Elizabeth, *d* of late Hon. Francis Maude; *S* uncle 1938; *m* 1919, Edith (*d* 1945), *d* of late George Berners Ruck Keene; two *s*; *m* 1948, Rosemary Grizel, *d* of late Rear-Adm. Archibald Cochrane, CMG, and *widow* of Major Thomas Clapton, DLI; one *s*. *Heir: s* Henry George Morton Peto [*b* 29 April 1920; *m* 1947, Frances Jacqueline, *d* of late Ralph Haldane Evers, Milan, and of Mrs Evers, Stow-on-the-Wold; two *s*]. *Address:* Balbeg, Straiton, Maybole, Ayrshire.

**PETO, Lt-Col Sir (James) Michael,** 2nd Bt, *cr* 1927; *b* 8 May 1894; *e s* of Sir Basil Peto, 1st Bt; *S* father, 1945; *m* 1920, Frances, *e d* of late Canon W. H. Carnegie, sub-Dean of Westminster; one *d*. *Educ:* Summer Fields, Oxford; Harrow School; Balliol College, Oxford; RMC, Sandhurst. 2nd Lt Coldstream Guards, 1915; served European War, France and Flanders, 1915-18 (despatches); Staff appointments HQ, London District, and HQ, East Anglian Area; retired as Major, 1931. Re-employed April 1939, as a DAQMG, HQ, London District; Lieut-Col and AQMG(M), HQ, London District, 1940; Military Liaison Officer, and ADTn(M), Ministry of War Transport, 1942-45; retired as Lieutenant-Colonel, 1945. *Publications:* Accidental Poems, 1947; Pebble Ridge, 1948. *Recreations:* travel and gardening. *Heir: b* Brigadier Christopher Henry Maxwell Peto, *qv*. *Address:* The Manor House, Yatton Keynell, near Chippenham, Wiltshire. *T:* Castle Combe 375.
*See also Sir Torquhil Matheson, Bt.*

**PETO, Sir Michael;** *see* Peto, Sir (J.) M.

**PETRE,** family name of **Baron Petre.**

**PETRE,** 17th Baron (*cr* 1603), **Joseph William Lionel Petre;** Captain Essex Regiment; *b* 5 June 1914; *s* of 16th Baron and Catherine (who *m* 2nd, 1921, Sir Frederic Carne Rasch, 2nd Bt, TD, *d* 1963) *d* of late Hon. John and late Lady Margaret Boscawen, Tregye, Falmouth, Cornwall; *S* father, 1915; *m* 1941, Marguerite, *d* of late Ion Wentworth Hamilton, Westwood, Nettlebed, Oxfordshire; one *s*. *Heir: s* Hon. John Patrick Lionel Petre, [*b* 4 Aug. 1942; *m* 1965, Marcia Gwendolyn, *o d* of Alfred Plumpton; one *s*]. *Address:* Ingatestone Hall, Essex.

**PETRE, Prof. E. O. G. T.;** *see* Turville-Petre.

**PETRE, Maj.-Gen. Roderic Loraine,** CB 1940; DSO 1917; MC; *o s* of late F. Loraine Petre, OBE; *b* 1887; *m* 1922, Katharine, *o d* of Herbert Bryans, Bradford Priory, Wilts; one *s* one *d*. *Educ:* Downside; Sandhurst. Joined S Wales Borderers, 1908; served siege and capture of Tsingtau, 1914, Gallipoli Campaign, 1915, Mesopotamia and capture of Baghdad, 1916-18 (despatches seven times, DSO, MC); Afghanistan, 1919; Operations in France, 1940 (CB); Bt Major, 1918; Major, 1928; Bt Lt-Col 1929; accelerated promotion into Dorset Regiment as Lt-Col 1932; commanded 2nd Bn The Dorset Regiment, 1932-35; Col 1935; Staff Officer, Sudan Defence Force, 1935-38; Comdt Senior Officers' School, Sheerness, 1938-39; Maj.-Gen., 1939; commanded 12th and 48th Divs and "Petreforce" (BEF), 1939-42; District Comd; 1942-44; retired pay, 1944. *Address:* c/o Glyn, Mills & Co., Kirkland House, Whitehall, SW1. *Club:* Army and Navy.

**PETRIE, Lady (Cecilia);** *d* of late F. J. G. Mason, Kensington; *m* 1926, Sir Charles Petrie, 3rd Bt, *qv*; one *s*. Mem. Kensington Borough Council (Queen's Gate Ward), 1946-62; Alderman since 1962; Mayor of the Royal Borough of Kensington, 1954-56. Member: (C) LCC, for S Kensington, 1949-65; Fulham & Kensington Hospital Management Committee, 1948-59 (Chairman, 1955-59); Chelsea and Kensington Hospital Management Cttee, 1959-; Board of Governors, Charing Cross Hospital, 1959-68; Member Board of Governors of Hospital for Diseases of the Chest, 1951-; Mem. Central Health Services Council, 1955-61; Dep.-Chm. of the London County Council, 1958-59; UK Delegate to United Nations Assembly, 14th Session, 1959; Mem.: SW Metropolitan Regional Hospital Board, 1959-65; London Exec. Council, Nat. Health Service, 1965-; Whitley Council Committee C; London Boroughs Assoc. MRSH. *Recreation:* reading detective stories. *Address:* 190 Coleherne Court, SW5. *T:* 01-373 6666.

**PETRIE, Sir Charles (Alexander),** 3rd Bt of Carrowcarden, *cr* 1918; CBE 1957; MA Oxon, FRHistS; Editor, Household Brigade Magazine since 1945; *b* 28 Sept. 1895; *s* of 1st Bt and Hannah, *d* of late William Hamilton; *m* 1st, 1920, Ursula Gabrielle (marr. diss., 1925; decd), *er d* of late Judge Dowdall, QC; one *s*; 2nd, 1926, Cecilia (*née* Mason) (*see* Lady Petrie); one *s*; *S* brother, 1927. *Educ:* privately; Corpus Christi College, Oxford. Historian; Corresponding Mem. of the Royal Spanish Academy of History; Pres. of Military Hist. Soc. of Ireland. Foreign Editor of the English Review, 1931-37; Associate Editor of Empire Review, 1940-41, Editor, 1941-43; Managing Editor, New English Review, 1945-50; served with RGA, 1915-19; attached War Cabinet Office, 1918-19; Official Lecturer to HM Forces, 1940-45. Corr. Mem. of the Institución Fernando el Católico, Zaragoza; Doctor (*hc*) Valladolid University, 1964; Comdr Order of Isabella the Catholic (Spain); Knight of Order of Civil Merit (Spain); Commendatore Order of Crown of Italy; Commander Order of George I (Greece); *Publications:* The History of Government, 1929; George Canning, 1930, new edn 1946; The Jacobite Movement, 1932, new edn, 1959;

History of Spain (with Louis Bertrand), 1934 (new edn 1957); The Four Georges: A Revaluation, 1935; The Stuarts, 1937; Life and Letters of Sir Austen Chamberlain (2 vols), 1939-40; Diplomatic History, 1713-1933, 1946; Earlier Diplomatic History, 1492-1713, 1949; Chapters of Life, 1950; The Marshal Duke of Berwick, 1953; The Carlton Club, 1955; Wellington: a Reassessment, 1956; The Spanish Royal House, 1958; The Powers Behind the Prime Ministers, 1959; The Victorians, 1960; The Modern British Monarchy, 1961; Philip II of Spain, 1963; King Alfonso XIII, 1963; Scenes of Edwardian Life, 1965; Don John of Austria, 1967; Great Beginnings, 1967; The Drift to World War, 1900-1914, 1968; contribs to Illustrated London News, 1958-. *Heir: s* Charles Richard Borthwick Petrie [*b* 19 Oct. 1921; *m* 1962, Jessie Ariana Borthwick Campbell]. *Address:* 190 Coleherne Court, SW5. *Clubs:* Carlton, 1900, Authors', Guards, Hurlingham; University (Dublin).

**PETRIE, Edward James,** CMG 1955; *b* 1907; retired from HM Treasury, Nairobi. Assistant Revenue Officer, Kenya, 1933; Assistant Treasurer, 1934; Senior Accountant, 1943; Assistant Financial Secretary, 1946; Financial Secretary, Barbados, 1948; Accountant-General, Kenya, 1951; Sec. to Treasury, Kenya, 1953-56; retd 1956. *Address:* 19 Stirling Road, Edinburgh 5.

**PETRIE, Joan Caroline;** Head of European Communities Information Unit, Foreign and Commonwealth Office, since 1969; *b* 2 Nov. 1920; *d* of James Alexander Petrie, Barrister-at-law, and Adrienne Johanna (*née* van den Bergh); *m* 1968, Maurice Edward Bathurst, *qv*; one step *s. Educ:* Wycombe Abbey Sch.; Newnham Coll., Cambridge (Mary Ewart Schol.). 1st cl. Med. and Mod. Langs Tripos, 1942, MA 1964. Entered Foreign Service, 1947: FO, 1947-48; 2nd Sec., The Hague, 1948-50; FO, 1950-54; 1st Sec., 1953; Bonn, 1954-58; FO (later FCO), 1958-; Counsellor 1969. Mem., UK Delegn to Colombo Plan Consultative Cttee, Jogjakarta, 1959. Adviser, British Group, Inter-Parly Union, 1962-68. Officer, Order of Leopold (Belgium), 1966. *Recreation:* music. *Address:* c/o Foreign and Commonwealth Office, SW1. *Club:* Oxford and Cambridge University.

**PETTY, Hon. Sir Horace (Rostill),** Kt 1964; BCom, FASA; Agent-General for State of Victoria, in London, 1964-69; *b* 29 March 1904; *m* 1st, 1930 (marr. diss.); two *s* two *d*; 2nd, 1959. *Educ:* South Yarra School; University High School; Melbourne University. Accountant and auditor (managerial appts in retail business field, etc.) from mid-twenties to 1939. Australian Army, 1940-44; Infty, Aust. Armd Div. and AHQ in North, rank Major. Mem. Municipal Council, City of Prahran, 1949- (Mayor, 1951-52). MLA for Toorak (Liberal) in Victorian Parl., 1952-64. (Victorian Govt) Minister of: Housing, July 1955-July 1961; Immigration, July 1956-Dec. 1961; Public Works, Victorian State Government, July 1961-Apr. 1964. Mem., RSSAILA. *Recreations:* golf, racing, motoring. *Address:* Leith Lodge, 595 Toorak Road, Toorak, Victoria 3142, Australia. *Clubs:* Devonshire, Eccentric; Richmond Golf; Stewards' (Henley); Naval and Military, Melbourne Cricket, Huntingdale Golf, Victoria Racing, Melbourne Rowing, RAC of Vic. (all Victorian).

**PETTY-FITZMAURICE;** *see* Mercer Nairne Petty-Fitzmaurice, family name of **Marquess of Lansdowne.**

**PEVSNER, Sir Nikolaus (Bernhard Leon),** Kt 1969; CBE 1953; FBA 1965; MA Cantab; MA Oxon; PhD; FSA; Hon. FRIBA; Hon. ARCA; Hon. FNZIA; Hon. Academician, Accademia di Belle Arti, Venice; Hon. Member, American Academy of Arts and Sciences; Emeritus Professor of History of Art, Birkbeck College, University of London; Art Editor, Penguin Books; Member of Editorial Board, The Architectural Review; *b* 30 Jan. 1902; *s* of late Hugo Pevsner; *m* 1923, Karola Kurlbaum (*d* 1963); two *s* one *d. Educ:* St Thomas's Sch., Leipzig; Univs of Leipzig, Munich, Berlin and Frankfort. PhD History of Art and Architecture, 1924; Asst Keeper, Dresden Gallery, 1924-28; Lectr, History of Art and Architecture, Goettingen Univ., 1929-33; Slade Prof. of Fine Art, Univ. of Cambridge, 1949-55; Fellow, St John's Coll., Cambridge, 1950-55, Hon. Fellow, 1967-; Slade Prof. of Fine Art, Univ. of Oxford, 1968-69. Chairman, Victorian Soc.; Member: Royal Fine Art Commn; Historic Buildings Council; Nat. Adv. Council for Art Educn; Nat. Council for Diplomas in Art and Design; British Council (Arts Panel); Council, Wm Morris Soc.; Adv. Bd for Redundant Churches. Hon. Fellow, Akademie der Wissenschaften Goettingen. Reith Lectr, BBC, 1955; Royal Gold Medal for Architecture (RIBA), 1967. Hon. Doctorates: Leicester, York, Leeds, Oxford, E Anglia, Zagreb. *Publications:* The Baroque Architecture of Leipzig, 1928; Italian Painting from the end of the Renaissance to the end of the Rococo (a vol. of the Handbuch der Kunstwissenschaft), 1927-30; Pioneers of the Modern Movement, from William Morris to Walter Gropius, 1936 (revised edn: Pioneers of Modern Design, Museum of Modern Art, New York, 1949; also foreign edns); An Enquiry into Industrial Art in England, 1937; German Baroque Sculpture (with S. Sitwell and A. Ayscough), 1938; Academies of Art, Past and Present, 1940; An Outline of European Architecture, Pelican Books, 1942, most recent edn, 1961 (also edns in numerous foreign langs); High Victorian Design, 1951; The Buildings of England (41 vols), 1951-; The Planning of the Elizabethan Country House, 1961; The Englishness of English Art, 1956; Sir Christopher Wren (in Italian), 1958; Sources of Modern Art, 1962 (re-issued as The Sources of Modern Architecture and Design, 1968); Dictionary of Architecture (with John Fleming and Hugh Honour), 1966; Studies in Art, Architecture and Design (2 vols), 1968. *Address:* 2 Wildwood Terrace, North End, NW3.

**PEYREFITTE, (Pierre-) Roger;** French author; *b* 17 Aug. 1907; *o s* of Jean Peyrefitte, landowner, and Eugénie Jamme; unmarried. *Educ:* Collège St Benoit, Ardouane, Hérault (Lazarist); Collège du Caousou, Toulouse, Hte. Garonne (Jesuit); Lycée de Foix, Ariège; Université de Toulouse; Ecole libre des Sciences Politiques, Paris. Bachelier de l'enseignement secondaire; Diplôme d'études supérieures de langue et de littérature française; Diplômé de l'Ecole libre des Sciences Politiques (major de la section diplomatique). Concours diplomatique, 1931; attached to Ministry of Foreign Affairs, 1931-33; Secretary, French Embassy, Athens, 1933-38; attached to Ministry of Foreign Affairs, 1938-40 and 1943-45. *Publications:* Les Amitiés Particulières, novel, 1944 (Prix Théophraste Renaudot, 1945): Mademoiselle de Murville, novel, 1947; Le Prince des neiges, play, 1947; L'Oracle, novel, 1948; Les Amours Singulières, 1949; La Mort d'une mère, 1950; Les Ambassades, novel, 1951; Du Vésuve à l'Etna, 1952; La Fin des Ambassades, novel, 1953; Les Clés de saint Pierre, novel, 1955; Jeunes Proies, 1956; Chevaliers de Malte,

1957; L'Exilé de Capri, novel, 1959; Le Spectateur Nocturne, play, 1960; Les Ambassades, play (adaptation of A. P. Antoine), 1961; Les Fils de la Lumière, 1962; La Nature du Prince, 1963; Les Juifs, 1965; Notre Amour, 1967; Les Américains, novel, 1968; Des Français, novel, 1970. *Recreations:* travel, walks, collecting antiques. *Address:* 9 Avenue du Maréchal Maunoury, 75 Paris XVIe, France.

**PEYTON, Rt. Hon. John Wynne William,** PC 1970; MP (C) Yeovil Division of Somerset since 1951; Minister for Transport Industries, Department of the Environment, since Oct. 1970; *b* 13 Feb. 1919; *s* of late Ivor Eliot Peyton and Dorothy Helen Peyton; *m* 1947, Diana Clinch (marr. diss., 1966); one *s* one *d* (and one *s* decd); *m* 1966, Mrs Mary Cobbold. *Educ:* Eton; Trinity College, Oxford. Commissioned 15/19 Hussars, 1939; Prisoner of War, Germany, 1940-45. Called to the Bar, 1945. Parly Secretary, Ministry of Power, 1962-64; Minister of Transport, June-Oct. 1970. Chm., General Electrical and Mechanical Systems, 1969-70. *Address:* 32 Chester Terrace, NW1. *T:* 01-935 6133; Lytes Cary Manor, Somerton, Somerset. *Club:* Boodle's.

**PEYTON, Sidney Augustus,** PhD; Librarian of Sheffield University, 1941-56; *b* 1891; *e s* of late Sidney Peyton, Newbury; *m* Muriel Kathleen Pearse. *Educ:* University Coll., Reading. Lectr, University Coll., Reading, 1919; Univ. Librarian, Reading, 1922-41. Hon. LittD Sheffield. *Publications:* Oxfordshire Peculiars (Oxford Record Society); Kesteven Quarter Sessions Minutes (Lincoln Record Society); Kettering Vestry Minutes (Northamptonshire Record Society); Northamptonshire QS Records, Introduction; various historical papers. *Recreation:* music. *Address:* 52 Woodholm Road, Sheffield S11 9HT. *T:* Sheffield 362094.

**PFEIFFER, Rudolf,** MA Oxon, DPhil Munich; DPhil *hc* Vienna; FBA 1949; Professor of Greek, University of Munich, 1929-37, and from 1951, Emeritus 1957; *b* 28 September 1889; *s* of late Carl Pfeiffer and late Elizabeth (*née* Naegele); *m* 1913, Lili (*d* 1969), *d* of late Sigmund and Mina Beer. *Educ:* Benedictine Abbey, St Stephan, Augsburg; Universities of Munich and Berlin. Sub-librarian, University Library, Munich, 1918; Lecturer, University of Munich, 1921; Professor extraordinarius, University of Berlin, 1923; Professor of Greek: Hamburg, 1923; Freiburg i. Br., 1927; Corpus Christi College, Oxford, 1938-51, University Lecturer, 1946, Senior Lecturer, 1948, Reader in Greek Literature, 1950. Ordinary Member of Bavarian Academy; Corresponding Member of Austrian Academy; Hon. Fellow of Athenian Scientific Society; Hon. Fellow Corpus Christi College, Oxford, 1959; Hon. Fellow Hellenic Society, 1961. Bavarian Order of Merit, 1959; Greek Order of Phœnix, 1959; Grand Cross of the Federal Republic of Germany, 1964. *Publications:* Augsburger Meistersinger und Homerübersetzer J. Spreng, 1914 and 1919; Callimachi Fragmenta nuper reperta, 1921, editio maior, 1923; Kallimachos-Studien, 1922; Humanitas Erasmiana, 1931; Die griechische Dichtung und die griechische Kultur, 1932; Die Diktyulkoi des Aischylos und der Inachos des Sophokles, 1937; Callimachus (complete edn) vol. I Fragmenta, 1949 (reprinted 1965), vol. II Hymni et Epigrammata, 1953 (repr. 1966); Von der Liebe zu den Griechen, 1958; Ausgewähite Schriften: Aufsätze und Vorträge zur griechischen Dichtung und zum Humanismus, 1960; Philologia Perennis, 1961; History of Classical Scholarship: From the Beginnings to the End of the Hellenistic Age, 1968; Von der Liebe zum Antike; zum 80 Geburtstag von R.P., 1969. Editor: U. von Wilamowitz, Kleine Schriften II, 1940. Numerous articles in periodicals on Greek and Latin literature, Erasmus, humanism. *Recreations:* music, walking. *Address:* Hiltenspergerstrasse 21, München 13, Germany. *T:* 372185.

**PHALP, Geoffrey Anderson,** CBE 1968; TD; Secretary, King Edward's Hospital Fund for London, since 1968; *b* 8 July 1915; *s* of late Charles Anderson Phalp and late Sara Gertrude Phalp (*née* Wilkie); *m* 1946, Jeanne Margaret, OBE, JP, *d* of late Emeritus Prof. G. R. Goldsborough, CBE, FRS; one *s* one *d*. *Educ:* Durham Sch.; Univ. of Durham (BCom). Served with RA (despatches), 1939-46. Asst Registrar, Med. Sch., King's Coll., Newcastle upon Tyne, 1946-49; Dep. House Governor and Sec., United Newcastle upon Tyne Hosps, 1949-51; Sec. and Principal Admin. Officer, United Birmingham Hosps, 1951-68. Member, Central Health Services Council and Standing Nursing Adv. Cttee. *Recreations:* fishing, gardening, music. *Address:* 86 Marryat Road, Wimbledon, SW19. *T:* 01-946 5132. *Club:* Savile.

**PHELAN, Maj.-Gen. Frederick Ross,** CB 1945; DSO 1919; MC 1916; VD 1931; *b* 8 Aug. 1885; *s* of Frederick Edward Phelan and Lillian Catherine Prevost; *m* 1910, Mary Marshall Johnston (*d* 1948); no *c*; *m* 1950, Vera Pearl Scott, ARRC. *Educ:* Public Schools, Montreal. Served European War, 1914-18 (despatches twice, MC, DSO, French Croix de Guerre); Post-war: commanded Canadian Grenadier Guards and Brigade of Canadian Guards; served War of 1939-45, Deputy Adjutant-General, Ottawa, 1940; Deputy Adjutant-General, London, 1940-41; Commander Canadian Reinforcement Units, Aldershot, 1941-43; General Officer Commanding Canadian and Newfoundland Forces, 1943; Dir Gen. Reserve Army, Canada, 1943-45; retired, 1945. CStJ. *Address:* The Priory, St Andrews East, PQ, Canada. *Club:* The Mount Royal (Montreal).

**PHELPS, Anthony John;** Under-Secretary, HM Treasury, since 1968; *b* 14 Oct. 1922; *s* of John Francis and Dorothy Phelps, Oxford; *m* 1949, Sheila Nan Rait (*d* 1967), *d* of late Colin Benton Rait, Edinburgh; one *s* two *d*. *Educ:* City of Oxford High Sch.; University Coll., Oxford. HM Treasury, 1946; Jun. Private Sec. to Chancellor of the Exchequer, 1949-50; Principal, 1950; Treasury Rep. in Far East, 1953-55; Private Sec. to the Prime Minister, 1958-61; Asst Sec., 1961. *Recreations:* music, watching sport. *Address:* 22 Woodcrest Road, Purley, Surrey. *T:* 01-660 1545.

**PHELPS, Richard Wintour;** General Manager, Skelmersdale New Town Development Corporation; *b* 26 July 1925; *s* of Rev. H. Phelps; *m* 1955, Pamela Marie Lawson; two *d*. *Educ:* Kingswood Sch.; Merton Coll., Oxford (MA). 14th Punjab Regt, IA, 1944-46. Colonial Admin. Service, Northern Region and Fed. Govt. of Nigeria, 1948-57 and 1959-61; Prin., HM Treasury, 1957-59 and 1961-65; Sen. Administrator, Hants CC, 1965-67. *Recreations:* reading, travel, bridge. *Address:* 4 Sandringham Road, Birkdale, Southport, Lancs. *T:* Southport 66607. *Club:* Royal Commonwealth Society.

**PHEMISTER, James,** MA, DSc, FRSE, FGS; FMSA; *b* 3 April 1893; 2nd *s* of John Clark Phemister and Elizabeth G. Crawford; *m* 1921, Margaret Clark, MA; two *s* one *d*. *Educ:* Govan High Sch.; Glasgow Univ. Served European War, RE and RGA; disabled 1917, and placed on retired list, 1918; teacher of Mathematics and Science, 1918-21; appointed Geological Survey, 1921; Petrographer, 1935-45; Curator, Museum of Practical Geology, 1945-46; Asst Dir Specialist Services, 1946-53; Pres. Mineralogical Soc., 1951-54; Pres. Glasgow Geol. Soc., 1961-64. Editor, Mineralogical Abstracts, 1959-66. *Publications:* papers on Petrological and Geophysical subjects. *Recreation:* swimming. *Address:* 19 Grange Terrace, Edinburgh 9.

**PHEMISTER, Prof. Thomas Crawford,** MSc (Chicago), PhD (Cantab), DSc (Glasgow); FRSE, FGS; Dr de l'Univ. de Rennes (hon. causa); Professor and Head of Department of Geology and Mineralogy, Aberdeen University, since 1937 (Vice-Principal 1963-66); *b* 25 May 1902; 4th *s* of John Clark Phemister and Elizabeth G. Crawford; *m* 1926, Mary Wood Reid, MA; three *d. Educ:* Allan Glen's School and University of Glasgow; St John's College, Cambridge; Chicago University. Assoc. Prof. of Geology and Mineralogy, Univ. of British Columbia, 1926-33; Field Officer, Geological Survey of Canada, 1928-30; University Demonstrator in Mineralogy and Petrology, Cambridge Univ., 1933-37. Served in Royal Engineers, War of 1939-45. Dean of Faculty of Science, Aberdeen University, 1945-48. Chm., Macaulay Inst. for Soil Research, 1958-. *Publications:* papers on mineralogical and petrological subjects. *Address:* Aberdeen University. *T:* Aberdeen 36489.

**PHILBIN, Most Rev. William J.;** *see* Down and Connor, Bishop of, (RC).

**PHILIP, William Shearer,** CMG 1961; MC 1918; President of Board of Management, Alfred Hospital, Melbourne, since 1948 (Member Board of Management, since 1935, Hon. Treasurer, 1939-48); Company Director; *b* Williamstown, Victoria, 18 Aug. 1891; *s* of Capt. William Philip, Aberdeen and Williamstown; *m* 1920, Irene Laura (*d* 1960), *d* of William Cross; two *s* two *d. Educ:* Scotch College, Melbourne. Flack and Flack and Price Waterhouse & Co., Chartered Accountants, 1909-56, Partner, 1925-56. Member Charities Board of Victoria, 1942-48, Chairman, 1946-47. Business Adviser, AAMC, 1940-45. *Recreations:* golf and fishing. *Address:* Glenshee, No 1 Macquarie Road, Toorak, Victoria 3142, Australia. *T:* 20.3973. *Clubs:* Melbourne, Australian and Royal Melbourne Golf (Melbourne).

**PHILIPPS,** family name of **Viscount St Davids** and **Baron Milford.**

**PHILIPPS, Hon. Hanning;** *see* Philipps, Hon. R. H.

**PHILIPPS, Hon. James Perrott,** TD; *b* 25 Nov. 1905; 3rd *s* of 1st Baron and *b* of 2nd Baron Milford, *qv*; *m* 1930, Hon. Elizabeth Joan, *d* of 1st Baron Kindersley; one *s* two *d. Educ:* Eton; Christ Church, Oxford. Member, Horserace Totalisator Board; Chairman, Tote Investors Ltd; Member of Lloyd's; Chairman: Newmarket Estates and Property Co. Ltd; Newmarket Racecourses Trust; Palace House Stables (Newmarket) Ltd; Dalham Forms Ltd. Mem., Jockey Club. Served War of 1939-45; Leicestershire Yeomanry and Shropshire Yeomanry (despatches). Major TA Reserve. High Sheriff of Suffolk, 1955-56. *Recreations:* shooting, fishing and racing. *Address:* Dalham Hall, Newmarket, Suffolk. *T:* Ousden 242. *Clubs:* Turf, Royal Automobile; Jockey (Newmarket).
*See also Hon. R. H. Philipps.*

**PHILIPPS, Hon. (Richard) Hanning,** MBE 1945; JP; Hon. Major Welsh Guards; HM Lieutenant of Pembrokeshire since 1958; Chairman, Milford Haven Conservancy Board, since 1963; Chairman: Northern Securities Trust Ltd; Dun & Bradstreet Ltd; Hon. President (formerly Chairman), Schweppes Ltd; Member, South Wales Regional Board, Lloyds Bank Ltd; *b* 14 Feb. 1904; 2nd *s* of 1st Baron and *b* of 2nd Baron Milford, *qv*; *m* 1930, Lady Marion Violet Dalrymple, JP, *d* of 12th Earl of Stair, KT, DSO; one *s* one *d. Educ:* Eton. Contested (Nat) Brecon and Radnor, 1939. Served War of 1939-45, NW Europe, 1944-45 (MBE). Vice-Lieutenant of Pembrokeshire, 1957. Hon. Colonel Pembroke Yeomanry, 1959. *Recreations:* painting, fishing, shooting, gardening. *Address:* Picton Castle, Haverfordwest, Pembrokeshire; 5 Connaught Place, W2. *Clubs:* Carlton, Pratt's.
*See also Hon. J. P. Philipps.*

**PHILIPS, Prof. Cyril Henry;** Professor of Oriental History, University of London, since 1946; Director, School of Oriental and African Studies, London, since 1957; Deputy Vice-Chancellor, University of London, 1969-70; *b* Worcester, 27 Dec. 1912; *s* of William Henry Philips; *m* 1939, Dorcas, *d* of John Rose, Wallasey; one *s* one *d. Educ:* Rock Ferry High School; Univs of Liverpool (MA) and London (PhD). Bishop Chavasse Prizeman; Gladstone Memorial Fellow. Frewen Lord Prizeman (Royal Empire Soc.); Alexander Prizeman (Royal Hist. Soc.); Asst Lectr, Sch. of Oriental Studies, 1937. Served in Suffolk Infantry, Army Education Corps, 1940-43; Commandant, Army School of Education, 1943. HM Treasury, Dept of Training, 1943-46. Colonial Office Mission on Community Development, Africa, 1947. Montague Burton Lectr, Univ. of Leeds, 1966. Chairman: UGC Cttee on Oriental, African and Slavonic Studies, 1965-70; UGC Cttee on Latin American Studies, 1966-70; Member: Social Development Cttee, Colonial Office, 1947-55; Colonial Office Research Council, 1955-57; University Grants Cttee, 1960-69; Commonwealth Education Commn, 1961-70; Postgraduate Awards Cttee (Min. of Education), 1962-64; Modern Languages Cttee (Min. of Education), 1964-67; Inter-Univ. Council, 1967-; Governor, Chinese Univ. of Hong Kong, 1965-. Hon. DLitt Warwick, 1967. *Publications:* The East India Company, 1940 (2nd edn 1961); Handbook of Oriental History, 1951 (2nd edn 1962); India, 1949; Correspondence of David Scott, 1951; Historians of India, Pakistan and Ceylon, 1961; The Evolution of India and Pakistan, 1962; Politics and Society in India, 1963; Fort William–India House Correspondence, 1964; History of the School of Oriental and African Studies, 1917-67, 1967; The Partition of India, 1970. *Address:* School of Oriental and African Studies, WC1. *T:* 01-580 9021.

**PHILIPS, Lt-Col John Lionel,** DSO 1917; late RA; *b* 1878; 3rd *s* of late G. H. Philips, MA, DL, JP, of Abbey Cwmhir, Radnorshire; *m* 1st, 1911, Nora, *d* of late J. Fitzmaurice, ICS; one *s* one *d*; 2nd, 1941, Shearme Van Kaughnet, *d* of late G. Wolferstan Thomas, Montreal, and of Mrs F. E. Meredith, London, England. *Educ:* Eton; New College, Oxford. Served European War, France, Mesopotamia, and Palestine, 1914-18 (despatches 4 times, DSO, Bt Lt-Col); retired pay, 1929. JP Radnorshire 1933, Sheriff 1935, DL 1938. *Address:* Little Abbey, Venns Lane, Hereford. *Club:* Army and Navy.

**PHILIPSON, Oliphant James;** *b* 9 Sept. 1905; 2nd *s* of late Hylton Philipson; *m* 1946, Helen Mabel, *d* of David Fell. *Educ:* Eton. Served

War of 1939-45, RNVR. *Address:* Manor House, Everton, near Lymington, Hampshire. *Clubs:* Carlton; Royal Yacht Squadron.

**PHILIPSON, Robin,** RSA 1962 (ARSA 1952), RSW 1954; Head of the School of Drawing and Painting, The College of Art, Edinburgh, since 1960; Secretary, Royal Scottish Academy, since 1969; *b* 17 Dec. 1916; son of James Philipson; *m* 1949, Brenda Mark; *m* 1962, Thora Clyne. *Educ:* Whitehaven Secondary School; Dumfries Academy; Edinburgh College of Art, 1936-40. Served War of 1939-45: King's Own Scottish Borderers, 1942-46, in India and Burma; attached to RIASC. Member of teaching staff, Edinburgh College of Art, 1947, Exhibits with Roland, Browse and Delbanco and Scottish Gallery, Edinburgh. Royal Fine Art Commn for Scotland, 1965. FRSA, 1965. *Address:* 23 Crawfurd Road, Edinburgh. *T:* 031-667 2373. *Club:* Scottish Arts (Edinburgh).

**PHILIPSON-STOW, Sir F. L.;** *see* Stow, Sir F. L. P.

**PHILLIMORE,** family name of **Baron Phillimore.**

**PHILLIMORE,** 3rd Baron, *cr* 1918, of Shiplake in County of Oxford; **Robert Godfrey Phillimore,** Bt, *cr* 1881; *b* 24 Sept. 1939; *s* of Capt. Hon. Anthony Francis Phillimore, 9th Queen's Royal Lancers (*e s* of 2nd Baron) and Anne, 2nd *d* of Maj.-Gen. Sir Cecil Pereira, KCB; *S* grandfather, 1947. *Heir: u* Major Hon. Claud Stephen Phillimore [*b* 15 Jan. 1911; *m* 1944, Anne Elizabeth, *e d* of Maj. Arthur Algernon Dorrien-Smith, DSO; one *s* one *d*]. *Address:* Coppid Hall, Henley-on-Thames, Oxon.

**PHILLIMORE, Rt. Hon. Sir Henry Josceline,** PC 1968; Kt 1959; OBE 1946; **Rt. Hon. Lord Justice Phillimore;** a Lord Justice of Appeal, since 1968; *b* 25 December 1910; *s* of Charles Augustus Phillimore and Alice Campion; *m* 1938, Katharine Mary, *d* of late Lieutenant-Commander L. C. Maude-Roxby, Royal Navy and Mrs Maude-Roxby; two *d. Educ:* Eton; Christ Church, Oxford. Called to Bar Middle Temple, 1934; QC 1952; Bencher, 1959; enlisted TA, July 1939; Commissioned, December 1939; served War of 1939-45; Colonel 1945; demobilised, 1945, and appointed Continental Secretary British War Crimes Executive; Junior Counsel Nuremberg, 1945-46; Recorder of Poole, 1946-54; Recorder of Winchester, 1954-59; Judge of High Court of Justice, Probate Divorce and Admiralty Division, 1959-62, Queen's Bench Division, 1962-68; Chm., Oxfordshire QS, 1962-68. Member, Royal Commn on Assizes and Quarter Sessions, 1967-. *Recreations:* fishing, shooting. *Address:* Queen Elizabeth Building, Temple, EC4. *Clubs:* Brooks's, Pratt's.

*See also Sir Richard Williams-Bulkeley, Bt.*

**PHILLIMORE, John Gore,** CMG 1946; a Managing Director of Baring Brothers & Co. Ltd, 1949; Director: Brascan Ltd, 1949 (formerly Brazilian Light & Power Co.); W. H. Smith & Son (Holdings) Ltd, 1954; Commonwealth Development Finance Co. Ltd, 1967, etc.; is a Rhodes Trustee; *b* 16 April 1908; 2nd *s* of late Adm. Sir Richard and Lady Phillimore, Shedfield, Hants; *m* 1951, Jill, *d* of Captain Mason Scott, Royal Navy retd, Buckland Manor Broadway, Worcs, and of Hon. Mrs Scott; two *s* two *d. Educ:* Winchester College; Christ Church, Oxon. Partner of Roberts, Meynell & Co., Buenos Aires, 1936-48; Representative of HM Treasury and Bank of England in South America, 1940-45. Commander, Orden de Mayo (Argentina). *Address:* The Postern, Tonbridge, Kent. *T:* 2178; 25 Lowndes Square, SW1. *T:* 01-235 3808. *Clubs:* White's, Beefsteak.

**PHILLIPS,** Baroness *cr* 1964 (Life Peeress); **Norah Phillips,** JP; a Baroness in Waiting (Government Whip) since 1965; General Secretary, National Association of Women's Clubs, since 1958; *b* 12 Aug. 1910; *d* of William and Catherine Lusher; *m* 1930, Morgan Phillips (decd); one *s* one *d* (*see* G. P. Dunwoody). *Educ:* Marist Convent; Hampton Training College. *Address:* 115 Rannoch Road, W6. *T:* 01-636 4066.

**PHILLIPS, Col Alan Andrew,** CIE 1946; VD; retired; *b* 18 Aug. 1889; *s* of Charles Addison Phillips and Annie Phillips (*née* Kerr); *m* 1st, 1915, Lucy Osborn (*d* 1952); two *s* two *d* (and one *s* killed on active service); 2nd, 1965, Peggie Crabtree, *o d* of late Charles Bell, Hexham. *Educ:* St Peter's School, York; Queen's College, Oxford. Indian State Railways, 1912-44, Chief Commercial Manager, North Western Railway, 1940-42; Government of India, War Transport Department, as Chief Controller of Railway Priorities, 1942-46. Auxiliary Force (India), 1912-46; Lt Col 1938; Hon. Col 1942; Hon. ADC to the C-in-C, India, 1936-46; retired, 1946. *Publications:* technical papers and magazine articles on Railway and Auxiliary Force matters. *Recreations:* shooting, fishing and natural history. *Address:* Kilncleuch, Langholm, Dumfriesshire. *T:* Langholm 341.

**PHILLIPS, Prof. Alban William Housego,** MBE 1946; Professor of Economics in the Australian National University since 1968; *b* 18 Nov. 1914; *s* of Harold Housego Phillips; *m* 1954, Beatrice Valda Bennett; two *d. Educ:* New Zealand State Schools; London School of Economics. Various posts in electrical engineering, 1930-40; served Royal Air Force (Technical Branch), 1940-46. Assistant Lecturer in Economics, London School of Economics, 1950-51; Lecturer in Economics, 1951-54; Reader in Economics, in the University of London, 1954-58; Tooke Prof. of Economic Science and Statistics, Univ. of London, 1958-67. *Publications:* articles in various economic journals. *Address:* Australian National University, Canberra, ACT 2600, Australia.

**PHILLIPS, Arthur,** OBE 1957; MA, PhD; JP; Barrister at Law (Middle Temple and Western Circuit); Chancellor, Diocese of Winchester; Deputy Chairman, Hampshire Quarter Sessions; President, Southern Rent Assessment Panel; Professor Emeritus, University of Southampton; *b* 29 May 1907; *e s* of Albert William Phillips and Agnes Phillips (*née* Edwards); *m* 1934, Kathleen Hudson; two *s* two *d. Educ:* Highgate School; Trinity College, Oxford. In chambers in Temple, 1929; joined Colonial Service, 1931, and served in Kenya: Dist Officer, 1931; Actg Resident Magistrate, 1933-35; Crown Counsel, 1936; Actg Solicitor-Gen., 1940 and 1946; Judicial Adviser, 1945; Mem. of Kenya Leg. Council, 1940. Served in Kenya Regt, Somaliland and Abyssinia, 1940-42; Chm. War Claims Commn, Br. Somaliland, 1942; retd from Colonial Service on medical grounds and practised at Bar, England, 1947-49. Reader in Law, LSE, Univ. of London, 1949-56; Prof. of English Law, Univ. of Southampton, 1956-67; Dean of Faculty of Law, 1956-62; Deputy Vice-Chancellor, 1961-63. Director of Survey of African Marriage and Family Life, 1948-52. Chairman Milk and Dairies Tribunal, South-Eastern Region, 1961-. JP Hants.; Chairman Winchester County Magistrates' Court, 1956-

61. Member, Church Assembly, 1965-70. Lay Reader, Diocese of Winchester, Counsellor to the Dean and Chapter of Winchester. *Publications:* Report on Native Tribunals (Kenya), 1945; (ed. and part-author) Survey of African Marriage and Family Life, 1953. *Address:* Church Cottage, Compton, Nr Winchester, Hants. *T:* Twyford 3295. *Clubs:* Royal Commonwealth Society; Hampshire (Winchester).

**PHILLIPS, Sir Charles;** *see* Phillips, Sir Edward Charles.

**PHILLIPS, Charles Garrett,** FRS 1963; DM; FRCP; Fellow of Trinity College, Oxford (1946), Professor of Neurophysiology in the University of Oxford since 1966 (Reader 1962-66); *b* 13 October 1916; *s* of Dr George Ramsey Phillips and Flora (*née* Green); *m* 1942, Cynthia Mary, *d* of late L. R. Broster, OBE, FRCS; two *d. Educ:* Bradfield; Magdalen College, Oxford; St Bartholomew's Hospital. Captain, RAMC, 1943-46. Hon. Sec., Physiological Society, 1960-66. Feldberg Prize, 1970. *Publications:* Papers on neurophysiology in Jl of Physiology, etc. *Address:* Trinity College, Oxford. *T:* 41801. *Club:* United University.

**PHILLIPS, Maj.-Gen. Charles George,** CB 1944; DSO 1919, Bar 1940; MC; *b* 7 July 1889; *s* of Major George Edward Phillips, DSO, RE (killed in action Somaliland Expedition, 1902), and L. V. C. Alluaud; *m* 1924, Norah Butler; three *d. Educ:* Repton; RMC, Sandhurst. 2nd Lt West Yorkshire Regiment, 1909; Lieut 1910; seconded for service Merehan Somali Expedition, Jubaland, Kenya, 1912-14; European War, served in German East Africa; Captain, 1914; temp. Lt-Col, 1916-19; commanded 3/2 KAR; commanded Column, Philcol, Portuguese East Africa, 1918; wounded, Njangao, 1917 (German East Africa); temp. Major, 1919; temp. Lt-Col, 1919-23; commanded 1st Batt. 1st King's African Rifles and OC Troops in Nyasaland; Major, 1924; Bt Lt-Col 1932; Lt-Col 1933; commanded 1st Battalion The West Yorkshire Regt (Prince of Wales Own), 1933-37; Col, 1935; Commander 146th (1st West Riding) Infantry Brigade TA, 1938; (Medals, AGS, DSO, MC, 1914-15 Star, General Service Medal, Allied Victory Medal, French Croix de Guerre (avec palme), Officer Military Order of Aviz); War of 1939-45 (3 medals, Bar to DSO); Comdr British Troops, Namsos, Norway, 1940; Northern Iceland, 1940-41; Gambia and Sierra Leone areas, 1942-44; Maj.-Gen. 1942; retired pay, 1944. *Address:* PO Box 2370, Nairobi, Kenya. *Club:* United Service.

**PHILLIPS, Prof. David Chilton,** FRS 1967; BSc, PhD (Wales); FInstP; Professor of Molecular Biophysics and Fellow of Corpus Christi College, Oxford, since Oct. 1966; *b* 7 March 1924; *o s* of late Charles Harry Phillips and of Edith Harriet Phillips (*née* Finney), Ellesmere, Shropshire; *m* 1960, Diana Kathleen (*née* Hutchinson); one *d. Educ:* Ellesmere C. of E. Schools; Oswestry Boys' High Sch.; UCW, Cardiff. Radar Officer, RNVR, 1944-47. UCW, 1942-44 and 1947-51. Post-doctoral Fellow, National Research Council of Canada, 1951-53; Research Officer, National Research Laboratories, Ottawa, 1953-55; Research Worker, Davy Faraday Research Lab., Royal Institution, London, 1955-66; Member MRC External Staff, 1960-66. UK Co-ordinator, Internat. Science Hall, Brussels Exhibition, 1958; Consultant, Royal Society Tercentenary Conversazione, 1960; Consultant, Apparatus Commn, Internat. Union of Crystallography, 1963-66; Director, British Biophysical Society Summer School in Molecular Biology and Biophysics, Oxford, 1966; Member European Molecular Biology Organization (EMBO), 1964; For. Hon. Member, Amer. Academy of Arts and Sciences, 1968; Hon. Mem., Amer. Society of Biological Chemists, 1969 (Lecturer, 1965); Almroth Wright Memorial Lecturer, 1966; Plenary Lecture, Internat. Biochem. Congress, Tokyo, 1967; Hassel Lecture, Oslo, 1968; Feldberg Prize, 1968. Member, Ed. Board, Journal of Molecular Biology, 1966-. *Publications:* papers in Acta Cryst. and other journals. *Address:* Molecular Biophysics Laboratory, Zoology Department, South Parks Road, Oxford OX1 3PS. *T:* Oxford 6789; 3 Fairlawn End, Upper Wolvercote, Oxford OX2 8AR. *T:* Oxford 55828; Corpus Christi College, Oxford.

**PHILLIPS, Maj.-Gen. Sir Edward,** KBE 1946 (CBE 1943); CB 1945; DSO 1919; MC; *b* 19 Dec. 1889; *s* of Edward Phillips, MB, Coventry. *Educ:* St Paul's Sch.; London Hospital; Durham Univ.; MB, BS; MRCS, LRCP, 1913. Entered RAM Corps, July 1914; Major, 1926; Lieut-Col, 1933; Colonel, 1941; Maj.-Gen., 1944; served France, 1914-18 (MC, DSO, despatches four times, Acting Lieut-Col); NW Frontier India, 1919; War of 1939-45 (CBE, CB, KBE); retired pay, 1949. Légion d'Honneur; Croix de Guerre; Ordre de la Couronne; Legion of Merit (USA). *Address:* c/o Glyn, Mills & Company, Whitehall, SW1.

**PHILLIPS, Sir (Edward) Charles,** Kt 1954; CBE 1946; Member of the East Africa Central Legislative Assembly, 1948-59; *b* 10 March 1888; *s* of Edward C. Phillips, Teddington, Middlesex; *m* 1st, 1915, Sylvia Maud Schunke (*d* 1944); one *s* one *d* (one *d* decd); 2nd, 1951, Audrey Jane Prytz; one *d. Educ:* privately. British-American Tobacco Co. Ltd, 1907-45; President: Mombasa Chamber of Commerce, 1935; Dar es Salaam Chamber of Commerce, 1938 and 1939; Member and later Chairman, Economic Control Board of Tanganyika, 1941-48; Member, Makerere College Council, 1941-49; Chairman: Tanganyika Packers Ltd, 1947-; Director: Savings & Loan Society Ltd, 1950-65; Wigglesworth & Co. (Africa) Ltd, 1949-64; Member of: East African Airways, 1940-61; Land Bank of Tanganyika, 1949-58; East African Industrial Council, 1948-59. MLC, 1940-59, MEC, 1940-58, Tanganyika. *Recreations:* previously: tennis, golf. *Address:* Belabbey, 41 Abbots Ride, Farnham, Surrey. *T:* Farnham 3118. *Clubs:* Lansdowne; Mombasa.

**PHILLIPS, Edwin William,** MBE 1946; Managing Director, Lazard Bros & Co. Ltd, since 1960; Chairman, Friends Provident & Century Life Office, since 1968; Member, South Eastern Gas Board, since 1967; *b* 29 Jan. 1918; *s* of C. E. Phillips, Chiswick; *m* 1951, P. M. Matusch; two *s. Educ:* Latymer Upper Sch. Joined Edward de Stein & Co., Merchant Bankers, 1934. Army, 1939-46; Major, Sherwood Rangers Yeomanry. Rejoined Edward de Stein & Co., 1946, Partner, 1954; merged into Lazard Bros & Co. Ltd, 1960. Dir, British Rail Property Bd, 1970. *Recreation:* cricket. *Address:* Send Barns, Send, Surrey. *T:* Ripley 3305. *Clubs:* Pratt's, MCC.

**PHILLIPS, Eric Lawrance,** CMG 1963; Secretary, Monopolies Commission, since 1969; *b* 23 July 1909; *s* of L. Stanley Phillips, London, NW1; *m* 1938, Phyllis Bray, Artist; two *s* one step *d. Educ:* Haileybury Coll.; Balliol Coll., Oxford (Scholar, BA). With Erlangers Ltd, 1932-39. Served War of 1939-45, Captain, RA. Principal, Board of Trade, 1945, Monopolies Commission, 1949; Asst Secretary, Monopolies Commission, 1951, Board of Trade, 1952; Under-Sec., Bd of

Trade, 1964-69. *Recreations:* looking at pictures, places and buildings. *Address:* 46 Platts Lane, NW3. *T:* 01-435 7873. *Club:* Royal Automobile.

**PHILLIPS, Frank Coles,** MA, PhD, FGS; Professor of Mineralogy and Petrology, University of Bristol, 1964-67, retired 1967; now Emeritus; *b* 19 March 1902; *s* of Nicholas Phillips and Kate Salmon; *m* 1929, Seonee Barker; one *s* one *d. Educ:* Plymouth Coll.; Corpus Christi Coll., Cambridge. 1st class, Natural Sciences Tripos, Part II (Geology), 1924; Amy Mary Preston Read Studentship, 1925; Fellow of Corpus Christi Coll., Cambridge, 1927-30; University Demonstrator in Mineralogy, 1928-32; Assistant Director of Studies in Natural Sciences, Corpus Christi College, 1931-46; University Lecturer in Mineralogy and Petrology, Cambridge, 1932-46; Lector in Mineralogy, Trinity Coll., 1945-46; Lecturer in Geology, University of Bristol, 1948-50; Reader in Petrology, 1950-64. Sedgwick Prize, 1937; Murchison Fund, Geological Society of London, 1937; Bolitho Gold Medal, Royal Geological Society of Cornwall, 1962. *Publications:* An Introduction to Crystallography, 1947 (revised edition, 1963); The Use of Stereographic Projection in Structural Geology, 1954 (2nd edition, 1960); revised (13th) edition of G. F. Herbert Smith's Gemstones, 1958; (with G. Windsor) trans. B. Sander, Einführung in die Gefügekunde der geologischen Körper, 1970. Papers on petrology and mineralogy communicated to scientific periodicals. *Recreations:* gardening, carpentry and mechanics. *Address:* Wains Way, Butt's Lawn, Brockenhurst, Hants. *T:* Brockenhurst 3000.

**PHILLIPS, Sir Fred (Albert),** Kt 1967; CVO 1966; Governor of St Kitts/Nevis/Anguilla, 1967-69; Special Representative, Cable and Wireless (West Indies); *b* 14 May 1918; *s* of Wilbert A. Phillips, Brighton, St Vincent; *m* 1942, Georgina, *d* of late Thomas Young; four *s* two *d. Educ:* London Univ. (LLB); Toronto Univ.; McGill Univ. (MCL); Hague Acad. of International Law. Called to the Bar, Middle Temple. Legal Clerk to Attorney-General of St Vincent, 1942-45; Principal Officer, Secretariat, 1945-47; Windward Island: Chief Clerk, Governor's Office, 1948-49; District Officer/Magistrate of District III, 1949-53; Magistrate, Grenada, and Comr of Carriacou, 1953-56; Asst Administrator and MEC, Grenada, 1957-58 (Officer Administrating the Govt, April 1958); Senior Asst Sec., Secretariat, Fedn of W Indies (dealing with constitutional development), 1958-60; Permanent Sec. (Sec. to Cabinet), 1960-62 (when Fedn dissolved); actg Administrator of Montserrat, 1961-62; Sen. Lectr, Univ. of W Indies and Sen. Resident Tutor, Dept of Extra-mural Studies, Barbados, 1962-63; Registrar, Coll. of Arts and Science, Univ. of W Indies, 1963-64; Sen. Res. Fellow, Faculty of Law and Centre for Developing Area Studies, McGill Univ., 1964-65; Guggenheim Fellow, 1965; Administrator of St Kitts, 1966-67. Has attended numerous conferences as a Legal or Constitutional Adviser. KStJ 1968. *Publications:* papers in various jls. *Recreations:* tennis, bridge. *Address:* Chambers, Kingstown, St Vincent, West Indies.

**PHILLIPS, Surgeon Rear-Adm. George,** CB 1961; retired 1961; *b* 1902; *s* of Dr G. Phillips; *m* 1930, Ernestine S., *d* of Surgeon Captain J. S. Orwin; one *s* one *d. Educ:* Dover Coll.; Edinburgh Univ. MB, ChB (Edinburgh), 1926; DLO England, 1936. Joined RN 1926; Surgeon Commander, 1938; MO i/c RN Hospital, Malta, 1943; Surgeon Captain, 1950; Surgeon Rear-Admiral, 1958; MO i/c RN Hospital, Trincomalee, 1950; MO i/c RN Hospital, Haslar, 1958; QHS 1958-61. CStJ 1960. *Recreations:* golf, fishing. *Address:* Whinacre, Yelverton, Devon. *T:* Yelverton 2519.

**PHILLIPS, Very Rev. Gordon Lewis;** Dean of Llandaff, since 1968; *b* 27 June 1911; *s* of Herbert Lewis and Margaret Gertrude Phillips. *Educ:* Cathedral Sch., Llandaff; Dean Close Sch., Cheltenham; Brasenose Coll., Oxford (scholar; exhibitioner; BA 1st cl. Lit. Hum., 1933; 3rd cl. Theology, 1935; MA 1937); Kelham Theological Coll. Deacon 1937; Priest 1938; Curate, St Julian, Newport, Mon, 1937-40; Rector: Northolt, Mddx, 1940-55; Bloomsbury, Diocese of London, 1956-68; Anglican Chaplain, London Univ., 1955-68; Examg Chaplain to Bishop of St Albans, 1957; Prebendary of Hoxton in St Paul's Cathedral, 1960-68; Proctor, Convocation of London, 1960-65; Mem., Standing Cttee on Anglican and Roman Catholic Relations; Select Preacher: Univ. of Oxford, 1942, 1964; Univ. of Cambridge, 1963. *Publications:* Seeing and Believing, 1953; Flame in the Mind, 1957; contrib. to Studies in the Fourth Gospel, 1957. *Address:* The Deanery, Llandaff, Cardiff.

**PHILLIPS, Sir Henry (Ellis Isidore),** Kt 1964; CMG 1960; MBE 1946; Managing Director, Standard Bank Finance and Development Corporation, since 1966; director of other public companies; *b* 30 Aug. 1914; *s* of late Harry J. Phillips, MBE; *m* 1st, 1941, Vivien Hyamson (marr. diss., 1965); two *s* one *d*; 2nd, 1966, Philippa Cohen. *Educ:* Haberdashers' Sch., Hampstead; University College, London. BA (London) 1936; MA 1939. Inst. of Historical Research, 1936-39. Commissioned in Beds and Herts Regt, 1939; served War of 1939-45, with 5th Bn, becoming Adjutant; POW, Singapore, 1942. Joined Colonial Administrative Service and appointed to Nyasaland, 1946 (until retirement in 1965); Development Secretary, 1952; seconded to Federal Treasury of Rhodesia and Nyasaland, 1953-57, Dep. Sec., 1956; Financial Sec., Nyasaland Govt, 1957-64, and Minister of Finance, 1961-64. FRHistS. *Recreations:* tennis, squash, photography and music; Associate Mem., MCC. *Address:* 34 Ross Court, Putney Hill, SW15. *T:* 01-789 1404. *Clubs:* Royal Commonwealth Society, Royal Societies.

**PHILLIPS, Herbert Moore,** CMG 1949; Assistant Secretary, Ministry of Labour and National Service, since 1942 (at present serving with UNESCO); *b* 7 Feb. 1908; *s* of Herbert Phillips and Beatrice Moore; *m* 1934, Martha Löffler (marr. diss.); one *d. Educ:* St Olave's; Wadham Coll., Oxford. Entered Administrative Class of Home Civil Service, 1931; Principal, Ministry of Labour, 1937; Asst Secretary, 1942; seconded to Foreign Service for three years, 1946-49, as Counsellor to Permanent Delegation of UK at seat of UN; Member of UK Delegations to UNRRA, ILO, World Health Organisation, Economic and Social Council and UN Assembly and Delegate to Economic Commn for Latin America, 1947-50; resumed duty as Asst Secretary, Overseas Branch, Ministry of Labour, 1949; Consultant, Economic Commn for Latin America, 1950-51; Economic Adviser, UNESCO. *Address:* c/o UNESCO, Place Fontenoy, Paris. *Club:* Oxford and Cambridge University.

**PHILLIPS, Horace,** CMG 1963; British High Commissioner in Tanzania, since 1968; *b* 31 May 1917; *s* of Samuel Phillips; *m* 1944, Idina Doreen Morgan; one *s* one *d. Educ:* Hillhead High Sch., Glasgow. Joined Board of Inland

Revenue, 1935. Served War of 1939-45, 1940-47. Transf. to FO, Oct. 1947; Acting Vice-Consul, Shiraz, Nov. 1947; Vice-Consul, Bushire, 1948 (Acting Consul, 1948); 1st Secretary and Consul, 1949; Kabul, Oct. 1949; Foreign Office, 1951; 1st Secretary, and Consul, Jedda, 1953; Counsellor, 1956; seconded to Colonial Office, Dec. 1956, as Protectorate Secretary, Aden, until Aug. 1960; Counsellor, British Embassy, Tehran, Oct. 1960; Deputy Political Resident in the Persian Gulf, at Bahrain, 1964-66; Ambassador to Indonesia, 1966-68. *Recreations:* swimming, languages, long-distance car driving especially in the Middle East. *Address:* c/o Foreign and Commonwealth Office, SW1.

**PHILLIPS, Ivan L.;** *see* Lloyd Phillips.

**PHILLIPS, Rev. Canon John Bertram,** MA (Cantab) 1933; DD (Lambeth), 1966; writer and broadcaster since 1955; *b* 16 Sept. 1906; *e s* of late Philip William Phillips, OBE, and late Emily Maud Powell; *m* 1939, Vera May, *o d* of William Ernest and May Jones; one *d. Educ:* Emanuel Sch., London; Emmanuel Coll. and Ridley Hall, Cambridge. Asst Master, Sherborne Prep. School for boys, 1927-28; Curate, St John's, Penge, London, 1930-33; freelance journalist and Editorial Secretary, Pathfinder Press, 1934-36; Curate, St Margaret's, Lee, London, 1936-40; Vicar of Good Shepherd, Lee, London, 1940-44; Vicar of St John's, Redhill, Surrey, 1945-55; Wiccamical Prebendary of Exceit in Chichester Cathedral, 1957-60. Canon of Salisbury Cathedral, 1964. Hon. DLitt, Exeter, 1970. *Publications:* Letters to Young Churches, 1947; Your God is too Small, 1952; The Gospels in Modern English, 1952; Making Men Whole, 1952; Plain Christianity, 1954; When God was Man, 1954; Appointment with God, 1954; The Young Church in Action, 1955; New Testament Christianity, 1956; The Church under the Cross, 1956; St Luke's Life of Christ, 1956; The Book of Revelation, 1957; Is God at Home?, 1957; The New Testament in Modern English, 1958; A Man Called Jesus, 1959; God our Contemporary, 1960; Good News, 1963; Four Prophets, 1963; Ring of Truth, 1967. *Recreations:* painting, photography, music, reading. *Address:* Golden Cap, 17 Gannetts Park, Swanage, Dorset. *T:* 3122.

**PHILLIPS, John Fleetwood Stewart,** CMG 1965; Ambassador to Jordan, since 1970; *b* 16 Dec. 1917; *e s* of late Major Herbert Stewart Phillips, 27th Light Cavalry, and of Violet Gordon, *d* of late Sir Alexander Pinhey, KCSI; *m* 1948, Mary Gordon Shaw, MB, BS; two *s* two *d. Educ:* Brighton; Worcester Coll., Oxford (Open Exhibition in Classics, MA). Served with 1st Bn, Argyll and Sutherland Highlanders in N Africa and Crete (wounded and captured, 1941). Appointed to Sudan Political Service, 1945; served in Kordofan and Blue Nile Provinces. HM Diplomatic Service, 1955, served in Foreign Office; Oriental Secretary in Libya, 1957; Counsellor, 1961; Consul-General at Muscat, 1960-63; Counsellor, British Embassy, Amman, 1963-66; Imperial Defence Coll., 1967; Dep. High Comr, Cyprus, 1968; Ambassador to Southern Yemen, 1969-70. *Recreations:* riding, fishing, birdwatching, shell-collecting. *Address:* c/o Foreign and Commonwealth Office, SW1; Southwood, Gordon Road, Horsham, Sussex. *T:* Horsham 2894. *Clubs:* Travellers', Royal Commonwealth Society.

**PHILLIPS, John Francis,** OBE 1957; Secretary and Chief Executive, Chartered Institute of Secretaries, since 1957; Deputy Chairman, Eggs Authority, since 1971; *b* 1911; *e s* of late F. W. Phillips and late Margaret (*née* Gillan); *m* 1937, Olive M. Royer; one *s* two *d. Educ:* Cardinal Vaughan Sch.; London Univ.; Trinity Hall, Cambridge. LLB (Hons) London; LLB (1st Cl. Hons), LLM Cantab. Barrister-at-law, Gray's Inn, 1944. Civil Servant (Lord Chancellor's Dept, Royal Courts of Justice), 1933-44; Parly Sec. and Asst Gen. Sec., Nat. Farmers' Union of England and Wales, 1945-57. Member: Council of Management, Private Patients' Plan, 1958-; Gen. Cttee, Bar Assoc. for Commerce, Finance and Industry, 1967-; (Minister's nominee), Council for Accreditation of Correspondence Colls, 1969-; British Egg Marketing Bd, 1969-71; Chm., Jt Cttee for Awards in Business Studies and Public Admin., 1968- (Mem. 1960-); Mem., Associated Examining Bd, GCE, 1958-; Governor, Christ's Hospital, 1967-; Mem., Bd of Governors, Crossways Trust, 1959- (Financial Advisor, 1966-); Deleg. to Internat. Labour Conf., 1950-56. FCIS 1958; FIArb 1966 (Council of Inst. 1967-); MBIM 1969 (Council of Inst. 1969-). *Publications:* The Agriculture Act, 1947, 1948; Heywood and Massey's Lunacy Practice, 1939; many articles on aspects of law relating to land and agriculture. *Recreation:* travel. *Address:* Devonshire House, Devonshire Street, W1; (office) 16 Park Crescent, W1. *T:* 01-580 4741. *Clubs:* United University, City Livery.

**PHILLIPS, John Grant,** CBE 1968; Governor and Chairman of Board, Reserve Bank of Australia, since 1968; *b* 13 March 1911; *s* of Oswald amd Ethel Phillips, Sydney; *m* 1935, Mary W. Debenham; two *s* two *d. Educ:* C of E Grammar Sch., Sydney; University of Sydney (BEc). Research Officer, NSW Retail Traders' Assoc., 1932-35; Econ. Asst, Royal Commn Monetary and Banking Systems, 1936-37; Econ. Dept, Commonwealth Bank of Australia, 1937-51; Investment Adviser, Commonwealth Bank, 1954-60; Dep. Governor and Dep. Chairman of Board, Reserve Bank of Australia, 1960-68. Leader, Australian Delegation to 6th Conf. GATT, Geneva, 1951; Member: Council, Macquarie Univ., 1967-; Australian Atomic Energy Adv. Cttee, 1969. *Address:* 3 Cyprian Street, Mosman, NSW 2088, Australia; Reserve Bank of Australia, 65 Martin Place, Sydney, NSW 2000, Australia. *T:* Sydney 2-0327. *Club:* University (Sydney).

**PHILLIPS, Prof. John Guest,** PhD, DSc; Professor of Zoology, University of Hull, since 1967; *b* 13 June 1933; *s* of Owen Gwynne Phillips and Dorothy Constance Phillips; *m* 1961, Jacqueline Ann Myles-White; two *s. Educ:* Llanelli Grammar Sch.; Univ. of Liverpool. BSc 1954, PhD 1957, Liverpool; DSc Hong Kong 1967. Commonwealth Fund Fellow, Yale Univ., 1957-59; Fellow, Davenport Coll., Yale Univ., 1957-59; Lectr in Zoology, Univ. of Sheffield, 1959-62; Milton Res. Assoc., Harvard Univ., 1960; Prof. of Zoology, Univ. of Hong Kong, 1962-67; Dean of Faculty of Science, Hong Kong, 1965-66. *Publications:* numerous papers in zoological, endocrinological and physiological jls. *Recreations:* gardening, squash rackets, music, travel. *Address:* Alberose, 54 Elveley Drive, West Ella, Yorks. *T:* Hull 654194.

**PHILLIPS, John Henry Hood,** MA; *b* 18 Aug. 1902; *e s* of late Surgeon-Captain J. E. Hood Phillips, RN, Portsmouth; *m* 1931, Winifred, *y d* of late S. T. Shovelton, CBE; two *s* one *d. Educ:* Weymouth Coll.; Keble Coll., Oxford (Modern History Exhibitioner, 1921); Oxford Univ. Dept of Education. Asst Master, King Edward VI School, Southampton, 1926-28; Divisional Education Officer, Middlesex CC,

1930-34; Asst Education Officer, Surrey CC, 1934-40; Dep. Education Officer, 1940-45; Sec. to Senate, Univ. of London, 1945-66. Mem. of Council, Boy Scouts' Assoc., 1947-68; Chm., Education Advisory Panel, 1945-58. Almoner, Christ's Hospital, 1947-, and Chm. Education Cttee; Chairman: Raynes Park Schools' Governors, 1949-58; Council, St Gabriel's Coll. of Educn, Camberwell, 1968-. *Publications:* The Heart of a Schoolboy, 1919; Hurrying Feet, 1924. *Address:* 7 St Cross Court, Winchester, Hants. *T:* Winchester 5162.
*See also O. H. Phillips.*

**PHILLIPS, Rt. Rev. John Henry Lawrence;** *see* Portsmouth, Bishop of.

**PHILLIPS, John Raymond,** MC 1945; QC 1968; *b* 20 Nov. 1915; *o* surv. *s* of David Rupert and Amy Isabel Phillips, Radyr, Glam; *m* 1951, Hazel Bradbury Evans, *o d* of T. John Evans, Cyncoed, Cardiff; two *s*. *Educ:* Rugby; Balliol Coll., Oxford (MA, BCL). Barrister, Gray's Inn, 1939; Arden Scholar; Bencher, 1965. Served 3rd Medium Regt, RA, 1940-45 (despatches). Practised at Bar, 1946-; Wales and Chester Circuit, 1939; Jun. Counsel, Inland Revenue (Rating Valuation), 1958-63; Jun. Counsel, Inland Revenue (Common Law), 1963-68. Dep. Chm., Glamorgan QS, 1964-. *Publication:* (ed) The Belsen Trial. *Address:* The Elms, Park Road, Teddington, Middx. *T:* 01-977 1584; 2 Crown Office Row, Temple, EC4. *T:* 01-353 1878. *Clubs:* Oxford and Cambridge University; Cardiff and County (Cardiff).

**PHILLIPS, Leonard George,** FRCS; Hon. Consulting Surgeon: Hospital for Women, Soho Square; Queen Charlotte's Hospital; Willesden General Hospital; Emeritus Consulting Surgeon, Croydon General Hospital; Examiner: London University; RCOG; *b* Dec. 1890. MRCS, LRCP, 1915; MB, BS 1916; BSc London, MS, FRCS, 1919; FRCOG 1938. Fellow, Royal Society of Medicine and Medical Society, London. *Publications:* contributions to medical journals and to Queen Charlotte's Practice of Obstetrics. *Recreations:* shooting, golf, gardening. *Address:* 39 Harley House, Regents Park, NW1. *T:* 01-935 3686; The Grove, Godmanchester, Hunts. *Clubs:* Devonshire; Melbourne (Melbourne).

**PHILLIPS, Sir Leslie (Walter),** Kt 1962; CBE 1947; Chairman T. A. Jones Co. Ltd, London Grain Brokers, 1943-70; Chairman, Baltic Exchange, 1963-65 (Vice-Chairman 1961-63); *b* 12 Aug. 1894; 2nd *s* of late Charles Phillips; *m* 1915, Mary, *d* of late John Corby; one *s*. President National Federation of Corn Trade Associations, 1949-52; President, London Corn Trade Assoc., 1959-60; Vice-Chairman, Sugar Board, 1966-68. Director of Freight, Ministry of Food, 1941-45; Controller of Freight and Warehousing, 1946-47. *Address:* Summerholme, Bexhill-on-Sea, Sussex. *T:* Bexhill 1211.

**PHILLIPS, Prof. Neville Crompton;** Vice-Chancellor and Rector, University of Canterbury, Christchurch, New Zealand; *b* 7 March 1916; 2nd *s* of Samuel and Clara Phillips, Christchurch, NZ; *m* 1940, Pauline Beatrice, 3rd *d* of Selby and Dorothy Palmer, Te Aratipi, Havelock North, NZ; one *s* two *d*. *Educ:* Dannevirke High Sch.; Palmerston North Boys' High Sch.; Canterbury University College; Merton Coll., Oxford. BA (NZ) 1936; MA 1938; NZ University Post-Grad. Schol. in Arts, Arnold Atkinson Prizeman, 1938; Journalist, Sun and Press, Christchurch, 1932-38; read PPE at Oxford, 1938-39; RA (Gunner, subseq. Major), 1939-46; service in Tunisia and Italy; Lecturer in History and Political Science, Canterbury University College, 1946-47; Senior Lecturer, 1948; Prof. of History and Political Science, 1949-62; Prof. of History, 1962-66; Emeritus Prof., 1966; Chairman, Canterbury Centennial Provincial Historical Cttee, 1948-66; Secondary Sch. Bds; 1st Pres., Canterbury Historical Assoc., 1953; Editorial Adviser, NZ War Histories, 1957-67; US Dept of State Leader Grantee, 1966; Council Mem., Canterbury Manufacturers' Assoc., 1967-; Christchurch Teachers' Coll. Council, 1968-. *Publications:* Italy, vol. 1 (The Sangro to Cassino), 1957; Yorkshire and English National Politics, 1783-84, 1961; articles, mainly on eighteenth-century English politics, in English and NZ jls. *Recreations:* reading history, watching cricket, things Italian. *Address:* 122 Straven Road, Christchurch 1, New Zealand. *T:* 47-559. *Clubs:* Canterbury, University (Christchurch).

**PHILLIPS, Prof. Owen Hood,** QC 1970; MA, BCL, Oxon; MA, LLB, Dublin; LLM Birmingham; JP; Barber Professor of Jurisprudence at the University of Birmingham, since 1946; *b* 30 Sept. 1907; *yr s* of late Surgeon-Captain J. E. Hood Phillips, RN, Portsmouth; *m* 1949, Lucy Mary Carden, 3rd *d* of late Arnold Philip, and formerly Lecturer in Physical Educn at University of Birmingham. *Educ:* Weymouth Coll.; Merton Coll., Oxford. Asst Lecturer in Laws, King's Coll., London, 1931-35; Lectr in General Jurisprudence, Univ. of Dublin (Trinity Coll.), 1935-37; Reader in English Law, Univ. of London, 1937-46; Vice-Dean of Faculty of Laws, King's Coll., London, 1937-40; Dean, Faculty of Law, and Dir, Legal Studies, Univ. of Birmingham, 1949-68; Public Orator, Univ. of Birmingham, 1950-62. Min. of Labour and National Service, 1940; Min. of Aircraft Production, 1940-45; adviser to Singapore Constitutional Commn, 1953-54; delegate to Malta Round Table Conf., 1955. Governor King Edward VI Schs, Birmingham (Bailiff, 1958-59); Pres., Soc. of Public Teachers of Law, 1963-64. JP Birmingham, 1961. *Publications:* Principles of English Law and the Constitution, 1939; Constitutional and Administrative Law, 4th edn 1967; Leading Cases in Constitutional and Administrative Law, 3rd edn, 1967; A First Book of English Law, 6th edn, 1970; Reform of the Constitution, 1970; contributions to various legal periodicals. *Address:* 24 Heaton Drive, Edgbaston, Birmingham 15. *T:* 021-454 2042; Mount Pleasant Cottage, Clee St Margaret, Shropshire.
*See also J. H. H. Phillips.*

**PHILLIPS, Prof. Owen Martin,** FRS 1968; Professor of Geophysics, Johns Hopkins University, since 1968; *b* 30 Dec. 1930; *s* of Richard Keith Phillips and Madeline Lofts; *m* 1953, Merle Winifred Simons; two *s* two *d*. *Educ:* University of Sydney; Cambridge Univ. ICI Fellow, Cambridge, 1955-57; Fellow, St John's Coll., Cambridge, 1957-60; Asst Prof., 1957-60, Assoc. Prof., 1960-63, Johns Hopkins Univ.; Asst Director of Research, Cambridge, 1961-64; Prof. of Geophysical Mechanics, Johns Hopkins Univ., 1963-68. Assoc. Editor Jl of Fluid Mechanics, 1964-; Mem. Council, Nat. Center of Atmospheric Research, Boulder, Colorado, 1964-; US Nat. Cttee Global Atmospheric Research Project, 1968. *Publications:* The Dynamics of the Upper Ocean, 1966; The Heart of the Earth, 1968; various scientific papers in Jl Fluid Mechanics, Proc. Cambridge Philos. Soc., Jl Marine Research, Proc. Royal Society, Deep Sea Research, Journal Geophys. Research.

*Address:* 23 Merrymount Road, Baltimore, Maryland 21210, USA. *T:* 433-7195.

**PHILLIPS, Patrick Edward,** TD 1955; RP 1954; ARWS 1968; Artist, Portrait Painter; *b* 17 March 1907; 2nd *s* of Lionel Charles Whitehead Phillips, Unsted Park, Godalming; *m* 1932, Susannah Catherine, *d* of late General Sir Reginald Byng Stephens, KCB, CMG, Church House, Lechlade, Glos; one *s* two *d*. *Educ:* Eton; Byam Shaw School of Art. Lieut, 98 (Surrey and Sussex Yeomanry) Field Bde, 1926; served War of 1939-45 (despatches); Major, RE, 1941; TARO retired, 1957. Principal of The Byam Shaw School of Drawing and Painting, 1946-55. *Address:* Gannets, Tolleshunt D'Arcy, Maldon, Essex. *T:* Tolleshunt D'Arcy 221. *Club:* Arts.

**PHILLIPS, Sir Philip David,** Kt 1967; CMG 1964; MM 1918; QC (Victoria) 1946; retired as Chairman, Commonwealth Grants Commission, Australia (1960-66); *b* 22 March 1897; *s* of Morris Mondle Phillips, Melbourne; *m* 1st; two *d*; 2nd, 1949, Olive Catherine, *d* of Henry Rosenthal, Melbourne. *Educ:* Melbourne C of E Grammar Sch.; Melbourne Univ. MA, LLM, 1922. Admitted to Vict. Bar, 1923; retired 1957. Chairman, Vict. Transport Regulation Board, 1934-37; Dep. Chairman, Commonwealth Liquid Fuel Control Board, 1940-45. S. Korman Special Lecturer, Melbourne Univ., 1957-. *Recreations:* lawn-bowls, woodwork. *Address:* Velden, Cromwell Street, Eltham, Victoria 3095, Australia. *T:* 4399015. *Clubs:* University (Sydney); Royal Automobile (Melbourne); Heidelberg Golf.

**PHILLIPS, Reginald Arthur,** CMG 1965; OBE 1951; Deputy Director-General, British Council, since 1966; *b* 31 Jan. 1913; *y s* of late James and Catherine Ann Phillips, Tredegar, Mon; *m* 1939, Doris Tate, *d* of William and Angelina Tate, São Paulo, Brazil; one *s* two *d*. *Educ:* Tredegar Grammar Sch.; Balliol Coll., Oxford (MA). Asst Master, St Paul's School, Brazil, 1936; Lecturer, Anglo-Brazilian Cultural Society, 1937-39. War of 1939-45: Intelligence Corps (Major), 1940-46. British Council: Latin America Dept, 1947; Home Div., 1948-54; Colonies Dept, 1954-57; Controller, Commonwealth Div., 1957-59; Controller, Finance Div., 1959-62; Assistant Director-General, 1962-66. *Recreations:* golf, walking, television. *Address:* 68 Leopold Road, Wimbledon, SW19. *T:* 01-946 2821. *Club:* Athenæum.

**PHILLIPS, Surgeon Rear-Adm. Rex Philip,** OBE 1963; QHS 1969; Medical Officer-in-Charge, Royal Naval Hospital, Plymouth, since Oct. 1969; *b* 17 May 1913; 2nd *s* of William John Phillips, late Consultant Anaesthetist at Royal Victoria Infirmary, Newcastle upon Tyne, and Nora Graham Phillips; *m* 1939, Gill Foley; two *s*. *Educ:* Epsom Coll.; Coll. of Med., Newcastle upon Tyne, Univ. of Durham (now Univ. of Newcastle upon Tyne). Qual. MB, BS 1937; Ho. Surg., Ingham Infirmary, S Shields, 1938. Joined RN, 1939; served War of 1939-45: HMS Rochester, 1939-41; Royal Marines, 1941-43; HMS Simba, 1943-45. HMS Excellent, 1945-47; qual. Dip. in Ophthalmology (London), 1948; HMS Implacable, Fleet MO, 1949-51; Specialist in Ophthalmology: HMS Ganges, 1951-53; Central Air Med. Bd, 1953-55; RN Hosp., Malta (Senior), 1955-57; Admty Adv. in Ophth. to Med. Dir-Gen., 1957-65; Surg. Captain 1963; SMO, RN Hosp., Malta, 1965-68; Staff MO to Flag Officer Submarines, 1968-69. *Recreations:* golf, bridge. *Address:* Langstone House, Langstone Village, Havant, Hants. *T:* Havant 4668. *Club:* United Service.

**PHILLIPS, Sir Robin Francis,** 3rd Bt, *cr* 1912; *b* 29 July 1940; *s* of Sir Lionel Francis Phillips, 2nd Bt, and Camilla Mary, *er d* of late Hugh Parker, 22 Chapel Street, Belgrave Square, SW1; *S* father, 1944. *Heir:* none. *Address:* 12 Manson Mews, Queen's Gate, Sw7.

**PHILLIPS, Hon. Sir Rowland (Ricketts),** Kt 1964; Chief Justice of Jamaica since 1963; *b* 30 Sept. 1904; *s* of George Augustus Phillips, Montego Bay, Jamaica, WI; *m* 1947, Enid Daphne Limonius; two *s* two *d*. *Educ:* Cornwall Coll., Jamaica. Called to Bar, 1941; Crown Counsel, Jamaica, 1943; Resident Magistrate, Jamaica, 1946; Puisne Judge: British Guiana, 1954-59; Jamaica, 1959-Oct. 1962; Judge, Court of Appeal, Jamaica, Oct.-Dec. 1962. *Address:* Supreme Court, Kingston, Jamaica, WI.

**PHILLIPS, Rt. Rev. Samuel Charles,** MA, LTh Durham; retired; *b* 6 May 1881; *s* of late Rt Rev. C. Phillips, DD, and Mrs Marianne Phillips; *m* 1923, Ayodele Pearse; one *s* three *d*. *Educ:* The CMS Grammar Sch., Freetown, Sierra Leone; Fourah Bay Coll., Sierra Leone. Tutor, CMS Grammar Sch., Lagos, 1905-06; Tutor, St Andrew's Coll., Oyo, 1907-08; Vice-Principal, Abeokuta Grammar Sch., 1908-14; Principal, Ijebu Ode Grammar Sch., 1914-18; Superintendent and Chairman Ondo Church District and Canon of the Cathedral, 1919-30; Pastor of St Paul's Cathedral, Breadfruit, Lagos, 1930-31; Canon Res. Cathedral Church of Christ, Lagos, Archdeacon of Lagos and Chairman of six District Church Councils, 1931-44; consecrated Asst Bishop of Lagos, 1944; resigned, 1956; Vicar-General, Dio. Lagos, 1952-56. Subsequently Organising Secretary, Nigeria Temperance Society. *Publications:* Christ or Mohammed (Lenten Addresses), 1944; Science Handmaid to the Bible. *Address:* PO Box 105, Oshogbo, Nigeria.

**PHILLIPS, Sydney William Charles,** CB 1955; Second Civil Service Commissioner, since 1968; *b* 1 Dec. 1908; *s* of late Frederick Charles and of Elizabeth Phillips; *m* 1932, Phyllis, *d* of late James Spence; two *s*. *Educ:* Bridport Grammar Sch.; University College, London. Administrative Asst, University College, Hull, 1932-37; Asst Registrar, Liverpool Univ., 1937-45; seconded to Min. of Works, 1941-43; Min. of Town and Country Planning, 1943-51 (Private Sec. to Minister, 1943-44); Asst Sec., 1944; Under-Sec., Min. of Housing and Local Govt, 1952-68. Fellow, UCL, 1969. *Recreations:* walking and gardening. *Address:* Innisfree, Higher Drive, Purley, Surrey. *T:* 01-660 8617. *Club:* United Service.

**PHILLIPS BROCKLEHURST, Charles Douglas Fergusson,** DL; *b* 17 March 1904; *o surv s* of late Lieut-Colonel R. W. D. Phillips Brocklehurst, DL, JP, Hare Hill, Macclesfield, and late Ida E., *d* of late Sir Patrick Heron Watson; unmarried. *Educ:* Eton; Christ Church, Oxford (BA). Served War of 1939-45 with Cheshire Yeo., Palestine and Syria, and 10 Armoured Division, Western Desert and Alamein; GSO1, Military Liaison, Albania; retired with hon. rank of Lt-Col, 1945. A Trustee of: Wallace Collection; Lady Lever Art Gallery; a Governor of Whitworth Art Gallery. DL 1952, Cheshire; High Sheriff of Cheshire, 1957. *Address:* Hare Hill, Macclesfield, Cheshire; 3 West Eaton Place, SW1. *T:* 01-235 4677. *Clubs:* White's, Beefsteak.

**PHILLIPSON, Prof. Andrew Tindal;** Professor of Veterinary Clinical Studies, Cambridge University, and Fellow of Churchill College, since Oct. 1963; *b* 19 Aug. 1910; *s* of John Tindal Phillipson and Cicely Gough Paterson;

*m* 1936, Rachel Margaret Young; three *s*. *Educ:* Christ's Coll., Finchley; St Catharine's Coll., Cambridge; Royal Veterinary Coll., London. BA Cambridge 1931, MA 1937; MRCVS London, 1936; Clement Stephenson Schol., 1936-39 (Award of Royal Veterinary College); Miss Aleen Cust Schol., 1938 and 1939 (Award of Royal College of Vet. Surg.); PhD Cambridge, 1941. Scientific Officer, Inst. of Animal Pathology, Cambridge, 1939-42; seconded to Agric. Res. Council's Unit of Animal Physiology, 1941, and taken on Council's Staff, 1942, to continue previous work on Physiol. of Digestion of the Ruminant (under direction of late Sir Jospeh Barcroft); Head of Physiol. Dept, Rowett Research Institute, 1947, and Dep. Director of Institute, 1952. FRSE 1953; Hon. Dr Vet. Sci., Royal Veterinary and Agricultural Coll., Copenhagen, 1958; Hon. Dr Vet. Med. University of Ghent, 1968. Dalrymple Champneys Cup and Medal, British Veterinary Assoc., 1959; Research Medal, Royal Agricultural Society of England, 1962. *Publications:* The Alimentary Tract of the Ruminant (with D. Benzie), 1957; various chapters contrib. to scientific books. Papers in: Journal Exper. Biology, Journal of Physiol., Quarterly Journal of Physiol., British Journal of Nutrition. Reviews in Biolog. Reviews, Annual Review of Biochem., Nutrition Abstracts and Review, etc. *Address:* Veterinary School, Madingley Road, Cambridge.

**PHILLPOTTS, Christopher Louis George,** CMG 1957; HM Diplomatic Service, retired; *b* 23 April 1915; *s* of Admiral Edward Montgomery Phillpotts, CB, and Violet Selina (*née* Cockburn); *m* 1942, Vivien Chanter-Bowden; one *s* one *d*. *Educ:* Royal Naval Coll., Dartmouth. Served in Royal Navy, 1932-43 (despatches twice). Joined Foreign Office, Nov. 1943. Appointed Vice-Consul, Malmö, March 1945; transferred Foreign Office, July 1945; Copenhagen, 3rd Secretary, 1947; 2nd Secretary, 1949; Foreign Office, 1951; Athens, 1st Secretary, 1953; Counsellor HM Embassy, Paris, 1957. Transferred Foreign Office, April 1962; Counsellor, Washington, 1964-66; Foreign and Commonwealth Office, 1966-70. *Recreation:* theatre. *Address:* 27 Merrick Square, SE1. *T:* 01-407 5995. *Clubs:* United Service, White's.

**PHILLPOTTS, (Mary) Adelaide Eden, (Mrs Nicholas Ross);** writer; *b* Ealing, Middlesex; *d* of late Eden Phillpotts; *m* 1951, Nicholas Ross. *Publications:* Illyrion and other Poems, 1916; Arachne: a Play, 1920; Savitri the Faithful, 1923, and Camillus and the Schoolmaster, 1923 (plays); Man, a Fable, 1922; The Friend, 1923; Lodgers in London, 1926, and Tomek, the Sculptor, 1927 (novels); Akhnaton (play), 1926; Yellow Sands (play, with Eden Phillpotts); A Marriage, 1928 (novel); The Atoning Years, 1929 (novel); Yellow Sands, 1930 (novel); The Youth of Jacob Ackner, 1931 (novel); The Founder of Shandon, 1932 (novel); The Growing World, 1934 (novel); Onward Journey, 1936 (novel); Broken Allegiance, 1937 (novel); What's Happened to Rankin?, 1938 (novel); The Gallant Heart, 1939 (novel); Laugh With Me, 1938 (play); The Round of Life (novel), 1940; Laugh with Me (novel), 1941; Our Little Town (novel), 1942; From Jane to John (novel), 1943; The Adventurers (novel), 1944; The Lodestar (novel), 1946; The Fosterling (novel), 1949; Stubborn Earth (novel), 1951; A Song of Man, 1959; Panorama of the World (travel), 1969. *Address:* Cobblestones, Kilkhampton, Bude, Cornwall.

**PHILO, Gordon Charles George,** CMG 1970; MC 1944; HM Diplomatic Service; Foreign and Commonwealth Office since 1969; *b* 8 Jan. 1920; *s* of Charles Gilbert Philo and Nellie Philo (*née* Pinnock); *m* 1952, Mavis (Vicky) Ella, *d* of John Ford Galsworthy and Sybel Victoria Galsworthy (*née* Strachan). *Educ:* Haberdashers' Aske's Hampstead Sch.; Wadham Coll., Oxford. Methuen Scholar in Modern History, Wadham Coll., 1938. Served War, HM Forces, 1940-46: Royal West African Frontier Force, 1942-43; Airborne Forces, Normandy and Europe, 1944-45; India 1945-46. Alexander Korda Scholar, The Sorbonne, 1948-49; Lectr in Modern History, Wadham Coll., 1949-50; Foundn Mem., St Antony's Coll., Oxford, 1950-51. Foreign Office, 1951; Russian course, Christ's Coll., Cambridge, 1952-53; Istanbul Third Sec., 1954-57; Ankara, Second Sec., 1957-58; FO, 1958-63; Kuala Lumpur, First Sec., 1963-67; FO, 1968; Consul-Gen., Hanoi, 1968-69. Kesatria Mangku Negara (Hon.), Order of Malaysia, 1968. *Recreations:* travel, writing. *Address:* 10 Abercorn Close, NW8. *T:* 01-286 9597.

**PHILP, Lieut-Colonel Robert,** MC, TD; Vice-Lieutenant, County of Clackmannan, since 1966; *s* of Major J. Philp, TD, JP; *m* 1924, Jane Black Adamson; one *d*. *Educ:* Dollar Academy. Served War 1914-18 (France), 1939-45 (India and Burma). DL Clackmannanshire, 1959; Sheriff-Substitute, 1962. *Address:* 1 Castle Park, Tulliallan, Kincardine, Alloa, Clackmannanshire.

**PHILPOTT, Air Vice-Marshal Peter Theodore,** CB 1966; CBE 1954 (OBE 1945); Director of Service Intelligence, Ministry of Defence, 1968-70; *b* 20 March 1915; *s* of late Rev. and Mrs R. G. K. F. Philpott, Worcester; *m* 1942, Marie, *d* of Charles Griffin, Malvern; two *d*. *Educ:* Malvern Coll.; RAF Coll., Cranwell, 1933; No. 31 Sqn, India, 1936-41; Staff Coll., Quetta, 1941; Directorate of Op. Trg., Air Ministry, 1942-44; OC, RAF, Horsham St Faith, 1945-46; JSSC, 1947; HQ, Fighter Command, 1948-51; OC, RAF Deversoir, 1952-54; DD Policy, Air Ministry, 1954-56; IDC Student, 1957; Director of Policy and Plans, Air Ministry, 1958-61; Senior RAF Directing Staff, Imperial Defence Coll., 1961-63; AOC No. 23 Group, Flying Training Comd, 1963-65; Head of British Defence Liaison Staff, Canberra, 1965-68. *Address:* c/o Lloyds Bank Ltd (Cox's and King's Branch), 6 Pall Mall, SW1. *Club:* Royal Air Force.

**PHILPS, Dr Frank Richard,** MBE 1946; Consultant in Exfoliative Cytology, University College Hospital, WC1, since 1960; *b* 9 March 1914; *s* of Francis John Philps and Matilda Ann Philps (*née* Healey); *m* 1941, Emma L. F. M. Schmidt; two *s* one *d*. *Educ:* Christ's Hospital, Horsham, Sussex. MRCS, LRCP, 1939; MB, BS, 1939; DPH 1947; MD London, 1952; FRCPath, 1966; Fellow, International Academy of Cytology, 1967. RAF Medical Service, 1940-46. Junior Hospital Appointments, UCH, 1950-54; Consultant Pathologist, Eastbourne, 1954-64; Research Asst, UCH, 1955-60. Producer, with wife, Wild Life Series of Educational Nature Films and films on pottery making, for Educational Foundation for Visual Aids; BBC Nature Film Prize, 1963; Council for Nature Film Prize, 1966. *Publications:* A Short Manual of Respiratory Cytology, 1964; Watching Wild Life, 1968. Papers on Cytology to several medical journals, 1954-67. *Recreations:* living in the country; watching wild animals and filming them. *Address:* Sharrods, Upper Dicker, Hailsham, Sussex. *T:* Hellingly 451.

**PHIPPS,** family name of **Marquess of Normanby.**

**PHIPPS, Gerald Hastings;** *b* 1882; *s* of late Eccleston A. E. Phipps; *m* 1912, Aline Maclean, *yr d* of Frank P. Purvis, formerly Professor of Naval Engineering, Tokyo Imperial Univ.; two *s* one *d*. *Educ:* Felsted School. HM Consular Service in Japan, 1903; Vice-Consul, 1915; Consul at Tamsui, Formosa, 1920; Honolulu, 1925; Kobe, 1932; HBM Consul-General, Seoul, Korea, 1934-41; retired, 1943. *Address:* 1 Downs View Road, Seaford, Sussex. *T:* 2125.

**PHIPPS, Maj.-General Herbert Clive,** CB 1951; DSO 1945; late RA; retired; *b* 3 Aug. 1898; *s* of Walter Tudway Phipps, Shepton Mallet, Somerset; *m* 1929, Rosalie Osborn, *d* of A. W. Marshall, Pinner, Middlesex; one *s* one *d*. *Educ:* Wellington; Royal Military Academy, Woolwich. Served European War, 1914-19, Royal Artillery; 2nd Lieut, 1916. Served War of 1939-45, France and British Liberation Army; Lieut-Colonel, 1940; Colonel, 1947; Maj.-General, 1951. Commander Royal Artillery, Guards Armoured Division, 1944; Commander 2nd AA Group, 1951-54; retired 1954. Colonel Comdt RA, 1955-64. *Address:* Dalton House, Hurstbourne Tarrant, Andover, Hants. *Club:* Army and Navy.

**PHIPPS, John Constantine;** Metropolitan Magistrate since 1959; *b* 19 Jan. 1910; *er s* of Sir Edmund Phipps, CB, and Margaret Percy, *d* of late Dame Jessie Phipps, DBE; *m* 1st, 1945, Priscilla Russell Cooke (*d* 1947); 2nd, 1949, Sheila (formerly Dilke; *née* Seeds) (from whom he obtained a divorce 1965); two *d*; 3rd, 1965, Hermione Deedes. *Educ:* Winchester Coll.; Trinity Coll., Oxford. Called to Bar, Middle Temple, 1933. RE (TA) 1938; War Office, 1940; Intelligence Corps, Captain, 1941, Major, 1943; Personal Asst to Lord Justice Lawrence (now Lord Oaksey), President of International Military Tribunal, Nuremburg, 1945-46. County of London Sessions: Prosecuting Counsel to Post Office, 1951-53, Junior Counsel to the Crown in Appeals, 1953-59, Prosecuting Counsel to the Crown, 1958-59; Recorder of Gravesend, 1957-59. *Address:* 26 Astell Street, SW3. *T:* 01-352 4014. *Club:* United University.

**PHIPPS, Vice-Adm. Sir Peter,** KBE 1964 (CBE 1962); DSC 1941 (Bar 1943); VRD 1945; retired, 1965; *b* 7 June 1909; *m* 1937, Jean Hutton; two *s* one *d*. *Educ:* Sumner Primary School; Christchurch Boys' High School. Joined staff of National Bank of NZ Ltd, 1927. Joined RNZNVR as Ord. Seaman, 1928; Sub-Lieut, 1930; Lieut, 1933. Served War of 1939-45 (American Navy Cross, 1943). Transferred to RNZN as Commander, 1945; Captain, 1952; Rear-Admiral, 1960. Chief of Naval Staff, NZ Naval Board, 1960-63; Chief of Defence Staff, New Zealand, 1963-65; Vice-Adm. 1964, retired 1965. *Recreations:* yachting, fishing; Dominion Comr for Sea Scouts. *Address:* 126 Motuhara Road, Plimmerton, New Zealand. *T:* Plimmerton 7240. *Clubs:* RNVR; Wellington (Wellington, NZ).

**PHIPPS, Rt. Rev. Simon Wilton;** *see* Horsham, Suffragan Bishop of.

**PHIPSON, Col Edward Selby,** CIE 1935; DSO 1916, MD (London) (Gold Medal), FRCP, FRSH, DPH, DTM&H; OStJ; Indian Medical Service, retired; *b* 10 March 1884; *s* of Ernest Thring Phipson and Ada Mary Yeats; *m* 1913, Mary, *d* of late Colonel Hugh Scott, JP, Lewes, Sussex; two *d*. *Educ:* King Edward's Sch., Birmingham; Birmingham Univ.; University College, London. Entered Indian Medical Service, 1908; served European War, 1914-17, Egypt and Gallipoli (despatches, DSO); afterwards held appointments of Assistant Health Officer, City of Bombay, 1917-18; Health Officer, Simla, 1918-23 and 1941-45 (re-employed); Port Health Officer, and Medical Officer in charge European General Hospital, Aden, 1923; Senior Medical Officer, Colony of Aden, 1937; Inspector-General of Civil Hospitals and Prisons, Assam, 1937-41. *Publications:* A Medical Survey of Aden, 1933, 1934; various contributions to Medical periodicals principally on Public Health and Tropical Diseases. *Address:* Greenwood Cottage, Heathcote Road, Camberley, Surrey. *T:* Camberley 21687.

**PIAGET, Jean;** Professor of Child Psychology and History of Scientific Thought, Geneva University, since 1929; Co-Director, Institut J. J. Rousseau (Institut des Sciences de l'Education), since 1933; *b* Neuchâtel, 9 Aug. 1896; *s* of Prof. Arthur Piaget; *m*; three *c*. *Educ:* Neuchâtel, Zürich and Paris Universities. Dr ès Sc., Neuchâtel, 1918. Joined Institut J. J. Rousseau (Inst. des Sciences de l'Education), 1921; Prof. of Philosophy, Univ. of Neuchâtel, 1926; Prof. of General Psychology, Univ. of Lausanne, 1937-54. Formerly: Pres., Swiss Soc. of Psychology; Co-editor, Revue Suisse de Psychologie; former Member Executive Council, UNESCO. Established, with the help of the Rockefeller Foundn and Swiss Foundn for Scientific Research, Internat. Centre of Genetic Epistemiology, Geneva. Dr *hc* Harvard Univ.; Hon. ScD Cambrdige 24 other Hon. Degrees. *Publications:* Le Langage et la Pensée chez l'enfant, 1923 (Eng. trans. 1926); Le Jugement et le raisonnement chez l'enfant, 1924 (Eng. trans. 1928); La Représentation du monde chez l'enfant (and Eng. trans.), 1929; La Causalité physique chez l'enfant, 1927 (Eng. Trans. 1930); Le Jugement moral chez l'enfant, 1932 (Eng. trans. 1950); La Naissance de l'intelligence chez l'enfant, 1936 (Eng. trans. 1952); La Construction du réel chez l'enfant, 1937 (Eng. trans. 1954); (with A. Szeminska) La Genèse du nombre chez l'enfant, 1941 (Eng. trans. 1952); La Formation du symbole chez l'enfant, 1946 (Eng. trans. 1951); Le Développement de la notion de temps chez l'enfant, 1946 (Eng. trans. 1970); (jointly) Le Développement des notions de mouvement et de vitesse chez l'enfant, 1946 (Eng. trans. 1970); (with B. Inhelder) La Représentation de l'espace chez l'enfant, 1948 (Eng. trans. 1956); (with B. Inhelder and A. Szeminska) La géométrie spontanée de l'enfant, 1948 (Eng. trans. 1960); Traité de logique, 1949; Introduction à l'épistémiologie génétique, 1950; (with B. Inhelder) La Genèse de l'idée de hasard chez l'enfant (Eng. trans. 1951); essai sur les transformations des opérations logiques, 1952; Logic and Psychology, 1953; (with B. Inhelder) De la logique de l'enfant à la logique de l'adolescent, 1955 (Eng. trans. 1958); La genèse des structures logiques élémentaires, classification et sériation, 1959 (Eng. trans. 1964); Les mécanismes perceptifs, 1961; Six études de psychologie, 1964 (Eng. trans. 1967); Sagesse et illusion de la philosophie, 1965; (with B. Inhelder) L'image mentale chez l'enfant, 1966; Biologie et connaissance, 1967; Logique et connaissance scientifique, 1967; Le structuralisme, 1968 (Eng. trans. 1970); (with B. Inhelder and H. Sinclair-de Zwart) Mémoire et intelligence, 1968; Psychologie et pédagogie, 1969; and 360 publications in scietific periodicals. *Address:* Ecole de psychologie et des sciences de l'éducation, Palais Wilson, Geneva, Switzerland; Pinchat s/Carouge, Geneva.

**PIATIGORSKY, Gregor,** Doctor of Music; Concert Artist (Violoncellist); *b*

Ekaterinoslav, Russia, 17 April 1903; *s* of Paul and Marie Piatigorsky; *m* 1936, Jacqueline, *d* of Baron Edouard de Rothschild; one *s* one *d*. *Educ:* Moscow Conservatory. Studied 'cello with Prof. de Glen. Concerts throughout Russia at age of nine. Left Russia in 1921, and has toured extensively in Europe, United States, Canada, South America, Mexico, Japan. Sonata Recitals with Rachmaninoff, Schnabel, Horowitz. Professor, Curtis Institute, Philadelphia until 1949; Doctor of Music Northwestern Univ., 1950. Director of Chamber Music, Berkshire Festival Music Center, USA. Introduced many first performances of Concertos and Sonatas by contemporary composers; founded Piatigorsky Scholarships for composition and violoncellists at Conservatoire de Paris, University of Chicago, and Peabody Conservatory, Baltimore. Has appeared in recitals and as soloist with all major Symphony Orchestras in England. Numerous recordings of Concerti, and Chamber Music. Holds hon. degrees in music and humanities. Hon. Mem. Royal Phil. Soc., London. Brandeis Gold Medal, 1954; Legion of Honour, France, 1955. *Publications:* Transcriptions of classics and modern works for 'cello and piano. *Address:* 400 South Bundy Drive, Los Angeles 49, California, USA. *Club:* Lotus (New York).

**PICACHY, Most Rev. Lawrence Trevor;** *see* Calcutta, Archbishop of, (RC).

**PICASSO, Pablo Ruiz;** Spanish painter and worker in Ceramics; *b* Malaga, Spain, 25 Oct. 1881; *m* 1st, 1917, Olga Koklova (*d* 1955); one *s*; 2nd, 1961, Jacqueline Roque. Has worked in Paris, 1901-; founder and leader of the Cubist School. Designer for Diaghilev Ballet, 1917-27; Director, Prado Gallery, Madrid, 1936-39; painted murals for Spanish Pavilion, Paris Exhibition, 1937. Exhibitions all over the World; British Exhibitions include: Gravures sur linoléum, Hanover Gallery, 1960; Paintings: Tate Gallery, 1960; Gimpel Fils, 1964; Paris, Grand Palais and Petit Palais, 1966; Sculpture, Tate Gallery, 1967. *Paintings:* Les Arlequins, L'Aveugle, La famille du singe, Femme à la mandoline, Guernica, Massacre in Korea, War and Peace; portraits of well-known people; still-life in galleries in London, Paris, Berlin, Philadelphia; *decorations for Russian ballets:* Parade, 1917; Tricorne, 1918; Pulcinella, 1919; *Publications:* The Dream and Life of General Franco, 1937; *plays:* Les Quatre Petites Filles, 1965 (Four Little Girls, 1970); Le Désir attrapé par la Queue, 1945 (Desire Caught by the Tail, 1970). *Address:* Villa Californie, Cannes, France; Galerie Louise Léris, 29 bis, Rue d'Astorg, Paris.

**PICCARD, Dr Jacques;** Scientist; consultant for Ocean Systems, Grumman Aerospace Corporation, New York; *b* Belgium, 1922; Swiss Citizen; *s* of late Prof. Auguste Piccard (explorer of the stratosphere, in lighter-than-air craft, and of the ocean depths, in vehicles of his own design); *m* 1953, Marie Claude (*née* Maillard); two *s* one *d*. *Educ:* Brussels; Switzerland. Grad., Univ. of Geneva, 1946; Dip. from Grad. Inst. of Internat. Studies. Asst Prof., Univ. of Geneva, 1946-48. With his father, he participated in design and operation of the first deep diving vessels, which they named the bathyscaph (deep ship); this vessel, like its successor, operated independently of a mother ship; they first constructed the FNRS-2 (later turned over to the French Navy) then the Trieste (ultimately purchased by US Navy); Dr J. Piccard piloted the Trieste on 65 successive dives (the last, 23 Jan. 1960, was the record-breaking descent to 35,800 feet in the Marianas Trench, off Guam in the Pacific Ocean). He built in 1963, the mesoscaph Auguste Piccard, the first civilian submarine, which made, in 1964-65, over 1,100 dives carrying 33,000 people into the depths of Lake Geneva; built (with Grumman) 2nd mesoscaph, Ben Franklin, and in 1969 made 1.500 miles/30 days drift dive in Gulf Stream. Hon. doctorate in Science, Amer. Internat. Coll., Springfield, Mass, 1962; Hon. DSc, Hopton Univ., 1970. Holds Distinguished Public Service Award, etc. *Publications:* technical papers, and a popularized account (trans. many langs) of the Trieste, Seven Miles Down (with Robert S. Dietz). *Address:* 19 avenue de l'Avenir, 1012 Lausanne, Switzerland. *T:* (021) 28 80 83, 28 80 88.

**PICKARD, Alexander,** CBE 1942; Town Clerk and Deputy-Judge and Registrar of Tolzey Court, Bristol, 1945-58, retired; *b* 27 Sept. 1897; *m* 1924 (wife *d* 1954); two *s*. *Educ:* King's School, Peterborough. Solicitor, 1924; Solicitor with Bradford Corpn, 1924-25; Senior Assistant Solicitor, Hull, 1925-30; Deputy Town Clerk, Hull, 1930-34; Town Clerk, Hull, 1934-45. Served Royal Navy, 1916-19. *Recreation:* gardening. *Address:* 7 Wedgwood Close, Northwood, Mddx. *T:* Northwood 27286.

**PICKARD, Sir Cyril (Stanley),** KCMG 1966 (CMG 1964); British High Commissioner in Pakistan since 1966; *b* 18 Sept. 1917; *s* of G. W. Pickard and Edith Pickard (*née* Humphrey), Sydenham; *m* 1941, Helen Elizabeth Strawson; three *s* one *d* (and one *s* decd). *Educ:* Alleyn's Sch., Dulwich; New Coll. Oxford. 1st Class Hons Modern History, 1939. Asst Principal, Home Office, 1939. War of 1939-45: Royal Artillery, 1940-41, Captain; appointment in Office of Minister of State, Cairo, 1941-44 Principal, 1943; with UNRRA in Middle East and Germany, 1944-45; transf. to Commonwealth Relations Office, 1948; Office of UK High Comr in India, New Delhi, 1950; Local Asst Sec., Office of UK High Comr, Canberra, 1952-55; Commonwealth Relations Office, Head of South Asian Dept, 1955-58; Deputy High Commissioner for the UK in New Zealand, 1958-61; Asst Under Sec. of State, CRO, 1962-66 (Acting High Commissioner in Cyprus, 1964). *Recreations:* gardening, cricket. *Address:* c/o British High Commission, Rawalpindi, West Pakistan.

**PICKARD, Rt. Rev. Stanley Chapman,** CBE 1968; an Assistant Bishop of Johannesburg since 1968; Provincial Executive Officer of the Province of S Africa since 1968; *b* 4 July 1910; *s* of John Chapman and Louisa Mary Pickard, Gloucester; unmarried. *Educ:* Grammar Sch., Birmingham. Studied pharmacy, 1928-32. Dorchester Theological College, 1933-36; Deacon, 1937; Priest, 1938; Curate St Catherine's, New Cross, SE14, 1937-39; joined UMCA, 1939; Kota Kota, Nyasaland, 1939-40; Likoma Island, Nyasaland, 1940-48; Archdeacon of Msumba, Portuguese East Africa, 1949-58; Bishop of Lebombo, 1958-68. *Recreations:* rowing, walking. *Address:* Box 1131, Johannesburg, S Africa.

**PICKAVANCE, Thomas Gerald,** CBE 1965; MA, PhD; Director of Nuclear Physics, Science Research Council, since 1969; Fellow, St Cross College, Oxford, 1967; *b* 19 October 1915; *s* of William and Ethel Pickavance, Lancashire; *m* 1943, Alice Isobel (*née* Boulton); two *s* one *d*. *Educ:* Cowley School, St Helens; Univ. of Liverpool. BSc (Hons Phys) 1937; PhD 1940. Research Physicist, Tube Alloys Project, 1941-46; Lecturer in Physics, University of Liverpool, 1943-46; Atomic Energy Research Establishment, Harwell: Head of Cyclotron Group, 1946-54; Head of Accelerator Group, 1954-57; Deputy Head of

General Physics Division, 1955-57; Dir, Rutherford High Energy Lab., SRC, 1957-69. Chm., European Cttee for Future Accelerators, 1970-. Hon. DSc, City Univ., 1969. *Publications:* papers and articles in learned journals on nuclear physics and particle accelerators. *Recreations:* motoring, travel, photography. *Address:* Craigellachie, Hinksey Hill Top, Oxford. *T:* (official) 01-242 1262; (home) Oxford 35243.

**PICKERING, Edward Davies;** Director, International Publishing Corporation, since 1966, and Chairman, IPC Magazines, since 1970; Chairman, The Daily Mirror Newspapers Ltd, since 1968; *b* 4 May 1912; 3rd *s* of George and Louie Pickering; *m* 1st, 1936, Margaret Soutter (marr. diss., 1947); one *d*; 2nd, 1955, Rosemary Whitton; two *s* one *d*. *Educ:* Middlesbrough High Sch. Chief Sub-Editor Daily Mail, 1939. Served Royal Artillery 1940-44; Staff of Supreme Headquarters Allied Expeditionary Force, 1944-45. Managing Editor: Daily Mail, 1947-49; Daily Express, 1951-57; Editor, Daily Express, 1957-62; Dir, Beaverbrook Newspapers, 1956-64; Editorial Dir, The Daily Mirror Newspapers Ltd, 1964-68; Dir, Scottish Daily Record and Sunday Mail Ltd, 1966-69; Chm., International Publishing Corporation Newspaper Div., 1968-70. Member Press Council, 1964-69. *Address:* Chase Warren, Haslemere, Surrey. *T:* Haslemere 2541. *Club:* Garrick.

**PICKERING, Frederick Pickering,** PhD (Breslau); Professor of German, University of Reading, since 1953; *b* Bradford, Yorkshire, 10 March 1909; *s* of late F. W. Pickering and Martha (*née* Pickering); *m* 1939, Florence Joan Anderson. *Educ:* Grange High School, Bradford; Leeds University (BA). Gilchrist Travelling Studentship; Germanic languages and literature at Breslau University (PhD). Lektor in English, 1931-32; Asst Lectr and Lectr in German, Univ. of Manchester, 1932-41. At a branch of Foreign Office, 1941-45. Head of German Dept, Univ. of Sheffield, 1945-53; Dean of the Faculty of Letters, Univ. of Reading, 1957-60. *Publications:* Medieval language, literature and art: Christi Leiden in einer Vision geschaut, 1952, an edn; Augustinus oder Boethius?, 1967; University German, 1968; Literature and Art in the Middle Ages, 1970; articles and reviews in English and German learned journals. *Recreations:* anything but reading. *Address:* Arborfield Court, Arborfield Cross, Berks. *T:* 350.

**PICKERING, Sir George Hunter,** Kt 1932; BA Oxon; Barrister-at-law (Inner Temple); *b* 7 Nov. 1877; 2nd *s* of George Pickering, Stone, Staffs; *m* 1917, Phyllis Mary Stubbs (*d* 1955); one *s* one *d*. *Educ:* Forest School; Hertford College, Oxford. Called to Bar, 1903; Member of the Western Circuit until 1907, when joined Mr O. Tonks, practising advocate in the BEA Protectorate; Town Magistrate, 1910; acted Judge of the High Court of Kenya, 1915-17, when appointed Judge and member of the Court of Appeal for Eastern Africa; Chief Justice of HBM's Court, Zanzibar, 1928-32; retired 1932. *Address:* South Cross, Bodicote, Banbury, Oxon.

**PICKERING, Sir George White,** Kt 1957; FRS 1960; MD, FRCP; Master of Pembroke College, Oxford, since 1969; Member: Council for Scientific Policy; Lord Chancellor's Committee on Legal Education; *b* 26 June 1904; *s* of George and Ann Pickering, Whalton, Northumberland; *m* 1930, Mary Carola, *y d* of late Sir A. C. Seward, FRS; one *s* three *d*. *Educ:* Dulwich College; Pembroke College, Cambridge (Scholar); St Thomas' Hospital (Scholar). 1st Class Honours Nat. Sci. Tripos, Pts I, 1925 and II, 1926; MB 1930; MD 1955; FRCP 1938; formerly Asst in Dept of Clinical Research and Lecturer in Cardio-vascular Pathology, University College Hospital, and Member of Scientific Staff MRC; Herzstein Lecturer, Stanford Univ. and Univ. of California, 1938; Sims British Commonwealth Travelling Prof., 1949; Member: UGC, 1944-54; MRC and Clinical Research Board, 1954-58; Prof. of Medicine, Univ. of London and Director of Medical Clinic. St Mary's Hosp., London, 1939-56; Regius Prof. of Medicine, Oxford Univ., Student of Christ Church, Master of God's House in Ewelme, and Physician to the United Oxford Hospitals, 1956-Dec. 1968; Pro-Vice-Chancellor, Oxford Univ., 1967-69; Emeritus Student of Christ Church, 1969. Mem., Standing Cttee on Legal Educn; Trustee: Beit Memorial Fellowship; Ciba Foundation. Pres. BMA, 1963-64. Stouffer Prize (jtly), 1970. Hon. degrees: DSc: Durham, 1957, Dartmouth (US), 1960; ScD, Trinity Coll., Dublin, 1962; MD: Ghent, 1948, Siena, 1965, Univ. W Aust., 1965; LLD: Manchester, 1964, Nottingham, 1965; DUniv. York, 1969. Hon. Fellow: Pembroke College, Cambridge, 1959; American College of Physicians; American Medical Association; RCP Edinburgh; RCP Ireland; Acad. of Medicine of Mexico; Hon. FRSM; Hon. Member: Assoc. of American Physicians; American Gastro-enterological Assoc.; Swedish Medical Soc.; Australian Med. Assoc.; Membre correspondant étranger, Soc. Med. des Hôpitaux de Paris; Foreign Hon. Member: Amer. Academy of Arts and Sciences; Czechoslovakian Med. Soc.; Hellenic Cardiac Soc.; Royal Belgian Acad. of Medicine; Danish Soc. for Internal Medicine; Foreign Associate, Amer. Nat. Acad. of Sciences, 1970. *Publications:* High Blood Pressure, 1955 (2nd edn, 1968); The Nature of Essential Hypertension, 1961; The Challenge to Education, 1967; Papers relating to vascular disease, high blood pressure, peptic ulcer, headache and education. *Recreations:* gardening, fishing. *Address:* Master's Lodgings, Pembroke College, Oxford. *T:* Oxford 43482. *Club:* Athenæum.

**PICKERING, Ian George Walker,** VRD (with clasp) 1952; MD; Director of Prison Medical Services, Home Office since 1963; *b* 24 Nov. 1915; *e s* of Geo. W. Pickering, Bradford, Yorks; *m* 1948, Jean 2nd *d* of John Bell Lowthian, MC and Bar; one *s* one *d*. *Educ:* Bradford Gram. Sch.; Leeds Univ. MB, ChB 1939; MD 1947; MRCP 1966. Various hosp. appts, 1939 and 1946-47. RNVR, 1939-46: at sea and appts RN Hosps, Plymouth and Sydney, NSW. Surgeon Lt-Comdr RNR, retd 1965. HM Prison Service, 1947; Senior MO, HM Prison and Borstal, Durham, 1955-63. Nuffield Travelling Fellow, 1961-62. Inspector of Retreats for Inebriates, 1963; Mem. Prison Bd, Home Office, 1967; Pres., British Acad. of Forensic Sciences, 1969-; Vice-President: 2nd Internat. Congress of Social Psychiatry, London, 1969; Oxford Postgrad. Fellowship in Psychiatry, 1966-; Member: Council, Soc. for Study of Addiction, 1967; Med. Council on Alcoholism, 1967; N of England Medico-Legal Soc., 1960-63, etc. *Publications:* articles in professional journals. *Recreation:* travel. *Address:* Drift House, Ockham Rd North, East Horsley, Surrey. *T:* East Horsley 2937. *Clubs:* Royal Automobile, RNVR; County (Durham).

**PICKETT, Thomas; Hon. Mr Justice Pickett;** Justice of Appeal, Court of Appeal for Zambia, since 1969; *b* 22 November 1912; *s* of John Joseph Pickett and Caroline Pickett (*née*

Brunt); *m* 1940, Winifred Irene Buckley, *yr d* of late Benjamin Buckley; no *c*. *Educ:* Glossop Grammar School; London University (LLB). Barrister-at-Law, Lincoln's Inn; called to Bar, 1948. Served in Army, 1939-50, retiring with permanent rank of Major. Dep. Asst Dir of Army Legal Services, 1948; Dist Magistrate, Gold Coast, 1950; Resident Magistrate, Northern Rhodesia 1955; Sen. Res. Magistrate, 1956; Acting Puisne Judge, 1960; Puisne Judge, High Courts of Northern Rhodesia, 1961-64, Zambia, 1964-69. Chairman: Tribunal on Detainees, 1967-; Electoral Commn (Supervisory); Delimitation Commn for Zambia, 1968-; Referendum Commn, 1969; Local Govt Commn, 1970. *Recreations:* walking, swimming. *Address:* High Court, PO Box RW 67, Lusaka, Zambia. *T:* Lusaka 51577. *Club:* Royal Over-Seas League.

**PICKFORD, Frank;** Assistant Under-Secretary of State, Employment Policy and General Division, Department of Employment and Productivity, since 1968; *b* 26 Oct. 1917; *s* of late Edwin Pickford, Bulwell, Nottingham; *m* 1944, May Talbot; two *s*. *Educ:* Nottingham High Sch.; St John's Coll., Cambridge. Entered Min. of Labour, 1939; Asst Private Sec. to Minister of Labour, 1941-43; Dir, London Office, Internat. Labour Office, 1951-56; Sec., NEDC, 1962-64; Under-Sec., Ministry of Labour, 1964. *Address:* 64 Westbere Road, NW2. *T:* 01-435 1207. *Club:* Reform.

**PICKFORD, Prof. (Lillian) Mary,** DSc; FRS 1966; Professor, Department of Physiology, University of Edinburgh, since 1966 (Reader in Physiology, 1952-66); *b* 14 Aug. 1902; *d* of Herbert Arthur Pickford and Lillian Alice Minnie Wintle. *Educ:* Wycombe Abbey Sch.; Bedford and University Colls, Univ. of London. BSc (1st cl., Gen.) 1924; BSc (2nd cl., Physiology Special) 1925; MSc (Physiology) 1926; MRCS, LRCP 1933; DSc London 1951. House Physician and Casualty Officer, Stafford Gen. Infirmary, 1935; Jun. Beit Memorial Research Fellow, 1936-39; Lectr, Dept of Physiology, Univ. of Edinburgh, 1939. Fellow, University Coll., London, 1968-. *Publications:* The Central Role of Hormones, 1969; papers in Jl Physiology, British Jl Pharmacology, Jl Endocrinology. *Recreations:* walking, travel, painting. *Address:* 10 Hatton Place, Edinburgh 9. *T:* 031-667 6011.

**PICKFORD, Mary;** actress; sometime partner in three producing companies in Hollywood: Comet, Triangle and Artists Alliance, and part owner, with others, of United Artists Corporation; sold holdings in United Artists, 1956; *b* Toronto, Canada, 8 April 1893 (family name Smith); mother a character actress; *m* 1st, Owen Moore (divorced, 1919); 2nd, 1920, Douglas Fairbanks (divorced, 1935); 3rd, 1937, Charles Buddy Rogers; one adopted *s* one adopted *d*. Debut on stage at 5; first marked success was in motion pictures, in Hearts Adrift; returned to stage in A Good Little Devil and Warrens of Virginia. Returned to motion pictures as star; best known pictures: Tess of the Storm Country, Stella Maris, Daddy Long Legs, Pollyanna, Rebecca of Sunny Brook Farm, Poor Little Rich Girl, Little Lord Fauntleroy, My Best Girl, etc.; also talking pictures Coquette (Academy of Motion Picture Arts and Sciences award), Taming of the Shrew, Kiki and Secrets. Mem. Bd Directors, Thomas Alva Edison Foundation; Mem. Edison Pioneers; Director, American Society for the Aged, Inc. Apptd Mem. Nat. Advisory Cttee for White House Conf. on Aging, 1959. Holds several awards both American and foreign, for public and political service and for war work. Holds Hon. Degrees. *Publications:* Why not try God?, 1934; The Demi Widow, 1935; My Rendezvous With Life, 1935; Sunshine and Shadow, 1956; many magazine articles. *Address:* Pickfair, Beverly Hills, California, USA.

**PICKFORD, Prof. Mary;** *see* Pickford, Prof. L. M.

**PICKFORD, Prof. Ralph William;** Professor of Psychology in the University of Glasgow, since Oct. 1955; *b* 11 Feb. 1903; *s* of William Pickford and Evelyn May Flower; *m* 1933, Alexis Susan Macquisten. *Educ:* Bournemouth School and Municipal Coll.; Emmanuel Coll., Cambridge. Emmanuel College: Exhibitioner, 1924, Sen. Schol. and Internal Research Student, 1927; BA 1927, MA 1930, PhD 1932. Goldsmiths' Company's Exhibitioner, 1925; Moral Sciences Tripos, First Class, 1927. Lecturer in Psychology and Acting Head of Dept, Aberdeen Univ., 1929. Asst in Psychology Dept, 1930, Lectr, 1935, Sen. Lectr and Acting Head of Psychology Dept 1947, Glasgow Univ. DLitt (Glasgow) 1947. Hon. Psychotherapist Notre Dame Child Guidance Clinic, 1947-, and Davidson Clinic, Glasgow, 1952-. First Pres., Experimental Psychology Group; Chm. and then Hon. Sec. Scottish Br. Brit. Psychological Soc.; Pres. Sect. J Brit. Assoc., 1958. Vice-Pres., Internat. Assoc. of Empirical Aesthetics; Hon. Mem. Soc. Française d'Esthétique; Mem., Council of Soc. Internat. de Psychopathologie de l'Expression. FBPsS. *Publications:* Individual Differences in Colour Vision, 1951; The Analysis of an Obsessional, 1954; (with R. Kherumian), Hérédité et Fréquence des Dyschromatopsies, 1959; (with G. M. Wyburn and R. J. Hirst), The Human Senses and Perception, 1963; Pickford Projective Pictures, 1963; Studies in Psychiatric Art, 1967; Monograph: The Psychology of Cultural Change in Painting, 1943. Many articles on Experimental, Social and Clinical Psychology, and the Psychology of Art. *Recreations:* painting, gardening, music. *Address:* Psychology Department, The University, Glasgow, W2. *T:* 041-339 8855.

**PICKLES, Sir John (Sydney),** Kt 1958; BSc, MIEE; *b* 2 August 1898; British: *m* 1925, Mary (*d* 1961), *d* of Bradford Pickton. *Educ:* Manchester University. The Yorkshire Electric Power Co., Leeds, 1921-31; County Electrical Engineer, Dumfries County Council, 1931-47; Chairman, South of Scotland Electricity Board, 1955-62. *Publications:* papers on Rural Electrification, read before Inst. of Electrical Engineers, 1937, 1946. *Club:* Royal Scottish Automobile (Glasgow).

**PICKLES, Wilfred,** OBE 1950; Radio Actor; *b* 13 Oct. 1904; *s* of Fred Pickles and Margaret Catterall; *m* 1930, Mabel Myerscough; *o s* decd. *Educ:* Parkinson Lane Sch., Halifax, Yorks. First broadcast, 1927, in Children's Hour; became regular broadcaster from the North; apptd N Regional Announcer, 1938, News Reader in London, 1942. First broadcast of Have a Go series, 1946. First Appearance on West End Stage The Gay Dog (comedy), Piccadilly Theatre, in 1952; first film, The Gay Dog, 1954; Television Series, Ask Pickles, 1954; Ride a Cock Horse, Comedy, Blackpool Season, 1957; Billy Liar (film), 1963; The Family Way (film), 1966. *Publications:* Between You and Me (autobiography), 1949; Personal Choice (poetry anthology), 1950; Sometime Never (Reminiscences), 1951; Ne'er forget the people (Portraits of the new Elizabethans), 1953; My North Countrie (anthology of North Country poems, prose, rhymes, jingles and stories), 1954; For Your

Delight (anthology of poetry), 1960. *Recreations:* tennis, golf. *Address:* 34 Farley Court, NW1. *T:* 01-935 8861. *Club:* BBC.

**PICKTHORN, Rt. Hon. Sir Kenneth (William Murray),** 1st Bt, *cr* 1959; PC 1964; LittD Cantab 1936; Fellow of Corpus Christi College, Cambridge since 1914; *b* 23 April 1892; *e s* of late Charles Wright Pickthorn, master mariner, and late Edith Maud Berkeley Murray; *m* 1924, Nancy Catherine, *d* of late Lewis Matthew Richards, barrister-at-law; two *s* one *d. Educ:* Aldenham School; Trinity College, Cambridge. 15th London Regiment and RAF in France and Macedonia; Dean of Corpus, 1919-27; Tutor, 1927-35. Pres., 1937-44. MP (C) Cambridge University, 1935-50, Carlton Division of Nottinghamshire, 1950-66. Parliamentary Sec., Ministry of Education, 1951-Oct. 1954. *Publications:* History of the Peace Conference, vol. i. ch. ii, The German Revolution and the Conditions which Prepared It, 1920; History of the British People, vol. vii., From 1914 to 1922, 1924; Some Historical Principles of the Constitution, 1925; Early Tudor Government, 1934; contributions to various periodicals. *Heir: s* Charles William Richards Pickthorn [*b* 3 Mar. 1927; *m* 1951, Helen, *d* of late Sir Jas. Mann, KCVO; one *s* two *d*]. *Address:* Quay Street, Orford, near Woodbridge, Suffolk. *T:* Orford 273. *Clubs:* Carlton, Army and Navy; University Pitt (Cambridge).
*See also N. A. Iliff.*

**PICOT, Francis Raymond,** CMG 1946; *b* Wellington, NZ, 7 June 1893; *s* of late John Picot; *m* 1917, Mavis, *d* of late Col George Hall, CMG, CBE, VD; one *s* one *d.* Bank of NSW, Wellington, 1910-17; Director of Internal Marketing, New Zealand, 1937; NZ Member Eastern Group Supply Council, India, 1940-41; Pacific Supply Council, Australia, 1941-42; late Commissioner of Supply, New Zealand. *Address:* 16 Benbow St, St Heliers, Auckland, NZ.

**PICOT, Jacques M. C. G.;** *see* Georges-Picot.

**PIDCOCK, Air Vice-Marshal Geoffrey Arthur Henzell,** CB 1948; CBE 1946; *b* 6 Nov. 1897; *s* of Arthur Pidcock, Eastbourne; *m* 1st, 1929, Evelyn Catherine (*d* 1965), *d* of William Hardacre, Hellifield, Yorks; one *d*; 2nd, 1965, Winifred Iris (Christine), *d* of Walter Humphry, Sudbury, Suffolk. *Educ:* Haileybury; Imperial Coll. of Science, City & Guilds Branch. Joined RFC 1916; service in France with Nos 1, 60 and 73 Squadrons; RAF 1918; service in India, Iraq and Middle East; specialised in Armament, 1924; Wing Comdr, 1937; service with Ordnance Bd, 1940-41; Dir of Armament Development, Ministry of Aircraft Production, 1941-44; Temp. Air Vice-Marshal, 1944; first RAF Pres., Ordnance Bd, 1945-47; Subst. Air Vice-Marshal, 1947; last Dir-Gen. of Armament, Air Ministry 1947-51; retired 1951; Head of Controls Division, Agence de Contrôle des Armements, Western European Union, Paris, 1955-63; Comdr USA Legion of Merit, Croix de Guerre (France), 1918. *Recreations:* reminiscence and travel. *Address:* Poynings, Winchester Road, Andover, Hants. *Club:* Royal Air Force.

**PIERCE, Francis William,** MA (Belfast and Dublin); Hughes Professor of Spanish, University of Sheffield, since 1953; Dean of the Faculty of Arts, 1964-67; *b* 21 Sept. 1915; *s* of late Robert Pierce, JP and Catherine Ismay Pierce; *m* 1944, Mary Charlotte Una, *o d* of late Rev. J. C. Black, Asyut, Upper Egypt; three *s. Educ:* Royal Belfast Academical Institution; Queen's University, Belfast. BA, 1st Cl. Hons, Spanish studies, QUB, 1938; Postgrad. Schol., Columbia Univ., New York, 1938-39; MA, QUB, 1939; Asst Lectr in Spanish, Univ. of Liverpool, 1939-40. Dep. to Prof. of Spanish, TCD, 1940-45; MA *jure officii,* Univ. of Dublin, 1943; Hughes Lectr in Spanish, Univ. of Sheffield, 1946. Visiting Professor: Brown Univ., Providence, RI, 1968; Case Western Reserve Univ., Cleveland, O, 1968. *Publications:* The Heroic Poem of the Spanish Golden Age: Selections, chosen with Introduction and Notes, 1947 (Oxford and New York); Hispanic Studies: Review and Revision, 1954; (ed) Hispanic Studies in Honour of I. González Llubera, 1959; La poesía épica del siglo de oro, 1961 (Madrid), 2nd edn 1968; The Historie of Aravcana, transcribed with introd. and notes, 1964; (ed with C. A. Jones) Actas del Primer Congreso Internacional de Hispanistas, 1964; (ed) Two Cervantes Short Novels, 1970. Articles and Reviews in Hispanic Review, Mod. Language Review, Bulletin of Hispanic Studies, Bulletin Hispanique, Erasmus, Estudis Romànics, Quaderni Ibero-Americani. *Address:* 16 Taptonville Crescent, Sheffield 10. *T:* Sheffield 64239.

**PIERCE, Rt. Rev. Reginald James;** *see* Athabasca, Bishop of.

**PIERCE-GOULDING, Lt-Col Terence Leslie Crawford,** MBE 1943; CD; Secretary, Commonwealth Press Union, since Oct. 1970; *b* 2 March 1918; *o s* of late Rev. Edward Pierce-Goulding and Christina; *m* 1964, Catherine Yvonne, *d* of John Welsh, Dunedin, NZ; one *s* one *d. Educ:* public and private schs, Edmonton, Alta. Royal Bank of Canada, 1935-39; enlisted British Army, 1940, 2nd Lieut Mddx Regt (DCO); transf. to Canadian Army overseas, 1941; Capt. Loyal Edmonton Regt, 1941-42; Staff Coll., 1943; GS03 (Ops), Canadian Planning Staff and HQ 1st Canadian Army, 1943-44; GSO2 (PR), HQ 21 Army Gp and BAOR, 1945-46; Sen. PRO, Central Comd HQ, 1947-48; Adviser to Perm. Canadian Delegn to UN, 1948-50; regtl and staff appts, Royal Canadian Regt and Army HQ, 1950-60; Chief Logistics Officer, UN Emergency Force (Middle East), 1962-63; Dir of Sen. Appts (Army), Canadian Forces HQ, 1963-66; Sen. Admin. Officer, Canadian Defence Liaison Staff (London), 1966-69, retd 1969. Canadian Internat. Development Agency, 1969-70. *Recreations:* golf, travel, photography, literature. *Address:* 22 Meadway, NW11. *T:* 01-455 2306. *Club:* Pathfinders.

**PIERCY,** family name of **Baron Piercy.**

**PIERCY,** 2nd Baron, *cr* 1945, of Burford; **Nicholas Pelham Piercy;** *b* 23 June 1918; *s* of 1st Baron Piercy, CBE; *S* father, 1966; *m* 1944, Oonagh Lavinia Baylay; two *s* three *d. Educ:* Eton; King's Coll., Cambridge (BA 1940, MA 1944). Lieut (A) RNVR (Fleet Air Arm), 1940; retd 1946. *Heir: s* Hon James William Piercy, *b* 19 Jan. 1946. *Address:* The Old Rectory, Elford, Tamworth, Staffs. *T:* Harlaston 233. *Club:* United University.

**PIERCY, Hon. Joanna Elizabeth;** *see* Turner, Hon. J. E.

**PIERCY, Hon. Penelope Katherine,** CBE 1968; Under-Secretary, Ministry of Technology, 1965-68; *b* 15 Apr. 1916; *d* of 1st Baron Piercy, CBE. *Educ:* St Paul's Girls' School; Somerville College, Oxford. War of 1939-45, various appointments, Military Intelligence. Foreign Office, 1945-47; Economist, Colonial Development Corp., 1948-54; Department of Scientific and Industrial Research, 1955-65 (Sen. Prin. Scientific Officer, 1960). *Address:*

Mawarden Court, Stratford-sub-Castle, Salisbury, Wilts. *T:* Salisbury 3976.

**PIERRE, Abbé; (Henri Antoine Grouès);** French priest; Founder of the Companions of Emmaüs; *b* Lyon, 5 Aug. 1912; 5th *c* of Antoine Grouès, Soyeux. *Educ:* Collège des Jésuites, Lyon. Entered Capuchin Monastery, 1930; studied at Capuchin seminary, Crest, Drôme, and Faculté de Théologie, Lyon. Secular priest, St Joseph Basilica, Grenoble. Served war of 1939-45 (Chevalier de la Légion d'Honneur, Croix de Guerre, Médaille de la Résistance); Alsatian and Alpine fronts; Vicar of the Cathedral, Grenoble; assumed name of Abbé Pierre and joined resistance movement, 1942; Chaplain of French Navy at Casablanca, 1944; of whole Free French Navy, 1945. Elected (Indep.) to 1st Constituent Assembly of 4th French Republic, 1945; elected as candidate of Mouvement Républicain Populaire to 2nd Constituent Assembly; re-elected 1946; contested (Indep.), 1951. Président de l'Exécutif du Mouvement Universel pour une Confédération Mondiale, 1947-51. Founded the Companions of Emmaüs, a movement to provide a roof for the "sanslogis" of Paris. *Publications:* 23 Mois de Vie Clandestine; L'Abbé Pierre vous Parle; Vers l'Homme; Feuilles Eparses. *Address:* 2 Avenue de la Liberté, Charenton-Val de Marne, France. *T:* 368.62.44.

**PIERRE, Sir (Joseph) Henry,** Kt 1957; FRCS; Consultant Surgeon, General Hospital, Port of Spain, Trinidad, WI, since 1950; Hon. Surgeon, Caura Tuberculosis Sanatorium, Trinidad; Hon. Surgeon, Mental Hospital, Trinidad; *b* 28 Oct. 1904; *s* of Charles Henry and Carmen M. Pierre; *m* 1939; one *s*; *m* 1962, Marjorie Boös; one *s*. *Educ:* Queen's Royal College, Trinidad. WI; St Bartholomew's Hosp., London; London Univ.; Royal Coll. of Surgeons, Edinburgh. Qualified in medicine, 1931; Casualty House Physician, St Bartholomew's Hosp., 1931; junior MO, Trinidad Medical Service, 1932; FRCSE 1939; FRCS 1959; Medical Officer, Grade A, 1945; Sen. Officer Surgeon, Gen. Hosp., San Fernando, 1945; Pres., Trinidad and Tobago Red Cross Soc.; Fellow Internat. Coll. of Surgeons, USA. Navy Meritorious Public Service Citation from US Govt, 1957. Coronation Medal, 1953. *Recreations:* photography, golf, yachting, tennis, horticulture. *Address:* 3 Maxwell Philip Street, St Clair, Port of Spain, Trinidad, West Indies. *T:* 24002. *Clubs:* West Indian, Royal Commonwealth Society; Yacht, Union, Country, St Andrew's Golf. (Hon mem.) Pointe-a-Pierre, UBOT (Trinidad, WI).

**PIERS, Sir Charles Robert Fitzmaurice,** 10th Bt, *cr* 1660; Lt-Comdr RCNVR; *b* 30 Aug. 1903; *s* of Sir Charles Piers, 9th Bt, and Hester Constance (Stella) (*d* 1936), *e d* of late S. R. Brewis of Ibstone House, Ibstone; *S* father, 1945; *m* 1936, Ann Blanche Scott, *o d* of late Capt. Thomas Ferguson (The Royal Highlanders); one *s* one *d*. *Educ:* RN Colleges, Osborne and Dartmouth. Served European War, 1939-45. *Heir: s* James Desmond Piers, *b* 24 July 1947. *Address:* Duncan, British Columbia, Canada.

**PIERSON, Warren Lee;** Chairman, All America Cable and Radio; Director: International Telephone and Telegraph Corporation; US Industries, Inc.; Vertientes-Camaguey Sugar Co., Cuba; Molybdenum Corporation of America; Ionics, Inc.; The Commercial Cable Co.; Trans World Airlines, Inc.; ITT World Communications Inc.; Unexcelled, Inc., etc; *b* Princeton, Minn, 29 Aug. 1896; *s* of Louis W. and Hilda Pearson Pierson; *m* 1927, Eleanor Mehnert; no *c*. *Educ:* Univ. of California (AB); Harvard Univ. (LLB). Pres. and Gen. Counsel, Export-Import Bank, 1936-45; Special Counsel: Export-Import Bank, 1934-36; Reconstruction Finance Corp., 1933-34; Mem. Nat. Emergency Council, 1934-36; Adviser to US Delegation: at 3rd meeting, Consultation of Ministers, Gen. Affairs Amer. Republics, Rio de Janeiro, 1942; at UN Monetary Conf., Bretton Woods NH, 1944; at Inter-American Conf. on Problems of War and Peace, Mexico City, 1945. US Member of Tripartite Commission on German Debts, 1951-53; Pres., International Chamber of Commerce, 1955. Has several Orders of foreign countries. *Address:* (office) 320 Park Avenue, New York, NY 10022. *T:* Plaza 2-6000; (home) 655 Park Avenue, New York, USA. *T:* (home) Rhinelander 4-1110; Further Lane, East Hampton, Long Island. *T:* (516) 324-1066. *Clubs:* Brook, Links (New York); Metropolitan (Washington); Bohemian (San Francisco); Maidstone (Long Island).

**PIGGOTT, Maj.-Gen. Francis James Claude,** CB 1963; CBE 1961; DSO 1945; *b* Tokyo, Japan, 11 Oct. 1910; *s* of late Maj.-Gen. F. S. G. Piggott, CB, DSO; *m* 1940, Muriel Joan, *d* of late Wilfred E. Cottam, Rotherham, Yorks; one *s* one *d*. *Educ:* Cheltenham; RMC Sandhurst. 2nd Lieut The Queen's Royal Regt, 1931; Language Officer, Japan, 1935-37; Captain, 1939; served 1939-45 in France (despatches), New Zealand, India and Burma (DSO); in Japan, UK and Egypt (OBE and Bt Lt-Col), 1946-52; attended 1st Course, Joint Services Staff Coll., 1947; Lt-Col comdg 1st Bn The Queen's Royal Regt, 1952, BAOR and Malaya; Colonel, War Office, 1954; Comd 161 Infantry Bde (TA), 1956; Dep. Director of Military Intelligence, War Office (Brigadier), 1958; Major-General, 1961; Assistant Chief of Staff (Intelligence), SHAPE, 1961-64; retired, 1964. Col, The Queen's Royal Surrey Regt, 1964-66; Dep. Col (Surrey) The Queen's Regt, 1967-69. *Recreations:* cricket and foreign travel. *Address:* Tocketts, Weeley, Essex. *T:* Weeley 232. *Clubs:* Army and Navy, MCC, Free Foresters.

**PIGGOTT, Colonel Joseph Clive,** CBE 1944; MC; DL (Warwickshire); *b* 2 February 1892; *s* of George Thomas Piggott; unmarried. *Educ:* Greenhill School, Moseley, Birmingham. Business career with Williams Brothers and Piggott Ltd, Birmingham, Brassfounders and Manufacturers of Brass and Copper Tubes. Commission with Coldstream Guards, 1915-19, and served in France with unit, Aug. 1915-Jan. 1919. Home Guard Comdr Warwickshire (Birmingham) Home Guard, 1941-45. *Recreations:* motoring and walking. *Address:* 35 Park Hill, Birmingham 13. *T:* 021-449 0347.

**PIGGOTT, Lester Keith;** Champion Jockey for eighth time at end of British Flat racing season of 1970 (also in 1960 and yearly since 1964); *b* 5 Nov. 1935; *s* of Keith Piggott and Iris Rickaby; *m* 1960, Susan Armstrong; two *d*. Selection of races won: the Derby (5 times): 1954 (on Never Say Die); 1957 (on Crepello); 1960 (on St Paddy); 1968 (on Sir Ivor); 1970 (on Nijinsky); many successes in other classic races. In several seasons since 1955 he has riden well over 100 winners a year, in this country alone; rides frequently in France. Won Washington, DC, International on Sir Ivor, 1968 (first time since 1922 an English Derby winner raced in USA), and on Karabas, 1969. *Recreations:* swimming, water skiing, golf. *Address:* Florizel, Newmarket, Suffolk. *T:* Newmarket 2584.

**PIGGOTT, Stuart,** FBA 1953; Abercromby Professor of Prehistoric Archæology,

University of Edinburgh, since 1946; *b* 28 May 1910; *s* of G. H. O. Piggott. *Educ:* Churchers Coll., Petersfield; St John's Coll., Oxford. On staff on Royal Commn on Ancient Monuments (Wales), 1929-34; Asst Dir of Avebury excavations, 1934-38; from 1939 in ranks and later as Intelligence Officer in Army in charge of military air photograph interpretation, South-East Asia. Conducted archæological excavations in southern England and carried out research on European prehistory up to 1942; in India, 1942-45; studied Oriental prehistory. Hon. DLittHum, Columbia, 1954. Fellow of Royal Soc. of Edinburgh, and of Soc. of Antiquaries; Mem. German Archæolog. Inst., 1953; Hon. Mem. Royal Irish Acad., 1956; Foreign Hon. Member American Academy of Arts and Sciences, 1960; advisory editor, Antiquity; Commissioner, Royal Commission on Ancient Monuments (Scot.). Trustee, British Museum, 1968-. Travelled in Europe and Asia. *Publications:* Some Ancient Cities of India, 1946; Fire Among the Ruins, 1948; British Prehistory, 1949; William Stukeley: an XVIII century Antiquary, 1950; Prehistoric India, 1950; A Picture Book of Ancient British Art (with G. E. Daniel), 1951; Neolithic Cultures of British Isles, 1954; Scotland before History, 1958; Approach to Archæology, 1959; (ed) The Dawn of Civilization, 1961; The West Kennet Long Barrow, 1962; Ancient Europe, 1965; Prehistoric Societies (with J. G. D. Clark), 1965; The Druids, 1968; numerous technical papers in archæological jls. *Recreations:* reading, cooking, travel. *Address:* The University, Edinburgh. *Clubs:* United University; Scottish Arts (Edinburgh).

**PIGOT, Brig.-Gen. Sir Robert,** 6th Bt, of Patshull, *cr* 1764; DSO 1916; MC (retired); Brevet Lieutenant Colonel Rifle Brigade; *b* 3 May 1882; *s* of Sir G. Pigot, 5th Bt, and Alice, *d* of Sir James Thompson Mackenzie, 1st Bt, of Glen Muick; *S* father, 1934; *m* 1913, Norah Beatrice Oakley, *y d* of C. Reginald Hargreaves, Remenham, Bucks; three *d.* Served European War 1914-18 (despatches, DSO, MC, Bt Maj., Bt Lieut-Col); Flying Officer RAFVR, 1939; resigned commn with rank of Wing Comdr, 1944. *Publication:* Twenty-five Years' Big-Game Hunting, 1928. *Heir: n* Maj.-Gen. Robert Anthony Pigot, *qv. Address:* Yarlington Lodge, Wincanton, Somerset.

**PIGOT, Maj.-Gen. Robert Anthony,** CB 1964; OBE 1959; Director, Executive Appointments Ltd; *b* 6 July 1915; *s* of late George Douglas Hugh Pigot and Hersey Elizabeth Pigot; *heir-pres.* to Brig.-Gen. Sir Robert Pigot, 6th Bt, *qv*; *m* 1942, Honor (*d* 1966), *d* of late Capt. Wilfred St Martin Gibbon; one *s* one *d*; *m* 1968, Sarah Anne Colville, *e d* of Mr David and Lady Joan Colville, The Old Vicarage, Dorton. *Educ:* Stowe Sch. Commissioned into the Royal Marines, 1934; served War of 1939-45 (despatches): Regimental service in RM Div. and Special Service Group; Staff appts in 3rd Commando Brigade in SE Asia; psc 1943-44; Directing Staff, Staff Coll., Camberley, 1946-47; Min. of Defence, 1953-54; Standing Group, NATO, Washington, 1954-57; Dep. Standing Gp Rep. with North Atlantic Council, Paris, 1958-59; Chief of Staff, Royal Marines, 1960-64; retd, Dec. 1964. Man. Director, Bone Brothers Ltd, 1964-66; Director, John Brown Plastics Machinery Ltd, 1965-66. *Recreations:* field sports (Jt Master, IW Foot Beagles) and yachting. *Address:* 7 Montpelier Place, SW7; Kensington Cottage, Bembridge, IW. *Clubs:* United Hunts; Royal Yacht Squadron; Bembridge Sailing; Royal Victoria Yacht; Seaview Yacht.

**PIGOT, Thomas Herbert,** QC 1967; *b* 19 May 1921; *e s* of late Thomas Pigot and of Martha Ann Pigot; *m* 1950, Zena Marguerite, *yr d* of late Tom and Dorothy Gladys Wall; three *d. Educ:* Manchester Gram. Sch. (Schol.); Brasenose Coll., Oxford (Somerset Schol.). BA (1st cl. hons Jurisprudence) 1941; MA 1946; BCL 1947. Commissioned Welch Regt, 1942; served N Africa with Royal Lincs Regt; wounded and taken prisoner, 1943; released, 1945. Called to Bar, Inner Temple, 1947; practised in Liverpool on Northern Circuit until 1967. *Recreations:* golf, watching Rugby football (both codes). *Address:* (home) 55 Westbourne Road, Birkdale, Southport, Lancs. *T:* Southport 67398; (professional) 2 Pump Court, Temple, EC4. *T:* 01-353 3106/7540. *Clubs:* Royal Automobile; Vincent's (Oxford); University (Liverpool); Royal Birkdale Golf; Waterloo Football.

**PIGOTT, Alan Desmond Frederick P.;** *see* Pemberton-Pigott.

**PIGOTT, Major Sir Berkeley,** 4th Bt, *cr* 1808; *b* 29 May 1894; *s* of Charles Berkeley, *e s* of 3rd Bt and Fanny Ada, *d* of Rev. W. P. Pigott; *S* grandfather, 1911; *m* 1919, Christabel, *d* of late Rev. F. H. Bowden-Smith, of Careys, Brockenhurst, Hants; one *s* two *d.* Served European War, 1914-18; Adjutant Ceylon Mounted Rifles and Ceylon Planters' Rifle Corps, 1924-28; retired pay, 1930; President, The National Pony Society, 1948; Chairman County Polo Association, 1948; Verderer of the New Forest, 1955-68; Chairman National Pony Society, 1961-62. *Heir: s* Berkeley Henry Sebastian Pigott; [*b* 24 June 1925; *m* 1954, Jean, *d* of J. W. Balls, Surlingham, Norfolk; two *s* one *d*]. *Address:* Wedge Hill Farm, Woodlands, Wimborne, Dorset.

**PIGOTT, Brig. Frank Borkman,** CB 1954; CIE 1946; late RE; *b* 1894. Served European War, 1914-18, in France, Belgium and the Balkans (wounded, despatches); War of 1939-45 (Burma star, medal). Formerly Deputy Engineer-in-Chief and Director of Works, Army Headquarters, India. Member of the Institution of Engineers, India; Associate Member of the Institution of Mechanical Engineers; Associate Member of the Institution of Electrical Engineers; Associate of City and Guilds of London Institute. *Address:* c/o Lloyds Bank, 6 Pall Mall, SW1.

**PIGOTT, Rt. Rev. Harold Grant,** CBE 1969; *b* 20 Aug. 1894; *s* of Robert and Rosalind Pigott. *Educ:* Antigua Gram. Sch.; Codrington Coll., Barbados. BA 1916, MA 1918. Head Master Parry Sch., Barbados and Curate St Lucy, 1917-21. St Vincent: Curate, Cath., 1921; then Rector of Barrouallie, 1921-26, and of Calliaqua, 1926-33. Archdeacon of St Vincent and St Lucia, 1929-45; Canon of Cath. St Vincent, 1929-62, and Rector of Georgetown, 1933-37, Grenada. Rector: St Andrew, 1937-45, St George, 1945-62; Archdeacon of Grenada, 1945-62. Bishop of Windward Islands, 1962-69. Coronation Medal, 1953. *Publication:* Daily Meditations on the Lenten Epistles, 1939. *Address:* Zion Hill, St Vincent, Windward Islands.

**PIGOTT, Harry,** MB, ChB; a Member of the National Assistance Board, 1957-66. *Educ:* Manchester University. MB, ChB. Manchester, 1926. Member of Manchester Corporation; Member, Management Committee, Regional Hospital Board, 1953. *Address:* Greenacre, Fletsand Road, Wilmslow, Cheshire.

**PIGOTT, Group Capt. J. R. W. Smyth-;** *see* Smyth-Pigott.

**PIGOTT, Air Vice-Marshal Michael Joseph,** CBE 1956; Director of Dental Services, RAF 1954-58; retired, 1958; *b* 16 May 1904; *m* 1938, Ethel Norah, *d* of Alfred Sutherland Blackman; one *d. Educ:* Blackrock College, Dublin; Nat. Univ. of Ireland; Nat. Dental Hosp. of Ireland. BDS 1925; FDSRCS 1948. Joined RAF 1930. Served War of 1939-45, Bomber Command; Inspecting Dental Officer: MEAF, 1945-48, Flying Trng Comd, 1948-49, Tech. Trng Comd, 1949-50; Principal Dental Officer, Home Comd 1950-54; Air Vice-Marshal, 1955. QHDS, 1950-58. *Address:* Oak Farmhouse, Carnon Downs, Truro, Cornwall. *T:* Perranarworthal 14.

**PIGOTT-BROWN, Sir William Brian,** 3rd Bt, *cr* 1902; *b* 20 Jan. 1941; *s* of Sir John Pigott-Brown, 2nd Bt (killed in action, 1942) and Helen (who *m* 1948, Capt. Charles Raymond Radclyffe), *o d* of Major Gilbert Egerton Cotton, Priestland, Tarporley, Cheshire; *S* father, 1942. *Heir:* none. *Address:* Orchard House, Aston Upthorpe, Berkshire; 25 Chapel Street, SW1.

**PIKE, Andrew Hamilton,** CMG 1956; OBE 1945; Minister for Lands and Mineral Resources, Tanganyika, 1957-59, retired; *b* 26 August 1903; *s* of late Canon William Pike Thurles, Co. Tipperary; *m* 1951, Catherine Provan Cathcart, *y d* of late Prof. E. P. Cathcart, CBE; four *s. Educ:* The Abbey, Tipperary; Trinity College, Dublin; University College, Oxford. Tanganyika: Administrative Officer (Cadet), 1927; Asst Dist Officer, 1930; Dist Officer, 1938; Dep. Provincial Comr, 1947; Provincial Comr, 1948; Senior Provincial Comr, 1951; Member for Lands and Mines, 1953. President Tanganyika Society, 1954-57; Member Editorial Board of "Tanganyika Notes and Records", until 1959. *Recreations:* tennis and golf. *Address:* Blatchfeld, Blackheath, near Guildford, Surrey. *T:* Bramley 2358.

**PIKE, Prof. Douglas Henry;** General-Editor, Australian Dictionary of Biography, 1962; Professor, Australian National University, 1964; *b* 3 Nov. 1908; *s* of Douglas and Louise Pike; *m* 1941, Olive Hagger; two *s. Educ:* China Inland Mission School, Chefoo, N China; University of Adelaide. BA 1947 (First Class Hons), MA 1951, DLitt 1957. Lecturer, 1948; Lecturer in History, Univ. of Western Australia, 1949-50; Reader in History, Univ. of Adelaide, 1951-60; Prof. of History, Univ. of Tasmania, 1961-63. *Publications:* Paradise of Dissent: South Australia, 1829-1857, 1957, 2nd edn 1967; Australia: The Quiet Continent, 1962, 2nd edn 1970; Charles Hawker, 1968; General Editor, Australian Dictionary of Biography, 1788-1850: vol. 1, A-H, 1966; vol. 2, I-Z, 1967; 1851-1891: vol. 1, A-C, 1969. *Address:* Australian National University, Canberra, ACT 2600, Australia.

**PIKE, Air Cdre James Maitland Nicholson,** CB 1963; DSO 1942; DFC 1941; RAF, retired; *b* 8 Feb. 1916; *s* of late Frank Pike, Glendarary, Achill Island, Co. Mayo, Eire, and Daphne (*née* Kenyon Stow), Worcester; *m* 1st, 1942; one *d*; 2nd, 1955, Amber Pauline Bettesworth Hellard; one *s* one step *d. Educ:* Stowe; RAF Coll., Cranwell. Commnd 1937; War Service: Aden, Middle East, UK (Coastal Command), Malta and Azores. Directing staff, RAF Staff Coll., 1945-47; Group Capt. 1955; Comd RAF Station, St Mawgan and RAF Station, Kinloss, 1955-57; SASO, RAF Malta, 1958-60; Air Cdre 1961; AOC, RAF Gibraltar, 1961-62; Imperial Defence College, 1963; Air Cdre Intelligence (B), Ministry of Defence, 1964; Dir of Security, RAF, 1965-69. *Recreations:* shooting, fishing, sailing. *Address:* Glendarary, Christmas Common, Watlington, Oxford. *Club:* Royal Air Force.

**PIKE, Miss Mervyn;** MP (C) Melton Division of Leicestershire since Dec. 1956; Company Managing Director since 1946; *b* 16 Sept. 1918; *d* of I. S. Pike, Company Director, Okehampton, Devonshire. *Educ:* Hunmanby Hall; Reading University. BA Hons Economics and Psychology, 1941. Contested (C): Pontefract, 1951; Leek, Staffordshire, 1955. Member West Riding CC 1955. Served in WAAF, 1941-46. Managing Director, Clokie & Co. Ltd, Castleford, 1946. Assistant Postmaster-General, 1959-63; Joint Parliamentary Under-Secretary of State, Home Office, 1963-64. Director, Watts, Blake, Bearne, 1964-. *Recreations:* racing, gardening, walking. *Address:* West Eaton House, West Eaton Place, SW1; Cold Overton, Oakham, Rutland. *Clubs:* Constitutional; United Hunts.

**PIKE, Sir Philip Ernest Housden,** Kt 1969; Chief Justice of Swaziland, since 1970; *b* 6 March 1914; *s* of Rev. Ernest Benjamin Pike and Dora Case Pike (*née* Lillie); *m* 2nd, 1959, Millicent Locke Staples; one *s* one *d* of 1st marriage. *Educ:* De Carteret School, and Munro Coll., Jamaica; Middle Temple, London. Barrister at Law, 1938. Crown Counsel, Jamaica, 1947-49; Legal Draftsman, Kenya, 1949-52; Solicitor General, Uganda, 1952-58; QC (Uganda) 1953; Attorney General, Sarawak, 1958-65; QC (Sarawak) 1958; Chief Justice, High Court in Borneo, 1965-68; Judge, High Court of Malawi, 1969-70, Actg Chief Justice, 1970. Coronation Medal, 1953. PNBS-Sarawak, 1965; Malaysia Commemorative Medal, 1967; PMN Malaysia 1968. *Recreations:* golf, photography. *Address:* The Chief Justice's Chambers, PO Box 19, Mbabane, Swaziland; 6 Mimosa Road, Westridge, Somerset West, Cape, S Africa.

**PIKE, Most Rev. Robert Bonsall;** *see* Meath, Bishop of.

**PIKE, Rt. Rev. St John Surridge;** DD *jure dig* 1958; an Assistant Bishop of Guildford and Vicar of St Mary the Virgin, Ewshot, since 1963; *b* 27 Dec. 1909; *s* of late Rev. Canon William Pike, Thurles, Co. Tipperary; *m* 1958, Clare, *d* of William Henry Jones; two *s* one *d. Educ:* The Abbey, Tipperary; Bishop Foy School, Waterford; Trinity Coll., Dublin (MA). Deacon, 1932; Priest, 1934; Curate of Taney, 1932-37; Head of Southern Church Mission, Ballymacarrett, Belfast, 1937-47; SPG Missionary, Diocese of Gambia, 1947-52; Rector of St George's, Belfast, 1952-57; Commissary for Gambia in N Ireland, 1954-57; Bishop of Gambia and the Rio Pongas, 1958-63. *Address:* The Vicarage, Ewshot, Farnham, Surrey. *T:* Crondall 206.

**PIKE, Sir Theodore (Ouseley),** KCMG 1956 (CMG 1953); *b* 1904; 3rd *s* of late Canon W. Pike, Thurles, Co. Tipperary; *m* 1934, Violet F., *d* of late Sir William Robinson, DL, JP; two *s* one *d. Educ:* The Abbey, Tipperary; Trinity Coll., Dublin; University Coll., Oxford. Colonial Administrative Service, Tanganyika, 1928-53. Governor and Commander-in-Chief, Somaliland Protectorate, 1954-59. Hon. LLD (Dublin). *Address:* c/o National & Grindlay's Bank, 23 Fenchurch Street, EC3.

**PIKE, Marshal of the Royal Air Force Sir Thomas (Geoffrey),** GCB 1961 (KCB 1955; CB 1946); CBE 1944; DFC 1942 and Bar, 1942; Deputy Supreme Allied Commander, Europe, 1964-67; *b* 29 June 1906; *s* of late Capt. S. R. Pike, RA; *m* 1930, Kathleen Althea, *e d* of Maj. H. Elwell; one *s* two *d. Educ:* Bedford School; RAF Coll., Cranwell. Joined RAF, 1923. Served War of

1939-45, Directorate of Organisation, Air Ministry; commanded a Fighter Squadron, 1941; Desert Air Force, 1943-45; AOC No 11 Group Fighter Command, 1950-51; DCS, HQ Air Forces Central Europe, 1951-53; Deputy Chief of the Air Staff, Dec. 1953-July 1956; Air Officer Commanding-in-Chief, Fighter Command, July 1956-Dec. 1959; Chief of the Air Staff, 1960-63. Squadron Leader, 1937; Group Captain, 1941; Air Commodore, 1944; Air Vice-Marshal, 1950; Air Marshal, 1955; Air Chief Marshal, 1957; Marshal of the RAF, 1962. Officer Legion of Merit (USA). *Address:* Little Wynters, Hastingwood, Harlow, Essex.

*See also Lt-Gen. Sir William Pike.*

**PIKE, Rt. Rev. V. J.;** *see* Sherborne, Bishop Suffragan of.

**PIKE, Lt-Gen. Sir William (Gregory Huddleston),** KCB 1961 (CB 1956); CBE 1952; DSO 1943; Chief Commander since 1969, and Commissioner-in-Chief since 1967, St John Ambulance; b 24 June 1905; *s* of late Captain Sydney Royston Pike, RA, and Sarah Elizabeth Pike (*née* Huddleston); *m* 1939, Josephine Margaret, *er d* of late Maj.-Gen. R. H. D. Tompson, CB, CMG, DSO, and Mrs B. D. Tompson; one *s* two *d. Educ:* Bedford School; Marlborough Coll.; RMA Woolwich. Lieutenant RA, 20th and 24th Field Brigades, RA and "A" Field Brigade, Indian Artillery, 1925-36; Staff College, Camberley, 1937-38; Command and Staff Appointments in UK, France and Belgium, North Africa, USA and Far East, 1939-50; CRA, 1st Commonwealth Div., Korea, 1951-52; idc 1953; Director of Staff Duties, War Office, 1954-57; Chief of Staff, Far East Land Forces, Oct. 1957-60; Vice-Chief of the Imperial General Staff, 1960-63; Col Comdt RA, 1962-70. Lieutenant of HM Tower of London, 1963-66. Jt Hon. Pres., Anglo-Korean Society, 1963-69. Hon. Col 277 (Argyll and Sutherland Highlanders) Regt RA (TA), 1960-67; Hon. Col Lowland Regt RA (T), 1967-70. Member Honourable Artillery Company; Governor and Member Administrative Board, Corps of Commissionaires, 1964. Officer, US Legion of Merit, 1953. KStJ 1967. *Recreations:* field sports and gardening. *Address:* Ganwells, Bentley, Hants. *T:* Bentley 2152; Rhos-y-Bayvil, Velindre, Crymmych, Pembs. *Club:* Army and Navy.

*See also Marshal of the Royal Air Force Sir Thomas Pike.*

**PILCHER, Sir John (Arthur),** KCMG 1966 (CMG 1957); Ambassador to Japan since 1967; *b* 16 May 1912; *s* of late Lt-Col A. J. Pilcher; *m* 1942, Delia Margaret Taylor; one *d. Educ:* Shrewsbury; Clare Coll., Cambridge; France, Austria and Italy. Served in Japan, 1936-39; China, 1939-41; Ministry of Information and Foreign Office, 1941-48; Italy, 1948-51; Foreign Office, 1951-54; Spain (Counsellor, Madrid), 1954-59; Philippines (Ambassador), 1959-63; Assistant Under-Secretary, Foreign Office, 1966-65; Ambassador to Austria, 1965-67. Grand Cross (Gold) Austrian Decoration of Honour, 1966. *Address:* British Embassy, Tokyo, Japan, *Club:* St James'.

**PILCHER, Robin Sturtevant,** MS, FRCS, FRCP; Emeritus Professor of Surgery, University of London; Professor of Surgery and Director of the Surgical Unit, University College Hospital, London, 1938-67; *b* 22 June 1902; *s* of Thorold and Helena Pilcher; *m* 1929, Mabel Pearks; one *s* one *d. Educ:* St Paul's Sch.; University Coll., London. Fellow University Coll., London. *Publications:* various surgical papers. *Address:* Swanbourne, 21 Church End, Haddenham, Bucks. *T:* 7248.

**PILDITCH, Sir Denys,** Kt 1944; CIE 1941; *b* 6 Oct. 1891; 2nd *s* of Frank Slater Pilditch; *m* 1919, Phyllis Charsley (*d* 1938), *d* of late John Roberts, Hinton Charterhouse, Somerset; one *d* (and one *s* decd); *m* 1948, Mary Joyce, *widow* of Arthur Yencken and *er d* of George Russell, Langi Willi, Linton, Vic, Aust. *Educ:* Tonbridge School. Joined Indian Police, UP, 1912; Temp. Commission, Indian Army, 1918-19; Superintendent, 1924; Central Intelligence Officer, Govt of India, 1936; Deputy Director, Intelligence Bureau, 1936; Director, Intelligence Bureau, 1939-45; Adviser to Secretary of State for India, 1947. King's Police Medal, 1933, Bar to Medal, 1935. *Address:* Bredfield Place, Woodbridge, Suffolk. *Club:* Royal Thames Yacht.

**PILDITCH, Sir Richard (Edward),** 4th Bt, *cr* 1929; *b* 8 Sept. 1926; *s* of Sir Philip Harold Pilditch, 2nd Bt, and Frances Isabella, *d* of J. G. Weeks, JP, Bedlington, Northumberland; *S* brother (Sir Philip John Frederick Pilditch, 3rd Bt) 1954; *m* 1950, Pauline Elizabeth Smith; one *s* one *d. Educ:* Charterhouse. Served War of 1939-45, with Royal Navy, in India and Ceylon, 1944-45. *Recreations:* shooting, fishing. *Heir: s* John Richard Pilditch, *b* 24 Sept. 1955. *Address:* 4 Fishermans Bank, Mudeford, Christchurch, Hants.

**PILE, Gen. Sir Frederick Alfred,** 2nd Bt, *cr* 1900; GCB 1945 (KCB 1941; CB 1938); DSO 1918; MC; LLD (Hon.) Leeds 1946; late Royal Tank Corps; *b* 14 Sept. 1884; *e s* of Sir T. D. Pile, 1st Bt, and Caroline Maude (*d* 1948), *d* of John M. Nicholson, JP, Dublin; *S* father, 1931; *m* 1st, 1915, Vera Millicent (whom he divorced, 1929), *d* of Brig.-Gen. Lloyd; two *s*; 2nd, 1932, Hester (*d* 1949), *o d* of late George Phillimore, BCL, Shedfield, Hants; 3rd, 1951, Molly Eveline Louise Mary (late Chief Comdr, ATS), *o d* of late Ralph Smyth, Newtown, Drogheda, County Louth, Ireland, *widow* of Brigadier Francis Wyville Home. RA 1904; Capt., 1914; Major, 1916; Bt Lt-Col, 1919; Lt-Col, 1927; Colonel, 1928; Maj.-Gen. 1937; Lieut-Gen, 1939; General 1941; served European War, 1914-18 (despatches, DSO, MC); Asst Dir of Mechanisation, War Office, 1928-32; Commander, Canal Brigade, Egypt, 1932-36; Commander, 1st Anti-Aircraft Division TA, 1937-39; GOC-in-C, Anti-Aircraft Command, 1939-45; Dir-Gen. Ministry of Works, 1945; Col-Comdt RA, 1945-52; Chairman: Cementation Co. Ltd, 1961-63 (Director, 1945-61); Fothergill & Harvey Ltd, 1956-64; Katherine Low Settlement, Battersea, 1951-63; Chartered Nurses' Soc.; Management Cttee, Herts Training School, 1950-67 (Mem. 1958-). *Heir: s* Frederick Devereux Pile, MC 1945; Col late Royal Tank Regt [*b* 10 Dec. 1915; *m* 1940, Pamela, *d* of Philip Henstock, Falkland Garth, Newbury; two *d*]. *Address:* Broom Manor, Cottered, Herts. *T:* Walkern 398. *Clubs:* Cavalry, Pratt's.

*See also J. D. Pile.*

**PILE, John Devereux;** Director, Imperial Tobacco Group Ltd, since 1967; Chairman and Managing Director, W. D. & H. O. Wills, since 1968; *b* 5 June 1918; 2nd *s* of Gen. Sir Frederick A. Pile, 2nd Bt, *qv*, and Lady Ferguson; *m* 1946, Katharine Mary Shafe; two *s* two *d. Educ:* Weymouth Coll., Dorset; Trinity Coll., Cambridge (BA). Service with RA, 1939-46 (Major). Joined Imperial Tobacco Group, 1946; Manager, W. D. & H. O. Wills and Wm Clarke & Son, Dublin, 1956-59; Chairman: Robert Sinclair Ltd, 1960-64; Churchmans, 1964-67. *Address:* Vale Court, Colerne, Chippenham, Wiltshire. *T:* Box 417.

**PILE, William Denis,** CB 1968; MBE 1944; Permanent Under-Secretary of State,

Department of Education and Science, since 1970; *b* 1 Dec. 1919; *s* of James Edward Pile and Jean Elizabeth Pile; *m* 1st, 1939, Brenda Skinner (marr. diss. 1947); 2nd, 1948, Joan Marguerite Crafter; one *s* two *d*. *Educ:* Royal Masonic School; St Catharine's College, Cambridge. Served Border Regt, 1940-45. Ministry of Education, 1947-50, 1951-66; Cabinet Office, 1950; Asst Under-Sec. of State: Dept of Education and Science, 1962; Ministry of Health, 1966; Dep. Under-Sec. of State, Home Office, 1967-70; Director-General, Prison Service, 1969-70. *Address:* The Manor House, Riverhead, near Sevenoaks, Kent. *T:* Sevenoaks 54498. *Clubs:* Oxford and Cambridge University; Hawks (Cambridge).

**PILKINGTON,** family name of **Baron Pilkington.**

**PILKINGTON,** Baron, *cr* 1968 (Life Peer), of St Helens; **Harry (William Henry) Pilkington,** Kt, *cr* 1953; DL; Chairman Pilkington Brothers Ltd since 1949; Director of other companies chiefly in the glass industry; Director of the Bank of England; Chancellor of Loughborough University of Technology since 1966; *b* 19 April 1905; *e s* of Richard Austin Pilkington and Hope (*née* Cozens-Hardy); *m* 1930, Rosamond Margaret Rowan (*d* 1953); one *s* one *d* (and one *d* decd); *m* 1961, Mrs Mavis Wilding. *Educ:* Rugby; Magdalene Coll., Cambridge. President: Federation of British Industries, 1953-55; Council of European Industrial Federations, 1954-57; Chairman: Royal Commn to consider pay of Doctors and Dentists, 1957-60; Cttee on Broadcasting, 1960-62; National Advisory Council for Education for Industry and Commerce, 1956-66; Econ. Develt Cttee for the Chemical Industry, 1967-; Mem. Council Manchester Business Sch., 1964-; Pres., Assoc. of Technical Institutions, 1966-68. DL Lancs, 1968. Hon. LLD: Manchester, 1959; Liverpool, 1963; Hon. DSc Loughborough, 1966; Hon. DCL Kent, 1968. *Recreations:* walking, gardening, tennis, cycling. *Address:* Windle Hall, St Helens, Lancs. *T:* 23423. *Club:* Oxford and Cambridge University.

**PILKINGTON, Sir Alastair;** *see* Pilkington, Sir L. A. B.

**PILKINGTON, Charles Vere;** retired as Chairman, Sotheby & Co.; *b* 11 Jan. 1905; *e s* of Charles Carlisle Pilkington and Emilia (*née* Lloyd); *m* 1936, Honor Chedworth (*d* 1961), *y d* of first and last Baron Kylsant; one *s*. *Educ:* Eton; Christ Church, Oxford, (MA). Dir, Sotheby & Co., Fine Art Auctioneers, 1927-58, Chm. 1953-58. Member of Council, Royal Musical Assoc., 1952-58; Member Business Cttee Musica Britannica. *Recreation:* music (harpsichord). *Address:* Casal da Nora, Colares, Portugal. *T:* 299253. *Clubs:* Travellers'; Eça de Queiroz.

**PILKINGTON, Canon Evan Matthias,** MA; Chaplain to the Queen since 1969; Canon Residentiary of Bristol Cathedral since 1968; *b* 27 Dec. 1916; *s* of Rev. Matthias Pilkington; *m* 1946, Elsie (*née* Lashley); four *s*. *Educ:* Worksop Coll.; Keble Coll., Oxford; Cuddesdon Theol. College. Curate of: Bottesford and Ashby, Scunthorpe, 1940; Holy Trinity, Southall, 1942; St John the Divine, Kennington, 1944; Vicar of: East Kirkby and Miningsby, Lincs, 1946; Holy Trinity, Upper Tooting, 1952; Kingston upon Thames, 1961. *Recreations:* walking, lettering. *Address:* 18 Percival Road, Clifton, Bristol BS8 3LN. *T:* Bristol 37969.

**PILKINGTON, Lawrence Herbert Austin,** CBE 1964; JP; Director, Pilkington Brothers Ltd, since 1935; *b* 13 Oct. 1911; 2nd *s* of Richard Austin and Hon. Hope Pilkington; *m* 1936, Norah Holden, Whitby, Ont., Canada; two *d*. *Educ:* Bromsgrove School; Magdalene College, Cambridge. Volunteer with Grenfell Mission, 1933-34. Joined Pilkington Brothers Limited, 1935. Chairman: Glass Delegacy, 1949-54; Glass Industry Research Assoc., 1954-58; British Coal Utilisation Research Assoc., 1963-68; Soc. of Acoustic Technology, 1963-; Member: Building Research Board, 1958-62; Wilson Cttee on Noise, 1960-63; President, Soc. of Glass Technology, 1960-64. JP Lancs, 1942. Hon. LLD, Sheffield, 1956. *Publications:* mainly on glass in various technical jls. *Recreations:* sailing, climbing, amateur radio, shooting. *Address:* The Holt, Foxhill, Frodsham, Cheshire. *T:* Frodsham 3304. *Club:* Royal Dee Yacht.

**PILKINGTON, Sir Lionel Alexander Bethune, (Sir Alastair),** Kt 1970; FRS 1969; Executive Director of Pilkington Brothers Ltd, St Helens, since 1955; Chairman, Fibreglass Ltd; *b* 7 Jan. 1920; *yr s* of late Col L. G. Pilkington and of Mrs L. G. Pilkington, Newbury, Berks; *m* 1945, Patricia Nicholls (*née* Elliott); one *s* one *d*. *Educ:* Sherborne School; Trinity Coll., Cambridge. War service, 1939-46. Joined Pilkington Brothers Ltd, Glass Manufacturers, St Helens, 1947; Production Manager and Assistant Works Manager, Doncaster, 1949-51; Head Office, 1952; Sub-Director, 1953. Mem., Central Adv. Council for Science and Technology, 1970-. Hon. DTech Loughborough Univ., 1968; Hon. Fellow, Manchester Inst. of Science and Technology, 1969. *Recreations:* gardening, sailing, music. *Address:* The Crossways, View Road, Rainhill, Prescot, Lancs. *T:* 051-426 4228.

**PILKINGTON, Margaret,** OBE 1956; Deputy Chairman, Whitworth Art Gallery, and Hon. Director, 1935-59; Founder Red Rose Guild of Craftsmen, 1920; Member of Manchester City Art Galleries Committee, since 1925; *b* 25 Nov. 1891; *d* of Lawrence Pilkington and Mary Gavin Stevenson. *Educ:* Croham Hurst School, South Croydon; Slade School of Art. President: Manchester Luncheon Club, 1963; Manchester Literary and Philosophical Society, 1964, 1965. JP Manchester, 1945. Hon. MA Manchester Univ., 1942. *Address:* Firwood, Alderley Edge, Cheshire. *T:* Alderley 2309. *Club:* University Women's.

**PILKINGTON, Captain Sir Richard Antony,** KBE 1961; MC 1940; *b* St Helens, 10 May 1908; *s* of Arthur Richard Pilkington and Marjorie, *d* of Sir Arthur Cope, KCVO, RA; *m* 1946, Rosemary (*née* Russell-Roberts); three *d*. *Educ:* Charterhouse; Oxford. Worked in Canada on a farm in 1928; joined Coldstream Guards in 1930; resigned Commission in 1935. Served War of 1939-45 (MC). Subsequently R of O, Coldstream Guards. MP (C) for Widnes, 1935-45, for Poole, 1951-64; PPS to Mr O. Stanley, Pres. Bd of Trade, 1939; Civil Lord of the Admiralty, 1942-45. Has travelled in Europe, Asia, Africa and America. *Recreations:* history, walking Roman roads, family genealogies, motor cars. *Address:* 14 Grove End Road, NW8.

**PILKINGTON, Dr Roger Windle;** Author; *b* 17 Jan. 1915; 3rd *s* of Richard Austin Pilkington and Hon. Hope (*née* Cozens-Hardy); *m* 1937, Theodora Miriam Jaboor; one *s* one *d*. *Educ:* Rugby; Freiburg, Germany; Magdalene Coll., Cambridge (MA, PhD). Research, genetics, 1937; Chm., London Missionary Soc., 1962; Chm. of Trustees, Homerton Coll., Cambridge, 1962; Chm. of Govs, Hall Sch., 1962; jt author, Sex and Morality Report, Brit. Council of Churches, 1966; Vice-Pres., River

Thames Soc., 1967; Master, Glass Sellers' Co., 1967. *Publications:* Males and Females, 1948; Stringer's Folly, Biology, Man and God, Sons and Daughters, 1951; How Your Life Began, 1953; Revelation Through Science, 1954; Jan's Treasure, In the Beginning, 1955; Thames Waters, The Facts of Life, 1956; Small Boat Through Belgium, The Chesterfield Gold, The Great South Sea, The Ways of the Sea, 1957; The Missing Panel, 1958; Small Boat Through Holland, Robert Boyle: Father of Chemistry, How Boats Go Uphill, 1959; Small Boat to the Skagerrak, World Without End, The Dahlia's Cargo, Don John's Ducats, 1960; Small Boat to Sweden, Small Boat to Alsace, The Ways of the Air, Who's Who and Why, 1961; Small Boat to Bavaria, Nepomuk of the River, Boats Overland, How Boats are Navigated, 1962; The River, (with Noel Streatfeild) Confirmation and After, Facts of Life for Parents, Small Boat to Germany, The Eisenbart Mystery, 1963; Heavens Alive, Small Boat Through France, 1964; Small Boat in Southern France, Glass, 1965; Small Boat on the Thames, The Boy from Stink Alley, 1966; Small Boat on the Meuse, Small Boat to Luxembourg, 1967; Small Boat on the Moselle, 1968; Small Boat to Elsinore, 1968; Small Boat in Northern Germany, 1969; Small Boat on the Lower Rhine, 1970; contribs to Guardian, Daily Telegraph, Times, Family Doctor, Yachting World, etc. *Recreations:* inland waterways, walking. *Address:* La Vielle Maison, The Bulwarks, St Aubin, Jersey, Channel Islands. *T:* Jersey Central 43760.

**PILKINGTON, Sir Thomas Henry Milborne-Swinnerton-,** 14th Bt, *cr* 1635; Director, Thos & James Harrison Ltd, since 1963; *b* 10 Mar. 1934; *s* of Sir Arthur W. Milborne-Swinnerton-Pilkington, 13th Bt and Elizabeth Mary (she *m* 1950, A. Burke), *d* of late Major J. F. Harrison, King's Walden Bury, Hitchin; *S* father 1952; *m* 1961, Susan, *e d* of N. S. R. Adamson, Durban, South Africa; one *s* two *d*. *Educ:* Eton College. *Recreations:* golf, cricket, racing. *Heir: s* Richard Arthur Milborne-Swinnerton-Pilkington, *b* 4 Sept. 1964. *Address:* King's Walden, Hitchin, Herts. *Clubs:* Cavalry, White's.

*See also Sir J. L. Armytage, Bt.*

**PILLAI, Sir (Narayana) Raghavan,** KCIE, *cr* 1946 (CIE 1939); CBE 1937; Padma Vibhushan, 1960; *b* 24 July 1898; *s* of M. C. Narayana Pillai, Trivandrum, S India; *m* 1928, Edith Minnie Arthurs; two *s*. *Educ:* Madras Univ.; Trinity Hall, Cambridge (schol.). BA (Madras) 1st Cl. English, 1918; Natural Sciences Tripos Pt 1 (Cambridge), 1st Cl., 1921; Law Tripos Pt 2, 1st Cl., 1922; ICS 1921; various appointments under the Government of Central Provinces and the Government of India. Secretary General, Ministry of External Affairs, New Delhi, 1952-60. Hon. DLitt Kerala University, 1953. Hon. Fellow, Trinity Hall, Cambrdige, 1970. *Recreation:* tennis. *Address:* 1022 St James's Court, SW1. *Clubs:* Oriental; Gymkhana (New Delhi).

**PIM, Captain Sir Richard (Pike),** KBE 1960; Kt 1945; VRD; DL; Inspector-General, Royal Ulster Constabulary, retired; National Governor for Northern Ireland, BBC, 1962-67; Member of Council, Winston Churchill Memorial Trust, 1965-69; Member, Ulster Transport Authority, 1962-64, retired; *b* Dunmurry, Co. Antrim, 1900; *yr s* of late Cecil Pim; *m* 1925, Marjorie Angel, 3rd *d* of late John ff. Young, Dungiven, Londonderry; two *s*. *Educ:* Lancing Coll., Sussex; Trinity College, Dublin. Served in RNVR in European War, 1914-18; Royal Irish Constabulary, 1921. Appointed to Civil Service, N Ireland, 1922; Asst Secretary, Ministry of Home Affairs (N Ireland), 1935; Staff of Prime Minister, Northern Ireland, 1938; in charge of Mr Churchill's War Room at Admiralty, 1939, and later of Map Room at Downing St; Capt. RNVR. North African Campaign (despatches). DL City of Belfast, 1957. Order of Crown of Yugoslavia; Legion of Merit, USA. *Address:* Mullagh, Killyleagh, Co. Down, Northern Ireland. *T:* Killyleagh 267. *Club:* Ulster (Belfast).

**PINAY, Antoine;** Minister of Foreign Affairs, France, 1955-56; Minister of Finance and Economic Affairs, France, 1958-60, resigned; leather manufacturer; *b* Department of the Rhône, 30 Dec. 1891. *Educ:* Marist Fathers' Sch., St-Chamond. Joined a tannery business there; became Mayor, 1929; later became gen. councillor, Dept of the Loire (Pres. 1949-). Was returned to Chamber of Deputies, 1936, Ind. Radical party; Senator, 1938; elected to 2nd Constituent Assembly, 1946; then to 1st Nat. Assembly; re-elected to Nat. Assembly as an associate of Ind. Republican group; Sec. of State for Economic Affairs, Sept. 1948-Oct. 1949; in several successive ministries, July 1950-Feb. 1952, he was Minister of Public Works, Transportation, and Tourism; Prime Minister of France, March-Dec. 1952. Served European War, 1914-18, in artillery as non-commnd officer (Croix de Guerre, Médaille Militaire). *Address:* Saint-Chamond, Loire, France.

**PINCHER, (Henry) Chapman;** Defence, Science and Medical Editor, Daily Express, since 1946; *b* Ambala, India, 29 March 1914; *s* of Maj. Richard Chapman Pincher, E Surrey Regt, and Helen (*née* Foster), Pontefract; *m* 1965, Constance Wolstenholme; one *s* one *d* (by previous *m*). *Educ:* Darlington Gram. Sch.; King's Coll., London; Inst. Educn; Mil. Coll. of Science. Carter Medallist, London, 1934; BSc (hons Botany, Zoology), 1935. Staff Liverpool Inst., 1936-40. Joined Royal Armoured Corps, 1940; Techn SO, Rocket Div., Min. of Supply, 1943-46. Granada Award, Journalist of the Year, 1964; Reporter of the Decade, 1966. *Publications:* Breeding of Farm Animals, 1946; A Study of Fishes, 1947; Into the Atomic Age, 1947; Spotlight on Animals, 1950; Evolution, 1950; (with Bernard Wicksteed) It's Fun Finding Out, 1950; Sleep, and how to get more of it, 1954; *novels:* Not with a Bang, 1965; The Giantkiller, 1967; The Penthouse Conspirators, 1970; original researches in genetics, numerous articles in scientific and agricultural jls. *Recreations:* fishing, shooting, natural history, country life; ferreting in Whitehall and bolting politicians. *Address:* Lowerhouse Farm, Ewhurst, Surrey.

**PINCKNEY, Charles Percy,** FRCP; Hon. Consulting Physician to: Pædiatric Department, St George's Hospital, SW1; Heritage Craft Schools and Hospitals, Chailey, Sussex; Windsor Group Hospitals, Windsor, Berks; *b* 28 April 1901; *er s* of late W. P. Pinckney, Dir of Rubber Cos; *m* 1934, Norah Manisty Boucher; one *s* one *d*. *Educ:* Radley College; Clare College, Cambridge (MA, MB, BCH). Qualified St George's Hospital, SW1. MRCS, LRCP 1925; FRCP 1941. Held various resident appointments St George's Hospital. Physician to King George Hospital, Ilford, 1931-59. *Publications:* articles in BMJ, Archives of Diseases in Children, and Medical Press, 1940-50. *Recreations:* tennis and ski-ing. *Address:* (private) 76 Albert Hall Mansions, SW7. *T:* 01-589 9351; (professional) 73 Harley Street, W1. *T:* 01-580 3533. *Club:* Hurlingham.

**PINDLING, Hon. (Lynden) Oscar;** Prime Minister and Minister of External Affairs of the Commonwealth of the Bahama Islands, since 1969; *b* 22 March 1930; *s* of Arnold Franklin and Viola Pindling; *m* 1956, Marguerite McKenzie; two *s* two *d*. *Educ:* Western Senior Sch., Nassau Govt High Sch.; London Univ. (LLB 1952; LLD 1970). Called to the Bar, Middle Temple, 1953. Practised as Lawyer, 1952-67. Parly Leader of Progressive Liberal Party, 1956; elected to Bahamas House of Assembly, 1956, re-elected 1962, 1967, and 1968. Worked for human rights and self-determination in the Bahamas; Mem., several delegns to Colonial Office, 1956-66; took part in Constitutional Conf., May 1963; Leader of Opposition, 1964; Mem., Delegns to UN Special Cttee of Twenty-four, 1965, 1966; Premier of the Bahamas and Minister of Tourism and Development, 1967; led Bahamian Delegn to Constitutional Conf., London, 1968. Chm., Commonwealth Parly Assoc., 1968. *Recreations:* swimming, boating, travel. *Address:* Office of the Prime Minister, Rawson Square, Nassau, Bahamas.

**PINDLING, Hon. Oscar;** *see* Pindling, Hon. L. O.

**PINE, John Bradley;** Antique business since 1968; *b* 2 Dec. 1913; *yr s* of Percival William Pine and late Maud Mary Pine (*née* Bradley); *m* 1st, 1945, Elizabeth Mary (Jayne) Hallett (*d* 1948); one *s*; 2nd, 1952, Ann Carney; one *s*. *Educ:* Douai School. Asst Solicitor, GWR, Eng., 1935-39; Mil. Service, 1939-45; a Sen. Prosecutor, CCG, 1945-47; Resident Magistrate and Crown Counsel, N Rhodesia, 1947-49; Called to Bar, 1950; Asst Attorney Gen., Gibraltar, 1949-54; QC (Bermuda), 1955; Attorney Gen., Bermuda, 1955-57; Actg Governor of Bermuda, 1956; QC (Nyasaland), 1958; Solicitor Gen., Nyasaland, 1958-60; Minister of Justice and Attorney Gen., Nyasaland, 1960-62, when replaced by an Elected Minister under self-governing Constitution; Legal Adviser to Governor of Nyasaland, July 1963, until Independence, July 1964; Parly Draftsman, Govt of N Ireland, 1965-66; Sec., Ulster Tourist Develt Assoc., 1967. *Recreations:* golf, antiques. *Address:* Loreto, Ballywilliam, Donaghadee, Co. Down, N Ireland. *T:* Donaghadee 3375. *Club:* Public Schools.

**PINE, Leslie Gilbert;** Author and Lecturer; *b* 22 Dec. 1907; *s* of Henry Moorshead Pine, Bristol, and Lilian Grace (*née* Beswetherick); *m* 1948, Grace V. Griffin; one *s*. *Educ:* Tellisford House Sch., Bristol; South-West London Coll., Barnes; London Univ. (BA). Asst Editor, Burke's Landed Gentry, 1935; subseq. Editor of Burke's Peerage and Landed Gentry and other reference books and then Managing Editor, The Shooting Times, 1960-64, and Shooting Times Library, 1962-64 (resigned as unable to agree with blood sports). Director L. & G. Pine & Co. Ltd, 1964-69. Censorship and Air Min., 1940; Min. of Labour, 1941; RAF 1942; Sqn Ldr 1945-46; served in N Africa, Italy, Greece and India (Intel. Branch). Barrister-at-Law, Inner Temple, 1953; Freeman, City of London, Liveryman of the Glaziers' Company, 1954. Prospective Parly Candidate (C) Bristol Central, 1956; contested seat, 1959; re-adopted, 1960; resigned and joined Liberal Party, 1962; Prospective Parly Candidate (L), S Croydon, 1963, resigned candidature, June 1964. Dioc. Lay Reader, London, 1939, Canterbury, 1961; received into Catholic Church, 1964. Corr. Mem. Inst. Internacional de Genealogica y Heraldica (Madrid) and of Gen. Socs in Belgium, Chile and Brazil; Gov., St And. Sch., S Croydon, 1960-64. A Vice-Pres. Clay Pigeon Shooting Assoc., 1961; FSA Scot., 1940; MJI, 1947 (Mem. Council, 1953-61); FJI 1957; Associate, Zool. Soc., London, 1961; FRSA 1961; Soc. of Authors, 1965; Augustan Soc., 1967; FRGS 1969; FRAS 1970. Member: RUSI; Royal Soc. St George. Has given over 600 lectures in Gt Britain, Ireland and Holland. *Publications:* The Stuarts of Traquair, 1940; The House of Wavell, 1948; The Middle Sea, 1950; The Story of Heraldry, 1952 (4th edn 1968, Japan, USA); Trace Your Ancestors, 1953; The Golden Book of the Coronation, 1953; They Came with The Conqueror, 1954; The Story of the Peerage, 1956; Tales of the British Aristocracy, 1956; The House of Constantine, 1957; Teach Yourself Heraldry and Genealogy, 1957; The Twilight of Monarchy, 1958; A Guide to Titles, 1959; Princes of Wales, 1959, new edn, 1970; American Origins, 1960, 1968; Your Family Tree, 1962; Ramshackledom, A Critical Appraisal of the Establishment, 1962; Heirs of the Conqueror, 1965; Heraldry, Ancestry and Titles, Questions and Answers, 1965; The Story of Surnames, 1965; After Their Blood, 1966; Tradition and Custom in Modern Britain, 1967; The Genealogist's Encyclopedia (USA and UK), 1969; The Story of Titles, 1969; International Heraldry, 1970. *Recreations:* reading, walking, gardening, badminton, archery, motoring; contributes articles to press. *Address:* Bodiam, High Street, Petworth, Sussex. *T:* 3112. *Clubs:* Royal Air Force, Press, Wig and Pen; Midhurst and Petworth Rotary (Sec.).

**PINEAU, Christian Paul Francis,** Officier Légion d'Honneur; Compagnon de la Libération; Croix de Guerre (French), Médaille de la Résistance (Rosette); French Statesman and Writer; *b* Chaumont (Haute-Marne), 14 Oct. 1904; *m* 1962, Mlle Blanche Bloys; one *d* (and five *s* one *d* of previous marriages). Minister of Food and Supplies, June-Nov. 1945; General Rapporteur to Budget Commission 1945-46; Chm. Nat. Assembly Finance Commn, 1946-47; Minister of Public Works, Transport, and Tourism (Schuman Cabinet), 1947-48, also (Marie Cabinet) July-Aug. 1948, also (Queuille Cabinet), Sept. 1948, also (Bidault Cabinet), Oct. 1949; Minister of Finance and Economic Affairs (Schuman Cabinet), Aug. 1946; Chm. Nat. Defence Credits Control Commn, 1951-55; Designated Premier, Feb. 1955; Minister for Foreign Affairs, Feb. 1956-June 1957. Holds GCMG (Hon.) Great Britain, and numerous other foreign decorations. *Publications: books for children:* Contes de je ne sais quand; Plume et le saumon; L'Ourse aux pattons verts; Cornerousse le Mystérieux; Histoires de la forêt de Bercé; La Planète aux enfants perdus; La Marelle et le ballon; La Bête à bêtises; *other publications;* The SNCF and French Transport; Mon cher député; La simple verité; L'escalier des ombres; economic and financial articles; contrib. to various papers. *Address:* 55 rue Vaneau, Paris 7e.

**PING, Aubrey Charles,** MInstT 1955; International Transport Consultant, Central Engineering Co. Ltd, since 1951; 1951; Director, HTS Management Holdings and HTS Management Consultants, since 1970; *b* 2 Dec. 1905; *s* of Thomas Walton Ping, Middleton Cheney, Oxon, and Hester Louisa (*née* Barden), Banbury, Oxon; *m* 1936, Constance, 2nd *d* of John and Rose Bryant, Finchley; three *s*. *Educ:* Manor Lane LCC School; Brockley County School. Railway clerk and official, 1922-43; various hon. Trade Union offices, 1926-43; broadcasting to French Transport Workers, 1941-43. Served War of 1939-45, Captain, Allied Commission, Italy, 1944; Major Exec. Officer and Chief Operations Branch, Allied Commission, Italy, 1945, Lt-Col Asst Director, Rome European Central Inland Transport Organisation, 1946; special purposes asst to Continental Supt,

British Rlys (Southern), 1947; Lecturer, International Transport, Southern Railway Training College, 1947-49. Director, Cyprus Airways, 1953-58. MInst Traffic Adminstration, 1953. Chairman: Air Terminals Ltd, 1958-69; British Air Services Ltd, 1966-69; Dep. Chm., BEA Helicopters Ltd, 1967-70. Director: Gibraltar Airways, 1952-70; Jersey Airlines Development Corporation, 1961; Cambrian Airways, 1963-69; Schreiner BEA Helicopters NV, 1968-70. BKS Air Transport, 1964-69. Mem. Bd, BEA, 1949-70; Chm. Jt Council for Civil Aviation, 1956. Dep. Chm., Airways Housing Trust, 1965-70; Chm. BEA Housing Assoc. and BEA Silver Wing Club, 1957-69. *Recreations:* reading, gardening, writing. *Address:* 903 London Road, Loudwater, Bucks. *Club:* Special Forces.

**PINK, Ven. Hubert Arthur Stanley,** MA; Archdeacon of Hampstead since 1964; Rector of St Andrew Undershaft since 1965; Examining Chaplain to the Bishop of London since 1964; *b* 22 Jan. 1905; *s* of Arthur Penrhyn Stanley and Edith Mary Pink. *Educ:* Ipswich Sch.; Selwyn Coll., Cambridge; Westcott House Theological Coll. Asst Master, Ipswich Sch., 1927-33; Chaplain, 1931-33; Asst-Curate: S Augustine, Ipswich, 1928-31; Whittlesford, 1933-35; Vicar of Canvey Island, 1935-38; Rector of Little Ilford, 1938-46; Dir of Religious Educn, Dio. Chelmsford, 1945-47; Gen. Sec., Nat. Soc. for Religious Educn, and Sec., C of E Sch. Council, 1947-51; Rector of Hackney, 1951-65; Prebendary of St Paul's, 1963-64. *Recreations:* walking, reading, scouting. *Address:* 35 Fox Lane, N13 4AD.

**PINK, Ralph Bonner,** CBE 1961; VRD 1951; MP (C) Portsmouth South since 1966; *b* 30 Sept. 1912; *s* of Frank Pink and Helen Mary (*née* Mumby); *m* 1939, Marguerite Nora Bannar-Martin; one *s* one *d*. *Educ:* Oundle School. Portsmouth City Council, 1948-; Lord Mayor of Portsmouth, 1961-62; JP for City of Portsmouth, 1950. Knight of Order of Dannebrog (Denmark). *Recreation:* yachting. *Address:* East Hill, Fareham, Hants. *Clubs:* Carlton, St Stephen's; Royal Albert Yacht (Portsmouth); Emsworth Sailing.

**PINKER, Rev. Martin Wallis,** OBE 1957; Chairman: Minister's Advisory Council (Canada) on Treatment of Offenders; Ontario Training Schools Advisory Board, 1958-63; (first) General Secretary, National Association of Discharged Prisoners' Aid Societies Inc., 1936-58; Director, Men's Division, Central After-Care Association, 1948-58; 2nd *s* of late Douglas Collyer Pinker and of Amelia Jane Wallis, Reading; *m* 1922, Lilian Hannah, *o d* of late Frederick and Betsy Eccles, Blackpool; one *s* one *d*. *Educ:* private study; Hartley Victoria Coll., Manchester. After training for business career, served European War, 1914-18, as Lieut Lancs Fus., India. Entered Primitive Methodist Ministry: ordained, 1922; served in London, Gravesend and Lymm (Cheshire) 1924-29; released from pastrol work, 1929, to become Organising Sec. of Discharged Prisoners' Aid Soc. at Strangeways Prison, Manchester. Mem. Jt Cttee to review work of Discharged Prisoners' Aid Socs (Maxwell Cttee), 1951; Internat. Prisoners' Aid Assoc. (Vice-Pres. 1951, Pres., 1954). Visited Germany at request of UN High Commn for Refugees, 1952. Has attended meetings of Congress of Correction, in USA and Canada; Founding Hon. Sec. Commonwealth Assoc. of Prisoners' Aid Societies. *Address:* Department of Correctional Services, Parliament Buildings, Toronto, Canada. *Club:* Empire (Canada).

**PINKERTON, Prof. John Henry McKnight;** Professor of Midwifery and Gynæcology, Queen's University, Belfast, since 1963; Gynæcologist, Royal Victoria Hospital, Belfast; Surgeon, Royal Maternity Hospital, Belfast; *b* 5 June 1920; *s* of late William R. and Eva Pinkerton; *m* 1947, Florence McKinstry, MB, BCh, BAO; four *s*. *Educ:* Royal Belfast Academical Institution; Queen's Univ., Belfast. Hyndman Univ. Entrance Scholar, 1939; MB, BCh, BAO Hons; Magrath Scholar in Obstetrics and Gynæcology, 1943. Active service in HM Ships as Surg.-Lt, RNVR, 1945-47. MD 1948; MRCOG 1949; FRCOG 1960: FZS 1960. Sen. Lectr in Obstetrics and Gynæcology, University Coll. of the West Indies, and Consultant Obstetrician and Gynæcologist to University Coll. Hosp. of the West Indies, 1953-59; Rockefeller Research Fellow at Harvard Medical Sch., 1956-57; Prof. of Obstetrics and Gynæcology, Univ. of London, at Queen Charlotte's and Chelsea Hosps and the Inst. of Obstetrics and Gynæcology, 1959-63; Obstetric Surgeon to Queen Charlotte's Hosp.; Surgeon to Chelsea Hosp. for Women. *Publications:* various papers on obstetrical and gynæcological subjects. *Address:* Department of Midwifery and Gynæcology, The Institute of Clinical Science, Grosvenor Road, Belfast BT12 6BJ. *T:* Belfast 40503.

**PINNELL, Leonard George,** CIE 1938; *b* 10 June 1896; *s* of Charles John Pinnell and Clara Matilda Wills; *m* 1924, Margaret Blake, *d* of Dr C. F. Coxwell; two *s*. *Educ:* City of London School; Balliol Coll., Oxford (Exhibitioner). Served European War, 1915-18, 10th Bedfordshire Regt, later Machine Gun Corps, Salonica; British Military Mission to USA (1917) and France; entered Indian Civil Service, 1920; served in Bengal, Survey and Settlement, Chief Manager Dacca Nawab Estate, and Districts; Private Sec. to the Governor, 1935; Sec. to the Governor, 1937-40 and 1945; Supervisor ICS Training, 1940-42; Acting PSV 1942; Dir Civil Supplies, Bengal, 1942; Comr Chittagong and Presidency Divs, 1943-44; Principal Officers' Training Course, 1944-45; Develt Comr and *ex officio* Addl Chief Sec., 1946; Chief Admin Officer Industrial and Commercial Finance Corp. Ltd, 1948-51; advisory mission to Greece, 1951; Domestic Bursar, St John's Coll., Oxford, 1953-60. *Address:* Little Chevremont, Woodham Road, Woking, Surrey. *T:* Woking 62858. *Club:* East India and Sports.

**PINNOCK, Frank Frewin,** CMG 1948; late Overseas Supplies Commissioner, Ministry of Food; *b* 28 Sept. 1902; *s* of Charles George and Florence Pinnock; *m* 1928, Rosalind Mary (*née* Scott); three *d*. *Educ:* City of London Sch. Formerly Director of several companies engaged in export and import of foodstuffs. Commissioned RAF, 1940; lent to Ministry of Food at Washington, 1941, and continued as Temporary Civil Servant until Oct. 1952. *Address:* The Small House, Lavant, Sussex.

**PINSENT, Gerald Hume Saverie,** CB 1949; CMG 1935; Comptroller-General, National Debt Office, 1946-51; *b* 25 May 1888; *s* of Ross and Alice Mary Pinsent; *m* 1st, 1915, Katharine Kentisbeare (*d* 1949), *d* of late Sir George Radford, MP; two *d*; 2nd, 1939, Margot (*d* 1950), *d* of Johann Georg von Bonin. *Educ:* King's Sch., Canterbury; Trinity Coll., Cambridge (Senior Scholar). BA 1910; MA 1912; 2nd Class Clerk in Treasury, 1911; Assistant Secretary, Treasury, 1931; Financial Adviser, HM Embassy, Berlin, 1932-39, HM Embassy, Washington, 1939-41; British Food Mission, Ottawa, 1942, 1943; Principal Assistant Secretary, Board of Trade, 1943.

Principal Assistant Secretary, Treasury, 1944. *Address:* The Flat, Litcham Hall, King's Lynn, Norfolk.
*See also Prof. Q. H. Gibson.*

**PINSENT, Roger Philip,** HM Consul-General, São Paulo, Brazil, since 1970; *b* 30 Dec. 1916; *s* of late Sidney Hume Pinsent; *m* 1941, Suzanne Smalley; one *s* two *d*. *Educ:* Downside Sch.; Lausanne, London and Grenoble Univs. London Univ. French Scholar, 1938; Prix Racine, 1939; BA Hons London, 1940. HM Forces, 1940-46; HM Diplomatic Service, May 1946; 1st Sec., HM Legation, Havana, 1948-50; HM Consul, Tangier, 1950-52; 1st Sec., HM Embassy, Madrid, 1952-53; FO, 1953-56; 1st Sec., Head of Chancery, HM Embassy, Lima (Chargé d'Affaires, 1958, 1959), 1956-59; Dep. Head of UK Delegation to the European Communities, Luxembourg, 1959-63; HM Ambassador to Nicaragua, 1963-67; Counsellor (Commercial), Ankara, 1967-70. *Recreations:* music, motoring, golf. *Address:* c/o Foreign and Commonwealth Office, King Charles Street, SW1. *T:* 01-839 8866. *Clubs:* St James'; Managua Cricket (Managua); Golf Club Grand Ducal, Luxembourg; Ankara Golf; San Fernando, Jockey (both São Paulo).

**PINSENT, Sir Roy,** 2nd Bt, *cr* 1938; *b* 22 July 1883; *e s* of Sir Richard Alfred Pinsent, 1st Bt, and Laura Proctor (*d* 1931), *d* of Thomas Ryland; *S* father, 1948; *m* 1918, Mary Tirzah (*d* 1951), *d* of Dr Edward Geoffrey Walls, Spilsby, Lincs; two *s* one *d*. *Educ:* Marlborough; University College, Oxford (BA). Admitted Solicitor, 1909; served European War, 1916-19, Lieut, RE. *Heir: s* Christopher Roy Pinsent [*b* 2 Aug. 1922; *m* 1951, Susan Mary, *d* of John Norton Scorer, Fotheringhay; one *s* two *d*]. *Address:* 5 St George's Square, SW1. *T:* 01-828 7282.

**PINTER, Harold,** CBE 1966; actor and playwright and director; *b* 10 Oct. 1930; *s* of J. Pinter; *m* 1956, Vivien Merchant, *qv*; one *s*. *Educ:* Hackney Downs Grammar Sch. Actor (mainly repertory), 1949-57. Shakespeare Prize, Hamburg, 1970. *Plays:* The Room, The Birthday Party (filmed, 1968), The Dumb Waiter, 1957; A Slight Ache, (radio) 1958, (stage) 1961; A Night Out (radio), A Night Out (television), The Caretaker (filmed, 1963), 1950; Night School (television), 1960; The Dwarfs (radio), 1960, (stage), 1963; The Collection (television), 1961, (stage), 1962; The Lover (television, stage), 1963 (Italia Prize for TV); Tea Party (television), 1964; The Homecoming, 1964; Landscape (radio), 1968, (stage), 1969; Silence (stage), 1969. *Screenplays:* The Caretaker, The Servant, 1962; The Pumpkin Eater, 1963; The Quiller Memorandum, 1966; Accident, 1967; The Birthday Party, 1968; The Go-Between, 1969; Langrishe Go-Down, 1970. *Publications:* The Caretaker, 1960; The Birthday Party, and other plays, 1960; A Slight Ache, 1961; The Collection, 1963; The Lover, 1963; The Homecoming, 1965; Tea Party, and, The Basement, 1967; Mac, 1968; Jt Editor, New Poems 1967, 1968; Landscape, and, Silence, 1969. *Recreations:* drinking and cricket. *Address:* 7 Hanover Terrace, NW1.

**PINTER, Mrs Harold;** *see* Merchant, Vivien.

**PIPER, David Towry,** CBE 1969; MA, FSA; FRSL; Director and Marlay Curator of the Fitzwilliam Museum, Cambridge, since 1967; Fellow of Christ's College, Cambridge, since 1967; *b* 21 July 1918; *s* of late Prof. S. H. Piper; *m* 1945, Anne Horatia Richmond; one *s* three *d*. *Educ:* Clifton Coll.; St Catharine's Coll., Cambridge. Served War of 1939-45: Indian Army (9th Jat Regt); Japanese prisoner-of-war, 1942-45. National Portrait Gallery: Asst-Keeper, 1946-64; Dir, Keeper and Sec., 1964-67. Slade Prof. of Fine Art, Oxford, 1966-67. Mem., Royal Fine Art Commn, 1970-. Trustee, Paul Mellon Foundn for British Art, 1969-70. *Publications:* The English Face, 1957; Catalogue of the 17th Century Portraits in the National Portrait Gallery, 1963; The Royal College of Physicians; Portraits (ed G. Wolstenholme), 1964; (ed) Enjoying Paintings, 1964; The Companion Guide to London, 1964; Shades, 1970; *novels* (*as Peter Towry*) *include:* It's Warm Inside, 1953; Trial by Battle, 1959. *Address:* c/o Fitzwilliam Museum, Trumpington Street, Cambridge. *T:* Cambridge 50023. *Club:* Athenæum.

**PIPER, John;** Painter and Writer; member of the Oxford Diocesan Advisory Committee since 1950; Royal Fine Art Commission since 1959; Trustee of the National Gallery since 1967; *b* 13 Dec. 1903; *s* of late C. A. Piper, Solicitor; *m* 1935, Mary Myfanwy Evans; two *s* two *d*. *Educ:* Epsom Coll.; Royal College of Art. Paintings, drawings, exhibited in London since 1925; Pictures bought by Tate Gallery, Contemporary Art Society, Victoria and Albert Museum, etc.; Series of watercolours of Windsor Castle commissioned by the Queen, 1941-42; windows for nave of Eton College Chapel commissioned 1958; windows and interior design, Nuffield College Chapel, Oxford, completed, 1961; window, Coventry Cathedral, completed, 1962; windows for King George VI Memorial Chapel, Windsor, 1969. Designed Tapestry for High Altar, Chichester Cathedral, 1966, and for Civic Hall, Newcastle upon Tyne. Designer for opera and ballet; a Trustee of Tate Gallery, 1946-53, 1954-61, 1968-; Arts council art panel, 1952-57. Hon. ARIBA, 1957; Hon. ARCA 1959; Hon. DLitt (Leicester), 1960, (Oxford) 1966. *Publications:* Wind in the Trees (poems), 1921; 'Shell Guide' to Oxfordshire, 1938; Brighton Aquantints, 1939; British Romantic Painters, 1942; Buildings and Prospects, 1949; (ed with John Betjeman) Buckinghamshire Architectural Guide, 1948; Berkshire Architectural Guide, 1949. *Relevant publication:* John Piper: Paintings, Drawings and Theatre Designs, 1932-54 (arr. S. John Woods), 1955. *Address:* Fawley Bottom Farmhouse, near Henley-on-Thames, Oxon.

**PIPER, Air Marshal Sir Tim, (Thomas William),** KBE 1968 (CBE 1958; OBE 1950); CB 1964; AFC 1941; *b* 11 Oct. 1911; *s* of late Thomas Edward Piper, Ackleton Hall, Worfield, Shropshire; *m* 1947, Betty Bedford, *d* of late William Bedford Mitchell, Irwin, Western Australia; no *c*. *Educ:* Trent College. Joined RAF, 1936; served War of 1939-45, in Bomber Command (UK); pow, 1941-45; OC, RAF Schwechat, Austria, 1946-47, Germany (Berlin Air Lift), 1948-49, Middle East, 1950-53; OC, RAF Dishforth, 1953-55; Group Captain, Plans, Transport Command, 1955-58; Director of Operational Requirements, Air Ministry, 1958-60; Chief of Staff, Near East Command, 1960-62; AOC No. 38 Group, RAF, 1962-64; Comdt, RAF Staff Coll., 1965-66; UK Mem., Permanent Military Deputies Group, Central Treaty Organisation, 1966-68; retd, 1968. Group Capt., 1953; Air Cdre, 1959; Air Vice-Marshal, 1960; Air Marshal, 1966; psa, 1947; jssc, 1950. *Recreations:* shooting, fishing. *Address:* Chirton Cottage, Chirton, Devizes, Wilts. *T:* Chirton 289. *Clubs:* United Service, Royal Air Force.

**PIPON, Vice-Admiral Sir James Murray,** KBE, *cr* 1937 (OBE 1919); CB 1935; CMG 1924; MVO 1921; Royal Navy, retired; *b* 25 Oct. 1882; *e s* of late Captain John P. Pipon, CB, CMG, RN; *m* 1921, Bertha Louisa Victoria,

2nd *d* of 1st Baron Roborough; one *s* two *d*. *Educ:* HMS Britannia. Comdr 1915; Captain 1920; Rear-Admiral, 1932; Naval Attaché to British Embassies at Paris, Brussels, etc., 1925-28; Chief of Staff to Commander-in-Chief, Plymouth, 1929-30; HMS Royal Sovereign, 1930-32; Commodore of RN Barracks, Devonport, 1932-34; Rear-Admiral in charge and Admiral Superintendent, HM Dockyard, Gibraltar, 1935-37; retired list, 1936; Senior British Naval Officer, Suez Canal, 1940-42; Flag Officer in charge Southampton, 1942-45. *Address:* Shepherds Crown, Compton Down, Winchester, Hants. *T:* Twyford (Hants) 3253. *Club:* United Service.

**PIPPARD, Professor (Alfred) Brian,** FRS 1956; Cavendish Professor of Physics, University of Cambridge, since 1971; President of Clare Hall, Cambridge, since 1966; *b* 7 Sept. 1920; *s* of late Prof. A. J. S. Pippard; *m* 1955, Charlotte Frances Dyer; three *d*. *Educ:* Clifton Coll.; Clare Coll., Cambridge. BA (Cantab) 1941, MA 1945. PhD 1949; ScD 1966. Scientific Officer, Radar Research and Development Establishment, Great Malvern, 1941-45; Stokes Student, Pembroke Coll., Cambridge, 1945-46; Demonstrator in Physics, University of Cambridge, 1946; Lecturer in Physics, 1950; Reader in Physics, 1959-60; John Humphrey Plummer Prof. of Physics, 1960-71. Visiting Prof., Institute for the Study of Metals, University of Chicago, 1955-56. Fellow of Clare Coll., Cambridge, 1947-66. Cherwell-Simon Memorial Lectr, Oxford, 1968-69. Hughes Medal of the Royal Soc., 1959; Holweck Medal, 1961; Dannie-Heineman Prize, 1969; Guthrie Prize, 1970. *Publications:* Elements of Classical Thermodynamics, 1957; Dynamics of Conduction Electrons, 1962; papers in Proc. Royal Soc., etc. *Recreation:* music. *Address:* Clare Hall, Cambridge.

**PIPPARD, Prof. Brian;** *see* Pippard, A. B.

**PIRATIN, Philip;** *b* 15 May 1907; *m* 1929, Celia Fund; one *s* two *d*. *Educ:* Davenant Foundation Sch., London, E1. Was a Member of Stepney Borough Council, 1937-49; MP (Com) Mile End Division of Stepney, 1945-50.

**PIRBHAI, Count Sir Eboo,** Kt 1952; OBE 1946; Director of Companies; *b* 25 July 1905; *m* 1925, Kulsambai; three *s* three *d*. *Educ:* Duke of Gloucester Sch., Nairobi. Representative of HH The Aga Khan in Africa. Member, Nairobi City Council, 1938-43. MLC Kenya, 1952-60; Member of various other official bodies; President Central Muslim Association; President Aga Khan Supreme Council, Africa. Given title of Count, created by HH The Aga Khan for Africa, 1954. Brilliant Star of Zanzibar, 1956. *Address:* PO Box 898, Nairobi, Kenya. *T:* 65049. *Clubs:* Reform, Lansdowne, Royal Commonwealth Society; Nairobi, Muthaiga (Kenya).

**PIRIE, Air Chief Marshal Sir George Clark,** KCB, *cr* 1951 (CB 1943); KBE, *cr* 1946 (CBE 1942); MC; DFC; LLD; Barrister-at-law; formerly RAF; *b* 28 July 1896; *m* 1926, Dora Kennedy; one *s* one *d*. Served European War, 1914-18; Deputy Director Operations, Air Ministry, 1936-37; Air Attaché, Washington, 1937-40; Middle East, 1941-43; Director-General Organisation, Air Ministry, 1943-45; Allied Air Commander-in-Chief, SE Asia, 1946-47; Inspector-General, RAF, 1948; Member, Air Council for Supply and Organisation, 1948-50; Head of Air Force Staff, British Joint Services Mission to US, 1950-51; retired RAF, 1951. Chairman, Air League of the British Empire, 1955-58. *Address:* 38 Albemarle, Wimbledon Parkside, SW19. *Clubs:* United Service, Royal Air Force.

**PIRIE, Group Captain Gordon Hamish,** CBE 1946; DL; JP; Alderman, City of Westminster, since 1963 (Councillor, 1949; Mayor, 1959-60; Leader of Council, 1961-69); *b* 10 Feb. 1918; *s* of Harold Victor Campbell Pirie and Irene Gordon Hogarth; *m* 1953, Margaret Joan Bomford; no *c*. *Educ:* Eton (scholar); RAF Coll., Cranwell. Permanent Commission, RAF, 1938. Served War of 1939-45: Dir of Ops, RNZAF, Atlantic and Pacific (despatches, CBE); retired as Group Captain, 1946. Comr No 1 (POW) Dist SJAB, 1960-69; Comdr St John Ambulance, London, 1969-. a Governor of Westminster Sch.; Vice-Pres., Engineering Industries Assoc., 1966-69; Mem., Council of Royal Albert Hall; a Trustee, RAF Museum; Vice-Chm., London Boroughs Assoc. DL, JP Co. of London. Liveryman, Worshipful Company of Girdlers. KStJ 1969. comdr, Legion of Honour, 1960. *Recreations:* motoring, bird-watching. *Address:* 7 Carysfort House, West Halkin Street, SW1. *T:* 01-235 1561; Cottage Row, Tarrant Gunville, Dorset. *T:* Tarrant Hinton 212. *Clubs:* Carlton, Royal Air Force; Royal Scottish Automobile (Glasgow).

**PIRIE, Sheriff Henry Ward;** Sheriff-Substitute of Lanarkshire and Glasgow since 1955; *b* 13 Feb. 1922; *o surv s* of late William Pirie, Merchant, Leith; *m* 1948, Jean Marion, *y d* of late Frank Jardine, sometime President of RCS of Edinburgh; four *s*. *Educ:* Watson's Coll., Edinburgh; Edinburgh Univ. MA 1944; LLB 1947. Served with Royal Scots; commnd Indian Army, 1944; Lieut, Bombay Grenadiers, 1944-46. Called to Scottish Bar, 1947. Sheriff-Substitute of Lanarkshire at Airdrie, 1954-55. OStJ 1967. *Recreations:* curling, golf, bridge. *Address:* Craigievar, Lenzie, Kirkintilloch, Dunbartonshire. *T:* Kirkintilloch 2494.

**PIRIE, Mrs John;** *see* Shaw, Anne Gillespie.

**PIRIE, Norman Wingate,** FRS 1949; Head of Biochemistry Department, Rothamsted Experimental Station, Harpenden, since 1947; *b* 1 July 1907; *yr s* of late Sir George Pirie, painter, Torrance, Stirlingshire; *m* 1931, Antoinette Patey; one *s*. *Educ:* Emmanuel Coll., Cambridge. Demonstrator in Biochemical Laboratory, Cambridge, 1932-40; Virus Physiologist, Rothamsted Experimental Station, Harpenden, 1940-46. Trades Union, ASTMS. Vice-Chm., Nat. Council for Civil Liberties; Mem., BBC Science Consultative Group. *Publications:* scientific papers on various aspects of Biochemistry but especially on separation and properties of macromolecules; articles on viruses, the origins of life, biochemical engineering, and the need for greatly extended research on food production and contraception. *Recreation:* politics. *Address:* Rothamsted Experimental Station, Harpenden, Herts. *T:* Harpenden 4671.

**PIRIE, Psyche;** Editor of Homes and Gardens (IPC Magazines), since 1968; *b* 6 Feb. 1918; *d* of late George Frederick Quarmby and of Mrs Dorothy Quarmby; *m* 1940, James Mansergh Pirie; one *d*. *Educ:* Kensington High Sch.; Chelsea Sch. of Art. Air Ministry, 1940-44. Teaching, Ealing Sch. of Art and Willesden Sch. of Art, 1944-46; Indep. Interior Designer, 1946-56; Furnishing Editor, Homes and Gardens, 1956-68. *Recreations:* conversation, cinema, theatre, junk shops; or doing absolutely nothing. *Address:* 9 Lansdowne Walk, W11. *T:* 01-727 5294.

**PIRIE-GORDON of Buthlaw, Christopher Martin,** CMG 1967; OBE 1949; HM Diplomatic Service, retired; *b* 28 Sept. 1911; *er s* late Harry Pirie-Gordon of Buthlaw, OBE, DSC, and Mabel Alicia, *d* of late George Earle Buckle, sometime Editor of The Times; unmarried; *S* father as 14th Laird of Buthlaw, 1969. *Educ:* Harrow; Magdalen Coll., Oxford. Palestine Admin Service, 1935; First Secretary and Consul, British Legation, Amman, 1946 (on secondment from Colonial Service); resigned, 1949; a Secretary to Order of St John of Jerusalem, 1950-51; entered Foreign Service, 1951; Asst Political Agent, Kuwait, 1952; Political Agent, Trucial States at Dubai, 1953; Eastern Dept, FO, 1955; Chargé d'Affaires, the Yemen, 1958; Consul, Innsbruck, 1960; Consul, Florence, and Consul-General, San Marino, 1963-70, retired 1970. CStJ 1967. *Recreations:* dining, wining and talking. *Address:* Polesacre, Lowfield Heath, Crawley, Sussex. *T:* Crawley 27697; Via Palestro 3, Florence, Italy. *T:* Florence 29.87.59. *Club:* Athenæum.

**PIRZADA, Syed Sharifuddin,** SPk; Attorney-General of Pakistan, 1965-66, and since 1968; *b* 12 June 1923; *s* of Syed Vilayat Ali Pirzada; *m* 1960; two *s* two *d. Educ:* University of Bombay. LLB 1945. Secretary, Provincial Muslim League, 1946; Managing Editor, Morning Herald, 1946; Prof., Sind Muslim Law Coll., 1947-55; Advocate: Bombay High Court, 1946; Sind Chief Court, 1947; West Pakistan High Court, 1955; Supreme Court of Pakistan, 1961; Senior Advocate Supreme Court of Pakistan; Foreign Minister of Pakistan, 1966-68. Represented Pakistan before International Tribunal on Rann of Kutch, 1965; Leader of Pakistan Delegations to Commonwealth Conf. and General Assembly of UN, 1966. Hon. Advisor, Constitutional Commn, 1960; Chairman, Pakistan Company Law Commn, 1961-62; Mem., Internat. River Cttee, 1961-; President: Pakistan Br., Internat. Law Assoc.; Karachi Bar Assoc., 1964; Pakistan Bar Council, 1966; Institute of International Affairs. Sitara-e-Pakistan, 1964. *Publications:* Evolution of Pakistan, 1963; Fundamental Rights and Constitutional Remedies in Pakistan. *Recreation:* bridge. *Address:* c/o Ministry of Foreign Affairs, Islamabad, Pakistan. *Clubs:* Sind (Karachi); Karachi Boat, Karachi Gymkhana.

**PISTON, Walter,** AB, Mus. Doc.; Professor of Music, Harvard University, 1944-Aug. 1960, retired; now Professor of Music Emeritus; *b* Rockland, Maine, USA, 20 Jan. 1894; *s* of Walter Piston and Leona Stover; *m* 1920, Kathryn Nason; no *c. Educ:* Harvard Univ., chiefly. Graduated Harvard Coll., 1924 (AB). Member faculty of music department at Harvard since 1926; John Knowles Paine Fellowship, 1924-26; studied in Paris with Nadia Boulanger; Guggenheim Fellowship; Member of American Academy of Arts and Letters and of American Academy of Arts and Sciences; numerous awards and commissions for compositions (Pulitzer prize, 1948, for Symphony No. 3); second Pulitzer prize, 1961, for Symphony No. 7; appointed to new Chair of Music at Harvard; Walter W. Naumberg Professor of Music, 1948. Hon. Doctor of Music, Harvard Univ., 1952. *Publications:* music: 8 Symphonies, 5 string quartets, ballet, orchestral works, various chamber music works, violin concerto, etc., all published, some recorded; books: Harmonic Analysis, 1933; Harmony, 1941; Counterpoint, 1947; Orchestration, 1955. *Address:* 127 Somerset Street, Belmont, Mass 02178, USA. *Club:* Harvard.

**PITBLADO, Sir David (Bruce),** KCB 1967 (CB 1955); CVO 1953; Second Permanent Secretary, Civil Service Department, since 1970; *b* 18 Aug. 1912; *o s* of Robert Bruce and Mary Jane Pitblado; *m* 1941, Edith, *yr d* of Captain J. T. and Mrs Rees Evans, Cardigan; one *s* one *d. Educ:* Strand Sch.; Emmanuel Coll., Cambridge; Middle Temple. Entered Dominions Office, 1935; Asst Private Secretary to Secretary of State, 1937-39; served in War Cabinet Office, 1942; transferred to Treasury, 1942; Under-Secretary, Treasury, 1949; Principal Private Secretary to the Prime Minister (Mr Clement Attlee, Mr Winston Churchill, and Sir Anthony Eden), 1951-56; Third Secretary, Treasury, 1960; Economic Minister and Head of UK Treasury Delegation, Washington, and Executive Dir for the UK, Internat. Monetary Fund and Internat. Bank for Reconstruction and Development, 1961-63; Deputy Sec., Ministry of Power, 1965-66, Permanent Sec., 1966-69, Permanent Sec. (Industry), Min. of Technology, 1969-70. *Address:* 23 Cadogan Street, SW3; Pengoitan, Borth, Cardiganshire. *Club:* Athenæum.

**PITCHFORD, Dr J. Watkins-;** *see* Watkins-Pitchford.

**PITCHFORTH, Harry;** Chief Executive, Metropolitan Water Board, since Oct. 1969; *b* 17 Jan. 1917; *s* of John William Pitchforth and Alice Hollas; *m* 1941, Edna May Blakebrough; one *s* one *d. Educ:* Heath Sch., Halifax; Queen's Coll., Oxford. 1st class Hons, School of Modern History, Oxford, 1939. Served War, 1940-45, Captain, RASC, and later Education Officer, 5 Guards Brigade. Ministry of Food, 1945; Principal Private Secretary, to Minister, Major G. Lloyd-George, 1952-54; seconded to National Coal Board, 1955-58; Ministry of Agriculture, Fisheries and Food: Regional Controller, 1957-61; Director of Establishments and Organisation, 1961-65; Under-Sec., HM Treasury, 1965-67; Controller of HM Stationery Office and the Queen's Printer of Acts of Parliament, 1967-69. *Recreations:* tennis, badminton, music. *Address:* 93 George V Avenue, Pinner, Middlesex. *T:* 01-863 1229. *Club:* Civil Service.

**PITCHFORTH, (Roland) Vivian,** RA 1953 (ARA 1942); ARCA (London); ARWS 1957; *b* 23 April 1895; *s* of Joseph Pitchforth, Wakefield; *m* 1932, Brenda Matthews. *Educ:* Wakefield Grammar Sch. Studied art at Wakefield and Leeds Schools of Art and Royal College of Art. Pictures in Public Collections: Tate Gallery, Aberdeen, Southport, Stoke, Preston, Rochdale, Salford, Bradford, Wakefield, Leeds, Liverpool, Manchester, Helsinki, Sydney Art Gallery, Australia, Hamilton Art Gallery, NZ; Night Transport in possession of Tate Gallery bought by Chantrey Bequest. One man exhibitions: Coolings, Lefevre, Redfern, Leicester and Wildenstein's Galleries, also in S Africa, 1946. Exhibited at New York Fair, Pittsburgh, Chicago, Canada, Australia, Warsaw, Brussels, Paris, Sweden, and most provincial Galleries in England. Official War Artist to Ministry of Information and later to the Admiralty. *Recreations:* sailing, billiards, chess. *Address:* Flat 17, 7 Elm Park Gardens, SW10. *Clubs:* Chelsea Arts, RA.

**PITMAN, Captain Charles Robert Senhouse,** CBE 1950; DSO 1917; MC; Indian Army (retired); Game Warden, Uganda Protectorate, 1925-May 1951; retired; Acting Game Warden, N Rhodesia (seconded for two years from Uganda), 1931-33; Member of Uganda Defence Force, 1940-44; OC Uganda Defence Force, 1941-44; seconded from Game

Department as Director, Security Intelligence, Uganda, 1941-46; *b* Bombay, 19 March 1890; *o s* of late C. E. Pitman, CIE; *m* 1924, Marjorie Fielding, *yr d* of late M. M. A. Duncan, Alpha, OFS. *Educ:* Royal Naval Sch., Eltham; Blundell's Sch., Tiverton; Royal Military Coll., Sandhurst (King's India Cadet). Gazetted to Indian Army as 2nd Lieut unattached, 1909; attached for one year to Royal Warwickshire Regt, 1st Bn; posted to 27th Punjabis, 1910; Lieut, 1911; Captain, 1915; served in Egypt, 1914-15; France, 1915; Mesopotamia, 1916-18 (wounded, despatches twice, MC, DSO); Palestine, 1918-20; resigned commn IA, 1921; Scientific Fellow, Zoological Soc. of London; Life Mem. and Vice-Pres. Fauna Preservation Soc.; Life Member: E Africa Natural History Soc.; Uganda Soc.; Nigerian Field Soc.; S African Ornithological Soc.; Wildfowl Trust; Wig and Pen Club; British Ornithologists' Union; British Ornithologists Club; Member: St George's (Hanover Square) Branch of British Legion; Officers' Assoc.; Royal Society of St George; Ornamental Pheasant Trust; Jersey Wildlife Preservation Trust; Royal Nat. Lifeboat Instn. *Publications:* A Game Warden among his Charges, 1931 (Penguin Edition, 1943); A Guide to the Snakes of Uganda, 1938; A Game Warden Takes Stock, 1942; Common Antelopes, 1956; contributor to: A New Dictionary of Birds, 1964, and to Oologist's Record, Bulletin, British Ornithologists' Club; Proc. Zoological Soc. of London; Uganda Journal, etc. *Recreation:* natural science. *Address:* c/o National Provincial Bank, Ltd, Exeter Bank Branch, 65 High Street, Exeter, Devon.

**PITMAN, Clement Fothergill,** MA; FMA 1952; Curator and Art Director, Nottingham Castle Museum and Art Gallery, Nottingham, 1929-59; *b* 1894; *er s* of late W. Hayward Pitman, one of HM's Lieutenants for City of London; *m* 1930, Nora Irene Greenwood (*d* 1966). *Educ:* privately; St JOhn's Coll., Oxford. Private Secretary to the Secretary of the War Trade Intelligence Department, 1919; Sometime Official Lecturer at the National Gallery; (University of London) Extension Lecturer on the History of European Art, 1926-30. Member of Nottingham University Court, 1948-59. *Publications:* Contributor to: Chambers's Encyclopædia, Vol. III, of The Concise Encyclopædia of Antiques; The Connoisseur. *Address:* Newhouse, St John's Road, Haywards Heath, Sussex. *T:* Haywards Heath 2186.

**PITMAN, Edwin James George,** BSc, MA, FAA; Emeritus Professor of Mathematics, University of Tasmania (Professor, 1926; retired, Dec. 1962); *b* Melbourne, 29 Oct. 1897; of English parents; *s* of late Edwin Edward Major Pitman and Ann Ungley Pitman; *m* 1932, Edith Elinor Josephine, *y d* of late William Nevin Tatlow Hurst; two *s* two *d*. *Educ:* South Melbourne Coll.; Ormond Coll., University of Melbourne. Enlisted Australian Imperial Forces, 1918; returned from abroad, 1919; BA with First Class Honours, Dixson scholarship and Wyselaskie scholarship in Mathematics; acting-Professor of Mathematics at Canterbury Coll., University of New Zealand, 1922-23; Tutor in Mathematics and Physics at Trinity Coll. and Ormond Coll., University of Melbourne, 1924-25; Visiting Prof. of Mathematical Statistics at Columbia Univ., NY, Univ. of N Carolina, and Princeton Univ., 1948-49; Visiting Prof. of Statistics: Stanford Univ., Stanford, California, 1957; Johns Hopkins Univ., Baltimore, 1963-64. Fellow, Inst. Math. Statistics, 1948; FAA 1954; Vice-Pres., 1960; Mem. International Statistical Institute, 1956; Pres., Australian Mathematical Soc., 1958-59; Hon. Fellow, Royal Statistical Soc., 1965; Hon. Life Mem. Statistical Soc. of Australia, 1966. *Address:* 301 Davey Street, Hobart, Tasmania 7000, Australia.

**PITMAN, Sir Hubert,** Kt 1961; OBE 1953; Member of Lloyd's since 1926; Chairman, H. Pitman & Co. Ltd, London, EC; *b* 19 Aug. 1901; *yr s* of W. H. Pitman, JP, sometime one of HM's Lieutenants for the City of London; unmarried. *Educ:* Repton. Member, Corporation of London, 1929-54; one of HM's Lieutenants for City of London, 1950-; Member LCC (Cities of London and Westminster), 1955-58; Alderman, 1954-63 (Sheriff, 1959-60) City of London. OStJ. Comdr Etoile Noire, France. *Recreation:* country. *Address:* 57 Porchester Terrace, W2. *T:* 01-262 6593; Danemore Park, Speldhurst, Kent. *T:* Speldhurst 29; 19 Leadenhall Street, EC3. *T:* 01-626 8070. *Club:* Carlton.

**PITMAN, Sir (Isaac) James,** KBE 1961; MA; Director: Boots Pure Drug Co. Ltd; Bovril Ltd; Equity & Law Life Assurance Society; Vice-Chairman (Chairman, Finance) of Committee of Management of University of London Institute of Education; Charter Pro-Chancellor, Bath University of Technology; Vice-President: British and Foreign School Society; British Association for Commercial and Industrial Education; National Association for Business Education; Member, National Union of Teachers; Chairman, Royal Society of Teachers Educational Trust, since 1949 (Chairman, Royal Society of Teachers, 1948-49). Proponent of Initial Teaching Alphabet, and its designer, for the better teaching of reading, also Member Committee of University of London Institute of Education and of National Foundation for Educational Research, conducting comparative researches into reasons for reading failure in earliest stages of learning; President, Simplified Spelling Society; Member Committee advising Public Trustee under Will of late George Bernard Shaw in carrying out his wishes for design and publication of a Proposed British Alphabet; *b* London, 14 Aug. 1901; *e s* of late Ernest Pitman; *gs* of late Sir Isaac Pitman; *m* 1927, Hon. Margaret Beaufort Lawson-Johnston (Order of Mercy), 2nd *d* of 1st Baron Luke of Pavenham; three *s* one *d*. *Educ:* Eton; Christ Church, Oxford, 2nd Class Hons Mod. Hist. Played Rugby football for Oxford v Cambridge, 1921, for England v Scotland, 1922; ran for Oxford v Cambridge, 1922; skied for Oxford v Cambridge, 1922; won Middle Weight Public Schools Boxing, 1919. Bursar, Duke of York's and King's Camp, 1933-39. Chairman, Sir Isaac Pitman and Sons Ltd, 1934-66. RAF 1940-43, Acting Sqdn Leader; Director of Bank of England, 1941-45; HM Treasury, Director of Organisation and Methods, 1943-45. MP (C) Bath, 1945-64. Hon. Pres., Parly Group for World Govt; Pres., Institute of Office Management, 1965-69. Hon. DLitt Hum Hofstra, NY; Hon. DLit: Strathclyde; Bath. *Address:* (office) 154 Southampton Row, WC1. *T:* 01-837 1608; 58 Chelsea Park Gardens, SW3. *T:* 01-352 7004; Holme Wood, Chisbridge X, Marlow, Bucks. *T:* Lane End 260. *Clubs:* Carlton; Harlequins, Achilles, Ski Club of Great Britain.

**PITT, Barrie (William Edward);** author and editor of military histories; *b* Galway, 7 July 1918; *y s* of John Pitt and Ethel May Pitt (*née* Pennell); *m* 1st, 1943, Phyllis Kate (*née* Edwards); one *s*; 2nd, 1953, Sonia Deirdre (*née* Hoskins). *Educ:* Portsmouth Southern Grammar Sch. Bank Clerk, 1935. Served War of 1939-45, in Army. Surveyor, 1946. Began writing, 1954. Information Officer, Atomic Energy Authority, 1961; Historical Consultant to BBC Series, The Great War, 1963; Editor, Purnell's History of the Second World War, 1964; Editor-in-Chief, Ballantine's Illustrated History of World War 2, 1967 (US Book Series); Editor, Purnell's History of the First World War, 1969. *Publications:* The Edge of Battle, 1958; Zeebrugge, St George's Day, 1918, 1958; Coronel and Falkland, 1960; 1918 The Last Act, 1962. Contrib. to: Encyclopaedia Britannica; The Sunday Times. *Recreations:* golf, travel. *Address:* Flat 4, Red Roofs, Bath Road, Taplow, Maidenhead, Berks. *T:* Maidenhead 32430. *Club:* Savage.

**PITT, Dr David Thomas,** MB, ChB Edinburgh, DCH London; JP; Member, for Hackney, Greater London Council (Dep. Chm., 1969-70) since 1964 (LCC 1961); Deputy Chairman, Community Relations Commission, since 1967; General Practitioner, London, since 1947; *b* St David's, Grenada, WI, 3 Oct. 1913; *m* 1943, Dorothy Elaine Alleyne; one *s* two *d*. *Educ:* St David's RC Sch., Grenada, WI; Grenada Boys' Secondary Sch.; Edinburgh Univ. First Junior Pres., Student Rep. Council, Edinburgh Univ., 1936-37. Dist Med. Officer, St Vincent, WI, 1938-39; Ho. Phys., San Fernando Hosp., Trinidad, 1939-41; GP, San Fernando, 1941-47; Mem. of San Fernando BC, 1941-47; Dep. Mayor, San Fernando, 1946-47; Pres., West Indian Nat. Party (Trinidad), 1945-47. Mem. Nat. Cttee for Commonwealth Immigrants, 1965-67; Chm., Campaign Against Racial Discrimination, 1965. JP 1966. Contested (Lab) Clapham (Wandsworth), 1970. *Recreations:* reading, watching television, watching cricket, listening to music, theatre. *Address:* 6 Heath Drive, NW3. *T:* 01-435 7532. *Clubs:* West Indian, Royal Commonwealth Society.

**PITT, Mgr George Edward,** CBE 1965; Parish Priest, St Joseph's, Wroughton, Wilts, since 1969; *b* 10 Oct. 1916; *s* of Francis Pitt and Anna Christina Oviedo. *Educ:* St Brendan's Coll., Bristol; Ven. English College, Rome. Priest, 1939; worked in Diocese of Clifton, 1940-43; joined Royal Navy as Chaplain, 1943; Principal Roman Catholic Chaplain, RN, 1963-69. Nominated a Domestic Prelate, 1963. *Recreation:* music. *Address:* 14 Wharf Road, Wroughton, Wilts. *T:* 330. *Club:* Army and Navy.

**PITT, Prof. Harry Raymond,** FRS 1957; BA, PhD; Vice-Chancellor, Reading University, since 1964; *b* 3 June 1914; *s* of H. Pitt; *m* 1940, Clemency Catherine, *d* of H. C. E. Jacoby, MIEE; four *s*. *Educ:* King Edward's Sch., Stourbridge; Peterhouse, Cambridge. Bye-Fellow, Peterhouse, Cambridge, 1936-39; Choate Memorial Fellow, Harvard Univ., 1937-38; Univ. of Aberdeen, 1939-42. Air Min. and Min. of Aircraft Production, 1942-45. Prof. of Mathematics, Queen's Univ., Belfast, 1945-50; Deputy Vice-Chancellor, Univ. of Nottingham, 1959-62; Prof. of Pure Mathematics, Univ. of Nottingham, 1950-64. Visiting Prof., Yale Univ., 1962-63. Hon. LLD, Aberdeen and Nottingham. *Publications:* Tauberian Theorems, 1957; Measure, Integration and Probability, 1963; mathematical papers in scientific journals. *Address:* The University, Reading, Berks.

**PITT, Colonel Robert Brindley,** CBE 1938; MC; TD; JP, DL; formerly Managing Director of Stothert and Pitt, Ltd, Engineers, Bath; *b* 18 April 1888; *m* 1920, Norah Helen Jacomb-Hood; three *s* one *d*. *Educ:* Rugby Sch.; Clare Coll., Cambridge. Served European War, France, Salonika and Russia, 1914-19. MIMechE. *Recreation:* farming. *Address:* 14 Royal Crescent, Bath. *Clubs:* Junior Carlton; Bath and County (Bath).

**PITT-RIVERS, Mrs Rosalind Venetia,** FRS 1954; Member of Scientific Staff, National Institute for Medical Research, London, NW7; *b* 4 March 1907; *d* of late Hon. Anthony Morton Henley, CMG, DSO, and of Hon. Sylvia Laura Henley (*née* Stanley); *m* 1931, Captain George Henry Lane Fox Pitt-Rivers (*d* 1966); one *s*. *Educ:* Notting Hill High Sch.; Bedford Coll., University of London. MSc London 1931; PhD London, 1939. *Address:* 23a Lyndhurst Road, Hampstead, NW3.

**PITTER, Ruth;** Poetess; *b* Ilford, Essex, 7 Nov. 1897; *d* of George Pitter, Elementary Schoolmaster. *Educ:* Elementary Sch.; Coborn Sch., Bow, E. Heinemann Foundation Award, 1954; Queen's Medal for Poetry, 1955. *Publications:* First Poems, 1920; First and Second Poems, 1927; Persephone in Hades (privately printed), 1931; A Mad Lady's Garland, 1934; A Trophy of Arms, 1936 (Hawthornden Prize, 1937); The Spirit Watches, 1939; The Rude Potato, 1941; The Bridge, 1945; Pitter on Cats, 1946; Urania, 1951; The Ermine, 1953; Still By Choice, 1966; Poems 1926-66, 1968. *Recreation:* gardening. *Address:* 71 Chilton Road, Long Crendon, near Aylesbury, Bucks. *T:* Long Crendon 373.

**PITTS, Sir Cyril (Alfred),** Kt 1968; General Manager, Overseas, of ICI Ltd, since 1968; *b* 21 March 1916; *m* 1942, Barbara; two *s* one *d*. *Educ:* St Olave's; Jesus Coll., Cambridge. Chairman of ICI Companies in India, 1964-68; President, Bengal Chamber of Commerce and Industry, 1967-68; President, Associated Chambers of Commerce and Industry of India, 1967-68. *Address:* 11 Queensmead, St John's Wood Park, NW8. *T:* 01-586 0871. *Clubs:* Oriental, Bengal (Calcutta).

**PITTS, William Ewart,** CBE 1963; Chief Constable, Derbyshire County Police, since 1953; *b* 18 Sept. 1900; *s* of William Pitts and Albenia Elizabeth (*née* Nicholls), Swansea; *m* 1923, Doris, *d* of Herbert Whiteley, Wakefield, Yorks; one *d*. *Educ:* Rowsley, Derbyshire. Served European War, Royal Navy, 1914-18. Liverpool City Police: Constable to Chief Superintendent, 1919-49; Bootle County Borough Police, Chief Constable, 1949-53. QPM 1956. *Recreations:* golf, fishing, swimming. *Address:* Coombs Road, Bakewell, Derbyshire. *T:* 2364.

**PITTS CRICK, R.;** *see* Crick, Ronald P.

**PITTS-TUCKER, Robert St John;** Secretary to Headmasters' Conference and Headmasters' Association since 1970; *b* 24 June 1909; *e s* of Walter Greame Pitts-Tucker, Solicitor, and Frances Elsie Wallace; *m* 1942, Joan Margery, *d* of Frank Furnivall, Civil Engineer, India, and Louisa Cameron Lees; three *s* one *d*. *Educ:* Haileybury (Schol.); Clare Coll., Cambrdige (Schol.). 1st cl. Class. Tripos, Pts I and II, 1930 and 1932. Asst Master, Shrewsbury Sch., 1932-44; Headmaster, Pocklington Sch., 1945-66; Dep. Sec. to HMC and HMA, 1966-69. Mem., House of Laity, Church Assembly, 1956-70; Diocesan Reader, York and St Albans; Mem., Ministry Cttee of ACCM; Mem., ER Yorks Educn Cttee, 1946-66; Vice-Chm., Yorks Rural Community Council, 1949-65; Mem., Secondary Schools Examination Council, 1954-57. *Publication:* (ed) Headmasters Association Review, 1966. *Recreations:* tennis, country walks, listening to music, gardening. *Address:* 29 Gordon Square, WC1. *T:* 01-387 4995. *Clubs:* Royal

Commonwealth Society, Hellenic Society; Union (Cambridge).

**PIXLEY, Norman Stewart,** CMG 1970; MBE 1941; VRD 1927; retired company director; Dean of the Consular Corps of Queensland since 1965; Hon. Consul for the Netherlands since 1948; *b* Brisbane, 3 May 1898; 2nd *s* of Arthur and Florence Pixley; *m* 1931, Grace Josephine, *d* of Arthur and Grace Spencer; twin *s* one *d*. *Educ:* Bowen House Sch.; Brisbane Grammar School. Served in RANR, 1913-46; Comdr, RANR, retd. Councillor, National Trust of Queensland; Pres., Qld Lawn Tennis Assoc., 1948-52; Pres., Brisbane Chamber of Commerce, 1952-53; Leader of Aust. Delegn to British Commonwealth Chambers of Commerce Conf., 1951; founded Qld Div. of Navy League, 1953 (Pres. until 1969). FRHistSoc Qld 1965 (Pres. 1968-). Kt, Order of Orange Nassau, 1964. *Publications:* papers on Australian history in Jl of Royal Hist. Soc. Qld, etc. *Recreations:* tennis, yachting, golf. *Address:* 147 Sherwood Road, Toowong, Brisbane, Queensland 4066, Australia. *T:* 701150. *Clubs:* Queensland, United Service, Royal Queensland Yacht Squadron, Tattersalls, Indooroopilly Golf (all Qld).

**PIZEY, Admiral Sir (Charles Thomas) Mark,** GBE 1957 (KBE 1953); CB 1942; DSO 1942; idc; RN retired; DL; *b* 1899; *s* of late Rev. C. E. Pizey, Mark and Huntspill, Somerset; *m* Phyllis, *d* of Alfred D'Angibau; two *d*. Served European War, 1914-18, Midshipman, Revenge, 1916-18; Lieut, 1920; HMS Danae Special Service Squadron World Cruise, 1921-22; Flag Lieut to Vice-Admiral Sir Howard Kelly, 2nd in command Mediterranean Fleet, 1929-30; Destroyer Commands Mediterranean and Home Fleets, 1930-39; War of 1939-45: Captain, 1939; Commanded HMS Ausonia, Atlantic Patrol and Convoys, 1939-40. Captain (D) 21st Destoyer Flotilla in HMS Campbell, Nore Command, Channel and North Sea Operations, 1940-42 (CB, DSO, despatches twice); commanded HMS Tyne and Chief Staff Officer to Rear-Admiral Destroyers, Home Fleet, Russian convoys, 1942-43 (bar to DSO); Director of Operations (Home) Admiralty Naval Staff, 1944-45; Chief of Staff to C-in-C Home Fleet, 1946; Imperial Defence Coll., 1947; Rear-Admiral, 1948; Chief of UK Services Liaison Staff, Australia, 1948-49; Flag Officer Commanding First Cruiser Squadron, 1950-51; Vice-Admiral, 1951; Chief of Naval Staff and Commander-in-Chief, Indian Navy, 1951-55; Admiral, 1954; Commander-in-Chief, Plymouth, 1955-58, retired. DL County of Somerset, 1962. *Address:* Abbots Barton, Seavington, Somerset. *Club:* United Service.

**PLACE, Rear-Adm. (Basil Charles) Godfrey,** VC 1944; CB 1970; DSC 1943; Personnel Director, Cunard Cargo Shipping, since 1970; *b* 19 July 1921; *s* of late Major C. G. M. Place, DSO, MC, and late Mrs Place; *m* 1943, Althea Annington, *d* of late Harry Tickler, Grimsby; one *s* two *d*. *Educ:* The Grange, Folkestone; RNC, Dartmouth. Midshipman, HMS Newcastle, 1939-40; 10th and 12th submarine flotillas, 1941-43; Lieut, 1942; HMS Cardigan Bay, 1946-48; staff of Flag Officer (Air) Home, 1950-51; Comdr, 1952; HMS Glory (801 Sqn), 1952-53; on Staff of Flag Officer, Flying Trng, 1953-55; Comdg HMS Tumult, 1955-56; Exec. Officer, HMS Theseus, 1956-57; Comdg HMS Corunna, 1957-58; Captain, 1958; Chief SO to Flag Officer Aircraft Carriers, 1958-60; Deputy Director of Air Warfare, 1960-62; Rothesay in command and Captain (D), 25th Escort Squadron, 1962-63; Commanding: HMS Ganges, 1963-65; HMS Albion, 1966-67; Adm. Comdg Reserves, and Dir-Gen., Naval Recruiting, 1968-70. Polish Cross of Valour, 1941. *Address:* 87 Bishop's Mansions, SW6; The Old Bakery, Corton Denham, Sherborne, Dorset. *Club:* Royal Commonwealth Society.

**PLAIDY, Jean;** *see* Hibbert, Eleanor.

**PLAMENATZ, John Petrov,** FBA 1962; Chichele Professor of Social and Political Theory, University of Oxford, since 1967; Official Fellow of Nuffield College, Oxford, 1951-67; *b* Cetinje, Montenegro, 16 May 1912; *s* of Peter Plamenatz and Ljubica Matanovitch; came to England, 1919; *m* 1943, Marjorie Hunter; no *c*. *Educ:* Clayesmore Sch.; Oriel Coll., Oxford Univ. MA 1937. University Lecturer in Social and Political Theory, Oxford, 1950-67. Fellow of All Souls Coll., Oxford, 1936-51, and 1967-. *Publications:* Consent, Freedom and Political Obligation, 1938; English Utilitarians, 1950; Revolutionary Movement in France, 1815-71, 1952; From Marx to Stalin, 1953; German Marxism and Russian Communism, 1954; On Alien Rule and Self-Government, 1960; Man and Society, Vols I and II, 1963; contributions to Political Studies, British Journal of Sociology, American Political Science Review, etc. *Recreation:* walking. *Address:* All Souls College, Oxford; Scotland Mount, Hook Norton, Banbury, Oxon.

**PLANT, Sir Arnold,** Kt 1947; Economist; Emeritus Professor; *b* London, 29 April 1898; 2nd *s* of late William C. Plant, FLA; *m* 1925, Edith Render, BA, London; two *s*. *Educ:* Strand Sch.; London School of Economics, University of London. Gerstenberg Scholar in Economics and Political Science, 1921; Bachelor of Commerce, 1922; BSc (Econ.), 1923; previously in engineering; Professor of Commerce and Dean of the Faculty of Commerce in the University of Cape Town, 1924-30 (Hon. LLD, 1968); Professor of Commerce in the University of London, at London School of Economics, 1930-65 (Hon. Fellow, 1967). Member: Council, Royal Economic Society; Cinematograph Films Council, 1938-69; Chairman: Industrial Injuries Advisory Council, 1955-67; Advertising Standards Authority, 1962-65; Colonial Social Science Research Council, 1955-62; Member, Overseas Research Council, 1959-64; Organiser for Ministry of Information, and first Director of Wartime Social Survey, 1940; Chairman, National Service Deferment Cttee for the Cinematograph Industry, Ministry of Labour, 1942-45; temporary civil servant, 1940-46 as Adviser to Ministerial Chairman of Interdepartmental Materials Cttee and Central Priority Cttee under Production Council (1940), Production Executive (1941), Min. of Production (1942-45), and on special duties in Cabinet Office, 1945-46; Member: BoT Cttee on a Central Institute of Management, 1945-46; Min. of Works Cttee on Distribution of Building Materials, 1946; Min. of Education Cttee on Commercial Education, 1946; Board of Trade Cttee on Film Distribution, 1949 (Chm.); Monopolies and Restrictive Practices Commission, 1953-56; Chm., Min. of Agriculture Cttee on Fowl Pest Policy, 1960-62. *Publications:* contributor to: London Essays in Economics in honour of Edwin Cannan, 1927; Tariffs: the Case Examined, 1931; Cambridge History of British Empire (South Africa Volume, 1936); Some Modern Business Problems (editor), 1937; The Population Problem, 1938; the scientific economic journals. *Address:* 19 Wildwood Road, NW11. *T:* 01-455 2863. *Club:* Reform.

**PLANT, Cyril Thomas Howe,** OBE 1965; General Secretary, Inland Revenue Staff Federation, since 1960; *b* Leek, Staffs, 27 Aug. 1910; *s* of late Sidney Plant and late Rose Edna Plant; *m* 1931, Gladys Mayers; two *s* one *d*. *Educ:* Leek High School. Entered Post Office, 1927; Inland Revenue, 1934; Asst Sec., Inland Revenue Staff Fedn, 1944; Chm. of Post Office and Civil Service Sanatorium Soc., 1950-; Mem. General Council TUC, 1964 (Mem. Economic, Internat. Cttees TUC, Adviser to UK Workers' Deleg. ILO, 1965-); UK Workers' Mem. of ILO Governing Body, Nov. 1969-; Chm. of Governors, Ruskin Coll., Oxford, 1967-; Treas., London Trades Council, 1952-; Mem., Civil Service Nat. Whitley Council, 1948-; Mem., Inland Revenue Departmental Whitley Council, 1938- (Chm. 1958-); Treas., Workers' Educational Assoc., 1969-. *Recreations:* horse racing, international activity. *Address:* Longridge, 19 Montacute Road, Lewes, Sussex. *T:* Lewes 2556. *Club:* English-Speaking Union.

**PLASKETT, Harry Hemley,** FRS 1936; MA (Oxon); Savilian Professor of Astronomy, Oxford, 1932-60, now Emeritus; *b* Toronto, 5 July 1893; *s* of John Stanley Plaskett, Victoria; *m* 1921, Edith Alice, *d* of John James Smith, barrister, Ottawa; one *s* one *d*. *Educ:* Ottawa Collegiate; Toronto Univ. (BA). Served CFA, France, 1917-18; Astronomer, Dominion Astrophysical Observatory, Victoria, 1919-27; Professor of Astrophysics, Harvard, 1928-32. Served anti-aircraft battery, 1939-40, and worked on experimental navigation for MAP, 1940-44 inc. Gold Medal, Royal Astronomical Society, 1963. Hon. LLD St Andrews, 1961. *Publications:* Papers on observational astrophysics in various journals and observatory publications. *Address:* 48 Blenheim Drive, Oxford OX2 8DQ.

**PLATNAUER, Maurice,** BLitt, MA; Hon. Fellow of Brasenose College, Oxford, since 1960; Hon. Fellow of New College since 1957; *b* 18 June 1887; *s* of Henry Maurice Platnauer and Marian Platnauer (*née* Wilson); unmarried. *Educ:* Shrewsbury Sch.; New Coll., Oxford. Assistant Master, Winchester Coll., 1910-15 amd 1919-22. Fellow of Brasenose Coll., 1922, Vice-Principal, 1936-56, Principal, 1956-60. Editor of Classical Quarterly, 1936-47. *Publications:* Septimus Severus, 1918; Claudian (Loeb Translation), 1922; (ed) Euripides, Iphigenia in Tauris, 1938; Latin Elegaic Verse, 1951; (ed) Aristophanes, Peace, 1964; Contributions to The Mind of Rome, 1926; New Chapters in Greek Literature, 1933; Greek Poetry and Life, 1938; Some Oxford Compositions, 1949; More Oxford Compositions, 1964. (ed) 50 Years of Classical Scholarship, 1954; articles in Classical Review, Classical Quarterly, etc. *Recreations:* travel, books, and music. *Address:* Brasenose College, Oxford. *T:* 48641. *Club:* Oxford and Cambridge University.

**PLATT,** family name of **Baron Platt.**

**PLATT,** Baron, *cr* 1967 (Life Peer), of Grindleford; **Robert Platt,** 1st Bt, *cr* 1959; MSc (Manchester); MD (Sheffield); FRCP; Professor of Medicine, Manchester University, and Physician, Royal infirmary, Manchester, 1945-65; President of the Royal College of Physicians, 1957-62; *b* London, 16 April 1900; *s* of William Platt and Susan Jane Willis; *m* 1922, Margaret Irene Cannon, MB, ChB, DPM; one *s* two *d*. *Educ:* private schools; Sheffield Univ. Physician, Royal Infirmary, Sheffield, 1931-45; Lt-Col, 1941-44, Brig., 1944-45, RAMC. Editor Quarterly Jl of Medicine, 1948-58. Member: Medical Research Council, 1953-57; Central Health Services Council; Cttee of Hallé Concerts Soc., 1947-53; Council Royal Manchester Coll. of Music; Medical Research Soc.; Chm., Clinical Research Board of Medical Research Council, 1964-67; Member: Medical Advisory Board, RAF; Royal Commn on Medical Educn, 1965; Hon. Mem. Assoc. of Physicians; Vice-Pres., Imperial Cancer Research Fund; Vice-Pres., British Assoc. Adv. Science, 1962; Chm., Manchester Chamber Concerts Soc., 1952-65; Membre d'honneur de la Société de Pathologie Rénale; Hon. Mem., Assoc. of American Physicians; Hon. Fellow, American Coll. of Physicians; Hon. Fellow, Royal Coll. of Gen. Practitioners; Hon. FRACP; Membre correspondant étranger, Soc. Méd. des Hôpitaux de Paris; Hon. Freeman, Worshipful Co. of Barbers; Hon. Fellow, Manchester Medical Soc.; Hon. FRSocMed; Fellow-Commoner, Christ's Coll., Cambridge; President: Eugenics Soc., 1965-68; Family Planning Assoc., 1968. Lumleian Lectr, RCP, London, 1952; Doyne memorial Lectr, Oxford, 1956; Watson Smith Lectr, RCP Edinburgh, 1958; Galton Lectr, London, 1961; Lilly Lectr, Amer. Coll. Physicians, 1961; Linacre Lectr, St John's Coll., Cambridge, 1963; Oslerian Orator, 1963; Rock Carling Fellow, 1963; Arthur Hall Lectr, Sheffield, 1965; Wiltshire Lectr, London, 1965; Harveian Orator, RCP, 1967. Hon. LLD: Sheffield, 1959; Belfast, 1959; Manchester, 1969; Hon. MD Bristol, 1959. *Publications:* Nephritis and Allied Diseases, 1934. Numerous papers to Quarterly Journal of Med., Clinical Science, etc., mostly on renal disease and genetics. *Recreation:* String Quartet playing ('cello). *Heir:* (to father's Btcy) *s* Hon. Peter Platt, Prof. of Music at Otago Univ., NZ [*b* 6 July 1924; *m* 1948, Jean Halliday Brentnall; one *s* two *d*]. *Address:* 53 Heathside, Hinchley Wood, Esher, Surrey. *Club:* Athenæum.

**PLATT, Sir Harry,** 1st Bt, *cr* 1958; Kt 1948; MD (Victoria), MS (London), FRCS; Hon. FACS; Hon. FRCS (Canada); Hon. FRCSE; Hon. FDS; President, National Fund for Research into Crippling Diseases, sing 1970; Past President, International Federation of Surgical Colleges (1958-66); President: Royal College of Surgeons, 1954-57; Central Council for the Disabled, 1969; Emeritus Professor of Orthopædic Surgery, University of Manchester; Surgical Director Ethel Hedley Hospital, Windermere; Hon. President, Société Internationale de Chirurgie Orthopédique et de Traumatologie; formerly Consultant Adviser: Ministry of Health, 1940-63; Ministry of Labour, 1952-64; Member: Central Health Services Council, 1948-57; Council English-Speaking Union; The Pilgrims; *b* Thornham, Lancashire, 7 Oct. 1886; *e s* of Ernest Platt; *m* 1916, Gertrude Sarah, 2nd *d* of Richard Turney; one *s* four *d*. *Educ:* Victoria Univ. of Manchester. University Gold Medal. MB, BS (London), 1909; Gold Medal for thesis MD (Vic), 1921; Hunterian Prof. of Surgery and Pathology, RCS, 1921; post-graduate study in USA, 1913-14 (Boston, New York, etc.); Pres. (1934-35) British Orthopædic Association; Captain RAMC (TF), 1915-19; Surgeon in charge of Special Military Surgical Centre (Orthopædic Hospital), Manchester. Hon. Degrees: DM, University of Berne, 1954; Dr, Univ. of Paris, 1966; LLD: Univs of Manchester, 1955, Liverpool, 1955, Belfast, 1955, Leeds, 1965. *Publications:* Monographs and articles on orthopædic surgery, medical education, hospital organisation, etc. *Recreations:* music, travel. *Heir:* *s* F(rank) Lindsey Platt, Barrister-at-Law [*b* 16 Jan. 1919; *m* 1951, Johanna Laenger]. *Address:* 14 Rusholme Gardens, Platt Lane, Manchester 14; 11 Lorne Street, Manchester 13. *T:* 061-273 3433, 061-

224 2427. *Clubs:* Travellers', Royal Automobile; St James's (Manchester).

**PLATT, James Westlake,** CBE 1965; *b* 13 June 1897; *s* of Rev. W. T. Platt, Auckland, NZ; *m* 1927, Veronica Norma Hope Arnold; four *s*. *Educ:* Auckland Grammar School; Balliol College, Oxford. Joined Royal Dutch/Shell Gp of Oil Cos, 1922; served in China and Argentine, 1922-45; Managing Director, Eagle Oil & Shipping Co., 1945-49; a Managing Director, Royal Dutch/Shell Group, 1949-57; Member, Drogheda Cttee on British Inf. Services Overseas, 1952-53; Chairman: Salaries Commission, Hong Kong Government, 1959; UK Advisory Council on Education for Management, 1960-67; Foundn for Management Educn, 1960-68; OECD. Internat. Gp to examine Develt of Management Studies in Europe, 1961-68; Governor, School of Oriental and African Studies, 1962-68. Hon. Fellow, Balliol Coll., 1963-. Hon. DSc, City Univ., 1969. *Address:* Anneville Lodge, Archirondel, Gorey, Jersey, CI. *T:* Jersey East 782. *Clubs:* Brooks's, Oxford and Cambridge University.

**PLATT, Kenneth Harry,** CBE 1966 (MBE 1944); Secretary, Institution of Mechanical Engineers, since 1961; *b* 14 March 1909; *m* 1956, Janet Heather Walters; one *d*. *Educ:* Shrewsbury School; Glasgow Univ. (BSc in Mech. Eng.). Lecturer, School of Mines, Treforest, 1936-38; Prof. of Mech. Engineering, Benares, India, 1938-39. War Service, RAOC and REME (Major), 1939-45. HM Inspectorate of Schools, 1946-48; Educn and Personnel Manager, Brush Elec. Eng. Co. Ltd, 1949-52; Instn of Mechanical Engineers, 1952-; Dep. Secretary, 1955. *Address:* 14 Riverside Road, Staines, Mddx. *T:* Staines 52101. *Clubs:* Royal Automobile, St Stephen's.

**PLATT, Gen. Sir William,** GBE, *cr* 1943; KCB, *cr* 1941 (CB 1939); DSO 1908; *b* 14 June 1885; *s* of late John Platt and Margaret Oudney Graham, 74 Whitehall Court, SW1; *m* 1921, Mollie Dendy *yr d* of late Dendy Watney; two *s*. *Educ:* Marlborough College; RMC Sandhurst. Entered Northumberland Fusiliers, 1905; Captain, 1914; Major, 1924; Lieut-Col, 1930; Col 1933; Maj.-Gen., 1938; Lt-Gen., 1941; General, 1943; served NW Frontier, India, 1908 (despatches, DSO); European War, 1914-18 (despatches, Bt Major, Bt Lt-Col on promotion to substantive rank of Major); commanded 2nd Bn Wiltshire Regt, 1930-33; General Staff Officer, 1st Grade, 3rd Division, Bulford, 1933-34; Commander 7th Infantry Brigade, 1934-38; ADC to the King, 1937-38. Commanded Troops in the Sudan and Commandant Sudan Defence Force, 1938-41; GOC-in-C East African Command, 1941-45; retd pay, 1945. Col, The Wiltshire Regiment, 1942-54. *Address:* 61/Fifteen, Portman Square, W1. *Club:* Athenæum.

**PLATT, Rev. William James;** General Secretary, British and Foreign Bible Society, 1948-60; Consultant, 1960-61; retired, 1961; *b* 2 May 1893; *s* of James and Mary Platt; *m* 1921, Hilda Waterhouse; one *d*. *Educ:* Rivington Grammar School; Didsbury Theological College, Manchester. Methodist Missionary in West Africa, 1916-30; Chairman and General Superintendent, Methodist District of French West Africa, 1925-30; joined Bible Society Staff as Secretary for Equatorial Africa, 1930; since 1948 has travelled extensively as General Secretary of Bible Society. Chairman of Council, United Bible Societies, 1954-57. Hon. DD, Knox College, Toronto, Canada, 1954. Officer of the Order of Orange Nassau, 1954; Commander, National Order of the Ivory Coast Republic, 1964. *Publications:* An African Prophet; From Fetish to Faith; Whose World?; Three Women in Central Asia; articles in religious and missionary publications. *Address:* Fraryhurst, 94 Downs Court Road, Purley, Surrey. *T:* 01-660 1041. *Club:* Royal Commonwealth Society.

**PLATTS-MILLS, John Faithful Fortescue,** QC 1964; Barrister-at-Law; *b* 4 Oct. 1906; *s* of John F. W. Mills and Dr Daisy Platts-Mills, Karori, Wellington, NZ; *m* 1936, Janet Katherine Cree; six *s*. *Educ:* Nelson College and Victoria University, NZ; Balliol College, Oxford (Rhodes Scholar). LLM (NZ), MA, BCL Oxon. MP (Lab) Finsbury, 1945-48, (Ind Lab) 1948-50. Pilot Officer, RAF, 1940; "Bevin Boy", 1944; collier, 1945. *Address:* Cloisters, Temple, EC4. *T:* 01-353 9333; New House, Uckfield, Sussex. *T:* Buxted 3238.

**PLAXTON, Ven. Cecil Andrew;** Archdeacon of Wiltshire; *b* 1902; *s* of Rev. J. W. Plaxton, Wells and Langport, Somerset; *m* 1929, Eleanor Joan Elisabeth Sowerby; one *s* one *d*. *Educ:* Magdalen College School, Oxford; St Edmund Hall, Oxford; Cuddesdon Theological College. BA 1924, MA 1928, Oxford; Deacon, 1926; Priest, 1927; Curate of Chard, 1926-28; Curate of St Martin, Salisbury, 1928-32; Vicar of Southbroom, Wilts, 1932-37; Vicar of Holy Trinity, Weymouth, 1937-51; Rural Dean of Weymouth, 1941-51; Rector of Pewsey, 1951-65; Canon of Salisbury and Prebend of Netheravon, 1949. Officiating Chaplain to the Forces, 1932-51. *Recreations:* archæology and travelling, music. *Address:* St Edmund's Way, Potterne Road, Devizes, Wilts. *T:* Devizes 3391.

**PLAYER, Denis Sydney,** CBE 1967; Chairman, Newall Engineering Group, since 1962 (Deputy Chairman, 1955); Chairman, Newall Machine Tool Co. Ltd, since 1964; *b* 13 Nov. 1913; *s* of Sydney Player and Minnie Emma Rowe; *m* 1940, Phyllis Ethel Holmes Brown; three *d*. *Educ:* England; Worcester Acad., Mass. Apprenticed to Newall Engrg Co. Ltd, 1930; spent a year with Federal Produce Corp., RI, before rejoining Newall Engrg on Sales side; Man. Dir, Optical Measuring Tools, 1940; formed Sales Div. for whole of Newall Engrg Gp, 1945. Joined Royal Artillery, 1939; invalided out, 1940. CEng, MIProdE. High Sheriff of Rutland, 1970-71. *Recreations:* yachting, vintage cars, fishing, shooting. *Address:* North Luffenham Hall, near Oakham, Rutland. *T:* North Luffenham 239. *Clubs:* Royal Automobile, Royal Thames Yacht, Royal Ocean Racing; Royal Scottish Automobile (Glasgow).

**PLAYFAIR, Sir Edward Wilder,** KCB 1957 (CB 1949); Director: National Westminster Bank Ltd; Glaxo Group Ltd; Tunnel Cement Ltd; Equity and Law Life Assurance Society Ltd; *b* 17 May 1909; *s* of late Dr Ernest Playfair *m* 1941, Dr Mary Lois Rae; three *d*. *Educ:* Eton; King's Coll. Cambridge. Inland Revenue, 1931-34; HM Treasury, 1934-46 and 1947-56 (Control Office for Germany and Austria, 1946-47); Permanent Under-Secretary of State for War, 1956-59; Permanent Sec., Ministry of Defence, 1960-61. Chairman, International Computers and Tabulators Ltd, 1961-65. Gov., Imperial Coll. of Science and Technology, 1958-; College Cttee of UCL, 1961- (Hon. Fellow, UCL, 1969); Trustee: The Observer Editorial Trust; National Gallery. *Address:* 12 The Vale, SW3. *T:* 01-352 4671. *Club:* Brooks's.

**PLAYFAIR, Maj.-Gen. Ian Stanley Ord,** CB 1943; DSO 1918; MC; *b* 10 Apr. 1894; *s* of late Col F. H. G. Playfair, Hampshire Regt; *m* 1930, Jocelyn, *o d* of Col L. N. Malan, OBE;

two *s. Educ:* Cheltenham College. Served European War, 1914-18 (despatches, MC and Bar, DSO); General Staff Officer, 2nd Grade, Staff College, Quetta, 1934-37; at Imperial Defence College, 1938; Commandant, Army Gas School, 1939; Director of Plans, War Office, 1940-41; Maj.-Gen. GS 11th Army Group, SE Asia Comd, 1943; retired pay, 1947. *Publication:* (official history) The Mediterranean and Middle East 1939-42: vol. 1, 1954; vol. 2, 1956; vol. 3, 1960; vol. 4, 1966. *Address:* 6 Park Road, Hythe, Kent.

**PLAYFAIR, Air Marshal Sir Patrick Henry Lyon,** KBE, *cr* 1940; CB 1931; CVO 1935; MC; *b* Edinburgh, 22 Nov. 1889; *s* of late John Playfair, MD, FRCPE; *m* 1937, Kate, *y d* of late Hayward James Strudwick; one adopted *s. Educ:* Cheltenham Coll.; Royal Military Acad., Woolwich. Entered RFA, 1910; seconded RFC (Military Wing), 1912; served European War in RFC and RAF; Air Officer Commanding No. 1 (Bomber) Group RAF, Abingdon, 1938-39; commanded Advanced Air Striking Force in France, 1939-40; AOC-in-C, India, 1940-42; retired list, 1942. DSM (USA); Legion of Honour (France). *Address:* St Mary's House, 56 Whiting Street, Bury St Edmunds, Suffolk. *Club:* Army and Navy.

**PLAYFORD, Hon. Sir Thomas,** GCMG 1957; MP, South Australia since 1933; Premier, Treasurer and Minister of Immigration of S Australia, Nov. 1938-March 1965; Minister of Industry and Employment, 1946-53; Leader of the Opposition, 1965-66; *b* 5 July 1896; *o s* of T. Playford, Norton's Summit, SA; *gs* of late Hon. T. Playford, sometime Premier of S Australia; *m* 1928, Lorna Beaman, *e d* of F. S. Clark; one *s* two *d. Educ:* Norton Summit Public School. Engaged in primary production (fruit grower); served European War 27th Bn AIF obtaining a Commission; entered SA Parliament, 1933, as one of representatives for District of Murray; elected as representative for Gumeracha District, 1938; Member of Liberal Country Party; Commissioner of Crown Lands, Minister of Repatriation and Irrigation, March 1938; succeeded Hon. R. L. Butler as Leader of Liberal Country Party, 1938. *Recreation:* horticulture. *Address:* House of Assembly, Parliament House, Adelaide, South Australia. *T:* 51-3241.

**PLEASENCE, Donald;** Actor; *b* 5 Oct. 1919; *s* of late Thomas Stanley and of Alice Pleasence; *m* 1st, 1940, Miriam Raymond; two *d*; 2nd, 1959, Josephine Crombie (marr. diss. 1970); two *d*; 3rd, 1970, Meira Shore; one *d. Educ:* The Grammar School, Ecclesfield, Yorkshire. Made first stage appearance at the Playhouse Theatre, Jersey, CI, May 1939; first London appearance, Twelfth Night, Arts Theatre, 1942. Served with RAF, 1942-46 (Flt Lieut); shot down and taken prisoner, 1944. Returned to stage in The Brothers Karamazov, Lyric, Hammersmith, 1946; Huis Clos, Arts Theatre; Birmingham Repertory Theatre, 1948-50; Bristol Old Vic, 1951; Right Side Up, and Saint's Day, Arts Theatre, 1951; Ziegfeld Theatre, New York (with L. Olivier Co.), 1951; played in own play, Ebb Tide, Edinburgh Festival and Royal Court Theatre, 1952; Stratford-on-Avon season, 1953. *Other London Appearances:* Hobson's Choice, 1952; Antony and Cleopatra, 1953; The Rules of the Game, 1955; The Lark, 1956; Misalliance, 1957; Restless Heart, 1960; The Caretaker, London, 1960, New York, 1961; Poor Bitos, London and New York; The Man in the Glass Booth, St Martin's, 1967 (London Variety Award for Stage Actor of the Year, 1968), New York, 1968-69. Many television appearances. Named Actor of the Year, 1958. *Films include:* The Beachcomber, Heart of a Child, Manuela, The Great Escape, Doctor Crippen, The Caretaker, The Greatest Story Ever Told, The Hallelujah Trail, Fantastic Voyage, Cul-de-Sac, The Night of the Generals, Eye of the Devil, Will Penny, The Mad Woman of Chaillot, Sleep is Lovely, Arthur! Arthur?; THX 1138; Wake in Fright; Soldier Blue. *Recreations:* boats, cars, very bad golf. *Address:* Strand on the Green, W14. *Clubs:* Royal Automobile, Pickwick.

**PLEASS, Sir Clement (John),** KCMG, *cr* 1955 (CMG 1950); KCVO 1956; KBE, *cr* 1953; MA; retired as Governor; *b* 19 November 1901; *s* of J. W. A. Pleass, Tiverton, Devon; *m* 1927, Sybil, *d* of Alwyn Child, Gerrard's Cross; one *s. Educ:* Royal Masonic School; Selwyn College, Cambridge. Joined Colonial Administrative Service, Jan. 1924; served in Nigeria, 1924-56. Lieut-Governor, 1952-54, Governor, 1954-56, Eastern Region of Nigeria, Mem., Colonial Development Corporation, 1957-. *Recreation:* golf. *Address:* Higher Barton, Malborough, near Kingsbridge, S Devon. *Club:* Royal Commonwealth Society.

**PLENDERLEITH, Harold James,** CBE 1959; MC 1918; BSc, PhD, Hon. LLD (St Andrews); FRSE; FSA; FMA; Director, International Centre for the Study of the Preservation and Restoration of Cultural Property (created by UNESCO), 1959-71; Keeper, Research Laboratory, British Museum, WC1, 1949-59; Member of Hon. Scientific Advisory Cttee, Nat. Gallery, since 1935; Chairman, 1944-58; Vice-Pres. of International Institute for the Conservation of Museum Objects, 1958 (Pres., 1965-67); Member, Directory Board of Museum Laboratories Cttee, International Council of Museums; *b* 19 Sept. 1898; *s* of Robert James Plenderleith, FEIS; *m* 1926, Elizabeth K. S. Smyth. *Educ:* Dundee Harris Acad.; St Andrews Univ. Professor of Chemistry, Royal Academy of Arts, London, 1936-58. Hon. Treas. Internat. Inst. for Conservation of Museum Objects, 1950-58. Rhind Lecturer (Edinburgh) 1954. Gold Medal, Society of Antiquaries of London, 1964. *Publications:* The Preservation of Antiquities, 1934; The Conservation of Prints, Drawings and Manuscripts, 1937; The Preservation of Leather Bookbindings, 1946; The Conservation of Antiquities and Works of Art, 1956: papers on allied subjects and on technical examinations of museum specimens in museum and scientific journals. *Recreations:* art and music. *Address:* 256 Via Cavour, 00184, Rome, Italy. *Club:* Athenæum.

**PLENDERLEITH, Thomas Donald,** RE 1961 (ARE 1951); Senior Art Master, St Nicholas Grammar School, Northwood, since 1956; *b* 11 March 1921; *s* of James Plenderleith and Georgina Ellis; *m* 1949, Joyce Rogers; one *s. Educ:* St Clement Danes; Ealing Sch. of Art; Hornsey Sch. of Art. Pilot, Bomber Command, RAF, 1941-46. Art Master, Pinner County Grammar Sch., 1948-56. Art Teacher's Diploma, 1947. *Recreations:* cricket, badminton. *Address:* 46 Sylvia Avenue, Hatch End, Mddx. *T:* 01-428 5019.

**PLEVEN, René Jean;** French Statesman; Compagnon de la Libération, 1943; Commandeur du Mérite Maritime, 1945; Député des Côtes-du-Nord since 1945; Minister of Justice, since 1969; Président du Conseil Général des Côtes-du-Nord, 1949; *b* 15 April 1901; *s* of Colonel Jules Pleven; *m* 1924, Anne Bompard (*d* 1966); two *d. Educ:* Faculté de Droit de Paris (LLD); Ecole Libre des Sciences Politiques. Company Director. Deputy chief of French Air Mission to USA, 1939. French National Committee and Comité

Français de Libération Nationale (Finances, Colonies, Foreign Affairs), 1941-44; Minister: of Colonies (Provisional Government), 1944; of Finances, 1944-46; of Defence, Nov. 1949 and 1952-54; Président du Conseil, July 1950, Aug. 1951-Jan. 1952; Vice-Président du Conseil, Feb. 1951; Minister of Foreign Affairs, 1958. Délégué à l'Assemblée parlementaire européenne, and Chm., Liberal Gp of this Assembly, 1956-69. Grand Officer Order of Leopold, 1945; Grand Croix Le Million d'éléphants, 1949; Grand Cross Etoile Polaire, 1950; Grand Cross: Orange-Nassau, 1950; Dannebrog, 1950; Nicham Alaouite, 1950; Vietnam, 1951. *Publications:* Les Ouvriers de l'agriculture anglaise depuis la guerre, 1925; Avenir de la Bretagne, 1962. *Recreation:* fishing. *Address:* 12 rue Chateaubriand, Dinan (Côtes-du-Nord), France.

**PLEYDELL-BOUVERIE,** family name of **Earl of Radnor.**

**PLIATZKY, Leo;** Under-Secretary, HM Treasury since 1967; *b* 1919; *m* 1948, Marian Jean Elias; one *s* one *d. Educ:* Manchester Grammar Sch.; City of London Sch.; Corpus Christi Coll., Oxford. First Cl. Classical Honour Mods, 1939. Served in RAOC and REME, 1940-45 (despatches). First Cl. Philosophy, Politics and Economics, 1946. Research Sec., Fabian Soc., 1946-47; Min. of Food, 1947-50; HM Treasury, 1950-. *Address:* 181 Dollis Hill Lane, NW2. *T:* 01-452 6037; 76 Pier Avenue, Southwold, Suffolk.

**PLIMMER, Sir Clifford (Ulric),** KBE 1967; Chairman: New Zealand Breweries Ltd; DRG(NZ) Ltd; Hay's-Wright Stephenson Ltd; *b* 25 July 1905; *s* of late Arthur Bloomfield Plimmer and Jessie Elizabeth (*née* Townsend); *m* 1935, Letha May (*née* Port); three *s* (and one *s* decd). *Educ:* Scots Coll., Wellington; Victoria Univ. of Wellington. Office Junior, 1922, Wright, Stephenson & Co. Ltd (stock and station agents, woolbrokers, gen. merchants, manufrs, car dealers, insurance agents, etc). Director: Cable Price Downer Ltd; New Zealand Breweries Ltd; Dunlop (NZ) Ltd and other NZ cos. Owns and operates a number of sheep and cattle farms in New Zealand. *Address:* 4 Massey Avenue, Lower Hutt, New Zealand. *T:* 63-590. *Clubs:* Wellington (Wellington); Northern, Wellesley (Auckland); Hutt, Hastings (NZ).

**PLIMSOLL, Sir James,** Kt 1962; CBE 1956; Australian Ambassador to the USA, since 1970; *b* Sydney, New South Wales, 25 April 1917; *s* of late James E. and Jessie Plimsoll; unmarried. *Educ:* Sydney High School; University of Sydney. Economic Department, Bank of New South Wales, 1938-42; Australian Army, 1942-47. Australian Delegation, Far Eastern Commission, 1945-48; Australian Representative, United Nations Commission for the Unification and Rehabilitation of Korea, 1950-52; Assistant Secretary, Department of External Affairs, Canberra, 1953-59; Australian Permanent Representative at the United Nations, 1959-63; Australian High Commissioner to India and Ambassador to Nepal, 1963-65; Secretary of Dept of External Affairs, Australia, 1965-70. *Address:* Australian Embassy, 1601 Massachusetts Avenue, NW, Washington, DC 20036, USA.

**PLOMER, William Charles Franklyn,** CBE 1968; FRSL; Writer; *b* 10 Dec. 1903. Served at Admiralty, 1940-45. President: The Poetry Society, 1968-; The Kilvert Society, 1968-. Hon. DLitt Durham. Queen's Gold Medal for Poetry, 1963. *Publications:* Turbott Wolfe, 1926; I Speak of Africa, 1927; Paper Houses, 1929; Sado, 1931; The Fivefold Screen, 1932; The Case is Altered, 1932; Cecil Rhodes, 1933; The Child of Queen Victoria, 1933; The Invaders, 1934; Ali the Lion, 1936; Visiting the Caves, 1936; (ed) Japanese Lady in Europe, by Haruko Ichikawa, 1937; (ed) Kilvert's Diary, 1938-40; Selected Poems, 1940; Double Lives, 1943; The Dorking Thigh, 1945; (ed) Curious Relations, by William D'Arfey, 1945; Four Countries, 1949; Museum Pieces, 1952; (with Benjamin Britten) Gloriana, 1953; A Shot in the Park, 1955; At Home, 1958; Collected Poems, 1960; (ed) A Message in Code, the Diary of Richard Rumbold, 1932-61, 1964; (with Benjamin Britten) Curlew River, 1964; (with Benjamin Britten) The Burning Fiery Furnace, 1966; Taste and Remember, 1966; (with Benjamin Britten) The Prodigal Son, 1968. *Address:* c/o Jonathan Cape, 30 Bedford Square, WC1.

**PLOURDE, Most Rev. Joseph Aurèle;** *see* Ottawa, Archbishop of, (RC).

**PLOW, Maj.-Gen. the Hon. Edward Chester,** CBE 1945; DSO 1944; CD 1950; DCL; Canadian Army (Retired); Director, Canadian Imperial Bank of Commerce, since 1963; *b* St Albans, Vermont, 28 September 1904; *s* of late John Plow and Hortense Harlow Plow (*née* Locklin); *m* 1937, Mary Nichols, *d* of late Thomas E. G. Lynch and M. Edith Lynch (*née* Nichols), Digby, NS; one *d. Educ:* Montreal schools; RMC Kingston. Commnd in RCHA, 1925; served in Canada and UK until 1939. Served War of 1939-45 (despatches twice): Italy and NW Europe; Artillery Staff Officer and Comdr; during latter part of War was Senior Artillery Officer, Canadian Army. Following the War served in various appts in Germany, Canada and the UK, and was GOC Eastern Command, Canada, 1950-58. Lieut-Governor of the Province of Nova Scotia, 1958-63. KStJ; Comdr, Order of Orange Nassau (Netherlands). Anglican. *Address:* Silver Birches, Oakfield, Halifax County, Nova Scotia, Canada. *Clubs:* Halifax; Oakfield Golf and Country; Saraguay.

**PLOWDEN,** family name of **Baron Plowden.**

**PLOWDEN,** Baron, *cr* 1959, of Plowden (Life Peer); **Edwin Noel Plowden,** KCB 1951; KBE 1946; Chairman of Tube Investments Ltd, since 1963; Director: Commercial Union Assurance Co. Ltd; National Westminster Bank Ltd; Chairman: Governing Body and Council, London Graduate School of Business Studies; Standing Advisory Committee on Pay of Higher Civil Service; Member, Civil Service College Advisory Council; Hon. Fellow, Pembroke College, Cambridge, 1958; *b* 6 Jan. 1907; 4th *s* of late Roger H. Plowden; *m* 1933, Bridget Horatia (*see* Lady Plowden); two *s* two *d. Educ:* Switzerland; Pembroke College, Cambridge. Temporary Civil Servant Ministry of Economic Warfare, 1939-40; Ministry of Aircraft Production, 1940-46; Chief Executive, 1945-46; Member of Aircraft Supply Council; Vice-Chairman Temporary Council Cttee of NATO, 1951-52; Chief Planning Officer and Chairman of Economic Planning Board, 1947-53. Adviser on Atomic Energy Organization, 1953-54; Chairman, Atomic Energy Authority, 1954-59; Visiting Fellow, Nuffield College, 1956-64; Chm. Cttee of Enquiry: Treasury control of Public Expenditure, 1959-61; organisation of Representational Services Overseas, 1963-64; Aircraft Industry, 1964-65. Hon. DSc Pennsylvania State Univ., 1958. *Address:* Martels Manor, Dunmow, Essex. *T:* Great Dunmow 2141; 7 Cottesmore Gardens, W8. *T:* 01-937 4238. *Club:* Brooks's.

**PLOWDEN, Lady, (Bridget Horatia),** JP; Co-opted Member, Education Committee, Inner London Education Authority, since 1967; Director, Trust Houses Forte Ltd; Chairman: Delves House Ltd; Working Ladies Guild; Professional Classes Aid Council; National Council for the Education of Gypsies and other Travellers; Chairman of Governors: Philippa Fawcett College of Education; Robert Montefiore Comprehensive School; President, Harding Housing Association; 2nd *d* of late Admiral Sir H. W. Richmond, KCB, and of Lady Richmond (Elsa, *née* Bell); *m* 1933, Baron Plowden, *qv*; two *s* two *d*. *Educ:* Downe House. Chairman, Central Advisory Council for Education (England) 1963-66; Vice-Chm., ILEA Schools Sub-Cttee, 1967-70. jp inner London Area Juvenile Panel, 1962-. Hon. LLD: Leicester, 1968; Reading, 1970. *Address:* Martels Manor, Dunmow, Essex. *T:* Great Dunmow, 2141; 7 Cottesmore Gardens, W8. *T:* 01-937 4238.

**PLOWMAN, Hon. Sir (John) Anthony,** Kt 1961; **Hon. Mr Justice Plowman;** Judge of the High Court of Justice (Chancery Division), since 1961; *b* 27 Dec. 1905; *e s* of late John Tharp Plowman (solicitor); *m* 1933, Vernon, 3rd *d* of late A. O. Graham, Versailles; three *d*. *Educ:* Highgate School; Gonville and Caius Coll., Cambridge. Solicitors Final (John Mackrell Prize), 1927; LLB London, 1927; LLB Cantab (1st Cl.), 1929; LLM Cantab 1956. Called to Bar, Lincoln's Inn, 1931 (Tancred and Cholmeley studentships; Buchanan Prize); QC 1954; Bencher of Lincoln's Inn, 1961. Served, 1940-45, Squadron-Leader, RAF. Member of General Council of the Bar, 1956-60. *Address:* Royal Courts of Justice, Strand, WC2; (home) Lane End, Bucks. *T:* Lane End 322. *Club:* Athenæum.

**PLOWRIGHT, Joan Ann, (Lady Olivier),** CBE 1970; Leading actress with the National Theatre since 1963; Member of the RADA Council; *b* 28 Oct. 1929; *d* of William Ernest Plowright and Daisy Margaret (*née* Burton); *m* 1st, 1953, Roger Gage (marr. diss.); 2nd, 1961, Sir Laurence Olivier, *qv*; one *s* two *d*. *Educ:* Scunthorpe Grammar School; Laban Art of Movement Studio; Old Vic Theatre School. First stage appearance in If Four Walls Told, Croydon Rep. Theatre, 1948; Bristol Old Vic and Mem. Old Vic Co., S Africa tour, 1952; first London appearance in The Duenna, Westminster, 1954; Moby Dick, Duke of York's, 1955; season of leading parts, Nottingham Playhouse, 1955-56; English Stage Co., Royal Court, 1956; The Crucible, Don Juan, The Death of Satan, Cards of Identity, The Good Woman of Setzuan, The Country Wife (transferred to Adelphi, 1957); The Chairs, The Making of Moo, Royal Court, 1957; The Entertainer, Palace, 1957; The Chairs, The Lesson, Phoenix, NY, 1958; The Entertainer, Royale, NY, 1958; The Chairs, The Lesson, Major Barbara, Royal Court, 1958; Hook, Line and Sinker, Piccadilly, 1958; Roots, Royal Court, Duke of York's, 1959; Rhinoceros, Royal Court, 1960; A Taste of Honey, Lyceum, NY, 1960 (Best Actress Tony Award); Chichester Festival: Uncle Vanya, The Chances, 1962; St Joan (Best Actress Evening Standard Award), Uncle Vanya, 1963; National Theatre: St Joan, Uncle Vanya, Hobson's Choice, opening season, 1963; The Master Builder, 1964; Much Ado About Nothing, 1967, 1968; Three Sisters, 1967, 1968; Tartuffe, 1967, 1968; The Advertisement, 1968; Love's Labour's Lost, 1968; The Merchant of Venice, 1970. Directed, Rites, 1969; produced, The Travails of Sancho Panza, 1969. *Films include:* Moby Dick, The Entertainer, Three Sisters. Appears on TV. *Recreations:* reading, music, entertaining. *Address:* c/o LOP Ltd, 8 Norfolk Street, WC2. *T:* 01-836 7932.

**PLUGGE, Capt. Leonard Frank,** BSc; FRAeS; FRAS; Politician, Scientist, Writer, Inventor, Painter and Sculptor; Hon. Colonel RE 29th (Kent) Cadet BN; *b* London; *o s* of Frank Plugge, Brighton; *m* Gertrude Ann, *o d* of Frederick Rowland, Muckleston, Kensington, and Muckleston, Shropshire; two *s* one *d*. *Educ:* at Dulwich; University Coll., London (BSc); Univ. of Brussels (Ingénieurs des Mines). Mem., Accademia di Belle Arti, Rome and Academy of Sciences, NY. Served European War, Lieut RNVR; Capt. RAF; Inter-Allied Aeronautical Commission of Control in Berlin; Aeronautical Delegate Spa Conference; Commission of Aeronautical Control, Paris; National Physical Laboratory, Teddington; Owens College, Manchester; Royal Aircraft Establishment, Farnborough; Imperial College of Science, South Kensington; Department of Scientific Research of Air Ministry; with Underground Railways Group of Companies; former MP (C) Chatham division of Rochester; Chairman Parliamentary Science Committee; Hon. Sec. Inter-Parliamentary Union; President International Broadcasting Club; Chairman, International Broadcasting Co., London, Imperial Broadcasting Corp., New York, and International Broadcasting Co., Toronto, Canada; created Army network, Radio International, first Radio programme for the British Expeditionary Forces in France. General Committee Radio Society of Great Britain; invented Radio two-way Telephone in Car, Television Glasses, Stereoscopic Cinematograph, Plugge Patent Auto Circuit; Member, Société Astronomique de France; Chevalier of the Légion d'Honneur; Commander of Dragon of Annam. *Publications:* Royal Aeronautical Society's Glossary of Aeronautical Terms (French Translation); Contributions on Travel and Radio to publications all over the world. *Recreations:* ice skating, yachting, yacht, MY Lennyann, Cannes; golf, tennis. *Address:* 15 Lowndes Square, SW1. *T:* 01-730 5523, 3545; Studio, Dolphin Square, SW1. *T:* 01-828 0680, 01-834 5115; The Wharf, Sutton-Courtenay. *T:* Sutton-Courtenay 47; 315 East 68 Street, New York. *T:* Rhinlander 4-7966. *Clubs:* Carlton, Authors', Royal Air Force, Royal Aero; Medway Yacht (Vice-Chairman).

**PLUMB, (Charles) Henry;** President of the National Farmers Union, since 1970; *b* 27 March 1925; *s* of Charles and Louise Plumb; *m* 1947, Marjorie Dorothy Dunn; one *s* two *d*. *Educ:* King Edward VI School, Nuneaton. National Farmers Union: Member Council, 1959; Vice-President, 1964, 1965; Deputy-President, 1966, 1967, 1968, 1969. Mem., Duke of Northumberland's Cttee of Enquiry on Foot and Mouth Disease, 1967-68; Vice-Pres. and Past Chm., Warwickshire County Fedn of Young Farmers' Clubs; Mem. Council, Animal Health Trust. FRSA 1970. *Recreations:* shooting, tennis. *Address:* Southfields Farm, Coleshill, Birmingham. *T:* Coleshill 63133; Agriculture House, Knightsbridge, SW1. *Club:* Farmers'; Coleshill Rotary (Hon. Member).

**PLUMB, John Harold;** FBA 1968; historian; Professor of Modern English History, University of Cambridge, since 1966; *b* 20 Aug. 1911; 3rd *s* of late James Plumb, Leicester. *Educ:* Alderman Newton's Sch., Leicester; University Coll., Leicester; Christ's Coll., Cambridge. BA London, 1st Class Hons History, 1933; PhD Cambridge, 1936; LittD Cambridge, 1957. Ehrman Research Fellow, King's Coll., Cambridge, 1939-46; FO, 1940-

45; Fellow of Christ's Coll., 1946-, Steward, 1948-50, Tutor, 1950-59. Vice-Master, 1964-68. Univ. Lectr in History, 1946-62; Reader in Modern English History, 1962-65; Chm. of History Faculty, 1966-68, Univ. of Cambridge. Trustee of National Portrait Gallery, 1961-; Syndic of the Fitzwilliam Museum, 1960-. FRHistS; FSA; FRSL 1969. Visiting Prof., Columbia Univ., 1960; Lectures: Ford's, Oxford Univ., 1965-66; Saposnekov, City College, NY, 1968; Guy Stanton Ford, Univ. of Minnesota, 1969. Hon. For. Mem., Amer. Acad. for Arts and Sciences, 1970. Hon. DLitt Leicester, 1968. Editor, History of Human Society, 1959-; European Advisory Editor to Horizon, 1959-. Historical Adviser, Penguin Books, 1960-. *Publications:* England in the Eighteenth Century, 1950; West African Explorers (with C. Howard), 1952; Chatham, 1953; (ed) Studies in Social History, 1955; Sir Robert Walpole, Vol. I, 1956, Vol. II, 1960; The First Four Georges, 1956; The Renaissance, 1961; Men and Places, 1962; Crisis in the Humanities, 1964; The Growth of Political Stability in England, 1675-1725, 1967; Death of the Past, 1969. *Contrib. to:* Man versus Society in Eighteenth Century Britain, 1968; Churchill Revised, 1969 (Churchill, The Historian). *Address:* Christ's College, Cambridge. *T:* 59601; The Old Rectory, Westhorpe, Stowmarket, Suffolk. *T:* Bacton 235. *Club:* Oxford and Cambridge University.

**PLUMBE, William John Conway;** HM Chief Inspector of Factories since 1967; *b* 17 Mar. 1910; *s* of Charles Conway Plumbe and Lilian Plumbe (*née* Lynham); *m* 1938, Margaret, *y d* of A. E. Paine, Sevenoaks; three *d*. *Educ:* King Edward VII, Sheffield; Sevenoaks School; Imperial College, London University. BSc, ACGI. Appointed HM Inspector of Factories, 1935. Service in HM Forces, 1943-46. HM Superintending Inspector of Factories, 1960-63; HM Deputy Chief Inspector of Factories, 1963-67. *Recreations:* gardening, country walking. *Address:* Culvennan, Hillydeal Rd, Otford, Kent. *T:* Otford 3517.

**PLUMLEY, Rev. Prof. Jack Martin;** Herbert Thompson Professor of Egyptology, University of Cambridge, since 1957; *b* 2 Sept. 1910; *e s* of Arthur Henry Plumley and Lily Plumley (*née* Martin); *m* 1938, Gwendolen Alice Darling; three *s*. *Educ:* Merchant Taylors' Sch., London; St John's Coll., Durham (BA, Univ. Hebrew Schol., MLitt); King's Coll., Cambridge (MA). Deacon 1933; Priest 1934; Curacies, 1933-41; Vicar of Christ Church, Hoxton, 1942-45, of St Paul's, Tottenham, 1945-47; Rector and Vicar of All Saints', Milton, Cambridge, 1948-57. Assoc. Lectr in Coptic, Univ. of Cambridge, 1949-57; Fellow Selwyn Coll., 1957. *Recreations:* music, rowing. *Address:* Selwyn College, Cambridge. *T:* 53570; 13 Lyndewode Road, Cambridge. *T:* 50328.

**PLUMMER, Baroness,** *cr* 1965 (Life Peeress); **Beatrice Plummer;** *b* 14 April 1903; *d* of Meyer Lapsker; *m* 1923, Leslie Arthur Plummer (later Sir Leslie Plummer, MP; *d* 1963). JP Essex, 1947. Member: Independent TV Authority, 1966; British Agricultural Export Council. *Recreation:* politics. *Address:* Berwick Hall, Toppesfield, Halstead, Essex; House of Lords, SW1; 31 Dorset Square, NW1.

**PLUMMER, Alfred,** BLitt Oxon; MSc (Econ.) London; MA, LLD Dublin; Hon. Librarian to the Worshipful Company of Weavers; *b* London, 2 Nov. 1896; *o s* of Alfred Plummer; *m* 1919, Minnie D. Goodey. *Educ:* Christ Church Sch., Brondesbury. Univ. training in Economics, Law and History at Trinity Coll., Dublin, London Univ. (London Sch. of Economics) and Oriel Coll., Oxford; enlisted in Honourable Artillery Company, 9 June 1915; active service in France, 1916-17; Lecturer in the Dept of Commerce in University Coll., Southampton, 1920-25; Vice-Principal of Ruskin Coll., Oxford, 1925-37; Head of Dept of Economics and Social Studies, City of Birmingham Commercial Coll., 1937-38; Head of Dept of Commerce, Languages and Social Studies, SW Essex Technical Coll., 1938-43; Vice Principle of SW Essex Technical Coll. and Headmaster of the County Technical Sch., 1944-45; Dir, Forest Training Coll., 1945-49; Inspector of Further Education, LCC, 1949-60; Staff Inspector, 1960-63. *Publications:* Exercises in Economics; Labour's Path to Power; The World in AgonyAn Economic Diagnosis; The Witney Blanket Industry; International Combines in Modern Industry; New British Industries in the 20th Century; Raw Materials or War Materials?; (with Richard Early) The Blanket Makers, 1669-1969; A History of Charles Early and Marriott (Witney) Ltd; various articles; contributor to the Encyclopædia of the Social Sciences. *Address:* 42 Gascoigne Gardens, Woodford Green, Essex.

**PLUMMER, (Arthur) Desmond (Herne),** TD 1950; JP; DL; Leader of the Greater London Council since 1967; *b* 25 May 1914; *s* of Arthur Herne Plummer and Janet (*née* McCormick); *m* 1941, Pat Holloway; one *d*. *Educ:* Hurstpierpoint Coll.; Coll. of Estate Management. Served 1939-46, Royal Engineers. Member: TA Sports Bd, 1953-; London Electricity Consultative Council, 1955-66; St Marylebone Borough Council, 1952-65 (Mayor, 1958-59); LCC, for St Marylebone, 1960-65; GLC, for Cities of London and Westminster, 1964- (Leader of Opposition, 1966-67); Member: Inner London Educn Authority, 1964-; South Bank Theatre Board, 1967-; Standing Conf. on SE Planning, 1967-; Transport Co-ordinating Council for London, 1967-69; Local Authorities Conditions of Service Adv. Bd, 1967-; Exec. Cttee, British Section of Internat. Union of Local Authorities; Exec. Cttee, Nat. Union Cons. and Unionist Assocs, 1967-; Chm., St Marylebone Conservative Assoc., 1965-66; Director: Portman Building Soc.; Nat. Employers' Mutual Gen. Insurance Assoc.; Nat. Employers' Life Assurance Assoc. Member of Lloyd's. Mem. Court, Univ. of London, 1967-. Liveryman, Worshipful Co. of Tin Plateworkers. FAI 1948; FRICS 1970; Hon. FFAS 1966. JP, Co. London, 1958-; DL Greater London, 1970-. *Publication:* Time for Change in Greater London, 1966; Report to London, 1970. *Recreations:* swimming (Capt. Otter Swimming Club, 1952-53); gardening, relaxing. *Address:* 4 The Lane, St Johns Wood, NW8. *Clubs:* Carlton, Royal Automobile, MCC.

**PLUMMER, Desmond;** *see* Plummer, A. D. H.

**PLUMMER, Norman Swift,** MD, FRCP; Senior Physician, and Physician in charge of Chest Clinic, Charing Cross Hospital since 1935; Physician to London Chest Hospital since 1947, to Bromley Hospital since 1948, to Edenbridge Hospital since 1946; *b* 10 June 1907; *s* of late Walter James Plummer and late Marianne Evelyn Clarence; *m* 1939, Helen Niven Wilson; one *s* three *d*. *Educ:* Kingswood Coll., Grahamstown; Guy's Hosp., Univ. of London; Amsterdam. Gold Medal in Medicine (Guy's), 1930; MD (London) 1933; FRCP 1941. Clin. Asst, Asst Ho. Surg., Out-Patient Officer, Ho. Phys. and Medical Registrar, Guy's Hosp., 1930-32; Post-Graduate Student, Kliniek Prof. Snapper, Amsterdam, 1932-33; Medical Registrar, Charing Cross

Hosp., 1933-35. Formerly: Consulting Physician: Oldchurch Hosp., Romford; The County Hosp. Chatham; All Saints' Hosp. Examr in Materia Medica, Soc. of Apothecaries of London, 1947-50; Lectr and Examr in Medicine, Univ. of London; Examr in Med., Conjt Bd, and MRCP. In RAMC, 1941-46; Brig. RAMC, Cons. Phys. to MEF. Royal Coll. of Physicians: Mem. Council 1965, Censor 1966, Senior Censor and Vice-Pres., 1970. Member: Association of Physicians; Thoracic Society; Fellow American Coll. of Chest Physicians. *Publications:* contributed to British Encyclopædia of Medical Practice, 2nd edn, 1952. Various medical papers in Guy's Hospital Reports, Lancet, BMJ, Thorax, Practitioner. *Address:* 118 Harley Street, W1. *T:* 01-486 2494, 01-788 5372. *Club:* Roehampton.

**PLUMPTRE,** family name of **Baron Fitzwalter.**

**PLUMTREE, Air Vice-Marshal Eric,** OBE 1946; DFC 1940; Air Officer Commanding, No 22 Group, RAF, since 1970; *b* 9 March 1919; *s* of William Plumtree, Plumbley Farm, Mosborough, Derbys, and Minnie Plumtree (*née* Wheatley); *m* 1942, Dorothy Patricia (*née* Lyall); two *s* (and one *s* decd). *Educ:* Eckington Grammar Sch. Served War of 1939-45: No 53 Army Co-op. Sqdn, 1940-41; No 241 FR Sqdn, 1942; OC No 169 FR Sqdn, 1943; Chief Instr, No 41, OTU, 1944; HQ, Fighter Command, 1945; Staff Coll., Haifa, 1946; Personal Staff Officer to C-in-C, MEAF, 1947-49; OC, No 54 (F) Sqdn, 1949-52; PSO to Chief of Air Staff, 1953-56; OC Flying Wing, Oldenburg, 1957-58; OC, Admin. Wing, Jever, 1958; JSSC, Latimer, 1959; OC, RAF Leuchars, 1959-61; Dep. Dir, Joint Planning Staff, 1962-63; IDC, 1964; Air Adviser to UK High Comr and Head of BDLS (Air), Ottawa, 1965-67; Dir, Air Plans, MoD (Air), 1968-69. *Recreations:* gardening, most sports. *Address:* Farcroft, Prospect Road, Market Drayton, Salop. *T:* Market Drayton 2680. *Club:* Royal Air Force.

**PLUNKET,** family name of **Baron Plunket.**

**PLUNKET,** 7th Baron, *cr* 1827; **Patrick Terence William Span Plunket;** CVO 1963 (MVO 1955); Lt-Col Irish Guards; Equerry to the Queen since 1952 (Equerry to King George VI, 1948-52); Deputy Master of HM Household, since 1954; *b* 8 Sept. 1923; *s* of 6th Baron and Dorothé Mabel (*d* 1938), *widow* of Capt. Jack Barnato, RAF; *S* father, 1938. *Educ:* Eton; Cambridge. A Trustee of the Wallace Collection and National Art Collections Fund. *Heir: b* Hon. Robin Rathmore Plunket, Capt. Rifle Brigade [*b* 1925; *m* 1951, Jennifer, *d* of late Bailey Southwell, Olivenhoutpoort, South Africa]. *Address:* Mount Offham, West Malling, Kent. *T:* W Malling 2195. *Club:* White's.

**PLUNKET GREENE, Mrs Alexander;** *see* Quant, Miss Mary.

**PLUNKETT,** family name of **Baron Dunsany,** of **Earl of Fingall,** and of **Baron Louth.**

**PLUNKETT, Brig. James Joseph,** CBE 1945; Colonel Commandant, Royal Army Veterinary Corps, 1953-59; *b* 1893; *m* 1951, Mrs Rachel Kelly, *d* of Eustace H. Bent, Lelant, Cornwall. *Educ:* Royal Dick Veterinary College. Commissioned, 1914; continuous military service. Director Army Veterinary and Remount Services, 1957-51; retired pay, 1951. *Recreation:* hunting. *Address:* Templeshanbo, near Enniscorthy, Co. Wexford, Eire. *Club:* Naval and Military.

**PLYMOUTH,** 3rd Earl of, *cr* 1905; **Other Robert Ivor Windsor-Clive;** Viscount Windsor (UK 1905); 15th Baron Windsor (England, *cr* 1529); DL; FRSA 1953; *b* 9 October 1923; *e s* of 2nd Earl and Lady Irene Charteris, *d* of 11th Earl of Wemyss; *S* father, 1943; *m* 1950, Caroline Helen, *o d* of Edward Rice, Dane Court, Eastry, Kent; three *s* one *d*. *Educ:* Eton. Pres., Nat. Museum of Wales, 1968-. DL County of Salop, 1961. *Heir: s* Viscount Windsor *qv*. *Address:* Oakly Park, Ludlow, Shropshire. *See also Dr Alan Glyn.*

**PLYMOUTH, Bishop of, (RC),** since 1955; **Rt. Rev. Cyril Edward Restieaux;** *b* 1910; *s* of Joseph and Edith Restieaux. *Educ:* English Coll., Rome; Gregorian University. Ordained, 1932; Curate at Nottingham, 1933; Parish Priest at Matlock, 1936; Hon. Canon of Nottingham, 1948; Vicar-General of Nottingham, 1951; Provost and Domestic Prelate to HH Pope Pius XII, 1955. *Publication:* Fifty Sermons, 1949. *Address:* Vescourt, Hartley, Plymouth.

**PLYMOUTH, Suffragan Bishop of,** since 1962; **Rt. Rev. Wilfrid Guy Sanderson;** *b* 17 Aug. 1905; *s* of late Wilfrid E. Sanderson; *m* 1934, Cecily Julia Mary Garratt; one *s* two *d*. *Educ:* Malvern College; Merton College, Oxford (MA). Ordained, 1931; Curate at S Farnborough, Hants, till 1934; Priest-in-charge of St Aidan's, Aldershot, 1934-37; Vicar of All Saints, Woodham, Surrey, 1937-46; Vicar of All Saints, Alton, Hants, 1946-54; Rector of Silverton, Devon, 1954-59; Archdeacon of Barnstaple, 1958-62; Rector of Shirwell, 1959-62. *Address:* Coltsfoot, Yeoland Lane, Yelverton, Devon. *T:* Yelverton 2308.

**PLYMOUTH, Archdeacon of;** *see* Matthews, Ven. F. A. J.

**POCHIN, Edward Eric,** CBE 1959; MA, MD, FRCP; Director, Department of Clinical Research, University College Hospital Medical School, London, since 1946; *b* 22 Sept. 1909; *s* of Charles Davenport Pochin; *m* 1940, Constance M. J., *d* of T. H. Tilly; one *s* one *d*. *Educ:* Repton; St John's Coll., Cambridge. Natural Science Tripos, Part I, 1st 1930, Part II (Physiology) 1st, 1931; Michael Foster Student, Strathcona Student, 1931-32; MA 1935; Gifford-Edmunds Prize, 1940; MD 1945; FRCP 1946. Mem. of Scientific Staff of Medical Research Council, 1941; Horton Smith Prize, 1945. Member: International Commn on Radiological Protection (Chm. 1962-69); Medical Research Soc., Physiological Soc., Assoc. of Physicians, Internat. Radiation Protection Assoc.; UK Deleg., United Nations Scientific Committee on Effects of Atomic Radiation. *Publications:* articles on thyroid disease and other medical subjects in scientific journals. *Recreation:* trivial painting. *Address:* University College Hospital Medical School, University Street, London, WC1. *Club:* Athenæum.

**POCHIN, Victor Robert,** CBE 1957; *b* 10 Sept. 1879; *o s* of late George William Pochin, DL, JP, Barkby Hall. *Educ:* Wellington; Trinity Coll., Cambridge. Barrister, Lincoln's Inn, 1907; Leicestershire CC 1913, County Alderman 1938-, Vice-Chm., 1924-60, Chm., 1960-61; JP 1906, DL 1925, Leicestershire; High Sheriff of Leicestershire, 1941; served European War, 1916-19, Leicestershire Yeomanry and First Life Guards. *Recreations:* fishing and shooting. *Address:* Barkby Hall, Leicestershire. *T:* Syston 2247. *Club:* United University.

**POCOCK, Carmichael Charles Peter;** CBE 1967; Managing Director of Royal Dutch/Shell Group of Companies since 1970; *b* 25 March

1920; *s* of Lt-Col (retd) Joseph Albert Pocock, Bristol; *m* 1943, Nina Alice Hilary (*née* Hearn); one *s* two *d*. *Educ:* Rossall School; Keble Coll., Oxford. Joined Royal Dutch/Shell Group in 1946 and served in Venezuela and London. Pres., Compania Shell de Venezuela, 1964; Regional Co-ordinator, East and Australasia, 1968. *Recreations:* sailing and mountain walking. *Address:* 9 Campden Hill Court, W8. *T:* 01-937 6204; Woodlands St Mary's House, near Newbury, Berkshire. *T:* Lambourn 510.

**POCOCK, Hugh Shellshear;** formerly: Director, Associated Iliffe Press Ltd; Chairman of Iliffe Electrical Publications Ltd; Managing Editor, The Electrical Review; (formerly Editor) of The Wireless World; retired Dec. 1962; *b* 6 May 1894; 3rd *s* of late Lexden Lewis Pocock, artist; *m* 1920, Mayda, *d* of late Serab Sēvian. *Educ:* Privately. Served European War, 1914-18: commissioned RE, 1915; served in Egypt, Mesopotamia, Persia, on wireless and intelligence work with rank of Capt. (despatches). Assisted in organisation of first short wave amateur transatlantic tests, 1921-22; organised first transatlantic broadcasting trials, 1923; proposed Empire Broadcasting on short wave in 1926, and urged its adoption in face of BBC opposition. Promoted and organised the National Wireless Register of technical personnel 1938, under Service auspices; CEng, FIEE; Life Senior Member of the Institute of Electrical and Electronics Engineers; Member of Honour, Union Internationale de la Presse Radiotechnique et Electronique. *Publications:* numerous articles relating to radio and electrical progress, technical and general. *Recreations:* genealogy and local history research. *Address:* 163 West Heath Road, NW3.

**POCOCK, Most Rev. Philip F.;** *see* Toronto, Coadjutor Archbishop of, (RC).

**POETT, Gen. Sir (Joseph Howard) Nigel,** KCB 1959 (CB 1952); DSO and Bar, 1945; idc; psc; Director, British Productivity Council, since 1966; *b* 20 Aug. 1907; *s* of late Maj.-General J. H. Poett, CB, CMG, CBE; *m* 1937, Julia, *d* of E. J. Herrick, Hawkes Bay, NZ; two *s* one *d*. *Educ:* Downside; RMC Sandhurst. 2nd Lieut, DLI, 1927; Operations, NW Frontier, 1930-31; Adjt 2nd Bn DLI, 1934-37; GSO2, 2nd Div., 1940; GSO1, War Office, 1941-42; Comd 11th Bn DLI, 1942-43; Comdr, 5th Parachute Bde, 1943-46; served North-West Europe, 1944-45; Director of Plans, War Office, 1946-48; idc 1948; Dep.-Commander, British Military Mission, Greece, 1949; Maj.-General, 1951; Chief of Staff, FARELF, 1950-52; GOC 3rd Infantry Division, Middle East Land Forces, 1952-54; Dir of Military Operations, War Office, 1954-56; Commandant, Staff Coll., Camberley, 1957-58; General Officer Commanding-in-Chief, Southern Command, 1958-61; Commander-in-Chief, Far East Land Forces, 1961-63. General, 1962. Colonel, The Durham Light Infantry, 1956-65. Silver Star, USA. *Address:* Swaynes Mead, Great Durnford, Salisbury, Wilts. *Clubs:* White's, Army and Navy, MCC.

**POITIER, Sidney;** actor, film and stage; *b* Miami, Florida, 20 Feb. 1924; *s* of Reginald Poitier and Evelyn (*née* Outten); *m* 1950, Juanita Hardy; three *d*. *Educ:* private tutors; Western Senior High Sch., Nassau; Governor's High Sch., Nassau. Served War of 1941-45 with 1267th Medical Detachment, United States Army. Started acting with American Negro Theatre, 1946. *Plays include:* Anna Lucasta, Broadway, 1948; A Raisin in the Sun, Broadway, 1959; *films include:* Cry, the Beloved Country, 1952; Red Ball Express, 1952; Go, Man, Go, 1954; Blackboard Jungle, 1955; Goodbye, My Lady, 1956; Edge of the City, 1957; Band of Angels, 1957; Something of Value, 1957; The Mark of the Hawk, 1958; The Defiant Ones, 1958 (Silver Bear Award, Berlin Film Festival, and New York Critics Award, 1958); Porgy and Bess, 1959; A Raisin in the Sun, 1960; Paris Blues, 1960; Lilies of the Field, 1963 (award for Best Actor of 1963, Motion Picture Academy of Arts and Sciences); The Bedford Incident, 1965; The Slender Thread, 1966; A Patch of Blue, 1966; Duel at Diablo, 1966; To Sir With Love, 1967; In the Heat of the Night, 1967; Guess Who's Coming to Dinner, 1968; For Love of Ivy, 1968. *Address:* c/o General Artists Corporation, 640 Fifth Avenue, New York City 19, NY, USA; Mount Vernon, New York, USA.

**POLAK, Cornelia Julia,** OBE 1964 (MBE 1956); HM Diplomatic Service, retired; *b* 2 Dec. 1908; *d* of late Solomon Polak and late Georgina Polak (*née* Pozner). Foreign Office, 1925-38; Asst Archivist, British Embassy, Paris, 1938-40; Foreign Office, 1940-47; Vice-Consul, Bergen, 1947-49; Consul, Washington, 1949-51; Foreign Office, 1951-55; Consul, Paris, 1955-57; Consul, Brussels, 1957-60; Foreign Office, 1960-63; Head of Treaty and Nationality Department, Foreign Office, 1963-67; Consul General, Geneva, 1967-69, retired; re-employed at FCO, 1969-70. *Address:* 24 Belsize Court, NW3.

**POLAND, Rear-Admiral Allan,** CBE 1943; DSO 1918; RN, retired; *b* 1888; *s* of William Poland, Blackheath; *m* 1912, Phyllis (*d* 1968), *d* of Dr R. A. Weston, Portsmouth; one *d* (and one *s* lost in HMS Thetis, 1939). Entered Navy, 1903; served in submarines and in command of submarine flotillas, 1910-37; Senior Naval Officer, Persian Gulf, 1937-39; Commodore Commanding East Indies Station, 1938 and 1939; ADC to the King, 1939; Commodore Commanding 9th Cruiser Squadron, 1939-40; Chief of Staff to Commander-in-Chief America and West Indies, 1940-42; Senior British Naval Officer Western Atlantic (Acting Vice-Admiral), 1942; Rear-Admiral, Alexandria, 1942-45; Naval Assistant to Director of Sea Transport, 1945-47. Grand Officer, Order of Humayun (Persia); Kt Comdr Order of Phœnix (Greece). *Address:* 35 Chiltley Way, Liphook, Hants. *T:* Liphook 2359.

**POLAND, Rear-Adm. Edmund Nicholas,** CB 1967; CBE 1962; Managing Director, John Bell (Fabrics of Scotland) Ltd, Biggar, since 1970; *b* 19 Feb. 1917; 2nd *s* of late Major Raymond A. Poland, RMLI; *m* 1941, Pauline Ruth Margaret Pechell; three *s* one *d* (and one *d* decd). *Educ:* Royal Naval Coll., Dartmouth. Served at sea during Abyssinian and Palestine crises, Spanish Civil War; War of 1939-45: convoy duties, Norwegian waters; Motor Torpedo Boats, Channel and Mediterranean; Torpedo Specialist, 1943; Staff Officer Ops to Naval Force Comdr, Burma; Sqdn T. Officer, HMS Royalist; HMS Hornet, 1946; Flotilla Torpedo and Anti-Submarine Officer of Third Submarine Flotilla, HMS Montclare; Air Warfare Div., Admiralty, 1950; British Naval Staff, Washington, 1953; jssc 1955; Directorate of Tactics and Ship Requirements, Admiralty; comd RN Air Station, Abbotsinch, 1956; Nato Standing Gp, Washington; Director of Under Sea Warfare (Naval), Ministry of Defence, 1962; Chief of Staff to C-in-C Home Fleet, 1965-68; retired. Commander, 1950; Capt., 1956; Rear-Adm., 1965. Man. Dir, Wellman Incandescent (Africa) Ltd, 1968-69; Manager, Organisation and Personnel, Middleburg Steel and Alloys Ltd, 1969-70. *Recreations:* golf, fishing.

*Address:* Easter Calzeat, Broughton, Biggar, Lanarkshire. *Clubs:* United Hunts', Golfers'.
*See also R. D. Poland.*

**POLAND, Richard Domville;** Under-Secretary, Ministry of Transport, since 1964; *b* 22 Oct. 1914; *er s* of late Major R. A. Poland, Royal Marine Light Infantry, and Mrs F. O. Bayly-Jones; *m* 1948, Rosalind Frances, *y d* of late Surgeon-Captain H. C. Devas; one *s* one *d*. *Educ:* RN Coll., Dartmouth. Joined Civil Service as Ops Officer in Air Ministry, Civil Aviation Dept, 1939; Private Secretary to Minister of Civil Aviation, 1944-48; Principal, 1946; Asst Secretary, 1953; Shipping Attaché, British Embassy, Washington, DC, 1957-60. *Address:* 63 High Street, Farnborough, Kent. *T:* Farnborough (Kent) 54531.
*See also Rear-Admiral E. N. Poland.*

**POLANI, Prof. Paul Emanuel,** MD, FRCP; DCH; Prince Philip Professor of Pædiatric Research in the University of London, and Director of Pædiatric Research Unit, Guy's Hospital Medical School, London, since Oct. 1960; Children's Physician and Geneticist to Guy's Hospital; Geneticist, Italian Hospital; *b* 1 Jan. 1914; first *s* of Enrico Polani and Elsa Zennaro; *m* 1944, Nina Ester Sullam; no *c*. *Educ:* Trieste, Siena and Pisa (Italy). MD (Pisa) 1938; MRCP (London) 1948; FRCP (London) 1961. National Birthday Trust Fund Fellow in Pædiatric Research, 1948; Assistant to Director, Dept of Child Health, Guy's Hospital Medical School, 1950; Research Physician on Cerebral Palsy and Director, Medical Research Unit, National Spastic Society, 1955; Consultant to WHO (Regional Office for Europe) on Pregnancy Wastage, 1959; Consultant, Nat. Inst. Neurol. Disability and Blindness, Nat. Inst. of Health, USA, 1959-. *Publications:* chapters in books on genetics, mental deficiency, psychiatry and pædiatrics; papers on genetics, congenital malformations and neurological disorders of children. *Recreations:* reading, horse riding, ski-ing. *Address:* Little Meadow, West Clandon, Surrey. *T:* Clandon 436.

**POLANYI, Prof. Michael,** FRS 1944; Hon. DSc: Princeton, 1946; Leeds, 1947; Manchester, 1966; Cambridge, 1969; Hon. LLD: Aberdeen, 1959; Notre Dame, 1965; Wesleyan, 1965; Toronto, 1967; Loyola, 1970; Professor Emeritus at Victoria University, Manchester, (Professor of Social Studies, 1948-Sept. 1958, retired); *b* Budapest, 12 March 1891; *m* 1921, Magda Kemeny; two *s*. *Educ:* Budapest; Karlsruhe. Privatdozent Technische Hochschule, Berlin, 1923; Member of Kaiser Wilhelm Institute für Physikalische Chemie, 1923; Life Member, 1929, resigned 1933; Prof. of Physical Chemistry, Victoria Univ., Manchester, 1933; Former Member National Society of Science, Letters and Arts in Naples, 1933; Riddell Lectr, Univ. of Durham, 1945; Lloyd Roberts Lectr, Manchester, 1946; Member of Max Planck Society, 1949; Alexander White Visiting Professor, Univ. of Chicago, 1950; Gifford Lectr, 1951-52, Univ. of Aberdeen; Visiting Prof., Univ. of Chicago, 1954. Lindsay Memorial Lectr, Keele, 1958; Eddington Lectr, Cambridge, 1960; Gunning Lectr, Edinburgh, 1960; Senior Research Fell., Merton Coll., Oxford, 1959-61; Distinguished Research Fell., Univ. of Virginia, 1961; McEnnerny Lectr, Berkeley, 1961; Foreign Hon. Member American Academy of Arts and Sciences, 1962; Terry Lectr, Yale, 1962; Member Internat. Acad. of Philosophy of Science, 1962; Fellow of Center for Adv. Study Behav. Sciences, Stanford, 1962-63; James B. Duke Vis. Prof., Duke Univ., 1964; Senior Fellow, Center of Advanced Studies, Wesleyan Univ., 1965; Alexander White Vis. Prof., Univ. of Chicago, 1967, 1968, 1969. *Publications:* Atomic Reactions, 1932; USSR Economics, 1935; Money and Unemployment (a diagrammatic film), 1939; The Contempt of Freedom, 1940; Patent Reform, 1944; Full Employment and Free Trade, 1945; Science Faith and Society, 1946; The Logic of Liberty, 1951; Personal Knowledge, 1958; The Study of Man, 1959; Beyond Nihilism, 1960; The Tacit Dimension, 1966; Knowing and Being, 1969; articles on plasticity, adsorption, crystal structure, chemical reaction kinetics, bond energies and polymerisation in German and British journals. *Address:* 22 Upland Park Road, Oxford. *T:* Oxford 58288. *Club:* Athenæum.

**POLE;** *see* Chandos Pole.

**POLE, Col Sir John Gawen Carew,** 12th Bart, *cr* 1628; DSO 1944; TD; JP; Lord-Lieutenant of Cornwall since 1962; Member of the Prince of Wales's Council, 1952-68; Director of Lloyds Bank since 1956 (Chairman Devon and Cornwall Committee, since 1956); Vice-Chairman, Westward Television Ltd, since 1960; Director: English China Clays Ltd, since 1963; Keith Prowse, since 1969; Member, Jockey Club (incorporating National Hunt Committee), since 1969 (Steward, 1953-56); Member Garden Society; *b* 4 March 1902; *e s* of late Lt-Gen. Sir Reginald Pole-Carew, KCB, of Antony, Cornwall, and Lady Beatrice Pole-Carew, *er d* of 3rd Marquess of Ormonde; *S* kinsman, 1926; *m* 1928, Cynthia Mary, OBE, 1959, *o d* of Walter Burns, North Mymms Park, Hatfield; one *s* two *d*. *Educ:* Eton; RMC, Sandhurst. Coldstream Guards, 1923-39; ADC to Commander-in-Chief in India, 1924-25; Comptroller to Governor-General, Union of S. Africa, 1935-36; Palestine, 1936; commanded 5th Bn Duke of Cornwall's LI (TA), 1939-43; commanded 2nd Bn Devonshire Regt, 1944; Colonel, Second Army, 1944-45; Normandy, France, Belgium, Holland, Germany, 1944-45 (despatches, Immediate DSO); raised and commanded post-war TA Bn, 4/5 Bn, DCLI, 1946-47; Hon. Col, 4/5 Bn DCLI (TA), 1958-60; Hon. Col DCLI (TA), 1960-67. Member: Central Transport Consultative Cttee for Great Britain, 1948-54; SW Electricity Consultative Council, 1949-52 (Vice-Chairman, 1951-52); Western Area Board, British Transport Commission, 1955-61. JP 1939, DL 1947, CA 1954-66, Cornwall; High Sheriff, Cornwall, 1947-48; Vice-Lt, Cornwall, 1950-62; Chairman Cornwall County Council, 1952-63. A Gentleman of HM Bodyguard of the Honourable Corps of Gentlemen-at-Arms, 1950-, Standard Bearer, 1968-. Prime Warden Worshipful Company of Fishmongers, 1969-70. *Recreations:* gardening, shooting, travel. *Heir:* *s* (John) Richard (Walter Reginald) Carew Pole [*b* 2 Dec. 1938; *m* 1966, Hon. Victoria Lever, *d* of 3rd Viscount Leverhulme, *qv*]. *Address:* Antony House, Torpoint, Cornwall. *T:* 406. *Clubs:* Guards, Pratt's, Turf, MCC.

**POLE, Sir Peter Van Notten,** 5th Bt, *cr* 1791; FASA; ACIS; Company Manager and Secretary; *b* 6 Nov. 1921; *s* of late Arthur Chandos Pole and Marjorie, *d* of late Charles Hargrave, Glen Forrest, W Australia; *S* kinsman, 1948; *m* 1949, Jean Emily, *d* of late Charles Douglas Stone, Borden, WA; one *s* one *d*. *Educ:* Guildford Grammar Sch. *Heir:* *s* Peter John Chandos Pole, *b* 27 April 1952. *Address:* 12 Lothian Street, Floreat Park, WA 6014, W Australia.

**POLKINGHORNE, Prof. John Charlton;** Professor of Mathematical Physics, University of Cambridge, since 1968; *b* 16 Oct. 1930; *s* of George Baulkwill Polkinghorne and

Dorothy Evelyn Polkinghorne (*née* Charlton); *m* 1955, Ruth Isobel Martin; two *s* one *d*. *Educ:* Elmhurst Grammar Sch.; Perse Sch.; Trinity Coll., Cambridge (MA 1956; PhD 1955). Fellow, Trinity Coll., Cambridge, 1954-; Commonwealth Fund Fellow, California Institute of Technology, 1955-56; Lecturer in Mathematical Physics, University of Edinburgh, 1956-58; Lecturer in Applied Mathematics, University of Cambridge, 1958-65; Reader in Theoretical Physics, University of Cambridge, 1965-68. *Publications:* (jointly) The Analytic S-Matrix, 1966; many articles on elementary particle physics in learned journals. *Recreation:* gardening. *Address:* 22 Rutherford Road, Cambridge. *T:* Trumpington 3321.

**POLLARD, Sir (Charles) Herbert,** Kt 1962; CBE 1957 (OBE 1946; MBE 1943); retired as City Treasurer, Kingston upon Hull, 1961; *b* 23 Oct. 1898; *s* of Charles Pollard; *m* 1922, Elsie (*d* 1970), *d* of Charles Crain; one *d*. *Educ:* Blackpool. City Treasurer, Kingston upon Hull, 1929-61; formerly held appointments in Finance Depts of Blackpool and Wallasey; Fellow, Inst. of Chartered Accountants; Member Council, Inst. of Municipal Treasurers and Accountants, 1944-61 (President Inst. 1952-53); Financial Adviser to Assoc. of Municipal Corporations, 1951-61; Member several cttees and working parties arranged by government departments on various aspects of education, housing, police and local authority finance; Trustee and Manager, Hull Savings Bank. Trustee: C. C. Grundy Trust; Hibbert Trust; John Gregson Trust. Chairman Hanover Housing Assoc.; Member: Nat. Savings Cttee, 1946-51; Nat. Savings Assembly; Blackpool and Fylde Hospital Management Cttee; Whittingham Hospital Management Cttee; Exec. Cttee, Royal Nat. Inst. for the Blind; Official delegate at International Confs on aspects of local government finance (including Education) in Rome and Geneva, held under auspices of International Union of Local Authorities (prepared British paper for this) and UNESCO Licentiate, London College of Music. Hon. Treas. and Member Council, General Assembly of Unitarian and Free Christian Churches, 1959-70 (President, 1956-57); Member, St John Council for Lancs. OStJ 1962. *Publications:* contrib. to: Local Government Finance and to other local government journals. *Recreations:* music, theatre; membership of voluntary service organisations. *Address:* 132 Clifton Drive South, Lytham St Anne's, Lancs. *T:* Lytham 7880. *Clubs:* National Liberal; Rotary (Hull and St Anne's).

**POLLARD, Graham;** *see* Pollard, H. G.

**POLLARD, (Henry) Graham;** author; *b* 7 March 1903; *e s* of Albert Frederick Pollard, first director of the Institute of Historical Research, London, and Catherine Susannah Lucy. *Educ:* Shrewsbury Sch.; University College, London; Jesus Coll., Oxford. Partner in Birrell & Garnett (Antiquarian Booksellers), 1924-38; Leverhulme Research Fellow, 1934-37; Reader in the History of Newspapers, Univ. of London, 1939-42; Board of Trade, 1942-59; Sandars Reader in Bibliography, Cambridge Univ., 1959; Lyell Reader in Bibliography, Univ. of Oxford, 1960-61; President, Bibliographical Society, London, 1960-61. Gold Medal, Bibliographical Soc., 1969. *Publications:* Catalogue of Type founders' Specimens, 1928; (with John Carter) An Inquiry into the Nature of Certain Nineteenth Century Pamphlets, 1934; (with John Carter) The Firm of Charles Ottley, Landon, & Co., 1948; T. J. Wise Centenary Studies, 1960; (with A. Ehrman) The Distribution of Books by Catalogue, Roxburghe Club, 1965. Contrib.: The Cambridge Bibliography of English Literature, 1940; The Library; The Fleuron; New Paths in Book Collecting, 1934; The Times Literary Supplement; The Book Collector; Bodleian Library Record; Oxoniensia. *Recreation:* book collecting. *Address:* Barton Manor, Barton Village Road, Headington, Oxford.

**POLLARD, Sir Herbert;** *see* Pollard, Sir C. H.

**POLLARD, Lt-Gen. Sir Reginald (George), KCVO 1970; KBE 1961 (CBE 1955); CB 1959; DSO 1942; psc; idc; retired;** *b* 20 Jan. 1903; *s* of late Albert Edgar Pollard, Bathurst, NSW; *m* 1925, Daisy Ethel, *d* of late A. H. Potter, Strathfield, NSW; two *s*. *Educ:* Bathurst High Sch.; Royal Military Coll., Duntroon. Lieut, Aust. Staff Corps, 1924; served War of 1939-45, France, Middle East, Syria (despatches), SE Asia, SW Pacific; Lieut-Colonel, 1941; Colonel, 1942; ADC to the King, 1951, to the Queen, 1952; Brigadier, 1953; Comd Aust. Army Component, British Commonwealth Forces, Korea, 1953; Maj.-General, 1954; QMG, AMF, 1954-57; Lt-Gen., 1957; GOC, Eastern Command, Australia, 1957-60; Chief of the General Staff, Australian Army, 1960-63; retired, 1963; Hon. Colonel, The Royal Australian Regt, 1965. Australian Secretary to The Queen, 1969; Dir-Gen., Royal Visit, 1970. *Recreation:* tennis. *Address:* Old Warburton Road, Wesburn, Victoria 3139, Australia. *T:* Yarra Junction 671321.

**POLLARD, Prof. Sidney;** Professor of Economic History, University of Sheffield, since 1963; *b* 21 April 1925; *s* of Moses and Leontine Pollak; *m* 1949, Eileen Andrews; two *s* one *d*. *Educ:* London School of Economics. University of Sheffield: Knoop Fellow, 1950-52; Asst Lecturer, 1952-55; Lecturer, 1955-60; Senior Lecturer, 1960-63. *Publications:* Three Centuries of Sheffield Steel, 1954; A History of Labour in Sheffield 1850-1939, 1959; The Development of the British Economy, 1914-1950, 1962; The Genesis of Modern Management, 1965; The Idea of Progress, 1968; (with D. W. Crossley) The Wealth of Britain, 1086-1966, 1968; articles in learned journals in field of economics, economic history and history. *Recreations:* walking, music. *Address:* 523 Fulwood Road, Sheffield S10 3QB. *T:* 303765. *Club:* National Liberal.

**POLLEN, Sir John Michael Hungerford,** 7th Bt of Redenham, Hampshire, *cr* 1795; *b* 6 April 1919; *s* of late Lieut-Commander John Francis Hungerford Pollen, RN; *S* kinsman, Sir John Lancelot Hungerford Pollen, 6th Bt, 1959; *m* 1st, 1941, Angela Mary Oriana Russi (marr. diss., 1956); one *s* one *d*; 2nd, 1957, Mrs Diana Jubb. *Educ:* Downside; Merton Coll., Oxford. Served War of 1939-45 (despatches). *Heir: s* Richard John Hungerford Pollen, *b* 3 Nov. 1946. *Address:* 3 Sherlock Mews, Baker Street, W1; Rodbourne, Malmesbury, Wiltshire. *T:* Malmesbury 2189.

**POLLINGTON, Viscount; John Christopher George Savile;** *b* 16 May 1931; *s* of 7th Earl of Mexborough, *qv*; *m* 1958, Elizabeth Hariot, *d* of 6th Earl of Verulam, *qv*; one *s* one *d*. *Address:* Dunnington Hall, York. *T:* Dunnington 273; 48 Belgrave Mews North, SW1. *T:* 01-235 4952. *Clubs:* Turf, Bath; All England Lawn Tennis and Croquet.

**POLLOCK,** family name of **Viscount Hanworth.**

**POLLOCK, David Linton;** Solicitor; *b* 7 July 1906; *yr s* of late Rev. C. A. E. Pollock, formerly President of Corpus Christi College,

Cambridge, and of Mrs G. I. Pollock; *m* 1st, 1933, Lilian Diana Turner; one *s*; 2nd, 1950, Margaret Duncan Curtis-Bennett (*née* Mackintosh). *Educ:* Marlborough Coll.; Trinity Coll., Cambridge. Partner in the firm of Freshfields, 1938-51; served with HM Treasury, 1939-40; War of 1939-45, Commander RNVR (despatches). Member of British Government Economic Mission to Argentina, 1946. Member of Council, Royal Yachting Assoc., 1950-65. Director: S. Pearson & Son Ltd; Legal & General Assurance Society Ltd; Vickers Ltd; National Westminster Bank Ltd; Pearson Longman Ltd. President, Société Civile du Vignoble de Château Latour. Member of Council, Marlborough College. *Recreation:* sailing. *Address:* 24 Tufton Court, Tufton Street, SW1. *T:* 01-222 6090; The Old Rectory, Wiggonholt, near Pulborough, Sussex. *T:* Pulborough 2531; (business) 17th Floor, Millbank Tower, SW1. *T:* 01-828 9020. *Clubs:* Royal Thames Yacht; Royal Yacht Squadron, Itchenor Sailing (Sussex).

**POLLOCK, Ellen Clara;** Actress and Director; President, The Shaw Society; Professor at RADA and Webber Douglas School of Acting; *m* 1st, 1929, Lt-Col L. F. Hancock, OBE, RE (decd); one *s*; 2nd, 1945, James Proudfoot, *qv*. *Educ:* St Mary's College, W2; Convent of The Blessed Sacrament, Brighton. First appeared, Everyman, 1920, as page in Romeo and Juliet. Accompanied Lady Forbes-Robertson on her S. African tour, and later visited Australia as Moscovitch's leading lady. West End successes include: Hit the Deck, Hippodrome, 1927; Her First Affaire, Kingsway, and Duke of York's, 1930; The Good Companions, Her Majesty's, 1931; Too True to be Good, New, 1933; Finished Abroad, Savoy, 1934; French Salad, Westminster and Royalty, 1934; The Dominant Sex, Shaftesbury and Aldwych, 1935. Open Air Theatre: Lysistrata; As You Like It. Seasons of Shaw's plays: at Lyric, Hammersmith, 1944, and with late Sir Donald Wolfit at King's, Hammersmith, 1953; three seasons of Grand Guignol plays at The Irving and Granville, Walham Green; Six Characters in Search of an Author, New Mayfair Theatre, 1963. Has acted in numerous films and TV, inc. Forsyte Saga. *Productions include:* Summer in December, Comedy Theatre, 1949; Miss Turner's Husband, St Martin's, 1949; The Third Visitor, Duke of York's, 1949; Shavings, St Martin's, 1951; Mrs Warren's Profession, Royal Court, 1956; A Matter of Choice, Arts, 1967. *Recreations:* motoring, swimming and cooking. *Address:* 28 Tedworth Square, SW3. *T:* 01-352 5082.

**POLLOCK, Sir George,** Kt 1959; QC; Director, British Employers' Confederation, 1954-65; *b* 15 March 1901; *s* of William Mackford Pollock; *m* 1922, Doris Evelyn Main; one *s* one *d*. Sub-editor Daily Chronicle, 1922-28; called to Bar, Gray's Inn, 1928; Bencher, 1948. QC 1951; Recorder of Sudbury, 1946-51. Served Army (Special Forces) 1940-44, Egypt, N Africa, Sicily and Italy (Colonel, Gen. Staff). Member: Governing Body, ILO, 1963-69; EFTA Consultative Cttee, 1966-69; Royal Commn on Trade Unions and Employers' Organisations. *Publication:* Life of Mr Justice McCardle, 1934. *Address:* 7a South Cliff Tower, Eastbourne, Sussex.

**POLLOCK, Sir George F(rederick),** 5th Bt, *cr* 1866; Artist-Photographer since 1963; *b* 13 Aug. 1928; *s* of Sir (Frederick) John Pollock, 4th Bt and Alix l'Estom (*née* Soubiran); *S* father, 1963; *m* 1951, Doreen Mumford, *o d* of N. E. K. Nash, CMG; one *s* two *d*. *Educ:* Eton; Trinity Coll., Cambridge. BA 1953, MA 1957. 2nd Lieut, 17/21 Lancers, 1948-49. Admitted Solicitor, 1956. FRPS; FRSA. Mem., London Salon of Photography; Hon. Mem., Photo Clubs du Val de Bièvre (Versailles), Lausanne and Germinal (Brussels). *Publications:* contrib. articles to ski-ing and photographic journals. *Recreation:* ski-ing. *Heir:* *s* David Frederick Pollock, *b* 13 April 1959. *Address:* Netherwood, Stones Lane, Westcott, near Dorking, Surrey. *T:* Dorking 5447. *Clubs:* Lansdowne, Ski Club of Great Britain, Kandahar; DHO (Wengen); Mardens (Klosters).

**POLLOCK, Sir George Seymour Montagu-;** 4th Bt, *cr* 1872; Lieutenant-Commander, RN (retired); *b* 14 Sept. 1900; *s* of Sir Montagu Frederick Montagu-Pollock, 3rd Bt, and Margaret Angela (*d* 1959), *d* of late W. A. Bell, Pendell Court, Blechingley; *S* father, 1938; *m* 1927, Karen-Sofie, *o c* of Hans Ludvig Dedekam, of Oslo; one *s* one *d*. *Educ:* Royal Naval Colleges, Osborne and Dartmouth. Entered RN, 1913; retired, 1920; With Unilever, 1920-64. Served in RN, War of 1939-45. *Heir:* *s* Giles Hampden Montagu-Pollock; *b* 19 Oct. 1928; *m* 1963, Caroline Veronica, *yr d* of Richard Russell; one *s* one *d*]. *Address:* Brooke House, Swallowcliffe, near Salisbury, Wilts. *T:* Tisbury 220.

*See also Sir William Montagu-Pollock.*

**POLLOCK, James Huey Hamill,** CMG 1946; OBE 1939; *b* 6 Aug. 1893; *s* of late William Charles Pollock; *m* 1919, Margaret Doris, OStJ (*d* 1962), *d* of late P. B. Kearns; two *s*. *Educ:* Royal School, Armagh. Served in Royal Irish Rifles, London Regt and Staff, 1914-20 (wounded, despatches); Dep. Governor, Ramallah, Palestine, 1920; Administrative Officer, Nigeria, 1923; Assistant Secretary, Nigerian Secretariat, Lagos, 1927; Administrative Officer, Palestine, 1930; District Commissioner, Haifa, 1939, Galilee, 1942; District Commissioner Jerusalem, 1944-48; Chief Civil Adviser to GOC British Troops in Palestine, 15 May 1948 till final withdrawal 30 June 1948. Colonial Office, 1949-52. Member, Senate of Northern Ireland, 1954-57; Deputy Speaker, 1956-57. Member Management Cttee, South Tyrone and Drumglass Hospitals, 1960-64. Lieutenant of Commandery of Ards, 1952-61. High Sheriff, Co. Tyrone, 1963. KJStJ. Commander of Order of George I of Greece, 1948. *Address:* 21 Queen Square, Bath, Somerset. *Clubs:* East India and Sports; Bath and County.

**POLLOCK, Martin Rivers,** FRS 1962; Professor of Biology, University of Edinburgh, since 1965; *b* 10 Dec. 1914; *s* of Hamilton Rivers Pollock and Eveline Morton Pollock (*née* Bell); *m* 1941, Jean Ilsley Paradise; two *s* two *d*. *Educ:* Winchester Coll., Trinity Coll., Cambridge; University College Hospital, London. BA Cantab, 1936; Senior Scholar, Trinity Coll., Cambridge, 1936; MRCS, LRCP 1939; MB, BCh Cantab 1940. House Appointments at UCH and Brompton Hospital, 1940-41; Bacteriologist, Emergency Public Health Laboratory Service, 1941-45; seconded to work on Infective Hepatitis with MRC Unit, 1943-45; apppointment to scientific staff, Medical Research Council, under Sir Paul Fildes, FRS, 1945-; Head of Division of Bacterial Physiology, Nat. Inst. for Medical Research, Mill Hill (MRC), 1949-65. *Publications:* articles in British Journal of Experimental Pathology, Biochemical Journal, Journal of Microbiology, etc. *Recreations:* sea cruising under sail and other types of adventurous travel, especially through deserts. *Address:* 30 Saxe-Coburg Place, Edinburgh 3. *T:* 031-332 1554.

**POLLOCK, Adm. Sir Michael (Patrick),** KCB 1969 (CB 1966); MVO 1952; DSC 1944; Chief of the Naval Staff and First Sea Lord, since 1971; *b* 19 Oct. 1916; *s* of late C. A. Pollock and of Mrs G. Pollock; *m* 1st, 1940, Margaret Steacy (*d* 1951), Bermuda; two *s* one *d*; 2nd, 1954, Marjory Helen Reece (*née* Bissett); one step *d*. *Educ:* RNC Dartmouth. Entered Navy, 1930; specialised in Gunnery, 1941. Served War of 1939-45 in Warspite, Vanessa, Arethusa and Norfolk, N. Atlantic, Mediterranean and Indian Ocean. Captain, Plans Div. of Admiralty and Director of Surface Weapons; comd HMS Vigo and Portsmouth Sqdn, 1958-59; comd HMS Ark Royal, 1963-64; Asst Chief of Naval Staff, 1964-66; Flag Officer Second in Command, Home Fleet, 1966-67; Flag Officer Submarines and Nato Commander Submarines, Eastern Atlantic, 1967-69; Controller of the Navy, 1970-71. Comdr, 1950; Capt., 1955; Rear-Adm., 1964; Vice-Adm., 1968; Adm., 1970. *Recreations:* sailing, tennis, golf, shooting, fishing, travel. *Address:* 350 Sea Front, Hayling Island, Hants. *T:* Hayling Island 3431. *Clubs:* Union (Malta); Naval (Portsmouth); Hayling Island Sailing.

**POLLOCK, Sir Ronald (Evelyn),** Kt *cr* 1947; *b* Kamptee, CP, India, 17 April 1891; *s* of Colonel E. Pollock, CBE, RA; *m* 1st, 1921, Margery (*d* 1959), *d* of late S. A. Fitze; one *d*; 2nd, 1963, Mrs Pamela Stent, *widow* of P. J. H. Stent, CIE, ICS, and *d* of late F. W. A. Prideaux, OBE. *Educ:* Harrow; Pembroke Coll., Cambridge. MA Cambridge. Called to Bar, Gray's Inn; ICS (retired). Judge of High Court, Nagpur, 1936-48; Acting Chief Justice, 1947; Chairman, Medical Appeal Tribunal, Southern Region, 1948-63. *Address:* 17 South Drive, Wokingham, Berks.

**POLLOCK, Sir William H. M.;** *see* Montagu-Pollock.

**POLLOK, Maj.-Gen. Robert Valentine,** CB 1940; CBE 1919; DSO 1917; late Irish Guards; *b* 14 Feb. 1884; 4th *s* of late John Pollok of Lismany, Ballinasloe, Co. Galway; *m* 1916, Sylvia Bettina, *d* of late George Fellows, Beeston Fields, Notts. *Educ:* Eton; Royal Military Coll., Sandhurst. Joined 15th Hussars, 1903; ADC to Lieutenant-Governor, United Provinces, India, 1908-12; ADC Governor-Gen. Australia, 1913-14. Served European War, 1914-18 (CBE, DSO, despatches, four times wounded): employed Australian Forces, Gallipoli (Adjutant and Staff Captain), 1914-15; transferred Irish Guards, 1916; Acting Major, 1917; Acting Lt-Col, 1917; Lt-Col, 1926; Bt Col, 1929; Col, 1930; Maj.-Gen., 1938; commanded 1st Bn Irish Guards, 1917-18, and 1926-30; Staff Coll., 1921; Brigade Major 1st Guards Brigade, 1922-25; Officer Commanding Regt and Regimental District, 1930-31; Commander 1st Guards Brigade, 1931-35; Commandant Senior Officers' Sch., Sheerness, 1935-38; General Officer comdg Northern Ireland District, 1938-40; Comdr 43rd (Wessex) Div. (TA); retired pay, 1941; re-employed as Colonel, General Staff, 1941; reverted to retired pay, 1941. *Address:* The Bridge House, Rathkeale, Co. Limerick, Eire. *T:* Rathkeale 11. *Club:* Cavalry.

**POLSON, Prof. Cyril John;** Professor of Forensic Medicine, University of Leeds, 1947-69, now Emeritus Professor; *b* 1901; *s* of William Polson, MB, CM, and A. D., *d* of Thomas Parker, JP, MInstCE, FRSE; *m* 1932, Mary Watkinson Tordoff (*d* 1961); one *d*; *m* 1963, G. Mary Pullan (BSc, MB, ChB, DObst, RCOG). *Educ:* Wrekin Coll.; Birmingham Univ. MB, ChB and MRCS, LRCP, 1924; MRCP 1926; FRCP, 1941; FCPath, 1964; MD 1929, Birmingham. Called to the Bar, Inner Temple, 1940. Assistant Lecturer, Univ. of Manchester, 1927; Univ. of Leeds: Lecturer in Pathology, 1928; Senior Lecturer in Pathology, and Pathologist to St J. Hospital, Leeds, 1945; Hon. Cons. Pathologist, Leeds (A Group) Hospitals, 1949; Hon. Member, N England Laryngological Society, 1948. Corr. Member la Société de Médecine Légale de France, 1950. Vice-President 2nd International Meeting in Forensic Medicine, NY, 1960; President British Association in Forensic Medicine, 1962-65; Hon. Mem., Leeds and West Riding Medico-Legal Society, 1970 (Pres. 1966). *Publications:* The Disposal of the Dead (senior author and editor), 2nd edn, 1962; The Essentials of Forensic Medicine, 2nd edn, 1965; Clinical Toxicology (with R. N. Tattersall), 2nd edn, 1969; The Scientific Aspects of Forensic Medicine, 1969; papers in scientific journals devoted to pathology and forensic medicine. *Recreations:* gardening, photography. *Address:* 16 Tewit Well Road, Harrogate. *T:* Harrogate 3434, Leeds 31897. *Club:* Authors'.

**POLSON, Milson George,** QC 1964; Practising Barrister since 1947; Chairman, Isle of Wight Quarter Sessions since 1967 (Deputy Chairman, 1964-67); Recorder of Exeter since 1966; *b* 3 June 1917; *s* of Caleb George Polson, Senghenydd, Glamorganshire; *m* 1939, Ida, *y d* of George Stephens, late Chief of Police, GW Railway Co.; one *s* one *d*. *Educ:* Caerphilly, Glam; London Univ. Glamorganshire County Council, 1935-37; Fulham Metropolitan Borough Council, 1937-39. Served War of 1939-45 (Defence and other Medals): Flt-Lt, Meteorologist, RAF; Europe, India, Burma, and China, 1939-46 (Burma Star). Called to the Bar, Lincoln's Inn, 1947; joined Inner Temple, *ad eundem*, 1961. Member: General Council of the Bar, 1967-70; Court of Exeter Univ., 1967. *Recreations:* travel, books, tennis, gardening. *Address:* 9 Charlbury Grove, Ealing, W5. *T:* 01-997 9578; Monk's Wall Cottage, Otterton, near Budleigh Salterton, Devon. *T:* Colaton Raleigh 374; 1 Crown Office Row, Temple, EC4. *T:* 01-353 9272. *Clubs:* Reform; Hampshire County (Winchester).

**POLTIMORE,** 6th Baron, *cr* 1831; **Hugh de Burgh Warwick Bampfylde;** Bt 1641; *b* 1888; *yr b* of 5th Baron Poltimore; *S* brother, 1967; *m* 1918, Margaret Mary, *d* of 4th Marquis de la Pasture; one *s* (and one *s* decd). *Educ:* Winchester; New Coll., Oxford. MA. Served East Africa, 1914-18. *Heir:* *g s* Mark Coplestone Bampfylde, *b* 8 June 1957. *Address:* The Ancient House, Peasenhall, Saxmundham, Suffolk. *Club:* St James'.

**POLUNIN, Nicholas,** MS (Yale); MA, DPhil, DSc (Oxon); FLS; FRGS; Editor (founding) of Biological Conservation, since 1967, and of Plant Science Monographs, since 1954; Guest Professor, University of Geneva, 1959-61; *b* Checkendon, Oxon, 26 June 1909; *e s* of late Vladimir and Elizabeth Violet (*née* Hart) Polunin; *m* 1st, 1939, Helen Lovat Fraser; one *s*; *m* 2nd, 1948, Helen Eugenie Campbell; two *s* one *d*. *Educ:* The Hall, Weybridge; Latymer Upper and privately; Oxford, Yale and Harvard Univs. Open Scholar of Christ Church, Oxford, 1928-32; First Class Hons Nat. Sci. Final Examination, Botany and Ecology; Goldsmiths' Senior Studentship for Research, 1932-33; Botanical tutor in various Oxford Colls, 1932-47; Henry Fellowship at Pierson Coll., Yale Univ., USA, 1933-34 (Sigma Xi); Departmental Demonstrator in Botany 1934-35, and Senior (Research) Scholar of New Coll., Oxford, 1934-36; Dept of Scientific and Industrial Research, Senior Research Award, 1935-38; Rolleston Memorial Prize, 1938; DSIR Special

Investigator, 1938; Research Associate, Gray Herbarium, Harvard Univ., USA, 1936-37, and subs. Foreign Research Associate; Fielding Curator and Keeper of the Univ. Herbaria, Oxford, and Univ. Demonstrator and Lectr in Botany, 1939-47; Oxford Univ. Botanical Moderator, 1941-45; Macdonald Prof. of Botany, McGill Univ., Canada, 1947-52 (Visiting Prof., 1946-47); Research Fellow, Harvard Univ., 1950-53; Lectr in Plant Science and Research Associate, Yale Univ., 1953-55; Project Dir, US Air Force, 1953-55, and Consultant to US Army Corps of Engineers; formerly Sen. Research Fell. and Lectr, New Coll., Oxford; Prof. of Plant Ecology and Taxonomy, Head of Dept of Botany, and Dir of Univ. Herbarium, etc., Baghdad, Iraq, Jan. 1956-58 (revolution); Prof. of Botany and Head of Dept, Faculty of Science (which he established as Dean), Univ. of Ife, Nigeria, 1962-66 (revolutions, etc). Leverhulme Res. Award, 1941-43; Arctic Inst. Res. Fellowship, 1946-48; Guggenheim Mem. Fellowship, 1950-52. Haley Lectr, Acadia Univ., NS, 1950; Visiting Lectr and Adviser on Biology, Brandeis Univ., Waltham, Mass, 1953-54. US Order of Polaris; Marie-Victorin Medal for services to Canadian botany; FRHS. Fellow; AAAS, Arctic Inst. NA, American Geographical Soc. Member or Leader, numerous scientific expeditions from 1930, particularly in arctic or sub-arctic regions, including Spitsbergen, Lapland (3 times), Iceland, Greenland, Canadian Eastern Arctic (5 times), Labrador-Ungava (many times), Canadian Western Arctic (including Magnetic Pole), Alaska, summer and winter flights over geographical North Pole; subsequently in Middle East and West Africa; Ford Foundation Award, Scandinavia and USSR, 1966-67. *Publications:* Russian Waters, 1931; The Isle of Auks, 1932; Botany of the Canadian Eastern Arctic, vol. I, Pteridophyta and Spermatophyta, 1940; vol. II, Thallophyta and Bryophyta (Ed.), 1947; vol. III, Vegetation and Ecology, 1948; Arctic Unfolding, 1949; Circumpolar Arctic Flora, 1959; Introduction to Plant Geography, 1960 (subseq. Amer. and other edns); Eléments de Géographie botanique, 1967; Plant Sciences in the Arctic and Subarctic (4 vols in prep.); papers chiefly on arctic and boreal flora, phytogeography, ecology, vegetation, aerobiology, and conservation; editor of International Industry, 1943-46, and of World Crops Books, 1954-69; associate editor, Environmental Pollution, 1969-. *Recreations:* travel and exploration, nature conservation, stock-markets. *Address:* 15 chemin F.-Lehmann, 1218 Grand-Saconnex, Geneva, Switzerland. *T:* (022) 561707; c/o New College, Oxford. *Clubs:* Reform; Harvard, Explorers, Torrey Botanical (New York City); Lake Placid (NY); New England Botanical (Boston); Canadian Field Naturalists' (Ottawa).

*See also O. Polunin.*

**POLUNIN, Oleg;** Assistant Master, Charterhouse School, since 1938; *b* 28 Nov. 1914; Russian father, British mother; *m* 1943, Lorna Mary Venning; one *s* one *d. Educ:* St Paul's Sch.; Magdalen Coll., Oxford. Served War of 1939-45, Intelligence Corps. Botanical Exploration and collecting, Nepal, 1949-52; Turkey, 1954-56; Karakoram, Pakistan, 1960; Kashmir; Iraq; Lebanon; Lecturer and Guide on Hellenic cruises and other tours, often off the beaten track. Founder member, past Chairman, and Secretary, Surrey Naturalists' Trust. *Publications:* (with A. J. Huxley) Flowers of the Mediterranean, 1965; Flowers of Europe, 1969. *Recreations:* travel, plant photography and collecting, pottery. *Address:* Dormers, Farncombe Hill, Godalming, Surrey.

*See also N. Polunin.*

**POLWARTH,** 10th Baron, *cr* 1690; **Henry Alexander Hepburne-Scott,** TD; DL; Member, Royal Company of Archers; a Scots Representative Peer, 1945-63; Chartered Accountant; Governor, Bank of Scotland; Chairman, General Accident, Fire & Life Assurance Corporation; President, Scottish Council (Development and Industry); Director of Imperial Chemical Industries Ltd, and other companies; *b* 17 Nov. 1916; *s* of late Hon. Walter Thomas Hepburne-Scott (*d* 1942); *S* grandfather, 1944; *m* 1st, 1943, Caroline Margaret (marr. diss. 1969), 2nd *d* of late Captain R. A. Hay, Marlefield, Roxburghshire, and Helmsley, Yorks; one *s* three *d*; 2nd, 1969, Jean, *d* of Adm. Sir Angus Cunninghame Graham, *qv*, and formerly wife of C. E. Jauncey, QC; two step *s* one step *d. Educ:* Eton Coll.; King's Coll., Cambridge. Served War of 1939-45, Captain, Lothians and Border Yeomanry. Former Partner, firm of Chiene and Tait, CA, Edinburgh. Chancellor, Aberdeen Univ., 1966. Hon. LLD: St Andrews Univ.; Aberdeen Univ.; DLitt Heriot-Watt Univ.; DUniv Stirling Univ. FRSE. DL Roxburgh, 1962. *Heir: s* Master of Polwarth, *qv. Address:* Harden, Hawick, Scotland. *T:* Hawick 2069; 22 Regent Terrace, Edinburgh EH7 5BS. *T:* 031-556 4690. *Clubs:* Brooks's, Caledonian; New (Edinburgh).

**POLWARTH, Master of; Hon. Andrew Walter Hepburne-Scott;** *b* 30 Nov. 1947; *s* and *heir* of 10th Baron Polwarth, *qv. Educ:* Eton; Trinity Hall, Cambridge. *Address:* Harden, Hawick, Scotland.

**POLYNESIA, Bishop in,** since 1969; **Rt. Rev. John Tristram Holland;** *b* 31 Jan. 1912; *s* of Rt Rev. H. StB. Holland; *m* 1937, Joan Theodora Arundell, *d* of Dr R. Leslie Ridge, Carlton House, Enfield, Mddx; three *d. Educ:* Durham School; University College, Oxford; Westcott House, Cambridge, BA 1933, MA 1937, Oxford. Deacon, 1935; Priest, 1936; Curate of St Peter's, Huddersfield, 1935-37; Commissary to Bishop of Wellington, 1936-37; Vicar of Featherston, 1938-41; CF (2 NZEF), 1941-45; Vicar of: St Peter's, Upper Riccarton, 1945-49; St Mary's, New Plymouth, 1949-51; Bishop of Waikato, 1951-69. *Address:* Bishop's House, Box 35, GPO, Suva, Fiji Islands.

**POMEROY,** family name of **Viscount Harberton.**

**POMFRET, Surgeon Rear-Adm. Arnold Ashworth,** CB 1957; OBE 1941; retired, 1957; *b* 1 June 1900; *s* of John and Eleanor Pomfret; *m* 1928, Carlene Blundstone; one *s* two *d. Educ:* Manchester Univ.; Postgraduate at London, Capetown and Oxford. MB, ChB (Manchester), 1922; DO (Oxon) 1934; DOMS (RCS&PEng), 1934. Senior Ophthalmic Specialist, RN. Last MO i/c Wei-Hai-Wei, 1940. Formerly Asst to MDG, 1944-45 and 1952-54. MO i/c RN Hospitals: Simonstown, 1946; Portland, 1948; Bermuda, 1950; MO i/c RN Hospital, Plymouth, and Command MO Plymouth, 1954-57. Gilbert Blane Medallist, 1934. Surgeon Comdr, 1934; Surgeon Captain, 1944; Surgeon Rear-Adm., 1954. QHS, 1954-57. CStJ 1957. *Recreations:* cricket, association football. *Address:* Passlands, Forton, Chard, Somerset.

**POMPIDOU, Georges Jean Raymond,** Grand Croix de la Légion d'Honneur; President of the French Republic, since June 1969; *b* 5 July 1911; *s* of late Prof. Léon Pompidou and of Marie-Louise (*née* Chavagnac); *m* Claude Cahour; one *s. Educ:* Lycée d'Albi; Lycée

Louis le Grand; Ecole Normale Supérieure; Ecole Libre des Sciences Politiques (Dipl. Agrégé des Lettres). Taught Literature: Lycée St Charles, Marseille, 1935-39; Lycée Henri IV, Paris, 1939-44. Infantry Officer, 1939-40. Chargé de Mission, Gen. de Gaulle's Cabinet, 1944-46; Dep. Director, Tourism, 1946-49; Member Council of State, 1946-54; Maître des Requêtes honoraire, 1957; Dir, Gen. de Gaulle's Cabinet, 1958-59; Mem., Constitutional Council, 1959-62; Prime Minister of France, 1962-68; Mem., Nat. Assembly, 1968-69; elected Pres. of Republic, 16 June 1969. Dir-Gen., Rothschild Bank, and several cos, 1956-62. *Publications:* Studies of Britannicus, 1944; Taine, 1947; Malraux, 1955; Anthologie de la Poésie Française, 1961. *Recreation:* hunting. *Address:* Palais de l'Elysée, Paris 8e, France.

**PONCET, André F.;** *see* François-Poncet.

**POND, Desmond Arthur,** MA, MD, FRCP, DPM; Professor of Psychiatry, University of London at The London Hospital Medical College, London, E1, since 1966; *b* 2 Sept. 1919; *o s* of Thomas Arthur and Ada Celia Pond; *m* 1945, Margaret Helen (*née* Jordan), MD; three *d*. *Educ:* John Lyon's, Harrow; St Olave's, SE1; Clare Coll., Cambridge; Universtiy College Hospital. Rockefeller Scholar, Duke Med. Sch., N Carolina, 1942-44; Sen. Lectr, Dept of Clin. Neurophysiology, Maudsley Hosp., and Cons. Psychiatrist, UCH, 1952-66; Goulstonian Lectr, RCP, 1961; Founder Mem., Inst. of Religion and Med., 1964; Mem., Archbishop's Gp on Divorce Law ('Putting Asunder'), 1964-66; Mem., MRC, 1968-; H. B. Williams Vis. Prof., Australian and New Zealand Coll. of Psychiatrists, 1968; Riddell Memorial Lectr, Univ. of Newcastle, 1971. *Publications:* various, on psychiatry and electroencephalography. *Recreations:* making music, gardens. *Address:* Yew Trees, 356 Dover House Road, Roehampton, SW15. *T:* 01-788 2903. *Club:* Athenæum.

**PONS, Lily;** Opera, concert, radio, film and recording star; of French birth; *m* 1938, André Kostelanetz, *qv*. *Educ:* Paris Conservatoire. Soprano. Past Member, Metropolitan Opera, Colon Teatre (Buenos Aires), Paris, Covent Garden, San Francisco, Rome, Chicago and Monte Carlo Opera Companies. *Radio:* Guest star on such popular air shows as Telephone Hour, Voice of Firestone, etc. *Moving Pictures:* Starred in RKO films: That Girl from Paris, I Dream Too Much, Hitting a New High. Officer, the French Legion of Honor; Chevalier of the Order of the Royal Crown of Brussels; Gold Medal of City of Paris; Order of Cross of Lorraine; Official Daughter LeClerc Div. *Recreation:* collection of Modern paintings. *Address:* Dallas, Texas.

**PONSONBY,** family name of **Earl of Bessborough** and of **Barons de Mauley, Ponsonby of Shulbrede,** and **Sysonby.**

**PONSONBY of Shulbrede,** 2nd Baron, *cr* 1930, of Shulbrede; **Matthew Henry Hubert Ponsonby;** *b* 28 July 1904; *s* of 1st Baron and Dorothea (*d* 1963), *d* of Sir Hubert Parry, 1st Bart and Lady Maud Parry; *S* father, 1946; *m* 1929, Hon. Elizabeth Bigham, *o d* of 2nd Viscount Mersey, PC, CMG, CBE; one *s* three *d*. *Educ:* Leighton Park School, Reading; Balliol College, Oxford. *Heir: s* Hon. Thomas Arthur Ponsonby [*b* 23 October 1930; *m* 1956, Ursula Mary, *yr d* of Commander Thomas Fox Pitt; one *s* three *d*]. *Address:* Shulbrede Priory, Haslemere, Surrey. *T:* Fernhurst 249.

**PONSONBY, Arthur Gordon;** *b* 14 June 1892; 2nd *s* of late Rev. Stewart Gordon Ponsonby; *m* 1938, Jacqueline, 2nd *d* of late Karl Kirdorf, Krefeld, Germany; one *s*. *Educ:* Marlborough; Trinity College, Cambridge. Interned in Ruhleben during the war, 1914-18; joined HM Consular service in 1920. HM Chargé d'Affairs, Monrovia, 1938-40; Consul-General at Rio de Janeiro, 1947-51; retd from HM Foreign Service, 1951. *Recreation:* gardening. *Address:* 26 Upper High Street, Thame, Oxon. *Club:* Royal Commonwealth Society.

**PONSONBY, Ashley Charles Gibbs,** MC 1945; Managing Director of Schroder, Wagg & Co. Ltd and Director of other companies; *b* 21 Feb. 1921; *o s* and *heir* of Col Sir Charles Edward Ponsonby, 1st Bt, *qv*; *m* 1950, Lady Martha Butler, *yr d* of 6th Marquess of Ormonde, *qv*; four *s*. *Educ:* Eton; Balliol College, Oxford. 2nd Lieut Coldstream Guards, 1941; served war 1942-45 (North Africa and Italy, wounded); Captain 1943; on staff Bermuda Garrison, 1945-46. A Church Commissioner since 1963. *Address:* Grimsdyke Farm, Woodleys, Woodstock, Oxon. *T:* Woodstock 7617. *Club:* Brooks's.

**PONSONBY, Col Sir Charles Edward,** 1st Bt *cr* 1956; TD; DL; *b* 2 Sept. 1879; *e s* of late Hon. Edwin Ponsonby; *m* 1912, Hon. Winifred Gibbs, *d* of 1st Baron Hunsdon; one *s* four *d*. *Educ:* Eton; Balliol College, Oxford. BA 1901; admitted a solicitor, 1904; Director of Companies; Chm. Royal Commonwealth Soc., 1954-57; President Royal African Soc., 1962; Past-Pres. Glass Manufacturers Federation; Mem. Council Joint African Board, Commonwealth Producers Organization, etc.; a Beit Trustee. Served European War, 1914-18, West Kent (QO) Yeomanry and 10th (Yeomanry) Battalion The Buffs in Gallipoli, Egypt, Palestine, and France (Croix de Guerre avec Palmes); commanded 97th (Kent Yeomanry) Brigade RA (T), 1930-36; Hon. Col 97th (Kent Yeomanry) Field Regt RA, 1942; and 297th (Kent Yeomanry) Lt AA Regt RA, 1942-49. MP (C) Sevenoaks, 1935-50; Parliamentary Private Sec. to Secretary of State for War and Secretary of State for Foreign Affairs (Rt Hon. Anthony Eden), 1940-45; Member Parly Delegs to Russia, 1945, Austria, 1948, Burma, 1950; Member Industrial Relations Mission to Nigeria, 1950. *Publications:* West Kent (QO) Yeomanry and 10th (Yeomanry) Bn The Buffs, 1914-19; History of Wootton; Ponsonby Remembers (autobiography); Wootton: Anatomy of an Oxfordshire Village, 1968. *Recreations:* archæology, writing, etc. *Heir: s* Ashley Charles Gibbs Ponsonby, *qv*. *Address:* Woodleys, Woodstock, Oxfordshire. *T:* Woodstock 422; 6 Eresby House, Rutland Gate, SW7. *T:* 01-589 3060. *Club:* Brooks's.

*See also Sir Edmund C. Bacon, M. A. Hamilton, J. E. Ramsden.*

**PONSONBY, Myles Walter,** CBE 1966; British Embassy, Rome, since 1969; *b* 12 Sept. 1924; *s* of late Victor Coope Ponsonby, MC and late Gladys Edith Ponsonby (*née* Walter); *m* 1951, Anne Veronica Theresa Maynard; one *s* two *d*. *Educ:* St Aubyn's, Rottingdean; Eton College. HM Forces (Captain, KRRC), 1942-49. Entered Foreign (subseq. Diplomatic) Service, 1951; served in: Egypt, 1951; Cyprus, 1952-53; Beirut, 1953-56; Djakarta, 1958-61; Nairobi, 1963-64; Hanoi (Consul-Gen.), 1964-65; FO, 1966-69. *Recreations:* shooting, gardening, travel. *Address:* c/o Foreign and Commonwealth Office, SW1; Godden House, Godden Green, Sevenoaks, Kent. *T:* Sevenoaks 61170. *Club:* Travellers'.

**PONSONBY, Robert Noel;** General Administrator, Scottish National Orchestra, since 1964; Artistic Advisor to International Arts Guild of the Bahamas since 1960; *b* 19 Dec. 1926; *o s* of late Noel Ponsonby, BMus, Organist Christ Church Cathedral, Oxford, and Mary White-Thomson (now Mrs L. H. Jaques, Winchester); *m* 1957, Una Mary (marr. diss.), *er d* of W. J. Kenny. *Educ:* Eton; Trinity Coll., Oxford. MA Oxon., Eng. Litt. Commissioned Scots Guards, 1945-47. Organ Scholar, Trinity Coll., Oxon., 1948-50; staff of Glyndebourne Opera, 1951-55; Artistic Director of the Edinburgh International Festival, 1955-60; with Independent Television Authority, 1962-64; Director, Commonwealth Arts Festival, Glasgow, 1965. *Publication:* Short History of Oxford University Opera Club, 1950. *Recreations:* fell-walking, English and Scottish painting, music. *Address:* 6 Kirklee Circus, Glasgow, W2. *Clubs:* Third Guards; Trinity Society; Scottish Arts (Edinburgh).

**PONTECORVO, Prof. Guido,** FRS 1955; FRS (Edinburgh) 1946; PhD (Edinburgh) 1941; DrAgr (Pisa) 1928; Member of the Scientific Staff, Imperial Cancer Research Fund, London, WC2; Visiting Professor: University College, London, since 1968; King's College, since 1970; *b* Pisa, Italy, 29 Nov. 1907; *s* of Massimo Pontecorvo and Maria (*née* Maroni); *m* 1939, Leonore Freyenmuth, Frauenfeld, Switzerland; one *d*. *Educ:* Pisa (Classics). Ispettorato Agrario per la Toscana, Florence, 1931-38; Inst. of Animal Genetics, Univ. of Edinburgh, 1938-40 and 1944-45; Dept of Zoology, Univ. of Glasgow, 1941-44; Dept of Genetics, Univ. of Glasgow, 1945-68 (Prof. 1955-68). Jesup Lectr, Columbia Univ., 1956; Messenger Lectr, Cornell Univ., 1957; Visiting Prof., Albert Einstein Coll. Med., 1965, 1966; Vis. Lectr, Washington State Univ., 1967; Royal Society, Leverhulme Overseas Vis. Prof., Inst. of Biophysics, Rio de Janeiro, 1969. Sec., Genetical Soc., 1945-51, Vice-Pres., 1954-57, 1966-69, Pres., 1964-66; Vice-Pres., Inst. of Biology, 1969-. For. Hon. Member: Amer. Acad. Arts and Sciences, 1958; Danish Royal Soc., 1966; Peruvian Soc. of Medical Genetics, 1969. Hon. DSc Leicester, 1968. Hansen Foundation Prize, 1961. *Publications:* Ricerche sull' economia montana dell' Appennino Toscano, 1933 (Florence); Trends in Genetic Analysis, 1958. Numerous papers in British, American, Swiss, French and Italian jls on Genetics. *Recreations:* mountaineering, alpine plants photography. *Address:* Flat 25, Cranfield House, 97 Southampton Row, WC1B 4HH. *T:* 01-636 9441.

**PONTEFRACT, Bishop Suffragan of,** since 1968; **Rt. Rev. William Gordon Fallows;** *b* 21 June 1913; *s* of William and Anne Joyce Fallows; *m* 1940, Edna Mary Blakeman; two *s* one *d*. *Educ:* Barrow Grammar School; St Edmund Hall, Oxford; Ripon Hall. BA 1935, MA 1939. Deacon, 1936; Priest, 1937; Curate of Holy Trinity, Leamington Spa, 1936-39; Vicar of Styvechale, Coventry, 1939-45; OCF 1941-44. Rural Dean of Preston, 1946-55; Proctor in Convocation, 1950-55; Archdeacon of Lancaster, 1955-59; Vicar of Preston, 1945-59; Principal of Ripon Hall, Oxford, 1959-68. Canon of Blackburn, 1952; Examining Chaplain to Bishop of Wakefield, since 1968; Chaplain to the Queen, 1953-68. Select Preacher, Univ. of Oxford, 1961. *Publication:* Mandell Creighton and the English Church, 1964. *Recreation:* fell walking. *Address:* Highfield, 306 Barnsley Road, Sandal, Wakefield. *T:* Wakefield 56935. *Club:* Authors'.

**PONTEFRACT, Archdeacon of;** *see* Henderson, Ven. E. C.

**PONTI, Signora Carlo;** *see* Loren, Sophia.

**PONTING, Brig. Theophilus John,** CSI 1947; CIE 1940; MC; psc; idc; IA, retired; *b* 1886. Served NW Frontier of India, 1908; European War, 1916-18, in Mesopotamia and Egypt (despatches, MC, French Croix de Guerre); retired, 1940. *Address:* Walldown, Whitehill, Bordon, Hants.

**POOL, Bernard Frank,** CB 1957; CBE 1951 (OBE 1944); Director of Navy Contracts, Admiralty, 1948-60, retired; Hon. Treasurer, Navy Records Society, since 1960; Councillor, Society for Nautical Research, since 1968; *b* 17 July 1896; *s* of late Augustus Frank Pool, CBE, and 1st wife, late Harriette Maude Mary Smith; *m* 1932, Hazel Violet, *d* of late Charles Ambrose; one *s* one *d*. *Educ:* Colfe Grammar School. LLB, BCom (London). Barrister-at-Law, Middle Temple, 1921. Assistant Contract Officer Admiralty, 1915; Assistant Director of Contracts, 1936; Deputy Director, 1940. *Publications:* Navy Board Contracts, 1660-1832, 1966; The Croker Papers (ed.), 1967; articles in The Mariner's Mirror, History Today. *Recreation:* naval history. *Address:* 81 Bromley Road, Shortlands, Bromley, Kent BR2 0AA. *T:* 01-460 6492. *Clubs:* Royal Commonwealth Society; Samuel Pepys.

**POOLE,** family name of **Baron Poole.**

**POOLE;** *see* Lane Poole and Lane-Poole.

**POOLE,** 1st Baron, *cr* 1958, of Aldgate; **Oliver Brian Sanderson Poole,** PC 1963; CBE 1945; TD; Member of Lloyd's; Director: S. Pearson & Sons Ltd; Whitehall Securities Corporation Ltd; Chairman, Lazard Bros & Co. Ltd; *b* 11 Aug., 1911; *s* of late Donald Louis Poole of Lloyd's and Mrs T. H. Minshall; *m* 1st, 1933, Betty Margaret Gilkison (marr. diss., 1951); one *s* three *d*; 2nd, 1952, Mrs Daphne Heber Percy (marr. diss., 1965); 3rd, 1966, Barbara Ann Taylor. *Educ:* Eton; Christ Church, Oxford. Life Guards, 1932-33; joined Warwickshire Yeomanry, 1934. Service in 1939-45 in Iraq, Syria, North Africa, Sicily and NW Europe (despatches thrice, MBE, OBE, CBE, US Legion of Merit, Order of Orange Nassau). MP (C) Oswestry Division of Salop, 1945-50. Conservative Party Organisation: Jt Hon. Treas., 1952-55; Chairman, 1955-57; Dep.-Chm., 1957-59; Jt Chm., May-Oct. 1963, Vice-Chm., Oct. 1963-Oct. 1964. Governor of Old Vic, 1948-63. *Heir: s* Hon. David Charles Poole, [*b* 6 Jan. 1945; *m* 1967, Fiona, *d* of John Donald, London SW6]. *Address:* 12 Egerton Terrace, SW3. *Clubs:* MCC, Buck's, Royal Yacht Squadron (Cowes).

*See also Sir Hugh Munro-Lucas-Tooth, Bt.*

**POOLE, John Hewitt Jellett,** MA, MAI, ScD; FTCD; Professor of Geophysics, University of Dublin, since 1934; *b* Dublin, 19 March 1893; *s* of T. H. Poole, Mayfield, Bandon, Co. Cork, and Maria Emily, *d* of Rev. J. H. Jellett, FRS, Provost of Trinity College, Dublin; unmarried. *Educ:* Mountjoy School, Dublin; Trinity College, Dublin. Pupil and Assistant on the GNR (I), 1916-19; served with Railway Corps in France, 1917; Research Assistant to Prof. John Joly, 1919; Assistant to Prof. W. E. Thrift, 1921-29; Lecturer in Physics, Dublin University, 1929; Commissioner of Irish Lights, 1927; Member: Royal Irish Academy, 1931; Physical Society, London, 1933; Council, Royal Dublin Society, 1933; Emergency Research Bureau, Ireland, 1941-45. Boyle Medallist, Royal Dublin Soc., 1947.

*Publications:* Papers in the Philosophical Magazine, Scientific Proceedings of Royal Dublin Society, etc., on Radioactivity of Rocks, Theories of Earth history, photo-electricity, etc. *Recreations:* yachting, tennis, walking. *Address:* Trinity College, Dublin; Ashbrook, Clontarf, Dublin.

**POOLE, Rev. Canon Joseph Weston;** Canon Residentiary, since 1963, and Precentor of Coventry, since 1958; *b* 25 March 1909; *s* of Rev. S. J. Poole and Mrs Poole (*née* Weston); *m* 1945, Esmé Beatrice Mounsey; three *s* two *d.* *Educ:* St George's School, Windsor; King's School, Canterbury; Jesus Coll., Cambridge (Organ Schol. and Class. Exhibnr); Westcott House, Cambridge. Curate of St Mary-at-the-Walls, Colchester, 1933; Sub-Warden of Student Movement House, 1935; Minor Canon and Sacrist of Canterbury, 1936; Precentor of Canterbury, 1937; Rector of Merstham, Surrey, 1949; Hon. Canon and Precentor of Coventry, 1958. *Recreations:* music, literature, typography. *Address:* The Precentor's House, 2 Spencer Road, Coventry. *T:* Coventry 73527.

**POOLE HUGHES, Rt. Rev. John R. W.;** *see* South-West Tanganyika, Bishop of.

**POORE, Sir Herbert Edward,** 6th Bt, *cr* 1795; *b* 1930; *s* of Sir Edward Poore, 5th Bt, and Amelia Guliemone; *S* father 1938. *Heir: u* Nasionceno Poore [*b* 1900; *m* Juana Borda (*d* 1943); three *s* three *d*]. *Address:* Curuzu Cuatia, Corrientes, Argentine Republic.

**POORE, Martin Edward Duncan,** MA, PhD; FInstBiol; Director, Nature Conservancy, since 1966; *b* 25 May 1925; *s* of T. E. D. Poore and Elizabeth McMartin; *m* 1948, Judith Ursula, *d* of Lt-Gen. Sir Treffry Thompson, *qv*; two *s*. *Educ:* Trinity Coll., Glenalmond; Edinburgh Univ.; Clare Coll., Cambridge. MA, PhD Cantab.; MA Oxon. Japanese interpreter, 1943-45. Nature Conservancy, 1953-56; Consultant Ecologist, Hunting Technical Services, 1956-59; Prof. of Botany, Univ. of Malaya, Kuala Lumpur, 1959-65; Dean of Science, Univ. of Malaya, 1964-65; Lectr, Forestry Dept, Oxford, 1965-66. *Publications:* papers on ecology and land use in various jls and scientific periodicals. *Recreations:* hill walking, natural history, music, gardening, photography. *Address:* Evenlode, Stonesfield, Oxon. *T:* Stonesfield 246. *Clubs:* Athenæum, United University.

**POPE, HH the;** *see* Paul VI.

**POPE, Andrew Lancelot,** CVO 1965; OBE 1959; Counsellor, HM Embassy, Bonn, since 1962; *b* 27 July 1912; *m* 1st, 1938 (marr. diss.); 2nd, 1948, Ilse Migliarina; one *step d.* *Educ:* Harrow School. Served War of 1939-45 (despatches): Lieut, Royal Fusiliers, 1939; POW 1940-45. Served in Mil. Govt and Allied High Commn in Germany, 1945-56; entered Foreign (subseq. Diplomatic) Service, 1959. Order of Merit (Germany), 1965; Order of Merit (Bavaria), 1970. *Recreations:* shooting, gardening. *Address:* Goldhill Grove, Lower Bourne, Farnham, Surrey. *T:* Farnham 21334. *Club:* Bath.

**POPE, Sir Barton;** *see* Pope, Sir Sidney Barton.

**POPE, Dudley Bernard Egerton;** Naval historian and author; *b* 29 Dec. 1925; *s* of late Sydney Broughton Pope and late Alice Pope (*née* Meehan); *m* 1954, Kathleen Patricia Hall; one *d.* *Educ:* Ashford (Kent). Served War of 1939-45: Midshipman, MN, 1941-43 (wounded and invalided). The Evening News: naval and defence correspondent, 1944-57, Dep. Foreign Editor, 1957-59; resigned to take up full-time authorship, 1959. Counsellor, Navy Record Soc., 1964-68. In 1965 created "Lt Ramage RN" series of historical novels covering life of naval officer in Nelson's day; cruising trans-Atlantic and Caribbean in own yacht, doing naval historical research, 1965-. *Publications: non-fiction:* Flag 4, the Battle of Coastal Forces in the Mediterranean, 1954; The Battle of the River Plate, 1956; 73 North, 1958; England Expects, 1959; At 12 Mr Byng was Shot, 1962; The Black Ship, 1963; Guns, 1965; *fiction:* Ramage (Book Society Choice) 1965; Ramage and the Drum Beat (Book Society Alternative Choice), 1967; Ramage and the Freebooters (Book of the Month Club Alt. Choice), 1969. *Recreations:* ocean cruising, skin-diving. *Address:* c/o Peter Janson Smith Ltd, 42 Great Russell Street, WC1. *Clubs:* Royal Ocean Racing; Ocean Cruising; Royal Temple Yacht.

**POPE, Sir George (Reginald),** Kt 1967; General Manager of The Times, 1965-67; Director: Times Newspapers Ltd, since 1967 (Deputy General Manager during 1967); Daltons Weekly Ltd; Kingsway Press Ltd; *b* 25 Mar. 1902; *s* of G. J. Pope; *m* 1930, Susie A. Hendy; one *s.* *Educ:* Clapham Parochial Sch. The Morning Post, 1916-37; The Daily Telegraph, 1937; The Times, 1937-. Treas., Methodist Press and Information Service; Mem. Cttee, British and Foreign Bible Soc., 1968-. Governor, St Mary's Hosp., Paddington. Pres. of the Advertising Assoc., 1962-63. Mackintosh Medal, 1953; Publicity Club of London Cup, 1961. *Recreation:* bowls. *Address:* 57 West Drive, Cheam, Surrey. *T:* 01-642 4754. *Club:* Royal Automobile.

**POPE, Air Vice-Marshal John Clifford,** CB 1963; CBE 1959; CEng, FIMechE; FRAeS; RAF (retired); *b* 27 April 1912; *s* of George Newcombe-Pope; *m* 1950, Christine Agnes, *d* of Alfred Hames, Chichester; one *s* two *d.* *Educ:* Tiverton Sch.; RAF Coll., Cranwell. Commnd, 1932; served with No. 3 Sqdn, 1933, Nos 27 and 29, on NW Frontier, 1933-36. War of 1939-45; Comd RAF Station, Cleave, 1940-42; served in Egypt and Palestine, 1943-46; Asst Dir Research and Devel., Min. of Supply, 1947-50; Dir of Engineering, RNZAF, 1951-53; Comd RAF Station, Stoke Heath, 1954-57; Sen. Tech. Staff Officer, No. 3 Gp Bomber Comd, 1957-59 and Flying Trg Comd, 1960-61; AOC and Comdt, RAF Technical College, 1961-63; Senior Technical Staff Officer, Transport Command, 1963-66. Life Vice-Pres., RAF Boxing Assoc. *Address:* The White House, Norton Road, Letchworth, Herts. *Club:* Royal Air Force.

**POPE, Rear-Adm. John Ernle;** Flag Officer, Western Fleet Flotillas, since 1969; *b* 22 May 1921; *s* of Comdr R. K. C. Pope, Homme House, Herefordshire. *Educ:* RN Coll., Dartmouth. Royal Navy, 1935. Served throughout War of 1939-45, in Destroyers. CO, HMS Decoy, 1962-64; Dir, Naval Equipment, 1964-66; CO, HMS Eagle, 1966-68; Rear-Adm. 1969. *Recreations:* sailing, shooting. *Address:* Homme House, Much Marcle, Herefordshire. *Club:* Army and Navy.

*See also Rear-Adm. M. D. Kyrle Pope.*

**POPE, Joseph Albert,** DSc, PhD (Belfast), WhSc; Vice-Chancellor, University of Aston in Birmingham, since 1969; *b* 18 October 1914; *s* of Albert Henry and Mary Pope; *m* 1940, Evelyn Alice Gallagher; one *s* two *d.* *Educ:* School of Arts and Crafts, Cambridge; King's College, London. Apprentice, Boulton & Pauls, Norwich, 1930-35. Whitworth Scholarship, 1935. Assistant Lecturer in Engineering, Queen's Univ., Belfast, 1938-44;

Assistant Lecturer in Engineering, Univ. of Manchester, 1944-45; Lecturer, then Senior Lecturer, Univ. of Sheffield, 1945-49; Professor of Mechanical Engineering, Nottingham University, 1949-60; Research Dir, Mirrlees Nat. Research Div., Stockport, 1960-69; Director: Mirrlees National Ltd, 1960-69; Tecquipment Ltd, 1960-; John Brown Ltd, 1970-. *Publications:* papers on the impact of metals and metal fatigue published in Proc. of Inst. of Mech. Engineers and Jl of Iron and Steel Inst. *Address:* 1 Arthur Road, Edgbaston, Birmingham 15. *T:* 021-454 7545.

**POPE, Lt-Gen. (retd) Maurice Arthur,** CB 1944; MC; CD; *b* Rivière du Loup, PQ, 29 Aug. 1889; *s* of late Sir Joseph Pope, KCMG, CVO, ISO, sometime Under-Secretary of State for External Affairs, Ottawa, and late Henriette Taschereau; *m* 1920, Comtesse Simonne du Monceau de Bergendal (Belgium); three *s* one *d*. *Educ:* Locally Ottawa; McGill University, BSc (Civil Engineering, 1911). Civil Engineer, Canadian Pacific Railway, 1911; European War, 1914-18 (MC, despatches); Cdn Battlefields Memorials Commission, Belgium and France, 1920-21; Staff College, Camberley, 1924-25; Staff Appts, Canada, 1926-31; War Office, 1931-33; Canada, 1933-35; Imperial Defence College, 1936; Sec., Chiefs of Staff Committee, Ottawa, 1938; Director Military Operations and Intelligence, Ottawa, 1939; Brigadier, General Staff, Cdn Military HQ, London, 1940; Vice-Chief of the General Staff, Ottawa, 1941; Chairman, Canadian Joint Staff Mission, Washington, DC, 1942-44; Military Staff Officer to the Prime Minister and Military Sec., Cabinet War Cttee, 1944-45; Head of Canadian Military Mission to Allied Control Council, Berlin, 1945-50; Ambassador to Belgium, 1950-53; Ambassador to Spain, 1953-56, retired. Hon. LLD. *Publication:* Soldiers and Politicians (memoirs), 1962. *Address:* 216 Manor Avenue, Ottawa, 2, Canada.

**POPE, Rear-Adm. Michael Donald K.;** *see* Kyrle Pope.

**POPE, Col Ronald James,** CMG 1969; Senior Directing Staff, Joint Services Staff College, since 1970; *b* 5 Aug. 1924; *s* of Albert Thomas Pope; *m* 1957, Charlotte Pflanz; one *d*. *Educ:* Llandaff School. Commissioned S Wales Borderers, 1943; Served D-day landings and NW Europe, 1944; subsequently Palestine, Eritrea, Cyprus; Instructor, Officer Cadet School, 1954-55; Staff Coll., 1956; Joint Services Staff Coll., 1961; Bde Major, 11 Infantry Brigade Group, 1962-65; CO 1st Bn, Guyana Defence Force, 1965-67; Chief of Staff, Guyana Defence Force, 1967-69. *Recreations:* fishing, other field sports, Rugby football. *Address:* Joint Services Staff College, Latimer, Chesham, Bucks. *T:* Little Chalfont 3325. *Club:* United Hunts.

**POPE, Sir (Sidney) Barton,** Kt 1959; *b* 18 Feb. 1905; *s* of Henry Pope, Northam, W Australia; *m* 1944, Ada Lilian, *d* of late J. B. Hawkins; two *s* two *d*. *Educ:* Pulteney Grammar School, S Australia. President S Aust. Chamber of Manufacturers, 1947-49; Director: S Australian Insurance Co. Ltd, S Aust.; Finance Corp. of Aust. Ltd, SA; Freighters Ltd. Patron, SA Assoc. for Mental Health. *Recreations:* cricket, golf. *Address:* 421 The Parade, Kensington Gardens, S Australia. *T:* 31-2502. *Club:* Naval, Military and Air Force (SA).

**POPE-HENNESSY, James,** CVO 1960; writer; *b* 20 Nov. 1916; *yr s* of late Major-General L. H. R. Pope-Hennessy, CB, DSO and late Dame Una Pope-Hennessy, DBE. *Educ:* Downside Sch.; Balliol College, Oxford. Editorial assistant, Sheed and Ward, publishers, 1937-38; private sec. to Governor of Trinidad and Tobago, 1939. War Office, 1940-44; British Army Staff, Washington, USA, 1944-45. Literary Editor, The Spectator, 1947-49. *Publications:* London Fabric, 1939; West Indian Summer, 1943; The Houses of Parliament, 1945; America is an Atmosphere, 1947; Monckton Milnes, The Years of Promise, 1950; Monckton Milnes: The Flight of Youth, 1851-1885, 1952; Aspects of Provence, 1952; The Baths of Absalom, 1953; Lord Crewe: The Likeness of a Liberal, 1955; Queen Victoria at Windsor and Balmoral, 1959; Queen Mary, 1959; Verandah, 1964; Sins of the Fathers, 1967; Half-Crown Colony, 1969. *Recreation:* travel. *Address:* 9 Ladbroke Grove, W11. *T:* 01-727 4293. *Club:* Beefsteak.

**POPE-HENNESSY, John Wyndham,** CBE 1959 (MBE 1944); FBA 1955; FSA; FRSL; Director and Secretary, Victoria and Albert Museum, since 1967 (Keeper, Department of Architecture and Sculpture, 1954-66); *b* 13 Dec. 1913; *er s* of late Major-General L. H. R. Pope-Hennessy, CB, DSO, and late Dame Una Pope-Hennessy, DBE. *Educ:* Downside School; Balliol Coll., Oxford. Joined staff of Victoria and Albert Museum, 1938. Served Air Ministry, 1939-45. Slade Professor of Fine Art, Univ. of Oxford, 1956-57; Clark Professor of Art, Williams College, Mass., USA, 1961-62; Slade Professor of Fine Art, and Fellow of Peterhouse, University of Cambridge, 1964-65. Member: Arts Council, 1968-; Ancient Momuments Bd for England, 1969-. Corresponding Member, Accademia Senese degli Intronati; Hon. Academician, Accademia del Disegno, Florence. Serena Medal of British Academy for Italian Studies, 1961; New York University Medal, 1965. *Publications:* Giovanni di Paolo, 1937; Sassetta, 1939; Sienese Quattrocento Painting, 1947; A Sienese Codex of the Divine Comedy, 1947; The Drawings of Domenichino at Windsor Castle, 1948; A Lecture on Nicholas Hilliard, 1949; Donatello's Ascension, 1949; The Virgin with the Laughing Child, 1949; edition of the Autobiography of Benvenuto Cellini, 1949; Paolo Uccello, 1950; Italian Gothic Sculpture in the Victoria and Albert Museum, 1952; Fra Angelico, 1952; Italian Gothic Sculpture, 1955; Italian Renaissance Sculpture, 1958; Italian High Renaissance and Baroque Sculpture, 1963; Catalogue of Italian Sculpture in the Victoria And Albert Museum, 1964; Renaissance Bronzes in the Kress Collection, 1965; The Portrait in the Renaissance, 1967; Essays on Italian Sculpture, 1968; Catalogue of Sculpture in the Frick Collection, 1970; Raphael (Wrightsman lectures), 1970. Contributed Burlington Magazine, etc. *Recreation:* music. *Address:* 41 Bedford Gardens, W8. *T:* 01-727 6160.

**POPHAM, Arthur Ewart,** CB 1954; FBA 1949; Hon. RE 1945; Keeper, Department of Prints and Drawings, British Museum, 1945-54; *b* Plymouth, 22 March 1889; *m* 1st, 1912, Brynhild Olivier; two *s* one *d*; 2nd, 1926, Rosalind Thornycroft. *Educ:* Dulwich Coll.; University Coll., London; King's College, Cambridge. Entered British Museum, 1912; served European War, 1914-18, Flight Lieutenant, RNAS, and Captain RAF, Egypt and Palestine; Hon. Secretary Vasari Society, 1925-35. Hon. Fellow, King's College, Cambridge, 1955. *Publications:* Catalogue of Dutch and Flemish Drawings in the British Museum Vol. V. 1932; The Drawings of Leonardo da Vinci, 1946; Catalogue of Italian Drawings of XV cent. in British Museum (with Philip Pouncey), 1950; Correggio's Drawings,

1957; Catalogue of Drawing of School of Parma in the British Museum, 1967. Contributions to Burlington Magazine and foreign periodicals. *Address:* 4 Canonbury Place, N1. *T:* 01-226 4640. *Club:* Athenæum.

**POPHAM, Margaret Evelyn,** CBE 1953; Principal Ladies' College, Cheltenham, Jan. 1937-July 1953; *d* of Rev. B. G. Popham. *Educ:* Blackheath High School; Westfield College, London Univ., BA Hons Classics; Camb. Teachers Dip.; Ont. Teachers Certif. Classical Mistress Co. Sch., Chatham, 1919-23; Classical and Senior Mistress, Havergal College, Toronto, Canada, 1923-30; Headmistress Ladies' College, Jersey, CI, 1930-32; Westonbirt School, 1932-37. Vice-Chm., Gabbitas-Thring Educational Trust, 1960-; Member: Westfield College Council, 1935-66; Independent Television Authority, 1954-56; ITA Children's Committee, 1956-60; Individual Freedom Society (Executive), 1954-; Commonwealth Migration Council (Exec.), 1956-66; Conservative Commonwealth Coun., and Conservative Women's National Advisory Committee, 1954-57, and 1960-; Canning House, 1955-65. South Kensington Conservative (Executive), 1958-62; European Union of Women (Executive), 1960-; National Broadcasting Development Committee, 1961-63; formerly Mem., Governing Body of Girls' Sch. Exec. *Publication:* (Memoirs) Boring-Never!, 1968. *Recreations:* literature and travelling; politics and Commonwealth questions. *Address:* 60 Stafford Court, W8. *T:* 01-937 2717. *Clubs:* Royal Commonwealth Society, Guide.

**POPJÁK, George Joseph,** FRS 1961; DSc (London), MD, FRIC; Professor of Biochemistry at University of California in Los Angeles, since 1968; *b* 5 May 1914; *s* of late George and Maria Popják, Szeged, Hungary; *m* 1941, Hasel Marjorie, *d* of Duncan and Mabel Hammond, Beckenham, Kent. *Educ:* Royal Hungarian Francis Joseph University, Szeged. Demonstrator at Department of Morbid Anatomy and Histology, University of Szeged, 1938-39; Br Council Scholar, Postgraduate Med. School of London, 1939-41; Demonstrator in Pathology, Dept of Pathology, St Thomas's Hosp. Med. School, London, 1941-43; Beit Mem. Fellow for medical research at St Thomas's Hosp. Med. School, London, 1943-47; Member scientific staff of Med. Research Council at Nat. Inst. for Med. Research, 1947-53; Director of Medical Research Council Experimental Radiopathology Research Unit, Hammersmith Hosp., 1953-62; Jt Dir, Chemical Enzymology Lab., Shell Res. Ltd, 1962-68; Assoc. Prof. in Molecular Sciences, Warwick Univ., 1965-68. Foreign member of Belgian Roy. Flemish Acad. of Science, Literature and Fine Arts, 1955; Hon. Mem., Amer. Soc. of Biological Chemists, 1968; (with Dr J. W. Cornforth, FRS) CIBA Medal of Biochemical Soc., 1965 (first award); Stouffer Prize, 1967; Davy Medal, Royal Soc., 1968. *Publications:* Chemistry, Biochemistry and Isotopic Tracer Technique (Roy. Inst. of Chemistry monograph), 1955; articles on fat metabolism in Jl Path. Bact., Jl Physiol., Biochemical Jl, etc. *Recreations:* music, modelling and gardening. *Address:* Depts of Psychiatry and Biochemistry, University of California at Los Angeles, Center for the Health Sciences, Los Angeles, Calif 90024, USA.

**POPLE, John Anthony,** FRS 1961; Professor of Chemical Physics, Carnegie-Mellon University, Pittsburgh, USA, since 1964; *b* 31 Oct. 1925; *e s* of Herbert Keith Pople and Mary Frances Jones, Burnham-on-Sea, Som.; *m* 1952, Joy Cynthia Bowers; three *s* one *d*. *Educ:* Bristol Grammar School; Cambridge University, MA, PhD. Mayhew Prize, 1948, Smith Prize, 1950, Cambridge; Fellow, Trinity College, 1951-58, Lecturer in Mathematics, 1954-58, Cambridge; Superintendent of Basic Physics Division, National Physical Laboratory, 1958-64. Marlow Medal, Faraday Society, 1958. Ford Visiting Professor, Carnegie Inst. of Technology, Pittsburgh, 1961-62. Fellow, Amer. Physical Soc., 1970. Langmuir Award, Amer. Chemical Soc., 1970. *Publications:* High Resolution nuclear magnetic resonance, 1959; Approximate Molecular Orbital Theory, 1970; scientific papers on molecular physics and theoretical chemistry. *Recreations:* music, travel. *Address:* Carnegie-Mellon University, Pittsburgh, PA 15213, USA.

**POPPER, Prof. Sir Karl Raimund,** Kt 1965; PhD (Vienna), MA (New Zealand), DLit (London), Hon. LLD (Chicago and Denver); FBA 1958; Hon. Mem. RSNZ 1965; Professor of Logic and Scientific Method in the University of London, 1949-69, and in Department of Philosophy, Logic, and Scientific Method (London School of Economics and Political Science), 1945-69; Emeritus Professor, 1969; *b* Vienna, 28 July 1902; *s* of Dr Simon Siegmund Carl Popper, Barrister, of Vienna, and of Jenny Popper (*née* Schiff); *m* 1930, Josefine Anna Henninger; no *c*. *Educ:* University of Vienna. Senior Lecturer in Philosophy, Canterbury University College, Christchurch (Univ. of NZ), 1937-45; Reader in Logic in Univ. of London, 1945-48. William James Lecturer in Philosophy, Harvard Univ., for 1950. Visiting Lecturer in Yale, Princeton, Chicago, and Emory Univs, 1950, 1956; Eleanor Rathbone Lectr, Bristol Univ., 1956; Fellow, Center for Advanced Study in the Behavioral Sciences, Stanford, Calif, 1956-57; Annual Philos. Lectr to Brit. Academy, 1960; Herbert Spencer Lectr, Oxford Univ., 1961; Shearman Memorial Lectr, University Coll. London, 1961; Visiting Prof. of Philosophy, Univ. of California Berkeley, and Minnesota Center for Phil. of Science, 1962; Indiana University, and Farnum Lectr, Princeton Univ., 1963, Vis. Prof., Institute for Advanced Studies, Vienna, 1964. Arthur H. Compton Memorial Lectr, Washinton Univ., 1965; Vis. Prof., Denver University, 1966; Vis. Fellow, The Salk Institute for Biological Studies, 1966-67; Kenan Univ. Prof., Emory Univ., 1969; Jacob Ziskind Vis. Prof. in Philosophy and the History of Thought, Brandeis Univ., 1969. Member: Editorial Bd: Foundations of Physics; British Jl Phil. of Science; Studi Internat. di Filosofia; Advisory Editorial Board, The Monist; Co-Editor: Ratio; Studies in the Foundations Methodology and Philosophy of Science; Methodology and Science; Rechtstheorie; Schriftenreihe Erfahrung und Denken; Ed. Correspond., Dialectica. Fellow, Internat. Acad. for Philos. of Science, 1948-; Chairman, Phil. of Science Group, 1951-53; President The Aristotelian Soc., 1958-59; President British Society for the Phil. of Science, 1959-61; Mem. Council, Assoc. for Symb. Logic, 1951-55. Foreign Hon. Mem., American Acad. of Arts and Sciences, 1966; Hon. Member, Harvard Chapter of Phi Beta Kappa, 1964. Prize of the City of Vienna for 'Geisteswissenschaften' (mental and moral sciences) 1965. *Publications:* (trans. into fourteen languages); Logik der Forschung, 1934, 1966, 1969; The Open Society and Its Enemies, 1945 (rev. and enlarged) 1950, 1952, 1957; rev., with new Addenda 1962, 1963; 5th ed., rev. 1966, 1969; Misère de l'historicisme, 1956, 1969; The Poverty of Historicism, 1957, 1960, 1961, 1963, 1966, 1969; The Logic of Scientific Discovery, 1959, 1960, 1962, 1965,

1968; On the Sources of Knowledge and of Ignorance, 1961; Conjectures and Refutations, 1963, 1965, 1969; Of Clouds and Clocks, 1966; articles in: Contemporary British Philosophy, vol. III, British Philosophy in the Mid-Twentieth Century, Ordo. vol. viii, Observation and Interpretation, Theories of History, Philosophical Problems of the Social Sciences, Philosophy of History, Human Understanding, Form and Strategy in Science, Mind Matter and Method, Quantum Theory and Reality, Problems in the Philosophy of Mathematics, Problems in the Philosophy of Science, The Problem of Inductive Logic, Logic Methodology and Philosophy of Science I and III, Akten d. XIV Internat. Kongresses f. Philos., Wien, Erziehung zur Freiheit, Gesetz und Wirklichkeit, Der Sinn der Geschichte, Geist und Gesicht der Gegenwart, Club Voltaire, Theorie und Realität, Logik der Sozialwissenschaften, Die Philosophie und die Wissenschaften, Versäumte Lektionen, Les Fondements Philosophiques des Systèmes Economiques, etc. Contrib. to: Mind, Economica, Proc. Royal Dutch Acad. of Sciences, Indagationes Mathematicæ, Proc. Brit. Acad., Nature Proc. Arist. Soc., Classical Review, The Listener, Ratio, The Indian Jl of Philos, Synthese, Proc. Fedn Am. Soc. Exper. Biology, L'Industria, La Scuola In Azione, Il Politico, etc. *Recreation:* music. *Address:* Fallowfield, Manor Road, Penn, Buckinghamshire. *T:* Penn 2126.

**POPPLEWELL,** family name of **Baron Popplewell.**

**POPPLEWELL,** Baron *cr* 1966 (Life Peer), of Sherburn-in-Elmet; **Ernest Popplewell;** *b* 10 Dec. 1899; *s* of J. W. and Alice Popplewell, Selby; *m* 1922, Lavinia Rainbow; one *s*. *Educ:* elementary. Railway signalman; NUR Trade Union Branch Secretary. Eighteen years membership Local Government Bodies. JP WR of Yorks. MP (Lab) Newcastle upon Tyne, West, 1945-66; Asst Whip (unpaid), 1946; Vice-Chamberlain of HM Household, 1947-51; an Opposition Whip, 1951, Deputy Chief Whip, 1955-Oct. 1959. Chairman: Labour Parly Transport Gp, 1959-65; Parly Nationalised Industries Cttee, 1964-66. Served War of 1914-18 with RMA (Belgian Croix de Guerre). *Address:* North View, Moor Lane, Sherburn-in-Elmet, nr Leeds. *T:* South Milford 213.

**POPPLEWELL, Oliver Bury,** QC 1969; Recorder of Burton-on-Trent, since 1970; Deputy Chairman, Oxfordshire Quarter Sessions, since 1970; *b* 15 Aug. 1927; *s* of Frank and Nina Popplewell; *m* 1954, Catharine Margaret Storey; four *s* (and one *s* decd). *Educ:* Charterhouse (Schol.); Queens' Coll., Cambridge (Class. exhibnr). BA 1950; LLB 1951. CUCC, 1949-51. Called to the Bar, 1951. *Recreations:* sailing, cricket, tennis. *Address:* Lime Tree Farm, Chartridge, Bucks. *T:* The Lee 356. *Clubs:* MCC; Hawks (Cambridge), Blakeney Sailing.

**PORBANDAR, Maharaja of, Lt-Col HH Maharaja Rana Saheb, Shri Sir Natwarsinhji Bhavsinhji,** KCSI, *cr* 1929; *b* 30 June 1901; *s* of HH the Rana Saheb Shri Bhavsinhji Bahadur of Porbandar; *m* 1st, 1920, Princess Rupaliba, MBE (*d* 1943), *d* of late Thakore Saheb of Limbdi, KCSI, KCIE; 2nd, 1954, Anantkunver. *Educ:* Rajkumar College, Rajkot; stood first in the Diploma Examination of the Chiefs' Colleges in 1918. Offically received by HH the Pope, at the Vatican, 1922. Captained first All-India Cricket Team which toured England 1932. *Publications:* 42 Compositions by N. Porbandar; Introspect: Three Essays; Values Reviewed; From the Flow of Life. *Recreations:* music, painting and writing. *Address:* Porbandar, Saurashtra, India; Firgrove, Ootacamund, S. India.

**PORCHER, Michael Somerville,** CMG 1962; OBE 1960; Assistant Secretary, Royal National Life-Boat Institution, since 1964; *b* 9 March 1921; *s* of late Geoffrey Lionel Porcher and Marjorie Fownes Porcher (*née* Somerville); *m* 1955, Mary Lorraine Porcher (*née* Tweedy); two *s*. *Educ:* Cheltenham College; St Edmund Hall, Oxford. Military Service, 1941-42. Joined Colonial Admin. Service: Sierra Leone; Cadet, 1942; Asst Dist, Comr, 1945; Dist Comr, 1951; British Guiana: Dep. Colonial Sec., 1952; Governor's Sec. and Clerk Exec. Council, 1953; Dep. Chief Sec., 1956. British Honduras: Colonial Secretary, 1960; Chief Secretary, 1961; retired, 1964. *Recreations:* fishing, shooting, sailing, riding. *Address:* Oaklands, Slinfold, near Horsham, Sussex.

**PORCHESTER, Lord; Henry George Reginald Molyneux Herbert,** DL; *b* 19 Jan. 1924; *o s* of 6th Earl of Carnarvon, *qv*; *m* 1956, Jean Margaret, *e d* of Hon. Oliver Wallop, Big Horn, Sheridan Co., Wyoming, USA; two *s* one *d*. Late Lieut RHG; retired pay, 1947. Hon Col, Hampshire Fortress Regt, RE (TA) 1963-67, retaining rank of Hon. Col. Racing Manager to the Queen, 1969-; Chairman: Game Research Assoc., 1960-67 (Vice-Pres., 1967-); Thoroughbred Breeders' Assoc., 1964-66. Member: Nature Conservancy, 1963-66; Sports Council, 1965 (Chm., Planning Cttee, 1965-); Forestry Commission, 1967; President: Amateur Riders' Assoc.; Hampshire Cricket Club, 1966-68; Jockey Club, 1964 (Chm., Race Planning Cttee, 1967-). DL Hampshire, 1965-; County Alderman, 1965- (CC Hants, 1954; Chm., CC Assoc. Planning Cttee, 1968-). *Address:* Milford Lake House, Burghclere, Newbury, Berks. *T:* Highclere 387. *Clubs:* White's, Portland.

*See also Earl of Portsmouth.*

**PORGES, Waldo William,** QC 1952; *b* 20 Sept. 1899; *s* of late Gustave Porges and Alice (*née* Pressfield); *m* 1926, Ann Forsyth McKechnie; one *d*. *Educ:* Eton; Christ Church, Oxford. Called to Bar, Lincoln's Inn, 1927. Bencher, 1957. *Publication:* Joint Editor, Temperley's Merchant Shipping Acts. *Address:* The Old Parsonage, Munslow, Craven Arms, Shropshire. *T:* Munslow 655.

**PORRITT, Sir Arthur (Espie),** 1st Bt *cr* 1963; GCMG 1967 (KCMG 1950); GCVO 1970 (KCVO 1957); CBE 1945 (OBE 1943); Governor-General of New Zealand, since Nov. 1967; *b* 10 Aug. 1900; *e s* of late E. E. Porritt, VD, MD, FRCS, Wanganui, New Zealand; *m* 1st, 1926, Mary Frances Wynne, *d* of William Bond; 2nd, 1946, Kathleen Mary, 2nd *d* of late A. S. Peck and of Mrs Windley, Spalding, Lincs; two *s* one *d*. *Educ:* Wanganui Collegiate School, NZ; Otago University, NZ; Magdalen College, Oxford (Rhodes Scholar); St Mary's Hospital, London. MA Oxon.; MCh Oxon. surgeon: St Mary's Hosp.; Hosp. of St John and St Elizabeth; King Edward VII Hosp. for Officers; Royal Masonic Hosp.; Consulting Surgeon: Princess Louise Kensington Hosp. for Children; Paddington Hosps; Royal Chelsea Hosp.; Civil Consulting Surgeon to the Army; Brigadier, RAMC, 21 Army Group; Surgeon-in-Ordinary to the Duke of York; Surgeon to HM Household; a Surgeon to King George VI, 1946-52; Sergeant-Surgeon to the Queen, 1952-67. Chairman: Medical Advisory Cttee, Ministry of Overseas Develt; Medical Services Review Cttee, 1958; Red Cross Comr for NZ in UK; Hon. Sec., Hunterian Soc., 1934-39 (Past Pres.); President: St Mary's Hosp. Med. Soc.; Royal College of Surgeons of England, 1960-63; BMA, 1960-61; RSM, 1966-67; Assoc. of Surgeons of Gt Britain and Ireland; Past Master, Soc. of Apothecaries, 1964-66; Mem. Council, Roy. Commonwealth Soc.; Pres., OUAC, 1925-26; holder of 100 yards and 220 yards hurdles records at Oxford and 100 yards Oxford v. Cambridge (9 9/10 seconds); represented Oxford in Athletics, 1923-26; Finalist Olympic, 100 metres (Bronze Medallist), Paris, 1924; Capt. NZ Olympic Team, Paris, 1924, Amsterdam, 1928, Manager Berlin, 1936; Mem., Internat. Olympic Cttee, British Olympic Council; Chm., British Empire and Commonwealth Games Federation. FRCS (Eng.); Fellow, Amer. Soc. of Clinical Surgery; Fellow, French Acad. of Surgery; Hon. FRACS; Hon. FRCS (Ed.); Hon. FACS; Hon. FRCS (Glasg.); Hon. FRCS (Can.); Hon. FCS (SAf); Hon. FRCS (I); Hon. FRCP; Hon. FRACP; Hon FRCOG; Hon. Fellow, Magdalen College, Oxford, 1961. BMA Gold Medal, 1964. Hon. LLD: St Andrews; New Zealand; Otago. Hon. MD Bristol; Hon. DSc Oxon. Legion of Merit (USA); KStJ. *Publications:* Athletics (with D. G. A. Lowe), 1929; Essentials of Modern Surgery (with R. M. Handfield-Jones), 1938, 6th edn 1956; various surgical articles in medical jls. *Recreations:* riding, golf, swimming; formerly athletics and Rugby football. *Heir: s* Jonathan Espie Porritt, *b* 6 July 1950. *Address:* Government House, Wellington, New Zealand. *Clubs:* Athenæum, Buck's.

**PORT ELIZABETH, BISHOP OF,** since 1970; **Rt. Rev. Philip Welsford Richmond Russell;** *b* 21 Oct. 1919; *s* of Leslie Richmond Russell and Clarice Louisa Russell (*née* Welsford); *m* 1945, Violet Eirene, *d* of Ven. Dr O. J. Hogarth, sometime Archdeacon of the Cape; one *s* three *d. Educ:* Durban High Sch.; Rhodes Univ. College (Univ. of South Africa), BA 1948; LTh 1950. Served War of 1939-45; MBE 1943. Deacon, 1950; Priest, 1951; Curate, St Peter's, Maritzburg, 1950-54; Vicar: Greytown, 1954-57; Ladysmith, 1957-61; Kloof, 1961-66; Archdeacon of Pinetown, 1961-66; Bishop Suffragan of Capetown, 1966-70. *Recreations:* tennis, fishing. *Address:* Bishop's House, 14 Buckingham Road, Port Elizabeth, Cape Province, South Africa.

**PORT MORESBY, Archbishop of, (RC),** since 1966; **Most Rev. Virgil Copas,** DD; Member of Religious Order of Missionaries of Sacred Heart (MSC); *b* 19 March 1915; *s* of Cornelius Copas and Kathleen (*née* Daly). *Educ:* St Mary's Coll. and Downlands Coll., Toowoomba, Queensland. Sec. to Bp L. Scharmach, Rabaul, New Britain, New Guinea, 1945-51; Religious Superior, Dio. of Darwin, Austr, 1954-60; Bishop of Port Moresby, 1960-66. *Address:* Archbishop's House, Catholic Missions, PO Box 82, Port Moresby, Papua and New Guinea, Oceania. *T:* 2653.

**PORT OF SPAIN, Archbishop of,** since 1968; **Most Rev. Anthony Pantin,** CSSp; *b* 27 Aug. 1929; *s* of Julian and Agnes Pantin, both of Trinidad. *Educ:* Sacred Heart Private Sch., Belmont Boys' Intermediate Sch., St Mary's Coll., Port of Spain; Seminary of Philosophy, Montreal Holy Ghost Missionary Coll., Dublin. Ordained Dublin, 1955; Guadeloupe, French West Indies, 1956-59; Fatima College, Port of Spain, 1959-64; Superior, St Mary's Coll., Port of Spain, 1965-68. *Address:* 27 Maraval Road, Port of Spain, Trinidad. *T:* 21103.

**PORTAL,** family name of **Viscount Portal of Hungerford.**

**PORTAL of Hungerford,** 1st Viscount, *cr* 1946, of Hungerford; 1st Baron, *cr* 1945; **Marshal of the Royal Air Force Charles Frederick Algernon Portal,** KG 1946; GCB 1942 (KCB 1940; CB 1939); OM 1946; DSO 1917; MC; Chairman, British Aircraft Corporation, 1960-68; *b* 21 May 1893; *s* of late E. R. Portal, Sulham, Pangbourne; *m* 1919, Joan Margaret, *y d* of Sir Charles Glynn Welby, 5th Bt; two *d. Educ:* Winchester; Christ Church, Oxford. Served European War, 1914-18 (despatches, DSO and bar, MC); Commd British Forces, Aden, 1934-35; Instructor Imperial Defence Coll., 1936-37; Director of Organization, Air Ministry, 1937-38; Air Member for Personnel on the Air Council, 1939-40; AOC-in-C Bomber Command, 1940; Chief of the Air Staff, 1940-45. Controller, Atomic Energy, Ministry of Supply, 1946-51. Director: Barclays Bank DCO, 1946-69; Barclays Bank Ltd, 1947-69; Portals Holdings Ltd, 1959-69; Whitbread Investment Co., 1962-. Chairman: King Edward VII Hospital, Midhurst, 1950-68. President, MCC, 1958-59. *Recreations:* fishing, stalking. *Heir: d* Hon. Rosemary Ann Portal, *b* 12 May 1923. *Address:* West Ashling House, Chichester, Sussex. *T:* West Ashling 216. *Club:* Travellers'.

**PORTAL, Sir Francis Spencer,** 5th Bt, *cr* 1901; DL; President, Portals Holdings Ltd; Director, Royal Exchange Assurance; *b* 27 June 1903; *s* of 4th Bt and late Mary, *d* of late Colonel William Mure, Caldwell, Ayrshire; *S* father, 1955; *m* 1st, 1930, Rowena (*d* 1948), *d* of late Paul Selby, Johannesburg; two *d*; 2nd, 1950, Jane Mary, *d* of late Albert Henry Williams, OBE, Flint House, Langston, Havant, Hants, and of Mrs E. G. Selwyn, The Quinton, Shawford, Hants; two *s* one *d. Educ:* Winchester; Christ Church, Oxford; McGill Univ., Montreal. Served War of 1939-45, Captain, late Welsh Guards, Guards Armoured Division (Croix de Guerre, 2nd Class Belgium). President and Chairman, YMCA Southern Region; Chairman, YMCA National Commn, 1968; Member, YMCA National Council. Master, Worshipful Co. of Clothworkers, 1970. High Sheriff of Hampshire, 1963, DL Hants, 1967-. *Recreations:* miscellaneous. *Heir: s* Jonathan Francis, *b* 13 Jan. 1953. *Address:* Burley Wood, Ashe, near Basingstoke, Hants. *T:* Overton 269. *Club:* Guards.

**PORTAL, Admiral Sir Reginald Henry,** KCB, *cr* 1949 (CB 1946); DSC 1916; *b* 6 Sept. 1894; *s* of late Edward Robert Portal, JP; DL; *m* 1926, Helen, *d* of late Frederick Anderson; two *s* two *d.* Served European War, 1914-19, with RN and RNAS (DSC); War of 1939-45 (despatches, CB); comd HMS York, 1939-41; HMS Royal Sovereign, 1941-42; Asst Chief of Naval Staff (Air), 1943-44; ADC to the King, 1943; Flag Officer Naval Air Stations (Australia), 1945; Naval representative on Joint Chiefs of Staff Cttee (Australia), 1946-47; Flag Officer, Air (Home), 1947-51; retired, 1951. *Address:* Savernake, Marlborough, Wilts.

**PORTARLINGTON,** 7th Earl of, *cr* 1785; **George Lionel Yuill Seymour Dawson-Damer;** Baron Dawson 1770; Viscount Carlow 1776; *b* 10 Aug. 1938; *er s* of Air Commodore Viscount Carlow (killed on active service, 1944) and Peggy (who *m* 2nd, 1945, Peter Nugent; she *d* 1963), *yr d* of late Charles Cambie; *S* grandfather, 1959; *m* 1961, Davina, *e d* of Sir Edward Windley, *qv*; two *s* one *d. Educ:* Eton. Page of Honour to the Queen, 1953-55. Director: G. S. Yuill & Co. Ltd, Sydney, 1964;

Cold Storage Holdings Ltd, London, 1965; Queensland Trading Holding Co. Ltd, Brisbane, 1967; Australian Stock Breeders Co. Ltd, Brisbane, 1966. *Heir: s* Viscount Carlow, *qv. Recreations:* shooting, fishing, ski-ing, books. *Address:* 55 Victoria Road, Bellevue Hill, Sydney, NSW 2023, Australia. *T:* 361965. *Club:* Union (Sydney).

**PORTEOUS, Alexander James Dow,** MA; Sydney Jones Professor of Education, University of Liverpool, 1954-63 (Professor of Education, 1938-54); retired Sept. 1963, now Professor Emeritus; Temporary Professor of Moral Philosophy, University of Edinburgh, 1963-64; *b* 22 July 1896; *s* of late John Dow Porteous, MA, former Rector of Knox Memorial Instituite, Haddington, and Agnes Paton Walker; *m* 1926, Eliza Murray Dalziel, MA (Hons Edinburgh), *e d* of late George Ross, Solicitor, Inverness; four *s* two *d. Educ:* Knox Memorial Institute, Haddington; Universities of Edinburgh and Oxford (Bible Clerk, Oriel College); Moray House Provincial Training College for Teachers, Edinburgh. Served in Army 1916-19, first with the Royal Scots; gazetted 2nd Lieut to the Royal Scots Fusiliers June 1918 and spent seven months on active service in France with the 11th Battalion; MA (Edinburgh) with First Class Honours in Classics, 1921 (Rhind Classical Scholarship, 1920, Guthrie Classical Fellowship, 1922); Ferguson Scholar in Classics, 1922; First Class in Literae Humaniores, Oxford, 1923; MA 1928; First Class Honours in Mental Philosophy (after Graduation) at Edinburgh University, and Diploma in Education, 1924; Shaw Fellow in Mental Philosophy in the University of Edinburgh, 1924-29; Assistant Lecturer in the Department of Logic and Metaphysics, Edinburgh University, 1924-26; Professor of Philosophy at Smith College, Northampton, Mass., USA, 1926-30; Associate Professor of Moral Philosophy, McGill University, Montreal, Canada, 1930-31; Professor, 1931-32; Lecturer in Ancient Philosophy, Edinburgh University, 1932-37; Reader, 1937-38. *Publications:* reviews and papers in philosophical journals. *Recreations:* swimming, golf. *Address:* 8 Osmaston Road, Prenton, Birkenhead, Cheshire. *T:* 051-608 3749.

**PORTEOUS, Christopher,** MA; Headmaster of Eltham College, since 1959; *b* 2 April 1921; *e s* of late Rev. Gilbert Porteous; *m* 1944, Amy Clunis, *d* of Theodore J. Biggs; one *s* three *d. Educ:* Nottingham High Sch. (Foundation Scholar); Emmanuel Coll., Cambridge (Senior Scholar). First Classes, with distinction, in Classical Tripos. Master of Classical Sixth, Mill Hill Sch., 1947-55; Asst Director, HM Civil Service Commission, 1955-59. *Recreations:* travel, the countryside. *Address:* Headmaster's House, Eltham College, SE9.

**PORTEOUS, Douglas Archibald,** CB 1950; retired; *b* 1891; *y s* of late Archibald Porteous, Glasgow. *Educ:* Glasgow High School. Fellow of the Faculty of Actuaries, 1920; Principal Actuary, Government Actuary's Dept, 1936; Deputy Government Actuary, 1946-53; retired, 1953. *Publication:* Pension and Widows' and Orphans' Funds, 1936. *Recreation:* golf. *Address:* Tusker House, 14 Godwin Road, Hastings, Sussex. *Club:* Reform.

**PORTEOUS, Rev. Norman Walker,** MA Edinburgh et Oxon, BD Edinburgh, DD St Andrews; *b* Haddington, 9 Sept. 1898; *yr s* of late John Dow Porteous, MA, formerly Rector of Knox Memorial Inst, Haddington, and Agnes Paton Walker; *m* 1929, May Hadwen, *y d* of late John Cook Robertson, Kirkcaldy; three *s* three *d. Educ:* Knox Memorial Institute, Haddington; Universities of Edinburgh, Oxford (Trinity College), Berlin, Tübingen and Münster; New Coll., Edinburgh. MA Edinburgh with 1st Class Honours in Classics; MA Oxon with 1st Class in Literæ Humaniores; BD Edinburgh with distinction in Old Testament; 1st Bursar at Edinburgh University, 1916; C. B. Black Scholar in New Testament Greek, 1920; John Edward Baxter Scholar in Classics, 1923; Ferguson Scholar in Classics, 1923; Senior Cunningham Fellow at New College and Kerr Travelling Scholar, 1927; served in army, 1917-19, commissioned 2nd Lieut, March 1918, served overseas with 13th Royal Scots; Ordained to Ministry of United Free Church of Scotland, 1929; Minister of Crossgates Church, 1929-31; Regius Professor of Hebrew and Oriental Languages in the University of St Andrews, 1931-35; Professor of Old Testament Language, Literature and Theology in the University of Edinburgh, 1935-37; Prof. of Hebrew and Semitic Languages, Univ. of Edinburgh, 1937-68; Principal of New Coll., and Dean of Faculty of Divinity, Univ. of Edinburgh, 1964-68; retd, 1968; now Emeritus Professor. Hon. DD St Andrews, 1944; Stone Lecturer, Princeton Theological Seminary, 1953; President, Soc. for Old Testament Study, 1954. *Publications:* Das Alte Testament Deutsch 23: Das Danielbuch 1962 (English edition, 1965); Living the Mystery: Collected Essays, 1967; contributions to: Theologische Aufsätze Karl Barth zum 50 Geburtstag, 1936; Record and Revelation, 1938; The Old Testament and Modern Study, 1951; Peake's Commentary on the Bible, 1962. *Address:* 3 Hermitage Gardens, Edinburgh. *T:* 031-447 4632.

**PORTEOUS, Colonel Patrick Anthony,** VC 1942; RA, retired 1970; *b* 1 Jan. 1918; *s* of late Brig.-General C. McL. Porteous, 9th Ghurkas, and Mrs Porteous, Fleet, Hampshire; *m* 1943, Lois Mary (*d* 1953), *d* of late Maj.-General Sir H. E. Roome, KCIE; one *s* one *d*; *m* 1955, Deirdre, *d* of late Eric King; three *d. Educ:* Wellington Coll.; Royal Military Acad., Woolwich. BEF France, Sept. 1939-May 1940, with 6th AA Regt, RA; Dieppe, Aug. 1942 (VC); No. 4 Commando, Dec. 1940-Oct. 1944; BLA June-Sept. 1944; 1st Airborne Div. Dec. 1944-July 1945; 6th Airborne Div., July 1945-March 1946; Staff Coll., Camberley, May-Nov. 1946; 16 Airborne Div. TA, Jan. 1947-Feb. 1948; 33 Airborne Lt Regt, RA, Feb. 1948-April 1949; No 1 Regular Commission Board, 1949; Instructor, RMA, Sandhurst, July 1950-July 1953; GHQ, Far East Land Forces, Singapore, Sept. 1953-July 1955; 1st Singapore Regt, RA, July-Dec. 1955; 14 Field Regt, RA, 1956-58; RAF Staff Coll., Jan. 1958-Dec. 1958; AMS, HQ Southern Comd, 1959-60; Colonel Junior Leaders Regt, RA, 1960-63; Colonel, General Staff War Office, later Ministry of Defence, 1963-66; Comdr Rheindahlen Garrison, 1966-69. *Recreation:* sailing. *Address:* Halnaker Cottage, Halnaker, Chichester, Sussex. *T:* Halnaker 335.

**PORTER, Mrs Adrian;** *see* Heaton, Rose Henniker.

**PORTER, Alfred Ernest,** CSI 1947; CIE 1942; *b* 2 Nov. 1896; *s* of F. L. Porter; *m* 1929, Nancy Florence (decd), *d* of late E. L. Melly; two *s. Educ:* Manchester Grammar Sch.; Corpus Christi Coll., Oxford. Manchester Regt, 1915; Machine Gun Corps, 1916; Indian Civil Service, 1922-48. *Address:* The Old Hall, Chawleigh, N Devon. *T:* Chulmleigh 280.

**PORTER, Sir Andrew M. H.;** *see* Horsbrugh-Porter.

**PORTER, Prof. Arthur,** MSc, PhD (Manchester); FRSC 1970; FIEE; Professor of Industrial Engineering, University of Toronto, Toronto, since 1961; Acting Director of Centre for Culture and Technology, 1967; Academic Commissioner, University of Western Ontario, London, since 1969; *b* 8 Dec. 1910; *s* of late John William Porter and Mary Anne Harris; *m* 1941, Phyllis Patricia Dixon; one *s*. *Educ:* The Grammar Sch., Ulverston; University of Manchester. Asst Lecturer, University of Manchester, 1936-37; Commonwealth Fund Fellow, Massachusetts Inst. of Technology, USA, 1937-39; Scientific Officer, Admiralty, 1939-45; Principal Scientific Officer, National Physical Laboratory, 1946; Prof. of Instrument Technology, Royal Military Coll. of Science, 1946-49; Head, Research Division, Ferranti Electric Ltd, Toronto, Canada, 1949-55; Professor of Light Electrical Engineering, Imperial College of Science and Technology, University of London, 1955-58; Dean of the College of Engineering, Saskatchewan Univ., Saskatoon, 1958. *Publications:* An Introduction to Servomechanisms, 1950; Cybernetics Simplified, 1969. Articles in Trans. Royal Society, Proc. Royal Society, Phil. Mag., Proc. Inst. Mech. Eng, Proc. IEE, Nature, etc. *Recreations:* gardening, golf. *Address:* Department of Industrial Engineering, University of Toronto, Toronto 5, Canada; Watendlath, Belfountain, Ontario. *T:* (519) 927-5323.

**PORTER, Air Vice-Marshal Cedric Ernest Victor,** CBE 1944; psa; *b* 12 Nov. 1893; *s* of late Joseph Francis Porter, OBE, JP, Helmsley, Yorks; *m* 1925, Vera Ellen, *d* of late Frank Baxendale, Framfield Place, Sussex; one *s*. *Educ:* Harrow Sch.; Cambridge Univ. Commissioned Essex Regt, Aug. 1914; Captain, 1916; RFC and RAF since May 1916; France, 1914-18; Palestine and Iraq, 1920-23; RAF Staff Coll., 1931; RAF Coll., Cranwell, 1932-34; Senior Air Staff Officer, Palestine and Transjordan, 1937-40; commanded RAF Sudan, 1940, Andover, 1941, 70 Group, 1941-43; 22 Group, 1943-46 (CBE, despatches twice); retired, 1946. *Recreations:* shooting, fishing, golf. *Address:* Pigeons Farm, Greenham, Newbury, Berks. *T:* Newbury 1214. *Club:* Royal Air Force.

**PORTER, Rt. Rev. David Brownfield;** *see* Aston, Bishop Suffragan of.

**PORTER, Eric (Richard);** actor; *b* London, 8 April 1928; *s* of Richard John Porter and Phoebe Elizabeth (*née* Spall). *Educ:* LCC and Wimbledon Technical College. First professional appearance with Shakespeare Memorial Theatre Company, Arts, Cambridge, 1945; first appearance on London stage as Dunois' Page in Saint Joan with the travelling repertory company, King's, Hammersmith, 1946; Birmingham Repertory Theatre, 1948-50; under contract to H. M. Tennant, Ltd, 1951-53. *Plays include:* The Silver Box, Lyric, Hammersmith, 1951; The Three Sisters, Aldwych, 1951; Thor, With Angels, Lyric, Hammersmith, 1951; title role in Noah, Whitehall, 1951; The Same Sky, Lyric, Hammersmith, 1952; Under the Sycamore Tree, Aldwych, 1952; season at Lyric, Hammersmith, directed by John Gielgud, 1953–plays: Richard II, The Way of the World, Venice Preserved; with Bristol Old Vic Company, 1954, and again 1955-56; parts included title roles in King Lear, Uncle Vanya, Volpone; with Old Vic Company, 1954-55: parts included Jacques in As You Like It, title role in Henry IV, Bolingbroke in Richard II, Christopher Sly in The Taming of the Shrew; Romanoff and Juliet, Piccadilly, 1956; A Man of Distinction, Edinburgh Festival and Princes, 1957; Time and Again, British tour with the Lunts, 1957, and New York in The Visit, 1958; The Coast of Coromandel, English tour, 1959; Rosmersholm, Royal Court, 1959, Comedy, 1960. (Evening Standard Drama Award as Best Actor of 1959); under contract to Royal Shakespeare Company, 1960-65; parts: Malvolio in Twelfth Night, Stratford, 1960, Aldwych, 1961; Duke in The Two Gentlemen of Verona, Stratford, 1960; Leontes in The Winter's Tale, Stratford, 1960; Ulysses in Troilus and Cressida, Stratford, 1960; Ferdinand in The Duchess of Malfi, Stratford, 1960, Aldwych, 1961; Lord Chamberlain in Ondine, Aldwych, 1961; Buckingham in Richard III, Stratford, 1961; title role in Becket, Aldwych, 1961, Globe, 1962; title role in Macbeth, Stratford, 1962; Iachimo in Cymbeline, Stratford, 1962; Pope Pius XII in The Representative, Aldwych, 1963. Stratford Season, 1964; Bolingbroke in Richard II; Henry IV in Henry IV Parts I and II; Chorus in Henry V; Richmond in Richard III; Stratford Season, 1965: Barabas in The Jew of Malta; Shylock in The Merchant of Venice; Chorus in Henry V, Aldwych, 1965; Ossip in The Government Inspector, Aldwych, 1966; Stratford Season, 1968; Lear in King Lear; Faustus in Dr Faustus (US tour, 1969); Paul Thomsen in My Little Boy–My Big Girl (also directed), Fortune, 1969. *Films:* The Fall of the Roman Empire, 1964; The Pumpkin Eater, 1964; The Heroes of Telemark, 1965; Kaleidoscope, 1966. Has also appeared many times on television, including Soames Forsyte in The Forsyte Saga, BBC (Best Actor Award, Guild of TV Producers and Directors, 1967). *Recreations:* walking, swimming. *Address:* c/o International Famous Agency, 11-12 Hanover Street, W1. *Club:* Buckstone.

**PORTER, George,** JP Liverpool; *b* 29 July 1884; *m* 1914; Florence Annie Pickburn; three *d*. *Educ:* Liverpool Elementary and Technical Schools. Councillor for Huyton, Lancs. Staff of Ministry of Labour and National Service during war period. MP (Lab) Central Division of Leeds, 1945-55. *Address:* 61 Stockbridge Lane, Huyton, Liverpool. *T:* 051-489 1094.

**PORTER, Prof. George,** FRS 1960; BSc (Leeds); MA, PhD, ScD, (Cambridge); FRIC; Director of the Royal Institution of Great Britain, and Fullerian Professor of Chemistry, since 1966; Honorary Professor of Physical Chemistry, University of Kent at Canterbury, since 1966; Visiting Professor, Department of Chemistry, University College, London, since 1967; *b* 6 Dec. 1920; *o s* of late John Smith Porter and of Alice Ann Porter, Stainforth, Yorks; *m* 1949, Stella Jean Brooke, *o d* of G. A. Brooke, Leeds, Kent, and of late Mrs J. Brooke; two *s*. *Educ:* Thorne Grammar Sch.; Leeds Univ.; Emmanuel Coll., Cambridge. Ackroyd Scholar, Leeds Univ., 1938-41. Served RNVR in Western Approaches and Mediterranean, 1941-45. Cambridge: Demonstrator in Physical Chemistry, 1949-52, Fellow of Emmanuel Coll., 1952-54; Hon. Fellow, 1967; Asst Director of Research in Physical Chemistry, 1952-54. Asst Director of British Rayon Research Assoc., 1954-55. Prof. of Physical Chemistry, University of Sheffield, 1955-63; Firth Prof. of Chemistry, University of Sheffield, 1963-66; Prof. of Chemistry, Royal Institution, 1963-66. Scientific Adviser to Gallaher Ltd, 1970-. Member: Aeronautical Research Council, 1964-66; Open Univ., 1969-. Pres., Chemical Soc., 1970- (Vice-Pres., 1968-70); Vice-Pres., Faraday Soc., 1965-67, 1970-. Pres., Comité Internat. de photobiologie, 1968-; Hon. Mem. NY Acad. of Sciences, 1968. Lectures: Tilden, 1958; Ramsen Meml, Amer. Chem. Soc., 1962; Liversidge, 1970. Hon.

Fellow, Inst. of Patentees and Inventors, 1970; Hon DSc: Utah, 1968; Sheffield, 1968; East Anglia, 1970. Corday-Morgan Medal, Chem. Soc., 1955; Nobel Prize (Jt) for Chemistry, 1967. *Publications:* Chemistry for the Modern World, 1962. Scientific papers in Proc. Royal Society, Trans. Faraday Society, etc. TV Series: Laws of Disorder, 1965-66; Time Machines, 1969-70. *Recreations:* ski-ing and sailing. *Address:* The Royal Institution, 21 Albemarle Street, WIX 4BS. *T:* 01-493 0669. *Clubs:* Athenæum, St James'.

**PORTER, Sir George Swinburne,** 3rd Bt, *cr* 1889; *b* 14 Dec. 1908; *o s* of Sir William Porter, 2nd Bt, and Mary Bousfield (*d* 1915), *d* of J. Steains; *S* father, 1935. *Educ:* Eton. *Heir:* none. *Address:* The Witch Inn, Sunte Avenue, Haywards Heath, Sussex.

**PORTER, Prof. Helen Kemp,** FRS 1956; DSc; FRIC; FRSE; Emeritus Professor, University of London; Second Secretary, Agricultural Research Council, since 1969; Fellow, Imperial College of Science and Technology; *b* 10 Nov. 1899; *d* of George Kemp Archbold and Caroline E. B. Archbold (*née* Whitehead); *m* 1937, William George Porter, MD, MRCP (decd); *m* 1962, Arthur St George Huggett, FRS, DSc, MB, BS (*d* 1968). *Educ:* Clifton High School for Girls, Bristol; University of London, Research Assistant, Food Investigation Board, 1922-32; DSc London, 1932. On staff of Research Institute of Plant Physiology, Imperial Coll., 1932-59; Reader in Enzymology, University of London, Imperial College of Science and Technology, 1957-59; Prof. of Plant Physiology, Imperial Coll. of Science and Technology, London Univ., 1959-64; Dir, ARC Unit of Plant Physiology, 1959-64. Hon. ARCS 1964. *Publications:* contributions to Annals of Botany, Biochemical Journal, Journal of Experimental Botany, etc. *Recreation:* needlework. *Address:* 49e Beaumont Street, W1N 1RE. *T:* 01-935 5862.

**PORTER, Ivor Forsyth,** CMG 1963; OBE 1944; Ambassador, UK Delegation to Geneva Disarmament Conference, since 1968 (Minister, 1967); *b* 12 Nov. 1913; *s* of Herbert and Evelyn Porter; *m* 1951, Ann, *o d* of late Dr John Speares (marr. diss., 1961); *m* 1961, Katerina, *o c* of A. T. Cholerton; one *s* one *d*. *Educ:* Barrow Grammar Sch.; Leeds Univ. (BA, PhD). Lecturer at Bucharest Univ., 1939-40; Temp. Secretary, at Bucharest Legation, 1940-41; Raiding Forces, 1941-45 (Major). Joined Foreign (subseq. Diplomatic) Service, May 1946, as 2nd Secretary in Sen. Branch; 1st Secretary 1948; transferred to Washington, 1951; Foreign Office, 1953; UK Delegation to NATO Paris as Counsellor and Head of Chancery, 1956; Nicosia, 1959 (Deputy Head UK Mission), Deputy High Commissioner, 1961-62, Cyprus; Permanent Rep. to Council of Europe, Strasbourg, 1962-65 (with personal rank of Minister); Dep. High Commissioner, Eastern India, 1965-66. *Recreations:* writing, walking. *Address:* 2 Plateau de Frontenex, Geneva, Switzerland. *Club:* Travellers'.

**PORTER, Maj.-General John Edmund L.;** *see* Leech-Porter.

**PORTER, Katherine Anne;** author, lecturer and teacher to students of writing, in Colleges and Universities in USA; *b* Texas, USA, 15 May 1890, family American (originating in Virginia) since 1648; *d* of Harrison Boone Porter, born in Kentucky, and Mary Alice Jones, Texas; *m* 1933, Eugene Dove Pressly (divorced); *m* 1938, Albert Russel Erskine, jun. (divorced); no *c*. *Educ:* private schools for girls in Louisiana and Texas. Guggenheim Foundation Fellowship, 1931-38; Gold Medal, Society for the Libraries of New York University, 1940; Fellow of Library of Congress, 1944 (Fellow of Regional American Literature). Lecturer to students of writing, Stanford Univ., California, 1948-49; Vice-President, Nat. Institute of Arts and Letters, New York, 1950; guest lecturer on Literature, Spring Semester, University of Chicago, 1951; one of reps of American Lit. to Internat. Festival of the Arts, Paris, 1952; Visiting Lecturer in Contemporary Poetry, University of Michigan, 1953-54; Fulbright Grant, Visiting Lecturer, University of Liège, 1954-55; Writer-in-residence, First Semester, University of Virginia, 1958-59; Glasgow Prof., Second Semester, Washington and Lee Univ., Va, 1959; Ewing Lecturer, University of California, Los Angeles (UCPA), 1960; Dept State grants (USIA) Lecturer on American Literature, Mexico, 1960, 1964; first Regents' Lecturer, University of California, Riverside, 1961. Appointed by President Lyndon B. Johnson as Member Commn on Presidential Scholars, 1964. Hon. DLit Woman's Coll., University of North Carolina, 1949; Hon. DLitt Hum, University of Michigan, 1954; Hon. DLitt Smith Coll., 1958, Maryville Coll., 1968; Hon. DHL, University of Maryland, 1966; Hon. Phi Beta Kappa, Univ. of Maryland, 1966. Doctor of Fine Arts, La Salle College. Emerson-Thoreau Bronze Medal for Service to Literature, American Academy of Arts and Sciences, 1962; Nat. Book Award for Fiction, 1966; Pulitzer Prize for Fiction, 1966; Gold Medal for Literature, National Inst. of Arts and Letters, 1967. *Publications: books:* Flowering Judas, 1930; Pale Horse, Pale Rider, 1939; The Leaning Tower, 1944; Ship of Fools, 1962; Collected Stories, 1965; *essays:* The Days Before, 1952; *translations:* Katherine Anne Porter's Old French Song Book, Paris, 1933; The Itching Parrot (from the Spanish), 1942. *Recreations:* old music, medieval history, reading; growing camellias, roses, irises. *Address:* Apt 1517, 6100 Westchester Park Drive, College Park, Md 20740, USA.

**PORTER, Air Marshal Sir Kenneth;** *see* Porter, Air Marshal Sir M. K. D.

**PORTER, Air Marshal Sir (Melvin) Kenneth (Drowley),** KCB 1967 (CB 1959); CBE 1945 (OBE 1942); Director of Technical Education Projects, University College, Cardiff, since 1970; *b* 19 Nov. 1912; *s* of late Edward Ernest Porter and late Helen Porter; *m* 1940, Elena, *d* of F. W. Sinclair; two *s* one *d*. *Educ:* No. 1 School of Technical Training, Halton; RAF Coll., Cranwell. Aircraft apprentice, RAF Halton; cadetship to RAF Coll., Cranwell; commissioned, 1932; Army Co-operation Sqdn, Fleet Air Arm, 1933-36, as PO and FO; specialised on Signals, 1936-37, Flt-Lieut; Sqdn Leader, 1939. Served War of 1939-45 (despatches thrice, OBE, CBE); Chief Signals Officer, Balloon Command, 1939; DCSO and CSO, HQ No. 11 Group, 1940-42; Temp. Wing Comdr, 1941; CSO, HQ 2nd TAF, 1943-45; Temp Gp Captain, 1943; Actg Air Commodore, 1944-45; CSO, HQ Bomber Command, 1945; Air Min. Tech. Plans, 1946-47, Gp Captain, 1946; Member Directing Staff, RAF Staff Coll., Andover, 1947-49; Senior Tech. Staff Officer, HQ No. 205 Group, 1950-52; Comdg Nos 1 and 2 Air Signallers Schools, 1952-54; CSO HQ 2nd ATAF, 1954-55; CSO, HQ Fighter Command, Actg Air Commodore, 1955-58, Air Cdr, 1958; Student Imperial Defence Coll., 1959; Commandant of No. 4 School of Technical Training, RAF St Athan, Glamorgan, and Air Officer Wales, 1960-61; Actg Air Vice-Marshal, 1961; Air Vice-Marshal, 1962; Director-General:

Ground Training, 1961-63; of Signals (Air), Ministry of Defence, 1964-66; AOC-in-C, Maintenance Command, 1966-70; Actg Air Marshal, 1966; Air Marshal, 1967. Member, Board of Governors, College of Aeronautics, 1964-. CEng 1966; FIEE; FRAeS; FBIM. Officer, Legion of Merit (US), 1945. *Recreation:* reading. *Address:* c/o Lloyds Bank Ltd, Cox's & King's Branch, 6 Pall Mall, SW1.

**PORTER, Hon. Sir Murray (Victor),** Kt 1970; Agent-General for Victoria in London since 1970; *b* 20 Dec. 1909; *s* of late V. Porter, Pt Pirie, SA; *m* 1932, Edith Alice Johnston, *d* of late C. A. Johnston; two *d*. *Educ:* Brighton (Victoria) Grammar Sch., Australia. Served War, 2nd AIF, 1941-45. MLA (Liberal) Sandringham, Victoria, 1955-70; Govt Whip, 1955-56; Asst Minister, 1956-58; Minister for: Forests, 1958-59; Local Govt, 1959-64; Public Works, 1964-70. *Recreations:* golf, swmming. *Address:* Victoria House, Melbourne Place, Strand, WC2. *T:* 01-836 2656. *Clubs:* East India and Sports; Royal Wimbledon Golf; Melbourne Cricket, Royal Melbourne Golf, Royal Automobile Club of Victoria.

**PORTER, Raymond Alfred James;** *b* 14 Oct. 1896; *o s* of Philip and Alice Porter; *m* 1922, Nellie, *er d* of George Edward Loveland; no *c*. *Educ:* Reigate Grammar Sch. Entered Lloyd's, 1912, Under-writing Member, 1934. Served European War, 1914-19, in Queen's Royal (West Surrey) Regt. Member, Cttee of Lloyd's, 1950-53, 1955-58, 1960-63 (Deputy Chairman of Lloyd's, 1961); Member, Cttee, Lloyd's Underwriters' Assoc., 1945-65 (Chairman, 1949-54, 1962); Chairman Joint Hull Cttee, 1958 and 1959. Member: Godstone RDC, 1946-60 and 1962-69 (Chairman, 1952-54); Surrey CC, 1955-58. *Address:* Mashobra, Limpsfield, Surrey. *T:* Oxted 2509.

**PORTER, Robert Stanley,** OBE 1959; Director-General, Economic Planning, Ministry of Overseas Development, since 1969; *b* 17 Sept. 1924; *s* of S. R. Porter; *m* 1st, 1953, Dorothea Naomi (marr. diss. 1967), *d* of Rev. Morris Seale; one *d*; 2nd, 1967, Julia Karen, *d* of Edmund A. Davies. *Educ:* St Clement Danes, Holborn Estate, Grammar Sch.; New Coll., Oxford. Research Economist, US Economic Cooperation Administration Special Mission to the UK, 1949; British Middle East Development Division: Asst Statistical Adviser, Cairo, 1951; Statistical Adviser and Economist, Beirut, 1955; Min. of Overseas Development: Dir, Geographical Div., Economic Planning Staff, 1965; Dep. Dir-Gen. of Economic Planning, 1967. *Publications:* articles in Oxford Economic Papers, Kyklos, Review of Income and Wealth. *Recreations:* music, theatre. *Address:* 25 Ashley Gardens, Ambrosden Avenue, SW1. *T:* 01-834 8613.

**PORTER, Rt. Hon. Robert Wilson;** PC (NI) 1969; QC (NI) 1965; MP (U) Lagan Valley, Parliament of N Ireland, since 1969 (Queen's University of Belfast, 1966-69); Minister of Home Affairs, Government of N Ireland, 1969-70; *b* 23 Dec. 1923; *s* of late Joseph Wilson Porter and late Letitia Mary (*née* Wasson); *m* 1953, Margaret Adelaide, *y d* of late F. W. Lynas; one *s* one *d* (and one *d* decd). *Educ:* Model Sch. and Foyle Coll., Londonderry; Queen's Univ., Belfast. RAFVR, 1943-46; Royal Artillery (TA), 1950-56. Foundation Schol., Queen's Univ., 1947 and 1948; LLB 1949. Called to Bar of N Ireland, 1950. Lecturer in Contract and Sale of Goods, Queen's Univ., 1950-51; Jun. Crown Counsel, Co. Londonderry, 1960-63, Co. Down, 1964-65; Counsel to Attorney-General for N Ireland, 1963-64 and 1965; Vice-Chairman, 1959-61, Chairman, 1961-66, War Pensions Appeal Tribunal for N Ireland. Minister of Health and Social Services, N Ireland, 1969; Parly Sec., Min. of Home Affairs, 1969. *Recreations:* gardening, golf. *Address:* Ardkeen, Marlborough Park North, Belfast 9, N Ireland. *T:* 666761. *Clubs:* Royal Air Force; Northern Counties (Londonderry).

**PORTER, Rodney Robert,** FRS 1964; Whitley Professor of Biochemistry University of Oxford, since 1967; *b* 8 Oct. 1917; *s* of Joseph L. and Isobel M. Porter; *m* 1948, Julia Frances New; two *s* three *d*. *Educ:* Grammar Sch., Ashton-in-Makerfield; Liverpool and Cambridge Universities. Scientific Staff at Nat. Inst. for Medical Research, Mill Hill, NW7, 1949-60; Pfizer Prof. of Immunology, St Mary's Hospital Medical Sch., London Univ., 1960-67. Mem., MRC, 1970-. Hon. Mem., Amer. Soc. of Biological Chemists, 1968; Hon. Foreign Mem., Amer. Acad. of Arts and Sciences, 1968. Award of Merit, Gairdner Foundation, 1966; Ciba Medal, Biochemical Society, 1967; Karl Landsteiner Memorial Award, Amer. Assoc. of Blood Banks, 1968. *Publications:* papers in Biochemical Journal and other learned journals. *Recreations:* walking, fishing. *Address:* Downhill Farm, Witney, Oxon.

**PORTER, Walter Stanley,** TD 1950; MA (Cantab); Headmaster of Framlingham College since Sept. 1955; *b* 28 Sept. 1909; *s* of late Walter Porter, Rugby; *m* 1937, Doreen, *o d* of B. Haynes, Rugby; one *d*. *Educ:* Rugby Sch.; Gonville and Caius Coll., Cambridge. Assistant Master and Officer Commanding Training Corps, Trent Coll., 1933-36; Felsted Sch., 1936-43; Radley Coll., 1944-55. FRSA 1968. *Recreations:* travel, amateur dramatics; formerly Rugby football, hockey. *Address:* Headmaster's House, Framlingham College, Suffolk. *T:* Framlingham 250. *Club:* Public Schools.

**PORTLAND,** 7th Duke of, *cr* 1716; **William Arthur Henry Cavendish-Bentinck,** KG 1948; Earl of Portland, Viscount Woodstock, and Baron of Cirencester, 1689; Marquess of Titchfield, 1716; Baron Bolsover, 1880; Lord Lieutenant of Nottinghamshire, 1939-62; Chancellor of Nottingham University, since 1954; *b* 16 March 1893; *e s* of 6th Duke and Winifred, DBE 1935 (*d* 1954), *d* of late Thomas Yorke Dallas-Yorke; *S* father 1943; *m* 1915, Hon. Ivy Gordon-Lennox (DBE 1958; Maid of Honour to Queen Alexandra, 1912-15), *o d* of late Lord Algernon Gordon-Lennox; one *d* (and one *d* decd). *Educ:* Eton. Lieutenant Royal Horse Guards; MP (U) Newark Division Notts, 1922-43; an Asst Whip, 1927; Junior Lord of the Treasury (unpaid), 1928-29 and 1931; commanded Notts Yeomanry (Sherwood Rangers), 1933-36. Hon. LLD, Nottingham, 1955. *Heir: kinsman* Major Sir Ferdinand William Cavendish-Bentinck, *qv*. *Address:* Welbeck Woodhouse, Worksop, Notts. *T:* Worksop 2460; Welbeck Abbey, Worksop; Langwell, Berriedale, Caithness.

**PORTLOCK, Rear-Admiral Ronald Etridge,** CB 1961; OBE 1947; DL; retired; *b* London, 28 June 1908; *o s* of Henry and Doris Portlock; *m* 1939, Angela, *d* of late Gerard Kirke Smith; no *c*. *Educ:* Royal Naval Coll., Dartmouth. Naval Cadet, 1922; Midshipman, 1926; Lieut-Commander, 1938; Commander, 1943; Captain, 1949; Rear-Admiral 1959. Served War of 1939-45 in HMS Ark Royal and King George V as Lieut-Commander; Admiralty as Commander. Post-war Mine Clearance in Far East, 1946-47; Captain, HM Underwater Detection Establishment, 1950-52; Chief of Staff to C-in-C, The Nore, 1953-54; in comd HMS Newfoundland, and Flag Captain to Flag

Officer; Second in Command Far East Station, 1955-56; Director of Underwater Weapons, Admiralty, 1957-58; Chief of Staff to the Commander-in-Chief, Far East Station, 1959-61, retired, 1961. ADC to the Queen, 1958. Director, Dwa Plantations Ltd. Chairman, Assoc. of Retired Naval Officers, 1965-67. DL Greater London, 1967. Royal Swedish Order of the Swords, 1954. *Address:* 1 Swan Court, Chelsea, SW3. *T:* 01-352 4390. *Club:* Royal Automobile.

**PORTMAN,** family name of **Viscount Portman.**

**PORTMAN,** 9th Viscount, *cr* 1873; **Edward Henry Berkeley Portman;** Baron 1873; *b* 22 April 1934; *s* of late Hon. Michael Berkeley Portman (*d* 1959) (*yr s* of 7th Viscount), and June Charles (*d* 1947); *S* uncle, 1967; *m* 1st, 1956, Rosemary Farris (marr. diss., 1965); one *s* one *d*; 2nd, 1966, Penelope Allin; two *s*. *Educ:* Canford; Royal Agricultural College. Farmer. *Recreations:* shooting, fishing, music. *Heir: s* Hon. Christopher Edward Berkeley Portman, *b* 31 July 1958. *Address:* Clock Mill, Clifford, Herefordshire. *T:* Clifford 235. *Clubs:* White's, Royal Aero.

**PORTSMOUTH,** 9th Earl of, *cr* 1743; **Gerard Vernon Wallop;** Viscount Lymington, Baron Wallop, 1720; Hereditary Bailiff of Burley, New Forest; Vice-Chairman, East Africa Natural Resources Research Council, since 1963; *b* 16 May 1898; *e s* of 8th Earl and Marguerite (*d* 1938), *d* of S. J. Walker, Kentucky; *S* father 1943; *m* 1st, 1920, Mary Lawrence (who obtained a divorce, 1936, and *m* 2nd, 1938, E. J. B. How), *d* of W. K. Post, Bayport, Long Island; one *s* one *d*; 2nd, 1936, Bridget, *o d* of late Captain P. B. Crohan, Royal Navy, Owipen Manor, Glos; one *s* two *d*. Served European War, 1916-19; MP (U) Basingstoke Division of Hants, 1929-34; Member of the Milk Marketing Board, July 1933; Vice-Chairman Hampshire War Agric. Cttee, 1939-47; Vice-President and Chairman Country Landowners Assoc., 1947-48. President, Electors Union, Kenya, 1953-55; MLC Kenya (Corporate Member for Agric.), 1957-60; Vice-Chairman, East African Natural Resources Research Council, 1963-. *Publications:* Git le Cœur, 1928; Ich Dien; The Tory Path, 1931; Horn, Hoof and Corn, 1932; Famine in England, 1938; Alternative to Death, 1943; British Farm Stock, 1950; A Knot of Roots (autobiog.), 1965. *Heir: s* Viscount Lymington, *qv*. *Address:* Over Wallop, Mt Elgon, Kitale, Kenya. *Clubs:* Buck's; Muthaiga Country (Nairobi).
*See also Viscount Chelsea, Lord Rupert Nevill, Lord Porchester.*

**PORTSMOUTH, Bishop of,** since 1960; **Rt. Rev. John Henry Lawrence Phillips;** *b* 2 Feb. 1910; *s* of Rev. H. L. Phillips, Wimborne, Dorset; *m* 1936, Morna, *d* of E. H. W. Wingfield-King, OBE; one *s* three *d*. *Educ:* Weymouth Coll., Trinity Hall, Cambridge. BA 1932; MA 1937; Ridley Hall, Cambridge, 1932-34. Deacon, 1934; priest, 1935. Curate of Christ Church, Harrogate, 1934-35; Curate of Methley, 1935-38; Rector of Farnley, Leeds, 1938-45; Surrogate, 1939-45; Chaplain RNVR, 1942-45; Director of Service Ordination Candidates, 1945-47; General Secretary Central Advisory Council of Training for the Ministry, 1947-49; Vicar of Radcliffe-on-Trent and of Shelford, 1949-57; Archdeacon of Nottingham, 1949-60; Rector of Clifton with Glapton, 1958-60. Chaplain to the Queen, 1959-60. *Recreations:* cricket, golf, Rugby football, etc. *Address:* Bishopswood, Fareham, Hants. *Club:* RNVR.

**PORTSMOUTH, Bishop of, (RC),** since 1965; **Rt. Rev. Derek John Harford Worlock;** *b* 4 Feb. 1920; 2nd *s* of Captain Harford Worlock and Dora (*née* Hoblyn). *Educ:* St Edmund's Coll., Ware, Herts. Ordained RC Priest, 1944. Curate, Our Lady of Victories, Kensington, 1944-45; Private Secretary to Archbishop of Westminster, 1945-64; Rector and Rural Dean, Church of SS Mary and Michael, London, E1, 1964-65. Privy Chamberlain to Pope Pius XII, 1949-53; Domestic Prelate of the Pope, 1953-65; *Peritus* at Vatican Council II, 1963-65; Consultor to Council of Laity, 1967-; Episcopal Secretary to RC Bishops' Conference, 1967-. Knight Commander of Holy Sepulchre of Jerusalem, 1966. *Publications:* Seek Ye First (compiler), 1949; Take One at Bedtime (anthology), 1962; English Bishops at the Council, 1965. *Address:* Bishop's House, Edinburgh Road, Portsmouth. *T:* 20894.

**PORTSMOUTH, Assistant Bishops of;** *see* Chamberlain, Rt Rev. Frank Noel, Woolmer, Rt Rev. L. H.

**PORTSMOUTH, Archdeacon of;** *see* Prior, Ven. Christopher.

**PORTSMOUTH, Provost of;** *see* Goff, Very Rev. E. N. P.

**PORTWAY, Col Donald,** CBE 1957; TD; DL; JP; MA; FICE; Hon. MIMI; Dean, Faculty of Engineering and Professor of Mechanical Engineering, University of Khartoum, 1957-61, retired; Hon. Fellow: Downing College, Cambridge; St Catharine's College, Cambridge; Emeritus Fellow Trumbull College, Yale University, USA; *b* 28 June 1887; *s* of late Ald. H. H. Portway, JP, Halstead, Essex; *m* 1919, Sophia Maud Grace, *niece* and adopted *d* of late J. A. Bezant, JP, Mettingham, Suffolk; one *d*. *Educ:* Felsted Sch.; Downing Coll., Cambridge (Senior Scholar). 1st Class Hons Mech. Sci. Tripos; Research in Mechanical Engineering, Cambridge Univ., 1911; Asst Master at RN Coll., Dartmouth, 1912; BEF 1914, 2nd Lieut to Major, RE; Fellow of St Catharine's Coll., Cambridge, and Lecturer in Engineering Dept, Cambridge Univ., 1919, subsequently Tutor, Senior Tutor and President of St Catharine's Coll., 14 years Proctor or Motor Proctor. Master of St Catharine's Coll., 1946-57. BEF 1939, as Bt Lieut-Colonel, RE (despatches), subsequently Colonel, General Staff. Army Cadet Comdt for Cambridgeshire and Isle of Ely, 1945-51; Sector Comdr, Home Guard, 1951-54. Joint Hon. Colonel University OTC Cambridge, 1950-57. *Publications:* Examples in Elementary Engineering, 1937; Science and Mechanization in Land Warfare, 1938; Military Science To-day, 1940; Talks to Future Officers, 1941; The Quest of Leadership, 1945; Korea, the Land of Morning Calm, 1953; Militant Don, 1963. *Recreations:* swimming, gardening; formerly winner 4 years running of Inter-Varsity Middleweights. *Address:* 33 Millington Road, Cambridge. *Clubs:* Royal Automobile; Hawks (Cambridge).

**POSKITT, Frederick Richard,** CBE 1962; Director, National Teachers' College, Kyambago, Uganda, since 1966; *b* 15 Aug. 1900; *s* of Frederick Hardy Poskitt and Kate Penlington Spencer; *m* 1936, Margaret Embree, *e d* of C. E. Turner, Woolton, Liverpool; two *s* one *d*. *Educ:* Kilburn Grammar Sch.; Downing Coll., Cambridge. Asst Master, Colchester Royal Grammar Sch., 1921-25; Head of History Dept, Manchester Grammar Sch., 1926-33; Headmaster, Bolton Sch., 1933-66. *Recreation:* travel. *Address:* PO Box 20012, Kampala, Uganda.

**POSNER, Michael Vivian;** Fellow and Director of Studies in Economics, Pembroke College, Cambridge, since 1960; *b* 25 Aug. 1931; *s* of Jack Posner; *m* 1953, Rebecca (*née* Reynolds); one *s* one *d*. *Educ:* Whitgift Sch.; Balliol Coll., Oxford. Research Officer, Oxford Inst. of Statistics, 1953-57; Asst Lecturer, then Lecturer in Economics, University of Cambridge, 1958-; Director of Economics, Ministry of Power, 1966-67; Economic Adviser to Treasury, 1967-69. *Publications:* (co-author) Italian Public Enterprise, 1966; books and articles on economics. *Recreation:* country life. *Address:* Okyamie, Bulmer, York. *T:* Whitwell-on-the-Hill 269. *Club:* Oxford and Cambridge University.

**POST, Col Kenneth Graham,** CBE 1945; TD; *b* 21 Jan. 1908; *s* of Donnell Post and Hon. Mrs Post; *m* 1st, 1944, Stephanie Bontē Wood (marr. diss., 1963); one *s* two *d*; 2nd, 1963, Diane Allen; two *s*. *Educ:* Winchester; Magdalen, Oxford. London Stock Exchange, 1929-37; 2nd Lieut, RA (TA) 1937; Norway, 1940; War Office, 1941-42; Ministry of Supply, 1943-44; Ministry of Works, 1945-47; Ministry of Housing, 1956-57; Ministry of Defence, 1957-59. Member Corby New Town Development Corporation, 1955-62; Director, Civic Trust, 1957-63. *Address:* 7 York Mansions, Prince of Wales Drive, SW11. *T:* 01-622 3760. *Club:* Pratt's.

**POSTAN, Michael,** FBA 1959; Professor of Economic History, 1938-65 (now Emeritus) and Fellow of Peterhouse, 1935-65 (now Hon. Fellow), Cambridge; Head of Section in MEW, 1939-42; the Official Historian of Munitions at the Offices of the War Cabinet since 1942; *b* Sept. 1899; *s* of Efim and Elena Postan, Tighina, Bessarabia; *m* 1937, Eileen Power (*d* 1940); *m* 1944, Lady Cynthia Rosalie Keppel, 2nd *d* of 9th Earl of Albemarle, *qv*; two *s*. Lecturer in History in University College (University of London), 1927-31; Lecturer in Economic History at London School of Economics, 1931-35; Lecturer in Economic History in University of Cambridge, 1935-38; Hon. President, Internat. Economic History Assoc. Hon. DLitt. *Address:* 2 Sylvester Road, Cambridge; Penrallt Goch, Festiniog, Merioneth. *Clubs:* United University, Alpine.

**POSTGATE, Raymond William;** Writer; *b* Cambridge, 6 Nov. 1896; *s* of Prof. J. P. Postgate, MA, DLitt, FBA; *gs* of Dr John Postgate; *m* 1918, Daisy, *d* of Rt Hon. George Lansbury; two *s*. *Educ:* Perse Sch., Cambridge; Liverpool Coll.; St John's Coll., Oxford. Eight years in Fleet Street, chiefly as Foreign sub-editor on the old Daily Herald; edited several Socialist journals; Departmental Editor, xivth edn, Encyclopædia Britannica; Civil Servant, 1942-50; European representative, Alfred A. Knopf Inc., NY, 1930-49; President, Good Food Club since 1949. *Publications:* The International During the War, 1918; The Bolshevik Theory, 1920; Revolution from 1789 to 1906, 1920; The Workers' International, 1920; The Builders' History, 1923; Out of the Past, 1922; History of the British Workers, 1926; Murder, Piracy and Treason, 1925; Pervigilium Veneris (ed. and trans. 1924); That Devil Wilkes, 1930; The Conversations of Dr Johnson, 1930; Robert Emmet, 1931; No Epitaph, 1932; Karl Marx, 1933; How to Make a Revolution, 1934; What to Do with the BBC, 1935; (with G. A. Vallance) Those Foreigners, 1937; Verdict of Twelve, 1940; Somebody at the Door, 1943; (with G. D. H. Cole) The Common People, 1746-1946, 1946; Life of George Lansbury, 1951; Plain Man's Guide to Wine, 1951 (15th rev. edn, 1970); The Ledger is Kept, 1953; The Story of a Year, 1848, 1955; An Alphabet of Wine, 1955; Mitsou by Colette (trs. 1957); Every Man is God, 1959; Outline of History, by H. G. Wells (latest revised edn 1970); Home Wine Cellar, 1960; Portuguese Wine, 1969; The Story of a Year, 1798, 1969; (ed and trans.) The Agamemnon of Aeschylus, 1970. Author and Editor, Good Food Guide, annually 1951-54; biennially since 1955 (latest edition, for 1969-70, 1969). *Recreation:* walking. *Address:* Red Lion Cottage, Blean, Kent. *T:* Blean 474. *Club:* Savile.

**POSTGATE, Richmond Seymour,** MA; Controller, Educational Broadcasting, BBC since 1965; *b* 31 Dec. 1908; *s* of Prof. J. P. Postgate, LittD, FBA, Classical Scholar, and Edith Postgate; *m* 1949, Audrey Winifred Jones; one *s* two *d*. *Educ:* St George's Sch., Harpenden, Herts; Clare Coll., Cambridge. Editorial staff of Manchester Guardian newspaper; teaching in Public and Elementary Schools; County LEA Administration; RAFVR. In BBC: Head of School Broadcasting, etc; Director-General, Nigerian Broadcasting Corporation, 1959-61. *Recreation:* walking. *Address:* 40 Clarendon Road, W11.

**POSTILL, Ronald,** TD 1943; MA; Tutor, Millfield School, since 1967; *b* 7 Feb. 1907; *er s* of late Harry Postill, Bridlington, Yorks, and S. Elizabeth Postill; *m* 1939, Yvonne D. P. Ebdy; one *s* one *d*. *Educ:* Bridlington Sch.; Trinity Coll., Cambridge. Open Exhibitioner in Natural Sciences; BA 1928; MA 1944. Asst Master: Aldenham Sch., 1928-30; Tonbridge Sch., 1930-39 and 1945; Headmaster, Victoria Coll., Jersey, 1946-67. Commissioned TA General List, 1928; comd Tonbridge Sch. OTC 1938-39; served War of 1939-45, Royal Signals; Comdt Royal Signals OCTU, 1944-45. King Haakon VII Liberty Cross (Norway), 1945. *Recreations:* criticising cricket (played for Hertfordshire, 1930-34); crosswords and cryptic puzzles. *Address:* Lavender Cottage, Charlton Adam, Somerton, Som. *T:* Charlton Mackrell 328.

**POTT, Col Douglas,** CIE 1929; DSO 1917; MC; Indian Army, retired; late 6th DCO Lancers; *b* 1888; *s* of late Colonel William Pott of Springfields, Steyning, Sussex. *Educ:* Wellington Coll. Served NW Frontier of India, 1908 (medal and clasp); European War, 1914-18 (despatches, DSO, MC); Instructor, Senior Officers' Sch., Belgaum, 1936-39; retired, 1939. *Address:* Thurston Old Vicarage, Bury St Edmunds, Suffolk. *Club:* Cavalry.

**POTT, Sir Leslie,** KBE 1962 (CBE 1957); *b* 4 July 1903; *s* of Charles Groves Pott; *m* 1937, Norma Lyons-Montgomery; one *s*. *Educ:* Manchester Grammar Sch.; Gonville and Caius Coll., Cambridge (Open Scholar). Entered Levant Consular Service, 1924; served at Casablanca, Damascus and Beirut, 1926-29; Moscow and Leningrad, 1930-35; Foreign Office, 1936-37; Piraeus and Athens, 1938-40; Consul at Baghdad, 1940-43; Foreign Office, 1943-45; Consul at Alexandria, 1946-47. Consul-General at Tabriz, 1947-50; Deputy High Commissioner for the UK at Bombay, 1950-52; Consul-General at Istanbul, 1952-55; at Marseilles, 1955-61, also to Monaco, 1957-61. Retired from HM Diplomatic Service, 1962. *Address:* Priory Cottage, Little Gaddesden, Herts. *T:* Little Gaddesden 3409. *Club:* Royal Automobile.

**POTTER, Arthur Kingscote,** CMG 1957; CBE 1946; *b* 7 April 1905; *s* of late R. E. Potter, Ridgewood, Almondsbury, Glos; *m* 1950, Hilda, *d* of late W. A. Butterfield, OBE; one *d*. *Educ:* Charterhouse; New Coll., Oxford (BA). Entered Indian CS, 1928. Financial Adviser,

Army in Burma, 1942 (despatches); Finance Secretary, Government of Burma, 1942-43; Financial Adviser (Brigadier), 11th Army Group, 1943, and Allied Land Forces, South-East Asia, 1943-44; Chief Financial Officer (Brig.), Military Administration of Burma, 1944-47; HM Treasury Representative in India, Pakistan and Burma, 1947-50; Asst Secretary, HM Treasury, 1950-56; Counsellor, UK Delegation to NATO, Paris, 1956-65. *Address:* c/o National Westminster Bank Ltd, 208 Piccadilly, W1V 0AB.

**POTTER, David Morris;** Coe Professor of American History, Stanford University, since 1961; Harold Vyvyan Harmsworth Professor of American History, and Fellow of Queen's College, Oxford, 1947-48; *b* Augusta, Georgia, 6 Dec. 1910; *s* of David Morris and Katie Brown Potter; *m* 1948, Dilys Mary Roberts (*d* 1969); one *d*. *Educ:* Emory (AB); Yale (MA, PhD). Instructor in History, University of Mississippi, 1936-38, and at Rice Inst., 1938-42. Yale Univ., Asst Professor, 1942-47; Associate Professor, 1947-49; Professor, 1949-50; Coe Prof., 1950-61. Editor, Yale Review, 1949-51; Fellow, Timothy Dwight Coll., 1942-61. Commonwealth Fund Lecturer, University College, London, 1963. *Publications:* Lincoln and his Party in the Secession Crisis, 1942; Trail to California; The Overland Journal of Vincent Geiger and Wakeman Bryarly, 1945; (with Jas H. Croushore) A Union Officer in the Reconstruction, 1948; (with T. G. Manning) Nationalism and Sectionalism in America, 1949; (with T. G. Manning) Government and the American Economy, 1949; People of Plenty: Economic Abundance and the American Character, 1954; The South and the Sectional Conflict, 1968. *Address:* Department of History, Stanford University, Stanford, California, USA.

**POTTER, Dennis (Christopher George);** playwright, author and journalist (freelance since 1964); *b* 17 May 1935; *e s* of Walter and Margaret Potter; *m* 1959, Margaret Morgan; one *s* two *d*. *Educ:* Bell's Grammar Sch., Coleford, Glos; St Clement Danes Grammar Sch.; New Coll., Oxford. Editor, Isis, 1958; BA (Hons) in PPE Oxon, 1959. BBC TV (current affairs), 1959-61; Daily Herald, feature writer, then TV critic, 1961-64; contested (Lab) East Herts, 1964; Leader writer, The Sun, Sept.-Oct. 1964, then resigned. First television play, 1965. Book critic, The Times, Oct. 1967-; Television critic, New Statesman, 1967; *television plays:* Vote Vote Vote for Nigel Barton (also at Bristol Old Vic, 1968); Stand Up Nigel Barton; Where the Buffalo Roam; A Beast with Two Backs; Son of Man, etc. *Publications:* The Glittering Coffin, 1960; The Changing Forest, 1962; The Nigel Barton Plays (paperback, 1968); Son of Man, 1970. *Recreations:* nothing unusual, i.e. the usual personal pleasures, sought with immoderate fervour. *Address:* Morecambe Lodge, Duxmere, Ross-on-Wye, Herefordshire. *T:* Ross-on-Wye 3199.

**POTTER, Douglas Charles Loftus; His Honour Judge Potter;** Judge of County Courts, since 1959; *b* 17 Dec. 1903; *s* of John Charles Potter, solicitor, Putney, and Caroline Annette Tidy Potter (*née* Onslow); *m* 1934, Margaret Isabel, *d* of Dr William Savile Henderson, Liverpool; one *d*. *Educ:* Radley; Trinity Coll., Oxford (MA). Rowed in winning crew, Ladies' Plate, Henley Regatta, 1923; Half-blue, OUAC, 3 miles, 1925. Barrister, Inner Temple, 1928; SE Circuit, Herts and Essex Sessions. Served War of 1939-45 in RAFVR, 1940-45. Judge of County Courts, 1959-: Willesden, Croydon and Kingston upon Thames. *Publications:* The Law Relating to Garages and Car Parks, 1939; The National Insurance Act, 1946, 1946. *Recreations:* walking, travel, reading, music, gardening. *Club:* Royal Automobile.

**POTTER, George Richard,** MA, PhD (Cambridge), FRHistS, FSA; retired as Professor of Medieval History, University of Sheffield, 1965; Emeritus Professor, since 1965; Temporary Professor, University of Warwick, 1968-69; *b* 6 Aug. 1900; *e s* of George Potter, Norwich; *m* 1927, Rachel, *y d* of M. Leon, Salisbury, Rhodesia; one *s* one *d*. *Educ:* King Edward VI Sch., Norwich; St John's Coll., Cambridge; Head of Department of History, University College, Leicester, 1925-27; Lecturer in Medieval History, Queen's Univ. of Belfast, 1927-31; Dean of the Faculty of Arts, 1939-42; External examiner for a number of Universities; Member Royal Commission on Historical Manuscripts; Vice-Chairman Universities Council for Adult Education, 1938-64; President, Historical Association, 1961-64. Cultural Attaché, British Embassy, Bonn, 1955-57. H. C. Lea Visiting Prof., University of Pennsylvania, 1966-67, 1967-68. Served with Royal Naval Volunteer Reserve, 1918-19. *Publications:* Sir Thomas More, 1925; The Autobiography of Ousâma, 1929; (with Bonjour and Offier) Short History of Switzerland, 1952; contribution to Cambridge Medieval History; advisory editor and contributor to Chambers's Encyclopædia; editor of New Cambridge Modern History, Vol. I; German Renaissance; various articles. *Recreations:* walking, travel. *Address:* Derwent Lane, Hathersage, Sheffield S30 1AS. *T:* Hathersage 428.

**POTTER, Sir Henry (Steven),** KCMG 1956 (CMG 1948); MA (Cantab); retired as British Resident, Zanzibar (1954-60); *b* 7 March 1904; *er s* of late Charles Edward Potter, MD; *m* 1929, Ruth Newton; one *s* one *d*. *Educ:* Shrewsbury Sch.; Queens' Coll., Cambridge. Colonial Administrative Service, District Officer, Kenya, 1926-44; Deputy Financial Secretary, Kenya, 1944-45; Financial Secretary, Uganda, 1945-48; Chief Secretary, Uganda, 1948-52; Chief Secretary, Kenya, 1952-54. KStJ 1958; Order of Brilliant Star of Zanzibar (1st Class), 1959. *Recreations:* golf, gardening. *Address:* Pen Pits, Penselwood, Wincanton, Somerset. *Club:* Nairobi (Kenya).

**POTTER, Howard Vincent;** retired as Director, Bakelite Ltd (1926-65) (Chairman, 1956-59); *b* 19 April 1888; 3rd *s* of Frederick John Potter; *m* 1915, Amy Parks; one *s* one *d*. *Educ:* University Sch.; King's Coll., London Univ. Pharmaceutical Chemist (Major degree), 1912; BSc (Hons). Research Chemist, 1913; Chemical Engineer, 1936; Managing Director, Bakelite Ltd, 1926, Chairman and Managing Director, 1946. CEng, FRIC, MIChemE, FPI. *Recreations:* gardening, photography. *Address:* 2 Chiltern Hills Road, Beaconsfield, Bucks. *T:* Beaconsfield 3398. *Clubs:* City Livery, Institute of Directors.

**POTTER, Sir Ian;** *see* Potter, Sir W. I.

**POTTER, Maj.-Gen. Sir John,** KBE 1968 (CBE 1963; OBE 1951); CB 1966; Director of Movements (Army), Ministry of Defence, Oct. 1966-Nov. 1968; retired; *b* 18 April 1913; *s* of late Major Benjamin Henry Potter, OBE, MC; *m* 1943, Vivienne Madge, *d* of late Captain Henry D'Arcy Medlicott Cooke; one *s* one *d*. Served War of 1939-45. Major-General, 1962; Colonel Comdt: RAOC, 1965-69; RCT, 1968-. Director of Supplies amd Transport, 1963-65. Transport Officer in Chief (Army), July 1965-June 1966. *Address:* c/o Lloyds Bank

Ltd, Cox's and King's Branch, 6 Pall Mall, SW1.

**POTTER, John Isidore,** MDS, LDS; late Professor of Dental Mechanics and Prosthetics, University College, Dublin; Member of ID Assoc.; Consultant Surgeon Dentist to St Patrick's Coll., Maynooth. *Address:* 113 Lower Baggot Street, Dublin.

**POTTER, Mrs Mary;** Artist; *b* 9 April 1900; *d* of John Arthur and Kathleen Mary Attenborough; *m* 1927, Stephen Potter, (marr. diss. 1955; he *d* 1969); two *s*. *Educ:* Private Sch.; Slade Sch. (Scholar). Paintings exhibited in London and provinces since 1921. One-man shows: Bloomsbury Gallery, 1931; Redfern Gallery, 1934 and 1949; Tooth's Gallery, 1939 and 1946; Leicester Gallery, 1951, 1953, 1954, 1957, 1961, 1963; New Art Centre, 1967, 1969. Retrospective Exhibition, Whitechapel Art Gallery, 1964. Pictures bought by the Tate Gallery, Arts Council, Manchester City Art Gallery, Contemporary Art Society, etc; and galleries in New York and Canada, and Australia. *Address:* Red Studio, Aldeburgh, Suffolk. *T:* Aldeburgh 2081.

**POTTER, Air Marshal Sir Patrick B. L.;** *see* Lee Potter.

**POTTER, Prof. Simeon,** PhD (Prague); FRSL; Professor Emeritus, Liverpool University; *b* London, 19 Jan. 1898; *y s* of George Potter and Matilda Holdsworth; *m* 1936, Doris Clara Mackay. *Educ:* Kilburn Grammar Sch.; Queen Mary Coll. and University Coll., London (MA); St John's Coll., Oxford (BLitt). Served European War in Royal Navy, Atlantic and Mediterranean, 1916-19; Asst Master, Harrow County Sch., 1921-24; Lecturer in English, University of Brno, 1924-31; broadcast frequently for Prague Radio, 1927-31; Lecturer in English and Adviser to Overseas Students, University of Southampton, 1931-45; Lecturer in English, University of Aarhus, 1934-35; Baines Professor of English Language and Philology, University of Liverpool, 1945-65. Guest Prof., Westfield Coll., London, 1967-68. Member Council, Philological Society, 1933-61; Jt Editor, The Language Library. *Publications:* Everyday English, 1927; An English Vocabulary, 1930; An English Grammar, 1932; The Winchester Bede, 1935; The Outlook in English Studies, 1946; Our Language, 1950; Cheshire Place-Names, 1955; Modern Linguistics, 1957; Language in the Modern World, 1960; English Life and Speech, 1964; Ed. Bradley, The Making of English, 1968; Changing English, 1969. Essays and reviews contributed to Philologica Pragensia, Anglia, Encyclopædia Britannica, Essays and Studies by Members of the English Association, Transactions of the Philological Society, Medium Aevum, Archivum Linguisticum, The Modern Language Review, The Review of English Studies, etc. *Address:* Maze Cottage, Hampton Court Road, East Molesey, Surrey. *T:* 01-977 2953.

**POTTER, Maj.-General Sir Wilfrid John;** *see* Potter, Maj.-General, Sir John.

**POTTER, Sir (William) Ian,** Kt 1962; Stockbroker, Melbourne, Australia; *b* 25 Aug. 1902; *s* of James William Potter and Maria Louisa (*née* McWhinnie); *m* 1955; two *d*. *Educ:* University of Sydney. Economist to Federal Treas., 1935-36; Commonwealth Rep. Rural Debt Adjustment Cttee, 1936; founded Ian Potter & Co., 1937; Principal Partner, 1937-67. served RANVR, 1939-44. Member: Cttee Stock Exchange of Melbourne, 1945-62; Melbourne University Council, 1947-; Commonwealth Immigration Planning Council, 1956-62; Nat. Art Gallery and Cultural Centre Bldg Cttee, 1960-. President, Australian Elizabethan Theatre Trust, 1964-66, Chairman, 1968-. *Publications:* contrib. articles on financial and economic subjects to learned journals and press. *Recreations:* yachting, tennis, golfing. *Address:* 30 Sargood Street, Toorak, Victoria 3142, Australia. *T:* 24 4308. *Clubs:* Melbourne, Australian, Royal Melbourne Golf (Melbourne); The Links (NY).

**POTTINGER, William George,** CVO 1953; Under-Secretary, Department of Agriculture and Fisheries for Scotland, since 1968; *b* 11 June 1916; *e s* of late Rev. William Pottinger, MA, Orkney, and Janet Woodcock; *m* 1946, Margaret Rutherfurd Clark McGregor; one *s*. *Educ:* George Watson's; High School of Glasgow; Edinburgh Univ.; Heidelberg; Queens' Coll., Cambridge (Major Scholar). Entered Scottish Home Dept, as Assistant Principal, 1939. Served War of 1939-45, RFA; France, N Africa, Italy (despatches), Lieut-Col RA. Principal, 1945; Private Secretary to successive Secretaries of State for Scotland, 1950-52; Asst Secretary, Scottish Home Dept, 1952; Under-Secretary: Scottish Home Dept, 1959-62; Scottish Home and Health Dept, 1962-63; Scottish Development Dept, 1963-64; Scottish Office, 1964-68. Secretary, Royal Commn on Scottish Affairs, 1952-54. *Publications:* papers and reviews. *Recreations:* squash rackets, golf and fishing. *Address:* Pelicans, Muirfield, Gullane, East Lothian. *T:* Gullane 2153. *Clubs:* Savile; New (Edinburgh).

**POTTLE, Frederick Albert,** BA Colby, MA, PhD Yale, Hon. LittD Colby, Rutgers, Hon. LHD Northwestern; Hon. LLD Glasgow; Sterling Professor of English, and Fellow Emeritus of Davenport College, Yale University; Public Orator, Yale University, 1942 and 1946; *b* Lovell, Maine, 3 Aug. 1897; *y s* of late Fred Leroy Pottle and Annette Wardwell Kemp; *m* 1920, Marion Isabel Starbird, Oxford, Maine; two *s*. *Educ:* Colby Coll. (*Summa cum laude*); Yale (John Addison Porter Prize). Served as private in Evacuation Hospital No 8, AEF, 1918-19; formerly Assistant Professor of English, University of New Hampshire; Editor of the Private Papers of James Boswell (succeeding the late Geoffrey Scott); Hon. member of Johnson Club; Vice-President, Johnson Society of London; Trustee: General Theological Seminary, 1947-68; Colby Coll., 1932-59, 1966-; Messenger Lecturer, Cornell Univ., 1941; Member of Joint Commission on Holy Matrimony of the Episcopal Church, 1940-46; Guggenheim Fellow, 1945-46, 1952-53; Chancellor Academy of American Poets, 1951-; Chairman of Editorial Cttee of Yale Editions of Private Papers of James Boswell, 1949-; Member Provinciaal Utrechtsch Genootschap van Kunsten en Wetenschappen, 1953-; Member American Academy of Arts and Sciences, 1957-; FIAL, 1958-; Member, American Philosophical Society, 1960. Wilbur Lucius Cross Medal, Yale, 1967; William Clyde DeVane Medal, Yale, 1969. *Publications:* Shelley and Browning, 1923; A New Portrait of James Boswell (with Chauncey B. Tinker), 1927; The Literary Career of James Boswell, 1929; Stretchers, the Story of a Hospital on the Western Front, 1929; The Private Papers of James Boswell: A Catalogue (with Marion S. Pottle), 1931; Vols 7-18 of The Private Papers of James Boswell, 1930-34; Boswell's Journal of a Tour to the Hebrides, from the Original Manuscript (with Charles H. Bennett), 1936, revised edition, 1963; Index to the Private Papers of James Boswell (with Joseph Foladare, John P. Kirby and others), 1937; Boswell and the Girl from Botany Bay, 1937; The Idiom of Poetry, 1941, revised and enlarged edition, 1946; Boswell's London Journal (1762-63), 1950; Boswell in Holland (1763-64), 1952; Boswell on the Grand Tour: Germany and Switzerland (1764), 1953; Boswell on the Grand Tour: Italy, Corsica and France, 1765 (with Frank Brady), 1955; Boswell in Search of a Wife, 1766-1769 (with Frank Brady), 1956; Boswell for the Defence, 1769-1774 (with William K. Wimsatt), 1959; Boswell: The Ominous Years, 1774-1776 (with Charles Ryskamp), 1963; James Boswell, The Earlier Years, 1966; Boswell in Extremes, 1776-1778 (with Charles McC. Weis), 1970; various articles. *Recreation:* gardening. *Address:* 35 Edgehill Road, New Haven, Conn 06511, USA. *Clubs:* Elizabethan (New Haven); Grolier, Ends of the Earth (New York).

**POTTS, Archie;** Director of Scientific and Technical Intelligence, Ministry of Defence, since 1964; *b* 28 Dec. 1914; *s* of late Mr and Mrs A. Potts, Newcastle upon Tyne; *m* 1951, Winifred Joan Bishop, MBE, *d* of late Mr and Mrs Reginald Bishop; two *s. Educ:* University of Durham. BSc (Hons) Physics, 1935. Research in Spectroscopy, King's Coll., University of Durham, 1936-39. War of 1939-45: Operational Research in Radar and Allied Fields, Fighter Command, amd N Africa and Italy, 1939-45; Hon. Sqdn Leader, RAFVR, 1943-45. Chief Research Officer, Fighter Command, 1946-51; Defence Research Staff, Min. of Defence, 1951-53; Scientific Adviser, Allied Air Forces Central Europe, 1954-56; Asst Scientific Adviser, Air Ministry, 1957; Dep. Director for Atomic Energy, Jt Intell. Bureau, 1957-63. FInstP 1945. *Recreation:* listening to music. *Address:* 2 Garrick Close, Richmond Green, Surrey. *T:* 01-948 1096. *Club:* Royal Air Force.

**POTTS, Prof. Edward Logan Johnston,** MSc; Professor of Mining, Department of Mining Engineering, University of Newcastle upon Tyne, since 1951; *b* Niddrie, Midlothian, 22 Jan. 1915; *s* of Samuel Potts; *m* 1940, Edith Mary, *d* of A. Hayton, Scarborough; one *s* one *d. Educ:* Coatbridge Grammar Sch., Lanarkshire; Gosforth Grammar Sch., Newcastle upon Tyne; King's Coll., University of Durham. BSc (dist.) 1939, 1st Class Hons (Dunelm) 1940; 1st Class Colliery Manager's Certif., 1941; MSc (Dunelm) 1945. Apprentice Mine Surveyor, Hazlerigg & Burradon Coal Co., Ltd, 1931-34. Asst to Chief Surveyor, Charlaw & Sacriston Collieries Co. Ltd, 1934-36; Certificated Mine Surveyor, 1936; Apprentice Mining Engineer, Wallsend & Hebburn Coal Co. Ltd, 1936-40; Cons. Mining Engineer, Northumberland, Durham, N Staffs; Surveyor to Northern "A" Regional cttee; prepared report on Northumberland and Cumberland Reserves and output, 1944; Reader in Mining, King's Coll., University of Durham, 1947; Mining Adviser: Northumberland Coal Owners' Assoc., 1947; Mickley Associated Collieries, 1949-51; Peterlee Development Corp. on mining subsidence, 1947-; Adviser to Kolar Gold Fields, S India, rock bursts in deep mining, 1955-. President, N of England Inst. Mining and Mech. Engineering, 1957-58. Consultant, Rock Mechanics, Australian Development, NT Australia. Research on photo-elasticity, etc; co-designer Dunelm circular fluorescent mine lighting unit. *Publications:* (jointly) Horizon Mining, 1953; papers on ventilation, mine lighting, strata control in Trans. Inst. Mining Eng., British Assoc. and other journals. *Recreations:* athletics, motoring. *Address:* University of Newcastle upon Tyne. *T:* Newcastle 28511; 4 Montagu Avenue, Gosforth, Newcastle upon Tyne 3. *T:* Newcastle 52171.

**POTTS, Thomas Edmund,** ERD 1957; Company Director; *b* 23 March 1908; *s* of late T. E. Potts, Leeds; *m* 1932, Phyllis Margaret, *d* of late J. S. Gebbie, Douglas, Isle of Man; one *s. Educ:* Leeds Modern School. Joined The British Oxygen Co. Ltd, 1928. Commissioned RE, Supp. R of O, 1938; served War of 1939-45, Madras Sappers and Miners in India, Eritrea, Western Desert, Tunisia, with 4th and 5th Indian Divs (despatches). Rejoined British Oxygen Co. Ltd, London, 1945; Managing Director, African Oxygen Ltd, Johannesburg, 1947; Director, British Oxygen Co. Ltd, 1955; Managing Director, The British Oxygen Co. Ltd, 1958-63; Pres. South African Instn of Welding, 1951; Vice-Pres., Inst. of Welding, 1963-64. *Recreation:* golf. *Address:* Budds Oak, Primrose Lane, Holyport, Berks. *T:* Maidenhead 26887. *Clubs:* Bath; Rand (Johannesburg); Temple Golf.

**POULETT,** family name of **Earl Poulett.**

**POULETT,** 8th Earl *cr* 1706; **George Amias Fitzwarrine Poulett;** Baron Poulett, 1627; Viscount Hinton of Hinton St George, 1706; *b* 23 June 1909; *s* of 7th Earl; *S* father, 1918; *m* 1st, 1935, Oriel Ross (whom he divorced in 1941); 2nd, 1941, Lorraine Lawrence (*d* 1961), of Svendborg, Denmark, and England; 3rd, 1968, Margaret Christine Ball. *Educ:* Eton. Served pupil apprenticeship as mechanical engineer at GWR Locomotive Works, Swindon, and Signal Factory, Reading. Technical Asst: to Chief Mechanical Engr, Woolwich Arsenal, 1940-41; to Director of Ordnance Factories (Small Arms), 1941-43. Assoc. Inst., Railway Signal Engineers; Assoc. Mem. Inst., British Engineers. Coronation Medal, 1953. *Heir:* none. *Address:* Lille Hus, Gorey, Jersey, Channel Islands. *T:* Jersey East 2270. Lille Hus, Dick's Point, Nassau, NP, Bahamas. *Club:* Carlton.

**POULTON, Lt-Col Henry Mortimer,** CIE 1942; late IA; Indian Political Service (retired); *b* 23 April 1898. First commission, 1917; joined Political Dept, 1922; Resident, Central India, 1946; retd, 1947. *Address:* Folly End, Milford on Sea, Hants. *T:* 3244.

**POUNCEY, Denys Duncan Rivers,** MA, MusB Cantab; FRCO; Organist and Master of the Choristers, Wells Cathedral, 1936-70; Conductor of Wells Cathedral Oratorio Chorus and Orchestra, 1946-66; Hon. Diocesan Choirmaster Bath and Wells Choral Association, 1946-70; *b* 23 Dec. 1906; *s* of late Rev. George Ernest Pouncey and late Madeline Mary Roberts; *m* 1937, Evelyn Cottier. *Educ:* Marlborough College; Queens' College, Cambridge. Asst to Dr Cyril Rootham, Organist and Choirmaster of St John's Coll., Cambridge, 1928-34; Organist and Choirmaster S Matthew's, Northampton, 1934-36; Founder and Conductor of Northampton Bach Choir. *Address:* Longstring, 23 Ash Lane, Wells, Somerset. *T:* Wells 3200.

**POUND, Sir Derek Allen,** 4th Bt, *cr* 1905; *b* 7 April 1920; *o s* of Sir Allen Leslie Pound, 3rd Bt, LLB, late sole member of legal firm of Pound & Pound, of Egham, and 1st wife, Margery (who obtained a divorce, 1925), 2nd *d* of Stephen G. Hayworth, Clapton Common; *m* 1942, Joan Amy, *d* of James Woodthorpe, Boston, Lincs; one *s* one *d. Educ:* Shrewsbury. Lieutenant Royal Artillery, 1941; transferred to Essex Regiment; released from Service, 1946. *Heir: s* John David Pound, [*b* 1 Nov. 1946; *m* 1968, Heather Frances O'Brien, *o d* of Harry Jackson Dean]. *Address:* 37 Great Cumberland Place, W1.

**POUND, Ezra,** PhB, MA, DLitt; American poet and composer; Fellow, Academy of American Poets, 1963; *b* 1885; *s* of H. L. and Isabel Weston Pound; *m* 1914, Dorothy Shakespear. *Educ:* University of Pennsylvania (MA, Fellow in Romanics); Hamilton College (PhD). Travel and study in Spain, Italy, and Provence, 1906-7; informally, literary executor for the late Ernest Fenollosa, work on the Japanese Noh drama and on Japanese and Chinese poetry, 1914; London Editor of The Little Review, 1917-19; formerly editor of the Exile. Contributor to Rassegna Monetaria, Criterion, Action, British Union Quarterly, Townsman, Hudson Review. A follower of Confucius and Ovid. Continued to speak on Rome Radio after Pearl Harbour on condition that he never be asked to say anything contrary to his conscience or contrary to his duties as an American citizen; a condition observed by the Italian Government. Is now resident in Italy. *Publications:* Poems A Lume Spento, 1908; Personæ, 1909; Exultations, 1909; Provença, 1910; Canzoni, 1911; Ripostes, 1912; Cathay, 1915; Lustra, 1916; Quia Pauper Amavi, 1919; Umbra (collected early poems), 1920; Hugh Selwyn Mauberley, 1920; Cantos I-XVI, 1925; Personæ (The Collected Poems), 1926; Cantos XVII-XXVII, 1928; XXX, 1930; Cantos 31-41, 1934; Fifth Decad of Cantos, 1937; Cantos 52-71, 1940; Pisan Cantos, 74-84, 1948; Section Rock-Drill, 85-95, 1955; Thrones 96-109 de los cantares, 1959. Music–two operas, Le Testament, 1919-21, partial performance, Paris, 1926; Guido Cavalcanti, 1931-32. Prose–The Spirit of Romance, 1910; Gaudier Brzeska, 1916; Pavannes and Divisions, 1918; Instigations, 1920; Indiscretions, 1923; Antheil and the Treatise on Harmony, 1924; Imaginary Letters, 1930; How to Read, 1931; Prolegomena, Vol. I, 1932; ABC of Economics, 1933; ABC of Reading, 1934; Make it New, 1934; Social Credit, an Impact, 1935; Jefferson and/or Mussolini, 1935; Polite Essays, 1936; Digest of the Analects, 1937; Guide to Kulchur, 1938; What is Money for?, 1939; Literary Essays, 1954; Pavannes and Divagations, 1958; Selected Cantos, 1967; Collected Shorter Poems, 1968. A number of these have been trans. into several languages. *Translations:* The Sonnets and Ballate of Guido Cavalcanti, 1912 and 1913; Certain Noble Plays of Japan, from the Fenollosa MSS, with Introduction by W. B. Yeats 1916; Noh, or Accomplishment, 1917; 12 Dialogues of Fontenelle, 1917; Gourmont's Physique de l'amour; The Ta Hio (Amer. version), 1928; Cavalcanti complete, definitive Text, 1932; The Classic Anthology defined by Confucius, 1954; Sophokles' Women of Trachis; Pea, Moscardino, 1956. *Written in Italian* (some trans. by others into English, etc): Confucio; Studio Integrale; L'Asse che non vacilla; Lavoro ed Usura; Natura Economica degli Stati Uniti; and numerous essays. German vols include: Masken; Frauen von Trachis. *Editor:* Catholic Anthology, 1915; Letters of John Butler Yeats, 1917; Profile, Active Anthology, 1933; The Chinese Written Character, by Ernest Fenollosa (ed with notes), 1936, etc. *Relevant publications:* The Letters of Ezra Pound (ed by D. D. Paige), 1951; The Translations of Ezra Pound, 1953; (by Charles Norman) Ezra Pound, 1969. Art books Scheiwiller Series: La Martinelli, 1956; Gaudier-Brzeska, Brancusi, 1957. *Recreation:* the public taste. *Address:* c/o Messrs Horne and Birkett, 19 Cowley Street, Westminster, SW1.

**POUNDER, Rafton John;** MP (UU) Belfast South, since Oct. 1963; *b* 13 May 1933; *s* of Cuthbert C. Pounder, Gefion, Ballynahatty, Shaw's Bridge, Belfast; *m* 1959, Valerie Isobel, *d* of late Robert Stewart, MBE, Cherryvalley, Belfast; one *s* one *d*. *Educ:* Charterhouse; Christ's College, Cambridge. Qualified as a Chartered Accountant, 1959. Chm. Cambridge Univ. Cons. and Unionist Assoc., 1954; Ulster rep. on Young Cons. and Unionist Nat. Adv. Cttee, 1960-63; Hon. Mem., Ulster Young Unionist Council, 1963; Member: UK delegn to Cons. Assembly of Council of Europe, and to Assembly of WEU, 1965-68; Exec. Ctte, Nat. Union of Cons. and Unionist Assocs, 1967-; Exec. Cttee, Ulster Unionist Council, 1967-; House of Commons Select Cttee on Public Accounts, 1970-; Vice-Chm., Cons, Parly Party's Technology Cttee, 1970-. Mem. CPA Delegn to: Jamaica and Cayman Is, Nov. 1966; Malawi, Sept. 1968. Hon. Secretary: Ulster Unionist Parly Party at Westminster, 1964-67; Cons. Parly Party's Power Cttee, 1969-70. Pres., Ulster Soc. for Prevention of Cruelty to Animals, 1968-. Dir, Progressive Building Soc. Lay Member, General Synod of the Church of Ireland, 1966-. *Recreations:* golf, reading, music. *Address:* 6 Bristow Park, Malone, Belfast 9, N Ireland. *T:* Belfast 669268. *Club:* Union Society (Cambridge).

**POUT, Harry Wilfrid,** OBE 1959; CEng, FIEE; Director, Admiralty Surface Weapons Establishment, since 1969; *b* 11 April 1920; British; *m* 1949, Margaret Elizabeth (*née* Nelson); three *d*. *Educ:* East Ham Grammar Sch.; Imperial Coll., London. BSc (Eng); ACGI 1940. RN Scientific Service, 1940; Admty Signal Estab. (later Admty Signal and Radar Estab.), 1940-54; Dept of Operational Research, Admty, 1954-59; idc 1959; Head of Guided Weapon Projects, Admty, 1960-65; Asst Chief Scientific Adviser (Projects), MoD, 1965-69. *Publications:* classified books; contribs to jls of IEE, RAeS, RUSI, etc. *Recreations:* mountaineering, gardening and do-it-yourself activities, amateur geology. *Address:* Oakmead, Fox Corner, Worplesdon, near Guildford, Surrey. *T:* Worplesdon 2223.

**POWDITCH, Alan (Cecil Robert),** MC 1944; JP; Secretary to the Board of Governors, St Mary's Hospital, W2, since 1950; *b* 14 April 1912; *s* of Cecil John and Annis Maudie Powditch; *m* 1942, Barbara Leggat; one *s* one *d*. *Educ:* Mercers School. Entered Hospital Service, 1933; Accountant, St Mary's Hospital, 1938. Served War of 1939-45, with 51st Royal Tank Regt, 1941-46. Dep. House Governor, St Mary's Hospital, 1947-50; Mem. of National Staff Cttee (Min. of Health) 1964. JP County of Middlesex 1965. *Recreations:* golf; interested in gardening when necessary. *Address:* Brentmore, Marlborough Park, Ducks Hill Road, Northwood, Mddx.

**POWELL, Alan Richard,** FRS 1953; retired; Research Manager, Johnson, Matthey and Co. Ltd, 1918-54; Research Consultant, 1954-59; *b* 6 March 1894; *s* of Alfred Powell and Ellen Brown; *m* 1st, 1914, Marguerite Tremmel (*d* 1956); one *s* three *d*; 2nd, 1960, Mildred Mary, *widow* of Arthur John Coleman. *Educ:* City of London School. Analytical chemist with G. T. Holloway & Co., Ltd, Poplar, 1913-18; Chief Chemist, 1916-18; started Research Laboratory with Johnson, Matthey and Co. Ltd, Hatton Garden, EC1 1918; more extensive Research Laboratories built at Wembley, 1938, extended, 1948, 1954. FIM 1947; FRIC 1948. *Publications:* Analysis of Ores and Minerals of the Rarer Elements (with late W. R. Schoeller), 1st edn 1918, 2nd edn 1940, 3rd edn 1954. Articles on Platinum Group Metals, etc. in Thorpe's Dictionary of Chemistry; articles on Rare Metals in Scott's Standard Methods of Chemical Analysis, 6th edn 1962. Chapter on Platinum Group Metals in Wilson's Comprehensive Analytical Chemistry, Vol. 10, 1961. Contributor to The Analyst, Journal of Applied Chemistry, Jl Chem. Soc., Bulletin Inst. Min. Met. Jl Inorg. Nucl. Chem. *Recreation:* gardening. *Address:* Red Roofs, Sycamore Road, Amersham, Buckinghamshire. *T:* Amersham 6308.

**POWELL, Anthony Dymoke;** CBE 1956; *b* 21 Dec. 1905; *o s* of late Lt-Col P. L. W. Powell, CBE, DSO; *m* 1934, Lady Violet Pakenham, 3rd *d* of 5th Earl of Longford, KP; two *s*. *Educ:* Eton; Balliol College, Oxford, MA. Served War of 1939-45, Welch Regt and Intelligence Corps, Major. A Trustee, National Portrait Gallery, 1962-. Orders of: the White Lion, (Czechoslovakia); the Oaken Crown and Croix de Guerre (Luxembourg); Leopold II (Belgium). *Publications:* Afternoon Men, 1931; Venusberg, 1932; From a View to a Death, 1933; Agents and Patients, 1936; What's become of Waring, 1939; John Aubrey and His Friends, 1948; Selections from John Aubrey, 1949; A Question of Upbringing, 1951 (first vol. of Music of Time series which follow); A Buyer's Market, 1952; The Acceptance World, 1955; At Lady Molly's, 1957 (James Tait Black Memorial Prize); Casanova's Chinese Restaurant, 1960; The Kindly Ones, 1962; The Valley of Bones, 1964; The Soldier's Art, 1966; The Military Philosophers, 1968; Books do Furnish a Room, 1971; *plays:* Afternoon Men (adapted by Riccardo Aragno), Arts Theatre Club, 1963. *Address:* The Chantry, near Frome, Somerset. *T:* Nunney 314. *Clubs:* Travellers', Pratt's.

**POWELL, (Arnold Joseph) Philip,** OBE 1957; FRIBA; Partner of Powell and Moya, Architects, since 1946; *b* 15 March 1921; *yr s* of late Canon A. C. Powell and late Mary Winnifred (*née* Walker), epsom and Chichester; *m* 1953, Philippa, *d* of Lt-Col C. C. Eccles, Tunbridge Wells; one *s* one *d*. *Educ:* Epsom Coll.; AA Sch. of Architecture (Hons Diploma). In private practice: with Michael Powell and Hidalgo Moya, 1946-50; with Hidalgo Moya, 1950-61; with Hidalgo Moya, Robert Henley and Peter Skinner, 1961-. *Works include:* Churchill Gdns flats, Westminster, 1948-62 (won in open competition); houses and flats at Gospel Oak, St Pancras, 1954; houses at: Chichester, 1950; Toys Hill, 1954; Oxshott, 1954; Baughurst, Hants, 1954; Skylon for Fest. of Britain, 1951 (won in open competition); British Pavilion, Expo 70, Osaka, Japan, 1970; Mayfield School, Putney, 1955; extensions, Brasenose Coll., Oxford, 1961, and Corpus Christi Coll., Oxford, 1969; picture gall. and undergrad. rooms, Christ Church, Oxford, 1967; new buildings, St John's Coll., Cambridge, 1967; Chichester Fest. Theatre, 1962; Public Swimming Baths, Putney, 1967; Mental Hosp. extensions at Fairmile, nr Wallingford, 1957 and Borocourt, nr Henley-on-Thames, 1964; Gen. Hosps at Swindon, Slough, High Wycombe and Wythenshawe. Has won numerous medals and awards for architectural work. Mem. Royal Fine Art Commn, 1969-. *Recreations:* travel, listening to music. *Address:* 16 The Little Boltons, SW10. *T:* 01-373 8620; 90 Tottenham Court Road, W1. *T:* 01-580 2794.

**POWELL, Arthur Barrington,** CMG 1967; Assistant Secretary, Ministry of Power, since 1955; *b* 24 April 1918; *er s* of late Thomas and Dorothy Powell, Maesteg, Glam; *m* 1945, Jane, *d* of late Gen. Sir George Weir, KCB, CMG, DSO; four *s* one *d*. *Educ:* Cowbridge; Jesus Coll. Oxford. Indian Civil Service, 1939-47; served in Province of Bihar. Asst Princ., Min. of Fuel and Power, 1947; Princ. Private Sec. to Minister, 1949-51; Petroleum Attaché, HM Embassy, Washington, 1962-64. *Address:* Hullhatch, Shamley Green, Guildford, Surrey. *T:* Bramley 2073. *Club:* Oxford and Cambridge University.

**POWELL, Baden-;** *see* Baden-Powell.

**POWELL, David;** Chairman and Chief Executive of Booker McConnell, since 1967; *b* 1914; *s* of Edward Churton Powell and Margaret (*née* Nesfield); *m* 1941, Joan Boileau (Henderson); one *s* four *d*. *Educ:* Charterhouse. Served 1939-46: Lt, Kent Yeomanry RA; Captain and Major on Staff. Qualifed as Chartered Accountant, 1939, admitted, 1943; in practice, 1946-47; joined Booker McConnell Ltd, 1947; Finance Dir, 1952; Dep. Chm. 1957; Man. Dir, 1966; Chm., Bookers Shopkeeping Holdings, 1956-63. Member: British-North American Cttee; Exec. Cttee, West India Cttee. *Recreations:* stalking, shooting, walking, gardening, reading. *Address:* Roughetts, Coldharbour Lane, Hildenborough, Kent. *T:* Hildenborough 3119. *Clubs:* Travellers', West Indian.

**POWELL, Dilys;** *see* Powell, E. D.

**POWELL, (Elizabeth) Dilys;** Film Critic of The Sunday Times since 1939; *yr d* of late Thomas and Mary Powell; *m* 1st, 1926, Humfry Payne, later Director of the British School of Archæology at Athens (*d* 1936); 2nd, 1943, Leonard Russell, *qv*; no *c*. *Educ:* Bournemouth High School; Somerville College, Oxford. Editorial Staff, Sunday Times, 1928-31 and 1936-41. Lived and travelled extensively in Greece, 1931-36. Member: Bd of Governors of British Film Institute, 1948-52; Independent Television Authority, 1954-57; Cinematograph Films Council, 1965-69; President, Classical Association, 1966-67. *Publications:* Descent from Parnassus, 1934; Remember Greece, 1941; The Traveller's Journey is Done, 1943; Coco, 1952; An Affair of the Heart, 1957. *Address:* 14 Albion Street, Hyde Park, W2. *T:* 01-723 9807.

**POWELL, Rt. Hon. Enoch;** *see* Powell, Rt Hon. J. E.

**POWELL, Frank John;** Metropolitan Police Magistrate, 1936-63; *b* 15 March 1891; *e s* of late Francis Cox Powell; *m* 1st, 1915, Irene Hesse (*d* 1955), *er d* of Arthur Wyatt; two *s* one *d*; 2nd, Joan (*d* 1965), *yr d* of F. L. Selley, MBE; 3rd, Betty Edelson. *Educ:* Rutlish; Inns of Court. Called to Bar, Middle Temple, 1921; contested (L) Kingston-on-Thames, 1929 and 1935; Queen's Westminster Rifles, 1910-14; King's Own Yorkshire LI, 1914-18; Captain and Adjutant. Magistrate: Greenwich and Woolwich, 1936-40; Tower Bridge, 1940-42; Clerkenwell, 1942-63. Member Chairmen's Panel, Metropolitan Juvenile Courts, 1946-52. Hon. Legal adviser New Malden Citizens Advice Bureau, 1939-46. Chm. 1950-53. Mem. House of Laity of Church Assembly, 1950-64. Chm. Nat. Assoc. of Homes and Hostels, 1955-60; Pres. Probation Officers Christian Fellowship, 1954-66; Mem. Council of Magistrates Association, 1942-60. *Publications:* The trial of Jesus Christ; Justice in Magistrates' Courts; The Roots of Crime (jointly), 1954. *Recreation:* golf. *Address:* 42 Queen's Park, West Drive, Bournemouth, Hants. *T:* Bournemouth 36730.

**POWELL, Herbert Marcus,** FRS 1953; BSc, MA; Professor of Chemical Crystallography, Oxford University, since 1964; *Educ:* St John's College, Oxford. MA Oxon 1931. Reader in Chemical Crystallography in the University of Oxford, 1944-64. Fellow of Hertford College.

*Address:* Chemical Crystallography Laboratory, South Parks Road, Oxford.

**POWELL, Rear-Adm. James,** DSO 1919; RN (retired); *b* 1887; *s* of late James Powell, of Lower Lockhams, Botley, Hants; *m* 1914, Gertrude Eileen, *d* of late Lt-Col F. Blenkinsop, IMS; one *s* three *d. Educ:* Eton; HMS Britannia. Lieut 1908; Lieut-Commander, 1916; Commander, 1922; Capt. 1929; served European War, 1914-19 (despatches, DSO); Captain-in-charge and King's Harbour Master, Portland, 1936-38; Captain-in-charge, Bermuda, 1938-40; Rear-Admiral, 1940; retired list, 1940; Commodore-in-charge, Bermuda, 1940-42; Commodore RNR of Convoy, 1942-43; Commodore Superintendent of Taranto Dockyard and other Italian Ports, 1944-45. Citizen and Merchant Taylor; Younger Brother of Trinity House. *Address:* Roman Villa, Twyford, Hants.

**POWELL, Rt. Hon. (John) Enoch,** PC 1960; MBE 1943; MA (Cantab); MP (C) Wolverhampton SW since 1950; *b* 16 June 1912; *s* of Albert Enoch Powell and Ellen Mary Breese; *m* 1952, Margaret Pamela (*née* Wilson); two *d. Educ:* King Edwards, Birmingham; Trinity College, Cambridge. Craven Scholar, 1931; First Chancellor's Classical Medallist; Porson Prizeman; Browne Medallist, 1932; BA (Cantab); Craven Travelling Student, 1933; Fellow of Trinity College, Cambridge, 1934-38; MA (Cantab) 1937; Professor of Greek in the University of Sydney, NSW, 1937-39; Pte and L/Cpl R Warwickshire Regt, 1939-40; 2nd Lieut General List, 1940; Captain, General Staff, 1940-41; Major, General Staff, 1941; Lieut-Col, GS, 1942; Col, GS, 1944; Brig. 1944; Dipl. OAS. Parliamentary Secretary, Ministry of Housing and Local Government, Dec. 1955-Jan. 1957; Financial Secretary to the Treasury, 1957-58; Minister of Health, July 1960-Oct. 1963. *Publications:* The Rendel Harris Papyri, 1936; First Poems, 1937; A Lexicon to Herodotus, 1938; The History of Herodotus, 1939; Casting-off, and other poems, 1939; Herodotus, Book VIII, 1939; Llyfr Blegywryd, 1942; Thucydidis Historia, 1942; Herodotus (translation), 1949; Dancer's End and The Wedding Gift (poems), 1951; The Social Services; Needs and Means, 1952; (jointly) One Nation, 1950; Change is our Ally, 1954; Biography of a Nation (with Angus Mande), 1955, 2nd edn 1970; Great Parliamentary Occasions; Saving in a Free Society, 1960; A Nation not Afraid, 1965; Medicine and Politics, 1966; The House of Lords in the Middle Ages (with Keith Wallis), 1968; Freedom and Reality, 1969; numerous political pamphlets. *Address:* 33 South Eaton Place, SW1. *T:* 01-730 0988. *Club:* Carlton.

**POWELL, Air Vice-Marshal John Frederick,** OBE 1956; Director of Educational Services, RAF, since 1967; *b* 12 June 1915; *y s* of Rev. Morgan Powell, Limpley Stoke, Bath; *m* 1939, Geraldine Ysolda, *e d* of late Sir John Fitzgerald Moylan, CB, CBE; four *s. Educ:* Lancing; King's Coll., Cambridge (MA). Joined RAF Educnl Service at No 1 Sch. of Techn Trng, 1937; Junior Lectr, RAF College, 1938-39; RAFVR (Admin. and Special Duties) ops room duties, Coastal Comd, 1939-45 (despatches); RAF Educn Br., 1946; Sen. Instructor in History, RAF Coll., 1946-49; RAF Staff Coll., 1950; Air Min., 1951-53; Sen. Tutor, RAF Coll., 1953-59; Educn Staff, HQ, FEAF, 1959-62; Min. of Def., 1962-64; Comd Educn Off., HQ Bomber Comd, 1964-66; OC, RAF Sch. of Educn, 1966-67; Air Commodore, 1967; Air Vice-Marshal, 1968. *Recreations:* beagling, choral music, tennis, squash. *Address:* 25d Cannon Place, NW3. *Club:* Royal Air Force.

**POWELL, Lawrence Fitzroy,** MA Oxon; Hon. DLitt Durham; Hon. DLitt Oxford, 1969; FRSL; Librarian of the Taylor Institution, Oxford University, 1921-49; *b* 9 Aug. 1881; *y s* of H. Powell and Anne Budd; *m* 1909, Ethelwyn Rebecca Steane (*d* 1941), a member of the staff of the Oxford Dictionary; one *s. Educ:* a London Board School and privately. Junior member of staff of Bodleian Library; member editorial staff of Oxford English Dictionary, 1902-16, 1919-21; served during European War at Admiralty, 1916-19; Examiner in Literary History for Library Association, 1930-33; Leverhulme Research Fellow, 1936; Lamont Lecturer, Yale University, 1961. Vice-President Bibliographical Soc.; Vice-Pres. Edinburgh Bibliographical Society; Member of Johnson Club; Pres. Johnson Society of London; Pres. Johnson Society of Lichfield; Hon. Mem. Mod. Lang. Assoc. of America; Hon. Fellow, Pembroke Coll., Oxford; Hon. Fellow, St Catherine's Coll., Oxford. *Publications:* Boswell's Life of Johnson, 4 vols, 1934; Boswell's Journal of a Tour to the Hebrides and Johnson's Diary of a Journey into North Wales, 2 vols, 1950 (new edition of vols 5 and 6, 1965); Boswell: Journal of a Tour to the Hebrides, 1958; (with W. J. Bate) an edition of Johnson's Adventurer, 1963 (Vol. 2 of the Yale Edition of Johnson's works), and other Johnsonian publications, etc; articles and reviews chiefly on 18th-century subjects. *Recreations:* walking, chess. *Address:* 228 Woodstock Road, Oxford. *T:* Oxford 58517. *Club:* Union Society (Oxford).

**POWELL, Michael;** film-director; *b* Bekesbourne, Canterbury, Kent, 30 Sept. 1905; *s* of Thomas William Powell and Mabel Corbett, Worcester; *m* 1943, Frances, *d* of J. J. Reidy, JP, MD; two *s. Educ:* King's School, Canterbury. In 1925 joined Rex Ingram's film company, Victorine Studios, Nice; dir. first film in England for Jerry Jackson, 1930; wrote and dir. The Edge of the World for Joe Rock, 1936; joined Korda, 1938: Spy in Black, Thief of Bagdad, The Lion Has Wings; with Emeric Pressburger, made sixteen films, among which 49th Parallel, Colonel Blimp, Matter of Life and Death, The Red Shoes, Tales of Hoffmann, Battle of the River Plate; recently dir. Age of Consent and The Tempest, both co-produced with James Mason. *Recreations:* walking, leaning on gates. *Address:* 8 Melbury Road, W14. *Club:* Savile.

**POWELL, Dame Muriel,** DBE 1968 (CBE 1962); Chief Nursing Office, Scottish Home and Health Department, since 1970; *b* 30 Oct. 1914; *d* of late Wallace George Powell and late Anne Elizabeth Powell, Cinderford, Glos. *Educ:* East Dean Grammar Sch., Cinderford; St George's Hosp., London. SRN 1937; SCM 1939; Sister Tutor Dipl., Battersea Coll. of Techn., 1941; Dipl. in Nursing, London Univ., 1942. Formerly: Ward Sister and Night Sister, St George's Hosp.; Sister, Co. Maternity Hosp., Postlip Hall, Glos. (War Emerg. Hosp.); District Nurse, Glos; Sister Tutor, Ipswich Borough Gen. Hosp.; Princ. Tutor, Manchester Royal Infirmary; Matron, St George's Hosp. London, 1947-70. Pres., Assoc. of Hosp. Matrons, 1958-63; Pres., Nat. Assoc. of State Enrolled Nurses, 1965-67; Dep. Pres., Royal Coll. of Nursing, 1963-64. Mem., Central Health Services Coun.; Chm., Standing Nursing Adv. Cttee, Min. of Health, 1958-69; Mem., Expert Adv. Panel on Nursing, WHO. *Recreation:* music. *Address:* Scottish Home and Health Dept, St Andrew's House, Edinburgh.

**POWELL, Prof. Percival Hugh,** MA, DLitt, Dr Phil.; Professor of German in the University of Leicester since 1958; *b* 4 Sept. 1912; 3rd *s* of late Thomas Powell and late Marie Sophia Roeser; *m* 1944, Dorothy Mavis Pattison (*née* Donald) (marriage dissolved, 1964); two *s* one adopted *d*; *m* 1966, Mary Kathleen (*née* Wilson); one *s*. *Educ:* University College, Cardiff; Univs of Rostock, Zürich, Bonn. 1st Class Hons German (Wales), 1933; Univ. Teachers' Diploma in Education, 1934; MA (Wales) Dist. 1936; Research Fellow of Univ. of Wales, 1936-38; Modern Languages Master, Towyn School, 1934-36; Dr Phil. (Rostock) 1938; Lektor in English, Univ. of Bonn, 1933-39; Asst Lectr, Univ. Coll., Cardiff, 1939-40; War Service, 1940-46 (Capt. Intelligence Corps); Lecturer in German, Univ. Coll., Leicester, 1946, Head of Department of German, 1954. Barclay Acheson Prof. of Internat. Studies at Macalester Coll., Minn., USA, 1965-66. DLitt (Wales) 1962. British Academy award, 1963; Fritz Thyssen Foundation Award, 1964; Leverhulme Trust Award, 1968. *Publications:* Pierre Corneilles Dramen in Deutschen Bearbeitungen, 1939; Critical editions of dramas of Andreas Gryphius, 1955-; articles and reviews in English and foreign literary jls. *Recreation:* music. *Address:* 7 Shanklin Avenue, Leicester. *T:* Leicester 708824.

**POWELL, Philip;** *see* Powell, A. J. P.

**POWELL, Ray Edwin;** *b* Table Grove, Illinois, 7 December 1887; *s* of late Joseph D. Powell and Sarah E. (*née* Anderson). *Educ:* Monmouth College; University of Illinois. Entered aluminium industry, 1909. Served War, in US Army, 1917-19; Captain. Settled in Canada, 1929. Hon. Chm. and Director, Aluminium Co. of Canada, Ltd; formerly director: Aluminium Ltd; Bell Telephone Co. of Canada; Bank of London and Montreal; Dominion Bridge Company, Ltd, etc, including many subsidiaries of Aluminium Ltd. Member Board of Governors: McGill Univ.; Univ. of Laval; Past Chancellor, McGill University, Montreal. Hon. DLitt, Monmouth Coll.; Hon. Dr of Laws, Univ. of Laval; Hon. LLD: McGill Univ., Queen's Univ. *Address:* 1336 Redpath Crescent, Montreal 25, Que., Canada. *Clubs:* Mount Royal, St James's, Mount Bruno (Montreal); Seigniory, Montebello (Quebec); University, Links (New York).

**POWELL, Major Sir Richard George Douglas,** 3rd Bt, *cr* 1897; MC 1944, Bar 1945; Welsh Guards; Director-General, Institute of Directors, since 1954; Director, Bovis Holdings Ltd; *b* 14 Nov. 1909; *o s* of Sir Douglas Powell, 2nd Bart, and Albinia Muriel, *e d* of W. F. Powell of Sharow Hall, Ripon; *m* 1933, Elizabeth Josephine, *o d* of late Lt-Col O. R. McMullen, CMG; one *s* two *d*. *Educ:* Eton College. *S* father, 1932. Served War of 1939-45 (MC and Bar). Croix Militaire 1st Class (Belgium), 1945; Assistant Military Attaché, British Embassy, Brussels, 1945-48. *Heir: s* Nicholas Folliott Douglas Powell [*b* 17 July 1935; *m* 1960, Daphne Jean, *yr d* of Major and Mrs George Errington, Monkton Ranch, Figtree, Southern Rhodesia; one *s* one *d*]. *Address:* Brightwell, Berkshire. *T:* Wallingford 3245. *Clubs:* Guards, Buck's.

**POWELL, Sir Richard (Royle),** GCB 1967 (KCB 1961; CB 1951); KBE 1954; CMG 1946; Deputy Chairman, Permanent Committee on Invisible Exports, since 1968; Chairman: Albright & Wilson, since 1969; Star Aluminium Co., since 1969; Director: Philip Hill Investment Trust; Hill Samuel Group; GEC-EE; *b* 30 July 1909; *er s* of Ernest Hartley and Florence Powell; unmarried. *Educ:* Queen Mary's Grammar Sch., Walsall; Sidney Sussex Coll., Camb. Entered Civil Service, 1931 and apptd to Admiralty; Private Sec. to First Lord, 1934-37; Member of British Admiralty Technical Mission, Canada, and of British Merchant Shipbuilding Mission, and later of British Merchant Shipping Mission in USA, 1940-44; Civil Adviser to Commander-in-Chief, British Pacific Fleet, 1944-45; Under-Secretary, Ministry of Defence, 1946-48. Dep. Sec., Admiralty, 1948-50; Dep. Sec., Min. of Defence, 1950-56; Permanent Secretary, Board of Trade, 1960-68 (Min. of Defence, 1956-59). *Address:* 56 Montagu Square, W1. *T:* 01-262 0911. *Club:* Athenæum.

**POWELL, Robert William;** Headmaster of Sherborne, 1950-70; retired; *b* 29 October 1909; *s* of late William Powell and Agnes Emma Powell; *m* 1938, Charity Rosamond Collard; one *s*. *Educ:* Bristol Grammar School; Christ Church, Oxford. Assistant Master, Repton, May-Dec. 1934; Assistant Master, Charterhouse, 1935. Served War of 1939-45, 1940-45. Housemaster of Gownboys, Charterhouse, 1946-50. *Recreations:* fishing, music. *Address:* Manor Farm House, Child Okeford, near Blandford, Dorset. *T:* Child Okeford 648. *Club:* United University.

**POWELL-COTTON, Christopher,** CMG 1961; MBE 1951; MC 1945; JP; Uganda CS, retired; *b* 23 Feb. 1918; *s* of Major P. H. G. Powell-Cotton and Mrs H. B. Powell-Cotton (*née* Slater); unmarried. *Educ:* Harrow School; Trinity College, Cambridge. Army Service, 1939-45: commissioned Buffs, 1940; seconded KAR, Oct. 1940; T/Major, 1943. Apptd to Uganda Administration, 1940, and released for Mil. Service. District Commissioner, 1950; Provincial Commissioner, 1955; Minister of Security and External Relations, 1961. Landowner in SE Kent. Dir, Powell-Cotton Museum of Nat. History and Ethnography. *Address:* Quex Park, Birchington, Kent. *T:* Thanet 41836. *Club:* MCC.

**POWELL-JONES, John Ernest;** Counsellor and Consul-General, British Embassy, Athens, since 1970; *b* 14 April 1925; *s* of late W. J. Powell-Jones; *m* 1st, 1949, Ann Murray (marr. diss. 1967); two *s* one *d*; 2nd, 1968, Pamela Sale. *Educ:* Charterhouse; University Coll., Oxford. Served with Rifle Bde, 1943-46. HM Foreign (now Diplomatic) Service, 1949; 3rd Sec. and Vice-Consul, Bogota, 1950-52; Eastern and later Levant Dept, FO, 1952-55; 2nd, later 1st Sec., Athens, 1955-59; News Dept, FO, 1959-60; 1st Sec., Leopoldville, 1961-62; UN Dept, FO, 1963-67; ndc Canada 1967-68; Counsellor, Political Adviser's Office, Singapore, 1968-69. *Recreations:* gardening, lawn tennis. *Address:* Gaston Gate, Cranleigh, Surrey. *T:* Cranleigh 4313. *Club:* Travellers'.

**POWER, Rear-Adm. Arthur Mackenzie,** MBE 1952; Admiral Superintendent, HM Dockyard, Portsmouth, 1968-71; Flag Officer, Spithead, 1969-71; *b* 18 June 1921; *s* of Admiral of Fleet Sir Arthur Power; *m* 1949, Marcia Helen Gell; two *s* one *d*. *Educ:* Rugby. Royal Navy, 1938; served War of 1939-45 and Korean War; specialised in gunnery; Captain, 1959; ADC to the Queen, 1968; Rear-Admiral, 1968. *Address:* Gunnsmead, South Road, Liphook, Hants.

**POWER, Beryl Millicent le Poer;** *b* Dunham Massey, Cheshire, 17 Sept. 1891. *Educ:* Oxford High School for Girls; Girton College, Cambridge. Organiser and speaker for National Union of Women's Suffrage Societies, 1912-14; Investigator appointed under the Trade Boards Act, Board of Trade and Ministry of Labour, 1915-22; Deputy

Chief Inspector of Trade Boards, 1923-29; holder of Laura Spelman Rockefeller Memorial Fellowship, studying technique of enforcement of Labour Laws in the United States of America, 1926-27; Member of Royal Commission on Indian Labour, 1929-31; Sec. Central Register of Persons with Scientific, Technical, Professional and Higher Administrative Qualifications, 1939-40; Asst Sec., Housing and Welfare, Ministry of Supply, 1941-45; UNRRA (China) Consultant in administration and welfare policies to Chinese National Relief and Rehabilitation Administration, 1945-47; seconded to ILO as Adviser on Employment and Youth Training to Chinese Ministry of Social Affairs, 1947-48; seconded to Economic Commission for Asia and the Far East, Thailand, 1949; retired from Civil Service (Min. of Labour and Nat. Service), 1951; Chm. Over Forty Assoc. for Women, 1955-62. *Address:* 42 Clarendon Road, W11. *Club:* University Women's.

**POWER, Mrs Brian St Quentin;** *see* Stack, (Ann) Prunella.

**POWER, Lieut-Col Gervase Bushe,** CIE 1916; MC; *b* 1883; *s* of late R. H. Power, Lismore, Co. Waterford; *m* 1953, Audrey Mary, *d* of Lt-Col E. M. A. Hogan, Indian Army (retired). *Educ:* Clifton Coll.; Royal Indian Engineering Coll., Coopers Hill. Indian Telegraphs Dept, 1905; Assistant Director Army Signals NW Frontier, 1919; served European War, Mesopotamia, 1915-19 (CIE, MC); Fourth Afghan War, 1919; resigned commission, 1919; Director of Telegraph Engineering, India, 1932-34; officiating Postmaster General, Madras, 1934; Postmaster General, Burma, 1935-36; retired, 1936. *Recreation:* gardening. *Address:* The Oast House, Tinley Lodge, Hildenborough, Kent. *T:* 3268.

**POWER, Sir John (Patrick McLannahan),** 3rd Bt, *cr* 1924, of Newlands Manor; Director, The Kingsway Offices Co. Ltd and other assoc. cos; Managing Director Arthur Beale Ltd, London and Chichester; *b* 16 March 1928; *s* of Sir Ivan McLannahan Cecil Power, 2nd Baronet, and Nancy Hilary, *d* of late Reverend J. W. Griffiths, Wentworth, Virginia Water; *m* 1st, 1957, Melanie (marr diss. 1967), *d* of Hon. Alastair Erskine, Glenfintaig House, Spean Bridge, Inverness-shire; two *s* one *d*; 2nd, 1970, Tracey, *d* of George Cooper, Amberley Place, Amberley, Sussex. *Educ:* Pangbourne Nautical Coll. Served RN, 1946-48, The Cunard Steamship Co. Ltd, London, 1945-58. *Recreations:* sailing, painting. *Heir: s* Alastair John Cecil Power, *b* 15 Aug. 1958. *Address:* Lippering House, Birdham, Chichester, Sussex. *Clubs:* Arts, Royal Ocean Racing, Royal London Yacht; Royal Naval Sailing Association; Island Sailing.
*See also Lord Cardross.*

**POWER, Adm. (retd) Sir Manley (Laurence),** KCB 1958 (CB 1955); CBE 1943 (OBE 1940); DSO 1944, Bar 1945; DL; *b* 10 Jan. 1904; *s* of Adm. Sir Laurence E. Power, KCB, CVO; *m* 1930, Barbara Alice Mary Topham; one *s* one *d*. *Educ:* RN Colleges, Osborne and Dartmouth. Naval Cadet, 1917; Midshipman, 1921; Sub-Lt 1924; Lt 1926; Lt-Comdr 1934; Comdr 1939; Capt. 1943; Rear-Adm. 1953; Vice-Adm. 1956; Admiral, 1960. Deputy Chief of Naval Staff, and Fifth Sea Lord, 1957-59; Commander-in-Chief, Portsmouth, Allied C-in-C, Channel, and C-in-C, Home Station (Designate), 1959-61; retired, 1961. CC, Isle of Wight, 1964-. DL, Hampshire, 1965. Officer of Legion of Merit (US); Croix de Guerre avec Palme (France). *Address:* Norton Cottage, Yarmouth, Isle of Wight. *T:* Yarmouth 401.

**POWER, Gen. Thomas Sarsfield,** DSM (US) 1945; Silver Star, 1945; Legion of Merit with one Oak Leaf Cluster, 1945; DFC 1944; Bronze Star 1945; Army Commendation Medal with one Oak Leaf Cluster, 1946, etc; Vice-Chairman, Eversharp Inc.; Director: Bucyrus-Erie Co.; Hedge Fund of America Inc.; *b* 18 June 1905; *s* of late Thomas S. and Mary Rice Power; *m* 1936, Mae Ayre of Newcastle upon Tyne, England; no *c*. *Educ:* Graduate Barnard Preparatory School, New York City, 1922. Commissioned 2nd Lieut US Army Air Corps. 1929. Served War, 1941-45: Exec. and Dep. Comdr 304th Bomb Wing, Italy, Jan.-Aug. 1944; Comdr, 314th Bomb Wing, Peterson Field, Colorado and Guam, 1944-45; Dep. Chief, Ops, US Strategic AF, Pacific, Aug.-Dec. 1945; HQ AAF, Washington, DC, Dec. 1945-March 1946; Asst Dep. Task Force Comdr for Air (Op. Crossroads) Bikini Atoll, Pacific, March-Sept. 1946. Dep. Asst Chief of Staff, Ops, HQUSAF, 1946-47; Chief, Training Div. and later Chief, Requirements Div., Dep. Chief of Staff, Ops, HQUSAF, 1947-48; Air Attaché, US Embassy, London, June-Oct. 1948; Vice C-in-C, Strategic Air Comd, Oct. 1948-April 1954; Comdr, Air Research and Development Comd, 1954-57; Commander-in-Chief, Strategic Air Command, United States Air Force, 1957-64, and, as additional duty, Director, Joint Strategic Target Planning Staff of Department of Defense, 1960-64. Kt of St Sylvester, 1964; Kt of St Brigette, 1967. French Croix de Guerre with Palm, 1949. *Recreations:* golf, fishing and holds the black belt in judo. *Address:* (office) 5933 W Slauson Avenue, Culver City, Calif 90232; (home) Thunderbird Country Club, Palm Springs, Calif 92262, USA.

**POWERSCOURT,** 9th Viscount, *cr* 1743; **Mervyn Patrick Wingfield;** Baron Wingfield, 1743; Baron Powerscourt (UK), 1885; Major, Royal Irish Fusiliers; late Lt 8th Hussars; *b* 22 Aug. 1905; *o s* of 8th Viscount Powerscourt and Sybil (*d* 1946), 2nd *d* of Walter Pleydell-Bouverie; *S* father 1947; *m* 1932, Sheila Claude, *o d* of Lt-Col Claude Beddington, 33 Grosvenor Street, W1; two *s* one *d*. *Educ:* RMC Sandhurst. Served War of 1939-45. *Heir: s* Hon. Mervyn Niall Wingfield [*b* 3 Sept. 1935; *m* 1962, Wendy Anne Pauline, *er d* of R. C. G. Slazenger; one *s* one *d*]. *Address:* Tarabeg, Dunsany, Co. Meath, Ireland. *T:* Tara 41. *Clubs:* Royal Thames Yacht; Royal Yacht Squadron (Cowes); Kildare Street (Dublin).
*See also Capt. Sir Terence Langrishe, Bt, Baron Templemore.*

**POWIS,** 5th Earl of, *cr* 1804; **Edward Robert Henry Herbert,** CBE 1945 (MBE 1938); TD; DL; psc; Viscount Clive, Baron Herbert, Baron Powis, 1804; Baron Clive, 1794; Baron Clive of Plassey in Ireland, 1762; Lieut-Colonel (Hon. Colonel) late Comdg 5th Bn KSLI, TA; late Major, KRRC; retired; *b* 19 May 1889; *e s* of Colonel Edward William Herbert, CB (*d* 1924), and *ggs* of 2nd Earl of Powis; *S* cousin, 1952; *m* 1932, Ella Mary, *d* of late Colonel W. H. Rathborne, Dublin. *Educ:* Eton; Christ Church, Oxford (MA). Joined KRRC 1909; served European War, 1914-19, France, Belgium; Staff Capt., 1917-18; DAQMG 1918; Iraq Ops, 1920-21. Captain, 1915; Major, 1927; retired, 1933; War of 1939-45 (CBE); Lieut-Colonel KSLI (TA) 1939; AAG War Office, Colonel, 1940. CC Salop, 1947-58, DL Salop, 1953. CStJ. *Heir: b* Hon. Christian Victor Charles Herbert [*b* 28 May 1904. Major late RAOC]. *Address:* 4 Green Street, W1. *T:* 01-499 8451. (Seat) Powis Castle, Welshpool. *T:* 3360. *Clubs:* Brooks's, United Service.

**POWLES, Sir Guy (Richardson),** KBE 1961; CMG 1954; ED 1944; first Ombudsman of New Zealand since Oct. 1962; *b* 5 April 1905; *s* of late Colonel C. G. Powles, CMG, DSO, New Zealand Staff Corps; *m* 1931, Eileen, *d* of A. J. Nicholls; two *s*. *Educ:* Wellington Coll., NZ; Victoria Univ. (LLB). Barrister, Supreme Court, New Zealand, 1929; served War of 1939-45 with NZ Military Forces, to rank of Colonel; Counsellor, NZ Legation, Washington, DC, USA, 1946-48; High Comr, Westerm Samoa, 1949-60, for NZ in India, 1960-62, Ceylon, 1961-62, and Ambassador of NZ to Nepal, 1961-62. President, NZ Inst. of Internat. Affairs, 1967-. Hon. LLD Victoria Univ. of Wellington, 1969. *Publications:* articles and speeches on international affairs and administrative law. *Address:* Office of the Ombudsman, Wellington, NZ.

**POWLETT;** *see* Orde-Powlett.

**POWLETT, Vice-Admiral Sir Peveril B. R. W. W.;** *see* William-Powlett.

**POWLETT, Rear-Adm. Philip Frederick,** CB 1961; DSO 1941 (and Bar 1942); DSC 1941; retired; Secretary, Friends of Norwich Cathedral; *b* 13 Nov. 1906; *s* of late Vice-Admiral F. A. Powlett, CBE; *m* 1935, Frances Elizabeth Sykes (*née* Elwell); two *s* one *d*. *Educ:* Osborne and Dartmouth. War of 1939-45 (DSC, DSO and Bar; Polish Cross of Valour, 1942); in command of destroyers and corvettes, Shearwater, Blankney, Cassandra. Deputy Director of Naval Air Organisation and Training, 1950; Senior Officer, Reserve Fleet, Clyde, 1952-53; Captain (F), 6th Frigate Squadron, 1954-55; Director (RN), Joint Anti-Submarine School, and Senior Naval Officer, Northern Ireland, 1956-58; Flag Officer and Admiral Superintendent, Gibraltar, 1959-62; retired, 1962. *Recreations:* fishing and sailing. *Address:* The Mill House, Lyng, Norwich, Norfolk, NOR 63X.

**POWNALL, Leslie Leigh,** MA, PhD; Clerk of the University Senate, University of London, since 1966; *b* 1 Nov. 1921; *y s* of A. de S. Pownall, Wanganui, New Zealand; *m* 1943, Judith, *d* of late Harold Whittaker, Palmerston North. *Educ:* Palmerston North Boys' High Sch.; Victoria University College, University of Canterbury, University of Wisconsin. Asst Master, Christchurch Boys' High Sch., 1941-46; Lecturer in Geography: Christchurch Teachers' Coll., 1946-47; Ardmore Teachers' Coll., 1948-49; Auckland University College, 1949-51; Senior Lecturer in Geography, 1951-60, Prof. of Geography, 1960-61, Vice-Chancellor and Rector, 1961-66, University of Canterbury. Consultant, Inter-University Council for Higher Educn Overseas, London, 1963; Consultant to Chm. of Working Party on Higher Educn in E Africa, 1968-69. Member Meeting, Council on World Tensions on Social and Economic Development (S Asia and Pacific), Kuala Lumpur, Malaysia, 1964; Member, Central Governing Body, City Parochial Foundation, London, 1967- (Mem., Finance and Gen. Purposes Cttee, and Grants Sub-Cttee); Governor, Internat. Students Trust, London, 1967-. *Publications:* New Zealand, 1951 (New York); geographic contrib. in academic journals of America, Netherlands and New Zealand. *Recreations:* music, literature. *Address:* The Senate House, University of London, WC1. *T:* 01-636 8000. *Clubs:* Canterbury, University (Christchurch, NZ).

**POWYS,** family name of **Baron Lilford.**

**POYNTER, (Frederick) Noel (Lawrence),** BA, PhD, FLA, FRSL; Director, Wellcome Institute of History of Medicine, since 1964; *b* 24 Dec. 1908; *s* of late H. W. Poynter; *m* 1st, 1939, Kate L. R. Marder (*d* 1966); no *c*; 2nd, 1968, Mrs Dodie Barry (*née* McClellan). *Educ:* King's and Univ. Coll. University of London. Asst Librarian, Wellcome Hist. Med. Lib., 1930; Chief Librarian, 1954. RAF, 1941-46. Founder Member and Hon. Secretary, Fac. of Hist. of Medicine, Society of Apothecaries of London, 1958-; Member, Council, Bibliographical Society, 1960-64, 1965-; Pres., Internat. Acad. of Hist. of Med., 1962-; Vice-Pres., British Society of Hist. of Med., 1965-; Gideon Delaune Lecturer, Society of Apothecaries, 1964. Has given Memorial lectures, in USA; Hon. Lecturer in History of Medicine, University of British Columbia, 1966-; Henry Cohen Lecturer in Medicine, University of Jerusalem, 1968. Hon. Member, Royal Society of Medicine (Hist. Section); also Hon. Member various foreign societies, Fellow, Internat. Acads of the Hist. of Science, Medicine and Pharmacy; Hon. DLitt, California; Hon. MD Kiel; Hon. Fellow, Huguenot Society of London. *Publications:* Selected Writings of William Clowes (1544-1604), 1948; A Seventeenth Century Doctor and his Patients: John Symcotts (joint), 1951; Bibliography, some Achievements and Prospects, 1961; A Short History of Medicine (joint), 1961; The Journal of James Yonge (1647-1721), 1963; Gideon Delaune and his Family Circle, 1965; The Evolution of Medical Education in Britain, 1966; Medicine and Culture, 1968. Ed. several medical works; Ed., Medical History (quarterly) also Current Work in the History of Medicine (quarterly); also numerous articles in periodicals. *Recreations:* painting, chamber music, French literature. *Address:* The Wellcome Institute of the History of Medicine, Euston Road, NW1. *T:* 01-387 4477; 33 Walsingham, Queensmead, NW8. *T:* 01-722 6744. *Club:* Athenæum.

**POYNTON, Sir (Arthur) Hilton,** GCMG 1964 (KCMG 1949; CMG 1946); Director, Overseas Branch, St John Ambulance, since 1968; *b* 20 April 1905; *y s* of late Arthur Blackburne Poynton, formerly Master of University College, Oxford; *m* 1946, Elisabeth Joan, *d* of Rev. Edmund Williams; two *s* one *d*. *Educ:* Marlborough Coll.; Brasenose Coll., Oxford. Entered Civil Service, Department of Scientific and Industrial Research, 1927; transferred to Colonial Office, 1929; Private Secretary to Minister of Supply (Lord Beaverbrook) and Minister of Production (Mr Lyttelton, now Lord Chandos), 1941-43; reverted to Colonial Office, 1943; Permanent Under-Secretary of State, CO, 1959-66. KStJ 1968. *Recreations:* music, travel. *Address:* Craigmillar, Stanhope Road, Croydon, Surrey. *T:* 01-688 3729. *Club:* Athenæum.

**POYNTON, Sir Hilton;** *see* Poynton Sir A. H.

**POYNTON, John Orde,** CMG 1961; MD; Consulting Bibliographer, University of Melbourne; *b* 9 April 1906; *o s* of Frederick John Poynton, MD, FRCP, and Alice Constance, *d* of Sir John William Powlett Campbell-Orde, 3rd Bt, of Kilmory; *m* 1965, Lola, *widow* of Group Captain T. S. Horry, DFC, AFC. *Educ:* Marlborough Coll.; Gonville and Caius Coll., Cambridge; Charing Cross Hospital. MA, MD (Cambridge); MRCS, LRCP; Horton-Smith prize, University of Cambridge, 1940. Sen. Resident Medical Officer, 1932-33; Health Officer, Fed. Malay States, 1936-37; Res. Officer Inst. for Med. Research, FMS, 1937-38, Pathologist, 1938-46; Pathologist, Inst. of Med. and Veterinary Science, S Australia, 1948-50, Director, 1950-61. *Publications:* The Great Sinderesis, 1947; Disjecta Medica, 1956; The

Sayings of Polylogy, 1960; monographs and papers on diseases prevalent in the tropics. *Recreation:* bibliognostics. *Address:* 31 Marne Street, South Yarra, Victoria 3141, Australia. *Club:* Marylebone Cricket.

**PRAGNELL, Anthony William,** OBE 1960; DFC 1944; Deputy Director-General (Administrative Services), Independent Television Authority, since 1961; *b* 15 Feb. 1921; *s* of William Hendley Pragnell and Silvia Pragnell; *m* 1955, Teresa Mary, *d* of Leo and Anne Monaghan, Maidstone; one *s* one *d*. *Educ:* Cardinal Vaughan Sch., London. Asst Examiner, Estate Duty Office, 1939. Joined RAF as aircrew cadet, 1942; Navigator, Bomber Command, one tour of ops with 166 Squadron; second tour with 109 Squadron (Pathfinder Force), 1943-46. Examiner, Estate Duty Office, 1946. LLB London Univ., 1949. Asst Principal, General Post Office, 1950; Asst Secretary, ITA, 1954; Secretary, ITA, 1955. *Recreations:* reading, music. *Address:* Ashley, Grassy Lane, Sevenoaks, Kent. *T:* Sevenoaks 51463.

**PRAIN, Alexander Moncur,** CBE 1964; Sheriff-Substitute of Perth and Angus at Perth since 1946; formerly Sheriff-Substitute of Lanarkshire at Airdrie; *b* Longforgan, Perthshire, 19 Feb. 1908; 2nd *s* of A. M. Prain, JP, and Mary Stuart Whytock; *m* 1936, Florence Margaret Robertson; one *s*. *Educ:* Merchiston Castle; Edinburgh Academy; Edinburgh Univ. Called to Scottish Bar, 1932; Army, 1940-43, Major, RAC. *Recreations:* fishing, reading. *Address:* Castellar, Crieff, Perthshire. *Club:* Royal Golfing (Perth).

**PRAIN, John Murray,** DSO 1940; OBE 1956; TD 1943 (two Bars); DL; *b* 17 Dec. 1902; *e s* of late James Prain, Hon. LLD St Andrews University, of Kincaple by St Andrews, Fife, and late Victoria Eleanor Murray; *m* 1934, Lorina Helen Elspeth, *o d* of late Colonel P. G. M. Skene, OBE, DL, of Halyards and Pitlour, Fife; one *s* one *d*. *Educ:* Charterhouse; Clare Coll., Cambridge, BA 1924. Director: Alliance Trust Co. Ltd; 2nd Alliance Trust Co. Ltd; Tayside Floorcloth Co. Ltd, 1946-69; The Scottish Life Assurance Co. Ltd; Royal Bank of Scotland; William Halley & Sons Ltd; Member Scottish Committee, Industrial and Commercial Finance Corporation, 1946-55; Chairman: Jute Importers Association, 1947-49; Assoc. of Jute Spinners and Manufacturers, 1950-52; Dundee District Cttee, Scottish Board for Industry, 1948-62. Member, Jute Working Party, 1946-48; part-time Member Scottish Gas Board, 1952-56; Member Employers' Panel Industrial Disputes Tribunal, 1952-59. Member, Employers' Panel, Industrial Court, 1959-. DL for County of Fife, 1958; Served in War of 1939-45, Fife and Forfar Yeomanry (wounded, despatches, DSO), and Staff (L/Lt-Col); Member Queen's Body Guard for Scotland, Royal Company of Archers; Hon. President, Fife and Kinross Area Council, British Legion (Scotland). *Address:* Mugdrum, Newburgh, Fife. *T:* Newburgh, Fife 367. *Clubs:* Cavalry; New (Edinburgh); Royal and Ancient (St Andrews).

**PRAIN, Sir Ronald (Lindsay),** Kt 1956; OBE 1946; Chairman, RST International Group of Companies, since 1950, including: Ametalco Inc.; Ametalco Ltd; Roan Selection Trust Ltd; RST International Metals Ltd; and other subsidiaries; Chairman: Bamangwato Concessions Ltd; Botswana RST Ltd; Merchant Bank (Zambia) Ltd; Director: Barclays Bank DCO (Zambian Local Board); Foseco Minsep Ltd; International Nickel Company of Canada Ltd; Minerals Separation Ltd; Monks Investment Trust Ltd; Pan-Holding SA; Bayhall Trust Ltd; Selection Trust Ltd; and other companies; *b* Iquiqui, Chile, 3 Sept. 1907; *s* of Arthur Lindsay Prain and Amy Prain (*née* Watson); *m* 1938, Esther Pansy, *d* of late Norman Brownrigg, Haslemere; two *s*. *Educ:* Cheltenham Coll. Controller (Ministry of Supply): Diamond Die and Tool Control, 1940-45; Quartz Crystal Control, 1943-45. First Chairman, Agricultural Research Council of Rhodesia & Nyasaland, 1959-63; First Chairman Merchant Bank of Central Africa Ltd, 1956-66; Chairman, Commonwealth Council of Mining & Metallurgical Institutions, 1961-; President, British Overseas Mining Assoc., 1952; President, Inst. of Metals, 1960-61; Member Council: Inst. of Race Relations; Overseas Develt Inst.; Overseas Mining Assoc. Hon. Pres., Copper Develt Assoc.; Hon. Member: Inst. of Metals; Inst. of Mining and Metallurgy. Life Member Council, Cheltenham College. ANKH Award, Copper Club, New York, 1964; Gold Medal, Inst. of Mining and Metallurgy, 1968; Platinum Medal, Inst. of Metals, 1969. *Publications:* Selected Papers (4 Vols). *Recreations:* cricket, real tennis, travel. *Address:* Waverley, St George's Hill, Weybridge, Surrey. *T:* Weybridge 42776; 43 Cadogan Square, SW1. *T:* 01-235 4900; Kafue House, 1 Nairobi Place, PO Box 851, Lusaka, Zambia. *T:* Lusaka 74070. *Clubs:* Brooks's, White's, MCC.

**PRAIN, Vyvyen Alice;** retired as Principal, Princess Helena College, Temple Dinsley, Herts, 1935-July 1958; *b* 11 Oct 1895; *d* of Hunter Douglas Prain and Ellen Flora Davis. *Educ:* Edinburgh Ladies' Coll.; Edinburgh Univ. Graduated MA (Hons) in History (second class) in 1918, having gained the Gladstone Memorial Prize for History and Political Economy, and three class medals; Trained for teaching at Cambridge Training Coll., and gained a First Class Teacher's Certificate in 1919; History Mistress at Princess Helena Coll., Ealing, 1919-24; History and Economics at Wycombe Abbey Sch., 1924-29; Principal of the Ladies' Coll., Guernsey, 1929-35. *Recreations:* needlework, reading, travelling. *Address:* 5 The Hexagon, Fitzroy Park, N6.

**PRASADA, Krishna,** CIE 1943; JP; ICS retired; Director-General, Posts and Telegraphs, New Delhi, 1945-53; *b* 4 Aug. 1894; *s* of Pandit Het Ram, CIE; *m* 1911, Bishan Devi (*d* 1950); three *s*. *Educ:* Bareilly; New Coll., Oxford. Joined ICS 1921; Joint Magistrate and subsequently a District Magistrate in UP. Services borrowed by Government of India in 1934, when he was appointed as Postmaster-General. Led Government of India deputations to International Tele-communications Conference, Cairo, 1938, Buenos Aires, 1952, and to International Postal Congress, Paris, 1947. Retired, 1954. Director, Rotary International, 1961-63. *Recreation:* tennis, Oxford Tennis Blue (1921) and played for India in the Davis Cup in 1927 and 1932. Won All India Tennis Championships. *Address:* L. 18/A, South Extension, II, New Delhi 49, India.

**PRATT,** family name of **Marquess Camden.**

**PRATT, Sir Bernard;** *see* Pratt, Sir E. B.

**PRATT, Rear-Adm. Charles Bernard,** CB 1961; retired; *b* 20 Feb. 1907; *s* of Rev. Charles Edward Pratt, Rector of Warbleton, Sussex, and Mrs Louisa Pratt; *m* 1945, Alice Margery, *d* of Charles Keeling, Sutton Coldfield, Warwicks; one *step d*. *Educ:* The King's Sch., Canterbury. Entered Navy, Special Entry cadet, 1925; Lieut, 1930; Lieut-Commander,

1938; Senior Engineer, HMS King George V, 1939-42; Commander, 1941; Captain, 1951; Commanding HMS Nuthatch, 1951-53; Chief of Staff to Flag Officer Reserve Aircraft, 1953-56; Naval Attaché, Rio de Janeiro, 1956-58; Rear Admiral, 1959; ADC to the Queen, Feb.-July 1959; Chief Staff Officer (Technical) to Flag Officer Air (Home), 1959-62; retired, 1962. *Address:* Christmas Lodge, Yapton, near Arundel, Sussex. *T:* Yapton 524.

**PRATT, Sir (E.) Bernard,** Kt 1941; *b* 4 July 1889; *s* of Edmund Hustwayte Pratt and Sophie Gertrude Goodall; *m* 1st, 1944, Florence Ellen Mary Adeline Spurgin (*née* Rideal) (*d* 1967); 2nd, 1968, D'Arcy La Roche Gatehouse, Cheltenham. *Educ:* Nottingham High Sch. *Recreations:* riding, shooting. *Address:* Lake Cottage, Prestbury, Glos. *T:* Cheltenham 7546. *Clubs:* Oriental, Royal Automobile.

**PRATT, Rev. Canon Francis William;** *b* 1900; *s* of Eliezer and Frances Elizabeth Pratt, Dunstable, Beds; *m* 1934, Phyllis May, *d* of Alexander and Kate Swift, Loughborough, Leics; three *s* (one *d* decd). *Educ:* St John's Coll., Durham; St Aidan's Coll. LTh 1927; BA 1928. Deacon, 1928; priest, 1929. Curate: St Margaret's, Leicester, 1928-30, Loughborough, 1930-34; Vicar, St Barnabas, New Humberstone, Leicester, 1934-44; Officiating Chaplain, Leicester City Mental Hospital, 1934-44; Vicar of Birstall, 1944-54; Rector of Wanlip, 1944-54; Curate-in-Charge, St John the Divine, Leicester, 1954-58; Chaplain, Leicester Cathedral, 1954-58. Hon. Chaplain to Bishop of Leicester, 1955-58; Surrogate, 1956; Second Canon Residentiary and Canon Treasurer, Leicester Cathedral, 1958-68; Master of Wyggeston Hospital, Leicester, 1957-68; retired, 1968. *Recreations:* walking and gardening. *Address:* Weybourne, Norfolk.

**PRATT, Hugh Macdonald; His Honour Judge Pratt;** County Court Judge, Circuit No 57 since Oct. 1947 (Circuit No 34, 1947); *b* 15 Sept. 1900; *o c* of late Sir John William Pratt; *m* 1928, Ingeborg, *e d* of late Consul Johannes Sundför, MBE, Haugesund, Norway; one *s*. *Educ:* Hillhead High Sch., Glasgow; Aske's Haberdashers' Sch., London; Balliol Coll., Oxford. Called to Bar, Inner Temple, 1924; practised London and Western Circuit; member General Council of the Bar; President, Hardwicke Society; contested Drake Div. of Plymouth, 1929; Dep. President War Damage (Valuation Appeals) Panel, 1946. Chairman, Devon Quarter Sessions, 1958-64. *Publications:* English trans. of Professor Axel Möller's International Law (Vol. I, 1931, Vol. II, 1935); trans. of various articles in Norwegian, Danish and Swedish on commercial and international law. *Recreations:* reading, gardening. *Address:* Portland Lodge, Pennsylvania, Exeter. *T:* Exeter 72859.

**PRATT, Very Rev. John Francis,** MA; Provost of Southwell, since 1970; *s* of late Rev. J. W. J. Pratt, Churchill, Somerset; *m* 1939, Norah Elizabeth, *y d* of late F. W. Corfield, Sandford, Somerset; two *d*. *Educ:* Keble Coll., Oxford; Wells Theological Coll. Priest, 1937. CF, 1st KSLI, 1941-46; (despatches, 1943); SCF, Cyprus, 1946. Vicar of: Rastrick, 1946-49; Wendover, 1949-59; Reading S Mary's (with All Saints, S Saviour's, S Mark's and S Matthew's), 1959-61; Vicar of Chilton with Dorton, 1961-70; Archdeacon of Buckingham, 1961-70. RD of Wendover, 1955-59; Chaplain to High Sheriff of Bucks, 1956, 1962. *Address:* The Residence, Southwell, Notts. *T:* Southwell 2593.

**PRATT, Rev. Ronald Arthur Frederick;** *b* 27 Aug. 1886; *s* of Charles Robert and Florence Maria Pratt; *m* 1925, Margaret Elam; no *c*. *Educ:* Tonbridge Sch.; Gonville and Caius Coll., Cambridge. Curate of Emmanuel, West Hampstead, 1910-13; of St Matthew's, Bethnal Green, E2, 1913-21; Chaplain RN (temp.), 1917-19; Vicar of Ossington, Newark on Trent, 1921-23; Vicar of St John, Long Eaton, Derbyshire, 1923-32; Vicar of St Barnabas, Derby, 1932-35; Archdeacon of Belize, British Honduras, CA, 1935-46. Missionary work in the Diocese of British Honduras, 1930-31. *Address:* 173 Old Dover Road, Canterbury, Kent.

**PRAWER, Prof. Siegbert Salomon;** Taylor Professor of German Language and Literature, University of Oxford, since 1969; Fellow of The Queen's College, Oxford, since 1969; *b* 15 Feb. 1925; *s* of Marcus and Eleonora Prawer; *m* 1949, Helga Alice (*née* Schaefer); one *s* two *d*. (and one *s* decd). *Educ:* King Henry VIII Sch., Coventry; Jesus Coll. (Schol.) and Christ's Coll., Cambridge. Charles Oldham Shakespeare Scholar, 1945, MA 1950, LittD 1962, Cantab; PhD Birmingham, 1953; MA 1969, DLitt 1969, Oxon. Adelaide Stoll Res. Student, Christ's Coll., Cambridge, 1947-48; Asst Lecturer, Lecturer, Sen. Lecturer, University of Birmingham, 1948-63; Prof. of German, Westfield Coll., London Univ., 1964-69. Visiting Professor: City Coll., NY, 1956-57; University of Chicago, 1963-64; Harvard Univ., 1968; Hamburg Univ., 1969. Hon. Director, London Univ. Inst. of Germanic Studies, 1966-68. *Publications:* German Lyric Poetry, 1952; Mörike und seine Leser, 1960; Heine's Buch der Lieder: A Critical Study, 1960; Heine: The Tragic Satirist, 1962; The Penguin Book of Lieder, 1964; (ed, with R. H. Thomas and L. W. Forster). Essays in German Langugage, Culture and Society, 1969; (ed) The Romantic Period in Germany, 1970; articles on German and English literature in many specialist periodicals and symposia. *Recreation:* theatre-going. *Address:* Taylor Institution, Oxford.

*See also Mrs R. P. Jhabvala.*

**PRAWER JHABVALA, Mrs Ruth;** *see* Jhabvala.

**PRAZ, Mario,** KBE (Hon.) 1962; LittD Florence, Dr Juris Rome; Hon. LittD Cambridge University, 1957; Professor of English Language and Literature, University of Rome, since 1934; retired (fuori ruolo), 1966; British Academy Gold Medallist for Anglo-Italian Studies, 1935; Italian Gold Medal, for cultural merits, 1958; national member of the Accademia dei Lincei; Hon. Member, Modern Language Association of America, 1954; *b* Rome 1896; *s* of Luciano Praz and Giulia Testa Di Marsciano; *m* 1934, Vivyan (marr. diss. 1947), *d* of late Leonora Eyles, and *step-d* of late D. L. Murray; one *d*. *Educ:* Rome; Florence. Came to England in 1923 to qualify for the title of *libero docente* in English Literature, which eventually he obtained in 1925; worked in the British Museum, 1923; Senior Lecturer in Italian at Liverpool Univ., 1924-32; Professor of Italian Studies at Manchester Univ., 1932-34; co-editor of La Cultura; editor of English Miscellany (Rome). Hon. LittD Aix-Marseille Univ., 1964; Hon. LittD, Paris Univ. (Sorbonne), 1967. *Publications:* I Saggi di Elia di Carlo Lamb, 1924; La Fortuna di Byron in Inghilterra, 1925; Poeti inglesi dell' Ottocento, 1925; Secentismo e Marinismo in Inghilterra, 1925; Machiavelli and the Elizabethans (British Academy Annual Italian Lecture), 1928; Penisola Pentagonale, 1928 (translated into English with the title Unromantic Spain, 1929); The Italian Element in English, 1929; La

Carne, la Morte e il Diavolo nella Letteratura Romantica, 1930 (translated into English with the title The Romantic Agony, 1933); Studi sul concettismo, 1934 (translated into English as Studies in Seventeenth-century Imagery, 1939, 2nd vol., 1948; revised enlarged edition in one vol., 1964); Antologia della letteratura inglese, 1936; Storia della letteratura inglese, 1937 (new rev. enlarged edition, 1960); Studi e svaghi inglesi, 1937; Gusto neoclassico, 1940 (rev. enlarged edition, 1959; translated into English as On Neoclassicism, 1968); Machiavelli in Inghilterra ed altri saggi, 1942 (rev. enlarged edition, 1962); Viaggio in Grecia, 1943; Fiori freschi, 1943; Ricerche anglo-italiane, 1944; La filosofia dell' arredamento, 1945 (rev. enlarged edition, 1964, in English as An Illustrated History of Interior Decoration, 1964); Motivi e figure, 1945; Prospettiva della letteratura inglese, 1947; Antologia delle letterature straniere, 1947; Cronache letterarie anglo-sassoni, Vols I, II, 1951, III, IV, 1966; Il Libro della poesia inglese, 1951; La Casa della Fama, Saggi di letteratura e d'arte, 1952; Lettrice notturna, 1952; La crisi dell'eroe nel romanzo vittoriano, 1952 (translated into English with the title The Hero in Eclipse in Victorian Fiction, 1956); Viaggi in Occidente, 1955; The Flaming Heart, Essays on Crashaw, Machiavelli, and other studies of the relations between Italian and English Literature, 1958; La Casa della Vita, 1958 (translated into English as The House of Life, 1964); Bellezza e bizzarria, 1960; I Volti del tempo, 1964; Panopticon Romano, 1967; Caleidoscopio shakespeariano, 1969; Mnemosyne: the parallel between literature and the visual arts, 1970; translations of Shakespeare's Measure for Measure and Troilus and Cressida, 1939, and of other works (by W. Pater, J. Austen, etc) general editor of standard Italian prose translation of Shakespeare's plays, 1943-47 and of Teatro elisabettiano, 1948; editor: works of Lorenzo Magalotti, 1945; D'Annunzio's selected works, 1966; contributions to literary and philological periodicals, both Italian and English. *Recreations:* travelling, Empire furniture. *Address:* Via Zanardelli 1, Rome, Italy; The University, Rome.

**PREBBLE, John Edward Curtis,** FRSL; Writer; *b* 23 June 1915; *o s* of late John William Prebble, Petty Officer, RN, and Florence (*née* Wood); *m* 1936, Betty, *d* of late Ernest Golby; two *s* one *d*. *Educ:* Sutherland Public Sch., Saskatchewan; Latymer Upper Sch., London. Entered journalism, 1934; in ranks with RA, 1940-45; Sergeant-reporter with No 1 British Army Newspaper Unit (Hamburg), 1945-46; reporter, columnist and feature-writer for British newspapers and magazines, 1946-60; novelist, historian, film-writer and author of several plays and dramatised documentaries for BBC TV. *Publications: novels:* Where the Sea Breaks, 1944; The Edge of Darkness, 1948; Age Without Pity, 1950; The Mather Story, 1954; The Brute Streets, 1954; The Buffalo Soldiers, 1959; *short stories:* My Great Aunt Appearing Day, 1958; *biography:* (with J. A. Jordan) Mongaso, 1956; *history:* The High Girders, 1956; Culloden, 1961; The Highland Clearances, 1963; Glencoe, 1966; The Darien Disaster, 1968; The Lion in the North, 1971. *Recreation:* serendipity. *Address:* Shaw Coign, Alcocks Lane, Burgh Heath, Surrey. *T:* Burgh Heath 55954. *Club:* Press.

**PRELOG, Prof. Dr Vladimir;** Professor of Organic Chemistry, Swiss Federal Institute of Technology, since 1951; *b* 23 July 1906; *m* 1933, Kamila Vitek; one *s*. *Educ:* Inst. of Technology, Prague. Chemist, Prague, 1929-34; Lecturer and Professor, University of Zagreb, 1935-41. Mem. Bd, CIBA Ltd, Basel. Privatdozent, Swiss Federal Inst. of Technology, Zürich, 1941. Mem. Leopoldina, Halle/Saale, 1963; Hon. Member: American Acad. of Arts and Sciences, 1960; Chem. Society, 1960; Nat. Acad. of Sciences, Washington, 1961; Foreign Member: Royal Society, 1962; Acad. of Sciences, USSR, 1966; Acad. dei Lincei, Roma 1965; Instiuto Lombardo, Milano, 1964. Dr *hc* Universities of: Zagreb, 1954; Liverpool, 1963; Paris, 1963; Bruxelles, 1969. Hon. DSc Cambridge, 1969. Davy Medal, Royal Society, 1967 A. W. Hofmann Medal, Gesell. deutsche Chem., 1967; Marcel Benoist Prize, 1965; Roger Adams Award, 1969. *Publications:* numerous scientific papers, mainly in Helvetica chimica acta. *Address:* (office) Universitätsstr. 6, 8006 Zürich, Switzerland. *T:* CH 051 326211; (home) Bellariastr. 41, 8038 Zürich. *T:* CH 051 457802.

**PREMINGER, Otto (Ludwig);** Producer-Director since 1928; *b* 5 Dec. 1906; *m* 1960, Hope Preminger (*née* Bryce); one *s* one *d* (twins). *Educ:* University of Vienna (LLD). Associate Professor, Yale Univ., 1938-41. *Films:* Margin for Error, 1942; A Royal Scandal, 1944; Laura, 1944; Fallen Angel, 1945; Centennial Summer, 1945; Forever Amber, 1947; Daisy Kenyon, 1948; Whirlpool, 1949; Where the Sidewalk Ends, 1950; The 13th Letter, 1950; Angel Face, 1952; The Moon is Blue, 1953; The River of No Return, 1953; Carmen Jones, 1954; The Man with the Golden Arm, 1955; Saint Joan, 1957; Bonjour Tristesse, 1958; Porgy and Bess, 1959; Anatomy of a Murder, 1959; Exodus, 1960; Advise and Consent, 1961; The Cardinal, 1963; In Harm's Way, 1965; Bunny Lake is Missing, 1965; Hurry Sundown, 1967; Skidoo, 1968; *plays include:* (director) Libel, Broadway, 1936; (prod. and dir) Outward Bound, Broadway, 1938; (leading rôle and director) Margin for Error, Broadway, 1939; (prod. and dir) My Dear Children, 1940; (prod. and dir) The Moon is Blue, Broadway, 1951; (prod. and dir) Critic's Choice, Broadway, 1960. *Recreation:* art collector. *Address:* 711 Fifth Avenue, New York 22, NY, USA. *T:* 838-6100.

**PRENDERGAST, John Vincent,** CMG 1968; CBE 1960; GM 1955; retired; *b* 11 Feb. 1912; *y s* of late John and Margaret Prendergast; *m* 1943, Enid Sonia, *yr d* of Percy Speed; one *s* one *d*. *Educ:* in Ireland; London Univ. (External). Local Government, London, 1930-39. War Service, 1939-46 (Major). Asst District Comr, Palestine Administration, 1946-47; Colonial Police Service, Palestine and Gold Coast, 1947-52; seconded Army, Canal Zone, on special duties, 1952-53; Colonial Police Service, Kenya, 1953-58 (Director of Intelligence and Security, 1955-58); Chief of Intelligence, Cyprus, 1958-60; Director, Special Branch, Hong Kong (retired as Dep. Comr of Police), 1960-66. Director of Intelligence, Aden, 1966-67. Colonial Police Medal, 1955; QPM 1963. *Recreations;* golf, squash, racing. *Address:* Casa Dielja, Ciampra Lane, Burmarrad, Malta GC. *Clubs:* East India and Sports, Special Foreces; Nairobi (Nairobi); Hong Kong (Hong Kong); Union, Malta Racing (Malta).

**PRENTICE, Rt. Hon. Reginald Ernest;** PC; JP; MP (Lab) East Ham (North) since May 1957; Alderman, GLC, since 1970; *b* 16 July 1923; *s* of Ernest George and Elizabeth Prentice; *m* 1948, Joan Godwin; one *d*. *Educ:* Whitgift Sch.; London School of Economics. Temporary Civil Servant, 1940-42; RA, 1942-46; commissioned 1943; served in Italy and Austria, 1944-46. Student at LSE, 1946-49. BSc (Econ). Member staff of Transport and

General Workers' Union, Asst to Legal Secretary; in charge of Union's Advice and Service Bureau, 1950-57; Minister of State, Department of Education and Science, 1964-66; Minister of Public Building and Works, 1966-67; Minister of Overseas Develt, 1967-69. JP County Borough of Croydon, 1961. *Publication:* (jt) Social Welfare and the Citizen, 1957. *Recreations:* walking, swimming, gardening. *Address:* 5 Hollingsworth Road, Croydon, Surrey. *T:* 01-657 0988.

**PRESCOTT, Hilda F. M.;** FRSL; *b* 22 Feb. 1896; *d* of late Rev. James Mulleneux Prescott and Margaret Prescott. *Educ:* Wallasey High Sch., Cheshire; Lady Margaret Hall, Oxford. MA Oxon; MA Manchester; research under late Prof. T. F. Tout. Jubilee Research Fellow at Royal Holloway Coll., 1958-60. Hon. DLitt Dunelm, 1957. *Publications:* The Unhurrying Chase, 1925; The Lost Fight, 1928; Flamenca, 1930; Son of Dust, 1932; Dead and not Buried, 1938; Spanish Tudor, 1940 (James Tait Black prize, 1941); The Man on a Donkey, 1952; Jerusalem Journey, 1954; Once to Sinai, 1957. *Address:* Orchard Piece, Charlbury, Oxon. *T:* Charlbury 342.

**PRESCOTT, James Arthur,** CBE 1947; FRS 1951; DSc; retired; Director, Waite Agricultural Research Institute, 1938-55; Professor of Agricultural Chemistry, University of Adelaide, 1924-55, Emeritus Professor since 1956; *b* 7 Oct. 1890; *e s* of Joseph Arthur Prescott, Bolton, Lancs; *m* 1915, Elsie Mason, Accrington, Lancs; one *s*. *Educ:* Ecole Littré, Lille; Accrington Grammar Sch.; Manchester Univ.; Leipzig Univ. Rothamsted Experimental Station; Chief Chemist and Superintendent of Field Experiments, Bahtim Experimental Station, Sultanic Agricultural Society of Egypt, 1916-24; Chief, Division of Soils, Commonwealth Council for Scientific and Industrial Research, 1929-47. Mem. Council and Scientific Adviser, Australian Wine Research Inst., 1954-69. Hon. DAgSc Melbourne, 1956. Hon. Member, Internat. Society of Soil Science, 1964. (Foundn) FAA 1954. *Publications:* various scientific, chiefly on soils, climatology and principles of crop production. *Address:* 82 Cross Road, Myrtle Bank, South Australia.

**PRESCOTT, John Leslie;** MP (Lab) Kingston upon Hull (East), since 1970; *b* 31 May 1938; *s* of John Herbert Prescott, JP, and Phyllis Prescott; *m* 1961, Pauline Tilston; two *s*. *Educ:* Ellesmore Port Secondary Modern Sch.; WEA; Ruskin Coll., Oxford (DipEcon/Pol Oxon); Correspondence Courses; Hull Univ. (BSc Econ). Trainee Chef, 1953-55; Steward, Passenger Lines, Merchant Navy, 1955-63; Ruskin Coll., Oxford, 1963-65; Recruitment Officer, General and Municipal Workers Union (temp.), 1965; Hull Univ., 1965-68. Contested (Lab) Southport, 1966; Full-time Official, National Union of Seamen, 1968-70. *Publication:* Not Wanted on Voyage, 1966. *Address:* 39 Gorsedale, Sutton Park, Hull, Yorks. *T:* 825461.

**PRESCOTT, Sir Mark,** 3rd Bt, *cr* 1938, of Godmanchester; Assistant Racehorse Trainer to J. A. J. Waugh, Newmarket; *b* 3 March 1948; *s* of late Major W. R. Stanley Prescott (MP for Darwen Div., 1943-51; 2nd *s* of Colonel Sir William Prescott, 1st Bt) and of Gwendolen (who *m* 2nd, 1952, Daniel Orme), *o c* of late Leonard Aldridge, CBE; *S* uncle, Sir Richard Stanley Prescott, 2nd Bt, 1965. *Educ:* Harrow. *Recreation:* steeplechasing. *Address:* 8 Western Esplanade, Hove, Sussex BN4 1WE. *T:* Brighton 44766; Heath House, Moulton Road, Newmarket, Suffolk. *T:* Newmarket 4935, Newmarket 2117. *Clubs:* Oriental; Subscription Rooms (Newmarket).

**PRESCOTT, Sir Stanley (Lewis),** Kt 1965; OBE 1957; MSc (Manchester); Vice-Chancellor, The University of Western Australia, since 1953; *b* 21 March 1910; *s* of J. Prescott, JP, Tetbury, Glos, England; *m* 1937, Monica M., *d* of Rev. H. A. Job; two *s* two *d*. *Educ:* Tetbury Grammar Sch.; University of Manchester; Lancashire College. Wild Prizeman in Pharmacology, University of Manchester, 1934. Professor of Physiology, Cheeloo Univ., Tsinan, North China, 1936. Commissioned Royal Australian Air Force, 1941; Sqdn Leader, and appointed CO, No. 1 Flying Personnel Research Unit, 1943-46. Master of Ormond Coll., University of Melbourne, Australia, 1946-53. Member Aitken Commn on University of Malaya, 1957; Chairman Commn on Nanyang Univ., Singapore, 1959; Commonwealth Consultant on Inter-University Council for Higher Education Overseas, 1960-; Chairman, Australian Vice-Chancellors' Cttee, 1964-65. Hon. LLD Western Australia. *Address:* The University of Western Australia, Nedlands, Western Australia 6009. *T:* 86-2481. *Club:* Weld (Western Australia).

**PRESLAND, John; (Gladys Bendit);** author and lecturer; *b* Melbourne, Australia; *d* of John Frederick Williams, Cape Colony and London, and Alice Emily Presland; *m* 1st, John Herbert Skelton (*d* 1942); two *s*; 2nd, 1943, Francis Edmund Bendit (*d* 1953). *Educ:* Queen's Coll., London; Girton Coll., Cambridge. BA (Cantab); Honours in Medieval and Modern Languages; Director of YMCA Employment Bureau for Disabled Soldiers, 1919; in charge of Women's Section of Central Council for Economic Information, also Lecturer, 1920-24; London University Extension Lecturer in Literature, 1924-27; Member of Seafarer's Education Service, 1924-48; one-time Lecturer for League of Nations Union, Ashridge Park, Empire Marketing Board, etc; Member of Home Office Advisory Cttee on Aliens, 1940; Member of Council and Chairman of Foreign Relief and Rehabilitation Cttee, Save the Children Fund; Member of Council of British Societies for Relief Abroad, 1942-45. *Publications:* Joan of Arc, 1909; Mary Queen of Scots, 1910; Manin and the Defence of Venice, 1911; The Deluge, Marcus Aurelius, 1912; Songs of Changing Skies; King Monmouth, 1915; Poems of London, 1918; Dominion, 1925; Frustration, 1926; Barricade, 1927; Escape MeNever, 1928; Mosaic, 1929; Satni, 1930; Albatross, 1931; Vae Victis: The Life of Ludwig von Benedek; Women and the Civilized State, 1934; Deedes Bey: A Study of Sir Wyndham Deedes, 1942; The Shaken Reed, 1945; Selected Poems, 1960. *Address:* 4 Marlborough Lodge, Hamilton Terrace, NW8. *T:* 01-624 4153.

**PRESS, John Bryant;** author and poet; Deputy Representative, British Council, Paris, and Assistant Cultural Attaché, British Embassy, Paris, since 1966; *b* 11 Jan. 1920; *s* of late Edward Kenneth Press and of Gladys (*née* Cooper); *m* 1947, Janet Crompton; one *s* one *d*. *Educ:* King Edward VI Sch., Norwich; Corpus Christi Coll., Cambridge, 1938-39 and 1945-46. Served War of 1939-45: RA, 1940-45. British Council: Athens, 1946-47; Salonika, 1947-50; Madras, 1950-51; Colombo, 1951-52; Birmingham, 1952-54; Cambridge, 1955-62; London, 1962-65. Gave George Elliston Poetry Foundation Lectures at Univ. of Cincinnati, 1962. FRSL 1959. *Publications:* The Fire and the Fountain, 1955; Uncertainties, 1956; (ed) Poetic Heritage, 1957; The Chequer'd Shade, 1958 (RSL

Heinemann Award); Andrew Marvell, 1958; Guy Fawkes Night, 1959; Herrick, 1961; Rule and Energy, 1963; Louis MacNeice, 1964; (ed) Palgrave's Golden Treasury, Book V, 1964; A Map of Modern English Verse, 1969; The Lengthening Shadows, 1971. Libretto, new version of Bluebeard's Castle, for colour television film of Bartok's opera, 1963. *Recreations:* travel (especially in France), theatre, opera, concerts, cinema; architecture and visual arts; watching football and cricket. *Address:* c/o British Council, 65 Davies Street, W1.

**PRESS, Dr Robert,** CBE 1962; Chief Scientific Officer, Cabinet Office, London (Member of Chief Scientific Adviser's Staff) since 1967; *b* 22 Feb. 1915; *s* of William J. Press; *m* 1946, Honor Elizabeth Tapp; no *c. Educ:* Regent House Secondary Sch., Co. Down; Queen's Univ., Belfast; Trinity Coll., Dublin Univ. BSc 1936, MSc 1937 QUB; PhD 1949 Dublin. Hon. Sec. Inst. of Physics and Physical Soc., 1966-. Physicist: War Dept Research, UK, 1941-43, and in India, 1944-46; on Staff of Scientific Adviser, Army Council, 1946-48; in Dept of Atomic Energy, Min. of Supply, 1948-51. Attaché at HM Embassy, Washington, 1951-55; MoD, 1955-58; Mem. British Delegn to Conf. for Discontinuance of Nuclear Tests, 1958-59. Dep. Chief Scientific Officer, MoD, 1960-62; Asst Chief Scientific Adviser (Nuclear), MoD, 1963-66. FPhysS 1950, FInstP 1961, FRSA 1967. *Publications:* Papers in: Nature, and Proc. Royal Soc., 1938, 1941; Scientific Proc. Royal Dublin Soc., 1939; Irish Jl of Med. Science, 1941. *Recreations:* photography, walking. *Address:* 8 Ardross Avenue, Northwood, Middlesex. *T:* Northwood 23707.

**PRESSBURGER, Emeric;** Author, Film Producer; *b* 5 Dec. 1902; one *d. Educ:* Universities of Prague and Stuttgart. Journalist in Hungary and Germany, author and writer of films in Berlin and Paris; came to England in 1935; formed jointly with Michael Powell, The Archers Film Producing Company, and Vega Productions Ltd, and made the following films: Spy in Black, 1938; 49th Parallel, 1940; One of our Aircraft is Missing, 1941; Colonel Blimp, 1942; I Know Where I'm Going, 1944; A Matter of Life and Death, 1945; Black Narcissus, 1946; The Red Shoes, 1947; Small Back Room, 1948; Gone to Earth, 1949; The Tales of Hoffmann, 1951; Oh Rosalinda!!, 1955; The Battle of the River Plate, 1956; Ill Met by Moonlight, 1956. Wrote and produced Miracle in Soho, 1957. Wrote, produced, and directed first film Twice Upon a Time, 1952. *Publications:* Killing a Mouse on Sunday (novel), 1961; The Glass Pearls (novel), 1966. *Recreations:* music, travel, and sports. *Address:* c/o Barclays Bank, 27 Regent Street, SW1.

**PRESSMAN, Mrs J. J.;** *see* Colbert, Claudette.

**PREST, Prof. Alan Richmond;** Professor of Economics (with special reference to the Public Sector), London School of Economics, since 1970; *b* 1 March 1919; *s* of F. and E. A. Prest; *m* 1945, Pauline Chasey Noble; two *s* one *d. Educ:* Archbishop Holgate's Sch., York; Clare Coll., Cambridge; Christ's Coll., Cambridge. Res. Worker, Dept of Applied Economics, Cambridge, 1946-48; Rockefeller Fellow, USA, 1948-49; University Lecturer, Cambridge, 1949-64; Fellow, Christ's Coll., Cambridge, 1950-64; Tutor, 1954-55, Bursar, 1955-64, Christ's Coll.; Prof. of Economics and Public Finance, 1964-68, and Stanley Jevons Prof. of Political Economy, 1968-70, University of Manchester. visiting Professor: Columbia Univ., New York, 1961-62; Univ. of Pittsburgh, 1969. President, Section F, British Association, 1967. *Publications:* War Economics of Primary Producing Countries, 1948; The National Income of Nigeria, 1950-51, (with I. G. Stewart), 1953; Consumers' Expenditure in the UK, 1900-19, 1954; Fiscal Survey of the British Caribbean, 1957; Public Finance in Theory and Practice, 1960; Public Finance in Under-Developed Countries, 1962; (ed) The UK Economy, 1966; (ed.) Public Sector Economics, 1968; Transport Economics in Developing Countries, 1969. Papers in various professional journals. *Address:* 21 Leeward Gardens, Wimbledon Hill, SW19. *Club:* Oxford and Cambridge University.

**PRESTON,** family name of **Viscount Gormanston.**

**PRESTON, Hon. Mrs Angela C.;** *see* Campbell-Preston.

**PRESTON, (Frederick) Leslie,** FRIBA; AADip; Partner in firm of Easton Robertson Preston and Partners, Architects; *b* 27 Nov. 1903; *m* 1927, Rita Lillian, *d* of late T. H. J. Washbourne; one *d. Educ:* Dulwich Coll.; Architectural Association Sch., London. Henry Jarvis Student, 1924; joined firm of Easton & Robertson, 1925, and engaged on: in London: Royal Horticultural Society's New Hall; Royal Bank of Canada; Metropolitan Water Board's Laboratories; in Cambridge: reconstruction of Old Library; Zoological laboratories; School of Anatomy; Gonville and Caius new buildings; in New York: British Pavilion, World's Fair, 1939. Hon. Citizen of City of New York, 1939. Served War of 1939-45, RAF, Wing Comdr, Airfield Construction Branch (despatches). *Principal works:* laboratories for Brewing Industry Research Foundation; laboratories for Coal Research Establishment, NCB, Cheltenham; Bank of England, Bristol; offices for Lloyds Bank, Plymouth; Birmingham; plans for development of Reading University: Faculty of Letters, Library, Windsor Hall, Depts of Physics and Sedimentology, Dept of Mathematics. Applied Physical Science Building, Palmer Building, Whiteknights House, Students Union, Animal Biology and Plant Buildings, Reading Univ.; additions to St Patrick's Hall and to Depts of Horticulture and Dairying, Reading Univ.; Buildings for Dulwich Coll.; office building for Salters' Co., London; Laboratories and Aquarium for Marine Biological Association, Plymouth; offices for Friends' Provident & Century Life Office, Dorking; Research Laboratories for Messrs Arthur Guinness Son & Co. (Park Royal) Ltd; University of Keele, Library; Midland Hotel, Manchester, alterations; University of Kent at Canterbury, Chemistry Laboratories, Biology Laboratories; Bank of England Printing Works Extension, Debden; Eagle Star Insurance Head Office, City; Plans for Aquarium, Rangoon Zoological Gardens. Member of RIBA Practice Cttee, 1951-55; Member Council of Architects' Registration Council of the UK, 1954-60. Governor of Westminster Technical College, 1957-67. Hon. DLitt, Reading, 1964. *Address:* 53 Bedford Square, WC1. *T:* 01-636 8121; Wichenford, Ashtead, Surrey. *Clubs:* Athenæum, Reform.

**PRESTON, Prof. George Dawson,** MA, ScD; Harris Professor of Physics at Queen's College, Dundee, in the University of St Andrews, 1943-66; now Emeritus; *b* 8 Aug. 1896; *s* of late Professor Thomas Preston, FRS, and Mrs K. M. Preston. MA, of Dublin; *m* 1923, Margaret Chrystal, MA; two *s* two *d. Educ:* Oundle Sch.; Gonville and Caius Coll., Cambridge. Served European War 7th Bn

Alexandra Princess of Wales' Own Yorkshire Regt, 1914-18. Metallurgy Division, National Physical Laboratory, 1921-43. FRSE; FInstP; FPhysS. *Publications:* papers on X-ray analysis of metals and alloys, electron diffraction and electron microscopy in Phil. Mag., Proc. Royal Society, Proc. Physical Society, etc. *Address:* Craigellie, Alyth, Perthshire. *T:* Alyth 325.

**PRESTON, Prof. Joseph Henry;** Professor of Fluid Mechanics, University of Liverpool, since Sept. 1955; Fellow, Queen Mary College, London, since Dec. 1959; *b* 1 March 1911; *s* of William and Jean Preston, Penruddock, Cumberland; *m* 1938, Ethel Noble, Bampton, Westmorland; one *s* one *d*. *Educ:* Queen Elizabeth Grammar Sch., Penrith, Cumberland; Queen Mary Coll., University of London. BSc Eng London 1932; 1851 Industrial Bursary, for practical training at Short Bros Ltd, Rochester, 1932-34; PhD (Aeronautics) London 1936; Asst Lecturer, Imperial Coll., 1936-38; Officer, Aero Division, National Physical Laboratory, Teddington, 1938-46; Lecturer in Aeronautics, Cambridge Univ., 1946-54 (MA Cantab); Reader in Engineering, at Cambridge, 1955. FRAeS. *Publications:* contributor to Phil. Mag.; Journal Royal Aero. Society; Engineer; Engineering; Aero. Engineer; Aero. Quarterly; Journal of Mechanics and Applied Maths; Reports and Memoranda of the Stationery Office. *Recreation:* mountaineering. *Address:* Department of Mechanical Engineering (Fluid Mechanics), The University, Liverpool. *Club:* Wayfarers (Liverpool).

**PRESTON, Sir Kenneth (Huson),** Kt 1959; President, Stone-Platt Industries Ltd; Director: Midland Bank Ltd; Philip Hill Investment Trust Ltd; *b* 19 May 1901; *e s* of late Sir Walter Preston, Tetbury, Glos; *m* 1922, Beryl Wilmot, *d* of Sir William Wilkinson; one *s* one *d*. *Educ:* Rugby; Trinity Coll., Oxford. *Recreations:* yachting, hunting. *Address:* Ilsom Farm, Tetbury, Gloucestershire. *T:* Tetbury 348. *Clubs:* Royal Thames Yacht; Royal Yacht Squadron (Vice-Commodore).

**PRESTON, Kerrison;** writer; *b* 21 May 1884; *s* of late Donald Preston, Solicitor, Bournemouth; *m* 1912, Evelyn Preston (second cousin) (*d* 1968); one *s* four *d* (and one *s* killed on active service, Tobruk, 1942). *Educ:* Rugby School. Practised as a family solicitor at Bournemouth, 1909-1949; held literary executorships, and many trusteeships. Founder and Governor Stanbridge School. Gave Blake Library to Westminster City, 1967. *Publications:* Blake and Rossetti, 1944; The Blake Collection of W. Graham Robertson, 1952; Letters from Graham Robertson, 1953; Blake's Fourfold Man; contributions to art magazines, etc. *Recreations:* books, pictures and grandchildren. *Address:* The Georgian House, Merstham, Surrey. *T:* Merstham 2647. *Clubs:* Authors'; Arts Theatre.

**PRESTON, Leslie;** *see* Preston, F. L.

**PRESTON, Adm. Sir Lionel (George),** KCB 1934 (CB 1916); *b* 27 Sept. 1875; *m* 1st, Emily Elizabeth Bryant, Bridgwater, Somerset; 2nd, Ivy Lilian Record, Sheppey, Kent. *Educ:* Stubbington House, Fareham. Entered Britannia, 1888; Lieut, 1897; served in Rosario, Boxer Rebellion, 1900; specially promoted to Commander, 1907, for seamanlike handling of HMS Bruiser in heavy weather off Malta, and on a dark night, when, by taking his ship alongside HMS Ariel, which was rapidly sinking, the majority of the officers and crew were saved; served European War, 1915-16 (CB, Officer of Legion of Honour, despatches, for proceeding at once in HMS Skipjack to the assistance of two trawlers which had been mined off Scarborough, and anchoring the ship in the mine-field to destroy several mines which the trawlers had swept up); Captain, 1914; Commanded Grand Fleet Mine-Sweeping Flotilla, 1914-17; Director of Mine-Sweeping Division, Admiralty, 1917-19; in charge of the direction of the clearance of Mines in British areas after war; in command of the Patrol, Mine-Sweeping Training and Fishing Protection Flotilla, 1919-20; CO, RN Signal School, Portsmouth, 1920-22; Comd HMS Eagle, 1923-25; Rear-Admiral, 1925; ADC, 1925-26; Comd Third Cruiser Squadron, 1926-28; Vice-Admiral, 1930; Fourth Sea Lord and Chief of Supplies and Transport, 1930-32; Comdt Imperial Defence Coll., 1933-34; Admiral, 1934; retired 1935; recalled to service Sept. 1939 as Adviser on Mine Sweeping; Director Small Vessels Pool (which organised a list of small craft, largely used later in Dunkirk operation), 1940-45; reverted to retired list, 1945. *Publication:* Sea and River Painters of the Netherlands in the XVII Century. *Address:* Murrel House, Dunstable, Beds.

**PRESTON, Myles Park;** Counsellor and Consul-General, HM Embassy, Djakarta, since 1969; *b* 4 April 1927; *s* of Robert and Marie Preston; *m* 1951, Ann Munro Betten; one *s* one *d*. *Educ:* Liverpool Inst. High Sch.; Clare Coll., Cambrdige. Instructor Lieut, RN, 1948-51; Asst Principal, Admty, 1951-53; CRO, 1953-54; 2nd Sec., British High Commn, New Delhi, 1954-56; 1st Sec., CRO, 1956-59; 1st Sec., Governor-General's Office and British High Commn, Lagos, 1959-62; CRO, 1962-64; 1st Sec., British High Commn, Kampala, 1964-67; Commonwealth Office and FCO, 1967-69. *Address:* 1 Duke Humphrey Road, Blackheath, SE3. *T:* 01-852 9039. *Club:* Travellers'.

**PRESTON, Peter Sansome;** Under-Secretary, Board of Trade, since 1969; *b* Nottingham, 18 Jan. 1922; *s* of Charles Guy Preston, Solicitor; *m* 1951, Marjory Harrison; one *s* three *d*. *Educ:* Nottingham High School. War Service, RAF, 1942-46; Board of Trade: Exec. Officer, 1947; Higher Exec. Off., 1950; Asst principal, 1951; Principal, 1953; Trade Comr, New Delhi, 1959; Asst Sec., 1964; idc 1968. *Publications'* several one-act plays. *Address:* 5 Greville Park Avenue, Ashtead, Surrey. *T:* Ashtead 72099.

**PRESTON, Prof. Reginald Dawson,** FRS 1954; Professor of Plant Biophysics, since 1953; Head, Astbury Department of Biophysics since 1962, University of Leeds; Chairman, School of Biological Sciences, since 1970; Dean of the Faculty of Science, 1955-58; *b* 21 July 1908; *s* of late Walter C. Preston, builder, and late Eliza Preston; *m* 1935, Sarah J. Pollard (decd); two *d* (one *s* decd); *m* 1963, Dr Eva Frei. *Educ:* Leeds University; Cornell University, USA. BSc (Hons Physics, Class I), 1929; PhD (Botany), 1931; 1851 Exhibition Fellowship, 1932-35; Rockefeller Foundation Fellowship, 1935-36. Lecturer, Botany Dept, Univ. of Leeds, 1936-46; Sen. Lectr, 1946-49; Reader, 1949-53. Mem. NY Acad. Sci., 1960. DSc 1943; FInstP 1944; FLS 1958; FIWSc 1960. *Publications:* Molecular Architecture of Plant Cell Walls, 1952; about 180 articles in Proc. Roy. Soc., Nature, Ann. Bot., Biochem. Biophys Acta, Jl Exp. Bot., etc. Editor: Proc. Leeds Phil. Soc. Sci. Sec.; Advances in Botanical Research; Associate Editor, Jl Exp. Bot. *Recreations:* walking, climbing, music. *Address:* 117 St Anne's Rd, Leeds 6, Yorks. *T:* 53248.

**PRESTON, Rev. Prof. Ronald Haydn;** Professor of Social and Pastorial Theology in the University of Manchester, since 1970; *b* 12 March 1913; *o s* of Haydn and Eleanor Jane Preston; *m* 1948, Edith Mary Lindley; one *s* two *d*. *Educ:* London School of Economics, University of London; St Catherine's Society, Oxford. BSc (Econ.) 1935, Cl. II, Div. I; Industrial Secretary of Student Christian Movement, 1935-38; BA Cl. I Theology, 1940; MA 1944; Curate, St John, Park, Sheffield, 1940-43; Study Secretary, Student Christian Movement, 1943-48; Warden of St Anselm Hall, University of Manchester, 1948-63; Lectr in Christian Ethics, Univ. of Manchester, 1948-70; Examining Chaplain to Bishop of Manchester, 1948-; Canon Residentiary of Manchester Cathedral, 1957-70. *Publications:* (jointly) Christians in Society, 1939; (jointly) The Revelation of St John the Divine, 1949; Ed. The Student Movement, 1943-48; reviews, etc. in The Guardian, Theology, etc. *Address:* 28 Rathen Road, Manchester M20 9GH. *T:* 061-445 3847.

**PRESTON, Col Rupert Lionel,** CBE 1945; Vice-Chairman, Royal Aero Club, 1970; Secretary-General, Royal Aero Club of the United Kingdom, 1945-63; *b* 1 Nov. 1902; *s* of Admiral Sir Lionel Preston, KCB; *m* 1932, Jean Mary, *d* of late F. B. Pitcairn and of Mrs Pitcairn; no *c*. *Educ:* Cheltenham College. Coldstream Guards, 1924-45. Assistant Provost Marshal, London, 1938-40; 11 Group RAF Defence Officer, 1940-43; comd RAF Regt 83 Group RAF, 1943-45 (despatches, 1945). Mem. Council Air Registration Boards, 1946-65; Vice-Pres. Fédération Aeronautique Internationale, 1961-64; AFRAeS; Vice-Patron, Guards Flying Club; Hon. Member Soc. of Licensed Aeronautical Engineers. Silver Medal of Royal Aero Club, 1964. Specialist in 17th century Seascape paintings of the Netherlands. *Publications:* How to become an Air Pilot, 1930, 7 edns. *Address:* 17 Coulson Street, SW3. *T:* 01-589 4989; 17 King Street, St James's, SW1. *T:* 01-930 1794. *Clubs:* Guards, Royal Aero; Wings (New York).

**PRESTON, Simon John;** Organist and Lecturer in Music, Christ Church, Oxford, since 1970; *b* 4 Aug. 1938. *Educ:* Canford Sch.; King's Coll., Cambridge (Dr Mann Organ Student). BA 1961, MusB 1962, MA 1964. Sub Organist, Westminster Abbey, 1962-67; Acting Organist, St Albans Abbey, 1967-68. *Recreations:* croquet, cinema. *Address:* Christ Church, Oxford.

**PRESTON, Sir Thomas (Hildebrand),** 6th Bt, *cr* 1815; OBE 1934; *b* 2 June 1886; *s* of William Thomas Preston, Gordon Highlanders, 2nd *s* of Sir Jacob Preston, 2nd Bt, Beeston Hall, Norfolk; *S* cousin, 1963; *m* 1913, Ella Henrietta v. Shickendantz; one *s* one *d*. *Educ:* Westminster; Trinity Hall, Cambridge. Conducted mining expeditions to Siberia and Caucasus; held many consular and diplomatic posts in Russia, Italy and Lithuania. One of HM Counsellors at Cairo, 1941; late Minister to Republic of Lithuania; seconded, 1947, as Resident Representative in Middle East, of Intergovernmental Committee on Refugees; retired, 1947; re-employed by FO on secretariat of Council of Foreign Ministers, 1948. Joined Messrs Thos de la Rue and Co., 1949. Associate and Offical lecturer, Brit. Atlantic Cttee (NATO). *Publications:* Before the Curtain, 1950; Composer of 2 ballets (performed publicly in London and elsewhere) and many other musical works. *Recreations:* tennis, golf, swimming. *Heir:* *s* Ronald Douglas Hildebrand Preston [*b* 9 Oct. 1916. *Educ:* Westminster; Trinity College, Cambridge]. *Address:* Beeston Hall, Beeston St Lawrence, Norwich, Norfolk. *Clubs:* St James', Royal Automobile; Norfolk (Norwich).

**PRESTT, Arthur Miller,** QC 1970; JP; *b* 23 April 1925; *s* of Arthur Prestt, Wigan; *m* 1949, Jill Mary, *d* of Graham Dawbarn, *qv*; one *s* one *d*. *Educ:* Bootham Sch., York; Trinity Hall, Cambridge (MA). Served 13th Bn Parachute Regt, BLA and Far East; Major Legal Staff, Singapore, 1947-48. Called to Bar, Middle Temple, 1949. Mental Health Review Tribunal, 1963-70; Dep. Chm., Cumberland QS, 1966-69, Chm., 1970-. Has held various appts in Scout Assoc.: Chm. SW Lancs Assoc., 1968-; Silver Acorn, 1970. JP Cumberland, 1966. *Address:* The Old Rectory, Eccleston, Chorley, Lancs. *T:* Eccleston (Lancs) 397; 2 Pump Court, EC4. *Club:* St James's (Manchester).

**PRESTWOOD, Viscount; John Richard Attlee;** *b* 3 Oct. 1956; *s* and *heir* of 2nd Earl Attlee, *qv*.

**PRETORIA, Bishop of,** since 1960; **Rt. Rev. Edward George Knapp-Fisher;** *b* 8 Jan. 1915; *s* of late Rev. George Edwin Knapp-Fisher and of Agatha Knapp-Fisher; *m* 1965, Joan, *d* of R. V. Bradley, Claremont, CP, SA. *Educ:* King's School, Worcester; Trinity College, Oxford. Assistant Curate of Brighouse, Yorks, 1939; Chaplain, RNVR, 1942; Chaplain of Cuddesdon College, 1946; Chaplain of St John's College, Cambridge, 1949; Vicar of Cuddesdon and Principal of Cuddesdon Theological College, 1952-60. Member, Anglican Roman-Catholic Preparatory Commission, 1967-68; Member, Jt Permanent Commn of the Roman Catholic Church and the Anglican Communion, 1969-. *Publications:* The Churchman's Heritage, 1952; Belief and Prayer, 1964; To be or not to be, 1968. *Recreation:* walking. *Address:* Bishop's House, 264 Celliers Street, Pretoria, South Africa.

**PRETTY, Air Marshal Sir Walter (Philip George),** KBE 1962 (CBE 1950; OBE 1942); CB 1957; Director, Redifon Ltd, since Oct. 1966; *b* 2 May 1909; *s* of William Pretty; *m* 1940, Betty Finlayson Methven, *d* of late Sir Harry Methven, KBE; one *s* three *d*. *Educ:* Alleyns Sch.; RAF Coll., Cranwell. Served War of 1939-45 (despatches twice, OBE); Director-General of Navigational Services, Min. of Civil Aviation, 1948; Dir of Electronics Research and Development, Min. of Supply, 1953; Director-General of Organisation, Air Ministry, 1958; Air Officer Commanding-in-Chief, Signals Command, 1961-64; Deputy Chief of the Defence Staff (Personnel and Logistics), Ministry of Defence, 1964-66. *Recreations:* golf, fishing. *Address:* c/o Redifon Ltd, Broomhill Road, Wandsworth, SW18; Chippings, Icklingham Road, Cobham, Surrey. *Club:* Royal Air Force.

**PREVETT, Comdr Harry,** OBE 1942; RN retired; Clerk to the Worshipful Company of Haberdashers, 1950-66; *b* 9 July 1900. Entered RN, 1917; Secretary to late Admiral Sir H. D. Pridham Wippell, KCB, CVO, 1936-47; retired, 1950.

**PREVIN, André (George);** American composer and conductor; *b*. Berlin, Germany, 6 April 1929; *s* of Jack Previn and Charlotte Epstein. *Educ:* Berlin and Paris Conservatoires and Univ. of California. American nationality, 1943. Recording artist of classical and jazz piano music, 1946-; composer of film scores for Metro-Goldwyn-Mayer, 1950-59. Served US Army, 1950-51. Music Dir, Houston Symphony Orchestra, 1967-69; Music Dir and Principal Conductor, London Symphony

Orchestra, 1968-. Acad. Award for Best Film Score: Gigi, 1958; Porgy and Bess, 1959; Irma la Douce, 1963; My Fair Lady, 1964. Exhibitor's Award, 1958, 1959, 1961, 1963; Award, Screen Composers Assoc., 1958; five awards, Nat. Gramophone Soc., three awards Downbeat Magazine, 1959. Major works include: Symphony for Srings, 1965; Overture to a Comdedy, 1966; Suite for Piano, 1967; Cello Concerto, 1968; Four Songs, Soprano and Orchestra, 1968; Violin Concerto, 1969; Two Serenades for Violin, 1969; Mouse Pieces, 1969; Guitar Concerto, 1970; other compositions: score for Coco, 1969. TV series of nine specials with LSO for BBC. *Recreations:* collecting contemporary art, fencing, American folk art. *Address:* c/o London Symphony Orchestra, 1 Montague Street, WC1.

**PREVOST, Captain Sir George James Augustine,** 5th Bart, *cr* 1805; *b* 16 Jan. 1910; *s* of Sir Charles Thomas Keble Prevost, 4th Bart, and Beatrice Mary, *o d* of Rev. J. A. Burrow of Tunstall, Kirkby Lonsdale; *S* father, 1939; *m* 1st, 1935, Muriel Emily (*d* 1939), *d* of late Lewis William Oram; one *s* one *d*; 2nd, 1940, Phyllis Catherine Mattock (from whom he obtained a divorce, 1949); 3rd, 1952, Patricia Betty Porter, Harpenden, Herts; two *s*. *Educ:* Repton. *Heir: s* Christopher Gerald Prevost, *b* 25 July 1935.

**PRICA, Srdja;** Ambassador of Yugoslavia to Italy, since 1967; *b* 20 Sept. 1905; *m* 1956, Vukica Tomanović-Prica. *Educ:* University of Zagreb, Yugoslavia. Newspaperman until 1946; Director of Department, Foreign Office, Belgrade, 1947-49; Asst Min., FO, Belgrade, 1949-51; Ambassador of Yugoslavia, Paris, 1951-55; Under-Sec. of State for Foreign Affairs, Belgrade, 1955-60; Ambassador to Court of St James's, 1960-65. Grand Officier, Légion d'Honneur (France); Egyptian, Italian, Swedish and Greek Orders. *Address:* c/o Department of External Affairs, Belgrade, Yugoslavia.

**PRICE, Prof. Albert Thomas,** DSc; FRAS; Professor of Applied Mathematics, University of Exeter (previously the University College of the South-West) 1952-68, now Emeritus; *b* 30 Jan. 1903; *e s* of Albert Thomas Price and Marie Lavinia (*née* Light); *m* 1947, Rose Ann Waterman; no *c*. *Educ:* Monmouth Sch.; Manchester University. Asst in Pure Mathematics, QUB, 1925-26; Asst Lecturer, 1926-30, Lecturer, 1930-46, and Asst Professor and Univ. Reader in Applied Mathematics, 1946-51, Imperial Coll. of Science and Technology, London; Professor and Head of Mathematics Dept, Roy. Technical Coll., Glasgow, 1951-52. Consultant to Admiralty, 1942-45. Guest investigator at Dept of Terrestrial Magnetism, Carnegie Instn, Washington, and at Inst. of Geophysics, Univ. of Calif, Los Angeles, 1952; Dean, Faculty of Science, Exeter Univ., 1954-58; Research Fellow, Univ. of Exeter, 1968-69. Internat. Geophysical Year Research Associate, Nat. Acad. of Sciences, Washington, DC, 1961-62. Consultant, Rand Corporation, Santa Monica, 1963. Chairman, Commn IV Internat. Assoc. Geomagnetism and Aeronomy, 1964-68; Member: Council of Royal Astronomical Soc., 1956-60; National Cttee for Geomagnetism and Aeronomy, 1946-; National Advisory Council on Education for Industry and Commerce, 1957-65; Regional Council for Further Educn for the South-West, 1953-65. Gold Medal, Royal Astronomical Soc., 1969. *Publications:* papers on applied mathematics and geomagnetism in Philosophical Transactions and Proc. Royal Soc., Proc. London Maths Soc., Quarterly Jl Mech. and Applied Maths, etc. *Recreation:* gardening. *Address:* 23 Butlers Court Road, Beaconsfield, Bucks. *T:* Beaconsfield 6584.

**PRICE, Sir A(rchibald) Grenfell,** Kt 1963; CMG 1933; DLitt (Adelaide), MA (Oxon); FRGS; Chairman Council, National Library of Australia, since 1960; MHR for Boothby, S Australia, 1941-43; Master, St Mark's College, University of Adelaide, 1925-57; University Lecturer in Geography, 1949-57; *b* Adelaide, 28 Jan. 1892; *s* of Henry Archibald Price, Banker, and Elizabeth Jane Price; *m* Kitty Pauline, *d* of C. W. Hayward, Solicitor, Adelaide; two *s* one *d*. *Educ:* St Peter's College, Adelaide, Magdalen College, Oxford. Housemaster St Peter's College, Adelaide, 1922-24; Member of Council, University of Adelaide, 1926-63; Macrossan Lecturer, University of Queensland, 1930; Chairman of Emergency Committee of S Australia, 1931-32; Research Fellowship, Rockefeller Foundation, 1932-33; Chm. SA Libraries Inquiry, 1936; Chm. Adv. Bd, Commonwealth Literary Fund, 1952-; Hon. Sec. Australian Humanities Research Council, 1956-59, Hon. Treasurer, 1959-; Cttee for Libraries, Austr. Adv. Cttee for Unesco, 1964-. *Publications:* Causal Geography of World, 1918; South Australians and their Environment, 1921; The Foundation and Settlement of South Australia, 1924; (with Sir D. Stamp) Longmans' Geography of the World (Australasian edition), 1928; Founders and Pioneers of South Australia, 1929; History and Problems of Northern Territory, Australia, 1930; White Settlers in the Tropics, 1939; Australia Comes of Age, 1945; White Settlers and Native Peoples, 1949; The Explorations of Captain James Cook in the Pacific (New York), 1957 and 1958; The Winning of Australian Antarctica: Sir Douglas Mawson's BANZARE Voyages 1929-30, 1962; The Western Invasions of the Pacific and its Continents, 1963; The Importance of Disease in History (Syme Oration, RACS), 1964; The Challenge of New Guinea: Australian Aid to Papuan Progress, 1965; A History of St Mark's College, University of Adelaide, 1967; The Skies Remember: the story of Ross and Kieth Smith; Edited, The Humanities in Australia, 1959; contributed to Cambridge History of the British Empire. *Recreation:* fishing. *Address:* 32 Edwin Terrace, Gilberton, South Australia; University House, Canberra. *Clubs:* Adelaide (SA), Commonwealth (Canberra); Australasian Pioneers (Sydney).

**PRICE, (Arthur) Leolin,** QC 1968; *b* 11 May 1924; 3rd *s* of late Evan Price and Ceridwen Price (*née* Price), Hawkhurst, Kent; *m* 1963, Hon. Rosalind Helen Penrose Lewis, *er d* of 1st Baron Brecon, *qv*; one *s* two *d*. *Educ:* Judd Sch., Tonbridge; Keble Coll., Oxford (Schol.; MA). War service, 1943-46 with Army: Capt., RA; Adjt, Indian Mountain Artillery Trng Centre and Depot, Ambala, Punjab, 1946. Treas., Oxford Union, 1948; Chm., Oxford Univ. Conserv. Assoc., 1948. Tutor (part-time), Keble Coll., Oxford, 1951-59. Called to Bar, Middle Temple, 1949; Barrister of Lincoln's Inn, 1959. QC Bahamas, 1969. Member: Editorial Cttee, Modern Law Review, 1954-65; Bar Council Law Reform Cttee, 1969-. *Publications:* articles and notes in legal jls. *Address:* 32 Hampstead Grove, NW3. *T:* 01-435 9843; 10 Old Square, Lincoln's Inn, WC2. *T:* 01-405 0758. *Club:* Carlton.

**PRICE, Aubrey Joseph;** *b* 29 October 1899; *s* of Joseph and Louise Price; *m* Margaret, *y d* of Capt. J. Roberton Harvey, RN; one *s* (and one *s* decd). *Educ:* City of Oxford School; Jesus College, Oxford (Ewelme Exhibitioner, Honours School of Nat. Science). Housemaster, Denstone Coll.; Sen. Science Master, Berkhamsted Sch.; Officer Commanding OTC; Headmaster, St Peter's Sch., York; Headmaster: Wellington School, Somerset, 1938-45; Royal Hospital Sch., Holbrook, 1945-47; Principal, Wymondham Training College, Norfolk, 1947-50; Warden, London Univ. Goldsmiths' Coll., 1950-53; Principal, Chester College, 1953-65, retd. Lieut Royal Naval Air Service, 1917-19. *Address:* Long Close, Winterbourne Earls, Salisbury, Wilts.

**PRICE, (Benjamin) Terence;** Director of Planning and Development, Vickers Ltd, since 1971; *b* 7 January 1921; *er s* of Benjamin and Nellie Price; *m* 1947, Jean Stella Vidal; one *s* one *d*. *Educ:* Crypt School, Gloucester; Queens' College, Cambridge (Scholar). Joined staff of Admiralty Signal Establishment, 1942; transferred to staff of C-in-C East Indies, 1945. Brief period as music studio manager BBC, 1946. Joined Atomic Energy Research Establishment, Harwell (Nuclear Physics Division), 1947; transferred to Atomic Energy Establishment, Winfrith, as Head of Reactor Development Division, 1959; Chief Scientific Officer, Ministry of Defence, 1960-63; Assistant Chief Scientific Adviser (Studies), Ministry of Defence, 1963-65; Director, Defence Operational Analysis Establishment, MoD, 1965-68; Chief Scientific Adviser, Min. of Transport, 1968-70. *Publication:* (with K. T. Spinney and C. C. Horton) Radiation Shielding, 1957. *Recreations:* sailing, ski-ing, making music. *Address:* Seers Bough, Wilton Lane, Jordans, Buckinghamshire. *T:* Chalfont St Giles 4589. *Club:* Athenæum.

**PRICE, Byron,** KBE (Hon.) 1948; Medal for Merit, US, 1946; *b* Topeka, Indiana, 25 March 1891; *s* of John Price and Emaline Barnes; *m* 1920, Priscilla Alden; no *c*. *Educ:* Wabash College (AB). In newspaper work, 1909; exec. news editor Associated Press, 1937-41, actg gen. man., 1939; US Dir of Censorship, Dec. 1941-Nov. 1945; on special mission to Germany as personal rep. of President Truman, 1945. Vice-Pres. Motion Picture Assoc. of America; Chm. Bd Assoc. Motion Picture Producers; Pres. Central Casting Corp.; 1st Vice-Pres. Educnl Film Research Inst.; Dir Hollywood Coordinating Cttee, 1946-47; Assistant Secretary-Gen., Administrative and Financial Services, United Nations, 1947-54; retired 1954. Served as 1st Lt, later Capt., Inf., US Army, 1917-19. Special Pulitzer citation for creation and administration of press and broadcasting censorship codes, 1944; Director General, Press Congress of the World, Columbia, Mo., 1959. Holds several hon. degrees. *Address:* Chestertown, Maryland, USA. *Clubs:* National Press, Gridiron (Washington); Chester River Yacht and Country.

**PRICE, Maj.-Gen. Cedric Rhys,** CB 1951; CBE 1945 (OBE 1943); Principal Staff Officer to Secretary of State for Commonwealth Relations, 1959-64; ADC to the Queen, 1954-57; *b* 13 June 1905; *o s* of late Colonel Sir Rhys H. Price, KBE, CMG, Highlands, Purley Downs; *m* 1935, Rosamund, *e d* of late Arthur W. Clifford, Dursley, Glos; two *d*. *Educ:* Wellington College; RMA Woolwich; Trinity College, Cambridge. Commissioned Royal Engineers, 1925; served in India, 1932-38; Staff College, 1938-39; Military Assistant Secretary, offices of War Cabinet, 1940-46; Secretary, British Joint Services Mission, Washington, USA, 1946-48; Secretary, Chiefs of Staff Cttee, Ministry of Defence, 1948-50; student, Imperial Defence College, SW1, 1951; Chief of Staff to Chairman of British Joint Services Mission, Washington, 1952-54; Brigadier, General Staff, Eastern Command, 1955-56; Director of Military Intelligence, War Office, 1956-59. *Recreations:* golf, tennis, riding. *Address:* March House, Ogbourne St George, Wilts. *T:* Ogbourne St George 200. *Club:* Army and Navy.

**PRICE, Maj.-Gen. Charles Basil,** CB 1945; DSO 1919; DCM 1915; VD; CD and Bar; retired from active management Canadian business; *b* 12 Dec. 1889; *s* of Charles Edward Burman Price, ARCO, and Catherine Durham Rogers; *m* 1915, Marjorie Meredith Holden Trenholme; one *s* (and one *s* killed in 1942 while serving with RCAF) four *d*. *Educ:* Montreal High School; Ottawa Collegiate Institute. Entered Bank of Montreal, Montreal, as junior clerk, 1905; with firm Evans & Evans, Ltd (Manufacturers' Agents), 1910-24; joined Elmhurst Dairy Ltd as Managing Director, 1924; joined Victoria Rifles of Canada Non-Permanent Active Militia, 1905; served in Flanders, 1914-19, with Royal Montreal Regt as CSM, Lieut, Captain, Major; Command Royal Montreal Regt Non-Permanent Active Militia, 1920-24, 1927-29; commanded 12th Inf. Bde Non-Permanent Active Militia, 1931-34; Commanded Duke of York's Royal Canadian Hussars, Non-Permanent Active Militia, Jan.-Oct. 1939; Command 3rd Inf. Bde Canadian Active Service Force, Sept. 1939; GOC 3rd Canadian Div. 1941; seconded to Canadian Red Cross Society as Overseas Commissioner, 1942; demobilised, 1945. President Canadian Club of Montreal, 1935-36; President Montreal Military Institute, 1937-38. Dominion President Canadian Legion, British Empire Service League, 1946-48 (Hon. Pres. 1948-61); Pres. Montreal Branch Royal Empire Society, 1946-49; Hon. Col Royal Montreal Regt, 1943-56; Hon. Col Comdt, Royal Canadian Infantry Corps, 1956-61. Patron, Montreal Br., Royal Commonwealth Soc., 1957-; Hon. Pres. Royal Canadian Legion, 1962-. Centennial Medal, 1967. *Recreation:* gardening. *Address:* Fayremead, Knowlton, PQ, Canada. *T:* Knowlton 243-6629. *Club:* United Services (Montreal).

**PRICE, Sir Charles (Keith Napier) Rugge-,** 9th Bt *cr* 1804; Section Head, Special Projects, Domtar Ltd; *b* 7 August, 1936; *s* of Lt-Col Sir Charles James Napier Rugge-Price, 8th Bt, and of Lady (Maeve Marguerite) Rugge-Price (*née* de la Peña); *S* father, 1966; *m* 1965, Jacqueline Mary (*née* Loranger); two *s*. *Educ:* Middleton College, Eire. 5th Regt Royal Horse Artillery, Germany and Wales, 1954-59. Actuarial Dept, William Mercers Ltd, Canada, 1959-60; Alexander and Alexander Services Ltd, Montreal, Canada, 1960-67; with Domtar Ltd, 1968-. *Heir: s* James Keith Peter Rugge-Price, *b* 8 April 1967. *Address:* 1525 Baker Street, Chambly, PQ, Canada. *T:* 514-658-6416.

**PRICE, Sir (Charles) Roy,** KCMG 1950 (CMG 1942); *b* 1 May 1893; *s* of late W. Sydney Price, Wellington, Somerset; *m* 1947, Nora Sara, *o d* of late Alexander Henderson, Edinburgh. *Educ:* Wellington School, Somerset; Univ. Coll., London. Unattached List TF 1915; Royal Garrison Artillery, 1915-18; served in France, 1916-18; entered Colonial Office, 1921; transferred to Dominions Office, 1925; Assistant Secretary, Imperial Wireless and Cable Conference, 1928; on Staff of UK Delegation to London Naval Conference, 1930, to Disarmament Conference, 1932-34, and to League of Nations Assembly, 1928, 1932-34, and 1939; Joint Secretary, Oversea Settlement Board, 1937-39; Assistant Secretary, Dominions Office, 1939; Deputy High Commissioner for UK in Union of South Africa, 1940-42; Deputy High Commissioner for UK in Australia, 1948-49; High Commissioner for UK in New Zealand, 1949-53. Fellow of University College, London. *Address:* c/o Lloyds Bank Ltd, 6 Pall Mall, SW1.

**PRICE, Christopher;** Education Correspondent, New Statesman; *b* 26 Jan. 1932; *s* of Stanley Price; *m* 1956, Annie Grierson Ross; two *s* one *d.* *Educ:* Leeds Grammar School; Queen's College, Oxford. Sec., Oxford Univ. Labour Club, 1953; Chm., Nat. Assoc. of Labour Student Organisations, 1955-56. Sheffield City Councillor, 1962-66; Dep. Chm., Sheffield Educn Cttee, MP (Lab) Perry Bar Division of Birmingham, 1966-70; PPS to Secretary of State for Education and Science, 1966-67. Editor, New Education, 1967-68. *Publications:* (Contrib.) A Radical Future, 1967; Crisis in the Classroom, 1968; articles in Socialist Commentary. *Address:* 96 Dovercourt Road, SE22. *T:* 01-693 8474.

**PRICE, Maj.-Gen. David;** *see* Price, Maj.-Gen. M. D.

**PRICE, David (Ernest Campbell),** MP (C) Eastleigh Division of Hampshire since 1955; Parliamentary Secretary, Ministry of Aviation Supply, since Oct. 1970; *b* 20 Nov. 1924; *o s* of Major Villiers Price; *m* 1960, Rosemary Eugénie Evelyn, *o d* of late Cyril F. Johnston, OBE; one *d.* *Educ:* Eton; Trinity College, Cambridge; Yale University, USA; Rosebery Schol., Eton; Open History Schol., Trinity College, Cambridge. Served with 1st Battalion Scots Guards, CMF; subsequently Staff Captain (Intelligence) HQ, 56 London Div., Trieste, 1942-46. Trin. Coll., Cambridge, BA Hons, MA. Pres. Cambridge Union; Vice-Pres. Fedn of Univ. Conservative and Unionist Assocs, 1946-48; Henry Fellow of Yale Univ., USA, 1948-49. Industrial Economist. Held various appts in Imperial Chemical Industries Ltd, 1949-62. Parly Sec., Board of Trade, 1962-64. Opposition Front-Bench spokesman on Science and Technology, 1964-70; Vice-Chm., Parly and Scientific Cttee, 1965-70, subseq. Vice-Pres. Parly Sec., Min. of Technology, June-Oct. 1970. British Representative to Consultative Assembly of the Council of Europe, 1958-61. Director, Assoc. British Maltsters, 1966-70. Governor, Middlesex Hospital, 1956-60. *Recreations:* cricket, walking, cooking. *Address:* 36 Sloane Court West, SW3. *T:* 01-730 3326. *Club:* Beefsteak.

**PRICE, Dennis;** Actor, since 1936; *b* 23 June 1915; *s* of Brig.-Gen. T. Rose Price and Mrs Dorothy Rose Price; *m* 1939, Joan Schofield; two *d.* *Educ:* Radley College, Berks; Worcester College, Oxford. Actor: Croydon and Oxford Repertory Theatres; appearances in several London theatre productions, also in USA. Has had numerous parts in films, and in television plays and programmes. *Recreation:* riding. *Address:* c/o The William Morris Agency, 4 Savile Row, W1. *Club:* Lord's Taverners.

**PRICE, Rt. Rev. Dudley William Mackay,** OSB, MA; Headmaster, Ampleforth Preparatory School, since 1966; Titular Abbot of St Mary's, York, since 1969; *b* 19 July 1899; 2nd and *e surv s* of late Sir Charles W. M. Price, DL. *Educ:* Radley College; Corpus Christi College, Oxford. History Scholar, 1917. Served European War, 1918-19, in France as 2nd Lt, Queen's Roy. Regt; called to Bar, Lincoln's Inn, 1923; South Wales Circuit, 1923-25; Director and Legal Adv., British-American Tobacco Co. (China) Ltd, and associated companies in Shanghai, 1925-33; entered Benedictine Order at Ampleforth Abbey, 1933; Priest, 1940; Senior History Master, 1943. House Master, 1951, Headmaster, 1954-64, Ampleforth College. *Address:* Gilling Castle, Gilling East, York. *T:* Ampleforth 328.

**PRICE, (Edith) Mary,** CBE 1956; Senior Land Registrar, HM Land Registry, 1953-58; *b* 14 Nov. 1897; *d* of late William Arthur Price and Edith Octavia, *d* of late William Smoult Playfair. *Educ:* Central Newcastle High School; Girton College, Cambridge. Post-Graduate Scholar, Bryn-Mawr College, Pennsylvania, USA, 1919-20; Social and Police Work in Boston and Detroit, USA, 1920-22. Called to the Bar, 1924; Member of the Inner Temple. *Address:* The Keeper's Cottage, Whitchurch Hill, Oxfordshire. *Club:* Voluntary Aid Detachment Ladies'.

**PRICE, Sir Frank (Leslie),** Kt 1966; DL; Chairman, Birmingham & Midland Investments Ltd; Chairman: Telford New Town Corporation, since 1968; British Waterways Board, since 1968; *b* 26 July 1922; *s* of G. F. Price; *m* 1944, Maisie Edna, *d* of Albert Davis, Handsworth; one *s.* *Educ:* St Matthias Church Sch., Birmingham; Vittoria Street Arts Sch. Elected to Birmingham City Coun., 1949; Alderman, 1958; Lord Mayor, 1964-65. Formerly Man. Dir, Murrayfield Real Estate Co.; Chm., W Midlands Sports Coun., 1965-69; Mem. W Midlands Economic Planning Coun.; Founder/Chm. Midlands Art Centre for Young People; Chm., Minister of Transport's Cttee on Roads in W Midlands Conurbation; Member: Council, Town and Country Planning Assoc.; Minister of Transport's Cttee of Inquiry into Major Ports, 1961; Court of Governors, Birmingham Univ.; Planning Cttee, Aston Univ. Fellow, Soc. of Valuers and Auctioneers; MInstT. DL Warwickshire, 1970. *Recreations:* painting, golf, inland cruising. *Address:* 50 Arthur Road, Edgbaston, Birmingham. *Club:* Reform.

**PRICE, Gwilym Ivor;** Chairman and Managing Director, Unigate Ltd, 1960-70; Chairman and Managing Director, United Dairies Ltd, since 1959; *b* 2 Oct. 1899; *er s* of late Sir William Price; *m* 1st, 1927, Nancye Freeman (*d* 1957); two *s*; 2nd, 1958, Margaret Ryrie Greaves. *Educ:* St Paul's School; Magdalene College, Cambridge. Served European War, 1914-18 in Army; commissioned. Director of United Dairies Ltd, 1931; Managing Director, 1936. *Address:* Ryrie Cottage, Coleshill, Bucks.

**PRICE, Henry Alfred,** CBE 1962; Managing Director of Price Topley & Co. Ltd, paper merchants; *b* 3 January 1911; *s* of James Wm and Louisa Rebecca Price; *m* 1938, Ivy May Trimmer; one *s* one *d.* *Educ:* Holloway County School. Joined paper trade, 1927. Member LCC, 1946-52; MP (C) West Lewisham, 1950-64. *Recreations:* music and sport. *Address:* 22 Cator Road, Sydenham, SE26. *T:* 01-778 3838.

**PRICE, Henry Habberley,** FBA 1943; MA, BSc; Professor Emeritus, University of Oxford, and Honorary Fellow of New College; *b* 1899; *s* of H. H. Price; unmarried. *Educ:* Winchester College; New College, Oxford (Scholar). Served in Royal Air Force, 1917-19; 1st Class in Lit. Hum. 1921; Fellow of Magdalen College, 1922-24; Assistant lecturer at Liverpool University, 1922-23; Fellow and Lecturer in Philosophy at Trin. Coll., 1924-35; Univ. Lectr in Philosophy, 1932-35; Wykeham Prof. of Logic, and Fell. New Coll., 1935-59. Pres. of Soc. for Psychical Research, 1939-40 and 1960-61. Visiting Professor at Princeton University, USA, 1948; Gifford Lecturer, Aberdeen University, 1959-60; Flint Visiting Prof., Univ. of California, Los Angeles, 1962; Boutwood Lecturer, Cambridge, 1965; Sarum Lectr, Oxford, 1970-71. Hon. DLitt, Dublin,

1953; Hon. LLD, St Andrews, 1954; Hon DLitt, Univ. of Wales, 1964. *Publications:* Perception; Hume's Theory of the External World; Thinking and Experience; Belief (Gifford Lectures); articles in Proc. Aristotelian Society and other philosophical periodicals. *Recreations:* aviation, painting and ornithology. Founder-member of Oxford University and City Gliding Club. *Address:* Hillside, Headington Hill, Oxford. *T:* Oxford 62988. *Club:* Royal Aero.

**PRICE, Herbert Spencer,** CBE 1956 (OBE 1946); Chief Constable of Bradford, 1940-57; *b* 19 Oct. 1892; *s* of Charles and Ann Price; *m* 1918, Florence (*d* 1948), *d* of Robert and Appaline Butterworth; one *s*. *Educ:* Skerton Council School; Storey Institute, Lancaster. Constable, Bradford, 1912; promoted through the ranks to Chief Constable; retired, Nov. 1957. King's Police Medal, 1951. *Address:* 421 Halifax Rd, Bradford. *T:* Bradford 676615.

**PRICE, Ven. Hetley;** *see* Price, Ven. S. H.

**PRICE, Very Rev. Hilary Martin Connop;** Rector and Provost of Chelmsford since 1967; *b* 1912; *s* of late Rev. Connop Lewis Price and late Shirley (*née* Lewis); *m* 1939, Dorothea (*née* Beaty-Pownall); one *s* two *d*. *Educ:* Cheltenham Coll.; Queens' Coll., Cambridge (MA); Ridley Hall, Cambridge. Asst Curate, St Peter's, Hersham, Surrey, 1936-40; Sen. Chaplain, Portsmouth Cathedral, 1940-41; Asst Curate, Holy Trinity, Cambridge, 1941-46; Chaplain, RAFVR, 1943-46; Vicar, St Gabriel's, Bishopwearmouth, 1946-56; Rector and Rural Dean, Newcastle-under-Lyme, 1956-67. Prebendary of Lichfield, 1964-67. Proctor in Convocation: of York for Durham Dio., 1954-56; of Canterbury for Lichfield Dio., 1962-67. *Address:* Provost's House, 7 Southborough Road, Chelmsford, Essex. *T:* 54530.

**PRICE, Comdr Hugh Perceval,** DSO 1940; OBE 1945; RN retired; Hydrographic Surveyor; *b* 19 May 1901; *s* of late Lt-Col Ivon Henry Price, DSO, LLD, Asst Insp.-Gen., Royal Irish Constabulary, and May Emily Kinahan; *m* 1925, Annie Grant Berry; one *s* one *d*. *Educ:* Monkstown Park School, Co. Dublin; Chesterfield School, Birr; RN Colleges, Osborne and Dartmouth. Entered RNC Osborne, 1915; HMS King George V, 1917; joined Surveying Service in 1925; employed on escort work and Hydrographic duties during war of 1939-45; retired list, 1946. *Recreation:* fishing. *Address:* 55 Tudor Avenue, Worcester Park, Surrey. *T:* 01-337 8966.

**PRICE, John Lister Willis,** CVO 1965; Counsellor, HM Diplomatic Service; Director of Information, NATO, since Dec. 1967; *b* 25 July 1915; *s* of Canon John Willis Price, Croughton, Brackley, Northants; *m* 1940, Frances Holland; one *s* one *d*. *Educ:* Bradfield; New College, Oxford. Military Service, 1940-46 (despatches), Lt-Col. Joined Foreign Office News Dept, 1946; apptd First Secretary, Paris, 1950; transf. to FO, 1952; to Sofia, 1956; FO, 1959; Head of British Information Services, Bonn, 1962-66; IDC 1967. *Recreations:* ski-ing, tennis. *Address:* 48 Avenue Prince Baudouin, Brussels 15. *Clubs:* Reform, Overseas, Ski Club of Gt Britain.

**PRICE, John Playfair;** *b* 4 July 1905; *s* of William Arthur Price and Edith Octavia Playfair; *m* 1932, Alice Elizabeth Kendall, Boston, Mass; two *d*. *Educ:* Gresham School; New College, Oxford. Hon. Exhib., New Coll., Oxford; Pres. Oxford Union Society. Diplomatic and Consular posts at Peking, Nanking, Tientsin, Canton, Chinkiang, Harbin (Manchuria), Katmandu (Nepal), Gangtok (Sikkim), Los Angeles, Kansas City, Tunis, Tangier, Lisbon, Santiago (Chile), and Geneva. Additional Judge, China, 1933-37; Foreign Office, 1938; 1st Secretary of Embassy, 1943; Consul-General for Khorasan, Sistan and Persian Baluchistan, 1948; retired from Foreign Service, 1950. Civil Service and Foreign Service Selection and Final Selection Boards, 1950; Dir and Chm. of Exec., Central African Rhodes Centenary Exhibition, 1951-52. *Address:* San Luis, Minorca, Spain.

**PRICE, (Joseph) Thomas;** MP (Lab) Westhoughton Division of Lancashire since June 1951; *b* Pendlebury, Lancs, 9 Oct. 1902; *e s* of William and Elizabeth Price; *m* 1933, Muriel Anna Wilcock; one *s* one *d*. *Educ:* St Peter's, Swinton; Salford Grammar School. Central Administration Staff, Distributive Workers Union (USDAW), 1921-51; Chief Legal Officer; Council Member, Association of Superannuation and Pension Funds, 1937-68; sometime secretary and treasurer, Labour Party organisation in Eccles Div. of Lancashire. Opposition Whip, 1953-64. *Publications:* numerous press articles and pamphlets. *Address:* House of Commons, SW1. *T:* Sale 5248.

**PRICE, Leolin;** *see* Price, A. L.

**PRICE, Leontyne;** Opera Prima Donna (Soprano); United States. *Educ:* Public Schools, Laurel, Mississippi; Central State College, Wilberforce, Ohio. Four Saints, 1952; Porgy and Bess, 1952-54. Operatic Debut on TV, 1955, as Tosca; Concerts in America, England, Australia, Europe. Operatic debut as Madame Lidouine in Dialogues of Carmelites, San Francisco, 1957; Covent Garden, Verona Arena, Vienna Staatsoper, 1958; Leonora in Il Trovatore, five rôles in Madame Butterfly, Donna Anna in Don Giovanni, Metropolitan, 1960-61; Salzburg debut singing soprano lead in Missa Solemnis, 1959; Aida in Aida, Liu in Turandot, La Scala, 1960; opened season at Metropolitan in 1961 as Minnie in Fanciulla del West; opened new Metropolitan Opera House, 1966, as Cleopatra in world premiere of Samuel Barber's Antony and Cleopatra; debut Teatre Dell'Opera, Rome, in Aida, 1967; debut Paris Opera, in Aida, 1968; debut Teatro Colon, Buenos Aires, as Leonora in Il Trovatore, 1969; opened season at Metropolitan Opera, in Aida, 1969. Has appeared on TV. Numerous recordings. Fellow, Amer. Acad. of Arts and Sciences. Hon. Dr of Music: Howard Univ., Washington, DC, 1962; Central State Coll., Wilberforce, Ohio, 1968; Hon. DHL, Dartmouth Univ., 1962; Hon. Dr of Humanities, Rust Coll., Holly Springs, Miss, 1968; Hon. Dr of Humane Letters, Fordham Univ., New York, 1969. Hon. Mem. Bd of Dirs, Campfire Girls, 1966. Presidential Medal of Freedom, 1966; Spingarn Medal, NAACP, 1965. Order of Merit (Italy), 1966. *Recreations:* cooking, dancing, shopping for clothes, etc, antiques for homes in Rome and New York. *Address:* 1133 Broadway (Suite 603), New York City, NY 10010, USA. *T:* Chelsea 3-0476.

**PRICE, (Llewelyn) Ralph;** Chairman, Honeywell Ltd; Vice-President, Honeywell Inc., USA; *b* 23 Oct. 1912; *s* of late L. D. Price, schoolmaster, and late Lena (*née* Dixon); *m* 1939, Vera Patricia Harrison; one *s* two *d*. *Educ:* Quarry Bank Sch., Liverpool. Chartered Accountant student, 1930-35; Sec. to Honeywell Ltd, 1936; Cost Investigator, Min. of Supply, 1943-46; private practice, 1946; Dir of Manufacturing (Scotland), Honeywell Ltd, 1947; Financial Dir, Honeywell, UK and

Europe, 1957; Dir, Computor Div., Honeywell, 1960; Managing Dir, Honeywell Ltd, 1965. Mem. Cttee, European League for Economic Co-operation; Mem. Council, Elec. Eng. Assoc. *Recreations:* golf, bridge, music. *Address:* Oakengates, Sandisplatt Road, Maidenhead, Berks. *T:* Maidenhead 28270. *Clubs:* Royal Automobile, Lansdowne; Temple Golf (Maidenhead); Stoke Poges Golf.

**PRICE, Mary;** *see* Price, E. M.

**PRICE, Maj.-Gen. (Maurice) David,** CB 1970; OBE 1956; *b* 13 Feb. 1915; *s* of Edward Allan Price and Edna Marion Price (*née* Turner); *m* 1938, Ella Lacy, *d* of H. L. Day; two *s* two *d*. *Educ:* Marlborough; RMA, Woolwich. 2nd Lt R Signals, 1935; POW, Singapore, 1942-45; Instructor, RMA, Sandhurst, 1946-49; GSO2, Staff College, 1949-51; AQMG, British Troops Egypt, 1954-56; Lt-Col 1955; Comdr, R Signals, 3 Div., 1956-59; Col 1961; Col GS, WO, 1959-61; Army Staff, Washington, 1961-63; Brig. 1965; Chief Signal Officer, Eastern Command, 1963-66; Director of Administrative Plans (Army) MoD, 1966-67; Vice-Quartermaster-Gen., MoD (Army), 1967-70. Col Comdt, Royal Corps of Signals, 1967-. *Recreation:* fishing. *Address:* The Cross, Chilmark, Salisbury, Wiltshire. *T:* Teffont 212. *Club:* Army and Navy.

**PRICE, Morgan Philips,** MA; JP; FRGS; landowner and farmer, Taynton, Glos; *b* Hillfield, Gloucester, 29 Jan. 1885; *s* of Major William Edwin Price, of Tibberton, landowner, MP Tewkesbury (1868-80), and Margaret, 2nd *d* of Robert Needham Philips, merchant, The Park, Prestwich, Manchester, MP Bury; *m* 1919, Elisa, *d* of Friedrich Balster, Halberstadt, Germany; one *s* one *d*. *Educ:* Harrow; Trinity College, Cambridge (Hons Science). Travelled in Central Asia, Siberia, Persia, Turkey, 1908-14; Liberal Candidate for Gloucester (City), 1911-14; correspondent of Manchester Guardian in Russia, 1914-18; joined ILP and Labour Party, 1919; correspondent of Daily Herald in Berlin, 1919-23; Parliamentary Labour Candidate for Gloucester (City), General Elections, 1922, 1923, and 1924; MP (Lab) Whitehaven Div. of Cumberland, 1929-31; Forest of Dean Div. of Glos, 1935-50; West Div. of Glos, 1950-59; PPS to Sir Charles Trevelyan, 1929-31; Forestry Commissioner 1942-45; Parliamentary Charity Comr, 1945-50. *Publications:* Siberia, 1912; Diplomatic History of the War, 1914; War and Revolution in Asiatic Russia, 1918; My Reminiscences of the Russian Revolution, 1918; Germany in Transition, 1923; Economic Problems of Europe, 1928; America after sixty years, 1936; Hitler's War and Eastern Europe, 1940; Russia through the Centuries, 1943; Russia Red or White, 1947; Through the Iron-Laced Curtain, 1949; A History of Turkey, 1956; Russia, Forty Years On, 1961; My Three Revolutions, 1969. *Recreations:* walking, shooting, hunting, study of agriculture and forestry. *Address:* The Grove, Taynton, near Gloucester. *T:* Tibberton 200. *Club:* Reform.

**PRICE, Norman Charles,** CB 1969; Deputy Chairman, Board of Inland Revenue since 1968; *b* 5 Jan. 1915; *s* of Charles William and Ethel Mary Price; *m* 1940, Kathleen Beatrice (*née* Elston); two *d*. *Educ:* Plaistow Grammar School. Entered Civil Service as Executive Officer, Customs and Excise, 1933; Inspector of Taxes, Inland Revenue, 1939; Secretaries' Office, Inland Revenue, 1951; Board of Inland Revenue, 1965. *Recreations:* music, history. *Address:* 3 Speed House, Barbican, EC2. *T:* 01-628 0369.

**PRICE, Norman Stewart,** CMG 1959; OBE 1946; *b* 9 Aug. 1907; *s* of late Lt-Col Ivon Henry Price, DSO, LLD, Asst Inspr-Gen., RIC, and May Emily (*née* Kinahan), Greystones, Ireland; *m* 1933, Rosalind Evelyn Noelle (*née* Ormsby); two *d*. *Educ:* Portora Royal School, Enniskillen; Exeter Sch.; Trinity Coll., Dublin. LLB 1929, BA Hons 1930. Cadet, Northern Rhodesia, 1930, District Officer, 1932, Provincial Comr, Northern Rhodesia, 1951-59; retired, 1959. Coronation Medal, 1953. *Recreations:* gardening; Captain Dublin University Harriers and Athletic Club, 1928-29; Half-Blue Oxford University Cross Country, 1929. *Address:* Overton 6 Wavell Road, Highlands, Salisbury, Rhodesia. *T:* Salisbury 46350.

**PRICE, Peter S.;** *see* Stanley Price.

**PRICE, Ralph;** *see* Price, L. R.

**PRICE, Sir Robert (John) G.;** *see* Green-Price.

**PRICE, Very Rev. Robert Peel;** Priest-in-charge, St Swithun's, Bournemouth, since 1968; Chaplain to the Queen since 1957; *b* 18 Sept. 1905. *Educ:* Dover College; Wadham College, Oxford (MA); Wells Theological College. Deacon, 1930; Priest, 1931; Curate of: Wimbledon, 1930-34; St Martin, Knowle, 1934-40; Cheam (in charge of St Oswald's), 1940-42; St Peter's, Bournemouth, 1942-45; Vicar of Christchurch with Mudeford, Diocese of Winchester, 1945-61; Hon. Canon of Winchester, 1950-61; Dean of Hereford, 1961-68, now Emeritus. *Address:* 1 Gervis Road, Bournemouth, Hants.

**PRICE, Brig. Rollo Edward Crwys,** CBE 1967; DSO 1961; *b* 6 April 1916; *s* of Eardley Edward Carnac Price, CIE; *m* 1945, Diana Budden; three *d*. *Educ:* Canford; RMC Sandhurst. Commissioned 2nd Lt in S Wales Borderers, 1936; War Service, Middle East and Italy, 1939-45; Lt-Col and seconded for service with Queen's Own Nigeria Regt, 1959-61; Col 1962; Comdr 160 Inf. Bde, 1964-67; Brig. 1966; Comdr, British Troops, Malta, 1968-69, retired. *Address:* The Old Rectory, Closworth, near Yeovil, Somerset. *T:* Yetminster 377. *Clubs:* United Service; Union (Malta).

**PRICE, Sir Rose (Francis),** 6th Bt, *cr* 1815; *b* 15 March 1910; *e s* of Sir Francis Price, 5th Bt, and Marjorie (*d* 1955), *d* of Sir W. Russell Russell, Hawkes Bay, NZ; *S* father, 1949; *m* 1949, Kathleen June, *yr d* of Norman W. Hutchinson, Melbourne, Australia; two *s*. *Educ:* Wellington; Trinity College, Cambridge. BA 1931. Served War of 1939-45, Capt. 4/11th Sikh Regt, 1940-45. *Heir: s* Francis Caradoc Rose Price, *b* 9 Sept. 1950. *Address:* Netherwood, Grays Park Road, Stoke Poges, Bucks. *Club:* Carlton.

**PRICE, Sir Roy;** *see* Price, Sir (Charles) R.

**PRICE, Ven. (Stuart) Hetley;** Archdeacon of Manchester since 1966; *b* 14 June 1922; *s* of F. L. Price, Loughborough; *m* 1952, Pamela Mary Cooper; one *s* one *d*. *Educ:* Loughborough Gram. Sch.; Corpus Christi Coll., Cambridge; Westcott House, Cambridge. Asst Curate, St Michael and All Angels, Bournemouth, 1945-48; Domestic Chaplain to Bp of Manchester, 1948-52; Asst Gen. Sec., SCM and Asst Curate, St Luke, Chelsea, 1952-55; Rector, Emmanuel Church, Didsbury, 1955-60; Residentiary Canon, Manchester Cathedral, 1960-. *Publication:* (with G. S. Wakefield) Unity at the Local Level, 1964. *Address:* 30

Rathen Road, Withington, Manchester M20 9GH. *T:* 061-445 4703. *Club:* Old Rectory (Manchester).

**PRICE, Terence;** *see* Price, B. T.

**PRICE, Thomas;** *see* Price, J. T.

**PRICE, Brig. Thomas Reginald,** DSO 1917; MC; *b* Woburn Sands, 15 Sept. 1894; *s* of Rev. T. J. Price, BA; *m* 1st, 1931, Christian Farquharson Gordon (*d* 1960), *yr d* of James Leask and Mrs M. E. Fraser; 2nd, 1969, Gwendolen, *e d* of C. S. Wicks. *Educ:* Kingswood School, Bath. Special Reserve Com. Northants Regt, 1915; Lt regular army, 1916; Captain 1923; Major, 1935; Lt-Col 1941; Brig. 1941; Royal Tank Corps, 1917; served in France, 1915-18 (DSO, MC 1917, bar to MC 1918, despatches thrice, wounded Loos, 1915. Somme, 1917, and German advance, 1918); in Nigeria, 1921-32; Lt-Col Commanding 1st Bn Nigeria Regiment, 1931-32; served War of 1939-45: Commandant Gold Coast, 1940; Commanded 31st Tank Bde, 1941-42; Commanded 1st Tank Bde, 1942-44; Brig. General Staff, Washington, 1945-48. *Recreations:* all outdoor games and sports. *Address:* Old Timbers, Dora's Green Lane, Dippenhall, Farnham, Surrey. *Club:* Naval and Military.

**PRICE, Major Vincent Walter,** QC 1933; MA; Barrister-at-Law, Price, Barrett, Mills, Finlayson, and Hollyer, Toronto; Past National President, United Nations Association in Canada; Director of several Canadian Companies including: A. R. Clarke & Co. Ltd (President and Director); Rennie Seeds Ltd; Breithampt Leather Co. Ltd (Chairman and Chief Executive Officer); W. B. Dack Ltd; Past Vice–President, World Federation, UNA; *b* 22 Aug. 1890; *s* of Rev. William Frederick and Sarah Penwarden Price; *m* 1924, Ruth Jeanette, *d* of late George Johnson Green and Laura Lawson Green, McAdam, New Brunswick; one *d*. *Educ:* McMaster University; Osgoode Hall, Toronto. Lecturer, Woodstock College, Woodstock, 1911-12; Master, Appleby School, Oakville, 1913-14; served Overseas with Canadian Expeditionary Force, 1915-18, rank of Lieutenant and Captain and Acting Adjutant, 123rd Battalion Royal Grenadiers, and Captain and Adjutant 4th Battalion Canadian Engineers (despatches twice), served with Royal Grenadiers, Toronto, 1920-27, and as Major, 2nd i/c Royal Regt of Canada (2nd Bn), 1940-44, now Major, Reserve; called to Bar of Ontario, 1920. President: English-Speaking Union of British Empire (Ontario Branch), 1932-47; UNA (Toronto Branch), 1945-47; Member National Executive UN Assoc. in Canada (Chm. 1947-48); Nat. Pres. Alliance Canadienne (AC-CA), 1957-58; Former Nat. Chm., Canadian Council for Reconstruction through UNESCO; Canadian Deleg. to 11th Gen. Conf. of UNESCO, Paris, 1960. Coronation Medal, 1937. *Publication:* Canada and World Security, 1945. *Recreations:* riding, fishing. *Address:* The Park Lane, Apt 303, 110 St Clair Avenue, W, Toronto 7, Canada. *T:* 924-3515; Wishwood Farm, Box 104, Rockwood, Ont. *T:* 856-9973. *Clubs:* University, Empire, Royal Canadian Military Institute also Cricket, Skating and Curling (Hon. Life Mem.) (Toronto).

**PRICE, Willard De Mille;** writer, editor; *b* Peterboro, Ontario, Canada, 28 July 1887; *s* of Albert Melancthon Price, and Estella Martin; *m* 1st, 1914, Eugenia Reeve (*d* 1929), Willoughby, Ohio; one *s*; 2nd, 1932, Mary Selden, New York. To United States, 1901; BA, Western Reserve Univ., Cleveland, Ohio, 1909; studied New York School of Philanthropy, 1911-12; MA, Columbia University, 1914; studied Journalism New York Univ. and Columbia; editorial staff, The Survey, New York, 1912-13; editoral secretary Board of Foreign Missions, Methodist Episcopal Church, 1915-19; editor World Outlook; manager of publication of Everyland and La Nueva Democracia; director periodical department of Interchurch World Movement and supervising editor various class and travel publications; Travel in 120 countries, particularly on expeditions for National Geographic Society and American Museum of Natural History, 1920-67. *Publications: books:* Ancient Peoples at New Tasks; The Negro Around the World; Study of American Influence in the Orient; Pacific Adventure; Rip Tide in the South Seas; Where Are You Going, Japan?; Children of the Rising Sun; Japan Reaches Out; Barbarian (a novel); Japan Rides the Tiger; Japan's Islands of Mystery; The Son of Heaven; Key to Japan; Roving South; Tropic Adventure; Amazon Adventure; I Cannot Rest from Travel; The Amazing Amazon; Journey by Junk; Underwater Adventure; Adventures in Paradise; Volcano Adventure; Innocents in Britain; Whale Adventure; Incredible Africa; African Adventure; The Amazing Mississippi; Elephant Adventure; Rivers I Have Known; America's Paradise Lost; Safari Adventure; Lion Adventure; Gorilla Adventure; Odd Way Round the World; Diving Adventure; The Japanese Miracle; contrib. to Spectator, Daily Telegraph, Saturday Evening Post, Encyc. Brit., etc. *Address:* 625 Verbena Lane, Cathedral City, California 92234, USA.

**PRICE, Prof. William Charles,** FRS 1959; Professor of Physics, University of London, at King's College, since 1955; *b* 1 April 1909; *s* of Richard Price and Florence Margaret (*née* Charles); *m* 1939, Nest Myra Davies; one *s* one *d*. *Educ:* Swansea Grammar Sch.; University of Wales (Swansea); Johns Hopkins University, Baltimore; Trinity Coll., Cambridge. BSc (Wales) 1930; Commonwealth Fellow, 1932; PhD (Johns Hopkins), 1934; Cambridge: Senior 1851 Exhibitioner, 1935, University Demonstrator, 1937-43, PhD (Cantab) 1937. Prize Fellow, Trinity Coll., 1938; ScD (Cantab) 1949; Meldola Medal of Inst. of Chem., 1938; Senior Spectroscopist, ICI (Billingham Div.), 1943-48; Research Associate, University of Chicago, 1946-47; Reader in Physics, University of London (King's Coll.) 1948. FKC 1970. FRIC 1944; FIP 1950. Co-editor, British Bulletin of Spectroscopy, 1950-. Hon. DSc Wales, 1970. *Publications:* research and review articles on physics and chemistry in scientific journals. *Address:* 38 Cross Way, Petts Wood, Kent. *T:* (King's College) 01-836 5454.

**PRICE, William George,** MP (Lab) Rugby Division of Warwickshire, since 1966; *b* 15 June 1934; *s* of George and Lillian Price; *m* 1963, Joy Thomas; one *s*. *Educ:* Forest of Dene Technical Coll.; Gloucester Technical Coll. Staff Journalist: Three Forest Newspapers, Cinderford, until 1959; Coventry Evening Telegraph, 1959-62; Birmingham Post & Mail, 1962-66. PPS to Sec. of State for Educn and Science, 1968-70. *Recreation:* sport. *Address:* Forestdene, Main Street, Frankton, Rugby. *T:* Marton 641.

**PRICE, William James,** CMG 1943; MInstCE; *b* 1884; *m* 1915, Margaret Restarick; one *s* one *d*. Ceylon PWD 1909-43; was Director of Public Works and Civil Aviation, Ceylon; retired, 1943. *Address:* Holcombe Hotel, 92 Heene Road, Worthing, Sussex.

**PRICE, William Thomas,** CBE 1960; MC 1917; BSc, FIAgrE; Principal, Harper Adams Agricultural College, Shropshire, 1946-62, retired 1962; *b* 15 Nov. 1895; *m* 1923, Fanny Louise (*d* 1964), *d* of Philip T. Dale, Stafford; no *c*; *m* 1965, Mrs Beryl E. Drew, *d* of T. W. Tayler, Northleach, Glos. *Educ:* Christ Coll., London; Reading Univ. Served European War, 1915-18, Royal Warwickshire Regt, RFC and RAF with rank of Captain. Lecturer in Dairy Husbandry, Staffordshire Farm Institute, 1920-22; Lecturer in Estate Management, Harper Adams Agricultural Coll., 1922-24; Wiltshire County Council: Lecturer in Agriculture, 1924-26; Organiser of Agricultural Education, 1926-46. Chief Exec. Officer, Wilts WAEC, 1939-46. President Shropshire and W Midland Agric. Society, 1963. David Black Award, 1961 (for greatest contrib. to British pig industry). Lecturer and broadcaster on agriculture. *Publications:* Wiltshire Agricultural Advisory Reports, 1939; The Housing of the Pig, 1953. Editor, The Pig, 1961; various articles on agricultural subjects. *Recreations:* fishing and travel. *Address:* Hambledon House, Park Road, Leamington Spa, Warwicks. *T:* Leamington Spa 24709. *Club:* Farmers'.

**PRICE THOMAS, Sir Clement,** KCVO, 1951; LLD; Hon. FRSocMed (1960); Hon. FACS; Hon. FRCSI; Hon. FRCSE; Honorary Consulting Surgeon to Westminster Hospital; Joint-Lecturer in Surgery at Westminster Hospital Medical School; Hon. Consulting Surgeon to Brompton Hospital for Diseases of the Chest; Consulting Surgeon to King Edward VII Sanatorium, Midhurst; Civilian Consultant in Thoracic Surgery, RAF, to Army, 1946-63; Adviser for Thoracic Surgery to Ministry of Health, 1946-63; President Welsh National School of Medicine, 1958-70; President Medical Protection Society; *b* Abercarn, Mon, 22 Nov. 1893; *m* 1925, Ethel Doris, *d* of Mortimer Ricks, Paignton, South Devon; two *s*. *Educ:* Caterham Sch.; University College of South Wales; Westminster Hospital (Scholar). Hughes Medal in Anatomy, Cardiff, Medical Sch.; MRCS; LRCP, 1921; FRCS, 1923; FRCP 1960; held all resident appointments, Westminster Hospital and Surgical Registrar, three years; Consulting Surgeon, Metropolitan Asylums Board (Mental Service), three years; served European War, 1914-18, RAMC, Gallipoli, Macedonia, and Palestine. President Royal Society Med., 1956-58; Tudor Edward's Memorial Lectr, RCP and RCS, 1959; Vicary Lecture, 1960; Bradshaw Lectr, RCS, 1963. Royal College of Surgeons: Mem. Council, 1952-64; Vice-Pres., 1962-64; ex-Mem., Court of Examiners. Hon. Fellow, American Assoc. for Thoracic Surgery; Member: Royal Norwegian Med. Society; Argentine Med. Society; Argentine Thoracic Society; Brazilian Tuberculosis Society; For. Member Académie de Chirurgie; Hon. Member: Internat. Surgical Society; Union Internationale Contra la Tuberculose; Polish Association of Surgeons; Ex-President Association of Surgeons of Great Britain and Ireland; Thoracic Society and Society of Thoracic Surgeons; Ex-President Royal Society Med. Hon. LLD Wales, 1953; Queen's Univ., Belfast, 1962; Hon. MD: Paris; Lisbon; Karachi, 1966; Athens, 1970. President: BMA, 1965-66; World Med. Assoc., 1965-66. Warsaw Decoration, 1960. *Publications:* Chapter on Chest in Malignant Disease and its Treatment by Radium, by Stanford Cade, 1940; Assoc. Editor and Contributor to "British Surgical Practice"; numerous articles on diseases of the chest and radium treatment in hospital reports and medical journals. *Recreations:* golf, photography. *Address:* Court Green, St Ann's Hill, Midhurst, Sussex.

**PRICE-WHITE, Lieut-Colonel David Archibald,** TD 1945; Solicitor with Edward Hughes & Co., Rhyl; *b* 5 Sept. 1906; *s* of Price Foulkes White and Charlotte Bell. *Educ:* Friars School; University College of North Wales. Admitted Solicitor (Hons), 1932; practised Solicitor, Bangor, 1933-39. Joined TA (RA), 1928; served 1939-45, France 1940, Middle East, Sicily, Italy, East Africa. MP (C) Caernarvon Boroughs, 1945-50. *Recreations:* cricket, Rugby, golf. *Address:* Dolanog, Pwllycrochan Avenue, Colwyn Bay, N Wales. *T:* Colwyn Bay 30758.

**PRICHARD, Sir John,** Kt, *cr* 1952; CBE 1941 (OBE 1927); JP; *b* 27 Jan. 1887; *s* of late W. Prichard, Wick, Glamorganshire; unmarried. Solicitor. Major, Royal Field Artillery, Territorial. First commission in RFA (T), 1911; served European War, Gallipoli, 1915, Mesopotamia, 1916-18 (despatches twice). Judge in Iraqi Courts, 1919-51; President Iraqi Supreme Court and Chief Justice, Iraq, 1938-51; retired, 1951. JP Co. Glamorgan, 1956. *Address:* West House, Wick, Glamorgan. *Club:* East India and Sports.

**PRICHARD, Montague Illtyd,** CBE 1965; MC 1944; Chairman and Managing Director of the several companies comprising the Perkins Engines Group in UK and overseas; a Director of Massey-Ferguson (Holdings) Ltd and Massey-Ferguson Italiana SpA, since 1959; Group Vice-President, Engines, Massey-Ferguson Ltd, Toronto; Director: Massey-Ferguson Finance Co. of Canada Ltd; Massey-Ferguson Ltd, Toronto, Canada; *b* 26 Sept. 1915; *s* of late George Montague Prichard; *m* 1942, Kathleen Georgana Hamill; two *s* one *d*. *Educ:* Felsted Sch., Essex. Served War of 1939-45 (despatches thrice, MC): Royal Engineers: Somaliland, India, Burma, Malaya and Far East, Lt-Col as CRE 20 Indian Division. R. A. Lister & Co. Ltd: Student Apprentice; then several years in India and Far East (overseas Org. Gp); appointed Director and Gen. Manager, Blackstone & Co. Ltd (part of Lister Group), 1950; Director, R. A. Lister & Co. Ltd, 1952. F. Perkins Ltd: Personal Asst to Man. Director, 1953; Director of Engineering, 1954; Dep. Man. Dir, 1956; Jt Man. Dir, 1958; Member: British Productivity Council; British National Export Council, 1965; Cttee of Management, British Road Federation; Vice-President, Society of Motor Manufacturers and Traders, 1966-70. Governor, Ashridge Management Coll. FInstMSM. *Address:* The Coach-House, Thornhaugh, Peterborough. *T:* Wansford 461. *Club:* East India and Sports.

**PRICHARD, Sir Norman (George Mollett),** Kt 1968; Member: Greater London Council; Inner London Education Authority; Vice-Chairman, Greater London Conference on Old People's Welfare, since 1966; *b* 14 April 1895; *er s* of late Rev. Alfred George Prichard and Mrs Margaret Prichard; *m* 1921, Winifred, *d* of late Thomas Edmund Just, Middlesbrough and London; one *s* one *d*. *Educ:* East Ham Grammar Sch.; Henry Thornton Sch.; King's Coll., London. Civil Servant, 1910-55. Religious and social work, 1908- (President, Wandsworth Free Church Federal Council, 1965-66). Called to Bar, Lincoln's Inn, 1924. MSc (London) in Psychology (Lecturer WEA, etc., 1929-46); Member Battersea Borough Council, 1927-65 (Mayor, 1935-36); Chairman of LCC, 1965-66, and of Finance, Housing and other LCC Cttees, 1953-65; Alderman LCC, 1950-52; Member LCC (N Hammersmith), 1952-65; Chairman,

London Boroughs Association, 1964-68; Member Greater London Council (Wandsworth), 1964-67, 1970- (Chairman, Establishment and Supplies Cttee, 1964-65); Member, Wandsworth London Borough Council, 1964-68; Chairman, Metropolitan Boroughs Standing Jt Cttee, 1949-65 (Organisation and Methods Cttee, 1950-61). Chairman of Governors: Hammersmith County Sch., 1965-67; Henry Thornton Sch., 1969-; Governor, Battersea Grammar Sch., 1967- (nominated by Univ. of London). Member: Local Government Manpower Cttee; Advisory Cttee on Recruitment for Civil Defence Services; Minister of Transport's Special Cttee on Parking. President, Bermondsey Band of Hope Union, 1967-; Hon. Treas., Nat. Peace Council; Hon. Supt, Battersea Special Services (founded by Rev. A. G. Prichard, 1908). Lecture Tours on London Local Government in Holland (1957), USA and Canada (1957, 1959, and 1961), which included visits to leading American Universities. Radio and TV interviews at home and abroad on local government subjects. Freeman, London Borough of Wandsworth, 1968. JP 1950. *Publications:* sections on psychology in various popular works, and contributions to legal and local government journals and to newspapers. *Recreations:* reading, gardening. *Address:* 4 Rusham Road, SW12. *T:* 01-673 5048. *Club:* Civil Service.

**PRICHARD, Air Commodore Richard Julian Paget,** CB 1963; CBE 1958; DFC 1942; AFC 1941; *b* 4 Oct. 1915; *o s* of Major W. O. Prichard, 24th Regt; unmarried. *Educ:* Harrow; St Catharine's Coll., Cambridge. Entered RAF, 1937; Air Armament Sch., Eastchurch and Manby, 1937-39; Flying Instructor, South Cerney, 1939-41; No. 21 (LB) Squadron, 1942-43; Staff Coll. (psa), 1943; AEAF, 1943-45; Chief Intelligence Officer, Burma and FEAF, 1946-47; Chief Flying Instructor, RAF Coll., Cranwell, 1947-49; Ministry of Defence, 1949-52; Instructor, RAF Staff Coll., 1953-55; Station Comdr, RAF Tengah, Singapore, 1956-58. IDC, 1959; Director Air Plans, Air Ministry, 1960-63; AOC No. 13 Scottish Sector, Fighter Command, 1963-64; AOC Northern Sector of Fighter Command, 1965-66; retired, 1966. US Legion of Merit, 1944. *Recreations:* tennis, fishing. *Address:* 42 Hillgate Place, W8. *Club:* Royal Air Force.

**PRICHARD, Ven. Thomas Estlin,** MA; Archdeacon of Maidstone and Residentiary Canon of Canterbury since 1968; *b* 20 Dec. 1910; 3rd *s* of Edgar and Eleanora Prichard; *m* 1937, Mildred Celina Frances Leale; four *d*. *Educ:* Clifton Coll.; Exeter Coll., Oxford. Curate of: Lambeth, 1934; Ashford, Kent, 1938; Vicar of: Boxley, 1943; St Peter in Thanet, 1954. *Recreation:* music. *Address:* 22 The Precincts, Canterbury, Kent. *T:* Canterbury 63056. *Club:* Vincent's (Oxford).

**PRICHARD-JONES, Sir John,** 2nd Bt, *cr* 1910; Captain, Reserve of Officers; *b* 20 Jan. 1913; *s* of 1st Bt and Marie, *y d* of late Charles Read; *S* father, 1917; *m* 1937, Heather, (from whom he obtained a divorce, 1950), *er d* of late Sir Walter Nugent, 4th Bt; one *s*; *m* 1959, Helen Marie Therese, *e d* of J. F. Liddy, 20 Laurence Street, Drogheda; one *d*. *Educ:* Eton; Christ Church, Oxford (BA Hons). Called to Bar, Gray's Inn, 1936. *Heir: s* David John Walter Prichard-Jones, BA (Hons) Oxon, *b* 14 March 1943. *Address:* Allenswood House, Lucan, Co. Dublin.

**PRICKARD, Thomas Francis Vaughan,** CVO 1935 (MVO 1926); late Surveyor-General and Deputy Receiver-General of the Duchy of Lancaster; *s* of late Rev. Wm Edward Prickard of Dderw, Radnorshire; *b* 1879; *m* 1905, Margaret Taunton (*d* 1968), *d* of late R. Taunton Raikes, Treberfydd, Breconshire; one *d*. *Educ:* Marlborough; King's Coll., Cambridge. JP Radnorshire, 1907; Sheriff of Radnorshire, 1933. *Recreations:* shooting, fishing. *Address:* Dderw, Rhayader, Radnor. *Club:* Leander.

*See also Sir J. S. Holland.*

**PRICKETT, Air Chief Marshal Sir Thomas (Other),** KCB 1965 (CB 1957); DSO 1943; DFC 1942; Air Member for Supply and Organisation, Ministry of Defence, 1968-70; *b* 31 July 1913; *s* of late E. G. Prickett; *m* 1942, Elizabeth Gratian, *d* of late William Galbally, Laguna Beach, Calif, USA; one *s* one *d*. *Educ:* Stubbington House Sch.; Haileybury Coll. Joined RAF, 1937; commanded RAF Tangmere, 1949-51; Group Captain operations, HQ Middle East Air Force, 1951-54; commanded RAF Jever, 1954-55; attended Imperial Defence Coll., 1956; Chief of Staff Air Task Force, 1956; Director of Policy, Air Ministry, 1957-58; SASO, HQ No 1 Group, 1958-60; ACAS (Ops) Air Ministry, 1960-63; ACAS (Policy and Planning) Air Ministry, 1963-64; AOC-in-C, NEAF, and Comdr British Forces in Cyprus, 1964-66; AOC-in-C, RAF Air Support Command, 1967-68. *Recreations:* polo, sailing, golf. *Address:* The Warren, Cutmill, Bosham, Sussex. *Club:* Royal Air Force.

**PRICKMAN, Air Cdre Thomas Bain,** CB 1953; CBE 1945; *b* 1902; *m* 1st, Ethel Serica (*d* 1949), *d* of John Cubbon, Douglas, IOM; 2nd, 1952, Dorothy (who *m* 1946, Group Captain F. C. Read, *d* 1949), *d* of John Charles Clarke, *Educ:* Blundell's Sch. Joined RAF, 1923. Served War of 1939-45, with Fighter Command; RAF Liaison staff in Australia, 1946-48; AOA, Home Command, 1950-54; retired, 1954. *Address:* Well Cottage, New Pond Hill, Cross-in-Hand, Sussex.

**PRIDEAUX, Humphrey Povah Treverbian,** OBE 1945; Chairman, NAAFI, 1965 (Director, 1956); Vice-President, The London Life Association Ltd, since 1965 (Director, 1964); a Deputy Chairman, Brooke Bond Liebig Ltd, since 1969 (Director, 1968); Director, w. H. Smith (Holdings) Ltd, since 1969; Chairman, Lord Wandsworth Foundation, since 1966; *b* 13 Dec. 1915; 3rd *s* of Walter Treverbian Prideaux and Marion Fenn (*née* Arbuthnot); *m* 1939, Cynthia, *er d* of Lieut-Colonel H. Birch Reynardson, *qv*; four *s*. *Educ:* St Aubyns, Rottingdean; Eton; Trinity Coll., Oxford (MA). Commissioned 3rd Carabiniers (Prince of Wales's Dragoon Guards) 1936; DAQMG Guards Armd Div., 1941; Instructor, Staff Coll., 1942; AQMG 21 Army Gp, 1943; AA QMG Guards Armd Div., 1944; Joint Planning Staff, War Office, 1945; Naval Staff Coll., 1948; Commandant School of Administration, 1948; Chiefs of Staff Secretariat, 1950; retired, 1953. *Recreation:* riding. *Address:* Summers Farm, Long Sutton, Basingstoke, Hants. *T:* Long Sutton 295. *Club:* Cavalry.

*See also J. F. Prideaux, W. A. Prideaux.*

**PRIDEAUX, John Francis,** OBE 1945; Chairman, Arbuthnot Latham Holdings Ltd, since 1969 (Chairman, Arbuthnot Latham & Co. Ltd, 1964-69, Director, 1936-69); Joint Deputy Chairman, National Westminster Bank Ltd, since 1969 (Director, 1955, Deputy Chairman, 1962-69, Westminster Bank Ltd); Chairman Westminster Foreign Bank Ltd, since 1969; Treasurer and Chairman, Board of Governors, St Thomas' Hospital, since 1964; *b* 30 Dec. 1911; 2nd *s* of Walter Treverbian Prideaux and Marion Fenn (*née* Arbuthnot); *m*

1934, Joan, *er d* of late Captain Gordon Hargreaves Brown, MC, and of late Lady Pigott Brown; two *s* one *d*. *Educ:* St Aubyns, Rottingdean; Eton. Joined Arbuthnot Latham & Co. Ltd, Merchant Bankers, 1930. Dep. Chm., Commonwealth Develt Corp., 1960-70. Middlesex Yeomanry, 1933; served War of 1939-45, Colonel Q, 2nd Army, 1944. Legion of Merit, USA, 1945. *Address:* Elderslie, Ockley, Surrey. *T:* Capel 2263. *Clubs:* Cavalry, Brooks's.

*See also H. P. T. Prideaux, W. A. Prideaux.*

**PRIDEAUX, Walter Arbuthnot,** MC 1945; TD 1948; Clerk of the Goldsmiths' Company since 1953; *b* 4 Jan. 1910; *e s* of Walter Treverbian Prideaux and Marion Fenn (*née* Arbuthnot); *m* 1937, Anne, *d* of Francis Stewart Cokayne; two *s* two *d*. *Educ:* Eton; Trinity Coll., Cambridge. Solicitor, 1934. Assistant Clerk of the Goldsmiths' Company, 1939-53. Kent Yeomanry, 1936-48. *Recreation:* rowed for Cambridge, 1930, 1931. *Address:* Saykers, Rusper, Horsham, Sussex. *T:* Rusper 331.

*See also H. P. T. Prideaux, J. F. Prideaux.*

**PRIDEAUX-BRUNE, Sir Humphrey Ingelram,** KBE 1943 (OBE 1931); CMG 1938; *b* 16 Nov. 1886; *m* 1920, Adah Louisa Anne (*d* 1947), *d* of late W. Montague Pollard-Urquhart, Castle Pollard, Co. Westmeath. *Educ:* Marlborough; University Coll., Oxford. Student Interpreter in China, 1911; one of HM Consuls in China, 1931; acting Chinese Counsellor, British Embassy, China, 1938-39; China Relations Officer in India, 1943; retired, 1945. *Address:* Thriftwood, Limpsfield, Surrey.

**PRIDHAM, Vice-Admiral Sir (Arthur) Francis,** KBE, *cr* 1946; CB 1940; *b* 3 June 1886; 2nd *s* of Edward Prideaux Brune Pridham; *m* 1911, Miriam Vidal (*d* 1969), *d* of Rev. Arthur Lewis; three *d*. Joined RN, 1901; served European War, 1914-19 as: Gunnery Officer of HMS Weymouth, Shannon and Marlborough; Captain, 1926; Imperial Defence Coll., 1927; commanded HM Ships Concord, Calliope, Curlew, Excellent, and Hood; ADC to the King, 1937; Rear-Admiral, 1938; Flag Officer, Humber Area, 1939-40; Vice-Admiral (retired), 1941; President of the Ordnance Board, 1941-45. Member of General Board, National Physical Laboratory, 1943-48. Imperial Russian Order of St Stanislas (2nd Class with Swords). Commander Legion of Merit (USA), 1946. *Publication:* Close of a Dynasty, 1956. *Address:* Woodhayne, Burley, Ringwood, Hants. *T:* Burley 2310. *Club:* United Service.

**PRIDHAM, Kenneth Robert Comyn;** Counsellor, British Embassy, Copenhagen, since 1968; *b* 28 July 1922; *s* of late Colonel G. R. Pridham, CBE, DSO, and Mignonne, *d* of late Charles Cumming, ICS; *m* 1965, Ann Rosalind, *d* of late E. Gilbert Woodward, Metropolitan Magistrate, and of Mrs Woodward. *Educ:* Winchester; Oriel Coll., Oxford. Lieut, 60th Rifles, 1942-46; served North Africa, Italy, Middle East (despatches). Entered Foreign (subseq. Diplomatic) Service, 1946; served at Berlin, Washington, Belgrade and Khartoum, and at the Foreign Office. *Address:* c/o Foreign and Commonwealth Office, SW1. *Club:* Travellers'.

**PRIDIE, Sir Eric (Denholm),** KCMG 1953 (CMG 1941); DSO 1918; OBE 1931; MB BS, London, MRCS, FRCP; Chief Medical Officer, Colonial Office, 1948-58, retired; *b* 10 Jan. 1896; *s* of Dr John Francis and Florence Pridie. *Educ:* St Bees Sch.; University of Liverpool. Served European War, 1914-18; France, 1915-16; Mesopotamia, 1917-18, with 6th and 7th Battalions King's Own Royal (Lancaster) Regt; Captain, 1917 (despatches, wounded, DSO); joined Sudan Med. Service, 1924; served in Kassala and Blue Nile Provinces; Asst Director, 1930; Director Sudan Medical Service, 1933-45; Member of Governor General's Council, 1934-45; President Central Board Public Health, Sudan, 1933-45, and Chairman School Council, Kitchener School of Medicine, 1933-45; Brigadier, Royal Army Medical Corps; DDMS Troops, Sudan and Eritrea, Middle East Forces, 1940-43 (despatches twice); Health Counsellor, British Embassy, Cairo, 1945-49, and Health Adviser British Middle East Office, 1946-49. Order of Nile 3rd Class. *Clubs:* Athenæum, Royal Commonwealth Society.

**PRIESTLEY, Dr Charles Henry Brian,** FAA 1954; FRS 1967; Chief of Division of Meteorological Physics, CSIRO, Australia, since 1946; *b* 8 July 1915; *s* of late T. G. Priestley; *m* 1946, Constance, *d* of H. Tweedy; one *s* two *d*. *Educ:* Mill Hill Sch.; St John's Coll., Cambridge. Served in Meteorological Office, Air Ministry, 1939-46; subseq. with CSIRO, Australia. MA (Cantab) 1942, ScD (Cantab) 1953. David Syme Prize, University of Melbourne, 1956. Member Exec. Cttee, International Assoc. of Meteorology, 1954-60, Vice-Pres., 1967-; Vice-President, Australian Acad. of Science, 1959-60; Member Advisory Cttee to World Meteorological Organisation, 1964-68 (Chairman, 1967). FRMetSoc (Buchan Prize, 1950 and Symons Medal, 1967, of Society); FInstP. *Publications:* Turbulent Transfer in the Lower Atmosphere, 1959; about 60 papers in scientific journals. *Recreation:* golf. *Address:* 11 Coonil Crescent, Malvern, SE4, Victoria, Australia. *T:* 50-5092.

**PRIESTLEY, Sir Gerald William,** KCIE 1946 (CIE 1943); *b* 12 Nov. 1888; *s* of James Henry Priestley; *m* 1919, Isobel Macleod Millar (*d* 1958); four *d*; *m* 1959, Evelyn May Ledward, Kloof. *Educ:* West Monmouthshire Sch., Pontypool; Trinity Coll., Cambridge. Entered ICS, 1912, in Madras; investigated Upper Bhavani and Tunga-bhadra Irrigation Projects, 1926 and 1934; Commissioner of Coorg, 1927; Member Board of Revenue, 1939; Chief Secretary to the Government of Madras, 1942; Adviser to Governor of Madras, 1945; retired, 1947. *Address:* c/o The Standard Bank, Kloof, Natal, South Africa.

**PRIESTLEY, John Boynton,** MA, LittD; LLD; DLitt; Author; *b* Bradford, 1894; *s* of Jonathan Priestley, schoolmaster; *m* Jacquetta Hawkes, *qv*; one *s* four *d* by previous marriages. *Educ:* Bradford; Trinity Hall, Cambridge. Served with Duke of Wellington's and Devon Regts, 1914-19. UK Delegate to UNESCO Conferences, 1946-47; Chairman of International Theatre Conf.: Paris, 1947, Prague, 1948; Chairman British Theatre Conf., 1948; President International Theatre Institute, 1949; Member of the National Theatre Board, 1966-67. *Publications:* Brief Diversions, 1922; Papers from Lilliput, 1922; I for One, 1923; Figures in Modern Literature, 1924; The English Comic Characters, 1925; George Meredith (English Men of Letters), 1926; Talking, 1926; Adam in Moonshine, 1927; Open House, 1927; Peacock (English Men of Letters), 1927; Benighted, 1927; The English Novel, 1927; Apes and Angels, 1928; English Humour, 1928; The Good Companions, 1929 (dramatised with E. Knoblock, 1931); The Balconinny, 1929; Town Major of Miraucourt; Angel Pavement, 1930; Self-Selected Essays, 1932; Dangerous Corner, play, 1932; Faraway, 1932; Wonder Hero, 1933, The Roundabout, play, 1933; Laburnum Grove, play, 1933; English Journey, 1934;

Eden End, 1934; Duet in Floodlight, play, 1935; Cornelius, play, 1935; Bees on the Boat Deck, play, 1936; They Walk in the City, 1936; Midnight on the Desert, 1937; Time and the Conways, play, 1937; I Have Been Here Before, play, 1937; People at Sea, play, 1937; The Doomsday Men, 1938; Music at Night, play, 1938; When We Are Married, play, 1938; Johnson Over Jordan, play, 1939; Rain upon Godshill, 1939; Let the People Sing, 1939; The Long Mirror, play, 1940; Postscripts, 1940; Out of the People, 1941; Goodnight, Children, play, 1942; Black-Out in Gretley, 1942; They Came to a City, play, 1943; Daylight on Saturday, 1943; The Man-Power Story, 1943; British Women go to War, 1943; Desert Highway, play, 1943; How Are They At Home?, play, 1944; Three Men in New Suits, 1945; An Inspector Calls, Ever Since Paradise, plays, 1946; The Secret Dream; Bright Day, 1946; Arts under Socialism; Theatre Outlook; Jenny Villiers; The Linden Tree, play, 1947; Home is Tomorrow, play, 1948; Summer Day's Dream, play, 1949; Delight (essays), 1949; libretto, The Olympians, opera, 1949; Last Holiday (film), 1950; Festival at Farbridge, 1951; (with Jacquetta Hawkes) Dragon's Mouth, play, 1952; The Other Place, 1953; The Magicians; Low Notes on a High Level, 1954; Mr Kettle and Mrs Moon, play, 1955; Journey Down a Rainbow (with Jacquetta Hawkes), 1955; The Glass Cage, play, 1957; Thoughts in the Wilderness, 1957; The Art of the Dramatist, 1957; Topside or the Future of England, 1958; Literature and Western Man, 1960; Saturn Over The Water, 1961; The Thirty-First of June, 1961; Charles Dickens: A Pictorial Biography, 1961; The Shapes of Sleep, 1962; Margin Released, 1962; A Severed Head (with Iris Murdoch), play, 1963; Sir Michael and Sir George, 1964; Man and Time, 1964; Lost Empires, 1965; The Moment–And Other Pieces (essays), 1966; Salt is Leaving, 1966; It's an Old Country, 1967; Trumpets Over the Sea, 1968; The Image Men, Vol. I, Out of Town, 1968, Vol. II, London End, 1968; Essays of Five Decades, ed Susan Cooper, 1969; The Prince of Pleasure and his Regency, 1969; The Edwardians, 1970. *Relevant publications:* J. B. Priestley: An Informal Study of His Work, by David Hughes, 1959; J. B. Priestley: the Dramatist, by Gareth Lloyd Evans, 1964; J. B. Priestley: portrait of an author, by Susan Cooper, 1970, etc. *Address:* Albany, Piccadilly, W1; Alveston, Warwickshire.

*See also Air Marshal Sir P. G. Wykeham.*

**PRIESTLEY, Mrs J. B.**; *see* Hawkes, Jacquetta.

**PRIESTLEY, Sir Raymond Edward,** Kt 1949; MC; MA (Cambridge); DSc, Melbourne, New Zealand and West Indies; LLD (St Andrews, Natal, Dalhousie, Birmingham); DLitt (Malaya); retired; *b* Tewkesbury, 1886; 2nd *s* of late J. E. Priestley, Tewkesbury; *m* 1915, Phyllis Mary (*d* 1961), *d* of late W. B. Boyd; two *d*. *Educ:* Tewkesbury Grammar Sch.; Bristol, Sydney and Cambridge Universities. Geologist, Shackleton Antarctic (Nimrod) Expedition, 1907-09; Scientist, Northern Party, Scott Antarctic Expedition, 1910-13; Adjutant, Wireless Training Centre, 1914-17; 46th Divisional Signal Company, France, 1918; Asst CSO 1st Army, 1919; SD 6 War Office, 1919, for writing History of Signal Service; Fellow of Clare Coll., Cambridge, 1923-34; Secretary General of the Faculties, Cambridge Univ., 1934; Vice-Chancellor Melbourne Univ., 1935-38; Principal and Vice-Chancellor, University of Birmingham, 1938-52. Chairman, Royal Commn on Civil Service, 1953-55; President of the British Association for the Advancement of Science, 1956. Director Falkland Islands Rear Base, 1955-59; President, Royal Geographical Society, 1961-63. Hon. Fellow of Clare Coll., Cambridge. Chevalier of the Belgian Crown. *Publications:* Geological Report, Shackleton Antarctic Expedition (with T. W. E. David); Antarctic Adventure; Scott's Northern Party; Breaking the Hindenburg Line (story of 46th Division); History of the Signal Service in France; Physiography and Glaciology Reports, Scott's Last Expedition, and other papers. *Address:* Barn Hill, Bredon's Norton, Tewkesbury, Glos.

**PRIMROSE,** family name of **Earl of Rosebery.**

**PRIMROSE, Lord; Neil Archibald Primrose,** DL; *b* 11 Feb. 1929; *o surv. s* of 6th Earl of Rosebery, *qv*; *m* 1955, Alison Mary Deirdre, *d* of Ronald W. Reid, 19 Lexden Road, Colchester, Essex; one *s* four *d*. *Educ:* Stowe; New Coll., Oxford. DL Midlothian, 1960. *Heir: s* Hon. Harry Ronald Neil Primrose, *b* 20 Nov. 1967. *Address:* 12 Orme Court, W2; Dalmeny House, South Queensferry, West Lothian.

**PRIMROSE, Sir John Ure,** 3rd Bt, *cr* 1903, of Redholme; farming in the Argentine; *b* 15 April 1908; *er s* of Sir William Louis Primrose, 2nd Bt, and Elizabeth Caroline (*d* 1951), *d* of Hugh Dunsmuir, Glasgow; *S* father, 1953; *m* Enid, *d* of James Evans Sladen, British Columbia; one *s*. *Educ:* Rugby; Sandhurst. Lieut, QO Cameron Highlanders, 1928-33. *Heir: s* Alasdair Neil Primrose [*b* 11 Dec. 1935; *m* 1958, Elaine Noreen, *d* of E. C. Lowndes, Buenos Aires; one *s* one *d*. *Educ.* St George's College, Buenos Aires]. *Address:* Puerto Victoria, Alto Parana, Misiones, Argentina.

**PRIMROSE, Sir John Ure,** Kt 1951; DL; JP; Lord Provost of Perth, 1945-54; Hon. Sheriff Substitute for Perth and Perthshire, 1949; Chairman: Scottish Motor Traction Co. Ltd, and of Subsidiary Companies, 1956; First Scottish American Trust, Second British American Trust, Third Scottish American Trust, Northern American Trust, Camperdown Trust, since 1969; *b* 22 Feb. 1900; *s* of Rev. Robert Primrose, Minister of Parish Church of Burnbank, Glasgow, and Catherine Wingate; *m* 1922, Helen Victoria Baker. *Educ:* Kelvinside Academy, Glasgow; Stanley House, Bridge of Allan, Perthshire. Served European War, Lieut in Royal Navy, 1914-18, demobilised 1919. Sgt.-Major Intelligence Corps, War of 1939-45. Took up farming, 1921; Chairman, Perth Branch NFU for 1935. Director: General Accident Fire & Life Assurance Corp. Ltd, General Buildings, Perth, 1948. Chairman, Board of Management for Perthshire General Hospitals, 1948-58. Aviation: ATC Scottish Consultative Cttee and Scottish Representative on ATC Consultative Cttee in London; Member: Aerodrome Owners Association of Great Britain (Chairman, 1939-43); Air Transport Advisory Council; Chairman, Scottish and Northern Ireland Cttee of the White Fish Authority, 1956-. Member Nyasaland Inquiry Commission, 1959. Formerly Member Scottish Advisory Council for Civil Aviation. *Recreations:* Rugby, yachting, golf, tennis. *Address:* Thistle Cottage, Lower Largo, Fife. *T:* Lundin Links 456. *Clubs:* Royal Perth Golfing Society (Perth); Clyde Corinthian Yachting (Glasgow).

**PRIMROSE, William,** CBE 1952; FGSM (Hon.); Viola Soloist; *b* 23 Aug. 1904; *s* of late John Primrose and of Margaret Primrose, both of Glasgow; *m* 1st, 1928, Dorothy (*d* 1951), *d* of John Friend of Exeter; two *d*; *m* 2nd, 1952, Alice Virginia French, Davenport, Iowa. *Educ:* Guildhall School of Music,

London; privately with Eugen Ysaye, Brussels. Violist with London String Quartet, 1930-35; First Violist with NBC Orchestra, New York, under Toscanini, 1937-42; since then exclusively as soloist. Professor, Viola and Chamber Music, Curtis Institute of Music, Philadelphia, 1940-50. Has toured extensively in US, Canada, Central and S. America, Great Britain, Western Europe and Israel. *Recreations:* chess, cricket and reading. *Club:* Savage.

**PRINCE, Professor Frank Templeton,** MA (Oxon); Professor of English, University of Southampton, since 1957; *b* Kimberley, South Africa, 13 Sept. 1912; 2nd *s* of late H. Prince and Margaret Templeton (*née* Hetherington); *m* 1943, Pauline Elizabeth, *d* of late H. F. Bush; two *d. Educ:* Christian Brothers' Coll., Kimberley, South Africa; Balliol Coll., Oxford. Visiting Fellow, Graduate Coll., Princeton, NJ, 1935-36. Study Groups Department, Chatham House, 1937-40. Served Army, Intelligence Corps, 1940-46. Department of English, Southampton Univ., 1946-. Visiting Fellow, All Souls Coll., 1968-69. *Publications:* Poems, 1938; Soldiers Bathing, 1954; The Italian Element in Milton's Verse, 1954; The Doors of Stone (poems), 1963; contributor to Review of English Studies. *Recreations:* music, etc. *Address:* 32 Brookvale Road, Southampton. *T:* Southampton 55457.

**PRINCE, Maj.-Gen. Hugh Anthony,** CBE 1960; retired as Chief, Military Planning Office, SEATO, Bangkok; *b* 11 Aug. 1911; *s* of H. T. Prince, FRCS, LRCP; *m* 1st, 1938, Elizabeth (*d* 1959), *d* of Dr Walter Bapty, Victoria, BC; two *s*; 2nd, 1959, Claude-Andrée, *d* of André Romanet, Château-de-Tholot, Beaujeu, Rhône; one *s. Educ:* Eastbourne Coll.; RMC, Sandhurst. Commissioned, 1931; served in 6th Gurkha Rifles until 1947; The King's Regt (Liverpool), 1947. *Recreations:* golf, gardening, antiques. *Address:* 13 Raphèle-les-Arles, France. *T:* Raphèle 93. *Club:* United Hunts.

**PRINCE, Leslie Barnett,** FCA; Senior Partner, Prince Simon and Co., Chartered Accountants; Director of Public Companies; *b* 27 May 1901; *s* of Sir Alexander William Prince, KBE, and Lady Prince (*née* Edith Jonas); *m* 1924, Norah Millie, *d* of Eliot Lewis, JP; one *s* two *d. Educ:* Clifton Coll.; Magdalene Coll., Cambridge (MA). Chartered Accountant; FCA 1930; London Chest Hospital Board, 1937-48; Hospital for Diseases of the Chest, Board of Management, 1948-61. Joint Chairman of Jewish Refugees Cttee, 1939-43; Director of Royal Ordnance Factories, Ministry of Supply, 1944-46. Member Court of Common Council, City of London, 1950-; Chairman: Rates Finance Cttee, 1957-65; Coal and Corn and Finance Cttee, Corporation of London, 1967; Coal, Corn and Rates Finance Cttee, 1968-. Sheriff of City of London, 1954-55. Deputy of Ward of Bishopsgate, 1970. Master, Worshipful Co. of Farriers, 1955-56. President: United Wards Club, 1957; Bishopsgate Ward Club, 1958. Companion of Star of Ethiopia, 1954; Commandeur Léopold II, 1963. *Recreation:* golf. *Address:* 21 Cadogan Gardens, SW3. *T:* 01-730 2957. *Clubs:* United University, Gresham, City Livery.

**PRINCE-SMITH, Sir (William) Richard,** 4th Bt, *cr* 1911; Landowner and Farmer; Chairman and Managing Director: Dependable Plant Hire; Tibthorpe Nominees Ltd; Clermont Farms; *b* 27 Dec. 1928; *s* of Sir William Prince-Smith, 3rd Bt, OBE, MC, and Marjorie, Lady Prince-Smith (*d* 1970); *S* father, 1964; *m* 1955, Margaret Ann Carter; one *s* one *d. Educ:* Charterhouse; Clare Coll., Cambridge (MA). BA (Agric.) 1951. *Recreations:* music, photography, shooting, yachting. *Heir: s* James William Prince-Smith, *b* 2 July 1959. *Address:* Morton Hall, Morton-on-the-Hill, Norwich, Norfolk NOR 58X. *T:* Great Witchingham 265. *Clubs:* Farmers'; Royal Norfolk and Suffolk Yacht; Norfolk Broads Yacht; Royal Thames Yacht.

**PRINGLE, Air Vice-Marshal Charles Norman Seton,** CBE 1967; MA, CEng, FRAeS; Air Officer Engineering, Strike Command, since 1970; *b* 6 June 1919; *s* of late Seton Pringle, OBE, FRCSI, Dublin; *m* 1946, Margaret, *d* of late B. Sharp, Baildon, Yorkshire; one *s. Educ:* Repton; St John's Coll., Cambridge. Commissioned, RAF, 1941; served India and Ceylon, 1942-46. Air Ministry, 1946-48; RAE, Farnborough, 1949-50; attached to USAF, 1950-52; appts in UK, 1952-60; STSO No 3 Group, Bomber Comd, 1960-62, and Air Forces Middle East, 1962-64; Comdt RAF St Athan and Air Officer Wales, 1964-66; MoD, 1967; IDC, 1968. Dir-Gen. of Engineering (RAF) MoD, 1969-70. *Recreations:* photography, ornithology, motor sport. *Address:* 8 Strangways Terrace, W14. *T:* 01-602 3356. *Club:* Royal Air Force.

**PRINGLE, John Martin Douglas;** *b* 1912; *s* of late J. Douglas Pringle, Hawick, Scotland; *m* 1936, Celia, *d* of E. A. Carroll; one *s* two *d. Educ:* Shrewsbury Sch.; Lincoln Coll., Oxford. First Class Literae Humaniores, 1934. Editorial Staff of Manchester Guardian, 1934-39. Served War of 1939-45 with King's Own Scottish Borderers, 1940-44; Assistant Editor, Manchester Guardian, 1944-48; Special Writer on The Times, 1948-52; Editor of The Sydney Morning Herald, 1952-57; Deputy Editor of The Observer, 1958-63; Managing Editor, Canberra Times, 1964-65; Editor, Sydney Morning Herald, 1965-70. *Publications:* China Struggles for Unity, 1938; Australian Accent, 1958; Australian Painting Today, 1963. *Address:* 27 Bayview Street, McMahon's Point, N. Sydney, NSW, Australia. *Club:* Travellers'.

**PRINGLE, Prof. J(ohn) Seton (Michael),** FRCS, FRCSI; Regius Professor of Surgery, University of Dublin, since 1961; Visiting Surgeon, Royal City of Dublin Hospital and Drumcondra Hospital; Consulting Surgeon: Rotunda Hospital; Stewart's Hospital; Royal Hospital for Incurables; *b* 12 July 1909; *s* of J. A. Pringle, KC; *m* 1st, 1939, B. Odlum; one *s* two *d*; 2nd, Mrs N. W. Cornwall (*née* Chaloner). *Educ:* Haileybury; Gonville and Caius Coll., Cambridge; Trinity Coll., Dublin. MB, BCh, BAO, Dublin, 1933; MB, BChir, Cambridge, 1933; FRCSI 1935; FRCS England 1937. Served with Royal Army Medical Corps, 1942-45 (Major). Visiting Surgeon, Mercer's Hospital, Dublin, 1938-45. *Publications:* contribs to Irish Journal of Medical Science, BMJ, etc. *Recreations:* sailing, shooting. *Address:* 33 Upper Fitzwilliam Street, Dublin 2, Ireland. *T:* Dublin 66711.

**PRINGLE, John William Sutton,** MBE 1945; FRS 1954; ScD 1955; Linacre Professor of Zoology, Oxford, and Fellow of Merton College, Oxford, since 1961; *b* 22 July 1912; *e s* of late John Pringle, MD, Manchester, and of Dorothy Emily (*née* Beney); *m* 1946, Beatrice Laura Wilson (*née* Gilbert-Carter); one *s* two *d. Educ:* Winchester Coll.; King's Coll., Cambridge (MA). University Demonstrator in Zoology, 1937-39; University Lecturer, 1945-59; Fellow of King's Coll., Cambridge, 1938-45; Telecommunications Research Establishment, 1939-44; Ministry of War

Transport, 1944-45; Fellow of Peterhouse, Cambridge, 1945-61, Emeritus Fellow, Oct. 1961-. Senior Tutor, 1948-57; Senior Bursar, 1957-59; Librarian, 1959-61; Reader in Experimental Cytology, Cambridge, 1959-61. American Medal of Freedom, 1945. *Publications:* Insect Flight, 1957; papers in Journal of Experimental Biology, Journal of Physiology, Philos. Trans. Royal Society. *Recreations:* gliding, canals. *Address:* 437 Banbury Road, Oxford OX2 8ED. *T:* 58470.

**PRINGLE, Dr Mia Lilly Kellmer;** Director, National Bureau for Co-operation in Child Care, since 1963; *d* of late Samuel and late Sophie Kellmer; *m* 1946, William Joseph Sommerville Pringle, BSc (*d* 1962); *m* 1969, William Leonard Hooper, BA Oxon. *Educ:* schools in Vienna; Birkbeck Coll., University of London. BA (Hons) 1944; Dip. Educ. Psychol. 1945; Fellowship, London Child Guidance Training Centre, 1945; PhD (Psych.) 1950. Teaching in Primary Schools, Middx and Herts, 1940-44; Educ. and Clin. Psychologist, Herts Child Guidance Service, 1945-50; University of Birmingham: Lecturer in Educ. Psych., 1950-54; Dep. Head, Dept of Child Study, 1954-63; Senior Lecturer in Educ. Psych., 1960-63. Member: Birmingham Educ. Cttee, 1957-63; Home Sec.'s Adv. Council on Child Care, 1966-; Consultative Panel for Social Develt, ODM, 1968-; Bd of Governors, Hosp. for Sick Children, Gt Ormond Street, 1969-; Research Consultant: on play needs, to Min. of Housing and Local Govt, 1968-; UN Research Inst. for Social Develt, 1967-69. FBPsS. *Publications:* The Emotional and Social Adjustment of Physically Handicapped Children, 1964; Deprivation and Education, 1965; Investment in Children (ed), 1965; Social Learning and its Measurement, 1966; Adoption–Facts and Fallacies, 1966; Caring for Children (ed), 1968; Able Misfits, 1970; co-author: 11,000 Seven-Year-Olds, 1966; Four Years On, 1967; Residential Child Care–Facts and Fallacies, 1967; Foster Care–Facts and Fallacies, 1967; The Community's Children, 1967; Directory of National, Voluntary Children's Organisations, 1968; The Challenge of Thalidomide, 1970; Living with Handicap; papers in journals of psychology and education. *Recreations:* reading, music, theatre-going, tennis, cooking. *Address:* (home) 68 Wimpole Street, W1. *T:* 01-935 3144; (office) Adam House, 1 Fitzroy Square, W1. *T:* 01-387 4263-5. *Club:* Royal Over-Seas League.

**PRINGLE, Dr Robert William,** OBE 1967; BSc, PhD; Chairman and Managing Director, Nuclear Enterprises Ltd, Edinburgh, since 1956; Vice-President, Nuclear Enterprises Inc. (California), since 1968; *b* 2 May 1920; *s* of Robert Pringle and Lillias Dalgleish Hair; *m* 1948, Carol Stokes; three *s* one *d*. *Educ:* George Heriot's Sch., Edinburgh; Edinburgh Univ. (Vans Dunlop Scholar in Natural Philosophy); Lecturer, Natural Philosophy, Edinburgh, 1945; Asst Professor of Physics, Manitoba, 1949; Prof. and Chairman of Physics, Manitoba, 1953. Nuclear Enterprises Ltd received Queen's Award to Industry, 1966. Member: Scottish Council, CBI (Cttee), 1966; University Court, Edinburgh Univ., 1967; Scottish Univs Industry Liaison Cttee, 1968; Bd, Edinburgh Univ. Centre for Industrial Liaison and Consultancy, 1968; Bd, Royal Observatory (Edinburgh), 1968; Bd, Astronomy, Space and Radio (SRC), 1970; Hon. Adviser, Nat. Museum of Antiquities of Scotland, 1969. FInstP 1948; Fellow, American Inst. Physics, 1950; FRSC 1955; FRSE 1964. *Publications:* papers on nuclear spectroscopy and nuclear geophysics in UK and US scientific journals. *Recreations:* golf, book-collecting, Rugby (Edinburgh, Edinburgh and Glasgow, Rest of Scotland, 1945-48), family. *Address:* Westridge, 91 Ravelston Dykes, Edinburgh 12. *T:* 031-337 2891. *Clubs:* Royal Society (Edinburgh); Murrayfield Golf.

**PRINGLE, Major Sir Steuart (Robert),** 10th Bt, *cr* 1683, Stichell, Selkirkshire; Major, Royal Marines; *b* 21 July 1928; *s* of Sir Norman H. Pringle, 9th Bt and Lady (Oonagh) Pringle (*née* Curran); *S* father, 1961; *m* 1953, Jacqueline Marie Gladwell; two *s* two *d*. *Educ:* Sherborne. Royal Marines; 2nd Lieut, 1946; Lieut, 1949; Captain, 1957; Major, 1964. *Heir:* *s* Simon Robert Pringle, *b* 6 Jan. 1959. *Address:* 40 Commando Royal Marines, BFPO 164. *Club:* United Hunts.

**PRINSEP, Col Evelyn Siegfried MacLeod,** CIE 1945; OBE 1923; retired; *b* 23 April 1892; *er s* of late Captain James Frederick MacLeod Prinsep, 56th Foot and Egyptian Army; *m* 1921, Clavdia, *d* of Ivan Komarov, Samara Province, Russia; one *s* one *d*. *Educ:* Wellington; RMC Sandhurst. 2nd Lieut IA, 1911; joined 11th KEO Lancers (Probyn's Horse), 1912; served European War, 1914-19 (despatches), in France, Belgium, Mesopotamia, Siberia; Knox's Mission, Siberia, 1919-20; Special Mission, Far East, 1921-22; GSO3 AHQ India, 1923-25; Private Secretary to Governor of Punjab, 1931; operations, North-West Frontier, 1936-37; Lt-Col, 1937; Commandant Probyn's Horse, 1938-41; AA and QMG Lucknow District, 1941-45; Colonel, 1941; retired, 1945. 1st class interpreter in Russian (1922 and re-qualified 1931). *Publications:* Freshwater Gates, 1946 (miscellany of own verse and prose stories); contrib. at various times to newspaper and quarterlies. *Recreations:* literature, languages; golf, tennis, skating. *Address:* 7 Park Mansions, Knightsbridge, SW1. *T:* 01-589 2290. *Clubs:* Cavalry; Roehampton.

**PRIOR, Sir (Charles) Geoffrey,** KCIE 1943 (CIE 1936); FRGS; retired Governor; *o s* of Richard Delabere Prior. *Educ:* Shrewsbury (Folliot Sandford English Prize, 1913, 1914); RMC, Sandhurst (Prize Cadetship). Battalion Commander, 1919-21; transferred to Indian Political Service, 1923; Under-Sec., Rajputana Agency, 1924-26; Sec., Persian Gulf Residency, 1927; Political Agent, Bahrain, 1929-32; received thanks: of Sec. of State for Air for services (exploration of E Arabian Air Route); of Govt of India for services (Bahrain Riots). Dep. Sec., FO, Delhi-Simla, 1933; Prime Minister, Alwar State, 1936-38; Polit. Resident, Persian Gulf, 1939-46; Mem., ME War Council, 1941-42; raised Persian Gulf Fighter Fund which presented ten Spitfires to HM Govt; represented India at Foreign Ministers Conf., 1945; Governor, Baluchistan, 1946, retired 1949; Resident Dir, British Bank of Iran and the Middle East; resigned, 1951. Lecture tour to US on behalf of HM Govt, 1953. Built Church of the Epiphany, Bushire. Pres., SA Nat. Equestrian Fedn, 1964-67. Jubilee Medal, 1935; Coronation Medal, 1937. *Recreations:* sailing, shooting. *Address:* c/o Barclays Bank, Adderley Street, Cape Town, S Africa. *Clubs:* Travellers', United Service; Civil Service (Capetown).

**PRIOR, Ven. Christopher,** CB 1968; Archdeacon of Portsmouth, since 1969; *b* 2 July 1912; *s* of late Ven. W. H. Prior; *m* 1945, Althea Stafford (*née* Coode); two *d*. *Educ:* King's Coll., Taunton; Keble Coll., Oxford; Cuddesdon Coll. Curate of Hornsea, 1938-41; Chaplain RN from 1941, Chaplain of the Fleet, 1966-69. Served in: HMS Royal Arthur, 1941; HMHS Maine, 1941-43; HMS Scylla, 1943-44: HMS

Owl, 1944-46; various ships, 1946-58; Britannia RNC, Dartmouth, 1958-61; HMS Blake, 1961-62; HM Dockyard, Portsmouth, 1963-66; QHC, 1966-69. *Recreations:* golf, walking. *Address:* Victoria Lodge, Osborn Road, Fareham, Hants. *T:* Fareham 3101.

**PRIOR, Sir Geoffrey,** *see* Prior, Sir C. G.

**PRIOR, Rt. Hon. James Michael Leathes,** PC 1970; MP (C) Lowestoft Division of Suffolk since Oct. 1959; Minister of Agriculture, Fisheries and Food, since 1970; Vice-Chairman of the Conservative Party, 1965; Farmer and Land Agent in Norfolk and Suffolk since 1951; *b* 11 Oct. 1927; 2nd *s* of late C. B. L. and A. S. M. Prior, Norwich; *m* 1954, Jane Primrose Gifford, 2nd *d* of late Air Vice-Marshal O. G. Lywood, CB, CBE; three *s* one *d*. *Educ:* Charterhouse; Pembroke College, Cambridge. 1st class degree in Estate Management, 1950; commissioned in Royal Norfolk Regt, 1946; served in India and Germany. PPS to Pres. of Bd of Trade, 1963, to Minister of Power, 1963-64, to Mr Edward Heath, Leader of the Opposition, 1965-70. Chm. Aston Boats Ltd, 1968-70; Director: F. Lambert and Sons Ltd, 1958-70; IDC Group, 1968-70; lately Dir, O. G. Lywood Ltd. *Recreations:* cricket, tennis, golf, gardening. *Address:* Old Hall, Brampton, Beccles, Suffolk. *T:* Brampton 278; 36 Morpeth Mansions, SW1. *T:* 01-834 5543. *Clubs:* Carlton; Farmers'; MCC; Butterflies Cricket.

**PRIOR-PALMER, Maj.-Gen. George Erroll,** CB 1952; DSO 1945; *b* 1903; *s* of Spunner Prior-Palmer, Co. Sligo and Merrion Square, Dublin, and Anne Leslie Gason, Kilteelagh, Co. Tipperary; *m* 1st, 1935, Katherine Edith, *d* of Frank Bibby; one *d*; 2nd, 1948, Lady Doreen Hersey Winifred Hope, *y d* of 2nd Marquess of Linlithgow, KT, GCSI, GCIE; one *s* one *d*. *Educ:* Wellington; RMC. 2nd Lt, 9th Lancers, 1923; Capt. 1930; Lt-Col 1941; Col 1946; Brig. 1943. Served in NW Europe, 1940 (despatches), and 1944-45. Mil. Attaché, British Embassy, Washington, 1946-48. Maj.-General, 1951; Commanding 6th Armoured Division, 1951-53; Commander British Army Staff and Military Member, British Joint Services Mission, Washington, 1953-56; Pres. Regular Commissions Board, 1956-57; retired, 1958. Joined British & Commonwealth Shipping Co. Ltd, 1958; Southampton Area Director, Union Castle Mail Steamship Co. Ltd, 1959-64; Manager, Cayzer Irvine & Co. Ltd, and Special Adviser to the British Commonwealth Group, 1964-65; Man. Dir, Overseas Containers Ltd, 1965-69. Legion of Honour, 1945; Croix de Guerre avec Palme, 1945. *Address:* Appleshaw House, Andover, Hampshire. *T:* Weyhill 333. *Clubs:* Cavalry, Royal Ocean Racing.
*See also Baron Farnham.*

**PRIOR-PALMER, Brig. Sir Otho (Leslie),** Kt 1959; DSO 1945; *b* 28 Oct. 1897; *s* of late Spunner Prior-Palmer, County Sligo, Ireland, and Merrion Square, Dublin, and Anne Leslie Gason, Kilteelagh, Co. Tipperary; *m* 1940, Sheila Mary Weller Poley (OBE 1958), Boxted Hall, Bury St Edmunds; one *s* two *d* (and one *d* by previous marr.); *m* 1964, Elizabeth, *d* of late Harold Henderson; two *s*. *Educ:* Wellington; RMC, Sandhurst. Commissioned 9th Lancers, 1916; commanded 2nd Northamptonshire Yeo., 1940-42; comd 30th Armoured Brigade, Mar.-Aug. 1942; 29th Armoured Brigade, 1942-43; 7th Armoured Brigade, 1943-45 (DSO); commanded latter during Italian Campaign; retd pay 1946, hon. rank of Brig. MP (C) Worthing Div. W Sussex, 1945-50, Worthing, 1950-64. Vice-Chm. Conservative Members' Defence Cttee, 1958-59; Past Chm. NATO Parliamentarians Defence Cttee. *Recreations:* ski-ing, sailing, all field sports, fishing. *Address:* Grange, Honiton, Devon. *T:* Broadhembury 377. *Clubs:* Pratt's; Royal Yacht Squadron (Cowes).

**PRITCHARD, Sir Asa Hubert,** Kt 1965; Merchant, retired; President, Asa H. Pritchard Ltd, Nassau; *b* 1 Aug. 1891; *s* of William Edward Pritchard, Bahamas; *m* 1915, Maud Pauline Pyfrom. *Educ:* Queen's College, Bahamas. MHA, Bahamas, 1925-62; Deputy Speaker, 1942-46; Speaker, 1946-62. Member: Board of Education, 1930-35; Electricity Board, 1940-46; Chm., Bahamas Develt Bd, 1946. *Address:* Breezy Ridge, PO Box 737, Nassau, Bahamas.

**PRITCHARD, Brig. Charles Hilary Vaughan;** *see under* Vaughan, Brig. C. H. V.

**PRITCHARD, Col Sir Derek (Wilbraham),** Kt 1968; Chairman, Carreras Ltd, since 1970; President, Institute of Directors, since 1968; *b* 8 June 1910; *s* of Frank Wheelton Pritchard and Ethel Annie Pritchard (*née* Cheetham); *m* 1941, Denise Arfor Pritchard (*née* Huntbach); two *d*. *Educ:* Clifton College, Bristol. Took over family business of E. Halliday & Son, Ltd, 1939. Called up in TA and served War of 1939-45; demob. as Col and joined Bd of E. K. Cole, Ltd, 1946. Joined Ind Coope Ltd, as Man. Dir of Grants of St James's Ltd, Wine Merchants, 1949. Director: Ind Coope Ltd, 1951; Ind Coope Tetley Ansell Ltd on merger of those companies, 1961; Allied Breweries Ltd, 1968-70; Pye of Cambridge Ltd; Guardian Royal Exchange Assurance Ltd; Caribbean Development Co. Ltd; George Sandeman Sons & Co. Ltd; J. & W. Nicholson & Co. Ltd; Midland Bank Ltd; Montagu Trust Ltd; Samuel Montagu Ltd; Thomas J. Deegan Co. of New York; The Jamaica Co. (Jamco Ltd); Pye Holdings Ltd; etc. Underwriting Member of Lloyd's. Dep. Chm., BNEC, 1965-66, Chm. 1966-68. *Recreations:* farming, fox hunting (Pytchley). *Address:* West Haddon Hall, near Rugby. *T:* West Haddon 210.

**PRITCHARD, E. E. E.;** *see* Evans-Pritchard.

**PRITCHARD, Sir Fred Eills,** Kt 1947; MBE 1942; Director, Inns of Court School of Law, 1958-68; *b* 23 June 1899; *s* of late Fred Pritchard, Liverpool; *m* 1931, Mabel Celia, *d* of late F. W. Gaskin, Liverpool; one *d*. *Educ:* Shrewsbury Sch.; Liverpool Univ. (LLM); Middle Temple; called to Bar, Middle Temple, 1923; practised on Northern Circuit in Liverpool, 1923-37; KC 1937; commission in RMA, 1917-19; commission in Royal Artillery, 1939; Major, and Deputy Judge Advocate, 1939-42; Lt-Col and Assistant Judge Advocate-General, 1942-45; Judge of the Salford Hundred Court of Record, 1944-47; Judge of Queen's Bench Division of High Court of Justice, 1947-53, resigned; Master of the Bench of the Middle Temple since 1946, Treasurer, 1964; Hon. Bencher, Gray's Inn, 1965-; Churchwarden St John's, St John's Wood; London Diocesan and St Marylebone Ruri Decanal Conf.; Mem. Coun. of Hawnes School Ltd; Mem. of House of Laity in National Assembly of Church of England, 1955-60; Chairman Appellate Tribunal for Conscientious Objectors under Nat. Service Act 1948, 1956-; Vice-Chm. Special Cttee for Southern Province under Reorganisation Areas Measure, 1944, 1956-; Chm. Cttee on the Rating of Charities, 1958-59; Chm. Special Grants Cttee, 1960; Mem. (apptd by LCJ), Governing Body Shrewsbury School, 1960-68 (Chm., 1960-68). A Church Commissioner, 1959-68; a Comr apptd by Min. of Aviation, Civil Aviation (Licensing) Regulations, 1960.

Hon. LLD Liverpool, 1956. *Publication:* The Common Calendar: a notebook on Criminal Law for Circuiteers. *Address:* 18 Hanover House, St John's Wood, NW8. *T:* 01-722 4932; 14 Chichester Court, Rustington, Sussex. *T:* Rustington 6002. *Clubs:* Constitutional, Public Schools; Middlesex County Cricket.

**PRITCHARD, Frederick Hugh Dalzel,** CBE 1961; Secretary-General, British Red Cross Society, 1951-70; *b* 26 Aug. 1905; *e s* of Gerald William and Alice Bayes Pritchard (*née* Dalzel), Richmond, Surrey; *m* 1935, Rosamond Wright Marshall; two *d. Educ:* Charterhouse School; Oriel College, Oxford. Admitted Solicitor, 1931. Partner in Pritchard Sons Partington & Holland, solicitors, London, 1933. Legal Adviser, War Organisation of British Red Cross Soc. and Order of St John, 1940. Exec. Asst to Vice-Chm., British Red Cross Soc., 1948. OStJ 1942. *Address:* Denver, Bulstrode Way, Gerrards Cross, Bucks. *T:* Gerrards Cross 83483.

**PRITCHARD, Hugh Wentworth,** CBE 1969; Partner in Messrs Sharpe Pritchard & Co., Solicitors and Parliamentary Agents, Westminster; Member of Council of Law Society, 1947-66; *b* 15 March 1903; *s* of late Sir Harry G. Pritchard; *m* 1934, Barbara Stableforth; two *s. Educ:* Charterhouse; Balliol College, Oxford. Admitted a solicitor, 1927; partner in Sharpe Pritchard & Co., 1928. Pres. Soc. of Parliamentary Agents, 1952-55; Member: Statute Law Committee, 1954; Committee on Administrative Tribunals and Enquiries, 1955; Council on Tribunals, 1958. Lay Reader, 1947. Served War of 1939-45, in England, France, Belgium and Germany; joined The Queen's as a private; commissioned in RAOC, attaining rank of Lt-Col. *Recreation:* golf. *Address:* 38 Russell Hill, Purley, Surrey CR2 2JA. *T:* 01-660 9029. *Clubs:* St Stephen's, London Rowing.

**PRITCHARD, Prof. John Joseph,** DM; FRCS; Professor of Anatomy in The Queen's University, Belfast, and Consultant in Anatomy to Northern Ireland Hospitals Authority, since 1952; *b* 9 Feb. 1916; *s* of Leonard Charles and Isobel Violet Pritchard, Adelaide, SA; *m* 1940, Muriel Rachel Edmunds; three *s* one *d. Educ:* St Peter's College, Adelaide; St Mark's College (University of Adelaide); Magdalen College, Oxford; St Bartholomew's Hospital, London. Rhodes Scholar, SA, 1934; BSc Adelaide, 1934; BA Hons Oxford, 1936; MRCS, LRCP 1940; MA Oxon, BM, BCh Oxon, 1940; DM Oxon, 1951; FRCS 1964. Ho. Phys., Mill Hill Emergency Hosp. and St Bartholomew's Hosp.; Demonstrator in Anatomy, University Coll., London, 1940; Asst Lectr, Lecturer, then Reader in Anatomy at St Mary's Hosp. Med. School, University of London, 1941-52. Vice-President, Anatomical Society of Great Britain and Ireland, 1953-56, 1958, President, 1967-69. Visiting Professor of Anatomy, Univ. of Illinois, 1965-66. *Publications:* articles on placental structure and function and bone growth and repair, chiefly in Jl of Anatomy, London. *Recreation:* conversation. *Address:* 75 Osborne Park, Belfast, Northern Ireland. *T:* 667206.

**PRITCHARD, John Michael,** CBE 1962; Musical Director, Glyndebourne Opera, since 1969, Principal Conductor since 1967; *b* 5 Feb. 1921; *s* of Albert Edward Pritchard and Amy Edith Shaylor. *Educ:* Sir George Monoux School, London; privately. Conductor: Derby String Orchestra, 1943-51; Music Staff, Glyndebourne Opera, 1947, Chorus master, 1949; Conductor, Jacques Orchestra, 1950-52; Asst to Fritz Busch, Vittorio Gui, 1950-51; Conductor Glyndebourne Festivals, 1952-68; Conductor and Musical Director, Royal Liverpool Philharmonic Orchestra, 1957-63; Musical Director, London Philharmonic Orchestra, 1962-66; Guest Conductor: Vienna State Opera, 1952-53, 1964-65; Covent Garden Opera, 1952-70; Edinburgh Internat. Festivals, opera and symphony concerts 1951-55, 1960, 1961, 1962, 1963; Aix-en-Provence Festival, 1963; Frankfurt Radio Orchestra, 1953; Cologne Radio Orchestra, 1953; Vienna Symphony Orchestra, 1953-55; Berlin Festival, 1954, 1964; Zürich Radio Orchestra, 1955, 1961; Santa Cecilia Orchestra, Rome, 1958; Orchestre Nationale, Brussels, 1958, 1965-67; Cracow Philharmonic Orch., 1961; Basel, Winterthur Orch., 1961, 1969; RIAS Orchestra, Berlin, 1961, 1966; Royal Philharmonic Soc., London, 1959, 1961, 1963, 1964, 1965, 1966, 1970; Wexford Festival, 1959, 1961; Oslo Philharmonic Orch., 1960, 1961, 1966; Pittsburgh Symphony Orch., 1963, 1964, and San Francisco Symphony, 1964; BBC Promenade Concerts, 1960, 1961, 1962, 1963, 1964, 1965, 1966, 1967, 1968; tour of Switzerland, 1962, 1966; of Australia, 1962; of Germany, 1963, 1966; with BBC Symph. Orch., 1968; tour of Jugoslavia, 1968; Georges Enesco Festival, Bucharest, 1964; Lausanne Festival, 1964; Berlin Philharmonic, 1964; New York Opera Assoc., 1964; Société Philharmonique, Brussels, 1965, 1967; Helsinki Philharmonic, 1966; Salzburg Festival, 1966; Teatro Colon, Buenos Aires, 1966; RAI Symphony Orch., Turin, 1967; Sjaellands Symphony Orch., Copenhagen, 1967-70; SABC Orchestra, Johannesburg, 1967-70; Scandinavian Tour, Glyndebourne Opera, 1967; Teatro San Carlo, Naples, 1969-70; Danish Radio Symph., 1968; Palermo Sinfonia, 1968; Munich State Opera, 1968-69; Athens Festival, 1968-70; Leipzig Gewandhaus, 1968-70; Dresden Staatskapelle, 1968-70; Berlin Radio, 1968-70; Chicago Civic Opera, 1969; London Philharmonic Tour, Far East, 1969; New Philharmonic Orch., Osaka, Tokyo, 1970; San Francisco Opera, 1970. *Recreations:* good food and wine, theatre. *Address:* Carters Corner Place, near Hailsham, Sussex. *Club:* Spanish.

**PRITCHARD, Sir Neil,** KCMG 1962 (CMG 1952); Ambassador in Bangkok, since 1967; *b* 14 January 1911; *s* of late Joseph and Lillian Pritchard; *m* 1943, Mary Burroughes, Pretoria, S Africa; one *s. Educ:* Liverpool Coll.; Worcester Coll., Oxford. Dominions Office, 1933; Private Secretary to Permanent Under-Sec., 1936-38; Assistant Secretary, Rhodesia-Nyasaland Royal Commission, 1938; Secretary, Office of UK High Commissioner, Pretoria, 1941-45; Principal Secretary, Office of UK Representative, Dublin, 1948-49; Assistant Under-Secretary of State, Commonwealth Relations Office, 1951-54; Dep. UK High Commissioner: Canada, 1954-57; Australia, 1957-60; Actg Dep. Under-Sec. of State, CRO, 1961; British High Comr in Tanganyika, 1961-63; Deputy Under-Secretary of State, Commonwealth Office (formerly CRO), 1963-67. *Recreation:* golf. *Address:* British Embassy, Bangkok, Thailand. *Club:* United University.

**PRITCHETT, Victor Sawdon,** CBE 1968; FRSL; Author and Critic; *b* 16 Dec. 1900; *s* of Sawdon Pritchett and Beatrice Martin; *m* Dorothy, *d* of Richard Samuel Roberts, Welshpool, Montgomeryshire; one *s* one *d. Educ:* Alleyn's School. Dir of New Statesman and Nation. Christian Gauss Lectr, Princeton Univ., 1953; Beckman Prof., Univ. California, Berkeley, 1962; Writer-in-Residence, Smith Coll., Mass, 1966; Vis. Professor: Brandeis Univ., Mass;

Columbia Univ.; Clark Lectr, 1969. *Publications:* Marching Spain; Clare Drummer; The Spanish Virgin; Shirley Sanz; Nothing Like Leather; Dead Man Leading; You Make Your Own Life; In My Good Books; It May Never Happen; The Living Novel; (with Elizabeth Bowen and Graham Greene) Why Do I Write?; Mr Beluncle; Books in General; The Spanish Temper; Collected Stories; When My Girl Comes Home (short stories); London Perceived; The Key to My Heart; New York Proclaimed; Foreign Faces; The Working Novelist; Dublin; A Cab at the Door (RSL Award); Blind Love (short stories); Meredith and English Comedy. *Address:* 12 Regent's Park Terrace, NW1. *Clubs:* Garrick, Savile.

**PRITT, Denis Nowell,** QC 1927; *b* 1887; *s* of late Harry Walter Pritt, Billericay, Essex; *m* 1914, Marie Frances, *d* of Walter Gough; one *d*. *Educ:* Winchester; London University; Germany; Switzerland; Spain; LLB London. Called to Bar, Middle Temple, 1909, retired from practice, 1960; MP (Soc.) N Hammersmith, 1935-50; Professor of Law, University of Ghana, 1965-66. Late Chm. of Howard League for Penal Reform and of Bentham Committee for Poor Litigants; President, Society for Cultural Relations with USSR; Pres., British Rumanian Friendship Assoc.; Joint Pres., Soc. for Friendship with Bulgaria; Hon. Pres. Internat. Assoc. of Democratic Lawyers; late Pres. Brit. Peace Cttee; Member of World Peace Council. Freedom of the city of Leipzig, 1957. Hon. LLD: Charles Univ., Prague, 1957; Sofia Univ., 1960; Humboldt Univ., Berlin, 1960; Moscow Univ., 1961. Lenin Peace Prize, 1954; Order of Georgi Dimitrov, 1964; Star of Internat. Friendship, 1965; Gold Medal of Czechoslovak Soc. for Internat. Relations, 1968. *Publications:* Light on Moscow, 1939; Must the War Spread?, 1949; Federal Illusion, 1940; Choose your Future, 1940; The Fall of the French Republic, 1940; USSR Our Ally, 1941; India Our Ally?; Revolt in Europe; A New World Grows; Star-Spangled Shadow, 1947; The State Department and the Cold War (New York), 1948; The Truth about the USSR; Russia is for Peace; Spies and Informers in the Witness-box, 1958; Liberty in Chains, 1962; The Labour Government, 1945-1951, 1963; Neo-Nazis, the Danger of War, 1966; The Autobiography of D. N. Pritt, Part 1, From Right to Left, 1965; Part 2, Brasshats and Bureaucrats, 1966; Part 3, The Defence Accuses, 1966; The Sale of Goods Act and the Partnership Act (India), 1966; Unrepentant Aggressors, 1969; Law, Class and Society, book I: Employers, Workers, and Trade Unions, 1970; many pamphlets; pt author of Twelve Studies in Soviet Russia; joint author of The Law versus the Trade Unions, 1958. *Address:* Barn End, Pamber Heath, Basingstoke, Hants. *T:* Silchester 319.

**PRITTIE,** family name of **Baron Dunalley.**

**PROBERT, Arthur Reginald;** MP (Lab) for Aberdare since Oct. 1954; *b* 1909; *s* of Albert John Probert, Penylan, Aberaman, Aberdare; *m* 1938, Muriel, *d* of late William Taylor, Abercwmboi, Glam; two *d*. *Educ:* elementary and grammar schools, Aberdare. Entered local government service, 1928; Housing Assistant, Aberdare Urban District Council. Secretary of Aberdare Trades and Labour Council, 1949-54; Member of the Executive Committee of Glamorgan Federation of Trades Councils, 1951-54; member of local employment and old age pensioners' welfare committees; Opposition Whip (Welsh), Oct. 1959-Feb. 1961; PPS to Minister of Technology, 1965-66. Served in Scotland, Germany and Denmark with Royal Air Force Volunteer Reserve, 1941-46. *Address:* Allt Fedw, Abernant, Aberdare, Glamorganshire; c/o House of Commons, SW1.

**PROBERT, Rhys Price;** Deputy Controller of Aircraft (RAF), Ministry of Technology, since 1968; *b* 28 May 1921; *s* of late Reverend Thomas and Margaret Jane Probert; *m* 1947, Carolyn Cleasby, Lancaster, NH, USA; three *s* one *d*. *Educ:* Jones' West Monmouth School; St Catharine's College, Cambridge. Royal Aircraft Establishment, 1942-44; Power Jets (Research and Development) Ltd, 1944-46; Applied Physics Laboratory, Johns Hopkins Univ., 1946-47; National Gas Turbine Establishment, 1947-63 (Dep. Dir, 1957); Director-General of Scientific Research/Air, Min. of Aviation, 1963-68. *Publications:* contribs to various scientific and technical jls. *Recreations:* squash, reading. *Address:* Fourways, Avenue Road, Farnborough, Hants. *Club:* Leander (Henley).

**PROBY, Major Sir Richard George,** 1st Bt *cr* 1952; MC 1917; landowner and farmer; Vice-Lieutenant of Huntingdonshire, 1957-66; *b* 21 July 1886; *s* of late Col D. J. Proby, Elton, and of Lady Margaret Proby (*née* Hely Hutchinson), *d* of 4th Earl of Donoughmore, PC; *m* 1911, Betty Monica (*d* 1967), *d* of late A. Hallam Murray; two *s* three *d* (and one *s* decd). *Educ:* Eton; Royal Military Acad., Woolwich. Lieutenant RFA, 1906-10; Captain Essex Yeomanry, 1913; Major 1919; served European War, 1914-19 (MC). Private sec. to Lord Ailwyn, 1st Chm. Agricultural Wages Bd, 1918. Chm. Hunts War Agric. Exec. Cttee, 1939, liaison officer to Min. of Agriculture, 1941-44 and 1952-55. Chm. Country Landowners' Assoc., 1943-46, Pres., 1947-51; an hon. Vice-Pres. Land Agents' Soc.; Mem. Coun. RASE; Chm. Forestry Cttee of Gt Britain, 1959; Chm. Eastern Provincial Area Conservative Assoc., 1938, Pres. 1960; Chm. Ex. Cttee of National Union of Conservative and Unionist Associations, 1943; Chm. National Union, 1946; Pres. National Union, 1958. Chm. Real Estate Panel of Eton College, 1952. Member Wilson Agricultural Reorganisation Cttee, 1955; JP Hunts; CC for Hunts; DL Hunts, 1952; High Sheriff, Hunts, Cambs, and the Isle of Ely, 1953; Pres. Roy. Forestry Society of England, Wales and Northern Ireland, 1955; Chm. Timber Growers Organization of England and Wales, 1959-, Pres. 1961; Mem. Exec. of Irish Landowners' Convention; Bledisloe Gold Medal for distinguished service to Agriculture, 1967. *Publications:* articles and letters on agricultural and forestry matters contributed to the Times, the Quarterly Review, etc. *Recreations:* riding, travelling, forestry. *Heir:* *s* Captain Peter Proby [*b* 4 Dec. 1911; *m* 1944, Blanche Harrison, *o d* of Lt-Col Henry Harrison Cripps, DSO; two *s* three *d*]. *Address:* Elton Hall, Peterborough, Northants. *T:* Elton 211; Eversham, Blackrock, Dublin. *T:* Dublin 887492. *Clubs:* Travellers', Constitutional, Roxburghe; Kildare Street (Dublin).

*See also Baron Inglewood, J. C. Moberly.*

**PROBYN, Air Commodore Harold Melsome,** CB 1944; CBE 1943; DSO 1917; *b* 8 Dec. 1891; *s* of late William Probyn; *m* 1920, Marjory (*d* 1961), *d* of late Francis Evance Savory. Served European War, 1914-17 (despatches, DSO); commanded: 208 (AC) Squadron, Egypt; No. 2 (AC), Squadron, Manston; 25 (Fighter) Squadron at Hawkinge; RAF School of Photography, 1932; No. 22 Group, RAF, 1932-34; Senior Personnel Staff Officer, Middle East, Cairo, 1934-35; Senior Engineer Staff Officer, Middle East, Cairo, 1935-37; No. 12 (Fighter) Group Royal Air Force,

Hucknall, Notts, 1937; served War of 1939-45 (despatches); commanded RAF Station, Cranwell, 1940-44; retired, 1944. *Address:* Nyeri, Kenya.

**PROCTER, Rev. Arthur Herbert,** VC; retired; *b* 11 Aug. 1890; *s* of Arthur Richard Procter and Ellen Cumpsty; *m* 1917; three *s*. *Educ:* St Aidan's College, Birkenhead. Clerk in provision trade, 1904-14; served in 5th King's Liverpool Regt, 1914-18; salesman in provision trade, 1918-26; ordained, 1927; Curate, Prescot Parish Church; Vicar of Bosley; Vicar of St Stephen's, Hyde, 1933-43; RAF Chaplain, 1941; Rector of St Mary's, Droylsden, 1946-51; Vicar of St Peters, Claybrooke, Rugby, 1951-63; Vicar of St John the Baptist, Bradworthy, 1963-65. *Recreations:* golf, cricket. *Address:* Clover Dell, 53 Mytton Oak Road, Shrewsbury, Shropshire.

**PROCTER, Dod,** RA 1942 (ARA 1934); Artist; *d* of Doctor Frederick Charles Shaw and Eunice Mary Richards; *m* 1912, Ernest Procter, ARA (*d* 1935); one *s*. *Educ:* Newlyn; Paris. *Works:* Tate Gallery, etc. *Address:* North Corner, Newlyn, Penzance, *T:* Penzance 2620.

**PROCTER, Evelyn Emma Stefanos,** MA; *b* 6 June 1897; *y d* of late Harold and Ada Louisa Procter. *Educ:* Cheltenham Ladies' College; Somerville College, Oxford. Hons Mod. Hist. Cl. 1, 1918; Mary Somerville Research Fellow, Somerville College, 1921-25; Tutor in History (1925) and Fellow of St Hugh's College, Oxford, 1926-46; University Lecturer in Medieval European History, 1933-39; Norman Maccoll Lecturer, University of Cambridge, 1948-49; Principal, St Hugh's College, Oxford, 1946-62, retd. Hon. Fell. St Hugh's College, Oxford, 1962. Chevalier de la Légion d'Honneur. *Publications:* Alfonso X of Castile; Patron of Literature and Learning, 1951; contributor to: Oxford Essays in Medieval History, presented to H. E. Salter, 1934; Homenaje a Rubió i Lluch, 1936; articles in Transactions of Royal Historical Society, Revue Hispanique, English Historical Review and Modern Language Review. *Recreation:* water-colour sketching. *Address:* Little Newland, Eynsham, Oxford.

**PROCTER, Norma;** Contralto Singer; *b* Cleethorpes, Lincolnshire, 1928. Studied under Roy Henderson and Alec Redshaw. Made first London appearance at Southwark Cathedral; debut at Covent Garden, in Gluck's Orpheus, 1961. Has sung at major British music festivals; other festivals: Santander, 1957; Vienna, 1958; Berlin, 1959. Numerous concerts and recitals throughout Europe; frequent broadcasts in Britain, Holland and Germany; has made many recordings. *Address:* 194 Clee Road, Grimsby, Lincolnshire; c/o Ibbs & Tillett Ltd, 124 Wigmore Street, W1.

**PROCTER-GREGG, Humphrey;** Emeritus Professor; Director, London Opera Centre, 1962-64; *b* Kirkby Lonsdale, 31 July 1895; *s* of Oliver Procter-Gregg, JP, and Florence Annie (*née* Hoare). *Educ:* King William's College; Peterhouse, Cambridge (Hist. and Organ Schol.); Royal College of Music (Opera Schol. and studentship to La Scala, Milan). MusB, MA. Hon. ARCM, FRCM. Became opera manager to Royal Coll. of Music, and stage-manager and/or producer to the Covent Garden, BNOC, and Carl Rosa Opera companies, also to Royal Manchester College of Music and BBC Opera Section; Dir, Carl Rosa Opera Company, 1958, Touring Opera, 1958. Professor of Music, University of Manchester, 1954-62, retired. Compositions include violin and clarinet sonatas, pianoforte music, songs and translations of operas. *Recreation:* painting. *Address:* 3 Oakland, Windermere, Westmorland.

**PROCTOR, Sir Dennis;** *see* Proctor, Sir P. D.

**PROCTOR, Ian Douglas Ben,** RDI 1969; FSIA 1969; Chairman, Ian Proctor Metal Masts Ltd, since 1959; freelance industrial designer since 1950; *b* 12 July 1918; *s* of Douglas McIntyre Proctor and Mary Albina Louise Proctor (*née* Tredwen); *m* 1942, Elizabeth Anne Gifford Lywood, *d* of Air Vice-Marshal O. G. Lywood, CB, CBE; three *s* one *d*. *Educ:* Gresham's Sch., Holt; London University. RAFVR (Flying Officer), 1941-47. Man. Dir, Gosport Yacht Co., 1947-48; Joint Editor Yachtsman Magazine, 1948-50; Daily Telegraph Yachting Correspondent, 1950-64. Yachtsman of the Year, 1965; Council of Industrial Design Award, 1967. *Publications:* Racing Dinghy Handling, 1948; Racing Dinghy Maintenance, 1949; Sailing: Wind and Current, 1950; Boats for Sailing, 1968. *Recreation:* sailing. *Address:* Fenmead, Brook Avenue, Warsash, Southampton. *Clubs:* Nash House; Hayling Island Sailing, Warsash Sailing, Hamble River Sailing, Aldenham Sailing.

**PROCTOR, Ven. Jesse Heighton,** MA (London); Archdeacon of Warwick, since 1958; Vicar of Sherbourne, Warwick, 1958-69; *b* 26 May 1908; *s* of Thomas and Sophia Proctor, Melton Mowbray; *m* 1938, Helena Mary Wood, *d* of John Thomas and Jessie Wood, Melton Mowbray; one *s* two *d*. *Educ:* County Grammar Sch. of King Edward VII, Melton Mowbray; Coll. of St Mark and St John, Chelsea, Univ. of London; St Andrew's Theological Training House, Whittlesford. Asst Master, Winterbourne Sch., Croydon, 1929-32; Sen. History Master, Melton Mowbray Gram. Sch., 1932-35; Deacon 1935, Priest 1936; Chap. and Tutor, St Andrew's, Whittlesford, 1935-38; Curate, St Philip's, Leicester, 1938-39; Vicar, Glen Parva and South Wigston, and Chap., Glen Parva Barracks, Leicester, 1939-46; Precentor of Coventry Cath., 1946-58; Hon. Canon of Coventry, 1947; Chaplain, Gulson Hosp., 1953-58; Sen. Examining Chap. to Bishop of Coventry, 1947-65; Canon Theologian of Coventry, 1954-59; Vice-Pres. CMS. Governor: Univ. of Warwick, 1966-68; City of Coventry Coll. of Educn, 1966-70. *Publications:* contrib. to Neville Gorton (SPCK), 1957. *Recreations:* journalism and the countryside. *Address:* Sherbourne Vicarage, Warwick. *T:* Barford 344. *Club:* National Liberal.

**PROCTOR, Sir (Philip) Dennis,** KCB 1959 (CB 1946); Director, Williams Hudson Ltd, since 1966; *b* 1 Sept. 1905; *s* of late Sir Philip Proctor, KBE; *m* 1st, 1936, Dorothy Varda (*d* 1951); no *c*; 2nd, 1953, Barbara, *d* of Sir Ronald Adam, Bt, *qv*; two *s* one *d*. *Educ:* Falconbury; Harrow; King's Coll., Cambridge. MA, 1929; entered Min. of Health, 1929; transferred to Treasury, 1930; Third Secretary, HM Treasury, 1948-50; resigned from Civil Service; joined the firm of A. P. Moller, Copenhagen, 1950; Man. Director, The Maersk Company Ltd, 1951-53; re-entered Civil Service, 1953; Dep. Sec., Min. of Transport and Civil Aviation, 1953-58; Permanent Sec., Min. of Power, 1958-65. Trustee of Tate Gallery, 1952; Chairman of the Tate Gallery, 1953-59. Hon. Fellow, King's Coll., Cambridge, 1968. *Address:* 43 Canonbury Square, N1. *T:* 01-226 4676. *Club:* Royal Automobile.

**PROCTOR-BEAUCHAMP, Rev. Sir I. C.;** *see* Beauchamp.

**PROFUMO, John Dennis,** OBE 1944; 5th Baron of the late United Kingdom of Italy; *b* 30 Jan. 1915; *e s* of late Baron Albert Profumo, KC; *m* 1954, Valerie Hobson, *qv*; one *s*. *Educ:* Harrow; Brasenose College, Oxford. Chief of Staff UK Mission in Japan, 1945. MP (C) Kettering Division, Northamptonshire, 1940-45; MP (C) Stratford-on-Avon Division of Warwickshire, 1950-63; Joint Parliamentary Secretary, Ministry of Transport and Civil Aviation, Nov. 1952-Jan. 1957; Parliamentary Under-Secretary of State for the Colonies, 1957-58; Parliamentary Under-Sec. of State, Foreign Affairs, Nov. 1958-Jan. 1959; Minister of State for Foreign Affairs, 1959-60; Secretary of State for War, July 1960-June 1963. Mem., Bd of Visitors, HM Prison, Grendon, 1968-. 1st Northamptonshire Yeomanry, 1939 (despatches). *Recreations:* shooting, cinematography. *Heir: s b* 30 Oct. 1955. *Club:* Boodle's.

*See also Baron Balfour of Inchrye.*

**PROKHOROV, Prof. Alexander Mikhailovich;** Physicist and Deputy Director, PN Lebedev Institute of Physics, Academy of Sciences of the USSR, Moscow; *b* Atherton, Australia, 11 July 1916; *s* of Mikhail Prokhorov; *m* 1941, Galina Alexeyevna (*née* Shelepina); one *s*. *Educ:* Leningrad State University; Lebedev Inst. of Physics. Corresponding Member, Academy of Sciences of the USSR (Department of Pure and Applied Physics), 1960-66, Full Member, 1966-; Professor, Moscow University, 1958-; Member, Communist Party of the Soviet Union, 1950-. Awarded Lenin Prize, 1959; Nobel Prize for Physics (jointly with Prof. N. G. Basov and Prof. C. H. Townes), 1964. *Publications:* contributions on non-linear oscillations, radiospectroscopy and quantum radio-physics. *Address:* P. N. Lebedev Institute of Physics, Academy of Sciences of the USSR, 53 Lenin Prospekt, Moscow, USSR.

**PROKHOROVA, Violetta;** *see* Elvin, V.

**PROKOSCH, Frederic;** Writer; *b* 17 May 1908; *s* of Eduard (Professor of Linguistics, Yale University) and Mathilde Prokosch. *Educ:* Yale University (PhD, 1933); King's College, Cambridge. Educated as a child in Wisconsin, Texas, Munich, Austria; travelled extensively all his life; research work in Chaucerian MSS, 1933-38 (PhD Dissertation: The Chaucerian Apocrypha). *Publications:* The Asiatics (novel), 1935; The Assassins (poems), 1936; The Seven Who Fled (novel), 1937; The Carnival (poems), 1938; Night of The Poor (novel), 1939; Death at Sea (poems), 1940; The Skies of Europe (novel), 1942; The Conspirators (novel), 1943; Some Poems of Hölderlin, 1943; Chosen Poems, 1944; Age of Thunder (novel), 1945; The Idols of the Cave (novel), 1946; The Medea of Euripides, 1947; The Sonnets of Louise Labé, 1947; Storm and Echo (novel), 1948; Nine Days to Mukalla (novel), 1953; A Tale for Midnight (novel), 1955; A Ballad of Love (novel), 1960; The Seven Sisters (novel), 1962; The Dark Dancer (novel), 1964; The Wreck of the Cassandra (novel), 1966; The Missolonghi Manuscript (novel), 1968. *Recreations:* squash racquets (Champion of France, 1938, 1939, Champion of Sweden, 1944), lawn tennis (Champion of Mallorca). *Address:* 44 Avenue de New York, Paris, 16, France. *Clubs:* Pitt (Cambridge); Yale (New York); France-Amérique (Paris).

**PROOPS, Mrs Marjorie,** OBE 1969; journalist; *d* of Alfred and Martha Rayle; *m* 1935; one *s*. *Educ:* Dalston Secondary Sch. Daily Mirror, 1939-45; Daily Herald, 1945-54; Daily Mirror, 1954-. Broadcaster, Television, 1960-. Mem., Council for the Unmarried Mother and Her Child. Woman Journalist of the Year, 1969. *Address:* 9 Sherwood Close, SW13.

**PROPHET, Prof. Arthur Shelley,** DDS; DpBact; FDSRCS; FFDRCSI; Professor of Dental Surgery, University of London, and Director of the Dental Department of University College Hospital Medical School, since October 1956; *b* 11 Jan. 1918; *s* of Eric Prophet and Mabel Wightman; *m* 1942, Vivienne Mary Bell; two *s*. *Educ:* Sedbergh School; University of Manchester. BDS Hons (Preston Prize and Medal), 1940; Diploma in Bacteriology (Manchester), 1948; DDS (Manchester) 1950; FDSRCS 1958; FFDRCS Ireland, 1964. Served in Royal Naval Volunteer Reserve (Dental Branch), 1941-46; Nuffield Dental Fellow, 1946-48; Lecturer in Dental Bacteriology, University of Manchester, 1948-54; Lecturer in Dental Surgery, QUB, 1954-56. Rep. of University of London on Gen. Dental Council, 1964-. Elected Mem. Bd, Faculty of Dental Surgery, RCS, 1964-; Member: Cttee of Management, Inst. of Dental Surgery, 1963-; Dental Sub-Cttee, UGC, 1968-. WHO Consultant, 1966. *Publications:* contrib. to medical and dental journals. *Recreation:* golf. *Address:* 40 Ollards Grove, Loughton, Essex. *T:* 01-508 3566.

**PROPPER, Arthur,** CMG 1965; MBE 1945; Corporate Planning Executive, Unigate Ltd, since 1970; *b* 3 Aug. 1910; 2nd *s* of late I. Propper; *m* 1941, Erica Mayer; one *d*. *Educ:* Owen's Sch.; Peterhouse, Cambridge (schol.). 1st class, Hist. Tripos, Pt 2. With W. S. Crawford Ltd (Advertising Agents), 1933-38, and the J. Walter Thompson Co. Ltd, 1939; Min. of Economic Warfare, 1940; transf. to Min. of Food, 1946 (subseq. to Min. of Agric., Fisheries and Food); established in Home Civil Service, 1949; Asst Sec., 1952; Mem. UK Delegn at Common Market negotiations, with rank of Under-Sec., 1962-63; seconded to Foreign Office, 1963; Counsellor (Agric.), UK Delegn to the European Communities, Brussels, and HM Embassy, Bonn, 1963-64; Under-Sec., Min. of Agriculture, Fisheries and Food, 1964-70. *Recreations:* the theatre, music, buying books, visiting Scotland. *Address:* 3 Hill House, Stanmore Hill, Middx. *T:* 01-954 1242. *Club:* United University.

**PROSSER, (Albert) Russell (Garness),** CMG 1967; MBE 1953; Adviser, Social Development, Ministry of Overseas Development, since 1967; *b* 8 April 1915; *s* of late Thomas Prosser; *m* 1957, Ruth Avalon Moore; one *s* (and one *s* decd). *Educ:* Godlys Sch.; London Sch. of Economics. Principal, Sch. of Social Welfare, Accra, 1947; Dep. Sec., Uganda, 1959; Permanent Secretary, Uganda, 1962; Adviser, Social Development, Kenya, 1963. Associated Mem., Inst. of Develt Studies, Univ. of Sussex. Editor, Clare Market Review, 1939-40. Golden Medallion, Belgian Govt, 1962. *Recreations:* angling, gardening. *Address:* 18b Wray Park Road, Reigate, Surrey. *T:* Reigate 42792.

**PROSSER, David Russell,** FJI; retired; Editor of the Western Mail, Cardiff, South Wales, 1942-56; *b* 30 October 1889; 2nd *s* of late John Lewis and Hannah Sowden Prosser; *m* 1913, Florence, 2nd *d* of Edwin Harris, Newport. *Educ:* Cardiff Technical College; University College of South Wales and Monmouthshire. Served on staffs of South Wales Echo, South Wales Daily News, Merthyr Express, Daily Dispatch, Manchester; active service European War, 1914-18, with Artists' Rifles OTC, Lieut 1st Bn Monmouthshire Regt (T);

with 5th Bn South Wales Borderers in France; Publicity Officer, Ministry of Labour (Appointments Dept) Wales, 1919-22. OStJ. *Publications:* The British Newspaper Press in Mid-Century, 1957; A National Trust for Promoting the Arts in Wales, 1959. Articles and reviews on history, economics and politics; investigated social conditions in South Wales for Third Winter of Unemployment Report (1922). *Recreations:* golf, angling, music. *Address:* 81a Station Road, Llanishen, Cardiff. *T:* Cardiff 752582.

**PROSSER, Raymond Frederick,** MC 1942; Under-Secretary, Marine Division, Board of Trade, since 1968; *b* 12 Sept. 1919; *s* of Frederick Charles Prosser and Jane Prosser (*née* Lawless); *m* 1949, Fay Newmarch Holmes; two *s* three *d*. *Educ:* Wimbledon Coll.; The Queen's Coll., Oxford (1938-39 and 1946). Served Royal Artillery (Field), 1939-45 (MC, despatches): service in Egypt, Libya, India and Burma; Major. Asst Principal, Min. of Civil Aviation, 1947; Sec., Air Transport Advisory Council, 1952-57; Private Sec. to Minister of Transport and Civil Aviation, 1959, and to Minister of Aviation, 1959-61; Counsellor (Civil Aviation), HM Embassy, Washington, DC, 1965-68. *Address:* Juniper House, Shalford Common, Shalford, Guildford, Surrey. *T:* Guildford 66498.

**PROSSER, Russell;** *see* Prosser, A. R. G.

**PROSSER, Thomas Vivian,** CBE 1963; Chairman and Managing Director, The National Building Agency, 1964-67; *b* 25 April 1908; *er s* of T. V. Prosser, Liverpool; *m* 1935, Florence Minnie (Billie), 2nd *d* of W. J. Boulton, Highworth, Wilts; one *s* one *d*. *Educ:* Old Swan Technical Institute (now West Derby High School); College of Technology, Liverpool. Pupil of A. E. Cuddy, LRIBA, Architect, 1924. Formerly: President, Liverpool Regional Fedn of Building Trades Employers, 1956; Pres., Nat. Fedn of Building Trades Employers, 1959-60. *Recreations:* gardening, reading. *Address:* Lavender Cottage, Brooms Lane, Kelsall, Cheshire. *T:* Kelsall 243. *Clubs:* Lyceum, Artists, Press (Liverpool).

**PROUD, Air Cdre Harold John Granville Ellis,** CBE 1946; *b* 23 Aug. 1906; *s* of late Ralph Henry Proud, Glasgow; *m* 1927, Jenefer Angela Margaret, *d* of late Lt-Col J. Bruce, OBE, 19th Lancers; two *d*. HAC (Inf.), 1924-26; commissioned RAF, pilot, 1926; Staff Coll., 1936; Comd No. 5 (Army Co-op) Sqdn, NW Frontier, India, 1937-38; Group Captain, 1942; Comd RAF Hurn (transport support for 1st Airborne Div.), 1942-43; AOA, Air HQ, India (actg Air Cdre), 1943-45; Director of Ground Defence, Air Min., 1946-47; Commandant RAF Regt Depot, 1947-49; Base Comdr, Far East Base, Singapore, 1949-51; Air Cdre, 1950; AOC 67 (NI) Gp and Senior Air Force Officer N Ire., 1951-54; Provost Marshal and Chief of Air Force Police, 1954; retired 1956. *Address:* Rectory Cottage, West Somerton, Norfolk. *T:* Winterton-on-Sea 628. *Club:* Royal Air Force.

**PROUDFOOT, Bruce Falconer;** Publicity Officer, Ulster Savings Committee, 1963-69; Editor, Northern Whig and Belfast Post, 1943-63; *b* 1903; 2nd *s* of G. A. Proudfoot, Edinburgh; *m* 1928, Cecilia, *er d* of V. T. T. Thompson, Newcastle on Tyne; twin *s*. *Educ:* Edinburgh Education Authority's Primary and Secondary Schools. Served with Edinburgh Evening Dispatch, Galloway Gazette (Newton-Stewart) and Newcastle Daily Chronicle before joining Northern Whig, 1925. *Recreation:* golf. *Address:* 10 Ophir Gardens, Belfast 15. *T:* 76368.

**PROUDFOOT, (George) Wilfred;** MP (C) Brighouse and Spenborough since 1970; owner, self-service stores; consultant in distribution; *b* 19 December 1921; *m* 1950, Margaret Mary, *d* of Percy Clifford Jackson, Pontefract, Yorks; two *s* one *d*. *Educ:* Crook Council Sch.; Scarborough Coll. Served War of 1939-45, NCO Fitter in RAF, 1940-46. Served Scarborough Town Council, 1950-58 (Chm. Health Cttee, 1952-58). MP (C) Cleveland Division of Yorkshire, Oct. 1959-Sept. 1964; PPS to Minister of State, Board of Trade, Apr.-July 1962, to Minister of Housing and Local Govt and Minister for Welsh Affairs (Rt Hon. Sir Keith Joseph, Bt, MP), 1962-64. Man. Dir, Radio 270, 1965-. *Recreations:* reading, photography, caravanning. *Address:* 278 Scalby Road, Scarborough, Yorkshire. *T:* Scarborough 63638/9. *Club:* Constitutional.

**PROUDFOOT, James,** RP 1947; ROI 1937; *b* 3 March 1908; *m* 1929, Editha May Gosman (divorced, 1936); one *s*; *m* 1945, Ellen Pollock, *qv*. *Educ:* Perth Academy; St Andrews. Studied Heatherleys (First Prize for a Still Life, all schools competing); Goldsmiths College, Paris. Elected National Society, 1932; United Artists, 1946; two one-man shows Scotland, one in London. Portrait of Peter Ustinov awarded Mention Honorable, Paris Salon, 1957. Produced some thousands alleged "silly drawings" mostly for private circulation. Illustrated two books poetry: one anthology, one humorous. Served War of 1939-45 as Sapper in Camouflage. *Recreations:* squash, snooker, table-tennis, walking, theatre-going. *Address:* 28 Tedworth Square, SW3. *Clubs:* Chelsea Arts, Savage.

**PROUDFOOT, Wilfred;** *see* Proudfoot, G. W.

**PROUDMAN, Joseph,** CBE 1952; MA, DSc, LLD, FRS; Professor Emeritus, University of Liverpool; Member Norwegian Academy of Science and Letters; Correspondant du Bureau des Longitudes, Paris; *b* 1888; *s* of John Proudman; *m* 1st, 1916, Rubina (*d* 1958), *d* of Thomas Ormrod; two *s* one *d*; 2nd, 1961, Mrs Beryl Gould. *Educ:* Widnes; University of Liverpool; Trinity College, Cambridge. Wrangler with Distinction, 1912; Smith's Prizeman, 1915; Adams Prizeman, 1923; Fellow of Trinity College, Cambridge, 1915-21; Professor of Applied Mathematics in University of Liverpool, 1919-33; Professor of Oceanography, 1933-54; Director of Liverpool Tidal Inst., 1919-45; Pro-Vice-Chancellor, Univ. of Liverpool, 1940-46; Pres. Internat. Assoc. of Physical Oceanography, 1951-54, Sec., 1933-48; Chairman of Advisory Committee on Research on Coastal Flooding, Ministry of Agriculture, Fisheries and Food, 1954-66; Chairman Sub-Committee on Growing Demand for Water, 1959-62 (Min. of Housing and Local Govt). JP Liverpool, 1941-54. A. Agassiz Medal of United States National Academy of Sciences, 1946; Hughes Medal of Royal Society, 1957. *Publications:* The Elements of Mechanics (with F. S. Carey) 1925; Dynamical Oceanography, 1953; scientific papers, mainly on Tides. *Address:* Edgemoor, Dewlands Way, Verwood, Dorset BH21 6JN. *T:* Verwood 2285.

**PRUDE, Mrs Walter F.;** *see* de Mille, Agnes George.

**PRUNTY, Prof. Francis Thomas Garnet,** FRCP; Professor of Chemical Pathology, University of London, at St Thomas's Hospital Medical School, since 1954; Physician, St Thomas' Hospital, since 1950; *b* 5 Jan. 1910; *s* of Frank

Hugh Prunty, and Una Elizah Newnham (*née* Marsden); *m* 1933, Rita Hepburn Stobbs; one *s* one *d*. *Educ:* St Paul's Sch.; Trinity Coll., Cambridge; St Thomas's Hospital Medical Sch. Senior Scholar, Trinity Coll., 1932; MA, Cambridge, 1936; MB, BChir, 1940; MD, 1944; Raymond Horton-Smith Prize, Cambridge, 1944; FRCP 1950. Research Fellow in Medicine, Harvard, USA, 1946-47; Asst in Medicine, Peter Bent Brigham Hospital, Boston, 1946-47; Rockefeller Travelling Fellow, 1946-47; Readership in Chem. Pathol., University of London, 1947; Humphrey Rolleston Lecturer, RCP, 1956. Late: Hon. Secretary Society for Endocrinology; President, Section of Endocrinology, Royal Society Med.; late Pres., International Society of Endocrinology. Life Governor, Imperial Cancer Research Fund (late Mem. Council); Socio Honorario, La Sociedad Medica de Occidente, Guatemala; Hon. Member, Roumanian Society of Endocrinology; co-editor, Steroids. *Publications:* The Chemistry and Treatment of Adrenocortical Diseases, 1964; A Laboratory Manual of Chemical Pathology (jointly), 1959; various articles in Medical and Biochemical journals. *Recreations:* travel, sailing. *Address:* 1 Lowndes Square, SW1. *T:* 01-235 4249. *Club:* Royal Thames Yacht.

**PRYCE, Professor Daniel Merlin;** Professor of Morbid Anatomy, St Mary's Hospital Medical School, University of London, 1954-67, now Emeritus; *b* 17 April 1902; *s* of Richard and Rachel Pryce, Troedyrhiw, S. Wales; *m* 1934, Mary Whelan; one *s* two *d*. *Educ:* Welsh National School of Medicine; St Mary's Hospital Medical Sch. St Mary's Hospital: Research Schol., Inoculation Dept, 1927; 2nd Asst Pathologist, 1928; Asst Chemical Pathologist, 1930; 1st Asst Pathologist, 1933; Reader in Morbid Anatomy, 1949. EMS Pathologist, Harefield and Amersham, 1939. *Publications:* (jointly) Ross's Post-Mortem Appearances, 6th edn, 1963; scientific papers in morbid anatomy, bacteriology and haematology. *Recreations:* sketching, mountaineering. *Address:* 11 Blomfield Road, W9. *T:* 01-286 5796.

**PRYCE, Edward Calcott,** CBE 1957 (OBE 1940); BA, LLB; Captain; Solicitor; retired; Sheriff, City of London, 1954; *b* 1885; *s* of David Pryce, Guilsfield, Mont; *m* 1911, Sylvia Middleton, Arbroath, Scotland (*d* 1967); no *c*. *Educ:* Welshpool and Aberystwyth. Qualified Solicitor, 1909. Served European War, 1914-18, and War of 1939-45. High Sheriff, Montgomeryshire, 1956. *Recreations:* gardening, shooting. *Address:* Bod Isaf, Guilsfield, Welshpool, Montgomeryshire. *T:* Guilsfield 362.

**PRYCE, Maurice Henry Lecorney,** FRS 1951; Professor of Physics, University of British Columbia, since 1968; *b* 24 Jan. 1913; *e s* of William John Pryce and Hortense Lecorney; *m* 1939, Susanne Margarete Born (marr. diss., 1959); one *s* three *d*; *m* 1961, Freda Mary Kinsey. *Educ:* Royal Grammar Sch., Guildford; Trinity Coll., Cambridge. Commonwealth Fund Fellow at Princeton, NJ, USA, 1935-37; Fellow of Trinity Coll., Cambridge, and Faculty Asst Lecturer, University of Cambridge, 1937-39; Reader in Theoretical Physics, University of Liverpool, 1939-45. Engaged on Radar research with Admiralty Signal Establishment, 1941-44, and on Atomic Energy Research with National Research Council of Canada, Montreal, 1944-45. University Lecturer in Mathematics and Fellow of Trinity Coll., Cambridge, 1945-46; Wykeham Professor of Physics, University of Oxford, 1946-54; Henry Overton Wills Professor of Physics, University of Bristol, 1954-64; Prof. of Physics, University of Southern California, 1964-68. Visiting Professor, Princeton Univ., NJ, USA, 1950-51. *Publications:* various on Theoretical Physics, in learned journals. *Recreations:* lawn tennis, sailing. *Address:* Physics Department, University of British Columbia, Vancouver 8, Canada. *Club:* Athenæum.

**PRYCE-JONES, Alan Payan,** TD; Book Critic, The New York Herald Tribune, since 1963; author and journalist; *b* 18 Nov. 1908; *s* of late Colonel Henry Morris Pryce-Jones, CB; *m* 1934, Thérèse (*d* 1953), *d* of late Baron Fould-Springer and of Mrs Frank Wooster, Paris; one *s*; *m* 1968, Mrs Mary Jean Kempner Thorne (*d* 1969), *d* of late Daniel Kempner. *Educ:* Eton; Magdalen Coll., Oxford. Formerly Asst Editor, The London Mercury, 1928-32; subseq. Times Literary Supplement; Editor, Times Literary Supplement, 1948-59; Trustee, National Portrait Gallery, 1950-61; Director, Old Vic Trust, 1950-61; Member Council, Royal College of Music, 1956-61; Program Associate, The Humanities and Arts Program, Ford Foundation, NY, 1961-63. Served War of 1939-45, France, Italy, Austria; Lieut-Colonel, 1945. *Publications:* The Spring Journey, 1931; People in the South, 1932; Beethoven, 1933; 27 Poems, 1935; Private Opinion, 1936; Nelson, an opera, 1954; Vanity Fair, a musical play (with Robin Miller and Julian Slade), 1962. *Recreations:* music, travelling. *Address:* 19 East 55th Street, New York NY 10022, USA. *Clubs:* Travellers', Garrick, Beefsteak, Pratt's, MCC; Century (New York).

**PRYDE, James Richmond Northridge,** CBE 1944; formerly General Manager of Poonmudi Tea and Rubber Co. Ltd, retired 1956; *b* 14 Aug. 1894; *s* of James Oliphant and Bessie Anne Pryde, Leighinmohr, Ballymena, N. Ireland; *m* 1921, Katharine, *d* of T. M. McNeil, St John's, Newfoundland; three *s* one *d*. *Educ:* St Bees Sch., Cumberland. Planting (entirely) since 1912. President, United Planters' Assoc. of Southern India, 1940-44. *Address:* Portland, Lorrha P.O., Co. Tipperary, Eire.

**PRYKE, Sir David Dudley,** 3rd Bt *cr* 1926; *b* 16 July 1912; *s* of Sir William Robert Dudley Pryke, 2nd Bt; *S* father 1959; *m* 1945, Doreen Winifred, *er d* of late Ralph Bernard Wilkins; two *d*. *Educ:* St Lawrence Coll., Ramsgate. Member, Common Council, Queenhithe Ward, 1960; Liveryman Turners' Company, 1961. *Heir:* *b* William Dudley Pryke [*b* 18 Nov. 1914; *m* 1940, Lucy Irene, *d* of late Frank Madgett; one *s* one *d*]. *Address:* 20 Plough Hill, Cuffley, Hertfordshire.

**PRYNNE, Brig. Harold Gordon Lusby,** CBE 1943 (OBE 1942); MC 1918; TD; *b* 8 May 1899; *s* of late William Henry Gordon Prynne; *m* 1950, Doris Elizabeth, *d* of Harry James Gully. *Educ:* University College Sch., London. Director of various private companies at home and abroad. Served European War, France, 1915-19 (MC), Kensington Regt (Territorial), Pte, Lieut, Captain, Major; DAQMG 56th Division; Regular Commn, 1919; DAQMG Rhine Army, 1919; Reserve of Officers, 1920; Brevet Major for services to Territorial Army, 1925; War of 1939-45 with Royal Pioneer Corps (despatches); Major, 1939; Lieut-Colonel, 1940; Colonel, 1942; Brigadier, 1942; Area Commandant, Middle East, 1942; Director of Pioneers and Labour Persia/Iraq, 1942-43; Middle East, 1943-44; Central Mediterranean Force, 1944-45. *Recreation:* travel. *Address:* Seven Coastguards, Kingsdown, Deal, Kent. *Club:* Public Schools.

**PRYNNE, Maj.-Gen. Michael Whitworth,** CB 1966; CBE 1962 (OBE 1944); Secretary, Association of Consulting Engineers, since 1969; *b* 1 April 1912; *e s* of late Lt-Col Alan H. L. Prynne and late Jeanette Annie (*née* Crosse); *m* 1940, Jean Violet, *d* of late Captain Geoffrey Stewart; one *s* three *d*. *Educ:* Bedford Sch.; RMA, Woolwich; St John's Coll., Cambridge. Commissioned into RE 1932. Served War of 1939-45: Persia and Iraq, North Africa and Italy (despatches); GSO1, HQ Eighth Army; Colonel, GS, HQ, ALFSEA; Joint Services Staff Coll., 1948; Military Attaché, Moscow, 1951-53; OC 39 Corps Engineer Regt, East Africa, 1953 (despatches); Colonel GS, HQ Northern Army Group, 1956; idc 1959; Dep.-Director War Office, 1960; Ministry of Defence, 1965-66. Chief of Staff, Headquarters Southern Command, 1964-65, and 1966-67; retired, 1967. *Address:* 4 Victoria Road, Kensington, W8. *T:* 01-937 6459. *Club:* Royal Ocean Racing.

**PRYOR, Norman Selwyn;** *b* 1896; *s* of Selwyn Robert Pryor, Plaw Hatch, Bishop's Stortford, Hertfordshire; *m* 1927, Nancy Mary, *d* of Kingsmill Henry Power, Sandpit Hall, Chobham, Surrey; three *d*. *Educ:* Eton; Trinity Coll., Cambridge. Served European War, 1914-19; Lieut, RFA (TF), 1916; Captain, 1918. DL 1956-68, JP, 1932-68, Essex; High Sheriff of Essex for 1957. *Address:* Manuden House, Manuden, Bishop's Stortford, Herts. *T:* Stansted 3282. *Club:* Oxford and Cambridge University.

**PRYS JONES, David;** *see* Jones, D. P.

**PUCKEY, Sir Walter (Charles),** Kt 1954; *b* 28 Dec. 1899; *s* of Thomas Edward Puckey, Fowey, Cornwall; *m* 1926, Alice Rebecca, *d* of Frederick Richards; no *c*. *Publications:* What is This Management?, 1944; So You're Going to a Meeting?, 1954; Management Principles, 1962; Organization in Business Management, 1963; The Board Room: a guide to the role and function of directors, 1969. *Recreations:* gardening and golf. *Address:* Greenlea, Batchworth Hill, Rickmansworth, Herts. *T:* Rickmansworth 3045; 17 Stratton Street, W1. *T:* 01-629 2494. *Club:* Savile.

**PUCKRIDGE, Geoffrey Martin,** CMG 1949; ED 1938; Colonial Administrative Service (retired); *b* 3 Oct. 1895; *s* of Rev. Oliver Puckridge. *Educ:* Exeter Sch. Devon Regt (TF) and RFC, 1914-20. Colonial Administrative Service, Gold Coast, 1921; Financial Secretary, Gold Coast, 1945-49. *Recreation:* golf. *Address:* Avon Cottage, Worton, Devizes, Wilts. *T:* Devizes 2824.

**PUDNER, Anthony Serle,** MBE 1952; Director, Engineering, Cable & Wireless Ltd, since Nov. 1969; *b* 10 June 1917; *s* of late Engr Captain W. H. Pudner, RN, and late Betty Macfarlane; *m* 1952, Johnie Johnson; one *s* one *d*. *Educ:* Imperial Service College. Joined Cable & Wireless Ltd, 1934; foreign service, 1938-60: Bermuda, CS Cable Enterprise, Greece, Haifa, Korea, Hong Kong, West Indies; Engr-in-Chief, 1965; Director: E African External Telecommunications Co., 1969; Trinidad & Tobago External Telecommunications Co., 1970. CEng; FIEE; FIERE (Vice-Pres. 1969); MIEEE. *Recreations:* music, tennis. *Address:* Kathony, Reigate Road, Epsom Downs, Surrey.

**PUDNEY, John Sleigh;** Poet, fiction writer, dramatist and journalist; *b* 19 Jan. 1909; *o s* of H. W. Pudney, farmer, and Mabel Elizabeth, *d* of H. C. Sleigh; *m* 1934, Crystal (marr. diss., 1955; she *m* 1955, L. R. Hale), *d* of Sir Alan Herbert; one *s* two *d*; *m* 1955, Monica Forbes Curtis, *d* of J. Grant Forbes. *Educ:* Gresham's Sch., Holt. Producer and writer on staff of BBC, 1934-37; Correspondent of News Chronicle, 1937-41; RAF, 1941-45. Book Critic Daily Express, 1947-48; Literary Editor, News Review, 1948-50; Director of Putnams, publishers, 1953-63. Contested (Lab) Sevenoaks Division, 1945. *Publications: verse:* Ten Summers, 1944; Selected Poems, 1945; Sixpenny Songs (poems), 1953; Collected Poems, 1957; The Trampoline, 1959; Spill Out (poems), 1967; Spandrels (poems), 1969; *collected stories:* It Breathed down my Neck, 1946; The Europeans, 1949; *novels:* Jacobson's Ladder, 1938; Estuary, 1947; Shuffley Wanderers, 1949; The Accomplice, 1950; Hero of a Summer's Day, 1951; The Net, 1952; A Ring for Luck, 1953; Trespass in the Sun, 1957; Thin Air, 1961; The Long Time Growing Up, 1971; *non-fiction:* The Green Grass Grew All Round, 1942; Who Only England Know, 1943; World Still There, 1945; The Thomas Cook Story, 1953; The Smallest Room, 1954; Six Great Aviators, 1955; The Seven Skies, 1959; Home and Away (autobiographical), 1960; A Pride of Unicorns, 1960; Bristol Fashion, 1960; The Camel, a monograph, 1964; The Golden Age of Steam, 1966; Suez, De Lesseps' Canal, 1968; *official:* The Air Battle of Malta, 1944; Atlantic Bridge, 1945; Laboratory of the Air, 1948; also books for boys and girls; *film scripts, etc.:* script writer for Travel Royal, 1952; Elizabeth is Queen, 1953; Welcome The Queen, 1954; May Wedding, 1960; joint author of screen play, Conflict of Wings, 1954; The Stolen Airliner, 1955; Blue Peter, 1955; The Concord, 1966; Mission of Fear, 1966; Ted, TV play, 1970. *Recreation:* bonfires. *Address:* 4 Macartney House, Chesterfield Walk, SE10. *T:* 01-858 0482. savile.

**PUGH, Sir Alun;** *see* Pugh, Sir J. A.

**PUGH, Harold Valentine,** CBE 1964; Chairman, Northern Ireland Joint Electricity Authority, 1967-70, retired; *b* 18 Oct. 1899; *s* of Henry John Valentine Pugh and Martha (*née* Bott); *m* 1934, Elizabeth Mary (*née* Harwood); two *s* one *d*. *Educ:* The High Sch., Murree, India; Manchester College of Technology. Trained Metropolitan-Vickers (asst engineer erection, 1925-30). Chief Engineer, Cory Bros, 1930-35; Deputy Superintendent and later Superintendent, Upper Boat Power Station, 1935-43; Generation Engineer, South Wales Power Company, 1943-44; Deputy Chief Engineer, Manchester Corporation Electricity Dept, 1944-48; Controller, British Electricity Authority, South Wales Division, 1948; Controller, British (later Central) Electricity Authority, London Division, 1951; Chairman: Eastern Electricity Board, 1957-63; South-Eastern Electricity Board, 1963-66. Director: Aberdare Holdings, 1966-70. AMCT; FIEE; MIMechE. *Recreations:* gardening, golf. *Address:* Clontaff, Doggetts Wood Lane, Chalfont St Giles, Bucks. *T:* Little Chalfont 2330.

**PUGH, Idwal Vaughan,** CB 1967; Permanent Under-Secretary of State, Welsh Office, since 1969; *b* 10 Feb. 1918; *s* of late Rhys Pugh and Elizabeth Pugh; *m* 1946, Mair Lewis; one *s* one *d*. *Educ:* Cowbridge Grammar Sch.; St John's Coll., Oxford. Army Service, 1940-46. Entered Min. of Civil Aviation, 1946; Alternate UK Rep. at International Civil Aviation Organisation, Montreal, 1950-53; Asst Secretary, 1956; Civil Air Attaché, Washington, 1957-59; Under Secretary, Min. of Transport, 1959; Min. of Housing and Local Govt, 1961; Dep. Sec., Min. of Housing and Local Govt, 1966-69. *Recreations:* golf, walking, piano. *Address:* 1 Great Ash, Lubbock

Road, Chislehurst, Kent. *T:* 01-467 1292. *Club:* Reform.

**PUGH, His Honour Sir (John) Alun,** Kt 1959; Judge of County Courts, retired; *b* 23 Jan. 1894; *o c* of Dr J. W. Pugh and Margaret Evans, Brighton; *m* 1915, Kathleen Mary, JP (*d* 1970), *o d* of late T. Edward Goodyear, Bromley, Kent; three *d* (one *s* decd). *Educ:* Brighton Coll.; Queen's Coll., Oxford (Open History Scholar). Welsh Guards, 1915-19, Lieut (wounded). Called to Bar, 1918, Inner Temple; joined South Wales Circuit. President, Hardwicke Society, 1924; Junior Editor, Butterworth's Workmen's Compensation Cases, 1927-39; Sole Editor 1939-42; Member Co. Court Rule Cttee, 1937-44, 1947-66, Chairman, 1963-66. Legal Adviser Ministry of Pensions, 1939-42; Judge of Circuit 32 (Norfolk), 1944-46, Circuit 37 (West London), 1947-48; Circuit 40 (Bow), 1948-50; Circuit 42 (Bloomsbury), 1950-66. Chairman, Norwich Licensing Area Planning Cttee, 1945-48; Member of Cttee on County Court Procedure, 1947-49; Member of Cttee on Funds in Court, 1958-59; President, Commn of Inquiry into Bahamas Police Force, 1962. *Address:* The Old Rectory, Dunsfold, Surrey. *T:* 444. *Club:* Reform.

**PUGH, John Stanley;** Editor, Liverpool Daily Post; *b* 9 Dec. 1927; *s* of John Albert and Winifred Lloyd Pugh; *m* 1953, Kathleen Mary; two *s* one *d*. *Educ:* Wallasey Grammar School. *Recreation:* golf. *Address:* 26 Westwood Road, Noctorum, Birkenhead, Cheshire.

**PUGH, Leslie Mervyn;** Stipendiary Magistrate for Liverpool since 1965; *b* 19 Nov. 1905; *s* of late Joseph and Harriette Pugh; *m* 1931, Elizabeth Gwladys Newcombe; two *d*. *Educ:* Wellington (Somerset). Admitted to Roll of Solicitors, 1928; Clerk: to Gower (Glam), RDC, 1931-40; to Swansea Justices, 1940-46; to Sheffield City Justices, 1946-57; to Hallamshire (WR), Justices, 1947-57; Stipendiary Magistrate, Huddersfield, 1957-65. President Justices' Clerks' Society, 1955-56; Member: Home Office Probation Advisory and Training Board, 1953-62; Departmental Cttee on Summary Trial of Minor Offences, 1954-55. *Publications:* Matrimonial Proceedings before Magistrates. *Recreations:* walking, gardening; Scout movement. *Address:* 17 St George's Road, Formby, near Liverpool L37 3HH. *T:* Formby 73426; Magistrates' Court, Dale Street, Liverpool. *Clubs:* Athenæum (Liverpool), University (Liverpool).

**PUGH, Prof. Leslie Penrhys,** CBE 1962; MA (Cantab); BSc (London), FRCVS; Emeritus Professor, Cambridge University; Professor of Veterinary Clinical Studies, Cambridge, 1951-63; Fellow of Magdalene Coll., Cambridge; Member, Agricultural Research Council, 1952-57; President, Royal College of Veterinary Surgeons, 1956; *b* 19 Dec. 1895; *s* of David Pugh and Emily Epton Hornby; *m* 1st, 1918, Paula Storie (*d* 1930); one *s* two *d*; 2nd, 1933, Betty Chandley; one *s* one *d*. *Educ:* Tonbridge; Royal Veterinary Coll.; London Univ. MRCVS 1917, BSc (London) 1917. FRCVS, 1923. General Practitioner in West Kent, 1919-50; Deputy Assistant Director of Veterinary Services (44th Home Counties Division TA), 1927; Major, 1927; Divisional Commandant Kent Special Constabulary (Sevenoaks Division), 1949. *Publication:* From Farriery to Veterinary Medicine, 1962. *Recreation:* gardening. *Address:* 69 South Cliff, Bexhill-on-Sea, Sussex. *T:* Bexhill 2047.

**PUGH, Maj.-Gen. Lewis (Owain),** CB 1957; CBE 1952; DSO 1945 (2 Bars, 1945, 1946); DL; JP; Indian Police Medal, 1940; Colonel, 2 King Edward VII's Own Goorkhas (The Sirmoor Rifles), 1956-69; Representative Colonel Brigade of 1958-69; Hon. Colonel 4th Battalion, The Royal Welch Fusiliers, since 1961; Vice-Lieutenant, Cardiganshire, since 1961; *b* 18 May 1907; *s* of late Major H. O. Pugh, DSO, DL; *m* 1941, Wanda, *d* of F. F. Kendzior, Kington Langley, Wilts; two *d*. *Educ:* Wellington Coll.; RMA, Woolwich. Commissioned Royal Artillery, 1927; Royal Horse Artillery, 1934; seconded Indian Police, 1936; Staff Coll., Quetta, 1940; North West Frontier, India, 1933. Served War of 1939-45: North West Frontier, India, 1940; Burma, 1942-45 (Special Service Forces, 1942-43) (despatches); Netherlands East Indies, 1946; Malaya, 1950-52 (despatches), and 1956-57. Comdr 33 Indian Inf. Bde, 1945; Comdr 26th Gurkha Inf. Bde, 1949-52; Dep. Director, Military Operations, War Office, 1953; Imperial Defence Coll., 1955; Chief of Staff, GHQ, Far East, 1956-57; General Officer Commanding 53 Welsh Infantry Division (TA), and Mid West District, 1958-61; retired, 1961. Colonel, 1951; Brigadier, 1955; Maj.-General, 1957. Vice-President: British Legion, Cards; Council for Protection of Rural Wales; President, ACF Recreational Cttee, Wales Area; formerly member: Council, Nat. Library of Wales; Council, Nat. Museum of Wales; Governing Body of the Church in Wales; Welsh Programme Advisory Cttee, ITA. Chm., Merioneth and Montgomery Bi-County Cttee, and Vice-Chm., N Wales Sub-Assoc., T&AVR; Mem., T&AVR Assoc., Wales and Monmouth. Deputy Chief Commissioner for Wales, St John Ambulance Bde. KStJ. Dato (1st Class), The Most Blessed Order of Stia Negara, Brunei. High Sheriff of Cardiganshire, 1964. *Recreations:* farming, polo, fishing. *Address:* Cymerau, Machynlleth, Mont, Wales. *T:* Glandyfi 230. *Club:* United Service.

**PUGH, Ralph Bernard,** MA; FSA; Professor of English History in the University of London, since 1968; Editor, Victoria History of Counties of England, since 1949; Supernumerary Fellow of St Edmund Hall, Oxford, since 1959 (Lecturer in Administrative History, 1952-59); *b* 1 Aug. 1910; *o c* of Bernard Carr and Mabel Elizabeth Pugh, Sutton, Surrey; unmarried. *Educ:* St Paul's Sch.; Queen's Coll., Oxford. 1st Class Hons, Modern History, 1932. Asst Keeper of Public Records, 2nd Cl. 1934, 1st Cl. 1946; Dominions Office, 1940-46, Acting Principal, 1941-46. Member, Institute for Advanced Study, Princeton, NJ, 1963-64, 1969-70. Wiltshire Archaeological and Nat. History Society: President, 1950-51, 1953-55; Vice-President, 1955-; Wiltshire Records Society (until 1967, Records Br. of Wilts Archaeological and Nat. History Society): Hon. Secretary and Editor, 1937-53; Chairman, 1953-67; President, 1967-; Vice-President, Selden Society, 1966-69. *Publications:* (ed) Abstracts of Feet of Fines for Wiltshire, Edw. I and II, 1929; (ed) Calendar of Antrobus Deeds, 1947; How to Write a Parish History, 1954; The Crown Estate, 1960; Records of the Colonial and Dominions Offices (PRO Handbooks), 1964; Itinerant Justices in English History, 1967; Imprisonment in Medieval England, 1968; (ed) Court Rolls of the Wiltshire Manors of Adam de Stratton, 1970. Articles in Victoria County History, Cambridge History of the British Empire and in learned periodicals. *Recreation:* sight-seeing. *Address:* 67 Southwood Park, N6. *T:* 01-340 5661. *Club:* Reform.

**PUGH, Roger Courtenay Beckwith,** MD; Pathologist to St Peter's Hospitals and the Institute of Urology, London, since 1955; *b* 23

July 1917; *y s* of late Dr Robert Pugh, Talgarth, Breconshire, and of late Margaret Louise Pugh (*née* Gough); *m* 1942, Winifred Dorothy, *yr d* of late Alfred Cooper and of Margaret Cooper (*née* Evans); one *s* one *d*. *Educ:* Gresham's Sch., Holt; St Mary's Hospital (University of London). MRCS, LRCP 1940; MB, BS, 1941; MD 1948; MCPath. 1964; FRCPath. 1967. House Surgeon, St Mary's Hospital and Sector Hospitals, 1940-42; War Service in RAF (Mediterranean theatre), 1942-46, Sqdn Leader; Registrar, Department of Pathology, St Mary's Hospital, 1946-48; Asst Pathologist and Lecturer in Pathology, St Mary's Hospital, 1948-51; Asst Morbid Anatomist, The Hospital for Sick Children, Great Ormond Street, 1951-54. Erasmus Wilson Demonstrator, RCS, 1959, 1961; Member: Board of Governors, St Peter's Hospitals; Pathological Society of Great Britain and Ireland; Assoc. of Clin. Pathologists; Internat. Society of Urology; Assoc. Member British Assoc. of Urological Surgeons. *Publications:* various contributions to Pathological, Urological and Paediatric Journals. *Recreations:* gardening, photography. *Address:* 19 Manor Way, Beckenham, Kent. *T:* 01-658 6294.

**PUGH, Rev. Canon T(homas) Jenkin,** TD 1946; Director, Archbishop's Mission to Holiday Camps and Caravan Sites, since 1969; Senior Chaplain in the Butlin Organisation, on staff of Archbishop of Canterbury, since 1947; Chaplain to the Queen since 1962; *b* 15 Nov. 1903; seventh *s* of Rees and Margaret Ann Pugh; *m* 1932, Marjorie Window (*d* 1970). *Educ:* Universities of Wales and London. Ordained, 1931. Vicar of Acton and Little Waldingfield, Suffolk. Chaplain, TA, with BEF, France, 1939-40; Far East, 1941-45; New Zealand, 1945-46. Canon of Lincoln Cathedral and Prebendary of Bedford Minor, 1955. MA Lambeth 1959. Member, Governing Body of the Church in Wales. *Recreation:* fishing. *Address:* Modwenna, Criccieth, N Wales. *T:* 2808. *Club:* Reform.

**PUGH, William David,** CBE 1965; FIM; FBIM; FIWM; JP; Deputy Chairman, English Steel Corporation Ltd, 1965-70 (Managing Director, 1955-65); Director of Personnel, British Steel Corporation (Midland Group), 1967-70; *b* 21 Nov. 1904; *s* of late Sir Arthur and Lady Pugh; *m* 1936, Mary Dorothea Barber; one *d*. *Educ:* Regent Street Polytechnic; Sheffield Univ. Joined Research Dept, Vickers Ltd, Sheffield, 1926, Director, Vickers Ltd, 1962-67; Chairman: The Darlington Forge Ltd, 1957-66; Taylor Bros & Co. Ltd, 1959-66; Director: (and alternate Chairman), Firth Vickers Stainless Steels Ltd, 1948-67; High Speed Steel Alloys Ltd, 1953-68; Industrial Training Council Service, 1960-67; British Iron and Steel Corp. Ltd, 1962-67; United Steel Cos Ltd, 1967-70; Sheffield Boy Scouts Holdings Ltd, 1965-; Iron and Steel Investments Ltd, 1964-68. Associate of Metallurgy (Sheffield University; Mappin Medallist). Hon. DMet (Sheffield), 1966. *Recreations:* gardening, golf, reading. *Address:* White Lodge, Church Lane, Dore, Sheffield. *T:* 364981. *Club:* Sheffield (Sheffield).

**PUGH, Rt. Rev. William Edward Augustus;** *see* Penrith, Bishop Suffragan of.

**PUGH, Sir William (John),** Kt 1956; OBE; FRS; BA, DSc (Wales), MSc (Manchester); Hon. DSc (Nottingham); Hon. LLD (Wales); MIME, FGS; lately Director, Geological Survey of Great Britain and Museum of Practical Geology (1950-60); Emeritus Professor of Geology, University of Manchester, since 1951; Fellow, Imperial College of Science and Technology, University of London, since 1960; *b* 28 July 1892; *s* of John and Harriet Pugh of Westbury; *m* Manon Clayton, 2nd *d* of J. Davies Bryan, LLD, Alexandria, Egypt; four *s*. *Educ:* County Sch., Welshpool; University College of Wales, Aberystwyth. Served European War with the Royal Welch Fusiliers, and attached to the General Staff 2nd and 4th Army HQ's, BEF, and GHQ British Army of the Rhine (OBE, French Croix de Guerre, despatches twice). Univ. Coll. of Wales, Aberystwyth: Prof. of Geology, 1919-31; Dean of Faculty of Science, 1929-31. University of Manchester: Prof. of Geology, 1931-50; Dean of the Faculty of Science, 1939-41; Pro-Vice-Chancellor, 1941-43; and Deputy Vice-Chancellor, 1943-50. Chairman University of Manchester Joint Recruiting Board, 1939-47; Manchester Educ. Cttee, 1947-50; Board of Governors, United Manchester Teaching Hospitals, 1948-50; Inter-University Council for Higher Education in the Colonies, 1946-50; Member Commission on Higher Education in Malaya, 1947. Late External Examiner, Universities of Birmingham, Cambridge, Dublin, Leeds, Oxford and Wales. President Section C (Geology), 1948; Member: Council British Assoc., 1951-57; Council Geological Society of London, 1933-38, 1947-50, 1957-62; Murchison Medal, 1952. Nature Conservancy, 1952-57. Council Royal Society, 1952. Geological Survey Board, 1940-44, 1946-50; Court and Council University College of Wales, Aberystwyth; Gov. Body Imperial College of Science and Technology. *Publications:* Papers dealing with the stratigraphy and tectonics of the Lower Palaeozoic rocks principally of Wales and published mainly in the Quarterly Journal of Geological Society of London. *Address:* 171 Oakwood Court, Kensington, W14. *T:* 01-602 2151. *Club:* Athenæum.

**PUGSLEY, Sir Alfred Grenvile,** Kt 1956; OBE 1944; FRS 1952; DSc; Professor of Civil Engineering, University of Bristol, 1945-68, now Emeritus; Pro-Vice-Chancellor, 1961-64; *b* May 1903; *s* of H. W. Pugsley, BA, FLS, London; *m* 1928, Kathleen M. Warner; no *c*. *Educ:* Rutlish Sch.; London Univ. Civil Engineering Apprenticeship at Royal Arsenal, Woolwich, 1923-26; Technical Officer, at the Royal Airship Works, Cardington, 1926-31; Member scientific and technical staff at Royal Aircraft Establishment, Farnborough, 1931-45, being Head of Structural and Mechanical Engineering Dept there, 1941-45. Visiting Lecturer on aircraft structures at Imperial Coll., London, 1938-40. Chairman of Aeronautical Research Council, 1952-57; President, Institution of Structural Engineers, 1957-58; Member, Advisory Council on Scientific Policy, 1956-59; Member of Various scientific and professional institutions and cttees. Hon. FRAeS, 1963; Hon. DSc Belfast, 1965; Hon. DUniv. Surrey, 1968. Structural Engineers' Gold Medal, 1968. *Publications:* The Theory of Suspension Bridges, 1957 (2nd edn 1968); The Safety of Structures, 1966; numerous Reports and Memoranda of Aeronautical Research Council; papers in scientific journals and publications of professional engineering bodies; articles and reviews in engineering press. *Address:* 4 Harley Court, Clifton Down, Bristol 8. *Club:* Athenæum.

**PUGSLEY, Rear-Admiral Anthony Follett,** CB 1944; DSO 1943; retired; *b* 7 Dec. 1901; *e s* of late J. Follett Pugsley, Whitefield, Wiveliscombe, Somerset; *m* 1931, Barbara, *d* of late J. Byam Shaw; one *s*. *Educ:* RN Colleges, Osborne and Dartmouth.

Midshipman, 1918; Commander, 1936; Captain, 1942; Rear-Admiral, 1952; retired, 1954. Served European War from May 1918; on Upper Yangtse, 1925-27, and in command HM Ships P.40, Antelope and Westcott, 1933-36; during War of 1939-45, in command HM Ships Javelin, Fearless, Paladin; Captain (D) 14th Flotilla, Jervis (despatches thrice, DSO and bar, Greek War Cross); took part in Normandy landing, 1944 (2nd bar to DSO); Naval Force Commander in assault on Walcheren, 1944 (CB); Captain (D) 19th Flotilla (Far East), 1945-46; Directing Staff, Senior Officers War Course, 1947-48; Naval Officer in charge, Londonderry and Director (RN) Joint Anti-Submarine School, 1948-50; in command HMS Warrior, 1951; Flag Officer, Malayan Area, Dec. 1951-Nov. 1953. *Publication:* Destroyer Man, 1957. *Address:* Javelin, Milverton, Somerset. *T:* Milverton 355.

**PUGSLEY, Sir Reuben (James),** Kt *cr* 1954; OBE 1939; JP; Director Weaver & Co. Ltd, Millers, Swansea, since 1939; *b* 3 March 1886; *m* 1907, Dora Gwendoline Owens; two *s*. *Educ:* St Monica's, Cardiff. Entered Flour Milling Industry, 1901. JP, City of Cardiff, 1926. *Recreation:* golf. *Address:* Summermead, Llandennis Avenue, Cyncoed, Cardiff. *T:* Cardiff 52478. *Club:* Cardiff and County (Cardiff).

**PULLAN, Ayrton George Popplewell,** MA; *b* 9 June 1879; *s* of Colonel Ayrton Pullan, Indian Staff Corps; *m* 1906, Kathleen Elizabeth Love (*d* 1968), *d* of G. D. Kempson; one *s* one *d*. *Educ:* Malvern Coll.; Trinity Coll., Oxford; Goldsmiths' Company Exhibitioner, 1899. 1st Class Classical Moderations, 2nd Class Lit Hum. Passed 7th Civil Service Examination, 1902; Assistant Collector, United Provinces, 1903; District Judge, 1918; Judge, Chief Court of Oudh, 1929; Judge, High Court of Judicature, Allahabad, India, 1931-33; barrister, Middle Temple; practised before Privy Council, 1935-52; Ministry of Labour and National Service, 1940-43. *Publications:* A Glossary of Indian Law Terms (Middle Temple Library); Index to Criminal Appeal Reports, Vols 1-34, 1952; (with D. W. Alcock) The Commercial Dictionary, 1953. *Recreations:* gardening, chess, embroidery. *Address:* The Dene, Forest Way, Tunbridge Wells, Kent. *T:* Tunbridge Wells 26579.

**PULLAN, John Marshall,** MChir, FRCS; Surgeon: St Thomas' Hospital, London; Bolingbroke Hospital, London; Consultant Surgeon, Royal Masonic Hospital, London; *b* 1 Aug. 1915; *e s* of William Greaves Pullan and Kathleen, *d* of Alfred Marshall, Otley, Yorkshire; *m* 1940, Leila Diana, *d* of H. C. Craven-Veitch, Surgeon; one *s* three *d*. *Educ:* Shrewsbury; King's Coll., Cambridge; St Thomas' Hospital, London. MA Cantab (1st Cl. Nat. Sc. Tripos) 1937; MB, BChir 1940; FRCS, 1942; MChir 1945. Teacher in Surgery, University of London; Examiner in Surgery, University of London, 1956; Member, Court of Examiners, RCS, 1964; Member, Board of Governors, St Thomas' Hospital. *Publications:* Section on Diseases of the Liver, Gall Bladder and Bile Ducts, in Textbook of British Surgery, ed Sir Henry Souttar, 1956; articles in surgical journals. *Address:* Palings, Warboys Road, Kingston Hill, Surrey. *T:* 01-546 5310; 3 Upper Wimpole Street, W1. *T:* 01-935 5873. *Club:* Flyfishers'.

**PULLAR, Hubert Norman,** CBE 1964; MA; HM Consul-General, Durban, Natal, since 1968; *b* 26 Dec. 1914; *y s* of late William Laurence and Christine Ellen Pullar, formerly of Uplands, Bridge-of-Allan, Stirlingshire; *m* 1943, Helen Alice La Fontaine; one *s* one *d*. *Educ:* Trin. Coll., Glenalmond; Trin. Coll., Oxford. Entered HM Consular Service, 1938. Served in Turkey, 1938-42; USA, 1943-46; Persia, 1946-48; Morocco, 1949-52; Foreign Office, 1952-54; Finland, 1954-56; Syria, 1956; Iraq, 1957-59; Antwerp, 1960-64; HM Consul-General, Jerusalem, 1964-67; Foreign Office, 1967-68. Order of Ouissam Alouite, Morocco, 1952. CStJ 1966. Coronation Medal, 1953. *Recreations:* golf, tennis, fencing (Oxford half-blue, 1936, 1937), Motoring, travel. *Address:* c/o Foreign and Commonwealth Office, SW1.

**PULLÉE, Ernest Edward,** CBE 1967; ARCA, ASIA, FSAE; Chief Officer, National Council for Diplomas in Art and Design, since 1967; *b* 19 Feb. 1907; *s* of Ernest and Caroline Elizabeth Pullée; *m* 1933, Margaret Fisher, ARCA, NEAC; one *s*. *Educ:* St Martin's Sch., Dover; Royal Coll. of Art, London. Principal: Gloucester Coll. of Art, 1934-39; Portsmouth Coll. of Art, 1939-45; Leeds Coll. of Art, 1945-56; Leicester Coll. of Art and Design, 1956-67. Pres., Nat. Soc. for Art Educn, 1945, 1959; Chm., Assoc. of Art Instns, 1959; Mem., Nat. Adv. Coun. for Art Educn, 1959; Mem., Nat. Coun. for Diplomas in Art and Design, 1961. Hon. DA (Manchester), 1961. *Publications:* contribs to professional and academic jls. *Recreation:* travel. *Address:* 91 Park Meadow, Hatfield, Herts. *T:* Hatfield 67937. *Club:* Chelsea Arts.

**PULLEIN-THOMPSON, Denis;** *see* Cannan, D.

**PULLEN, William Reginald James,** MVO 1966; LLB; FCIS; JP; Receiver-General, since 1959, Chapter Clerk since 1963 and Registrar since 1964, Westminster Abbey; *b* 17 Feb. 1922; *er s* of late William Pullen and Lillian Pullen (*née* Chinn), Falmouth; *m* 1948, Doreen Angela Hebron; two *d*. *Educ:* Falmouth Gram. School; King's College, London; private study. Served War of 1939-45; Flt Lt, RAFVR (admin and special duties) SE Asia. Asst to Chief Accountant, Westminster Abbey, 1947; Dep. Registrar, 1951; Sec. Westminster Abbey Appeal, 1953. Westminster City Council, 1962-65; Gov. Grey Coat Hosp.; Gov., Queen Anne's Sch., Caversham. Freeman, Worshipful Co. of Wax Chandlers. OStJ 1969. *Recreations:* reading, walking, cooking. *Address:* 4b Dean's Yard, Westminster, SW1. *T:* 01-222 4023. *Club:* Royal Commonwealth Society.

**PULLEYBLANK, Prof. Edwin George,** PhD; Head, Department of Asian Studies, University of British Columbia, since 1968; *b* Calgary, Alberta, 7 Aug. 1922; *s* of W. G. E. Pulleyblank, Calgary; *m* 1945, Winona Ruth Relyea, Arnprior, Ont; one *s* two *d*. *Educ:* Central High School, Calgary; University of Alberta; University of London. BA Hons Classics, Univ. of Alberta, 1942; Nat. Research Council of Canada, 1943-46. School of Oriental and African Studies, Univ. of London: Chinese Govt Schol., 1946; Lectr in Classical Chinese, 1948; PhD in Classical Chinese, 1951; Lectr in Far Eastern History, 1952; Professor of Chinese, University of Cambridge, 1953; Prof. of Chinese, Univ. of British Columbia, 1966. Fellow of Downing Coll., Cambridge, 1955. *Publications:* The Background of the Rebellion of An Lu-Shan; articles in Asia Major, Bulletin of School of Oriental and African Studies, etc. *Address:* Department of Asian Studies, University of British Columbia, Vancouver 8, BC, Canada.

**PULLICINO, Dr Anthony Alfred;** High Commissioner for Malta in London since 1970; *b* 14 March 1917; *s* of late Sir Philip Pullicino; *m* 1944, Edith Baker; three *s* two *d*. *Educ:* St

Aloysius Coll., Malta; Royal Univ. of Malta; Melbourne University. BA 1939, LLD 1943, Malta; LLB Melbourne 1963. Served in Royal Malta Artillery, 1944-45 (Lieut). MLA Malta, 1951-55 (Speaker, 1951-52). Mem. Council, CPA, attending sessions in London 1952, Nairobi 1953. Practised as Solicitor, Melbourne, 1963-65; High Comr for Malta in Canberra, 1965-69. *Recreation:* golf. *Address:* 15 Upper Belgrave Street, SW1. *T:* 01-235 6229. *Club:* Casino Maltese (Malta).

**PULLING, Martin John Langley,** CBE 1958 (OBE 1954); Chairman: The Ferrograph Co. Ltd; Rendar Instruments Ltd; Director, Compagnie Générale d'Electricité Internationale (UK) Ltd; *b* 30 May 1906; *o s* of late Rev. Augustine J. Pulling and Dorothea Fremlin Key; *m* 1939, Yvonne Limborgh, Antwerp, Belgium; no *c. Educ:* Marlborough College; King's College, Cambridge (Scholar). Mech. Scis. Tripos, BA 1928; MA 1943. Various posts in radio industry, 1929-34; joined BBC Engrg Div., 1934; retired as Dep. Dir of Engrg, 1967. Was Chm. of Technical Cttee (of European Broadcasting Union) responsible for development of "Eurovision" from its inception in 1952 until 1962. FIEE 1967 (MIEE 1945, AMIEE 1935); Chm., Electronics and Communications Section, IEE, 1959-60; Mem. Coun., IEE, 1963-66; MITE 1966. *Address:* 6 Cadogan House, 93 Sloane Street, SW1. *T:* 01-235 1739. *Club:* Savile.

**PULLINGER, Francis Alan,** CBE 1970; Chairman since 1961 and Managing Director since 1958, G. N. Haden & Sons Ltd; *b* 22 May 1913; *s* of William Pullinger; *m* 1st, 1946, Felicity Charmian Gotch Hobson (decd); two *s* one *d*; 2nd, 1966, Jacqueline Louise Anne Durin. *Educ:* Marlborough Coll.; Balliol Coll., Oxford (MA). Joined G. N. Haden & Sons Ltd as engineer at Trowbridge, 1934; transf. to London Office, 1935; Manager, Bristol Office, 1946; Director, G. N. Haden, 1949. *Recreations:* mountaineering, sailing, beagling. *Address:* Barnhorn, Meadway, Berkhamsted, Herts. *T:* Berkhamsted 3206. *Clubs:* Alpine, Travellers'.

**PULVERTAFT, Prof. Robert James Valentine,** OBE 1944; MD Cantab; FRCP; FC Path; Emeritus Professor of Clinical Pathology, University of London (Professor, 1950-62); Visiting Professor of Pathology, Makerere University College; Visiting Professor of Pathology, University of Ibadan, W Nigeria; President Association of Clinical Pathologists, 1953; Director of Laboratories, Westminster Hospital, until 1962; Lieutenant-Colonel RAMC, 1943, serving Middle East Forces; subsequently Assistant Director of Pathology, Northern Command and MEF; lately Hon. Consultant in Pathology to the Army at Home; *b* 14 Feb. 1897; *s* of Rev. T. J. Pulvertaft and B. C. Denroche; *m* E. L. M. Costello; one *s* two *d. Educ:* Westminster School; Trinity College, Cambridge (Classical Scholar); St Thomas' Hosp. Lt 3rd Royal Sussex 1915-19; served with 4th Royal Sussex (Palestine); seconded to RFC as observer (Palestine) and pilot in 205 Squadron RAF (France); Senior Exhibitioner and Scholar, Nat. Science, Trinity College Cantab. 2nd class Part II Tripos Nat. Science (Physiology); Entrance University Scholar St Thomas' Hospital; Asst Bacteriologist, VD Dept St Thomas' Hospital; Pathologist to Units, St Thomas' Hosp., 1923-32; Plimmer Research Fellow in Pathology, 1929-32; EMS Sept.-Nov. 1939; National Institute Medical Research, 1939-40. Examiner in Pathology, Univs of Cambridge, Oxford, London, Trinity College, Dublin, National University of Ireland, Liverpool University; also for the Conjoint Board and Royal Army Medical Coll. *Publications:* Studies on Malignant Disease in Nigeria by Tissue Culture; various papers on bacteriology and pathology, particularly in relation to the study of living cells by cinemicrography. *Address:* Hedges, Stour Row, Dorset.

**PUMPHREY, John Laurence,** CMG 1963; British High Commissioner to Zambia, since 1967; *b* 22 July 1916; *s* of late Charles Ernest Pumphrey and Iris Mary (*née* Moberly-Bell); *m* 1945, Jean, *e d* of Sir Walter Buchanan Riddell, 12th Bt; four *s* one *d. Educ:* Winchester; New College, Oxford. Served War of 1939-45 in Army. Foreign Service from 1945. Head of Establishment and Organisation Department, Foreign Office, 1955-60; Counsellor, Staff of British Commissioner-General for SE Asia, Singapore, 1960-63; Counsellor, HM Embassy, Belgrade, 1963-65; Deputy High Commissioner, Nairobi, 1965-67. Military Cross, 3rd Class (Greece), 1941. *Address:* c/o Foreign and Commonwealth Office, King Charles Street, SW1. *Club:* Brooks's.

**PUNGAN, Vasile;** Ambassador of Socialist Republic of Rumania to the Court of St James's since 1966; *b* 2 Nov. 1926; *m* 1952, Liliana Niţă; one *d. Educ:* Inst. of Econs, Bucharest. Dr in Econ. Scis and Univ. Prof.; Dean of Faculty, Agronomical Inst. Nicolae Bălcescu, Bucharest, 1954; Gen. Dir, Min. of Agric. and Forestry, 1955-58; Counsellor, Rumanian Embassy, Washington, 1959-62; Dir and Mem. Foreign Office Coll., 1963-66. Alternate Mem., Central Cttee of Romanian Communist Party, 1969. Holds orders and medals of Socialist Republic of Rumania. *Address:* 1 Belgrave Square, SW1. *T:* 01-235 7738.

**PURCELL, Denis;** *see* Purcell, J. D.

**PURCELL, Prof. Edward Mills,** PhD; Gerhard Gade University Professor, Harvard University, since 1960; *b* 30 Aug. 1912; *s* of Edward A. Purcell and Mary Elizabeth Mills; *m* 1937, Beth C. Busser; two *s. Educ:* Purdue University; Harvard University. PhD Harvard, 1938; Instructor in Physics, Harvard, 1938-40; Radiation Laboratory, Mass. Inst. of Technology, 1940-45; Associate Professor of Physics, Harvard, 1945-49; Professor of Physics, 1949-60. Senior Fellow, Society of Fellows, Harvard, 1950-. (Jointly) Nobel Prize in Physics, 1952. Hon. DEng Purdue, 1953; Hon. DSci Washington Univ., St Louis, 1963. *Publications:* Principles of Microwave Circuits, 1948; Physics for Students of Science and Engineering, 1952; Electricity and Magnetism, 1965. Papers in Physical Review, Astrophys. Jl. *Address:* 5 Wright Street, Cambridge, Mass, USA. *T:* 547-9317. *Club:* Cosmos (Washington, DC).

**PURCELL, (John) Denis;** Metropolitan Magistrate, Clerkenwell Magistrates' Court, since 1963; *b* 7 Dec. 1913; *s* of John Poyntz Purcell and Dorothy Branston, Newark; *m* 1951, Pauline Mary, *e d* of Rev. Hiram Craven, Painswick, Glos; two *s. Educ:* Marlborough; Wadham College, Oxford. Called to Bar, Gray's Inn, 1938; SE Circuit; Sussex QS. Served War of 1939-45: commnd from HAC, 1939, to Shropshire Yeo., 1940; ADC to GOC-in-C, Western Command, 1941; Staff Capt., Western Command; GSO3, Italy; DAAG, HQ British Troops, Palestine. Actg Dep. Chm., London QS, 1962. *Recreations:* back-yard gardening, racing. *Address:* 1 Cheltenham Terrace, SW3. *T:* 01-730 2896.

**PURCELL, Ven. William Henry Samuel,** MA; Archdeacon of Dorking, since 1968; *b* 22 Jan.

1912; *m* 1941, Kathleen Clough, Leeds; two *s*. *Educ:* King Edward VI School, Norwich; Fitzwilliam House, Cambridge (MA). Asst Curate, St Michael's, Headingley, Leeds, 1937; Minor Canon of Ripon Cathedral, 1940; Vicar: St Matthew, Holbeck, Leeds, 1943; St Matthew, Chapel Allerton, Leeds, 1947; St Martin's, Epsom, 1963. Rural Dean of Epsom, 1965. Hon. Canon of Ripon Cathedral, 1962; Hon. Canon of Guildford Cathedral, 1968. *Recreations:* walking, travel. *Address:* 4 Orchardleigh, St Nicholas Hill, Leatherhead, Surrey. *T:* Leatherhead 5708.

**PURCELL-BURET, Captain Theobald John Claud,** CBE 1942; DSC 1917; retired Commodore of Royal Mail Fleet; *b* London, 18 June 1879; *s* of John Claud Buret, London and Geneva, and Alice Maria, *e d* of late Theobald John Purcell, Kilkenny, Eire; assumed by royal licence 1941 additional surname of Purcell; *m* 1st, 1907, Maud (*d* 1936), *y d* of late Leonard Huckle, Bristol; one *d*; 2nd, 1941, Hon. Winifred Elspeth Guthrie (*d* 1965), *o d* of 1st Baron Forres, PC. *Educ:* Victoria Coll., Jersey. Entered Merchant Service, 1894; master mariner, 1916; Commodore Royal Mail Fleet, 1939-42; retired 1942. Younger Brother of Trinity House. *Publications:* The Wanderer, and other Poems, 1951 (Dublin). *Address:* Ballyfoyle, Christchurch Road, Winchester, Hants. *Club:* Royal Commonwealth Society.

**PURCHAS, Rev. Canon Alban C.,** MA; retired as Vicar of Methven, Christchurch, NZ (1951-55); Chaplain to St George's Church Hospital, 1958; Hon. Canon of Christchurch Cathedral, 1949; *b* 8 Oct. 1890; *s* of Canon Henry T. Purchas, MA, and Lily E. Cox; *m* 1917, *d* of Rev. C. A. Tobin, Vicar of Burwood, Christchurch; two *s* three *d* (and one *s* killed in action, Italy, 1944). *Educ:* Christ's College, Christchurch, NZ. Deacon, 1914; Priest, 1915; Assistant Curate Parish of Geraldine, 1914-17; Chaplain, Christ's College, 1917-19; Vicar, Kumara, 1919-24, and with Hokitika, 1921-24; Akaroa, 1924-28; Holy Trinity, Lyttleton, 1928-32; Rangiora, 1932-39; Cashmere Hills, 1939-44; Fendalton, 1947-51. Archdeacon of Rangiora and Westland, 1934-44; Canon Missioner and Youth Organiser for Dio. Christchurch, NZ, 1944-47; Archdeacon of Christchurch, 1944-49. *Recreation:* gardening. *Address:* 48 Cholmondeley Avenue, Christchurch 2, NZ.

**PURCHAS, Francis Brooks,** QC 1965; Barrister-at-Law; Deputy Chairman of East Sussex Quarter Sessions, since 1966; Recorder of Canterbury, since 1969; *b* 19 June 1919; *s* of Capt. Francis Purchas, 5th Royal Irish Lancers and Millicent Purchas (*née* Brooks); *m* 1942, Patricia Mona Kathleen, *d* of Lieut Milburn, Canada; two *s*. *Educ:* Summerfields Sch., Oxford; Marlborough Coll.; Trinity Coll., Cambridge. Served RE, 1940-46: North Africa, 1943 (despatches); Hon. Lt-Col retd (Africa Star, Italy Star, 1939-45 Medal; Defence Medal, 1939-45 Star). Allied Mil. Commission, Vienna. Called to Bar, Inner Temple, 1948; practised at Bar, 1948-65, and continuing. Mem. of Livery, Worshipful Co. of Broderers, 1962. *Recreations:* shooting, golf, photography. *Address:* The Thatched House, Roundwood Lane, Haywards Heath, Sussex. *T:* Lindfield 3256; 1 Harcourt Buildings, Temple, EC4. *T:* 01-353 0375. *Clubs:* East India and Sports; Hawks (Cambridge).

**PURDEN, Roma Laurette, (Laurie Purden; Mrs J. K. Kotch);** Editor of Good Housekeeping since 1965; *b* 30 Sept. 1928; *d* of George Cecil Arnold Purden and Constance Mary Sheppard; *m* 1957, John Keith Kotch; two *d*. *Educ:* Harecroft Sch., Tunbridge Wells. Editor of: Housewife, 1954-57; Home, 1957-62; House Beautiful, 1963-65. *Address:* 11 Abbey Gardens, NW8.

**PURDIE, Rev. Albert B.,** OBE; MA, PhD; *b* 27 Aug. 1888; 3rd *s* of Arthur Purdie, London. *Educ:* St Edmund's, Ware; Christ's College, Cambridge. Priest, 1914; Hons Classical Tripos, 1921; Diploma of Classical Archæology, 1922; PhD (Fribourg) 1934; Army Chaplain, 1914-19; in France with 48th Divn 1915-16; Senior Catholic Chaplain of the British Salonika Force at Salonika and Constantinople, 1918-19 (despatches, OBE, Order of St Sava); Housemaster at St Edmund's, Ware, 1922-33; Assistant Headmaster, 1926-29; Headmaster, 1929-36; Chaplain, RAF, 1940-44. *Publications:* A Pilgrim-Walk in Canterbury, 1910; Poems, 1918; Life of Blessed John Southworth, 1930; Latin Verse Inscriptions, 1935; contributions to various journals. *Address:* Barclay's Bank, Goring Road, West Worthing, Sussex.

**PURDIE, Cora Gwendolyn Jean, (Wendy);** *see* Campbell-Purdie.

**PURDY, Robert John,** CMG 1963; OBE 1954; Bursar, Gresham's School, Holt, since 1965; retired from HM Overseas Civil Service, 1963; *b* 2 March 1916; 2nd *s* of late Lt-Col T. W. Purdy, Woodgate House, Aylsham, Norfolk; *m* 1957, Elizabeth (*née* Sharp); two *s* one *d*. *Educ:* Haileybury College; Jesus College, Cambridge (BA). Served 1940-46 with 81 West African Division Reconnaissance Regt, 3rd and 4th Burma Campaigns (despatches, Major). Appointed to Colonial Administrative Service, Northern Nigeria, 1939; promoted Resident, 1956; Senior Resident, Staff Grade, 1957. Resident, Adamawa Province, 1956; Senior Resident, Plateau Province, 1958-61; Senior Resident, Sokoto Province, 1961-63, retd. *Recreations:* shooting, fishing, gardening. *Address:* Spratt's Green House, Aylsham, Norwich NOR 07Y. *T:* Aylsham 2147.

**PURSEY, Comdr Harry;** RN, retired; Journalist and Lecturer; *b* 1891; *e s* of late G. Pursey, Sidmouth, Devon. *Educ:* elementary school; Royal Hosp. School, Greenwich (Navy's orphanage). Joined Navy as seaman boy, HMS Impregnable, Devonport, 1907, and first naval officer from lower deck to become MP. Specialised in torpedo and mining. Served European War, 1914-18, Dover Patrol, Grand Fleet, HMS Revenge (Battle of Jutland), Eastern Mediterranean (despatches). Commissioned 1917. Black Sea and Turkish operations, 1919-20; Mad Mullah campaign, Somaliland, 1920 (Africa General Service Medal and clasp); Mesopotamia, 1920. Serving in HMS Eagle when Spanish trans-Atlantic flying-boat salved in mid-Atlantic, 1929. HMS Hood, 1931-33; retired list, 1936. Press correspondent in Spain during Civil War, 1937. Ministry of Information National Speaker, 1940-41. MP (Lab) Hull East, 1945-70. Contributed to The Times, Brassey's Naval Annual, British, Dominion and American Press. *Address:* 43 Farnaby Road, Shortlands, Bromley, Kent. *T:* 01-460 0361.

**PURVES, James Grant;** HM Consul-General, Hamburg, since 1967; *b* 15 May 1911; *s* of Alexander Murray and Elizabeth Purves; *m* 1947, Mary Tinsley; three *s* one *d*. *Educ:* Universities of St Andrews and Freiburg-im-Breisgau. Research, 1933-35; Market Research, 1935-36; Secretary, Central Council for Health Education, 1936-39; German Section, BBC, 1939-45. 1st Secretary, Foreign Service: in Berne, Warsaw, Tel Aviv, Bangkok;

Consul in Luanda, Lille, Johannesburg; Counsellor, HM Embassy, Berne, 1965-67. *Recreations:* swimming, tennis, travel. *Address:* Long Roof, Walberswick, Southwold, Suffolk. *T:* Southwold 2242. *Clubs:* Royal Automobile; Anglo-German (Hamburg); Grande Société (Berne).

**PUSEY, Nathan Marsh,** PhD; President, Harvard University, 1953-June 1971; *b* Council Bluffs, Iowa, 4 April 1907; *s* of John Marsh Pusey and Rosa Pusey (*née* Drake); *m* 1936, Anne Woodward; two *s* one *d. Educ:* Harvard University, USA. AB 1928, AM 1932, PhD, 1937. Assistant, Harvard, 1933-34; Sophomore tutor, Lawrence Coll., 1935-38; Asst Prof., history and literature, Scripps Coll., Claremont, Calif., 1938-40; Wesleyan Univ.: Asst Prof., Classics, 1940-43, Assoc. Prof., 1943-44; Pres., Lawrence Coll., Appleton, Wisconsin, 1944-53. Trustee, Carnegie Foundn for Advancement of Teaching; Pres., Assoc. of American Univs. Hon. LLD: Wesleyan Univ., 1944; Ripon Coll., 1945; Yale Univ., 1953; Columbia Univ., 1954; Brown Univ. 1954; Princeton Univ., 1954; Boston Univ., 1955; Northeastern Univ., 1955; Williams Coll., 1955; Jewish Theol. Sem., 1955; Tufts Univ., 1955; Univ. of Pa., 1956; Johns Hopkins Univ., 1957; North-Western Univ., 1958; Univ. of Calif., 1958; Rockefeller Inst., 1959; St Louis Univ., 1959; University of North Carolina and Oberlin College, 1960; Marquette University, 1963; Wheaton College, 1964; Dickinson College, 1965; Lehigh University, 1965; Hon. LHD: Coe Coll., 1948; Lawrence Coll., 1954; Colgate Univ. and Boston Coll., 1963; Univ. of Mass., 1968; Loyola Univ., 1970; D de l'U, Univ. of Montreal, 1958; LittD, Morehouse Coll., 1962; Univ. of Wisconsin, 1967; Hon. DD, Pacific Sch. of Religion, 1966; also hon. degrees from abroad. Officier de la Légion d'Honneur, 1958. *Publication:* The Age of the Scholar, 1963. *Address:* 17 Quincy Street, Cambridge, Mass 02138, USA.

**PUSINELLI, Miss Doris,** RI 1934; PS; Artist, of British birth. *Recreations:* painting, writing. *Address:* Crede House, Bosham, Sussex. *T:* Bosham 2294.

**PUSINELLI, Frederick Nigel Molière,** CMG 1966; OBE 1963; MC 1940; HM Overseas Civil Service, retired; *b* 28 April 1919; second *s* of S. Jacques and T. May Pusinelli, Frettenham, Norfolk and Fowey, Cornwall; *m* 1941, Joan Mary Chaloner, *d* of Cuthbert B. and Mildred H. Smith, Cromer, Norfolk and Bexhill-on-Sea, Sussex; one *s* one *d. Educ:* Aldenham School; Pembroke College, Cambridge (BA Hons in law). Commissioned RA 1939; served BEF, 1940; India/Burma, 1942-45; Major, 1942; Staff College, Quetta, 1945. Administrative officer, Gilbert and Ellice Islands Colony, 1946-57: Sec. to Govt, Co-operative Societies officer, District officer, District Commissioner, Actg Resident Commissioner, 1955-57. Transferred to Aden, 1958; Dep. Financial Sec. and frequently Actg Financial Sec. till 1962; Director of Establishments, 1962-68, and Assistant High Commissioner, 1963-68, Aden and Federation of South Arabia. Member E African Currency Board, 1960-62. Salaries Commissioner: British Virgin Islands, 1968; Montserrat, 1969; St Lucia and St Vincent, 1970; Classification Comr, Barbados, 1969; Chairman, Salaries Commission: Antigua, 1969; Dominica, 1970. *Publication:* Report on Census of Population of Gilbert and Ellice Islands Colony, 1947. *Recreations:* dinghy racing, carpentry. *Address:* Routledge Cottage, Westbourne, Emsworth, Hants. *T:* Emsworth 2915. *Clubs:* Royal Commonwealth Society; Royal Yachting Assoc., Cambridge University Cruising, Emsworth Sailing.

**PUTT, S(amuel) Gorley,** OBE 1966; MA; Fellow and Senior Tutor, Christ's College, Cambridge, since 1968; Chairman, English Association, since 1964 (Member of Executive Council, since 1963); *b* 9 June 1913; *o c* of late Poole Putt and late Ellen Blake Gorley, Brixham. *Educ:* Torquay Grammar School; Christ's College, Cambridge; Yale University. 1st Class English Tripos Pts I and II, MA 1937, Cambridge; Commonwealth Fund Fellow, MA 1936, Yale. BBC Talks Dept, 1936-38; Warden and Sec., Appts Cttee, Queen's Univ. of Belfast, 1939-40; RNVR, 1940-46, Lieut-Comdr; Warden and Tutor to Overseas Students and Director International Summer School, Univ. Coll., Exeter, 1946-49; Warden of Harkness House, 1949-68 and Director, Div. of International Fellowships, The Commonwealth Fund, 1966-68. Vis. Prof., Univ. of Massachusetts, 1968. Member: English-Speaking Union, London Cttee, 1952-57; UK-US Educational Commn: Travel Grants Cttee, 1955-64; Observer, 1966-68; Committee of Management, Inst. of US Studies, London Univ., 1965-69. FRSL 1952. *Publications:* Men Dressed As Seamen, 1943; View from Atlantis, 1955; (ed) Cousins and Strangers, 1956; Coastline, 1959; Scholars of the Heart, 1962; (ed) Essays and Studies, 1963; A Reader's Guide to Henry James, 1966. *Address:* Christ's College, Cambridge. *T:* Cambridge 59601. *Club:* Athenæum.

**PUTTICK, Lt-Gen. Sir Edward,** KCB 1946 (CB 1942); DSO 1918; idc; *b* 26 June 1890; *s* of John Prior Puttick, London, and Rachel Orpen, Kilgarvan, Kenmare, Ireland; *m* 1919, Irene Lillian Dignan (decd), Auckland; three *d. Educ:* Waitaki Boys' High School, Oamaru, NZ. Served European War, 1914-18: Capt. to Lt-Col, Samoa, Egypt, France, Belgium; Commander (temp.) 3rd New Zealand Rifle Brigade, 1917 (severely wounded); Commandant NZRB Reserve Depot, Brocton Stafford, 1918; Asst Quartermaster-General, New Zealand, 1919-29; Commandant Special Expedition to Fiji during Indian riots, 1920; Staff Officer in charge No. 1 Regtl District Auckland, 1929-33; GSO Christchurch, 1933-34, Lt-Col, 1933; Quartermaster-General, NZ Military Forces, Wellington, NZ, 1934-36; at Imperial Defence College and Imperial Conference, 1937; Colonel, 1937; ADC (addit) to the King, 1938-41; Adjutant and Quartermaster-General and 2nd Military Member of the Army Board, Army Headquarters, Wellington, NZ, 1938-39; Officer Commanding Central District, Wellington, NZ, 1939; Comdr 4th NZ Infantry Brigade, NZ Expeditionary Force, Egypt, 1940-41; Operations Greece, 1941; Comd NZ Forces, Crete, May 1941; GOC New Zealand Forces, 1942-45, and Chief of New Zealand General Staff, 1941-45 (Greek Military Cross, 1st Class, Bar to DSO, Commander Legion of Merit (USA)); Prime Ministers' Conf. (London), 1944; Maj.-Gen. 1941; Lt-Gen. 1942. Commanded New Zealand Contingent in Victory March, London, 1946; retired, 1946. Gold Staff Officer at Coronation of King George VI, 1937. *Publication:* 25 Battalion: Official History of New Zealand in the Second World War, 1939-1945, 1960. *Recreations:* cricket, shooting, fishing. *Address:* Wallis Street, Raglan, NZ.

**PYATT, Rt. Rev. William Allan;** *see* Christchurch, Bishop of.

**PYE, Norman;** Professor of Geography since 1954, University of Leicester (Pro-Vice-Chancellor, 1963-66); Dean, Faculty of

Science, 1957-60; *b* 2 November 1913; *s* of John Whittaker Pye and Hilda Constance (*née* Platt); *m* 1940, Isabella Jane (*née* Currie); two *s*. *Educ:* Wigan Grammar School; Manchester University. Manchester University: BA Hons Geography Class I, 1935, Diploma in Education Class I, 1936; Asst Lecturer, Dept of Geography, 1936-37; St Catharine's Coll., Cambridge, 1937-38; Assistant Lecturer in Geography, Manchester Univ., 1938-46. Seconded to Hydrographic Dept, Admiralty, for War Service, 1940-46. Lecturer in Geography, 1946-53, Sen. Lecturer, 1953-54, Manchester Univ. Editor, "Geography". Member Corby Development Corp., 1965. Mem. Council, Royal Geographical Soc., 1967. *Publications:* research papers and articles in learned journals. *Recreations:* travel, music, gardening, walking. *Address:* 127 Spencefield Lane, Evington, Leicester. *T:* Thurnby 5167.

**PYKE, Air Commodore Alan,** CB 1961; OBE 1951; Royal Air Force (Retired); *b* 5 September 1911; *s* of late Arthur Oakley Pyke, Gillingham, Kent. *Educ:* Ashton-under-Lyne; Royal Air Force College, Cranwell. Joined RAF, 1927. Served War of 1939-45, Fighter Command and Maintenance Command; jssc; psa; CEng, FIMechE. *Recreations:* golf, gardening. *Address:* Oakley, Bate's Lane, Helsby, Cheshire. *Club:* Royal Air Force.

**PYKE, Cyril John,** CMG 1951; *b* 1892; *s* of Richard John Pyke, Midgham, Berks; *m* 1917, Gladys, *e d* of F. W. Pote, Exeter; one *s* two *d* (and one *s* decd). *Educ:* King's College, London; Trinity Hall, Cambridge. Civil Service Administrative Class, 1921; Assistant Secretary, Ministry of Supply, 1939; Deputy Director of Finance, Ministry of Supply, 1940; Principal Assistant Secretary, 1942; Economic Adviser to Government of Malaya, 1945; Head of Finance and Economics Department, Foreign Office Administration of African Territories, 1949. *Address:* The Barn Cottage, Salford Road, Aspley Guise, Bucks.

**PYKE-LEES, Walter Kinnear;** Registrar, General Medical Council, 1951-70; *b* 17 Dec. 1909; *m* 1944, Joan Warburton, *d* of G. F. Stebbing, FRCS, FFR, and Margaret Warburton Stebbing; two *d*. *Educ:* Liverpool College; Wadham College, Oxford. Clerk of the Council's Dept, LCC, 1933-37; Asst Sec., GMC, 1937; seconded to HM Treasury, 1940-45; Asst Sec., GMC, 1945-51. Mem. Exec. Cttee, English Assoc., 1950-62. Mem. Council, Britain-Burma Soc., 1968-. *Publications:* History and Present Work of the General Medical Council, 1958; *as Peter Leyland:* The Naked Mountain (verse), 1951; The English Association Book of Verse (anthology, with M. Alderton Pink), 1953. *Recreations:* golf, chess. *Address:* 7 Burghley Road, Wimbledon, SW19. *T:* 01-946 5727.

**PYKE-NOTT, Comdr Sir James (Grenvile),** Kt 1952; CMG 1949; RN (retired); *b* 28 April 1897; *s* of John Moëls Pyke-Nott, Mill House, Dumbleton, nr Evesham, Worcs and Dora Florence Geraldine, *d* of Bennet Rothes Langton, Langton Hall, Langton, Spilsby, Lincs; *m* 1949, Joan Mary Lee, *d* of late Rev. W. M. L. Evans. *Educ:* Orleton Preparatory School, Scarborough; Royal Naval Colleges, Osborne and Dartmouth. Served in Royal Navy in European War, 1914-18, and in War of 1939-45. Appointed to Colonial Administrative Service, 1924; served in Nigeria; Chief Commissioner, Eastern Provinces, 1948-52, Lieut-Governor, Eastern Region, 1952, Nigeria; retired, 1952. *Recreations:* shooting and golf. *Address:* 7 Carroll Avenue, Merrow, near Guildford, Surrey.

**PYM, Sir Charles (Evelyn),** Kt 1959; CBE 1939 (OBE 1919); DL; *b* 11 Jan. 1879; 2nd *s* of late Horatio Noble Pym, Foxwold, Kent, and Sarah Juliet, *d* of Edmund Backhouse, MP; *m* 1905, Violet C. (*d* 1927), *o d* of Frederick Lubbock, Emmetts, Kent; three *s* one *d*. *Educ:* Eton; Magdalen College, Oxford. Late Captain 5th Lancers, Major Suffolk Yeo.; served S African War, 1901-02; Gallipoli and Egypt, 1915-16; France, 1917-19 (despatches twice, OBE); JP, DL Kent; Kent County Council, 1925-65; County Alderman, 1935-; Vice-Chairman, 1936-49; Chairman, 1949-52. Comdr St John of Jerusalem. *Recreations:* shooting, walking. *Address:* Foxwold, Brasted, Kent. *T:* Westerham 3724. *Clubs:* Junior Carlton, Bath; Kent County (Maidstone).

**PYM, Rt. Hon. Francis Leslie,** PC 1970; MC 1945; MP (C) Cambridgeshire since 1961; Parliamentary Secretary to the Treasury and Government Chief Whip since 1970; *b* 13 Feb. 1922; *s* of late Leslie Ruthven Pym, MP, and Iris, *d* of Charles Orde; *m* 1949, Valerie Fortune Daglish; two *s* two *d*. *Educ:* Eton; Magdalene Coll., Cambridge. Served War of 1939-45 (despatches, 1944 and 1945, MC): 9th Lancers, 1942-46; African and Italian campaigns. Contested (C) Rhondda West, 1959. Asst Govt Whip (unpaid), Oct. 1962-64; Opposition Whip, 1964-67; Opposition Dep. Chief Whip, 1967-70. Mem. Herefordshire County Council, 1958-61. *Address:* Everton Park, Sandy, Beds. *T:* Sandy 80376. *Clubs:* Carlton, Cavalry.

**PYM, William St John,** CBE 1946; *b* 5 June 1889; 4th *s* of late Walter Ruthven Pym, Bishop of Bombay; *m* 1st, 1920, Catherine Gardner; two *d*; 2nd, 1947, Eleanor Shelmerdine; one *d*. *Educ:* Rossall; Trinity College, Cambridge. Junior Examiner, Board of Education, 1914. Served European War with RGA in France, 1915-17. War Cabinet Secretariat, 1917-19; Fellow, Tutor and Assistant Bursar, Trinity Hall, Cambridge, 1919-23; HM Inspector of Schools, 1923-33; Chief Inspector of Schools under LCC, 1933-36; Head of Staff Division of BBC, 1936-49; Director of Personnel Bureau, UNESCO, 1950-51. *Address:* The Outlook, Cooden, Sussex.

**PYMAN, Gen. Sir Harold (English),** GBE 1963 (CBE 1944; MBE 1941); KCB 1958 (CB 1946); DSO 1942; MA; *b* 12 March 1908; *yr s* of late H. E. Pyman, W Hartlepool; *m* 1933, Elizabeth McArthur; two *s* one *d*. *Educ:* Fettes Coll.; Clare Coll., Cambridge (MA). Gazetted to Royal Tank Regiment, 1929; North-West Frontier Campaign, 1937; Capt. 1938; student at Staff College, Quetta, 1939; Instructor at Staff College, Quetta, 1939-41; psc†; Western Desert, 1941 (despatches); GSO I, 7 Armoured Division (DSO); CO 3rd Royal Tank Regt (bar to DSO); Brigadier General Staff, Home Forces, 1943-44; Brigadier General Staff 30 Corps for Normandy invasion (CBE); Chief of Staff Second Army, 1944-45 (despatches); Chief of General Staff ALFSEA and Acting Maj.-Gen., 1945-46 (CB, US Legion of Merit, Commander); Chief of Staff, GHQ, MELF, 1946-49; Maj.-Gen., 1949; GOC 56 (London) Armoured Division TA, 1949-51; Director-General, Fighting Vehicles, Ministry of Supply, 1951-53; GOC 11th Armoured Division, BAOR, 1953-55; Director of Weapons and Development, War Office, April 1955-May 1956; Lieut-General, 1957; General Officer Commanding 1st Corps, BAOR, 1956-58; Deputy Chief of the Imperial General Staff, 1958-61; General, 1961; Commander-in-Chief, Allied Forces, Northern Europe, 1961-63; retired 1964. Late Hon. Col, Berkshire and Westminster Dragoons (2nd Company of London Yeo.) TA; Col Comdt: The Royal

Tank Regt, 1958-65; The Royal Armoured Corps, 1963-66. *Recreations:* books, his garden and his writing; horticultural exhibitor. *Address:* Chitterwell, Sampford Arundel, Wellington, Somerset. *Club:* Somerset County (Taunton).

**PYMAN, Lancelot Frank Lee,** CMG 1961; HM Consul-General, San Francisco, since Oct. 1963; *b* 8 August 1910; *s* of late Dr F. L. Pyman, FRS, and of Mrs I. C. Pyman; *m* 1936, Sarah Woods Gamble. *Educ:* Dover College; King's College, Cambridge (Exhibitioner). Entered Levant Consular Service, 1933; various posts in Persia, 1933-38; Consul, Cernauti, Roumania, 1939-40; Vice-Consul, Beirut, Lebanon, 1940-41. Served with HM Forces in Levant States, 1941. Asst Oriental Secretary, HM Embassy, Tehran, Dec. 1941-44; Foreign Office, 1944-48; Consul, St Louis, Missouri, Dec. 1948-49; Oriental Counsellor, Tehran, Dec. 1949-Sept. 1952; Counsellor, British Embassy, Rio de Janeiro, 1952-53; Consul-General, Tetuan, 1953-56; Counsellor, British Embassy, Rabat, 1956-57; HM Consul-General, Zagreb, 1957-61; HM Consul-General, Basra, March-Dec. 1961. Ambassador to the Somali Republic, 1961-63. *Recreations:* listening to music, tennis, golf. *Address:* c/o Foreign and Commonwealth Office, SW1.

**PYRAH, Prof. Leslie Norman,** CBE 1963; retired as Senior Consultant Surgeon, Department of Urology, Leeds General Infirmary (1950-64); Hon. Director, Medical Research Council Unit, Leeds General Infirmary, 1956-64; Professor of Urological Surgery, Leeds University, 1956-64, now emeritus; *b* 11 April 1899; *s* of Arthur Pyrah; *m* 1934, Mary Christopher Batley; two *s* one *d. Educ:* University of Leeds; School of Medicine, Leeds. Hon. Asst Surgeon, Leeds Gen. Infirmary, 1934; Hon. Consultant Surgeon, Dewsbury Infirmary, Leeds Public Dispensary, Goole Hosp., and Lecturer in Surgery, Univ. of Leeds, 1934; Hon. Cons. Surgeon, St James' Hosp., Leeds, 1941; Surgeon with charge of Out-patients, Leeds Infirmary, 1944; Weild Lectr, Royal Faculty Physicians and Surgeons, Glasgow, 1955; Ramon Guiteras Lectr, Amer. Urological Assoc., Pittsburgh, USA, 1957; Pres., Section of Urology, Royal Soc. Med., 1958; Litchfield Lectr, Univ. of Oxford, 1959; Hunterian Orator, RCS, 1969. Chm., Specialist Adv. Cttee in Urology, Jt Royal Colls of Surgeons of GB and Ireland. Pres., British Assoc. of Urological Surgeons, 1961, 1962; Pres. Leeds and W Riding Medico-Chirurgical Soc., 1959. Mem. Council (elected), Royal College of Surgeons of England, 1960-68. Hon. Mem. Soc. Belge de Chirurgie, 1958; Corresponding Member: Amer. Assoc. of Genito-Urinary Surgeons, 1962; Amer. Soc. of Pelvic Surgeons, 1962; Australasian Soc. of Urology, 1963. St Peter's Medal (British Assoc. of Urological Surgeons) for outstanding contributions to urology, 1959. DSc (*hc*) Leeds, 1965. *Publications:* numerous, in British Journal of Surgery, British Journal of Urology, Proc. Royal Soc. Med., Lancet, BMJ. Contrib. British Surgical Progress, 1956. *Recreations:* tennis, music. *Address:* Fieldhead, Westwood Lane, Leeds 16. *T:* 52777; (consulting rooms) 27 Clarendon Road, Leeds 2. *T:* Leeds 23144. *Club:* Athenæum.

# Q

**QUANT, Miss Mary, (Mrs A. Plunket Greene),** OBE 1966; RDI 1969; Director of Mary Quant Group of companies since 1955; *b* 11 Feb. 1934; *d* of Jack and Mildred Quant; *m* 1957, Alexander Plunket Greene; one *s. Educ:* 13 schools; Goldsmiths' College of Art. Fashion Designer. Maison Blanche Rex Award (US), 1964; Sunday Times Internat. Award, 1964; Piavola d'Oro Award (Italy), 1966; Annual Design Medal, Inst. of Industrial Artists and Designers, 1966. FSIA 1967. *Publication:* Quant by Quant, 1966. *Address:* 3 Ives Street, SW3. *T:* 01-584 8781.

**QU'APPELLE, Archbishop of,** since 1970; **Most Rev. George Frederick Clarence Jackson;** Metropolitan of Rupert's Land; *b* 5 July 1907; *s* of James Sandiford Jackson; *m* 1939, Eileen de Montfort Welborn; two *s* two *d. Educ:* University of Toronto. Deacon, 1934; Priest, 1935, Diocese of Niagara. Diocese of: Toronto, 1937-38; Chester, 1938-46; Niagara, 1946-58; Qu'Appelle, 1958-. Hon. Canon, Christ Church Cathedral, Hamilton, Ontario, 1952; Dean of Qu'Appelle, 1958; Bishop of Qu'Appelle, 1960. DD (*hc*) 1959. *Recreations:* curling, gardening. *Address:* 1501 College Avenue, Regina, Saskatchewan, Canada. *T:* Regina 522-1294.

**QUARONI, Pietro,** Grand Cross of Order of Merit (GCOM, Italy); Grand Cross Crown (GCCI, Italy); MC (British); President-General, Italian Red Cross; *b* 3 October 1898; *s* of Giuseppe Quaroni and Sofia Pia von Seitz; *m* 1928, Larissa Cegodaeff; two *s. Educ:* Rome University. Began Italian Diplomatic career, 1920. Appointments: Constantinople, 1920; Buenos Aires, 1923; Moscow, 1925; Tirana, 1928; Ministry of Foreign Affairs, Rome, 1932; expert at Stresa Conference, 1935; Consul-General, Salonika, 1935; Italian Minister, Kabul, 1936; Ambassador, Moscow, 1944; Member of Italian Delegation at Peace Conf.; Ambassador, Paris, 1947-58; Ambassador, Bonn, 1958-61; Ambassador, London, 1961-64. Pres., Italian Radio Television, 1964-69. Grand Cross Légion d'Honneur (France), 1958; Grand Cross, Order of Merit (Germany), 1961. *Publications:* Memoirs of an Ambassador, 1954; Diplomatic Bag, 1956 (Eng. trans. 1966); The World of an Ambassador; Problems of Foreign Policy; Europe at the Crossway; Russian and China; Editor, Affari Esteri (quarterly). *Address:* Via Alberico II 4, Rome, Italy; Italian Red Cross, via Toscana 12, Rome, Italy. *Club:* Circolo Caccia (Rome); Jockey (Paris).

**QUARRELL, Prof. Arthur George,** ARCS, DSc, PhD (London); Professor of Metallurgy and Warden of Sorby Hall, Sheffield University; Vice-President: Iron and Steel Institute; Institution of Metallurgists; *b* 30 Oct. 1910; *m* 1934, Rose Amy Atkins; one *s* (and two *s* decd). *Educ:* College Secondary School, Swindon; Imperial College of Science and Technology. University of Sheffield, Department of Metallurgy: Assistant Lecturer, 1937-39; Lecturer, 1940-45. British Non-Ferrous Metals Research Association: Senior Metallurgist, Oct. 1945-March 1946; Research Manager, March 1946-Sept. 1950; Prof. of Physical Metallurgy, Sheffield Univ., 1950-55; Dean of the Faculty of Metallurgy, 1950-55, 1962-64. Pro-Vice-Chancellor of Sheffield Univ., 1958-62. Pres., Instn of Metallurgists, 1970-71. *Publications:* Physical Examination of Metals, 1940, 2nd edn 1961; Papers in Proc. Roy. Soc., Proc. Phys Soc., Jl Inst. Metals, Jl Iron and Steel Inst.

*Recreations:* gardening and other manual activities. *Address:* 58 Endcliffe Vale Road, Sheffield S10 3EW. *T:* 65857.

**QUARTERMAINE, Sir Allan (Stephen),** Kt 1956; CBE 1943; MC; BSc; FICE; *b* 9 November 1888; *s* of late Charles Stephen Quartermaine; *m* 1914, Gladys E. H. Siddons (*d* 1956); one *s*. *Educ:* University College, London (Hons Graduate, Chadwick Scholar, and Fellow). Hertfordshire CC, Surveyor's Department; Tees Side Bridge and Engineering Works; Great Western Railway; Royal Engineers, Egypt and Palestine, 1915-19 (despatches, MC); Commanded No. 1 Bridging Company, RE, SR, 1925; Director-General, Aircraft Production Factories, 1940; Chief Engineer, Great Western Railway and Western Region, British Railways, 1940-51; President Institution of Civil Engineers, 1951-52; Mem. Departmental Cttee on Coastal Flooding, 1953-54; Mem. Royal Fine Art Commission, 1954-60; Chm. Council for Codes of Practice, British Standards Institution, 1954-58; Mem. Hydraulics Research Board, DSIR, 1954-58. Hon. Member Institution of Royal Engineers; Chm. Civil Engineering Scholarship Trust, 1958-64. *Address:* 53 Westminster Gardens, SW1. *T:* 01-834 2143. *Club:* Athenæum.

**QUASTEL, Juda Hirsch,** CC (Canada) 1970; FRS 1940; DSc London; PhD Cantab; ARCS London; FRIC; FRSC; Professor of Neurochemistry, University of British Columbia, Canada, since 1966; *b* 2 Oct. 1899; *e s* of late Jonas and Flora Quastel, Sheffield, Yorks; *m* 1931, Henrietta Jungman, MA; two *s* one *d*. *Educ:* Central Secondary School, Sheffield; Imperial College of Science, London University; Trinity College, Cambridge. Commenced research in biochemistry in Cambridge University, Oct. 1921; awarded Senior Studentship by Royal Commissioners for Exhibition of 1851, 1923; Demonstrator and lecturer in biochemistry, Cambridge Univ. 1923; Fellow of Trinity College, Cambridge, 1924; Meldola Medallist 1927; Beit Memorial Research Fellow, 1928; Director of Research, Cardiff City Mental Hospital, 1929-41; Rockefeller Foundation Fellow, 1936; Director of ARC Unit of Soil Metabolism, 1941-47; Prof. of Biochemistry, McGill Univ., Montreal, 1947-66; Director: McGill-Montreal Gen. Hosp. Research Inst., 1947-65; McGill Unit of Cell Metabolism, 1965-66. Member of Council of Royal Institute of Chemistry, 1944-47; Member: Water Pollution Research Board, 1944-47; Bd of Governors, Hebrew Univ., Jerusalem, 1950; Pres., Montreal Physiological Soc., 1950; Pres. Canadian Biochemical Soc., 1963; Canadian Microbiological Soc. Award, 1965. Member, British, Can. and Amer. scientific societies; Consultant, Montreal General Hosp., Children's Memorial Hosp., and Jewish General Hosp., Montreal; Mem. Staff, Vancouver Gen. Hosp. Leeuwenhoek Lectr, Royal Society, 1954; Bryan Priestman Lectr, Univ. New Brunswick, 1956; Kearney Foundation Lectr, Univ. Calif., 1958; Royal Society Leverhulme Visiting Professor, in India, 1965-66. Fellow: NY Academy of Science, 1954; Amer. Assoc. for Advancement of Science, 1964. Hon. Fellow: Japanese Pharmacological Soc., 1963; Canadian Microbiological Soc., 1965; N Pacific Soc. of Neurology and Psychiatry, 1966. Hon. DSc McGill, 1964; Hon. PhD Jerusalem, 1970. *Publications:* since 1923 mainly on subjects of biochemical interest; author and co-editor: Neurochemistry, 1955- (1963); Methods in Medical Research, Vol. 9, 1961; Chemistry of Brain Metabolism, 1962; Metabolic Inhibitors, Vols 1 and 2, 1963, 1964. *Address:* Neurochemistry Section, Kinsmen Laboratories, University of British Columbia, Vancouver, Canada; 4585 Langara Avenue, Vancouver, Canada.

**QUAYLE, (John) Anthony,** CBE 1952; Actor; *b* 7 September 1913; *s* of Arthur Quayle and Esther Quayle (*née* Overton); *m* 1947, Dorothy Hyson; one *s* two *d*. *Educ:* Rugby. First appeared on stage, 1931; acted in various London productions between then and 1939, including several appearances at Old Vic; also acted in New York. Served War of 1939-45, Royal Artillery. After 1945 became play-producer as well as actor, being responsible for production of Crime and Punishment, The Relapse, Harvey, Who is Sylvia. Director, Shakespeare Memorial Theatre, 1948-56, where he has produced The Winter's Tale, Troilus and Cressida, Macbeth, Julius Caesar; King Lear (with John Gielgud), Richard II, Henry IV, Part I (with John Kidd), Henry V, Othello and Measure for Measure. Among parts played at Stratford are: The Bastard, Petruchio, Claudius, Iago, Hector in Troilus and Cressida; Henry VIII, 1949; Antony and Henry VIII, 1950; Falstaff in Henry IV, Parts I and II, 1951; Coriolanus; Mosca in Volpone, 1952; Othello, Bottom in a Midsummer Night's Dream, Pandarus in Troilus and Cressida, 1954; Falstaff in The Merry Wives of Windsor; Aaron in Titus Andronicus, 1955. Took Shakespeare Memorial Theatre Company to Australia, 1949, 1953. Played Tamburlaine, New York, 1956; acted in A View from the Bridge, Comedy Theatre, 1956; Made a tour of Europe in Titus Andronicus, 1957; directed and acted in The Firstborn, New York, 1958; acted in: Long Day's Journey into Night, Edinburgh Festival and London, 1958; Look After Lulu!, Royal Court, 1959; Chin-Chin, Wyndham's, 1960; The Right Honourable Gentleman, Her Majesty's, 1964; Incident at Vichy, Phœnix, 1966; Galileo, New York, 1967; Halfway Up The Tree, New York, 1967; Sleuth, St Martin's, 1970; The Idiot, National Theatre, 1970. Directed: Lady Windermere's Fan, 1967; Tiger at the Gates, New York, 1968. *Films:* Saraband for Dead Lovers, Hamlet, Oh Rosalinda, Battle of the River Plate, The Wrong Man, Woman in a Dressing Gown, The Man Who Wouldn't Talk, Ice Cold in Alex, Serious Charge, Tarzan's Greatest Adventure, The Challenge, The Guns of Navarone, HMS Defiant, Lawrence of Arabia, The Fall of the Roman Empire, Operation Crossbow, A Study in Terror, Incompreso, MacKenna's Gold, Before Winter Comes, Anne of the Thousand Days. *Publications:* Eight Hours from England, 1945; On Such a Night, 1947. *Address:* 22 Pelham Crescent, SW7.

**QUAYLE, Richard William,** OBE 1948; Special Commissioner of Income Tax, 1953-66; Member, London Rent Assessment Panel, since 1967; *b* 9 Aug. 1901; *o s* of late Richard Smith Quayle; *m* 1926, Ursula Mary Heron Ryan, *o d* of Arthur Heron Ryan Tenison, FRIBA; one *d*. *Educ:* Charterhouse; Magdalen College, Oxford. Called to Bar, Inner Temple, 1925. Entered Office of Solicitor of Inland Revenue; Assistant Solicitor of Inland Revenue, 1950. *Recreation:* fishing. *Address:* St Peter's Cottage, Westcott, Dorking, Surrey. *T:* Dorking 5311. *Clubs:* Oxford and Cambridge University, MCC; Royal Tennis Court (Hampton Court).

**QUEBEC, Cardinal Archbishop of,** since 1965; **His Eminence Cardinal Maurice Roy,** DD (Laval), DPh (Inst. Angelicum); Archbishop of Quebec since 1947; Primate of Canada since 1956; elevated to the Sacred College of Cardinals and given titular church of Our Lady of the Blessed Sacrament and the Holy Canadian Martyrs, 1965; *b* 25 Jan. 1905; *s* of late Ferdinand Roy. *Educ:* Seminary of Quebec and Laval Univ., Quebec; Collegium Angelicum, Rome; Institut catholique and Sorbonne, Paris. Priest, 1927; Professor of: Dogmatic Theology, 1930-35; Apologetics, 1935-36; Sacramentary Theology, 1936-39; Students' Chaplain, 1936-37. Hon. Capt.-Chaplain Royal 22nd Regt 1939; Hon. Major and Chief Chaplain Canadian Base Units at Aldershot, 1941; Hon. Lt-Col, Chaplain HQ First Cdn Corps (England and Italy), 1941; Sicily and Italy Campaigns, 1943; Hon. Col, Asst Prin. Chaplain 1st Cdn Army, 1944; France, Belgium, Germany, Holland campaigns, 1944-45 (despatches). Rector Grand Seminary of Quebec, 1945; Bishop of Three-Rivers, 1946; Bishop Ordinary to Cdn Armed Forces (Military Vicar), 1946. Central Commission preparatory to Council Vatican II, June 1962; Council Vatican II Commission on Sacred Theology, Dec. 1962; Sacred Congregations of the Council and of Seminaries and Universities, 1965; Chairman: Concilium De Laicis; Pontifical Commission, Justitia et Pax, Rome. OBE, 1945; Chevalier of the Legion of Honour, 1947; Commander of the Order of Leopold and Croix de Guerre with palm, 1948; Commander of the Order of Orange Nassau, Holland, 1949; Knight Grand Cross, Equestrian Order to the Holy Sepulchre of Jerusalem, 1965; Bailiff Grand Cross of Honour and Devotion, Sovereign Order of Malta, 1965. *Address:* Archevêché de Québec, Québec, Canada.

**QUEBEC, Bishop of,** since 1960; **Rt. Rev. Russel Featherstone Brown;** *b* Newcastle upon Tyne, 7 Jan. 1900; *s* of Henry John George Brown and Lucy Jane Ferguson; *m* 1940, Priscilla Marian Oldacres (*d* 1948); three *s*. *Educ:* Bishop's Univ., Lennoxville, PQ, Canada. BA (Theo.) 1933. RAF, 1918-19; business, 1919-29; University, 1929-33; Deacon, 1933; Priest, 1934; Curate, Christ Church Cathedral, Montreal, 1933-36; Priest-in-Charge, Fort St John, BC, 1936-40; Rector of Sherbrooke, PQ, 1940-54; Canon, Holy Trinity Cathedral, Quebec, 1948; Rector, St Matthew's, Quebec, PQ, 1954-60; Archdeacon of Quebec, 1954-60. Hon. DCL Bishop's Univ., Lennoxville, 1961; Hon. DD, Montreal Diocesan Theological College, 1968. *Address:* Bishopthorpe, Quebec 4, PQ, Canada.

**QUEEN, Ellery;** *see* Dannay, Frederic and Lee, Manfred B.

**QUEENSBERRY,** 12th Marquess of, *cr* 1682; **David Harrington Angus Douglas;** late Royal Horse Guards; Viscount Drumlanrig and Baron Douglas, 1628; Earl of Queensberry, 1633; Bt (Nova Scotia), 1668; Professor of Ceramics, Royal College of Art, since 1959; *b* 19 Dec. 1929; *s* of 11th Marquess of Queensberry and late Cathleen Mann; *S* father, 1954; *m* 1st, 1956, Mrs Ann Radford; one *d*; 2nd, 1969, Alexandra, *d* of Guy Wyndham Sich; one *s* one *d*. *Educ:* Eton. *Heir: half-b* Lord Gawain Archibald Douglas, *b* 24 May 1948. *Address:* 5 Sutherland House, Marloes Road, W8.

**QUEENSLAND, NORTH, Bishop of,** since 1953; **Rt. Rev. Ian (Wotton Allnutt) Shevill,** MA (Sydney); *b* 2 May 1917; *s* of Erson James Shevill; *m* 1959, Dr June (*d* 1970), *d* of Basil Stephenson, Worthing; two *s*. *Educ:* Scot's Coll., Sydney; Sydney Univ.; School of Oriental and African Studies, London Univ.; Moore Theological Coll., Sydney. BA, 1939, MA, 1945, Sydney; ThL, ThD, 1953, Moore Theol. Coll. Deacon, 1940; Priest, 1941; Curate of St Paul, Burwood, 1940-45; Organising Secretary of the Australian Board of Missions, for Province of Queensland, 1946-47; Education Secretary, Society for the Propagation of Gospel, 1948-51. *Publications:* New Dawn in Papua, 1946; Pacific Conquest, 1948; God's World at Prayer, 1951; Orthodox and other Eastern Churches in Australia, 1964; Half Time, 1966; Going it with God, 1969. *Address:* Bishop's Lodge, Townsville, N Queensland, Australia.

**QUEGUINER, Jean;** Légion d'Honneur, 1970; Deputy Secretary-General, Inter-Governmental Maritime Consultative Organization (IMCO) since 1968; *b* 2 June 1921; *s* of Etienne Queguiner and Anne Trehin; *m* 1952, Marguerite Gaillard; one *s* one *d*. *Educ:* Lycée Buffon, Collège Stanislas and Faculté de Droit, Paris; Coll. of Administration of Maritime Affairs, St Malo. Head of Maritime Dist of Caen, 1953; Dep. Head of Coll. of Admin. of Maritime Affairs, 1955; Head of Safety of Navigation Section, 1963; Vice-Chm. of Maritime Safety Cttee of Inter-Govtl Maritime Consultative Organization, 1965-68. *Publications:* Législation et réglementation maritime, 1955; Le code de la mer, 1965; La croisière cotière, 1967; Le code fluvial à l'usage des plaisanciers, 1970. *Recreation:* sailing. *Address:* (office) 101-104 Piccadilly, W1. *T:* 01-499 9040; (home) 32 Melton Court, Old Brompton Road, SW7. *Club:* Royal Automobile.

**QUENET, Sir Vincent (Ernest),** Kt 1962; Judge President of Appellate Division, High Court of Rhodesia, 1964-70; *b* 14 Dec. 1906; *y s* of George Alfred Quénet, Worcester, CP, SA; *m* 1938, Gabrielle, *d* of Hon. Norman Price; three *s*. *Educ:* Worcester High Sch.; University of Cape Town. Advocate of Supreme Court of SA and Barrister-at-law, Middle Temple. Practised at Johannesburg Bar, QC; Judge of: High Court of S Rhodesia, 1952-61; Fed. Supreme Court, Federation of Rhodesia and Nyasaland, 1961-64. *Address:* Tiger Valley, Borrowdale, Salisbury, Rhodesia. *T:* 8872813. *Clubs:* Rand (Johannesburg); Salisbury (Rhodesia).

**QUENINGTON, Viscount; Michael Henry Hicks Beach;** *b* 7 Feb. 1950; *s* and *heir* of 2nd Earl St Aldwyn, *qv*. *Address:* Williamstrip Park, Cirencester, Glos.; 13 Upper Belgrave Street, SW1.

**QUENNELL, Joan Mary,** MBE 1958; JP; MP (C) Petersfield since 1960; *b* 23 Dec. 1923; *o c* of late Walter Quennell, Dangstein, Rogate. *Educ:* Dunhurst and Bedales Schools. War Service, WLA and BRCS. Vice-Chairman, Horsham Division Cons. Assoc., 1949 (Chairman, 1958-61); W Sussex CC, 1951-61. Served on Finance, Local Government, Selection and Education Cttees, etc; also as Governor various schools and colleges; Governor, Crawley Coll., Further Education, 1956-69; Member Southern Reg. Council for Further Education, 1959-61; Member Reg. Adv. Council, Technological Education (London and Home Counties), 1959-61. Parliamentary Private Secretary to the Minister of Transport, 1962-64; Member: Select Cttee on Public Accounts, 1970-. JP (W Sussex), 1959-. *Recreations:* swimming, reading, gardening, the theatre. *Address:* House of Commons, SW1.

**QUENNELL, (Mrs) Marjorie,** Hon. ARIBA; illustrator; *b* Bromley Common, Kent; *d* of Allen Courtney; *m* 1904, Charles Henry Bourne Quennell, Architect (*d* 1935); one *s* (*see* Peter Quennell) (one *d* decd, and one *s* decd, War of 1939-45). *Educ:* Oakhurst, Shortlands; various art schools. Curator of the Geffrye

Museum till 1941. *Publications:* (with C. H. B. Quennell) A History of Everyday Things in England, Part I, 1918; Part II, 1919; Part III, 1933; Part IV, 1934; Everyday Life in the Old Stone Age, 1921; New Stone, Bronze, and Early Iron Ages, 1922; Roman Britain, 1924; Anglo-Saxon Viking and Norman Times, 1926; Everyday Things in Homeric Greece, 1929; Everyday Things in Archaic Greece, 1931; Everyday Things in Classical Greece, 1932; The Good New Days, 1936. *Recreation:* painter. *Address:* 6 Wallands Crescent, Lewes, Sussex.

**QUENNELL, Peter;** *b* March 1905; *s* of Marjorie, *qv* and C. H. B. Quennell (*d* 1935). *Educ:* Berkhamsted Grammar Sch.; Balliol Coll., Oxford. Editor, History To-day; edited The Cornhill Magazine, 1944-51. *Publications:* Poems; Baudelaire and the Symbolists; A Superficial Journey; Byron, The Years of Fame; Byron in Italy; Caroline of England; Four Portraits; John Ruskin, The Portrait of a Prophet; Spring in Sicily; The Singular Preference; Hogarth's Progress; The Sign of the Fish; Shakespeare: The Poet and his Background; Alexander Pope: The Education of Genius; translation of Memoirs of the Comte de Gramont; Private Letters of Princess Lieven to Prince Metternich, edited with introduction; (ed) Byron: A Self-Portrait (Letters and Diaries, 1798-1824), 2 vols; (ed) Mayhew's London Labour and the London Poor, in three vols of selections; (ed) The Memoirs of William Hickey. *Address:* Bracken House, 10 Cannon Street, EC4. *Club:* White's.

**QUEREJAZU CALVO, Roberto;** Cross of the Chaco and Award of Military Merit (Bolivia); Bolivian Ambassador to the Court of St James's 1966-70, and to the Court of the Hague, 1966-70; *b* 24 Nov. 1913; *m* 1944, Dorothy Lewis; one *s* one *d*. *Educ:* Sucre Univ., Bolivia. Director of Minister's Cabinet, Legal Dept, and Political Dept, Bolivian Foreign Service, 1939-42; First Secretary, Embassy in Brazil, 1943; Secretary-General, Bolivian Delegn to UN, 1946; Bolivian Embassy, London: Counsellor, 1947; Chargé d'Affaires, 1948-52; Bolivian Rep.: to UN Conference on Tin, 1951; to Interamerican Conference for De-Nuclearization of Latin America, Mexico, 1964; Bolivian Delegate: XX UN General Assembly, 1965; 2nd Interamerican Conference Extraord., Rio de Janeiro, 1965; Under-Secretary of State for Foreign Affairs, Bolivia, 1966. Holds foreign awards. *Publication:* Masamaclay (History of Chaco War), 1966. *Recreation:* tennis. *Address:* 98 Great Brownings, Dulwich, SE21.

**QUICK SMITH, George William,** CBE 1959; Chief Executive and Member of National Freight Corporation since 1968; Chairman, Skyways Coach-Air Ltd; *b* 23 Aug. 1905; *s* of George Windsor Smith and Maud Edith (*née* Quick); *m* 1934, Ida Muriel Tinkler; no *c*. *Educ:* Univ. of London (LLB). Barrister-at-law, Inner Temple. FCIS; MInstT (past Vice-Pres.). Various positions in shipping, 1922-35; Sec. of various assocs and Mem. of joint negotiating and other bodies connected with road transport; British employers deleg. to various internat. confs including ILO, 1935-48; First Legal Adviser and Sec. and later Mem. of Board of British Road Services, 1948-59; Adviser on Special Projects, British Transport Commn, 1959-62; Chief Sec. and now Chief Exec. of Transport Holding Co., 1962-. Dir various road haulage cos; Trustee various transport benevolent funds; Master of Carmen's Co., 1967-68; Freeman of City of London. Churchwarden, All Saints Margaret Street, London, 1960-. Mem. Governing Body, SPCK, 1967-. *Publications:* various books and papers on road transport and road transport law; Commentary on Transport Act 1947. *Recreations:* contrasting variations of work. *Address:* 8 Cambridge Gate, Regents Park, NW1. *T:* 01-935 1626. *Club:* City Livery.

**QUIGLEY, Hugh,** MA; Economist and Farmer; *b* Stirling, 6 Aug. 1895; *e s* of James and Catherine Quigley, Stirling, afterwards Lanark; *m* Marion Sommerville, *y d* of Joseph Dyer, Kilbank, Lanark; one *s* one *d*. *Educ:* Lanark Grammar Sch.; Glasgow Univ.; Naples Univ.; Munich Univ. War Service, 1915-18; MA, 1st Class Hons in French, German, Italian, Glasgow Univ., 1919; Carnegie Research Fellow in Modern Languages, 1919-21; Economist in Research Department of Metropolitan-Vickers Electrical Company, 1922-24; Head of Economic and Statistical Department of the British Electrical and Allied Manufacturers' Assoc., 1924-30; Chief Statistical Officer, Central Electricity Board, 1931-43. *Publications:* Lombardy, Tyrol, and the Trentino, 1925; The Land of the Rhone, 1927; Passchendaele and the Somme, 1928 (revised edn, 1965); Lanarkshire in Prose and Verse, 1929; Electrical Power and National Progress, 1925; Towards Industrial Recovery, 1927; Republican Germany (with R. T. Clark), 1928 (repr. 1968); German History from 1900 to 1931 (chap. in German Studies ed. Jethro Bithell), 1932; Part translator of R. Liefmann: Cartels, Concerns and Trusts, 1932; Power Resources of the World (for World Power Conference), 1929; Combines and Trusts in the Electrical Industry, 1927; The Electrical Industry of Great Britain, 1929; (both for the British Electrical and Allied Manufacturers' Association); Housing and Slum Clearance in London (with I. Goldie), 1934; Italian Criticism in the 18th Century; The Influence of English Philosophy and the Development of Aesthetics, based on Imagination; Antonio Conti (chapter in Mélanges Hauvette); The Highlands of Scotland, 1936; A Plan for the Highlands, 1936; End Monopoly Exploitation, 1941; New Forest Orchard, 1947; A Small Community: Melchet, 1970. *Recreation:* painting. *Address:* Melchet Park, Romsey, Hants.

**QUILL, Colonel Raymond Humphrey,** CBE 1947; DSO 1947; MVO (4th Class) 1934; Colonel (retired), Royal Marines; *b* 4 May 1897; *s* of late Maj.-General Richard Henry Quill, CB, MD; unmarried. *Educ:* Wellington Coll.; Cheltenham. Joined Royal Marines, 1914. Served European War, 1914-19. Major, RM, 1934; Lieut-Colonel, 1943; Colonel, 1944. Served War of 1939-45. ADC to the King, 1948-50; retired, 1950. Legion of Merit, USA, 1948. Fellow, British Horological Institute, 1954-. *Publication:* John Harrison: The man who found Longitude, 1967. *Recreations:* athletics, fishing, horology. *Address:* 104 Marsham Court, Westminster, SW1. *T:* 01-828 3730. *Clubs:* Boodle's, Royal Thames Yacht, Royal Automobile.

**QUILTER, Sir Anthony (Raymond Leopold Cuthbert),** 4th Bt, *cr* 1897; Landowner since 1959; *b* 25 March 1937; *s* of Sir (John) Raymond (Cuthbert) Quilter, 3rd Bt and Margery Marianne (*née* Cooke); *S* father 1959; *m* 1964, Mary Elise, *er d* of late Colonel Brian (Sherlock) Gooch, DSO, TD; one *s* one *d*. *Educ:* Harrow. Is engaged in farming. *Recreations:* shooting, golf. *Heir: s* Guy Raymond Cuthbert Quilter, *b* 13 April 1967. *Address:* Methersgate Hall, Woodbridge, Suffolk. *T:* Woodbridge 16.

**QUIN;** *see* Wyndham-Quin.

**QUIN, Rt. Rev. George Alderson;** *see* Down and Dromore, Bishop of.

**QUINE, Prof. Willard Van Orman;** American author; Professor of Philosophy, since 1948, and Edgar Pierce Professor of Philosophy, since 1956, Harvard University; *b* Akron, Ohio, 25 June 1908; *s* of Cloyd Robert and Hattie Van Orman Quine; *m* 1st, 1930, Naomi Clayton; two *d*; 2nd, 1948, Marjorie Boynton; one *s* one *d*. *Educ:* Oberlin Coll., Ohio (AB); Harvard Univ. (AM, PhD). Harvard: Sheldon Travelling Fellow, 1932-33 (Vienna, Prague, Warsaw); Jun. Fellow, Society of Fellows, 1933-36 (Sen. Fellow, 1949-, Chairman, 1957-58); Instructor and Tutor in Philosophy, 1936-41; Assoc. Professor of Philosophy, 1941-48; Chairman, Dept of Philosophy, 1952-53. Visiting Professor, Universidade de São Paulo, Brazil, 1942. Lieut, then Lieut-Commander, USNR, active duty, 1942-46. Consulting editor, Journal of Symbolic Logic, 1936-52; Vice-President, Association for Symbolic Logic, 1938-40; President, 1953-55; Vice-President, Eastern Division, American Philosophical Assoc., 1950; President, 1957; Corres. Fellow, British Academy, 1959-. FAAS, 1945 (Councillor, 1950-53); American Philosophical Society, 1957- (Councillor, 1966-); Institut Internat. de Philosophie, 1953-; Acad. Internat. de Philosophie de Science, 1960; Instituto Brasileiro de Filosofia, 1963-; Trustee, Institute for Unity of Science, 1949-; Syndic, Harvard University Press: 1951-53; 1954-56, 1959-60, 1962-66. George Eastman Visiting Prof., Oxford Univ., 1953-54; Vis. Professor: Univ. of Tokyo, 1959; Rockefeller Univ., 1968; Collège de France, 1969. A. T. Shearman Lecturer, University of London, 1954; Gavin David Young Lectr in Philosophy, Univ. of Adelaide, 1959; John Dewey Lectr, Columbia Univ., 1968. Member Institute for Advanced Study, Princeton, USA, 1956-57. Fellow: Centre for Advanced Study in the Behavioural Sciences, Palo Alto, California, 1958-59; Centre for Advanced Studies, Wesleyan Univ., Conn, 1965. Hon. degrees: MA Oxon, 1953; DLitt Oxon, 1970; LittD: Oberlin, 1955; Akron, 1965; Washington, 1966; Temple, 1970; LLD Ohio State, 1957; DesI Lille, 1965; LHD Chicago, 1967. N. M. Butler Gold Medal, 1970. *Publications:* A System of Logistic, 1934; Mathematical Logic, 1940, rev. edn 1951; Elementary Logic, 1941, rev. edn 1965; O sentido da nova logica, 1944 (São Paulo): Methods of Logic, 1950, rev. edn 1959; From a Logical Point of View, 1953, rev. edn 1961); Word and Object, 1960; Set Theory and its Logic, 1963, revised edn 1969; Ways of Paradox and Other Essays, 1966; Selected Logic Papers, 1966; Ontological Relativity and Other Essays, 1969; Philosophy of Logic, 1970; (with J. S. Ullian) The Web of Belief, 1970. Contributions to Journal of Symbolic Logic; Journal of Philosophy; Philosophical Review; Mind; Rivista di Filosofia; Scientific American; NY Review of Books; Library of Living Philosophers. *Recreation:* travel. *Address:* 38 Chestnut Street, Boston, Mass 02108, USA. *T:* 742-2813.

**QUINLAN, Maj.-Gen. Henry,** CB 1960; *b* 5 Jan. 1906; *s* of Dr Denis Quinlan, LRCP, LRCS (Edinburgh), of Castletownroche, Co. Cork; *m* 1936, Euphemia Nancy, *d* of John Tallents Wynyard Brooke of Shanghai, and Altrincham, Cheshire; two *s* two *d*. *Educ:* Clongowes Wood Coll., Sallins, Co. Kildare. BDS 1926; FFD RCS (I) 1964. Royal Army Dental Corps; Lieut, 1927; Captain, Dec. 1930; Major, 1937; Lieut-Colonel, Dec. 1947; Colonel, 1953; Maj.-General, Oct. 1958; Director Army Dental Service, 1958-63; QHDS 1954-64, retired; Colonel Comdt Royal Army Dental Corps, 1964-66. Officer OStJ 1958. *Address:* Whitebridge, Redlands Lane, Crondall, Hants. *T:* Crondall 239.

**QUINN, Most Rev. Austin;** *see* Kilmore, Bishop of, (RC).

**QUINN, Professor David Beers,** DLit (QUB), PhD (London), MRIA, FRHistS, FRAI; Andrew Geddes and John Rankin Professor of Modern History, University of Liverpool, since 1957; *b* 24 April 1909; *o s* of late David Quinn, Omagh and Belfast, and Albertina Devine, Cork; *m* 1937, Alison Moffat Robertson, MA, *d* of late John Ireland Robertson, Edinburgh; two *s* one *d*. *Educ:* Clara (Offaly) No. 2 National Sch.; Royal Belfast Academical Institution; Queen's Univ., Belfast; King's Coll., University of London. University Schol., QUB, 1928-31 (1st Class Hons in Medieval and Modern History, 1931); PhD London, 1934. Asst Lecturer, 1934, and Lecturer, 1937, University College, Southampton; Lecturer in History, QUB, 1939-44; seconded to BBC European Service, 1943; Prof. of History, University College, Swansea, 1944-57; DLit (QUB), 1958. Secretary, Ulster Society for Irish Historical Studies, 1939-44; Member: Council of Hakluyt Society, 1950-54, 1957-60 (Vice-President, 1960-); Council of Royal Historical Society, 1951-55, 1956-60 (Vice-President, 1964-68); Fellow, Folger Shakespeare Lib. (Washington, DC), 1957, 1959, 1963-64; Leverhulme Res. Fellow, 1963; British Council Visiting Scholar, NZ, 1967; Harrison Vis. Prof., Coll. of William and Mary, Williamsburg, Va, 1969-70. Hon. DLitt, Newfoundland, 1964. *Publications:* The Port Books or Petty Customs Accounts of Southampton for the Reign of Edward IV, 2 vols, 1937-38; The Voyages and Colonising Enterprises of Sir Humphrey Gilbert, 2 vols, 1940; Raleigh and the British Empire, 1947; The Roanoke Voyages, 1584-90, 2 vols, 1955; (with H. A. Cronne and T. W. Moody) Essays in British and Irish History in Honour of J. E. Todd, 1949; (with Paul Hulton) The American Drawings of John White, 1577-1590, 1964; (with R. A. Skelton) R. Hakluyt's Principall Navigations (1589), 1965; The Elizabethans and the Irish, 1966; Richard Hakluyt, Editor, 1967; North American Discovery, 1970; contribs on Irish history and the discovery and settlement of N. America in historical journals. *Address:* 9 Knowsley Road, Cressington Park, Liverpool L19 0PF. *T:* 051-427 2041.

**QUINNELL, Air Commodore John Charles,** CB 1943; DFC 1918; *b* 7 Jan. 1891; *er s* of late John B. Quinnell, Edenburn, Gortatlea, Co. Kerry, Ireland; *m* 1923, Atwell (*d* 1945), *d* of late James McFarlane, Fifeshire, Scotland; no *c*; *m* 1948, Mildred Joan, *widow* of Major Cyril Drummond, Cadland Fawley, Southampton, and *d* of late Horace Humphreys. *Educ:* Royal Sch., Dungannon, Co. Tyrone. Commissioned RA 1914; seconded RFC 1915; transferred RAF, 1918. Served European War, 1914-19 (despatches, DFC); RAF Staff Coll., 1924; Imperial Defence Coll., 1929; AOC No. 6 Auxiliary Group, 1935-38, and of No. 6 Group 1939; Senior Air Staff Officer, Advanced Air Striking Force, 1939-40 (despatches); AOC a Group, RAF, 1942; retired, 1945. *Recreations:* shooting, yachting. *Address:* Nelson's Place, Fawley, Southampton, Hants. *T:* Fawley, Hants 202. *Clubs:* Turf, Royal Thames Yacht; Royal Yacht Squadron.

**QUIRK, Prof. (Charles) Randolph,** MA, PhD, DLit (London); FIL; Quain Professor of English Language and Literature, University College, London, since 1968; *b* 12 July 1920; *s* of late Thomas and Amy Randolph Quirk,

Lambfell, Isle of Man; *m* 1946, Jean, *d* of Ellis Gauntlett Williams; two *s*. *Educ:* Cronk y Voddy Sch.; Douglas High Sch., IOM; University College, London. Served RAF, 1940-45; Assistant Lecturer in English, University College, London, 1947-50; Lecturer in English, Univ. Coll., London, 1950-54; Commonwealth Fund Fellow, Yale Univ. and University of Michigan, 1951-52; Secretary, Communication Research Centre, University Coll., London, 1953-54; Reader in English Language and Literature, University of Durham, 1954-58; Professor of English Language in the University of Durham, 1958-60; Professor of English Language in the University of London, 1960-68; Special University Lectures, London, 1960; Director, University of London, Summer School of English, 1962-67; Member: Senate, Univ. of London, 1970-; Admin. Board, British Inst. in Paris; Chm., Cttee of Enquiry into Speech Therapy Services. Fellow, UCL, 1970-. *Publications:* General Editor, English Language Series; The Concessive Relation in Old English Poetry, 1954; Studies in Communication (with A. J. Ayer and others), 1955; An Old English Grammar (with C. L. Wrenn), 1955, revised edn, 1958; Charles Dickens and Appropriate Language, 1959; The Teaching of English (with A. H. Smith), 1959, revised edn, 1964; The Study of the Mother-Tongue, 1961; The Use of English (with Supplements by A. C. Gimson and J. Warburg), 1962, enlarged edn, 1968; Prosodic and Paralinguistic Features in English (with D. Crystal), 1964; A Common Language (with A. H. Marckwardt), 1964; Investigating Linguistic Acceptability (with J. Svartvik), 1966; Essays on the English Language–Mediaeval and Modern, 1968; (with S. Greenbaum) Elicitation Experiments in English, 1970; contrib. to: Proc. 8th Internat. Congress of Linguists, 1958; Language and Society (Festschrift for Arthur M. Jensen), 1961; Proc. 9th International Congress of Linguists, 1962; English Teaching Abroad and the British Universities (ed G. Bullough), 1961; Dictionaries and that Dictionary (ed J. H. Sledd and W. R. Ebbitt), 1962; World Book Encyclopædia Dictionary (ed C. L. Barnhart), 1963; Early English and Norse Studies (Festschrift for A. H. Smith), 1963; (ed Lady Birkenhead) Essays by Divers Hands, 1969; Essays and Studies, 1970; papers in linguistic and literary journals. *Address:* 62 Talbot Road, Highgate, N6. *T:* 01-340 1460. *Club:* Athenæum.

**QUIRK, John Stanton S.**; *see* Shirley-Quirk.

**QUIRK, Ronald Charles,** OBE 1955; Member of Council, Stock Exchange, London, since 1950 (Deputy Chairman, 1964-67); *b* 11 Jan. 1908; *s* of George Henry Quirk and Ethel Jane Sargent; *m* 1932, Joan Reed; one *s* two *d*. *Educ:* Whitgift. Joined Geo. D. Atkin & Co. (stockjobbers), 1923; admitted into partnership, 1931; Director, Akroyd & Smithers, 1970. Joined RNVR 1940; served in Combined Operations until 1946. *Address:* White Lodge, Hillcroft Avenue, Purley, Surrey. *T:* 01-660 2685. *Clubs:* City of London; Island Sailing (Cowes); Royal Yachting Association; Lee-on-Solent Sailing.

**QVIST, George,** FRCS; Surgeon, Royal Free Hospital, since 1946, Willesden General Hospital, since 1956, Royal National Throat, Nose and Ear Hospital, since 1950; *b* 13 April 1910; *s* of Emil and Emily Qvist; *m* 1958, Dr Frances Gardner, *qv*. *Educ:* Quintin Sch.; Univ. Coll. Hosp. MB, BS Lond., 1933; FRCS 1934. Surgical Registrar, Royal Free Hospital, 1939-41; Surgeon Emergency Medical Service, 1941-44; Surgical Specialist and O/C Surgical Division, Lieutenant-Colonel RAMC, 1944-46. Member of Council, RCS; Member of Court of Examiners, RCS, 1951-57; Past President, Hunterian Society. *Publications:* Chapter in Maingot's Mangement of Abdominal Operations; various papers on surgical subjects. *Address:* 72 Harley Street, W1. *T:* 01-580 5265; Fitzroy Lodge, Fitzroy Park, Highgate, N6. *T:* 01-340 5873.

# R

**RABAUL, Archbishop of, (RC),** since 1966; **Most Rev. John Hoehne;** *b* Herbern, Germany, 12 Aug. 1910; *s* of M. Hoehne, Herbern. *Educ:* Germany. Dir, Native Seminary, 1939-45; Parish Priest, Namatanai, New Ireland, 1945-49; Dir, St Mary's, Vuvu, 1949-50; Dir, Kininigunan, 1951-56; Manager General of Catholic Mission, Vunapope, 1956-63; Vicar Apostolic from 1963. *Publications:* contribs to Zeitschrift fuer Neue Missionswissenschaft. *Recreation:* native psychology. *Address:* Archbishop's House, PO Box 414, Rabaul, Papua and New Guinea.

**RABBI, The Chief;** *see* Jakobovits, Rabbi Dr Immanuel.

**RABI, Prof. Isidor Isaac,** PhD; University Professor Emeritus, Columbia University, NY; Member: Naval Research Advisory Committee; (US Mem.) Science Committee of United Nations; President's Science Advisory Commission; General Advisory Committee, Arms Control and Disarmament Agency; Consultant to General Advisory Committee, Atomic Energy Commission; etc; *b* Rymanov, Austria, 29 July 1898; *s* of David and Scheindel Rabi; *m* Helen Newmark; two *d*. *Educ:* Cornell University (BChem 1919); Columbia University (PhD, 1927). Lecturer, Physics, Columbia University, New York, 1929; then various posts, there, 1930-50, when Higgins Professor of Physics until 1964, University Professor, 1964-67. Associate Director, Radiation Laboratory, Massachusetts Institute of Technology, Cambridge, Mass, 1940-45. Member: National Academy of Sciences; American Physics Soc., etc. Holds numerous honorary doctorates; awarded medals and prizes, 1939 onwards, including Nobel prize in physics, 1944, Atoms for Peace Award (jointly), 1967. *Publications:* My Life and Times as a Physicist, 1960; communications to The Physical Review, 1927-; contrib. to scientific jls on magnetism, quantum mechanics, nuclear physics, and molecular beams. *Recreations:* The theatre, travel, walking. *Address:* Columbia University, New York, NY, USA. *T:* 280-3368. *Clubs:* Athenæum (London); Cosmos (Washington).

**RABORN, Vice-Adm. William Francis, Jr,** DSM 1960; Silver Star 1945; Bronze Star Medal 1951; Commendation Medal 1954; National Security Medal, 1966, etc; United States Naval Officer, retired; *b* Decatur, Texas, 8 June 1905; *s* of William Francis, Sr, and Mrs Cornelia V. Raborn (*née* Moore); *m* 1955, Mildred T. Terrill; one *s* one *d*. *Educ:* US Naval Acad., Annapolis, Md (BS); Naval War Coll., Newport, RI. Ensign, USN, 1928; Naval Aviator, 1934; Sea duty, 1928-40; Aviation Gunnery Sch., 1940-42; Exec. Off., USS Hancock, 1943-45; Chief Staff Comdr Task Force 58, W Pacific, 1945-47; Ops Off. Comdr for Air W Coast, 1947-49; R & D Guided Missiles, 1949-50; Guided Missile Div., Office

1954-55; Asst Chief of Staff to C-in-C, Atlantic Fleet, 1955; Dir, Office of Special Projects, Polaris program, 1955; Dep. Chief, Naval Ops (Develt), 1962; retd from USN, 1963; Vice-Pres., Program management Aerojet Gen. Corp., Azusa, Calif, 1963-65; Director of Central Intelligence, USA, 1965-66; Industrial Consultant, Aerojet Gen. Corp. *Address:* (home) 1606 Crestwood Lane, McLean, Virginia 22101, USA; (business) c/o Aerojet General Corporation, 1120 Connecticut Avenue, NW, Washington, DC 20036, USA. *Clubs:* Army-Navy, Metropolitan (Washington, DC); Chevy Chase (Md); Burning Tree (Bethesda, Md); Canyon Country (Palm Springs, Calif); Jonathan (Los Angeles, Calif).

**RABY, Sir Victor Harry,** KBE 1956; CB 1948; MC; Deputy Under-Secretary of State, Department of the Permanent Under-Secretary of State for Air, 1946-57, retired December 1957; *b* 1897; *s* of Harry Raby, Menheniot, Cornwall; *m* 1921, Dorothy Alys, *d* of Rodney Buzzard, Ditchling, Sussex; one *s*. *Educ:* Grey College, Bloemfontein, S Africa. Served European War, 1914-19, with London Regt (MC). *Address:* The Red House, Fordens Lane, Holcombe, Dawlish, Devon. *Club:* Royal Automobile.

**RACE, Robert Russell,** CBE 1970; FRS 1952; PhD Cantab, MRCS, FRCP; Director, Medical Research Council Blood Group Unit, Lister Institute, SW1, since 1946; *b* 28 Nov. 1907; *e s* of late Joseph Dawson Race and late May Race (*née* Tweddle), Kensington; *m* 1st, 1938, Margaret Monica (*d* 1955), *d* of late J. R. C. Rotton, MVO; three *d*; 2nd, Ruth Ann, *d* of late Rev. H. Sanger, Urunga, NSW. *Educ:* St Paul's School; St Bartholomew's Hosp.; Trinity Hall, Cambridge. Asst Pathologist, Hosp. for Consumption and Diseases of the Chest, Brompton, 1935-37; Asst Serologist, Galton Laboratory, UC, London, 1937-39; Asst Dir then Dir, Galton Laboratory Serum Unit, at Dept of Pathology, Cambridge, 1939-46. Hon. MD, Univ. of Turku, 1970. Oliver Memorial Award for Blood Transfusion, 1948; Carlos J. Finlay Medal, Republic of Cuba, 1955; Landsteiner Memorial Award, jointly with Ruth Sanger, 1957; Oehlecker Medal, Deutsche Gesellschaft für Bluttransfusion, 1970. Kruis van Verdeinst, Netherlands Red Cross, 1959. MD (*hc*), University of Paris, 1965. *Publications:* (with Ruth Sanger) Blood Groups in Man, 1950, 1954, 1958, 1962, 1968. Many papers in genetical and medical journals. *Address:* 22 Vicarage Road, East Sheen, SW14. *T:* 01-876 1508.

**RACZYNSKI, Count Edward,** Dr Juris; Chairman: The Polish Institute and Sikorski Museum, since 1966; Polish Cultural Foundation, since 1970; *b* 19 Dec. 1891; *s* of Count Edouard Raczynski and Countess Rose Potocka; *m* 1st, 1925, Joyous (*d* 1930), *d* of Sir Arthur Basil Markham, 1st Bt, and Lucy, CBE, *d* of Captain A. B. Cunningham, late RA; 2nd, 1932, Cecile (*d* 1962), *d* of Edward Jaroszynski and Wanda Countess Sierakowska; three *d*. *Educ:* Universities of Krakow and Leipzig; London School of Economics and Political Science. Entered Polish Ministry of Foreign Affairs, 1919; served in Copenhagen, London, and Warsaw; Delegate to Disarmament Conference, Geneva, 1932-34; Polish Minister accredited to the League of Nations, 1932-34; Polish Ambassador to the Court of St James's, 1934-45; Acting Polish Minister for Foreign Affairs, 1941-42; Minister of State in charge of Foreign Affairs, Cabinet of Gen. Sikorski, 1942-43; Chief Polish Rep. on Interim Treasury Cttee for Polish Questions, 1945-47; Hon. Chief Polish Adviser, Ministry of Labour and National Service, 1952-Dec. 1956; Chairman, Polish Research Centre, London, 1940-67. Grand Officier of the Order of Polonia Restituta, Grand Cross of the Crown of Rumania, etc. *Publications:* In Allied London: Diary 1939-45 (in Polish); In Allied London: (Wartime Diaries), (in English), 1963; Rogalin and its Inhabitants (in Polish), 1963; Pani Róża (in Polish), 1969. Book of Verse (in Polish). *Recreations:* tennis, golf, skating, ski-ing. *Address:* 8 Lennox Gardens, SW1; 5 Krakowskie Przedmieście, Warsaw, Poland. *Club:* St James'.

**RADCLIFFE,** family name of **Viscount Radcliffe.**

**RADCLIFFE,** 1st Viscount, *cr* 1962; **Cyril John Radcliffe,** PC 1949; GBE 1948 (KBE 1944); FBA 1968; Baron (Life Peer) *cr* 1949; a Lord of Appeal in Ordinary, 1949-64; *b* 30 Mar. 1899; *s* of Alfred Ernest Radcliffe and Sybil Harriet Cunliffe; *m* 1939, Antonia, *d* of 1st Baron Charnwood. *Educ:* Haileybury; New College, Oxford (Hon. Fellow, 1949). Fellow of All Souls College, Oxford, 1922-37; Eldon Law Scholar, 1924; called to Bar, Inner Temple, 1924, Bencher 1943. QC 1935. Appts at Ministry of Information, 1939-41; Director General, Ministry of Information, 1941-45; Vice-Chairman Gen. Council of the Bar, 1946-49; Chairman Punjab and Bengal Boundary Commissions, 1947; Chairman Royal Commission on Taxation of Profits and Income, 1952; Chairman BBC General Advisory Council, 1952-55; Chairman, British Commonwealth International Newsfilm Agency Trust, 1957-; Constitutional Commissioner, Cyprus, 1956; Chm. Cttee of inquiry into the Monetary and Credit System, 1957-59; Chairman of Committee of Inquiry into Security Procedures and Practices, 1961; Chairman of Tribunal of Inquiry into the Vassall Case, 1962; Chairman, Privy Councillors' Inquiry into Daily Express and D Notices, 1967. Chairman Board of Trustees, British Museum, 1963-68 (Trustee, 1957-69); Trustee, British Museum (Natural History), 1963-69; Chancellor of University of Warwick, 1966-; Life Trustee: Shakespeare Birthplace Trust; Sir John Soane's Museum; Mem. Court of Univ. of London, 1958-63; Chm. Bd of Governors, School of Oriental and African Studies, London Univ., 1960-. Reith lecturer, BBC, 1951; Montagu Burton lecture, Glasgow University, 1953; Lloyd Roberts lecture, Roy. Soc. Med., 1955; Rosenthal Foundation lecturer, 1960; Rede Lecture, Cambridge, 1961; Romanes Lecture, Oxford, 1962; Oration, London School of Economics, 1965; Carr-Saunders Lecture, Inst. of Race Relations, 1969. Hon. MICE; Hon. Fell. Inst. of Bankers. Hon. LLD: Univ. of Wales, 1957; Univ. of St Andrews, 1959; Northwestern Univ., Illinois, USA, 1960; Univ. of Sussex, 1963; Univ. of Manchester, 1965; Hon. DCL, Oxford, 1961. Hon. DLitt, Univ. of Warwick, 1967. *Publications:* The Problem of Power (Reith Lectures, 1951); The Law and its Compass (Rosenthal Foundation Lectures), 1960; Not in Feather Beds, 1968. *Heir:* none. *Address:* 5 Campden Hill Gate, Duchess of Bedford Walk, W8. *T:* 01-937 0321; Hampton Lucy House, Warwick.

**RADCLIFFE, Sir Everard;** *see* Radcliffe, Sir Joseph B. E. H.

**RADCLIFFE, Hugh John Reginald Joseph,** MBE 1944; Deputy Chairman, London Stock Exchange, 1967-June 1970; *b* 3 March 1911; 2nd *s* of Sir Everard Radcliffe, 5th Bt; *m* 1937, Marie Therese, *d* of late Maj.-Gen. Sir Cecil Pereira, KCB, CMG; five *s* one *d*. *Educ:* Downside. Kt Comdr St Silvester (Papal),

1965. *Address:* Beetle Cottage, Carthouse Lane, Horsell, Surrey.

*See also Sir J. B. E. H. Radcliffe, Bt.*

**RADCLIFFE, Sir (Joseph Benedict) Everard (Henry),** 6th Bt *cr* 1813; MC 1945; Captain, late 60th Rifles; *b* 10 March 1910; *s* of Sir Everard Joseph Radcliffe, 5th Bt and Daisy (*d* 1943), *d* of Captain H. Ashton Case; *S* father, 1969; *m* 1st, 1937, Elizabeth (marr. diss. 1968), *e d* of Gilbert Butler, Utica, New York; one *d* (one *s* decd); 2nd, 1968, Marcia Anne Helen, *y d* of Major David Turville Constable Maxwell, Bosworth Hall, Husbands Bosworth, Rugby. *Educ:* Downside; RMC, Sandhurst. ADC to Governor and C-in-C, Bermuda, 1936-39. Served War of 1939-45 (MC, prisoner-of-war). *Heir: b* Hugh John Reginald Joseph Radcliffe, *qv. Address:* Rudding Park, Harrogate, Yorks.

**RADCLYFFE, Sir Charles E. M.;** *see* Mott-Radclyffe.

**RADFORD, Adm. Arthur William,** DSM (US); Legion of Merit; US Navy, retired; Director: Witco Chemical Company Inc.; Molybdenum Corporation of America; US Freight Company; Dashaveyor Co.; Chairman of Board, Imodco, USA; *b* Chicago, Ill, 27 Feb. 1896. *Educ:* Naval Acad. Commissioned Ensign, 1916; served with Atlantic and Pacific Fleets, 1918-19; Flt Trg, 1920; with Bureau of Aeronautics, Navy Dept, 1921-23; Aircraft Sqdns, Battle Fleet, and air units attached to USS Colorado and Pennsylvania; Naval Air Station, San Diego, 1927-29; with USS Saratoga, 1929-30; on staff, Comdr Aircraft, Battle Sqdn, US Fleet, 1931-32; Bureau of Aeronautics, 1932-35; served USS Wright (navigator), 1935, Saratoga, 1936-37; in comd Naval Air Stn, Seattle, 1937-40; served USS Yorktown, 1940-41; Director of Aviation Trg, Bureau of Aeronautics, Navy Dept, 1941-43; served in Pacific, 1943-44; Asst Dep. Chief of Naval Operations for Air, 1944; C-in-C, US Pacific Fleet, 1949-53; Chairman of the Joint Chiefs of Staff, 1953-57, retd. *Address:* Apartment S-501, 550 N Street, SW, Washington, DC 20024, USA.

**RADFORD, Courtenay Arthur Ralegh,** FBA 1956; *b* 7 Nov. 1900; *o s* of late Arthur Lock and Ada M. Radford; unmarried. *Educ:* St George's School, Harpenden; Exeter College, Oxford. BA 1921; MA 1937; Inspector of Ancient Monuments in Wales and Monmouthshire, 1929-34; Director of the British School at Rome, 1936-39; Member of Royal Commission on Ancient Monuments in Wales and Monmouthshire, 1935-46; Member of Royal Commission on Historical Monuments (England), 1953; supervised excavations at Tintagel, Ditchley, Castle Dore, the Hurlers, Whithorn, Glastonbury, Birsay and elsewhere; FSA 1928 (Vice-Pres. 1954-58); FRHistS 1930; President: Prehistoric Soc., 1954-58; Roy. Archæological Inst., 1960-63; Cambrian Archæological Assoc., 1961; Soc. of Medieval Archæology, 1969. Hon. DLitt Glasgow, 1963; Univ. of Wales, 1963. *Publications:* Reports on the Excavations at Tintagel, Ditchley, Whithorn, etc.; various articles on archæological subjects. *Address:* Culmcott, Uffculme, Devon. *Club:* Athenæum.

**RADFORD, Air Cdre Dudley Spencer,** CB 1957; DSO 1944; DFC 1940; AFC 1943; Divisional Personnel Officer, Hawker Siddeley Aviation Ltd, Avro Whitworth Division; *b* 21 Sept. 1910; *s* of late John Francis Radford and of Alice Radford; *m* 1943, Pamela Biddulph Corr (*née* Padley); two *d. Educ:* Bedford School. Pilot training, 1932; No. III Fighter Sqdn, 1933-35; trained as flying instructor, 1936, instructional duties, 1936-38; Asst Adjt No 600 City of London Sqdn, 1938; Adjutant No 616 S Riding Sqdn, 1939; OC No 8 Sqdn, Aden, 1940-41; Chief Instructor: No 1 Flying Instructors' School, 1942; No 3 Advanced Flying Unit, 1943; OC No 10 Bomber Sqdn, 1944; RN Staff College course, 1944-45; Group Capt. Trng, HQ Transport Comd, 1945-46; Officer Comdg: RAF Spitalgate, 1947; RAF Wittering, 1948; RAF Liaison Officer, S Rhodesian Govt, 1949-50; Dep. Dir Postings, Air Ministry, 1951-53; idc 1954; Dir of Tactical and Air Transport Ops, 1955-56; Commandant, Central Reconnaissance Establishment, 1957-59; retired 1959. Officer, Order of Leopold (Belgium), 1947. *Address:* c/o Lloyds Bank Ltd, 6 Pall Mall, SW1. *Club:* Royal Air Force.

**RADFORD, Ronald Walter,** MBE 1947; Commissioner (and Secretary) Customs and Excise since 1965; Deputy Chairman of the Board since 1970; *b* 28 Feb. 1916; *er s* of late George Leonard Radford and of Ethel Mary Radford; *m* 1949, Jean Alison Dunlop Strange; one *s* one *d. Educ:* Southend-on-Sea High Sch.; St John's Coll., Cambridge (Schol., Wrangler, MA). Joined ICS, 1939; Dist Magistrate and Collector, Shahabad, Bihar, 1945; on leave, prep. to retirement from ICS, 1947; Admin. Class, Home CS, and posted to HM Customs and Excise, 1947; Asst Sec., 1953. *Address:* King's Beam House, Mark Lane, EC3. *T:* 01-626 1515. *Clubs:* Reform, Civil Service.

**RADHAKRISHNAN, Sir Sarvepalli,** OM (Hon.) 1963; Kt 1931; FBA 1939, Hon. Fellow 1962; FRSL 1951; MA (Madras 1909; Oxford 1936); DCL (Hon.) 1952, Oxford; LittD (Hon.) 1953, Cambridge; LLD (Hon.) 1948, London, etc; President, the Republic of India, 1962-67; *b* 5 September 1888; *m* S. Sivakamamma; one *s* five *d. Educ:* Madras Christian College. Asst Professor of Philosophy, Presidency College, Madras, 1911-16; Prof. of Philosophy, Presidency College, 1916-17; University Prof. of Philosophy, Mysore, 1918-21; George V Prof. of Philosophy, Calcutta Univ., 1921-31 and 1937-41; Vice-Chancellor, Andhra Univ., Waltair, 1931-36, and of Benares Hindu Univ., 1939-48; Spalding Prof. of Eastern Religions and Ethics, Oxford, 1936-52; Professor Emeritus, 1952; Hon. Fellow of All Souls College; Hon. Prof. Moscow University, 1956; Indian Ambassador to USSR, 1949-52; Vice-Pres. of the Republic of India, 1952-62. Upton Lectr, Manchester Coll., Oxford, 1926 and 1929-30; Haskell Lectr in Comparative Religion, Univ. of Chicago, 1926; Gen. Pres. Third Session Indian Philosophical Congress, Bombay, 1927; Chairman Executive Council Indian Philosophical Congress, 1925-37; Pres. Post Graduate Council in Arts, 1927-31; Hibbert Lecturer, 1929; Member: International Committee on Intellectual Co-operation of the League of Nations, Geneva, 1931-39; Constituent Assembly of India, 1947-49; Leader of Indian Deleg. to UNESCO, 1946-52, and member Exec. Board UNESCO, 1946-51 (Chm. 1948-49), Pres. Gen. Conf., 1952-54, 1958; Chm. Univs. Commn, Govt of India, 1948-49. Hon. Fell. Roy. Asiatic Soc. of Bengal; Pres. Indian PEN 1949-, Vice-President, International PEN 1956-; President, Sahitya Akademi (National Academy of Letters), 1964-68; Chancellor of Delhi University, 1953-62. Hon. Member Rumanian Academy of Science. German Order pour le mérite, 1954; Goethe Plaquette, 1959; German Booksellers' Peace Prize, 1961. *Publications:* The Reign of Religion in Contemporary Philosophy, 1920; Indian Philosophy in the Library of Philosophy, vol. i 1923; vol. ii 1927; 2nd edn 1930 and 1931; The Philosophy of the Upanishads, 1924, 2nd edn

1935; The Hindu View of Life, 1927, translated into French and German, etc; The Religion we Need, 1928; Kalki, or The Future of Civilization, 1929, 2nd edition, 1934: An Idealist View of Life, 1932; East and West in Religion, 1933; (ed jtly) Contemporary Indian Philosophy, 1936; Eastern Religions and Western Thought, 1939, 2nd edn; (ed) Mahatma Gandhi, 1939; India and China, 1944; Education, Politics and War, 1944; Religion and Society, 1947; Is this Peace?, 1945; The Bhagavadgītā, 1948; Dhammapada, 1950; The Principal Upanishads, 1953; Recovery of Faith, 1955; East and West: Some Reflections, 1955; (ed jtly) A Source Book of Indian Philosophy, 1957; Brahma Sūtra, 1960; Fellowship of the Spirit, 1961; Religion in a Changing World, 1967; The Radhakrishnan Reader, 1969; article on Indian Philosophy in Ency. Brit., 14th edn, and others on Philosophy and Religion in Mind, International Journal of Ethics, Hibbert Journal, etc. *Recreation:* light reading. *Address:* 30 Edward Elliot Road, Mylapore, Madras 4, India.
*See also Dr S. Gopal.*

**RADICE, Edward Albert,** CBE 1946; *b* 2 Jan. 1907; *s* of C. A. Radice, ICS and Alice Effie (*née* Murray), DSc; *m* 1936, Joan Keeling; one *s* one *d*. *Educ:* Winchester Coll.; Magdalen Coll., Oxford. 1st Cl. Hons Maths Mods and Lit. Hum., DPhil, Oxford. Commonwealth Fund Fellow, Columbia Univ., New York, 1933-35; Assistant Professor of Economics, Wesleyan University, Middletown, Conn., 1937-39; League of Nations Secretariat, 1939; Ministry of Economic Warfare, 1940-44; Foreign Office, 1944-50; Control Commn for Germany, 1950; Counsellor, British Embassy, Copenhagen, 1950-52; Economic Adviser, MoD, 1952-65; Dir of Economic Intelligence, MoD, 1966-69. *Publications:* (jt) An American Experiment, 1936; Fundamental Issues in the United States, 1936; Savings in Great Britain, 1922-35, 1939; contribs to Econometrica, Oxford Economic Papers. *Address:* 2 Talbot Road, Oxford. *T:* Oxford 55573.
*See also I. de L. Radice.*

**RADICE, Fulke Rosavo,** CBE 1959; MA; late Vice-Director International Bureau of Universal Postal Union (1946-58); *b* Naples, 8 Feb. 1888; British subject; *s* of Albert Hampden Radice, Thistleborough, NI and Adelaide Anna Teresa (*née* Visetti); *m* 1917, Katharine Stella Mary Speck, *d* of late Canon J. H. Speck and Mrs Speck (*née* Dalrymple); two *s* (and one *s* killed fighting in French Maquis, 1944). *Educ:* Bedford School (Scholar); Brasenose Coll., Oxford (open scholarship in History; 2nd Cl. Hons Mods (classical), 1909; 1st Cl. Mod. History, 1911). Home Civil Service, 1911; Secretary's Office, Gen. Post Office, 1911-46. Head of Brit. Secretariat of Universal Postal Union Congress, 1929, Head of Congress Secretariat at UPU Congresses, 1947, 1952, 1957. Served European War, 1914-18, in France, Salonica, Egypt, Italy; War of 1939-45 in Home Guard. *Publications:* articles in Nineteenth Century and After, and in History. *Recreations:* rifle shooting (Oxford half blue, Oxford long range; English XX, 1909, 1910; King's Prize at Bisley, gold and silver medals, 1910; record score); Rugby football; ski-ing; freemasonry; historical studies. *Address:* 39 Monbijoustrasse, Berne, Switzerland. *T:* Berne 251985; c/o Coutts & Co., 440 Strand, WC2. *Clubs:* Bath; Grande Société (Berne).

**RADICE, Italo de Lisle,** CB 1969; Secretary and Comptroller General, National Debt Office, since 1969; *b* 2 March 1911; *s* of Charles Albert Radice, ICS, and Alice Effie (*née* Murray); *m* 1935, Betty Dawson; three *s* (and one *d* decd). *Educ:* Blundell's School; Magdalen College, Oxford (demy). 1st Cl. Hons Classical Mods, 2nd Cl. Lit Hum (Oxon), 2nd Cl. PPE. admitted Solicitor, 1938; Public Trustee Office, 1939; Military Government East and North Africa, Italy, and Germany, 1941-46; Treasury, 1946, Under-Secretary, 1961-68. *Recreation:* opera going. *Address:* 65 Cholmeley Crescent, N6. *T:* 01-348 4122; Old Post Office, Berrick Salome, Oxford.
*See also E. A. Radice.*

**RADLEY, Sir Gordon;** *see* Radley, Sir W. G.

**RADLEY, Oswald Alfred,** CBE 1945; MC 1918; *b* 18 June 1887; *s* of A. W. Radley, Congleton, Cheshire; *m* 1929, Joan, *d* of James Laithwood, Alcumlow Hall, Congleton, Cheshire; one *s* one *d*. *Educ:* Trent Coll. Served European War, 1914-19, 7th Bn Cheshire Regt and as Staff Capt. (wounded, despatches). ARP Controller, Leeds, 1941-45. President: Leeds Law Society, 1937; Town Planning Institute, 1940; Soc. of Town Clerks, 1948-50; Town Clerk of Leeds, 1938-52. *Address:* 1 Oatlands Drive, Harrogate. *T:* Harrogate 83515. *Club:* Leeds (Leeds).

**RADLEY, Sir (William) Gordon,** KCB 1956; Kt 1954; CBE 1946; PhD, CEng, FIEE; Director-General, General Post Office, 1955-60; *b* 18 Jan. 1898; *s* of late William A. Radley, OBE, Blackheath; *m* 1938, Dorothy Margaret, *d* of late J. G. Hines, Wandsworth Common; one *s* one *d*. *Educ:* Leeds Modern School; Faraday House Electrical Engineering College, PhD London. Served European War, 1914-18, in Royal Engineers. Apprentice Bruce Peebles Ltd, Edinburgh; entered GPO Engineering Dept, 1920; Controller of Research, 1944-49; Deputy Engineer-in-Chief, 1949-51; Engineer-in-Chief, 1951-54; retired as Dir-Gen. and entered industry, 1960. Chairman: Marconi Co., 1961-65; Marconi Internat. Marine Co., 1961-; English Electric Computers Ltd, 1963-68; Director: English Electric Co. and various subsids, 1960-68; Canadian Marconi Co., 1961-67. Chairman: Electro-Acoustics Cttee, Medical Research Council, 1944-49; Materials Cttee, Radio Research Board, 1948-52; Measurements Section, Institution of Electrical Engineers, 1944-45, Vice-Pres., 1951-56, Pres. 1956-57; Pres. British Electrical and Allied Industries Research Assoc., 1957-58; Vice-Pres., and Mem., Nat. Exec., Abbeyfield Soc.; Mem., British Churches Housing Trust. Hon. FIERE, 1964; Hon. FIEE, 1969. Hon. Mem., Société Royale Belge des Electriciens, 1957. Christopher Columbus Internat. Prize for Communications, 1955; Faraday Medal, IEE, 1958. Comdr, Order of Merit, Research and Invention, France, 1965. *Publications:* numerous scientific papers. *Recreation:* walking. *Address:* 13 Gills Hill, Radlett, Herts. *T:* Radlett 5904.

**RADLEY-SMITH, Eric John,** MS; FRCS; Surgeon: Royal Free Hospital, London; Brentford Hospital; Epsom Hospital; Neurosurgeon, Royal National Throat, Nose and Ear Hospital. *Educ:* Paston; King's College, London; King's College Hospital. MB, BS (Hons, Distinction in Medicine, Surgery, Forensic Medicine and Hygiene), 1933; MS, London, 1936; LRCP, 1933; FRCS 1935 (MRCS 1933). Served War of 1939-45, Wing Comdr i/c Surgical Div. RAFVR. Formerly: Surgical Registrar, King's Coll. Hosp.; House Surgeon, National Hosp. for Nervous Diseases, Queen Square. Examnr in Surgery, Univs of London and West Indies. Mem. Court, RCS. Mem. Assoc. of British Neurosurgeons; Fellow, Assoc. of Surgeons of Great Britain. *Publications:* papers in medical journals. *Recreations:* football and farming. *Address:* 27 Harley Street, W1. *T:* 01-580 2923; Colley Cottage, Reigate Heath, Surrey. *T:* Reigate 44532.

**RADNOR,** 8th Earl of, *cr* 1765; **Jacob Pleydell-Bouverie;** Bt 1713-14; Viscount Folkestone, Baron Longford, 1747; Baron Pleydell-Bouverie, 1765; *b* 10 Nov. 1927; *e s* of 7th Earl of Radnor, KG, KCVO, and Helen Olivia, *d* of late Charles R. W. Adeane, CB; *S* father, 1968; *m* 1st, 1953, Anne (marriage dissolved, 1962), *d* of Donald Seth-Smith, Njoro, Kenya and Whitsbury Cross, near Fordingbridge, Hants; two *s;* 2nd, 1963, Margaret Robin, *d* of late Robin Fleming, Catter House, Drymen; three *d* (including twins). *Educ:* Harrow; Trinity Coll. Cambridge. Degree in Agriculture. In Argentine, 1948-50. *Heir: s* Viscount Folkestone, *qv. Address:* Longford Castle, Salisbury, Wilts. *T:* Bodenham 232.

**RADO, Prof. Richard;** Professor of Pure Mathematics, University of Reading, since 1954; *b* 28 April 1906; 2nd *s* of Leopold Rado, Berlin; *m* 1933, Luise, *e d* of Hermann Zadek, Berlin; one *s. Educ:* University of Berlin (DPhil); University of Göttingen; University of Cambridge (PhD). Lecturer, Sheffield Univ., 1936-47; Reader, King's College, Univ. of London, 1947-54. London Mathematical Society: Mem. of Council, 1948-57; Hon. Sec., 1953-54; Vice-President, 1954-56. FIMA. *Publications:* articles in various journals on topics in pure mathematics. *Recreations:* music, reading, walking. *Address:* 14 Glebe Road, Reading. *T:* 81281.

**RADZINOWICZ, Sir Leon,** Kt 1970; Ma, LLD; Fellow of Trinity College, Cambridge, since 1948; Wolfson Professor of Criminology, University of Cambridge, since 1959, and Director of the Institute of Criminology, since 1960; Associate Fellow, Silliman College, Yale, since 1966; Adjunct Professor of Law and Criminology, Columbia Law School, since 1966; *b* Poland, 15 Aug. 1906; *m* 1933, Irene Szereszewski (marriage dissolved, 1955); *m* 1958, Mary Ann, *d* of Gen. Nevins, Gettysburg, Pa, USA; one *s* one *d;* naturalised British subject, 1947. *Educ:* Warsaw, Paris, Geneva and Rome. University of Paris, 1924-25; Licencié en Droit, Univ. of Geneva, 1927; Doctor of Law, Rome, 1928; LLD Cambridge, 1951. Lecturer, University of Geneva, 1928-31; Doctor of Law, Cracow, 1929; Reported on working of penal system in Belgium, 1930; Lectr, Free Univ. of Warsaw, 1932, and Asst Prof., 1936. Came to England on behalf of Polish Ministry of Justice to report on working of English penal system, 1938; Asst Dir of Research, University of Cambridge, 1946-49; Director, Department of Criminal Science, University of Cambridge, 1949-59; Walter E. Meyer Research Professor of Law, Yale Law School, 1962-63; Visiting Prof. and Carpentier Lecturer, Columbia Law School, Visiting Professor: Virginia Law School, 1968-69 and 1970; Univ. of Pennsylvania, 1970; Rutgers Univ., 1970. Member, Conseil de Direction de l'Assoc. Intern. de Droit Pénal, Paris, 1947-; Vice-Pres. Internat. Soc. of Social Defence, 1956-; Head of Social Defence Section, UN, New York, 1947-48. Mem. Roy. Commission on Capital Punishment, 1949-53; Mem. Advisory Council on the Treatment of Offenders, Home Office, 1950-63, Chm. Sub-Cttee on Maximum Security in Prisons, 1967-68; Mem. Advisory Coun. on the Penal System, 1966-; Pres. Brit. Acad. of Forensic Sciences, 1960-61; Vice-Pres., 1961-; First Chm. Council of Europe Sci. Cttee, Problems of Crime, 1963-70; Mem. Royal Commn on Penal System in Eng. and Wales, 1964-66; Consultant, President's Nat. Commn on Violence, Washington, 1968-69. Hon. LLD Leicester, 1965. Coronation Medal, 1953. Chevalier de l'Ordre de Léopold, Belgium, 1930. James Barr Ames Prize and Medal, Faculty of Harvard Law School, 1950. *Publications:* In Search of Criminology, 1961 (Italian edn 1965; French edn 1965); The Need for Criminology, 1965; Ideology and Crime (Carpentier Lectures), 1966, (Italian edn 1968); The Dangerous Offender (Frank Newsam Memorial Lecture), 1968; Editor of series: English Studies in Criminal Science, now Cambridge Studies in Criminology, 26 vols; History of English Criminal Law, Vol. I, 1948 (under auspices of Pilgrim Trust), Vols II and III, 1956, Vol. IV, 1968 (under auspices of Rockefeller Foundation); numerous articles in English and foreign periodicals. *Address:* 21 Cranmer Road, Cambridge. *T:* 56867; 7 West Road, Cambridge. *Club:* Athenæum.

**RAE, Sir Alexander (Montgomery) Wilson,** KCMG 1960 (CMG 1945); MD; Chief MO Colonial Office, 1958-60; *b* 31 Jan. 1896; *s* of late Rev. Robert Rae and Kate Wilson; *m* 1924, Elizabeth Harper, MB, ChB, DPH; one *d. Educ:* George Heriot's School; Univ. of Edinburgh. MB, ChB 1921; MD 1929; Resident Medical Officer, North Wales Sanatorium, 1922; West African Medical Staff, 1924-45; Senior Medical Officer, Gambia, 1935-37; Deputy Director of Medical Services, Gold Coast, 1938; Deputy Director of Medical Services, Nigeria, 1939; Deputy Medical Adviser to Secretary of State for the Colonies, 1944. Lieut, Scottish Horse and Imperial Camel Corps, 1914-18. Retired, 1960. *Address:* Field House, Ramsey, Isle of Man. *T:* Ramsey 3414.

**RAE, John Malcolm,** MA, PhD; Headmaster of Westminster School, since 1970; *b* 20 March 1931; *s* of Dr L. John Rae, radiologist, London Hospital, and Blodwen Rae; *m* 1955, Daphné Ray Simpson, *d* of John Phimester Simpson; two *s* four *d. Educ:* Bishop's Stortford Coll.; Sidney Sussex Coll., Cambridge. MA Camb. 1958; PhD 1965. 2nd Lieut Royal Fusiliers, 1950-51. Asst Master, Harrow School, 1955-66; Dept of War Studies, King's Coll., London, 1962-65; Headmaster, Taunton School, 1966-70. JP Middlesex, 1961-66. *Publications:* The Custard Boys, 1960; (jtly, film) Reach for Glory (UN Award); Conscience and Politics, 1970. *Recreations:* writing, swimming, children. *Address:* 17 Dean's Yard, SW1. *T:* 01-222 6904. *Clubs:* Public Schools; Hawks (Cambridge).

**RAE, Sir Robert,** Kt 1958; CB 1952; BAgr, CDA (Edinburgh); retired as Director of National Agricultural Advisory Service, (1948-59); *b* 9 June 1894; *s* of late Rev. Robert Rae and Kate Wilson; *m* 1926, Constance Alma (*d* 1965), *e d* of late George King; no *c. Educ:* George Heriot's School, University, Edinburgh; East of Scotland College of Agriculture, Edinburgh. Trooper, Scottish Horse, 1914-15; Lieutenant, 1915-16; attached 21st (E of I) Lancers, 1917-19; Lecturer in Agriculture, East Anglian Institute of Agriculture, Chelmsford, Essex, 1920-21; Vice-Principal and County Advisory Officer, Hertfordshire Institute of Agriculture, St Albans, 1921-25; Lecturer in charge of Department of Crop and Animal Husbandry, The Queen's University, Belfast, 1925-32; Professor of Crop and Animal Husbandry, The Queen's University of Belfast, 1932-33; Head of Crop and Animal Husbandry Research Division, Ministry of Agriculture, Northern Ireland, 1925-33; Joint Director of the Agricultural Research Institute, Hillsborough, Co. Down, 1926-33; Professor of Agriculture, University of Reading, 1933-44; Agricultural Attaché,

British Embassy, Washington, 1944-45; Under Secretary, Ministry of Agriculture, Fisheries and Food, 1946. *Publications:* articles in agricultural journals. *Address:* Brendon, Lezayre Road, Ramsey, Isle of Man. *T:* Ramsey 3461.

**RAE, Air Vice-Marshal Ronald Arthur R.;** *see* Ramsay Rae.

**RAE, Lt-Col William,** DSO 1916; Retired; *b* 15 Jan. 1883; *s* of William Rae, MA, Advocate, Aberdeen, and Joan Anderson; *m* 1936, Edith Marion, *e d* of late Lt-Col L. St John Brodrick; two *s*. *Educ:* Aberdeen University (MA, BL). Went to Canada, 1907; Capt. Seaforth Highlanders of Canada, Vancouver, BC, on organisation, 1910; Canadian Expeditionary Force, 1914-19 (despatches 4 times; wounded). Lt-Col Comdg 4th Canadian Inf. Bn, 1916, GSO1. Hon. Overseas Director, Canadian Legion War Services, 1940-45 (Dominion Award of Merit). Hon. Lt-Col, The Canadian Scottish (Princess Mary's), Victoria, BC, 1967-. Man. Dir, The Commonwealth Trust Ltd, retired, 1949. Master, Worshipful Company of Plumbers, City of London, 1945 and 1953. French Croix de Guerre, 1918; Volunteer Decoration (Canada) 1921. *Recreations:* gardening, rifle-shooting (Canadian Rifle Team, Bisley, 1919). *Address:* 3065 Surrey Road, Victoria, BC, Canada. *Clubs:* Athenæum; Vancouver (Vancouver, BC); Union (Victoria, BC).

**RAEBURN, Sir Edward Alfred,** 3rd Bt, *cr* 1923; Chairman: Raeburn Developments Ltd; Nina Breddal Ltd; *b* 18 May 1919; *s* of Sir W. Norman Raeburn, 2nd Bt, CBE, KC, and Mary Irene Lennard; *S* father, 1947; *m* 1950, Joan, *d* of Frederick Hill, Boston, USA, formerly of Bexley, Kent; one *s*. *Educ:* Uppingham School; Christ Church, Oxford. Served War of 1939-45, RA 1939-46, taking part in N and E African campaigns; final rank Captain. Liveryman of Worshipful Company of Shipwrights. *Recreations:* gardening, fishing. *Heir:* *s* Michael Edward Norman Raeburn, *b* 12 Nov. 1954. *Address:* Smallacre, St Catherine's, Hook Heath, Woking, Surrey. *T:* Woking 5534.

**RAEBURN, Prof. John Ross,** BSc (Agric.), PhD, MS; Strathcona-Fordyce Professor of Agriculture, Aberdeen University, since Sept. 1959; Principal, North of Scotland College of Agriculture, since 1963; *b* 20 Nov. 1912; *s* of late Charles Raeburn and Margaret (*née* Ross); *m* 1941, Mary, *o d* of Alfred and Kathrine Roberts; one *s* three *d*. *Educ:* Manchester Grammar School; Edinburgh and Cornell Universities. Professor of Agricultural Economics, Nanking University, 1936-37; Research Officer, Oxford University, 1938-39; Ministry of Food Divisional statistician, 1939-41, Head Agricultural Plans Branch, 1941-46; Senior research officer, Oxford University, 1946-49; Reader in Agricultural Economics, London University, 1949-59. Visiting Professor, Cornell, 1950. Consultant to UN. Member: Agricultural Mission to Yugoslavia, 1951; Mission of Enquiry into Rubber Industry, Malaya, 1954; Colonial Economic Research Committee, 1949-61; Scottish Agricultural Improvement Council, 1960-; Verdon-Smith Committee, 1962-64. Hon. MA Oxford, 1946. Fellow, Royal Society of Edinburgh, 1961. Vice-President, International Association of Agricultural Economists; President, Agric. Econ. Society, 1966-67. FInstBiol 1968. *Publications:* Preliminary economic survey of the Northern Territories of the Gold Coast, 1950; (jtly) Problems in the mechanisation of native agriculture in tropical African Territories, 1950; research bulletins and contributions to agricultural economic journals. *Recreations:* gardening, travel. *Address:* School of Agriculture, Aberdeen.

**RAEBURN, Walter Augustus Leopold,** QC 1947; MA (Oxon); LLM (London); Occasional Additional Judge, Central Criminal Court, since 1959; Recorder of West Ham, 1949-65; *b* London, 5 Jan. 1897; *s* of late H. L. Regensburg, of London Stock Exchange (who emigrated to England, 1881, naturalised British 1887); *m* 1925, Dora, *y d* of Hedley Williams, Hastings; four *s* three *d*. *Educ:* University College School; Charterhouse; Christ Church, Oxford. Studied at London Univ., 1947-49. Assumed present surname on leaving school, 1915; Queen's (Royal West Surrey) Regt and RAF, 1915-19 (wounded on Somme, 1916); read History at Oxford, 1919-21; called to Bar, 1922; Bencher, Middle Temple, 1955; joined Labour Party, 1923; Prospective Parly Candidate, 1925-27; foundation member Soc. of Labour Candidates (now Labour Parly Assoc.); London Press Exchange, 1928-30; foundation member of Haldane Club (now Haldane Soc.), Chm. 1935-37; resigned 1949, to found and join Soc. of Labour Lawyers; Past Chm. Tribunal of Inquiry under Prevention of Fraud (Investments) Act, 1939 (now Licensed Dealers Tribunal); Chairman: Mental Health Review Tribunal for NE Metropolitan Region, 1960-63; Performing Right Tribunal, 1958-69; Med. Appeal Tribunal, London, 1960-65, London North, 1966-1969; on panel of Chairmen for NE Metropolitan Region, 1963-. Frequently appointed to sit as Special Commissioner in Divorce, 1954-; Mem. General Cttee of Rainer Foundation (formerly London Police Court Mission); Mem., two Cttees concerned with welfare of discharged prisoners; Mem., Executive Cttee of the Grotius Soc., 1949-60; Mem., British Institute of International and Comparative Law, 1960-; Mem., Probation Advisory and Training Board, 1953-62; Vice-President Royal Philanthropic Society's School; President Surrey Branch, Nat. Assoc. of Probation Officers, 1953-; Manager, Mayford (LCC) Approved School, 1954-65; Vice-Chm. Govs, Isaac Newton (LCC) Comprehensive School, 1958-67; Governor, Port Regis Preparatory Sch., 1947-. Manager, Trinity Church (Hampstead) Primary School, 1967-. *Publications:* articles in legal and social sci. jls. *Recreations:* voluntary activities shown above. *Address:* 2 Crown Office Row, Temple, EC4. *T:* 01-583 2681; 30 Maresfield Gardens, NW3. *T:* 01-435 2570.

**RAEBURN, Maj.-Gen. William Digby Manifold,** CB 1966; DSO 1945; MBE 1941; Chief Instructor (Army), Imperial Defence College, 1968-70; *b* 6 Aug. 1915; *s* of late Sir Ernest Manifold Raeburn, KBE, and of Lady Raeburn; *m* 1960, Adeline Margaret (*née* Pryor). *Educ:* Winchester; Magdalene College, Cambridge (MA). Commnd into Scots Guards, 1936; comd 2nd Bn Scots Guards, 1953; Lieut-Col Comdg Scots Guards, 1958; Comdr, 1st Guards Bde Group, 1959; Comdr, 51st Infty Bde Group, 1960; Director of Combat Development (Army), 1963-65; Chief of Staff to C-in-C, Allied Forces, N Europe, 1965-68. *Recreations:* ski-ing, golf, shooting, sailing. *Address:* 45 Wilton Crescent, SW1. *Clubs:* White's, Pratt's; Royal Yacht Squadron.

**RAFFRAY, Sir Philippe,** Kt, *cr* 1946; CBE 1942; London Representative, Mauritius Chamber of Agriculture, 1946-55, retired; Member of Executive Council, Mauritius, 1943-46; Elected member of Legislative Council 1916-

46; *b* Mauritius, 1888; 4th *s* of late O. Raymond Raffray; *m* 1918, Marguerite, *d* of Victor de K/vern, KC (Mauritius); one *s* three *d*. *Educ:* Royal College, Mauritius. Called to Bar, Middle Temple, 1912; Licentiate-in-Law, Paris, 1912. Mauritius Volunteer Artillery, 1915-18. KC (Mauritius), 1932. Member Mauritius Delegation to London, 1932; Special Delegate to Colonial Office *re* Sugar Industry, 1945. FRSA 1949. *Address:* 12 Bis, Rue Dublineau, Tours, France. *Clubs:* Athenæum, Curepipe (Mauritius).

**RAGG, Air Vice-Marshal Robert Linton,** CB 1949; CBE 1945; AFC 1927; RAF retired; *b* 9 April 1901; *o s* of Robert Stewart Ragg, MA (Oxon), and Margaret Elizabeth Christie; *m* 1928, Louie Margaret Moir. *Educ:* Dragon School, Oxford; Dulwich College. Pilot Officer, RAF, 1921; served in Iraq, 1922-24; Experimental Pilot at Royal Aircraft Establishment, Farnborough, 1925-29; Pilcher Memorial Prize, RAeS, 1926; graduated RAF Staff Coll., Andover, 1937; Command Navigation Officer, Bomber Comd, 1939-40; SASO No 15 Gp, 1943-44 (despatches); Deputy AOC No 222 Gp 1944-45 (despatches); AOA, BAF, SEA (later Air HQ India), 1945-46 (despatches); AOC No 63 Gp, RAF, 1946-48; SASO, Transport Command, RAF, 1948-49; Senior Air Staff Officer, Far East Air Force, 1949-51; Director-General of Personnel (II), Air Ministry, Feb.-Sept. 1952; AOC No 18 Gp, RAF (Pitreavie Castle, Dunfermline, Fife) and Sen. Air Force Officer, Scotland, and Air Comdr, Northern Sub-Area, Allied Atlantic Command, NATO, Sept. 1952-March 1955. Bursar, Gordonstoun School, 1955-57; one of HM Comrs, Queen Victoria School, Dunblane, 1955-57; County Comr for Scouts, Cornwall, 1958-62. Mem. Bd of Governors Truro Cathedral School. Order of Cloud and Banner (Chinese), 1945. *Address:* Rockbarton, Shepton Beauchamp, Ilminster, Somerset. *Club:* Royal Air Force.

**RAGLAN,** 5th Baron, *cr* 1852; **FitzRoy John Somerset;** JP; Crown Estate Commissioner, since 1970; Chairman, Cwmbran Development Corporation, since 1970; *b* 8 Nov. 1927; *er s* of 4th Baron and Hon. Julia Hamilton, CStJ, *d* of 11th Baron Belhaven and Stenton, CIE; *S* father, 1964. *Educ:* Westminster; Magdalen College, Oxford; Royal Agricultural College, Cirencester. Captain, Welsh Guards, RARO; JP Monmouthshire, 1958. *Heir: b* Hon. Geoffrey Somerset [*b* 29 Aug. 1932; *m* 1956, Caroline Rachel Hill; one *s* two *d*]. *Address:* Cefntilla Court, Usk, Monmouthshire. *Clubs:* Beefsteak, Bugatti Owners, Vintage Sports Car; Usk Farmers'.

**RAHIMTOOLA, Sir Fazal Ibrahim,** Kt *cr* 1946; CIE 1939; MLC; BA; JP; Director: Ahmedabad Advance Mill, Ltd; Tata Power Co. Ltd; Tata Iron & Steel Co., Ltd; Bharat Line, Ltd (Chairman); The Swadeshi Mills, Ltd; Overseas Communications Service (Government of India); New Swadeshi Sugar Mills Ltd; Sultania Cotton Manufacturing Co., Ltd; Dhrangadhra Chemical Works Ltd; Fazalbhai Ibrahim & Co. Prvt Ltd; *b* 21 Oct. 1895; *s* of late Sir Ibrahim Rahimtoola, GBE, KCSI; *m* 1920, Jainabai, *d* of Alimahomed Fazalbhoy. *Educ:* St Xavier's High Sch. and Coll., Bombay; Poona Law Coll. (1st LLB). Mem., Bombay Municipal Corp., 1919-30; Trustee, Bombay Port Trust, 1921-36. Appt by Govt of India on Govt Securities Cttee; Rep. of Bombay Municipal Corp. on BB & CI Rly Advisory Council till 1930; Sec. Indian Imperial Citizenship Assoc.; Mem. Standing Finance Cttee for Railways, Rly Bd; Mem. Haj Inquiry Cttee, 1929; Chm. Reception Cttee of Bombay Presidency Muslim Educ. Conf.; Pres. Urdu Newspapers Assoc.; Rep. Bombay Govt on Cttee of the Sir Harcourt Butler Technological Inst., to advise Govt of UP; Mem. Central Broadcasting Advisory Council till 1930; Mem. Standing Cttee for Haj; Elected Mem., Central Legislative Assembly, 1925-30; appt Actg Pres., Indian Tariff Bd, 1932; Pres. Indian Tariff Bd, 1935; Elected MLA, 1937. Conducted several enquiries, 1930-38, as Mem. and Pres., Indian Tariff Board. Chairman or Mem. numerous Bombay Cttees both during War of 1939-45 and later. Delegate to Indian States on Eastern Group Conf.; Mem. War Risk Insurance Claims Cttee, Govt of India; Mem. Central Food Council and its Standing Cttee; Director, National War Front; Mem. Post-War reconstruction Cttee for Agricultural Research; Chm. Indian Fisheries Cttee; Mem. Price-Fixation Cttee of Govt of India; Mem. Gregory Foodgrains Policy Cttee; Mem. Industrial Policy Cttee (Planning Dept); Mem. All-India Council for Technical Educn; Mem. Nat. Commn for India and its Science Sub-Commn (Unesco); Elected Mem. Bombay Leg. Council, 1948; Sheriff of Bombay, 1950; Deleg. to Unesco Conf., Florence, 1950; Deleg. Internat. Engineering Confs, New Delhi, 1951; Deleg. Symposium for Utilisation of Industrial Wastes; Chm. Deep-sea Fisheries Station, Bombay, Govt of India; Mem. Central Exec. Cttee, Tuberculosis Assoc. of India; Deleg. Govt of India on Fourth Commonwealth TB and Health Conf., London, 1955; Chm., Cttee of Hosts, 38th Internat. Eucharistic Congress. Mem. East India Assoc., London; FRSA. Late Hon. Magistrate. Hon. Consul-Gen. for Thailand in Bombay. Jubilee and Coronation Medals. *Address:* Ismail Buildings, Hornby Road, Fort, Bombay, India. *Clubs:* (Pres.) Matheran, Poona (India).

**RAHIMTOOLA, Habib Ibrahim,** BA, LLB, FRPS (Gt Br.); Chairman, Pakistan Government Shipping Rates Advisory Board since 1959; Diplomatist, Pakistan; *b* 10 March 1912; *s* of late Sir Ibrahim Rahimtoola, GBE, KCSI, CIE, and Lady Kulsum Rahimtoola (*née* Mitha); *m* Zubeida, *d* of Sir Sultan Chinoy, *qv*; two *s* one *d*. *Educ:* St Xavier's School and College and Govt Law Coll., Bombay. High Commissioner for Pakistan in London, 1947-52; Ambassador for Pakistan to France, 1952-53; Governor of Sind Province, 1953-54, of Punjab Province, June-Nov. 1954; Minister for Commerce, Central Govt, Nov. 1954-Aug. 1955; Minister for Commerce and Industries, 1955-56. President: Fed. of Muslim Chambers of Commerce and Industry, New Delhi, 1947-48; Bombay Provincial Muslim Chamber of Commerce, 1944-47; Bombay Provincial Muslim League Parly Board for Local Bodies, 1945-47; Young Men's Muslim Association, 1946-47; Bombay Muslim Students' Union, 1946-47-48. Director, Rotary Club, 1944-46; Chairman Membership Committee, 1945-46, Classification Cttee, 1944-45; Member: Govt of India Food Delegation to UK and USA, 1946; Govt of India Policy Cttee on Shipping; Govt of Bombay Housing Panel; Civil Aviation Conference, Govt of India, 1947; Cttee on Trade Policy, Govt of India, 1947; Indian Delegation to Internat. Trade and Employment Conference, Geneva, 1947; alternate Leader Indian Delegation Special Cereals Conference, Paris, 1947; Delegate or Leader of Pakistan Delegations: Inter-Allied Reparations Agency, Brussels, 1947-48-49-50-51; FAO, Geneva, 1947; Dollar Talks, London, 1947; Internat. Trade and Employment Conf., Geneva, 1947; Freedom of Information Conf., Geneva, 1948; Safety of Life at Sea (1948), and Sterling Balance (1948, 1949, 1950, 1951) Confs, London; Prime Ministers'

Conferences, London, 1948, 1949, 1951; Foreign Ministers' Conference, Ceylon, 1950; ILO, 1950; Commonwealth Finance Ministers' Conf., 1949-52; SE Asia Conf. on Colombo Plan, 1950; Commonwealth Talks on Japanese Peace Treaty, London, 1950; General Agreement on Tariffs and Trade Conf., 1950-52; Supply Ministers' Conf., London, 1951; UNESCO, Paris, 1953; Afro-Asian Conf., Bandung, 1955; Leader Pakistan Trade Delegation to Brit. E Africa, 1956; Leader, Flood Control Conf., New Delhi, 1956; Chm. Karachi Development Authority, 1958-60; Chm. Water Co-ordination Council, 1958-60. Chm., or Dir, numerous companies. Internat. Counsellor, Lions Internat.; Chairman: Karachi Race Club; Pak-Japan Cultural Assoc.; Royal Commonwealth Soc. (Pakistan); Pakistan Ceylon Assoc.; Dep. Chm. Jockey Club of Pakistan; President: Photographic Society of Pakistan; Karachi AA. FRSA; FRPS, FRAS; FRES. *Recreations:* photography, horse racing, golf, tennis. *Address:* Bandenawaz Ltd, Oriental Building, McLeod Rd, PO Box 4792, Karachi 2, Pakistan. *T:* 221267; Kulib 1, Rahimtoola Road, Karachi 8. *T:* 42125. *Clubs:* MCC, International Sportsmen's, Royal Automobile; Sind, Boat, Golf, Gymkhana (Karachi); Willingdon (Bombay).

**RAHMAN, Shaikh Abdur,** HPk 1957; Chief Justice Supreme Court of Pakistan, 1st March-4th June 1968, retired; *b* 4 June 1903; *s* of Sh. Ghulam Ali; *m* 1934, Mumtaz Jehan Mohammad Deen; three *s* one *d*. *Educ:* Punjab Univ. (MA); Oxford Univ. (BA Hons). Entered ICS 1928; served as Asst Comr, Sub-divl Officer, and then as Dist and Sessions Judge in various Districts of Punjab, up to May 1945; Legal Remembrancer and Sec. Legislative Dept, Punjab, up to May 1946; Judge, High Court, Lahore, May 1946; Mem., Bengal Boundary Commn at partition of India and Pakistan, 1947; Custodian of Evacuee Properties, 1947-51; Vice-Chancellor, Punjab Univ., 1950-51; Chief Justice: Lahore High Court, 1954; High Court of W Pakistan, 1955; Judge Supreme Court of Pakistan, 1958. Chairman Agartala case Special Tribunal (latter part), 1968; finally retd Feb. 1969. Member: Punjab Univ. Syndicate; Governing Body, Central Islamic Research Inst.; Dir, Inst. of Islamic Culture, Lahore; Pres., Pakistan Arts Council, Lahore, 1949-, etc. Holds hon. doctorates. *Publications:* Tarjuman-i-Asrar (trans. into Urdu verse of Sir Mohammad Iqbal's Persian, Asrari-Khudi), 1952; Hadith-i-Dil (collection of addresses in Urdu), 1963; Safar (collection of original poems in Urdu), 1964. *Recreations:* writing and participation in cultural activities. *Address:* 65 Main Gulberg, Lahore, West Pakistan. *T:* Lahore 80109. *Club:* Gymkhana (Lahore).

**RAHMAN PUTRA, Tunku (Prince) Abdul;** *see* Abdul Rahman Putra.

**RAIKES, Maj.-Gen. Sir Geoffrey Taunton,** Kt 1960; CB 1938; DSO 1916; DL, retired as Lord Lieutenant for Brecknock (1948-59); *b* 7 April 1884; 4th *s* of late Robert Taunton Raikes of Treberfydd, Breconshire, and 2nd wife, Rosa Margaret, 4th *d* of Henry William Cripps, QC, Beechwood, Gt Marlow; *m* 1923, Dorothy Amabel Wilson (*d* 1952), *o d* of late Arthur Wilson-Fox, CB, and Mrs Wilson-Fox, of Ridgeway House, Northaw; three *d*. *Educ:* Radley College; Sandhurst. Entered Army, 1903; employed with Egyptian Army, 1913-15; served European War, 1914-18 (despatches, DSO and two bars, Bt Major, Bt Lieutenant-Colonel, Croix de Guerre); Chief Instructor in Military History and Tactics, RMA, 1928-30; commanded 1st Batt. South Wales Borderers, 1931-34; Instructor (Class Y) Senior Officers' School, Sheerness, 1934-35; Commander 9th Infantry Brigade, 1935-37; Maj.-Gen., 1937; retired pay, 1938; Commander Territorial Army Div., 1939-40. *Address:* Treberfydd, Bwlch, Breconshire; c/o Glyn, Mills & Co., Holt's Branch, Whitehall, SW1. *Club:* Army and Navy.

**RAIKES, Sir (Henry) Victor (Alpin MacKinnon),** KBE 1953; *b* 19 Jan. 1901; *s* of late H. St John Raikes, CBE, KC; *m* 1940, Audrey Elizabeth Joyce, *o d* of A. P. Wilson, Repton; two *d*. *Educ:* Westminster School; Trinity Coll., Cambridge (BA). Called to Bar, Inner Temple, 1924; contested (C) Ilkeston Division of Derbyshire, 1924 and 1929; MP (C) SE Essex, 1931-45; MP (C) Wavertree Division of Liverpool, 1945-50, Garston Division of Liverpool, 1950-57 (Ind C 1957). Flight Lieut RAFVR, 1940-42. JP Derbyshire, 1927. Kt of Malta, Order of St John of Jerusalem, 1970. *Address:* 8 Gledhow Gardens, SW5. *Clubs:* Carlton, MCC.

**RAIKES, Rear-Adm. Iwan Geoffrey,** CBE 1967; DSC 1943; Naval Secretary, since 1970; *b* 21 April 1921; *s* of Adm. Sir Robert Henry Taunton Raikes, KCB, CVO, DSO, and Lady (Ida Guinevere) Raikes; *m* 1947, Cecilia Primrose Hunt; one *s* one *d*. *Educ:* RNC Dartmouth. Entered Royal Navy, 1935; specialised in Submarines, 1941; Commander, Dec. 1952; Captain, Dec. 1960; Rear-Admiral, Jan. 1970. *Recreations:* shooting, fishing, sailing, skiing, tennis. *Address:* Aberyscir Court, Brecon, S Wales. *Club:* United Service.

**RAIKES, Sir Victor;** *see* Raikes, Sir H. V. A. M.

**RAILTON, Brig. Dame Mary,** DBE 1956 (CBE 1953); *b* 28 May 1906; *d* of late James and Margery Railton. *Educ:* privately. Joined FANY, 1938; commissioned in ATS, 1940; WRAC 1949; Director WRAC, 1954-57; Deputy Controller Commandant, 1961-67. *Address:* 1 Frogmore Cottages, Great Bedwyn, Marlborough, Wilts.

**RAILTON, Reid Antony,** BSc, MIMechE; Consulting Engineer; *b* 24 June 1895; *s* of Charles W. Railton, Alderley Edge, Cheshire; *m* 1928, Margaret Audrey Hensman; one *s* one *d*. *Educ:* Rugby; Manchester Univ. RAeC Pilot's Certificate, 1915; served apprenticeship with Leyland Motors Ltd, 1915-17; served with RNVR Motor Boat Section, 1918; studied Factory Layout in USA, 1920; Asst to Chief Engineer Leyland Motors Ltd, 1921-23; Managing Director of Arab Motors Ltd, Letchworth, 1925-27; Designer of the first motor cars to exceed the officially-timed speeds of four, five, and six miles per minute. Designer late John Cobb's Railton car which held world's speed record for twenty-five years. As late Sir Malcolm Campbell's engineering consultant, was responsible for his boat Blue-Bird II, which for many years held world's speed record at 141 mph. In similar capacity was responsible for late John Cobb's boat, Crusader, the first boat to exceed speed of 200 mph. *Publications:* Papers before Instn Auto. Engrs, Instn Mech. Engrs and Soc. Automotive Engrs (USA). *Address:* 241 The Uplands, Berkeley, S Calif 94705, USA.

**RAILTON, Dame Ruth,** DBE 1966 (OBE 1954); Founder and Musical Director of the National Youth Orchestra and National Junior Music School, 1947-65; Professor, Chopin Conservatoire, Warsaw; Governor, Royal Ballet School; *b* 14 Dec. 1915; *m* 1962, Cecil Harmsworth King, *qv*. *Educ:* St Mary's School,

Wantage; Royal Academy of Music, London. Director of Music or Choral Work for many schools and societies, 1939-49. FRAM 1956; Hon. FRMCM 1959; Hon. FRCM 1965; Hon. FTCL 1969. Hon. LLD Aberdeen Univ., 1960. *Recreations:* interested in everything. *Address:* The Pavilion, Hampton Court, East Molesey, Surrey.

**RAINBIRD, George Meadus;** Director of Thomson Publications Ltd since 1969; author and publisher; *b* 22 May 1905; *s* of Leonard Rainbird and Sarah (*née* Meadus); *m* 1st, 1926, Eva Warner (marr. diss.); one *s* three *d*; 2nd, 1939, Joyce Trinder (*d* 1970); two *s* one *d*. *Educ:* local grammar school. Founded publishing house, George Rainbird Ltd, 1951; acquired Zaehnsdorf Ltd and Wigmore Bindery Ltd, 1954-56; merged with Thomson Organization, 1965. Chairman: Thos Nelson & Sons Ltd; George Rainbird Ltd; Rainbird Reference Books Ltd; Sphere Books Ltd; Dir, Hamish Hamilton Ltd. Chm., International Wine and Food Society. *Publications:* Escape to Sunshine, 1952; A Pocket Book of Wine, 1963; Sherry and the Wines of Spain, 1966. *Recreations:* books, gardens and wine. *Address:* Whichford House, Shipston-on-Stour, Warwicks. *T:* Long Compton 285; K1 Albany, W1. *T:* 01-723 9042. *Clubs:* Savile, Saintsbury.

**RAINE, Kathleen Jessie, (Mrs Madge);** Poet; *b* 1908; *o d* of George Raine, schoolmaster, and of Jessie Raine; *m* Charles Madge (marriage dissolved); one *s* one *d*. *Educ:* Girton College, Cambridge. *Publications:* Stone and Flower, 1943; Living in Time, 1946; The Pythoness, 1949; The Year One, 1952; Collected Poems, 1956; The Hollow Hill (poems), 1965; Defending Ancient Springs (criticism), 1967; Blake and Tradition (Andrew Mellon Lectures, Washington, 1962), Princeton 1968, London 1969; (with George Mills Harper) Selected Writings of Thomas Taylor the Platonist, Princeton and London, 1969. Contributions to literary journals. *Address:* 47 Paultons Square, SW3. *Club:* University Women's.

**RAINER, Luise;** Actress; *b* Vienna, 12 Jan.; *d* of Heinz Rainer; *m* 1937, Clifford Odets, (*d* 1963) (from whom she obtained a divorce, 1940); *m* 1945, Robert, *s* of late John Knittel; one *d*. *Educ:* Austria, France, Switzerland and Italy. Started stage career at age of sixteen; later was discovered by Metro-Goldwyn-Mayer talent scout in Vienna; came to Hollywood; appeared in Escapade; starred in The Great Ziegfeld, The Good Earth, Emperor's Candlesticks, Big City, Toy Wife (Frou Frou); received Motion Picture Academy of Arts and Sciences Award for the best feminine performance in 1936 and 1937. *Recreation:* walking. *Address:* 34 Eaton Mews North, SW1. *T:* 01-235 4263.

**RAINS, Prof. Anthony John Harding,** MS, FRCS; Professor of Surgery in the University of London at Charing Cross Hospital Medical School, since Oct. 1959; Hon. Surgeon Charing Cross Hospital; *b* 5 Nov. 1920; *s* of late Dr Robert Harding Rains and Mrs Florence Harding Rains; *m* 1943, Mary Adelaide Lillywhite; three *d*. *Educ:* Christ's Hospital School, Horsham; St Mary's Hospital, London. MB, BS London, MRCS, LRCP 1943. Ho. Surg. and Ho. Phys. St Mary's, 1943. RAF, 1944-47. Ex-Service Registrar to Mr Handfield-Jones and Sir Arthur Porritt, 1947-48. FRCS 1948; Res. Surgical Officer, Bedford County Hosp., 1948-50; Lectr in Surgery, Univ. of Birmingham, 1950-54, Sen. Lectr, 1955-59. MS (London) 1952. Hon. Consulting Surgeon, United Birmingham Hospitals, 1954-59. Mem. Court of Examiners, RCS. Sir Arthur Keith medal, RCS. Editor, Annals of RCS. *Publications:* Gallstones: Causes and Treatment; Urgencies and Emergencies for Nurses; (ed with Dr P. B. Kunkler) The Treatment of Cancer in Clinical Practice; ed Bailey and Love's Short Practice of Surgery; articles on the surgery of the gall bladder, on the formation of gall stones, inguinal hernia and arterial disease. *Recreations:* music, country garden, painting. *Address:* Charing Cross Hospital Medical School, 62 Chandos Place, WC2. *T:* 01-836 7788.

**RAINSFORD, Surg. Rear-Adm. (retd) Seymour Grome,** CB 1955; FRCPath 1964; Research Fellow in Hæmophilia, Wessex Regional Hospital Board, 1967; *b* 24 April 1900; *s* of Frederick Edward Rainsford, MD, Palmerstown Hse, Co. Dublin; *m* 1929, Violet Helen (*née* Thomas), Plymouth. *Educ:* St Columba's College, Co. Dublin; Trinity College, Dublin. MB, BCh, BAO 1922, Dublin; Joined RN as Surg. Lieut, 1922; MD 1932, DPH 1937, ScD, 1939, Dublin; MRCP 1949. North Persian Forces Memorial Medal, for research on Mediterranean Fever, 1933; Gilbert Blane Gold Medal for research on Typhoid Fever, 1938; Chadwick Gold Medal and Prize for research on typhoid vaccine and on blood transfusion in the Royal Navy, 1939. Surgeon Rear-Adm. 1952; Deputy Medical Director-General of the Royal Navy, 1952-55. Chevalier de la Légion d'Honneur, 1948; CStJ 1955. *Publications:* papers on typhoid fever and other tropical diseases, haematology, blood transfusion and physiological problems concerned in diving and submarine escape, in Jl Hygiene, Lancet, BMJ and Journal RN Med. Serv. *Recreations:* shooting, golf. *Club:* Army and Navy.

**RAIS, Tan Sri Abdul J.;** *see* Jamil Rais.

**RAISMAN, Sir (Abraham) Jeremy,** GCMG 1959; GCIE 1945 (CIE 1934); KCSI 1941 (CSI 1938); Kt 1939; Director, Lloyds Bank Europe Ltd; Deputy Chairman, Lloyds and Scottish Finance Ltd since 1958; Director: Commonwealth Trust Ltd; National and Grindlay's Bank; *b* 19 March 1892; *m* 1925, Renée Mary Kelly; two *s*. *Educ:* Leeds High School and University; Pembroke College, Oxford. MA (1st Class Mods 1st Lit Hum); John Locke Scholar in Moral Philosophy, 1915; joined ICS 1916; served in Bihar and Orissa till 1922; Customs Department Bombay and Calcutta, 1922-28; Commissioner of Income-Tax, Punjab and NWFP, 1928-31; Joint Secretary, Commerce Department, Government of India, 1931-34; Member Central Board of Revenue, 1934; Director, Reserve Bank of India, 1938; Secretary, Finance Dept, 1938-39; Finance Member of Govt of India, 1939-45; and Vice-President, Govr-Genl's Executive Council, 1944. Chairman, British Indian delegation to International Monetary Conference, Bretton Woods, USA, June-July 1944; retired from India, 1945; led UK Treasury Mission to India and Pakistan, Jan.-Feb. 1948; adviser to Govt of Pakistan on distribution of Central and Provincial revenues, Nov.-Dec. 1951; Chairman: Fiscal Commn for Federation of Rhodesia and Nyasaland, 1952; Nigeria Fiscal Commn, 1957-58; Economic and Fiscal Commn for East Africa, 1960-61. Comr, Public Works Loans Board, 1947, Chairman, 1948-70. vice-Chm., Lloyds Bank Ltd, 1947-53, Dep.-Chm., 1953-63. Hon. LLD Leeds. Hon. Fellow of Pembroke College, Oxford. *Address:* 71 Lombard Street, EC3. *T:* 01-626 1500; Fieldhead, Shamley Green, Surrey. *T:* Bramley 3128. *Clubs:* Athenæum, Reform.

**RAISON, Timothy Hugh Francis;** MP (C) Aylesbury since 1970; Editorial Consultant,

IPC Magazines; *b* 3 Nov. 1929; *s* of Maxwell and late Celia Raison; *m* 1956, Veldes Julia Charrington; one *s* three *d*. *Educ:* Dragon Sch., Oxford; Eton (King's Schol.); Christ Church, Oxford (Open History Schol.). Editorial Staff: Picture Post, 1953-56; New Scientist, 1956-61; Editor, Crossbow, 1958-60; Editor, New Society, 1962-68. Member: Youth Service Develt Coun., 1960-63; Central Adv. Coun. for Educn, 1963-66; Adv. Cttee on Drug Dependence, 1966-; (co-opted) Inner London Educn Authority Educn Cttee, 1967-70; Richmond upon Thames Coun., 1967-. Nansen Medal (for share in originating World Refugee Year), 1960. *Publications:* Why Conservative?, 1964; (ed) Youth in New Society, 1966; (ed) Founding Fathers of Social Science, 1969; various political pamphlets. *Recreations:* cricket, golf, tennis, painting. *Address:* 2 Mill Hill Road, Barnes, SW13. *T:* 01-876 2840; The Vicarage, Aston Abbotts, Bucks. *Clubs:* Carlton, Beefsteak, MCC.

**RAISTRICK, Harold,** FRS 1934; ScD (Cantab); DSc (Leeds); FRIC; MChemA; formerly Professor of Biochemistry, University of London and formerly Director of Division of Biochemistry and Chemistry in relation to Public Health, London School of Hygiene and Tropical Medicine (1929-56); retired 1956; Professor Emeritus since 1956; *b* Pudsey, Yorkshire, 26 Nov. 1890; *s* of late Mark Walker Raistrick; *m* 1917, Martha Louisa (*d* 1945), *d* of Jonathan Coates, Pudsey, Yorkshire; two *d*; *m* 1947, Betty Helen, *d* of Edward Young, London. *Educ:* Central High School, Leeds; Univ. of Leeds; University of Cambridge. On Research Staff of School of Biochemistry, University of Cambridge, 1914-21; in charge of Biochemical Department, Nobel's Explosives Co. Ltd, Stevenston, Ayrshire (Imperial Chemical Industries, Limited), 1921-29. Bakerian Lecturer, Royal Society, 1949; Flintoff Medallist, Chemical Society, 1963. *Publications:* various papers on microbiological chemistry in Biochemical Journal, Journal of Chemical Society and Philosophical Transactions of Royal Society, British Journal of Experimental Pathology, and the Lancet. *Recreations:* angling, golf and walking. *Address:* Belfairs, Sea Drive, Felpham, Bognor Regis, Sussex. *T:* Middleton-on-Sea 3150.

**RAITZ, Vladimir Gavrilovich;** Chairman, Horizon Holidays Ltd and all Companies within Horizon Group, since 1949; *b* 23 May 1922; *s* of Dr Gavril Raitz and Cecilia Raitz; *m* 1954, Helen Antonia (*née* Corkrey); three *d*. *Educ:* Mill Hill Sch.; London University. BSc(Econ.), Econ. History, 1942. British United Press, 1942-43; Reuters, 1943-48; founded Horizon Holidays, to operate first inclusive tour air charters out of UK, 1949. Member: NEDC for Hotels and Catering Industry, 1968; Cinematograph Films Council, 1969-. *Recreations:* reading, ski-ing. *Address:* 12 Chelsea Square, SW3. *T:* 01-352 2241. *Club:* Reform.

**RAJAGOPALACHARYA, Chakravarti;** *b* Hosur, Salem District, India, 1878; *s* of Chakravarti Ventatārya and Singāramma; *m* 1899, Alamelamangamma; four *c*. *Educ:* Central Coll., Bangalore; Presidency Coll. and Law Coll., Madras. Joined Bar, 1900; practised at Salem, India, 1900-19; joined Mahatma Gandhi's Satyagraha campaign and non-co-operation movement, 1919-20; Gen. Sec. Indian Nat. Congress, 1921-22 (Mem. Working Cttee, 1922-47); Sec. Prohibition League of India, 1930; Prime Minister, Madras, 1937-39; associated with Indian Freedom Movement since 1906; induced All India Congress Cttee to offer co-operation in war effort, 1940; underwent imprisonment in connection with Indian Freedom Movement five times during 1921 to 1942; asst, Mahatma Gandhi in the Gandhi-Jinnah talks, 1944; Member Interim Govt of India, 1946-47; Governor of West Bengal, 1947-48; acted as Gov.-Gen., India, Nov. 1947; Governor-General of India (in succession to Earl Mountbatten of Burma), June 1948-Jan. 1950; retd to inaugurate Indian Union Republic; Home Minister for India, 1950-51; Chief Minister, Govt of Madras, 1952-54. Founded Swatantra Party to oppose Congress Party, defending individual freedom and private enterprise, 1959. *Publications:* Fatal Cart and other stories, Prohibition Manual, 1935; Way Out (booklet), 1942; Reconciliation (booklet), 1942; Marcus Aurelius and Socrates in Tamil, Tamil Essays, Mahabharat, Ramayana in story chapters (translated into almost all Indian languages). Upanishads for lay readers and Bhagavat Gita Selections and Notes. Hinduism, Doctrine and Way of Life. Ed. Mahatma Gandhi's Young India during latter's incarceration, 1922. *Address:* Nowroji Road, Madras 31, India.

**RAJAH, Arumugam Ponnu;** (first) High Commisioner for Republic of Singapore in United Kingdom since 1966; *b* Negri Sembilan, Malaysia, 23 July 1911; *m* Vijaya Lakshmi; one *s* one *d*. *Educ:* St Paul's Inst., Seremban; Raffles Instn, Singapore; Oxford Univ. (BA). Barrister-at-law, Lincoln's Inn. City Councillor, Singapore: nominated, 1947-49; elected, 1949-57; MLA, Singapore, 1959-66, Speaker, 1964-66. Mem. Bd of Trustees, Singapore Improvement Trust, 1949-57; Mem., Raffles Coll. Coun. and Univ. of Malaya Coun., 1955-63; Chm., Public Accounts Cttee of Legislative Assembly, 1959-63. *Address:* 2 Wilton Crescent, SW1.

**RAJAPAKSE, Sir Lalita (Abhaya),** Kt, *cr* 1952; QC (Ceylon); BA, LLD (London); High Commissioner for Ceylon in Great Britain, 1967-69; *b* 3 May 1900; *s* of Adrian de Abrew Rajapakse and Agnes Rajapakse; *m* 1935, Rose Thelma Chrysobel Gunasekera; one *s* two *d*. *Educ:* St Joseph's College, Colombo; University Coll., London (BA 1922, LLB 1923, LLD 1925, Fellow, 1968). Called to English Bar, Lincoln's Inn, 1924 (Benchers' rights at Bench Table, 1968-69). Called to Ceylon Bar, 1925; Lectr, 1926, Examiner, 1927, Ceylon Law Coll. Mem. of Council of Legal Education (Ceylon), 1939; Founded Revata Coll. Balapitiya, Ceylon, 1933. KC 1944, QC 1952 (Ceylon); Member of University Council, University of Ceylon, 1946. Commissioner of Assize, Supreme Court, Ceylon, 1947; Member of Senate, Ceylon Parliament, 1947, Leader of Senate, 1949; Minister of Justice, Ceylon, 1947-53. Ambassador of Ceylon in France, 1965-66. Mem. Ceylon Delegn, Commonwealth Conf. on Foreign Affairs, 1950; Chairman Gal Oya Commission, 1956; Mem. Univ. Council: Vidyodaya Univ., Ceylon, 1959-; Vidyalankara Univ., Ceylon, 1959-; Pres., All Ceylon Buddhist Congress, 1961-64. *Recreations:* tennis, swimming, agriculture. *Address:* Lumbini, Horton Place, Colombo, Ceylon. *T:* Colombo 95885.

**RAKE, Alfred Mordey,** CBE 1953; *b* 27 March 1906; *s* of Dr H. V. Rake, Fordingbridge, Hants; *m* 1st, 1930, Gwendolen (*d* 1944), *d* of late Edward Craig-Hall, Hove, Sussex; three *s*; 2nd, 1947, Jean Mary, *d* of late F. G. Kingsland, Thornton Heath, Surrey; two *d*. *Educ:* King's School, Canterbury; Corpus Christi College, Cambridge. 1st Cl. Hons Classical Tripos Pt 1, 1927; Cauldwell Scholar, 1927; 1st Cl. Hons (with distinction) Classical Tripos Pt II, 1928; Asst Principal, Min. of

Transport, 1930; Private Sec. to Parliamentary Sec., 1935; Principal, 1936; Asst Sec., 1941; transferred to Min. of Fuel and Power, 1946; Under Secretary, 1955; retired, 1966. *Recreation:* gardening. *Address:* The White House, Whimple, Devon. *T:* Whimple 560.

**RALEIGH, Nigel Hugh C.;** *see* Curtis-Raleigh.

**RALFS, Maj.-Gen. Bertram George,** CB 1965; Royal Marines, retired; *b* 1 June 1905; *s* of late George Spencer Ralfs; *m* 1929, Daisy Harrison; one *d. Educ:* Portsmouth Gram. Sch. Royal Marines: Probationary 2nd Lt, 1923; Capt. 1935, Bt Maj. 1940, Maj. 1942, Lt-Col 1948, Col 1953; Maj.-Gen. 1962. Served in battleships Malaya, Barham, Warspite, Queen Elizabeth, Valiant and Nelson, also in Cruiser Devonshire; Superintendent of Applied Ballistics, 1953-57; Chief Inspector of Naval Ordnance, 1959-62; President, Ordnance Board, 1964-65; retd 1965. Pres., Instn of Engineering Inspection, 1964-66. Chairman: NATO Ballistics Group, 1953-58; NATO Standardisation of Ballistic Atmosphere Cttee, 1956-58; National Council for Quality and Reliability, 1964-66. *Address:* Hanover House, Tonbridge, Kent. *T:* Tonbridge 61647. *Club:* United Service.

**RALLI, Sir Godfrey (Victor),** 3rd Bt, *cr* 1912; TD; Chairman G. & L. Ralli Investment & Trustee Co. Ltd, since 1962; *b* 9 Sept. 1915; *s* of Sir Strati Ralli, 2nd Bt, MC; *S* father 1964; *m* 1st, 1937, Nora Margaret Forman (marriage dissolved, 1947); one *s* two *d*; 2nd, 1949, Jean, *er d* of late Keith Barlow. *Educ:* Eton. Joined Ralli Bros Ltd, 1936. Served War of 1939-45 (despatches), Captain, Berkshire Yeomanry RA. Director and Vice-Chairman, Ralli Bros Ltd, 1946-62; Director, Guardian Assce; Chm., Greater London Fund for the Blind. *Recreations:* fishing, golf. *Heir: s* David Charles Ralli, *b* 5 April 1946. *Address:* 62 Sheffield Terrace, W8. *T:* 01-727 4106. *Clubs:* City of London, Cavalry, White's.

**RALPH, Ronald Seton,** MRCS, LRCP, DPH; retired; late Consultant Pathologist Battersea and Putney Group of Hospitals; Hon. Pathologist, Eltham and Mottingham Cottage Hospital; *b* Saugor, India, 22 July 1895; *s* of late Col A. C. Ralph, DSO; *m* 1918, Marjorie, *d* of late Dr Joseph Bott, Richmond, Surrey; one *s. Educ:* Dover College; Guy's Hospital. Late Director of Clinical Research Assoc. Laboratories; late Clinical Pathologist, St John's Hospital, Lewisham, SE13; late Assistant Bacteriologist, Guy's Hospital, and late Physician in Charge of Diseases of the Skin, St John's Hospital, SE13. *Publications:* various on medical subjects in Lancet, Medical World, and Journal of Clinical Research. *Address:* Cotswold, Haywards Heath, Sussex. *T:* Haywards Heath 3446.

**RALSTON, Col Alexander Windeyer,** CMG 1918; DSO 1917; Hon. Colonel, Retired; List Barrister-at-law (non-practising); Chairman War Pensions Entitlement Appeal Tribunal for Commonwealth of Australia, 1929-42; JP for NSW; *b* Croydon, Sydney, NSW, 27 Nov. 1885; *e s* of late A. G. Ralston, KC; *m* 1927, Florence Mary, *o d* of late H. G. Currie, London; two *s* three *d. Educ:* Sydney Grammar School; University of Sydney; BA, LLB and Diploma in Military Science. Admitted to Bar, 1909; joined Australian Naval and Military Expeditionary Force as Capt. 1914; present at capture of Rabaul, Herbertshohe, Madang, Quieta, and in command of expedition to southern end of New Ireland; joined AIF March 1915 as Major and was in Gallipoli, 1915, to evacuation, becoming 2nd in command of 19th Batt. in Oct. 1915; arrived in France March 1916; promoted Lt-Col and to command 20th Batt. 16 June 1916; 2nd Australian Machine Gun Batt., March 1918 to Aug. 1919 (despatches 4 times, CMG, DSO); Hon. Col, Retired List, 1943. Colonial Auxiliary Forces Officers Decoration, VD. *Recreations:* fishing, reading. *Address:* Knowle, 489 New South Head Road, Double Bay, Sydney, NSW. *T:* 36 5153. *Clubs:* Imperial Service, Royal Sydney Golf (non-playing) (Sydney).

**RAM, Jagjivan;** Minister of Defence, India, since 1970; *b* Arrah, Bihar, 5 April 1908; *m* 1935, Indrani Devi; one *s* one *d. Educ:* Banaras Hindu Univ.; Calcutta Univ. (BSc). Appeared before Hammond Commn, 1936; started Agricl Lab. Movement in Bihar and formed Bihar Provincial Khet Mazdoor (Agricl Lab.) Sabha, 1937; Parly Sec., Bihar Govt, 1937-39; jailed in 1940 and 1942 and released in Oct. 1943 on med. grounds; Vice-Pres., Bihar Br. of All India TUC, 1940-46; Sec., Bihar Provincial Congress Cttee, 1940-46; Labour Minister of interim Govt, Sept. 1946-May 1952; appeared before Cabinet Mission, 1946, as accredited leader of Scheduled Castes and rep. their case. Leader, Indian Delegn to ILO Conf., Geneva, 1947; Chm., Preparatory Asia Regional Conf. of ILO, Oct.-Nov. 1947; Leader, Indian Delegn to 33rd Session of ILO Conf. 1950 (Chm. Conf.); Communication Minister, Govt of India, 1952-56; Minister for: Transport and Railway, Dec. 1956-Apr. 1957; Railways, 1957-62; Transport and Communications, 1962-63; Labour, Employment and Rehabilitation, 1966 (AN); Leader, Indian Delegn to Asian Labour Ministers' Conf., Manila, 1966; Minister of Food, Agriculture, Community Develt and Co-op., 1967-70 (also charge Min. of Labour, Employment and Rehabilitation, Nov. 1969-1970). Leader, Indian Delegns: FAO Conf., Rome, 1967; World Food Congress, the Hague, 1970. Member: All India Congress Cttee, 1940- (of its Central Parly Bd 1950-); Exec. Cttee, Hindustan Mazdoor Sewak Sangh, 1947-; Disciplinary Action Cttee of Congress Working Cttee (since constituted); All India Congress Working Cttee, 1948-; Congress Economic Planning Sub Cttee; Gandhi Smarak Nidhi; Indian Inst. of Public Admin.; Governing Bodies, several colls and educnl instns. Trustee, Nehru Memorial Trust, etc. Past Pres. of several Trades Unions. Hon. Dr of Sciences (Vikram Univ., Ujjain). *Address:* (home) 6 Hastings Road, New Delhi 11, India. *T:* 376555; (office) Ministry of Defence, New Delhi, India. *T:* 376990.

**RAM CHANDRA,** CIE 1933; MBE 1919; MA (Punjab); MA (Cantab); a Trustee of The Tribune (English daily newspaper in Punjab), since 1949, President of Board of Trustees, since 1967; Syndic and Fellow of Punjabi University, Patiala since 1962; *b* 1 March 1889; *m* 1917; one *s* one *d. Educ:* Government College, Lahore (Fuller Exhibitioner); Trinity College, Cambridge (Senior Scholar and Wrangler, b star). Assistant Professor of Mathematics, Government College, Lahore, 1908-10; joined ICS, 1913; served in Punjab as Assistant Commissioner in various districts; Colonisation Officer, 1915; Under-Secretary, 1919-21; Settlement Officer, 1921-25; Director of Land Records, 1924; Deputy Commissioner, 1925; Secretary to Punjab Government, Transferred Department, 1926-27; Home Secretary to Punjab Government, 1928; Deputy Secretary to Govt of India, Department of Education, Health, and Lands, 1928; Joint Secretary, 1932; Secretary, 1935; Member Council of State, 1935; Member, Punjab Legislative Council, 1936; Finance Secretary to Punjab Govt, 1936-37;

Commissioner, 1938-39; Sec. to Punjab Govt, Medical and Local Govt Depts, 1939-41; Chief Controller of Imports, India, 1941-44; Leader of Indian Delegation to Egypt for Cotton Conference, 1943; Secretary to Government of India, Commerce Dept, 1944-45; Secretary to Govt of India, Defence Dept, 1945-46; Financial Comr, Punjab, 1946-48; Chairman, Punjab (India) Public Service Commission, 1948-53; Mem., Punjab Legislative Council (elected by Graduates' Constituency), 1954-60; Fellow of Panjab Univ., Chandigarh, 1947-68, Syndic, 1949-64. Chief Comr, Scouts and Guides, Punjab, 1955-68. *Recreation:* gardening. *Address:* Forest Hill, Simla 2, India. *T:* 2129.

**RAMAGE, Captain Cecil Beresford,** MC; *b* 17 Jan. 1895; *o s* of John Walker Ramage, Edinburgh; *m* 1921, Cathleen Nesbitt, *qv*; one *s* one *d. Educ:* Edinburgh Academy; Pembroke College, Oxford (open Classical Scholar); President Oxford Union Society; commissioned in the Royal Scots, 1914; served Gallipoli, Egypt, Palestine, until 1919 (despatches, Order of the Nile); contested Newcastle on Tyne, General Election, 1922; MP (L) Newcastle on Tyne (West Division), 1923-24; contested Southport, 1929, Barrister-at-Law, Middle Temple, 1921; subseq. Oxf. Circuit. *Recreations:* golf, tennis.

**RAMAGE, James Granville William;** British High Commissioner in The Gambia, since 1968; *b* 19 Nov. 1919; *s* of late Rev. George Granville Ramage and Helen Marion (*née* Middlemass); *m* 1947, Eileen Mary Smith; one *s* two *d. Educ:* Glasgow Acad.; Glasgow University. Served in HM Forces, 1940-46 (despatches). Entered HM Foreign Service, 1947; seconded for service at Bombay, 1947-49; transf. to Foreign Office, 1950; First Sec. and Consul at Manila, 1952-56; South-East Asia Dept, FO, 1956-58; HM Consul at Atlanta, Ga, 1958-62; Gen. Dept, FO, 1962-63; HM Consul-General, Tangier, 1963-67. *Recreations:* music, photography. *Address:* c/o Foreign and Commonwealth Office, SW1; 4 Merton Hall Road, Wimbledon, SW19. *T:* 01-542 5492.

**RAMAGE, Sir Richard (Ogilvy),** Kt 1958; CMG 1943; *b* 5 Jan. 1896; *s* of John T. Ramage, Shipbuilder; *m* 1932, Dorothy Frances Broome; no *c. Educ:* Edinburgh Academy. Royal Engineers, 1914-19; Administrative Service, Nigeria, 1920-35 (Dep. Resident, 1934); Assistant to Lieutenant-Governor, Malta, 1935-39; Under-Sec. Gold Coast, 1939-42; Colonial Secretary, Sierra Leone, 1942-50; Acting Governor, Sierra Leone, on various occasions; retired 1951. Employed on special duties, 1951-55 (British Honduras, Mauritius, Aden, Gambia, Western Pacific High Commission, Kingdom of Tonga and Jamaica); Chairman: Public Service Commn, Uganda, 1955-59, Police Service Commn, 1957-59, retired; Member ILO Cttee of Experts on Social Policy in Non-Metropolitan Territories, 1951-58. Chm. Post Election (Constitution) Cttee, Tanganyika, 1959; Chm. Economy Commission, Uganda, 1960; Comr to examine arrangements for localisation in E African Post and Telecommunications Administration, and East Africa High Commission, 1961; reported on Civil Services of Basutoland, Bechuanaland and Swaziland, 1961; advised on the public service in relation to constitutional development, Aden and South Arabian Federation, 1962 and 1963; a UK Observer, Malta Referendum, 1964. Reported on the Public Service, State of Brunei and British Honduras, 1965. Arbitrator, Aden Port Trust and Senior Staff and Pilots, 1965. Salaries Commissioner for the Seychelles, 1967; Adviser on localisation of Civil Service, Fiji, 1968; Adviser on salaries etc, Civil Service, Kingdom of Tonga, 1969. OStJ. *Recreations:* golf, travel. *Address:* Spilsby House, Ottery St Mary, Devon. *Clubs:* East India and Sports, Royal Commonwealth Society.

**RAMAN, Sir (Chandrasekhara) Venkata,** Kt, *cr* 1929; MA; Hon. DSc; Hon. PhD, Hon. LLD; Nobel Laureate in Physics; Director, Raman Research Institute, Bangalore; *b* 7 Nov. 1888. *Educ:* Presidency College, Madras. BA 1st class, 1904, and University medal; MA 1st class, and joined Indian Finance Department, 1907; Curzon Research Prizeman, 1912; Sir Rashbehari Ghosh Travelling Fellow and British Association Lecturer, 1924; Research Associate, California Institute of Technology, Pasadena, 1924; Mateucci medallist, Rome, 1929; Hughes Medallist of Royal Society, 1930; Franklin Medallist, 1942. Foreign Associate: Paris Acad. of Sciences, 1949; Pontifical Acad. of Sciences, 1961; Academies of Science, USSR, 1962; Hungary, Czechoslovakia, 1963; Romania, 1966. FRS 1924-68. Pres., Indian Acad. of Sciences, 1934. Hon. Member, Société Philomathique de Paris; Hon. Fellow, Optical Society of America, Franklin Institute, Royal Irish Academy, Zürich Physical Society, Royal Philosophical Society, Glasgow, and Royal Society of New Zealand. *Publications:* Molecular Diffraction of Light; Mechanical Theory of Bowed Strings and Violin-Tone; Diffraction of X-rays; Theory of Musical Instruments, and many scientific papers in the Philosophical Magazine and the Physical Review, Nature, The Astrophysical Journal, the Proceedings of the Royal Society, and of the Indian Academy of Sciences. *Address:* Raman Research Institute, Hebbal Post, Bangalore 6, India.

**RAMBAHADUR LIMBU, Corporal (Gurkha),** VC 1966; *b* Nov. 1939; *s* of late Tekbir Limbu; *m* 1st, 1960, Tikamaya Limbuni (*d* 1966); two *s*; 2nd, 1967, Punimaya Limbuni; two *s*. Army Cert. of Educn 1st cl. Enlisted 10th Princess Mary's Own Gurkha Rifles, 1957; served on ops in Borneo (VC). *Recreations:* football, volley-ball, badminton, basketball. *Address:* 10th PMO Gurkha Rifles, Minden Barracks, Penang, Malaysia; c/o VC Association, 807 Nelson House, Dolphin Square, SW1. *Clubs:* VC and GC Association, Royal Society of St George (England).

**RAMBERT, Dame Marie (Dame Marie Dukes),** DBE 1962 (CBE 1953); Founder and Director of Ballet Rambert; Lecturer and teacher; Director, New Ballet Rambert Company since 1966; *b* Warsaw, 1888; *m* 1918, Ashley Dukes (*d* 1959); two *d. Educ:* Warsaw, Paris. Trained by Enrico Cecchetti; Member of Diaghilev's Russian Ballet Company, 1912-13; opened Rambert School of Ballet, 1920; Produced first ballet, Tragedy of Fashion, by Frederick Ashton, 1926; first season of Ballet Rambert at Lyric Theatre, Hammersmith, 1930. Jupiter recording, On Ballet, 1960. Radio and Television personality. Queen Elizabeth Coronation Award, 1956; Diploma, Regional College of Art, Manchester, 1960; FRSA 1963; Hon. DLitt, Univ. of Sussex, 1964. Légion d'Honneur, 1957. *Publications:* (trans.) Ulanova: Her Childhood and Schooldays, 1962; (collaborated) Dancers of Mercury: The Story of Ballet Rambert, 1960. *Recreation:* reading. *Address:* 19 Campden Hill Gardens, W8. *T:* 01-727 5946; Mercury Theatre, Ladbroke Road, W11. *T:* 01-727 5700.

**RAMGOOLAM, Sir Seewoosagur,** Kt 1965; LRCP, MRCS; Premier and Minister of

Finance, Mauritius; *b* 1900; *m*; one *s* one *d*. *Educ:* Royal Coll., Curepipe; University Coll. and University Coll. Hosp., London. Municipal Councillor, 1940-53, 1956-60; Deputy Mayor of Port Louis, 1956; Mayor of Port Louis, 1958; Member: Legislative Assembly, 1940; Executive Council, 1948; Liaison Officer for Education, 1951-56; Ministerial Secretary to the Treasury, 1958-60; Minister of Finance, 1960; elected Leader of the House, 1960; Chief Minister and Minister of Finance, 1961; Premier, 1964. Editor, Indian Cultural Review. *Recreations:* art and literature. *Address:* 85 Desforges Street, Port Louis, Mauritius. *T:* 20460.

**RAMPHAL, Hon. Sir Shridath Surendranath,** Kt 1970; CMG 1966; QC (Guyana); Minister of State and Attorney-General, Guyana; Member, International Commission of Jurists, since 1970; *b* 1928; *m*. *Educ:* King's Coll., London (LLM 1952). Called to the Bar, Gray's Inn, 1951. Colonial Legal Probationers' Schol.; Arden Prize; Atkin Prize. Crown Counsel, British Guiana, 1953-54; Asst to Attorney-Gen., 1954-56; Legal Draftsman, 1956-58; First Legal Draftsman, West Indies, 1958-59; Solicitor-Gen., British Guiana, 1959-61; Asst Attorney-Gen., West Indies, 1961-62. *Address:* Chambers of the Attorney-General, Georgetown, Guyana.

**RAMPTON, Jack Leslie,** CB 1969; Deputy Secretary, Ministry of Technology (formerly Ministry of Power), since 1968; *b* 10 July 1920; *s* of Leonard Wilfrid Rampton and Sylvia (*née* Davies); *m* 1950, Eileen Joan (*née* Hart); one *s* one *d*. *Educ:* Tonbridge Sch.; Trinity Coll., Oxford. Treasury, 1941; Asst Priv. Sec. to successive Chancellors of the Exchequer, 1942-43; Priv. Sec. to Financial Sec., 1945-46; Economic and Financial Adv. to Comr-Gen. for SE Asia and to British High Comr, Malaya, 1959-61; Under-Secretary, HM Treasury, 1964-68. *Recreations:* gardening, games, photography, travel; Oxford Squash V (Capt.) 1939-40; Authentic, 1940. *Address:* 17 The Ridgeway, Tonbridge, Kent. *T:* Tonbridge 2117. *Club:* Vincent's (Oxford).

**RAMSAY,** family name of **Earl of Dalhousie.**

**RAMSAY, Lord; James Hubert Ramsay;** *b* 17 Jan. 1948; *er s* and *heir* of 16th Earl of Dalhousie, *qv*. *Educ:* Ampleforth. 2nd Bn Coldstream Guards, commnd 1968. *Address:* Brechin Castle, Brechin; Dalhousie Castle, Bonnyrigg, Midlothian. *Club:* Turf.

**RAMSAY, Maj.-Gen. Sir Alan (Hollick),** Kt 1961; CB 1946; CBE 1942; DSO 1943; retired as Director of Education, Victoria, Australia, 1960; *b* 12 March 1895; *s* of Charles Ramsay and Frances Hollick; *m* 1924, Edna Mary Watson; one *s* one *d*. *Educ:* Melbourne High School; University of Melbourne (BSc, DipEd). Served in Middle East, New Guinea and New Britain with AIF (CBE, DSO, CB). *Recreations:* fishing, bowls. *Address:* 45 Allenby Avenue, East Malvern, Melbourne, Australia. *T:* 25.3585. *Club:* Naval and Military (Melbourne).

**RAMSAY, Adm. Hon. Sir Alexander Robert Maule,** GCVO 1938 (KCVO 1932); KCB 1937 (CB 1934); DSO 1916; *b* 29 May 1881; *s* of 13th Earl of Dalhousie and Ida, *d* of 6th Earl of Tankerville; *m* 1919, Princess Victoria Patricia Helena Elizabeth (*see* Lady Patricia Ramsay), *d* of 1st Duke of Connaught, KG; one *s* (Alexander Arthur Alfonso David Maule Ramsay of Mar; *b* 21 Dec. 1919; *m* 1956, Hon. Flora Fraser, *o d* and *heiress* of 19th Lord Saltoun, *qv*; three *d*). *Educ:* Royal Naval College, Dartmouth. Served Dardanelles, 1914-15 (DSO, promoted Captain); Naval ADC to the King, 1931; late Naval Attaché in Paris; Rear-Adm., 1931; Commodore of Royal Naval Barracks at Portsmouth, 1929-31; Rear-Admiral Aircraft Carriers, 1933-36; Vice-Admiral, 1936; Commander-in-Chief East Indies, 1936-38; Fifth Sea Lord and Chief of Naval Air Service, 1938-39; Admiral, 1939. *Recreation:* sport and games. *Address:* Ribsden Holt, Windlesham, Surrey. *Club:* United Service.

**RAMSAY, Sir Alexander William Burnett,** 7th Bt, *cr* 1806, of Balmain (also *heir-pres* to Btcy of Burnett, *cr* 1626 (Nova Scotia), of Leys, Kincardineshire, which became dormant, 1959, on death of Sir Alexander Edwin Burnett of Leys, and was not claimed by Sir Alexander Burnett Ramsay, 6th Bt, of Balmain); *b* 4 Aug. 1938; *s* of Sir Alexander Burnett Ramsay, 6th Bt and Isabel Ellice, *e d* of late William Whitney, Woodstock, New South Wales; *S* father, 1965; *m* 1963, Neryl Eileen, *d* of J. C. Smith Thornton Trangie; one *s*. *Heir:* *s* Alexander David Ramsay, *b* 20 Aug. 1966. *Address:* Bullbah, Warren, New South Wales, Australia.

**RAMSAY, Arthur;** *see* Ramsay, James A.

**RAMSAY, Clyde Archibald,** CMG 1969; MBE 1960; JP (Barbados); Chief Establishments Officer Civil Service, Barbados, since 1962; also Head of Civil Service since 1967; *b* 8 April 1914; *s* of late Alan C. and Wilhelmina Ramsay; *m* 1943, Thelma Ione, *d* of Alfred and Rowena Pragnell; two *s*. *Educ:* Combermere Secondary Sch., Barbados. Joined Civil Service, 1932; Asst Auditor-Gen., 1957; Local Govt Comr, Chief Registering Officer and Supervisor of Elections, 1959; Chief Establishments Officer and Chm. of Whitley Council, Barbados, 1962. Vice-Pres., Barbados Boy Scouts' Assoc. JP 1961. *Recreation:* swimming. *Address:* Hargate, Hastings, Christ Church, Barbados. *T:* 77790.

**RAMSAY, Henry Thomas,** CBE 1960; Director, Safety in Mines Research Establishment, Ministry of Technology (formerly Ministry of Power), Sheffield, 1954-70, retired; *b* 7 Dec. 1907; *s* of Henry Thomas and Florence Emily Ramsay, Gravesend, Kent; *m* 1953, Dora Gwenllian Burgoyne Davies; one *s* one *d*. *Educ:* Gravesend Junior Techn. Sch.; thereafter by evening study. Jun. Asst in laboratories at Henleys Telegraph Works, Gravesend, 1923-28; Student Asst at Research Labs of GEC, 1928-32; apptd to Leading Scientific Staff, 1932; Sen. Prin. Scientific Officer, RAE, 1948-54. Dep. Scientific Officer, Safety in Mines Research Estabt (for 6 weeks until Dir), 1954. *Publications:* contrib. to: trans of Instn of Electrical Engrs; Jl of Inst. of Mining Engrs; other technical jls. *Recreations:* riding, reading. *Address:* 1 Hilltop Road, Dronfield, Derbyshire. *T:* Dronfield 3011.

**RAMSAY, Comdr Hugh Malcolm,** CBE 1941; Royal Australian Navy (retired); *b* 28 Feb. 1884; *s* of late James and late Mary Margaret Ramsay, Melbourne, Australia; *m* 1911, Gertrude Emily, *d* of late Godfrey Leslie, Melbourne; two *s* two *d*. War of 1914-18, served in HMA ships Pioneer and Brisbane, in Australian, East African, and Mediterranean waters. Held various senior administrative posts in Department of Navy, Melbourne, 1920-48. *Address:* Rycroft Hall, 109 Park St, South Yarra, Melbourne, Australia. *T:* BM 1085. *Club:* Naval and Military (Melbourne).

**RAMSAY, J(ames) Arthur,** MBE 1945; FRS 1955; Fellow of Queens' College, Cambridge, since 1934; Professor of Comparative Physiology, University of Cambridge, since

1969 (Reader, 1959); *b* 6 Sept. 1909; *s* of late David Ramsay and Isabella Rae Ramsay (*née* Garvie), Maybole, Ayrshire; *m* 1939, Helen Amelie, *d* of late Oscar Dickson, Stockholm; one *s* one *d*. *Educ:* Fettes College; Gonville and Caius College, Cambridge. University Demonstrator and Fellow of Queens', 1934. Major RA Coast and Anti-Aircraft Defence Experimental Establishment, 1939-45. Joint Editor, Journal of Experimental Biology, 1952-. *Publications:* Physiological Approach to the Lower Animals, 1952; The Experimental Basis of Modern Biology, 1965. Papers in Jl of Experimental Biology. *Recreations:* mountaineering, ski-ing. *Address:* Orchard, Selwyn Gardens, Cambridge. *T:* Cambridge 56135.

**RAMSAY, Sir Neis Alexander,** 12th Bt of Bamff, *cr* 1666; Farmer since 1953; Landowner and Farmer since 1959; *b* 4 Oct. 1909; *s* of Sir James Douglas Ramsay, 11th Bt, MVO, TD, JP; *S* father 1959; *m* 1st, 1940, Edith Alix Ross Hayes (marriage dissolved, 1950), *d* of C. F. Hayes, Linksfield, Johannesburg; 2nd, 1952, Rachel Leanore Beatrice Drummond, *d* of late Colonel C. B. Urmstom, Glenmorven; no *c*. *Educ:* Winchester; Trinity College, Cambridge. 2nd Lt Gordon Highlanders, 1933-34; British South African Police, 1934-35; Lieutenant, South African Engineer Corps, 1939-45; Mining in South Africa, 1936-50; Returned to UK, 1950. *Recreations:* shooting and golf. *Heir: kinsman* George William Neil Ramsay, *b* 30 May 1907. *Address:* Bamff, Alyth, Perthshire. *T:* Alyth 382. *Clubs:* New (Edinburgh); Royal Perth Golfing Society (Perth).

**RAMSAY, Norman James Gemmill;** Puisne Judge of High Court for Zambia, 1964-68, retired; *b* 26 Aug. 1916; *s* of late James Ramsay and late Mrs Christina Emma Ramsay; *m* 1952, Rachael Mary Berkeley Cox, *d* of Sir Herbert Charles Fahie Cox, *qv*; two *s*. *Educ:* Merchiston Castle Sch.; Edinburgh Univ. (MA, LLB). Writer to the Signet, 1939; Advocate, Scotland, 1956. War Service, RN, 1940-46; Lt (S), RNVR. Colonial Legal Service, Northern Rhodesia: Administrator-General, 1947; Resident Magistrate, 1956; Sen. Resident Magistrate, 1958; Puisne Judge of High Court, 1964. Mem., Victoria Falls Trust, 1950-58. *Recreations:* rowing, sailing, squash racquets. *Address:* D'Arcy House, by Dalkeith, Midlothian.

**RAMSAY, The Lady Patricia, (Victoria Patricia Helena Elizabeth),** CI, 1911; VA 1902; RWS, RWA, NEAC; *b* 17 March 1886; *y d* of TRH The Duke and Duchess of Connaught and Strathearn; *m* 1919, Admiral The Hon. Sir Alexander Ramsay, *qv*; one *s*. On her marriage she renounced, by Royal permission, the style and title of "HRH" and "Princess", and adopted that of "Lady", with precedence before Marchionesses of England. Colonel-in-Chief, Princess Patricia's Canadian Light Infantry. DGStJ. *Address:* Ribsden Holt, Windlesham, Surrey. *T:* Bagshot 2157.

**RAMSAY, Robert Anstruther,** MA, MChir, MB Cantab; FRCS; Consulting Surgeon to Metropolitan Hospital and to Belgrave Hospital for Children; *b* Montreal, Canada, 18 Feb. 1887; *s* of Robert Anstruther Ramsay and Catherine Hamilton Duff; *m* 1914, Marguerite Renée de Miniac; two *s* one *d*. *Educ:* Caius College, Cambridge; St Bartholomew's Hospital. *Publications:* Various papers on Surgical Subjects. *Address:* 9 Place des Ternes, Paris 17. *T:* Carnot 8340; c/o Bank of Montreal, 9 Waterloo Place, SW1. *Club:* United University.

**RAMSAY, Thomas Meek,** CMG 1965; Chairman: The Kiwi International Company Ltd, Melbourne, since 1967; The Kiwi Polish Co. Pty Ltd, Melbourne, since 1966 (Managing Director, since 1956); *b* Essendon, Victoria, 24 Nov. 1907; *s* of late William Ramsay, Scotland; *m* 1941, Catherine Anne, *d* of John William Richardson, Adelaide, SA; four *s* one *d*. *Educ:* Malvern Grammar; Scotch Coll.; Melbourne Univ. (BSc). CMF: AIF, 1940-41 (Lt); Asst Controller, Min. of Munitions, 1941-45. Chairman: The Victoria Portland Cement Co. Pty Ltd; Norwich Union Life Insurance Soc. (Aust. Bd); Industrial Design Council of Australia. Director: Australian Consolidated Industries Ltd Group; Associated Portland Cement Manufacturers (Aust.) Ltd Group; Collie (Aust.) Ltd Group; Overseas Corp. (Aust.) Ltd Group; Rocla Industries Ltd; First National City Trust Co. (Bahamas) Ltd. President: Associated Chambers of Manufactures of Australia, 1962-63 (now Mem. Exec.); Victorian Chamber of Manufrs, 1962-64 (now Mem. Exec. and Coun.); Member: Manufacturing Industries Adv. Coun.; Consumers Protection Council (Vic); Netherlands Australia Trade and industrial Develt Council; Victoria Promotion Cttee; Selection Cttee, Industrial Sir Winston Churchill Fellowships. FRHistS of Queensland, 1964; FRHistS of Victoria, 1965; FAIM; Fellow: Inst. of Directors; Scottish Antiquarian Soc. *Recreations:* gardening, golf, Australian historical research. *Address:* 23 Airlie Street, South Yarra, Victoria 3141, Australia. *T:* 26 1751. *Clubs:* Oriental (London); Athenæum, Australian (Melbourne).

**RAMSAY-FAIRFAX-LUCY, Major Sir B. F. C.;** *see* Fairfax-Lucy.

**RAMSAY RAE, Air Vice-Marshal Ronald Arthur,** CB 1960; OBE 1947; National Playing Fields Association, since 1963; *b* 9 Oct. 1910; *s* of late George Ramsay Rae, Lindfield, NSW, and late Alice Ramsay Rae (*née* Haselden); *m* 1939, Rosemary Gough Howell, *d* of late Charles Gough Howell, KC, Attorney General, Singapore; one *s* one *d*. *Educ:* Sydney, New South Wales, Australia. Served Australian Citizen Force and then as Cadet, RAAF, at Point Cook, 1930-31; transf. to RAF, 1932; flying duties in UK and Middle East with Nos 33 and 142 Sqdns until 1936; Advanced Armament Course; Armament officer in Far East, 1938-42; then Comdr RAF Tengah, Singapore; POW, 1943-45; Grp Capt. in comd Central Gunnery Sch., Leconfield, Yorks, 1946; despatches, 1946. RAF Staff Coll., Andover, 1948; Dep. Dir Organisation (Estab.), Middle East; in comd RAF North Luffenham and then RAF Oakington (206 Advanced Flying Sch.); Commandant, Aircraft and Armament Exptl Estab., Boscombe Down, 1955-57; Dep. Air Sec., Air Min., 1957-59; Air Officer Commanding No 224 Group, Royal Air Force, 1959-62, retd. AFRAeS 1956. *Recreations:* cricket, golf, tennis, winter sports (Cresta Run and ski-ing). *Address:* Commonwealth Bank of Australia, Strand, WC2; Little Wakestone, Bedham, Fittleworth, W Sussex. *Club:* Royal Air Force.

**RAMSBOTHAM,** family name of **Viscount Soulbury.**

**RAMSBOTHAM, Rt. Rev. John Alexander;** Assistant Bishop of Newcastle, since 1968; *b* 25 Feb. 1906; *s* of late Rev. Alexander Ramsbotham and of late Margaret Emily Ramsbotham; *m* 1933, Eirian Morgan Owen; three *s* two *d*. *Educ:* Haileybury College; Corpus Christi College, Cambridge; Wells

Theological College. Travelling secretary, 1929-30, Missionary secretary, 1930-33, Student Christian Movement; Chaplain, 1933-34. Vice-Principal, 1934-36, Wells Theol. Coll.; Priest-Vicar Wells Cathedral, 1933-36; Warden, College of the Ascension, Selly Oak, 1936-40; Rector of Ordsall, Notts, 1941-42; Vicar of St George's, Jesmond, Newcastle on Tyne, 1942-50; Bishop Suffragan of Jarrow, 1950-58, also Archdeacon of Auckland and Canon of Durham; Bishop of Wakefield, 1958-67. *Publication:* Belief in Christ and the Christian Community, 1949. *Recreation:* music. *Address:* Deneholme, Allendale Road, Hexham, Northumberland. *T:* Hexham 2607. *Club:* Royal Commonwealth Society.

**RAMSBOTHAM, Hon. Peter Edward,** CMG 1964; High Commissioner for the UK in Nicosia, since 1969; *b* 8 Oct. 1919; *yr s* of 1st Viscount Soulbury, *qv*; *m* 1941, Frances Blomfield; two *s* one *d*. *Educ:* Eton College; Magdalen College, Oxford. HM Forces, 1943-46 (Croix de Guerre, 1945). Control Office for Germany and Austria from 1947; Regional Political Officer in Hamburg; entered Foreign Office, Oct. 1948; Political Division of Allied Control Commission, Berlin, Nov. 1948; transferred to Foreign Office, 1950; 1st Secretary, 1950; transferred to UK delegation, New York, 1953; Foreign Office, 1957; Counsellor, 1961; Head of Chancery, British Embassy, Paris, 1963-67; Foreign Office, 1967-69. *Address:* 34 Edwardes Square, W8. *T:* 01-603 9928.

**RAMSBOTTOM, John,** OBE 1919; MA; *b* Manchester, 25 Oct. 1885; *m* 1917, Beatrice (*d* 1957), *d* of Henry Westwood Broom; one *d*. *Educ:* Emmanuel Coll., Cambridge; Manchester University. Asst, Brit. Mus. (Nat. Hist.), 1910, Dep. Keeper, 1928-30, Keeper of Botany, 1930-50. Protozoologist (civilian) HM Salonika Forces, 1917-19, Capt. attached RAMC, 1918 (despatches thrice; MBE, 1918, OBE 1919). Hon FRHS, 1912; Veitch Memorial Medal, 1944, VMH 1950; Dean Hole Medal (Nat. Rose Soc.), 1950. Gen. Sec. Brit. Mycological Soc., 1923-45, Pres. 1924, 1946; Botanical Sec., Linnean Soc., 1923-38, Pres. 1938-41; Linnean Gold Medal, 1965. President: Sect. K, Brit. Assoc., 1936, Sect. X, 1947; Mycology and Bacteriology, Internat. Botanical Congress, 1950, Protection of Nature, 1954; Medical Mycology, Internat. Congress of Microbiology, 1950; S London Botanical Inst., 1938-68; Soc. Bibliography Nat. Hist., 1942-; British Soc. for Mycopathology, 1964-67; Member: Lawes Agricultural Trust Cttee, 1938-; Internat. Office for Protection of Nature, 1948. Hon. Mem. of various societies and academies. Holds hon. doctorates: Coimbra, 1938; Uppsala, 1957. Grande Médaille, Geoffrey-St Hilaire, 1949. *Publications:* Handbook of the Larger British Fungi, 1923 (often repr.); Enemies of the Rose, 1925 (1956); A Book of Roses, 1939; Fungi: An Introduction to Mycology, 1929; Edible Fungi, 1943 (1948); Poisonous Fungi, 1945; Mushrooms and Toadstools, 1953. *Address:* 49 Nassau Road, Barnes, SW13; British Museum (Nat. Hist.), Cromwell Road, SW7.

**RAMSDEN, Caryl Oliver Imbert,** CMG 1965; CVO 1966; *b* 4 April 1915; *s* of late Lt-Col J. V. Ramsden; *m* 1945, Anne, *d* of Sir Charles Wickham, *qv*; one *s*. *Educ:* Eton; New Coll., Oxford. Served in Royal Regiment of Artillery, 1937-49; Assistant Military Attaché, Bucharest, 1947-49. Entered HM Foreign Service, 1949, retired 1967; Private Secretary to Prime Minister, 1957; Consul-General, Hanover, 1957-59; Counsellor, Rio de Janeiro, 1959; acted as Chargé d'Affaires, 1960; Counsellor, Brussels 1962. Commander of the Star of Ethiopia, 1954; Commander, Order of Leopold, 1966. *Recreation:* golf. *Address:* The Old Rectory, Burton Agnes, near Driffield, E Yorks. *Clubs:* Cavalry; Ganton Golf.

**RAMSDEN, Sir Geoffrey Charles Frescheville,** Kt 1948; CIE 1942; *b* 21 April 1893; *s* of Colonel H. F. S. Ramsden, CBE, and Hon. Edwyna Fiennes; *m* 1930, Margaret Lovell, *d* of late Rev. J. Robinson; no *c*. *Educ:* Haileybury College; Sidney Sussex Coll., Cambridge (MA). Served in the Army, 1914-19; Capt. 1st Bn Royal Sussex Regt, NW Frontier (India) 1915-19; joined ICS 1920; Secretary Indian Tariff Board, 1923-25; Deputy Commissioner of Jubbulpore, 1926 and 1931-34, and of various other Districts; Commissioner, Jubbulpore Div., 1936 and 1941-44, and Chhatisgarh Div., 1937-40; Development Adviser to Governor, 1945; Financial Comr CP and Berar, 1941-45 and 1946-47; retd, 1948. *Recreations:* travel, photography, tennis and fishing. *Address:* Fynescourt, Grayshott, Hindhead, Surrey. *T:* Hindhead 449. *Club:* Royal Over-Seas League.

**RAMSDEN, Sir Geoffrey William P.,** Bt; *see* Pennington-Ramsden.

**RAMSDEN, Prof. Herbert,** MA, Dr en Filosofia y Letras; Professor of Spanish Language and Literature, University of Manchester, since 1961; *b* 20 April 1927; *s* of Herbert and Ann Ramsden; *m* 1953, Joyce Robina Hall, SRN, ONC, CMB; three *s* (incl. twin *s*) twin *d*. *Educ:* Sale Grammar Sch.; Univs of Manchester, Strasbourg, Madrid and Sorbonne. National Service, Inf. and Intell. Corps, 1949-51 (commnd). Travel, study and research abroad (Kemsley Travelling Fellow, etc), 1951-54; Univ. of Manchester: Asst Lectr in Spanish, 1954-57; Lectr in Spanish, 1957-61; Chm. of MA Cttee, 1964-65; Pres., Philological Club, 1966-68. *Publications:* An Essential Course in Modern Spanish, 1959; Weak-Pronoun Position in the Early Romance Languages, 1963; (ed. with critical study) Azorín, La ruta de Don Quijote, 1966; Angel Ganivet's Idearium español: A Critical Study, 1967; articles in Bulletin of Hispanic Studies, Modern Language Review, Modern Languages, etc. *Recreations:* family, hill-walking, foreign travel. *Address:* Grove House, Grove Lane, Cheadle Hulme, Cheshire. *T:* 061-439 4306.

**RAMSDEN, Rt. Hon. James Edward,** PC 1963; MP (C) Harrogate Div. of W Riding of Yorkshire since March 1954; *b* 1 Nov. 1923; *s* of Capt. Edward Ramsden, MC, and Mrs Ramsden, OBE, Breckamore Hall, Ripon; *m* 1949, Juliet Barbara Anne, *y d* of Col Sir Charles Ponsonby, Bt, *qv*; three *s* two *d*. *Educ:* Eton; Trinity College, Oxford (MA). Commissioned 1942; served North-West Europe with Rifle Brigade, 1944-45. Parliamentary Private Secretary to Home Secretary, November 1959-October 1960; Under-Sec. and Financial Sec., War Office, Oct. 1960-Oct. 1963; Sec. of State for War, 1963-64; Minister of Defence for the Army, April-Oct. 1964. Director, UK Board, Colonial Mutual Life Assurance Society, 1966-. *Address:* Old Sleningford Hall, nr Ripon, Yorks. *T:* North Stainley 229. *Clubs:* Carlton, Brooks's, MCC.

**RAMSEY, Sir Alfred (Ernest),** Kt 1967; Manager, Football Association World Cup Team, since 1963; *b* Dagenham, 1920; *m* 1951, Victoria Phyllis Answorth, *d* of William Welch. *Educ:* Becontree Heath School. Started playing for Southampton and was an International with them; transferred to

Tottenham Hotspur, 1949; with Spurs (right back), 1949-51; they won the 2nd and 1st Division titles in successive seasons. Manager of Ipswich Town Football Club, which rose from 3rd Division to Championship of the League, 1955-63. Played 31 times for England. *Address:* c/o Football Association, 22 Lancaster Gate, W2.

**RAMSEY, Most Rev. and Rt. Hon. Arthur Michael;** *see* Canterbury, Archbishop of.

**RAMSEY, Rt. Rev. Ian Thomas;** *see* Durham, Bishop of.

**RAMSEY, Rt. Rev. K. V. R.;** *see* Hulme, Suffragan Bishop of.

**RAMSEY, Leonard Gerald Gwynne,** Editor of The Connoisseur since 1951; *b* 17 March 1913; *s* of late L. B. Ramsey, London Stock Exchange; *m* 1941, Dorothy Elizabeth, *y d* of late W. J. McMillan, Belfast; one *s* one *d. Educ:* Radley College. Commissioned Oxfordshire and Buckinghamshire Light Infantry (T), 1938; invalided out of Army, 1944; on General Staff, War Office, 1941-44, and other staff appointments. Public Relations Officer, The National Trust, 1946-49; Press Officer at Board of Trade and Colonial Office, 1950-51. Member of several Committees associated with ecclesiastical art and charitable matters. FSA 1949. *Publications:* (ed) The Connoisseur Encyclopædia of Antiques, 5 vols, 1954-60; (ed. with Ralph Edwards) The Connoisseur Period Guides, 6 vols, 1956-59; Montague Dawson, marine artist, a biography, 1967; (ed with Helen Comstock) The Connoisseur's Guide to Antique Furniture, 1969. *Recreations:* historic buildings, works of art, work. *Address:* 231 Grove End Gardens, NW8; Church Cottage, Cockfield, Bury St Edmunds, Suffolk. *Club:* East India and Sports.

**RAMSEY, Prof. Norman Foster, Jun.;** Higgins Professor of Physics, Harvard University, since 1947; Chairman Harvard Nuclear Physics Committee, 1948-60; *b* 27 Aug. 1915; *s* of Brig.-Gen. and Mrs Norman F. Ramsey; *m* 1940, Elinor Stedman Jameson; four *d. Educ:* Columbia Univ.; Cambridge Univ. (England). Carnegie Fellow, Carnegie Instn of Washington, 1939-40; Assoc., Univ. of Ill., 1940-42; Asst Prof., Columbia Univ., 1942-45; Research Assoc., MIT Radiation Laboratory, 1940-43; Cons. to Nat. Defense Research Cttee, 1940-45; Expert Consultant to Sec. of War, 1942-45; Grp Leader and Assoc. Div. Head, Los Alamos Lab. of Atomic Energy Project, 1943-45; Chief Scientist of Atomic Energy Lab. at Tinian, 1945; Assoc. Prof., Columbia Univ., 1945-47; Head of Physics Dept, Brookhaven Nat. Lab., 1946-47; Assoc. Prof., Harvard Univ., 1947-50; John Simon Guggenheim Fell., Oxford Univ., 1953-54. Dir Harvard Nuclear Lab., 1948-50, 1952; Science Adviser, NATO 1958-59; Fell. Amer. Phys. Soc. and Amer. Acad. of Arts and Sciences; Nat. Acad. of Sciences; Amer. Philos. Soc.; Sigma Xi; Phi Beta Kappa. Bd of Directors, Varian Associates, 1964-66; Bd of Trustees: Associated Univs; Brookhaven Nat. Lab., 1952-55; Carnegie Endowment for Internat. Peace; Univ. Research Assoc. (Pres., 1966-); Air Force Sci. Adv. Bd, 1948-54; Dept of Defense Panel on Atomic Energy, 1953-59; Bd of Editors of Review of Modern Physics, 1953-56; Chm. Exec. Cttee for Camb. Electron Accelerator, 1956-63; Coun. Amer. Phys. Soc., 1956-60. Gen. Adv. Cttee, Atomic Energy Commn, 1960-. Chm., High Energy Accelerator Panel of President's Sci. Adv. Cttee and AEC, 1963. Presidential Certificate of Merit, 1947; E. O. Lawrence Award, 1960. Hon. MA Harvard, 1947; Hon. ScD Cambridge, 1953; Hon. DSc: Case Western Reserve, 1968; Middlebury Coll., 1969. *Publications:* Experimental Nuclear Physics, 1952; Nuclear Moments, 1953; Molecular Beams, 1956; Quick Calculus, 1965; and numerous articles in Physical Review and other scientific jls. *Recreations:* tennis, ski-ing, walking, sailing, etc. *Address:* 55 Scott Road, Belmont, Mass 02178, USA. *T:* Ivanhoe 4.35.53, Belmont. *Club:* Authors' (London).

**RAMSEY, Robert John;** Director of Labour Relations, Ford Motor Company Ltd, since 1969; *b* 16 Aug. 1921; *m* 1949, Arlette Ikor; one *s* one *d. Educ:* Royal Liberty Sch., Romford. Joined Ford Motor Co. Ltd, as student, 1937. Served War of 1939-45: RAF Air Crew, Flt-Lt, 1942-46; POW, 1944-45. Rejoined Ford Motor Co. Ltd, 1946; Industrial Relations Manager, 1958. *Recreations:* reading, theatre, hill walking, boating. *Address:* Le Revard, 50 Warren Road, Leigh-on-Sea, Essex. *T:* Southend 557289.

**RANASINHA, Sir Arthur (Godwin),** Kt 1954; CMG 1949; CBE 1948; diplomat and civil servant, Ceylon; *b* 24 June 1898; *s* of W. P. Ranasinha, Proctor and Notary, Oriental Scholar, and Mary Ann (*née* de Alwis); *m* 1921, Annette Hilda (*d* 1968), *d* of Mudalyar de Alwis, Negombo, Ceylon; two *d* (one *s* decd). *Educ:* S Thomas' College, Colombo; Trinity Hall, Cambridge. Ceylon University, Scholar, 1917; ICS, 1920. BA (Hons in History) London, 1920. Entered Ceylon Civil Service, 1921; Police Magistrate: Point Pedro, 1923; Balapitiya, 1923; Jaffna, 1926. District Judge: Avisawella, 1928; Badulla, 1930; Asst Govt Agent, Colombo, 1932; Sec. to Minister for Agriculture and Lands, 1933; Public Trustee, 1936; Custodian of Enemy Property, 1939; Superintendent of Census, 1944; Sec. to Leader of State Council on political mission to London, 1945; Commissioner of Lands, 1946; Permanent Secretary, Min. of Agriculture and Lands, 1947-50; Secretary to the Cabinet and Deputy Secretary, Treasury, 1950-51; Permanent Secretary, Ministry of Finance, Secretary to Treasury and Secretary to Cabinet, 1951-54; Governor, Central Bank of Ceylon, 1954-59; Ambassador for Ceylon in Italy and Greece, 1959-61; Chairman: People's Bank Commn, 1965-66; Taxation Commn, 1966-67; Tea Commn, 1967-68. Knight Grand Cross, Order of Merit of the Italian Republic, 1961. *Recreations:* chess, racing, tennis, etc. *Address:* Rangiri, Lady McCallum's Drive, Kandy, Ceylon.

**RANCE, Maj.-Gen. Sir Hubert (Elvin),** GCMG 1948; GBE 1946 (OBE 1940); CB 1946; Colonel Commandant Royal Corps of Signals, 1953-62; *b* 17 July 1898; *s* of Frederick Hubert Rance; *m* 1927, Mary Noël Guy; one *s* one *d. Educ:* Wimbledon College; RMC, Sandhurst. Worc. Regiment, 1916-26. 4th Bn Worcs Regiment, BEF, France, Oct. 1916-April 1917; R Signals, 1926-44; Adjt 2 Div. Signals, 1927-30; GSO3 War Office (Military Training), 1936-38; Instructor Staff College, Camberley, 1938-39; Asst Dir BEF and GSO1, BEF, France, 1939-40; OC 4 Div. Signals, BEF, France, April-June 1940, evacuated Dunkirk, continued in command till Oct. 1940 (despatches, OBE); GSO1 War Office (Military Training), 1940-41; Deputy Director Military Training (Brig.), 1941-42; Director of Technical Training WO (Brig.), 1942-43; Brig. General Staff, Western Command, 1943-45; Director of Civil Affairs, Burma (Maj.-Gen.), 1945-46 (CB); Deputy Commander South-Western District, Taunton, 1946; Governor of Burma, 1946-48; retired pay, 1947. Chairman Standing Closer Assoc. Cttee, British West

Indies, 1948-50; British co-Chairman Caribbean Commission, 1948-50; Governor and C-in-C of Trinidad and Tobago, 1950-55. *Recreations:* cricket, tennis, and shooting. *Address:* The Old Farm, Frensham, Surrey. *T:* Frensham 2164. *Club:* Army and Navy.

**RANCHHODLAL, Sir Chinubhai Madhowlal,** 2nd Bt, *cr* 1913; *b* 18 April 1906; *s* of 1st Bt and Sulochana, *d* of Chunilal Khushalrai; *S* father, 1916; *m* 1924, Tanumati, *d* of Jhaverilal Bulakhiram Mehta of Ahmedabad. Father was first member of Hindu community to receive a baronetcy. *Heir: s* Udayan, *b* 25 July, 1929. *Address:* Shantikunj, PO, Shahibag, Ahmedabad, Bombay, India. *T:* 2061. *TA:* Shantikunj. *Club:* Willingdon (Bombay).

**RANDALL, Sir Alec Walter George,** KCMG, *cr* 1949 (CMG 1944); OBE 1920; Delegate to International Conference on Atomic Energy Agency, 1956, and International Conference on Law of the Sea, 1958; *b* 27 July 1892; *s* of George and Clara Randall; *m* 1915, Dr Amy Jones (*d* 1966); one *s* three *d. Educ:* Queen Elizabeth's Grammar Sch., Barnet; University Coll., London. Entered Foreign Office, 1920; 2nd Sec. HM Legation to Holy See, 1925-30; 1st Secretary HM Legation, Bucharest, 1930-33; served in Foreign Office, 1933-35; 1st Secretary HM Legation, Copenhagen, 1935-38; Counsellor in Foreign Office, 1938-45; Ambassador to Denmark, 1947-52 (Minister, 1945-47); retired from Foreign Service, 1953. Alternate Delegate to UN Assembly and Economic and Social Council, New York and Geneva, 1953-57. Fellow of UCL, 1948. *Publications:* Vatican Assignment, 1956; Discovering Rome, 1960; The Pope, the Jews and the Nazis, 1963. *Address:* 9 Master Close, Oxted, Surrey. *T:* Oxted 2276. *Club:* Reform.

**RANDALL, Rev. Edmund Laurence;** Warden, St Barnabas' Theological College, since 1964; *b* 2 June 1920; *s* of Robert Leonard Randall and Grace Annie Randall (*née* Young); unmarried. *Educ:* Dulwich College; Corpus Christi College, Cambridge. BA 1941. MA 1947. Served War, 1940-45, with Royal Artillery (AA). Corpus Christi Coll., 1938-40 and 1945-47. Wells Theological College, 1947-49. Deacon, 1949; Priest, 1950. Assistant Curate at St Luke's, Bournemouth, 1949-52; Fellow of Selwyn College, Cambridge, 1952-57; Chaplain, 1953-57; Residentiary Canon of Ely and Principal of Ely Theological Coll., 1957-59; Chaplain, St Francis Theological Coll., Brisbane, 1960-64. *Recreations:* travel, motoring. *Address:* St Barnabas' Theological College, Belair, South Australia 5052, Australia. *Club:* Naval, Military and Air Force, South Australia.

**RANDALL, Harry Enos;** *b* 1899; *s* of Henry Randall, Penge; *m* 1925, Rose Nellie, *d* of Joseph Nicholson, Isle of Man; one *s* two *d.* Served on executive of Workers' Educational Association. Joined Post Office, 1914. Organising Secretary of Union of Post Office Workers, 1940-55. MP (Lab) Clitheroe Division of Lancashire, 1945-50, Gateshead West, Dec. 1955-1970; Asst Govt Whip (unpaid), 2-23 Feb. 1950; British Delegate to Council of Europe and Western European Union, 1958-60; UK Representative, Exec. Cttee, UN High Commission Programme for Refugees, 1965-. *Address:* Hillside, Arundel Road, Newhaven, Sussex. *T:* Newhaven 4542; 16 Verlands Close, Niton, near Ventnor, Isle of Wight. *T:* Niton 570.

**RANDALL, Sir John (Turton),** Kt 1962; FRS 1946; FInstP; DSc (Manchester); Professor of Biophysics in the University of London (King's College), 1961-70, now Emeritus Professor; Honorary Professor in the University of Edinburgh; Fellow of King's College, London, since 1960; *b* 23 March 1905; *o s* of late Sidney and Hannah Cawley Randall; *m* 1928, Doris Duckworth; one *s. Educ:* University of Manchester (Graduate Research Scholar and Prizeman, 1925; MSc 1926, DSc 1938). Research physicist, Research Laboratories of General Electric Company Ltd, 1926-37; Warren Research Fellow of Royal Society, 1937-44; Hon. Member of the staff, University of Birmingham, 1940-43; Research in University of Birmingham for Admiralty, 1939-43, on cavity magnetron; Temporary Lecturer in Cavendish Laboratory, Cambridge, 1943-44; Professor of Natural Philosophy, United College of St Salvator and St Leonard, University of St Andrews, 1944-46; Wheatstone Prof. of Physics in University of London (King's College), 1946-61; Dir, MRC Biophysics Research Unit, 1947-70; Chm., Sch. of Biological Sciences, King's Coll., Univ. of London, 1963-69. Awarded (with H. A. H. Boot) Thomas Gray Memorial Prize of Royal Society of Arts (1943) for discovery of the cavity magnetron. Duddell Medallist, Physical Society of London, 1945; Hughes Medallist, Royal Society, 1946; John Price Wetherill Medal of Franklin Inst. of State of Pennsylvania, 1958. Lectr Rockefeller Inst. for Med. Research, New York, 1956-57; Gregynog Lectr, Univ. Coll. of Wales, Aberystwyth, 1958; Visiting Prof. of Biophysics, Yale University, 1960. John Scott Award, City of Philadelphia, 1959. *Publications:* The Diffraction of X-rays by Amorphous Solids, Liquids and Gases, 1934; (Editor) The Nature and Structure of Collagen, 1953; (Jt Editor) Progress in Biophysics, 1950-55; papers in various scientific journals on structure in glasses and liquids, the luminescence of solids, the cavity magnetron; and, since 1946, the biophysics of connective tissues, problems of fine structure and the morphogenesis of cellular organelles. *Address:* Department of Zoology, University of Edinburgh, West Mains Road, Edinburgh EH9 3JT; 16 Kevoch Road, Lasswade, Midlothian. *Club:* Athenæum.

**RANDALL, John William,** CBE 1963; Hon. President: The Dickinson Robinson Group Ltd, since 1968 (Chairman, John Dickinson & Co. Ltd, 1955-68); The Dickinson Robinson Group Africa (Pty) Ltd; *b* 20 May 1891; *s* of late John T. and late Ellen A. Randall; *m* 1921, Lillian Anne Reeves; no *c. Educ:* Hemel Hempstead Church of England School. John Dickinson & Co. Ltd: Secretary, 1928; Financial Director, 1936; Managing Director, 1945. *Recreation:* farming. *Address:* Hawridge Court, Chesham, Bucks. *T:* Cholesbury 240.

**RANDALL, Michael Bennett;** Managing Editor, (News), The Sunday Times, since 1967; *b* 12 Aug. 1919. *Educ:* St Peter's, Seaford; Canford. Asst Editor, Sunday Chronicle, 1952-53; Editor, Sunday Graphic, 1953; Asst Editor, Daily Mirror, 1953-56; Asst Editor, News Chronicle, 1956-57; Asst Editor, Daily Mail, 1957-61; Deputy Editor, Daily Mail, 1961-63; Editor, Daily Mail, 1963-66. *Address:* 6 Spencer House, Vale of Health, Hampstead, NW3. *T:* 01-435 9011.

**RANDALL, Sir Richard (John),** Kt 1964; BEcon; ACIS; Secretary to the Treasury, Commonwealth of Australia; *b* 13 Oct. 1906; *s* of G. Randall, Birkdale, Queensland; *m* 1945, Nora Barry, *d* of T. J. Clyne; two *s* one *d. Educ:* Wynnum High School; University of Sydney (BEcon, 1st cl. hons). Carnegie Research Scholar, Sydney University, 1937; Research Office, Premier's Office, Sydney, 1937-39;

Commonwealth Treasury, 1940. Served with AIF, 1941-45. *Recreations:* golf, fishing. *Address:* 5 Throsby Crescent, Narrabundah, Canberra, ACT 2604, Australia. *Club:* Royal Canberra Golf.

**RANDALL, Terence George,** CBE 1959 (OBE 1946); Deputy Clerk of the LCC, 1947-65, Children's Officer, 1962-65, retired; *b* 5 May 1904; *s* of George Arthur and Kate Amelia Randall; *m* 1928, Ivy Diana Allen; two *s. Educ:* St Bonaventure's Grammar School, Forest Gate; City of London School; Birkbeck College, London University. BA 1927. Entered clerical staff of London County Council, 1921; promoted to administrative grade, 1926. Was concerned with all sides of the Council's work, especially with housing, town planning, civil defence, staff management, the coordination of work involving several departments, and latterly child care. *Recreations:* reading, walking, and gardening. *Address:* Green End, Willow Close, Hutton, Essex. *T:* Brentwood 1242.

**RANDALL LANE, Henry Jerrold;** *see* Lane, H. J. R.

**RANDELL, John Bulmer;** Physician for Psychological Medicine, Charing Cross Hospital, WC2, since 1949; *b* 25 Aug. 1918; 2nd *s* of Percy G. Randell and Katie E. Bulmer; *m* 1944, Margaret Davies; one *d. Educ:* The College, Penarth; Welsh Nat. School of Medicine. BSc (Wales) 1938; MB, BCh (Wales) 1941; MD 1960. MO, Cefn Coed Hosp., 1941; MO, Sully Hosp., 1941-42; Temp. Surg. Lieut, RNVR, 1942-46; DPM 1945. First Asst MO, York Clinic, Guy's Hosp., 1946-48; MRCP 1947; FRCP 1964; Psychotherapist, St George's Hosp., 1948-51; Asst Psychiatrist, St Thomas' Hosp., 1949-59. *Recreations:* golf and photography. *Address:* 118 Harley Street, W1. *T:* 01-486 2494. *Clubs:* Savile, Royal Automobile, Players.

**RANDLE, Herbert Niel,** CIE 1947; FBA 1950; MA 1909; DPhil 1926; *b* 1880; *o s* of Nathaniel Randle; *m* 1915, Edith Joan (*d* 1967), *o d* of William Chaffey Whitby; (one *s,* VC posthumous 1944) two *d. Educ:* Dulwich Coll.; Hertford Coll., Oxford (Scholar). 1st Class Classical Mods, 1901; 1st Class Lit Hum 1903; Indian Educational Service, 1905-27; Prof. of Philosophy, University of Allahabad, 1926; Asst Librarian, India Office, 1927; Librarian, India Office, 1933-45; re-employed until 1949. *Publications:* Sense-data and Sensible Appearances (Mind, 1922); Fragments from Dinnāga (Royal Asiatic Society), 1926; Indian Logic in the Early Schools, 1930; articles in Orientalist publications. *Address:* 1 Denbigh Gardens, Richmond, Surrey. *T:* 01-940 3592.

**RANDOLPH, Cyril George;** *b* 26 June 1899; *s* of late Felton Randolph; *m* 1927, Betty Dixey; one *d. Educ:* Christ's Hospital. A Man. Dir, Glyn, Mills & Co., 1941-64; Chairman: Sun Life Assurance Society, 1953- (Director, 1943-); General Funds Investment Trust, 1965- (Director, 1964-); Household & General Insurance Co. Ltd, 1965-. Almoner, Christ's Hospital. *Recreation:* golf. *Address:* 3 Belgrave Place, SW1. *T:* 01-235 2626. *Clubs:* Brooks's; New Zealand Golf (West Byfleet); Aldeburgh.
*See also Ven. T. B. Randolph.*

**RANDOLPH, John Hugh Edward;** Stipendiary Magistrate of Leeds since 1965; *b* 14 Oct. 1913; *s* of late Charles Edward Randolph and Phyllis Randolph; *m* 1959, Anna Marjorie (*née* Thomson). *Educ:* Bradford Gram. Sch.; Leeds University. Called to Bar, Middle Temple, 1946; practised on NE Circuit until 1965. Deputy Chairman: E Riding QS, 1958-63; W Riding QS, 1963-. *Recreation:* golf. *Address:* 28 Arthurs Avenue, Harrogate, Yorks. *T:* 67577. *Club:* Leeds (Leeds).

**RANDOLPH, Peter,** CBE 1966; Chairman, Wilkinson Sword Ltd, since 1966; *b* 21 April 1920; *s* of Harry Beckham Randolph and Margaret Isabel (*née* Adams); *m* 1943, Edith Ripley; four *s. Educ:* St Paul's School; London University. Started in law before War. Wilkinson Sword Ltd: joined as accountant, 1946; Director and Secretary, 1948; Marketing Dir, 1949; Administration Dir, 1952; Asst Man. Dir, 1954; Jt Man. Dir, 1957; Man. Dir, 1960; Dep. Chairman, 1965. FBIM. *Recreations:* travelling, meteorology, yachting. *Address:* Diss Park, Gerrards Cross, Bucks. *Clubs:* Arts, City Livery, Little Ship; Tamesis.

**RANDOLPH, Ven. Thomas Berkeley;** Archdeacon of Hereford, 1959-70, Archdeacon Emeritus, since 1970; Canon Residentiary of Hereford Cathedral, 1961-70; *b* 15 March 1904; *s* of Felton George Randolph, Barrister-at-law, and Emily Margaret Randolph, Chichester, Sx; *m* 1935, Margaret, *d* of Rev. H. C. R. F. Jenner, Vennwood, Hereford and Wenvoe, Glam; two *s* one *d. Educ:* Christ's Hospital; Queen's College, Oxford (Scholar). BA (2nd Class Theology) 1927; MA 1932; Cuddesdon Coll., 1927; Curate of St Mary's, Portsea, 1928-33; Chaplain (Eccles. Est.) St Paul's Cathedral, Calcutta, 1934-37; Vicar of Eastleigh, 1938-46; Vicar of St Mary the Virgin with All Saints, St Saviour's, St Mark's and St Matthew's, Reading, 1946-59. Proctor in Convocation for the Diocese of Oxford, 1950-55; Hon. Canon of Christ Church, Oxford, 1957-59; Vicar of Wellington, Hereford, 1959-61. *Recreation:* golf. *Address:* 14 Heatherwood, Midhurst, Sussex. *T:* Midhurst 2765.
*See also C. G. Randolph.*

**RANDRUP, Michael;** Manager, British Aircraft Corporation, Saudi Arabia; *b* 20 April 1913; *s* of Soeren Revsgaard and Alexandra Randrup, Skive, Denmark; *m* 1941, Betty Perry (*d* 1949); one *s* one *d*; *m* 1954, Florence May Dryden. *Educ:* King's School, Canterbury; Chelsea College of Aeronautics. Learned to fly, 1934; RAF, 1940-46; OC Engine Research Flight RAE, 1945; Chief Test Pilot, D. Napier & Son Ltd, 1946-60. Aircraft Altitude World Record, 1957; Britannia Trophy, 1958; Derry Richards Mem. Trophy, 1958. *Address:* PO Box 1732, Riyadh, Saudi Arabia. *Club:* Royal Aero.

**RANFURLY,** 6th Earl of, *cr* 1831; **Thomas Daniel Knox,** KCMG 1955; Baron Welles, 1781; Viscount Northland, 1791; Baron Ranfurly (UK) 1826; Deputy Chairman, Inchcape & Co. Ltd; Chairman: Regis Property Holdings Ltd; Colonial Mutual Life Assurance Soc. Ltd (London Board); Director: Antony Gibbs & Sons (Insurance) Ltd; Anton Underwriting Agencies Ltd; Madame Tussauds Ltd; *b* 29 May 1913; *s* of late Viscount Northland (killed in action, 1915) and Hilda, *d* of late Sir Daniel Cooper, 2nd Bt; *S* grandfather 1933; *m* 1939, Hermione, *e d* of G. R. P. Llewellyn, Baglan Hall, Monmouth Road, Abergavenny, Mon; one *d. Educ:* Eton; Trinity Coll., Cambridge. ADC to Gov.-Gen. of Australia, 1936-38; served European War of 1939-45 (prisoner). Governor and C-in-C, Bahamas, 1953-56. Chairman London Scout Council, 1957-65; Chief Scout's Commissioner, Greater London, 1965-. President, Shaftesbury Homes and "Arethusa" Training Ship, 1959-; A Governor, London Clinic, 1969-. *Heir: kinsman* Gerald Françoys Needham Knox [*b* 4 Jan. 1929; *m* 1955, Rosemary, *o d* of late Air Vice-Marshal Felton Vesey Holt, CMG, DSO; two *s* two *d*]. *Address:* Great Pednor,

Chesham, Bucks. *T:* Gt Missenden 2155. *Clubs:* White's; Jockey (Newmarket).

**RANGANATHAN, Shiyali Ramamrita,** MA, DLitt, LT, FLA; Padmasri, National Research Professor in Library Science since 1965, and Hon. Professor Documentation Research and Training Centre, Bangalore 3, since 1962; President Indian Library Association, 1944-53; Professor of Library Science, University of Delhi, 1947-53; *b* Shiyali, India, 9 Aug. 1892; *e s* of N. Ramamritam and D. Sitalakshmi; *m* 1929, Sarada; one *s*. *Educ:* Hindu High School, Shiyali; Madras Christian College; Teachers' Coll., Saidapet; University Coll., London. Hon. DLitt: Delhi Univ., 1948; Pittsburgh Univ., 1964. Margaret Mann Award of ALA, 1970. Lectr in Maths in Govt Colls of Madras, 1917-20; Asst Prof. of Maths, Presidency Coll., Madras, 1920-23; Univ. Librarian, and Head of Library School, Madras, 1924-44; Univ. Librarian and Professor of Library Science, Benares Hindu Univ., 1945-47. Sec., Maths and Science Section, Madras Teachers' Guild, 1922-24; Treas., Indian Math. Soc., 1928-34; Sec. Madras Library Assoc., 1928-57 (Pres., 1957-67); Sec., Indian Adult Educn Assoc., 1949-52 (Vice-Pres., 1953); Sec., Library Service Section, All Asia Educnl Conf., 1930; Hon. Vice-Pres. Brit. Library Assoc.; Hon. Fellow, Internat. Fed. for Documentation, Hon. Chm., FID/CR; Travel in Europe, 1924-25 and in Europe, America and Asia, 1948 onwards. Member: Nat. Central Library Cttee of Government of India; Chairman, Lib. Committee, University Grants Commission, Lib. Sc. Course Cttee, India; Internat. Advisory Cttee of Library Experts of UN; Internat. Bibliog. Cttee UNESCO, 1951-54; Faculty of UNESCO's Internat. School of Librarianship, 1948; Indian National Commn for UNESCO. Founder: Sarada Ranganathan Professorship in Lib. Scis, Univ. of Madras, 1957; Sarada Ranganathan Endowment for Lib. Scis, 1963. *Publications:* Five Laws of Library Science, 1931, 2nd edn, 1957; Colon Classification, 1933, 6th edn, 1960; Classified Catalogue Code, 1934, 5th edn, 1964; Library Administration, 1935, 2nd edn, 1959; Prolegomena to Library Classification, 1937, 3rd edn 1967; Theory of Library Catalogue, 1938; Reference Service and Bibliography, 1940; Bibliography of Reference Books and Bibliographies, 1941; School and College Libraries, 1942; Library Classification: Fundamentals and Procedure, 1943; Elements of Library Classification, 1945; 3rd edn, 1961; Dictionary Catalogue Code, 1945, 2nd edn, 1952; Education for Leisure, 1945, 4th edn, 1961; Library Organisation, 1946, 3rd edn, 1963; Library Development Plan for the Allahabad University, 1947; Classification and International Documentation, 1948; Preface to Library Science, 1948; Library Development Plan for India, 1950; Library Catalogue: Fundamentals and Procedure, 1950; Library Tour, 1948, Europe and America, 1950; Classification, Coding and Machinery for Search, 1950; Classification and Communication, 1951; Library Manual, 1951, 2nd edn, 1960; Documentation Problems, 1951; Philosophy of Library Classification, 1951; Library Book-Selection, 1952, 2nd edn 1966; Social Bibliography, 1952; Social Education Literature, 1952; Union Catalogue of periodicals in South Asia, Vol. I Science, 1953; Depth Classification, 1953; Library Legislation, 1953; Heading and Canons, 1955; Classification of Management, 1956; Library Plan for Bengal, 1958; Library Plan for Kerala, 1960; Social Science Research and Libraries, 1960; Reference Service, 1961; Documentation and its Facets, 1963; Colon Classification: A Descriptive Account, 1965. Ed. of Library Science with a slant to Documentation. *Address:* Sarada, 100 Main Road 4, Bangalore 3, India. *T:* 3657.

**RANGER, James;** *b* 1889; *s* of Richard H. and Mary S. Ranger; *m* 1915, Mabel Annie Thorogood; three *d*. *Educ:* Stock Street Council School, Plaistow, E. MP (Lab) Ilford South, 1945-50. *Address:* 29 Meadow Close, SW20.

**RANK,** family name of **Baron Rank.**

**RANK,** 1st Baron *cr* 1957, of Sutton Scotney; **Joseph Arthur Rank,** JP; Hon. Life President, Ranks Hovis McDougall Ltd, since 1969 (Chairman, 1952-69); President, The Rank Organisation Ltd, since 1962 (Chairman, 1941-62); Vice-President Animal Health Trust; *b* 22 Dec. 1888; *s* of late Joseph and Emily Voase Rank; *m* 1917, Hon. Laura Ellen Marshall, *d* of 1st and last Baron Marshall of Chipstead; two *d*. *Educ:* Leys School, Cambridge. Hon. LLD, Southampton, 1967. *Recreations:* golf and shooting. *Heir:* none. *Address:* Sutton Manor, Sutton Scotney, Hants.

**RANK, Benjamin Keith,** CMG 1955; MS, FRCS; FRACS; FACS; Consulting Plastic Surgeon, Royal Melbourne Hospital, Repatriation Department, Victoria Eye and Ear Hospital, Queen Victoria Hospital, etc, and in Tasmania; Surgeon in charge Reparative Surgery, Peter McCallum Clinic, Melbourne; *b* 14 Jan. 1911; *s* of Wreghitt Rank and Bessie Rank (*née* Smith); *m* 1938, Barbara Lyle Facy; one *s* three *d*. *Educ:* Scotch College, Melbourne; Ormond College, University of Melbourne. MB, BS Melbourne, 1934; Resident Medical Officer, Royal Melbourne Hospital, 1935-36; MS (Melb.), 1937; MRCS, LRCP 1938; Resident Surgical Officer, London County Council, 1938-39 (St James' Hospital, Balham); FRCS 1938; Assistant Plastic Surgeon (EMS) at Hill End (Bart's), 1939-40; AAMC, 1940-45; Officer i/c AIF Plastic Surgery Unit in Egypt, and later at Heidelberg Military Hospital, Victoria, Australia (Lt-Col); Hon. Plastic Surgeon, Royal Melbourne Hosp., 1946-66. Carnegie Fellow, 1947. Member: Dental Board of Victoria 1949-; BMA State Council, 1950-60; Chm. Exec. Cttee, RACS (Pres., 1966-68); Chm., Cttee of Management, Victorian Plastic Surgery Unit (Preston Hosp.); Mem. Council, International House, Univ. of Melbourne; Sir Arthur Sims Commonwealth Travelling Prof., Roy. Coll. of Surgeons of England, 1958. 87th Mem., James IV Assoc. of Surgeons; Pres., British Assoc. of Plastic Surgeons, 1965. Pres., 5th Internat. Congress of Plastic Surgery, Melbourne, 1971. FRACS 1943; Hon. FACST 1952; RACS 1965; Hon. FRCS Canada; Hon. DSc Punjabi Univ., 1970; Hon. Member: Société Française de Chirurgie Plastique; Indian Association of Surgeons. *Publications:* (jointly) Surgery of Repair as applied to Hand Injuries, 1953. Papers in British, American and Australian Surgical Jls. *Recreations:* golf, gardening. *Address:* Mill Hill, Vine Street, Heidelberg, Victoria, Australia. *Clubs:* Melbourne, Army and Navy (Melbourne); Tasmanian (Hobart); Peninsula Golf.

**RANK, Joseph McArthur;** Chairman, Ranks Hovis McDougall Ltd, since 1969; *b* 24 April 1918; *s* of late Rowland Rank and of Margaret McArthur; *m* 1946, Hon. Moira (who *m* 1940, Peter Anthony Stanley Woodwark, killed in action, 1943; one *d*), *d* of 3rd Baron Southborough, *qv*; one *s* one *d*. *Educ:* Loretto. Joined Mark Mayhew Ltd, 1936. Served RAF, 1940-46. Personal Pilot to Air C-in-C, SEAC, 1945; Jt Man. Dir, Joseph Rank Ltd, 1955-65;

Dep. Chm. and Chief Exec., Ranks Hovis McDougall Ltd, 1965-69, Exec. Chm., 1969-. Pres., Nat. Assoc. of British and Irish Millers, 1957-58. Chm., Millers Mutual Assoc., 1969-; Chm. Council, British Nutrition Foundation, 1968-69; Dir, Royal Alexandra and Albert Sch., 1952-; Friend of the Royal Coll. of Physicians, 1967-; Council, Royal Warrant Holders Assoc., 1968-. *Recreations:* boating, travelling. *Address:* Landhurst, Hartfield, Sussex. *T:* Hartfield 293. *Clubs:* Royal Air Force; Poole Harbour Yacht.

**RANKEILLOUR,** 4th Baron *cr* 1932, of Buxted; **Peter St Thomas More Henry Hope;** *b* 29 May 1935; *s* of 3rd Baron Rankeillour and Mary Sibyl, *d* of late Col Wilfrid Ricardo, DSO; *S* father, 1967; unmarried. *Educ:* Ampleforth College; privately. *Recreations:* hunting, shooting, genealogy, boating. *Heir: cousin* Michael Richard Hope [*b* 21 Oct. 1940; *m* 1964, Elizabeth Rosemary, *e d* of Col F. H. Fuller; one *d*]. *Address:* Achaderry House, Roy Bridge, Inverness-shire. *T:* Spean Bridge 206. *Club:* Highland (Inverness).

**RANKIN, Andrew,** QC 1968; *b* 3 Aug. 1924; *s* of William Locke Rankin and Mary Ann McArdle, Edinburgh; *m* 1st, 1944, Winifred (marriage dissolved, 1963), *d* of Frank McAdam, Edinburgh; two *s* two *d* (and one *s* decd); 2nd, 1964, Veronica, *d* of George Aloysius Martin, Liverpool. *Educ:* Royal High Sch., Edinburgh; Univ. of Edinburgh; Downing Coll., Cambridge. Served War of 1939-45 (Gen. Service Medal, 1939-45 Star): Sub-Lt, RNVR, 1943. BL (Edin.) 1946; BA, 1st cl. hons Law Tripos (Cantab), 1948. Royal Commonwealth Soc. Medal, 1942; Cecil Peace Prize, 1946; Lord Justice Holker Exhibn, Gray's Inn, 1947-50; Lord Justice Holker Schol., Gray's Inn, 1950-53; Univ. Blue, Edin., 1943 and 1946 and Camb., 1948. Lectr in Law, Univ. of Liverpool, 1948-52. Called to Bar, Gray's Inn, 1950. *Publications:* (Ed., 4th edn) Levie's Law of Bankruptcy in Scotland, 1950; various articles in UK and foreign legal jls. *Recreations:* swimming, travel by sea, racing (both codes), watching soccer (especially Liverpool FC). *Address:* Chelwood, Pine Walks, Prenton, Cheshire. *T:* 051-608 2987; 2 Hare Court, Temple, EC4. *T:* 01-353 0076.

**RANKIN, Dame Annabelle (Jane Mary),** DBE 1957; Senator for the State of Queensland, Australia (elected, 1946; took seat, 1947); Minister of Housing, Commonwealth of Australia, since 1966; *b* Brisbane; *d* of Mrs A. Rankin, Brisbane, and late Col C. D. W. Rankin, former Qld MLA for many years and sometime Minister for Railways; unmarried. *Educ:* Childers and Howard State Schools, Queensland; Glennie Memorial School, Toowoomba, Queensland. Clerk in Trustee Company; State Sec., Queensland Girl Guides' Assoc. War Service: YWCA Assistant Commissioner for Queensland, attached to Australian Women's Services, 1943-46. Appointed Organiser, Junior Red Cross, Queensland, 1946. First Queensland woman to enter Federal Parliament; Member, Parliamentary Standing Committee on Broadcasting, 1947; Whip of Senate Opposition, 1947; Government Whip in the Senate, 1951-66. Vice-President, Liberal Party of Australia, Queensland Division, 1949. Member of Public Works Committee, 1950; Member of Australian delegation to Commonwealth Parliamentary Association Conference, Ottawa, 1952. *Recreations:* motoring, reading. *Address:* The Senate House, Parliament Buildings, Canberra, ACT; 26 Glen Road, Toowong, Brisbane, Queensland, Australia. *T:* Brisbane U4824. *Clubs:* Moreton, Lyceum (Brisbane).

**RANKIN, Sir Hugh (Charles Rhys),** 3rd Bt, *cr* 1898; FSA (Scot.) 1948; Representative to District Council Perth CC (Eastern District), 1949, Perth CC 1950; Councillor for Boro' of Rattray and Blairgowrie, 1949; joined RASC as 2nd Lieut, May 1940, at age of 41 years; Captain 1940-45, India; sheep farming and is a judge of sheep at prominent shows; formerly Senior Vice-President of the Western Islamic Association; a former Vice-President of Scottish National Liberal Association; *b* 8 Aug. 1899; *er s* of Sir Reginald Rankin, 2nd Bt, and Hon. Nest Rice (*d* 1943), 2nd *d* of 6th Baron Dynevor; changed his names by Scotch law in July 1946 to above; *S* father, 1931; *m* 1932, Helen Margaret (*d* 1945), *e d* of Sir Charles Stewart, KBE, 1st Public Trustee, and *widow* of Capt. Colin Campbell, Scots Guards; *m* 1946, Robina Kelly, FSA (Scot.), Crieff, Perthshire. *Educ:* Harrow. Served in 1st Royal Dragoon Guards in Sinn Feinn Campaign, 1920-22; ex-Pres. Clun Forest Sheep Breeders Assoc., 1928, and their representative to National Sheep Breeders Association that year; in 1938 was a representative on committee of British sheep breeders in London appointed to petition Government *re* sheep industry. Runner-up All Britain Sheep Judging Competition (6,000 entrants), 1962. A writer on agricultural stock; expert on Highland problems; was Brit. Rep., 1937, to 1st all European Muslim Congress at Geneva; a practising Non-Theistic Theravada Buddhist since 1944, and performed Holy Buddhist Pilgrimage, Nov. 1944, the 2nd Britisher to do so; Vice-Pres. World's Buddhist Assoc., 1945. Joined Labour Party 1939 and holds extreme political views; is a Dominion Home Ruler for Scotland, member Scottish National Party; joined Scottish Communist Party, 1945; Welsh Republican Nationalist and Welsh speaker. Mem. Roy. Inst. and Roy. Soc. of Arts; is Hereditary Piper of the Clan Maclaine. News of the World Kt of the Road (for courtesy in motor driving). Broadsword Champion of British Army (Cavalry), 1921. *Publications:* articles in agricultural publications, etc. *Recreations:* golf (holds an amateur record amongst golfers of Gt Britain in having played on 382 separate courses of UK and Eire), shooting, coarse fishing, hunting, motoring, cycling on mountain tracks to tops of British mountains (Pres. Rough Stuff Cycling Assoc., 1956); study of ancient track ways; bowls, tennis, archæology, study of domestic animals, speaking on politics, especially *re* Scottish Home Rule and Highland problems. *Heir: nephew* Ian Niall Rankin [*b* 19 Dec. 1932; *s* of Arthur Niall Talbot Rankin and of Lady Jean Rankin, *qv*; *m* 1959, Alexandra, *o d* of Adm. Sir Laurence Durlacher, *qv*; one *s* one *d*]. *Address:* c/o Messrs Hooper, Holt & Keen, Solicitors, 2a High Street, Redhill, Surrey. *Club:* Royal and Ancient Golf (St Andrews).

**RANKIN, Lady Jean (Margaret),** DCVO 1969 (CVO 1957); Woman of the Bedchamber to Queen Elizabeth The Queen Mother, since 1947; *b* 15 Aug. 1905; *d* of 12th Earl of Stair; *m* 1931, Niall Rankin (*d* 1965), *s* of Sir Reginald Rankin, 2nd Bt; two *s*. Governor, Thomas Coram Foundation. Order of Orange-Nassau, Netherlands, 1950. *Address:* House of Treshnish, Calgary, Isle of Mull. *T:* Dervaig 249; 3 Catherine Wheel Yard, SW1.

*See also Sir Hugh C. R. Rankin, Bt.*

**RANKIN, John;** MP (Lab-Co-op) Govan Division of Glasgow since 1955 (Tradeston Division of Glasgow, 1945-55); Teacher; *s* of George Rankin and Henrietta Henderson; *m* 1st, Jessie Roy Turnbull (*d* 1965), Barrhead; two *s* three *d*; 2nd, 1968, M. C. Parsons. Educ: Allan Glen School; Glasgow University (MA).

Propagandist and Lecturer for Scottish Labour College, Co-operative Movement and Labour Party. Chairman of Glasgow ILP, 1925-28; Vice-Chairman, Eastwood Parish Council, 1928-29. *Recreation:* golf, Eastwood Golf Club (Captain, 1942). *Address:* 55 Holeburn Road, Glasgow S3. *T:* 041-637 2625; 122c New Kent Road, SE1.

**RANKIN, John Mitchell,** QC 1969; *b* 20 April 1924; *yr s* of late Very Rev. Provost H. M. Rankin, St Ninian's Cathedral, Perth, Scotland; *m* 1949, Heather Hope, *o d* of late H. K. Cox, Snaigow, Perthshire; two *s* two *d. Educ:* Trinity Coll., Glenalmond; Keble Coll., Oxford. Served in Royal Navy, 1942-46 (Lt RNVR, 1945). BA Oxon 1949; called to Bar, Middle Temple, 1950. Dir, Norland Nursery Training Coll., Ltd. *Recreations:* painting and graphic arts. *Address:* 1 Brick Court, Temple, EC4. *T:* 01-853 8558. *Clubs:* Travellers', Naval and Military.

**RANKIN, Prof. Robert Alexander,** MA, PhD, ScD; Professor of Mathematics, Glasgow University, since 1954; *b* 27 Oct. 1915; *s* of late Rev. Prof. Oliver Shaw Rankin, DD, and late Olivia Teresa Shaw; *m* 1942, Mary Ferrier Llewellyn, *d* of late W. M. Llewellyn and K. F. Llewellyn, JP; one *s* three *d. Educ:* Fettes; Clare Coll., Cambridge. Wrangler, 1936; Fellow of Clare College, 1939-51; Ministry of Supply (work on rockets), 1940-45; Faculty Asst Lecturer, Cambridge Univ., 1945-48; Univ. Lecturer, Cambridge, 1948-51; Asst Tutor, Clare Coll., 1947-51; Praelector, Clare Coll., 1949-51; Mason Professor of Pure Mathematics at Birmingham University, 1951-54. Mathematical Sec. and Editor of Proceedings of Cambridge Philosophical Soc., 1947-51; Hon. Pres. Glasgow Gaelic Soc., 1957-; Pres. Edinburgh Mathematical Soc., 1957-58; Mem., Special Cttee, Advisory Coun. on Educn in Scotland, 1959-61; Vis. Prof., Indiana Univ., 1963-64; Vice-Pres. Roy. Soc. of Edinburgh, 1960-63; Chairman: Scottish Mathematical Council; Clyde Estuary Amenity Council. Keith Prize, RSE, 1961-63. *Publications:* Matematicheskaya Teorija Dvizhenija Neupravljaemykh Raket, 1951; An Introduction to Mathematical Analysis, 1963; papers on the Theory of Numbers, Theory of Functions, Rocket Ballistics and Gaelic Subjects in various journals. *Recreations:* hill-walking; Gaelic studies. *Address:* 10 The University, Glasgow W2. *T:* 041-339 2641; Cromla Cottage, Corrie, Isle of Arran.

**RANKINE, Sir John (Dalzell),** KCMG 1954 (CMG 1947); KCVO 1956; *b* 8 June 1907; *o s* of late Sir Richard Rankine, KCMG; *m* 1939, Janet Grace, *d* of Major R. L. Austin, Clifton, Bristol; one *d. Educ:* Christ's College, Christchurch, New Zealand; Exeter College, Oxford. BA 1930; entered Colonial Administration Service as Cadet, Uganda, 1931; Asst Sec. East African Governor's Conference, 1939; First Asst Sec., 1942; Asst Colonial Sec., Fiji, 1942; Colonial Sec., Barbados, 1945; Chief Secretary, Kenya, 1947-51; Chairman, Development and Reconstruction Authority. British Resident, Zanzibar, 1952-54; administered Govts of Barbados and Kenya on various occasions; Governor, Western Region, Nigeria, 1954-60. KStJ 1958. Brilliant Star of Zanzibar (1st Class), 1954. *Recreations:* tennis, squash, golf. *Address:* Quarriers, Wadhurst, Sussex. *T:* Wadhurst 3159. *Clubs:* Athenæum, MCC, Queen's.

**RANKING, Robert Duncan; His Honour Judge Ranking;** County Court Judge, since 1968; *b* 24 Oct. 1915; *yr s* of Dr R. M. Ranking, Tunbridge Wells, Kent; *m* 1949, Evelyn Mary Tagart (*née* Walker); one *d. Educ:* Cheltenham Coll.; Pembroke Coll., Cambridge (MA). Called to Bar, 1939. Served in Queen's Own Royal W Kent Regt, 1939-46. Dep. Chm. E Sx QS, 1962; Dep. Chm., Agricultural Land Tribunal (S Eastern Area), 1963. *Address:* 2 Hungershall Park, Tunbridge Wells, Kent. *T:* 27551.

**RANNIE, Prof. Ian;** FRCPath 1964; FI Biol 1964; Professor of Pathology (Dental School), University of Newcastle upon Tyne, since Oct. 1960; *b* 29 Oct. 1915; *o s* of James Rannie, MA, and Nicholas Denniston McMeekan; *m* 1943, Flora Welch; two *s. Educ:* Ayr Academy; Glasgow University. BSc (Glas), 1935; MB, ChB (Glas), 1938; BSc Hons Pathology and Bacteriology (Glas), 1939; Hutcheson Research Schol. (Pathology), 1940. Assistant to Professor of Bacteriology, Glasgow, 1940-41; Lecturer in Pathology, 1950-60, King's College, Univ. of Durham. Consultant Pathologist, United Newcastle upon Tyne Hospitals, 1948-. *Publications:* papers on various subjects in medical journals. *Recreation:* golf. *Address:* 5 Osborne Villas, Newcastle upon Tyne NE2 1JU. *T:* 813163. *Club:* Royal Societies.

**RANSFORD, Col Sir Alister John,** Kt 1946; CIE 1936; RE (retired); CStJ; Bursar, Loretto School, Musselburgh, 1948-59; *b* 5 Jan. 1895; *s* of late T. D. Ransford, FRCS, LRCP, Bath; *m* 1927, Lucy Torfrida, 4th *d* of late William Walford, Greens Norton Park, Towcester; one *s* one *d. Educ:* Fettes College; Royal Military Academy, Woolwich. 2nd Lieut RE, 1914; served European War, France and Belgium (despatches, 1914-15 star, two medals); India, Military Engineering Services, 1922; Finance Dept., Govt of India, HM's Mint, Bombay, 1924; Mint Master, His Majesty's Mint, Bombay, 1931-47; Major, 1929; Lt-Col, 1937; Col, 1940; retired, 1949. *Address:* Great Oak Corner, Eardisley, Hereford.

**RANSOM, Charles Frederick George,** CMG 1956; OBE 1950; Research Fellow, Centre for Contemporary European Studies, University of Sussex, since 1968; *b* 9 July 1911; *s* of late Charles Edward Ransom and Elizabeth Ransom, Harrow, Middlesex; *m* 1943, Eileen Mary Emily, *d* of late Rt Rev. A. I. Greaves, Bishop Suffragan of Grimsby, DD; two *s* one *d. Educ:* Harrow CGS; University College, London (Ricardo Scholar, 1933-35). Schoolmaster and Univ. Extra-Mural Lecturer, 1936-40. Served in UK and Italy, York and Lancaster Regt (Major), 1940-46. FO 1946; First Sec., HM Embassy, Rome, 1958-61; FO Supernumerary Fellow, St Antony's Coll., Oxford, 1966-67. *Publications:* articles on European affairs. *Recreations:* music, literature, gardening. *Address:* Ladyfield, Etchingham, Sussex. *T:* 216. *Club:* Reform.

**RANSOME, Maj.-Gen. Robert St George Tyldesley,** CB 1946; CBE 1944; MC 1940; *b* 22 June 1903; *s* of Dr A. S. Ransome; *m* 1947, Kathleen, *widow* of Brig. C. Leslie-Smith, IA. *Educ:* Winchester Coll.; Royal Military College, Sandhurst. Joined Royal Fusiliers, 1924; Instructor, Royal Military College, Sandhurst, 1935-37; Staff College, 1938-39; BEF 1939-40 (despatches, MC); Instructor, Senior Staff College, 1940; served in Mediterranean, Middle East, 1941-43; commanded 11th Battalion Royal Fusiliers, 1942. Visited Middle East, Quebec, S Africa, Yalta, Potsdam, Italy, France, etc, 1943-45; Vice-QMG to the Forces (Maj.-Gen.), 1946; idc 1947; BGS, GHQ Far East, 1948; Comdr Scottish Beach Bde (TA), 1950; Malaya, 1950 (despatches); Services Adviser, UK High

Commission, Germany, 1954-55; Chief (Maj.-Gen.), Jt Services Liaison Organisation, BAOR, 1955-58, retd. Deputy Colonel, Royal Fusiliers, 1962-63. *Recreations:* gardening, shooting, military history. *Address:* Wilford Cottage, Melton, Suffolk. *Clubs:* Army and Navy, MCC.

**RAO, Calyampudi Radhakrishna,** FRS 1967; Director, Research and Training School, Indian Statistical Institute, since 1964; *b* 10 Sept. 1920; *s* of C. D. Naidu and A. Laksmikantamma; *m* 1948, C. Bhargavi Rao; one *s* one *d. Educ:* Andhra Univ. (MA, 1st Class Maths); Calcutta Univ. (MA, 1st Class Statistics; Gold Medal); PhD, ScD, Cambridge. Superintending Statistician, Indian Statistical Institute, 1943-49; Professor and Head of Division of Theoretical Research and Training, Indian Statistical Institute, 1949-64. Co-editor, Sankhya, Indian Jl of Statistics, 1964-. Member, Internat. Statistical Inst., 1951 (Mem. Statistical Educn Cttee, 1958-61, 1965-; Treasurer, 1962-65); Chm., Indian Nat. Cttee for Statistics, 1962-; Fell., Nat. Inst. of Sciences of India, 1953; Fell., Inst. of Math. Statistics, USA, 1958. Hon. Fellow, Royal Stat. Soc., 1969; Shanti Swarup Bhatnagar Memorial Award, 1963; Guy Medal in Silver, Royal Stat. Soc., 1965; Meghnad Saha Gold Medal, 1969. Hon. DSc: Andhra; Leningrad. *Publications:* (with Mahalanobis and Majumdar) Anthropometric Survey of the United Provinces, 1941, a statistical study, 1949; Advanced Statistical Methods in Biometric Research, 1952; (with Mukherjee and Trevor) The Ancient Inhabitants of Jebal Moya, 1955; (with Majumdar) Bengal Anthropometric Survey, 1945, a statistical study, 1959; Linear Statistical Inference and its Applications, 1965; (with A. Matthai and S. K. Mitra) Formulae and Tables for Statistical Work, 1966. *Address:* 538 Yojana Bhavan, Parliament Street, New Delhi 1, India.

**RAPER, Vice-Adm. Robert George,** CB 1968; Director-General, Ships, since 1968 (Deputy Director-General, Oct. 1967-May 1968); Chief Naval Engineer Officer, since 1968; Senior Naval Representative, Bath, since 1968; *b* 27 Aug. 1915; *s* of Major Robert George Raper and Ida Jean (*née* MacAdam Smith); *m* 1940, Frances Joan St John (*née* Phillips); one *s* two *d. Educ:* RNC Dartmouth; RN Engineering College, Keyham; Advanced Engineering Course RNC Greenwich. Sen. Engineer, HMS Edinburgh, 1940 until ship was sunk, 1942 (despatches); Turbine Research Section, Admiralty, 1942-45; Engineer Officer, HMS Broadsword, Battleaxe, Crossbow, 1945-47; Comdr, 1947; Engineer-in-Chief's Dept, Admiralty, 1948-51; Engr Officer, HMS Birmingham, 1952-54; lent to RCN, 1954; Technical Sec. to Engineer-in-Chief of the Fleet, 1955-57; Capt. 1957; IDC 1958; in command HMS Caledonia, 1959-61; Dep. Dir of Marine Engineering, Admiralty, 1961-63; CSO (T) to Flag Officer Sea Training, 1963-65; Dir, Marine Engineering, MoD (Navy Dept), 1966-67. *Recreations:* carpentry; playing at golf, tennis, cricket. *Address:* Innoch's Lodge, Hinton Charterhouse, Nr Bath, Somerset. *T:* Limpley Stoke 3125. *Club:* United Service.

**RAPHAEL, Chaim,** CBE 1965 (OBE 1951); Research Fellow, University of Sussex, since 1969; Head of Information Div.: HM Treasury, 1959-68; Civil Service Dept, 1968-69. *Publications:* Memoirs of a Special Case, 1962; The Walls of Jerusalem, 1968; *novels:* (under pseudonym Jocelyn Davey): The Undoubted Deed, 1956; The Naked Villany, 1958; A Touch of Stagefright, 1960; A Killing in Hats, 1964. *Recreation:* America. *Address:* 142 Ebury Street, SW1; 30 The Course, Lewes, Sussex. *T:* Lewes 5786. *Clubs: Reform, Jack's.*

**RAPHAEL, Prof. David Daiches,** MA, DPhil; Professor of Philosophy, Reading University, since 1970; *b* 25 Jan. 1916; 2nd *s* of late Jacob Raphael and of Sarah Warshawsky, Liverpool; *m* 1942, Sylvia, *er d* of late Rabbi Dr Salis Daiches and of Flora Levin, Edinburgh; two *d. Educ:* Liverpool Collegiate School; University College, Oxford (scholar). 1st Class, Classical Moderations, 1936; Hall-Houghton Junior Septuagint Prizeman, 1937; 1st Class, Literae Humaniores, 1938; Robinson Senior Scholar of Oriel College, Oxford, 1938-40; Passmore Edwards Scholar, 1939. Served in Army, 1940-41. Temporary Assistant Principal, Ministry of Labour and National Service, 1941-44; temp. Principal, 1944-46. Professor of Philosophy, University of Otago, Dunedin, NZ, 1946-49; Lecturer in Moral Philosophy, Univ. of Glasgow, 1949-51; Senior Lecturer, 1951-60; Edward Caird Prof. of Political and Social Philosophy, Univ. of Glasgow, 1960-70. Visiting Professor of Philosophy, Hamilton Coll., Clinton, NY (under Chauncey S. Truax Foundation), and Univ. of Southern California, 1959; Mahlon Powell Lectr, Indiana Univ., 1959; Vis. Fellow, All Souls Coll., Oxford, 1967-68. Ind. Mem. Cttee on Teaching Profession in Scotland (Wheatley Cttee), 1961-63; Ind. Mem., Scottish Agricultural Wages Board, 1962-. Mem. Academic Adv. Cttee, Heriot-Watt Univ., Edinburgh, 1964-; Mem. Cttee on Distribution of Teachers in Scotland (Roberts Cttee), 1965-66; Independent Member Police Advisory Board for Scotland, 1965-70; Member Social Sciences Adv. Cttee, UK Nat. Commission, UNESCO, 1966-; Academic Mem., Bd of Governors, Hebrew Univ. of Jerusalem, 1969-. *Publications:* The Moral Sense, 1947; Edition of Richard Price's Review of Morals, 1948; Moral Judgement, 1955; The Paradox of Tragedy, 1960; Political Theory and the Rights of Man, 1967; British Moralists 1650-1800, 1969; Problems of Political Philosophy, 1970. Articles in jls of philosophy and of political studies. *Address:* Department of Philosophy, University of Reading, Reading.

**RAPHAEL, Prof. Ralph Alexander,** FRS 1962; PhD (London), DSc (London); FRSE; ARCS; DIC; FRIC; Regius Professor of Chemistry, Glasgow University, since 1957; *b* 1 Jan. 1921; *s* of Jack Raphael; *m* 1944, Prudence Marguerite Anne, *d* of Col P. J. Gaffikin, MC, MD; one *s* one *d. Educ:* Wesley College, Dublin; Tottenham County School; Imperial College of Science and Technology. Chemist, May & Baker Ltd, 1943-46. ICI Research Fellow, Univ. of London, 1946-49; Lecturer in Organic Chemistry, Univ. of Glasgow, 1949-54; Professor of Organic Chemistry, Queen's University, Belfast, 1954-57. Meldola Medallist, Royal Institute of Chemistry, 1948; Tilden Lectr, Chem. Soc., 1960, Corday-Morgan Vis. Lectr, 1963; Roy. Soc. Vis. Prof., 1967. Vice-Pres. Chemical Soc., 1967-; Mem., Academic Adv. Bd, Warwick Univ. *Publications:* Chemistry of Carbon Compounds, Vol. IIA, 1953; Acetylenic Compounds in Organic Synthesis, 1955. Papers in Journal of Chemical Society. *Recreations:* music, bridge, badminton. *Address:* Department of Chemistry, The University, Glasgow, W2; 18 Kilmardinny Grove, Bearsden, Glasgow. *T:* 041-942 3864. *Club:* Athenæum.

**RAPHOE, Bishop of,** (RC), since 1965; **Most Rev. Anthony C. MacFeely;** *b* 4 Feb. 1909. *Educ:* St Columb's Coll., Londonderry; St Patrick's Coll., Maynooth; Irish Coll., Rome. Priest,

1932; Prof., St Columb's Coll., Oct. 1934; Pres., St Columb's Coll., 1950; Parish Priest, Strabane, Co. Tyrone, 1959-65. *Recreation:* walking. *Address:* Ard Eunan, Letterkenny, Co. Donegal, Ireland.

**RAPP, Sir Thomas (Cecil),** KBE, *cr* 1950; CMG 1945; MC; *b* Saltburn-by-the-Sea, 1893; *m* 1922, Dorothy, *d* of John Clarke; one *d* (and one *d* decd). *Educ:* Coatham School; Sidney Sussex College, Cambridge. Served European War (Duke of Wellington's Regiment TF), 1914-18, retiring with rank of Major; an assistant in Levant Consular Service, 1919; Acting Vice-Consul, Port Said, 1920; Vice-Consul, Cairo, 1922; Rabat, 1927; Consul, Sofia, 1931; Moscow, 1932; Zagreb, 1936; Consul-General at Zagreb, Jugoslavia, 1939-41. Captured by German armed forces and interned in Germany, 1941-43; Consul-General, Tabriz, 1943-44; Salonica, 1944-45; Minister to Albania (did not proceed), 1946; Deputy head and subsequently head of British Economic Mission to Greece, 1946-47; Ambassador to Mexico, 1947-50; Head of British Middle East Office, Cairo, 1950-53. *Recreation:* walking. *Address:* York Cottage, Sandgate, Kent. *T:* Folkestone 38594. *Club:* Athenæum.

**RASCH, Sir Richard Guy Carne,** 3rd Bt, *cr* 1903; a Member of HM Body Guard, Honourable Corps of Gentlemen-at-Arms, since 1968; *b* 10 Oct. 1918; *s* of Brigadier G. E. C. Rasch, CVO, DSO (*d* 1955); *m* 1st, 1947, Anne Mary, *d* of late Major J. H. Dent-Brocklehurst; one *s* one *d*; 2nd, 1961, Fiona Mary, *d* of Robert Douglas Shaw; *S* uncle, 1963. *Educ:* Eton; RMC, Sandhurst. Major, late Grenadier Guards. Served War of 1939-45; retired, 1951. *Recreations:* shooting, fishing. *Heir: s* Simon Anthony Carne Rasch, *b* 26 Feb. 1948. *Address:* 45 Cheyne Court, Chelsea, SW3. *T:* 01-352 7770; Woodhill, Danbury, Essex. *Clubs:* White's, Guards.

**RASH, Mrs D. E. A.;** *see* Wallace, Doreen.

**RASHLEIGH, Sir Harry (Evelyn Battie),** 5th Bt, *cr* 1831; *b* 17 May 1923; *er s* of late Captain Harry Rashleigh, JP (3rd *s* of 3rd Bt) and Jane Henrietta, *d* of late E. W. Rashleigh, Stoketon, Saltash, Cornwall; *S* kinsman 1951; *m* 1954, Honora Elizabeth Sneyd, *d* of G. S. Sneyd, The Watch House, Downderry, Cornwall; one *s* three *d*. *Educ:* Wellington Sch., Som. Served War of 1939-45, Westminster Dragoons, 1941-45; 79th Armoured Div. Experimental Wing, 1945-46. Mechanical Engineer with John Mowlem & Co. Ltd, UK, 1947-48; John Mowlem & Co. Ltd, Tanganyika, East Africa, 1948-50; Earth Moving & Construction Ltd., Tanganyika, East Africa, 1948-51, 1954-65. Farmer. *Recreations:* shooting, sailing. *Heir: s* Richard Harry Rashleigh, *b* 8 July 1958. *Address:* Holdstrong, Coryton, Nr Okehampton, Devon. *T:* Lydford 319. *Club:* Royal Fowey Yacht.

**RASHLEIGH BELCHER, John;** *see* Belcher, J. R.

**RASMINSKY, Louis,** CBE 1946; Governor, Bank of Canada, since 1961; *b* 1 Feb. 1908; *s* of David and Etta Rasminsky; *m* 1930, Lyla Rotenberg; one *s* one *d*. *Educ:* University of Toronto; London School of Economics. Financial Section, League of Nations, 1930-39; Chairman, Foreign Exchange Control Board, Canada, 1940-51; Deputy Governor, Bank of Canada, 1956-61. Executive Director, International Monetary Fund, 1946-62; Executive Director, International Bank, 1950-62. Hon. LLD Univ. of Toronto, 1953; Hon. DHL Hebrew Union Coll., 1963. Hon. Fell., London Sch. of Economics, 1960. *Recreations:* golf, fishing. *Address:* 440 Roxborough Avenue, Rockcliffe Park, Ont, Canada. *T:* SH 9-7704. *Clubs:* Cercle Universitaire d'Ottawa (Ottawa); Five Lakes Fishing (Wakefield, PQ).

**RASMUSSEN, Professor Steen Eiler;** Architect; Professor of Architecture, Royal Academy of Fine Arts, Copenhagen, 1938-68; *b* Copenhagen, 9 Feb. 1898; *s* of General Eiler Rasmussen; *m* 1934, Karen Margrete Schrøder; two *d*. *Educ:* Metropolitanskolen; Royal Academy of Fine Arts, Copenhagen. Three first prizes in town planning competitions, 1919. Mem. Danish Roy. Acad. of Fine Arts, 1922; Lecturer at Architectural Sch. of the Academy, 1924; Architect to Municipal Town Planning Office, Copenhagen, 1932-38. Pres. Copenhagen Regional Planning Cttee, 1945-58. Visiting Professor in USA: Massachusetts Inst. of Technology, 1953, Yale, 1954, Philadelphia, 1958, Berkeley, 1959. Lethaby Professor, Roy. College of Art, London, 1958. Designed: Tingbjerg Housing Estate, Copenhagen, 1953-; Schools, Town Hall. Hon. Corr. Member: RIBA London, Bavarian Acad. of Fine Arts, 1958; American Institute of Architects, 1962; Hon. Royal Designer for Industry, London, 1947; Hon. Dr: Technische Hochschule Munich; Univ. of Lund. *Publications:* London, the Unique City, 1937; Towns and Buildings, 1951; Experiencing Architecture, 1959. *Recreation:* to doze in a chair thinking of future books. *Address:* Dreyersvej 9, 2960 Rungsted Kyst, Denmark. *T:* 863510.

**RATCLIFFE, John Ashworth,** CB 1965; CBE 1959 (OBE 1947); FRS 1951; MA; Director of Radio and Space Research Station, Slough, Oct. 1960-Feb. 1966; *b* 12 Dec. 1902; *s* of H. H. Ratcliffe, Rawtenstall, Lancs; *m* 1930, Nora Disley; two *d*. *Educ:* Giggleswick School; Sidney Sussex College, Cambridge. Taught Physics at Cambridge and Research in Radio Wave Propagation, 1924-60; Reader in Physics, Cambridge University, 1947-60; Fellow of Sidney Sussex College, 1927-60, Hon. Fellow 1962. President: Physical Society, 1959-60; Section A, British Association, 1964; Chairman, Electronics Board, IEE, 1962-63; Vice-Pres., IEE, 1963-66, Pres., 1966. FIEE, FIEEE. War Service with Telecommunications Research Establishment (TRE), Malvern. Faraday Medal, 1966; Royal Medal (Roy. Soc.), 1966. *Publications:* numerous papers in scientific journals on Radio Wave Propagation. *Address:* 193 Huntingdon Road, Cambridge. *Club:* Athenæum.

**RATCLIFFE, Reginald,** CB 1959; MBE 1943; Chief Executive, Machine Tool Division, Staveley Industries, 1965-68, retired; *b* 8 Jan. 1908; *s* of Elias Ratcliffe, Birkenhead; *m* 1933, Vera George; one *s* one *d*. *Educ:* Liverpool Univ. BEng 1930. MEng 1933; Carlton Stitt Medallist, 1930. Entered Royal Arsenal, Woolwich, as Technical Assistant, 1930; Royal Ordnance Factory, Nottingham, 1938; Dir of Instrument Production, Min. of Supply, 1954; Royal Ordnance Factories: Dep. Controller 1956-59; Controller 1959-64; Deputy Master General of the Ordnance (Production) 1964. President, Institution of Production Engineers, 1963-65. *Publications:* various contributions to technical journals. *Recreations:* tennis, swimming. *Address:* 43 Martins Drive, Ferndown, Dorset BH22 9SG. *T:* Ferndown 4081.

**RATHBONE, John Francis Warre,** CBE 1966; TD 1950; Secretary of National Trust for Places of Historic Interest or Natural Beauty, 1949-68; President, London Centre of the

National Trust, since 1968; *b* 18 July 1909; *e s* of Francis Warre Rathbone and Edith Bertha Hampshire, Allerton Beeches, Liverpool. *Educ:* Marlborough; New College, Oxford. Solicitor, 1934. Served War of 1939-45; AA Comd and staff (Col 1945). Dir Ministry of Justice Control Branch, CCG (British Element), 1946-49. Member Bd of Governors: Univ. Coll. Hosp.; Brit. Inst. of Recorded Sound. Chm., Mutual Households Assoc. Ltd; Mem., Adv. Cttee, Landscape Treatment of Trunk Roads. *Recreations:* music, travel. *Address:* 10 St Andrew's Place, Regent's Park, NW1. *T:* 01-935 1066. *Club:* Travellers'.

**RATHBONE, Monroe Jackson;** President, Standard Oil Co. (NJ), 1954-65, Director, 1949-65, retired; *b* Parkersburg, W Va, 1 March 1900; *s* of Monroe Jackson Rathbone and Ida Virginia (*née* Welch); *m* 1922, Eleanor Groves; one *s* one *d*. *Educ:* Parkersburg High School; Lehigh University, Bethlehem, Pa (Chem. E.). Served US Army (2nd Lieut), 1918-19. Joined Standard Oil Co. of Louisiana, 1921; Chemical Engineer, asst to Gen. Superintendent, 1926-31; Gen. Superintendent, 1931-33; Asst Gen. Manager, Manufacturing Dept, 1933-36; Vice-Pres. and Gen. Manager i/c manufacturing operations, 1935-36; President, 1936-44; President and Director, Esso Standard Oil Co., 1944-49. Hon. Director American Petroleum Institute; Pres., Bd of Trustees, Lehigh Univ. Chm., Nat. Fund for Medical Educn. Vice-Chm., Council for Financial Aid to Education. Dir, Deafness Research Foundation. Comdr, Order of St Olaf, Norway; Comdr, Order of Orange-Nassau, Netherlands; Kt, Order of Leopold, Belgium; Palladium Medal, Soc. Industrielle du Chemie; Gold Medal, Amer. Petroleum Inst.; Gold Medal, Wharton Alumni Assoc., Univ. of Pennsylvania; Award of Merit, Amer. Inst. Consulting Engineers; Humanitarian Award, Deafness Research Foundation. Holds numerous hon. degrees. *Address:* 10 Glendale Road, Summit, New Jersey 07901, USA; 1 Rockefeller Plaza, NYC 10020, USA. *Clubs:* University, River (New York); Baton Rouge; Baltusrol Golf; Augusta National Golf.

**RATHBONE, Very Rev. Norman Stanley;** Dean of Hereford since 1969; *b* 8 Sept. 1914; *er s* of Stanley George and Helen Rathbone; *m* 1952, Christine Olive Gooderson; two *s* two *d*. *Educ:* Lawrence Sheriff Sch., Rugby; Christ's Coll., Cambridge; Westcott House, Cambridge. BA 1936, MA 1939. St Mary Magdalen's, Coventry: Curate, 1938; Vicar, 1945; Canon Theologian, Coventry Cathedral, 1954; Canon Residentiary and Chancellor, Lincoln Cathedral, 1959. *Address:* The Deanery, Hereford. *T:* Hereford 2525.

**RATHCAVAN,** 1st Baron, *cr* 1953, of The Braid, Co. Antrim; **(Robert William) Hugh O'Neill,** Bt, *cr* 1929, PC (Ireland 1921, Northern Ireland 1922, Gt Brit. 1937); Hon. LLD, Queen's University Belfast; HM Lieutenant for County Antrim, 1949-59; *b* 8 June 1883; *o surv. s* of 2nd Baron O'Neill; *m* 1909, Sylvia, *d* of Walter A. Sandeman of Morden House, Royston; three *s*. *Educ:* Eton; New Coll., Oxford, BA. Bar, Inner Temple, 1909; contested Stockport, 1906; MP (UU) Mid-Antrim, 1915-22, Co. Antrim, 1922-50, North Antrim, 1950-52; MP for County Antrim in the Parliament of Northern Ireland, 1921-29; first Speaker of the House of Commons of Northern Ireland, 1921-29; Chairman Cons Private Members' (1922) Committee, 1935-39; Parl. Under-Sec. of State for India and for Burma, 1939-40; late Lt North of Ireland Imperial Yeomanry; late Captain Royal Irish Rifles and Major (general list); served in European War, 1915-18, France and Palestine. *Recreations:* shooting, fishing. *Heir: s* Hon. Phelim Robert Hugh O'Neill, *qv*. *Address:* Cleggan Lodge, Ballymena, Co. Antrim. *T:* Aughafatten 209; 28 Queen's Gate Gardens, SW7. *T:* 01-584 0358. *Clubs:* Carlton; Ulster (Belfast).

*See also Hon. Sir Con D. W. O'Neill.*

**RATHCREEDAN,** 2nd Baron, *cr* 1916; **Charles Patrick Norton,** TD; *b* 26 Nov. 1905; *er s* of 1st Baron and Marguerite Cecil (*d* 1955), *d* of Sir Charles Huntington, 1st Bart, MP; *S* father, 1930; *m* 1946, Ann Pauline, *er d* of late Surgeon Capt. William Bastian, RN; two *s* one *d*. *Educ:* Wellington Coll.; Lincoln Coll., Oxford, MA. Called to Bar, Inner Temple, 1931; admitted Solicitor, 1936; Major 4th Battalion Oxford and Buckinghamshire Light Inf., TA; served France, 1940; prisoner of war, 1940-45. Master, Founders' Co., 1970. *Recreations:* tennis, golf. *Heir: s* Hon. Christopher John Norton, *b* 3 June 1949. *Address:* Bellehatch Park, Henley-on-Thames, Oxon. *T:* Henley 4160.

**RATHDONNELL,** 5th Baron, *cr* 1868; **Thomas Benjamin McClintock Bunbury;** Lieutenant, RN; *b* 17 Sept. 1938; *o s* of William, 4th Baron Rathdonnell and Pamela, *e d* of late John Malcolm Drew; *S* father 1959; *m* 1965, Jessica Harriet, *d* of George Gilbert Butler, Scatorish, Bennettsbridge, Co. Kilkenny; two *s*. *Educ:* Charterhouse; Royal Naval College, Dartmouth. *Heir: s* William Leopold McClintock Bunbury, *b* 6 July 1966. *Address:* Lisvanagh, Rathvilly, County Carlow, Ireland. *T:* Rathvilly 4.

**RATTER, John,** CBE 1945 (OBE 1944); ERD 1953; Railway Engineer, World Bank, Washington DC, since 1970; *b* 15 May 1908; *s* of George Dempster Ratter, South Shields; *m* 1937, Eileen Cail, Knaresborough, Yorkshire; two *s* one *d*. *Educ:* St Peters School, York; Durham University. BSc; MICE. Various appointments as civil engineer with London and North Eastern Railway and London Passenger Transport Board, 1929-39; War of 1939-45: served with Royal Engineers, France, Africa and Italy, and in War Office; Deputy Director of Transportation, CMF, with rank of Colonel. Various appointments with LNE Railway and LPTB and Railway Exec., 1945-53; Chief Civil Engineer, British Transport Commission, 1953-54; Technical Adviser, BTC, 1954-58; Member: BTC, 1958-62, British Railways Board, 1963-70. Pres., Internat. Union of Railways, 1960-62. Legion of Merit (USA), 1944; Légion d'Honneur (France), 1963; Order of Merit, German Federal Republic, 1968; Comdr, Order of Leopold II, Belgium, 1969. *Address:* 2601 Woodley Place NW, Washington DC 20008, USA. *Club:* United Service.

**RATTIGAN, Terence Mervyn,** CBE 1958; *b* 10 June 1911; unmarried. *Educ:* Harrow (Scholar); Trinity College, Oxford (Scholar in Modern History). Playwright. First Episode, Comedy, London, 1934, and New York; French without Tears, Criterion, London, 1936, and New York; After the Dance, St James's, London, 1939; Flare Path, Apollo, London, 1942, and New York; While the Sun Shines, London, 1943, and New York; Love in Idleness, Lyric, London, 1944; (O Mistress Mine, New York, 1945); The Winslow Boy, Lyric, 1946, and USA, 1947, Haymarket, 1970; Playbill (The Browning Version and Harlequinade), Phoenix, 1948, New York, 1949; Adventure Story, St James's, 1949; French Without Tears (revived), Vaudeville, 1949; Who is Sylvia?, Criterion, 1950; The Deep Blue Sea, Duchess, 1952, New York, 1952; The Sleeping Prince, Phoenix, 1953,

New York, 1956, St Martin's, 1968; Separate Tables, St James's, 1954, New York, 1956; Variation on a Theme, Globe, 1958; Ross, Haymarket, 1960, New York, 1961; Man and Boy, Queen's, 1963, New York, 1963; A Bequest to the Nation, Haymarket, 1970. *Films:* French without Tears, Quiet Wedding, The Day will Dawn, Uncensored, Way To The Stars, Journey Together, While The Sun Shines, The Winslow Boy, The Browning Version, The Sound Barrier, The Final Test, The Deep Blue Sea, The Prince and the Showgirl, Separate Tables; The VIP's; The Yellow Rolls-Royce; Conduct Unbecoming. *Publications:* above plays. *Recreation:* watching cricket. *Address:* c/o Dr Jan Van Loewen Ltd, 81-83 Shaftesbury Avenue, W1. *Clubs:* St James'; Royal and Ancient; MCC.

**RAU, Santha Rama, (Mrs Faubion Bowers);** free-lance writer since 1945; *b* Madras, India, 24 Jan. 1923; *d* of late Sir Benegal Rama Rau, CIE; *m* 1952, Faubion Bowers; one *s*. *Educ:* St Paul's Girls' School, London, England; Wellesley College, Mass., USA. Feature writer for the Office of War Information, New York, USA, during vacations from college, 1942-45. Hon. doctorate: Bates College, USA, 1961; Russell Sage College, 1965; Phi Beta Kappa, Wellesley College, 1960. *Publications:* Home to India, 1945; East of Home, 1950; This is India, 1953; Remember the House, 1955; View to the South-East, 1957; My Russian Journey, 1959; A Passage to India (dramatization), 1962; Gifts of Passage, 1962. Many articles and short stories in New Yorker, Art News, Horizon, Saturday Evening Post, Reader's Digest, etc. *Recreations:* baseball, tennis. *Address:* 10D Mafatlal Park, Bhulabhai Desai Road, Bombay, India.

**RAVEN, Rear-Adm. John Stanley,** CB 1964; BSc, FIEE; Registrar, Institution of Electrical Engineers; *b* 5 Oct. 1910; *s* of Frederick William Raven; *m* 1935, Nancy, *d* of William Harold Murdoch; three *s*. *Educ:* Huddersfield College; Leeds University (BSc). Temp. RNVR Commission, 1939; transferred to RN, 1946; retired, 1965. *Recreation:* painting. *Address:* 57 Kitcheners Meads, Fishpool Street, St Albans, Herts. *T:* St Albans 62240.

**RAVEN, Dame Kathleen (Dame Kathleen Annie Ingram),** DBE 1968; SRN 1936; SCM 1938; Chief Nursing Officer in the Department of Health and Social Security (formerly Ministry of Health), since 1958; *b* 9 Nov. 1910; *o d* of late Fredric William Raven and Annie Williams Mason; *m* 1959, Professor John Thornton Ingram, *qv*. *Educ:* Ulverston Grammar School; privately; St Bartholomew's Hosp., London; City of London Maternity Hospital. St Bartholomew's Hospital: Night Superintendent, Ward Sister, Administrative Sister, Assistant Matron, 1936-49; Matron, Gen. Infirmary, Leeds, 1949-57; Dep. Chief Nursing Officer, Min. of Health, 1957-58. Mem. Gen. Nursing Council for England and Wales, 1950-57; Mem. Council and Chm. Yorkshire Br., Roy. Coll. of Nursing, 1950-57; Mem. Central Area Advisory Bd for Secondary Education, Leeds, 1953-57; Area Nursing Officer, Order of St John, 1953-57; Mem. Exec. Cttee Assoc. of Hospital Matrons for England and Wales, 1955-57; Mem. Advisory Cttee for Sister Tutor's Diploma, Univ. of Hull, 1955-57; Internal Examr for Diploma of Nursing, Univ. of Leeds, 1950-57; Mem. Area Nurse Trg Cttee, 1951-57; Mem. Area Cttee Nat. Hosp. Service Reserve, 1950-57; Mem. Central Health Services Council, 1957-58; Mem. Council and Mem. Nursing Advisory Bd, Brit. Red Cross Soc., 1958; Mem. Cttee of St John Ambulance Assoc., 1958; Mem. National Florence Nightingale Memorial Cttee of Great Britain and Northern Ireland, 1958; Mem. WHO Expert Advisory Panel on Nursing, 1961. Officer (Sister) Order of St John, 1963. *Recreations:* painting, reading, travel. *Address:* 29 Harley Street, W1. *T:* 01-580 3765; Jesmond, Burcott, Wing, Leighton Buzzard, Bedfordshire. *T:* Wing 244.
*See also R. W. Raven.*

**RAVEN, Martin Owen,** MA, MD, MRCP; retired; Hon. Consulting Physician, Ramsgate General Hospital; *b* 4 July 1888; *s* of Thomas F. and Margaret M. Raven; *m* 1920, Sibyl (*d* 1969), *d* of Sherwood Mockett, St Peter's, Kent; one *s* two *d*. *Educ:* Uppingham; Trinity College, Oxford. House Surgeon, House Physician, St Mary's Hospital; Naval Surgeon, 1914-18; Physician, Ramsgate Hospital, 1926; Physician at Southport Emergency Hospital, 1941-45; Physician, Ramsgate and Margate General Hospital, 1949. *Publications:* Treatment of Rheumatism in Childhood (Modern Technique in Treatment, vol. ii); Diabetes Mellitus in Childhood, 1924; Rheumatic Diseases of Childhood, 1926; Medical Treatment in the Welfare State, 1951; Intradermal injection of influenza virus vaccine in Herpes Zoster, 1965; Reflections on Retirement, 1969, etc. *Address:* East Cliff House, Broadstairs, Kent. *T:* Thanet 63700.

**RAVEN, Ronald William,** OBE 1946; TD; FRCS 1931; Consulting Surgeon, Westminster Hospital and Royal Marsden Hospital, since 1969; Surgeon, French Hospital, London, since 1936; Cons. Surgeon (General Surgeon) Eversfield Chest Hospital since 1937; Cons. Surgeon Star and Garter Home for Disabled Sailors, Soldiers and Airmen since 1948; *b* 28 July 1904; *e s* of late Fredric William Raven and Annie Williams Mason, Coniston, Lancs. *Educ:* Ulverston Grammar School; St Bartholomew's Hospital Medical College, Univ. of London. St Bart's Hosp.: gained various prizes and surgical schol.; resident surgical appts, 1928-29; Demonstrator in Pathology, St Bart's Hosp., 1929-31; Registrar Statistics Nat. Radium Commn, 1931-34; jun. surgical appts, 1931-35; Asst Surg. Gordon Hosp., 1935; Asst Surg. Roy. Cancer Hosp., 1939-46, Surg. 1946-62; Jt Lectr in Surgery, Westminster Med. Sch., Univ. of London, 1951-69; Surgeon, Westminster (Gordon) Hosp., 1947-69; Sen. Surgeon, Royal Marsden Hosp. and Inst. of Cancer Research, Royal Cancer Hosp., 1962-69. Arris and Gale Lectr, 1933; Erasmus Wilson Lectr, 1935, 1946 and 1947; Hunterian Prof., 1948, RCS; Fell. Assoc. of Surg. of Great Britain; Member Internat. Soc. of Surgery; Fell. Roy. Soc. Med. (Past Pres. Section of Proctology); Mem. Council, RCS of England; Pres., Assoc. of Head and Neck Oncologists of Great Britain; Chairman Council and late Chm. Exec. Cttee Marie Curie Memorial Foundation; Chm. Joint National Cancer Survey Committee; Vice-President and Chairman Council of Epsom Coll.; late Chairman Conjoint Cttee; late Mem. Bd of Governors Royal Marsden Hosp.; Mem. Council of Queen's Institute of District Nursing; Mem. (late Chm.), Cttee of Management Med. Insurance Agency. Surg. EMS, 1939; joined RAMC, 1941, and served in N Africa, Italy and Malta (mentioned); o/c Surg. Div. (Lt-Col); and o/c Gen. Hosp. (Col), 1946; Lt-Col RAMC (TA); o/c Surg. Div. Gen. Hosp., 1947; Col RAMC (TA); o/c No 57 (Middlesex) General Hospital (TA), 1953-59; Colonel TARO, 1959-62; Hon. Colonel RAMC. OStJ 1946. Hon. Professor National Univ. of Colombia, 1949; Hon. MD Cartagena, 1949; Corr. For. Member: Soc. of Head and Neck Surgeons of USA; Roman Surg. Soc.; Soc. Surg. of Bogotá; Société de Chirurgie de Lyon; Mem. Nat. Acad. Med. of Colombia;

Mem. NY Acad. of Sciences; Soc. of Surgeons of Colombia; Italian Soc. Thoracic Surg.; Malcolm Morris Memorial Lectr, 1954; Blair Bell Memorial Lectr, 1960; Elizabeth Matthai Endowment Lectures, Madras University, 1965; First W. Emory Burnett Honor Lecture, Temple Univ., USA, 1966; Edith A. Ward Mem. Lecture, 1966. Visiting Professor Surgery, Ein-Shams University, Cairo, 1961. Surgical missions to: Colombia, 1949; Saudi Arabia, 1961, 1962. Chevalier de la Légion d'Honneur, 1952. *Publications:* Treatment of Shock, 1942; Surgical Care, 1st edn 1942, 2nd edn 1952; Cancer in General Practice (jointly), 1952; Surgical Instruments and Appliances (jointly), 1952; War Wounds and Injuries (Jt Editor and Contrib.), 1940; chapters on Shock and Malignant Disease in Encyclopædia British Medical Practice, 1952, 1955, 1962-69; Handbook on Cancer for Nurses and Health Visitors, 1953; Cancer and Allied Diseases, 1955; Cancer of the Pharynx, Larynx and Oesophagus and its Surgical Treatment, 1958; Editor and contributor to Cancer (7 vols), 1957-60; ed, Cancer Progress, 1960 and 1963; Contrib. chapts in Operative Surgery (Rob and Rodney Smith), 1956-57; Jt Editor, The Prevention of Cancer, 1967. Papers on surgical subjects, especially relating to Cancer in British and foreign journals. *Recreations:* philately (medallist Internat. Stamp Exhibn, London, 1950), music, ceramics and pictures, travel. *Address:* 29 Harley Street, W1. *T:* 01-580 3765; Manor Lodge, Wingrave, Aylesbury, Bucks. *T:* Aston Abbots 287; Byethorn, L'Iklin, Naxxar, Malta. *T:* 23536.

*See also Dame Kathleen Raven.*

**RAVEN, Simon (Arthur Noël);** author, critic and dramatist since 1957; *b* 28 Dec. 1927; *s* of Arthur Godart Raven and Esther Kate Raven (*née* Christmas); *m* 1951, Susan Mandeville Kilner (marriage dissolved); one *s*. *Educ:* Charterhouse; King's Coll., Cambridge (MA). Research, 1951-52; regular commn, King's Shropshire Light Inf., 1953-57 (Capt.): served in Kenya; resigned, 1957. Member, Horatian Society. *Publications: novels:* The Feathers of Death, 1959; Brother Cain, 1959; Doctors Wear Scarlet, 1960; Close of Play, 1962; The Rich Pay Late, 1964; Friends in Low Places, 1965; The Sabre Squadron, 1966; Fielding Gray, 1967; The Judas Boy, 1968; Places Where They Sing, 1970; *general:* The English Gentleman, 1961; Boys Will be Boys, 1963; Royal Foundation and Other Plays, 1965; contribs to Observer, Spectator, Punch, etc. BBC TV Plays: Royal Foundation, 1961; The Scapegoat, 1964; Sir Jocelyn, 1965; Dramatisation: Huxley's Point Counter-Point, 1968; Trollope's The Way We Live Now, 1969; ABC TV Play, The Gaming Book, 1965. *Recreations:* cricket, travel, reading. *Address:* c/o Anthony Blond Ltd, 56 Doughty Street, WC1. *Club:* Butterflies Cricket.

**RAVENSDALE,** 3rd Baron *cr* 1911; **Nicholas Mosley,** MC 1944; *b* 25 June 1923; *e s* of Sir Oswald Mosley, 6th Bt, *qv*, and late Lady Cynthia Mosley; is *heir* to father's baronetcy; *S* to Aunt's Barony, 1966; *m* 1947, Rosemary Laura Salmond; three *s* one *d*. *Educ:* Eton; Balliol College, Oxford. Served in the Rifle Brigade, Captain, 1942-46. *Publications:* (as Nicholas Mosley): Spaces of the Dark, 1951; The Rainbearers, 1955; Corruption, 1957; African Switchback, 1958; The Life of Raymond Raynes, 1961; Meeting Place, 1962; Accident, 1964; Experience and Religion, 1964; Assassins, 1966; Impossible Object, 1968. *Heir: s* Hon. Shaun Nicholas Mosley, *b* 5 August 1949. *Address:* 9 Church Row, Hampstead, NW3. *T:* 01-435 8222.

**RAVENSDALE, Thomas Corney,** CMG 1951; retired; *b* 17 Feb. 1905; *s* of late Henry Ravensdale and late Lilian (*née* Corney); *m* (marriage dissolved); two *s*; *m* 1965, Mme Antoine Watteau (*née* Ricard). *Educ:* Royal Masonic Sch., Bushey, Herts; St Catharine's Coll., Cambridge. Acting Vice-Consul, Smyrna, 1928; 3rd Secretary, British Embassy, Ankara, 1929-34; 2nd Asst Oriental Sec., The Residency, Cairo, 1934-37; Vice-Consul, Bagdad, 1937-42; 1st Asst Oriental Sec., Brit. Embassy, Cairo, 1942-47; Oriental Counsellor, Cairo, 1948-51; Political Adviser, British Residency, Benghazi, 1951; Couns., Brit. Embassy in Libya, 1952-55; Ambassador to Dominican Republic, 1955-58; Insp. Foreign Service Establishments, 1958-60; Ambassador to the Republics of Dahomey, Niger, Upper Volta and the Ivory Coast, 1960-63. *Recreation:* gardening. *Address:* The Cottage, 13 rue de Penthièvre, Petit Andely, (27) Les Andelys, France. *Club:* Athenæum.

**RAVENSWORTH,** 8th Baron *cr* 1821; **Arthur Waller Liddell,** Bt 1642; Radio Engineer, British Broadcasting Corporation, since 1944; *b* 25 July 1924; *s* of late Hon. Cyril Arthur Liddell (2nd *s* of 5th Baron) and Dorothy L., *d* of William Brown, Slinfold, Sussex; *S* cousin 1950; *m* 1950, Wendy, *d* of J. S. Bell, Cookham, Berks; one *s* one *d*. *Educ:* Harrow. *Heir: s* Hon. Thomas Arthur Hamish Liddell, *b* 27 Oct. 1954. *Address:* Eslington Park, Whittingham, Alnwick, Northumberland. *T:* Whittingham 239.

**RAWCLIFFE, Prof. Gordon Hindle,** MA, DSc, FIEE; Professor of Electrical Engineering, University of Bristol, since 1944; *b* Sheffield, 2 June 1910; *e s* of late Rev. J. Hindle Rawcliffe, Gloucester; *m* 1st, Stella Morgan (marriage dissolved); two *d*; 2nd, 1952, Sheila Mary Wicks, MA Oxon; two *d*. *Educ:* St Edmund's School, Canterbury; Keble College, Oxford. 1st Class Hons Engineering Science, 1932. Metropolitan-Vickers Electrical Co. Ltd, Manchester (now AEI Ltd), 1932-37; Lecturer in Electrical Engineering, University of Liverpool, 1937-41; Head of Electrical Engineering Department, Robert Gordon's Technical College, Aberdeen, and Lecturer-in-charge of Electrical Engineering, Univ. of Aberdeen, 1941-44. Instn of Electrical Engineers: Chairman Western Centre, 1956-57; Council, 1956-58, 1966-69; Utilization Section Committee, 1960-62; Power Divisional Board, 1963-65, and 1969-; Hunter Meml Lecture, 1970. Many patents and inventions relating to Electrical Machinery, including 2-speed P.A.M. induction motor. Consultant to: AEI/English Electric Machines Ltd; Brush Electrical Eng. Co. Ltd, 1955-69; Lancashire Dynamo Co. Ltd, 1958-67; Westinghouse Electric Corp., E Pittsburgh, USA; Reyrolle-Parsons, and other organisations. Lecture and Consulting tours in USA and Canada, 1961, Hungary, 1962, Turkey, 1963, Australia and NZ, 1964, Japan and Far East, 1965, S Africa (Bernard Price Meml Lecture), 1965, Czechoslovakia, 1966, Far East, Australia and USA, 1967, Middle and Far East, 1968, Bulgaria and Poland, 1968. *Publications:* numerous papers in Proceedings of Institution of Electrical Engineers (Premiums 1938, 1940, 1956, 1963, 1964, 1966) and other scientific and technical jls, etc. *Recreations:* exploring the West of England; travel, reading and music. *Address:* Engineering Laboratories, University Walk, Bristol BS8 1TR; 28 Upper Belgrave Road, Clifton, Bristol BS8 2XL; *T:* 24161 and 37940. *Club:* Athenæum.

**RAWDEN-SMITH, Rupert Rawden;** Metropolitan Stipendiary Magistrate since

1967; *b* 24 Sept. 1912; *s* of late Dr Hoyland Smith; *m* 1941, Mollie Snow; one *s* one *d*. *Educ:* Rossall School; King's College, London University (LLB). Barrister, Middle Temple, 1939; Recorder of Sunderland, 1961-67. *Recreation:* shooting. *Address:* 97 Church Road, Wimbledon, SW19. *T:* 01-946 4325.

**RAWES, Francis Roderick,** MBE 1944; MA; Headmaster of St Edmund's School, Canterbury, since 1964; *b* 28 Jan. 1916; *e s* of late Prescott Rawes and of Susanna May Dockery; *m* 1940, Dorothy Joyce, *d* of E. M. Hundley, Oswestry; two *s* one *d*. *Educ:* Charterhouse; St Edmund Hall, Oxford. Asst Master at Westminster School, 1938-40 and 1946-64; Housemaster, 1947-64. Served in Intelligence Corps, 1940-46: GSO3 (I) 13 Corps; GSO1 (I) HQ 15 Army Group and MI14 War Office. *Address:* St Edmund's School, Canterbury, Kent. *T:* Canterbury 64496.

**RAWLINGS, Margaret, (Lady Barlow);** Actress; *b* Osaka, Japan, 5 June 1906; *d* of Rev. G. W. Rawlings and Lilian Boddington; *m* 1st, 1927, Gabriel Toyne, actor (marriage dissolved 1938); no *c*; 2nd, 1942, Robert Barlow (*see* Sir Robert Barlow); one *d*. *Educ:* Oxford High School for Girls; Lady Margaret Hall, Oxford. Left Oxford after one year, and joined the Macdona Players Bernard Shaw Repertory Company on tour, 1927; played Jennifer in the Doctor's Dilemma and many other parts; toured Canada with Maurice Colbourne, 1929; First London engagement Bianca Capello in The Venetian at Little Theatre in 1931, followed by New York; played Elizabeth Barrett Browning, in The Barretts of Wimpole Street in Australia and New Zealand; Oscar Wilde's Salome at Gate Theatre; Liza Kingdom, The Old Folks at Home, Queen's; Mary Fitton in This Side Idolatry, Lyric; Jean in The Greeks had a word for it, Liza Doolittle in Pygmalion and Ann in Man and Superman, Cambridge Theatre, 1935; Katie O'Shea in Parnell, Ethel Barrymore Theatre, New York 1935, later at New, London; Lady Macbeth for OUDS 1936; Mary and Lily in Black Limelight, St James' and Duke of York's, 1937-38; Helen in Trojan Women, Karen Selby in The Flashing Stream, Lyric, 1938-39, and in New York; Revival of Liza in Pygmalion, Haymarket, 1939; You of all People, Apollo, 1939; A House in the Square, St Martin's, 1940; Mrs Dearth in Dear Brutus, 1941-42; Gwendolen Fairfax in the Importance of Being Earnest, Royal Command Perf., Haymarket, 1946; Titania in Purcell's Fairy Queen, Covent Garden, 1946; Vittoria Corombona in Webster's The White Devil, Duchess, 1947; Marceline in Jean-Jacques bernard's The Unquiet Spirit, Arts, 1949; Germaine in A Woman in Love, tour and Embassy, 1949; The Purple Fig Tree, Piccadilly, 1950; Lady Macbeth, Arts, 1950; Spring at Marino, Arts, 1951; Zabina in Tamburlaine, Old Vic, 1951-52; Lysistrata in The Apple Cart, Haymarket, 1953; Countess in The Dark is Light Enough, Salisbury and Windsor Repertory, 1955; Paulina and Mistress Ford, Old Vic, 1955-56; Title Rôle in Racine's Phèdre, Theatre in the Round, London and tour, 1957-58; Sappho in Sappho, Lyceum, Edinburgh, 1961; Ask Me No More, Windsor, 1962; Title role in Racine's Phèdre, Cambridge Arts, 1963; Ella Rentheim in John Gabriel Borkman, Duchess, 1963; Jocasta in Œdipus, Playhouse (Nottingham), 1964; Gertrude in Hamlet, Ludlow Festival, 1965; Madame Torpe in Torpe's Hotel, Yvonne Arnaud Theatre, Guildford, 1965; Mrs Bridgenorth, in Getting Married, Strand, 1967; Carlotta, in A Song at Twilight, Windsor, 1968. *Films:* Roman Holiday; Beautiful Stranger; No Road Back. *Television:* Criss Cross Quiz; Somerset Maugham Hour; Sunday Break; Compact; Maigret; Planemakers; solo performance, Black Limelight, Armchair Theatre, 1969. Innumerable broadcasts, incl. We Beg to Differ, and, Brains Trust; poetry recitals; recordings of: Keats, Gerard Manley Hopkins, Alice in Wonderland; (Marlowe Soc.) King Lear, Pericles; New English Bible Gospels. *Publication:* (Trans.) Racine's Phèdre, 1961, (US, 1962). *Recreation:* poetry. *Address:* Rocketer, Wendover, Bucks. *T:* Wendover 2234. *Club:* Arts Theatre.

**RAWLINS, Colin Guy Champion,** OBE 1965; DFC 1941; Director of Zoos, Zoological Society of London, since 1966; *b* 5 June 1919; *s* of R. S. C. Rawlins and Yvonne Blanche Andrews; *m* 1946, Rosemary Jensen; two *s* one *d*. *Educ:* Prince of Wales Sch., Nairobi; Charterhouse; Queen's Coll., Oxford (BA). Served with RAF, 1939-46: Bomber Comd, NW Europe; POW, 1941-45; Sqdn-Leader. HM Overseas Civil Service, 1946-66: Administrative Officer, Northern Rhodesia (later Zambia); appointments at Headquarters and in field; Provincial Commissioner, Resident Secretary. FCIS 1967. *Recreations:* aviation, most outdoor sports, current affairs. *Address:* c/o Zoological Society of London, Regent's Park, NW1; Birchgrove, Earl Howe Road, Holmer Green, Bucks. *Club:* Royal Aero.

**RAWLINS, Evelyn Charles Donaldson,** CMG 1932; CBE 1930; *b* 27 Feb. 1884; *s* of W. Donaldson Rawlins, KC, White Waltham Grove, Bucks; *m* 1908, Suzanne, *d* of E. Kappes; one *s*. *Educ:* Eton; Trinity College, Cambridge. Acting Consul-General, Beirut, 1907; HM Vice-Consul at Adana, 1910; Acting Consul-General in Crete, 1911, and at Beirut, 1913; Consul at Canea, 1915; Member of International Consular Commission on Foreign Claims in Crete; attached to AHQ Salonica Expeditionary Force, 1915; active service with Navy, 1915-17; attached to Serbian Commercial Mission, 1918, and Greek Commercial Mission, 1918; Chief Commissioner on British Commercial Mission to Morocco, 1918; Commercial Secretary (Grade I) for Greece and Serbia, 1919; in charge of British Economic Mission to Jugoslavia, 1919; Commercial Secretary (Grade I) at Berne, 1922; transferred to Prague, 1923, and to Budapest, 1924; transferred to Rome with rank of Commerical Counsellor, 1926; Director of Exhibitions Division, Department of Overseas Trade, 1930; Commissioner-General to HM Government at International Exhibition, Antwerp, 1930, and British Empire Trade Exhibition, Buenos Aires, 1931; Commercial Counsellor, British Legation, Vienna, 1932-34; British Embassy, Berlin, 1934-37; Minister to Bolivia, 1937-40; Retired from Diplomatic Service; Greek Order of Redeemer (Gold Cross). *Address:* c/o Standard Bank, Northumberland Avenue, WC2.

**RAWLINS, His Honour Percy Lionel Edwin,** MA, LLB, Cantab; County Court Judge, 1947-67; Circuit No 36 (Berks Glos & Oxon), 1962-67; *b* 14 April, 1902; *s* of F. P. F. M. Rawlins, Solicitor, and F. Rawlins; *m* 1930, Katharine M. E. Fearnley-Sander; one *s* one *d*. *Educ:* Highgate School; Selwyn College, Cambridge. Honours Law Tripos, Cambridge, 1924; called to Bar, 1926, Midland Circuit; Major attached ACA, 1944-46; Legal Officer, Villach, Austria, 1945-46; VP Educational Interchange Council, 1950; Fell. Corporation of SS Mary and Nicolas, 1951. *Recreation:* gardening. *Address:* The Well House, Christmas Common, Watlington, Oxon. *T:* Watlington 577.

**RAWLINSON, Sir Anthony Henry John,** 5th Bt *cr* 1891; *b* 1 May 1936; *s* of Sir Alfred Frederick Rawlinson, 4th Bt and of Bessie Ford Taylor, *d* of Frank Raymond Emmatt, Harrogate; *S* father, 1969; *m* 1960, Penelope Byng Noel (marr. diss. 1967), 2nd *d* of Rear-Adm. G. J. B. Noel, RN; one *s* one *d*. *Educ:* Millfield School. *Heir:* *s* Alexander Rawlinson, *b* 1964. *Address:* 4 Mona Road, Darling Point, Sydney, NSW, Australia.

**RAWLINSON, Anthony Keith;** Under-Secretary, HM Treasury, since 1968; *b* 5 March 1926; *s* of late Alfred Edward John Rawlinson, Bishop of Derby 1936-59, and Mildred Ansley Rawlinson (*née* Ellis); *m* 1956, Mary Hill; three *s*. *Educ:* Maidwell Hall; Eton; Christ Church, Oxford. Eton: King's Schol., 1939, Newcastle Schol., 1944, Captain of Sch. 1944; Christ Church, Open Schol. (classics), 1944. Gren. Gds (Lieut), 1944-47. Oxford: 1st Cl. Honour Mods (classics), 1949, 2nd Cl. Lit. Hum., 1951. Entered Civil Service by open competition as Asst Principal, 1951; Min. of Labour and Nat. Service, 1951-53; transferred to Treasury, 1953; Principal, 1955; seconded to Atomic Energy Authority as Private Sec. to Chairman, 1958-60; returned to Treasury, 1960; Asst Sec., 1963; Under-Sec., 1968. *Publications:* articles and reviews in mountaineering jls. Editor, Climbers' Club Jl, 1955-59. *Recreation:* mountaineering (Pres. OU Mountaineering Club, 1949-50). *Address:* 105 Corringham Road, NW11. *T:* 01-458 3402. *Clubs:* Oxford and Cambridge University, Alpine (Hon. Sec., 1963-66).

**RAWLINSON, Sir Joseph,** Kt 1962; CBE 1953; MEng, FINstCE, FIMechE, FIMunE; Chief Engineer and County Surveyor, London County Council, 1947-62; *b* 16 April 1897; *m* 1923, Gertrude Moseley Maggs; one *s* one *d*. *Educ:* Liverpool University. Served European War, 1914-18, with Liverpool Scottish and RAF; Engineer with Public Works Contractor on Construction of Roads and Sub-aqueous Tunnels; Asst City Engineer, Liverpool, 1930-35; City Engineer, Westminster, 1936-47. Hon. Citizen, City of Winnipeg, Canada, 1959. *Publications:* Reclamation of Mersey Foreshore for Promenade at Otterspool (Proceeding of Royal Sanitary Inst.), 1933; (with W. R. Davidge) City of Westminster Plan. *Recreations:* motoring and golf. *Address:* 26 Sanderstead Hill, Sanderstead, Surrey. *Club:* Royal Automobile.

**RAWLINSON, Rt. Hon. Sir Peter (Anthony Grayson),** PC 1964; Kt 1962; QC 1959; MP (C) Epsom Division of Surrey since 1955; Attorney General since 1970; *b* 26 June 1919; *o surv. s* of Lt-Col A. R. Rawlinson, OBE, and Ailsa Grayson Rawlinson; *m* 1st, 1940, Haidee Kavanagh; three *d*; 2nd, 1954, Elaine Dominguez, Newport, Rhode Island, USA; two *s* one *d*. *Educ:* Downside; Christ's Coll., Cambridge (Exhibitioner). Served in Irish Guards, 1939-46; N Africa, 1943 (despatches); demobilized with rank of Major, 1946. Called to Bar, Inner Temple, 1946. Bencher, 1962. Contested (C) Hackney South, 1951. Recorder of Salisbury, 1961-62; Solicitor-General, July 1962-Oct. 1964. Opposition Spokesman: for Law, 1964-65, 1968-70; for Broadcasting, 1965; Vice-Chm., Legal Cttee, 1966; Chm., Parly Legal Cttee, 1967. Member of Council, Justice, 1960-62, 1964; Trustee of Amnesty, 1960-62; Member, Bar Council, 1966-68; Mem. Senate, Inns of Court, 1968. *Recreations:* the theatre and painting. *Address:* 55 Chelsea Square, SW3; 12 King's Bench Walk, Temple, EC4. *T:* 01-353 1400. *Clubs:* White's, Pratt's, MCC.

**RAWSON, Christopher Selwyn Priestley;** JP; Chairman and Managing Director, Christopher Rawson Ltd; Chairman, brown & Sons Ltd, since 1965; *b* 25 March 1928; *e s* of Selwyn Gerald Caygill Rawson, OBE, Comdr RN (retd) and Dr Doris Rawson, MB, ChB (*née* Brown); *m* 1959, Rosemary Ann Focke; two *d*. *Educ:* The Nautical College, Pangbourne, Berks. Navigating Apprentice, Merchant Service, T. & J. Brocklebank Ltd, 1945-48. Sheriff of the City of London, 1961-62; Member of Court of Common Council (Ward of Bread Street) 1963-. Chm. Governors, The Elms Sch., Colwall, near Malvern, Worcs, 1965-. Chm., Port and City of London Health Cttee, 1967-70. Silver Medal for Woollen and Worsted Raw Materials, City and Guilds of London Institute, 1951; Livery of Clothworkers Company, 1952; Freeman, Company of Watermen and Lightermen, 1966; ATI 1953; Associate of RINA 1957; AIMarE 1962. Comdr National Order of Senegal, 1961; Comdr, National Order of The Ivory Coast, 1962; Comdr Order of the Star of Africa, 1962. *Recreations:* shooting, sailing. *Address:* 56 Ovington Street, SW3. *T:* 01-589 3136; 10/11 Lime Street, EC3. *T:* 01-626 1801. *Clubs:* City of London, Royal Thames Yacht, Royal Automobile, City Livery.

**RAWSON, Maj.-Gen. Geoffrey Grahame,** CB 1941; OBE; MC; *b* 2 Dec. 1887; *s* of Edward Creswell Rawson, ICS, and Marion Duffield; *m* 1919, Ella Cane (*d* 1967); two *s*. *Educ:* Cheltenham Coll.; RMA Woolwich. Commissioned Royal Engineers, 1908; transferred Royal Corps of Signals, 1920; DAAG War Office, 1921; Chief Instructor School of Signals, 1932; Deputy Director Staff Duties, War Office, 1937; Director of Signals, War Office, 1941; Inspector of Signals, 1942; Colonel Comdt Royal Signals, 1944-50. Lt-Col, Royal Signals, 1928; Colonel, 1931; Brigadier, 1937; Major-General, 1941; served European War, 1914-18, with BEF in France and in Salonika (Brevet Major, Legion of Honour 5th Class, OBE, MC, despatches five times); ADC to the King, 1938-41; retired pay, 1944. *Address:* 15 Collingham Road, SW5. *Club:* United Service.

**RAWSON, Sir Stanley Walter,** Kt 1953; *b* 9 October 1891; *s* of Frank H. Rawson, Sheffield; *m* 1922, Phyllis (*d* 1967), *d* of A. Freer, Bargate; two *s*. *Educ:* King Edward's School, Sheffield; Queen's Coll., Oxford, 1st Cl. Hon. Mods, 1911, Lit Hum 1913, History, 1914. Fellow of All Souls, 1914-21. Asst Sec., Bolckow Vaughan & Co. Ltd, 1916; Comptroller: Dorman Long & Co. Ltd, 1929; John Brown & Co. Ltd, 1934 (Vice-Chairman, 1953-59). Director-General Machine Tools, Ministry of Supply, 1951-53. Chm., Robert Fraser and Partners, 1960-61. *Publications:* contributions to Journal of Royal Economic Society. *Recreations:* golf and reading. *Address:* 28 Eton Court, Eton Avenue, NW3.

**RAWSTHORNE, Alan,** CBE 1961; Composer; *b* Haslingden, Lancashire, 2 May 1905; *s* of Hubert Rawsthorne, MRCS; *m* 1st, 1934, Jessie Hinchliffe, violinist; 2nd, 1954, Isabel Lambert. *Educ:* Sandringham School, Southport, Lancs; Royal Manchester College of Music (Fellow, 1943). Did not begin serious study of music till the age of 20, owing to parental opposition; previously a student of dentistry and architecture; entered Royal Manchester Coll. of Music 1926, and subsequently spent some time abroad. Taught at Dartington Hall, 1932-34, and worked as musician to the School of Dance-mime there; returned to London, 1934. Compositions performed at International Soc. for Contemporary Music festivals, London 1938 and 1946; Warsaw 1939; Brussels 1950; contributed articles on Music to Life and Letters, 1934-35. Joined the Army (Royal Artillery) March 1941. Hon. DMus: Belfast, 1969; Liverpool, 1969. *Publications:* Variations for 2 Violins, 1938; Symphonic Studies, 1939; String Quartet No 1, 1939; Piano Concerto, 1942; The Creel (piano duet), 1942; Street Corner Overture, 1944; Cortèges (Fantasy-Overture), 1945; Violin Concerto, 1948; Quartet for Clarinet and strings; Sonata for cello and piano; Sonatina for piano; Concerto for String Orchestra; Concerto for oboe and strings; symphony; 2nd piano concerto; A Canticle of Man (chamber cantata); Sonata for viola and piano; Practical Cats (for Speaker and Orchestra); String Quartet No 2; Madame Chrysanthème (ballet); 2nd Violin Concerto, 1956; Sonata for violin and piano, 1957; symphony No 2, 1959; Overture, Hallé, 1958; Concerto for 10 Instruments, 1961; Improvisations on a theme by Constant Lambert, 1961; Mediaeval Diptych (for Baritone and Orchestra); Trio (for piano, violin and cello); Divertimento for Chamber Orchestra; Lament for a Sparrow (for tenor, chorus and harp), 1962; Quintet for Piano and Wind; Carmen Vitale (Cantata for soprano, chorus and Orchestra); Elegiac Rhapsody (for String Orchestra), 1964; Symphony No 3, 1964; Tankas of the Four Seasons, 1965; Suite for Brass Band; String Quartet No 3, 1965; Cello Concerto, 1966; The God in the Cave (for Chorus and Orchestra), 1966; Ballade (for piano), 1967; Concerto for two pianos and orchestra, 1968; Quintet for piano and strings, 1968; Suite for harp, flute and viola, 1968; Triptych for full orchestra, 1969; some songs and piano music. *Recreation:* chess. *Address:* c/o Oxford University Press, 44 Conduit Street, W1.

**RAY, Rt. Rev. Chandu;** Co-ordinating Officer for Asian Evangelism since 1969; *b* 14 April 1912; Pakistani parentage; *m* Anita Joy (*née* Meggitt); two *s* three *d*. *Educ:* D. J. Sind Coll., Karachi; Bishop's Coll., Calcutta. Bursar, Bishop Cotton Sch., Simla. Deacon, 1943; Priest, 1943. Vicar, St Philip's Church, Hyderabad, 1944; Sec., British and Foreign Bible Soc. in Pakistan, 1948; Canon of Lahore Cathedral, 1954; Archdeacon of Karachi, 1956; Asst Bishop of Lahore and Bishop in Karachi, 1957; first Bishop of Karachi, 1963-69. Hon. Dr of Sacred Theology, Wycliff, Toronto; Hon. Dr of Divinity, Huron, London. *Publications:* (trans) Old Testament in Sindhi Language, 1954; (revised 2nd edn) New Testament in Sindhi, 1955. *Recreations:* hockey, cricket, tennis. *Address:* 2 Canning Rise, Singapore 6. *T:* 24918.

**RAY, Cyril;** journalist; Editorial Staff, The Observer, since 1962; Vice-President, Editorial Advisory Council, The Good Food Guide, since 1968; *b* 16 March 1908; *e s* of Albert Benson Ray (who changed the family name from Rotenberg, 1913), and Rita Ray; *m* 1953, Elizabeth Mary, JP, *o d* of late Rev. H. C. Brocklehurst; one *s*. *Educ:* elementary sch., Bury, Lancs; Manchester Grammar Sch. (foundn schol.); Jesus Coll., Oxford (open schol.). Manchester Guardian, 1936-44; War Correspondent: 5th Destroyer Flotilla, 1940; N African Landings, 1942; 8th Army, Italy (despatches); for BBC: US 82nd Airborne Div., Nijmegen, 1944; US 3rd Army, 1944-45. UNESCO and other missions, Italy, Greece, East, Central and S Africa, 1945-50. Sunday Times, 1949-56 (Moscow Correspondent, 1950-52); Asst Editor, The Spectator, 1958-62; Wine Correspondent: The Director, 1958-; The Observer, 1959-; Chairman, Directors' Wine Club, 1962-; Founder and First Chairman, Circle of Wine Writers; Trustee, Albany, 1967-. Much occasional broadcasting, 1940-62, including The Critics, 1958-62. Vice-Chm., Cranbrook Labour Party. *Publications:* (ed) Scenes and Characters from Surtees, 1948; From Algiers to Austria: The History of 78 Division, 1952; The Pageant of London, 1958; Merry England, 1960; Regiment of the Line: The Story of the Lancashire Fusiliers, 1963; (ed) The Gourmet's Companion, 1963; (ed) Morton Shand's Book of French Wines, 1964; (ed) Best Murder Stories, 1965; The Wines of Italy, 1966 (Bologna Trophy, 1967); In a Glass Lightly, 1967; Lafite: The Story of Château Lafite-Rothschild, 1968. Editor, The Compleat Imbiber, approx. annually, 1956- (Wine and Food Soc.'s first André Simon Prize, 1964). *Recreation:* riding. *Address:* Delmonden Manor, Hawkhurst, Kent. *T:* Hawkhurst 2029; Albany, Piccadilly, W1. *T:* 01-734 0270. *Clubs:* Athenæum, Brooks's, Buck's, MCC, Special Forces; Kildare Street (Dublin).

**RAY, Frederick Ivor,** CB 1958; CBE 1953; BSc (Eng); FIEE; Telecommunications Consultant; *b* 18 Jan. 1899; *s* of Frederick Pedder Ray; *m* 1923, Katherine (*d* 1968), *d* of Hubert Abdy Fellowes, Newbury; two *s*. *Educ:* Bournemouth School; Faraday House Electrical Engineering College. Served European War, 1917-19, RE. Entered GPO Engineering Dept, 1922; Sectional Engineer, 1932-35; Telephone Manager, Scotland West, 1935-39; Telecommunications Controller, NW Region, 1939; Controller Telephones, London, 1940-44; Assistant Secretary, 1944-48; Regional Director, London, 1948-56; Director of Inland Telecommunications, 1956-61; Director, International Press Communications Committee, 1965-67; Commonwealth Press Union Adviser on Telecommunications, 1963-67. *Recreations:* fishing, caravanning, golf. *Address:* 19 Shepherds Road, Watford. *T:* 23113.

**RAY, Gordon Norton;** President of the John Simon Guggenheim Memorial Foundation, since 1963; *b* New York City, 8 Sept. 1915; *s* of Jesse Gordon and Jessie Norton Ray; unmarried. *Educ:* University of Indiana (AM); Harvard Univ. (AM, PhD). Instructor in English, Harvard, 1940-42; Guggenheim Fellow, 1941-42, 1946, 1956-57. Lt, US Navy, serving abroad aicraft carriers Belleau Wood and Boxer, Pacific, 1942-46; Professor of English, 1946-60, Head of Dept, 1950-57, Vice-President and Provost, 1957-60, University of Illinois. Associate Secretary General, Guggenheim Foundn, 1960-61; Sec.-Gen., 1961-63. Rockefeller Fellow, 1948-49; Member US Educational Commn in UK, which established Fulbright program, 1948-49. Lowell Lectures, Boston, 1950; Berg Professor, New York Univ. 1952-53; Professor of English, 1962-. Member Commission on Trends in Education, Mod. Lang. Assoc., 1953-59, Trustee 1966-; Advisor in literature, Houghton Mifflin Co., 1953-. Advisory Bd, Guggenheim Foundation, 1959-60, Trustee, 1963-; Trustee, Pierpont Morgan Library, 1970-. LittD: Monmouth Coll., 1959; Syracuse Univ., 1961; Duke Univ., 1965; Illinois Univ., 1968; LLD: New York Univ., 1961; Tulane Univ., 1963; Univ. of Calif, 1968; Columbia Univ., 1969; LHD, Indiana Univ., 1964. FRSL 1948. Fellow, Amer. Acad. of Arts and Sciences, 1962. *Publications:* Letters and Private Papers of Thackeray, 4 vols, 1945-46; The Buried Life, 1952; Thackeray: The Uses of Adversity, 1955; Henry James and H. G. Wells, 1958; Thackeray: The Age of Wisdom, 1958; etc; contrib. to magazines and learned jls. *Recreations:* book-collecting, travel. *Address:* 25 Sutton Place South, New York, NY 10022, USA. *Clubs:* Athenæum (London); Harvard,

Grolier (President, 1965-69), Century (New York).

**RAY, Reginald Edwin Anthony,** CIE 1941; *b* 15 May 1891; *s* of late George Anthony Ray, East Dulwich; *m* 1920, Marion Huggan, Pudsey, Yorks; two *s* one *d*. *Educ:* City of London School. Joined Indian Police, 1910; Deputy Inspector General, Intelligence Branch, Bengal, 1937-43; Comr of Police, Calcutta, 1943-46; retired 1946. Indian Police Medal, 1933; King's Police Medal, 1944. *Address:* 52 Canonbury Park North, N1. *T:* 01-226 3602.

**RAY, Satyajit;** Padmashree, 1957; Padmabhushan, 1964; Indian film producer and film director since 1953; *b* 2 May 1921; *s* of late Sukumar and Suprabha Ray (*née* Das); *m* 1949, Bijoya (*née* Das); one *s*. *Educ:* Ballygunge Govt School; Presidency College, Calcutta. Joined British advertising firm, D. J. Keymer & Co., as visualiser, 1943; Art Director, 1950. In 1952, started first feature film, Pather Panchali, finished in 1955 (Cannes Special Award, 1956, San Francisco, best film, 1957). Left advertising for whole-time film-making, 1956. Other films: Aparajito, 1957 (Venice Grand Prix, 1957, San Francisco, best direction); Jalsaghar, 1958; Devi, 1959; Apur Sansar, 1959 (Selznick Award and Sutherland Trophy 1960); Teen Kanya (Two Daughters), 1961; Kanchanjangha, 1962; Mahanagar, 1963; Charulata, 1964; The Coward and The Holy Man (Kapurush-O-Mahapurush), 1965; The Hero (Nayak), 1965; Goopy Gyne and Bagha Byne, 1969. Founded first Film Society in Calcutta, 1947. Composes background music for own films. *Publications:* film articles in Sight and Sound, Sequence. (Editor, 1961-) children's magazine Sandesh, with contributions of stories, poems. *Recreations:* listening to Indian and Western classical music, and reading science-fiction. *Address:* 3 Lake Temple Road, Calcutta 29, India. *T:* 46-1817.

**RAY, Ted;** Theatrical and BBC Entertainer; *s* of Chas Olden, comedian, and of Margaret Ellen Kenyon; *m* 1933, Dorothy Sybil Stevens; two *s*. *Educ:* Liverpool Collegiate School. Became successively clerk, ship's steward and dance band violinist. First stage appearance, Palace Theatre, Prescot, Lancs, 1927. First London appearance, London Music Hall, Shoreditch, 1930. Toured South Africa thrice; Royal Command Performances: London Palladium, 1948; London Coliseum, 1949; Empire, Leicester Sq., 1950; London Palladium, 1952. Interested in theatre charities (King Water Rat, 1949 and 1950). Began 1st radio series, Ray's a Laugh, 1949; Resident MC of BBC Calling All Forces, 1950. Television: The Ted Ray Show, BBC, 1955; I Object, Jackanory; Jokers Wild, 1969-70. *Films:* Meet Me Tonight, 1952; Escape by Night, 1953; My Wife's Family, 1956; The Crowning Touch, 1957; Carry on Teacher, 1959; Please Turn Over, 1959. *Publications:* Autobiography: Raising the Laughs, 1952; My Turn Next, 1963. *Recreations:* golf, swimming, motoring, boxing. *Address:* 30 Broad Walk, N21. *Clubs:* Crews Hill Golf; Temple Golf.

**RAYBOULD, Clarence,** Hon. DMus, FRCO, Hon. RAM, FBSM; Hon. FTCL; Bard of Wales; Past Director of Senior Orchestra, Royal Academy of Music; *b* 1886, English; *m* 1940, Evelyn Brodhurst Vaughan. *Educ:* King Edward's School, and University, Birmingham. Conductor Beecham Opera Co. and Royal Opera, Covent Garden, for nine years; Musical adviser and conductor, Columbia Gramophone Co. 1927-31; composed, arranged and conducted for the first British film to have its own music, and a number of other early British documentaries; Chief Asst Conductor of BBC Symphony Orch., 1936-45; has conducted much British music, some for the first time, in many European cities, and in America. Hon. DMus, Univ. of Wales, 1954. *Works:* an opera and a number of pianoforte, violoncello and clarinet works, chamber music and part-songs, some of which published. *Address:* Crannies, 12 North Street, Northam, N Devon. *T:* Bideford 2517.

**RAYBOULD, Prof. Sidney Griffith,** PhD; Professor of Adult Education, 1953-69, and Director of Extra-Mural Studies, 1946-69, University of Leeds; *b* 10 Nov. 1903; *s* of Albert and Margaret Raybould; *m* 1933, Nina Marjorie (*née* Calvert); two *s* two *d*. *Educ:* Middlesbrough High School; University College, Nottingham. Teacher, Middlesbrough Local Education Authority, 1925-35; Staff Tutor, Univ. of Leeds, 1936-46. Visiting Director of Extra-Mural Studies, Univ. Coll., Ibadan, Nigeria, 1954-55; Visiting Director of Extra-Mural Studies, University Coll. of the West Indies, 1960-61; Vis. Dean of Degree Studies in Extension, McMaster Univ., Hamilton, Ontario. New Zealand Prestige Fellow, 1964, 1966. Member: Central Advisory Council for Education (England), 1950-61; General Advisory Council, BBC, 1952-59; Inter-University Council for Higher Education Overseas, 1955-69; Council on Overseas Colleges of Arts, Science and Technology, 1955-62; Vice-President of the WEA, 1949-57. Hon. LLD, McMaster University, 1962. *Publications:* The WEA: The Next Phase, 1949; The English Universities and Adult Education, 1951; Adult Education at a Tropical University, 1957; Trends in English Adult Education (Ed.), 1958; (contributor): Universities in Adult Education, 1952; University Extramural Education in England, 1945-62, 1964; Encyclopædia Britannica; British Jl of Educational Studies. *Recreations:* reading, biography, walking, watching cricket. *Address:* 49 Kent Road, Harrogate, Yorks. *T:* Harrogate 68719. *Club:* Reform.

**RAYLEIGH,** 5th Baron *cr* 1821; **John Arthur Strutt;** *b* 12 April 1908; *e s* of 4th Baron Rayleigh, FRS, and late Mary Hilda, 2nd *d* of 4th Earl of Leitrim; *S* father 1947; *m* 1934, Ursula Mary, *o d* of Lieut-Colonel R. H. R. Brocklebank, DSO and Charlotte Carissima, *o d* of General Sir Bindon Blood, GCB, GCVO. *Educ:* Eton; Trinity College, Cambridge. *Heir:* *b* Hon. Charles Richard Strutt, *qv*. *Address:* Terling Place, Chelmsford, Essex. *T:* Terling 235; 18 Hyde Park Square, W2. *T:* 01-723 9813.

**RAYMER, Michael Robert,** OBE 1951; HM Overseas Civil Service, retired, 1962; Principal, Ministry of Defence; *b* 22 July 1917; *surv s* of Rev. W. H. Raymer, MA; *m* 1948, Joyce Marion Scott; two *s* one *d*. *Educ:* Marlborough College (Foundation Scholar); Jesus College, Cambridge (Rustat Schol.). BA (Hons) 1939. Administrative Officer, Nigeria, 1940-49 and 1952-55. Served in Royal W African Frontier Force, 1940-43. Colonial Sec. to Govt of the Falkland Islands, 1949-52; Prin. Estab. Officer, N Nigeria, 1954; Controller of Organisation and Establishments, to Government of Fiji, 1955-62. *Recreation:* gardening. *Address:* 174 Ballards Way, Croydon, Surrey CR0 5RG.

**RAYMOND, Ernest;** novelist; Knight Officer of the Order of Merit of the Italian Republic; FRSL; President, Dickens Fellowship, 1971; *b* 31 December 1888; *s* of William Bell Raymond; *m* 1st, Zoe Irène Maude (marriage dissolved), *d* of late Capt. Doucett, RNR, Younger Brother of Trinity House; one *s* one *d*; 2nd,

Diana Joan, *o d* of late William Thomas Young, Professor of Literature, University of London; one *s*. *Educ:* Colet Court; St Paul's School; Chichester Theological College; LTh Durham University, 1914; 1st Class, Universities Preliminary to Holy Orders, 1914. Assistant Master at Glengorse, Eastbourne, 1908-11; at St Christopher's, Bath, 1911-12; ordained, 1914; resigned Orders, 1923; attached to 10th Manchester Regiment, 1915-17; 9th Worcester Regiment, 1917-19; served in Gallipoli, Egypt, France, Mesopotamia, Persia, and Russia; demobilised, 1919; Awarded gold medal of Book Guild, 1936, for novel: We, the Accused. *Publications:* Tell England, 1922; Rossenal, 1922; Damascus Gate, 1923; Wander light, 1924; The Shout of the King, 1924, Daphne Bruno, I, 1925; Daphne Bruno, II, 1926; Morris in the Dance, 1927; The Old Tree Blossomed, 1928; Through Literature to Life, 1928; The Berg (play), 1929; A Family that Was, 1929; The Jesting Army, 1930; Mary Leith, 1931; The Multabello Road (play), 1932; Once in England (trilogy), 1932; Newtimber Lane, 1933; Child of Norman's End, 1934; We, the Accused, 1935; Don John's Mountain Home, 1936; The Marsh, 1937; In the Steps of St Francis, 1938; The Miracle of Brean, 1939; A Song of the Tide, 1940; The Last to Rest, 1941; Was There Love Once?, 1942; The Corporal of the Guard, 1943; For Them that Trespass, 1944; Back to Humanity (with Patrick Raymond), 1945; The Five Sons of Le Faber, 1945; The Autobiography of David—, (edited), 1946; The Kilburn Tale, 1947; In the Steps of the Brontës, 1948; Gentle Greaves, 1949; The Witness of David –, Welcome, 1950; A Chorus Ending, 1951; Two Gentlemen of Rome, The Story of Keats and Shelley, 1952; The Chalice and the Sword, 1952; To the Wood no more, 1954; The Nameless Places, 1954; The Lord of Wensley, 1956; The Old June Weather, 1957; The City and the Dream, 1958; The Quiet Shore, 1958; The Visit of Brother Ives, 1960; Paris, City of Enchantment, 1961; Mr Olim, 1961; Thc Chatelaine, 1962; One of our Brethren, 1963; Late in the Day, 1964; The Tree of Heaven, 1965; The Mountain Farm, 1966; The Bethany Road, 1967; autobiography: The Story of My Days, 1968; Please You, Draw Near, 1969; Good Morning, Good People, 1970; poems and articles in periodicals. *Recreations:* climbing, watching cricket, travelling. *Address:* 22 The Pryors, East Heath Road, Hampstead, NW3. *T:* 3716. *Club:* Garrick.

**RAYMOND, Harold,** OBE, MC, MA; *b* 1887; *s* of Cuthbert and Ellen Martha Raymond, Rose Lawn, Worcester; *m* 1920, Vera, *d* of Rev. T. M. Everett, Vicar of Ruislip, and *widow* of Capt. R. G. Tasker, Worcestershire Regiment; one *s*. *Educ:* Worcester King's School; Pembroke College, Oxford (Scholar, Hon. Mods and Lit Hum). Assistant Master, Oundle School, 1912-14; served European War, 1914-18; 2nd Lieut 10 Worc. Regt, 1914; Captain, 1915; Staff Captain 58 Brigade, 1916-17; Major, General Staff, DAAG, 19 Division, 1918-19 (despatches thrice, OBE, MC); partner in Chatto & Windus, 1919-53; Chairman of Chatto & Windus Ltd, 1953-54; originated, and in 1926 proposed, the Book Tokens scheme, which was finally adopted by the British Book Trade in 1932; retired 1956. *Address:* Biddenden Place, Biddenden, Kent. *Club:* Athenæum.

*See also A. G. Tasker.*

**RAYMOND, Sir Stanley (Edward),** Kt 1967; MInstT, FBIM; Chairman, Gaming Board for Great Britain, since 1968; b 10 Aug. 1913; *s* of late Frederick George and Lilian Grace Raymond; *m* 1938, Enid, *d* of Capt. S. A. Buley, Polruan-by-Fowey; one *s*. *Educ:* Orphanage; Grammar Sch., Hampton, Mx. Entered Civil Service, 1930. Asst Sec., Soc. of Civil Servants, 1939-45. War service in Royal Artillery, 1942-45; Lieutenant-Colonel on demobilisation. London Passenger Transport Board, 1946; British Road Services, 1947; BTC, 1955; Director of Establishment and Staff, 1956; Chief Commercial Manager, Scottish Region, British Railways, 1957 and Asst Gen. Manager, 1959; Traffic Adviser, BTC, 1961; Chm. Western Railway Board, and General Manager, Western Region, British Railways, 1962-63; Member, 1963, a Vice-Chm., 1964-65, and Chm., 1965-67, British Railways Bd. Mem. Council, BIM. *Recreation:* walking. *Address:* 124 Chiltern Court, Baker Street, NW1; 26 Cavendish House, Brighton, Sussex.

**RAYMONT, Professor John Edwin George;** Professor of Biological Oceanography, University of Southampton, since 1964; Deputy Vice-Chancellor, 1966-68; *b* 6 April 1915; *s* of Walter and Ellen Raymont; *m* 1945, Joan Katharine Brigit Sloan; one *s* two *d*. *Educ:* Hele's School and University College, Exeter. First Class Hons London External Degree in Zoology, 1936. Henry Fellow, Harvard Univ., USA, 1937-38. AM Harvard 1938; DSc Univ. of Exeter, 1960. Assistant Lecturer in Zoology, University College, Exeter, 1938-39; Lecturer in Zoology, University of Edinburgh, 1939-46; Prof. of Zoology, Univ. of Southampton, 1946-64. Mem. Wessex Regional Hosp. Bd (1959-), and Chm. Planning and Developments Cttee; Chm., Southampton Group Hosp. Management Cttee. Fell., Indian Acad. of Sciences, 1967-. Mem. Council, Marine Biological Assoc. of UK, 1968. *Publications:* Plankton and Productivity in the Oceans, 1963; on physiology of copepods, marine fish cultivation and marine benthos in Proc. Roy. Soc. of Edin., Biological Bulletin, Jl of Marine Biolog. Assoc., Limnol. and Oceanogr., Int. Revue ges. Hydrobiol., Deep-Sea Research, etc. *Address:* Biscayne, 2 Glenwood Avenue, Southampton. *T:* Southampton 67677.

**RAYNE, Edward;** Chairman and Managing Director of H. & M. Rayne Ltd, since 1951; President of Rayne-Delman Shoes Inc., since 1961; Member, Board of Governors, Genesco Inc., 1967; Chairman of Incorporated Society of London Fashion Designers, since 1960; Member of Export Council for Europe, since 1962; Vice-Chm., Consumer Goods Cttee, 1970-; President: Royal Warrant Holders Association, 1964; British Footwear Manufacturers' Federation, 1965; *b* 19 Aug. 1922; *s* of Joseph Edward Rayne and Meta Elizabeth Reddish (American); *m* 1952, Phyllis Cort; two *s*. *Educ:* Harrow School. Harper's Bazaar Trophy, 1963. Fellow, British Boot and Shoe Inst., 1959. *Recreations:* golf and bridge. *Address:* 15 Grosvenor Square, W1. *T:* 01-493 2871. *Clubs:* Portland, St James'; Travellers' (Paris).

**RAYNE, Sir Max,** Kt 1969; Chairman, London Merchant Securities, Ltd, since 1960; *b* 8 Feb. 1918; *er s* of Phillip and Deborah Rayne; *m* 1st, 1941, Margaret Marco (marr. diss., 1960); one *s* two *d*; 2nd, 1965, Lady Jane Antonia Frances Vane-Tempest-Stewart, *er d* of 8th Marquess of Londonderry; one *s* two *d*. *Educ:* Central Foundation Sch. and University Coll., London. Served RAF 1940-45. Founder Dir, Brit. Commercial Property Investment Trust, Ltd, 1948; Chairman: Invergordon Distillers (Holdings), Ltd, 1965-; Carlton INdustries Ltd, 1967-; Director: New River Co. Ltd, 1962-; British Lion Holdings Ltd, 1967-; Rimmel Ltd, 1968-; LRC International Ltd,

1970-, and other companies. Governor: St Thomas' Hosp., 1962-; Royal Ballet Sch., 1966-; Yehudi Menuhin Sch., 1966-; Malvern Coll., 1966-; Centre for Environmental Studies, 1967-; Member: Gen. Council, King Edward VII's Hosp. Fund for London; Council, St Thomas's Hospital Medical School, 1965-; Jewish Welfare Bd, 1966-; Nat. Theatre Board, 1970-; Chm., London Festival Ballet Trust, 1967-; Trustee, E Grinstead Research Trust, 1967-. Founder Patron, The Max Rayne Foundation (created, 1962, to continue philanthropic work of Max Rayne Charitable Trust in fields of education, research, med. and gen. welfare, the arts, etc). Hon. Fellow: University Coll., London, 1966; Darwin Coll., Cambridge, 1966. Hon. LLD London, 1968. *Address:* 33 Duke Street, W1. *T:* 01-935 3555.

**RAYNER, Vice-Admiral Herbert Sharples,** DSC 1941, Bar 1944; CD 1946 (on institution); Royal Canadian Navy, retired; Chief of Naval Staff (Canada), 1960-64; *b* 16 Jan. 1911; *s* of Harold Rayner and Annie May (*née* Suitter); *m* 1936, Betty Bachelier Graham (*née* Snook); three *s* three *d*. *Educ:* Hutton Grammar School, Preston, Lancs; St Catharine's Collegiate Institute, St Catharine's, Ont. Cadet, RCN, 1928; Capt. 1948; Rear-Adm., 1955; Vice-Adm., 1960. Served War of 1939-45 (DSC and Bar, despatches twice): Comd HMCS St Laurent, 1940-42; SO Operations to CO Atlantic Coast, 1942-43; i/c destroyer Huron, 1943-44; Dir of Plans, Naval HQ, 1944-45; Capt. (D) Halifax, 1945; Comd destroyer Nootka, 1946; Comd RCN Air Section, Dartmouth, NS, 1947; Commandant, Canadian Services Coll., BC, 1948-49; Imperial Defence College, UK, 1950; Sec., Chiefs of Staff Cttee, Nat. Defence HQ, Canada, 1951; Co-ordinator of Joint Staff, 1951; Comd HMCS Magnificent, 1953; Chief of Naval Personnel, 1955; Flag Officer, Pacific Coast, 1957. Chevalier, Legion of Honour; Croix de Guerre, 1946. *Recreations:* walking and climbing; photography. *Address:* 9 Loch Isle Road, RR8, Ottawa, Ontario, Canada. *T:* 828-0101. *Clubs:* Canadian Alpine, Adirondack Mountain, University (Ottawa).

**RAYNER, Rt. Rev. Keith;** *see* Wangaratta, Bishop of.

**RAYNER, Brigadier Sir Ralph,** Kt 1956; DL; *s* of Reverend George Rayner, Bradshaw, near Queensbury, Yorks; *m* 1931, Elizabeth, *d* of late S. A. Courtauld; three *s* one *d*. Served France, 1915; Afghan War, 1919 (despatches); British Mission to Kabul, 1920; NW Frontier, 1924; France, 1939 (despatches); Germany, 1945; Hon. Col Wessex Signals, 1948. Chairman: Western Area, Conservative Assoc., 1955-61; Royal Soc. St George, 1954-64. MP (U) Totnes Division of Devonshire, 1935-55. Freeman of the City of London. DL Devon, 1952; High Sheriff of Devon, 1958; Mem., Devon CC, 1964. *Address:* Ashcombe Tower, near Dawlish, Devon. *T:* Dawlish 3178; 1 Egerton Gardens, SW3. *T:* 01-584 6208. *Clubs:* Carlton, Buck's, Pratt's, Pilgrims.

**RAYNHAM, Viscount; Charles George Townshend;** *b* 26 Sept. 1945; *s* and *heir* of 7th Marquess Townshend, *qv*. *Educ:* Eton. *Address:* Raynham Hall, Fakenham, Norfolk. *T:* Fakenham 2133. *Club:* White's.

**RAYNOR, Prof. Geoffrey Vincent,** FRS 1959; MA, DPhil, DSc Oxon; Deputy Principal, University of Birmingham, and Professor of Physical Metallurgy, since 1969; *b* 2 Oct. 1913; *y s* of late Alfred Ernest Raynor, Nottingham; *m* 1943, Emily Jean, *er d* of late Dr Geo. F. Brockless, London; three *s*. *Educ:* Nottingham High School; Keble Coll., Oxford, 1st cl. Hons, School of Natural Science (Chemistry), Oxford, 1936. Research Assistant, Oxford University, 1936; Departmental Demonstrator in Inorganic Chemistry, 1937-45; DSIR. Senior Research Award, 1938-41. Metallurgical research for Ministry of Supply and Ministry of Aircraft Production, 1939-45; ICI Research Fellow, Univ. of Birmingham, 1945-47; Beilby Memorial Award, 1947; Reader in Theoretical Metallurgy, Univ. of Birmingham, 1947-49; Prof. of Metal Physics, 1949-54; Prof. of Physical Metallurgy, 1954-55; Feeney Prof. of Physical Metallurgy, and Head of Dept of Physical Metallurgy and Science of Materials, Univ. of Birmingham, 1955-69; Dean, Faculty of Science and Engineering, 1966-69. Vice-President: Inst. of Metals, 1953-56; Instn of Metallurgists, 1963-66; Pres., Birmingham Metallurgical Assoc., 1965-66. Walter Rosenhain Medal of Inst. of Metals, 1951; Visiting Professor of Metallurgy, Chicago University, 1951-52. Fellow New York Acad. of Science, 1961. Battelle Visiting Prof. Ohio State Univ., 1962. Heyn Medal of Deutsche Gesellschaft für Metallkunde, 1956. Member several metallurgical research committees. *Publications:* Introduction to the Electron Theory of Metals, Inst. of Metals monograph and report series, No. 4, 1947; contrib. to Butterworth's scientific publications: Progress in Metal Physics, 1949, and Metals Reference Book, 1949; The Structure of Metals and Alloys (with W. Hume-Rothery), 1954; The Physical Metallurgy of Magnesium and its Alloys, 1959; scientific papers on theory of metals and alloys in Proc. Royal Soc., Philosophical Mag., Trans. Faraday Soc., and metallurgical journals. *Recreations:* rowing and sculling. *Address:* 94 Gillhurst Road, Harborne, Birmingham B17 8PA. *T:* 021-429 3176.

**RAZZALL, Leonard Humphrey;** a Master of the Supreme Court (Taxing) since 1954; *b* 13 Nov. 1912; *s* of Horace Razzall and Sarah Thompson, Scarborough; *m* 1936, Muriel (*d* 1968), *yr d* of late Pearson Knowles; two *s*. *Educ:* Scarborough High Sch. Admitted solicitor, 1935; founded firm Humphrey Razzall & Co., 1938. Served in Royal Marines, 1941-46, Staff Captain. Contested (L) Scarborough and Whitby Division, 1945. *Recreations:* travel, cricket. *Address:* 10 Tudor Way, Gunnersbury Avenue, W3. *T:* 01-992 2088. *Clubs:* National Liberal, English-Speaking Union.

**REA,** family name of **Baron Rea.**

**REA,** 2nd Baron, *cr* 1937, of Eskdale; **Philip Russell Rea,** PC 1962; OB 1946; MA; DL; JP; 2nd Bt, *cr* 1935; a Deputy Speaker, House of Lords; merchant banker, company director; Underwriter at Lloyd's; *b* London, 7 Feb. 1900; *e s* of 1st Baron Rea of Eskdale and Evelyn (*d* 1930), *d* of J. J. Muirhead; *S* father, 1948; *m* 1922, Lorna Smith (*see* Lorna Rea); one *d* (one *s* decd). *Educ:* Westminster; Christ Church, Oxford; Grenoble Univ. Grenadier Guards, 1918-19; served War of 1939-45: KRRC, attached Special Forces, 1940-46 (Lt-Col; despatched; OBE). FO, 1946-50; Chief Liberal Whip, House of Lords, 1950-55; Dep. Lord Chm. of Cttees, 1950-60; Dep. Lord Speaker, 1950-; Liberal Leader, House of Lords, 1955-67; Pres., Liberal Party, 1955. Leader, British Parly Delegn to Burma and Indonesia, 1954; UK Deleg. to Council of Europe, Strasbourg, 1957; Mem. Parly Delegn to USA, and to Hong Kong and Ceylon, 1958. Member: Cumberland Develt Council, 1950-60; BBC Adv. Council, 1957-62; Political Honours Scrutiny Cttee, 1962-; Lord

Chancellor's Adv. Cttee, Inner London; Outward Bound Trust Council. President: Fell Dales Assoc., 1950-60; Special Forces Club; Elizabethan Club, 1965-66. Trustee, Nat. Liberal Club, Pres. 1966-. Governor, Westminster Sch. DL Cumberland, 1955, Greater London, 1966-; JP London, 1966-. Officer, Order of Crown (Belgium); Chevalier, Legion of Honour, and Croix de Guerre with palm (France); Grand Commandeur, Ordre de Mérite (France). Hon. Adm. Louisiana, USA. *Heir: n* John Nicolas Rea, MB [*b* 6 June 1928; *m* 1951, Elizabeth Anne, *d* of late W. H. Robinson; four *s*]. *Address:* 5 St John's House, 30 Smith Square, SW1. *T:* 01-222 6565. *Clubs:* Guards, Garrick, Grillions, Special Forces, National Liberal.

*See also M. J. S. Clapham, J. B. Herbert.*

**REA, James Taylor,** CMG 1958; HM Overseas Civil Service, retired; *b* 19 Oct. 1907; *s* of Rev. Martin Rea, Presbyterian Minister, and Mary Rea (*née* Fisher); *m* 1934, Catharine, *d* of Dr W. H. Bleakney, Whitman College, Walla Walla, Washington, USA; one *s* one *d. Educ:* Royal School, Dungannon; Queen's University, Belfast (BA); St John's College, Cambridge (MA), 1931-58: HM Colonial Administrative Service (now known as HM Overseas Civil Service) serving throughout in Malaya and Singapore. Principal offices held: Asst Sec., Chinese Affairs, Fedn of Malaya, 1948; Dep. Comr for Labour, Fedn of Malaya, 1949; Dep. Malayan Establishment Officer, 1950; Dep. Pres., 1952-55, Pres., 1955-58, City Council, Singapore. Retired, 1958. Mem., N Ireland Housing Trust, Vice Chm., 1970-. Indep. Mem.: Catering Wages Council, N Ireland, 1965; Retail Bespoke Tailoring Wages Council, 1965-; Laundry Wages Council, 1965-; Shirtmaking Wages Council, 1965. Nominated Member General Dental Council, under Dentist Act, 1957, Nov. 1961. Chm. Hotel Grants Advisory Cttee, N Ireland, 1963. Mem. Downpatrick Hosp. Management Cttee, 1966-. *Address:* Craigduff, Downpatrick, N Ireland. *T:* Seaforde 258.

**REA, Lorna; (The Lady Rea);** Writer; *b* Glasgow, 12 June 1897; *d* of late Lewis O. Smith, merchant; *m* 1922, Philip Russell Rea (*see* Baron Rea); one *d. Educ:* St James's, West Malvern; Newnham College, Cambridge (Hons). WVS (London Region), 1940-45. *Publications:* Six Mrs Greenes, Rachel Moon, The Happy Prisoner, First Night, The Armada, Six and Seven, and other publications. *Address:* 5 St John's House, Smith Square, Westminster, SW1. *T:* 01-222 6106.

**REA, Robert Lindsay-,** BSc, MD, MCh FRCS; *b* 1881; *s* of Robert Rea, Belfast; *m* Mary Eleanor, *d* of late James Waddell, Glasgow; two *s* two *d. Educ:* Belfast Model Sch. and Belfast Technical Sch.; Queen's Univ., Belfast; Middlesex Hospital; Université de Paris. Fellow of Royal Society of Medicine; Hon. Member of Ophthalmological Society of United Kingdom; supervised X-ray work of 4th Army, BEF, in France, 1918. Consulting Surgeon to Western Ophthalmic Hospital; Consulting Surgeon to West End Hosp. for Neurology and Neuro-Surgery, London; retired 1966. *Publications:* Affections of the Eye in General Practice; Neuro-ophthalmology; various papers on Ophthalmic subjects in medical journals. *Recreation:* golf. *Address:* 7 Tenby Mansions, W1. *T:* 01-935 2357. *Club:* Moor Park (Rickmansworth).

**READ, Alfred Burgess,** RDI 1940; ARCA; FSIA; Design Consultant; Sqdn Ldr RAFVR, Italy (despatches twice); *b* 29 May 1899; *s* of late I. Read, Willingdon, Sussex; *m* 1924, Phyllis Barbara Walker, Harrogate, Yorks; two *s* one *d. Educ:* Eastbourne Grammar School; Eastbourne School of Art; Royal College of Art, South Kensington. 2nd Lieut, Welsh Guards, 1918-19; Royal College of Art, South Kensington, 1920-23; Diploma of Royal College of Art, 1923; Rural Industries Bureau Travelling Scholarship to Italy, 1924; Ayrton Premium from Institution of Electrical Engineers, 1933; Design Consultant, Troughton and Young (Lighting) Ltd. *Publication:* Lighting the Home, 1938. *Recreation:* painting. *Address:* West Riding, Milton Abbas, Blandford Forum, Dorset. *T:* Milton Abbas 410. *Clubs:* Arts, Chelsea Arts.

**READ, Col Alfred Howard,** CB 1952; OBE 1939; TD; DL; MEng; CEng, FIEE; *b* 25 Aug. 1893; *er s* of Alfred Read, Huyton, Lancs. *Educ:* Birkenhead Institute; Liverpool Univ. Served European War with RE, 1914-19; transf. Roy. Corps of Signals, 1921; served War of 1939-45, in France and Belgium; Col 1942. Mil. Member, Middx T and AFA, 1936-54. DL Greater London, 1965 (Middx, 1948-65). Director of Overseas Telecommunications, Post Office, 1950-54; retired, 1954; Telecommunications Attaché, British Embassy, Washington, 1954-60. *Address:* Thatched House, Thurne, Norfolk. *T:* Potter Heigham 316. *Club:* Conservative (Great Yarmouth).

**READ, Lt-Gen. Sir Anthony;** *see* Read, Lt-Gen. Sir J. A. J.

**READ, Vice-Adm. Arthur Duncan,** CB 1944; *b* 1889; *m* 1922, Rosamond Vere, *d* of late W. H. Monckton; three *d.* Joined Royal Navy, 1904; Captain, 1932; Rear-Admiral, 1942; Flag Officer, Ceylon, 1942-43; commanded a Cruiser Squadron, 1943-45; retired, 1945. *Address:* Brewers Wood, Shorne Ridgeway, near Gravesend, Kent. *T:* Shorne 2328.

*See also M. L. M. Chavasse.*

**READ, Rev. David Haxton Carswell,** MA, DD; Minister of Madison Avenue Presbyterian Church, New York City, USA, since 1956; regular broadcaster; *b* Cupar, Fife, 2 Jan. 1910; *s* of John Alexander Read and Catherine Haxton Carswell; *m* 1936, Dorothy Florence Patricia Gilbert; one *s. Educ:* Daniel Stewart's College, Edinburgh. Edinburgh Univ.; Univs of Montpeller, Strasbourg, Paris, and Marburg; New Coll., Edinburgh. MA Edin. (first class Hons in Lit.) 1932; BD (dist. in Dogmatics) 1936. Ordained Minister of the Church of Scotland, 1936; Minister of Coldstream West Church, 1936-39. CF, 1939-45 (despatches; POW, 1940-45, Germany). Minister of Greenbank Parish, Edinburgh, 1939-49; first Chaplain, Univ. of Edinburgh, 1949-55; Chaplain to the Queen in Scotland, 1952-55. Member: Bd of Dirs, Union Theological Seminary; Bd of Preachers, Harvard Univ.; Inst. for Religious and Social Studies, etc. Guest Lectr and Preacher in USA, Scotland and Australia. Hon. DD: Edinburgh, 1956; Yale, 1959; Lafayette Coll., 1965; Hope Coll., 1969; Hon. LittD Coll. of Wooster, 1966. *Publications:* The Spirit of Life, 1939; The Church to Come (trans. from German), 1939; Prisoners' Quest, Lectures on Christian doctrine in a POW Camp, 1944; The Communication of The Gospel, Warrack Lectures, 1952; The Christian Faith, 1955 (New York, 1956); I am Persuaded, 1961 (New York, 1962); Sons of Anak, 1964 (New York); God's Mobile Family, 1966 (New York); Whose God is Dead?, 1966 (Cin); Holy Common Sense, 1966 (Tenn); The Pattern of Christ, 1967 (New York); The Presence of Christ, 1968 (NJ); Christian Ethics, 1968 (New York, 1969); Virginia Woolfe Meets

Charlie Brown, 1968 (Mich). Articles and sermons in Atlantic Monthly, Scottish Jl of Theology, Expository Times, etc. *Recreations:* languages; drama; travel, especially in France. *Address:* 1165 Fifth Avenue, New York, NY, USA. *Club:* The Century (New York).

**READ, Gen. Sir (John) Antony (Jervis),** KCB 1967 (CB 1965); CBE 1959 (OBE 1957); DSO 1945; MC 1941; Quartermaster-General, since 1969; *b* 10 Sept. 1913; *e s* of late John Dale Read, Heathfield, Sussex; *m* 1947, Sheila, *e d* of late F. G. C. Morris, London, NW8; three *d*. *Educ:* Winchester; Sandhurst. Commissioned Oxford and Bucks Lt Inf., 1934; seconded to Gold Coast Regt, RWAFF, 1936; comd 81 (WA) Div. Reconnaissance Regt, 1943; comd 1 Gambia Regt, 1944; war service Kenya, Abyssinia, Somaliland, Burma; DAMS, War Office, 1947-49; Company Comd RMA Sandhurst, 1949-52; AA&QMG 11 Armd Div., 1953-54; comd 1 Oxford and Bucks Lt Inf., 1955-57; comd 3 Inf. Bde Gp, 1957-59; Comdt School of Infantry, 1959-62; GOC Northumbrian Area and 50 (Northumbrian) Division (TA), 1962-64; Vice-Quarter-Master-General, Min. of Defence, 1964-66; GOC-in-C, Western Comd, 1966-69. Colonel Commandant: Army Catering Corps, 1966; The Light Division, 1968; Small Arms School Corps, 1969. Governor, Royal Sch. for Daughters of Officers of the Army, 1966. *Address:* c/o National Westminster Bank, 94 Kensington High Street, W8. *Club:* Army and Navy.

**READ, John Emms,** FCA 1947; Chief Executive and Group Managing Director (UK), Electric and Musical Industries Ltd, since 1967; *b* 29 March 1918; *s* of late William Emms Read and of Daysie Elizabeth (*née* Cooper); *m* 1942, Dorothy Millicent Berry; two *s*. *Educ:* Brighton, Hove and Sussex Grammar Sch. Served Royal Navy, 1939-46 (rank of Comdr (S) RNVR); Admiral's Secretary: to Asst Chief of Naval Staff, Admty, 1942-45; to Brit. Admty Technical Mission, Ottawa, Canada, 1945-46. Ford Motor Co. Ltd, 1946-64 (Admin. Staff Coll., Henley, 1952), Dir of Sales, 1961-64; Electric and Musical Industries Ltd, 1965-. Dir, Capitol Industries Inc., and other Associated Cos. Mem. Court Brunel Univ., 1969. *Recreations:* music, sports. *Address:* 16 Somers Crescent, Hyde Park, W2. *T:* 01-402 5758.

**READ, John Erskine,** SM 1967; BA Dalhousie; BA, BCL, Oxon; KC 1925; Hon. Fellow, University College, Oxford; Hon. Master of the Bench, Gray's Inn; Judge, International Court of Justice, 1946-58; retired; Lecturer on Constitutional Law, University of Ottawa; Member, Appeals Committee Opium Protocol, since 1963; *b* Halifax, NS, 5 July 1888; *s* of Dr H. H. Read; *m* 1915, Diana Willes, *d* of late Sir Thomas Willes Chitty, 1st Bt, KC; two *s*. *Educ:* Halifax City Schs; Halifax County Acad.; Dalhousie University; Columbia Univ. New York; University College, Oxford (Rhodes Scholar). Admitted to the Bar of Nova Scotia, 1913; practised law with Harris, Henry, Rogers & Harris, later with Henry, Rogers, Harris & Stewart, until 1920; served with the Canadian Field Artillery, 1914-18 (despatches, wounded and invalided from the Service with the rank of Captain and Acting Major, 1918); Lecturer at the Dalhousie Law School, 1914; retired from firm of Henry, Rogers, Harris & Stewart, 1920, to accept Professorship of Law at Dalhousie Law School; Dean of the Dalhousie Law School and George Munro Professor of Law, Dalhousie University, 1924; Legal Adviser Department of External Affairs, Canada, 1929; member of the Conference of Commissioners on Uniformity of Legislation in Canada, 1924-46. Hon. LLD: Dalhousie; McMaster; Alberta; Hon. DCL: Oxon; Acadia. *Publications:* The Rule of Law on the International Plane; Cases on Canadian Constitutional Law; Documents relating to Dominion and Provincial Constitutions; various articles in law publications. *Recreation:* golf. *Address:* 81 Dunmurray Boulevard, Agincourt, Ont, Canada. *Club:* University (Ottawa).

**READ, Maj.-Gen. John Hugh Sherlock,** OBE 1944; Assistant Chief of the Defence Staff (Policy), Ministry of Defence, since 1970; *b* 6 Sept. 1917; *s* of late Group Captain John Victor Read, Blunham, Bedfordshire, and Chacewater, Cornwall, and Elizabeth Hannah (*née* Link); *m* 1942, Mary Monica Wulfhilde Curtis, *d* of late Henry Curtis, Spofforth, Yorks, and Harrogate; two *s* one *d*. *Educ:* Bedford School; RMA Woolwich; Magdalene Coll., Cambridge. BA (Cantab.) 1939. MA (Cantab.) 1944. Commissioned 2nd Lt RE, 1937. Served UK, France, Belgium, Egypt, Palestine, Greece, Austria at regimental duty and on staff, 1939-45, and UK, Austria, Germany, Hong Kong, 1945-57; GSO1, Singapore Base Dist, 1957; CO, Training Regt, RE, 1959; IDC, 1962; Min. of Defence (War Office), 1963; Comdr, Training Bde, RE, 1963; Asst Comdt, RMA, 1966-68; Director of Military Operations, MoD, 1968-70. *Recreations:* fishing, shooting, gardening. *Address:* Fullbrook Farm, Elstead, Surrey. *T:* Elstead 3312; Flat 4, Church Close, Church Street, Kensington, W8. *T:* 01-937 1863. *Club:* East India and Sports.

**READ, Prof. Margaret (Helen),** CBE 1949; MA (Cantab), PhD (London); *b* 5 Aug. 1889; *d* of Mabyn Read, MD, Worcester, and Isabel Margaret Lawford. *Educ:* Roedean School, Brighton; Newnham College, Cambridge. Social work in India, 1919-24; lecturing on international affairs in Gt Britain and USA, 1924-30; LSE, student of anthropology and occasional lecturer, 1930-34; Research Fellow, Internat. African Inst. and field work in N Rhodesia and Nyasaland, 1934-39; Asst Lecturer, LSE, 1937-40; Univ. of London Inst. of Educ., Prof. and Head of Dept of Educ. in Tropical Areas, 1940-55; Prof. of Educ., Univ. Coll., Ibadan, Nigeria, 1955-56; occasional Consultant to WHO, 1956-62; Consultant to Milbank Memorial Fund, New York, 1964, 1965, 1966, 1967, 1968, 1969. Vis. Prof., Cornell Univ., 1951-52, Northwestern Univ., 1955, Michigan State Univ., 1960, Yale Univ. Medical School, 1965, 1966, 1967, 1968. Associate of Newnham College, Cambridge. *Publications:* Indian Peasant Uprooted, 1931; Africans and their Schools, 1953; Education and Social Change in Tropical Areas, 1955; The Ngoni of Nyasaland, 1956; Children of their Fathers, 1959; Culture, Health and Disease, 1966; articles in Africa, Bantu Studies, Journal of Applied Anthropology, Annals of the American Academy, etc. *Recreations:* gardening, music. *Address:* 9 Paradise Walk, Chelsea, SW3. *T:* 01-352 0528. *Club:* Royal Commonwealth Society.

**READ, Prof. Thomas Talmage,** MChD; FRCS; FDSRCS; HDD; LRCP; Professor Emeritus of Clinical Dental Surgery and Warden of Dental School and Hospital, University of Leeds (Professor 1931); Consultant, United Leeds Teaching Hospitals and Leeds Regional Hospital Boards; Consulting Oral Surgeon, Leeds Education Committee; *b* 22 Nov. 1893; *s* of Robert Patrick Read and Rachel Read (*née* Macmillan); *m* 1950, Pamela Margaret Robinson; two *s* two *d*. *Educ:* Shawlands Academy; Glasgow High School; Anderson's College; Glasgow Royal Infirmary and

University; Glasgow Dental School and Middlesex Hospital. John Burns Gold Medal, Wallace Prize and Dall Prize, and medals in many branches of medicine and dentistry, and in metallurgy. From 1918-31; Res. Surg., Glasgow Royal Infirmary; Res. Surg. Officer, Glasgow Eye Infirmary; Res. MO, Roy. Samaritan Hosp.; Visiting Dental Surgeon, Glasgow Dental Hosp.; Lectr in Special Anatomy, Materia Medica and Bacteriology, Glasgow Dental School; Hon. Sec., Glasgow Odontol Soc. and W Scotland Branch, British Dental Assoc. From 1931: Founder Pres. Leeds Scientific Film Soc.; former Pres. Pathology Club and Leeds sect. British Dental Assoc.; Founder Pres. Oral Surgery Club. During War of 1939-45, Cons. i/c Maxillo-Facial Centre, St James's Hosp., Leeds; MO i/c First Aid Post 21, Leeds and mem. Manpower War Cttee. Member Dental Educ. Advisory Council, Br. Dental Hosps Assoc., United Leeds Hosp. Bd and General Dental Council; Chm. of Advisory Technical Panel, Leeds Regional Hosp. Bd; Pres. Dental Implant Soc.; Vice-Pres. Inst. of Br. Surgical Technicians; Member: BMA; Br. Dental Assoc.; Assoc. of Plastic Surgeons; West Riding Medico-Chirurgical Soc.; Royal Soc. Med. Vice-Dean, Founder Fellow and Mem. Bd of Dental Faculty, Royal Coll. of Surgeons. Former External Examiner, Univs of Manchester, Bristol, Liverpool, Durham and RCS; now External Examiner, Univ. of Glasgow and Queen's Univ. Belfast. Hon. Fell. British Assoc. of Oral Surgeons. Has produced several original films. *Publications:* Dental Operations (Demonstrations of Operative Surgery), 1954; numerous articles in medical and dental journals on various aspects of Maxillo-Facial and Oral Surgery, Oral Bacteriology and Pathology. *Recreations:* golf; scientific film production. *Address:* Fairlands, Foxhill Drive, Leeds 16. *T:* Leeds 52906. *Clubs:* Leeds, Alwoodley Golf (Leeds).

**READE, Sir Clyde Nixon,** 12th Bt *cr* 1661; *b* 1906; *s* of Sir George Reade, 10th Bt; *S* brother, Sir John Reade, 11th Bt, 1958; *m* 1st, 1930, Trilby (*d* 1958), *d* of Charles McCarthy; 2nd, 1960, Alice Martha Asher; five *step d.* Is a Royal Arch Mason. *Address:* 225 East Ash Street, Mason, Michigan, USA.

**READER, (William Henry) Ralph,** CBE 1957 (MBE 1942); theatrical producer, author, composer and actor; *b* 25 May 1903; *s* of William Henry and Emma Reader, Crewkerne, Somerset. *Educ:* Crewkerne; Cardiff. Started as clerk in office in Sussex; went to Ireland with same firm; returned to England; went to America to study for the stage; appeared in numerous productions, then took up producing; after 6 years returned to London to produce shows there; in 1928 appeared in Good News at Carlton Theatre, Haymarket; has produced about six Drury Lane productions, including Jack and the Beanstalk 1936, Rise and Shine 1937, also about six shows at the London Hippodrome including Yes Madam and Please Teacher; starred in The Gang Show Film, also in Limelight with Anna Neagle; appeared with The Gang at the London Palladium in the Royal Command Variety Performance, produced Daily Express Pageant, Albert Hall, London, Battle for Freedom; Hearts of Oak Naval Pageant for Daily Express, 1945; British Legion Festival of Remembrance, annually, 1944-; RAF Pageant, Per Ardua Ad Astra, 1945, all at Albert Hall, London; produced Wings for Air Council, 1947; produced Out of the Blue, June 1947, season show, Grand, Blackpool; appeared in The Gang Show, Stoll Theatre. Produced (with all star cast) Pilgrim's Progress, Covent Garden, 1948, also in 1969. Was Officer in charge of RAF Gang Shows (official RAF entertainment units). Instituted Nat. Light Opera Company, 1950. Appeared in film Derby Day; took first entertainment to the Troops in Malaya; appeared in Meet the Gang. Produced Coronation Pageant, Royal Albert Hall, Pageant of Nursing, Royal Festival Hall, Centenary Rally of YMCA Sports de Paris, Rotary Pageant, Royal Albert Hall; Produced Wild Grows the Heather, London Hippodrome, 1956; produced Voyage of the Venturer, Youth Festival, English Ranger Pageant, Royal Albert Hall, 1956; appeared Royal Command Performance, 1957; prod. 1st Amer. Gang Show, Chicago, 1958; prod. Lord Mayor's Show, 1958; wrote music, book and lyrics of Summer Holiday, musical play, prod. Scarborough Open Air Theatre, 1960; Produced Gang Show in US, 1958, 1959, 1960, 1961; prod. World Refugee Finale, Albert Hall, 1960; wrote play, The Hill, prod. 1960; appd in Here Comes the Gang, touring Gt Britain, 1961; appeared in: Royal Command Perf., London Palladium, 1937, 1957, 1964; The Story of Mike, 1961; wrote and produced 4 One-Act Plays (We Present), 1962; staged ensembles for film, The Lonely Stage, 1962; prod. Burma Reunion, also The Voyage of the Venturer (wrote book and music), Royal Albert Hall, 1962; prod. Flying High for ITV 1962; wrote and appd in All for the Boys, London, 1963; prod. El Alamein Re-union, Royal Albert Hall, 1963; wrote play, Happy Family, also played lead, 1964. Produced at Royal Albert Hall: The Old Contemptibles; Burma Re-union. Writer and producer: yearly editions of the Gang Show; The Pathfinders, Toronto, 1965; musical play, You can't go wrong if you're right, 1967. Prod. "Dr Barnardo Centenary", Royal Albert Hall, 1966 (his 120th presentation there). Prod. and appd in Babes in the Wood, 1968. Appears on BBC TV, Radio, ITV, US and Canadian TV. Compèred Radio Series "Startime", also, for Overseas BBC, "A Star Remembers". Subject of This Is Your Life, 1967. Illuminated Address from State of Illinois, for Services to Boyhood throughout the World, 1964. Life Member, Boy Scouts of America. *Publications:* Good Turns; The Road to Where; Gang Show Music and Sketches; Music and Book of Boy Scout, performed at Albert Hall; More Sketches: Great Oaks, Oh Scouting is a Boy, The Wingate Patrol; We'll Live Forever; The Story of Mike; Leave it to Pete; The Gang Show Story; All for the Boys; *autobiography:* It's been terrific. *Recreations:* motoring, writing, football. *Address:* Round Corners, 2 Sherrock Gardens, Hendon, NW4.

**READER HARRIS, (Muriel) Diana;** Headmistress, Sherborne School for Girls, Dorset, since 1950; President, Church Missionary Society, since 1969; *b* Hong Kong, 11 Oct. 1912; *er d* of late Montgomery Reader Harris. *Educ:* Sherborne School for Girls; University of London (external student). BA 1st Class Honours (English), 1934; Asst Mistress, Sherborne School for Girls, 1934, and House Mistress, 1938. Organised Public Schools and Clubs Camps for Girls, 1937-39; in charge of group evacuated from Sherborne to Canada, 1940; joined staff of National Association of Girls' Clubs, 1943; Member Dorset Educ. Cttee, 1952-70; Chm. Christian Consultative Cttee Nat. Assoc. of Mixed Clubs and Girls' Clubs, 1952-68; Chm. Outward Bound Girls' Courses, 1954-59. Mem. Exec. Cttee Church Missionary Soc. 1953 (Chm. 1960-63); Mem. Women's Consultative Cttee, Min. of Labour, 1958. Gov., Greycoat Hospital, 1944-48. Member: Standing Research and Advisory Cttee, 1949, Administrative Council, 1955-67, King George's Jubilee Trust; Council, Nat. Youth

Orchestra of Great Britain, 1951-62; Council, Outward Bound Trust, 1956-64; Independent Television Authority, 1956-60; Exec. Cttee, Association of Headmistresses, 1953-58, 1960; Pres., 1964-66; Pres. Assoc. of Headmistresses of Boarding Schools, 1960-62; Member: Cttee on Agricultural Colls, Min. of Agric., 1961-64; Archbishop's Council on Evangelism, 1966-68; Schools Council, 1966. FRSA 1964. *Address:* White Lodge, Sherborne, Dorset. *T:* Sherborne 2044. *Club:* English-Speaking Union.

**READHEAD, James (Templeman),** 3rd Bt, *cr* 1922 (but discontinued style of Sir and the use of his title, 1965); Lieutenant late King's Own Yorkshire Light Infantry, TA; *b* 12 Feb. 1910; *s* of late Stanley Readhead, Stanhope House, Westoe, South Shields, and late Hilda Maud, *d* of Thomas John Templeman, Weymouth, Dorset; *S* uncle, 1940; *m* 1946, Hilda Rosemary, *o d* of George Henry Hudson, The Manor, Hatfield, nr Doncaster, Yorks; one *d*. *Educ:* Repton School. Electrical Engineer. *Recreations:* various.

**READING,** 3rd Marquess of, *cr* 1926; **Michael Alfred Rufus Isaacs,** MBE 1945; MC 1940; Earl of Reading, *cr* 1917; Viscount Erleigh, *cr* 1917; Viscount Reading, *cr* 1916; Baron, *cr* 1914; Member of the London Stock Exchange since 1953; *b* 8 March 1916; *o s* of 2nd Marquess of Reading, PC, GCMG, CBE, MC, TD, QC, and Eva Violet (*see* Eva Marchioness of Reading); *S* father 1960; *m* 1941, Margot Irene, *yr d* of Percy Duke, OBE, Watts Close, Tadworth, Surrey; three *s* one *d*. *Educ:* Eton; Balliol College, Oxford. Served 1939-46, Queen's Bays and Staff (Major). *Heir:* *s* Viscount Erleigh, *qv*. *Address:* Staplefield Grange, Staplefield, near Haywards Heath, Sussex. *T:* Handcross 253; 18 Eccleston Square Mews, SW1. *T:* 01-828 5330. *Club:* City of London.

*See also Baron Melchett, Sir Solly Zuckerman.*

**READING, Eva Marchioness of; (Eva Violet Mond),** CBE 1957; JP; Past President National Council of Women (Vice-President, 1953-57; President Oct. 1957-59); *b* 6 Aug. 1895; *e d* of 1st Baron Melchett, PC, FRS; *m* 1914, 2nd Marquess of Reading, PC, GCMG, CBE, MC, TD, QC (*d* 1960); one *s* (*see* 3rd Marquess of Reading) two *d*. *Educ:* private schools. Chm. Sun Babies Day Nursery, Hoxton, 1929-39; Mem. General Nursing Council, 1935-37; Chm. Council Nat. Soc. of Day Nurseries, 1939; Advisor to Min. of Health on Child Care, 1940-45; Chm. Violet Melchett Mothercraft Home and Infant Welfare Centre, 1946-68; Member Exec., World Jewish Congress, 1941- (Pres., British Section); Committee of Honour, International Council of Women, 1957. FRSH. *Publications:* Little One's Log; In the Beginning. *Recreation:* gardening. *Address:* Flat 8, 30 Cadogan Place, SW1. *T:* 01-235 7755; Cumberland House, Thakeham, W Sussex. *T:* West Chiltington 2103.

**READING, Dowager Marchioness of, (Stella),** Baroness (Life Peer), *cr* 1958, under title of Baroness Swanborough, GBE 1944 (DBE 1941); CStJ 1939; Chairman and Founder of Women's Royal Voluntary Service (formerly WVS), since 1938; Member: Factory and Welfare Board, 1940; National Savings Central Cttee, 1941-48; Central Housing Advisory Cttee; National Advisory Committee on Employment of older men and women; *d* of Charles Charnaud; *m* 1931, 1st Marquis of Reading (*d* 1935); Governor of the BBC, 1946; Vice-Chm., 1947-51; Chm., Personal Service League, 1932-38; Vice-Chm., Imp. Relations Trust, 1936-68; Member: Broadcasting Commission, 1935; Council of the Freedom from Hunger Campaign; Chairman Advisory Council on Commonwealth Immigration, 1962-65; Mem., Council of the University of Sussex. JP Deal and Walmer, 1932-37. hon. DLit Reading, 1947; Hon. Dr of Laws: Smith Coll., USA, 1956; Yale Univ., USA, 1958; Univ. of Manitoba, Canada, 1960; Hon. LLD Leeds, 1969. American National Achievement Award for Women, 1948; American Red Cross Civilian Service Bar and Silver Medal. Dame of Justice and Grace, Order of St John, 1951. Grand Officer in the Order of Orange Nassau, 1952. *Address:* 16 Lord North Street, SW1; Swanborough Manor, Lewes, Sussex.

**READING, Suffragan Bishop of,** since 1955; **Rt. Rev. Eric Henry Knell,** MA Oxon; *b* 1 April 1903; *s* of Edward Henry and Edith Helen Knell; unmarried. *Educ:* Trinity College, Oxford. Assistant Curate of St Barnabas, Southfields, 1928; Domestic Chaplain to Bishop of Lincoln, 1933; in charge of Trinity College, Oxford, Mission in Stratford, E15, 1936; Vicar of Emmanuel, Forest Gate, 1941; Vicar of Christ Church, Reading, 1945. Archdeacon of Berkshire, 1955-67. *Address:* The Well House, Upper Basildon, Berkshire. *T:* Upper Basildon 378.

**READING, Major-General Arnold Hughes Eagleton,** CBE 1946; DL; *b* 3 April 1896; *s* of Rev. M. A. Reading, Heilbron, OFS, S Africa; *m* 1933, Phoebe Ruth Elisabeth Powell. *Educ:* Cranleigh School. 2nd Lieut Royal Marines, Aug. 1914; Maj.-Gen. 1946; retired list 1947. DL Somerset, 1955. *Address:* The Stone House, Sellicks Green, Taunton, Som. *T:* Blagdon Hill 280. *Club:* Army and Navy.

**READING, Joseph Lewis,** CMG 1963; Secretary, Movement of Exports EDC, National Economic Develoment Office; Consultant to Vocational Guidance Association; *b* 5 Aug. 1907; *s* of J. W. Reading, New Malden, Surrey; *m* 1934, Dorothy Elaine, *d* of Reginald Fitch, Esher and London Stock Exchange; three *s* one *d*. *Educ:* King's College School, Wimbledon; London University, BSc (Eng.) 1929; ACGI 1929. Entered Civil Service as Consular Cadet in Dept of Overseas Trade, 1932; Principal, Min. of Economic Warfare, 1939-44; Asst Secretary, Min. of Production, 1944-45; Board of Trade, since 1945; Director, British Industries' Fair, 1952-55; Establishment Officer (Overseas), 1955-63; Economic Adviser to British High Comr and Senior British Trade Comr in NZ, 1963-67. *Recreations:* gardening, fishing. *Address:* Church Cottage, Milton-on-Stour, Gillingham, Dorset. *T:* Gillingham (Dorset) 2929.

**READMAN, Maj.-Gen. Edgar Platt,** CBE 1942 (OBE 1939); TD 1939; RAOC Retd; retired as Managing Director English Steel Corporation Tool Co., Manchester, 1958; *b* 12 Aug. 1893; *s* of Ernest W. Readman, Sheffield; *m* 1919, May, *d* of Marriot Stillwell, Leeds; one *d*. *Educ:* Sheffield Central School. Served European War, 1914-19, with Tank Corps; transferred RAOC, 1923, TA; Lt-Col 1934; Brigadier, 1940; Subs. Major-General, 1944; retired, 1951. Returned to industry, 1945. *Address:* Cedarcroft, Blackford Hill, Henley-in-Arden, Warwickshire. *T:* Henley-in-Arden 2326.

**REARDON-SMITH, Sir William;** *see* Smith.

**REAVELL, (James) Arthur,** MSc, MIMechE, MIChemE, FInstF, FIM; retired from business, 1963, as President (late Chairman, Founder) of Kestner Evaporator and Engineering Co., Ltd; *b* 10 June 1872; *s* of

George and Martha Rose Reavell; *m* 1898, Emma Mabel Clowes (*decd*); two *s* one *d* (and one *s* decd); *m* 1941, Winifred Ethel Haydon. *Educ:* Alnwick Gram. Sch.; Silcoates Coll., Wakefield. Engineering experience in England and USA; Gen. Manager of Blake Knowles Pump Works, Ltd, and Wheeler Condenser and Engineering Co.; for many years member of Council of Society of Chemical Industry, a founder of Chemical Engineering Group and Chairman 1920-24, also 1932-33; a founder of Institution of Chemical Engineers, President 1929-31; an original member of Chemical Plant Manufacturers' Association, Chairman 1927-30; President of Combustion Appliance Makers' Association, 1937-39; Vice-President British Coal Utilisation Research Association, 1939; FCS; Member of Executive of National Physical Laboratory, 1931-36; Chairman of Chemical Engineering Industry Section of British Standards Institution since its inception in 1931-52. Hon. MSc Witwatersrand, 1964. *Publications:* Many technical papers in transactions of Institution of Chemical Engineers, of Society Chemical Industry, Chemical Engineering Group, and other technical bodies. *Recreations:* gardening, fishing and shooting. *Address:* Waylands, Beckenham, Kent. *T:* 01-650 1941; Pollards, Four Elms, nr Edenbridge, Kent.

**REAY,** 14th Baron, *cr* 1628, of Reay, Caithness, and Baron Mackay of Ophemert and Zennewijnen, Holland; **Hugh William Mackay;** Bt of Nova Scotia, 1627; Chief of Clan Mackay; *b* 19 July 1937; *s* of 13th Baron Reay and Charlotte Mary Younger; *S* father, 1963; *m* 1964, Hon. Annabel Therèse Fraser, *y d* of 17th Baron Lovat, *qv*; one *s* one *d*. *Educ:* Eton; Christ Church. *Recreations:* none. *Heir: s* the Master of Reay, *qv*. *Address:* 11 Wilton Crescent, SW1. *T:* 01-235 7171; Ophemert, Holland. *T:* 281. *Clubs:* St James', Turf, Beefsteak.

**REAY, Master of; Aeneas Simon Mackay,** *b* 20 March 1965; *s* and *heir* of 14th Baron Reay, *qv*.

**REAY, Basil;** *see* Reay, S. B.

**REAY, George Adam,** CBE 1958 (OBE 1949); Director, Torry Research Station, Department of Scientific and Industrial Research, 1958-64; retd; *b* 31 May 1901; *er s* of Adam Reay and Helen Glass Cownie, Aberdeen; *m* 1928, Tina Mary Margaret, *d* of Sinclair Pottinger Shewan and Ann Law, Fetlar, Shetland; one *s* one *d*. *Educ:* Robert Gordon's College, Aberdeen; University of Aberdeen; Emmanuel College, Cambridge. MA, BSc (Aberdeen), 1921, 1923; PhD (Cantab) 1927; FRIC 1948; FRSE 1955; Senior Kilgour Schol., Aberdeen; Carnegie Research Fellow, Cambridge. Research Officer of Food Investigation Organisation, of DSIR, 1927-57; at Torry Research Station, 1929-64; Officer in Charge, 1937, Superintendent, 1946. Hon. Research Lecturer in Fish Technology at Aberdeen Univ., 1946-64; Chairman, FAO Liaison Cttee on Fishery Products Technology, 1950-64; Mem., Food Science Cttee of Roy. Coll. of Science and Technology, Glasgow, 1957-64; Mem., FAO Panel of Fisheries Experts, 1962-; Mem., White Fish Authority Research and Development Policy Committee, 1962-64. *Publications:* scientific and technical papers, reviews, reports, etc, concerning handling, processing, transport and preservation for food, of fish, from catching to consumption. *Recreations:* music, fishing, walking. *Address:* 27 Salisbury Terrace, Aberdeen. *T:* Aberdeen 20842.

**REAY, (Stanley) Basil,** OBE 1957; Secretary, The Lawn Tennis Association, since 1948; Hon. Secretary, The International Lawn Tennis Federation and the Davis Cup Competition; Wing Comdr, RAFVR; *b* 2 Feb. 1909; *s* of Robert and Maud Reay (*née* Cox), Stockton on Tees; *m* 1935, Beatrice Levene; one *s* one *d*. *Educ:* Queen Elizabeth Grammar School, Hexham; St John's College. Schoolmaster in England, 1929-32; Min. of Education, Egypt, 1932-39. Chairman Inter-Services Language Training Cttee, 1945-47. Served RAF, 1939-47, chiefly in ME (Wing Comdr, 1944). Commandeur, Ordre de Merite Sportif (France), 1960. *Recreations:* travel and sports. *Address:* Molende, Molember Road, East Molesey, Surrey. *Clubs:* Royal Automobile, RAF Reserves; All England (Wimbledon); International Lawn Tennis Clubs of Great Britain, USA, France, Italy, Sweden and Denmark.

**REBACK, Mrs Marcus;** *see* Caldwell, Taylor.

**REBBECK, Dr Denis,** CBE 1952; MA, MSc, PhD, BLitt; DL, JP; CEng, FICE, FIMechE, MRINA, MIMarE, MInstT; *b* 22 Jan. 1914; *er s* of late Sir Frederick Ernest Rebbeck, KBE; *m* 1938, Rosamond Annette Kathleen, *e d* of late Henry Jameson, Bangor, Co. Down; four *s*. *Educ:* Campbell Coll., Belfast; Pembroke Coll., Cambridge. BA (Hons) Mech. Sciences Tripos, 1935; MA (Cantab) 1939; MA (Dublin) 1945; BLitt (Dublin) 1946; MSc (Belfast) 1946; PhD (Belfast) 1950; Part-time Post-grad. Research. Harland & Wolff, Ltd: Director, 1946-70; Dep. Man. Director, 1953; Man. Dir, 1962-70; Chm., 1965-66. Director: Iron Trades Employers' Insurance Association Ltd and Iron Trades Mutual Insurance Co. Ltd, 1950- (Vice-Chm., 1969-); Belships Co. Ltd, 1970-; Colvilles Ltd, 1963-67; Brown Brothers & Co. Ltd, 1967-68; Shipbuilding Corporation Ltd, 1963-; National Commercial Bank of Scotland Ltd, 1965-69; Royal Bank of Scotland Ltd, 1969-; John Kelly Ltd, 1968- (Dep. Chm., 1968; Chm., 1969); The British Ship Research Assoc. (Trustees) Ltd; National Shipbuilders Security, Ltd, 1952-58. Special Consultant, Swan Hunter Group Ltd, 1970-. Belfast Harbour Commissioner, 1962-. Member Research Council, and Chairman, Design Main Committee, British Ship Research Association; Pres., Shipbuilding Employers' Fedn, 1962-63; Member: Northern Ireland Economic Council; Lloyd's Register of Shipping General Cttee, 1962- and Technical Cttee, 1964-; Management Board, Shipbuilders & Repairers National Assoc.; Management Board, Engineering Employers Fedn, 1963-; Council, Royal Institution of Naval Architects, 1964-; Council for Scientific Research and Development in NI, 1948-59; Member Inst. of Engineers and Shipbuilders in Scotland; Past Chm. and Trustee, Belfast Savings Bank; Cambridge Univ. Engineers' Assoc.; Science Masters' Assoc. (Pres. NI Branch, 1954-55); NI Grammar Schools Careers Assoc. (Pres., 1964-65); Life Mem. Brit. Assoc. for the Advancement of Science; National Playing Fields Assoc. (NI Exec. Cttee); Member Drummond Technical Investigation Cttee, 1955-56; Member Lord Coleraine's Committee to enquire into Youth Employment Services in NI, 1957-58; Member, Sir John Lockwood's Cttee on Univ. and Higher Techn. Educn in Northern Ireland, 1963-64; Queen's Univ., Better Equipment Fund Exec. Cttee; Vice-Pres. of Belfast Savings Council; Visitor, Linen Industry Research Assoc., DSIR, 1954-57; President NI Society of Incorporated Secretaries, 1955-70; Pres. Glencraig Curative Schools, NI, 1953-70; Past Mem. Council: Instn Mech. Engineers; Inst. Marine Engineers; Pres. Belfast Assoc. of Engineers, 1947-48; Chm. NI Assoc., Instn Civil Engineers, 1952-53; Member of the

Court of Assistants, Worshipful Company of Shipwrights. Vice-Pres., Queen's Univ. Guild, 1951-65; Board Governors Campbell Coll., Belfast, 1952-60 (Vice-Chm. 1957-60); Mem. T and AFA for Belfast, 1947-65; Dep.-Chm. NI Festival of Britain, 1948-51; papers read before British Association, Institution Civil Engineers, etc; Akroyd Stuart Award, Inst. Marine Engineers, 1943. JP County Borough of Belfast, 1949; DL County of the City of Belfast, 1960. *Recreations:* golf, sailing. *Address:* The White House, Craigavad, Holywood, County Down, N Ireland. *T:* Holywood 2294. *Clubs:* Royal Yacht Squadron, Royal Automobile, City Livery, Den Norske; Cambridge Union; Ulster (Belfast); Shippingklubben (Oslo); Royal Norwegian Yacht; Royal North of Ireland Yacht (Cultra, Co. Down); Royal Ulster Yacht (Rear-Commodore, 1965-67) (Bangor, Co. Down).

**REBBECK, Rear-Adm. Sir Edward;** *see* Rebbeck, Rear-Adm. Sir L. E.

**REBBECK, Rear-Admiral Sir (Leopold) Edward,** KBE 1956; CB 1954; retired; *b* 26 July 1901; *s* of Edward Wise Rebbeck, Bournemouth; *m* Clara Margaret Allen, *e d* of R. G. Coombe, Ceylon; two *s* two *d*. *Educ:* Pembroke Lodge; Royal Naval Colls Osborne and Dartmouth. Served European War in HMS Erin; HM Yacht Victoria and Albert, 1932-35; War of 1939-45; HMS Birmingham, and as Assistant Naval Attaché, USA. Commanding Officer, RN Air Station Anthorn, 1946; Fleet Engineer Officer to C in C Mediterranean, 1949. ADC to King George VI, 1951-52; ADC to the Queen, 1952; Rear-Admiral Reserve Aircraft, 1952-55, retired. Vickers Group, 1956-66. Member Inst. of Met.; Member Soc. Naval Architects and Marine Engineers (New York). *Recreations:* golf, motoring. *Address:* Stubb Hill House, Iping, Nr Midhurst, Sussex. *T:* Milland 238. *Clubs:* Army and Navy, Royal Automobile.

**RECKITT, (Hon.) Lt-Col Basil Norman;** TD 1946; DL; Director, Reckitt and Colman Ltd (Chairman, 1966-70); *b* 12 Aug. 1905; *s* of Frank Norman Reckitt, Architect, and Beatrice Margaret Hewett; *m* 1st, 1928, Virginia Carre-Smith (*d* 1961); three *d*; 2nd, 1966, Mary Holmes (*née* Peirce), *widow* of Paul Holmes, Malham Tarn, near Settle. *Educ:* Uppingham; King's Coll., Cambridge (MA). Joined Reckitt & Sons Ltd, 1927; Dir, Reckitt & Colman Ltd, 1938. 2nd Lieut, 62nd HAA Regt (TA), 1939; Bde Major, 39th AA Brigade, 1940; CO 141 HAA (M) Regt, 1942; Military Government, Germany, 1944-45. Deputy Chairman, Reckitt & Colman Holdings Ltd, 1964. Chairman: The Scout Assoc., E Riding Scout County; E Riding Playing Fields Assoc.; Life Governor, Hymers College; Trustee, Hull Trustee Savings Bank; Mem. Council, Hull Univ. DL for Kingston upon Hull and E Riding of Yorks, 1961. Sheriff of Hull, 1970-71. Hon. LLD, Hull University, 1967. *Publications:* History of Reckitt & Sons Ltd, 1951; Charles I and Hull, 1952. *Recreations:* riding and walking. *Address:* The Elms, Roos, Nr Hull, E Yorkshire. *T:* Burton Pidsea 223. *Club:* United Hunts.

**RECKNELL, George Hugh;** retired as Actuary and Manager, and Director National Mutual Life Assurance Society, 1956; *b* 17 Oct. 1893; *s* of George Samuel Recknell; *m* 1st, Eileen Mary (*d* 1961), *y d* of late Dr Walter Paterson; two *d*; 2nd, 1962, Jean Addison, lately Matron, Guy's Hosp. *Educ:* Christ's Hosp. Fellow of the Faculty of Actuaries, 1915 (Vice-Pres., 1950-53); Lt 12th Cameronians attached Royal Engineers Signals Service, France, 1916; Palestine and Syria, 1917-19; Fellow Institute of Actuaries, 1923 (Vice-Pres. 1941-45); Chm. for many years of Harrow Nat. Savings Cttee; Gov. of Guy's Hosp., 1954-63; Investment Adviser to BOAC and BEA Jt Pension Fund, 1955-67; Chm. First Irish Investments Ltd. Director City General Insurance Co. Ltd, 1958-65. *Publications:* Contributions on Actuarial and Financial subjects in various jls; A History of King Street and Cheapside; A History of the Actuaries Club; Steyning: History and Descriptive Survey. *Recreations:* reading and showing my house to visitors. *Address:* Chantry Green House, Steyning, Sussex. *T:* Steyning 2239. *Clubs:* United Service, Actuaries; West Sussex Golf.

**REDCLIFFE MAUD,** family name of **Baron Redcliffe-Maud.**

**REDCLIFFE-MAUD,** Baron *cr* 1967 (Life Peer), of City and County of Bristol; **John Primatt Redcliffe Redcliffe-Maud,** GCB 1955 (KCB 1946); CBE 1942; Master of University College, Oxford, since 1963; *b* 3 Feb. 1906; *yr s* of late John Primatt Maud, Bishop of Kensington, and late Elizabeth Diana Furse; *m* 1932, Jean, *yr d* of late J. B. Hamilton, Melrose; one *s* two *d*. *Educ:* Eton (King's Scholar); New College, Oxford (Open Classical Scholar); Harvard College, USA. Henry P. Davison Scholar from Oxford Univ. to Harvard College, 1928-29; AB Harvard, 1929; Junior Research Fellow, 1929, University College, Oxford; Fellow and Dean, 1932-39; Rhodes Travelling Fellowship to Africa, 1932; University Lecturer in Politics, 1938-39; Councillor Oxford City, 1930-36; invited by Johannesburg City Council to write municipal history of city; Tutor to Colonial Administrative Services Course, Oxford, 1937-39; Master of Birkbeck College, University of London, 1939-43; Deputy Secretary, later Second Secretary, Ministry of Food, 1941-44; Second Secretary, Office of the Minister of Reconstruction, 1944-45; Secretary, Office of Lord President of the Council, 1945; Permanent Secretary, Ministry of Education, 1945-52; mem. Economic Planning Board, 1952-58; Permanent Secretary, Ministry of Fuel and Power, 1952-59; British Ambassador in South Africa, 1961-63 (High Commissioner, 1959-61), and High Commissioner for Basutoland, Bechuanaland Protectorate and Swaziland, 1959-63. High Bailiff of Westminster, 1967-. UK deleg. to Confs on Food and Agric., Hot Springs, 1943, UNRRA, Atlantic City, 1943, and UNESCO, 1946, 1947, 1948, 1949, 1950 (President Executive Board, 1949-50). Chm., Council, Royal Coll. of Music. Trustee, Cassel Educational Trust, 1963. Chairman: Local Govt Management Cttee, 1964-67; Royal Commn on Local Govt in England, 1966-69. Pres., Royal Inst. of Public Administration, 1969. Hon. Fellow, New Coll., Oxford, 1964; Fellow, Eton Coll., 1964. Hon. LLD: Witwatersrand, 1960; Natal, 1963; Leeds, 1967; Nottingham, 1968; Hon. DSocSc Birmingham, 1968. Sen. Fell., RCA, 1961; FRCM, 1964. *Publications:* English Local Government, 1932; City Government: The Johannesburg Experiment, 1938; Chapter in Oxford and the Groups, 1934; Chapter in Personal Ethics, 1935; Johannesburg and the Art of Self-Government, 1937; Chapter in Education in a Changing World, 1951. *Address:* The Master's Lodgings, University College, Oxford. *Clubs:* Savile; Eton Ramblers.

**REDDAWAY, Arthur Frederick John,** CMG 1959; OBE 1957; Director, Council for the Advancement of Arab-British Understanding; *b* 12 April 1916; *s* of Arthur Joseph Reddaway, Chartered Accountant, and Thirza May King;

*m* 1945, Anthoula, *d* of Dr Christodoulos Papaioannou, Nicosia; two *s*. *Educ:* County High School, Ilford; University of Reading. Colonial Administrative Service, Cyprus, 1938; Imperial Defence College, 1954; Administrative Sec., Cyprus, 1957-60; Dep. Comr-General, UNRWA for Palestine Refugees, 1960-68. *Address:* 19 Woodsyre, Sydenham Hill, SE26. *Club:* East India and Sports.

**REDDAWAY, George Frank Norman,** CBE 1965 (MBE 1946); HM Diplomatic Service; Assistant Under-Secretary of State, Foreign and Commonwealth Office, since 1970; *b* 2 May 1918; *s* of late William Fiddian Reddaway and late Kate Waterland Reddaway (*née* Sills); *m* 1944, Jean Brett; two *s* three *d*. *Educ:* Oundle School; King's College, Cambridge. Scholar Modern Langs, 1935; 1st Class Hons Mod. Langs Tripos Parts 1 and 2, 1937 and 1939. Served in Army, 1939-46; psc Camberley, 1944. Foreign Office, 1946; Private Secretary to Parliamentary Under Secretary of State, 1947-49; Rome, 1949; Ottawa, 1952; Foreign Office, 1955; Imperial Defence College, 1960; Beirut, 1961; Counsellor, Office of the Political Adviser to the C-in-C, Far East, Singapore, 1965-66; Counsellor (Commercial), Khartoum, 1967-69. *Recreations:* tennis, walking. *Address:* c/o Foreign and Commonwealth Office, SW1. *Club:* Oxford and Cambridge University.

**REDDAWAY, William Brian;** FBA 1967; Professor of Political Economy, University of Cambridge, since 1969; Fellow of Clare Coll., Cambridge, since 1938; Member, National Board for Prices and Incomes, since 1967; Editor, Economic Journal, since 1971; *b* 8 January 1913; *s* of late William Fiddian Reddaway and late Kate Waterland Reddaway (*née* Sills); *m* 1938, Barbara Augusta Bennett; three *s* one *d*. *Educ:* Oundle Sch.; King's Coll., Cambridge; Maj. schol. natural science; 1st cl. Maths tripos, part I, 1st cl. 1st div. Economics tripos, part II; Adam Smith Prize; MA. Assistant, Bank of England, 1934-35; Research Fellow in Economics, University of Melbourne, 1936-37; Statistics Division, Board of Trade (final rank Chief Statistician), 1940-47; University Lectr in Economics, 1939-55, Reader in Applied Economics, 1957-65, Dir of Dept of Applied Economics, 1955-69, Univ. of Cambrdige. Economic Adviser to OEEC, 1951-52; Visiting Economist, Center for International Studies, New Delhi, 1959-60; Vis. Lectr, Economic Develt Inst. (Washington), 1966-67; Consultant, Harvard Develt Adv. Service (in Ghana), 1967. Mem. of Royal Commn on the Press, 1961-62. *Publications:* Russian Financial System, 1935; Economics of a Declining Population, 1939; (with C. F. Carter, Richard Stone) Measurement of Production Movements, 1948; The Development of the Indian Economy, 1962; Effects of UK Direct Investment Overseas, Interim Report, 1967, Final Report, 1968; Effects of the Selective Employment Tax, First Report, 1970; articles in numerous economic journals. *Recreations:* ski-ing, skating, walking. *Address:* 4 Adams Road, Cambridge. *T:* 50041.

**REDDICK, Ven. Percy George,** MA Oxon; Archdeacon of Bristol, 1950-67; Canon Residentiary, Bristol Cathedral, 1955-62; Hon. Canon, 1962-67; *b* 9 November 1896; *s* of Henry Reddick and Elisabeth (*née* Powell); *m* 1st, 1922, Edith Annie Cropper, one *d*; 2nd, 1944, Elsie Maud Thomas. *Educ:* St Edmund Hall and Wycliffe Hall, Oxford. Served European War, King's Royal Rifles, 1915-17 (General Service and Victory Medal); invalided. Oxford, 1919-23. Curate: St Michael's, Southfields, 1923-25; Holy Trinity, Sydenham, 1925-30; Vicar: St Saviour, Herne Hill, 1930-40; Downend, 1940-43; Diocesan Secretary, Bristol, 1943-50; Chaplain to Bishop of Bristol and Diocesan Chaplain, 1943-50; Hon. Canon Bristol Cathedral, 1946-50; Examining Chaplain to Bishop of Bristol. *Recreation:* woodwork. *Address:* 24 Henleaze Road, Westbury-on-Trym, Bristol. *T:* Bristol 628820.

**REDDISH, Sir Halford (Walter Lupton),** Kt 1958; FCA; Chairman and Chief Executive, The Rugby Portland Cement Co. Ltd and subsidiary companies; Director: Scottish Union and National Insurance Co. (London Board); Norwich Union Insurance Societies (London Board); Hawker Siddeley Group Ltd; Alfred Herbert Ltd; Granada Group Ltd; Meldrum Investment Trust Ltd; Underwriting Member of Lloyd's; President of Rugby Conservative Association; Member of Council, Institute of Directors; Freeman of the City of London in the Livery of the Pattenmakers; *b* 15 Aug. 1898; *s* of Henry Lupton Reddish; *m* Valerie, *e d* of Arthur Grosart Lehman Smith, MRCS, LRCP. *Educ:* Rugby School. Served European War, 1914-18. Gold Medallist and Inst. Prizeman, Inst. Chartered Accountants, 1920. *Recreations:* business, chess. *Address:* Welton House, near Daventry. *T:* Daventry 2525; Dorchester Hotel, W1. *T:* 01-629 8888; (office) Rugby. *T:* Rugby 2244. *Club:* Carlton.

**REDESDALE,** 5th Baron, *cr* 1902; **Clement Napier Bertram Mitford;** Partner in: Redeclean since 1964; Redecraft; Director: Glenfleet Ltd; Leisure Arts Ltd; Great Gardens of England (Selling Centres) Ltd; *b* 28 Oct. 1932; *o s* of late Hon. E. R. B. O. Freeman-Mitford, 5th *s* of 1st Baron; *S* uncle, 1963; *m* 1958, Sarah Georgina Cranston Todd; one *s* six *d*. *Educ:* Eton. DipPA. Joined Colin Turner (London) Ltd, 1953; joined Erwin Wasey (Advertising), 1955, Associate Director, 1960-64. Pres., Guild of Cleaners and Launderers, 1968-70. *Heir:* *s* Hon. Rupert Bertram Mitford, *b* 18 July 1967. *Address:* 2 St Mark's Square, NW1. *T:* 01-722 1965. *Club:* Lansdowne.

**REDFERN, Sir (Arthur) Shuldham,** KCVO 1939; CMG 1945; *b* 13 June 1895; *er s* of Dr J. J. Redfern; *m* 1925, Ruth Marion Grimshaw; one *s*. *Educ:* Winchester; Trinity College, Cambridge. Served European War, 1914-19, Major Royal Flying Corps and RAF, 1918; joined Sudan Political Service, 1920; successively Assistant District Commissioner in Provinces of Khartoum, Darfur, Blue Nile; Dep. Governor of Blue Nile Province, 1927; Assistant Civil Secretary, Khartoum, 1929; Commissioner Port Sudan, 1932; Governor Kassala Province, 1934; Secretary to Governor-General of Canada, 1935-45; British Council, 1947-51. CStJ; Officer of Order of the Nile, 1925. *Publications:* articles in Canadian papers. *Recreations:* music, painting. *Address:* 32 Sheffield Terrace, W8. *T:* 01-229 1323. *Club:* Athenæum.

**REDFERN, Philip;** Deputy Director, Office of Population, Censuses and Surveys, since 1970; *b* 14 Dec. 1922; *m* 1951, Gwendoline Mary Phillips; three *d*. *Educ:* Bemrose Sch., Derby; St John's Coll., Cambridge. Wrangler, Mathematical Tripos, Cambridge, 1942. Asst Statistician, Central Statistical Office, 1947; Chief Statistician, Min. of Education, 1960; Dir of Statistics and Jt Head of Planning Branch, Dept of Educn and Science, 1967. *Address:* Northanger Cottage, Bookhurst Hill, Cranleigh, Surrey.

**REDGRAVE, Sir Michael (Scudamore),** Kt 1959; CBE 1952; Actor; *b* 20 March 1908; *s* of G. E. ("Roy") Redgrave, actor, and Margaret Scudamore, actress; *m* 1935, Rachel Kempson; one *s* two *d*. *Educ:* Clifton Coll.; Magdalene Coll., Cambridge. MA; formerly modern language master Cranleigh Sch. Liverpool Repertory Theatre, 1934-36; Country Wife, As You Like It, Hamlet, etc, Old Vic Season, 1936-37; Richard II, School for Scandal, Three Sisters, Queen's Theatre, 1937-38; White Guard, Twelfth Night, Phœnix Theatre, 1938-39; Family Reunion, Westminster Theatre, 1939; Beggar's Opera, Haymarket Theatre, 1940; Thunder Rock, Globe Theatre, 1940; The Duke in Darkness, St James's Theatre, 1942; A Month in the Country, Parisienne, St James's Theatre, 1943; Uncle Harry, Garrick Theatre, 1944; Jacobowsky and the Colonel, Piccadilly, 1945; Macbeth, Aldwych, 1947; Macbeth, National Theatre, New York, 1948; The Father, Embassy, 1948, and Duchess, 1949; A Woman in Love, Embassy, 1949; Love's Labour's Lost, She Stoops to Conquer, A Month in the Country, Hamlet, with Old Vic Theatre Co., New, 1949-50; played Hamlet at Switzerland and Holland Festivals, also at Kronborg Castle, Elsinore, 1950; Richard II, Henry IV Parts 1 and 2, Henry V, The Tempest, Memorial Theatre, Stratford-on-Avon, 1951; solo performance of Shakespeare, Holland Festival, 1951; Winter Journey, St James's, 1952; Rockefeller Foundation Lecturer, Bristol Univ., 1952; Shylock, Antony and King Lear, Stratford-on-Avon, 1953; Antony, Princes, 1953, and Amsterdam, Brussels and Paris, 1954; Tiger at the Gates, Apollo, 1955, and Plymouth, New York, 1955; Theodore Spencer Memorial Lecturer, Harvard Univ., 1956; The Sleeping Prince, Coronet, New York, 1956; A Touch of the Sun, Saville, 1958; Hamlet and Benedick, Stratford-on-Avon, 1958; played Hamlet with Shakespeare Memorial Theatre Co., in Russia, 1958; The Aspern Papers, Queen's, 1959; The Tiger and the Horse, Queen's, 1960; solo performances of Shakespeare and of Hans Andersen, Bath Festival, 1961; The Complaisant Lover, Barrymore, NY, 1961; Uncle Vanya, Chichester Festival, 1962; Out of Bounds, Wyndham's, 1962; Uncle Vanya, Chichester Festival, 1963; joined National Theatre, 1963 (first production, Oct. 1963); Claudius in Hamlet; Uncle Vanya, Hobson's Choice, The Master Builder; A Month in the Country, Y. Arnaud and Cambridge Theatres, also Samson Agonistes (YA), 1965; entered films, 1938. *Films:* The Lady Vanishes, The Stars Look Down, Kipps, Jeannie, Thunder Rock, The Way to the Stars, Dead of Night, The Captive Heart, The Man Within, Fame is the Spur, Mourning Becomes Electra, The Browning Version, The Importance of being Earnest, The Green Scarf, Dam Busters, The Night My Number Came Up, Confidential Report, 1984, Time without Pity, The Happy Road, The Quiet American, Shake Hands with the Devil, Wreck of the Mary Deare; No, my darling daughter!, The Innocents, The Loneliness of the Long-Distance Runner, Young Cassidy, The Hill, The Heroes of Telemark, Oh What a Lovely War!, The Battle of Britain, Goodbye Mr Chips, Connecting Rooms, etc. Producer: Werther, Glyndebourne, 1966, 1969; La Bohème, Glyndebourne, 1967. Joined Royal Navy, 1941; discharged on medical grounds, 1942. President, English-Speaking Board; President, Questors Theatre; Director of Festival, Yvonne Arnaud Theatre, Guildford, 1965. FRSA; Hon. DLitt (Bristol), 1966. Commander Order of Dannebrog, 1955. *Publications:* The Seventh Man (play), 1936; Actor's Ways and Means, 1953; Mask or Face, 1958; The Aspern Papers (play), 1959; The Mountebank's Tale (novel), 1959; Circus Boy (play), 1963. *Relevant Publication:* Michael Redgrave, Actor, by Richard Findlater, 1956. *Address:* c/o Christopher Mann Ltd, 140 Park Lane, W1. *Club:* Garrick.

*See also Vanessa Redgrave.*

**REDGRAVE, Vanessa,** CBE 1967; Actress since 1957; *b* 30 Jan. 1937; *d* of Sir Michael Redgrave, *qv*; *m* 1962, Tony Richardson, *qv* (marriage dissolved, 1967); two *d*. *Educ:* Queensgate School; Central School of Speech and Drama. Frinton Summer Repertory, 1957; Touch of the Sun, Saville, 1958; Midsummer Night's Dream, Stratford-on-Avon, 1959; Look on Tempests, 1960; The Tiger and the Horse, 1960; Lady from the Sea, 1960; Royal Shakespeare Theatre Company: As You Like It, 1961; Taming of the Shrew, 1961; Cymbeline, 1962; The Seagull, English Stage Company, 1964; The Prime of Miss Jean Brodie, Wyndham's, 1966. *Films:* Morgan–A Suitable Case for Treatment, 1966 (Cannes Fest. Award, Best Actress 1966); The Sailor from Gibraltar, 1967; Blow-Up, 1967; Camelot, 1967; Red White and Zero, 1967; Charge of the Light Brigade, 1968; Isadora, 1968; A Quiet Place in the Country, 1968; The Seagull, 1969. Has appeared on TV. *Publication:* Pussies and Tigers (anthology of writings of school children), 1963.

**REDINGTON, Frank Mitchell,** MA, FIA; Chief Actuary, Prudential Assurance Co. Ltd, 1950-68, Director since 1968; *b* 10 May 1906; *e s* of late William David and Lily Redington; *m* 1938, Katie Marianne Rosenfeld; one *s* one *d*. *Educ:* Liverpool Institute; Magdalene College, Cambridge (MA). Entered Prudential, 1928; FIA 1934; Chairman, Life Offices Association, 1956-57; President, Institute of Actuaries, 1958-60 (Gold Medal of Inst., 1968). *Publications:* contributions to Jl of Inst. of Actuaries and foreign actuarial journals. *Address:* 10 Rose Walk, St Albans, Herts. *T:* St Albans 54722.

**REDMAN, Maj.-Gen. Denis Arthur Kay,** CB 1963; OBE 1942; Colonel Commandant, REME, 1963-68; Director, Electrical and Mechanical Engineering, War Office, 1960-63, retd; *b* 8 April 1910; *s* of late Brig. A. S. Redman, CB; *m* 1943, Penelope, *d* of A. S. Kay; one *s* one *d*. *Educ:* Wellington Coll.; London Univ. BSc (Eng) 1st class Hons (London); FCGI, MIMechE, AMIEE. Commissioned in RAOC, 1934; served in Middle East, 1936-43; transferred to REME, 1942; Temp. Brig., 1944; DDME 1st Corps, 1951; Comdt REME Training Centre 1957-59. Graduate of Staff Coll., Joint Services Staff Coll. and Imperial Defence Coll. *Recreations:* normal. *Address:* Caerleon, 8 Murdoch Road, Wokingham, Berks. *T:* Wokingham 84. *Club:* Army and Navy.

**REDMAN, Lt-Gen. Sir Harold,** KCB *cr* 1953 (CB 1947); CBE 1944; *b* 25 August 1899; *s* of late A. E. Redman, Shawford, Winchester; *m* 1st, 1947, Patricia Mary (*d* 1951), *d* of late Brig. John Leslie Weston, CBE, DSO; one *d*; 2nd, 1953, Barbara Ann, *d* of late J. R. Wharton, Haffield, nr Ledbury; one *s* one *d*. *Educ:* Farnham; RMA, Woolwich. Commissioned into R Artillery, 1917; served in France and Germany, 1918 (BWM, VM); Waziristan, 1923-24 (NWF medal); Staff College, Camberley, 1929-30; transferred to KOYLI 1929; GSO 3 War Office, 1932-34; Bt Major, 1935; Brigade Major (3rd Division), 1934-36; GSO 2 Senior Officer School, 1937-38; GSO 2 Staff College, 1938-39; Bt Lt-Col 1939; War Cabinet Secretariat, 1939-40; Col 1942; Comd 7 Bn KOYLI 1940-41; Comd 151 (DLI) Infantry Bde Feb.-Dec. 1941; BGS Eighth

Army, 1941-42; Comd 10 Ind. Motor Bde 1942-43; Secretary Combined Chiefs of Staff (Brig.), 1943-44; Deputy Commander French Forces of the Interior (Maj.-Gen.), Aug.-Sept. 1944; SHAEF Mission to French High Command, 1944-45; Head British Military Mission (France), 1945-46; CGS, ALFSEA, 1946-48; Director of Military Operations, War Office, 1948-51; Principal Staff Officer to Deputy Supreme Allied Commander, Europe, 1951-52; Vice-Chief of the Imperial General Staff, 1952-55; Governor and Commander-in-Chief, Gibraltar, 1955-58, retired. Director and Secretary The Wolfson Foundation, 1958-67. Col KOYLI, 1950-60. *Recreation:* gardening. *Address:* King's Worthy Court, near Winchester, Hants. *T:* Winchester 3672. *Club:* United Service.

**REDMAN, Sir (Herbert) Vere,** Kt 1961; CMG 1951; OBE 1943; HM Foreign Service, retired; *b* 14 Oct. 1901; 2nd *s* of Charles D. Redman, Brockley, London; *m* 1925, Madeleine Aline (*d* 1970), *e d* of Colonel François Mathieu, Rouen, France. *Educ:* St Dunstan's College, Catford; University of London. Lecturer in English, Tokyo University of Commerce, 1927-33; Editorial Associate, Japan Advertiser, 1930-35; Assoc. Editor, Japan Advertiser, 1935-38; Tokyo Correspondent: Daily Mail (London), 1933-39, The Sun, Baltimore, USA, 1935-39; Press Attaché, British Embassy, Tokyo, 1939-41; Director, Far East Div., Ministry of Information, London, 1942-46; Counsellor (Information), British Embassy, Tokyo, Japan, 1946-61; retired from HM Foreign Service, 1962. Officier d'Académie (French), 1938; Order of the Rising Sun 3rd Cl. (Japan), 1964. *Publications:* Japan in Crisis, 1935; The Problem of the Far East, (with Sobei Mogi), 1936; This Language Learning Business (with H. E. Palmer), 1934. *Recreation:* swimming. *Address:* Le Rocher, Goult, Vaucluse, France. *T:* Goult 46. *Clubs:* Tokyo, American, Josui Kai (Tokyo).

**REDMAN, Roderick Oliver,** FRS 1946; MA, PhD; Professor of Astrophysics and Director of the Observatories, Cambridge University, since 1947; *b* 17 July 1905; *s* of Roderick George Redman and Elizabeth, *née* Stone; *m* 1935, Annie Kathleen, *d* of J. A. Bancroft, Annapolis Royal, NS, Canada; three *s* one *d*. *Educ:* Marling School, Stroud; St John's Coll., Cambridge. Asst Astronomer, Dominion Astrophysical Observatory, Victoria, BC, 1928-31; PhD 1929; Asst Director, Solar Physics Observatory, Cambridge, 1931-37; University Lecturer in Astrophysics, 1933-37; Fellow of St John's College, Cambridge, 1932-39, 1947-; Chief Assistant, Radcliffe Observatory, Pretoria, South Africa, 1937-47. President of the Royal Astronomical Society, 1959-61. *Publications:* scientific papers. *Recreations:* music, gardening. *Address:* The Observatories, Cambridge. *T:* Cambrdige 65681.

**REDMAN, Sydney,** CB 1961; Deputy Under-Secretary of State (Navy), Ministry of Defence, since 1964; *b* 12 Feb. 1914; *s* of John Barritt Redman and Ann Meech; *m* 1939, Barbara Mary Grey; one *s* two *d*. *Educ:* Manchester Gram. Sch.; Corpus Christi Coll., Oxford. Principal Private Sec. to Secretary of State for War, 1942-44. Asst Under-Secretary of State, War Office, 1957-63; Asst Under-Secretary of State, Ministry of Defence, 1964 (Under-Sec., 1963-64). *Address:* Littlehurst, Birch Avenue, Haywards Heath, Sussex. *T:* Haywards Heath 3738. *Club:* United University.

**REDMAN, Sir Vere;** *see* Redman, Sir H. V.

**REDMAYNE,** family name of **Baron Redmayne.**

**REDMAYNE,** Baron *cr* 1966 (Life Peer), of Rushcliffe; **Martin Redmayne;** Bt *cr* 1964; PC 1959; DSO 1944; DL; Deputy Chairman, Harrods Ltd; Director: House of Fraser Ltd; Boots Pure Drug Co. Ltd; *b* 16 Nov. 1910; *s* of Leonard Redmayne; *m* 1933, Anne Griffiths; one *s*. *Educ:* Radley. Commanded 14th Bn The Sherwood Foresters, Italy, 1943; formed and commanded 66 Inf. Bde, 1944-45; Hon. Brig., 1945. MP (C) Rushcliffe Div. of Notts, 1950-66. A Govt Whip, 1951; A Lord Comr of the Treasury, 1953-59; Dep. Govt Chief Whip, 1955-59; Parly Sec. to Treasury and Govt Chief Whip, Oct. 1959-64; Opposition Chief Whip, Oct.-Nov. 1964. JP Nottingham, 1946-66; DL Notts, 1954. *Recreations:* golf, fishing. *Heir:* (to Baronetcy only): *s* Hon. Nicholas Redmayne [*b* 1 Feb. 1938; *m* 1963, Ann Saunders; one *s* one *d*]. *Address:* 27 Hans Place, SW1. *T:* 01-584 1525. *Clubs:* Carlton, Buck's.

**REDMOND, James,** FIEE; Director of Engineering, BBC, since 1968; *b* 8 Nov. 1918; *s* of Patrick and Marion Redmond; *m* 1942, Joan Morris; one *s* one *d*. *Educ:* Graeme High Sch., Falkirk. Radio Officer, Merchant Navy, 1935-37 and 1939-45; BBC Television, Alexandra Palace, 1937-39; BBC: Installation Engr, 1949; Supt Engr Television Recording, 1960; Sen. Supt Engr TV, 1963; Asst Dir of Engrg, 1967. MIEE 1960. *Recreation:* golf. *Address:* 43 Cholmeley Crescent, Highgate, N6. *T:* 01-340 1611.

**REDMOND, Robert Spencer,** TD 1953; MP (C) Bolton (West) since 1970; Director, Ashley Associates Ltd (Managing Director, 1969-70); *b* 10 Sept. 1919; *m* 1949, Marjorie Helen Heyes; one *s*. *Educ:* Liverpool Coll. Served War, Army, 1939-46: commissioned The Liverpool Scottish, 1938; transferred, RASC, 1941; Middle East, Junior Staff Sch., 1943; DAQMG, HQ Special Ops (Mediterranean), 1943-45; released, rank of Major, 1946. Conservative Agent, 1947-56 (Wigan, 1947-49, Knutsford, 1949-56). Managing Dir, Heyes & Co. Ltd, Wigan, 1956-66; Ashley Associates Ltd: Commercial Manager, 1966-69; Managing Dir, 1969-70; Dir, 1970-. Pres., Alderley Edge British Legion, 1968-; Chm. (and Founder), NW Export Club, 1958-60. *Publication:* past contrib. FBI Review. *Recreation:* meeting people. *Address:* Ballytrent, Horseshoe Lane, Alderley Edge, Cheshire. *T:* Alderley Edge 3197. *Club:* Special Forces.

**REDPATH, John Thomas,** CB 1969; MBE 1944; FRIBA; Director General of Research and Development, Ministry of Public Building and Works, since Dec. 1967; *b* 24 Jan. 1915; *m* 1st, 1939, Kate (*née* Francis) (*d* 1949); one *d*; 2nd, 1949, Claesina (*née* van der Vlerk); three *s* one *d*. *Educ:* Price's Sch.; Southern Coll. of Art. Served with RE, 1940-47. Asst Architect: Kent CC, 1936-38; Oxford City Coun., 1938-40; Princ. Asst Architect, Herts, CC, 1948-55; Dep. County Architect, Somerset CC, 1955-59; Chief Architect (Abroad), War Office, 1959-63; Dir of Development, Min. of Public Building and Works, 1963-67. *Publications:* various articles in architectural jls. *Recreation:* golf. *Address:* Ministry of Public Building and Works, Lambeth Bridge House, SW1. *Club:* Reform.

**REDSHAW, Leonard;** Assistant Managing Director, Vickers Ltd, and Chairman, Vickers Ltd Shipbuilding Group, since 1968; *b* 15 April 1911; *s* of late Joseph Stanley Redshaw, Naval Architect; *m* 1939, Joan Mary, *d* of Wm White, London; one *s* one *d*. *Educ:* Barrow Grammar Sch.; Univ. of Liverpool. 1st cl. Hons degree in naval architecture; 1851 Roy. Comr's exhibn post grad. Schol., Master's degree. Joined the Management Staff of Vickers-Armstrongs, 1936; Asst to Shipbuilding Manager, 1950; Special Dir, 1953; when Vickers-Armstrongs (Shipbuilders) Ltd was formed he was apptd Shipbuilding Gen. Man. of Yards at Barrow-in-Furness and Newcastle, 1955; Dir, Vickers-Armstrongs (Shipbuilders) Ltd, 1956, Deputy Managing Director, 1961; Builders' Chief Polaris Exec., 1963; Man. Dir, Vickers Ltd Shipbuilding Group, 1964; Special Dir, Vickers Ltd, 1965; Dir, Vickers Ltd, 1967; Chm., Vickers Ltd Shipbuilding Group, 1967. Director: Rolls Royce & Associates, Ltd, Derby, 1966; British Hovercraft Corp. Ltd; British Hovercraft Corp. (Manufacturing) Ltd; Shipbuilding Corp Ltd. Chm., tech. Cttee, Lloyd's Register of Shipping and Mem., Lloyd's General Cttee. Member: Council, Brit. Shipbuilding Research Assoc.; NE Coast Instn of Engrs and Shipbuilders; Council, RINA; NW Economic Planning Council; Shipbuilders and Repairers Nat. Assoc. (Mem., Shipbuilding Management Bd and Ind. Relations Bd; Vice-Chm., Warship Cttee). FInstW. *Publications:* British Shipbuilding–Welding, 1947; Application of Welding to Ship Construction, 1962. *Recreations:* gliding, fishing. *Address:* Netherclose, Ireleth, Askam-in-Furness. *T:* Dalton-in-Furness 2529.

**REDSHAW, Prof. Seymour Cunningham,** DSc (Wales), PhD (London), FICE, FIStructE, FRAeS; Beale Professor and Head of Civil Engineering Department, University of Birmingham, 1950-69; Dean of Faculty of Science, 1955-57; Member of Aeronautical Research Council, 1955; a Governor of Coll. of Aeronautics, 1951-69; *b* 20 March 1906; *s* of Walter James Redshaw and Edith Marion Cunningham; *m* 1935, Mary Elizabeth Jarrold; three *s*. *Educ:* Blundell's School; University of Wales. Technical Assistant, Bristol Aeroplane Co. Ltd, 1927-31; Asst Designer General Aircraft Ltd, 1931-32; Member of Staff: Imperial College, London, 1933-35; Building Research Station, 1936-40; Boulton Paul Aircraft Ltd, 1940-50: Chief Engineer, 1945; Director, 1949. Mem. Adv. Cttee on Building Research, 1965-67; Mem. Council, Univ. of Aston, 1966-67; Chm., Acad. Adv. Cttee, and Mem. Council, Univ. of Bath, 1966. Hon. DSc, Bath. *Publications:* numerous papers in scientific and engineering journals. *Address:* West Gate, Brewood, Staffs. *T:* Brewood 274. *Clubs:* Athenæum, Savage, National Liberal.

**REDWOOD, Sir Thomas Boverton,** 2nd Bt, *cr* 1911; TD; *b* 15 October 1906; *s* of late Bernard Boverton Redwood (*d* 1911) and Gladys Dora (*d* 1965), *d* of William J. P. Sherwen, Hensingham, Whitehaven (she *m* 2nd, 1914, Esmond Robinson); *S* grandfather, 1919; *m* 1933, Ruth (from whom he obtained a divorce, 1943), *y d* of late Mrs Creighton; one *s*; *m* 1944, Ursula, *d* of late Rev. H. P. Hale; two *s* one *d* (and one *s* decd). *Educ:* Harrow. *Heir:* *s* Capt. Peter Boverton Redwood, KOSB [*b* 1 Dec. 1937; *m* 1964, Gilian, *d* of J. L. Waddington Wood; two *d*]. *Address:* Dolphin Cottage, 37 Kersey Road, Flushing, Falmouth, Cornwall.

**REECE, Sir Alan;** *see* Reece, Sir L. A.

**REECE, Courtenay Walton;** Puisne Judge, Hong Kong, 1952-61, retired; *b* 4 Dec. 1899; 3rd *s* of H. Walter Reece, KC (Barbados); *m* 1927, Rosa U. E. Parker (*d* 1956); two *d*. *Educ:* Harrison College and Codrington College, Barbados; Jesus College, Oxford (BA). Called to Bar, Middle Temple, 1925; Police Magistrate, Barbados, 1926; Registrar, Barbados, 1931; Magistrate, Nigeria, 1938; Crown Counsel, Nigeria, 1939; Senior Crown Counsel, Nigeria, 1946; Puisne Judge, Nigeria, 1949. *Recreations:* motor-boating, swimming, carpentry, fishing. *Address:* 108 Macdonnell Road, 7th Floor, Hong Kong. *Club:* Royal Hong Kong, Jockey.

**REECE, Francis Bertram,** CBE 1958; Metropolitan Magistrate, 1943-61 (Bow St, 1948-61); *b* 1888; *s* of late Rev. Canon J. F. Reece; *m* 1st, 1914, Gladys Catherine (*d* 1939), *d* of late Ephraim Wood, DL, JP, Pabo Hall, Conway; one *d*; 2nd, 1940, Dorothy Alice Macbeth, *widow* of Captain W. A. Low, 19th Hussars, *d* of Dr A. Macbeth Elliot. *Educ:* Rossall; St John's Coll., Cambridge (Classical Exhibitioner). Barrister, Inner Temple, 1914. Contested (C) Aberavon Div. of Glam., 1929. Chairman: Poisons Bd (Home Office), 1946-58; Preventive Detention Adv. Bd. Recorder of Birkenhead, 1935-43. *Address:* Snowdenham Cottage, Bramley, Surrey. *T:* 3145. *Clubs:* Garrick, Carlton, Oxford and Cambridge University; Royal and Ancient (St Andrews); Royal Mid-Surrey Golf.

**REECE, Sir Gerald,** KCMG 1950; CBE 1943 (OBE 1937); Scottish Chairman, Howard League for Penal Reform, since 1961; Chairman of Managers, Loaningdale Approved School, since 1968; *b* 10 Jan. 1897; *s* of Edward Mackintosh Reece; *m* 1936, Alys Isabel Wingfield, *d* of Dr H. E. H. Tracy; one *s* two *d* (and one *s* decd). *Educ:* Rugby School. Commissioned Sherwood Foresters, 1915; served France and Belgium (wounded thrice). Solicitor Sup. Court, England, 1921; entered Kenya Administrative Service, 1925; seconded as HBM's Consul for Southern Abyssinia, 1934; Senior Political Officer, Borana Province of Ethiopia, 1941; Officer in Charge, Northern Frontier of Kenya, 1939-45; Provincial Commissioner, Kenya, 1945-48; Military Governor, British Somaliland, 1948; Governor and Commander-in-Chief, Somaliland Protectorate, 1948-53. *Address:* Bolton Old Manse, near Haddington, East Lothian. *T:* Gifford 351.

**REECE, Sir (Louis) Alan,** Kt 1964; CMG 1963; Chairman: Trinidad and Tobago Electricity Board; Boundaries Commission; Elections Commission; Industrial Development Corporation; British West Indian Airways; Secretary to the Cabinet and Permanent Secretary to the Prime Minister, Trinidad and Tobago, 1961-63, retd; *b* 1906; *s* of Claud Austin Reece. *Educ:* Queen's Royal College, Trinidad. *Address:* c/o Whitehall, St Clair, Port of Spain, Trinidad.

**REED, Adrian Harbottle;** HM Diplomatic Service; Counsellor (Commercial) and Consul-General, Helsinki, since Dec. 1968; *b* 5 Jan. 1921; *s* of Harbottle Reed, MBE, FRIBA, and Winifred Reed (*née* Rowland); *m* 1947, Doris Davidson Duthie; one *s* one *d*. *Educ:* Hele's Sch., Exeter; Emmanuel Coll., Cambridge. Royal Artillery, 1941-47. India Office, 1947; Commonwealth Relations Office, 1947; served in UK High Commission: Pakistan, 1948-50; Fedn of Rhodesia and Nyasaland, 1953-56; British Embassy, Dublin, 1960-62; CO, 1962-68. *Address:* Wistaria Cottage, Shamley Green, Surrey. *T:* Bramley 3135.

**REED, Sir Carol,** Kt, *cr* 1952; Film Producer and Director; *b* 30 December 1906; *m* 1943, Diana Wynyard (marr. diss., 1947; she *d* 1964); *m* 1948, Penelope Dudley Ward; one *s*. *Educ:* King's School, Canterbury. First appearance on the stage Dec. 1924 at Empire Theatre, Leicester Square; acted small parts until joined Edgar Wallace as actor and stage-director in 1927; left theatre and went into Film Production, 1930. Has directed Midshipman

Easy, Laburnum Grove, A Girl in the News, Bank Holiday, Penny Paradise, Who's Your Lady Friend, Talk of the Devil, Climbing High, A Girl Must Live, The Stars Look Down, Night Train to Munich, Kipps, The Young Mr Pitt, The Way Ahead, A Letter from Home, The New Lot, Odd Man Out, The Fallen Idol, The Third Man, An Outcast of the Islands, The Man Between, A Kid for Two Farthings, Trapeze, The Key, Our Man in Havana, The Running Man, The Agony and The Ecstasy, Oliver!. Joined Army in 1941; directed film for SHAEF, Anglo-American Picture of the War from "D" Day to "VE" Day, entitled The True Glory. Golden Thistle Award, 1967. *Address:* 213 Kings Road, Chelsea, SW3.

**REED, David;** MP (Lab) Sedgefield Division of Co. Durham since 1970; *b* 24 April 1945; *s* of Wilfred Reed and Elsie Swindon; *m* 1970, Jacqueline Mary Woodley. *Educ:* West Hartlepool Grammar Sch. Journalist: Northern Echo, 1963-64; Imperial Chemical Industries, 1964-65; Public Relations Officer: NE Development Council, 1966-68; Vickers Ltd, 1968-70. *Publications:* many articles in national newspapers and other jls, on regional affairs. *Recreations:* working 18 hours a day during the week and relaxing completely at week-ends. *Address:* 52 West Heath Court, Northend Road, NW11. *T:* 01-458 3309.

**REED, Douglas;** Writer; *b* London, 1895. Relatively unschooled. At 13 publisher's office-boy, at 19 bank clerk; infantry and air force war service, 1914-18 (wounded twice, despatches); newspaper clerk, 1921; sub-editor The Times, 1924; Assistant Berlin Correspondent of The Times, 1929-35; The Times Central European Correspondent, 1935-38; subsequently independent writer; War Correspondent, Normandy, 1944; travelling in Africa, US and Canada, 1947-64. *Publications:* The Burning of The Reichstag, 1934; Insanity Fair, 1938; Disgrace Abounding, 1939; A Prophet at Home, 1941; All Our Tomorrows, 1942; Lest We Regret, 1943; From Smoke to Smother, 1948; Somewhere South of Suez, 1950; Far and Wide, 1951; The Battle for Rhodesia, 1966; *novels:* Galanty Show, 1947; Reasons of Health, 1949; Rule of Three, 1950. *Address:* c/o Jonathan Cape Ltd, 30 Bedford Square, WC1.

**REED, Edward John;** Clerk to the Clothworkers' Company of the City of London since 1963; *b* 2 Sept. 1913; *o c* of late Edward Reed; *m* 1939, Rita Isabel Venus Cheston-Porter; one *s* one *d. Educ:* St Paul's School. Admitted Solicitor, 1938. Territorial Service with HAC; commnd 1940; served BEF and BAOR with 63 (WR) Medium Regt RA; Capt. 1942. Clerk to Governor of Mary Datchelor Girls' Sch., 1963; Chm. of Metropolitan Society for the Blind and Indigent Blind Visiting Society, 1965. CStJ 1968. Chevalier, Order of Leopold with Palm, and Croix de Guerre with Palm, Belgium, 1944. *Recreations:* sailing, photography. *Address:* Clothworkers' Hall, Dunster Court, Mincing Lane, EC3. *T:* 01-626 6336.

**REED, Hon. Sir Geoffrey (Sandford),** Kt 1953; retired; *b* 14 March 1892; *s* of late Rev. William Reed; *m* 1918, Kathleen Jennie Matthews; one *s* one *d. Educ:* Prince Alfred College, Adelaide; Adelaide University (LLB). Called to South Australia Bar, 1914; Law Society of South Australia: Hon. Sec., 1924-27; Mem. Statutory Cttee, 1929-35; Vice-Pres. 1934. Lectr in Private Internat. Law and Law of Evidence and Procedure, Adelaide Univ., 1928-34. Actg Judge, Supreme Court of SA, April 1935-July 1937; KC 1937. Chm. SA Nat. Security Advisory Cttee, 1941-45; Chm. or Comr, a number of Roy. Commissions and Bds of Inquiry, State and Commonwealth Govts, 1943-48; Judge, Supreme Court of S Australia, 1943-62. Dir-Gen. of Security, Commonwealth of Australia, March 1949-June 1950. *Recreation:* golf. *Address:* 17 Briar Avenue, Medindie, SA 5081, Australia. *Club:* Adelaide (Adelaide).

**REED, Henry;** poet, critic, and radio-dramatist; *b* 22 Feb. 1914; *s* of Henry Reed and Mary Ann Ball. *Educ:* King Edward VI School, Aston Birmingham; Birmingham University. Journalism and teaching, 1937-41; served in Army, 1941-42; Foreign Office, 1942-45. Since 1945 engaged in broadcasting, journalism, and writing of radio-scripts. *Publications:* A Map of Verona (poems), 1946; Moby Dick (a radio version of Melville's novel), 1947; The Novel since 1939 (British Council pamphlet), 1947. *Address:* c/o Messrs Jonathan Cape, Ltd, 30 Bedford Square, WC1. *Club:* Savile.

**REED, Laurance Douglas;** MP (C) Bolton East since 1970; *b* 4 Dec. 1937; *s* of Douglas Austin Reed and Mary Ellen Reed (*née* Philpott). *Educ:* Gresham's Sch., Holt; University Coll., Oxford (MA). Nat. Service, RN, 1956-58; Oxford (Law), 1960-63; worked and studied on Continent (Brussels, Bruges, Leyden, Luxembourg, Strasbourg, Paris, Rome, Bologna, Geneva), 1963-66; Public Sector Research Unit, 1967-69. Member: Soc. for Underwater Technology; British Council of European Movement. *Publication:* Europe in a Shrinking World, 1967. *Recreations:* gardening, painting, roller-skating. *Address:* 19 Blenheim House, Carslake Avenue, Bolton, Lancs. *T:* Bolton 45326. *Club:* St Stephen's.

**REED, Maurice Ernest,** CBE 1951 (MBE 1948); The Deputy Master in Lunacy, The Court of Protection, since 1950; *b* 27 Feb. 1908; *yr s* of late Mr Justice Haythorne Reed, Chief Justice, Nyasaland; *m* 1932, Isabel Sidonie Lincoln-Reed; one *d. Educ:* King's College School, Wimbledon; Emmanuel College, Cambridge. Called to Bar, Gray's Inn, 1932; Legal Assistant, Law Officers Dept, 1935-48; Legal Secretary, 1948-50. *Address:* The White Cottage, Towersey, Oxon. *T:* Thame 229.

**REED, Michael,** CB 1962; *b* 7 July 1912; Registrar General since 1963; Director, Office of Population Censuses and Surveys, since 1970; *s* of late Richard and Winifred Reed; *m* 1st, 1939, Marcia Jackson; two *d*; 2nd, 1950, Hermione Jeanne, *d* of Dr P. Roux, Kimberley, SA; one *s* one *d. Educ:* Christ's Hospital; Jesus College, Cambridge. Entered Ministry of Health, 1935; Private Secretary to Minister, 1942-45; Under-Secretary, Ministry of Health, 1956-58, Cabinet Office, 1958-61, Ministry of Health, 1961-63. *Address:* Manor House, Cooksbridge, Sussex. *Club:* Athenæum.

**REED, Sir Nigel (Vernon),** Kt 1970; **Hon. Mr Justice Reed;** CBE 1967 (MBE 1945); TD 1950; Chief Justice of the Northern States of Nigeria, since 1968; *b* 31 Oct. 1913; *s* of Vernon Herbert Reed, formerly MP and MLC New Zealand, and of Eila Mabel Reed; *m* 1945, Ellen Elizabeth Langstaff; one *s* two *d. Educ:* Wanganui Collegiate School, NZ; Victoria University College, NZ; Jesus College, Cambridge. LLB (NZ) and LLB (Cantab). Called to the Bar, Lincoln's Inn, 1939. Military Service, 1939-45, Lt-Col 1944. Appointed to Colonial Legal Service, 1946; Magistrate, Nigeria, 1946; Chief Magistrate, Nigeria, 1951; Chief Registrar, High Court of the Northern Region of Nigeria, 1955; Judge, High Court of the Northern Region of

Nigeria, 1956; Sen. Puisne Judge, High Court of Northern Nigeria, 1964. *Address:* High Court, Kaduna, Nigeria.

**REED, Philip Dunham;** Chairman of the Board, Federal Reserve Bank of New York, 1960-65; *b* Milwaukee, Wisconsin, 16 Nov. 1899; *s* of William Dennis Reed and Virginia Brandreth Dunham; *m* 1921, Mabel Mayhew Smith; one *s* one *d*. *Educ:* University of Wisconsin (BS in Electrical Engineering); Fordham Univ. (LLB). Hon. LLD, Union Coll. and Brooklyn Poly. Inst., Hon. DEng Rensslaer Poly. Inst.; Hon. Dr of Commercial Science, New York Univ. 1950; Hon. Dr of Laws, Univ. of Wisconsin, 1950. Swarthmore Coll., 1954. With General Electric Co. (Law Dept), 1926-; Asst to Pres. and Dir, 1937-39; Chm. of Bd, 1940; resigned Chairmanship Dec. 1942 to continue war work in England; re-elected Chm. of Bd, 1945-58; Chm., Finance Cttee, General Electric Co., NY, 1945-59, Director Emeritus, 1968-. Chm. of Bd of Internat. General Electric Company, 1945 until merger with parent co., 1952. Director: American Express Co.; American Express Internat. Banking Corp.; Eurofund Inc.; Otis Elevator Company; Kraftco Corp., 1958-70; Scott Paper Co., 1958-66; Metropolitan Life Insurance Co.; Tiffany & Co.; Bigelow-Sanford Inc.; Bankers Trust Co.; Metropolitan Opera Assoc. Inc., 1945-53; Mem. Business Advisory Council for Dept of Commerce, 1940- (Vice-Chm. 1951-52); US Adv. Commn on Information, 1948-61; Member: Executive Commn, Payroll Savings Adv. Cttee for US Treasury Dept, 1946-56; Dir, Council on Foreign Relations, 1946-69; Trustee: Carnegie Endowment for Internat. Peace, 1945-53; Cttee for Economic Development (and Member Research and Policy Cttee); Member of the Visiting Cttee, Graduate School of Business Admin., Harvard Univ., 1940-60; Director, Ford Foundation Fund for Advancement of Education, 1951-53; Consultant to US Deleg., San Francisco Conf. on World Organization; Chm. US Associates (now US Council), Internat. Chamber of Commerce, 1945-Jan. 1948; mem. Exec. Cttee, US Council, ICC; Hon. Pres. Internat. Chamber of Commerce (Pres., 1949-51); Chm. US Side of Anglo-American Productivity Council, 1948-52; Vice-Chm. Eisenhower Exchange Fellowships, 1953-; Chm. Finance Cttee, 1955-56. Mem. President's Cttee on Information Activities Abroad, 1960; Mem. Cttee on the Univ. and World Affairs (Ford Foundn), 1960; Trustee of Kress Foundn, 1960-65. Entered War work, 1941, with Office of Production Management, Washington, and its successor the War Production Board (Chief of Bureau of Industry Branches responsible for organising and converting peacetime industries to war production). Went to London, July 1942, as Deputy Chief of Economic Mission headed by W. Averell Harriman; Chief of Mission for Economic Affairs, London, with rank of Minister, Oct. 1943-31 Dec. 1944. Special Ambassador to Mexico, 1958. President's Certificate of Merit Award, 1947; Comdr Légion d'Honneur (France), 1951 (Officer, 1947). *Address:* 375 Park Avenue, New York, NY 10022, USA; (home) Rye, NY. *Clubs:* University, The Links (NY City); Apawamis, Shenorock Shore (Rye, NY); Blind Brook (Port Chester, NY); Augusta National Golf (Augusta, Ga); Bohemian (San Francisco); Mill Reef (Antigua, WI).

**REED, Stanley William;** Director, British Film Institute, since 1964; *b* 21 Jan. 1911; *s* of Sidney James Reed and Ellen Maria Patient; *m* 1937, Alicia Mary Chapman; three *d*. *Educ:* Stratford Gram. Sch.; Coll. of St Mark and St John, Chelsea. Teacher in E London schools, 1931-39. In charge of school evacuation parties, 1939-45. Teacher and Visual Aids Officer, West Ham Education Cttee, 1939-50. British Film Institute: Educn Officer, 1952-56; Sec., 1956-64. *Publications:* The Cinema, 1952; How Films are Made, 1955; A Guide to Good Viewing, 1961. Neighbourhood 15 (film, also Dir). *Recreations:* opera and exploring London's suburbs. *Address:* 54 Felstead Road, Wanstead, E11. *T:* 01-989 6021.

**REED, Rt. Rev. Thomas Thornton;** *see* Adelaide, Bishop of.

**REEKIE, Henry Enfield;** Headmaster of Felsted School, 1951-68; *b* Hayfield, Derbyshire, 17 Oct. 1907; *s* of John Albert Reekie and Edith Dowson; *m* 1936, Pauline Rosalind, *d* of Eric W. Seeman; one *s* three *d*. *Educ:* Oundle; Clare College, Cambridge. Asst Master, Felsted School, 1929, Housemaster, 1933, Senior Science Master, 1945; Headmaster, St Bees School, 1946. *Recreations:* ski-ing, outdoor games. *Address:* Tarn House, Lake Street, Mark Cross, Crowborough, Sussex. *T:* Mayfield 3100. *Club:* Public Schools.

**REES, Arthur Morgan,** OBE 1963; QPM 1970; DL; Chief Constable, Staffordshire County and Stoke-on-Trent Constabulary, since 1968; *b* 20 Nov. 1912; *s* of Thomas and Jane Rees, The Limes, Llangadog; *m* 1943, Dorothy Webb; one *d*. *Educ:* Llandovery Coll.; St Catharine's Coll., Cambridge. BA 1935, MA 1939. Metropolitan Police, 1935-41; RAF (Pilot), 1941-46 (Subst. Sqdn Ldr; Actg Wing Comdr); Metropolitan Police, 1946-57; Chief Constable: Denbighshire, 1957-64; Staffordshire, 1964-67. Trustee and Board of Governors, Llandovery College. DL Staffs, 1967. CStJ 1969. *Recreations:* former Rugby International for Wales (14 caps), Cambridge Rugby Blue, 1933 and 1934; Chairman: Crawshays Welsh Rugby XV, 1970; Midlands Sports Adv. Cttee. *Address:* Burnden House, 150 Weston Road, Stafford. *T:* (home) Stafford 2025, (office) Stafford 3311. *Clubs:* Royal Air Force, East India and Sports; Hawks (Cambridge).

**REES, Brian,** MA Cantab; Headmaster, Merchant Taylors' School, since 1965; *b* 20 Aug. 1929; *s* of late Frederick T. Rees; *m* 1959, Julia, *d* of Sir Robert Birley, *qv*; two *s* three *d*. *Educ:* Bede Grammar Sch., Sunderland; Trinity Coll., Cambridge (Scholar). 1st cl. Historical Tripos, Part I, 1951; Part II, 1952. Eton College; Asst Master, 1952-65; Housemaster, 1963-65. *Recreations:* music, painting. *Address:* Merchant Taylors' School, Sandy Lodge, Northwood, Middlesex. *T:* Northwood 21850. *Clubs:* Athenæum, Savile.

**REES, Prof. Brinley Roderick,** MA Oxon, PhD Wales; Professor of Greek, University of Birmingham since 1970; *b* 27 Dec. 1919; *s* of John David Rees and Mary Ann (*née* Roderick); *m* 1951, Zena Muriel Stella Mayall; two *s*. *Educ:* Christ Coll., Brecon; Merton Coll., Oxford (Postmaster). 1st Cl., Class. Hons Mods and Hon. Mention, Craven and Ireland Schols, 1946. Welch Regt, 1940-45. Asst Classics Master, Christ Coll., Brecon, 1947; Cardiff High Sch., 1947-48; Asst Lectr in Classics, University Coll. of Wales Aberystwyth, 1948-49; Lectr 1949-56; Sen. Lectr in Greek, Univ. of Manchester, 1956-58; Prof. of Greek, University Coll. of South Wales and Monmouthshire, 1958-70. Governor: Manchester Grammar School, 1957-58; Christ College, Brecon, 1961-; Cardiff Training College, 1963-67; Member Council, Hellenic Society, 1958-61, 1965-68; Hon. Secretary, Classical Association, 1963-

69, Vice-Pres., 1969-; Dean of the Faculty of Arts, 1963-65; Dean of Students, 1967-68. FRSA 1968. *Publications:* The Merton Papyri, Vol. II (with H. I. Bell and J. W. B. Barns), 1959; The Use of Greek, 1961; Papyri from Hermopolis and other Byzantine Documents, 1964; (with M. E. Jervis) Lampas: a new approach to Greek, 1970; Classics: an outline for intending students, 1970; articles and reviews in various classical and other jls. *Address:* 1 Russell Road, Birmingham B13 8RA.

**REES, Hon. Sir (Charles William) Stanley,** Kt 1962; TD 1949; DL; **Hon. Mr Justice Rees;** Judge of High Court of Justice, Probate, Divorce and Admiralty Division, since 1962; Chairman, East Sussex Quarter Sessions, since 1964 (Deputy Chairman 1959-64); *b* 30 Nov. 1907; *s* of Dr David Charles Rees, MRCS, LRCP, and Myrtle May (*née* Dolley); *m* 1934, Jean Isabel Munro Wheildon; one *s*. *Educ:* St Andrew's College, Grahamstown, S Africa; University College, Oxford. BA, BCL (Oxon). Called to the Bar, 1931; Bencher, Inner Temple, 1962. 2nd Lt 99th Regt AA RA (London Welsh), 1939; JAG's office in Home Commands, 1940-43; Lt-Col in charge JAG's Branch, HQ Palestine Command, 1944-45; released from military service as Hon. Lt-Col, 1945. QC 1957; Recorder of Croydon, 1961-62; Commissioner of Assize, Stafford, Dec. 1961. DL County of Sussex, 1968. Member Governing Body, Brighton College. *Recreations:* fishing, walking, gardening. *Address:* Royal Courts of Justice, Strand, WC2; Lark Rise, Lyoth Lane, Lindfield, Sussex. *Club:* Oxford and Cambridge University.
*See also Harland Rees.*

**REES, Prof. David,** FRS 1968; Professor of Pure Mathematics, University of Exeter, since 1958; *b* 29 May 1918; *s* of David and Florence Gertrude Rees; *m* 1952, Joan Sybil Cushen; four *d*. *Educ:* King Henry VIII Grammar School, Abergavenny; Sidney Sussex College, Cambridge. Manchester University: Assistant Lecturer, 1945-46, Lecturer, 1946-49; Cambridge University: Lecturer, 1949-58; Fellow of Downing College, Cambridge, 1950-58, Hon. Fellow, 1970-. *Publications:* papers on Algebraic topics in British and foreign mathematical journals. *Recreations:* reading and listening to music. *Address:* 6 Hillcrest Park, Exeter EX4 4SH. *T:* Exeter 59398.

**REES, David Morgan,** CBE 1956; CEng; JP; *b* 29 March 1904; *s* of late Rees Rees, JP, Pencoed, Glam.; *m* 1935, Marjorie Griffith; one *s* one *d*. *Educ:* Llandovery Coll.; Birmingham University. Mining Engineer, qualified Birmingham University. Mining in Wales, 1930-36; Agent, BA Colliery, 1936-46. Area General Manager, East Midlands Division, 1947-52; Chairman South Western Division, National Coal Board, 1952-61. Mem., Council for Wales and Mon., 1953-56. Commander (Brother), Order of St John. JP Newcastle, Carmarthenshire, and Bridgend, Glam. *Address:* Four Winds, Danygraig, Porthcawl, Glam. *T:* Porthcawl 490. *Clubs:* Cardiff and County (Cardiff); Royal Porthcawl Golf (Porthcawl).

**REES, Mrs Dorothy Mary,** CBE 1964; Member, Central Training Council, 1964-67; *b* 1898; widow. *Educ:* Elementary and Secondary Schools. Formerly: school teacher; Member of Barry Borough Council. Alderman of Glamorgan CC; for. Mem. Nat. Advisory Committee for National Insurance; Member: Joint Education Committee for Wales (Chm., Technical Educn Sub-Cttee); Welsh Teaching Hospitals Board. Liaison Officer, Ministry of Food, during War of 1939-45. MP (Lab) Barry Division of Glamorganshire, 1950-51; formerly Parliamentary Private Secretary to the Minister of National Insurance. *Address:* 341 Barry Road, Barry, Glam.

**REES, Sir Frederick (Tavinor),** Kt, *cr* 1954; CBE 1950; MC 1917; TD 1938; *b* 24 Feb. 1890; *s* of late I. Rees, Maesteg, Glam. *Educ:* Queen's Coll., Taunton; Univ. of Wales (BSc 1912); St Bartholomew's Hospital, London. MRCS, LRCP, 1914; House Physician, St Bartholomew's Hosp., 1914; served European War, 1914-18, Major RAMC (MC immediate award); Territorial Army, Lieut-Col, 1921; Colonel, AMS (TA), 1932; ADMS 53rd (Welsh) Division, 1932-36; Hon. Colonel Medical Units, 53rd (Welsh) Division, 1938-45. Ministry of Pensions Medical Staff, 1919; Commissioner of Medical Services, Wales Region; Director of Medical Services HQ, 1941; Dep. Director-General, 1942-49; Director-General of Medical Services, Ministry of Pensions, 1949-53. CStJ 1927. *Recreations:* gardening, fishing. *Address:* 30 Gordon Road, Ealing, W5. *T:* 01-997 2435.

**REES, Professor Garnet;** Professor of French, University of Hull, since 1957; *b* 15 March 1912; *o s* of William Garnet and Mabel Rees; *m* 1941, Dilys, *o d* of Robert and Ellen Hughes; two *d*. *Educ:* Pontardawe Grammar School; University College of Wales, Aberystwyth; University of Paris. BA (Wales), 1934; MA (Wales), 1937; Docteur de l'Université de Paris, 1940; Fellow of Univ. of Wales, 1937-39; Asst Lecturer in French, Univ. Coll., Aberystwyth, 1939-40. Served War of 1939-45, in Roy. Regt of Artillery (Captain, Instructor in Gunnery), 1940-45. Lecturer in French, Univ. of Southampton, 1945-46; Sen. Lecturer in French, Univ. Coll., Swansea, 1946-57. Officier des Palmes Académiques (France), 1961. Chevalier de la Légion d'Honneur, 1967. *Publications:* Remy de Gourmont, 1940; articles on modern French literature and bibliography in learned journals. *Recreations:* gardening and motoring. *Address:* The University of Hull; 88 Newland Park, Hull. *T:* 407810.

**REES, Geraint;** *see* Rees, R. G.

**REES, Goronwy;** *see* Rees, Morgan Goronwy.

**REES, Harland,** MA, MCh, FRCS; Urological Surgeon, King's College Hospital; Surgeon and Urological Surgeon, Hampstead General Hospital; *b* 21 Sept. 1909; *yr s* of Dr David Charles Rees, MRCS, LRCP, and Myrtle May (*née* Dolley); *m* 1950, Helen Marie Tarver; two *s* one *d*. *Educ:* St Andrew's Coll., Grahamstown, S Africa; University Coll., Oxford; Charing Cross Hospital. Rhodes Scholar, Oxford University. Served RAMC, 1942-46; OC Surgical Div. 53, Indian General Hospital. Adviser in Surgery, Siam (Thailand). Examiner in Surgery, University of Cambridge, 1963-. *Publications:* articles and chapters in various books and journals, 1952-63. *Recreations:* walking, cultivation of trees; Rugby football, Oxford *v* Cambridge, 1932-33. *Address:* 149 Harley Street, W1. *T:* 01-935 4444; Kensworth Gorse, Kensworth, near Dunstable, Beds. *T:* Whipsnade 411. *Club:* Vincent's (Oxford).
*See also Hon. Sir C. W. S. Rees.*

**REES, Hugh;** *see* Rees, J. E. H.

**REES, Sir Hugh Ellis;** *see* Ellis-Rees.

**REES, (John Edward) Hugh;** Chartered Surveyor, Chartered Auctioneer and Estate Agent; *b* 8 Jan. 1928; *s* of David Emlyn Rees,

The Mirador, Swansea; *m* 1961, Jill Dian Milo-Jones; two *s*. *Educ:* Parc Wern School, Glanmor School, Swansea; Bromsgrove School. Served in Army (commissioned RA), 1946-48. MP (C) Swansea, West Division, Oct. 1959-64; PPS to Parliamentary Sec. for Housing and Local Govt and to Minister of State, Board of Trade, 1961; Assistant Government Whip, 1962-64. FRICS, FAI. *Address:* Sherwood, 35 Caswell Road, Newton, Swansea, Glamorgan.

**REES, Llewellyn;** *see* Rees, (Walter) L.

**REES, Merlyn;** MP (Lab) South Leeds since June 1963; *b* Cilfynydd, South Wales, 18 Dec. 1920; *s* of late L. D. and E. M. Rees; *m* 1949, Colleen Faith (*née* Cleveley); three *s*. *Educ:* Elementary Schools, S Wales and Wembley, Middx; Harrow Weald Grammar School; Goldsmiths' Coll., Univ. of London; London School of Economics; London Univ. Institute of Education. Nottingham Univ. Air Sqdn; Served RAF, 1941-46; demobilised as Sqdn Ldr. Teacher in Economics and History, Harrow Weald Grammar School, 1949-60. Organised Festival of Labour, 1960-62. Lecturer in Economics, Luton Coll. of Technology, 1962-63; PPS to Chancellor of the Exchequer, 1964; Parly Under-Sec. of State, MoD (Army), 1965-66; MoD (RAF), 1966-68; Home Office, 1968-70. Contested (Lab) Harrow East, Gen. Elections 1955 and 1959 and By-Election, 1959. *Recreation:* reading. *Address:* 50 Cedar Drive, Hatch End, Pinner, Middx.

**REES, (Morgan) Goronwy;** *b* 29 Nov. 1909; *yr s* of Rev. Richard Jenkyn Rees and Apphia Mary James; *m* 1940, Margaret Ewing Morris; three *s* two *d*. *Educ:* High School for Boys, Cardiff; New Coll., Oxford. Fellow of All Souls, 1931; Leader Writer, The Manchester Guardian, 1932; Asst Editor, The Spectator, 1936. War of 1939-45: Gunner, 90 Field Regt RA, 1939; commissioned Royal Welch Fusiliers, 1940. Director of a firm of general engineers and coppersmiths, 1946. Estates Bursar, All Souls College, Oxford, 1951. Principal, University College of Wales, Aberystwyth, 1953-57. *Publications:* The Multi-Millionaires: Six Studies in Wealth, 1961; The Rhine; St Michael: a history of Marks & Spencer, 1969; *novels:* A Summer Flood, 1932; A Bridge to Divide Them, 1937; Where No Wounds Were; *translations:* (with Stephen Spender) Danton's Death, by Georg Büchner, 1939; Conversations with Kafka, 1939; *reminiscences:* A Bundle of Sensations, 1960; The Great Slump, 1970. *Address:* 41 Royal Crescent, W11. *T:* 01-603 5114.

**REES, Peter Wynford Innes,** QC 1969; MP (C) Dover since 1970; *b* 9 Dec. 1926; *s* of late Maj.-Gen. T. W. Rees (Indian Army), Goytre Hall, Abergavenny; *m* 1969, Mrs Anthea Wendell, *d* of Major H. J. M. Hyslop, late Argyle and Sutherland Highlanders. *Educ:* Stowe; Christ Church, Oxford. Served Scots Guards, 1945-48. Called to the Bar, 1953; Oxford Circuit. Contested (C): Abertillery, 1964 and 1965; Liverpool, West Derby, 1966. *Address:* 39 Headfort Place, SW1; Goytre Hall, Abergavenny, Monmouthshire; 5 Church Street, St Clement's, Sandwich, Kent. *Club:* Guards.

**REES, Richard Geraint;** Metropolitan Police Magistrate since Dec. 1956; *b* 5 May 1907; *s* of Rev. Richard Jenkyn Rees, MA, and Apphia Mary Rees, Aberystwyth; *m* 1st, 1938, Mary Davies; one *s*; 2nd, 1950, Margaret Grotrian; one *d*. *Educ:* Cardiff High School; University College of Wales, Aberystwyth; St John's College, Cambridge. LLB 1st Cl. Hons, Univ. Coll. of Wales, 1929, BA 1st Cl. Parts I and II Law Tripos, 1930 and 1931; Barrister, Inner Temple, 1932 (Certificate of Honour). Practised on S Wales Circuit, 1934-39. Commissioned Welsh Guards, Nov. 1939; DAAG London Dist, 1943-44; Assistant Director Army Welfare Services, Lt-Col, British Army Staff, Paris, 1944-45. Practised in London and on Wales and Chester Circuit, 1946-56. Despatches, Bronze Star (USA) 1946. *Recreation:* gardening. *Address:* 10 Crossway, Walton-on-Thames, Surrey. *T:* Walton-on-Thames 21913. *Club:* Reform.

**REES, Hon. Sir Stanley;** *see* Rees, Hon. Sir C. W. S.

**REES, Thomas Ifor,** CMG 1942; Hon. LLD, BA (University of Wales); *b* 16 Feb. 1890; *s* of John Thomas Rees and Elizabeth Davies; *m* 1918, Betty Phillips; one *s* two *d*. *Educ:* Aberystwyth (County School and University College). Graduated, 1910; passed competitive examination and appointed Vice-Consul in the Consular Service, 1913; appointed to Marseilles same year; Acting Consul-General there, 1914; transferred to Caracas, 1914; acting as Chargé d'Affaires, 1916; Consul at Managua, Nicaragua, 1921; given rank of Chargé d'Affaires *ad interim*, 1922; transferred to Bilbao, Spain, 1925; transferred to Mexico City in 1932, with local rank of Consul-General; transferred with same rank to Havana, 1934; Chargé d'Affaires at Havana, 1934. 1935, and 1936; HM Special Envoy for inauguration of President Gomez, 1936; HM Consul-General, Milan, 1937-38; Mexico City, 1938-43; Special Ambassador for inauguration of President Hertzog, 1947; British Minister to Bolivia, 1944-47, Ambassador, 1947-49. Hon. LLD (Wales), 1950; retired, 1950. *Publications:* In and Around the Valley of Mexico, 1953; Sajama, 1960; Illimani, 1964. *Recreations:* photography and gardening. *Address:* Bronceiro, Bowstreet, Cardiganshire. *T:* 229.

**REES, (Walter) Llewellyn,** MA; Actor and Theatre Administrator; Honorary President of International Theatre Institute since 1951; *b* 18 June 1901; *s* of Walter Francis Rees and Mary Gwendoline Naden; *m* 1961, Madeleine Newbury; one *s* one *d*. *Educ:* King Edward's School, Birmingham; Keble College, Oxford. Private Tutor, 1923-26; studied at RADA, 1926-28; Actor, 1928-40; Gen. Sec. of British Actors' Equity Assoc., 1940-46; Jt Secretary: London Theatre Council, 1940-46, Prov. Theatre Council, 1942-46; Sec. of Fed. of Theatre Unions, 1944-46; Governor of the Old Vic, 1945-47; Drama Director, Arts Council of Great Britain, 1947-49; Administrator of the Old Vic, 1949-51; Administrator of Arts Theatre, 1951-52; General Administrator, Donald Wolfit's Company, 1952-58; Chairman Executive Committee of International Theatre Institute, 1948-51; returned to West End Stage, 1956, as Bishop of Buenos Aires in The Strong are Lonely, Theatre Royal, Haymarket; Olmeda in The Master of Santiago, Lyric Theatre, Hammersmith, 1957; Polonius in Hamlet, Bristol Old Vic, 1958; Dean of College in My Friend Judas, Arts Theatre, 1959; Mr Brandy in Settled out of Court, Strand Theatre, 1960-61; Justice Worthy in Lock Up Your Daughters, Mermaid Theatre and Her Majesty's, 1962-63; Sir Henry James in the Right Honourable Gentleman, Her Majesty's, 1964-65. Many film and television appearances. *Recreation:* travel. *Address:* 7 The Hermitage, SW13.

**REES, Professor William;** Emeritus Professor of the History of Wales and Head of Department of History at University College, Cardiff; *b* 14

Dec. 1887; *s* of Daniel and Margaret Rees; *m* 1914, Agnes Price; no *c*. *Educ:* Brecon County School; Univ. Coll., Cardiff; LSE, University of London. BA Hons (Wales), 1909; MA (Wales), 1914; DScEcon (London), 1920; Hon. DLitt (Wales), 1969; FSA; FRHistS; formerly Vice-Pres. and Mem. of Council; formerly Fellow of Univ. of Wales and Prof. of the History of Wales and Head of the Department of History, University College, Cardiff; O'Donnell Lecturer in Celtic Studies, Univ. of Wales, 1957 and Univ. of Oxford, 1959-60; President: Cambrian Archæological Assoc., 1960-61; Cardiff Naturalists' Soc., 1949-50; Member: Board of Celtic Studies, University of Wales; former Mem. Ancient Monuments Board for Wales; Member of Court and Council: National Museum of Wales; Welsh Folk Museum; Mem. Court, Nat. Library of Wales; Editor S Wales and Monmouth Record Soc.; Mem. various Editorial Boards; former Mem. Exec., Standing Conference of Local History. Chairman Exec., Welsh National Council of UNA, 1945-56. Mem., UNESCO Nat. Co-operating Body for the Social Sciences, 1952-62. KStJ 1963. *Publications:* South Wales and the March, a Social and Agrarian Study, 1924, rept. 1967; The Making of Europe; Historical Map of South Wales and the Border in the Fourteenth Century, 1933; An Historical Atlas of Wales; Caerphilly Castle; The Union of England and Wales; The Order of St John of Jerusalem; The Charters of Newport (Mon), The Duchy of Lancaster Lordships in Wales, 1954; A Breviat of Glamorgan, 1954; Cardiff. A History of the City, 1962, repr. 1969; Survivals of Ancient Celtic Custom in Mediæval England, in, Angles and Britons, 1963; The Black Death in Wales, in, Essays in Mediæval History, 1968; Industry before the Industrial Revolution, 2 vols 1968. Contributor to Dictionary of National Biography, Encyclopædia Britannica, Encyclopedia Americana, and Chambers's Encyclopædia; numerous papers, cartographical and bibliographical studies. List of published works in Mediæval Lordship of Brecon, Brecknock Museum, Brecon, 1968. *Address:* 2 Park Road, Penarth, Glam. *T:* Penarth 701465.

**REES, William Linford Llewelyn,** FRCP; Professor of Psychiatry, St Bartholomew's Hospital Medical College, University of London, since 1966; Physician in charge of Department of Psychological Medicine, St Bartholomew's Hospital, since 1959; Lecturer in Psychological Medicine, St Bartholomew's Medical College, since 1958; Recognised Clinical Teacher in Mental Diseases, Institute of Psychiatry, University of London, since 1956; *b* 24 Oct. 1914; *e s* of late Edward Parry Rees and Mary Rees, Llanelly, Carmathenshire; *m* 1940, Catherine, *y d* of late David Thomas, and of Angharad Thomas, Alltwen, Glam; two *s* two *d*. *Educ:* Llanelly Grammar School; University Coll., Cardiff; Welsh Nat. Sch. of Medicine; The Maudsley Hosp.; Univ. of London. BSc 1935; MB, BCh 1938; DPM 1940; MRCP 1942; MD 1943; FRCP 1950. David Hepburn Medal and Alfred Hughes Medal in Anatomy, 1935; John Maclean Medal and Prize in Obstetrics and Gynaecology, 1937, etc. Specialist, EMS, 1942; Dep. Med. Supt, Mill Hill Emergency Hosp., 1945; Asst Physician and Postgrad. Teacher in Clinical Psychology, The Maudsley Hosp., 1946; Dep. Physician Supt, Whitchurch Hosp., 1947; Regional Psychiatrist for Wales and Mon, 1948; Consultant Physician, The Bethlem Royal Hosp. and The Maudsley Hosp., 1954-66. Hon. Consultant, Royal Sch. for Deaf Children. Lectures to Univs and Learned Socs in Europe, USA, Asia, Australia and S America. Examiner: Diploma Psychological Medicine, RCP, 1964-69; MRCP, RCP, RCPE and RCPGlas, 1969-; MB and DPM, Univ. of Leeds, 1969-. Pres., Soc. for Psychosomatic Research, 1957-58. Vice-Pres., Section of Psychiatry, RSM, 1968. Treasurer, World Psychiatric Assoc., 1966-. Member: Clinical Psychiatry Cttee, MRC, 1959-; Council, Royal Medio-Psychological Assoc. (Chm., Research and Clinical Section, 1957-63); Soc. for Study of Human Biology; Asthma Research Council; Clinical Trials Cttee, Dunlop Cttee on Safety of Drugs; Psycholoigcal Medicine Group, BMA, 1967-; Bd of Advanced Med. Studies, Univ. of London, 1966-69; Higher Degrees Cttee, Univ. of London. Founder Mem., Internat. Coll. of Neuro-psychopharmacology. Hon. Member Learned Socs in USA, Sweden, Venezuela, East Germany and Australia. FRSM; Fellow, Eugenics Soc.; Distinguished Fellow, Amer. Psychiatric Assoc., 1968. Governor, The Behtlem Royal Hosp. and The Maudsley Hosp. Co-Editor, Jl of Psychosomatic Research. *Publications:* (with Eysenck and Himmelweit) Dimensions of Personality, 1947; Short Textbook of Psychiatry, 1967. Chapters in: Modern Treatment in General Practice, 1947; Recent Progress in Psychiatry, 1950; Schizophrenia: Somatic Aspects, 1957; Psychoendocrinology, 1958; Recent Progress in Psychosomatic Research, 1960; Stress and Psychiatric Disorders, 1960. Papers in: Nature, BMJ, Jl of Mental Sci., Jl of Psychosomatic Research, Eugenics Review, etc. Contribs to Med. Annual, 1958-68. *Recreations:* swimming, tennis, photography, fishing. *Address:* Penbryn, 62 Oakwood Avenue, Purley, Surrey. *T:* 01-660 8575. *Club:* Athenæum.

**REES-DAVIES, William Rupert;** MP (C) Isle of Thanet since March 1953; Barrister-at-law; *b* 19 Nov. 1916; *o s* of late Sir William Rees-Davies, KC, DL, JP, formerly Chief Justice of Hong Kong and Liberal MP for Pembroke and of late Lady Rees-Davies; *m* 1959, Jane, *d* of Mr and Mrs Henry Mander; two *d*. *Educ:* Eton; Trinity Coll., Cambridge; Eton Soc., Eton XI, 1934-35; Eton Victor Ludorum; Cambridge Cricket XI, 1938; Honours in History and Law. Called to Bar, Inner Temple, 1939. Commissioned HM Welsh Guards, 1939; served War of 1939-45 (discharged disabled with loss of arm, 1943). Contested (C) South Nottingham in 1950 and 1951. Chairman, All Party Cttee on Tourism, House of Commons, 1966-69. *Recreations:* collecting pictures and antiques. *Address:* 6 Victoria Square, SW1. *T:* 01-828 3357. *Clubs:* MCC; Hawks, University Pitt (Cambridge).

**REES-JONES, Geoffrey Rippon,** MA Oxon; Principal, King William's College, Isle of Man, since 1958; *b* 8 July 1914; *er s* of W. Rees-Jones, BA, Ipswich; *m* 1950, Unity Margaret McConnell, *d* of Major P. M. Sanders, Hampstead; one *s* one *d*. *Educ:* Ipswich School (scholar); University College, Oxford (open scholar). Assistant Master, Eastbourne College, 1936-38, Marlborough College, 1938-54 (Housemaster, C2, 1946-54); Headmaster, Bembridge School, 1954-58; served War mainly in Commandos, 1940-45; Commandant, Commando Mountain Warfare School, 1943; Staff College, Camberley, 1944 (sc); Brigade Major, 4 Commando Bde, 1944-45 (despatches). *Recreations:* sailing, cricket, golf, fives; Oxford Rugby 'blue', 1933-35, Wales XV, 1934-36. *Address:* King William's College, Isle of Man. *T:* Castletown 2551.

**REES-MOGG, William;** Editor of The Times since 1967; Director of The Times Ltd, since 1968; Member, Executive Board, Times Newspapers Ltd, since 1968; *b* 14 July 1928; *s* of late Edmund Fletcher Rees-Mogg and Beatrice Rees-Mogg (*née* Warren), Temple Cloud, Somerset; *m* 1962, Gillian Shakespeare Morris, *d* of T. R. Morris; two *s* two *d*. *Educ:* Charterhouse; Balliol Coll., Oxford (Brackenbury Scholar). President, Oxford Union, 1951. Financial Times, 1952-60, Chief Leader Writer, 1955-60; Asst Editor, 1957-60; Sunday Times, City Editor, 1960-61; Political and Economic Editor, 1961-63; Deputy Editor, 1964-67. Contested (C) Chester-le-Street, Co. Durham, By-election 1956; General Election, 1959. Treasurer, Institute of Journalists, 1960-63, 1966-68, Pres., 1963-64; Vice-Chm. Cons. Party's Nat. Advisory Cttee on Political Education, 1961-63. Vis. Fellow, Nuffield Coll., Oxford, 1968-. *Recreation:* book collecting. *Address:* 3 Smith Square, SW1. *T:* 01-222 1030, 01-930 8232; Ston Easton Park, near Bath. *Clubs:* Carlton, Garrick.

**REES-THOMAS, Mrs William;** *see* Darwin, Ruth.

**REES-THOMAS, William,** CB 1950; MD (London); FRCP (England); DPM (Cantab); Medical Senior Commissioner Board of Control, 1932, retired; *b* Bailea, Senny, Breconshire, S Wales, 15 June 1887; *m* 1st, 1917, Muriel (*decd*), *o d* of Rev. F. Hodgson Jones; one *s* one *d*; 2nd, 1948, Ruth Darwin, *qv*. *Educ:* County School, Brecon; Cardiff University; Charing Cross Hospital. MB, BS (hons) London, 1909; MD (London), 1910; MRCP 1913; FRCP, 1933; DPM (Cantab), 1914; Alfred Sheen Prize, 1906; Alfred Hughes Memorial Medal, 1907; Llewelyn Prize, 1909; Murchison Scholar (RCP), 1912; Gaskell Prize and Gold Medal, 1913; Certificate Psychiatry Royal Medico Psychological Association; Distinguished Psychiatry RCP; Fellow Royal Society of Medicine; Member BMA and Royal Medico-Psychological Association; late House Physician Charing Cross hospital; Deputy Superintendent East Sussex Mental Hospital; Medical Superintendent Rampton State Institution; KHP, 1944-47. *Publications:* various. *Recreations:* golf, photography. *Address:* High Hackhurst, Abinger Hammer, Dorking, Surrey.

**REES-WILLIAMS,** family name of **Baron Ogmore.**

**REESE, Surg. Rear-Adm. John Mansel,** CB 1962; OBE 1953; *b* 3 July 1906; *s* of late Dr D. W. Reese, and late Mrs A. M. Reese; *m* 1946, Beryl (*née* Dunn); two *d* (and one *s* decd). *Educ:* Epsom Coll.; St Mary's Hosp. Med. Sch., London University. MRCS, LRCP 1930; DPH 1934. Entered Royal Navy, Jan. 1931; Naval Medical Officer of Health, Orkney and Shetland Comd, 1942-44; Naval MOH, Ceylon, 1944-46; Admiralty, 1947-53; Medical Officer-in-Charge RN Hospital, Plymouth, 1960-63; QHP 1960-63. Surgeon Comdr, 1943; Surgeon Captain, 1954; Surgeon Rear-Adm., 1960; retd 1963. FRSTM&H. Sir Gilbert Blane Gold Medal, 1939. Member Gray's Inn, 1953. CStJ 1961. *Address:* Wentworth, Links Road, Budleigh Salterton, S Devon.

**REESE, (John) Terence;** bridge expert, author and journalist; *b* 28 Aug. 1913; *s* of John and Anne Reese; *m* 1970, Alwyn Sherrington. *Educ:* Bilton Grange; Bradfield Coll. (top scholar); New Coll., Oxford (top class. scholar). Worked at Harrods, 1935-36; left to follow career as bridge expert and journalist. Edited various bridge magazines, became bridge correspondent of the Evening News, 1948 and of the Observer, 1950. Winner of numerous British, European and World Championships. *Publications:* The Elements of Contract, 1938; Reese on Play, 1948; The Expert Game, 1958; Play Bridge with Reese, 1960; Story of an Accusation, 1966; *with Albert Dormer:* The Acol System Today, 1961; The Play of the Cards, 1967; Bridge for Tournament Players, 1969; and many others. *Recreations:* golf, greyhound racing. *Address:* 18a Woods Mews, Park Lane, W1. *T:* 01-629 5553. *Clubs:* Curzon House, Crockford's; Sunningdale Golf, Berkshire Golf, Aldeburgh Golf.

**REEVE, Rt. Rev. Arthur Stretton;** *see* Lichfield, Bishop of.

**REEVE, (Charles) Trevor; His Honour Judge Reeve;** County Court Judge, since 1968; *b* 4 July 1915; *o s* of William George Reeve and Elsie (*née* Bowring), Wokingham; *m* 1941, Marjorie, *d* of Charles Evelyn Browne, Eccles, Lancs. *Educ:* Winchester College; Trinity College, Oxford. Commissioned 10th Royal Hussars (PWO) 1940; served BEF, CMF (Major) 1940-44; Staff College, Camberley, 1945. Called to Bar (Inner Temple), 1946; Bencher, 1965; QC 1965. *Recreations:* golf, dancing. *Address:* 95 Abingdon Road, Kensington, W8. *T:* 01-937 7530. *Clubs:* Garrick; Royal North Devon Golf (Westward Ho!); Sunningdale Golf.

**REEVE, Major-General John Talbot Wentworth,** CB 1946; CBE 1941; DSO 1919; *b* 1891; *e s* of Charles Sydney Wentworth Reeve; *m* 1st, 1919, Sybil Alice (*d* 1949), 4th *d* of Sir George Agnew, 2nd Bt; one *d* (one *s* killed in North Africa, June 1942); 2nd, 1950, Mrs Marjorie Frances Wagstaff (*see* Mrs M. F. Reeve). *Educ:* Eton; Royal Military College, Sandhurst. Served European War, 1914-19 (despatches, DSO); commanded 1st Bn The Rifle Brigade, 1936-38; Commander Hong Kong Infantry Brigade, 1938-41; DAG Home Forces, 1942-43; Commander Sussex District, 1943-44; DAG, MEF, 1944-46; retd pay, 1946. *Address:* Livermere Lodge, near Bury St Edmunds, Suffolk. *T:* Honington 376. *Club:* Army and Navy.

**REEVE, Mrs Marjorie Frances Wentworth,** CBE 1944; TD 1950; JP; *d* of late Charles Fry, Bedford; *m* 1st, Lieutenant-Commander J. K. Laughton, Royal Navy (*d* 1925); one *s*; 2nd, Major-General C. M. Wagstaff, CB, CMG, CIE, DSO (*d* 1934); 3rd, 1950, Major-General J. T. Wentworth Reeve, *qv*. Joined ATS, 1938; served with BEF, and in Middle East and BAOR; late Controller ATS. Was i/c Public Welfare Section of Control Commission for Germany (BE); Principal in Board of Trade (Overseas) till 1950; Swedish Red Cross Medal in Silver, 1950; County Director, BRCS, 1953-57; Dep. Pres. Suffolk BRCS, 1957. JP (W Suffolk), 1954. *Address:* Livermere Lodge, near Bury St Edmunds, Suffolk. *T:* Honington 376. *Club:* Army and Navy.

**REEVE, Trevor;** *see* Reeve, C. T.

**REEVES, Rt. Rev. Ambrose;** *see* Reeves, Rt Rev. R. A.

**REEVES, James,** MA; free-lance author, editor and broadcaster since 1952; *b* 1 July 1909; *er s* of Albert John and Ethel Mary Reeves; *m* 1936, Mary (*née* Phillips) (*d* 1966); one *s* two *d*. *Educ:* Stowe; Cambridge. Schoolmaster and lectr in teachers' training colleges, 1933-52. *Publications:* The Wandering Moon, 1950; The Blackbird in the Lilac, 1952; English Fables and Fairy Stories, 1954; Pigeons and Princesses; The Critical Sense, 1956; Prefabulous Animiles, 1957; Mulbridge Manor; Teaching Poetry; The Idiom of the People, 1958; Exploits of Don Quixote, 1959;

The Everlasting Circle; Collected Poems, 1960; A Short History of English Poetry, 1961; Ragged Robin, 1961; Fables from Æsop, 1961; (ed) A Golden Land, 1958; (ed) Great English Essays, 1961; (ed) Penguin Book of Georgian Poetry, 1962; Sailor Rumbelow and Britannia, 1962; The Strange Light, 1964; Three Tall Tales, 1964; The Questioning Tiger (poems), 1964; The Pillar-Box Thieves; Understanding Poetry; ed, Cassell Book of English Poetry, 1965; The Road to a Kingdom, 1965; The Secret Shoemakers, 1966; Selected Poems, 1967; The Cold Flame, 1967; (ed jtly) A New Canon of English Poetry, 1967; Rhyming Will, 1967; (ed jtly) Homage to Trumbull Stickney, 1968; The Trojan Horse, 1968; (ed) The Christmas Book, 1968; (ed) One's None, 1968; Subsong; Poems, 1969; Commitment to Poetry, 1969; Heroes and Monsters, 1969; The Angel and the Donkey, 1969; Mr Horrox and the Gratch, 1969; (ed) The Poets and Their Critics, Vol. III, 1969; (ed jtly) Selected Poems of Andrew Marvell, 1969; (jtly) Inside Poetry, 1970; (ed) Chaucer: lyric and allegory, 1970; Maeldun the Voyager, 1971; How to Write Poems for Children, 1971. *Recreation:* music. *Address:* Flints, Rotten Row, Lewes, Sussex. *T:* Lewes 2579.

**REEVES, Marjorie Ethel,** MA (Oxon), PhD (London); FRHistS; Vice-Principal, St Anne's College, Oxford, 1951-62, 1964-67; *b* 17 July 1905; *d* of Robert J. W. Reeves and Edith Saffery Whitaker. *Educ:* The High School for Girls, Trowbridge, Wilts. St Hugh's Coll., Oxford; Westfield Coll., London. Asst Mistress, Roan School, Greenwich, 1927-29; Research Fellow, Westfield Coll., London, 1929-31; Lecturer, St Gabriel's Trng Coll., London, 1931-38; Tutor, later Fellow of St Anne's College, 1938-. Member: Central Advisory Council, Min. of Educn, 1947-61; Academic Planning Bd, Univ. of Kent; Academic Advisory Cttee, University of Surrey; Educn Council, ITA; British Council of Churches. Formerly Member: School Broadcasting Council. *Publications:* Growing Up in a Modern Society, 1946; (ed, with L. Tondelli, B. Hirsch-Reich) Il Libro delle Figure dell'Abate Gioachino da Fiore, 1953; Three Questions in Higher Education (Hazen Foundation, USA), 1955; Moral Education in a Changing Society (ed W. Niblett), 1963; ed, Eighteen Plus: Unity and Diversity in Higher Education, 1965; The Influence of Prophecy in the later Middle Ages: a study in Joachimism, 1969; Higher Education: demand and response (ed W. R. Niblett), 1969; Then and There Series: The Medieval Town, 1954, The Medieval Village, 1954, Elizabethan Court, 1956, The Medieval Monastery, 1957, The Norman Conquest, 1958, Alfred and the Danes, 1959; The Medieval Castle, 1960, Elizabethan Citizen, 1961; contributions on history in Speculum, Medieval and Renaissance Studies, Sophia, Recherches de Théologie, etc, and on education in Times Educational Supplement, New Era, etc. *Recreations:* music, gardening, bird-watching. *Address:* St Anne's College, Oxford. *T:* Oxford 57417. *Club:* University Women's.

**REEVES, Rt. Rev. (Richard) Ambrose;** Rector of St Michael's, Lewes, since 1968 (Priest in Charge, 1966-68); Assistant Bishop in the Diocese of Chichester, since 1966; *b* 6 Dec. 1899; *m* 1931, Ada Margaret van Ryssen; one *s* two *d* (and one *s* decd). *Educ:* Sidney Sussex Coll., Cambridge. 2nd class Historical Tripos, Part I, 1923, BA (2nd class Moral Science Tripos, Part II), 1924, MA 1943. College of the Resurrection, Mirfield, 1924; Gen. Th. Seminary, New York, 1926. Deacon, 1926; Priest, 1927; Curate of St Albans, Golders Green, 1926-31; Rector of St Margaret, Leven, 1931-35; licensed to officiate in the Diocese of Gibraltar and permission to officiate in the Diocese of London (N and C Eur.), 1935-37; Vicar of St James Haydock, 1937-42; Rector of St Nicholas City and Dio. Liverpool, 1942-49; Canon of Liverpool Cathedral, 1944-49; Proctor in Convocation, Liverpool, 1945-49; Bishop of Johannesburg, 1949-61; Assistant Bishop of London, 1962-66. General Secretary, Student Christian Movement of Great Britain and Ireland, 1962-65; Secretary, World Student Christian Federation, Geneva, 1935-37. Sub-Prelate Ven. Order of St John of Jerusalem, 1953; STD, Theological Seminary, NY, 1954. Pres., Anti-Apartheid Movement, 1970-. Fellow, Ancient Monuments Soc., 1957; Hon. Fellow, Sidney Sussex Coll., Cambridge, 1960. *Publications:* Shooting at Sharpeville: the Agony of South Africa, 1960; South Africa–Yesterday and Tomorrow, 1962; Let the facts speak (Christian Action), 1962; Calvary Now, 1965. *Address:* St Michael's Rectory, Lewes, Sussex. *T:* Lewes 4723.

**REFSHAUGE, Maj.-Gen. Sir William (Dudley),** Kt 1966; CBE 1959 (OBE 1944); ED 1965; Commonwealth Director-General of Health, Australia, since 1960; *b* 3 April 1913; *s* of late F. C. Refshauge, Melbourne; *m* 1942, Helen Elizabeth, *d* of late R. E. Allwright, Tasmania; four *s* one *d*. *Educ:* Hampton High Sch.; Scotch Coll., Melbourne; Melbourne University. MB, BS (Melbourne) 1938; FRCOG 1961; FRACS 1962; FRACP 1963; Hon. FRSH 1967; Fellow Australian College of Medical Administrators, 1967. Served with AIF, 1939-46; Lt-Col, RAAMC (despatches four times). Medical Supt, Royal Women's Hosp., Melbourne, 1948-51; Col, and Dep. DGAMS, Aust., 1951-55; Maj.-Gen., and DGAMS, Aust., 1955-60; QHP, 1955-64. Chairman: Council, Aust. Coll. of Nursing, 1958-60 (Chm. Educn Cttee, 1951-58); Nat. Health and MRC, 1960-; Nat. Fitness Council, 1960-; Nat. Tuberculosis Adv. Council, 1960-; Prog. and Budget Cttee, 15th World Health Assembly, 1962; Admin., Fin. and Legal Cttee 19th World Health Assembly; Exec. Bd, WHO, 1969-70. Member: Council, Aust. Red Cross Soc., 1954-60; Mem. Nat. Blood Transfusion Cttee, ARCS 1955-60; Nat. Trustee, Returned Services League Aust., 1961-; Mem. Bd of Management, Canberra Grammar Sch., 1963-68. *Publications:* contribs to Australian Med. Jl, NZ Med. Jl, etc. *Recreations:* bowls, gardening. *Address:* Dept of Health, Canberra, ACT 2605, Australia. *Clubs:* Melbourne, Naval and Military, Cricket (Melbourne); University (Sydney); Commonwealth (Canberra); Bowling (Canberra).

**REGINA, Archbishop of, (RC),** since 1948; **Most Rev. Michael C. O'Neill,** OBE 1944; MM 1918; *b* 15 Feb. 1898; Irish Canadian. *Educ:* St Michael's College, University of Toronto; St Augustine's Seminary, Toronto. Overseas Service, Signaller, CFA, European War, 1916-19. St Joseph's Seminary, Edmonton; Professor, 1928-39; Rector, 1930-39. Overseas Service, Canadian Chaplain Services, War of 1939-45; Principal Chaplain (Army) Overseas, (RC), 1941-45; Principal Chaplain (Army), (RC), 1945-46. Hon. LLD, Toronto, 1952. *Address:* 3225 13th Avenue, Regina, Sask, Canada. *T:* 525-9877. *Club:* East India and Sports.

**REICHENBACH, Henry-Béat de F.;** *see* de Fischer-Reichenbach.

**REICHSTEIN, Prof. Tadeus,** Dr ing chem; Ordentlicher Professor, Head of Department of Organic Chemistry, University of Basel, 1946-60; *b* Wloclawek, Poland, 20 July 1897; *s* of Isidor Reichstein and Gustava Brockmann; *m* 1927, Henriette Louise Quarles van Ufford; one *d.* *Educ:* Oberrealschule and Eidgenössische Technische Hochschule, Department of Chemistry, Zürich. Assistant, ETH, Zürich, 1922-34; professor of organic chemistry, ETH, Zürich, 1934; head of department of pharmacy, University of Basel, 1938. Dr *hc* Sorbonne, Paris, 1947, Basel 1951, Genf 1967, ETH, Zürich, 1967, Abidjan 1967, London 1968, Leeds 1970; Marcel Benoit Prize, 1948; (jointly) Nobel Prize for Medicine, 1950; Cameron Prize, 1951; Foreign Member Royal Society, 1952; Copley Medal, Royal Soc., 1968. *Publications:* numerous papers. *Recreations:* swimmer, skier, devoted gardener, mountain-climber. *Address:* Institut für Organische Chemie der Universität, St Johanns-Ring 19, CH 4000, Basel, Switzerland. *T:* (061) 44 90 90.

**REID,** Baron (Life Peer), *cr* 1948, of Drem; **James Scott Cumberland Reid,** PC 1941; CH 1967; QC 1932; LLD Edinburgh; FRSE; a Lord of Appeal in Ordinary since 1948; *b* 1890; *s* of late James Reid, WS, Drem, East Lothian; *m* 1933, Esther May, *d* of late C. B. Nelson and *widow* of G. F. Brierley. *Educ:* Edinburgh Acad.; Jesus Coll., Cambridge. Admitted to Scots Bar, 1914; served European War, 1914-19, 8th Royal Scots and Machine Gun Corps; in practice in Advocate since 1919; MP (U) Stirling and Falkirk Burghs, 1931-35; Hillhead division of Glasgow, 1937-48; Solicitor-General for Scotland, 1936-41; Lord Advocate, 1941-45; Dean of Faculty of Advocates, 1945-48. Chairman, Malaya Constitutional Commission, 1956-57. Hon. Fellow Jesus College, Cambridge. Hon. Bencher, Gray's Inn. *Address:* Danefold, West Grinstead, Horsham, Sussex; 4 South Square, Gray's Inn, WC1. *Club:* Athenæum.

**REID, Capt. Alec S. C.;** *see* Cunningham-Reid.

**REID, Colonel A(ndrew) McKie,** MC 1916; TD 1942; FRCS; Hon. Ophthalmic Surgeon United Liverpool Hospitals; late Lecturer in Ophthalmology, University of Liverpool; Lecturer, School of Tropical Medicine, Liverpool; *b* 14 April 1893; *s* of late James Reid and late Janet McKie; *m* 1st, 1927, Clodagh (*d* 1945), *d* of late Major R. Wyman, TD, JP; one *s* one *d*; 2nd, 1966, Jessie, JP Liverpool 1968, *d* of late Prosper Marsden, MSc. *Educ:* Liverpool (Pres. Guild of Undergraduates, Univ. of Liverpool, 1920); London; Vienna. Served European War, 1914-18 (wounded, MC immediate award), in King's Regiment and Machine Gun Corps, France and Italy, 1915-19; POW 1918. MB, ChB (distinction in Public Health), Liverpool, 1921; House Physician, Liverpool Roy. Infirmary; House Surgeon, London Hosp.; Clin. Asst, Moorfields Eye Hosp.; Dip. Ophth. Med. and Surgery, 1923; FRCS 1925; post-grad. study, Vienna, 1925-26; Cons. Ophth. Surgeon, Liverpool, 1926-39. Commanded Liverpool Univ. OTC, 1932-38. Formed 1st W Gen. Hosp. RAMC, 1939; served: Norway (ADMS), 1940; Africa and India 1942-45; resumed consulting practice, 1946. Member: Univ. Court, 1930, and Faculty of Med., 1945, Univ. of Liverpool; Court of Examiners, RCS, 1949; Examiner, QUB, 1948; Pres.: Section of Ophth., BMA, 1950; N of England Ophth. Soc., 1948; Liverpool Med. Institution, 1958-59; Vice-Pres., Section of Ophth., RSM, 1951-54; Vice-Pres. Ophth. Soc. of UK; Member: Faculty of Ophthalmologists (Treas.), 1954; Med. Advisory Council Regional Bd, 1950-53; Bd of Governors, United Liverpool Hosps, 1956; Governor: Liverpool Blue Coat Hospital, 1952-; Liverpool Coll. of Art; Hon. Treas. Liverpool Cons. Assoc., 1956 (Dep. Chm. 1959); Mem., Liverpool City Council, 1961; Chm. Health Cttee, 1962; Chm., Roy. Liverpool Philharmonic Soc., 1967. OStJ 1961. *Publications:* chapters in: Well's Surgery for Nurses, 1938; Manson's Tropical Medicine, 16th and 17th edns; Rob and Smith's Clinical Surgery; articles in British Jl Ophthal., BMJ, Practitioner. *Recreations:* music, travel, fishing. *Address:* 86 Rodney Street, Liverpool 1. *T:* 051-709 3030. *Clubs:* Athenæum; Racquet (Liverpool).

**REID, Archibald Cameron,** CMG 1963; CVO 1970; Deputy High Commissioner in the Kingdom of Tonga since 1970; *b* 7 Aug. 1915; *s* of William Reid; *m* 1941, Joan Raymond Charlton; two *s* two *d.* *Educ:* Fettes; Queen's College, Cambridge. Apptd Admin. Officer, Class II, in Colony of Fiji, 1938; Admin. Officer, Class I, 1954; British Agent and Consul, Tonga, 1957-59; Sec. for Fijian Affairs, 1959-65; British Comr and Consul, Tonga, 1965-70. *Recreations:* hill walking, painting, golf. *Address:* 2a Ramsay Garden, Edinburgh, 1. *T:* 031-225 6541; British High Commission, Tonga.

**REID, Charles William,** BSc (Econ); ASAA; *b* 29 May 1895; *s* of Charles and Ada Reid; *m* 1924, Gladys Ellen Edith Dudley; two *d.* *Educ:* Latymer Upper School; Holloway County School; University of London. War Office, 1914; Queen's Westminster Rifles, 1915-19 (served overseas, wounded twice). Exchequer and Audit Department, 1919-38; Exports Credit Guarantee Dept, 1938-39; Ministry of Supply, 1939-40; Ministry of Supply Mission, USA, 1940-46, Director of Requirements and Secretary-General; Ministry of Supply, Overseas Disposals, 1946-48; Dep. Financial Adviser. Control Commn, Germany, 1948-50; Min. of Works, Comptroller of Accounts, 1950-54; Under-Secretary for Finance, 1954-56; retired, 1956. Incorporated Accountant, 1926. Medal of Freedom (USA), 1947. *Recreations:* travel and sports. Athletics purple, Univ. of London; represented Great Britain in first athletics match with France, 1921. *Address:* Pynes, Edington, Near Bridgwater, Somerset. *T:* Chilton Polden 320.

**REID, Major-General Denys Whitehorn,** CB 1945; CBE 1942; DSO 1918; MC 1916; Indian Army, retired; *b* 24 March 1897. Served European War, 1915-18, with Seaforth Highlanders (wounded, despatches twice, MC and bar, DSO); War of 1939-45 in Middle East and commanded 10th Indian Division in Italy (wounded, Bar to DSO, CBE, CB); late 5th Mahratta Light Infantry; retd, 1947. *Address:* Lane End Cottage, Sampford Arundel, Nr Wellington, Somerset. *T:* Greenham 465. *Club:* Naval and Military.

**REID, Desmond Arthur;** Chairman: R. K. Harrison & Co. Ltd, since 1947; R. K. Harrison, J. I. Jacobs (Insurance) Ltd; Yeoman Investment Trust Ltd; Deputy Chairman, Prudential Assurance Co. Ltd, since 1968 (Director, 1960); *b* 6 Feb. 1918; *s* of late Col Percy Lester Reid, CBE, DL, and late Mrs Katharine Marjorie Elizabeth Reid; *m* 1939, Anne, *d* of late Major J. B. Paget and of

Mrs J. B. Paget, London SW7; one *s. Educ:* Eton. Joined Lloyd's, 1936. Irish Guards, 1939-45 (wounded in Normandy, 1944; Major). Returned Lloyd's, 1946 (Member). Director: Selection Croissance; Edger Investments Ltd; General Consolidated Investment Trust Ltd; London & St Lawrence Investment Co. Ltd; Moorgate Investment Co. Ltd; Practical Investment Co. Ltd; Prudential Unit Trust Managers Ltd; Prudential Nominees Ltd; Prudential Staff Deferred Annuity Fund Ltd; Suburban & Counties Properties Ltd, and subsidiaries. Councillor, Chelsea Bor. Council, 1945-52 (Chm. Finance Cttee, 1950-52). Chm., Inst. of Obstetrics and Gynæcology; Vice-Pres., Insurance Inst. of London; Mem., The Livery of Merchant Taylors. *Recreations:* shooting, gardening. *Address:* 155 Old Church Street, SW3. *T:* 01-352 0478. *Clubs:* White's, City of London; Travellers' (Paris).

**REID, Professor Donald Darnley,** MD; DSc; FRCP; Professor of Epidemiology, London School of Hygiene and Tropical Medicine, University of London, since 1959, and Director of Department of Medical Statistics and Epidemiology since 1961; *b* 6 May 1914; *s* of late Donald Reid and Mary Darnley; *m* 1939, Christine Macleod, MA, *d* of late Dr D. J. Macleod, OBE; two *d. Educ:* Royal Academy, Inverness; Universities of Aberdeen and London. House appointments Roy. Northern Infirmary, Inverness, 1937-38; served War of 1939-45, in Med. Branch RAF, first in Bomber Command then in research section, Directorate-Gen. of Med. Services, 1939-46. Lecturer, 1946-50; Reader in Epidemiology and Vital Statistics, London Sch. of Hygiene and Trop. Med., 1956-59. Vis. Assoc. Prof. of Biostatistics, Univ. of California, 1948-49; Milroy Lectr, RCP, 1958; Sydney Watson Smith Lectr, RCPE 1962; Cutter Lectr, Harvard, 1969. Past Pres., section of Epidemiology and Preventive Med., RSM; (former Chm. Med. sect.) Roy. Stat. Society; Consultant in Epidemiology to RAF; Chm., Epidemiology Panel, Med. Service, NCB; Member: US Public Health Service Joint US-UK Board on Cardiorespiratory Disease; Member consultant panel for WHO on Cardiovascular Diseases. *Publications:* contrib. to medical text books, also journals on epidemiological methods, especially in mental and cardiorespiratory diseases. *Recreations:* photography, music. *Address:* 20 Ormond Crescent, Hampton, Middlesex. *T:* 01-979 1050.

**REID, Sir Douglas Neilson,** 2nd Bt, *cr* 1922; JP; farmer; Member Royal Company of Archers (Queen's Body Guard for Scotland); *b* 12 Feb. 1898; *s* of Sir Hugh Reid, 1st Bt, and Marion Maclune (*d* 1913), *y d* of late John Bell, Shipowner, Craigview, Prestwick, Ayrshire; *S* father 1935; *m* 1926, Margaret Brighton Young Maxtone; one *s* one *d. Educ:* Loretto; Clare College, Cambridge. Served European War, 1916-18 with HLI and RFC; served as Flying Officer in RAFVR, 1939-41. *Recreations:* shooting, fishing, natural history, etc. *Heir: s* Hugh Reid, *b* 27 Nov. 1933. *Address:* Tullich, Lochcarron, Ross-shire. *T:* Lochcarron 216; Auchterarder House, Perthshire. *T:* 2632. *Clubs:* Royal Scottish Automobile (Glasgow); Shikar.

**REID, Sir Edward (James),** 2nd Bt, *cr* 1897; KBE 1967 (OBE 1946); a Director of the Bank of Scotland since 1967; Hon. President, Clan Donnachaidh Society; Member Council, Scottish Craft Centre; *b* 20 April 1901, godson of King Edward VII; *er s* of Sir James Reid, 1st Bt, and Hon. Susan Baring (*d* 1961), formerly Maid of Honour to Queen Victoria, *d* of 1st Baron Revelstoke; *S* father, 1923; *m* 1930, Tatiana, *d* of Col Alexander Fenoult, formerly of Russian Imperial Guard; one *s* one *d*. Page of Honour to the King, 1911-17; Scholar, King's College, Cambridge; Browne Medallist, 1920, 1921 and 1922; First Class Pt II Classical Tripos, 1922. Director of Baring Bros & Co. Ltd, 1926-66; Chairman of Provident Mutual Life Assurance Association, 1963-66 (Director 1938-66); Chairman of British and Chinese Corporation Ltd, 1946-66; Member of London Committee of Hongkong and Shanghai Banking Corp., 1946-66; (Director 1941-46 while Head Office was in London); Chairman, Accepting Houses Committee, 1946-66; Chairman Directors, Royal Caledonian Schools, Bushey, 1947-66; Commissioner for Income-Tax, City of London, 1938-66. Governor of Guy's Hosp., 1937-48. Member Executive Cttee Finland Fund, 1939-40. Treasurer of the Infants Hosp., Vincent Square, 1938-46. Chairman, British Banking Committee for German Affairs, 1948-62. President, Institute of Bankers, 1962-64; Hon. Fellow 1967; Pres., Overseas Bankers' Club, 1964-65. A Vice-Pres., Liverpool Sch. Trop. Medicine and Highland Soc. of London. FSA Scot., 1967. Order of the Rising Sun (Second Class), Japan 1964. *Heir: s* Alexander James Reid [*b* 6 December 1932; *m* 1955, Michaela Ann, *yr d* of Olaf Kier; one *s* three *d*]. *Address:* 16 Buckingham Terrace, Edinburgh EH4 3AD. *Clubs:* Caledonian; Scottish Arts (Edinburgh).

*See also Admiral Sir Peter Reid.*

**REID, Air Vice-Marshal Sir (George) Ranald Macfarlane,** KCB, *cr* 1945 (CB 1941); DSO 1919; MC and bar; Extra Gentleman Usher to the Queen, 1959; Gentleman Usher to the Queen, 1952 (formerly to King George VI, 1952); *s* of late George Macfarlane Reid, Queensland and Prestwick; *m* 1934, Leslie Livermore Washburne, *d* of late Hamilton Wright, Washington, DC, USA, and *g d* of Senator William Washburne; one *s* one *d. Educ:* Routenburn; Malvern Coll. Regular Officer, 1914-46 in: 4th (SR) Argyll and Sutherland Highlanders; 2nd Black Watch; RFC and RAF. Served European War, 1914-18 (wounded, despatches, MC and Bar, DSO); Egypt, 1919-21; Sudan, 1927-29; RAF Staff Coll., 1930; Imperial Defence Coll., 1932; Air Attaché, British Embassy, Washington, 1933-35; AOC Halton, 1936-38; Air Officer Commanding British Forces, Aden, 1938-41; Air Officer Administration Flying Training Command; AOC 54 Group; AOC West Africa, 1944-45; retired from Royal Air Force, 1946. *Address:* c/o Lloyds Bank Ltd, 6 Pall Mall, SW1. *Clubs:* Royal Air Force; Weld (Perth, Western Australia).

**REID, George Smith;** Sheriff-Substitute of Ayr and Bute, at Ayr, since 1948; *b* 29 Feb. 1904; *yr s* of John Mitchell Reid, manufacturer, Glasgow; *m* 1935, Marion Liddell Boyd; two *s* two *d. Educ:* Hutchesons' Grammar School, Glasgow; Glasgow University. MA 1925, LLB 1927. Called to Scottish Bar, 1935. *Recreations:* swimming, golf. *Address:* 10 Wheatfield Road, Ayr. *T:* 67858.

**REID, Rev. George Thomson Henderson,** MC 1945; Minister of West Church of St Andrews, Aberdeen, since 1955; Chaplain to the Queen in Scotland since 1969; *b* 31 March 1910; *s* of Rev. David Reid, DD; *m* 1938, Anne Guilland Watt, *d* of late Principal Very Rev. Hugh Watt, DD, Edinburgh; three *s* one *d*. *Educ:* George Watson's Boys' Coll.; Univ. of Edinburgh. MA 1932, BD 1935, Edinburgh. Served as Chaplain to 3rd Bn Scots Guards, 1940-45, Sen. Chaplain to 15th (S) Div., 1945. Minister at: Port Seton, E Lothian, 1935-38; Juniper Green, Edinburgh, 1938-49; Claremont Church, Glasgow, 1949-55. Hon. DD Aberdeen, 1969. *Recreations:* golf, bird-watching, painting. *Address:* 6 Moray Place, Aberdeen. *T:* Aberdeen 34216.

**REID, Harold Alexander,** CIE 1944; retired; *b* 31 Dec. 1891; *s* of Alexander Reid, Rutherglen, Lanarkshire, Scotland; *m* 1922, Ella, *d* of Robert Gray, Bishopbriggs, Glasgow; one *d*. *Educ:* Royal Technical College, Glasgow. Assistant Locomotive Superintendent, South Indian Railway, 1914; Chief Mechanical Engineer, South Indian Railway, 1932-45. *Recreation:* golf. *Address:* 6 Montpellier Court, Lansdown Road, Cheltenham, Glos. *T:* 23655. *Club:* New (Cheltenham).

**REID, Harold Martin Smith;** Deputy High Commissioner, Malawi, since 1970; *b* 27 Aug. 1928; *s* of late Marcus Reid and late Winifred Mary Reid (*née* Stephens); *m* 1956, Jane Elizabeth Harwood; one *s* three *d*. *Educ:* Merchant Taylors' Sch.; Brasenose Coll., Oxford. Entered HM Foreign Service, 1953; served in: FO, 1953-54; Paris, 1954-57; Rangoon, 1958-61; FO, 1961-65; Adviser on External Relations to Governor of British Guiana, and subseq. Dep. High Comr, British High Commn, Georgetown, Guyana, 1965-68; First Sec., Bucharest, 1968-70. *Recreations:* painting and drawing; tennis. *Address:* c/o Foreign and Commonwealth Office, SW1; 1 Rockwells Gardens, SE19. *T:* 01-670 6151. *Club:* Oxford and Cambridge.

**REID, James,** MBE 1953; Editor, Dumfries and Galloway Standard, 1919-54; *b* Insch, Aberdeenshire, 11 Feb. 1873; *y s* of Alexander Reid; *m* 1903, Annie Crawford, *d* of John Whyte, Glasgow; two *d*. *Educ:* Insch, Aberdeen. Left teaching for journalism and served on various papers in Glasgow and Dundee; editor of Northern Chronicle, Inverness, 1911-19; toured Canada, 1924; Chairman of Dumfriesshire Liberal Assoc., 1931-47. *Recreation:* gardening. *Address:* Criffel, 1 Southerton Crescent, Kirkcaldy, Fife. *T:* Kirkcaldy 4529.

**REID, John,** CB 1967; Chief Veterinary Officer, Ministry of Agriculture, Fisheries and Food, 1965-70; *b* 14 May 1906; *s* of late John Reid, Callander, Perthshire; *m* 1933, Molly Russell; one *d*. *Educ:* McLaren High Sch., Callander; Royal (Dick) Veterinary Coll., Edinburgh. MRCVS 1929; DVSM 1931. Asst Veterinary Officer, Midlothian County Council, 1931; Asst Veterinary Officer, Cumberland County Council, 1932; Ministry of Agriculture and Fisheries: Divisional Veterinary Officer, 1938; Superintending Veterinary Officer, 1952; Ministry of Agriculture, Fisheries and Food: Regional Veterinary Officer, 1958; Deputy Chief Veterinary Officer, 1960; Director of Veterinary Field Services, 1963. Mem. ARC, 1965-70. Vice-Chm., FAO European Commn for Control of Foot-and-Mouth Disease, 1967-70. *Recreations:* gardening, hill walking and fishing. *Address:* Owl's Green Cottage, Dennington, Woodbridge, Suffolk. *T:* Badingham 205. *Club:* Farmers'.

**REID, John Kelman Sutherland,** CBE 1970; TD 1961; Professor of Christian Dogmatics, University of Aberdeen, since 1961; *b* 31 March 1910; *y s* of late Reverend Dr David Reid, Calcutta and Leith, and of late Mrs G. T. Reid (*née* Stuart); *m* 1950, Margaret Winifrid Brookes. *Educ:* George Watson's Boys' College, Edinburgh; Universities of Edinburgh (MA and BD), Heidelberg, Marburg, Basel, and Strasbourg. MA 1st Cl. Hons Philosophy, 1933. Prof. of Philosophy in Scottish Church Coll., Univ. of Calcutta, 1935-37; BD (dist. in Theol.), 1938, and Cunningham Fellow. Ordained into Church of Scotland and inducted into Parish of Craigmillar Park, Edinburgh, 1939. CF, chiefly with Parachute Regt, 1942-46. Jt Ed. Scot. Jl Theol. since inception, 1947; Hon. sec. Jt Cttee on New Translation of the Bible, 1949-; Prof. of Theology and Head of Department of Theology, University of Leeds, 1952-61. Hon. DD (Edinburgh), 1957. *Publications:* The Authority of Scripture, 1957; Our Life in Christ, 1963; Christian Apologetics, 1969. Translation of: Oscar Cullmann's The Earliest Christian Confessions, 1949; Baptism in the New Testament, 1952; Calvin's Theological Treatises, ed and trans. 1954; Jean Bosc's The Kingly Office of the Lord Jesus Christ, 1959; Calvin's Concerning the Eternal Predestination of God, ed and trans., 1961. *Address:* Don House, 46 Don Street, Aberdeen. *Clubs:* Army and Navy; Mortonhall Golf (Edinburgh); Royal Aberdeen Golf (Aberdeen).

**REID, Adm. Sir (John) Peter (Lorne),** GCB 1961 (KCB 1957; CB 1946); CVO 1953; Vice-Admiral of the United Kingdom and of the Admiralty since 1966; *b* 10 Jan. 1903; 2nd *s* of Sir James Reid, 1st Baronet of Ellon, and of Susan, *d* of 1st Baron Revelstoke; *m* 1933, Jean, *o d* of Sir Henry Dundas, 3rd Bt of Arniston, and of Beatrix, *d* of 12th Earl of Home; one *s* one *d*. *Educ:* Royal Naval Colleges, Osborne and Dartmouth. Lieut 1925; Comdr 1935; Captain 1941; Rear-Adm. 1951; Vice-Adm. 1954; Adm. 1958. Served War of 1939-45 (CB despatches twice); commanded HMS Dido, 1947, HMS Cleopatra, 1948-49; Chief of Staff to the C-in-C Portsmouth, 1951-53. Rear-Adm. (Review) on Staff of C-in-C Portsmouth, 1953; Flag Officer (Air) Mediterranean, and Flag Officer Second in Command, Mediterranean Fleet, 1954-55; Third Sea Lord, and Controller of the Navy, 1956-61, retd, 1961. Rear-Admiral of the United Kingdom and of the Admiralty, 1962-66. Director, Richardsons, Westgarth and Co. Ltd. President British Legion, Scotland. DL, East Lothian, 1962; Vice-Lieutenant, 1964, 1967; Vice-Convener, E Lothian CC, 1969-. *Address:* Membland, Haddington, East Lothian. *T:* Gifford 207. *Clubs:* Army and Navy, Caledonian.

*See also Sir David Montgomery, Bt, Sir Edward Reid, Bt.*

**REID, Louis Arnaud,** MA, PhD, DLitt; Professor Emeritus of Philosophy of Education, Institute of Education, London University, (Professor 1947-62); *b* Ellon, Aberdeenshire, 18 Feb. 1895; *s* of late Rev. A. H. Reid and late Margaret C. Miller; *m* 1920, Gladys Kate, *y d* of late W. H. Bignold; two *s*; *m* 1957, Frances Mary Holt, *d* of Denys Horton; two *step d*. *Educ:* Aberdeen Grammar School; Leys Sch., Camb.; University of Edinburgh. Studied engineering, 1913; RE 1914; discharged, 1915; 1st Cl. Hons in Mental Philosophy, 1919; medallist, English Essays; University verse prizeman; Cousin prizeman in Fine Art; medallist in Moral Philosophy; Bruce of Grangehill and Falkland prizeman in Advanced Metaphysics; Vans Dunlop scholar in Moral Philosophy; Lord Rector's prizeman; Hamilton Philosophical Fellow; Mrs Foster

Watson Memorial Prizeman; Lecturer in Philosophy in University College, Aberystwyth, 1919-26; Visiting Professor Stanford University, California, 1927; Independent Lecturer in Philosophy University of Liverpool, 1926-32; Prof. of Philosophy Armstrong Coll. (now Univ. of Newcastle upon Tyne), 1932-47. Visiting Prof., Univ. of British Columbia, 1951; Vis. Prof. of Philosophy, Univ. of Oregon, 1962-63; Vis. Prof., Chinese Univ. of Hong Kong, 1966-67. Ext. Examiner, Univs of Liverpool, Sheffield, Leeds, Edinburgh, Aberdeen, Glasgow, London, W Indies, Hong Kong. *Publications:* Knowledge and Truth, An Epistemological Essay, 1923; A Study in Aesthetics, 1931; Creative Morality, 1936; Preface to Faith, 1939; The Rediscovery of Belief, 1945; Ways of Knowledge and Experience, 1960; Philosophy and Education, 1961; Meaning in the Arts, 1970; articles in Mind, Hibbert Journal, Proceedings of the Aristotelian Society, Times Ed. Supp., etc. *Address:* 50 Rotherwick Road, NW11. *T:* 01-455 6850. *Clubs:* Athenæum, PEN.

**REID, Malcolm Herbert Marcus;** Commercial Counsellor, HM Embassy, Madrid, since 1967; *b* 2 March 1927; *s* of late Marcus Reid and Winifred Stephens; *m* 1956, Eleanor, *d* of late H. G. Evans, MC; four *s*. *Educ:* Merchant Taylors' Sch.; St John's Coll., Oxford. Served in Navy, 1945-48 and in RNVR, 1949-53. Entered Board of Trade, 1951. Private Secretary to Permanent Secretary, 1954-57; Trade Comr in Ottawa, 1957-60; Board of Trade, 1960-63; Private Secretary to successive Prime Ministers, 1963-66. *Recreation:* National Hunt racing. *Address:* 26 Ashley Close, Walton-on-Thames, Surrey. *T:* 27363; Plaza Canovas del Castillo 3, Madrid, Spain. *Club:* Oxford and Cambridge University.

**REID, May,** CBE 1920; *b* Bombay, 1 May 1882; *e d* of late Edward Jervis Reid. *Educ:* privately; Bedford College. Assistant and Acting County Secretary, London Branch British Red Cross Society, 1914-23; Secretary to Lord Queenborough, 1923-28; Assistant Sec. National Christian Council of India, 1932-41. *Address:* 4 Bywater Street, SW3. *T:* 01-589 3270.

**REID, Sir Norman (Robert),** Kt 1970; DA (Edinburgh); FMA; FIIC; Director, the Tate Gallery, since 1964; *b* 27 December 1915; *o s* of Edward Daniel Reid and Blanche, *d* of Richard Drouet; *m* 1941, Jean Lindsay Bertram; one *s* one *d*. *Educ:* Wilson's Grammar School; Edinburgh Coll. of Art; Edinburgh Univ. Served War of 1939-46, Major, Argyll and Sutherland Highlanders. Joined staff of Tate Gallery, 1946; Deputy Director, 1954; Keeper, 1959. Fellow, International Institute for Conservation (IIC) (Secretary General, 1963-65; Vice-Chm., 1966); British Rep. Internat. Committee on Museums and Galleries of Modern Art, 1963-; President, Penwith Society of Arts; Member: Council, Friends of the Tate Gall., 1958- (Founder Mem.); Arts Council Art Panel, 1964-; Inst. of Contemporary Arts Adv. Panel, 1965-; Contemporary Art Soc. Cttee, 1965-; "Paintings in Hospitals" Adv. Cttee, 1965-69; British Council Fine Arts Cttee, 1965- (Chm. 1968-); Culture Adv. Cttee of UK Nat. Commn for Unesco, 1966-; Univ. of London, Bd of Studies in History of Art, 1968; Cttee, The Rome Centre, 1969. Hon. DLitt, East Anglia, 1970. Officer of the Mexican Order of the Aztec Eagle. *Address:* The Tate Gallery, Millbank, SW1. *T:* 01-828 4444; 50 Brabourne Rise, Park Langley, Beckenham, Kent. *T:* 01-650 7088.

**REID, Patrick Robert,** MBE 1940; MC 1943; Windett, Reid, Burrows & Bonar Law Ltd and Development Contractors Ltd, since 1963; *b* 13 Nov. 1910; *s* of John Reid, CIE, ICS, and Alice Mabel Daniell; *m* 1943, Jane Cabot; three *s* two *d*. *Educ:* Clongowes Wood College, Co. Kildare; Wimbledon College; King's College, London University. BSc (London) 1932; AMICE, 1936; Pupilage, Sir Alex Gibb & Partners, 1934-37. Served War of 1939-45, BEF, France, Capt. RASC 2nd Div., Ammunition Officer, 1939-40; POW Germany, 1940-42; Asst Mil. Attaché, Berne, 1943-46; First Sec. (Commercial), British Embassy, Ankara, 1946-49; Chief Administrator, OEEC, Paris, 1949-52. Prospective Parl. Candidate (C) Dartford and Erith, 1953-55. Director, Richard Costain (Projects) Ltd, 1959-62; Dir, Richard Costain (Middle East) Ltd, 1959-62. W. S. Atkins & Partners, Consulting Engineers, 1962-63. *Publications:* The Colditz Story, 1953; The Latter Days, 1955; (with Sir Olaf Caroe and Sir Thomas Rapp) From Nile to Indus, 1960; Winged Diplomat, 1962. Economic Survey Northern Nigeria, 1962. *Recreations:* ski-ing, yachting, gardening. *Clubs:* St James', Lansdowne.

**REID, Admiral Sir Peter;** *see* Reid, Sir J. P. L.

**REID, Air Vice-Marshal Sir Ranald;** *see* Reid Sir G. R. M.

**REID, Robert,** QC (Scotland) 1961; President, Industrial Tribunals for Scotland, since 1965; *b* 5 Sept. 1922; *s* of late Robert Reid and of Mary Forsyth, Inverness; *m* 1946, Sheila Stuart Fraser (*d* 1951); *m* 1962, Jane (late Lynch or Thomson); one *s*. *Educ:* Inverness Royal Academy; Edinburgh University (BL). Passed Advocate, 1949. *Recreations:* poetry, gardening. *Address:* 33 Regent Terrace, Edinburgh. *T:* 031-556 1783. *Clubs:* Arts, Edinburgh University Staff (Edinburgh).

**REID, Dr Robert Douglas;** *b* 6 Sept. 1898; *s* of John and Maud Helen Reid; unmarried. *Educ:* Wells Cathedral School; St John's College, Oxford; Bristol University. Army 1917-19, Somerset Light Infantry in Flanders and Ireland; Assistant Master at Downside School, 1923-24; Canford School, 1924-28; Housemaster at Worksop College, 1928-33; Headmaster Kings School, Taunton, 1933-37. Somerset County Council, 1958-66; Member Wells City Council. Doctor of Philosophy, Oxon; BSc Bristol. *Publications:* Cathedral Church of St Andrew at Wells; Diary of Mary Yeoman; Notes on Practical Chemistry; A Concise General Science, 1949. *Recreations:* archæology, lawn tennis. *Address:* 8 Chamberlain Street, Wells, Somerset. *T:* 2494.

**REID, Thomas Bertram Wallace,** MA (Oxon), MA, LLB (Dublin), MA (Manchester), L ès L (Montpellier); Officier d'Académie; Professor Emeritus, University of Oxford, and Emeritus Fellow of Trinity College, Oxford; *b* 10 July 1901; *e s* of late Thomas E. Reid, MBE, JP, Little Castledillon, Armagh; *m* 1942, Joyce M. H. Smalley; one *s*. *Educ:* Armagh Royal School; Trinity Coll., Dublin. Foundation Scholar, Hutchinson Stewart Literary Scholar, First Senior Moderator in Modern Literature, Prizeman in Old French and Provençal, Irish, and Law. Lecteur d'Anglais, Univ. of Montpellier, 1924-26; Asst Master, Frome County School, 1926-29; Assistant Lecturer in French, University of Manchester, 1929-35; Lecturer, 1935-45; Prof. of Romance Philology, 1945-58; Dean of the Faculty of Arts, 1950-51; Pro-Vice-Chancellor, 1957-58; Prof. of the Romance Languages, Univ. of Oxford, and Fell. Trinity Coll., Oxford, 1958-68. Vis. Prof., Univ. of Toronto, 1969-70.

Pres., Anglo-Norman Text Society. *Publications:* The Yvain of Chrestien de Troyes (ed.), 1942; Twelve Fabliaux (ed.), 1958; Historical Philology and Linguistic Science, 1960; The Romance of Horn by Thomas, ed. M. K. Pope, Vol. II (revised and completed), 1964; articles and reviews on linguistic subjects in Modern Lang. Review, Medium Aevum, French Studies, etc. *Address:* 37 Blandford Avenue, Oxford. *T:* Oxford 58112.

**REID, Whitelaw;** President and Director, Reid Enterprises; Chairman and Director, The Drinx Plus Company Inc. (formerly called Roadsides Inc.); *b* 26 July 1913; *s* of late Ogden Reid and Mrs Ogden Reid; *m* 1st, 1948, Joan Brandon (marr. diss., 1959); two *s*; 2nd, 1959, Elizabeth Ann Brooks; one *s* one *d*. *Educ:* Lincoln Sch., NYC; St Paul's Sch., Concord, New Hampshire; Yale Univ. (BA). New York Herald Tribune: in various departments, 1938-40; foreign correspondent, England, 1940; Assistant to Editor, 1946; Editor (and Pres., 1953-55), 1947-55; Chm. of Bd, 1955-58; Director, 1946-65; Pres., Herald Tribune Fresh Air Fund, 1946-62, Dir 1962-. Served War of 1939-45, 1st Lieut, USNR. Pres., Reid Foundation; formerly Dir, Farfield Foundn; Director: Freedom House; Korean Soc. Inc. Chm., NY State Cttee on Public Employee Security Procedure, 1956-57. Member: Nat. Commn for Unesco, 1955-60; President's Citizen Advisers on the Mutual Security Program, 1956-57; Yale Alumni Board (Vice-Chm., 1962-64), Yale Univ. Council (Chm., Publications Cttee, 1965-70); Council on Foreign Relations; Nat. Inst. of Social Sciences. Fellow, Pearson Coll., Yale, 1949-. *Address:* (business) Drinx Plus Company, Rutherford Industrial Park, Veterans Boulevard, at Route 3, Rutherford, NJ; (home and office) Ophir Farm, Purchase, New York, USA. *Clubs:* Century, Overseas Press, Silurians, Pilgrims, NY Young Republican, Amateur Ski (New York); Metropolitan (Washington); St Regis Yacht; Manursing Is.

**REID, Flight Lt William,** VC 1943; National Cattle and Sheep Adviser (based at Head Office, Spillers Ltd, Old Change House, EC4) Spillers Ltd, Nov. 1959; Agriculture Adviser, The MacRobert Trust, Douneside, Tarland, Aberdeenshire, from 1950; *b* 21 Dec. 1921; *s* of late William Reid, Baillieston, Glasgow; *m* 1952, Violet Gallagher, 11 Dryburgh Gdns, Glasgow, NW1; one *s* one *d*. *Educ:* Coatbridge Secondary Sch.; Glasgow Univ.; West of Scotland Coll. of Agriculture. Student of Metallurgy, Sept. 1940; BSc (Agric.), 1949; Post-Graduate World Travelling Scholarship for 6 months, to study Agric. and Installations in India, Australia, NZ, USA and Canada, 1949-50. Joined RAF 1941; trained in Lancaster, Calif, USA. Won VC during a trip to Düsseldorf, 3 Nov. 1943, when member of 61 Squadron; pilot RAFVR, 617 Squadron (prisoner); demobilised, 1946; recalled to RAF for 3 months, Dec. 1951. Joined RAFVR, commissioned Jan. 1949, 103 Reserve Centre, Perth. *Recreations:* golf, shooting, fishing, etc. *Address:* Morven, 68 Upper Hall Park, Berkhamsted, Herts. *T:* Berkhamsted 2541. *Club:* Royal Air Force Reserves.

**REID, William,** CBE 1962; PhD, DSc; *b* 20 June 1906; *o s* of late Sir Charles Carlow Reid; *m* 1935, Sheila Janette Christiana Davidson; one *s* one *d*. *Educ:* Dollar Acad.; Dunfermline High School. Early underground practical experience in coal mining attached to The Fife Coal Co. Ltd, and in the Ruhr and US. BSc (Mining and Metallurgy) 1929, and PhD (Mining) 1933, Univ. of Edinburgh. Held various mining appointments with The Fife Coal Co. Ltd, 1922-42; apptd Gen. Works Manager and Dir, 1942. Leader of Ministry of Fuel and Power Technical Mission to the Ruhr Coalfield, 1945; apptd in the Scottish Div. Nat. Coal Board, Prod. Dir, 1947, Deputy Chairman, 1950, Chairman, 1952; Board Member for Production, NCB, 1955-57; Chm., Durham Div., NCB, 1957-63; Chm., Northumberland and Durham Div., NCB, 1964-67, Regional Chm., 1967-69. Leader of NCB Technical Mission to coalfields of Soviet Union, 1956. Chm., Northern Regional Marketing Cttee, Nat. Marketing Council, 1966. Member: N Reg. Econ. Planning Council, 1965; Port of Tyne Authority, 1968. Chairman: Northern Brick Co.; Associated Heat Services (N) Ltd; Dep. Chm., Victor Products (Wallsend) Ltd. Vice-Chm., council, Univ. of Durham, 1964. President: Mining Inst. of Scotland, 1951-52; IMinE, 1956-57. Hon. DCL Durham, 1970. *Publications:* numerous papers related to industry, particularly coal mining. *Recreation:* golf. *Address:* Norwood, Picktree Village, Chester-le-Street, Co. Durham. *T:* Chester-le-Street 2260. *Club:* Union (Newcastle upon Tyne).

**REID, William,** FSA; Director, National Army Museum, since 1970; *b* Glasgow, 8 Nov. 1926; *o s* of Colin Colquhoun Reid and Mary Evelyn Bingham; *m* 1958, Nina Frances Brigden. *Educ:* Glasgow and Oxford. Commnd RAF Regt, 1946-48. Joined staff of Armouries, Tower of London, 1956; Asst Keeper 1st Class, 1964. Organising Sec., 3rd Internat. Congress of Museums of Arms and Military History, London, Glasgow and Edinburgh, 1963; Sec.-Gen., Internat. Assoc. of Museums of Arms and Military History, Rome, 1969. *Publications:* contribs to Connoisseur, Guildhall Miscellany, Jl of Arms and Armour Soc. and other British and foreign jls. *Recreations:* the study of armour and arms, music, ornithology, travel. *Address:* 66 Ennerdale Road, Kew, Richmond, Surrey. *T:* 01-940 0904. *Club:* United University.

**REID-ADAM, Randle,** CBE 1953 (OBE 1947); *b* 16 Jan. 1912; *s* of late James and of Helen Reid-Adam; *m* 1942, Rita Audrey Carty; two *d*. *Educ:* Oundle; Trinity Hall, Cambridge. Appointed to Department of Overseas Trade, 1933. Commercial Secretary, British Embassy, Washington, 1940. Served in Foreign Service posts at Cairo, New York, Cologne, Stockholm, San Francisco and Panama; retired 1964. *Address:* Draycott, Nr Moreton-in-Marsh, Glos.

**REIDHAVEN, Viscount, (Master of Seafield); James Andrew Ogilvie-Grant-Studley-Herbert;** *b* 30 Nov. 1963; *s* and *heir* of Earl of Seafield, *qv*.

**REIDY, Joseph Patrick Irwin,** FRCS; Consulting Plastic Surgeon: Westminster Hospital since 1948; Stoke Mandeville Hospital, Bucks, since 1951 (Director, Plastic Surgery, since 1957); Oldchurch Hospital, Romford, since 1946; Consulting Plastic Surgeon (Hon.), St Paul's Hospital, WC, since 1959; *b* 30 October 1907; 2nd *s* of late Dr Jerome J. Reidy, JP, MD, Co. Limerick and London and of Alderman Mrs F. W. Reidy, JP (*née* Dawson), Castle Dawson, Co. Derry; *m* 1943, Anne (*d* 1970), *e d* of late T. Johnson, and of late Mrs T. Johnson, County Durham; three *d*. *Educ:* Stonyhurst College, Lancs; St John's Coll., Cambridge; London Hospital. MA (Nat. Sci. Trip.) (Cantab); MD, BCh (Cantab); FRCS. Casualty Officer and Ho. Phys., Poplar Hosp., 1932; Ho. Surg. and Casualty Officer, London Hosp., 1933; Ho. Surg., Leicester Roy. Inf., 1934; General Practitioner, 1934-37. Surgeon H. Div., Metropolitan Police, 1934-37. Hon. Dem. of Anatomy, Med. Sch., Middx Hosp., 1938; Civilian Surg., RAF Hosp., Halton, Bucks,

1939; Res. Surg. Officer; EMS, Albert Dock Hosp., 1939-40; EMS, St Andrew's Hosp., Billericay, 1940-42; Chief Asst, Plastic Surgery, St Thomas' Hosp., 1943-48. Cons. Plastic Surgeon, Essex Co. Hosp., Colchester, 1943-46; Senior Grade Surgeon, Plastic Surg. Unit, Min. of Pensions: Stoke Mandeville Hosp., Bucks, 1942-51; Queen Mary's Hosp., Roehampton, 1942-51. Consulting Plastic Surgeon: Middlesex CC, 1944-48; Nelson Hosp., Kingston, 1948-50; Metropolitan ENT Hosp., 1948-50; West Middlesex Hosp.; Lord Mayor Treloar Hosp., Alton, 1953-56. Hon. Chief MO, Amateur Boxing Association, 1948; Hon. Secretary and Treas. United Hospitals Rugby Football Club, 1957-62. Liveryman Soc. of Apothecaries; BMA; Freeman of City of London; FRSocMed; FMedSoc Lond.; Fellow Hunterian Soc.; Pres., Chiltern Medical Soc., 1958-60; Pres., Brit. Assoc. of Plastic Surgeons, 1962. Member British Assoc. of Surgeons. Hunterian Professor, RCS 1957, 1968. Member, Brit. Acad. of Forensic Sciences; Lecturer, London Univ., 1952; Purkinje Medal, Czechoslovak Acad. of Sciences, 1965. *Publications:* contrib. since 1944 to: Proc. Roy. Soc. Med., Medical Press, West London Medico-Chirurgical Journal, British Journal of Plastic Surgery, BMJ, Medical History 2nd World War, Monograph Plastic Surgery and Physiotherapy, Annals RCS, etc. *Recreation:* gardening. *Address:* 147 Harley Street, W1. *T:* 01-935 4444; Icknield House, Askett, Bucks. *T:* Princes Risborough 6258. *Clubs:* Royal Over-Seas League; Cork and County (Cork).

**REIGATE,** Baron *cr* 1970 (Life Peer), of Outwood, Surrey; **John Kenyon Vaughan-Morgan;** Bt 1960; PC 1961; *b* 2 Feb. 1905; *yr s* of late Sir Kenyon Vaughan-Morgan, DL, OBE, MP and late Lady Vaughan-Morgan; *m* 1940, Emily, *d* of late W. Redmond Cross and of Mrs Cross, New York City; two *d*. *Educ:* Eton; Christ Church, Oxford. Mem. Chelsea Borough Council, 1928; Member of London County Council for Chelsea, 1946-52; Chm. East Fulham Conservative and Unionist Assoc., 1935-38 (Pres. 1945); MP (C) Reigate Div. of Surrey, 1950-70. Parly Sec., Min. of Health, 1957; Minister of State, BoT, 1957-59. Dir, Morgan Crucible Co. Ltd. Chm. Bd of Govs, Westminster Hosp., 1963- (Mem., 1960). Dep. Chm., South Westminster Justices. Mem., Court of Assistants, Merchant Taylors Co. (Master 1970). Served War of 1939-45; Welsh Guards, 1940; GSO2, War Office; GSO1, HQ 21 Army Group (despatches). *Address:* Ashcroft, Outwood, Surrey. *T:* Smallfield 2043; 36 Eaton Square, SW1. *T:* 01-235 6506. *Clubs:* Carlton, Brooks's, Hurlingham.

**REILLY, Sir (D'Arcy) Patrick,** GCMG 1968 (KCMG 1957; CMG 1949); OBE 1942; Chairman: British and French Bank, since 1969; United Bank for Africa, since 1969; Trident Insurance Co., since 1969; *b* 17 March 1909; *s* of late Sir D'Arcy Reilly, Indian Civil Service; *m* 1938, Rachel Mary, *d* of late Brigadier-General Sir Percy Sykes, KCIE, CB, CMG; two *d*. *Educ:* Winchester; New Coll., Oxford. 1st class Hon. Mods, 1930, Lit Hum 1932. Laming Travelling Fellow, Queen's College, 1932; Fellow of All Souls College, 1932-39, 1969-; Diplomatic Service, 1933; Third Secretary, Tehran, 1935-38; Ministry of Economic Warfare, 1939-42; First Secretary, Algiers, 1943; Paris, 1944; Athens, 1945. Counsellor, HM Foreign Service, 1947; Counsellor at Athens, 1947-48; Imperial Defence College, 1949; Assistant Under-Secretary of State, Foreign Office, 1950-53; Minister in Paris, 1953-56; Dep. Under-Sec. of State, Foreign Office, Oct. 1956; Ambassador to the USSR, 1957-60; Dep. Under-Sec. of State, Foreign Office, 1960-64; Official Head of UK Delegation to UN Conference on Trade and Development, 1964; Ambassador to France, 1965-68. Chairman: London Chamber of Commerce Standing Cttee for Common Market countries; London Univ. Management Cttee, British Inst. in Paris; Member: Council, Bedford Coll., London Univ.; Exec. Cttee, INSEAD, Fontainbleau. *Address:* 5 Penywern Road, SW5. *T:* 01-373 8838; Hampden Cottage, Ramsden, Oxon. *T:* Ramsden 348. *Club:* Athenæum.

**REILLY, Noel Marcus Prowse,** CMG 1958; Deputy Head of UK Treasury Delegation, Washington, and Alternate Director for the UK, International Bank for Reconstruction and Development, International Finance Corporation and International Development Association, 1962-65, retired; *b* 31 Dec. 1902; *s* of late Frederick Reilly and late Ellen Prowse; *m* 1st, 1927, Dolores Albra Pratten (marr. diss., 1963); one *s* one *d*; 2nd, 1963, Dorothy Alma Rainsford. *Educ:* University Coll. Sch.; Gonville and Caius College, Cambridge. Schoolmaster, Boston, Massachusetts, USA, 1924; business in New Zealand, 1926, England, 1928; Secretary, Area Cttee for National Fitness for Oxon, Bucks, and Berks, 1938; Press Censor, Ministry of Information, 1939; Principal, HM Treasury, 1946; 1st Cl. Hons Economics, London, 1946; Economic Counsellor, Persian Gulf, 1953-59; Financial Counsellor, HM Embassy, Washington, 1960-65. *Publication:* The Key to Prosperity, 1931. *Recreations:* ski-ing, sailing, canoeing. *Address:* North Sandwich, New Hampshire 03259, USA.

**REILLY, Sir Patrick;** *see* Reilly, Sir D. P.

**REILLY, Sir Paul,** Kt 1967; Director, Council of Industrial Design, since 1960; *b* 29 May 1912; *s* of late Prof. Sir Charles Reilly, formerly Head of Liverpool Sch. of Architecture; *m* 1st, 1939, Pamela Wentworth Foster; one *d*; 2nd, 1952, Annette Stockwell. *Educ:* Winchester; Hertford College, Oxford; London School of Economics. Salesman and Sales Manager, Venesta Ltd, 1934-36; Leader Page Editor and Features Editor, News Chronicle, 1936-40. RAC, 1940; RNVR 1941-45. Editorial Staff, Modern Plastics, New York, 1946; Co-Editor, British Plastics Encyclopædia, 1947; Chief Information Officer, Council of Industrial Design, 1948; Deputy Director, 1954. Member: Council, Royal Society of Arts, 1959-62, 1963; Council, BTA, 1960-70; Council, Royal College of Art, 1963-70; BBC General Advisory Council, 1964-; British Nat. Export Council, 1966-; Design Panel, British Railways Bd, 1966-; British Council Fine Arts Adv. Cttee, 1970-; GLC Historic Buildings Bd, 1967-; Post Office Stamp Adv. Cttee, 1967-, Design Adv. Cttee, 1970-; Governing Body, City of Birmingham Polytechnic, 1970-; Governor: Hammersmith Coll. of Art and Building, 1948-67; Camberwell Sch. of Art and Crafts, 1948-; Central Sch. of Art and Design, 1952-; Hon. Fellow: Society of Industrial Artists, 1959; Royal Coll. of Art, 1965; Royal Inst. of British Architects, 1965; Hon. Assoc. Manchester Coll. of Art, 1963; Hon. Member, Art Workers Guild, 1961; Corresponding Mem., Svenskaslöjdforeningen, 1956. Comdr, Royal Order of Vasa (Sweden), 1961. Bicentenary Medal, RSA, 1963. *Publications:* An Introduction to Regency Architecture (Art and Technics), 1948. *Recreation:* looking at buildings. *Address:* 3 Alexander Place, SW7. *T:* 01-589 4031. *Clubs:* Athenæum, United University.

**REINDORP, Rt. Rev. G. E.;** *see* Guildford, Bishop of.

**REINERS, William Joseph;** Director of Research and Information, Ministry of Public Building and Works, since 1963; *b* 19 May 1923; *s* of late William and Hannah Reiners; *m* 1952, Catharine Anne Palmer; three *s* one *d*. *Educ:* Liverpool Collegiate Sch.; Liverpool Univ. RAE Farnborough, 1944-46; Min. of Works, 1946-50; Head, Building Operations and Economics Div., Building Research Station, 1950-63. *Publications:* various on building operations and economics. *Address:* Valais, Berks Hill, Chorleywood, Herts. *T:* Chorleywood 3293.

**REINHARDT, Max;** Managing Director, Bodley Head Group of Publishers, since 1957; Chairman and Managing Director, Max Reinhardt Ltd and HFL (Publishers) Ltd, since 1948; *b* 30 Nov. 1915; *s* of Ernest Reinhardt and Frieda Reinhardt (*née* Darr); *m* 1st, 1947, Margaret Leighton (marr. diss. 1955), *qv*; 2nd, 1957, Joan, *d* of Carlisle and Dorothy MacDonald, New York City; two *d*. *Educ:* English High Sch. for Boys, Istanbul; Ecole des Hautes Etudes Commerciales, Paris; London School of Economics. Acquired HFL (Publishers) Ltd, 1947; founded Max Reinhardt Ltd, 1948, which bought: The Bodley Head Ltd, 1956; T. Werner Laurie Ltd, 1957; The Nonesuch Library, 1961; Hollis & Carter, 1962; Putnam & Co. and Bowes & Bowes, 1963. Mem. Council: Publishers' Assoc., 1963-69; Royal Academy of Dramatic Art, 1965-. *Recreations:* squash racquets, tennis, swimming, bridge. *Address:* 16 Pelham Crescent, SW7. *T:* 01-589 5527. *Clubs:* Savile, Hurlingham, Royal Automobile.

**REISS, Sir John (Anthony Ewart),** Kt 1967; Chairman of Associated Portland Cement Manufacturers Ltd since 1957; *b* 8 April 1909; *m* 1st, 1938, Marie Ambrosine Phillpotts; one *s* one *d*; 2nd, 1951, Elizabeth Booth-Jones (*née* MacEwan); two *d*. *Educ:* Eton. Cotton, Banking, Insurance, 1928-34. Joined Associated Portland Cement Manufacturers, 1934; Dir, 1946; Managing Director, 1948. BEM 1941. *Recreations:* shooting, cricket. *Address:* Baggrave Hall, Hungarton, Leics. *T:* Hungarton 229. *Club:* Buck's.

**REITH,** family name of **Baron Reith.**

**REITH,** 1st Baron, *cr* 1940, of Stonehaven; **John Charles Walsham Reith,** KT 1969; PC 1940; GCVO 1939; GBE 1934; Kt 1927; CB (Mil) 1945; TD 1947; DCL, Oxford, 1935; LLD, Aberdeen, 1933, Manchester, 1933 and Glasgow, 1951; Hon. Fellow, Worcester College, Oxford, 1962; CEng, FICE; Hon. FRIBA; Hon. MRICS; Hon. MTPI; Hon. FIMunE; Hon. FILA; Member, Queen's Body Guard for Scotland, The Royal Co. of Archers; Lord Rector of the University of Glasgow, 1965-68; Lord High Commissioner, General Assembly of Church of Scotland, 1967, 1968; *b* 1889; 5th *s* of Very Reverend George Reith, DD of Aberdeen and Glasgow, and Adah Mary Weston, London; *m* 1921, Muriel Katharine, *y d* of late John Lynch Odhams; one *s* one *d*. *Educ:* Glasgow Acad.; Gresham's Sch., Holt; Royal Tech. Coll., Glasgow; MSc (Lafayette). Served five years' engineering apprenticeship in Glasgow; London, engineer with S. Pearson & Son, Ltd, 1913; to the Front with 5th SR (Cameronians), 1914; Major RE, 1915 (wounded); America, in charge of contracts for munitions for Great Britain, 1916-17; Admiralty, Department of Civil Engineer-in-Chief, 1918; in charge of liquidation of ordnance and engineering contracts for Ministry of Munitions, 1919; General Manager, Wm Beardmore & Co., Ltd, Coatbridge, 1920; first General Manager, BBC, 1922; Managing Director, 1923; Director-General, 1927-38; Chairman, Imperial Airways, 1938-39, and first Chairman of British Overseas Airways Corporation, 1939-40; Minister of Information, 1940; Minister of Transport, 1940; first Minister of Works, 1940-42, leading to Ministry of Works and Planning; Lieutenant-Commander, RNVR, Coastal Forces, 1942; Extra Naval Assistant to 3rd Sea Lord, 1943; Captain, RNVR, Director of Combined Operations Material Dept, Admiralty, 1943-45. 45,000 miles air tour of Commonwealth and Empire, Chairman: Commonwealth Telecom. Conf., 1945; Commonwealth Telecom. Board, 1946-50; New Towns Cttee, 1946; Hemel Hempstead Development Corp., 1947-50; National Film Finance Corp., 1948-50; Colonial Development Corp., 1950-59; State Building Soc., 1960-64; Vice-Chm., British Oxygen Co. Ltd, 1956-66; Dir, Phœnix Assurance Co. Ltd, 1953-68. MP (Nat) Southampton, 1940. *Publications:* Into the Wind, 1949; Wearing Spurs, 1966. *Heir: s* Hon. Christopher John Reith, MA (Agric) [*b* 1928; *m* 1969, Penelope Margaret Ann, *er d* of late H. R. Morris, Beeston, Notts. *Educ:* Eton; Worcester Coll., Oxford. Royal Navy, 1946-48]. *Clubs:* Athenæum; New (Edinburgh), Western (Glasgow).

**REITH, Douglas,** QC (Scotland) 1957; *b* 29 June 1919; *s* of William Reith and Jessie McAllan; *m* 1949, Elizabeth Archer Stewart; one *s* one *d*. *Educ:* Aberdeen Grammar School; Aberdeen University (MA, LLB). Became Member of Faculty of Advocates in Scotland, 1946. Served in Royal Signals, 1939-46. Standing Junior Counsel in Scotland to Customs and Excise, 1949-51; Advocate-Depute, Crown Office, Scotland, 1953-57; Pres., Pensions Appeal Tribunal (Scotland), 1958-64; Chm., Nat. Health Service Tribunal (Scotland), 1963-65; A Commissioner for the purposes of the National Insurance Acts, 1961-. *Address:* 11 Heriot Row, Edinburgh 3. *T:* 031-556 6966. *Club:* New (Edinburgh).

**REITLINGER, Gerald Roberts,** BLitt; Writer on contemporary history and the history of art; Editor and publisher of Drawing and Design, 1927-29; *b* London, 2 March 1900; 3rd *s* of Albert Reitlinger; *m* 1945; one *d*. *Educ:* Westminster School; Christ Church, Oxford. Studied art, Slade School and Westminster School of Art; exhibited paintings at New English Art Club; London Group, British Artists exhibitions; National Society, etc; directed with Professor D. Talbot Rice, Oxford Univ. Expedition to Hira, Iraq, 1931-32; served RA, 1939-41; lectr to HM Forces, 1942-45. *Publications:* A Tower of Skulls, 1932; South of the Clouds, 1939; The Final Solution, 1953 (rev. edn, 1967); The SS, Alibi of a Nation, 1956; The House built on Sand; Conflicts of German policy in Russia, 1939-45, 1960; The Economics of Taste: The Rise and Fall of Picture Prices, 1961; The Economics of Taste, Part Two; Objets d'Art, 1760-1960, 1963; Part Three: The Art market in the 1960s, 1970; book reviews and articles, Daily Telegraph, Observer, Commentary, Connoisseur, Antiques Year Book, Financial Times, New York Times, etc; numerous archæological monographs in Iraq; Ars Islamica, Royal Central Asian Society Journal, The Burlington Magazine, Ars Orientalis, OCS Bulletin, etc. *Address:* Woodgate House, Beckley, Rye, Sussex. *Club:* Savile.

**RELTON, Rev. Herbert Maurice,** DD; Curate-in-Charge, Sibton, Saxmundham, Suffolk, 1953-58, retired; *b* 15 August 1882; *s* of late Rev.

Frederick Relton, FKC, FRHistS; *m* 1911, Grace Lydia, (*d* 1965), *d* of late John Parkhouse, of Mayfield, Pinner, Middlesex. *Educ:* City of London School; King's Coll., Univ. of London. BD 1907; with Hons, 1910; DD 1916; Deacon, 1907; Priest, 1908; Curate of St John Baptist, Pinner, 1907-10; Lecturer in Dogmatic Theology, King's Coll. for Women, 1911-12; Curate of Christ Church, Brondesbury, 1910-15; S Andrew Undershaft, 1915-17; Vicar of Isleworth, Middlesex, 1917-27; Vicar of All Saints, Ennismore Gardens, 1930-51; Assistant Diocesan Inspector of Church Schools, London Diocese, 1915-19; Lecturer in Dogmatic Theology, KCL, 1918-24; Prof. of Dogmatic Theology, KCL, 1925-48; Hon. Secretary, Board of Studies in Theology, London University, 1923-27; Chairman of the Board, 1934-35; Dean of the Faculty of Theology, 1935; Professor of Biblical and Historical Theology, University of London, 1931-48; Examiner in Theology, Universities of London, Manchester, Durham, etc; Proctor in Convocation for Diocese of London, 1930-36 and for Univ. of London, 1936-50. Fellow of King's College, London, 1922. *Publications:* A Study in Christology, 1916; The Catholic Conception of the Incarnation, 1924; Some Postulates of a Christian Philosophy, 1925; messages from a Troubled Church to a World in Trouble, 1933; Church and State, 1936; Religion and the State, 1937; Cross and Altar; 1947; Studies in Christian Doctrine, 1960; contributor to King's College Lectures on Immortality; contributor to Psychology and the Church; contributor to Confirmation, vol. i, 1926; editor of and contributor to the New Prayer Book, King's College Lectures, 1927; contributor to Dogma, 1929; numerous articles, reviews, etc, on Theological subjects and the Philosophy of Religion. *Recreations:* chess, fishing. *Address:* The Old Vicarage, Bramfield, Halesworth, Suffolk. *T:* Bramfield 210.

**REMEZ, Aharon;** Ambassador of Israel to the Court of St James's 1965-70; *b* 8 May 1919; *m* 1952, Rita (*née* Levy); one *s* three *d*. *Educ:* Herzliah Grammar Sch., Tel Aviv. Volunteered for service with RAF, and served as fighter pilot in Gt Brit. and in European theatre of war; after end of war with British Occupation forces in Germany. Mem., kibbutz Kfar Blum, 1947-. Dir Planning and of Ops and subseq. Chief of Staff, and C-in-C Israel Air Force (rank Brig.-Gen.), 1948-51; Head of Min. of Defence Purchasing Mission, USA, 1951-53; Aviation Adviser to Minister of Def., 1953-54; Mem. Bd of Dirs, Solel Boneh Ltd, and Exec. Dir, Koor Industries Ltd, 1954-59; MP (Israel Lab Party) for Mapai, 1956-57; Admin. Dir, Weizmann Inst. of Science, Rehovot, 1959-60. Dir, Internat. Co-op. Dept, Min. for Foreign Affairs, Jerusalem, 1960; Adviser on Internat. Co-operation to Min. for Foreign Affairs, also Consultant to OECD, 1964-65. Chm., Nat. Council for Civil Aviation, 1960-. *Recreations:* handicrafts, sculpture. *Address:* 8 San Martin Street, The Cottages, Jerusalem, Israel.

**REMNANT,** family name of **Baron Remnant.**

**REMNANT,** 3rd Baron *cr* 1928, of Wenhaston; **James Wogan Remnant,** Bt 1917; *b* 23 October 1930; *s* of 2nd Baron and of Dowager Lady Remnant; *S* father, 1967; *m* 24 June, 1953, Serena Jane Loehnis, *o d* of Sir Clive Loehnis, *qv*; three *s* one *d*. *Educ:* Eton. Director: Touche, Remnant & Co.; Australia and New Zealand Banking Group; National Provident Institution for Mutual Life Assurance; Ultramar Ltd; Union Discount Co. of London (Dep. Chm.); Atlas Electric & General Trust, and other cos. Fellow of the Institute of Chartered Accountants. *Heir: s* Hon. Philip John Remnant, *b* 20 December 1954. *Address:* Bear Place, Hare Hatch, Reading RG10 9XR. *Clubs:* City of London, Bath.

**RENALS, Sir Stanley,** 4th Bt, *cr* 1895; is in the Merchant Navy; *b* 20 May 1923; 2nd *s* of Sir James Herbert Renals, 2nd Bt; *S* brother, Sir Herbert Renals, 3rd Bt, 1961; *m* 1957, Maria Dolores Rodriguez Pinto, *d* of late José Rodriguez Ruiz; one *s*. *Educ:* City of London Freemen's School. *Heir: s* Stanley Michael Renals, *b* 14 January 1958. *Address:* 47 Baden Road, Brighton, Sussex.

**RENAUD, Madeleine, (Mme Jean-Louis Barrault);** Chevalier de la Légion d'Honneur; actress; formed Madeleine Renaud-Jean-Louis Barrault Company, 1947, Co-director and player leading parts; *b* Paris, 21 Feb. 1903; *d* of Prof. Jean Renaud; *m* 1940, Jean-Louis Barrault, *qv*. *Educ:* Lycée Racine; Conservatoire de Paris (Ier Prix de Comédie). Pensionnaire, Comédie Française, 1921-47. Has appeared in classical and modern plays, and in films. Commandeur des Arts et Lettres. *Publications:* novels, short stories, plays. *Address:* 18 Avenue du Président Wilson, Paris 16e.

**RENAULT, Mary** (pseudonym of **Mary Challans**); *b* 4 Sept. 1905; *er d* of late Dr Frank Challans, and of Clementine Mary Newsome Challans (*née* Baxter). *Educ:* Clifton High School, Bristol; St Hugh's Coll. Oxford (MA Oxon). Radcliffe Infirmary, Oxford. Completed nursing training in 1937; returned to nursing, 1939, until end of War. Went to live in South Africa, 1948. FRSL 1959. Nat. Pres., PEN Club of S Africa, 1961. *Publications:* Purposes of Love, 1939; Kind Are Her Answers, 1940; The Friendly Young Ladies, 1944; Return to Night, 1946; North Face, 1948; The Charioteer, 1953; The Last of the Wine, 1956; The King Must Die, 1958; The Bull from the Sea, 1962; The Lion in the Gateway, 1964; The Mask of Apollo, 1966; Fire from Heaven, 1970. *Recreations:* conversation and dogs. *Address:* Delos, Glen Beach, Camps Bay, Cape, South Africa. *T:* 399226.

**RENDALL, Peter Godfrey;** Headmaster, Bembridge School, Isle of Wight, since 1959; *b* 25 April 1909; *s* of Godfrey A. H. Rendall and Mary Whishaw Rendall (*née* Wilson); *m* 1944, Ann McKnight Kauffer; two *s* one *d*. *Educ:* Rugby School; Corpus Christi College, Oxford. Assistant Master: Felsted School, Essex, 1931-34; Upper Canada College, Toronto, 1934-35; Felsted School, Essex, 1935-43. Served War of 1939-45, RAF, 1943-46, Flight-Lieut. Second Master, St Bees School, Cumberland, 1946-48; Headmaster Achimota School, Gold Coast, 1949-54; Assistant Master, Lancing College, 1954-59. Diocesan Lay-Reader. Coronation Medal, 1953. *Recreations:* reading, gardening, carpentry, painting. *Address:* Bembridge School, Isle of Wight. *T:* Bembridge 2733. *Club:* Royal Commonwealth Society.

**RENDALL, Philip Stanley,** MBE 1964; DL; retired as Managing Director of Courtaulds Ltd (1943-61), and as Deputy Chairman (1949-61); *b* 7 July 1895; *s* of late Dr Stanley Rendall and Claire Louise Rendall; *m* 1923, Louise Gwendoline, 2nd *d* of James Calcott; two *d*. *Educ:* Shrewsbury. Served European War, 1914-18, in France. Joined Courtaulds Ltd, 1920; Director, 1937. Chairman, Lustre Fibres Limited, 1946-57; formerly Chairman, British Nylon Spinners Ltd, Chairman, British Celanese Ltd, 1960-61 (Vice-Chm., 1957-60).

High Sheriff of Warwickshire, 1949-50. Commandant, Warwickshire Special Constabulary, retired. DL Co. Warwick, 1967. Chevalier de la Légion d'Honneur, 1957. *Recreations:* golf, tennis. *Address:* 47 Kenilworth Road, Leamington Spa. *T:* Leamington Spa, 183. *Club:* Leamington Tennis Court (Leamington).

**RENDEL, Sir George William,** KCMG, *cr* 1943 (CMG 1932); *b* 1889; *y s* of George Wightwick Rendel, Civil Engineer and Professional Civil Lord of the Admiralty; *m* 1914, Geraldine, OBE 1943 (*d* 1965), *d* of Gerald Beresford FitzGerald; two *s* two *d*. *Educ:* Downside; Queen's College, Oxford (Classical scholar, 1st Class, Mod. Hist. 1911). Entered Diplomatic Service, 1913; served in Berlin, Athens, Rome, Lisbon and Madrid; Head of the Eastern Department, Foreign Office, 1930-38; HM Envoy Extraordinary and Minister Plenipotentiary to Bulgaria, 1938-41; British Minister and (later) Ambassador to the Yugoslav Govt in London, 1941-43; Employed in Foreign Office and UK Representative on European Cttee of UNRRA, 1944-47; attended UNRRA Confs, Atlantic City, Montreal, Geneva, etc; UK Representative for Refugee questions on Econ. and Social Council of UN and on various other confs and UN Cttees in London, New York, Geneva, Lausanne, etc, 1945-47; British Ambassador to Belgium, 1947-50 (also Minister to Luxembourg, 1947-49); Chief United Kingdom Delegate on Austrian Treaty Commission in Vienna, 1947, and for negotiation of Treaty of Brussels, 1948; Montreux Straits Conference, 1936; crossed Arabia from the Persian Gulf to Red Sea (with Lady Rendel), visiting Hasa and Riyadh at the invitation of King Ibn Saud, 1937; negotiated agreement with Italy on Red Sea and Middle East, March 1938; visited the Belgian Congo, officially (with Lady Rendel), returning via East Africa, 1948. Retired on pension, 1950. Re-employed by the Foreign Office as Leader of UK Deleg. to Internat. High-frequency Broadcasting Conf., Rapallo, 1950, and as UK Mem. (and Chm.) of Tripartite Commn on German Debts, 1951-53; Chm. Commission on Constitutional Development in Singapore, 1953-54; UK Mem. of Saar Referendum Commission, 1955; Special Ambassador to Lima and La Paz for inaugurations of Presidents of Peru and Bolivia, 1956. Re-employed by the Foreign Office in connection with the Anglo-Egyptian Financial Agreement, 1959-64. Chm., Singer & Friedlander Ltd, 1957-68. *Publication:* The Sword and the Olive; Recollections of Diplomacy and the Foreign Service, 1913-54, 1957. *Recreations:* travelling, sketching, music. *Address:* 48 Lowndes Square, SW1. *Club:* Travellers'.

**RENDELL, Sir William,** Kt 1967; General Manager, Commonwealth Development Corporation, since 1953; *b* 25 Jan. 1908; *s* of William Reginald Rendell and Hon. Janet Marion Rendell; *m* 1st, 1946, Simone Nicole (*née* Dubois) (marr. diss. 1950); one *s*; 2nd, 1950, Annie Henriette Maria (*née* Thorsen). *Educ:* Winchester; Trinity Coll., Cambridge. FCA. partner, Whinney Murray & Co., 1947-52. *Recreations:* shooting, fishing, sailing. *Address:* 10 Montpelier Place, SW7. *T:* 01-584 8232.

**RENDLESHAM,** 8th Baron, *cr* 1806; **Charles Anthony Hugh Thellusson;** Royal Corps of Signals; *b* 15 March 1915; *s* of Lt-Col Hon. Hugh Edmund Thellusson, DSO (3rd *s* of 5th Baron); *S* uncle, 1943; *m* 1st, 1940, Margaret Elizabeth (who obtained a divorce, 1947; she *m* 1962, Patrick P. C. Barthropp) *d* of Lt-Col Robin Rome, Monk's Hall, Glemsford; one *d*; 2nd, 1947, Clare, *d* of Lt-Col D. H. G. McCririck; one *s* three *d*. *Educ:* Eton. *Heir: s* Hon. Charles William Brooke Thellusson, *b* 10 Jan. 1954. *Address:* 28 Walham Grove, SW6.
*See also Sir William Goring, Bt.*

**RENFREW, Thomas,** CBE 1952 (MBE 1943); Chief Inspector of Constabulary for Scotland, 1965-66; *b* 18 June 1901; *s* of late Thomas Renfrew, and late Hannah Lennox; *m* 1928, Agnes Dunbar Allan (decd); three *d*. *Educ:* Eastbank Academy, Glasgow; Glasgow University (BL). Joined City of Glasgow Police, 1919; transferred to Lanarkshire Constabulary, 1926; Inspector, 1928; Superintendent, 1938; Chief Constable of Lanarkshire, 1945-58, and of Hamilton, 1949-58; Inspector of Constabulary for Scotland, 1958-65. *Address:* 4 Hillpark Gardens, Edinburgh 4. *T:* 031-336 2629.

**RENNELL,** 2nd Baron, *cr* 1933, of Rodd, Herefordshire; **Francis James Rennell Rodd,** KBE 1944; CB 1943; JP; MA (Oxon); *quondam* Visiting Fellow, Nuffield College, Oxford (1947-59); Vice-Lieutenant, Herefordshire; Director, Morgan, Grenfell & Co., and other public companies; *b* 25 Oct. 1895; *e s* of 1st Baron and Lilias (*d* 1951), *d* of J. A. Guthrie, Craigie, Forfar; *S* father, 1941; *m* 1928, Mary Constance, *d* of 1st Baron Bicester; four *d*. *Educ:* Eton; Balliol Coll., Oxford. Served in RFA in France, 1914-15; Intelligence Officer in Italy, 1916; Staff Officer in Libya, Egypt, Sinai, Palestine, and Syria, 1917-18 (despatches, Italian Order of St Maurice and Lazarus); entered Diplomatic Service, 1919; served in Rome, Sofia, where was Chargé d'Affaires, and Foreign Office; resigned, 1924; Stock Exchange, 1926-28; Bank of England, 1929-32; Manager, Bank for International Settlements, 1930-31. Served 1939-44 (despatches, CB, KBE); Major-General, Civil Affairs Administration in Middle East, E Africa, and Italy. Exploration in S Sahara during 1922 and 1927, for which RGS awarded Cuthbert Peake Grant and Founder's Medal, 1929. Mem. Bd, BOAC, 1954-65. President, RGS, 1945-48; Hon. Vice-Pres., RGS; Trustee of London Museum; Mem. Council, Brit. School in Rome; Mem. Council, British Association for Advancement of Science; Conservative. Hon. LLD (Manchester), 1962. *Publications:* People of the Veil; General William Eaton; British Military Administration of African Territories, 1940-45; Valley on the March; and articles in periodicals. *Recreations:* geography and farming. *Heir: b* Hon. Gustaf Guthrie Rennell Rodd, OBE [*b* 13 July 1905; *m* 1st, 1932, Yvonne Mary (marr. diss. 1948), *d* of late Sir Charles Murray Marling, GCMG, CB; one *s* (one *s* decd); 2nd, 1948, Claude Rosemary Calvert (marr. diss. 1966), *d* of Archibald W. D. Dove.]. *Address:* 23 Great Winchester St, EC2; The Rodd, nr Presteigne, Radnorshire. *T:* Presteigne 362. *Club:* Beefsteak.
*See also Baroness Emmet of Amberley.*

**RENNERT, Guenther,** Dr jur; Opera and Theatre Producer; Director, Bavarian State Opera, Munich, since 1967; *b* 1 April 1911; *m* 1956, Elisabeth Rennert (*née* Abegg); one *s* three *d*. *Educ:* Germany. Asst Prod., films, operas and plays, 1933-35; Producer in Frankfurt, 1935-37; Wuppertal, 1937-39; Head Producer: Charlottenburg Opera House, 1942-45, Munich, 1945-46; Dir of Opera and Dir State Opera House, Hamburg, 1946-56; Artistic Counsellor and Head of Production of Glyndebourne Festival Opera, 1959-67. Productions (Opera): Mozart, Wagner, Verdi, Rossini, Britten, Berg, Stravinski; Productions at: Salzburg Festival, 1948-;

Edinburgh Festival, 1952-; Glyndebourne Festival, 1959-; New York Metropolitan Opera; Metropolitan National Company; San Francisco; London (Covent Garden); Hamburg; Stuttgart; Milan (Scala), 1954-; Munich (Staatsoper), 1962-. Prodns (Theatre): Shakespeare, O'Neill, Gogol, Schehade, Giraudoux, Brecht, MacLeish, Frisch, Hauptmann; Prodns in: Vienna (Burg Theater); Berlin (Schillertheater); Stuttgart (Staatstheater). Mem., Akademie der Künste, Berlin, 1961-. Brahms-Medaille, Hamburg, 1956. *Publications:* Bearbeitungen der Opern: Iphigenia in Aulis (Gluck); Der Türke in Italien (Rossini); Die Liebesprobe (Rossini); Jephta (Handel); Verlobung im Kloster (Prokoviev); translations of Puccini. *Address:* 8033 Krailling, Schwalbenweg 11a, Germany. *Club:* Rotary.

**RENNIE, Sir Alfred (Baillie),** Kt 1960; formerly a Federal Justice of the West Indies Federation (1958-62); *b* 18 March 1896; *s* of James Malcolm and Mary Jane Rennie; *m* 1925, Patricia Margaret O'Gorman; one *s* two *d*. *Educ:* Wolmer's School, Kingston, Jamaica; King's College, London. Lieut, British West Indies Regt, 1916-19. Called to the Bar, 1922; practised in Jamaica and Bermuda, 1922-29; Clerk of the Courts, Jamaica, 1929-33; Resident Magistrate, 1933-34; Crown Solicitor, 1934-49; Judge of Supreme Court of Jamaica, 1949-58. *Recreation:* shooting. *Address:* 1 Waterloo Road, Kingston 10, Jamaica.

**RENNIE, Archibald Louden;** Registrar General for Scotland since 1969; *b* 4 June 1924; *s* of John and Isabella Rennie; *m* 1950, Kathleen Harkess; four *s*. *Educ:* Madras Coll.; St Andrews University. Experimental Officer, Mine Design Dept, Admty, 1944-47; Dept of Health for Scotland, 1947-62; Private Sec. to Sec. of State for Scotland, 1962-63; Asst Sec., Scottish Home and Health Dept, 1963-69. *Recreations:* Scottish literature, sailing. *Address:* 38 Blacket Place, Edinburgh 9. *T:* 031-667 1359. *Clubs:* Royal Commonwealth Society; Scottish Arts (Edinburgh).

**RENNIE, Compton Alexander,** CMG 1969; Nuclear Energy Consultant since 1968; Director, Nuclear Power and Reactors Division, International Atomic Energy Agency, Vienna, since 1970. *b* 12 Dec. 1915; *s* of George Malcolm Rennie, Southampton; *m* 1941, Marjorie Dorothy Pearson; no *c*. *Educ:* Sutton Valence Sch., Kent; Sidney Sussex Coll., Cambridge. Radar Officer, TRE, Malvern, 1940-45. Atomic Energy Research Estabt, Harwell, 1945-59: Overseas Liaison Officer, 1955; Dep. Head, Reactor Div., 1957; Head, High Temperature Reactor Div., 1958; Atomic Energy Estabt, Winfrith, Dorset, and chief Exec. of OECD High Temperature Reactor Project (Dragon Project), 1959-68. ford Foundn Atoms for Peace Award, 1969. *Recreations:* golf, sailing, gardening. *Address:* 33 Stowell Crescent, Wareham, Dorset. *T:* Wareham 2671.

**RENNIE, Sir Gilbert (McCall),** GBE 1954; KCMG 1949 (CMG 1941); Kt 1946; MC; MA, Hon. LLD (Glasgow); *b* 24 Sept 1895; *yr s* of late John Rennie; *m* 1929, Jean Marcella Huggins; two *s* one *d*. *Educ:* Stirling High School; Glasgow Univ. Served European War, 1915-19, KOSB, Capt.; Ceylon Civil Service, 1920-37; Financial Sec., Gold Coast, 1937-39; Chief Secretary, Kenya, 1939-47; Governor and C-in-C Northern Rhodesia, 1948-54; High Comr in UK for Fedn of Rhodesia and Nyasaland, 1954-61. Chm., UK Cttee for Freedom from Hunger Campaign, 1965-; Joint Treasurer, Royal Society of Arts, 1965-70. KStJ. *Recreations:* gardening, fishing, golf. *Address:* 7 Beech Hill, Hadley Wood, Barnet, Herts. *Club:* Royal Commonwealth Society.

**RENNIE, John Chalmers;** Town Clerk of Aberdeen, 1946-68; *b* 16 April 1907; *s* of late John Chalmers Rennie, Pharmacist, Wishaw; *m* 1937, Georgina Stoddart, *d* of late Henry Bell, Engineer and Ironfounder, Wishaw; one *s*. *Educ:* University of Glasgow. Town Clerk Depute, Motherwell and Wishaw, 1929-43; Town Clerk Depute, Aberdeen, 1943-46. *Recreation:* motoring. *Address:* 34 Morningfield Road, Aberdeen. *T:* Aberdeen 36904. *Club:* Royal Northern (Aberdeen).

**RENNIE, Sir John (Ogilvy),** KCMG 1967 (CMG 1956); Deputy Under-Secretary of State, Foreign and Commonwealth Office; *b* 13 Jan. 1914; *o s* of late Charles Ogilvy Rennie and Agnes Annette Paton; *m* 1938, Anne-Marie Celine Monica Godat (*d* 1964); one *s*; *m* 1966, Mrs Jennifer Margaret Rycroft; one *s*. *Educ:* Wellington College; Balliol College, Oxford. Kenyon & Eckhardt Inc., New York, 1935-39; Vice-Consul, Baltimore, 1940; British Press Service, New York, 1941; British Information Services, 1942-46; Foreign Office, 1946-49; First Secretary (Commercial) HM Embassy, Washington, 1949-51; First Secretary HM Embassy, Warsaw, 1951-53; Counsellor, Foreign Office, 1953; Head of Information Research Dept, FO, 1953-58; Minister (Commercial), British Embassy: Buenos Aires, 1958-60; Washington, 1960-63; Asst Under Sec. of State, FO, 1964-65; on loan to Civil Service Commission during 1966. *Recreations:* electronics, painting (Exhibitor RA, 1930, 1931; Paris Salon, 1932). *Address:* c/o Foreign and Commonwealth Office, SW1. *Clubs:* Bath, Brooks's.

**RENNIE, Sir John Shaw,** GCMG 1968 (KCMG 1962; CMG 1958); OBE 1955; Deputy Commissioner-General, United Nations Relief and Works Agency for Palestine Refugees, since 1968; *b* 12 Jan. 1917; *s* of late John Shaw Rennie, Saskatoon, Sask, Canada; *m* 1946, Mary Winifred Macalpine Robertson; one *s*. *Educ:* Hillhead High School; Glasgow University; Balliol College, Oxford. Cadet, Tanganyika, 1940; Asst District Officer, 1942; District Officer, 1949; Deputy Colonial Secretary, Mauritius, 1951; British Resident Commr, New Hebrides, 1955-62; Governor and C-in-C of Mauritius, 1962-March 1968, Governor-General, March-Aug. 1968. *Address:* c/o UNRWA, Beirut, Lebanon. *Club:* Royal Commonwealth Society.

**RENNY, Brig. George Douglas,** CBE 1959; DSO 1945; *b* 30 Dec. 1908; *s* of late Lt-Col G. S. Renny and late Mrs E. M. P. Renny; *m* 1937, Mary Helen Louise (*née* Wortham); three *d*. *Educ:* Cheltenham; RMC Sandhurst. Commissioned in Kings Own Scottish Borderers, 1928; served in India, 1930-37, with Regt and as ADC; Camberley Staff College; Brigade Major with 51st Highland Div. in France, 1940 (despatches); Lt-Colonel Gen. Staff, War Office, 1943; landed in Normandy 6 June, 1944, comdg 1st Bn Kings Own Scottish Borderers (wounded, despatches); comd 5/7 Bn Gordon Highlanders, 51st Highland Div., France and Holland; comd 156 West Scottish Bde (52 Lowland Div.) in operations ending at Bremen, 1945; Chief Secretary in British Military Government Land North Rhine/Westphalia, 1946; Brig.-General Staff, Eastern Command, 1949; student Imperial Defence College, 1952, comd 2nd Inf. Brigade (Suez Canal Zone & UK), 1953-56; Deputy Director Personnel Services, War Office, 1957-59; Group Staff Adviser, The Morgan Crucible Co, 1959-69; Consultant, Robert Lee &

Partners, 1970-. *Recreations:* fishing, sailing, genealogy, reading. *Address:* The Old Rectory, Newbourne, East Suffolk. *Club:* Army and Navy.

**RENOIR, Jean;** Chevalier de la Légion d'Honneur; Croix de Guerre; Commandeur de l'Ordre des Arts et Lettres; Film director, producer and writer, since 1924, and Stage, since 1953; *b* Paris, 15 Sept. 1894; *s* of Pierre Auguste Renoir, painter, and Aline (*née* Charigot); *m* 1944, Dido Freire; one *s* (by previous marriage). *Educ:* Sainte-Croix College, Neuilly; The University, Aix-en-Provence. Served War of 1914-18 (Croix de Guerre), Cavalry Officer and Air Force Pilot. Served one semester as Regents' Professor, University of California, Berkeley, USA, 1960. Subsequently concerned with ceramics, Motion pictures, and stage (directed, Shakespeare's Julius Caesar at Arles, 1954; author and dir, Orvet, French adaptation Clifford Odets Le Grand Couteau). Numerous films including: La Chienne; La Bête Humaine; La Grande Illusion (one of 12 best films of all times, Brussels Fair, 1958); La Règle du Jeu; The Southerner; The River; The Golden Coach; French Can-Can; Elena et Les Hommes; Le Testament du Dr Cordelier; Le Déjeuner sur l'Herbe, Le Caporal Epinglé, 1962; Le petit théâtre de Jean Renoir, 1969. Louis Delluc Prize, 1937; NY Critics award, 1941; Golden Lion awards, 1937, 1946, 1951; Golden Laurel Trophy, 1958; Osella d'oro, Venice, 1968; Grand Prix de l'Académie du Cinéma, 1956. Hon. Dr of Fine Arts, Univ. of California, 1963; Fellow American Acad. of Arts and Sciences, 1964; Sociétaire, Soc. des Auteurs et Compositeurs Dramatiques; Mem., Federazione Internazionale dei Cavalieri del Cinema; Hon. Mem. Royal Acad. of Arts. *Publications:* Orvet, 1953; Renoir, My Father, 1962 (Prix Charles Blanc, Académie Française 1963); The Notebooks of Captain Georges, 1966. *Recreation:* Art collector. *Address:* 1273 Leona Drive, Beverly Hills, Calif 90210, USA; 7 Avenue Frochot, Paris IX.

**RENOUF, Vice-Adm. Edward de Faye,** CB 1944; CVO 1931; RN; *b* 1888; *s* of late Edward Binet Renouf, Jersey, CI. *Educ:* HMS Britannia. Joined RN 1903; served European War, 1914-19; Naval Attaché, Buenos Aires, 1930-33; commanded HMS Orion, 1934-36; on Staff of RN War Coll. Greenwich, 1936-38; commanded HMS Sheffield, 1938-40; commanded Cruiser Squadron, 1940-41; retired, 1943. *Address:* Manleys, St Peters, Jersey, CI.

**RENOUVIN, Pierre;** Membre de l'Institut de France, 1946; Grand Croix de la Légion d'honneur; Croix de guerre; Hon. Professor Faculté des Lettres de Paris; Doyen, Faculté des Lettres, 1955-58; *b* 9 Jan. 1893; *s* of Georges Renouvin and Marguerite Dalican; *m* 1918, Marie-Thérèse Gabalda; one *s* two *d*. *Educ:* Lycée Louis le Grand and Sorbonne, Paris. Agrégé d'histoire et de géographie, 1912; L en droit, 1913. Served European War, 1914-18, as Lt Infantry (twice wounded). On staff, Lycée d'Orléans, 1919-20; Docteur ès Lettres, 1921; Lecturer on History of 1914-18 War, Sorbonne, 1922; Professor of Contemporary History, Sorbonne, 1932-65; Professor: Ecole libre des Sciences politiques, 1938; Institut d'Etudes politiques, 1944. Dir, Revue historique, 1940. Pres. Fondation nationale des Sciences politiques, 1959; President de la Commission de publication des documents diplomatiques français (1932-1939); Vice-Pres.: Commission des Archives diplomatiques; Dr *hc* Univs of Rome, Liège, Padua and Cambridge. Corresp. Member: British Acad., 1952; Acad. nac. de la Historia (Buenos-Aires); Membre associé: Académie royale de Belgique, 1961; Accademia nazionale dei Lincei, 1966. *Publications:* Les Assemblées provinciales de 1787, 1921; Les Formes du gouvernement de Guerre 1914, 1925; La Crise européenne et la première guerre mondiale, 1934 (5th edn 1969); La Question d'Extrême-Orient, 1840-1940, 1946; Le XIXe Siècle (I L'Europe des Nationalités et l'éveil de nouveaux mondes; II L'apogée de l'Europe); Les crises du XXe Siècle: la première guerre mondiale; la seconde guerre mondiale (ces volumes forment les tomes V, VI, VII et VIII, de l'Histoire des relations internationales), 1954-58; (jt) Introduction à l'histoire des relations internationales, 1964; L'armistice de Rethondes (Nov. 1918), 1968; articles in Revue d'histoire de la guerre mondiale, Revue historique, etc. *Address:* 2 Boulevard Saint-Germain, Paris 5. *T:* Danton 77.07.

**RENSHAW, Sir (Charles) Stephen (Bine),** 2nd Bt, *cr* 1902; *s* of 1st Bt and Mary Home (*d* 1937), *d* of A. F. Stoddard, Broadfield, Renfrewshire; *b* 9 Dec. 1883; *S* father, 1918; *m* 1st, 1911, Edith Mary (marriage dissolved, 1939), 4th *d* of late Rear-Adm. Sir Ed. Chichester, 9th Bt of Youlston, Devonshire; one *s* two *d*; 2nd, 1939, Mace Caroline, *d* of late Major Wynn-Tetley. *Heir:* *s* Charles Maurice Bine Renshaw [*b* 7 Oct. 1912; *m* Isabel Popkin (marr. diss. 1947); one *s* one *d* (and one *s* decd)]. *Address:* Great Fransham, E Dereham, Norfolk. *T:* Wendling 206.

**RENTON, Rt. Hon. Sir David (Lockhart-Mure),** PC 1962; KBE 1964; TD; QC 1954; MA; BCL; DL; MP (Nat L), 1945-50, (Nat L and C), 1950-68, (C) since 1968, Huntingdonshire; Recorder of Guildford, since 1968; *b* 12 Aug. 1908; *s* of late Dr Maurice Waugh Renton, The Bridge House, Dartford, Kent, and Eszma Olivia, *d* of late Allen Walter Borman, Alexandria; *m* 1947, Claire Cicely, *y d* of late Walter Duncan; three *d*. *Educ:* Stubbington; Oundle; University College, Oxford. BA (Hons Jurisprudence), 1930; BCL, 1931; MA. President, Oxford University Liberal Club, 1930-31. Called to Bar, Lincoln's Inn, 1933; South-Eastern Circuit; elected to General Council of the Bar, 1939; Bencher, Lincoln's Inn, 1962. Commnd RE (TA), 1938; transferred to RA 1940; served throughout War of 1939-45; Capt. 1941; Major, 1943; served in Middle East, 1942-45. Parliamentary Secretary, Min. of Fuel and Power, 1955-57, Ministry of Power, 1957-58; Joint Parliamentary Under-Secretary of State, Home Office, 1958-61; Minister of State, Home Office, 1961-62; Recorder of Rochester, 1963-68; Vice-Chm. (Admin.) and Chm. Finance Cttee, Council of Legal Educn, 1968-70. Mem., Senate of Inns of Court, 1967-69. DL Huntingdonshire, 1962, Huntingdon and Peterborough, 1964. *Recreations:* outdoor sports and games, gardening. *Address:* Moat House, Abbots Ripton, Huntingdon. *T:* Abbots Ripton 227; Westminster Gardens, SW1. *T:* 01-828 5836; 5 King's Bench Walk, Temple, EC4. *T:* 01-353 2882/4. *Clubs:* Carlton, Pratt's.

**RENTON, Brigadier (Hon. Maj.-Gen.) James Malcolm Leslie,** CB 1948; DSO 1941; (Bar 1942) OBE 1927 (MBE 1925); JP; DL; *b* 18 March 1898; *s* of late Major Alexander Leslie Renton; unmarried. *Educ:* Eton Coll.; RMC, Sandhurst. 2nd Lt Rifle Brigade, 1916; severely wounded, 1917; DAAG Iraq Levies, 1922-27; commanded 2nd Batt. Rifle Brigade, 1940-41 (DSO); 7th Motor Brigade Group, 1942 (Bar to DSO); 7th Armoured Division, 1942; Senior Officers' School, 1943-44; Head of the British Military Mission to the Iraq Army and Inspector-General, 1944-48; retired

1948. Iraqi Order of the Rafidain, 3rd Class, 1945, 2nd Class, 1948, JP West Sussex, 1949; DL Sussex, 1956; Dep. Comr for Sussex, St John's Ambulance Bde, 1950, Comr, 1952-54. Mem. Brit. Deleg. to Coronation of King Feisal II of Iraq, 1953. Chm. Council, Anglo-Iraqi Soc., 1954-58. KStJ 1961 (CStJ 1951). *Recreations:* travelling and music. *Address:* Rowfold Grange, Billingshurst, Sussex. *T:* Billingshurst 2067. *Club:* Army and Navy.

**RENWICK,** family name of **Baron Renwick.**

**RENWICK,** 1st Baron *cr* 1964, of Coombe; **Robert Burnham Renwick,** Bt *cr* 1927; KBE 1946; Partner W. Greenwell & Co., 2 Finch Lane, EC, Stockbrokers; Chairman or Director of several companies; Chairman, Institute of Directors; *b* 4 Oct. 1904; *s* of Sir Harry Renwick, 1st Bt, and Frederica Louisa (*d* 1927), *d* of Robert Laing, Stirling; *S* father, 1932; *m* 1st, 1929, Dorothy Mary (marriage dissolved, 1953), *er d* of late Major Harold Parkes, The Dial House, Alveston, Stratford-on-Avon; one *s* three *d*; 2nd, 1953, Mrs John Spencer, *widow* of Major J. O. Spencer, *o d* of late Sir Reginald Clarke, CIE. *Educ:* Eton; Trinity College, Oxford. Controller of Communications, Air Ministry, 1942-45; Controller of Communications Equipment, Min. of Aircraft Production, 1942-45; late Chm. Co. of London Electric Supply Co. and its Group of Companies. *Heir: s* Hon. Harry Andrew Renwick [*b* 10 Oct. 1935; *m* 1965, Sally, *d* of late Capt. K. S. B. Lucking and of Mrs M. P. Stormonth-Darling, Lednathie, Glen Prosen, Angus; two *s*]. *Address:* Herne's Cottage, Windsor Forest, Berks. *T:* Winkfield Row 2832. *Clubs:* White's, Buck's.
*See also Hon. J. F. H. Baring.*

**RENWICK, Sir Eustace Deuchar,** 3rd Bt *cr* 1921; Shipowner, retired; *b* 27 Nov. 1902; *s* of Sir John Renwick, 2nd Bt, and Ethel, *d* of James Deuchar; *S* father, 1946; *m* 1934, Diana Mary, *e d* of Col Bernard Cruddas, DSO; two *s* one *d*. *Educ:* Uppingham. Served War of 1939-45, RAFVR 1940-45, Sqdn-Ldr 1942 (despatches). *Recreations:* golf, hunting. *Heir: s* Richard Eustace Renwick [*b* 13 Jan. 1938; m 1966, Caroline Anne, *er d* of Major Rupert Milburn; two *s*]. *Address:* Whalton, nr Morpeth, Northumberland. *T:* Whalton 215. *Clubs:* Army and Navy, northern Counties (Newcastle).
*See also Sir J. N. Milburn, Bt.*

**RENWICK, George Russell,** MA; Headmaster, Dover College, 1934-54, retired; *b* 7 Aug. 1901; *s* of George Edward Renwick and Helen Isabella Russell; *m* 1927, Isabella Alice Watkins; one *s* three *d*. *Educ:* Charterhouse; New College, Oxford. Assistant Master, Stowe School, 1924-25; Charterhouse, 1926-34; OUAC 1923, 1924; British Olympic Team, 1924. Councillor, Dover Borough Council, 1946-50. *Address:* The Old Parsonage, Sidlesham, nr Chichester. *Club:* (former Commodore) Royal Cinque Ports Yacht (Dover).

**RENWICK, Sir John,** Kt 1968; JP; Senior Partner in Renwick, Blandford, Wilson & Co., Solicitors, Sheffield and Eckington; *b* 16 Nov. 1901; *s* of James David and Mary Beatrice Renwick; *m* 1933, Margaret Rachel, *d* of Alfred Stanley and Rachel Fawcett; one *s* one *d*. *Educ:* King Edward VII School, Sheffield; Sidney Sussex College, Cambridge (MA, LLB). Admitted a Solicitor, 1927, practising, since, at 12 East Parade, Sheffield, and Eckington, Nr Sheffield. Mem. Council, Law Society, 1949- (Pres. 1967-68); Chm., Trustee Savings Banks Inspection Cttee, 1954-; Trustee, Sheffield Savings Bank, 1948-. Hon. LLD Sheffield, 1968. *Recreations:* walking, gardening and carpentry. *Address:* Saint Cross, Ridgeway, Nr Sheffield. *T:* Eckington (Derbyshire) 3114. *Club:* Sheffield (Sheffield).

**RENWICK, William Lindsay;** Regius Professor of Rhetoric and English Literature, University of Edinburgh, 1945-59; now Emeritus Professor; *b* Glasgow, 6 Jan. 1889; *s* of W. K. Renwick, Glasgow; *m* Margaret, *d* of Robert Lang. *Educ:* Glasgow University; Toulouse; the Sorbonne; Merton College, Oxford. MA Glasgow, 1910, and Clark Scholar, 1912; served with the Cameronians (Scottish Rifles), 1914-19; BLitt Oxon, 1920; Lecturer in Glasgow University; Joseph Cowen Professor of English Language and Literature, King's College, Newcastle upon Tyne, in the University of Durham, 1921-45; Visiting Professor, China, 1943-44; DLitt (Glasgow), 1926; D(*hc*), Bordeaux, 1934; FBA 1946; LLD (Glasgow), 1953. *Publications:* Edmund Spenser, An Essay on Renaissance Poetry, 1925; Spenser's Works, 1928; John of Bordeaux, 1936; (with H. Orton) The Beginnings of English Literature, 1939; English Literature 1789-1815, 1963. *Address:* Arthur Lodge, 60 Dalkeith Road, Edinburgh 9. *T:* 031-667 5163.

**REPTON, Suffragan Bishop of,** since 1965, **Rt. Rev. William Warren Hunt,** MA; *b* 22 Jan. 1909; *s* of Harry Hunt, Carlisle; *m* 1939, Mollie, *d* of Edwin Green, Heswall, Cheshire; four *d*. *Educ:* Carlisle Grammar School; Keble College, Oxford; Cuddesdon Theological College, Oxford. Deacon 1932; Priest 1933; Curate: Kendal Parish Church, 1932-35; St Martin-in-the-Fields, London, 1935-40. Chaplain to the Forces, 1940-44. Vicar, St Nicholas, Radford, Coventry, 1944-48; Vicar, Holy Trinity, Leamington Spa, 1948-57, and Rural Dean of Leamington; Vicar and Rural Dean of Croydon, 1957-65. Hon. Canon Canterbury Cathedral, 1957. *Recreations:* golf, vicarage lawn croquet (own rules); travel, reading. *Address:* Underwood, Baslow Road, Bakewell, Derbyshire DE4 1AB. *T:* Bakewell 2339. *Club:* Royal Over-Seas League.

**RESTIEAUX, Rt. Rev. Cyril Edward;** *see* Plymouth, Bishop of, (RC).

**REUTER, Prof. Gerd Edzard Harry,** MA Cantab; Professor of Mathematics, Imperial College of Science and Technology, London, since 1965; *b* 21 Nov. 1921; *s* of Ernst Rudolf Johannes Reuter and Gertrud Charlotte Reuter (*née* Scholz); *m* 1945, Eileen Grace Legard; one *s* three *d*. *Educ:* The Leys School and Trinity College, Cambridge. Mem. of Dept of Mathematics, Univ. of Manchester, 1946-58; Professor of Pure Mathematics, Univ. of Durham, 1959-65. *Publications:* Elementary Differential Equations and Operators, 1958; articles in various mathematical and scientific jls. *Address:* Department of Mathematics, Imperial College of Science and Technology, Exhibition Road, SW7.

**REVANS, Prof. Reginald William,** PhD; MIMinE; Senior Research Fellow, European Association of Management Training Centres, since 1965; *b* 14 May 1907; *s* of Thomas William Revans, Principal Ship Surveyor, Board of Trade; *m* 1st, 1932, Annida Aquist, Gothenburg (marriage dissolved, 1947); three *d*; 2nd, 1955, Norah Mary Merritt, Chelmsford; one *s*. *Educ:* Battersea Grammar School; University Coll., London; Emmanuel Coll., Cambridge. BSc London, PhD Cantab, Commonwealth Fund Fellow, Univ. of Michigan, 1930-32; Research Fellow, Emmanuel Coll., Cambridge, 1932-35; Dep. Chief Education Officer, Essex CC, 1935-45;

Dir of Education, Mining Assoc. of Gt Britain, 1945-47 and NCB, 1947-50; Research on management of coalmines, 1950-55; Prof., Industrial Admin., Univ. of Manchester, 1955-65. Hon. DSc Bath, 1969. *Publications:* Report on Education for Mining Industry, 1945; Education of the Young Worker, 1949; Standards for Morale, 1964; Science and the Manager, 1965; The Theory and Practice of Management, 1965; various in professional magazines upon application of analytical methods to understanding of industrial morale. *Recreations:* British Olympic Team, 1928; holder of Cambridge undergraduate long jump record, 1929-62. *Address:* 53 rue de la Concorde, Brussels 5. *Club:* National Liberal.

**REVELSTOKE,** 4th Baron *cr* 1885; **Rupert Baring;** *b* 8 Feb. 1911; *o s* of 3rd Baron and Maude (*d* 1922), *d* of late Pierre Lorillard; *S* father, 1934; *m* 1934, Flora (who obtained a divorce 1944), 2nd *d* of 1st Baron Hesketh; two *s. Educ:* Eton. 2nd Lt Royal Armoured Corps (TA). *Heir: s* Hon. John Baring, *b* 2 Dec. 1934. *Address:* Lambay Island, Rush, Co. Dublin, Ireland.

**REVERDIN, Prof. Olivier,** DrLitt; Professor of Greek, University of Geneva, since 1958; President, Consultative Assembly of Council of Europe, since 1969 (Member since 1964); Deputy (Liberal) for Geneva, Swiss National Council, since 1955; *b* 15 July 1913; *m* 1936, Renée Chaponnière; two *s* one *d. Educ:* Geneva, Paris and Athens. LicLitt 1935. Foreign Mem., French Sch. of Archaeology, Athens, 1936-38; Attaché Swiss Legation, Service of Foreign Interests, Rome, 1941-43; Privatdocent of Greek, Univ. of Geneva, 1945-57; Parly Redactor, 1945-54; Chief Editor 1954-59, Manager 1954-67, Journal de Genève. Mem. 1963-, Pres. 1968-, Swiss National Research Council; Mem., Swiss Science Council; Pres., Fondation Hardt pour l'étude de l'antiquité classique, Geneva, 1959-. *Publications:* La religion de la cité platonicienne, 1945; La guerre du Sonderbund, 1947; La Crète, berceau de la civilisation occidentale, 1960; Connaissance de la Suisse, 1966. *Address:* 8 rue des Granges, 1204 Geneva, Switzerland. *T:* 022-24-31-26.

**REVINGTON, Air Commodore Arthur Pethick,** CB 1950; CBE 1945 (OBE 1940); retired; *b* 24 June 1901; *s* of late Cdr G. A. Revington, RN; *m* 1946, Joan, *widow* of Cuthbert William Prideaux Selby. *Educ:* Plymouth College; RAF College, Cranwell. Served War of 1939-45 (despatches thrice); AOC No 4 Gp, 1946-47; AOC No 47 Gp, 1948-50; Sen. Air Liaison Officer, United Kingdom Service Liaison Staff, Canada, 1950-53; retired 1954. *Address:* Trescoll, Newton Ferrers, South Devon. *T:* 465.

**REX, Marcus,** CMG 1941; *b* 11 Sept. 1886; *s* of A. B. Rex, Shanghai; *m* 1930, Mary Lilian (*d* 1948), *e d* of Sir Mark Sheldon, KBE; one *d. Educ:* Highgate School; Trinity Coll., Cambridge. Cadet Malayan Civil Service, 1910; Financial Adviser and Treasurer FMS, 1932; Controller of Rubber, Malaya, 1934; Acting Chief Secretary to Government, FMS, 1935; Acting British Resident, Perak, 1936; Financial Secretary FMS, 1937; British Resident, Perak, 1938; retired. *Address:* PO Box 316, Queanbeyan, NSW, australia. *Clubs:* East India and Sports; Union (Sydney).

**REY, Jean;** Member, Commission of the European Economic Community, since 1958 (President, 1967-70); *b* Liège, 15 July 1902; *s* of Arnold Rey, Protestant Pastor. *Educ:* Athénée and Univ. of Liège (Dr of Law). Advocate, Court of Appeal, Liège, 1926. Served War of 1939-45 (Croix de Guerre, Commem. Medal); POW, Germany, 1940-45. Councillor, Liège, 1935-58; Mem. for Liège, Chamber of Deputies, 1939-58; Minister of Reconstruction, 1949-50; Minister of Economic Affairs, 1954-58; Delegate; 3rd Gen. Assembly, UN, Paris, 1948; 1st Assembly, 1949 and 5th Assembly, 1953, Council of Europe; Mem., Commn to study European Problems, 1952. Dir, Philips Electrical Gp 1971-; Pres., Sofina, 1971-. Hon. DCL, Oxon, 1968. Grand Officer, Order of Leopold; Grand Cross, Order of Orange Nassau; Grand Cordon, Order of Lion of Finland; Comdr, Order of Crown of Oak; Grand Cordon, Order of Phœnix (Greece), *Address:* 235 rue de la Loi, 1040 Brussels, Belgium.

**REYES, Narciso G.,** Bintang Mahaputera 1964; Philippine Permanent Representative to the United Nations, since 1970; *b* Manila, 6 Feb. 1914; *m. Educ:* Univ. of Sto Tomas (AB). Mem., English Faculty, Univ. of Sto Tomas, 1935-36; Assoc. Ed., Philippine Commonweal, 1935-41; Nat. Language Faculty, Ateneo de Manila, 1939-41; Assoc. Ed., Manila Post, 1945-47; Assoc. News Ed., Evening News, Manila, 1947-48; Man. Ed., Philippine Newspaper Guild Organ, 1947-48; various advisory and UN posts, 1948-; Dir, Philippine Information Agency, 1954-55; Minister-Counsellor, Bangkok, 1956; Public Relations Dir, SEATO, 1956-58; Minister, later Amb., Burma, 1958-62; Amb. to Indonesia, 1962-67. Mem. various delegns and missions, incl. sessions of UN; Philippine Rep. to UN Commn for Social Devt, 1967- (Vice-Chm., 1967; Chm., 1968); Special UN Rep. on Social Develt, 1968. Outstanding Alumnus, Univ. of Sto Tomas, 1969. *Publications:* essays, poems and short stories. *Address:* 13 East 66th Street, New York, USA.

**REYNARDSON, Lt-Col Henry T. Birch,** CMG 1933; *b* 24 Feb. 1892; *s* of late W. J. Birch Reynardson, Adwell House, Tetsworth; *m* 1st, 1917, Diana Helen (*d* 1962), *d* of late Hon. E. Ponsonby; two *s* two *d*; 2nd, 1965, Frances Straker. *Educ:* Eton; Christ Church, Oxford. Entered Army, Oxford and Bucks Light Infantry, 1913; served in India, 1913-14; Mesopotamia, 1914-15; retired on grounds of ill-health as result of wounds 1927; Secretary to Governor-General of Union of South Africa, 1927-33. High Sheriff of Oxfordshire, 1958. *Address:* Box House, Bampton, Oxon. *Club:* Army and Navy.

**REYNOLDS, Alan Lowe,** CMG 1957; OBE 1951; retired; *b* 19 Aug. 1897; *m* 1925, Hilda Quinn; two *s. Educ:* Milton School, S Rhodesia. S Rhodesian Govt Service, 1915-57; Magistrate in various places; Secretary for Justice and Defence, S Rhodesia, 1948; Secretary for Justice, Internal Affairs and Housing, S Rhodesia, 1953-57. *Recreations:* fishing, golf. *Address:* 288 Cambridge Road, Greendale, Salisbury, Rhodesia. *T:* 44574. *Clubs:* Bulawayo (Bulawayo); Salisbury, Royal Salisbury Golf (Salisbury, Rhodesia).

**REYNOLDS, Alan (Munro);** painter, maker of reliefs, and printmaker; *b* 27 April 1926; *m* 1957, Vona Darby. *Educ:* Woolwich Polytechnic Art School; Royal College of Art (Scholarship and Medal). One man exhibitions: Redfern Gall., London, 1952, 1953, 1954, 1956, 1960, 1962, 1964; Durlacher Gall., New York, 1954, 1959; Leicester Galleries, London, 1958; represented at Carnegie (Pittsburgh) International, USA, 1952, 1955, 1958, 1961; Works shown at Internat. Exhibn, Rome, 1955 (where he was awarded one of the three equal prizes). These works were subsequently shown at the Musée d'Art

Moderne, Paris, and at Brussels. Took part in British Council Exhibition in Oslo and Copenhagen, 1956. Works in: Tate Gallery; Victoria and Albert Museum; Nat. Gall. of S Australia (Adelaide); Nat. Gall. of New Zealand; Nat. Gall. of Victoria (Melbourne); Nat. Gall. of Canada; Museum of Modern Art, New York; Contemporary Art Society; British Council; Felton Bequest; Arts Council of GB; Bristol City Art Gall.; Rothschild Foundation; Wakefield City Art Gall.; Manchester City Art Gall.; The Graves Art Gall., Sheffield; Nottingham Castle Museum; Birmingham City Art Gall.; Fitzwilliam Museum, Cambridge; Museum of Modern Art, São Paulo, Brazil; Leeds Art Gall.; Toledo Art Gall., Ohio, USA; Barnes Foundation, USA; Oriel College, Oxford; Warwick Univ.; Museum and Art Gallery, Brighton; Museum and Art Gallery, Plymouth. One-man exhibitions: Aldeburgh, Suffolk, 1965; Redfern Gallery, 1966, 1970. Council of Industrial Design Award, 1965; Arts Council of Great Britain Purchase Award, 1967. *Relevant Publication:* The Painter, Alan Reynolds, by J. P. Hodin, 1962. *Address:* Briar Cottage, High Street, Cranbrook, Kent.

**REYNOLDS, (Arthur) Graham;** Keeper of the Department of Prints and Drawings since 1961 (of Engraving, Illustration and Design, 1959-61), and of Paintings, Victoria and Albert Museum, since 1959; *b* Highgate, 10 Jan. 1914; *o s* of late Arthur T. Reynolds and Eva Mullins; *m* 1943, Daphne, *d* of late Thomas Dent, Huddersfield. *Educ:* Highgate School; Queens' College, Cambridge. Joined staff of Victoria and Albert Museum, 1937. Seconded to Ministry of Home Security, 1939-45. *Publications:* Twentieth Century Drawings, 1946; Nicholas Hilliard and Isaac Oliver, 1947; Van Gogh, 1947; Nineteenth Century Drawings, 1949; Thomas Bewick, 1949; An Introduction to English Water-Colour Painting, 1950; Gastronomic Pleasures, 1950; Elizabethan and Jacobean Costume, 1951; English Portrait Miniatures, 1952; Painters of the Victorian Scene, 1953; Catalogue of the Constable Collection, Victoria and Albert Museum, 1960; Constable, the Natural Painter, 1965; Victorian Painting, 1966; Turner, 1969. Editor of series English Masters of Black and White. Contributions to Burlington Magazine, etc. *Address:* 14 Airlie Gardens, W8. *T:* 01-727 5449. *Club:* Athenæum.

**REYNOLDS, Barbara,** MA Cantab; BA (Hons), PhD London; writer, lexicographer; Reader in Italian Studies, University of Nottingham, since Oct. 1969; *b* 13 June 1914; *d* of late Alfred Charles Reynolds; *m* 1939, Lewis Thorpe, *qv*; one *s* one *d*. *Educ:* St Paul's Girls' Sch.; UCL. Asst Lectr in Italian, LSE 1937-40. Chief Exec. and Gen. Editor, The Cambridge Italian Dictionary, 1948-; Mem. Coun. Senate, Cambridge Univ., 1961-62. University Lecturer in Italian Literature and Language, Cambridge, 1945-62 (Faculty Assistant Lecturer, 1940-45); Warden of Willoughby Hall, Univ. of Nottingham, 1963-69; Reader in Italian, Univ. of Nottingham, 1966-69. Silver medal for Services to Italian culture (Italian Govt), 1964; Edmund Gardner Prize, 1964. *Publications:* (with K. T. Butler) Tredici Novelle Moderne, 1947; The Linguistic Writings of Alessandro Manzoni: a Textual and Chronological Reconstruction, 1950; The King of Italy and the Corporation of London, 1953; rev. edn with introd., Dante and the Early Astronomers, by M. A. Orr, 1956; The Cambridge Italian Dictionary, Vol. I, Italian-English, 1962; (with Dorothy L. Sayers) Paradise: a translation into English triple rhyme, from the Italian of Dante Alighieri, 1962; (with Lewis Thorpe) Guido Farina, Painter of Verona, 1967; La Vita Nuova (Poems of Youth); trans. of Dante's Vita Nuova, 1969; numerous articles on Italian literature in learned jls. *Recreations:* travel; family life. *Address:* 26 Parkside, Wollaton Vale, Nottingham. *T:* Nottingham 255114. *Club: University Women's.*

**REYNOLDS, Clyde Albert M.;** *see* Marshall-Reynolds.

**REYNOLDS, Sir David James,** 3rd Bt, *cr* 1923; Member of Lloyds Insurance; *b* 26 Jan. 1924; *er s* of Sir John Francis Roskell Reynolds, 2nd Bt, MBE, JP and Milicent (*d* 1931), *d* of late Major James Orr-Ewing and late Lady Margaret Orr-Ewing; *S* father 1956; unmarried. *Educ:* Downside. Active service in Army, 1942-47, Italy, etc; on demobilisation, Captain 15/19 Hussars. *Recreation:* sport. *Heir: half-brother* John Julian Reynolds [*b* 25 Feb. 1942; *m* 1966, Carolyne Anne, *d* of Captain Hector and Lady Jean Christie, of Jervaulx Abbey, Ripon, Yorks]. *Address:* 11 Queen's Gate Terrace, SW7. *T:* 01-584 9914.

**REYNOLDS, Doris Livesey, (Mrs Arthur Holmes),** DSc, FRSE, FGS; Honorary Research Fellow, Bedford College, since 1962; *b* 1 July 1899; *d* of Alfred Reynolds and Louisa Margaret Livesey; *m* 1939, Arthur Holmes, FRS. *Educ:* Palmer's School, Grays, Essex; Bedford College, London University. Assistant in Geology, Queen's Univ., Belfast, 1921-26; Dem. in Geology, Bedford Coll., London Univ., 1927-31; Lectr in Petrology, University Coll., London Univ., 1931-33; Lectr in Petrology, Durham Colls, Durham Univ., 1933-43. Hon. Research Fellow of the University of Edinburgh, 1943-62. Leverhulme Fellowship to investigate the geology of the Slieve Gullion volcano, 1946-48. Lyell Medallist, Geological Soc., London, 1960. *Publications:* Elements of Physical Geology, 1969; on the origin of granite and allied subjects in Quart. Journ. Geol Soc., Proc. Roy. Irish Acad., Roy. Soc. of Edin., Geological Magazine, etc. *Address:* 6 Albany, 20 St John's Avenue, Putney, SW15.

**REYNOLDS, Eric Vincent,** MA; TD 1948; Headmaster of Stowe, 1949-58, retired; *b* 30 April 1904; *o s* of late Arthur John and Lily Reynolds; unmarried. *Educ:* Haileybury College; St John's College, Cambridge. Modern and Mediæval languages Tripos, Parts 1 and 2; Lector in English at University of Leipzig, 1926-27; MA 1930. Assistant Master: Rugby School, 1927-31; Upper Canada College, Toronto, 1931-32; Rugby School, 1932-49 (Housemaster, 1944-49). CO, Rugby School JTC, 1938-44. *Recreations:* ski-ing and mountaineering. *Address:* 48 Lemsford Road, St Albans, Herts. *T:* 53599.

**REYNOLDS, Eva Mary Barbara;** *see* Reynolds, Barbara.

**REYNOLDS, Frank Arrowsmith,** LLB; HM Consul-General, Seville, since 1969; *b* 30 March 1916; *s* of late Sydney Edward Clyde Reynolds and Bessie (*née* Foster); *m* 1938, Joan Marion Lockyer; one *s* two *d*. *Educ:* Addey and Stanhope Sch.; London University. Army, 1941-46 (Lieut, RE). District Officer, Tanganyika, 1950; Commonwealth Office, 1962. *Recreations:* music, sailing. *Address:* c/o Foreign and Commonwealth Office, SW1. *Clubs:* Royal Bombay Yacht; Chichester Yacht; Pineda (Seville).

**REYNOLDS, Graham;** *see* Reynolds, A. G.

**REYNOLDS, Guy Edwin K.;** *see* King-Reynolds.

**REYNOLDS, Major-General Jack Raymond,** OBE 1945; ERD 1948; Director of Movements (Army), Ministry of Defence, since 1968; *b* 10 June 1916; *s* of Walter Reynolds and Evelyn Marion (*née* Burrows); *m* 1940, Joan Howe Taylor; one *s* one *d*. *Educ:* Haberdashers' Aske's. Student Apprentice, AEC Ltd, 1934. Commissioned RASC (SR), 1936. Served War of 1939-45, France, Middle East and Italy (despatches). CRASC 7th Armoured Div., 1955-57; GSO 1 War Office, 1958-60; Col GS; UK Delegn to NATO Standing Group, Washington, DC, 1960-62; DDST, Southern Command, 1962-64; Commandant, RASC Training Centre, 1964-65; Imperial Defence College, 1966; Dep. Quarter-Master-General, BAOR, 1967-68. MInstT 1966. *Recreation:* shooting. *Address:* Inglehurst, Malthouse Lane, Tadley, Hants. *Club:* Army and Navy.

**REYNOLDS, James; Hon. Mr Justice Reynolds;** Judge of the High Court, Eastern Region of Nigeria, 1956; *b* Belfast, May, 1908; *yr s* of late James Reynolds and late Agnes Forde (*née* Cully); *m* 1946, Alexandra Mary Erskine Strain; two *s* two *d*. *Educ:* Belfast Roy. Acad.; Queen's Univ., Belfast. Called to Bar of N Ire., 1931; practised at N Ire Bar, 1931-40. Colonial Legal Service as Crown Counsel in Hong Kong, 1940. Prisoner-of-war in Japanese hands, 1941-45. Returned to Hong Kong, 1946; apptd District Judge, 1953. *Address:* c/o Ministry of Overseas Development, Eland House, Stag Place, SW1.

**REYNOLDS, Paul Kenneth Baillie,** CBE 1957 (OBE 1950); TD 1943; President, Royal Archæological Institute, 1963-66; *b* 28 Feb. 1896; *s* of late Louis Baillie Reynolds, London Stock Exchange, and late Mrs Baillie Reynolds, novelist; *m* 1925, Janetta (*d* 1945), *d* of Sir Louis Stuart, CIE; two *s* one *d*. *Educ:* Winchester College; Hertford College, Oxford (MA). Lieut RFA (TF), 1915-19; served RA (TA), 1927-39; Major RA, 1939-45. Pelham Student, British School at Rome, 1921-23; Asst Master, Winchester, 1924; Lectr in Ancient History, Univ. College of Wales, Aberystwyth, 1924-34; Inspector of Ancient Monuments for England, Ministry of Works, 1934-54; Chief Inspector of Ancient Monuments, Ministry of Works, 1954-61. Has taken part in excavating Roman sites. FSA 1929. *Publications:* The Vigiles of Imperial Rome, 1926; articles on Ancient History and Excavation Reports in Journals of Hellenic and Roman Studies, Archaeologia Cambrensis, etc. *Address:* Fyfers, Drinkstone Green, Bury St Edmund's, Suffolk. *T:* Rattlesden 233. *Club:* Oxford and Cambridge University.

**REYNOLDS, Richard S., Jr;** Chairman: Directors, Reynolds Metals Co., USA; Board and Executive Committee, Robertshaw Controls Co.; Director: British Aluminium Ltd; Reynolds TI Aluminium Ltd; Manufacturers Hanover Trust Co., NYC; Central National Bank, Richmond, Va; *b* Winston-Salem, NC, 27 May 1908; *e s* of R. S. and Louise Parham Reynolds; *m* 1933, Virginia Sargeant; two *s*. *Educ:* Davidson College; Wharton School of Finance, Univ. of Pennsylvania (BS). Became Mem. New York Stock Exchange, 1930, and with two partners, formed banking firm of Reynolds & Co. which he left, 1938, to join Reynolds Metals Co. as asst to the President. He served as treasurer of Reynolds, 1938-44; Vice-Pres. and Treasurer, 1944-48; President, 1948-63. Member: Business Council; National Export Expansion Council; Bd of Trustees, Univ. of Pennsylvania; Bd of Graduate School of Business of Univ. of Virginia; Bd of Univ. of Richmond. Hon. Mem., Amer. Inst. of Architects. *Recreation:* fox hunting (joint master of hounds, Deep Run Hunt Club). *Address:* Reynolds Metals Company, 6601 West Broad Street, Richmond, Va, USA. *T:* Atlantic 2-2311. *Clubs:* Commonwealth, Richmond, Rotunda (Richmond, Va); Country Club of Virginia; Farmington Country Club; Brook, Pinnacle (New York); Metropolitan (Washington and New York).

**REYNOLDS, Major-General Roger Clayton,** CB 1944; OBE 1941; MC 1916; *b* 26 Jan. 1895; *s* of late Lewis William Reynolds and Fanny Matilda Clayton; *m* 1st, 1918, Marjorie Grace McVeagh (*d* 1938); one *s* one *d*; 2nd, 1952, Mrs August Oddleifson, Rochester, New York, USA. *Educ:* Bradfield College; RMA, Woolwich. 1st Commission RA, Aug. 1914; served European War, 1914-18 (MC, 1914 Star); Staff College, Camberley, 1928-29; Staff Captain Delhi Independent Brigade, 1931; DAAG, AHQ, India, 1932-36; GSO 1 War Office, 1939-40; AA Brigade Comd 1941-42; comd 3rd AA Group, Bristol, 1942-44; Comd 1 AA Group London, 1944-47; retired pay, 1948. *Recreations:* Bradfield College 1st XI Soccer, cricket; RMA, 1st XI Soccer; Staff College 1st team hockey, tennis. *Address:* The Old Orchard, Avon, New York State 14414, USA. *Club:* Army and Navy.

**REYNOLDS, Seymour John Romer,** MA, MB, BChir (Cambridge) 1936; MRCS, LRCP, 1935; DMRE 1938; Physician to Radiological Department, Charing Cross Hospital, 1945; Dean of Charing Cross Hospital Medical School, 1962; Consultant Radiologist: Kingston Hospital Group; New Victoria Hospital, Kingston-upon-Thames; *b* 26 April 1911; *s* of late Russell J. Reynolds, CBE, FRCP; *m* 1939, Margaret Stuart McCombie; one *s*. *Educ:* Westminster School; Trinity Coll., Cambridge; Charing Cross Hosp. Med. School. Formerly: House Surgeon, House Physician and Clin. Asst at Charing Cross Hosp.; Univ. Demonstrator in Anatomy, Cambridge Univ., 1937; Radiologist: Victoria Hosp., Kingston-upon-Thames, 1939; Prince of Wales Gen. Hosp., Tottenham, 1939; Highlands Hosp.; Hackney Hosp.; Epsom Hosp. 1943; Queen Mary's Hosp., Roehampton, 1946. *Recreations:* gardening, visiting art galleries. *Address:* Camelot, Renfrew Road, Kingston Hill, Surrey. *T:* 01-942 3808.

**REYNOLDS, William Vaughan;** Principal, St Marylebone Literary Institute, 1965-70, retired. *b* 10 May 1908; *yr s* of late William Reynolds, MBE, editor of The Midland Daily Telegraph; *m* 1932, Gertrude Mabel, *yr d* of late Arthur Charles Flint; four *s*. *Educ:* King Henry VIII School, Coventry; St Edmund Hall, Oxford. First class in Final Hons School of Eng. Lang. and Lit., 1930; BLitt, 1931; MA 1934; Senior Exhibitioner, St Edmund Hall, 1930-31. Assistant Lecturer in English Literature, University of Sheffield, 1931-34; Lecturer, 1934-41. Deputy Regional Officer, Ministry of Information (NE Region), 1941-45; Sec., East and West Ridings Industrial Publicity Cttee, 1943-45. Joined staff of The Birmingham Post as Leader-writer and Editorial Asst, 1945; served in London office, 1949; Editor, 1950-64, retired. Mem. British Cttee, Internat. Press Inst., 1952-64; Pres., Rotary Club of Birmingham, 1962-63; Mem., Church Information Adv. Cttee, 1966-. *Publications:* Selections from Johnson, 1935; articles contributed to The Review of English Studies and to Notes and Queries; literary and dramatic reviews in various periodicals and newspapers. Has broadcast frequently in Gt Britain and US. *Recreations:* motoring, cats, theatre going, and reading. *Address:* Little

East Church Cottage, Cheriton Bishop, Exeter, Devon. *T:* Cheriton Bishop 321. *Club:* Athenæum.

**RHIND, Donald,** CMG 1962; OBE 1947; *b* 26 September 1899; *er s* of late Thomas Rhind, MRCS, LRCP; *m* 1939, Annemarie Eugenia Ludovica von Ferrari und Brunnerfeld; one *s* one *d*. *Educ:* Aldenham School; Bristol University (BSc). Economic Botanist, Burma, 1923-45; Civil Affairs Service, Burma (Lieutenant-Colonel), 1945; Senior Economic Botanist, Burma, 1946-47; Director of Agriculture, Ceylon, 1947-50; Secretary for Agriculture and Forestry Research, West Africa, 1951-53; Secretary for Colonial Agricultural Research, 1953-61; Adviser on Agricultural Research, Department of Technical Co-operation, 1961-64, Min. of Overseas Development, 1964-67; Agricultural Research Coordinator, SEATO, 1968-69. FLS, FIBiol. *Publications:* The Grasses of Burma, 1945; numerous scientific papers on tropical agriculture. *Address:* 1 The Briars, Upper Richmond Road, Putney, SW15. *T:* 01-788 9512.

**RHINE, Professor Joseph Banks,** PhD; Executive Director of Foundation for Research on the Nature of Man, Durham, NC, USA, since 1964; *b* 29 September 1895; *m* 1920, Louisa Ella Weckesser; one *s* three *d*. *Educ:* Ohio Northern; Wooster; Univ. of Chicago. Research, Plant Physiology, Boyce Thompson Inst., 1923-24; Instructor, Plant Physiology, Botany Dept, West Virginia Univ., 1924-26; Duke University: Instructor, Philosophy and Psychology, 1928; Asst Prof., Psychol., 1930; Assoc. Prof., Psychol., 1934, Professor, 1937-50. *Publications:* Extrasensory Perception, 1934; New Frontiers of the Mind, 1937; (co-author) Extrasensory Perception After Sixty Years, 1940; The Reach of the Mind, 1947; New World of the Mind, 1953; (co-author) Parapsychology, Frontier Science of the Mind, 1957; Parapsychology, From Duke to FRNM, 1965; (co-ed) Parapsychology Today, 1968; (co-ed) Progress in Parapsychology, 1970. *Recreations:* music, nature, and family life. *Address:* Box 6847, College Station, Durham, NC 27708, USA.

**RHODES,** family name of **Baron Rhodes.**

**RHODES,** Baron *cr* 1964, of Saddleworth (Life Peer); **Hervey Rhodes,** PC 1969; DFC and Bar; Lord Lieutenant of Lancaster since 1968; *b* 12 August 1895; *s* of John Eastwood and Elizabeth Ann Rhodes; *m* 1925, Ann Bradbury; two *d*. *Educ:* Greenfield, St Mary's Elementary Sch.; Huddersfield Technical College. Woollen worker pre-1914; joined King's Own Royal Lancs, 1914, commissioned, seconded to Flying Corps (wounded, DFC and Bar). Discharged from Hospital, 1921. Commenced business as woollen manufacturer. Served on Local Authority. Chairman of Urban District Council, 1944-45. Chairman, Saddleworth War Charities. Commanded 36th West Riding Bn Home Guard. Contested Royton Division of Lancs, 1945; MP (Lab) Ashton-under-Lyne, 1945-64; PPS, Min. of Pensions, 1948; Parliamentary Secretary, Board of Trade, 1950-51, 1964-67. Freedom of Borough of Ashton-under-Lyne, 1965, and of Saddleworth, Yorks. KStJ 1969. Hon. DTech Bradford, 1966. *Address:* Cribbstones, Delph, near Oldham, Lancs. *T:* Saddleworth 4500.

**RHODES, Rev. Canon Cecil;** Canon Residentiary of St Edmundsbury Cathedral, since Oct. 1964; *b* Preston, Lancs, 5 Oct. 1910; *s* of James Rhodes; *m* 1940, Gladys, *d* of H. B. Farlie; one *s* two *d*. *Educ:* Preston Gram. Sch.; St Peter's Hall, Oxford; Wycliffe Hall, Oxford (MA). Deacon, 1936. Priest, 1937. Curate, St Stephen, Selly Hill, Birmingham, 1936-38; Asst Editor and Youth Sec., The Pathfinder, 1938-40; Jt Editor, Light and Life Publications, 1941-44; Diocesan Chaplain-in-charge, St Mary, Pype Hayes, Birmingham, 1940-44; Vicar: St Luke, Tunbridge Wells, 1944-49; St Augustine, Edgbaston, Birmingham, 1949-64; Birmingham Diocesan Adviser for Stewardship, 1960-64; Hon. Canon of Birmingham, 1961-64. Diocesan Dir of Lay Training, Diocese of St Edmundsbury and Ipswich; Chairman: Diocesan Lay Responsibility Cttee; Diocesan Information Cttee. Founder and Editor, Church News, 1946-; Jt Editor, The Pilgrim, C of E youth magazine, 1949-50; regular contributor to The Birmingham Post, 1950-64. *Recreations:* writing, books, travel. *Address:* Abbey Precincts, Bury St Edmunds, Suffolk. *T:* Bury St Edmunds 3530.

**RHODES, Rev. Clifford Oswald,** MA Oxon; Rector of Somerton, Oxfordshire, since 1958; *b* 12 April 1911; *s* of Rev. Edward Rhodes; *m* 1941, Elizabeth, *e d* of H. R. Bowden; one *s* three *d*. *Educ:* The Grange Grammar Sch., Bradford; St Peter's Coll., Oxford. Journalism, 1934-37; Wycliffe Hall, Oxford, 1937-38; Curate, St Luke's Church, Wythenshawe, Manchester, 1938-40; CF 1940-45; Editor of the Record, 1946-49. Hon. Chaplain, St Bride's, Fleet Street, 1952-; Lectr, St Margaret's, Lothbury, EC2, 1954-. Licence to preach, from Oxford Univ., 1957. Editor of the Church of England Newspaper, 1949-59; Director and Secretary, the Modern Churchmen's Union, 1954-60; Editor of Business, 1960-63; Account Executive, Gilbert McAllister and Partners Ltd, public relations consultants, 1963-65. Editorial Director, Harcourt Kitchin and Partners Ltd, 1964. *Publications:* The New Church in the New Age, 1958; Musical Instruments and the Orchestra, 1968; The Awful Boss's Book, 1968; (ed) Authority in a Changing Society, 1969; contrib. to many newspapers and periodicals and learned jls. *Recreations:* the arts and country life. *Address:* The Rectory, Somerton, Oxfordshire OX5 4NF. *T:* Fritwell 255.

**RHODES, Geoffrey William;** MP (Lab and Co-op) East Newcastle since 1964; *b* 7 Nov. 1928; *s* of Harold and late Alice May Rhodes, Leeds; *m* 1954, Marise Evelyn, *d* of late Prof. H. Victor Wiseman, Exeter; one *s* one *d*. *Educ:* Cockburn High Sch., Leeds; Univ. of Leeds. BA Hons 1952, MA (Local Govt) 1954, Pres. of Union, 1954, Leeds University. Mem., Leeds City Council, 1953-58. Head of Dept of Business Studies, Leigh Technical Coll., Lancs, until election to Parliament. Parliamentary Private Secretary to: Minister of Housing and Local Govt, 1965-66; Leader of House of Commons, 1966-67. Chm., Parly Labour Party Educ. Cttee, 1966-67; Mem., Consultative Cttee, Council of Europe, 1967-. *Recreations:* philately, cricket, reading. *Address:* 33 Southlands, High Heaton, Newcastle upon Tyne.

**RHODES, Brig.-Gen. Sir Godfrey Dean,** Kt, *cr* 1934; CB 1943; CBE 1919; DSO 1917; late RE; Chief Scout for Kenya; *b* Victoria, BC, July 1886; *s* of H. Rhodes, Vancouver, BC; *m* 1915, M. J. Topping; two *s* one *d*. *Educ:* Trinity College School, Port Hope, Canada; RMC, Kingston, Canada. Commission in RE 1907; Lt 1909; Capt. 1914; Major, 1924; retired, 1926; Adjutant to Railway Construction Troops, France, 1914-15; Commanding Railway Construction Coy Peninsula and Salonika, 1915-16; temp. Major, 1916; temp. Lt-Col 1916, Asst Director of Railways,

Salonika; temp Col 1917, Director of Railways, Salonika; Brig.-Gen. 1919; served European War, 1914-19 (despatches thrice, DSO, CBE, Legion of Honour (Officer), Order of Redeemer (Greek), Order of White Eagle (Serbian), Brevet Major); War of 1939-45; Director of Transportation Persia, Oct. 1941; Brig.; Sept. 1942 DQMG (Mov. and Tn) Paiforce; Regional Port Dir, Calcutta, under Govt of India, 1945 (CB, despatches thrice). Chief Engineer and Special Comr of Works, Govt of Kenya, 1948-51; Formerly: General Manager Kenya and Uganda Rlys and Harbours; Chief Rep. Africa Office, Sir Alex. Gibb and Partners, Consulting Engineers. KStJ. Comr SJAB. *Recreations:* general. *Address:* c/o Lloyds Bank, Ltd, 6 Pall Mall, SW1; PO Box 5077, Nairobi, Kenya.

**RHODES, Sir John (Christopher Douglas),** 4th Bt, *cr* 1919; *b* 24 May 1946; *s* of Sir Christopher Rhodes, 3rd Bt, and of Mary Florence, *d* of late Dr Douglas Wardleworth; *S* father, 1964. *Heir: b* Michael Philip James Rhodes, *b* 3 April 1948. *Address:* 86 High Street, Blakeney, Holt, Norfolk. *T:* Cley 260.

**RHODES, John Ivor McKinnon;** Minister (Treasury Adviser), United Kingdom Mission to the United Nations, since 1966; *b* 6 March 1914; *s* of late Joseph Thomas Rhodes and late Hilda (*née* McKinnon); *m* 1939, Eden Annetta (*née* Clark); one *s* one *d*. *Educ:* Leeds Modern School. Exec. Officer, WO, 1933; Financial Adviser's Office, HQ British Forces in Palestine, 1938; Major 1940; Asst Comd Sec., Southern Comd, 1944; Financial Adviser, London District, 1946; Principal 1947, Asst Sec. 1959, HM Treasury. Member: UN Adv. Cttee on Administrative and Budgetary Questions; UN Cttee on Contributions; UN Pension Board. *Recreations:* tennis, badminton, cycling in Central Park. *Address:* 55 East 72nd Street, New York, NY 10021, USA. *T:* 212-RE7-0614; c/o FCO, SW1. *Club:* Royal Commonwealth Society.

**RHODES, Marion,** RE 1953 (ARE 1941); Etcher, Painter in Water Colour and Oils; *b* Huddersfield, Yorks, 1907; *d* of Samuel Rhodes and Mary Jane Mallinson. *Educ:* Greenhead High School, Huddersfield; Huddersfield Art School; Leeds College of Art; The Central School of Arts and Crafts, London. Art Teachers' Certificate (Univ. of Oxford), 1930; teaching posts, 1930-67; pt-time lecturer in Art at Berridge House Training Coll., 1947-55. SGA 1936, Hon. Life Mem., 1969; FRSA 1944; Member, Manchester Acad. of Fine Art, 1955; Paris Salon: Honourable Mention, 1952; Bronze Medal, 1956; Silver Medal 1961; Gold Medal, 1967. Exhibited from 1934 at: Royal Academy, Royal Scottish Academy, The Paris Salon, Walker Art Gallery, Towner Art Gallery, Atkinson Art Gallery, Southport, Brighton, Bradford, Leeds, Manchester and other provincial Art Galleries, also USA and S Africa. Etching of Jordans' Hostel and drawing of The Meeting House purchased by Contemporary Art Soc. and presented to British Museum; other works in the Print Room, British Museum; work also purchased by Bradford Corporation Art Gallery, Brighouse Art Gallery, Stoke-on-Trent Education Committee's Loan Scheme, and South London (Camberwell) Library's Committee. Fellow, Ancient Monuments Soc. Hon. Mem., Tommasso Campanella Acad., Rome (Silver Medal, 1970). *Recreations:* gardening and geology. *Address:* 2 Goodwyn Avenue, Mill Hill, NW7. *T:* 01-959 2280. *Club:* English-Speaking Union.

**RHODES, Peregrine Alexander;** Counsellor, British Embassy, Rome, since 1970; *b* 14 May 1925; *s* of Cyril Edmunds Rhodes and Elizabeth Jocelyn Rhodes; *m* 1st, 1951, Jane Marion Hassell (marr. diss.); two *s* one *d*; 2nd, 1969, Margaret Rosemary Page. *Educ:* Winchester Coll.; New Coll., Oxford. Served with Coldstream Guards, 1944-47. Joined FO, 1950; 2nd Sec., Rangoon, 1953-56; Private Sec. to Minister of State, 1956-59; 1st Sec., Vienna, 1959-62; 1st Sec., Helsinki, 1962-65; FCO, 1965-68, Counsellor 1967; Inst. for Study of Internat. Organisation, Sussex Univ., 1968-69. *Recreations:* photography, reading. *Address:* British Embassy, Rome. *Club:* Travellers'.

**RHODES, Prof. Philip,** FRCS, FRCOG; Professor of Obstetrics and Gynæcology, St Thomas's Hospital Medical School, University of London, since 1964, Dean, since 1968; *b* 2 May 1922; *s* of Sydney Rhodes, Dore, Sheffield; *m* 1946, Mary Elizabeth Worley, Barrowden, Rutland; three *s* two *d*. *Educ:* King Edward VII Sch., Sheffield; Clare Coll., Cambridge; St Thomas's Hospital Medical School. BA(Cantab) 1943, MB, BChir(Cantab) 1946; FRCS 1953; MRCOG 1956; FRCOG 1964. Major RAMC, 1948-50. Medical appointments held in St Thomas' Hosp., Folkestone, Harrogate, Chelsea Hosp. for Women, Queen Charlotte's Hosp., 1946-58; Consultant Obstetric Physician, St Thomas' Hosp., 1958-63; Governor: Dulwich College, 1966; St Thomas' Hosp., 1969-. Mem., SW Metropolitan Regional Hosp. Board, 1967-. *Publications:* Fluid Balance in Obstetrics, 1960; Introduction to Gynæcology and Obstetrics, 1967; Reproductive Physiology for Medical Students, 1969; Woman: A Biological Study, 1969; articles in Jl of Obstetrics and Gynæcology of the British Empire, Lancet, Practitioner. *Recreations:* reading, gardening, photography, anthropology, sociology. *Address:* 37 Alleyn Road, Dulwich, SE21. *T:* 01-670 1342.

**RHODES JAMES, Robert Vidal;** *see* James R. V. R.

**RHYL,** Baron *cr* 1970 (Life Peer), of Holywell, Southampton; **(Evelyn) Nigel (Chetwode) Birch,** PC 1955; OBE 1945; *b* 1906; *s* of late Gen. Sir Noel Birch, GBE, KCB, KCMG, 11 Kensington Gore, SW7; *m* 1950, Hon. Esmé Glyn, *d* of 4th Baron Wolverton. *Educ:* Eton. Partner in Cohen Laming Hoare until May 1939 when retired to study politics. Territorial Army officer before the war. Served War of 1939-45 in KRRC and on Gen. Staff; Lt-Col 1944; served in Great Britain and Italy. MP (C) Flintshire, 1945-50, West Flint, 1950-70; Parly Under-Sec. of State, Air Ministry, 1951-52; Parliamentary Sec., Ministry of Defence, 1952-54; Minister of Works, Oct. 1954-Dec. 1955; Sec. of State for Air, Dec. 1955-17 Jan. 1957; Economic Sec. to the Treasury, 1957-58, resigned. Pres., Johnson Soc., Lichfield, 1966-. *Publication:* The Conservative Party. *Recreations:* reading history; gardening; shooting; fishing. *Address:* 73 Ashley Gardens, SW1; Holywell House, Swanmore, Hants. *Clubs:* Brooks's, Pratt's, White's.

**RHYMES, Rev. Canon Douglas Alfred;** Canon Residentiary and Librarian, Southwark Cathedral, 1962-69, Hon. Canon, since 1969; Vicar of St Giles, Camberwell, since 1968; *b* 26 March 1914; *s* of Peter Alfred and Jessie Rhymes; unmarried. *Educ:* King Edward VI School, Birmingham; Birmingham Univ.; Ripon Hall Theological College, Oxford. BA (2nd Cl. Hons 1st Div.) Philosophy 1939. Asst Curate, Dovercourt, Essex, 1940-43; Chaplain to the Forces, 1943-46; Asst Curate, Romford, Essex (in charge of St George's,

Romford and St Thomas', Noak Hill), 1946-49; Priest-in-charge, Ascension, Chelmsford, 1949-50; Sacrist, Southwark Cathedral, 1950-54; Vicar, All Saints, New Eltham, SE9, 1954-62. Director of Lay Training, Diocese of Southwark. *Publications:* (part author) Crisis Booklets, Christianity and Communism, 1952; Layman's Church, 1963; No New Morality, 1964; Prayer in the Secular City, 1967. *Recreations:* theatre, conversation, country walks, golf. *Address:* The Vicarage, St Giles Centre, Camberwell, SE5. *T:* 01-703 3316.

**RHYS,** family name of **Baron Dynevor.**

**RHYS, Keidrych;** poet and writer; editor (founder) of magazine Wales, 1937-60; *b* Bethlehem, Llandilo, 26 Dec. 1915; *m* 1st, 1939, Lynette Roberts, poet and novelist, of Buenos Aires; one *s* one *d*; 2nd, 1956, Eva Smith; one *s. Educ:* Bethlehem; Llangadog; Llandovery Grammar Sch., etc. Literary and other journalism, London, etc, 1935. Served in Army (London Welsh AA) (1939-45 medals); with Ministry of Information, London, 1943-44; War Correspondent (France, Belgium, Holland, Germany), 1944-45. Public Relations Consultant, various charities and organisations, 1950-54; Welsh columnist and correspondent, The People, 1954-60. London Editor, Poetry London-New York, 1956-60. Vice-President International Musical Festival and Eisteddfod; Executive Committee (writers' group); Chairman Friends of Wales Soc.; Vice-Pres. Carmarthen Arts Club; Carmarthenshire County Drama Cttee and Rural Community Council. *Publications:* The Van Pool and other poems, 1941; Poems from the Forces, 1942; More Poems from the Forces, 1943; Modern Welsh Poetry, 1945; Angry Prayers, 1952; The Expatriates, 1964; Poems; Contributor to: Wales, Times Lit. Supp., New Statesman, anthologies, and to European and American jls. *Recreations:* Welsh National affairs, wine and food, talking to right friends, lecturing, theatre. *Address:* 40 Heath Street, NW3. *T:* 01-794 2970. *Clubs:* Press; Y Wasg.

**RHYS WILLIAMS, Sir Brandon (Meredith),** 2nd Bt, *cr* 1918; MP (C) Kensington South, since March 1968; Consultant, Management Selection Ltd, since 1963; Assistant Director, Spastics Society, 1962-63; lately with Imperial Chemical Industries Ltd; *b* 14 Nov. 1927; *s* of Sir Rhys Rhys Williams, 1st Bt, DSO, QC, and Lady (Juliet) Rhys Williams, DBE (*d* 1964); *S* father, 1955; *m* 1961, Caroline Susan, *e d* of L. A. Foster, Greatham Manor, Pulborough, Sussex; one *s* two *d. Educ:* Eton. Served in Welsh Guards, 1946-48 (Lt). Contested (C) Pontypridd Parly Div., 1959, and Ebbw Vale Div., 1960 and 1964. *Publications:* The New Social Contract, 1967; More Power to the Shareholder?, 1969; Redistributing Income in a Free Society, 1969. *Heir: s* Arthur Gareth Ludovic Rhys Williams, *b* 9 Nov. 1961. *Address:* 32 Rawlings Street, SW3. *T:* 01-584 0636; Miskin Manor, Pontyclun, Glamorgan. *T:* Llantrisant 204. *Clubs:* Brooks's, White's; Cardiff and County (Cardiff).

**RIABOUCHINSKA, Tatiana (Mme Lichine);** Ballerina of Russian Ballet; *b* 23 May 1916; *d* of Michael P. Riabouchinsky, Moscow (Banker), and Tatiana Riabouchinska (*d* 1935), Dancer of Moscow Imperial School of Dance; *m* 1942, David Lichine, *qv.*, one *d. Educ:* Cour Fénelon, Paris. Trained first by her mother; then by Volinine (dancer of the Moscow Imperial Grand Theatre); then by Mathilde Kchesinska. First appeared as child dancer with Balieff's Chauve Souris in London, 1931; joined new Russian Ballet (de-Basil), 1932, and danced with them in nearly all countries of Western Europe, Australia and N and S America. Contribution to books on dancing by: Andre Levinson, Arnold L. Haskell, Irving Deakin, Rayner Heppenstall, Kay Ambrose, Prince Peter Lieven, Cyril W. Beaumont, Cyril Brahms, Adrian Stokes, A. V. Coton, Ninette de Valois, etc. *Address:* 965 Oakmont Drive, Los Angeles 49, California, USA.

**RIALL, Air Cdre Arthur Bookey,** CBE 1956 (OBE 1953); RAF Regiment, retired; General Secretary, National Rifle Association, since 1968; *b* 7 Dec. 1911; *o s* of Major M. B. Riall, OBE, and Mrs S. M. Riall (*née* Lefroy); *m* 1950, Pamela Patricia Hewitt; five *s* one *d. Educ:* Charterhouse; RMC, Sandhurst. Commissioned E Yorks Regt, 1932; served in India with 1st Bn until 1939 when posted as Instr to Small Arms Sch.; Staff Coll., 1941; staff appts until Home posting, 1944; served 2nd Bn NW Europe (wounded, despatches); seconded to RAF in Iraq, for service with Iraq Levies, 1947; transf. RAF Regt, 1948; Chief Instr, RAF Regt Depot, 1951-53; commanded RAF levies, until their disbandment, 1953-55 and RAF Regt Depot, Catterick, 1955-59; Staff appts in UK and Cyprus, 1959-61; Air Cdre, 1963; apptd Dir of Ground Defence, RAF, 1963; retd Dec. 1966, and joined staff of NRA. *Recreations:* hunting (Master, Royal Exodus Hunt, until disbandment in 1955), target rifle shooting, ornithology (Vice-Pres., RAF Ornith. Soc.). *Address:* Long Acre, Aldershot Road, Church Crookham, Hants. *T:* Fleet 5666. *Club:* Naval and Military.

**RIBBANS, Prof. Geoffrey Wilfrid,** MA; Gilmour Professor of Spanish, University of Liverpool, since 1963; Editor, Bulletin of Hispanic Studies, since 1964; *b* 15 April 1927; *o s* of Wilfrid Henry Ribbans and Rose Matilda Burton; *m* 1956, Magdalena Cumming (*née* Willmann), Cologne; one *s* two *d. Educ:* Sir George Monoux Grammar Sch., Walthamstow; King's Coll., Univ. of London. BA Hons Spanish 1st cl., 1948; Univ. of London Postgrad. Studentship; MA 1953. Asst Lectr, Queen's Univ., Belfast, 1951-52; Asst, St Salvator's Coll., Univ. of St Andrews, 1952-53; Univ. of Sheffield: Asst Lectr, 1953-55; Lectr, 1955-61; Sen. Lectr, 1961-63. First Director, Centre for Latin-American Studies, Univ. of Liverpool, 1966-70; Andrew Mellon Vis. Prof., Univ. of Pittsburgh, 1970-71. *Publications:* Catalunya i València vistes pels viatgers anglesos del segle XVIIIè, 1955; Niebla y Soledad: estudios sobre Unamuno y Machado, 1970; numerous articles on Spanish literature in specialised jls. *Recreations:* travel, fine art. *Address:* The Knowle, 18 Pine Walks, Prenton, Birkenhead, Cheshire L42 8NE. *T:* 051-608 3909.

**RICARDO, Sir Harry (Ralph),** Kt 1948; FRS 1929; LLD Birmingham, 1943; consulting engineer; Chairman and Technical Director (1919-64; retired), Ricardo and Company Ltd, Consulting Engineers; *b* London, 26 Jan. 1885; *s* of Halsey Ralph Ricardo, architect and artist, and C. J. *d* of Sir Alexander Rendel; *m* Beatrice Bertha Hale; three *d. Educ:* Rugby School; Trinity College, Cambridge. Joined the staff of Rendel, Palmer and Tritton, consulting engineers, as mechanical engineer, dealing with locomotives, steam plant, and Diesel engines, 1906-15! designed petrol engines for the Tanks and acted as Consulting Engineer to Mechanical Warfare Dept, 1916; Consulting Engineer to the Air Ministry on aero engines, 1918; engaged on research work into and the design of high-speed internal combustion engines; Pres. Institution of Mechanical Engineers, 1944-45; Hon. Fellow, Trinity Coll., Cambrdige, 1968; Hon. DSc, Univ. of Sussex, 1970; Rumford Medal, Royal

Soc., 1944; James Watt Medal, IMechE 1953. *Publications:* The High Speed Internal Combustion Engine, 2 vols, 1st edn 1923, 5th edn 1968; Engines of High Output, 1926; Memories and Machines: the Pattern of my Life, 1968; technical papers. *Recreations:* sailing and gardening. *Address:* Woodside, Graffham, nr Petworth, Sussex. *T:* Graffham 205. *Club:* Athenæum.

**RICE**; *see* Spring Rice, family name of Baron Monteagle of Brandon.

**RICE, David Talbot,** CBE 1968 (MBE 1942); TD; MA, BSc, DLitt, FSA; Hon. RSA; Watson-Gordon Professor of the History of Fine Art, University of Edinburgh, 1934; Lieutenant-Colonel TA (retired); *b* 11 July 1903; *s* of late Henry Charles Talbot Rice and late Cecil Mary Lloyd; *m* 1927, Tamara Abelson; one *s* two *d*. *Educ:* Eton; Christ Church, Oxford. Has travelled extensively in the Near East, principally to study Byzantine and Islamic art and archæology; excavated in Constantinople, 1927-32, and 1952-54; various expeditions to Cyprus, Asia Minor, Iraq and Iran; helped with the Persian Exhibition, London, 1931; organised Byzantine Exhibition in Edinburgh and London, 1958. Lectr on Byzantine and Near Eastern art at the Courtauld Institute, London, 1932-38. Corresponding Member German Archæological Institute. Member of ITA, 1958-63; Member of Arts Council, 1963-68, and Reviewing Cttee, 1967. *Publications:* Byzantine Glazed Pottery, 1930; Byzantine Art, 1935; (with R. Byron) The Birth of Western Painting, 1930; edited Russian Art, 1935; (with Gabriel Millet) Byzantine Painting at Trebizond, 1936; The Icons of Cyprus, 1937; The Background of Art, 1939; Byzantine Painting, 1948; English Art 871-1100, 1952; Teach Yourself to Study Art, 1955; The Beginnings of Christian Art, 1957; Second Report on Walker Trust excavations, Constantinople, 1958; The Art of Byzantium, 1959; Art of the Byzantine Era, 1963; Islamic Art, 1965; The Church of Hagia Sophia, Trebizond, 1968; numerous articles in periodicals. *Recreations:* travel, country life. *Address:* 20 Nelson Street, Edinburgh. *T:* 031-556 7100; The Pigeon House, Foss Bridge, Glos. *T:* Fossebridge 230. *Clubs:* United University; Edinburgh Arts.

**RICE, George Ritchie,** CMG 1947; OBE 1927; *b* 31 July 1881; *s* of late John Norman Rice; *m* 1911, Elvina, *d* of late Charles Moore, Messing, Essex; one *d*; *m* 1956, Helen Woodman, Bexhill. *Educ:* Wilson's School; King's College, London. Civil Service; War Office, 1899; trans. to Army Accounts Dept, 1905; Chief Accountant, 1926; Financial Adviser, GOC China, 1927-29; GOC Egypt, 1934-35; GOC Palestine, 1936; joined Ministry of Supply, 1939; Director of Clothing and Textiles, 1939-43; Dep. Director-Gen. Equipment and Stores, 1943-45; Director-Gen. Disposals Mission, Middle East, 1945-46; Ministry of Supply, Special Representative for S Africa, 1946-47; Ministry of Supply, Director of Sales, Hamburg, 1947-50; retired from Civil Service, 1950. *Address:* 16 Westville Road, Bexhill-on-Sea. *T:* 489. *Club:* National.

**RICE, Roderick Alexander,** FACCA; Executive Director, Cable & Wireless Ltd, since 1965; *b* 7 April 1922; *s* of Samuel Richard Rice and Katrine Alice Rice; *m* 1965, Monica McClean; three *s*. *Educ:* Brockley County Grammar Sch. Cable & Wireless Ltd: Asst Chief Accountant, 1959; Dep. Chief Accountant, 1961; Chief Accountant, 1962; Executive Director, 1965. Jordan Star of Independence, 1965. *Recreations:* bowls, cricket, gardening. *Address:* 10 Beverley Close, Camberley, Surrey. *T:* Camberley 26731. *Clubs:* Royal Commonwealth Institute; (Chairman) Exiles (Richmond).

**RICE, Wilfred Eric,** CBE 1948 (OBE 1942); Chairman and life governing director, Rice & Son Ltd, building contractors; *b* 25 May 1898; *s* of late Sir Frederick Gill Rice, one-time MP for Harwich, Essex; *m* 1923, Vera Lillian Lampard, MBE, 1944, *d* of late W. B. Lampard. *Educ:* Dulwich College. Served European War, 1914-18, Lieut 3rd London Regt (severely wounded). Entered family business of Rice & Son Ltd, 1919. Past President: London Master Builders Assoc., 1942-43; London Rotary Club, 1944-45. Chairman: Hotel and Catering Trades Advisory Cttee (Min. of Labour), 1947-60; Disabled Persons Advisory Cttee, Brixton, 1948-59; Local Employment Cttee, Brixton, 1935-47; West London Road Safety Cttee, 1946-62; Deputy Chm. Westminster Bench, 1957-67. JP London since 1943. Member Conscientious Objectors Tribunal, 1941-44. Master, worshipful Company of Innholders; Liveryman, Worshipful Company of Paviors. Mayor of the City of Westminster, 1950-51. Comdr Royal Order of Dannebrog (Denmark); Officer of Order of Orange Nassau (Holland), 1950. *Address:* 3 Buckingham Gate, SW1. *T:* 01-834 2831; 10 The Beach, Walmer, Kent. *T:* Deal 5516.

**RICE-JONES, His Honour Benjamin Rowland,** BA, LLB Hons Cambridge; retired as County Court Judge, Circuit No 56 (1952-60); *b* 19 June 1888; *s* of J. E. and E. M. Rice-Jones; *m* 1916, Nancy (*d* 1966), *d* of H. Shelmerdine; one *d*. *Educ:* Temple Grove Sch.; Clifton Coll.; Christ's College, Cambridge. Called to Bar, Inner Temple, 1912 (Certificate of Honour); joined Northern Circuit. Assistant Judge at the Liverpool Court of Passage; Judge, Circuit No. 12, 1945-52. Served in HM Forces, 1914-19, Inns of Court OTC, 2/2 Lancs Battery RGA, TF, 1/1 West Riding Battery RGA TF (wounded at Ypres). *Address:* Kinross, West Hill Lane, Budleigh Salterton, Devon. *T:* 3214.

**RICE-OXLEY, Douglas George,** MC 1918; TD 1924; MB; BS(London); MRCS; LRCP (1909); Surgeon in Ordinary to late Princess Beatrice; *b* 1885; 2nd *s* of late Sir Alfred James Rice-Oxley, CBE, MD; *m* 1916, Estelle Mortimer, *d* of late Mortimer Miller and Mrs Arthur Sidgwick; two *s*. *Educ:* Dulwich College; London Hospital. Lt-Col RAMC, TA; served European War, 1914-19, 56th Div. BEF, 1916-19 (despatches, MC, Allied, Victory and Territorial War Medals); re-employed, 1939-45; Officer i/c Medical Div. 7 General Hospital, BEF, 1939-40 (1939-43 Star); Consulting Physician, Princess Louise Kensington Hospital for Children; Hon. Medical Adviser Coal Owners' Benevolent Assoc.; Ex-Pres. West London Medico-Chirurgical Society; Vice-Pres. Chelsea Clinical Society; Hon. Medical Secretary Royal British Nurses Association; late House Physician, House Surgeon, Resident Anæsthetist, and Senior Clinical Assistant London Hospital; King's Jubilee Medal, 1935; Coronation Medal, 1937. *Publications:* contributions to various medical papers. *Recreations:* gardening, bridge. *Address:* 16 Fonnereau Road, Ipswich. *T:* Ipswich 52354.

**RICH, Sir Almeric (Frederic Conness),** 6th Bt, *cr* 1791; *b* 9 Feb. 1897; *o s* of Sir Almeric E. F. Rich, 5th Bt, and Louise (*d* 1932), *d* of Hon. John Conness, Mattapan, Mass, USA; *S* father 1948. Lt RGA, 1914-19. HM Borstal Service, 1932-61. *Clubs:* Royal Societies; Phyllis Court (Henley-on-Thames).

**RICH, Prof. Edwin Ernest,** MA; LittD; Vere Harmsworth Professor of Naval and Imperial History, Cambridge, 1951-70; Master of St Catharine's College, Cambridge, since 1957 (Fellow since 1930); Hon. Fellow: Trumbull College, Yale; Selwyn College, Cambridge; Worcester College, Oxford; *b* 4 August 1904; *s* of George Edwin and Rose Rich, Brislington, Bristol; *m* 1934, Adele, *d* of Laurence Blades; one *d*. *Educ:* Colston's School, Bristol; Selwyn College, Cambridge. *Publications:* Staple Courts of Bristol, 1931; Ordinances of the Merchants of the Staple, 1935; The Hudson's Bay Company, 1670-1870, 1958-59; Gen. Ed. Hudson's Bay Record Soc., 1937-60; Montreal and the Fur Trade, 1966; The Fur Trade and the Northwest, 1967. *Recreations:* caravanning, ski-bobbing, golf. *Address:* St Catharine's College, Cambridge. *T:* 59445. *Clubs:* Leander, Royal Commonwealth Society.

**RICH, Maj.-Gen. Henry Hampton,** CB 1943; Indian Army, retired; *b* 30 March 1891; *s* of late Col H. H. Rich, RA; *m* 1st, 1925, Joyce Clelie Campbell Elliott (*d* 1968); one *s* one *d*; 2nd, 1969, Margaretta, widow of Lt-Col A. G. Shea. Educ: Aldenham School; Royal Military College, Sandhurst. 2nd Lieutenant 1911; joined 120th Rajputana Infantry, 1912; European War, 1914-18 (Siege of Kut-al-Amara); North-West Frontier of India; Staff College, Camberley, 1924-25; Major, 2/6th Rajputana Rifles, 1926; Instructor Staff College, Quetta, 1931-34; commanded 1st Bn Burma Rifles, DSD Army HQ India, 1937-39; commanded Nowshera Brigade, 1940-41; 14th Indian Div., 1941-42; Assam District, 1942; re-constituted Burma Army, 1943-44; retired, 1944. Maj.-Gen. 1942. Serving Brother, Order of St John of Jerusalem. *Address:* Flat 6, 10 Elm Park Gardens, SW10. *T:* 01-352 3783.

**RICH, Jacob Morris,** MA, LLB; Secretary South African Jewish Board of Deputies; Associate Secretary, Co-ordinating Board of Jewish Organisations for Consultation with Economic and Social Council of UN; *b* Longton, Stoke-on-Trent, 4 March 1897; *m* 1940, Sylvia Linken; two *d*. *Educ:* Hanley High School; Fitzwilliam Hall, Cambridge. Served in Palestine with Jewish Battalions of the Royal Fusiliers during European War; Secretary to the Board of Deputies of British Jews, 1926-31; Secretary of the Joint Foreign Committee of the Board of Deputies of British Jews and the Anglo-Jewish Association, 1930-31; Hon. Secretary Jewish Historical Society of England, 1924-31; Editor, The Jewish Chronicle, 1931-36; Member, Royal Institute of International Affairs. *Address:* 17 Campbell Rd, Parktown West, Johannesburg, S Africa.

**RICH, John Rowland;** Counsellor and Head of Chancery, British Embassy, Prague, since 1969; *b* 29 June 1928; *s* of Rowland William Rich, *qv*; *m* 1956, Rosemary Ann, *yr d* of Bertram Evan Williams, Ferndown, Dorset; two *s* one *d*. *Educ:* Sedbergh; Clare Coll., Cambridge (Foundn Exhibnr 1948). BA 1949, MA 1954. HM Forces, 1949-51; FO, 1951-53; 3rd, later 2nd Sec., Addis Ababa, 1953-56; 2nd, later 1st Sec., Stockholm, 1956-59; FO, 1959-63; 1st Sec. (Economic) and Head of Chancery, Bahrain (Political Residency), 1963-66; FCO, 1966-69. *Recreations:* motoring, walking, gardening, tennis. *Address:* c/o Foreign and Commonwealth Office (Prague), SW1; 23 Embercourt Road, Thames Ditton, Surrey. *T:* 01-398 1205. *Club:* Travellers'.

**RICH, Rowland William;** Principal, City of Leeds Training College, 1933-63; *b* 1901; *s* of William Henry Rich of Weston-super-Mare; *m* 1926, Phyllis Mary, *e d* of Charles Linstead Chambers of Southgate; one *s* one *d*. *Educ:* Brighton Grammar School; University College, London; London Day Training College, BA (Hons English), 1921, Teachers' Diploma, 1922, MA (Education), 1925; PhD 1934; English master and housemaster, Newport (Essex) Grammar School, 1922-25; Lecturer in Education, University of Durham (Durham Division), 1925-30; Professor of Education, University College, Hull, 1930-33; Tutor to extra-mural tutorial classes (WEA) in English Literature, Social History and Psychology; Vice-Chairman, Association of Tutors in Adult Education, 1931-33; President Training College Association, 1938; Chairman, Association of Teachers in Colleges and Departments of Education, 1946; Member National Advisory Council on Training and Supply of Teachers, 1950-56. *Publications:* The Training of Teachers in the Nineteenth Century, 1933; The Teacher in a Planned Society, 1949; contributor to Adult Education in Practice, 1934, Britain Today, 1943, Education in Britain, 1944. *Recreations:* gardening, walking. *Address:* 65 Cheriton Road, Winchester, Hants. *T:* Winchester 3654.
*See also J. R. Rich.*

**RICHARD, Ivor Seward;** MP (Lab) Barons Court since 1964; Barrister-at-Law; *b* 30 May 1932; *s* of Seward Thomas Richard, mining and electrical engineer, and Isabella Irene Richard; *m* 1962, Alison Mary Imrie; one *s* one *d* (and one *s* by former marriage). *Educ:* St Michael's Sch., Bryn, Llanelly; Cheltenham Coll.; Pembroke Coll. (Wightwick Scholar), Oxford. BA Oxon (Jurisprudence) 1953; called to Bar, 1955. Practised in chambers, London, 1955-. Parly Candidate, S Kensington, 1959. Delegate: Assembly, Council of Europe, 1965-68; Western European Union, 1965-68; PPS, Sec. of State for Defence, 1966-69; Parly Under-Sec. (Army), Min. of Defence, 1969-70. Member: Fabian Society; Society of Labour Lawyers; Inst. of Strategic Studies; Royal Inst. of Internat. Affairs. Governor, Atlantic Inst. *Publications:* Articles in various political jls. *Recreations:* playing Bach, watching football matches (Chelsea), talking. *Address:* 47 Burntwood Grange Road, SW18. *T:* 01-870 1473.

**RICHARDS,** family name of **Baron Milverton.**

**RICHARDS, Audrey Isabel,** CBE 1955; FBA 1967; Hon. Fellow, Newnham College, Cambridge (Fellow, 1956); Smuts Reader in Anthropology, Cambridge University, 1961-67; *b* 1899. *Educ:* Downe House Sch.; Newnham Coll., Cambridge (MA); PhD (Lond.). Field work: in Northern Rhodesia, 1930-31, 1933-34, 1957; in Northern Transvaal, 1939-40; in Uganda, 1950-55. Lecturer in Social Anthropology, London School of Economics, 1931-33; 1935-37; Reader in Social Anthropology, London Univ. 1946-50; Director, East African Institute of Social Research, Makerere College, Kampala, Uganda, 1950-56; Cambridge University, 1956-67. Member: Colonial Res. Cttee, 1944-47; Colonial Social Science Res. Council, 1944-50 and 1956-62; Committee for scientific research in Africa South of Sahara, 1954-56. President: Royal Anthropological Institute, 1959-61; African Studies Assoc., 1964-65. *Publications:* Hunger and Work in a Savage Tribe, 1932; Land, Labour and Diet in N Rhodesia, 1939; (ed) Economic Development and Tribal Change, 1954; Chisungu, a study of girls' initiation ceremonies in N Rhodesia, 1956; (ed) East African Chiefs, 1960; papers in Africa, African Studies and African Affairs. *Recreations:* walking, travel. *Address:* Crawley Cottage, Elmdon, Saffron Walden, Essex. *Club:* Royal Commonwealth Society.

**RICHARDS, Ceri Giraldus,** CBE 1960; painter; Member: London Group, 1937; Surrealist Group, 1937; Objective Abstraction Group, Zwemmer's, 1934; *b* Swansea, 6 June 1903. *Educ:* County School, Gowerton, Swansea; Swansea School of Art; Royal College of Art, S Kensington. Oil paintings acquired by the Tate Gallery and Public Galleries in many parts of the world. Exhibits in Marlborough New London Gallery; also in many Galleries abroad; was one of five British artists exhibited at San Paulo II Bienal, 1953-54; exhibited at Venice Biennale, 1962. A Trustee of the Tate Gallery, 1958-65. *Address:* 12 Edith Grove, Chelsea, SW10.

**RICHARDS, Charles Anthony Langdon,** CMG 1958; *b* 18 April 1911; *s* of T. L. Richards, Bristol, Musician; *m* 1937, Mary Edith Warren-Codrington; two *s*. *Educ:* Clifton Coll.; Brasenose Coll., Oxford. Appointed Colonial CS, Uganda, 1934; Major, 7th King's African Rifles, 1939-41: duties in Mauritius, 1941-46; District Officer, Uganda, 1946-50; Commissioner for Social Development, Tanganyika, 1950-53; Commissioner for Community Development, Uganda, 1953-54; Resident, Buganda, Oct. 1954-60; Minister of Local Government, Uganda, 1960-61. *Recreation:* gardening. *Address:* The Wall House, Oak Drive, Highworth, Wilts.

**RICHARDS, Brig. Collen Edward Melville,** CBE 1944; DSO, MC; late East Lancashire Regiment; Commander Gold Coast Regiment, 1939; *m* 1927, Violet Abigail (*d* 1967), *d* of William Briggs, Stoke Bishop, Bristol. Served European War, 1914-18 (wounded, despatches thrice, DSO, MC); Middle East, 1941 (Bar to DSO); retired pay, 1946; BSc (Hons) London. *Address:* Applecot, Budleigh Salterton, S Devon.

**RICHARDS, Rev. Canon Daniel;** Vicar of Llangynwyd with Maesteg, 1931-66, of Grouped Parish of Troedyrhiw Garth, Maesteg, 1950-60; Rural Dean of Margam, 1941-66; Residentiary Canon of Llandaff Cathedral since 1949; Precentor of Llandaff Cathedral, 1961-67; *b* 13 February 1892; *s* of John and Elizabeth Richards; *m* 1919, Hilda Roberts; one *s* (and one *s* killed 1944). *Educ:* St David's College, Lampeter, Cards. LD 1915, Mathews Scholar, 1928-29, BA and BD 1929; Curate of St Mary's Church, Court Henry, Carms, 1915-18; Curate of St Mary's Church, Burry Port, Carms, 1918-24; Rector of Llangeitho, Cards, 1924-31; SPCK Hon. Group Secretary for Dioceses of St David's, Swansea and Brecon, Llandaff and Monmouth, 1966-. Fellow of Philosophical Society of England, 1942. *Address:* Llandre, 26 Brynteg Avenue, Bridgend, Glamorgan. *T:* Bridgend 5117.

**RICHARDS, Denis Edward;** First Secretary (Press), UK Negotiating Delegation, Brussels, since 1970; *b* 25 May 1923; *m* 1947, Nancy Beryl Brown; two *d*. *Educ:* Wilson's Grammar Sch., London; St Peter's Coll., Oxford. Lieut RNVR, 1941-46; Colonial Service (HMOCS), 1948-60: District Admin. and Min. of Finance, Ghana (Gold Coast); HM Diplomatic Service, 1960-: CRO, 1960; Karachi, 1961-63; FO (News Dept), 1964-68; Brussels (NATO), 1969; Brussels (UK Negotiating Delegn), 1970. *Recreations:* music, amateur dramatics. *Address:* 32 Avenue Brugmann, 1060 Brussels, Belgium. *T:* 44 17 86; 20 Meadow Hill, Purley, Surrey. *T:* 01-660 8306.

**RICHARDS, Denis George;** author; *b* 10 Sept. 1910; *s* of late George Richards and Frances Amelia Gosland; *m* 1940, Barbara, *d* of J. H. Smethurst, Heaton, Bolton; four *d*. *Educ:* Owen's Sch.; Trinity Hall, Cambridge (Scholar). BA 1931 (1st Cl. in both Parts of Historical Tripos); MA 1935; Asst Master, Manchester Grammar School, 1931-39; Senior History and English Master, Bradfield Coll., 1939-41; Narrator in Air Ministry Historical Branch, writing confidential studies on various aspects of the air war, 1942-43; Sen. Narrator, 1943-47; Hon. Sqdn Ldr RAFVR, 1943-47; engaged in writing, under Air Min. auspices, an official History of the Royal Air Force in the Second World War, 1947-49; was established in Admin. Civil Service, Principal, Department of Permanent Under Secretary of State for Air, 1949-50; Principal, Morley College, 1950-65; Longman's Fellow in Univ. of Sussex, 1965-68. *Publications:* An Illustrated History of Modern Europe, 1938; Modern Europe (1919-39 section for revised edn of work by Sydney Herbert), 1940; (with J. W. Hunt) An Illustrated History of Modern Britain, 1950; (with late Hilary St G. Saunders) Royal Air Force 1939-45—an officially commissioned history in 3 volumes, 1953-54 (awarded C. P. Robertson Memorial Trophy, 1954); (with J. Evan Cruikshank) The Modern Age, 1955; Britain under the Tudors and Stuarts, 1958; Offspring of the Vic: a History of Morley College, 1958; (with Anthony Quick) Britain 1714-1851, 1961; (with J. A. Bolton) Britain and the Ancient World, 1963; (with Anthony Quick) Britain, 1851-1945, 1967; (with Anthony Quick) Twentieth Century Britain, 1968. *Recreations:* music, pictures, the open air, travel in the more civilized parts of Europe, the lighter tasks in the garden. *Address:* 16 Broadlands Road, N6. *T:* 01-340 5259. *Clubs:* Arts; PEN.

**RICHARDS, Prof. Dickinson W.,** MD; Professor of Medicine, Columbia University, New York, 1947-61; Emeritus, 1961; *b* 30 Oct. 1895; *s* of Dickinson W. Richards and Sally Richards (*née* Lambert); *m* 1931, Constance Burrell Riley; four *d*. *Educ:* Yale University (BA); Columbia University (MD). Career in practice and teaching of medicine; medical research, 1925-61. Member: Nat. Acad. of Sciences, 1957; Amer. Acad. of Arts and Sciences, 1968. Hon. Doctor of Science: Yale, 1957; Columbia, 1966. Nobel laureate in medicine and physiology, 1956. Chevalier Legion of Honour (France), 1963. *Publications:* papers on research in cardiac and pulmonary physiology, 1927-70. Ed. and co-author: Circulation of the Blood: Men and Ideas, 1964. *Address:* College of Physicians and Surgeons, 630 West 168th Street, New York, NY 10032, USA. *T:* (New York) 579-3667. *Club:* Century (New York).

**RICHARDS, Edgar Lynton, (Tony Richards);** MBE 1954; MC 1944, Bar 1945; TD 1953; Senior Partner, Fuller & Co., since 1968; Member, Monopolies Commission, since 1965; *b* 21 April 1912; *s* of late Thomas Edgar Richards, ARIBA, MICE, and Enid Marie (*née* Thomas); *m* 1937, Barbara Lebus; three *s* one *d*. *Educ:* Harrow. Served War of 1939-45, Special Services; commissioned Northamptonshire Yeomanry; France, Africa, Burma (MC and Bar, despatches). Member: Stock Exchange, London, 1939-; Stock Exchange Council, 1955-68; holds various directorships. Chm. of Trustees, American Museums in Britain; Governor, House of Citizenship. *Recreations:* ski-ing, fishing, tennis. *Address:* Heydonbury, Heydon, Cambs. *Club:* Bath, Gresham, MCC.

**RICHARDS, Sir Edward (Trenton),** Kt 1970; CBE 1967; Deputy Government Leader, House of Assembly, Bermuda, since 1968; Member of Government responsible for Immigration, Labour, Social Security; *b* 4 Oct. 1908; 2nd *s* of late George A. Richards and

Millicent Richards, British Guiana; *m* 1940, Madree Elizabeth Williams; one *s* two *d*. *Educ:* Collegiate Sch.; Queen's Coll., Guyana; Middle Temple. Secondary School-teacher, 1930-43; called to Bar, 1946. Elected to House of Assembly, Bermuda, 1948; served numerous Select Cttees of Parliament; served on Commns; Member, Exec. Council, 1963-. Served on many Govt Boards; Chairman: Public Transportation Board; Transport Control Board. Bermuda Representative: CPA Conf., Lagos, 1962; Guyana's Independence Celebrations, 1966; Mem., Constitution Conf., 1966. Magistrate, 1958. Chm., Berkeley Educational Soc., 1956-. Senior Vice-Pres., Bermuda Football Assoc. Hon. LLD, Wilberforce, USA, 1960. *Recreations:* music, reading, walking. *Address:* Wilton, Keith Hall Road, Warwick East, Bermuda. *T:* 1-5985. *Clubs:* Somerset Cricket, Warwick, Blue Waters Anglers (Bermuda).

**RICHARDS, Elfyn John,** OBE 1958; FRAeS; FIMechE; Vice-Chancellor of Loughborough University, since 1967; *b* Barry, Glamorgan, South Wales, 28 Dec. 1914; *s* of Edward James Richards, Barry, schoolmaster, and of Catherine Richards; *m* 1941, Eluned Gwenddydd Jones, Aberporth, Cardigan; three *d*. *Educ:* Barry County School; Univ. Coll. of Wales, Aberystwyth (BSc); St John's Coll., Cambridge (MA). DSc (Wales), 1959. Research Asst, Bristol Aeroplane Company, 1938-39; Scientific Officer, National Physical Laboratory, Teddington, 1939-45, and Secretary, various Aeronautical Research Council sub-cttees; Chief Aerodynamicist and Asst Chief-Designer, Vickers Armstrong, Ltd, Weybridge, 1945-50; Prof. of Aeronautical Engineering, 1950-64, and Dir, Inst. of Sound and Vibration Research, 1963-67, Univ. of Southampton, also Aeronautical Engineering Consultant. Member: Science Research Council; Noise Adv. Council; Noise Research Council, ARC; Construction Research and Adv. Council; Inland Transport and Develt Council; Gen. Adv. Council of BBC (Chm. Midlands Adv. Council, 1968-); Cttee of Scientific Advisory Council; Wilson Cttee on Problems of Noise. Aeronautical consultant to Vickers Armstrong Ltd, Westlands Ltd. Taylor Gold Medal of the Royal Aeronautical Soc., 1949; James Watt Medal of the Institution of Civil Engineers, 1963. *Publications:* many reports and memoranda of Aeronautical Research Council; articles and lectures in Roy. Aeronautical Soc. *Recreations:* swimming, walking. *Address:* Vice-Chancellor's Lodge, Loughborough University. *Club:* Athenæum.

**RICHARDS, Francis Brooks,** CMG 1963; DSC and Bar, 1943; HM Minister, Bonn, since 1969; *b* 18 July 1918; *s* of Francis Bartlett Richards; *m* 1941, Hazel Myfanwy Williams; one *s* one *d*. *Educ:* Stowe School; Magdalene College, Cambridge. Served with RN, 1939-44 (Lieut-Comdr RNVR). HM Embassy: Paris, 1944-48; Athens, 1952-54; First Sec. and Head of Chancery, Political Residency, Persian Gulf, 1954-57; Assistant Private Secretary to Foreign Secretary, 1958-59; Counsellor (Information), HM Embassy, Paris, 1959-64; Head of Information Policy Dept, 1964-65, and of Jt Inf. Policy and Guidance Dept, FO/CRO, 1965-66; seconded to Cabinet Office, 1966-68. Chevalier, Légion d'Honneur and Croix de Guerre (France), 1944. *Recreations:* sailing, gardening. *Address:* The Ranger's House, Farnham, Surrey. *T:* Farnham (Sy) 6764. *Club:* Royal Ocean Racing.

**RICHARDS, Frank Roydon,** MA, BMus Oxon; Hon. LLD Glasgow; retired as Rector of Glasgow Academy (1932-59); *b* 16 Jan. 1899; *s* of Frank Herbert Richards and Edith Alice Philips; *m* 1927, Nancy Warry; one *s* two *d* (and one *s* decd). *Educ:* Christ's Hosp.; Queen's Coll., Oxford (Scholar). 1st Class Classical Mods 1920, 2nd Class Literae Humaniores, 1922; Asst Master Glasgow Acad., 1922-24; Grecians Tutor, Christ's Hosp., 1924-28; Headmaster, Bridlington School, 1928-32; 2nd Lt RGA (SR) BEF France, 1918; OTC Lieut 1919; Capt. 1925. *Recreation:* music. *Address:* Arntemplar, Killearn, Glasgow. *T:* Killearn 391.

**RICHARDS, George Edward Fugl,** CBE 1949; BA, LLB Cantab; *b* 5 Dec. 1891; *s* of Ernest Adolphus Richards and Lavinia Thomson Fraser. *Educ:* Portsmouth Grammar School; Chicago University; Downing Coll., Cambridge. Private Sec. to Hon. Gideon Murray (later Lord Elibank) and R. Popham Lobb (later Nicholson), successive Administrators of St Vincent, BWI; Barrister-at-Law, Middle Temple, 1922; Acting Magistrate, Grenada, BWI, 1925-27; St Lucia, BWI, 1927-28; Magistrate, Dominica, BWI, 1928-31; Crown Attorney, Dominica, 1931-35; Chief Justice, St Lucia, 1935-40; Senior Puisne Judge of Supreme Court of Windward Is and Leeward Is, BWI, 1940-48; retired, Dec. 1948. *Address:* St Vincent, West Indies.

**RICHARDS, Maj.-Gen. George Warren,** CB 1945; CBE 1944; DSO 1942, Bar, 1943; MC 1918; DL; *b* 4 July 1898; *s* of late John Richards, Llewynderw Hall, Welshpool; *m* 1930, Gwen Laird; two *d*. *Educ:* Oswestry; Sandhurst; commissioned into RW Fus., 1916; attached to MGC, 1917; Tank Corps, 1920. Retired from Army, 1949. DL Monmouthshire, 1965. *Address:* Trewarren, Llandewi Rhydderch, Nr Abergavenny, Mon.

**RICHARDS, Sir Gordon,** Kt 1953; Racing Manager, since 1970 (Jockey, retired 1954, then Trainer, 1955-70); *b* 5 May 1904; *s* of Nathan Richards; *m*; two *s*. Started life as a clerk; went as a stable apprentice to Mr Martin G. Hartigan, 1919; has headed the list of winning jockeys, 1925, 1927-29, 1931-33, 1938-40, 1942; 259 winners in 1933, breaking Fred Archer's Record; passed Archer's record total of 2,749 winners, 26 April 1943; passed own record with 269 winners, 1947; rode 4000th winner 4 May 1950; broke world record with 4,500 winners 17 July 1952. Won the 1953 Derby on Pinza. *Publication:* My Story, 1955. *Recreations:* shooting, watching football. *Address:* Barclays Bank Ltd, High Street, Marlborough, Wilts.

**RICHARDS, Very Rev. Gwynfryn;** Dean of Bangor since 1962; Archdeacon of Bangor, 1957-62; Rector of Llandudno, 1956-62; *b* 10 Sept. 1902; *er s* of Joshua and Elizabeth Ann Richards, Nantyffyllon, Glam; *m* 1935, Margery Phyllis Evans; one *s* one *d*. *Educ:* Universities of Wales, Oxford and Boston. Scholar, Univ. Coll., Cardiff, 1918-21; BSc (Wales), 1921; Jesus Coll., Oxford, 1921-23; Certificate, School of Geography, Oxford, 1922; BA 1st Cl. Hons School of Natural Science, 1923; MA 1928. In industry (USA), 1923-25. Boston Univ. Sch. of Theology, 1926-28; STB First Cl., 1928; Scholar and Travelling Fellow, 1928-29; Oxford, 1928-29; St Michael's Coll., Llandaff, 1929-30; deacon, 1930; priest, 1931. Curate of: Llanrhos, 1930-34; Aberystwyth, St Michael, 1934-38; Rector of Llanllyfni, 1938-49; Vicar of Conway with Gyffin, 1949-56. Canon of Bangor Cathedral, 1943-62, Treas., 1943-57; Examining Chaplain to Bp of Bangor, 1944-; Rural Dean of Arllechwedd, 1953-57. Pantyfedwen Lectr, Univ. Coll., Aberystwyth, 1967. *Publications:* Ffurfiau Ordeinio Holl Eglwysi Cymru, 1943;

Yr Hen Fam, 1952; Ein Hymraniadau Annedwydd, 1963; contrib. to Journal of the Historical Society of the Church in Wales and various symposia. *Recreations:* gardening, photography, local history. *Address:* The Deanery, Bangor, Caerns. *T:* 3425.

**RICHARDS, Brigadier Hugh Upton,** CBE 1943; DSO 1944; *b* 1894; *s* of J. Richards; *m* Florence Matilda (*d* 1964), *d* of J. McLeod; one *s*; *m* 1966, Mrs Irene Mary Olver, *widow* of Cecil Paul Olver. Served European War, 1914-19, with Worcestershire Regiment; Lieutenant, 1917; Captain, 1931; Bt Major, 1934; Major, 1936; transfd West Yorkshire Regt, 1936; Lt-Col 1939; Col 1942; Brig. 1940; commanded 4 Bn Nigeria Regt 1933-34, Sierra Leone Bn 1939, and 3 (West African) Inf. Bde, 1940-44. Campaign Palestine, 1936 and 1938 and Burma. *Address:* Pencombe Hall, Bromyard, Herefordshire. *Club:* Army and Navy.

**RICHARDS, Ivor Armstrong,** CH 1964; MA; LittD; University Professor (Emeritus, 1963), Harvard University, Cambridge, Massachusetts, USA (Professor 1944); Fellow of Magdalene College, Cambridge, 1926, Hon. Fellow, 1964; *b* 26 Feb. 1893; *s* of late W. Armstrong Richards, Sandbach, Cheshire; *m* 1926, Dorothy Eleanor, *e d* of John J. Pilley. *Educ:* Clifton; Magdalene College, Cambridge. Class I, Moral Sciences Tripos, Part I, 1915. college Lecturer in English and Moral Sciences, 1922; Visiting Professor Tsing Hua University, Peking, 1929-30; Visiting Lecturer, Harvard University, 1931; Director, The Orthological Institute (Basic English) of China, 1936-38. Hon. LittD Harvard, 1944. Corresponding Fellow of the British Academy, 1959. Loines Poetry Award, 1962; Emerson-Thoreau Medal, Amer. Acad. of Arts and Sciences, 1970. *Publications:* Foundations of Aesthetics (with C. K. Ogden and James Wood), 1921; The Meaning of Meaning (with C. K. Ogden), 1923; Principles of Literary Criticism, 1924; Science and Poetry, 1925; Practical Criticism, 1929; Mencius on the Mind, 1931; Coleridge On Imagination, 1934; Interpretation in Teaching, 1938; How to Read a Page, 1942; The Republic of Plato (a simplified version), 1942; Basic English and its Uses, 1943; Speculative Instruments, 1955; Goodbye Earth and other Poems, 1958; The Screens and other Poems, 1960; Tomorrow Morning, Faustus!, 1962; Why So, Socrates?, 1963; So Much Nearer: Essays Toward a World English, 1968; Design for Escape: World Education through Modern Media, 1968; Poetries & Sciences, 1970. *Recreations:* mountaineering, travel. *Address:* 1000 Memorial Drive, Cambridge, Mass 02138, USA. *Club:* Alpine.

**RICHARDS, James Maude;** CBE 1959; Executive editor Architectural Review since 1959 (joint editor since 1946); Member editorial board Architects' Journal, 1947-61; Architectural Correspondent, The Times, since 1947; Hoffman Wood Professor of Architecture, Leeds University, 1957-59; *b* 13 Aug. 1907; 2nd *s* of late Louis Saurin Richards and Lucy Denes (*née* Clarence); *m* 1st, 1936, Margaret (marr. diss., 1948), *d* of late David Angus; (one *s* decd) one *d*; 2nd, 1954, Kathleen Margaret (Kit), *widow* of late Morland Lewis and 2nd *d* of late Henry Bryan Godfrey-Faussett-Osborne, Queendown Warren, Sittingbourne, Kent; one *s*. *Educ:* Gresham's School, Holt; AA School of Architecture. ARIBA, AADipl 1930. Studied and practised architecture in Canada and USA, 1930-31, London and Dublin, 1931-32; Asst Editor, The Architects' Jl, 1933; The Architectural Review, 1935; Editor, Publications Div., 1942, Director of Publications, Middle East, Cairo, 1943-46, MOI; Gen. Editor, The Architectural Press, 1946. Member: exec. cttee Modern Architectural Research Gp, 1946-54; AA Council, 1948-51, 1958-61; Advisory Council, Inst. of Contemporary Arts, 1947-68; Architecture Council, Festival of Britain, 1949-51; British Cttee, Internat. Union of Architects, 1950-66; Royal Fine Art Commn, 1951-66; Fine Art Cttee, Brit. Council, 1954-; Council of Industrial Design, 1955-61; Min. of Transport (Worboys) Cttee on traffic signs, 1962-63. World Soc. of Ekistics, 1965-; Vice-Pres. Nat. Council on Inland Transport, 1963-. Broadcaster, television and sound (regular member, BBC Critics panel, 1948-68). Hon. AILA, 1955. Chevalier (First Class), Order of White Rose of Finland, 1960; Gold Medal, Mexican Institute of Architects, 1963. *Publications:* Miniature History of the English House, 1938; (with late Eric Ravilious) High Street, 1938; Introduction to Modern Architecture, 1940; (with John Summerson) The Bombed Buildings of Britain, 1942; Edward Bawden, 1946; The Castles on the Ground, 1946; The Functional Tradition in Early Industrial Buildings, 1958; New Building in the Commonwealth, 1961; An Architectural Journey in Japan, 1963; Guide to Finnish Architecture, 1966. *Recreations:* travel and topography; work. *Address:* 94 Cheyne Walk, Chelsea, SW10. *T:* 01-352 9874. *Club:* Athenæum.

**RICHARDS, Rt. Rev. John Richards,** DD (Lambeth); *b* 3 March 1901; *s* of Thomas and Elizabeth Richards, Llanbadarn, Fawr, Aberystwyth; *m* 1929, Katherine Mary, *d* of W. E. and M. Hodgkinson, Inglewood, St Michael's, Tenterden; one *s* one *d*. *Educ:* Ardwyn School, Aberystwyth; Univ. College of Wales; St Michael's College Llandaff. BA 1922 (2nd Cl. Hons Mod. Langs); MA 1955; DD 1956. Deacon, 1924; priest, 1925; Curate of Pembrey w Burry Post, 1924-27; CMS missionary in Iran, 1927-45, at Shiraz, 1927-36, at Yezd, 1938-42, at Isfahan, 1942-45; Archdeacon in Iran, 1937-45. Mem. of Near East Christian Paiforce, 1942-45; Vicar of Skewen, 1945-52, Vicar of St Catherine, Pontypridd, 1952-54; Canon of St Andrew in Llandaff Cathedral, 1949-54; Dean of Bangor, 1955-56; Vicar of St James', Bangor, and Canon of Bangor Cathedral, 1954-55; Bishop of St David's, 1956-March 1971. Mem. of Governing Body of the Church in Wales, 1948. Chaplain and Sub-Prelate, Order of St John, 1961. *Publications:* The Religion of the Baha'is, 1932; The Open Road in Persia, 1932; Baha'ism, 1965. *Address:* Lluest Wen, Llanbadarn Road, Aberystwyth.

**RICHARDS, Hon. Mrs Noel Olivier,** MD; Hon. Consulting Physician, Westminster Children's Hospital, 1958, retired; *b* 1892; *d* of 1st and last Baron Olivier; *m* 1920, William Arthur Richards, FRCS; one *s* four *d*. *Educ:* Bedales School; University College, London; London School of Medicine for Women, MB, BS 1917; LRCP, MRCS 1917; MD London 1921; MRCP 1922. Formerly: Consultant Physician, Westminster Children's Hosp.; Pædiatrician Westminster Med. School; Physician, Children's Department, Elizabeth Garrett Anderson Hospital; Out-patients' Physician and Senior Resident Medical Officer, Victoria Hospital for Children. *Publication:* (jt) Healthy Babies, 1940. *Recreation:* Natural History. *Address:* Greenoge, 40 Swakeleys Road, Ickenham, Uxbridge. *T:* Ruislip 39211.

**RICHARDS, His Honour Norman Grantham Lewis,** OBE 1945; QC 1955; an Official Referee of the Supreme Court since September 1963; Dep. Chairman of Middlesex Quarter Sessions, 1962-65; *b* 29 Dec. 1905; *s* of L. M.

Richards and Gertrude E. Richards; *m* 1930, Helen Nina Colls; one *d. Educ:* Charterhouse; Trinity College, Cambridge. Barrister-at-Law, 1928, Wales and Chester Circuit. Served War of 1939-45 (despatches twice, OBE). Recorder of Merthyr Tydfil, 1960-63. *Recreations:* golf, cricket. *Address:* 35 Ormonde Gate, Chelsea, SW3. *T:* 01-352 7874. *Clubs:* St James's, Portland.

**RICHARDS, Prof. Owain Westmacott,** FRS 1959; MA, DSc (Oxford); Professor of Zoology and Applied Entomology, Imperial College, London, 1953-67, now Emeritus; Fellow of Imperial College, 1969; *b* 31 Dec. 1901; 2nd *s* of H. M. Richards, MD; *m* 1931, Maud Jessie (*d* 1970), *d* of Eng. Capt. C. M. Norris, RN; two *d. Educ:* Hereford Cathedral School; Brasenose College, Oxford. Exhibitioner, 1920, and Senior Hulme Schol., Brasenose Coll.; Christopher Welch Schol., Oxford Univ., 1924. Research Asst, Dept of Entomology, Imperial College, 1927; Lecturer, 1930; Reader, 1937. Hon. Mem. Société Entomologique d'Egypte; Hon. Fellow, Royal Entomological Soc. of London; Hon. Mem. Nederlandsche Entomologische Vereeniging; Hon. Member British Ecological Society. *Publications:* The Variations of Animals in Nature (with G. C. Robson), 1936; The Social Insects, 1953; Imms' General Textbook of Entomology, 9th edn (with R. G. Davies), 1957. *Recreation:* entomology. *Address:* 89 St Stephen's Road, Ealing, W13.

**RICHARDS, Raymond,** MA, FSA, FRHistS; Past Chairman, Ancient Monuments Society; Trustee: Historic Churches Preservation Trust; Historic Cheshire Churches Preservation Trust; Friends of Ancient English Churches; *b* Macclesfield, 19 July 1906; *er s* of late Thomas Edward Richards and Lucy Mary, *d* of late William Kersall Gatley, Gatley, Cheshire; *m* 1940, Monica, *y d* of late John Relf, Liverpool and Brightling, Sussex; two *s.* Chairman: Cheshire Cttee, Nat. Register of Archives (Historical Manuscripts Commission); Southport Repertory Company, in Association with Arts Council of Gt Britain, 1948-51; Past President, Macclesfield and District Field Club. Member: Chester Diocesan Faculties Advisory Committee; Central Council for Care of Churches, 1948-58; Parochial Church Libraries Sub-Cttee, 1950-51; House of Laity, Church Assembly; Patron, Living and Manor of Gawsworth, Cheshire. Governor Keele University. Hon. MA Liverpool, 1948. *Publications:* Old Cheshire Churches, 1947; St Winifred's Chapel, Holywell, 1948; High Legh Chapels, 1950; The Lesser Chapels of Cheshire, Part 1, 1951; Part 2, 1953; The Manor of Gawsworth, 1955. *Recreation:* yachting. *Address:* Gawsworth Hall, Gawsworth, Cheshire. *T:* Macclesfield 4643. *Clubs:* Athenæum; Athenæum (Liverpool); Royal Mersey Yacht; Dublin University (Dublin).

**RICHARDS, Dr Rex Edward,** DSc Oxon 1970; FRS 1959; Dr Lee's Professor of Chemistry, Oxford, 1964-Oct. 1970; Warden of Merton College, Oxford, since 1969; *b* 28 Oct. 1922; *s* of H. W. and E. N. Richards; *m* 1948, Eva Edith Vago; two *d. Educ:* Colyton Grammar School, Devon; St John's College, Oxford. Senior Demy, Magdalen College, Oxford, 1946; MA; DPhil; Fellow, Lincoln College, Oxford, 1947-64, Hon. Fellow, 1968; Research Fellow, Harvard University, 1955; Fellow Exeter College, 1964-69; Hon. Fellow, St John's Coll., Oxford, 1968. Member: Chemical Society Council, 1957; Faraday Society Council, 1963. Tilden Lectr, 1962. Corday-Morgan Medal of Chemical Soc., 1954. *Publications:* various contributions to scientific journals. *Recreation:* family. *Address:* Warden's Lodgings, Merton College, Oxford. *T:* Oxford 49651.

**RICHARDS, Rt. Rev. Ronald Edwin;** *see* Bendigo, Bishop of.

**RICHARDS, Tony;** *see* Richards, E. L.

**RICHARDS, William John,** CB 1956; CBE 1952; Director, Staff College for Further Education, 1961-63, retired; *b* 6 July 1903; *s* of late Stephen Richards, Solva, Pembrokeshire; *m* 1929, Nelia, *d* of Albert Porter, Preston, Lancs; one *s* one *d. Educ:* St David's Grammar Sch.; Victoria University, Manchester (BSc Eng.). On Research staff at Royal Aircraft Establishment, Farnborough, 1925-41; Head of Physics and Instruments Dept at RAE, 1937-41; Deputy Director of Scientific Research (Armaments), Ministry of Aircraft Production, 1942-46; Chief Superintendent Telecommunications Research Establishment, Ministry of Supply, Malvern, 1946-53; Director of the Royal Radar Establishment, Ministry of Aviation (formerly Supply), at Malvern, 1953-61. *Recreations:* education, architecture. *Address:* 23 Priory Road, Malvern, Worcs. *T:* Malvern 5304.

**RICHARDSON, Very Rev. Alan,** MA (Liverpool); MA, DD (Oxon); Dean of York since 1964; *b* 17 Oct. 1905; *s* of late William and Annie Richardson; *m* 1933, Phyllis Mary (*née* Parkhouse); no *c. Educ:* Liverpool University; Exeter College, Oxford; Ridley Hall, Cambridge. Intercoll. Secretary, Student Christian Movement, Liverpool University, 1928-31; Curate, St Saviour, Liverpool, 1928-30; Asst Chaplain, Liverpool Cathedral, 1930-31; Chaplain, Ripon Hall, Oxford, 1931-33; Tutor of Jesus Coll., Oxford, 1934; Vicar of Cambo, Northumberland, 1934-38; Study Sec., Student Christian Movement, 1938-43; Sixth Canon of Durham Cathedral, 1943-53; Sub-Dean, 1953; Professor of Christian Theology, University of Nottingham, 1953-64; Hon. Canon, Derby Cathedral, 1953-64. Visiting Professor, Berkeley Div. School, Newhaven, Connecticut, 1949. Examining Chaplain to Bishop of Sheffield, 1939-62, to Archbishop of York, 1948-61, to Bishop of Southwell, 1953-64. Bampton Lecturer, Oxford, 1962. Hon. DD (Glasgow), 1952. *Publications:* Creeds in the Making, 1935; Miracle Stories of the Gospels, 1941; Preface to Bible Study, 1943; Christian Apologetics, 1947; Science, History and Faith, 1950; (ed) Theological Word Book of the Bible, 1950; Biblical Doctrine of Work, 1952; Genesis I-XI, 1953; Introduction to the Theology of the New Testament, 1958; The Bible in the Age of Science, 1961; History, Sacred and Profane (Bampton Lectures), 1964; Religion in Contemporary Debate, 1966; (ed) A Dictionary of Christian Theology, 1969, etc. *Recreations:* piano, fell walking, dogs. *Address:* The Deanery, York. *Club:* Royal Commonwealth Society.

**RICHARDSON, Alexander Stewart,** CBE 1943; BSc; *b* 17 May 1897; *e s* of late Alexander Stewart Richardson and Susan Hamilton Horsburgh; *m* 1931, Kathleen Margaret, *o d* of late Angus McColl, Inverness; one *s* one *d. Educ:* Edinburgh University. Military Service, 1916-19; Agricultural Officer, Tanganyika Territory, 1924; Senior Agricultural Officer, 1930; Deputy Director of Agriculture, Uganda, 1937; Director of Agriculture, Nyasaland, 1940-44; MLC 1940; Chairman Supply Board and Controller of Essential Supplies and Prices, 1941 and 1942; Controller of Production and Food, 1943. Member of

Executive and Legislative Councils; Officer in general charge of Supplies, Prices and Distribution of Commodities; Uganda Govt Rep. on East African Production and Supply Council; Leader of East African Cotton deleg. to New Delhi, India, 1946; retired, 1947; Director of Agriculture, Uganda, 1944-47. *Recreations:* golf, shooting, fishing. *Address:* 24 Drummond Road, Inverness. *T:* 33497.

**RICHARDSON, Councillor Arthur;** *b* 31 Jan. 1897; *s* of Thomas and Annie Eliza Richardson; unmarried. *Educ:* St Mary's Church of England School, Hull. With Messrs Rank Ltd, Flourmillers, Hull, 1912-29; business on own account as Licensee of Public House. Member: Hull Board of Guardians, 1922-30; Hull City Council, 1929-; Alderman 1946, retired 1949; elected Councillor again, 1949; Lord Mayor of Kingston-upon-Hull, and Admiral of the Humber, 1953-54. Coronation Medal, 1953. *Recreations:* swimming, politics. *Address:* c/o City Offices, Kingston upon Hull.

**RICHARDSON, Charles Arthur;** Agent General for Province of Nova Scotia in UK and Europe, since 1969; *b* 10 Oct. 1918; *s* of John Richardson, Sydney, Nova Scotia, Canada; *m* 1945, Barbara Vaughan, Newport, Monmouthshire; three *s*. *Educ:* Sydney Academy, Sydney, NS, Canada. Served in War of 1939-45: European Theatre, with North Nova Scotia Highlanders, Infantry, Canadian Army Third Division. Canadian Banking, 1936-69: Sen. Manager, Maritime Provinces, Toronto-Dominion Bank, Halifax, NS. *Recreations:* golf, swimming. *Address:* Province of Nova Scotia, 60 Trafalgar Square, London WC2. *T:* 01-930 6864. *Clubs:* Royal Automobile (London); Ashburn Golf (Halifax, NS).

**RICHARDSON, Gen. Sir Charles (Leslie),** GCB 1967 (KCB 1962; CB 1957); CBE 1945; DSO 1943; Master-General of the Ordnance, 1966-71; ADC (General) to the Queen 1967-70; *s* of late Lieutenant-Colonel C. W. Richardson, RA, and Mrs Richardson; *m* 1947, Audrey Styles (*née* Jorgensen); one *s* two *d*. *Educ:* Wellington College; Royal Military Acad., Woolwich (King's Medal); Cambridge Univ. (BA). Commissioned Royal Engineers, 1928; Exhibitioner, Clare College, Cambridge, 1930, 1st Cl. Hons Mech Sciences Tripos. Served France and Belgium, 1939-40; GSO1 Plans HQ, Eighth Army, 1942; BGS Eighth Army, 1943; Deputy Chief of Staff Fifth US Army, 1943; BGS Plans, 21st Army Group, 1944; Brigade Commander, 1953-54; Commandant, Royal Military College of Science, 1955-58; General Officer Commanding Singapore District, 1958-60; Director of Combat Development, War Office, 1960-61; Director-General of Military Training, 1961-63; General Officer Commanding-in-Chief, Northern Command, 1963-65. Quartermaster General to the Forces, 1965-66. Legion of Merit (US), 1944. Colonel Commandant: Corps of Roy. Engineers, 1962-; RAOC, 1967-. *Address:* The Stables, Betchworth, Surrey. *Club:* Army and Navy.

**RICHARDSON, Brigadier (Retd) Charles Walter Philipps,** DSO and Bar 1945; *b* 8 Jan. 1905; *s* of W. J. Richardson and E. C. Philipps; *m* 1st, 1932, Joan Kathleen Constance Lang (from whom he obtained a divorce, 1946); one *s*; 2nd, 1946, Hon. Mrs Averil Diana Going; one *s*. *Educ:* RNC Osborne and Dartmouth; RMC Sandhurst. 2nd Lieut KOSB, 1924; served in Egypt, China and India; Bde Maj. 52nd (Lowland) Div., 1942; Comdr 6th Bn KOSB 15th (Scottish) Div., 1944-46; Colonel 1946; Comdt, Tactical Wing, School of Infantry, Warminster, 1947-48; GSO(1) Singapore District, 1948-49; Deputy Comdt Malay Regt, 1949; Dir Amphibious Warfare Trg, 1951; Comdr 158 Inf. Bde (TA), 1952; Brig. 1952; Dep. Comdr Lowland District, 1955-57. Retired 1957. Order of Leopold and Belgian Croix de Guerre, 1945. *Recreations:* shooting, fishing. *Address:* Ashe Warren House, Overton, Hants. *T:* Overton 215. *Club:* Army and Navy.

**RICHARDSON, Sir Egerton (Rudolf),** Kt 1968; CMG 1959; Ambassador of Jamaica to the United States, since 1967; *b* 15 Aug. 1912; *s* of James Neil Richardson and Doris Adel Burton; *m* (wife *d* 1966); one *s* one *d*. *Educ:* Calabar High School, Kingston, Jamaica; Oxford University. Entered Civil Service, 1933; Secretary Land Policy Co-ordinating Committee, 1943-53; Asst Treasurer, 1944-47; Asst Secretary Secretariat, 1947-51; Principal Asst Sec., 1951-53; Permanent Sec., Min. of Agric. and Lands, 1953-54; Under-Sec. Finance, 1954-56; on secondment, CO, London, 1953-54; Financial Secretary, Jamaica, 1956-62; Ambassador and Permanent Representative at UN, 1962-67. *Recreations:* swimming, tennis, golf; astronomy. *Address:* Jamaican Embassy, 1666 Connecticut Avenue NW, Washington, DC 20009, USA. *Club:* Constant Spring Golf (St Andrew, Jamaica).

**RICHARDSON, Sir Eric;** *see* Richardson, Sir J. E.

**RICHARDSON, Sir Frank;** *see* Richardson, Sir (H.) Frank.

**RICHARDSON, Major-General Frank McLean,** CB 1960; DSO 1941; OBE 1945; MD; Director Medical Services, BAOR, 1956-61; *b* 3 March 1904; *s* of late Col Hugh Richardson, DSO, and of Elizabeth Richardson; *m* 1944, Sylvia Innes, *d* of Col S. A. Innes, DSO; two *s* one *d*. *Educ:* Glenalmond; Edinburgh Univ. MB, ChB 1926. MD 1938. Joined RAMC, 1927; Captain 1930; Major 1936; Lt-Col 1945; Col 1949; Brig. 1956; Maj.-Gen. 1957. Honorary Surgeon to the Queen, 1957-61. Hon. Col 51 (H) Div. Dist RAMC, TA, 1963-67. *Address:* c/o Glyn Mills & Co., Kirkland House, SW1; The Shaws, Barnton, Edinburgh 4.

**RICHARDSON, Prof. Frederick Denys,** FRS 1968; BSc, PhD, DSc; FIM; MIMM; MIChemE; Professor of Extraction Metallurgy, Imperial College of Science and Technology, London University, since 1957; *b* 17 Sept. 1913; *y s* of late Charles Willerton Richardson, Bombay; *m* 1942, Irene Mary, *o d* of late George E. Austin, Birkdale; two *s*. *Educ:* privately; University College, London; Princeton University, USA. Commonwealth Fund Fellow, 1937-39; RNVR 1939-46; Commander, 1942; Deputy Director Miscellaneous Weapon Development, Admiralty, 1943-46; Superintending Chemist, British Iron and Steel Research Association, 1946-50; Nuffield Fellow and Director Nuffield Research Group, Imperial College, 1950-57; Member of Council, Iron and Steel Inst., 1962; Vice-Pres., Inst MM, 1968; Charter Fellow, Metallurgical Soc.; American Inst. of Mining and Metallurgical Engineers, 1963. Sir George Beilby Memorial Award for researches on the thermo-dynamics of high temperature systems, 1956; Bessemer Gold Medal of Iron and Steel Inst. for contribs to kinetics and thermodynamics of metallurgical processes, 1968. Howe, Hatfield, May and Wernher Lectures, 1964-67. *Publications:* Papers on chemical and metallurgical research in scientific jls. *Recreations:* riding, fishing, gardening. *Address:* Imperial College, Prince Consort Road, SW7. *Clubs:* Athenæum, Royal Automobile.

**RICHARDSON, George Barclay;** Fellow of St John's College, Oxford, since 1951 and University Reader in Economics, since 1969; Member, Monopolies Commission, since 1969; *b* 19 Sept. 1924; *s* of George and Christina Richardson; *m* 1957, Isabel Alison Chalk; two *s*. *Educ:* Aberdeen Central Secondary Sch. and other schs in Scotland; Aberdeen Univ.; Corpus Christi Coll., Oxford. BSc Physics and Maths, 1944 (Aberdeen); PPE 1949 and MA (Oxon). Admty Scientific Res. Dept, 1944; Lieut, RNVR, 1945. Intell. Officer, HQ Intell. Div. BAOR, 1946-47; Third Sec., HM Foreign Service, 1949; Student, Nuffield Coll., Oxford, 1950. Mem., Economic Develt Cttee for Electrical Engineering Industry, 1964-. *Publications:* Information and Investment, 1960; Economic Theory, 1964; articles in academic jls. *Address:* 3 Wellington Place, Oxford. *Club:* United University.

**RICHARDSON, George Wigham;** Underwriting Member of Lloyd's; Shipowner and Shipbuilder; Director, Wigham-Richardson & Bevingtons Ltd, and other companies; *b* 12 April 1895; 2nd *s* of Sir Philip Wigham Richardson, 1st Bt, and *heir pres.* to Sir W. W. Richardson, 2nd Bt, *qv*; *m* 1st, 1923, Adela Nancy (marr. diss., 1937), *d* of late A. O. Davies; 2nd, 1944, Barbara, *d* of late Harry Clements Ansell, Sutton Coldfield; three *d*. *Educ:* Rugby School. Served European War in Flanders and France, 1915-18, and with Army of Occupation in Germany, 1918-19 (despatches). Prime Warden of Worshipful Company of Shipwrights, 1943. *Address:* H3 Albany, W1. *TA:* Armadores, London. *T:* 01-734 1861 and 01-283 5250. *Clubs:* Carlton, Constitutional, City of London.

**RICHARDSON, Colonel (Hon.) Gerald,** CMG 1954; OBE 1947; *b* 27 Feb. 1907; *s* of Frederick William and Gertrude Richardson; *m* 1939, Phyllis Vida Richardson (*née* Browne); no *c*. *Educ:* West Bridgford High School, Nottingham. Metropolitan Police (Detective Supt), 1927-43; seconded to HM Forces (Army) with rank of Major; special police duties, Sicily and Italy, 1943-45; formerly Inspector-General of Police and Director of Public Safety, British-United States Zone, Free Territory of Trieste and Commissioner of Police (CID), Tangier. Lieut-Col, 1945; Col, 1947. US Medal of Freedom with Bronze Palm. *Recreations:* rowing and swimming. *Address:* c/o Lloyds Bank Ltd, 58 High St, NW10.

**RICHARDSON, Gordon (William Humphreys),** MBE 1944; Chairman: J. Henry Schroder Wagg & Co. Ltd since 1962; Schroders Ltd since 1966; J. Henry Schroder Banking Corporation (New York), 1967-70; Member, Court of the Bank of England, since 1967; *b* 25 Nov. 1915; *er s* of John Robert and Nellie Richardson; *m* 1941, Margaret Alison, *er d* of Canon H. R. L. Sheppard; one *s* one *d*. *Educ:* Nottingham High School; Gonville and Caius College, Cambridge (BA, LLB). Commnd S Notts Hussars Yeomanry, 1939; Staff Coll., Camberley, 1941; served until 1946. Called to Bar, Gray's Inn, 1946; Mem. Bar, Council, 1951-55; ceased practice at Bar, Aug. 1955-. Industrial and Commercial Finance Corp. Ltd, 1955-57; Director: J. Henry Schroder & Co., 1957-; Lloyds Bank Ltd, 1960-67; Bank of England, 1967-71; Legal and General Assurance Soc., Ltd, 1956-70 (Vice-Chm. 1959-70). Mem. Company Law Amendment Committee (Jenkins Committee), 1959-62; Chm. Cttee on Turnover Taxation, 1963. Member Court of London University, 1962-65. *Address:* 64 Chelsea Square, SW3. *T:* 01-352 1308. *Club:* Brooks's.
*See also Sir John Riddell, Bt.*

**RICHARDSON, Graham Edmund;** Rector, Dollar Academy, Clackmannanshire, since Sept. 1962; *b* 16 July 1913; *s* of H. W. Richardson, BSc, MIEE, AMIMechE, Studland, Dorset; *m* 1939, Eileen Cynthia, *d* of Lewis Beesly, FRCSE, Brightwalton, Newbury, Berks; one *s* one *d*. *Educ:* Tonbridge School; Strasbourg University; Queen's College, Oxford. Asst Master, Fettes College, Edinburgh, 1935-55; Housemaster, 1946-55; Headmaster, Melville College, Edinburgh, 1955-62. Mem., Scottish Adv. Cttee, ITA. *Address:* Devon Lodge, Dollar, Clackmannanshire.

**RICHARDSON, Prof. Harold Owen Wilson,** DSc, PhD; FRSE; Hildred Carlile Professor of Physics, Bedford College, University of London, since 1956; *b* 1907; *e s* of late Sir Owen Richardson; *m* 1st, 1930, Jean Rosemary Campbell (marr. diss., 1940); one *d*; 2nd, 1955, Sylvia Camroux Topsfield. *Educ:* University College School; King's College, London. BSc (London); PhD (Cantab); DSc (Edinburgh). Research student, Cavendish Lab., Cambridge (Trinity Coll.), 1928-30; part-time Demonstrator at King's Coll., London, 1930-31; Demonstrator, Bedford Coll., London, 1931-35; Asst Lectr, Univ. of Leeds, 1935-36; Asst Lecturer and Lecturer, Univ. of Liverpool, 1936-46; Experimental Officer, Projectile Development Establishment, Min. of Supply, 1940-42; Lecturer in Natural Philosophy, Univ. of Edinburgh, 1946-51, Reader, 1951-52; Prof. of Physics, Univ. of Exeter, 1952-56. Member Fabian Society. Warden of Reed Hall, Univ. Coll. of the South-West, 1953-55. Regional Scientific Adviser to the Home Office, 1953-56. *Publications:* papers on radioactivity, the magnetic focusing of electrons and the design of magnets. *Address:* Bedford College, Regent's Park, NW1.

**RICHARDSON, Sir Henry;** *see* Richardson, Sir J. H. S.

**RICHARDSON, Henry Gerald,** FBA 1952; lately Secretary, Tithe Redemption Commission. *Educ:* Westminster City School; London School of Economics. MA, BSc. *Publications:* The Early Statutes, 1934; Rotuli Parliamentorum Anglie *hactenus inediti*, 1935; Select Cases of Procedure Without Writ, 1941; Parliaments and Councils of Mediaeval Ireland, 1947; The Irish Parliament in the Middle Ages, 1952; Fleta, 1956; Parliaments and Great Councils of Medieval England, 1961; The Administration of Ireland (1172-1377), 1963; The Governance of Mediæval England from the Conquest to Magna Carta, 1963; Law and Legislation from Æthelberht to Magna Carta, 1966 (the above with G. O. Sayles); Memoranda Roll 1 John, 1943; The English Jewry under Angevin Kings, 1960; The Coronation in Mediaeval England (Traditio), 1961; Bracton, 1964; many articles in Brit. and Amer. historical and legal publications. *Address:* The Grange, Goudhurst, Kent. *T:* Goudhurst 415.

**RICHARDSON, Sir (H.) Frank,** Kt, *cr* 1953; *b* 1901; *s* of William Thomas and Louisa Jane Richardson; *m* 1949, Marjorie Amy Hislop; four *s* two *d*. *Educ:* All Saints Gram. Sch., St Kilda, Vict.; Univ. of Tasmania, Australia. Deputy Chairman: Business Board, Defence Department, Commonwealth of Australia, 1941-47; Commonwealth Disposals Commission, Australia, 1944-49. Past Chairman of various Department Stores, etc., in Australia; now Director of Proprietary companies. Life Governor, Retail Traders Assoc. of Victoria. Mem. Council, The Australian National University, 1953-. *Recreations:* tennis, golf. *Address:* 40

Heyington Place, Toorak, Victoria 3142, Australia. *T:* 20.40.30. *Club:* Athenæum (Melbourne, Australia).

**RICHARDSON, Hugh Edward,** CIE 1947; OBE 1944; *b* 22 Dec. 1905; *s* of Hugh Richardson, DSO, MD, and Elizabeth, *née* McLean; *m* 1951, Huldah Rennie (*née* Walker). *Educ:* Trinity College, Glenalmond; Keble College, Oxford. Entered Indian Civil Service, 1930; SDO, Tamluk, Midnapore Dist, Bengal, 1932-34; entered Foreign and Political Service of Govt of India, 1934; APA Loralai, Baluchistan, 1934-35; British Trade Agent, Gyantse, and O-in-C British Mission, Lhasa, 1936-40; service in NWFP, 1940-42; 1st Sec. Indian Agency-General in China, Chungking, 1942-43; Dep. Sec. to Govt of India, EA Dept, 1944-45; British Trade Agent, Gyantse, and O-in-C, British Mission, Lhasa, 1946-47; Indian Trade Agent, Gyantse and Officer-in-charge, Indian Mission, Lhasa, 1947-50. Retd from ICS, 1950. *Publication:* Tibet and its History, 1962. *Recreations:* golf, angling. *Address:* c/o National and Grindlay's Bank Ltd, 13 St James's Square, SW1. *Club:* Royal and Ancient Golf (St Andrews).

**RICHARDSON, Ian;** actor; *b* 7 April 1934; *s* of John Richardson and Margaret Drummond; *m* 1961, Maroussia Frank; two *s*. *Educ:* Tynecastle; Edinburgh; Univ. of Glasgow. Studied for stage at Coll. of Dramatic Art, Glasgow (James Bridie Gold Medal, 1957). Joined Birmingham Repertory Theatre Co. 1958 (leading parts incl. Hamlet); joined Shakespeare Memorial Theatre Company, Stratford-on-Avon, 1960 (Arragon, Sir Andrew Aguecheek); became long-term contract player there, Nov. 1960 (theatre re-named Royal Shakespeare Company, 1961). First appearance in London, as Count Malatesti in The Duchess of Malfi, Aldwych, Dec. 1960; has played leading parts for Royal Shakespeare Co., 1961 onwards; in 1964: Edmund in King Lear, prior to touring this, and The Comedy of Errors, in Europe and USSR, and making his first appearance (May) in New York (State Theatre), repeating Antipholus of Ephesus in The Comedy of Errors; (Aug.) Herald in Marat/Sade, Aldwych; (Oct.) Ithamore in The Jew of Malta; (Dec.) Ford in The Merry Wives of Windsor; in 1965: (May) Antipholus of Syracuse, Royal Shakespeare; (July) Eino Silakka in Squire Puntila and His Servant Matti, Aldwych; (Aug.) Chorus in Henry V and Vendice in The Revengers Tragedy; (Nov.) again, Marat, Aldwych, and (Dec.) Martin Beck Theatre, NY; in 1966: Coriolanus; Bertram in Alls Well That Ends Well, and Malcolm in Macbeth; (Nov.) touring latter two plays in USSR and returning with them to Aldwych; in 1968: (Apr.) Cassius in Julius Caesar, and Ford in The Merry Wives of Windsor; (May) ret. Aldwych in both plays; (Aug.) again Royal Shakespeare; in 1969: Pericles and, again, Ford; (Nov.) again, Vendice in The Revengers Tragedy, at Aldwych; in 1970: toured Japan and appeared in 4 Stratford productions. *Recreations:* music, swimming. *Address:* 40 Buckingham Palace Mansions, Buckingham Palace Road, SW1. *T:* 01-730 1177.

**RICHARDSON, Joanna,** MA Oxon; FRSL; author; *o d* of Frederick Richardson and Charlotte Elsa (*née* Benjamin). *Educ:* The Downs School, Seaford; St Anne's College, Oxford. Mem. Council, Royal Soc. of Literature, 1961-. *Publications:* Fanny Brawne: a biography, 1952; Rachel, 1956; Théophile Gautier: his Life and Times, 1958; Sarah Bernhardt, 1959; Edward FitzGerald, 1960; The Disastrous Marriage: a Study of George IV and Caroline of Brunswick, 1960; My Dearest Uncle: a Life of Leopold, First King of the Belgians, 1961; (ed) FitzGerald: Selected Works, 1962; The Pre-Eminent Victorian: a study of Tennyson, 1962; The Everlasting Spell: a study of Keats and his Friends, 1963; (ed) Essays by Divers Hands (trans. Royal Soc. Lit.), 1963; introd. to Victor Hugo: Choses Vues (The Oxford Lib. of French Classics), 1964; Edward Lear, 1965; George IV: a Portrait, 1966; Creevey and Greville, 1967; Princess Mathilde, 1969; The Bohemians, 1969; Verlaine, 1971; Imperial Paris, 1971. Contributor, BBC. Has also written for The Times, The Times Literary Supplement, Sunday Times, Spectator, New Statesman, New York Times Book Review, French Studies, Modern Language Review, Keats-Shelley Memorial Bulletin, etc. *Recreations:* antique-collecting, sketching. *Address:* 55 Flask Walk, NW3. *T:* 01-435 5156.

**RICHARDSON, Rt. Rev. John;** *see* Nicobar Islands, Bishop of.

**RICHARDSON, Sir (John) Eric,** Kt 1967; CBE 1962; PhD, BEng, CEng, FIEE, AMIMechE, FBHI, FPS; FRSA; Director, The Polytechnic of Central London, 1969-70; *b* 30 June 1905; *e surv. s* of late William and Mary Elizabeth Richardson, Birkenhead; *m* 1941, Alice May, *d* of H. M. Wilson, Hull; one *s* two *d* (and one *d* decd). *Educ:* Birkenhead Higher Elementary Sch.; Liverpool Univ. BEng 1st Cl. Hons, 1931, PhD 1933, Liverpool. Chief Lectr in Electrical Engineering, 1933-37, Head of Engineering Dept, 1937-41, Hull Municipal Technical Coll.; Principal: Oldham Municipal Technical Coll., 1942-44; Royal Technical Coll., Salford, 1944-47; Northampton Polytechnic, London, EC1, 1947-56; Dir Nat. Coll. of Horology and Instrument Technology, 1947-56; Dir of Educn, Regent Street Polytechnic, W1, 1957-69. Hon. Secretary Association of Technical Institutions, 1957-67, Chairman, 1967-68; Pres. Assoc. of Principals of Technical Instns, 1961-62; Deputy Chairman, Council for Overseas Colleges of Arts, Science and Technology, 1949-62; Member: Council for Technical Education and Training in Overseas Countries, 1962-; UK Adv. Cttee on Educn for Management, 1961-66; Governing Council of Nigerian Coll. of Art, Science and Technology, 1953-61; Council, Univ. Coll., Nairobi, 1961-70; Provisional Council, Univ. of East Africa, 1961-63; Governing Body, College of Aeronautics, Cranfield, 1956-59; Council of British Horological Institute, 1951-; Gen. Optical Council, 1959-; Science and Technol Cttee of CNAA, 1965-; Electrical Engrg Bd of CNAA (Chm.); Industrial Trg Bd for Electricity Supply Industry, 1965-; Council, RSA 1968- (Chm. Exams Cttee, 1969-); Council and Exec. Cttee, Leprosy Mission, 1970-; Council and Exec. Cttee, City and Guilds of London Inst., 1969- (Chm. Policy and Overseas Cttees; Vice-Chm. Technical Educn Cttee; Jt Hon. Sec., 1970-). Chairman: Africa Evangelical Fellowship (SAGM), 1950-70; Nat. Young Life Campaign, 1949-64; Council, Inter-Varsity Fellowship of Evangelical Unions, 1966-69; Governors of London Bible Coll., 1970-. *Publications:* paper in IEE Jl (Instn Prize); various papers on higher technological education in UK and Nigeria. *Recreations:* gardening, photography. *Address:* 25 Delamere Road, Ealing, W5. *T:* 01-567 1588.

**RICHARDSON, John Eric,** MS; FRCS; Surgeon: The London Hospital since 1949; The Royal Masonic Hospital since 1960; King Edward VII's Hospital for Officers since 1960; St Andrews Hospital, Dollis Hill, since 1965; Prince of Wales Hospital, Tottenham, N15,

1958-65; Consultant Surgeon to the Navy; *b* Loughborough, 24 February 1916; *s* of late C. G. Richardson, MD, FRCS; *m* 1943, Elisabeth Jean, *d* of late Rev. John Webster; one *s* one *d*. *Educ:* Clifton College; London Hospital. MB, BS London (Hons and Distinction, Pathology), 1939; MRCS, LRCP 1939. Andrew Clarke Prize, London Hosp., 1939. Resident Appointments, London Hospital and Poplar Hospital, 1939-41; Surgeon Lieut RNVR (Surgical Specialist), 1941-46; Surgical Registrar, London Hosp., 1946-47; Rockefeller Travelling Fellow, 1947-48; Research Fellow in Surgery, Harvard Univ., 1947-48; Fellow in Clinical Surgery, Massachusetts Gen. Hosp., Boston, Mass, 1947-48. Hunterian Prof., RCS, 1953. Examr in Surgery to Soc. of Apothecaries, London, 1959-67 and Univ. of London, 1962-63, 1965-66. *Publications:* contrib. to Lancet and BMJ on gastro-enterology and endocrine disease. *Address:* 90 Harley Street, W1. *T:* 01-935 2186; 10 Middle Field, NW8. *T:* 01-722 1101. *Clubs:* Garrick, Royal Lymington Yacht.

**RICHARDSON, Ven. John Farquhar,** MA; Archdeacon of Derby since 1952; Chaplain to The Queen since 1952; First Residentiary Canon of Derby Cathedral since 1954; *b* 23 April 1905; 2nd *s* of late William Henry Richardson and Gertrude Richardson (*née* Walker); *m* 1936, Elizabeth Mary, *d* of Henry Roy Dean; one *s* two *d*. *Educ:* Winchester; Trinity Hall, Cambridge; Westcott House, Cambridge. Curate of Holy Trinity, Cambridge, 1929-32; Chaplain of Repton School, 1932-35; Curate of St Martin-in-the-Fields, 1935-36; Vicar of Christ Church, Hampstead, 1936-41; Rector of Bishopwearmouth, 1941-52; Rural Dean of Wearmouth, 1947-52. Proctor in Convocation, 1950-52; Hon. Canon of Durham, 1951-52; Hon. Chaplain to the Queen, 1952. *Recreation:* golf. *Address:* 22 Kedleston Road, Derby DE3 1GU. *T:* Derby 46990. *Clubs:* Royal Automobile; Jesters; Hawks (Cambridge).

**RICHARDSON, Sir (John) Henry (Swain),** Kt 1941; Director, Yule Catto & Co. Ltd, East India Merchants; Past Director, The Chartered Bank; *b* 18 June 1889; *o s* of late John Richardson, Ashford, Kent; *m* 1920, Olga, 2nd *d* of George John Stavridi, of Geneva and Calcutta; one *d*. Served European War, 1914-19, in Mesopotamia and India with 5th Buffs and XIth Rajputs; Senior Deputy Chairman, Andrew Yule & Co. Ltd, 1936-41; Vice-Pres. Bengal Chamber of Commerce, 1939, and Pres., 1940; Pres. Associated Chambers of Commerce of India, 1940, Member, Council of State, Govt of India, 1939-41; Member, Legislative Assembly, Govt of India, and Leader, European Group, 1942-45. *Recreation:* music. *Address:* Fairlawn, Hall Place Drive, Queen's Road, Weybridge, Surrey. *Club:* Oriental.

**RICHARDSON, Sir John (Samuel),** 1st Bt, *cr* 1963; Kt 1960; MVO 1943; MD, FRCP; Physician: St Thomas' Hospital, since 1949; King Edward VII's Hospital for Officers since 1964; Cons. Physician to Metropolitan Police since 1957 and London Transport Board since 1964; Hon. Consultant Physician to the Army since 1964; Member, Army Medical Advisory Board, Ministry of Defence, 1965; Member, General Medical Council, since 1967; *b* 16 June 1910; *s* of Major John Watson Richardson, Solicitor, and Elizabeth Blakeney, *d* of Sir Samuel Roberts, 1st Baronet, both of Sheffield; *m* 1933, Sybil Angela Stephanie, *d* of A. Ronald Trist, Stanmore, and the late Mrs Trist; two *d*. *Educ:* Charterhouse; Trinity College, Cambridge. MB, BChir (Cambridge), 1936; MRCP 1937; FRCP, 1948; MD (Cambridge), 1940. Major, RAMC (temp.), 1939; Lt-Col, RAMC (temp.), 1942; 1st asst, Medical Professorial Unit, St Thomas' Hosp., 1946; Physician to Out-Patients, St Thomas' Hosp., 1947-68; Examiner in Medicine: Univs of Cambridge, London, Manchester and Ireland; Royal College of Physicians, Conjoint Bd; Bd of Governors, St Thomas' Hospital, 1953-59 and 1964-. Pres., BMA, 1970-; Member Council: Association of Physicians, 1956-59; Royal Society of Medicine (Hon. Librarian, 1957-63, Pres., Section of Medical Educn, 1967-68, Pres., 1969), 1957-66, 1967-; RCP, 1957-60, 1967-; National Representative of UK, Internat. Soc. of Internal Medicine, 1958-66, Pres., 1966-; Chm., Jt Consultants Cttee, 1967-; Mem., Gen. Med. Council, 1968-; Member Council: Med. Soc. of London (Hon. Sec. and Vice-Pres., 1956-, and Lettsomian Lecturer, 1963); Roy. Med. Foundn, 1960-70; Bedford Coll., 1960-62; Mem. Court, Apothecaries' Company, 1960- (Junior Warden, 1969); Mem. of Cutlers' Company. CStJ 1970. *Publications:* The Practice of Medicine, 2nd Ed., 1960; Connective Tissue Disorders, 1963; Anticoagulant Prophylaxis and Treatment (jointly), 1965; papers on endocrinological and general medical subjects in Quarterly Jl of Medicine, Jl of Physiology, Lancet, BMJ, Practitioner, etc. *Heir:* none. *Address:* Alvechurch, 1 Hillcrest Road, W5. *T:* 01-997 6988. *Club:* Athenæum.

**RICHARDSON, Prof. Leopold John Dixon,** OBE 1965; MA; Professor (Hon.) of Classical Literature, TCD, 1963; Member, Royal Irish Academy, 1965; retired as Professor of Greek, University College, Cardiff, 1946-58; Research Associate (Hon.) University College, London, 1964-66; Hon. Secretary, Classical Association, 1943-63; *b* 3 Aug. 1893; *o s* of late William Hamilton Irwin Richardson and late Sara Ann Dagg; *m* 1925, Frances Petticrew Patton (*d* 1955); two *d*. *Educ:* The High School, Dublin; Trinity College, Dublin. Classical Sizarship, Classical Foundn Schol.; Sen. Moderatorship with Gold Medal in Classics and in Mental and Moral Science, and Univ. Studentship in Classics, 1916; Vice-Chancellor's Prizeman, Greek Prose, Greek Verse, Latin Verse; Berkeley, Tyrrell and Vice-Chancellor's Medallist; Ferrar, William Roberts, Hebrew and Sanskrit Prizeman; Fellowship Prizeman, 1929. MA 1920; MA (Wales) 1942. Member of Council: Philological Soc., 1944-50; Roman Soc., 1949-52; Hellenic Soc., 1955-58. Editor: Proc. of Classical Assoc., 1948-63; Studies in Mycenaean Inscriptions and Dialect, 1959-. Asst to Prof. of Greek, Queen's Univ., Belfast, 1922-23; Dep. Prof., 1923-24; Lectr in Latin, Univ. Coll., Cardiff, 1925-46. *Publications:* Ta Indika, 1929; various articles in English, Irish and foreign learned journals. *Address:* 1 Howell's Crescent, Llandaff, Glam. *T:* Cardiff 561078; 75 Wellington Road, Dublin 4. *T:* 689542. *Club:* University (Dublin).

**RICHARDSON, Sir Leslie Lewis,** 2nd Bt, *cr* 1924; Director of Companies; *b* 14 August 1915; *s* of Sir Lewis Richardson, 1st Bart, CBE, head of the firm of L. Richardson & Co. of London, Port Elizabeth, New York and Boston, and Phoebe, *o d* of Isaac Isaacs; *S* father 1934; *m* 1946, Joy Patricia, twin *d* of P. J. Rillstone, Johannesburg; two *s* one *d*. *Educ:* Harrow. Served with South African Artillery, 1940-44, in the Union and North Africa. *Heir:* *s* Anthony Lewis Richardson, *b* 5 Aug. 1950. *Address:* The Richardson Building, Market Square, Port Elizabeth, South Africa; Yellowwoods, Witteklip, Cape Province, South Africa.

**RICHARDSON, Linetta de Castelvecchio,** MA; Serena Professor of Italian at University of Birmingham, 1921-46; *yr d* of late Francesco and the Comtesse Joséphine Palamidessi de Castelvecchio; *m* 1929, Rev. Canon Robert Douglas Richardson, *qv*. Bronze medallist of the Regio Conservatorio di St Anna in Pisa. Lecturer and Head of Italian Department at King's College, London, 1916-21. *Address:* Greenfields, Upton Lovel, nr Warminster, Wilts. *T:* Codford St Mary 229.

**RICHARDSON, Group Capt. Michael Oborne,** RAF, retired; Commandant, Star and Garter Home for Disabled Sailors, Soldiers and Airmen, since 1967; *b* Holmfirth, Yorks, 13 May 1908; *s* of Rev. Canon G. L. Richardson, MA, BD, and Edith Maria (*née* Ellison); *m* 1935, Nellie Marguerita, *d* of Walter Ross Somervell, Elizavetgrad, Russia; one *s* one *d*. *Educ:* Lancing Coll.; Keble Coll., Oxford; Guy's Hospital. BA 1929; MRCS, LRCP 1938; DPH 1955; MA Oxon 1963; DPhysMed 1964. Oxford House, Bethnal Green, 1930. Commissioned RAF, 1939; served at Kenley; War Service included HQ Fighter Comd (Unit), S Africa, Western Desert, Malta, Sicily, Italy (despatches). Post-war service in Germany and Aden and comdt various hosps and Medical Rehabilitation Units. OStJ 1965. *Recreations:* the countryside. *Address:* Ancaster House, Richmond Hill, Surrey. *T:* Richmond 1473; The Old Thatched Cottage, Love Lane, Shaftesbury, Dorset. *T:* Shaftesbury 2392. *Club:* Royal Air Force.

**RICHARDSON, Sir Ralph David,** Kt 1947; Actor; President: National Youth Theatre, since 1959; Greater London Arts Association, since 1969; *b* Cheltenham, Glos, 1902; *s* of Arthur Richardson and Lydia Russell; *m* 1st, 1924, Muriel Hewitt (*d* 1942); no *c*; 2nd, 1944, Meriel Forbes-Robertson; one *s*. *Educ:* Xaverian Coll., Brighton; privately. Made his first appearance on the stage at Brighton, 1921; toured in the Provinces in Shakespeare Repertory for four years; joined the Birmingham Repertory Theatre in 1925; first London appearance in 1926 at the Haymarket Theatre as Arthur Varwell in Yellow Sands; season of plays at the Court Theatre in 1928; toured in South Africa in 1929; from 1930 to 1932 played two seasons at the Old Vic and two seasons at the Malvern summer theatre; Too True To Be Good at the New Theatre and For Services Rendered at the Queens in 1933, followed by Wild Decembers and Sheppey; Eden End and Cornelius at the Duchess Theatre in 1935, and played Mercutio in Romeo and Juliet in the USA in 1936; Promise, Bees on the Boatdeck and The Amazing Dr Clitterhouse, until 1937; in 1938, The Midsummer Night's Dream and Othello at the Old Vic; Johnson over Jordan, Sept. 1939, joined Fleet Air Arm as sub/Lieut RNVR; Lieut (A) RNVR 1940; Lt-Comdr RNVR 1941. Released from Naval Service, June 1944, to act for and direct Drama of Old Vic Theatre Company; Old Vic 1st Season, 1944-45: played Peer Gynt, Bluntschli in Arms and the Man, Uncle Vanya, Henry VII in Richard the Third, toured Germany and visited Comédie Française in Paris. Old Vic 2nd season, 1945-46: played Falstaff in Henry IV, parts 1 and 2, Bluntschli in Arms and the Man, Tiresias in Oedipus Rex, Lord Burleigh in The Critic. Visited New York for six weeks' season. Old Vic 3rd Season, 1946-47: played Cyrano in Cyrano de Bergerac, the Inspector in An Inspector Calls, Face in The Alchemist, produced Richard II (playing Gaunt): Dr Sloper in The Heiress, Haymarket, 1949; David Preston in Home at Seven, Wyndham's 1950; Vershinin in Three Sisters, Aldwych, 1951; Stratford-on-Avon Season, 1952; Macbeth, Volpone, The Tempest; The White Carnation (playing John Greenwood), Globe, 1953; A Day by the Sea, Haymarket, 1954; Sleeping Prince and Separate Tables, Australian and New Zealand Tour, 1955; The Waltz of the Toreadors (New York), 1957; Flowering Cherry, Haymarket, 1958; The Complaisant Lover, Globe, 1959; The Last Joke, 1960; The School for Scandal, Haymarket and US Tour, 1962; Six Characters in search of an Author, May Fair, 1963; The Merchant of Venice and A Midsummer Night's Dream, South American and European Tour, 1964; Carving a Statue, Haymarket, 1964; You Never Can Tell, 1966; The Rivals, 1966, 1967; Merchant of Venice, 1967; What the Butler Saw, 1969. *Films:* made his first film, The Ghoul, in 1933; other films include: Things to Come; The Man Who Could Work Miracles; Bulldog Drummond; South Riding; Divorce of Lady X; The Citadel; Four Feathers; Q Planes; Night of the Fire; The Silver Fleet; The Volunteer; School for Secrets; Anna Karenina, The Fallen Idol, The Heiress (Hollywood); Outcast of the Islands; Home at Seven; The Holly and the Ivy; The Sound Barrier; The Passionate Stranger; Oscar Wilde; Exodus; Spartacus; Long Day's Journey into Night; Woman of Straw; Dr Zhivago, 1965; The Wrong Box, 1966; Gordon of Khartoum, 1966; Twelfth Night, 1968; Battle of Britain, 1968; Oh! What a Lovely War, 1968; The Bed-Sitting Room, 1968; The Looking-Glass War, 1968; Mr Micawber in David Copperfield, 1969; A Run on Gold, 1969; Home, 1970. Hon. DLitt Oxon, 1969. Order of St Olaf (Norway), 1970. *Publications:* articles in magazines and newspapers. *Recreations:* drawing, squash racquets, tennis. *Address:* 1 Chester Terrace, Regent's Park, NW1. *Clubs:* Athenæum, Beefsteak, Savile.

**RICHARDSON, Robert Augustus;** HM Chief Inspector of Schools, Department of Education and Science, since Sept. 1968; *b* 2 Aug. 1912; *s* of late Ferdinand Augustus Richardson and Muriel Emma Richardson; *m* 1936, Elizabeth Gertrude Williamson; one *d*. *Educ:* Royal College of Art. Schoolmaster, 1934; Headmaster, Sidcup School of Art, 1937. Served in Royal Navy, 1941-46. Principal: Folkestone Sch. of Art, 1946; Maidstone Coll. of Art, 1948. Dept of Education and Science: HM Inspector of Schools, 1958; HM Staff Inspector, 1966. ARCA 1934. *Recreations:* theatre, music. *Address:* 68 Highfield Drive, Hurstpierpoint, Sussex. *T:* Hurstpierpoint 2186.

**RICHARDSON, Rev. Canon Robert Douglas,** DD, BLitt, MA; *b* 26 February 1893; *er s* of late Frederick Richardson; *m* 1929, Professor Linetta P. de Castelvecchio (*see* Richardson, Linetta de Castelvecchio). *Educ:* Hertford College and Ripon Hall, Oxford. Served European War, 1914-18, in RN; Curate of Stourport-on-Severn; Succentor of Birmingham Cathedral; Vicar of Four Oaks and Vicar of Harborne; Select Preacher, Cambridge University; sometime External Lectr in Biblical Studies to Univ. of Birmingham; Examining Chaplain to Bishop of Birmingham, 1932-53; Canon Emeritus of Birmingham Cathedral; Principal of Ripon Hall, Oxford, 1948-52; Rector of Boyton with Sherrington, 1952-67. *Publications:* The Conflict of Ideals in the Church of England, 1923; The Gospel of Modernism, 1933; Sectional Editor of Webster's Dictionary (1934 edn); A Revised Order of Holy Communion, 1936. Christian Belief and Practice, 1940. A Further Inquiry into Eucharistic Origins (in the English edn of Lietzmann's Mass and Lord's Supper), publ. in fascicles, 1953-; The Psalms as Christian Prayers and Praises, 1960; contrib. to various

Theological Jls. *Address:* Greenfields, Upton Lovel, nr Warminster, Wilts. *T:* Codford St Mary 229.

**RICHARDSON, Maj.-Gen. Roland,** CB 1944; MC; *b* 25 March 1896. 2nd Lt Indian Army, 1915; Capt. 1918; Major, 1932; Bt Lt-Col 1935; Lt-Col 1937; Col 1940; Temp. Maj.-Gen. 1943; Maj.-Gen. 1944; psc; retired 1948. *Address:* Chisaro, Cashel, Rhodesia.

**RICHARDSON, Ronald Frederick,** MBE 1945; Chairman, North Western Electricity Board, since 1964; *b* 1913; *s* of Albert F. Richardson and Elizabeth Jane (*née* Sayer); *m* 1946, Anne Elizabeth McArdle; two *s. Educ:* Coopers' Company's School; Northampton Engineering Inst.; Polytechnic Inst.; Administrative Staff College. Served War of 1939-45: Major, Field Park Company RE, 1942-46. Callenders Cables, 1929-36; Central London Electricity, 1936-39, 1946-48; London Electricity Board, 1948-52; British Electricity Authority, 1952-57; South Western Electricity Board, 1957-63. Chm., Nat. Inspection Council for Electrical Installation Contracting, 1969-70; Member: North West Economic Planning Council, 1965-70; Court of Manchester Univ., 1969-; Council of Salford Univ., 1970-. *Recreations:* music, the open air. *Address:* Four Gables, Leycester Drive, Slade Lane, Mobberley, Knutsford, Cheshire. *T:* Mobberley 3131. *Clubs:* Royal Automobile; St James's (Manchester).

**RICHARDSON, Sir Simon Alaisdair S.;** *see* Stewart-Richardson.

**RICHARDSON, Tony;** Director, Woodfall Film Productions Ltd, since 1958; *b* 5 June 1928; *s* of Clarence Albert and Elsie Evans Richardson; *m* 1962, Vanessa Redgrave, *qv* (marr. diss., 1967); two *d. Educ:* Wadham College, Oxford. *Plays* directed or produced: Look Back in Anger; The Chairs; Pericles and Othello (Stratford); The Entertainer; Semi-Detached; Luther; The Seagull; St Joan of the Stockyards; Hamlet. *Films* directed or produced: Look Back in Anger, 1958; The Entertainer, 1959; Saturday Night and Sunday Morning (prod.), 1960; Taste of Honey, 1961; The Loneliness of the Long Distance Runner (prod. and dir.), 1962; Tom Jones (dir.), 1962; Girl with Green Eyes (prod.), 1964; The Loved One (prod.), 1965; Mademoiselle (dir.), 1965; The Sailor from Gibraltar (dir.), 1965; Red and Blue (dir.) 1966; The Charge of the Light Brigade (dir.), 1968; Laughter in the Dark (dir.), 1969; Hamlet (dir.), 1969; Ned Kelly (dir.), 1969. *Recreations:* directing plays and films. *Address:* 11a Curzon Street, W1. *T:* 01-493 7613.

**RICHARDSON, William Eric,** CEng, FIEE, FBIM; Chairman, South Wales Electricity Board, since 1968; Member, Electricity Council, since 1968; *b* 21 May 1915; *o s* of William Pryor and Elizabeth Jane Richardson, Hove, Sussex; *m* 1946, Helen Lilian Hall; one *s. Educ:* Royal Masonic Sch., Bushey. Engineer with Brighton Corp., 1934-37; Southampton Corp., 1937-39; Norwich Corp., 1939-46; Distribution Engr with Newport (Mon) Corp., 1946-48; Area Engr with S Wales Electricity Bd, 1948-57; Area Manager, 1957-65; Chief Commercial Engr, 1965-67; Dep. Chm., 1967-68. *Recreations:* sailing, golf, gardening. *Address:* Beaumont, 92 Allt-yr-yn Avenue, Newport, Monmouthshire. *T:* Newport (Mon) 64388.

**RICHARDSON, Sir William (Robert),** Kt 1967; Chief Executive Officer, Cooperative Press Ltd, since 1967; *b* 16 Jan. 1909; *s* of Thomas and Constance Margaret Richardson; *m* 1932, Gladys Gillians; one *s* two *d. Educ:* various public elem. schs, Newcastle upon Tyne; evening classes; Cooperative College. Editor, Cooperative News, 1938; Editor, Reynolds News, later changed name to Sunday Citizen, 1942-67, when paper closed. Mem. Post Office Users' Nat. Council, 1969-. *Recreation:* reading. *Address:* 6 Alders Road, Disley, Cheshire. *T:* Disley 3758.

**RICHARDSON, William Rowson,** CMG 1948; formerly Under-Secretary, Ministry of Education; *b* 1 Jan. 1892; *s* of George and Maria Richardson, Leeds; *m* 1922, Margaret Hadfield, *d* of late J. N. Marsden, Lisbon; one *s* one *d.* Chevalier 1st Class Order of St Olaf, 1948. *Address:* Lark Rise, Stonards Brow, Shamley Green, Nr Guildford. *T:* Bramley 2114.

**RICHARDSON, Sir William Wigham,** 2nd Bt, *cr* 1929; MBE 1919; JP, CA; *b* 12 June 1893; *e s* of Sir Philip Wigham Richardson, 1st Bt; *S* father 1953; *m* 1921, Katharine Elizabeth (*d* 1945), *d* of late Howard John Elphinstone; no *c. Educ:* Rugby School; abroad. Served European War, 1914-19. ADC to Governor and C-in-C, Barbados, 1918-20. JP (Tunbridge Wells), 1940; CC Kent, 1946; CA Kent, 1950. *Heir: b* George Wigham Richardson, *qv. Address:* 4 Calverley Park, Tunbridge Wells. *T:* 1819. *Club:* Union, Royal Automobile.

**RICHARDSON-BUNBURY, Sir (Richard David) Michael,** *see* Bunbury.

**RICHES, Sir Derek (Martin Hurry),** KCMG 1963 (CMG, 1958); Ambassador to Lebanon, 1963-67, retired; *b* 26 July 1912; *s* of late Claud Riches and Flora Martin; *m* 1942 Helen Barkley Hayes, Poughkeepsie, NY, USA; one *d. Educ:* University College School; University College, London. Appointed Probationer Vice-Consul, Beirut, Dec. 1934. Subsequently promoted and held various appts, Ethiopia and Cairo; Foreign Office, 1944; promoted one of HM Consuls serving in FO, 1945. Kabul, 1948 (in charge, 1948 and 1949); Consul at Jedda, 1951 (Chargé d'Affaires, 1952); Officer Grade 6, Branch A, Foreign Service and apptd Trade Comr, Khartoum, 1953. Attached to Imperial Defence College, 1955; returned to Foreign Office, 1955; Counsellor in the Foreign Office, Head of Eastern Department, 1955; British Ambassador in Libya, 1959-61; British Ambassador to the Congo, 1961-63. *Address:* 48 The Avenue, Kew Gardens, Surrey. *Club:* Royal Automobile.

**RICHES, Sir Eric (William),** Kt 1958; MC; MS (London), FRCS; Emeritus Surgeon and Urologist to Middlesex Hospital; Hon. Consultant Urologist to Hospital of St John and St Andrew; formerly Consulting Urologist to the Army and to Ministry of Pensions Spinal Injury Centre; Urologist, St Andrew's Hospital, Dollis Hill; lately Urologist, Royal Masonic Hospital; Hon. Curator, Historical Surgical Instruments Collection, Royal College of Surgeons, 1962; *b* Alford, Lincolnshire, 29 July 1897; *s* of William Riches; *m* 1st, 1927, Annie M. S. (*d* 1952), *d* of late Dr A. T. Brand, Driffield, E Yorks; two *d*; 2nd, 1954, Susan Elizabeth Ann, *d* of Lt-Col L. H. Kitton, MBE, MC; one *d. Educ:* Christ's Hospital; Middlesex Hospital. Served European War, 10th Lincoln and 11th Suffolk Regt, Capt. and Adjutant (MC); Senior Broderip Scholar and Lyell Gold Medallist, Middlesex Hospital, 1925. Past Vice-President, Royal College of Surgeons, Member of Court of Examiners, 1940-46; Hunterian Professor 1938 and 1942, Jacksonian Prizeman, 1942; Bradshaw Lecturer, 1962; Gordon-Taylor Lecturer,

1967. Hon. Fellow Royal Society of Medicine, 1966, lately Hon. Librarian, ex-President Clinical Section, Section of Urology, and Section of Surgery. Past-President Medical Society of London; Lettsomian Lecturer, 1958, Orator, 1970; Senior Fellow Association of Surgeons of Great Britain and Ireland; Past President Hunterian Society, Orator, 1967; Vice-President, Internat. Soc. of Urology (Pres. XIII Congress, 1964); Hon. Fellow and Past Pres. of British Assoc. of Urological Surgeons; St Peters medallist, 1964; Member Association Française d'Urologie; Honorary Member: Urological Society of Australasia; Canadian Urological Assoc.; Swedish Urological Soc.; American Urological Assoc.; Ramon Guiteras Lectr, 1963; Hon. Associate Mem. French Academy of Surgery, 1961; Emeritus Mem. Internat. Soc. of Surgery; Treas. British Journal of Surgery; Past chm., Ed. Cttee, British Jl of Urology; Mem. of Biological and Medical Cttee, Royal Commission on Population. Visiting Professor, Urol.; University of Texas and State University of New York, 1965; Visiting Professor and Balfour Lecturer, University of Toronto, 1966. Treasurer, Christ's Hospital, and Chm., Council of Almoners, 1970-. *Publications:* Modern Trends in Urology, Series 1, 1953, Series 2, 1960, Series 3, 1969; Tumours of the Kidney and Ureter, 1964; various articles on Surgery and Urology in Scientific journals; contributor to Text Book of Urology, British Surgical Practice, and to Encyclopædia of Urology. *Recreations:* golf, music, photography. *Address:* 22 Weymouth Street, Portland Place, W1N 3FA. *T:* 01-580 4800.

**RICHES, General Sir Ian (Hurry),** KCB 1960 (CB 1959); DSO 1945; *b* 27 Sept. 1908; *s* of C. W. H. Riches; *m* 1936, Winifred Eleanor Layton; two *s*. *Educ:* Univ. Coll. Sch., London. Joined Royal Marines, 1927; Major, 1946; Lt-Colonel, 1949; Colonel, 1953; Maj.-Gen., 1957; Lt-Gen. 1959; General 1961. Maj.-Gen., RM, Portsmouth Group, 1957-59; Commandant-General, Royal Marines, 1959-62; Regional Dir of Civil Defence, 1964-68; Representative Col Comdt, 1967-68. *Address:* c/o National Provincial Bank, Lancaster Gate, W2.

**RICHES, Rt. Rev. Kenneth;** *see* Lincoln, Bishop of.

**RICHES, Hon. Lindsay Gordon,** CMG 1967; MP (South Australian Parliament) since 1933; Mayor of Port Augusta City, South Australia, since 1936; *b* 18 Feb. 1904; *s* of F. W. Riches, Bordertown, S Austr.; *m* 1933, Evelyn Frances Higginson; one *s* two *d*. *Educ:* Bordertown Public School. Editor, The Transcontinental Newspaper, Port Augusta, 1928-38; Member S Austr. Parliament: for Newcastle, 1933-38; for Stuart, 1938-; Speaker of S Australian Parliament, 1965-68. *Recreations:* football, tennis, swimming, church activities. *Address:* 77 Flinders Terrace, Port Augusta, South Australia. *T:* 2487.

**RICHMOND,** 9th Duke of, *cr* 1675, **and GORDON,** 4th Duke of, *cr* 1876; **Frederick Charles Gordon-Lennox;** Earl of March, Baron Settrington, Duke of Lennox, Earl of Darnley, Baron Methuen, 1675; Earl of Kinrara, 1876; Duke d'Aubigny (France), 1683-84; Hereditary Constable of Inverness Castle; Flight Lieut, RAFVR; *b* 5 Feb. 1904; *o surv s* of 8th Duke and Hilda, CBE, *qv*, *d* of late Henry Arthur Brassey, Preston Hall, Kent; *S* father, 1935; *m* 1927, Elizabeth Grace, *y d* of late Rev. T. W. Hudson; two *s*. *Educ:* Eton; Christ Church, Oxford. *Heir:* *s* Earl of March, *qv*. *Address:* Carne's Seat, Goodwood, Chichester, Sussex.

*See also Sir Alastair Coats, Bt, C. G. Vyner.*

**RICHMOND and GORDON, Hilda Madeleine, Duchess of,** DBE, *cr* 1946 (CBE 1919); JP; *e d* of late Henry A. Brassey, Preston Hall, Aylesford; *m* 1893, 8th Duke of Richmond and Gordon (*d* 1935); one *s* two *d*.

**RICHMOND, Archdeacon of;** *see* Turnbull, Ven. John William.

**RICHMOND, Sir Alan (James),** Kt 1969; Director, Lanchester Polytechnic, Coventry, since 1970; *b* 12 Oct. 1919. Trained and employed Engineering Industry, 1938-45; London Univ., BSc(Eng) 1945, PhD 1954; Lecturer, Battersea Polytechnic, 1946-55; Head of Engineering Dept, Welsh Coll. of Advanced Technology, 1955-58; Principal, Lanchester College of Technology, Coventry, 1959-69. FIMechE. *Publications:* (with W. J. Peck) Applied Thermodynamics Problems for Engineers, 1950; Problems in Heat Engines, 1957; various reviews and articles. *Recreations:* gardening, reading. *Address:* 25 Asthill Grove, Coventry CV3 6HN. *T:* Coventry 29198. *Club:* Royal Commonwealth Society.

**RICHMOND, Sir John (Christopher Blake),** KCMG 1963 (CMG 1959); Lecturer, School of Oriental Studies, University of Durham, since 1966; *b* 7 September 1909; *s* of E. T. Richmond, FRIBA, and M. M. Richmond (*née* Lubbock); *m* 1939, D. M. L. Galbraith; two *s* three *d*. *Educ:* Lancing College; Hertford College, Oxford; University College, London. Various archaeological expeditions, 1931-36; HM Office of Works, 1937-39; served War, Middle East, 1939-46; Dept of Antiquities, Palestine Govt, 1946-47; HM Diplomatic Service, Baghdad, 1947; Foreign Office, 1951; Counsellor, British Embassy, Amman, 1953-55; HM Consul-General, Houston, Texas, 1955-58; Foreign Office, 1958-59; Counsellor, British Property Commission, Cairo, 1959; HM Ambassador to Kuwait, 1961-63 (Political Agent, Kuwait, 1959-61); Supernumerary Fellow of St Anthony's College, Oxford, 1963-64; Ambassador to Sudan, 1965-66. *Address:* c/o Messrs Coutts & Co., 15 Lombard St, EC3.

**RICHMOND, Sir John (Frederick),** 2nd Bt, *cr* 1929; *b* 12 Aug. 1924; *s* of Sir Frederick Henry Richmond, 1st Bt (formerly Chm. Debenham's Ltd and Harvey Nichols & Co. Ltd), and Dorothy Agnes, *d* of Frances Joseph Sheppard; *S* father 1953; *m* 1965, Mrs Anne Moreen Bentley; one *d*. *Educ:* Eton; Jesus Coll., Cambridge. Lt 10th Roy. Hussars; seconded Provost br., 1944-47. *Address:* Shimpling Park Farm, Bury St Edmunds, Suffolk. *Club:* Cavalry.

**RICHMOND, Vice-Adm. Sir Maxwell,** KBE 1957 (OBE 1940); CB 1954; DSO 1942; RN retired; *b* 19 Oct. 1900; *e s* of Robert Richardson Richmond and Bernadette Richmond (*née* Farrell); *m* 1929, Jessie Messervy Craig; one *s* three *d* (and one *s* decd). *Educ:* New Zealand State Schools; Westminster. Cadet Royal Navy 1918; Lieutenant 1922; specialised navigation; held various (N) posts, 1926-36. Comdr 1936; HMS Hostile in Comd, 1936-38; Staff Coll., 1939; HMS Basilisk in Comd, 1939-40; Dover Patrol, Norway and Dunkirk; Operations, Admty, 1940-41; HMS Bulldog as Sen. Officer Escort Gp, 1942, Atlantic and Russian Convoys; Capt. 1942; Chief Staff Officer to Cdre, Londonderry, 1943; HMS Milne as Capt. (D) 3rd Dest. Flot., 1944-46; Home Fleet, Russian Convoys and Flank Force, Mediterranean; Asst Chief of Supplies, Admty, 1946-48; Naval

Liaison Officer, Wellington, NZ, 1948-50; Sen. Naval Officer, N Ire., 1951; Rear-Adm. 1952; Deputy Chief of Naval Personnel (Training), 1952-55; Flag Officer (Air), Mediterranean, and Flag Officer Second-in-Command, Mediterranean Fleet, 1955-Oct. 1956. Order of the Red Banner (Russian) 1942; Croix de Guerre (French) 1945. *Recreations:* sailing and tramping. *Address:* 29 Parkside Street, Auckland 5, New Zealand. *Club:* United Service.

**RICHMOND, Oliffe Legh,** MA; *b* 13 Sept. 1881; *s* of late D. C. Richmond, CB; *m* 1st, 1919, Beryl (*d* 1929), *d* of late Very Rev. C. E. T. Griffith; one *s* one *d*; 2nd, 1934, Ursula, *d* of late Rev. Charles Winser. *Educ:* Fonthill; Eton (Newcastle Medallist and Wilder Divinity Prizeman); King's College, Cambridge. Sir William Browne's Medal for Latin Ode, 1902; Craven Research Student, 1904-6; Fellow of King's College, Cambridge, 1905-15; Classical Lecturer, 1911-14; Professor of Latin in the Univ. College of South Wales and Monmouthshire, 1914-19; served with His Majesty's Forces as Intelligence Officer in War Office and at Italian Headquarters, 1916-19; Professor of Humanity in Edinburgh University, 1919-48. *Publications:* The Temples of Apollo and Divus Augustus on Roman Coins (in Essays and Studies presented to William Ridgeway, 1913); The Augustan Palatium, Journal of Roman Studies, 1914, vol. 2; Propertius 1928; Rawalpindi, and other verses in wartime, 1941; Song of Freedom, and other verses in war-time, 1942; Challenge to Faith, 1945; Thames Symphony, 1947; Two Ancient Love-tales, 1949; The Farther View, 1950. *Address:* 3 Silchester Hall, near Reading, Berks. *T:* Silchester 269.

**RICHNELL, Donovan Thomas;** Director and Goldsmiths' Librarian, University of London Library, since 1967; *b* 3 Aug. 1911; *o s* of Thomas Hodgson Richnell and Constance Margaret Richnell (*née* Allen); *m* 1957, Renée Norma Hilton; one *s* one *d*. *Educ:* St Paul's School; Corpus Christi Coll., Cambridge; University Coll., London. BA, FLA. Library Asst, Royal Soc. Med., 1934-35; Asst Librarian, Nat. Library of Scotland, 1935-46; Sub-Librarian, Royal Soc. Med., 1946-49; Dep. Librarian, London Univ. Library, 1949-60; Librarian, Univ. of Reading, 1960-67. Sec. to Regional Comr for Civil Defence, Scotland, 1939-40. Royal Navy, 1942-46; Lieut (sp.) RNVR. Detached service with US Army X Corps, New Guinea and Philippines, 1944-45 (US Bronze Star, Philippines campaign, 1945). Library Association: Mem. Council, 1962-; President 1970; Hon. Sec., U and R Section, 1961-65; National and University Libraries Committee: Chm., 1962-66; Aslib: Mem. Council, 1951-; Hon. Sec., 1957-63; Chm. of Council, 1968-. Mem. Library Adv. Council for England, 1966-. Mem. Nat. Central Library Exec. Cttee, 1964-. *Publications:* various articles. *Recreations:* music, theatre. *Address:* 3 Upper Staithe, Chiswick, W4.

**RICHTER, Gisela M. A.;** Curator Emeritus, Department of Greek and Roman Art, Metropolitan Museum of Art, NY; Curator, 1925-48; *b* London, 1882; *d* of late Jean Paul Richter. *Educ:* Maida Vale High School; Girton College, Cambridge; British School of Archæology, Athens. LittD (Cambridge University and TCD); Hon. LHD (Smith College); Hon. DFA (Rochester Univ.); Hon. DLitt (Oxford Univ.); Hon. PhD (Basle Univ.). Hon. Member of Society for the Promotion of Hellenic Studies; Hon. Fellow Society of Antiquaries, London; Member: Archæological Institute of America (Executive Committee, 1944-46); President New York Soc., 1941-48; German Archæological Inst.; Soc. for the Promotion of Roman Studies; American Philosophical Soc.; Council, L'Association Internationale d'Archéologie Classique; Member: Accademia pontificia archeologica, Rome; Accademia Nazionale dei Lincei; Accademia delle Scienze, etc., Naples; Corr. Fellow British Acad.; Fellowship Awards Cttee Internat. Fedn of Univ. Women; Vis. Cttee to Dumbarton Oaks, 1952-65 and Museum of Fine Arts, Boston; Advisory Cttee, Guggenheim Foundation, 1948-52; Managing Cttee, American School of Classical Studies, Athens; Fellow American Numismatic Society; Fellow, Metropolitan Museum of Art; Hon. Fell., Somerville College, Oxford, Girton College, Cambridge; Associate Editor American Journal of Archæology; Visiting Lecturer, Columbia University; Ryerson Memorial Lecturer at Yale Univ., 1938; Mary Flexner Lecturer at Bryn Mawr Coll., 1941-42; Charles Beebe Martin lecturer at Oberlin College, 1943. Trustee American Friends of Greece. Achievement Award, Amer. Assoc. Univ. Women, 1944; Medal, Amer. Acad., Rome, 1965; Gold Medal, Archaeological Inst. of America, 1968. *Publications:* Catalogue of Greek, Roman, and Etruscan Bronzes, 1915; Catalogue of Engraved Gems of the Classical Style, 1920; Handbook of the Classical Collection of the Metropolitan Museum, 1917, 6th edn 1930; Craft of Athenian Pottery, 1923; Ancient Furniture, 1926; The Sculpture and Sculptors of the Greeks, 1929, 4th edn 1970; Animals in Greek Sculpture, 1930; Shapes and Names of Athenian Vases (with M. J. Milne), 1930; Red-figured Athenian Vases in the Metropolitan Museum (drawings by Lindsley F. Hall), 1936; Augustan Art (with Christine Alexander), 1939; Handbook of the Etruscan Collection, 1940; Roman Portraits, I and II, 1941; Kouroi (with photographs by Gerard M. Young), 1942; Ancient Gems, from Evans and Beatty Collections, 1942; Archaic Attic Gravestones, 1944; Greek Painting, 1944, 2nd edn 1949; Attic Red-Figured Vases, A Survey, 1946, 2nd edn, 1958; Roman Portraits, 1948; Archaic Greek Art against its Historical Background, 1949; Three Critical Periods in Greek Sculpture, 1951; Attic Black-Figured Kylikes (fascicule 2 of Metropolitan Museum of Art, Corpus Vasorum Antiquorum), 1952; Handbook of the Greek Collection of the Metropolitan Museum, 1953; Catalogue of Greek Sculptures in the Metropolitan Museum, 1954; Ancient Italy, 1955; Greek Portraits (Collection Latomus XX), 1955; Catalogue of Engraved Gems in the Metropolitan Museum, 1956; Catalogue of Greek and Roman Antiquities in the Dumbarton Oaks Collection, 1956; A Handbook of Greek Art, 1959, 6th edn 1969; Greek Portraits II (Collection Latomus XXXVI), 1959; Greek Portraits III (Collection Latomus XLVIII), 1960; Kouroi, Archaic Greek Youths, 1960 (3rd edn 1970); The Archaic Gravestones of Attica, 1961; Greek Portraits IV (Collection Latomus, 1962); The Portraits of the Greeks (3 vols) 1965; The Furniture of the Greeks, Etruscans, and Romans, 1966; Korai, Archaic Greek Maidens, 1968; The Engraved Gems of the Greeks, Etruscans and Romans: Part I, 1968; Part II, 1970; Perspective in Greek and Roman Art, 1970; articles in archæological jls. *Address:* 81 Viale delle Mura Gianicolensi, Rome. *Clubs:* University Women's (London); English-Speaking Union (New York).

**RICHTER, Sviatoslav;** pianist; *b* Zhitomir, Ukraine, 20 March 1915; *m* Nina Dorliak. *Educ:* Moscow State Conservatoire. Gave first piano recital at age of nineteen and began to give concerts on a wide scale in 1942. Appeared at the Royal Albert Hall and the Royal Festival Hall, London, 1961; Royal Festival Hall, 1963, 1966. Was recently awarded Lenin Prize, and also holds the title of "Peoples' Artist of the USSR"; Order of Lenin, 1965. *Recreations:* walking, ski-ing and painting. *Address:* c/o Victor Hochhauser Ltd, 4 Holland Park Avenue, W11.

**RICKARDS, David Ayscough,** CBE 1960; MA; Headmaster, Welbeck College, since 1953; *b* 27 Sept. 1912; *s* of late G. W. Rickards, MP for Skipton, 1933-43, and Katharine Rigby; *m* 1937, Kathleen Louise Cochran; one *d. Educ:* Sedbergh School; Pembroke College, Cambridge (MA). Asst Master, Blundell's Sch., 1934-39; Housemaster, Blundell's School, 1939-40. Served War of 1939-45: commission in Duke of Wellington's Regt, 1940; Staff Captain 3rd Inf. Bde, 1940-41; student at Staff Coll., Camberley, 1942; DAQMG, South Eastern Command, HQ, 1943; DAQMG (Plans), HQ Second Army, 1944; Lt-Col Instructor, Staff College, Camberley, 1945-46. Again Housemaster, Blundell's School, 1946-53. Hon. Major TARO. *Recreations:* Cambridge Blue for cross-country running. Half-Blue for Athletics (3 miles); ocean racing, golf, shooting. *Address:* Welbeck College, Worksop, Notts. *T:* Worksop 3308 (house), 3326 (office); Thorborough, Grove Hill, St Mawes, Cornwall. *T:* St Mawes 376. *Clubs:* Public Schools; Royal Ocean Racing; Hawks (Cambridge); Achilles.

**RICKARDS, Maj.-Gen. Gerald Arthur,** DSO 1918; MC; late RA; *b* 24 Oct. 1886; *s* of late A. G. Rickards, KC, 20 Southwell Gardens, SW7; *m* 1920, Stella Evelyn, 2nd *d* of late Lt-Col H. G. Ricardo, DSO, Gatcombe, Minchinhampton, Glos; four *d. educ:* Eton; RMA Woolwich. 2nd Lieut RFA, 1906; Lieut 1909; Capt., 1914; Major, 1917; Lt-Col, 1935; Col., 1938; acting Maj.-Gen., 1940; Temp. Maj.-Gen., 1941; served European War (France), 1915-19 (despatches twice, MC, DSO); commanded "A" Indian Field Artillery Brigade at Bangalore, 1935-38; commanded 44th AA Brigade, 1938-40; 12th AA Division, 1940-42; retired (Hon. Maj.-Gen.), 1942; Senior Hon. Branch Visitor, SSAFA, 1944-50. Chm. Tetbury RDC, 1950-60. DL Glos, 1953. Order of Aviz (Portugal) 2nd Class, 1919. *Recreations:* all games and sports. *Address:* Elm House, Fletching, Uckfield, Sussex. *T:* Newick 2332. *Clubs:* Army and Navy, MCC.

**RICKARDS, Oscar Stanley Norman,** CBE 1945; Grand Officer in the Order of Orange-Nassau, 1947; Haakon VII Liberty Cross, 1947; Director of Victualling, Admiralty, 1941-58; *b* 14 Nov. 1893; *s* of Thomas Rickards and Laura Rose Short; *m* 1925, Sylvia Annie Dean; one *d. Educ:* University College School, Hampstead. Joined Admiralty, 1913. *Address:* Little Thresholds, Hawkshill Way, Esher, Surrey. *T:* 64914.

**RICKENBACKER, Edward Vernon;** retired as Chairman of Board, Eastern Air Lines Inc., USA (1953-63); *b* Columbus, Ohio, 8 Oct. 1890; *s* of Elizabeth and William Rickenbacker; *m* 1922, Adelaide Frost Durant; two *s. Educ:* Studied mechanical engineering and drafting with International Correspondence School. Engaged in automobile racing, 1910-17; served US Army Air Corps, 1917-19 (officially credited with 26 enemy planes; Croix de Guerre, Legion of Honour, DSC with 9 Oak leaves, Congressional Medal of Honour; Medal of Merit, War of 1939-45). Vice-President Rickenbacker Motor Co., 1921-26; Cadillac Motor Car Company Sales Manager, La Salle Division, 1928-29; Vice-President General Aviation Manufacturing Corp., 1929; Vice-President American Airways, 1932; Vice-President North American Aviation Inc. 1933; General Manager Eastern Air Lines, 1935; (President, 1938-53; Chairman of the Board, 1953-63). Many Hon. Degrees from Univs and Colls in USA. *Publications:* Fighting the Flying Circus, 1919; Seven Came Through, 1943; Rickenbacker: an autobiography, 1967. *Address:* 45 Rockefeller Plaza, New York, NY 10020, USA. *T:* LT 1-7576, New York City.

**RICKETT, Sir Denis Hubert Fletcher,** KCMG 1956 (CMG 1947); CB 1951; Vice-President, International Bank for Reconstruction and Development, since 1968; *b* 27 July 1907; *s* of late Hubert Cecil Rickett, OBE, JP; *m* 1946, Ruth Pauline (MB, BS, MRCS, LRCP), *d* of late William Anderson Armstrong, JP; two *s* one *d. Educ:* Rugby School; Balliol College, Oxford. Fellow of All Souls College, Oxford, 1929-49. Joined staff of Economic Advisory Council, 1931; Offices of War Cabinet, 1939; Principal Private Secretary to Right Honourable Oliver Lyttelton, when Minister of Production, 1943-45; Personal Assistant (for work on Atomic Energy) to Rt Hon. Sir John Anderson, when Chancellor of the Exchequer, 1945; transferred to Treasury, 1947; Principal Private Secretary to the Rt Hon. C. R. Attlee, when Prime Minister, 1950-51; Economic Minister, British Embassy, Washington, and Head of UK Treasury and Supply Delegation, 1951-54; Third Secretary, HM Treasury, 1955-60, Second Secretary, 1960-68. *Recreation:* music. *Address:* 11 Hanover Terrace, NW1. *T:* 01-262 4797. *Clubs:* Athenæum, St James'.

**RICKETTS, Maj.-Gen. Abdy Henry Gough,** CBE 1952; DSO 1945; DL; *b* 8 Dec. 1905; *s* of Lt-Col P. E. Ricketts, DSO, MVO, and L. C. Ricketts (*née* Morant); *m* 1932, Joan Warre, *d* of E. T. Close, Camberley; one *s* one *d. Educ:* Winchester. Sandhurst, 1924; Durham LI, 1925; Shanghai Defence Force, 1927; NW Frontier, India (medal and clasp), 1930; Burma "Chindit" campaign, 1944-45; Gen. Service Medal and clasp, Malaya, 1950; comd British Brigade, Korea, 1952; Comdr (temp. Maj.-Gen.), Cyprus District, 1955-56. Col, Durham LI, 1965-68; Dep. Col, The Light Infantry (Durham), 1968-. DL Somerset, 1968. Officer, Legion of Merit (USA), 1953. *Address:* The Old Rectory, Pylle, Shepton Mallet, Som. *T:* Ditcheat 248. *Club:* United Service.

**RICKETTS, Michael Rodney,** MA; Headmaster, Sutton Valence School, since Sept. 1967; *b* 29 Sept. 1923; *er s* of late Rt Rev. C. M. Ricketts, Bishop of Dunwich, and of Mrs Ricketts; *m* 1958, Judith Ann Caroline de Courtenay Corry; two *s* two *d. Educ:* Sherborne; Trinity Coll., Oxford. Served War of 1939-45: in 8th Army with 60th Rifles, 1942-47. Trinity Coll., Oxford, 1947-50; Asst Master and Housemaster, Bradfield Coll., 1950-67. *Recreations:* cricket, shooting, country activities. *Address:* Headmaster's House, Sutton Valence School, near Maidstone, Kent. *T:* Sutton Vallence 2281. *Clubs:* Public Schools, MCC.

**RICKETTS, Sir Robert (Cornwallis Gerald St Leger),** 7th Bt, *cr* 1828; Solicitor; *b* 8 Nov. 1917; *s* of Sir Claude Albert Frederick Ricketts, 6th Bt, and Lilian Helen Gwendoline (*d* 1955), *o d* of Arthur M. Hill, late 5th Fusiliers; *S* father 1937; *m* 1945, Anne Theresa, *d* of late Rt Hon. Sir Richard Stafford Cripps, PC, CH, FRS, QC; two *s* two *d. Educ:* Haileybury; Magdalene College, Cambridge (2nd Cl. Hons in History and Law, BA 1939, MA 1943). Served War of 1939-45 (Captain, Devon Regiment); Personal Assistant to Chief of Staff, Gibraltar, 1942-45; ADC to Lieutenant-Governor of Jersey, 1945-46. Partner in Wellington and Clifford, 1950. FRSA. Hon. Citizen, Mobile, USA, 1970. *Heir:* *s* Robert Tristram Ricketts, *b* 17 April 1946. *Address:* Forwood House, Minchinhampton, Glos. *TA* and *T:* Brimscombe 2160. *Club:* New (Cheltenham).

**RICKFORD, Richard Braithwaite Keevil,** MD (London), BS, FRCS, FRCOG; Physician in charge, Obstetric Department, St Thomas' Hospital, London, since 1946; Surgeon, Chelsea Hospital for Women, since 1950; Gynæcologist, Oxted Hospitals, since 1952; Dean, Institute of Obstetrics and Gynaecology; *b* 1 June 1914; *e s* of late L. T. R. Rickford; *m* 1939, Dorothy, *d* of late Thomas Lathan; three *s* (and one *s* decd). *Educ:* Weymouth College; University of London. Various surgical, obstetric and gynæcological appointments at Norfolk and Norwich Hospital and St Thomas' Hospital. Examiner to: Universities of London, Cambridge and Glasgow; Royal Coll. of Obstetricians and Gynæcologists; Conjoint Board; Central Midwives Board. *Publications:* contributions to medical journals. *Recreations:* winter sports, sailing. *Address:* 100 Harley Street, W1. *T:* 01-935 8422; 25 Stormont Road, Highgate, N6. *T:* 01-340 9700. *Clubs:* Ski Club of Great Britain; Royal Dart Yacht (Kingswear, Devon).

**RICKS, Sir John (Plowman),** Kt 1964; Solicitor to the Post Office since 1953; *b* 3 April 1910; *s* of late James Young Ricks; *m* 1936, May Celia, *d* of late Robert William Chubb; three *s*. *Educ:* Christ's Hosp.; Jesus Coll., Oxford. Admitted Solicitor, 1935; entered Post Office Solicitor's Department, 1935; Assistant Solicitor, Post Office, 1951. *Address:* Solicitor's Office, The Post Office, 23 Rowland Street, W1P 6HS; 5 Hillside Gardens, Barnet, Herts. *T:* 01-449 6114.

**RIDDELL, Prof. Athol George,** MBE 1944; FRCS; Professor of Surgery, University of Bristol, since 1964; *b* 31 Jan. 1917; *s* of John Wood Riddell; *m* 1946, Valerie Constance Wiltshire; two *s*. *Educ:* Harvey Grammar School, Folkestone; University College Hospital, London. MB, BS, London 1940; FRCS 1948; MS London 1954. Served War of 1939-45: RAF Medical Service, 1940-46 (Squadron Leader). John Marshall Fellow, Univ. of London, 1948-49; Res. Asst Surgeon, University Coll. Hosp., 1950-52; Fellow, Harvard Coll., 1952-54; Reader in Surgery, Univ. of Manchester, 1955-64. *Publications:* Surgery for Portal Hypertension (Taylor, Recent Advances in Surgery), 1960; numerous contribs to surgical jls. *Recreations:* gardening, golf. *Address:* Corbys, Castle Road, Clevedon, Somerset. *T:* Clevedon 2568.

**RIDDELL, Sir John Charles Buchanan-,** 13th Bt, *cr* 1628; Chartered Accountant; with International Bank for Reconstruction and Development, Washington DC; *b* 3 Jan. 1934; *o s* of Sir Walter Buchanan Riddell, 12th Bt, and Hon. Rachel Beatrice Lyttelton (*d* 1965), *y d* of 8th Viscount Cobham; *S* father 1934; *m* 1969, Sarah, *o d* of Gordon Richardson, *qv*. *Educ:* Eton; Christ Church, Oxford. *Heir: cousin,* Gervase Robert Riddell-Carre [*b* 30 Oct. 1906; *m* 1940, Eileen Inez Tweedie; two *s*]. *Address:* Hepple, Morpeth, Northumberland. *TA:* Hepple. *Clubs:* Brooks's, Beefsteak; Northern Counties (Newcastle).
*See also J. L. Pumphrey.*

**RIDDELL, Victor Horsley,** MA, MD; FRCS; Consulting Surgeon, St George's Hospital, London; *e s* of Robert George Riddell, MD, FRCSEd, and Annie Wilson. *Educ:* Clifton; Cambridge; St George's Hospital, London (Allingham Schol. and Brackenbury prize in Surgery). Hunterian Professor, RCS; Consultant Surgical Adviser, Civil Aviation Dept (medical branch), Bd of Trade; Examiner in Surgery to Universities of: Cambridge (1952-62), Leeds (1952), Birmingham (1953), and London (1946); President: Chelsea Clinical Society, 1954-55; St George's Hosp. Medical School and Sports Club, 1954-56; St George's Hosp. Hunterian Society, 1956; Representative of RCS on Surgical Mission to USSR, 1957; Leader of British Council Surgical Mission to Near East, Cyprus, Jordan, Irak and Iran, 1960; James IV Assoc. of Surgeons Visitor to India, 1963; guest surgeon, New Delhi and Bankok, 1970. Moynihan Fellow, Assoc. of Surgeons; Treasurer (Great Britain) Internat. Soc. of Surgery, 1950-60; Fellow Assoc. of Surgeons; FRSocMed (Council, 1952); Fellow Med. Soc. London; Fellow Hunterian Soc. *Publications:* on diseases of the thyroid and breast to medical journals and books. *Recreation:* cricket (Cambridge XI, 1926). *Address:* 97 Harley Street, W1. *T:* 01-935 5259. *Clubs:* Athenæum, MCC.

**RIDDELL, William John Brownlow,** MD, FRCP Glasgow, FRSEd, DOMS; Emeritus Professor of Ophthalmology, Glasgow University; Consulting Ophthalmic Surgeon, Western Infirmary, Glasgow, since 1964; *b* 1899; *s* of late Brownlow Riddell, MD; *m* 1932, Anna Ellinor, *y d* of late John Ferguson, Lenzie; one *s* one *d*. *Educ:* Glasgow Academy; Glasgow Univ.; Royal London Opthalmic Hospital (Moorfields). Midshipman, RNVR, 1917-19; Lucien Howe Lecturer, Harvard, 1946; Charles H. May Lecturer, New York Academy of Medicine, 1946; President Section of Ophthalmology, Royal Society of Medicine, 1951-53; Pres., Ophthalmological Section, BMA, 1954; Convocation Lecturer, Univ. of Cincinnati, 1954; Vice-President Ophthalmological Soc. of UK, 1951-54; Senate Assessor on University Court, 1955-63; Pres. Scottish Ophthalmological Club, 1961-63; Deputy Master, Oxford Ophthalmolgical Congress, 1963-65. Vice-Pres., Faculty of Ophthalmologists, 1963-65; Member: General Optical Council, 1963-; Comitē Exēcutif, Assoc. Internat. de Prophylaxie de la Cēcitē, 1963-69. *Publications:* Papers on Ophthalmological subjects and Human Heredity. *Address:* 24 Gladstone Place, Aberdeen AB1 6XA. *Club:* Athenæum.

**RIDDELL-WEBSTER, General Sir T. S.;** *see* Webster.

**RIDDELSDELL, Mildred,** CBE 1958; Deputy Under-Secretary of State, Department of Health and Social Security (formerly Ministry of Social Security), since 1966; *b* 1 Dec. 1913; 2nd *d* of Rev. H. J. Riddelsdell. *Educ:* St Mary's Hall, Brighton; Bedford Coll., London. Entered Min. of Labour, 1936; Asst Sec., Min. of National Insurance, 1945; Under Secretary, 1950; On loan to United Nations, 1953-56; Secretary, National Incomes Commission, 1962-65; Ministry of Pensions and National Insurance, 1965, Social Security, 1966. *Recreation:* gardening. *Address:* 18 Park Close, Bladon, Oxon; 25 Chepstow Crescent, W11. *T:* 01-727 5906.

**RIDDLE, Hugh Joseph, (Huseph),** RP 1960; Artist; Portrait Painter; *b* 24 May 1912; *s* of Hugh Howard Riddle and Christine Simons Brown; *m* 1936, Joan Claudia Johnson; one *s* two *d*. *Educ:* Harrow; Magdalen, Oxford; Slade School of Art; Byam Shaw School of Art and others. *Recreations:* sailing, ski-ing, swimming, tennis. *Address:* (Studio) 8/49 Roland Gardens, SW7; 10 Cristowe Rd, SW6. *T:* 01-736 4540.

**RIDDOCH, John Haddow,** CMG 1963; Under-Secretary, Board of Trade, 1966-69, retired; *b* 4 Feb. 1909; *s* of Joseph Riddoch, Gourock, Renfrewshire; *m* 1938, Isobel W. Russell; one *s* two *d*. *Educ:* Greenock Acad.; Glasgow Univ. Entered Inland Revenue Dept (Inspectorate of Taxes), 1932; Asst Principal in Air Ministry (Dept of Civil Aviation), 1939; Principal, 1942; Asst Sec., Min. of Civil Aviation, 1945; Under-Sec., Min. of Transport and Civil Aviation, 1957, Min. of Aviation, 1959; United Kingdom Representative on the Council of the ICAO, 1957-62 (First Vice-Pres. of Council, Oct. 1961-62); Under-Secretary, Ministry of Aviation, 1962-66. *Recreations:* music, gardening. *Address:* 10 The Fairway, New Barnet, Herts.

**RIDE, Sir Lindsay (Tasman),** Kt 1962; CBE 1944 (OBE 1942); ED (4 clasps) 1948; MA, DM, BCh Oxon, MRCS, LRCP; JP; Emeritus Professor of Physiology, University of Hong Kong, 1965; *b* 10 Oct. 1898; *s* of Rev. William and Eliza Mary Ride; *m* 1st, 1925, M. M. L. Fenety; two *s* two *d*; 2nd, 1954, V. M. Witchell. *Educ:* Scotch College, Melbourne; Ormond College, Melbourne; New College, Oxford; Guy's Hospital, London. Served Aust. Imp. Forces, 1916-19 (twice wounded). CO Hong Kong Field Amb., 1941; prisoner-of-war, escaped, 1942; Col Comdt Brit. Army Aid Gp, China, 1942-45; Brig., Comdt Roy. Hong Kong Volunteer Defence Corps, 1948-62. Victorian Rhodes Schol., 1922; Sen. Science Schol., Guy's Hosp., 1925; Prof. of Physiology, Univ. of Hong Kong, 1928-52; Dean, Medical Faculty, 1930-32, 1935-39; Vice-Chancellor, 1949-65; Research Associate, Inst. of Social Studies and Humanities, Chinese Univ. of Hong Kong, 1965-67. Foundation Member, Association of Southeast Asian Institutions of Higher Learning, 1957, Vice-Pres. 1963-64; Chm. Assoc. of Univs of Brit. Commonwealth, 1960-61; Vice-Pres., Hong Kong Brit. Roy. Asiatic Soc., 1961; Chairman: Music Soc. of Hong Kong; 2nd UNESCO SE Asian Regional Meeting on Scientific Research; Life Mem. Court of Univ. of Hong Kong, 1965-; Mem., Kowloon Riots Commn of Enquiry, 1966. Hon. LLD: Toronto, 1951; Melbourne, 1957; London, 1963; Hong Kong, 1965. Hon. RAM 1962. Hon. Col, HK Regt 1968. *Publications:* Genetics and the Clinician, 1939; Robert Morrison, The Scholar and the Man, 1957; Biographical Note on James Legge, 1961; various articles on human genetics in learned journals. *Recreations:* cricket, tennis, music; formerly rowing and athletics. *Address:* 8a Stanley Beach Rd, Stanley, Hong Kong. *T:* H93246. *Clubs:* Athenæum; Vincent's (Oxford); Leander (Henley); Hong Kong.

**RIDEAL, Sir Eric (Keightley),** Kt 1951; MBE; FRS 1930; FKC 1963; DSc London, MA Cantab; PhD Bonn; FRIC, MRI; Hon. DSc (Dublin, Birmingham, Belfast, Turin, Bonn); DTech, Brunel; Senior Research Fellow, Imperial College of Science and Technology; Fellow: King's College, London; Trinity Hall, Cambridge; *b* 11 April 1890; *s* of late Samuel Rideal; *m* 1921, Margaret (*d* 1964), *d* of late William H. Jackson, of Princeton, New Jersey; one *d*. *Educ:* Oundle Sch.; Trinity Hall, Cambridge (Scholar); Bonn. Gold Medal, Society of Engineers, 1913; visited Ecuador 1913 for Govt on Sanitation of Guyaquil and Quito; Capt. RE European War; Invalided to Munitions Inventions Board from France; research for Dept on Fixation of Atmospheric Nitrogen; Part time lecturer University College, London; Visiting Professor of Physical Chemistry, University of Illinois, USA, 1919-20; Professor of Colloid Science, Cambridge University, 1930-46; Fullerian Professor of Chemistry, the Royal Institution and Director of Davy Faraday Research Laboratory, 1946-49; Professor of Physical Chemistry, King's Coll., Univ. of London, 1950-55; Cantor Lecturer; Past President Faraday Society; Past Pres. Society of Chemical Industry; Past Chm. Chemical Council; Past Pres. Chemical Soc.; For. Mem. Spanish Roy. Soc. Physical Chemistry; Davy Medal of Roy. Soc., 1951; Chm. Advisory Council on Scientific Research and Technical Development, Min. of Supply, 1953-58. *Publications:* Water Supplies; Recent Developments in Catalytic Chemistry, 1921; Colloid Chemistry, 1924; Disinfection and Disinfectants (with S. Rideal); Electrometallurgy; Ozone; Catalysis in Theory and Practice (with H. S. Taylor); An Introduction to Surface Chemistry; Interfacial Phenomena (with L. Davies); Concepts in Catalysis, 1968; contributions to various scientific journals. *Recreation:* gardening. *Address:* 22 Westbourne Park Road, W2; The Spinney, West Runton, Cromer, Norfolk. *Club:* Athenæum.
*See also Peter Raymond Oliver.*

**RIDEALGH, Mrs Mabel;** General Secretary of Women's Co-operative Guild, 1953-63; *b* 11 Aug. 1898; *d* of M. A. Jewitt, Wallsend-on-Tyne, Northumberland; *m* 1919, Leonard, *s* of W. R. Ridealgh, Sunderland, Durham; one *s* one *d*. National Pres. Women's Co-op. Guild, 1941-42; Hon. Regional Organiser Bd of Trade (Make-do and Mend), 1942-44; MP (Lab) Ilford North, 1945-50. *Address:* 2 Eastwood Rd, Goodmayes, Ilford, Essex. *T:* 01-599 8960.

**RIDEHALGH, Arthur;** *b* 10 April 1907; 4th *s* of late James and Amelia Ridehalgh, Oaklands, Barrowford, Lancs; *m* 1935, Ellen Dugdale Lonsdale, 2nd *d* of late Joseph and Anne Elizabeth Lonsdale, Higher Causeway, Barrowford, Lancs; one *d*. *Educ:* Terra Nova Prep. Birkdale; Sedbergh; Wadham Coll., Oxford (BA). Barrister-at-Law, Gray's Inn, 1929; joined Northern Circuit, 1929; Crown Attorney and Magistrate, St Kitts, Leeward Islands, 1935; Crown Counsel, Gold Coast, 1939; Solicitor-General, Nigeria, 1946; Attorney-General, Hong Kong, 1952; retired from HM Overseas Service, 1962; KC (Nigeria), 1949; QC (Hong Kong), 1953. *Address:* Lilac Cottage, Llanfair Talhaiarn, Abergele, Denbighshire.

**RIDGE, Anthony Hubert;** Deputy Director-General, International Bureau, Universal Postal Union, Bern, since 1964; *b* 5 Oct. 1913; *s* of Timothy Leopold Ridge and Magdalen (*née* Hernig); *m* 1938, Marjory Joan Sage; three *s* one *d*. *Educ:* Christ's Hospital; Jesus College, Cambridge. Asst Principal in GPO and Ministry of Home Security, 1937-42; Principal in Ministry of Home Security and GPO, 1942-47; Principal Private Sec. to PMG, Secretary to Post Office Board, 1947-49; Dep. Regional Director, London Postal Region, 1949-51; Asst Secretary, mainly in international Postal Service, 1951-60; Director of Clerical Mechanization and Buildings, and Member of Post Office Board, GPO, 1960-63. *Recreations:* music, languages, transport, gardening. *Address:* Staple, Postling, Hythe, Kent. *T:* Lyminge 87315; Weltpostverein, Bern, Switzerland. *Clubs:* Christ's Hospital, United University.

**RIDGERS, John Nalton Sharpe;** Chairman of Lloyd's, 1963 (Deputy Chairman, 1962); Director, London Trust Co. Ltd, 1963; *b* 10

June 1910; 4th *c* and *o s* of Sharpe Ridgers; *m* 1936, Barbara Mary, *o d* of Robert Cobb; five *d*. *Educ:* Wellington College. Entered Lloyd's, 1928; underwriting member, 1932. Member Cttee Lloyd's Underwriters' Association, 1951-61, 1964-69, Chm. 1961; Member Joint Hull Cttee, 1957-69, Dep. Chm., 1968, Chm., 1969. Mem. Cttee of Lloyd's, 1957-60, 1962-65. *Recreations:* rackets, squash and lawn tennis. *Address:* Watlynge, Dyants Lane, Bitchet Green, near Sevenoaks, Kent. *T:* Sevenoaks 61353. *Club:* City of London.

**RIDGWAY, Gen. Matthew Bunker,** DSC (with Oak Leaf Cluster); DSM (with 3rd Oak Leaf Cluster); Silver Star (with Oak Leaf Cluster); Legion of Merit; Bronze Star Medal (with Oak Leaf Cluster); Purple Heart; Chairman of The Mellon Institute of Industrial Research 1955-60, retired; *b* 3 March 1895; *s* of Thomas Ridgway and Ruth Starbuck Bunker; *m* 1930; one *d*; *m* 1947, Mary Anthony; one *s*. *Educ:* United States Military Academy, 1913-17. Inf. School (Company Officers' Course), 1924-25; Mem. Am. Electoral Commn, Nicaragua, 1927-28; Mem. Commn on Bolivian-Paraguayan boundary dispute, 1929; Inf. School (Advanced Course), 1929-30; Liaison Officer to Govt in Philippine Is, Tech. Adviser to Gov.-Gen., 1932-33; Comd and Gen. Staff School, 1933-35; Asst Chief of Staff, 6th Corps Area, 1935-36; Dep. Chief of Staff, Second Army, 1936; Army War College, 1936-37; Assistant Chief of Staff, Fourth Army, 1937-39; accompanied Gen. Marshall on special mission to Brazil, 1939; War Plans Div., War Department Gen. Staff, 1939-42; Asst Div. Comdr, 82nd Inf. Div., 1942; Comdr 1942; Comdg Gen. 82nd Airborne Div., Sicily, Italy, Normandy, 1942-44; Comdr 18th Airborne Corps, Belgium, France, Germany, 1944-45; Comdr Luzon Area Command, 1945; Comdr Medit. Theater, and Dep. Supreme Allied Comdr, Medit., 1945-46; Senior US Army Member Military Staff Cttee, UN, 1946-48; Chm. Inter-Am. Defense Bd, 1946-48; C-in-C Caribbean Command, 1948-49; Dep. Army Chief of Staff for Admin., 1949-50 (and Chm. Inter-Am. Defense Bd, 1950); Comdg Gen. Eighth Army in Korea, 1950-51; Comdr UN Comd in Far East, C-in-C of Far East Comd and Supreme Comdr for Allied Powers in Japan, 1951-52; Supreme Allied Comdr, Europe, 1952-53; Chief of Staff, United States Army, 1953-55, retired. Hon. KCB 1955 (Hon. CB 1945); holds many American and foreign decorations. *Address:* 918 W Waldheim Road, Fox Chapel, Pittsburgh, Pa 15215, USA.

**RIDING, George A.,** MA; Headmaster, Aldenham School, 1933-July 1949; *b* 1 April 1888; *s* of Daniel A. Riding and Anne Deighton; *m* Aideen Maud, *d* of T. W. Rolleston, *g d* of late Rev. Stopford Brooke; two *s*. *Educ:* Manchester Grammar School (Scholar); University of Manchester (MA English Language and Literature); New College, Oxford, 1st Class Honours, Modern Languages (French and German), 1921, Heath Harrison Travelling Scholarship, 1920; President, Oxford University French Club, 1920; Assistant Master, Mill Hill School, 1914-15; Rugby School, 1921-28 (Sixth Form Master); served with Northumberland Fusiliers (wounded); Registrar, King's Lancashire Military Convalescent Hospital, 1917-18; Captain in Rugby School OTC; Headmaster, Warwick School, 1928-33. Member of House of Laity, Church Assembly, 1944. Member of Council, Inc. Assoc. of Head Masters, 1942-44. Foundation Member of Hispanic Council. Member School Broadcasting Council, 1947-58; Chairman Secondary Programmes Committee, 1947-54. Chairman: Cornwall Modern Churchmen's Union, 1950; Truro Divisional Liberal Association, 1950-51; Cornwall Liberal Council, 1950; Minack Theatre Society, 1960-66; E Cornwall Society for the Mentally Handicapped, 1960-66. Carried out (with headmaster of Fettes Coll.) survey of pre-service educn in Pakistan, 1951. *Publications:* Blackie's Longer French Texts; Les Trois Mousquetaires; La Bête dans les Neiges; contrib. to Naval Review, Spectator. *Address:* Colona, Port Mellon, Mevagissey, St Austell, Cornwall. *T:* Mevagissey 3440.

**RIDING, Laura** (now Jackson); *b* New York City, 16 Jan. 1901; American mother and naturalised (Austrian-born) father (Nathaniel S. Reichenthal); *m* 1941, Schuyler B. Jackson (American writer; poetry-editor of Time, 1938-43). *Educ:* American public schools; Cornell University. First published poems in American poetry magazines; member of group of Southern poets, The Fugitives; went to England in 1926, remaining abroad until 1939; engaging in writing and allied activities, seeking a single terminology of truth to supersede our confused terminological diversity (*eg*, as Editor of Epilogue, a critical miscellany), operating Seizin Press with Robert Graves, collaborating in writing with him, and others. Has since renounced poetry as humanly inadequate and concentrated on direct linguistic handling of truth-problem, studying ways to intensify people's consciousness of word-meanings; working long with husband on definitional project now beginning to assume book-form. *Publications include:* Contemporaries and Snobs, 1927; Anarchism Is Not Enough, 1928; Experts are Puzzled, 1930; Progress of Stories, 1935; Trojan Ending, 1937; The World and Ourselves, 1938; Collected Poems, 1938; Lives of Wives, 1939; The Telling (a personal evangel–complete magazine publication, Chelsea, USA), 1967; Selected Poems: in five sets, 1970; contribs to magazines. *Address:* Wabasso, Florida 32970, USA.

**RIDLER, Anne (Barbara);** author; *b* 30 July 1912; *o d* of late H. C. Bradby, housemaster of Rugby School, and Violet Milford; *m* 1938, Vivian Ridler, *qv*; two *s* two *d*. *Educ:* Downe House School; King's College, London; and in Florence and Rome. *Publications: poems:* Poems, 1939; A Dream Observed, 1941; The Nine Bright Shiners, 1943; The Golden Bird, 1951; A Matter of Life and Death, 1959; Selected Poems (New York), 1961; *plays:* Cain, 1943; The Shadow Factory, 1946; Henry Bly and other plays, 1950; The Trial of Thomas Cranmer, 1956; Who is my Neighbour?, 1963; *biography:* Olive Willis and Downe House, 1967; Editor: Shakespeare Criticism, 1919-35; A Little Book of Modern Verse, 1941; Best Ghost Stories, 1945; Supplement to Faber Book of Modern Verse, 1951; The Image of the City and other essays by Charles Williams, 1958; Shakespeare Criticism 1935-60, 1963; Poems of James Thomson, 1963; Thomas Traherne, 1966; (with Christopher Bradby) Best Stories of Church and Clergy, 1966. *Recreations:* music; the theatre; the cinema. *Address:* 14 Stanley Road, Oxford.

**RIDLER, Vivian Hughes,** MA Oxon 1958 (by decree; Corpus Christi College); Printer to the University of Oxford since Oct. 1958; *b* 2 Oct. 1913; *s* of Bertram Hughes Ridler and Elizabeth Emmeline (*née* Best); *m* 1938, Anne Barbara Bradby (*see* A. B. Ridler); two *s* two *d*. *Educ:* Bristol Gram. Sch. Appren. E. S. & A. Robinson, Ltd, 1931-36. Works Manager University Press, Oxford, 1948; Assistant Printer, 1949-58. Pres., British Federation of Master Printers, 1968-69. Professorial Fellow, St Edmund Hall, 1966. *Recreations:* printing, theatre, cinema, cinematography. *Address:* 14 Stanley Road, Oxford. *T:* Oxford 47595.

**RIDLEY**, family name of **Viscount Ridley.**

**RIDLEY**, 4th Viscount, *cr* 1900; **Matthew White Ridley,** TD 1960; DL; Baron Wensleydale, *cr* 1900; Bt 1756; *b* 29 July 1925; *e s* of 3rd Viscount Ridley; *S* father, 1964; *m* 1953, Lady Anne Lumley, 3rd *d* of 11th Earl of Scarbrough, KG, PC, GCSI, GCIE, GCVO; one *s* three *d. Educ:* Eton; Balliol College, Oxford. Captain, Coldstream Guards, 1946; Bt-Col Northumberland Hussars (TA). Chairman: North Eastern Housing Assoc. Ltd, 1959-; Northumberland County Council. Director: Northern Rock Building Society; Tyne Tees Television; Martins Bank (NE) Ltd. Mem. Council of Newcastle University, 1966-. JP 1957, CC 1958, CA 1963, DL 1968, Northumberland. *Heir: s* Hon. Matthew White Ridley, *b* 7 Feb. 1958. *Address:* Blagdon, Seaton Burn, Northumberland. *T:* Stannington 236. *Clubs:* Turf, Beefsteak; Northern Counties (Newcastle upon Tyne).
*See also Hon. Nicholas Ridley.*

**RIDLEY, Arnold;** dramatic author, actor, and producer; *b* Bath, 7 January 1896; *s* of late William Robert Ridley and Rosa Morrish; *m* Althea Parker; one *s. Educ:* Bristol University. Formerly a schoolmaster; enlisted, 1915; served in ranks; was severely wounded, Somme, 1916, and discharged 1917; rejoined HM Forces Oct. 1939, served on PR Staff with acting rank of Major BEF, France, 1939-40; joined Birmingham Repertory Company, 1918, and played various parts for several seasons; later with: Plymouth Repertory Company; White Rose Players, Harrogate; Oxford Repertory Theatre Company; original Walter Gabriel in stage version of The Archers; frequent appearances on Television (Harry Crane in BBC series Starr and Co.; The Vicar in Crossroads; Private Godfrey in Dad's Army); also Broadcasts; Doughy Hood in The Archers, BBC; author of the following produced plays: The Brass God, 1921; The Ghost Train, 1925; The Burnett Mystery, 1926; The God o' Mud, 1926; The Wrecker (with Bernard Merivale), 1927; Keepers of Youth, 1929; The Flying Fool (with Merivale), 1929; Third Time Lucky, 1929; Recipe for Murder, 1932; Headline, 1934; Half-a-Crown (with Douglas Furber), 1934; Glory Be, 1934; Needs Must, 1938; Out Goes She (with Merivale), 1939; Peril at End House (with Agatha Christie), 1940; Happy Holiday (with Eric Maschwitz), 1954; Tabitha (with Mary Cathcart Borer), 1955; The Running Man (with Anthony Armstrong), 1955; Murder Happens, 1945; Easy Money, 1947; Trifles Light as Air (with St Vincent Troubridge), 1949; East of Ludgate Hill, 1950; The Dark Corridor (with Richard Reich), 1950; Beggar My Neighbour, 1951; You, My Guests!, 1956; Shadows on the Sand (with Borer), 1956; Geranium, 1957; Bellamy (with Anthony Armstrong), 1959; High Fidelity (with Cedric Wallis), 1964; prod. the following plays: Sunshine House, Little Theatre 1933; Rude Awakening, Shilling Theatre, 1934; Flood Tide, Phœnix Theatre, 1938; Producer, Malvern Company, 1942-44. Wrote and directed film Royal Eagle, 1935; other films include: East of Ludgate Hill, 1935; Blind Justice, 1935; The Last Chance, 1936; The Seven Sinners, 1936. *Publications:* Keepers of Youth, 1929; various short stories and articles. *Recreations:* Rugby football and cricket; takes active interest in Bath Rugby Club, served as hon. match sec. several years and elected president, 1950-, and Life Member, 1963. *Address:* c/o Hughes Massie & Co., 18 Southampton Place, WC1. *Clubs:* Savage, Dramatists'.

**RIDLEY, Mrs Betty;** *see* Ridley, Mrs M. B.

**RIDLEY, Edward Alexander Keane,** CB 1963; Principal Assistant Solicitor, Treasury Solicitor's Department, 1956-69, retired; *b* 16 April 1904; *s* of late Major Edward Keane Ridley, Dudswell House, near Berkhamsted, Herts, and late Ethel Janet Ridley, *d* of Alexander Forbes Tweedie; unmarried. *Educ:* Wellington College; Keble College, Oxford. Admitted Solicitor, 1928. Entered Treasury Solicitor's Department, 1934. *Recreation:* music. *Address:* c/o Coutts & Co., 440 Strand, WC2.

**RIDLEY, Frederick Thomas,** FRCS; Hon. Consulting Surgeon, Moorfields Eye Hospital, 1968; *b* 14 June 1903; *s* of Frederick William Ridley and Ellen Smith; *m* 1940, Josephine Rose Ansell (marr. diss.); two *d; m* 1965, Pauline Cartier Bourgeois, *widow, d* of Arthur J. B. Cartier, Asst US Attorney, Boston, Mass. *Educ:* King Edwards, Birmingham; Univ. of Birmingham. BSc Birmingham 1922; MB, BS London 1925; LMSSA London 1925; LRCP 1926; MRCS 1926; FRCS 1928. Formerly: House Surg. (Ophth., Gynæc. and Gen.), Queen's Hosp., Birmingham; Pathologist, Central London Ophth. Hosp.; Lectr in Pathology, DO Oxon; Hon. Research Asst, Wright-Fleming Inst., St Mary's Hosp., 1930; Lectr, Inst. of Ophth., Univ. of London, 1947; Hon. Cons. Surgeon: Western Ophth. Hosp., 1926; Central London Ophth. Hosp., 1928; Cons. Surgeon, Moorfields Eye Hosp., 1928; Dir, Contact Lens Dept, 1950; Senior Surgeon, 1961, retd 1968. Pres., Section of Ophthalmology, RSM, 1963-64, Hon. Mem. 1970; Pres., 2nd Internat. Corneo-Plastic Conf., RCS, 1967. Chm., Listening Library. FRSM; Member: Ophth. Soc. of UK; Oxford Ophth. Congress. Middlemore Lectr 1951; Doyne Memorial Lecture, 1954; Edward Nettleship Prize and Gold Medal, 1963; Sight Foundn Award, Baylor Univ., 1966. *Publications:* (jt) Mayou's Diseases of the Eye, 1933; (jt) Student's Guide to Fundus Appearances, 1933; (jt) Modern Trends in Ophthalmology, 1940; many addresses, chapters in books, and papers in scientific jls. *Recreation:* formerly farming. *Address:* 80 Harley Street, W1. *T:* 01-580 4141. *Club:* Oriental.

**RIDLEY, Mrs Michael;** *see* Ridley, Mrs (Mildred) Betty.

**RIDLEY, Mrs (Mildred) Betty, (Mrs Michael Ridley)**; (Hon.) MA (Lambeth) 1958; a Church Commissioner, since 1959; *b* 10 Sept. 1909; *d* of late Rt Rev. Henry Mosley, sometime Bishop of Southwell; *m* 1929, Rev. Michael Ridley (*d* 1953), Rector of Finchley; three *s* one *d. Educ:* North London Collegiate School; Cheltenham Ladies' College. Member: Central Board of Finance; ACCM; Missionary and Ecumenical Council, Church Assembly; Bd of Govs of Church Comrs; National Assembly of Church of England, 1945-; General Synod of Church of England, 1970-; Vice-Pres. British Council of Churches, 1954-56; Chm., Redundant Churches Cttee. *Recreation:* choral singing. *Address:* 99 Warwick Way, SW1. *T:* 01-834 5367.

**RIDLEY, Hon. Nicholas,** AMICE; MP (C) Cirencester and Tewkesbury Division of Gloucestershire since Oct. 1959; Parliamentary Under-Secretary of State, Department of Trade and Industry, since Oct. 1970; *b* 17 Feb. 1929; *yr s* of 3rd Viscount Ridley, CBE, TD; *m* 1950, Hon. Clayre

Campbell, 2nd *d* of 4th Baron Stratheden and Campbell, *qv*; three *d*. *Educ:* Eton; Balliol College, Oxford. Civil Engineering Contractor, Brims & Co. Ltd, Newcastle upon Tyne, 1950-59, Director, 1954-70; Dir, Heenan Group Ltd, 1961-68. Contested (C) Blyth, Gen. Election, 1955; PPS to Minister of Education, 1962-64; Delegate to Council of Europe, 1962-66; Parly Sec., Min. of Technology, June-Oct. 1970. *Recreations:* painting, architecture and fishing. *Address:* Old Rectory, Naunton, Cheltenham, Glos. *T:* Guiting Power 252; 212 Lambeth Road, SE1. *T:* 01-928 3441.

**RIDLEY, Nicholas Harold Lloyd,** MD, FRCS; Surgeon, Moorfields Eye Hospital since 1938; Surgeon in charge Ophthalmic Department, St Thomas' Hospital, since 1946; Hon. Consultant in Ophthalmology to the Army since 1965; *b* 10 July 1906; *s* of late N. C. Ridley, MB (London), FRCS, Royal Navy retired, Leicester; *m* 1941, Elisabeth Jane, *d* of late H. B. Wetherill, CIE; two *s* one *d*. *Educ:* Charterhouse; Pembroke Coll., Cambridge; St Thomas' Hospital, London. MB 1931, MD 1946, Cambridge; FRCS 1932. Late Hon. Ophthalmic Surgeon, Royal Buckinghamshire Hospital, Temp. Major RAMC. Hon. Cons. in Ophthalmology to Min. of Defence (Army), 1964-71; Vice-Pres., Ophthalmological Soc. of UK; Member: Oxford Ophthalmological Congress; Ophthalmic Section (late Vice-Pres.), Royal Soc. Med.; Advisory Panel, WHO, 1966-71; Hon. Fellow International College of Surgeons, Chicago, 1952; Hon. Member: Peruvian Ophthalmic Society, 1957. Ophthalmological Society of Australia, 1963; Hon. Member, Irish Ophthalmological Society. *Publications:* Monograph on Ocular Onchocerciasis; numerous contrib. in textbooks and medical journals on intraocular acrylic lens surgery and other subjects. *Recreation:* fly-fishing. *Address:* 53 Harley Street, W1. *T:* 01-580 1077. *Club:* Flyfishers'.

**RIDLEY, Sir Sidney,** Kt 1953; Emeritus Fellow, St John's College, 1969 (Fellow, 1962); Indian Civil Service, retired; *b* 26 March 1902; *s* of John William and Elizabeth Janet Ridley; *m* 1929, Dorothy Hoole; three *d*. *Educ:* Lancaster Royal Grammar Sch.; Sidney Sussex Coll., Cambridge. MA Cantab, MA Oxon. Joined ICS, 1926; Finance Secretary, Govt of Sind, 1936; Secretary to the Agent-General for India in South Africa, 1936-40; Chief Secretary, Govt of Sind, 1944; Commissioner: Northern Division, Ahmedabad, 1946; Central Div., Poona, 1947; Revenue Commissioner in Sind and Secretary to Government, 1947-54. Representative of W Africa Cttee in Ghana, Sierra Leone and the Gambia, 1957-60; Domestic Bursar, St John's Coll., Oxford, 1960-68. *Recreation:* golf. *Address:* 26 Museum Road, Oxford. *Club:* East India and Sports.

**RIDLEY, Rear-Adm. William Terence Colborne,** CB 1968; OBE 1954; Admiral Superintendent, HM Dockyard, Rosyth, since Sept. 1966; *b* 9 March 1915; *s* of late Capt. W. H. W. Ridley, RN and late Vera Constance (*née* Walker); *m* 1938, Barbara Allen; one *s*. *Educ:* Emsworth House; RNC, Dartmouth (Robert Roxburgh Prize); RNEC, Keyham. HMS Exeter, 1936; HMS Valiant, 1939; HMS Firedrake, 1940 (despatches twice); E-in-C Dept Admty, 1941; HMS Indefatigable, 1944; Admty Fuel Experimental Stn, 1947; Seaslug Project Officer, RAE Farnborough, 1950; HMS Ark Royal, 1956; E-in-C Dept Admty, Dreadnought Project Team, 1958; CO, RNEC, 1962; Staff of C-in-C Portsmouth, 1964. Lt-Comdr 1944; Comdr 1947; Capt. 1957; Rear-Adm. 1966. FIMechE, MIMarE. *Recreations:* gardening, botany, caravanning, do-it-yourself. *Address:* Castlandhill House, Rosyth, Fife. *Clubs:* United Service; Royal Naval (Portsmouth).

**RIDOLFI, Marchese Roberto, (Marquis of Montescudaio);** author; Professor at University of Florence; *b* 12 Sept. 1899; *m* 1st, 1922, Countess Maria Giulia Bocchi Bianchi; one *s* one *d*; 2nd, 1960, Maria Caprioli. *Educ:* Pisa. Member of Superior Board of Archives, 1929-42; Editor of: Rivista Storica degli Archivi, 1929-33; La Bibliofilia, 1943; Director of the Centro per lo studio dei Paleotipi at University of Florence, Italy; Editor of National Editions of Works of Savonarola; Associate-Editor of Belfagor. Hon. degrees: Doctor of Letters (Univ. of Pisa), 1960; DLitt (Univ. of Oxford), 1961. *Publications:* Studi savonaroliani, 1935; Opuscoli de storia letteraria, 1942; Vita di Girolamo Savonarola, 1952 (English trans., London, 1959); Vita di Niccolò Machiavelli, 1954 (English trans., London, 1963); Memorie di uno studioso, 1956; Vita di Giovanni Papini, 1957; Vita di Francesco Guicciardini, 1960 (Eng. trans. London, 1968); Il libro dei sogni, 1962; La parte davanti, 1966; I Ghiribizzi, 1968; Studi sulle commedie del Machiavelli, 1968, etc. *Recreation:* book collecting. *Heir:* *s* Cosimo Ridolfi, *b* 6 April 1929. *Address:* Via delle Campora, 49, Florence, Italy. *T:* 220141.

**RIDSDALE, Julian Errington;** MP (C), Harwich Division of Essex, since Feb. 1954; *b* 8 June 1915; *m* 1942, Victoire Evelyn Patricia Bennett; one *d*. *Educ:* Tonbridge; Sandhurst. 2nd Lieutenant, Royal Norfolk Regiment, 1935; attached British Embassy, Tokyo, 1938-39; served War of 1939-45: Royal Norfolk Regt, Royal Scots, and Somerset Light Infantry; GSO3, Far Eastern Sect., War Office, 1941; GSO2, Joint Staff Mission, Washington, 1944-45; retired from Army with rank of Major, 1946. Contested SW Islington (C), LCC, 1949, N Paddington (C), Gen. Elec., 1951. PPS to Parly Under-Sec. of State for Colonies, 1957-58; PPS to Minister of State for Foreign Affairs, 1958-60; Parly Under-Sec. of State: for Air and Vice-President of the Air Council, 1962-64; for Defence for the Royal Air Force, Ministry of Defence, April-Oct. 1964. Pres., British Japanese Parly Group, 1964-; Vice-Chm., UN Parly Assoc., 1966-. Master, Skinners' Co., 1970-71. *Recreations:* tennis, chess, gardening, travelling, and sailing. *Address:* Fiddan, St Osyth, Essex. *T:* St Osyth 367; 12 The Boltons, SW10. *T:* 01-373 6159. *Clubs:* Carlton, MCC, Hurlingham; Frinton Tennis.

**RIEFLER, Winfield William;** retired; Assistant to Chairman, Board of Governors, Federal Reserve System, 1948-Dec. 1959; Secretary, Federal Open Market Committee 1952-Dec. 1959; *b* Buffalo, NY, 9 Feb. 1897; *s* of Philip D. Riefler and Clara Gartner; *m* 1924, Dorothy Miles Brown; two *s*. *Educ:* Amherst College (AB 1921, LHD (Hon.) 1944); Brookings Grad. School (PhD 1927). Foreign Trade Officer, Department of Commerce, Buenos Aires, Argentina, 1921; 1923; division of research and statistics Federal Reserve Board, 1923-33; Exec. Sec. Cttee on Bank Reserves, 1930-32; Chairman Central Statistical Board, 1933-35, Economic Adviser: to Executive Council, 1933-34, to National Emergency Council, 1934-35; Professor, School of Economics and Politics of Institute for Advanced Study, 1935-48; Assistant to Secretary of the Treasury, 1939; on leave of absence to Act as Minister to London (Special Assistant to Ambassador) in charge of Economic Warfare, 1942-44; Trustee, Institute for Advanced Study, 1936-41; Director, National Bureau of Economic

Research, 1936-42, 1945-48; Special Adviser, US Dept of Treasury, 1937; Alternate Member Finance Cttee, League of Nations, 1937-46; Director, Foreign Policy Assoc., 1938-40; Director, Federal Reserve Bank of Philadelphia, 1941-42; Chm., League of Nations Deleg. on Economic Depressions, 1945; Chm., Social Science Research Council Com. on Social and Economic Aspects of Atomic Energy, 1945; Director, Council on Foreign Relations, 1945-50; Chm., 20th Century Fund Com. on Foreign Economic Relations, 1946; Consultant, US Select Cttee on Foreign Aid, 1947; Member, UN Subcommn on Employment and Economic Stability, 1947-50; Member, Business Advisory Council, 1947- (Graduate Mem. 1955-61); Trustee Foreign Service Educational Foundation, 1948-60. Member: American Economic Association; American Statistical Association (Pres. 1941); Royal Economic Soc., London. *Publication:* Money Rates and Money Markets in the United States, 1930. *Address:* 430 Island Circle, Sarasota, Florida 33581, USA. *Club:* Cosmos (Washington).

**RIEGER, Sir Clarence (Oscar Ferrero),** CBE 1965; FRACS, FRCSE; *b* 23 Nov. 1897; *s* of Oscar Paul Philip and Sarina Rieger; *m* 1923, Bessie Eileen, *d* of Charles Ernest Main; two *s* one *d*. *Educ:* Adelaide High Sch.; Univ. of Adelaide. MBBS Adelaide 1919; FRCSE 1932; FRACS 1957. Served War of 1939-45: Major, AAMC, AIF. Adelaide Children's Hospital: Hon. Surgeon, 1939; Hon. Cons. Surg., 1958; Pres. and Chm. Bd, 1958. Member: Branch Council, BMA, 1946-61 (Pres., 1949-51); Med. Bd of SA, 1952-; Fed. Council BMA, 1950-61; Fed. Council AMA, 1962-64 (Vice-Pres., 1964-67); President: First Aust. Med. Congress, 1962; AMA, 1967-70; BMA, 1968. FAMA, 1964; FBMA 1970; Hon. FACMA, 1970. Gold Medal, AMA, 1969. Hon. LLD Aberdeen, 1969. *Publications:* contrib. (1950-) to: Med. Jl Aust., BMJ, NZ Med. Jl. *Recreations:* golf, gardening, bowls. *Address:* 7 Austin Crescent, St George's, South Australia 5064, Australia. *T:* 79-6454. *Clubs:* Adelaide, Naval, Military and Air Force (Adelaide); Kooyonga Golf (Lockleys).

**RIEU, Emile Victor,** CBE 1953; Hon. LittD (Leeds) 1949; FRSL; Editor of the Penguin Classics, 1944-64; Academic and Literary Adviser to Methuen & Co. Ltd since 1936; *b* 10 Feb. 1887; *y s* of Dr C. P. H. Rieu; *m* 1914, Nelly Lewis, *d* of H. T. Lewis, Pembrokeshire; two *s* two *d*. *Educ:* St Paul's School (scholar); Balliol College, Oxford (scholar). Manager, Oxford University Press, Bombay, 1912; 2nd Lieut 105th Mahratta Light Inf., 1918; Educational Manager, Methuen & Co., 1923, Managing Director, 1933-36. Major, Home Guard, 1943. President, Virgil Society, 1951; Vice-President, RSL, 1958; Benson Medal (RSL), 1968. *Publications:* A Book of Latin Poetry, 1925; Cuckoo Calling, 1933; The Penguin Odyssey, 1945; Virgil: The Pastoral Poems, 1949; The Penguin Iliad, 1950; The Four Gospels, a New Translation, 1952; A Puffin Quartet of Poets (part author), 1958; The Penguin Argonautica (Voyage of Argo), 1959; The Flattered Flying Fish and other poems, 1962. *Recreations:* carpentry, mountains, petrology. *Address:* 31 Hurst Avenue, N6. *T:* 01-340 4178. *Club:* Athenæum.

**RIGBY, Lt-Col Sir (Hugh) John (Macbeth),** 2nd Bt, *cr* 1929; ERD and 2 clasps; Director, Executors of James Mills Ltd; *b* 1 Sept 1914; *s* of Sir Hugh Mallinson Rigby, 1st Bt, and Flora (*d* 1970), *d* of Norman Macbeth; *S* father, 1944; *m* 1946, Mary Patricia Erskine Leacock; four *s*. *Educ:* Rugby; Magdalene Coll., Cambridge. Lt-Col RCT, retd, 1967. *Heir: s* Anthony John Rigby, *b* 3 Oct. 1946. *Address:* Ridgehill, Sutton, near Macclesfield, Cheshire. *T:* Sutton 353.

**RIGBY, Sir Ivo (Charles Clayton),** Kt 1964; **Hon. Mr Justice Rigby;** Chief Justice of Hong Kong and of Brunei, since 1970; *b* 2 June 1911; *s* of late James Philip Clayton Rigby and late Elisabeth Mary Corbett; *m* 1st, 1938, Agnes Bothway; 2nd, Kathleen Nancy, *d* of late Dr W. E. Jones, CMG; no *c*. *Educ:* Magdalen College School, Oxford. Called to the Bar (Inner Temple), 1932; Magistrate, Gambia, 1935-38; Chief Magistrate, Crown Counsel, and President of a District Court, Palestine, 1938-48; Assistant Judge, Nyasaland, 1948-54; President of Sessions Court, Malaya, 1954-55; Puisne Judge, Malaya, 1956-61; Senior Puisne Judge, Hong Kong, 1961-70. *Publications:* The Law Reports of Nyasaland, 1934-1952. *Recreations:* squash, cricket and bridge. *Address:* The Courts of Justice, Hong Kong. *Clubs:* Bath, East India and Sports; Hong Kong.

**RIGBY, Norman Leslie;** Co-ordinator of Industrial Advisers, HM Government, based on Ministry of Technology, since 1969; *b* 27 June 1920; *s* of Leslie Rigby and Elsie Lester Wright; *m* 1950, Mary Josephine Calderhead; two *d* (one *s* decd). *Educ:* Cowley Sch., St Helens. Served RAF, 1939-45, War Intell. Officer to Free French Air Force. Management Trainee, Simon Engineering Group, 1946-48; Marketing Exec., Procter & Gamble Ltd, 1948-55; Marketing Dir, Macleans Ltd (Beecham Group), 1955-59; Nabisco Ltd: Marketing Dir 1959; Man. Dir 1960; Vice-Chm. . 1962; Chm. 1964; seconded to Govt as Industrial Adviser, 1968. FBIM and Mem. Council 1967. *Recreations:* gardening, tennis, golf. *Address:* 38 West Common Way, Harpenden, Herts. *T:* Harpenden 5448.

**RIGG, Harry Sibson Leslie,** QC 1960; Recorder of Wigan since 1964; *b* 8 Nov. 1915; *s* of Sibson Eric Rigg and Annie Louise (*née* Green); *m* 1939, Nina Marjorie (*née* Booth); one *d*. *Educ:* Charterhouse; Lincoln College, Oxford. Manchester Regiment, Staff Captain, 1939-44. Barrister, Lincoln's Inn, 1944. Master of the Bench, 1966. Contested (C) Edge Hill Division of Liverpool, May 1955. *Recreations:* art (oil painting), music, golf. *Address:* 2 Paper Buildings, Temple, EC4; Fern Hill, Goldrings Road, Oxshott, Surrey. *Club:* Royal Mid-Surrey.

**RIGG, Sir Theodore,** KBE, *cr* 1938; MA, MSc, Hon. DSc, FRIC; FNZIC; FRSNZ; retired; *b* 6 April 1888; *s* of John and Hannah Rigg; *m* 1919, Esther Mary White (*d* 1959); two *d*; *m* 1966, Kathleen Maisey Curtis, DSc. *Educ:* Wellington Coll.; Victoria Univ. Coll., Wellington; Cambridge Univ. MSc 1st Class Hons Phys. Chem., Jacob Joseph Scholar, 1851 Exhibitioner; MA Cantab 1924. War Relief work, France, Serbia and Russia, 1914-19; Agricultural Chemist Cawthron Institute, 1920; Member Research Council, NZ Dept of Sci. and Ind. Research, 1926-54; Asst Dir, 1928, Director, Cawthron Institute, 1934-56; Liversidge Lecturer, ANZAAS, 1936; Chairman NZ Research Council, 1943-54; President NZ Inst. of Chemistry, 1942-43; Member Nelson Catchment Board, 1945-55; NZ Delegate Empire Science Conferences, London, 1946; Hon. DSc Univ. of W Australia, 1947; Chairman Tobacco Research and Hop Research Cttees, DSIR, 1948-56; Organising Chairman Soils, Agriculture and Forestry Div., 7th Pacific Science Conf., NZ, 1949. Fellow Royal Hort. Soc. NZ, 1950; President, ANZAAS, 1954-55. Hon. Fellow, NZIC, 1956; Hon. DSc NZ Univ., 1957. Silver Jubilee

Medal, 1935; Coronation Medal, 1953. *Publications:* numerous publications dealing with soil and fertilizer research. *Address:* 5 Taupata Street, Stoke Nelson, New Zealand.

**RIGNOLD, Hugo Henry;** conductor; Musical Director and Principal Conductor, City of Birmingham Symphony Orchestra, 1960-68; *b* 15 May 1905; *s* of Hugo Charles Rignold, conductor, and Agnes Mann, Opera singer; *m* 1st, 1934, Rita Mary Gaylor; one *d*; 2nd, 1941, Phyllis Stanley; one *d*; 3rd, 1948, Patricia Horton. *Educ:* St Mary's and Kelvin College, Winnipeg, Canada. Royal Opera House, Covent Garden, 1947-48; Liverpool Philharmonic Soc., 1948-54; Edinburgh Festival (Midsummer Night's Dream) and American Tour following, 1954-55. Guest appearances: Holland, Italy, Switzerland, etc., and important orchestras in UK, 1955; opened Festival Cape Town, S Africa, Sept. 1955, returning there for season, 1956-57; Musical Director of the Royal Ballet, 1957-60. Hon. ARAM 1949. Hon. FRAM 1952. *Recreations:* golf, cricket, motor racing; antique furniture. *Address:* 1 Holford Road, Hampstead, NW3.

**RILEY, Bridget Louise;** Artist; *b* 24 April 1931; *d* of John Riley and Louise (*née* Gladstone). *Educ:* Cheltenham Ladies' College; Goldsmiths' School of Art; Royal College of Art. ARCA 1955. AICA critics Prize, 1963; Stuyvesant Bursary, 1964. Mem., RSA. One-man shows: London, 1962, 1963, 1969; New York, Los Angeles, 1965; New York, 1967. Exhibited in group shows: England, France, Israel, America, Germany, Italy. Represented Britain: Paris Biennale, 1965; Venice Biennale, 1968 (awarded Chief internat. painting prize). Public collections include: Tate Gallery, Victoria and Albert Museum, Arts Council, British Council, Museum of Modern Art, New York, Museum of Modern Art, Pasadena, Ferens Art Gallery, Hull, Allbright Knox, Buffalo, USA, Museum of Contemporary Art, Chicago, Ulster Museum, Ireland. *Address:* 7 Royal Crescent, W11. *T:* 01-603 4469.

**RILEY, Rt. Rev. Charles Lawrence,** CBE 1942 (OBE 1920); VD; retired as Bishop of Bendigo, Victoria (1938-57), and as Chaplain-General to AMF (1942-57); Hon. Canon of St George's Cathedral, Jerusalem, 1950-57; *b* 10 Oct. 1888; *s* of Most Rev. Charles Owen Leaver Riley, sometime Archbishop of Perth, and Elizabeth Merriman; *m* 1916, Lucille Mary Lefroy; two *s* two *d*. *Educ:* Hale School, Perth, WA; Gonville and Caius Coll., Cambridge (Govt of W Australia Scholar, Exhibitioner). BA 1909; LLB 1910; MA 1913; Deacon 1912; Priest 1914; Curate of Stoke-on-Trent, 1912-14; Rector of St Hilda, Perth, WA, 1914-21; of St Mary, West Perth, 1921-30; Archdeacon of Northam, 1930-38; Canon of St George's Cathedral, Perth, 1933-38; Senior Chaplain to AIF, 1940-41. *Address:* Lennard Street, Waterman's Bay, WA6020, Australia. *Club:* Union (Cambridge).

**RILEY, Harry Lister,** DSc, ARCS, DIC, FRIC; Consultant; *b* 7 Sept. 1899; *s* of late Arthur Riley, Keighley, Yorks; *m* 1924, Marion, *o c* of David Belfield; two *s* one *d*. *Educ:* The Grammar School, Keighley; Imperial College of Science and Technology (Royal College of Science). Served with 9th Bn KOYLI, 1917-19. Beit Scientific Research Fellow, 1921-23; Demonstrator, and later Lecturer in Chemistry at the Royal College of Science, South Kensington, SW7, 1923-32; Professor of Inorganic and Physical Chemistry, King's Coll. (Univ. of Durham), Newcastle on Tyne, 1932-47; Hon. Secretary and Dir of Research to the Northern Coke Research Committee; Jubilee Memorial Lecturer, Society of Chemical Industry, 1938-39; Director of Chemical Research and Development, United Steel Companies Ltd, 1947-64; Dir of carbonization research, Nat. Coal Board, 1947. *Publications:* various research publications in The Journal of the Chemical Society, the Philosophical Magazine, the Geological Magazine, and the Proceedings of the Royal Society, etc. *Recreation:* golf. *Address:* 4 First Turn, Wolvercote, Oxford OX2 8AH. *T:* Oxford 56385.

**RILEY, Norman Denbigh,** CBE 1952; Keeper, Department of Entomology, British (Museum) Natural History, 1932-Nov. 1955; retired; *b* 1890; *m* 1920, Edith Vaughan; one *s* one *d*. *Educ:* Dulwich College. Demonstrator in Entomology, Imperial College of Science, 1911; entered Museum, 1911. Served as Captain in ASC and The Queens in France, 1914-19 (despatches). Fellow Royal Entomological Society of London (Vice-Pres. 1929, 1940; Treas., 1939-40; Sec., 1926-29, 1941-51; Pres., 1951-52). *Publications:* numerous papers on Lepidoptera. *Address:* 7 McKay Road, Wimbledon, SW20.

**RILEY, Ralph,** FRS 1967; DSc; Director, since 1971, and Head of Cytogenetics Section, since 1954, Plant Breeding Institute, Cambrdige; Special Professor of Botany, University of Nottingham, since 1970; *b* 23 Oct. 1924; *y c* of Ralph and Clara Riley; *m* 1949, Joan Elizabeth Norrington; two *d*. *Educ:* Audenshaw Gram. Sch.; Univ. of Sheffield. Infantry Officer, 6 KOSB, 2 Royal Ulster Rifles and 1 S Lancs, 1943-47; Univ. of Sheffield, 1947-52; Research worker, Plant Breeding Inst., Cambridge, 1952-; National Research Council/Nuffield Foundn Lectr at Canadian Univs, 1966; Fellow of Univ. Coll., Cambrdige. William Bate Hardy Prize, Cambrdige Phil. Soc., 1969. *Publications:* scientific papers and articles on genetics of chromosome behaviour, plant cytogenetics and evolution and breeding of crop plants especially wheat. *Address:* Glebe House, 116 Shelford Road, Trumpington, Cambridge. *T:* Trumpington 3267.

**RIMINGTON, Claude,** FRS 1954, MA, PhD Cantab, DSc London; Emeritus Professor of Chemical Pathology, University of London; Head of Department of Chemical Pathology, University College Hospital Medical School, 1945-67; *b* 17 Nov. 1902; *s* of George Garthwaite Rimington, Newcastle-on-Tyne; *m* 1929, Soffi, *d* of Clemet Andersen, Askeröy, Lyngör, Norway; one *d*. *Educ:* Emmanuel College, Cambridge. Benn W. Levy Research Scholar, Univ. of Cambridge, 1926-28; Biochemist, Wool Industries Research Association, Leeds, 1928-30; Empire Marketing Board Senior Research Fellow, then Scientific Research Officer, Division of Veterinary Services, Govt of Union of South Africa, at Onderstepoort Veterinary Research Laboratory, Pretoria, 1931-37; Biochemist, National Institute for Medical Research, Medical Research Council, London, 1937-45. Hon. FRCP Edinburgh, 1967; Hon. Mem. Brit. Assoc. of Dermatology, 1967. Graham Gold Medal, Univ. of London, 1967. *Publications:* (with A. Goldberg), Diseases of Porphyrin Metabolism, 1962; numerous biochemical and scientific papers. *Recreations:* sailing, languages, Scandinavian literature. *Address:* c/o Department of Chemical Pathology, University College Hospital Medical School, University Street, WC1. *T:* 01-387 5861.

**RIMOUSKI, Archbishop of, (RC),** since 1964; **Most Rev. Louis Levesque,** ThD; *b* 27 May 1908; *s* of Philippe Levesque and Catherine Levesque (*née* Beaulieu). *Educ:* Laval Univ. Priest, 1932;

Bishop of Hearst, Ontario, 1952-64. Chm., Canadian Cath. Conf., 1965-67; Mem. Congregation Bishops, Rome, 1968-. *Address:* Archevêché de Rimouski, PQ, Canada.

**RING, Lindsay Roberts,** JP; Chairman, Ring & Brymer (Birchs) Ltd; *b* 1 May 1914; *y s* of George Arthur Ring and Helen Rhoda Mason Ring (*née* Stedman); *m* 1940, Hazel Doris, *d* of A. Trevor Nichols, CBE; two *s* one *d. Educ:* Dulwich Coll.; Mecklenburg, Germany. Served 1939-45, Europe and Middle East, Major RASC. Underwriting Member of Lloyd's, 1964. Fellow, Hotel and Catering Inst.; Chm., Hotel and Catering Trades Benevolent Assoc., 1962-; Mem., Bd of Verge of Royal Palaces. Governor, Farringtons Sch. Freeman, City of London, 1935; Mem. Court of Assistants, Armourers' and Brasiers' Co.; Common Councilman, City of London (Ward of Bishopsgate), 1964-68; Alderman (Ward of Vintry), 1968; Sheriff, City of London, 1967-68; JP Inner London, 1964. OStJ 1968. *Address:* Chalvedune, Wilderness Road, Chiselhurst, Kent. *T:* 01-467 3199. *Clubs:* East India and Sports, City Livery.

**RINGHAM, Reginald,** CBE 1958; MIMinE; *b* 30 April 1894; *s* of John Charles Ringham; *m* 1923, Doris Clare Fletcher; one *d. Educ:* Oundle. Entered Mining Industry, 1913, as student under Sir Arthur Markham, 1st Bt; joined Staveley Coal and Iron Co. Ltd, 1922, and served with them in various capacities, becoming Gen. Manager of the Collieries, 1938. Since nationalisation of the mines has served in E Midlands Div. as Area Gen. Manager, Production Director, and Dep. Chm.; Chm. E Midlands Div., National Coal Board, 1951-60. OStJ 1941. *Address:* Elizabeth House, Southwold, Suffolk. *T:* 3154.

**RINK, George Arnold,** QC 1956; Bencher of Lincoln's Inn; *b* 21 April 1902; *s* of late M. Rink; *m* 1949, Margaret Joan Suttill, MB, BS (*widow* of Francis Suttill, DSO), Director of the Medical Department of British Council. *Educ:* Charterhouse; University College, Oxford. 1st Cl. Hon. Mods, and Lit. Hum.; BCL; Barrister, Lincoln's Inn, 1926, and has been in practice since then, except for period in Civil Service, 1939-44. Chm., Tribunal of Inquiry under Prevention of Fraud (Investments) Act, 1968-. Trustee of Charterhouse in Southwark, 1948-66. Member Board of Governors, Royal Free Hospital, 1955-64, Middlesex Hospital, 1964-70. Member, Advisory Council, Science of Science Foundation, 1966-. *Publications:* articles in professional journals. *Recreations:* opera, ski-ing, walking; formerly fencing (Oxford half blue, 1924). *Address:* 17 Old Buildings, Lincoln's Inn, WC2. *T:* 01-405 5017; 173 Oakwood Court, W14. *T:* 01-602 2143. *Club:* Athenæum.

**RIPLEY, Sir Hugh,** 4th Bt *cr* 1880; Director, John Walker & Sons Ltd, Scotch Whisky Distillers; *b* 26 May 1916; *s* of Sir Henry William Alfred Ripley, 3rd Bt, and Dorothy (*d* 1964), *e d* of late Robert William Daker Harley; *S* father 1956; *m* 1946, Dorothy Mary Dunlop Bruce-Jones; one *s* one *d. Educ:* Eton. Served in Africa and Italy with 1st Bn KSLI (despatches twice, American Silver Star); retired regular Major. *Recreations:* golf, fishing, shooting. *Heir: s* William Hugh Ripley, *b* 13 April 1950. *Address:* House in the Wood, Wentworth, Surrey. *T:* Wentworth 2100; Bedstone, Bucknell, Shropshire. *Club:* Boodle's.

**RIPLEY, Sydney William Leonard,** DL; Mem. Greater London Council (Kingston-upon-Thames Borough) from 1964; Joint Deputy Leader, Conservative Opposition, 1964-66; *b* 17 July 1909; *o s* of late Leonard Ripley; *m* 1934, Doris Emily, *d* of late William Gray; one *s* two *d. Educ:* King's School, Canterbury; London. Served War of 1939-45, with RAF, Flight-Lieut (despatches). Contested (C) Ipswich, 1950, Watford, 1951; Chairman Malden and Coombe Conservative Assoc., 1938-49, Pres., 1950-; Vice-Pres., Kingston Division, 1955-. Chairman Leonard Ripley and Co. Ltd and other printing companies. Member, Malden and Coombe Borough Council, 1938-48, formerly Chm. Finance Cttee; DL Surrey 1960; DL Greater London, 1966; JP 1959-69, CC 1946, CA 1955, Surrey (Chairman, Finance Cttee, 1962-64); Vice-Chm. Surrey CC, 1956-59; Chm. General Purposes Cttee, 1952-59; Chm. Surrey County Council, 1959-62; Mem., Surrey Jt Standing Cttee, 1959-65; County Council rep. on Metrop. Water Bd, 1956-65; County Councils Assoc., 1958-65; Surrey T&AFA, 1959-65; Governor Westminster Hosp., 1963-65; GLC rep. on Surrey T&AFA, 1965-; London Tourist Board, 1965-68. Chm., SW Regional Hosp. Bd, 1963-65. Freeman, City of London. *Recreations:* golf, swimming, tennis. *Address:* 2 Thames Side, Thames Ditton, Surrey. *T:* 01-398 5005. *Club:* Carlton.

**RIPON, Bishop of,** since 1959; **Rt. Rev. John Richard Humpidge Moorman,** MA, DD, Cambridge; LittD Leeds; St Bonaventure, USA; FSA; Hon. Fellow of Emmanuel College; *b* Leeds, 4 June 1905; 2nd *s* of late Professor F. W. Moorman; *m* 1930, Mary Caroline, *d* of late G. M. Trevelyan, OM; no *c. Educ:* Gresham's School, Holt; Emmanuel College, Cambridge. Curate of Holbeck, Leeds, 1929-33; of Leighton Buzzard, 1933-35; Rector of Fallowfield, Manchester, 1935-42; Hon. and Examining Chaplain to Bishop of Manchester, 1940-44; Vicar of Lanercost, 1945-46, and Examining Chaplain to Bishop of Carlisle, 1945-59; Principal of Chichester Theological Coll. and Chancellor of Chichester Cathedral, 1946-56; Prebendary of Heathfield in Chichester Cathedral, 1956-59; Delegate-observer to 2nd Vatican Council, 1962-65. Hale Memorial Lectr, Evanston, USA, 1966. Chairman, Anglican members, Anglican-Roman Catholic Preparatory Commn, 1967-69; Member, Jt Permanent Commn of the Roman Catholic Church and the Anglican Communion, 1969-. *Publications:* Sources for the Life of S Francis of Assisi, 1940; Church Life in England in the Thirteenth Century, 1945; A New Fioretti, 1946; B. K. Cunningham, a Memoir, 1947; S Francis of Assisi, 1950; The Grey Friars in Cambridge (Birkbeck Lectures), 1952; A History of the Church in England, 1953; The Curate of Souls, 1958; The Path to Glory, 1960; Vatican Observed, 1967; A History of the Franciscan Order, 1968. *Recreations:* country life, music. *Address:* Bishop Mount, Ripon, W Yorks. *T:* Ripon 2045.

**RIPON, Dean of;** *see* Le Grice, Very Rev. F. E.

**RIPPON, Rt. Hon. (Aubrey) Geoffrey (Frederick);** PC 1962; QC 1964; MP (C) Hexham, since 1966; Chancellor of the Duchy of Lancaster, since 1970; *b* 28 May 1924; *o s* of late Arthur Sydney Rippon, Surbiton, Sy; *m* 1946, Ann Leyland, *d* of Donald Yorke, MC, Prenton, Birkenhead, Cheshire; one *s* three *d. Educ:* King's College, Taunton; Brasenose College, Oxford (Hulme Open Exhibitioner; MA). Secretary and Librarian of the Oxford Union, 1942; Pres. Oxford University Conservative Assoc., 1942; Chm., Federation of University Conservative Associations, 1943. Called to the Bar, Middle Temple, 1948 (Robert Garraway Rice Pupillage Prizeman). Member Surbiton Borough Council, 1945-54;

Alderman, 1949; Mayor, 1951-52; Member: LCC (Chelsea), 1952-61 (Leader of Conserv. Party on LCC, 1957-59). Court, Univ. of London, 1958-, President: British Section of the Council of European Municipalities; The Enterprise Assoc.; London Mayors' Assoc.; Jt President, Commonwealth League for Economic Co-operation (Chm. British Section, 1969-70); Chm. Conservative National Advisory Committee on Local Government, 1957-59; Vice-Pres., Council of Europe's Local Government Conference, 1957 and 1958; Contested (C) Shoreditch and Finsbury, General Elections, 1950 and 1951; MP (C) Norwich South, 1955-64. PPS, Min. of Housing and Local Govt, 1956-57, Min. of Defence, 1957-59; Parly Sec., Min. of Aviation, 1959-61; Jt Parly Sec., Min. of Housing and Local Govt, Oct. 1961-July 1962; Minister of Public Building and Works, 1962-64 (Cabinet, 1963-64); Minister of Technology, 1970. Formerly: Chm., Holland, Hannen & Cubitts; Dep. Chm., Drake & Gorham; Dir, Fairey Co. Ltd; Dir, Bristol Aeroplane Co. Ltd. *Publications:* (Co-author) Forward from Victory, 1943; The Rent Act, 1957; various pamphlets and articles on foreign affairs, local government and legal subjects. *Recreations:* cricket, golf, walking. *Address:* 39 Cadogan Square, SW1. *T:* 01-235 5204; Ellwood House, Barrasford, Hexham, Northumberland. *T:* Humshaugh 215; *Clubs:* Carlton, MCC; Northern Conservative and Unionist (Newcastle upon Tyne).

**RIPPON, Rt. Hon. Geoffrey;** *see* Rippon, Rt Hon. A. G. F.

**RISK, Thomas Neilson;** Partner, Maclay Murray & Spens, Solicitors, Glasgow, since 1950; Chairman, Standard Life Assurance Company, since 1969; Director, British Linen Bank; *b* 13 Sept. 1922; *s* of late Ralph Risk, CBE, and of Margaret Nelson Robertson; *m* 1949, Suzanne Eiloart; four *s*. *Educ:* Kelvinside Academy; Glasgow Univ. *Recreations:* shooting, sailing. *Address:* 18 Boclair Crescent, Bearsden, Dunbartonshire. *T:* 041-942 0392. *Clubs:* Western (Glasgow); Royal Northern Yacht (Rhu, Dunbartonshire).

**RISSON, Maj.-Gen. Sir Robert Joseph Henry,** Kt 1970; CB 1958; CBE 1945 (OBE 1942); DSO 1942; ED 1948; Chairman Melbourne and Metropolitan Tramways Board, 1949-70; Chairman, National Fitness Council of Victoria since 1961; Chairman, Victorian Committee, Duke of Edinburgh's Award Scheme; *b* 20 April 1901; *s* of late Robert Risson *m* 1934, Gwendolyn, *d* of late C. A. Spurgin; no *c*. *Educ:* Gatton High Sch.; Univ. of Queensland. BE (Civil); FICE; FIEAust; MInstT; FAIM. Served AIF, War of 1939-45: GOC 3 Div. (Australian), 1953-56; Citizen Military Forces Member Australian Military Board, 1957-58. Chief Commissioner, Boy Scouts, Victoria, 1958-63; Pres., Instn Engineers, Australia, 1962-63. OStJ 1966. *Address:* 39 Somers Street, Burwood, Victoria 3125, Australia. *Clubs:* Australian (Melbourne); Naval and Military (Melbourne); United Service, Johnsonian (Brisbane).

**RITCHARD, Cyril;** actor; *b* Sydney, NSW, 1 Dec. 1898; *s* of Herbert Trimnell-Ritchard and Margaret (*née* Collins); *m* Madge Elliott (*d* 1955), actress. *Educ:* St Aloysius College, Sydney, New South Wales; Sydney University. Various light comedy parts, 1917-24; went to USA, 1924; first appearance on London stage in Bubbly, Duke of York's, 1925; in various productions, 1925-31, including Charlot's Revue and the Co-Optimists of 1930; Australia, 1932-36; returned to England, 1936; played the leading part in Nine Sharp (Revue), Little, 1938-39; The Little Review, Little, 1939; produced The New Ambassadors' Revue, Ambassadors', 1941; appeared in Big Top, His Majesty's, 1942; The Importance of Being Earnest (Algernon Moncrieffe), Phœnix, 1942; The Merry Widow (Prince Danilo), His Majesty's, 1943, on tour abroad for the Forces, 1943-44, Coliseum, 1944; Gay Rosalinda, Palace, 1945; returned to Australia, taking various parts at Theatre Royal, Sydney, 1946; Love for Love (Tattle), New York, 1947; The Relapse (Sir Novelty Fashion), Lyric, Hammersmith, Dec. 1947, Phœnix, Jan. 1948, and in USA 1950. Since 1948 has directed and played in USA, London, etc. Recent successes include: The Millionairess (Adrian Blenderbland), New, and in New York, 1952; High Spirits, London Hippodrome, 1953; Captain Hook in Musical of Peter Pan, Winter Garden, New York, 1954; (directed) Tales of Hoffman, New York Metropolitan Opera, 1955; Eisenstein in Rosalinda, Civic Light Opera Co., Los Angeles and San Francisco, 1956; (directed and played Don Andres), Offenbach's La Perichole, Metropolitan Opera House, New York, also (directed) Reluctant Debutante, Henry Miller Theatre, New York, Dec. 1956 (directed and played in) Visit to a Small Planet (Kreton), Booth Theatre, New York, 1957; (directed and starred in) The Pleasure of his Company, USA, 1958-60, touring Australia, 1960; (directed and starred in) The Happiest Girl in the World, New York, 1961; The Roar of the Greasepaint–the Smell of the Crowd, New York, 1965; appeared in Half a Sixpence (film), 1967; directed and played in, Midsummer Night's Dream, Stratford, Connecticut, 1967. Directed new versions of The Marriage of Figaro and Gypsy Baron, Metropolitan Opera, 1958-59; starred in Romulus, Music Box Theater, New York; and in revival of La Perichole, Metropolitan Opera House; played Phineas Fogg in musical version of Around the World in 80 days, St Louis Municipal Opera and Kansas City Starlight Theater. Has also appeared in films and starred in several TV spectaculars. *Address:* 135 Central Park West, New York City, USA.

**RITCHIE,** family name of **Baron Ritchie of Dundee.**

**RITCHIE OF DUNDEE,** 3rd Baron, *cr* 1905, **John Kenneth Ritchie,** PC 1965; Chairman of the Stock Exchange, 1959-65 (Deputy Chairman, 1954-59 and 1965-); Senior Partner, Norris Oakley Richardson & Glover, Stockbrokers; Director: English Association of American Bond & Shareholders Ltd (Chairman); Hutchinson Ltd; *b* 22 Sept. 1902; 2nd and *e surv s* of 2nd Baron Ritchie of Dundee and Sarah Ruth (*d* 1950), 4th *d* of L. J. Jennings, MP; *S* father 1948; *m* 1945, Joan Beatrice (*d* 1963), *d* of late Rev. H. C. L. Tindall; no *c*. *Educ:* RNC, Osborne; Winchester; Magdalen College, Oxford. Served War of 1939-45, KRRC (Captain), 1940-45. Chairman Poplar Hospital, 1948; Chairman Bow Group of Hospitals Management Cttee, 1948-58; Mayor of Winchelsea, 1934. *Heir: b* Hon. Colin Neville Ower Ritchie [*b* 9 July 1908; *m* 1943, Anne Petronill (Huntley), *d* of H. C. Burra, Rye. *Educ:* Trinity College, Oxford (BA)]. *Address:* 40 Thurloe Square, SW7. *T:* 01-589 9730; Lower Bosney, Iden, Sussex. *T:* Iden 282. *Clubs:* Brooks's, City of London, All England Lawn Tennis.

**RITCHIE, Albert Edgar;** Under-Secretary of State for External Affairs, Canada, since 1970; *b* 20 Dec. 1916; *m*; two *s* two *d*. *Educ:* Mount Allison Univ., New Brunswick (BA) 1938); Queen's College, Oxford (Rhodes Scholar, 1940; BA). Deputy Under-Secretary of State for External Affairs, Canada, 1964-66; Canadian Ambassador to USA, 1966-70. Hon. LLD: Mount Allison Univ., 1966; St Thomas Univ., 1968. *Address:* (home) 16 Carlyle Avenue, Ottawa 1, Ont, Canada; (office) East Block, Ottawa 2, Ont. *T:* 992-4803. *Club:* Rideau (Ottawa).

**RITCHIE, Anthony Elliot,** MA, BSc, MD; FRSE; Secretary and Treasurer, Carnegie Trust for the Universities of Scotland, since 1969; *b* 30 March 1915; *s* of late Prof. James Ritchie; *m* 1941, Elizabeth Lambie Knox, MB, ChB, *y d* of John Knox, Dunfermline; one *s* three *d*. *Educ:* Edinburgh Academy; Aberdeen and Edinburgh Universities. MA (Aber), 1933; BSc 1936, with Hunter Memorial Prize. MB, ChB (Edin.) 1940. Carnegie Research Scholar, Physiology Dept, Edin. Univ., 1940-41; Asst Lect. 1941; Lect. 1942. Ellis Prize in Physiology, 1941; Gunning Victoria Jubilee Prize, 1943; MD (Edin.) with Gold Medal Thesis, 1945; senior lecturer grade, 1946. Lecturer in Electrotherapy, Edin. Royal Infirmary, 1943-48; Chandos Prof. of Physiology, Univ. of St Andrews, 1948-69; Dean, Faculty of Science, 1961-66. Hon. Physiologist Gogarburn Nerve Injuries Hospital, 1941-46; Honeyman Gillespie Lecturer, 1944; hon. Consultant in Electrotherapy, Scot. E Regional Hospital Board, 1950-69; Fellow Royal Soc. of Edinburgh, 1951 (Council RSE 1957-60; Secretary to Ordinary Meetings, 1960-65, Vice-President, 1965-66; General Secretary, 1966-); Scientific Adviser, Civil Defence, 1961-; Adv. Cttee on Med. Research, Scotland, 1961-, Vice-Chm., 1967-69; Chairman: Scottish Cttee on Science Educn, 1970-; Central Cttee, Scottish Nat. Blood Transfusion, 1970-; Scottish Universities Entrance Bd, 1963-69; St Leonard's Sch., St Andrews, 1968-69. Examiner, Chartered Soc. of Physiotherapy, Pharmaceutical Soc. of Great Britain, and RCSE. RAMC (TA) commission, 1942-44. Hon. FCSP, 1970. *Publications:* (with J. Lenman) Clinical Electromyography, 1970; medical and scientific papers on nerve injury diagnosis and medical electronics. *Recreations:* reading, mountaineering, motor cars. *Address:* 12 Ravelston Park, Edinburgh EH4 3DX. *T:* 031-332 6560. *Clubs:* Caledonian; Royal and Ancient (St Andrews); New (Edinburgh).

**RITCHIE, Charles Stewart Almon;** Canadian High Commissioner in London since 1967; *b* 23 Sept. 1906; *s* of William Bruce Almon Ritchie, KC and Lilian Constance Harriette Ritchie (*née* Stewart), both of Halifax; *m* 1948, Sylvia Catherine Beatrice Smellie; no *c*. *Educ:* University of King's College; Ecole Libre des Sciences Politiques, Paris. BA, MA Oxford 1929, MA Harvard, 1930. Joined Dept of External Affairs, 3rd Sec. Ottawa, 1934; 3rd Sec., Washington, 1936; 2nd Sec., London, 1939; 1st Sec., London, 1943; 1st Sec., Ottawa, 1945; Counsellor, Paris, 1947; Asst Under-Secretary of State for External Affairs, Ottawa, 1950, Deputy Under-Secretary of State for External Affairs, 1952; Ambassador to Federal Republic of Germany, Bonn, and Head of Military Mission, Berlin, 1954; Permanent Rep. to UN, New York 1958; Ambassador of Canada to the United States, 1962; Ambassador and Permanent Representative of Canada to the North Atlantic Council, 1966-67. Hon. DCL, Univ. of King's College, Halifax, NS; Hon. Fellow, Pembroke College, Oxford. *Address:* Canada House, Trafalgar Square, SW1. *T:* 01-930 9741. *Club: Brooks's.*

**RITCHIE, Sir Douglas;** *see* Ritchie, Sir J. D.

**RITCHIE, Rear-Adm. George Stephen,** CB 1967; DSC 1942; ADC to the Queen, 1965; Hydrographer of the Navy, 1966-71; *b* 31 Oct. 1914; *s* of Sir (John) Douglas Ritchie, *qv*; *m* 1942, Mrs Disa Elizabeth Smith (*née* Beveridge); three *s* one *d*. *Educ:* RNC, Dartmouth. Joined RN Surveying Service, 1936; attached Eighth Army, 1942-43; served in HM Survey Ship Scott for invasion of Europe, 1944; comd HMS Challenger on scientific voyage round world, 1950-51; comd HM New Zealand Survey Ship Lachlan and NZ Surveying Service, 1953-56; comd HM Surveying Ship Dalrymple, Persian Gulf, 1959; comd HM Surveying Ship Vidal, West Indies and Western Europe, 1963-65. *Publications:* Challenger, 1957; The Admiralty Chart, 1967; papers on navigation and oceanography in various jls. *Recreations:* writing, painting, gardening, hunting. *Address:* Sharpe House, Wiveliscombe, Somerset. *T:* Wiveliscombe 218. *Club:* Reform.

**RITCHIE, Harry Parker,** CMG 1966; HM Overseas Civil Service; Minister of Finance, Fiji, since 1967; *b* 3 June, 1919; *s* of W. S. Ritchie; *m* 1949, Mary Grace, *née* Foster; two *s*. *Educ:* Royal Belfast Academical Institution; Queen's University, Belfast. Served War of 1939-45 (Captain). Administrative Cadet, Bechuanaland Protectorate, 1946; Swaziland, 1948; District Officer, 1953; seconded to Office of High Commissioner, as Assistant Secretary, 1954; Deputy Financial Secretary, Fiji, 1957, Financial Secretary, 1962-67. *Recreations:* golf, reading. *Address:* Financial Secretary's Office, Suva, Fiji. *Club:* Royal Over-Seas League.

**RITCHIE, Horace David;** Professor of Surgery, University of London, and Director of the Surgical Unit at The London Hospital, since 1964; *b* 24 Sept. 1920; *m*; three *s*. *Educ:* Universities of Glasgow, Cambridge and Edinburgh. *Publications:* contribs to various scientific journals. *Address:* 129 Burbage Road, Dulwich Village, SE21.

**RITCHIE, Sir James Edward Thomson,** 2nd Bt, *cr* 1918 (2nd creation); TD 1943 (2 clasps); FRSA; Chairman M. W. Hardy & Co. Ltd and associated companies; Director: Wm Ritchie & Son (Textiles) Ltd; Guardian Assurance Group (Local London Director); Member Court of Assistants, Merchant Taylors' Co. (Master, 1963-64); *b* 16 June 1902; *s* of 1st Baronet and Ada Bevan, *d* of late Edward ap Rees Bryant; *S* father, 1937; *m* 1st, 1928, Esme Phyllis (*d* 1939), *o d* of late J. M. Oldham, Ormidale, Ascot; 2nd, 1936, Rosemary, *yr d* of late Col. Henry Streatfeild, DSO, TD; two *d*. *Educ:* Rugby; The Queen's Coll., Oxford. Joined Inns of Court Regt, 1936; commissioned, 1938; served 1939-45 (CMF 1944-45), various staff and regimental appts; Lt-Col 1945; re-commissioned, 1949, to command 44 (Home Counties) Div. Provost Co. RCMP (TA); retired 1953. Co-opted Mem. Kent TA&AFA (Mem. General Purposes Cttee), 1953-68. Pres., British Legion, Ashford (Kent) Br; Patron, Ashford and Dist Caledonian Society; Chm. Finance and General Purposes Cttee and joint Hon. Treas., London School of Hygiene and Tropical Medicine, Univ. of London, 1951-61; Mem. Bd of Management and Finance and Gen. Purposes Cttee, 1964-67. *Heir: half-b* William Peter Emerton Ritchie, *b* 1918. *Address:* Lees House, Willesborough, Ashford, Kent. *T:* Ashford 24037. *Club:* Army and Navy.

**RITCHIE, (James) Martin;** Chairman and Chief Executive, The Bowater Paper Corporation Ltd; *b* 29 May 1917; *s* of late Sir James Ritchie,

CBE and Lady Ritchie (*née* Gemmell); *m* 1939, Noreen Mary Louise Johnston; three *s*. *Educ:* Strathallan Sch., Perthshire. Joined Andrew Ritchie & Son Ltd, Glasgow, corrugated fibre container manufrs, 1934; Dir, 1938. TA Officer, 1938; served War of 1939-45: HAA Regt; Capt. 1941; psc 1943; DA&AQMG, MEF, Middle East, 1944-45 (Maj.). Rejoined Andrew Ritchie & Son Ltd, then part of Eburite Organisation; Man. Dir, 1950; Gen. Man., Bowater-Eburite Ltd, on merger with Bowater Organisation, 1956; Bowater Paper Corp. Ltd: Dir, 1959; Man. Dir, 1964; Dep. Chm. and Man. Dir, 1967; Chm. 1969. *Recreations:* golf, fishing. *Address:* The Grove, Denham, Bucks. *T:* Denham 2945. *Clubs:* Denham Golf; Winged Foot Golf (Mamaroneck, NY).

**RITCHIE, John,** MBE 1944; Master of the Supreme Court of Judicature (Queen's Bench Division) since 1960; *b* 7 Feb. 1913; *e s* of W. Tod Ritchie, JP, Rector of Hutchesons' Grammar School, Glasgow; *m* 1936, Nora Gwendolen Margaret, *yr d* of Sir Frederic G. Kenyon, GBE, KCB, FBA; one *s* two *d*. *Educ:* Glasgow Academy; Magdalen College, Oxford. BA 1935; MA 1948. Called to the Bar, Middle Temple, 1935; practised in London and on South-Eastern Circuit, 1935-60; Recorder of King's Lynn, 1956-58. Served War of 1939-45 (MBE, Belgian Croix de Guerre, despatches twice): BEF 1940; BLA 1944-45; private, Royal Fusiliers, 1939; commissioned Queen's Own Cameron Highlanders, 1940; Major, 1942. Belgian Croix de Guerre, 1944. *Recreations:* cricket; tennis; painting; rose-growing; wine-tasting. *Address:* Kirkstead, Godstone, Surrey. *T:* Godstone 335; Royal Courts of Justice, Strand, WC2. *T:* 01-405 7641. *Club:* Caledonian.

**RITCHIE, Sir (John) Douglas,** Kt, *cr* 1941; MC; *b* 28 Nov., 1885; *s* of John Walker Ritchie, Collieston, Aberdeenshire, and Mary Southern; *m* 1913, Margaret Stephen (OBE 1946, JP, Officer of the Order of Orange-Nassau), *d* of James Allan, Methlick, Aberdeenshire; one *s*. *Educ:* Manchester Grammar School; Manchester Univ. Served European War in France in 4th Gordon Highlanders and Tank Corps (MC); Town Clerk of Burnley, 1920-23; Solicitor to the Port of London Authority, 1923-26; Solicitor and Secretary to the Port of London Authority, 1927-38; Deputy General Manager, 1938; Gen. Manager, 1938-46; Vice-Chm., Port of London Authority, 1946-55. Mem. Aberdeen County Council, 1955-65; Pres., Dock and Harbour Authorities Assoc., 1954-56; Pres. of Burns Club of London, 1934-35; Chief Executive of London Port Emergency Cttee, 1939-46; Member of Inland Transport War Council; Col. Engineer and Railway Staff Corps RE (TA). *Recreations:* sailing, fishing. *Address:* Collieston, Aberdeenshire. *T:* Collieston 216. *Club:* Royal Northern (Aberdeen).

*See also Rear-Adm. G. S. Ritchie.*

**RITCHIE, Sir John (Neish),** Kt 1961; CB 1955; Principal and Dean of the Royal Veterinary College, University of London, 1965-70; *b* 19 Jan. 1904; *m* 1930, Florina Margaret Drummond; two *s* two *d*. *Educ:* Turriff, Aberdeenshire; Royal (Dick) Veterinary Coll., Edinburgh; Edinburgh Univ. MRCVS 1925; DVSM 1926; BSc 1927; FRSE 1957. Asst Vet. Officer, City of Edinburgh, 1927-29; Co. Vet. Officer, Midlothian, 1929-35; Sen. Vet. Officer, Dept of Agric. for Scotland, 1935-38; Suptg Inspector, Min. of Agric. and Fisheries, 1938-45; Dep. Chief Vet. Officer, 1945; Chief Veterinary Officer, Ministry of Agriculture, Fisheries and Food, 1952-65. Hon. FRCVS, 1955; Hon. degrees: DVSc (Liv.) 1961; LLD (Toronto) 1962, (Edin.) 1965; Bledisloe Vet. Award, 1961; BOCM Poultry Award, 1964. Member: ARC; Scientific Adv. panel to Minister of Agric., Fisheries and Food, 1965-68; Council, Roy. Coll. of Veterinary Surgeons, 1951-70 (President, 1959-61, Vice-President, 1958-59, 1961-62). Chm., European Commn for the Control of Foot-and-Mouth Disease, 1959-65; Member Gov. Body: Houghton Poultry Research Stn, 1965-68; Animal Virus Research Inst., Pirbright, 1951-65; Wye Coll., Univ. of London; Chairman, FAO/WHO Expert Panel on Vet. Educn. *Publications:* Articles on vet. subjects in several jls. *Recreation:* painting. *Address:* c/o Royal Bank of Scotland Ltd, 115 Regent Street, W1A 3DD. *Clubs:* Athenæum, Farmers'.

**RITCHIE, Kenneth Gordon,** CMG 1968; Counsellor, Foreign and Commonwealth Office, since 1970; *b* 19 Aug. 1921; *s* of Walter Ritchie, Arbroath; *m* 1951, Esme Stronsa Nash. *Educ:* Arbroath High Sch.; St Andrews Univ. (MA). Joined FO, 1944; Embassy, Ankara, 1944-47; Foreign Office, 1947-49; Khorramshahr, 1949-50; Tehran, 1950-52; Djakarta, 1952-55; Foreign Office, 1955-57; Peking, 1957-62; Santiago, 1962-64; Elisabethville, 1965-66; Dep. High Commissioner, Lusaka, 1966-67; High Commissioner, Guyane, 1967-70. *Recreations:* cinephotography, model railways. *Address:* c/o Foreign and Commonwealth Office, King Charles Street, SW1.

**RITCHIE, Martin;** *see* Ritchie, J. M.

**RITCHIE, Gen. Sir Neil Methuen,** GBE 1951 (KBE 1945; CBE 1940); KCB 1947 (CB 1944); DSO 1917; MC 1918; retired; Chairman of the Mercantile and General Reinsurance Co. of Canada Ltd; Chairman and Director, Macdonald-Buchanan Properties Ltd; Director: Grosvenor-Laing (Langley-Park) Ltd; Toromont Industrial Holdings Ltd; Electra Investments (Can.) Ltd; Tanqueray Gordon & Co. (Can.) Ltd; *b* 29 July 1897; 2nd *s* of late Dugald Ritchie of Restholme, Liss, Hants; *m* 1937, Catherine, *d* of James A. Minnes, Kingston, Ontario; one *s* one *d*. *Educ:* Lancing; RMC, Sandhurst. 2nd Lieut The Black Watch, 1914; Lieutenant 1915; Capt. 1917; Bt Major, 1933; Major, 1934; Bt Lt-Col 1936; Lt-Col The King's Own Royal Regt 1938; Col 1939; Brigadier 1939; Acting Maj.-General 1940; Temp. Major-General 1941; Maj.-Gen. 1943; Temp. Lt-Gen. 1944; Lt-Gen. 1945; General 1947; served European War, 1914-19; France, 1915; Mesopotamia, 1916-17; Palestine, 1918 (despatches, DSO, MC); Palestine, 1938-39 (despatches); Gen. Staff Officer, 3rd Grade, War Office, 1923-27; Staff College, Camberley, 1929-30; GSO2, Northern Command, India, 1933-37; GSO1, 1939; Brigadier, General Staff, 1939; Comdr 51st Highland Division, 1940-41; Deputy Chief of Staff Middle East, 1941; Commander of 8th Army, Libya, acting rank of Lieut-General, 1941; Comd 52nd Lowland Division, 1942-43; Comd 12 Corps BLA, 1944-45; GOC-in-C Scottish Command and Governor of Edinburgh Castle, 1945-47; C-in-C, Far East Land Forces, 1947-49; Commander British Army Staff, Washington, and Military Member of Joint Services Mission 1950-51; ADC General to the King, 1948-51; retired pay, 1951. Colonel, The Black Watch (Royal Highland Regiment), 1950-52. Queen's Body Guard for Scotland. Virtuti Militari (Poland), 1945; Comdr Legion of Honour, Croix de Guerre (France), 1945; Kt Comdr Orange Nassau (Holland), 1945; Comdr Order of Merit (USA), 1945. KStJ 1963. *Address:*

Dalavich House, RRI, Ashburn, Ontario, Canada. *T:* 416 649 2513. *Clubs:* Boodle's, MCC, Caledonian, I Zingari, Free Foresters; New (Edin.); Mount Royal (Montreal); York, Toronto (Toronto).

**RITCHIE, Sir Thomas Malcolm,** Kt 1951; Chartered Engineer; FIE Australia; Director: Crompton Parkinson (Australia) Pty Ltd; Noyes (Australia) Pty Ltd and Associated Companies; *b* 11 June 1894; *s* of Thomas Ritchie, Ivanhoe, Vic; *m* 1924, Phyllis Elizabeth Brown. *Educ:* Melbourne. Diplomas in Electrical and Mechanical Engineering. Man. Dir Metropolitan Vickers (Aust.) Pty Ltd, 1923-29; Gen. Mgr Australian Electrical Mfg Co. Ltd, 1929-32; Works Director, Aust. General Elec. Co. Ltd, 1932-34; Chm. and Man. Dir Noyes Bros (Sydney) Ltd, 1934-54; Chm., British Insulated Callenders Cables (Australia) Ltd, 1953-59; Business Administrator, NSW, Min. of Munitions, 1940-45; Mem. Bd of Governors, Fairbridge Farm Schools of NSW, 1945-53; Mem. of Electricity Advisory Cttee to Govt of NSW, 1935-46; Federal Pres., The Liberal Party of Australia, 1945-47 and 1949-51. *Recreations:* golf, bowls. *Address:* Trelm, Moss Vale, NSW 2577, Australia; Royal Sydney Golf Club, Rose Bay, Sydney. *T:* Moss Vale 321. *Clubs:* Union, Australian (Sydney); Johnsonian (Brisbane, Qld), etc.

**RITCHIE, Major-General Walter Henry Dennison,** CB 1953; CBE 1944 (OBE 1940); Chairman, Earls Court Ltd; *b* 28 April 1901; *s* of Henry Montague Ritchie, Perth; *m* 1930, Gladys Stella, *d* of William Craven, Southsea; one *s* one *d*. *Educ:* St John's Coll., Southsea. 2nd Lieut RASC, 1925; served War of 1939-45, in France, N Africa, Italy; Maj. 1939; Brig. 1943; Maj.-Gen. 1953; Director of Quartering, War Office, 1953-54; Director of Supplies and Transport, War Office, 1954-57; retired. Col Comdt, RASC, 1959-64; Hon. Col. 101 AER Regt, RCT, 1965-67. Officer Legion of Merit, USA 1945. *Club:* Army and Navy.

**RITCHIE-CALDER;** family name of **Baron Ritchie-Calder.**

**RITCHIE-CALDER,** Baron, *cr* 1966, of Balmashannar (Life Peer); **Peter Ritchie Ritchie-Calder,** CBE 1945; MA (Edinburgh) 1961; author and journalist; Chairman, Metrication Board, since 1969; *b* 1 July 1906; *s* of David Lindsay Calder and Georgina Ritchie, Forfar, Angus; *m* 1927, Mabel Jane Forbes, *d* of Dr David McKail, Glasgow; three *s* two *d*. *Educ:* Forfar Academy. Police court reporter, Dundee Courier (1922), D. C. Thomson Press (London office, 1924, Glasgow, 1925), Daily News (1926-30), Daily Chronicle (1930), Daily Herald (1930-41). Author, scientific, social and political journalist and broadcaster (radio and television). Science Editor, News Chronicle, 1945-56. Dept of FO, 1941-45; Editorial Staff, New Statesman, 1945-58; Montague Burton Professor of International Relations, Edinburgh University, 1961-67. Charles Beard lectr, Ruskin College, Oxford, 1957; Member Council British Association, Pres. Section X, 1955; Fell. Amer. Assoc. for Advancement of Science; Fabian Executive; Secretary of H. G. Wells' Debate, and Viscount Sankey Cttee, on New Declaration of the Rights of Man, 1940; Mem. British delegn to Unesco (Paris, 1946, Mexico City, 1947, 1966, 1968); special adviser at FAO Famine Conf. (Washington, 1946); Desert survey for Unesco, 1950; chief, special UN Mission to SE Asia, 1951; Mission (UN auspices) to Arctic, 1955; Member UN Secretariat, at Peaceful Uses of Atomic Energy Confs, 1955 and 1958, and Member WHO group on mental aspects of Atomic Energy, 1957; Consultant-Editor, UN Science and Technology Conference, Geneva, 1963; Chm. Chicago University study group on Radiation in the Environment, 1960; Special UN Mission to Congo, 1960; 2nd UN Mission to SE Asia, 1962. Associate, Center for the Study of Democratic Institutions, California, 1965; Chairman Association of British Science Writers, 1949-55. President: Mental Health Film Council; National Peace Council; Fellow of World Academy of Arts and Science; Danforth Foundation Lecturer, USA, 1965. UK Commn for WHO; UK Commn for Unesco; Cons., OXFAM; Vice-Pres. Workers' Educational Assoc., 1958-68; Member: Gen. Council, Open Univ., 1969-; Community Relations Commn, 1968-. Kalinga Internat. Award for science writing, 1960; Victor Gollanz Award for service to humanity, 1969. *Publications:* Birth of the Future, 1934; Conquest of Suffering, 1935; Roving Commission, 1935; Lesson of London, 1941; Carry on, London, 1941; Start Planning Britain Now, 1941; Men against the Desert, 1951; Profile of Science, 1951; The Lamp is Lit, 1951; Men against Ignorance, 1953 (UNESCO); Men Against the Jungle, 1954; Science in Our Lives, 1954 (USA); Science Makes Sense, 1955; Men against the Frozen North, 1957; Magic to Medicine, 1958; Medicine and Man, 1958; Ten Steps Forward: The Story of WHO, 1958; The Hand of Life: The Story of the Weizmann Institute, 1959; The Inheritors, 1960; Agony of the Congo, 1961; Life-Savers, 1961; Common Sense about a Starving World, 1962; Living with the Atom, 1962; World of Opportunity (for United Nations), 1963; Two-Way Passage, 1964; The Evolution of the Machine, 1968; Man and the Cosmos, 1968; Leonardo and the Age of the Eye, 1970. *Recreation:* carpentry. *Address:* 1 Randolph Place, Edinburgh 3. *T:* 031-225 5565. *Clubs:* Savile; Scottish Arts, University Staff, Press (Edinburgh).

*See also N. D. R. Calder.*

**RITSON, Sir Edward Herbert,** KBE, *cr* 1950; CB 1945; LLB; *b* 1892; *s* of late Edward E. Ritson, Liverpool; *m* 1922, Norah, *d* of David Halley, Broughty Ferry; one *s*. *Educ:* Liverpool Institute; London Univ. Entered Civil Service, 1910; Deputy Chairman, Board of Inland Revenue, 1949-57. *Address:* The Small House, Dinton, Salisbury, Wilts. *T:* Teffont 209. *Club:* East India and Sports.

**RITSON, Muriel;** CBE 1936; Controller (Scot.) (retd), Ministry of National Insurance; *b* 1885; *d* of John Fletcher Ritson and Agnes Jane Catto. *Educ:* Greenock Academy; Germany. Social Worker and Rent Collector, Glasgow Workman's Dwgs Coy. Ltd, 1908-11; Secretary Women's Friendly Society of Scotland, 1911-19; Member Scottish Board of Health, 1919-29; Controller Health and Pensions Insurance, Department of Health, Scotland, 1929-45. Member Ryan Committee of Enquiry into Health Insurance; Committee on Admission of Women to Diplomatic and Consular Service; Beveridge Comm. on Social Insurance. *Address:* 8 Eton Terrace, Edinburgh.

**RIVERDALE,** 2nd Baron, *cr* 1935; **Robert Arthur Balfour,** Bt 1929; DL; President, Balfour Darwins Ltd, since 1969 (Chairman, 1961-69); Director: National Westminster Bank Ltd, Eastern Region, since 1969; Yorkshire Television Ltd, since 1967; The Sheffield Steelmakers Ltd, since 1952 (Chairman, 1958-65); *b* Sheffield, 1 Sept. 1901; *er s* of 1st Baron Riverdale, GBE; *S* father, 1957; *m* 1st, 1926, Nancy Marguerite (*d* 1928), *d* of late Rear-Adm. Mark Rundle, DSO; one *s*; 2nd, 1933,

Christian Mary, *er d* of late Major Rowland Hill; one *s* one *d*. *Educ:* Aysgarth; Oundle. Served with RNVR, 1940-45, attaining rank of Lt-Comdr. Joined Arthur Balfour & Co. Ltd, 1918; Dir, 1924; Man. Dir, 1949; Chm. and Man. Dir, 1957-61; Exec. Chm. 1961-69. Director: National Provincial Bank, 1964-69 (Local Bd, 1949-69); Light Trades House Ltd, 1956-65. The Association of British Chambers of Commerce: Mem. Exec. Council, 1950-; Vice-Pres., 1952-54; Dep. Pres., 1954-57; Pres., 1957-58; Chm., Overseas Cttee, 1953-57. President: Nat. Fedn of Engineers' Tool Manufacturers, 1951-57 (Hon. Vice-Pres., 1957-; Representative on Gauge and Tool Adv. Council, 1946-64); Sheffield Chamber of Commerce, 1950 (Jt Hon. Sec., 1957-); Milling Cutter and Reamer Trade Assoc., 1936-54 (Vice-Pres., 1954-57); Twist Drill Traders' Assoc., 1946-55; Chm., British Council, Aust. Assoc. of British Manufacturers, 1954-57 (Vice-Chm., 1957-65; Hon. Mem., 1965-); Member: Management and Tech. Cttee, High Speed Steel Assoc., 1947-65; British Nat. Cttee of Internat. Chamber of Commerce Adv. Cttee, 1957-58; Nat. Production Adv. Cttee, 1957-58; Consultative Cttee for Industry, 1957-58; Standing Cttee, Crucible and High Speed Steel Conf., 1951-64; Western Hemisphere Exports Council (formerly Dollar Exports Council), 1957-61; Governor, Sheffield Savings Bank, 1948-58 (Patron, 1958-); Master Cutler, 1946; Trustee, Sheffield Town Trust, 1958-; Guardian of Standard of Wrought Plate within City of Sheffield, 1948-; Belgian Consul for Sheffield area, 1945-. JP, City of Sheffield, 1950-66; DL, West Riding of Yorkshire, and for City and County of York, 1959-. Is a Churchman and a Conservative. Chevalier of Order of the Crown, Belgium, 1956. *Recreations:* yachting, yacht designing, shooting. *Heir: s* Hon. Mark Robin Balfour [*b* 16 July 1927; *m* 1959, Susan Ann, *e d* of R. P. Phillips, Ranmoor, Sheffield; one *s* two *d*. *Educ:* Aysgarth; Trinity College School, Ontario, Company Director]. *Address:* Ropes, Grindleford, via Sheffield. *T:* Grindleford 408. *Clubs:* Bath, Royal Cruising; Sheffield (Sheffield).

**RIVERINA, NSW, Bishop of,** since 1966; **Rt. Rev. John Basil Rowland Grindrod;** *b* 14 Dec. 1919; *s* of Edward Basil and Dorothy Gladys Grindrod; *m* 1949, Ailsa W., *d* of G. Newman; two *d*. *Educ:* Repton School; Queen's College, Oxford; Lincoln Theological College. BA 1949; MA 1953. Deacon, 1951; Priest, 1952, Manchester. Curate: St Michael's, Hulme, 1951-54; Bundaberg, Qld, 1954-56; Rector: All Souls, Ancoats, Manchester, 1956-60; Emerald, Qld, 1960-61; St Barnabas, N Rockhampton, Qld, 1961-65; Archdeacon of Rockhampton, Qld, 1960-65; Vicar, Christ Church, S Yarra, Vic, 1965-66. *Address:* Bishop's Lodge, Narrandera, NSW, Australia. *T:* Narrandera 177.

**RIVERS, Alfred Peter,** FCA, FCIS; Chairman, Hovis-McDougall Ltd, since 1965 (Deputy Chairman and Managing Director, 1957-65); Director, Ranks Hovis McDougall Ltd, since 1962; *b* 7 April 1906; *s* of late Peter McKay Rivers and Grace Skinner; *m* 1934, Louise, *d* of late Charles Masters; one *s* one *d*. *Educ:* Addiscombe New Coll. and privately. Chairman of Hovis Ltd, and subsidiaries. Director: Scottish Union & National Insurance Co., 1959; Norwich Union Insurance Group (London Board), 1964. Member: UK Adv. Council on Education for Management, 1961-65; Council, Chartered Inst. of Secretaries, 1957 (Pres., 1970); Bd of Governors, King's Coll. Hosp., 1958-; Economics and Business Studies Bd, Council for Nat. Acad. Awards, 1965-69; NEDC for Food Manufacturing Industry, 1968-; Council, Chest and Heart Assoc., 1968-. Chairman: Fitton Trust, 1958-; Nat. Appeal Cttee, Shaftesbury Soc., 1962-68; Nat. Appeal Cttee, Voluntary Research Trust for King's Coll. Hosp. and Med. Sch., 1962-; Triad Trust, 1967-; Flour Adv. Bureau, 1968-. *Recreations:* music and humour. *Address:* Elmcourt, Sutton Lane, Banstead, Surrey. *T:* Burgh Heath 56363. *Clubs:* Gresham, Royal Automobile.

**RIVERS, Georgia;** *see* Clark, Marjorie;

**RIVERS, Mrs Rosalind V.;** *see* Pitt-Rivers.

**RIVETT-CARNAC, Sir Henry George Crabbe,** 7th Bt, *cr* 1886; *b* 18 Jan. 1889; *e s* of late Rev. Sir Clennel George Rivett-Carnac, 6th Bart, and Emily Louisa (*d* 1894), *d* of late Rev. George Crabbe; *S* father, 1932. Formerly in Burma Police. *Heir: nephew* Rev. Thomas Nicholas Rivett-Carnac, *b* 3 June 1927.

**RIVETT-DRAKE, Brig. Dame Jean (Elizabeth),** DBE 1964 (MBE 1947); Director, Women's Royal Army Corps, 1961-64, retd; *b* 13 July 1909; *d* of Comdr Bertram Gregory Drake and of late Dora Rivett-Drake. *Educ:* St Mary's Hall, Brighton; Paris; Royal Academy of Music (LRAM piano). Served War of 1939-45 (despatches, 1946); driver, 1st London Motor Transport Co., Women's Transport Service (FANY), 1940; commnd ATS, 1942; served with BLA and 3 Port Staging Camp, Calais, 1945-47. Comdt Warr. Offrs' and Non-Commnd Offrs' Sch., 1947-48; Dep. Pres. No 10 Regular Commns Bd, 1948-49; Asst Dep. Dir: Home Counties Dist, 1949-52; London Dist, 1952-54; Far ELF, 1954-56; Dep. Dir: WO, 1957-60; Eastern Comd, 1960-61. Hon. ADC to the Queen, 1961-64. *Address:* 87 Hove Park Road, Hove 4, Sussex. *T:* Brighton 505839; c/o Barclays Bank Ltd, 119/120 St George's Road, Kemp Town, Brighton 7, Sussex. *Club:* English-Speaking Union.

**RIVINGTON, Gerald Chippindale;** Chairman of Rivingtons (Publishers) Ltd; Chairman of the Governors of Harrow School, 1953-64; Member of Board of Referees (Finance), 1932-69; *b* 13 Dec. 1893; *s* of Charles Robert Rivington, JP, DL, Castle Bank, Appleby, Westmorland; *m* 1915, Margaret Stewardson Summersby (*d* 1951). *Educ:* Harrow. Served European War, 1914-18, Border Regt, Capt. 1914; France, 1915-16; invalided, 1916. Vice-Pres., Publishers' Association, 1929-31. Liveryman, Stationers' and Newspaper Makers' Company; Renter Warden, 1920. *Recreation:* books. *Address:* 96 Rivermead Court, Hurlingham, SW6. *Club:* Garrick.

**RIX, Brian Norman Roger;** Actor-Manager since 1948; *b* 27 Jan. 1924; *s* of H. D. Rix; *m* 1949, Elspet Jeans Macgregor-Gray; two *s* two *d*. *Educ:* Bootham Sch., York. Stage career: joined Donald Wolfit, 1942; first West End appearance, Sebastian in Twelfth Night, St James's, 1943; White Rose Players, Harrogate, 1943-44. Served War of 1939-45, RAF and Bevin Boy. Became Actor Manager, 1948; ran repertory cos at Ilkley, Bridlington and Margate, 1948-50; toured Reluctant Heroes and brought to Whitehall Theatre, 1950-54; Dry Rot, 1954-58; Simple Spymen, 1958-61; One For the Pot, 1961-64; Chase Me Comrade, 1964-66; went to Garrick Theatre, 1967, with repertoire of farce: Stand By Your Bedouin; Uproar in the House; Let Sleeping Wives Lie; after 6 months went over to latter, only, which ran till 1969; then followed She's Done It Again, 1969-70. Entered films, 1951: subsequently made nine, including Reluctant Heroes, 1951, Dry Rot, 1956. Signed long-term BBC, TV contract to present farces on

TV, 1956 (renewed). *Recreations:* cricket, amateur radio (G2DQU). *Address:* York House, Roedean Crescent, SW15. *T:* 01-876 1085. *Clubs:* Lord's Taverners' (Pres. 1970); Leander (Hon. Mem.).

**ROACH, Air Vice-Marshal Harold Jace,** CB 1946; CBE 1944; AFC; Polonia Restituta 3rd cl. (Poland), 1944; FIMechE; *b* 8 May 1896; *m* 1927, Emile Blanche Fuller; one *d. Educ:* Lower School of John Lyon, Harrow. Apprenticed Cromptons, Chelmsford; enlisted in RNAS 1915; served in France, 1916-17; Air Ministry, 1917-20; Halton, 1920-24; Henlow, 1924-26; Irak, 1927-29; No. 10 Group, 1930-32; HQ Coastal Command, 1933; Grantham, 1934; Gosport, 1936; Far East, Singapore, 1937-41; 41 Group, 1942; HQ Bomber Command, 1942-46; RAF Station, St Athan, 1946-47; AOC No. 43 Group, Maintenance Command, 1947-48; AOC No. 41 Group, Maintenance Comd, 1948; retd 1951. *Recreations:* swimming, hockey. *Address:* Woodcot, Goodworth Clatford, Andover, Hants. *T:* 2885.

**ROACH, Harry Robert,** MA Cantab; Headmaster, Hymers College, Hull, since 1951; *b* 4 Sept. 1906; *m* 1943, Blanche Hortense Sinner; one *s* one *d. Educ:* St Olave's Grammar School, London; Clare College, Cambridge. Assistant Master: Aldenham School, 1928-38; King's School, Canterbury, 1938-42; Eton College, 1945-46; Head Master, King Edward VI Grammar School, Five Ways, Birmingham, 1946-51. Served War of 1939-45, in Intelligence Corps, 1942-45. *Publication:* Six Plays of Racine, 1951. *Recreations:* reading and acting. *Address:* Hymers College, Hull. *T:* Hull 41363.

**ROAD, Sir Alfred,** Kt *cr* 1953; CBE 1950; Inland Revenue, retired; *b* 10 Jan. 1891; *s* of late Alfred Road, MBE; *m* 1915, Gladys Mabel (*d* 1966), *d* of David Rees Thomas; two *s* one *d. Educ:* Borden Grammar School. Entered Inland Revenue as Assistant Surveyor of Taxes, 1910; Surveyor, 1915; served in charge of Sudbury, Holloway, Enfield, City 6 Districts, and in charge of Departmental Claims Branch; Principal Inspector, Somerset House, 1939; Dep. Chief Inspector of Taxes, 1947-52, Chief Inspector, 1952-56. *Recreations:* gardening, motoring. *Address:* 31 Cornwall Road, Cheam, Surrey. *T:* 01-642 8300.

**ROARK, Helen Wills;** *b* California, 1905; *d* of Dr Clarence A. Wills (surgeon) and Catherine A. Wills; *m* 1st, 1929, Frederick Schander Moody (marr. diss. 1937); 2nd, 1939, Aidan Roark. *Educ:* Anna Head School, Berkeley, California; University of California; Phi Beta Kappa (Scholarship Society). *Publications:* three books on tennis; Mystery Book, 1939; articles in various magazines and periodicals. *Recreations:* American Lawn Tennis Championship, 1923-24-25-27-28-29 and 1931; English Lawn Tennis Championship, 1927-28-29-30-32-33-35-38; French, 1927-28-29-30; has held exhibitions of drawing and paintings at Cooling Galleries, London, 1929 (drawings); Grand Central Art Galleries, New York, 1930 (drawings), 1936 (flower paintings in oil); Berheim-Jenne Galleries, Paris, 1932 (etchings). *Address:* 564 Park Avenue, New York City, NY, USA. *Clubs:* All England Lawn Tennis; Colony, West Side Lawn Tennis (New York); Burlingame Country (California).

**ROB, Prof. Charles Granville,** MC 1943; Chairman, Department of Surgery, University of Rochester School of Medicine and Professor of Surgery, University of Rochester, New York, since 1960; *b* 4 May 1913; *s* of Joseph William Rob, OBE, MD; *m* 1941, Mary Dorothy Elaine Beazley; two *s* two *d. Educ:* Oundle School; Cambridge Univ.; St Thomas's Hospital. FRCS 1939; MChir Cantab, 1941. Lt-Col RAMC Surgeon, St Thomas' Hospital, 1948; Professor of Surgery, London University, 1950-60; formerly Surgeon and Director ot the Surgical Professorial Unit, St Mary's Hospital; Consultant Vascular Surgeon to the Army. *Publications:* various surgical. *Recreations:* mountaineering. ski-ing. *Address:* 260 Crittenden Boulevard, Rochester 20, NY, USA. *Club:* Alpine.

**ROB, John Vernon,** CMG 1961; Served in the Foreign and Commonwealth Office (formerly Commonwealth Office), 1967, retired 1969; *b* 17 Dec. 1915; 2nd *s* of late Dr J. W. Rob; *m* 1942, Bridget Anne Elisabeth Freeman (marr. diss., 1946); one *d. Educ:* Oundle Sch.; St John's Coll., Cambridge. Entered Consular Service, 1939. Served in the Army, 1940-45. Returned to Foreign Service, 1945; served in Sofia, 1949-51; attached Canadian National Defence College, 1951-52; Foreign Office, 1952-55; Counsellor, UK High Commission, New Delhi, 1955-58, Warsaw, 1959-60; Ambassador to Congo Republic, Central African Republic and Republics of Gabon and Chad, 1960-62; served in Foreign Office as HM Inspector of Foreign Service Establishments, 1962-65; British High Commissioner in Singapore, 1965-67. *Recreations:* reading and walking. *Address:* c/o Mildland Bank Ltd, Walton-on-Thames, Surrey.

**ROBARTES;** *see* Agar-Robartes, family name of Viscount Clifden.

**ROBARTS, Basil;** Chief General Manager since 1963, and Director since 1964, Norwich Union Insurance Group; *b* 13 Jan. 1915; *s* of late Henry Ernest Robarts and Beatrice Katie (*née* Stevens); *m* 1941, Sheila Margaret Cooper Thwaites; one *s* one *d. Educ:* Gresham's Sch., Holt. Served Army, 1939-45 (Lt-Col, RA). Joined Norwich Union Life Insce Soc., 1934; Gen. Man. and Actuary, 1953. Director: Scottish Union & Nat. Insce Co., Co., 1959; Norwich Union Life and Fire Insce Socs, 1964; Maritime Insce Co., 1968. Institute of Actuaries: Fellow (FIA), 1939; Treas., 1965-67; Gen. Commissioner of Income Tax, 1958-; Chm., British Insce Assoc., 1969-. *Recreations:* tennis, sailing, music. *Address:* 466 Unthank Rd, Norwich. *T:* Norwich 51135. *Clubs:* United Service; Norfolk (Norwich).

**ROBARTS, David John;** Chairman, National Westminster Bank Ltd, since 1969 (Deputy Chairman, 1968-69; Chairman of National Provincial Bank Ltd, 1954-68); Director of Robert Fleming & Co. Ltd; Director of other companies; Chairman, Committee of London Clearing Bankers and President, British Bankers' Association, 1956-60 and 1968-70; *b* 1906; *e s* of Capt. Gerald Robarts; *m* 1951, Pauline Mary, *d* of Colonel Francis Follett, and *widow* of Clive Stoddart; three *s* one *d. Educ:* Eton; Magdalen College, Oxford. Church Commissioner, 1957-65. High Sheriff of Buckinghamshire, 1963. *Address:* 7 Smith Square, Westminster, SW1. *T:* 01-222 2428; Lillingstone House, Buckingham. *T:* Lillingstone Dayrell 202. *Clubs:* Pratt's; New (Edinburgh).

**ROBARTS, Eric Kirkby;** Chairman and Managing Director, Express Dairy Co. Ltd; *b* 20 Jan. 1908; *s* of Charles Martin Robarts and Flora Robarts (*née* Kirkby); *m* 1930, Iris Lucy Swan; five *d. Educ:* Bishops Stortford Coll.; Herts Inst. of Agriculture. Ran family business, C. M. Robarts & Son, until Aug. 1942. Joined Express Dairy Co. Ltd, 1942: Dir,

1947; Man. Dir, 1960; Dep. Chm., 1966; Chm., 1967. FBIM. *Recreations:* hunting, shooting. *Address:* Frithcote, Watford Road, Northwood, Middx. *T:* Northwood 22533. *Club:* Farmers'.

**ROBATHAN, Rev. Canon Frederick Norman,** OBE 1945; MA; Hon. CF (1st Cl.); Canon Emeritus of Ely Cathedral, since 1960; *b* 4 Jan. 1896; *s* of Reverend Thomas Frederick and Edith Jane Robathan, St Andrew's College, Gorakpur, India; *m* 1922, Renée Wells (JP 1947-53); one *s* (and one *s* decd). *Educ:* King's School, Chester; Dean Close Sch., Cheltenham; St Edmund Hall, Oxford (MA); Wycliffe Hall, Oxford. Served as Commissioned Officer, European War, 1914-19 (campaign medals), France, 1915-16. Ordained, 1921; Curate, Quarry Bank, Staffs, 1921; Priest Vicar, Truro Cathedral, 1923-25; Priest Vicar, Lincoln Cathedral, 1925-28; Chaplain HM Prison, Lincoln, 1926-28; Minor Canon and Sacrist and Junior Cardinal, St Paul's Cathedral, 1928-34; Chaplain Guy's Hosp., 1932-33; Minor Canon, Westminster Abbey, 1934-37, and Chaplain, Westminster Hospital; Rector of Hackney, 1937-45, and Chaplain East London Hospital, CF, RARO, 1923. War of 1939-45 (campaign medals); BEF 1940; Evacuation, Dunkirk, 1940; Sen. Chaplain 43 Div., 1941; Army Technical Sch., Arborfield, 1941; Sen. Chaplain Royal Garrison Church, Aldershot, 1942; Dep. Asst Chaplain-Gen. 12th Corps, 1943; Asst Chaplain-Gen. 21 Army Grp., 1944; Normandy Landings, 1944 (despatches). Vicar of Brighton, Sussex and Canon and Prebendary of Waltham in Chichester Cathedral, 1945-53; Canon Residentiary and Treasurer, Ely Cathedral, 1953-59; Vicar of Cardington, Bedford, 1959. Sen. Chaplain Army Cadet Force, Cambs, 1954-59. Councillor, Bedford RDC, 1960. Chaplain to High Sheriff of Beds., 1962; Rector of Charleton with Buckland tout Saints, Kingsbridge, S Devon, 1962-66. Hon. Priest Vicar, Truro Cathedral, 1967. Coronation Medal, 1937. *Recreations:* rowing, hockey, cricket, antiquaries. *Address:* Myrtle Court, Mevagissey, Cornwall. *T:* Mevagissey 2233.

**ROBB, Sir Douglas;** *see* Robb, Sir G. D.

**ROBB, Sir (George) Douglas,** Kt 1960; CMG 1956; FRCS; FACS (Hon.); FRACS; Chancellor, University of Auckland, 1961-68; *b* 29 April 1899; *s* of John and Agnes Robb, Melbourne and Auckland; *m* 1935, Helen Seabrook, Auckland; one *s* two *d*. *Educ:* Auckland Grammar School; Auckland University College; Otago University. MB 1922, MD 1929, ChM 1938, Otago. Post-graduate study in London, 1923-28; FRCS (Eng.), 1926; FRS NZ, 1961. Surgical practice in Auckland, 1928; Sen. Thoracic Surgeon, Green Lane Hosp., Auckland, 1942-64, retired. Chairman, New Zealand Medical Council, 1969- (Mem. 1941-); New Zealand Medical Research Council, 1951-62; Vice-President, Auckland Medical Research Foundation; President BMA, 1961-62. LLD (Hon.): Queen's, Belfast, 1962; Univ. of Auckland, 1969. FRCP 1966. *Publications:* Medicine and Health in New Zealand, 1941; Hospital Reform in NZ, 1949; University Development in Auckland, 1957; Medical Odyssey, 1967. *Recreation:* sea fishing. *Address:* 41 Symonds Street, Auckland, NZ. *Clubs:* Northern, University (Auckland).

**ROBB, Professor James Christie;** Professor of Physical Chemistry, University of Birmingham, since 1957; *b* 23 April 1924; *s* of James M. Robb, Rocklands, The House of Daviot, Inverurie, Aberdeenshire; *m* 1951, Joyce Irene Morley; three *d*. *Educ:* Daviot School; Inverurie Academy; Aberdeen University. BSc Hons, 1945, PhD, 1948, Aberdeen; DSIR Senior Research Award, 1948-50. ICI Fellow, Birmingham Univ., 1950-51; on Birmingham Univ. staff, 1951-. DSc, Birmingham, 1954. *Publications:* scientific contrib. to Proc. Royal Soc., Trans. Faraday Soc., etc. *Recreations:* badminton, motoring, photography. *Address:* 42 School Road, Moseley, Birmingham 13. *T:* 021-449 2610.

**ROBB, Leonard Arthur,** CMG 1933; MVO 1954; JP; retired; *b* 4 Dec. 1891; *s* of David Arthur Robb and Agnes Eliza Allen; *m* 1923; one *s* one *d*. *Educ:* Stratford District High School, NZ. Served with AIF in Gallipoli, Egypt, and France. Retired as Official Secretary to the Governor of New South Wales. *Recreations:* tennis, surfing. *Address:* 1 Wapiti, Superba Parade, Mosman, NSW, Australia. *T:* XM 5803.

**ROBB, Michael Antony Moyse,** CMG 1961; Deputy Director, Central Bureau for Educational Visits and Exchanges, since 1970; *b* Cairo, Egypt, 8 April 1914; *s* of late George Robb (Ministry of Education, Cairo, and later representative of Messrs Macmillan); *m* 1943, Brenda Patience Shankland (widow, *née* Robinson); two step *s* one *s* one *d*. *Educ:* Malvern College; Germany, France, Spain. Passed into Consular Service, 1936; Probationer Vice-Consul, British Consulate-General, New York, Nov. 1936; confirmed as Vice-Consul, 1939; HBM Vice-Consul, Miami, Fla, 1941; Acting Consul, Atlanta, in 1943 and 1944. Served in Foreign Office, 1945-Dec. 1947; Foreign Service Officer Grade 7, 1945; First Secretary (Information), at British Embassy, the Hague, 1948; Counsellor (Information), at British High Commission, later British Embassy, Bonn, 1951; Foreign Service Officer Grade 6, 1953; Counsellor, British Embassy, Rio de Janeiro, 1955-59; Foreign Service Inspector, Foreign Office, 1959-61; Minister (Information) at British Embassy, Washington, 1961-65; Minister, British Embassy, Pretoria, 1965-69. *Address:* 46 Fitzjohn's Avenue, NW3. *T:* 01-435 5689. *Club:* Travellers'.

**ROBB, Nesca Adeline,** DPhil, author; *b* 27 May 1905; *d* of late Charles Robb, Managing Director, J. Robb & Co. Ltd, Belfast, and Agnes Mabel, *d* of Dr Wilberforce Arnold, Belfast. *Educ:* Richmond Lodge, Belfast; Somerville College, Oxford. BA (1st Cl. Mod. Lang.) 1927; MA 1931; DPhil 1932. Research, voluntary social work, 1928-33; coaching at Oxford, 1934-38; senior English teacher, Italian Institute, London, 1938-39. Advisory Officer and Registrar, Women's Employment Federation, London, 1940-44. Since then has lived in N Ireland and taken varied part in local affairs: Cttee of National Trust, Northern Ireland; Internat. PEN, Belfast Centre (Chm., 1950-51, 1961-62); Pres., Irish PEN, 1968-69; Chm., USPCA, Bangor Br. Has lectured for Society for Italian Studies, British Council, Anglo-Netherlands Soc., National Trust, etc., and written poems, articles and broadcast scripts. FRSL 1948; Lid van de Maatschappij der Nederlandse Letterkunde, 1963. *Publications:* Neoplatonism of the Italian Renaissance, 1935; Poems, 1939; An Ulsterwoman in England, 1942; Four in Exile, 1948; William of Orange: A Personal Portrait, Vol. I 1650-1673, 1962, Vol. II 1674-1702, 1966; A History of Richmond Lodge School, 1969; contribs to Encyc. Brit. (new edn). *Recreations:* travel, music, cookery. *Address:* 10 Raglan Road, Bangor, Co. Down, Northern Ireland. *T:* Bangor 5991. *Club:* University Women's.

**ROBB, Ven. Percy Douglas;** Archdeacon of Kingston-upon-Thames since 1953; Vicar of St Peter with All Saints, Petersham, since 1963; *b* 7 Aug. 1902; *s* of Percy Robb and Agnes Jane Black (*née* Thomson); unmarried. *Educ:* Bedford Sch.; Pembroke Coll., Oxford; Westcott House, Cambridge. BA Oxon 1925, MA 1928. Deacon 1926, priest 1927, diocese of Southwark; Curate of Lambeth, 1926-31; Rector of St Paul with St Mark, Deptford, 1931-44; Rural Dean of Greenwich, 1941-44; Vicar of Lewisham, 1944-55; Vicar of St Andrew's, Coulsdon, 1955-63; Hon. Canon of Southwark, 1951-53. Proctor in Convocation of Southwark, 1950-51 and 1953-. *Address:* The Vicarage, Petersham, Surrey. *T:* 01-940 2488. *Club:* United University.

**ROBB, William,** NDA, FRSE; *b* 1885; *e s* of late William Robb, Rochsolloch, Airdrie; *m* 1924, Agnes Logan, *e d* of late Archibald Steel, Prestwick, Ayrshire; two *d. Educ:* Airdrie Academy; West of Scotland Agricultural College, Glasgow. Assist, Agriculture Department, The University of St Andrews, 1913-16 and 1919-20; War Service, Royal Engineers, 1916-19; Assistant Director, Scottish Society for Research in Plant Breeding, 1921-25; Director of Research, 1925-50, retired. *Recreation:* golf. *Address:* 24 Downie Terrace, Edinburgh EH12 7AU.

**ROBBE-GRILLET, Alain,** Literary Consultant, Writer and Cinéaste; Editions de Minuit, Paris, since 1955; *b* 18 Aug. 1922; *s* of Gaston Robbe-Grillet and Yvonne Canu; *m* 1957, Catherine Rstakian. *Educ:* Lycée Buffon, Paris; Lycée St Louis, Paris; Institut National Agronomique, Paris. Engineer: Institut National de la Statistique, 1945-49; Institut des Fruits et Agrumes Coloniaux, 1949-51. *Films:* L'Immortelle, 1963; Trans-Europ-Express, 1967; L'Homme qui ment, 1968; L'Eden et Après, 1970. *Publications:* Les Gommes, 1953 (The Erasers, 1966); Le Voyeur, 1955 (The Voyeur, 1959); La Jalousie, 1957 (Jealousy, 1960); Dans Le Labyrinthe, 1959 (In the Labyrinth, 1967); L'Année Dernière à Marienbad, 1961 (Last Year in Marienbad, 1962); Instantanés, 1962 (Snapshots, and, Towards a New Novel, 1965); L'Immortelle, 1963; Pour un Nouveau Roman, 1964; La Maison de Rendez-vous, 1965. *Address:* 18 Boulevard Maillot, Neuilly-sur-Seine, France. *T:* 722 31.22.

**ROBBINS,** family name of **Baron Robbins.**

**ROBBINS,** Baron *cr* 1959 (Life Peer), of Clare Market; **Lionel Charles Robbins,** CH 1968; CB 1944; FBA 1942; MA Oxon, BSc (Econ.); Lecturer in Economics at the London School of Economics; Chairman of the Financial Times since 1961; Director: Pearson Longman Ltd, since 1967; Longman Group of Publishing Companies, since 1968; First Chancellor of Stirling University, since 1968; *b* 22 Nov. 1898; *e s* of late Rowland Richard Robbins, CBE; *m* 1924, Iris Elizabeth, *d* of late A. G. Gardiner; one *s* one *d. Educ:* Southall County Sch.; Univ. Coll., London; London School of Economics. Served European War, 1916-19 (RFA); Lecturer New College, Oxford, 1924; Lecturer London School of Economics, 1925-27; Fellow and Lecturer New College, Oxford, 1927-29; Professor of Economics in the University of London, at London School of Economics, 1929-61. Chairman: Cttee on Higher Education, 1961-64; Court of Governors, London School of Economics, 1968-. Director of the Economic Section of Offices of the War Cabinet, 1941-45; President of Royal Economic Society, 1954-55. Trustee: National Gallery, 1952-59, 1960-67, 1967-; Tate Gall., 1953-59, 1962-67; Dir Royal Opera House, Covent Garden; Mem. Planning Board for Univ. of York; President British Academy, 1962-67. Member: Accademia dei Lincei, Rome; American Philosophical Society; American Acad. of Arts and Sciences; Foreign Associate, National Acad. of Education, America. Hon. DLitt (Dunelm, Exeter, Strathclyde, Sheffield, Heriot-Watt); Hon. LHD (Columbia); Hon. LLD (Cantab, Leicester, Strasbourg, CNAA); Hon. Dr of Laws, Calif; Hon. Doutor en Ciências Econômicas e Financeiras Universidade Técnica de Lisboa; Hon. DSc (Econ.) London; Hon. DUniv: York; Stirling; Hon. Dr, RCA; Hon. Fellow: Univ. Coll. London; Manchester Coll. of Science and Technology; LSE; London Grad. Sch. of Business Studies. *Publications:* An Essay on the Nature and Significance of Economic Science; The Great Depression; Economic Planning and International Order; The Economic Basis of Class Conflict and other Essays in Political Economy; The Economic Causes of War; The Economic Problem in Peace and War, 1947; The Theory of Economic Policy in English Classical Political Economy, 1952; The Economist in the Twentieth Century and other Lectures in Political Economy, 1954; Robert Torrens and the Evolution of Classical Economics; Politics and Economics, 1963; The University in the Modern World, 1966; The Theory of Economic Development in the History of Economic Thought, 1968; The Evolution of Modern Economic Theory, 1970; articles in Economic Jl, Economica, Lloyds Bank Review, etc. *Address:* 10 Meadway Close, NW11. *Club:* Reform.

**ROBBINS, Edgar Carmichael,** CBE, 1957; Solicitor since 1945 and Legal Adviser since 1959 to The British Broadcasting Corporation; *b* 22 March 1911; *s* of John Haldeman Robbins; *m* 1936, Alice Eugenia, *d* of Rev. Herbert Norman Nash; two *s* two *d. Educ:* Westminster Sch.; London Univ. (LLB). Admitted a solicitor, 1933, Employed by The British Broadcasting Corporation, 1934-. *Publications:* William Paston, Justice, 1932; The Cursed Norfolk Justice, 1936. *Address:* 30 Royal Avenue, Chelsea, SW3. *T:* 01-730 5767. *Club:* Athenæum.

**ROBBINS, Prof. Frederick C.,** MD; Bronze Star (US Army), 1945; Professor of Pediatrics, Case Western Reserve University School of Medicine, Cleveland, since 1952, Dean of the School, since 1966; *b* 25 Aug. 1916; *s* of William J. Robbins and Christine Chapman Robbins; *m* 1948, Alice Havemeyer Northrop; two *d. Educ:* University of Missouri (AB); University of Missouri Medical School (BS); Harvard Medical School (MD). US Army, 1942-46; rank on discharge, Major. Various posts in the Children's Hospital, Boston, from 1940, finishing as Chief Resident in Medicine, 1948; Sen. Fellow in Virus Diseases, National Research Council, 1948-50; Research Fellow in Pediatrics, Harvard Med. Sch., 1948-50; Instr in Ped., 1950-51, Associate in Ped., 1951-52, at Harvard Medical School; Dir, Department of Pediatrics, Cleveland Metropolitan General Hospital, 1952-66. Associate Research Div. of Infectious Diseases, the Children's Medical Center, Boston, 1950-52; Research Fellow in Ped., the Boston Lying-in Hospital, Boston, Mass, 1950-52; Asst to Children's Medical Service, Mass Gen. Hosp., Boston, 1950-52. Visiting Scientist, Donner Lab., Univ. of California, 1963-64. Pres., Soc. for Pediatric Research, 1961-62. First Mead Johnson Award, 1953; Nobel Prize in Physiology and Medicine, 1954; Award for Distinguished Achievement (Modern Medicine), 1963; Med. Mutual

Honor Award for 1969. Hon. Dr of Science: John Carroll University, 1955; Univ. of Missouri, 1958; Hon. Dr of Laws, Univ. of New Mexico, 1968. *Publications:* numerous in various jls, primarily on subject of viruses and infectious diseases. *Recreations:* music, tennis, sailing. *Address:* 2467 Guilford Road, Cleveland Heights, Ohio 44106, USA. *T:* 321-0885; (office) Case Western Reserve University School of Medicine, 2109 Adelbert Road, Cleveland, Ohio 44106, USA. *T:* 216 368-2820.

**ROBBINS, Jerome;** Choreographer; Associate Artistic Director, New York City Ballet, since 1949; Director, Ballets: USA, since 1958; *b* New York, 11 Oct. 1918; *s* of Harry and Lena Robbins. *Educ:* Woodrow Wilson High School, Weehawken, NJ; New York University. Studied ballet with Antony Tudor and Eugene Loring, and Modern, Spanish and oriental dance. First stage experience with Sandor-Sorel Dance Center, New York, 1937; dancer in chorus of American musicals, 1938-40; Theatre Ballet, 1940-44 (soloist 1941), London season, 1946; formed own company, Ballets: USA, 1958, Best Known ballets include: Fancy Free; Interplay; Facsimile (for Ballet Theatre); Age of Anxiety; The Cage; Afternoon of a Faun; The Concert; NY Export, Op. Jazz; Move; Events; Les Noces. Has created choreography for musicals including: On the Town, 1945; High Button Shoes, 1947; Call Me Madam, 1950; The King and I, 1951; Peter Pan, 1954; Bells Are Ringing, 1956; West Side Story, 1957; Fiddler on the Roof, 1964 (Dir and Choreo.) (won Tony Award, 1965). *Address:* 17 51st Street, Weehawken, New Jersey, USA.

**ROBBINS, Richard Michael;** Member, London Transport Executive, since 1970 (Member, London Transport Board, 1965-70); *b* 7 Sept. 1915; *er s* of late Alfred Gordon Robbins and Josephine, *d* of R. L. Capell, Northampton; *m* 1939, Rose Margaret Elspeth, *er d* of late Sir Robert Reid Bannatyne, CB, Lindfield, Sussex; one *s* two *d*. *Educ:* Westminster Sch. (King's Schol.); Christ Church, Oxford (Westminster Schol.; MA); Univ. of Vienna. Joined London Passenger Transport Board, 1939. War service, RE (Transportation), 1939-46: Persia and Iraq, 1941-43; GHQ, MEF, 1943-44; Major, AML (Greece), 1944-45. Rejoined London Transport, 1946; Sec. to Chm., 1947-50; Sec., London Transp. Exec., 1950-55; Sec. and Chief Public Relations Off., 1955-60; Chief Commercial and Pub. Rel. Off., 1960-65. Mem. Council, Inst. of Transport, 1957-60 and 1962-64 (Chm., Metrop. Sect., 1962-63; Hon. Librarian, 1969-); Pres., Omnibus Soc., 1965; Chm., Middx Victoria County History Council, 1963-; Chm., Middx Local History Council, 1958-65; Mem. Council, British Archæol. Assoc., 1957-60; President: London and Middx Archæol. Soc., 1965- (Mem. Council, 1951-56 and 1960-65); Greater London Industrial Archæol. Soc., 1969-; Rly Students Assoc., 1967-68. Fellow, Royal Statistical Soc., 1951; FSA 1957 (Mem. Council, 1965-67, 1970-). Governor, Museum of London, 1968-; Trustee, London Museum, 1970-. *Publications:* The North London Railway, 1937; 190 in Persia, 1951; The Isle of Wight Railways, 1953; Middlesex, 1953; (ed) Middlesex Parish Churches, 1955; The Railway Age, 1962; (with T. C. Barker) History of London Transport, vol. 1, 1963; George and Robert Stephenson, 1966; Points and Signals, 1967; Joint Editor, Journal of Transport History, 1953-65; contribs to transport and historical jls. *Recreations:* exploring cities and suburbs; travelling abroad and in branch railway trains; concert-going. *Address:* 129 Chiltern Court, Baker Street, NW1. *T:* 01-486 1412. *Clubs:* Reform.

**ROBBINS, Brig. (Hon.) Thomas,** CB 1945; CBE 1945; MC 1918; Croix de Guerre (France) 1918. Served European War, 1914-19, with Liverpool Scottish, BEF, 1914, and 6(T) Bn Lancashire Fusiliers; seconded to Intelligence Corps. Intelligence Officer 62 (WR) Division, France and Germany, 1917-19 (despatches thrice); Captain RARO, 1919; War of 1939-45, asst Comdt Intelligence Training Centre and Politico-Military Course, Cambridge; British Army Staff, Washington, DC, and Military Intelligence Training Centre, US Army, Camp Ritchie, Md (Col GSOI), 1942; First Comdt Civil Affairs Staff Centre, Wimbledon; Brigadier, 1943; Chief Staff Officer for Civil Affairs, HQ 21 Army Group, 1943-45; served in NW Europe, 1944-45; retired, 1945. British Commercial Commissioner and 2nd Commercial Secretary, HBM Embassy, Berlin, 1919-20. Officer Legion of Merit (USA); Officier Légion d'Honneur (France); Commander Order of the Cross, Leopold II (Belgium); Citoyen d'Honneur de la Commune de Cornac, Lot, 1966. *Address:* c/o The English Rooms, Funchal, Madeira.

**ROBENS,** family name of **Baron Robens of Woldingham.**

**ROBENS OF WOLDINGHAM,** Baron *cr* 1961, of Woldingham (Life Peer); **Alfred Robens,** PC 1951; Chairman, National Coal Board since 1961; Chancellor, University of Surrey, since 1966; a Director: Bank of England, since 1966; Times Newspapers Ltd, since 1967; *b* 18 Dec. 1910; *s* of George and Edith Robens; *m* 1937, Eva, *d* of Fred and Elizabeth Powell. *Educ:* Manchester Secondary Sch. Official of Union of Distributive and Allied Workers, 1935-45; Manchester City Councillor, 1942-45. MP (Lab) Wansbeck Div. of Northumberland, 1945-50, and for Blyth, 1950-60. Parliamentary Private Secretary to Minister of Transport, 1945-47; Parliamentary Secretary, Ministry of Fuel and Power, 1947-51; Minister of Labour and National Service, April-Oct. 1951. Chm. Foundation on Automation and Employment, 1962; Member: NEDC, 1962-; Royal Commn on Trade Unions and Employers' Assocs, 1965-68. Chairman: Jt Steering Cttee for Malta, 1967; Jt Econ. Mission to Malta, 1967. Member: Council of Manchester Business School, 1964- (Dep. Chm.); Court of Governors, LSE, 1965. Governor, Queen Elizabeth Training Coll. for the Disabled, 1951-; Chairman: Bd of Govs, Guy's Hosp., 1965-; Cttee on Safety, 1970; Fellow, Manchester Coll. of Science and Technology, 1965-. Hon. DCL, Univ. of Newcastle upon Tyne, 1964; Hon. LLD, Leicester Univ., 1966. Hon. MInstM, 1968. *Publications:* Human Engineering, 1970; sundry articles to magazines, journals and newspapers. *Recreation:* gardening. *Address:* Walton Manor, Walton-on-the-Hill, Surrey. *Club:* Reform.

**ROBERGE, Guy,** QC (Can.); Agent General for Government of Province of Quebec in United Kingdom since 1966; *b* 26 Jan. 1915; *s* of P. A. Roberge and Irène Duchesneau; *m* 1957, Marie Raymond; one *s* one *d*. *Educ:* Laval Univ., Quebec. Called to Bar, 1937; Mem., Quebec Legislative Assembly, 1944-48; Mem., Restrictive Trade Practices Commn of Canada, 1955-57; Chm. and Chief Exec. Officer, Nat. Film Bd of Canada, 1957-66. Hon. DCL, Bishop's Univ., 1967. *Address:* Quebec House, 12 Upper Grosvenor St, W1. *T:* 01-629 4155; (home) 6 Ilchester Place, W14. *T:* 01-602 2213. *Clubs:* Travellers'; Quebec Garrison (Quebec City); Rideau (Ottawa).

**ROBERTHALL,** family name of **Baron Roberthall.**

**ROBERTHALL,** Baron *cr* 1969 (Life Peer), of Silverspur, Queensland, and Trenance, Cornwall; **Robert Lowe Roberthall,** KCMG 1954; CB 1950; MA; Principal Hertford College, Oxford, 1964-67, Hon. Fellow since 1969; advisory director to Unilever and adviser to Tube Investments, since 1961; Member of Economic Planning Board, 1947-61; *b* New South Wales, 6 March 1901; *s* of late Edgar Hall and Rose Helen, *d* of A. K. Cullen; changed surname to Roberthall by deed poll, 1969; *m* 1932, Laura Margaret (marr. diss. 1968), *d* of G. E. Linfoot; two *d*; *m* 1968, Perilla Thyme, *d* of Sir Richard Southwell, *qv*. *Educ:* Ipswich, Qld; Univ. of Queensland; Magdalen College, Oxford. BEng, Queensland, 1922; Rhodes Scholar, 1923-26 (First in Modern Greats, 1926); Lecturer in Economics, Trinity College, 1926-47; Fellow, 1927-50; Hon. Fellow, 1958; Junior Dean, 1927; Dean, 1933-38; Bursar, 1938-39; Proproctor, 1933; Ministry of Supply, 1939-46; British Raw Materials Mission, Washington, 1942-44; Adviser, Board of Trade, 1946-47; Director Economic Section, Cabinet Office, 1947-53; Economic Adviser to HM Government, 1953-61. Fellow of Nuffield College, 1938-47, Visiting Fellow, 1961-64. Mem. of Economic and Employment Commn UN, 1946-49; Chm., OEEC Gp of Economic Experts, 1955-61; UK Mem., Commonwealth Economic Cttee, 1961-67; Vice-Pres. Roy. Economic Society (Hon. Secretary, 1948-58; President, 1958-60); Pres., Business Economists' Group, 1968-. Rede Lecturer, Cambridge University, 1962. Hon. DSc, University of Queensland. *Publications:* Earning and Spending, 1934; The Economic System in a Socialist State, 1936; various articles, etc on economics. *Recreations:* walking, gardening. *Address:* 34 Maunsel Street, SW1. *T:* 01-834 6108. *Club:* Travellers'.

**ROBERTS,** family name of **Baron Clwyd.**

**ROBERTS, Albert,** JP; DL; MP (Lab) Normanton Division of West Riding of Yorkshire since 1951; *b* 14 May 1908; *s* of Albert Roberts and Annie Roberts (*née* Ward); *m* 1932, Alice Ashton; one *s* one *d*. *Educ:* Woodlesford School; Normanton and Whitwood Technical College, Yorks. Safety Board, Mines Inspector, 1941-51. Chairman: Anglo-Spanish Parly Cttee; Anglo-South Korean Parly Group; Dep. Chm., british Group, Inter-Parly Union, 1967-. Governor, United Leeds Hospitals; Exec. Mem., Yorkshire Area Heart Foundn. DL, W Riding, Yorks, 1967. Order of Isabela la Catolica (Spain), 1967. *Recreations:* cricket, bowls. *Address:* Cordoba, 14 Aberford Road, Oulton-Woodlesford, near Leeds. *T:* Rothwell 2303.

**ROBERTS, Dr Albert,** MSc, PhD; MIMinE, MIMM, AMInstCE, FGS, CEng; Director, Postgraduate School of Mining, University of Sheffield, since 1956; *b* 25 April 1911; British; *m* 1938, May Taberner; two *s* one *d*. *Educ:* Wigan Mining and Techn. College. Mining Engr, Wigan Coal Corp., 1931-35, 1938-40; Ashanti Goldfields Corp., 1935-38; Lectr: Sunderland Techn. Coll., 1940-45; Nottingham Univ., 1945-55; Sheffield Univ., 1955. Ed., Internat. Jl of Rock Mechanics and Mining Sciences, 1964-68. *Publications:* Geological Structures, 1946; Underground Lighting, 1959; Mine Ventilation, 1959; Mineral Processing, 1965. *Recreations:* gardening, photography, music, fishing. *Address:* 1 Abbeydale Park Rise, Sheffield. *T:* Sheffield 362183; 8 The Garth, Bull Bay, Anglesey. *T:* Amlwch 612.

**ROBERTS, Angus Thomas;** Principal Assistant Solicitor to General Post Office since 1965; *b* 28 March 1913; *s* of Edward Roberts and Margaret (*née* Murray); *m* 1940, Frances Monica, *d* of late Frederick and late Agnes Bertha Cane; two *s*. *Educ:* Felsted School. Admitted Solicitor, 1936. Entered Post Office Solicitor's Dept, 1939. Served in Royal Navy, 1941-46 (Lieut, RNVR). Asst Solicitor to GPO, 1951. *Recreations:* golf, gardening. *Address:* The Tithe Barn, Old Church Lane, Stanmore, Middx. *T:* 01-954 1276. *Club:* Stanmore Golf.

**ROBERTS, Prof. Arthur Loten;** Livesey Professor of Coal Gas and Fuel Industries, since 1947, and Chairman of the Houldsworth School of Applied Science, University of Leeds; Pro-Vice-Chancellor, 1967-69; *b* 1 April 1906; *s* of Arthur James Roberts, Hull, and Alice Maude Loten, Hornsea, E Yorks; *m* 1941, Katherine Mary Hargrove; one *s* one *d*. *Educ:* Christ's Hospital; Univ. of Leeds. BSc 1928, PhD 1930, Assistant Lecturer, Lecturer, Senior Lecturer, Leeds Univ. Part-time mem. North-Eastern Area Gas Board, 1950-; Mem. Gas Council Research Cttee, 1951-; Hon. Sec. Advisory Research Cttee of Gas Council and University; Chairman Joint Refractories Cttee of British Ceramic Research Assoc. and the Gas Council; Mem. other Cttees of the Council; Pres. British Ceramic Society, 1957-58; Member of Technology Sub-Cttee, University Grants Cttee, 1960-. FRIC, FInstF, Fellow Inst. Ceram., Hon. MInstGasE. *Publications:* numerous contributions to chemical, ceramic and fuel jls. *Recreations:* painting, pianoforte, garden. *Address:* Hillside, 6 King's Road, Bramhope, Leeds, Yorks. *T:* Leeds 674977.

**ROBERTS, Prof. Benjamin Charles,** MA Oxon; Professor of Industrial Relations, London School of Economics, University of London, since 1962; *b* 1 Aug. 1917; *s* of Walter Whitfield Roberts and Mabel Frances Roberts; *m* 1945, Veronica Lilian Vine-Lott; two *s*. *Educ:* LSE; New Coll., Oxford. Research Student, Nuffield Coll., Oxford, 1948-49; Part-time Lectr, Ruskin Coll., Oxford, 1948-49; London Sch. of Economics: Lectr in Trade Union Studies, 1949-56; Reader in Industrial Relations, 1956-62; Mem. Ct of Govs, 1964-69. Vis. Prof: Princeton Univ., 1958; MIT 1959; Univ. of Calif., Berkeley, 1965. Assoc., Internat. Inst. of Labour Studies, Geneva, 1966-; Mem. Council: Inst. Manpower Studies; Foundn for Automation and Employment. Editor, British Jl of Industrial Relations, 1963-. Pres., British Univs Industrial Relations Assoc., 1965-68; Pres., Internat. Industrial Relations Assoc., 1967-. *Publications:* Trade Unions in the New Era, 1947; Trade Union Government and Administration in Great Britain, 1956; National Wages Policy in War and Peace, 1958; The Trades Union Congress, 1868-1921, 1958; Trade Unions in a Free Society, 1959; (Ed.) Industrial Relations: Contemporary Problems and Perspectives, 1962; Labour in the Tropical Territories of the Commonwealth, 1964; (Ed.) Manpower Planning and Employment Trends 1966; (with L. Greyfié de Bellecombe) Collective Bargaining in African Countries, 1967; (Ed.) Industrial Relations: Contemporary Issues, 1968; (with John Lovell) A Short History of the TUC, 1968; also Evidence to Royal Commn on Trade Unions, 1966, and Report to ILO on Labour and Automation: Manpower Adjustment Programmes in the United Kingdom, 1967. *Recreations:* gardening; wining, dining and talking; rummaging through junk shops. *Address:* 28 Temple Fortune Lane, NW11. *T:* 01-458 1421.

**ROBERTS, Rev. Prof. Bleddyn Jones,** MA, DD; Professor of Hebrew, University College of North Wales, Bangor, since 1953; *b* 21 April 1906; *s* of late Thomas and Sophia Jones Roberts, Penycae, Wrexham, Denbs; *m* 1943, Miriam Eluned, MB, BCh, *d* of late Rev. John Davies, and Mrs A. Davies (*née* David), Aberystwyth, Cards. *Educ:* Ruabon Grammar School; Univ. Coll. of N Wales; Leipzig Univ. 1st Class Hons BA (Wales), 1928; BD (Wales) 1934; MA (Wales) 1936; DD (Wales) 1953. Asst Lecturer in Hebrew, Manchester University, 1934-36; Asst Lecturer, Bangor, 1936-37; Professor of Hebrew, United (Presbyterian) Theological College, Aberystwyth, 1937-46; Senior Lecturer in Biblical Studies, Univ. Coll. of N Wales, 1946-53; Past Examiner in Universities of Sheffield, Dublin, Manchester, Glasgow; Mem., Translation Panel of New English Bible, 1949-69; President, Society OT Study, 1964; Director of New Welsh Bible, 1964. *Publications:* Patrymau Llenyddol y Beibl, 1950; The Old Testament Text and Versions, 1951; Some Observations on the Damascus Document and the Dead Sea Scrolls, 1952; The Dead Sea Scrolls and Old Testament Scriptures, 1953; Sgroliau'r Mor Marw, 1956; The Second Isaiah Scroll from Qumrän, 1959; The Canon of the Old Testament: A Suggestion, 1963; Diwinyddiaeth yr Hen Destament, 1964; Jeremeia, Proffwyd Gofidiau, 1967; contributor to: The Interpreter's Dictionary of the Bible; Grant and Rowley Dictionary of the Bible; Peake's Commentary on the Bible; Bulletin of the John Rylands Library; Y Traethodydd; Jl of Theological Studies; Diwinyddiaeth; Jl of New Testament Studies. *Address:* 2 St Oswald's, Victoria Drive, Bangor, Caerns. *T:* Bangor 4630.

**ROBERTS, Brian Birley,** CMG 1969; PhD; Head of Polar Regions Section, Foreign and Commonwealth Office (formerly Foreign Office) (half time), since 1946; Senior Principal Scientific Officer since 1968; Research Associate, Scott Polar Research Institute, Cambridge (half-time), since 1960 (Research Fellow (half-time), 1946-60); *b* 23 Oct. 1912; *y s* of late Charles Michael Roberts, MB, BS; unmarried. *Educ:* Uppingham Sch.; Emmanuel Coll., Cambridge. MA 1934, PhD 1940. Leader, Cambridge Expedns to Iceland, 1932, and E Greenland, 1933; Mem., British Graham Land Expedn, 1934-37 (Polar Medal, 1940); Special adviser on cold climate equipment to Controller of Ordnance Services, WO, 1940-41; Bruce Memorial Prize of RSE, of Royal Phys. Soc. Edinburgh and RSGS, 1940; Admty, NID, 1941-43; Jt Editor, Polar Record, 1942-; FO Res. Dept, 1944-67 (half-time 1946-); Co-founder and Editor, Jl of Glaciology, 1947; Back Award of RGS, 1948; Mem., Op. Lyon, Canadian Arctic, 1949; Mem. Norwegian-British-Swedish Antarctic Expedn, 1950-51; exch. visit to USSR Arctic orgs, 1956; UK Deleg. to Wash. Antarctic Conf., 1959, and subseq. Antarctic Treaty Consultative Meetings: Canberra, 1961; Buenos Aires, 1962; Brussels, 1964; Santiago, 1966; Paris, 1968; Tokyo, 1970; Official UK Observer with US Op. Deep Freeze, 1960-61; Pres., Antarctic Club, 1963-64; Mem. French Expedn to sub-Antarctic islands in S Indian Ocean, 1964. Fellow of Churchill Coll., Cambridge, 1965. *Publications:* Iceland papers, 1939; Handbook on clothing and equipment required in cold climates, 1941; Organization of polar information, 1960; Illustrated glossary of snow and ice, 1966; (ed) Edward Wilson's Birds of the Antarctic, 1967; numerous papers in scientific periodicals. *Recreations:* ornithology, glaciology, small islands. *Address:* 41 Causewayside, Fen Causeway, Cambridge. *T:* Cambridge 55506. *Club:* Travellers'.

**ROBERTS, Brian Richard;** Editor, The Sunday Telegraph, since 1966 (Managing Editor, 1961-66); *b* 16 Sept. 1906; *e s* of late Robert Lewis Roberts, CBE; *m* 1935, Elisabeth Franziska Dora, *er d* of late Dr Leo Zuntz, Berlin; one adopted *s*. *Educ:* Merchant Taylors' Sch.; St John's Coll., Oxford (MA). Editorial staff, Oxford Mail, 1930-33; Daily Mail, 1933-38 (Night Editor, 1936-38); Joined The Daily Telegraph, 1939 (Night Editor, 1944-57, Chief Asst Editor 1957-60). Pres., Inst. of Journalists, 1954-55; Vice-Pres., Guild of Agricultural Journalists; Mem. Governing Body, Northern Polytechnic, London, 1946- (Chm. 1956-); Chm., Formation Cttee, Polytechnic of N London, 1970; Chm. of Council, Assoc. of Technical Institutions, 1964-65, Hon. Treasurer, 1967-. *Recreation:* agriculture. *Address:* Old Foxhunt Manor, Waldron, Nr Heathfield, Sussex. *T:* Horam Road 2618. *Club:* United University.

*See also C. H. Roberts and Rev. R. L. Roberts.*

**ROBERTS, Bryan Clieve,** CMG 1964; QC; BA Oxon; Attorney-General of Malawi since Sept. 1964; Permanent Secretary to Office of the President and Secretary to Cabinet since 1965; Head of Malawi Civil Service; Chairman: Army Council; Police Council; National Security Committee; National Intelligence Committee; National Development and Planning Coordination Committee; *b* 22 March 1923; *s* of late Herbert Roberts, MA, and of Doris Evelyn Clieve; *m* 1958, Pamela Dorothy, *d* of late Major Charles Knight. *Educ:* Whitgift School; Magdalen Coll., Oxford (BA Hons). Served War of 1939-45: commissioned in RA and RHA, 1941-46; active service in Normandy, Belgium, Holland and Germany, 1944-45. Called to Bar, Gray's Inn, 1950; in chambers in Temple, 1950-51; Legal Asst, Treasury Solicitor's Dept, 1951-53. Crown Counsel, N Rhodesia, 1953-60; Dir of Public Prosecutions, N Rhodesia, 1960-61; QC 1961; Nyasaland: Solicitor-Gen. and Perm. Sec. to Min. of Justice, 1961; Solicitor-General, 1961-64; Minister of Justice, 1962-63; Mem., Nyasaland Legislative Council, 1961-63; Officer of the Order of Menelik II of Ethiopia, 1965; Comdr, Nat. Order of Republic of Malagasy, 1969. *Recreations:* golf, music. *Address:* Office of the President and Cabinet, Zomba, Malawi. *Clubs:* United Hunts; Royal Commonwealth Society.

**ROBERTS, Cecil Edric Mornington,** Hon. LLD; *b* 18 May 1892. *Educ:* Mundella Grammar School. Literary Editor Liverpool Post, 1915-18; Naval Correspondent with the Grand Fleet, Dover Patrol, Milford Convoy; accredited correspondent with Royal Air Force; accredited by War Office as correspondent with the British Armies on Western Front for Newspaper Society and Reuter; with Allied Armies in march to the Rhine; Assistant Director Munitions Overseas Transport, and Statistical Officer, American Dept, British Ministry of Munitions; Examining Officer to Civil Liabilities Commission, 1919; Editor, Nottingham Journal, 1920-25; lecture tour USA and Canada, 1920, 1924, 1926, 1929, 1936, 1939; Parliamentary candidate (L) Nottingham, East Division, 1922; British Mission, USA, 1940-46. Hon. Freeman, City of Nottingham; Hon. Citizen of Alassio, Italy; Gold Medal and Diploma, City of Rome. *Publications:* The Trent, 1912; Phyllistrata and other Poems, 1913; Through Eyes of Youth; Poems, 1914; Youth of Beauty; Poems, 1915; Collected War Poems, 1916; Twenty-Six Poems; The Chelsea Cherub (novel), 1917; Charing Cross, 1918;

Poems, 1918; Training the Airmen, Poems, collected American edition, 1919; edited Raemaker's Cartoons; The People's Atlas, 1920; A Tale of Young Lovers, Poetic Drama (produced Compton Comedy Company, 1921), 1922; Scissors, 1922; Sails of Sunset, 1924; The Love Rack, 1925; Little Mrs Manington, 1926; The Right to Kiss, a comedy (produced Dean Co., 1926); Sagusto; Diary of Russell Beresford, 1927; David and Diana, 1928; Indiana Jane; Pamela's Spring Song, 1929; Havana Bound, 1930; Half Way, 1931; Bargain Basement, 1931; Spears Against US, 1932; Life of Sir Alfred Fripp, 1932; Pilgrim Cottage, 1933; Gone Rustic; The Guests Arrive, 1934; Volcano, 1935, Gone Afield, 1936; Gone Sunwards, 1936; Victoria Four-Thirty, 1937; They wanted to live, 1938; Spears Against Us (a drama, produced Liverpool Rep. Co.), 1939; And so to Bath, 1940; A Man Arose, 1941; One Small Candle, 1942; So Immortal a Flower, 1944; And So to America, 1946; Eight for Eternity, 1948; And So To Rome, 1950; Terrace in the Sun, 1951; One Year of Life, 1952; The Remarkable Young Man, 1954; Portal to Paradise, 1955; Love is Like That, 1957; Selected Poems, 1960; Wide Horizon, 1962; The Grand Cruise, 1963; A Flight of Birds, 1965; The Growing Boy (autobiog.), 1967; The Years of Promise, 1968; The Bright Twenties, 1969. *Recreations:* travel. *Address:* Grand Hotel, Rome, Italy. *Clubs:* Athenæum, Royal Automobile.

**ROBERTS, Rear-Adm. Cedric Kenelm;** CB 1970; DSO 1952; Flag Officer Naval Flying Training since 1968; *b* 19 April 1918; *s* of F. A. Roberts; *m* 1940, Audrey, *d* of T. M. Elias; four *s*. *Educ:* King Edward's Sch., Birmingham. Joined RN as Naval Airman 2nd Cl., 1940; commnd Temp. Sub-Lt (A), RNVR, 1940; sunk in HMS Manchester, 1942, Malta Convoy; interned in Sahara; released, Nov. 1942; Personal Pilot to Vice-Adm. Sir Arthur Lyster, 1943; HMS Trumpeter, Russian Convoys, 1944; perm. commn as Lt RN, HMS Vindex, Pacific, 1945; CO 813 Sqdn, 1948; Naval Staff Coll., 1949; CO 767 Sqdn, 1950-51; CO 825 Sqdn, 1951-52; CO, RNAS Eglinton, 1958-59; Chief Staff Officer: FONFT, 1959-61; FOAC, 1961-62; Capt., HMS Osprey, 1962-64; Capt., RNAS Culdrose, 1964-65; Chief Staff Officer (Ops), Far East Fleet, 1966-67. Comdr 1952; Capt. 1958; Rear-Adm. 1968. *Recreations:* sport, shooting, sea fishing. *Address:* Myrtle House, Ham Street, Baltonsborough, Somerset. *T:* Baltonsborough 343.

**ROBERTS, Charles Stuart;** Head of Caribbean Department, Foreign and Commonwealth Office, since 1970; *b* 24 May 1918; *s* of late Charles William Roberts and of Dorothy Roberts; *m* 1946, Margaret Ethel Jones; one *s* two *d*. *Educ:* Merchant Taylors' School. Entered Colonial Office, 1936. Naval Service (Lieut RNVR), 1940-46. Economic and Financial Adviser, Leeward Is, 1955-57; transferred to HM Diplomatic Service (Counsellor), 1966; British Govt Representative, W Indies Associated States, 1967-70. *Recreations:* chess, crosswords. *Address:* Gordon Lea, Montacute Road, Tunbridge Wells, Kent. *T:* Tunbridge Wells 25553.

**ROBERTS, Colin Henderson,** FBA 1947; Secretary to Delegates of Oxford University College since 1934; *b* 8 June 1909; *s* of late Robert Lewis Roberts, CBE; *m* 1947, Alison Muriel, *d* of Reginald Haynes and Phyllis Irene Barrow; one *d*. *Educ:* Merchant Taylors' School; St John's College, Oxford (MA). 1st Cl., Hon. Class. Mods, 1929; 1st Cl., Lit. hum. 1931; Sen. Schol., St John's Coll., 1931-34; Craven Univ. Fellow, 1932-34. Studied Berlin Univ., 1932; Univ. of Michigan, Near East Research (Egypt), 1932-34; Dept of Foreign Office, 1939-45. Lecturer in Classics, St John's College, Oxford, 1939-53; tutor, 1946-53; University Lecturer in Papyrology, 1937-48; Reader, 1948-53. Delegate of Oxford Univ. Press, 1946-53; FBA 1947; Visiting Mem. of Inst. for Advanced Study, Princeton, NJ, 1951-52; Sandars Reader in Bibliography, University of Cambridge, 1960-61. *Publications:* An Unpublished Fragment of the Fourth Gospel, 1935; Catalogue of the Greek Papyri in the Rylands Library, Manchester, Vol. III, 1938, Vol. IV (with E. G. Turner), 1952; part editor of the Oxyrhynchus Papyri, Parts XVIII-XX, 1941-52 and XXII, 1954; The Antinoopolis Papyri, 1950; The Merton Papyri (with H. I. Bell), 1948; The Codex, 1955; The Greek Bookhand, 1955. *Recreation:* walking. *Address:* Cutts End Point, Cumnor, Oxford. *T:* Cumnor 2797. *Club:* Athenæum.

*See also B. R. Roberts and Rev. R. L. Roberts.*

**ROBERTS, Cyril Alfred,** CBE 1947 (MBE 1944); Chairman, Woodall-Duckham Ltd, since 1970; *b* 4 June 1908; *s* of late A. W. Roberts; *m* 1932, Christine Annabel Kitson, *d* of late Hon. E. C. Kitson, Leeds; three *s* one *d*. *Educ:* Eton; Trinity Coll., Oxford. Called to the Bar, 1932, and practised until 1939. Served War of 1939-45, HM Forces, 1939-46; France, 1940; Western Desert, 1941-42; Instructor, Staff Coll., Haifa, 1943; War Office, Army Council Secretariat, 1943-45; Brigadier AG Co-ordination, 1945-46. Asst Sec. National Coal Board, 1946-47; Under-Secretary, 1947-51; Secretary, 1951-59; Member of the Board, 1960-67. Chm., Institute of Cardiology, 1967-; Mem. Bd of Governors, Nat. Heart Hospital; Mem. Bd, Woodall-Duckham Group Ltd. Adviser to Minister of Defence on Resettlement from the Forces, 1968-. FBIM. *Address:* 11 Gerald Road, SW1. *T:* 01-730 5506; Bury Gate House, Pulborough, Sussex. *T:* Bury 440. *Club:* Turf.

**ROBERTS, David Arthur;** Counsellor; Head of Accommodation Department, Foreign and Commonwealth Office, since 1968; *b* 8 Aug. 1924; *s* of late Rev. T. A. Roberts and of Mrs. T. A. Roberts; *m* 1st, 1951, Nicole Marie Fay (*d* 1965); two *d*; 2nd, 1968, Hazel Faith Arnot. *Educ:* Hereford Cathedral Sch.; Jesus Coll., Oxford. Joined Army, 1943-46. HM Foreign Service, Dec. 1947. Served: Baghdad, 1948-49; Tokyo, 1949-51; FO, 1951-53; Alexandria, 1953-55; Khartoum, 1955-58; FO, 1958-60; Dakar, 1960-61; FO, 1962-63; Damascus, 1963-66; Political Agent in the Trucial States, Dubai, 1966-68. *Address:* 15 Basingbourne Close, Fleet, Hampshire. *Club:* Reform.

**ROBERTS, Denys K.;** *see* Kilham Roberts.

**ROBERTS, Denys Tudor Emil,** CBE 1970 (OBE 1960); QC (Gibraltar 1960, Hong Kong 1964); Attorney-General of Hong Kong since Sept. 1966; *b* 19 Jan. 1923; *s* of William David and Dorothy Elizabeth Roberts; *m* 1949, Brenda Dorothy; one *s* one *d*. *Educ:* Aldenham; Wadham Coll., Oxford, 1942 and 1946-49 (MA 1948, BCL 1949); served with Royal Artillery, 1943-46, France, Belgium, Holland, Germany, India (Captain); English Bar, 1950-53; Crown Counsel, Nyasaland, 1953-59; Attorney-General, Gibraltar, 1960-62; Solicitor-Smuggler's Circuit; Beds and Roses; The Elwood Wager; The Bones of the Wajingas; How to Dispense with Lawyers. *Recreations:* cricket, writing. *Address:* Attorney-General's Chambers, Hong Kong; High Point, Beaucroft Lane, Colehill, Wimborne, Dorset. *Clubs:* MCC; Hong Kong (Hong Kong).

**ROBERTS, Rev. Canon Edward Eric,** JP; Canon Residentiary, Vice–Provost of Southwell Cathedral and Personal Chaplain to the Bishop of Southwell, since 1968; Canon, 1964; Southwell Diocesan Director of Education since 1961; *b* 29 April 1911; *o s* of late Edward Thomas Roberts and of Mrs Charlotte Roberts, Liverpool; *m* 1938, Sybil Mary (*née* Curren); two *d. Educ:* Univ. of Liverpool; St Augustine's Coll., Canterbury. Youth Officer: City of Oxford LEA, 1938-43; Wallasey CB, LEA, 1943-44; Training Officer, Church of England Youth Council, 1944-52; Southwell Diocesan Dir of Further Educn, 1952-61. JP, City of Nottingham, 1958-. *Recreation:* photography. *Address:* 13 Farthingate Close, Southwell, Notts. *T:* Southwell 2295.

**ROBERTS, Dr Edward Frederick Denis;** Librarian, National Library of Scotland, since 1970; *b* 16 June 1927; *s* of Herbert Roberts and Jane Spottiswoode Roberts (*née* Wilkinson); *m* 1954, Irene Mary Beatrice (*née* Richardson); one *s* one *d. Educ:* Royal Belfast Academical Institution; Queen's University of Belfast. BA (1st cl. Hons Modern History) 1951; PhD 1955. Research Assistant, Dept of History, Queen's Univ. of Belfast, 1951-55; National Library of Scotland: Asst Keeper, Dept of Manuscripts, 1955-66; Secretary of the Library, 1966-67; Librarian, Trinity College Dublin, 1967-70. Sec., 1965-69, Pres., 1969-, Cttee on Rare and Precious Books and Documents, Internat. Fedn of Library Assocs. *Recreations:* reading, cinema, travel. *Address:* National Library of Scotland, Edinburgh EH1 1EW. *T:* 031-225 4104.

**ROBERTS, Rt. Rev. Edward James Keymer;** *see* Ely, Bishop of.

**ROBERTS, Eirlys Rhiwen Cadwaladr;** Head of Research and Editorial, Consumers' Association (Which?), since 1958; Research Director for Research Institute of Consumer Affairs; *b* 3 Jan. 1911; *d* of Dr Ellis James Roberts and Jane Tennant Macaulay; *m* 1941, John Cullen (marriage dissolved); no *c. Educ:* Clapham High School; Girton College, Cambridge. BA (Hons) Classics. Sub-editor in Amalgamated Press; Military, then Political Intelligence, 1943-44 and 1944-45; Public Relations in UNRRA, Albanian Mission, 1945-47; Information Division of the Treasury, 1947-57. Mem., Consumers' Cttees for GB, England and Wales. *Publication:* Consumers, 1966. *Recreations:* climbing, ice-skating, reading detective novels. *Address:* 8 Lloyd Square, WC1. *T:* 01-837 2492.

**ROBERTS, Emrys;** Barrister-at-Law; Director: English Calico Ltd; Yates Duxbury & Sons Ltd; Chairman, Mid-Wales Development Corporation, since 1968; *b* 22 Sept. 1910; *s* of late Owen Owens Roberts and of Mary Grace Williams, both of Caernarvon; *m* 1948, Anna Elisabeth Tudor; one *s* one *d. Educ:* Caernarvon; Aberystwyth; Gonville and Caius Coll., Cambridge; Geneva. MA (Cantab); LLB (Wales); 1st Class, Parts I and II, Law Tripos, Cambridge, 1933; 1st Class Hons, University of Wales, 1931, S. T. Evans Prize; Solicitor, 1936, 1st Class Hons, Clements Inn Prize. Squadron Leader RAF, 1941-45 (MBE). Called to Bar, Gray's Inn, 1944. MP (L) for Merioneth, 1945-51; Member of Parliamentary Delegations to Yugoslavia, Representative at Council of Europe, 1950 and 1951. Chm. of Council, Nat. Eisteddfod of Wales, 1964-67; Vice-Pres. Hon. Soc. of Cymmrodorion. *Publications:* (jointly) The Law of Restrictive Trade Practices and Monopolies; articles in periodicals. *Address:* Pennant, Hale, Cheshire. *T:* 061-980 3003.

**ROBERTS, Major-General Frank Crowther,** VC 1918; DSO 1915; OBE; MC; *b* 2 June 1891; *s* of Rev. Frank Roberts, Vicar of St John, Southall; *m* 1932, Winifred Margaret, *y d* of late John Downing Wragg. Entered Army, 1911; Capt. 1915; Major, 1927; Lt-Col 1936; Col 1938; Major-General, 1939; served European War, 1914-18 (wounded, despatches, DSO, VC, MC 1917); Southern Kurdistan, 1930-31 (Bt Lt-Col); Inspector, General Staff Branch, Iraq Army, 1931; GSO II N Ireland District, 1935-36; commanded 1st Bn Royal Warwickshire Regt, 1936-38; Commander, Poona (Independent) Brigade Area, India, 1938-39; retired pay, 1939; Commander South Midland Division TA, 1939. *Address:* Four Winds, Bretry, Nr Burton-on-Trent.

**ROBERTS, Sir Frank (Kenyon),** GCMG 1963 (KCMG 1953; CMG 1946); GCVO 1965; Advisory Director of Unilever; Adviser on International Affairs to Lloyd's; Director, Dunlop Co. Ltd; President: British Atlantic Committee, since 1968; Atlantic Treaty Association, since 1969; Chairman, European Atlantic Group, since 1970; *b* Buenos Aires, 27 Oct. 1907; *s* of Henry George Roberts, Preston, and Gertrude Kenyon, Blackburn; *m* 1937, Celeste Leila Beatrix, *d* of late Sir Said Shoucair Pasha, Cairo, Financial Adviser to Sudan Government; no *c. Educ:* Bedales; Rugby; Trinity College, Cambridge (Scholar). Entered Foreign Office, 1930; served HM Embassy, Paris, 1932-35 and at HM Embassy, Cairo, 1935-37; Foreign Office, 1937-45; Chargé d'Affaires to Czechoslovak Govt, 1943; British Minister in Moscow, 1945-47; Principal Private Secretary to Secretary of State for Foreign Affairs, 1947-49; Deputy High Commr (UK) in India, 1949-51; Deputy-Under Secretary of State, Foreign Office, 1951-54; HM Ambassador to Yugoslavia, 1954-57; United Kingdom Permanent Representative on the North Atlantic Council, 1957-60; Ambassador: to the USSR, 1960-62; to the Federal Republic of Germany, 1963-68. Mem., FCO Review Cttee on Overseas Representation, 1968-69. Grand Cross, German Order of Merit, 1965. *Address:* 25 Kensington Court Gardens, W8. *Clubs:* Brooks's, Royal Automobile.

**ROBERTS, Brig. Geoffrey P. H.;** *see* Hardy-Roberts.

**ROBERTS, George Charles L.;** *see* Lloyd-Roberts.

**ROBERTS, Maj.-Gen. George Philip Bradley,** CB 1945; DSO 1942; MC 1941; late RTR; *b* 5 Nov. 1906; *m* 1936, Désirée, *d* of Major A. B. Godfray, Jersey; two *s* two *d. Educ:* Marlborough; RMC, Sandhurst. 2nd Lieut Royal Tank Corps, 1926; served War of 1939-45 (MC, DSO and two Bars, CB, despatches thrice); Officier Légion d'Honneur; Croix de Guerre avec palmes. Commander 11th Armoured Div., 1943-46; Comdr 7th Armoured Div., 1947-48; Dir, Royal Armoured Corps, War Office, 1948-49; retired pay, 1949. Hon. Col Kent and County of London Yeomanry Squadron, The Royal Yeomanry Regt, T&AVR, 1949-70. JP County of Kent, 1960-70. *Address:* Se Serra Mitjana, Calonge, Majorca; c/o Glyn, Mills & Co., Kirkland House, Whitehall, SW1. *Club:* Army

**ROBERTS, Sir Gilbert,** Kt 1965; FRS 1965; BScEng; Consultant, Freeman, Fox and Partners, since 1969; *b* 18 Feb. 1899; *s* of Henry William Roberts; *m* 1925, Elizabeth Nada Hora; two *d. Educ:* City and Guilds Coll., London. Flt-Lt 73 Sqdn RFC, 1917-18. Asst to Sir Ralph Freeman on design of Sydney Harbour Bridge; in bridge dept of Dorman Long and Co. Ltd, 1926-35; worked on design of numerous bridges, develt of welded constrn and Chromador high tensile structural steel; joined Sir William Arrol & Co. Ltd, Glasgow: in charge of constrn and develt, 1936; Dir and Chief Engnr, 1945; joined Freeman, Fox and Partners as partner responsible for design of Severn Bridge on behalf of jt consg engrs, 1949; designed Forth Road Bridge for same consultants; invented and patented design of present Severn Bridge. Designer of: Auckland Harbour Bridge; Volta Bridge, Ghana; new Maidenhead Bridge and others; also radio-telescopes for CSIRO (Aust.) and NRC (Can.). Inventor of 500-ton Goliath Crane designed for Babcock's power station work; designer of other welded crane structures. FInstW; FICE; FIStrucE; Fell., AmSocCE; Fell., Imperial College; FCGI, Telford Gold Medal, ICE, 1967; Royal Medal, Royal Soc., 1968; James Watt Medal, ICE, 1969; MacRobert Award, 1969. *Publications:* numerous papers and articles on engineering subjects. *Address:* 42 Wynnstay Gardens, Allen Street, W8. *Club:* Athenæum.

**ROBERTS, Capt. Gilbert Howland,** CBE 1944; RD 1964; Royal Navy (retired); *b* 11 Oct. 1900; *s* of Colonel Sir Howland Roberts, 12th Baronet, and Elizabeth Marie La Roche; *m* 1930 (marriage dissolved); one *s* one *d*; *m* 1947, Jean Winifred Warren; one *d*. *Educ:* Westminster; Royal Naval Colleges, Osborne and Dartmouth. Served European War, 1916-18; specialised in gunnery, 1922; Medal of Royal Humane Society, 1922; Commander, 1935; Staff of HM Tactical School, 1935-36; command HMS Fearless, 1937-38; invalided, 1938; rejoined Royal Navy, 1940; served since in HMS Excellent and on Staff of C-in-C Western Approaches as Director Tactical School (CBE, Order of Polonia Restituta); Captain, 1942. Commodore Royal Norwegian Navy, Naval Assistant to Norwegian Naval C-in-C, 1946- 47; lent Royal Canadian Navy for duty and lecture tour, 1955; Comd HMS Vivid, RNR, 1956-64. Lees-Knowles Lecturer, Military History, Cambridge Univ., 1951. CC Devon, 1957; Alderman, Torbay County Borough, 1967. Order of St Olaf; Officer of the Legion of Honour. *Recreation:* gardening. *Address:* Little Priors, Watcome, Torquay.

**ROBERTS, Rt. Hon. Goronwy Owen,** PC 1968; MA; MP (Lab) for Caernarvon Division of Caernarvonshire since 1950 (Caernarvonshire, 1945-50); Fellow, University of Wales, since 1938; *b* 20 Sept. 1913; *yr s* of E. E. and Amelia Roberts, Bethesda, Caernarvonshire; *m* 1942, Marian Ann, *yr d* of David and Elizabeth Evans, Tresalem, Aberdare; one *s* one *d*. *Educ:* Universities of Wales and London; on Continent. Exhibitioner, BA; MA; Univ. of Wales; Research at King's College, London, and on the Continent, 1937-39. Served in Infantry, 1941; Army Reserve, 1941-. Youth Education Officer to Caernarvonshire Education Authority, 1941-44. Mem., House of Commons Panel of Chairmen, 1963-64; Minister of State, Welsh Office, 1964-66; Dept of Education and Science, 1966-67; Minister of State, FCO, 1967-69, Bd. of Trade, 1969-70. Writes and broadcasts on literary and political matters. Mem. Court of Governors of University Coll. of Wales and National Museum of Wales, Fabian Society; Trustee, Oppenheimer Trust for Ex-Servicemen. Chm., Regional Economic Council for Wales, 1965-. Formerly: Chm. Hughes and Son Ltd, Publishers, Wrexham; Lectr in Educn, Univ. Coll., Swansea. FRSA 1968. *Recreations:* walking, music, collecting Year Books. *Address:* House of Commons, SW1.

**ROBERTS, Gwilym Edffrwd;** Director, Methods Advisory Services Ltd; *b* 7 Aug. 1928; *s* of William and Jane Ann Roberts; *m* 1954, Mair Griffiths; no *c*. *Educ:* Brynrefail Gram. Sch.; UCW (Bangor). Industrial Management, 1952-57; Principal Lecturer, Hendon College of Technology, 1957-66; MP (Lab) South Bedfordshire, 1966-70. industrial Consultant, Market and Operational Research, 1957-. *Recreations:* cricket, table tennis, journalism. *Address:* 60 Swasedale Rd, Luton, Beds. *T:* 53893.

**ROBERTS, Rev. Harold,** PhD (Cambridge); Principal, Richmond College, Surrey (University of London), 1955-68; Chair of Systematic Theology and Philosophy of Religion, Richmond College, 1940-68; President of the Methodist Conference, 1957; *b* Ashley, Cheshire; *s* of E. J. and A. Roberts; *m* 1926, Edna Tydvil Thomas, BA (*d* 1964). *Educ:* Hulme Gram. Sch., Manchester; Univ. Coll., Bangor; Wesley House and Jesus College, Cambridge. BA 1st Class Hons Philosophy 1920, MA 1921, Univ. Coll., Bangor. Asst Tutor, Wesley House, Camb., 1924-26; Minister: Liverpool (Waterloo), 1926-29; Oxford, 1929-34; Chair of Systematic Theology and Philosophy of Religion, Wesley College, Headingley, 1934-40; Minister, Ipswich (Museum St), 1941-45. Univ. of London: Member of Senate, 1951-59, Dean of Faculty of Theology, 1953-56; Examiner in Theology, Univ. of London, Queen's Univ., Belfast, Univ. of Wales, etc. Cato Lecturer, Australia, 1950; Fernley-Hartley Lecturer, 1954; Tipple Lecturer, Drew Univ., USA, 1956. Member of Central Cttee World Council of Churches, 1954-62; Pres. of World Methodist Coun., 1956-61; Jt Chm., Anglican-Methodist Unity Commn, 1967; Select Preacher, Univ. of Cambridge, 1958. Hon. DD Trinity College, Dublin, 1961. *Publications:* part-author: The Doctrine of the Holy Spirit, 1938; The Message and Mission of Methodism (Ed.), 1945; Jesus and the Kingdom of God, 1955; Anglican-Methodist Conversations, 1963. *Address:* Flat 16, Dalegarth, Hurst Park Avenue, Cambridge. *T:* 55220. *Club:* Athenæum.

**ROBERTS, Sir Harold (Charles West),** Kt 1953; CBE 1948; MC 1916; *b* 23 May 1892; *s* of T. B. and Elizabeth Roberts, Stoke-on-Trent; *m* Alice May, *d* of A. T. Bourne, Trentham, Staffs; no *c*. *Educ:* Newcastle School; Birmingham University. Trained as a mining engineer in North Staffordshire. Served European War, in France and Italy, Middlesex Regiment, 1916-18; in India, Indian Army, 1918-19. BSc 1921. HM Inspector of Mines, 1922; senior Inspector, 1936; Chief Inspector of Training, Ministry of Fuel and Power, 1943; Deputy Chief Inspector of Mines, 1945; HM Chief Inspector of Mines, 1951-58, retired. *Recreations:* golf and walking. *Address:* Layfield, Cavendish, Suffolk.

**ROBERTS, (Herbert) John,** CMG 1965; MP Zambia, since 1964, (Ind) Zambia National Assembly since 1966; *b* 22 Nov. 1919; *m* 1946, Margaret Pollard; three *s* one *d*. *Educ:* Holy Trinity, Weymouth; Milton, Bulawayo. Served War of 1939-45; Somaliland, Ethiopia, Burma. Elected MLC, 1954; Leader of Northern Rhodesia United Federal Party, 1959-63; Founder of National Progress Party, 1963; Min. of Labour and Mines, 1959-61; Leader of Opposition (NR), 1961-64; Leader of Opposition (Zambia), 1964-65; disbanded Nat. Progress Party, 1966. *Address:* PO Box 1299, Lusaka, Zambia.

**ROBERTS, Sir Howard;** *see* Roberts, Sir J. R. H.

**ROBERTS, (Ieuan) Wyn (Pritchard);** MP (C) Conway since 1970; Parliamentary Private Secretary to Secretary of State for Wales, since 1970; *b* 10 July 1930; *s* of late Rev. E. P. Roberts and Margaret Ann; *m* 1956, Enid Grace Williams; three *s. Educ:* Harrow; University Coll., Oxford. Sub-editor, Liverpool Daily Post, 1952-54; News Asst, BBC, 1954-57; TWW Ltd: News, Special Events and Welsh Language Programmes Producer, 1957-59; Production Controller, 1959-60; Exec. Producer, 1960-68; Welsh Controller, 1964-68; Programme Exec., Harlech TV, 1969. Mem. of Gorsedd, Royal National Eisteddfod of Wales, 1966. Member, Court of Governors: Nat. Library of Wales; Nat. Museum of Wales; University Coll. of Wales, Aberystwyth, 1970-. *Recreation:* gardening. *Address:* Tan y Gwalia, Conway, Caerns. *T:* Tyn y Groes 371. *Clubs:* Savile; Cardiff and County (Cardiff).

**ROBERTS, Sir James Denby,** 2nd Bt, *cr* 1909; OBE 1959; JP; *b* 3 June 1904; *e s* of late Bertram Foster Roberts and Gertrude, *o d* of Sir Ellis Denby, JP; *S* grandfather, 1935; *m* 1927, Irene Charlotte D'Orsey, *yr d* of William Dunn, MB, CM, JP; three *s* one *d* (and one *s* decd). *Educ:* Rugby; University College, Oxford (MA). Member, Central Agricultural Executive Committee; Council Member, RASE. Chairman: Scottish Soc. for Research in Plant Breeding; Mem., Nature Conservancy Cttee, 1965. *Recreations:* fishing, shooting. *Heir: s* William James Denby Roberts, *b* 10 Aug. 1936. *Address:* Strathallan Castle, Auchterarder, Perthshire. *T:* 2131. *Club:* Athenæum.

**ROBERTS, Sir (James Reginald) Howard,** Kt, *cr* 1949; CBE 1946; JP 1947, DL 1949; Solicitor; *b* 2 Jan. 1891; *s* of James Reginald Roberts, Liverpool, and Mary Barron Muir; *m* 1950, Joan Blackstone-Smith, Egham; (two *s* one *d* by former marriage). *Educ:* Reading School. Articled to Town Clerk, Sheffield, 1908; Asst Solicitor, Stoke-on-Trent, 1913; war service, 1914-18; Assistant Solicitor, Liverpool, 1920; Asst Prosecuting Solicitor, Liverpool, 1921; Assistant Town Clerk, Liverpool, 1922; Deputy Town Clerk, Liverpool, 1927; Town Clerk, Kingston-upon-Hull, 1929; Solicitor to LCC 1934-36; Solicitor and Parliamentary Officer to LCC, 1936-47; Clerk of London County Council, 1947-56; Clerk of Lieutenancy of County of London and Hon. Clerk to Advisory Committee on JPs for County of London, 1947-56; Regional Co-ordinating Officer for Civil Defence Vehicles, London Civil Defence Region, 1939-45; Solicitor to the National Fire Service (London Region), 1941-45; Vice-President: Royal Inst. PA; Nat. Fire Service Benevolent Fund; Past President Royal Society for the Prevention of Accidents; Legal Mem. of Town Planning Inst., Pres. 1947. Mem., Surrey CC. Officer of Legion of Honour, 1950; Officer of Order of Orange Nassau, 1950; Chevalier of Order of Dannebrog, 1951; Chevalier of Royal Order of North Star, 1954; Chevalier of Order of the Star of Ethiopia, 1954; Chevalier of Portuguese Military Order of Christ. *Publications:* The National Fire Service; The Law relating to Town and Country Planning. *Recreation:* fishing. *Address:* Burford, Englefield Green, Surrey. *Club:* Savage.

**ROBERTS, Dame Jean,** DBE 1962; DL; JP; *m* 1922, Cameron Roberts (decd), Headmaster of Albert Senior Secondary Sch., Springburn; one *d. Educ:* Albert Sch.; Whitehill Sch. Taught at Bishopstreet School and later in a special school for handicapped children. Representative of Kingston Ward in Corp. of City of Glasgow from Nov. 1929-May 1966; DL 1964, JP 1934, Glasgow; Sen. Magistrate; held the following posts as first woman to do so: Convener of Electrical Cttee; Dep. Chm. of the Corp; Leader of the Labour Group; City Treasurer; Lord Provost of the City of Glasgow and Lord Lieut of the county of the City of Glasgow, 1960-63. Vice-Chairman of the Scottish National Orchestra. Chairman, Cumbernauld Develt, Corp., 1965-. Member: Scottish Arts Council, 1963; Arts Council of Gt Britain, 1965-68. Since 1930: apptd by Secretary of State for Scotland to serve on many Advisory Cttees dealing with Local Govt, Social and Economic matters in Scotland. Order of St Olav, 1962. *Recreations:* music and public service. *Address:* 35 Beechwood Drive, Glasgow, W1. *T:* 041-334 1930.

**ROBERTS, John;** *see* Roberts, H. J.

**ROBERTS, John Alexander Fraser,** CBE 1965; FRS 1963; MA Cantab; MD, DSc (Edinburgh); FRCP; Geneticist, Paediatric Research Unit, Guy's Hospital Medical School, SE1, 1964; Hon. Clinical Geneticist, Guy's Hospital; Consultant in Medical Genetics: Royal Eastern Counties Hospital, Colchester; United Bristol Hospitals; *b* 8 Sept. 1899; *er s* of late Robert Henry Roberts, Foxhall, Denbigh, and late Elizabeth Mary; *m* 1941, Doris, *y d* of late Herbert and Kate Hare; two *d. Educ:* Denbigh Gram. Sch.; privately; Gonville and Caius Coll., Cambridge; Univs of Edinburgh, Wales and Bristol. 2nd Lieut Royal Welch Fusliliers, 1918-19; War of 1939-45: Surgeon-Comdr RNVR and Cons. in Med. Statistics, RN, 1942-46. Research Asst, Inst. of Animal Genetics, Univ. of Edinburgh, 1922-28; Biologist, Wool Industries Research Assoc., 1928-31; Macaulay Research Fellow, Univ. of Edinburgh, 1931-33; Dir, Burden Mental Research Dept, Stoke Park Colony, Bristol, 1933-57; Lectr in Med. Genetics, London School of Hygiene and Trop. Med., 1946-57; Dir, Clinical Genetics Research Unit (MRC), Inst. of Child Health, Univ. of London, and Hon. Consultant in Med. Genetics, The Hospital for Sick Children, Gt Ormond St, 1957-64. President: Royal Anthropological Inst. of Gt Britain and Ire., 1957-59; Biometric Society (British Region), 1960-62; Section of Epidemiology and Preventive Medicine, RSM, 1960-62. Lectures: Charles West, RCP, 1961; Leonard Parsons, Univ. of Birmingham, 1963; Donald Paterson, Univ. of British Columbia (and Vis. Prof.), 1967. *Publications:* An Introduction to Medical Genetics, 5th edn 1970; papers in medical, biological and genetical journals. *Recreation:* mountain walks. *Address:* 13 Ruvigny Mansions, Embankment, SW15. *T:* 01-788 1210; Foxhall, Denbigh. *Club:* Athenæum.

**ROBERTS, John Eric,** DSc (Leeds), FInstP; Emeritus Professor of Physics, University of London, 1969; Physicist to Middlesex Hospital, W1, 1946-69; Consultant Adviser in Physics, Department of Health and Social Security; *b* Leeds, 1907; *e s* of late James J. Roberts, Normanton, Yorks; *m* Sarah, *o d* of late Thomas Raybould, Normanton, Yorks; two *d. Educ:* Normanton Grammar School; University of Leeds (Brown Scholar). BSc (Physics Hons), Leeds, 1928; Univ. Research Scholar, PhD 1930; Research Assistant in Physics, University of Leeds, 1930; Assistant Physicist, Royal Cancer Hospital, 1932; Senior Asst Physicist, Middlesex Hosp., 1937; Joel Prof. of Physics Applied to Medicine, Univ. of London, 1946-69; Regional Adviser, ME, Internat. Atomic Energy Agency, 1963. FInstP. 1938; DSc (Leeds), 1944. Pres., British Inst. of Radiology, 1951-52; Pres.

Hospital Physicists Assoc., 1950-51; Editor, Physics in Medicine and Biology, 1956-60; Editor, British Jl of Radiology, 1964-67. Hon. Mem., Fac. of Radiologists. *Publications:* Nuclear War and Peace, 1956; scientific papers in various journals. *Address:* Windrush, Malthouse Lane, Ludham, Great Yarmouth, Norfolk. *T:* Potter Heigham 459.

**ROBERTS, Air Vice-Marshal John Frederick,** CB 1967; CBE 1960 (OBE 1954); with Deloitte, Plender, Griffiths & Co., Chartered Accountants, Swansea, since 1969; *b* 24 Feb. 1913; *y s* of late W. J. Roberts, Pontardawe; *m* 1942, Mary Winifred (*d* 1968), *d* of late J. E. Newns; one *s*. *Educ:* Pontardawe Gram. Sch., Glam. Chartered Accountant, 1936. Joined RAF, 1938; service in Middle East, 1942-45; Mem. Directing Staff, RAF Staff Coll., Bracknell, 1954-56; SASO, RAF Record Office, 1958-60; Dep. Comptroller, Allied Forces Central Europe, 1960-62; Stn Comdr RAF Uxbridge, 1963; Dir of Personal Services I, Min. of Def. (Air), 1964-65; Dir-Gen. of Ground Training (RAF), 1966-68; retd, 1968. *Recreations:* cricket, golf, cabinet-making. *Address:* Cefneithrym, 1 Lon Cadog, Sketty, Swansea. *T:* Swansea 23-763. *Clubs:* Royal Air Force, MCC; Ffynone (Swansea).

**ROBERTS, John Morris;** Fellow and Tutor, Merton College, Oxford, since 1953; Editor, English Historical Review, since 1967; *b* 14 April 1928; *s* of late Edward Henry Roberts and late Dorothy Julia Roberts, Bath, Som.; *m* 1964, Judith Cecilia Mary, *e d* of late Rev. James Armitage and Monica Armitage; one *s* one *d*. *Educ:* Taunton Sch.; Keble Coll., Oxford (Schol.). National Service, 1949-50; Prize Fell., Magdalen Coll., Oxford, 1951-53; Commonwealth Fund Fell., Princeton and Yale, 1953-54; Princ. of Postmasters, Merton Coll., 1955-60; Sen. Proctor, 1967-68; Sub-Warden, Merton Coll., 1968-69, acting Warden, 1969-70. Mem., Inst. for Advanced Study, Princeton, 1960-61; Vis. Prof., Univ. of S Carolina, 1961; Sec. of Harmsworth Trust, 1962-68. *Publications:* French Revolution Documents, 1966; Europe 1880-1945, 1967; (Gen. Editor) Purnell's History of the 20th Century; articles and reviews in learned jls. *Recreation:* music. *Address:* Merton College, Oxford. *Club:* Oxford and Cambridge University.

**ROBERTS, John Reginald,** CBE 1943; *b* 28 June 1893; *s* of William Rowe and Ada Mary Roberts; *m* 1925, Hilda Mary Redshaw; one *s*. *Educ:* Liverpool College; Ducie Avenue Secondary School, Manchester; Manchester College of Technology (Associate). European War, 1914-18; in France with Royal Engineers. Ex Engineer PWD, Nigeria, 1921; Sen. Hydraulic Engineer PWD, Gold Coast (now Ghana), 1929; Dep. Director of Public Works Gold Coast (now Ghana), 1937; Director of Public Works, 1939-45; Regional Engineer, NW Region, Ministry of Housing and Local Govt, 1946-56. *Address:* 90 Bramhall Lane South, Bramhall, Stockport.

**ROBERTS, Kate Winifred J.;** *see* Jones-Roberts.

**ROBERTS, Sir Leslie,** Kt 1952; CBE 1942; Chairman since 1950 (Managing Director until 1961), Manchester Ship Canal Co.; *s* of William Roberts; *m* 1st, 1922, Christine Marjorie Stott (*decd*); one *s* one *d*; *m* 2nd, 1948, Marjorie Adele Gibson (*d* 1968). Has spent all his business life in shipping, first in London and later in Liverpool and Manchester. Was Asst Manager of White Star Line, Liverpool; joined Frederick Leyland & Company Ltd as one of the Joint Managers; General Manager, 1929; Deputy General Manager of Manchester Ship Canal Co., 1934; Gen. Manager, 1936. Rep. Liverpool Steamship Owners' Assoc. on Mersey Docks and Harbour Bd; Chm., Bridgewater Estates Ltd; Director: Manchester Liners Ltd, 1947; Williams, Deacon's Bank Ltd, 1950-70; former Dir, National Boiler & General Insurance Co. Ltd and vulcan Boiler & General Insurance Co. Ltd. *Address:* Windy How, Broadway, Hale, Cheshire. *T:* 061-980 3032; Ship Canal House, King Street, Manchester M2 4WX. *TA:* Canal Manchester. *T:* 061-832 2244.

**ROBERTS, Prof. Michael,** FBA 1960; Professor of Modern History, The Queen's University, Belfast, since 1954; Dean of the Faculty of Arts, 1957-60; *b* 21 May 1908; *s* of Arthur Roberts and Hannah Elizabeth Landless; *m* 1941, Ann McKinnon Morton; one *d*. *Educ:* Brighton College; Worcester College, Oxford. Gladstone Memorial Prizeman, 1931; A. M. P. Read Scholar (Oxford), 1932. Procter Visiting Fell., Princeton Univ., USA, 1931-32; Lecturer, Merton Coll., Oxford, 1932-34; DPhil, Oxford, 1935; Professor of Modern History, Rhodes Univ., S Africa, 1935-53. Lieut, SA Int. Corps, 1942-44. British Council Representative, Stockholm, 1944-46. Public Orator, Rhodes University, 1951-53; Hugh Le May Visiting Fell., Rhodes Univ., 1960-61; A. L. Smith Lecturer, Balliol Coll., Oxford, 1962; Enid Muir Memorial Lecturer, Univ. of Newcastle upon Tyne, 1965; Creighton Lecturer in History, Univ. of London, 1965; Stenton Lectr, Univ. of Reading, 1969. Hon. Fellow, Worcester Coll., Oxford, 1966; Vis. Fellow, All Souls Coll., Oxford, 1968-69. MRIA 1968. For. Member: Roy. Swedish Acad. of Letters. History and Antiquities; Royal Swedish Academy of Science; Hon. Mem. Samfundet för utgivande av handskrifter rörande Skandinaviens historia. FRHist Society; Fil dr (*hc*) (Stockholm), 1960. Chevalier, Order of North Star (Sweden), 1954. *Publications:* The Whig Party, 1807-1812, 1939; (with A. E. G. Trollip) The South African Opposition, 1939-1945, 1947; Gustavus Adolphus: A History of Sweden, 1611-1632, Vol. I, 1953, Vol. II, 1958; Essays in Swedish History, 1967; The Early Vasas: A History of Sweden 1523-1611, 1968; Sweden as a Great Power 1611-1697, 1968; Sverige och Europa, 1969; Gustav Vasa, 1970; trans. from Swedish of works by Nils Ahnlund, F. G. Bengtsson; articles in EHR, History, Historical Jl; Past and Present; South African Archives Yearbook, etc. *Recreation:* music. *Address:* Raheen House, Spa, Ballynahinch, Co. Down, N Ireland. *T:* Ballynahinch 2270.

**ROBERTS, Michael (Hilary Arthur);** MP (C) Cardiff (North) since 1970; *b* 1927; *s* of Rev. T. A. Roberts (formerly Rector of Neath); *m* 1952, Eileen Jean Evans; two *s* one *d*. *Educ:* Neath Grammar School; Cardiff University College. First Headmaster of the Bishop of Llandaff High School, 1963-70. *Address:* Ashgrove Farm, Whitchurch, Cardiff. *T:* Cardiff 66527.

**ROBERTS, Brig. Michael Rookherst,** DSO 1944; Historian, Cabinet Office, 1956-68; *b* 24 Oct. 1894; *s* of R. G. S. Roberts, Mount Rivers, Carrigaline, Co. Cork; *m* 1919, Isabel, 3rd *d* of James Fisher, JP, ship owner, Barrow in Furness; one *s* one *d*. *Educ:* West Buckland; RMC Sandhurst. Served European War, 1914-18, with Lancashire Fusiliers and 113th Inf., IA (France and S Persia); Waziristan, 1920; 2nd Lt 1914; Bt Major, 1931; Asst Mil. Sec., 1931; Comdt 2/10th Gurkha Rifles, 1937; GSO1, Nepalese Contingent, 1940; Brig. 1940; Comd bde of 7th Indian Div., Arakan, 1943-44 (despatches); Colonel, 10th Princess Mary's Own Gurkha Rifles, 1957-59. Chm. Gurkha

Brigade Assoc., 1955-67; Gov., West Buckland School, 1954 (Chm., 1960-68). Fellow Royal Historical Soc., 1960; Chm. Canterbury Soc., 1969-. *Publications:* Golden Arrow (history of 7th Indian Division), 1952; joint author, Official History, War Against Japan, Vol. II, 1958, Vol. III, 1962, Vol. IV, 1965, Vol. V, 1969; completed Connell, Wavell: Supreme Commander, 1969; articles to Royal United Service Institution Journal, Army Quarterly, Economist; Dictionary of National Biography. *Address:* Merton Lodge, Nackington, Canterbury, Kent. *T:* 65212. *Club:* Army and Navy.

**ROBERTS, Norman Stafford,** MA, DPA; Headmaster, Taunton School, since Sept. 1970; *b* 15 Feb. 1926; *s* of Walter S. Roberts, LLM and Florence E. Roberts (*née* Phythian), Calderstones, Liverpool; *m* 1965, Beatrice, *o d* of late George and Winifred Best, Donaghadee, Co. Down; one *s* one *d*. *Educ:* Quarry Bank High Sch., Liverpool; Hertford Coll., Oxford (Open Exhibnr, History). Served in RA, Egypt and Palestine, 1945-47 (Lieut). 2nd cl. hons PPE 1950; DipEd Oxford 1951; DPA London 1951. Asst Master, Berkhamsted Junior Sch., 1951-55; House Master, Sixth Form Master, Berkhamsted Sch., 1955-59; Walter Hines Page Scholar to USA, 1959; Senior History Master, CO CCF (Hon. Major 1965), Monkton Combe Sch., 1959-65, Housemaster 1962-65; Schoolmaster Student, Merton Coll., Oxford, 1964; Headmaster, Sexey's Sch., Bruton, 1965-70. *Recreations:* foreign travel, bridge, hockey, tennis. *Address:* The Gables, Private Road, Staplegrove, Taunton, Somerset. *T:* Taunton 2588. *Club:* Public Schools.

**ROBERTS, Sir Norman (Stanley),** KBE *cr* 1953 (OBE 1936; MBE 1920); CMG 1950; *b* 20 July 1893; British; *m* 1st, 1921, Olga Taskin (marriage dissolved, 1931); one *s*; 2nd, 1945, Marie Elder, *d* of General Baron de Rauch. Served European War, 1914-19, with Rifle Brigade. Entered Foreign Office, 1920; First Secretary (Commercial), Tehran, 1945, Counsellor (Commercial) 1946; Counsellor (Commercial) Stockholm, Dec. 1948; Minister, Commercial, 1950-52, Minister, 1952-53, Tokyo; retd, June 1954. Negotiated agreement with Japanese Govt about payment of indemnity to former Allied prisoners of war, Dec. 1954. Director: Alva Steamship Co. Ltd, Navigation & Coal Trade Co. Ltd, Anglo Australian Navigation Co. Ltd; Chm., Japan Soc. of London, 1964-67. Order of the Rising Sun (2nd Class), Japan, 1959. *Address:* 46 Princes Gate, SW7. *T:* 01-589 1317. *Clubs:* United Service, MCC.

**ROBERTS, Gen. Sir Ouvry Lindfield.** GCB 1953 (KCB 1952; CB 1946); KBE 1950 (CBE 1944); DSO 1941; President of Grosvenor Laing (BC) Limited (Canada), 1955-60; formerly Director: Grosvenor/Laing (BC) Ltd; Grosvenor/Laing (Langley Park) Ltd; Grosvenor International Ltd; Redhill Investment Corporation Ltd; Macdonald Buchanan Properties Ltd; *b* 3 April 1898; *m* 1924, Elsie Nora Eileen Webster (*d* 1955); two *s*; *m* 1955, Joyce Mary Segar, *yr d* of Eric W. Scorer, OBE, Coombe Hurst, Lincoln; two *s* one *d*. *Educ:* Cheltenham College; Royal Military Academy, Woolwich; King's Coll., Cambridge (MA). RE, commissioned 1917; Comdg 23 Ind. Div., 1943-45; Comdg 34 Ind. Corps, 1945; Vice-Adjutant-Gen. War Office, 1945-47; GOC Northern Ireland District, 1948-49; GOC-in-C Southern Command, 1949-52; Quarter-master-General to the Forces, 1952-55; ADC General to the Queen, 1952-55; Colonel Commandant, Corps of Royal Engineers, 1952-62. Administrative Officer, Univ. of BC, 1961-68. *Recreations:* cricket (Army, Quidnung); hockey (Cambrdige, Army, Wales). *Address:* 17 Third Acre Rise, Oxford. *T:* Cumnor 2562. *Clubs:* Oriental, MCC.

**ROBERTS, Sir Peter Geoffrey,** 3rd Bt, *cr* 1919; *b* 23 June 1912; *yr* and *o surv s* of Sir Samuel Roberts, 2nd Bt and Gladys Mary (*d* 1966), *d* of W. E. Dring, MD, Tenterden, Kent; *S* father 1955; *m* 1939, Judith Randell Hempson; one *s* four *d*. *Educ:* Harrow; Trinity College, Cambridge. Barr.-at-Law, Inner Temple, 1935. Maj. Coldstream Guards. MP (C) Ecclesall Div. of Sheffield, 1945-50; (C-L) Heeley Div. of Sheffield, 1950-66. Chairman: Wellman Engineering Corp., Ltd; Newton Chambers & Co., Ltd; Curzonia Knitwear Ltd; The Wombwell Investment Co. Ltd; Cam Rotors Ltd; Director: Guardian Assurance Co. Ltd; Guardian Royal Exchange Assurance Ltd; Williams Deacon's Bank Ltd; Williams & Glyn's Bank Ltd; Hadfields Ltd. past Chm., Conservative Members' Committee on Fuel and Power; Past Pres., Soc. of British Gas Industries (Pres., 1963). Master Cutler, Sheffield, 1957. High Sheriff of Hallamshire, 1970-71. *Publication:* Coal Act, 1938. *Heir: s* Samuel Roberts, *b* 16 April 1948. *Address:* 11 Mount Street, W1. *T:* 01-499 4242; Redholme, Sandygate Road, Sheffield, Yorshire S10 5UA. *T:* Sheffield 32700; Cockley Cley Hall, Swaffham, Norfolk. *T:* Swaffham 308. *Clubs:* Carlton, Brooks's; Sheffield (Sheffield).

**ROBERTS, Lieut-Comdr Peter Scawen Watkinson,** VC 1942; DSC 1942; RN retired; *b* 28 July 1917; *yr s* of George Watkinson Roberts, 82 King William Street, EC4; *m* 1940, Brigid Victoria, *yr d* of S. J. Lethbridge, Plymouth; one *s* one *d*. *Educ:* King's School, Canterbury. Entered Royal Navy, 1935; Sub-Lieut 1938; Lieut 1940; Lt-Comdr 1947. HMS Shropshire, 1936-38; Submarines, Sept. 1939; HMS: Tribune, 1940; Thrasher, 1941; Beagle, 1941-42; Vernon, 1943-45; Black Prince, 1945-46; Defiance, 1946-48; Eagle, 1948; Gorregan, 1950; Apollo, 1952; Cardigan Bay, 1953; Dingley, 1955; Vernon, 1956 (HM Underwater Countermeasures and Weapons Estabt, 1957); Drake, 1959. Retired list, 1962. *Address:* The Coach House, Membland, Newton Ferrers, S Devon. *T:* Newton Ferrers 346. *Clubs:* Royal Burnham Yacht (Burnham-on-Crouch); Royal Naval Sailing Association.

**ROBERTS, Richard (David Hallam);** Headmaster, Wycliffe College, Stonehouse, since 1967; *b* 27 July 1931; *s* of Arthur Hallam Roberts, Barrister-at-law, sometime Attorney-General, Zanzibar, and Ruvé Constance Jessie Roberts; *m* 1960, Wendy Ewen Mount; three *s*. *Educ:* King's Sch., Canterbury; Jesus Coll., Cambridge. Commissioned into RA 6th Field Regt, 1952. Asst Master, King's Sch., Canterbury, 1956; Housemaster, 1957; Head of Modern Language Dept, 1961; Senior Housemaster, 1965. *Address:* The Headmaster's House, Wycliffe College, Stonehouse, Glos GL10 2JQ. *Club:* Leander (Henley-on-Thames).

**ROBERTS, Rear-Adm. Richard Douglas,** CEng; FIMechE; Rear-Admiral Engineering on staff Flag Officer Naval Air Command, since 1969; *b* 7 Nov. 1916; *s* of Rear-Adm. E. W. Roberts and Mrs R. E. Roberts (*née* Cox); *m* 1943, Mary Norma Wright; one *s* one *d*. *Educ:* RNC Dartmouth; RNEC Keyham. Frobisher, 1934; RNEC Keyham, 1935-38 (qual. Marine Eng); HM Ships: Kent, 1938-40; Exeter, 1941; Bermuda, 1942; Mauritius, 1943-45; RNEC Manadon, 1945 (qual. Aero Eng); RNAY Donibristle, 1946 (AMIMechE); RNAS Worthy Down, 1947; RNAS Yeovilton, 1948-49; Staff of Rear-Adm. Reserve Aircraft, 1949-

50; Comdr, 1950; RN Staff Coll., 1951; RNAY Fleetlands, 1952-53 (Production Man.); HMS Newfoundland, 1954-56 (Engr Officer); Engr-in-Chief's Dept, Bath, 1956-60; Captain 1960; RNAY Belfast, 1961-62 (Supt); idc, 1963 (MIMechE); Dir, Fleet Maintenance, 1964-66; Dir, Naval Officer Appts (E), 1966-68; Rear-Adm. 1969. MBIM 1967. *Recreations:* sailing (RNSA, 1936) fishing. *Address:* Staff of FONAC, Wykeham Hall, Lee-on-Solent, Hants. *Clubs:* Army and Navy, Royal Over-Seas League, Victoria League; Lee-on-Solent Yacht.

**ROBERTS, Robert David Valpo;** Member of the Electricity Council since 1967; *b* 5 July 1906; *e s* of David Roberts and Jane Anne Roberts (*née* Evans); *m* 1939, Maureen Elizabeth (*née* Gresty); no *c. Educ:* Dolgellau Gram. Sch.; London Sch. of Economics and Political Science (BCom). South American Jl, 1927-35; Leonard Hill Ltd, 1935-36; Asst Sec., S Wales and Mon Council of Social Service, 1936-40; Districts Officer, Miners' Welfare Commn, 1940-48; Sec., Nat. Jt Adv. Coun. of Electricity Supply Industry, 1949-57; Dep. Industrial Relations Adviser, Electricity Coun., 1957-60; Industrial Relations Adviser, Electricity Coun., 1960-66. Member: Nat. Jt Adv. Council, Dept of Employment and Productivity (formerly Min. of Labour), 1960-; Nat. Adv. Council on Educn for Industry and Commerce, Dept of Educn and Science, 1970-. Mem. Court, Univ. of Wales Inst. of Science and Technology, 1970-. *Publications:* (with Sir Ronald Edwards) Status, Productivity, and Pay: a major experiment; (booklet) Miners Welfare Looks Forward; (booklet, with T. E. M. McKitterick) Workers and Management: The German Codetermination Experiment; articles on aspects of industrial relations in Brit. Jl of Industrial Relations and The Listener. *Recreation:* fishing. *Address:* Mynthurst Barn, Leigh, Reigate, Surrey. *T:* Norwood Hill 465. *Club:* Flyfishers'.

**ROBERTS, Rev. Roger Lewis,** MA Oxon; Chaplain, the Queen's Chapel of the Savoy, and Chaplain of the Royal Victorian Order, since Nov. 1961; Chaplain to the Queen, since 1969; *b* 3 Aug. 1911; 3rd *s* of late Robert Lewis Roberts, CBE; *m* 1935, Katie Agnes Mary Perryman; one *s. Educ:* Highgate School; Exeter College, Oxford. 1st Class Hon. Mods, 1931; 1st Class Lit. Hum., 1933; Charles Oldham Prize, 1933; BA 1933; MA 1938; Sixth Form Master, The Liverpool Institute, 1933-34; Sixth Form Master, Rugby School, 1934-40; enlisted RRA, 1940; Army Educational Corps, 1941-43 (Major). Headmaster, Blundell's Sch., 1943-47; Deacon, Exeter, 1946; Priest, St Albans, 1948; Assistant Priest, Cathedral and Abbey Church of St Alban, 1948-49. Vicar of Sharnbrook, Bedfordshire, 1949-54. Vicar of the Guild Church of All Hallows, London Wall, 1954-58, of St Botolph without Aldersgate, 1958-61. Warden, The Church of England Men's Society, 1957-61 (Gen. Sec. 1954-57, Vice-Pres. 1962-). Member of editorial staff, The Church Times, 1950-(Editor, 1960-68). Chaplain: Instn of Electrical Engineers, 1961-; Worshipful Co. of Glaziers, 1967-. *Recreation:* walking. *Address:* The Queen's Chapel of the Savoy, Strand, WC2; 97 Corringham Road, Golders Green, NW11. *T:* 01-455 2118. *Club:* Oxford and Cambrdige University.

*See also B. R. Roberts and C. H. Roberts.*

**ROBERTS, Sir Stephen (Henry),** Kt 1965; CMG 1956; MA, DSc (Econ.) London, LittD (Melbourne), LLD (Bristol, British Columbia, McGill); DCL (Durham); DLit (New England); Vice-Chancellor and Principal, University of Sydney, 1947-67; Challis Professor of Modern History, 1929-47; Dean of Faculty of Arts, 1941-47; Chairman of Professorial Board, 1944-45 and 1946-47; Acting Vice-Chancellor, 1947; *b* Maldon, Victoria, 15 Feb. 1901; *m* 1927, Thelma Asche, *d* of late John Asche, Toorak, Victoria; three *d. Educ:* Castlemaine; Melbourne; London; Paris. Lecturer, Research Fellow Melbourne Univ., 1920-25; Research in London and France, 1925-29 and in Germany, 1935-37 and 1953; Chairman, Australian Vice-Chancellors' Committee, 1952-53; Chairman, New South Wales State Cancer Council, 1952-68. Commander: Royal Danish Order of Dannebrog, 1950; Order of the Cedar of Lebanon, 1962; Royal Greek Order of the Phoenix, 1964; Commander, Order of Merit (Italy), 1967; Officer, Legion of Honour (France), 1967; Hon. DLitt Sydney, 1967. *Publications:* History of Australian Land Settlement, 1923; Population Problems of the Pacific, 1925; French Colonial Policy, 1870-1925, 1928; The Squatting Age in Australia, 1932; History of Modern Europe, 1933; The House that Hitler built, 1937; Problems of Modern France, 1937; Contributor to Cambridge History of the Empire, to Cyclopedia of the Social Sciences and to Encyclopedia Britannica Year-Book; Part-author of Australia and the Far East, 1935, and The Australian Mandate in New Guinea; many writings on French regionalism. *Recreations:* travel, philately, history of wine. *Address:* 16 Wyuna Road, Point Piper, Sydney, NSW 2027, Australia.

**ROBERTS, Most Rev. Thomas d'Esterre,** SJ, DD; *b* 1893. Entered Society of Jesus, 1909; Priest, 1925; Rector of St Francis Xavier's College, Liverpool, 1935-37; Archbishop of Bombay, (RC), 1937-50, retired, 1950. *Publication:* Black Popes, 1954. *Relevant Publication:* Archbishop Roberts, SJ, His Life and Writings, by D. A. Hurn, 1966. *Address:* 114 Mount Street, W1. *T:* 01-493 7811.

**ROBERTS, Col Sir Thomas Langdon Howland,** 6th Bt, of Glassenbury and Brightfieldstown, Co. Cork, *cr* 1809 (claimant to 13th Baronetcy *cr* 1620); CBE 1964; DL; Roy. Artillery (retd); late King's Regt, and VIth KAR; Hon. Colonel 499 (M) HAA Regiment RA (TA), 1949; Actg Col Comdr, No. 4 Sector, County of London Home Guard, 1952-56; Commandant County of London ACF, 1956-63; *b* 18 June 1898; *s* of 12th Bt and Elizabeth Marie (*d* 1949), *d* of late W. T. La Roche, MD, New Jersey, USA; *S* father, 1917; *m* 1930, Evelyn Margaret, *o d* of late H. Fielding-Hall, Burma Commission; two *s* one *d. Educ:* Westminster School; RMA, Woolwich. Capt. 1928; Major, 1938; Lt-Col 1941. President, County of Kent SS&AFA, 1964-; Vice-Chm., Roy. Cambridge Home for Soldiers' Widows, 1961-68; Hon. Sec., Royal Artillery Officers' Sports Fund, 1951-; Hon. Treas, Army Guild of St Helena, 1958-; Hon. Treas, Officers' Families Fund, 1964-67. DL, County of London (Wandsworth), 1962-. *Recreations:* sailing, shooting, riding, stamp collecting. *Heir:* *s* Gilbert Howland Rookehurst Roberts, Lt TARO, BA Cambridge [*b* 31 May 1934; *m* 1958, Ines, *o d* of late A. Labunski; one *s* one *d*]. *Address:* Furzebank, Shorne, Ridgeway, near Gravesend, Kent. *Clubs:* Army and Navy; RA Yacht; RE Yacht.

**ROBERTS, Sir Walter St Clair Howland,** KCMG, *cr* 1951 (CMG 1937); MC; *b* 14 Dec. 1893; *m* 1st, 1924, Helen Cecil Ronayne (*d* 1951), *o c* of late Colonel A. W. Weekes, DSO, OBE, RE; 2nd, Cecily (*d* 1964), *widow* of H. E. Ormond. *Educ:* Winchester; Brasenose Coll., Oxford. Prisoner of War, 1914-16; served with RFA, 1917-19 (MC). Entered Foreign Office,

1919; Head of Western Europe Dept, 1936-39, and POW Dept, 1941-45; Ambassador to Peru, 1945-48; Minister to Roumania, 1949-51; Minister to Holy See, 1951-53. *Address:* Leaton Lodge, Bomere Heath, Shropshire.

**ROBERTS, Walter S.;** *see* Stewart-Roberts.

**ROBERTS, Wilfrid,** JP; *b* 28 Aug. 1900; *s* of Charles and Lady Cecilia Roberts, Boothby, Brampton, Cumberland; *m* 1928, Anne Constance Jennings; three *d*. *Educ:* Gresham School; Balliol College, Oxford. MP (L) North Cumberland, 1935-50; joined Labour Party, July 1956. *Address:* Boothby, Brampton, Cumberland.

**ROBERTS, Sir William,** Kt 1938; CIE 1934; BSc; LLD (hc); Member of Council of British Cotton Growing Association, Manchester; Emeritus Director BCGA Pb Ltd and Man. Dir RCA Ltd; Member Boyd Orr Agricultural Inquiry Committee, Pakistan, 1951-52; *b* 17 Feb. 1884; *s* of John and Ann Roberts; *m* 1919, E. M. Jones, Llangefni; Anglesey; one *s* two *d*. *Educ:* Llangefni County School; UCNW Bangor; Leipzig University. BSc, with 1st Class Hons in Chemistry in 1906; LLD (hc), Wales, 1952. Joined Indian Agricultural Service, 1906; Professor of Agriculture, Lyallpur, 1909-21; Principal, 1916-21. Member Indo-Japanese and Indo-British Trade Cttees, 1934 and 1938. *Publications:* Punjab Agriculture–Text Book of, revised edn, 1947 and 1951. *Recreations:* tennis, fishing. *Address:* Caer Menai, Bangor, N Wales. *Clubs:* Sind (Karachi), Punjab (Lahore).

**ROBERTS, William;** RA 1966 (ARA 1958); artist; member of the London Group; *b* London, 1895. *Educ:* St Martin's School of Art; Slade School, London University. Worked at Omega Workshops under Roger Fry before 1914-18 War. Joined Vorticist Gp, 1914 (started by Wyndham Lewis). London Group, 1915. Official War Artist during European War, 1914-18 and War of 1939-45. Three paintings acquired by the Tate Gallery. Retrospective Exhibition, Tate Gallery, 1965; Exhibition, d'Offay Couper Gallery, 1969.

**ROBERTS, Col William Quincey,** CBE 1958 (OBE 1952); DSO 1944 (Bar, 1945); MVO 1955; TD; DL; Land Steward, Duchy of Cornwall, since 1948; *b* 5 Aug. 1912; *s* of late C. M. Roberts, MVO, Woodland Place, Bathwick Hill, Bath; *m* 1938, Janet Finnimore Hughes, *d* of late E. E. Hughes, Bath; three *d*. *Educ:* Tonbridge School. Asst Land Steward, Duchy of Cornwall, 1933. Commissioned Somerset LI (TA), 1933; Captain 1939; Major 1940; 2 i/c 6th Bn, 1942; served NW Europe, 1944-45; 2 i/c 4 Som. LI 1944; Lt-Col 1944; Comdr, 5 Bn Wilts Regt, 1944, 4 Bn Dorset Regt, 1944-45, and 4 Bn Somerset LI, 1947-52; Bt-Col 1952; Col 1954; Dep.-Comdr 130 Inf. Bde (TA), 1953-58. ADC to the Queen, 1956-61. Hon. Col: The Somerset Light Infantry, 1960-67; Somerset Yeomanry and Light Infantry, 1967- . JP Somerset, 1949; DL 1958; High Sheriff, 1969-70. Hon. Show Dir, Bath and West Southern Counties Soc., 1957-. Fell. Land Agents' Soc., 1947. *Recreations:* all field sports. *Address:* Stonewalls, Newton St Loe, Nr Bath, Somerset. *T:* Newton St Loe 246. *Clubs:* Army and Navy; Bath and County (Bath).

**ROBERTS, Col William Richter,** CBE 1944; retired Civil Servant; *b* 12 Jan. 1888; *s* of William Roberts, Buckhurst Hill, Essex; *m* 1922, Alice Katharine, *d* of Major Fasson, Shoreham, Sussex; two *d*. *Educ:* Bancroft's School, Woodford Wells. Surveying Staff, GPO; Surveyor of Western District, England; Deputy Regional Director, Home Counties Region, GPO, 1949; served European War with Army Postal Services, 1914-19 (despatches); demobilised with rank of Lt-Col; Order of Crown of Roumania; War of 1939-45 with Army Postal Services, France, 1939-40, MEF 1941-43 (despatches, OBE, CBE); BLA 1944-45 (despatches twice, Officer, Legion of Merit, USA, French médaille de Reconaissance, en vermeil). *Recreations:* botany, fishing. *Address:* The Gables, 9 Mill Lane, Shoreham-by-Sea, Sussex. *Club:* Royal Commonwealth Society.

**ROBERTS, Wyn;** *see* Roberts, I. W. P.

**ROBERTS-JONES, Ivor,** ARA 1969; sculptor; Teacher of sculpture, Goldsmiths' College School of Art; *b* 2 Nov. 1913; *s* of William and Florence Robert-Jones; *m* 1940, Monica Florence Booth; one *d* (one *s* decd). *Educ:* Oswestry Grammar Sch.; Worksop Coll.; Goldsmiths' Coll. Art Sch.; Royal Academy Schs. Served in RA, 1939-46; active service in Arakan, Burma. One-man Exhibition of Sculpture, Beaux Arts Gall., 1957. Works purchased by: Tate Gallery; Arts Council of Gt Brit.; Welsh Arts Council; Beaverbrook Foundation, New Brunswick; Nat. Mus. of Wales. Public commissions: Augustus John Memorial, Fordingbridge; Saint Francis, Lady Chapel, Ardleigh, Essex; Apsley Cherry Garrard, Wheathampstead, etc. Exhibited at: The John Moore, Leicester Galls, Royal Academy, Arts Council travelling exhibitions, etc. Work is in many private collections. *Publications:* poetry published in Welsh Review, Poets of the Forties, etc. Sculpture illustr. in British Art since 1900 by John Rothenstein; British Sculptors, 1947; Architectural Review, etc. *Recreation:* sailing. *Address:* 31 St James's Gardens, W11. *T:* 01-603 9614. *Club:* Cruising Association.

**ROBERTS-WEST, Lt-Gen. Sir M. M. A.;** *see* West.

**ROBERTS-WRAY, Sir Kenneth Owen,** GCMG 1960 (KCMG 1949; CMG 1946); QC 1959; Legal Adviser, Commonwealth Relations Office (Dominions Office until 1947) and Colonial Office, 1945-60, retired; *b* 6 June 1899; *s* of late Captain Thomas Henry Roberts-Wray, CB, OBE, VD, RNVR, sometime ADC to King George V, and late Florence Grace Roberts-Wray; *m* 1st, 1927, Joan Tremayne Waring (*d* 1961); three *s*; 2nd, 1965, Lady (Mary Howard) Williams, *widow* of Sir Ernest Williams, JP. *Educ:* University Tutorial Coll.; RMA, Woolwich; Merton College, Oxford (1st Class Hons School of Jurisprudence). 2/Lt RA 1918; Lieutenant, 1919; retired on account of wounds, 1920. Called to Bar 1924 (Certificate of Honour); Professional Legal Clerk, Minister of Health, 1926, Asst Chief Clerk, 1929; 2nd Asst Legal Adviser, Dominions Office and Colonial Office, 1931; Asst Legal Adviser, 1943. Chairman: Law Officers Conf., WI, 1944; Judicial Advisers Confs, Uganda, 1953, Nigeria, 1956. DCL Oxon, 1967; Hon. LLD Birmingham, 1968. *Publications:* part author of The Law of Collisions on Land, 1925; (Contrib.) Changing Law in Developing Countries (ed Anderson), 1963; Commonwealth and Colonial Law, 1966; articles on Colonial Law in legal publications. *Recreations:* golf, photography. *Address:* The Old Golf House, Forest Row, Sussex. *T:* Forest Row 2588; 5 King's Bench Walk, Temple, EC4. *T:* 01-353 2882/2884. *Clubs:* Oxford and Cambridge; Royal Ashdown Forest Golf.

**ROBERTSHAW, Vice-Adm. Sir Ballin Illingworth,** KBE 1958 (CBE 1944; OBE 1943);

CB 1955; *b* 11 Sept. 1902; *s* of late Sydney Robertshaw and Gladys Gwendoline Robertshaw; *m* 1st, 1932, Hannah Catherine Luard (*d* 1948); two *s* two *d*; 2nd, 1949, Margaret MacLaren. *Educ:* RN Colls Osborne and Dartmouth. RN Coll., Osborne, 1916; HMS Centurion, Midshipman, 1920; HMS Eagle, Sub Lt and Lt, 1924-26; specialized in Navigation at HMS Dryad, 1927; served HMS Cornflower, 1927-30; HMS Wallace, 1932; HMS Resolution, 1933-36; RN Staff College, 1936; Commander, HMS York, 1938; in command HMS Wallace, 1940; Admiralty, 1941; Staff of C-in-C Med. 1942-43; Captain, 1943; Invasion of Normandy, 1944; in command, HMS Cleopatra, 1944-46; Naval Asst to Second Sea Lord, 1949-51; in command HMS Implacable, 1952; Rear-Admiral, 1953; Chief-of-Staff to C-in-C, Portsmouth, 1953-55; Vice-Admiral, 1956; Chief of Allied Staff, Mediterranean, 1955-58; retired 1958. *Address:* Moonhills Gate, Beaulieu, Hants. *T:* Beaulieu 340. *Clubs:* United Service, Royal Cruising, Royal Ocean Racing.

**ROBERTSHAW, Wilfrid,** MA; Director of Bradford City Art Gallery and Museums, 1939-58; *b* 11 May 1893; *s* of late Jonathan and Emma Robertshaw; *m* 1920, Doris, *d* of late Edward and Janet Smith; one *d* (one *s* decd). *Educ:* Bradford; Leeds University. Librarian and Asst Keeper, Yorkshire Museum, York, 1915-19; Chief Asst, Bradford Public Libraries, 1919-26; Dep. Dir, Bradford City Art Gallery and Museums, 1926-39. Hon. Sec.: Assoc. of Assistant Librarians (Yorkshire Div.), 1922-23; Bradford Historical and Antiquarian Soc., 1926-34, Pres., 1934-35, 1955-57; Hon. Editor, The Bradford Antiquary, 1935-; Hon. Sec., Bradford Diocesan Area Cttee, Nat. Register of Archives, 1950-70; Mem., Exec. Cttee, WR Yorks (N Section) Cttee, Nat. Register of Archives, 1954-67; Mem., Bradford Diocesan Adv. Cttee for the Care of Churches, 1965-; Hon. Member: Bradford Arts Club; Bradford Historical and Antiquarian Soc. *Publications:* Official Handbook of Bolling Hall Museum, 1954; Centenary History of St Philip's Church School, Bradford, 1964; (ed.) West Yorkshire Deeds, 1931-36; Registers of the Independent Chapel of Kipping in the parish of Bradford, 1937-54; forewords to art exhibition catalogues; reviews, articles and papers in Librarian and Book World, etc., Studio and other art jls, and periodicals and newspapers. *Recreations:* research into art, social history and genealogy; music. *Address:* 1241 Thornton Road, Thornton, Bradford, Yorks. *T:* Thornton 3277.

**ROBERTSON,** family name of **Baron Robertson of Oakridge.**

**ROBERTSON OF OAKRIDGE,** 1st Baron *cr* 1961, of Oakridge; **Gen. Brian Hubert Robertson,** Bt, *cr* 1919, of Welbourn; GCB 1952 (CB 1943); GBE 1949 (CBE 1942); KCMG 1947; KCVO 1944; DSO 1919; MC; DL; *b* 22 July 1896; *e s* of late FM Sir William Robertson, Bt, GCB, GCMG, GCVO; *S* father, 1933; *m* 1926, Edith, *d* of late J. B. Macindoe, Glasgow; one *s* two *d*. Served European War, 1914-19 (despatches, DSO, MC); Waziristan Expedition, 1922-23 (despatches, Bt Major); retired pay, 1933; Managing Director, Dunlop South Africa Ltd, 1935; served Middle East, 1941-43 (CBE, CB); Chief Administrative Officer to General Alexander, C-in-C Italy, 1944-45; (KCVO); restored to the Active List Oct. 1945; Lt-Gen. 1946; Dep. Mil. Gov., CCG, 1945-47; Gen. 1947; C-in-C and Mil. Gov., 1947-49; UK High Commissioner, Allied High Commission, Germany, 1949-50; Commander-in-Chief, MELF, 1950-53, retd Nov. 1953. ADC Gen. to King George VI, 1949-52 and to the Queen, Feb.-June 1952. Chairman: British Transport Commission, 1953-61; ITA General Advisory Council, 1965-68. Director, Dunlop Co. Ltd, 1961-69; Vice-Pres., International Sleeping Car Co. President: Forces Aid Society; Lord Roberts Workshops; Regular Forces Employment Association; Anglo-German Assoc.; Vice-President, Gloucester Association of Boys' Clubs. Colonel Commandant RE, 1950-60. REME, 1951-61; Hon. Col RE (AER, Tn), 1956-66; Hon. Col Engr and Ry Staff Corps, RE (TA), 1961-70. DL Gloucestershire, 1965; Master, Salters' Company, 1965. Hon. LLD Cambridge; CStJ; Comdr Legion of Honour; Comdr US Legion of Merit. *Heir: s* Major Hon. William Ronald Robertson, late Royal Scots Greys [*b* 8 Dec. 1930. *Educ:* Charterhouse]. *Address:* Iles Green, Far Oakridge, Gloucestershire. *Clubs:* United Service, Buck's.

*See also Sir W. P. M. Vincent, Bt.*

**ROBERTSON, Hon. Lord; Ian Macdonald Robertson,** TD 1946; a Senator of the College of Justice in Scotland (with judicial title of Lord Robertson) since 1966; *b* 30 Oct. 1912; *s* of late James Robertson and Margaret Eva Wilson, Broughty Ferry, Angus, and Edinburgh; *m* 1938, Anna Love Glen, *d* of late Judge James Fulton Glen, Tampa, Florida, USA; one *s* two *d*. *Educ:* Merchiston Castle School; Balliol College, Oxford; Edinburgh University. BA Oxford (Mod. Greats), 1934; LLB Edinburgh 1937; Vans Dunlop Schol. in Law, Edinburgh 1937. Member Faculty of Advocates, 1939; Advocate-Depute, 1949-51; QC (Scot.), 1954; Sheriff of Ayr and Bute, 1961-66; Sheriff of Perth and Angus, 1966. Chairman Medical Appeals Tribunal, 1957-63; Scottish Jt Council for Teachers' Salaries, 1965; Member Court of Session Rules Council, 1955-58; External Examiner in law subjects, Aberdeen, Glasgow, Edinburgh and St Andrews Universities; Member Committee on Conflicts of Jurisdiction affecting Children, 1958; Gov. of Merchiston Castle School, 1954; Assessor on Court of Edinburgh Univ., 1967. Served War of 1939-45, 8th Bn The Royal Scots (The Royal Regt); commd 1939; SO (Capt.), 44th Lowland Brigade (15th Scottish Division), Normandy and NW Europe (despatches). *Publication:* From Normandy to the Baltic, 1945. *Recreation:* golf. *Address:* 49 Moray Place, Edinburgh 3. *T:* 031-225 6637. *Clubs:* New; Honourable Company of Edinburgh Golfers.

*See also Sir James W. Robertson.*

**ROBERTSON, Alan,** OBE 1965; FRS 1964; BA; DSc; Deputy Chief Scientific Officer, ARC Unit of Animal Genetics, Edinburgh; *b* 21 Feb. 1920; *s* of late John Mouat Robertson and Annie Grace; *m* 1947, Margaret Sidney, *y d* of late Maurice Bernheim; two *s* one *d*. *Educ:* Liverpool Institute; Gonville and Caius College, Cambridge. Operational Research Section, Coastal Command, RAF, 1943-46. ARC Unit of Animal Genetics, Edinburgh, 1947-. Hon. Prof., Edinburgh Univ., 1967. Hon. Dr rer nat Univ. of Hohenheim, 1968. Gold Medal, Royal Agric. Soc., 1958. *Publications:* papers in scientific jls. *Recreations:* gardening, tennis. *Address:* 47 Braid Road, Edinburgh 10. *T:* 031-447 4239. *Club:* Farmers'.

**ROBERTSON, Alec;** *see* Robertson, A. T. P.

**ROBERTSON, Sir Alexander,** Kt 1961; DCM 1916. Formerly Metropolitan Police: Assistant Commissioner, 1956-58, Deputy Commissioner, 1958-61; retired 31 Oct. 1961. *Recreations:* golf, fishing. *Address:* Dunkeld,

Wansunt Road, Bexley, Kent. *T:* Crayford 21878.

**ROBERTSON, Prof. Sir Alexander,** Kt 1970; CBE 1963; William Dick Professor of Animal Health, University of Edinburgh, since 1953; Director: Veterinary Field Station, since 1969; Centre for Tropical Veterinary Medicine, since 1970; *b* 3 Feb. 1908; *m* 1936, Janet McKinlay; two *d. Educ:* Stonehaven Mackie Acad.; Aberdeen University; and Royal (Dick) Veterinary College, Edinburgh. MA Aberdeen, 1929; BSc Aberdeen, 1930; PhD Edinburgh, 1940; MRCVS, 1934. Demonstrator in Anatomy, Royal (Dick) Veterinary College, Edinburgh, 1934; Vet. Inspector, Min. of Agriculture, 1935-37; Sen. Lectr in Physiology, 1938-44, Prof. of Vet. Hygiene, 1944-53, Director, 1951-54, Royal (Dick) School of Veterinary Studies, Univ. of Edinburgh; Dean of Faculty of Vet. Medicine, Univ. of Edinburgh, 1964-70. Exec. Officer for Scotland, Farm Livestock Emergency Service, 1942-47. FRSE, 1945; FRIC, 1946; FRSH, 1950; FRZSScot, 1952; Mem. Departmental Cttee on Foot and Mouth Disease, 1952-54; Pres. Brit. Vet. Assoc., 1954-55; Vice-Pres. Roy. Zoological Soc. of Scotland, 1959-; Mem. Governing Body, Animal Virus Research Inst., Pirbright, 1954-62; Mem. Council Royal Coll. of Veterinary Surgeons, 1957- (Treasurer, 1964-67; Vice-Pres., 1967-68, 1969-70; Pres., 1968-69); Mem. Departmental Cttee of Inquiry into Fowl Pest, 1960-61; Mem. Governing Body Rowett Research Institute, 1962-; Chairman: Sci. Adv. Panel, Pig Industry Develt Authority, 1962-68; Research Adv. Cttee, Meat and Livestock Commn, 1969-; Member: FAO/WHO Expert Panel on Veterinary Educn, 1962-; East African Natural Resources Research Council, 1963-; Mem. Council, RSE, 1963-65, Vice-Pres., 1969-. *Publications:* (Ed.) International Encyclopædia of Veterinary Medicine; numerous articles in veterinary and other scientific journals. *Recreations:* gardening, motoring, hill climbing. *Address:* 205 Mayfield Road, Edinburgh 9. *T:* 031-667 1242. *Clubs:* Caledonian, Farmers'; New (Edinburgh).

**ROBERTSON, Alexander Thomas Parke; (Alec Robertson);** FRAM, 1945; *b* 3 June 1892; *s* of J. R. S. Robertson, MD, and Elizabeth Macrory. *Educ:* Bradfield College, Berks; Royal Academy of Music. Began professional career as organist of Frensham Parish Church, 1914; Farnham Parish Church, 1914. Served European War, 1914-18, commissioned Hampshire Regt 1914; went India, 1914, Palestine, for active service, 1917. Joined The Gramophone Co. (His Master's Voice) in 1920 to develop educational use of the gramophone by means of lectures, building up repertoire, etc.; head of this Education Dept, 1925. Went to Rome to study theology, church music, etc., at Collegio Beda, 1930. Joined BBC in Gramophone Dept, 1940, Music Dept, 1941, finally Talks Dept, 1944; Specialist Talks Producer (Music), British Broadcasting Corporation, 1944-53; retired, 1953; besides organising output of music talks, became well known as a broadcaster. An authority on plainchant and early church music; writer, lecturer, and adjudicator. *Publications:* The Interpretation of Plainchant, 1937; Dvořák, 1945; Contrasts, Arts and Religion, 1947; Sacred Music, 1950; More than Music (autobiography), 1961; Catholic Church Music, 1961; Schubert's Songs (in symposium), 1946; ed. Chamber Music (Pelican), 1956; Jt ed., Pelican History of Music in 3 vols, 1961-66; Requiem, 1967; Church Cantatas of J. S. Bach, 1970; contrib. to Chambers's Encyc., Grove's Dictionary of Music and Musicians (new edn), and to musical and other journals. *Address:* Apsley Cottage, near Pulborough, Sussex. *T:* Coolham 359.

**ROBERTSON, Algar Ronald Ward,** CMG 1953; CBE 1948; ED; FRGS; *b* 8 Sept. 1902; *s* of late Hume Robertson, Elmhurst, Wimbledon Common; *m* 1st, 1931, Carol Rhys (marr. diss., 1954), *d* of late H. R. Maunsell; one *d*; 2nd, 1955, Marjorie Mary, *d* of F. W. Lovatt Smith, Magham Down, Sussex. *Educ:* Dean Close School, Cheltenham. Assistant Treas., Gold Coast, 1929-36; Deputy Treasurer, British Guiana, 1936-39; Financial Secretary, Fiji, 1940-48, Trinidad and Tobago, 1948-53, Nigeria, 1953-54; Federation of Nigeria, 1954-56. *Recreations:* polo, golf, tennis. *Address:* Maplestone Farm, Broad Oak, near Rye, Sussex. *T:* Brede 261. *Club:* Naval and Military.

**ROBERTSON, Andrew,** FRS 1940; *Educ:* Manchester Univ., DSc; Fairbairn Prize. Demonstrator in Engineering, Manchester University; Vulcan Fellow, University of Manchester; Major (Tech.), RAF; Prof. of Mechanical Engineering, Bristol Univ., 1919-46; President, Institution of Mechanical Engineers, 1945-46; Pres. Section G British Assoc., 1950; Principal of Bristol Merchant Venturers' Technical College, 1924-49. Hon. LLD Bristol, 1959; Hon. DSc Bath, 1969. *Publications:* Papers chiefly on Strength of Materials in Proc. Roy. Soc., Inst. Civil Engineers; Section G, British Association. *Address:* 15 Cranleigh Gardens, Bristol 9.

**ROBERTSON, Bryan Charles Francis,** OBE 1961; Director, Whitechapel Art Gallery, London, 1952-68; Author, Broadcasting and Television, etc.; *b* 1 April 1925; *yr s* of A. F. Robertson and Ellen Dorothy Black; unmarried. *Educ:* Battersea Grammar School. Worked and studied in France and Germany, 1947-48; Director, Heffer Gallery, Cambridge, 1949-51. Mem. Arts Council Art Panel, 1958-61; Mem. Contemporary Art Soc. Cttee, 1958- US Embassy Grant to visit United States, 1956; Lectr on art, Royal Ballet School, 1958; Ford Foundn Grant for research for writing, 1961; British Council Lecture Tour, SE Asia and Australian State Galleries, 1960. Since 1953 has organized major exhibitions at Whitechapel, including Turner, Hepworth, Moore, Stubbs, John Martin, Rowlandson and Gillray, Bellotto, Mondrian, de Stäel, Nolan, Davie, Smith, Malevich, Pollock, Richards, Australian Painting, Rothko, Tobey, Vaughan, Guston, Poliakof, Caro, Medley, etc. *Publications:* Jackson Pollock, a monograph, 1960; Sidney Nolan, a monograph, 1961; (with Sir Kenneth Clark and Colin MacInnes) Robert Motherwell, a monograph, 1964; contribs (art criticism) to London Magazine, Art News (US), Spectator, New Statesman, Twentieth Century, Listener, Cambridge Review, Museums Jl, etc. *Address:* 73 Barnsbury Street, N1. *Club:* Savile.

**ROBERTSON, Catherine Christian,** MA; Headmistress of George Watson's Ladies' College, 1926-45; *b* 10 Dec. 1886; *d* of late Alexander Robertson, Perth, and Mary Macfarlane Duncan, Edinburgh. *Educ:* privately; Perth Academy; University of Edinburgh. Graduated in Arts, with Hons in English Literature and Language, Class II, 1910; Cherwell Hall, Oxford; Diploma of Education, 1911; George Scott Travelling Scholar, 1911. Head of the English Department, Edinburgh Ladies: Coll., 1919-26; travel in America as Chautauqua Scholar of the English-Speaking Union (first Scotswoman to hold this award), 1925. President, Association of Headmistresses,

Scottish Branch, 1941-42; Vice-Chairman of Council, Girls' Training Corps, Scotland, 1942. *Recreations:* walking, foreign travel, music. *Address:* 6 Bruntsfield Crescent, Edinburgh 10. *T:* 031-447 1266. *Club:* Ladies' Caledonian (Edinburgh).

**ROBERTSON, Maj.-Gen. Cecil Bruce,** CB 1948; CBE 1946; MC 1918; DL; JP; *b* 8 March 1897; *er s* of late W. Bruce Robertson, 26 Kensington Palace Gdns, London, W, and of Mrs Bruce Robertson; *m* 1925, Sheila Mary, *d* of late Brig.-Gen. F. A. MacFarlan, CB; two *s* one *d*. *Educ:* Cheltenham; RMC Sandhurst. Commnd 2nd Lt The Argyll and Sutherland Highlanders, 1914. GSO2 HQ1 Corps, 1939-40; GSO1, 45 Div., 1940-41; Bde Commander 44 Div., 1941-42; DD of O (O) War Office, 1943; Director of Combined Operations (Military), 1943-45; BGS Southern Command, 1945-47; Chief of Staff Southern Command, 1947-48. Temp. Major-Gen., 1947; retired, 1948. DL Devon, 1954; JP 1955. *Recreations:* shooting, fishing. *Address:* The Glebe House, Chudleigh, Devon. *T:* Chudleigh 2223. *Club:* Army and Navy.

**ROBERTSON, Prof. Charles Martin;** FBA 1967; Lincoln Professor of Classical Archæology and Art, University of Oxford, since 1961; Fellow of Lincoln College; *b* 11 Sept. 1911; *s* of late Professor Donald Struan Robertson, FBA, FSA, and Petica Coursolles Jones; *m* 1942, Theodosia Cecil Spring Rice; four *s* two *d*. *Educ:* Leys School, Cambridge; Trinity College, Cambridge. BA Cambridge, 1934, MA 1947; student at British School of Archæology, Athens, 1934-36; Asst Keeper, Dept of Greek and Roman Antiquities, British Museum, 1936-48 (released for service, War of 1939-45, 1940-46); Yates Professor of Classical Art and Archæology in the Univ. of London (Univ. Coll.), 1948-61. Corresp. Mem., German Archæological Inst., 1953; Ordinary Mem., 1953; Chm., Man. Cttee, British School at Athens, 1958-68. Mem., Inst. for Advanced Study, Princeton, 1968-69. *Publications:* Why Study Greek Art? (Inaugural Lecture), 1949; Greek Painting, 1959; The Visual Arts of the Greeks (in The Greeks), 1962; Between Archæology and Art History (Inaugural Lecture), 1963; Crooked Connections (poems), 1970. Articles, notes and reviews since 1935, in British and foreign periodicals. *Address:* Sheepstead House, Abingdon, Berks. *T:* Frilford Heath 252.

**ROBERTSON, Douglas William,** CMG 1947; DSO 1918; MC 1918; *b* 30 Nov. 1898; 2nd *surv s* of late Rev. J. A. Robertson, MA; *m* 1924, Mary Eagland (*d* 1968), *y d* of late W. E. Longbottom, Adelaide; no *c*. *Educ:* George Watson's College, Edinburgh. 2nd Lt KRRC, 1917; France, 1918 (wounded, MC, DSO, despatches); Administrative Service, Uganda, 1921-50; Resident of Buganda, 1945; Secretary for African Affairs, Uganda, 1947-50, retired, 1950. *Address:* 3a Ravelston Park, Edinburgh. *Clubs:* East India and Sports; New (Edinburgh).

**ROBERTSON, Edith Anne;** *b* Glasgow, 1883; *e d* of Robert Stewart of Clarewood, Limpsfield; *m* 1919, Rev. Professor J. A. Robertson (*d* 1955); three *d*. *Publications:* Songs of Pilgrimage and Battle, 1916; The Life and Letters of St Francis Xavier, Missionary, Mystic, Explorer, 1917; Poems, Second Book, 1919; Life of St Francis Xavier in the Modern Series of Missionary Biographies, 1930; He is Become My Song, 1930; Poems frae the Suddron o Walter de la Mare made ower intil Scots, 1955; Voices Frae the City o Trees, 1955; Collected Ballads and Poems in the Scots Tongue, 1967; Translations into the Scots Tongue of Poems of G. M. Hopkins, 1968; Forest Voices, and other poems in English, 1968. Author of historical play, Lady Jonet Douglas. *Address:* c/o Post Office, Dalry, Castle-Douglas, Kirkcudbrightshire, Scotland. *Club:* PEN.

**ROBERTSON, Francis Calder F.;** *see* Ford Robertson.

**ROBERTSON, George Paterson;** Executive Director, National and Commercial Banking Group Ltd, since 1969; *b* 28 March 1911; 2nd *s* of Alexander Peterson Robertson and Helen Allan Guthrie; *m* 1941, Mary Martin Crichton; one *d* (one *s* decd). *Educ:* Allan Glen's Sch., Glasgow. Commissioned RAF Accountant Branch, 1940-46; Cashier and Gen. Manager, The Royal Bank of Scotland, 1965-68; Director: The Royal Bank of Scotland, 1967-68; Glyn Mills & Co., 1965-68; Williams Deacon's Bank Ltd, 1965-68; Scottish Agricultural Securities Corp. Ltd, 1965-68. Pres., Inst. of Bankers in Scotland, 1967-69; Vice-Pres., British Bankers' Assoc., 1968-69; Past Hon. Treasurer: Earl Haig Fund (Scotland), 1965-68; Officers' Assoc. (Scottish Br.), 1965-68; Scottish Veterans' Garden City Assoc. Inc., 1965-68. *Address:* 3 Kings Court, Beckenham, Kent. *T:* 01-650 5414. *Clubs:* Caledonian, New (Edinburgh); Western (Glasgow).

**ROBERTSON, H. Rocke,** CC (Canada); CM, FRCS(C), FRCSE, FACS, FRSC; Principal and Vice-Chancellor of McGill University, 1962-70; Dec. 1962; *b* 4 Aug. 1912; *s* of Harold Bruce Robertson and Helen McGregor Rogers; *m* 1937, Beatrice Roslyn Arnold; three *s* one *d*. *Educ:* St Michael's Sch., Victoria, BC; Ecole Nouvelle, Switzerland; Brentwood College, Victoria, BC; McGill University. Montreal Gen. Hospital: rotating, 1936; pathology, 1937-38; Clin. Asst in Surg., Roy. Infirmary, Edinburgh, 1938-39; Demonstr in Anat., Middx Hosp. Med. Sch., 1939; Jun. Asst in Surg., Montreal Gen. Hosp., 1939-40; Chief of Surgery: Shaughnessy Hosp., DVA, Vancouver, 1945-59 (Prof. of Surg., Univ. of BC, 1950-59); Vancouver Gen. Hosp., 1950-59; Montreal Gen. Hosp., 1959-62 (Prof. of Surg., McGill University, 1959-62). Mem. Nat. Research Coun., 1964. Dir, Bell Telephone Co. of Canada, 1965-. Hon. DCL, Bishop's Univ., 1963; Hon. LLD: Manitoba, 1964; Toronto, 1964; Victoria, 1964; Glasgow, 1965; Michigan, 1967; Dartmouth, 1967; Hon. DSc: Brit. Columbia, 1964; Memorial, 1968; Dr de l'Univ., Montreal, 1965. FRSA 1963. *Publications:* numerous in scientific journals and text books. *Recreations:* tennis, fishing, gardening, golf. *Address:* McGill University, Montreal, PQ, Canada. *T:* 392-5347. *Clubs:* Mount Royal, University, Faculty, Indoor Tennis (Montreal).

**ROBERTSON, Maj.-Gen. Ian Argyll, of Brackla,** CB 1968; MBE 1947; MA; Representative in Scotland of Messrs Spink & Son, since 1969; *b* 17 July 1913; 2nd *s* of John Argyll Robertson and Sarah Lilian Pitt Healing; *m* 1939, Marjorie Violet Isobel Duncan; two *d*. *Educ:* Winchester Coll.; Trinity Coll., Oxford. Commnd Seaforth Highlanders, 1934; Brigade Major: 152 Highland Bde, 1943; 231 Infantry Bde, 1944; GSO2, Staff College, Camberley, 1944-45; AAG, 15 Indian Corps, 1945-46; GSO1, 51 Highland Div., 1952-54; Comdg 1st Bn Seaforth Highlanders, 1954-57; Comdg Support Weapons Wing, 1957-59; Comdg 127 (East Lancs) Inf. Bde, TA, 1959-61; Nat. Defence College, Delhi, 1962-63; Comdg School of Infantry, 1963-64; Commanding 51st Highland Division, 1964-66; Director of Army Equipment Policy, Ministry of Defence,

1966-68; retd. *Recreations:* golf, fishing, shooting. *Address:* Brackla House, Nairn. *T:* Cawdor 220. *Clubs:* Army and Navy, MCC; Vincent's (Oxford).

**ROBERTSON, Ian (Gow),** MA Oxon; Keeper of Western Art, Ashmolean Museum, Oxford, and of Hope Collection of Engraved Portraits, 1962-68; Fellow of Worcester College, Oxford; *b* Killearn, Stirlingshire, 20 Sept. 1910; *er s* of John Gow Robertson and Margaret Stewart. *Educ:* The King's School, Canterbury. Studied art at continental centres, in US and in public and private collections in UK. Assistant Keeper in Dept of Fine Art, Ashmolean Museum, 1931. Ministry of Home Security, 1939-41; served in Royal Navy, 1941-46. Senior Assistant Keeper, Ashmolean Museum, 1949. *Recreations:* gardening, listening to music. *Address:* 15 Gledhow Gardens, SW5. *Club:* RNVR.

**ROBERTSON, Ian Macbeth,** MVO 1956; Under-Secretary, Scottish Education Department, since 1966; *b* 1 Feb. 1918; *s* of late Sheriff-Substitute J. A. T. Robertson; *m* 1947, Anne Stewart Marshall. *Educ:* Melville College; Edinburgh University. Served War of 1939-45 in Middle East and Italy; Royal Artillery and London Scottish, Captain. Entered Dept of Health for Scotland, 1946. Private Secretary to Minister of State, Scottish Office, 1951-52 and to Secretary of State for Scotland, 1952-55. Asst Secretary, Dept of Health for Scotland, 1955; Assistant Under-Secretary of State, Scottish Office, 1963-64; Under-Secretary, Scottish Development Department, 1964-65. *Address:* 19 Palmerston Road, Edinburgh 9. *T:* 031-667 5432. *Clubs:* Naval and Military; New (Edinburgh).

**ROBERTSON, Ian Macdonald;** *see* Robertson, Hon. Lord.

**ROBERTSON, James,** CBE 1969; MA; FRCM; Hon. FTCL; Hon. GSM; Hon. RAM; Director, London Opera Centre, since 1964; *b* 17 June 1912; *s* of Ainslie John Robertson and Phyllis Mary Roughton; *m* 1949, Rachel June Fraser; two *s*. *Educ:* Winchester College; Trinity College, Cambridge; Conservatorium, Leipzig; Royal College of Music, London. On musical staff, Glyndebourne Opera, 1937-39; Conductor, Carl Rosa Opera, Co., 1938-39; Conductor, Canadian Broadcasting Corp., 1939-40; Air Ministry, 1940-42; RAFVR (Intelligence), 1942-46. Director, Sadler's Wells Opera Company, 1946-54; Conductor of National Orchestra of New Zealand Broadcasting Service, Sept. 1954-Nov. 1957. Conductor, Touring Opera, 1958; Adviser on Opera, Théâtre de la Monnaie, Brussels, 1960-61; Artistic and Musical Director, New Zealand Opera Co., 1962-63. *Recreation:* languages. *Address:* 29 Warwick Rd, W5.

**ROBERTSON, Maj.-Gen. James Alexander Rowland,** CB 1958; CBE 1956 (OBE 1949; MBE 1942); DSO 1944 (Bar 1945); Administrative Official, National Canine Defence League, since 1969; *b* 23 March 1910; *s* of Colonel James Currie Robertson, CIE, CMG, CBE, IMS, and Catherine Rowland Jones; *m* 1949, Ann Madeline Tosswill (*d* 1949). *Educ:* Aysgarth School; Epsom College, RMC, Sandhurst. Commissioned 2 Lieutenant IA, 1930, attached 1st KOYLI; posted 6th Gurkha Rifles, 1931; Instructor Sch. of Physical Training, 1936-37; Staff Coll., Quetta, July-Dec. 1941; Bde Major 1 (Maymyo) Bde, Jan.-June, 1942; Bde Major, 106 I Inf. Bde, 1942-44; Comdr 1/7 Gurkha Rifles, 1944-45; Comdr 48 Ind. Inf. Bde, 1945-47; GSO 1, Instr Staff Coll., Quetta, June-Nov., 1947; Comdr 1/6th Gurkha Rifles, 1947-48; GSO 1 Gurkha Planning Staff, March-June, 1948; GSO 1 Malaya comd, June-Nov. 1948; BGS 1948-49. GSO 1, War Office, 1950-52; Col GS, 1 Corps, Germany, 1952-54; Comdr 51 Indep. Bde, 1955-57; Commander 17 Gurkha Division Overseas Commonwealth Land Forces, and Maj.-Gen. Brigade of Gurkhas, 1958-61; GOC Land Forces, Middle East Command, 1961-63; Gurkha Liaison Officer, War Office, 1963-64, retd. Personnel Dir, NAAFI, 1964-69. Colonel, 6th Queen Elizabeth's Own Gurkha Rifles, 1961-69; Chm. Gurkha Brigade Assoc., 1968. *Recreations:* fishing and an outdoor life. *Club:* Army and Navy.

**ROBERTSON, Sir James (Anderson),** Kt 1968; CBE 1963 (OBE 1949; MBE 1942); Chief Constable of Glasgow since 1960; *b* Glasgow, 8 April 1906; *s* of James Robertson, East Haugh, Pitlochry, Perthshire and later of Glasgow, and Mary Rankin Anderson, Glasgow; *m* 1942, Janet Lorraine Gilfillan Macfarlane, Largs, Ayrshire; two *s* one *d*. *Educ:* Provanside Sch., Glasgow and Glasgow Univ. BL 1936. Joined City of Glasgow Police, 1926; Dep. Chief Constable, 1943. Zone Police Comdr (Designate) (Civil Defence). Chairman, Glasgow Standing Conf. of Voluntary Youth Organisations. Queen's Police Medal, 1961. OStJ 1964. *Recreations:* golf and gardening. *Address:* Police Headquarters, Glasgow. *T:* 041-522 3500; 3 Kirklee Road, Glasgow, W. *T:* 041-339 4400.

**ROBERTSON, James Cassels;** Vice-Lieutenant of Dunbartonshire since 1968; Director, William Robertson Shipowners Ltd, Glasgow; *b* 19 May 1921; *yr s* of late William Francis Robertson and of Harriett Willis Cassels; *m* 1947, Joan, *er d* of late Lt-Comdr E. Kirkpatrick-Crockett, RN, and of Leila Bootiman; two *s* one *d*. *Educ:* Winchester. Served in RNVR, 1940-46. DL Dunbartonshire, 1965. Chm., Scottish and Ulster Area, British Shipping Fedn, 1968. *Recreation:* yachting. *Address:* Rossland, Helensburgh, Dunbartonshire. *T:* Helensburgh 4573. *Clubs:* Royal Thames Yacht; Royal Yacht Squadron (Cowes); Royal Northern Yacht (Rhu) (Cdre).

**ROBERTSON, James Geddes,** CMG 1961; Under-Secretary, Ministry of Housing and Local Government (formerly Department of Economic Affairs), since 1965; Chairman, Northern Economic Planning Board, since 1965; *b* 29 Nov. 1910; *s* of late Captain A. M. Robertson, Portsoy, Banffshire; *m* 1939, Marion Mitchell Black; one *s* one *d*. *Educ:* Fordyce Academy, Banffshire; George Watson's College, Edinburgh; Edinburgh University. Kitchener Schol., 1928-32, MA 1st cl. Hons History (Edinburgh), 1932. Entered Ministry of Labour as Third Class Officer, 1933; Principal, 1943; on exchange to Commonwealth Dept of Labour and Nat. Service, Australia, 1947-49; Asst Sec., Min of Labour, 1956; Member of Government Delegations to Governing Body and Conference of ILO, 1956-60, and Social Cttee, Council of Europe, 1953-61; Training Department, Ministry of Labour, 1963-65; Served War of 1939-45, RAF 1942-45. *Address:* Woodside, Wylam, Northumberland. *T:* Wylam 2112.

**ROBERTSON, Maj.-Gen. James Howden,** QHDS 1967; Director, Army Dental Service, since 1970; *b* 16 Oct. 1915; *s* of John and Marion Robertson, Glasgow and Creetown; *m* 1942, Muriel Edna, *d* of Alfred Jefferies, Elgin; two *s* one *d*. *Educ:* White Hill Sch., Glasgow; Glasgow Dental Hospital. LDS, RFPS(G) 1939; FDS, RCSE 1957. Lieut, Army Dental

Corps, 1939; Captain 1940; Major 1943; Lt-Col 1954; Col 1962; Brig. 1967; Maj.-Gen. 1970. Served in UK and Norway, 1939-44, Europe, 1944-50; Senior Specialist in Dental Surgery, 1957; Middle East, 1958-61; Consultant, CMH Aldershot, 1962-67; Consulting Dental Surgeon to the Army, 1967-70. OStJ 1969. *Publications:* various articles in medical and dental jls on oral and maxillo-facial surgery. *Recreations:* wildfowling, fishing, gardening. *Address:* Struan House, Echobarn Lane, Wrecclesham, Farnham, Surrey. *T:* 6876.

**ROBERTSON, Sir James (Wilson),** KT 1965; GCMG 1957 (KCMG 1953); GCVO 1956; KBE 1948 (MBE 1931); Director, Barclays Bank DCO, since 1961; *b* 27 Oct. 1899; *e s* of late James Robertson, Broughty Ferry, Angus and Edinburgh, and late Mrs Robertson, Glenlyon, Spylaw Bank Road, Colinton, Midlothian; *m* 1926, Nancy, *er d* of H. S. Walker, Huddersfield; one *s* one *d*. *Educ:* Merchiston Castle School, Edinburgh; Balliol College, Oxford. BA 1922, MA 1930; Honorary Fellow of Balliol, 1953. Oxford University Rugby XV, 1921. Officer Cadet, 1918-19; 2nd Lieutenant, Black Watch, 1919; entered Sudan Political Service, 1922; Assistant Dist Commissioner and Dist Comr, 1922-36. Jebel Aulia compensation commission, 1936. Sub-Governor White Nile Province, 1937; Dep. Governor Gezira Province, 1939; actg Governor Gezira Province, 1940-41. Asst Civil Secretary, 1941; Deputy Civil Secretary, 1942; Civil Secretary Sudan Government, 1945-53; Chairman British Guiana Constitutional Commission, 1953-54; Director, Uganda Co. Ltd, 1954-55 and 1961-69; Governor-General and Commander-in-Chief of Federation of Nigeria, 1955-60 (first Governor-General and Commander-in-Chief of the Independent Federation of Nigeria, Oct.-Nov. 1960). Comr to examine the question of Kenya Coastal Strip, Oct. 1961. Chairman: Commonwealth Inst., 1961-68; Central Coun. Roy. Over-Seas League, 1962-67; Sudan British Pensioners' Assoc., 1961-67; Coun. for Aid to African Students, 1961-; Pres. Overseas Service Pensioners' Assoc., 1961-; Pres. Britain-Nigeria Assoc., 1961-; a Governor, Queen Mary Coll., Univ. of London, 1961-; Mem. Council, Royal Commonwealth Society for the Blind; Deputy Chairman, Nat. Cttee for Commonwealth Immigrants, 1965-68. Hon. LLD Leeds University, 1961. FRSA 1964. Wellcome Medal, Royal African Society, 1961. Order of the Nile, 4th Class, 1934. KStJ 1955. *Address:* The Old Bakehouse, Cholsey, near Wallingford, Berkshire. *T:* Cholsey 234; Douglas Cottage, Killichonan, Rannoch Station, Perthshire. *T:* Bridge of Gaur 242. *Club:* Athenæum.

*See also Hon. Lord Robertson.*

**ROBERTSON, John;** MP (Lab) Paisley since 1961; *b* 3 Feb. 1913; *s* of William Robertson; *m* 1939; two *s* three *d*. *Educ:* elementary and secondary schools. Formerly District Secretary and Assistant Divisional Organizer of the Amalgamated Engineering Union, West of Scotland. Mem., Lanarkshire County Council, Motherwell and Wishaw Town Council, 1946-52. Member of Labour Party, 1943-; contested (Lab) Scotstoun Division of Glasgow, General Election, Oct. 1951. *Recreations:* politics, painting, bowling and Trade Union. *Address:* 260 Ladywell Road, Motherwell, Lanarkshire. *T:* Motherwell 62391.

**ROBERTSON, John Monteath,** CBE 1962; FRS 1945; FRIC, FInstP, FRSE; MA, PhD, DSc (Glasgow); Gardiner Professor of Chemistry, University of Glasgow, 1942-70; Director of Laboratories since 1955; *b* 24 July 1900; *s* of William Robertson and Jane Monteath, of Nether Fordun, Auchterarder; *m* 1930, Stella Kennard Nairn, MA; two *s* one *d*. *Educ:* Perth Academy; Glasgow University. Commonwealth Fellow, USA, 1928; Member staff of Davy Faraday Laboratory of Royal Institution, 1930; Senior Lecturer in Physical Chemistry, University of Sheffield, 1939; Scientific Adviser (Chemical) to Bomber Command, 1941; Hon. Scientific Adviser to RAF, 1942. George Fisher Baker Lecturer, Cornell Univ., USA, 1951; Visiting Prof., Univ. of California, Berkeley, USA, 1958. Member, University Grants Committee, 1960-65; President, Chemical Society, 1962-64. Davy Medal, Royal Soc., 1960; Longstaff Medal, Chemical Society, 1966. Corresp. Member Turin Academy of Sciences, 1962. Hon. LLD Aberdeen; Hon. DSc Strathclyde. *Publications:* Organic Crystals and Molecules, 1953; papers and articles on chemical, physical, and X-ray diffraction subjects in Proc. Royal Soc., Jl of Chem. Soc., etc. *Address:* 42 Bailie Drive, Bearsden, near Glasgow. *T:* 041-942 2640. *Club:* Athenæum.

**ROBERTSON, Col John Richard Hugh,** OBE 1951; Chief Inspecting Officer of Railways, Ministry of Transport, since 1969; *b* 18 Nov. 1912; *s* of Col James C. Robertson, CMG, CIE, CBE, IMS, and Catherine Mary Jones; *m* 1940, Elizabeth, *d* of W. Froggatt, MC; two *s*. *Educ:* Wellington Coll.; RMA, Woolwich; Trinity Hall, Cambridge Univ. RMA, Woolwich, 1931 (Prize Cadet, Cadet Schol., Army Schol., and Sword of Honour; boxing, athletics and pentathlon teams); RE, 1932; Trinity Hall, Cambridge, 1933; BA (Hons, Mech. Sci. Tripos), 1935. Served War of 1939-45: BEF, 1939; Norway, 1940; psc, 1941; AQMG, MECTC, 1943; AQMG CTC, India and SORE, DCO, India, 1944; Comd 46 Ind. Beach Gp, 1945. AQMG, Malaya, Chief Instructor Transptn Trg Centre, UK, 1946; JSSC, AAG AG3, War Office, 1947; Chief Instructor, Greek Staff Coll., 1950; CO, ME Transptn Regt, RE, 1952; Chief Instr (Tactics), SME, Chatham, 1954; AAG, MPI, War Office, 1957; Inspecting Officer of Railways, 1959. MInstT 1969. *Recreations:* fishing, wildfowling. *Address:* Little Green, Frensham, Surrey. *T:* Frensham 2775. *Clubs:* United Service, United Hunts.

**ROBERTSON, Lewis (Findlay),** CBE 1969; Chairman, Scottish Arts Council, since 1970; Member, Arts Council of Great Britain, since 1970; Member, Monopolies Commission, since 1969; *b* 28 Nov. 1922; *s* of John Farquharson Robertson and Margaret Arthur; *m* 1950, Elspeth Badenoch; three *s* one *d*. *Educ:* Trinity Coll., Glenalmond. Accountancy training; RAF Intelligence; Industrialist. Chm., 1968-70, and Man. Dir, 1965-70, Scott & Robertson Ltd. Member of Court, Univ. of Dundee, 1967-70; Chm. Eastern Regional Hosp. Bd (Scotland), 1960-70; Trustee (Exec. Cttee), Carnegie Trust for Univs of Scotland; Mem. Provincial Synod, Episcopal Church of Scotland; Auditor, Diocese of Brechin, Mem. Cttee of Enquiry, Pharmaceutical Industry, 1965-67. *Recreations:* music and words. *Address:* Westdene, Perth Road, Dundee DD2 1LS. *Clubs:* Caledonian; New (Edinburgh); Eastern (Dundee).

**ROBERTSON, Muriel,** FRS 1947; MA, DSc (Glasgow); LLD (Glasgow) 1948; Protozoologist, Lister Inst., 1915-61; *b* 8 April 1883; *d* of Robert Andrew Robertson and Elizabeth Ritter. *Educ:* privately; Glasgow Univ. Carnegie Research Sch., 1905-06; Carnegie Research Fellow, 1907-10; Asst to late Prof. Minchin, 1909-10; on Staff Lister Inst., 1910-11; Protozoologist to Uganda Protectorate, 1911-14. *Publications:* numerous papers on Protozoology and bacteriology in various scientific journals. *Recreations:* sketching and walking. *Address:* Dogleap, Limavady, Co. Londonderry, Northern Ireland. *Club:* Cowdray.

**ROBERTSON, Commandant Dame Nancy (Margaret),** DBE 1957 (CBE 1953; OBE 1946); retired as Director of Women's Royal Naval Service (Dec. 1954-April 1958); *b* 1 March 1909; *er d* of Rev. William Cowper Robertson and Jessie Katharine (*née* McGregor). *Educ:* Esdaile School, Edinburgh; Paris. Secretarial work, London and Paris, 1928-39; WRNS, 1939. Formerly Superintendent Training, WRNS. *Recreations:* needlework, gardening. *Address:* Rose Cottage, Buckland Common, Tring, Herts. *T:* Cholesbury 354.

**ROBERTSON, Prof. Noel Farnie,** BSc Edinburgh; MA Cantab; PhD Edinburgh; FRSE; Professor of Agriculture and Rural Economy, University of Edinburgh, and Principal, East of Scotland College of Agriculture, since 1969; *b* 24 Dec. 1923; *o s* of James Robertson and Catherine Landles Robertson (*née* Brown); *m* 1948, Doreen Colina Gardner; two *s* two *d*. *Educ:* Trinity Academy, Edinburgh; University of Edinburgh; Trinity College, Cambridge. Plant Pathologist, West African Cacao Research Institute, 1946-48; Lecturer in Botany, University of Cambridge, 1948-59; Prof. of Botany, Univ. of Hull, 1959-69. *Address:* Boghall Farmhouse, Biggar Road, Edinburgh EH10 7DX. *T:* 031-445 3194.

**ROBERTSON, Patrick Allan Pearson,** CMG 1956; *b* 11 Aug. 1913; *s* of A. N. McI. Robertson; *m* 1939, Penelope Margaret Gaskell (*d* 1966); one *s* two *d*. *Educ:* Sedbergh School; King's College, Cambridge. Cadet, Tanganyika, 1936; Asst Dist Officer, 1938; Clerk of Exec. and Legislative Councils, 1945-46; Dist Officer, 1948; Principal Asst Sec., 1949; Financial Sec., Aden, 1951; Asst Sec., Colonial Office, 1956-57; Chief Sec., Zanzibar, 1958; Civil Sec., Zanzibar, 1961-64; Deputy British Resident, Zanzibar, 1963-64; retired, 1964. Associate Member, Commonwealth Parliamentary Association. Freeman, City of London. *Recreations:* golf, tennis, fishing. *Address:* Inver Lodge, Rosmuc, Co. Galway, Eire. *T:* Rosmuc 4. *Club:* Royal Commonwealth Society.

**ROBERTSON, Ronald Mackintosh;** Director, British Investment Trust Ltd, since 1969 (Manager, 1939-70); *b* 23 March 1905; *s* of late Lt-Col F. M. B. Robertson, DSO, The Black Watch, and late Gertrude Sanderson; *m* 1944, Mary Frances, *e d* of Col T. S. Irwin, Justicetown, Carlisle. *Educ:* Eton. Served War of 1939-45 with Lothians and Border Yeomanry until 1942 (wounded, 1940). Thereafter Military Police (Staff). Chairman: Electronic Trust Ltd; Technology Investments Ltd; Director: Royal Bank of Scotland Ltd; Hill Samuel British Trust; Hill Samuel International Trust. *Recreations:* shooting, racing. *Address:* Linnhous, Livingston, West Lothian. *T:* West Calder 242. *Clubs:* Boodle's; MCC.

**ROBERTSON, Prof. Rutherford Ness,** CMG 1968; FRS 1961; DSc; PhD; FAA; Master, University House, Australian National University, since 1969; *b* 29 Sept. 1913; *o c* of Rev. J. Robertson, MA, and Josephine Robertson; *m* 1937, Mary Helen Bruce Rogerson; one *s*. *Educ:* St Andrew's Coll., NZ; Univ. of Sydney; St John's Coll., Cambridge. Sydney Univ. Science Res. Schol., 1934-35, Linnean Macleay Fell., 1935-36. Exhibn of 1851 Res. Schol., 1936-39; Res. at Botany Sch., Cambridge, in plant physiology, 1936-39, PhD 1939; Asst Lectr, later Lectr, Botany Sch., Univ. of Sydney, 1939-46; Sen. Res. Offr, later Chief Res. Offr, Div. of Food Preservation, CSIRO, 1946-59 (res. in plant physiol. and biochem.); Sydney University: jointly in charge of Plant Physiol. Unit, 1952-59, Hon. Res. Associate, 1954-59; Visiting Prof., Univ. of Calif, Los Angeles, 1958-59; Kerney Foundn Lectr, Univ. of Calif, Berkeley, 1959; Mem. Exec., CSIRO 1959-62; DSc Sydney 1961; Prof. of Botany, Univ. of Adelaide, 1962-69, now Emeritus. Pres. Linnean Soc. of NSW, 1949; Hon. Sec. Austr. Nat. Res. Council, 1951-55; Corresp. Mem., Amer. Soc. of Plant Physiologists, 1953; FAA 1954; Clarke Memorial Medal, Roy. Soc. of NSW, 1955; Pres., Australian Academy of Science, 1970 (Sec. Biological Sciences, 1957-58); Foreign Associate, US National Academy of Sciences, 1962; Farrer Memorial Medal, 1963; Pres., Aust. and NZ Assoc. for the Advancement of Science, 1964-66. Chm., Aust. Research Grants Cttee, 1965-69. Hon. DSc: Tasmania, 1965; Monash 1970; Hon ScD Cambrdige, 1969. ANZAAS Medal, 1968. *Publications:* (with G. E. Briggs, FRS, and A. B. Hope) Electrolytes and Plant Cells, 1961; Protons, Electrons, Phosphorylation and Active Transport, 1968; various scientific papers on plant physiology and biochemistry. *Recreations:* riding, water colours. *Address:* University House, Australian National University, Canberra, ACT 2600, Australia. *Club:* Adelaide (Adelaide).

**ROBERTSON, Vernon Alec Murray,** CBE 1943; MC 1917, Bar 1918; *b* 29 Dec. 1890; *o s* of Alexander Robertson, Calcutta; *m* 1st, 1915, Ivy Kathleen (*decd*), *y d* of C. J. Cooper, Clapham Park, SW; one *s* two *d*; 2nd, 1934, Gertrude Ruth, *widow* of C. E. H. Morton, Bank Manager. *Educ:* Dover College; Crystal Palace School of Practical Engineering. Civil Engineer on Railway Work. Articled to late D. Gravell, MInstCE, 1909-12; SE & C Rly Engineers Department, 1912-19; GE Railway District Engineer, 1919; Underground Railways of London as Civil Engineer, 1928; Chief Engineer (Civil) LPTB, 1938; Engineer-in-Chief, 1940-43; Chief Civil Engineer to Southern Rly Co., 1944-48, British Rlys, Southern Region, 1948-51, retd 1951; Partner and consultant, Sir William Halcrow & Partners, Chartered Civil Engineers, Westminster, 1951-64. Served European War as NCO in London Scottish; commissioned RE 1915; France with BEF 1915-19 (despatches, MC and Bar); demob. as Major RE 1919; Past Col Comdg Engineer and Railway Staff Corps RE. Past Pres. InstCE; Past Pres. and Fellow, Permanent Way Institution; Hon. FSE; Hon. Mem. American Railway Engineering Association. *Recreation:* fishing. *Address:* 25 Chalfont Court, NW1. *T:* 01-935 5950. *Clubs:* Athenæum, Royal Automobile.

**ROBERTSON, Air Cdre William Duncan,** CBE 1968; Royal Air Force; Director of Operations Air Defence and Overseas since 1969; *b* 24 June 1922; *s* of William and Helen Robertson, Aberdeen; *m* 1st, 1952, Doreen Mary (*d* 1963), *d* of late Comdr G. A. C. Sharp, DSC, RN (retd); one *s* one *d*; 2nd, 1968, Ute, *d* of late Dr R. Koenig, Wesel, West Germany. *Educ:* Robert Gordon's Coll., Aberdeen. Sqdn Comdr, No 207 Sqdn, 1959-61. Gp Dir, RAF Staff Coll., 1962-65; Station Comdr, RAF Wildenrath, 1965-67; Dep. Dir, Administrative Plans, 1967; Dir of Ops (Plans), 1968. *Recreations:* golf, tennis. *Address:* Culter

Lodge, Milltimber, Aberdeenshire. *Club:* Royal Air Force.

**ROBERTSON, William Walter Samuel,** CBE 1957 (OBE 1950); Director, GoConCrete Ltd; Member, Eastern Electricity Board; *b* 3 July 1906; *s* of W. H. A. and A. M. Robertson (*née* Lane); *m* 1935, Kathleen Elizabeth Chawner East; one *s* two *d*. *Educ:* Bedford School; King's College, London. BSc (Eng.) First Class Hons, 1926. Apprenticeship to W. H. A. Robertson & Co. Ltd (Director, 1929) and to Torrington Mfg Co., USA, 1926-28. Regional Controller and Chm. of North Midland Regional Bd for Production, 1943-45; Chairman, Eastern Regional Bd for Industry, 1949-64 (Vice-Chm., 1945-49); Member Advisory Committee, Revolving Fund for Industry, 1955-58. MIMechE, 1943; MIPE, 1945. High Sheriff of Bedfordshire, 1963. Governor, St Felix School, Southwold. *Recreations:* rowing, golf, Rugby football. *Address:* Oakley House, Oakley, Beds. *T:* Oakley 2895. *Clubs:* Royal Automobile; Leander (Henley-on-Thames).

**ROBERTSON-JUSTICE, James Norval Harald;** Rector of the University of Edinburgh, 1957-60, 1963-66; *b* 15 June 1905; *o s* of late James Norval Justice, DSc, MIMM. *Educ:* Marlborough Coll.; Bonn University (Dr Phil, Nat. Sci.). Career undistinguished but varied, comprising some three score jobs in different parts of the world. Inventor of the rocket propelled net method of catching wildfowl for marking. LLD (Hon.) Edinburgh, 1960. *Publications:* various papers on ornithology, ecology and conservation. *Recreation:* falconry. *Address:* Spinningdale, Sutherland. *T:* Whiteface 223. *Clubs:* The Goat; Highland (Inverness).

**ROBESON, Paul Le Roy;** concert singer and actor; *b* Princeton, New Jersey, 9 April 1898; *s* of Rev. William D. Robeson and Louisa Bustill; *m* Eslanda Cardozo Goode (*d* 1965); one *s*. *Educ:* Rutgers Coll. (Scholar), BA; Columbia Univ., New York, LLB; Rutgers University, Hon. MA. Made first appearance on stage in New York, 1921; first appearance on concert platform in New York in 1925, as singer of negro folk music which, together with his associate Lawrence Brown, he has played a leading part in developing; first appearance in London in Emperor Jones, 1925. Makes annual international concert tours with Lawrence Brown. Played the leading roles in Taboo, Emperor Jones, All God's Chillun, Black Boy, in New York; sang Ol' Man River in the Show Boat at Drury Lane, 1928; played title role in Othello at the Savoy, 1930; title role in Hairy Ape at Ambassadors, 1932; role of Jim Harris in All God's Chillun at Piccadilly, 1933; title role in film of Emperor Jones, 1933; role of Bosambo in film of Sanders of the River, 1935; title role in Stevedore at Embassy, 1935; title role in John Henry in New York, 1940; title role in Othello in USA, 1943-44 and 1944-45 and at Royal Shakespeare Theatre, Stratford-on-Avon, 1959. Hon. Dr Phil, Humboldt Univ., Berlin, 1960. Member: Phi Beta Kappa and Cap and Skull, Rutgers; Alpha Phi Alpha and Sigma Tau Sigma fraternities. *Publication:* Here I Stand, 1958. *Address:* c/o H. Lee Lurie, 10 E 40th Street, New York City.

**ROBEY, Douglas John Brett,** CMG 1960; Ambassador and Permanent United Kingdom Representative to the Council of Europe, since 1969; *b* 7 Aug. 1914; *s* of late E. J. B. and Margaret Robey; *m* 1943, Elizabeth, *d* of Col David D. Barrett, US Army (retd); two *s* one *d*. *Educ:* Cranleigh School; St John's College, Oxford; Ecole des Sciences Politiques, Paris. BA (History); Editor of The Cherwell. Joined HM Foreign Service, 1937. Served in China, USA, Paris, Berlin, Baghdad; Consul-Gen., Chicago, 1966-69. *Publication:* The Innovator 1945. *Recreations:* reading, writing, and the Niebelung Ring. *Address:* UK Delegation, 10 rue du Général de Castelnau, Strasbourg, France. *Club:* Travellers'.

**ROBEY, Edward George,** BA, LLB; Barrister-at-Law; a Metropolitan Magistrate since 1954; *s* of late Sir George Robey, CBE, and his first wife, the late Ethel Haydon; *m* 1942, Denise, *d* of late Denis Williams, Virginia Water. *Educ:* Westminster School; Jesus Coll., Cambridge. Called to Bar, Inner Temple, 1925; professional staff of Director of Public Prosecutions, 1932-50; apptd to Attorney-General's Executive for prosecution of the Major War Criminals at Nuremberg, 1945. *Recreation:* music. *Address:* 11 Shrewsbury House, Cheyne Walk, SW3. *T:* 01-352 2403. *Club:* Garrick.

**ROBICHAUD, Most Rev. Norbert;** *see* Moncton, Archbishop of, (RC).

**ROBIESON, Sir William,** Kt 1948; MA, LLD (Glasgow); JP; Editor of the Glasgow Herald, 1937-55; Chancellor's Assessor, Glasgow University, since 1956; *b* Fossoway, Kinross-shire, 29 May 1890; *s* of William D. Robieson, Schoolmaster; *m* 1919, Mabel Graham, *e d* of John Mackenzie, Sandbank, Argyll; one *d*. *Educ:* Dollar Academy; University of Glasgow. MA, Glasgow, 1912, First Class Honours in History; Assistant to Professor of History in the University of Glasgow, 1913-14; joined Editorial Staff of Glasgow Herald, 1914, and returned there, 1919, after serving with Cameron Highlanders and with Gold Coast Regt of West African Frontier Force; Assistant Editor of Glasgow Herald, 1926; Member of Royal Commission on Population, 1944-49; Trustee, National Galleries of Scotland, 1949-67, and National Museum of Antiquities of Scotland, 1954-66. *Address:* 9 Clarence Drive, Glasgow, W2. *T:* 041-339 5964.

**ROBIN, Ian (Gibson),** FRCS; Consulting ENT Surgeon: Royal Northern Hospital, since 1937; St Mary's Hospital, Paddington, since 1948; Princess Louise (Kensington) Hospital for Children, since 1948; *b* 22 May 1909; *s* of Dr Arthur Robin, Edinburgh, and Elizabeth Parker; *m* 1939, Shelagh Marian, *d* of late Colonel C. M. Croft; one *s* two *d*. *Educ:* Merchiston Castle School; Clare College, Cambridge. MA, MB, BCh Cantab 1933; LRCP 1933; FRCS 1935. Guy's Hosp.; late House Phys.; Sen. Science Schol., 1930; Treasurer's Gold Medals in Clinical Surgery and Medicine, 1933; Arthur Durham Travelling Schol., 1933; Charles Oldham Prize in Ophthalmology, 1933; Registrar and Chief Clin. Asst, ENT Dept., 1935-36; House Surgeon, Roy. Northern Hosp., 1934; late Consult. ENT Surgeon, Potters Bar Hosp., Forest Hosp., 1938-46, Roy. Chest Hosp., 1939-44. Surgeon EMS, Sector III London Area, 1939-45. Late Vice-Chm., Royal Nat. Institute for the Deaf. Member Hunterian Soc.; Council of Nat. Deaf Children's Soc.; Council of Brit. Assoc. of Otolaryngologists; Past Pres., Laryng. Section, RSM, 1967-68; Vice-Pres., Otolog. Section, RSM, 1967-68, 1969; late Examiner for DLO of RCS of England. Lectures: Yearsley, 1968; Jobson Horne, 1969. Mem., Royal Water-Colour Soc. *Publications:* (jt) Diseases of Ear, Nose and Throat (Synopsis Series), 1957; papers in various med. treatises, jls, etc. *Recreations:* golf, gardening, sketching; formerly athletics and Rugby. *Address:* Stowe House, 3 North

End, Hampstead, NW3. *T:* 01-458 2292; Harley Street, W1. *T:* 01-580 3625. *Clubs:* Hawks (Cambridge); Achilles (Great Britain); Hampstead Golf.

**ROBINS, Mrs Denise;** *b* Whitehall Court, SW1; *m*; three *d*; *m* 1939, Lt-Col R. O'Neill Pearson. *Educ:* Staten Island, USA; Convent, Upper Norwood, SE. Entered Dundee Courier Office, Dundee, 1914; became a Free Lance writer, and published numerous serials and short stories; first novel published in 1924. *Publications:* 154 books including House of the 7th Cross, The Noble One, Khamsin, etc.; *historical novels:* (as Harriet Gray) notably Gold for the Gay Masters and Dance in the Dust; *autobiography:* Stranger than Fiction. *Recreations:* music, books, travel. *Address:* 27 Muster Green, Haywards Heath, Sussex. *T:* Haywards Heath 50580.

**ROBINS, Sir Reginald Edwin,** Kt *cr* 1945; CMG 1938; OBE; MInstT; *b* 29 April 1891; *s* of Thomas Henry Robins, late of Basingstoke, Hants; *m* 1914, Adeline Annie (*d* 1964), *d* of Edward Ayling, Bentworth, Hants; one *s* one *d*. *Educ:* Queen Mary's School, Basingstoke; London School of Economics. Entered service of Great Western Railway, 1908; special training under Great Western training scheme for officers, 1920; London School of Economics, 1919-24; Brunel Medallist; entered Colonial Service, Kenya and Uganda Railways, 1925; General Manager, Tanganyika Railways and Ports Services, 1936-42; Kenya and Uganda Railways and Harbours, 1942-48; Commr for Transport, East Africa High Commission, 1948-53. *Recreation:* golf. *Address:* Kenton, Linkside West, Hindhead, Surrey.

**ROBINS, Prof. Robert Henry;** Professor of General Linguistics, University of London, since 1965; Head of Department of Phonetics and Linguistics, School of Oriental and African Studies, University of London, since 1970; *b* 1 July 1921; *s* of John Norman Robins, medical practitioner, and Muriel Winifred (*née* Porter); *m* 1953, Sheila Marie Fynn. *Educ:* Tonbridge Sch.; New Coll., Oxford. Oxford, 1940-41 and 1945-48, MA 1948; DLit London 1968. Lectr in Linguistics, Sch. of Oriental and African Studies, London, 1948-55; Reader in General Linguistics, Univ. of London, 1955-64. Research Fellow, Univ. of California, 1951; Vis. Professor: Washington, 1963; Hawaii, 1968; Minnesota, 1971. Hon. Sec., Philological Soc., 1961-; British Representative, CIPL, 1970-. *Publications:* Ancient and Mediaeval Grammatical Theory in Europe, 1951; The Yurok Language, 1958; General Linguistics: an introductory survey, 1964; A Short History of Linguistics, 1967; articles in Language, TPS, BSOAS, Lingua, Foundations of Language, Man, etc. *Recreations:* gardening, travel. *Address:* 65 Dome Hill, Caterham, Surrey. *T:* Caterham 43778. *Club:* Royal Commonwealth Society.

**ROBINSON,** family name of **Baron Martonmere.**

**ROBINSON, Sir Albert (Edward Phineas),** Kt 1962; *b* 30 December 1915; *s* of late Charles Phineas Robinson (formerly MP Durban, S Africa) and of late Mabel V. Robinson; *m* 1944, Mary Judith Bertish; four *d*. *Educ:* Durban High School; Universities of Stellenbosch, London, Cambridge and Leiden; MA (Cantab). Barrister, Lincoln's Inn. Served War of 1939-45, in Imperial Light Horse, Western Desert, N Africa, 1940-43. Member Johannesburg City Council, 1945-48 (Leader United Party in Council, 1946-47); MP (United Party), S African Parl., 1947-53; became permanent resident in Rhodesia, 1953. Exec. Dir, Anglo American Corp. of SA Ltd; Director: Anglo American Corp., Rhodesia Ltd; Zambian Anglo American Ltd. Deputy Chairman: General Mining and Finance Corporation, South Africa; Highveld Steel and Vanadium Corporation; Director, Founders Bldg Soc.; Director (in Rhodesia) of Bd of Standard Bank; Director, in Rhodesia and South Africa, of various Mining, Financial and Industrial Companies. Chm. Central African Airways Corp., 1957-61. Member, Monckton Commission, 1960; High Commissioner in the UK for the Federation of Rhodesia and Nyasaland, 1961-63. *Recreations:* people, music and conversation. *Address:* Rumbavu Park, PO Box 2341, Salisbury, Rhodesia. *Clubs:* Carlton (London); Salisbury (Salisbury, Rhodesia); City (Capetown).

**ROBINSON, Maj.-Gen. Alfred Eryk,** CB 1949; DSO 1940; JP; DL; *b* 19 Sept. 1894; *s* of late A. H. Robinson, JP, Derwent House, West Ayton, Scarborough; *m* 1942, Ailison Campbell, *d* of late P. C. Low, Dowrich House, Sandford, Crediton, and *widow* of Major S. H. Birchall Wood, R Deccan Horse. *Educ:* RMC, Sandhurst. Joined Green Howards, Aug. 1914; Lieut-Colonel, 1st Bn Green Howards, 1939; Col 1942; Temp. Maj.-Gen. 1943; retired, 1948. Colonel, The Green Howards, 1949-59. N Riding of Yorkshire: DL, 1952, JP 1953. *Address:* Derwent House, West Ayton, Scarborough, Yorks. *T:* West Ayton 2130. *Club:* United Service.

**ROBINSON, Sir Arnet,** Kt 1963; President, Coast Lines Ltd, and Associated Companies (formerly Chairman, and Chairman of Executive Committee); *b* 24 April 1898; 2nd *s* of Francis and Amy Robinson, Stanmore Middlesex; *m* 1928, Beatrice E. Baber; two *s* one *d*. *Educ:* Westminster (King's Scholar). Chm. Mersey Docks and Harbour Board, 1954-62; President Dock and Harbour Authorities Association, 1961-63; Vice-Pres. and Member Cttee of Management RNLI. Served European War, 1914-18, 60th Rifles (SR) and attached RAF; War of 1939-45, HG, Cheshire Regt. Chm. Coasting and Short Sea Shipping Control Cttee, Liverpool Area, 1939-47; Chm. Liverpool Steam Ship Owners Assoc., 1946 (Chm. Coastwise Section, 1943-44 and 1948); Vice-Chm., Gen. Council of British Shipping, 1946; Chm. Coasting Liner Sect., Chamber of Shipping, 1948-50. OStJ. *Recreation:* yachting. *Address:* White Gables, St Margarets Rd, Hoylake, Cheshire. *T:* 051-632 4453. *Clubs:* Junior Carlton, MCC; Royal Yacht Squadron; Royal Liverpool Golf.

**ROBINSON, Arthur Napoleon Raymond;** Minister of External Affairs, Trinidad and Tobago Government, since 1967; *b* 16 Dec. 1926; *s* of late James Alexander Andrew Robinson, Headmaster, and Emily Isabella Robinson; *m* 1961, Patricia Rawlins; one *s* one *d*. *Educ:* Bishop's High Sch., Tobago; St John's Coll., Oxford. LLB (London); MA (PPE) Oxon. Called to Bar, Inner Temple; in practice, 1956-61. Treas., People's Nat. Movt (governing Party) 1956; Mem. Federal Parlt, 1958; Mem. for Tobago East, 1961; Minister of Finance, 1961-66; Dep. Political Leader of Party, 1966; Actg Prime Minister (during his absence), April and Aug. 1967. Member: Legal Commn on US Leased Areas under 1941 Agreement, 1959; Industrial Develt Corp., 1960; Council, Univ. of West Indies, 1960-62. *Publications:* articles and addresses. *Address:* (office) Knowsley, Queen's Park West, Port of Spain, Trinidad, W Indies. *T:* 34241.

**ROBINSON, Austin;** *see* Robinson, E. A. G.

**ROBINSON, Basil William;** Keeper, Department of Metalwork, Victoria and Albert Museum since 1966; *b* 20 June 1912; *o c* of William Robinson and Rebecca Frances Mabel, *d* of Rev. George Gilbanks; *m* 1st, 1945, Ailsa Mary Stewart (*d* 1954); 2nd, 1958, Oriel Hermione Steel; one *s* one *d*. *Educ:* Winchester (Exhibitioner); CCC Oxford. BA 1935; MA, BLitt, 1938. Asst Keeper, Victoria and Albert Museum, 1939. Min. of Home Security, 1939-40. Served as Capt., 2nd Punjab Regt, India, Burma, Malaya, 1943-46. Deputy Keeper, V. and A. Museum, 1954. Pres., Royal Asiatic Soc., 1970; Vice-Pres., Arms and Armour Soc., 1953; Hon. Pres., Tō-ken Soc. of Great Britain, 1967. *Publications:* A Primer of Japanese Sword-blades, 1955; Persian Miniatures, 1957; Japanese Landscape Prints of the 19th Century, 1957; A Descriptive Catalogue of the Persian Paintings in the Bodleian Library, 1958; Kuniyoshi, 1961; The Arts of the Japanese Sword, 1961; Persian Drawings, 1965; part-author, vols 2 and 3, Catalogue of Persian MSS and Miniatures in the Chester Beatty Library, 3 vols, 1958-62; Persian Miniature Painting, 1967; numerous booklets, articles and reviews on Persian and Japanese art. *Recreations:* catch singing (founder and Chairman, Aldrich Catch Club); cats. *Address:* 41 Redcliffe Gardens, SW10. *T:* 01-352 1290. *Club:* Hurlingham.

**ROBINSON, Air Vice-Marshal Bruce,** CB 1968; CBE 1953; Air Officer Commanding No 24 Gp, RAF, 1965-67; retired, 1967; *b* 19 Jan. 1912; *s* of late Dr G. Burton Robinson, Cannington, Somerset; *m* 1940, Elizabeth Ann Compton, *d* of Air Commodore D. F. Lucking; one *s* one *d*. *Educ:* King's School, Bruton. Commissioned in SR of O, The Somerset Light Infty, 1931-33; Commissioned in RAF, 1933; No 16 (Army Co-op. Sqdn), 1934-37; Specialist Engineer course, 1937-39. Served War of 1939-45: Technical duties in Fighter and Bomber Commands, UK Senior Technical Staff Officer, Rhodesian Air Training Group, 1946-48; on loan to Indian Air Force (Director of Technical Services), 1951-53; Commandant, No 1 Radio School, RAF Locking, 1953-55; Sen. RAF Officer at Wright Patterson Air Force Base, Dayton, Ohio, 1958-60; Commandant No 1 Sch. of Technical Training, RAF Halton, Bucks, 1961-63. Director of RAF Aircraft Development, Min. of Aviation, 1963-65. *Recreations:* golf, sailing, painting, writing. *Address:* Bent Hollow, Bromeswell, Woodbridge, Suffolk. *T:* Eyke 295.

**ROBINSON, Christopher John;** Master of the Choristers and Organist of Worcester Cathedral since Sept. 1963; Conductor, City of Birmingham Choir since 1963; *b* 20 April 1936; *s* of Prebendary John Robinson, Malvern, Worcs; *m* 1962, Shirley Ann, *d* of H. F. Churchman, Sawston, Cambs; one *s* one *d*. *Educ:* St Michael's Coll., Tenbury; Rugby; Christ Church, Oxford. MA, BMus, FRCO. Assistant Organist of Christ Church, Oxford, 1955-58; Assistant Organist of New College, Oxford, 1957-58; Music Master at Oundle School, 1959-62; Assistant Organist of Worcester Cathedral, 1962-63. *Recreations:* cricket, fishing, motoring. *Address:* 13 College Green, Worcester. *T:* 23555.

**ROBINSON, Rt. Rev. Christopher J. G.;** *see* Bombay, Bishop of.

**ROBINSON, Mrs Clare;** *see* Panter-Downes, M. P.

**ROBINSON, Rt. Rev. Cuthbert Cooper,** DD; *b* 26 May 1893; *s* of Rev. John Cooper Robinson, DD, and Betsy Poynton; *m* 1920, Jean A. Bryce, *d* of Dr P. H. Bryce, Ottawa; two *s* two *d* (one *d* decd). *Educ:* University of Toronto (BA); Wycliffe College, Toronto. Canadian Army, 1914-19 (Lieut). Deacon, 1920; Educational work in Japan, 1920-38; Priest, 1938; Rector of Geraldton, 1939-43; Rector of Forest, 1943-44; Rector of Noranda, 1944-48; Rector of Timmins, 1948-54. Canon, 1947; Dean of Moosonee, 1948; Bishop of Moosonee, 1954-63, retired. Hon. DD 1949. *Address:* 58 Catherine Avenue, Aurora, Ontario, Canada.

**ROBINSON, Commodore David Samuel,** CBE 1941; RD; RNR (retired); *b* 20 Dec. 1888; *s* of James Samuel and Eleanor Robinson; *m* 1st; one *s* one *d*; 2nd, 1939, Margaret Gwendoline Keyes; one *s*. *Educ:* Hull Trinity House Navigation School. Master mariner (extra), 1913; joined Cunard Steamship Company Ltd, 1913; Sub-Lieut RNR, 1914; on active service throughout War of 1914-18, light cruisers; continued in Cunard Atlantic passenger service to outbreak of War, 1939, serving in Queen Mary and in new Mauretania; served War of 1939-45 (CBE); on retired list RNR, 1944; Marine Superintendent Cunard White Star Line in New York, 1944-53; retired 1953. *Address:* The Oaks, Ebford, Topsham, Devon.

**ROBINSON, Sir Dove-Myer,** Kt 1970; Mayor of Auckland, New Zealand, 1959-65, and since 1968; *b* Sheffield, 15 June 1901; 6th *c* of Moss Robinson and Ida Robinson (*née* Brown); of Jewish race; *m* 1st, Bettine Williams; 2nd, Thelma Ruth Thompson; one *s* five *d*. *Educ:* primary schools in Sheffield, Manchester, London and Devonport (Auckland, NZ). Mem., Auckland City Council, 1952-59; Chm., Auckland Metropolitan Drainage Bd, 1953-55; Chm., Auckland Airport Cttee, 1959-61; Mem., Auckland Univ. Council, 1952-; Chm., Auckland Regional Authority, 1963-65, Mem., 1963-, Chm. Rapid Transit Cttee, 1968-; Vice-Pres., NZ Municipal Assoc., 1959-65, 1968-; President: Auckland Rugby League, 1964-; NZ Anti-Fluoridation Soc., 1954-; Auckland Festival Soc., 1959-65, 1968-. Fellow, NZ Inst of Management; Mem., Inst. Water Pollution Control, etc; MRSH. *Publications:* Utilization of Town and Country Wastes, Garbage and Sewage, 1946; Passenger Transport in Auckland, 1969; numerous leaflets and pubns on Pollution, Conservation, Fluoridation, Nutrition, Local and Regional Govt, Town Planning, Rapid Transit, etc. *Recreations:* golf, fishing, boating, photography, motoring, local government. *Address:* (private) 12a Aldred Road, Remuera, Auckland 5, New Zealand. *T:* 53693; (office) Auckland City Council Civic Administration Building, Civic Square, Auckland. *T:* 14650. *Clubs:* Remuera Golf, Rugby League, etc (Auckland, NZ).

**ROBINSON, Prof. (Edward) Austin (Gossage),** CMG 1947; OBE 1944; FBA 1955; Emeritus Professor of Economics, Cambridge University since 1966 (Professor, 1950-65); Fellow of Sidney Sussex College, Cambridge, since 1931; Secretary of Royal Economic Society, 1945-70; Joint Editor of Economic Journal, 1944-70; *b* 20 Nov. 1897; *s* of late Rev. Canon Albert Gossage Robinson; *m* 1926, Joan (*see* Prof. J. V. Robinson), *d* of late Major-General Sir Frederick Maurice, KCMG, CB; two *d*. *Educ:* Marlborough College (Scholar); Christ's College, Cambridge (Scholar). BA 1921; MA 1923; RNAS and RAF (Pilot), 1917-19; Fellow of Corpus Christi Coll., Cambridge, 1923-26; Tutor to HH The Maharaja of Gwalior, 1926-28; University Lecturer, Cambridge, 1929-49; Asst Editor of Economic Journal, 1934, Joint Editor, 1944; Member of Economic Section, War Cabinet Office, 1939-42; Economic Adviser and Head of Programmes Division,

Ministry of Production, 1942-45; Member of British Reparations Mission, Moscow and Berlin, 1945; Economic Adviser to Board of Trade, 1946; returned to Cambridge, Sept. 1946. Mem. of Economic Planning Staff, 1947-48; Treasurer of International Economic Association, 1950-59, President 1959-62; Mem. Council, DSIR, 1954-59; Dir of Economics, Min. of Power, 1967-68. Chairman: Council Nat. Inst. of Economic and Social Research, 1949-62; European Energy Advisory Commn, OEEC, 1957-60; Exec. Cttee, Overseas Develt Inst. *Publications:* The Structure of Competitive Industry, 1931; Monopoly, 1941; Economic Consequences of the Size of Nations, 1960; Economic Development of Africa South of the Sahara, 1964; Problems in Economic Development, 1965; The Economics of Education (with J. E. Vaizey), 1966; Economic Development in South Asia, 1970; contributor to: Modern Industry and the African, 1933; Lord Hailey's African Survey, 1938; articles in Economic Journal, etc. *Address:* Sidney Sussex College, Cambridge; 62 Grange Road, Cambridge. *T:* Cambridge 57548. *Club:* Reform.

*See also Bishop of Bombay.*

**ROBINSON, Edward G.;** Actor, Film Actor, and Radio Entertainer; *b* Rumania, 12 Dec. 1893; *s* of M. and S. Goldenberg; *m* 1st, 1927, Gladys Lloyd Cassell (marr. diss. 1956); one *s*; 2nd, 1958, Jane Adler. *Educ:* Townsend Harris High Sch.; City of New York Coll.; Columbia Univ.; American Acad. of Dramatic Arts, NY. Stage appearances include: Paid in Full, 1913; Under Fire, 1915; Under Sentence, 1916; The Pawn, 1917; The Little Teacher, 1918; Night Lodging, 1919; Poldekin, Samson and Delilah, 1920; The Idle Inn, The Deluge, Banco, 1922; Peer Gynt, The Adding Machine, A Royal Fandango, 1923; The Firebrand, 1924; Androcles and The Lion, The Man of Destiny, 1925; The Goat Song, The Chief Thing, Henry-Behave, 1926; Juarez and Maximilian, Ned McCobb's Daughter, The Brothers Karamazov, Right You Are if You Think You Are, 1926-27; The Racket, 1927; The Man with Red Hair, 1928; Kibitzer, 1929; Mr Samuel, 1930; Darkness at Noon, Season 1951-52 (toured US); The Middle of the Night (Broadway), 1956-58 (3 yrs). *Films include:* The Bright Shawl (silent film), 1923, The Hole in the Wall, The Night Ride, East is West, The Widow from Chicago, A Lady to Love, Outside the Law, Smart Money, Little Cæsar, Five Star Final, The Hatchet Man, Two Seconds, Tiger Shark, Little Giant, Silver Dollar, I Loved a Woman, Dark Hazard, Man with Two Faces, The Whole Town's Talking, Bullets or Ballots, Kid Galahad, A Slight Case of Murder, I am the Law, The Amazing Dr Clitterhouse, Blackmail, Confessions of a Nazi Spy, The Life of Dr Ehrlich, Brother Orchid, A Dispatch from Reuter's, Man Power, The Sea Wolf, Unholy Partners, Tales of Manhattan, Night before Christmas, Flesh and Fantasy, Double Indemnity, Destroyer, Mr Winkle Goes to War, Woman in the Window, Scarlet Street, The Stranger, Our Vines have Tender Grapes, The Red House, All my Sons, Key Largo, Night has a Thousand Eyes, House of Strangers, My Daughter Joy, Operation X, Actors and Sin, Vice Squad, The Big Leaguer, The Glass Web, Black Tuesday, Violent Men, Tight Spot, Bullet for Joey, Illegal, The Darkest Hour, The Ten Commandments, Nightmare, Hell on Frisco Bay, Hole in the Head, Seven Thieves, Pépé, My Geisha, Two Weeks in Another Town, Sammy Going South, The Prize, Robin and the Seven Hoods, Good Neighbour Sam, Cheyenne Autumn, The Outrage, Cincinnati Kid, The Biggest Bundle of Them All, Peking Blonde, Grand Slam, Never a Dull Moment, Mackenna's Gold, Operation St Peter, Song of Norway, The Old Man Who Cried Wolf. Served European War, 1917-18, with United States Navy; War of 1941-45, with Office of War Information (broadcasts from England in 9 languages to Continental underground). Chevalier Légion d'Honneur, 1952; Officier de l'Instruction Publique, 1953. Townsend Harris Medal (CCNY); James K. Hackett Medal (CCNY); Eleanor Roosevelt Humanitarian Award, 1963. *Recreations:* languages, music, pipes, painting, travelling, collecting art. *Publication:* The Kibitzer (with J. Swerling), 1929. *Address:* 910 Rexford Drive, Beverly Hills, Calif, USA. *Clubs:* Lambs (NY); Masquers (Hollywood).

**ROBINSON, Edward Stanley Gotch,** CBE 1952; MA; FSA; FBA 1942; *y s* of late Edward Robinson, Sneyd Park, Bristol; *m* 1917, Pamela Comfrey, *o d* of late Sir Victor Horsley, CB, FRS; two *s* four *d*. *Educ:* Clifton College (Scholar); Christ Church Oxford (Scholar). First Class Class. Mod. and Lit. Hum.; Barclay Head Prize for Numismatics, 1910; Student of the British School at Athens, 1910; Asst in British Museum, 1912; Dep. Keeper, 1936; Keeper of Coins and Medals, British Museum, 1949-52, retired. Lt, 3rd Northants Regt, 1914; served in France, 1915-16 (twice wounded); in Home Office, 1917-19; Huntington Medallist American Numismatic Society, 1935; Medallist of Royal Numismatic Society, 1942; Hon. Curator of Greek Coins, Ashmolean Museum, Oxford; Hon. Student of Christ Church, Oxford, since 1955; corresponding member: Deutsches Archaeologisches Institut and the American, Vienna, and Zagreb Numismatic Socs. Hon. DLitt, Oxford, 1955. *Publications:* Cyrenaica, in British Museum Catalogue of Greek Coins, 1927; Locker-Lampson (1923) and Woodward (1928) Collections of Greek Coins; (ed. and part author) Sylloge Nummorum Græcorum, 1931 (in progress); contrib. archæological periodicals. *Address:* 89 Great Russell Street, WC1; Iwerne Stepleton, Blandford, Dorset. *Club:* Athenæum.

*See also E. W. Maude.*

**ROBINSON, Eric,** OBE 1969; Conductor and TV Personality; *b* 13 Dec. 1908; *s* of Percy and Carrie Robinson. *Educ:* Watford Grammar School; Royal College of Music. Joined BBC Theatre Orchestra (violinist), 1923. Army volunteer, 1940; latter years of service devoted to directing and recording shows for the Troops. Appointed to BBC Television Service, 1947, where he conducted shows of every type, particularly Music for You. Programmes include: (TV) Eric Robinson presents, 1967-; (Radio) Melodies for You, 1967-; Records for You, 1960-. Director of some 14 companies inc. IBC Sound Recording Studios. *Publication:* Conducted Personally, 1955. *Recreation:* rose growing. *Address:* 28/30 Market Place, W1. *T:* 01-580 9694. *Club:* Savage.

*See also Stanford Robinson.*

**ROBINSON, Sir (Ernest) Stanley,** Kt 1969; CBE 1966; President of the Barbados Senate since 1966 (Member since 1964); sugar planter; *b* 18 Jan. 1905; *s* of Samuel Stanley Robinson and Hannagh Eliza Robinson; *m* 1926, Annie Carmen Yearwood; one *s* two *d*. *Educ:* Harrison Coll., Barbados; Warwick Sch., England; St John's Coll., Cambridge. MHA Barbados, 1928-32, 1937-46; MLC, 1952-64; Mem. Barbados Privy Council. Founder Mem., Barbados Sugar Producers Assoc.; Dir, West Indies Sugar Assoc.; Chm., Plantations Ltd, Bridgetown, Barbados; Director: Foursquare Sugar Estates Ltd; Foursquare Factory Ltd; Constant Estates Ltd; Barbados

Light & Power Co.; General Traders Ltd (Chm.); Vaucluse Factory Ltd; Vaucluse Estates Ltd. *Recreations:* swimming, shooting. *Address:* Constant Estates Ltd, St George, Barbados, West Indies. *Clubs:* Royal Over-Seas League; Barbados Yacht.

**ROBINSON, Forbes;** Principal Artist (Bass), Royal Opera House, Covent Garden, since 1954; *b* Macclesfield, 21 May 1926; *s* of Wilfred and Gertrude Robinson; *m* 1952, Marion Stubbs; two *d*. *Educ:* King's Sch., Macclesfield. St Paul's Coll., Cheltenham (teacher's trg), 1943-45. Capt. in RAEC, 1946-48. Loughborough Coll. (Hons Dipl., Phys. Educn), 1949-50; La Scuola di Canto (Scala, Milan), 1952-53. Promenade Debut, 1957. Guest artist with Dublin, Handel, Sadler's Wells, Scottish and Welsh National Opera Cos. Has sung at Festivals at Aldeburgh, Barcelona, Edinburgh, Holland, Leeds, Lucerne, Portugal and Schwetzingen. Has also sung in Argentina, Belgium, Denmark, Germany, Luxembourg, Sweden, and USA. First British singer to sing Don Giovanni at Royal Opera House, Covent Garden, for 100 years. Awarded Opera Medal for 1963, for creating King Priam (Tippett). *Recreations:* walking, swimming. *Address:* 225 Princes Gardens, W3. *T:* 01-992 5498. *Club:* Savage.

**ROBINSON, Major Sir Frederick Villiers Laud,** 10th Bt, *cr* 1660; late 3rd Northamptonshire Regt; *b* 4 December 1880; *o s* of 9th Bt and Madeleine Caroline, *e d* of Frederick Sartoris of Rushden, Northants; *S* father, 1893; *m* 1st, 1913, Eileen (who obtained a divorce, 1933; she *d* 1965), *e d* of Harry Higham; one *s* (and one *s* killed in action North Africa, 1941); 2nd, 1933, Frances Joyce, *er d* of Arthur Tyrwhitt Drake, Crendle, Sherborne, Dorset. Served European War, 1914-18 (wounded twice, MC, Croix de Guerre). Owns about 2100 acres. *Heir: s* Michael Frederick Laud Robinson, Northamptonshire Yeomanry; [*b* 23 Jan. 1914; *m* 1st, 1941, Elizabeth (marr. diss. 1966), *er d* of Brig. Charles Bridge, CMG, DSO, MC; one *s* one *d*; 2nd, 1966, Joan Isabel, *d* of Vernon James Reveley, and *widow* of Hon. John Breckinridge Fermor-Hesketh]. *Address:* Cranford Hall, Kettering, Northants. *T:* Cranford 217.

**ROBINSON, Sir George (Gilmour),** Kt, *cr* 1955; *b* 30 Aug. 1894; *s* of George Thomas Robinson and Ada Violet Gallier; *m* 1942, Muriel Alice Fry. *Educ:* Repton; Trinity College, Oxford. (MA). Served European War, 1914-19. Called to Bar, 1924, and practised. Resident Magistrate, Kenya, 1930-38; Puisne Judge, Northern Rhodesia, 1938-46; Puisne Judge, Nigeria, 1947-52; Chief Justice, Zanzibar, 1952-55; retired 1955. *Recreations:* shooting, golf, sailing. *Address:* The Old House, Southwold, Suffolk. *T:* 2374.

**ROBINSON, Gleeson Edward,** CB 1945; MC; LLD (London); Hon. Captain, RFA; *s* of Rev. John Robinson, Dudley; *m* 1945, Frances Elizabeth (*d* 1966), *widow* of P. J. Horsley. *Educ:* King Edward's Sch., Birmingham; London University. Solicitor, London, 1904-15; Royal Field Artillery, 1915-19, served in France (despatches, MC and Bar); Barrister-at-Law, Middle Temple, 1920; Secretary of Clearing Office (Enemy Debts), 1920-25; British Member of Anglo-German Mixed Arbitral Tribunal established under Treaty of Versailles, 1925-30; Traffic Comr (Metropolitan Area), 1931-46; Chm. Road Rail Traffic Appeal Tribunal, 1946-49. *Publication:* Public Authorities and Legal Liability. *Recreations:* golf, fishing. *Address:* La Falaise, Noirmont Lane, Ouaisne, Jersey, CI. *T:* Central 41461.

**ROBINSON, Mrs Gower;** *see* Bloom, Ursula.

**ROBINSON, Maj.-Gen. Guy St George,** CB 1945; DSO 1918; MC 1915; psc; *b* 2 April 1887; *s* of St George Charles Woodhouse Robinson, solicitor, Sligo, Ireland, and Isabella Carson, *sister* of late Baron Carson; *m* 1917, Eva Suzanne Hadra (*d* 1959). *Educ:* Malvern; Sandhurst. Joined Northamptonshire Regiment, 1907; posted to 1st Bn, 1908, Poona; went to Aden with Bn, 1908-10, and returned to England (Devonport), 1911; went to France, Aug. 1914 (wounded, MC); Adjutant 1st Northamptonshire Regt, April-Nov. 1915; 2nd in command, April-July 1917; Lt-Col in command, July 1917-April 1919 (despatches twice, DSO, MC); Instructor RMC, Sandhurst, 1919-23; Staff College, Camberley, 1924-25; Commanded Regimental Depôt, Northampton, 1926-27; Staff, 1928-31; 2nd Bn, Aldershot, 1932; Lt-Col 1933; commanded 2nd Bn Northamptonshire Regiment, 1933-35; Col 1935; Assistant Commandant, Hythe Wing, Small Arms School, 1935-37; Commander Rangoon Brigade Area, 1937-40; Brigade Commander, Home Forces, 1941; Area Commander, 1942; District Commander, 1943; Col of Northamptonshire Regt 1943-53; retired pay, 1944. *Address:* Saltwood Cottage, Hythe, Kent.

**ROBINSON, Sir Harold (Ernest),** Kt 1955; Managing Director of Woodford Lodge Estates Limited, Trinidad, 1944-61; *b* 9 Oct. 1905; *s* of Ernest Augustus Robinson and Rita Mabel (*née* Fitt); *m* 1929, Clarice Graeme (*née* Yearwood); two *s* three *d*. *Educ:* Lancing; Stowe; Magdalene Coll., Cambridge. Joined Staff of Usine St Madeleine Sugar Estate Ltd, San Fernando, Trinidad, 1927; joined staff of Woodford Lodge Estates Ltd, 1929. *Recreation:* flying. *Address:* c/o H. E. Robinson & Co. Ltd, 4 Edward Street, Port of Spain, Trinidad, WI. *Clubs:* West Indian; Union (Port of Spain, Trinidad).

**ROBINSON, Harold George Robert,** OBE 1961; CEng, MIEE; Head of Research Planning Division (Chief Scientific Officer), Ministry of Technology, since 1969; *b* 2 April 1924; *s* of Harold Arthur Robinson and Winifred Margaret (*née* Ballard); *m* 1955, Sonja (*née* Lapthorn); two *s*. *Educ:* Portsmouth Northern Grammar Sch.; Imperial Coll., London Univ.; California Inst. of Technology. WhSch 1944; BSc 1948; FCGI 1970. Joined RAE as Scientific Officer, 1948; Head of Satellite Launcher Div., Space Dept, RAE, 1961; Head of Avionics Dept, RAE, 1965. Bronze Medal, RAeS, 1961. *Publications:* various scientific and technical papers, contribs to books, primarily on rocket and space research. *Recreations:* sailing, painting. *Address:* Wildroots, Brackendale Road, Camberley, Surrey. *T:* Camberley 23771.

**ROBINSON, Prof. Joan Violet,** FBA 1958; Professor of Economics, University of Cambridge, 1965-Oct. 1971; *b* 31 Oct. 1903; *d* of late Major-General Sir Frederick Maurice, KCMG, CB; *m* 1926, E. A. G. Robinson, *qv*; two *d*. *Educ:* St Paul's Girls' School, London; Girton Coll., Cambridge. Economics Tripos, 1925; Faculty Asst Lectr in Economics, Cambridge Univ., 1931; Univ. Lectr, 1937; Reader, 1949. *Publications:* Economics of Imperfect Competition, 1933; Essays in the Theory of Employment, 1937; Introduction to the Theory of Employment, 1937; Essay on Marxian Economics, 1942; Collected Economic Papers, Vol. I, 1951; The Rate of Interest and Other Essays, 1952; The Accumulation of Capital, 1956; Collected Economic Papers, Vol. II, 1960; Essays in The

Theory of Economic Growth, 1963; Economic Philosophy, 1963; Collected Economic Papers, Vol. III, 1965; Economics: An Awkward Corner, 1966; The Cultural Revolution in China, 1969; Freedom and Necessity, 1970; articles, etc in Economic Journal, etc. *Address:* 62 Grange Road, Cambridge. *T:* 57548.

**ROBINSON, John Armstrong,** CMG 1969; UK Negotiating Delegation, Brussels, since 1970; Head of European Economic Integration Department, Foreign and Commonwealth Office, 1968-70; *b* 18 Dec. 1925; *m* 1952 Marianne Berger; one *s* one *d.* HM Forces, 1944-46; Foreign Office, 1949-50; Second Secretary, Delhi, 1950-52; Foreign Office, 1952-53; Helsinki, 1953-56; Second later First Secretary, Paris, 1956-58; Foreign Office, 1958-61; First Secretary in UK Delegation to European Communities, Brussels, 1962-67; Counsellor, Foreign Office, 1967; Appointed Member of team of nine officials for negotiations on British entry into the Common Market, 1970. *Address:* c/o Foreign and Commonwealth Office, SW1.

**ROBINSON, Rt. Rev. John Arthur Thomas,** MA, BD, DD, PhD; Lecturer in Theology, Trinity College, Cambridge, since 1969; Fellow, and Dean of Chapel, Trinity College, since 1969; also Assistant Bishop of Southwark, since 1969; *b* 15 June 1919; *s* of Reverend Canon Arthur William Robinson, DD and Mary Beatrice Robinson; *m* 1947, Ruth (*née* Grace); one *s* three *d. Educ:* Marlborough College; Jesus and Trinity Colleges, Cambridge; Westcott House, Cambridge. BA 1942 (1st class Theology); MA 1945; PhD 1946; BD 1962; DD 1968. Curate of St Matthew, Moorfields, Bristol, 1945-48; Chaplain, Wells Theological College, 1948-51; Fellow and Dean, Clare College, Cambridge, 1951-59; Assistant Lecturer in Divinity, Cambridge University, 1953-54; Lecturer in Divinity, 1954-59; Bishop Suffragan of Woolwich, 1959-69. Examining Chaplain to Archbishop of Canterbury, 1953-59; Six Preacher, Canterbury Cathedral, 1958-68; Proctor in Convocation, Diocese of Southwark, 1960-70. Vis. Prof. and Noble Lectr, Harvard, 1955; Vis. Prof., Union Theological Seminary, Richmond, VA, 1958; Lectures: Reinicker, Va Seminary, 1958; Purdy, Hartford Seminary, Conn, 1964; Thorp, Cornell University, 1964; Lilley, Wabash Coll., Indiana, 1966; West, Stanford Univ., 1966; Hulsean, Cambridge, 1970. *Publications:* In the End God, 1950 (rev. edn, 1968); The Body, 1952; Jesus and His Coming, 1957; On Being the Church in the World, 1960, rev. edn 1969; Christ Comes In, 1960; Liturgy Coming to Life, 1960; Twelve New Testament Studies, 1962; Honest to God, 1963; Christian Morals Today, 1964; The New Reformation?, 1965; But That I Can't Believe!, 1967; Exploration into God, 1967; Christian Freedom in a Permissive Society, 1970; *contrib. to:* Christian Faith and Communist Faith, 1953; Becoming a Christian, 1954; The Historic Episcopate, 1954; Jesus Christ, History, Interpretation and Faith, 1956; New Ways with the Ministry, 1960; Bishops, 1961; The Interpreter's Dictionary of the Bible (article: Resurrection in the NT), 1962; Layman's Church, 1963; The Roads Converge, 1963; The Honest to God Debate, 1963; The Authorship and Integrity of the New Testament, 1965; The Restless Church, 1966; Theologians of our Time, 1966; Theological Freedom and Social Responsibility, 1967; Sermons from Great St Mary's, 1968; articles in learned journals, mainly on New Testament subjects. *Address:* Trinity College, Cambridge CB2 1TQ. *T:* Cambridge 58201.

**ROBINSON, Sir John Beverley,** 7th Bt, *cr* 1854; *b* 3 Oct. 1913; *s* of Sir John Beverley Robinson, 6th Bt, and Constance Marie, *d* of Robert W. Pentecost; *S* father 1954. *Heir: kinsman* Christopher Robinson, QC [*b* 22 Jan. 1909; *m* 1933, Neville Taylor, *e d* of Rear-Adm. W. R. Gherardi, US Navy; three *s* one *d*]. *Address:* 63 Park Road, Grimsby Beach, Ontario, Canada.

**ROBINSON, Sir John (Edgar),** Kt 1958; Chairman Frederic Robinson Ltd and associated companies since 1933; *b* 20 March 1895; *s* of William Robinson, Stockport and Wilmslow and Priscilla (*née* Needham); *m* 1926, Gwendolen Harriet May, *d* of Sydney Herbert Evans, London; three *s. Educ:* Stockport Grammar School; Manchester University (LLB). Qualified as Solicitor, 1918; entered family business of Frederic Robinson, Ltd, 1918. President Stockport Chamber of Commerce, 1947. Held various offices in Conservative Party, 1945-; Chairman Knutsford Division Conservative Assoc., 1949-52, Deputy President, 1952-. *Recreation:* sailing. *Address:* Wellfield, Dean Row, Wilmslow, Cheshire. *T:* Wilmslow 23384. *Clubs:* Royal Welsh Yacht (Caernarvon); South Caernarvonshire Yacht.

**ROBINSON, John Foster,** CBE 1968; TD; Chairman, The Dickinson Robinson Group Ltd, since 1968 (Deputy Chairman 1966); *b* 2 Feb. 1909; *s* of late Sir Foster Gotch Robinson; *m* 1935, Margaret Eve Hannah Paterson; two *s* two *d. Educ:* Harrow; Christ Church, Oxford. Dir, E. S. & A. Robinson Ltd, 1943, Jt Man. Dir 1948; Chm., E. S. & A. Robinson (Holdings) Ltd, 1961; Dir, Eagle Star Insurance Co. Ltd, 1968; Chm., SW Regional Board, National Westminster Bank Ltd, 1969. *Recreations:* shooting, fishing, golf. *Address:* St George's Hill, Easton-in-Gordano, Bristol BS20 0PX. *T:* Pill 2108. *Clubs:* Portland, Houghton; Clifton, Bristol, Constitutional (Bristol).

**ROBINSON, Rev. Canon Joseph,** MTh, AKC; Canon Residentiary and Librarian of Canterbury Cathedral since 1968; Examining Chaplain to the Archbishop of Canterbury since 1968; *b* 23 Feb. 1927; *er s* of Thomas and Maggie Robinson; *m* 1953, Anne Antrobus; two *s* two *d. Educ:* Upholland Grammar Sch., Lancs; King's Coll., London. BD (1st cl. Hons); AKC (1st cl.) 1951; MTh 1958. Deacon, 1952; Priest, 1953; Curate, All Hallows, Tottenham, 1952-55; Minor Canon of St Paul's Cathedral, 1956-68; Sacrist, 1958-68; Lectr in Hebrew and Old Testament Studies, King's Coll., London, 1959-68. Golden Lectr, 1963; St Antholin Lectr, 1964-67. Chaplain, Worshipful Co. of Cutlers, 1963-; Sub Chaplain, Order of St John of Jerusalem, 1965-. *Publications:* articles in: Church Quarterly Review, Expository Times, Church Times; many reviews in various jls. *Recreation:* reading. *Address:* 12 The Precincts, Canterbury, Kent. *T:* Canterbury 61954. *Club:* Athenæum.

**ROBINSON, Kathleen Marian, (Mrs Vincent F. Sherry; Kathleen M. Sherry);** FRCS, FRCOG, MD; Obstetrician, and Gynæcologist, Royal Free Hospital since 1946; Obstetrician, Queen Charlotte's Hospital, since 1946; *b* 25 May 1911; *d* of late James Robinson and Ruth Robinson (*née* Edmeston); *m* 1946, Vincent Francis Sherry; one *s* two *d. Educ:* Penrhos College, Colwyn Bay; Royal Free Hospital School of Medicine, London University. MB, BS, 1936; MRCS, LRCP 1936; MD London 1940; FRCS 1940; MRCOG 1941; FRCOG 1953. House Surgeon: Royal Free Hospital; Samaritan Hospital, Royal Marsden Hospital, Queen Charlotte's Hospital. Resident

Obstetrician, Queen Charlotte's Hospital. Recognised Teacher of the London University. FRSM; FRHS. *Publications:* contributor to Queen Charlotte's Text Book of Obstetrics, also to Practical Motherhood and Parentcraft. *Recreation:* gardening. *Address:* 17 Herondale Avenue, Wandsworth Common, SW18. *T:* 01-874 8588; 148 Harley Street, W1. *T:* 01-935 1900.

**ROBINSON, Rt. Hon. Kenneth,** PC 1964; Director, Social Policy, British Steel Corporation, since 1970; *b* Warrington, Lancs, 19 March 1911; *s* of late Clarence Robinson, MRCS, LRCP; *m* 1941, Helen Elizabeth Edwards; one *d. Educ:* Oundle Sch. Insurance Broker at Lloyd's, 1927-40. Served War of 1939-45, RN 1941-46; Ord. Seaman, 1941; commissioned, 1942; Lieut-Comdr RNVR, 1944; served Home Fleet, Mediterranean, Far East and Pacific. Company Secretary, 1946-69. MP (Lab) St Pancras N, 1949-70; Asst Whip (unpaid), 1950-51, an Opposition Whip, 1951-54; Minister of Health, 1964-68; Minister for Planning and Land, Min. of Housing and Local Govt, 1968-69. *Publications:* Wilkie Collins, a Biography, 1951; Policy for Mental Health, 1958; Patterns of Care, 1961; Look at Parliament, 1962; *Recreations:* looking at paintings, reading, listening to music. *Address:* British Steel Corporation, 33 Grosvenor Place, SW1; 12 Grove Terrace, NW5.

**ROBINSON, Kenneth Dean,** MA Oxon; Headmaster, Bradford Grammar School, since 1963; *b* 9 March 1909; *s* of late Rev. Arthur Edward and late Mary Edith Robinson; *m* 1936, Marjorie Belle Carter, Bradford, Yorks; two *s* two *d. Educ:* Bradford Grammar Sch.; Corpus Christi Coll., Oxford (Scholar). Classical Honour Mods Class I, Litt Hum. Class II. Sixth Form Classical Master, St Edmund's, Canterbury, 1932-34; Head of Classical Dept, Wellington College, Berks, 1934-41; Intelligence Corps, 1941-45; Asst to Director of Education, Shire Hall, Reading, Berks, 1945-46; Headmaster, Birkenhead Sch., Cheshire, 1946-63. Classics panel Secondary Sch. Examinations Council, 1948-50; Pres. Liverpool Br., Class. Assoc., 1958; Council, IAHM, 1949-53; HMC Cttee, 1956-60; Chm. NW Div., HMC, 1958-59; Chm. Direct Grant Cttee, HMC, 1958-59, Mem., 1967-70; Chm. Op. Res. Sect. Div. XII, IAHM, 1952-60; Chm. Div. XII, IAHM, 1961-62; Mem. Council, 1962-63; Mem. Court, Univ. of Bradford. *Publications:* (with R. L. Chambers) Septimus: a First Latin Reader, 1936; The Latin Way, 1947. *Recreations:* gardening, chess, painting, canals, teaching, growing beards on country holidays. *Address:* The Clock House, Frizinghall, Bradford 9, Yorks. *T:* Bradford 44538.

**ROBINSON, Kenneth Ernest,** JP, MA, FRHistS; Vice-Chancellor, University of Hong Kong, since 1965; *b* 9 March 1914; *o s* of late Ernest and Isabel Robinson, Plumstead, Kent; *m* 1938, Stephanie, *o d* of late William Wilson, Westminster; one *s* one *d. Educ:* Monoux Grammar School, Walthamstow; Hertford College, Oxford (Scholar, 1st Cl. PPE; 1st Cl. Mod. Hist.; Beit Senior Schol. in Colonial History); London School of Economics. Colonial Office, 1936; Asst Sec. 1946; resigned 1948. Fellow of Nuffield Coll., and Reader in Commonwealth Govt, Oxford, 1948-57; Director of the Institute of Commonwealth Studies and Professor of Commonwealth Affairs, Univ. of London, 1957-65. Leverhulme Research Fellow, 1952-53; Visiting Lecturer, School of Advanced International Studies, Johns Hopkins Univ., USA, 1954; Carnegie Travel Grant, East, Central and South Africa, 1960; Reid Lecturer, Acadia Univ., 1963; Visiting Professor, Duke Univ., NC, 1963. Editor, Journal of Commonwealth Political Studies, 1961-65; Special Commonwealth Award (Min. of Overseas Development), 1965. Member: (part-time) Directing Staff, Civil Service Selection Board, 1951-56; Colonial Economic Research Committee, 1949-62; Colonial Social Science Research Council, 1958-62; Mem. Council: Overseas Development Institute, 1960-65; Royal Inst. of Internat. Affairs, 1962-65; Internat. African Inst., 1960-65; African Studies Assoc., UK, 1963-65; Assoc. of Commonwealth Univs, 1967-68. Governor, LSE, 1959-65. Corresp. Mem., Académie des Sciences d'Outre-Mer, Paris. Hon. LLD Chinese Univ. of Hong Kong, 1969. *Publications:* (with W. J. M. Mackenzie) Five Elections in Africa, 1960; (with A. F. Madden) Essays in Imperial Government presented to Margery Perham, 1963; The Dilemmas of Trusteeship, 1965; (with W. B. Hamilton & C. D. Goodwin) A Decade of the Commonwealth 1955-64 (USA), 1966. Contrib. to Africa Today (USA), 1955; Africa in the Modern World (USA), 1955; University Cooperation and Asian Development (USA), 1967; L'Europe du XIXe et du XXe Siècle, Vol. 7 (Italy), 1968; papers in learned jls. *Address:* The Lodge, 1 University Drive, Hong Kong; The Old Rectory, Westcote, Oxon. *Clubs:* Oxford and Cambridge University, Royal Commonwealth Society; Hong Kong, Hong Kong Country, and Royal Hong Kong Jockey.

**ROBINSON, Sir Leslie (Harold),** KBE 1957; CB 1952; Industrial Adviser to J. Henry Schroder Wagg since 1964; Vice-Chairman: George Cohen 600 Group; Ransome & Marles Bearing Co.; Director: Renold Chains; A. Reyrolle & Co.; National Film Finance Corporation; British Lion Films; Hall-Thermotank; General Refractories; Chairman, NEDC Electrical Engineering Committee, since 1964; *b* 19 Oct. 1903; *s* of George and Blanche Robinson; *m* 1938, Isobel, *d* of George William Steele; no *c. Educ:* Owen's School; Peterhouse, Cambridge. BA 1925; teaching, 1926-37: HMI Board of Education, 1937; Ministry of Supply, 1939; Under Secretary, 1948; Deputy-Secretary, Ministry of Supply, 1953; Second Secretary, Board of Trade, 1955-63, retired. Member: General Council, BNEC, 1967-; Export Guarantees Adv. Council, 1969-. Chairman: London Univ. Halls of Residence Cttee, 1964-; Univ. of London Cttee of Student Accommodation. *Recreations:* opera, drinking wine, lawn tennis. *Address:* White House, Esher Close, Esher, Surrey. *T:* Esher 63114. *Club:* Royal Automobile.

**ROBINSON, Group Captain Marcus,** CB 1956; AFC 1942 and Bar 1944; DL; Chairman, Robinson, Dunn & Co. Ltd since 1966 (Director since 1939); Director: RD (Chemicals & Wood Processes) Ltd; McDougalls Timber Co. Ltd since 1958; Thomson & Balfour Ltd since 1966; *b* 27 May 1912; *s* of Wilson and Eileen Robinson; *m* 1st, 1941, Mrs Mary Playfair (marriage dissolved, 1951); 2nd, 1953, Mrs Joan E. G. O. Weatherlake (*née* Carter); one *s* one *d. Educ:* Rossall. Commissioned AAF, 602 Sqdn, 1934; Squadron Ldr, 1940, commanding 616 Squadron; Wing Comdr, 1943; Group Capt., 1945; re-formed 602 Squadron, 1947; Member Air Advisory Council, Air Ministry, 1952-56; Chairman Glasgow TA and AFA, 1953-56; Chairman Glasgow Rating Valuation Appeals Cttee, 1963 (Dep. Chm., 1958-63). Deputy Chm. Earl Haig Fund Glasgow and SW Scotland, 1961-. DL Glasgow, 1955. *Recreations:* ski-ing, sailing. *Clubs:* Western (Glasgow), Royal Northern Yacht (Rhu).

**ROBINSON, Air Commodore Maurice Wilbraham Sandford,** CBE 1943; Royal Air Force; *b* 20 Sept. 1910; *s* of late Josiah Robinson; *m* 1936, Margaret Gwendolen Phelps; one *s* two *d*. *Educ:* Liverpool College. Entered RAF Cadet College, Cranwell, 1929; commissioned RAF, 1930. Retired, March 1958. *Address:* Gwern Borter, Ro Wen, Conway, Caerns. *Club:* Royal Air Force.

**ROBINSON, Sir Montague Arnet;** *see* Robinson, Sir Arnet.

**ROBINSON, Sir Niall B. L-;** *see* Lynch-Robinson.

**ROBINSON, Nigel Francis Maltby;** Metropolitan Stipendiary Magistrate since 1962; *b* 5 Nov. 1906; *s* of Francis George Robinson, OBE, Ilkeston, Derbyshire; *m* 1933, Flora, *d* of John McKay, Sutton, Surrey. *Educ:* Lancing; Hertford College, Oxford (MA, BCL). Called to Bar, Middle Temple, 1928; Practised Midland Circuit, 1928-62. Served Royal Artillery, 1940-45. JP and Dep. Chairman, Quarter Sessions for Derbyshire, 1958-64; JP and Dep. Chm., Nottinghamshire Quarter Sessions, 1961-66. *Address:* Greenwich Magistrates' Court, Blackheath Road, SE10. *T:* 01-692 3129. *Clubs:* Flyfishers'; Nottingham and Nottinghamshire United Services.

**ROBINSON, Very Rev. Norman;** Provost of Blackburn Cathedral since 1961; *b* 18 Feb. 1905; *s* of Thomas and Margaret Robinson (*née* Cullen); unmarried. *Educ:* Ulverston Grammar School; Liverpool University; Ridley Hall, Cambridge. BSc. 1st class Hons Maths, Derby Scholar, 1927; Dip. Educ. 1928. Senior Mathematics Master, Quarry Bank School, Liverpool, 1928-35. Deacon, 1934; priest, 1935; Curate: Mossley Hill, Liverpool, 1934-35; Holy Trinity, Southport, 1935-37; Lancaster Priory, 1937-40; Vicar of: Newbarns and Hawcoat, 1940-48; Penrith, 1948-59; Hon. Canon, Carlisle, 1954; Rector of West Derby, Liverpool, 1959-61. *Recreations:* music, theatre, books. *Address:* Broomfield, Preston New Road, Blackburn, Lancs.

**ROBINSON, Sir Norman De Winton,** Kt 1958; *b* 9 March 1890; *s* of Frederick Farquhar Robinson and Caroline Margaret Turner; *m* 1916, Edna Jeanne Smibert; one *d* (and one *s* killed in action, 1943). *Educ:* Melbourne Church of England Gram. Sch. Australian Knitting Mills Ltd, 1907-23; Yarra Falls Ltd, Abbotsford, 1923-66; Chm., Norwich Union Fire Insurance Society, Melbourne, 1942. Coronation Medal, 1953. *Recreations:* racing, golf. *Address:* 2a Hopetoun Road, Toorak, Victoria 3142, Australia. *T:* UY7898. *Clubs:* Athenæum (Melbourne); Peninsula Golf; VRC, VATC, MVRC (racing clubs).

**ROBINSON, Rev. Prof. Norman Hamilton Galloway,** MA (Glasgow); BD (Edinburgh); DLitt (Glasgow); DD (Edinburgh); Professor of Divinity and Systematic Theology in the University of St Andrews; *b* 7 October 1912; *e s* of late George Robinson and late Barbara Fraser, Troon, Ayrshire; *m* 1936, Mary Elizabeth, *o d* of Christopher Johnston, Portrush; two *s* two *d*. *Educ:* Ayr Academy; Universities of Glasgow, Oxford and Edinburgh. Minister of: Sandsting Parish Church, Shetland, 1939-43; South Church, Fraserburgh, Aberdeenshire, 1943-48; High Kirk of Rothesay, 1948-54; Prof. of Divinity and Dean of Faculty, Rhodes Univ., Grahamstown, SA, 1954-56; Prof. of Systematic Theology, 1956-67, of Divinity and Systematic Theology, 1967-, Univ. of St Andrews. Dean of Faculty of Divinity, Univ. of St Andrews, 1958-62; Examiner in Divinity, Universities of: Natal, 1954-55, South Africa, 1954-56, Aberdeen, 1960-62, Edinburgh, 1962-65, Newcastle upon Tyne, 1965-67, Glasgow, 1967-. Special Lectr in Christian Ethics, Assembly's Coll., Belfast, 1960-61; Guest Lecturer: Institute of Theology, Princeton Theol Seminary, USA, 1966; Graduate Summer Session, Anglican Theol and Union Colls, Vancouver, Canada, 1966. Gov. of Strathallan School. *Publications:* Faith and Duty, 1950; The Claim of Morality, 1952; Christ and Conscience, 1956; contribs to: Theologians of Our Time, 1966; Dictionary of Christian Theology, 1969; Talk of God, 1969; articles and reviews in Philosophy, The Philosophical Quarterly, Theology, The Expository Times, Hibbert Jl, Scottish Journal of Theology, etc. *Recreation:* golf. *Address:* Arcan, Tay Street, Newport-on-Tay, Fife. *T:* 2253.

**ROBINSON, Oliver John;** Editor, Good Housekeeping, 1947-65, Editor-in-Chief, 1965-67; *b* 7 April 1908; *s* of late W. Heath and Josephine Constance Robinson; *m* 1933, Evelyn Anne Laidler. *Educ:* Cranleigh Sch. Art Editor, Good Housekeeping, 1930; Art Editor, Nash's, 1933. Temporary commission, Queen's Royal Regt, 1941; Camouflage Development and Training Centre, 1942; Staff Officer, War Office, 1944. *Address:* 92 Charlbert Court, St John's Wood, NW8. *T:* 01-722 0723. *Club:* Savage.

**ROBINSON, Sir Robert,** OM 1949; Kt *cr* 1939; FRS; Commandeur de la Légion d'Honneur; MA, FRIC; DSc (Victoria); Hon. DSc Oxford, London, Liverpool, Wales, Dunelm, Sheffield, Belfast, Nottingham, Delhi, Bristol, Sydney, Zagreb, Strathclyde, Hokkaido; Hon. ScD Cantab; Hon. LLD Birmingham, Edinburgh, St Andrews, Glasgow, Liverpool, Manchester; Hon. DPharm Madrid and Paris; Hon. DLL Brussels; Hon. MICE; Hon. Fellow of Magdalen College, Oxford, since 1956; Hon. Fellow of Weizmann Institute of Science, Rehovot, Israel; Director: Shell Chemical Co. Ltd since 1955, Shell Research Ltd, since 1967; President, British Association for the Advancement of Science, 1955; President, Society of Chemical Industry, 1958-59; Hon. or Foreign member of many academies and scientific societies; *b* 13 Sept. 1886; *s* of W. B. Robinson, surgical dressing manufacturer, and Mrs Robinson of Field House, Chesterfield; *m* 1st, 1912, Gertrude Maud Walsh, MSc (*d* 1954), *d* of T. M. Walsh, The Hollies, Winsford; one *s* one *d*; 2nd, 1957, Stearn Sylvia (*née* Hershey), Hillstrom, of NY. *Educ:* Fulneck School, nr Leeds; University of Manchester. Prof. of Organic Chemistry (Pure and Applied), Univ. of Sydney, NSW, 1912-15; Heath Harrison Professor of Organic Chemistry, Liverpool, 1915; Director of Research, British Dyestuffs Corporation, Ltd, 1920; Professor of Chemistry, St Andrews, 1921; Professor of Organic Chemistry, Manchester, 1922-28; Professor of Organic Chemistry, University College, London, 1928-30; Waynflete Professor of Chemistry, Oxford University, 1930-55; Bakerian Lecturer, Royal Society, 1929; President Chemical Society, 1939-41; Longstaff Medallist Chemical Society; Davy Medallist of Royal Society, 1930; Royal Medallist, 1932; President of Royal Society, 1945-50; Paracelsus Medallist of the Swiss Chemical Soc., 1939; Copley Medallist, 1942; Albert Gold Medal, RSA, 1947; Hofmann Medal, German Chem. Society, 1957. Hon. Member Parl and Sci. Committee, 1949; Hon. Member Chemists' Club of New York; Member: Roumanian Academy of Sciences; Soviet Academy of Sciences, 1966. Hon.

Freeman of Borough of Chesterfield, 1947; Franklin Medal of Franklin Institute, Philadelphia, 1947; Nobel Prize for Chemistry, 1947; Priestley Medal, American Chemical Society, 1953; Flintoff Medal, Chem. Soc. 1960. Order of the Rising Sun, 2nd class (Japan). *Publications:* numerous scientific papers, mainly in the Journal of the Chemical Society. *Recreations:* mountaineering, chess. *Address:* Grimms Hill Lodge, Great Missenden, Bucks. *T:* Great Missenden 2465; Shell Chemical Co. Ltd, Shell Centre, Downstream Building, SE1. *Clubs:* Athenæum, Alpine.

*See also Rt Rev. W. L. M. Way.*

**ROBINSON, Dr Ronald Edward,** CBE 1970; DFC 1944; Fellow of St John's College, Cambridge, since 1949; Smuts Reader in History of the British Commonwealth since 1966; *b* 3 Sept. 1920; *e s* of William Edward and Ada Theresa Robinson, Clapham; *m* 1948, Alice Josephine Denny; two *s* two *d*. *Educ:* Battersea Grammar Sch.; St John's Coll., Cambridge. Major Scholar in History, St John's Coll., 1939; BA 1946, PhD 1949, Cantab. Research Officer, African Studies Branch, Colonial Office, 1947-49; Lectr in History, Univ. of Cambridge, 1953-66; Mem., Bridges Cttee of Trng in Public Administration, 1961-62; Tutor, St John's Coll., Cambridge, 1961-66; Chm., Cambridge Confs on Problems of Developing Countries, 1961-70. *Publications:* Africa and the Victorians, 1961; Developing the Third World, 1971; articles in Cambridge History of the British Empire, Vol. III, 1959, and The New Cambridge Modern History, Vol. XI, 1963; reports on Problems of Developing Countries, 1963-71; articles and reviews in learned jls. *Recreations:* cricket, tennis. *Address:* Thorneycreek, Herschel Road, Cambridge. *T:* Cambridge 61621. *Clubs:* Royal Commonwealth Society; Hawks (Cambridge).

**ROBINSON, Ronald Henry Ottywell Betham,** MA, MB, BCh, FRCS; retired as Senior Surgeon and Urologist, St Thomas's, SE, and Consultant Urologist, Ministry of Pensions and St Helier Hospital; *b* 16 May 1896; *s* of Henry Betham Robinson, MD, MS, FRCS; *m* Audrey, *er d* of late Col G. K. Walker, CIE, OBE; one *d*. *Educ:* Malvern; King's College, Cambridge (Senior Scholar); St Thomas's Hospital (University Scholar). Temporary Surgeon Lieutenant Royal Navy during European War, and Surg. Lieut Comdr RNVR (retd); Member of International Soc. of Urology; Past Pres. of the British Association of Urological Surgeons; Hon. Sec. Royal Society of Medicine (Past Pres. Urological Section, Past Vice-Pres. Surgical Section); Fellow Assoc. of Surgeons; Member Society of Thoracic Surgeons; Arris and Gale Lecturer, Royal College of Surgeons; Member Council, RCS (Eng.); late Chairman, Court of Examiners, RCS (Eng.); Examiner in Surgery, Univ. of Cambridge and Univ. of Malaya. Past Master of the Worshipful Company of Cordwainers. OStJ. *Publications:* Articles on Surgery and Urology in Text-book and Journals. *Recreations:* golf, travel. *Address:* The Glen, Leigh Hill Road, Cobham, Surrey. *T:* Cobham 2003. *Club:* United University.

**ROBINSON, Stanford;** Orchestral, Choral and Opera Conductor; Lecturer on musical subjects; *b* Leeds, 5 July 1904; *s* of James Percy and Carrie Robinson; *m* Lorely Dyer; one *d*. *Educ:* Stationers' Company's School; Royal College of Music, London, and abroad. British Broadcasting Corporation, 1924-66; Chorus Master until 1932, during which time formed the BBC choral activities in London, including the BBC Singers, the Choral Society, and the BBC Chorus; during the period also conducted the Wireless Orchestra extensively in all kinds of programmes, symphonic and otherwise; Conductor of BBC Theatre Orchestra, 1932-46; Music Dir Variety Dept, 1932-36; Dir Music Productions, producing and conducting all studio performances of opera besides operetta and other musical feature programmes, 1936-46; Opera Director and Associate Conductor of the BBC Symphony Orchestra, 1946-49; Conductor Opera Orch. and Opera Organiser, BBC, 1949-52. Toured Australia and New Zealand, conducting ABC and NZBC orchestras in numerous cities, 1966-67; Chief Conductor, Queensland Symphony Orchestra, 1968-69. Hon. ARCM; Hon. GSM. *Publications:* Orchestral Music, part songs, choral arrangements and songs. *Recreations:* gardening, photography. *Address:* 40 Menelik Road, NW2. *T:* 01-794 3423. *Club:* Savage.

*See also Eric Robinson.*

**ROBINSON, Sir Stanley;** *see* Robinson, E. S.

**ROBINSON, Sydney Allen;** General President, National Union of Boot and Shoe Operatives, 1947-70, retired; Member, Monopolies Commission, since 1966; *b* 13 Aug. 1905; *m* 1940, Grace Mary Lack; one *s* one *d*. *Educ:* Clophill Elementary School, Bedfordshire. National Union of Boot and Shoe Operatives: Full-time Branch Officer, 1939; National Organiser, 1947; Assistant General Secretary, 1949. *Recreations:* gardening, adult education. *Address:* 45 Fourth Avenue, Wellingborough, Northants. *T:* Wellingborough 2956.

**ROBINSON, Rt. Rev. Walter Wade;** *see* Dunedin, Bishop of.

**ROBINSON, Sir Wilfred (Henry Frederick),** 3rd Bt, *cr* 1908; Vice-Principal, Diocesan College School, Rondebosch, South Africa; *b* 24 Dec. 1917; *s* of Wilfred Henry Robinson (*d* 1922) (3rd *s* of 1st Bt), and Eileen (*d* 1963), *d* of Frederick St Leger, Claremont, SA; *S* uncle, Sir Joseph Benjamin Robinson, 2nd Bt, 1954; *m* 1946, Margaret Alison Kathleen, *d* of late Frank Mellish, MC, Bergendal, Gansbaai, Cape Province, SA; one *s* two *d*. *Educ:* Diocesan Coll., Rondebosch; St John's Coll., Cambridge, MA 1944. Served War of 1939-45, Devonshire Regt and Parachute Regt, Major. *Heir: s* Peter Frank Robinson, *b* 1949. *Address:* 44 Kildare Road, Newlands, Cape, S Africa. *Clubs:* Lansdowne; Western Prov. Sports (Cape Town).

**ROBINSON, Major-General William Arthur,** CB 1964; OBE 1944; retired; MA; MD; *b* 2 March 1908; *s* of late Sir William Robinson, DL, JP; *m* 1934, Sheela, *d* of J. R. Yarr, Newbury, Berks; two *s*. *Educ:* Wesley College and Trinity College, Dublin. MA, MD, 1934. Commissioned RAMC, 1931; served in Egypt and Sudan, 1932-37; Instructor and MO Army Gas School, 1938-41; Adviser in Chemical Warfare, 1941-43; Comd 200 Fd Ambulance (Egypt, Sicily and NW Europe), 1943-44; ADMS: 3 (Brit.) Inf. Div., NW Europe, 1945-46; Lt-Col Assistant Director-General Army Medical Dept (AMD1) War Office, 1946-49; jssc 1949; OC Hospital, E Africa, 1950-51; ADMS HQ Cyrenaica Dist (Colonel, ADMS 1 Bn Div., 1951-52, ADG (AMD1), War Office, 1952-54; DDMS Malta, 1954-57; Commandant, Depot and TE RAMC, 1958-60; Major-General, 1960; Deputy Director-General, Army Medical Services, 1960-61; DDMS Southern Command, 1961; DMS, Far East Land Forces, 1963-65; QHS, 1960-65. Col Comdt, RAMC, 1966-. *Recreations:* cross-country running (sen. colours); sailing, hockey, golf. *Address:* Lechlade, Horton Heath, Eastleigh, Hants.

**ROBINSON, Rev. W(illiam) Gordon,** PhD; Principal, Northern Congregational College, 1958-68; Principal, Lancashire Independent College, Manchester, 1943-58; *b* 19 May 1903; *m* 1932, Phyllis King; one *s* one *d*. *Educ:* Universities of Liverpool (BA), Manchester (BD, PhD), Oxford (MA). Congregational minister: Gatley, Cheshire, 1929-32; Oldham, 1932-43; Tutor, Lancashire Independent College, 1929-33; Manchester University: Lecturer in New Testament, 1943-51; Lecturer in Ecclesiastical History, 1951-70; Secretary, Faculty of Theology, 1948-58, Tutor, 1958-68; Chairman, Lancashire Congregational Union, 1946 and 1956; Chairman, Congregational Union of England and Wales, 1955-56. *Publications:* Introduction to the New Testament, 1949; Our Heritage of Free Prayer, 1950; William Roby, 1766-1830, 1954; New Testament Treasure, 1954; Decision, Challenge, Victory, 1954; History of the Lancashire Congregational Union, 1955; Catchwords, Character and The Calendar, 1957; The Gospel and the Church, 1958; Jonathan Scott, 1961; Benjamin Waugh, 1961; Historians of Israel, 1962; New Testament Detection, 1964; The Bible and History (Jtly), 1968; Living Words and Their Meaning, 1968; The Literature of the New Testament, 1970. *Address:* Craigneish, Highfield Road, Grange-over-Sands, Lancashire. *T:* Grange-over-Sands 3214.

**ROBOROUGH,** 2nd Baron, *cr* 1938, of Maristow; **Massey Henry Edgcumbe Lopes;** Bt, *cr* 1805; JP; Brevet Major Reserve of Officers Royal Scots Greys; *b* 4 Oct. 1903; *o s* of 1st Baron and Lady Albertha Louisa Florence Edgcumbe (*d* 1941), *d* of 4th Earl of Mount Edgcumbe; *S* father 1938; *m* 1936, Helen, *o d* of late Colonel E. A. F. Dawson, Launde Abbey, Leicestershire; two *s* one *d*. *Educ:* Eton Coll.; Christ Church, Oxford (BA). Served in Royal Scots Greys, 1925-38; served again 1939-45. ADC to Earl of Clarendon, when Governor of Union of South Africa, 1936-37. CA Devon; DL 1946; Vice-Lieutenant of Devon, 1951; Lord Lieutenant of Devon, 1958-; Member of Duchy of Cornwall Council, 1958-68; High Steward of Barnstaple. Chairman Dartmoor National Park; Chairman Devon Outward Bound. Hon. LLD Exeter, 1969. KStJ. *Heir: s* Hon. Henry Massey Lopes [*b* 2 Feb. 1940; *m* 1968, Robyn, *e d* of John Bromwich, Melbourne, Aust.; one *s*]. *Address:* Bickham House, Roborough, S Devon. *T:* Yelverton 478. *Clubs:* Cavalry, St James'.
*See also Baron Carnock, Vice-Adm. Sir J. M. Pipon.*

**ROBSON, Air Vice-Marshal Adam Henry,** CB 1949; OBE 1938; MC; MSc; PhD; RAF retd; *b* 3 Aug. 1892; *s* of J. Robson, Low Fell, Co. Durham; *m* 1917, Vera Mary, *d* of late Robert Purvis, Solicitor, South Shields; two *s*. *Educ:* Armstrong College, Newcastle upon Tyne; King's College, University of London. Asst Sec., Dorset County Educ. Cttee, 1920-23; Entered RAF Educational Service in 1923; Dir of Educational Services, RAF, 1944-52. Mem. Exec. Cttee and Coun., Nat. Inst. of Adult Educn, 1947-52; Mem. Exec. Cttee and Coun. Nat. Foundn of Educl Research, 1947-52; Mem. Governing Body, Sch. of Oriental and African Studies, London Univ., 1948-52; Director, Hungarian Students Resettlement, World Univ. Service, London, 1957-58. Mem., Hampshire County Youth Adv. Cttee, 1961-67. Served in Durham Light Infantry, 1914-19 (MC and bar, despatches). *Address:* Wey Cottage, Bentley, Farnham, Surrey. *T:* Bentley 2264.

**ROBSON, Denis Hicks,** QC 1955; **His Honour Judge Robson;** County Court Judge, Circuit No 20, since 1957; Chairman, Northamptonshire Quarter Sessions, since 1970; *b* 7 Jan. 1904; *s* of late Robert Robson, ISO, and Helen Julia, *d* of late James J. Hicks, KCSG; *m* 1931, Mary Grace (*d* 1947), *e d* of late Sir William Orpen, KBE; one *s* one *d*; *m* 1960, Hon. Elizabeth (*widow* of John Cockburn Millar), *d* of late Lord Atkin, PC. *Educ:* Douai School; Trinity Hall, Cambridge. Called to the Bar, Inner Temple, 1927; North Eastern Circuit. War of 1939-45, commissioned in RASC, 1940; Military Department of Judge Advocate General's Office, 1942-45; Major, 1944; Recorder of Doncaster, 1950-53; Recorder of Middlesbrough, 1953-57. *Address:* Wakerley Manor, Oakham, Rutland. *T:* Morcott 224.

**ROBSON, Dame Flora,** DBE 1960; *b* South Shields, 28 March 1902; *d* of David Mather Robson and Eliza McKenzie, Royal Academy of Dramatic Art (Bronze medal). Hon. DLitt: Durham, Wales. Order of Finland's White Rose and Finland's Lion. First appearance on stage, 1921; in All God's Chillun, 1933; Old Vic Season, 1934; Touchwood and Mary Read, Dragoon and Pirate; Close Quarters, 1935; Mary Tudor, 1936; Lady Brooke in Autumn, St Martin's Theatre; Thérèse Raquin in Guilty, Lyric Theatre, Hammersmith, 1944; Man about the House, Piccadilly; Message from Margaret, Duchess; Lady Macbeth, New York, 1948; Captain Brassbound's Conversion (Shaw), Lyric Hammersmith, 1948; Alicia Christie in Black Chiffon, Westminster, 1949; Paulina in The Winter's Tale, Phœnix, 1951; Miss Giddens in The Innocents, Her Majesty's, 1952; Sister Agatha in The Return, Duchess, 1953; Rachel in No Escape; Sarah in A Kind of Folly, Duchess, 1955; Mrs Smith in Suspect, Royal Court, 1955; Janet Holt in The House by the Lake, Duke of York's, 1956-58; Mrs Alving in Ghosts, Old Vic, 1958; Miss Tina in The Aspern Papers, Queen's, 1959; and tour, S Africa, 1960; Grace Rouarte in Time and Yellow Roses, St Martin's, 1961; Miss Moffat in The Corn is Green, in S Africa, S Rhodesia and at Flora Robson Playhouse, Newcastle upon Tyne, 1962; tour, Close Quarters, 1963; Mrs Borkman in John Gabriel Borkman, Duchess, 1962; The Trojan Women, Edinburgh Festival, 1966; tour, Brother and Sister; Miss Prism in The Importance of Being Earnest, Haymarket, 1968; Ring Round The Moon, 1969; The Old Ladies, 1969. *Films:* Empress Elizabeth of Russia in Catherine the Great, 1933; Queen Elizabeth in Fire Over England; Mrs Blair in Farewell Again; Ellen Dean in Wuthering Heights; Mary Rider in Poison Pen; Ftata Teeta in Cæsar and Cleopatra; Sister Phillippa in Black Narcissus; Nell Dawson, MP, in Frieda; Countess Von Platen in Saraband for Dead Lovers; Mary Rackham in Tall Headlines; Melita in Malta Story; The Nurse in Romeo and Juliet; Donna McKenzie in High Tide at Noon; Mrs Haggard in The Gipsy and the Gentleman; Olivia in Innocent Sinners; The Empress of China in 55 Days at Peking; Miss Gilchrist in Murder at the Gallop; Young Cassidy; Guns at Batasi; Those Magnificent Men in their Flying Machines; Seven Women; The Shuttered Room; Cry in the Wind; Eye of the Devil; Fragment of Fear; I think you are dying, young man. *Relevant Publication:* Flora Robson by Janet Dunbar, 1960. *Address:* Marine House, 14 Marine Gardens, Brighton 7, Sussex.

**ROBSON, Vice-Adm. (retd) Sir Geoffrey;** *see* Robson, Vice-Adm. Sir W. G. A.

**ROBSON, Professor Hugh Norwood,** MB, ChB, FRCP, FRCP(Ed), FRACP; Vice-Chancellor, University of Sheffield, since 1966; Professor Emeritus, University of Adelaide, since 1965; *b* 18 Oct. 1917; *s* of late Hugh and Elizabeth Robson; *m* 1942, Alice Eleanor, *o d* of A. McD Livingstone, CIE, MC, MA, BSc, and late Gladys Livingstone, Berkhamsted, Herts; one *s* two *d*. *Educ:* Dumfries Academy; University of Edinburgh. Surg-Lieut RNVR, Western Approaches, Normandy, Arakan, Malaya, 1942-46. Clinical Tutor, Royal Infirmary, Edinburgh, 1946; Lecturer, Dept of Medicine, Univ. of Edinburgh, 1947-50; Sen. Lectr, Dept of Medicine, Univ. of Aberdeen, 1950-53; Prof. of Medicine, Univ. of Adelaide, S Australia, 1953-65. Member: Nat. Health and Med. Research Council of Australia, 1957-65; New Guinea Med. Research Council, 1962-65; Australian Drug Evaluation Cttee, 1963-65; Inter-Univ. Council for Higher Educn Overseas, 1967-; Central Cttee on Postgraduate Med. Educn, GB, 1968- (Chm.); British Cttee of Award for Harkness Fellowships (Commonwealth Fund), 1968-; Special Steels Div. Adv. Bd, BSC, 1970-; Cttee of Vice-Chancellors and Principals of Univs of UK, 1970-. Trustee, Nuffield Provincial Hosps Trust, 1966-. *Publications:* papers on hæmatological and other subjects in Brit., Amer. and Aust. med. jls. *Recreations:* reading, carpentry and golf. *Address:* Vice-Chancellor's Office, University of Sheffield, Sheffield S10 2TN. *T:* Sheffield 78555. *Clubs:* Athenæum; Sheffield (Sheffield).

**ROBSON, Professor Emeritus James,** MA, DLitt (Glasgow), DD (Hon. St Andrews); MA (Hon. Manchester); *b* 1890; *s* of Rev. Charles Robson; *m* 1919, Annie, *d* of John Cunningham, Dunblane; one *s* one *d*. *Educ:* Inverness Royal Acad.; Stirling High School; Glasgow University; Trinity College, Glasgow. Assistant to Hebrew Professor, Glasgow Univ., 1915-16. Served with YMCA in Mesopotamia and India, 1916-18. Lecturer in English, Forman Christian College, Lahore, 1918-19; Missionary at Sheikh Othman, Aden, 1919-26; Minister at Shandon, Dunbartonshire, 1926-28; Lecturer in Arabic, 1928-48, Reader in Arabic, 1948-49, Glasgow Univ.; Prof. of Arabic, the Univ. of Manchester, 1949-58; Recording Secretary, Glasgow University Oriental Soc., 1931-49; Secretary, 1959-68. External Examiner for Hons Degree: Manchester, 1933-36; 1942-45; 1961-64; Edinburgh, 1945-47; 1952-54; 1961-63; St Andrews, 1957-60; Aberdeen, 1960-62; Glasgow, 1960, 1962; London, 1955-66; and for PhD on occasion at Cambridge, Melbourne, etc. *Publications:* Ion Keith-Falconer of Arabia, 1923; Christ in Islam, 1929; Tracts on listening to Music, 1938; Ancient Arabian Musical Instruments, 1938; An introduction to the science of Tradition, 1953; Mishkāt al-masābih (trans and notes), 4 vols, 1963-65; ed, Islam section in A Dictionary of Comparative Religion, 1970; articles in learned journals. *Recreation:* gardening. *Address:* 17 Woodlands Drive, Glasgow, C4. *T:* 041-332 4088.

**ROBSON, Prof. John Michael;** Professor of Pharmacology, Guy's Hospital Medical School, London University, 1950-68, now Emeritus; *b* 13 Dec. 1900; *m* 1930, Sarah Benjamin. *Educ:* Leeds Central High School; Leeds University. Qualified MB, ChB, 1925; MD, 1930; DSc, 1932. Lecturer in Pharmacology, Edinburgh University, 1934; Reader in Pharmacology, Guy's Hospital Medical School, 1946. *Publications:* Recent Advances in Sex and Reproductive Physiology, 1934 (2nd edn 1940, 3rd edn 1947); Chapter in Endocrine in Theory and Practice, 1937; Chapter in The Practice of Endocrinology, 1948; (with C. A. Keele) Recent Advances in Pharmacology, 1950, 2nd edn 1956, 3rd edn (with S. Stacey) 1962, 4th edn, 1968; papers in British Journal of Pharmacol., Journal Physiol., Lancet, British Medical Journal, etc. *Recreations:* bridge, detective stories. *Address:* 2 Brunel House, Cheyne Walk, SW10. *T:* 01-352 8473.

**ROBSON, Sir Kenneth,** Kt 1968; CBE 1959; FRCP; Physician: St George's Hospital, SW1, since 1938; Brompton Hospital, SW3, since 1947; King Edward VII Hospital for Officers; King Edward VII Sanatorium, Midhurst; Civil Consultant-in-Medicine, Royal Air Force, since 1949; Chief Medical Referee (UK) Confederation Life Assoc.; *b* 1909; *y s* of late John Ajmer and Katherine Robson. *Educ:* Bradfield; Christ's College, Cambridge; Middlesex Hospital. Davis and Cree Prizes in Medicine; 2nd Broderip Schol., 1933; qualified, 1933; Resident Posts and Registrarships at Middlesex and Brompton Hospitals. MA, MD, BChir Cantab; MRCP 1935, FRCP 1943. Goulstonian Lectr, RCP, 1944; Examr, 1949-57; Censor, 1959; Registrar, 1961. Examr in Med.: Univs Camb., London, Durham. RAFVR Med. Br., 1938; whole time service, 1939-46; Wing Comdr-in-charge of Med. Divs at hosps in England and India; Air Cdre, Consultant-in-Medicine to RAF in India and Far East; toured Medical Estabs for HM Colonial Office in N Caribbean Is and Br Honduras, 1959; Visitor for RCP and RCS to Medical Faculty, Univ. of Khartoum, 1963; RCP Visitor, Australia and New Zealand, 1965, S Africa, 1969. Mem. Assoc. of Physicians and of Thoracic Society (President 1965; Secretary 1947-60); Corresp. Fellow, Amer. Coll. of Physicians; Hon. Fellow, S African Coll. of Physicians. *Publications:* contributions to text books and various scientific jls mostly in connection with the chest. *Recreations:* amateur cinematography; watching professional football. *Address:* 34 Sydney Street, SW3. *T:* 01-352 3852; Tatham's, Danehill, Sussex. *Clubs:* Athenæum, Royal Air Force; Royal Ashdown Forest Golf.

**ROBSON, Lawrence William,** FCA, FCWA, JDipMA; Senior Partner, Robson, Rhodes & Co., 24-28 Moorgate, EC2; *b* 8 Aug. 1904; *e s* of late Michael William Robson and of Jane Robson, Norton-on-Tees, Co. Durham; *m* 1940, Inga-Stina Arvidsson, Stockholm; one *s* two *d*. *Educ:* Stockton Grammar School. Financial Adviser, UNRRA, 1944-46, and IRO, 1946; Chm. of several engineering cos; Member: Lloyd's; Court of Guardian Assurance Co. Ltd; London Transport Executive; Council, Inst. of Chartered Accountants in England and Wales, 1949-69; Anglo-Amer. Productivity Team, 1949; Liberal Party Organisation (Pres., 1953-54); Herbert Cttee of Inquiry into efficiency and organisation of elect. supply industry, 1954-56; Economic Policy Cttee, FBI, 1956-62; Britain in Europe Cttee (Chm. 1958-64); Adv. Cttee on Censuses of Production, 1961-67; Council, BIM, 1961-; Anglo-Swedish Soc. (Chm.); European Atlantic Gp (Vice-Pres., 1969-); Council of European Movement, 1969-. Pres., Inst. Cost and Works Accountants, 1950-51; Liveryman, Worshipful Cos of Farmers, Painter-Stainers and Shipwrights. *Publications:* papers on accountancy, management, political and economic subjects. *Recreations:* ski-ing, cricket, sailing and shooting. *Address:* Kiddington Hall, Woodstock, Oxon. *T:* Enstone 398. *Club:* Boodle's.

**ROBSON, Sir Thomas (Buston),** Kt, *cr* 1954; MBE 1919; FCA; Partner in Price Waterhouse

& Co., Chartered Accountants, 1934-66; Chairman, Renold Ltd, since 1967; *b* Newcastle upon Tyne, 4 Jan. 1896; *s* of late Thomas Robson, Langholm, Dumfriesshire, and Newcastle upon Tyne; *m* 1936, Roberta Cecilia Helen, *d* of late Rev. Archibald Fleming, DD, St Columba's Church of Scotland, Pont St, SW1; two *d*. *Educ:* Rutherford College, Newcastle upon Tyne; Armstrong Collge, University of Durham. BA Hons, Modern History, 1920; MA 1923. Served European War, 1914-18, with British Salonika Force in Macedonia; Captain RGA; MBE, despatches 1919; articled with Sisson & Allden, Chartered Accountants, Newcastle upon Tyne, 1920; W. B. Peat gold medal in final examination of Inst. Chartered Accountants in England and Wales, 1922; joined staff of Price Waterhouse & Co., London, 1923; ACA, 1923, FCA, 1939; Mem. Council of Inst., 1941-66 (Vice-Pres. 1951-52; Pres., 1952-53); rep. Inst. at overseas mtgs of accountants; FCA (Ont.); CA (Rhodesia). Internat. Associate of American Institute of Certified Public Accountants: Member: Committee on Amendment of Census of Production Act, Bd of Trade, 1945; Central Valuation Bd for Coal Industry, 1947; Accountancy Advisory Cttee on Companies Act, Bd of Trade, 1948-68 (Chm. 1955-68); Cttee of Inquiry into London Transport Exec., Min. of Transport and Civil Aviation, 1953; Chm. Cttees of Inquiry into Coal Distribution Costs, Min. of Fuel and Power, 1956 and Min. of Commerce, N Ireland, 1956; Mem. Advisory Cttee on Replacement of the "Queen" ships, Min. of Transport and Civil Aviation, 1959; Chm. Economic Development Cttee for Paper and Board Industry under National Economic Development Council, 1964-67. Vice-Pres. Union Européenne des Experts Comptables, Economiques et Financiers, 1963-64; Mem. Transport Tribunal, 1963-69. *Publications:* Garnsey's Holding Companies and their Published Accounts, 3rd edn, 1936; The Construction of Consolidated Accounts, 1936; Consolidated and other Group Accounts, 1st edn, 1946, 4th edn, 1969; numerous papers and addresses on professional subjects. *Recreations:* walking and reading; for many years an active worker in Boy Scout movement (Vice-Pres., Gr London Central Scout Council). *Address:* (Home) 23 Brompton Square, SW3. *T:* 01-589 6553; (Office) 3 Frederick's Place, Old Jewry, EC2. *T:* 01-606 6044. *Club:* Athenæum.

**ROBSON, Professor William;** Professor of Biochemistry, King's College, London University, 1958-60, Professor Emeritus, 1961; *b* 15 Feb. 1893; *s* of William Robson, Cramlington, Northumberland; *m* 1924, Anne Wallace, *d* of Alexander Kerr, JP, Forres, Morayshire. *Educ:* Morpeth Gram. Sch.; King's Coll., London. Royal Flying Corps, 1916; commissioned and "wings" awarded, 1917. BSc (Hons) London 1920. Asst Dept. of Medical Chemistry, Univ. of Edinburgh, 1920; Research Assistant, Dept of Therapeutics, Univ. of Edinburgh, 1922; PhD Edinburgh 1924; Lecturer in Physiological Chemistry, King's College, London, 1927; Reader in Biochemistry, King's College, London, 1931; DSc London 1930. Secretary, Biochemical Society, 1942-47. Fellow Rockefeller Foundation at Rockefeller Inst., NY, 1924, FKC 1955. *Publications:* Essentials of Chemical Physiology, 11th Edn, 1929, 12th Edn, 1933; papers in Jl of Chemical Society, Biochemical Journal. *Address:* 40 Waggon Road, Hadley Wood, Barnet, Herts. *T:* 01-449 2824.

**ROBSON, William Alexander;** Professor Emeritus of Public Administration in the University of London (London School of Economics and Political Science) (Professor, 1947-62); Barrister-at-law; Hon. Fellow, London Sch. of Economics; *b* 14 July 1895; *s* of late J. Robson; *m* 1929, Juliette Alvin, *qv*; two *s* one *d*. *Educ:* Univ. of London (London School of Economics and Political Science); BSc (Economics) First Class Honours, 1922; PhD 1924; LLM 1928. Served European War, 1914-18, as Lieutenant on active service in Royal Flying Corps and RAF; called to Bar, Lincoln's Inn, 1922; Lecturer at the London School of Economics from 1926; Reader in Administrative Law, 1933-46; Visiting Professor, University of Chicago, 1933, University of N Carolina, 1951, University of Patna, 1953, and other Indian Univs, Univ. of California, Berkeley, 1957; Indian Institute of Public Administration, 1960; Internat. Christian Univ., Tokyo, 1969. Principal, Mines Department, 1940-42; Ministry of Fuel and Power, 1942-43; Asst Sec., Air Ministry, 1943-45; Ministry of Civil Aviation, 1945; Member: Council, Town and Country Planning Assoc.; Deptl Cttee on Admin. of Greater London Plan; Vice-President: Royal Inst. of Public Administration; Cttee on Training in Public Administration for Overseas Countries: Political Studies Assoc. Pres., Internat. Political Science Assoc., 1950-53. Chairman, Gr London Gp, LSE. Noranda Lectr, Expo 1967. Founder and Joint Editor, The Political Quarterly. Consultant to Govts of Lebanon, Nigeria, Turkey, and Tokyo Metropol. Govt. Docteur de l'Univ. (*hc*); Lille, 1953; Grenoble, 1955; Paris, 1955; Algiers, 1959; Hon. DLitt: Dunelm, 1963; Manchester, 1964; Hon. DSocSci, Birmingham, 1970. *Publications:* From Patronage to Proficiency in the Public Service, 1922; The Relation of Wealth to Welfare, 1924; Justice and Administrative Law, 1928; Civilisation and the Growth of Law, 1935; The Town Councillor (with C. R. Attlee), 1925; contributor to London Essays in Economics, 1927; Modern Theories of Law, 1938; The Development of Local Government, 1931; The Law of Local Government Audit, 1930; A Century of Municipal Progress (contributor and Joint Editor), 1935; The British Civil Servant, (contributor and editor), 1937; Public Enterprise (contributor and editor), 1937; The Government and Misgovernment of London, 1939; The British System of Government, 1940; Social Security (contributor and editor), 1943; Planning and Performance, 1943; Population and the People, 1945; British Government since 1918 (contributor), 1950; Problems of Nationalised Industry, 1952; The Teaching of Political Science (Unesco), 1954; Great Cities of the World, 1955; The Civil Service in Britain and France, 1956; Nationalised Industry and Public Ownership, 1960; The Governors and the Governed, 1964; The Heart of Greater London, 1965; Local Government in Crisis, 1966; Politics and Government at Home and Abroad, 1967. Editor, Politics Section, Hutchinson University Library. *Recreations:* walking and tennis. *Address:* 48 Lanchester Road, N6. *T:* 01-883 1331. *Clubs:* Athenæum, Campden Hill Tennis.

**ROBSON, Vice-Adm. Sir (William) Geoffrey (Arthur),** KBE 1956; CB 1953; DSO 1940 (Bar 1941); DSC 1941; Lieutenant-Governor and Commander-in-Chief of Guernsey, 1958-64; *b* 10 March 1902; *s* of Major John Robson; *m* 1st, 1925, Sylvia Margaret Forrester (*d* 1968); one *s*; 2nd, 1969, Elizabeth Kathleen, widow of Lt-Col V. H. Holt. *Educ:* RN Colleges, Osborne and Dartmouth. Midshipman, HMS Malaya, 1918; served in Destroyers, 1922-37. Commanded Rowena, 1934; Wren, 1935-36; RN Staff Course, 1937; RAF Staff Course,

1938. Served War of 1939-45 (despatches thrice, DSO and Bar, DSC): Comd HMS Kandahar, 1939-41; Combined Operations, 1942-43; Commanded the 26th Destroyer Flotilla, 1944, in HMS Hardy; Captain of Coastal Forces (Nore), 1945; HMS Superb in command, 1945-47; Comd HMS Ganges, 1948-50; President of Admiralty Interview Board, 1950-51; Flag Officer (Flotillas), Home Fleet, 1951-53; Flag Officer, Scotland, 1952-56; Commander-in-Chief, South Atlantic, 1956-58; retd, 1958. Commander of the Order of St Olav (Norway). *Recreations:* shooting, fishing, and golf. *Address:* Fyrish House, Evanton, Ross-shire; Amat, Ardgay, Ross-shire. *Club:* Army and Navy.

**ROBSON, William Michael;** Director: Booker McConnell Ltd, since 1955; The Standard Bank Ltd (a Dep. Chm.), since 1965; The Standard Bank Finance & Development Corp. Ltd (Chm.), since 1966; Standard and Chartered Banking Group Ltd, since 1970; *b* 31 Dec. 1912; *e s* of late Col the Hon. Harold Burge Robson, TD, DL, JP, Pinewood Hill, Witley, Surrey and late Ysolt Robson (*née* Leroy-Lewis); *m* 1st, 1939, Audrey Isobel Wales (*d* 1964), *d* of late Maj. William Dick, Low Gosforth Hall, Northumberland; two *s* one *d*; 2nd, 1965, Frances Mary Wyville, *d* of late James Anderson Ramage Dawson, Balado House, Kinross, and *widow* of Andrew Alexander Nigel Buchanan (he *d* 1960). *Educ:* Eton; New College, Oxford. Served War of 1939-45: with Grenadier Guards (Maj. 1944), England and Europe BAOR. A Vice-Chm., Victoria League for Commonwealth Friendship, 1962-65. Dir British South Africa Co., 1961-66 (Vice-Chm., Jt East & Central African Bd, 1956-63); Mem., BNEC, Africa, 1965-. High Sheriff of Kent, 1970. *Address:* 28 Smith Terrace, Chelsea, SW3. *T:* 01-352 2177; Hales Place, Tenterden, Kent. *T:* Tenterden 2932. *Clubs:* Brooks's, Pratt's, MCC, Band of Brothers.

**ROBSON BROWN, Sir William,** Kt 1957; British parentage; *m* 1st, 1922, Elsie Irene Thomas (*d* 1968); two *d*; 2nd, 1969, Mrs Kay Sanders. *Educ:* Armstrong College, Newcastle upon Tyne. Served European War, 1914-18, in RFC and RAF. MP (C) Esher Division of Surrey, 1950-70. Lifetime experience in steel industry; authority on management labour relations in industry. Pres., Society of Commercial Accountants; Mem. Council, Confederation of British Industry. Chm. Governors of Brooklands County Technical Coll. Pres. The Marlow Foundation. *Publications:* The Tinplate Industry; Industrial Democracy at Work; Management and Society. *Address:* Churchfields, Weybridge, Surrey.

**ROBSON-SCOTT, Prof. William Douglas,** MA Oxon, DrPhil Vienna; Hon. Director, Institute of Germanic Studies, since 1968; *b* 9 Aug. 1901; *s* of late Thomas William Robson-Scott and Florence Jane (*née* Lang); *m* 1947, Elaine Davies; one *d*. *Educ:* Rugby Sch.; University Coll., Oxford; Univs of Berlin and Vienna. 1st cl. hons English, Oxon, 1923. Lektor, Univ. of Berlin, 1933-37; seconded to War Office, 1939-45; Birkbeck Coll., Univ. of London: Lectr in German, 1939-61; Reader, 1961-66; Prof. of German Language and Literature, 1966-68, Emer. Prof. 1968. *Publications:* German Travellers in England 1400-1800, 1953; The Literary Background of the Gothic Revival in Germany, 1965; various articles in learned jls. *Recreations:* hill-walking, travel. *Address:* 19 Dorset Square, NW1. *T:* 01-262 2877.

**ROCH, Muriel Elizabeth Sutcliffe,** BA; Headmistress, School of S Mary and S Anne, Abbots Bromley, Staffs, since 1953; *b* 7 Sept. 1916; *d* of late Rev. Sydney John Roch, MA Cantab, Pembroke and Manchester. *Educ:* Manchester High Sch.; Bedford Coll., London; Hughes Hall, Cambridge. Teaching appointments at: Devonport High School, 1939-41; Lady Manners, Bakewell, 1941-44; Howells School, Denbigh, 1944-47; Talbot Heath, Bournemouth, 1947-53. Mem. Exec. Cttee, Assoc. of Head Mistresses. *Recreations:* motoring, travel. *Address:* S Anne's Croft, Abbots Bromley, Staffs. *T:* Abbots Bromley 381. *Club:* English-Speaking Union.

**ROCHDALE,** 1st Viscount *cr* 1960; 2nd Baron 1913; **John Durival Kemp,** OBE 1945; TD; DL Cumberland; Director: Kelsall & Kemp Ltd, Rochdale (Chm.); Williams and Glyn's Bank, since 1970; *b* 5 June 1906; *s* of 1st Baron and Lady Beatrice Egerton, 3rd *d* of 3rd Earl of Ellesmere; *S* father, 1945; *m* 1931, Elinor Dorothea Pease (CBE 1964; JP); one *s* (one *d* decd). *Educ:* Eton; Trin. Coll., Cambridge. Hons degree Nat. Science Tripos. Served War of 1939-45 (despatches); attached USA forces in Pacific with rank of Col, 1944; Temp. Brig., 1945. Hon. Col 251 (Westmorland and Cumberland Yeomanry) Field Regiment, RA, TA, late 851 (W&CY) Field Bty, RA, 1959-67. Director: Consett Iron Co. Ltd, 1957-67; Williams Deacon's Bank Ltd, 1960-70. President National Union of Manufacturers, 1953-56; Member, Dollar Exports Council, 1953-61; Western Hemisphere Exports Council, 1961-64; a Gov. of the BBC 1954-59; Pres., British Legion, NW Area, 1955-61; Mem. Central Transport Consultative Cttee for GB, 1953-57; Chairman: Docks and Harbours Committee of Inquiry, 1961; Cotton Board, 1957-62; National Ports Council, 1963-67; Cttee of Inquiry into Shipping, 1967-70. *Heir: s* Hon. St John Durival Kemp [*b* 1938; *m* 1960, Serena Jane, *d* of Michael Clark-Hall and Mrs George Trotter; two *s* two *d*]. *Address:* Lingholm, Keswick, Cumberland. *T:* Keswick 72003. *Club:* Lansdowne.

*See also Sir John D. Barlow, Sir V. B. J. Seely, Duke of Sutherland.*

**ROCHDALE, Archdeacon of;** *see* Ballard, Ven. A. H.

**ROCHE,** family name of **Baron Fermoy.**

**ROCHE, James Michael;** Chairman of Board of Directors and Chief Executive Officer, General Motors Corporation, since Nov. 1967; *b* 16 Dec. 1906; *s* of Thomas E. and Gertrude Agnes (Buel) Roche; *m* 1929, Louise McMillan; two *s* one *d*. *Educ:* LaSalle Univ., Chicago. Statistician, Cadillac Motor Car Div., Chicago Sales and Service Br., 1927; Asst to Chicago Br. Man., Cadillac, 1928; Asst Regional Business Man., NY, Cadillac, 1931; Asst Man., Cadillac Business Management Dept, Detroit, 1933; Man., Nat. Business Management, Cadillac, 1935; Dir of Personnel, Cadillac, 1943; Dir of Personnel and Public Relations, Cadillac, 1949; Gen. Sales Man., Cadillac, 1950; Gen. Man. of Cadillac and Vice-Pres., Gen. Motors Corp., 1957; Vice-Pres., Distribution Staff, Gen. Motors Corp., 1960; Exec. Vice-Pres., Gen. Motors, 1962; Pres. and Chief Operating Off., Gen. Motors Corp., 1965. Hon. Dr of Laws: John Carrol Univ., Ohio, 1963; Fordham Univ., NY, 1966; Michigan State Univ., 1968; Hon. Dr of Science, Judson Coll., Ill, 1965; Hon. Dr of Laws, Eastern Michigan Univ., 1969. Kt of Malta (Amer. Chapter), 1951. *Recreations:* music, reading, fishing. *Address:* Bloomfield Hills, Michigan 48013, USA; 860 Fifth Avenue, New York, NY 10021, USA. *Clubs:* Detroit, Economic (Detroit); Links, University, Economic (NY); Detroit Athletic,

Orchard Lake Country, Bloomfield Hills Country.

**ROCHE, Sir Standish O'Grady,** 4th Bt, *cr* 1838; DSO 1942; Lt-Comdr RN retd; *b* 13 March 1911; *s* of 3rd Bt and Sybil (*d* 1950), *o d* of Col Julius Dyson-Laurie, Gloucester Pl., W; *S* father, 1914; *m* 1946, Evelyn Laura, *o d* of Major W. Andon; two *s*. ADC to Gov.-General of New Zealand, 1935-37. Croix de Guerre (1945). *Heir: s* David O'Grady Roche, *b* 21 Sept. 1947. *Address:* Rua Heliodoro Salgado 9, Santo Amaro de Oeiras, Portugal.

**ROCHE, Hon. Thomas Gabriel,** QC 1955; Recorder of the City of Worcester since 1959; *b* 1909; *yr s* of late Baron Roche, PC. *Educ:* Rugby; Wadham Coll., Oxford. Called to the Bar, Inner Temple, 1932. Served War of 1939-45 (Lt-Col 1944, despatches). Church Commissioner, 1961-65; Member, Monopolies Commission, 1966-69. *Address:* Chadlington, Oxford. *Club:* United University.

**ROCHESTER,** 2nd Baron, of the 4th creation, *cr* 1931, of Rochester in the County of Kent; **Foster Charles Lowry Lamb;** Personnel Manager (Education and Training), Mond Division, Imperial Chemical Industries Ltd, since 1965; Chairman, West Cheshire Boy Scouts' Association; Chairman Northwich and District Local Employment Committee; *b* 7 June 1916; *s* of 1st Baron Rochester, CMG, and Rosa Dorothea, *y d* of late W. J. Hurst, JP, Drumaness, County Down; *S* father 1955; *m* 1942, Mary Carlisle, *yr d* of T. B. Wheeler, CBE, Aspley Guise, Bucks; two *s* one *d* (and one *d* decd). *Educ:* Mill Hill; Jesus College, Cambridge. BA 1937; MA 1941. Served War of 1939-45: Captain 23rd Hussars; France, 1944. *Heir: s* Hon. David Charles Lamb [*b* 8 Sept. 1944; *m* 1969, Jacqueline Stamp. *Educ:* Shrewsbury Sch.; Univ. of Sussex]. *Address:* The Hollies, Hartford, Northwich, Cheshire. *T:* Northwich 74733. *Club:* National Liberal.
*See also Hon. K. H. L. Lamb.*

**ROCHESTER, Bishop of,** since 1961; **Rt. Rev. Richard David Say,** DD (Lambeth) 1961; Lord High Almoner, since 1970; *b* 4 Oct. 1914; *s* of Commander Richard Say, OBE, RNVR, and Kathleen Mary (*née* Wildy); *m* 1943, Irene Frances (JP), *e d* of Seaburne and Frances Rayner, Exeter; one *s* two *d* (and one *s* decd). *Educ:* University Coll. Sch.; Christ's College, Cambridge (MA); Ridley Hall, Cambridge. Ordained deacon, 1939; priest, 1940. Curate of Croydon Parish Church, 1939-43; Curate of St Martin-in-the-Fields, London, 1943-50; Asst Sec. Church of England Youth Council, 1942-44; Gen. Sec., 1944-47; Gen. Sec. British Council of Churches, 1947-55; Church of England delegate to World Council of Churches, 1948, 1954 and 1961. Select Preacher, University of Cambridge, 1954 and University of Oxford, 1963; Rector of Bishop's Hatfield, 1955-61; Hon. Canon of St Albans, 1957-61. Domestic Chaplain to Marquess of Salisbury and Chaplain of Welfield Hospital, 1955-61; Hon. Chaplain of The Pilgrims, 1968-. Vice-Chm., Missionary and Ecumenical Council of the National Synod; Dep. Chm., Redundant Churches Cttee. Entered House of Lords, 1969. Chaplain and Sub-Prelate, Order of St John. *Recreations:* sailing and travel. *Address:* Bishopscourt, Rochester. *T:* Medway 42721. *Club:* United University.

**ROCHESTER, Assistant Bishop of;** *see* Russell, Rt Rev. J. K.

**ROCHESTER, Dean of;** *see* Betts, Rt Rev. S. W.

**ROCHESTER, Archdeacon of;** *see* Stewart-Smith, Ven. D. C.

**ROCHESTER, Prof. George Dixon,** FRS 1958; FInstP; Professor of Physics, University of Durham, since 1955; *b* 4 Feb. 1908; *s* of Thomas and Ellen Rochester; *m* 1938, Idaline, *o d* of Rev. J. B. Bayliffe; one *s* one *d*. *Educ:* Wallsend Grammar School; Universities of Durham, Stockholm and California. BSc, MSc, PhD (Dunelm). Earl Grey Memorial Scholar, Armstrong College, Durham University, 1926-29; Earl Grey Fellow, at Stockholm Univ., 1934-35; Commonwealth Fund Fellow at California Univ., 1935-37; Manchester University: Asst Lectr, 1937-46; Lectr, 1946-49; Sen. Lectr, 1949-53; Reader, 1953-55. Scientific Adviser in Civil Defence for NW Region, 1952-55. C. V. Boys Prizeman of the Physical Society of London, 1956; Symons Memorial Lecturer of the Royal Meteorological Soc., 1962. Member Council for National Academic Awards, 1964-. Second Pro-Vice-Chancellor, Univ. of Durham, 1967-69, Pro-Vice-Chancellor, 1969-70. *Publications:* (with J. G. Wilson) Cloud Chamber Photographs of the Cosmic Radiation, 1952. Scientific papers on cosmic rays and spectroscopy. *Recreations:* gardening, travel. *Address:* Physics Department, University of Durham, Durham.

**ROCHETA, Dr Manuel Farrajota;** Military Order of Christ of Portugal; Ambassador for Portugal in Madrid, since 1968; *b* 6 Aug. 1906; *s* of Manuel and Rosa Rocheta; *m* 1933, Maria Luiza Belmarco Rocheta; one *d*. *Educ:* Lisbon University. Entered Diplomatic Service, 1931; Assistant Consul Hamburg, 1934; Consul Copenhagen, 1935-39; First Sec. and Chargé d'Affaires ai, Bucarest, 1943-45; First Sec. and Chargé d'Affaires ai, Dublin, 1945; First Secretary, Washington, 1946, Counsellor, 1947, Minister-Counsellor, 1950 (Chargé d'Affaires, 1 Nov. 1946-31 March 1947 and 11 Feb. 1950-6 June 1950); Asst Dir-Gen. of Political Dept, Foreign Affairs Ministry, Lisbon, 1951; Minister-Plen. and Dir-Gen. of Political Dept, Foreign Ministry, Lisbon, 1954; Minister in Bonn, 1956, Ambassador, 1956-58; Ambassador: to Rio de Janeiro, 1958-61; to the Court of St James's, 1961-68. Doctor in Law, Univ. of Bahia, Brazil. Knight Grand Cross of Royal Victorian Order, Gt Brit. (Hon. GCVO) 1955, and holds Grand Cross of several foreign orders. *Recreations:* walking and swimming. *Address:* The Portuguese Embassy, Madrid, Spain.

**ROCHFORT, Capt. C. B.;** *see* Boyd-Rochfort.

**ROCKE, John Roy Mansfield;** Vice-Chairman, Booker McConnell Ltd, since 1962; *b* 13 April 1918; *s* of late Frederick Gilbert Rocke and late Mary Susan Rocke; *m* 1948, Pauline Diane Berry; no *c*. *Educ:* Charterhouse; Trinity Coll., Cambridge (BA). War Service, Grenadier Guards, 1940-46 (Maj.). Orme & Eykyn (Stockbrokers), 1946-50; Booker McConnell Ltd, 1950- (Dir, 1954). Mem., British Nat. Export Coun. and Chm., BNEC (Caribbean), 1965-68; Chm., Nat. Econ. Development Cttee for the Food Manufacturing Industry, 1967-. *Address:* 22 Bruton Street, W1. *T:* 01-629 3393; Pendomer Manor, Pendomer, near Yeovil, Somerset. *Club:* Guards.

**ROCKEFELLER, David,** Chairman and Chief Executive, Chase Manhattan Bank, since 1969 (Director, 1956; Vice-Chairman, 1957; President and Chairman of Executive Committee, 1961); Chairman of Chase International Investment Corporation since 1961; *b* New York City, 12 June 1915; *s* of John Davison and Abby Greene (Aldrich)

Rockefeller; *m* 1940, Margaret, *d* of Francis Sims McGrath, Mount Kisco, NY; two *s* four *d*. *Educ:* Lincoln School of Columbia University's Teachers College; Harvard Univ. (BS); London School of Economics; Univ. of Chicago (PhD). Asst Regional Dir, US Office of Defense Health and Welfare Services, 1941. Served in US Army, N Africa and France, 1942-45 (Captain). Joined Chase National Bank, NYC, as Asst Manager, Foreign Dept, 1946; Asst Cashier, 1947; Second Vice-Pres., 1948; Vice-Pres., 1949; Senior Vice-Pres., 1952; Exec. Vice-Pres., Chase Manhattan Bank (formed by merging of Chase Nat. Bank and Bank of Manhattan Co.), 1955. President and Trustee, Sealantic Fund, Inc.; Trustee, Rockefeller Brothers Fund, Inc.; President, Rockefeller Family Fund; Chairman: Chase Manhattan Bank Foundation; Council for Latin America; Downtown–Lower Manhattan Assoc., Inc.; Chm. Bd of Trustees: Museum of Modern Art; Rockefeller Univ.; Chm. and Dir, Internat. Exec. Service Corps; Dir and Mem. Finance Cttee, Rockefeller Center, Inc.; Co-Chm., Task Force on Housing, Reconstruction and Investment of Urban Coalition; Founding mem. Business Cttee for the Arts; Director and Vice-President, Council on Foreign Relations, Inc.; Director, Hills Realty Co., Inc.; Member: Economic Policy Cttee, American Bankers Assoc. (Trustee, Foundation for Educn in Economics); Business Council; Advisory Bd, Brazilian American Cultural Institute; Advisory Cttee, Internat. Monetary Arrangements; Near East Emergency Donations; Harvard Univ.: Mem. Cttee on Univ. Resources. Gold Medal, Nat. Inst. of Social Sciences, 1967. Hon. LLD: Columbia Univ., 1954; Bowdoin Coll., 1958; Jewish Theological Seminary, 1958; Williams Coll., 1966. Holds civic awards; Officer, Legion of Honour, 1955. *Recreation:* sailing. *Address:* Room 5600, 30 Rockefeller Plaza, New York, NY 10020, USA. *Clubs:* Century, Harvard, Knickerbocker, Links, University (New York).

*See also John D. Rockefeller, L. S. Rockefeller, N. A. Rockefeller.*

**ROCKEFELLER, James Stillman;** Director, First National City Trust Co. (Bahamas) Ltd; Vice-President and Director, Indian Spring Land Co.; Director of: Kimberly-Clark Corp.; National Cash Register Co.; Pan-American World Airways; Cranston (RI) Print Works Co.; Monsanto Company; *b* New York, 8 June 1902; *s* of William Goodsell Rockefeller and Elsie (*née* Stillman); *m* 1925, Nancy Carnegie; two *s* two *d*. *Educ:* Yale University (BA). With Brown Bros & Co., NYC, 1924-30; joined National City Bank of New York (later First Nat. City Bank), 1930; Asst Cashier, 1931; Asst Vice-Pres. 1933; Vice-Pres., 1940-48; Sen. Vice-Pres., 1948-52; Exec. Vice-Pres., 1952; Pres. and Director, 1952-59; Chairman, 1959-67. Rep. Greenwich (Conn.) Town Meeting, 1933-42. Served as Lieutenant-Colonel in US Army, 1942-46. Member Board of Managers, Memorial Hospital for Cancer and Allied Diseases, NY; Trustee of Estate of William Rockefeller; Trustee American Museum of National History. *Address:* First National City Bank, 399 Park Avenue, New York, NY 10022, USA. *Clubs:* Links, Down Town Assoc., Union League, Fifth Avenue (New York); Metropolitan (Washington, DC); Field (Greenwich, Conn).

**ROCKEFELLER, John Davison,** 3rd, OBE (Hon.) 1948; Chairman, Rockefeller Foundation, since 1952 (Trustee of Foundation since 1931); *b* 21 March 1906; *s* of late John Davison Rockefeller, Jr, FRS, and Abby Greene Aldrich; *m* 1932, Blanchette Ferry Hooker; one *s* three *d*. *Educ:* Loomis School, Windsor, Conn.; Princeton Univ., Princeton, NJ (BS). Lt-Comdr, USNR, working with Combined Civil Affairs Cttee and State-War-Navy Co-ordinating Cttee, 1942-45. Consultant to the Dulles Mission to Japan on Peace Settlement, 1951; Adviser, US Delegation, Japanese Peace Treaty Conf., San Francisco, 1951. Established Rockefeller Public Service Awards, 1951. Chairman: Nat. Policy Panel on World Population and Quality of Human Develt; Commn on Population Growth and the American Future; Population Council (founder); Greater New York Fund Campaign, 1949; Agricultural Development Council (founder); Japan Soc. (Pres. 1952-70); President: The JDR 3rd Fund (founder); Amer. Youth Hostels, 1948-51. Trustee: Rockefeller Brothers Fund (Pres., 1940-55; Chm., Performing Arts Panel, 1963-65); Princeton Univ. (emeritus); United Negro College Fund (Hon. Chm.; Chm., Nat. Council, 1958-65); Colonial Williamsburg Inc., 1934-54 (Chm., 1939-53); Educational Broadcasting Corp., 1962-64; General Education Bd, 1932-65 (Chm., 1952-65); Internat. House, NYC, 1930-49; Lincoln Center for the Performing Arts (Hon. Chm.; Chm., 1961-70); Riverside Church, 1930-49, now Hon. Trustee; Rockefeller Inst. (now Rockefeller Univ.), 1932-39. Director: Phelps Meml Hosp. (Hon. Dir, 1953-68); Foreign Policy Assoc., 1954-61; NY Life Ins. Co., 1949-59; Rockefeller Center Inc., 1932-63. Special Tony Award, American Theater Wing, 1960; Lasker Award in Planned Parenthood, 1961; Gold Baton Award, Amer. Symphony Orch. League, 1963; Handel Medallion, NYC, 1964; Silver Plaque, Fedn of Jewish Philanthropies of NY, 1964; Presidential Citation, 1967 (for Rockefeller Public Service Awards); Margaret Sanger Award for Public Service in Family Planning, 1967; Gold Medal, Nat. Inst. of Social Sciences, 1967; Soc. for the Family of Man Award, Protestant Council, 1968. Grand Cordon, Order of Sacred Treasure, Japan, 1954; Most Noble Order of the Crown of Thailand, 1st cl, 1960; Order of Sikatuna, Philippines, 1967; Grand Cordon, Order of Rising Sun, Japan, 1968. *Recreations:* riding, golf, sailing. *Address:* 1 Beekman Place, New York City 10022, USA; (office) 30 Rockefeller Plaza, New York City 10020. *Clubs:* Century Association, University (New York); Metropolitan (Washington, DC).

*See also David Rockefeller, L. S. Rockefeller, N. A. Rockefeller.*

**ROCKEFELLER, Laurance Spelman;** Chairman, Caneel Bay Plantation Inc.; Director, Rockefeller Center Inc.; *b* New York, 26 May 1910; *s* of John Davison Rockefeller, Jr, FRS and Abby Greene Aldrich; *m* 1934, Mary French; one *s* three *d*. *Educ:* Lincoln School of Teachers College; Princeton University (BA). War service, Lt and Lt-Comdr, USNR, 1942-45. Chm., New York State Coun. of Parks; Trustee: Rockefeller Bros Fund; Amer. Cttee Internat. Wildlife Protection; Jackson Hole Preserve, Inc. (Pres.); Alfred P. Sloan Foundation Inc.; Memorial Sloan-Kettering Cancer Center (Chm.); American Conservation Assoc. (Pres.); New York Zoological Soc. (Pres.); National Board of YWCA of USA; National Geographic Soc.; Sealantic Fund, Inc. (Vice-Pres.); Life Mem. of Corp., Massachusetts Institute of Technology; Mem., Advisory Council, Dept of Philosophy, Princeton Univ.; Public Mem., Public Land Law Review Commn. Chm., Citizen's Adv. Cttee on Recreation and Natural Beauty; Nat. Recreation and Park Assoc. Gold Medal, Nat. Inst. of Social Sciences, 1967. Comdr, Royal Order of the Lion, Belgium, 1950. *Address:* Room 5600, 30

Rockefeller Plaza, New York, NY 10020, USA; 834 Fifth Avenue, New York, NY 10021. *Clubs:* River, Princeton, University, Downtown Association, Brook, Seawanhaka Yacht, Sleepy Hollow, Knickerbocker (all in USA).

*See also David Rockefeller, John D. Rockefeller, N. A. Rockefeller.*

**ROCKEFELLER, Nelson Aldrich;** Governor of New York State, elected in Nov. 1958, re-elected 1962, 1966; Chairman of Special Commission on Civil Defense; Mem. Advisory Commn on Intergovernmental Relations; International Basic Economy Corp.: Chm., 1958; Pres., 1947-53, 1956-58; Dir, 1947-53, 1956-58; *b* 8 July 1908; *s* of late John D. Rockefeller, Jr, FRS, and Abby Greene Aldrich; *m* 1st, 1930, Mary Todhunter Clark (marr. diss. 1962); two *s* two *d* (and one *s* decd); 2nd, 1963, Margaretta Fitler Murphy; two *s*. *Educ:* Dartmouth College (AB). Chase National Bank; Clerk, New York, London and Paris branches, 1931; Rockefeller Center, Inc.: Director, 1931-58; Pres., 1938-45, 1948-51; Chm., 1945-53 and 1956-58; Rockefeller Brothers Fund, Inc.: Pres., 1956-58; Trustee, 1940-; Museum of Modern Art (NY City): Pres., 1939-41, 1946-53; Chm., 1957-58; Trustee, 1932-. Co-ordinator of Inter-American Affairs, 1940-44; Asst Sec. of State, 1944-45; Amer. Internat. Assoc. for Economic and Social Development: Founder; Pres., 1946-53, 1957-58; Dir, 1946-53, 1956-; International Development Advisory Bd (Chm. 1950-51); President's Advisory Cttee on Govt Organization, Chairman, 1952-58; Under Secretary, Department of Health, Education and Welfare, USA, 1953-54; Special Assistant to the President, USA, 1954-55. Museum of Primitive Art (NY City): Founder and Pres., 1954-, Trustee, 1954-. Director, University of the Andes Foundation, Gold Medal, Nat. Inst. of Social Sciences, 1967. Holds various Hon. Degrees in Law and Humane Letters, Awards (US), also Foreign Orders. Citation by Nat. Conf. of Christians and Jews for work in field of human relations, 1948; Thomas F. Cunningham Award for contrib. toward betterment of Inter-American Relations, 1964. *Address:* Pocantico Hills, North Tarrytown, New York, USA. *Clubs:* Century Association, University (NY); Cosmos (Washington, DC); Seal Harbour Yacht (Maine).

*See also David Rockefeller, John D. Rockefeller, L. S. Rockefeller.*

**ROCKHAMPTON,** Bishop of, since 1963; **Rt. Rev. Donald Norman Shearman;** *b* 6 Feb. 1926; *s* of Stewart and Marie Shearman, Sydney; *m* 1952, Stuart Fay, *d* of late Chap. F. H. Bashford; three *s* three *d*. *Educ:* Fort St and Orange High Schools; St John's Theological College, Morpeth, NSW. Served War of 1939-45: air crew, 1944-46. Theological College, 1948-50. Deacon, 1950; Priest, 1951. Curate: of Dubbo, 1950-52; of Forbes, and Warden of St John's Hostel, 1953-56; Rector of Coonabarabran, 1957-59; Director of Promotion and Adult Christian Education, 1959-62; Canon, All Saints Cathedral, Bathurst, 1962; Archdeacon of Mildura and Rector of St Margaret's, 1963. *Recreations:* fire-arms and related subjects. *Address:* Lis Escop, Rockhampton, Queensland 4700, Australia. *T:* 2-3755.

**ROCKLEY,** 2nd Baron, *cr* 1934, of Lytchett Heath; **Robert William Evelyn Cecil;** Brig. (retired) RA; *b* 28 Feb. 1901; *s* of 1st Baron and Hon. Alicia Margaret Amherst, CBE (*d* 1941), *d* of 1st Baron Amherst of Hackney; *S* father 1941; *m* 1933, Anne, *d* of late Adm. Hon. Sir Herbert Meade-Fetherstonhaugh, GCVO, CB, DSO; two *s* one *d*. *Educ:* Christ Church, Oxford; Yale, USA (Davison scholar). Engineer; Director of: National Provincial Bank Ltd, Foreign & Colonial Trust; Clerical, Medical and General Life Assurance Society; Ministry of Supply, 1939-43; Military Governor 1944-45. *Recreations:* shooting, fishing. *Heir: s* Hon. James Hugh Cecil [*b* 5 April 1934; *m* 1958, Lady Sarah, *e d* of 7th Earl Cadogan, *qv*; one *s* two *d*]. *Address:* Lytchett Heath, Poole, Dorset; Clive House, 5 Connaught Place, W2. *Clubs:* Carlton, Pratt's.

**ROCKSAVAGE, Earl of; David George Philip Cholmondeley;** *b* 27 June 1960; *s* and *heir* of 6th Marquess of Cholmondeley, *qv*.

**ROCYN-JONES, Arthur,** MB, BS (London), FRCS; Consulting Surgeon to Royal National Orthopædic Hospital; Emeritus Consultant Orthopædic Surgeon: West End Hospital for Neurology and Neurosurgery; Fulham and Kensington Hospital Group; Consulting Orthopædic Surgeon to West Suffolk General Hospital, Glan Ely Hospital and to the Prince of Wales Hospital, Cardiff; *b* Rhymney, Monmouthshire; *y s* of David and Catherine Rocyn Jones; *m* Margaret, *d* of late Rev. D. J. Llewelyn, Vicar of Beaufort; one *d*. *Educ:* Lewis' School, University College, Cardiff (Monmouth Scholar); Univ. College, London; London Hospital. House Surgeon, Royal Infirmary, Cardiff; Senior House Surgeon and afterwards Surgical Registrar, Royal National Orthopædic Hospital; Fellow Roy. Soc. Med. (Hon. Mem. and Ex-Pres. of Orthopædic Section); Emeritus Fell., Brit. Orthopædic Association; Member Société Internationale de Chirurgie Orthopédique; Member of Council Hon. Society of Cymmrodorion; Member Cambrian Archæological Assoc.; Mem. Gen. Cttee British and Foreign Bible Soc. *Publications:* The Evolution of Orthopædic Surgery in Great Britain; and other papers in scientific journals. *Address:* 146 Harley Street, W1. *T:* 01-935 2378; Bryntirion, 151 Stanmore Hill, Stanmore, Middlesex. *T:* 01-954 1788.

**RODD,** family name of **Baron Rennell.**

**RODDAN, Gilbert McMicking,** CMG 1957; Deputy Agricultural Adviser, Department of Technical Co-operation, 1961 (to Secretary of State for Colonies, 1956); retired 1965; *b* 13 May 1906; *m* 1934, Olive Mary Wetherill; two *d*. *Educ:* Dumfries Academy; Glasgow and Oxford Universities; Imperial College of Tropical Agriculture, Trinidad. Colonial Service, 1930-56. *Address:* Wayland, Edinburgh Road, Peebles. *Club:* Royal Commonwealth Society.

**RODEN,** 9th Earl of, *cr* 1771; **Robert William Jocelyn;** Baron Newport, 1743; Viscount Jocelyn, 1755; a baronet of England, 1665; Captain Royal Navy; retired; *b* 4 Dec. 1909; *S* father 1956; *m* 1937, Clodagh, *d* of late Edward Kennedy, Bishopscourt, Co. Kildare; three *s*. Retired 1960. *Heir: s* Viscount Jocelyn, *qv*. *Address:* Bryansford, Co. Down. *T:* Newcastle 3469.

**RODERICK, Caerwyn Eifion;** MP (Lab) Brecon and Radnor since 1970; *b* 15 July 1927; *m* 1952, Eirlys Mary Lewis; one *s* two *d*. *Educ:* Maes-y-Daerwen County Sch., Ystradgynlais; University Coll. of North Wales, Bangor. Asst Master: Caterham Sch., Surrey, 1949-52; Chartesey Sch., LCC, 1952-54; Sen. Maths Master, Boys' Grammar Sch., Brecon, 1954-57; Method Study Engineer, NCB, 1957-60; Sen. Maths Master, Hartridge High Sch., Newport, Mon, 1960-69; Lecturer, Coll. of

Educn, Cardiff, 1969-70. *Address:* 29 Charlotte Square, Rhiwbina, Cardiff. *T:* Cardiff 68269.

**RODERICK, Rev. Charles Edward Morys;** Chaplain to the Queen since 1962; Vicar of St Michael's, Chester Square, London, since 1953; *b* 18 June 1910; *s* of Edward Thomas and Marion Petronella Roderick; *m* 1940, Betty Margaret Arrowsmith; two *s*. *Educ:* Christ's College, Brecon; Trinity College, Oxford (MA). Schoolmaster, 1932-38; training for ordination, 1938-39; ordained, 1939; Curate, St Luke's Parish Church of Chelsea, 1939-46; Chaplain to the Forces, 1940-45; Rector of Denham, Bucks, 1946-53. HCF. *Address:* 4 Chester Square, SW1. *T:* 01-730 8889.

**RODGER, Alec (Thomas Alexander),** MA Cantab, FBPsS; Professor of Occupational Psychology, University of London, at Birkbeck College, since 1960 (Reader in Psychology, 1948-60); Chairman, Psychology Board, Council for National Academic Awards; Adviser to Management Selection (Group) Ltd; *b* 22 Nov. 1907; *e s* of late T. Ritchie Rodger, OBE; unmarried. *Educ:* Scarborough College; Gonville and Caius College, Cambridge (Yatman Exhibitioner). Nat. Inst. Industrial Psychology, 1929-47 (Head of Vocational Guidance Dept 1936-47; concurrently Psychologist, WO, 1940-41, and Senior Psychologist to the Admlty, 1941-47). (Estab.) Sen. Psychologist to Admlty, 1947-48, and first Member of Civil Service Psychologist Class. Mem. Psychology Cttee, MRC, 1946-56; Mem. Human Factors Panel, Govt Cttee on Industrial Productivity, 1948-51; Editor, Occupational Psychology, 1948-68; Adviser, Min. of Labour, 1948-68; Chm. Working Party on Personnel Selection Methods, Min. of Defence, 1950-51; Mem., Min. of Health's Adv. Cttee for Management Efficiency in the NHS, 1964-66; Gen. Sec., British Psychological Soc., 1948-54, Pres. 1957-58; Pres. Section J. British Association, 1955; Founder-Dir, MSL Group, 1956-70. Fellow, Amer. Psychological Association, 1968. Governor, Birkbeck College, 1964-68. *Publications:* A Borstal Experiment in Vocational Guidance, 1937; Occupational Versatility and Planned Procrastination, 1961. Contrib. to Chambers's Encyclopædia; The Study of Society; Current Trends in British Psychology; Society, Problems and Methods of Study; Educational and Occupational Selection in West Africa; Readings in Psychology; and to various periodicals. *Recreations:* music, motoring abroad. *Address:* Birkbeck College, Malet Street, WC1. *Clubs:* Arts Theatre, Royal Automobile.

**RODGER, Allan George,** OBE 1944; Under-Secretary, Scottish Education Department, 1959-63, retired; *b* Kirkcaldy, 7 Jan. 1902; *s* of Allan Rodger, Schoolmaster, and Annie Venters; *m* 1930, Barbara Melville Simpson; one *s* one *d*. *Educ:* Pathhead Primary School, Kirkcaldy; Kirkcaldy High School; Edinburgh University (MA (Hons) Maths, BSc, MEd, Dip Geog). Teacher, Viewforth School, Kirkcaldy, 1926-29; Lecturer, Moray House Training Coll. and Univ. Dept of Educ. (Edinburgh), 1929-35; HM Inspector of Schools, 1935-45, with special duties in regard to geography, special schools, and training colleges (seconded to special administrative duties in Education Dept, 1939-45); Asst Secretary, Scottish Educ. Dept, 1945-59. Served on Educational Commission for Govts of Uganda and Kenya, 1961. Chairman of various Govt Cttees on Scottish Educ. matters. *Publications:* contrib. to Jl of Educational Psychology and other educational journals. *Recreations:* reading, music, gardening. *Address:* 72 Duddingston Road West, Edinburgh EH15 3PT. *T:* 031-661 1746.

**RODGER, Rt. Rev. Patrick Campbell;** *see* Manchester, Bishop of.

**RODGER, Thomas Ferguson,** CBE 1967; FRCP (Glasgow), FRCP (Edinburgh); Professor of Psychological Medicine, University of Glasgow, since 1948; Consulting Psychiatrist, Western Infirmary and Southern General Hospital, Glasgow; Hon. Consulting Psychiatrist to the Army in Scotland; External Examiner, Edinburgh and Leeds Universities; *b* 4 Nov. 1907; *m* 1934, Jean Chalmers; two *s* one *d*. *Educ:* North Kelvinside School, Glasgow; Glasgow University. BSc, 1927; MB, ChB, with Commendation, 1929; MRCP Ed., 1939; FRCP Ed., 1947, Glas. 1962; FRFPS(G) 1958. FBPsS. Past Pres., Roy. Medico-Psychological Assoc. Asst, Dept of Psychiatry, Johns Hopkins Univ., Baltimore, 1931-32; Dep. Superintendent, Glasgow Roy. Mental Hosp., and Assistant Lecturer in Psychiatry, Glasgow Univ., 1933-40; War of 1939-45: Specialist in Psychiatry, RAMC, 1940-44; Consultant in Psychiatry, Army Medical Services, SEAC and India, 1944-45; Commissioner, General Board of Control for Scotland, 1945-48. *Publications:* (jointly) Notes on Psychological Medicine, 1962; Psychology in Relation to Medicine, 1963; articles in medical journals on psychiatric subjects. *Address:* 25 Campbell Drive, Bearsden, near Glasgow. *T:* 041-942 3101.

**RODGERS, Air Commodore Alexander Mitchell,** CB 1957; *b* 24 July 1906; *m* 1934, Agnes Mary Collier; one *s* one *d*. *Educ:* Forfar Acad.; St Andrews Univ. BSc 1928. Commissioned in RAF, 1931; passed flying training course as pilot, 1932; passed radio course, Cranwell, 1935; in India during 1935-38; RAF Staff College, 1939; served War of 1939-45: France, 1939-40, UK 1940-41, North Africa, Sicily, Italy, 1941-45; Transport Command, 1945-46; Commanded St Mawgan, Hendon, Defford, 1946-51; Europe, 1951-53; Commandant RAF Watton, 1953-57; retired 1957; ATC Liaison Officer, RAF Flying Training Comd, 1957-70. American Bronze Star. *Recreations:* shooting, fishing. *Address:* Farnborough, near Banbury, Oxon. *T:* Farnborough 266. *Club:* Royal Air Force.

**RODGERS, Mrs Barbara Noel;** Reader in Social Administration, Manchester University, since 1965; *b* 1912; *d* of F. S. Stancliffe, Wilmslow, Cheshire; *m* 1950, Brian Rodgers; no *c*. *Educ:* Wycombe Abbey Sch.; (Exhibitioner) Somerville Coll., Oxford (MA). Social work and travel, 1935-39; Jt appt with Manch. and Salford Council of Social Service and Manchester Univ. (practical work Tutor and special Lectr), 1939-45. Lectr 1945, Sen. Lectr, 1955, and Reader, 1965, Manchester Univ.; Teaching Fellowship in Grad. Sch. of Social Work, Toronto Univ., 1948-49. Mem. various wages councils, 1950-, of National Assistance Bd, 1965, and of Supplementary Benefits Commn, 1966. Served and serving on numerous voluntary welfare organisations. *Publications:* (co-author) Till We Build Again, 1948; (co-author) Portrait of Social Work, 1960; A Follow Up Study of Manchester Social Administration Students, 1940-60, 1963; Careers of Social Studies Graduates, 1964; (co-author) Comparative Social Administration, 1968. Numerous articles in learned jls mainly on social services in America, France and Canada. *Recreations:* walking, bird watching, travel. *Address:* The Old Vicarage, Goostrey, Crewe, Cheshire. *T:* Holmes Chapel 2397.

**RODGERS, David John,** CBE 1933; *b* 27 March 1890; *s* of Richard Broomhead Rodgers and Janet Thomson. Entered Consular Service, 1913; Vice-Consul, Buenos Aires, 1914; Vice-Consul, Strasburg, 1921; Consul, Brest, 1922, Madrid, 1923; Chargé d'Affaires, Salvador and Guatemala, 1928; Consul, Liège, 1932, Palermo, 1936; Consul-General, Barcelona, 1938, New Orleans, 1940, Mexico, 1944; appointed Minister to Nicaragua, 1947, but could not proceed thither owing to injuries in accident; retd 1949. *Address:* 27 Loughrigg Av., Ambleside, Westmorland.

**RODGERS, Gerald Fleming;** *b* 22 Sept. 1917; *s* of Thomas Fleming Rodgers and Mary Elizabeth (*née* Gillespie); *m* 1965, Helen Lucy, *y d* of Dr Wall, Coleshill; one *s*. *Educ:* Rugby; Queens' Coll., Cambridge. Served War of 1939-45, Army, 1939-46. Foreign (subseq. Diplomatic) Service, 1947; served at: Jedda, 1947-49; British Middle East Office, Cairo and Fayid, 1949-53; FO, 1953-59; Peking, 1959-61; UK Delegation to OECD, 1961-64; Djakarta, 1964-65; Counsellor, Paris, 1965-67. *Address:* Laurelcroft, North Street, Kilsby, Rugby, Warwickshire. *T:* Crick 314.

**RODGERS, Prof. Harold William,** OBE 1943; FRCS 1933; Professor of Surgery, Queen's University of Belfast, since 1947; *b* 1 Dec. 1907; *s* of Major R. T. Rodgers; *m* 1938, Margaret Boycott; one *s* three *d*. *Educ:* King's College School; St Bartholomew's Hospital. St Bartholomew's Hospital: House Surgeon, Demonstrator in Anatomy, Chief Asst, Casualty Surgeon, Senior Asst Surgeon. Served War of 1939-45, RAMC, North Africa, Italy, France; Hon. Lieut-Col. Nuffield Medical Visitor to African Territories; WHO Vis. Prof. to India; Fellow Roy. Institute of International Affairs; Vice-Pres. Intervarsity Fellowship; FRC Soc.; Past President: British Society of Gastro-enterology; Christian Medical Fellowship; British Surgical Research Soc.; Past Chairman, Ct of Examiners of RCS; Pres. YMCA (Belfast). District Surgeon, St John's Ambulance Brigade. OStJ 1968. *Publications:* Gastroscopy, 1937; General articles in surgical and medical journals. *Recreations:* painting, sailing, travel. *Address:* 51 Myrtlefield Park, N Ireland. *T:* 667765.

**RODGERS, Sir John (Charles),** 1st Bt, *cr* 1964; MP (C) Sevenoaks Division of Kent since 1950; *b* 5 Oct. 1906; *o s* of Charles and Maud Mary Rodgers; *m* Betsy, JP, East Sussex, *y d* of Francis W. Aikin-Sneath, JP, and of Louisa, *d* of Col W. Langworthy Baker; two *s*. *Educ:* St Peter's, York; Ecole des Roches, France; Keble College, Oxford (scholar). MA. Sub-Warden, Mary Ward Settlement, 1929; Lecturer and Administrative Assistant, University of Hull, 1930; Foreign Office, 1939 and 1944-45; Special Mission to Portugal, December 1945; Director Commercial Relations Division, Ministry of Information, 1939-41; Director Post-War Export Trade Development, Dept of Overseas Trade, 1941-42; Deputy Head Industrial Information Div., Min. of Production, 1942-44; Foundation Gov. of Administrative Staff Coll.; Exec. Council Member, Foundation for Management Education; BBC General Advisory Council, 1946-52; Hon. Secretary Smuts Memorial Committee, 1953; Chm. Cttee on Litter in Royal Parks, 1954; Exec. Cttee of British Council, 1957-58; Governor, British Film Institute, 1958; Member Tucker Cttee on Proceedings before Examining Justices, 1957; Leader, Parliamentary Panel, and on Exec. and Coun., Inst. of Dirs, 1955-58; Vice-Chm. Exec. Cttee Political and Economic Planning (PEP), 1962-68; Exec. London Library, 1963-; PPS to Rt Hon. Viscount Eccles (at Ministries of Works, Education and Board of Trade), 1951-57; Parliamentary Sec., Bd of Trade, Oct. 1958-Oct. 1960. UK Delegate to Gen. Assembly, Council of Europe, and to WEU, 1969-. Chm., New English Library Ltd; Dep. Chm., J. Walter Thompson Co. Ltd, 1936-70; Dir other companies; Pres. Inst. of Practitioners in Advertising, 1967-69; Master, Worshipful Company of Masons, 1968-69; Freeman of the City of London. FBIM; FSS; FIS; FRSA. Knight Grand Cross, Order of Civil Merit (Spain), 1965. *Publications:* Mary Ward Settlement: a history, 1930; The Old Public Schools of England, 1938; The English Woodland, 1941; Industry looks at the New Order (joint), 1941; English Rivers, 1948; One Nation (joint), 1950; York, 1951; ed. Thomas Gray, 1953; Change is our Ally (joint), 1954; Capitalism–Strength and Stress (joint), 1958. *Recreations:* travel, theatre. *Heir: s* John Fairlie Tobias Rodgers, *b* 2 July 1940. *Address:* House of Commons, SW1; 72 Berkeley House, Hay Hill, W1. *T:* 01-629 5220; The Dower House, Groombridge, Kent. *T:* 213. *Clubs:* Brooks's, Pratt's, Royal Thames Yacht.

**RODGERS, Richard;** American composer and producer; President and Producing Director, Lincoln Center for the Performing Arts, Music Theatre; *b* New York, 28 June 1902; *m* 1930, Dorothy Feiner; two *d*. *Educ:* Columbia University; Institute of Musical Art, New York. Musical scores include: Lido Lady (London) 1926; One Dam Thing After Another (London) 1927; Evergreen (London) 1930; America's Sweetheart, 1931; Jumbo, 1935; On Your Toes, 1936; Babes in Arms, 1937; I'd Rather Be Right, 1937; I Married An Angel, 1938; The Boys From Syracuse, 1938; Too Many Girls, 1939; Higher and Higher, 1940; Pal Joey, 1940; Oklahoma, 1943 (Pulitzer Award, 1944); Carousel, 1945; Allegro, 1947. Wrote music for: Love Me Tonight (film); Ghost Town (ballet), 1939; State Fair (film), 1945. Co-producer: By Jupiter, 1942 (wrote music); I Remember Mama, 1944; Annie Get Your Gun, Happy Birthday, 1946; John Loves Mary, Show Boat, 1947; South Pacific, 1949 (wrote score) (Pulitzer Prize, 1950); The Happy Time, 1950; The King and I, 1951 (wrote score); Pipe Dream, 1955 (wrote score); The Sound of Music, 1959 (wrote score); Flower Drum Song, 1960 (wrote score); Producer: No Strings, 1962 (wrote score); Do I Hear a Waltz?, 1965 (wrote score). TV series: Churchill, The Valiant Years; Victory at Sea; TV Specials; Cinderella, 1957; Androcles and the Lion, 1967. President Dramatists' Guild, 1943-47. Member: Authors League of America; Nat. Assoc. for Amer. Composers and Conductors; Nat. Inst. of Arts and Letters. Hon. Degrees: Drury Coll., 1949; Columbia, 1954; Univ. of Massachusetts, 1954; Univ. of Bridgeport, 1962; Univ. of Maryland, 1962; Hamilton Coll., 1965; Brandeis Univ., 1965. *Address:* c/o Rodgers & Hammerstein, 598 Madison Avenue, New York, NY 10022, USA.

**RODGERS, William Thomas;** MP (Lab) Stockton-on-Tees since 1962; *b* 28 Oct. 1928; *s* of William Arthur and Gertrude Helen Rodgers; *m* 1955, Silvia Szulman; three *d*. *Educ:* Sudley Road Council Sch.; Quarry Bank High School, Liverpool; Magdalen College, Oxford. General Secretary, Fabian Society, 1953-60. Contested (Lab) Bristol West, March 1957; Parly Under-Sec. of State: Dept of Econ. Affairs, 1964-67, Foreign Office, 1967-68; Leader, UK delegn to Council of Europe and Assembly of WEU, 1967-68; Minister of State: BoT, 1968-69; Treasury, 1969-70. Borough Councillor, St Marylebone, 1958-62. *Publications:* Hugh Gaitskell, 1906-1963 (ed),

1964; (jt) The People into Parliament, 1966; pamphlets, etc. *Address:* 48 Patshull Road, NW5. *T:* 01-485 9997.

**RODHAM, Brig. Cuthbert Harold Boyd,** CBE 1953 (OBE 1934); DSO and Bar, 1945; MC 1921; Director of Sports, Government of Pakistan, since 1963; *b* 1900; *s* of late Rear-Adm. H. Rodham, CMG. *Educ:* Dover Coll. Entered Indian Army, 2/18 Roy. Garhwal Rifles, 1919; Capt. 1925; Bt Major, 1936; Major, 1937; Lt-Col 1942; Col 1943; Brig. 1944. Served Afghanistan, 1919; NWF of India, 1919-21; Mahsud campaign, 1920 (wounded, despatches, MC); Waziristan Operations, 1922-23; Mahsud Operations, 1930. Indian Coronation Contingent, 1937. War of 1939-45 (despatches 3 times, DSO and Bar); French Indo-China Occupation Force, 1945-46; Director of Infantry, GHQ India, 1946-47; Brigade Commander, Pakistan Army, 1948-51, Director of Infantry, 1951-57; Deputy Chief of General Staff, Pakistan Army, 1957-63, retd. Order of Quaid-i-Azam, Pakistan, 1959. *Recreation:* shooting. *Address:* Flashman's Hotel, The Mall, Rawalpindi, Pakistan; c/o Grindlay's Bank, The Mall, Lahore, Pakistan.

**RODNEY,** family name of **Baron Rodney.**

**RODNEY,** 8th Baron, *cr* 1782; **George Bridges Harley Guest Rodney;** Bt 1764; late Captain Royal Scots Greys; *b* 2 Nov. 1891; *s* of 7th Baron; *S* father, 1909; *m* 1917, Lady Marjorie Lowther (*d* 1968), *y d* of 6th Earl of Lonsdale; two *s* two *d* (and *e s* killed in War). *Educ:* Eton: Oxford. *Heir:* *s* Hon. John Francis Rodney [*b* 28 June 1920; *m* 1951, Regine, *yr d* of late Chevalier Pangaert d'Opdorp, Belgium; one *s* one *d*]. *Address:* Cottesmore Lodge, Park Drive, Albert Head, RRI, Victoria, BC, Canada.

**RODRIGO, Prof. Joseph Lionel Christie,** CMG 1956; *b* 31 July 1895; *s* of J. A. G. and Catherine Rodrigo; *m* 1922, Evelyn Fernando; two *s* three *d. Educ:* Royal and Trinity Colleges, Ceylon; Balliol College, Oxford. BA (London) 1917; BA (Oxon.) 1920; MA 1925; Barrister, Gray's Inn, 1921. Editor of Ceylon Morning Leader, 1921-26; Headmaster, Wesley College, Colombo, 1926-28; Asst Lecturer in Classics, Univ. College, Colombo, 1928, Lecturer, 1930, Reader, 1931; Prof. of Western Classics, Univ. of Ceylon, 1945-57, Emeritus Prof., 1960; Dean, Faculty of Arts, University of Ceylon, 1952-57; Education Officer Ceylon High Commn, London, 1957-59. Chm. Bd of Governors, CMS Schools in Ceylon, 1942-49, 1959-; Dir YMCA, 1922-49; President: Classical Assoc. of Ceylon; Oxford Soc., Ceylon Br., 1961-. *Recreation:* free-lance journalism. *Address:* 23/3 Guildford Crescent, Colombo, Ceylon. *Club:* Sinhalese Sports' (Ceylon).

**RODRIGO, Sir (Senapathige Theobald) Philip,** Kt 1953; OBE 1952; Gate-Mudaliyar 1947; Senator, Parliament of Ceylon, since 1950; *b* 22 Aug. 1899; *s* of Chevalier Mudaliyar John Rodrigo and Helena Roslin Fernando; *m* 1st, 1920, Mary Dorothy (*d* 1929); 2nd, 1930, Elizabeth Mary, both daughters of Simon Salgado; one *s* six *d. Educ:* De La Salle Coll. and St Benedict's Coll. Merchant and Planter; Partner S. T. P. Rodrigo & Bros; Managing Director: Eastern Ocean Steamship Supply Co.; New Imperial Lighterage Co.; Senior Partner: Dominion Trading Co.; Dominion Hotel Co., Colombo; Director: Gen. Insce Co.; United Lanka Rubber & Coconut Co. Pres. etc., various organisations. JP 1938. *Recreations:* billiards, painting, gardening. *Address:* Wasala Walauwa, Rodrigo Place, Mutwal, Colombo, Ceylon. *T:* 4563, 3589 & 3876; Claremont, Nuwara Eliya, Ceylon.

**RODRIGUES, Sir Alberto,** Kt 1966; CBE 1964 (OBE 1960; MBE 1948); General Medical Practitioner, Hong Kong; Senior Unofficial Member Executive Council since 1964; Pro-Chancellor and Chairman of Executive Council, University of Hong Kong; *b* 5 November 1911; *s* of late Luiz Gonzaga Rodrigues and late Giovanina Remedios; *m* 1940, Cynthia Maria da Silva; one *s* two *d. Educ:* St Joseph's College and University of Hong Kong. MBBS Univ. of Hong Kong, 1934; Post graduate work, London and Lisbon, 1935-36; Medical Practitioner, 1937-40; also Medical Officer in Hong Kong Defence Force. POW, 1940-45. Medical Practitioner, 1945-50; Post graduate work, New York, 1951-52; Resident, Winnipeg Maternity Hosp. (Canada), 1952-53; General Medical Practitioner, 1953-. Member: Urban Council (Hong Kong), 1940-41; 1947-50; Legislative Council, 1953-60; Executive Council, 1960-. Med. Superintendent, St Paul's Hospital, 1953-. Officer, Ordem de Cristo (Portugal), 1949; Chevalier, Légion d'Honneur (France), 1962; Knight Grand Cross, Order of St Sylvester (Vatican), 1966. *Recreations:* cricket, hockey, tennis, swimming, badminton. *Address:* St Paul's Hospital Annexe, Causeway Bay, Hong Kong. *T:* 760017. *Clubs:* Hong Kong, Royal Hong Kong Jockey, Hong Kong Country, Lusitano, Recreio (all Hong Kong).

**RODWELL, Air Commodore Robert John,** CB 1947; RAF; retired; *b* 13 Jan. 1897; 3rd *s* of late J. B. Rodwell, Exmouth, Devon; *m* 1919, M. H. Livock; two *d. Educ:* St Edmund's Coll., Ware. Enlisted Hampshire Regiment, 1914; 2nd Lieut Devonshire Regiment, 1916; transferred to RFC as Pilot, 1917; served European War, 1914-18, India, Egypt, France (Croix de Guerre); regular commission, RAF, 1919; served in Ireland, Egypt, Iraq, Palestine, 1920-25; Adjt Staff Coll., 1925-28; specialised and qualified as Engineer Officer, 1928-30; served in Iraq, 1932-34; Iraq and Sudan, 1934-36; on transfer to Tech. Branch Staff Duties and Command of Tech. Training Schools in Tech. Training Command, 1936-48; President RAF Central Trade Test Board, 1947; Group Capt. 1940; Air Commodore, 1948; retired, 1952. *Address:* Kingsley, Chine Walk, Ferndown, Dorset.

**ROE, Frederic Gordon,** FSA, FRHistS; *b* 24 Sept. 1894; *s* of late Fred Roe, RI, RBC, and Letitia Mabel, *e d* of Sydney W. Lee; *m* 1921, Eleanor Beatrice, *o d* of late Cecil Reginald Grundy; one *d. Educ:* Westminster School; in Art under his father, and at the Chelsea School of Art. Joined The Connoisseur, 1913; Art Critic, 1919; Assistant Editor, 1921-32; Acting-Editor, March-June 1926; Editor, 1933; Director, Connoisseur Ltd, 1931-34; Gunner, 1212 Battery, RFA, 1917-19; Art Critic, Daily Mail, 1920 (resigned 1921); Member, Junior Art Workers' Guild, 1920-23; restored to Westminster Abbey Muniments Wren's Original designs for the restoration of the Abbey, 1927; Hon. Member Society of Pewter Collectors, 1933-; Art Critic, The Artist, 1935-36; ARP Warden (and higher grades), 1940-45; Odhams Press Book Dept, 1943-44. FRSA 1968. *Publications:* Henry Bright of the Norwich School, 1920; Charles Bentley, 1921; Dictator of the Royal Academy (Joseph Farington, RA), 1921; David Cox, 1924—original MS of this book is in the National Museum of Wales, Cardiff; Sporting Prints of the 18th and early 19th centuries, 1927; The Life and Times of King Edward the Eighth, 1937; Coronation Cavalcade, 1937; Catalogue of Paintings in the Nettlefold

Collection (with C. R. Grundy), 1937-38; Etty and the Nude (with W. Gaunt), 1943; The Nude from Cranach to Etty and beyond, 1944; The Bronze Cross, 1945; Cox the Master, 1946; English Period Furniture, 1946; Rowlandson, 1947; Sea Painters of Britain, 1947-48; Old English Furniture, 1948; Clarence below the Basement (for children), 1948; English Cottage Furniture, 1949, 2nd edn, 1950, rev. edn., 1961; Britain's Birthright, 1950; Victorian Furniture, 1952; Windsor Chairs, 1953; The Victorian Child, 1959; The Georgian Child, 1961; The British Museum's Pictures (with J. R. F. Thompson), 1961; Home Furnishing with Antiques, 1965; Victorian Corners, 1968; Women in Profile: a study in Silhouette, 1970; much work in over 70 vols of The Connoisseur; also British Racehorse, Concise Encyclopædia of Antiques, etc. *Recreations:* walking, reading, genealogical research. *Address:* 19 Vallance Road, Alexandra Park, N22. *T:* 01-888 4029.

**ROE, Brig. William C.;** *see* Carden Roe.

**ROEBUCK, Roy Delville;** journalist; *b* 1929; *m* 1957, Dr Mary Ogilvy Adams; one *s*. *Educ:* state schools and various newspapers. Served RAF, 1948-50 (National Service). Joined Labour Party, 1945; MP (Lab) Harrow East, 1966-70. Member: Commonwealth Parly Assoc. Delegn to Malawi, 1968; Select Cttees on Parly Comr for Administration, 1968-69, on Estimates, 1969-70; Fabian Soc.; Co-operative Party; Nat. Union of Journalists; NUGMW. Contested (Lab) Altrincham and Sale, 1964 and Feb. 1965. *Address:* 15 Old Forge Close, Stanmore, Middx. *T:* 01-954 2251.

**ROGAN, Rev. William Henry;** Minister of Humbie, East Lothian, since 1969; Chaplain to the Queen since 1966; *b* 1908; *s* of late Rev. John Rogan and Christian Ann McGhie; *m* 1940, Norah Violet Henderson, Helensburgh; one *s* two *d*. *Educ:* Royal High Sch. of Edinburgh; Univ. of Edinburgh. MA 1928; BD 1931. Asst, St Cuthbert's Parish Church, Edinburgh, 1930-32; Minister: Whithorn Parish, 1932; St Bride's Parish, Helensburgh, 1936-50; Paisley Abbey, 1950-69. Supt, Church of Scotland Huts and Canteens in Orkney and Shetland, 1941-42; Army Chaplain, 1943-46. Select Preacher: Glasgow Univ., 1960-65; Aberdeen Univ., 1959-66; St Andrews Univ., 1959; Convener, Church of Scotland Youth Cttee, 1965-70. Founder and formerly Chm., Soc. of Friends of Paisley Abbey. Hon. DD Edinburgh, 1963. *Recreation:* angling. *Address:* The Manse, Humbie, East Lothian. *T:* Humbie 223. *Club:* Liberal (Edinburgh).

**ROGERS, Rt. Rev. Alan F. B.;** *see* Edmonton, Suffragan Bishop of.

**ROGERS, Prof. C(laude) Ambrose,** FRS 1959; Astor Professor of Mathematics in the University of London, 1958; *b* 1 Nov. 1920; *s* of late Sir Leonard Rogers, KCSI, CIE, FRS; *m* 1952, Mrs J. M. Gordon, *widow* of W. G. Gordon, and *d* of F. W. G. North; two *d*. *Educ:* Berkhamsted School; University Coll., London; Birkbeck Coll., London. BSc, PhD, DSc (London, 1941, 1949, 1952). Experimental officer, Ministry of Supply, 1940-45; lecturer and reader, University College, London, 1946-54; Prof. of Pure Mathematics, Univ. of Birmingham, 1954-58. *Publications:* Packing and Covering, 1964; Hausdorff Measures, 1970; articles in various mathematical journals. *Recreation:* string figures. *Address:* Dept of Mathematics, University College, WC1; 8 Grey Close, NW11. *T:* 01-455 8027.

**ROGERS, Claude Maurice,** OBE 1959; painter; Member of the London Group (President, 1952-65); Professor of Fine Art, Reading University, since 1963; Lectr, Slade Sch. of Fine Arts, London Univ., 1955-63; Member: Arts Panel, Arts Council of Great Britain, 1957-63; Nat. Council for Diplomas in Art and Design, and Chairman Fine Art Panel, since 1961; British Cttee, Internat. Assoc. of Artists, UNESCO (Vice-Chm.); Fell., University Coll., London; *b* 24 Jan. 1907; *e c* of late David de Sola Rogers, LDS, RCS; *m* 1937, Elsie, *e d* of late Jethro Few, Kingston, Jamaica; one *s*. *Educ:* St Paul's; Slade Sch. of Fine Art, London University. With Victor Pasmore and William Coldstream founded School of Drawing and Painting, 316 Euston Rd, 1937-39. Royal Engineer, 1941-43 (Corporal). Examiner to Ministry of Education for Diploma Examination in Art, 1949-56. Exhibitions: one-man exhibns: London Artists' Assoc., 1933; Leicester Galls, 1940, 1947, 1954, 1960; Exhibitor UNESCO Exhib., Paris, 1946; Carnegie Internat., 1936 and 1950; with British Council in America, Canada, S Africa, Sweden, Italy, etc.; with Arts Council (Four Contemporary British Painters, The Euston Road School and some others, Second Anthology 1951, Sixty Pictures for '51; etc.). Retrospective Exhibition, 1955, Newcastle, Manchester, Bristol, Leicester, etc. Represented in Tate Gallery, Victoria and Albert Museum, Ashmolean Museum, Fitzwilliam Museum; Commonwealth galleries. Works also acquired by: Chantry Bequest, Contemporary Art Society, Arts Council, Ministry of Works. *Address:* 36 Southwood Lane, Highgate, N6. *T:* 01-348 1997; The Old Rectory, Somerton, near Bury St Edmunds, Suffolk. *T:* Hawkedon 231.

**ROGERS, Brig. Edgar William,** CIE 1944; BSc; late Indian Army; *b* 14 July 1892; *o surv. s* of late Francis Rogers, Stamford, Lincs; *m* 1920, Marjorie, *y d* of late John Harper, Ipswich; one *s*. *Educ:* Bracondale Sch., Norwich; King's Coll., London. 2nd Lt The Duke of Wellington's Regt, 1914; transferred IAOC, 1928; Bt Lt Col 1936; Director of Armaments, GHQ India, 1942-46; retired 1947. Hampshire CC, 1955-58; Alton UDC, 1952-58. *Address:* 29 Marley Avenue, New Milton, Hampshire. *T:* New Milton 1221.

**ROGERS, Rev. Edward;** General Secretary, Methodist Christian Citizenship Department, since 1950; President, Methodist Conference, 1960; Moderator, Free Church Federal Council, 1968; *b* 4 Jan. 1909; *s* of Capt. E. E. Rogers, Fleetwood; *m* 1937, Edith May, *o d* of A. L. Sutton, Plaistow. *Educ:* Baines's Poulton-Le-Fylde Grammar School; Manchester University. Kitchener Scholar, Shuttleworth Scholar, Hulme Hall, Manchester. MA (Econ. and Pol.) 1931; Hartley Coll.; BD, 1933. Methodist Circuit Minister: East London Mission, Bakewell, Birmingham (Sutton Park), Southport, 1933-50. Fernley Lecturer, 1951; Ainslie Lecturer, 1952; Beckly Lecturer, 1957. Organising Director, Methodist Relief Fund, 1953-; Chairman, Inter-Church Aid and Refugee Service, British Council of Churches, 1960-64; Chairman: Standing Commn on Migration, 1964-; Churches Cttee on Gambling Legislation, 1967-; Exec. Council, UK Immigrants Adv. Service, 1970-; Select Committee on Cruelty to Animals, 1963. *Publications:* First Easter, 1948; A Commentary on Communism, 1951; Programme for Peace, 1954; God's Business, 1957; That They Might Have Life, 1958; The Christian Approach to the Communist, 1959; Church Government, 1964; Living Standards, 1964; Law, Morality and Gospel, 1969.

*Recreations:* travel, indiscriminate reading. *Address:* 6 Green Court Gardens, Croydon, Surrey. *T:* 01-654 5573.

**ROGERS, Ven. Evan James Gwyn;** Archdeacon of Doncaster since 1967; *b* 14 Jan. 1914; *s* of John Morgan Rogers and Margaret Rogers; *m* 1943, Eleanor Mabel, *d* of Capt. J. H. Evans; one *s* one *d*. *Educ:* St David's, Lampeter; Wycliffe Hall, Oxford. Vicar: Hamer, 1943; St Catharine's, Wigan, 1947; Diocesan Missioner, Dio. Liverpool, 1953; Hon. Chaplain to Bp of Liverpool, 1953; Hon. Canon, Liverpool Cathedral, 1957; Vicar of Coniston Cold, 1960; Dir of Educn, Dio. Bradford, 1960; Exam. Chaplain to Bp of Sheffield, 1963; Vice-Chm. Standing Conf., WR Educn Cttee, 1963; Hon. Canon of Bradford, 1964. *Publications:* Do This in Remembrance, 1950; Dr Barnardo, 1951; (with Canon F. L. M. Bennett) A Communion Book, 1951; contrib. to West Riding New Agreed Syllabus, 1966. *Address:* High Melton Vicarage, near Doncaster, Yorks. *T:* Mexborough 2345.

**ROGERS, George Henry Roland,** CBE 1965; *b* 1906; *m*; one *s* one *d*. *Educ:* Willesden Elementary School; Middlesex CC Schools. A railway clerk. Member Wembley Borough Council, 1937-41. Served War of 1939-45, Royal Corps of Signals, 1942. MP (Lab) North Kensington, 1945-70; Chairman, London Group of Labour Members, 1949-54; Opposition London Whip, 1954-64; a Lord Commissioner of the Treasury, October 1964-January 1966. PPS to Min. of Supply, 1947-49 and to Minister of State for Foreign Affairs, 1950; Delegate to UN Assembly 1950; Delegate to Council of Europe and Western European Union, 1961-63. Hon. Sec. Parliamentary Painting Group. *Address:* High Pines, Hundred Acre Lane, Wivelsfield Green, Sussex.

**ROGERS, Graham; His Honour Judge Rogers;** Assistant Judge of the Mayor's and City of London Court, and Commissioner of the Central Criminal Court, since 1969; Chairman, London Licensing Planning Committee, since 1967; a Deputy Chairman, City of London Quarter Sessions, since 1969; *b* 10 June 1907; 2nd *s* of late Alfred Rogers, Moseley; unmarried. *Educ:* Repton Sch.; King's Coll., Cambridge (BA 1929; MA 1936). Called to Bar, Inner Temple, 1930; practised Oxford Circuit and Birmingham, 1930-39; served War of 1939-45; Major, 45th AA Battalion RE (TA), 1939; transferred to RA, 1940; UK and NW Europe, 1939-46; demobilised with rank of Colonel (TD and 2 clasps). Judge of Control Commission Supreme Court (later Allied High Commn Court), Germany, 1947; Chief Judge, 1952. Recorder of Liverpool, 1954-56; Chairman, Medical Appeal Tribunals, 1956-59; Metropolitan Magistrate, 1959-61; Additional Judge of the Mayor's and City of London Court, 1961-64; Additional Judge, Central Criminal Court, 1964-69. *Address:* Mayor's and City of London Court, Guildhall, EC2. *Clubs:* United Service, United University.

**ROGERS, Hugh Charles Innes,** MA, FIMechE; Chairman, Avon Rubber Co., since 1968; Director, United Builders Merchants Ltd, since 1969; Director, Bristol and West Building Society; *b* 2 November 1904; *s* of late Hugh Innes Rogers, OBE, MIEE; *m* 1930, Iris Monica Seymour; one *s* three *d*. *Educ:* Marlborough; Clare College, Cambridge. Brecknell Munro & Rogers, 1926-31 (Chairman and Jt Man. Dir, 1931-41); SW Reg. Controller, Min. of Supply, 1941; SW Reg. Controller, Min. of Production and Chm. of Regional Bd, 1942-44; Dep. Controller (Production) in Admiralty, 1944-46; Chief Engineer, Imperial Tobacco Co. Ltd, Bristol, 1948; a Deputy Chairman of Imperial Tobacco Co. Ltd, Bristol, 1964-67, Dir, 1949-67; Dir, British American Tobacco Co., 1964-67. Member Bristol University Council, 1938, Chairman 1968-. Chairman SW Regional Housing Bd, 1952-53; Chairman SW Regional Council, FBI, 1954. *Recreations:* sailing, shooting, tennis, farming. *Address:* Beach House, Bitton, near Bristol. *T:* Bitton 3127. *Club:* East India and Sports.

**ROGERS, John,** OBE 1918; FRIC; *b* 24 May 1878; *s* of Richard and Sarah Rogers; *m* 1st, 1905, M. K. Allan; one *d*; 2nd, 1939, M. K. Garnett. *Educ:* Board Sch.; Technical Coll., Glasgow. Research Chemist, Ardeer Factory, 1899; Nobel's: Technical Supt, 1908, Tech. Manager, 1918, Tech. Dir, 1920; ICI: Tech. Dir, 1926, Dep. Chm., 1940, Chm., 1951-53, retired; formerly Dep. Chm. African Explosives and Chemical Industries Ltd; formerly Director ICI (Australia and New Zealand) Ltd, Cape Explosives Works Ltd; Pres. Society of Chemical Industry, 1951-52. Hon. LLD, St Andrew's Univ., 1952. *Address:* 29 Eaton Square, SW1. *Clubs:* Athenæum, Chemical.

**ROGERS, Lindsay;** *b* Baltimore, Maryland, 23 May 1891; *s* of George Wilson Rogers and Emma K. Gore; *m* 1917, Oona Carolyn Staples (*d* 1965); no *c*. *Educ:* Johns Hopkins Univ., AB 1912, PhD 1915, LLD 1948; Univ. of Maryland, LLB, 1915. Associate Professor of Political Science, Univ. of Virginia, 1915-20; Lecturer on Government, Harvard University, 1920-21; Associate Professor of Government, Columbia Univ., 1921, and Burgess Professor of Public Law, 1929-59; Moreland Comr, State of NY, 1928; Page Barbour Lecturer Univ. of Virginia, 1932; Visiting Professor on the Walgreen Foundation, Univ. of Chicago, 1939; Deputy Administrator, National Industrial Recovery Administration, 1933-34; Chairman, Board of Labour Review, Federal Emergency Administration of Public Works, 1934-37; Assistant Director of ILO, 1942-47. Consultant, US Senate Committee on Foreign Relations, 1952-53 and 1956-62. Visiting Professor: Political Science, Johns Hopkins University, 1960; Occidental College, 1962-63. James Lecturer, University of Illinois, 1955. Member: Bar, US Supreme Court; Amer. Philosophical Soc. *Publications:* The Postal Power of Congress, 1916; America's Case against Germany, 1917; The New Constitutions of Europe (with H. L. McBain), 1922 (Japanese translation); The American Senate, 1926 (new edn, 1968); Crisis Government, 1934 (Czech transl.); The Pollsters, 1949. *Recreation:* contract bridge. *Address:* 88 Morningside Drive, New York, NY 10027. *Clubs:* Athenæum; Century (New York); Cosmos (Washington).

**ROGERS, Martin Hartley Guy;** British Deputy High Commissioner, Bombay, since 1968; *b* 11 June 1925; *s* of late Rev. Canon T. Guy Rogers and Marguerite Inez Rogers; *m* 1959, Jean Beresford Chinn; one *s* three *d*. *Educ:* Marlborough Coll.; Jesus Coll., Cambridge. CRO, 1949; 2nd Sec., Karachi, 1951-53; CRO, 1953-56 and 1958-60; seconded to Govt of Fedn of Nigeria, 1956-57; ndc 1960-61; 1st Sec., Ottawa, 1961-62; Adviser to Jamaican Min. of External Affairs, 1963; CRO, later Commonwealth Office, 1963-68. *Recreations:* golf, tennis. *Address:* c/o Foreign and Commonwealth Office, King Charles Street, SW1. *Club:* Oxford and Cambridge University.

**ROGERS, Maurice Arthur Thorold;** Secretary, Royal Insititution, since 1968; Joint Head, Head Office Research and Development Department, ICI, since 1962; *b* 8 June 1911; *s* of A. G. L. Rogers; *g s* of Prof. J. E. Thorold Rogers; *m* 1947, Margaret Joan (*née* Cravan); one *s* two *d. Educ:* Dragon Sch.; Westminster Sch.; University Coll., London. 1st Class hons BSc (Chem.) UCL 1932, PhD (Chem.) 1934. Chemist, ICI Dyestuffs Div., 1934-45; Head of Academic Relations Dept, 1946-58; Head of Head Office Research Dept, ICI, 1958-62. *Publications:* numerous papers in: Jl of Chem. Soc.; Nature; etc. *Recreations:* Chm. (and Founder) of a local Preservation Soc.; gardening. *Address:* Learig, Hitcham Road, Burnham, Bucks. *T:* Burnham 61588.

**ROGERS, Murray Rowland Fletcher; Hon. Mr Justice Rogers;** Member, Courts of Appeal for the Seychelles, St Helena, The Falkland Islands Colony and Dependencies, and the British Antarctic Territory, since 1965; *b* 13 Sept. 1899; *s* of Geoffrey Pearson and Adeline Maud Rogers; *m* 1924, Dorothy Lilian Bardsley (*d* 1950); one *s* one *d. Educ:* St Edward's School; RMC, Sandhurst; 2nd Lieut 8th Hussars, 1918-21; Liverpool Univ. (BA 1924). Schoolmaster until 1929; called to Bar, Gray's Inn, 1929; Northern Circuit until 1937; Magistrate, Nigeria, 1937-42; Chief Magistrate, Palestine, 1942-47; District Judge, Malaya, 1947-49; President Sessions Court, Malaya, 1949-52; Judge of Supreme Court, Sarawak, N Borneo and Brunei, 1952-63, retd. *Address:* Flat 10, 2 Mountview Road, N4. *Clubs:* Athenæum; Artists' (Liverpool).

**ROGERS, Prof. Neville William,** DLit London; Professor of English, Ohio University, since 1964; *b* 5 Jan. 1908; *s* of Leonard George and Carrie Elizabeth Rogers (*née* Jennings). *Educ:* Rossall Sch.; Birkbeck Coll., London; studied French, Italian and German abroad. BA Gen. 1932, BA Hons cl. II Classics, 1934, London. Intell. Officer, RAF, Middle East and Italy, 1942-46. Asst Master, various prep. schs, 1927-32; Headmaster, Wellesley Sch., Croydon, 1932-34; Asst Master: King Edward VI Sch., Stafford, 1935-39; St Marylebone Grammar Sch., 1939-52; Leverhulme Fellow at Oxford, working on Shelley MSS, 1952-55; Sen. Res. Fellow and Lectr, Univ. of Birmingham, 1956-62; Vis. Professor: Michigan, 1959; Washington, St Louis, UCLA, 1960; Brandeis, 1962-64; has lectured at many US and French univs. Has broadcast in English, Italian and French. Mem., Kennedy Scott's Philharmonic Choir, 1933-39; Founder Mem., London Philharmonic Choir (Vice-Chm. 1947-48); Mem. Cttee: British-Italian Soc., 1947-; Keats Shelley Memorial Assoc., 1946-. FRSL. *Publications:* Keats, Shelley and Rome, 1949 (4th edn 1970); Shelley at Work, 1956 (2nd edn 1968); (ed with Archibald Colquhoun) Italian Regional Tales of the Nineteenth Century, 1961; (ed) The Esdaile Poems, 1966; (ed and annotated) Selected Poetry of Shelley, 1968; contribs to Encycl. Britannica, Times Lit. Supp., Times Educnl Supp., Twentieth Century, Review of English Studies, Mod. Lang. Review, Keats-Shelley Memorial Bulletin, Keats-Shelley Jl, Book Collector, Ulisse, Il Ponte. *Recreations:* literature, languages, music, travel. *Address:* 22 Clavering Avenue, SW13. *T:* 01-748 1358; Ohio University, Athens, Ohio, USA. *Clubs:* Authors', National Liberal.

**ROGERS, Maj.-Gen. Norman A. C.;** *see* Coxwell-Rogers.

**ROGERS, Maj.-Gen. Norman Charles,** FRCS 1949; Director of Army Surgery since 1969; Hon. Surgeon to the Queen since 1969; *b* 14 Oct. 1916; *s* of Wing Comdr Charles William Rogers, RAF, and Edith Minnie Rogers (*née* Weaver); *m* 1954, Pamela Marion (*née* Rose); two *s* one *d. Educ:* Imperial Service Coll.; St Bartholomew's Hosp. MB, BS London; MRCS, LRCP 1939. Emergency Commn, Lieut RAMC, Oct. 1939; 131 Field Amb. RAMC, Dunkirk (despatches); RMO, 4th Royal Tank Regt, N Africa, 1941-42; Italy, 1942-43 (POW); RMO 1st Black Watch, NW Europe, 1944-45 (wounded, despatches twice). Ho. Surg., St Bartholomew's Hosp., 1946-47; Registrar (Surgical) Appts, Norwich, 1948-52; Sen. Registrar Appts, Birmingham, 1952-56; granted permanent commn, RAMC, 1956; surgical appts in mil. hospitals: Chester, Dhekelia (Cyprus), Catterick, Iserlohn (BAOR), 1956-67; Command Consultant Surgeon, BAOR, 1967-69. *Publications:* contribs on surgical subjects. *Recreations:* gardening, history. *Address:* 29 Ponsonby Terrace, SW1. *T:* 01-834 7915. *Club:* Army and Navy.

**ROGERS, Mrs P. E.;** *see* Box, B. E.

**ROGERS, Paul;** actor; *b* Plympton, Devon, 22 March 1917; *s* of Edwin and Dulcie Myrtle Rogers; *m* 1st, 1939, Jocelyn Wynne (marr. diss. 1955); two *s*; 2nd, 1955, Rosalind Boxall; two *d. Educ:* Newton Abbot Grammar School, Devon. Michael Chekhov Theatre Studio, 1936-38. First appearance on stage as Charles Dickens in Bird's Eye of Valour, Scala, 1938; Stratford-upon-Avon Shakespeare Memorial Theatre, 1939; Concert Party and Colchester Rep. Co. until 1940. Served Royal Navy, 1940-46. Colchester Rep. Co. and Arts Council Tour and London Season, Tess of the D'Urbervilles, 1946-47; Bristol Old Vic, 1947-49; London Old Vic (incl. tour S Africa and Southern Rhodesia), 1949-53; also at Edinburgh, London and in USA, 1954-57; London, 1958; tour to Moscow, Leningrad and Warsaw, 1960. Roles with Old Vic include numerous Shakespearean leads. Other parts include: Sir Claude Mulhammer in The Confidential Clerk, Edinburgh Festival and Lyric, London, 1953; Lord Claverton in The Elder Statesman, Edinburgh Fest. and Cambridge Theatre, London, 1958; Mr Fox in Mr Fox of Venice, Piccadilly, 1959; Johnny Condell in One More River, Duke of York's and Westminster, 1959; Nickles in JB, Phœnix, 1961; Reginald Kinsale in Photo Finish, Saville, 1962; The Seagull, Queen's, 1964; Season of Goodwill, Queen's, 1964; The Homecoming, Aldwych, 1965; Timon of Athens, Stratford-upon-Avon, 1965; The Government Inspector, Aldwych, 1966; Henry IV, Stratford-upon-Avon, 1966; Max in The Homecoming, New York, 1967 (Tony Award and Whitbread Anglo-American Award); Plaza Suite, Lyric, 1969; The Happy Apple, Apollo, 1970; Sleuth, St Martin's, 1970, etc. Appears in films and television. *Publication:* a Preface to Folio Soc. edition of Shakespeare's Love's Labour's Lost, 1959. *Recreations:* gardening, carpentry, books. *Address:* 9 Hillside Gardens, Highgate, N6. *T:* 01-340 2656.

**ROGERS, Rev. Percival Hallewell,** MBE 1945; Headmaster Portora Royal School, Enniskillen, since 1954; *b* 13 Sept. 1912; *m* 1940, Annie Mary Stuart, 2nd *d* of Lt-Col James Morwood; two *s* one *d. Educ:* Brentwood School; St Edmund Hall, Oxford. BA Class II, Hons English, Oxford, 1935; Diploma in Education, 1936; MA 1946. Two terms of teaching, Westminster School; Master in charge of English, Haileybury, 1936; served War, 1940-45 (despatches twice, MBE): RA, Major; DAA QMG; Bishop's College, Cheshunt, 1946; ordained, 1947; Asst Chaplain and English Master, Haileybury, 1947;

Chaplain and English Master, 1949. *Publication:* Editor and contrib. to A Guide to Divinity Teaching (SPCK), 1962. *Address:* Portora Royal School, Enniskillen, N Ireland. *T:* Enniskillen 2069. *Clubs:* Ulster (Belfast); Friendly Brothers (Dublin); Royal Over-Seas League (London and Belfast).

**ROGERS, Sir Philip,** KCB 1970 (CB 1965); CMG 1952; Permanent Under-Secretary of State, Department of Health and Social Security, since 1970; *b* 19 Aug. 1914; *s* of William Edward and Sarah Jane Rogers; *m* 1940, Heather Mavis Gordon; one *s* one *d. Educ:* William Hulme's Grammar School, Manchester; Emmanuel Coll., Cambridge. Apptd to administrative class of Home Civil Service, as an Asst Principal in Colonial Office, 1936; seconded to be Private Secretary to Governor of Jamaica, Jan.-Dec. 1939; Asst Secretary, Colonial Office, 1946-53; Assistant Under-Secretary of State, Colonial Office, 1953-61; Under-Secretary, Department of Technical Co-operation, 1961-64; Dep. Sec. of Cabinet, 1964-67; Third Secretary, Treasury, 1967-68; Dep. Secretary, 1968-69, Second Permanent Secretary, 1969-70, Civil Service Dept. *Recreation:* gardening. *Address:* 48 Bathgate Road, Wimbledon, SW19. *T:* 01-946 7330. *Club:* Oxford and Cambridge University.

**ROGERS, Sir Philip (James),** Kt 1961; CBE 1952; Chairman, Tobacco Research Council, since 1963; *b* 1908; *s* of late James Henry Rogers; *m* 1939, Brenda Mary Sharp, CBE, *d* of late E. T. Sharp. *Educ:* Blundell's Sch. Served War (RWAFF and Intell. Corps), 1940-44. MLC, Nigeria, 1947-51; MLC, Kenya, 1957-62; Elected Representative, Kenya, East African Legislative Assembly, 1962 and 1963. President: Nig. Cham. Comm., 1948 and 1950 (Vice-Pres. 1947 and 1949); Nairobi Cham. Comm., 1957 (Vice-Pres. 1956); AAA of Nig., 1951; Dir, Nig. Elec. Corp., 1951; Governor, Nig. Coll. of Technology, 1951; Member: Nig. Exec. Cttee, Rd Transport Bd, 1948-51; Central Coun. Red Cross Soc. of W Africa, 1950-51; Trades Adv. Cttee, Nig., 1950 and 1951-; Wages Adv. Bd, Kenya, 1955-61; EA Industrial Council, 1954-63; EA Air Licencing Appeals Trib., 1958-60; EA Air Adv. Coun., 1956-60; Kenya Road Authority, 1957-61; Provl Council, Univ. of E Africa, 1961-63; Gov. Coun., Roy. Tech. Coll. of E Africa, 1957-58 (Chm. 1958/59/60). Chairman: East African Tobacco Co. Ltd, 1951-63; Rift Valley Cigarette Co. Ltd, 1956-63; EA Rd Fedn, 1954-56; Kenya Cttee on Study and Trg in USA, 1958-63; Bd of Govs, Coll. of Social Studies, 1960-63; Nairobi Special Loans Cttee, 1960-63; Af. Teachers' Service Bd, 1956-63; Coun., Royal College (now Univ. Coll., Nairobi), 1961-63; Trustee, Outward Bound Trust of Kenya, 1959-63; Rep. of Assoc. Chams of Comm. & Indust. of Eastern Africa; Mem. of Industrial Tribunals, England and Wales, 1966. Governor, Plumpton Agric. Coll., 1967. Chm., Federation of Sussex Amenity Socs, 1968-; Mem., E Sussex Educn Cttee. *Address:* Brislands, Newick, Sussex. *Club:* Naval and Military.

**ROGERS, Thomas Edward,** CMG 1960; MBE 1945; Ambassador to Colombia, since 1970; *b* 28 Dec. 1912; *s* of T. E. Rogers and Lucy Jane Browne; *m* 1950, Eileen Mary, *d* of R. J. Speechley; no *c. Educ:* Bedford Sch.; Emmanuel Coll., Cambridge (Exhibnr); School of Oriental Studies, London. Selected for Indian Civil Service, 1936, and for Indian Political Service, 1941. Served in Bengal, 1937-41; in Persian Gulf, 1941-45, at Bushire, Bandar Abbas and Bahrein; Political Agent, Quetta, 1947. Entered Foreign Service, 1948: FO, 1948-50; Bogota, 1950-53; jssc, 1953-54; Coun. (Comm.), Madrid, 1954-58; Coun. (Econ.), Belgrade, 1958-62; Minister (Econ.), Buenos Aires, 1963-65; Dep. UK High Comr, Canada, 1966-70. *Recreation:* travel. *Address:* c/o Foreign and Commonwealth Office, SW1. *Clubs:* Oxford and Cambridge University; Country (Bogota).

**ROGERS, William Pierce;** Secretary of State, United States of America, since 1969; *b* 23 June 1913; *s* of Harrison A. and Myra Beswick Rogers; *m* 1937, Adele Langston; three *s* one *d. Educ:* Canton High School, Canton, New York; Colgate University; Cornell Law School. Law firm of Cadwalader, Wickersham and Taft, NY City, 1937; an asst District Attorney in NY County, 1938; US Navy, 1942-46; Dist Attorney's Office in New York, 1946; Chief Counsel, Senate Investigating Cttee, 1947; Counsel, Senate Permanent Investigating Cttee, 1949; law firm of Dwight, Royall, Harris, Koegel and Caskey, offices in New York and Washington, 1950; Dep. Attorney-General, 1953; Attorney-General of the US, 1957-61. Partner, law firm of Royall, Koegel, Rogers & Wells, 1961-69. Holds several hon. degrees in Law, from Univs and Colls in the USA, 1956-60. Mem. Bar Assocs in the USA. US Representative: to 20th Session of UN General Assembly, 1965; on UN Ad Hoc Cttee on SW Africa, 1967; Mem., President's Commn on Law Enforcement and Administration of Justice, 1965-67. *Recreations:* golf, tennis, swimming. *Address:* Department of State, Washington, DC 20520, USA; 870 United Nations Plaza, New York, NY 10017; 7007 Glenbrook Road, Bethesda, Md 20014. *Clubs:* Metropolitan (Washington); Burning Tree (Bethesda); The Recess, Racquet and Tennis, The Sky (NYC).

**ROIJEN, Jan Herman Van;** Grand Cross, Order of Orange Nassau; Commander, Order of the Netherlands Lion; Netherlands Ambassador to the United Kingdom, 1964-70; Netherlands Ambassador to the Icelandic Republic, 1964-70; Netherlands Permanent Representative to Council of Western European Union, 1964-70; *b* Istanbul, 10 April 1905; *s* of Jan Herman van Roijen (sometime Netherlands Min. to USA), and (American-born) Albertina Winthrop van Roijen; *m* 1934, Anne Snouck Hurgronje; two *s* two *d. Educ:* Univ. of Utrecht. Doctor in Law, 1929. Joined Foreign Service, 1930; Attaché to Neths Legn, Washington, 1930-32; Min. of For. Affairs, 1933-36; Sec. to Neths Legn, Tokyo, 1936-39; Chief of Polit. Div. of Min. of For. Affairs, 1939. Jailed during German occupation; escaped to London, 1944. Minister without Portfolio, 1945; Minister of For. Affairs, March-July 1946; Asst Deleg. and Deleg. to UN Conf. and Assemblies, 1945-48; Ambassador to Canada, 1947-50. Leader, Neths Delegn to bring about Netherlands-Indonesian Round Table Conf., Batavia, 1949; Dep. Leader, Neths Delegn at Round Table Conf., The Hague, 1949. Ambassador to the United States, 1950-64. Leader, Neths Delegn in negotiations with Indonesia about W New Guinea, Middleburg (Va.) and New York, 1962. Holds several hon. doctorates in Laws, of Univs and Colls in USA; Gr. Cross, Order of Oak Crown, Luxembourg; Gr. Cross, Order of Falcon, Iceland; Comdr, Order of British Empire (CBE); Comdr, Order of Holy Treasure, Japan. *Recreations:* reading, theatre, golf. *Address:* Blankenburgh, 38 Buurtweg, Wassenaar, Netherlands. *Clubs:* St James', Turf, Beefsteak; Century Assoc. (NY); De Haagsche (The Hague).

**ROLFE, Rear-Adm. (Retd) Henry Cuthbert Norris,** CB 1959; *b* 1908; *s* of Benedict Hugh Rolfe, MA Oxon; *m* 1931, Mary Monica Fox; one *s* two *d. Educ:* Pangbourne Nautical

College. Joined Royal Navy, 1925. Served War of 1939-45: HMS Hermes, 1939; South-East Asia, 1944; Staff of Director of Air Warfare, Admiralty, 1947; Commanded HMS Veryan Bay, 1948; service with Royal Canadian Navy, 1949; Commanded HMS Vengeance, 1952; Commanded RN Air Station, Culdrose, 1952; Commanded HMS Centaur, 1954-56; Commanded RN Air Station, Ford, 1956-57; Asst Chief of Naval Staff (Warfare) 1957-60; Regional Director, Northern Region, Commonwealth Graves Commission, 1961-64, retd. Naval ADC to the Queen, 1957; Rear-Admiral, 1957. Liveryman, Worshipful Company of Coachmakers and Coach Harnessmakers, 1962. *Address:* 85 High Street, Market Lavington, Wiltshire.

**ROLFE, Hume B.;** *see* Boggis-Rolfe.

**ROLL, Sir Eric,** KCMG 1962 (CMG 1949); CB 1956; a Director of the Bank of England, since 1968; *b* 1 Dec. 1907; *yr s* of Mathias and Fany Roll; *m* 1934, Winifred, *o d* of Elliott and Sophia Taylor; two *d*. *Educ:* on the Continent; Univ. of Birmingham. BCom 1928; PhD 1930; Gladstone Memorial Prize, 1928; Univ. Research Scholarship, 1929. Prof. of Economics and Commerce, Univ. Coll. of Hull, 1935-46 (leave of absence 1939-46). Special Rockefeller Foundation Fellow, USA, 1939-41. Member, later Dep. Head, British Food Mission to N America, 1941-46; UK Dep. Member and UK Exec. Officer, Combined Food Board, Washington, until 1946; Asst Sec., Ministry of Food, 1946-47; Under-Secretary, HM Treasury (Central Economic Planning Staff), 1948; Minister, UK Delegation to OEEC, 1949. Deputy Head, United Kingdom Delegation to North Atlantic Treaty Organization, Paris, 1952; Under Secretary Ministry of Agriculture, Fisheries and Food, 1953-57; Executive Dir, International Sugar Council, 1957-59; Chm., United Nations Sugar Conf., 1958; Deputy Secretary, Ministry of Agriculture, Fisheries and Food, 1959-61; Deputy Leader, UK Delegation for negotiations with the European Economic Community, 1961-63; Economic Minister and Head of UK Treasury Delegation, Washington, 1963-64, also Exec. Dir for the UK International Monetary Fund and International Bank for Reconstruction and Development; Permanent Under-Sec. of State, Dept of Economic Affairs, 1964-66. Chm. Book Development Council, 1967-. Exec. Dir, S. G. Warburg & Co. Ltd, 1967-; Dir, Times Newspapers Ltd, 1967-; also other Directorships. Hon. DSc, Hull, 1967; Hon DSocSci, Birmingham, 1967. *Publications:* An Early Experiment in Industrial Organization, 1930; Spotlight on Germany, 1933; About Money, 1934; Elements of Economic Theory, 1935; Organized Labour (collaborated), 1938; The British Commonwealth at War (collaborated), 1943; A History of Economic Thought, 1954; The Combined Food Board, 1957; The World After Keynes, 1968; articles in Economic Journals, Economica, American Economic Review, etc. *Recreations:* motoring, reading. *Address:* D2 Albany, Piccadilly, W1. *Clubs:* Athenæum, Brooks's.

**ROLL, Rev. Sir James William (Cecil),** 4th Bt, *cr* 1921; Vicar of St John's, Becontree, since 1958; *b* 1 June 1912; *s* of Sir Cecil Ernest Roll, 3rd Bt, and Mildred Kate (*d* 1926), *d* of William Wells, Snaresbrook; *S* father, 1938; unmarried. *Educ:* Chigwell School, Essex; Pembroke College, Oxford; Chichester Theological College. Deacon, 1937. Curate East Ham Parish Church, 1944-58. *Heir:* *b* Gordon Wells Roll, *b* 4 Nov. 1913. *Address:* St John's Vicarage, 34 Castle Road, Dagenham, Essex. *T:* 01-592 5409; 53 Chalkwell Avenue, Westcliff on Sea, Essex. *T:* Southend on Sea 75526.

**ROLLASON, Prof. Ernest Clarence,** MSc, PhD, FIM; Hanson Professor of Metallurgy, Chairman of School of Metallurgy, and Head of Department of Industrial Metallurgy, University of Birmingham, since 1969; *b* 16 March 1908; *m* 1935, Norah Sylvia Palmer-Whorton; one *s* (one *d* decd). *Educ:* Dudley Grammar School; University of Birmingham. Bean Cars Ltd; County Technical College, Wednesbury, Lecturer, 1930-35; Senior Lecturer, Metallurgy Dept, Univ. of Birmingham, 1935-40; Director and Research Manager, Murex Welding Processes Ltd, 1940-51; Henry Bell Wortley Professor of Metallurgy, University of Liverpool, 1951-56. *Publications:* Metal Spraying, 1938; Metallurgy for Engineers, 1939 (3rd edn, 1961); scientific papers in technical jls. *Address:* 83 Farquhar Road, Edgbaston, Birmingham 15. *T:* 021-454 3443.

**ROLLESTON, Col (retd) William Lancelot,** CMG 1958; OBE 1943; *b* 25 June 1905; *s* of Hector Rolleston, Wellington, NZ; *m* 1932, Audrey Joyce Upton; one *s* one *d*. *Educ:* Winchester; Royal Military Academy, Woolwich. Royal Engineers, 1925-46; Colonial Service: Singapore and North Borneo, 1947-50; Tanganyika, 1950-59 (Minister for Communications and Works, 1957-59); Hon. Colonel: 6th Bn King's African Rifles, 1958-59, 2/6th Bn King's African Rifles, 1954-59. Secretary, W Africa Cttee, 1961-70. *Address:* Timberyard Cottage, Beaulieu, Hants. *T:* Beaulieu 388. *Club:* United Hunts.

**ROLLO,** family name of **Baron Rollo.**

**ROLLO,** 13th Baron, *cr* 1651; **Eric John Stapylton Rollo;** Baron Dunning, 1869; JP; *b* 3 Dec. 1915; *s* of 12th Baron and Helen Maud (*d* 1928), *o c* of Frederick Chetwynd Stapylton of Hatton Hill, Windlesham, Surrey; *S* father, 1947; *m* 1938, Suzanne Hatton; two *s* one *d*. *Educ:* Eton. Served War of 1939-45, Grenadier Guards, retiring with rank of Captain. JP Perthshire, 1962. *Heir:* *s* Master of Rollo, *qv*. *Address:* Pitcairns, Dunning, Perthshire. *T:* Dunning 202. *Club:* Guards.

**ROLLO, Master of; Hon. David Eric Howard Rollo;** *b* 31 March 1943; *s* and *heir* of 13th Baron Rollo, *qv*. *Educ:* Eton. Capt. Grenadier Guards. *Address:* Pitcairns, Dunning, Perthshire. *T:* Dunning 202. *Clubs:* Guards, Turf.

**ROLPH, C. H.;** *see* Hewitt, Cecil R.

**ROLT, Lionel Thomas Caswall;** Author; *b* 11 Feb. 1910; *s* of Lionel Caswall Rolt and Jemima Alice (*née* Timperley). *Educ:* Cheltenham College. Mechanical Engineer, 1926-41; Ministry of Supply, 1941-45. Author, 1945-. Co-founder Inland Waterways Association, 1946; Founder and Vice-President, Talyllyn Railway Preservation Society, 1950; Chairman, Talyllyn Railway Co., 1963-68; Member: Inland Waterways Redevelopment Advisory Cttee, 1959-62; Science Museum Adv. Council, 1963-; Exec. Cttee, Soc. for the History of Technology (USA), 1969- (Mem. Adv. Council, 1963-69); Vice-President, Newcomen Society; Hon. MA, Newcastle Univ., 1965. FRSL; CIMechE. *Publications:* Narrow Boat, 1944; High Horse Riderless, 1946; Sleep No More, 1947; Worcestershire, 1948; Green and Silver, 1949; Inland Waterways of England, 1950; Horseless Carriage, 1950; The Thames from Mouth to Source, 1951; Lines of Character, 1952; Railway Adventure, 1953; Winterstoke, 1954;

The Clouded Mirror, 1955; Red for Danger, 1955; Pictorial History of Motoring, 1956; Isambard Kingdom Brunel, 1957; Thomas Telford, 1958; George and Robert Stephenson, 1960; The Cornish Giant, 1960; Great Engineers, 1961; James Watt, 1962; Thomas Newcomen, 1963; A Hunslet Hundred, 1964; Tools for the Job, 1965; The Aeronauts, 1966; The Mechanicals, 1967; Navigable Waterways, 1969; Waterloo Ironworks, 1969; (ed) Best Railway Stories, 1969; Victorian Engineering, 1970. *Recreations:* motoring in vintage cars; railways and interest in history of engineering generally. *Address:* The Cottage, Stanley Pontlarge, Winchcombe, Glos. *T:* Winchcombe 594. *Clubs:* United Motor Sports, Vintage Sports Car.

**ROMAINS, Jules,** de l'Académie Française; Grand Officier de la Légion d'Honneur; Homme de Lettres; *b* Saint-Julien Chapteuil, 26 Aug. 1885; *m* 1936, Mdlle Lise Dreyfus. *Educ:* Paris, Ecole Normale Supérieure. Professeur de Philosophie, pendant dix ans, dans différents lycées de la province et de Paris; depuis 1919, carrière exclusivement littéraire: poète, auteur dramatique, romancier, etc. *Publications:* La Vie Unanime; Europe; Les Copains; Mort de Quelqu'un; Lucienne. Le Dieu des corps. Quand le navire . . .; Les Hommes de Bonne Volonte (27 volumes, 1932-46; traduction anglaise par Gerard Hopkins); L'Homme Blanc; Une Vue des Choses; Bertrand de Ganges, Le Moulin et l'Hospice, Salsette decouvre l'Amérique, Violation de Frontières, Le Fils de Jerphanion, Une Femme singulière, Le Besoin de voir clair, Mémoires de Mdme Chauverel, Un Grand honnête Homme, Pour Raison garder, Portraits d'Inconnus, etc.; *plays:* Knock; Le Dictateur; Le Trouhadec; Musse; Cromedeyre-le-Vieil; Donogoo; Grâce encore pour la Terre! *Address:* 6 rue de Solférino, Paris, VII, France.

**ROMANES, Professor George John,** PhD; Professor of Anatomy, Edinburgh University since Oct. 1954; Chairman Board of Management, Edinburgh Royal Infirmary, since 1959; *b* 2 Dec. 1916; *s* of George Romanes, BSc, AMICE, and Isabella Elizabeth Burn Smith; *m* 1945, Muriel Grace Adam, Edinburgh; four *d. Educ:* Edinburgh Academy; Christ's College, Cambridge (BA, PhD); Edinburgh University (MB, ChB). Marmaduke Sheild Scholar in Human Anatomy, 1938-40; Demonstrator in Anatomy, Cambridge, 1939; Beit Memorial Fellow for Medical Research, Cambridge, 1944-46; Lectr in Neuroanatomy, Edinburgh, 1946; Prof. of Anatomy, Edinburgh, 1954. Commonwealth Fund Fell., Columbia Univ., NY, 1949-50. Mem. Anatomical Soc. of Gt Brit. and Ireland; Mem. Amer. Assoc. of Anatomists; Assoc. Mem. Amer. Neurological Assoc. FRSE 1955; FRCSE 1958. *Publications:* (ed) Cunningham's Textbook and Manuals of Anatomy; various papers on the anatomy and development of the nervous system in Jl of Anatomy and Jl of Comparative Neurology. *Recreations:* angling and curling. *Address:* 197 Colinton Road, Edinburgh, 11. *T:* 031-443 1101.

**ROMANIS, William Hugh Cowie,** JP, MA, MB, MChir Cantab, FRCS, LRCP, FRS (Edinburgh), FZS, FRAS; Barrister-at-Law; Consulting Surgeon to St Thomas's Hospital; Surgeon to Royal Masonic Hospital; Consulting Surgeon to the City of London Hospital for Diseases of the Chest, Royal Masonic Institute for Girls, Wimbledon, Sevenoaks, Wrotham, Woking, Kingston, and Okehampton Hospitals; *b* Godalming, 8 Nov. 1889; *e s* of Rev. William Francis John Romanis, MA Cantab, Preacher of the Charterhouse, EC, and Annie Ellen Cowie; *m* 1916, Dorothy Elizabeth, *d* of Rev. Canon Robert Burnet, Chancellor of Ferns Cathedral, Co. Wexford; one *s* two *d. Educ:* Charterhouse (Scholar, Captain of School); Trinity College, Cambridge (Mathematical Scholar); 1st cl. Mathematical Tripos (Part I.); 1st cl. Natural Science Tripos (Part I.); St Thomas's Hospital. Served European War in RAMC at Casualty Clearing Stations Nos 6 and 44; Examiner in Surgery, Universities of Cambridge, London, Glasgow; Mem. Court of Examiners, RCS; Member British Acad. Forensic Sciences. JP Surrey (Chm. Godalming Petty Sessions). CStJ. *Publications:* Science and Practice of Surgery (two vols); Surgical Emergencies in Practice; Synopsis of Surgical Diagnosis; Surgery of Exophthalmic Goitre, Lancet; Surgery in the Treatment of Phthisis, Lancet; Gastric Ulcer, The Acute Abdomen, Practitioner; and other scientific papers. *Recreations:* criminology, model engineering. *Address:* 149 Harley Street, W1. *T:* 01-935 4444; The Rough, Hurtmore, Godalming. *T:* 22518. *Clubs:* United University; Guildford County.

*See also R. E. W. Harland.*

**ROME, Maj.-Gen. Francis David,** CB 1955; CMG 1959; CBE 1949; DSO 1944; retired; *b* 11 Sept. 1905; *er s* of late Francis James Rome; *m* 1936, Sybil Parry, 2nd *d* of late Lieut-Colonel Henry Carden, DCLI; no *c. Educ:* Cheltenham Coll.; RMC, Sandhurst. Commander: 111 Indian Infantry Brigade, Special Force, SEAC, 1944-45 (DSO); 3rd Parachute Bde, 1946-47; 1st Parachute Bde, 1947-48 (CBE). Served War of 1939-45, France, 1939-40, SEAC, 1943-45; Palestine, 1946-48; Malaya, 1950-51; Deputy Adjutant General, GHQ Far East Land Forces, 1950-53; General Officer Commanding, 16th Airborne Division (Territorial Army), 1953-56; General Officer Commanding, Berlin (British Sector), 1956-59. Colonel, The Royal Fusiliers, 1954-59. *Recreations:* shooting, fishing. *Address:* Sevenhampton House, Highworth, Swindon, Wilts. *T:* Highworth 511. *Club:* Army and Navy.

**ROMILLY,** family name of **Baron Romilly.**

**ROMILLY,** 4th Baron, *cr* 1865; **William Gaspard Guy Romilly,** Hon. MA Oxon 1943; *b* 8 March 1899; *o c* of 3rd Baron and Violet Edith, *o sister* of Sir Philip H. B. Grey Egerton, 12th Bt, and *niece* of Lord Londesborough; *S* father, 1905; *m* 1st, 1929, Hon. Diana Joan Sackville-West (marriage dissolved, 1944), *o d* of 4th Baron Sackville, KBE; 2nd, 1944, Dora (*d* 1960), *d* of late Reginald Morris; 3rd, 1966, Elizabeth, *widow* of Capt. Lionel Cecil, and *er d* of late Charles M. Clover. *Educ:* Eton; Sandhurst. Coldstream Guards, 1917-23; served in France in European War; Reserve of Officers, 1923. Rejoined Coldstream Guards, September 1939; served until 1945 and granted honorary rank of Major. Member of Malborough and Ramsbury Rural District Council, 1949-(Chairman, 1964-67). *Heir:* none. *Address:* Bridge House, Chilton Foliat, near Hungerford, Berks. *T:* Hungerford 2328.

**ROMNEY,** 6th Earl of, *cr* 1801; **Charles Marsham;** Bt, 1663; Baron of Romney, 1716; Viscount Marsham, 1801; DL and JP for Norfolk; *b* 9 July 1892; *o s* of 5th Earl of Romney and Anne (*d* 1936), *d* of late Sir Edward H. Scott, 5th Bt; *S* father, 1933; *m* 1918, Marie, *e d* of late Adm. Sir Colin Keppel, GCVO, KCIE, CB, DSO. *Educ:* Eton; RMC, Sandhurst. Served European War, 1914-18 (wounded); Commandant Guards Depôt,

1928-31; Lt-Col, commanding 2nd Bn Coldstream Guards 1934-36; retired pay, 1936; Commandant Guards Depôt again, 1939-44. Life Vice-Pres., National Council of YMCA's; President: Marine Soc.; Debtor's Relief Funds Charity. *Heir: cousin,* Michael Henry Marsham [*b* 22 Nov. 1910; *m* 1939, Frances Aileen, *o d* of late J. R. Landale, IA]. *Address:* Gayton Hall, King's Lynn, Norfolk. *T:* Gayton 259.
*See also Sir R. L. Hare.*

**RONALD, E. B.;** *see* Barker, Ronald Ernest.

**RONALD, Mrs Edmund;** *see* Templeton, Mrs Edith.

**RONALD, Sir Nigel Bruce,** KCMG, *cr* 1946 (CMG 1934); CVO 1935; *b* 20 Dec. 1894; *s* of late Arthur Wilson Ronald. *Educ:* Winchester; Magdalen College, Oxford. Liverpool Regiment (TF) 1914-17; Grenadier Guards (SR), 1917-20; 3rd Secretary HM Diplomatic Service 1920; 2nd Secretary 1922; Private Secretary to Parliamentary Under-Secretary, 1927; Assistant Private Secretary to Foreign Secretary, 1929-34; 1st Secretary, 1930; Counsellor, 1939; Assistant Under-Secretary, 1942; Ambassador to Portugal, 1947-54. *Address:* The Lodge, Broadwindsor, Dorset. *T:* 243. *Club:* Travellers'.

**RONALDS, Andrew John,** CBE 1961 (OBE 1951); *b* 4 Feb. 1897; *s* of General John Romanenko and Mary (*née* Drentin); *m* 1918, Nathalie, *d* of General Nicolas Woronow and Catherine (*née* Genishta); no *c. Educ:* Imperial Corps of Pages, St Petersburg. Served European War, 1914-18, with Russian Army, 4th Guards Rifles, Imperial Family's Own (twice wounded, Major); attached British Mil. Mission in S Russia, 1919-20; served at British Vice-Consulate, Dubrovnik, 1926-29. Entered British Consular Service, 1936, established in Foreign Service, 1947; served at Belgrade, Sarajevo, Split (captured by enemy forces, 1941), Lisbon, Lourenço Marques, Athens, Naples, Venice, Beira and Bilbao; Consul General at Tananarive, Madagascar, 1956; Ambassador to Malagasy Republic (Madagascar), 1960-61; retired August 1961. On special service with Armed Forces in ME and Central Mediterranean, 1943-45 (despatches). Imperial Order of St George, 4th Class (Russia). *Recreations:* music, walking. *Address:* c/o Lloyds Bank, Ltd, 112 Kensington High Street, W8. *Clubs:* Civil Service; Societã Dell'Unione (Venice).

**RONALDSHAY, Earl of; Lawrence Mark Dundas;** *b* 28 Dec. 1937; *e s* of 3rd Marquess of Zetland, *qv*; *m* 1964, Susan, 2nd *d* of Guy Chamberlin, Shefford House, Great Shefford, and late Mrs Chamberlin; two *s* one *d. Educ:* Harrow School; Christ's College, Cambridge. Late 2nd Lieut, Grenadier Guards. *Heir: s* Lord Dundas, *qv. Address:* Hill House, Cheriton, Alresford, Hampshire. *T:* Bramdean 377.

**ROOKE, Daphne Marie;** author; *b* 6 March 1914; *d* of Robert Pizzey and Marie Knevitt; *m* 1937, Irvin Rooke; one *d. Educ:* Durban, S Africa. *Publications:* A Grove of Fever Trees, 1950; Mittee, 1951; Ratoons; The South African Twins, 1953; The Australian Twins, 1954; Wizards' Country; The New Zealand Twins, 1957; Beti, 1959; A Lover for Estelle, 1961; The Greyling, 1962; Diamond Jo, 1965; Boy on the Mountain, 1969. *Recreation:* breeding of Boxer dogs. *Address:* Bardouroka, NSW 2315, Australia.

**ROOKE, Denis Eric,** CBE 1970; BSc (Eng.); Member for Production and Supply, The Gas Council; *b* 2 April 1924; *yr s* of F. G. Rooke; *m* 1949, Elizabeth Brenda, *d* of D. D. Evans, Ystradgynlais, Brecon; one *d. Educ:* Westminster City Sch.; Addey and Stanhope Sch.; University Coll., London. Served with REME, UK and India, 1944-49 (Major). Joined staff of S Eastern Gas Bd as Asst Mechanical Engr in coal-tar by-products works, 1949; Dep. Man. of works, 1954; seconded to N Thames Gas Bd, 1957, for work in UK and USA on liquefied natural gas; mem. technical team which sailed in Methane Pioneer on first voyage bringing liquefied natural gas to UK, 1959; S Eastern Gas Bd's Development Engr, 1959; Development Engr, Gas Council, 1960; Dir of Production and Supplies, Jan. 1966; Mem. (full-time), Gas Council, Aug. 1966. *Publications:* papers to Instn of Gas Engrs, World Power Conf., World Petroleum Conf., etc. *Recreations:* photography, listening to music. *Address:* 23 Hardy Road, Blackheath, SE3. *Club:* English-Speaking Union.

**ROOKE, James Smith,** CMG 1961; OBE 1949; Minister (Economic), British Embassy, Paris, since 1968; *b* 6 July 1916; *s* of Joseph Nelson Rooke and Adeline Mounser (*née* Woodgate); *m* 1938, Maria Theresa Rebrec, Vienna; one *s* two *d. Educ:* Workington Grammar Sch.; University College, London; Vienna Univ. Apptd to Dept of Overseas Trade, 1938. Military service, 1940-45, KRRC and AEC. Second Secretary (Commercial), British Embassy, Bogotá, 1946; UK Delegation to ITO Conf., Havana, 1947; Dep. UK Commercial Rep., Frankfurt, 1948; First Secretary (Commercial), British Embassy, Rome, 1951; Consul (Commercial), Milan, 1954; Deputy Consul-General (Commercial), New York, 1955-59; HM Counsellor (Commercial) British Embassy, Berne, 1959-63, Rome, 1963-66; Minister (Commercial), British High Commn, Canberra, 1966-68. *Recreations:* climbing, tennis, ski-ing. *Address:* British Embassy, 35 rue du Faubourg St Honoré, Paris 8. *Club:* Devonshire.

**ROOKS, Major-Gen. Lowell W.,** CB (Hon.) 1947; US Army, retd; Fund-Raising Co-ordinator UN International Children's Emergency Fund, since 1949; *b* 11 April 1893; *s* of Albert Rooks and Ruth Naomi Richardson; *m* 1920, Martha Caroline Phillips; two *d. Educ:* University of Washington, Seattle, Washington, USA. Served European War, 1914-18, entering military service 1917; participated in fighting in Vosges Mountains and Meuse-Argonne offensive, France, 1918; later Instructor at Infantry School and Command and Gen. Staff School; War of 1939-45, Chief of Training Div., Army Ground Forces until 1942; Chief of Staff, Second Corps, UK, 1942; participated in Assualt Landings at Oran, Algeria, Nov. 1942; Asst Chief of Staff, G3, AFHQ, under Gen. Eisenhower Dec. 1942; later Dep. Chief of Staff, AFHQ; transferred to European theatre and commanded 90th Div. in final phases of Battle of the Bulge and cracking of Siegfried Line; returned to Gen. Eisenhower's Staff at SHAEF where exercised primary role in planning operations resulting in crossing of Rhine, isolation and capture of Ruhr, advance to Elbe and thrust through Bavaria into Austria; shortly after VE Day, i/c Allied Party sent to Flensburg, Germany, to establish control over self-styled Actg German Govt headed by Grand Admiral Doenitz and German High Command, headed by Field Marshal Keitel; later acted to place all members of this "Government" under arrest; returned to US 1945; Deputy Director-General, UNRRA, Jan. 1946; Director-General UN Relief and Rehabilitation Admin., 1947-48 (when organisation liquidated);

Distinguished Service Medal with Oak-leaf Cluster; Silver Star Citation, Legion of Merit and Bronze Star; British Companion of the Order of the Bath; French Legion of Honour and Croix de Guerre with Palm; Brazilian Order of Military Merit; Belgian Croix de Guerre with Palm, and Belgian Commander of the Order of the Crown with Palm. *Recreations:* golf, fishing and hunting. *Address:* Box 106, Tucson Road, Nogales, Arizona, USA. *T:* 0187J5. *Clubs:* Army Navy Town, Army Navy Country (Washington, DC).

**ROOM, Thomas Gerald,** FRS 1941; Professor of Mathematics, Sydney University, 1935-68, now Emeritus; *b* 10 Nov. 1902; 2nd *s* of E. W. Room, OBE, JP; *m* 1937, Jessie, *d* of C. F. Bannerman; one *s* two *d. Educ:* Alleyn's School; St John's Coll., Cambridge (ScD). Asst Lectr, Liverpool University, 1925; Fellow of St John's College, Cambridge, 1927; Lecturer in Mathematics, Cambridge University, 1929; Visiting Prof. of Mathematics: Univ. of Washington, 1948; Univ. of Tennessee, 1949; Univ. of Sussex, 1966; Westfield Coll., Univ. of London, 1969-70. Fellow Sydney University Senate and Dean of Faculty of Science, 1952-56, 1960-65. Member Inst. for Advanced Study, Princeton, NJ, 1949 and 1957-58; Visiting Lectr, Univ. of Princeton, 1958. Pres., Austr. Mathematical Soc., 1950-62. *Publication:* Geometry of Determinantal Loci, 1939; The Sorting Process, 1966; A Background to Geometry, 1967. *Recreations:* gardening; Boy Scouts (Rover Section). *Address:* High Walden, St Ives, NSW, Australia. *T:* (Sydney) JJ2798.

**ROOME, Rear-Admiral Henry Stewart,** CBE 1949; *b* 7 May 1896; *s* of late Eng. Rear-Adm. G. W. Roome, CBE; *m* 1921, Aileen D. M. L., *d* of Comdr C. T. Scott, RIM; two *s* one *d. Educ:* RN Colleges; Osborne, Dartmouth, Keyham. Midshipman, HMS Bellerophon, 1913; acting Sub-Lt 1915. Served European War in Grand Fleet Destroyers, 1916-18 (despatches); Lieut, 1917; RN Coll., Keyham, 1918; Lieut (E) 1919; Comdr (E), 1928; Capt. (E), 1940. ADC to the King, 1946-47; Rear-Adm. (E), 1947. Served War of 1939-45, HM Dockyards, Devonport and Sheerness; and at Admiralty; Manager Engineering Department, HM Dockyard, Portsmouth, 1945-50; retired, 1950. *Address:* Moorlands, Moorland Avenue, Barton-on-Sea, Hants.

**ROONEY, Major-General Sir Owen (Patrick James),** KBE 1959 (CBE 1951; OBE 1943); CB 1957; *b* 1900, *s* of late Captain Owen Rooney, Royal Artillery; *m* 1924, Una Colman, *d* of Charles Guilfoyle Doran, Queenstown, County Cork; one *s* one *d. Educ:* Haberdashers' Aske's School; RMA, Woolwich. Army Officer from 1919, when commissioned in RFA; RAPC, 1924; Egypt, Sudan and Palestine, 1932-37; served War of 1939-45, France, N Africa and Italy; BAOR, 1951-54; Maj.-Gen. 1955; Paymaster-in-Chief, War Office, 1955-59; retired. Col Comdt Royal Army Pay Corps, 1960-63. *Recreation:* formerly Hon. Vice-Pres., Football Assoc., 1959-61. Army Football Assoc. (Vice-Pres.). *Address:* Flat 9, Westfield Park House, Spencer Road, Ryde, Isle of Wight. *Club:* Army and Navy.

**ROOT, Frederick James,** CB 1952; Deputy Secretary, Ministry of Public Building and Works (previously Ministry of Works), 1959-66; *b* 2 July 1906; *s* of late Alan and Elizabeth A. Root; *m* 1941, Margaret Eleanor Barbour, *d* of late Dr G. F. Barbour Simpson, Edinburgh; two *d. Educ:* Christ's Hosp.; Merton Coll., Oxford. Entered Civil Service, 1928; Private Secretary to successive First Commissioners of Works, 1933-37, and to successive Ministers of Works, 1940-43. *Address:* Scotsdene, Haslemere, Surrey. *T:* Haslemere 3750. *Clubs:* Athenæum, Royal Automobile.

**ROOT, Rev. Prof. Howard Eugene;** Professor of Theology, University of Southampton, since 1966; *b* 13 April 1926; *s* of late Howard Root and Flora Hoskins; *m* 1952, Celia Holland; two *s* two *d. Educ:* Univ. of Southern California; St Catherine's Coll. and Magdalen Coll., Oxford; Ripon Hall, Oxford. BA S Calif 1945; BA Oxon 1951; MA Oxon 1970; MA Cantab 1953. Teaching Fellow, 1945-47; Instructor, American Univ., Cairo, 1947-49; Sen. Demy, Magdalen Coll., Oxford, and Liddon Student, 1952-53. Deacon, 1953; Priest, 1954. Curate of Trumpington, 1953; Asst Lectr in Divinity, Cambridge, 1953-57; Lectr, 1957-65; Fellow, Emmanuel Coll., Cambridge, 1954-65, Chaplain, 1954-56, Dean, 1956-65. Wilde Lectr Oxford Univ., 1957-60; Senior Denyer and Johnson Scholar, Oxford, 1963-64. Exam. Chaplain to Bishops of Ripon, Southwark, and Bristol; Official Anglican Observer at Second Vatican Council, 1963-65; Consultant, Lambeth Conf., 1968. Chm., Archbishops' Commn on Marriage, 1968-; Member: Academic Coun., Ecumenical Inst., Jerusalem, 1966-; Anglican-RC Preparatory Commn, 1967-68; Archbishops' Commn on Christian Doctrine, 1967-; Internat. Roman Catholic-Anglican Jt Commn, 1969-. Hon. Chaplain, Winchester Cathedral, 1966-67; Canon Theologian of Winchester, 1967-. Editor (with H. Chadwick and H. F. D. Sparks), Jl of Theological Studies, 1969-. *Recreations:* music, theatre, poetry, fiction. *Address:* Department of Theology, The University, Southampton. *T:* 56331.

**ROOTES,** family name of **Baron Rootes.**

**ROOTES,** 2nd Baron *cr* 1959; **William Geoffrey Rootes;** Chairman since 1970, Chrysler United Kingdom (lately Rootes Motors Ltd); *b* 14 June 1917; *er s* of 1st Baron Rootes, GBE; *S* father, 1964; *m* 1946, Marian, *widow* of Wing Comdr J. H. Slater, AFC, and *d* of late Lt-Col H. R. Hayter, DSO; one *s* one *d. Educ:* Harrow; Christ Church, Oxford. Served War of 1939-45 in RASC (France, E Africa, Western Desert, Libya, Tunisia and Italy), demobilised, Actg Major, 1946. Rejoined Rootes Group, 1946: Man. Dir, 1962-67; Dep. Chm., 1965-67; Chm. 1967-70. Dir, First Nat. City Trust Co. (Bahamas) Ltd. Pres., Motor & Cycle Trades Benevolent Fund, 1968-70. Member: Nat. Adv. Council, Motor Manufrg Industry; Nat. Economic Development Cttee, Motor Manufacturing Industry; Council and Management Committee, Soc. Motor Manufacturers and Traders Ltd (Pres., 1960-61); BNEC (Chm., American Cttee); Council, CBI; Council, Inst. of Dirs; Council, Warwick Univ. (Chm., Appointments Bd); Pres., Motor Ind. Research Assoc. FBIM 1965; FRSA. *Recreations:* shooting, tennis, ski-ing. *Heir: s* Hon. Nicholas Geoffrey Rootes, *b* 12 July 1951. *Address:* Rootes Motors Ltd, Devonshire House, Piccadilly, W1; North Standen House, Hungerford, Berks; Glenalmond House, Glenalmond, Perthshire. *Clubs:* Buck's, St James'.

**ROOTES, Sir Reginald (Claud),** Kt, *cr* 1946; *b* 20 Oct. 1896; *s* of late William and Jane Rootes; *m* 1st, 1922, Ruth Joyce, *d* of late Harding Bensted; one *s*; 2nd, 1938, Nancy Norris, *d* of late J. C. Beadle. *Educ:* Cranbrook Sch., Kent, Civil Service, Admiralty, 1915-18. Pres. Society of Motor Manufacturers and Traders, 1945-46, Dep. Pres., 1946-50; Past Pres. Motor Industry Research Assoc. *Recreations:*

various. *Address:* Polla House, Hothfield, Ashford, Kent. *T:* Ashford 1495. *Club:* Buck's.

**ROOTH, Ivar;** *b* Stockholm, 2 Nov. 1888; two *s* two *d. Educ:* Universities of Uppsala and Berlin. Governor of Central Bank of Sweden, 1929-48; Assistant Manager and solicitor of Stockholm Mortgage Bank; Director of Bank for International Settlements; Chairman of the Board and Managing Director of the International Monetary Fund, 1951-56. Hon. PhD Uppsala, 1962. *Address:* 13 Larsbergsvagen, Lidingö 1, Sweden.

**ROOTHAM, Jasper St John,** MA; Managing Director, Lazard Bros & Co. Ltd; Chairman, Standard Industrial Trust, since 1970; *b* 21 Nov. 1910; *s* of Dr Cyril Bradley and Rosamond Margaret Rootham; *m* 1944, Joan McClelland; one *s* one *d. Educ:* Tonbridge Sch. (Judd Schol.); St John's Coll., Cambridge (Maj. Schol.). 1st cl. Class. Tripos Pts I and II. Entered Civil Service, 1933; Min. of Agric., 1933-34; CO, 1934-36; Treasury, 1936-38; Pte Sec. to Prime Minister, 1938-39; Treasury, 1939-40; resigned to join Army, 1940; served Middle East, Balkans, Germany (despatches); demobilized, 1946 (Col); entered Bank of England as Actg Asst Adviser, 1946; Adviser to Governor, 1957; Chief of Overseas Dept, 1962; Asst to Governor, 1964; retd, 1967. Director: Agricultural Mortgage Corp.; British Sugar Corp; Chm., DEK Printing Machines Ltd. A Governor, Overseas Coll., Farnham Castle. *Publications:* Miss Fire, 1946; Demi-Paradise, 1960; poems. *Recreations:* music, country life. *Address:* Lower Farm, Hadstock, Cambridge. *T:* Linton 566. *Clubs:* Athenæum, Overseas Bankers'.

**ROOTS, William Lloyd,** QC 1959; TD; MA (Oxon.); *b* 10 Sept. 1911; *s* of Neville Roots; *m* 1939, Elizabeth Colquhoun Gow Gray; one *s. Educ:* Tonbridge School; Brasenose College, Oxford. Called to Bar, Middle Temple, 1933; Master of the Bench, 1965. Surrey and Sussex Yeomanry, RA (TA), 1939-46. Alderman, Royal Borough of Kensington, 1953-59; Chairman, Fulham and Kensington Hospital Management Cttee, 1952-55; MP (C) Kensington South, 1959-67, resigned. Dep. Chm., Dorset QS 1960-. *Publications:* a number of books on Local Government Law. *Recreations:* travel, fishing. *Address:* 2 Mitre Court Buildings, Temple, EC4. *T:* 01-236 4488. *Clubs:* Carlton, 1900, United and Cecil, Hurlingham.

**ROPER;** *see* Trevor-Roper.

**ROPER, Captain Edward Gregson,** CBE 1959; DSO 1942; DSC; Capt. RN retd; *b* 12 April 1910; *s* of late John Gregson Roper, OBE; *m* 1933, Sylvia, *d* of E. F. L. Hopkins; one *d. Educ:* Oundle. Joined Royal Navy, 1928; served War of 1939-45 (DSC, DSO): Comd HMS Velox, 1940-42; Impulsive, 1942-43; Comdr, 1943; Comd 18th Destroyer Flotilla, 1944-45. Captain, 1950; Comd HMS Ocean, 1955-56; Royal Naval College, Greenwich, 1956-59; retired, 1959. *Address:* Polmayne, St Minver, Cornwall. *Clubs:* United Service; Royal Yacht Squadron (Naval Member).

**ROPER, Edward Ridgill;** DSO 1918; MC; VD; QC; formerly President of Courts of Appeal for Botswana, Lesotho and Swaziland; Judge of the Supreme Court of South Africa, 1946-55; former Member of Parliament, Union of South Africa, Wynberg Division; *b* 30 Oct. 1885; *s* of late Rev. Thomas Roper, Kroonstad, Orange Free State; *m* 1919, Gladys Frances, *e d* of F. W. Farrow, Walton-on-Thames; one *d. Educ:* Kingswood College, Grahamstown; Victoria College, Stellenbosch; Diocesan College, Rondebosch; BA, LLB, Maynard Scholar and Ebden Prizeman, University of Cape of Good Hope. Admitted to Cape Bar, 1910; 2nd Lt Cape Garrison Artillery, 1909; Capt. 1912; temp. Capt. RFA 1915; temp. Major, 1917; Officer Commdg Cape Garrison Artillery, 1921-24; served German SW Africa, South African Rebellion, Egypt, France and Belgium, Italy (DSO, MC, VD, Croix de Guerre, despatches, wounded thrice); Officer Commanding 32nd Field Regt, South African Artillery, 1942. Pres., S Af. Red Cross, 1958, 1959, 1961, 1962; Pres., Boy Scouts Assoc. of South Africa, 1967. *Recreation:* gardening. *Address:* 1 Kent Road, Dunkeld West, Johannesburg, S Africa. *Club:* Rand (Johannesburg).

**ROPER, Sir Harold,** Kt, *cr* 1945; CBE 1943; MC; MP (C) North Cornwall, 1950-59; *b* 2 Sept. 1891; *s* of Arthur Charles Roper, FRCS, MRCP, Exeter; *m* 1929, Norah Keys, Edinburgh; four *d. Educ:* Blundell's; Sidney Sussex Coll., Cambridge. Varsity Boat, 1913. European War, France and Italy, 1915-18, 8th Devons, Capt. (MC); General Manager, Burmah Oil Co. Ltd 1936-45; despatches, 1942. Member: Burma Legislative Council, 1935-36; Burma Senate, 1937-42; Chm. Burma Chamber of Commerce, 1940. Mem. Devon CC, 1961-68. *Address:* Gorse Hill, Ilsham Marine Drive, Torquay, Devon.

**ROPER, John Charles Abercromby,** CMG 1969; MC; Ambassador to Luxembourg, since 1970; *b* 8 June 1915; *s* of late Charles Roper, MD, and of Mrs Roper; *m* 1st, 1945, Valerie Armstrong-MacDonnell (marr. diss.); two *d*; 2nd, 1960, Kathryn, *d* of late Edgar Bibas, New York. *Educ:* Harrow; Universities of Cambridge and Princeton (Commonwealth Fellow). Served 1939-46, Scots Guards and Special Forces, Major (MC). HM Diplomatic Service, 1946; Athens, 1947-51; Foreign Office, 1951-54; Washington, 1954-59. Seconded to Min. of Defence and apptd Dep. Commandant (Civil) of NATO Defence College, Paris, 1960-62; Asst Sec., Cabinet Office, 1962-64; Counsellor, UK Delegn to OECD, 1964-70. *Address:* British Embassy, Luxembourg; Island of Hydra, Greece. *Clubs:* Guards, Special Forces; Travellers' (Paris).

**ROPER, John (Francis Hodgess);** MP (Lab and Co-op) Farnworth since 1970; *b* 10 Sept. 1935; *e s* of Rev. Frederick Mabor Hodgess Roper and Ellen Frances (*née* Brockway); *m* 1959, Valerie Hope, *er d* of late Rt Hon. L. John Edwards, PC, OBE, MP, and Mrs D. M. Edwards; one *d. Educ:* William Hulme's Grammar Sch., Manchester; Reading Sch.; Magdalen Coll., Oxford; Univ. of Chicago. Nat. Service, commnd RNVR, 1954-56; studied PPE, Oxford, 1956-59 (Pres. UN Student Assoc., 1957; organised Univ. referendum on Nuclear Disarmament); Harkness Fellow, Commonwealth Fund, 1959-61; Research Fellow in Economic Statistics, Univ. of Manchester, 1961; Asst Lectr in Econs, 1962, Lectr 1964, Faculty Tutor 1968. Contested (Lab) High Peak (Derbs), 1964. Vice-Chm., Nat. Exec. Cttee, UNA, 1965-; Cons. for Council of Europe, 1965-66. Research Adviser (part-time), DEA in NW, 1967-69; Dir, Hyde Equitable Co-op. Soc., 1964-; Dir, Co-op. Wholesale Soc., 1969-; Exec. Cttee, Manchester and Salford Council of Social Service, 1965-; Council, Manchester Statistical Soc., 1968-. *Publications:* (with Lloyd Harrison) Towards Regional Co-operatives, 1967; The Teaching of Economics at University Level, 1970; articles and reviews in Co-operative jls and Manchester School. *Recreations:* reading, travel. *Address:* House of

Commons, SW1. *Clubs:* Farnworth and Kearsley Labour (Kearsley, Lancs).

**ROPER-CURZON,** family name of **Baron Teynham.**

**ROPNER, Sir Guy;** *see* Ropner, Sir W. G.

**ROPNER, John Raymond;** Director: Sir R. Ropner & Co. (Management) Ltd; National Westminster (formerly National Provincial) Bank, since 1953; and other companies; *b* 8 May 1903; *s* of William Ropner; *m* 1928, Joan Redhead; two *s* one *d*. *Educ:* Harrow; Clare College, Cambridge (BAEcon 1925). Durham Heavy Bde, RA (TA), 1922-28; joined Sir R. Ropner & Co. Ltd, 1925; Ministry of War Transport, North Western Europe, 1944-45. High Sheriff of Durham, 1958. Member, Shipping Advisory Panel, 1962. Order of Oranje-Nassau, 1947. *Recreations:* gardening, fishing, shooting; formerly golf (Cambridge blue, 1925). *Address:* Middleton Lodge, Middleton Tyas, Richmond, Yorks. *T:* Barton (Yorks) 212. *Club:* Bath.

**ROPNER, Colonel Sir Leonard,** 1st Bt *cr* 1952; MC; TD; BA; DL, JP; Director: Sir R. Ropner & Company Ltd, Shipowners; British Shipowners' Assoc., and other cos; Member of Council of Chamber of Shipping of the United Kingdom since 1928, and of Tramp Shipping Committee since 1935; *b* 26 February 1895; *e s* of William Ropner, JP, and *g s* of late Sir Robert Ropner, Bt, VD, DL, JP; *m* 1932, Esmé, *y d* of late Bruce Robertson; one *s* two *d*. *Educ:* Harrow; Clare College, Cambridge (Scholar). Commissioned in the Royal Artillery, 1914; later commanded a battery in France for two years (MC); Officer, commanding Durham Heavy Brigade RA (TA), 1919-28, Hon. Col 426 Coast Regt RA, TA, 1928-56, Hon. Col 132 Corps Engineer Regt TA, 1956-58; Member Durham County T&AFA 1920-61 (Vice-Chm. 1948-52). MP (C) Sedgefield Div. of Durham, 1923-29, Barkston Ash, W R Yorks, 1931-64; Parliamentary Private Secretary to Secretary of State for War, 1924-28; Temp. Chm. of Cttees, 1945-58; Hon. Treasurer, Conservative and Unionist Films Association, 1930-47, Chairman, 1947-59; Chairman, Conservative Shipping and Ship-building Committee, 1946-64; Hon. Treasurer of Primrose League, 1952-64. Member of English Consultative Committee under the Forestry Acts, 1932-36; Forestry Commissioner, 1936-45; Assistant Controller, Ministry of Supply Timber Control, Sept. 1939; Forestry Commission Timber Supply Department, 1940; Dep. Dir Home Grown Timber Production, Ministry of Supply, 1941. Re-joined RA as 2nd Lt 1941; later Lt-Col Comdg Regt RA, and Col HQ 21st Army Group, Belgium and Germany. County Comr, St John Ambulance Bde, N Riding of Yorkshire, 1950-66. DL, JP Durham. KStJ. *Heir: s* John Bruce Woollacott Ropner [*b* 16 April 1937; *m* 1961, Anne Melicent, *d* of late Sir Ralph Delmé-Radcliffe; two *d*]. *Address:* Thorp Perrow, Bedale, Yorkshire. *T:* Bedale 2710. *TA:* Bedale. *Clubs:* Carlton, Bath, Buck's; Durham County (Durham); Yorkshire (York).

**ROPNER, Sir Robert (Desmond),** Kt 1959; Director: Ropner Holdings Ltd; Sir R Ropner & Co. Ltd, and assoc. cos; BP Tanker Co. Ltd; BP Clyde Tanker Co. Ltd; Airvert Ltd; Airtech Ltd; Hozelock Ltd; Croft Autodrome Ltd; *b* 2 July 1908; 4th *s* of William Ropner, JP, and *gs* of Sir Robert Ropner, 1st Bt, VD, DL, JP; *m* 1st, 1932, Dorothy Beecroft Sheila (marriage dissolved, 1946), *d* of Sir Edmund Beecroft Lacon, 5th Bt; two *s*; 2nd, 1947, Sibyl (*d* 1969), *d* of late Thomas O. Carter. *Educ:* Harrow; Clare College, Cambridge (BA). Mem. Ministry of Transport Ships Licensing Cttee, 1947; Chm. Tramp Shipping Sub-Cttee of Shipping Advisory and Allocations Committee, 1947; Member Council, Chamber of Shipping of the UK, and various Committees, 1941- (Pres. 1958-59; Chairman Deep Sea Tramp Section, 1951-53); Mem., General Council British Shipping, 1941-, Chm., 1958-59; Member, Shipping Advisory Panel, 1962; Mem., Exec. Council, Shipping Federation Ltd; Past Chm. North of England Protecting and Indemnity Assoc. *Recreations:* forestry, motoring. *Address:* Camp Hill, Bedale, Yorkshire. *T:* Sinderby 262; Flat 2c, Sloane Avenue Mansions, SW3. *T:* 01-584 9585. *Clubs:* City of London, Boodle's.

**ROPNER, Sir Robert Douglas,** 4th Bt, *cr* 1904; *b* 1 Dec. 1921; *o s* of Sir (E. H. O.) Robert Ropner, 3rd Bt; *S* father, 1962; *m* 1943, Patricia Kathleen, *d* of W. E. Scofield, W. Malling, Kent; one *s* one *d*. *Educ:* Harrow, Formerly Capt., RA. *Heir: s* Robert Clinton Ropner, *b* 6 Feb. 1949.

**ROPNER, Sir (William) Guy,** Kt, *cr* 1947; Director Sir R. Ropner & Co. Ltd and other companies; *b* 14 June 1896; *s* of William Ropner; *m* 1921, Margarita Gray; two *s* one *d*. *Educ:* Harrow. European War, 1914-18, joined Durham Royal Garrison Artillery, 1914, and served in France with Siege Batteries; joined Sir R. Ropner & Co. Ltd, 1919; War of 1939-45, entered Ministry of Shipping, 1939, and served in various capacities throughout war, including Dep. Director Ship Management Div., Head of Convoy Section and Minister's Rep. in Canada; President Chamber of Shipping, 1950; Chairman General Council of British Shipping, 1950; Deputy Chairman, Lloyd's Register of Shipping, 1950-60. *Recreations:* gardening. *Address:* Hillside, Patrick Brompton, Bedale, Yorks. *T:* Constable Burton 206. *Clubs:* Royal Motor Yacht; Royal Thames Yacht.

**ROSA, John Nogueira,** OBE 1947; BCom; Deputy Managing Director, M. Golodetz Ltd, International Merchants, EC3; *b* Durban, South Africa, 17 Jan. 1903; *s* of John Michael and Maria Magdalena Nogueira Rosa; *m* 1929, Eileen, *d* of James Moncrieff Anderson; no *c*. *Educ:* South Africa; London School of Economics and Political Science. Ottoman Bank, Istanbul, 1924-28; Helbert, Wagg & Co. Ltd, Private Bankers, London, 1929-41; HM Treasury Rep. in Syria and the Lebanon, 1941-42; Colonial Office, London, 1942-47; Member Colonial Office Mission to East and Central Africa to investigate production of groundnuts, 1946; Helbert, Wagg & Co., Ltd, 1947, resigned 1947; late Member Boards Overseas Food Corp., The Queensland-British Food Corp., and Colonial Development Corporation, 1948-51. *Recreation:* travel. *Address:* 11a Troy Court, W8. *T:* 01-937 6729.

**ROSAY, Françoise;** Actress; *widow* of Jacques Feyder, director; three *s*. Started career as singer, taking important rôles at National Opera in Paris. Title rôle in Madam Tic-Tac, Winter Garden, London, 1950; Trespass, Globe Theatre. Entered films in France, 1927, and had immediate successes. Went to England in 1944, having contracts with Ealing Studios. French films include: La Kermesse héroique, Carnet de bal, Une Femme Disparaît, Drôle de Drame. Eng. Lang. films include: The Half Way House, Johnny Frenchman, Saraband for Dead Lovers, Quartet, The Naked Heart, That Lady, Me and the Colonel. *Address:* 195 Rue de l'Université, Paris.

**ROSCOE, Air Cdre Peter Henry,** CB 1967; FCA; *b* 1912. Dept of Air Member for Personnel, 1963-67; Dir of Personnel (Ground) Min. of Defence (RAF), 1966; retired 1967. *Address:* Fairhaven, Tan-y-Bryn Road, Holyhead, Anglesey.

**ROSE, Sir Alan (Edward Percival),** KCMG 1955; Kt 1950; QC (Ceylon), 1948; MA, LLB Cantab; Chief Justice (1st) of the State of Singapore, 1958-63; *b* 8 October 1899; *yr s* of late Charles Edward James Rose; unmarried. *Educ:* Aldenham Sch.; Trinity Coll., Cambridge. 2nd Lieut 1st Bn Rifle Brigade, BEF, 1918-19; called to Bar, Inner Temple, 1923; entered Colonial Legal Service, 1929; Chief Police Magistrate, Fiji, 1929; Crown Counsel, Northern Rhodesia, 1931; Solicitor-General, Palestine, 1936; Puisne Judge, Palestine, 1939; Chm., Commissions of Inquiry into loss of SS Patria, 1940; and into corruption in Customs Dept, 1942; acted as Chief Justice, 1944; Judge of Supreme Court, Ceylon, 1945; acted as Legal Secretary, Ceylon, 1946 and 1947; Attorney-Gen. (1st) Dominion of Ceylon, 1947-51; Officer Administering Govt of Ceylon, Mar.-June 1952, July-Sept. 1953; Chief Justice of the Dominion of Ceylon, 1951-55, retired 1955. Chm. Commn of Inquiry into affairs of Nairobi City Council, 1956; Chm. Medical Appeal Tribunal, Midland Region, 1957-58, 1963-68, London (South), 1968-. *Address:* 9 Hove Place, Hove 3, Sussex. *T:* Brighton 733666. *Club:* Bath.

**ROSE, Sir Alec (Richard),** Kt 1968; Fruit Merchant since 1957; *b* 13 July 1908; *s* of Ambrose Rose; *m* 1st, 1931, Barbara Kathleen (*née* Baldwin); two *s* two *d*; 2nd, 1960, Dorothy Mabel (*née* Walker). *Educ:* Simon Langton Boys School, Canterbury. Farming in Canada, 1928-30; Haulage Contractor, 1930-39; served RNVR, 1939-45; Market Gardener, 1945-57. Pres., British Junior Exploration Soc., 1969-. Member: Fruiterers Co.; Worshipful Co. of Basketmakers; Worshipful Co. of Shipwrights. Freedom of Portsmouth, 1968. Blue Water Medal, Cruising Club of America, 1969. *Publication:* My Lively Lady, 1968. *Recreation:* sailing (inc. circumnavigation of world, 1968). *Address:* 38 Osborne Rd, Southsea, Hants. *T:* Portsmouth 26036. *Clubs:* City Livery; Portsmouth County, Royal Naval (Portsmouth); Royal Yacht Squadron, Royal Albert Yacht, Royal Naval Sailing Assoc.; Eastney Cruising Assoc.

**ROSE, Rt. Rev. Alfred Carey Wollaston,** MA; an Assistant Bishop in the Diocese of Canterbury since 1957; Sub-Prelate of Order of St John of Jerusalem; *s* of late Rev. A. Rose, Vicar of Wilstead, Beds; *m* 1920, Lois, *d* of late Charles Garton of Banstead, Surrey; four *s*. *Educ:* Marlborough; Worcester College, Oxford. Curate of St Mary, Somers Town, 1909-14; temporary Chaplain RN, 1914-19, HMS London, 1914-16, HMS Tyne, 1917-18, HMS Marlborough, 1918-19; Sub-Warden Bishops Hostel, Lincoln, 1919-20; Warden, 1921-27; Vicar of Haigh, Lancs, 1920-21; Prebendary of Lincoln Cathedral, 1927-28; Vicar and Rural Dean of Brighton, 1928-34; Prebendary of Waltham in Chichester Cathedral, 1928; Examining Chaplain to the Bishop of Chichester, 1928-34; Chaplain to the King, 1933-34. Suffragan Bishop of Dover, 1935-56. *Recreation:* golf. *Address:* Glebe House, St Stephen's Green, Canterbury, Kent. *T:* Canterbury 63673.

*See also C. M. Rose.*

**ROSE, Bernard William George,** MusB Cantab 1938, MA Oxon, Cantab, DMus Oxon 1955, FRCO; Fellow, Organist, Informator Choristarum, Magdalen College, Oxford, since 1957; University Lecturer in Music since 1950; Choragus in the University, 1958-63; *b* Little Hallingbury, Herts, 9 May 1916; *s* of William and Jessie Rose; *m* 1939, Molly Daphne, JP, 5th *d* of D. G. Marshall, MBE, Cambridge; three *s*. *Educ:* Salisbury Cathedral Sch.; Royal Coll. of Music; St Catharine's Coll., Cambridge. Organ Scholar, St Catharine's, Cambridge, 1935-39; Stewart of Rannoch Scholar in Sacred Music, Cambridge, 1935-39; Organist and Conductor of the Eaglesfield Musical Soc., The Queen's Coll., Oxford, 1939-57, Fellow, 1949. Served with 4th Co. of London Yeomanry (Sharpshooters), 1941-44, Adjutant 1942 (PoW 1943-44). Council: Royal Coll. of Organists. *Publications:* contrib. Proc. Roy. Mus. Assoc., 1955; various church music compositions and edns of church music; edns of Anthems of Thomas Tomkins; (ed) Early English Church Music, Vols 5 and 9; Hallische Händel Ausgabe, 'Susanna'; General Editor, Novello Church Music. Reviews in Music and Letters, articles in Musical Times. *Recreations:* climbing, sailing. *Address:* Appleton Manor, near Abingdon, Berks. *T:* Cumnor 2919.

**ROSE, Christine Brooke;** *see* Brooke-Rose.

**ROSE, Clive Martin,** CMG 1967; British Embassy, Washington, since 1969; *b* 15 Sept. 1921; *s* of Rt Rev. Alfred Carey Wollaston Rose, *qv*; *m* 1946, Elisabeth Mackenzie, *d* of late Rev. Cyril Lewis, Gilston; two *s* three *d*. *Educ:* Marlborough College; Christ Church, Oxford. Rifle Bde, 1941-46 (Maj.; despatches): served in Europe, 1944-45; India, 1945; Iraq, 1945-46. Commonwealth Relations Office, 1948; Office of Deputy High Comr, Madras, 1948-49; Foreign Office, 1950-53; UK High Commn, Germany, 1953-54; British Embassy, Bonn, 1955; FO, 1956-59; 1st Sec. and HM Consul, Montevideo, 1959-62; FO, 1962-65; Commercial Counsellor, Paris, 1965-67; Imp. Defence Coll., 1968. *Address:* 10 Woodsford Square, Addison Road, W14. *T:* 01-603 0100. *Club:* Travellers'.

**ROSE, (Edward) Michael,** CMG 1955; Director and Secretary, East Africa and Mauritius Association, since 1969; *b* 18 Oct. 1913; *s* of Frank Atcherley Rose and Marian Elizabeth Darling Harris; unmarried. *Educ:* Rugby; St John's College, Cambridge. Entered Diplomatic Service, 1937; served Oslo 1940, Algiers, 1944, Copenhagen 1945-48; Deputy to GOC British Sector of Berlin, 1952-55; Counsellor, Foreign Office, 1955-60; Minister, Bonn, 1960-63; Ambassador to the Congo (Leopoldville), 1963-65; Asst Under-Sec., Foreign Office, 1965-67; Dep. Sec., Cabinet Office, 1967-68. Fellow, Center for Internat. Affairs, Harvard Univ., 1958-59. *Recreations:* golf, gardening. *Address:* 2 Godfrey Street, SW3; Ovington Grange, Clare, Suffolk. *Club:* Travellers'.

**ROSE, Eliot Joseph Benn, (Jim Rose);** Editorial Director, Westminster Press Ltd, since 1970; *b* 7 June 1909; *s* of Colonel E. A. Rose, *qv*; *m* 1946, Susan Pamela Gibson; one *s* one *d*. *Educ:* Rugby; New College, Oxford. Served War of 1939-45, RAF, Wing-Comdr. Literary Editor, The Observer, 1948-51; Director: International Press Institute, Zürich, 1952-63; Survey of Race Relations in Britain, 1963-68. Legion of Merit (US). *Publication:* Colour and Citizenship, 1969. *Address:* 37 Pembroke Square, W8. *T:* 01-937 3772. *Club:* Bath.

**ROSE, Lieut-Colonel Ernest Albert,** CBE 1919 (OBE 1919); BSc, FIMechE; late Honorary Colonel 2/7th Battalion Queen's Royal

Regiment; *b* 1879; *m* Dula, *e d* of Eliot Lewis, JP, Liverpool; two *s* one *d* (and one *d* decd). *Educ:* Liverpool College; Liverpool University. Formerly General Manager of New Arrol-Johnston Car Co. Ltd; a pioneer of motoring in England; chief Engineer to the Pioneer Motor Traction Co. formed in 1903 at Liverpool, the Road Carrying Co. Ltd; for many years Director of Delaunay Belleville Motors, Ltd; a Member of the General Council of the Royal Automobile Club; served European War, 1914-19 (despatches, OBE, CBE, Order of Crown of Italy). *Recreations:* golf and motoring. *Address:* Old Kiln, Churt, nr Farnham, Surrey. *Club:* Bath. *See also E. J. B. Rose.*

**ROSE, Sir Francis Cyril,** 4th Bt, *cr* 1872; Painter and Author; *b* 18 Sept. 1909; *e s* of 3rd Bt and Laetitia, *d* of late Comte Rouy de Labadesse; *S* father, 1915; *m* 1st, 1943, Frederica Dorothy Violet (marr. diss. 1966), *d* of late General Sir Frederick Carrington, KCB, KCMG; 2nd, 1967, Mrs Beryl Davis, *widow* of Squadron Leader Basil Montefiore Davis, RAF. *Educ:* St Anthony's Preparatory School, Eastbourne; Beaumont College. Served War of 1939-45; RAF 1940-42 (invalided out). Artistic Adviser Edinburgh Tapestry Co. Ltd, 1948-50; Artistic Consultant Roosen Silks Ltd. Exhibns: Paris, 1933, New York, Chicago and London, 1934; Petit Palace, Paris, 1938 (official show); represented British Modern Art (with Group), Salon d'Automne, Paris, 1939; Reid and Lefevre, London, 1944; Exhibition of Paintings organised by US Army (441st Troop Carrier Group) Gallery Pierre Colle, Paris, Feb. 1945; Wallpaper designs, History of Wallpaper Exhibition, Suffolk Gallery, London, 1945; Cotton Board Flower Painting Exhibition, Manchester, 1945; Redfern Gallery, London, 1945; Associated American Artists, NY, 1947; Gimpel Fils, London, 1949 and 1952; Passedoit Gallery, NY, 1950; Gallery Pierre Colle, Paris, 1950; Molton Gallery, 1961; Preston Gallery, Bolton, Lancs, 1964; Upper Grosvenor Galleries, 1967; retrospective exhibition, GLC London Gall. and Royal Pavilion, Brighton, 1966. Costumes and Scenery for Cupid and Psyche Ballet at Sadler's Wells, 1939; for La Peri, ballet given by Serge Lifar, Monte Carlo ballets, 1946; sets for Trigon, Arts Theatre, 1964. Textile designs for the Cotton Board, 1944; Artistic adviser for 1947-48, Mount Row Prints Ltd. *Publications:* The White Cow and other Chinese Tales, 1945; The Shadowy Pine Tree, 1945; Your Home, 1946. Illustrations; The World is Round, 1939, Paris France, 1940, by Gertrude Stein; Gertrude Stein's First Reader, and 3 plays, Maurice Fridberg, 1946; Autobiography: Saying Life, 1961; Drinking at Home, 1964; Gertrude Stein and Painting, 1968. *Heir: cousin,* Sir Julian Rose, Bt, *qv*. *Address:* 56 Fountain House, Park Lane, W1. *T:* 01-629 0457.

**ROSE, Francis Leslie,** OBE 1949; FRS 1957; PhD; DSc; FRIC; Research Manager, Imperial Chemical Industries Ltd, Pharmaceuticals Division, since 1954; Honorary Reader in Organic Chemistry, University of Manchester Institute of Science and Technology; *b* 27 June 1909; *s* of late Frederick William and Elizabeth Ann Rose Lincoln; *m* 1935, Ailsa Buckley; one *s*. *Educ:* City Sch., Lincoln; Univ. of Nottingham. BSc (London) Hons Chemistry, 1930; PhD (Lond.) 1934; DSc (Nottingham) 1950; research chemist ICI Ltd, 1932; gold medallist, Society of Apothecaries, 1948; Tilden Lecture, Chem. Soc., 1951; Member, Court of Governors, Manchester University and Court of Governors, Univ. of Manchester Inst. of Science and Technology. Mem., Home Office Forensic Science Cttee. *Publications:* numerous scientific papers on chemotherapeutic themes, mainly in Jl of Chem. Soc., Brit. Jl of Pharmacol., Biochem. Jl, etc. *Recreations:* music, in particular the organ; sailing. *Address:* 26 Queensway, Heald Green, Cheadle, Cheshire. *T:* 061-437 2876. *Club:* Athenæum.

**ROSE, Dame Hilda Nora;** *see* Lloyd, Dame H. N.

**ROSE, Sir Hugh,** 2nd Bt, *cr* 1935; TD, 1945; DL; Director: Bank of Scotland; Scottish Provident Institution; Securities Trust of Scotland Ltd; A. B. Fleming (Holdings) Ltd; Member of Committee of Management, Edinburgh Savings Bank; *b* 16 Dec. 1902; *s* of late Sir Arthur Rose, 1st Bt, DSO, and Mary (*d* 1939), *d* of late Robert Weir, JP, DL, Edinburgh; *S* father, 1937; *m* 1930, Marjorie, *d* of T. Leslie Usher; one *d* (and two *s* decd). *Educ:* Edinburgh Academy; Harrow; Trinity College, Cambridge. Major RA, TA, 1941, Italy (despatches). Commissioner General Board of Control for Scotland, 1936-62. County Comr for Boy Scouts for Edinburgh and Leith, 1946-50; Mem., Council on Tribunals, 1958-62; Chm. Mental Welfare Commission for Scotland, 1962-65. Lieut, Royal Company of Archers (Queen's Body Guard for Scotland). DL Edinburgh, 1958. *Address:* 14 Mortonhall Road, Edinburgh. *Clubs:* Caledonian; New (Edinburgh).

**ROSE, Jack,** CMG 1963; MBE 1954; DFC 1942; *b* 18 Jan. 1917; *s* of late Charles Thomas Rose; *m* 1st, 1940, Margaret Valerie (*d* 1966), 2nd *d* of late Alec Stuart Budd; two *s*; 2nd, 1967, Beryl Elizabeth, 4th *d* of late A. S. Budd. *Educ:* Shooters Hill School; London University. Served RAF, 1938-46 (Wing Commander). Joined Colonial Administrative Service, N Rhodesia, 1947; Private Secretary to Governor of Northern Rhodesia, 1950-53; seconded to Colonial Office, 1954-56; Administrative posts, Northern Rhodesia, 1956-60; Administrator, Cayman Islands (seconded), 1960-63; Assistant to Governor, British Guiana, 1963-64 (Actg Governor and Dep. Governor for periods). *Recreations:* gardening, Rugby football, fishing. *Address:* Oakhill, Church Road, Stone Street, Sevenoaks, Kent. *T:* Sevenoaks 61791. *Clubs:* Royal Air Force, Royal Air Force Reserves.

**ROSE, Jim;** *see* Rose, E. J. B.

**ROSE, Sir Julian (Day),** 4th Bt *cr* 1909; *b* 3 March 1947; 3rd and *o surv. s* of Sir Charles Henry Rose, 3rd Bt and of Phoebe, *d* of 2nd Baron Phillimore (*d* 1947); *S* father, 1966. *Educ:* Stanbridge School. *Address:* Hardwick House, Whitchurch-on-Thames, Oxfordshire. *See also Sir Francis Rose, Bt.*

**ROSE, Michael;** *see* Rose, Edward Michael.

**ROSE, Morris James Alexander,** DFC 1945; Sheriff-Substitute of Aberdeen, Kincardine and Banff at Aberdeen and Stonehaven since 1968; *b* 21 Feb. 1923; *er s* of late Alexander Alistair Rose, Glasgow, and Eileen May McClure, *d* of late James Howe McClure, Glasgow; *m* 1953, Jennifer Jane Moncrieff, *yr d* of William Wallace Moncrieff, Troon; one *s* one *d*. *Educ:* Kelvinside Academy; Uppingham Sch.; Glasgow Univ. Served with RAFVR, 1941-46. Admitted to Faculty of Advocates, 1952. *Recreation:* golf. *Address:* Sheriff's Chambers, Aberdeen.

**ROSE, Paul (Bernard);** MP (Lab) Blackley Division of Manchester since 1964; *b* 26 Dec. 1935; *s* of Arthur and Norah Rose; *m* 1957, Eve Marie-Thérèse; one *s* one *d*. *Educ:* Bury Gram. Sch.; Manchester Univ.; Gray's Inn. LLB

(Hons) Manch., 1956; Barrister-at-Law, 1957. Legal and Secretarial Dept, Co-op. Union Ltd, 1957-60; Lectureship, Dept of Liberal Studies, Royal Coll. of Advanced Technology, Salford, 1961-63; Barrister-at-Law, practising on northern circuit, 1963-65. PPS to Minister of Transport, 1967-68. Chairman: NW Regional Sports Council, 1966-68; Parly Labour Home Office Group; Campaign for Democracy in Ulster. Delegate to Council of Europe and WEU. *Publications:* Handbook to Industrial and Provident Societies Act, 1960; Guide to Weights and Measures, 1965; The Manchester Martyrs, 1970. Contrib. to many periodicals on political and legal topics. *Recreations:* sport, theatre. *Address:* House of Commons, SW1.

**ROSE, Captain Sir Philip (Humphrey Vivian),** 3rd Bt, *cr* 1874; RA, enlisted 1939; *gs* of Sir Philip Rose, Rayners, Penn, 2nd Bt (whom he succeeded in 1919), and *s* of late Capt. Philip Vivian Rose, 3rd Batt. Oxfords. Light Infantry, and Maude Winifred, 2nd *d* of William Gillilan, 6 Palace Gate, W8; *b* 16 Mar. 1903; *m* 1927, Joan, *yr d* of late Dr Martin Richardson; (one *s* killed in aircraft accident at Downside on 15 May 1943) two *d. Heir: cousin,* Ronald Paul Lancaster Rose, *b* 31 July 1907 [*m* 1st, 1933, Shelagh Grant Lindsay (marr. diss., 1937), *d* of Major Curtis; one *s*; 2nd, 1938, Peggy Gleitzman; 3rd, 1948, Emily Lavender, *d* of late Capt. H. V. Hare, and *widow* of Tom E. Montgomery]. *Address:* Tylers Cottage, Peterley Corner, Great Missenden, Bucks. *T:* Great Missenden 2215.

**ROSE, Reginald L. S.;** *see* Smith-Rose.

**ROSE, Prof. Richard;** Professor of Politics, University of Strathclyde, since 1966; *b* 9 April 1933; *o s* of Charles Imse and Mary Conely Rose, St Louis, Mo, USA; *m* 1956, Rosemary J., *o d* of late James Kenny, Whitstable, Kent; two *s* one *d. Educ:* Clayton High Sch., Mo; Johns Hopkins Univ., BA (Distinction, Phi Beta Kappa) comparative drama, 1953; London Sch. of Economics, 1953-54; Oxford University, 1957-60, DPhil (Lincoln and Nuffield Colls). Political public relations, Mississippi Valley, 1954-55; Reporter, St Louis Post-Despatch, 1955-57; Lecturer in Govt, Univ. of Manchester, 1961-66. Election Correspondent, The Times, 1964, 1966; 1970. Pres., Scottish Political Studies Assoc., 1967-68. Psephologist, Indep. Television News, 1970. *Publications:* The British General Election of 1959 (with D. E. Butler), 1960; Must Labour Lose? (with Mark Abrams) 1960; Politics in England, 1964; (ed) Studies in British Politics, 1966, rev. edn 1969; Influencing Voters, 1967; (ed) Policy Making in Britain, 1969; People in Politics, 1970. Contrib. academic journals in Europe and America. *Recreations:* architecture (historical, Britain; modern, America), music. *Address:* Department of Politics, McCance Building, Richmond Street, Glasgow C1. *T:* 041-552 4400; Bennochy, 1 East Abercromby Street, Helensburgh, Dunbartonshire. *T:* Helensburgh 2164. *Club:* Reform.

**ROSE, Wilfred Andrew;** Ambassador of Trinidad and Tobago to Brazil, since 1969; *b* 4 Oct. 1916; *s* of James Emmanuel Rose and Eleanora Rose; *m* 1944, Pamphylia Marcano; one *s. Educ:* Tranquility Boys' Intermediate Sch.; Queen's Royal Coll.; Imperial Coll. of Tropical Agriculture, Trinidad (DipAgr); Coll. of Estate Management, London; London University. Agric. Technologist, Food Control Dept, during War of 1939-45. Subseq. Cane Farmers' Superintendent; Estate Manager; Housing Manager, Planning and Housing Commission, Trinidad and Tobago. Editor, Jl of Agricl Soc. of Trinidad and Tobago. Member: Roy. Soc. of Health; Agricl Soc. of Trinidad and Tobago (Life); W India Cttee; Chartered Auctioneers' and Estate Agents' Inst. (Associate). West Indies National Party; People's National Movement (several cttees). Chm., Commn of Enquiry on Road Passenger Transport. Elected Member for St Ann's, Trinidad, Federal Elections of the West Indies, 1958. Minister of Communications and Works, Federal Govt, West Indies, 1958-62 (twice acted as Dep. Prime Minister); High Commissioner for Trinidad and Tobago: in Canada, 1962-64; in UK, 1964-69, Ambassador to EEC, 1965-69, and Ambassador to UN Agencies, Europe, and Permanent Representative to GATT, 1965-68; led West Indies delegn to various confs; Rep. of Govt, frequently abroad. Chm., Commonwealth Rhodesia Sanctions Cttee, 1968-69; Vice-Chm., UNCTAD II, New Delhi, 1968; Member: Commonwealth Telecommunications Bd, 1964-68; Commonwealth Telecommunications Council, 1968. Freeman, City of London, 1967. *Publications:* articles on agriculture in the Trinidad Press, 1942-45. *Recreations:* agriculture, horse-riding, golf. *Address:* (home) Avenida Francisco Bhering, 169 Arpoador, Rio de Janeiro, Brazil; Embassy of Trinidad and Tobago, Praia do Russel 694, Rio de Janeiro. *Clubs:* West Indian, United Service, Travellers' (all in London; Gávea Golf and Country (Rio de Janeiro).

**ROSE-MILLER, Brig. G. P.;** *see* Miller.

**ROSEBERY,** 6th Earl of, *cr* 1703; **Albert Edward Harry Meyer Archibald Primrose,** KT 1947; PC 1945; DSO 1918; MC; LLD 1954; FRCSE 1955; Bt 1651; Viscount Rosebery, Baron Primrose and Dalmeny, 1700; Viscount of Inverkeithing, Baron Dalmeny and Primrose, 1703; Baron Rosebery (UK), 1828; Earl of Midlothian, 1911; Viscount Mentmore of Mentmore, 1911; Baron Epsom of Epsom, 1911; Lord Lieutenant for Midlothian, 1929-64; *b* 8 Jan. 1882; *e s* of 5th Earl and Hannah, *o d* of Baron Meyer de Rothschild (*d* 1890); *S* father, 1929; *m* 1st, 1909, Lady Dorothy A. M. A. Grosvenor (whom he divorced, 1919; she *m* 2nd, Captain R. B. Brassey; 3rd, 1929, C. Hilton-Green and 4th, Commander Mack; *d* 1966), *y d* of late Lord Henry Grosvenor and Dora Mina, *e d* of James A. Erskine Wemyss, of Wemyss Castle and Torrie House, Fifeshire; one *d*; 2nd, 1924, Eva, Lady Belper (DBE, *cr* 1955 LLD (Edin.) 1957), *d* of 2nd Baron Aberdare; one *s. Educ:* Eton; Sandhurst. Captained Surrey XI, 1905, 1906, 1907; played for Scotland *v* Australians, 1906; late 2nd Lieut Grenadier Guards; MP (L) Midlothian, 1906-10; served European War, 1914-18 (wounded, DSO, MC). Capt. Royal Company of Archers. A Steward of Jockey Club 1929, 1945; Pres. Thoroughbred Breeders' Assoc., 1932-57. Regional Commr for Scotland, 1941-45; Secretary of State for Scotland, 1945; Member of Royal Commn on Justice of the Peace, 1946-48; Chairman Departmental Cttee on Export and Slaughter of Horses, 1949; Pres., National Liberal Party, 1945-47; Chm., The Royal Fine Art Commission for Scotland, 1952-57; Chm., Scottish Tourist Bd, 1955-65. Pres. Roy. Zoological Soc. of Scotland, 1942-64; Pres. Royal Scot Corporation, 1947-. *Heir: s* Lord Primrose, *qv. Address:* Dalmeny House, South Queensferry, West Lothian. *T:* South Queensferry 555; Mentmore, Leighton Buzzard. *T:* Leighton Buzzard 2147; Cleveland House, Newmarket. *T:* Newmarket 2483. *See also Hon. H. A. V. Smith.*

**ROSEHILL, Lord; Robert Andrew Carnegie;** Landowner, Farmer; *b* 24 June 1926; *yr s* and *heir* of 12th Earl of Northesk, *qv*; *m* 1949, Jean Margaret, *yr d* of Captain (John) Duncan George MacRae, Ballimore, Otter Ferry, Argyll; one *s* two *d* (and one *s* decd). *Educ:* Pangbourne RNR Coll.; Tabor Naval Acad., USA. Served with Royal Navy, 1942-45. *Recreations:* shooting, motor racing. *Heir: s* Hon. David John MacRae Carnegie, *b* 3 November 1954. *Address:* Fair Oak, Rogate, Sussex.

**ROSENBERG HOFFMAN, Anna;** *see* Hoffman, Anna Rosenberg.

**ROSENFELD, Prof. Léon;** Professor at Nordic Institute for Theoretical Atomic Physics, Copenhagen, since 1958; Editor-in-chief, Nuclear Physics, since 1956; *b* 14 Aug. 1904; *s* of Léon Rosenfeld and Jeanne Pierre; *m* 1933, Yvonne Cambresier; one *s* one *d*. *Educ:* University of Liège, Belgium. PhD, Liège, 1926; Asst Univ. of Göttingen, 1928; Lecturer, Univ. of Liège, 1930; Prof., Univ. of Liège, 1937; Prof., Univ. of Utrecht, 1940; Prof. of Theoretical Physics, Univ. of Manchester, 1947-58. Chevalier de l'Ordre de Léopold, 1938; Member: International Acad. of History of Science, 1966; (Corresp. Mem., 1947-66); Roy. Danish Acad. of Sciences and Letters, 1951; Brazilian Acad. of Sciences, 1959; Roy. Belgian Acad. of Sciences, Letters and Fine Arts, 1959; German Acad. of Sciences in Berlin, 1969; Chm., Danish National Committee for History and Philosophy of Science, 1964; Doctor, *hc*: Univ. of Brussels, 1965; Univ. of Copenhagen, 1965. Laureate of Prix Francqui, 1949. *Publications:* Niels Bohr, an Essay, (Amsterdam), 1945; De ontsluiting van de Atoomkern, (Amsterdam) 1946; Nuclear Forces, (Amsterdam) 1948; Theory of Electrons, (Amsterdam) 1951. Papers on quantum theory, nuclear physics, history of science. *Address:* Carl Plougsvej 9/II, Copenhagen V. *T:* Vester 8987.

**ROSENHEAD, Prof. Louis,** CBE 1954; FRS 1946; DSc (Leeds); PhD (Cantab.); Prof. of Applied Mathematics, The University, Liverpool, since 1933; Public Orator, University of Liverpool, since 1968; Pro-Vice-Chancellor, University of Liverpool, 1961-65; formerly Fellow of St John's College, Cambridge; *b* 1 Jan. 1906; *s* of Abraham Rosenhead and Helen Nelson; *m* 1932, Esther Brostoff; two *s*. *Educ:* Leeds Central High School; The University of Leeds; St John's College, Cambridge (Strathcona Research Student); The University of Göttingen. BSc (Leeds 1st Class Hons); PhD (Leeds); Senior Research Student of the Dept of Scientific and Industrial Research, 1929; PhD (Cantab.) 1930; DSc (Leeds) 1935; Senior Research Student of Royal Exhibition of 1851; Lecturer, Applied Mathematics at the University College of Swansea, 1931. Temporarily attached Min. of Supply, 1940-45. Mem. of various Govt Scientific Committees since 1939. *Publications:* Index of Mathematical Tables, 2nd edn 1962 (part-author); Compressible Airflow; Tables, 1952 (part-author); Compressible Airflow: Graphs, 1954 (part-author); Laminar Boundary Layers, 1963 (editor); Scientific Publications in the Proceedings of the Royal Society, Proceedings of the Cambridge Philosophical Society, Monthly Notices of the Royal Astronomical Society, etc. *Address:* 30 Wheatcroft Road, Liverpool L18 9UF. *T:* 051-427 6033.

**ROSENHEIM,** family name of **Baron Rosenheim.**

**ROSENHEIM,** Baron *cr* 1970 (Life Peer); **Max Leonard Rosenheim,** KBE 1967 (CBE 1955); MA, MD, FRCP; Professor of Medicine, University of London, and Director, Medical Unit, University College Hospital Medical School, since 1950; *b* 1908; *s* of late Ludwig Rosenheim, London. *Educ:* Shrewsbury School; St John's Coll., Cambridge; University College Hospital. Appointments on junior staff, University College and Westminster Hospitals, 1932-38; Bilton Pollard Travelling Fellowship (University Coll. Hosp.), 1939; working as Research Assistant at Massachusetts General Hospital, Boston, USA; First Assistant, Medical Unit University Coll. Hosp., 1939. RAMC, 1941-46; served in Middle East and Italy with rank of Lt-Col. Cons. Physician (local Brig.) South-East Asia Command, 1945-46; Physician, University College Hosp., 1946-50. Sir Arthur Sims Commonwealth Travelling Prof., 1958; Sir Ernest Finch Visiting Professor, Sheffield Univ. 1967. Mem. Med. Research Council, 1961-65; Pres., Royal Coll. of Physicians, London, 1966-. Hon. Member: Assoc. of American Physicians, 1959; Swedish Med. Soc., 1968; For. Hon. Mem. Amer. Acad. of Arts and Sciences, 1961; Hon. Fellow: University Coll., London, 1967; American Coll. of Physicians, 1967; Royal Aust. Coll. of Physicians, 1968; Royal Coll. of Physicians of Edinburgh, 1968; Royal Coll. of Physicians of Canada, 1969; Royal Irish Coll. of Physicians, 1969; Royal Coll. of Gen. Practitioners, 1969; St John's Coll., Cambridge, 1969. Hon. DSc: Univ. of Wales, 1969; Birmingham, 1970; Ceylon, 1970. *Publications:* contribs to various medical journals. *Address:* University College Hospital Medical School, University Street, WC1. *T:* 01-387 5861; 39 Eton Avenue, NW3. *T:* 01-794 3320. *Clubs:* Athenæum, Savile; United Hospitals Sailing.

**ROSENMAN, Samuel Irving;** Lawyer, US; Member firm Rosenman Colin Kaye Petschek Freund & Emil; *b* Texas, 13 Feb. 1896; *s* of Sol Rosenman and Ethel Paler; *m* 1924, Dorothy Reuben; two *s*. *Educ:* Columbia University. AB 1915; LLB 1919; admitted to New York Bar, 1920; Member New York State Legislature, 1922-26, Bill Drafting Commissioner, 1926-28; Counsel to Gov. Franklin D. Roosevelt, 1929-32; apptd Justice, NY Supreme Court, 1932, re-apptd, 1933; later elected for 14-year term; resigned, to be Special Counsel: to President Roosevelt, 1943-45; to President Truman, April 1945-Feb. 1946; resigned to resume practice of law. Trustee: Franklin D. Roosevelt Library, Harry S. Truman Library; Member: Assoc. of Bar of NYC (President, 1964-66); Board of Dirs of Amer. Judicature Soc.; Amer. Bar Assoc.; NY State Bar Assoc.; Presidential Steel Industry Fact-finding Board; Presidential Maritime industry Bd, 1961; Exec. Cttee of Lawyers' Cttee for Civil Rights (set up at request of Presidents Kennedy and Johnson); Chm. Presidential Emergency Railway Bd, 1963. Phi Beta Kappa, Delta Sigma Rho, Phi Epsilon Pi. Democrat. Jewish religion. Awarded Medal for Merit by President Truman; Officer of French Legion of Honour. *Publications:* Public Papers and Addresses of Franklin D. Roosevelt, 1928-45; Working with Roosevelt, 1952. *Address:* 575 Madison Avenue, New York, NY 10022, USA. *T:* Murray Hill 8-7800.

**ROSENTHAL, Erwin Isak Jacob,** LittD, DrPhil, MA; Reader in Oriental Studies, University of Cambridge, since 1959; Fellow of Pembroke College; *b* 18 Sept. 1904; *y s* of Moses and Amalie Rosenthal; *m* 1933, Elizabeth Charlotte Marx; one *s* one *d*. *Educ:* Heilbronn; Universities of Heidelberg, Munich, Berlin. Goldsmid Lectr in Hebrew, Lectr in North-Semitic Epigraphy, Head of Dept of Hebrew, University Coll., Univ. of London, 1933-36; Special Lectr, Semitic Langs and Lits, Univ. of

Manchester, 1936-44, Nat. Service: RASC, 1944-45; attached FO, 1945; German Sect., FO, 1946-48. Lectr, Central Advisory Coun. for Educn, HM Forces, 1940-44; Tutor, Adult Educn, Univ. Tutorial Class, WEA, London, 1946-48 (Part-time); Univ. Lectr in Hebrew, Cambridge, 1948-59. Vis. Professor: Columbia Univ., 1967-68; El Colegio de Mexico, 1968. *Publications:* Ibn Khalduns Gedanken über den Staat, 1932; Law and Religion (Vol. 3 Judaism and Christianity), 1938 (ed and contrib.); Saadya Studies, 1943 (ed and contrib.); Averroes' Commentary on Plato's Republic, 1956, 1966, 1969 (ed and trans.); Political Thought in Medieval Islam, 1958, 1962, 1968; Griechisches Erbe in der jüdischen Religionsphilosophie des Mittelalters, 1960; Judaism and Islam, 1961; Islam in the Modern National State, 1965; Studia Semitica (1: Jewish Themes; 11: Islamic Themes), 1970; articles in learned jls; Festschriften. *Recreations:* music, walking, travelling. *Address:* Pembroke College and 199 Chesterton Road, Cambridge. *T:* 57648.

**ROSENTHAL, Harold David;** Editor of Opera since 1953; Lecturer and Broadcaster since 1950; *b* 30 Sept. 1917; *s* of Israel Victor Rosenthal and Leah Samuels; *m* 1944, Lillah Phyllis Weiner; one *s* one *d*. *Educ:* City of London School; University College, London (BA); Inst. of Education, London. Asst Editor, Opera, 1950-53; Archivist, Royal Opera House, Covent Garden, 1950-56. Member: Arts Council Patrons of Music Fund Cttee, 1960-; Council, Friends of Covent Garden, 1962-; Chairman, Music Section, Critics' Circle of Gt Britain, 1965-67. *Publications:* Sopranos of Today, 1956; Two Centuries of Opera at Covent Garden, 1958; A Concise Oxford Dictionary of Opera (with John Warrack), 1964; Great Singers of Today, 1966; Mapleson Memoires (ed and annotated), 1966; The Opera Bedside Book, 1965; Opera at Covent Garden, 1967. *Recreations:* travel, food; collecting playbills, prints, programmes, etc. *Address:* 6 Woodland Rise, N10 3UH. *T:* 01-883 4415.

**ROSEVEARE, Sir Martin P(earson),** Kt 1946; Hon. Fellow of St John's College, Cambridge, since 1952; *b* 24 April 1898; *s* of late Canon R. P. Roseveare, late Vicar of Lewisham; *m* 1921, Edith Mary Pearse (marr. diss., 1958); one *s* three *d* (and one *d* decd); *m* 1958, Olivia Margaret Montgomery. *Educ:* Marlborough College; St John's College, Cambridge (scholar). Maths Tripos, Part I, Class 1, 1919; Part II wrangler (b), 1921; Schoolmaster, Repton School, 1921-23; Haileybury College, 1923-26; Board of Education, HM Inspector of Schools, 1927; Staff Inspector of Mathematics, 1939. Loaned to Ministry of Information, 1939, Ministry of Food, 1939-44 and 1946 (acting Assistant Sec., 1940, acting Principal Assistant Sec. 1942); Senior Chief Inspector, Ministry of Education, 1944-57, retired; Headmaster Mzuzu School, Nyasaland, 1957-63; Principal, Soche Hill College, Malawi, 1964-67; Schoolmaster, Marymount School, Mzuzu, Malawi, 1967-70. Served European War, RFA, Lt 1916-19, France, Belgium, Italy (wounded despatches). *Recreations:* hockey, camping. *Address:* Box 29, Mzuzu, Malawi.

**ROSEVEARE, Rt. Rev. Reginald Richard,** CBE 1968; *b* 18 May 1902; 6th *c* of Rev. Canon Richard Polgreen and Mary Isobel Roseveare; unmarried. *Educ:* Sedbergh School. Clerk and Assistant Salesman to W. J. & H. Thompson, Tea and Rubber Brokers, London, 1920-24; at Kelham Theological College, 1924-29; made Profession in Society of the Sacred Mission, Kelham, 1928; Deacon, 1929; Priest, 1930; Asst Curate, St George, Nottingham, 1929-34; Chaplain, HM Borstal Inst., Nottingham, 1932-34; Tutor, Kelham Theological College, 1934-37; Priest-in-Charge of Mission District of Parson Cross, Sheffield, 1937-39; Vicar of St Cecilia, Parson Cross, Sheffield, 1939-52; Member of Sheffield City Education Committee, 1941-50; Proctor in Convocation, 1950-52; Rural Dean of Ecclesfield, 1943-52; Canon Residentiary of Sheffield Cathedral, 1945-52; Provincial SSM, S Africa, 1952-56; Bishop of Accra, 1956-67. Expelled by Ghana Govt, 13 Aug. 1962; allowed to return, 13 Nov. 1962. *Publications:* A Parish Communion Book, 1938; Getting Married in Church, 1944. *Address:* Kelham, Newark, Notts.

**ROSEVEARE, Robert William;** Secretary, British Steel Corporation, since 1967; *b* 23 Aug. 1924; *s* of William Leonard Roseveare, MC and Marjory C. Roseveare; *m* 1954, Patricia Elizabeth, *d* of Guy L. Thompson, FRCS, Scarborough; one *s* three *d*. *Educ:* Gresham's Sch., Holt; St John's Coll., Cambridge (MA). Served in Fleet Air Arm, 1943-46. Home Civil Service, Admin. Class, 1949. Asst Private Sec. to Minister of Power, 1952-54; Prin., 1954; seconded to Cabinet Office, 1958-60; British Embassy, Washington, 1960-62; Asst Sec., Min. of Power, 1964; seconded to British Steel Corp., 1967. *Recreation:* walking. *Address:* Elm Tree Cottage, Ox Lane, Harpenden, Herts. *T:* Harpenden 3071.

**ROSIER, Air Chief Marshal Sir Frederick (Ernest),** KCB 1966 (CB 1961); CBE 1955 (OBE 1943); DSO 1942; Deputy Commander-in-Chief, Allied Forces, Central Europe, since 1970; *b* 13 Oct. 1915; *s* of E. G. Rosier; *m* 1939, Hettie Denise Blackwell; three *s* one *d*. *Educ:* Grove Park School, Wrexham. Commissioned RAF, 1935; 43 (F) Sqdn, 1936-39. Served War of 1939-45 in France, UK, Western Desert and Europe. OC Horsham St Faith, 1947; exchange duties with USAF, 1948-50; Instructor at Jt Services Staff College, 1950-52; Gp Capt. Operations at Central Fighter Establishment, 1952-54; Gp Capt. Plans at Fighter Command, 1955-56; ADC to the Queen, 1956-58; idc 1957; Director of Joint Plans, Air Ministry, 1958; Chm. Joint Planning Staff, 1959-61; AOC Air Forces Middle East, 1961-63; Senior Air Staff Officer, HQ Transport Command, 1964-66; Air Officer C-in-C, RAF, Fighter Command, 1966-68; UK Mem., Permanent Military Deputies Group, Central Treaty Organisation, Ankara, 1968-70. Commander, Order of Orange Nassau, 1947. *Address:* Deputy Commander-in-Chief, HQ AFCENT, British Forces Post Office 28. *Club:* Royal Air Force.

**ROSIER, Rt. Rev. Stanley Bruce;** *see* Willochra, Bishop of.

**ROSKELL, Professor John Smith,** MA, DPhil; FBA 1968; Professor of Medieval History, University of Manchester, since 1962; *b* Norden, Rochdale, 2 July 1913; *s* of late John Edmund and of Lucy A. Roskell; *m* 1942, Evelyn Liddle; one *s* one *d*. *Educ:* Rochdale Municipal Secondary School; Accrington Grammar Sch.; University of Manchester; Balliol College, Oxford. Asst Lecturer in History, Manchester University, 1938; Lecturer, 1945; Senior Lecturer, 1950-52; Professor of Medieval History, University of Nottingham, 1952-62. Pres., Lancashire Parish Register Soc., 1962. Royal Navy, 1940-45; Lieut RNVR, 1942-45. *Publications:* The Knights of the Shire of the County Palatine of Lancaster (1377-1460), Chetham Society, 1937; The Commons in the Parliament of 1422, 1954; The Commons and their Speakers in English Parliaments, 1376-1523, 1965; articles in English Historical Review, Bulletin of the Institute of Historical Research, etc. *Recreation:* cricket. *Address:* 42 Barcheston Road, Cheadle, Cheshire. *T:* 061-428 4630.

**ROSKILL, Sir Ashton (Wentworth),** Kt 1967; QC 1949; MA Oxon; Chairman, Monopolies Commission, since 1965 (Part-time Member, 1960-65); *b* 1 Jan. 1902; *e s* of late John Roskill, KC, and Sybil Mary Wentworth, *d* of late Ashton Dilke, MP; *m* 1st, 1932, Violet Willoughby (*d* 1964), *d* of late Charles W. Waddington, CIE; one *s* one *d*; 2nd, 1965, Phyllis Sydney, *y d* of late Sydney Burney, CBE. *Educ:* Winchester; Exeter Coll., Oxford (Schol.), 1st class hons Modern History, 1923; Barrister-at-Law, Inner Temple, 1925, Certificate of Honour, Council of Legal Education. Attached War Office, Intelligence Staff, 1940-45, Bencher, Inner Temple, 1958. *Address:* 8 King's Bench Walk, Temple, EC4. *T:* 01-353 2734; Cox's Newtown, Newbury, Berks. *T:* Newbury 328. *Club:* Reform.

**ROSKILL, Hon. Sir Eustace Wentworth,** Kt 1962; **Hon. Mr Justice Roskill;** Judge of the High Court of Justice, Queen's Bench Division, since 1962; Chairman, Hampshire Quarter Sessions, since 1960; Chairman, Commission on the Third London Airport, since 1968; *b* 6 Feb. 1911; *y s* of late John Roskill, KC and of late Sybil Mary Wentworth, *d* of Ashton Wentworth Dilke, MP; *m* 1947, Elisabeth Wallace Jackson, 3rd *d* of late Thomas Frame Jackson, Buenos Aires; one *s* two *d*. *Educ:* Winchester College (exhibnr); Exeter Coll., Oxford (exhibnr). 1st Cl. hons, Hon. Sch. of Mod. Hist. Oxford, BA 1932; MA 1936; Harmsworth Law Schol. Middle Temple, 1932; called to Bar, Middle Temple, 1933. Worked at Ministries of Shipping and War Transport, 1939-45. JP Hants, 1950; Dep. Chm. Hants QS, 1951-60; QC 1953; Bencher, 1961; Comr of Assize (Birmingham), 1961. Vice-Chm., Parole Bd., 1967-69. Hon. Fellow, Exeter College, Oxford, 1963. JP Hants 1950. *Recreations:* music, swimming, gardening. *Address:* Heatherfield, Newtown, Newbury, Berks. *T:* Newbury 606; New Court, Temple, EC4. *T:* 01-353 8870; Royal Courts of Justice, Strand, WC2. *Clubs:* Reform; Hampshire (Winchester).

**ROSKILL, Captain Stephen Wentworth,** DSC 1944; MA Cantab; FRHistS; late RN; Fellow of Churchill College, Cambridge, 1961, Life Fellow, 1970; *b* 1 Aug. 1903; *s* of John Henry Roskill, KC, and Sybil Mary Dilke, *d* of Ashton Wentworth Dilke, MP; *m* 1930, Elizabeth, *d* of Henry Van den Bergh; four *s* three *d*. *Educ:* RN Colleges, Osborne and Dartmouth. RN, 1917-48; Gunnery Specialist, 1928; Commander, 1938; Captain, 1944. Served at sea as Commander HMS Warspite, 1939; Naval Staff, 1939-41; Commander and Captain, HMNZS Leander, 1941-44; Senior Observer, Bikini Atomic Bomb Trials, 1946; Dep. Director of Naval Intelligence, 1946-48; invalided, 1948; Cabinet Office, Official Naval Historian, 1949-60. Officer Legion of Merit (USA). Lees Knowles Lecturer, Cambridge, 1961; Distinguished Visitor Lecturer, US Naval Academy, Annapolis, 1965; Richmond Lecturer, Cambridge, 1967. Navy Records Society: Councillor, 1956-66, and 1968-70; Vice-Pres., 1966-68, 1970-. *Publications:* The War at Sea (official history), Vol. I, 1954, Vol. II, 1957; HMS Warspite, 1957; The Secret Capture, 1959; The War at Sea, Vol. III, Part I, 1960; The Navy at War, 1960; the War at Sea, Vol. III, Part II, 1961: The Strategy of Sea Power, 1962; A Merchant Fleet in War, 1962; The Art of Leadership, 1964; Naval Policy between the Wars, Vol. I, 1968; Documents relating to the Naval Air Service 1908-1918, 1969; Hankey, Man of Secrets, vol. 1, 1877-1918, 1970. *Recreations:* all country pursuits, painting. *Address:* Blounce Farm, South Warnborough, Basingstoke, Hants. *T:* Long Sutton 234. *Club:* Travellers'.

**ROSMER, Milton;** *b* 4 Nov. 1882; *s* of William and Miriam Lunt (father professionally known as Arthur Milton); *m* Irene Rooke (*d* 1958), actress; no *c*. *Educ:* Manchester Gram. School. Began with Osmond Tearle's Shakespeare Co.; toured in Drury Lane Production of The Best of Friends, Martin Harvey's Co., two years; Miss Horniman's Co., Gaiety, Manch., four years; Ben Greet Players in America, three years playing: Everyman, Romeo, Oberon, Mark Antony, Orlando, etc. Produced under own management The Fugitive (John Galsworthy), also new plays by Stanley Houghton, Harold Brighouse, etc. at Prince of Wales, Court, Criterion Theatres, etc., London. Directed Everyman Theatre, Hampstead, three years; Director Stratford-on-Avon Shakespeare Festival Company for 1943; produced number of plays in London, The Green Bay Tree, The Father, The Devil's Disciple, etc. Acted leads in many of Galsworthy's, Shaw's, Masefield's, Ibsen's plays. Starred in silent films as Heathcliff in Wuthering Heights, Jan Ridd in Lorna Doone, etc. Dir films for Gaumont Brit. (for three years), London Films, etc. Played many leading parts in BBC and TV Played as Sgt Rough in Gaslight, Apollo Theatre; Hjaimar, The Wild Duck, St James's Theatre; Cassius, Julius Caesar, St James's; Gen. Burgoyne (and prod. the play), Devil's Disciple, Piccadilly Theatre; Dr Ferguson, One Bright Day, Apollo, and a large number of leading parts in London, the Provinces, America and Canada. *Address:* Box Tree, Hawridge, Chesham, Bucks. *T:* Cholesbury (Bucks) 297.

**ROSOMAN, Leonard Henry,** RA 1969 (ARA 1960); FSA; Tutor, Royal College of Art, since 1957; *b* 27 Oct. 1913; *s* of Henry Rosoman; *m* 1963, Jocelyn, *d* of Bertie Rickards, Melbourne, Australia. *Educ:* Deacons Sch., Peterborough; Durham Univ. Teacher of Drawing and Painting, Reimann Sch. of Art, London, 1938-39; Official War Artist to Admiralty, 1943-45; Teacher: Camberwell Sch. of Art, London, 1947-48; (Mural Painting) Edinburgh Coll. of Art, 1948-56; Chelsea School of Art, 1956-57; Tutor, Royal Coll. of Art, 1957-. One Man Shows: St George's Gallery, London, 1946 and 1949; Roland, Browse and Delbanco Gallery, London, 1954, 1957, 1959, 1965 and 1969. Works bought by: HM Govt, Arts Council, British Council, York Art Gall., Contemporary Art Soc., Adelaide Art Gallery, VA Museum. Executed large mural paintings for: Festival of Britain, 1951; British Pavilion, Brussels World Fair, 1958; Harewood House, 1959; Mem. Soc. of Internat. Artists; FSIA; Hon. ARCA. *Recreation:* travelling as much as possible. *Address:* 7 Pembroke Studios, Pembroke Gardens, W8. *T:* 01-603 3638.

**ROSS, Bishop of, (RC);** *see under* Cork, Bishop of, (RC).

**ROSS, Alan;** author, publisher and journalist; Editor of London Magazine; Managing Director, Alan Ross Ltd, Publishers; *b* Calcutta, 6 May 1922; *o s* of late John Brackenridge Ross, CBE and Clare, *d* of Captain Patrick Fitzpatrick, Indian Army; *m* 1949, Jennifer, *d* of Sir Geoffrey Fry, 1st and last Bt, KCB, CVO; one *s*. *Educ:* Haileybury; St John's College, Oxford. RN 1942-47; general service, Arctic and North Seas, 1942-44; Asst Staff Officer, Intelligence, 16th Destroyer Flotilla, 1944; on staff of Flag

Officer, Western Germany, 1945, and Interpreter to British Naval Commander-in-Chief, Germany, 1946. British Council, 1947-50; on staff of The Observer 1950-. Toured Australia as correspondent, with MCC, 1954-55, 1962-63; toured South Africa, 1956-57, 1964-65; toured West Indies, 1960, 1968. Atlantic Award for Literature (Rockefeller Foundation), 1946. *Publications:* The Derelict Day, 1947; Time Was Away, 1948; The Forties, 1950; The Gulf of Pleasure, 1951; Poetry 1945-50, 1951; The Bandit on the Billiard Table, 1954 (revised edition South to Sardinia, 1960); Something of the Sea, 1954; Australia 55, 1956; Abroad (ed), 1957; Cape Summer and the Australians in England, 1957; To Whom It May Concern, 1958; The Onion Man, 1959; Through the Caribbean, 1960; The Cricketer's Companion (ed), 1960; Danger on Glass Island, 1960; African Negatives, 1962; Australia 63, 1963; West Indies at Lord's, 1963; (ed) London Magazine Book of Stories, 1964; North from Sicily, 1965; Poems 1942-67, 1968. Several trans and introductions. Contrib. to various jls in England and America. *Recreations:* travel, sport (played cricket and squash for Oxford University and Royal Navy), collecting pictures, racing. *Address:* 5 Pelham Crescent, SW7. *T:* 01-589 8984; Clayton Manor, near Hassocks, Sussex. *T:* Hassocks 3666. *Clubs:* Garrick, MCC; Vincent's (Oxford).

**ROSS, Alan Strode Campbell,** MA Oxon, MA Birmingham; Professor of Linguistics, University of Birmingham, since Oct. 1951 (Professor of English Language, 1948-51); *b* 1 February 1907; *er s* of late Archibald Campbell Carne Ross, Penzance and Brecon, and Millicent Strode Cobham; *m* 1933, Elizabeth Stefanyja, *yr d* of late Bronislas Olszewski, Warsaw; one *s*. *Educ:* Lindisfarne, Blackheath; Naish House, Burnham-on-Sea; Malvern College; Christ College, Brecon. Henry Skynner Scholarship in Astronomy, Balliol College, Oxford, 1925; First Class Hons School of English Lang and Lit., Oxford, 1929; Asst Lecturer in English Lang., Leeds Univ., 1929. Lecturer, 1936. Foreign Office, 1940-45. Lecturer in English Lang., Univ. of Birmingham, 1946, Reader, 1947. Corresp. member of Suomalais-ugrilainen Seura. *Publications:* The Dream of the Rood (with B. Dickins), 1934; Studies in the Accidence of the Lindisfarne Gospels, 1937; The Numeral-Signs of the Mohenjo-daro Script, 1938; The Terfinnas and Beormas of Ohthere, 1940; Ginger, 1952, Urs Graf edn of the Lindisfarne Gospels (with others), 1956-60; Etymology, 1958; Essentials of German Grammar, 1963; (with F. G. Healey) Patience Napoléon, 1963; (with A. W. Moverley) The Pitcairnese Language, 1964; Essentials of English Grammar, 1964; (with N. F. C. Owen) I. I. Revzin, Models of Language (translated from Russian), 1966; Arts v. Science (ed), 1967; (ed) What are U, 1969; How to pronounce it, 1970. Articles in Acta Philologica Scandinavica, Archivum Linguisticum, Biometrika, Englische Studien, Geographical Journal, Journal English and Germanic Philology, Journal Roy. Statistical Soc., Mathematical Gazette, Moderna Sprak, Mod. Lang. Notes, Mod. Lang. Rev., Nature, Neuphilologische Mitteilungen; Studia germanica; Zeitschrift für vergleichende Sprachforschung. Noblesse Oblige (ed. N. Mitford); Saga-Book of Viking Soc., Trans of Philological Soc., etc. Part-ed Leeds Studies in English (I-IV); Ed. English Philological Studies. *Recreations:* land-rovering, stamp-collecting, patience, croquet. *Address:* Department of Linguistics, PO Box 363, University of Birmingham, Birmingham 15. *Club:* Oxford and Cambridge University.

**ROSS, Brig.-Gen. Alexander,** CMG 1919; DSO 1917; VD; QC; LLD (Sask); Barrister; Judge of District Court of Yorkton, Saskatchewan, 1921-55, retired; *b* Forres, Scotland, 2 Dec. 1880; *m* 1909, Harriet Beatrice Scott of Qu'Appelle, Saskatchewan, Canada; no *c*. *Educ:* Public and High Schools in Saskatchewan. Called to Bar of Saskatchewan, 1901; KC 1913; Lieut in Canadian Militia, 1908; went overseas as Major Second-in-Command of 28 Batt CEF, May 1915; arrived in France Sept. 1915; promoted to command Battalion, Sept. 1916, and to command 6th Canadian Infantry Brigade, Oct. 1918; served European War, 1915-18 (despatches seven times, CMG, DSO and bar); appointed to command the 21st Infantry Brigade Canadian Militia with rank Col. (Hon. Brig.-General), 1921; retired list, 1954. *Address:* 45 Darlington St, Yorkton, Saskatchewan, Canada. *T:* 32681.

**ROSS, Alexander,** CMG 1946; formerly Deputy Minister of National Defence, Canada; *m* 1919, (Eileen Ivy) Joan, *d* of Francis M. Coppin, London. *Educ:* Glasgow High School. Served European War, 1914-18, with Canadian Army in France (wounded); Chartered Accountant, Canadian Farm Loan Board, 1929-42; Financial Superintendent, Canadian Military Headquarters, London, 1942-44. *Club:* Rideau (Ottawa).

**ROSS, Alexander;** Chairman, United Dominions Trust Ltd, since 1963 (Director, 1955; Vice-Chairman, 1962); Deputy Chairman, Eagle Star Insurance Co. Ltd; Chairman, Australia and New Zealand Banking Group Ltd; *b* 2 Sept. 1907; *s* of late William Alexander Ross and of Kathleen Ross; *m* 1933, Nora Bethia Burgess; two *s* two *d*. *Educ:* Mount Albert Gram. Sch.; Auckland University Coll., Auckland, NZ. Joined Nat. Bank of NZ, 1927, and Reserve Bank of NZ on its establishment in 1934; Dep. Gov., 1948-55. Rep. NZ on numerous occasions overseas, including Sterling Area Conf. in Australia, 1954. Rep. NZ in rowing, at Empire Games, 1930; managed NZ team to Empire Games, Vancouver, 1954; NZ rowing selector for Olympic and Empire Games; Chairman: British Commonwealth Games Fedn, 1968-; Cttee for Exports to NZ, 1965-67; East European Trade Council, 1967-69; Vice-Pres., British Export Houses Assoc., 1968-; Member: BNEC, 1965-69; National Research Development Corp., 1966-; New Zealand Soc. (Past Pres.); Cttee of Directors, Royal Caledonian Schools, 1964-69; Council, Dominion Students' Hall Trust. *Recreations:* riding, rowing, golf. *Address:* 36 Fairacres, Roehampton Lane, SW15. *T:* 01-876 3802. *Clubs:* Brooks's, Royal Automobile; Leander.

**ROSS, Alfred William,** OBE 1955; MA, MIEE; Chief of Naval Research, Ministry of Defence, since 1968; *b* 13 Sept. 1914; *m* 1946, Margaret Elizabeth Wilson; three *d*. *Educ:* King Edward VI School, Stourbridge; Christ's Coll., Cambridge. Joined HM Signal Sch., Portsmouth, 1936. Worked on Radar during War at Admiralty Signal and Radar Establishment. Defence Research Policy Staff, Ministry of Defence, 1946-47; Chief Superintendent, Army Operational Research Group, 1951-56. Director, Naval Physical Research, Ministry of Defence, 1956-68. *Publications:* scientific papers on radar, electronics and operational research. *Recreation:* golf. *Address:* 336 Fir Tree Road, Epsom Downs, Surrey. *T:* Burgh Heath 56774. *Clubs:* Golfers'; Banstead Downs Golf.

**ROSS, Allan Dawson,** BSc, PhD (Edinburgh), FICE, FRSE; Professor of Civil Engineering at University of London, King's College, since

1946; *b* 22 Feb. 1909; 4th *s* of Robert and Anne Ross, Dublin; *m* 1935, Isabel Goodburn; one *d.* *Educ:* Peebles High School; University of Edinburgh. Bursar of The Royal Commission for the Exhibition of 1851. Held civil engineering appointments in road and railway construction, 1929-32; Assistant to late Prof. Sir T. Hudson Beare, Univ. of Edinburgh, 1932-34; Education Officer, Air Ministry, 1934-35; Lecturer in Civil and Mechanical Engineering, University of London, King's College, 1935-46. *Publications:* various papers published in journals of learned and technical institutions. *Address:* 4 Northfield Avenue, Pinner, Middx. *T:* 01-866 2988.

**ROSS, Sir Archibald (David Manisty),** KCMG 1961 (CMG 1953); Ambassador to Sweden since 1966; *b* 12 Oct. 1911; *s* of late J. A. Ross, Indian Civil Service, and Dorothea, *e d* of late G. Eldon Manisty, Bengal Civil Service; *m* 1939, Mary Melville, *d* of Melville Macfadyen; one *s* one *d* (and one *s* decd). *Educ:* Winchester; New College, Oxford (MA). 1st Class Hon. Mods 1932, Lit. Hum. 1934; Gaisford Greek Verse Prize, 1932; Laming Travelling Fellow, Queen's College, 1934-35. Diplomatic Service, 1936; Third Secretary: Berlin, 1939, Stockholm, 1939-44; First Secretary: Foreign Office, 1944-47, Tehran, 1947-50; Counsellor, Foreign Office, 1950-53; HM Minister, Rome, 1953-56; Assistant Under Secretary of State for Foreign Affairs, 1956-60; Ambassador to Portugal, 1961-66. *Address:* British Embassy, Stockholm, Sweden; c/o Foreign and Commonwealth Office, SW1. *Clubs:* Travellers', Leander.

**ROSS, Hon. Sir Bruce;** *see* Ross, Hon. Sir D. B.

**ROSS, Prof. Claud Richard,** MA; Consultant, Organisation for European Economic Co-operation and Development, Paris, since 1969; *b* 24 March 1924; *o s* of late Claud Frederick Ross and Frances Muriel Ross, Steyning, Sussex; *m* 1954, Leslie Beatrice, *d* of Oliver Arnell and late Dr H. M. Arnell, Kitale, Kenya; two *d.* *Educ:* Ardingly Coll.; Hertford Coll., Oxford (Open Schol., Mod. Hist.). Served in Royal Engineers, 1942-47. 1st cl. PPE, 1950. Fellow of Hertford Coll., 1951-63; Lectr in Economics, Oxford Univ., 1951-52 and 1955-63; Economic Section, HM Treasury, 1952-55; Junior Proctor, Oxford Univ., 1958-59; Bursar, Hertford Coll., 1959-63; Prof. of Economics and Dean of Social Studies, Univ. of East Anglia, 1963-69, Pro-Vice-Chancellor, 1964-68. Adviser, Bankers' Mission to India and Pakistan, 1960. Represented HM Treasury on OECD Working Party on Policies for Economic Growth, 1961-68. Leader, British Economic Mission to Tanzania, 1965; Member: East Anglia Economic Planning Council, 1966-69 (Dep. Chm., 1967-69); Jt Mission for Malta, 1967. *Publications:* Financial and Physical Problems of Development in the Gold Coast (with D. Seers), 1952; articles on economics. *Address:* c/o OECD, 2 rue André Pascal, Paris 16e; Southend House, Loddon, Norfolk.

**ROSS, Sir David;** *see* Ross, Sir W. D.

**ROSS, Donald MacArthur,** QC (Scotland) 1964; *b* 29 March 1927; *s* of late John Ross, Dundee; *m* 1958, Dorothy Margaret, *d* of late William Annand, Kirriemuir; two *d.* *Educ:* Dundee High School; Edinburgh University. MA (Edinburgh) 1947; LLB with distinction (Edinburgh) 1951. National Service with The Black Watch (RHR), 2nd Lt, 1947-49. Advocate, 1952. Standing Junior Counsel in Scotland to: Min. of Labour and Nat. Service, 1959-62; Scottish Development Dept (Highways), 1962-64; Junior Legal Assessor to Edinburgh Burgh and Dean of Guild Courts, 1958-64. Vice-Dean of the Faculty of Advocates, 1967-. Member: Scottish Cttee of Council on Tribunals; Cttee on Privacy, 1970; Bd of Management, Royal Infirmary, Edinburgh, and associated hosps. *Recreations:* shooting, gardening. *Address:* 9 India Street, Edinburgh 3; 33 Lauder Road, Edinburgh 9. *T:* 031-667 5731.

**ROSS, Hon. Sir (Dudley) Bruce,** Kt 1962; retired; *b* 21 May 1892; *s* of William Alexander Ross and Annie Isabella Ross, Adelaide, S Australia; *m* 1st, 1920, Margaret Eleanor Waterhouse (decd); one *s* three *d*; 2nd, 1954, Agnes Jessie Linklater. *Educ:* Queen's School, St Peter's College and University of Adelaide, S Australia. LLB (Adelaide) 1914. KC 1945. Judge of Supreme Court of S Australia, 1952-62. Pres. Law Society of S Australia, 1948-49; Vice-Pres., Law Council of Australia, 1948-49; Chancellor, Dioceses of Adelaide and Willochra, 1944-69; Member Council of Governors, St Peter's Coll., Adelaide, 1948-60; Pres. Church of England Boys' Home, 1943-; Pres., Kindergarten Union of SA, 1962-. Served European War, 1914-18, with 5th Division, AIF. *Recreation:* bowls. *Address:* 19 Sherbourne Road, Medindie Gardens, SA 5081, Australia. *T:* ML2178. *Clubs:* Adelaide, Naval, Military and Air Force (Adelaide).

**ROSS, Hon. Frank Mackenzie,** CMG 1946; MC 1918; Hon. LLD; Hon. Co-Chairman, Canada Cement Lafarge Ltd; Chairman of the Board: International Paints (Canada) Ltd, Montreal; Grosvenor-Laing (BC) Ltd, Vancouver, and other companies in Group; Canadian Allied Property Investments Ltd, Vancouver, and other companies in Group; President and Director, West Coast Shipbuilders Ltd, Vancouver; Director of several other Companies; *b* Glasgow, Scotland, 14 April 1891; *s* of David and Grace (Archibald) Ross, both of Ross-shire; *m* 1945, Phyllis Gregory Turner, SM 1967, CBE 1946, LLD. *Educ:* Royal Academy, Tain, Scotland. Served European War, 1914-18, with 8th Battalion, Canadian Army (MC). Formerly Dir.-Gen. of Production of Naval Armaments and Equipment, Department of Munitions and Supply, Canada. Lieutenant-Governor of the Province of British Columbia, 1955-60. Hon. degrees from Universities of: New Brunswick, 1956; British Columbia, 1958; St Francis Xavier, Nova Scotia, 1961; Aberdeen, 1961. KStJ 1956. *Address:* 2002 Robson Street, Vancouver 5, BC, Canada; (business) 1101 West 6th Avenue, Vancouver 9, BC. *Clubs:* St James's (Montreal); Vancouver, University, Faculty, Terminal City (Vancouver).

**ROSS, Rear-Adm. George Campbell,** CB 1952; CBE 1945; CEng, MIMechE; AFRAeS; retired; *b* 9 Aug. 1900; *s* of late Sir Archibald Ross, KBE; *m* 1st, 1929, Alice Behrens; 2nd, 1950, Lucia Boer (marr. diss. 1969); two *d.* *Educ:* Royal Naval Colleges, Osborne and Dartmouth. Served European War, 1914-18, Home Fleet. Engineering Courses at RN College, Greenwich, and RNE College, Keyham, 1919-21; HMS Hawkins, Flagship China Station, 1921-24; RNE Coll., Lecturer in Marine Engineering, 1924-27; HMS Effingham, Flagship East Indies Station, 1927-29; HM Dockyard, Chatham, 1929-31; HMS Rodney, 1931-33; Comdr 1933; Asst Naval Attaché, Embassy, Tokyo, 1933-36; HMS Manchester, 1937-39; Engineer-in-Chief's Dept, Admiralty, 1939-41; HMS Nelson, 1941-43 (Staff Engineer Officer to Flag Officer, Force "H", Malta Convoy, N Africa and Sicily); Capt. 1943; Aircraft Maintenance and Repair Dept, Admiralty, 1943-47; ADC to the King, 1948-49; Chief of Staff to Rear-Admiral

Reserve Aircraft, 1948-49; Rear-Adm. (E) 1949; Director of Aircraft Maintenance and Repair, Admiralty, 1949-53; retd, Oct. 1953. Joined Hawker Siddeley group, Nov. 1953, and retd Sept. 1965. Dir, Columbia Industrial Develts; Consultant to Grieveson Grant, Stockbrokers, and other cos. Chairman, Combined Services Winter Sports Assoc., 1951-67. Freedom and Livery of Worshipful Company of Carmen. *Recreations:* fishing, ski-ing, painting. *Address:* 11 Redcliffe Close, Old Brompton Road, SW5. *T:* 01-373 0609. *Clubs:* Hurlingham, Army and Navy.

**ROSS, Sir Henry (James),** Kt, *cr* 1952; Life President, The Distillers' Company Ltd, Edinburgh; *b* 14 March 1893; *s* of William Henry Ross, OBE, and Annie Gilmour Pollok Dalgleish; *m* 1917, Blanche Alix Jowett Newbould (*d* 1950); two *s*. *Educ:* George Watson's College, Edinburgh; The Leys School, Cambridge; Institut Tilly, Berlin. Distillers' Company Ltd; joined as trainee, 1910; Director, 1925; Chm. Management Cttee, 1946; Dep. Chm., 1947; Chm., 1948-58. *Recreations:* yachting and fishing. *Address:* 27 Learmonth Terrace, Edinburgh.

**ROSS, James,** QC 1966; Deputy Chairman of Quarter Sessions, Parts of Lindsey, since 1968; Recorder of Coventry since 1968; *b* 22 March 1913; *s* of John Stuart Ross, FRCSE; *m* 1939, Clare Margaret, *d* of Alderman Robert Cort-Cox, Stratford-on-Avon; one *d*. *Educ:* Glenalmond; Exeter Coll., Oxford. BA Oxon 1934. Admitted Solicitor, 1938; called to Bar, Gray's Inn, 1945. Legal Member, Mental Health Review Tribunal, Birmingham Region, 1962; Deputy Chairman, Agricultural Land Tribunal, East Midland Area, 1963. *Recreation:* sailing. *Address:* 2 Dr Johnson's Buildings, Temple, EC4. *T:* 01-353 5371. *Clubs:* Union (Birmingham); Leicestershire (Leicester); Nottinghamshire (Nottingham); Bar Yacht, Island Cruising, Royal Yachting Association.

**ROSS, Sir James Paterson,** 1st Bt, *cr* 1960; KCVO 1949; Surgeon to the Queen, 1952-64, retd; Professor of Surgery, University of London, 1935-60, Emeritus Professor, 1960; Director, British Post-graduate Medical Federation, 1960-66; Consulting Surgeon, St Bartholomew's Hospital; President Royal College of Surgeons of England, 1957-60; *b* 26 May 1895; *s* of James Ross and May Paterson; *m* 1924, Marjorie Burton Townsend; two *s*. *Educ:* Christ's College, Finchley; St Bartholomew's Hospital Medical College (Entrance Scholarship in Science). Treasurer's Prize and Junior Scholarship Anatomy and Physiology, St Bartholomew's, 1914; Sergeant RAMC(T), 1914-15; Temp. Surgeon Lieutenant, Royal Navy, 1917-19; Gold Medal, University of London MB Examination, 1920; FRCS(Eng.), 1922. Associate in Surgery (Neurological Clinic) Peter Bent Brigham Hospital, Boston, USA; MS London, 1928; Reader in Surgery, Univ. of London; Jacksonian Prize Essay, Hunterian Prof., Royal College of Surgeons; Examiner in Surgery, Universities of London, Edinburgh, Glasgow, Belfast, Wales, Manchester, Bristol and Aberdeen. Sims Commonwealth Travelling Prof., 1957. FACS (Hon.), 1953, FRACS (Hon.), 1957. LLD (Hon.), Glasgow, 1957; FRCSEd (Hon.), 1959; FFR (Hon.) 1959; FRCSGlas. (Hon.) 1959; FDS (Hon.) 1964. *Publications:* The Surgery of the Sympathetic Nervous System (with G. E. Gask), 1934; (Jt Editor) British Surgical Practice (with Sir E. Rock Carling), 1947; several papers on surgical subjects in Medical Press. *Heir:* *s* James Keith Ross, RD, MS, FRCS [*b* 9 May 1927; *m* 1956, Jaqueline Annella Clarke; one *s* three *d*]. *Address:* Flat H, 14 John Spencer Square, Canonbury, N1. *T:* 01-359 1122.

**ROSS, James Stiven,** CBE 1951; Principal of Westminster Training College, 1940-53; *b* Brechin, Angus, 4 Nov. 1892; *s* of James Donaldson Ross and Isabella Small Galloway; unmarried. *Educ:* Brechin High School; University College, Dundee (University of St Andrews); Dundee Training College. MA (1st Cl. Hons Maths) St Andrews, 1914; BSc St Andrews, 1915; MA Lond., 1923. Enlisted June 1915; released Oct. 1915, to take up work as Chemist at HM Factory, Oldbury (1915-18). Westminster Training College: Lecturer in Mathematics, 1919; Lecturer in Education, 1921; Vice-Principal, 1930. Fellow: British Psychological Society; The Royal Philharmonic Society; The College of Preceptors. *Publications:* Groundwork of Educational Psychology, 1930; Groundwork of Educational Theory, 1942; Basic Psychology, 1946; The Religious Basis of Education, 1948. *Recreations:* music, walking. *Address:* Westminster, North Latch, Brechin, Angus. *T:* 2605.

**ROSS, Kenneth Brebner,** OBE 1952; Former Managing Director: Steels Process Plants Ltd, Eastcote, Middlesex; Archibald Low & Sons Ltd, Kirkintilloch, Scotland; retired; *b* Aliwal North, S Africa, 28 March 1901; *s* of Edward Ross and Annie Stretch Brebner; *m* 1947, Lilian Frances Powell; no *c*. *Educ:* Grey Coll. School, Bloemfontein; Grey University College, Bloemfontein; Exeter College (OFS Rhodes Scholar, 1923), Oxford (Hons. Chem.). Joined Anglo-Iranian Oil Co., 1926; General Refineries Manager, Abadan Refinery, 1951; Director, Costain-John Brown, 1952-54; Director of Operations in Production Group of UK Atomic Energy Authority, 1954-61. *Recreation:* golf. *Address:* Little Gables, Redwood Road, Sidmouth, Devon. *Club:* East India and Sports.

**ROSS, Leonard Q.;** *see* Rosten, Leo C.

**ROSS, Malcolm Keir;** Headmaster of Crown Woods School, London, since 1957; *b* 8 June 1910; *m* 1937, Isabel Munkley; two *d*. *Educ:* Grangefield Grammar Sch., Stockton-on-Tees; Keble Coll., Oxford. Schoolmaster: Gordonstoun, 1933-34; Haverfordwest Grammar Sch., 1934-36; Bromley Grammar Sch., 1936-40; war service with RAF, 1940-45; Warden of Village Coll., Sawston, Cambs, 1945-57. Member: C of E Bd of Educn; Cttee of Enquiry into conditions of service life for young servicemen, 1969. FRSA. *Recreations:* gardening, reading. *Address:* 11 Birchwood Avenue, Sidcup, Kent. *T:* 01-300 6431.

**ROSS, Rear-Admiral Maurice James,** CB 1962; DSC 1940; retired; *b* 31 Oct. 1908; *s* of Basil James Ross and Avis Mary (*née* Wilkinson); *m* 1946, Helen Matheson McCall; one *d*. *Educ:* Charterhouse. Entered Royal Navy, 1927; Lieut, 1931; Lieut-Comdr, 1939; Comdr, 1943; Captain, 1951; Rear-Adm., 1960. Specialised in gunnery, 1935; served War of 1939-45, in HM Ships Somali and Cleopatra, at HMS Excellent, and Admiralty; comd HMS Hart on Far East Station, 1947-48; subsequently held appointments at Admiralty, Singapore, and Washington: Director of Tactical, Ship Requirements and Staff Duties Div., Naval Staff, 1958-59; Assistant Chief of Naval Staff (Warfare), 1960-63. *Address:* 19 Eaton Mews North, SW1. *T:* 01-235 5567; Monk's Cottage, Leaveland, near Faversham, Kent. *T:* Challock 227. *Club:* United Service.

**ROSS, Mrs Nicholas;** *see* Phillpotts, M. Adelaide Eden.

**ROSS, Prof. Peter McGregor;** Professor of Engineering, University of Cambridge, since 1970; *b* 25 June 1919; *s* of William McGregor Ross and Isabel Ross (*née* Abraham); *m* 1950, Sylvia Robson Gripper, *d* of Laurence A. and Jean E. Gripper; two *s* one *d*. *Educ:* St Christopher Sch., Letchworth; Ulverston Grammar Sch.; St John's Coll., Cambridge. Graduate Apprentice and Asst Engineer with London Power Co., 1941-46; Chief Designer, Gas Turbine Dept, John Brown & Co. (Clydebank) Ltd, 1946-54; Head of Mechanical R&D Dept, C. A. Parsons & Co. Ltd, Newcastle upon Tyne, 1954-61; Chief Development Engineer, Tube Investments, Ltd, 1962-64; Technical Dir, W. H. A. Robertson & Co., Ltd, Bedford, 1965-66; Engineering Dir, Loewy Robertson Engineering Co., Bournemouth, 1966-68; Dir of Research, Davy Ashmore Ltd, 1968-69. Visiting Prof., Univ. of Aston, 1966-68. Fellow of University Coll., Cambridge, 1970-. *Recreation:* sailing. *Address:* University Engineering Department, Trumpington Street, Cambridge CB2 1PZ. *T:* Cambridge 66466; 15 Clarkson Road, Cambridge. *T:* Cambridge 65924. *Club:* Royal Over-Seas League.

**ROSS, Robert,** MA, FLS, FRMS; Keeper of Botany, British Museum (Natural History), since Oct. 1966; *b* 14 Aug. 1912; *e s* of Robert Ross, Pinner, Middx; *m* 1939, Margaret Helen Steadman; one *s* three *d*. *Educ:* St Paul's Sch.; St John's Coll., Cambridge. Asst Keeper, British Museum (Natural History), 1936; Principal Scientific Officer, 1950; Deputy Keeper, 1962. Royal Microscopical Society: Hon. Librarian, 1947-51; Hon. Editor, 1953-; Vice-Pres., 1959-60. Administrator of Finances, Internat. Assoc. of Plant Taxonomy, 1964-69; Sec., Gen. Cttee for Plant Nomenclature, 1964-69, Chm., 1969-. Pres., British Phycological Soc., 1969-. *Publications:* various papers in scientific jls on botanical subjects. *Recreations:* morris dancing (Bagman, Morris Ring of England, 1946-50); walking. *Address:* 9 Vincent Close, Bromley, Kent BR2 9ED. *T:* 01-460 7269.

**ROSS, Stanley Graham,** DSO 1918; MC; BA, MD (McGill), FRCP; *b* Dundas, Ontario, Canada, 29 April 1888; *e s* of late James Ross, MD, and Beatrice Dudgeon Graham; *m* 1930, Jean Lesley, *d* of late Arthur L. Drummond, Montreal, Canada; three *s* one *d*. *Educ:* Hamilton Collegiate Institute; McGill University. Resident Physician Royal Victoria Hospital 1913-14; served overseas 1915-19 CEF (despatches twice, DSO, MC, 1914-15 star, two medals); Major in CAMC 1917; post-graduate work in London 1919-20, in the Johns Hopkins Hospital, Baltimore, 1920-22; Member of the American Pediatric Society; Member of the Canadian Pediatric Society. *Address:* 65 Rosemount Crescent, Westmount, Montreal, Canada. *Club:* University (Montreal).

**ROSS, Mrs Thomas A.;** *see* Runge, N. C.

**ROSS, Col. Walter John Macdonald,** CB 1958; OBE 1955; MC 1946; TD 1946 and 2 Bars; DL; JP; Landed Proprietor and Farmer; *b* 1914; *s* of late Major Robert Ross of Ledgowan, Ross-shire, and Marion, *d* of late Walter Macfarlane, DL, JP; *m* 1940, Josephine May, 2nd *d* of late Malcolm Cross, and of late Evelyn Cross of Earlston House, Borgue; two *s* one *d*. *Educ:* Loretto. Commissioned RA (TA), 1935. Served War of 1939-45, UK and NW Europe. Comd 5 KOSB (TA), 1951-55; Deputy Comd 157 (L) Inf. Bde, 1955-59. Underwriting Member of Lloyd's. DL 1960 and JP 1958, Stewartry of Kirkcudbright. Royal Humane Society Parchment for Saving Life, 1963. Member of Royal Company of Archers, Queen's Body Guard for Scotland. County Councillor (Vice-Convener), Stewartry of Kirkcudbright. *Recreations:* shooting, fishing. *Address:* Netherhall, Bridge-of-Dee, Kirkcudbrightshire. *T:* Bridge-of-Dee 208. *Clubs:* New (Edinburgh); Western (Glasgow).

**ROSS, Rt. Hon. William,** PC 1964; MBE; MA; MP (Lab) Kilmarnock Division Ayr and Bute since 1946; *b* 7 April 1911; *s* of W. Ross, Ayr; *m* 1948, Elizabeth Jane Elma Aitkenhead, Ayr; two *d*. *Educ:* Ayr Academy; Glasgow University. MA 1932; Schoolmaster. Served War of 1939-45, HLI, R Signals, Major; India, SACSEA. Contested Ayr Burgh, General Election, 1945. Secretary of State for Scotland, 1964-70. Chairman, Regional Economic Advisory Council for Scotland, 1965-. *Recreation:* golf. *Address:* 10 Chapelpark Road, Ayr. *T:* Ayr 5673.

**ROSS, William Alexander,** CBE 1951 (OBE 1946); FRIBA; retired, 1960; *b* 27 June 1891; *s* of William Thomson Ross, Alva, Clackmannanshire, and Louisa Jane (*née* Bevan), London; *m* 1918, Elspeth Stuart Ramsay Colquhoun (*d* 1970). *Educ:* St Michael's School, Highgate; Regent St Polytechnic London. Gold medallist (Polytechnic). Royal Academy School of Architecture, 1912-14; articled to G. A. Mitchel, ARIBA, and employed as chief architectural asst on rebuilding of Regent St Polytechnic; Architectural Asst to J. Lyons & Co. on Regent Palace Hotel, etc., 1912; Draughtsman, H. M. Office of Works, 1912; Bronze Medallist, Nat. Competition, South Kensington, for Architectural Design, 1912. Served European War, 1914-18; RNVR, 1914; Sub-Lt RNAS, 1916; Capt. RAF, 1918; demobilised, 1919. Lecturer in Architectural Design, Polytechnic, 1920-31; Asst Architect, HM Office of Works, 1919, War Office, 1927; Architect, War Office, 1928; Senior Architect, then superintending Architect, Ministry of Works, 1941; Dep. Director of Works and Services (Scotland), 1943; Director of Works and Services (Scotland), Ministry of Works, 1944-53; retired from Civil Service, 1953. Hon. Associate Instn of Royal Engineers. Silver Jubilee Medal, 1935; Coronation Medals, 1937 and 1953. *Address:* 5 The Garth, Holden Road, N12. *T:* 01-445 2392.

**ROSS, Sir (William) David,** KBE 1938 (OBE 1918); Commander, First Class, of Order of St Olav; Grand Officer, Order of Polonia Restituta; MA, DLitt; Hon. LLD (Edinburgh and Manchester); Hon. Litt D (Dublin); Hon. LHD (Columbia): Hon. DLit (London); Hon. Doctor (Paris and Oslo); Hon. Fellow of Merton, Balliol and Oriel Colleges, and of Trinity College, Dublin; FBA; Member American Philosophical Society, Académie des Sciences Morales et Politiques, and American Academy of Arts and Sciences; Provost of Oriel College, Oxford, 1929-47; Vice-Chancellor, 1941-44; Pro-Vice-Chancellor, 1944-47; *b* Thurso, Caithness, 15 April 1877; *s* of late John Ross, MA, Principal, Maharajah's Coll., Travancore; *m* 1906, Edith Helen (*d* 1953), *d* of John Ogden, Manchester; four *d*. *Educ:* Royal High School, Edinburgh; Edinburgh Univ., MA, 1895; Balliol College, Oxford (Exhibitioner); First Class Classical Mods, 1898; Jenkyns Exhibitioner, Balliol, 1900; First Class Lit. Hum., 1900; Lecturer of Oriel College, Fellow of Merton College, 1900-2; Fellow and Tutor, Oriel College, 1902-29; Deputy White's Professor of Moral

Philosophy, Oxford University, 1923-28; Secretary of NE Coast Armaments Committee, 1915-16; served in Ministry of Munitions, 1916-19; Major, Special List, 1918-19; late Chm. several Wages Councils; Pres. Classical Assoc., 1932; Pres. of British Academy, 1936-40; Pres. of Aristotelian Society, 1939-40; Gifford Lecturer, Univ. of Aberdeen, 1935-36; Visiting Prof., Columbia Univ., 1938-39; Chairman of Council, British (now Royal) Institute of Philosophy, 1940; Pres. Union Académique Internationale, 1947; Chm. of Departmental Cttees on Woollen Textile Trade in Yorkshire, 1936, on Health of Cotton Cardroom Workers, 1937, and on the Fair Wages Clause, 1937; Member of Departmental Committee on Holidays with Pay, 1937; Member of Appellate Tribunal for Conscientious Objectors, 1940-41; Member of Nat. Arbitration Tribunal, 1941-52; Chm. of Civil Service Arbitration Tribunal, 1942-52; Chm., Royal Commission on the Press, 1947-49. *Publications:* Joint Editor, and later Editor, of Oxford Translation of Aristotle, Metaphysics, 1908; Ethics, 1925; and Select Fragments, 1952; Aristotle, 1923; edition of Aristotle, Metaphysics, 1924; Physics, 1935; Analytics, 1949; Fragmenta Selecta, 1954; Parva Naturalia, 1955; De Anima, 1956 and 1961; Politics, 1957; Topics and Sophistici Elenchi, 1958; Rhetoric, 1959; Aristotle, Selections, 1927; edition of Theophrastus, Metaphysics, 1929; The Right and the Good, 1930; Foundations of Ethics, 1939; Plato's Theory of Ideas, 1951; Kant's Ethical Theory, 1954. *Address:* 17 Bradmore Road, Oxford. *T:* Oxford 57864.

*See also Sir John Miller Martin.*

**ROSS SKINNER, Lt-Col Harry Crawley,** DSO 1918; MC; Highland Light Infantry; *b* 1896; *er s* of late Sir Harry Ross Skinner; *m* 1927, Joan, *er d* of late Francis Crawley, Stockwood, Luton, Beds; one *s.* Served European War, 1914-18 (despatches, DSO, MC); retired, 1932; served War of 1939-45. *Address:* Warmwell House, Dorchester, Dorset. *T:* Warmwell 279. *Clubs:* Caledonian, Lansdowne.

**ROSS WILLIAMSON, Hugh,** FRSL; Writer; *b* 1901; *e s* of late Rev. Hugh Ross Williamson and Grace Winifred Walker; *m* 1941, Margaret Joan Cox; one *s* one *d.* Asst Editor, The Yorkshire Post, 1925-30; Editor of The Bookman, 1930-34; Acting Editor of the Strand Magazine, 1934-35; Director of London General Press, 1936-42, and 1968-. Anglican Priest, 1943-55; reconciled to Catholic Church, 1955. *Publications:* The Poetry of T. S. Eliot, 1932; John Hampden, 1933; King James I, 1936; Who is for Liberty?, 1939; George Villiers, Duke of Buckingham, 1940; AD 33, 1941; Captain Thomas Schofield, 1942; Charles and Cromwell, 1946; The Arrow and the Sword, 1947; The Silver Bowl, 1948; Four Stuart Portraits, 1949; The Seven Christian Virtues, 1949; The Gunpowder Plot, 1951; Sir Walter Ralegh, 1951; Jeremy Taylor, 1952; Canterbury Cathedral, 1953; The Ancient Capital, 1953; Historical Whodunits, 1955; James by the Grace of God–, 1955; The Great Prayer, 1955; The Walled Garden (autobiography), 1956; The Day they killed the King, 1957; Enigmas of History, 1957; Beginning of the English Reformation, 1957; The Sisters, 1958; The Challenge of Bernadette, 1958; The Day Shakespeare Died, 1962; Sixty Saints of Christendom, 1960; A Wicked Pack of Cards, 1961; The Flowering Hawthorn, 1962; Guy Fawkes, 1964; The Butt of Malmsey, 1967; The Marriage made in Blood, 1968; A Matter of Martyrdom, 1969; The Cardinal in Exile, 1969; The Cardinal in England, 1970; The Florentine Woman, 1970. *Plays:* In a Glass Darkly, 1932; Rose and Glove, 1934; The Seven Deadly Virtues, 1935; Monsieur Moi, 1935; Various Heavens, 1936; Mr Gladstone, 1937; Paul, a Bond-slave, 1945; Queen Elizabeth, 1946; Odds beyond Arithmetic, 1947; Fool's Paradise, 1949; The Cardinal's Learning, 1950; Gunpowder, Treason and Plot, 1951; Diamond cut Diamond, 1952; His Eminence of England, 1953; The Mime of Bernadette, 1958; Test of Truth, 1958; Heart of Bruce, 1959; Teresa of Avila, 1961; (with Ian Burford) Quartet for Lovers, 1962; Pavane for a Dead Infanta, 1968. *Club:* Savage.

**ROSSE,** 6th Earl of, *cr* 1806; **Laurence Michael Harvey Parsons,** MBE 1945; Bt 1677; Baron Oxmantown, 1792; MRIA, FSA (London and Ireland); FRAS; FRSA; Hon. ARIBA; (Hon.) LLD (Dublin and Belfast); Pro-Chancellor of Univ. of Dublin since 1965 (Vice-Chancellor, 1949-65); Chairman, London Prudential Investment Trust; *b* 28 Sept. 1906; *s* of 5th Earl and Lois, *d* of Sir Cecil Lister-Kaye, 4th Bart, and Lady Beatrice Lister-Kaye (she *m* 2nd, 5th Viscount de Vesci); *S* father, 1918; *m* 1935, Anne, *o d* of Lt-Col Leonard Messel, OBE, Nymans, Staplefield, Sussex; two *s.* *Educ:* Eton; Christ Church, Oxford (MA). Chairman: Standing Commission on Museums and Galleries; Properties Cttee; National Trust; Internat. Dendrology Soc.; Trustee, Historic Churches Preservation Trust. President: Friends of the National Collections of Ireland; Ancient Monuments Society; Irish Architectural Records Association; Royal Hortic. Soc. of Ireland, 1959-69; Adelaide Hospital; Furniture History Soc.; Georgian Group (Chm., 1946-68); Member: Arts Council of Ireland and of Nat. Monuments Adv. Coun. of Ireland; Adv. Council, Victoria and Albert Museum and Science Museum; Min. of Transport Trunk Roads Adv. Cttee. Served War of 1939-45 (MBE). *Publication:* (with Colonel E. R. Hill) The Story of the Guards Armoured Division, 1941-45, 1956. *Heir; s* Lord Oxmantown, *qv.* *Address:* Womersley Park, Doncaster, Yorks. *T:* Wentbridge 282; 18 Stafford Terrace, W8. *T:* 01-937 5857; Birr Castle, Co. Offaly. *T:* Birr 23. *Clubs:* Brooks's, Royal Automobile; Kildare Street (Dublin).

*See also Earl of Snowdon.*

**ROSSETTI, Harold Ford,** CB 1959; Director, London Office, International Labour Organisation, since 1970; *b* 19 Feb. 1909; *s* of Gabriel Arthur Madox Rossetti and Dora Brandreth Lewis; *m* 1933, Joan, *er d* of Rev. G. H. Holley; two *s* one *d.* *Educ:* Bolton School; Gonville and Caius College, Cambridge. Asst Principal, Customs and Excise, 1932; transferred to Min. of Labour, 1934; Student, Imperial Defence College, 1947; Head of Manpower Div., OEEC, Paris, 1951-55; Deputy Secretary, Ministry of Labour, 1959-63; Deputy Under Sec. of State, Dept of Educn and Science, 1963-69. Head of UK Delegn, Internat. Labour Conf., and Mem., Governing Body, ILO, 1960-63. Mem., South Bank Theatre Board, 1967-69. *Publication:* The Darkling Plain (novel), 1936. *Address:* Church Farm, Great Glemham, Saxmundham, Suffolk. *T:* Rendham 477. *Club:* Travellers'.

**ROSSI, Hugh Alexis Louis;** MP (C) Hornsey since 1966; an Assistant Government Whip, since 1970; *b* 21 June 1927; *m* 1955, Philomena Elizabeth Jennings; one *s* four *d.* *Educ:* Finchley Catholic Gram. Sch.; King's Coll., Univ. of London (LLB). Solicitor with Hons, 1950; Partner in London practice. Mem. Hornsey Borough Coun., 1956-65 (Chm. Housing Cttee); Dep. Mayor of Hornsey, 1964-65; Whip and Dep. Leader of Coun.; Mem. Haringey Coun., 1965-68 (Leader of

Opposition, 1965-66); Middlesex CC, 1961-65 (Chm. Building Cttee). Jt Sec., Cons. Party Housing Cttee, 1968-70; Vice-Chm., Cons. Party Legal Cttee, 1970-. Knight of Holy Sepulchre. *Recreations:* gardening, family. *Address:* 16 Beech Drive, N2. *T:* 01-883 8222.

**ROSSLYN,** 6th Earl of, *cr* 1801; **Antony Hugh Francis Harry St Clair-Erskine;** Bt 1666; Baron Loughborough, 1795; Captain King's Royal Rifle Corps; underwriting member of Lloyd's; Director of R. F. Kershaw Ltd; *b* 18 May 1917; *s* of late Lord Loughborough (*d* 1929) and Sheila (who obtained a divorce, 1926, and *m* 2nd, 1928, Sir John Milbanke, 11th Bt, 3rd, 1954, Prince Dimitri of Russia; she *d* 1969), *o d* of Harry Chisholm, Australia; *S* grandfather, 1939; *m* 1955, Athenais De Mortemart (marriage dissolved, 1962), *o d* of late Duc De Vivonne and Mme M. V. Ollivier, La Ferme Ste Barbe, Arcangues, BP, France; one *s* one *d*. *Educ:* Eton; Magdalen Coll., Oxford. Served with GHQ Liaison Regt (Phantom) and attached to 3rd Canadian Infantry Division (despatches). *Heir: s* Lord Loughborough, *qv*. *Address:* Stonerwood Park, Petersfield, Hants. *T:* Petersfield 3433. *Clubs:* White's, Royal Automobile, MCC; New (Edinburgh); Royal and Ancient (St Andrews); Kildare Street (Dublin); Travellers' (Paris).

**ROSSMORE,** 7th Baron, *cr* 1796; **William Warner Westenra;** *b* 14 Feb. 1931; *o s* of 6th Baron and of Dolores Cecil, *d* of late Lieut-Col James Alban Wilson, DSO, West Burton, Yorks; *S* father, 1958. *Educ:* Eton; Trinity Coll., Cambridge (BA). 2nd Lieut, Somerset LI. *Heir:* none. *Address:* Rossmore Park, Co. Monaghan, Eire. *T:* Monaghan 47.

**ROST, Peter Lewis;** MP (C) Derbyshire (South-East) since 1970; Member, London Stock Exchange; *b* 19 Sept. 1930; *s* of Frederick Rosenstiel and Elisabeth Merz; *m* 1961, Hilary Mayo; one *s* two *d*. *Educ:* various primary schs; Aylesbury Grammar Sch. National Service, RAF, 1948-50; Birmingham Univ. (BA Hons Geog.), 1950-53. Investment Analyst and Financial Journalist with Investors Chronicle, 1953-58; firstly Investment Advisor, 1958, and then, 1962, Mem. London Stock Exchange and Partner with present firm. *Recreations:* tennis, ski-ing, gardening, antique map collecting. *Address:* Norcott Court, Berkhamsted, Herts. *T:* Berkhamsted 6123.

**ROSTAL, Professor Max;** Professor at the Guildhall School of Music, London, 1944-58; Professor of the Master-Class, State Academy of Music, Cologne, since 1957; Professor of the Master-Class, Conservatoire, Berne, Switzerland, since 1958; *b* 7 Aug. 1905; *m* 1946, Karoline T. J. (*née* Reichsedle von Hohenblum-Simitsch); two *d*. *Educ:* State Acad., Vienna (Prof. Rosé); State Academy, Berlin (Prof. Flesch). Concert artist since age of 6; gave concerts in all parts of the world; at age of 23 Assistant to Prof. Flesch; Professor at State Academy of Music, Berlin, 1928-33. Lived in London, 1934-58; now residing in Berne, Switzerland. Has made various recordings for HMV, Decca, Argo, Concert Hall Soc., and Deutsche Grammophon Companies. FGSM 1945. Bundesverdienstkreuz 1st Class, German Federal Govt, 1968. *Publications:* many compositions, transcriptions, arrangements, editions. *Recreations:* motoring, photography, reading. *Address:* 3005 Berne, Weststrasse 12, Switzerland. *T:* Berne 031/43.16.30.

**ROSTAND, Jean;** Biologist and Writer; *b* 30 Oct. 1894; *s* of Edmond Rostand and Rosemonde Gérard; *m* 1920, Andrée Mante; one *s*. *Educ:* Sorbonne. Member of the French Academy. *Publications:* Les Chromosomes; La Vie des Crapauds; Pensées d'un Biologiste; Ce que je crois; Pages d'un moraliste; L'Aventure humaine; Aux Sources de la Biologie, etc. *Recreation:* chess. *Address:* 29 rue Pradier, Ville d'Avray, Seine-et-Oise, France. *T:* 926-4331.

**ROSTEN, Leo C.,** (pseudonym: **Leonard Q. Ross**); Special Editorial Advisor, Look Magazine, since 1949; *b* 11 April 1908; *s* of Samuel C. and Ida F. Rosten; *m* 1st, 1935, Priscilla Ann Mead (decd); one *s* two *d*; 2nd, 1960, Gertrude Zimmerman. *Educ:* University of Chicago (PhD); London School of Economics. Research Assistant, Political Science Dept, Univ. of Chicago, 1933-35; Fellow, Social Science Research Council, 1934-36; Grants from Rockefeller Foundation and Carnegie Corporation, 1938-40. Dir, Motion Picture Research Project, 1939-41. Spec. Consultant, Nat. Defense Advisory Commn, Washington, 1939; Chief, Motion Picture Branch, Office of Emergency Management; Chief, Motion Picture Div., Office of Facts and Figures, Washington, 1941-42; Dep. Dir, Office of War Information, Washington, 1942-45; Special Consultant, Sec. of War, Washington, 1945; special mission to France, Germany, England, 1945. Faculty Associate, Columbia Univ., 1953-; Lectr in Political Science, Yale Univ., 1955, New School for Social Research, NY, 1959. Ford Visiting Professor in Political Science, Univ. of California (Berkeley), USA, 1960-61. Wrote film screenplays: Sleep, My Love; The Velvet Touch; Walk East on Beacon; The Dark Corner, etc. Member: Amer. Acad. of Political and Social Science; Amer. Assoc. for Advancement of Science; National Book Cttee; Nat. Council, Authors League of America; Authors Guild of America; Educational Policies Cttee of Nat. Educational Assoc. Phi Beta Kappa, 1929; Freedom Foundation's Award, 1955, George Polk Memorial Award, 1955, etc. *Publications:* The Education of H*y*m*a*n K*a*p*l*a*n, 1937; The Washington Correspondents, 1937; The Strangest Places, 1939; Hollywood: The Movie Colony, The Movie Makers, 1941; The Dark Corner, 1945; Guide To The Religions of America (Ed.), 1957; The Return of H*y*m*a*n K*a*p*l*a*n 1959; Captain Newman, MD, 1961; The Story Behind the Painting, 1961; The Many Worlds of Leo Rosten; The Leo Rosten Bedside Book, 1965; A Most Private Intrigue, 1967; The Joys of Yiddish, 1968; A Trumpet for Reason, 1970; People I have Loved, Known or Admired, 1970. Contributions learned journals. *Recreations:* photography; travel. *Address:* c/o Look Magazine, 488 Madison Avenue, New York, NY 10022, USA. *T:* 750-7333. *Clubs:* Authors' (London); Cosmos (Washington), Chaos (New York).

**ROSTOW, Eugene Victor;** Sterling Professor of Law, Yale University; *b* 25 Aug. 1913; *s* of Victor A. and Lillian H. Rostow; *m* 1933, Edna B. Greenberg; two *s* one *d*. *Educ:* Yale Coll.; King's Coll., Cambridge; Yale Law Sch. Practised law, New York, 1937-38; Yale Law Faculty, 1938-, Asst to Asst Sec. of State Acheson, 1942-44; Asst to Exec. Sec., Economic Commn for Europe, UN, Geneva, 1949-50; Dean of Yale Law School, 1955-65; Under-Sec. of State for Political Affairs, 1966-69. Pitt Prof., Cambridge, 1959-60; Eastman Prof., Oxford, 1970-71. Chevalier, Legion of Honour (France), 1960; Grand Cross, Order of the Crown (Belgium), 1969. *Publications:* A National Policy for the Oil Industry, 1948; Planning for Freedom, 1959; The Sovereign Prerogative, 1962; Law, Power and the

Pursuit of Peace, 1968; contribs to legal and economic jls. *Address:* 208 St Ronan Street, New Haven, Conn 06511, USA. *T:* 203-776-3906; Peru, Vermont 05152, USA. *T:* 802-824-6627. *Clubs:* Century (New York); Elizabethan, Lawn (New Haven).
*See also W. W. Rostow.*

**ROSTOW, Walt Whitman;** Professor of Economics and of History, University of Texas at Austin, Texas, since 1969; Special Assistant to the President, The White House, 1966; *b* 7 Oct. 1916; 2nd *s* of Victor and Lillian Rostow; *m* 1947, Elspeth, *o d* of Milton J. and Harriet Vaughan Davies; one *s* one *d*. *Educ:* Yale (BA 1936; PhD 1940); Oxford (Rhodes Scholar). Social Science Research Council Fellow, 1939-40; Instructor, Columbia Coll., 1940-41; Office Strategic Services, 1941-45 (Army of the United States, 1943-45, Major; Legion of Merit; Hon. OBE); Assistant Chief Division German-Austrian Economic Affairs; Department of State, 1945-46; Harmsworth Professor American History, Oxford, 1946-47; Special Assistant to Executive Secretary, Economic Commission for Europe, 1947-49; Pitt Professor of American History, Cambridge, 1949-50; Professor of Economic History, Massachusetts Institute of Technology, 1950-65. Deputy Special Assistant to the President (USA) for National Security Affairs, Jan. 1961-Dec. 1961; Counselor and Chairman, Policy Planning Council, Department of State, 1961-66; US Mem., Inter-Amer. Cttee on Alliance for Progress, 1964-66. Member: Royal Economic Society, England; American Academy of Arts and Sciences, 1957. Hon. LLD: Carnegie Inst. of Tech., Pittsburgh, 1962; Univ. Miami, 1965; Univ. Notre Dame, 1966; Middlebury Coll., 1967. Medal of Freedom, with distinction, 1969. *Publications:* The American Diplomatic Revolution, 1947; Essays on the British Economy of the Nineteenth Century, 1948; The Process of Ecomonic Growth, 1952; (with A. D. Gayer and A. J. Schwartz) The Growth and Fluctuations of the British Economy, 1790-1850, 1953; (with A. Levin and others) The Dynamics of Soviet Society, 1953; (with others) The Prospects for Communist China, 1954; (with R. W. Hatch) An American Policy in Asia, 1955; (with M. F. Millikan) A Proposal: Key to An Effective Foreign Policy, 1957; The Stages of Economic Growth, 1960; The United States in the World Arena, 1960; The Economics of Take-off into Sustained Growth (ed), 1963; View from the Seventh Floor, 1964; A Design for Asian Development, 1965; various articles contributed to: The Economist, Economic Journal, Economic History Review, Journal of Econ. History, American Econ. Review, etc. *Address:* 1 Wild Wind Point, Austin, Texas 78746, USA. *Clubs:* Elizabethan (New Haven, Conn, USA); Cosmos (Washington, DC).
*See also E. V. Rostow.*

**ROSTRON, Sir Frank,** Kt 1967; MBE 1954; FIEE; Director, Ferranti Ltd, Hollinwood, Lancs, 1958-68; *b* 11 Sept. 1900; *s* of late Samuel Ernest and Martha Rostron, Oldham; *m* 1929, Helen Jodrell Owen; one *s* one *d*. *Educ:* Oldham High Sch.; Manchester Coll. of Tech. Ferranti Ltd, 1917-68: successively inside and outside technical sales; Instrument Sales Manager; Export Sales Manager; Director. Served War of 1939-45: Electrical Engineer Officer, RAF; released with rank of Squadron Leader. President, Manchester Chamber of Commerce, 1956 and 1957. Director: National and Vulcan Boiler and General Insurance Co. Ltd, 1961-70; Aron Meters Ltd, 1961-68; McKechnie Brothers Ltd, 1966-. Chairman: Cotton Board, 1963-67 (Independent Member, 1959); Cotton and Allied Textiles Industry Training Board, 1966-67; Textile Council, 1967-68. *Address:* 5 Brocklehurst Drive, Prestbury, Macclesfield, Cheshire. *T:* Prestbury 89577. *Club:* Royal Air Force.

**ROSTROPOVICH, Mstislav;** 'cellist; *b* 1927; *m* Gälina Vishnevskaya, *qv*. *Educ:* State Conservatoire, Moscow. Has played in many concerts in Russia and abroad from 1942; first performance of Shostakovich's 'cello concerto (dedicated to him), Edinburgh Festival, 1960. Series of concerts with London Symphony Orchestra under Gennadi Rozhdestvensky, Festival Hall, 1965 (Gold Medal). Mem. Union of Soviet Composers, 1950-. Lenin Prize, 1964. Hon. MusD St Andrews, 1968. *Address:* Union of Soviet Composers, Moscow, USSR.

**ROTBLAT, Prof. Joseph,** CBE 1965; MA, DSc (Warsaw); PhD (Liverpool); DSc (London); FInstP; Professor of Physics in the University of London, at St Bartholomew's Hospital Medical College, since 1950; Physicist to St Bartholomew's Hospital; Editor, Physics in Medicine and Biology; Secretary-General, Pugwash Conferences on Science and World Affairs; *b* 4 Nov. 1908; *e s* of late Z. Rotblat, Warsaw. *Educ:* University of Warsaw, Poland. Research Fellow of Radiological Laboratory of Scientific Society of Warsaw, 1933-39; Asst Director of Atomic Physics Institute of Free Univ. of Poland, 1937-39; Oliver Lodge Fellow of Univ. of Liverpool, 1939-40; Lecturer and afterwards Senior Lecturer in Dept of Physics, Liverpool Univ., 1940-49; Director of Research in nuclear physics at Liverpool Univ., 1945-49; work on atomic energy at Liverpool Univ. and Los Alamos, New Mexico. Pres., Hosp. Physicists' Assoc; Vice-Pres., British Inst. of Radiology. Member, Polish Academy of Sciences, 1966. *Publications:* (part-author) Progress in Nuclear Physics, 1950; (with Chadwick) Radio-activity and Radioactive Substances, 1953; Atomic Energy, a Survey, 1954; Atoms and the Universe, 1956; Science and World Affairs, 1962; Aspects of Medical Physics, 1966; Pugwash, the First Ten Years, 1967; papers on nuclear physics and radiation biology in Proceedings of Royal Society. Radiation Research, Nature, etc. *Recreations:* recorded music, travel. *Address:* 8 Asmara Road, West Hampstead, NW2. *T:* 01-435 1471. *Club:* Athenæum.

**ROTH, Professor Klaus Friedrich,** FRS 1960; Professor of Pure Mathematics (Theory of Numbers) at Imperial College of Science and Technology, since 1966; *b* 29 Oct. 1925; *s* of late Dr Franz Roth and Mathilde Roth (*née* Liebrecht); *m* 1955, Melek Khairy, BSc, PhD. *Educ:* St Paul's Sch.; Peterhouse, Cambridge; Univ. College, London. BA (Cambridge, 1945); MSc, PhD (London, 1948, 1950). Asst Master, Gordonstoun School, 1945-46. Member of Dept of Mathematics, University College, London, 1948-66; title of Professor in the University of London conferred 1961. Visiting Lecturer, 1956-57, Vis. Prof., 1965-66, at Mass Inst. of Techn., USA. Fields Medal awarded at International Congress of Mathematicians, 1958. Foreign Hon. Mem., Amer. Acad. of Arts and Sciences, 1966. *Publications:* papers in various mathematical jls. *Recreations:* chess, cinema. *Address:* Department of Mathematics, Imperial College, Exhibition Road, SW7; 24 Burnsall Street, SW3. *T:* 01-352 1363.

**ROTH, Professor Martin,** MD (London); FRCP; DPM; Professor of Psychological Medicine, University of Newcastle upon Tyne, since 1956; Physician, Royal Victoria Infirmary, Newcastle upon Tyne; Clinical Director, Department of Psychiatry, Newcastle General

Hospital; Hon. Director, MRC Group devoted to study of relationship between functional and organic mental disorders; *b* 6 Nov. 1917; *s* of Samuel Simon and late Regina Roth; *m* 1945, Constance Heller; three *d. Educ:* University of London, St Mary's Hospital. Formerly: Senior Registrar, Maida Vale, and Maudsley Hosps; Physician, Crichton Royal Hosp., Dumfries; Director of Clinical Research, Graylingwell Hosp.; Visiting Assistant Professor, in the Department of Psychiatry, McGill University, Montreal, 1954; Consultant, WHO Expert Cttee on Mental Health Problems of Ageing and the Aged, 1958; Mayne Vis. Prof., Univ. of Queensland, 1968. Pres., Section of Psychiatry, RSM, 1968-; Member: Royal Medico-Psychological Association; (Burlingame Prize, 1951); MRC, 1964-68; Clinical Research Board, MRC, 1964-70. Hon. Mem., Société Royale de Médicine Mentale de Belgique. *Publications:* (with Mayer-Gross and Slater) Clinical Psychiatry, 1954, (with Slater) 3rd edn 1969; *contrib. to:* Schizophrenia, Somatic Aspects, 1957; Social and Genetic Influences on Life and Death, 1967; papers on psychiatric aspects of ageing, neurosis, schizophrenia, in various psychiatric and medical journals. *Recreations:* music, conversation, literature, travel. *Address:* Elmfield Lodge, Elmfield Road, Gosforth, Newcastle upon Tyne NE3 4BA. *T:* Gosforth 5-4019. *Club:* Athenæum.

**ROTH, Air Commodore Victor Henry Batten,** CB 1959; CBE 1949; RAF, retd; *b* 7 June 1904; *s* of late Victor Roth; *m* 1948, Catherine Lang, *d* of late John McNaught Colquhoun. *Educ:* London Sch. of Economics (BCom.). Commnd in RAF, 1929; Home Aircraft Depot, 1929-31; No. 2 Maintenance Unit, 1931-32; Air HQ, Iraq, 1933; Aircraft Depot, Iraq, 1934; No. 2 Maintenance Unit, 1935; Equipt Staff, Air Min., 1935-43; OC No. 312 Maintenance Unit, SEAC, 1943-44; Sen. Equipt Staff Officer, No. 226 Gp, SEAC, 1944; HQ Base Air Forces, SE Asia, 1944-45; Mil. Staff Coll., Quetta, 1945-46; Dir of Administrative Plans, Air Min., 1946-49; Equipt Staff, Air Min., 1949-51; Sen. Equipt Staff Officer, FEAF, 1951-52; Imperial Defence Coll., 1953; OC No. 61 Maintenance Unit, 1954-55; Dir of Equipt (D), Air Min., 1955-59; Sen. Air Staff Officer, No. 40 Gp, 1959-61; AOC No. 40 Gp (acting Air Vice-Marshal), 1961; Comdt RAF Supply Control Centre, 1961-62; retired, Jan. 1963. King's Commendation, 1941. Mem., Thingoe Rural District Council, 1964-. *Address:* 1 Sharp's Green, Horringer, Bury St Edmunds, Suffolk. *T:* Horringer 332.

**ROTHA, Paul;** Film Producer and Director; Author; Journalist; Managing Director, Paul Rotha Productions Ltd, since 1941; *b* London, 3 June 1907. *Educ:* Highgate School; Slade School of Art, London. Painter and designer; Art Critic to The Connoisseur, 1927-28; specialised in the production of documentary films, starting with Empire Marketing Board; has made documentary films for Unesco, The Times, Shell-Mex, Imperial Airways, Manchester Corporation, Scottish Office, National Council of Social Service, Gas Industry, Royal National Life-Boat Institution, Central Electricity Board, National Book Council, Vickers-Armstrong, Orient Line, etc, Gold Medals for Films at Venice Film Festival (1934), Brussels Film Festival (1935) and Leipsig Film Festival (1962); British Film Academy Awards, 1947 and 1952. Visited US under auspices of Rockefeller Foundation, 1937-38, to lecture on documentary films, 1953-54; Simon Senior Research Fellow, Univ. of Manchester, 1967-68; Head of Documentary at BBC Television; Producer and/or Dir: The Silent Raid (feature), Life of Adolf Hitler, World Without End (co-dir), Cradle of Genius, Cat and Mouse (feature), No Resting Place (feature), The World is Rich, The Challenge of Television (BBC), A City Speaks, Total War in Britain, Land of Promise, Children of the City, World of Plenty, Contact, To-Day We Live, Cover to Cover, The Future's in the Air, The Face of Britain, New Worlds for Old, The Fourth Estate, etc. *Publications:* The Film Till Now, 1930, new edns 1949, 1960, 1967; Celluloid; The Film To-Day, 1931; The Documentary Film, 1936, new edns 1939 and 1952; (with Roger Manvell) Movie Parade, 1936, new edn, 1950; (with E. Anstey and others) Shots in the Dark, 1951; (ed) Portrait of a Flying Yorkshireman, 1952; Television in the Making, 1956; Rotha on the Film, 1958; Letting Go, 1962; (with Basil Wright and A. Calder-Marshall) The Innocent Eye: a biography of Robert Flaherty, 1963. *Address:* c/o John Farquharson Ltd, 15 Red Lion Square, WC1.

**ROTHENSTEIN, Sir John (Knewstub Maurice),** Kt 1952; CBE 1948; PhD (London); Hon. LLD (New Brunswick; St Andrews); Director of the Tate Gallery, 1938-64; Writer; Hon. Fellow Worcester College, Oxford, 1963; Member: British Council, since 1938; Advisory Committee on Decoration of Westminster Cathedral, since 1953; Council, Friends of the Tate Gallery, since 1958; Advisory Council, Oxford Museum of Modern Art, since 1966; *b* London, 11 July 1901; *e s* of Sir William Rothenstein and Alice Mary, *e c* of Walter John Knewstub, of Chelsea; *m* 1929, Elizabeth Kennard Whittington, 2nd *d* of Charles Judson Smith, of Lexington, Kentucky; one *d. Educ:* Bedales School; Worcester College, Oxford (MA); University College, London (PhD). Assistant Professor of Art History in the University of Kentucky, 1927-28; Assistant Professor in the Department of Fine Arts, University of Pittsburgh, 1928-29; Director: City Art Gallery, Leeds, 1932-34; City Art Galleries and Ruskin Museum, Sheffield, 1933-38; Member: Executive Committee, Contemporary Art Society, 1938-65; Art Panel, Arts Council of Great Britain, 1945-52, and 1953-56. Rector, University of St Andrews, 1964-67. Vis. Prof. in Dept of Fine Arts, Fordham Univ., USA, 1967-68; Vis. Prof. of History of Art: Agnes Scott Coll., Ga, USA, 1969-70; Brooklyn Coll., City Univ., NY, 1971. Editor, The Masters, 1965-67. Knight Commander, Mexican Order of the Aztec Eagle, 1953. *Publications:* The Portrait Drawings of William Rothenstein, 1889-1925, 1926; Eric Gill, 1927; The Artist of the 1890's, 1928; Morning Sorrow: a novel, 1930; British Artists and the War, 1931; Nineteenth Century Painting, 1932; An Introduction to English Painting, 1933; The Life and Death of Conder, 1938; Augustus John (Phaidon British Artists), 1944; Edward Burra (Penguin Modern Painters), 1945; Manet, 1945; Modern Foreign Pictures in the Tate Gallery, 1949; Turner, 1949; London's River, 1951 (with Father Vincet Turner, SJ); Modern English Painters, vol. I, Sickert to Smith, 1952, vol. II, Lewis to Moore, 1956; The Tate Gallery, 1958; Turner, 1960; British Art since 1900; an Anthology, 1962; Sickert, 1961; Paul Nash, 1961; Augustus John, 1962; Matthew Smith, 1962; Turner (with Martin Butlin), 1963; Francis Bacon (with Ronald Alley), 1964; *autobiography:* Summer's Lease (I), 1965; Brave Day, Hideous Night (II), 1966; Time's Thievish Progress (III), 1970. Hon. Editor, Museums Journal, 1959-61; (ed) Sixteen Letters from Oscar Wilde, 1930. *Address:* Beauforest House, Newington, Warborough, Oxon. *T:* Warborough 482; 8 Tryon Street,

Chelsea, SW3. *T:* 01-584 7849. *Clubs:* Athenæum, Chelsea Arts (Hon. Mem.).
*See also Baron Dynevor.*

**ROTHENSTEIN, Michael;** Painter and printmaker; *b* 1908; *yr s* of late Sir William Rothenstein; *m* 1936, Betty Desmond Fitz-Gerald (marr. diss., 1957); one *s* one *d*; *m* 1958, Diana, 2nd *d* of late Comdr H. C. Arnold-Forster, CMG. Exhibitions: Redfern Gallery; Zwemmer Gallery; St George's Gallery; Hamilton Gallery; New Vision Centre; Gallery One; Grabowski Gallery. Retrospective exhibn, Kunstnernes Hus, Oslo, 1969. Works acquired by: Museum of Modern Art and Brooklyn Museum, New York; Tate Gallery; British Museum; Victoria and Albert Museum; Library of Congress, Washington; British Council; Arts Council; museums of: Sydney; Victoria; Dallas; Boston; Cincinnati; Lugano; etc. Exhibited: São Paulo Biennial, 1951; Xylon, Zürich, 1956, 1960; Cincinnati Biennial, 1954, 1960; Ljublyana Biennial of Graphic Art, 1957, 1961, 1963; Albertina, Vienna (Prints), 1963; Internat. Triennale, Grechen, 1961, 1964, 1967; 8th Internat. Exhibition, Lugano; 4th Internat. Print Exhibn, Tokyo, 1966; Trust House Award, 1963; Gold Medal, first internat. Engraving Biennale, Buenos Aires. *Publications:* Frontiers of Printmaking, 1966; Relief Printing, 1970. *Address:* Columbia House, Stisted, Braintree, Essex. *T:* Braintree 25444.

**ROTHERHAM, Air Vice-Marshal John Kevitt,** CB 1962; CBE 1960; Director-General (Engineering), RAF, 1967-69; retired; *b* 28 Dec. 1910; *s* of Colonel Ewan Rotherham; *m* 1st, 1936, Joan Catherine Penrose (*d* 1940); one *d*; 2nd, 1941, Margot Susan Hayter. *Educ:* Uppingham; Exeter College, Oxford. Joined RAF with Univ. perm. commn, 1933; 17 (F) Squdn, 1934; 605 (B) Sqdn, 1936; School of Aeronautical Engineering, Henlow, 1936; post-grad. course, Imperial Coll., 1938; 43 (M) Group, 1939; Kidbrooke, 1940; MAP 1941; 41 (M) Group, 1942; HQ Flying Training Comd, 1946; exchange posting with USAF, 1947; Air Ministry, 1948; Joint Services Staff Coll., 1951; No 205 Group, Middle East, 1952; Air Ministry, 1954; seconded to Pakistan Air Force, 1957; Senior Technical Staff Officer, Transport Command, RAF, 1960-63; AOC No 24 (Training) Group, Technical Training Command, RAF, 1963-65; Senior Tech. Staff Officer, Bomber Command, 1965-67. AFRAeS 1949, FRAeS 1967. *Recreations:* sailing, ski-ing, golf. *Address:* Hiltons, Golf Links Road, Ferndown, Dorset. *Clubs:* Royal Air Force; Royal Motor Yacht; Parkstone Yacht.
*See also R. J. S. McDowall.*

**ROTHERHAM, Leonard,** CBE 1970; DSc; FRS 1963; CEng, FIEE, FInstF, FIM, FInstP; Vice-Chancellor, Bath University of Technology, since 1969; *b* 31 Aug. 1913; *m* 1937, Nora Mary Thompson; one *s* two *d*. *Educ:* Strutt School, Belper; University College, London. Physicist, Brown Firth Research Laboratories, 1935-46; Head of Metallurgy Dept, RAE Farnborough, 1946-50; Dir, R&D, UKAEA, Industrial Group, Risley, 1950-58. Mem. for Research, Central Electricity Generating Bd, 1958-69; Head of Research, Electricity Supply Industry and Electricity Council, 1965-69. Chm., Adv. Cttee for Scientific and Technical Information, 1970-. Mem., Central Adv. Council for Science and Technology, 1968-. Fellow UCL, 1959; Hon. Fellow, Inst. of Welding, 1965; Hon. Life Mem., American Society of Mechanical Engineers, 1963; President, Instn of Metallurgists, 1964; Inst. of Metals, 1965; Member of Council, Royal Society, 1965-66. *Publications:* Creep of Metals, 1951; various scientific and technical papers; also lectures: Hatfield Memorial, 1961; Coal Science, 1961; Calvin Rice (of Amer. Soc. of Mech. Engrs), 1963; 2nd Metallurgical Engineering, Inst. of Metals, 1963. *Address:* Bath University of Technology, Bath, Somerset. *Club:* Athenæum.

**ROTHERMERE,** 2nd Viscount, *cr* 1919, of Hemsted; **Esmond Cecil Harmsworth,** Baron, *cr* 1914; Bt *cr* 1910; Chairman: Daily Mail and General Trust Ltd; Associated Newspapers Ltd; *b* 29 May 1898; *o surv s* of 1st Viscount and Mary Lilian (*d* 1937), *d* of George Wade Share; *S* father, 1940; *m* 1st, 1920, Margaret Hunam (from whom he obtained a divorce, 1938), *d* of late William Redhead; one *s* two *d*; 2nd, 1945, Lady O'Neill (marr. diss., 1952; she *m* 1952, late Ian L. Fleming), *widow* of 3rd Baron O'Neill and *e d* of Hon. Guy Charteris; 3rd, 1966, Mrs Mary Ohrstrom, *d* of Kenneth Murchison, Dallas, Texas; one *s*. *Educ:* Eton. Commission in Royal Marine Artillery, 1917; ADC to Prime Minister in Paris (Peace Conference), 1919; MP (U) Isle of Thanet, 1919-29. Mem., Adv. Council, Min. of Information, 1939; Chm., Newspaper Proprietors Assoc., 1934-61. Chancellor, Newfoundland Univ., 1952-61. DCL Bishop's University, PQ, 1954. *Recreations:* tennis and racquets. *Heir:* *s* Hon. Vere Harold Esmond Harmsworth [*b* 27 Aug. 1925; *m* 1957, Mrs Patricia Evelyn Beverley Brooks, *d* of John William Matthews; one *s* two *d*]. *Address:* Warwick House, St James's, SW1. *Clubs:* Buck's, White's.
*See also Sir Neill Cooper-Key, Earl of Cromer.*

**ROTHERWICK,** 2nd Baron *cr* 1939; **Herbert Robin Cayzer;** Bt 1924; *b* 5 Dec. 1912; *s* of 1st Baron Rotherwick; *S* father 1958; *m* 1952, Sarah-Jane, *o d* of Sir Michael Nial Slade, 6th Bt; three *s* one *d*. *Educ:* Eton; Christ Church, Oxford (BA). Supplementary Reserve Royal Scots Greys, 1938; served War of 1939-45 with them in Middle East. Deputy Chairman British & Commonwealth Shipping Co. Ltd, and Director of other and associated companies. *Heir:* *s* Hon. (Herbert) Robin Cayzer, *b* 12 March 1954. *Address:* Cornbury Park, Charlbury, Oxfordshire. *T:* Charlbury 311; Lanfine, Newmilns, Ayrshire; 51 Eaton Square, SW1. *Club:* Turf.

**ROTHERY, William H.;** *see* Hume-Rothery.

**ROTHES,** 20th Earl of, *cr* before 1457; **Malcolm George Dyer-Edwardes Leslie;** Baron Leslie and Ballenbreich, 1457; Representative Peer for Scotland, 1931-59; Deputy Chairman, British Electric Traction Co. Ltd; Chairman, National Mutual Life Assurance Society; Director, Omnium Investment Co. Ltd; *b* 8 Feb. 1902; *e s* of 19th Earl and Noel Lucy Martha (*d* 1956) (who *m* 2nd, 1927, Col Claud Macfie, DSO, *d* 1963), *d* of T. Dyer Edwardes, Prinknash Park, Gloucester; *S* father, 1927; *m* 1926, Beryl, *o d* of J. Lionel Dugdale, of Crathorne Hall, Crathorne, Yorks; one *s* two *d*. *Educ:* Eton. Member of Royal Coy of Archers (Queen's Body Guard for Scotland); 2nd Lt (General List), 1939–Major (General List), 1941. Director of Tyres, Ministry of Supply, 1942-45. *Heir:* *s* Lord Leslie, *qv*. *Address:* Strawberry House, Chiswick Mall, W4. *Club:* Travellers'.
*See also Hon. John W. Leslie.*

**ROTHMAN, Sydney;** Chairman of Rothmans Tobacco (Holdings) Ltd since 1953, and Director of sundry related companies (Chairman and Managing Director Rothmans Ltd 1929-53); *b* 2 December 1897; *s* of Louis and Jane Rothman; *m* 1929, Jeannette Tropp; one *s* one *d*. *Educ:* Highgate School. Joined L.

Rothman & Company, 1919, Partner, 1923, Rothmans Ltd. Ministry of Supply, 1941-45. *Recreation:* golf. *Address:* 33 Bryanston Square, W1. *Clubs:* Royal Automobile; Ham Manor (Angmering).

**ROTHNIE, Alan Keir,** CMG 1967; HM Diplomatic Service; Consul-General, Chicago, since 1969; *b* 2 May 1920; *s* of late John and Dora Rothnie, Aberdeen; *m* 1953, Anne Cadogan Harris, *d* of Euan Cadogan Harris, *qv*; two *s* one *d*. *Educ:* Montrose Acad.; St Andrews University. Served RNVR, 1939-45. Entered Diplomatic Service, Nov. 1945; Foreign Office, 1945-46; 3rd Sec., HM Legation, Vienna, 1946-48; 2nd Sec., HM Embassy, Bangkok, 1949-50; FO 1951-53; 1st Sec. HM Embassy, Madrid, 1953-55; Asst Political Agent, Kuwait, 1956-58; FO, 1958-60; Middle East Centre for Arab Studies, Shemlan, 1960-62 (Chargé d'Affaires, HM Embassy, Kuwait, 1961); Commercial Counsellor: HM Embassy, Baghdad, 1963-64; HM Embassy, Moscow, 1965-68. *Recreations:* cricket, lawn tennis, ski-ing. *Address:* 6 Newlands Road, Rottingdean, Sussex BN2 7GD. *T:* Brighton 32598; British Consulate General, 33 North Dearborn Street, Chicago, Illinois 60602, USA. *Clubs:* White's, MCC.

**ROTHSCHILD,** family name of **Baron Rothschild.**

**ROTHSCHILD,** 3rd Baron, *cr* 1885; **Nathaniel Mayer Victor Rothschild;** Bt 1846; GM 1944; FRS 1953; PhD; ScD; Head of Central Policy Review Staff in the Cabinet Office, since 1970; *b* 31 Oct. 1910; *s* of late Hon. (Nathaniel) Charles Rothschild, 2nd *s* of 1st Baron Rothschild; *S* uncle, 1937; *m* 1st, 1933, Barbara (divorced, 1946), *o d* of late St John Hutchinson, KC; one *s* two *d*; 2nd, 1946, Teresa, MBE, MA, JP, *d* of late R. J. G. Mayor, CB; one *s* two *d* (and one *s* decd). *Educ:* Harrow, Trinity Coll., Cambridge. Fellow of Trinity Coll., Cambridge, 1935-39, Hon. Fellow, 1961. War of 1939-45: Military Intelligence (despatches, American Legion of Merit, American Bronze Star). Director, BOAC, 1946-48; Assistant Dir of Research, Dept of Zoology, Cambridge, 1950-70; Vice-Chm., Shell Research Ltd, 1961-63, Chm., 1963-70; Chm., Shell Research NV, 1967-70; Director: Shell Internationale Research MIJ, 1965-70; Shell Chemicals UK Ltd, 1963-70; Shell International Gas, 1969-70; Research Co-ordinator, Royal Dutch Shell Group, 1965-70. Member: BBC General Advisory Council, 1952-56; Council for Scientific Policy, 1965-67; Central Adv. Council for Science and Technology, 1969-; Chairman, Agricultural Research Council, 1948-58. Hon. Fellow: Bellairs Research Inst. of McGill Univ., Barbados, 1960; Weizmann Inst. of Science, Rehovoth, 1962; University Coll., Cambridge, 1966. Hon. DSc: Newcastle, 1964; Manchester, 1966; Technion, Haifa, 1968. *Publications:* Scientific papers; Fertilization; A Classification of Living Animals. *Heir: s* Hon. (Nathaniel Charles) Jacob Rothschild, [*b* 29 April 1936; *m* 1961, Serena, *er d* of Sir Philip Dunn, *qv*; three *d*]. *Address:* 11 Herschel Road, Cambridge.

*See also Hon. M. Rothschild.*

**ROTHSCHILD, Edmund Leopold de,** TD; Senior Partner, N. M. Rothschild & Sons, since 1960 (Partner since 1946); *b* 2 Jan. 1916; *s* of Lionel Nathan de Rothschild and Marie Louise Beer; *m* 1948, Elizabeth Edith Lentner; two *s* two *d*. *Educ:* Harrow Sch.; Trinity Coll., Cambridge. Major, RA (TA). Served France, North Africa and Italy, 1939-46 (wounded). Dep. Chairman: Brit. Newfoundland Corp. Ltd, 1963-69; Churchill Falls (Labrador) Corp. Ltd, 1966-69. Trustee, Queen's Inst. of Dist. Nursing; Mem. Council, Royal Nat. Pension Fund for Nurses; Pres., Assoc. of Jewish Ex-Servicemen and Women; Jt Treasurer: Council of Christians and Jews; Friends of the Hebrew Univ. of Jerusalem. Hon. LLD, Memorial Univ. of Newfoundland, 1961. *Publication:* Window on the World, 1949. *Recreations:* gardening, fishing, shooting, cine-photography, hunting butterflies. *Address:* Inchmery House, Exbury, Southampton SO4 1AE. *T:* Blackfield 3345. *Clubs:* White's, St James'; United Services (Montreal). *See also L. D. de Rothschild.*

**ROTHSCHILD, Baron Guy (Edouard Alphonse Paul) de;** Officier de la Légion d'Honneur, 1959; Officier de l'Ordre du Mérite National Mauritanien, 1963; President: Banque Rothschild, since 1968; Société Minière et Métallurgique de Penarroya, since 1964; Five Arrows Securities; Second Continuation Ltd; Partner, N. M. Rothschild & Sons; Director: Francarep; Le Nickel; SAGA; Rothschild Intercontinental Bank Ltd; New Court Securities Corp.; Franco-Britannique de Participations; European Property Co Ltd; Femmes d'Aujourd'hui; Rio Tinto-Zinc Corp. Ltd; Compagnie du Nord (President, Executive Committee); *b* 21 May 1909; *s* of late Baron Edouard de Rothschild and of the Baronne de Rothschild (*née* Germaine Halphen); *m* 1st, 1937, Baronne Alix Schey de Koromla (marriage dissolved, 1956); one *s*; 2nd, 1957, Baronne Marie-Hélène de Zuylen de Nyevelt (who *m* 1st, Comte François de Nicolay; one *s* and one step *s*. *Educ:* Lycées Condorcet et Louis le Grand, Facultés de Droit et des Lettres (Licencié en Droit). Served War of 1939-45 (Croix de Guerre). Chevalier du Mérite Agricole, 1948. Associé de MM de Rothschild Frères, 1936-67; Pres., Compagnie du Chemin de Fer du Nord, 1949-68. Pres., Fonds Social Juif Unifié. Mem., Société d'Encouragement. *Recreation:* haras et écurie de courses, golf. *Address:* 10 rue de Courcelles, Paris 8, France. *Clubs:* Nouveau Cercle, Automobile Club de France, Cercle Interallié.

**ROTHSCHILD, Leopold David de;** Partner, N. M. Rothschild & Sons, since 1956; *b* 12 May 1927; *yr s* of Lionel de Rothschild and Marie Louise Beer. *Educ:* Lockers Park; Bishops Coll. Sch., Canada; Harrow; Trinity Coll., Cambridge. Chm., Rothschild Intercontinental Bank Ltd, 1969; Director of Bank of England, 1970. Chm., Latin American Section, London Chamber of Commerce, 1968. Chm., English Chamber Orchestra and Music Soc. Ltd, 1963; Director of Sadlers Wells Trust. *Recreations:* music, sailing. *Address:* New Court, St Swithin's Lane, EC4. *T:* 01-626 4356. *Clubs:* Brooks's; Royal Yacht Squadron.

*See also E. L. de Rothschild.*

**ROTHSCHILD, Hon. Miriam, (Hon. Mrs Miriam Lane);** *b* 5 Aug. 1908; *e d* of Hon. N. C. Rothschild and Rozsika de Wertheimstein; *m* 1943, Capt. George Lane, MC (marriage dissolved, 1957); one *s* three *d* (and one *s* one *d* decd). *Educ:* home. Member: Zoological and Entomological Research Coun.; Marine Biological Assoc.; Royal Entomological Soc.; Systematics Assoc.; Soc. for Promotion of Nature Reserves, etc.; Ed., Novitates Zoologica, 1938-41; Mem., Publications Cttee, Zoological Soc.; Foreign Office, 1940-42; Trustee, British Museum of Natural History, 1967. Hon. Fellow, St Hugh's Coll., Oxford. Hon. DSc, Oxford. Defence Medal (1940-45). *Publications:* Catalogue Rothschild Collection of Fleas (5 vols), British Museum; (with Theresa Clay) Fleas, Flukes and

Cuckoos; numerous contribs to scientific jls. *Recreations:* riding, ski-ing, squash rackets, tennis, shooting. *Address:* Ashton, Peterborough, Northants. *Clubs:* Queen's, British Ornithological, Entomological.

*See also Baron Rothschild.*

**ROTHWELL, Harry,** BA, PhD Cantab; Professor of History, University of Southampton (formerly Hartley University College), 1945-68; Emeritus, 1968; Dean of the Faculty of Arts, 1949-52; Vice-President, Historical Association; *b* 8 September 1902; *s* of Harry Rothwell and Emma Watson; *m* 1935, Martha Annabella Goedecke; two *d. Educ:* Barnsley Grammar School; Manchester University; St John's College, Cambridge. 1st Class Hons in History, Prizeman and Faulkner Fellow, Manchester, 1925; Mullinger Schol., St John's Coll., Cambridge, 1925-28; Senior Asst to Keeper of Western Manuscripts, Bodleian Library, 1928-29; Lectr in Medieval History, Univ. of Toronto, Toronto, 1929-31; Lecturer in Medieval and European History, Edinburgh Univ., 1931-45; Lieut (Sp) RNVR and Director of Naval Studies, Edinburgh Univ., 1942-45. Past Pres., Hampshire Field Club and Archæological Soc. *Publications:* The Chronicle of Walter of Guisborough, 1957, articles and reviews in professional journals. *Address:* Hill House, Knapp, Ampfield, Nr Romsey, Hants. *T:* Braishfield 666.

**ROUGHTON, Francis John Worsley,** FRS 1936; MA, PhD (Cambridge); Fellow (since 1923) and Lecturer (1929-47) of Trinity College, Cambridge; John Humphrey Professor of Colloid Science in the University of Cambridge, 1947-66, Emeritus Professor, 1966; *b* 6 June 1899; *s* of John Paul Roughton, MRCS, LRCP, JP, and Caroline Margaret Worsley; *m* 1925, Alice Isabella, *e d* of late Prof. B. Hopkinson, CMG, FRS; one *s* one *d. Educ:* Winchester College (Scholar); Trinity College, Cambridge (Scholar). 1st Class Nat. Sci. Tripos Part I, 1919 BA (Cantab) 1920, Michael Foster Student 1921, George Henry Lewes Student 1921, Gedge Prize 1922, Dunn Lecturer in Bio-Chemistry (Cambridge) 1923. Rolleston Prize (Oxford), 1924; Lecturer in Physico-Chemical Physiology (Cambridge), 1927; Visiting Research Fellow in War Science and Medicine at Harvard and Columbia Univs, 1942-45. Rockefeller travelling fellow in USA, 1929; Harvey Lectr, New York, 1943; Hanna Lectr, Western Reserve Univ., 1944; Norman Bauer Lectr, Logan Univ., Utah, 1962; Vis. Prof. at Univ. of Calif. and Pennsylvania, 1967. Secretary of Physiology Section of British Association, 1931-34; formerly Director of Hopkinson House Ltd and Vincent House Ltd; Mem. Cttee of Vincent Housing Assoc. Co-editor of Biochemical Journal, 1935-41. Hon. Member: New York Acad. of Sciences; Amer. Physiological Soc.; British Gelatine and Glue Research Assoc.; Royal Danish Acad. of Sciences and Letters. Hopkins Memorial Medal, Biochemical Soc., 1969. *Publications:* Papers in Scientific Journals on Physiological, Biochemical and Physico-Chemical Subjects (especially on the Chemistry of Respiration). *Recreations:* walking, biography, genealogy, family history and fiction. *Address:* Ellerslie, 9 Adams Road, Cambridge. *T:* Cambridge 53890.

*See also Rev. A. R. Woolley.*

**ROUGIER, George Ronald,** CBE 1967; QC 1959; Barrister-at-Law; Chairman, Cambridgeshire and Isle of Ely QS, since 1965; Deputy Chairman, Essex QS, since 1963; *b* 6 June 1900; 2nd *s* of Charles Joseph Rougier, Odessa, and Jean Crookston; *m* 1925, Georgette Heyer, *qv*; one *s. Educ:* RNC Osborne and Dartmouth; Marlborough Coll.; Roy. Sch. of Mines. Entered Navy as Cadet, 1913; Marlborough, 1915. Mining Engineer, 1922-31. Called to Bar, 1939; Bencher of the Inner Temple, 1966; retired from the Bar, 1968. Chm., General Optical Council, 1961. *Recreations:* golf, bridge. *Address:* Flat 4, 60 Jermyn Street, SW1. *Club:* Garrick.

**ROULLIER, Jean Georges,** Commander Legion of Honour, 1958; Chairman, Merchant Navy Social Institutions in France, since 1968; *b* 10 Dec. 1898; *s* of Jean-Baptiste Victor Roullier and Marie-Eugénie Vacher; *m* 1930, Marie-Louise Jeanne Sevestre; two *s* two *d. Educ:* Lycée Henri IV, Paris; Facultés des Lettres et de Droit, Paris (Licencié). Sec. Gen. Dept of Wartime Shipping, France, 1940; Director, Min. of Merchant Marine, 1950-63; Vice-Chm., Higher Council of Merchant Marine, 1950-63; Chairman, Council of Intergovernmental Maritime Consultative Organization, 1959-63, Sec.-Gen., 1963-67. *Publication:* Les Transports Maritimes de la France en Guerre, 1945. *Address:* Place du Jeu de Paume, 91 Dourdan, France. *T:* 492-77-82.

**ROULSTON, Air Commodore Jack Fendick,** CBE 1945; DSO 1943; DFC 1940; RAF; *b* 14 Jan. 1913; *s* of H. E. Roulston, Summerstrand, Port Elizabeth, S Africa; *m* 1939, Joan Redmayne, *o d* of J. A. Carman, MD, Nairobi, Kenya; two *s* one *d. Educ:* Queen's Coll. and Univ. of Capetown, SA. Commissioned in RAF, 1936; Squadron Leader comdg 223 Sqdn, 1940; Wing Commander comdg 55 Sqdn, 1942; Group Captain comdg 232 Wing, 1943; RAF Staff College, 1946; Group Capt. Opns Far East Air Force, 1952; RAF Flying College, 1954; Directorate of Operational Requirements, Air Ministry, 1955; Commander Air Task Group, Task Force Grapple, 1958-60; Commandant the Aeroplane and Armament Experimental Establishment, Boscombe Down, Wilts, 1960-65, retd. *Recreations:* golf, shooting, fishing. *Address:* Chilmark, near Salisbury, Wilts. *T:* Teffont 384. *Club:* Royal Air Force.

**ROUPELL, Brigadier George Rowland Patrick,** VC 1915; CB 1956; DL; Colonel, The East Surrey Regiment, 1954-59; *b* 7 April 1892; *s* of late Col F. F. Rouppell, CO of 1st East Surrey Regt; *m* 1921, Doris Phoebe (*d* 1958), twin *d* of late Capt. Mowbray L. Sant; one *s* one *d*; 2nd, 1959, Mrs Rachel Kennedy, *d* of late R. A. Bruce, Yeovil, Somerset. *Educ:* Rossall; Sandhurst. Entered army, 1912; Major, 1928; Lieutenant-Colonel, 1935; Colonel, 1939; served European War, 1914-18 (despatches thrice, wounded twice, VC, French Croix de Guerre, Order of St George, 4th Class); North Russia, 1919; General Staff Officer, 2nd grade, Royal Military Coll., Kingston, Canada, 1929-31; Commanded Depot, The East Surrey Regt, Kingston-on-Thames; GSO 2nd Grade, China Command, 1934-35; commanded 1st Batt. The East Surrey Regt, 1935-39; served War of 1939-45; commanded 36 Inf. Bde and 105 Inf. Bde; retired pay, 1946; psc 1922. DL Surrey, 1953. Member of Order of St George, 4th Class (Russian). *Address:* Little Chartham, Shalford, Surrey. *T:* Guildford 62429. *Club:* Army and Navy.

**ROUS,** family name of **Earl of Stradbroke.**

**ROUS, Sir Stanley (Ford),** Kt, *cr* 1949; CBE 1943; JP; Secretary of the Football Association, 1934-61 (now Hon. Vice-President); President Fédération Internationale de Football Association, since Sept. 1961; *b* 25 April 1895; *s* of George Samuel and Alice Rous; *m* 1924, Adrienne Gacon (*d* 1950). *Educ:* Sir John Leman School, Beccles; St Luke's College, Exeter. Served European

War, 1914-18, in France and Palestine, 272nd Brigade RFA (East Anglian); Assistant Master, Watford Grammar School, 1921-34; Member Paddington Borough Council, 1943-47; Past Pres. Paddington and Marylebone Rotary Club: Chairman Central Council for Physical Recreation. JP Paddington Div., 1950. Mem. King George's Jubilee Trust, King George VI Foundation. Chm., Arts Educ. Trust; Governor, St Luke's Coll., Exeter, Dir, Humphries Holdings Ltd; Mem., BBC Adv. Council. Liveryman Worshipful Co. of Loriners. Chevalier de l'Ordre Grand-Ducal de la Couronne de Chêne de Luxembourg; Chevalier de la Légion d'Honneur; Commendatore, Ordine Al Merito della Repubblica Italiana; Commander, Order of Ouissam Alaouite (Morocco), 1968. *Publications:* (jtly) The Football Association Coaching Manual; Recreative Physical Exercises and Activities for Association Football and other Games Players. *Recreation:* tennis. *Address:* 115 Ladbroke Road, W11. *T:* 01-727 4113. *Clubs:* Royal Automobile, MCC; All England Lawn Tennis and Croquet, Hurlingham.

**ROUSE, Sir Anthony (Gerald Roderick),** KCMG 1969 (CMG 1961); OBE 1945; British Consul-General in New York since 1966; *b* 9 April 1911; *s* of late Lt-Col Maxwell Rouse and of Mrs Rouse, Eastbourne; *m* 1935, Beatrice Catherine Ellis. *Educ:* Harrow; Heidelberg Univ. Joined HAC 1935; RA (T) 1938; 2 Lt 1940; transf. to Intelligence Corps; served MEF and CMF on staff of 3rd Corps (commendation); Lt-Col 1944. Entered Foreign Service, 1946; First Secretary (Information), Athens, 1946; Foreign Office, 1949. British Embassy, Moscow, 1952-54; Counsellor, 1955; Office of UK High Commissioner, Canberra, 1955-57; HM Inspector of Foreign Service Establishments, 1957-59; Counsellor (Information) British Embassy, Bonn, 1959-62; British Deputy Commandant, Berlin, 1962-64; HM Minister, British Embassy, Rome, 1964-66. *Address:* c/o Foreign and Commonwealth Office, SW1. *Club:* United Service.

**ROUSE, Arthur Frederick,** CMG 1949; *b* 25 Sept. 1910; *s* of late G. A. Rouse, Reading; *m* 1937, Helena, *y d* of late Rev. L. Klamborowski, Clare, Suffolk. *Educ:* Reading School; St John's College, Oxford. White Scholar of St John's, 1928; 1st Cl. Hons Classical Moderations, 1929; 2nd Cl. Literae Humaniores, 1932. Assistant Master Edinburgh Academy, 1932; entered Home Civil Service by competitive exam. starting as Asst Principal in Ministry of Labour, 1933; Private Sec. to Parl. Secretary, 1936-38; accompanied British Delegation to Internat. Labour Conf., 1936-37; Principal, Ministry of Labour, 1938, Asst Secretary, 1944; Dep. Chief, Manpower Division, CCG (British Element), 1945-46; UK Govt Rep. on various Internat. Cttees, 1946-49, including OEEC Manpower Cttee, Chairman of ILO European Manpower Cttee; Special Asst on Manpower to Dir-Gen. of ILO, 1949-50; Head of Latin American Immigration Field Office of ILO, 1950-51; Chairman of Beatrice Intensive Conservative Area Cttee, 1956; Senior Research Fellow, Univ. Coll. of Rhodesia and Nyasaland, 1957-62; Chairman, Wages Advisory Board for Nyasaland, 1960-62. Public administration and industrial consultant. *Recreations:* farming and travel. *Address:* Alicedale Farm, Beatrice, Rhodesia.

**ROUSE, E(dward) Clive,** MBE 1946; Medieval Archæologist; Specialist in Mural and Panel Paintings; Lecturer; *b* 15 October 1901; *s* of late Edward Foxwell Rouse (Stroud, Gloucestershire and Acton, Middlesex) and late Frances Sarah Rouse (*née* Sams). *Educ:* Gresham's School; St Martin's School of Art. On leaving school studied art and medieval antiquities, 1920-21; FSA London, 1937 (Mem. of Coun., 1943-44); FRSA 1968. President: Royal Archæological Institute, 1969 (Vice-Pres., 1965); Bucks Archaeological Soc., 1969. Liveryman, Fishmongers' Company, 1962. Hon. MA Oxon 1969. Served War of 1939-45, RAFVR (Intelligence); Flight-Lt, 1941-45; MBE for special services at Central Interpretation Unit, Medmenham. *Publications:* The Old Towns of England, 1936 (twice reprinted); Discovering Wall Paintings, 1968; (jointly) Guide to Buckinghamshire, 1935; contributor to: The Beauty of Britain, 1935; Collins' Guide to English Parish Churches, 1958. Papers in Archæologia, Antiquaries' Journal, Archæological Journal, and publications of many County Archæological Societies. *Recreation:* travel. *Address:* Oakfield, North Park, Gerrards Cross, Bucks. *T:* Gerrards Cross 82595.

**ROUTH, Augustus Crosbie;** *b* 7 Aug. 1892; *s* of late Augustus Routh, Manager of Imperial Ottoman Bank, Salonica; *m* 1917, Ethel Madeleine Martin, The Steyne, Worthing; one *d* (and one *s* killed in action, 1941, one *d* decd). *Educ:* abroad; Edinburgh; LSE, London. Shipping Clerk, Consulate-General, Smyrna, 1910, Chief Clerk, 1920; General Consular Service, 1920; Acting Consul-General, Marseilles, Strasbourg, Milan, Genoa, and Monrovia at various dates: Consul at Istanbul, 1934; Actg Consul-Gen., Tripoli, 1935; Consul at Benghazi, 1936; Actg Consul-General, Marseilles, 1937; re-appointed Consul at Istanbul, 1938; Acting Consul-General, Antwerp, 1940; Chargé d'Affaires and Consul-General, Monrovia, Liberia, 1941; promoted Consul-General at Nice, France, 1944; HM Minister, Haiti, 1946-50; retired, 1950. Coronation Medal, 1937. *Address:* 16 Hailsham Road, Worthing, Sussex. *T:* Worthing 49250.

**ROUTLEDGE, Alan;** Deputy Head, Communications Department, Foreign and Commonwealth Office (formerly Foreign Office), and Head, Cypher and Signals Branch, Diplomatic Wireless Service, since 1967; *b* 12 May 1919; *s* of George and Rose Routledge, Wallasey, Cheshire; *m* 1949, Irene Hendry, Falkirk, Stirlingshire; one *s* (and one *s* decd). *Educ:* Liscard High Sch., Wallasey. Served Army, Cheshire (Earl of Chester's) Yeomanry, 1939-46. Control Commn for Germany, 1946-51; Diplomatic Wireless Service of FO (now Foreign and Commonwealth Office), 1951-. *Recreations:* cricket, golf, English history. *Address:* 10 St Margaret's Close, Orpington, Kent. *T:* Orpington 23900. *Clubs:* Civil Service; Knoll Country (Orpington).

**ROW, Commander Sir Philip (John),** KCVO 1969 (CVO 1965; MVO 1958); OBE 1944; RN Retired; an Extra Equerry to the Queen since 1969; Deputy Treasurer to the Queen, 1958-68. *Address:* Clare Lodge, Ewshot, Farnham, Surrey.

**ROWALLAN,** 2nd Baron, *cr* 1911; **Thomas Godfrey Polson Corbett,** KT 1957; KBE 1951; MC; TD; DL; Lieutenant-Colonel (retired) Royal Scots Fusiliers; *b* 19 Dec. 1895; *o surv s* of 1st Baron and Alice Mary (*d* 1902), *o d* of John Polson, of Castle Levan, Gourock; *S* father, 1933; *m* 1918, Gwyn Mervyn, *d* of J. B. Grimond, St Andrews; four *s* (and one killed in action, 1944) one *d. Educ:* Eton. Served European War, 1914-18: Gallipoli, Egypt, Palestine and France (wounded, MC); also France, 1940, comdg a Bn of Royal Scots

Fusiliers; retired 1944. Chief Scout British Commonwealth and Empire, 1945-59. Governor, National Bank of Scotland, 1951-59; Governor of Tasmania, 1959 until April 1963. Hon. Col Roy. Tasmania Regt, 1961-63. Mem., The Pilgrims Soc. Hon. LLD, McGill Univ., 1948, Glasgow Univ., 1952, Birmingham Univ., 1957. Freeman of the City of Edinburgh, 1957. KStJ, 1959. *Heir: s* Captain Hon. Arthur Cameron Corbett, Royal Artillery; TA [*b* 17 Dec. 1919; *m* 1945, Eleanor Mary (marriage dissolved, 1962), *o d* of late Capt. George Boyle, The Royal Scots Fusiliers; one *s* three *d. Educ:* Eton]. *Address:* Rowallan, Kilmarnock, Scotland. *Club:* Brooks's.

**ROWAN, Carl T.;** Syndicated columnist, correspondent, Chicago Daily News; radio and TV commentator, Post-Newsweek Broadcasting; Roving Editor, Reader's Digest; *b* 11 August 1925; *s* of Thomas D. and Johnnie B. Rowan; *m* 1950, Vivien Murphy; two *s* one *d. Educ:* Tennessee State University; Washburn University; Oberlin Coll.; University of Minnesota. Mem. Staff of Minneapolis Tribune, 1948-61; Dept of State, 1961-63; US Ambassador to Finland, 1963-64; Director, United States Information Agency, Washington, DC, 1964-65. Hon. DLitt: Simpson Coll., 1957; Hamline Univ., 1958; Oberlin Coll., 1962; Dr of Humane Letters: Washburn Univ., 1964; Talladega Coll., 1965; St Olaf Coll., 1966; Knoxville Coll., 1966; Dr of Laws: Howard Univ., 1964; Alfred Univ., 1964; Temple Univ., 1964; Atlanta Univ., 1965; Allegheny Coll., 1966; Dr of Public Admin., Morgan State Coll., 1964. *Publications:* South of Freedom, 1953; The Pitiful and the Proud, 1956; Go South to Sorrow, 1957; Wait Till Next Year, 1960. *Recreations:* tennis, golf and bowling, singing and dancing. *Address:* 2832 Ellicott Street North-West, Washington, DC, USA. *Clubs:* Federal City, Indian Spring, (Washington, DC).

**ROWAN, Sir Leslie;** *see* Rowan, Sir T. L.

**ROWAN, Sir (Thomas) Leslie,** KCB 1949 (CB 1946); CVO 1947; Chairman, Vickers Ltd, since 1967 (Deputy Chairman, 1966-67), and Managing Director since 1962; Director and Deputy Chairman, British Aircraft Corp., since 1962; Director: Barclays Bank Ltd; Canadian Vickers Ltd; Vickers Australia; Legal and General Assurance; President, Overseas Development Institute, since 1967 (Chairman, 1960-67); Deputy Chairman, British National Export Council; *b* 22 February 1908; *s* of Rev. Thomas Rowan, Dromore, Co. Sligo, and Hannah Josephine Birrel, Halifax, Yorks; *m* 1944, Catherine Patricia, 3rd *d* of Brig. R. H. A. D. Love; two *s* two *d. Educ:* Panchgani (India); Tonbridge; Queens' College, Cambridge (Hon Fellow, 1954). Entered Colonial Office, 1930; Treasury, 1933; Assistant Private Secretary to Chancellor of Exchequer, 1934-37; Asst and later Principal Private Secretary to Prime Minister (Mr Churchill), 1941-45, (Mr Attlee), 1945-47; Permanent Sec., Office of Minister for Economic Affairs, 1947; Second Secretary, HM Treasury, 1947-49; Economic Minister in the Embassy, Washington, 1949-51; Second Secretary, HM Treasury, 1951-58, retired. Mem., Nat. Defence Industries Council, 1969-. Captained England (1937, 1938 and 1947), Cambridge (1929 and 1930) and Civil Service at Hockey. *Publication:* contrib. to Action This Day–Working with Churchill, 1968. *Recreations:* games. *Address:* 16 The Vale, Chelsea, SW3. *T:* 01-352 2668. *Clubs:* Senior United Service; Hawks (Cambridge).

**ROWAN-LEGG, Allan Aubrey;** Agent General for Ontario in the UK since 1968; *b* 19 May 1912; *m* 1944, Daphne M. Ker; three *d.* Dir, Vice-Pres. and Gen. Sales Man., Interlake Fuel Oil Ltd, and Interlake Steel Products, 1955-57; Pres. and Dir, Superior Propane Ltd, Northern Propane Gas Co., 1957-63; Dir, Vice-Pres. and Gen. Man., Garlock of Canada Ltd, and Yale Rubber Mfg Co. of Canada Ltd, 1963-64; Regional Dir for Ont., Canadian Corp. for 1967 World Exhibn, 1964-67. Freeman of City of London, 1969. Canada Centennial Medal. *Recreations:* yachting, golfing, swimming, curling. *Address:* (office) Ontario House, 13 Charles II Street, SW1. *T:* 01-930 6404; (home) Flat 6, 12 Reeves Mews, Park Place, W1. *Clubs:* Junior Carlton, Canadian Veterans Assoc. in UK, Royal Automobile, The Pilgrims; Royal Canadian Yacht (Toronto).

**ROWBOTHAM, Edgar Stanley,** MD, MRCP, FFARCS, DA; Retired Cons. (late Senior) Anæsthetist, Royal Free Hospital, London; *b* 8 May 1890; *s* of Dr E. J. Rowbotham and Gertrude Wootton; *m* 1915, May Levesley (*d* 1969); no *c*; *m* 1969, Beatrice Mary Howard. *Educ:* King's College, London; Charing Cross Hospital. Served European War, 1914-18, RAMC (despatches twice); served 1939-44. Bronze Star US Forces, 1945. *Publications:* Anæsthesia in Operations for Goitre, 1945; numerous in medical journals. *Recreations:* golf, sailing. *Address:* Caminho Velho da Ajuda 24, Funchal, Madeira. *T:* 2 67 18.

**ROWE, Albert Percival,** CBE 1942; Medal for Merit (USA), 1946; Hon. LLD Melbourne 1955; Vice-Chancellor of the University of Adelaide, 1948-58, retired; *m* 1932, Mary Gordon Mathews. Chief Superintendent Telecommunications Research Establishment, 1938-45; Deputy Controller of Research and Development, Admiralty, 1946-47; Chairman of the Defence Advisory Committee and Defence Scientific Adviser to the Australian Government, 1947-48. Fellow, Imperial College Sci. and Tech., 1957. *Publications:* One Story of Radar, 1948; If the Gown Fits, 1960; Astronomy and Cosmology, 1968. *Address:* 6 Firs Close, College Grove, Malvern, Worcs.

**ROWE, Eric George,** CMG 1955; *b* 30 June 1904; *s* of late Ernest Kruse Rowe; *m* 1931, Gladys Ethel, *d* of late Charles Horace Rogers, ARCA. *Educ:* Chatham House School, Ramsgate; St Edmund Hall Oxford. Assistant Master, Queen Mary's Grammar School, Walsall, 1926-27. Entered Colonial Service, Tanganyika; Administrative Officer (Cadet), 1928; Asst District Officer, 1930; District Officer, 1940; Provincial Commissioner, 1948; Senior Provincial Commissioner, 1952; Minister for Local Government and Administration, Tanganyika, 1958; Supervisor, Overseas Services Courses, Oxford, 1959-69. *Publication:* paper in Ibis. *Recreation:* ornithology. *Address:* Manor Farm, East Hanney, Berks. *T:* West Hanney 229. *Club:* Royal Commonwealth Society.

**ROWE, Henry Peter;** Parliamentary Counsel since 1962; *b* 18 Aug. 1916; 3rd *s* of Dr Richard Röhr and Olga Röhr, Vienna; *m* 1947, Patricia, *yr d* of W. R. King, London; two *s* one *d. Educ:* Vienna; Gonville and Caius Coll., Cambridge. War service, Pioneer Corps, RAC, Military Govt, British Troops, Berlin, 1941-46. Called to Bar, Gray's Inn, 1947. Joined Parliamentary Counsel Office, 1947; Commonwealth Fund Travelling Fellowship in US, 1955; with Law Commn, 1966-68. *Recreations:* music, reading, walking. *Address:* 19 Paxton Gardens, Woking, Surrey. *T:* Byfleet 43816.

**ROWE, Sir Michael (Edward),** Kt 1963; CBE 1946; QC 1945; President of the Lands Tribunal, since 1966; *b* 24 December 1901; *s* of late John Tetley Rowe, Archdeacon of Rochester; *m* 1927, Elizabeth, *d* of Basil Guy, Stonaford House, Launceston; three *d. Educ:* Marlborough College; Trinity College, Cambridge (MA, LLB). Barrister, Gray's Inn, 1925; Bencher, 1945; Treasurer, 1961. 2nd Lt Queen's Roy. Regt, 1940; Staff Capt. 1941; released to become Asst Sec. War Damage Commission; Deputy Secretary, 1944-45; returned to practice, Jan. 1946; Member, General Claims Tribunal, 1946; Member of Council of Royal Institution of Chartered Surveyors, 1949-60; Member, Committee Inland Waterways, 1956-58; Deputy-Chairman Local Government Commission for England, 1958-65. Former Editor, Ryde on Rating. *Recreations:* gardening. *Address:* Hunter's End, S Chailey, Sussex.

**ROWE, Norbert Edward,** CBE 1944; CEng; FIMechE; Vice-President, Engineering De Havilland Aircraft of Canada, 1963-67, retired, 1967; *b* 18 June 1898; *s* of Harold Arthur and Jane Rowe, Plymouth, Devon; *m* 1929, Cecilia Brown; two *s* two *d. Educ:* City and Guilds (Engineering) Coll. Whitworth Exhibition, 1921; BSc Eng. London, 1st Cl. Hons, 1923; Associate of City and Guilds Institute, 1923; DIC 1924; FRAeS 1944; Air Ministry; Royal Aircraft Establishment, 1924, Junior Technical Officer, 1925; Testing Establishment, Technical Officer, 1926; Senior Technical Officer, 1937; Testing Establishment, Chief Technical Officer, 1937; Headquarters, Asst Director, 1938; Ministry of Aircraft Production Headquarters, Deputy Director, Research and Develt of Aircraft, 1940; Director of Technical Development, Ministry of Aircraft Production, 1941-45; Director-General of Technical Development, 1945-46; Controller of Research and Special Developments, British European Airways Corporation (on resignation from Civil Service), 1946-51; Technical Director Blackburn and General Aircraft Ltd, E Yorks, 1952-61; Joint Managing Director of the Blackburn Aircraft Company, 1960-61; Director, Hawker Siddeley Aviation, 1961-63. Member: Air Registration Bd, 1968; Aeronautical Research Council, 1969. Fellow Inst. Aeronautical Sciences of Amer., 1953; FCGI 1954. Pres. Royal Aeronautical Society, 1955-56, Hon. Fellow 1962. Pres. Helicopter Assoc. of GB, 1959-60. Hon. Fellow, Canadian Aerospace Inst., 1965. *Address:* 1 Potters Way, Laverstock, Salisbury, Wilts. *Clubs:* Athenæum.

**ROWE, Norman Francis;** one of the Special Commissioners of Income Tax since 1950; *b* 18 May 1908; *o s* of late Frank Rowe and Eva Eveline (*née* Metcalfe), Watford; *m* 1941, Suzanne Marian (marr. diss., 1964), *o d* of D. S. Richardson; one *s*; *m* 1965, Vittoria, *yr d* of P. Cav. Tondi. *Educ:* Sherborne. Chartered Accountant, 1931-37; Called to Bar, Lincoln's Inn, 1940; Mem. of Western Circuit. Served War of 1939-45 (despatches); RAF, 1940-45, serving in UK, Middle East, India, Burma and Ceylon; demobilised with rank of Squadron Leader. Freeman, City of London; Liveryman, Worshipful Co. of Glaziers and Painters of Glass. *Publications:* author of Schedule C and Profits Tax sections of Simon's Income Tax, 1st edn. *Recreations:* fishing, yachting. *Address:* Vittoria House, 1 Ashfield Close, Petersham, Surrey. *T:* 01-948 1807. *Clubs:* United Service, Bar Yacht, Little Ship; London Corinthian Sailing; Island Cruising (Devon).

**ROWE, Norman Lester,** FDSRCS (Eng.), FDSRCS (Edinburgh), FDSRCS (Glasgow), LRCP, MRCS, LMSSA (London), HDDRCS (Edinburgh); Consultant in Oral Surgery to: Westminster Hospital; Plastic & Oral Surgery Centre, Queen Mary's Hospital, Roehampton (Westminster Hospital Teaching Group); Eastman Dental Hospital; Hon. Consultant in Oral & Maxillo-facial Surgery, North West Surrey Group, South West Metropolitan Regional Hospital Board; Civilian Consultant to the Royal Navy and the Army; Hon. Lecturer in Oral Surgery, Institute of Dental Surgery; Recognised Teacher in Oral Surgery, University of London; Member, Board of Faculty of Dental Surgery, Royal College of Surgeons (Vice-Dean, 1967); Examiner, Royal College of Surgeons, and Royal College of Surgeons of Glasgow; *b* 15 Dec. 1915; *s* of late A. W. Rowe, OBE and of L. L. Rowe; *m* 1938, Cynthia Mary Freeman; one *s* one *d. Educ:* Malvern College; Guy's Hospital. Gen. Practice, 1937-41; Capt. RADC, 1941-46. Formerly Senior Registrar, Plastic and Jaw Injuries Unit, Hill End Hosp., St Albans, 1947, and consultant in Oral Surgery, Plastic and Oral Surgery Centre, Rooksdown House, Park Prewett, Basingstoke, 1948-59. Webb-Johnson Lectr, RCS, 1967-69. Foundn Fellow, Brit. Assoc. of Oral Surgeons, Pres., 1969-70; Fellow and Sec.-Gen., Internat. Assoc. of Oral Surgeons; Associate Mem., Brit. Assoc. of Plastic Surgeons. FRSM. *Publications:* Fractures of the Facial Skeleton (jtly), 1955, 2nd Edn, 1968. Various articles in British and Foreign Medical and Dental Jls. *Address:* Brackendale, Holly Bank Road, Hook Heath, Woking, Surrey. *T:* Woking 60008. *Club:* Royal Naval Medical.

**ROWE, Owen John Tressider,** MA; Headmaster of Epsom College, since 1970; *b* 30 July 1922; *e s* of late Harold Ridges Rowe and of Emma Eliza (*née* Matthews), Lymington, Hampshire; *m* 1946, Marcelle Ljufliny Hyde-Johnson; one *s* one *d. Educ:* King Edward VI School, Southampton; Exeter College, Oxford (Scholar, MA); 1st Cl. Hons in Classical Hon. Mods, 1942. Served War of 1939-45, Lieut in Roy. Hampshire Regt, 1942-45. 1st Cl. Hons in Lit Hum, Dec. 1947; Assistant Master: Royal Grammar School, Lancaster, 1948-50; Charterhouse, 1950-60 (Head of Classical Dept); Officer Comdg Charterhouse CCF, 1954-60; Headmaster of Giggleswick School, 1961-70. Governor, Welbeck College. *Recreation:* golf. *Address:* Epsom College, Epsom, Surrey. *T:* Epsom 23621. *Club:* Public Schools.

**ROWE, Prof. Peter Noël,** DSc (Eng), MIChemE, CEng; Ramsay Memorial Professor of Chemical Engineering, and Head of Department, University College, London, since Oct. 1965; *b* 25 Dec. 1919; *e s* of Charles Henry Rowe and Kate Winifred (*née* Storry); *m* 1952, Pauline Garmirian; two *s. Educ:* Preston Grammar Sch.; Manchester Coll. of Technology; Imperial Coll., London. Princ. Scientific Officer, AERE, Harwell, 1958-65. *Publications:* scientific articles in Trans. IChemE, Chem. Eng. Science, etc. *Address:* Pamber Green, Upper Basildon, Reading, Berks. *T:* Upper Basildon 382.

**ROWE, Peter Whitmill,** MA; Headmaster of Cranbrook School, Kent, since 1970; *b* 12 Feb. 1928; British; *s* of Gerald Whitmill Rowe, chartered accountant, one-time General Manager of Morris Commercials Co. Ltd; *m* 1952, Bridget Ann Moyle; two *s* one *d. Educ:* Bishop's Stortford College; St John's College, Cambridge. BA 1950; MA (Hons) 1956. VI Form History Master, Brentwood School, Essex, 1951-54; Senior History Master,

Repton School, Derbys, 1954-57; Headmaster of Bishop's Stortford Coll., Herts, 1957-70. JP, Bishop's Stortford, 1968-70. *Recreation:* cricket (Gentlemen of Herts). *Address:* School House, Cranbrook, Kent. *T:* Cranbrook 2163.

**ROWE, Robert Stewart,** CBE 1969; Director, Leeds City Art Gallery and Temple Newsam House, since 1958 (and also of Lotherton Hall since 1968); *b* 31 Dec. 1920; *s* of late James Stewart Rowe and of Mrs A. G. Gillespie; *m* 1953, Barbara Elizabeth Hamilton Baynes; one *s* two *d*. *Educ:* privately; Downing Coll., Cambridge; Richmond Sch. of Art. Asst Keeper of Art, Birmingham Museum and Art Gallery, 1950-56; Dep. Dir, Manchester City Art Galls, 1956-58. *Publications:* Adam Silver, 1965; articles in Burlington Magazine, Museums Jl, etc. *Recreations:* gardening, walking, reading. *Address:* Grove Lodge, Shadwell, Leeds 17. *T:* Leeds 656365.

**ROWELL, Sir Andrew (Herrick),** Kt 1948; MA, FIA; retired as Director of Clerical, Medical and General Life Assurance Society (Deputy Chairman, 1955-66); *b* 12 March 1890; *s* of Jabez Rowell and Eliza Tooke; *m* 1922, Olive Gwendoline Bessie Coles (*d* 1956); one *s* one *d*. *Educ:* Wellingborough Sch.; St John's Coll., Cambridge. Served European War, 1915-18; Fellow of the Institute of Actuaries, 1922; President, 1946-48. *Address:* Calumet, Beaconsfield, Bucks. *T:* Beaconsfield 3329.

**ROWELL, Sir (Herbert Babington) Robin,** Kt, *cr* 1952; CBE 1948; AFC 1918; DL 1944, Co. Durham; late of R. & W. Hawthorn, Leslie & Co. Ltd, Hebburn-on-Tyne, (Director 1929, Chairman, 1943-65); *b* 28 May 1894; *s* of late Sir Herbert Babington Rowell, KBE, The Manor House, Newcastle on Tyne, and late Lady Mary Dobree Rowell, Redesmouth House, Bellingham, Northumberland; *m* 1924, Hilda, *d* of Oswald Dobell, Neston, Cheshire; two *d*. *Educ:* Repton. Served European War, 1914-18, with RE, RFC and RAF, 1914-19; Capt. 1916; retd 1920. Chm. of Council, British Shipbuilding Research Assoc., 1951-52; Vice-President Institution of Naval Architects; President: Shipbuilding Conference, 1948; Shipbuilding Employers' Federation, 1941-42; North East Coast Institution of Engineers and Shipbuilders, 1946-48; Chairman Tyne Shipbuilders Association, 1942-47. Hon. DSc Dunelm. *Recreations:* shooting, golf. *Address:* Wylam Cottage, Wylam, Northumberland. *T:* Wylam 2207.

**ROWELL, Sir Robin;** *see* Rowell, Sir H. B. R.

**ROWELL, Lieut-Gen. Sir Sydney Fairbairn,** KBE, *cr* 1953 (CBE 1941); CB 1946; retired; *b* 15 December 1894; *s* of Col James Rowell, CB, VD, Lockleys, S Australia; *m* 1919, Blanche May, *d* of J. S. Murison, Exeter, South Australia; one *d*. *Educ:* Adelaide High School; Royal Military College, Duntroon (graduated 1914). Served with AIF, Gallipoli, 1915; Capt. Australian Staff Corps, 1920; Major, 1925; Lt-Col, 1935; attended Staff College, Camberley, 1925-26; GSO 44th (Home Counties) Division, 1935-36; attended Imperial Defence College, 1937; Director of Military Operations, Army HQ, Melbourne, 1938; Colonel and GSO 1 6th Australian Division, AIF, 1939; Brigadier and BGS 1st Australian Corps, AIF, 1940; served in Libya, Greece and Syria, 1941; Maj.-Gen. and Deputy Chief of General Staff at Army HQ, Melbourne, 1941; Lt-Gen. and Corps Comdr, April 1942; GOC New Guinea Force, Aug. 1942; GOC, AIF, Middle East and Australian Liaison Officer at GHQ, Middle East Forces, Feb. 1943; Director of Tactical Investigation, War Office, 1944-45; Chief of General Staff, Australia, 1950-54 (Vice-Chief, 1946-50); retired Dec. 1954. *Address:* 39 Kensington Road, South Yarra, Victoria, Australia.

**ROWETT, Geoffrey Charles;** Director and General Manager, Times Newspapers Ltd, since 1967; *b* 1 Aug. 1925; *s* of Frederick Charles and Nell Rowett; *m* 1951, Joyce Eddiford; two *s*. *Educ:* Roundhay Sch., Leeds. Articled to Blackburns, Robson Coates & Co., Leeds and London. FCA, FCWA, CA(SR), JDipMA, MIMC. Midland Bank Executor & Trustee Co. Ltd, 1941; Royal Navy, 1943-46; Blackburns, Robson Coates & Co., 1947; Deloitte, Plender Griffiths Annan & Co., 1952; Production-Engineering SA (Pty) Ltd, 1954; P-E Consulting Group Ltd, 1964; Thomson Newspapers Ltd, 1965; Man. Dir, Sunday Times, 1965. *Address:* Printing House Square, EC4. *T:* 01-236 2000. *Clubs:* Royal Automobile; New (Johannesburg).

**ROWLAND, David Powys;** Stipendiary Magistrate, Merthyr Tydfil, since 1961; Deputy Chairman of Quarter Sessions: Glamorgan since 1961; Breconshire since 1964; *b* 7 Aug. 1917; *s* of late Henry Rowland, CBE, Weston-super-Mare; *m* 1st, 1946, Joan (*d* 1958), *d* of late Group Capt. J. McCrae, MBE, Weston-super-Mare; one *s* one *d*; 2nd, 1961, Jenny, *d* of Percival Lance, Swanage, and *widow* of Michael A. Forester-Bennett, Alverstoke; one *s* one *d*. (and one step-*d*). *Educ:* Cheltenham Coll.; Oriel Coll., Oxford (BA). Lieut, Royal Welch Fusiliers, 1940-46. Called to Bar, Middle Temple, 1947. Mem. Nat. Adv. Coun. on Training of Magistrates, 1964-. *Recreations:* fly-fishing, gardening, golf. *Address:* 53 St Tydfil's Court, Merthyr Tydfil. *T:* Merthyr Tydfil 3768; 8 Tivoli Road, Cheltenham. *T:* Cheltenham 56514. *Club:* Cardiff and County (Cardiff).

**ROWLAND, Herbert Grimley;** Special Commissioner of Income Tax since 1965; *b* 10 Feb. 1905; *s* of Frank Rowland, MRCS, LRCP, and Josephine Mary (*née* Quirke); *m* 1938, Margaret Jane Elizabeth, *yr d* of Robert Crawford Higginson and Mary Higginson; one *d*. *Educ:* Nautical Coll., Pangbourne; Peterhouse, Cambridge. Called to Bar, 1928; admitted Solicitor, 1933; private practice, Solicitor, 1933-40; joined Office of Solicitor of Inland Revenue, 1940; Princ. Asst Solicitor of Inland Revenue, 1961; Acting Solicitor of Inland Revenue, 1965. *Recreation:* golf. *Address:* Chantry Meadow, Chantry View Road, Guildford, Surrey. *T:* Guildford 66827. *Clubs:* Worplesdon Golf, Bramley Golf.

**ROWLANDS, Sir Alun;** *see* Rowlands, Sir R. A.

**ROWLANDS, Edward;** *b* 23 Jan. 1940; *e s* of W. S. Rowlands; *m* 1968, Janice Williams, Kidwelly, Carmarthenshire; one *s*. *Educ:* Rhondda Grammar Sch.; Wirral Grammar Sch.; King's Coll., London. BA Hons History (London) 1962. Research Asst, History of Parliament Trust, 1963-65; Lectr in Modern History and Govt, Welsh Coll. of Adv. Technology, 1965-. MP (Lab) Cardiff North, 1966-70; Parly Under-Sec., Welsh Office, 1969-70. *Recreations:* badminton, cricket. *Address:* 35 Vandon Court, Petty France, SW1. *T:* 01-222 5085; 6 Claerwen Drive, Cardiff. *T:* Cardiff 757570.

**ROWLANDS, Air Marshal John Samuel,** GC 1943; OBE 1954; Air Officer Commanding-in-Chief, Headquarters Maintenance Command, since 1970; *b* 23 Sept. 1915; *s* of late Samuel and Sarah Rowlands; *m* 1942, Constance Wight; two *d*. *Educ:* Hawarden School; University of Wales (BSc Hons). Joined RAFVR, 1939;

permanent commission in RAF, 1945. British Defence Staff, Washington, 1961-63; Imperial Defence College, 1964; Royal Air Force College, Cranwell, 1965-68; First Director General of Training, RAF, 1968-70. *Recreations:* photography, tennis, motoring. *Address:* c/o Lloyd's Bank, 346 Strand, WC2. *Club:* Royal Air Force.

**ROWLANDS, Sir (Richard) Alun,** KBE 1946 (CBE 1944; OBE 1920); MD (London); BSc and Hon. LLD (Wales); FRCP; Hon. Consulting Physician to The London Hospital, Poplar Hospital, Claybury Mental Hospital and Barnardo's Homes; Consulting Physician to Royal Navy; *b* 12 Sept. 1885; *s* of late Richard Rowlands, Bryngwran, Anglesey; *m* 1962, Mrs Lucienne Delva, *widow* of Dr J. P. Delva. *Educ:* Beaumaris Grammar School; University College of North Wales; London Hospital. Demonstrator of Physiology and Asst to Lecturer on Cardiac Research, 1911-13, and Medical Tutor, 1914-1920, London Hosp. Med. Coll.; Medical Registrar, London Hosp., 1914-20; late Examiner in Medicine for Conjoint Board and Univs of London and Liverpool; temp. Surgeon Rear-Admiral, RN, 1939-46; Regional Adviser in Medicine (EMS Region 6), 1940-46. Sen. Mem. Assoc. of Physicians of Great Britain and Ireland; Mem. Physiological Soc.; FRSocMed (Pres., Sect. of Medicine, 1951-53). *Publications:* papers in Medical and Scientific Journals. *Recreations:* golf and walking. *Address:* 82 Campden Hill Court, Kensington, W8. *T:* 01-937 9160. *Club:* Athenæum.

**ROWLANDSON, Sir Graham;** *see* Rowlandson, Sir Stanley Graham.

**ROWLANDSON, Sir (Stanley) Graham,** Kt 1956; MBE 1943; JP; FCA; Senior Partner, S. Graham Rowlandson & Co., Chartered Accountants; Chairman, The Finance & Industrial Trust Ltd; Member GLC for London Borough of Enfield, since 1964; Chairman, Establishment Committee, since 1967; *b* 25 Aug. 1908; *s* of late H. Stanley Rowlandson, Claremont, Enfield, Middx; *m* 1938, Vera Elworthy, *d* of late Ernest Alfred Lane, Woodside Pk, N; two *s* one *d*. *Educ:* Mill Hill Sch.; Blois, France. Member, Enfield UDC, 1934-46 (Chm., 1940-42; Chm. Finance Cttee, 1937-45; Leader, Cons. Group and Council, 1937-40, 1942-45); Middlesex CC, 1942-46, 1947-51, 1959-65, CA, 1951-58, High Sheriff 1958 (Vice-Chm. Establishment Cttee 1949-51, Chm. 1951-55; Chm. Finance Cttee 1949-51, Vice-Chm. 1951-55; Dep. Leader, 1951, 1964-65; Leader, 1951-54; Vice-Chm. CC 1954-55, Chm. 1955-56; Chm. Health Cttee, 1956-58, 1961-65; Mem., Standing Jt Cttee, 1951-58, 1961-65); Chairman: Finance Cttee, GLC, 1969-; Establishments Cttee, 1967-69; Member: Gen. Purposes Cttee, Supplies Cttee (Leader of Opposition), of GLC, 1964-67; Rep. on Local Govt Training Bd of GLC, 1967-, Chm. Finance Cttee, 1967-; Member: Local Govt Computer Centre, 1967; Exec. Coun. CCs Assoc., 1955-58; Local Authorities Management Services and Computer Cttee, 1969-; Jt Hon. Treas., Middx Assoc., 1965-69, Vice-Pres., 1969-; Vice-Chm., Home Counties N Local Govt Adv. Cttee, 1959-64; Greater London Area Local Govt Adv. Cttee, 1964-, Dep. Chm., 1964-; Mem., Nat. Local Govt Adv. Cttee, 1960-; Common Councilman, City of London, for Coleman St Ward, 1961; Chm., Port and City of London Health and Welfare Cttees, 1964-67. Contested (C) N Tottenham, 1937 and 1938; Chairman: Enfield W Cons Assoc., 1949-52; Enfield Bor. Cons. Assoc., 1952-64 (Pres. 1964-); Nat. Union of Cons. and Unionist Assocs: Vice-Chm. Home Counties N Prov. Area, 1953-54, 1961-64; Mem. Nat. Exec. Cttee, 1964-; Mem. Finance and GP Cttee, Greater London Area, 1964- (Dep. Chm., 1964-69; Chm. Middx Parly and Local Govt Gps, 1953-54; Mem. Middx Exec. Council, 1951-53, 1962-63. Chm., Enfield Savings, 1940-45; Mem., Nat. Savings London Reg. Adv. Cttee, 1942-46; Mem., Admin. Coun., Lord Mayor's Nat. Air Raid Distress Fund, 1940-54. Governor: Roy. Nat. Orthopædic Hosp., 1948-52; Med. Coll., St Bartholomew's Hosp., 1966-; Member: Gen. Coun., King Edward's Hosp. Fund for London, 1956-; NE Met. Reg. Hosp. Bd, 1952- (Chm. 1956-); Ct of Govs, London Sch. of Hygiene and Tropical Med., 1957-58; Bd of Governors: St Bartholomew's Hosp., 1957-, London Hosp., 1960-, Hammersmith and St Mark's Hosps, 1960-, Moorfields Eye Hosp., 1961-; VP International Cultural Exchange from 1964; Vice-Chm., Enfield Gp Hosp. Man. Cttees, 1948-53; Member: Whitley Coun. for Health Services, 1957-64; Nat. Cons Coun. on Recruitment of Nurses and Midwives, 1963-64; Council of Fed. Superannuation Scheme for Nurses and Hospital Officers, 1965-; Nat. Old People's Welfare Council, 1959-; Adv. Council on Overseas Services Resettlement Bureau, 1968-; Finance Committee, International Society for Rehabilitation of Disabled, 1958 (Chm., 1964-67; Vice-Chm. Brit. Cttee 1963-); Vice-Chairman: Council for Professions supp. to Medicine, 1961-; Nat. Baby Welfare Council, 1961-63; Hon. Treasurer: UK Cttee, WHO, 1963-; Infantile Paralysis Fellowship, 1949-52 (Chm. 1952-57); Vice-Pres., Edmonton and Enfield Br, British Diabetic Assoc., 1960; Trustee, Westminster Philanthropic Soc., 1960-. Mem. Court, Univ. of Essex, 1965-; Gov., Mill Hill Sch., 1952-58, 1961-; Vice-Pres., Internat. Cultural Exchange, 1964-; Mem. Council RSA, 1966-; Pres., Boy Scouts Assoc., Enfield Br., 1958-; Vice-President: London Scout Council, 1956-65; Co. of Greater London N Scout Council, 1965-; Pres., Middx Table Tennis Assoc., 1957-; Mem. Council, Royal Warrant Holders' Assoc., 1958-59. Worshipful Co. of Masons: Mem. Ct of Assts; Renter Warden, 1962; Upper Warden, 1963; Master, 1964; Liveryman, Paviors' Co. Coleman St Ward Club: Vice-Chm., 1965; Chm., 1966. *Recreations:* racing (race-horse owner), writing. *Address:* Salisbury House, EC2. *T:* 01-628 8566; 18 Grosvenor Square, W1. *T:* 01-449 2010; Harmer Green End, Digswell, Herts. *T:* Welwyn 5141. *Club:* Old Millhillians (Pres. 1965-66).

**ROWLEY, John Vincent d'Alessio;** General Manager, Bracknell New Town Development Corporation, since 1955; *b* 12 Sept. 1907; 2nd *s* of late Ven. Hugh Rowley, Archdeacon of Kingwilliamstown, S Africa; *m* 1936, Violet Maud (*d* 1969), *d* of S. H. Day, Grahamstown, S Africa; one *s*. *Educ:* St Andrews Coll., Grahamstown; Trinity Coll., Oxford (Rhodes Schol.). BA 1929; Oxford Univ. Rugby XV, 1929. Entered Sudan Political Service, 1930; Asst District Comr and District Comr, 1930-49; seconded Sudan Defence Force, 1940-42; Dep. Gov., Kordofan Province, 1950-52; Asst Financial Sec., 1952-53; Governor, Darfur Province, 1953-55. *Recreations:* music, gardening, golf. *Address:* Craigholm, Harmans Water, Bracknell, Berks. *T:* Bracknell 5447. *Club:* United University.

**ROWLEY, Sir Joshua Francis,** 7th Bt, *cr* 1786; DL; *b* 31 Dec. 1920; *o s* of 6th Bt and Margery Frances Bacon; *S* father, 1962; *m* 1959, Hon. Celia Ella Vere Monckton, 2nd *d* of 8th Viscount Galway; one *d*. *Educ:* Eton; Trinity College, Cambridge. Grenadier Guards, 1940-46. Deputy Secretary, National Trust, 1952-55. Director, Essex & Suffolk Insurance Co.,

1962. DL Suffolk, 1968. *Address:* The Cottage, Stoke-by-Nayland, Suffolk. *T:* Nayland 400. *Clubs:* Boodle's, Pratt's, MCC.

**ROWLEY, Sir William Joshua,** 6th Bt, *cr* 1836; late Lt-Col Lancashire Fusiliers; breeder of racehorses; *b* 15 April 1891; *s* of George Charles Erskine Rowley, 3rd Bt (*d* 1922) and his 2nd wife Amy Isabel (*d* 1961), OBE 1918, 3rd *d* of William Foster Batt, Abergavenny; *S* nephew 1953; *m* 1st, 1917, Beatrice Gwendoline Kirby (marriage dissolved, 1940); two *s* one *d*; 2nd, 1940, Margaret Sheila, *o d* of late Harold Camp, Stamford, Conn., USA; two *d*. *Educ:* Wellington College; RMC, Sandhurst. Joined Lancashire Fusiliers, 1910; served European War, 1914-19, France (wounded, 1914 star with clasp, 2 medals); War of 1939-45, Western Command, HQ (two medals). *Heir: s* Charles Robert Rowley [*b* 15 March 1926; *m* 1952, Astrid Pennington Cleife, *d* of Sir Arthur Massey, *qv*; one *s* one *d*]. *Address:* Widdington House, Widdington, near Newport, Essex. *T:* Newport 288.

**ROWLEY-CONWY,** family name of **Baron Langford.**

**ROWLINSON, Professor John Shipley,** FRS 1970; BSc, MA, DPhil Oxon; FRIC; MIChemE; Professor of Chemical Technology, University of London (Imperial College), since 1961; *b* 12 May 1926; *er s* of Frank Rowlinson and Winifred Jones; *m* 1952, Nancy Gaskell; one *s* one *d*. *Educ:* Rossall School (Scholar); Trinity College, Oxford (Millard Scholar). Research Associate, Univ. of Wisconsin, USA, 1950-51; ICI Research Fellow, Lecturer, and Senior Lecturer in Chemistry, University of Manchester, 1951-60. Hon. Treas., Faraday Society, 1968-; Member, Sale Borough Council, 1956-59. Meldola Medal, Roy. Inst. of Chemistry, 1954; Marlow Medal, Faraday Soc., 1957. *Publications:* Liquids and Liquid Mixtures, 1959, 1969; The Perfect Gas, 1963; Physics of Simple Liquids (joint editor), 1968; (trans. jtly) The Metric System, 1969; papers in Trans Faraday Soc. and other journals. *Recreation:* climbing. *Address:* 19 Burdett Avenue, SW20. *T:* 01-946 2989; Imperial College of Science and Technology, SW7. *T:* 01-589 5111.

**ROWNTREE, Sir Norman Andrew Forster,** Kt 1970; CEng; FInstCE; Member and Director of Water Resources Board, since 1964; *b* 11 March 1912; *s* of Arthur Thomas Rowntree, London, and Ethel, *d* of Andrew Forster; *m* 1939, Betty, *d* of William Arthur Thomas; two *s* one *d*. *Educ:* Tottenham County Sch.; London Univ. (BSc(Eng)). Consulting Engineer, 1953-64. Past Pres., Inst. of Water Engineers. Fellow and Mem. Council, Inst. of Civil Engineers. *Address:* 43 Kingswood Road, Tadworth, Surrey. *T:* Tadworth 3562; Water Resources Board, Reading Bridge House, Reading, Berks. *Club:* St Stephen's.

**ROWSE, Alfred Leslie,** MA, DLitt; FBA 1958; Fellow of All Souls College, Oxford; *b* St Austell, Cornwall, 4 Dec. 1903. *Educ:* Elementary and Grammar Schools, St Austell; Christ Church Oxford (Douglas Jerrold Scholar in English Literature). Fellow of the Royal Society of Literature; President of the English Association, 1952; Raleigh Lecturer, British Academy, 1957; Trevelyan Lecturer, Cambridge, 1958; Beatty Memorial Lecturer, McGill University, 1963. Pres., Shakespeare Club, Stratford-upon-Avon, 1970-71. *Publications:* Politics and the Younger Generation, 1931; Mr Keynes and the Labour Movement, 1936; Sir Richard Grenville of the Revenge, 1937; Tudor Cornwall, 1941; Poems of a Decade, 1931-41; A Cornish Childhood, 1942; The Spirit of English History, 1943; Poems Chiefly Cornish, 1944; The English Spirit: Essays in History and Literature, 1944, rev. edn 1966; West Country Stories, 1945; The Use of History, 1946; Poems of Deliverance, 1946; The End of an Epoch, 1947; The England of Elizabeth, 1950; The English Past, 1951 (rev. edn, as Times, Persons, Places, 1965); Translation and completion of Lucien Romier's History of France, 1953; The Expansion of Elizabethan England, 1955; The Early Churchills, 1956; The Later Churchills, 1958; Poems Partly American, 1958; The Elizabethans and America, 1959; St Austell: Church, Town, Parish, 1960; All Souls and Appeasement, 1961; Ralegh and the Throckmortons, 1962; William Shakespeare: A Biography, 1963; Shakespeare's Sonnets, Ed., with Introd. and Commentary, 1964; Christopher Marlowe: A Biography, 1964; A Cornishman at Oxford, 1965; Shakespeare's Southampton: Patron of Virginia, 1965; Bosworth Field and the Wars of the Roses, 1966; Poems of Cornwall and America, 1967; Cornish Stories, 1967; A Cornish Anthology, 1968; The Cornish in America, 1969; abridged edn J. A. Froude, The Two Chiefs of Dunboy, with foreword, 1969. *Address:* All Souls College, Oxford. *T:* Oxford 49641-2; Trenarren House, St Austell, Cornwall. *T:* St Austell 2053.

**ROXBEE COX,** family name of **Baron Kings Norton.**

**ROXBURGH, Air Vice-Marshal, Henry Lindsay,** CBE 1966; Commandant, RAF Institute of Aviation Medicine; *b* 5 Dec. 1909; *s* of John Roxburgh, Galston, Ayrshire and Cape Town, and Edith Mary Roxburgh (*née* Smithers), Kenilworth, Cape; *m* 1944, Hermione Babington (*née* Collard); one *s* two *d*. *Educ:* George Watson's College, Edinburgh; Edinburgh University. BSc 1932; PhD 1934; MB, ChB 1940; FRCP (Edinburgh) 1966. Medical Branch, Royal Air Force, 1941-. Service mainly at RAF Inst. of Aviation Med.: research undertaken in various aspects of aviation physiology and related subjects. Apptd Prof. in Aviation Medicine, 1966. Chairman, Aero-Space Medical Panel of Advisory Gp of Aero-Space Research and Development, Paris, 1965-67. FRAeS 1965. *Publications:* papers in field of aviation medicine. *Recreation:* gardening. *Address:* Manor Cottage, 54 Church Road, Fleet, Hampshire. *Club:* Pathfinder.

**ROXBURGH, Sir James;** *see* Roxburgh, Sir T. J. Y.

**ROXBURGH, Vice-Adm. John Charles Young,** CB 1969; CBE 1967; DSO 1943; DSC 1942 (Bar, 1945); Flag Officer Submarines and NATO Commander Submarines, Eastern Atlantic, since Nov. 1969; *b* 29 June 1919; *s* of Sir (Thomas) James (Young) Roxburgh, *qv*; *m* 1942, Philippa, 3rd *d* of late Major C. M. Hewlett, MC; one *s* one *d*. *Educ:* RNC, Dartmouth. Naval Cadet, 1933; Midshipman, 1937; Sub-Lt 1939; Lt 1941; Lt-Comdr 1949; Comdr 1952; Capt. 1958; Rear-Adm. 1947; Vice-Adm. 1970. Served in various ships, 1937-39; joined Submarine Br., 1940; served in ops off Norway, in Bay of Biscay and Mediterranean, 1940-42; comd HM Submarines H43, United and Tapir, 1942-45 in ops in Mediterranean and off Norway; HMS Vanguard, 1948-50; comd HM Submarine Turpin, 1951-53; HMS Triumph, 1955; HMS Ark Royal, 1955-56; comd HMS Contest, 1956-58; Brit. Jt Services Mission, Wash., 1958-60; comd 3rd Submarine Sqdn and HMS Adamant, 1960-61; idc 1962; Dep. Dir of Defence Plans (Navy), Min. of Def., 1963-65;

comd HMS Eagle, 1965-67; Flag Officer: Sea Training, 1967-69; Plymouth, 1969. *Recreations:* golf, sailing, walking, music. *Address:* Dolphin House, Gosport, Hants. *Clubs:* East India and Sports; Royal Naval (Portsmouth).

**ROXBURGH, Sir Ronald Francis,** Kt 1946; Judge of High Court of Justice, Chancery Division, 1946-60, retired; *b* 19 Nov. 1889; *o s* of Francis Roxburgh and Annie Gertrude Mortlock; *m* 1st, 1935, Jane Minney (*d* 1960), *yr d* of Archibald H. and Lady Frances Gordon-Duff; one *d*; 2nd, 1966, Mrs Dorothea Mary Hodge. *Educ:* Harrow; Trinity College, Cambridge. Classical Tripos Part I, Class I, Division II, 1911. Whewell International Law Scholar, 1912; called to Bar, Middle Temple, 1914; KC 1933; Bencher of Lincoln's Inn, 1938, Treasurer, 1957. *Publications:* Prisoners of War Information Bureau in London, 1915; International Conventions and Third States, 1917; The Origins of Lincoln's Inn, 1963; (ed) The Black Books of Lincoln's Inn, vol. v, 1968; edited Oppenheim's International Law (3rd edn), 1920-21. *Recreations:* walking, travel. *Address:* 8 Old Square, Lincoln's Inn, WC2. *T:* 01-242 4748; Holman's House, Stone-in-Oxney, Tenterden, Kent. *T:* Wittersham 321.

**ROXBURGH, Sir (Thomas) James (Young),** Kt 1954; CIE 1932; MA Cantab; *b* 2 March 1892; *y s* of T. Y. Roxburgh, London; *m* 1918, Mona Heymerdinguer; one *s* one *d*. *Educ:* Merchant Taylors'; Magdalene Coll., Cambridge. Entered Indian Civil Service, 1915; served IARO, 1916-19; Chief Presidency Magistrate, Calcutta, 1923-31; Secretary, Judicial Department, and Legal Remembrancer, to Government of Bengal, 1937-39; Puisne Judge, High Court, Calcutta, retired, 1952. Chm. Medical Appeal Tribunal, under the Industrial Injuries Act, 1952-64. Called to Bar, Lincoln's Inn, 1932. *Address:* 50 Courtfield Gardens, SW5. *T:* 01-370 3454. *Club:* East India and Sports.

*See also Vice-Adm. J. C. Y. Roxburgh.*

**ROXBURGHE,** 9th Duke of, *cr* 1707; **George Victor Robert John Innes-Ker,** Baron Roxburghe, 1600; Earl of Roxburghe and Kelso; Viscount Broxmouth; Baron Ker, 1616; Bt (Scot.) 1625; Marquess of Bowmont and Cessford, 1707; Earl of Innes (UK), 1837; Hon. Major, late RHG; *b* 7 Sept. 1913; *o s* of 8th Duke and May (*d* 1937), *o d* of Ogden Goelet; *S* father, 1932; *m* 1st, 1935, Lady Mary Evelyn Hungerford Crewe-Milnes (marriage dissolved, 1953), 4th *d* of 1st Marquess of Crewe, KG, PC; 2nd, 1954, Mrs Elisabeth Church; two *s*. *Educ:* RMC, Sandhurst. Owns about 80,000 acres. *Heir:* *s* Marquis of Bowmont and Cessford, *qv*. *Address:* Floors Castle, Kelso. *Clubs:* Turf, Jockey.

**ROY, Andrew Donald;** Deputy Director, Economic Service, HM Treasury, since 1969; *b* 28 June 1920; *er s* of late Donald Whatley Roy, FRCS, FRCOG, and late Beatrice Anne Roy (*née* Barstow); *m* 1947, Katherine Juliet Grove-White; one *s* two *d*. *Educ:* Malvern Coll. (Scholar); Sidney Sussex Coll., Cambridge (Scholar). Maths Trip. Pt I 1939 and Econ. Trip. Pt II 1948, Class I hons. Served War of 1939-45: Royal Artillery, in UK, India and Burma (8 Medium Regt). Cambridge Univ.: Jun. Research Worker, Dept of Applied Econ., 1948-49; Asst Lecturer, 1949-51; Lecturer, 1951-64; Jun. Proctor, 1956-57; Sidney Sussex Coll.: Fellow, 1951-64; Tutor, 1953-56; Sen. Tutor, 1956-62. Economic Section, HM Treasury: Economic Consultant, 1962-64; Sen. Economic Adviser, 1964-69. *Publications:* British Economic Statistics (with C. F. Carter), 1954; articles in economic and statistical jls. *Address:* 15 Rusholme Road, Putney, SW15. *T:* 01-789 3180. *Clubs:* Oxford and Cambridge University.

**ROY, Sir Asoka Kumar,** Kt 1937; Director: Jardine Henderson Ltd; Bengal Coal Co. Ltd; The Titaghur Paper Mills Co. Ltd; Anglo-India Jute Mills Co. Ltd; Braithwaite & Co. (India) Ltd, and several other companies; *b* 9 Sept. 1886; *s* of late Akshoy Kumar Roy Chaudhury of Taki and late Shoroshi Bala Roy Chaudhurani; *m* 1908, Charu Hashini, 4th *d* of late Taraprasad Roy Chaudhury; one *s* one *d*. *Educ:* Doveton College, Presidency College and Ripon College, Calcutta. MA, BL (Calcutta); Vakil, Calcutta High Court, 1908; called to Bar, Middle Temple, 1912 (First Class Honoursman at the Final Bar Examination); Standing Counsel, Bengal, 1929; twice acted as a Judge of the High Court of Calcutta; Advocate-General of Bengal, 1934-43; Law Member, Governor-General's Council, India, 1943-46. *Recreations:* gardening and walking. *Address:* 3 Upper Wood Street, Calcutta, India. *Clubs:* Calcutta, Royal Calcutta Turf (Calcutta).

**ROY, Catherine Murray,** CBE 1940; RRC 1918; MM; *d* of Rev. John Roy, MA. *Educ:* High School for Girls, Glasgow; Esdaile, Edinburgh. Trained at the Western Infirmary, Glasgow, 1905-9; joined QAIMNS 1909; served in European War in France, 1914-19 (despatches, MM, RRC); Médaille Militaire des Epidémies, 1918; Matron-in-Chief, Queen Alexandra's Imperial Military Nursing Service, 1938-40. *Address:* 28 Charing Cross Mansions, Glasgow C3. *Club:* Royal Over-Seas League.

**ROY, Ian;** Assistant Under-Secretary of State, Home Office, since 1963 (Principal Finance Officer, 1963-67, Fire Department since 1967); *b* 2 Aug. 1912; *o s* of late John Roy and Annie Froude Marshall; *m* 1939, Betty Louise Blissett; one *s* two *d*. *Educ:* Manchester Grammar School; Peterhouse, Cambridge. Assistant Inspector of Taxes, 1935; Assistant Principal, Home Office, 1936; Private Secretary to Permanent Under-Secretary of State, 1938; to Parliamentary Under-Secretary of State, 1939-40; Asst Secretary, 1947. *Address:* Flat 47, Cholmeley Lodge, Cholmeley Park, Highgate, N6. *T:* 01-340 3143.

**ROY, James Alexander;** Professor Emeritus; *s* of Rev. William and Elizabeth Fisher Roy; *m* 1952, Margaret Gordon Fleming, Hampstead, London. *Educ:* Edinburgh and Giessen Universities. MA 1st Class Hons English Lang. and Lit; Reader in English, Giessen Univ., 1906-8; Lectr English Lang. and Literature, St Andrews Univ., 1908-20; Prof. of English, Queen's Univ., Kingston, Canada, 1920-50; Guest Prof., Giessen, 1921, Univs of Berlin, Münster, and Göttingen, 1936 and 1937; Lectr in Scottish Literature, Queen's Univ., 1944-45; Vis. Prof., Queen's Univ., 1960; Sometime Examr in English to United Free Ch. of Scotland Theol Coll. Awarded Plaque of Honour by City of Kingston, 1960. Army, 1915-19; Artillery, and Intelligence Staff, GHQ, 1918; first Intell. Officer, Capt. XVII Corps HQs; attached as Educational Officer to GHQ Peace Conf. Staff, Paris, 1919; Mem. Inter-allied Commn of Control, Teschen, Silesia, 1919 (despatches). Guest of Czechoslovakian Govt, 1946; Charter member and past Governor of Dominion Drama Festival, Ottawa; Past Chairman: Canada Club of Edinburgh; Edinburgh Br., Royal Commonwealth Soc.; Past Mem. of Council, Victoria League in Scotland. *Publications:* The Dream of the Rood, 1910; Cowper and his Poetry, 1914; Pole and Czech in Silesia, 1920;

Christ in the Strand and other Poems, 1922; The Minister of Balglass (serialized), 1925; Joseph Howe: A Study in Achievement and Frustration, 1935; James Matthew Barrie, An Appreciation, 1937; Is there a Scottish Literature?, 1945; Forbes of Culloden (St Andrew's Day Lecture), 1945; (autobiography) The Heart is Highland, 1947; The Scot and Canada, 1947; Kingston: The King's Town, 1952; ("Brother André" in) Our Sense of Identity, 1954. Contributor to: Edinburgh Review, Scottish Field, Times Literary Supplement, Toronto Quarterly, Queen's Quarterly, Dalhousie Review, etc. *Recreations:* walking, motoring and book collecting. *Address:* 17 South Learmonth Gardens, Edinburgh 4. *Clubs:* Royal Commonwealth Society, English-Speaking Union; New (Edinburgh).

**ROY, His Eminence Cardinal Maurice;** *see* Quebec, Cardinal Archbishop of.

**ROY, Maurice;** Grand Officier, Légion d'Honneur; Professor at Ecole Polytechnique, Paris, 1947-69; Président: Committee on Space Research; International Union of Theoretical and Applied Mechanics; *b* 7 Nov. 1899; *m* 1932, Maritchu Nebout; one *s*. *Educ:* Ecole Polytechnique; Ecole Nat. Sup. des Mines. Ingénieur Général des Mines (retd); Contrôle Technique des Chemins de Fer, 1922-35; Director General: Mechanical Industry, 1935-40; Office Nat. de la Recherche Aéronautique, 1949-62; Professor successively at French Nat. Engineering Schs (Ponts et Chaussées, Génie Rural, Aéronautique), and at Ecole Polytechnique. Membre de l'Institut (Académie des Sciences), 1949 (Pres. 1966). Foreign Member: US Nat. Acad. of Sci.; Austrian Acad. of Sci.; Hon. FRAeS. Dr *hc* Bruxelles, Aachen, Saarbrucken, Québec, Oxford. *Publications:* books on Thermodynamics, Mechanics, Aviation and Propulsion; scientific and technical papers. *Recreations:* literature, golf. *Address:* 86 Avenue Niel, Paris 17e, France. *T:* 824-0102.

**ROYALL, Kenneth Claiborne,** DSM 1945 (US); LLD; lawyer; *b* Goldsboro, NC, 24 July 1894; *s* of George Claiborne Royall and Clara Howard Jones; *m* 1917, Margaret Best; one *s* one *d*. *Educ:* Univ. of North Carolina (AB); Harvard Law School (LLB). Associate Editor Harvard Law Review, 1915-17. Admitted to North Carolina Bar, 1916; law practice Goldsboro, NC, 1919-30, Raleigh and Goldsboro, NC, 1931-42, Royall, Gosney and Smith; law practice New York and Washington, DC, 1949-58, Dwight, Royall, Harris, Koegel and Caskey; Royall, Koegel, Harris and Caskey, 1958-61; Royall, Koegel and Rogus, 1961. State Senator, NC, 1927; Presidential Elector (NC), 1940. 2nd and 1st Lt Field Artillery, 1917-19, overseas, 1918-19; Col. and Brig.-Gen., 1942-45; service overseas 1944 and 1945; Under-Secretary of War, 1945-47; Secretary of War, 1947; Secretary of the Army, 1947-49. Member: N Carolina Bar Assoc. (Pres. 1929-30); New York and American Bar Assocs; American Law Institute. *Address:* 1040 Fifth Avenue, New York City, USA. *Clubs:* Links, Blind Brook, Recess (New York); Chevy Chase, Burning Tree, Army and Navy Country (Washington).

**ROYCE, David Nowill;** Commercial Inspector, Foreign and Commonwealth Office, since 1968; *b* 10 Sept. 1920; *s* of Bernard Royce and Ida Christine (*née* Nowill); *m* 1942, Esther Sylvia Yule; two *s* one *d*. *Educ:* Reading School; Vienna University. Served HM Forces, 1940-46. Major, Intelligence Corps, 1946; Asst Principal, Foreign Office, German Section, 1948; Foreign Service, 1949; First Secretary: Athens, 1953; Saigon, 1955; Foreign Office, 1957; Head of Chancery, Caracas, 1960; Counsellor (Commercial), Bonn, 1963; Counsellor (Commercial) and Consul-Gen., Helsinki, 1967-68. *Recreations:* tennis, swimming, sailing. *Address:* 5 Sprimont Place, SW3. *T:* 01-589 9148.

**ROYDEN, Sir John Ledward,** 4th Bt *cr* 1905; Director, Duncan Fox & Co. Ltd since 1945; *b* 31 Dec. 1907; *s* of Sir Ernest Royden, 3rd Bt, Hill Bank, Frankby, Cheshire; *S* father, 1960; *m* 1936, Dolores Catherine Coward; two *s* two *d*. *Educ:* Winchester Coll.; Magdalen College, Oxford. Duncan Fox & Co. Ltd, 1930-39. Ministry of Economic Warfare, 1939-45; Member, Willingdon Mission to South America, 1940-41. Order of Merit (Chile), 1945. *Recreations:* gardening (rhododendrons), shooting. *Heir:* *s* Christopher John Royden [*b* 26 Feb. 1937; *m* 1961, Diana Bridget, *d* of Lt-Col J. H. Goodhart, Kirby Moorside, Yorkshire; one *s*]. *Address:* Netherfield Place, Battle, Sussex. *T:* 84. *Club:* Carlton.

**ROYDS, John Caress,** MA Cantab; Headmaster of Uppingham School since 1965; *b* 1920; 3rd *s* of Rev. Edward Thomas Hubert Royds, BA. *Educ:* Monkton Combe School, Bath; Queens' College, Cambridge. II 1 hons History, 1947. Military service with British and Indian Armies, 1940-46. Assistant master, Bryanston School, Dorset, 1947-61, House-master, 1951-61; Headmaster, General Wingate School, Addis Ababa, 1961-65. *Address:* The School House, Uppingham, Rutland. *T:* 2216. *Club:* Royal Commonwealth Society.

**ROYLE,** family name of **Baron Royle.**

**ROYLE,** Baron, *cr* 1964, of Pendleton (Life Peer); **Charles Royle,** JP; *b* 23 Jan. 1896; *m* 1919, Florence Smith; one *d*. *Educ:* elementary; Stockport Grammar School. Engaged in Retail Meat Trade; President Manchester and Salford Meat Traders' Assoc., 1942-43; Meat Agent Ministry of Food, 1939-45. Ex-Member Stockport Borough Council; Past Chairman Stockport Labour Party; Vice-President Magistrates Association; President, East Sussex Branch, Probation Officers' Assoc. Contested Lancaster, 1935; MP (Lab) West Salford, 1945-64; a Lord Comr of the Treasury, 1950-51; one of the Opposition Whips, 1951-64; a Dep. Speaker and a Dep. Chm. of Cttees, House of Lords. Pres., Brit.-Caribbean Assoc.; Vice-Pres., Assoc. of Municipal Corporations; Director: Alliance Building Society; Chm., General Surety & Guarantee Co. Ltd. Hon. Fellow Inst. of Architects and Surveyors. JP Brighton, 1959. *Recreation:* golf. *Address:* 45 Hovedene, Cromwell Road, Hove, Sussex.

**ROYLE, Anthony Henry Fanshawe;** MP (C) Richmond, Surrey, since Oct. 1959; Parliamentary Under-Secretary of State, Foreign and Commonwealth Office, since 1970; *b* 27 March 1927; *s* of Sir Lancelot Royle, *qv*; *m* 1957, Shirley Worthington; two *d*. *Educ:* Harrow; Sandhurst. Capt., The Life Guards (Germany, Egypt, Palestine and Transjordan), 1945-48; served with 21st Special Air Service Regt (TA), 1948-51. Parliamentary Private Secretary: to Under-Sec. of State for the Colonies, July-Oct. 1960; to Sec. of State for Air, 1960-62; to Minister of Aviation, 1962-64; Vice-Chm., Cons. Parly Foreign Affairs Cttee, 1965-67; Tory Opposition Whip, 1967-70. Dir, British Match Corp., 1969-70. *Address:* 47 Cadogan Place, SW1; The Chapter Manor, South Cerney, Gloucestershire. *Clubs:* Pratt's, White's, Carlton.

**ROYLE, Rev. Canon Arthur;** Hon. Canon (Emeritus) Ely Cathedral, 1965; *b* 23 April 1895; *s* of Thomas White Royle, Maidstone, Kent; unmarried. *Educ:* Maidstone Grammar School; Keble College, Oxford (MA). Curate, St John Evangelist, East Dulwich, 1924-30; Vicar of St Paul, Newington, 1930-42; Rural Dean of Newington, 1935-42, Surrogate, 1935-42; Rector of Orton Longueville, Hunts, 1942-66; Rector of Alwalton, Hunts, 1943-66; Hon. Canon of Ely, 1947-54; Rural Dean of Yaxley, 1947-54; Archdeacon of Huntingdon, 1954-65. Member: Norman Cross RDC 1948-64; Huntingdon Educn Cttee, 1953-65; Huntingdon CC 1958-65. *Address:* The College of St Mark, Audley End, Saffron Walden, Essex. *T:* Saffron Walden 3127.

**ROYLE, Prof. Joseph Kenneth;** Head of Department of Mechanical Engineering, University of Sheffield, since 1966; *b* 3 April 1924; *s* of J. Royle, Accrington, Lancs; *m* 1955, P. R. Wallwork; one *s* two *d*. *Educ:* Manchester University. Royal Aircraft Estabt, 1944-48; Manchester Univ., 1949-61; Vis. Assoc. Prof., MIT, 1961-62; Sen. Lectr, Univ. of Manchester Inst. of Science and Technology, 1962-64; Dept of Mech. Engrg, Univ. of Sheffield, 1964-. *Publications:* contribs to Proc. IMechE, etc. *Recreations:* gardening, music. *Address:* Anselm, Over Lane, Baslow, Derbyshire. *T:* Baslow 3149.

**ROYLE, Sir Lancelot (Carrington),** KBE, 1944; Director, Bryant & May Ltd; *b* 31 May 1898; *y s* of Reverend Vernon Peter Fanshawe and Eleanor Agnes Royle, Stanmore Park, Stanmore, Middlesex; *m* 1922, Barbara Rachel Haldin; two *s* one *d*. *Educ:* Stanmore Park; Harrow School; RMA Woolwich. Left Woolwich, 1918; France, 113 Army Brigade, RFA, 1918; Cologne, 1918-21; Army Champion, 100 yds, 1920; resigned commission, 1921; took up appointment with Van den Berghs, Ltd, subsequently by amalgamation, Lever & Unilever, Ltd; recalled, War of 1939-45; served with 56th Heavy Battery, RA, 1940; appointed member Macharg/Royle Committee by Treasury, 1940. Gov. of Harrow School, 1947-62. Chairman: Navy, Army and Air Force Institutes, 1941-53; Allied Suppliers Ltd, 1947-58; Lipton Ltd, 1952-59; Lipton (Overseas) Ltd, 1959-63. Director: British Match Corp. Ltd, 1961-68; Liebigs Extract of Meat Co. Ltd, 1961-68; Oxo Ltd, 1961-68. *Recreations:* athletics (Olympic Games, 1924), football, cricket. *Address:* 31 Elsworthy Road, Primrose Hill, NW3. *T:* 01-722 5445. *Club:* Army and Navy.

*See also A. H. F. Royle.*

**ROYSTON, Viscount; Philip Simon Prospero Lindley Rupert Yorke;** *b* 20 April 1938; *o s* of 9th Earl of Hardwicke, *qv*; *m* 1968, Virginia Anne, *d* of Geoffrey Lyon; one *d*. *Educ:* Eton; McGill University, Montreal. *Recreation:* shooting. *Address:* 9 Fernshaw Road, SW10. *T:* 01-352 0891. *Clubs:* Turf, White's; Puffins (Edinburgh).

**ROZHDESTVENSKY, Gennadi Nikolaevich;** Principal Conductor, Bolshoi Theatre, 1965-70; *b* 1931; *m* Nina Vladimirovna Timofeyeva, Soviet ballet dancer. Studied piano at Moscow Conservatoire; started conducting at 18. Conductor Bolshoi Theatre, 1956-60 (Assistant Conductor, 1951); Chief Conductor, USSR Radio and Television Symphony Orchestra, 1960-65. Guest conductor, Europe, Israel, America. Merited Artist of the RSFSR. *Recreation:* photography. *Address:* c/o Victor Hochhauser Ltd, 4 Holland Park Avenue, W11.

**RUBBRA, Edmund,** CBE 1960; MA Oxon, DMus; Hon. LLD Leicester; FRAM 1970; FGSM 1968; composer pianist; Professor of Composition at Guildhall School of Music, since 1961; Senior Lecturer in Music, Oxford University, 1947-68; Fellow, Worcester College, Oxford, 1963; *b* Northampton, 23 May 1901. *Educ:* Northampton; University of Reading; Royal College of Music. Orchestral works include: Eight symphonies; Festival Overture; Sinfonia Concertante for piano and orchestra; Concertos for piano, violin, and viola; Soliloquy for cello and small orchestra; Improvisation for Violin and orchestra; Improvisations on Virginal Pieces by Giles Farnaby; Variations for Brass Band; Brahms-Handel Variations scored for full orchestra. Opera, Bee-bee-bei. Chamber works include: Sonatas for violin and piano, cello and piano, oboe and piano; 2 Piano Trios; three string quartets; Lyric Movement for piano and string quartet; Phantasy for two violins and piano; Introduction and Fugue for piano; Eight Preludes for piano; Prelude and Fugue on a Theme by Cyril Scott for piano; Pezzo Ostinato for harp solo; Discourse for harp and 'cello; The Buddha Suite for flute, oboe and string trio; Meditazioni for recorder and harpsichord; Fantasia on a Theme of Machaut for recorder and string quartet; Notturno for four recorders; Passacaglia sopra Plusieurs Regrets for recorder and harpsichord; Sonatina for recorder and harpsichord; 3 works for unaccomp. violin, viola and cello. Vocal works include: 7 Motets; 7 Madrigals; Mass and Festival Gloria for double choir; 4-part Mass; 3-part Mass; Missa Brevis for 3-part treble choir and organ; The Morning Watch for choir and orchestra; The Dark Night of the Soul for Choir and orchestra; Song of the Soul for choir, strings, harp and timpani; In die et nocte canticum for choir and orchestra; Inscape for choir, strings and harp; Veni, Creator Spiritus, for Choir and Brass; 3 Psalms for low voice and piano; Advent Cantata for baritone, choir and small orchestra; Amoretti for tenor and string quartet; 5 Spenser Sonnets for tenor and string orchestra; 4 Medieval Latin Lyrics for baritone and string orchestra; The Jade Mountain, five songs for harp and voice; Magnificat and Nunc Dimittis for choir and organ; Te Deum for choir, solo, and orchestra; Cantata, in Honorem Mariae Matris Dei, for choir, boys' voices, soprano and alto soli, and orchestra; Ode to the Queen for Voice and orchestra; Tenebrae settings for unaccompanied choir; Two Sonnets by William Alabaster for voice, viola and piano; Cantata Pastorale for voice, recorder, harpsichord and cello; Autumn for 3-part female choir and piano; The Beatitudes for 3-part female choir unaccompanied; Anthems: Up O my soul; And when the Builders; Lord, with what care; The Givers for 4-part unaccompanied choir; Cantata di camera Crucifixus pro nobis; Te Deum for 8-part unaccompanied choir; Lauda Sion, for unaccompanied double choir; Creature-Songs to Heaven, for 3-part treble voices, piano and strings; numerous songs. *Publications:* Counterpoint: A Survey; Holst: A monograph; ed Casella, The Evolution of Music, rev. and enl. edn. *Address:* Lindens, Bull Lane, Gerrards Cross, Bucks. *T:* Gerrards Cross 84650.

**RUBINSTEIN, Arthur;** pianist; *b* Lodz, Poland, January 1888; *m* 1932, Aniela Mlynarska; two *s* two *d*. *Educ:* under Joachim, Prof. Heinrich Barth, Robert Kahn and Max Bruch. Gave many concerts in Russia, Poland, Germany, Austria; made first appearance in Spain in 1915, followed by 120 concerts in Spain alone; later in Latin America, where made 13 tours; since 1924 has toured Europe extensively;

again in US, 1937, and became American Citizen. Toured Far East. Since 1945, every year, has made tours in US and all Western Europe (but refused to play in Germany, 1914- ). In 1961 gave 10 recitals at Carnegie Hall, New York, in 4 weeks' time, all for 10 different charities. Appeared Festival Hall, London, 1954, 1955, 1956, 1957, 1960, 1962, 1963, 1965, 1968, 1969, 1970. Holds several foreign Orders. Doctor *hc*: Yale Univ.; Brown Univ.; Northwestern Univ.; Hon. Member: Acad. Santa Cecilia, Rome; Acad. of Brazil; Gold Medal, Beethoven, Roy. Phil. Society. *Address:* 22 square de l'avenue Foch, Paris 16ieme.

**RUBINSTEIN, Harold Frederick;** Solicitor; Member of the firm of Rubinstein Nash & Co.; *b* London, 18 March 1891; *s* of late J. S. Rubinstein, Solicitor; *m* 1920, Lina Lowy (*d* 1939); two *s* (and one died on active service, RAF, 31 Aug. 1943). *Educ:* Cheltenham College; France and Germany. *Author of plays produced and/or published including:* Consequences, 1913; The Spirit of Parsifal Robinson, 1919; Old Boyhood, 1919; Shakespeare (with Clifford Bax), 1921; What's Wrong with the Drama? (five one-act plays), 1923; Exodus (with Halcott Glover), 1923; Peter and Paul, 1924; Churchill (with A. J. Talbot), 1925; Revanche, 1925; The House, 1926; Plays Out of Time, 1930; The Dickens of Gray's Inn, 1931; Israel Set Free (five one-act plays), 1936; Johnson Was No Gentleman, 1937; Hated Servants (eight one-act plays), 1944; The Fifth Gospel, 1946; Six London Plays (with Vera Arlett). 1950; Bernard Shaw in Heaven, 1952; Unearthly Gentleman (Trilogy of plays about Shakespeare), 1965. *Also published:* The English Drama, 1928; ed Great English Plays, 1928; Four Jewish Plays, 1948; (with J. C. Trewin) The Drama Bedside Book, 1966. *Recreation:* homework. *Address:* 6 Raymond Buildings, Gray's Inn, WC1. *T:* 01-242 8404.

**RUBRA, Edward John,** MRCS, LRCP; Anæsthetist and General Practitioner; *b* 23 July 1902; 2nd *s* of Dr H. H. Rubra, Crouch End; *m* 1927, Alice Eliza, *d* of Ernest Lindus, Dulwich; two *s*. *Educ:* Brighton College; King's College, London; Westminster Hospital (Guthrie Scholar). House Surgeon and Resident Medical Officer, Westminster Hospital; late Hon. Anæsthetist, University College Hospital, Westminster Hospital, Golden Square Throat Hospital, Throat Department, Brompton Hospital; late Anæsthetist, Dental Department, London Hospital and Islington Clinic; served War of 1939-45 (despatches), Lt-Col, Adviser in Anæsthetics, Southern Command, India. *Recreation:* study of Norman Architecture. *Address:* 66 Crouch Hall Road, Crouch End, N8. *T:* 01-340 2529; 6 Church End, Walkern, Herts. *T:* Walkern 313.

**RUCK, Berta, (Mrs Oliver Onions);** novelist; *b* 1878; *d* of Col and Mrs A. A. Ruck; *m* 1910, Oliver Onions (George Oliver) (*d* 1961); two *s*. *Educ:* St Winifred's School, Bangor, Wales. Studied art at the Slade School (scholarship), and at Calorossi's, Paris. Afterwards took to writing articles and short stories, first novel published 1914. Has lectured under Adult Education for HM Forces, and has recently broadcast. TV programme Yesterday's Witness, 1970. *Publications:* over 100 books, including: His Official Fiancée; The Lad with Wings; The Girls at his Billet; Sir or Madam and many other novels, the latest being Tomboy in Lace, She Danced in the Ballet, Love and Apron-Strings, Hopeful Journey, Song of the Lark, Marriage is a Blind Date, Fantastic Holiday, The Men in Her Life!; We All Have Our Secrets; Romance and a Film Star; A Wish A Day; A Smile for the Past (memoirs); Romantic after-thought, Love and A Rich Girl; Sherry and Ghosts; Runaway Lovers; Rendezvous at Zagarelli's; Shopping for a Husband; A Trickle of Welsh Blood. *Recreations:* was an ice-breaker, and liked air travel; is now over 90 but fit. *Address:* Bryntegwel, Aberdovey, Merioneth, Wales. *T:* Aberdovey 286.

**RUCK KEENE, Vice-Admiral Philip,** CB 1948; CBE 1942; DSO 1945; *b* 11 Nov. 1897; *s* of Rev. E. R. Ruck Keene; *m* 1923, Marguerite Evelyn Constance Agatha Gyles; one *d*. *Educ:* Haileybury College. Royal Navy, mainly in submarines; Rear-Adm. 1946; ADC to the King, 1946; Flag Officer in Charge, Ceylon, 1946-47; Director of Naval Training, 1947-49; retired, 1949. Legion of Merit (USA); Order of King George of Greece. *Recreations:* mountaineering, ski-ing, fishing. *Address:* Sonnberg, Kitzbühel, Tirol, Austria. *Club:* RN Ski and Mountaineering.

**RUCKER, Sir Arthur Nevil,** KCMG 1942; CB 1941; CBE 1937; Chairman of Stevenage New Town Corporation, 1962-66 (Vice-Chairman, 1956-62); *b* 20 June 1895; *o s* of late Sir Arthur Rucker, FRS, and Lady Rucker of Everington House, nr Newbury; *m* 1922, Elsie Marion Broadbent; two *s* two *d*. *Educ:* Marlborough; Trinity College, Cambridge. Served European War (12th Suffolk Regiment, Lieutenant), 1915-18; entered Civil Service as Assistant Principal, 1920; Private Secretary to successive Ministers of Health, 1928-36; Director of Establishments and Public Relations, Ministry of Health, 1937-39; Principal Private Secretary to Prime Minister, 1939-40; seconded for special duties, 1941, returned to Ministry of Health as Deputy Secretary, 1943; Deputy Director-General, IRO, 1948. Deputy Agent-General of the UN Korean Reconstruction Agency, 1951; Member Commonwealth War Graves Commission, 1956-69. Hon. LLD Wales, 1965. *Address:* Manor Farm House, Yattendon, Berks. *T:* Yattendon 205. *Club:* Athenæum.

**RUDD, Surgeon Rear-Adm. Eric Thomas Sutherland,** CB 1958; CBE 1954; FRCSEd; *b* 19 Feb. 1902; *s* of late Rev. Canon Thomas Ernest Rudd; *m* 1930, Enid Marjorie (*d* 1968), *d* of Capt. Hubert Vaughan-Jones, CBE, RN; one *s* one *d*. *Educ:* Royal Sch., Armagh; Trinity Coll., Dublin. BA 1923; MB, BCh, BAO Dublin, 1925; FRCS Edinburgh, 1930. Sen. Fell. of Association of Surgeons of Great Britain and Ireland. Late Surgical Specialist, Royal Navy; Surg. Rear-Adm., 1955; Hon. Surgeon to the Queen, 1955-58; Medical Officer-in-Charge, Royal Naval Hospital, Haslar, and on Staff of Commander-in-Chief, Portsmouth, 1955-58, retd. Retired as House Governor, King Edward VII Convalescent Home for Officers, Osborne, Isle of Wight, 1965. *Recreations:* shooting, fishing, golf. *Address:* Fort Norris, East Cowes, Isle of Wight. *T:* Cowes 3107. *Club:* Royal Yacht Squadron.

**RUDD, G(eoffrey) Burkitt (Whitcomb),** BA; LLB; Puisne Judge, Kenya, 1951-69, retired; *b* 29 May 1908; *s* of late T. A. Rudd; *m* 1936, Guenda Mary de Clifton Parmiter; four *s* one *d*. *Educ:* St Columba's College; Dublin University (TCD). Called to Bar, King's Inns, 1932; Resident Magistrate, Kenya, 1936-44; Acting Chief Justice, Aden, 1944; Judge of the Supreme Court, Aden, 1945-51; has acted as Chief Justice, Kenya. *Recreations:* shooting, fishing, riding. *Address:* The Old Rectory, Clonoulty, Goolds Cross, Co. Tipperary, Ireland.

**RUDDERHAM, Rt. Rev. J. E.;** *see* Clifton, Bishop of, (RC).

**RUDDLE, Lt-Col Sir (George) Kenneth (Fordham),** Kt 1957; TD; DL; *b* 17 May 1903; *o s* of late George Ruddle; *m* 1930, Nancy Margaret, *er d* of late H. G. Allen, Woburn Sands, Beds; one *s* two *d* (and one *d* decd). *Educ:* Repton. Chairman of family brewing business, G. Ruddle & Co. Ltd; Mem., Exec. Cttee of National Union of Conservative and Unionist Assocs, 1951-62, 1964-67; Chm. E Midland area of Nat. Union of Cons and Unionist Assocs, 1951-57. Alderman, Rutland CC; Chairman, 1958-70; DL Co. of Rutland 1938-; High Sheriff of Rutland, 1938. Former Vice-Chm., Leics and Rutland T&AFA; Dep. Vice-Chm., Leics and Rutland Police Authority; Pres. Rutland County Scouts Council; Pres. Rutland Horticultural Soc. *Recreations:* cricket, gardening. *Address:* Islington Lodge, Langham, Oakham, Rutland. *T:* Oakham 2944. *Clubs:* Carlton, MCC, No. 10 Club (Institute of Directors).

**RUDÉ, Prof. George Frederick Elliot;** Professor of History, Flinders University of South Australia, since Oct. 1968; *b* 8 Feb. 1910; *s* of Jens Essendrop Rude, Norway, and Amy Geraldine Elliot Rude, England; *m* 1940, Doreen, *d* of J. W. De la Hoyde, Dublin; no *c*. *Educ:* Shrewsbury Sch.; Trinity Coll., Cambridge. Dr of Letters (Adelaide), 1967. Taught at: Stowe Sch., Bucks, 1931-35; St Paul's Sch., London, 1936-49; Sir Walter St John's Sch., London, 1950-54; Holloway Sch., London, 1954-59; Univ. of Adelaide: Sen. Lectr in History, 1960-63; Prof. of History, 1964-67. Leverhulme Vis. Prof., Univ. of Tokyo, Sept.-Nov. 1967; Vis. Prof., Univ. of Stirling, 1968. Mem., Australian Research Grants Cttee, 1969. Alexander Prize, Roy. Hist. Soc., 1955. FRHistSoc. 1957; Fellow, Australian Humanities Res. Coun., 1963. *Publications:* The Crowd in the French Revolution, 1959; Wilkes and Liberty, 1962; Revolutionary Europe 1783-1815, 1964; The Crowd in History, 1964; (ed) The Eighteenth Century 1715-1815, 1965; (ed) Robespierre, 1967; (with E. J. Hobsbawm) Captain Swing, 1969; contribs to Eng. Hist. Review, Eng. Econ. Hist. Review, Revue Historique, Past and Present, etc. *Recreations:* swimming, reading, public speaking. *Address:* School of Social Sciences, Flinders University of South Australia, Bedford Park, Adelaide, South Australia 5042, Australia.

**RUDGARD, Ven. Richard Cuthbert,** OBE 1944; TD 1950; Rector of Ellisfield and Farleigh Wallop, Basingstoke, since 1960; Archdeacon of Basingstoke and Canon of Winchester since 1958; *b* 28 Dec. 1901; *e s* of Canon R. W. and Mrs E. M. Rudgard; *m* 1st, 1933, Mary M. McLean (decd); one *s*; 2nd, 1939, Maisie M. Cooke. *Educ:* Radley College; St Augustine's College, Canterbury. With Melanesian Mission, 1922-33. Assistant Priest, Heene, Worthing, 1934; Rector of Newbold Pacey with Moreton Morrell, 1936-45; Rector of Eversley, 1946-60; Rural Dean of Odiham, 1953-59. War of 1939-45 (despatches thrice); Chaplain to the Forces, TA, 1939; SCF 1st Armoured Division, 1942, N Africa; DACG 13 Corps, 1943, Sicily and Italy; Personal Chaplain to Chaplain General, 1944-46. DACG (TA) Southern Command, 1947-56. Hon. Chaplain to the Queen, 1954-56. *Recreations:* riding and tennis. *Address:* Ellisfield Rectory, Basingstoke, Hants. *T:* Herriard 217.

**RUDOE, Wulf;** Director of Statistics and Research, Department of Health and Social Security (formerly Ministry of Health), since 1966; *b* 9 March 1916; *m* 1942, Ellen Trilling; one *s* one *d*. *Educ:* Central Foundation School; Peterhouse, Cambridge (Open Schol. and Research Schol.). Mathematics Tripos Pt III, 1938, Distinction. Royal Aircraft Establishment, 1939. Operational Research, RAF, 1939-45. Operational Research in Building Industry, Min. of Works, 1946-48, Principal Scientific Officer 1948; Board of Trade, Statistician 1948, Chief Statistician 1952. Fellow Inst. of Statisticians; Mem. Council, 1962- and Hon. Treasurer, 1965-, Roy. Statistical Soc. *Recreations:* walking, travel, languages. *Address:* 72 North End Road, NW11. *T:* 01-455 2890.

**RUEFF, Jacques,** Grand' Croix de la Légion d'Honneur; Croix de Guerre (3 citations); French Economist; Member of French Academy and of Academy of Moral and Political Sciences; Chancellor of the French Institute; Member of Economic and Social Council; *b* 23 Aug. 1896; *m* 1937, Christiane Vignat; two *d*. *Educ:* École Polytechnique, Paris. Inspector of Finance, 1923; Mem. Secretariat, League of Nations, 1927-30; Financial Attaché, London, 1930-34; Asst Director, later Director, Treasury, Ministry of Finance, 1934-39; Counsellor of State, 1937; Vice-Governor, Bank of France, 1939-41, resigned; Econ. Adviser to Commander-in-Chief Germany, 1945; Delegate to Reparations Commn, Moscow, and Pres., Inter-Allied Reparations Agency, 1946; Judge, Court of Justice of European Steel and Coal Community, 1952; Judge, Court of European Communities, 1958-62; Pres., Cttee for Reform of French Financial Situation, 1958; Vice-Pres., Cttee for Removal of Economic Obstacles, 1960. Foreign Associate: Nat. Acad. of Lincei, Rome; Roy. Acad. of Sciences, Letters and Fine Arts, Belgium. Grand Cross and Grand Officer of several foreign orders. *Publications:* Des Sciences physiques au Sciences morales, 1921; Theorie des Phénomènes monétaires, 1927; L'ordre social, 1946; Epître aux Dirigistes, 1949; L'âge de l'inflation, 1963; Le lancinant problème des balances de paiement, 1965; Les Dieux et les Rois, 1967. *Recreation:* golf. *Address:* 51 rue de Varenne, Paris 7e, France *T:* Littré 36-01; Berville, par Conteville, Eure. *Club:* Saint-Cloud.

**RUEGGER, Paul J.;** Swiss diplomat and jurist; *b* 14 August 1897; *s* of Prof. J. Ruegger; *m* 1932, Countess Isabella Salazar y Munatones (*d* 1969). *Educ:* College Lucerne; Univs of Lausanne, Munich, and Zürich (Doctor of Law). Attaché at Swiss Foreign Office and Sec. Swiss Advisory Cttee for League of Nations and post-war problems, 1918; Secretary of the Swiss Delegation to the League of Nations, 1920-25 (technical adviser, 1923-25); Sec. Swiss Delegation to Internat. Econ. Conf. of Genoa, 1922; Asst Prof. of Internat. Law, Univ. of Geneva, 1922-24; Legal Adviser to Swiss Delegation Conference for control of trade of arms, etc., 1925; Deputy Registrar Permanent Court of International Justice, 1926-28; Counsellor Swiss Legation in Rome, 1929-31; Head of Political Office Foreign Affairs Dept in Berne, 1931-33; 1st Counsellor of the Swiss Legation in Paris, 1933-36; Swiss Minister in Rome, 1936-42; Swiss Minister to Great Britain, 1944-48. Head of the Swiss Delegation for establishment of a Convention between Switzerland and UN on diplomatic privileges and immunities of UNO establishments in Switzerland; member of Swiss Deleg. to last League of Nations Assembly, Geneva, 1946; President Internat. Committee of Red Cross, 1948-55, Chm. 1968- ; Chm. ILO Committee on Forced Labour, 1956-60. Prof. of Human Rights, Univ. of

Strasbourg, 1964. Member of: Perm. Court of Arbitration; Curatorium of Acad. of Internat. Law, at the Hague; Inst. of Internat. Law; Commissions of Conciliation: between Switzerland and USA; between Switzerland and Spain; between France and the Netherlands; between Sweden and Denmark (Chm). UN Nansen Medal Award Cttee; Ambassador, 1957; Chm. Swiss Deleg. to UN Conf. on Law of the Sea, Geneva, 1958 and 1960, and to UN Confs on Diplomatic Relations and Immunities, Vienna, 1961; on Consular Relations and Immunities, Vienna, 1963; on Law of Treaties, Vienna, 1968 and 1969; Chm. Cttee of UN Atomic Energy Agency, Vienna, on Civil Liability and Internat. Responsibility for Nuclear Hazards, 1959-62; Chm. ILO Arbitral Commn, Ghana-Portugal, 1961-62; Pres., prep. UN Conf., 1964, and of conf. of plenipotentiaries, New York, on transit trade and land-locked countries, 1965. *Publications:* The Nationality of Corporations in International Law, 1918; Terms of Civil Law in International Law, 1920; The Responsibility of States for Crimes committed on their Territory, 1923; The Practice of International Conciliation Committees, 1929; Foreign Administration as Institutional Function of Intercourse between States, 1934; The Economic Foundations of International Law, 1931; The Juridical Aspects of the Organisation of the International Red Cross, 1953; Swiss Neutrality and European Integration, 1953; etc. *Address:* Villa il Pino, 267 Via Bolognese, Florence, Italy; 5 rue Gautier, Geneva, Switzerland. *Clubs:* St James'; Circolo dell' Unione (Florence).

*See also Baron Armstrong.*

**RUFF, William Willis,** DL; Clerk of the Surrey County Council since 1952; *b* 22 Sept. 1914; *s* of late William Ruff, Whitby, Yorks; *m* 1939, Agnes, *d* of late Howard Nankivell; two *s*. *Educ:* Durham School. Served War of 1939-45: Royal Signals, North Africa and India, 1940-45; Capt., 1942; Maj., 1943. Asst Solicitor: Scarborough Corp., 1937; Heston and Isleworth Corp., 1938; Surrey County Council: Asst Solicitor, 1939; Senior Asst Solicitor, 1947; Asst Clerk, 1948; Deputy Clerk, 1951. Chm., Soc. of Clerks of Peace and of Clerks of County Councils, 1969-71. DL Surrey, 1964. *Recreations:* music and cricket. *Address:* (home) Clare Hill, Deepdene Park Road, Dorking, Surrey. *T:* Dorking 2406; (office) County Hall, Kingston upon Thames, Surrey. *T:* 01-546 1050. *Club:* United Service.

**RUGBY,** 2nd Baron, *cr* 1947, of Rugby; **Alan Loader Maffey;** *b* 16 April 1913; *s* of 1st Baron Rugby, GCMG, KCB, KCVO, CSI, CIE, and of Dorothy Gladys (OBE 1919), *d* of late Charles Lang Huggins, JP, Hadlow Grange, Buxted; *S* father, 1969; *m* 1947, Margaret, *d* of Harold Bindley; four *s* two *d*. *Educ:* Stowe. Served War of 1939-45, RAF. *Heir:* *s* Hon. John Richard Maffey, *b* 28 Aug. 1949. *Address:* Grove Farm, Frankton, near Rugby, Warwicks.

**RUGG, Sir (Edward) Percy,** Kt 1959; JP; DL; Councillor for Royal Borough of Kensington and Chelsea, Greater London Council, 1964-70; Leader of Conservative Party, on the Council, 1964-66; Chairman of Council, 1967-68; Councillor for Chelsea, LCC (Alderman, 1958-61; Leader of Conservative Party, on the LCC 1959-65); *b* 14 Jan. 1906; *s* of Albert Henry and Louise Rugg; *m* 1933, Elizabeth Frances Symes; two *s* one *d*. *Educ:* Leys Sch. Solicitor, 1929. Hertfordshire County Council, 1940-45. Chairman: Hertford Division Conservative Association, 1948-52; Ware Rural District Council, 1949-54; Junior Carlton Club Political Council, 1954-57; Commercial Law and International Arbitration Committee of British National Committee of International Chamber of Commerce, 1957-; Gen. Purposes Cttee, GLC, 1969-70; Heathrow Airport Consultative Cttee, 1969-70; Pres. East Herts Conservative Assoc., 1961-. Member: London Tourist Bd, 1968-; BTA, 1969-. JP, Herts, 1949-; DL Greater London, 1967-. Dep. Kt Pres., Hon. Soc. of Knights of Round Table. *Recreations:* shooting, fishing. *Address:* 97 Rivermead Court, Hurlingham, SW6. *T:* 01-736 3996. *Clubs:* City Livery, Hurlingham.

**RUGG, Sir Percy;** *see* Rugg, Sir E. P.

**RUGGE-PRICE, Sir C. K. N.;** *see* Price.

**RUGGLES-BRISE, Col Sir John Archibald,** 2nd Bt, *cr* 1935; CB 1958; OBE 1945; TD; JP; Lord Lieutenant of Essex since 1958; Pro-Chancellor, University of Essex, since 1964; *b* 13 June 1908; *er s* of Colonel Sir Edward Archibald Ruggles-Brise, 1st Bt, MC, TD, DL, JP, MP, and Agatha (*d* 1937), *e d* of J. H. Gurney, DL, JP, of Keswick Hall, Norfolk; *S* father, 1942. *Educ:* Eton. Served AA Comd, 1939-45. Member of Lloyd's; West End Dir, Commercial Union Assurance. Pres., CLA, 1957-59; Church Comr 1959-64; Chm., Council of the Baronetage, 1958-63. DL 1945, JP 1946, Vice-Lieutenant, 1947, Co. Essex. Hon. Freeman of Chelmsford. Governor of Felsted and Chigwell Schools. KStJ. *Recreation:* shooting. *Heir:* *b* Capt. Guy Edward Ruggles-Brise, TD, DL [*b* 15 June 1914; *m* 1940, Elizabeth, *o d* of James Knox, Smithstone House, Kilwinning, Ayrshire; three *s*. Captain 104th (Essex Yeo.) Field Brigade RHA (TA); served War of 1939-45 (prisoner)]. *Address:* Spains Hall, Finchingfield, Essex. *T:* Great Bardfield 266. *Club:* Carlton.

**RUIZ SOLER, Antonio, (Antonio);** Cross of the Order of Isabella the Catholic, 1951; Comdr Order of Civil Merit, 1964; Spanish dancer; *b* Seville, 4 November 1921. Studied at the Realito Dance Academy. First stage appearance at the age of eight; subsequently toured North and South America Southern and Western Europe, and Scandinavia. First stage appearance in Great Britain, Edinburgh Festival, 1950; London dĕbut, Cambridge Theatre, 1951. Golden Medal, Fine Arts, 1952. Formed Ballet Company, 1953; dĕbut in Generalife Theatre, Granada, presenting his Ballet in Europe, S and N America. Has also appeared in many festivals in Spain. Appearances with Ballet in London: Stoll, 1954; Palace, 1956; Coliseum, 1958; Royalty, 1960; Drury Lane, 1963. Gala perf. in Washington to President Kennedy, Ed Sullivan Show in New York, appearances Europe, 1963. Festivals of Spain, 1964-65; Madrid Season, 1965; N Amer. tour, 1965; Ed Sullivan Show, 1965. Appears on TV. Gold Medal, Swedish Acad. of Dancing, 1963; Medal of Min. of Information and Tourism, Madrid, 1963.

**RUMBALL, Air Vice-Marshal Sir (Campion) Aubrey,** KBE 1960 (CBE 1954; OBE 1945); FRCP; Senior Consultant in Medicine, RAF, Medical Branch, 1951-66; *b* 26 Dec. 1904; *s* of Frederick William Rumball; *m* 1931, Margaret, *d* of George Williams, Tydd St Giles, Cambridgeshire. *Educ:* Dulwich Coll.; Guy's Hosp. LDSRCS Eng 1926; MRCS Eng, LRCP Lond., 1930; DTM & H Eng. 1937; DPM 1939; MRCP 1947; FRCP Lond. 1952. Served War of 1939-45, France and Middle East (OBE); Medical Specialist to Nos 1, 2, and 5 RAF Hosps. QHP 1952-66 (KHP 1948-

52). FRSM; Hon. Treasurer, Royal Society of Medicine, 1959-65; Member Council, 1965-66; Hon. Fellow, 1969. Cade Gold Medal, RCS, 1956. *Publications:* contributions to BMJ, Lancet, Brit. Heart Jl, etc. *Recreations:* fishing and motoring. *Address:* The Lodge, High Beech, St Leonard's-on-Sea, East Sussex. *Club:* Royal Air Force.

**RUMBOLD, Sir Algernon;** *see* Rumbold, Sir H. A. F.

**RUMBOLD, Sir Anthony;** *see* Rumbold, Sir H. A. C.

**RUMBOLD, Rev. Canon Charles Robert;** Chaplain, St Mary's Diocesan School for Girls, 1951-66; Dean of Pretoria, 1933-50. *Educ:* Bishops' College, Cheshunt. Deacon, 1921; Priest, 1922; Rector of Arcadia, 1928-33. *Address:* Irene Homes, Irene, Transvaal, S Africa.

**RUMBOLD, Sir (Horace) Algernon (Fraser),** KCMG 1960 (CMG 1953); CIE 1947; *b* 27 Feb. 1906; *s* of late Colonel William Edwin Rumbold, CMG; *m* 1946, Margaret Adél, *d* of late Arthur Joseph Hughes, OBE; two *d*. *Educ:* Wellington College; Christ Church, Oxford. Assistant Principal, India Office, 1929; Private Sec. to Parliamentary Under-Secretaries of State for India, 1930-33, and to Permanent Under-Secretary of State, 1933-34; Principal, 1934; Asst Sec., 1943; transferred to Commonwealth Relations Office, 1947; Deputy High Commissioner in the Union of South Africa, 1949-53; Asst Under Sec. of State, CRO, 1954-58; Deputy Under Secretary of State, Commonwealth Relations Office, 1958-66; retired, 1966. *Recreations:* golf, tennis. *Address:* Shortwoods, West Clandon, Surrey. *T:* Clandon 757. *Club:* Travellers'.

**RUMBOLD, Sir (Horace) Anthony (Claude),** 10th Bt, *cr* 1779; KCMG 1962 (CMG 1953); KCVO 1969; CB 1955; HM Diplomatic Service, retired; *b* 7 March 1911; *s* of Right Hon. Sir Horace Rumbold, 9th Bt, GCB, GCMG, MVO, and Etheldred, Lady Rumbold, CBE (*d* 1964), 2nd *d* of Sir Edmund Fane, KCMG; *m* 1937. Felicity Ann, *yr d* of late Lt-Col F. G. Bailey and of Lady Janet Bailey, Lake House, Salisbury, Wilts; one *s* three *d*. *Educ:* Eton; Magdalen College, Oxford (BA). Third Sec. in the Foreign Office, 1935; transferred to Washington, 1937; Second Secretary, 1940; transferred to Foreign Office, 1942; served on staff of Resident Minister, Mediterranean, 1944; First Sec., 1945; transferred Prague, 1947; transferred to Foreign Office as Counsellor, 1949; transferred to Paris as Counsellor, 1951; appointed Principal Private Secretary to Foreign Secretary, 1954; Assistant Under-Secretary of State, Foreign Office, 1957; British Minister in Paris, 1960-63; Ambassador to Thailand and UK Representative on the Council of SEATO, 1965-67; Ambassador to Austria, 1967-70. Commander of the Order of St Olaf, 1955. *Heir: s* Henry Rumbold, *b* 24 Dec. 1947. *Address:* Hatch House, Tisbury, Wilts. *T:* Tisbury 238. *Club:* Travellers'.

*See also Viscount Esher, H. W. Farmar.*

**RUMSEY, Harry Victor,** CB 1953; Senior Lecturer in Mathematics, Royal Military Academy, Sandhurst, 1953-68; *b* 27 Nov. 1898; *s* of Edward Victor Rumsey and Mina Esler; *m* 1939, Sarah Fox. *Educ:* The King's School, Macclesfield; Selwyn College, Cambridge (MA). Served European War, 1914-18, Border Regiment, Private (MM), Royal Navy as Instructor Lieutenant, 1922; retired as Instructor Captain, 1953. *Address:* Highways, Harcombe Cross, Axminster, Devon. *T:* Axminster 2017.

**RUNCIE, Rt. Rev. Robert Alexander Kennedy;** *see* St Albans, Bishop of.

**RUNCIMAN,** family name of **Viscount Runciman of Doxford.**

**RUNCIMAN OF DOXFORD,** 2nd Viscount, *cr* 1937; **Walter Leslie Runciman,** Baron Runciman, *cr* 1933, of Shoreston; Bt, *cr* 1906; OBE 1946; AFC; DL; Chairman: Walter Runciman & Co. Ltd; Anchor Line Ltd; John Tann Security Ltd; Director of other cos; Chairman of Trustees, National Maritime Museum; *b* 26 Aug. 1900; *er s* of 1st Viscount Runciman of Doxford, PC, and Hilda (*d* 1956), MP (L) St Ives, 1928-29, *d* of J. C. Stevenson; *S* father 1949; *m* 2nd, 1932, Katherine Schuyler, *y d* of late Wm R. Garrison, New York; one *s*. *Educ:* Eton (King's Scholar); Trinity College, Cambridge (Scholar). Chm., North of England Shipowners Association, 1931-32 and 1970-71; Chairman of Council, Armstrong College, University of Durham, 1935-37; Director-General of British Overseas Airways Corporation, 1940-43; Air Commodore and Air Attaché, Tehran, 1943-46. Pres. Chamber of Shipping of the UK, and Chm. General Council of British Shipping, 1952; Mem. Air Transport Advisory Council, 1946-54, Vice-Chm., 1951-54; President, RINA, 1951-61; Mem. Shipping Advisory Panel, 1962. Chm., Cttee on Horticultural Marketing, 1955-56. DL Northumberland, 1961. Hon. DCL, Durham. *Recreations:* sailing, shooting. *Heir: s* Hon. Walter Garrison Runciman [*b* 10 Nov. 1934. *Educ:* Eton (Oppidan Schol.); Trinity Coll., Cambridge (Scholar; fellow, 1959-63); *m* 1963, Ruth, *o d* of late Joseph Hellman, Johannesburg; one *s* two *d*]. *Address:* 10 Southwick Place, W2. *T:* 01-723 6882; Doxford, Chathill, Northumberland. *Clubs:* Brooks's; Royal Yacht Squadron (Cdre).

*See also Hon. Sir Steven Runciman.*

**RUNCIMAN, Hon. Sir Steven; (James Cochran Stevenson),** Kt 1958; FBA 1957; MA; *b* 7 July 1903; 2nd *s* of 1st Viscount Runciman of Doxford, PC. *Educ:* Eton (King's Schol.); Trinity College, Cambridge (Schol.). Fellow of Trinity College, Cambridge, 1927-38 (Hon. Fellow 1965); Lecturer at the University of Cambridge, 1932-38; Press Attaché, British Legation, Sofia, 1940; British Embassy, Cairo, 1941; Professor of Byzantine Art and History in Univ. of Istanbul, 1942-45; Rep. Brit. Council in Greece, 1945-47. Waynflete Lectr, Magdalen Coll., Oxford, 1953-54; Gifford Lectr, St And., 1960-62; Alexander White Prof., Univ. of Chicago, 1963; Birkbeck Lectr, Trinity Coll., Cambridge, 1966; Wiles Lectr, Queen's Univ., Belfast, 1968. Mem. Advisory Council, Victoria and Albert Museum, 1957; Chm., Anglo-Hellenic League, 1951-67; Trustee, British Museum, 1960-67; Pres. British Inst. of Archæology at Ankara; For. Mem., American Philosophical Soc.; Corresp. Mem. Real Academia de Historia, Madrid. Hon. LittD Camb.; Hon. LLD Glasgow; Hon. DLitt: Durham; St Andrews; Hon. LitD London. Hon. DPhil Salonika; Hon. DD Wabash, USA; Hon. DHL Chicago. Knight Commander, Order of the Phœnix (Greece), 1961. *Publications:* The Emperor Romanus Lecapenus, 1929; The First Bulgarian Empire, 1930; Byzantine Civilization, 1933; The Medieval Manichee, 1947; A History of the Crusades, Vol. I, 1951, Vol. II, 1952, Vol. III, 1954; The Eastern Schism, 1955; The Sicilian Vespers, 1958; The White Rajahs, 1960; The Fall of Constantinople, 1453, 1965; The Great Church in Captivity, The Last Byzantine

Renaissance, 1970; contributions to various Historical Journals. *Address:* Elshieshields, Lockerbie, Dumfriesshire. *Club:* Athenæum.

**RUNCORN, Prof. Stanley Keith,** FRS 1965; Professor of Physics and Head of the School of Physics, University of Newcastle upon Tyne, since 1963, and in the University of Durham (King's College), 1956-63; *b* 19 November 1922; *s* of W. H. Runcorn, Southport, Lancs; unmarried. *Educ:* King George V Sch., Southport; Gonville and Caius Coll., Cambridge. ScD 1963. Radar Research and Devel. Establishment (Min. of Supply), 1943-46; Asst Lecturer, 1946-48, and Lecturer, 1948-49, in Physics, Univ. of Manchester; Asst Dir of Research in Geophysics, Cambridge Univ., 1950-55; Research Geophysicist, Univ. of California at Los Angeles, 1952 and 1953; Fellow of Gonville and Caius Coll., Cambridge, 1948-55; Visiting Scientist, Dominion Observatory, Ottawa, 1955; Vis. Prof. of Geophysics: Cal. Inst. of Tech., 1957; Univ. of Miami, 1966; Pa State Univ., 1967; Florida State Univ., 1968; J. Ellerton Becker Senior Visiting Fellow, Australian Academy of Science, 1963; Rutherford Memorial Lectr (Kenya, Tanzania and Uganda), 1970. Mem., Natural Environment Research Council, 1965-. Napier Shaw Prize, Royal Met. Soc., 1959. Hon. DSc Utrecht, 1969. *Publications:* scientific papers. *Recreations:* usual. *Address:* University of Newcastle upon Tyne, Newcastle upon Tyne NE1 7RU.

**RUNDALL, Sir Francis (Brian Anthony),** GCMG 1968 (KCMG 1956; CMG 1951); OBE 1944; Ambassador to Japan, 1963-67; *b* 11 Sept. 1908; *s* of late Lieutenant-Colonel Charles Frank Rundall, CMG, DSO; *m* 1935, Mary, *d* of late Frank Syrett, MD; one *s* one *d*. *Educ:* Marlborough College; Peterhouse, Cambridge. Entered General Consular Service, 1930; served in Antwerp, Colon, Panama, Boston, Barcelona, Piraeus; Consul, New York, 1944; transferred Foreign Office, 1946; HM Inspector of Foreign Service Establishments, 1949-53. Chief Administrative Officer, UK High Commission in Germany during 1953; Consul-General in New York, 1953-57; Ambassador to Israel, 1957-59; Deputy Under-Secretary of State, Foreign Office, 1959-63. *Address:* Lime Tree Cottage, Church Oakley, Basingstoke, Hants. *T:* Oakley 217. *Club:* Travellers'.

**RUNGE, Norah Cecil, (Mrs Thomas A. Ross),** OBE 1918; Alderman LCC, 1937-61; *b* London, 1884; *d* of late Lawrence Hasluck; *m* 1st, 1906, J. J. Runge (*d* 1935); one *s* one *d* (and two *s* decd); 2nd, 1939, Thomas Arthur Ross, MD, FRCP (*d* 1941). *Educ:* privately. Supt of the Soldiers' and Sailors' Free Buffet, Paddington Station, 1915-19; President of the Rotherhithe Conservative and Unionist Association, 1932-46; Vice-Chairman of Central Women's Advisory Committee of Conservative and Unionist Associations, 1941-42, of the London Conservative Union Council, 1940-47; Chm. of the London Area Women's Advisory Committee, 1938-43, Pres. 1943-45; Member of Civil Defence, Bermondsey; worked for Red Cross POW Dept., 1941-45. MP (U) Rotherhithe, 1931-35; contested Rotherhithe, 1935 and 1945. Chairman Horton Hospital Management Committee, 1948-52; Member of Board of Governors of Bethlem Royal, and Maudsley Hosp., 1948-60. Dep. Chm. LCC, 1951-52. *Address:* St John's House, Smith Square, SW1. *T:* 01-222 1563.

*See also Baron Drumalbyn.*

**RUOFF, Theodore Burton Fox,** CB 1970; CBE 1962; Chief Land Registrar since 1963; *b* 12 April 1910; *s* of late Percy Ruoff and late Edith Crane; *m* 1947, Marjorie Alice, *er d* of late George Mawson, Worthing; no *c*. *Educ:* Clarence School, Weston-super-Mare; King Edward VI School, Bury St Edmunds. Admitted as a solicitor, 1933; 2nd class Hons; Hertfordshire Law Society prizeman; Nuffield Fellowship in Australia and New Zealand, 1951-52; Senior Land Registrar of HM Land Registry, 1958. *Publications:* An Englishman Looks at the Torrens System, 1957; Concise Land Registration Practice, 1959; Rent charges in Registered Conveyancing, 1961; Land Registration Forms, 1962; Curtis and Ruoff's The Law and Practice of Registered Conveyancing (2nd edn, 1965); regular contribs to Australian Law Jl, Conveyancer and Property Lawyer, etc. *Recreations:* sketching, painting; indifferent golf, gardening. *Address:* Flat One, 83 South Hill Park, Hampstead, NW3. *T:* 01-435 8014. *Clubs:* Travellers', MCC.

**RUPERT'S LAND, Metropolitan of;** *see* Qu'Appelle, Archbishop of.

**RUPERT'S LAND, Bishop of,** since 1970; **Rt. Rev. Barry Valentine,** MA, BD, LTh, DD; *b* 26 Sept. 1927; *s* of Harry John Valentine and Ethel Margaret Purkiss; *m* 1952, Mary Currell Hayes; three *s* one *d*. *Educ:* Brentwood Sch.; St John's Coll., Cambridge; McGill Univ., Montreal. Curate, Christ Church Cath., Montreal, 1952; Incumbent, Chateauguay-Beauharnois, 1954; Dir, Religious Educn, Dio. Montreal, 1957; Rector of St Lambert, PQ, 1961; Exec. Officer, Dio. Montreal, 1965; Dean of Montreal, 1968; Bishop Coadjutor of Rupert's Land, 1969; Chancellor, St John's Coll., Winnipeg, 1970. Hon. DD: St John's Coll., Winnipeg, 1969; Montreal Dio. Theol. Coll., 1970. *Recreations:* music, theatre, walking, reading; over-aged and bibulous cricket. *Address:* Anglican Centre, 302, 257 Smith Street, Winnipeg 1, Manitoba, Canada. *T:* 204-942 7371. *Clubs:* Winnipeg Squash Racquet; Taverners Cricket.

**RUPP, Rev. Prof. Ernest Gordon,** MA, DD Cantab; FBA 1970; Dixie Professor of Ecclesiastical History, University of Cambridge, since 1968; Principal, Wesley House, Cambridge, since 1967; *b* 7 Jan. 1910; *m* 1938, Marjorie Hibbard; one *s*. *Educ:* Owen's School, EC; King's College, London (BA); Wesley House, Cambridge; Universities of Strasbourg and Basel. Methodist Minister, Chislehurst, Kent, 1938-46; Wesley House, Cambridge, 1946-47; Richmond College, Surrey, 1947-52; Birkbeck Lectr, Trinity Coll., Cambridge, 1947; Lecturer in Divinity, Cambridge Univ., 1952-56; Prof. of Ecclesiastical History, Univ. of Manchester, 1956-67. President of the Methodist Conference, 1968-69; Mem., Central Cttee of World Council of Churches, 1969. Fellow, Emmanuel Coll., 1968; Hon. Fellow: Fitzwilliam College, 1969; King's Coll., London, 1969. Hon. DD Aberdeen; Hon. Dr Théol, Paris. *Publications:* Studies in the English Protestant Tradition, 1947; Luther's Progress to the Diet of Worms, 1951; The Righteousness of God (Luther studies), 1953; Some Makers of English Religion, 1957; The Old Reformation and the New, 1967; Patterns of Reformation, 1969. *Address:* Principal's Lodge, Wesley House, Cambridge.

**RUSBY, Norman Lloyd,** MA, DM Oxon, FRCP; Consulting Physician: London Hospital since 1970 (Physician, 1946-70); London Chest Hospital since 1970 (Physician, 1936-70); King Edward VII Hospital, Midhurst; Benenden Chest Hospital (Civil Service); Consulting Physician in Diseases of the Chest to the Royal

Navy; *b* 26 October 1905; *s* of Dr Edward L. M. Rusby, Streatham; *m* 1941, Elizabeth, *e d* of F. A. Broadhead, Nottingham; three *s*. *Educ:* Lancing College; St John's College, Oxford; St Thomas's Hospital. Medical Registrar and Tutor, British Postgraduate Medical School, Hammersmith, 1937-39. Member Standing Advisory Committee on Tuberculosis to Min. of Health, 1940-44; Editor of Tubercle, 1938-44; Hon. Colonel RAMC; Local Brigadier, Consulting Physician Middle East Land Forces, 1946. Nuffield visitor to East Africa, 1950, 1953. Examiner in Medicine: University of London, 1951-56; University of Cambridge, 1957-60; Royal College of Physicians, 1962-68. Mitchell Lecturer, RCP, 1967. Vice-Chairman of Council, Chest and Heart Assoc.; Member: Assoc. of Physicians of Gt Britain and Ireland; Thoracic Society; Board of Governors: Hospitals for Diseases of the Chest, 1962-67; London Hospital, 1967-70. *Publications:* (Jt Editor) Recent Advances in Respiratory Tuberculosis, 6th edn 1968; contributions to various journals, chiefly on diseases of the chest. *Address:* 112 Harley Street, W1. *T:* 01-935 2007; 21 Windmill Hill, Hampstead, NW3. *T:* 01-794 6889. *Club:* United University.

**RUSE, Prof. Harold Stanley,** MA (Oxon), DSc (Edinburgh), FRSE; Professor of Pure Mathematics in the University of Leeds, 1946-70, now Professor Emeritus; Head of Department of Mathematics, 1946-68; Chairman, School of Mathematics, and Head of Department of Pure Mathematics, 1968-70; *b* 12 Feb. 1905; 3rd *s* of late Frederick and Lydia Ruse, Hastings; unmarried. *Educ:* Hastings Gram. Sch.; Jesus Coll., Oxford. Bruce of Grangehill Research Schol., University of Edin., 1927-28; Lectr in Mathematics, Univ. of Edin., 1928-37; Sen. Mathematical Schol., Oxford, 1929; Rockefeller Research Fellow, Princeton Univ., USA, 1933-34; Pres. Edinburgh Mathematical Soc., 1935-36; Keith Prize, Royal Soc. of Edin., 1935-37; Prof. of Mathematics, Univ. Coll., Southampton, 1937-46. Visiting Fellow, Princeton, 1952-53. *Publications:* (with A. G. Walker and T. J. Willmore) Harmonic Spaces, 1962; research papers on relativity, differential geometry and algebra. *Address:* The University, Leeds LS2 9JT; 10 Oak Bank, 13 Shaw Lane, Leeds LS6 4DH. *T:* (residence) 56085.

**RUSHBROOK WILLIAMS, L. F.;** *see* Williams.

**RUSHBROOKE, Vice-Adm. Edmund Gerard Noel,** CBE 1942; DSC 1917; retired; *b* 15 Dec. 1892; *s* of Capt. William Henry Rushbrooke, JP (Cosford, Thursley, Surrey, and Whitepoint, Queenstown, Ireland), and of Mrs Margaret Mary Rushbrooke; *m* 1st, 1926, Ada Stott Moncrieff; one *d* (decd); 2nd, 1937, Marjorie Wentworth Foster (*d* 1970). *Educ:* RNC, Osborne and Dartmouth. Served War of 1914-18, in Destroyers as Sub-Lt and Lieut (DSC, Croix de Guerre, Board of Trade Life Saving Medal). Comdr, 1928; Capt., 1936. Chief of Intelligence Staff, China Station, 1937; served War of 1939-45; in Command: HMS Guardian, 1939; HMS Argus, 1940; HMS Eagle, 1941; Director of Naval Intelligence, 1942-46; Rear-Adm., 1945; retired 1947; Vice-Adm. on retired list, 1948. US Legion of Merit, 1946. *Address:* 14 Royal Crescent, Bath, Somerset. *Club:* MCC.

**RUSHBROOKE, Prof. G(eorge) Stanley,** MA, PhD; FRSE; Professor of Theoretical Physics, University of Newcastle upon Tyne, since 1951; *b* 19 January 1915; *s* of George Henry Rushbrooke and Frances Isobel Rushbrooke (*née* Wright), Willenhall, Staffs; *m* 1949, Thelma Barbara Cox. *Educ:* Wolverhampton Grammar School; St John's College, Cambridge. Schol. St John's Coll., Camb., 1933-37; Research Asst, Bristol Univ., 1938-39; Senior DSIR award and Carnegie Teaching Fellowship, 1939-44, UC Dundee, Univ. of St Andrews; Lectr in Mathematical Chemistry, The Univ., Leeds, 1944-48; Sen. Lectr in Theoretical Physics, Oxford, Univ. and Lecturer in Mathematics, University Coll., Oxford, 1948-51; Visiting Prof., Dept of Chemistry, Univ. of Oregon, USA, 1962-63; Vis. Prof. of Physics and Chemistry, Rice Univ., Houston, 1967. *Publications:* Introduction to Statistical Mechanics, 1949; research papers in scientific journals. *Address:* The University, Newcastle upon Tyne NE1 7RU.

**RUSHFORD, Antony Redfern,** CMG 1963; HM Diplomatic Service; Deputy Legal Adviser, Foreign and Commonwealth Office, since 1969; *b* 9 February 1922. *Educ:* Taunton School; Trinity College, Cambridge. RAFVR, 1943-47, Sqdn Ldr, 1946. Admitted a Solicitor, 1944 (removed from roll at own request, 1957). BA, LLB 1948; MA 1951; Student, Inner Temple, 1957. Colonial Office: Legal Asst, 1949-54; Senior Legal Assistant, 1954-60; Assistant Legal Adviser, 1960-66; Legal Counsellor, FCO (formerly CO), 1966-69. Foundn Mem. Exec. Council, Royal Commonwealth Soc. for the Blind, 1969-. *Address:* 9 Hertford Street, Mayfair, W1Y 7DY. *T:* 01-499 4276; 9 Moorland Avenue, Barton on Sea, New Milton, Hants BH25 7DB. *T:* New Milton 325.

**RUSHOLME,** 1st Baron, *cr* 1945, of Rusholme; **Robert Alexander Palmer;** Chairman, London Midland Area Board, British Railways, 1955-60; Chairman, Board of Survey, Inland Waterways, 1954; *b* 29 November 1890; *s* of William Palmer and Elizabeth Green; unmarried. *Educ:* St Mary's School, Ashton-on-Mersey. Late Pres. of Internat. Co-operative Alliance; JP, Manchester. Served in Manchester Regiment, 1914-18, Egypt, Belgium, France. Member: Central Price Regulation Cttee, 1939-45; Retail Trade Cttee, 1941-42; Min. of Labour Cttee for Business Training, 1944; Cttee on Proceedings in Matrimonial Causes, 1946-47; British Transport Commission, 1947-59; Central Transport Consultative Cttee, 1948-59; Road Haulage Disposal Board, 1953; Cttee on Organisation of Crown Lands, 1954-55; Chm. Coastal Shipping Advisory Cttee, 1947-56; Dir Thos Cook & Son Ltd and associated cos, 1949-67. *Publications:* pamphlets and articles on Co-operation and allied subjects. *Address:* Rusholme Gardens, Manchester 14. *T:* 061-224 9596.

**RUSHTON, Frederick Alan;** Member of North Regional Board, National Westminster Bank Ltd; Director, Northern Counties Board, Legal and General Assurance Society Ltd, since 1969; formerly Chief General Manager and Director, District Bank Ltd, Manchester; *b* 15 Feb. 1905; *s* of Frederick and Elizabeth Rushton; *m* 1931, Eirene Williams; two *s*. *Educ:* University Sch., Southport, Lancs. Dir, Westminster Hambro Trust Managers Ltd. Governor, Manchester Grammar Sch.; Mem. Court, Univ. of Manchester. *Recreations:* golf, gardening. *Address:* Gortmore, Broadway, Hale, Cheshire. *T:* 061-980 4809.

**RUSHTON, Martin A.,** CBE 1960; Professor Emeritus of Dental Medicine in the University of London; *b* 29 March 1903; *s* of W. Rushton; *m* 1949, Dorothy (*née* Whiteside); one *d*. *Educ:* Caius College, Cambridge; Guy's Hospital. Additional Dental Surgeon to Guy's Hospital; Hon. Consulting Dental Surgeon to St

Thomas' Hosp.; Dental Surgeon i/c Maxillo-facial Unit, Basingstoke, 1939-46. Dean, Faculty of Dental Surgery, RCS, 1959-62. Pres., BDA, 1964-65. Hon. degrees: OdontD Stockholm, 1958; LLD: Toronto, 1959; Belfast, 1965; DOdont Copenhagen, 1964; DSc Wales 1969. FRCS 1964. Colyer Gold Medal, RCS, 1968. *Address:* Alcala, Kippington Road, Sevenoaks, Kent. *T:* 55627.

**RUSHTON, William Albert Hugh,** FRS 1948; ScD, PhD, MA, MRCS, LRCP; Fellow, Trinity College, Cambridge, since 1938 (Director of Medical Studies, 1938-63); Distinguished Research Professor in Psychobiology, Florida State University, Tallahassee, since 1968; *b* 8 December 1901; *er s* of William and Alice Rushton, Harley Street and Hampstead, London; *m* 1930, Marjorie, 2nd *d* of Norman Kendrick, Cardiff; two *s* two *d*. *Educ:* Gresham's, Holt; Emmanuel Coll., Cambridge; University Coll. Hosp., London; Stokes Student Pembroke Coll., Cambridge, 1927; Johnson Fellow, Univ. Pennsylvania, 1929; Research Fellow, Emmanuel Coll., 1931; Lectr in Physiology, Cambridge University, 1935-53; Reader, 1953-65; Prof. of Visual Physiology, Cambridge Univ., 1966-68. Hon. Member: American Academy of Arts and Sciences, 1963; Swedish Royal Soc., 1968. Ferrier Lectr, Roy. Soc., 1962. First Prentice Medallist, Amer. Acad. Optometry, 1963; Silliman Lecturer, Univ. Yale, 1966; Feldberg Prize, 1967; Waynflete Lectr, Magdalen Coll., Oxford, 1968. Hon. DSc Case Western Reserve Univ., 1969. *Publications:* papers in Jl of Physiology, Proc. Roy. Soc., etc. *Recreation:* music (viola and bassoon). *Address:* Trinity College, Cambridge; Shawms, Conduit Head Road, Cambridge. *T:* 54742.

**RUSK, Dean;** Secretary of State, USA, 1961-69; *b* 9 February 1909; *s* of Robert Hugh Rusk and Frances Elizabeth Clotfelter; *m* 1937, Virginia Foisie; two *s* one *d*. *Educ:* Davidson College, North Carolina; St John's College, Oxford. Assoc. Prof. of Government and Dean of Faculty, Mills Coll., 1934-40; US Army, 1940-46; Special Asst to Secretary of War, 1946; US Dept of State, 1947-51; Asst Sec. of State for UN Affairs; Dep. Under Sec. of State; Asst Sec. of State for Far Eastern Affairs; President, The Rockefeller Foundation, 1952-61, Distinguished Fellow, 1969-. Hon. Fellow, St John's Coll., Oxford, 1955. Hon. LLD: Mills Coll., Calif, 1948; Davidson Coll., 1950; Univ. of Calif, 1961; Emory Univ., Georgia, 1961; Princeton Univ., NJ, 1961; Louisiana State Univ. 1962; Amherst Coll., 1962; Columbia Univ., 1963; Harvard Univ., 1963; Rhode Island Univ., 1963; Valparaiso Univ., 1964; Williams Coll., 1964; Univ. of N Carolina, 1964; George Washington Univ., 1965; Oberlin Coll., 1965; Maryville Coll., 1965; Denver Univ., 1966; Erskine Coll., 1967. Hon. DCL Oxford, 1962; Hon. LHD: Westminster Coll., 1962; Hebrew Union Coll., 1963; Hardin-Simmons Univ., 1967. Cecil Peace Prize, 1933. Legion of Merit (Oak Leaf Cluster). *Address:* 4980 Quebec Street NW, Washington, DC 20016, USA. *Club:* Century (New York).

**RUSK, Robert Robertson,** MA (Glasgow), BA (Cambridge), PhD (Jena); retired as Director to The Scottish Council for Research in Education, 1958; *b* 1879; *m* Florence (*d* 1953), *e d* of late Mr and Mrs George Lowe, Lurgan House, Co. Westmeath; one *d*. *Educ:* Ayr Grammar Sch.; Ayr Acad.; Univs of Glasgow, Jena, Cambridge. Formerly Lectr on Education in the University of Glasgow, retd, 1951. *Publications:* Experimental Education; The Doctrines of the Great Educators; The Religious Education of the Child; the Training of Teachers in Scotland; An Historical Review; The Philosophical Bases of Education; Research in Education; An Introduction; A History of Infant Education; Outline of Experimental Education. *Recreation:* golf. *Address:* Arniston, 51 Old Edinburgh Road, Inverness. *T:* Inverness 32643.

**RUSSELL;** *see* Hamilton-Russell.

**RUSSELL,** family name of **Duke of Bedford, Earl Russell, Baron Ampthill, Baron de Clifford,** and **Baron Russell of Liverpool.**

**RUSSELL,** 4th Earl *cr* 1861; **John Conrad Russell;** Viscount Amberley, 1861; *b* 16 Nov. 1921; *er s* of 3rd Earl Russell, OM, FRS, and Dora Winifred, MBE, *d* of late Sir Frederick Black, KCB; *S* father, 1970; *m* 1946, Susan Doniphan (marr. diss. 1954), *d* of late Vachel Lindsay; two *d*. *Educ:* Dartington Hall School; University of California, Los Angeles; Harvard University. Served War of 1939-45, in RNVR, 1943-46; Temp. Admin. Asst, FAO of the United Nations, Washington, DC, 1946-47; temp. Admin. Asst, HM Treasury, 1947-49. *Heir: half-brother* Hon. Conrad Sebastian Robert Russell [*b* 15 April 1937; *m* 1962, Elizabeth Franklin, *e d* of Horace Sanders; one *s*]. *Address:* Carn Voel, Porthcurno, Nr Penzance, Cornwall.

**RUSSELL, Hon. Lord; Albert Russell,** QC (Scotland) 1931; Senator of College of Justice in Scotland, 1936-60; *b* 1884; *s* of late Sir William F. Russell, Glasgow; *m* 1913, Florence Muir, *d* of late Thomas Galloway, of Auchendrane, Ayrshire; one *s* three *d*. *Educ:* Glasgow Academy; Glasgow University (MA, LLB). Admitted to the Faculty of Advocates, 1908; served in Royal Engineers, 1915-18; Advocate Depute, 1928-29; MP (U) Kirkcaldy Burghs, 1931-35; Solicitor-General for Scotland, 1935-36. *Address:* 3 Glenorchy Road, North Berwick, East Lothian. *Club:* Northern (Edinburgh).

*See also A. M. G. Russell.*

**RUSSELL OF LIVERPOOL,** 2nd Baron, *cr* 1919; **Edward Frederick Langley Russell,** CBE 1945 (OBE 1943); MC; Barrister-at-Law, Gray's Inn, 1931; *b* 10 April 1895; *o s* of Richard Henry Langley Russell and Mabel Younge; *S* grandfather, 1920; *m* 1st, 1920, Constance Claudine (marr. diss., 1933), *yr d* of late Col Philip Cecil Harcourt Gordon, CMG; one *s* one *d*; 2nd, 1933, Joan Betty (marr. diss., 1946), *d* of late Dr David Ewart, OBE, MD, FRCS, Chichester; one *d*; 3rd, 1946, Alix, *o d* of Marquis de Bréviaire d'Alaincourt, and *widow* of Comte Bernard de Richard d'Ivry. *Educ:* Liverpool Coll.; St John's Coll., Oxford. Served European War, 1914-18 (MC and two bars); War of 1939-45 (despatches, OBE, CBE); Brig. (retd); ADJAG, BEF, 1939-40; DJAG, HQ First Army, 1942-43; Allied Force HQ, 1943-45; GHQ Middle East Forces, 1945-46; HQ BAOR, 1946-47, 1948-51; Assistant Judge Advocate General, 1951-54. Officier de la Légion d'Honneur, 1960. *Publications:* The Scourge of the Swastika, 1954; Though the Heavens Fall, 1956; The Knights of Bushido, 1958; That Reminds Me, 1959; If I forget Thee, 1960; The Royal Conscience, 1961; The Trial of Adolf Eichmann, 1962; The Tragedy of the Congo, 1962; South Africa Today–and Tomorrow?, 1963; The Knight of the Sword, 1964; Deadman's Hill, 1965; Caroline the Unhappy Queen, 1967; Return of the Swastika?, 1968; Henry of Navarre, 1969. *Heir: s* Hon. Langley Gordon Haslingden Russell, MC 1945, late Captain Grenadier Guards [*b* 14 Sept. 1922; *m* 1951, Kiloran Margaret, *d* of Hon. Sir Arthur Howard, *qv*; three *s* three *d*].

*Address:* 35 Dinard, France. *Club:* Wig and Pen.

**RUSSELL, Alan;** A Managing Director of J. Henry Schroder Wagg & Co. Ltd; Director: Alexanders Discount Co. Ltd; Legal and General Assurance Society Ltd; IBM United Kingdom Ltd; National Westminster Bank Ltd; Schroders Ltd; Turner & Newall & Co. Ltd; Yorkshire Bank Co. Ltd; *b* 5 Dec. 1910; *s* of late Hon. Cyril Russell; *m* 1st, 1937, Grace Evelyn Moore (decd); one *d*; 2nd, 1944, Jean Patricia, *widow* of Wing Comdr J. R. Cridland, AAF, and *d* of late Stafford Croom Johnson, JP; one step *s* one *s*. *Educ:* Beaumont. Served War of 1939-45, in Army, London Scottish, Lt-Col, attached US Army, Europe, 1941-45. *Address:* 23 Rutland Gate, SW7. *Clubs:* Bath, MCC.

**RUSSELL, Albert;** *see* Russell, Hon. Lord.

**RUSSELL, Albert Muir Galloway,** QC (Scot.) 1965; *b* 26 Oct. 1925; *s* of Hon. Lord Russell, *qv*; *m* 1954, Margaret Winifred, *o d* of T. McW Millar, FRCS(E), Edinburgh; two *s* two *d*. *Educ:* Edinburgh Academy; Wellington College; Brasenose College, Oxford. BA (Hons) Oxon, 1949; LLB (Edin.), 1951. Lieut, Scots Guards, 1944-47. Member of Faculty of Advocates, 1951-. *Recreation:* golf. *Address:* 11 Tipperlinn Road, Edinburgh 10. *T:* 031-447 3511.

**RUSSELL, Alexander Smith,** MC; MA, DSc; Emeritus Student of Christ Church, Oxford, since 1955; Governor of St Paul's School and St Paul's Girls' School, 1933-61; Elder in Presbyterian Church since 1930; *b* Musselburgh, Scotland, 31 May 1888; 2nd *s* of late John Russell, HM Inland Revenue; *m* 1st, 1919, Mary (*d* 1942), 4th *d* of late John Higginson, Dunmurry, Co. Antrim; three *d*; 2nd, 1956, Norma (*née* Hull Lewis), Fellow and Librarian of Somerville College, *widow* of J. E. Hodgson. *Educ:* Woodside School and High School, Glasgow; Universities of Glasgow, Berlin, and Manchester. MA (Glas.) 1908 with 2nd Class Hons, in Math. and Nat. Phil., BSc 1909; carried out research work in Chemistry, especially in Radio-activity, in the laboratories of F. Soddy in Glasgow, 1909-10, of W. Nernst in Berlin, 1910-11, and of Lord Rutherford in Manchester, 1911-13; held from the University of Glasgow successively, 1908-13, the Thomson, Mackay Smith, Carnegie Research, and 1851 Exhibition Research Scholarships, and the Carnegie Research Fellowship; DSc (Glas.) 1913; Lecturer in Physics at Westminster Training College, 1913-14; Lecturer in Physical Chemistry at the University of Sheffield, 1919-20; Student and Tutor of Christ Church, Oxford, 1920-55; Censor, 1938-46; Member of Hebdomadal Council, 1943-55. Served with army in France, 1915-18, with RGA, later attached RE (Capt. RGA, wounded, despatches, MC). MA (Oxon.) 1920. *Publications:* many research papers in the Philosophical Magazine, Proceedings of Royal Society, Phys Zeit, etc.; literary contributions to Manchester Guardian, Quarterly Review, Nineteenth Century, The Listener, etc.; first editor of Discovery; (with S. J. Johnstone) The Rare Earth Industry, 1915; An Introduction to the Chemistry of Radio-Active Substances, 1922; (with B. H. Streeter and others) Adventure, 1927; Incandescent Electric Lamps, 1937; (with others) The Annual Report of the Chemical Society. *Recreations:* house-work, drawing, book collecting. *Address:* 12 Frenchay Road, Oxford. *T:* Oxford 56275.

**RUSSELL, Anna;** International Concert Comedienne; *b* 27 Dec. 1911; *d* of Col C. Russell-Brown, CB, DSO, RE, and Beatrice M. Tandy; single. *Educ:* St Felix School, Southwold; Royal College of Music, London. Folk singer, BBC, 1935-40; Canadian Broadcasting Corp. programmes, 1942-46; Radio interviewer, CBC, 1945-46; Debut, Town Hall, New York, as concert comedienne, 1948; Broadway show, Anna Russell and her Little Show, 1953; Towns of USA, Canada, Great Britain, Australia, New Zealand, the Orient and South Africa, 1948-60. Television, Radio Summer Theatre, USA. *Publications:* The Power of Being a Positive Stinker (NY); The Anna Russell Song Book. *Recreation:* gardening. *Address:* (office) 119 W 57th Street, New York, USA. *Club:* Zouta International (USA, Toronto Branch, Internat. Mem.).

**RUSSELL, Archibald Edward,** CBE 1954; FRS 1970; Joint Chairman, Concorde Executive Committee of Directors, 1965-69; Vice-Chairman, BAC-Sud Aviation Concorde Committee, 1969-70, retired; *b* 30 May 1904; *m*; one *s* one *d*. *Educ:* Fairfield Secondary Sch.; Bristol Univ. Joined Bristol Aeroplane Co. Ltd, 1926; Chief Technician, 1931; Technical Designer, 1938; Chief Engineer, 1944; Dir, 1951; Tech. Dir, 1960-66; Chm., British Aircraft Corporation, Filton Div., 1967-69 (Man. Dir, 1966-67). Wright Bros Memorial Lecture, Washington, 1949; 42nd Wilbur Wright Memorial Lecture, London, 1954; RAeS British Gold Medal, 1951; Hon. DSc Bristol, 1951. CEng; FIAeS; Hon FRAeS 1967. *Publications:* papers in R&M Series of Aeronautical Research Cttee and RAeS Journal. *Address:* 22 Old Sneed Park, Stoke Bishop, Bristol 9. *T:* 682748. *Club:* Royal Aero.

**RUSSELL, Rev. Arthur Colin,** CMG 1957; ED; MA; Parish Minister of Aberlemno, since 1959; *b* 1906; *e s* of late Arthur W. Russell, OBE, WS; *m* 1939, Elma (*d* 1967), *d* of late Douglas Strachan, Hon. RSA; three *d*. *Educ:* Harrow; Brasenose College, Oxford. Barrister-at-law, Inner Temple. Cadet, Gold Coast (now Ghana), 1929; Asst Dist Comr, 1930; Dist Comr, 1940; Judicial Adviser, 1947; Senior, 1951; Regional Officer, 1952; Permanent Sec., Min. of Education and Social Welfare, 1953; Governor's Secretary, 1954; Chief Regional Officer, Ashanti, 1955-57, retd. *Address:* Aberlemno, Forfar, Angus. *T:* Aberlemno 265. *Club:* New (Edinburgh).

**RUSSELL, Audrey;** Broadcaster, Radio and Television; *o d* of late John Strangman Russell and Muriel Russell (*née* Metcalfe), Co. Dublin; unmarried. *Educ:* privately, in England, and France. Trained Central School of Speech and Drama; Poetry Society's Gold Medal, 1934; Minshall Cup for Verse Speaking in Foreign Languages, 1932 and 1936. First stage appearance in London in Victoria Regina, Lyric, 1937; under Gilbert Miller's management, 1937-39. National Fire Service, 1939-42; joined war-time staff, BBC, 1942; accredited BBC war correspondent overseas, 1944-45; news reporter, BBC, 1946-51. Commentaries on State occasions have included: Princess Elizabeth's wedding; Funeral of King George VI at Windsor; the Coronation of Queen Elizabeth II in Westminster Abbey; Weddings: Princess Margaret's; Princess Alexandra's; Duke of Kent's; Funeral of Sir Winston Churchill in St Paul's; BBC Commentator, 1953-: on Commonwealth Tours of the Queen and Duke of Edinburgh to Bermuda, NZ, Australia, Uganda, Malta, Canada, Nigeria, India, Pakistan, Ghana, Sierra Leone, Tanganyika; visits of Queen Elizabeth the Queen Mother to Central and E Africa; State Visits include: Oslo, 1955; Stockholm, 1956; Lisbon, Paris,

Copenhagen, USA, 1957; Amsterdam, 1958; Nepal, Iran, Italy, 1961; W Germany, 1965; Austria, 1969. Royal Maundy Distribution broadcasts, 1952-; numerous TV appearances in connection with history and art. Vice-Chm. Council, Morley College. FRSA. Freeman of City of London, 1967. *Recreations:* painting in oils, and visiting art galleries. *Address:* 117 Kenilworth Court, SW15. *Club:* Oxford and Cambridge University.

**RUSSELL, Barbara Winifred,** MA; Headmistress, Berkhamsted School for Girls, 1950-July 1971; *b* 5 Jan. 1910; *er d* of Lionel Wilfred and Elizabeth Martin Russell. *Educ:* St Oran's School, Edinburgh; Edinburgh University; Oxford University, Dept of Education. History Mistress, Brighton and Hove High School, 1932-38; Senior History Mistress, Roedean School, 1938-49. *Recreations:* reading, walking, travel. *Address:* Disney Lodge, Berkhamsted, Herts. *T:* Berkhamsted 2168. *Club:* Royal Over-Seas League.

**RUSSELL, Ben Harold;** Vice-President, Scientific Development Corporation, since 1964; Chairman, SDC (GB) Ltd, since 1964; Associate Director, The Dorchester Hotel, since 1964; Director, Cunard House Ltd, 1962-63; *b* 13 Nov. 1891; *o s* of late John and Clara Russell; *m* 1926, Evelyn Scotney White (*d* 1967), Melbourne, Australia; one *s*; 2nd, 1968, Elizabeth Gertrude Boor. *Educ:* privately; Christ Church, Cheltenham. Served War of 1914-18 (despatches). Entered service of Cunard Steamship Co. Ltd, 1906, Dir 1947-62, Dep. Gen. Manager, 1947-56; Director: Cunard White Star Ltd, 1947-56; Cunard House Ltd, 1962-63. Member of Board, Travel Assoc., 1946-50; Member Board British Travel and Holidays Assoc. (as rep. British Liner Cttee) on formation of Board, 1950-64, first Vice-President, 1964; Member of the London Tourist Board on formation, 1962 (Vice-Chairman, 1965, Chairman, 1966-68, Vice-President, 1968); Rep. International Chamber of Shipping at UN Conf. on Tourism, Rome, 1963. Member Board of Governors, University College Hospital, 1951-66; Member Whitley Councils for the Health Services (GB) Medical Council, 1953-66; Vice-President, Institute of Travel Managers; Chairman, US Sect., London Chamber of Commerce, 1964-68; Vice-Chm., Exec. Assoc. of Great Britain, 1941-43; Mem. Inst. of Directors; Liveryman, Worshipful Company of Shipwrights; Freeman, City of London. Member, The Pilgrims. FRSA. Meritorious Service Medal, 1917; Chevalier Order of Orange-Nassau, 1947. *Address:* 32 Knightsbridge Court, Sloane Street, SW1. *T:* 01-235 2895. *Clubs:* United Service, Canada, Saints and Sinners.

**RUSSELL, Brian Fitzgerald,** MD, FRCP; Physician, Department of Dermatology, The London Hospital, 1951-69; Physician, St John's Hospital for Diseases of the Skin, 1947-69; Civilian consultant in Dermatology to the Royal Navy, 1955-69; past Dean, Institute of Dermatology; *b* 1 Sept. 1904; *s* of Dr John Hutchinson Russell and Helen Margaret (*née* Collingwood); *m* 1932, Phyllis Daisy Woodward; three *s* one *d*. *Educ:* Merchant Taylors' School. MD (London) 1929; FRCP 1951; DPH (Eng.) 1943. Medical First Asst, London Hosp., 1930-32; general medical practice, 1933-45; Dermatologist, Prince of Wales's Hosp., Tottenham, 1946-51; Asst Physician, Dept of Dermatology St Bartholomew's Hosp., 1946-51. President: St John's Hosp. Dermatological Soc., 1958-60; Dermatological Sect., RSM, 1968-69; Corr. Mem.: American Dermatological Soc.; Danish Dermatological Soc. *Publications:* St John's Hospital for Diseases of the Skin, 1863-1963, 1963; (with Eric Wittkower) Emotional Factors in Skin Diseases, 1953; Section on Dermatology in Price's Medicine (ed by Bodley Scott), 1970. *Recreation:* rustication. *Address:* Parsonage Farm Cottage, Arkesden, Saffron Walden. *T:* Clavering 379. *Club:* Chesterford Country.

**RUSSELL, Sir Charles Ian,** 3rd Bt, *cr* 1916; partner in Charles Russell & Co., Hale Court, Lincoln's Inn, WC2; Captain, RHA (despatches); *b* 13 March 1918; *s* of Captain Sir Alec Charles Russell, 2nd Bt, and Monica (who *m* 2nd, 1942, Brig. John Victor Faviell, CBE, MC), *d* of Hon. Sir Charles Russell, 1st Bt; *S* father, 1938; *m* 1947, Rosemary, *er d* of late Sir John Prestige; one *s* one *d*. *Educ:* Beaumont College; University College, Oxford. Admitted Solicitor, 1947. *Recreations:* golf, bridge. *Heir: s* Charles Dominic Russell, *b* 28 May 1956. *Address:* 12a Albert Court, SW7. *T:* 01-584 2651; Hidden House, Sandwich, Kent. *Clubs:* Garrick; Royal St George's (Sandwich).

**RUSSELL, Rt. Hon. Sir Charles (Ritchie),** PC 1962; Kt 1960; **Rt. Hon. Lord Justice Russell;** a Lord Justice of Appeal since 1962; *b* 12 Jan. 1908; *s* of Francis Xavier, Baron Russell of Killowen, Lord of Appeal in Ordinary (*s* of Charles Baron Russell of Killowen, Lord Chief Justice of England) and Mary Emily Ritchie (*d* of 1st Baron Ritchie of Dundee, former Chancellor of Exchequer); *m* 1933, Joan Elisabeth, *d* of late Dr J. A. Torrens, MD, FRCP; two *s* one *d*. *Educ:* Beaumont; Oriel College, Oxford. Called to Bar, Lincoln's Inn, 1931; QC 1948; Bencher, 1952. Army, 1939-45; RA (Airborne) (despatches, French Croix de Guerre with star). Attorney-General to the Duchy of Cornwall, 1951-60; Judge of Chancery Division, High Court of Justice, 1960-62. President, Restrictive Practices Court, 1961-62 (Member, 1960-62). *Recreation:* golf. *Address:* Brook House, Storrington, Sussex. *T:* Storrington 2138. *Clubs:* Garrick, Beefsteak.

**RUSSELL, Professor Charles Scott,** FRCSE; Professor of Obstetrics and Gynæcology, University of Sheffield, since 1950; *b* 27 March 1912; *s* of late Prof. William Russell and Mrs Beatrice Russell (*née* Ritchie); *m* 1939, Eveline Campbell; four *d*. *Educ:* Edinburgh Acad.; Edinburgh Univ. MB, ChB Edinburgh, 1935; FRCSE 1939; MRCOG 1940; MD 1950; FRCOG 1954. House Surgeon, Canterbury, 1935-36; House Physician, Edinburgh, 1936; General Practice, Dunfermline, 1937; House Surgeon: Royal Maternity and Simpson Memorial Hospital, 1937; Royal Infirmary, Edinburgh, 1938; Research Asst and First Asst, Nuffield Dept of Obstetrics and Gynæcology, Univ. of Oxford, 1939-46; Asst Director, Dept of Obstetrics and Gynæcology, Univ. of Manchester, and Resident Obstetrician and Gynæcologist, St Mary's Hosps, Manchester, 1947-49; Reader in Obstetrics and Gynæcology, Univ. of Manchester, 1949-50. *Publications:* Vesico-Vaginal Fistulas and Related Matters, 1962; The World of a Gynæcologist, 1968; papers in Lancet, Jl of Obst. and Gynæc. of Brit. Empire and others. *Recreations:* gardening, bee-keeping. *Address:* 6 Cavendish Road, Sheffield 11. *T:* 52454.

**RUSSELL, Rev. David Syme,** MA, BD, DLitt; General Secretary, Baptist Union of Great Britain and Ireland, since 1967; *b* 21 Nov. 1916; second *s* of Peter Russell and Janet Marshall Syme; *m* 1943, Marion Hamilton Campbell; one *s* one *d*. *Educ:* Scottish Baptist Coll., Glasgow; Trinity Coll., Glasgow; Glasgow

Univ. (MA, BD, DLitt); Regent's Park Coll.; Oxford Univ. (MA, BLitt). Minister of Baptist Churches: Berwick, 1939-41; Oxford, 1943-45; Acton, 1945-53. Principal of Rawdon Coll., Leeds, and lectr in Old Testament languages and literature, 1953-64; Joint Principal of the Northern Baptist College, Manchester, 1964-67. *Publications:* Between the Testaments, 1960; Two Refugees (Ezekiel and Second Isaiah), 1962; The Method and Message of Jewish Apocalyptic, 1964; The Jews from Alexander to Herod, 1967; contrib. to Encyc. Britannica, 1963. *Recreation:* woodwork. *Address:* 48 Chiltern Road, Sutton, Surrey. *T:* 01-642 2071.

**RUSSELL, David Sturrock W.**; *see* West-Russell.

**RUSSELL, Dorothy Stuart,** MD (London); MA (Oxon); ScD (Cantab); LLD (Glasgow); DSc (McGill); FRCP; retired 1960; Director of Bernhard Baron Institute of Pathology, London Hospital; Professor of Morbid Anatomy in University of London, 1946-60, Emeritus Professor, 1960; Hon. Fellow: Girton College, Cambridge; St Hugh's College, Oxford; *b* 27 June 1895; 2nd *d* of late Philip Stuart Russell, Sydney, NSW, and Alice Louisa, *d* of William Cave. *Educ:* Perse High School for Girls, Cambridge; Girton College, Cambridge; London Hospital. Natural Sciences Tripos, Part I, Class I, 1918; Gilchrist Studentship, Girton College, 1918; Sutton Prize in Pathology and Clinical Obstetrics and Gynæcology Prize, London Hospital, 1921; Junior Beit Fellow, 1923-26, attached to Bernhard Baron Institute of Pathology, London Hospital, and subsequently with grants from Medical Research Council; Rockefeller Travelling Fellow, 1928-29, at Boston, Mass, and Montreal; Medical Research Council, Scientific Staff, 1933-46. Attached to Nuffield Dept of Surgery, Oxford, 1940-44; returned to London Hospital, Oct. 1944. John Hunter Medal and Triennial Prize, Royal College of Surgeons, 1934, for work on the kidney and the brain; Oliver-Sharpey Prize, RCP, 1968, for research. *Publications:* Tumours of the Nervous System; papers in pathology to various journals. *Address:* Holcombe End, Westcott, Dorking, Surrey.

**RUSSELL, Lt-Gen. Sir Dudley,** KBE 1950 (CBE 1944); CB 1945; DSO 1942; MC; late IA, retired; *b* 1 Dec. 1896; *m* 1929, Elizabeth, *d* of Sandys Birket Foster, New York, USA. Served Eritrea and Abyssinia, 1941 (OBE); Western Desert, 1942 (DSO); Italy, 1944-45 (CBE, CB, Commander Order of the American Legion of Merit); Chief British Adviser to Indian Army, 1948-54; retd 1954. *Address:* c/o Barclays Bank, Nassau, Bahamas. *Club:* United Service.

**RUSSELL, Sir (Edward) Lionel,** Kt 1962; CBE 1953; *b* 8 May 1903; *s* of Edward and Kate Russell, Bristol. *Educ:* Clifton College; Christ's College, Cambridge. Lecturer in English, Univ. of Lund, Sweden, 1925-31; Assistant Master, Charterhouse, 1932-35; Asst Director of Education, Liverpool, 1935-38; Asst Education Officer, Birmingham, 1938-46; Chief Education Officer, Birmingham, 1946-68. Member: Univ. Grants Cttee, 1954-63; Council for Nat. Academic Awards; Nat. Adv. Council on Educn for Industry and Commerce; Nat. Cttee for Commonwealth Immigrants, 1965-68; Chairman: Inquiry into Adult Educn in England and Wales, 1969- Centre for Educnl Develt Overseas; Youth Employment Service Training Bd. Pres., Assoc. of Chief Education Officers, 1955-57. Hon. ACT Birmingham, 1962; Hon. DEd CNAA, 1969. *Address:* 24 Tyndall's Park Road, Bristol 8. *T:* Bristol 37121. *Club:* Athenæum.

**RUSSELL, Edward Walter,** CMG 1960; MA Cantab, PhD Cantab; Professor of Soil Science, Reading University, 1964-70; *b* Wye, Kent, 27 Oct. 1904; *e s* of late Sir (Edward) John Russell, OBE, FRS; *m* 1933, Margaret, *y d* of late Sir Hugh Calthrop Webster; one *s* two *d*. *Educ:* Oundle; Gonville and Caius College, Cambridge. Soil Physicist, Rothamsted Experimental Station, Harpenden, 1930-48; Reader in Soil Science, Oxford Univ., 1948-55; Director, East African Agriculture and Forestry Research Organisation, 1955-64. Member: Scientific Council for Africa, 1956-63; Agricultural Research Council of Central Africa, 1959-64. Pres., British Soc. of Soil Science, 1968-70. FInstP; FIBiol; FIAgrE. For. Corr. Mem., French Acad. of Agriculture, 1969. Hon. Councillor, Consejo Superior de Investigations Cientificas, Madrid, 1970. Hon DSc, Univ. of East Anglia, 1970. *Publications:* 8th and 9th Editions of Soil Conditions and Plant Growth; contrib. on physics and chemistry of soils to agricultural and soil science journals. *Address:* 31 Brooklyn Drive, Emmer Green, Reading, Berks RG4 8SR. *T:* Reading 72934. *Clubs:* Athenæum, Farmers'.

**RUSSELL, Evelyn Charles Sackville;** Metropolitan Stipendiary Magistrate since 1961; *b* 2 Dec. 1912; *s* of late Henry Frederick Russell and late Kathleen Isabel, *d* of Richard Morphy; *m* 1939, Joan, *er d* of Harold Edward Jocelyn Camps; one *d*. *Educ:* Douai School; Château de Mesnières, Seine Maritime, France. Hon. Artillery Co., 1938. Served War of 1939-45, Royal Artillery, in UK, N Africa, Italy and Greece. Called to the Bar (Gray's Inn), 1945. *Recreations:* tennis, racing. *Address:* The Gate House, Coopersale, Epping, Essex. *T:* Epping 2568.

**RUSSELL, Sir Frederick (Stratten),** Kt 1965; CBE 1955; DSC, DFC; FRS 1938; BA Cantab; Secretary to Marine Biological Association of the United Kingdom and Director of the Plymouth Laboratory, 1945-65, retd; *b* Bridport, 3 Nov. 1897; *y s* of late William Russell, MA Oxon, Newquay, and late Lucy Binfield, *d* of Henry Newman, Liverpool; *m* 1923, Gweneth, MBE, *d* of late John and late Mary Barnhouse Moy Evans; one *s*. *Educ:* Oundle School; Gonville and Caius College, Cambridge. Served European War, RNAS and RAF, 1916-18 (DSC, DFC, French Croix de Guerre); Interallied Belgian Coast Defence Committee, 1919; Assistant Director of Fisheries Research to Government of Egypt, 1922-23; on scientific staff of Marine Biological Association's Laboratory, Plymouth, Devon, since 1924; Great Barrier Reef Expedition, 1928-29; served War of 1939-45 as Wing Comdr on Air Staff Intelligence, 1940-45. Colonial Fisheries Advisory Cttee, 1945-61; Min. Overseas Devlt Fisheries Advisory Panel, 1961-; National Oceanographic Council, 1950-65; Chairman, Advisory Panel on biological research to Central Electricity Generating Board, 1962-; Trustee, Nat. Maritime Museum, 1965-; Pres. Devonshire Association, 1953. Editor, Journal of Marine Biological Association, 1945-65; Advances in Marine Biology, 1962-. LLD (Hon.) Glasgow, 1957; DSc (Hon.): Exeter, 1960; Birmingham, 1966. Coronation Medal. Linnean Soc. Gold Medal, 1961. Hon. Fellow, Gonville and Caius Coll., Cambridge. For. Mem. Roy. Danish Acad.; Hon. Mem. Physiological Soc.; Challenger Soc. *Publications:* The Seas (with C. M. Yonge), 1928; The Medusae of the British Isles, 1953, vol. II, 1970; numerous Scientific publications on biology of marine plankton invertebrates and fishes, in Scientific Journals, and on marine biology in Britannica Book of The Year, 1949-. *Recreations:* angling, sketching. *Address:* Wardour, Derriford, 295 Tavistock Road, Plymouth, Devon PL6 8AA. *T:* Plymouth 72887; The Laboratory, Citadel Hill, Plymouth. *T:* Plymouth 67105.

**RUSSELL, Sir George Michael,** 7th Bt, *cr* 1812; *b* 30 Sept. 1908; *s* of Sir Arthur Edward Ian Montagu Russell, 6th Bt, MBE and late Aileen Kerr, *y d* of Admiral Mark Robert Pechell; *S* father, 1964; *m* 1936, Joy Frances Bedford, *d* of late W. Mitchell, Irwin, Western Australia; two *d. Educ:* Radley, Berkshire, England. *Heir: half-b* Arthur Mervyn Russell, *b* 7 Feb. 1923.
*See also Baron Broughshane.*

**RUSSELL, Maj.-Gen. George Neville,** CB 1946; CBE 1943; Royal Engineers (retired); Chairman: Sutton Dwellings Trust; *b* 19 Oct. 1899; *m* 1st, 1927, Iris Mills, Wimbledon; two *d*; 2nd, 1946, Jocelyn Delia Harvie Bennett; one *s* two *d. Educ:* Rugby; Woolwich; Cambridge. Director of Movements, GHQ, Middle East, 1942-43; DQMG (Movements and Transportation), GHQ, New Delhi, 1944-45; Transportation Adviser to Special Commissioner in SE Asia, 1946-47; Chairman British Road Services, 1948-59. Member: Eastern Area Board, British Transport Commn, 1957-62 (Chm., 1961-62); British Railways Board, 1962-64; Institute of Transport (President, 1958-59). *Address:* Drayton Wood House, Hastoe, near Tring, Herts. *Club:* Army and Navy.

**RUSSELL, Gerald Francis Morris,** MD, FRCP, FRCPE, DPM; Professor of Psychiatry, Royal Free Hospital School of Medicine, since 1971; *b* Grammont, Belgium, 12 Jan. 1928; 2nd *s* of late Maj. Daniel George Russell, MC, and of Berthe Marie Russell (*née* De Boe); *m* 1950, Margaret Taylor, MB, ChB; three *s. Educ:* Collège St Jean Berchmans, Brussels; George Watson's Coll., Edinburgh (Dux); Univ. of Edinburgh (Mouat Schol. in Practice of Physic). MD (with commendation), 1957. RAMC Regimental Med. Off., Queen's Bays, 1951-53; Neurological Registrar, Northern Gen. Hosp., Edin., 1954-56; MRC Clinical Res. Fellow, 1956-58; Inst. of Psychiatry, Maudsley Hospital: 1st Asst, 1959-60; Senior Lectr, 1961-70; Dean, 1966-70; Bethlem Royal and Maudsley Hospital: Physician, 1961-70, Hon. Physician, 1971-; Mem. Bd of Governors, 1966-70. Vice-Chm., Educn Cttee, Royal Medico-Psychological Assoc., 1969 (Mem. Council, 1966-); Sec. of Sect. of Psychiatry, Roy. Soc. Med., 1966-68; Mem. Ed. Bd, Brit. Jl of Psychiatry, 1966-; Mem. European Soc. for Clinical Investigation, 1968-. Corr. Fellow, Amer. Psychiatric Assoc., 1967. *Publications:* contrib. to Studies in Psychiatry (ed M. Shepherd and D. L. Davies), 1968; articles in med. jls on psychiatry, neurology, nutrition and education. *Recreations:* roses, music, swimming. *Address:* Royal Free Hospital School of Medicine, 8 Hunter Street, WC1.

**RUSSELL, Sir Gordon;** *see* Russell, Sir S. G.

**RUSSELL, Admiral Hon. Sir Guy (Herbrand Edward),** GBE, *cr* 1953 (CBE 1943); KCB, *cr* 1951 (CB 1948); DSO 1944; RN retired; *b* 14 April 1898; 2nd *s* of 2nd Baron Ampthill; *m* 1939, Hon. Elizabeth Blades, *d* of 1st Baron Ebbisham, GBE; two *s* one *d. Educ:* Osborne and Dartmouth. Served European War, 1914-18, at Gallipoli and Jutland (despatches); afterwards saw service in Black Sea, Mediterranean, East Indies, East Africa, and China Station; psc 1929; Comdr 1931; Capt. 1936; Rear-Adm. 1945; Vice-Adm. 1948; Adm. 1952; idc 1937; attached Cabinet Office, 1938 and 1939; War of 1939-45, commanded HMS Protector, HMS Cumberland, HMS Nelson, and HMS Duke of York (despatches, DSO); Chief of Staff to Field-Marshal Lord Gort, VC, at Gibraltar and Malta, 1942 (CBE). Naval Instructor, Imperial Defence College, 1946-48; FO Commanding 2nd Cruiser Squadron, 1948-49; Admiral Commanding Reserves, 1949-51; C-in-C, Far East Station, 1951-53; a Lord Commissioner of the Admiralty, Second Sea Lord, and Chief of Naval Personnel, 1953-55; Commandant Imperial Defence College, 1956-58, retired; First and Principal ADC to the Queen, 1954-58. Chairman: Nat. Assoc. of Boys' Clubs, 1958-63; Missions to Seamen, 1960-65; Radley College Council, 1965-69. *Recreations:* all games, shooting, etc. *Address:* The Old Vicarage, Shamley Green, near Guildford, Surrey. *Clubs:* United Service, Royal Automobile.

**RUSSELL, Gyrth,** RI; ROI; Member Royal Society Marine Artists; *b* 13 April 1892; *s* of Hon. Justice B. Russell, Supreme Court of Nova Scotia, and Louise Coleman Russell; *m* 1911, Gladys Harman Webster; two *s* one *d*; divorced 1933; *m* 1942, Ronagh Alexandra Slee. *Educ:* Public Schools of Nova Scotia; studied Art in Boston and at Académie Julien and Académie Colarossi, Paris, 1913-14. Exhibited widely in Britain and America; represented in the Imperial War Museum, the National Gallery of Canada and the Nova Scotia Museum of Fine Arts; appointed Official War Artist for the Canadian Government, with hon. rank of Lieut, 1917; represented by eighteen works in the Canadian War Memorial Exhibition, Burlington House, 1919. Served in RN Patrol Service, 1940-43. *Publications:* See and Paint, 1957; (with L. du G. Peach) Unknown Devon, 1926; An Introduction to Oil Painting, 1959. Occasional contrib. to The Artist and The Studio. *Address:* 1 Kymin Terrace, Penarth, Glam. *T:* Penarth 709362. *Club:* Little Ship.

**RUSSELL, Henry Stanway; His Honour Judge Russell;** County Court Judge since 1965; *b* 27 April 1910; *s* of William Stanway Russell and Dorothy Sophia Taylor; *m* 1937, Norah Patricia Knight Tapson; two *d. Educ:* Haileybury College; Merton College, Oxford. Called to Bar Inner Temple, 1934; Western Circuit, 1934. 1st Derbyshire Yeomanry RAC (Lieut). Served Tunisia and Italy, 1942-44. Capt., Judge Advocate General's Dept., 1945; Dep. Chm., Cornwall QS, 1963. *Address:* The Manor, Hinton Bluett, Temple Cloud, Nr Bristol. *T:* Temple Cloud 259.

**RUSSELL, Professor James Knox,** MD; ChB; FRCOG; Professor of Midwifery and Gynæcology, and Postgraduate Sub-Dean, University of Newcastle upon Tyne; Consulting Obstetrician, Princess Mary Maternity Hospital; Consultant Gynæcologist, Royal Victoria Infirmary, Newcastle upon Tyne, since 1956; *b* 5 Sept. 1919; *s* of James Russell, Aberdeen; *m* 1944, Cecillia V. Urquhart, MD, DCH, *o d* of Patrick Urquhart, MA; three *d. Educ:* Aberdeen Grammar School; University of Aberdeen. MB, ChB 1942, MD 1954, Aberdeen; MRCOG 1949; FRCOG 1958. First Assistant to Prof. of Obstetrics and Gynæcology, Univ. of Durham, 1950; Senior Lecturer in Obstetrics and Gynæcology, Univ. of Durham, 1956; Consultant Obstetrician, Princess Mary Maternity Hosp., 1956; Consultant Gynæcologist, Royal Victoria Infirmary, Newcastle upon Tyne, 1956. Hon. Obstetrician, MRC Unit on Reproduction and Growth; Examiner in Obstetrics and

Gynæcology, Univs of London, Birmingham, and Liverpool. Served War, 1943-46, as Medical Officer in RAF, UK and Western Europe. *Publications:* various papers on obstetrical and gynæcological subjects to learned journals. *Recreations:* photography and gardening. *Address:* 8 Woodlands, Gosforth, Newcastle upon Tyne. *T:* Gosforth 53698. *Club:* Royal Societies.

**RUSSELL, John;** Art critic of The Sunday Times, since 1950; *b* 1919; *o s* of Isaac James Russell and Harriet Elizabeth Potter; *m* 1st, 1946, Alexandrine Apponyi (marr. diss., 1950); one *d*; 2nd, 1956, Vera Poliakoff. *Educ:* St Paul's Sch.; Magdalen Coll., Oxford (BA). Hon. Attaché, Tate Gall., 1940-41; MOI, 1941-43; Naval Intell. Div., Admty, 1943-46. Regular contributor, The Sunday Times, 1945-; London corresp. Art News, New York, 1956-; European corresp., Art in America, New York, 1956-. Mem. art panel, Arts Council, 1958-68. Organised Arts Council exhibns: Modigliani, 1964, Rouault, 1966 and Balthus, 1968 (all at Tate Gallery); Pop Art (with Suzi Gablik), 1969 (at the Hayward Gallery). *Publications:* books include: Shakespeare's Country, 1942; Switzerland, 1950; Logan Pearsall Smith, 1950; Erich Kleiber, 1956; Paris, 1960; Seurat, 1965; Private View (with Bryan Robertson and Lord Snowdon), 1965; Max Ernst, 1967; Henry Moore, 1968; Ben Nicholson, 1969; Pop Art Redefined (with Suzi Gablik), 1969; *translations:* from André Gide, Roger Martin du Gard, Jules Supervielle and Claude Lévi-Strauss. *Recreations:* walking about in small towns anywhere between Lübeck and Périgueux, or in the USA. *Address:* 5 Westmoreland Street, W1. *T:* 01-486 1786. *Club:* Travellers'.

**RUSSELL, Air Vice-Marshal John Bernard,** CB 1964; CBE 1960 (OBE 1954); DSO 1943; UK Representative on Council of International Civil Aviation Organization, Montreal, since 1969; *b* 13 April 1916; *m* 1937, Dorothy Mary Lucas; one *s* one *d*. *Educ:* Marwood's Sch., Sandwich. Commissioned, RAF, 1935; Specialist Navigator, 1939; served War of 1939-45, 502 and 172 Squadrons and Staff appointments in Coastal Comd, 1940-44; Staff Coll., 1944; Middle East, 1944-45; Directing Staff, 1945-48; British Jt Services Mission, Washington, 1948-50; Air Ministry, 1951-54; HQ No. 19 Group, 1954-57; RAF Malta, 1957-59; Director of Operations (Maritime, Navigation and Air Traffic Control), 1960-63; SASO, RAF Coastal Command, 1963-66; Controller, Nat. Air Traffic Control Services, BoT, 1966-69. *Recreation:* golf. *Address:* 912 International Aviation Building, 1080 University Street, Montreal 101, Canada; 1 Stanley Road, Deal, Kent.

**RUSSELL, Rt. Rev. John Keith;** Assistant Bishop of Rochester since 1965; Vicar of King Charles the Martyr, Tunbridge Wells, since 1965; *b* 4 Aug. 1916; *s* of Rev. B. Russell and A. M. Russell; *m* 1941, Doreen Glen Johnston; one *s* three *d*. *Educ:* Shrewsbury School; Christ's College, Cambridge; Ridley Hall, Cambridge. Assistant Curate, Shirley, Southampton, 1940-45; Tutor, Buwalasi College, Uganda, and Mass Literacy Field Worker, Upper Nile Diocese, 1946-48; Rural Dean, Masaba Deanery, Upper Nile Diocese, 1948-52; Education Secretary, Mbale Archdeaconry, Upper Nile Dio., 1948-55; Asst Bishop on Upper Nile, Uganda, 1955-60; Bishop of Northern Uganda, 1961-64. Chm., Jt Social Work Council for Canterbury and Rochester Dioceses, 1968-. *Publication:* Men without God?, 1966. *Recreations:* cricket, football, music. *Address:* King Charles's Vicarage, Tunbridge Wells, Kent.

**RUSSELL, Sir John (Weir),** Kt 1958; *b* 1893; *s* of Samuel Russell, ICS, and Maud Morrison (*née* Parr); *m* 1st, 1920, Lucy Ellen Mead; one *s* one *d*; 2nd, 1932, Mary Catherine Davies (*née* Stewart). *Educ:* Winchester; New College, Oxford. European War, 1914-18; L.-Corp. King Edward's Horse, 1914; 2nd Lt, Lt, Capt., RFA President, Oxford Union, 1920. Barrister-at-Law, Inner Temple, 1922. War of 1939-45: Major, General Staff Intelligence, War Office; Lt-Col Comdg Special Communications Unit. Chairman, London Conservative Union, 1953-55. Governor: Old Vic; Sadler's Wells; Morley Coll.; Chm., Vic-Wells Assoc.; Trustee City Parochial Foundation; Vice-President Shakespeare Fellowship; Pres. Fifth Army (1916-18) Old Comrades Assoc.; Pres. Salonica Reunion Assoc.; Chairman Osteopathic Association Clinic. Registrar Imperial Society of Knights Bachelor. *Recreations:* golf, reading, fishing. *Address:* 57 Rivermead Court, SW6. *T:* 01-736 6783; 4 Brick Court, Temple, EC4. *T:* 01-353 4870. *Clubs:* Carlton, Junior Carlton, Garrick; Hurlingham.

**RUSSELL, Sir John (Wriothesley),** GCVO 1968 (KCVO 1965); CMG 1958; HM Ambassador to Spain, since 1969; *b* 23 Aug. 1914; *s* of late Sir Thomas Russell Pasha, KBE, CMG; *m* 1945, Aliki Diplarakos, Athens, Greece; one *s* one *d*. *Educ:* Eton; Trinity Coll., Cambridge. Entered HM Diplomatic Service, 1937; 3rd Sec.: Foreign Office, 1937, Vienna, 1937, Foreign Office, 1938, Moscow, 1939; 2nd Sec., Washington, 1942; 1st Sec.: Warsaw, 1945, Foreign Office, 1948; First (actg) Dir-Gen., Brussels Treaty Orgn, London, 1948. Rome, 1950; Counsellor, 1953, and Dir Gen. British Information Services, New York; Counsellor, HM Embassy, Teheran, 1956-59. Foreign Office Spokesman (Head of News Dept, Foreign Office) 1959-62; Ambassador: to Ethiopia, 1962-66; to Brazil, 1966-69. Joint-Master, West Street Hunt, 1960-. Coronation Medal, 1953. *Address:* c/o Foreign and Commonwealth Office, SW1; 80 Chester Square, SW1; The Vine Farm, Northbourne, Deal, Kent. *Clubs:* Beefsteak, Garrick, White's.

**RUSSELL, Ken;** film director since 1958; *b* 3 July 1927; *s* of A. H. Russell; *m* 1957, Shirley Ann Kingdon; four *s* one *d*. *Educ:* Nautical Coll., Pangbourne. Merchant Navy, 1945; RAF, 1946-49. Ny Norsk Ballet, 1950; Garrick Players, 1951; free-lance photographer, 1951-57; Film Director, BBC, 1958-66; free-lance film director, 1966; *Films:* Elgar; Bartok; Debussy; Henri Rousseau; Isadora Duncan; Delius; Richard Strauss; French Dressing; The Billion Dollar Brain; Women in Love; The Music Lovers. *Recreation:* music.

**RUSSELL, Mrs Leonard;** *see* Powell, (E.) Dilys.

**RUSSELL, Leonard;** Associate Editor and Chief Literary Editor, Sunday Times; Director, Times Publications Ltd; *b* 26 July 1906; 2nd *s* of Thomas and Mary Russell; *m* 1943, Elizabeth Dilys Powell, *qv*; no *c*. *Publications:* Edited: Parody Party, 1936; Press Gang, 1937; English Wits, 1940; founded The Saturday Book, 1941, and edited it annually until 1951; (with Nicolas Bentley) The English Comic Album, 1948; The Russell Reader, 1956. *Address:* 14 Albion Street, Hyde Park, W2. *T:* 01-723 9807; Slaugham Manor, Slaugham, Sussex. *T:* Handcross 555.

**RUSSELL, Leonard James,** MA, BSc, DPhil; FBA 1954; Hon LLD Glasgow; Emeritus Professor of Philosophy, Univ. of Birmingham, since 1951; *b* 1884; *s* of late Rev. E. T. Russell; *m* 1911, Alice, *d* of late Robert

Green; one *s* one *d*. *Educ:* Univ. of Glasgow; Emmanuel Coll., Cambridge. Lecturer in Logic, Univ. Glasgow, 1910; Prof. of Philosophy, University of Bristol, 1923-25; Professor of Philosophy, University of Birmingham, 1925-50; Dean of the Faculty of Arts, 1937-40; Acting Dean, 1941-43; Acting Professor of Philosophy for the summer quarter of 1932, Stanford University, California; President of the Aristotelian Society, 1932-33; President of Mind Association, 1932-33; Nuffield Foundation Visiting Lectureship to Australia, 1951. Sponsor, University College of N Staffordshire, 1949-52; Visiting Professor of Philosophy, Emory Univ., Atlanta, Ga, 1962-63, 1966. *Publications:* An Introduction to Logic, 1914 (Japanese trans., 1950); An Introduction to Philosophy, 1929. *Address:* 50 Weoley Park Road, Selly Oak, Birmingham B29 6RB. *T:* 021-472 2148.

**RUSSELL, Hon. Leopold Oliver,** CBE 1970 (OBE 1944); TD; Director-General, Cement and Concrete Association since 1958; *b* 26 Jan. 1907; 4th *s* of 2nd Baron Ampthill, GCSI, GCIE; *m* 1935, Rosemary Wintour (marr. diss., 1954); no *c*. *Educ:* Eton. Weekly newspaper publishing company, 1925-38; served War of 1939-45, 5th Battalion Beds and Herts Regiment TA; Gen. Staff appts HQ 18th Div., Eastern Command, South-Eastern Command, GHQ Home Forces, HQ 21st Army Group, and CCG; released with rank of Brigadier; Asst Sec. to Board of Trade, 1946-47; Director, British Institute of Management, 1947-56. *Address:* 17 Onslow Square, SW7. *T:* 01-589 0891; The Old Rectory, Kettlebaston, Bildeston, Suffolk. *T:* Bildeston 314. *Clubs:* Brooks's, Buck's, Beefsteak, Pratt's.

**RUSSELL, Sir Lionel;** *see* Russell, Sir E. L.

**RUSSELL, Martin Guthrie,** CBE 1970; Deputy Chairman, Prison Commission, since 1960; *b* 7 May 1914; *s* of William James Russell and Bessie Gertrude Meades; *m* 1951, Moira May Eynon, *d* of Capt. Richard Threlfell; one *d*. *Educ:* Alleyn's School; Sidney Sussex, Cambridge (MA). Asst Principal, Home Office, 1937; Asst Private Sec. to Lord Privy Seal, 1942; Principal, Home Office, 1942; seconded to Treasury, 1949-51 and 1952-54; Asst Sec. 1950; Estabt Officer, Prison Commn, 1954. *Recreations:* gardening, sailing, ski-ing. *Address:* 4 Camden Road, Sutton, Surrey. *T:* 01-642 5090. *Club:* Oxford and Cambridge University.

**RUSSELL, Brigadier Nelson,** CB 1949; DSO 1943; MC 1916; *b* 7 July 1897; *s* of Nelson Russell, Strathmore, Lisburn, N Ireland; *m* 1926, Edith, *d* of A. T. Allan, Highfield, Lisburn, N Ireland; no *c*. *Educ:* Campbell College, Belfast. Served European War, France and Belgium, 1914-18; 2nd Lt The Royal Irish Fusiliers, 1915. Egypt, India, Sudan, Palestine, 1919-39; Bde Major, 1937-40; Lt-Col, GSO2, 1940; Tunisia, Sicily, Italy, 1939-45; Comdr: The Irish Brigade, 1942-44; Belfast Sub-Area, 1945; Belfast Garrison, 1946; Ulster Indep. Inf. Bde Gp, 1947-50; retired, 1950. Appointed Serjeant-at-Arms to Parliament of Northern Ireland, 1951. *Recreations:* shooting, fishing, golf and gardening. *Address:* The Manor House, Tollymore, Newcastle, N Ireland. *Club:* Ulster (Belfast).

**RUSSELL, Prof. Peter Edward Lionel Russell;** (surname formerly Wheeler); King Alfonso XIII Professor of Spanish and Director of Portuguese Studies, Oxford, since 1953; *b* 24 Oct. 1913; *er s* of Hugh Bernard Wheeler and Rita Muriel (*née* Russell), Christchurch, NZ. *Educ:* Cheltenham College; Queen's College, Oxford. Laming scholar of Queen's College, 1931; de Osma student, 1934; First Class Final Honour School of Modern Langs 1935. Lecturer of St John's College, 1937-53 and Queen's College, 1938-45. Enlisted, 1940; commissioned (Intelligence Corps) Dec. 1940; Temp. Lt-Col, 1945; specially employed in Caribbean, W Africa and SE Asia, 1942-46. Fellow of Queen's College, 1946-53, and Univ. Lectr in Spanish Studies, 1946-53; Fellow of Exeter Coll., 1953; Norman Maccoll Lectr, Cambridge, 1969. Member: Portuguese Academy of History, 1956; UGC Cttee on Latin-American Studies in British Univs, 1962-64. *Publications:* As Fontes de Fernão Lopes, 1941 (Coimbra); The English Intervention in Spain and Portugal in the Time of Edward III and Richard II, 1955; Prince Henry the Navigator, 1960; (with D. M. Rogers) Hispanic Manuscripts and Books in the Bodleian and Oxford College Libraries, 1962. Articles and reviews in Modern Language Review, Medium Aevum, Bulletin of Hispanic Studies, etc. *Recreations:* photography and travel. *Address:* 23 Belsyre Court, Woodstock Road, Oxford. *T:* Oxford 56086. *Club:* United University.

**RUSSELL, Rt. Rev. Philip Welsford Richmond;** *see* Port Elizabeth, Bishop of.

**RUSSELL, Richard Drew,** RDI 1944; Professor of Furniture Design, Royal College, of Art, 1948-64; Professor Emeritus, 1964; Consultant Industrial Designer; *b* 21 Dec. 1903; *s* of Sydney Bolton Russell and Elizabeth Russell (*née* Shefford); *m* 1933, Marian Pepler; two *s* one *d*. *Educ:* Dean Close School, Cheltenham. Trained at Architectural Association School; joined Gordon Russell Ltd, 1929, eventually becoming Director in charge of design; joined Murphy Radio Ltd as staff industrial designer, 1934; set up in private practice in London as consultant industrial designer 1936; joined RNVR to work on camouflage of ships, 1942; resumed private practice in London as designer, 1946. FSIA, 1946. *Recreation:* gardens. *Address:* 17 Hamilton Terrace, NW8. *T:* 01-286 0957; 115 Crawford Street, W1H 1AG. *T:* 01-935 4188. *Club:* Arts.

**RUSSELL, Ritchie;** *see* Russell, W. R.

**RUSSELL, Robert Christopher Hamlyn;** Director, Hydraulics Research Station, Ministry of Technology, since 1965; *b* Singapore, 1921; *s* of Philip Charles and Hilda Gertrude Russell; *m* 1950, Cynthia Mary Roberts; one *s* two *d*. *Educ:* Stowe; King's Coll., Cambridge. Asst Engineer: BTH Co., Rugby, 1944; Dunlop Rubber Co., 1946; Sen. Scientific Officer, later PSO, then SPSO, in Hydraulics Research Station, 1949-65; Director, 1965-. Visiting Prof., Univ. of Strathclyde, 1967. *Publications:* Waves and Tides, 1951; papers on civil engineering hydraulics. *Address:* 29 St Mary's Street, Wallingford, Berks. *T:* Wallingford 3323.

**RUSSELL, Sir Robert Edwin,** Kt, *cr* 1946; CSI 1941; CIE 1934; MA; Indian Civil Service, retired; *b* 21 April 1890; *s* of Robert Russell, Fellow of Trinity College, Dublin; *m* Esther Rhona, *d* of Lt-Colonel J. G. P. Murray, IMS; one *s* two *d*. *Educ:* Campbell College, Belfast; Trinity College, Dublin. Entered ICS, 1912; military service, 1915-19; District Magistrate and Collector, Bihar, 1920-38; Secretary to Government, Revenue Dept, 1927-31; Chief Secretary, 1934-35, 1938-39; Adviser to the Governor of Bihar, India, 1939-45; Asst Sec., Dept of Health for Scotland, 1947-55, retd. A

Vice-Pres., National Trust for Scotland. Hon. MTPI. *Address:* 43 Grange Road, Edinburgh 9. *T:* 031-667 3386. *Club:* New (Edinburgh).

**RUSSELL, Robert Tor,** CIE 1930; DSO 1917; Chief Architect, Government of India; retired 1941; Chief Planning Inspector, Ministry of Housing and Local Government; retired 1954; *b* 1888; *s* of S. B. Russell, Gosmore, Hitchin; *m* 1921, Ethel Frances, MBE, *d* of H. Hatch, ICS, Hitchin; one *s* one *d.* Served Mesopotamia, 1916-19 (despatches, DSO). *Address:* Millhayes, Bickleigh, Tiverton, Devon.

**RUSSELL, Prof. Roger Wolcott;** Vice Chancellor, Academic Affairs, University of California, Irvine, since 1967 (Prof. of Psychobiology and Psychology); *b* 30 Aug. 1914; *s* of Leonard Walker and Sadie Stanhope Russell, Worcester, Mass, USA; *m* 1945, Kathleen Sherman Fortescue; one *s* one *d. Educ:* Worcester (Mass, USA) Public Schools; Clark Univ. (Livermore Schol., Clark Fellow in Psychology); BA 1935, MA 1936; Peabody Coll. (Payne Schol.); University of Virginia (Du Pont Research Fellow); PhD 1939; DSc Univ. of London, 1954. Instructor in Psychology: Univ. of Nebraska, 1939-41, Michigan State Coll., 1941; Research Psychologist, USAF Sch. of Aviation Medicine, 1941-42; Officer USAF, 1942-46; Asst Prof. in Psychol., Univ. of Pittsburgh, 1946-47; Assoc. Prof. of Psychol., Univ. of Pittsburgh and Res. Fellow in Neurophysiol., Western Psychiatric Inst., 1947-49; Fulbright Advanced Research Schol. and Director, Animal Research Lab., Institute of Psychiatry, Univ. of London, 1949-50; Prof. of Psychology and Head of Dept of Psychol., University Coll., London 1950-57 (on leave of absence, 1956-57); Dean of Advanced Studies, Indiana Univ., 1966-67 (Prof. and Chm. Dept of Psychology, 1959-66). Executive Sec. of the American Psychological Assoc., 1956-59, Board of Directors, 1963-65, Pres. Div. 1, 1968-69; Mem., USPHS Advis. Cttee in Psychopharmacology, 1957-63, 1967-70; Member: Nat. Research Coun. (USA), 1958-61, 1963-65, 1967-; Army Sci. Adv. Panel (USA), 1958-66; Sec.-Gen. Internat. Union of Scientific Psychology, 1960-66 (Vice-Pres., 1966-69; Pres., 1969-); Aust.-Amer. Educ. Found. Vis. Prof., Dept of Psychol., Univ. of Sydney, 1965-66; Vis. Erskine Fellow, Univ. of Canterbury, NZ, 1966. Mem., Soc. for Neurosciences. Bronze Star Medal (USA), 1945. Army Commendation Medal (USA), 1946. *Publications:* (ed) Frontiers in Psychology, 1964; (ed) Frontiers in Physiological Psychology, 1966; research papers on experimental psycho-pathology, Physiological, child and social psychology, psychopharmacology. *Recreations:* golf, tennis. *Address:* University of California at Irvine, Irvine, California 92664, USA. *T:* 714-833-5105. *Club:* Cosmos (Washington, DC).

**RUSSELL, Sir Ronald (Stanley),** Kt 1964; MA Cantab; MP (C) Wembley South since 1950; author and journalist; *b* 1904; *s* of late J. Stanley Russell, Seahouses, Northumberland; *m* Ena Glendenning, *d* of late Alfred Forrester, FRIBA, Grove Hill, Middlesbrough; one *s* one *d. Educ:* Haileybury; Caius Coll. Cambridge. On Staff of Newcastle Chronicle Limited, 1929-31; Reuter's Ltd, 1931-35; Lecturer on Economics of Coal Industry, 1935-39. Served War of 1939-45 in coast artillery, and as staff officer. Research Secretary Empire Economic Union, 1945-51. Mem. LCC for Norwood, 1946-52; contested (C) Shettleston Div. of Glasgow, 1935; Coatbridge Div. of Lanarkshire, 1945. Parliamentary Private Secretary to Rt Hon. Duncan Sandys, MP, 1951-55. Sponsored the Pet Animals Bill and piloted it through all its stages in the Commons, 1951, also Opticians Bill, 1957-58; Mem. UK Delegation to Council of Europe and Western European Union, 1957-66. Dep.-Chairman, General Optical Council, 1959-; Chairman, Commonwealth Producers' Organisation, 1960-63 and 1964-; Member Chairman's Panel of House of Commons, 1959-; Jt Hon. Sec., Conservative Private Member's Cttee, 1957-61; Hon. Treasurer, 1961-; Hon. Sec. Animal Welfare Group, 1960-. Besides Commonwealth and foreign affairs, keenly interested in transport problems; member of London and Home Counties Traffic Advisory Cttee 1946-52. *Publications:* Imperial Preference, 1947; Government Bulk Buying, 1948; Tariff Preferences in Western Europe, 1949; Commonwealth Co-operation, 1952-53, 1952. *Recreations:* riding, swimming, photography, travel. *Address:* 29 Acacia road, St John's Wood, NW8. *T:* 01-722 5700; Crumstone, Seahouses, Northumberland. *Clubs:* Carlton, Constitutional, Press.

**RUSSELL, Rosalind, (Mrs F. Brisson);** film actress; *d* of James R. and Clara McKnight Russell; *m* 1941, Frederick Brisson; one *s. Educ:* Marymount College; Barnard College. Hon. Dr Fine Arts, Univ. of Portland, 1967. *Films include:* Craig's Wife; Night Must Fall; His Girl Friday; My Sister Eileen; Take a Letter, Darling; Roughly Speaking; Sister Kenny; Mourning Becomes Electra; The Velvet Touch; Tell it to the Judge; Woman of Distinction; Never Wave at a Wac; The Girl Rush; Picnic; Auntie Mame; A Majority of One; Five Finger Exercise; Gypsy; Oh Dad, Poor Dad, Mama's Hung You in the Closet and I'm Feeling so Sad; Life with Mother Superior; Where Angels Go . . . Trouble Follows; Rosie!; The Unexpected Mrs Pollifax; *plays:* Bell, Book and Candle; Broadway musical comedy, Wonderful Town; Auntie Mame. TV Spectacular, Wonderful Town. *Recreations:* riding, swimming, tennis, golf. *Address:* 6505 Wilshire Boulevard, Los Angeles 48, California, USA. *Clubs:* Bel Air Country (Los Angeles), Eldorado Country (Palm Desert, Calif).

**RUSSELL, Sir (Sydney) Gordon,** Kt 1955; CBE 1947; MC; RDI; FSIA; *b* London, 20 May 1892; *e s* of late S. B. Russell, Snowshill, Glos. and Elizabeth Russell; *m* 1921, Constance Elizabeth Jane Vere, *d* of late Dr F. A. V. Denning, Sligo; two *s* one *d* (and one *s* decd). *Educ:* Campden Grammar School. Served European War with Worcestershire Regiment, 1914-19 (MC). Designer, Managing Director, Gordon Russell Ltd, 1926-40, later Director, now Chairman; Partner Russell & Sons, 1919-46, now Chm. The Lygon Arms Ltd (Broadway). Mem. Art Workers Guild, 1926, Master, 1962; RDI, 1940, Master of the Faculty, 1947-49; Member Utility Furniture Advisory Cttee and Furniture Production Cttee (Bd of Trade), 1942 and Chm. of Bd of Trade Design Panel, 1943-47; Specialist Assessor for Nat. Diploma in Design to Min. of Educ., 1938-53; served on jury of Internat. Low-Cost Furniture Competition, Museum of Modern Art, New York, 1948; Original Member Exec. Cttee, Festival of Britain, 1951; Member: Art Panel of Arts Council, 1948-53, Fine Arts Cttee of British Council, 1948-58, Council of Roy. Soc. of Arts, 1947-49 and 1951-55; Original Mem. Council of Industrial Design, 1944, Dir, 1947-59, Mem., 1960-; Mem. Council, Royal Coll. of Art, 1948-51, and 1952-63; Mem. Council Royal Sch. of Needlework, 1951-68; Mem. Design Panel, Brit. Railways Bd, 1956-66; Pres. Design and Industries Assoc., 1959-62; Member, National Council for Diplomas in Art and Design, 1961-

68. First FSIA, 1945; FRSA, 1949; First Hon. DesRCA, 1952, Senior Fellow, 1960; Hon. ARIBA, 1953, Hon. Fellow, 1965; Hon. AILA, 1955; Hon. LLD, Birmingham Univ., 1960; Hon. DUniv. York, 1969. Mem. Hon. Cttee for Internat. Exhibition of architecture and industrial design, Hälsingborg, Sweden, 1955; Mem. Higher Jury, XIIth Milan Triennale Exhibition, 1960. Officer, Swedish Royal Order of the Vasa, 1954; Commander, Norwegian Royal Order of St Olav, 1957. Gold Albert Medal, RSA, 1962. *Publications:* The Story of Furniture (Puffin), 1947; The Things We See: Furniture (Penguin), 1948; Looking at Furniture, 1964; (autobiography) Designer's Trade, 1968; and articles, lectures and broadcasts on design and country life. *Recreations:* gardening and hand-work of many kinds. *Address:* Kingcombe, Chipping Campden, Glos. *T:* 253. *Club:* Arts.

**RUSSELL, Col (Hon. Brig.) Valentine Cubitt,** DSO 1918; MC; late Suffolk Regiment; *b* 14 Feb. 1896; *y s* of late Stuart Arthur Russell, Kensington; *m* 1918, Mabel Hannah, *d* of Alexander Brewster, Liverpool. Served European War, 1914-18 (despatches twice, DSO, MC and bar, Belgian Croix de Guerre); War of 1939-45 (despatches), temp. Brig. 1941; Col 1941; retired, 1947. *Address:* 92 Gordon Avenue, Stanmore, Middlesex HA7 3QS. *T:* 01-954 1311.

**RUSSELL, (William) Ritchie,** CBE 1952; MD, FRCP; Consultant Neurologist: to United Oxford Hospitals, 1945-70; to Army, 1948-69; Professor of Clinical Neurology, Oxford Univ., 1966-70; *b* 7 Feb. 1903; *s* of Professor William Russell, MD; *m* 1932, Jean Stuart Low; one *s* one *d. Educ:* Edinburgh Academy; Edinburgh Univ. MBChB, 1926; MD(Edin.), 1932; FRCPEd, 1933; FRCP, 1943; MA Oxon, 1946; DSc Oxon, 1955. Asst Physician, Royal Infirmary, Edinburgh, 1934; Lecturer in Neurology: University of Edinburgh, 1938; Oxford University, 1949-66. Served RAMC, 1940-45; Consultant Neurologist (Brig.), MEF, 1943. Editor of Jl of Neurol., Neurosurg, Psychiat., 1948-69. KStJ 1957. *Publications:* Poliomyelitis, 2nd Edn 1956; Brain-Memory-Learning, 1959; Traumatic Aphasia, 1961. Research papers on neurological subjects in medical journals. *Address:* 31 Belsyre Court, Woodstock Road, Oxford OX2 6HU. *T:* 57445. *Club:* Athenæum.

**RUSSELL, William Robert;** Chairman and Managing Director, Shaw Savill & Albion Co. Ltd, since 1968; *b* 6 Aug. 1913; *s* of William Andrew Russell and Mary Margaret Russell; *m* 1940, Muriel Faith Rolfe; one *s* one *d. Educ:* Wakefield Road Central, East Ham. Served War of 1939-45: Mine-Sweeping and Anti-Submarine vessels; Commissioned, 1942; appointed to command, 1943. Joined Shaw Savill & Albion Co. Ltd, 1929; Director, 1958; Manager, 1959; General Manager, 1961; Deputy Chairman, 1966; Director: Furness Withy & Co. Ltd; Geo. Thompson & Co. Ltd (Chm.); Thames Stevedoring Co. (1965) Ltd; Ocean Port Services Ltd; Crusader Shipping Co. Ltd; Aberdeen & Commonwealth Line Ltd; Economic Insurance Co. Ltd; Dolphin Line Ltd; Cairn Line of Steamships Ltd. Chairman: British Council, Australian British Trade Assoc.; Cttee of European Nat. Shipowners' Assocs, 1969-; Member: Council of Chamber of Shipping; Exec. Cttee, British Shipping Fedn. *Recreations:* gardening, golf. *Address:* Westland, Uvedale Road, Limpsfield, Oxted, Surrey. *T:* Oxted 3080. *Club:* RNVR.

**RUSSELL SCOTT, Charles;** *see* Scott, C. R.

**RUSSELL-SMITH, Dame Enid, (Mary Russell),** DBE 1953; MA; Principal of St Aidan's College, Durham University, 1963-70; Hon. Lecturer in Politics since 1964; *b* 3 March 1903; *d* of late Arthur Russell-Smith, of Hartfield, Sussex. *Educ:* St Felix Sch., Southwold, Suffolk; Newnham Coll., Cambridge. Modern Languages Tripos (French and German). Entered Civil Service as Assistant Principal in Ministry of Health, 1925. Deputy Secretary, Ministry of Health, 1956-63. Chm., Sunderland Church Commn. Associate Fellow, Newnham College. *Address:* 3 Pimlico, Durham. *Club:* University Women's.

**RUSSO, Sir Peter (George),** Kt 1964; CBE 1953 (OBE 1939); JP; Barrister-at-Law; Minister of Housing and Economic Development, Gibraltar Council, 1964-68; *b* 1899; *s* of George Russo; *m* 1926, Margot, *d* of late John A. Imossi, Gibraltar; one *d.* Mem. various Govt bodies and cttees; Dir of several local cos; Trustee, John Mackintosh Foundn; past Chm. City Council, former Mem. Exec. Council, Gibraltar. JP Gibraltar, 1947-. *Address:* 2 Red Sands Lane, Gibraltar. *T:* Gibraltar A622. *Club:* Royal Gibraltar Yacht (past Cdre).

**RUTHERFORD, Professor Andrew;** Regius (Chalmers) Professor of English Literature, University of Aberdeen, since 1968; *b* Helmsdale, Sutherland, 23 July 1929; *s* of Thomas Armstrong Rutherford and Christian P. Rutherford (*née* Russell); *m* 1953, Nancy Milroy Browning, *d* of late Dr Arthur Browning; two *s* one *d. Educ:* Helmsdale Sch.; George Watson's Boys' Coll.; Univ. of Edinburgh; Merton Coll., Oxford. MA Edinburgh Univ., First Cl. Hons Eng. Lang. and Lit., James Elliott Prize, and Vans Dunlop Schol., 1951; Carnegie Schol., 1953; BLitt Oxford, 1958. Commnd Seaforth Hldrs, 1952; served with Somaliland Scouts, 1952-53; 11th Bn Seaforth Hldrs (TA), 1953-58. Asst Lectr in English, Univ. of Edinburgh, 1955; Lectr, 1956-64; Vis. Assoc. Prof., Univ. of Rochester (NY), 1963; Sen. Lectr, Univ. of Aberdeen, 1964; Second Prof. of English, Univ. of Aberdeen, 1965-68. Lectures: Byron Foundn, Nottingham Univ., 1964; Chatterton, British Acad., 1965; Stevenson, Edinburgh Univ., 1967. Chm., English Bd, Council for Nat. Academic Awards; Mem. Central Cttee on English, Scottish Education Dept. *Publications:* Byron: A Critical Study, 1961; (ed.) Kipling's Mind and Art, 1964; (ed.) Byron: The Critical Heritage, 1970; articles in learned journals. *Address:* Department of English, Taylor Building, King's College, Aberdeen; 150 Hamilton Place, Aberdeen. *T:* Aberdeen 23868.

**RUTHERFORD, Gideon Campbell,** CB 1948; JP; engaged in farming; Chairman Sutherland Territorial Forces, Major; Hon. Sheriff-Substitute for Sutherland; *b* 2 April 1888; *s* of late John Rutherford, Kildonan, Sutherland; *m* 1917, Laura Gordon; two *s* two *d. Educ:* Helmsdale Higher Grade School. Farming at Kildonan Sheep Farm until 4th Aug. 1914; served European War; mobilised with 5th Seaforths in France (wounded 1916); two years in Hospital. Bought Estate of Proncy, Dornoch, 1924. *Recreation:* fishing. *Address:* Proncy, Dornoch, Sutherland. *T:* 54.

**RUTHERFORD, Herman Graham,** CBE 1966; QPM 1957; DL; Chief Constable of Surrey, 1956-68; retired, 1968; *b* 3 April 1908; *m* 1940, Dorothy Weaver; three *s* one *d. Educ:* Grammar School, Consett, County Durham. Metropolitan Police, 1929-45; Chief Constable: of Oxfordshire, 1945-54; of Lincolnshire, 1954-56. Barrister, Gray's Inn,

1941. Served Army, Allied Military Government, 1943-45, Lt-Colonel. DL Surrey, 1968. *Recreation:* sailing. *Address:* Hankley Farm, Elstead, Surrey. *T:* Elstead 2200. *Clubs:* Tatty Bogle, Little Ship.

**RUTHERFORD, Dame Margaret,** DBE 1967 (OBE 1961); ARCM, LRAM (Eloc.); actress; *b* London, 11 May 1892; *d* of William Rutherford and Florence Nicholson; *m* 1945, Stringer Davis. *Educ:* Wimbledon Hill School; Raven's Croft, Seaford, Sussex. Formerly taught pianoforte and elocution. Studied for stage at Old Vic, where made first theatrical appearance, 1925. Subsequently played in repertory at Oxford and Croydon, and with Greater London Players; West End successes from 1933, notably Bijou in Spring Meeting and Madame Arcati in Blithe Spirit; toured on the Continent, Sept. 1944, for ENSA; toured USA and Canada with John Gielgud, 1947, as Lady Bracknell in the Importance of being Earnest; subsequently played Miss Whitchurch in The Happiest Days of your Life, Apollo Theatre; Madame Desmortes in Ring round the Moon, 1950; Constance Hargreaves in Miss Hargreaves, Royal Court Theatre; Lady Wishfort in The Way of the World, Lyric, Hammersmith; The White Queen in Alice Through the Looking Glass, Princes, 1954; The Duchess in Time Remembered, Lyric, Hammersmith, and New Theatre, 1954-55; Mirabelle in A Likely Tale, Globe Theatre, 1956; Lady Wishfort in The Way of the World, Saville Theatre, 1956; Lady Bracknell in The Importance of Being Earnest, Irish Festival, 1957; Australian Tour for Elizabethan Theatre Trust, 1957-58; Minerva Goody in Farewell, Farewell Eugene, Garrick Theatre, 1959; Mrs Candour in The School for Scandal, Haymarket, 1962; The Solid Gold Cadillac, Saville, 1965; The Clandestine Marriage, Chichester, 1966; Mrs Malaprop in The Rivals, Haymarket, 1966. First appearance in films, 1936, in Dusty Ermine. *Films include:* Blithe Spirit, Miranda, Passport to Pimlico, Her Favourite Husband, The Happiest Days of Your Life, The Importance of Being Earnest, Castle in the Air, Curtain Up, Miss Robin Hood, Innocents in Paris, Runaway Bus, Trouble in Store, Mad about Men, Aunt Clara, An Alligator named Daisy, The Smallest Show on Earth, Just my Luck, I'm All Right Jack, On the Double, "Murder" she Said, Mouse on the Moon, Murder at the Gallop, The VIP's, Murder Most Foul, Murder Ahoy, Chimes at Midnight, A Countess from Hong Kong, Arabella. Has also appeared on Television, notably in 3 plays repeated frequently all over the world: Day after Tomorrow; The Two Wise Virgins of Hove; The Kidnapping of Mary Smith. Awarded Gold Medallion, Ingenio et arte, Denmark, 1955. For role in film, The VIP's, awarded: Golden Globe for Best Supporting Actress (Foreign Press Assoc., Hollywood), 1964; Best Film Actress Silver Medal (Variety Club of Gt Britain), 1964; Oscar as Best Supporting Actress, 1964; Gold Medal Una Vita per il Cinema (Consorzio Stampa Cinematografica, Rome), 1967. *Address:* c/o Film Rights Ltd, 113-117 Wardour Street, W1. *T:* 01-437 7151; Gerrards Cross, Bucks.

**RUTHERFORD, Brig. Thomas John,** CBE 1945; ED; retired as National Chairman, Farm Credit Corporation (1959-63); *b* Leith, Ontario, Canada, 16 Jan. 1893; *s* of Malcolm Rutherford; *m* 1919, Helen Sibbald; three *s* one *d.* Engaged in farming at Leith, Ont.; joined Grey Regt, September 1912; proceeded overseas, 1916; served in France and Belgium with 4th Canadian Mounted Rifles (wounded, despatches); demobilised, 1919. Contested House of Commons, Grey North, 1921; Local Registrar Supreme Court and Surrogate Regist. and Sheriff, Co. Grey, 1923; Lt-Col to command Grey Regt, 1925; Col to command 22nd Cdn Inf. Bde, 1932; R of O, 1936; reverted to Major, 1939, to command a company of the Grey and Simcoe Foresters; Lt-Col to command the Grey and Simcoe Foresters (Overseas Unit), 1940; Brig. to command 1st Canadian Armoured Brigade, 1941; commanded Canadian Armoured Corps Reinforcement Units (UK) and Senior Adviser Canadian Armoured Corps, UK, 1943; Dep. Comdr, Canadian Forces, Netherlands, and Canadian Repatriation Units, UK, 1946. Dir-Gen. of Rehabn, Can., 1946; Nat. Dir, Soldier Settlement and Veterans' Land Act, 1947-62. Hon. Col, Grey and Simcoe Foresters. *Publications:* Scouts and Patrols; Production-line Farming. *Address:* RR1, Owen Sound, Ont, Canada. *Club:* Canadian Mil. Inst.

**RUTHNASWAMY, Miriadas,** CIE 1930; MA Cantab; MP, Council of States, New Delhi, since 1962; *b* Madras Royapuran, 15 Aug. 1885; *s* of Rai Bahadur M. I. Ruthnaswamy, officer on old Nizam's Railway; *m* 1914, Marie Dhyrianathan; four *s* five *d. Educ:* St Joseph's Coll., Cuddalor; St Joseph's Coll., Trichinopoly; Nizam's Coll., Hyderabad; Madras Univ.; Downing Coll., Cambridge. Barrister-at-Law, Gray's Inn. Asst Prof. of English and History, Baroda Coll., 1913-18; Prof. of History, Pachiappa's Coll., 1918-27, Principal, 1921-27; Principal, Law Coll., Madras, 1928-30; Mem. Madras Public Services Commission, 1930-42; Vice-Chancellor, Annamalai University, 1942-48. Member: Mun. Corp., Madras, 1921-24; Madras Legisl. Council, 1922-26 (Pres. 1925-26); Indian Legsl. Assembly, 1927. Founded Catholic Union of India, 1925. Padma Bhushan Award. *Publications:* The Political Philosophy of Mr Ghandi, 1922; The Making of the State, 1935; Influences in British Administrative System, 1937; India from the Dawn, 1949; Principles and Practices of Public Administration, 1953, 1956, 1959, 1962, 1970; Principles and Practice of Foreign Policy, 1962; India after God, 1964. *Recreations:* walking, conversation. *Address:* Cathedral View, San Thome Road, Madras 4, India; 8 Allenby Road, New Delhi.

**RUTHVEN,** family name of **Earl of Gowrie.**

**RUTHVEN OF CANBERRA and DIRLETON, Viscount; Patrick Leo Brer Ruthven;** *b* 4 Feb. 1964; *s* and *heir* of 2nd Earl of Gowrie, *qv.*

**RUTHVEN OF FREELAND, Lady,** 10th in line, Scot. *cr* 1651; **Bridget Helen Monckton** (The Dowager Viscountess Monckton of Brenchley), CBE 1947; *b* 27 July 1896; *e d* of 9th Lord Ruthven, CB, CMG, DSO and Jean Leslie (*d* 1952), *d* of Norman George Lampson; *S* father 1956; *m* 1st, 1918, 11th Earl of Carlisle (marr. diss., 1947; he *d* 1963); one *s* one *d*; 2nd, 1947, (as Sir Walter Monckton), 1st Viscount Monckton of Brenchley, PC, GCVO, KCMG, MC, QC (*d* 1965). Joined ATS, 1938, as Sen. Comdr; promoted Controller, 1941; Dir Women's Auxilliary Corps (India), 1944-46, with rank of Sen. Controller. Governor, St George's Hosp., 1952-69; Mem. SE Metropolitan Regional Hosp. Board, 1953-; Governor, Bethlem Royal Hosp. and the Maudsley Hosp., 1957-; Member: St Francis and Lady Chichester Hosp. Management Cttees, 1959-68; Mid-Sussex Hosp. Management Cttee, 1965-68; Hellingley Hosp., Hailsham, 1970; Chm. Nat. Assoc. of Leagues of Hosp. Friends, 1962. *Heir: s* Earl of Carlisle, *qv. Address:* 113 Eaton Square, SW1.

**RUTLAND,** 10th Duke of, *cr* 1703; **Charles John Robert Manners,** CBE 1962; Marquess of Granby, 1703; Earl of Rutland, 1525; Baron Manners of Haddon, 1679; Baron Roos of Belvoir, 1896; 2nd Lieut Grenadier Guards; *b* 28 May 1919; *e s* of 9th Duke and Kathleen, 3rd *d* of late F. J. Tennant; *S* father, 1940; *m* 1946, Anne Bairstow Cumming (marr. diss. 1956), *e d* of late Major Cumming Bell, Binham Lodge, Edgerton, Huddersfield; one *d*; *m* 1958, Frances Helen, *d* of Charles Sweeny and of Margaret, Duchess of Argyll; two *s* one *d* (and one *s* decd). *Educ:* Eton; Trinity Coll., Cambridge. Owns 18,000 acres; minerals in Leicestershire and Derbyshire; picture gallery at Belvoir Castle. *Heir: s* Marquis of Granby, *qv*. *Address:* Belvoir Castle, Grantham; Haddon Hall, Derby.
*See also Marquess of Anglesey, Sir R. G. M. Throckmorton, Bt, Earl of Wemyss.*

**RUTT, Rt. Rev. Cecil Richard;** *see* Taejon (Korea), Bishop of.

**RUTTER, Herbert Hugh,** CB 1967; *b* 25 Dec. 1905; *m* 1948, Maureen Elsie, *d* of Donald A. Gooch; one *d*. *Educ:* Harris Coll., Preston; Manchester Univ.; (BA), LLM London. Admitted Solicitor, 1931; Public Trustee Office, 1931; Tithe Redemption Commn, 1936; Asst Solicitor to Min. of Agric., Comrs of Crown Lands and Forestry Commn, 1948; Dep. Legal Adviser, Min. of Agric., Fsheries & Food, 1960; retd 1967. *Publications:* contrib. legal jls. *Address:* Willows, Burton Bradstock, Bridport, Dorset. *T:* Burton Bradstock 341. *Club:* Civil Service.

**RUTTER, John Cleverdon;** Stipendiary Magistrate for the City of Cardiff since 1966; Deputy Chairman, Glamorgan Quarter Sessions, since 1969; *b* 18 Sept. 1919; 2nd *s* of Edgar John Rutter; *m* 1951, Jill, *d* of Maxwell Duncan McIntosh; one *s* one *d*. *Educ:* Cardiff High Sch.; Univ. Coll., of SW of England, Exeter (Open Schol.); Keble Coll., Oxford. MA Oxon; LLB London. Royal Artillery, 1940-45; commnd 1941; served overseas. Called to the Bar, Lincoln's Inn, 1948; practised Wales and Chester Circuit, 1948-66. A Legal Member, Mental Health Review Tribunal for Wales Region, 1960-66. An Assistant Recorder of: Cardiff, 1962-66; Merthyr Tydfil, 1962-66; Swansea, 1965-66. *Recreations:* golf, cricket, reading. *Address:* Law Courts, Cardiff. *T:* Cardiff 23139.

**RUTTER, Air Vice-Marshal (Retd) Norman Colpoy Simpson,** CB 1965; CBE 1945; idc; jssc; psa; Sen. Tech. Staff Officer, Bomber Command, 1961-65; *b* 1909; *s* of Rufus John Rutter; *m* 1936, Irene Sophia, *d* of late Colonel A. M. Lloyd; one *s* one *d*. Air Cdre, 1957; Air Officer Commanding and Commandant of the Royal Air Force Technical College, Henlow, 1959-61. CEng, FIMechE; FRAeS. *Address:* c/o Grindlay's Bank, 13 St James's Square, SW1.

**RUTTER, W(illiam) Arthur,** CBE 1949 (OBE 1944); FRIBA; retired; *b* Cardiff, 8 Jan. 1890; *s* of William Rutter; *m* 1915, Amy, *d* of William Dyche, BA, Cardiff; one *s* three *d*. Chief Architect to the Ministry of Works, 1946-51. *Address:* Millmeadow Cottage, Bramley, Surrey.

**RUTTLE, Henry Samuel; His Honour Judge Ruttle;** Judge of County Courts, Westminster (Circuit 44) since 1964 (Lambeth (Circuit 48), 1959-64); *b* 10 Nov. 1906; *yr s* of late Michael Ruttle, Portlaw, Co. Waterford, Ireland; *m* 1943, Joyce Mayo Moriarty (*d* 1968), *yr d* of late J. O. M. Moriarty, Plymouth; one *s* two *d*. *Educ:* Wesley College, Dublin and Trinity College, Dublin. BA (Moderatorship in Legal and Political Science) and LLB, 1929; LLD 1933; MA 1950. Called to the Bar, Gray's Inn, 1933; practised in Common Law: London and Western Circuit. Served War of 1939-45: RAFVR, 1940-45; Squadron Leader. Deputy Judge Advocate Judge Advocate General's Office. Resumed practice at Bar, 1945. Member of Church Assembly, 1948-55; Member of General Council of the Bar, 1957-59; Deputy Chairman Agricultural Land Tribunal (SW Area), 1958-59. JP, Co. Surrey, 1961. *Recreations:* Rugby football (Leinster Inter-Provincial, 1927; Captain London Irish RFC, 1935-36; Middlesex County); fly-fishing. *Address:* West Lodge, West Side, Wimbledon Common, SW19.

**RUWENZORI, Bishop of;** *see* Uganda, Rwanda and Burundi, Archbishop of.

**RYAN, Alfred Patrick,** CBE 1946; *b* 1900; *s* of Frederick and Charlotte Kate Ryan; *m* 1926, Rachel Rosa, *d* of C. E. Montague; one *d*. *Educ:* Whitgift; Balliol Coll., Oxford. 2nd Lt RFA. Editorial Staff, Manchester Guardian and Daily Telegraph; Empire Marketing Board Secretariat; Publicity Manager, Gas, Light & Coke Co. Squadron Leader, RAFVR, 1939-40. Editor of the BBC News Services, 1940-47; joined The Times 1947; Asst Editor and Literary Editor until 1968; now writing continuation of the official History of The Times. *Publications:* Lord Northcliffe, 1953; Islands Apart (America), 1954; Mutiny at the Curragh, 1956. *Address:* c/o The Times, EC4. *Clubs:* United University, Garrick, Beefsteak; St Stephen's Green (Dublin).

**RYAN, Arthur James,** CBE 1953; Regional Director, London Postal Region, 1949-60, retired; *b* 10 Oct. 1900; *e s* of late Stephen James Ryan, Little Common, Bexhill on Sea, Sx; *m* 1925, Marjorie, *y d* of late George James Dee; two *d*. *Educ:* City of London College and privately. Clerk, Headquarters, GPO London, 1918; Asst Surveyor, GPO, Class II, 1926, Class I, 1935; served in N Wales, Eastern Counties, South Western District; Chief Superintendent, then Assistant Controller, 1936, Controller (Mails and Transport), 1941, London Postal Region; Assistant Secretary, Min. of Fuel and Power (on loan), 1941; Dep. Regional Director, London Postal Region, 1944; Member of Post Office Board, 1950. *Recreations:* golf, gardening. *Address:* Daymer Cottage, Cooden Drive, Bexhill-on-Sea, Sussex. *T:* Cooden 2277. *Club:* Royal Automobile.

**RYAN, (Christopher) Nigel (John);** Editor, Independent Television News, since 1968; *b* 12 Dec. 1929; *s* of Brig. C. E. Ryan, MC, RA and Joyce Mary Dodgson. *Educ:* Ampleforth Coll.; Queen's Coll., Oxford (BA). Joined staff of Reuters, London, 1954; Corresp. in Rome, 1957-60; Congo Corresp., 1960; joined Independent Television News as Roving Corresp., 1961; Editor, Reporting '66 and Reporting '67; freelance scriptwriter. *Publications:* trans. novels by Georges Simenon from French; other trans. of Auguste le Breton and Solange Fasquelle. *Address:* 7a Park Walk, SW10.

**RYAN, Cornelius John;** Writer; Roving Editor, Reader's Digest, since 1965; *b* Dublin, Ireland, 5 June 1920; *s* of John Joseph Ryan and Amelia (*née* Clohisey); naturalised US citizen, 1950; *m* 1950, Kathryn Ann Morgan; one *s* one *d*. *Educ:* Christian Brothers' Sch., Dublin; Irish Acad. Music. Reporter: Reuter's News Agency, London, 1941-42; Daily Telegraph, London, 1943; War Correspondent, Europe, Pacific, 1943-47 (war medals); Jerusalem, 1946-47;

Time and Life, NY, also St Louis Post Despatch, 1946-47; Contribs Ed. Time, 1947-49; Mem. Special Projects Dept, prod. TV show Newsweek, 1949-50; Sen. Editor Collier's, NY, 1956; Staff Writer, Reader's Digest, NY, 1962-65. Consultant, Pan Amer. World Airways; Director: D. J. Ryan & Co., Dublin; Ryan Holdings Co., Dublin; State Nat. Bank of Connecticut; Nat. Bd, Boys' Clubs of America; Trustee, Correspondents Fund, Overseas Press Club. Hon. Research Fell., Econs and Social Scis, Manchester Univ., 1964. *Publications:* (with Frank Kelley) Star Spangled Mikado, 1948; MacArthur, 1951; (with Dr Von Braun and others) Across the Space Frontier, 1952; (with Dr Von Braun and others) Conquest of the Moon, 1954; One Minute to Ditch, 1957; The Longest Day, 1959; The Last Battle, 1966. *Recreations:* golf, fishing, shooting. *Address:* Old Branchville Road, Ridgefield, Conn 06877, USA. *T:* 438-2335. *Clubs:* New York Athletic, Waccabuc Country, Player's (New York); National Press of America (Washington, DC); Union Interalliée (Paris).

**RYAN, Sir Derek Gerald,** 3rd Bt, *cr* 1919; *b* 9 July 1922; *s* of Sir Gerald Ellis Ryan, 2nd Bt, and Hylda Winifryde Herapath; *S* father 1947; *m* 1947, Penelope Anne Hawkins; one *s* three *d*. Has become a US citizen. *Educ:* Harrow. Served War of 1939-45. Lieut Grenadier Guards, 1941-45. *Heir: s* Derek Gerald Ryan, Junior, *b* 25 March 1954. *Address:* Eagle Head, Manchester, Massachusetts, USA.

**RYAN, Most Rev. Finbar,** OP, MA, DD, LLD; *b* 4 March 1882; *s* of Edward and Matilda Ryan, Cork, Ireland. *Educ:* Christian Brothers Coll., Cork; Clongowes Wood Coll., Sallins; Roy. and Nat. Univs of Ireland; Minerva Univ. Rome. Ordained 1905; Dominican Provincial, 1921-26, 1930-34; Titular Archbishop of Gabula and Coadjutor of Port of Spain, 1937-40; Archbishop of Port of Spain, 1940-66; Titular Archbishop of Villa Magna. Assistant Pontifical Throne and Vatican Count, 1950; Grand Officer Supreme Order of Christ, 1950; Trinity Cross, Trinidad and Tobago, 1969. *Publications:* Our Lady of Fatima, 1939; Ed. The Irish Rosary, 1908-20. *Address:* Bon Secours Hospital, Cork, Eire.

**RYAN, Rt. Rev. Hugh Edward;** Titular Bishop of Nigizubi, since 1967; *b* Kyabram, Victoria, 25 April 1888. Ordained, 1916. Bishop of Townsville, 1938-67. *Address:* Villa Vincent, Fulham Rd, Townsville, Queensland, Australia.

**RYAN, John,** CBE 1949; MC 1916; MA (Cantab), BSc (London); Chairman, Centre for Interfirm Comparison Ltd; Member, Board, Oversea Service Ltd; Past Member, Western Area Board, BTC; *b* 27 July 1894; *m* 1922, Mabel McEwen; three *s* one *d*. *Educ:* Wolverhampton Grammar School; Gonville and Caius Coll., Cambridge. Mathematical Tripos, 1914. Served European War, 1914-18; Major, Royal Signals; Cmd Guards Signals Company (despatches, MC). Chm. British Closures Manufacturers' Assoc.; Fellow, Assoc. of Incorporated Statisticians; Hon. Vice-Pres. Inst. of Sheet Metal Engineering; Member Council Scientific and Industrial Film Assoc.; Fellow: International Academy of Management; British Institute of Management. Chm., Lloyd Thomas Charity; Vice-Chm., Industrial Christian Fellowship; Treasurer, Ealing Civic Soc. Member: Livery of Merchant Taylors' Company; Pilgrims of Great Britain; Conseiller d'honneur, Comité Internationale d'Organisation Scientifique (CIOS); Hon. President of CECIOS (European Council of CIOS). *Address:* 30 Amherst Road, Ealing, W13. *T:* 01-997 5190. *Clubs:* Reform, English-Speaking Union.

**RYAN, John;** *b* 30 April 1940; *m* 1964, Eunice Ann Edmonds; one *s*. *Educ:* Lanark Grammar School; Glasgow University. Member, National Association of Labour Student Organisations, 1958-62; formerly Youth Organiser, Lanark City Labour Party; Member, Executive Committee, North Paddington Labour Party, 1964-66. Contested (Lab) Buckinghamshire South, 1964; MP (Lab) Uxbridge, 1966-70. Member, Fabian Society, 1961-; Dir, Tribune, 1969-. Associate Member, Market Research Society. *Recreations:* golf, walking. *Address:* 77 Randolph Avenue, W9. *T:* 01-286 4381.

**RYAN, John Francis,** FFARCS; Consulting Anæsthetist, St Thomas's Hospital; *b* 1894; *s* of John Ryan, OBE, and Ellen Rebecca Ryan; *m* 1924, Frances Emmeline Perry; three *d*. *Educ:* Merchant Taylors' School; St Thomas' Hosp. MRCS, LRCP 1917; MB, BS London 1919; DA Eng. 1939; FFARCS Eng 1949. Formerly Anæsthetist, Nat. Hosp. for Paralysed and Epileptic; Evelina Hosp. for Children. European War, 1914-18, Temp. Surg. RN; War of 1939-45, Temp. Surg. Lt-Comdr RNVR, Specialist in Anæsthetics, RN. FRSocMed; Fellow Assoc. of Anæsthetists of Gt Brit. and Ire. *Publications:* contribs to med. jls. *Recreations:* gardening, golf. *Address:* The Rookery, Burton Bradstock, Dorset. *T:* Burton Bradstock 256. *Clubs:* RNVR, Lansdowne.

**RYAN, Rt. Rev. Joseph F.;** *see* Hamilton, Bishop of, (RC).

**RYAN, Nigel;** *see* Ryan, C. N. J.

**RYBURN, Rev. Hubert James,** CMG 1959; MA (Oxon and NZ), BD (Union); Chancellor of University of Otago since 1955; *b* 19 April 1897; *s* of Very Rev. Robert Middleton Ryburn and Anna Jane Steadman; *m* 1931, Jocelyn Maud Dunlop, *d* of Professor F. W. Dunlop; two *s* two *d*. *Educ:* Otago University; Oxford University; Union Theological Seminary, NY. Rhodes Scholar, 1921-24. Ordained a minister of the Presbyterian Church of New Zealand, 1926; Minister: Bay of Islands, 1926-29; St Andrews', Dunedin, 1929-41; Master of Knox College, Dunedin, 1941-63. Member: Council of Otago University, 1946-; Senate of Univ. of NZ, 1948-61; Pro-Chancellor of Univ. of Otago, 1954-55; Chancellor, 1955-. Hon. LLD (Otago). *Recreation:* fishing. *Address:* St Margaret's College, Dunedin, NZ. *T:* 88-429.

**RYCROFT, Sir Richard Newton,** 7th Bt, *cr* 1784; *b* 23 Jan. 1918; *yr s* of Sir Nelson Edward Oliver Rycroft, 6th Bt, and Ethel Sylvia (*d* 1952), *d* of late Robert Nurton, Odcombe, Yeovil; *S* father 1958; *m* 1947, Ann, *d* of late Hugh Bellingham-Smith, Alfriston, Sussex, and Mrs Harvey Robarts; two *d*. *Educ:* Winchester; Christ Church, Oxford (BA). Served War of 1939-45: Bedfordshire and Hertfordshire Regt, on special service work in Balkans (Major, despatches); Knight's Cross of Royal Order of Phœnix with Swords (Greece). *Heir: uncle* Henry Richard Rycroft, OBE, DSC, Comdr RN retd [*b* 28 Dec. 1911; *m* 1941, Penelope Gwendolen, *d* of late Lt-Col C. S. B. Evans-Lombe; one *s* three *d*]. *Address:* Winalls Wood House, Stuckton, Fordingbridge, Hampshire. *T:* Fordingbridge 2263.
*See also Viscount FitzHarris.*

**RYDER,** family name of **Earl of Harrowby.**

**RYDER, Don;** *see* Ryder, Sydney Thomas.

**RYDER, Eric Charles,** MA, LLB; Barrister-at-Law; Professor of English Law in the University of London (University College) since 1960; *b* 28 July 1915; *er s* of late Charles Henry Ryder, solicitor, Hanley, Staffs, and of Ellen Miller; *m* 1941, Nancy Winifred Roberts; no *c. Educ:* Hanley High School; Gonville and Caius College, Cambridge (scholar). BA (Law Tripos Parts I and II, 1st Cl.), 1936; LLB (1st Cl.) 1937; MA 1940; Tapp Law Scholar, Gonville and Caius College, 1937; called to Bar, Gray's Inn, 1937; practice at Chancery Bar. Ministry of Food, 1941-44; Lecturer in Law, King's College, Newcastle upon Tyne, 1944; Dean of Faculty of Law, Univ. of Durham, 1947-60; Professor of Law, Univ. of Durham (King's College), 1953-60. Practised as conveyancing counsel, Newcastle upon Tyne, 1944-53. *Publications:* Hawkins and Ryder on the Construction of Wills, 1965; contrib. to legal periodicals. *Address:* 19 Langton Ave, Whetstone, N20. *T:* 01-445 1588.

**RYDER, Sir Gerard,** Kt 1969; CB 1964; Solicitor to the Board of Trade since 1960; *b* 24 May 1909; *s* of late Frederick and Elizabeth Ryder, both of Manchester; *m* 1936, Eileen McCarthy; two *s* four *d* (and one *d* decd). *Educ:* Xaverian College, Manchester; Manchester University. Admitted Solicitor, 1932; private practice, 1932-42. Mines Dept (Board of Trade) and Min. of Fuel and Power, 1942-45. Board of Trade: Senior Legal Asst, 1945; Asst Solicitor, 1948; Principal Assistant Solicitor, 1957. *Address:* 1 Furze Hill, Purley, Surrey. *T:* 01-660 8525.

**RYDER, Peter Hugh Dudley,** MBE 1944; Managing Director, Thomas Tilling Ltd, 1957-68; *b* 28 April 1913; *s* of Hon. Archibald Dudley Ryder and Eleanor Frederica Fisher-Rowe; *m* 1940, Sarah Susannah Bowes-Lyon; two *s* one *d. Educ:* Oundle School. Provincial Newspapers Ltd, Hull and Leeds, 1930-33; Illustrated Newspapers Ltd, 1933-39; seconded from TA to Political Intell. Dept of FO, 1939-45 (Lt-Col 1944); Jt Man. Dir, Contact Publications Ltd, 1945; Man. Dir, Daimler Hire Ltd, 1950; Commercial Dir, James A. Jobling & Co. Ltd, Sunderland, 1953; Chairman: James A. Jobling & Co. Ltd, 1957-62 and 1967-68; Heinemann Gp of Publishers Ltd, 1961-68; Director: District Bank Ltd, 1961-69; Cornhill Insce Co. Ltd, 1965-68. Mem. Council, BIM, 1966-69 (Mem. Bd of Fellows, 1968-69); Mem. Bd of Govs, Ashridge Management Coll., 1968. *Recreations:* home life, many forms of sport and games. *Address:* The Spanish House, Wardija, Malta. *Club:* Royal Automobile.

**RYDER, Captain Robert Edward Dudley,** VC 1942; RN (retired); *b* 16 Feb. 1908; *s* of late Col C. H. D. Ryder, CB, CIE, DSO; *m* 1941, Hilare Myfanwy Green-Wilkinson; one *s* one *d. Educ:* Hazelhurst, Frant; Cheltenham College. Entered RN 1926; commanded Yacht Tai Mo Shan, 1933-34, on passage from Hong-Kong to Dartmouth; a member of British Graham Land Expedition to the Antarctic, 1934-37, in command of the Research Yacht Penola (Polar Medal with Clasp); commanded Naval forces in attack on St Nazaire, March 1942 (VC); took part in attack on Dieppe, Aug. 1942 (despatches); retd list, 1950. MP (C) Merton and Morden, 1950-55. *Publications:* The Attack on St Nazaire, 1947; Coverplan, 1953. *Address:* c/o Lloyds Bank, Cox's & King's Branch, 6 Pall Mall, SW1.

**RYDER, Sydney Thomas, (Don Ryder);** Chairman and Chief Executive, Reed International Ltd (formerly Reed Group Ltd), since 1968; *b* 16 Sept. 1916; *s* of John Ryder; *m* 1950; one *s* one *d. Educ:* Ealing. Editor, Stock Exchange Gazette, 1950-60; Jt Man. Dir, 1960-61, Sole Man. Dir, 1961-63, Kelly Iliffe Holdings, and Associated Iliffe Press Ltd; Dir, Internat. Publishing Corp., 1963-70; Man. Dir, Reed Paper Gp, 1963-68. Member: Council, BIM, 1970-; Court, Cranfield Inst. of Technology, 1970-; Nat. Materials Handling Cttee (Pres., 1970-). *Recreations:* sailing, squash, chess. *Address:* 12 Gloucester Square, W2. *T:* 01-262 4773.

**RYDGE, Sir Norman,** Kt 1966; CBE 1955; Chairman of Directors; The Greater Union Organisation Pty Ltd; Carlton Investments Ltd; Union Theatres Investments Ltd; Director: Amalgamated Holdings Ltd; City Mutual Life Assce Soc. Ltd; General Television Corp., and many other Australian companies; *b* 18 Oct. 1900; *s* of William Rydge and Margaret McSweeney; *m* 1950, Phoebe Caroline McEwing; three *s* (and one *s* decd). *Educ:* Fort Street High School. Comr, Rural Bank of NSW; Pres. of Trustees, Mus of Applied Arts and Sciences; Hon. Life Governor: Royal Prince Alfred Hosp. (Sydney); Royal Children's Hosp. and Alfred Hosp. (Melb.); Australian Inst. of Management. Founder of Rydge's Business Journal, 1927. *Publications:* Federal Income Tax Law; Federal Land Tax Law; The Law of Income Tax in NSW; Employers' Endowment Tax; Commonwealth Income Tax Acts; Australasian Executorship Law and Accounts; The NSW Income Tax Management Act; Australasian edition of Stevens' Mercantile Law. *Recreations:* boating, gardening. *Address:* 55 Wunulla Road, Point Piper, NSW, Australia. *T:* 36-6314. *Clubs:* Tattersall's, American National, Australian Golf, Royal Motor Yacht (all Sydney).

**RYDON, Professor Henry Norman,** DSc, PhD (London), DPhil Oxon, FRIC; Professor of Chemistry, University of Exeter, since 1957; *b* 24 March 1912; *o s* of late Henry William Rydon and Elizabeth Mary Anne (*née* Salmon); *m* 1st, 1937, Eleanor Alice Tattersall (*d* 1968); one *d*; 2nd, 1968, Lovis Elna Hibbard (*née* Davies). *Educ:* Central Foundation Sch., London; Imperial Coll., London. BSc (London), 1931; PhD (London), 1933; DSc (London), 1938; DPhil (Oxon.), 1939. Demonstrator in Organic Chemistry, Imperial College, London, 1933-37; Demonstrator in Chemistry, Birkbeck College, London, 1933-37; 1851 Exhibition Senior Student, Oxford University, 1937-40; Chemical Defence Experimental Station, Porton, 1940-45; Member Scientific Staff, Medical Research Council, Lister Institute, 1945-47; Reader in Organic Chemistry, Birkbeck Coll., London, 1947-49; Asst Prof. and Reader in Organic Chemistry, Imperial Coll., London, 1949-52; Professor of Chemistry and Director of the Chemical Laboratories, Manchester College of Science and Technology, 1952-57. Member Council: Chem. Society, 1947-50, 1951-52, 1954-57, 1964-67; Roy. Inst. of Chemistry, 1955-58, 1959-62, 1963-66; Soc. of Chemical Industry, 1961-63; Regional Scientific Adviser for Civil Defence, Home Office, 1951-52, 1955-57. Meldola Medal, Roy. Inst. of Chemistry, 1939; Harrison Memorial Prize, Chem. Soc., 1941. *Publications:* papers in Jl of Chem. Soc. and other scientific jls, 1933-. *Recreations:* travel and motoring. *Address:* Harts Close, Broadclyst, Exeter EX5 3AX. *T:* Broadclyst 399. *Club:* Royal Automobile.

**RYLAH, Hon. Sir Arthur (Gordon),** KBE 1968; CMG 1965; ED; Chief Secretary, and Deputy Premier of Victoria since 1955; MLA for Kew, Victoria, since 1949; *b* 3 Oct. 1909; *s* of W. R. Rylah; *m* 1937, Ann Flora (decd) (*née*

Flashman); one *s* one *d*. *Educ:* Trinity Grammar Sch.; Trinity Coll., Melbourne Univ. (BA, LLB). Solicitor and Member of firm of Rylah & Rylah. *Recreation:* tennis. *Address:* Ferrier Street, Macedon, Victoria, Australia. *Clubs:* Athenæum, Naval and Military, Victoria Racing, Royal South Yarra Lawn Tennis (Melbourne).

**RYLAND, Albert William Cecil,** CB 1965; Joint Deputy Chairman and Chief Executive, Post Office Corporation, since 1969; *b* 10 Nov. 1913; *s* of late A. E. Ryland, OBE; *m* 1946, Sybil, *d* of late H. C. Wookey; one *s* one *d*. *Educ:* Gosforth County Grammar School. Assistant Traffic Superintendent, GPO, 1934; Asst Surveyor, GPO, 1938. Served War of 1939-45 in Royal Engineers (Postal Section), Middle East and Central Mediterranean. Principal, GPO, 1949; Principal Private Secretary to PMG, 1954; Asst Secretary, GPO, 1955; Director of Establishments and Organisation, GPO, 1958; Director of Inland Telecommunications, GPO, 1961-65; Dep. Director-General, 1965-67; Man. Dir, Telecommunications, GPO, 1967-69. CompIEE. Hon. CGIA. *Address:* 60 Devonshire Way, Shirley, Croydon, Surrey CRO 8BR. *T:* 01-777 6504. *Club:* Reform.

**RYLAND, Charles Mortimer Tollemache S.;** *see* Smith-Ryland.

**RYLAND, Judge John,** CIE 1946; RIN (retired); Judge for British Columbia, 1969; *b* 31 March 1900; *s* of late W. J. Ryland, Surbiton; *m* 1938, Lucy Lenore, *d* of J. W. Bryden, Victoria, BC; two *s*. *Educ:* King's College School; HMS Conway. *Address:* Royston, BC, Canada.

**RYLANDS, George Humphrey Wolferstan,** CBE 1961; MA; Fellow of King's College, Cambridge; Sometime Dean, Bursar, College Lecturer, and Director of Studies; University Lecturer in English Literature (retd); *b* 23 October 1902; *s* of Thomas Kirkland Rylands. *Educ:* Eton (King's Scholar); King's Coll., Cambridge (Scholar). Chm. of Directors and Trustees of the Arts Theatre, Cambridge; Governor of the Old Vic; Chm. of Apollo Soc., 1943-68. Member: Cheltenham Coll. Council; Council of RADA; Director: Tennent Productions Ltd; LP recording of the Shakespeare canon, for the British Council. *Publications:* Words and Poetry, 1928; Shakespeare the Poet (in a Companion to Shakespeare Studies), 1934; Poems; The Ages of Man, a Shakespeare Anthology, 1939; Shakespeare's Poetic Energy (British Academy Lecture, 1951). *Address:* King's College, Cambridge. *T:* Cambridge 50411. *Clubs:* Athenæum, Reform.

**RYLE, George Bodley,** CBE 1960; *b* 4 March 1902; *y s* of late Reginald John Ryle, MD, JP, and Catherine Ryle (*née* Scott); *m* 1934, Margaret Bevan; one *s* three *d*. *Educ:* Brighton College; St Catherine's, Oxford. Entered Forestry Commission, 1924; Dep. Director Gen., 1963; retired 1965. Seconded as Divisional Officer, Home Timber Production Dept, Ministry of Supply, 1939-46; as Chief Control Officer, North German Timber Control, Control Commission for Germany, 1946-47; Conservator, Forestry Commission, 1947-54; Dir of Forestry for Wales, 1954-58; Dir of Forestry for England, 1958-63. Apptd Verderer of the New Forest, 1966. *Publications:* Forest Service, 1969; numerous in Forestry, Quarterly Journal of Forestry and Empire Forestry Review. *Recreations:* walking the hills; entomology. *Address:* The White Cottage, Bank, Lyndhurst, Hants.

**RYLE, Gilbert;** *b* 19 Aug. 1900; *s* of Reginald John Ryle, MD, and Catherine Scott; unmarried. *Educ:* Brighton Coll.; Queen's Coll., Oxford. Classical Scholar, Queen's Coll., Oxford; 1st Classes in Classical Hon. Mods Lit Hum, and Philosophy, Politics and Economics; Captain Queen's Coll. Boat Club; Trial Eights, 1923; Lecturer, Christ Church, Oxford, 1924; Student and Tutor in Philosophy, Christ Church, Oxford, 1925; sometime Jun. and Sen. Censor of Christ Church and Jun. Proctor of the University; Waynflete Professor of Metaphysical Philosophy, Oxford, 1945-68. War of 1939-45, commissioned Welsh Guards, 1940, ending as Major. Hon. Student of Christ Church; Hon. Fellow, Queen's Coll., Oxford; Hon. Fellow, Magdalen Coll., Oxford. For. Hon. Mem., Amer. Acad. of Arts and Sciences, 1968; Hon. DLitt: Univ. of Birmingham; Univ. of Warwick, 1969; Hull, 1970. *Publications:* The Concept of Mind, 1949; Dilemmas, 1954; Plato's Progress, 1966; also various articles and reviews in *Mind*, Aristotelian Society Proceedings and Philosophy; also Inaugural Lecture, Philosophical Arguments, 1945; Editor of *Mind*. *Address:* Magdalen College, Oxford; Yarm, North Street, Islip, Oxon. *T:* Kidlington 3277. *Clubs:* Travellers', Leander.

**RYLE, Kenneth Sherriff,** CBE 1964; MC 1945; Secretary to the Church Commissioners for England since 1969; *b* 13 April 1912; *s* of Herbert Ryle, CVO, OBE; *m* 1941, Jean Margaret Watt; one *s* one *d*. *Educ:* Cheltenham Coll. Chartered Accountant, 1936; Queen Anne's Bounty, 1936-48. Served in RA, 1940-45: India, Persia, Middle East, Sicily, Italy, Germany; Captain 1944. Church Commissioners, 1948- (Dep. Sec., 1964-69). *Recreation:* golf. *Address:* 47 Albyfield, Bickley, Kent. *T:* 01-467 6319. *Clubs:* Naval and Military; Chiselhurst Golf.

**RYLE, Sir Martin,** Kt 1966; FRS 1952; Professor of Radio Astronomy, Cambridge, since 1959; *b* 27 Sept. 1918; *s* of late Prof. J. A. Ryle, MD, FRCP, and Mrs Miriam Ryle (*née* Scully); *m* 1947, Ella Rowena Palmer; one *s* two *d*. *Educ:* Bradfield Coll.; Christ Church, Oxford. Telecommunications Research Establishment, 1939-45; ICI Fellowship, Cavendish Laboratory, Cambridge, 1945-48; University Lecturer in Physics, Cambridge, 1948-59. Fellowship, Trinity Coll., Cambridge, 1949-. Hughes Medal, Royal Society, 1954; Gold Medal, Royal Astronomical Soc., 1964; Henry Draper Medal, Nat. Academy of Sciences (US), 1965. Hon. DSc: Strathclyde, 1968; Oxford, 1969. *Publications:* papers in: Proc. Roy. Soc., Proc. Physical Soc., Monthly Notices of Roy. Astronomical Soc. *Recreation:* sailing. *Address:* 5a Herschel Road, Cambridge. *T:* 56670.

**RYLEY, Air Vice-Marshal Douglas William Robert,** CB 1956; CBE 1944; retired, 1962; *b* 11 November 1905; *y s* of late Lachlan Macpherson Ryley, OBE, Ichapur, India and Palta, Bournemouth; *m* 1932, Madeline Doreen, *d* of late William Lloyd-Evans, Postlip, Glos; one *d*. *Educ:* Bedford School; RAF College, Cranwell. Commissioned in RAF 1925; India, 1929-34; Air Armament School, 1935; HQ RAF Far East, 1937; Woolwich Arsenal, 1939; UK Tech. Mission, USA, 1941; UK Tech. Mission, Canada, 1943; Ordnance Board, 1944; Superintendent EE Pendine, 1945; OC 10 S of TT, 1947; STSO No. 3 Group, 1948; AOC and Comdt, RAF Tech. Coll., Henlow, 1949; STSO HQ Coastal Comd, 1952; Dir of Armament Engineering, Air Min., 1954; Dir of Guided Weapons Engineering, Air Min., 1957; AOA, HQ Maintenance Command, 1958. *Recreations:* golf and shooting. *Address:* Foresters, Over Wallop, Stockbridge, Hants.

**RYMAN, Hon. Mrs (John);** *see* Summerskill, Dr the Hon. S. C. W.

**RYMER-JONES, Brig. John Murray,** CBE 1950 (OBE 1941); MC 1917, and Bar 1918; QPM 1959; retired as Assistant Commissioner Metropolitan Police (1950-59); Secretary, Drinking Fountain Association, since 1959; Committee Member, Royal Humane Society, since 1957; *b* 12 July 1897; *s* of John and Lilian Rymer-Jones; *m* 1930, Gertrude Alice Wobey; one *s* two *d*. *Educ:* Felsted School; RMA, Woolwich. Commissioned RFA 1916; served European War: France and Flanders, 1916-18; Army of Rhine, 1919. Ireland, 1920; Plebiscite, Upper Silesia, 1921; HQ British Army in Egypt, 1921-25; HQ Shanghai Defence Force, 1927-28; Company Commander and Instructor, RMA, Woolwich, 1929-33; retired as Captain, RA. Joined Metropolitan Police as Chief Inspector, 1934; Superintendent, 1935; Chief Constable, 1936; Inspector-General and Brigadier commanding Palestine Police, 1943-46. Commander Metropolitan Police, 1946-50. Area Comr, St John Ambulance, North Kent, 1963-66. Commander of St John of Jerusalem, 1952; Chevalier, Légion d'Honneur, 1950; *Recreations:* talking and music. *Address:* 24 Brookway, Blackheath, SE3.

**RYMILL, Hon. Sir Arthur (Campbell),** Kt 1954; MLC, South Australia, since 1956; Chairman of Directors, The Bank of Adelaide, since 1953; Member of Principal Board, Australian Mutual Provident Society; Director of public companies in South Australia; *b* 8 Dec. 1907; *s* of late Arthur Graham Rymill, North Adelaide; *m* 1934, Margaret Earle, *d* of Roland Cudmore; two *d*. *Educ:* Queen's Sch. and St Peter's Coll., Adelaide; Univ. of Adelaide. Barrister and Solicitor, 1930. Mem. Adelaide City Council, 1933-38, 1946-64; Lord Mayor of Adelaide, 1950-54. Pres., S Australian Liberal and Country League, 1953-55; First Pres., Nat. Trust of S Australia; Vice-Pres., Aust. Elizabethan Theatre Trust, 1954-63; Mem., Found. Bd of Govs, Adelaide Festival of Arts; Vice-Pres., Adelaide Children's Hosp. Won Australasian Unlimited Speedboat Championship, 1933; rep. S Austr. in Australasian Polo Championships, 1938 and 1951. Served War of 1939-45, 2nd AIF: enlisted Private, 2/7th Field Regt, later commissioned. *Recreations:* almond growing, violin playing, golf. *Address:* 39 Brougham Place, North Adelaide, South Australia. *Clubs:* Adelaide (Adelaide); Melbourne (Melbourne); Royal Adelaide Golf, Royal SA Yacht Squadron.

# S

**SABBEN-CLARE, Ernest E.,** MA Oxon, BA London; Information Officer to University of Oxford, since 1970; *b* 11 Aug. 1910; *s* of late Mr and Mrs J. W. Sabben-Clare; *m* 1938, Rosamond Dorothy Mary Scott; two *s* one *d*. *Educ:* Winchester Coll. (schol.); New College, Oxford (schol.). 1st cl. Mod. Hist., Oxford, 1932. Asst Master, Winchester Coll., 1932-34; Asst Dist Officer, Tanganyika, 1935-40; seconded Colonial Office, 1940-47; Lt, 10th Essex Bn Home Guard; Colonial Attaché, British Embassy, Washington, and Comr, Caribbean Commn, 1947-49; Nigerian Govt, 1950-55; Permanent Sec., Min. of Commerce, 1953-55; 1st cl. French, London Univ. (external), 1954; Asst Master, Marlborough Coll., 1955-60, Under-Master from 1957; Headmaster, Bishop Wordsworth's School, Salisbury, 1960-63; Headmaster, Leeds Grammar School, 1963-70. *Publication:* Editor, Wilts Archaeological and Natural History Magazine, 1956-62. *Recreations:* caravanning, walking, reading, theatre-going. *Address:* The Registry, University of Oxford, Broad Street, Oxford. *Club:* Athenæum.

**SABIN, Professor Albert Bruce;** Legion of Merit (US) 1945; President, Weizmann Institute of Science, Rehovot, Israel, since 1970; *b* 26 Aug. 1906; *s* of Jacob Sabin and Tillie Krugman; *m* 1935, Sylvia Tregillus (*d* 1966); two *d*; *m* 1967, Jane Blach Warner. *Educ:* New York Univ. (MD). Ho. Phys., Bellevue Hosp., NY, 1932-33; Nat. Research Council Fellow, Lister Inst., London, 1934; Rockefeller Inst. for Med. Research, NY, 1935-39; Associate Prof. of Research Pediatrics, Univ. of Cincinnati, 1939-43; active duty, US Army, 1943-46; Distinguished Service Prof. of Research Pediatrics, Univ. of Cincinnati Coll. of Medicine and The Children's Hosp. Research Foundn, 1946-69. Mem. Nat. Acad. of Sciences of the USA; Fellow, Amer. Acad. of Arts and Sciences; Mem. and Hon. Mem. of various Amer. and foreign societies; Corr. Mem. British Paediatric Association. Holds hon. degrees; awards include: Feltrinelli Prize ($40,000) of Accad. dei Lincei, Rome, 1964; Lasker ($10,000) Prize for Clinical Research, 1965. Gold Medal, Royal Soc. of Health, 1969. Hon. FRSH London. *Publications:* numerous papers on pneumococcus infection, poliomyelitis, encephalitis, virus diseases of nervous system, toxoplasmosis, sandfly fever, dengue, other topics relating to various infectious diseases and virus-cancer relationships. *Recreations:* reading and music. *Address:* Weizmann Institute of Science, Rehovot, Israel. *Club:* New York Univ. (NY).

**SABINE, Neville Warde,** CMG 1960; CBE 1957; *b* 6 April 1910; *s* of late John William Sabine; *m* 1954, Zoë Margherita Bargna; two *d*. *Educ:* Manchester Grammar School; Brasenose College, Oxford. BA Hons. (Oxon) 1934. Colonial Service (Colonial Audit Dept) 1934; served Gold Coast, Malaya, Uganda, Leeward Islands, and N Borneo. Served War of 1939-45, Gold Coast Regt, 1939-40; Singapore RA (V), 1940-42; British Military Administration, Malaya, 1945-46. Auditor-General, Ghana, 1954-64; Secretary, Central Bd of Finance of Church of England, 1964-. *Recreations:* bridge and tennis. *Address:* 11 Windlesham Road, Brighton. *T:* Brighton 732157. *Club:* Royal Commonwealth Society.

**SABITI, Most Rev. Erica;** *see* Uganda, Rwanda and Burundi, Archbishop of.

**SACHER, Harry;** Director, Marks and Spencer Ltd, 1932-62, retired; *b* London, 3 Sept. 1881; *s* of Jacob and Esther Sacher; *m* 1915, Miriam (Hon. Fellow, St Hilda's College, Oxford; Hon. Fellow, Weizmann Inst. of Science), *d* of Michael and Hannah Marks, Manchester; two *s*. *Educ:* Central Foundation School, London; University Coll., London; New Coll., Oxford; Berlin Univ.; Sorbonne. Ed. Staff, Manchester Guardian, 1905-9 and 1915-19 and Daily News, 1909-15; called to Bar, 1909; practised in Palestine, 1920-30; Member of Executive of World Zionist Organisation, 1927-31. Hon. Fellow, New College, Oxford, 1958; Hon. Fellow, University College, London, 1961; Hon. Fellow, Weizmann Institute of Science, 1962; Hon. LLD Hebrew Univ. of Jerusalem, 1966. *Publications:* Israel, the Establishment of a State; Zionist Portraits; Edited Zionism and the Jewish Future; Palestine. *Address:* 37 Grosvenor Square, W1. *T:* 01-499 3720. *Club:* Savile.

**SACHS, Major-General Albert,** CB 1955; CBE 1952; Hon. consultant Pathologist, Queen Victoria Hospital, East Grinstead; *b* 18 May 1904; *s* of late John Sachs, JP, Pretoria, South Africa; *m* 1930, Olga Alice, KIH, OStJ, *d* of late John Winter le Chasseur, Jersey, CI. *Educ:* Pretoria High School; Trinity Coll., Dublin. BA (Hons), 1926; MB, ChB, 1926; MD 1931; MSc 1935; MRCP, 1953; FRCP 1965; FCPath 1964. Joined RAMC, 1927; Lt-Col, 1942; Col., 1945; Brigadier, 1949; Major-General, 1953. Mohmand Ops, NWFP, India (Medal and Clasp), 1933; served War of 1939-45, India, Madagascar, Middle East, Persia, Iraq and Italy; Reader in Pathology, Roy. Army Med. Coll., 1949; Dir of Path., and Cons. Path. to Army, WO, 1949-53; Deputy Director Medical Services, UK Command, 1953-56; retired, 1956; Hon. Col 44 (HC) Infantry Division RAMC (TA), 1957-62; Col Commandant, RAMC, 1964-69. FRSM; Fellow, Royal Soc. Trop. Med. and Hyg.; Member: Assoc. Clin. Pathologists; Path. Soc. of Gt Britain & Ireland; Cons. Path. Group, BMA; British Society for Immunology; British Association in Forensic Medicine; Assoc. Member British Association of Plastic Surgeons. KHP, 1951; QHP, 1952-56. Mem., Royal Philatelic Soc., London. OStJ 1956. *Publications:* articles in Journals of RAMC, IAMC, Roy. United Services Inst.; Proc. Roy. Soc. Med.; Proc. Roy. Soc. Trop. Med. and Hyg.; monthly Bulletin of Min. of Health and Laboratory Service; The Practitioner. *Recreations:* swimming, tennis and philately. *Address:* The Patch, Baldwins Hill, Nr East Grinstead, Sussex. *T:* East Grinstead 21570. *Club:* United Service.

**SACHS, Rt. Hon. Sir Eric,** PC 1966; Kt 1954; MBE 1941; TD; **Rt. Hon. Lord Justice Sachs;** a Lord Justice of Appeal since 1966; Judge, High Court of Justice, since 1954 (Probate, Divorce and Admiralty Division, 1954-60; Queen's Bench Division, 1960-66); *b* London, 23 July 1898; *o s* of late Edwin O. Sachs, FRS (Edinburgh), 5 Ulster Tce, Regent's Park; *m* 1934, Hon. Margaret, 2nd *d* of Baron Goddard of Aldbourne, *qv*; one *s* one *d*. *Educ:* Charterhouse; Christ Church, Oxford. Served European War, 1917-19, Lieut RA (wounded); recommissioned as 2nd Lieut Aug. 1939; Capt. 1939; Major and DAAG 1940; Lt-Col and AAG 1941; Brig. (specially employed) 1942-45. Called to Bar, Middle Temple, 1921; KC 1938; QC 1952; Leader of the Oxford Circuit, 1952-54; Bencher, 1947, Treasurer, 1967; Recorder of Dudley, 1938-43; Recorder of Stoke-on-Trent, 1943-54; Commissioner of Assize, 1946 (Western Circuit), 1948 (S-Eastern Circuit) and 1953 (Birmingham); Special Commission to Gold Coast (Appeals from Enquiry into Customs, Supplies and Currency Control Depts). 1947; Mem. of Gen. Council of the Bar (Exec. Cttee), 1946-53; Mem. of Legal Aid Committees (Legal Aid Act, 1949), 1948-53; Gresham Lecturer on Law, 1948-49. Brig. (late RA, TARO). *Publication:* Legal Aid, 1951. *Recreations:* travel. *Address:* Royal Courts of Justice, Strand, WC2; Queen Elizabeth Building, Temple, EC4. *T:* 01-583 1145; Walland Oast, Wadhurst, Sussex. *T:* 2080. *Clubs:* Athenæum, Hurlingham, MCC.

**SACKETT, A. B.,** MC; MA Oxon; retired as Headmaster Kingswood School, Bath (1928-59); *b* 1895; *m* 1925, Dorothy E. Salter; four *s* one *d*. *Educ:* Kingswood School, Bath; Merton College, Oxford. Served European War, Gallipoli, Egypt, France, 1915-18; Capt. Northumberland Fusiliers, attached 1/5 Lancashire Fusiliers; Housemaster Christ's Hospital, 1922-28. World Methodist Council, 1951-66; Chairman of Governors, Bath Academy of Art, 1959-64. *Address:* Tudor Lodge, Greenway Lane, Bath.

**SACKS, Mrs Samuel;** *see* Landau, M. E.

**SACKVILLE,** family name of **Earl De la Warr.**

**SACKVILLE,** 6th Baron, *cr* 1876; **Lionel Bertrand Sackville-West;** *b* 30 May 1913; *s* of late Hon. Bertrand George Sackville-West, *y b* of 4th Baron and Eva Adela Mabel Inigo (*d* 1936), *d* of late Maj.-Gen. Inigo Richmond Jones, CB, CVO; *S* cousin, 1965; *m* 1953, Jacobine Napier, *widow* of Capt. John Hichens, RA, and *d* of J. R. Menzies-Wilson; five *d*. *Educ:* Winchester; Magdalen Coll., Oxford. Formerly Capt. Coldstream Gds; served War, 1939-42 (POW). Member of Lloyd's, 1949. *Heir: b* Hugh Rosslyn Inigo Sackville-West, MC [*b* 1 Feb. 1919; *m* 1957, Bridget Eleanor, *d* of Capt. Robert Lionel Brooke Cunliffe, *qv*; two *s* three *d*]. *Address:* Knole, Sevenoaks, Kent.

**SACKVILLE, Col Nigel V. S.;** *see* Stopford Sackville.

**SACKVILLE-WEST,** family name of **Baron Sackville.**

**SAGAN, Françoise,** pen-name of Françoise Quoirez; authoress; *b* France, 21 June 1935; *y c* of Paul Quoirez; *m* 1958, Guy Schoeller (marr. diss. 1960); *m* 1962, Robert James Westhoff; one *s*. *Educ:* convent and private school. Published first novel at age of 18. Has written some songs and collaborated in scheme for ballet Le Rendez-vous Manqué, produced Paris and London, 1958. *Publications:* (all trans into Eng., usually French title): Bonjour Tristesse, 1954; Un Certain Sourire, 1956 (filmed, 1958); Dans un mois, dans un an, 1957 (Eng. trans Those Without Shadows, 1958); Aimez-vous Brahms . . . . 1959 (Eng. trans. 1960); Château en Suède (play), 1960; Les Violons, parfois . . . (play), 1961; La Robe Mauve de Valentine (play), 1963; Toxique . . . (tr. 1965); La Chamade (tr. 1966) (film, 1970); Le Cheval Evanoui (play), 1966; Le Garde du cœur, 1968 (tr., The Heart-Keeper, 1968). *Address:* c/o M. René Julliard, 30 rue de l'Université, Paris 7e.

**SAGITTARIUS;** *see* Katzin, Olga.

**SAINER, Leonard;** Senior Partner, Titmuss, Sainer & Webb; *b* 12 Oct. 1909; *s* of Archer and Sarah Sainer. deputy Chairman: Sears Holdings Ltd; British Shoe Corporation Ltd; Sears Engineering Ltd; Lewis Investment Trust Ltd; Selfridges Ltd; Bentley Engineering Group Ltd. *Address:* (business) 2 Serjeants' Inn, EC4; (home) 15 Chesterfield House, South Audley Street, W1.

**SAINSBURY,** Baron, *cr* 1962, of Drury Lane (Life Peer); **Alan John Sainsbury;** President of J. Sainsbury Ltd, since 1967 (Chairman, 1956-67); *b* 13 Aug. 1902; *er s* of John Benjamin and Mabel Miriam Sainsbury; *m* 1st, 1925. Doreen

Davan Adams (marriage dissolved 1939); three *s*; 2nd, 1944, Anne Elizabeth Lewy; one *d*. *Educ:* Haileybury. Joined Grocery and Provision Firm of J. Sainsbury, Ltd (founded by his grandparents), 1921. Served on many war-time consultative committees of Ministry of Food; Member Williams' Committee on Milk Distribution, 1947-48; Member, Food Research Advisory Cttee, 1960- (Chm., 1965-); Mem. NEDC Cttee for the Distributive Trades, 1964-68; Chm, Cttee of Inquiry into Relationship of Pharmaceutical Industry with National Health Service, 1965-67. President: Multiple Shops' Fedn, 1963-65; The Grocers' Inst., 1963-66; Internat. Assoc. of Chain Stores, 1965-68; The Royal Inst. of Public Health and Hygiene, 1965-70; Pestalozzi Children's Village Trust, 1963-; a Vice-President, Assoc. of Agriculture, 1965-; Royal Society for the Encouragment of Arts, Manufactures and Commerce, 1962-66; Mem., Court of Univ. of Essex, 1966-; Governor, City Literary Inst., 1967-69; Chm. of Trustees, Overseas Students Adv. Bureau. Liberal candidate, Sudbury Div. of Suffolk, Gen. Elections of 1929, 1931 and 1935. Joined Labour Party, 1945. *Address:* J. Sainsbury Ltd, Stamford House, Stamford Street, SE1. *T:* 01-928 3355; Flat 8, 34 Bryanston Square, W1.

*See also Hon. J. D. Sainsbury.*

**SAINSBURY, Edward Hardwicke;** TD 1945; Judge, High Court of Lagos, 1960-63, and of Southern Cameroons, 1961-63 (Speaker, House of Assembly, 1958-63, Chm., Public Service Commn, 1961-63, S (Cameroons); *b* 17 Sept. 1912; *e s* of Henry Morgan Sainsbury, and *g s* of James C. Hardwicke, a pioneer of technical and other education in S Wales; *m* 1946, Ann, 2nd *d* of Kenneth Ellis, Tunbridge Wells; one *s* one *d*. *Educ:* Cardiff High School; University of S Wales and Monmouth. Solicitor in private practice, 1935; commissioned (TA) 1936; Prosecuting Solicitor, Cardiff, 1938, Sen. Pros. Solicitor, 1939. Served War of 1939-45; Adjutant, 77th HAA Regt, 1940; comd 240 HAA Battery Gibraltar, 1944; demobilised Nov. 1945. Hong Kong: Asst Crown Solictor, 1946; commissioner for revision of the laws of Hong Kong, 1947; magistrate, 1948; registrar, High Court, 1949; sen. magistrate, Kowloon, 1951; Barrister, Inner Temple, 1951; Land Officer and crown counsel, Hong Kong, 1952; legal draftsman, Nigeria, 1953; Principal Legal Draftsman, Fed. of Nigeria, 1958. President, Commonwealth Parliamentary Assoc., Southern Cameroons, 1959-63. Solicitor and Partner, Dawson, Hart & Co., Uckfield, 1963; District Notary Public. *Publication:* (jointly) Revised Laws of Hong Kong, 1948. *Recreations:* squash, golf. *Address:* Little Gassons, Fairwarp, Uckfield, Sussex. *T:* Nutley 2100. *Club:* East India and Sports.

**SAINSBURY, Hon. Mrs John;** *see* Linden, Anya.

**SAINSBURY, Hon. John Davan;** Chairman, J. Sainsbury Ltd, since 1969 (Vice-Chairman, 1967-69); Director, Covent Garden Opera House, since 1969; *b* 2 Nov. 1927; *e s* of Baron Sainsbury, *qv*; *m* 1963, Anya Linden, *qv*; two *s* one *d*. *Educ:* Stowe School; Worcester College, Oxford. Director, J. Sainsbury Ltd, 1958. Hon. Sec., Contemporary Art Soc.; Governor, Royal Ballet School; Chm., Friends of Covent Garden, 1969-. *Address:* c/o Stamford House, Stamford Street, SE1. *T:* 01-928 3355. *Club:* Garrick.

**SAINSBURY, Richard Eric,** CBE 1964; Director-General, Electronics and Weapons Production, Ministry of Technology, since 1967 (Ministry of Aviation, 1961-67); *b* 15 Sept. 1909; 2nd *s* of E. A. Sainsbury and F. W. Sainsbury (*née* Hill), Trowbridge, Wilts; *m* 1936, Margaret (*née* Horne); one *s*. *Educ:* Lewisham School, Weston-super-Mare; Bristol University. Grad. in Engineering, 1932; time-study with J. Lucas, 1934; subseq. with various firms; Ministry of Aircraft Production, 1940, Deputy Director, 1943; Joint Services Staff College, 1947; Director Instrument and Radio Production, Ministry of Supply, 1950; Imperial Defence College, 1959; Director, Guided Weapons Production, 1960; Coronation Medal, 1953. *Recreations:* walking, reading, skiing. *Address:* The Old Brick Cottage, Sutton Place, Abinger Hammer, near Dorking, Surrey. *T:* Dorking 730450.

**SAINSBURY, Sir Robert,** Kt 1967 (for services to the arts); Joint President, J. Sainsbury Ltd; *b* 24 Oct. 1906; *s* of late John Benjamin Sainsbury and late Mabel Lydia (*née* Van den Bergh); *m* 1937, Lisa Ingeborg (*née* Van den Bergh; second cousin); one *s* three *d*. *Educ:* Haileybury Coll.; Pembroke Coll., Cambridge (MA). ACA, 1930, FCA, 1935. Joined J. Sainsbury Ltd, 1930; Dir, 1934; Jt Gen. Man., 1938; Dep. Chm., 1956; Chm. 1967; Jt Pres., 1969. Mem. Art Panel of Arts Council. Trustee, Tate Gall., 1959- (Vice-Chm. 1967, Chm., 1969); Mem. Vis. Cttee to Primitive Art Dept, Metropolitan Museum of Art, NY; Treas. Inst. of Med. Social Workers, 1948-; Past Governor, St Thomas' Hospital. *Address:* 5 Smith Square, SW1. *T:* 01-222 7252; The Old Vicarage, Bucklebury, Berks. *T:* Yattendon 204.

**SAINSBURY, Air Vice-Marshal T. A. L.;** *see* Langford-Sainsbury.

**SAINT, Charles Frederick Morris,** CBE 1919; MD, MS Durham, FRCS; Hon. FRACS; Hon. FRSocMed; Hon. Fellow Greek Surgical Society; Hon. FCS (SAf), 1967; Hunterian Professor, RCS England, 1949; Emeritus Professor of Surgery, University, Cape Town; retired; *b* 1886. Formerly Major RAMC; served European War, 1914-19 (despatches, CBE). *Publications:* Surgical Note Taking, 5th Edn (with Prof. J. H. Louw), 1960; (Joint) An Introduction to Surgery, 4th Edn, 1948; An Introduction to Clinical Surgery, 1945, 2nd Edn, 1940. *Address:* Sark, CI.

**SAINT, Sir John;** *see* Saint, Sir S. J.

**SAINT, Capt. Peter J. J.;** *see* Johnston-Saint.

**SAINT, Sir (Sidney) John,** Kt, *cr* 1950; CMG 1946; OBE 1942; BSc, PhD (London); MSc (Reading); FRIC; Dir, Sugar Technological Laboratory, Barbados, 1949-63, retd; *b* 16 Sept. 1897; *m* 1923, Constance Elizabeth Hole; two *s* one *d*. *Educ:* Beaminster Grammar School; Reading University. Served with RAF, 1916-19; Salter's Research Fellow, 1920-22; Lecturer in Agricultural Chemistry, Leeds

University, 1922-27; Chemist, Department of Agriculture, Barbados, 1927-37; Director of Agriculture Barbados, 1937-49; Chm., BWI Sugar Cane Breeding Station, 1937-49; Competent Authority and Controller of Supplies, Barbados, 1939-46; Pres., Barbados Technologists Assoc., 1939-42, 1950-63; Gen. Chm., Internat. Soc. of Sugar Cane Technologists, 1950-53; Chairman: Barbados Public Service Commn, 1952-57; Barbados Development Bd, 1956-59; Interim Federal Public Service Commn, 1956-59. Pres. Museum and Hist. Soc., 1946-59. MEC, 1947-61; PC (Barbados), 1961-63. Hon. Freeman, City of Bridgetown, Barbados, 1963. *Publications:* numerous papers on soils, manuring of tropical crops and sugar technology. *Address:* Selwyn, St George's Lane, Hurstpierpoint, Sussex. *T:* Hurstpierpoint 2335.

**SAINT, Dr Stafford Eric,** CVO 1956; Medical Practitioner, 1931-70; *b* 13 April 1904; *s* of Sir Wakelin Saint; *m* 1931, Isabel Mary Fulford; two *s* one *d*. *Educ:* King's School, Ely; The London Hospital. MRCS Eng., LRCP Lond., 1926. JP Bucks, 1948-68. *Address:* 28 The Uplands, Gerrard's Cross, Bucks.

**ST ALBANS,** 13th Duke of, *cr* 1684; **Charles Frederic Aubrey de Vere Beauclerk,** OBE 1945; Earl of Burford and Baron of Heddington, 1676; Baron Vere, 1750; Hereditary Grand Falconer of England; Hereditary Registrar, Court of Chancery; Chairman: Grendon Securities Ltd; Industrial Midlands Investment Trust; Travelworld Olympic Ltd; Director: James Archibald Productions Ltd; Herbert Greaves Ltd; Amalgamated Developers Ltd; Member, Advisory Council, Centre for Educational Television Overseas; *b* 16 Aug. 1915; *s* of Aubrey Topham Beauclerk and Gwendolen, *d* of late Sir Frederic Hughes; *S* kinsman, 1964; *m* 1st, Nathalie Chatham (who obtained a divorce, 1947), *d* of late P. F. Walker; one *s*; 2nd, 1947, Suzanne Marie Adele, *d* of late Emile William Fesq, Mas Mistral, Vence, AM, France; three *s* one *d*. *Educ:* Eton; Magdalene Coll., Cambridge (MA). Served War of 1939-45 in Infantry, Military Intelligence and Psychological Warfare; Col, Intelligence Corps. Controller Inf. Services, Allied Commn for Austria, 1946-50. Central Office of Information: Chief Books Editor, 1951-58; Chief Films Production Officer, 1958-60; Dir, Films Div., 1960-64. *Heir: s* Earl of Burford, *qv*. *Address:* 57 Oakley Street, Chelsea, SW3. *T:* 01-352 8008. *Clubs:* St James's, Brooks's.

**ST ALBANS, Bishop of,** since 1970; **Rt. Rev. Robert Alexander Kennedy Runcie,** MC 1945; *b* 2 Oct. 1921; *s* of Robert Dalziel Runcie and Anne Runcie; *m* 1957, Angela Rosalind, *d* of J. W. Cecil Turner; one *s* one *d*. *Educ:* Merchant Taylors', Crosby; Brasenose Coll., Oxford (Squire Minor Schol.); Westcott Hse, Cambridge. BA (1st Cl. Hons, Lit. Hum.), MA Oxon, 1948. Served Scots Guards, War of 1939-45 (MC). Deacon, 1950; Priest, 1951; Curate, All Saints, Gosforth, 1950-52; Chaplain, Westcott House, Cambridge, 1953-54; Vice-Principal, 1954-56; Fellow, Dean and Asst Tutor of Trinity Hall, Cambridge, 1956-60; Vicar of Cuddesdon and Principal of Cuddesdon Coll., 1960-69. Canon and Prebendary of Lincoln, 1969. Teape Lectr, St Stephen's Coll., Delhi, 1962. Select Preacher: Cambridge, 1957, Oxford, 1959. *Recreations:* travel, reading novels. *Address:* Abbey Gate House, St Albans, Herts. *T:* St Albans 53305. *Club:* Athenæum.

**ST ALBANS, Dean of;** *see* Kennaby, Very Rev. Noel Martin.

**ST ALBANS, Archdeacon of;** *see* Snell, Ven. B. C.

**ST ALDWYN,** 2nd Earl, *cr* 1915, of Coln St Aldwyns; **Michael John Hicks Beach;** Viscount Quenington, *cr* 1915; Bt, *cr* 1619; Viscount St Aldwyn, *cr* 1906; PC 1959; KBE 1964; TD 1949; DL, JP; *b* 9 Oct. 1912; *s* of Visc. Quenington, Roy. Glos. Hussars Yeo. (*d* 1916; *o s* of 1st Earl) and Marjorie (*d* 1916), *d* of late H. Dent Brocklehurst, Sudeley Castle, Gloucs; *S* grandfather, 1916 (his father having been killed in action a week previously); *m* 1948, Diana Mary Christian (she *m* 1st, 1939, Major Richard Patrick Pilkington Smyly, MC; marriage annulled, 1942), *o d* of late Henry C. G. and Mrs Mills; three *s*. *Educ:* Eton; Christ Church, Oxford. Major Royal Glos Hussars Yeomanry, 1942. Parliamentary Secretary, Ministry of Agriculture and Fisheries, 1954-58; Captain of Gentlemen-at-Arms and Government Chief Whip in the House of Lords, 1958-64, 1970-; Opposition Chief Whip, House of Lords, 1964-70. DL 1950, JP 1952, Glos. KStJ; Vice-Chancellor, Order of St John, 1969-. *Heir: s* Viscount Quenington, *qv*. *Address:* Williamstrip Park, Cirencester, Gloucestershire. *T:* Coln St Aldwyns 226; 13 Upper Belgrave Street, SW1. *T:* 01-235 8464. *Clubs:* Buck's; Royal Yacht Squadron.
*See also Brig. Sir Charles Dillwyn-Venables-Llewelyn, Bt, Sir Richard Keane, Bt.*

**ST ANDREWS, Earl of; George Philip Nicholas Windsor;** *b* 26 June 1962; *s* of HRH the Duke of Kent and HRH the Duchess of Kent.
*See under Royal Family.*

**ST ANDREWS AND EDINBURGH, Archbishop of, (RC),** since 1951; **His Eminence Cardinal Gordon Joseph Gray,** MA (Hon.) St Andrews; Hon. DD St Andrews, 1967; *b* 10 August 1910; 2nd *s* of Francis William and Angela Gray. *Educ:* Holy Cross Acad., Edinburgh; St John's Seminary, Wonersh. Assistant-Priest, St Andrews, 1935-41; Parish Priest, Hawick, 1941-47; Rector of Blairs College, Aberdeen (Scottish National Junior Seminary), 1947-51. Cardinal, 1969. *Address:* St Bennet's, 42 Greenhill Gardens, Edinburgh 10. *T:* 031-447 3337.

**ST ANDREWS, DUNKELD AND DUNBLANE, Bishop of,** since 1969; **Rt. Rev. Michael Geoffrey Hare Duke;** *b* 28 Nov. 1925; *s* of A. R. A. Hare Duke, Civil Engineer; *m* 1949, Grace Lydia Frances McKean Dodd; one *s* three *d*. *Educ:* Bradfield Coll.; Trinity Coll., Oxford. BA 1949, MA 1951. Sub-Lt, RNVR, 1944-46. Deacon, 1952; Priest, 1953; Curate, St John's Wood Church, 1952-56; Vicar, St Mark's, Bury, 1956-62; Pastoral Dir, Clin. Theol. Assoc., 1962-64; Vicar, St Paul's, Daybrook, and Pastoral Consultant to Clin. Theol. Assoc., 1964-69; OCF, E Midland Dist HQ, 1968-69. Mem. Editorial Bd, Contact Magazine, 1962-. *Publications:* Understanding the Adolescent, 1969; (jointly): The Caring Church, 1963; First Aid in Counselling, 1968. Contributor to: Expository Times, Blackfriars, New Christian, Church Quarterly Review, Church Times, Contact. *Address:* Bishop's House, Fairmount Road, Perth, Perthshire. *T:* Perth 21580.

**ST ANDREWS, DUNKELD, and DUNBLANE, Dean of;** *see* Irvine, Very Rev. Thomas Thurstan.

**ST ARNAUD (Victoria), Bishop of,** since 1951; **Rt. Rev. Allen Ernest Winter;** *b* 8 Dec. 1903; *o s* of Ernest Thomas and Margaret Winter, Malvern, Vic; *m* 1939, Eunice Eleanor, 3rd *d* of Albert and Eleanor Sambell; three *s* two *d*. *Educ:* Melbourne C of E Grammar School; Trinity Coll., Univ. of Melbourne (BA 1926,

MA 1928); University College, Oxford (BA 1932, MA 1951); Australian College of Theology (ThL 1927, ThD 1951 iur. dig.). Deacon, 1927, priest, 1928, Melbourne; Curate, Christ Church, S Yarra, 1927-29; on leave, Oxford, 1929-32; Curate, St James', Ivanhoe, 1932-35; Minister of Sunshine, 1935-39; Incumbent of St Luke's, Brighton, Melb., 1939-48; Chaplain, AIF, 1942-46; Incumbent of Christ Church, Essendon, 1948-49; Canon-Residentiary and Rector of All Saints' Cathedral, Bathurst, 1949-51. *Address:* Bishopsholme, St Arnaud, Victoria 3478, Australia.

**ST ASAPH, Dean of;** *see* Charles, Very Rev. Harold John.

**ST AUBYN,** family name of **Baron St Levan.**

**ST AUBYN, Sir J. M.;** *see* Molesworth-St Aubyn.

**ST AUDRIES,** 2nd Baron, *cr* 1911; **Alexander Peregrine Fuller-Acland-Hood,** Bt, *cr* 1809, also Bt of Hartington, *cr* 1806; *e s* of 1st Baron, and Hon. Mildred Rose Eveleigh-de-Moleyns (*d* 1949), 2nd *d* of 4th Baron Ventry; *b* 24 Dec. 1893; *S* father, 1917. *Educ:* Eton; Magdalen Coll., Oxford (MA). Lieut Somerset LI and Gren. Gds (during war only). JP 1923-47, CC 1937-52, Somerset. Patron of 3 livings. CStJ. *Heir:* (to Baronetcies only) *kinsman* Alexander William Fuller-Acland-Hood [*b* 5 March 1901; *m* 1925, Mary Jessup; one *d* (one *s* decd). Naturalized American citizen, 1926]. *Address:* Fairfield, Stogursey, Bridgwater. *T:* Nether Stowey 251.

**ST BONIFACE, Archbishop of, (RC),** since 1955; **Most Rev. Maurice Baudoux,** STD, PhD, Dès L; *b* Belgium, 1902. *Educ:* Prud'homme convent, Saskatchewan; St Boniface College, Manitoba; St Joseph's Seminary, Alberta; Grand Seminary, Quebec. Priest, 1929; Curate then Pastor, Prud'homme, Sask; Domestic Prelate, 1944; First Bishop of Saint Paul in Alberta, 1948; Coadjutor-Archbishop of Saint Boniface, 1952. *Address:* Archbishop's Residence, 151 Cathedral Avenue, St Boniface 6, Manitoba, Canada.

**ST CLAIR,** family name of **Baron Sinclair.**

**ST CLAIR, Malcolm Archibald James,** farmer; *b* 16 Feb. 1927; *o s* of late Maj.-Gen. George James Paul St Clair, CB, CBE, DSO and late Charlotte Theresa Orme Little; *m* 1955, Mary-Jean Rosalie Alice, *o d* of Wing-Comdr Caryl Liddell Hargreaves, Broadwood House, Sunningdale; two *s*. *Educ:* Eton. Served with Royal Scots Greys, 1944-48. Formerly Hon. Sec. to Sir Winston Churchill. Contested (C) Bristol South-East, 1959; MP (C) Bristol South-East, 1961-63. Lt Col Comdg, Royal Gloucestershire Hussars (T). *Recreation:* hunting. *Address:* Upton House, Tetbury, Glos. *Clubs:* Cavalry, Turf, White's.

**ST CLAIR-ERSKINE,** family name of **Earl of Rosslyn.**

**ST CLAIR-FORD, Capt. Sir Aubrey,** 6th Bt, *cr* 1793; DSO 1942; RN, retired; *b* 29 Feb. 1904; *e s* of late Anson and Elsie St Clair-Ford; *S* cousin 1948; *m* 1945, Anne, *o d* of Harold Christopherson, Penerley Lodge, Beaulieu, Hants; one *s* one *d*. *Educ:* Stubbington House; RNC, Osborne and Dartmouth. Served War of 1939-45 (despatches, DSO and bar); Korean War of 1950-53 (despatches, Officer, Legion of Merit, US). *Heir:* *s* Anson St Clair-Ford, *b* 16 March 1952. *Address:* Corner House, Sandle Copse, Fordingbridge, Hants. *Club:* Army and Navy.
*See also Maj.-Gen. Sir Peter St Clair-Ford.*

**ST CLAIR-FORD, Maj.-Gen. (retd) Sir Peter,** KBE 1961 (CBE 1953); CB 1954; DSO 1943 and Bar 1944; idc; psc; General Secretary of the Officers' Association, 1963-66; *b* 25 Nov. 1905; *s* of late Anson St Clair-Ford and Elsie (*née* Adams); unmarried. *Educ:* Dover College; Royal Military College, Sandhurst. Commissioned into KOYLI, 1925; Somaliland Camel Corps, 1932-39; France, 1939; Staff College, Camberley, 1940 (psc); various Staff appts, UK, 1940-43; Comd 1 Bn KOYLI, 1943-44, Italy and Palestine; Comd 3 Inf. Bde, 1944-46, Italy and Palestine; Comd 129 Inf. Bde (TA), 1947-48; BGS Southern Command (UK), 1948-49; Imperial Defence College (idc), 1950; BGS, FARELF, 1951-52; Training Adviser to Pakistan Army, 1952-54; Commander 1 Federal Division, Malaya, 1954-57; Deputy Chief of Staff, Headquarters Allied Land Forces Central Europe, 1958-60; retd, 1960. *Recreations:* shooting, golf, racing. *Address:* Cotswold Lodge, Littlestone, Kent. *Club:* East India and Sports.
*See also Capt. Sir Aubrey St Clair-Ford, Bt.*

**ST CYRES,** Viscount; **John Stafford Northcote;** *b* 15 Feb. 1957; *s* and *heir* of 4th Earl of Iddesleigh, *qv*.

**ST DAVIDS,** 2nd Viscount, *cr* 1918; **Jestyn Reginald Austen Plantagenet Philipps;** Baron, *cr* 1908; Bt, *cr* 1621; Lt RNVR; Founder and Warden, Regents Boat Club, Floating Youth Club for Boys and Girls; *b* 19 Feb. 1917; *s* of 1st Viscount and Elizabeth Frances (*see* Elizabeth, Viscountess St Davids), *d* of late Hon. Paulyn F. C. Rowdon-Hastings, of The Manor House, Ashby-de-la-Zouch; *S* father, 1938; *m* 1938, Doreen Guinness (marr. diss., 1954; she *d* 1956), *o d* of Captain Arthur Jowett, Toorak, Melbourne, Australia; one *s* four *d*; *m* 1954, Elisabeth Joyce, *e d* of Dr E. A. Woolf, Hove, Sussex (marr. diss., 1959); *m* 1959, Evelyn Marjorie, *d* of late Dr J. E. G. Harris, Bray, Berks. *Educ:* Eton; Trinity Coll., Cambridge. *Heir:* *s* Hon. Colwyn Jestyn John Philipps, *b* 30 Jan. 1939. *Address:* 15 St Mark's Crescent, Regent's Park, NW1.

**ST DAVIDS, Elizabeth, Viscountess; Elizabeth Frances Philipps;** (Baroness Strange of Knokin, *cr* 1299, Baroness Hungerford, *cr* 1426, Baroness de Moleyns, *cr* 1445, all in her own right; *S* on termination of abeyance, 1921); *b* 19 June 1884; 2nd *d* of late Major Hon. Paulyn Francis Cuthbert Rawdon-Hastings; *m* 1916, 1st Viscount St Davids [*d* 1938); one *s* one *d*. *Heir:* (to Baronies of Strange of Knokin, Hungerford, and de Moleyns) *s* Viscount St Davids, *qv*. *Address:* 15 St Mark's Crescent, Regent's Park, NW1.

**ST DAVID'S, Dean of;** *see* Jenkins, Very Rev. T. E.

**ST DAVID'S, Archdeacon of;** *see* Tree, Ven. R. J.

**SAINT-DENIS, Michel Jacques** (pseudonym **Jacques Duchesne**) Officier de la Légion d'Honneur; actor; dramatic author; producer; Consultant Director of the Royal Shakespeare Theatre Company, since 1966 (Director, 1962-); Co-Director, Juilliard School Drama Division, New York, since 1968; *b* Beauvais, France, 13 Sept. 1897; *s* of Charles Saint-Denis and Marguerite Copeau; *m* 1923, Marie Ostroga (marriage dissolved); one *s* one *d*; *m* Suria Magito. *Educ:* College Rollin, Paris; Lycée de Versailles. Served European War, 1914-18 (Croix de Guerre). Began career as private secretary to Jacques Copeau (his uncle by marriage), at Théâtre du Vieux Colombier, subsequently becoming stage-manager, then stage-director and asst producer at the same theatre; first appearance as an actor, 1922, as Curio in Twelfth Night; remained for ten years with Copeau and Les Copiaux in Burgundy and wrote his first plays in collaboration with Jean Villard; in 1930 founded and was director and producer for La Compagnie des Quinze; he also acted in the plays produced; made first appearance in London as Lucas in Le Médecin Malgré Lui, in 1927, at the St James's; appeared at Arts and New Theatres, 1931; toured with his company in Europe; founded the London Theatre Studio, Islington, 1935 (Managing Director); produced Noah, with John Gielgud, New Theatre, 1935; Sowers of the Hills, Westminster, 1935; The Witch of Edmonton, with Dame Edith Evans, Old Vic, 1936; Macbeth, with Sir Laurence Olivier, Old Vic, 1937; Three Sisters, with Dame Peggy Ashcroft, Sir John Gielgud, Michael Redgrave, Sir Alec Guinness, Queens, 1938; The White Guard, Phœnix, 1938; Twelfth Night, with Michael Redgrave, Phœnix, 1938; The Marriage of Blood, with Martita Hunt, Savoy, 1939; Weep for the Spring, 1939; also produced shows at the London Theatre Studio, including The Electra of Sophocles, and The Alcestis of Euripides. Served War of 1939-45 (Rosette de la Résistance): mobilised in Infanterie Coloniale, 1939-40; Officier de liaison at English GHQ; Head of French Section, BBC, under pseudonym Jaques Duchesne, 1940-44; instigation of English Service of Radiodiffusion française, 1944-45. Foundation of Old Vic Theatre Centre and School, 1946; Director-General, 1946-52. Productions for the Old Vic since 1945, include: Œdipus Rex, with Sir Laurence Olivier; A Month in the Country, with Michael Redgrave; Electra, with Dame Peggy Ashcroft; King John, etc. Supervised (with Pierre Sonrel) complete reconstruction of stage and auditorium for re-opening of Old Vic, Waterloo Road, 1951. Foundation, under French Govt auspices, of Centre National Dramatique de l'Est. Strasbourg (Dir.-Gen., 1952-57). Has visited Russia; Canada at invitation of Canadian govt, to study foundation of Canadian Theatre and Theatre-school (opening Montreal, Nov. 1960), and US at invitation of Rockefeller Foundation, 1958. Inspecteur Général des Spectacles, 1959-; Special Consultant for foundation of Repertory Theatre and Drama School, Lincoln Square, New York, 1960; Co-Director, Royal Shakespeare Theatre, Stratford-on-Avon, 1962. Produced: Oedipus Rex, Sadler's Wells, 1960; The Cherry Orchard, Aldwych, 1965; Squire Puntila and his Servant Matti, Aldwych, 1965. Internat. Award, 1969, of Internat. Theatre Inst. and Amer. Educnl Theatre. Hon. DLitt Birmingham Univ., 1962; Hon. LHD Dartmouth College, Hanover, USA, 1962. Hon. Fellow, Royal College of Art, 1963. CBE (Hon.); Chevalier de l'Ordre de Léopold. *Publications:* Theatre: The Rediscovery of Style, 1960; articles in theatrical jls, etc. *Recreations:* travelling, driving, music, fishing. *Address:* 2 Bloomfield Terrace, SW1.

**ST EDMUNDSBURY and IPSWICH, Bishop of,** since 1966; **Rt. Rev. Leslie Wilfrid Brown,** CBE 1965; *b* 10 June 1912; *s* of Harry and Maud Brown; *m* 1939, Annie Winifred, *d* of Hon. R. D. Megaw, Belfast; one *d*. *Educ:* Enfield Gram. School; London College of Divinity (London Univ.). BD 1936, MTh 1944, DD 1957. MA Cantab. hon. causa, 1953. Deacon, Curate St James' Milton, Portsmouth, 1935; priest, 1936. Missionary, CMS, 1938 to Cambridge Nicholson Instn, Kottayam, Travancore, S India. Fellow Commoner and Chaplain, Downing College, Cambridge, 1943; Kerala United Theological Seminary, Trivandrum: tutor, 1945, Principal, 1946, and from 1951. Chaplain, Jesus Coll., Cambridge and Select Preacher before Univ. of Cambridge, 1950, 1967, Oxford, 1967. Archbishop of Uganda, Rwanda and Burundi, 1961-65; Bishop of Namirembe, 1960-65 (of Uganda, 1953-60; name of diocese changed). Hon. Fellow, Downing Coll., Cambridge, 1966. DD (*hc*) Trinity Coll., Toronto, 1963. Chaplain and Sub-Prelate, Order of St John, 1968. *Publications:* The Indian Christians of St Thomas, 1956; The Christian Family, 1959; God as Christians see Him, 1961; Relevant Liturgy, 1965. *Address:* Bishop's House, 14 Park Road, Ipswich. *T:* Ipswich 52829. *Club:* Royal Commonwealth Society.

**ST EDMUNDSBURY and IPSWICH, Assistant Bishop of;** *see* Hollis, Rt. Rev. A. M.

**ST EDMUNDSBURY and IPSWICH, Provost of;** *see* Waddington, Very Rev. J. A. H.

**ST GEORGE, Sir Robert Alan,** 7th Bt, *cr* 1766; now Religious Lay Brother; *b* 20 March 1900; *s* of Sir Theophilus John St George, 6th Bt, and Florence Emma, *d* of late John Venderplank, Natal; *S* father, 1943. *Educ:* St Charles Coll., Maritzburg. Served RAF, 1918; War of 1939-45, Middle East (prisoner). *Heir:* *b* Rev. Denis Howard, *b* 6 Sept. 1902. *Address:* St Joseph's Scholasticate, Cedara, Natal, SA.

**ST GERMANS,** 9th Earl of, *cr* 1815; **Nicholas Richard Michael Eliot;** Baron Eliot, 1784; Major, Duke of Cornwall's Light Infantry; *b* 26 Jan. 1914; *er s* of 8th Earl of St Germans, KCVO, OBE, and of Helen Agnes Post (*d* 1962) (*d* of Lady Barrymore and late Arthur Post, New York, USA); *S* father 1960; *m* 1st, 1939, Helen Mary (marr. diss., 1947; she *d* 1951), *d* of late Lt-Col Charles Walter Villiers, CBE, DSO, and late Lady Kathleen Villiers; one *s* one *d*; 2nd, 1948, Mrs Margaret Eleanor Eyston (marr. diss., 1959), *o d* of late Lt-Col William Francis George Wyndham, MVO; 3rd, 1965, Mrs Mary Bridget Lotinga, *d* of late Sir Shenton Thomas and of Lady Thomas, SW7. *Educ:* Eton. Joined Duke of Cornwall's Light Infantry, 1937. Served War of 1939-45: attached Royal Armoured Corps. *Heir:* *s* Lord Eliot, *qv*. *Club:* St James'.
*See also Earl of Shelburne.*

**ST HELENA, Bishop of,** since 1967; **Rt. Rev. Edmund Michael Hubert Capper,** OBE 1961; LTh (Dur.); *b* 12 March 1908; *e s* of Arthur Charles and Mabel Lavinia Capper; unmarried. *Educ:* St Joseph's Academy, Blackheath; St Augustine's College, Canterbury. Deacon, 1932, Priest, 1933. Royal Army Chaplains' Dept, 1942-46 (EA); Archdeacon of Lindi and Canon of Masasi Cathedral, 1947-54; Archdeacon of Dar es Salaam, 1954-58. Provost of the Collegiate Church of St Alban the Martyr, Dar es Salaam, Tanganyika, 1957-62; Canon of Zanzibar, 1954-62; Member, Universities' Mission to Central Africa, 1936-62; Chairman, Tanganyika British Legion Benevolent Fund, 1956-62; President, Tanganyika British Legion, 1960-62; Chaplain, Palma de Mallorca, 1962-67. *Publications:* Be Confirmed, 1960. Various missionary booklets and pamphlets. *Recreations:* swimming and walking. *Address:* Bishopsholme, St Helena Island, South Atlantic. *Clubs:* Royal Commonwealth Society; Exiles (Ascension); British (Palma).

**ST HELENS,** 1st Baron *cr* 1964; **Michael Henry Colin Hughes-Young,** MC 1944; *b* 28 Oct. 1912; *s* of late Brig.-Gen. H. G. Young, CIE, DSO; *m* 1939, Elizabeth Agnes Blakiston-Houston (*d* 1956); one *s* three *d* (and *er s* decd). *Educ:*

Harrow; Sandhurst. Joined Black Watch, 1932; attached French Army, 1934; seconded King's African Rifles, 1935; Abyssianian War and Invasion of Europe, 1940 and 1944; retired as Lt-Col, 1947. Contested (C) St Helens, 1951; Conservative Central Office, 1948-55; MP (C) Wandsworth Central, 1955-64; Parliamentary Private Secretary to Minister of State, Board of Trade, 1956-58 and Assistant Whip (unpaid), 1956-58; Dep. Govt Chief Whip, 1959-64; a Lord Commissioner of the Treasury, 1958-62; Treasurer of HM Household, 1962-64. *Heir:* *s* Hon. Richard Francis Hughes-Young, *b* 4 Nov. 1945. *Address:* Marchfield, Binfield, Berks. *T:* Bracknell 3338. *Club:* Carlton.

**ST JOHN,** family name of **Baron St John of Bletso,** and of **Viscount Bolingbroke.**

**ST JOHN of BLETSO,** 19th Baron, *cr* 1558, 16th Bt, 1660; **John Moubray Russell St John;** *b* 3 Aug. 1917; *o s* of 18th Baron and Evelyn Geraldine (*d* 1918), *d* of late Captain Andrew Hamilton Russell; *S* father, 1934. *Heir: cousin,* Rev. Oliver John Frank Lockwood St John, DSC, Comdr RN retd [*b* 31 March 1914; *m* 1938, Elva Rosemary, *d* of Dr A. J. Skinn, Hong Kong; four *d.* Served War of 1939-45 (DSC and Bar). Vicar of St George's, Tyldesley, Lancs].

**ST JOHN, Geoffrey Robert,** MC; *s* of late H. P. St John and *d* of Hon. Pascoe Charles Glyn; *b* 4 Jan. 1889; *heir pres* to Viscount Bolingbroke, *qv; m* 1st, 1914, Gwendolen I. (who obtained a divorce, 1924), *o c* of H. Okeden, Stutton House, Suffolk; 2nd, 1925, Katharine M. (who obt. a div., 1940; she *d* 1958), *o d* of A. S. J. Musgrave, Abbeylands, Settle, Yorks; two *s* one *d*; 3rd, 1941, Mary Violet Handley Mills (*d* 1951), *niece* and *adopted d* of late John Mills, Maffra, Vic, Australia; 4th, 1957, Brynhildr, *d* of late Harold Archdall Vicars and *widow* of W. Bryant Purkis. *Educ:* Marlborough; Magdalen Coll., Oxford. Served with Royal Fusiliers, European War, 1914-19 (despatches, MC). Secretary of the Over 45's Association, from 1957. *Address:* Haytos Lodge, Newport, Essex. *T:* Newport (Essex) 650.

**ST JOHN, Oliver Charles Beauchamp,** CMG 1963; with Foreign Office, 1948-68; *b* 23 Oct. 1907; *s* of late Lt-Col Sir Henry Beauchamp St John, KCIE, CBE, and late Olive Amy Herbert; *m* 1935, Elizabeth Mary Lambton (*d* 1957); one *s* three *d*; *m* 1966, Mrs Mary Maxwell-Gumbleton. *Educ:* Charterhouse; RMC, Sandhurst. XXth Lancers, IA, 1928-32; Indian Political Service, 1932-47; numerous appts in IPS including Asst Private Sec. to Viceroy, 1932-34; Prime Minister, Alwar State, 1936; Political Agent, Western Kathiawar, 1937; Sec. to Governor, NWFP, 1942-46; Dep. Comr, Hazara, 1947-48. *Recreations:* shooting, fishing, riding, golf. *Address:* Curtle Cottage, Beaulieu, Hants. *T:* Beaulieu 268. *Clubs:* Naval and Military, Hurlingham.

**ST JOHN, Maj.-Gen. Roger Ellis Tudor,** CB 1965; MC 1944; *b* Hexham on Tyne, 4 Oct. 1911; *s* of late Major B. T. St John, Craigveigh, Aboyne, Aberdeenshire; *m* 1943, Rosemary Jean Douglas Vickers, Englefield Green, Surrey; one *s* three *d. Educ:* Wellington College; RMC Sandhurst. Joined Fifth Fusiliers, 1931; served War of 1939-45 (despatches, MC), in Hong Kong, UK and NW Europe; Bde Major 11 Armoured Div., 1944-45; GSO 2 Instructor Camberley Staff Coll., 1945-46; AA and QMG 1st Division, Tripoli, 1948-50; comd 1st Bn Royal Northumberland Fusiliers, 1953-55 (despatches), Mau Mau Rebellion; AMS Mil. Secretary's Branch, War Office, 1955-57; Comdr 11 Inf. Bde Group, BAOR, 1957-60; Asst Commandant, Camberley Staff Coll., 1960-62; Commander, British Army Staff, Military Member, British Defence Staffs, and Military Attaché, Washington, 1963-65; President, Regular Army Commissions Board, 1965-67; retired, 1967. Colonel, Royal Northumberland Fusiliers, 1965-68. Personnel Adminr, Urwick, Orr and Partners Ltd, Management Consultants. *Address:* Harelaw, Gorse Hill Road, Virginia Water, Surrey. *Club:* Army and Navy.

**ST JOHN PERSE;** *see* Leger, M.-R. A. St-L.

**ST JOHN-STEVAS, Norman Antony Francis;** MP (C) Chelmsford, since Oct. 1964; Author, Barrister and Journalist; *b* London, 18 May 1929; *o s* of late Stephen S. Stevas, civil engineer and company director, and Kitty St John O'Connor, Duarrigle Castle, County Cork; unmarried. *Educ:* Ratcliffe; Fitzwilliam, Cambridge; Christ Church, Oxford; Yale. Scholar, Clothworkers Exhibnr, 1946, 1947; BA (Cambridge) (1st cl. hons in law), 1950, MA 1954; President, Cambridge Union, 1950; Whitlock Prize, 1950; MA 1952, BCL 1954 (Oxon); Sec. Oxford Union, 1952. Contested (C) Dagenham, Gen. Election, 1951; Barrister, Middle Temple, 1952; Blackstone and Harmsworth schol., 1952; Blackstone Prize, 1953. Lecturer, Southampton University, 1952-53, King's Coll., London, 1953-56, tutored in jurisprudence, Christ Church, 1953-55, and Merton, 1955-57, Oxford. Founder member, Inst. of Higher European Studies, Bolzano, 1955; PhD (Lond.) 1957; Yorke Prize, Cambridge Univ., 1957; Fellow Yale Law School, 1957; Fulbright Award, 1957; Fund for the Republic Fellow, 1958; Dr of Sc. and Law (Yale), 1960; Lecture tours of USA, 1958-68. Regents' Prof., Univ. of California at Santa Barbara, 1969; Deleg. Council of Europe and WEU, 1967-71. Legal Adviser to Sir Alan Herbert's Cttee on book censorship, 1954-59; joined The Economist, 1959, to edit collected works of Walter Bagehot and became legal, ecclesiastical and political correspondent. Sec., Cons. Parly Home Affairs Cttee, 1969-. Member: Conservative National Advisory Committee on Education, 1961; Fulbright Commission, 1961. Founder Mem., Christian-Social Inst. of Culture, Rome, 1969. Editor The Dublin (Wiseman) Review, 1961. KSt Lazarus of Jerusalem, 1963. Cav., Order of Merit (Italian Republic), 1965. FRSL, 1966. *Publications:* Obscenity and the Law, 1956; Walter Bagehot, 1959; Life, Death and the Law, 1961; The Right to Life, 1963; Law and Morals, 1964; The Literary Works of Walter Bagehot, vols, I, II, 1966, The Historical Works, Vols III, IV, 1968; The Agonising Choice, 1971. Contrib. to: Critical Quarterly, Modern Law Review, Criminal Law Review, Law and Contemporary Problems, Twentieth Century, Times Lit. Supp., Dublin Review. *Recreations:* reading, talking, listening (to music), travelling, walking, appearing on television. *Address:* 1 Hampstead Square, NW3. *T:* Hampstead 7080. *Clubs:* Garrick, Beefsteak.

**ST JOHN'S (Newfoundland), Archbishop of, (RC),** since 1951; **Most Rev. Patrick James Skinner,** CJM; *b* 1904. *Educ:* St Bonaventure's College, St John's; Holy Heart Seminary, Halifax; Eudist Seminary, Gros Pin, PQ; Laval University, Quebec. Priest, 1929; consecrated, as Auxiliary to Archbishop of St John's, Newfoundland, 1950. *Address:* Basilica Residence, Bonaventure Avenue, St John's, Newfoundland.

**ST JOHN'S** (S Africa), **Bishop of,** since 1956; **Rt. Rev. James Leo Schuster;** *b* 18 July 1912; *s* of Rev. Harold Vernon Schuster and Elsie Jane (*née* Roberton); *m* 1951, Ilse Henriette Emmy Gottschalk; three *s* two *d* (and one *s* decd). *Educ:* Lancing; Keble Coll., Oxford. Deacon, 1937; Priest, 1938; Asst Missioner, Clare Coll. Mission, Rotherhithe, 1937-38; Chaplain St Stephen's House, Oxford, 1938-40; CF (EC), 1940-46; wounded, 1942; despatches, 1943. Chaplain, St Stephen's House, Oxford, 1946-49; Principal St Bede's College, Umtata, 1949-56. *Address:* Bishopsmead, PO Box 163, Umtata, CP, South Africa. *T:* Umtata 74.

**ST JOHNSTON, Colonel Sir (Thomas) Eric,** Kt 1967; CBE 1952 (OBE 1945); QPM 1958; MA Cantab; HM Chief Inspector of Constabulary for England and Wales, 1967-70; invited by Government of Victoria, Australia, to examine and report on efficiency of the Police Force in the State, 1970; *b* 7 Jan. 1911; *o s* of late T. G. St Johnston, Edgbaston, Warwicks; *m* 1st, 1937, Joan (marr. diss. 1969), *d* of late Alwyn Wharton, MD, Oldham, Lancs; one *s* two *d*; 2nd, 1969, Margaret Emily Jameson Till, widow of Lt-Col S. Jameson Till, MC. *Educ:* Bromsgrove School, Worcestershire; Corpus Christi, Cambridge. Late RA (TA), 1929-35; employed in rank of Colonel for special duties, War Office, 1943, and as staff officer, SHAEF, 1944; member staff of King's Camp, 1932 *et seq*; employed on civil staff at New Scotland Yard, 1932-35; Barrister, Middle Temple, 1934; Metropolitan Police College, 1935 (winner of Baton of Honour); Inspector, Metropolitan Police, 1936-40; Chief Constable of Oxfordshire, 1940-44, of Durham County, 1944-50, of Lancashire, 1950-67. Visited USA as guest of US Government, 1953; Visiting Lecturer, Univ. of California, 1953; Visiting Lectr to Israeli Police, 1955; British Council Lecturer in Australia and New Zealand, 1966; idc, 1957. Freeman of City of London and Liveryman of Vintners' Company, 1956; Chevalier de Tastevin, 1965. Chairman, Christian Police Trust Corp. Ltd, 1954-67. Dep. Chm., Sail Training Assoc. Endowment Trustee, Bromsgrove School. Hon. Col 33rd (Lancs and Cheshire) Signal Regt (V), 1967-70. hon. MA Manchester, 1961. Mem., Chapter Gen, Order of St John, 1968-69; KStJ 1966 (CStJ, 1960). Legion of Honour and Croix de Guerre (France). *Publications:* contrib. to Police periodicals in UK, and USA. *Recreations:* shooting and sailing. *Address:* 2 Ennismore Gardens Mews, SW7. *T:* 01-584 9158. *Clubs:* United Service, MCC; Royal Ocean Racing.

**ST JUST,** 2nd Baron, *cr* 1935, of St Just in Penwith; **Peter George Grenfell;** *b* 22 July 1922; *s* of 1st Baron and Florence, *e d* of late George W. Henderson; *s* father, 1941; *m* 1st, 1949, Leslie (marriage dissolved, 1955), *d* of late Condé Nast, New York; one *d*; 2nd, 1956, Maria Britneva; two *d. Educ:* Harrow. Served War, 1941-46, 60th Rifles. *Address:* 82 Whitelands House, Chelsea, SW3. *T:* 01-730 6672; Wilbury Park, Newton Tony, near Salisbury, Wilts. *T:* Cholderton 664. *Clubs:* Buck's, White's, House of Lords Yacht.

**ST LAURENT, Rt. Hon. Louis Stephen,** CC (Canada) 1967; PC 1946; LLD, QC 1915; Prime Minister of Canada, 1948-57; Leader of Canadian Liberal Party, 1948-58; MP Quebec-East, 1942-58; *b* Compton, Que, 1 Feb. 1882; *s* of J. B. M. St Laurent and Mary Anne Broderick; *m* 1908, Jeanne (*d* 1966), *d* of P. F. Renault, Beauceville, Quebec; two *s* three *d. Educ:* St Charles College, Sherbrooke; Laval University, Quebec (BA). Called to Bar of Quebec, 1905; Prof. Law Faculty, Laval Univ., 1914; formerly of St Laurent, Gagne, Devlin, and Taschereau, now of St Laurent, Monast, Desmeules and Walters, advocates, 500 E Grande Allée, Quebec, Que; Pres. Canadian Bar Assoc., 1930-32, now Hon. Life Pres. Minister of Justice and Attorney-General, 1941-46 and 1948; Minister of External Affairs, 1946-48. Chairman Can. Delegation to UN General Assembly, 1946, 1947. Liberal; Roman Catholic; Hon. LLD: Laval Univ. 1915; Queen's Univ., 1930; Univ. of Manitoba, 1935; Univ. of Montreal, 1943; Bishop's Coll., 1943; Dalhousie Univ., 1947; Univ. of Ottawa, 1947; Dartmouth Univ., 1948; McGill Univ., 1949; Rensselaer Polytechnic Inst., 1949; St Louis Univ. 1950; St Lawrence Univ., 1950; Univ. of Toronto, 1950; Univ. of Western Ont, 1951; Northwestern Univ., 1951; Univ. of BC, 1952; London Univ., 1952; St Francis Xavier Univ., 1953; Peshawar Univ., 1954; Delhi Univ., 1954; Univ. of Sask, 1963; RMC of Canada, 1964; Hon. DCL: Mount Allison, 1952; Oxford Univ., 1953. Freedom of City of London, 1955. *Address:* 201 East Grand Allee, Quebec, Canada. *Clubs:* Garrison (Quebec); Cercle Universitaire, University (Montreal); Rideau Country (Ottawa).

**ST LEGER,** family name of **Viscount Doneraile.**

**ST LEONARDS,** 3rd Baron (*cr* 1852), **Frank Edward Sugden;** *b* 11 Nov. 1890; *o surv s* of late Hon. Henry Frank Sugden and Edith, *e d* of Abraham Bowman of Stangrove, Edenbridge; *S* uncle, 1908. *Educ:* Westminster; Christ Church Oxford. Late Lt Royal Horse Guards (Reserve). Owns about 4600 acres. *Heir: kinsman,* John Gerard Sugden, *b* 3 Feb. 1950. *Club:* St James'.

**ST LEVAN,** 3rd Baron (*cr* 1887), **Francis Cecil St Aubyn,** Bt, *cr* 1866; JP; DL; late Major Gren. Guards; Colonel Home Guard; *b* 18 April 1895; *s* of late Hon. A. J. D. Stuart St Aubyn; *S* uncle 1940; *m* 1916, Hon. Clementina Gwendolen Catharine Nicholson, *o d* of 1st Baron Carnock; three *s* two *d. Educ:* Eton; Sandhurst. Served European War, 1914-15 (wounded); rejoined Grenadier Guards 1939-42. DL for County of Cornwall, 1961. *Heir: s* Hon. John Francis Arthur St Aubyn, DSC 1944; Lieut RNVR, *b* 23 Feb. 1919. *Address:* St Michael's Mount, Marazion, Cornwall. *T:* 22. *Clubs:* Travellers', Army and Navy; Royal Cornwall Yacht.

*See also Earl Amherst.*

**ST OSWALD,** 4th Baron, *cr* 1885; **Rowland Denys Guy Winn,** MC 1951; DL; Member of Lloyd's since 1956; Vice-Chairman of Central and Eastern European Commission of the European Movement; Editorial Director, Tom Stacey Ltd; *b* 19 Sept. 1916; *s* of 3rd Baron St Oswald and Eva, *d* of Charles Greene; *S* father 1957; *m* 1st, 1952, Laurian (from whom he obtained a divorce, 1955), *o d* of Sir Roderick Jones, KBE; 2nd, 1955, Marie Wanda, *y d* of late Sigismund Jaxa-Chamiec, Zorawia, Warsaw; no *c. Educ:* Stowe Sch.; Universities of Bonn and Freiburg. Reuter's Corresp. for Spain, 1935; Daily Telegraph Corresp. and War Corresp., 1936 (condemned to death, Sept. 1936); Corresp. in Middle East, 1938, in Balkans 1939. Enlisted Army, 1939; served Middle East (8th King's Royal Hussars), 1941-44; Far East, 1945 (despatches). Resided Spain, 1946-50. Volunteered to serve in Korea, 1950; 8th King's Roy. Irish Hussars, 1950-51. Contested (C) Dearne Valley Div., 1955; adopted as Conservative candidate, Pudsey Div., 1957. A Lord-in-Waiting to the Queen, 1959-62; Jt Parly Sec. to Min. of Agriculture, Fisheries and Food, 1962-64; PPS to Sec. of State for Defence and to Lord Privy Seal, 1970-. Chairman, Mid-Yorkshire Conservative Assoc., 1965; President: W Riding of Yorks

Playing Fields Assoc., 1970-; British Assoc. Industrial Editors, 1964-70; Yorks Region Nat. Soc. Mentally Handicapped Children; Yorkshire Area Young Conservatives; Ackworth, Upton, Hemsworth and Wrangbrooke Branches, British Legion; Vice-President: W Riding British Legion; Anglo-Polish Soc., 1969. Trustee and Pres., Northern Cttee of Cheshire Foundn Homes for the Sick. Pres., Soc. of Yorkshiremen in London, 1960-61; Trustee Huddersfield Branch, Coldstreamers' Assoc.; Patron of Wakefield Trinity Football Club; Pres., Yorkshire Agric. Soc., 1968. Hon. Col 150 (Northumbrian) Regt RCT (V), 1967-. DL West Riding, Yorks, 1962. Croix de Guerre and Order of Leopold (Belgium), 1951; Légion d'Honneur and Croix de Guerre (France), 1945. *Publications:* Lord Highport Dropped at Dawn, 1949; My Dear, it's Heaven, 1950; Carmela, 1954 (USA 1955). *Recreations:* the company of his wife; talking and writing to friends. *Heir: b* Capt. Hon. Derek Edward Anthony Winn [*b* 9 July 1919; *m* 1954, Denise Eileen Charlotte, *o d* of Wilfrid Haig Loyd; one *s* one *d*]. *Address:* Nostell Priory, Wakefield, Yorks. *T:* Crofton 394; White Lodge, Gilston Road, SW10. *T:* 01-373 3660. *Clubs:* Cavalry, Garrick, Press. Special Forces, Beefsteak, Pratt's.

**ST PATRICK'S (DUBLIN), Dean of;** *see* Armstrong, Very Rev. J. W.

**ST PAUL'S, Dean of;** *see* Sullivan, Very Rev. M. G.

**ST VINCENT,** 7th Viscount (*cr* 1801); **Ronald George James Jervis;** *b* 3 May 1905; *o surv s* of 6th Viscount and Marion Annie (*d* 1911), *d* of James Brown, JP, Orchard, Carluke, Scotland; *S* father, 1940; *m* 1945, Phillida, *o d* of Lt-Col R. H. Logan, Taunton; two *s* one *d*. *Educ:* Sherborne. JP Somerset, 1950-55. *Heir: s* Hon. Edward Robert James Jervis, *b* 12 May 1951. *Address:* Avranche Manor, St Lawrence, Jersey, CI.

**ST VINCENT FERRERI,** 8th Marquis of, **Alfio Testaferrata Ghâxaq** (Marquis Testaferrata ); *b* 1911; *s* of Daniel Testaferrata Bonici Ghâxaq and Agnese (*d* 1941), *d* of Baroncino Nicola Galea di San Marciano; *S* father, 1945. *Educ:* Stonyhurst College, Blackburn; University Coll., Oxford. Sometime Mem., Cttee of Privileges of Maltese Nobility; Member Royal Numismatic Society; Membre de la Société suisse de Numismatique. Hereditary Knight of the Holy Roman Empire; Patrician of Rome, Messina, and Citta di Castello. *Address:* 29 Villegaignon Street, Mdina, Malta, GC. *T:* Rabat 74139. *Club:* Casino Maltese (Valletta).

**SAINTONGE, Rolland A. A. C. de;** *see* Chaput de Saintonge.

**SALAM, Professor Abdus,** Sitara-i-Pakistan, 1959; FRS 1959; PhD; Professor of Theoretical Physics at the Imperial College of Science and Technology in the University of London since 1957; Director, International Centre for Theoretical Physics, Trieste, since 1964; Science Adviser to the President of Pakistan, since 1961; Member, UN Advisory Cttee on Science and Technology; *b* 29 Jan. 1926. *Educ:* Govt Coll., Lahore, Pakistan (MA); St John's Coll., Camb. (BA, PhD). Fellow, St John's Coll., Cambridge, 1951-56; Professor of Mathematics, Government College, Lahore, 1951-54; Lecturer in Mathematics, University of Cambridge, 1954-56. Has made contributions to the theory of elementary particles. Fellow, Royal Swedish Acad. of Sciences, 1970. Hon. DSc Panjab University, Lahore, Pakistan, 1957. Hopkins Prize, Cambridge Philosophical Soc., 1957; Adams Prize, Cambridge Univ., 1958; Maxwell Medal and Prize, Institute of Physics and the Physical Soc., 1962; Hughes Medal, Royal Society, 1964; Atoms for Peace Award, 1968. *Address:* Imperial College of Science and Technology, Prince Consort Road, SW7; International Centre for Theoretical Physics PO Box 586, 34100 Trieste, Italy. *Club:* Athenæum.

**SALAMAN, Myer Head,** MD; Research Pathologist, Royal College of Surgeons, since 1968; *b* 2 August 1902; *e s* of Redcliffe N. Salaman, MD, FRS and Nina Salaman; *m* 1926, Esther Polianowsky; one *s* three *d*. *Educ:* Clifton College; Bedales School; Trinity College, Cambridge; London Hospital Medical College. Natural Science Tripos Pts I and II, Cambridge, 1921-25; London Hosp.: Clinical training, 1927-30; House Appts, 1931-32; Research on Viruses, 1932-34, and Lister Inst. (Junior Beit Mem. Fellow) 1935-38; Cancer Research, St Bartholomew's Hosp., 1939; Asst Pathologist, Emergency Public Health Service, 1940-42; Cancer and Virus Research, Strangeways Lab., 1942-43; Temp. Major, RAMC, 1943-46. Engaged in Cancer Research at the London Hospital, 1946-48; Dir, Dept of Cancer Research, London Hosp. Med. Sch., 1948-67. MA 1926, MD 1936 Cantab; MRCS, LRCP, 1930; Dipl. Bact. London, 1936. FRSocMed. *Publications:* papers on virus diseases, and on cancer, in Jour. Pathology and Bacteriology, Proc. Roy. Soc. (B), Brit. Jour. Cancer, etc. *Recreation:* walking. *Address:* 21 Argyll Road, W8. *T:* 01-937 1374; Dept of Pathology, Royal College of Surgeons of England, Lincoln's Inn Fields, WC2. *T:* 01-405 3474. *Club:* Athenæum.

*See also H. B. Barlow.*

**SALE, Geoffrey Stead;** Director of Studies, RMA, Sandhurst, Camberley, since 1967; *b* 6 Aug. 1907; *s* of Frederic W. R. Sale, Solicitor, Carlisle, and Ivy I. Davidson; *m* 1938, Olivia Jean Bell-Scott (*d* 1950), Edinburgh; one *s* three *d*. *Educ:* Berkhamsted School; Lincoln College, Oxford (MA). Diploma in Education; Assistant Master and Housemaster, Fettes College, Edinburgh, 1931-46; Headmaster, King's School, Bruton, 1946-57; Headmaster, Rossall School, 1957-67. FRSA, 1953. Captain TA (General List). Member, House of Laity, Church Assembly, 1960. *Publication:* Four Hundred Years a School (History of King's School). *Recreations:* walking, photography, writing. *Address:* Oak Grove House, RMA Sandhurst, Camberley, Surrey. *T:* Camberley 23701. *Club:* Oxford and Cambridge University.

**SALE, John Lewis,** CIE 1930; FICE; Public Works Dept, retired 1934; *b* 24 Aug. 1885; *s* of late Sir Stephen George Sale, KCIE; *m* 1924, Helen Caroline Ommanney, *d* of late Sir Ralph Sneyd Pearson, CIE; three *s*. *Educ:* Marlborough; RIEC, Cooper's Hill. Served European War, 1915-19; JP (Berks); CC 1937; CA 1950. *Address:* Priors Hold, Wantage, Berks. *T:* 161.

**SALE, Richard;** Headmaster of Brentwood School since 1966; *b* 4 Oct. 1919; *e s* of late Richard and of Rachel Sale; *m* 1943, Elizabeth Thérèse Bauer; four *s* one *d*. *Educ:* Repton Sch. (Schol.); Oriel Coll., Oxford. Commissioned, KSLI, 1940; served War of 1939-45: Canada and Normandy; demobilised, rank of Major, 1946. Asst Master, Repton Sch., 1946-61; Housemaster of The Priory, 1953-61; Headmaster, Oswestry School, Shropshire, 1962-66. Member: Army Scholarship Board; Council, Football Association. Governor, Moreton Hall School. FRSA 1969. *Recreations:* cricket (Oxford Blue;

Warwickshire, 1939, 1946, 1947; Derbyshire, 1949-54), golf, fives (Oxford Blue), and other games. *Address:* Roden House, Brentwood, Essex. *T:* Brentwood 8036. *Clubs:* MCC; Vincent's (Oxford).

**SALE, Brigadier Walter Morley,** CVO 1952; OBE 1944; Extra Equerry to the Queen, since 1961; *b* 1903; *s* of Charles Sale, late of Aston Rowant House, Oxon; *m* 1928, Hon. Ismay Hilda Margaret FitzRoy, *d* of 4th Baron Southampton, OBE; one *s* one *d*. *Educ:* RN Colls, Osborne and Dartmouth; New Coll., Oxford (BA). Royal Horse Guards: joined 1924; Captain, 1930; Major, 1936; Lt-Col, 1940; Brig. 1945. Served on staff with Guards Armoured Division and in Command of 1st Household Cavalry Regt (despatches twice). Equerry to the Queen, 1954; Crown Equerry, 1955-61. Croix de Guerre with Palm, 1945; Chevalier Order of Leopold II with Palm (Belgium), 1945. *Recreation:* shooting. *Address:* Heveningham House, Halesworth, Suffolk. *T:* Ubbeston 348. *Club:* Turf.

**SALES, William Henry,** BSc (Econ.) Hons. London; Chairman, Yorkshire (late NE) Division of the National Coal Board, 1957-67, retired (Member, National Coal Board, 1953-57); *b* 26 April 1903. *Educ:* pit; Fircroft; London School of Economics. Miners' Welfare Scholarship. Varied career; pit; boys' clubs; WEA Lecturer; schoolmaster. Dep. Labour Director, East Midlands Division, NCB, 1947-51; Deputy Chairman, North-Western Division, 1951-53. Chm. Church of England Industrial Council, 1967-. Hon. Fellow, LSE, 1960. *Publications:* various papers in Economic and Sociological Journals. *Address:* Handley Cross, Cantley, Doncaster, Yorks. *T:* Doncaster 55547.

**SALFORD, Bishop of, (RC),** since 1964; **Rt. Rev. Thomas Holland,** DSC 1944; DD (Gregorian); *b* 11 June 1908; *s* of John Holland and Mary (*née* Fletcher). *Educ:* Upholland; Valladolid; Rome. PhD Valladolid, 1929; DD Gregorian, Rome, 1936. Taught theology: Spain, 1936-42; Lisbon, 1942-43. Chaplain, RN, 1943-46; Port Chaplain, Bombay, 1946-48; CMS, 1948-56; Secretary to Apostolic Delegate, 1956-60; Coadjutor Bp of Portsmouth, 1960-64. Privy Chamberlain to the Pope, 1958. Member of Vatican Secretariat for Promoting Christian Unity, 1961-, for Unbelievers, 1965-. *Publication:* Great Cross, 1958. *Address:* Wardley Hall, Worsley, Manchester M28 5ND. *T:* 061-794 2825-6.

**SALFORD, Auxiliary Bishop of, (RC);** *see* Burke, Rt Rev. Geoffrey.

**SALINGER, Jerome David;** American author; *b* New York City, 1919; *m*; one *s* one *d*. *Educ:* Manhattan public schools; Military Academy, Paris. Served with 4th Infantry Division, US Army, 1942-46 (Staff Sergeant). Travelled in Europe, 1937-38. Started writing at age of 15; first story published, 1940. *Publications:* The Catcher in the Rye, 1951; For Esme–with Love and Squalor, 1953; Franny and Zooey, 1962; Raise High the Roof Beam, Carpenters and Seymour: an Introduction, 1963. *Address:* c/o Harold Ober Associates, 40 East 49th Street, New York 17, NY USA.

**SALINGER, Pierre (Emil George);** Politician, Journalist; Deputy Chairman, Gramco (UK) Ltd, since 1970; Director: Gramco Management Company; Gramco International SA; National General Productions Inc.; *b* San Francisco, 14 June 1925; *s* of Herbert and Jehanne Salinger; *m* 2nd, 1957, Nancy Brook Joy (marr. diss., 1965); two *s* one *d*; 3rd, 1965, Nicole Gillmann, Paris, France; one *s*. *Educ:* Lowell High School, San Francisco; State Coll., San Francisco; Univ. of San Francisco. Served War, 1942-45, with US Navy. With San Francisco Chronicle, 1942-55; Guest Lectr, Mills Coll., Calif, 1950-55; Press Officer, Democratic Presidential Campaign (Calif), 1952; West Coast Editor, Contributing Editor, Collier's Magazine, 1955-56; Investigator, Senate Labor Rackets Cttee, 1957-59; Press Sec. to President Kennedy (when Senator), 1959-61, and to President of the United States, 1961-64; appointed to serve as a US Senator, 4 Aug. 1964-2 Jan. 1965. Trustee, Robert F. Kennedy Meml Foundn; Mem., Adv. Council, Johns Hopkins University Center, Bologna, Italy. *Publications:* articles on county jail conditions in California, 1953; A Tribute to John F. Kennedy, Encyclopedia Britannica, 1964; With Kennedy, 1966; A Tribute to Robert F. Kennedy, 1968. *Address:* 59 Chester Square, SW1.

**SALISBURY,** 5th Marquess of, *cr* 1789; **Robert Arthur James Gascoyne-Cecil;** KG 1946; PC 1940; FRS; Baron Cecil 1603; Viscount Cranborne, 1604; Earl of Salisbury, 1605; late Lt 5th (Res.) Batt. Grenadier Guards; Chancellor, Order of the Garter, since 1960; Lord President of the Council, 1952-57; Leader of the House of Lords, 1942-45 and 1951-57; High Steward of Hertford, since 1947; Chancellor, University of Liverpool, since 1951; Chairman of the Royal Commission on Historical Monuments, since 1957; Director: Westminster Bank Ltd, 1957-68; British South Africa Company, 1957-61; Trustee of the National Gallery, 1959-66; *b* 27 August 1893; *e s* of 4th Marquess of Salisbury, KG, GCVO, and Lady Cicely Alice Gore (*d* 1955), *d* of 5th Earl of Arran; *S* father 1947; *m* 1915, Elizabeth Vere, *e d* of late Lord Richard Cavendish, PC, CB, CMG; one *s*. *Educ:* Eton; Christ Church, Oxford. MP (U) South Dorset, 1929-41; Parliamentary Under-Sec. of State for Foreign Affairs, 1935-38; Paymaster-General, 1940; Secretary of State for Dominion Affairs, 1940-42; called to House of Lords as Baron Cecil of Essendon, 1941; Secretary of State for the Colonies, 1942; Lord Privy Seal, 1942-43, 1951-52; Secretary of State for Dominion Affairs, 1943-45; Secretary of State for Commonwealth Relations, 1952. *Heir: s* Viscount Cranborne, *qv*. *Address:* Hatfield House, Hatfield, Hertfordshire. *T:* Hatfield 62702; Cranborne Lodge, Cranborne, Dorset. *T:* Cranborne 225; 2 Swan Walk, Chelsea, SW3. *T:* 01-352 6666. *Clubs:* Carlton, Turf, Buck's.

*See also Lord David Cecil, Duke of Devonshire, Dowager Duchess of Devonshire, Baron Harlech, Dowager Lady Harlech, Earl of Selborne.*

**SALISBURY, Bishop of,** since 1963; **Rt. Rev. Joseph Edward Fison;** *b* 18 March 1906; *s* of Frederick Flint Fison and Ethel Mary Fison; *m* 1944, Monica Irene Stober; two *s* two *d*. *Educ:* Orley Farm Prep. School; Shrewsbury School; The Queen's College, Oxford; Wycliffe Hall, Oxford. 2nd Cl. Hon. Mods, 2nd Cl. Lit Hum, 1st Cl Theol.; BA Oxon 1929, MA 1934, BD 1950. Taught at English Mission Coll., Cairo, 1930-33; ordained Deacon and Priest, 1934; Tutor and Chaplain, Wycliffe Hall, Oxford, 1934-37; Curate, St Aldate's Church, Oxford, 1937-40; Chaplain to Forces, 1940-45; Senior Chaplain, Jerusalem, 1943-45; Canon Residentiary of Rochester Cathedral, 1945-52; Canon Residentiary and Sub-Dean of Truro Cathedral and Rector of St Mary's Truro, 1952-59; Vicar of St Mary the Great with St Michael and All Angels, Cambridge, 1959-63. Lectured in USA, 1956; Select Preacher, Cambridge Univ., 1957; Hon. Canon of Ely

Cathedral, 1961-63. Chairman, Churches' Council of Healing, 1964-68. Pres. Council, Marlborough Coll.; Governor: Sherborne Sch.; St Mary's, Calne; Bryanston Sch. Hon. DD Aberdeen Univ., 1958. *Publications:* The Blessing of the Holy Spirit, 1950; Understanding the Old Testament, 1952; The Christian Hope, 1954; The Faith of the Bible, 1957 (Penguin); Fire upon the Earth, 1958. Contributor to: The Gospel of Grace, 1936; The Triumph of God, 1948; Steps to Christian Understanding (ed R. J. W. Bevan), 1958; Lenten Counsellors, 1962. Editor of and Contributor to: On the Move to Unity, 1962. Article on Haggai in Encyclopædia Britannica (written for new edn). *Address:* South Canonry, 71 The Close, Salisbury, Wilts. *T:* Salisbury 4031. *Clubs:* Old Salopian, Oxford Society, Automobile Association; Cambridge Union Society.

**SALISBURY, Assistant Bishop of;** *see* MacInnes, Most Rev. Angus Campbell.

**SALISBURY, Dean of;** *no new appointment at time of going to press.*

**SALISBURY (Rhodesia), Archbishop of; Most Rev. Francis Markall,** SJ; Metropolitan of Province of Rhodesia since Nov. 1956; *b* 24 Sept. 1905; *e s* of late Walter James Markall and Alice Mary Gray, London. *Educ:* St Ignatius' College, London. Entered Society of Jesus, 1924; continued classical and philosophical studies, 1926-31; Assistant Master, Stonyhurst College, 1931-34; theological studies, 1934-38; Missionary in Rhodesia, 1939-56; Titular Archbishop of Cotieo and Coadjutor with right of succession to Archbishop of Salisbury, April 1956. *Address:* Archbishop's House, PO Box 8060, Causeway, Rhodesia. *Club:* Salisbury (Salisbury).

**SALISBURY, Sir Edward James,** Kt 1946; CBE 1939; FRS 1933; DSc, Hon. LLD (Edinburgh and Glasgow); VMH; FLS; Director, Royal Botanic Gardens, Kew, 1943-56; Vice-Chairman, Agricultural Improvement Council, 1944-56; Chairman, Joint Committee of AIC and ARC, 1944-59); Mem. Cttee on Higher Agricultural Educn, 1944; Scientific Advisory Cttee to Cabinet, 1943-45; Vice-Pres. RHS; Hon. Adviser Ministry of Labour; Vice-Chm. Cttee on Colonial Agricultural Research, 1945; Fullerton Prof. of Physiology, Royal Instn, 1947-52; Leader of British Delegation to Australian Conference on Plant and Animal Nutrition, 1949; *b* 16 April 1886; *y s* of J. Wright Salisbury, of Limbrick Hall, Harpenden; *m* Mabel (*d* 1956), *d* of J. Elwin-Coles. *Educ:* University College School and University College, London. Gold Medal in Botany, BSc Hons Botany, Research Medal, Quain Student University College, DSc; Senior Lecturer East London College, 1914-18; Lecturer University College, 1918; Reader in Plant Ecology, 1924; formerly Quain Professor of Botany, Univ. of London, University Coll.; Fellow of University Coll., 1920; Vice-Pres., Royal Society, 1943, 1948-55 (Biological Secretary, 1945-55); Pres. SE Union Sci. Societies, 1932; President British Ecological Society, 1928; Pres. Herts NHS, 1922-25; Pres. Norfolk and Norwich Nat. Soc., 1931; VP Linnean Society, 1928; Pres. Section K British Association, 1937; Pres. School Nature Study Union, 1938-44; Pres. Science Masters' Association, 1955; Hon. Sec. British Ecological Soc., 1917-32; Veitchian Gold Medal, 1936; Master's Memorial Lecturer, 1937, 1962; Symonds Memorial Lecturer, 1939; Amos Memorial Lecturer, 1950; Des Vœux Lecturer, 1954; Hon. Fellow Botanical Society of Edinburgh, 1938; Fellow Queen Mary College, London University, 1938; formerly Governor: Royal Holloway College; Queen Mary Coll.; East Malling Research Station; Trustee Lawes Agricultural Trust; Chm. Commonwealth Bursaries Cttee, 1953-66; Mem. of Senate, Univ. of London, 1934-44; Mem. Univ. Grants Cttee, 1944-49; Percy Sladen Trustee, 1939-66; Member of Agricultural Research Council, 1940-44; President: Sussex Naturalists' Trust, 1961-68; Bee Research Assoc., 1964. Hon. Member: Brit. Ecological Soc., 1958; Botanical Soc. of British Isles, 1968. Hon. FInstBiol. Royal Medal of Royal Society, 1945; Hon. Freeman, Worshipful Co. of Gardeners, 1951; VMH 1953. *Publications:* numerous technical papers; article Ecology, in Encyclopædia Britannica; An Introduction to the Study of Plants, 1914, 9th edn 1928; An Introduction to the Structure and Reproduction of Plants, 1920, 2nd edn 1927; Elementary Studies in Plant Life, 1915, 8th edn 1926; Botany for Medical Students, 1921, 3rd edn 1928; The East Anglian Flora, 1933; The Living Garden, 1935, 2nd edn 1942, German Edition 1936, American Edition 1936; Plant Form and Function, 1938-54; The Reproductive Capacity of Plants, 1942; Flowers of the Woods, 1946; Downs and Dunes, 1952; Weeds and Aliens, 1961; The Biology of Garden Weeds, 1962. *Recreations:* walking, gardening. *Address:* Croindene, Strandway, Felpham, Bognor Regis, Sussex.

**SALISBURY, Harrison Evans;** Assistant Managing Editor, New York Times; *b* 14 Nov. 1908; *s* of Percy Pritchard Salisbury and Georgiana Evans Salisbury; *m* 1st, 1933, Mary Hollis (marr. diss.); two *s*; 2nd, 1964, Charlotte Young Rand. *Educ:* Univ. of Minnesota (AB). United Press, 1930: London Manager, 1943; Foreign Editor, 1945. New York Times: Moscow Corresp., 1949-54; National Editor, 1962; Asst Man. Editor, 1964. Pulitzer Prize, International Correspondence, 1955. Holds hon. doctorates. *Publications:* Russia on the Way, 1946; American in Russia, 1955; The Shook-up Generation, 1958; To Moscow–And Beyond, 1960; Moscow Journal, 1961; The Northern Palmyra Affair, 1962; A New Russia?, 1962; Russia, 1965; Orbit of China, 1967; Behind the Lines–Hanoi 1967; The Soviet Union–The 50 Years, 1967; The 900 Days, the Siege of Leningrad, 1969; The Coming War Between Russia and China, 1969. *Address:* 349 East 84th Street, New York City, NY 10028, USA. *T:* 249-1818. *Clubs:* Century Association. The Players (New York); National Press (Washington, DC).

**SALISBURY-JONES, Maj.-Gen. Sir (Arthur) Guy,** GCVO 1961 (KCVO 1953); CMG 1949; CBE 1945; MC; DL; Extra Equerry to the Queen since 1962; *b* 4 July 1896; *s* of late Arthur Thomas Salisbury-Jones; *m* Hilda, *widow* of Maj. Guy Yerburgh, Irish Guards, and *d* of Rt Hon. Sir Maurice de Bunsen, Bt, PC, GCMG, GCVO, CB; one *s* one *d*. *Educ:* Eton. Joined Coldstream Guards, 1915; served European War, 1914-18 (twice wounded, MC and Bar); student at Ecole Spéciale Militaire, St Cyr, 1920-21; Liaison Officer in Syria, 1924-26; Jebel Druze Campaign, 1925-26 (French Croix de Guerre); China, 1927; Staff College, 1932-34; Staff London District, 1935-38; commanded 3rd Battalion Coldstream Guards, in Palestine, 1938-39 (despatches); served in Syria, Italian Somaliland, Greece and Crete, 1939-41 (despatches); was Head of Military Mission to South Africa, 1941-44; Supreme HQ Allied Exped. Force, 1944-45; Head of British Military Mission to France and Military Attaché, Paris, 1946-49; ADC to the King, 1948-49; retired, 1949; HM Marshal of the Diplomatic Corps, 1950-61. Chm.,

Franco-British Soc., 1963-67. Wine Grower. DL Hampshire, 1965. Order of Red Banner USSR, Order of White Lion Czechoslovakia, Grand Officier Legion of Honour, Croix de Guerre. *Publication:* So Full a Glory–A Life of Marshal de Lattre de Tassigny, 1954. *Address:* Mill Down, Hambledon, Hants. *T:* Hambledon 475. *Clubs:* Guards, Turf, Pratt's, Leander.
*See also Baron Saye and Sele.*

**SALK, Jonas Edward,** BS, MD; Fellow and Director, Salk Institute for Biological Studies, since 1963; Visiting Professor-at-Large, University of Pittsburgh, 1963; *b* New York, 28 Oct. 1914; *s* of Daniel B. Salk; *m* 1st, 1939, Donna Lindsay (marr. diss. 1968); three *s*; 2nd, 1970, Françoise Gilot. *Educ:* NY University College of Medicine; Coll. of New York City (BS). Fellow, NY Univ. Coll. of Medicine, 1935-40; Mount Sinai Hosp., NYC, 1940-42; Nat. Research Council Fellow, Sch. of Public Health, Univ. of Michigan, 1942-43, Research Fellow in Epidemiology, 1943-44, Research Assoc., 1944-46, Asst Professor, 1946-47; Assoc. Prof. of Bacteriology and Director of Virus Research, School of Medicine, Univ. of Pittsburgh, 1947-49, Research Prof., 1949-54. Consultant in epidemic diseases to: Sec. of War, 1944-46, Sec. of Army, 1947-54; Commonwealth Professor of Experimental Medicine, 1957-62 (Professor of Preventive Med., Sch. of Med., Univ. of Pittsburgh, USA, and Chairman of the Department, 1954-57). Specialist in polio research; developed antipoliomyelitis vaccine, 1954. Member: Amer. Epidemiological Soc., Soc. of Amer. Bacteriologists, etc. Fellow: Amer. Public Health Assoc., Amer. Soc. for Advancement of Science. *Address:* 2444 Ellentown Road, La Jolla, Calif, USA.

**SALMON, Cyril,** QC 1970; *b* 27 Aug. 1924; *s* of Jack and Freda Salmon; *m* 1948, Patrice Ruth Tanchan; one *s* one *d*. *Educ:* Northampton Sch.; Trinity Hall, Cambridge. Called to Bar, Middle Temple, 1947. Dep.-Chm., Lindsay Quarter Sessions, 1970. *Recreations:* surveying history and literature. *Address:* 1 Hare Court, Temple, EC4. *T:* 01-353 5324.

**SALMON, Rt. Hon. Sir Cyril (Barnet),** PC 1964; Kt 1957; **Rt. Hon. Lord Justice Salmon;** a Lord Justice of Appeal since 1964; *b* 28 Dec. 1903; *s* of late Montagu Salmon; *m* 1st, 1929, Rencie (*d* 1942), *d* of late Sidney Gorton Vanderfelt, OBE; one *s* one *d*; 2nd, 1946, Jean, Lady Morris, *d* of late Lt-Col D. Maitland-Makgill-Crichton. *Educ:* Mill Hill; Pembroke College, Cambridge. BA 1925; called to Bar, Middle Temple, 1925; QC 1945; Bencher 1953; Recorder of Gravesend, 1947-57; Judge of High Court of Justice, Queen's Bench Division, 1957-64. Chm., Royal Commission on the Working of the Tribunals of Inquiry (Evidence) Act, 1921, 1966-. Commnd Royal Artillery, 1940. 8th Army HQ Staff, 1943-44. JP (Kent), 1949. Commissioner of Assize, Wales and Chester Circuit, 1955; Governor of Mill Hill School. Hon. Fellow, Pembroke College, Cambridge. *Recreations:* golf, shooting. *Address:* 1 Melina Place, St John's Wood, NW8. *T:* 01-286 9758; The Old Drum, Sandwich, Kent. *T:* Sandwich 2244. *Clubs:* Athenæum, St James'.

**SALMON, Air Vice-Marshal Sir Cyril John Roderic;** *see* Salmon, Air Vice-Marshal Sir Roderic.

**SALMON, Geoffrey Isidore Hamilton,** CBE 1954; Chairman of J. Lyons & Co. Ltd since 1968; *b* 14 Jan. 1908; *s* of Harry Salmon and Lena (*née* Gluckstein); *m* 1936, Peggy Rica (*née* Jacobs); two *s* one *d*. *Educ:* Malvern Coll.; Jesus Coll., Cambridge (BA). Hon. Catering Adviser to the Army, 1959-. *Address:* 10 Stavordale Lodge, Melbury Road, W14. *T:* 01-602 3425.

**SALMON, Sir Julian,** Kt 1969; CBE 1957 (OBE 1943); Chairman, General Industrial Plastics (Holdings) Ltd, since 1969; Deputy Chairman of J. Lyons & Co. Ltd, 1965-69; Chairman, Hotel and Catering Industry Training Board; Member, Central Training Council; Vice-President of the Hotel and Catering Institute; Member of the Board of Governors, Charing Cross Hospital; *b* 29 Aug. 1903; *s* of late Sir Isidore Salmon, CBE, MP; *m* 1930, Anne Handelman. *Educ:* Repton; Jesus College, Cambridge. BA, LLB, 1924. Served War of 1939-45, RAFVR (Wing Comdr). Hon. Catering Adviser to the Royal Air Force, 1949-; Chairman of the Managers, Finnart House School, Weybridge. *Address:* 54 Melbury Court, W8. *T:* 01-602 3203. *Club:* Junior Carlton.

**SALMON, Dame Nancy (Marion);** *see* Snagge, Dame Nancy.

**SALMON, Air Vice-Marshal Sir Roderic,** KBE 1968 (OBE 1945); CB 1959; RAF; Secretary, Diocese of St Edmundsbury and Ipswich, since 1968; *b* 21 Aug. 1911; *s* of Edmund Frederick and Edna Salmon; *m* 1939, Hilda (*née* Mitchell); one *s* two adopted *d*. *Educ:* Howard Gardens High School, Cardiff; City of Cardiff Technical College. Commissioned in Royal Air Force, 1935; No 2 Squadron, 1936; No 70 Squadron, 1936-38; Air Ministry, Directorate of Movements, 1939-43; Second Tactical Air Force (Senior Movements Staff Officer), 1944-46 (despatches); RAF Staff College (Student), 1946; CO No 33 Maintenance Unit, 1947; No 57 Maintenance Unit, 1947-49; Member of the Directing Staff, Joint Services Staff College, 1949-51; Head of Logistics Planning, HQ Allied Air Forces, Central Europe, 1951-53; CO No 16 Maintenance Unit, 1953-54; Imperial Defence College, 1955: HQ No 40 Group (Operations Staff), 1956-59; Director of Equipment (A), Air Ministry, 1959-62; Senior Air Staff Officer, HQ Maintenance Command, 1962-64; Dir-Gen. of Equipment (RAF), MoD, 1964-68; retd, 1968. *Recreations:* gardening, fishing and tennis. *Address:* Damer Close, (Crossways), Little Bealings, Woodbridge, Suffolk. *T:* Kesgrave 2408.

**SALMON, Sir Samuel (Isidore),** Kt 1960; President, J. Lyons & Company Ltd, since 1968 (Chairman, 1965-68); Chairman, Palace Hotel Ltd; Director, Cadogan Investments Ltd; *b* 18 Oct. 1900; *s* of late Sir Isidore Salmon, CBE, DL, JP, MP, and of Lady Salmon; *m* 1937, Lallah Wendy, *d* of Alexander and Hannah Benjamin; one *s* one *d*. *Educ:* Bedales School, Petersfield; Jesus College, Cambridge (MA). LCC Member for Cities of London and Westminster, 1949-65; Deputy Chairman, LCC, 1959-60; (elected) GLC Mem. for City of Westminster, 1964-67; Mayor of London Borough of Hammersmith, 1968-69. Vice-Chm., Metropolitan Water Bd, 1970. Governor, Regent Street Polytechnic, 1950-. *Recreations:* bridge, reading. *Address:* 14 Carlos Place, W1. *T:* 01-629 7000. *Clubs:* Carlton, 1900, Leander.

**SALMON, Very Rev. Thomas Noel Desmond Cornwall;** Dean of Christ Church, Dublin, since 1967; *b* Dublin, 5 Feb. 1913; *s* of Francis Allen Cornwall Salmon, BDS, and Emma Sophia, *d* of Dr Hamilton Jolly, Clonroche, Co. Wexford; unmarried. *Educ:* privately; Trinity College, Dublin; BA 1935, MA, BD. Deacon 1937; Priest 1938. Curate Assistant: Bangor, Co. Down, 1937-40; St James' Belfast,

1940-42; Larne, Co. Antrim, 1942-44; Clerical Vicar, Christ Church Cathedral, 1944-45; Curate Assistant, Rathfarnham, Dublin, 1945-50; Incumbent: Tullow, Carrickmines, 1950-62; St Ann, Dublin, 1962-67. Asst Lectr in Divinity School, TCD, 1945-63; Examining Chaplain to Archbishop of Dublin, 1949-. *Recreations:* in younger days Rugby football (Monkstown FC Dublin) and swimming; now walking, gardening and reading. *Address:* 13 Merlyn Park, Ballsbridge, Dublin 4. *T:* 694780.

**SALMON, Col William Alexander,** OBE 1956; Assistant Ecclesiastical Secretary to Lord Chancellor (appointed 1964), and to Prime Minister, since 1965; *b* 16 Nov. 1910; *o s* of late Lt-Colonel W. H. B. Salmon, late IA; *m* 1939, Jean Barbara Macmillan, *o d* of late J. V. Macmillan, DD, OBE (Bishop of Guildford, 1934-49); one *s* two *d*. *Educ:* Haileybury College; RMC, Sandhurst. Commissioned 2nd Lt HLI 1930; ADC to Governor of Sind, 1936-38. Served during War of 1939-45: France, 1939; Middle East, Italy, Greece, Bde Major, 1942; GSO2 HQ Aegean Force, 1943; CO, 2nd Bn Beds and Herts Regt, 1945-46. CO, 2nd Bn Royal Irish Fusiliers, 1946-47; GSO1 (Trng), HQ Scottish Command, 1947-49; Chief of Staff to Lt-Gen. Glubb Pasha, HQ Arab Legion, 1950-53; CO 1st Bn HLI, 1953-55; Col, GS (O and T Div.) SHAPE, 1957-59; AQMG (QAE2), The War Office, 1959-62; AAG (AG14), The War Office, 1962-63; retd 1963. Hashemite Order of El Istiqlal (2nd Cl.), 1953. *Recreations:* shooting, fishing, gardening, stamp collecting. *Address:* Carnanton, Camden Park, Tunbridge Wells, Kent. *T:* Tunbridge Wells 27008. *Club:* United Service.

**SALOP, Archdeacon of;** *see* Austerberry, Ven. S. D.

**SALT, Dame Barbara,** DBE 1963 (CBE 1959; MBE 1946); with Foreign and Commonwealth Office, London; *b* 30 Sept. 1904; *d* of Reginald J. Salt, *y s* of Sir Thomas Salt, 1st Bt (sometime MP for Stafford and Chairman of Lloyds Bank) and of Maud Fanny (*née* Wigram). *Educ:* The Downs School, Seaford, Sussex; Munich Univ., Germany. Served with HM Consulate-General, Tangier, 1942-46; Principal in Foreign Office, 1946-49; First Secretary (Commercial), Moscow, 1950-51; First Secretary, Washington, 1951-55; Counsellor, Washington, 1955-57; Counsellor and Consul-General at the British Embassy, Tel Aviv, Israel, 1957-60; HM Minister, UK Permanent Delegation to Ten Power Disarmament Committee, Geneva, 1960; British representative on the Economic and Social Council of the United Nations, 1961-62; appointed HM Ambassador to Tel Aviv, 1962 (did not proceed); Leader, UK Delegation, Anglo/Israel Financial Negotiations, 1963-64; Leader, UK delegn to Anglo-Roumanian Negotiations, London, 1966. Hon. Pres., Israel Art Students Scholarship Fund, 1966; Hon. Chairman, Voluntary Overseas Service Assoc., 1966-69. Patron, Monopeds Assoc.; co-Patron, Rowenstall Rovers Football Club. *Recreations:* reading, gardening, motoring. *Address:* 17B, Montagu Square, W1. *T:* 01-935 8624. *Club:* New Century.

**SALT, Sir David Shirley,** 5th Bt, *cr* 1869; *b* 14 June 1930; *s* of 4th Bt and Stella Houlton, 2nd *d* of Richard Houlton Jackson, MRCS, LRCP, Bakewell, Derbyshire; *S* father 1953; *m* 1955, Margaret Gillian, *d* of H. Alwyn Lenox, 31 Markham Square, SW3. *Educ:* Stowe. *Heir: b* Anthony Houlton Salt [*b* 15 Sept. 1931; *m* 1957, Prudence Meath Baker; four *d*]. *Address:* c/o Lloyd's, EC3.
*See also Baron Glanusk.*

**SALT, George,** FRS 1956; ScD; Fellow of King's College, Cambridge, since 1933; Reader in Animal Ecology, University of Cambridge, since 1965; *b* Loughborough, 12 Dec. 1903; *s* of late Walter Salt and Mary Cecilia (*née* Hulme), Calgary, Alberta; *m* 1939, Joyce Laing, Newnham Coll. and Stockton-on-Tees; two *s*. *Educ:* Crescent Heights Collegiate Inst., Calgary; Univ. of Alberta (BSc); Harvard Univ. (SM, SD); Univ. of Cambridge (PhD, ScD). National Research Fellow, Harvard Univ., 1927-28; Entomologist, Imperial Inst. Entom, 1929-31; Royal Soc. Moseley Research Student, 1932-33; Univ. Lectr in Zoology, Cambridge, 1937-65; Fellow of King's Coll., Cambridge, 1933-, Dean, 1939-45, Tutor for Advanced Students, 1945-51. Visiting Prof. Univ. of California, Berkeley, 1966. On biological expedns in NW Canada and Rocky Mts, Cuba, Republic of Colombia, E Africa, Pakistan. *Publications:* The Cellular Defence Reactions of Insects, 1970; papers in scientific jls on insect parasitism and ecology. *Recreations:* mountaineering, gardening, calligraphy and illumination. *Address:* King's College, Cambridge; 21 Barton Road, Cambridge. *T:* Cambridge 55450.

**SALT, Maj.-Gen. Harold Francis,** CB 1932; CMG 1919; DSO 1918; late RA; psc; *b* 30 Dec. 1879; *y s* of late Sir Thomas Salt, 1st Bt; *m* 1914, Phyllis Dulce (*d* 1965), *d* of late Major E. D. Cameron, RFA; two *d*. *Educ:* RIEC, Coopers Hill. Joined Army, 1900; Lieut 1901; Capt. 1908; Major, 1914; Brevet Lt-Colonel, 1918; Bt-Col 1919; Col 1921; Maj.-Gen., 1931; GSO 3rd Grade, Scottish Command, 1914; Brigade Major, RA, 11th Division 1915; GSO 2nd Grade, 10th Division, 1916-17; GSO, 1st Grade, 10th Division, 1917-18; Brigadier-General, General Staff, 21st Corps, 1918-19; Instructor Senior Officers' School, Belgaum, India; Asst-Commandant, Royal Military Academy, Woolwich, 1925-29; Comdr RA 54th (East Anglian) Division, TA 1930-31; Comdr Territorial Army Air Defence Formations 1931-35; Deputy Adjutant General (Director of Organization) Army HQs, India, 1935-36; Deputy Quartermaster General, Army HQ India, 1936-39; retired pay, 1939; served European War Gallipoli (Suvla Bay), Salonika, Palestine, and Syria (despatches thrice, DSO, CMG, Order of the Nile, 3rd Class). *Address:* Newhouse Farm, Ilton, Ilminster, Somerset. *T:* Ilminster 2498.

**SALT, Sir Michael;** *see* Salt, Sir T. M. J.

**SALT, Sir (Thomas) Michael (John),** 4th Bt, *cr* 1899; *b* 7 Nov. 1946; *s* of Lt-Col Sir Thomas Henry Salt, 3rd Bt, and Meriel Sophia Wilmot, *d* of late Capt. Berkeley C. W. Williams and Hon. Mrs Williams, Herringston, Dorchester; *S* father 1965. *Educ:* Eton. *Heir: b* Anthony William David Salt, *b* 5 Feb. 1950. *Recreation:* shooting. *Address:* Shillingstone House, Shillingstone, Dorset.

**SALTER,** family name of **Baron Salter.**

**SALTER,** 1st Baron, *cr* 1953, of Kidlington; **(James) Arthur Salter;** PC 1941; GBE, *cr* 1944; KCB, *cr* 1922 (CB 1918); *b* Oxford, 15 March 1881; *s* of late James E. Salter, Oxford; *m* 1940, Mrs Arthur Bullard (*d* 1969), *widow* of Arthur Bullard, of Washington, DC. *Educ:* Oxford High School; Brasenose College, Oxford. Transport Department, Admiralty, 1904; Assistant Secretary National Health Insurance Commission, England, 1913; Director of Ship Requisitioning, 1917; Secretary of Allied Maritime Transport Council and Chairman of Allied Maritime Transport Executive, 1918; Supreme Economic Council, 1919; General Secretary Reparation Commission, 1920-22;

Director Economic and Finance Section League of Nations, June 1919-Jan. 1920, and 1922-31; Missions to India, 1930, China, 1931 and 1933; Chairman Road-Rail Conference, 1932; Gladstone Professor of Political Theory and Institutions, Oxford University, 1934-44; Chairman of Railway Staff National Tribunal, 1936-39. MP (Ind), Oxford University, 1937-50; Parliamentary Secretary to Ministry of Shipping, 1939-41; Joint Parliamentary Secretary to Ministry of War Transport, 1941, and Head of British Merchant Shipping Mission, Washington, 1941-43; Senior Deputy Director-General UNRRA, 1944; Chancellor of the Duchy of Lancaster, 1945; Chairman Advisory Council of International Bank, 1947-48. MP (C) Ormskirk Division of Lancashire, 1951-53; Minister of State for Economic Affairs, 1951-Nov. 1952; Minister of Materials, Nov. 1952-53. Officier de la Couronne Belgique, 1919; Commandeur de la Légion d'Honneur, 1920; Commendatore Order of the Crown of Italy, 1922; Brilliant Jade (China), 1937; Hon. Fellow BNC and Fellow of All Souls; Hon. DCL Oxford and hon. doctorates at Manchester, Vienna, Harvard, Columbia, McGill, University of California, Amherst. *Publications:* Allied Shipping Control; An Experiment in International Administration, 1921; Recovery, 1932; The Framework of an Ordered Society, 1933; The United States of Europe, 1933; World Trade and its Future, 1936; Security, 1939; Personality in Politics, 1947; Memoirs of a Public Servant, 1961; Slave of the Lamp, 1967. *Heir:* none. *Address:* West House, 35 Glebe Place, Chelsea, SW3. *T:* 01-352 7091; All Souls College, Oxford. *Club:* Reform.

**SALTER, Vice-Admiral Jocelyn Stuart Cambridge,** CB 1954; DSO 1942 (Bar 1951); OBE 1942; *b* 24 Nov. 1901; *s* of late Henry Stuart Salter, of Messrs Lee, Bolton & Lee (Solicitors); *m* 1935, Joan, *d* of late Rev. C. E. C. de Coetlogon, of the Indian Ecclesiastical Establishment; one *s* one *d*. *Educ:* Royal Naval Colleges, Osborne and Dartmouth. Joined Royal Navy, 1915; Midshipman, 1917; served European War in HMS Ramillies, Grand Fleet, 1917-19; Lieut 1923; Comdr 1937; Comd HMS Foresight in Force H, and in Home Fleet, 1941-42; Capt. 1942. Comd 16th Dest. Flotilla, 1944-45; Comd HMS Jamaica, 1950-51 (served with UN Fleet in Korean waters); served on staff of SHAPE, 1951; ADC, 1951; Rear-Admiral, 1952; Vice-Admiral, 1954; Flag Officer, Malta, and Admiral Superintendent HM Dockyard, Malta, 1952-54; Admiral Superintendent HM Dockyard, Portsmouth, 1954-57; retired, 1957. Mem., Court of Assistants, Haberdashers' Company, Warden, 1958, 1963, 1968. Norwegian Haakon VII Liberty Cross, 1946; United States Bronze Star medal, 1950. *Address:* Folly House, Hambledon, Hampshire. *T:* Hambledon 732. *Clubs:* United Service; Royal Naval (Portsmouth).

**SALTER DAVIES, Roy Dicker;** *see* Davies.

**SALTOUN,** 19th Lord, *cr* 1445, of Abernethy; **Alexander Arthur Fraser,** MC; a Representative Peer for Scotland, 1935-63; *b* 8 March 1886; *e s* of 18th Lord and Mary (*d* 1940), *o d* of Thomas Arthur Grattan-Bellew, MP; *S* father, 1933; *m* 1920, Dorothy, *e d* of Sir Charles Welby, 5th Bt; one *d* (one *s* killed in action). Late Sub-Lieutenant Forfar and Kincardine Artillery Militia: Captain, retired, 3rd Battalion Gordon Highlanders; prisoner of war, 1914-18. *Heiress: d* Hon. Flora Marjory Fraser [*b* 18 Oct. 1930; *m* 1956, Captain Alexander Ramsay, Grenadier Guards, *o s* of Adm. Hon. Sir Alexander Ramsay, *qv*; three *d*]. *Address:* Cairnbulg Castle, Fraserburgh; Cross Deep, Twickenham. *Clubs:* Athenæum; New (Edinburgh).

**SALTZMAN, Charles Eskridge,** DSM 1945 (US); Legion of Merit (US) 1943; Partner, Goldman, Sachs & Co. (investment banking) since 1956; Director: Continental Can Company, Inc.; A. H. Robins Co., Inc.; *b* 19 Sept. 1903; *s* of Maj.-Gen. Charles McKinley Saltzman and Mary Saltzman (*née* Eskridge); *m* 1st, 1931, Gertrude Lamont (marr. diss.); one *s*; 2nd, 1947, Cynthia Southall Myrick (marr. diss.); two *d* (one *s* decd). *Educ:* Cornell Univ.; US Mil. Acad.; Magdalen College, Oxford University. BS (US Mil. Acad.); BA, MA (Rhodes Scholar) (Oxford Univ.). Served as 2nd Lt, Corps of Engrs, US Army, 1925-30; commissioned 1st Lieut, NY National Guard, 1930; Lieutenant-Colonel 1940; on active duty in US Army, 1940-46, serving overseas, 1942-46; Brigadier-General 1945; relieved from active duty, 1946; Maj.-Gen. AUS (Retd). With NY Telephone Co., 1930-35; with NY Stock Exchange, 1935-49 (Asst to Exec. Vice-Pres., later Sec. and Vice-Pres.). Asst Sec. of State, 1947-49; Partner Henry Sears & Co., 1949-56; Under-Sec. of State for Admin., 1954-55. Pres., English-Speaking Union of the US, 1961-66; Mem. Pilgrims of the United States. Member, Director, or Trustee of many boards, societies and religious, medical and educational institutions. Order of British Empire (OBE), 1943; holds other foreign decorations. *Address:* (home) 101 E 69th Street, New York, NY 10021, USA. *T:* RE 4 5400; (office) 55 Broad Street, New York, NY 10004. *T:* (212) 676-8000. *Clubs:* Century Association, Recess, River, Union, University (New York); Army and Navy, Metropolitan (Washington); Cold Spring Harbor Beach.

**SALUSBURY-TRELAWNY, Sir J. B.;** *see* Trelawny.

**SALZMAN, Louis Francis,** CBE 1955; MA, FSA; *b* 26 March 1878; *s* of Dr F. W. Salzman, Brighton; *m* 1904, Maud, *d* of Rev. G. M. Russell; two *s* two *d*. *Educ:* Haileybury; Pembroke College, Cambridge. Editor, Victoria County Histories, 1934-49; Hon. editor, Sussex Archæological Society, 1909-59 (Pres., 1954-56); Master St George's School, Harpenden and Captain 4th Herts Cadets, 1916-18. Hon. DLitt, Sussex, 1965. *Publications:* Henry II, 1914; English Industries of the Middle Ages, 1913 and 1923; Medieval Byways, 1913; More Medieval Byways, 1926; The Girdle of Venus, a play, 1922; English Life in the Middle Ages, 1926; England in Tudor Times, 1926; A Survey of English History, 1930; English Trade in the Middle Ages, 1931; A Documentary History of Building in England Down to 1540, 1951 and 1967; A Random Scrap Book, 1957; Edward I, 1968, etc. *Address:* 12 Houndean Rise, Lewes, Sussex. *T:* 4882.

**SAMBELL, Most Rev. Geoffrey Tremayne;** *see* Perth (Australia), Archbishop of.

**SAMMAN, Peter Derrick,** MD, FRCP; Physician to Dermatological Department, Westminster Hospital, since 1951, and St John's Hospital for Diseases of the Skin since 1959; Consultant Dermatologist, Orpington and Sevenoaks Hospitals, since 1951; Dean, Institute of Dermatology, 1965-70; *b* 20 March 1914; *y s* of Herbert Frederick Samman and Emily Elizabeth Savage; *m* 1953, Judith Mary Kelly; three *d*. *Educ:* King William's Coll., IOM; Emmanual Coll., Cambridge; King's Coll. Hosp., London. BA (Nat. Scis. Tripos), 1936; MB, BChir Cantab 1939; MRCP 1946; MA, MD Cantab 1948; FRCP 1963. House

Surg., King's Coll. Hosp., 1939; Sqdn Ldr, RAFVR, 1940-45; House Phys. and Registrar, King's Coll. Hosp., 1946; Sen. Dermatological Registrar and Tutor in Dermatology, United Bristol Hosps, 1947-48; Sen. Registrar, St John's Hosp. for Diseases of the Skin, 1949-50. FRSocMed; Mem. Brit. Assoc. of Dermatology; Hon. Mem., Dermatological Soc. of S Africa. *Publications:* The Nails in Disease, 1965; chapters in Textbook of Dermatology (ed Rook, Wilkinson and Ebling), 1968; various articles in med. jls. *Recreation:* gardening. *Address:* 18 Sutherland Avenue, Orpington, Kent. *T:* Orpington 20839.

**SAMPLES, Reginald McCartney,** DSO 1942; OBE 1963; Head of British Government Office, and Senior British Trade Commissioner, Toronto, Canada, since 1969; *b* 11 Aug. 1918; *o s* of William and Jessie Samples; *m* 1947, Elsie Roberts Hide; two *s* one step *d*. *Educ:* Rhyl Grammar Sch.; Liverpool Univ. (BCom). Served, 1940-46; RNVR (Air Branch); torpedo action with 825 Sqn against German ships Scharnhorst, Gneisenau and Prinz Eugen in English Channel (wounded, DSO); Lieut (A). Central Office of Information (Economic Editor, Overseas Newspapers), 1947-48. CRO (Brit. Inf. Services, India), 1948; Economic Information Officer, Bombay, 1948-52; Editor-in-Chief, BIS, New Delhi, 1952; Dep.-Dir, BIS, New Delhi, 1952-56; Dir, BIS, Pakistan (Karachi), 1956-59; Dir, BIS, Canada (Ottawa), 1959-65, OBE; Counsellor (Information) to Brit. High Comr, India, and Dir, BIS, India (New Delhi), 1965-68; Under-Sec. of State, Commonwealth Office, 1968. *Recreations:* tennis, golf. *Address:* c/o Foreign and Commonwealth Office, SW1. *Club:* RNVR.

**SAMPSON, Anthony (Terrell Seward);** writer and journalist; *b* 3 Aug. 1926; *s* of Michael Sampson and Phyllis, *d* of Sir Albert Seward, FRS; *m* 1965, Sally, *d* of Dr P. G. Bentlif, Jersey, and of Mrs G. Denison-Smith, Islip, Oxon; one *s* one *d*. *Educ:* Westminster School; Christ Church, Oxford. Served with Royal Navy, 1944-47; Sub-Lieut, RNVR, 1946. Editor of Drum Magazine, Johannesburg, 1951-55; Editorial staff of The Observer, 1955-66. Editor, The Observer Magazine, 1965-66. Associate Prof., Univ. of Vincennes, Paris, 1968-. *Publications:* Drum, a Venture into the New Africa, 1956; The Treason Cage, 1958; Commonsense about Africa, 1960; (with S. Pienaar) South Africa: two views of Separate Development 1960; Anatomy of Britain, 1962; Anatomy of Britain Today, 1965; Macmillan: a study in ambiguity, 1967; The New Europeans, 1968. *Recreation:* gardening. *Address:* 27 Ladbroke Grove, W11. *T:* 01-727 4188; 2 Valley Farm, Walberswick, Suffolk. *T:* Southwold 2080. *Clubs:* Beefsteak, Savile.

**SAMPSON, Jack;** *see* Sampson, Jacob Albert.

**SAMPSON, Jacob Albert, (Jack Sampson);** Chairman, United Drapery Stores Ltd, since 1966; *b* 15 March 1905; *m* 1927, Cissie Okin; one *d*. Entered family shoe business, 1920; joined Great Universal Stores Ltd, 1938 (Dir, 1942); resigned, 1946, to become Managing Dir of John Blundell Ltd, a subsidiary of United Drapery Stores Ltd; Dir, United Drapery Stores Ltd, 1947 (Managing Dir, 1959; Chm., 1966). *Address:* United Drapery Stores Ltd, 364-366 Kensington High Street, W14.

**SAMSON, Sir Frederick;** *see* Samson, Sir W. F.

**SAMSON, Otto William,** PhD (Hamburg), FMA, FRAS, FRGS, FRAI; Wellcome Research Fellowship, 1965-67; Curator, Horniman Museum and Library, 1947-65; *b* Hamburg, 1 March 1900; *s* of Martin Samson and Mathilde Kallmes; *m* 1948, Muriel Elizabeth Williams (*née* Richards). *Educ:* Universities of Freiburg im Breisgau, Berlin, Munich, Hamburg. Assistant Keeper, Museum of Ethnography, Hamburg, 1928-30; Keeper, Far Eastern Dept, 1930-33; Ethnographical research for Hamburg Museum in China, 1931-32; Research work, physical anthropology, Galton Lab., Univ. of London, 1933; awarded Tweedie Exploration Fellowship for archæology and anthropology, Univ. of Edinburgh, travelling in India, Tibet, Burma, 1935-37; research work on Djebel Moya osteological material, Galton Lab., Univ. of London, 1937-39; Ethnographical Dept, British Museum, 1939, temp. Asst Keeper, 1942-47. Hon. Librarian, Royal Anthropological Inst., 1942-46. *Recreations:* reading and walking. *Address:* 1a Taymount Rise, SE23. *T:* 01-699 8245.

**SAMSON, Sir (William) Frederick,** Kt 1962; Mayor of Fremantle since 1951; *b* 12 Jan. 1892; *s* of Michael and Mary Samson; *m* 1935, Daphne Alice Marks; no *c*. *Educ:* Christian Brothers College, Fremantle and Perth; University of W Australia. On construction reservoir and sewer mains, Metropolitan Water Supply, Sewerage and Drainage Dept, Perth, 1913-18; Surveyor with Crossland and Hardy, Perth, 1919-24; Partnership with late W. H. Shields, Engineering and Surveying, 1925-31; since 1931, Real Estate Agent. Fellow Commonwealth Inst. of Valuers. Chm., Home Building Soc. Inc.; Mem. State Electricity Commn, WA; past Pres. Rotary Club of Fremantle; Mem. WA Cricket Assoc. Cricket Cttee, 1913-47; past Pres. Fremantle Cricket Club, Fremantle Horticultural Soc.; President: Fremantle Chamber of Commerce; WA Rifle Assoc. First Freeman, City of Fremantle. *Recreations:* rifle shooting, gardening, photography. *Address:* 61 Ellen Street, Fremantle, Western Australia 6160. *T:* 5 2553; (Office) 5 Queen Street, Fremantle, Western Australia. *T:* 1316. *Clubs:* Naval, Military and Air Force (Perth); Commercial, Exchange (Fremantle).

**SAMUEL,** family name of **Viscounts Bearsted** and **Samuel.**

**SAMUEL,** 2nd Viscount, *cr* 1937, of Mount Carmel and of Toxteth, Liverpool; **Edwin Herbert Samuel,** CMG 1947; Colonial Service, retired; Visiting Professor in Public Administration, Graduate School of Public and International Affairs, University of Pittsburgh, since 1970; Principal of the Institute of Public Administration in Israel; *b* 11 Sept. 1898; *e s* of 1st Viscount Samuel, PC, GCB, OM, GBE, and Beatrice (*d* 1959), *y d* of Ellis A. Franklin; *S* father, 1963; *m* 1920, Hadassah Goor; two *s*. *Educ:* Westminster School; Balliol Coll., Oxford (BA); Commonwealth Fund Fellow, Columbia University, 1931-32. 2nd Lieut RFA and GSI, GHQ, EEF, 1917-19; District Officer: Jerusalem, Ramallah, and Jaffa, 1920-27; Assistant Secretary, Government of Palestine, 1927-30; Assistant District Comr, Galilee, 1933-34; Deputy Comr for Migration, 1934-39; Postal and Telegraph Censor, Jerusalem, 1939-42; Chief Censor and (from 1944) Press Censor, 1942-45; Director of Broadcasting, 1945-48; Visiting Professor in Middle East Govt, Dropsie College, Philadelphia, 1948-49; European Director of the Conquest of the Desert, International Exhibition, Jerusalem, 1951-53; Sen. Lectr in British Institutions, Hebrew Univ., Jerusalem, 1954-69; Visiting Lectr in Public Administration, Univ. of the

Witwatersrand, 1955; Visiting Prof. in Political Science, Graduate School of Public Affairs, Albany State Univ. of New York, 1963; Vis. Prof., Dept of Urban Affairs, Univ. of Miami, Fla, 1971. A Director: the Jewish Chronicle, London, 1951-; Vallentine Mitchell (publishers), London, 1965-; Ellern Investment Corp. Ltd, Tel Aviv, 1964-; Moller Textile Corporation, Nahariya, 1965-; Adviser to the Magen David Adom (Israel Nat. Red Cross Society) on publicity and public relations, 1957-; President of Professional and Technical Workers' Aliya (PATWA), Gt Brit.; Mem. of Council: Anglo-Israel Assoc., London; Anglo-Jewish Assoc., London; Labour Friends of Israel, London; (British) Friends of the Hebrew University; The Bridge, etc. *Publications:* A Primer on Palestine, 1932; Handbook of the Jewish Communal Villages, 1938 and 1945; The Children's Community of Mishmar HaEmek, 1942; The Theory of Administration, 1947; Problems of Government in the State of Israel, 1956; British Traditions in the Administration of Israel, 1957; Anglo-Israel Relations, 1948-1968: a catalogue, 1969; A Lifetime in Jerusalem: memoirs, 1970; A Cottage in Galilee (short stories), 1957; A Coat of Many Colours (short stories), 1960; My Friend Musa (short stories), 1963; The Cucumber King (short stories), 1965; Capt. Noah and His Ark (illustrated children's story), 1965; His Celestial Highness (short stories), 1968; The Man Who Liked Cats (short stories), 1971. *Heir: s* Prof. The Hon. David Herbert Samuel, MA, PhD [*b* 8 July 1922; *m* 1st, 1950, Esther Berelowitz (marr. diss., 1957), Cape Town; one *d*; 2nd, 1960, Mrs Rinna Dafni, *d* of late Meir Grossman, Israel; one *d*]. *Address:* House of Lords, SW1; 15 Rashba Road, Jerusalem, Israel. *T:* 33871.

**SAMUEL, Adrian Christopher Ian,** CMG 1959; CVO 1963; Group Overseas Co-ordinator, Constructors John Brown Ltd; *b* 20 Aug. 1915; *s* of late George Christopher Samuel and Alma Richards; *m* 1942, Sheila, *er d* of late J. C. Barrett, Killiney, Co. Dublin; three *s* one *d*. *Educ:* Rugby Sch.; St John's Coll., Oxford. Entered HM Consular Service, 1938; served at Beirut, Tunis and Trieste. Served War, 1940-44, in Royal Air Force. Returned to HM Foreign Service and served at HM Embassies in Ankara, Cairo and Damascus; First Secretary, 1947; Counsellor, 1956; Principal Private Secretary to the Secretary of State for Foreign Affairs, Oct. 1959-63; Minister at HM Embassy, Madrid, 1963-65; resigned 1965. Dir, British Chemical Engrg Contractors Assoc., 1966-69. *Recreations:* golf, shooting, sailing and reading. *Address:* Miswells House, Turners Hill, Sussex. *T:* Turners Hill 285. *Clubs:* Garrick, Lansdowne.

**SAMUEL, Sir Harold,** Kt 1963; FRICS; Hon. Fellow: Magdalene College, Cambridge, 1961; University College, London, 1968; Chairman: The Land Securities Investment Trust Ltd; The Central London Housing Trust for the Aged; Member, Covent Garden Market Authority, since 1961; *b* London, 23 April 1912; *s* of late Vivian and Ada Samuel; *m* 1936, Edna Nedas; two *d* (and one *d* decd). *Educ:* Mill Hill School; College of Estate Management. Member: Crown Estate Commissioners Regent St Cttee, 1963-; Land Commission, 1967-70; Special (Rebuilding) Cttee, RICS; Court of The City Univ.; Court of Univ. of Sussex; Court of Univ. Coll. of Swansea; Court of Patrons, RCS; a Vice-Pres., British Heart Foundation; Trustee, Mill Hill Sch.; Director, Railway Sites Ltd (British Rail), 1962-65. *Recreations:* swimming, horticulture, agriculture. *Address:* 75 Avenue Road, Regent's Park, NW8; Wych Cross Place, Forest Row, East Sussex. *Club:* Devonshire.

**SAMUEL, Herbert Dawkin;** Director of Greenwich Hospital, Admiralty, 1959-64, retired; *b* 21 Jan. 1904; *o s* of Alfred Samuel, Llanelly; *m* 1936, Evelyn Mary, *d* of Col H. J. Barton, RE; two *s*. *Educ:* Clifton Coll.; Merton Coll., Oxford; Heidelberg University. 1st cl. Hons, Mod. Langs; Laming Fellow, Queen's Coll., Oxford, 1925-27. Entered Consular Service, 1927; Actg Vice-consul, Genoa, 1927, Paris, 1929. Asst Master: Repton School, 1930; Harrow School, 1931; Dist. Inspector, Bd of Education, 1938. Entered Admiralty as Principal, 1939; Under-Secretary, 1956. Coronation Medal, 1953. *Address:* 2 Highlands Drive, St Leonard's-on-Sea, Sussex.

**SAMUEL, Sir Jon (Michael Glen),** 5th Bt, *cr* 1898; *b* 25 Jan. 1944; *o s* of Sir John Oliver Cecil Samuel, 4th Bt, and of Charlotte Mary, *d* of late R. H. Hoyt, Calgary, Canada; *S* father, 1962; *m* 1966, Antoinette Sandra, *d* of late Capt. Antony Hewitt, RE, 2nd SAS Regt, and of Mrs K. A. H. Casson, Frith Farm, Wolverton, Hants. *Educ:* Radley; London Univ. Dir, Enfield Automotive, 1967. *Recreations:* motor racing, water ski-ing. *Address:* Birchwood, Beech Close, Cobham, Surrey. *T:* Cobham 3882.

**SAMUEL, Hon. Peter Montefiore,** MC 1942; TD 1951; Banker; Deputy Chairman, Hill, Samuel Group; Chairman, Dylon International Ltd; *b* 9 Dec. 1911; second *s* of 2nd Viscount Bearsted and Dorothea, *e d* of late E. Montefiore Micholls; *b* and *heir-pres.* to 3rd Viscount Bearsted, *qv*; *m* 1st, 1939, Deirdre du Barry (marr. diss. 1942); 2nd, 1946, Hon. Elizabeth Adelaide Pearce Serocold, *d* of Baron Cohen, *qv*; two *s* one *d*. *Educ:* Eton; New College, Oxford (BA). Served Warwickshire Yeo, Middle East and Italy, 1939-45. Dep. Chm., Hill, Samuel & Co. Ltd. Director: Shell Transport & Trading Co. Ltd; Samuel Properties Ltd; Mayborn Products Ltd. (Chairman); Trades Union Unit Trust Managers Ltd. President, Norwood Home for Jewish Children; Trustee, Whitechapel Art Gallery. *Recreations:* golf, fishing, shooting. *Address:* Flat 14, 12 Hill Street, W1. *T:* 01-629 5191; Farley Hall, Farley Hill, near Reading, Berkshire. *T:* Eversley 3242; Phones, Newtonmore, Inverness-shire. *T:* Newtonmore 212. *Club:* White's.

**SAMUELS, Albert Edward,** LLB; JP; Chairman, redhill and Netherne Group Hospital Management Committee, since 1968; Legal Member, London Rent Assessment Panel; *b* 12 May 1900; *er s* of John Samuels and Esther Stella Samuels; *m* 1934, Sadie Beatrice, BSc (Econ.); one *s*. *Educ:* Sir Walter St John's School; University of London (King's College). Admitted a Solicitor, 1921. Elected to Battersea Borough Council, 1922; Councillor, 1922-25; Alderman, 1925-31. Contested LCC Election, 1925. Mem. Metropolitan Water Bd, 1925-28, 1941-46. Mem. of LCC, 1928-31, 1934-37, 1946-49 and 1952-65 (for Bermondsey); Chairman: Public Control Cttee, 1934-37, 1946-48 and 1952-55; Establishment Cttee, 1955-58, 1960-65; Jt Cttee of Members and Staff 1955-58; Interim Staff Panel, 1960-65; Chairman, LCC, 1958-59; (elected) Member, Greater London Council, 1964-67 (Chm. Public Health Services Cttee). Vice-Chm. Jt Cttee of LCC and QS 1934-36, 1947-48. Pres. Sir Walter St John's Old Boys' Assoc., 1956-57. JP (County of London) 1933. Comdr Order of Merit of Italian Republic, 1958; Kt Comdr of the Order of Merit of the Federal Republic of Germany,

1958. *Recreations:* reading, walking and golf. *Address:* The Chantry, Cronks Hill, Reigate, Surrey. *T:* 3717; 292 High Holborn, WC1. *T:* 01-405 5455. *Clubs:* Athenæum, Royal Automobile; Reigate Heath Golf.

**SAMUELS, Sir Alexander,** Kt 1963; CBE 1956; JP, FRSA, MInstT, AMIMechE; Member, (part-time) British Waterways Board, since 1966, and Covent Garden Market Authority, since 1961; *b* 15 Sept. 1905. *Educ:* Elementary Sch. Mem., Shoreditch Borough Council, 1945-61; Chairman: London and Home Counties Traffic Advisory Cttee, 1946-61; Special Enquiry into London Traffic Congestion, 1951; Working Party for Car Parking, 1953; Cttee for Speed limit Enquiry, 1954; Special Survey Cttee on use of Parking Meters, 1956; London Travel Cttee, 1958; Operations Group of the Transport Co-ordinating Council for London, 1966; Dep. Chm., Nat. Road Safety Advisory Council, 1965-66; Vice-Pres., London Accident Prevention Council, 1956; Member: Departmental Cttee Road Safety, 1957-64; Adviser to the Minister of Transport on London Traffic Management, 1961-65, on Road Traffic, 1965-66. *Recreation:* golf. *Address:* Redcroft, 19 Hartsbourne Avenue, Bushey Heath, Herts. *T:* 01-950 1162. *Clubs:* Royal Automobile, Reform.

**SAMUELS, Professor Michael Louis;** Professor of English Language, University of Glasgow, since 1959; *b* 1920; *s* of Harry Samuels, OBE, MA, barrister-at-law, and Celine Samuels (*née* Aronowitz), London; *m* 1950, Hilary, *d* of late Julius and Ruth Samuel, Glasgow; one *d*. *Educ:* St Paul's School; Balliol College, Oxford. Domus Exhibitioner in Classics, Balliol College, Oxford, 1938-40 and 1945-47; MA 1947 (First Class Hons English Lang. and Lit.). Worked for Air Ministry (Maintenance Command), 1940-45. Research Fellow, University of Birmingham, 1947-48; Assistant in English Language, University of Edinburgh, 1948-49; Lecturer in English Language, Univ. of Edinburgh, 1949-59. *Publications:* articles and reviews in Trans Philological Soc., Medium Aevum, Review of English Studies, Archivum Linguisticum, English Studies, English and Germanic Studies. *Address:* 4 Queen's Gate, Dowanhill, Glasgow, W2. *T:* 041-334 4999.

**SAMUELSON, Sir Francis Henry Bernard,** 4th Bt, *cr* 1884; *b* 22 Feb. 1890; *s* of late Sir Francis (Arthur Edward) Samuelson, 3rd Bt, and Fanny Isabel (*d* 1897), *e d* of William Merritt Wright, St John, New Brunswick, Canada; *S* father, 1946; *m* 1913, Margaret Kendall, *d* of late H. Kendall Barnes; three *s* two *d*. *Educ:* Eton; Trinity College, Cambridge. *Heir:* *s* (Bernard) Michael (Francis) Samuelson [*b* 17 Jan. 1917; *m* 1952, Janet Amy, *yr d* of Lt-Comdr L. G. Elkington, Chelsea; one *s* two *d*]. *Address:* Midway House, Partridge Green, Sussex.

**SAN VINCENZO FERRERI, Marquis of;** *see* St Vincent Ferreri.

**SANCTUARY, Gerald Philip;** Executive Director, Sex Information and Education Council of the United States, since 1969; *b* 22 Nov. 1930; *s* of John Cyril Tabor Sanctuary, MD and Maisie Toppin Sanctuary (*née* Brooks); *m* 1956, Rosemary Patricia L'Estrange, Dublin; three *s* one *d*. *Educ:* Bryanston Sch.; Law Soc.'s Sch. of Law. National Service Pilot, 1953-55; Asst Solicitor, Kingston, 1955-56; Partner in Hasties, Solicitors, Lincoln's Inn Fields, 1957-62; Field Sec., Nat. Marriage Guidance Council, 1963-65, Nat. Secretary 1965-69. *Publications:* Marriage Under Stress, 1968; Divorce - and After, 1970. *Recreation:* amateur drama. *Address:* c/o SIECUS, 1855 Broadway, New York, NY 10023, USA.

**SANDARS, George Edward Russell,** CMG 1951; MBE 1933; *b* 19 Oct. 1901; *s* of Rev. Canon George Russell Sandars and Mary Lambart Wyld; *m* 1937, Vera Margaret Molyneux-Seel; no *c*. *Educ:* Winchester; New College, Oxford. Joined Sudan Political Service, 1924; Private Secretary to Governor General, 1933-37; Sudan Agent in Cairo, 1941-45; Governor of Blue Nile Province, 1948-51. Sec., Inst. of Brewing, 1951-64. *Address:* Red Cottages, Dogmersfield, nr Basingstoke, Hants. *T:* Fleet 4801. *Club:* Athenæum.

**SANDARS, John Eric William Graves,** OBE 1945; TD 1944; JP, DL; Chairman and Managing Director Sandars & Co. Ltd, Maltsters, Gainsborough; Director: Vaux & Associated Breweries Ltd, Sunderland; Gainsborough Malting Co. Ltd, Gainsborough; J. Pidcock & Co. Ltd, Maltsters, Nottingham; R. & W. Paul (Maltsters) Ltd, Ipswich; *b* 26 Feb. 1906; *s* of late John Drysdale Sandars, JP, DL, and of late Hon. Maud Evelyn Sandars (*née* Graves); *m* 1932, Margaret Mary Katherine Clare Elwes; one *d*. *Educ:* Eton; Trinity College, Cambridge. MA, Cambridge, 1965. Commissioned into Notts (Sherwood Rangers) Yeomanry TA, 1927. Served War of 1939-45; Middle East, 1939-43 (despatches twice); France and Germany, 1944-45 (American Bronze Star, 1944, OBE), with rank of Lieutenant-Colonel. Served on Lincs (Lindsey) CC, 1937, County Agricultural Executive Cttee, 1948. JP 1936. High Sheriff of Lincolnshire, 1949; DL 1950; County Alderman, 1953. Chairman, Maltsters Association of Great Britain, 1952-55. Chm., 1928-38, Pres., 1969, Gainsborough Div., Conservative and Unionist Assoc. *Recreation:* shooting. *Address:* Gate Burton Hall, Gainsborough, Lincs. *T:* Torksey 248. *Clubs:* Boodle's, Cavalry, MCC.

*See also Sir James McEwen, Bt.*

**SANDARS, Vice-Admiral Sir (Reginald) Thomas,** KBE 1962; CB 1959; MIMechE; *b* 20 September 1904; *s* of Canon George Russell Sandars and Mary Lambert (*née* Wyld); *m* 1935, Elizabeth Audrey Crewdson; three *s*. *Educ:* RN Colleges Osborne and Dartmouth. Joined RN as cadet, 1918; specialised in engineering, 1924; Rear-Admiral, 1956; Deputy Chief of Naval Personnel, 1957-58; Director of Fleet Maintenance, Admiralty, 1958-59; Vice-Admiral, 1960; Director-General of Dockyards and Maintenance, 1959-62; and Chief Naval Engineer Officer, 1960-62; retired, 1962. *Address:* Woodlands, Wrecclesham, near Farnham, Surrey *T:* Farnham 6076. *Club:* Army and Navy.

**SANDBACH, Prof. Francis Henry,** FBA 1968; Fellow of Trinity College, Cambridge, since 1927; *b* 23 Feb. 1903; *s* of late Prof. F. E. and Ethel Sandbach; *m* 1932, Mary Warburton Mathews; one *s* one *d* (and one *s* decd). *Educ:* King Edward's Sch., Birmingham; Trinity Coll., Cambridge. Browne Schol., 1922; Craven Schol., 1923; Chancellor's Medallist, 1925; Charles Oldham Class. Schol., 1925. Asst Lectr, Manchester Univ., 1926-28; Lectr in Classics, Univ. of Cambridge, 1929-67; Brereton Reader in Classics, 1951-67; Prof. of Classics, 1967-70. Junior Proctor, 1940-41; Trinity Coll.: Lecturer in Classics, 1929-63; Tutor, 1945-52; Sen. Tutor, 1952-56. *Publications:* (jtly) Plutarch's Moralia, vol. ix, 1961, vol. xi, 1965, vol. sv, 1969; Plutarchus Moralia, vol. vii, 1967; articles in class. jls.

*Address:* 2 Hedgerley Close, Cambridge. *T:* 53152.

**SANDERS, Air Chief Marshal Sir Arthur Penrose Martyn,** GCB 1955 (KCB 1952; CB 1944); KBE 1946 (CBE, 1942); *b* 17 March 1898; *s* of late Rev. Preb. H. Martyn Sanders; *m* 1928, Edith Mary, *d* of late H. A. Olivier; two *d.* *Educ:* Haileybury Coll.; Royal Military College, Sandhurst. Royal Flying Corps, 1916-18; RAF 1918; Egypt, 1921-25; psa 1927; Aden, 1932-33; idc 1934; Director Ground Defence, Air Ministry, 1940-42; Asst Chief of Staff (Air), Allied Force Headquarters, for operation Torch, Sept.-Dec. 1942; AO i/c A, Bomber Command, 1943-45; Commandant, RAF Staff College, 1945-47; AOC-in-C, BAFO, Germany, 1947-48; Vice-Chief of the Air Staff, 1948-50; Deputy Chief of the Air Staff, 1950-52; Commander-in-Chief, Middle East Air Force, 1952-53; Commandant Imperial Defence College, 1954-55; ADC to the Queen, 1954-55; retired from RAF Jan. 1956. Mem., North Thames Gas Bd, 1956-64; Ind. Chm., Fiji Sugar Bd, Jan.-July, 1962; Chm., League of Remembrance, 1959-. Order of Red Star (USSR), 1944; Polonia Restituta, 2nd Class (Poland), 1945; Legion of Merit, Commander (USA), 1947. *Recreations:* fishing, gardening. *Address:* c/o Barclays Bank Ltd, 1 Pall Mall East, SW1. *Clubs:* Royal Air Force, Junior Army and Navy.

**SANDERS, Christopher Cavania,** RA 1961 (ARA 1953); RP 1968; ARCA 1928; Artist-Painter; *b* near Wakefield, 25 Dec. 1905; *s* of Alfred B. Sanders; *m* 1931, Barbara L. Stubbs (ARCA 1928) (*d* 1967), *d* of Francis F. Stubbs, Isleworth and Felpham; two *s* two *d.* *Educ:* Ossett Grammar Sch.; Wakefield Sch. of Art; Leeds Coll. of Art; Royal Coll. of Art. Gold Medallist, Paris Salon, 1955. *Recreation:* sailing. *Address:* 6 Firs Drive, Cranford, Hounslow, Middx. *T:* 01-759 0395.

**SANDERS, Cyril Woods,** CB 1959; Board of Trade; Lord of the Manor of Kavenham-Stoke-Wereham and Wretton in Norfolk; *b* 21 Feb. 1912; *er s* of Cyril Sturgis Sanders and Dorothy (*née* Woods); *m* 1944, Kate Emily Boyes; one *s* three *d.* *Educ:* St Paul's Sch.; Queen's Coll., Oxford. BA Oxon 1934, Lit. Hum. Joined General Post Office as Assistant Principal, 1934; transferred to Board of Trade, 1935; Principal, 1940; Principal Private Secretary to President, Board of Trade, 1941-42; Assistant Secretary, 1944; Under-Secretary, 1952. *Recreations:* walking, sailing, painting. *Address:* 42 Smith St, Chelsea, SW3. *T:* 01-352 8053; Old Pollard. Whistley Green, Hurst, Berks; Canower, Cashel, Connemara, Eire. *Clubs:* Ski Club of Gt Britain; Island Cruising (Devon).

**SANDERS, Sir Harold (George),** Kt 1963; MA, PhD; Deputy Chairman, University Grants Committee, 1964-67 (Member, 1949-55); *b* 9 Oct. 1898; *s* of W. O. Sanders, JP, Wollaston, nr Wellingborough; *m* 1923, Kathleen Penson Plunkett; one *s* one *d.* *Educ:* Wellingborough School; St John's College, Cambridge. Assistant (Physiology), Animal Nutrition Inst., School of Agriculture, Cambridge, 1922-29; University Lecturer (Agriculture), Cambridge, 1929-44; Fellow, St John's College, Cambridge, 1938-44; Executive Officer, Herts War Agricultural Executive Committee, 1941-44; Prof. of Agriculture, Reading Univ., 1945-54; Chief Scientific Adviser (Agriculture) to Ministry of Agriculture, Fisheries and Food, 1955-64. Served European War, 1917-19, 2nd Lt RFA (France). *Publications:* An Outline of British Crop Husbandry, 1939, 3rd Edn, 1958; (with G. Eley) Farms of Britain, 1946. *Address:* Orchard Close, Theale, Berks. *T:* Theale 264. *Club:* Farmers'.

**SANDERS, John Derek;** Organist and Master of the Choristers, Gloucester Cathedral, since 1967; *b* 26 Nov. 1933; *s* of Alderman J. T. Sanders, JP, CA and Mrs E. M. Sanders (*née* Trivett); *m* 1967, Janet Ann Dawson; one *s.* *Educ:* Felsted Sch., Essex; Royal Coll. of Music; Gonville and Caius Coll., Cambridge. ARCM 1952; FRCO 1955; MusB 1956; MA 1958. Dir of Music, King's Sch., Gloucester, and Asst Organist, Gloucester Cathedral, 1958-63; Organist and Master of the Choristers, Chester Cathedral, 1964-67. Dir of Music, Cheltenham Ladies' Coll., 1968-. Conductor of Three Choirs Festival, 1968. *Publication:* Festival Te Deum, 1962. *Recreations:* gastronomy, travelling. *Address:* 20 College Green, Gloucester. *T:* 24764.

**SANDERS, Terence Robert Beaumont,** CB 1950; DL; Chairman, Buckland Sand and Silica Co. Ltd; Engineering Adviser to the British Standards Institution, since 1952; closely associated with work of International Organisation for Standardization; Chairman, ISO/STACO, since 1964; Director, GHP Group; *b* 2 June 1901; *yr s* of late Robert Massy Dawson Sanders, Charleville Park, Co. Cork, and Hilda Beaumont, Buckland Court, Surrey; *m* 1st, 1931, Marion (*d* 1961), *er d* of late Colonel A. W. Macdonald, DSO, Spean Bridge: five *s*; 2nd, 1965, Deborah, *y d* of late Daniel C. Donoghue of Philadelphia. *Educ:* Eton; Trinity Coll. Cambridge. Fellow of CCC, Cambridge, 1924, Estates Bursar, 1935, Life Fellow, 1945; sometime Univ. Lectr in Engineering, Cambridge Univ. Commissioned TA, 1923, RA; Capt. 1928, Maj. 1939; Herts Yeo. 1939-42. Min. of Supply, 1944; Asst Chief Engineer, Armament Design and later Principal Dir of Tech. Development (Defence); demobilised, 1945, with rank of Colonel. Entered Scientific Civil Service, 1946, Retired 1951. Mem., S-E Gas Bd, 1961-69. Rowed in Univ. Boat Race, 1922; won Henley Stewards' Cup, 1922, 1923, 1924; Grand, 1929; Olympic IVs, 1924; Hon. Treas., CUBC, 1928-39. FICE, FIMechE, FInstW. High Sheriff, Surrey, 1967; DL Surrey, 1967. *Publication:* Centenary History of Boat Race. *Recreations:* rowing, shooting, farming. *Address:* Slough House, Buckland, Surrey. *Clubs:* Brooks's, Farmers', Leander.

**SANDERSON,** family name of **Baron Sanderson of Ayot.**

**SANDERSON OF AYOT,** 1st Baron, *cr* 1960; **Basil Sanderson,** MC 1916; Director, British Maritime Trust Ltd; *b* 19 June 1894; *s* of late Harold Arthur Sanderson (Chairman 1913-29 of White Star Line and other Shipping Companies) and Maud Blood, New York; *m* 1927 Evelyn Constance (*d* 1940), *d* of J. Bruce Ismay, and Florence Schefflyn, New York; twin *s* one *d.* *Educ:* Rugby; Trinity Coll., Oxford. Served European War, 1914-18; commissioned Duke of Lancaster's Own Yeomanry, GSO3 1st Inf. Div., Bde Major 126 Inf. Bde, GSO2 41st Inf. Div. (despatches twice, Bt-Major, MC and bar, Belgian Croix de Guerre); joined White Star Line, Liverpool, 1919, thence 1921 Geo. Thompson & Co. Ltd, and finally 1927 Shaw Savill & Albion Co. Ltd as Manager; Man. Director, 1945-59; Chairman, 1947-63; Director, 1963-68. Director:' Bank of England, 1943-65; Furness Withy & Co. Ltd, 1945-65; Finance Corporation for Industry, 1953-66. Member Committee of Lloyd's Register, 1927-; Chairman: London General Shipowners Society, 1933-34; Nat. Council of Port Labour Employers, 1934-40; Shipping Fedn, 1934-50 (Pres., 1950-63); President: Internat. Shipping

Fedn, 1934-51; British Employers' Confederation, 1938-39; Mem. of Economic Planning Board, 1957-62. War of 1939-45; Dir Shipping in Port, Min. of Shipping, 1939-41; Head of Port and Transit Control, Min. of War Transport, 1941-45, when returned to City. High Sheriff, County of London, 1948-49. US Medal of Freedom with Silver Palm. *Publication:* Ships and Sealing Wax (autobiography), 1967. *Recreations:* tennis, gardening. *Heir:* *er* twin *s* Dr Hon. Alan Lindsay Sanderson [*b* 12 Jan. 1931; *m* 1959, Gertrude Bochsler, Zürich; one *s* three *d*. *Educ:* Uppingham]. *Address:* Ayot Bury, Welwyn, Herts. *T:* Welwyn 4360. *Club:* Bath.

**SANDERSON, Air Marshal Sir (Alfred) Clifford,** KBE, *cr* 1953 (CBE 1942); CB 1948; DFC; retired; *b* 19 February 1898; *s* of late Alfred Sanderson, Hayes, Kent; *m* 1923, Hazel Evelyn, *yr d* of late Capt. Bernard Daly, The Bedfordshire Regt, Templeogue, Co. Dublin; two *d*. *Educ:* Dulwich College. Commissioned RFC 1916; Served in France, with 16 and 46 Sqdns, 1917 and 1918; Ireland, 1919-22; India, NW Frontier, 1924-29; Palestine, 1938-40; Malta, 1940-41; Egypt, 1942-43; Director, Administration and Plans, 1943-45; AOC, Burma, 1946-47; Air Officer i/c Administration at Air Command, Far East, 1947-48; Air Officer Commanding Malaya, 1948-49; Director-General of Personnel, Air Ministry, 1949-52; Commander-in-Chief, Far East Air Forces, 1952-54; retd Feb. 1955. *Address:* 24 Hovedene, Hove, Sussex.

**SANDERSON, Sir Bryan;** *see* Sanderson, Sir F. P. B.

**SANDERSON, Air Marshal Sir Clifford;** *see* Sanderson, Air Marshal Sir A. C.

**SANDERSON, Sir (Frank Philip) Bryan,** 2nd Bt, *cr* 1920; Lt-Comdr RNVR; *b* 18 Feb. 1910; *s* of Sir Frank Bernard Sanderson, 1st Bt, and Amy Edith (*d* 1949), *d* of David Wing, Scarborough; *S* father 1965; *m* 1933, Annette Irene Caroline (*d* 1967), *d* of late Col Korab Laskowski, Warsaw, (*g d* of General Count de Castellaz); two *s* one *d*. *Educ:* Stowe; Pembroke College, Oxford. Served War of 1939-45 with Fleet Air Arm. A Member of Lloyd's. Chairman, Humber Fishing and Fish Manure Co., Hull. *Recreation:* shooting. *Heir:* *s* Frank Linton Sanderson [*b* 21 Nov. 1933; *m* 1961, Margaret Ann, *o d* of John C. Maxwell; two *s* three *d*]. *Address:* Lychgate Cottage, Scaynes Hill, Sussex. *Club:* Junior Carlton.

**SANDERSON, His Honour Kenneth Francis Villiers,** CMG 1957; retired as Judge of Local Court, Adelaide, SA (1950-58); *b* 30 March 1895; *s* of Francis V. Sanderson and Fannie A. Klingender; three *s*. *Educ:* St Peter's College, Adelaide. Admitted to Bar of South Australia, 1918; appointed Stipendiary Magistrate, 1927. *Recreations:* yachting and field sports. *Address:* No 3 Hexham Avenue, Myrtle Bank, South Australia 5064, Australia. *T:* 79.4880. *Club:* Royal SA Yacht Squadron (S Australia).

**SANDERSON, Captain Lancelot,** CIE 1942; RIN, retired; Captain, RN Emergency List; *b* 1889; *s* of late Herbert Elsworth Sanderson; *m* 1919, Anna St John, *d* of late William Sloane; two *d*. *Educ:* HMS Worcester. Joined RIN 1911; served European War, 1914-19; Surveyor-in-Charge, Marine Survey of India, 1935-39; Naval Officer-in-Charge, Calcutta, 1939-43; Chief of Personnel, Naval Headquarters, New Delhi, 1944-45; retired 1946. *Address:* 30 Beeches Close, Saffron Walden, Essex. *T:* Saffron Walden 3405.

**SANDERSON, Very Rev. Roy;** *see* Sanderson, Very Rev. W. R.

**SANDERSON, Rt. Rev. Wilfrid Guy;** *see* Plymouth, Suffragan Bishop of.

**SANDERSON, Very Rev. (William) Roy;** Parish Minister at Stenton and Whittingehame since 1963; Chaplain to the Queen in Scotland, since 1965; *b* 23 Sept. 1907; *er s* of late Arthur Watson Sanderson, Leith, and late Ethel Catherine Watson, Dundee; *m* 1941, Annie Muriel Easton, Glasgow; three *s* two *d*. *Educ:* Cargilfield Sch.; Fettes Coll.; Oriel Coll., Oxford; Edinburgh University. BA 1929, MA 1933, Oxon. Ordained, 1933. Asst Minister, St Giles' Cath., Edin., 1932-34; Minister: at St Andrew's, Lochgelly, 1935-39; at the Barony of Glasgow, 1939-63. Moderator of Glasgow Presbytery, 1958; Convener of Assembly Cttees: on Religious Instruction of Youth, 1950-55; on Deaconesses, 1956-61; Panel of Doctrine, 1960-65; on Gen. Administration, 1967-. Convener of Business Cttee and Leader of General Assembly of the Church of Scotland, 1965-66, 1968-69-70. Moderator of Gen. Assembly of the Church of Scotland, May 1967-May 1968. Chairman of BBC Scottish Religious Advisory Committee, 1961-; Member Central Religious Advisory Cttee of BBC and ITA, 1961-. Governor, Fettes Coll., Edinburgh, 1967-. Hon. DD, Glasgow, 1959. *Publication:* Responsibility (Moderatorial address), 1967. *Recreations:* golf, reading. *Address:* Whittingehame Manse, Haddington, East Lothian. *T:* Stenton 225. *Club:* Overseas (Edinburgh).

**SANDES, Lt-Col Edward Warren Caulfeild,** DSO 1919; OBE 1959; MC 1916; RE retired; *b* 1880; *o s* of late Col H. T. T. Sandes, RA; *m* 1919, Sylvia Mary, *d* of late Henry Francis Sneyd-Kynnersley; one *s* one *d*. *Educ:* Monkton Combe Sch.; RMA, Woolwich. Commissioned, 1899; Lieut, 1902; Captain, 1908; Major, 1916; Lt-Colonel, 1925; served in military employment in India, 1902-10; Prof. of Civil Engineering, Thomason Coll., Roorkee, India, 1910-15; Principal, Thomason Coll., 1921-30; served European War (Mesopotamia), 1915-16 (DSO, MC, French Croix de Guerre with palms); was in the besieged garrison of Kut-el-Amarah (despatches thrice) and a prisoner of war in Turkey for 2½ years after the surrender of Kut; retired, 1931. Fowke Memorial Medal for Architectural Design, SME Chatham, 1901; Gold Medal, Institution of Royal Engrs, 1964. *Publications:* In Kut and Captivity, 1919; Tales of Turkey, 1924; The Military Engineer in India, Vol. I, 1933; Vol. II, 1935; The Royal Engineers in Egypt and the Sudan, 1937; The Indian Sappers and Miners, 1948; From Pyramid to Pagoda (The W Yorks Regt History), 1952; The Indian Engineers, 1939-47, 1957; Biographies; articles in RE Journal. *Address:* Ryelands, Buxton Road, Weymouth. *T:* Weymouth 6357. *Clubs:* Naval and Military; Royal Dorset Yacht (Weymouth).

**SANDFORD,** 2nd Baron, *cr* 1945, of Banbury; **Rev. John Cyril Edmondson,** DSC 1942; Conservative Peer in House of Lords, since 1959; Parliamentary Under-Secretary of State, Department of the Environment, since Oct. 1970; *b* 22 Dec. 1920; *e s* of 1st Baron Sandford; *S* father, 1959; *m* 1947, Catharine Mary Hunt; two *s* two *d*. *Educ:* Eton Coll.; Royal Naval Coll., Dartmouth; Westcott House, Cambridge. Served War of 1939-45: Mediterranean Fleet, 1940-41; Home Fleet, 1942; Normandy Landings, 1944 (wounded); Mediterranean Fleet, HMS Saumarez, 1946 (wounded). Staff of RN Coll., Dartmouth, 1947-49; HMS Vengeance, 1950; HMS

Cleopatra, 1951-52; Staff Commander-in-Chief Far East, 1953-55; Commander of Home Fleet Flagship, HMS Tyne, 1956; retired 1956. Ordained Deacon in Church of England, 1958; Parish of St Nicholas, Harpenden, 1958-63; Exec. Chaplain to Bishop of St Albans, 1965-68. Opposition Whip, House of Lords, 1966-70; Parly Sec., Min. of Housing and Local Govt, June-Oct. 1970; Chairman: Hertfordshire Council of Social Service, 1966-69; Westminster Council of Social Service, 1969-70; Church Army Board, 1969-70; Mem., Adv. Council on Penal Reform, 1968-70. *Recreation:* ski-ing. *Heir: s* Hon. James John Mowbray Edmondson, *b* 1 July 1949. *Address:* 6 Smith Square, Westminster, SW1. *T:* 01-222 5715. *Clubs:* United Service; Ski Club of Gt Britain.

**SANDFORD, Brigadier Daniel Arthur,** CBE 1942 (OBE 1941); DSO 1916; late Royal Garrison Artillery; *b* 1882; *s* of late Ven. E. G. Sandford, Archdeacon of Exeter; *m* 1918, Christine, CBE 1966, *o d* of H. S. Lush, High Croft Terr., Brighton; two *s* four *d. Educ:* St Paul's; RMA, Woolwich. 2nd Lt RGA 1900; Sudan Govt Administration, 1910-13; HM Consul at Addis Ababa, Abyssinia, 1914; served Sudan, 1910 (medal and clasp); European War, 1914-18 (wounded, despatches, DSO and bar, Legion of Honour); retired pay, 1922; resident in Abyssinia, 1920-36, farming; Adviser to Governor of Maji Province, Ethiopia, 1935; resident in England during Italian occupation of Ethiopia; joined Officers' Emergency Reserve, Sept. 1939; June 1940, Head of Mission 101 (with rank of Col) which entered Ethiopia to assist patriots 6 months before British troops; Principal Military and Political Adviser to Emperor Haile Selassie with rank of Brig., Feb. 1941; reverted to Unemployed List to become Principal Adviser to the Ministry of Interior, Ethiopian Government, Apr. 1942; Personal Adviser to Emperor, 1944; Director General of Addis Ababa Municipality, 1945-48. Now resident in Ethiopia, farming and, with wife, interested in a Community Development project. Haile Selassie Medal of Ethiopia with palm, 1942; Comdr Order of Selassie, 1951. *Address:* Addis Ababa, Ethiopia; c/o Lloyds Bank, 6 Pall Mall, SW1. *Club:* Royal Commonwealth Society.

**SANDFORD, Sir Folliott Herbert,** KBE, *cr* 1949; CMG 1944; Registrar of Oxford University, and Fellow, New College, Oxford, since 1958; *b* 28 Oct. 1906; *s* of late W. C. Sandford, Barrister-at-Law; *m* 1935, Gwendoline Alexander Masters; no *c. Educ:* Winchester; New Coll., Oxford (1st Class Greats, 1st Class Law); Geneva. Entered Air Ministry, 1930; Principal Private Secretary to successive Secretaries of State (Viscount Swinton, Sir Kingsley Wood, Sir Samuel Hoare, and Sir Archibald Sinclair), 1937-40; attached to RAF Ferry Command, Montreal, 1941-42; Secretary, Office of Resident Minister, West Africa, 1942-44; Assistant Under-Secretary of State, Air Ministry, 1944-47; Deputy Under-Secretary of State, Air Ministry, 1947-58. Renter Warden, Skinners' Company, 1958. *Address:* 5 South Parks Road, Oxford; Damsel's Mill, Painswick, Glos. *Club:* Reform.

**SANDFORD, Kenneth Stuart;** Reader Emeritus in Geology, University of Oxford; Emeritus Fellow, University College, Oxford; *b* 9 Dec. 1899; *y s* of Horatio Sandford, JP, and Lizzie, *d* of Jonathan Adlington; *m* 1929, Grace Audrey Rob Prestwich (*d* 1965); one *d. Educ:* King's School, Rochester; University College, Oxford (Gunsley Scholar). 2nd Lieut RFA (Temp. Regular Army); Major, RA (Y), 1936, TD 1940; BA (1st Class Honours Natural Science), Burdett-Coutts Scholar, 1921, DPhil 1923, MA 1925, DSc 1934 (Oxford); Geological Society of London: FGS, Daniel-Pidgeon Fund, 1924, Council, 1943-47, 1950-54; Oxford University Arctic Expedition and member of sledging party in North East Land, 1924; geological research in Nile Valley and adjoining deserts, 1925-33 (Brit. Sch. of Archæology in Egypt and Oriental Institute, Univ. of Chicago); Libyan Desert Expedition (Major R. A. Bagnold), 1932; Royal Geographical Society: Murchison Grant, 1932; Council, 1934-37, 1939-43, 1962-66, Vice-Pres., 1967-; University Demonstrator in Pleistocene Geology (Oxford), 1927; in Geology, 1935; Reader, 1948. Senior Treas., OU Exploration Club, 1935-47, Vice-Pres., 1947-54, 1957-65, Pres., 1954-57; Editor, Geologists' Assoc., 1948-51, 1968-; Vice-Pres., Brit. Glaciolog. Soc., 1951-61; Hon. Foreign Member: Svenska Sällskapets für Antropologi och Geografi, 1939; Société belge de Géologie, de Paléontologie, et d'Hydrologie, 1948; Corr. Mem., Fouad I Desert Inst., and of Geological Soc., Egypt, 1950. Bolitho Gold Medal, Royal Geolog. Soc. of Cornwall, 1934. *Publications:* Papers in British and foreign scientific journals, and memoirs. *Address:* Department of Geology and Mineralogy, Parks Road, Oxford and Foxcombe Corner, Boars Hill, Oxford. *T:* Oxford 35179.

**SANDFORD SMITH, Richard Henry,** FCIS; Chairman, Eastern Gas Board, since 1970; *b* 29 March 1909; *s* of late Dr H. Sandford Smith; *m* 1936, Dorothy Hewitt, *y d* of late Rev. J. F. Hewitt; one *s. Educ:* Haileybury Coll. London Stock Exchange, 1926. Qualified as Chartered Secretary and awarded Sir Ernest Clarke Prize, 1932. Joined Gas Light & Coke Co., 1932; Sec., SE Gas Corp. Ltd, 1939-49; Sec., SE Gas Bd, 1949-56 (Dep. Chm., 1956-69). Mem., Auxiliary Hosps Cttee of King Edward's Hosp. Fund for London. *Recreations:* theatre, golf, gardening. *Address:* 60 The Marlowes, St John's Wood Park, NW8. *Club:* Bath.

**SANDHURST,** 5th Baron, *cr* 1871; (**John Edward**) **Terence Mansfield,** DFC 1944; Managing Director, Leslie Rankin Ltd, Jersey; *b* 4 Sept. 1920, *er s* of 4th Baron Sandhurst, OBE, and Morley Victoria (*née* Upcher; *d* 1961); *S* father 1964; *m* 1947, Janet Mary, *er d* of late John Edward Lloyd, NY, USA; one *s* one *d. Educ:* Harrow. Served RAFVR, 1939-46: Bomber Command (as Navigator and Bombing Leader): 149 Sqdn, 1941; 419 (RCAF) Sqdn, 1942; 12 Sqdn, 1943-45. 1946-55: Metropolitan Special Constabulary 'C' Div., Sergeant, 1949-52; long service medal, 1955. Hon. ADC to Lieutenant-Governor of Jersey. *Recreation:* golf. *Heir: s* Hon. Guy Rhys John Mansfield, *b* 3 March 1949. *Address:* Les Fougères, St John, Jersey, CI. *Clubs:* MCC, Pathfinder; United (Jersey).

*See also Viscount Parker.*

**SANDIE, Brigadier John Grey,** DSO 1940; MC; *b* 14 June 1897; *s* of late R. L. Sandie; *m* 1951, Stella Marian, *d* of late Robert Ives, Erpingham House, near Norwich. *Educ:* Shrewsbury; Royal Military College, Sandhurst. Regular Army; served European War, 1916-18 (MC; despatches twice; Croix de Guerre; wounded twice); Sudan Defence Force, 1928-35 (Staff G3 1934); served War of 1939-45, took part in the Dunkirk withdrawal (despatches, DSO); Commanded 1st Bn Loyal Regiment, 1940-42; Commander 159 Inf. Bde; North West Europe Campaign; Commandant Small Arms School, Hythe, 1944-47; retired, 1947. *Recreations:* shooting, photography. *Address:* The Old Rectory, Washford Pyne, Black Dog, near Crediton, Devon. *T:* Witheridge 335. *Club:* Naval and Military.

**SANDILANDS,** family name of **Baron Torphichen.**

**SANDILANDS, Francis Edwin Prescott,** CBE 1967; Chief Executive since 1958, Director since 1965 and Vice-Chairman since 1968, Commercial Union Assurance Co. Ltd; *b* 11 December 1913; *s* of late Lieut-Col Prescott Sandilands, DSO, RM, and late Gladys Baird Murton; *m* 1939, Susan Gillian Jackson; two *s*. *Educ:* Eton; Corpus Christi College, Cambridge. MA 1938. Served War of 1939-45, Royal Scots Fusiliers and General Staff, UK and NW Europe (Lt-Col; despatches). Joined Ocean Accident and Guarantee Corporation Ltd, 1935, Manager, 1955; General Manager, then Chief General Manager Commercial Union Assurance Co. Ltd, 1958; Chm., Trade Indemnity Co. Ltd, 1966-; Director: British Aviation Insurance Co. Ltd; Finance Corporation for Industry; Trafalgar House Investments Ltd; Watling Street Properties Ltd; Chairman: London Salvage Corps, 1962-63; British Insurance Assoc., 1965-67; Pres., Insurance Inst. of London, 1969-70 (Dep. Pres., 1968-69). Mem. Cambridge Univ. Appts Bd, 1963-66. Governor, Summer Fields School, Oxford. *Recreations:* gardening, medieval studies. *Address:* 14 Sloane Avenue, SW3. *T:* 01-589 5287; Thackers, Geldeston, near Beccles, Suffolk. *T:* Kirby Cane 226. *Club:* Brooks's.

**SANDON, Viscount; Dudley Danvers Granville Coutts Ryder,** TD; a Managing Director, Coutts and Co. since 1949; Director: National Westminster Bank Ltd (National Provincial Bank, 1964-69); United Kingdom Provident Institution; Olympia Ltd; *b* 20 Dec. 1922; *er s* of 6th Earl of Harrowby, *qv*; *m* 1949, Jeannette Rosalthé, *yr d* of Captain Peter Johnston-Saint, *qv*; one *s* one *d*. *Educ:* Eton. Lt-Col RA. OC 254 (City of London) Field Regt, RA (TA), 1962-64. Served War of 1939-45: 59 Inf. Div., 5 Para. Bde, in NW Europe (wounded); India and Java (pol. offr), 56 Armoured Div., 1941-45. Mem. Kensington Borough Council, 1950-65, Kensington and Chelsea BC 1965-. Hon. Treasurer: Family Welfare Assoc., 1951-65; Central Council for the Care of Cripples, 1953-60; South Kensington Conservative Association, 1953-56; Pres., Wolverhampton SW Conservative and Unionist Assoc., 1959-68. General Commissioner for Income Tax; Mem., Lord Chancellor's Adv. Investment Cttee for Court of Protection. Manager, Fulham and Kensington Hosp. Group, 1953-56; Chairman: Inst. of Psychiatry; Board of Governors Bethlem Royal and Maudsley Hospitals, 1965-; a Deputy Chairman: Teaching Hospitals Assoc. London Postgraduate Cttee; Member: Bd of Govs of Univ. of Keele, 1956-58; Exec. Cttee London area Conservative Assoc., 1949-50; Council, Timber Growers' Organisation, 1961-62. Chm., Staffordshire Soc., 1957-59 (Hon. Treas., 1947-51). OC 254 (City of London) Field Regt, RA (TA), 1962-64. *Heir: s* Hon. Dudley Adrian Conroy Ryder, *b* 18 March 1951. *Address:* 5 Tregunter Road, SW10. *T:* 01-373 9276; Sandon Hall, Stafford. *T:* Sandon 338.

**SANDON, Frank,** MA Cantab; Life Fellow, Royal Statistical Society; Fellow, Institute of Statisticians; Fellow, Institute of Mathematics, and its Applications; Associate, British Psychological Society; *b* 3 June 1890; *e s* of late Robert Sandon, HM Examiner of Patents, and Louisa Rudkins Watts; *m* 1919, Sophie, 2nd *d* of Carl Gugenheim and of late Laura Maison; no *c*. *Educ:* Burghley Road Board School; Owen's School, Islington (Foundation Scholar and Leaving Exhibitioner); Corpus Christi College, Cambridge (Scholar and Prizeman. Wrangler, 1912); Diploma (with distinction) in Education, Oxford, 1925; Higher Division Clerk, Home Office, 1913-19; Friends' Ambulance Unit, BEF, 1916-19; Mathematics and Form Master, Sheffield CSS, 1919-20; Roan School, 1920-21; Highgate School, 1921-23; West Ham Secondary School, 1923-29; Devonport High School for Boys, 1937-41; Head Master: Corporation Grammar School, Plymouth, 1929-37; Millom Grammar School, Millom Technical School and Millom Commercial School (Millom County Secondary School, Millom, Cumberland), 1941-50; Mathematics Master, King Edward's School, Aston, 1955-57; Edgbaston High School, 1957-58; Lordswood Technical School for Girls, 1958-59; Hon. Lectr Working Men's Coll., 1914-16; Lectr in Statistics, LCC, 1920-29; Principal, Millom Institute, 1942-50; Lectr, Coll. of Commerce, Birmingham, 1955-59; Examiner: NUJMB, 1927-29, 1932-33; London Univ.; SEC, 1928-31, 1940-41; Oxford Locals and Cambridge Locals, 1938-40, 1945; Oxford and Cambridge Schools Examination Bd, 1941-47; Education Committees of LCC, 1930 and 1938, Birmingham, 1930-41, and Wiltshire, 1940; International Inst. Exams Enquiry, 1934; Civil Service Commn since 1941; Chief Examiner, Somerset, 1945-48, 1955-59; Chief Examiner, Birmingham, 1941-50; Selection Officer, Birmingham, 1951-55; Founder-Pres. Plymouth Branch, Math. Assoc. *Publications:* Mathematical statistical, and pedagogical articles, notes, reviews, etc; Every-Day Mathematics, 1920; Wightman's Mathematical Tables, 1921; Wightman's Arithmetical Tables, 1921; miscellaneous press articles on swimming, rambling, etc. *Recreations:* swimming (CUSC, Blue, 1910-12; British team, Olympic Games, Stockholm, 1912; Hon. Rep. Plymouth and Penzance, Royal Life Saving Society), fell walking, and rambling (Gen. Cttee Holiday Fellowship; Founder Pres., Plymouth Group; Founder Treasurer, Devon and Cornwall YHA). *Address:* 726 Enterprise House, King's Head Hill, Chingford, E4 7NF.

**SANDOVER, Sir (Alfred) Eric,** Kt 1967; MC 1916; Chairman of Directors, Sandovers O'Connor Pty Ltd, since 1953; Chairman, Swan Portland Cement, since 1956; Chairman, Welded Mesh Pty Ltd; Director of other companies; *b* 11 Feb. 1897; *s* of Alfred Sandover, MBE, and Rosalind Sandover; *m* 1923, Kathleen Barber, OBE, *d* of Maj.-Gen. G. W. Barber, CMG, DSO; two *s* one *d*. *Educ:* St Peter's Coll., Adelaide. Served European War, 1914-18: E Surrey Regt; 6th Sherwood Foresters, Somme, 1916; served War of 1939-45: 44 Bn AIF and on Staff, Land HQ, Australian Army. Mem. Cttee, Employers' Fedn of Australia, 1950-; Mem. Cttee, Chamber of Commerce of Australia, 1935-; Past Pres., Hardware Assoc. of Australia; Patron, Mentally Incurable Children Assoc.; Business Adviser, Ngala Mothercraft Home, etc. Mem. Shire Coun. of Peppermint Grove for 25 years. *Recreations:* riding horses (formerly MFH West Australian Hunt Club); golf, swimming, deep-sea fishing, etc. *Address:* 29 Leake Street, Peppermint Grove, West Australia 6011. *T:* 3-2101. *Clubs:* (Past Pres.) Weld, (Past Pres.) Naval, Military and Air Force, Karrinyup Golf, West Australian Turf, WA Hunt, etc. (all Perth).

**SANDREY, John Gordon,** FRCS; Consultant Surgeon, St Peter's Hospital for Stone; Consultant Urologist to the Royal Navy, etc; *b* 20 May 1903; *m* 1932, Eulie Barbara Johnston; one *d*. *Educ:* Sydney, Australia; MB ChM Sydney, 1926; MRCS, LRCP, 19[illegible] FRCS 1930. Temporary Surgeon-Capt[illegible]

RNVR, 1940-46. Mem. de la Soc. Internat. d'Urol.; FRSocMed. Formerly Surgical Registrar, Royal Prince Alfred Hospital, Sydney, and Resident Surgical Officer, St Mark's and St Peter's Hospital. *Publications:* contributions to medical journals from 1943. *Address:* 27 Pont Street, SW1. *T:* 01-235 7494.

**SANDS, Percy Cooper,** MA; JP; *b* 3 Feb. 1883; *s* of John and Annie Maria Sands; *m* 1909, Olive Clara Cowley; one *s* two *d. Educ:* Nottingham High School; St John's College, Cambridge (Scholar; Fellow). Composition Master of the City of London School, EC, 1906-14; Headmaster, Pocklington School, 1915-44; Thirlwall Medal, Cambridge University, 1907. *Publications:* Client Princes of the Roman Empire; Gods and Heroes; Literary Genius of the Old Testament; Literary Genius of the New Testament; Forty-five Talks for Bible Classes; Modern Illustrations of the Gospel; Men of God; Sons of God; Witnesses of God; History of Pocklington School. *Address:* The Balk, Pocklington, York. *T:* Pocklington 2187.

**SANDS, Sir Stafford (Lofthouse),** Kt 1964; CBE 1955; Member of the House of Assembly, Bahamas, 1937-67; Minister for Tourism and Finance, Bahamas, 1963-67; *b* 1913; *s* of late Stafford Sands, The Knowle, Montagu Foreshore, Nassau, Bahamas; *m* 1st, 1937, Winifred Maude (marr. diss., 1961), *d* of late Sir Walter Kingsbury Moore, CBE; 2nd, 1965, Ulli, *d* of late Lauri Castren, Helsinki, Finland. *Educ:* Winnwood Sch., NY, USA. Called to the Bar, Bahamas, 1935; Bd of Educn, Bahamas, 1937-38; Member: Marketing Committee, 1941; Agricultural and Marine Products Board, 1943; Health Board, 1944-46; Broadcasting Committee, 1944-45; War-Time Supplies Commission, 1944-45; Public Board of Works, 1945-46; Executive Council, 1945-46; Economic Supplies Board, 1946; Airports Board, 1947-52; Town Planning Committee, 1952; Co-ordination Committee, 1954; Chm., Development Board, 1950-63. *Address:* Waterloo, East Bay Street, Nassau, Bahamas; Hermanos Becquer 8, Madrid 6, Spain.

**SANDWICH,** 10th Earl of, *cr* 1660; Viscount Hinchingbrooke and Baron Montagu of St Neots, 1660 [Disclaimed his Peerages for life, 24 July 1964]; *see under* Montagu, A. V. E. P.

**SANDYS,** 7th Baron, *cr* 1802; **Richard Michael Oliver Hill;** DL; Landowner; *b* 21 July 1931; *o s* of late Lt-Col the Lord Sandys and of Lady Sandys; *S* father, 1961; *m* 1961, Patricia Simpson Hall, *d* of late Captain Lionel Hall, MC. *Educ:* Royal Naval College, Dartmouth. Lieutenant in The Royal Scots Greys, 1950-55. FRGS. DL Worcestershire, 1968. *Heir: cousin,* Marcus Tufton Hill, *b* 13 March 1931. *Address:* Ombersley Court, Droitwich, Worcestershire. *T:* Ombersley 220. *Club:* Cavalry.

**SANDYS, Rt. Hon. Duncan Edwin,** PC 1944; MP (C) Streatham Division of Wandsworth since 1950; *b* 24 Jan. 1908; *o s* of Captain George Sandys, formerly MP for Wells, and Mildred, *d* of Duncan Cameron, Ashburton, New Zealand; *m* 1st, 1935, Diana (marr. diss., 1960; she *d* 1963), *d* of late Rt Hon. Sir Winston Churchill; one *s* two *d*; 2nd, 1962, Marie-Claire, *d* of Adrien Schmitt, Paris, and formerly Viscountess Hudson; one *d. Educ:* Eton; Magdalen Coll., Oxford (MA). Entered Diplomatic Service, 1930; served in Foreign Office and British Embassy, Berlin; MP (C) for Norwood Div. of Lambeth, 1935-45; Member Nat. Exec. of Conservative Party, 1938-39; Commissioned in Territorial Army (Royal Artillery), 1937; served in Expeditionary Force in Norway, 1940; Lt-Col 1941; disabled on active service, 1941; Financial Secretary to War Office, 1941-43; Parliamentary Secretary, Ministry of Supply, 1943-44; Chairman of War Cabinet Cttee for defence against German "V" weapons, 1943-45; Minister of Works, 1944-45; founded European Movement, 1947, Chm. International Executive until 1950; Chm., Parly Council of European Movement, 1950-51 and since 1968; Mem. of European Consultative Assembly at Strasbourg, 1950-51 and since 1965; Mem. of General Advisory Council of BBC, 1947-51; Director, Ashanti Goldfields Corporation, 1947-51, and since 1966; Minister of Supply, Oct. 1951-Oct. 1954; Minister of Housing and Local Govt, Oct. 1954-Jan. 1957; Minister of Defence, Jan. 1957-Oct. 1959; Minister of Aviation, Oct. 1959-July 1960; Secretary of State for Commonwealth Relations, July 1960-Oct. 1964, and for the Colonies, July 1962-Oct. 1964. Pres. of Civic Trust, which he founded in 1956; Pres., Europa Nostra, 1969-. Hon. Fellow, RIBA, 1968. Grand Cross, Order of Merit, Italy, 1960. *Address:* 86 Vincent Square, SW1. *T:* 01-834 5886. *Clubs:* Carlton, Pratt's.
*See also P. Dixon, D. Walters.*

**SANDYS, George Owen,** JP. DL, Co. Lancaster; *b* 17 July 1884; *er* twin *s* of Lieut-Col Edwin Del Sandys, 58th Northamptonshire Regt; *m* 1914, Dulcie Edythe Angela, *o d* of late Sir E. P. W. Redford, CB; one *s* one *d. Educ:* Bedford Grammar School; Royal Military College, Sandhurst. Served in 1st Royal Scots (The Royal Regiment), 1903-12; in the Westmorland and Cumberland Yeo., 1912-19, when was placed in the TF Reserve Class 1 as a Major. Served in 2nd County of Lancaster (North Lonsdale) Bn Home Guard, 1940, Lt-Col from 1941; succeeded in the family estates his cousin the late Col Thomas Myles Sandys (for many years MP for Bootle Division of Liverpool), 1911; High Sheriff of Lancashire, 1925-26. *Address:* 6/9 Wilbraham Place, SW1. *T:* 01-730 7544; Graythwaite Hall, Ulverston, Lancs. *T:* Newby Bridge 333. *Clubs:* Carlton, Beefsteak.

**SANER, Robert Morton,** CVO 1966; CBE 1962 (OBE 1946; MBE 1941); *b* 30 December 1911; *o s* of late Major A. E. Saner; *m* 1943, Katharine Mary Gordon; two *d. Educ:* Westminster Sch.; Christ Church, Oxford. ICS, 1935; served in United Provinces; Under Sec., Defence Department, Government of India, 1940; Deputy Secretary and Chief Administrative Officer, General Headquarters, New Delhi, 1943-45; served with Resettlement Directorate, 1945-47. Retired from Indian Civil Service and entered Foreign (subseq. Diplomatic) Service, 1947. Served in Madras, 1947-50; Foreign Office, 1950-52; Budapest, 1953-55; NATO Defence College, 1955; Counsellor and Consul-General, Djakarta, 1955-59; Counsellor, Buenos Aires, 1960-64; Consul-General, Antwerp, 1964-70. Acted as Chargé d'Affaires, 1953, 1954, 1956, 1958, 1959, 1960. Member, Skinners' Company. Commander, Order of Leopold II (Belgium). *Recreations:* riding, golf. *Address:* c/o National & Grindlay's Bank, 13 St James's Square, SW1.

**SANGAR, Owen Jermy,** CBE 1951; MC 1918; retired from Forestry Commission; *b* 20 May 1893; *s* of late Isaac Twigg and late Cordelia Charlotte Sangar, Lowestoft, Suffolk; *m* 1920, Eveline Mary, *d* of Walter Reginald Dickinson, West Wickham, Kent; one *d. Educ:* Felsted Sch.; Univ. of Washington, USA. British Columbia Forest Service, 1913-14. Served European War (despatches twice): Canadian Field Artillery, 1915; RGA and RA (staff appt), 1916-19; retired as Captain. Forestry Commission, 1919-58; Asst Comr, England

and Wales, 1938-45; Director, England, 1946-58. Chairman, FAO's European Commission for Forestry and Forest Products, 1948-52. Pres. Soc. of Foresters of Gt Brit., 1948-49. *Publications:* various papers and articles for Forestry Conferences and in technical journals. *Address:* Gweath, Mullion, S Cornwall. *T:* Mullion 481.

**SANGER, Frederick,** CBE 1963; FRS 1954; on staff of Medical Research Council since 1951; *b* 13 Aug. 1918; *s* of Frederick Sanger, MD, and Cicely Sanger; *m* 1940, M. Joan Howe; two *s* one *d*. *Educ:* Bryanston; St John's College, Cambridge. BA 1939; PhD 1943. From 1940, research in Biochemistry at Cambridge University; Beit Memorial Fellowship for Medical Research, 1944-51; Corday-Morgan Medal and Prize of Chemical Society, 1951; Fellowship at King's College, Cambridge, 1954. For. Hon. Mem., Amer. Acad. of Arts and Sciences, 1958; Hon. Mem. Amer. Society of Biological Chemists, 1961; Foreign Assoc., Nat. Acad. of Sciences, 1967. Hon. DSc Leicester, 1968. Nobel Prize for Chemistry, 1958; Alfred Benson Prize, 1966; Royal Medal, Royal Soc., 1969. Hon. DSc Oxon, 1970. *Publications:* papers on Chemistry of Insulin and Nucleic Acid Structure in Biochemical and other journals. *Address:* 252 Hills Road, Cambridge. *T:* Cambridge 47065.

**SANGER, Gerald Fountaine,** CBE 1954; JP; Director: Daily Mail and General Trust Ltd; London General Cab Co. Ltd (Chairman, 1951-57); British Movietonews Ltd; West Country Holdings Ltd; News Holdings Ltd; F. Hewitt & Son (1927) Ltd; *b* 23 May 1898; *s* of late William Sanger, CB; *m* 1922, Margaret Hope, *d* of late G. H. Munroe, of Chessington Place, Surrey; two *s* one *d*. *Educ:* Shrewsbury School; Keble College, Oxford, MA. Lieut Royal Marine Artillery, 1917-19; Private Secretary to Hon. Esmond Harmsworth, 1921-29; Editor of British Movietone News, 1929-54; Admin. Dir Associated Newspapers Ltd, 1954-63. Capt. The Queen's Royal Regt, 1939; Hon. Sec., Old Salopian Club, 1942-55, Chm., 1955-57, Pres., 1963-64; Hon. Production Adviser, Conservative and Unionist Films Assoc., 1948-59; Chm., Dorking Division of Surrey Conservative and Unionist Association, 1949-52, President, 1958-63. JP Surrey, 1949. Surrey CC (Horsleys Division), 1965. *Recreation:* tennis. *Address:* Willingham Cottage, Send, Surrey. *T:* Ripley 2142. *Clubs:* Carlton, Garrick.

**SANGSTER, John Young;** Director, Birmingham Small Arms Company Ltd, since 1951 (Chairman, 1956-61); *b* 29 May 1896; *s* of late Charles Sangster; *m* 1st, 1923, Kathleen, *d* of late Robert Burns; one *d*; 2nd, 1951, Phyllis, *d* of Frederick Hamer; 3rd, 1963, Margery, *d* of late Robert Cheney Hart. *Educ:* Hurstpierpoint Coll. Served 14th Royal Warwickshire Regt, 1914-18. The Rover Co. Ltd, 1919-23; Chairman: Ariel Motors Ltd, 1923-45; Triumph Engineering Co. Ltd, 1936-64; The Daimler Co. Ltd, 1956-60. Pres. Cycle & Motor Cycle Assoc., 1953-54. *Recreations:* motoring, ski-ing, yachting. *Address:* 51 South Street, W1. *T:* 01-499 7594. *Club:* Royal Thames Yacht.

**SANSBURY, Rt. Rev. (Cyril) Kenneth,** MA Cantab; Hon. DD (Trinity College, Wycliffe College, Toronto); General Secretary of the British Council of Churches since 1966; Assistant Bishop, Diocese of London, since 1966; *b* 21 Jan. 1905; *s* of late Cyril J. Sansbury; *m* 1931, Ada Ethelreda Mary, *d* of late Captain P. B. Wamsley; one *s* two *d*. *Educ:* St Paul's School; Peterhouse, Cambridge; Westcott House, Cambridge. 2nd cl. Classical Tripos, 1926; 1st cl. Theological Tripos, Pt I 1927 and Pt II 1928. Curate of St Peter's, Dulwich Common, 1928-31 and Wimbledon, 1931-32; SPG Missionary, Numazu, Japan, 1932-34; Prof. at Central Theological Coll. and British Chaplain at St Andrew's, Tokyo, 1934-41; Chaplain to HM Embassy, Tokyo, 1938-41; Chaplain, RCAF, 1941-45; Warden, Lincoln Theological Coll., 1945-52; Canon and Prebendary of Asgarby in Lincoln Cathedral, 1948-52; Warden, St Augustine's College, Canterbury (Central College of the Anglican Communion), 1952-61; Commissary: to Bishop of Jamaica, 1950-61; to Bishop of Caledonia, 1953-61; Proctor in Convocation: for Lincoln, 1950-55; for Canterbury, 1955-61. Examining Chaplain: to Bishop in S Tokyo, 1935-41; to Bishop of Lincoln, 1946-53; to Bishop of Edinburgh, 1947-59; to Bishop of Bradford, 1956-61; to Archbishop of Canterbury, 1959-61. Hon. Canon of Canterbury, 1953-61; Select Preacher, Univ. of Cambridge, 1957. Bishop of Singapore and Malaya, 1961-66. Member, Advisory Committee of Conference of European Churches, 1967-. Hon. Fellow, St Augustine's College, Canterbury, 1961. *Publication:* Truth, Unity and Concord, 1967. *Address:* British Council of Churches, 10 Eaton Gate, SW1. *T:* 01-730 9611; (home) 8 Cliveden Place, SW1. *T:* 01-730 3033. *Club:* Royal Over-Seas League.
*See also Canon G. R. Sansbury.*

**SANSBURY, Canon Graham Rogers,** MA; Vicar of Grantham since 1958; Chaplain to the Queen since 1969; Canon of Lincoln Cathedral since 1961; *b* 4 Aug. 1909; *s* of Cyril and Sophie Sansbury; *m* 1935, Cecily, *d* of Prof. Bompas Smith; one *s* one *d* (and one *d* decd). *Educ:* Dulwich Coll.; Peterhouse, Cambridge; Westcott House, Cambridge. Curate: St Peter St Helier, Southwark, 1932-35; Old Malden, 1935-38; Chaplain, Kolar Gold Field, South India, 1938-44; Priest i/c St Michael's, North Hull, 1945-48; Rector of Skegness, 1948-58; Rural Dean of Grantham, 1958-69. *Publications:* The Paul Report: A Study Guide, 1964; contrib. to The Paul Report Considered. *Recreations:* cine-photography, walking, gardening. *Address:* The Vicarage, Grantham, Lincs. *T:* Grantham 3710. *Club:* Royal Commonwealth Society.
*See also Rt Rev. C. K. Sansbury.*

**SANSOM, Lt-Gen. Ernest William,** CB 1943; DSO 1919; CD; *b* 18 Dec. 1890; *m* 1st, 1917, Eileen Curzon-Smith (*d* 1927); two *d*; 2nd, 1929, Lucy Aymor Waddell; one *d*. *Educ:* Public schools, New Brunswick; Commercial Coll., Fredericton, NB; Univ. of Toronto; Staff Coll., Camberley, Surrey. Joined 71st York Regt, Canadian Militia, 1906; Lieut, 1907; Canadian Expeditionary Force during European War, 1914-19; Commanded 16th Canadian Machine Gun Company, 2nd Bn and 1st Bn Canadian Machine Gun Corps; Permanent Active Militia, from 1920; Organised and Commanded Royal Canadian Machine Gun Brigade until 1923; Army Staff College, Camberley, 1924-25; GSO2, Halifax, NS, 1926-27; GSO2, Defence HQ, Ottawa, 1928-30; AA and QMG, Military District No. 12, 1931-34; GSO1, Military District No. 4, Montreal, 1935-36; Director of Military Training for Canada, 1937-39; proceeded overseas 1939 with 1st Canadian Division as AA and QMG; Commanded 2nd Inf. Bde and served as DAG at Canadian Military HQ, London, July-Nov., 1940; Commanded 3rd Canadian Div., 1940-41; 5th Canadian Armoured Division, 1941-43; 2nd Canadian Corps, 1943-44; returned to Canada, Feb. 1944, on sick leave; Inspector-General Canadian Army Overseas, Jan. 1945; retired, May 1945. Hon. ADC to Governor-General of

Canada, 1948. Progressive-Conservative candidate York-Sunbury general election, June 1945 (defeated), also by-election 1947. Past President: Fredericton Soc. of St Andrew; Fredericton Br., Royal Canadian Legion; Hon. Pres., Fredericton Garrison Club; Life Mem., Canadian Rehabilitation Council for Disabled; Director, New Brunswick Br.: Canadian Paraplegic Assoc.; St John Ambulance Assoc.; Hon. Vice Pres., United Empire Loyalists Assoc. of Canada. OStJ. *Recreations:* fishing, shooting and gardening. *Address:* Fredericton, New Brunswick, Canada.

**SANSOM, George Samuel,** MC, DFC; DSc; Honorary Research Assistant, Department of Embryology, University College, London; *b* London, 7 Aug. 1888; *s* of S. G. C. Sansom and Annie Sansom; *m* 1921, D. V. Dodgson; three *s*. *Educ:* Wellington Coll.; University Coll, London. BSc 1911; Derby Scholar, Zoology, 1912. British Red Cross in Flanders, 1914; Royal Air Force Balloon Observer in France, 1915-18 (MC, DFC). Fellow of University Coll., London, 1930. *Recreations:* formerly rock-climbing, flying; now pistol shooting. *Address:* Kennel Moor, Godalming, Surrey.

**SANSOM, William;** FRSL; Author; *b* 18 Jan. 1912; 3rd *s* of Ernest Brooks Sansom and Mabel Clark, Barrow; *m* 1954, Ruth, *d* of Norman Grundy, FCA, Tunbridge Wells; one *s* (and one step *s*). *Educ:* Uppingham School; and variously in Europe. Has written regularly for literary periodicals in England; books translated into many foreign languages; awarded Travel Scholarship in 1946, literary bursary in 1947, by the Society of Authors. *Publications:* Fireman Flower, 1944; Three, 1946; Westminster in War, 1947; Something Terrible, Something Lovely, 1948; South, 1948; The Equilibriad, 1948; The Body (novel), 1949; The Passionate North, 1950; The Face of Innocence (novel), 1951; A Touch of the Sun, 1952; Pleasures Strange and Simple, 1953; A Bed of Roses (novel), 1954; Lord Love Us (ballads), 1954; A Contest of Ladies, 1956; The Loving Eye (novel), 1956; Among the Dahlias, 1957; The Icicle and the Sun, 1958; The Cautious Heart (novel), 1958; Blue Skies, Brown Studies, 1960; The Last Hours of Sandra Lee (novel), 1961; The Stories of William Sansom, 1963; Away to it All, 1964; The Ulcerated Milkman, 1966; Goodbye (novel), 1966; Grand Tour Today, 1968; Christmas, 1968. *Recreation:* watching. *Address:* c/o The Elaine Greene Agency, 42 Great Russell Street, WC1.

**SANTA CRUZ, Marques de,** *cr* 1569; **José Fernandez Villaverde y Roca de Togores;** Grand Cross of Carlos III; Grand Cross of Isabel La Catolica; Grand Cross of Merito Naval; Knight of Calatrava; Spanish Ambassador to Court of St James's since 1958; *b* 4 April 1902; *s* of Raimundo F. Villaverde, Marqués de Pozo Rubio and Angela, Marquesa de Pozo Rubio, Grandee of Spain; *m* 1942, Casilda de Silva y Fernandez de Henestrosa, Marquesa de Santa Cruz, Duquesa de San Carlos; three *s* one *d*. *Educ:* privately in Madrid; University of Madrid; New College, Oxford. Entered Diplomatic Service, 1921; Attaché: London, 1921, Rome, 1923; Secretary Legation; Vienna, 1927, Stockholm, 1933, London, 1934; Minister-Counsellor Embassy, London, 1944; Minister: Copenhagen, 1948, The Hague, 1950. Chm. Spanish Delegn, 7th Session The Hague Conf. on Private Internat. Law, 1951; Ambassador to Cairo, 1953; Under Secretary of State for Foreign Affairs, 1955. Representative of Spain on Exec. Council of Latin Union, 1955; Spanish Deleg. to 11th and 12th Gen. Assembly of UN, 1956 and 1957; Chm. of Spanish Delegn to XLVI Conf. of Inter-Parly Union, 1957. Hon. Fellow, New College, Oxford 1959. Holds several foreign decorations. *Recreations:* riding, shooting, golf. *Heir:* *s* Alvaro Villaverde, Marqués del Viso; *b* 3 Nov. 1943. *Address:* 24 Belgrave Square, SW1. *T:* 01-235 8363. *Clubs:* Beefsteak, White's; Nuevo (Madrid).

**SANTA CRUZ, Victor (Rafael Andrés),** GCVO (Hon.) 1965; Ambassador of Chile to the Court of St James's since 1959; *b* 7 May 1913; *s* of Don Gregorio Santa Cruz and Doña Matilde Serrano; *m* 1937, Doña Adriana Sutil Alcalde; two *s* two *d*. *Educ:* Stonyhurst; Instituto Nacional, Chile. Law degree, Chile, 1937; Prof. of Civil Law, in Chile, 1941; elected MP, Chilean Parliament, 1945. *Recreation:* golf. *Address:* 92 Eaton Place, SW1. *T:* 01-235 1047. *Clubs:* White's, Turf, Beefsteak; Club de la Union (Santiago).

**SARAGAT, Giuseppe;** President of the Italian Republic, since 1964; *b* 19 Sept. 1898; *s* of Giovanni Saragat and Ernestina Stratta; *m* 1922, Giuseppina Bollani (*d* 1961); one *s* one *d*. *Educ:* University of Economic and Commercial Science, Turin. Served European War, 1915-18 (Lieut); joined Italian Socialist Party, 1924; Member, Exec. Office, Italian Socialist Party, 1925; left Italy for Vienna, Paris and south of France during fascist period, 1926-43; imprisoned by Nazi occupation authorities in Rome, escaped, 1943; Minister without portfolio, 1944; Italian Ambassador in Paris, 1945-46; Pres., Constituent Assembly, 1946; founded Italian Workers Socialist Party (later called Social Democratic Party), 1947; Deputy Prime Minister, 1947-48; Member of Parliament, 1948-64; Deputy Prime Minister and Minister of Merchant Marine, 1948; Secretary of the Social Democratic Party, 1949-54, 1957-64; Deputy Prime Minister, 1954-57; Chm., Standing Cttee for Foreign Affairs, Chamber of Deputies, 1963; Minister of Foreign Affairs, 1963-64. *Publications:* L'umanesimo marxista, 1944; Socialismo e libertà, 1944; Per la difesa delle classi lavoratrici, 1951; Il problema della pace, 1951; L'unità socialista, 1956; Per una politica di centrosinistra, 1960; Quaranta anni di lotta per la democrazia, 1965. *Address:* Palazzo del Quirinale, Rome.

**SARAJČIĆ, Ivo;** Yugoslav Ambassador to the Court of St James's, 1966-70; *b* 10 March 1915; *s* of Ivan and Elizabeth Sarajčić; *m* 1944, Marija Godbar; three *s*. *Educ:* Univ. of Philosophy, Zagreb. Participated in War of Liberation from (beginning) 1941 (Partizan Remembrance Medal); held various prominent political positions. Subsequently: Secretary, Presidium of Nat. Assembly of Croatia; Editor-in-Chief of Borba; Asst Minister of Educn; Dir of Information Office of Yugoslav Govt; MEC, Croatia; also Mem. Central Cttee of League of Communists of Croatia, Mem. Federal Assembly, Mem. Council for Foreign Affairs and Internat. Relations. Yugoslav Diplomatic Service, 1959-: Ambassador to Austria, 1960-63; Asst Sec. of State for Foreign Affairs, 1963-66. *Address:* c/o Ministry of Foreign Affairs, Belgrade, Yugoslavia.

**SARELL, Captain Richard Iwan Alexander,** DSO 1939; RN retd; *b* 22 Feb. 1909; *s* of late Philip Charles Sarell; *m* 1961, Mrs Ann Morgan (*née* Keenlyside). *Educ:* Royal Naval Coll., Dartmouth. Entered RNC Dartmouth, 1922; Comdr 1943; Capt. 1948; specialised in Gunnery, 1934; DSO for action against enemy submarines while in command of HMS Broke, 1939. despatches, 1943. Naval Attaché, Moscow and Helsinki, 1949-51; student

Imperial Defence Coll., 1952; Defence Research Policy Staff, 1954; retd 1957. *Recreations:* fishing, riding. *Address:* 43 Rivermead Court, Ranelagh Gardens, SW6. *Club:* Boodle's.

**SARELL, Sir Roderick (Francis Gisbert),** KCMG 1968 (CMG 1958); Ambassador to Turkey, since 1969; *b* 23 Jan. 1913; *y s* of late Philip Charles Sarell, HM Consular Service and of Ethel Ida Rebecca, *d* of late John Dewar Campbell; *m* 1946, Pamela Muriel, *d* of late Vivian Francis Crowther-Smith; three *s. Educ:* Ashdown House, Sussex; Radley; Magdalen College, Oxford. HM Consular Service, 1936; Vice-Consul, Persia, 1937; Italian East Africa, 1939; Iraq, 1940; 2nd Secretary, Addis Ababa, 1942; 1st Secretary, HM Foreign Service, 1946; Rome, Bucharest, 1946; Foreign Office, 1949; Acting Counsellor, 1952; Counsellor and Consul-General, Rangoon, 1953; Consul-General, Algiers, 1956-59; Head of Southern Dept, Foreign Office, 1959-61, General Dept, 1961-63; Ambassador to Libya, 1964-69. Coronation medal, 1953. *Recreations:* swimming, ski-ing, walking. *Address:* British Embassy, Ankara, Turkey; The Littens, Hampstead Norris, Newbury, Berks. *T:* Yattendon 274. *Clubs:* Athenæum, Oriental, Royal Over-Seas League; Leander.

**SARGAN, Prof. John Denis;** Professor of Econometrics, London School of Economics and Political Science, since 1964; *b* 23 Aug. 1924; *s* of H. and G. A. Sargan; *m* 1953, Phyllis Mary Millard; two *s* one *d. Educ:* Doncaster Grammar Sch.; St John's Coll., Cambridge. Asst. Lectr, Lectr and Reader, Leeds Univ., 1948-63; Reader, LSE, 1963-64. *Address:* 119 Highfield Way, Rickmansworth, Herts.

**SARGANT, Sir Edmund;** *see* Sargant, Sir H. E.

**SARGANT, Sir (Henry) Edmund,** Kt 1969; President of the Law Society, 1968-69; Partner in Radcliffes and Co. (formerly Radcliffes and Hood St Barbe Sladen and Wing), since 1930; *b* 24 May 1906; *s* of Rt Hon. Sir Charles Henry Sargant, Lord Justice of Appeal, and Amelia Julia Sargant, RRC; *m* 1930, Mary Kathleen Lemmey, 3rd *d* of Tom Lemmey, DD, Housemaster, subseq. Second Master, Wellington College, Berks; one *s. Educ:* Rugby School; Trinity College, Cambridge (MA). 3rd Cl. Hons Solicitors' final examination; admitted 1930. Served War of 1939-45 in RAF, Provost and Security Branch; (W Africa; Middle East; Acting Wing Comdr). Member, Council, Law Society, 1951-; Chm., Disciplinary Cttee of Architects Registration Council, 1964, 1965, 1966. Master, Worshipful Co. of Merchant Taylors, 1954. *Recreations:* gardening, cine photography. *Address:* 1 Harley Gardens, The Boltons, SW10. *T:* 01-373 4269. *Club:* United University. *See also M. C. Nourse.*

**SARGANT, William Walters,** MA, MB Cantab, FRCP, DPM; Physician in charge of Department of Psychological Medicine, St Thomas' Hospital, London, since 1948; *b* 1907; *s* of Norman T. C. Sargant, Highgate; *m* 1940, Margaret Heriot Glen. *Educ:* Leys School; St John's College, Cambridge. Geraldine Harmsworth Schol., St Mary's Hosp., 1928; Asst to Medical Professorial Unit, St Mary's Hosp., 1932-34; MO and Phys., Maudsley Hosp., 1935-49; Rockefeller Travelling Fellowship and Research Fellow, Harvard Medical Sch., USA, 1938-39; Asst Clinical Dir Sutton Emergency Hosp., 1939-47; Visiting Prof. of Neuropsychiatry, Duke Univ. Med. Sch., USA, 1947-48; Registrar Royal Medico-Psychological Assoc.; Pres., Section of Psychiatry, Royal Society of Medicine, 1956-57; Examiner in Psychological Medicine, Conjoint Board of England, 1960-63; Associate Secretary, World Psychiatric Assoc., 1961-66. Lectures: Ernest Parsons Memorial, Amer. Soc. of Biological Psychiatry, 1964; Herman Goldham Internat., New York Coll. of Med., 1964; Watson Smith, RCP, 1966; Maudsley, RMPA, 1968; Belisle Memorial, Michigan, 1968. *Publications:* Physical Methods of Treatment in Psychiatry, 1944, 4th edn, 1963; Battle for the Mind, 1957; The Unquiet Mind, 1967. Various papers on psychiatric topics, in medical jls. *Recreation:* (formerly) Barbarians RFC, St Mary's Hosp. RFC (Capt.) and Middlesex Co. RFC. *Address:* 23 Harley Street, W1. *T:* 01-636 5161. *Club:* Savage.

**SARGEAUNT, Bertram Edward,** MVO 1920; OBE 1918; FSA; Government Secretary and Treasurer, Isle of Man, 1910-44; *b* 1877; *s* of late Captain F. A. Sargeaunt, Royal Navy, and Alice Caroline, *sister* of 1st Baron Fisher of Kilverstone, Admiral of the Fleet; *m* 1910, Kathleen Hamilton (*d* 1962), *e d* of late Robert Thornewill, Craythorne, Burton-on-Trent; one *d. Educ:* Bedford School. Staff, Royal United Service Institution, Whitehall, 1899-1910. Late Captain, 12th London Regiment. Officer of the Order of St John of Jerusalem. A trustee of Manx Museum, 1922-53, and a Church Commissioner for Isle of Man, 1943-53. Organised and presided at centenary luncheon held in London in 1955 for sons and daughters of those who served in the Crimean War, 1854-1856; also Golden Jubilee Luncheon held in London, 1958, for TA Officers who served as such in 1908; administered internment camps for 26,000 prisoners in the first World War and 16,000 in the Second World War. *Publications:* The Royal Monmouthshire Militia; The Isle of Man and the Great War; The Royal Manx Fencibles; A Military History of the Isle of Man. *Address:* Ladymead, Hurstpierpoint, Sussex. *T:* Hurstpierpoint 2159. *Club:* Royal Societies.

**SARGEAUNT, Henry Anthony,** CB 1961; OBE 1949; Scientific Consultant, United Nations, since 1968; *b* 11 June 1907; *o s* of Lt-Col Henry Sargeaunt and Norah Ierne Carden; *m* 1939, Winifred Doris Parkinson; two *s* one *d. Educ:* Clifton Coll.; University Coll., Reading (London Univ.); Cambridge Univ. Rhodes Research Grant, 1939-42; served with HM Forces, 1944-46: France, 1944; Staff Capt. with 21 Army Group, 1944; Supt Operational Research Group (ORG) (W&E), Min. of Supply, 1946; Supt, Army ORG, 1947-50; Dep. Scientific Adviser, 1950-52, Scientific Adviser, to Army Council, 1952-55; Asst Scientific Adviser to Supreme Allied Commander in Europe, Sept. 1955-57; Dep. Science Adviser, NATO, 1958-59; re-apptd Scientific Adviser to Army Council, 1959; Dep. Chief Scientist (B), War Office, 1960-62; Chief Scientific Adviser, Home Office, 1962-67. *Recreations:* yachting, horse-racing, bird-watching. *Address:* Alderley, Cumnor, near Oxford. *Club:* Junior Army and Navy.

**SARGEAUNT, Margaret Joan,** MA, BLitt; Principal of Queen Elizabeth College (formerly King's College of Household and Social Science), University of London, 1947-66; *b* 29 July 1903; *d* of Rev. William Drake Sargeaunt and Florence Thursby. *Educ:* Godolphin School, Salisbury; St Hugh's College, Oxford. First Class Hons in Eng. Lang. and Lit., 1925; Diploma in Educn with distinction, 1926; BLitt (Oxon), 1931. Asst Mistress at Wycombe Abbey School, 1926-29; Lecturer in Education, Univ. of Sheffield, 1931-37; Adviser of Women Students and Warden of Masson Hall, Univ. of Edinburgh,

1937-47. Hon. Fellow, Queen Elizabeth Coll., 1966. *Publications:* John Ford, 1935, US edn, 1966; various articles and notes (Review of English Studies). *Recreation:* walking. *Address:* The Tangle, Ibstone, High Wycombe, Bucks. *T:* Turville Heath 383.

**SARGENT, Ven. Alexander,** MA; Archdeacon of Canterbury, 1942-68, and Canon Residentiary of Canterbury Cathedral, 1939-68, Hon. Canon since 1968; *b* 9 May 1895; *s* of Frederick George Sargent and Florence Crundall. *Educ:* King's School, Canterbury; St Edmund Hall, Oxford; Cuddesdon Theological Coll. Deacon, 1919; Priest, 1920; Curate of St Margarets-at-Cliffe, 1919; of All Saints, Maidstone, 1921; Chaplain of Cuddesdon Theological College, 1923; Sub-Warden of St Paul's College, Grahamstown, 1927; Resident Chaplain to the Archbishop of Canterbury, 1929-39; Archdeacon of Maidstone, 1939-42; Commissary to the Bishop of Grahamstown, 1931; Six Preacher in Canterbury Cathedral, 1933; Select Preacher, Univ. of Oxford, 1949-51. *Address:* Starr's House, The Precincts, Canterbury, Kent. *T:* Canterbury 65960. *Club:* Athenæum.

**SARGENT, Sir Donald,** KBE 1961; CB 1951; Secretary, Supplementary Benefits Commission and Deputy Secretary, Ministry of Social Security, 1966-68, retired; Chairman: Civil Service Retirement Fellowship, since 1968; Corporation of Insurance Brokers Society of Pension Consultants, since 1970; Vice-Chairman, Hospital Savings Association, since 1970; *b* 11 Dec. 1906; *s* of late S. G. Sargent; *m* 1944, Dorothy Mary, *d* of late E. Raven, CB; one *s*. *Educ:* King Edward's School, Birmingham; Trinity College, Cambridge. BA (Classical Tripos, 1st Cl.), 1928. Asst Principal, GPO, 1929; Private Sec. to Director General, 1935-37; Principal, 1937; Home Office, ARP Dept, 1938-41; Principal Private Secretary to PMG, 1941-44; Asst Sec., GPO, 1944; Dep. Chief Administrative Officer, CCG, 1946-47; idc, 1948; Director of Personnel and Accommodation, GPO 1949-53; Director of Postal Services, 1953-55; Deputy Director General, 1955-59; Secretary, National Assistance Bd, 1959-66. Dir, Abbeyfield Soc., 1968-70. *Recreations:* mountaineering, sailing, music. *Address:* 1 Croham Valley Road, Croydon, Surrey. *T:* 01-657 4023.

**SARGENT, Rt. Rev. Douglas Noel;** *see* Selby, Bishop Suffragan of.

**SARGENT, Sir John Philip,** Kt, *cr* 1946; CIE 1941; MA (Oxon); Hon. DLitt (Patna, Delhi, Osmania, Travancore, Jadavpur); *b* 27 Dec. 1888; *s* of George Sargent and Bertha White; *m* 1923, Ruth (*d* 1933), *d* of R. C. Taunton; one *s*. *Educ:* St Paul's School; Oriel College, Oxford. Inspector of Schools, East Riding (Yorks) CC, 1913-20; served European War, 1914-18, Royal Artillery; Assistant Education Officer, Birmingham, 1920-27; Director of Education, Southend-on-Sea, 1927-31; Director of Education, Essex CC, 1931-38; Educational Commissioner with Govt of India, 1938-42; Educational Adviser to Govt of India, 1943-48; Sec., Education Department, Govt of India, 1945-48; Director, Commonwealth II Dept, British Council, 1948-52; Warden of Missenden Abbey Adult Educn Coll., 1953-57. Pres., Association of Directors and Secretaries for Education, 1936; Pres., Education Section, British Association, 1938. *Recreations:* golf, walking. *Address:* 8 Lillington Avenue, Leamington Spa, Warwicks. *Clubs:* Oriental; Vincent's (Oxford).

**SARGENT, Sir (Sidney) Donald;** *see* Sargent, Sir Donald.

**SARGOOD, Richard;** Trade Union Officer; retired; *b* 31 July 1888; *m* 1919, Sarah Lilian Deane; one *d*. *Educ:* Kennington Road LCC School; Evening Continuation School. Trade Union Official since 1919; Member Camberwell Borough Council, 1923-29; Vice-Chm. LCC, 1951-52 (Member 1934-65). MP (Lab) for West Bermondsey, 1945-50; formerly Chairman: Mental Hospitals Committee of LCC, Supplies Cttee, Parliamentary Cttee, Fire Brigade Cttee; (till 1965) Staff Appeals Committee, LCC; Mem. Camberwell Youth Employment Cttee. *Recreations:* walking, reading, keenly interested in amateur football. *Address:* 3 Gillbrook Cottages, Woodbury, South Devon EX5 1LH. *T:* Woodbury 446.

**SARKODEE-ADOO, Julius; Mr Justice Sarkodee-Adoo;** Chief Justice, Republic of Ghana, 1964-66 (Judge, Supreme Court, Republic of Ghana, 1960; Puisne Judge, Ghana, 1956); *b* 18 Sept. 1908; *e s* of late Julius Sarkodee-Adoo, Merchant, Koforidua (New Juaben), and Emma Apeakorama, Afwerase, Akwapim; *m* 1941, Florence Flatteau, Akuse, Ghana; three *s* three *d*. *Educ:* Methodist Primary Sch., Koforidua; Wesleyan Boys' High Sch., Freetown, Sierra Leone; University of London, King's College. Called to Bar, Inner Temple, 1932; enrolled in Supreme Court of Gold Coast (now Ghana), 1934; Legal Practitioner, 1934-56; Chm., Cttee of Enquiry into the Ga, Akwapim, Abeadzi, Gomoa Assin, Teshie and Osu Stool Disputes; Mem. Representational and Electoral Reform Commn; Chm. Cttee of Enquiry into Mines Disputes, 1953-56; Mem. Judicial Service Commn, 1957-59. Formerly Director Ghana Commercial Bank. *Recreation:* tennis. *Address:* Florrie Villa, PO Box 283, Accra, Ghana.

**SARNOFF, David,** Hon. DSc, Hon. DLit, Hon. DSc Comm., Hon. Dr of Laws, Hon. Dr of Humane Letters; Chairman of the Board, RCA Corporation (formerly Radio Corporation of America), 1947-70, now Hon. Chairman; *b* Uzlian, Minsk, Russia, 27 Feb. 1891; *m* 1917, Lizette Hermant; three *s*. *Educ:* New York Public Schools; Pratt Institute. Went to USA 1900. Messenger boy, Commercial Cable Co., 1906; Office boy, Marconi Wireless Telegraph Co. of America, 1906; Junior telegraph operator, Marconi Co., 1907; Wireless operator, Nantucket Island, 1908; Manager, Marconi Station, Sea Gate, 1909; Wireless operator, SS Harvard, SS Beothic in Arctic, 1910-11; John Wanamaker's, New York, 1911-12; Chief Radio Inspector, Marconi Co., 1913; Contract Manager, 1914; Asst Traffic Manager, 1915-16; Commercial Manager, 1917-19; Radio Corp. of America (later RCA Corporation): Commercial Manager, 1919-20; General Manager, 1921; Vice-Pres., 1922; Exec. Vice-Pres., 1929; Pres., 1930; Chm. and Chief Exec. Officer, 1947; Chm., 1966-70. Lt-Col Signal Corps Reserve, US Army, 1924; Col, 1931; Brig.-Gen., 1944; now Brig.-Gen. AUS, retd. Trustee: Thomas A. Edison Foundn; Educ. Alliance; Trustee Emeritus: Pratt Inst.; New York Univ.; Member: Inst. of Electrical and Electronics Engineers (Fellow); British Instn of Radio Engineers (Hon.); Newcomen Soc. of England; Roy. Soc. of Arts, London (Fellow); Weizmann Inst. of Science, Israel (Hon. Fellow); member of many other engineering and scientific institutes and societies. Collaborated with Owen D. Young in reparations settlement in Paris, 1929. Order of Polonia Restituta Officers Grade, 1924; Cross of Chevalier of Legion of Honour (France),

1935, Cross of Officer, 1940, Cross of Comdr, 1947; Officer of Order of Oaken Crown of Grand Duchy of Luxembourg, 1935; Order of the Rising Sun, Japan, 1960; Legion of Merit, US War Dept, 1944; Medal for Merit, 1946; US Treasury's Silver Medal Award, 1946; Citation from UN, 1949. Gold Medal of French Union of Inventors, 1954. James Forrestal Memorial Medal, Nat. Security Ind. Assocn, 1956; Decoration for Exceptional Civilian Service, US Army, 1956. Commander, Order of Merit of the Italian Republic, 1959. Christopher Columbus Internat. Award, Italy, 1959; Medallion of Valor, Commendation Award, Israel, 1960. *Address:* 30 Rockefeller Plaza, New York, NY 10020, USA. *Clubs:* Army and Navy (Washington); India House (NY); Metropolitan (Washington).

**SAROYAN, William;** writer; *b* Fresno, California, 31 Aug. 1908; *s* of Armenak Saroyan (*d* 1911) and Takoohi Saroyan (*d* 1950), of Bitlis, Armenia, who emigrated to America in 1905 and 1907; *m* 1943, Carol Marcus (marriage dissolved 1949); one *s* one *d*. *Educ:* Fresno public schools until fifteen years of age; public libraries; movie and vaudeville theatres; streets. Began selling newspapers when seven; from that year until his twenty-second year worked at a variety of jobs; since twenty-second year has done very little but loaf and write; began to write when nine years old; writing was constantly interrupted or delayed by work; this displeased him, so he stopped working; has no intention of ever working again, as it bores him. *Religion:* living. *Party:* William Saroyan. *Publications:* The Daring Young Man on the Flying Trapeze, 1934; Inhale and Exhale, 1936; Three Times Three, 1936 (US only); The Gay and Melancholy Flux, 1936 (England only); Little Children, 1937; Love, Here Is My Hat, 1938; The Trouble with Tigers, 1938; Peace, It's Wonderful, 1939; My Heart's in the Highlands (play), 1939; The Time of Your Life (play), 1939; Love's Old Sweet Song (play), 1939; My Name is Aram, 1940; Saroyan's Fables (US only), 1941; The Beautiful People (play), 1941; Sweeney in the Trees (play), 1941; Across the Board on Tomorrow Morning (play), 1941; The Human Comedy (novel), 1943; Get Away Old Man (play), 1943; Dear Baby (stories), 1944; The Adventures of Wesley Jackson (novel), 1946; Jim Dandy, Fat Man in a Famine (play), 1947; Don't Go Away Mad (play), 1949; Sam Ego's House (play), 1949; A Decent Birth, A Happy Funeral (play), 1949; The Twin Adventures, 1950, A Novel and a Diary (US only); The Assyrian (short stories), 1950; Rock Wagram (novel), 1951; Tracy's Tiger (novel), 1952; The Laughing Matter (novel), 1953; The Bicycle Rider in Beverly Hills (memoir), 1952; Mama I Love You, 1957; The Whole Voyald (short stories), 1957; Papa You're Crazy, 1958; The Cave Dwellers (play), 1959; Sam, the Highest Jumper of Them All (play, written and directed for Theatre Workshop), 1960; Talking To You (one act play, Duke of York's), 1962; Short Drive, Sweet Chariot (autobiographical), 1964; One Day in the Afternoon of the World (novel), 1965; Not Dying, 1966; (with A. Rothstein) Look At Us, 1967; I Used to Believe I Had Forever, Now I'm Not So Sure (Short Stories), 1968; Letters from 74 Rue Taitbout, or Don't Go, But If You Must, Say Hello to Everybody, 1969. *Recreations:* everything. *Address:* 2729 W Griffith Way, Fresno, California, USA.

**SARRAUTE, Nathalie;** writer; *b* Ivanowo, Russia, 18 July 1902; *d* of Ilya Tcherniak and Pauline Chatounowski; *m* 1925, Raymond Sarraute; three *d*. *Educ:* Sorbonne; Ecole de Droit de Paris; Oxford. *Publications:* Tropismes, 1939 (trans. Tropisms, 1964); Portrait d'un inconnu, 1948 (Portrait of a Man Unknown, 1959); Martereau, 1953 (trans. 1964); L'Ere du soupçon, 1956 (The Age of Suspicion, 1964); Le Planétarium, 1959 (The Planetarium, 1962); Les Fruits d'or, 1963 (The Golden Fruits, 1965); Entre la vie et la mort, 1968 (Between Life and Death, 1969); (*plays*): Le Silence, Le Mensonge, 1967 (Silence, and The Lie, 1969); Isma, 1970. *Address:* 12 Avenue Pierre I de Serbie, Paris 16e, France. *T:* Kléber 93-83.

**SARSFIELD-HALL, Edwin Geoffrey,** CMG 1933; Order of the Nile 3rd class (Comdr); FRGS; DL; JP; *b* 24 April 1886; *s* of Edwin Hall, JP, DL, Blackrock, Co. Cork and Ada Georgina Shekleton; took additional family surname of Sarsfield by Deed Poll, 1908; *m* Ethel Robin, OBE, *er d* of Edward Clowes, Betchworth, Surrey; (one *s* killed on active service, 1944) one *d*. *Educ:* Clifton College; Dublin University; Cambridge University. MA, LLB, BL; Barrister, Irish Bar; joined Sudan Political Service, 1908; Settlement Officer and District Judge, Legal Dept, 1913-16; Assistant Political and Intelligence Officer, Darfur Expedition, 1916, rank of Kaimakam (Lt-Col) in Egyptian Army (despatches twice, Order of the Nile); temp. duty with Egyptian Expeditionary Force, Palestine, 1917; Dist Comr, Darfur Province, 1917-21; Deputy Governor, Kordofan Province, 1921; Governor, 1926; Governor, Khartoum Province, 1929-36; retired, 1936; District Commissioner for Special Area of West Cumberland, 1937-38. Director Workington Iron & Steel Co., 1938-51; Director West Cumberland Industrial Development Co., 1937-57. A Dep. Chm., Cumberland Quarter Sessions, 1956-61. Hon. Major Border Regiment. DL Cumberland, 1955. *Recreations:* golf, shooting, painting. *Address:* Skiddaw Lodge, Keswick, Cumberland. *Clubs:* Naval and Military; Sudan (Khartoum).

**SARTRE, Jean-Paul;** Author; *b* Paris, 5 June 1905. *Educ:* Paris; La Rochelle. Degree in Philosophy, 1930. Professor at Havre, French Institute at Berlin, Lycée Henry IV at Paris. Wrote philosophical works first, then novels and plays. Mobilised, 1939, served in Army, 1939-40, prisoner of war, 1940-41, returned from Germany and took part in resistance movement, 1941-44. Prof. of philosophy until 1944 when resigned to become founder and editor of Les Temps Modernes. Refused Nobel Prize for Literature, 1964 (saying that he had always refused to accept all official distinctions). *Publications:* Imaginaire, 1936; Imagination, 1937; Nausée, 1937; le Mur, 1938; les Mouches, Huis-Clos, l'Être et le Néant, 1943; les Chemins de la liberté, 1944-45; Morts sans sépulture, La Putain respectueuse, 1946; The Age of Reason, 1947; Reprieve, 1947; Le Diable et le Bon Dieu, 1948; Iron in the Soul, 1950; The Psychology of Imagination, 1951; Les Mains sâles, 1952; Œuvres Complètes, 1952; Nekrassov, 1953 (Edinburgh Fest., 1957); Les Sequestrés d'Altona, 1959; Critique de la Raison dialectique, 1961; Words (memoirs), 1964; Baudelaire, 1964; Saint Genet, Actor and Martyr, 1964 (Eng. trans. by B. Frechtman); Situations, 1965 (trans. B. Eisler); Literary and Philosophical Essays, 1968; The Communists and Peace, 1969; The Spectre of Stalin, 1969, etc. *Address:* c/o Hamish Hamilton Ltd, 90 Great Russell Street, WC1.

**SARUM, Archdeacon of;** *see* Wingfield Digby, Ven. S. B.

**SASKATCHEWAN, Bishop of,** since 1960; **Rt. Rev. William Henry Howes Crump;** *b* London, Ontario, Canada, 13 March 1903; *m* 1932, Betty Margaret Dean Thomas; one *s* one *d*. *Educ:* London, Ontario; University of Western Ontario; Huron College; Trinity College, Toronto. Ordained deacon, 1926; Curate, Wawanesa, Manitoba, 1926; Priest, 1927. Rector: Glenboro, Manitoba, 1927; Holland, Manitoba, 1931; Boissevain, Manitoba, 1933; St Aidan's, Winnipeg, 1933-44; Christ Church, Calgary, 1944-60. Canon of St Paul, Diocese of Calgary, 1949. *Address:* 675 20th Street West, Prince Albert, Sask, Canada.

**SASKATOON, Bishop of,** since 1950; **Rt. Rev. Stanley Charles Steer;** *s* of S. E. and E. G. Steer; *m* 1936, Marjorie Slater. *Educ:* Guildford Gram. Sch.; Univ. of Saskatchewan (BA), Oxford Univ. (MA). Hon. DD: Wycliffe Coll., Toronto, 1947, Emmanuel Coll., Saskatoon, 1952; St Chad's Coll., Regina, 1964. Missionary at Vanderhoof, BC, 1929; Chaplain, St Mark's Church, Alexandria, 1931; Chaplain, University Coll., Oxford, 1932-33; St John's Hall, Univ. of London: Tutor, 1933; Vice-Principal, 1936. Chaplain, The Mercers' Company, City of London, 1937; Principal, Emmanuel Coll., Saskatoon, 1941; Hon. Canon of St John's Cathedral, Saskatoon, and CF (R of O), 1943. *Recreation:* tennis. *Address:* 1104 Elliott Street, Saskatoon, Sask, Canada. *T:* 653-0890.

**SATTERLY, Air Vice-Marshal Harold Vivian,** CB 1949; CBE 1943; DFC 1941; RAF retired; Director, Grampian Travel Ltd; *b* 24 May 1907; *s* of late Ernest Satterly, Exmouth, Devon; *m* 1935, Mary Gavin, *d* of late Col A. L. Lindesay, St Andrews, Fife; one *s* two *d*. *Educ:* Hele's School, Exeter; Exmouth; RAF Halton, Air Officer Comdg, 205 Group, Middle East Air Forces, 1952-54; ACAS (Operational Requirements), Air Ministry, 1954-57; Air Officer Commanding 64 (Northern) Group, 1957-59. Air Commodore, 1948; Air Vice-Marshal, 1952. Retired, 1959. *Recreations:* various. *Address:* Tullich, Forest Lane, Hightown Hill, Ringwood, Hants. *T:* Ringwood 4756. *Club:* Royal Air Force.

**SATTERTHWAITE, Rt. Rev. John Richard;** *see* Fulham, Suffragan Bishop of.

**SAUDI ARABIA, HM the King of; HM Malik Faisal bin Abdul Aziz al Saud,** Hon. GBE, 1932; Hon. KCMG, 1926; Viceroy of the Hejaz since 1926; *b* 1905; 2nd *s* of Abdul Aziz al Saud, King of Saudi Arabia, and *b* of King Ibn Sa'ud. Has made many visits to Europe and the US, notably in 1939 and 1946 when he represented Saudi Arabia at London discussions on Palestine. Represented Saudi Arabia at San Francisco Conf., 1945, and has subsequently attended meetings of UN Gen. Assembly in New York. On the death of his father and accession of his elder brother, he was declared Crown Prince, 1953; proclaimed King, Nov. 1964. Prime Minister and Minister of Foreign Affairs, 1953-60; was granted full control of finances and internal and external affairs also of Armed Forces of Saudi Arabia by a decree of his brother, 24 March 1958, until Dec. 1960. *Address:* Riyadh, Saudi Arabia.

**SAUGMAN, Christian Ditlev Trappaud,** Comdr of the Order of Dannebrog, 1961 (Kt 1948, 1st class, 1955); Hon. KBE 1955 (Hon. CBE 1948); Managing Director; barrister; Member of board of British Import Union, Copenhagen, since 1934 (President, 1945-60); *b* 16 June 1895; *s* of late Fritz Saugman and Anna Adele (*née* Hansen); *m* 1920, Vera Schmidt; one *s*. *Educ:* Herlufsholm public sch.; Univ. of Copenhagen, Bachelor of law (Copenhagen), 1918. Junior partner W. Schmidt, 1918, sole proprietor, 1921; established associated export firms, London, 1933, New York, 1936. Delegate of Danish wholesale assoc., 1930, Vice-chm., 1938-40. council member, 1947, Vice-chm., of council, 1949, Pres., 1960-65. Mem., Cttee of the Stock Exchange; Pres. British Exhibn of Copenhagen, 1948 and 1955. Chm. Danish assoc. of race-horse breeders until 1950; Member: state export cttee; Danish cttee of internat. chamber of commerce, 1951; council of the port of Copenhagen; President of Council, Freeport of Copenhagen; President, Kraks Foundation (Danish Who is Who); Member of Council Otto Mønsteds Company; several government committees. FRSA 1962. *Recreations:* farming and riding. *Address:* Sælvgade 22, Copenhagen. *Club:* Royal Danish Automobile.

**SAUL, Bazil Sylvester W.;** *see* Wingate-Saul.

**SAUMAREZ,** family name of **Baron de Saumarez.**

**SAUNDBY, Air Marshal Sir Robert Henry Magnus Spencer,** KCB 1956 (CB 1942); KBE, *cr* 1944; MC 1917; DFC 1926; AFC 1919; FRES 1950; DL; *b* 26 April 1896; *s* of late Robert Saundby, MD, LLD, FRCP, and Mary Edith Spencer; *m* Joyce Mary Rees-Webbe; one *s* two *d*. *Educ:* King Edward's Sch., Birmingham. Served European War of 1914-18; 2nd Lt Royal Warwickshire Regt, 1914; transf. to Royal Flying Corps, 1915; France and Flanders, 1916-17 (MC; wounded, despatches; AFC); served in Iraq, Aden, and Egypt, 1922-26 (DFC); RAF Staff College Course, 1928; Air Staff, Wessex Bombing Area HQ, 1929-30; Air Staff, Air Ministry, 1931-32; idc Course, 1933; Instructor at RAF Staff College, 1934-36; Deputy Director of Operations, Air Ministry, 1937; Director of Operational requirements, Air Ministry, 1938-39; Asst Chief of Air Staff (T), 1940; Senior Air Staff Officer, Bomber Comd, 1941-42; Dep. AOC-in-C, Bomber Comd, RAF, 1943-45 (despatches thrice); retd, 1946; Life Vice-Pres., RAF Assoc.; Chairman Nat. Council, 1945-58; President, Metropolitan Area, British Legion, 1947-62, Patron, 1962; Chairman, Berkshire T and AFA, 1956-61; Vice-Chm. Council T and AF Assocs, 1947-60; Mem., Minister of Pensions' Central Adv. Cttee, 1948-66; Chm., Exec. Cttee, Central Council for the Care of the Disabled, 1953-55; Member Council, Air League of British Empire, 1949-62, Vice-Pres., 1962; Pres., Berkshire, Buckinghamshire, and Oxfordshire Naturalists' Trust; Officer, Legion of Honour, France, 1945; Commander, Legion of Merit, USA, 1946; Grand Officer, Order of Leopold II (Belgium) and Belgian Croix de Guerre with Palm, 1947. DL County of Berkshire, 1960. *Publications:* Flying Colours, 1918; edited the Book of the Piscatorial Society, 1836-1936, 1936; A Fly-Rod on Many Waters, 1961; Air Bombardment, the Story of its Development, 1961; numerous articles in newspapers and journals. *Recreations:* fly-fishing and entomology. *Address:* Oxleas, Burghclere, near Newbury, Berkshire. *T:* Burghclere 389. *Clubs:* Royal Air Forces, Flyfishers', Pathfinders'.

**SAUNDERS, Rt. Rev. Charles John Godfrey;** retired; *b* 15 Feb. 1888; *s* of Rev. S. T. H. Saunders, Rector of St Helen's, Bishopsgate, and M. F. Ll. Saunders; *m* 1916, Mildred Robinson, *d* of Louis Hebblethwaite, Hull; one *s* two *d*. *Educ:* Merchant Taylors' School; St John's College, Oxford (Scholar); Cuddesdon College. Pusey and Ellerton Schol. 1907; BA (3rd Cl. Th. Hon.) and Hall Houghton Septuagint (Jun.) Prize, 1909; MA 1916. Deacon, 1911; Priest, 1912, Lucknow; SPG

Cawnpore, 1911-16; Chaplain, Roorkee, 1917; Cawnpore, 1918; Chakrata, 1921; Staff Chaplain, Army Headquarters, India, 1921-25; Metropolitan's Chaplain, Calcutta, 1925-28; Bishop of Lucknow, 1928-38; Rector of Uckfield, 1938-42; Barcombe, 1942-47; Vicar of West Lavington, Midhurst, 1947-53; Assistant Bishop Diocese of Chichester, 1939-53; Canon of Middleton in Chichester Cathedral, 1943-53; on staff of St Matthew's Church, Moorfields, Bristol, as Assistant to Chaplain of Bristol Royal Infirmary, Oct. 1953-Dec. 1958; Chaplain to the Lord Mayor of Bristol, 1961-65. Grand Chaplain of England, 1940. *Recreations:* Oxford University swimming team, 1909; running, tennis. *Address:* 2 Grange Road, Clifton, Bristol BS8 4EA.

**SAUNDERS, Christopher Thomas,** CMG 1953; Economist, at UN's Economic Commission for Europe, since 1965; *b* 5 Nov. 1907; *s* of Thomas Beckenn Avening Saunders, clergyman, and Mary Theodora Slater; *m* 1947, Cornelia Jacomijntje Gielstra; one *s*. *Educ:* Craig School, Windermere; St Edward's School; Christ Church, Oxford. BA 1929; MA 1932; University of Liverpool: Social Survey of Merseyside, 1930-33; University of Manchester: Economic Reseach Dept, 1933-35; Joint Committee of Cotton Trade Organisations, Manchester, 1935-40; Cotton Control, 1940-44; Combined Production and Resources Board, Washington, 1944-45; Min. of Labour, 1945-47; Central Statistical Office, 1947-57; Dir, Nat. Inst. of Econ. and Social Research, 1957-64. *Publications:* Red Oxford (with M. P. Ashley), 1929; Social Survey of Merseyside (collaborated in), 1934; Seasonal Variations in Employment, 1936. Articles in Economic Jl, Jl of Roy. Statistical Soc., The Manchester School. *Recreations:* walking and other forms of travel; painting. *Address:* c/o Palais des Nations, Geneva, Switzerland. *Club:* Reform.

**SAUNDERS, Henry George Boulton;** Organist and Choirmaster to the Hon. Society of Benchers at Gray's Inn; Organist and Master of the Choir to the Household Division; General Inspector of Education, Surrey County Council, from 1962; *b* Devonport, Feb. 1914; *m* 1943, Kathleen Mary, *d* of Major S. Brandle, MC, London; one *s* two *d*. *Educ:* Grammar Sch., Kilburn; Royal Acad. of Music (Thomas Threlfall Organ Scholar). DMus Durham; BMus Durham and London; Grad. Royal Schs of Music, London, 1935; FRCO (La Fontaine prize, 1935); FRAM; Worshipful Company of Musicians Silver Medal, 1937; Organist and Choirmaster at St Saviour's, Hampstead, 1934-35; Music Master Trinity County Sch., Wood Green, 1935-46; Inspector of Secondary Schs, City of Leicester, 1946-62. *Publication:* Read and Sing, 1959. *Recreations:* gardening, riding. *Address:* Principal's Lodge, St Margaret's Drive, Twickenham, Mddx. *T:* 01-892 2009; Grays, 9 Star Hill Drive, Churt, Surrey. *T:* Headley Down 2458.

**SAUNDERS, Air Chief Marshal Sir Hugh (William Lumsden),** GCB 1953 (KCB 1950; CB 1943); KBE 1945 (CBE 1941); MC, DFC; MM; Chairman, HM Forces Savings Committee, since 1956; *b* 1894; *s* of Frederick William Saunders, Transvaal; *m* 1923, Phyllis Margaret, *d* of Major P. W. Mabbett, Bidborough, Kent; one *s* (and one *s* decd). *Educ:* Marist Brothers' School, Johannesburg. Served European War, 1914-19, with Witwatersrand Rifles and South African Horse; transf. RFC 1917; Group Capt. 1939; Air Commodore, 1941; temp. Air Vice-Marshal, 1942; Air Marshal, 1947; Air Chief Marshal, 1950; Chief of Air Staff, New Zealand, 1939-41; AOC, No. 11 Group, Fighter Command, 1942-44; Director-General of Postings, Air Ministry, 1944-45; Air Marshal Commanding RAF Burma, 1945-46; AOC-in-C, Bomber Command, 1947; Air Council Member for Personnel, 1947-49; Inspector-General of the RAF, 1949-50; Commander-in-Chief Air Forces Western Europe, Jan.-April 1951. Air Deputy to Supreme Allied Commander Europe, 1951-53; Special Air Adviser to Royal Danish Air Force, 1954-56; Chief Co-ordinator of Anglo-American hospitality activities in UK, 1956-59. A Vice-Chm., Nat. Savings Cttee, 1956-70. Order of Polonia Restituta, 2nd Class (Poland); Commander Order of Merit (US); Officier Légion d'Honneur (France); Grand Cross of Dannebrog (Denmark). *Address:* c/o Barclays Bank, DCO, Goodenough House, 33 Old Broad Street, EC2. *Club:* Royal Air Force.

**SAUNDERS, John Anthony Holt,** CBE 1970; DSO 1945; MC 1944; JP; Chairman, The Hongkong and Shanghai Banking Corporation, since 1964; *b* 29 July 1917; *s* of late E. B. Saunders; *m* 1942, Enid Mary Durant Cassidy; two *d*. *Educ:* Bromsgrove. Joined The Hongkong and Shanghai Banking Corp., 1937. Served War of 1939-45, in British Army, 1940-45 (despatches, MC, DSO): East Surrey Regt in N Africa, Sicily and Italy, and commanded 2nd Bn Lancashire Fusiliers at Argenta Gap, Italy, 1945. Rejoined The Hongkong and Shanghai Banking Corp., 1945, and served in Singapore and Hong Kong. Chm., Hongkong and Shanghai Banking Corp. of California, 1962; Director, Mercantile Credits Ltd, Sydney, 1964; Chairman, Mercantile Bank, 1966-. MEC, Hong Kong Govt; Chm. of Stewards, Royal Hong Kong Jockey Club; Treas., Univ. of Hong Kong. Hon. DSocSc (Hong Kong) 1969. Comdr, Order of Prince Henry the Navigator (Portugal), 1966. *Recreations:* golf, sailing. *Address:* 37 Plantation Road, Hong Kong. *T:* 96144; The Dairy House, Maresfield, Sussex. *Clubs:* MCC, Oriental; Royal Hong Kong Golf.

**SAUNDERS, Sir Owen (Alfred),** Kt 1965; FRS 1958; MA, DSc; Hon. MIMechE; FInstP; FInstF; FRAeS; Hon. FCGI; Life Member of ASME; Emeritus Professor of Mechanical Engineering, University of London, Imperial College (Professor, 1946; Head of Department, 1946-65; Pro-Rector, 1964-67, Acting Rector, 1966-67); Vice-Chancellor, University of London, 1967-69; *b* 24 September 1904; *s* of Alfred George Saunders and Margaret Ellen Jones, *m* 1935, Marion Isabel McKechney; one *s* two *d*., *Educ:* Emanuel School; Birkbeck College, London; Trinity College, Cambridge (Senior Scholar). Scientific Officer, Dept of Scientific and Industrial Research, 1926; Lecturer in Applied Mathematical Physics, Imperial College, 1932; Clothworkers' Reader in Applied Thermodynamics, Univ. of London, 1937; on loan to Directorate of Turbine Engines, MAP, 1942-45. Dean, City and Guilds Coll., 1955-64. Past Pres., Institution of Mechanical Engineers. Chairman: British Flame Research Cttee; Naval Engineering Research and Development Cttee; Nuclear Safety Advisory Cttee, 1966-. Director, International Research and Development Ltd. *Publications:* The Calculation of Heat Transmission, 1932; An Introduction to Heat Transfer, 1950; various scientific and technical papers in Proceedings of Royal Society, Phil. Mag., Physical Society, Engineering, and the Institutions. *Recreations:* music, golf. *Address:* Oakbank, Sea Lane, Middleton, Sussex. *T:* Middleton 2966. *Club:* Athenæum.

**SAUNDERS-DAVIES, Rt. Rev. David Henry;** *b* 1894; *o s* of Rev. James Davies and Mary Saunders Davies, Liverpool; *m* 1920, Catherine, *d* of John and Ellen Livingstone Price; one *s* one *d*. *Educ:* Liverpool College; Christ College, Brecon; RMC Sandhurst; Queens' College, Cambridge. Ryle Prize, 1920; BA 1920; MA 1923. Deacon, 1921, Priest, 1922. Curate of St John, Birkenhead, 1921-24; of St John, Reading, 1925-26; licensed to officiate in Diocese of Chester, 1926-28; Vicar of Hollingworth, 1928-31; Rector of Mobberley, 1931-45; Surrogate, 1931; Rural Dean of Knutsford, 1937-42; served War of 1939-45: Chaplain RAFVR, 1940-41; Assistant Chaplain-in-Chief, RAF, Middle East, 1942-45 (despatches); Hon. Canon of Chester, 1945-; Proctor in Convocation, 1945-51; Rector of Malpas, 1945-46; Rural Dean of Stockport, 1948-51; Rector of Stockport, 1946-55; Suffragan Bishop of Stockport, 1951-65; Hon. Asst Bishop of Worcester, 1965-68. Licence, Diocese of Rochester, 1968. *Recreation:* fishing. *Address:* 41 Dornden Drive, Langton Green, Tunbridge Wells, Kent. *T:* Langton 2547.

**SAUNDERS-JACOBS, Brig. John Conrad,** CBE 1945; DSO 1944; Indian Army, retired; *b* 12 Nov. 1900; *s* of George Saunders-Jacobs; *m* 1930, Sylvia, *e d* of Col H. Drury Shaw, DSO; one *d*. *Educ:* University College, London; RMC, Sandhurst. Joined Royal Garhwal Rifles in India, 1921; Co. comd, RMC, Sandhurst, 1937-38; Bt Major, 1938; War of 1939-45: GSO1, NWF, India, 1941-42; bn, bde and actg div. comdr, Middle East, Italy and Greece, 1942-46. Staff Coll., Quetta, 1934-35; Imperial Defence Coll., London, 1946; Asst Comdt, Staff Coll., Quetta, 1947; GHQ India, Dir of Mil. Operations, Delhi, 1947; retired, 1948. UK delegate to UN Special Cttee on the Balkans, 1948; Official mil. historian, Cabinet Office, 1949-50; export agent, London, 1950-53; RO II, War Office, 1954; civil servant, 1958. *Recreations:* walking, gardening, current affairs. *Address:* Firlands, West Chiltington, Pulborough, Sussex. *T:* West Chiltington 3197.

**SAVA, George; (George Alexis Milkomanovich Milkomane);** Author and Consulting Surgeon; *b* 15 Oct. 1903; *s* of Col Ivan Alexandrovitch and Countess Maria Ignatiev; *nephew* of Prince Alexander Milkomanovich Milkomane; *m* 1939, Jannette Hollingdale; two *s* two *d*. *Educ:* Public Schools in Bulgaria and Russia. Entered Russian Imperial Naval Academy in 1913; after the Revolution studied in various medical schools, Univ. of Paris, Florence, Rome, Munich, Berlin and Bonn; domiciled in this country since 1932; further medical education at Manchester, Glasgow and Edinburgh; naturalised British subject in 1938; Research scholarships in medicine and surgery, University of Rome, Libero Docente (Professorship) of Univ. of Rome, 1954. Grand Chev. of the Crown of Bulgaria; Commendatore dell' Ordine al Merito Della Repubblica Italiana, 1961. *Publications: autobiog. medical:* The Healing Knife, 1937; Beauty from the Surgeon's Knife, 1938; A Surgeon's Destiny, 1939; Donkey's Serenade, 1940; Twice the Clock Round, 1941; A Ring at the Door, 1941; Surgeon's Symphony, 1944; The Knife Heals Again, 1948; The Way of a Surgeon, 1949; Strange Cases, 1950; A Doctor's Odyssey, 1951; Patients' Progress, 1952; A Surgeon Remembers, 1953; Surgeon Under Capricorn, 1954; The Lure of Surgery, 1955; A Surgeon at Large, 1957; All this and Surgery too, 1958; Appointments in Rome, 1963; A Surgeon in New Zealand, 1964; A Surgeon in Cyprus, 1965; A Surgeon in Australia, 1966; The Gates of Heaven are Narrow, 1968; *political and historical books:* Russia Triumphant, 1944; A Tale of Ten Cities, 1944; They Stayed in London, 1943; Valley of Forgotten People, 1942; The Chetniks, 1943; Rasputin Speaks, 1941; School for War, 1943; War Without Guns, 1944; *novels:* Land Fit for Heroes, 1945; Link of Two Hearts, 1945; Gissy, 1946; Call it Life, 1946; Alias Doctor Holtzman, 1968. *Recreations:* tennis, golf, riding, aviation. *Address:* 9 Pembridge Place, W2. *Club:* PEN.

**SAVAGE, Albert Walter,** CMG 1954; Director-General (retired), Colonial Civil Aviation Service; *b* 12 June 1898; *s* of William Albert Savage, Wheathampstead, Herts; *m* 1923, Lilian Marie Gertrude Storch; one *s* one *d*. *Educ:* Northern Polytechnic, Northampton Institute and Sheffield University. Apprentice, Grahame White Flying School, 1914-16. Served European War, 1914-18, RFC, 1916 to end of war. Aeronautical Inspection Directorate, Air Ministry, UK 1921-34, India, 1934-36; seconded to Egyptian Govt as Chief Technical Inspector, Civil Aviation Dept, Cairo, 1936-46; Colonial Civil Aviation Service, 1946-; Director of Civil Aviation, W Africa, 1946-49; Director-General of Civil Aviation, Malaya/Borneo territories, 1949-54; Civil Aviation Adviser, Government of Jordan, 1954-55; Director of Civil Aviation, Leeward and Windward Islands, 1956-60. Director of Civil Aviation, Sierra Leone, 1961-62. *Recreations:* golf, tennis and squash. *Address:* 6 Whitecroft Way, Beckenham, Kent. *T:* 01-650 2027. *Club:* Royal Aero.

**SAVAGE, Sir Alfred William Lungley,** KCMG 1951 (CMG 1948); Chairman, West African Currency Board, 1956-69; *b* 5 May 1903; *y s* of late Charles Savage, Gillingham, Kent; *m* 1931, Doreen, 2nd *d* of James Hopwood, OBE, Bulawayo, Rhodesia; one *s* one *d*. *Educ:* Owens School, London. Entered Home Civil Service, 1920; Asst Treasurer, Govt of N Rhodesia, 1928; Dep. Treas., Govt of Fiji, 1935; Dep. Treas., 1939, Dep. Financial Sec., 1940, Under-Sec., 1945, Govt of Palestine; Dep. Financial Sec., Govt of Nigeria, 1946; Financial Sec., 1948; Governor and C-in-C, Barbados, 1949-53; British Guiana, 1953-55; Crown Agent for Overseas Governments, 1955-63. *Address:* 10 Tay Street, Newport on Tay, Fife.

**SAVAGE, Sir (Edward) Graham,** Kt, *cr* 1947; CB 1935; *b* 31 Aug. 1886; *s* of Edward Graham Savage and Mary Matilda Dewey; *m* 1911; two *s* one *d*. *Educ:* Upper Sheringham School; King Edward VI Middle School, Norwich; Downing College, Cambridge. Tutor Bede College, Durham; Assistant Master, St Andrew's College, Toronto; Tewfikieh School, Cairo; Lecturer, Khedivial Training College, Egypt; served R W Kent Regt Gallipoli and France, 1914-19; Assistant Master, Eton College; District Inspector, Board of Education, 1919-27; Staff Inspector for Science, 1927; Divisional Inspector NW Division, 1931-32; Chief Inspector, of Technical Schools and Colleges, 1932; Senior Chief Inspector, 1933-40. Education Officer to the LCC, 1940-51, retired. Chm. League of the Empire, 1947-62; Chm. Simplified Spelling Society, 1949; President Science Masters' Assoc., 1952-53, Chief Assessor to Industrial Fund for Advancement of Science Teaching in Schools, 1956; Chm., Board of Building Education, 1956-66; Mem. Council and Exec. Cttee, City and Guilds of London Institute, 1963 (Vice-Chairman, 1967, Vice-President, 1967). Hon. Fellow, Inst. of Builders, 1966. *Publication:* The Planning and Equipment of School Science Blocks, 1964. *Recreations:* walking, gardening. *Address:* Barbary, Maresfield Park, Uckfield, Sussex. *T:* Uckfield 2586.

**SAVAGE, Rt. Rev. Gordon David,** MA; *b* 14 April 1915; *s* of Augustus Johnson Savage and Louisa Hannah Atkinson; *m* 1938, Eva Louise, *y d* of H. J. Jessen, Copenhagen; one *s* two *d*. *Educ:* Reading Sch.; Tyndale Hall, Bristol; St Catherine's, Oxford. MA Oxon, 1949. Was a Librarian before ordination, 1932-37; deacon, 1940, priest, 1941; Chaplain, Lecturer and Tutor, Tyndale Hall, Bristol, 1940-44; General Secretary Church Society, London, 1945-52; Curate-in-Charge of the City Church, Oxford, 1948-52; Proctor in Convocation, 1951-61; Vicar of Marston, Oxford, 1952-57; Archdeacon of Buckingham and Vicar of Whitchurch, Bucks, 1957-61; Suffragan Bishop of Buckingham, 1960-64; Bishop of Southwell, 1964-70. *Address:* c/o Barclays Bank Ltd, High Street, Oxford.

**SAVAGE, Sir Graham;** *see* Savage, Sir E. G.

**SAVARESE, Signora Fernando;** *see* Elvin, Violetta.

**SAVERNAKE, Viscount; Michael Sydney Cedric Brudenell-Bruce;** Lt RHG, 1946; Member London Stock Exchange since 1954; *b* 31 March 1926; *e s* of 7th Marquess of Ailesbury, *qv*; *m* 1st, 1952, Edwina Sylvia de Winton (from whom he obtained a divorce, 1961), *yr d* of Lt-Col Sir (Ernest) Edward de Winton Wills, 4th Bt, *qv*; one *s* two *d*; 2nd, 1963, Juliet Adrienne, *d* of late Hilary Lethbridge Kingsford and of Mrs Latham Hobrow, Hove; two *d*. *Educ:* Eton. *Heir:* *s* Hon. David Michael James Brudenell-Bruce, *b* 12 Nov. 1952. *Address:* Sturmy House, Savernake Forest, Marlborough, Wilts. *T:* Burbage (Wilts) 479. *Club:* Carlton.

**SAVILE,** family name of **Earl of Mexborough.**

**SAVILE,** 3rd Baron, *cr* 1888; **George Halifax Lumley-Savile;** DL; JP; *b* 24 Jan. 1919; *s* of 2nd Baron and Esme Grace Virginia (*d* 1958), *d* of J. Wolton; *S* father, 1931. *Educ:* Eton. Served in 1939-45 War in Duke of Wellington's Regiment, and attached Lincolnshire Regiment during the Burma Campaigns. DL W Riding, Yorks, 1954. Is Patron of two livings. Owns about 18,000 acres. JP Borough of Dewsbury, 1955. SBStJ. *Recreations:* music and shooting. *Heir:* *b* Hon. Henry Leoline Thornhill Lumley-Savile [*b* 2 Oct. 1923; *m* 1st, 1946, Presiley June (marriage dissolved, 1951), *o d* of Major G. H. E. Inchbald, Halebourne House, Chobham, Surrey; one *s*; 2nd, 1961, Caroline Jeffie (*d* 1970), *o d* of Peter Clive, California, USA, and Elizabeth Clive, 58 Queens' Gate, SW7. Served War of 1939-45, in Grenadier Guards, Italy (wounded)]. *Address:* Gryce Hall, Shelley, Huddersfield. *T:* Kirkburton 2774; Walshaw, Hebden Bridge, Yorks. *T:* Hebden Bridge 2275. *Club:* St James'.

**SAVILL, David Malcolm,** QC 1969; *b* 18 Sept. 1930; *s* of Lionel and Lisbeth Savill, Selsfield, East Grinstead; *m* 1955, Mary Arnott (*née* Eadie); one *s* two *d*. *Educ:* Marlborough Coll.; Clare Coll., Cambridge. 2nd Lieut Grenadier Guards, 1949-50. BA (Hons) Cambridge, 1953. Called to the Bar, Middle Temple, 1954. *Recreations:* cricket, golf, gardening. *Address:* The Priory, Knaresborough, Yorks. *T:* Knaresborough 2309. *Clubs:* Leeds (Leeds); County (Durham).

**SAVILL, Sir Eric (Humphrey),** KCVO, *cr* 1955 (CVO 1950; MVO 1938); CBE 1946; MC, MA Cantab, FRICS; Director of the Gardens, Windsor Great Park (Deputy Ranger of Windsor Great Park, 1937-59; Director of Forestry and of Gardens for Crown Estate until retired, January 1963); *b* 20 October 1895; *s* of late Sir Edwin Savill. *Educ:* Malvern Coll.; Magdalene Coll., Cambridge. At outbreak of European War joined Univ. and Public School Corps as a Private; Commissioned to Devonshire Regt 1915, Captain 1916; served in France with 8th and 2nd Bns (wounded); joined firm of Alfred Savill & Sons, chartered Surveyors, 1920; Partner, 1926. Mem. Bd Management: Hosp. for Sick Children, Gt Ormond St, 1926-42; King Edward VII Hosp., Windsor, 1933-46; Mem. Min. of Transport Adv. Cttee on Landscape Treatment of Trunk Roads, 1954-69 (Chm., 1962-69). Gold Veitch Memorial Medal, The Royal Horticultural Society, 1963; Gold Medal, The Royal Forestry Soc. of England, Wales and Northern Ireland, 1963. *Recreations:* gardening, shooting, fishing. *Address:* The Garden House, The Great Park, Windsor. *T:* Egham 4617.

**SAVILL, Colonel Kenneth Edward,** DSO 1945; DL; *b* 8 August 1906; *s* of Walter Henry Savill and May Marriott; *m* 1935, Jacqueline Salusbury Hughes; two *d* (and one *d* decd). *Educ:* Winchester College; RMC Sandhurst. 2nd Lieut, 12th Royal Lancers, 1926; Capt., King's Dragoon Guards, 1936; served War of 1939-45, France, 1939-40; N Africa and Italy, 1943-45; comd Queen's Bays, 1947-50; Col 1950; retd 1954. A Gentleman-at-Arms, HM Bodyguard, 1955-. CC Hampshire, 1961-; High Sheriff of Hampshire, 1961; DL Hampshire, 1965. Col, 1st The Queen's Dragoon Guards, 1964-68. *Recreations:* hunting, shooting. *Address:* Chilton Manor, Alresford, Hants. *T:* Preston Candover 246. *Clubs:* Cavalry; Hampshire (Winchester).

**SAVILLE, (Leonard) Malcolm;** Author; Editor of General Books, George Newnes Ltd and C. Arthur Pearson Ltd, 1957-66; *b* 21 February 1901; *s* of Ernest Vivian Saville and Fanny Ethel Hayes; *m* 1926, Dorothy May McCoy; two *s* two *d*. *Educ:* Private Schools. Has written original stories for Children's Film Foundation; seven stories adapted as serials for BBC. *Publications:* books for children (as Malcolm Saville): King of Kings; Jane's Country Year; Adventure of the Lifeboat Service; Country Scrapbook for Boys and Girls; Open Air Scrapbook for Boys and Girls; Seaside Scrapbook for Boys and Girls; Coronation Gift Book; Mystery at Witchend; Seven White Gates; The Gay Dolphin Adventure; The Secret of Grey Walls; Lone Pine Five; The Elusive Grasshopper; The Neglected Mountain; Saucers Over the Moor; Wings Over Witchend; Lone Pine London; The Secret of the Gorge; Mystery Mine; Sea Witch Comes Home; Not Scarlet but Gold; Treasure at Amorys; Man with Three Fingers; Rye Royal; Strangers at Witchend; All Summer Through; Christmas at Nettleford; Spring Comes to Nettleford; The Secret of Buzzard Scar; Redshank's Warning; Two Fair Plaits; The Sign of the Alpine Rose; The Luck of Sallowby; Strangers at Snowfell; The Ambermere Treasure; The Master of Maryknoll; The Buckinghams at Ravenswyke; The Long Passage; A Palace for the Buckinghams; Trouble at Townsend; The Riddle of the Painted Box; The Flying Fish Adventure; The Secret of the Hidden Pool; Young Johnnie Bimbo; The Fourth Key; Susan, Bill and the Wolfdog; Susan, Bill and the Ivy-clad Oak; Susan, Bill and the Vanishing Boy; Susan, Bill and the Golden Clock; Susan, Bill and the Dark Stranger; Susan, Bill and the Saucy Kate; Susan, Bill and the Brightstar Circus; Susan, Bill and the Pirates Bold; Treasure at the Mill; Four and Twenty

Blackbirds (repr. as The Secret of Galleybird Pit); The Thin Grey Man; Malcolm Saville's Country Book; Malcolm Saville's Seaside Book; Three Towers in Tuscany; The Purple Valley; Dark Danger; White Fire; Power of Three; The Dagger and the Flame; Come to London; Strange Story; Come to Devon; Come to Cornwall; Come to Somerset; See How It Grows; Good Dog Dandy. *Recreations:* walking, watching cricket, reading. *Address:* Little Toft, 28 Hartfield Rd, Seaford, Sussex. *T:* Seaford 4349. *Club:* Savage.

**SAVILLE, Malcolm;** *see* Saville, Leonard Malcolm.

**SAVIN, Lewis Herbert,** MD, MS, London (University Medal in Ophthalmology), MRCP. FRCS; Fellow, King's College, London, 1953; Hunterian Professor Royal College of Surgeons of England, 1943; FRSM (Member Council Ophthalmic Section, 1943; Vice-President 1955); *b* 1901; *e s* of late Lewis Savin, MRCS, Yunnan, and of late Kate C. Savin; *m* 1931, Mary Helen, *e d* of late Walter Griffith, Wimbledon; two *s* one *d. Educ:* Christ's Hosp.; King's Coll., London; King's Coll. Hosp (Warneford Entrance Scholarship, Warneford and Barry Prizes). House Physician and House Surg. to the City of London Hosp. for Diseases of Heart and Lungs, 1924; 1st Assistant Medical Officer to St Marylebone Hospital, 1927; Medical Superintendent Seamen's Hospital, Greenwich, 1928; House Surgeon to Royal Eye Hospital, 1923; afterwards clinical assistant, pathologist, assistant Surgeon, Surgeon, Senior Surgeon, Royal Eye Hospital, SE1, resigning 1956. Ophthalmic Surgeon, Metropolitan Hospital, 1929-34; Consulting Ophthalmic Surgeon, Maudsley Hospital, 1937-39; Consulting Ophthalmic Surgeon to the LCC General Hospitals, 1936-48, and to Whipps Cross Hospital, 1931-47; Ophthalmologist to Horton War Hospital (MInistry of Health Emergency Medical Service), 1939-47; Consulting Ophthalmic Surgeon, King's College Hospital, 1966 (Asst Ophthalmic Surgeon, 1931; Senior Ophthalmic Surgeon, 1945-66). Hon. Secretary Ophthalmological Soc. of UK, 1937-39 (Member Council, 1939-42; Vice-President, 1957); Emeritus Lecturer in Ophthalmology, King's Coll. Hosp. Med. Sch.; Examr under Conjoint Examining Bd for DOMS Part I, 1941-46; Examiner in DO, 1949; Staff Examiner in Ophthalmology, Univ. of London, 1952. Vice-Pres. sect. of ophth, Roy. Soc. Med., 1956-57; President Faculty of Ophthalmologists, 1957. *Publications:* Medical and Ophthalmic contributions to Lancet, British Journal of Ophthalmology (The Effect of Aluminium and its Alloys on the Eye: a Report presented to Vision Committee of Medical Research Council, 1947), and Transactions of Ophthalmological Society of the United Kingdom. *Address:* 20 Wimpole Street, W1. *T:* 01-580 3919.

**SAVORY, Hubert Newman,** MA, DPhil Oxon, FSA, FMA; Keeper of Archæology, National Museum of Wales, Cardiff, since 1956; *b* 7 Aug. 1911; *s* of William Charles Newman Savory and Alice Amelia (*née* Minns); *m* 1949, Priscilla Valerie Thirkell; four *s* two *d. Educ:* Magdalen College Sch., Oxford; St Edmund Hall, Oxford Univ. BA Oxon 1934 (Lit. Hum. 1st Cl.); DPhil Oxon 1937; Randall MacIver Student in Iberian Archæology, 1936-38. Assistant, 1938, Asst Keeper, 1939, Dept of Archæology, National Museum of Wales. Member, Royal Commn on Ancient Monuments (Wales and Monmouthshire), 1970-. Conducted excavations of various Welsh cromlechs, round barrows, hill-forts, etc. Served War of 1939-45, in Army, 1940-45. *Publications:* Spain and Portugal: The Prehistory of the Iberian Peninsula, 1968; contrib. to Proc. of Prehistoric Soc.; Archæologia Cambrensis, etc. *Recreations:* walking, gardening. *Address:* 31 Lady Mary Road, Cardiff. *T:* Cardiff 753106.

**SAVORY, Lt-Gen. Sir Reginald Arthur,** KCIE, *cr* 1947; CB 1944; DSO 1941; MC; psc; late Indian Army; *b* 26 July 1894; *s* of A. L. Savory, Bramham Gardens, London, *m* 1st, 1922, Myrtle Estelle Richardson (*d* 1965); no *c*; 2nd, 1969, Marie Nikolaevna McIlwraith (*née* Zurabova). *Educ:* Uppingham; Hanover; Sandhurst. First Commission, 1914; served European War, Egypt, Gallipoli (wounded, despatches, MC), Persia, Mesopotamia, Siberia; Kurdistan, 1923; Brevet Major, 1929; North-West Frontier, India, 1930 (despatches); Instructor, Indian Mil. Acad., 1932-34; Brevet Lt-Col 1934; Waziristan, 1937 (despatches); War of 1939-45, commanded 11th Indian Infantry Brigade, 1940-41, Middle East (DSO); GOC Eritrea, 1941 (despatches); Maj.-Gen. 1943; commanded 23rd Indian Div. 1942-43 (despatches); Director of Infantry (India), 1943.45; GOC Persia and Iraq, 1945-46; Lt-Gen. 1947. Adjutant-General in India, 1946-47; retired 1948. Col, Sikh Light Infantry, 1947-56. DL Somerset, 1952-60; JP Somerset, 1952-60; CC Somerset, 1952-59; County Alderman, Somerset, 1959-60; Chm. T & AFA, Somerset, 1953-59. *Publication:* His Britannic Majesty's Army in Germany, during the Seven Years War, 1966. *Address:* Richmond Cottage, Seale, near Farnham, Surrey. *Club:* United Service.

**SAW, Prof. Ruth Lydia;** Professor Emeritus in Aesthetics, University of London, 1964; *b* 1 August 1901; *d* of Samuel James and Matilda Louisa Saw (*née* Horner). *Educ:* County School for Girls, Wallington, Surrey; Bedford College, University of London. Lecturer in Philosophy, Smith Coll., Northampton, Mass., USA, 1927-34; Lecturer in Philosophy: Bedford College, 1939-44; Birkbeck College, 1939-46, Reader in Philosophy, 1946-61; Prof. of Aesthetics in Univ. of London, 1961-64, and Head of Dept of Philosophy, Birkbeck Coll. British Society of Aesthetics: Founder Mem. and Chm. Council, 1960; Vice-Pres., 1963; Pres., 1969; Pres., Aristotelian Soc., 1965. *Publications:* The Vindication of Metaphysics, 1951; Leibniz, 1954; Aesthetics, 1970; sections (William of Ockham, Leibniz), in A Critical History of Western Philosophy. Contrib. to Proc. Aristotelian Soc., Philosophy, Brit. Jl of Aesthetics. *Recreations:* gardening, the theatre; interested in illuminated manuscripts, early gardening and botany books. *Address:* 72 Grosvenor Avenue, Carshalton, Surrey. *T:* Wallington 8898. *Club:* Women's Farm and Garden.

**SAWBRIDGE, Henry Raywood,** CBE 1960; retired from HM Foreign Service, 1964; Deputy Director, Centre of Japanese Studies, University of Sheffield, 1964-66; *b* 1 Nov. 1907; 2nd *s* of Rev. John Edward Bridgman Sawbridge; *m* 1947, Lilian, *d* of late William Herbert Wood; one *s* one *d. Educ:* Eton; Trinity Coll., Oxford. Entered HM Consular Service, 1931, and served in Japan, Korea and at FO; served with Australian Forces, 1943; HM Consul-General, Yokohama, 1949; Chargé d'Affaires, Korea, 1950; HM Consul-General, Geneva, 1953; Counsellor at Foreign Office, 1960. Coronation Medal, 1953. *Recreations:* shooting, fishing. *Address:* The Moorings, Kingsgate, Kent. *Club:* Travellers'.

**SAWYER, Charles;** Senior partner, Taft, Stettinus and Hollister, Attorneys at Law; *b* 10 Feb. 1887; *s* of Edward Milton and Caroline

Butler Sawyer; *m* 1st, 1918, Margaret Sterrett Johnston (*d* 1937); three *s* two *d*; 2nd, 1942, Elizabeth L. de Veyrac. *Educ:* Oberlin College, Oberlin, Ohio (BA); University of Cincinnati (LLB). Elected to City Council, Cincinnati, Ohio, 1911; Lieut Governor of Ohio, 1932; Democratic Candidate for Governor of Ohio, 1938; Ambassador to Belgium and Minister to Luxembourg, 1944; Secretary of Commerce, 1948-53. Hon. LLD: University of Cincinnati; Bryant College; Franklin and Marshall College; Miami University; Oberlin College. Hon. JD University of Cincinnati. *Publication:* Concerns of a Conservative Democrat, 1968. *Address:* Fountain Avenue, Glendale, Ohio 45246, USA. *Clubs:* Queen City, Cincinnati Country (Cincinnati); Chevy Chase (Maryland); Everglades, Bath and Tennis (Palm Beach, Fla).

**SAWYER, John Stanley,** MA; FRS 1962; Director of Research, Meteorological Office, since 1965; *b* 19 June 1916; *s* of late Arthur Stanley Sawyer and of Emily Florence Sawyer (*née* Frost), Bladon, Oxford; *m* 1951, Betty Vera Beeching (*née* Tooke), *widow*; one *d*. *Educ:* Latymer Upper Sch., Hammersmith; Jesus Coll., Cambridge. Entered Meteorological Office, 1937; appointments: Calshot, 1938; Thorney Island, 1939; HQ 16 Group RAF, 1942; Air Command SE Asia, 1943; Research 1946-. Actg Pres., Commn for Atmospheric Sciences, World Meteorological Organisation, 1968-; Pres., Royal Meteorological Soc., 1963-65 (Hugh Robert Mill Medal 1956, Buchan Prize 1962). *Publications:* Ways of the Weather, 1958; scientific papers largely in Quart. Jl Roy. Met. Soc. *Address:* 8 Sherring Close, Bracknell, Berks. *T:* Bracknell 23380.

**SAWYERR, Rev. Prof. Canon Harry Alphonso Ebun,** CBE 1963 (MBE 1954); Principal, Fourah Bay College, since 1968, and Professor of Theology since 1962; Vice-Chancellor, University of Sierra Leone, since 1970 (Pro-Vice-Chancellor, 1968-70); *b* 16 Oct. 1909; *s* of Rev. Obrien Alphonso Dandeson Sawyerr and Mrs Cleopatra Florence Omodele Sawyerr; *m* 1935, Edith Kehinde Lavinia Edwin; one *d*. *Educ:* Prince of Wales Sch.; Fourah Bay Coll.; St John's Coll., Durham. BA 1933; MA 1936; MEd 1940. Fourah Bay Coll.: Tutor 1933-45; Lectr 1948-52; Chaplain 1948-56; Sen. Lectr 1952-62; Vice-Principal 1956-58 and 1964-68. Sec., Theological Advisers Board, Province of W Africa, 1952-58; Mem., World Council of Churches Commn on Faith and Order, 1962-. Select Preacher, UC Ibadan, 1961; Chm., Board of Teacher Trng, 1960-63; Leader, Sierra Leone Delegn to 3rd Commonwealth Educn Conf., 1964; Editor, Sierra Leone Bulletin of Religion, 1962-68; Select Preacher, Fourah Bay Coll., UC Sierra Leone, 1964; Pres., Milton Margai Trng (now Teachers) Coll., 1960-69. 1st Prize, Thomas Cochrane Essay Comp., 1960. Sierra Leone Independence Medal, 1961. Hon. DD Durham, 1970. *Publications:* Creative Evangelism, 1968; (with W. T. Harris) The Springs of Mende Belief and Conduct, 1968; God: Ancestor or Creator?, 1970; (contrib.) Biblical Revelation and Traditional Beliefs (ed K. Dickson and P. Ellingworth), 1969; articles in Scottish Jl of Theology, Church Quarterly, East Asia Jl of Theology, Internat. Review of Missions, Numen, Sierra Leone Bulletin of Religion. *Recreations:* motor driving, walking, gardening. *Address:* Fourah Bay College, University of Sierra Leone, Mount Aureol, Freetown, Sierra Leone. *T:* 7-300.

**SAXTON, John Arthur,** DSc, PhD, CEng, FIEE, FInstP; Director, Radio and Space Research Station, Science Research Council, since 1966; Visiting Professor of Physics, University College, London, since 1968; *b* 28 June 1914; *s* of late H. and L. E. Saxton; *m* 1939, Kathleen Florence Crook, BA, *d* of late Alfred H. Crook, OBE, MA; one *s* one *d*. *Educ:* Loughborough Grammar School; Imperial Coll., London Univ. (Royal Sch.). 1st Class Hons Phys 1935; Imperial Coll., Governors' Prize for Physics, 1935. Demonstrator Physics Dept, Imperial Coll., 1936-38; Mem. Scientific Staff, DSIR, at Nat. Phys. Laboratory, 1938-52, and at Radio Research Station, 1952-64; Dep. Dir Radio Research Station, 1960-64; Director, United Kingdom Scientific Mission, Washington, DC, USA, and Scientific Counsellor at the British Embassy there, 1964-66. Admin. Staff Coll., Henley-on-Thames, 1955; Special Lectr, Imperial Coll., 1948-58; Vis. Prof. of Elec. Engrg, Univ. Texas, 1961-62. Mem. Council, Instn of Elec. Engrs, 1949-52, 1962-64, 1966-; Chm., Elec. Div. Bd, IEE, 1969-70. Delegate to several confs of Internat. Radio Consultative Cttee and Internat. Scientific Radio Union, 1953-; Chairman: URSI Commn II, 1966-69; CCIR Study Gp V, 1970-. *Publications:* numerous papers in scientific jls on radio wave propogation and dielectric Studies. *Address:* Radio and Space Research Station, Ditton Park, Slough, Bucks. *T:* Slough 24411. *Club:* Athenæum.

**SAXTON, Rev. William Isaac,** CB 1946; OBE 1936; MA; Instructor Captain, RN (retired); *b* Cropwell Butler, Notts, 16 Nov. 1891; *s* of W. I. Saxton, Sen., and Mathilde F. E. Saxton; *m* 1920, Juliette Morton Turner; three *s*. *Educ:* Nottingham High School; King's College, Cambridge (Exhibitioner, Natural Science Tripos Parts I and II, 2nd Cl.); Ripon Hall, Oxford. Joined Navy as Naval Instructor, 1915; HMS Indomitable, 1916-18, present at Jutland, served subsequently in HMS Warspite, RNE Coll., Keyham, Boys' Training Service; Instr Comdr 1929; Instr Capt. 1936; Fleet Education Officer, Home Fleet and Mediterranean; Deputy Director, Education Department, 1944; Director, Education Department, Admiralty, 1945-48; retired from RN, 1948; Director of Education in the Indian Navy, 1948-53. Deacon and Priest, 1954; Vicar of West Farleigh, 1954-70. *Address:* Brook Cottage, Mill Lane, Wateringbury, Maidstone, Kent. *T:* Wateringbury 306.

**SAY, Rt. Rev. Richard David;** *see* Rochester, Bishop of.

**SAYE AND SELE,** 21st Baron *cr* 1447 and 1603; **Nathaniel Thomas Allen Fiennes;** *b* 22 September 1920; *s* of Ivo Murray Twisleton-Wykeham-Fiennes, 20th Baron Saye and Sele, OBE, MC, and Hersey Cecilia Hester, *d* of late Captain Sir Thomas Dacres Butler, KCVO; *S* father, 1968; *m* 1958, Mariette Helena, *d* of Maj.-Gen. Sir Guy Salisbury-Jones, *qv*; three *s* one *d* (and one *s* decd). *Educ:* Eton; New College, Oxford. Served with Rifle Brigade, 1941-49 (despatches twice). Chartered Surveyor. Partner in firm of Laws and Fiennes; Dep. Chm., Daniel Thwaites & Co. *Heir:* *s* Hon. Richard Ingel Fiennes, *b* 19 August 1959. *Address:* Broughton Castle, Banbury, Oxon. *T:* Banbury 2624.

*See also Very Rev. Hon. O. W. Fiennes.*

**SAYER, Vice-Adm. Sir Guy (Bourchier),** KBE 1959; CB 1956; DSC 1943; retired as Flag Officer Commanding Reserve Fleet (1958-59); *b* 2 January 1903; 3rd *s* of late William Feetham and late Edith Alexandra Sayer, E Finchley, London, N; *m* 1925, Sylvia Rosalind Pleadwell, *d* of late Maj.-Gen. R. C. Munday, CB, RAF, and late Mrs Olive Munday, Hartley, Plymouth, Devon; twin *s*. *Educ:* Cholmeley House, Highgate; RN Colleges Osborne and

Dartmouth. Naval Cadet, 1916; Midshipman, 1920; Sub-Lieut, 1923; Lieut-Comdr, 1933; Comdr Dec. 1937; Capt. 1944; Rear-Adm., 1953. Vice-Controller of the Navy and Director of Naval Equipment, Admiralty, 1953-56; Flag Officer, Home Fleet Training Squadron, 1956-57; Vice-Adm. 1957; retired, 1959. *Publication:* The History of HMS Vernon, 1929. *Recreations:* estate maintenance, walking. *Address:* Old Middle Cator, Widecombe-in-the-Moor, Devon. *T:* Widecombe 228. *Club:* United Service.

**SAYERS, Sir Edward (George),** Kt 1965; CMG 1956; MD, FRCP, FRACP, Hon. FACP, Hon. FRCPE, FRS (NZ); DTM&H; Formerly Dean of the Medical Faculty and Professor of Therapeutics, University of Otago, New Zealand, 1959-67; *b* 10 Sept. 1902; *s* of Henry Hind Sayers; *m* 1928, Jane Lumsden, *d* of Wm Grove, MD; two *s* four *d. Educ:* Christ's College, Christchurch; Otago University; Otago Medical School, 1920-24; MB, ChB (NZ), 1924. House Physician, Wellington Hospital, 1925; Student and House Physician, London Sch. of Tropical Medicine, DTM&H 1926; Medical Missionary, British Solomon Is, 1927-34; MRCP, 1935. Consulting Physician, Auckland (NZ), 1935-39; FRACP 1938. Served War of 1939-45, Middle East and Pacific, 1939-44; OC Medical Div. 1st NZ Gen. Hosp., Egypt and Greece; Cons. Physician NZ Forces in Pacific; OC 4 New Zealand Gen. Hosp. (Colonel); Cons. Physician, Auckland, NZ, 1945-59; Pres. RACP, 1956-58. Chm. NZ Med. Council, 1956-64; Mem. NZ Med. Research Council, 1959-67. Col Comdt, Royal NZMC, 1963-67. Pres., NZ Branch, BMA, 1963; Fellow Christ's College (NZ); Mem. Council, Univ. of Otago, 1959-67. FRCP 1949; Hon. FACP, 1957; Hon. FRCPE, 1960; FRS (NZ), 1961. Legion of Merit (USA), 1944, KStJ. *Publications:* articles in med. jls. *Recreation:* fishing. *Address:* PO Box 5219, Dunedin, New Zealand. *Club:* Fernhill (Dunedin).

**SAYERS, Sir Frederick,** Kt 1941; CIE 1937; KPM 1927; *b* 22 July 1885; *s* of Hugh T. Sayers, Cashel, Co. Tipperary; *m* 1909, Elizabeth (*d* 1960), *d* of J. Boyan MD. *Educ:* Foyle College, Londonderry, Trinity College, Dublin. Joined Indian Police, Madras, 1906; Acting Inspector-General, 1936 and 1937; Deputy Inspector-General of Police, and Commissioner of Police, Madras, 1936-37; Inspector-General of Police, Madras, 1937; retired, 1940; Adviser to Secretary of State for India, 1942-47. King's Police Medal (Gallantry), 1927; General Service Medal, 1921 (Malabar Rebellion). *Address:* Camlagh, Greystones, Co. Wicklow, Eire.

**SAYERS, Prof. James,** MSc, PhD Cantab; Professor of Electron Physics, University of Birmingham, since 1946; *b* 2 Sept. 1912; *s* of late J. Sayers; *m* 1943, Diana Ailsa Joan Montgomery; two *s* one *d. Educ:* Ballymena Academy; University of Belfast; St John's College, Cambridge. Fellow of St John's College, Cambridge, 1941-46. Research for Admiralty in Univ. of Birmingham, 1939-43, on micro-wave radar; Member of British Group of Atomic Scientists transferred to work on the US Manhattan Project, 1943-45. Award by the Royal Commission on Awards to Inventors, 1949. British delegate to Internat. Scientific Radio Union, Zürich, 1950. *Publications:* papers in Proc. Royal Soc., Proc. Phys. Soc., and in the reports of various Internat. Scientific Conferences, on Upper Atmosphere Physics and the Physics of Ionized Gases. *Recreations:* tennis, cine-photography. *Address:* 25 Twatling Road, Barnt Green, Worcestershire. *T:* 021-445 1548.

**SAYERS, (Matthew Herbert) Patrick,** OBE 1945; retired Major-General late RAMC; MD; FRCPath; Consulting Pathologist, HM Factory Inspectorate, Department of Employment and Productivity; late Hon. Physician to HM The Queen; Director of Army Pathology and Consulting Pathologist to the Army, 1964-67; *b* 17 Jan. 1908; *s* of late Herbert John Ireland Sayers, Musician, and late Julia Alice Sayers (*née* Tabb); *m* 1935, Moira, *d* of Robert Dougall; two *s* one *d. Educ:* Whitgift School; St Thomas' Hospital, London. MRCS, LRCP 1932; MB, BS London 1933; MD London 1961; FCPath 1964. Commissioned Lieutenant RAMC, 1935; served India and Far East, 1936-46: Asst Dir of Pathology, HQ 14th Army, 1942-44; Dep. Dir of Pathology, Allied Land Forces, SE Asia, 1945. Asst Dir-Gen., War Office, 1948; OC The David Bruce Laboratories, 1949; Asst Dir of Pathology, Middle East Land Forces, 1953; Editor, Journal RAMC, 1955-61; Dep. Dir of Pathology, Far East Land Forces, 1961-64. CStJ. *Publications:* contribs to scientific jls on scrub typhus and immunology. *Recreations:* gardening, music, cricket, field sports. *Address:* Providence Cottage, The Common, Lingfield, Surrey. *T:* Lingfield 2496. *Clubs:* Army and Navy; MCC.

**SAYERS, Patrick;** *see* Sayers, M. H. P.

**SAYERS, Richard Sidney,** FBA 1957; Emeritus Professor of Economics with special reference to Money and Banking, University of London (Cassel Professor of Economics, 1947-68); *b* 1908; *s* of S. J. Sayers; *m* 1930, Millicent Hodson; one *s* one *d. Educ:* St Catharine's Coll., Cambridge. Asst Lectr in Economics, London Sch. of Economics, 1931-35; Lectr in Economics, Exeter, Corpus Christi and Pembroke Colleges, Oxford, 1935-45; Fellow of Pembroke College, Oxford, 1939-45; Ministry of Supply, 1940-45; Economic Adviser, Cabinet Office, 1945-47. Member: Radcliffe Committee on the Working of the Monetary System, 1957-59; OECD Cttee on Fiscal Measures, 1966-68; Monopolies Commission, 1968. Pres. Section F, Brit. Assoc., 1960; Vice-Pres., Brit. Academy, 1966-67. Hon. Fellow: St Catharine's Coll., Cambridge; Inst. of Bankers. Hon. DLitt Warwick, 1967; Hon. DCL Kent, 1967. *Publications:* Bank of England Operations, 1890-1914, 1936; Modern Banking, 1938 (7th Edn 1967); American Banking System, 1948; (ed) Banking in the British Commonwealth, 1952; (jt editor with T. S. Ashton) Papers in English Monetary History, 1953; Financial Policy, 1939-45, 1956; Central Banking after Bagehot, 1957; Lloyds Bank in the History of English Banking, 1957; (ed) Banking in Western Europe, 1962; (ed) Economic writings of James Pennington, 1963; A History of Economic Change in England, 1880-1939, 1967; Gilletts in the London Money Market, 1867-1967, 1968.

**SAYLE, Robert,** MA; *b* 26 Feb. 1889; 2nd *s* of late John Sayle, Kirk Michael, Isle of Man; *m* 1916, Elizabeth Stewart Mackay, Liverpool; two *d. Educ:* King William's College, IOM; Chester College; St Edmund Hall, Oxford. Second Class, Honour School of English; House Master and Chief English Master, City of Oxford School; Headmaster of Coleshill Grammar School, Warwickshire, 1929-30; of the City of Bath Boys' School, 1934-39; of the Nelson School, Wigton, 1930-34, and again 1939-52. *Address:* Moanee Mollagh, Kirk Michael, Isle of Man. *T:* Kirk Michael 243.

**SAYLES, Prof. George Osborne,** MA, DLitt; FBA; MRIA; *b* 20 April 1901; *s* of Rev. L. P. Sayles and Margaret Brown, Glasgow; *m* 1936, Agnes, *d* of George Sutherland, Glasgow; one *s* one *d*. *Educ:* Ilkeston Grammar Sch.; Glasgow Univ.; University Coll., London. Open Bursar, Ewing Gold Medallist, First Cl. Hons History, Glasgow Univ., 1923; Carnegie Res. Schol., University Coll., London, 1923-24; Asst, 1924, Lectr, 1925 and Sen. Lectr, 1934-35, in History, Glasgow Univ.; Leverhulme Res. Fellow, 1939; Professor of Modern History in the Queen's University, Belfast, 1945-53; Burnett-Fletcher Professor of History in the Univ. of Aberdeen, 1953-62; Kenan Prof. of History, New York Univ., 1967; Vis. Prof., Louvain Univ., Belgium, 1951; Woodward Lectr, Yale Univ., USA, 1952; Fellow, Folger Library, Washington, 1960-61. Chm. Advisory Cttee, Official War History of Northern Ireland, 1949; Member: Commission Internationale pour l'Histoire des Assemblées d'Etats; Advisory Historical Committee, Official Histories of War (Gt Brit.), 1950; Irish Manuscripts Commn, Dublin, 1949; Scottish Cttee on History of Scottish Parliament, 1937; Council of Stair Soc. (Scotland); Inst. for Advanced Study, Princeton, NJ, 1969. Vice-Pres. Selden Soc., London, 1953. Intelligence Officer (voluntary) to District Commissioner for Civil Defence SW Scotland, 1939-44; HG Glasgow, 12th Bn 1940. Hon. LittD (Trinity College, Dublin). James Barr Ames Medal, Faculty of Law, Harvard Univ., 1958. *Publications:* Author, Editor or Joint Editor (with H. G. Richardson, *qv*) of: The Early Statutes, 1934; Rotuli Parliamentorum Anglie Hactenus Inediti, 1935; Select Cases in Court of King's Bench: under Edward I (3 vols), 1936-39; Edward II (1 vol.), 1956; Edward III (2 vols), 1958, 1965; Richard II, Henry IV, Henry V (1 vol.), 1971; Select Cases in Procedure without Writ, 1943; Parliaments and Councils of Medieval Ireland, 1947; Medieval Foundations of England, 1948, 3rd edn 1964, American edn, 1950; Irish Parliament in the Middle Ages, 1952; The Irish Parliament in 1782, 1954; Fleta, 1955; Parliaments and Great Councils in Medieval England, 1961; Governance of Medieval England, 1963; The Administration of Ireland, 1172-1377, 1964; Law and Legislation in Medieval England, 1966. Articles and Reviews in Eng. Hist. Review, Scot. Hist. Review, Law Quarterly Review, Proc. RIA, etc. *Recreations:* travel, motoring. *Address:* Warren Hill, Crowborough, Sussex. *T:* 61439.

**SCADDING, John Guyett,** MD (London), FRCP; Professor of Medicine in the University of London, at Institute of Diseases of the Chest (Dean of Institute, 1946-60, Director of Studies, 1950); Physician, Brompton Hospital, since 1939; Hon. Associate Physician, Hammersmith Hospital, since 1963; Hon. Consultant in Diseases of the Chest to the Army at Home since 1953; Chairman Industrial Medical Panel, National Coal Board, since 1951; *b* 30 August 1907; *e s* of late John William Scadding and Jessima Alice Guyett; *m* 1940, Mabel Pennington; one *s* two *d*. *Educ:* Mercers' School; Middlesex Hospital Medical School, University of London. MRCS, LRCP, 1929; MB, BS (London), 1930. Resident appts, Middx Hosp., Connaught Hosp., Walthamstow, and Brompton Hosp., 1930-35; MRCP 1932; MD (London, Univ. gold medal), 1932; First Asst, Dept of Med., Brit. Postgrad. Med. Sch., 1935; FRCP 1941; RAMC 1940-45 (Lt-Col, O i/c Med. Div.); Phys., Hammersmith Hosp., and Sen. Lectr in Medicine, Postgrad. Med. Sch. of London, 1946-62; Mem. Central Health Services Council, and Standing Medical Advisory Cttee, 1954-66; Mem. Clinical Research Board, 1960-65. Royal College of Physicians: Bradshaw Lectr, 1949; Mitchell Lectr, 1960; Tudor Edwards Lectr, 1970; Councillor, 1949-52; Censor, 1968-70; Lettsomian Lectr, Med. Soc. of London, 1955. Editor, Thorax, 1946-59. Pres., British Tuberculosis Assoc., 1959-61. *Publications:* Sarcoidosis, 1967; contributions to textbooks and articles, mainly on respiratory diseases, in medical journals. *Recreations:* music, pottering about. *Address:* Institute of Diseases of the Chest, Brompton, SW3. *T:* 01-352 8144; 19 South Square, NW11. *T:* 01-455 8229. *Club:* Athenæum.

**SCAMP, Sir (Athelstan) Jack,** Kt 1968; DL, JP; Personnel Director, GEC Ltd, since 1962; Director: AEI, since 1967; Urwick, Orr & Partners, since 1969; New Opportunities Association, since 1969; Associate Professor of Industrial Relations, University of Warwick, since 1970; *b* 22 May 1913; 2nd *s* of Edward Henry and Jane Scamp; *m* 1939, Jane, *d* of John Kendall; one *s* one *d*. *Educ:* Birmingham. Chief Personnel Officer, Plessey Co. Ltd, 1953-58; Personnel Dir, Massey-Ferguson (UK) Ltd, 1958-62. Mem. of the Industrial Court since 1964; Chairman, Motor Industry Joint Labour Council, 1965-69; Member Lord Devlin Cttee of Inquiry Docks, Oct. 1964; seconded to Dept of Economic Affairs as Industrial Adviser, Feb. 1965-April 1966. Dir, Fairfields (Glasgow) Ltd, 1967-68. Chairman, Courts of Inquiry: Footplate Staff, British Railways, 1965; Transporter Drivers, Longbridge Group of Delivery Agents, 1966; Transporter Drivers, Motor Vehicle Collections Ltd, 1966; Maintenance Workers, Birmingham Aluminium Castings Ltd, 1967; British Airline Pilots' Assoc., 1967; Dispute at Liverpool Docks, 1967; Time Workers at Pressed Steel Fisher Ltd, 1968; Sewing Machinists, Ford Motor Co., 1968; Demarcation Dispute, Vickers Shipyard, Barrow-in-Furness, 1969; Chairman: Inquiry into Employment of Coal Trimmers in NE Ports, 1967; Inquiry into Employment of Coal Trimmers, Immingham, June 1970; Council Workers' Pay Dispute, Oct. 1970. Gov., William Temple College, 1967-. CIEE, 1967. DL Warwicks, 1967. *Recreations:* Association football, cricket and tennis. *Address:* Flax Hill, Ufton, Harbury, Leamington Spa, Warwicks. *T:* Harbury 799. *Club:* Rugby Town (Rugby).

**SCANLAN, Most Rev. Mgr J. D.;** *see* Glasgow, Archbishop of, (RC).

**SCANLON, Hugh Parr;** President, Amalgamated Union of Engineering and Foundry Workers, since 1968; Member: TUC General Council, since 1968; TUC Economic Committee, since 1968; *b* 26 Oct. 1913; *m* 1943, Nora; two *d*. *Educ:* Stretford Elem. Sch.; NCLC. Apprentice, Instrument Maker, Shop Steward-Convener, AEI, Trafford Park; Divisional Organiser, AEU, Manchester, 1947-63; Mem. Exec. Coun., AEU, London, 1963-67. *Recreations:* golf, swimming, gardening. *Address:* 30 Crown Woods Way, Eltham, SE9. *T:* 01-850 8833. *Club:* Eltham Warren Golf.

**SCARBOROUGH, Prof. Harold;** Professor of Medicine, Ahmadu Bello University, Zaria, Nigeria, since 1970; Dean of Faculty of Medicine; *b* 27 March 1909; British; unmarried. *Educ:* Bridlington School, Yorks; Edinburgh University; St Mary's Hospital Medical School; Harvard University. Clinical Tutor, Royal Infirmary of Edinburgh and Assistant, Dept of Therapeutics, Edinburgh Univ., 1933-38; Beit Memorial Research Fellow and Demonstrator in Pharmacology, Edinburgh Univ., 1938-39; Beit Memorial Research Fellow, Medical Unit, St Mary's

Hosp., London, 1945-47; Rockefeller Travelling Fellow at Harvard Medical School, 1947-48; Reader in Medicine, University of Birmingham, 1949-50; Prof. of Medicine in Welsh Nat. Sch. of Medicine, Univ. of Wales, 1950-70; formerly: Dir, Med. Unit, Cardiff Royal Infirmary; Chm., Div. of Medicine, United Cardiff Hosps. *Publications:* (part author) Textbook of Physiology and Biochemistry, 1950; papers in BMJ, Lancet, Quart. Jl Med., and other medical and scientific journals. *Recreations:* gardening, the theatre. *Address:* Faculty of Medicine, Ahmadu Bello University, Zaria, Nigeria. *Club:* Athenæum.

**SCARBROUGH,** 12th Earl of, *cr* 1690; **Richard Aldred Lumley;** Viscount Lumley (Ire.), 1628; Baron Lumley, 1681; Viscount Lumley, 1690; *b* 5 Dec. 1932; *o s* of 11th Earl of Scarbrough, KG, PC, GCSI, GCIE, GCVO, and of Katharine Isobel, Countess of Scarbrough, DCVO, *d* of late R. F. McEwen; *S* father, 1969; *m* 1970, Lady Elizabeth Ramsay, *d* of Earl of Dalhousie, *qv*. *Educ:* Eton; Magdalen College, Oxford. 2nd Lt 11th Hussars, 1951-52; formerly Lt Queen's Own Yorkshire Dragoons. ADC to Governor and C-in-C, Cyprus, 1956. *Address:* Sandbeck Park, Rotherham, Yorks. *T:* Doncaster 742210; 4 Wilton Street, SW1. *T:* 01-235 4454. *Clubs:* White's, Pratt's, Beefsteak.

**SCARFE, Prof. Francis Harold,** OBE; FRSL; Author; Director, British Institute in Paris, since 1959, and Professor of French in the University of London, since 1965; *b* 18 September 1911; *s* of John James Scarfe and Margaret Ingham Dobson; *m* 1938, Margarete M. Geisler; one *s*. *Educ:* Universities of Durham, Cambridge and Paris. RAOC and RAEC, 1941-46; Lt-Col, 1945. Supervisor of Studies and Secretary, Extension Lectures Committee, University of Oxford, 1946-47; Senior Lecturer in French University of Glasgow, 1947-59. Chevalier des Arts et Lettres. *Publications: poetry:* Inscapes, 1940; Poems and Ballads, 1941; Underworlds, 1950; *criticism:* Auden and After, 1942; W. H. Auden, 1949 (Monaco); The Art of Paul Valéry, 1954; La vie et l'œuvre de T. S. Eliot, 1964 (Paris); *editions:* Baudelaire, 1961; Chénier, 1961; André Chénier, his Life and Work, 1965; *novels:* Promises, 1950; Single Blessedness, 1951; Unfinished Woman, 1954; various translations. *Address:* 6 rue de la Sorbonne, Paris 5e, *T:* Danton 80-86.

**SCARFE, Gerald;** artist; *b* 1 June 1936. *Educ:* scattered (due to chronic asthma as a child). Punch, 1960; Private Eye, 1961; Daily Mail, 1966; Sunday Times, 1967; cover artist to illustrator, Time Magazine, 1967; animation and film directing for BBC, 1969-. Has taken part in exhibitions: Grosvenor Gall., 1969 and 1970; Pavillon d'Humour, Montreal, 1967; Expo '70, Osaka, 1970. One-man exhibitions of sculptures and lithographs: Waddell Gall., New York, 1968 and 1970; Grosvenor Gall., 1969; Vincent Price Gall., Chicago, 1969. *Publications:* Gerald Scarfe's People, 1966. *Recreations:* drawing, painting and sculpting. *Address:* 10 Cheyne Walk, SW3.

**SCARFOGLIO, Carlo;** literary and political writer; *b* 16 Oct. 1887; *s* of Edoardo Scarfoglio and Matilde Serao; *m* Virginia Daleggio, Constantinople; one *s*. *Educ:* Collegio Cicognini, Prato, Tuscany; Rome University. Started as foreign correspondent for the Mattino of Naples (his father's property); was in London, 1909-11; then was correspondent in the Tripoli and the Balkan Wars; specialised in Eastern and International affairs, always for the Stampa of Turin and the Mattino of Naples; was correspondent, European War, from the Anglo-French and from the Turkish front; assumed temporary editorship of the Mattino, and subsequently of the Nazione, of Florence; was Editor of last paper four years; left it to assume joint editorship of the Mattino until the sale of this family concern in 1928; left active journalism at that date, and has turned to literature and to political studies. After the fall of Mussolini (25 July 1943), called to the editorship of the Nazione of Florence. Left it within a month, in order to avoid collaborating with the Germans, who had occupied the town. Contributor to Milano-Sera, of Milan, also to Paese-Sera, of Rome, mainly on the Southern question and on foreign affairs; Editor of I Rinnovamento d' Italia, weekly, Rome, and co-editor of La Pace, monthly, Rome. Now literary rather than journalistic. *Publications:* Idee Sulla Ricostruzione, 1920; Bidental, 1934; Russian Tour, 1934; England and the Continent, 1939; La Vera Croce, an historical novel (publ. in Eng. and Amer. as The True Cross); Ro-Ma, an inquiry on pre-olympic cults and civilisations, 1939; Davanti a questa guerra, 1941; Possiamo essere nazionalisti?; Il mezzogiorno e l' unitã d' Italia, 1953; I Racconti della Torre, 1962. *Recreations:* travelling, motoring, alpineering, swimming. *Address:* Viale Parioli 54, Rome.

**SCARLETT,** family name of **Baron Abinger.**

**SCARLETT, Lt-Col Henry A.;** *see* Ashley-Scarlett.

**SCARLETT, Sir Peter (William Shelley Yorke),** KCMG 1958 (CMG 1949); KCVO 1955; *b* 30 March 1905; *s* of late William James Yorke Scarlett, Fyfield House, Andover; *m* 1934, Elisabeth, *d* of late Sir John Dearman Birchall, TD, MP, Cotswold Farm, Cirencester; one *s* three *d*. *Educ:* Eton; Christ Church, Oxford. Apptd to Foreign Office as a Third Secretary, 1929; Cairo, 1930; Bagdad, 1932; Lisbon, 1934; promoted a Second Secretary, 1934; acted as Chargé d'Affaires, Riga, 1937 and 1938. Attached to representative of Latvia at coronation of King George VI, 1937; Brussels, 1938; promoted actg First Sec., 1940; captured by enemy forces, 1940; returned to UK and resumed duties at Foreign Office, 1941; Paris, 1944; Allied Forces Headquarters, Caserta, 1946; Counsellor, Foreign Office, 1947; Inspector of HM Diplomatic Service Establishments, 1950; British Permanent Representative on the Council of Europe, Strasbourg, 1952; HM Ambassador to Norway, 1955; HM Minister to the Holy See, 1960-65, retired. Chairman, Cathedrals Advisory Committee, 1967. *Address:* Rudhall, Ross-on-Wye, Herefordshire. *Clubs:* Brooks's, Junior Carlton.

**SCARMAN, Hon. Sir Leslie (George),** Kt 1961; OBE 1944; **Hon. Mr Justice Scarman;** Judge of the High Court of Justice (Probate, Divorce, and Admiralty Division), since 1961; *b* 29 July 1911; *s* of George Charles and Ida Irene Scarman; *m* 1947, Ruth Clement; one *s*. *Educ:* Radley College; Brasenose College, Oxford. Classical Scholar, Radley, 1925; Open Classical Scholar, Brasenose Coll., 1930; Hon. Mods 1st cl., 1932; Lit. Hum. 1st cl., 1934; Harmsworth Law Scholar, Middle Temple, 1936, Barrister, 1936; QC 1957. Chm., Law Commission, 1965- ; Chm., Univ. of London Court, 1970, Dep. Chm., 1966-70; Vice-Chm., Statute Law Cttee, 1967-. Mem. Arts Council, 1968-70. Hon. Fellow, Brasenose College, Oxford, 1966. Hon. LLD: Exeter, 1965; Glasgow, 1969. RAFVR, 1940-45. Order of Battle Merit (Russia), 1945. *Recreation:* golf. *Address:* 77 Cadogan Square, SW1.

**SCARR, John Geoffrey Fearnley;** *b* 12 July 1910; 2nd *s* of late William Harcourt Scarr and Lydia (*née* Harrop); *m* 1945, Dorothy Edna Terry; two *d*. *Educ:* King's School, Ely; Trinity College, Cambridge (MA Hons, LLB). Called to the Bar, Lincoln's Inn, 1935; practised Northern Circuit and Lancashire Palatine Court. Served throughout War of 1939-45: Far East and War Office; major. Colonial Service; Resident Magistrate and Coroner, N Rhodesia, 1953; Chief Judicial Comr, Western Pacific High Commn Territories, 1959; Judge of the Supreme Court, Nassau and Bahamas, 1961-65; Acting Chief Justice on several occasions; Chancellor Dio. Nassau and the Bahamas, 1962-64; Deputy Chairman, Bahamas Constituencies Commn, 1964; Legal Staff of Law Commn, 1965-66. *Publications:* The Law and Practice of Land Registration 1938; (ed) Northern Rhodesia Law Reports, 1949-54; contrib. to legal journals. *Recreations:* golf, music, sailing. *Address:* Littlegate, The Crescent, Shiplake, Henley-on-Thames, Oxon. *T:* Wargrave 2201; Baycroft, Montagu Bay, Box 437, Nassau, Bahamas. *T:* Nassau 2-4195. *Club:* Royal Nassau Sailing.

**SCARSDALE,** 2nd Viscount, *cr* 1911; **Richard Nathaniel Curzon,** TD; Baron Scarsdale, 1761; Bt Scotland, 1636, England, 1641; Hon. Colonel Royal Artillery; Director Arthur Woolacott and Rappings Ltd, Blackfriars House, EC; *b* 3 July 1898; *s* of late Col Hon. Alfred Nathaniel Curzon; *S* uncle, Marquess Curzon, as Viscount Scarsdale, 1925; *m* 1st, 1923, Mildred Carson Dunbar (who obtained a divorce, 1946; she *d* 1969), *d* of late William Roland Dunbar of Huyton, Cheshire; four *d*; 2nd, 1946, Mrs Ottilie Margarete Julie Harris, *e d* of late Charles Pretzlik, Lowfield Park, Crawley, and of Mrs Pretzlik, Ovington Mansions, 22 Ovington Square, SW2. *Educ:* Eton; RMC, Sandhurst. Lieut Royal Scots Greys; Capt. Derbyshire Yeomanry; Major RA. Served in France, Belgium and Germany, 1918-19, and in Middle East, 1941-43. Mem. Derbyshire TA Assoc.; Hon. Col RA (TA). Vice-Pres. and Admin. Steward, Brit. Boxing Board of Control. County Dir and a Vice-Pres., St John Ambulance Assoc. and Brigade for Derbyshire. KStJ. *Heir:* cousin, Francis John Nathaniel Curzon, *qv*. *Address:* Kedleston, Derby. *T:* Duffield 2386. *Clubs:* Buck's, Lansdowne, MCC, Royal Automobile.

*See also Sir R. A. Cary, Bt, Sir Dudley Cunliffe-Owen, Bt.*

**SCARTH of Breckness, Col Henry William;** Lord Lieutenant of Orkney, since 1966; JP; Hon. Sheriff Substitute for Orkney since 1959; *b* 19 June 1899; *o s* of late Pillans Scarth and Madelena H. Sharbau; *m* 1st, 1927, Mary Beatrix Robertson (*d* 1955); one *d* (one *s* decd); 2nd, 1960, Kathleen Edgar. *Educ:* St Paul's. Served European War, 1914-18, France and N Russia, Lt (actg Capt.) Scots Guards. Succeeded as 11th Laird, 1929. Hon. Col RA (TA) Orkney and Zetland Unit. County Clerk, Roxburgh, 1935-40; Civil Defence Comr, Orkney and Zetland, 1940-44; Dep. Dir Allied Commn for Austria, 1945-47; Chairman: Orkney CC; Orkney Hosp. Bd, 1957-65; Pres. Orkney T & AVR; Mem., Highlands and Islands Consult. Coun. DL 1954, CC 1955, JP, Orkney. Vice-Lieutenant, Orkney, 1965-66. Cross of St Anne (2nd Cl.), Cross of St Stanislaus (3rd Cl.) (Russia), 1919. *Recreations:* shooting, fishing. *Address:* Skaill House, Orkney. *T:* Sandwick 501. *Clubs:* Guards; New (Edinburgh).

**SCATCHARD, Vice-Adm. John Percival,** CB 1963; DSC 1941; first Bar, 1944; second Bar, 1945; *b* 5 Sept. 1910; *s* of Dr James P. Scatchard, MB, BS, Tadcaster, Yorks; *m* 1943, Edith Margaret Niven; one *d*. *Educ:* Aysgarth School, Yorkshire; RNC Dartmouth. Joined RN, 1924; served War of 1939-45, in HMS Kashmir–Garth and Termagent; Captain (D) Portsmouth, 1951-52; Captain 5th Destroyer Squadron, 1957-58; Director Naval Equipment, Admiralty, 1959-60; Commandant, Joint Services Staff College, Latimer, Bucks, 1960-62; Flag Officer, Second-in-Command, Far East Fleet, 1962-64; retd list, 1964. *Recreations:* riding, gardening, sailing. *Address:* Reachfar, Warsash, near Southampton, Hants. *Club:* Royal Thames Yacht.

**SCHAEFFER, Professor Claude Frederic Armand;** Officier Légion d'Honneur, 1947; Hon. Professor, Collège de France; Member of French Academy; Director of Archæological Expeditions of Ras Shamra (Syria) and Enkomi (Cyprus); Member of National Council of Scientific Research; Member Higher Council of Archaeological Research, Ministry of Cultural Affairs; *b* Strasbourg, Alsace, 6 March 1898; *s* of Henri Schaeffer, industrialist, and Mme Schaeffer (*née* Wiernsberger); *m* 1924, Odile, *d* of Prof. Robert Forrer, archæologist and collector; one *s* two *d*. *Educ:* Univ. Strasbourg. Keeper: Archæological Museum, Strasbourg, 1924-33; Coin Cabinet, Univ. Strasbourg, 1926-33; Museum of Nat. Antiquities, Château de St-Germain-en-Laye, 1933-56; Fellow of St John's Coll., Oxford, 1941-45; Hon. Fellow, 1955-. Captain of Corvette, Free French Naval Forces, England, 1940-45. Director of Research, Nat. Centre of Scientific Research, 1946-54; Prof. of European Pre-history and Nat. Archæology, Ecole de Louvre, 1951-54. Vice-Pres., Commn des Fouilles et Missions Archéologiques, Min. of Foreign Affairs, 1952-69. Life Mem., Cttee of Honour, Internat. Union of Prehistoric and Protohistoric Sciences, 1964. Is Member or Hon. Mem. of a number of socs. DrLit *hc* Oxford, 1942; Dr of Law *hc* Glasgow, 1948; Gold Medal: Soc. of Antiquaries of London, 1958; Soc. of Sciences, Famagusta, 1965. Foreign Member, Royal Academy of Denmark. Hon. Citizen: Famagusta, 1970; Latakia, 1950. Holds other foreign awards. *Publications:* Les Haches néolithiques du Musée de Haguenau, 1924; Les Tertres funéraires préhistoriques dans la forêt de Haguenau, Vol. I, Les Tumulus de l'Age du Bronze, 1926; Un Dépôt d'outils et un trésor de bronzes de l'époque galloromaine, découverts à Seltz, 1927; Les Tertres funéraires préhistoriques dans la forêt de Haguenau, Vol. II, Les Tumulus de l'Age du Fer, 1930; Le Casque romain de Drusenheim, 1932; Missions en Chypre, 1936; The Cuneiform Texts of Ras Shamra-Ugarit, 1939; Ugaritica, I, 1939; Stratigraphie comparée et chronologie de l'Asie Occidentale, vol. I, 1948; Ugaritica II, 1949; Enkomi-Alasia, I, 1952; Ugaritica III, 1956; IV, 1962; V, 1968; VI, 1969; Enkomi-Alasia, II, 1970; also very numerous contributions to learned journals, etc. *Recreations:* travel, exploration, mountains. *Address:* Le Castel Blanc, 14 Rue Turgot, St-Germain-en-Laye, 78 France. *T:* 963.13.47; La Chaumière, Fréland, Haut Rhin, France; L'Escale, La Croix-Valmer, 83 Var, BP16. *T:* 97.62.14.

**SCHAPERA, Prof. Isaac,** MA (Cape Town) 1925; PhD (London) 1929; DSc (London) 1939; FBA 1958; FRSSAf 1934; Emeritus Professor University of London (London School of Economics), 1969; *b* Garies, South Africa, 23 June 1905; 3rd *s* of late Herman and Rose Schapera. *Educ:* S African Coll. Sch., Cape Town; Universities of Cape Town and

London. Prof. of Social Anthropology, Univ. of Cape Town, 1935-50; Prof. of Anthropology, Univ. of London (LSE), 1950-69, now Emeritus. Many anthropological field expeditions to Bechuanaland Protectorate, 1929-50. Chairman Association of Social Anthropologists of the British Commonwealth, 1954-58; President, Royal Anthropological Inst., 1961-63. *Publications:* The Khoisan Peoples of South Africa, 1930; A Handbook of Tswana Law and Custom, 1938; Married Life in an African Tribe, 1940; Native Land Tenure in the Bechuanaland Protectorate, 1943; Migrant Labour and Tribal Life, 1948; The Ethnic Composition of Tswana Tribes, 1952; The Tswana, 1953; Government and Politics in Tribal Societies, 1956; Praise Poems of Tswana Chiefs, 1965; Tribal Innovators, 1970. Editor: Western Civilization and the Natives of South Africa, 1934; The Bantu-speaking Tribes of South Africa, 1937; David Livingstone's Journals and Letters, 1841-56 (6 vols), 1959-63, etc. Contrib. to many learned journals. *Address:* c/o Standard Bank, Northumberland Avenue, WC2.

**SCHAPIRO, Prof. Leonard Bertram,** LLB; Professor of Political Science, with Special Reference to Russian Studies, London School of Economics and Political Science, University of London, since 1962; *b* Glasgow, 22 April 1908; *s* of Max Schapiro and Leah (*née* Levine); *m* 1943, Isabel Margaret, *d* of Don Salvador de Madariaga, *qv*; no *c*. *Educ:* St Paul's Sch.; University Coll., London. Called to Bar, Gray's Inn, 1932; practised at Bar, London and Western Circuit, 1932-39; BBC Monitoring Service, 1940-42; War Office, 1942-45; Intell. Div., German Control Commn, 1945-46 (Maj.); practised at Bar, 1946-55; Dept of Politics, LSE, 1955-. For. Hon. Mem., Amer. Acad. of Arts and Sciences, 1967. *Publications:* The Origin of the Communist Autocracy, 1955; The Communist Party of the Soviet Union, 1960; The Government and Politics of Soviet Russia, 1965; Rationalism and Nationalism in Russian Nineteenth Century Political Thought, 1967; numerous contribs to learned jls, symposia, etc. *Recreations:* music, travel, mediæval art. *Address:* 27 Southwood Lawn Rd, Highgate, N6. *T:* 01-340 1669. *Club:* Reform.

**SCHAPIRO, Meyer;** University Professor, Columbia University, since 1965; *b* Shavly, Lithuania, 23 Sept. 1904; *s* of Nathan Menahem Schapiro and Feige Edelman; *m* 1928, Dr Lillian Milgram; one *s* one *d*. *Educ:* Boys' High Sch., Brooklyn; Columbia University. PhD Columbia, 1929. Columbia University: Lectr, Dept of Art History and Archæology, 1928; Asst Prof., 1936; Assoc. Prof., 1948; Prof., 1952; University Prof., 1965. Visiting Lecturer: Institute of Fine Arts, NY University, 1931-36; New School for Social Research, NY, 1938-50; Vis. Prof.: Univ. of London, 1947, 1957; Univ. of Jerusalem, 1961; Messenger Lectr, Cornell Univ., 1960; Patten Lectr, Indiana Univ., 1961; Charles Eliot Norton Prof., Harvard Univ., 1966-67; Slade Prof. of Fine Art, Oxford Univ., 1968. Guggenheim Fellow, 1939, 1943; Fellow: Amer. Acad. of Arts and Sciences, 1952; Inst. for Advanced Study in Behavioral Sciences, Palo Alto, 1962-63; Amer. Philosophical Soc., 1969; Mediaeval Acad., 1970. Bd of Editors: Jl of History of Ideas; Semiotica; Dissent. Award for Distinction, Amer. Council of Learned Socs, 1960. *Publications:* The Romanesque Sculpture of Moissac, 1931; Van Gogh, 1950; Cézanne, 1952; The Parma Ildefonsus, 1964; articles in collective books and in Art Bulletin, Gazette des Beaux-Arts, Jl Warburg and Courtauld Insts, Jl History of Ideas, Jl Architectural Historians, Kritische Berichte, Amer. Jl Sociology, Partisan Review, Encounter, etc. *Address:* 279 West 4th St, New York, NY 10014, USA.

**SCHARRER, Irene,** FRAM; pianist; *m* 1915, S. Gurney Lubbock, MA (*d* 1958); one *s* one *d*. *Educ:* Royal Academy of Music; studied under Tobias Matthay. Has appeared at Queen's Hall Symphony Concerts; London Symphony Concerts; Royal Philharmonic Concerts, London; New Symphony Orchestral Concerts; Nikisch Symphony Concerts; Leipzig Gewandhaus; Berlin Philharmonic Orchestra; Royal Albert Hall Sunday Concerts; Liverpool Philharmonic; Norwich Philharmonic; Richter Hallé Concerts, Manchester, and in all the musical centres of Great Britain; has toured in Europe and America. *Address:* 61 Addison Road, W14. *T:* 01-937 0848.

**SCHERGER, Air Chief Marshal Sir Frederick (Rudolph Williams),** KBE 1958 (CBE 1950); CB 1954; DSO 1944; AFC 1940; Chairman Australian National Airlines Commission, 1966; *b* 18 May 1904; *o s* of Frederick H. Scherger and Sarah (*née* Chamberlain), Ararat, Victoria, Australia; *m* 1929, Thelma Lilian Harricks; one *d*. *Educ:* Ararat High School; Royal Military College, Australia. Grad. Dec. 1924; seconded to RAAF Jan. 1925; completed flying course, Dec. 1925. Various flying training and squadron appts, 1926-35; RAF Staff Coll. Course, 1935; RAF attachments, 1936; Director of Training, RAAF, 1937-40; AOC No. 10 Group, RAAF, 1943-44; AOC 1st TAF, RAAF, 1945-46; idc, 1946; Deputy Chief of Air Staff, RAAF, 1947-51; Head Australian Joint Services Staff, Washington, 1951-52; Air Officer Commanding, RAF, Malaya, 1953-54; Air Member for Personnel, RAAF, 1954-57. CAS, RAAF, 1957-61; Chairman, Chiefs of Staff, 1961-66. *Recreations:* golf, shooting, motoring. *Address:* 37 Kensington Road, South Yarra, Vic 3141, Australia. *Clubs:* Melbourne, Naval and Military (Melbourne).

**SCHIAPARELLI, Mme Elsa;** couturière; *b* Rome; *m* (marriage dissolved); one *d*. Early career as film script writer and translator for an importing firm, US; later engaged in free-lance writing and gold sculpturing, Paris; became a French citizen; set up first couture establishment, Rue de la Paix, 1929; moved into larger premises, with separate perfume business, Place Vendôme, 1935. During War of 1939-45, lectured in USA; raised funds for France and worked as nurses' aid in Bellevue Hosp., New York. Reopened establishment Place Vendôme, 1945; established Schiaparelli Parfum Inc., NY, and in 1949 opened a New York branch to manufacture her creations on mass-production basis. *Publication:* Shocking Life, 1954. *Address:* 21 Place Vendôme, Paris, France.

**SCHILD, Heinz Otto,** FRS 1966; MD, PhD, DS; FIBiol; Professor of Pharmacology, University of London, at University College, since 1961; *b* Fiume, 18 May 1906; *s* of Hermann Schild and Thekla (*née* Spiegel); *m* 1938, Mireille Madeleine Haquin; three *d*. *Educ:* Universities of Munich, Berlin and Edinburgh. MD Munich, 1931; PhD Edinburgh, 1935; DSc London, 1950. Assistant, Pharmacology Dept, Univ. of Edinburgh, 1936; Demonstrator, 1937, Lecturer, 1942, Reader, 1945, Dept of Pharmacology, University Coll., London; Dean, Faculty of Med. Sciences, University Coll., 1964-67. Chm., Scientific Adv. Bd, Asthma Res. Council; Member WHO Visiting Team of Medical Scientists to SE Asia, 1952; Examiner, Univs of Leeds, Liverpool, Oxford,

Edinburgh, West Africa, West Indies, Makerere College. *Publications:* (joint) Applied Pharmacology, 1968; papers in Journal of Physiology, British Journal of Pharmacology, Immunology, Lancet, Nature. *Recreation:* walking slowly. *Address:* Mole Ridge, St Mary's Road, Leatherhead, Surrey. *T:* Leatherhead 3773.

**SCHILLER, Prof. Dr Karl;** Federal Minister of Economics, Bonn, since Dec. 1966; Member of Deutscher Bundestag since 1965; Professor of Political Economy, University of Hamburg, and Director of Institute for Foreign Trade and Overseas Economy, since 1947; *b* 24 April 1911; *s* of Carl and Maria Schiller; one *s* three *d*. *Educ:* Univs of Kiel, Frankfurt, Berlin. Research Asst, Institut für Weltwirtschaft, Kiel, 1935-39; Lectr, Univ. of Kiel, 1945-46; Rector, Univ. of Hamburg, 1956-58. Senator for Economic Affairs and Transportation, Hamburg, 1948-53; Mem., Bürgerschaft Hamburg, 1949-57; Senator for Economics, West Berlin, 1961-65. *Publications:* Sozialismus und Wettbewerb, 1955; Neueste Entwicklungen in der Theorie der Wirtschaftspolitik, 1958; Zur Wachstumsproblematik der Entwicklungsländer, 1960; Der konom und die Gesellschaft, 1964, etc. *Address:* Bundesministerium für Wirtschaft, 53 Bonn, West Germany. *T:* 761.

**SCHILLING, Professor Richard Selwyn Francis,** MD (London); DSc (London); FRCP; DPH; DIH; Professor of Occupational Health, London School of Hygiene and Tropical Medicine, University of London, since 1960; Director, TUC Centenary Institute of Occupational Health since 1968; *b* 9 Jan. 1911; *s* of late George Schilling and of Florence Louise Schilling, Kessingland, Suffolk; *m* 1937, Heather Maude Elinore Norman; one *s* two *d*. *Educ:* Epsom College; St Thomas' Hospital. Obstetric house physician, St Thomas' Hosp., 1935; house physician, Addenbrooke's Hosp., Cambridge, 1936; Asst Industrial MO, ICI (metals) Ltd, Birmingham, 1937; Medical Inspector of Factories, 1939-42. Served War of 1939-45, Captain RAMC, France and Belgium, 1939-40. Sec. Industrial Health Research Board of Med. Research Council, 1942-46; Nuffield Fellow in Industrial Health, 1946-47; Reader in Occupational Health, Univ. of Manchester, 1947-56; Milroy Lecturer, RCP, 1956; Mackenzie Lecturer, BMA, 1956; Cantor Lecturer, Roy. Soc. of Arts, 1963; C-EA Winslow Lecturer, Yale Univ., 1963. Former Pres., Assoc. of Industrial Medical Officers; Former Pres. British Occupational Hygiene Soc.; Former President Occup. Med. Sect. of Roy. Soc. Med. WHO Consultant, 1956-69; Member, Committee of Inquiry into Trawler Safety, 1968. FRSA 1964. *Publications:* (ed) Modern Trends in Occupational Health, 1960; original papers on Byssinosis (respiratory disease of textile workers) and other subjects in occupational health in BMJ, Lancet, Brit. Jl of Industrial Medicine, and foreign journals. *Recreations:* fishing, tennis and golf. *Address:* 32 Inner Staithe, Hartington Rd, W4. *T:* 01-994 2469.

**SCHILSKY, Eric,** RA 1968 (ARA 1957); RSA 1956 (ARSA 1952); sculptor; Head of the School of Sculpture, Edinburgh College of Art, 1946-69, retired; *b* Southampton, Oct. 1898; *m* Victorine Anne Foot, SSA, DA (Edinburgh), *d* of Major Hammond-Foot, RE; one *d*. *Educ:* Slade School of Art London. Formerly on teaching staff of Westminster School of Art and subsequently Central School of Arts, London. *Address:* 16a Meadow Place, Edinburgh 9.

**SCHLESINGER, Arthur (Meier), Jr;** writer; educator; Schweitzer Professor of the Humanities, City University of New York since 1966; *b* Columbus, Ohio, 15 Oct. 1917; *s* of late Arthur Meier and of Elizabeth Bancroft Schlesinger; *m* 1940, Marian Cannon; two *s* two *d*. *Educ:* Harvard; Peterhouse, Cambridge. AB (Harvard), 1938; Henry Fellow, Peterhouse, Cambridge, 1938-39. Soc. of Fellows, Harvard, 1939-42; US Office of War Information, 1942-43; US Office of Strategic Services, 1943-45; US Army, 1945. Mem. Adlai Stevenson Campaign Staff, 1952, 1956. Professor of History, Harvard University, 1954-61 (Associate, 1946-54); Special Assistant to President, 1961-64. Film Reviewer: Show, 1962-65; Vogue (US), 1966-. Member of Jury, Cannes Film Festival, 1964. Holds Hon. Doctorates, 1950-. Pulitzer Prize: History, 1945; Biography, 1965; Nat. Inst. of Arts and Letters, Gold Medal for History, 1967. *Publications:* Orestes A. Brownson: a Pilgrim's Progress, 1939; The Age of Jackson, 1945; The Vital Center, 1949, (in UK) The Politics of Freedom, 1950; The General and the President (with R. H. Rovere), 1951; Guide to Politics (with Quincy Howe), 1954; (co-editor) Harvard Guide to American History, 1954; The Age of Roosevelt: I: The Crisis of the Old Order, 1957; II: The Coming of the New Deal, 1959; III: The Politics of Upheaval, 1960; The Politics of Hope, 1962; A Thousand Days: John F. Kennedy in the White House, 1965; The Bitter Heritage, 1967; The Crisis of Confidence: Ideas, Power & Violence in America, 1969; articles to magazines and newspapers. *Address:* 166 E 61st Street, New York City; (office) 33 W 42nd Street, New York City. *T:* 790-4261. *Clubs:* Century, Harvard (New York), Federal City (Washington).

**SCHLESINGER, Bernard,** OBE 1946; MA, MD, FRCP; Consulting Physician to University College Hospital, Hospital for Sick Children, Great Ormond Street, and Royal Northern Hospital; originally Consulting Paediatrician to the Army; now retired; *b* 23 Nov. 1896; *s* of late Richard Schlesinger; *m* 1925, Winifred Henrietta, *d* of late H. Regensburg, London; two *s* one *d* (and two *d* decd). *Educ:* Uppingham; Emmanuel Coll., Cambridge. Served European War, 1914-18 as a Private, and in War of 1939-45, as Brigadier, Consulting Physician, NW Army and Central Command, India Command. Fell. of Assoc. of Physicians, Brit. Pædiatric Assoc. (Pres., 1953-54); Fell., Roy. Soc. of Med. (Pres., Pædiatric Sect, 1960-61). Milroy Lectr, 1938. Dawson Williams Prize, 1961. *Publications:* numerous articles and books on Diseases of Children and Researches on Rheumatism. *Recreation:* squash racquets. *Address:* Oliver's Cottage, Boxford, near Newbury, Berks. *T:* Boxford 206. *Clubs:* East India and Sports, Anglo-Belgian.

*See also J. R. Schlesinger.*

**SCHLESINGER, John Richard,** CBE 1970; film director; *b* 16 Feb. 1926; *s* of Bernard Schlesinger, *qv*. *Educ:* Uppingham; Balliol Coll., Oxford (BA). Directed: films for Monitor and Tonight (BBC TV), 1958-60; Terminus, for British Transport Films, 1960; A Kind of Loving, 1961; Billy Liar, 1962-63; Timon of Athens, and Days in the Trees, for Royal Shakespeare Co., 1964-66; Darling, 1964-65; Far from the Madding Crowd, 1966-67; Midnight Cowboy, 1968-69. Soc. of TV and Film Academy Award for Best Director, also Director's Guild of America Award and an American Oscar, for Midnight Cowboy; Golden Lion Award, Venice Film Festival 1961, for Terminus; Golden Bear Award, Berlin Film Festival 1962, for A Kind of

Loving; New York Critics Award, for Darling. *Recreations:* gardening, travel, music, antiques. *Address:* c/o Michael Oliver, Berger Oliver & Co., 40 Piccadilly, W1. *T:* 01-734 7421.

**SCHMIDT-ISSERSTEDT, Hans,** Dr phil; Generalmusikdirektor; Chief Conductor, North German Radio, Hamburg, since 1945; *b* Berlin, 5 May 1900; *m* Helga Swedlund; two *s* (and one *s* decd). *Educ:* Humanistisch. Gym., Berlin; Hochschule für Musik, Berlin; Univs of Berlin, Heidelberg and Münster. Sen. Conductor, Rostock, Darmstadt, Hamburg; Opera Director, German Opera House, Berlin; Chief Conductor, Stockholm Philharmonic Orchestra, 1955-64. Guest Conductor in all important orchestral societies of Old and New Worlds. Mem., Swedish Royal Academy of Music; Hon. Mem., Royal Academy of Music, 1970. Mem., Order of Crown of Bulgaria; Comdr, Order of Cross of Vasa (Sweden), 1964. *Publications:* Hassan gewinnt (three-act opera); orchestral, chamber and vocal music, etc. *Address:* North German Radio, Rothenbaumchaussee 132, Hamburg 13, Germany. *T:* 44-19-31.

**SCHNEIDER, Dr William George,** FRS 1962; FRSC 1951; President, National Research Council of Canada, Ottawa, since 1967; *b* Wolseley, Saskatchewan, 1 June 1915; *s* of Michael Schneider and Phillipina Schneider (*née* Kraushaar); *m* 1940, Jean Frances Purves; two *d. Educ:* University of Saskatchewan; McGill University; Harvard University. BSc 1937, MSc 1939, University of Saskatchewan; PhD (in physical chem.), 1941, McGill Univ. War research under contract of US Office of Scientific Research and Development and US Navy at Woods Hole Oceanographic Inst., Woods Hole, Mass, USA, 1943-46 (US Navy Certificate of Merit, 1946). Joined Nat. Research Council, Division of Pure Chemistry, Ottawa, 1946; Vice-President (Scientific), 1965-67. Hon. DSc, York University, 1966. *Publications:* (with J. A. Pople and H. J. Bernstein) High Resolution Nuclear Magnetic Resonance, 1959; scientific papers in chemistry and physics research jls. *Recreations:* tennis, ski-ing. *Address:* National Research Council of Canada, Ottawa 7, Canada. *T:* 993-2024.

**SCHNEIDERHAN, Frau Wolfgang;** *see* Seefried, Irmgard.

**SCHNYDER, Felix;** Ambassador of Switzerland to the United States, since 1966; *b* 5 March 1910; Swiss; *s* of Maximilian Schnyder and Louise (*née* Steiner); *m* 1941, Sigrid Bucher; one *d. Educ:* University of Berne. Barrister, 1938; activities in private enterprise, 1938-40; joined Federal Political Dept, 1940; assigned to Swiss Legation in Moscow, 1947-49; Counsellor of Legation, Head of Swiss Delegation in Berlin, 1949-54; First Counsellor, Swiss Legation in Washington, 1954-57; Swiss Minister in Israel, 1957; Permanent Observer for Switzerland at UN in New York, 1958-61; Swiss Delegate to Technical Assistance Cttee; Swiss Delegate to Exec. Board of UNICEF (Chm. 1960); UN High Comr for Refugees, 1961-65. *Recreations:* ski-ing, mountaineering, reading (history and politics), chess and bridge. *Address:* 2900 Cathedral Avenue NW, Washington, DC 20008, USA. *T:* HO 2-1811.

**SCHOFIELD, Alfred Norman;** CBE 1967; Town Clerk, Southampton, 1953-68, retd; *b* 2 May 1903; *s* of Alfred Schofield and Mary Schofield (*née* Nodes); *m* 1929, Bessie Agnes Fyfe Hartley; two *s* one *d. Educ:* Woodhouse Grove School; Sheffield University. LLM Sheffield (Frederick Clifford Post Grad. Schol.) 1926. Admitted Solicitor, 1926. Asst Solicitor, Sheffield Corp. 1927; Asst Town Clerk, Rotherham, 1929; Town Clerk: Worksop, 1932; Watford, 1940; War Service: Judge Advocate General's Dept (Army); Pres. Mil. Court, Jerusalem, 1944-46; rank Lt-Col (despatches). Past Pres. Soc. of Town Clerks; First Pres. Commonwealth Assoc. of Town Clerks. *Publications:* Bye Laws of Local Authorities, 1939; Teach Yourself Beekeeping, 1942; Local Government Elections, 1948; Parliamentary Elections, 1949; Housing Law and Practice, 1951; House Purchase through Local Authorities, 1953; The Councillor, 1950. All the above have had several editions. Consulting Editor, Local Government Forms and Precedents. *Recreations:* azalea and heather propagation, beekeeping. *Address:* Belvedere Lodge, Bassett Green Road, Southampton SO2 3NE. *T:* 69048. *Clubs:* Press, National Liberal; Trojans (Southampton).

**SCHOFIELD, Bertram,** CBE 1959; MA, PhD, LittD; Keeper of Manuscripts and Egerton Librarian, British Museum, 1956-61; *b* 13 June 1896; *m* 1928, Edith, *d* of Arthur William and Edith Emily Thomas; one *s* two *d. Educ:* University Sch., Southport; University of Liverpool (Charles Beard and University Fellow); Sorbonne, Ecole des Chartes and Ecole des Hautes Etudes, Paris; Emmanuel College, Cambridge (Open Research Student). Served European War, with Roy. Wilts Yeomanry, 1917-19. Asst Keeper, Dept of MSS, British Museum, 1922; Deputy-Keeper, 1947; Keeper, 1956. Seconded to Min. of Economic Warfare, 1940-42, and for special duties with Inter-Services Intelligence and Combined Ops, HQ, 1942-44. Member: Bd of Studies in Palæography, University of London: Committee of Inst. of Historical Research, 1951-61; Council of Royal Historical Society, 1956-59; Canterbury and York Society; Vice-Pres. British Records Assoc., 1956-61; Governor: North London Collegiate School and Camden High Sch. for Girls, 1955-64. *Publications:* Muchelney Memoranda (Somerset Record Soc.), 1927; (with A. J. Collins) Legal and Manorial Formularies, 1933; The Knyvett Letters, 1949; contrib. to Musical Quarterly, Music Review, Music and Letters. British Museum Quarterly, Studies presented to Sir Hilary Jenkinson, 1957; Musik in Geschichte und Gegenwart, etc. *Recreations:* gardening and music. *Address:* 4 Farm Close, Kidlington, Oxford. *T:* Kidlington 4110.

**SCHOFIELD, Vice-Admiral (Retd) Brian Betham,** CB 1949; CBE 1943; *b* 11 Oct. 1895; *s* of Thomas Dodgshon Schofield and Margaret Annie Bradley; *m* 1st, 1922, Doris Sibyl Ambrose (marr. diss., 1941); one *s* (and one *s* decd); 2nd, 1941, Norah Kathleen Handley (*née* Beatty) (*d* 1946); 3rd, 1946, Grace Mildred Seale; two *d. Educ:* RN Colleges, Osborne and Dartmouth. Midshipman, 1913 (Dogger Bank action); Lieut-Comdr 1925; Comdr 1931; Capt., 1938; Rear-Admiral, 1947; Vice-Adm., 1950; Naval Attaché at The Hague and Brussels, 1939-40; commanded HMS King George V, 1945-46; despatches, 1946. Retired list, 1950. King George VI Coronation medal. Officer of Legion of Merit (USA). *Publications:* The Royal Navy Today, 1960; The Russian Convoys, 1964; British Seapower, 1967; The Rescue Ships (with L. F. Martyn), 1968. *Address:* Holme, Lower Shiplake, Henley-on-Thames, Oxon. *T:* Wargrave 2809.

**SCHOFIELD, (Edward) Guy;** FJI; Journalist; Director: United Newspapers Publications Ltd; United Newspapers Ltd; Sheffield

Newspapers Ltd; Yorkshire Post Newspapers Ltd; *b* 10 July 1902; *s* of Frank Garside Schofield and Fanny Atkinson; *m* 1st, Norah Ellett (*d* 1935); one *d*; 2nd, Ellen Clark. *Educ:* Leeds Modern School. Leeds Mercury, 1918-25; Daily Dispatch, Manchester, 1925-27; Evening Chronicle, Manchester, 1929-30; Chief Sub-Editor, Evening Standard, London, 1931-38; Editor: Yorkshire Evening News, 1938-43; The Evening News, London, 1943-50; Daily Mail, London, 1950-54; Dir of Associated Newspapers Ltd, 1947-55. Member of Press Council, 1953-55; Chairman British Committee, International Press Institute, 1953-55; Director of Publicity, Conservative Party Headquarters, 1955-57; Deputy Editor, The Yorkshire Post, 1957-59; Editor, Weekly Post, 1960-61. *Publications:* The Purple and the Scarlet, 1959; Crime Before Calvary, 1960; In the Year 62, 1962; Why Was He Killed?, 1965. *Address:* Pear Tree Cottage, Sinnington, York. *Club:* Authors'.

**SCHOFIELD, Guy;** *see* Schofield, E. G.

**SCHOFIELD, Ivor Frederick Wentworth,** CMG 1957; ED 1943; *b* 5 July 1904; *s* of Charles William and Jane Schofield; *m* 1937, Gladys May Powell. *Educ:* King's School, Worcester; Hertford Coll., Oxford. Cadet, Admin. Service, Nigeria, 1927; Resident, 1949; Adminstrative officer, Staff Grade, Nigeria (Western Region), 1954; Commissioner of Inland Revenue, Western Region, Nigeria, 1958; retired 1959; re-engaged on contract as Comr of Inland Rev. until Dec. 1960; Administrator of Income Tax, Southern Cameroons, 1960-61; Comr of Income Tax, The Gambia (UNO, Opex), 1964-66; Adviser on Income Tax, The Gambia (UNO), 1967-70. Served War of 1939-45: Royal West African Frontier Force, 1940-42; British Military Administration, Tripolitania, 1942-43; British Military Administration, Dodecanese (Temp. Lt-Col) 1943-45 (despatches). *Recreation:* gardening. *Address:* Goshen, Route de Saint, St Martin's, Guernsey, Channel Islands. *T:* Guernsey 37428.

**SCHOFIELD MORRIS, R.;** *see* Morris, Robert S.

**SCHOLDERER, (Julius) Victor,** CBE 1961; MA, Hon. DLitt (Durham and University of Wales); FBA 1948; *b* Putney, 9 Oct. 1880; *s* of Otto Scholderer, artist, of Frankfort-on-Main, and Luise Steurwaldt; *m* 1913, Frida Marie (*d* 1950), *d* of Wirkl. Geh. Oberbaurat Otto Semler, Berlin. *Educ:* St Paul's School; Trinity College, Oxford (scholar). Gaisford Prize (Greek verse), 1900; 1st Classical Mods; 2nd Lit. Hum.; entered British Museum, 1904; Deputy Keeper in the Department of Printed Books, 1930-45; has worked on the Catalogue of Books printed in the XVth Century now in the British Museum since 1905 and has edited parts v-viii; worked part-time on preparation of Short Title Catalogues of books printed in Italy, in Germany and in the Netherlands up to 1600 now in the British Museum; Sandars Reader in Bibliography, Univ. of Cambridge, 1930; designer of the New Hellenic Greek type; President, Bibliographical Society, 1946-48; gold medal of the Society, 1951; Hon. Member, Gutenberg-Gesellschaft; Hon. Fellow of Pierpont Morgan Library. *Publications:* Greek Printing Types, 1465-1927; Hand-list of Incunabula in National Library of Wales; Johann Gutenberg, Inventor of Printing, 1963; Fifty Essays in Fifteenth- and Sixteenth-Century Bibliography, 1966; papers and articles on early printing published in Transactions of the Bibliographical Society, The Library, Gutenberg-Jahrbuch and elsewhere; part editor of Sir William Osler's Incunabula Medica, 1923; The Avenue and other verses, 1959; Women of Troy, 1965; Reminiscences, 1970. *Address:* British Museum, Bloomsbury, WC1.

**SCHOLEFIELD, Charles Edward,** QC 1959; *b* 15 July 1902; *e s* of Edward Scholefield, Castleford, Yorks; *m* 1966, Catherine Helene (formerly Childs), *o d* of Reginald and Marguerite Blyth; one step *s*; one step *d*. *Educ:* St Peter's School, York. Admitted a Solicitor, 1925; Barrister, Middle Temple, 1934; North Eastern Circuit. Served in Royal Army Pay Corps, 1940-45; Captain, 1943-45. Chm., Council of Professions akin to Medicine, 1966. Master of the Bench of the Middle Temple, 1966. *Publications:* (ed) 11th and 12th edns, Lumley's Public Health. *Recreations:* cricket and Rugby football (watching only now); walking; Sherlock Holmes Society of London; Society of Yorkshiremen in London (Past Chairman). *Address:* Gray's Inn Chambers, Gray's Inn, WC2. *T:* 01-242 5226; 135 Surrenden Road, Brighton, Sussex. *Club:* Reform.

**SCHOLES, Alwyn Denton; Hon. Mr Justice Scholes;** Senior Puisne Judge, Hong Kong, 1970-71; *b* 16 Dec. 1910; *s* of Denton Scholes and Mrs Scholes (*née* Birch); *m* 1939, Juliet Angela Ierne Pyne; one *s* four *d*. *Educ:* Cheltenham College; Selwyn College, Cambridge. Legal Tripos Parts I and II, Cantab, 1932, 1933. Called to the Bar, 1934; practised at the Bar in London and on Midland Circuit, 1934-38; apptd District Magistrate, Gold Coast, 1938; Acting Crown Counsel and Solicitor General, Gold Coast, 1941; apptd Magistrate, Hong Kong, 1948; First Magistrate: Kowloon, 1949; Hong Kong, 1949. Appointed District Judge, Hong Kong, 1953, Puisne Judge, Hong Kong, 1958. *Recreations:* tennis, walking and swimming. *Address:* 74 Peak Road, Hong Kong. *T:* 96606 (Hong Kong); Western Field, Manor Road, Sidmouth, Devon. *Clubs:* Royal Commonwealth Society; Hong Kong Cricket (Hong Kong).

**SCHOLES, Hubert;** Under-Secretary, Ministry of Technology (formerly Ministry of Power), since 1968; *b* 22 March 1921; *s* of late Hubert Scholes and Lucy (*née* Carter); *m* 1949, Patricia Caldwell; one *s*. *Educ:* Shrewsbury Sch.; Balliol Coll., Oxford. Served RA, 1940-45. Asst Principal, Min. of Fuel and Power, 1946; Principal, 1950; Ministry of Housing and Local Govt, 1956-57; Principal Private Sec. to Minister of Power, 1959-62; Asst Sec., 1962. *Address:* Fir Tree Lodge, Jumps Road, Churt, Farnham, Surrey. *T:* Frensham 2315.

**SCHOLES, Joseph,** CB 1945; OBE 1918; *b* 4 Sept. 1889; *s* of John Scholes, Radcliffe, Lancs; *m* 1915, Edna Horrocks. *Educ:* Manchester Grammar School; Trinity College, Cambridge. Wrangler, Mathematical Tripos, 1911; entered GPO through Higher Division, 1912; Assistant Director of Vegetable Supplies, Ministry of Food, 1916-20; Postmaster-Surveyor, Glasgow, 1936; Regional Director, GPO 1939; Principal Officer to Regional Commissioner, Ministry of Home Security, 1940-43; Assistant Director-General (Personnel) GPO, 1946-49; retired. *Address:* Church Orchard, North Newton, Bridgwater, Somerset. *T:* North Petherton 338.

**SCHOLTE, Lieut-Col Frederick Lewellen,** OBE 1919; FIMechE; late RFC; retired Consulting Engineer; *b* 1890; *m* Hilda May (*d* 1969), *d* of James Gardner, Skelmorlie, Ayrshire; one *s* two *d*. *Educ:* Highgate School. *Address:* 6 Alvanley Court, Finchley Rd, NW3. *T:* 01-435

5685. *Clubs:* Royal Automobile, Royal Air Force.

**SCHON, Sir Frank,** Kt 1966; Chairman, National Research Development Corporation, since 1969 (Member, since 1967); *b* 18 May 1912; *o s* of Dr Frederick Schon and Henriette (*née* Nettel); *m* 1936, Gertrude Secher; two *d. Educ:* Rainer Gymnasium, Vienna II; University of Prague; University of Vienna (studied law externally). Co-founder: Marchon Products Ltd, 1939; Solway Chemicals Ltd, 1943; Chairman and Managing Director of both until May 1967; Director, Albright & Wilson Ltd, 1956-67; Non-executive Director, Associated Portland Cement Manufacturers Ltd, 1967-. Mem. of Council: King's College, Durham, 1959-63; University of Newcastle upon Tyne, 1963-66. Member of Court, Univ. of Newcastle upon Tyne, 1963-. Chm. Cumberland Development Council, 1964-68; Member: Northern Economic Planning Council, 1965-68; Industrial Reorganisation Corp., 1966-71; Adv. Council of Technology, 1968; part-time Mem., Northern Gas Bd, 1963-66. Hon. Freeman of Whitehaven, 1961. Hon. DCL Durham, 1961. *Recreations:* golf, reading. *Address:* Spaniards Field, Wildwood Rise, NW11. *T:* 01-455 3729.

**SCHÖNER, Dr Josef A,** GCVO (Hon.) 1966; Austrian Ambassador to the Court of St James's, 1966-70; *b* 18 Feb. 1904; *s* of Andreas Schöner and Lina (*née* Eder); *m* 1965, Henriette (*née* Welz); no *c. Educ:* Grammar Sch., Vienna; Univ. of Vienna; Dr jur and Dr rer pol. Entered Austrian Foreign Service, 1933; Attaché, Austr. Legation, Washington, 1934; Ministry for Foreign Affairs, Vienna, 1934-38; dismissed by German authorities after Anschluss; returned to Foreign Service, 1945; Counsellor, Austr. Leg., London, 1947; Washington, 1947-50; Chief of Austr. Liaison Offices in Germany (Bonn); Envoy Extraordinary and Minister Plenipotentiary, 1952; Head, Dept of Political Affairs, Vienna, 1953-55; Secretary-General for Foreign Affairs, Vienna, 1955-58; Austr. Ambassador, Bonn, 1958-66. Holds Austrian Grand Decoration with Star in Silver, Grand Cross of foreign Orders and other decorations. *Recreations:* sailing, photography, painting and sculpture. *Address:* 13 Seilerstaette, 1010 Wien, Austria. *Club:* Union Yacht (Austria).

**SCHONLAND, Sir Basil (Ferdinand Jamieson),** Kt 1960; CBE 1945; FRS 1938; MA, PhD, MIEE (SA); Hon. ScD (Cantab, Capetown, Rhodes); Hon. DSc (Southampton); Hon. LLD (Natal); Hon. Fellow, of Gonville and Caius Coll., Cambridge, 1959; *b* Grahamstown, SA, 5 Feb. 1896; *s* of late Prof. S. Schonland; *m* 1923, Isabel Marian Craib; one *s* two *d. Educ:* St Andrew's College and Rhodes College, Grahamstown; Gonville and Caius College, Cambridge. Served European War with BEF France, 1915-18, Capt. RE (Signals) (OBE, despatches); Brig. South African Corps of Signals, 1941-44; Supt, Army Operational Research Group (Ministry of Supply), 1941-44; Brig. (Scientific Adviser) to C-in-C 21st Army Group, BLA, 1944 (CBE); George Green Student and Exhibitioner Caius College, Cambridge, Research work in Cavendish Laboratory, 1920-22; Lecturer and later Professor of Physics, University of Cape Town, 1922-36; Pres., SA CSIR, 1945-50; Dir, Bernard Price Inst. of Geophysics and Carnegie-Price Prof. of Geophysics, Univ. of the Witwatersrand, Johannesburg, 1937-54; Dep. Dir, AERE, Harwell, 1954-58, Dir, 1958-60; Dir, Research Gp, UKAEA, 1960-61, retired; Halley Lecturer, University of Oxford, 1937; Chree Lecturer and Medallist, Physical Society of London, 1943; Hughes Medal of Royal Soc., 1945; Elliott-Cresson Medal of Franklin Institute, 1950; Faraday Medallist, IEE, 1962. *Publications:* Atmospheric Electricity, 1932, 2nd edn 1953; The Flight of Thunderbolts, 1950, 2nd edn 1964; The Atomists (1805-1933), 1968; papers in scientific journals on Cathode and Cosmic rays, Wireless and Lightning. *Recreation:* gardening. *Address:* The Down House, Shawford, Nr Winchester, Hants. *T:* Twyford 2221. *Club:* Athenæum.

**SCHOTZ, Benno,** RSA 1937; artist-sculptor; Queen's Sculptor in Ordinary for Scotland since 1963; *b* 1891; *s* of Jacob Schotz; *m* 1927, Milly Stelmach; one *s* one *d. Educ:* Pärnu, Estonia; Glasgow. BSc 1965. Head of Sculpture and Ceramics Departments, Glasgow School of Art, 1938-60. Originally studied engineering at Darmstadt and Glasgow Royal Technical Coll.; then took up sculpture; at Glasgow Art School; first one-man show in 1926 at Reid and Lefèvre's in Glasgow; second 1929; first London one-man show at the Lefèvre Galleries, 1930; one-man show in Dundee, 1935, Edinburgh, 1945, Jerusalem and Haifa Municipal Galleries, 1954-55; Edinburgh Festival, 1955; Royal Fine Art Institute Rooms, Glasgow, 1957; Exhibition by Arts Council of Great Britain (Scottish Cttee) in Edinburgh, Aberdeen, Dundee, Perth, Stirling, 1962; Glasgow, 1963; represented in Public Galleries in Glasgow, Edinburgh, Aberdeen, Perth, Dundee, Paisley, Stoke-on-Trent, Belfast, Jerusalem, Tel-Aviv and New Zealand; modelled many personalities in the arts and politics; Bust of Keir Hardie in House of Commons, 1956. Has a number of carvings on buildings in Glasgow and elsewhere; sculpture groups in churches and schools; 23 foot high Group Town Centre piece in Glenrothes, etc. Hon. LLD Strathclyde, 1969. Hon. FRIAS 1969. *Address:* 2 Kirklee Road, Glasgow W2. *T:* 041-339 9963. *Club:* Glasgow Art (Glasgow).

**SCHRAM, Emil;** Chairman of Board, Peru Trust Co.; *b* Peru, Indiana, 23 November 1893; *s* of Emil Alexander Schram and Katharine Graf; *m* 1914, Mabel Miller; three *s. Educ:* Peru High School. Book-keeper, J. O. Cole, Peru, Ind., 1910-15; manager Hartwell Land Trust, Hillview, Ill., 1915-33; Chairman National Drainage Assoc., 1931-33; chief, drainage, levee and irrigation div., Reconstruction Finance Corp., 1933-36; Director, 1936-41; Chm., 1939-41; President, New York Stock Exchange, 1941-51; Director: Cities Service Co.; Associates Investment Co.; Home Insce Co.; Indiana National Bank; CTS Corp. Valley Farms, Inc.; Hon. Mem. Business Council. Hon. degrees: Dr of Law: New York Univ.; Univ. of Vermont; Franklin College; Indiana Univ. *Recreations:* golf and fishing. *Address:* Hillcrest, RR1, Peru, Ind 46970, USA. *T:* 473 9100. *Club:* Columbia (Indianapolis).

**SCHRAM, Prof. Stuart Reynolds;** Professor of Politics (with reference to China) in the University of London, and Head of Contemporary China Institute, School of Oriental and African Studies, since 1968; *b* 27 Feb. 1924; *s* of Warren R. Schram and Nada Stedman Schram. *Educ:* West High Sch., Minneapolis, Minn; Univ. of Minnesota (BA, 1944); Columbia Univ. (PhD 1954). Dir, Soviet and Chinese Section, Centre d'Etude des Relations Internationales, Fondation Nationale des Sciences Politiques, Paris, 1954-67. *Publications:* Protestantism and Politics in France, 1954; La théorie de la "révolution permanente" en Chine, 1963; The Political Thought of Mao Tse-Tung, 1963, rev. edn 1969; Le marxisme et l'Asie 1853-1964, 1965, rev. and enl. English edn 1969; Mao Tse-tung,

1966, 2nd rev. edn 1971; *translations:* Mao Zedong, une étude de l'éducation physique, 1962; Mao Tse-tung, Basic Tactics, 1966; introd. and notes to Quotations from Chairman Mao Tsetung, 1967. *Recreations:* concert- and theatre-going, walking in the country, fishing. *Address:* Contemporary China Institute, 24 Fitzroy Square, W1. *T:* 01-387 9044.

**SCHREIBER, Brig. Derek,** MVO 1935; late 11th Hussars; *b* 7 May 1904; 2nd *s* of late Captain C. S. Schreiber, and late Hon. Mrs Schreiber, Marlesford Hall, Woodbridge, Suffolk; *m* 1945, Viscountess Clive; one *d. Educ:* Harrow; RMC, Sandhurst. Joined 11th Hussars, 1923; Adjutant, 1930-33; Equerry to Duke of Gloucester, 1934-35; Commander 50 Indian Tank Brigade, 1943-44; Chief of Staff to Duke of Gloucester, 1944-46. *Recreations:* hunting, polo, aviation. *Address:* Bellasis House, Dorking, Surrey. *T:* Betchworth 3339; 59 Cadogan Place, SW1. *T:* 01-235 7454. *Club:* Cavalry.

*See also Baroness Darcy de Knayth.*

**SCHREIBER, Lieut-Gen. Sir Edmond Charles Acton,** KCB, *cr* 1944 (CB 1942); DSO 1914; DL; late Royal Artillery; *b* 30 April 1890; *s* of late Brigadier-General Acton L. Schreiber, CB, CMG, DSO; *m* 1916, Phyllis, *o d* of late Major C. P. Barchard; two *d.* Entered army, 1909; Capt., 1915; Bt Major, 1918; Maj., 1927; Bt Lt-Col, 1930; Lt-Col, 1937; Col 1938; Maj.-Gen. 1940; temp. Lt-Gen. 1941; Lt-Gen. 1944; served European War, 1914-18 (despatches, DSO, Bt Maj.); GSO2 Staff College, 1930-33; GSO2 War Office, 1934-37; GSO1 Senior Officers' School, Sheerness, 1938; Brigadier RA, Southern Command, 1938-39; Comdr 45 Div. 1940, 5 Corps, 1941, First Army, 1942; GOC-in-C Western Command, 1942-44; GOC-in-C South-Eastern Command, 1944; Governor and Commander-in-Chief of Malta, 1944-46; retired, 1947. National President, Old Contemptibles Association, 1960. DL Devon, 1948. KStJ, 1944. *Address:* Devoncourt Hotel, Exmouth, Devon. *Club:* Army and Navy.

**SCHREIBER, Mrs Gaby;** Consultant designer; specialist in interior and industrial design; Chairman: Gaby Schreiber & Associates; Convel Designers Ltd; Convel Ltd; Convel Design International, sprl, Brussels; *d* of Gunther George Peter Wolff; *m* Leopold Schreiber (*d* 1961). *Educ:* studied art and later stage and interior design in Vienna, Florence, Berlin and Paris, Consultancies have included: Allen and Hanbury (Surgical Engineering) Limited; BOAC; Divs of Dunlop Rubber Gp; Bartrev Gp of Cos; Hawker Siddeley Aviation Ltd (for the Queen's Flight and RAF); Rank Organisation Ltd; Peter Robinson Ltd; West Cumberland Hosp.; Newcastle Regional Hosp. Bd; Crown Agents; Cunard Steamship Co. Ltd; Myers & Co.; National Westminster Bank; Marquess of Londonderry; designed Exhibn Stands in Britain, Europe and USA. Member CoID, 1960-62 (Mem. Design Awards Cttee, 1961); Judge on Indep. Panel, to select Duke of Edinburgh's Prize for Elegant Design, 1960 and 1961; FSIA (Chm., Consultant Designers Gp; Past Chm., Internat. Relations Cttee). Has broadcast and appeared on TV. *Publications:* contribs on industrial and interior design and on colour to art and technical pubns; her work has appeared in internat. books and jls on design. *Recreations:* gardening, farming, golf, paintings, drawings. *Address:* 9 Eaton Square, SW1. *T:* 01-235 4656.

**SCHRODER, Ernest Melville,** CMG 1970; Director: Adelaide Cement Holdings Ltd; Quarry Industries Ltd; Adelaide Motors Investments Ltd; *b* 23 Aug. 1901; *s* of Harold Schroder and Florence L. A. Schroder (*née* Stimson); *m* 1928, Winsome Dawson; two *s* one *d. Educ:* Newcastle (NSW) High Sch.; Newcastle Techn. College. Chief Chemist: Kandos Cement Co., Sydney, 1927-30; Australian Cement Ltd, Geelong, 1930-44; Man. Dir, Adelaide Cement Ltd, Adelaide, 1944-68, retd. Pres., SA Chamber of Manufacturers, 1963-64, 1964-65; Vice-Pres., Assoc. Chamber of Manufrs of Aust., 1964-65; Pres., Cement and Concrete Assoc. of Aust., 1953-54, 1960-61; State Cttee Mem., CSIRO, 1954-; Mem., CSIRO Adv. Council, 1955-61. FRACI; AIEAust; MAIMM; FAIM. *Recreations:* golf, gardening. *Address:* 32 Coreega Avenue, Springfield, South Australia 5062. *T:* Adelaide 796452. *Clubs:* Adelaide, Naval Military and Air Force of South Australia (Adelaide).

**SCHULTZ, Sir Leo, (Joseph Leopold),** Kt 1966; OBE 1945; Alderman, City of Kingston upon Hull, since 1926; *b* 4 Feb. 1900; *s* of Solomon Schultz; *m* 1928, Kate, *d* of George Pickersgill; one *s. Educ:* Hull. *Recreation:* cricket. *Address:* 6 Newland Park, Hull. *T:* 42253.

**SCHUMANN, Maurice;** Chevalier de la Légion d'Honneur; Compagnon de la Libération; Croix de Guerre (1939-45); Minister for Foreign Affairs, France, since June 1969; writer and broadcaster; *b* Paris, 10 April 1911; *s* of Julien Schumann and Thérèse Michel; *m* 1944, Lucie Daniel; one *s* two *d. Educ:* Lycées of Janson-de-Sailly and Henry IV; Faculty of Letters, Univ. of Paris (Licencié ès Lettres). Attached to l'Agence Havas in London and later Paris, 1935-39; Chief Official Broadcaster, BBC French Service, 1940-44; Liaison Officer with Allied Expeditionary Forces at end of war; Mem. Provisional Consultative Assembly, Nov. 1944-July 1945; Deputy for Nord, 1945-67 and 1968; Mem. Constituent Assemblies, Oct. 1945-May 1946 and June-Nov. 1946. A Founder, Popular Republican Movement (MRP); Deputy of this group, 1945 (Pres., 1945-49; Hon. Pres., 1949-); Minister for Foreign Affairs, 1951-54; Pres., For. Affairs Cttee of Nat. Assembly, 1959; Minister of State (Prime Minister's Office), Arpil-May 1962; Minister of State, in charge of scientific res. and atomic and spacial questions, 1967-68; Minister of State for Social Affairs, 1968-69. Has been Pres. of various organisations, incl. Internat. Movement for Atlantic Union, 1966-. *Publications:* Le Germanisme en marche, 1938; Mussolini, 1939; Les problèmes Ukrainiens et la paix européenne, 1939; Honneur et Patrie, 1945; Le vrai malaise des intellectuels de gauche, 1957; Le Rendezvous avec quelqu'un (novel), 1962; La Voix du couvrefeu (novel), 1964; many articles etc (under pseudonym of André Sidobre) to l'Aube (Paris daily), Le Temps présent and La Vie catholique, etc. *Address:* Ministère des Affaires Etrangères, 37 Quai d'Orsay, Paris 7e, France.

**SCHUSCHNIGG, Dr Kurt von;** Professor, St Louis University, USA, 1948-67; *b* Riva (South Tyrol), 14 Dec. 1897; *s* of late Artur von Schuschnigg, Austrian General; *m* 1st, 1924, Herma Masera (*d* 1935); one *s*; 2nd, 1938, Countess Czernin. *Educ:* Stella Matutina College, Feldkirch; Innsbruck University. Member Austrian Parliament, 1927; Minister for Justice, 1932; Chancellor of Austria, 1934-38. *Publications:* Dreimal Oesterreich, 1937 (Farewell, Austria, 1938); Requiem in Rot-Weiss-Rot, 1945 (Zürich, Milan, New York); Im Kampf mit Hitler: die Ueberwindung der Anschussidee, 1969, London 1970. *Address:* Mutters, near Innsbrück, Austria.

**SCHUSTER, Sir (Felix) James (Moncrieff),** 3rd Bt, *cr* 1906; OBE 1955; TD; *b* 8 January 1913; *o* *s* of Sir Victor Schuster, 2nd Bt, and Lucy, *d* of W. B. Skene, Pitlour-Halyards, Fife; *S* father, 1962; *m* 1937, Ragna, *er d* of late Direktor Sundø, Copenhagen; two *d. Educ:* Winchester. Served War of 1939-45, with The Rifle Brigade (Middle East and Combined Operations). Lt-Col comdg London Rifle Brigade. Rangers (RB), TA, 1952-; Bt-Colonel, 1955. *Heir:* none. *Address:* Little Swanborough, near Lewes, Sussex. *Club:* Bath.

**SCHUSTER, Sir George Ernest,** KCSI 1931; KCMG 1926; CBE 1918; MC; Member Oxfordshire County Council; Chairman, Board of Governors, United World College of the Atlantic; Deputy President, International Council, United World Colleges; *b* 1881; *s* of late Ernest Schuster, KC; *m* 1908, Hon. Gwendolen, *d* of Lord Parker of Waddington; one *s* (and one killed in action, 1941). *Educ:* Charterhouse (Scholar); New College, Oxford (Classical Exhibitioner), 1st Class in Greats, 1903. Barrister-at-Law, 1905; partner in Schuster Son & Co.; and Director of Numerous companies, 1906-14; served European War, 1914-18, with QO Oxfordshire Hussars and on Staff in France; North Russia, 1919, AA and QMG, Murmansk Force, Lt-Col TF Reserve (despatches four times, MC. CBE); travelled Central Europe to report on economic conditions for Anglo-Danubian Assoc. Ltd, 1920; Chief Assist to Organiser of International Credits under League of Nations, 1921; Member of Advisory Committee to Treasury under Trade Facilities Act, 1921-2; Financial Secretary Sudan Government, 1922-27; Chairman of Advisory Committee to Colonial Secretary on East African Loans, 1926-28; Economic and Financial Adviser, Colonial Office, 1927-28; Member of East African Commission on Closer Union, 1928; Finance Mem. of Executive Council of Viceroy of India, 1928-34; Chairman of Joint Committee of Inquiry into the Anglo Argentine Meat Trade, 1935-38; Mem. of Colonial Development Advisory Cttee, 1936-38; MP (L Nat) Walsall, 1938-45; Member of Select Committee on National Expenditure, 1939-45. Member of Govt Cttee on Industrial Productivity and Chairman of Cttee's Panel on Human Relations, 1947-51; Mem. and Treas. of Medical Research Council, 1947-51; Visited Malta at request of Malta Govt to advise on economic and financial policy, 1950 and 1956-57. Chm., Oxford Regional Hosp. Bd, 1951-63. Hon. DCL Oxford. *Publications:* India and Democracy, 1941; Christianity and Human Relations in Industry, 1951. *Recreations:* all country sports. *Address:* Nether Worton House, Middle Barton, Oxon. *Clubs:* Athenæum, Brooks's.

**SCHUSTER, Sir James;** *see* Schuster, Sir F. J. M.

**SCHUSTER, Rt. Rev. James Leo;** *see* St John's (S Africa), Bishop of.

**SCHWARTZ, George Leopold,** BA, BSc (Econ.): Deputy City Editor Sunday Times, Economic Adviser Kemsley Newspapers, 1944-61; *b* 10 Feb. 1891; *s* of late Adolph George Schwartz, Philadelphia; *m* 1927, Rhoda Lomax (*d* 1966). *Educ:* Varndean Sch.; St Paul's Coll., Cheltenham; London School of Economics. Teacher, LCC, 1913; Secretary London Cambridge Economic Service, 1923; Cassel Lecturer in University of London, 1929. Editor Bankers' Magazine, 1945-54. Hon. Fellow, London School of Economics. *Publications:* (with F. W. Paish) Insurance Funds and their Investment, 1934; Bread and Circuses, 1959. Articles and pamphlets. *Recreation:* detesting government. *Address:* 28 Spencer Drive, N2. *T:* 01-455 7423. *Club:* Reform.

**SCHWARZ, Rudolf;** Principal Conductor, Northern Sinfonia Orchestra, Newcastle upon Tyne, and Guest Conductor of Bergen Orchestra, Norway, since 1964; *b* 29 April 1905; Austrian (British subject, 1952); *m* 1950, Greta Ohlson; one *s* (and one *step d* and one *step s*). *Educ:* Vienna. Conductor, Opera House, Düsseldorf, 1923-27; Conductor, Opera House, Karlsruhe, 1927-33; Musical Director, Jewish Cultural Organisation, Berlin, 1936-41; Conductor, Bournemouth Municipal Orchestra, 1947-51; Conductor, City of Birmingham Symphony Orchestra, 1951-57; Chief Conductor of the BBC Symphony Orchestra, 1957-62. Hon. RAM; Hon. GSM. *Address:* 24 Wildcroft Manor, Putney Heath, SW15.

**SCHWARZ-BART, André;** French writer; *b* Metz, Lorraine, France, 1928; 2nd *s* of parents from Poland. *Educ:* self-educated; Sorbonne. Joined French Resistance at 15. Has worked in a factory and in Les Halles, Paris, while writing. *Publication:* Le Dernier des Justes, 1959 (Prix Goncourt, 1959; Eng. trans., 1960). *Address:* c/o Editions du Seuil, 27 rue Jacob, Paris VIe.

**SCHWARZENBERG, Dr Johannes Erkinger,** GCVO (Hon.) 1966; Minister Plenipotentiary of Sovereign Order of Malta to Italy, since 1969; *b* 31 Jan. 1903; *m* 1931, Kathleen, Vicomtesse de Spoelberch; one *s* one *d. Educ:* Univ. of Vienna (Doctor of Law). Civil servant, Ministry of the Interior, Austria, 1928; Attaché, Federal Chancellery, Foreign Affairs, 1930; Secretary, Austrian Legation, Rome, 1933, Berlin, 1935; left diplomatic career, 1938; Director and Delegate, Internat. Cttee of Red Cross, Geneva, 1940-46; re-entered Austrian diplomatic career as Counsellor in Paris, 1946; Austrian Minister in Rome, 1948; Austrian Ambassador: in Rome, 1950; in London, 1955-65; to Holy See, 1965-68. Commander's Cross in gold, Austrian Order of Merit, 1955, Grand Cross of the Italian Order of Merit, 1955, and other decorations. *Address:* 32 via Botteghe Oscure, 00186 Rome, Italy.

**SCHWARZENBERGER, Prof. Georg;** Professor of International Law in the University of London since 1962; Dean, Faculty of Laws, University College, London, 1965-67 (Vice-Dean, 1949-55 and 1963-65); Director, London Institute of World Affairs since 1943; Barrister-at-Law, Gray's Inn, since 1955; *b* 20 May 1908; *o s* of Ludwig and Ferry Schwarzenberger; *m* 1931, Suse Schwarz; one *s*. *Educ:* Karls-Gymnasium, Heilbronn aN; Univs of Heidelberg, Frankfurt, Berlin, Tübingen, Paris and London. Dr Jur. (Tübingen) 1930; PhD (London) 1936. Sec. London Inst. of World Affairs (formerly New Commonwealth Inst.) 1934-43; Lectr in Internat. Law and Relations, University Coll., London, 1938-45; Sub-Dean and Tutor, Faculty of Laws, 1942-49; Reader in Internat. Law, 1945-62. Co-Editor (with G. W. Keeton) of: The Library of World Affairs, 1946-; The Year Book of World Affairs, 1947-; Current Legal Problems, 1948-. Member, Permanent Finnish-Netherlands Conciliation Commission. *Publications:* The League of Nations and World Order, 1936; Power Politics: A Study of World Society (1st edn 1941, 3rd edn 1964); International Law and Totalitarian Lawlessness, 1943; International Law as Applied by International Court and Tribunals, 1945 (Vol. I, 3rd edn 1957, Vol. II, 1968); A Manual of International Law, 1947 (5th edn 1967); The Fundamental Principles of International Law, Hague

Academy of Internat. Law (Receuil, Vol. 87), 1955; The Legality of Nuclear Weapons, 1958; The Frontiers of International Law, 1962; The Inductive Approach to International Law, 1965; The Principles and Standards of International Economic Law, Hague Acad. of Internat. Law (Recueil, Vol. 117), 1966; Foreign Investments and International Law, 1969; International Law and Order, 1971. *Recreations:* gardening, swimming. *Address:* University College, London, WC1; (private) 4 Bowers Way, Harpenden, Herts. *T:* Harpenden 3497.

**SCHWARZKOPF, Elisabeth;** Opera and Concert Singer; *b* 9 Dec. 1915; *o d* of Gymnasial-direktor Friedrich Schwarzkopf and Elisabeth (*née* Fröhlich); *m* Walter Legge. *Educ:* High School for Music, Berlin. Vienna State Opera; Royal Opera, Covent Garden; La Scala, Milan, since 1950; San Francisco Opera, since 1955. Appears regularly at most International Festivals; Bayreuth Festival, 1951. Inauguration Piccolo Teatro della Scala, Dec. 1955. Appeared (in Der Rosenkavalier) Metropolitan Opera, New York, 1964. *Film:* Der Rosenkavalier, 1962. Lilli Lehmann Medal (Salzburg), 1950; first Premio Orfeo d'oro, Mantua. *Recreations:* music, tennis, gardening, ski-ing, mountaineering.

**SCHWEITZER, Pierre-Paul;** Commandeur de la Légion d'Honneur; Croix de Guerre (1939-45); Médaille de la Résistance avec rosette; Inspecteur Général des Finances; Managing Director and Chairman of the Board, International Monetary Fund since Sept. 1963; *b* 29 May 1912; *s* of Paul Schweitzer and Emma Munch; *m* 1941, Catherine Hatt; one *s* one *d*. *Educ:* Univs of Strasbourg and Paris; Ecole Libre des Sciences Politiques. Joined French Treasury, 1936; Inspecteur des Finances, 1939; Dep. Dir for Internat. Finance, French Treasury, Paris, 1946; Alternate Executive Director, Internat. Monetary Fund, Washington, 1947; Sec.-Gen. for European Economic Cooperation in the French Administration, Paris, 1948; Financial Counsellor, French Embassy, Washington, 1949; Director, Treasury, Paris, 1953; Dep. Governor of the Banque de France, Paris, 1960-63. Hon. LLD: Yale, 1966; Harvard 1966; Leeds, 1968; New York, 1968. *Address:* (home) 1717 Foxhall Road NW, Washington, DC 20007; (office) 19th and H Streets, NW, Washington, DC 20431, USA. *T:* Executive 3 63 62.

**SCHWINGER, Prof. Julian,** AB, PhD; Higgins Professor of Physics, Harvard University, since 1966 (Professor since 1947); *b* 12 Feb. 1918; *s* of Benjamin Schwinger and Belle Schwinger (*née* Rosenfeld); *m* 1947, Clarice Carrol. *Educ:* Columbia University. Nat. Research Council Fellow, 1939-40; Research Associate, University of California at Berkeley, 1940-41; Instructor, later Assistant Professor, Purdue University, 1941-43; Member Staff: Radiation Laboratory, MIT, 1943-46; Metallurgy Laboratory, University of Chicago, 1943; Associate Professor of Physics, Harvard University, 1945-47. Member, Board of Sponsors, Bulletin of the Atomic Scientists. Member: Nat. Acad. of Scis; Amer. Acad. of Arts and Scis; Amer. Phys. Soc.; Amer. Assoc. for Advancement of Science; NY Acad. of Sciences; Civil Liberties Union. Guggenheim Fellow, 1970. Awarded Nobel Prize for Physics (with R. Feynman and S. Tomonaga), 1965; many other awards and medals. Hon. DSc: Purdue University, 1961; Harvard, 1962; Columbia, 1966. *Publications:* Quantum Electrodynamics (editor), 1958; (with D. Saxon) Discontinuities in Wave Guides, 1968; Particles and Sources, 1969; Quantum Kinematics and Dynamics, 1970; Particles, Sources and Fields, 1970. *Recreations:* swimming, ski-ing, driving, and being one of the world's worst pianists. *Address:* Harvard University, Department of Physics, Cambridge, Mass 02138, USA; 256 Slade Street, Belmont, Mass 02178, USA.

**SCICLUNA, Sir Hannibal Publius,** Kt 1955; MBE 1935; MA (*hc* Oxon, 1938); LLD (*hc* Malta, 1966); FSA (London, 1946, Scotland 1959); *b* 15 February 1880; *s* of late Joseph Scicluna and Carmen (*née* Galdes); *m* 1st, 1903, Amalia (*née* Lanfranco) (*d* 1947); two *s* (and one *s* decd) three *d*; 2nd, 1959, Margaret Helen Jarvis (*née* Cadzow). *Educ:* St Ignatius College; Royal Malta University. Entered Malta Civil Service, 1902; Solicitor, 1905; Secretary and Registrar of Malta University, 1913-20; Solicitor and Clerk, Crown Advocate's Office and Min. of Justice, 1916-23; Secretary to Legal Sec., Malta Imp. Govt, 1921-23; Rep. of Malta Govt Emigration Cttee in Devastated Regions, France, 1920 (Officier d'Académie, France); Mem. Antiquities Cttee, Malta, 1922; Librarian of Roy. Malta Library, 1923; Malta Rep. Internat. Cttee of Hist. Sciences, 1931; Dir Malta Museum, 1937; Dep. Comr BRCOStJ Joint War Organisation, 1940; Pres. Malta Cttee BRCS, 1952; Archivist and Librarian, Sov. Mil. Order of Malta, 1955 (Rome). Frequent delegate for Malta at internat. congresses, etc. King's Jubilee Medal, 1935; Coronation Medal, 1937. KStJ 1938; Distinguished Service Medal, OStJ; Kt Grand Cross of Magistral Grace with Riband, Order of St John of Jerusalem and of Malta, 1959; Chevalier Officier Legion Hon., 1950; Coronation Medal, 1953. Kt Grand Cross of Merit of Order of Malta, 1956; Kt Commander Order of St Gregory the Great, 1956; Kt Grand Cross Hospitaller and Military Order of St Lazarus of Jerusalem, 1967; Kt of Honour, Order of House of Lippe, 1962; Grand Cross with Riband of Constantinian Order of St George, 1963. *Publications:* The Archives of the SM Order of Malta, 1912; The French Occupation of Malta (1798-1800), 1923; The Order of St John of Jerusalem, 1929; The Book of Deliberations of the Venerable Tongue of England, 1949; The Church of St John in Valletta, 1955; The Order of St John of Jerusalem and Places of Interest in Malta and Gozo, 1969; numerous historical and documentary. *Recreations:* travel; formerly football (Association), riding, tennis, swimming, boating. *Address:* Villa St Martin, Malta, GC. *T:* St Paul's 73428; The Cloisters, 27 Mrabat Street, Sliema, Malta, GC. *T:* Sliema 30493; Samuelston, East Saltoun, Pencaitland, East Lothian. *T:* Pencaitland 252. *Clubs:* Casino Maltese (Valletta); Malta Union (Sliema, Malta, GC).

**SCLATER-BOOTH,** family name of **Baron Basing.**

**SCOBLE, (Arthur William) John;** Chairman, Economic Planning Board, South West Region (Bristol), since 1965; *b* Plymouth, 11 Jan. 1910; *er s* of Arthur and Mabel Scoble, Plymouth; *m* 1935, Constance Aveline, *d* of Samuel Robbins, Bristol; three *d*. *Educ:* Sexey's Sch., Bruton, Somerset. Entered Civil Service, 1930; HM Customs and Excise, 1930-35; special duties, HM Customs and Excise, 1935-40; Special duties, Min. of Supply, 1940-44; Min. of Nat. Insce, 1945-50; jssc 1950; Min. of Works: Regional Dir, Newcastle, 1951-54; Secretariat (Asst Sec.), 1954-59; UN, Buenos Aires, 1960-61; Min. of Works HQ, 1962-64; Dept of Economic Affairs, 1965-. *Address:* Longwood House, Failand, Bristol. *T:* Long Ashton 2092.

**SCOFIELD, (David) Paul,** CBE 1956; Actor; Associate Director, National Theatre, since 1970; *b* 21 Jan. 1922; *s* of Edward H. and M. Scofield; *m* 1943, Joy Parker (actress); one *s* one *d*. *Educ:* Varndean Sch. for Boys, Brighton. Theatre training, Croydon Repertory, 1939; London Mask Theatre School, 1940. Shakespeare with ENSA, 1940-41; Birmingham Repertory Theatre, 1942; CEMA Factory tours, 1942-43; Whitehall Theatre, 1943; Birmingham Repertory, 1943-44-45; Stratford-upon-Avon, 1946-47-48. Mem., Royal Shakespeare Directorate, 1966-68. London theatres: Arts, 1946; Phoenix, 1947; Adventure Story, and The Seagull, St James's, 1949; Ring Round the Moon, Globe, 1950; Much Ado About Nothing, Phœnix, 1952; The River Line, Edin. Fest., Lyric (Hammersmith), Strand, 1952; John Gielgud's Company, 1952-53: Richard II, The Way of the World, Venice Preserved, etc; A Question of Fact, Piccadilly, 1953-54; Time Remembered, Lyric, Hammersmith, New Theatre, 1954-55; Hamlet, Moscow, 1955; Paul Scofield-Peter Brook Season, Phœnix Theatre, 1956; Hamlet, The Power and the Glory, Family Reunion; A Dead Secret, Piccadilly Theatre, 1957; Expresso Bongo, Saville Theatre, 1958; The Complaisant Lover, Globe Theatre, 1959; A Man For All Seasons, Globe Theatre, 1960, New York, 1961-62; Coriolanus and Love's Labour's Lost, at Shakespeare Festival Season, Stratford, Ont., 1961; King Lear: Stratford-on-Avon, Aldwych Theatre, 1962-63, Europe and US, 1964; Timon of Athens, Stratford-on-Avon, 1965; The Government Inspector, also Staircase, Aldwych, 1966; Macbeth, Stratford-on-Avon, 1967, Russia, Finland, 1967, Aldwych, 1968; The Hotel in Amsterdam, Royal Court, 1968; Uncle Vanya, Royal Court, 1970. *Films:* The Train, 1964; A Man for All Seasons, 1966 (from the play); King Lear, 1969. Hon. LLD Glasgow, 1968. *Relevant Publication:* Paul Scofield, by J. C. Trewin, 1956. *Address:* The Gables, Balcombe, Sussex. *T:* 378.

**SCOFIELD, Paul;** *see* Scofield, (D.) P.

**SCOGINGS, Very Rev. Frank,** LTh; retired as Dean of Natal, (1946-60), and Vicar Gen. (1948-60). LTh, University of Durham, 1914. Deacon, 1914; priest, 1915. Curate of St Augustine, Penhalonga, 1914-16; St Michael, Salisbury, 1916-21; St John, Bulawayo, 1921-26; Priest-in-Charge of St Michael's Mission, Salisbury, 1927-28; St Faith's Native Mission, Durban, 1928-36; Vicar of St Saviour's Cathedral, Pietermaritzburg, Diocese of Natal, 1936; Sub-Dean, 1936-46; Canon of Natal, 1944. *Address:* 6 Taunton Road, Maritzburg, Natal, South Africa.

**SCOLLAN, Thomas;** engineer; trade union organiser for distributive workers. Former President Scottish Trade Union Congress. MP (Lab) Western Renfrew, 1945-50. *Address:* 9 Barlogan Avenue, Glasgow SW2.

**SCOONES, General Sir Geoffry (Allen Percival),** KCB 1947; KBE 1944 (OBE 1935); CSI 1942; DSO 1917; MC; *b* 1893; *e s* of late Major Fitzmaurice Scoones, formerly Royal Fusiliers; *m* 1918, Angela Maud, *e d* of late Rev. Spencer R. A. Buller, RD; one *s* two *d*. *Educ:* Wellington College, RMC Sandhurst. Commandant 2nd Battn 8th Gurkha Rifles, Indian Army, 1935; Director of Military Operations and Intelligence, India, 1941-42; Major-General, 1942; GOC 4 Corps, Burma, 1942-44; GOC-in-C Central Command, India, 1945-46; General, 1946; Principal Staff Officer, Commonwealth Relations Office, 1947-53; ADC to the King, 1947-49; United Kingdom High Commissioner in New Zealand, 1953-57. *Address:* The Old Mill House, Wendover, Bucks. *Club:* United Hunts.

**SCOONES, Major-General Sir Reginald (Laurence),** KBE, *cr* 1955 (OBE 1941); CB 1951; DSO 1945; late Royal Armoured Corps; Director, The Brewers' Society, 1957-69; *b* 18 Dec. 1900; *s* of late Major Fitzmaurice Scoones, Royal Fusiliers; *m* 1933, Isabella Bowie, *d* of John Nisbet, Cumbrae Isles, Scotland; one *d*. *Educ:* Wellington College; RMC, Sandhurst. 2nd Lt R Fus., 1920; transferred Royal Tank Corps, 1923; attd Sudan Defence Force, 1926-34; served War of 1939-45, Middle East and Burma; Lt-Col 1941; Brig. 1942; Maj.-Gen. 1950; Major-General Commanding British Troops Sudan and Commandant Sudan Defence Force, 1950-54. *Recreations:* riding, golf, tennis. *Address:* Casa Pandora, Montes da Luz, Lagos, Algarve, Portugal. *Club:* United Hunts.

**SCOPES, Sir Frederick,** Kt 1954; Chairman: Chamberlin and Hill Ltd; Solid Smokeless Fuels Federation; Deputy Treasurer, Nottingham University; *b* 24 Feb. 1892; *o s* of Harry and Alice D. Scopes; *m* 1st, 1916, Effie Theresa (*d* 1962); two *s*; 2nd, 1964, Ellen Frederica, *d* of late Capt. H. P. Wallis, RHA (formerly Mrs Downe). *Educ:* King Edward's Schools, Camp Hill and New St, Birmingham; Corpus Christi College, Oxford (Modern History Scholar). MA. Chairman, The Stanton Ironworks Co. Ltd, 1957-62 (Man. Dir 1942-57). President, The Joint Iron Council, 1948-54; OStJ. Liveryman, Worshipful Company of Founders. *Address:* 6 Clarendon Terrace, Brighton BN2 1FD. *T:* Brighton 62168. *Club:* Bath.

**SCOPES, Sir Leonard Arthur,** KCVO 1961; CMG 1957; OBE 1946; Member, United Nations Joint Inspection Unit, Geneva; *b* 19 March 1912; *s* of late Arthur Edward Scopes and Jessie Russell Hendry; *m* 1938, Brunhilde Slater Rolfe; two *s* two *d*. *Educ:* St Dunstan's College; Gonville and Caius College, Cambridge (MA). Joined HM Consular Service, 1933; Vice-Consul: Antwerp, 1933, Saigon, 1935; Canton, 1937; Acting Consul, Surabaya, 1941; Vice-Consul, Lourenço Marques, 1942; Consul, Skoplje and Ljubljana, 1945; Commercial Secretary, Bogota, 1947; Assistant in United Nations (Economic and Social) Department of Foreign Office, 1950; Counsellor, Djakarta, 1952; Foreign Service Inspector, 1954; HM Ambassador to Nepal, 1957-62; HM Ambassador to Paraguay, 1962-67. *Recreation:* golf. *Address:* Room D516, Palais des Nations, CH-1211 Geneva 10, Switzerland.

**SCORRER, Aileen Mona,** CBE 1953; Chief Inspector, Children's Department, Home Office, 1950-65; *b* 26 Feb. 1905; *d* of late G. H. Scorrer, Sussex, and late Mina Drury. *Educ:* Huyton College, Liverpool; Royal Holloway College, London. *Address:* Coverdale, Susan Wood, Chislehurst, Kent BR7 5NG. *T:* 01-467 3407.

**SCOTHORNE, Prof. Raymond John,** BSc, MD Leeds; MD Chicago; FRSE; FRCSGlas; Professor of Anatomy in the University of Newcastle upon Tyne, since 1960; *b* 1920; *s* of late John Scothorne and of Lavinia Scothorne; *m* 1948, Audrey, *o d* of Rev. Selwyn Gillott, Oxford; one *s* two *d*. *Educ:* Royal Grammar School, Newcastle upon Tyne; Universities of Leeds and Chicago, BSc (Hons) 1st cl. (Leeds), 1941; MD (Chicago), Rockefeller Student, 1941-43; MB (Hons) 1st cl. (Leeds), 1944; MD (with Distinction) (Leeds), 1951. Demonstrator and Lecturer in Anatomy, 1944-50, Univ. of Leeds; Sen. Lecturer in

Anatomy, 1950-60, Univ. of Glasgow. Hon. Sec., Anat. Soc. of Great Britain and Ireland, 1967-; Mem., Med. Sub-Cttee, UGC, 1967-. Struthers Prize and Gold Medal in Anatomy, Univ. of Glasgow, 1957. *Publications:* papers on embryology and histology. *Address:* School of Medicine, University of Newcastle upon Tyne; 52 Errington Road, Ponteland, Northumberland. *T:* Ponteland 3518.

**SCOTLAND, Rear-Adm. John Earl,** CB 1964; DSC 1943; Regional Sales Director, Upper Clyde Shipbuilders, since 1968; *b* 24 Aug. 1911; *s* of Capt. W. R. Scotland, RN and Gwladys Lewis, Sydney, New South Wales; *m* 1940, Eileen Anne Studholme Brownrigg; one *s* two *d. Educ:* Cranbrook School, Sydney, New South Wales; Royal Naval Coll., Dartmouth. Qual. Gunnery Officer, 1938; HMS Dunedin, 1939; HMS Curacoa, 1940; HMS Jamaica, 1941-43; HMS King George V, 1945; in command HMS Modeste, 1946; Comdr 1946; in comd HMS Gravelines, 1951; Captain, 1953; in comd Gunnery School, Devonport, 1953; in comd HMS Vigilant and Dartmouth Training Sqdn, 1955 Naval Attaché, Rome, 1957; in comd HMS Lion, 1960; Rear-Adm. 1962; Flag Officer Middle East, 1962-64; Senior Naval Member, Ordnance Board, 1965-67, Pres., 1967-68. Officer, Order of Merit of the Republic of Italy. *Recreations:* painting, tennis, water ski-ing. *Address:* 9 Tite Street, SW3. *Clubs:* United Service; Royal Yacht Squadron (Naval Member).

**SCOTT,** family name of **Earl of Eldon.**

**SCOTT;** *see* Hepburne-Scott, family name of **Baron Polwarth.**

**SCOTT, MONTAGU-DOUGLAS-,** family name of **Duke of Buccleuch.**

**SCOTT, Prof. Alexander Whiteford,** CBE 1960; Professor of Chemical Engineering, University of Strathclyde, Glasgow, since 1955; Hon. Engineering Consultant to Ministry of Agriculture, Fisheries and Food, 1946-62; *b* 28 January 1904; *s* of Alexander Scott, Glasgow; *m* 1933, Rowena Christianna (*d* 1970), *d* of John Craig, Glasgow; one *s. Educ:* Royal College of Science and Technology, Glasgow. BSc, PhD, ARCST, Glasgow. FIMechE, MIChemE, Hon. MIHVE. *Address:* 9 Rowallan Road, Thornliebank, Glasgow. *T:* 041-638 2968. *Club:* Authors'.

**SCOTT, Maj.-Gen. Anthony Gerald O'Carroll,** CB 1951; CBE 1946 (OBE 1945); DL; *b* 22 June 1899; *s* of late Brigadier-General P. C. J. Scott, CB, and Mrs F. K. Scott (*née* Carroll); *m* 1926, Helena, *d* of Francis R. James, Hereford; one *d. Educ:* Wellington College; RMA, Woolwich. Gazetted 2nd Lt RFA, 1918; served European War, 1914-18, with Chestnut Troop, RHA; RFA, 1919-21; seconded King's African Rifles (local Capt.), 1921-26; Adjutant Beds Yeo., 1927-31; Instructor in Gunnery, School of Artillery, 1932; student Staff College, Camberley, psc, 1934-35; India, 1936; Staff Officer, RA, Western Comd, India, 1937; Instructor, Staff College, Quetta, 1938; BGS, 15 Indian Corps, Arakan, Burma, 1942; CRA 25 Indian Div., 1943; Comdr 53 Indian Inf. Bde, 1944; BGS Eastern Comd, UK, 1945; Comd Sussex AA Bde, 1948; Commander Hamburg District, 1950-51; Commander, Singapore Base District, 1951-54; retired 1954. Vice-Pres., British Falconers' Club (Pres., 1956-66); MBOU. DL Bedfordshire, 1955; CC 1955-70. *Publications:* occasional articles in sporting papers. *Recreations:* hunting, fishing, shooting, falconry, training gun dogs, gardening. *Address:* Mill Lane, Pavenham, Bedfordshire.

**SCOTT, Archibald Gifford,** CIE 1942; *b* 21 April 1889; *s* of late William Gifford Scott, MB, and Caroline (*née* Strickland), Newton Abbot, Devon; *m* 1932, Kathleen, *d* of late H. J. Burton-Jones, Boulters, Maidenhead, Berks. *Educ:* Bromsgrove. King's Police Medal, 1931. Inspector-General of Police, Central Provinces and Berar, 1941-44. *Recreations:* fishing, shooting, golf. *Address:* Leigh Peverell, Doddiscombsleigh, nr Exeter. *Clubs:* East India and Sports; Royal Bombay Yacht.

**SCOTT, Sir (Arleigh) Winston,** GCMG 1967; Governor-General of Barbados since 1967; *b* 27 March 1900; *m* 1936, Rosita May Hynam; three *d. Educ:* Harrison College, Barbados; Howard University, USA. BSc 1921; MD 1925; LRCP, LRCS (Edin.), LRFPS (Glas.), 1926; O et A Chir, NY Ophthalm. Hosp., 1931. Physician and Surgeon, Woodside Nursing Home, 1934-67. Member Senate, Barbados, 1964-66; appointed to Privy Council of Barbados, 1966. KStJ 1967. *Recreation:* reading. *Address:* Government House, St Michael, Barbados. *T:* 92646. *Club:* Rotary International (Barbados).

**SCOTT, Audrey;** *see* Scott, M. Audrey.

**SCOTT, Sir (Charles) Hilary,** Kt 1967; Solicitor; *b* Bradford, 27 March 1906; *s* of late Lieutenant-Colonel C. E. Scott and of Mrs M. E. M. Scott, of Bradford; *m* 1932, Beatrice Margery, *d* of late Reverend Canon Garrad; one *s* two *d. Educ:* Sedbergh Sch. Articled with Wade & Co., Bradford. Qual. as Solicitor (Class 2 Hons) 1930; Partner Slaughter & May, London. Served in RNVR, 1940-45 (Lieut-Comdr); President of the Law Society, 1966 (Mem. Council, 1948-; Vice-Pres. 1965-66); Member: Nat. Film Finance Corp., 1948- (Chm. 1964-69); Jenkins Cttee on Company Law, 1959-62; Panel of Judges of The Accountant Awards for company accounts, 1961-69; London Adv. Bd of Salvation Army; Noise Adv. Council. Trustee, Glyndebourne Arts Trust. Director: Tarmac Derby Ltd; Equity & Law Life Assurance Society Ltd; London Board, Bank of Scotland; The Inveresk Paper Co. Ltd. FRSA. *Recreations:* travel, music. *Address:* Knowle House, Bishop's Walk, Addington, Surrey. *T:* 01-654 3638. *Club:* Junior Carlton.

*See also M. Audrey Scott, G. M. C. Thornely.*

**SCOTT, Charles Peter,** CMG 1964; OBE 1948; Assistant Under-Secretary of State, Foreign and Commonwealth Office, since 1970; *b* 30 Dec. 1917; *er s* of late Rev. John Joseph Scott and late Dorothea Scott (*née* Senior); *m* 1954, Rachael, *yr d* of C. W. Lloyd Jones, *qv*; one *s* two *d. Educ:* Weymouth Coll.; Pembroke Coll., Cambridge. Indian Civil Service: Probationer, 1939; appointed to Madras Presidency, 1940; Asst Private Sec. to Viceroy, 1946-47. Entered HM Diplomatic Service, 1947, Second Sec., Tokyo, 1948; First Sec., 1949; Foreign Office, 1950; Private Sec. to Gen. Lord Ismay at NATO, Paris, 1952; First Sec., Vienna, 1954; First Sec. at British Information Services, NY, 1956; Counsellor and Consul-General, Washington, 1959; Student at IDC, 1962; Head of UK Mission to European Office of the United Nations, Geneva, 1963; Minister at HM Embassy, Rome, 1966-69; Temp. Vis. Fellow at Centre for Contemporary European Studies, Univ. of Sussex, 1969-70. *Recreations:* fishing, walking. *Address:* c/o Foreign and Commonwealth Office, Whitehall, SW1; c/o Coutts & Co., 440 Strand, WC2. *Club:* United University.

**SCOTT, C(harles) Russell,** MA Cantab; JP; Headmaster of Cranbrook School, 1929-60; retired; *b* 8 Feb. 1898; *s* of late Russell Scott and Susanna Laetitia Worthington; *m* 1923, Irene Keightley, 2nd *d* of late Harold Rankin, JP, Rochford, Essex; three *s* one *d*. *Educ:* Bedales School; Haileybury Coll.; St John's Coll., Cambridge (Exhibitioner in Science). 2nd Lt RGA, 1917; BEF France with 529 Siege Battery RGA, Lieut Nov. 1918; Asst in Kent County Education Office, 1921-22; Asst Education Secretary, Cambridgeshire, 1922-27; first Hon. Secretary Cambridgeshire Festival of Music; Assistant Master Tonbridge School, 1927-29; Hon. Secretary Committee for *Music and the Community*, 1933 (the Cambridgeshire Report on the Teaching of Music); Chairman of Standing Conference for Amateur Music, 1946-63, Rural Music Schools Assoc., 1958-62, Kent Council of Social Service, Advisory Committee on Amateur Opera, 1948-63, Kent County Music Cttee, 1932-65, and Kent Rural Music School, 1964-67. *Recreations:* music, social work. *Address:* The Quarry, Wrotham, Kent. *T:* Fairseat 453.

**SCOTT, Ven. Claud Syms;** Archdeacon of Suffolk, 1962-70; Vicar of Hoxne with Denham St John, 1962-70; *b* 31 Aug. 1901; *s* of Claud Syms and Margaret Elizabeth Scott; *m* 1930, Grace Maud Savery. *Educ:* Brentwood Sch.; Trinity Coll., Oxf. BA 1923, MA 1927. Deacon, 1926; Priest, 1927; Asst Curate, St Luke, Bedminster, 1926-30; Curate-in-charge, All Hallows Conventional District, Ipswich, 1930-38; Vicar of Exning with Landwade, 1938-54; Rural Dean of Newmarket, 1946-54; Hon. Canon of St Edmundsbury, 1953; Rector of Stradbroke with Horham and Athelington, 1954-58; Rector of St Mary Stoke, Ipswich, 1958-62; Rural Dean of Ipswich, 1958-Dec. 1961. Master, Worshipful Company of Armourers and Brasiers, 1951. *Address:* 68 Lowestoft Road, Reydon, Southwold, Suffolk.

**SCOTT, Cyril;** Musical Composer, Librettist, and Author; *b* Oxton, Cheshire, 1879; *s* of Henry and Mary Scott; *m* 1921, Rose Laure, novelist, *er d* of Cav. Uff. Robert Allatini. First Symphony performed in Darmstadt at age of 20; orchestral and chamber works performed in Vienna, Berlin, Petrograd, Paris, Budapest, Brussels, New York, etc. *Publications:* numerous songs, piano works, violin works, chamber, choral, and orchestral works, including Neapolitan Rhapsody, 1960; concertos: Piano Concerto, Violin Concerto, Concerto for 2 Violins, Cello Concerto, Concerto for 2 Pianos; operas called The Alchemist, The Shrine, etc; a ballet, The Incompetent Apothecary; Cantatas, Nativity Hymn, selected by the Carnegie Trust for publication; La Belle Dame sans Merci, first performed at Leeds Festival, 1934; Summerland; Mirabelle; Neptune, symphonic poem; Symphony entitled the Muses; 4 String Quartets, No. 4, 1968; *Poetry:* The Celestial Aftermath; The Vales of Unity; The Voice of the Ancient; *Prose:* Music: Its Secret Influence throughout the Ages, 1969; Memoirs, entitled My Years of Indiscretion; An Outline of Modern Occultism; The Ghost of a Smile; Doctors, Disease and Health; Cancer Prevention, 1968; Victory Over Cancer, 1969; Health, Diet and Commonsense, 1969; (autobiography) Bone of Contention, 1969. *Recreations:* transcendental philosophy and mysticism, therapeutical research. *Address:* c/o Boosey & Hawkes, 295 Regent Street, W1; c/o Elkin & Co., 27 Soho Square, W1; c/o Thorsons Publishers Ltd, 37/38 Margaret Street, W1.

**SCOTT, David;** Clerk of Select Committees, House of Commons, since Nov. 1970; *b* 6 Sept. 1916; *er s* of late Sir Basil Scott and late Gertrude, MBE, 2nd *d* of Henry Villiers Stuart of Dromana, MP; *m* 1951, Hester Mary (MA Edinburgh; BA Oxon), *y d* of late Gilbert Ogilvy of Winton and Pencaitland; one *s* three *d*. *Educ:* Stowe; New College, Oxford (MA). War Service 1939-45: Argyll and Sutherland Highlanders (SR), Reconnaissance Corps and Highland Light Infantry; T/Capt., 1941; Asst to Political Adviser for Khuzistan, Iran, 1944; Actg Vice Consul, Ahwaz, 1944-45. Clerk, House of Commons, 1946; Deputy Principal Clerk, 1962; Clerk of Standing Cttees, 1966-70. *Recreation:* fishing. *Address:* 22 Blomfield Road, W9. *T:* 01-286 3279; Glenaros, Aros, Isle of Mull. *T:* Aros 37. *Clubs:* Travellers', Pratts; Puffins (Edinburgh).

**SCOTT, David Aubrey,** CMG 1966; Assistant Under-Secretary of State, Foreign and Commonwealth Office, since 1970; *b* 3 Aug. 1919; *s* of late Hugh Sumner Scott and of Barbara E. Scott, JP (*née* Jackson); *m* 1941, Vera Kathleen, *d* of late Major G. H. Ibbitson, MBE, RA; two *s* one *d*. *Educ:* Charterhouse; Birmingham University. Served War of 1939-45, Royal Artillery, 1939-47; Chief Radar Adviser, British Military Mission to Egyptian Army, 1945-47, Major. Appointed to CRO, 1948; Asst Private Secretary to Secretary of State, 1949; Pretoria, 1951-53; seconded to Cabinet Office, 1954-56; Asst Sec., Malta Round Table Conf., 1955; Secretary-General, Malaya and Caribbean Constitutional Confs, 1956; Singapore, 1956-58; Asst Sec., Monckton Commn, 1960; Dep. Brit. High Comr, Fedn of Rhodesia and Nyasaland, 1961-63; Imperial Defence College, 1964; Deputy British High Commissioner in India, 1965-67; British High Comr in Uganda, and Ambassador to Rwanda (non-resident), 1967-70. *Recreations:* sailing, bird-watching. *Address:* 23 Petersham Mews, SW7. *Clubs:* East India and Sports, Royal Over-Seas League.

**SCOTT, David Aylmer,** FRS 1949; FRSC; MA, PhD; Research Member, Connaught Medical Research Laboratories, University of Toronto, 1922, retd; *b* 2 Oct. 1892; *s* of James Robert Scott and Mary Ann Scott (*née* McKenzie), Kincardine, Ont.; *m* 1928, Bertha Collett Herington, BA; two *d*. Control Chemist, British Chemical Co.; Research Chemist, British Acetones; Research Chemist, Riordon Pulp and Paper Co.; Nat. Research Council Scholarship, 1921-22; worked with Sir Charles Harington at University College Hosp., London, 1928-29. Member; Biochemical Soc.; American Soc. of Biological Chemists; Canadian Physiological Soc.; Toronto Biochemical Soc. Flavelle Medal, Royal Soc. of Canada, 1954; Banting Medal, American Diabetes Assoc., 1964. *Publications:* mainly concerned with Insulin, Heparin, and Carbonic Anhydrase. *Recreation:* golf. *Address:* 16 Browside Avenue, Forest Hill, Toronto. *T:* Hu 3-1837. *Clubs:* York, University of Toronto Faculty, York Downs Golf and Country (Toronto).

**SCOTT, Sir David John Montagu Douglas,** KCMG, *cr* 1941 (CMG 1935); OBE 1919; *b* 7 March 1887; *s* of Adm. Lord Charles Scott, GCB; *m* 1918, Dorothy Charlotte Drummond (*d* 1965); one *s* (killed during the War, 1941); *m* 1970, Valerie Finnis. *Educ:* Eton; Christ Church, Oxford. Joined 3rd Batt. the Royal Scots, 1906; entered the Foreign Office, 1911; served in France, Flanders and Salonika, 1914-18 (wounded, despatches, Legion of Honour, OBE); re-joined Foreign Office, 1919; Assistant Under-Secretary of State for

Foreign Affairs, 1938-44; Deputy Under-Secretary of State in the Foreign Office, 1944; retired, 1947. *Recreations:* fishing, shooting, gardening. *Address:* Boughton House, Kettering, Northants. *T:* Kettering 82279. *Club:* Travellers'.

**SCOTT, Sir Donald;** *see* Scott, Sir R. D.

**SCOTT, Donald;** *see* Scott, W. D.

**SCOTT, Professor Douglas Frederick Schumacher;** Professor of German in the University of Durham (late Durham Colleges), since 1958; *b* Newcastle under Lyme, Staffs, 17 Sept. 1910; *o s* of Frederick Scott and Magdalena (*née* Gronbach); *m* 1942, Margaret, *o d* of late Owen Gray Ellis, Beaumaris, Anglesey, and Helen (*née* Gibbs); two *d. Educ:* Queen Mary's Grammar School, Walsall, Staffs; Dillmann-Real-gymnasium Stuttgart, Germany; University of Tübingen, Göttingen (Dr phil.); University College, London (MA). Part-time Assistant, German Dept, University Coll., London, 1935-37; Lecturer in charge German Dept, Huddersfield Technical Coll., 1937-38; Lecturer in German, King's Coll., Newcastle, 1938-46; released for service with Friends' Ambulance Unit, 1940-46; Lecturer in German, King's Coll., London, 1946-49; Reader and Head of Dept of German, The Durham Colls, 1949-58. *Publications:* Some English Correspondents of Goethe, 1949; W. v. Humboldt and the Idea of a University, 1960; articles and reviews on German lit. and Anglo-German literary relations in various English and German Journals. *Recreations:* music, travel. *Address:* 6 Fieldhouse Terrace, Durham. *T:* Durham 4518. *Club:* Penn.

**SCOTT, Col Sir Douglas Winchester,** 2nd Bt *cr* 1913; *b* 4 Feb. 1907; *s* of Admiral Sir Percy Scott, KCB, KCVO, LLD, 1st Bt, and Roma, *e d* of Sir Frederic Dixon Hartland, 1st Bt; *S* father, 1924; *m* 1933, Elizabeth Joyce, 2nd *d* of W. N. C. Grant, Lyne Place, Virginia Water, Surrey; two *s* one *d. Educ:* Harrow; RMC Sandhurst. Comd 3rd Hussars, 1944; Comd 9th Lancers, 1947; Hon. Col 3rd Hussars, 1955-58; Col Queen's Own Hussars, 1962-65. Treasurer Thomas Coram Foundation, 1958, Vice-Pres. 1970. *Heir: s* Anthony Percy Scott [*b* 1 May 1937; *m* 1962, Caroline Teresa Anne, *er d* of Edward Bacon; two *s* one *d*]. *Address:* 9 Pont Street Mews, SW1; Habyn Hill, Rogate, nr Petersfield, Hants. *Club:* Cavalry.

**SCOTT, Sir Edward Arthur Dolman,** 8th Bt, *cr* 1806; resident in South Australia; *b* 14 Dec. 1905; *e s* of Sir Douglas Edward Scott, 7th Bt, and Florence Ada, *d* of W. Wilderman; *S* father 1951; *m*; one *d. Educ:* Reading Grammar School. *Heir: b* Douglas Francis Scott, *b* 6 Aug. 1907. *Address:* 8 Alice Street, South Plympton, S Australia.

**SCOTT, Rt. Rev. Edward Walter;** *see* Kootenay, Bishop of.

**SCOTT, Elisabeth Whitworth,** AADip, FRIBA, retired; architect; *b* 1898; *d* of Bernard Scott, Surgeon. *Educ:* Redmoor School, Bournemouth; Architectural Association Schools. Won competition for designing new Shakespeare Memorial Theatre, Stratford-on-Avon, 1928. *Recreations:* music, theatre, country. *Address:* 12a Mount Pleasant Road, Poole, Dorset.

**SCOTT, Sir Eric,** Kt 1965; OBE 1958; President, The Pharmacy Guild of Australia (formerly Federated Pharmaceutical Service Guild of Australia), since 1947; *b* 11 Dec. 1891; *s* of W. G. Scott, Hawthorn, Victoria, Aust.; *m* 1914, Eva Caroline, *d* of R. J. Poulton; one *s* two *d. Educ:* Wesley College, Melbourne, Victoria. Pharmaceutical Chemist, 1927. State President, Federated Pharmaceutical Service Guild of Australia (Victorian Branch), 1931-47; President, Pharmaceutical Society of Victoria, 1955-60; Member of Commonwealth and State Pharmaceutical Benefits Committees under National Health Act, 1954-. Hon. Mem., Society of Great Britain, 1970. *Recreations:* golf, gardening, cooking. *Address:* Woorak, 64 Heyington Place, Toorak, Victoria 3142, Australia. *T:* 20-4883. *Clubs:* Commonwealth (Canberra); Royal Automobile, Athenæum (Victoria).

**SCOTT, Ethleen Mary,** MA; retired as Principal of St Aidan's College, University of Durham, (1961-63); *b* 25 Nov. 1896; *d* of Rev. H. R. Scott, MA, DD, and Jennie Hill Scott. *Educ:* Walthamstow Hall, Sevenoaks, Kent; Royal Holloway College, University of London. BA Hons in French, Cl. I 1919; MA (with dist.) 1923; LRAM 1919; ARCM 1942. French Mistress, Queen Elizabeth's Girls' Grammar School, Barnet, 1921-25; Lecturer in French, Royal Holloway College, 1925-28; Lecturer in French, Durham Colleges in the University of Durham, 1928-47; Principal of St Aidan's Society, 1947-61. *Recreations:* music, gardening. *Address:* Whitegates, Westbere, Canterbury, Kent.

**SCOTT, Francis Clayton;** *b* 6 Aug. 1881; *s* of Sir James William Scott, 1st Bt, and Anne Jane, *d* of John Haslam of Gilnow Hall, Bolton-le-Moors; *m* 1911, Gwendolen Frieda Martha, *d* of late George Jager of Lingdale, Birkenhead; one *s* one *d. Educ:* Bedales; Oriel College, Oxford (BA). Formerly Chairman of the Provincial Insurance Company Limited of Kendal and London, founded by his father. Founder and former Chairman of Brathay Hall Centre, Ambleside; High Sheriff of Westmorland, 1934. *Recreations:* shooting, fishing, yachting. *Address:* Matson Ground, Windermere. *T:* 3162. *Club:* Brooks's.

**SCOTT, Francis Reginald,** CC (Canada) 1967; QC (Quebec) 1961; BA (Bishop's, Oxon); BLitt (Oxon); BCL McGill; Visiting Professor, French Canada Studies Program, McGill University; *b* Quebec, PQ, 1 Aug. 1899; *s* of Archdeacon Frederick George and Amy Scott; *m* 1928, Marian Mildred Dale; one *s. Educ:* Quebec High School; Bishop's College, Lennoxville, Que.; Magdalen College, Oxford; McGill University, Montreal. Rhodes Scholar, 1920; taught school at Quebec High School, Bishops College School, Lower Canada College, 1920-24; admitted to Bar of Province of Quebec, 1927; assistant professor of Federal and Constitutional Law, McGill University, 1928; Professor of Law, 1934; Dean of Law Faculty, 1961-64. Chairman National Council of Co-operative Commonwealth Federation, 1942-50; legal adviser to Govt of Saskatchewan at the Constitutional Conference, 1950 and 1960; UN Technical Assistance Resident Rep. to Burma, 1952; Mem. Roy. Commn on Bilingualism and Biculturalism, 1963; Past-Pres. League for Social Reconstruction; Guggenheim Fellowship, 1940; FRSC, 1947; Lorne Pierce Medal Roy. Soc. Canada, 1962; Molson Award 1965. Hon. degrees: Dalhousie; Manitoba; Queen's; UBC; Osgoode Hall; Montreal; Sir George Williams; Toronto; Laval; Bishop's. *Publications:* Canada Today, Her National Interests and National Policy, 1938; Civil Liberties and Canadian Federalism, 1959; *poetry:* Overture, 1945; Events and Signals, 1954; The Eye of The Needle, 1957; Signature, 1964; Selected Poems, 1966. Co-author of Social Planning for Canada, 1935;

Democracy Needs Socialism, 1938; Make This your Canada, 1943; (ed, with A. J. M. Smith) New Provinces, Poems of Several Authors, 1936; The Blasted Pine, 1957; articles on constitutional and political subjects. *Address:* 451 Clarke Avenue, Montreal 6, Que, Canada. *Club:* McGill Faculty (Montreal).

**SCOTT, Sir George (Edward),** Kt 1967; CBE 1963 (OBE 1941); KPM; Chief Constable of the West Riding Constabulary, 1959-68, and of the West Yorkshire Constabulary, 1968-69, retired; *b* 6 June 1903; *s* of late Frederick William Scott; *m* 1926, Lilian, *d* of Matthew Brown, Norwich; one *s* one *d*. *Educ:* City of Norwich School. Joined Norwich City Police, as Cadet, 1918; Dep. Chief Constable, Norwich, 1933-36; Chief Constable: Luton, 1936-44; Newcastle upon Tyne, 1944-48; Sheffield, 1948-59. County Director (Hon.) of St John Ambulance Association, Surrey. President: Northern Police Convalescent Home; Northern Police Orphans Trust; Dep. Pres., RoSPA. King's Police Medal, 1949; KStJ 1966 (CStJ 1957). *Recreations:* golf, sailing. *Address:* White Lodge, Barham Close, Weybridge, Surrey. *Clubs:* National Liberal; St John.

**SCOTT, George Edwin;** Television Commentator, Broadcaster, Journalist; *b* 22 June 1925; *s* of late George Benjamin Scott and Florence Hilda Scott; *m* 1947, Shelagh Maud Isobel Maw; two *s* one *d*. *Educ:* Middlesbrough High School; New College, Oxford. Northern Echo, 1941-42; Yorkshire Post, 1942-43; RNVR, 1943-46; New College, Oxford, 1946-48 (Founder and Editor of Oxford Viewpoint); Daily Express, 1948-53; Truth, 1953-57; Deputy Editor, 1954; Editor, 1954-57 (ceased publication). Contested (L) Middlesbrough East, March 1962, Middlesbrough West, June 1962, Wimbledon, 1964. Chairman, Political Division, Liberal Party, 1962-63. Mem., Panorama team, 1958-59; Chairman/Interviewer: TWW, 1959-67; Rediffusion, 1966-68; broadcasts regularly. *Publications:* Time and Place (autobiographical), 1956; The RCs 1967; Reporter Anonymous, 1968; contrib. column, Liberal View, Daily Mirror, 1962-64; contribs to Spectator, Punch, and other jls. *Recreations:* theatre, cricket and watching others gardening. *Address:* 26 Vineyard Hill Road, Wimbledon Park, SW19. *T:* 01-946 5899. *Club:* Reform.

**SCOTT, Prof. George Ian,** CBE 1968; FRCSE; FRCPE; FRSE; Hon. Surgeon Oculist to the Queen in Scotland; Professor of Ophthalmology, University of Edinburgh, since 1954; Adviser in Ophthalmology, SE Regional Hospital Board, since 1954; Ophthalmic Surgeon, Royal Infirmary, Edinburgh, since 1953; *b* 15 March 1907; *s* of late George John Scott; *m* 1946, Maxine, *d* of late A. D. Vandamm; one *s*. *Educ:* Edinburgh Acad.; Univ. of Edinburgh. MA 1929; MB, ChB 1933; FRCS Edin. 1937; FRS Edin. 1954. Served War of 1939-45, RAMC; Command Ophthalmologist, Scottish Command, 1939; Mem. Advisory Ophthalmic Panel, Ministry of Supply, 1941; Consultant Ophthalmologist, MEF, 1942; Brig. RAMC, 1942. Asst Ophthalmic Surgeon, Royal Infirmary, Edinburgh, 1946; Mem. Vision Cttee, MRC, 1946; Visiting Consultant, Western General and Bangour Hosps, 1949; Consultant in Neuro-Ophthalmology to Department of Neuro-Surgery, Edinburgh, 1954. Member, International Council of Ophthalmology, 1963; Past President: Faculty of Ophthalmologists; RCS of Edin.; Member Association of British Neurologists; President Ophthalmological Soc. of United Kingdom; FRSoc.Med. (former Vice-President Section of Ophthalmology); Hon. Col RAMC; Hon. Consultant in Ophthalmology to Army in Scotland. *Publications:* papers in British Journal of Ophthalmology, Nature, Lancet, British Medical Journal, British Journal of Radiology, Proc. Roy. Soc. Med., Trans. Ophthalmological Soc., United Kingdom, and The American Journal of Opthalmology. *Address:* 20 Heriot Row, Edinburgh 3. *T:* 031-225 6943. *Clubs:* Garrick; New (Edinburgh); Royal Societies.

**SCOTT, Rev. G(uthrie) Michael;** Anglican priest Diocese of Chichester, since 1950; *b* 30 July 1907; *s* of Rev. Perceval Caleb Scott and Ethel Maud (*née* Burn); unmarried. *Educ:* King's College, Taunton; St Paul's College, Grahamstown, S Africa; Chichester Theological College. Ordained, 1930; Curate St Mary, Slaugham, Sussex, 1930-32; St Stephen's, Gloucester Rd, S Kensington, 1932-34. Domestic Chaplain to Bishop of Bombay, 1935-37; Chaplain, St Paul's Cathedral, Calcutta, 1937-38; Kasauli, 1938-39. Enlisted RAF 1940, invalided 1941. Returned to S Africa, 1943; St Alban's Coloured Mission and Chaplain St Joseph's Orphanage, Johannesburg, 1943-46; General License: Diocese of Johannesburg, 1946-50, Chichester, 1950-. In 1947 appealed to United Nations on behalf of two tribes of SW African Mandated Territory; attended sessions of General Assembly at Chiefs' request and was granted hearing by Fourth Cttee 1949, 1950 and 1955; Question referred to International Court of Justice. Took part in formation of Africa Bureau, 1952. Nagaland Peace Mission, 1964-66. *Publications:* Shadow over Africa, 1950; Attitude to Africa (Penguin), 1951; African Episode, 1954; Orphans' Heritage, 1958; A Time to Speak (autobiography), 1958; The Nagas in Search of Peace, 1966. *Recreations:* walking, reading, sailing, theatre, etc. *Address:* c/o Lloyds Bank, 6 Pall Mall, SW1.

**SCOTT, Henry Cooper,** QC 1961; Recorder of Leeds, since 1970; Chairman, East Riding Quarter Sessions, since 1958; Chancellor, Diocese of Bradford and of Ripon since 1957; *b* 14 March 1915; *s* of late C. Paley Scott, KC, and Ruth, *d* of Rev. S. C. Scott, Chester; *m* 1947, Anne, *d* of late A. C. Bennett, Knaresborough; three *s*. *Educ:* Uppingham; Selwyn Coll., Cambridge. BA 1936; MA 1957. Called to Bar, 1939; Bencher, Inner Temple, 1968. Served War of 1939-45, Army (TA) (1939-45, Burma, Defence, etc, medals); demobilised 1946 as Major. Recorder of: York, 1961-65; Kingston upon Hull, 1965-69; Sheffield, 1969-70. Mem., Parole Bd, 1967-70. *Address:* West End, Crayke, York. *T:* Easingwold 490.

**SCOTT, Brig. Sir Henry (Lawrence),** Kt, *cr* 1947; CB 1932; DSO 1917 and Bar, 1920; MC; psc; *b* 6 April 1882; *m* Winifred Ethel (*d* 1931); one *s* (*er s* killed in action, Waziristan, 1937) two *d*. 2nd Lt Dorset Regt, 1902; Indian Army, 1903; Lt 1904; Capt. 1911; Major, 1917; Bt Lt-Col 1919; Lt-Col 1926; Col 1927; Instructor, Senior Officers School, India, 1921-23; Comd. 1st Bn 4th PWD Gurkha Rifles; AA and QMG, 1929-31; Commander Kohat Bde, 1932-35; served European War, 1914-18; Mesopotamia, 1920-21 (despatches nine times, DSO, and bar, MC); ADC to the King, 1934-35, retired 1935; Chief of Staff Jammu and Kashmir, 1936-47. *Address:* Box 187, Grahamstown, CP, S Africa.

**SCOTT, Sir (Henry) Maurice,** Kt 1966; CBE 1957; DFC 1945; Speaker, Legislative Council of Fiji, 1958-66; *b* 23 July 1910; *s* of Sir Henry Milne Scott, QC; *m* 1963, Allerdina Fenna Gatty; two *s*. *Educ:* Wanganui Collegiate Sch.,

NZ; Magdalen Coll., Oxford. Called to Bar, Gray's Inn, 1936; joined legal firm of Wm Scott & Co., Suva, 1939. Enlisted Fiji Mil. Forces; resigned and joined 208 Sqdn RAF as pilot; served in W Desert, Palestine, Iraq, Italy. Re-joined Wm Scott & Co., 1947. Elected European Mem. for Northwestern Div. Fiji Legislative Coun.; Sen. Mem. 1956. Chairman: Burns Philp (South Sea) Co. Ltd; Fiji Times & Herald Ltd; Fiji Industries Ltd; Pacific Fishing Co. Ltd; Lepers' Trust Bd; President: Fiji Show Assoc.; Fiji Rugby Union; Returned Soldiers and Ex-Servicemen's Assoc. of Fiji; Director: Queensland Insce Co. Ltd; Fiji Tobacco Co. Ltd; Sidney Cooke Ltd, etc. Rep. Fiji: Festival of Britain, 1951; Coronation, 1953; Independence Celebrations, Malaya, 1957. Consul for Netherlands in Fiji, Tonga and Pitcairn Island. *Recreations:* swimming, fishing. *Address:* Raivolita, Tamavua, Fiji. *T:* 22084. *Clubs:* Defence, Royal Suva Yacht (Fiji).

**SCOTT, Sir Hilary;** *see* Scott, Sir C. H.

**SCOTT, Sir Ian Dixon,** KCMG 1962 (CMG 1959); KCVO 1965; CIE 1947; *b* Inverness, 6 March 1909; *s* of late Thomas Henderson Scott, OBE, MICE, and Mary Agnes Dixon, Selkirk; *m* 1937, Hon. Anna Drusilla Lindsay, *d* of 1st Baron Lindsay of Birker, CBE, LLD; one *s* four *d*. *Educ:* Queen's Royal College, Trinidad; Balliol College, Oxford (MA); London School of Economics. Entered Indian Civil Service, 1932; Indian Political Service, 1935; Assistant Director of Intelligence, Peshawar, 1941; Principal, Islamia College, Peshawar, 1943; Deputy Private Secretary to the Viceroy of India, 1945-47. Worked in John Lewis & Co. Ltd, 1948-50. Appointed to Foreign Service, 1950; First Secretary, Foreign Office, 1950-51; British Legation, Helsinki, 1952; British Embassy, Beirut, 1954; Counsellor, 1956; Chargé d'Affaires, 1956, 1957, 1958; idc 1959; Consul-General, then Ambassador to the Congo, 1960-61; Ambassador to Sudan, 1961-65, to Norway, 1965-68. Director: H. Clarkson (Holdings), 1968-; Clarksons Holidays Ltd, 1968-; Cavell & Rufford (Holdings) Ltd, 1968-. *Publication:* Tumbled House, 1969. *Recreation:* sailing. *Address:* Ash House, Alde Lane, Aldeburgh, Suffolk.

**SCOTT, Major-General James Bruce,** CB 1944; DSO 1942; MC 1918; late IA; *b* 25 Dec. 1892; *s* of late James Scott, CIE, Westfield, Dorking; *m* 1923, Nancy Claridge, *d* of W. R. Davies, JP; two *s*. *Educ:* Exeter School; RMC Sandhurst. 2nd Lieut, Unattached List, Indian Army, 1912; Captain 1916; Major, 1929; Bt Lieut-Colonel 1934; Lt-Col 1936; Bde Comdr, Brig., 1939; Maj.-Gen. 1941. GSO2 AHQ, India, 1931-35; Commander 1/8 Gurkha Rifles, 1935-39; Comdr 1st Burma Bde, 1939-41; Comdr 1st Burma Div., 1941-42; Inspector of Infantry (India), 1942-43; Comdr Peshawar Dist, 1943-46. Despatches 4 times. *Address:* 177 Rivermead Court, SW6. *T:* 01-736 2961. *Clubs:* United Service, Hurlingham.

**SCOTT, Prof. James Henderson;** Professor of Dental Anatomy, Queen's University of Belfast, since 1964; *b* 8 Nov. 1913; *s* of late John and Nell Scott, Dundalk, Ireland; *m* 1945, Olive Marron; one *s* three *d*. *Educ:* Dundalk Gram. Sch.; Methodist Coll., Belfast. Joined RC Church, 1939. Lectr, 1946, Reader, 1956, Queen's Univ., Belfast. Lecture tours: S Africa, 1957; US, 1960. Howard Mummery Prize for Dental Research, 1963. FFD (Founder Mem.), RCS Ire., 1963. *Publications:* (with N. B. B. Symons) Introduction to Dental Anatomy, 1952, 5th edn 1967; (with A. D. Dixon) Anatomy for Students of Dentistry, 1959, 2nd edn 1966; The Christian Vision, 1964; Essentials of Oral Anatomy, 1967; Dento-facial Development and Growth, 1967; contribs to Jl of Anatomical Soc., Trans European Orthodontic Soc., Amer. Jl of Orthodontics, Amer. Jl of Physical Anthropology. *Recreations:* poetry, politics and polemics. *Address:* 30 Malone Heights, Belfast 9, N Ireland. *T:* Belfast 612320.

**SCOTT, J(ames) M(aurice),** OBE 1945; MA; Author and explorer; *b* 13 Dec. 1906. *Educ:* Fettes College; Clare College, Cambridge. *Publications:* Gino Watkins, 1935; Land of Seals, 1949; Bright Eyes of Danger, 1950; Hudson of Hudson's Bay, 1950; Other Side of the Moon, 1950; Snowstone, 1950; Vineyards of France, 1950; Captain Smith and Pocahontas, 1953; Man Who Made Wine, 1953; Heather Mary, 1953; Sea-wyf and Biscuit, 1955; White Magic, 1955; Choice of Heaven, 1959; The Tea Story, 1964; The Book of Pall Mall, 1965; Dingo, 1966; The Devil You Don't, 1967; In a Beautiful Pea-Green Boat, 1968; The White Poppy, 1968; From Sea to Ocean, 1969. *Recreations:* mountain walking, sailing. *Address:* Thatched Cottage, Yelling, Hunts.

**SCOTT, James Steel,** MD, FRCSEd; Professor of Obstetrics and Gynæcology, University of Leeds, since 1961; *b* 18 April 1924; *s* of late Dr Angus M. Scott and Margaret Scott; *m* 1958, Olive Sharpe; two *s*. *Educ:* Glasgow Academy; University of Glasgow. MB, ChB 1946. Service in RAMC, 1946-48. MRCOG 1953. Obstetric Tutor, Liverpool University, 1954; Lecturer, 1958; Senior Lecturer, 1960. MD, FRCSEd 1959. *Publications:* contrib. to Lancet, Brit. Med. Jl, Jl of Obst. and Gynæc. of Brit. Empire, Amer. Jl of Obst. and Gynæc., etc. *Recreation:* sailing. *Address:* 24 Long Causeway, Leeds 16.

**SCOTT, Sir James (Walter),** 2nd Bt, *cr* 1962; *b* 26 Oct. 1924; *e s* of Sir Jervoise Bolitho Scott, 1st Bt, and Kathleen Isabel, *yr d* of late Godfrey Walter, Malshanger, Basingstoke; *S* father 1965; *m* 1951, Anne Constantia, *e d* of Lt-Col Clive Austin, Roundwood, Micheldever, Hants; three *s* one *d* (and one *d* decd). *Educ:* Eton. Lt-Col The Life Guards, formerly Grenadier Guards, retired 1969. Served War of 1939-45: NW Europe, 1944-45. Palestine, 1945-46; ADC to Viceroy and Gov.-Gen. of India, 1946-48; Malaya, 1948-49; Cyprus, 1958, 1960, 1964; Malaysia, 1966. Underwriting Member of Lloyd's. Liveryman, Worshipful Co. of Mercers. *Heir:* *s* James Jervoise Scott, *b* 12 Oct. 1952. *Address:* Rotherfield Park, Alton, Hampshire. *T:* Tisted 204. *Club:* Guards.

**SCOTT, Brig. John,** DSO 1919; OBE 1958; *b* 1887; *m* 1st, 1913, Sybil, *d* of late Sir Frederic Hewitt, MVO, MD; two *s*; 2nd, 1933, Hester Mary, *d* of Arthur Hogan. *Educ:* St Andrews University (MA 1907). Served European War, 1914-18 (despatches twice, DSO); commanding Royal Artillery 15th (Scottish) Div., 1939-40; GSO 1 Home Guard, 12th Corps 1940-41; Commander Gravesend Sub Area, 1941-42; Training Officer Inverness-shire Home Guard, 1942-44. CC Worcestershire, 1949, Alderman, 1965. Chm. S Worcestershire Conservative Assoc., 1950-56. *Recreations:* travelling, golf. *Address:* Combermere, 25 Avenue Road, Malvern, Worcs. *T:* Malvern 4601.

**SCOTT, Sir John A. G.;** *see* Guillum Scott.

**SCOTT, John Dick;** Author; Editor, Finance and Development, 1963; *b* 26 Feb. 1917; *o s* of late Alexander Scott, OBE, and of Margaret

Gourlay Allardice; *m* 1941, Helen Elisabeth, *y d* of late Sir Edmund Whittaker, FRS, and of Lady Whittaker; two *s. Educ:* Stewart's Coll., Edinburgh; Edinburgh Univ. (MA, Hons History). Assistant Principal, Ministry of Aircraft Production, 1940; attached to Cabinet Office for Work on official History of the War, 1944. Literary editor of the Spectator, 1953-56. *Publications:* The Cellar, 1947; The Margin, 1949; The Way to Glory, 1952; The End of an Old Song, 1954; (with Richard Hughes) The Administration of War Production, 1956; Life in Britain, 1956; Siemens Brothers, 1958; Vickers: A History, 1962; The Pretty Penny, 1963. *Address:* Apartment 101, 1517 30th Street, NW, Washington, DC 20007, USA. *T:* 338-3015. *Club:* Garrick.

**SCOTT, John Waugh,** MA, DPhil, LLD (Glasgow); Professor of Logic and Philosophy, University College, Cardiff, 1920-44, Professor Emeritus since 1944; *b* 9 Nov. 1878; 2nd *s* of Gavin Stewart Scott, Hallhill, Lesmahagow, Lanarkshire; *m* 1913, Margaret Green (*d* 1956); two *d. Educ:* Hamilton Academy; University of Glasgow. Graduated with First-Class Honours in Mental Philosophy, 1903; Lecturer in Moral Philosophy in the University of Glasgow, 1905-20; Mills Lecturer in Philosophy, University of California, 1921-22; Contributor to Encyclopaedia Britannica; at various dates has held external examinerships in Philosophy in seven British Universities; LLD University of Glasgow, 1944. Originated and conducted "The Homecrofts" experiment, Cheltenham, 1928-56. Hon. Secretary of the National Homecroft Association, 1925-43. *Publications:* Syndicalism and Philosophical Realism; Unemployment, a Suggested Policy; Self-Subsistence for the Unemployed; Barter; Edited, from reliquiae of A. A. Bowman, A Sacramental Universe, designed and supervised A Synoptic Index to the Proceedings of the Aristotelian Society, Vol. I, 1900-49, Vol. II 1949-59, Vol. III, 1959-69; sundry articles on philosophical and social subjects; sundry notes contrib. to The New Age (under pseudonym W. D. Law). *Recreations:* long ago: walking; today: pestering modern economists for an authoritative ruling on C. B. Phipson's The Science of Civilisation. *Address:* Welkin, Crossford, Carluke, Lanarkshire.

**SCOTT, Laurence Prestwich;** Chairman of the Manchester Guardian & Evening News Ltd, since 1949; *b* 10 June 1909; *s* of John Russell and Alice Olga Scott; *m* 1939, Constance Mary Black (*d* 1969); two *s* one *d*; *m* 1970, Jessica Mary Crowther Thompson. *Educ:* Rugby; Trinity College, Cambridge. Director, Anglia Television Ltd; Chm., UK Section, Commonwealth Press Union; Dir, Press Assoc. and Reuters, 1948-55, 1956-60. Mem., Council of Manchester University (Dep. Chm., 1957-70); Trustee, Civic Trust for the North West. *Address:* Westow Lodge, Alderley Edge, Cheshire.

**SCOTT, M. Audrey;** Headmistress of the Perse School for Girls, Cambridge, 1947-67, retired; *b* 22 Oct. 1904; *d* of late Lieutenant-Colonel C. E. Scott, solicitor, and Mrs C. E. Scott, Bradford. *Educ:* Queen Margaret's School, Scarborough (now at Escrick); Newnham College, Cambridge. Teaching at Benenden School, Kent, 1926-29; Atherley School, Southampton, 1929-31; Edgbaston Church College, 1931-40; Thornbury Grammar School, Glos, 1941-43; Headmistress, Yeovil High School, Jan. 1944-Aug. 1947. Association of Headmistresses: Exec. Cttee, 1956-62; Chm., Foreign and Commonwealth Education Cttee, 1960-62; Pres., Six Counties Branch, 1959-61. *Address:* 14 Storey's Way, Cambridge. *T:* 55030.

*See also Sir Hilary Scott.*

**SCOTT, Colonel Sir Malcolm S.;** *see* Stoddart-Scott.

**SCOTT, Sir Maurice;** *see* Scott, Sir H. M.

**SCOTT, Rev. Michael;** *see* Scott, Rev. G. M.

**SCOTT, Michael,** MVO 1961; Counsellor, British High Commission, Nicosia, since 1968; *b* 19 May 1923; *yr s* of late John Scott and of Kathleen Scott; *m* 1944, Vivienne Sylvia Vincent-Barwood (marriage dissolved, 1967); three *s. Educ:* Dame Allan's School; Durham Univ. Served War with Durham Light Infantry, 1941; 1st Gurkha Rifles, 1943-47, Captain. Appointed to Colonial Office, 1949; transferred to CRO, 1957; First Secretary, Karachi, 1958-59; Deputy High Commissioner, Peshawar, Pakistan, 1959-62; Director, British Information Services in India, New Delhi, 1963-65; Commonwealth Office, 1965-68. *Address:* c/o Foreign and Commonwealth Office, SW1.

**SCOTT, Maj.-Gen. Michael Frederick,** JP; Farmer; *b* 25 Oct. 1911; *s* of Col F. W. Scott, Romsey, Hants; *m* 1961, Laila Wallis (*née* Tatchell). *Educ:* Harrow. Apprenticed as Mechanical Engr to John I. Thornycroft Co. Basingstoke, 1932-35; commnd Lieut, RAOC, 1936; transf. REME 1942. Served: India, 1938-44; Palestine, 1947-48; Germany, 1951-54; Cyprus, 1955-58. Inspector, REME, 1960-63; Commandant Technical Group, REME, 1963-65 (retd); Col Comdt, REME, 1968-. FIMechE. JP Somerset, 1967. *Recreations:* sailing, shooting, country pursuits. *Address:* Parsonage Farm, South Barrow, Yeovil, Somerset. *T:* North Cadbury 417. *Club:* Royal Ocean Racing.

**SCOTT, Most Rev. Moses Nathaniel Christopher Omobiala;** *see* West Africa, Archbishop of.

**SCOTT, Nicholas Paul,** MBE 1964; JP; MP (C) Paddington South since 1966; Parliamentary Private Secretary to Chancellor of the Exchequer, since 1970; *b* 1933; *e s* of P. J. Scott; *m* Elizabeth Robinson; one *s* two *d*. *Educ:* Clapham College. Served Holborn Borough Coun., 1956-59 and 1962-65; contested (C) SW Islington, 1959 and 1964; Nat. Chm., Young Conservatives, 1963; Vice-Chm., Conservative Parly Labour Cttee, 1967-70. Chairman: Westminster Community Relations Council, 1967-; Paddington Churches Housing Trust, 1970-. Nat. President, PEST. Man. Dir, E. Allom & Co., 1968-70; Chm., Creative Consultants Ltd, 1969-. JP London, 1961. *Recreations:* cricket, squash. *Address:* 20 Victoria Square, SW1. *T:* 01-828 3823; Eight, Compton Bassett, Wilts. *T:* Calne 3010. *Club:* Carlton.

**SCOTT, Prof. Norman Carson,** BA, BSc; Professor Emeritus of Phonetics in the University of London, Hon. Fellow, School of Oriental and African Studies, since 1966; *b* 14 March 1899; *m* 1st, 1920, Mildred Cardew; one *s*; 2nd, 1940, Mary Simkins. *Educ:* Alleyn's School, Dulwich; King's College, London. Asst Master in grammar schools, 1925-37; part-time lecturer in Phonetics of French, Institut Français du Royaume-Uni, 1935-39; lecturer in phonetics, University Coll., London, 1937-44; lecturer in phonetics, 1944-47, Reader in phonetics, 1947-60, Professor of phonetics, 1960-66, School of Oriental and African Studies, University of London. Hon. Secretary, Philological Society, 1951-60;

President, 1963-65, Vice-President, 1970. *Publications:* (with M. Simkins) French Sentence Tables for Schools, 1939; English Conversations in Simplified Phonetic Transcription, 1942; A Dictionary of Sea Dayak, 1956; contrib. to learned journals. *Address:* 9 Gonnerston, St Albans, Herts.

**SCOTT, Sir Oliver (Christopher Anderson),** 3rd Bt, of Yews, Westmorland, *cr* 1909; Radiobiologist, 1954-66, Director, British Empire Cancer Campaign Research Unit in Radiobiology, 1966-69; *b* 6 November 1922; *s* of Sir Samuel H. Scott, 2nd Bt and Nancy Lilian (*née* Anderson); *S* father 1960; *m* 1951, Phoebe Ann Tolhurst; one *s* two *d. Educ:* Charterhouse; King's College, Cambridge. Clinical training at St Thomas' Hosp., 1943-46; MRCS, LRCP, 1946; MB, BCh, Cambridge, 1946; Surgeon-Lieutenant RNVR, 1947-49. Chm., Finance Cttee, British Cancer Council, 1970. High Sheriff of Westmorland, 1966. *Publications:* contributions to scientific books and journals. *Recreations:* skiing and walking. *Heir: s* Christopher James Scott, *b* 16 Jan. 1955. *Address:* 31 Kensington Square, W8. *T:* 01-937 8556. *Club:* Brooks's.

**SCOTT, Oliver Lester Schreiner;** Physician-in-Charge, Skin Department, Charing Cross Hospital, since 1957; Consultant Dermatologist, South West Metropolitan Regional Hospital Board, since 1951; *b* London, 16 June 1919; *s* of Ralph Lester Scott, FRCS (Ed.), and Ursula Hester Schreiner; *m* 1943, Katherine Ogle Branfoot; two *d. Educ:* Diocesan College, Cape Town; Trinity College, Cambridge; St Thomas's Hospital, London. MRCS, LRCP 1942; MA, MB, BChir, (Cantab) 1943; MRCP (London) 1944. FRCP 1964. Med. Specialist, RAF Med. Branch, 1944-46. Mem. Coun. of Royal Med. Foundn of Epsom Coll., 1953-; Mem. Bd of Governors, and Vice-Dean of Med. Sch., Charing Cross Hospital; Vice-Chm., Med. Insurance Agency. *Publications:* section on skin disorders in Clinical Genetics, ed. A. Sorsby; medical articles in Lancet, British Journal of Dermatology, etc. *Recreation:* fishing. *Address:* 114 Harley Street, W1. *T:* 01-935 0621; South Lodge, South Side, Wimbledon Common, SW19. *T:* 01-946 6662.

**SCOTT, Paul Henderson;** Counsellor and Consul-General, Vienna, since 1968; *b* 7 Nov. 1920; *s* of Alan Scott and Catherine Scott (*née* Henderson), Edinburgh; *m* 1953, Beatrice Celia Sharpe; one *s* one *d. Educ:* Royal High School, Edinburgh; Edinburgh University (MA). HM Forces, 1941-47 (Major RA). Foreign Office, 1947-53; First Secretary, Warsaw, 1953-55; First Secretary, La Paz, 1955-59; Foreign Office, 1959-62; Counsellor, Havana, 1962-64; Canadian National Defence College, 1964-65; British Deputy Commissioner General for Montreal Exhibition, 1965-67. Grosse Goldene Ehrenzeichen, Austria, 1969. *Recreations:* skiing, sailing. *Address:* c/o Foreign and Commonwealth Office, SW1. *Club:* Royal St Lawrence Yacht (Montreal).

**SCOTT, Rev. Dr Percy;** Principal of Hartley Victoria College, Manchester, since 1959; *b* 14 Nov. 1910; *s* of Herbert and Emma Scott; *m* 1937, Christa Schleining; one *s* two *d. Educ:* Lincoln City School; London and Marburg Universities. Richmond College, London, 1931-35; Marburg, 1935-37; Minister at: Exeter, 1937-39; Stockton-on-Tees, 1939-45; Leeds, 1945-47; Tutor in Systematic Theology at Hartley Victoria College, 1947-; Member, Faculty of Theology, Manchester Univ., 1953-. *Publications:* John Wesley's Lehre von der Heiligung, 1938; (trans.) Day by Day we Magnify Thee (Luther), 1950; other translations from German; signed reviews in The Expository Times and London Quarterly; articles. *Recreation:* sport. *Address:* Hartley Victoria College, Manchester 16. *T:* 061-881 3593. *Club:* Rotarian (Manchester South).

**SCOTT, Peter,** OBE 1948; Hon. ATPI; *o s* of Peter Scott and Mary Harriet Wycherley; *m* 1st, 1925, Lilian Dove (*d* 1935); 2nd, 1938, Richenda Payne; no *c. Educ:* privately; School of Architecture, Liverpool University. Served European War, Palestine, Captain Royal Field Artillery; after demobilisation, varied business experience; Asst Sec. Home Service Committee, Society of Friends, 1926-28; Joint Sec., 1928-34; organised relief work in S Wales, 1928; originator of the Brynmawr Experiment and Subsistence Production Societies for older unemployed men in S Wales and Lancs. *Address:* The Old Coach House, East House, Adderbury, Banbury, Oxon. *T:* Adderbury 304.

**SCOTT, Peter Markham,** CBE 1953 (MBE 1942); DSC 1943; Artist; Rector of Aberdeen University, 1960-63; Admiral of Manx Herring Fleet, 1962-65; Lt-Comdr RNVR, retired; *b* 14 Sept. 1909; *s* of Captain Robert Falcon Scott, CVO, RN, and Kathleen Bruce (she *m* 2nd, 1922, Edward Hilton Young, later 1st Baron Kennet, PC, GBE, DSO, DSC, who *died* 1960; she *died* 1947); *m* 1st, 1942, Elizabeth Jane (marriage dissolved, 1951), *d* of David Howard; one *d;* 2nd, 1951, Philippa, *d* of late Comdr F. W. Talbot-Ponsonby, RN; one *s* one *d. Educ:* Oundle; Trinity College, Cambridge (MA); Munich State Academy; Royal Academy Schools, London. Exhibited paintings Royal Acad. since 1933; held Exhibitions of oil paintings at Ackermann's Galleries, Bond Street, also New York; specialises in bird-painting and portraits; lectures and nature feature programmes on BBC television. Won international 14-foot Dinghy Championship for Prince of Wales Cup, 1937, 1938, and 1946. Represented Great Britain at Olympic Games, 1936 in single-handed sailing (bronze medal). Served in destroyers in Battle of Atlantic, and Light Coastal Forces in Channel, 1939-45 (despatches thrice, MBE, DSC and Bar). Founder and Hon. Director, Wildfowl Trust; Vice-Pres. and Chm. Trustees, World Wildlife Fund; President: Home Counties Nth Young Conservatives, 1946-48; Glos Assoc. of Youth Clubs; Internat. Yacht Racing Union, 1955-69; Vice-President: British Gliding Assoc.; Inland Waterways Assoc.; Camping Club of Great Britain; Bristol Gliding Club; Member Council: Boy Scout Association; Officers Association; British Gliding Assoc.; British Schools Exploring Society; Royal Yachting Assoc.; Winston Churchill Memorial Trust. Chairman: Survival Service Commn, Internat. Union for the Conservation of Nature and Natural Resources; Internat. Ornithological Committee; Fauna Preservation Society; Olympic Yachting Committee, 1947-48; Internat. Jury for Yachting, Olympic Games: 1956, Melbourne; 1960, Naples; 1964, Japan; Mexico, 1968; Joint Rules Committee to Unify European and American Yacht Racing Rules, 1953-54. Explored unmapped Perry River area in Canadian Arctic, May-August 1949; Leader of ornithological expedition to Central Highlands, Iceland, to mark wild geese, 1951, 1953; Expeditions to Australasia and Pacific, 1956-57, West Indies, Panama, Ecuador and Galapagos Is, 1959. Gliding: International Gold Badge, 1958; International Diamond badge, 1963; National Gliding Champion, 1963; Chm., British Gliding Assoc., 1968-70. Hon. LLD University of Exeter, 1963; Hon. LLD Univ. of Aberdeen,

1963. Cherry Kearton New Medal, RGS, 1967; Albert Medal, RSA, 1970. *Publications:* Morning Flight, 1935; Wild Chorus, 1938; The Battle of the Narrow Seas, 1945; Portrait Drawings, 1949; Key to Wildfowl of the World, 1949 (coloured key, 1958); Wild Geese and Eskimos, 1951; (with James Fisher) A Thousand Geese, 1953; (with Hugh Boyd) Wildfowl of the British Isles, 1957; The Eye of the Wind (autobiography), 1961; (with Philippa Scott) Animals in Africa, 1962. Illustrated Lord Kennet's A Bird in the Bush, Michael Bratby's Grey Goose and Through the Air, Paul Gallico's The Snow Goose, Ian Pitman's And Clouds Flying, Richard Perry's Turn of the Tide, Countryside Character, Adventures Among Birds, Three Schoolboys, Handbook of British Birds, Vol. III, L. A. Knight's The Morlo, Ray Gregorson's Lemuel, Jean Delacour's Waterfowl of the World, W. A. Cadman's Tales of a Wildfowler; Editor and illustrator of Annual Reports of Wildfowl Trust from 1948. *Recreations:* exploring, bird-watching, yacht racing, gliding. *Address:* New Grounds, Slimbridge, Glos. *Clubs:* Savile, Royal Thames Yacht; Royal Yacht Squadron, Island Sailing (Cowes); Explorers, Boone and Crockett (New York).

**SCOTT, Ralph Roylance,** CMG 1939; MC; MB; MRCS; DPH; retired; *b* 10 July 1893; *o s* of late Ernest Scott, Tynemouth. *Educ:* Blundell's School; Durham University. RAMC (SR), 1914; Active Service, 1916-19; Colonial Medical Service, 1919; Director of Medical Services, Tanganyika, 1935-45. *Publications:* Introduction to the Study of Preventive Medicine, 1939; Glossary of Scientific Terms, 1929; Contrib. E. A. Med. Jl, 1963. *Recreation:* music. *Address:* PO Karen, Nairobi, Kenya. *Club:* Nairobi.

**SCOTT, Brig. Raymond S.,** CIE 1934; Indian Army, retired; *s* of A. S. B. Scott, Crondall, Hants; *m* 1911, Phyllis Freda Hildesley; one *s* one *d.* 32nd Lancers Indian Army, and Army Remount Department; Director of Remounts, India, 1930-34. *Recreations:* riding, racing. *Address:* Water Hall, Ifield, Sussex. *T:* Crawley 20002. *Club:* Cavalry.

**SCOTT, Prof. Richard;** Professor of General Practice, University of Edinburgh, since 1963; *b* 11 May 1914; *s* of Richard Scott and Beatrice Scott (*née* Aitken); *m* 1938, Mary Ellen Maclachlan; three *s* two *d. Educ:* Beath High Sch.; Edinburgh Univ. MB, ChB 1936; MD (with commendation) 1938; Lewis Cameron Postgrad. Prize, 1938; DPH Edin. 1946 (class medal); FRCGP 1967. General Practice, 1936-39. War Service, 1939-46 (Lieutenant-Colonel RAMC). Lecturer in Public Health and Social Medicine, Edin. Univ., 1946; Sen. Lectr and Dir General Practice Teaching Unit, 1951; subseq. Reader in General Practice. Mem. Foundn Steering Cttee, Coll. of GPs 1951; James Mackenzie Lectr, 1964. Hon. Sec. Scottish Council, Roy. Coll. of General Practitioners, 1952-. Consultant and Technical Advisor, WHO. *Publications:* Contrib. to scientific and medical jls. *Recreation:* caravanning. *Address:* 24 Fountainhall Road, Edinburgh 9. *T:* 031-667 4244.

**SCOTT, Sir (Robert) Donald,** Kt, *cr* 1955; landowner and farmer; *b* 19 May 1901; *s* of late William Scott, Newcastle upon Tyne; *m* 1930, Olive Anna Daphne, *d* of late J. J. Russell, Ballygasson House, Co. Louth; two *d. Educ:* Mill Hill School; Magdalene Coll., Cambridge (MA). Liaison Officer to Minister of Agriculture, 1942-46, 1955-64, for Northern Region; Member Northumberland Rivers Catchment Board, 1942-46; MP (C) Wansbeck Division of Northumberland, 1940-45; Penrith and The Border Division of Cumberland, 1950-55; Member of the Speaker's Conference on Electoral Reform, 1944; Jt Parliamentary Sec. to Min. of Agriculture and Fisheries, May-July 1945; Chm. of Ministry of Agriculture Hill Sheep Advisory Committee for England and Wales, 1945-46; Member Hill Farming Advisory Cttee for Eng., Wales and N Ireland, 1946-50; Assistant Agriculture Adviser, Ministry of Agriculture, 1945-46; Vice-Chairman Northern Area Conservative Assocs, and Chairman Northumberland County Conservative Assocs, 1945-50; Chairman Conservative Political Education Cttee, 1949-50: Member Royal Commission on Common Land, 1955-58; Governor of Conservative Coll. of the North. *Recreation:* shooting. *Address:* Caistron, Thropton, via Morpeth, Northumberland. *TA* and *T:* Hepple 218. *Clubs:* Constitutional, Farmers'.

**SCOTT, Very Rev. Robert Forrester Victor,** DD Univ. of Edinburgh, 1944; CF; Minister of Auchterhouse Parish, 1960-68; retired, 1968; *b* 11 August 1897; *s* of Rev. William Frank Scott and Henrietta Porteous Hardy; *m* 1924, Phyllis Lee (*d* 1969), *d* of Frank Scott Graves; one *s* two *d. Educ:* Morrison's Acad., Crieff; Roy. High Sch., Edinburgh; Edinburgh Univ. On leaving school, served with 13th Bn The Royal Scots, France, 1916-19; ordained to Parish of Strathmiglo, Fife, 1923; inducted to St Andrew's Parish, Dundee, 1926; inducted as Colleague and Successor to late Very Rev. John White, CH, DD, LLD, The Barony, of Glasgow, 1935; Minister of St Columba's Church of Scotland, Pont St, SW1, 1938-60; Moderator of the General Assembly of the Church of Scotland, May 1956-May 1957; Mem. Advisory Council, BBC, 1958-62; Chm. West London Cttee for Protection of Children, 1947-60. Presbyterian Chaplain, The Royal Hospital, Chelsea, 1956-60. Officer of the Order of Orange-Nassau, 1948. *Publications:* articles in newspapers and periodicals. *Recreation:* fishing. *Address:* 34 Learmouth Avenue, Edinburgh 4. *Club:* Caledonian.

**SCOTT, Sir Robert (Heatlie),** GCMG 1958 (KCMG 1954; CMG 1950); CBE 1946; JP; Lord Lieutenant of Peebleshire since 1968; Permanent Secretary, Ministry of Defence, 1961-63, retired; *b* Peterhead, Scotland, 20 September 1905; *s* of T. H. Scott, OBE, MInstCE; *m* 1933, Rosamond Dewar Durie; one *d. Educ:* Queen's Royal College, Trinidad; New College, Oxford. Called to the Bar, Gray's Inn, 1927. Joined HM Consular Service in China, 1927; served in Peking, Shanghai, Canton, Hong Kong, Singapore; Assistant Under-Secretary of State, Foreign Office, 1950-53; Minister British Embassy, Washington, 1953-55; Commissioner-General for the UK in South-East Asia, 1955-59; Commandant, Imperial Defence College, 1960-61. JP 1968. *Address:* Lyne Station House, by Peebles, Peeblesshire.

**SCOTT, Robin;** *see* Scutt, R. H.

**SCOTT, Sir Ronald B.;** *see* Bodley Scott.

**SCOTT, Sheila (Christine),** OBE 1968; Aviator; Competitive Pilot since 1959; *b* 27 April 1927; *d* of Harold R. Hopkins, Worcester, and Edith Hopkins (*née* Kenward); *m* 1945, Rupert Leaman Bellamy (marr. diss. 1950). *Educ:* Alice Ottley School, Worcs. VAD, RN, 1945; acting, 1946-59, with Repertory Companies at Watford, Aldershot and Windsor; small parts in films, TV and West End Stage. Started flying, 1959; obtained British and USA commercial licences; Racing Pilot: first race won 1960 national air races (De Havilland Trophy, etc); Holder of 99 World Class Records (Aviation), incl. Round the World in class CIc and in open feminine classes; London to Capetown and Capetown to London; N Atlantic (western crossing direct); S Atlantic, Brazil to W Africa; winner of many air races; won female Light Aircraft prize, Transatlantic Air Race London-New York May 1969; won Ford Woman's Prize, London-Sydney Air Race, Dec. 1969. Founder and 1st Gov., Brit. Section, Ninety Nines Inc., 1964. Life Mem. and Hon. Diploma, Academia Romana vel Sodalitis Quirinale. Silver Award of Merit, Brit. Guild of Air Pilots and Navigators, 1966, Liveryman, 1968; Isabella D'Este Award (Italy), 1966; Silver Medal, Royal Aero Club, 1967; Harmon Trophy, 1967; Britannia Trophy, 1968. *Publication:* I Must Fly, 1968. *Recreations:* sailing and ballooning (Founder, British Balloon and Airships Club). *Address:* 593 Park West, W2. *T:* 01-262 7733. *Club:* Royal Aero.

**SCOTT, Rev. Sidney;** *see* Scott, Rev. (Walter) S.

**SCOTT, Sir Terence Charles Stuart M.;** *see* Morrison-Scott.

**SCOTT, Thomas Frederick McNair,** MA Cantab, MD Cantab, MRCS; FRCP; Senior Physician The Children's Hospital of Philadelphia, 1940-69, now Professor Emeritus; Professor of Pediatrics, University of Pennsylvania, 1966, now Professor Emeritus; *b* 18 June 1901; *e s* of Robert Frederick McNair Scott, MB, ChB (Edin.), and Alice Nystrom; *m* 1936, Mary Dwight Baker, PhD (Radcliffe), *o d* of late Clarence Dwight Baker, Wisconsin, USA; one *s* one *d*. *Educ:* Cheltenham College; Caius College, Cambridge (Scholar). Natural Science Tripos Pt I Class I, Part II (Physiology) Class II; Junior University Entrance Scholarship to St George's Hospital, 1924; Brackenbury Prize in Medicine, 1926; Qualified conjoint board, 1927; MRCP, 1928; FRCP 1953; Casualty Officer, House Surgeon, House Physn, Resident Obst. Asst, Medical Registrar, at St George's Hospital, 1927-29; House Physician Queens Hospital for Children, 1930; Research Fellow of Medicine, Harvard University, Mass, USA, 1930-31; Instructor in Pædiatrics Johns Hopkins University, Baltimore, Md, USA, 1931-34; Assistant Resident Physician at Hospital of Rockefeller Institute for Medical Research, New York, USA, working on Virus diseases, 1934-36; Assistant Physician i/c of Children's Out-patients, Lecturer in Children's Diseases, at St George's Hospital, SW1, Assistant Physician at Queens Hospital for Children, E2, 1936-38; Prof. of Pediatrics, Temple Univ. Med. Sch., Philadelphia, 1938-40; Research Prof. of Pediatrics, Univ. of Pennsylvania, 1940-66. *Publications:* Papers on Cytology and Blood diseases, Lead poisoning in children, Virus diseases of the central nervous system, Herpetic stomatitis in children, Virus diseases of the skin. *Address:* 401 South Taney, Philadelphia, Pa, USA; Children's Hospital, 18th and Bainbridge Street, Philadelphia, Pa 19146, USA.

**SCOTT, Maj.-Gen. Thomas Patrick David,** CB 1956; CBE 1945; DSO 1943, and Bar, 1945; *b* 1 March 1905; *o s* of late Lieutenant-General Sir Thomas E. Scott, KCB, CIE, DSO; *m* 1936, Peggy Winifred, *d* of late Capt. Robert McGregor Bowen-Colthurst, Killinadrish, Co. Cork; three *d*. *Educ:* Blundell's; RMC Sandhurst. 2nd Lt Royal Irish Fusiliers, 1924, Adjt, 1933-36; Instructor, RMC, 1936-38; student, Staff College, 1939; OC 1st Royal Irish Fusiliers, 1942-43; Comdr, 38th Irish Brigade, 1944-47; Comdt, Senior Officers School, 1948-50; Commander 107 Ulster Bde Gp (TA), 1950-52; DAG, MELF, 1952-54; Training Adviser to Commander-in-Chief, GHQ, Pakistan, 1954-56; GOC 42 (Lancs) Div. TA and North-West District, 1956-59. Colonel The Royal Irish Fusiliers (Princess Victoria's), 1960-68; Dep. Col Royal Irish Rangers, 1968-. Chairman, Co. Armagh TA&AFA, Dec. 1959-67. High Sheriff, Co. Tyrone, 1966. *Recreation:* fishing. *Address:* Rossfad House, Ballinamallard, Co. Fermanagh, N Ireland. *T:* Killadeas 243. *Clubs:* United Service, Ski Club of Great Britain.

**SCOTT, Sir Walter,** 4th Bt, *cr* 1907; *b* 29 July 1918; *s* of Sir Walter Scott, 3rd Bt, and Nancie Margot, *d* of S. H. March; *S* father, 1967; *m* 1945, Diana Mary, *d* of J. R. Owen; one *s* one *d*. *Educ:* Eton; Jesus College, Cambridge. Served 1st Royal Dragoons, 1939-46; Temp. Major, 1945. JP East Sussex, 1963. *Recreations:* field sports. *Heir: s* Walter John Scott, *b* 24 Feb. 1948. *Address:* Eckington Manor, Ripe, Lewes, Sussex. *T:* Ripe 204. *Club:* Oxford and Cambridge University.

**SCOTT, Sir Walter,** Kt 1966; CMG 1960; Governing Director, W. D. Scott and Co. Pty Ltd, since 1938; *b* 10 Nov. 1903; *s* of Alexander and Selina Scott; *m* 1931, Dorothy Ada Ransom; two *s*. *Educ:* Modern School, Perth, WA. Chm., Austr.: Decimal Curr. Bd; Industr. Design Coun.; Productivity Coun.; Member: Secondary Industries Commn, 1944-50; Aust. Aluminium Production Commn, 1944-52; Roy. Commn on Collinsville, 1954-55; Chairman: Motor Car Production Adv. Cttee, 1945-50; Cttee of Investigation, NSW Coal Prices, 1954; Decimal Currency Cttee, 1959-60. World Pres. Internat. Cttee for Scientific Management (CIOS), 1958-60. Wallace Clark Award (for services to Internat. Management) (USA), 1957; Henry Robinson Towne Lectr, 1961; John Storey Award, 1962; Frank and Lillian Gilbreth Award, 1963; Vice-Chancellor, Internat. Acad. of Management, 1965; Fellow International Academy of Management. Gold Medal, Conseil Internat. pour l'Organisation Scientifique, 1966. *Publications:* Budgetary Control, 1937; Cost Accounting, 1944; Greater Production, 1950; Australia and the Challenge of Change, 1957. *Address:* The Anchorage, 5 Milson Road, Cremorne Point, NSW, Australia. *T:* 90-7569. *Clubs:* Union, Royal Sydney Yacht Squadron, American National, Rotary (Sydney, NSW).

**SCOTT, Rev. (Walter) Sidney;** Clergyman (licensed to officiate Dioceses of London and Winchester since 1946, Portsmouth since 1953 and Guildford since 1958); Author and Lecturer; *b* 2 November 1900; *o s* of late Walter Samuel Scott, KC; *m* 1937, Margaret, *o d* of John E. Jefferson Hogg, OBE, JP, DL, Norton House, Co. Durham; no *c*. *Educ:* St Columba's College, Dublin; Trinity College, Dublin (BA 1st Class and Respondent; MA); University of Alberta, Canada (BA); Université de Nancy, France, (D d'Univ., avec mention très honorable); Wells Theological College. Curate of Writtle, Essex, 1929-31; Precentor (1931-41) and Priest-in-Charge (1941-46) of St Peter's, Cranley Gardens, SW. British Chaplain of Ostend, 1937; High Sheriff's Chaplain, Sussex, 1940 and 1941; Mem. of Bd, American Students' Center, Paris, 1955-. At various times temporary Chaplain of Paris, Antwerp, Dinard, Amsterdam, Oslo, etc. Officier d'Académie (France), 1939; Officier de l'Instruction Publique (France), 1949; Chevalier de la Légion d'Honneur (France), 1958; Médaille d'Honneur (Chinon) 1963; Freedom of Vaucouleurs, France, 1949, etc. *Publications:* Worship and Drama, 1938; Prayers and

Intercessions, 1939; A War-Time Compline, 1940; Little Chelsea, 1941; The Athenians, 1943; Harriet and Mary, 1944; Shelley at Oxford, 1944; The Fantasticks, 1945; A Clowder of Cats, 1945; John Donne, 1946; Georgian Theatre, 1946; Pride of London (with Walter Scott and Joan Stevenson) 1947; Bygone Pleasures of London, 1948; (ed) New Shelley Letters, 1948; (ed) Gilbert White's Antiquities of Selborne, 1949; A Selborne Handbook, 1950; (ed) Hogg's Alexy Haimatoff, 1952; (ed) Letters of Maria Edgeworth and A. L. Barbauld, 1953; A Journal of the Terror, 1955; Green Retreats, 1955; The Trial of Joan of Arc, 1956; L'Art du Culte selon la coutume de l'Eglise d'Angleterre, 1957; (ed) Gilbert White's Natural History of Selborne, 1962; A Crusading Dean, 1967. *Recreation:* book collecting. *Address:* Shortfield House, Frensham, Surrey. *T:* 2566. *Club:* Athenæum.

**SCOTT, Major-General Sir William (Arthur),** KCMG 1959; CB 1950; CBE 1943; *b* 25 March 1899; *s* of Herbert Ernest and Jane Scott; *m* 1927, Dulcie Buchanan; two *d. Educ:* privately; RMA, Woolwich. Commissioned RE 1917; France and Belgium, 1918; transferred to Royal Signals, 1921; Waziristan, 1921-23; Razmak FF, 1923 (MBE 1924); France, 1940; N Af., 1942 (CBE); Sicily and Italy, 1943-45. Dir of Signals, War Office, 1948-52; Dir of Weapons and Development, War Office, 1952-55; retired, 1955. Late Col Comdt Royal Signals; Master of Signals, 1961-70. *Address:* Stapleton, Budleigh Salterton, Devon. *T:* Budleigh Salterton 3123. *Club:* United Service.

**SCOTT, William Clifford Munro,** MD; Consulting Psychiatrist, Montreal Children's Hospital, and Montreal General Hospital; *b* 11 March 1903; *o s* of late Rev. Robert Smyth Scott and late Katherine Munro Hopper; *m* 1934, Emmy Luise (marr. diss.), *er d* of late Hugo Böcking; two *s*; *m* 1970, Evelyn Freeman Fitch. *Educ:* Parkdale Collegiate, Toronto; University of Toronto. BSc (Med.), MD (Tor.), DPM (London), LMSSA. James H. Richardson Fellow, Department of Anat., 1922-24; Lectr in Anat. and Physiol., Margaret Eaton Sch. of Phys. Educ., Toronto, 1923-25; Post-Grad. Educ. in Psychiatry: Johns Hopkins Med. Sch., 1928-29; Boston Psychopathic Hosp., Harvard Univ. Med. Sch., 1929-30; Commonwealth Fund Fellow, Dept of Psychiatry, Harvard Univ., 1930-33; studied at Nat. Hosp., Queen Sq., London, 1931-32, and at Inst of Psycho-Analysis, London, 1931-33. Staff positions Maudsley Hosp., 1933-35, Cassel Hosp., 1935-38; private practice, 1938-. EMS Psychiatrist, Min. of Health, London, Sheffield and S Wales, 1939-46; Psychiatric Cons. to St Dunstan's, 1945. Mem. Cttee of Management, Inst. of Psychiatry (Univ. of London), 1951-53; Med. Dir London Clinic of Psycho-Analysis, 1947-53; Senior Psychotherapist, Bethlem Royal Hosp. and Maudsley Hosp., 1948-54; Teacher Inst. of Psychiatry (Univ. of London), 1948-54; Associate Professor in charge of Training in Psycho-Analysis, Department of Psychiatry, McGill University, Montreal, 1954-59; Post-Grad. Teacher (Psychiatry and Psycho-Analysis), 1945-. Chm. Psychotherapy and Social Psychiatry Section, Roy. Medico-Psychological Assoc., 1952-54; Pres. Brit. Psycho-Analytical Soc., 1953-54; Mem. Bd Dirs, Inst. of Psycho-Analysis, 1947-54 (Chm. 1954); Director of Canadian Inst. of Psycho-Analysis, 1965-67. FBPsS; ex-Chm. Med. Sect. and Mem. Council, Brit. Psychological Soc.; ex-Mem. Cttee Sect. Psychiatry; Roy. Soc. Med.; Amer. Psychiatric Assoc.; Vice-Pres., Psychiatric Sect., BMA, 1952 and 1955; Asst Ed. Internat. Jl Psycho-Analysis; ex-Asst Ed., Brit. Jl Med. Psychology. *Publications:* chiefly in Brit. Jl of Med. Psychol. and Internat. Jl of Psycho-Analysis. *Recreations:* people and books. *Address:* 1260 McGregor Avenue, Montreal, PQ, Canada.

**SCOTT, (William) Donald,** CBE 1968; MA (Oxon); BSc (Yale); *b* 22 May 1903; *s* of late Reverend William Scott and Sara Jane (*née* Platt); *m* 1928, Muriel Barbara, *d* of late Louis F. Rothschild, NYC; two *s* one *d. Educ:* Taunton Sch., Taunton; Univ. College, Oxford (open scholar); Yale University, USA (Henry P. Davison Scholar). Hercules Powder Co., USA and Rotterdam, 1926-28; British Paint & Lacquer Co., Cowley, Oxford, 1928-35; ICI Ltd: Nobel Div., 1935-41; Dyestuffs Div., 1941-43; Southern Sales Region, Dep. Regional Manager, 1943-45; Regional Manager, 1945-51; Billingham Div., Jt Man. Dir, 1951-55; Main Board Director, 1954-65. Director, 1952-60, and Chairman, 1956-60, Scottish Agricultural Industries Ltd; Chm., Home Grown Cereals Authority, 1965-68; Director: Canadian Industries Ltd, 1957-62; Glaxo Group Ltd, 1965-68; Laporte Industries Ltd, 1965-68. Mem., Western Hemisphere Exports Council, 1961-64. FRSA 1968. *Recreations:* cricket, golf. *Address:* c/o Miss B. J. Scott, 4 Cumberland Terrace, Regent's Park, NW1. *T:* 01-935 0068. *Clubs:* Savile, Beefsteak, Royal Automobile, MCC; Royal and Ancient (St Andrews).

**SCOTT, Prof. William Douglas R.;** *see* Robson-Scott.

**SCOTT, Rev. W(illiam) Gardiner,** MA; Minister and Warden of Scots Memorial Church and Hospice, Jerusalem, Israel, since 1966; *b* 23 February 1906; *o s* of late William Gardiner Scott, Portsoy, Banffshire; *m* 1953, Darinka Milo, *d* of late Milo Glogovac, Oakland, Calif; one *d. Educ:* Grange School, B'oness, West Lothian; Edinburgh University and New College, Edinburgh. In catering business, 1926-30; graduated in Arts, Edin., 1934; Theological Travel Scholarship to Palestine, 1936; travelled as ship's steward to America and India, 1936; ordained to Ministry of Church of Scotland, 1939; Sub-Warden 1939, Deputy Warden 1940, New College Settlement, Edinburgh; enlisted as Army Chaplain, 1941; served in Egypt, 1942-44 and developed community centre at RA Depot, Cairo and initiated publication of weekly Scots newspaper, The Clachan Crack; founded Montgomery House, Alexandria, as community centre for all ranks of allied troops, 1943; served in Palestine as Church of Scotland Chaplain for Galilee and district, 1944-46; Senior Chaplain at Scottish Command, 1946-47; Warden of Student Movement House, London, 1947-49; Chaplain at Victoria Univ. Coll., Wellington, NZ, 1950-54; locum tenens St John's West Church, Leith, 1955; Minister: of Church of Scotland, Jerusalem, 1955-60; Parish of Abernethy, 1960-66. *Recreations:* travel, gardening, cooking, walking. *Address:* St Andrew's Hospice, Church of Scotland, Jerusalem, Israel.

**SCOTT, William George,** CBE 1966; Painter; *b* 15 Feb. 1913; *e s* of William John and Agnes Scott; *m* 1937, Hilda Mary Lucas; two *s. Educ:* Enniskillen; Belfast Sch. of Art; Roy. Acad. Schools, London. Exhibitions: Leger Gallery, 1942, 1944, 1946; Leicester Gall., 1948, 1951; Hanover Gall., 1953, 1956, 1961, 1963, 1965, 1967; Martha Jackson Gallery, NY, 1954, 1958; Venice Biennale, 1958; VIth Sao Paulo Biennial, 1953 and 1961, Brazil, Exhibited in British Council Exhibns in Europe; *works exhibited in:* Tate Gall.; Victoria and Albert

Museum; Paris; New York; Toledo, USA; S Africa; Canada; Australia; S America. *Address:* 13 Edith Terrace, Chelsea, SW10. *T:* 01-352 8044.

**SCOTT, Sir Winston;** *see* Scott, Sir A. W.

**SCOTT BLAIR, George William,** MA (Oxon), DSc (London); FRIC; FInstP; *b* 23 July 1902; *s* of late James and Jessie Scott Blair; *m* 1927, Margaret Florence Riddelsdell; no *c. Educ:* Charterhouse; Trinity College, Oxford. Ten years on Research Staff at Rothamsted Experimental Station; sometime Fellow on Rockefeller Foundation at University of Cornell; Head of Chemistry, later Physics Department National Institute for Research in Dairying, University of Reading, 1937-67; retired. Consultant rheologist. Poiseuille Gold Medal, Internat. Soc. of Haemorheology, 1969; Gold Medal, Brit. Soc. of Rheology, 1970. Membre d'honneur, Groupe française de Rhéologie, 1970. *Publications:* An Introduction to Industrial Rheology, 1938; A Survey of General and Applied Rheology, 1943; 2nd edn, 1949; Measurements of Mind and Matter, 1950; (ed) Foodstuffs: their Plasticity, Fluidity, and Consistency, 1953; (with Prof. M. Reiner) Agricultural Rheology, 1957; Elementary Rheology, 1969; papers in various scientific journals, 1925-67. *Recreations:* music, modern languages, philosophy of science. *Address:* Grist Cottage, Iffley, Oxford.

**SCOTT-BROWN, Walter Graham,** CVO 1945; BA (Hon. Nat. Sci. Tripos), MD, BCh Cambridge; FRCS, FRCSE; Consulting Surgeon Throat, Nose and Ear Department Royal Free Hospital and late Surgeon at Royal National Throat, Nose and Ear Hospital; late Consulting Aurist and Laryngologist at East Grinstead Cottage Hospital and at the Maxillo-facial unit; and Lecturer to University of London; late Lecturer at Royal National Hospital; Fellow Royal Society Medicine and Member Otological and Laryngological Section; Fellow Medical Society of London; engaged in consulting practice in London as oto-rhino-laryngologist; *e s* of late George A. Brown; *m* 1926, Margaret Affleck, *d* of G. K. Bannerman, High Wycombe; one *s* three *d. Educ:* Corpus Christi College, Cambridge; St Bartholomew's Hospital, London. Served European War, 1916-18 (despatches, wounded); France and Italy T Battery RHA and Captain and Adjutant 14th Brigade RHA 1918; Exhibitioner Corpus Christi College, Cambridge, 1919; Shuter Scholar St Bartholomew's Hospital, 1922; House Surgeon and Clinical Assistant in Ear, Nose and Throat Dept St Barts; Copeman Medallist for Scientific Research, Cambridge, 1932; Dorothy Temple Cross Research Fellowship (travelling), 1932, Berlin, Vienna, Stockholm, Copenhagen, etc. *Publications:* Allergic affections of the Nose, 1945; (ed and contrib.) Diseases of the Ear, Nose and Throat, 2nd edn 1965; Methods of Examination in Ear, Nose and Throat, 1953; Broncho-oesophageal fistula, Cavernous sinus thrombosis: a fatal complication of minor facial sepsis, and other scientific and clinical publications. *Recreations:* fishing, painting. *Address:* 61 Harley Street, W1. *T:* 01-580 1831; Little Down, Ropley, Hants. *T:* 2314.

**SCOTT-ELLIOT, Aydua Helen,** CVO 1970 (MVO 1958); retired 1970; *b* 1909; *d* of late Lewis Alexander Scott-Elliot and of Princess Eydua Odescalchi. *Educ:* St Paul's Girls' School and abroad. Temp. Asst Civilian Officer, Admty, 1941-46; Keeper of Prints and Drawings, Royal Library, Windsor Castle, 1946-69. *Publications:* articles in Burlington Magazine, Apollo, etc. *Recreation:* gardening. *Address:* Shaldon, Station Road, Mayfield, Sussex. *T:* Mayfield 2079. *Club:* University Women's.

**SCOTT ELLIOT, Major-General James,** CB 1954; CBE 1945 (OBE 1940); DSO 1943, Bar 1944; HM Lieutenant of the County of Dumfries, 1962-67; *b* 6 Nov. 1902; *s* of late Lt-Col W. Scott Elliot, DSO and Marie Theresa Scott Elliot (*née* Lyon); *m* 1932, Cecil Margaret Du Buisson; one *s* two *d. Educ:* Wellington College; Sandhurst. 2nd Lieut KOSB, 1923; Capt. Argyll and Sutherland Highlanders, 1936; psc 1937-38; Major, 1940; served in Egypt, China, India, Malta, Palestine. War of 1939-45: France, N Africa, Sicily, Italy; Temp. Lt-Col 1941; Temp. Brig. 1944; despatches, 1945; Germany, 1946-47; War Office, 1948-49; Major-General, 1954; GOC 51st (Highland) Division and Highland Dist, 1952-56; retd, 1956. Colonel King's Own Scottish Borderers, 1954-61. President: Dumfries and Galloway Natural History and Antiquarian Soc., 1962-65; Soc. of Antiquaries of Scotland, 1965-67; Brit. Soc. of Dowsers, 1966-. *Club:* Army and Navy.

**SCOTT-ELLIOT, Walter Travers;** *b* 9 Oct. 1895; *o s* of Wm Scott Elliot, Arkleton, Dumfriesshire, and Maude, *o c* of Robert Boyle Travers, Farsid, Co. Cork; *m* 1948, Dorothy Alice, *d* of late William Nunn, Calcutta. *Educ:* Eton. 2nd Lieut Coldstream Guards, Special Reserve, 1914; Capt. 1917; retired, 1919. Subsequently joined Bombay Company Ltd, East India Merchants; Managing Director, 1927. Served on Headquarters, Ministry of Labour, 1941-45; MP (Lab) Accrington, 1945-50; PPS to Sec. of State for War, 1946-47. *Recreations:* shooting and travelling. *Address:* 22 Richmond Court, Sloane Street, SW1. *Club:* Reform.

**SCOTT-ELLIS,** family name of **Baron Howard de Walden.**

**SCOTT FOX, Sir (Robert) David (John),** KCMG 1963 (CMG 1956); HM Diplomatic Service, retired; Special Representative of the Secretary of State for Foreign and Commonwealth Affairs, since 1970; *b* 20 June 1910; *yr s* of late Judge John Scott Fox, KC, and late Agnes Maria Theresa, *d* of Hermann Hammer; *m* 1951, Brigitte, *d* of Pierre Taton; three *d. Educ:* Eton; Christ Church, Oxford; Fellow Queen's College. Entered HM Diplomatic Service, 1934. Served Berlin, 1937; Prague, 1937-39; Rio de Janeiro, 1940-44; Foreign Office, 1944-49; Counsellor at Jedda, 1949-51; Chargé d'Affaires there in 1949 and 1950; transferred to Ankara, Counsellor, 1951; Chargé d'Affaires there, 1951, 1952, 1953 and 1954; Minister (Economic and Social Affairs) to UK Delegation to UN, 1955-58; Minister to Roumania, 1959-61; Ambassador to Chile, 1961-66; Ambassador to Finland, 1966-69. *Address:* 47 Eaton Terrace, SW1. *T:* 01-730 5505. *Club:* Travellers'.

**SCOTT-HOPKINS, Major James Sidney Rawdon;** MP (C) Derbyshire West, since Nov. 1967 (North Cornwall, 1959-66); *b* 29 Nov. 1921; *s* of Col R. Scott-Hopkins, DSO, MC and late Mrs Scott-Hopkins; *m* 1946, Geraldine Elizabeth Mary Hargreaves; three *s* one *d. Educ:* Eton; Oxford. Army, 1939-50; farming, 1950-59. Joint Parliamentary Secretary, Ministry of Agriculture, Fisheries and Food, 1962-64. *Recreations:* riding, shooting. *Address:* 63 Crompton Court, SW7. *T:* 01-589 5335. *Clubs:* Carlton, Farmers', St Stephen's.

**SCOTT-MALDEN, (Charles) Peter,** CB 1966; Deputy Secretary, Ministry of Transport, since 1968; *b* 29 June 1918; *e s* of late Gilbert Scott Scott-Malden and of Phyllis Dorothy Scott-Malden (*née* Wilkinson); *m* 1941, Jean Honor Chamberlain Silver, *yr d* of late Lieut-Colonel J. P. Silver, CBE, DSO, RAMC; two *s* two *d*. *Educ:* Winchester Coll. (Schol.); King's College, Cambridge (major Scholar). Entered Ministry of Transport, 1939. War of 1939-45; RAMC 1940-41; Glider Pilot Regiment, 1942-45. Assistant Secretary, Ministry of Transport, 1949. Under-Secretary, 1959. Attended course at Imperial Defence College, 1956 (idc). *Recreations:* music, golf. *Address:* 23 Burdon Lane, Cheam, Surrey. *T:* 01-642 7086. *Club:* Royal Automobile.

**SCOTT-MALDEN, Air Vice-Marshal (Francis) David (Stephen),** DSO 1942; DFC 1941; RAF (Retd); Ministry of Transport since 1966; *b* 26 Dec. 1919; *s* of late Gilbert Scott Scott-Malden and of Phyllis Dorothy Wilkinson; *m* 1955, Anne Elizabeth Watson; two *s* two *d*. *Educ:* Winchester Coll. (Scholar; Goddard Scholar, 1938); King's Coll., Cambridge (Scholar, Sir William Browne Medal for Greek Verse, 1939). Joined Cambridge University Air Squadron, Nov. 1938; called up into RAFVR as Pilot Officer, Oct 1939; flying on operations, 1940-42, as Pilot Officer, Flight Lt, Squadron Leader, and Wing Comdr (DFC and Bar, DSO, Norwegian War Cross; Commander, Order of Orange Nassau, 1945). Visited International Youth Assembly at Washington, DC, as rep. of English Universities, and toured USA as member of United Nations delegation, Sept.-Nov. 1942. RAF Selection Board (Dep. Pres.), 1946; on staff of RAF College, 1946-48; Central Fighter Establishment, 1948; RAF Staff Coll., Bracknell, 1951; psa; RAF Flying Coll., 1954-55; pfc; Jt Planning Staff, Min. of Defence, 1955-57; Group Capt. 1958; Imperial Defence College, 1957-59; idc. Dep. Dir Plans, Air Ministry, 1959-61; Air Cdre 1962; Air Vice-Marshal, 1965. *Recreations:* shooting, fishing, sailing. *Address:* Moray House, Fairway, Merrow, Guildford, Surrey. *T:* Guildford 63311.

**SCOTT-MALDEN, Peter;** *see* Scott-Malden, C. P.

**SCOTT-MILLER, Commander Ronald,** VRD 1942; RNVR (Retired); *b* 1 Nov. 1904; *s* of late Colonel Walter Scott-Miller, DL; *m* 1932, Stella Louise Farquhar, *d* of late Farquhar Deuchar, Shortridge Hall, Northumberland. *Educ:* Aldro School, Eastbourne; Uppingham. Joined London Division, RNVR, as Midshipman, 1924; War of 1939-45 (despatches): HMS Dunedin, Northern Patrol, 1939; HMS London, Atlantic, Russian Convoys, 1940-43; Combined Operations, Mediterranean, NW Europe, 1943-45. Commander, 1943; retired, 1946. MP (C) King's Lynn Division of Norfolk, 1951-59; Parliamentary Private Secretary: to Financial Secretary to Treasury, Dec. 1953-July 1954; to Minister of Transport, 1954-56; to Minister of Pensions and National Insurance, 1956-59. Trustee of Uppingham School, 1954-59. Freeman of the City of London, and Liveryman of Worshipful Company of Butchers, 1926. US Legion of Merit (Legionaire), 1943. *Recreations:* shooting, sailing. *Address:* 19 rue Guimard, Brussels 4, Belgium. *Clubs:* United Hunts, RNVR.

**SCOTT-MONCRIEFF, Adm. Sir Alan (Kenneth),** KCB 1955 (CB 1952); CBE 1952; DSO 1942, Bar 1943; DL; *s* of Robert Lawrence Scott-Moncrieff and Victoria Troutbeck; *m* 1923, Norah Doreen Vereker; one *d*. *Educ:* RN Colleges, Osborne and Dartmouth. Joined HMS Orion, as Midshipman, 1917; Comd HMS Enchantress, 1939-40; Comd HMS Faulkner, Capt. "D" 8th Flotilla, 1942-43 (despatches twice). Imperial Defence College, 1948; Comd HMS Superb, 1949; Flag Officer Comd Fifth Cruiser Sqdn, 1951-52. Korean War (CBE, despatches); Adm. Comd. Reserves, 1953-55; C-in-C, Far East Station, 1955-57. Retired, 1958. A Younger Brother of Trinity House. Chm., Red Ensign Club, Stepney; Chm., Victory Ex-Services Club. DL County of London, 1962. King Haakon Medal (Norway), 1945; Comdr Legion of Merit (US), 1952. *Address:* 62 Cranmer Court, SW3. *Club:* United Service.

**SCOTT-MONCRIEFF, Joanna Constance;** Producer, BBC Religious Broadcasting, 1964; *b* 7 Sept. 1920; *y d* of late Rev. C. W. Scott-Moncrieff, MA, and Constance E. H. Lunn; *m* 1961, Noel John Horne Baker; one *d*. *Educ:* St Swithun's Sch., Winchester; Sorbonne, Paris. Social work, 1941; Political Warfare Executive, 1941-45; joined BBC, 1945; Deputy Editor, Woman's Hour, 1950; Editor, 1956-64. *Publications:* Woman's Hour Book, 1953; BBC Book of Woman's Hour, 1957. *Recreation:* weeding. *Address:* Berins Hill, Ipsden, Oxon.

**SCOTT-SMITH, Catharine Mary,** MA Cantab; Principal of Beechlawn Tutorial College, Oxford, since Sept. 1966; *b* 4 April 1912; *d* of Edward Montagu Scott-Smith and Catharine Lorance (*née* Garland). *Educ:* Wycombe Abbey School, Bucks; Girton College, Cambridge. Classics Mistress: St Katharine's School, Wantage, 1933-37; Godolphin School, Salisbury 1937-41; Classics Mistress and house-mistress, Headington School, Oxford, 1941-47, Second Mistress, 1946-47; Classics Mistress and house-mistress, Wycombe Abbey School, Bucks, 1947-55. Second Mistress, 1951-54; Headmistress of Westonbirt School, Tetbury, Gloucestershire, 1955-64. Member Council: Berkhamsted School for Girls; Headington School, Oxford. *Address:* Graystones, Fairlight, Hastings, Sussex. *T:* Pett 3071. *Club:* University Women's.

**SCOTT-TAGGART, John,** MC; Wing Commander; Barrister-at-law; *b* Bolton, Lancashire, 1897; *s* of Wm Scott-Taggart, MIMechE, consulting engineer. *Educ:* Bolton School; Technological Institutions; King's College, University of London; Law at University College, London. Specialised in radio engineering and patent work; served European War, 1914-19 (despatches, MC); Head of the Patent Department, Radio Communication Company, Ltd, 1920; founded 1922 and later became sole proprietor of the Radio Press, Ltd; served War of 1939-45 with RAF, France, 1939-40 (despatches). Staff Officer, Air Ministry, immediately responsible for all Radar training in RAF, 1940-41; Senior Technical Officer, No. 73 Wing and, as such, was technically responsible for all radar stations in two-thirds of England and Wales, 1943-45 (despatches); Admiralty Signal and Radar Establishment, 1951-59. Has acted as Patent Adviser to radio concerns on both sides of the Atlantic. Has taken out numerous patents relating to valve manufacture, radio receiving and transmitting circuits, and allied matters since 1918; CEng; Fellow of the Institute of Radio Engineers; FIEE; MIMechE; FInstP; Fellow American Institute of Electrical Engineers. Cavaliere Ufficiale of Order Al Merito della Repubblica Italiana, 1963 (for services to art). *Publications:* Textbooks: Manual of Modern Radio; Book of Practical Radio; Thermionic Tubes in Radio Telegraphy and Telephony; Elementary Textbook on Wireless Vacuum Tubes; Radio Valves and How to Use Them; Wireless Valves Simply Explained; Practical Wireless Valve

Circuits, etc; Italian Maiolica, 1970; Spanish Pottery and Porcelain, 1970; over five hundred articles in technical press; papers read before learned societies (twice at Brit. Assoc.). *Recreation:* collection of paintings, sculpture and ceramics. *Address:* 96 Gregories Rd, Beaconsfield, Bucks.

**SCOTTER, Maj.-Gen. William Norman Roy,** OBE 1965; MC 1945; Chief of Staff, Southern Command, since 1970; *b* 9 Feb. 1922; *s* of Claude Norman Scotter, Carlisle, and Hilda Marie (*née* Turner); *m* 1947, Jean, *d* of Rev. D. S. Stiven, MC, DD; one *s* two *d. Educ:* St Bees Sch., Cumberland. Scots Guards, 1941-42; RMA Dehra Dun, 1942; commnd 7th Gurkha Rifles, 1942; served in Burma, 1944-45, 1/7th Gurkha Rifles (MC); 2nd Bn Border Regt, 1946-47, 1/2 Goorkhas, Malaya, 1948-51; psc 1951; NATO Northern Flank, 1952-54; 1st Bn Border Regt, 1954-56; HQ 6 Bde, 1956-58; jssc 1959; Instructor Camberley, 1960-63; MoD, 1963-65; CO 1 King's Own Royal Border Regt, 1965-67; Comdr 19 Inf. Bde, 1967-69; ndc 1969-70. MBIM. *Recreations:* ball games and sawing logs. *Address:* c/o Midland Bank Ltd, Court Square, Carlisle, Cumberland.

**SCOVELL, Rowley Fielding;** Managing Director, Currie Line Limited, 1944-67; *b* 29 Nov. 1902; *s* of late Rowland Hill Scovell; *m* 1944, Amy Stansmore Huddart, *widow* of Lieut-Comdr G. P. Huddart, RN; one *s. Educ:* Rugby; Trinity Coll., Cambridge. Joined Currie Line Ltd, 1923. Regional Shipping Representative, E Scotland, Min. of War Transport, 1940-46; Shipping Adviser to Turkish Government, June-Dec., 1943. Director Standard Life Assurance Company (Chm., 1957-60). *Recreation:* golf. *Address:* Bowerhouse, Dunbar, Scotland. *T:* Dunbar 2293. *Clubs:* Boodle's; New (Edinburgh).

**SCOWEN, Eric Frank,** MD, DSc; FRCP, FRCS, FRCPE; FRCPath; Director, Medical Professorial Unit, since 1955; Physician to St Bartholomew's Hospital since 1946; Professor of Medicine, University of London, since 1961 (Reader in Medicine, 1938-61); Chairman, Council of Imperial Cancer Research Fund, since 1967; *b* 22 April 1910; *s* of Frank Edward Scowen and Eleanor Betsy (*née* Barnes) (*d* 1969). *Educ:* City of London School; St Bartholomew's Hospital Medical College. St Bartholomew's Hospital: House Physician, 1931, Second Assistant, 1933, to Medical Professorial Unit; Baly Research Fell. in Clin. Med., 1933; First Asst to Med. Professorial Unit, 1935; Asst Dir of Med. Prof. Unit, and Asst Phys, 1937; Rockefeller Research Fell. to Columbia Univ., New York, 1937. Chairman: Cttee on Safety of Drugs, 1969- (Mem., 1963); British Pharmacopœia Commission, 1963-69. *Publications:* various in medical and scientific journals. *Address:* 44 Lincoln's Inn Fields, WC2. *T:* 01-405 4480. *Club:* Athenæum.

**SCRAGG, Air Vice-Marshal Sir Colin,** KBE 1963 (CBE 1953; MBE 1940); CB 1960; AFC 1942, Bar to AFC 1949; retired; *b* 8 Sept. 1908; *s* of late Lt A. Scragg, KRRC; *m* 1932, Phyllis Kathleen Rayner, Southampton; one *s* two *d. Educ:* King Edward VI School, Southampton. No. 1 (Fighter) Squadron, 1931-34; served in a succession of flying training schools, including 34 FTS Canada, until 1943; War of 1939-45, Comd No. 166 (Bomber) Squadron, 1943-44 (pow, Germany). Transport Command Development Unit, 1946-49; Dep. Director, Operational Requirements, Air Min., 1950-53, Director, 1955-58; idc 1954; AOC No. 23 Training Group, 1958-60; Deputy Controller Aircraft (RAF), Ministry of Aviation, 1960-64. Order of Orange Nassau (Netherlands), 1945. *Address:* Wedgwood, Pine Walk, Chilworth, Southampton. *T:* Southampton 69110. *Club:* Royal Air Force.

**SCRIMGEOUR, James,** CMG 1959; OBE 1944; *b* 8 June 1903; *s* of late Alexander Carron Scrimgeour and Helen May Scrimgeour (*née* Bird); *m* 1928, Winifred, *d* of late Stephen Ward Giles; one *s. Educ:* Loretto School; Clare College, Cambridge. Member of Stock Exchange, 1929-69. Auxiliary Air Force, 1938-45; Air staff, Air Ministry, 1942-45. Chm., Hume Holdings Ltd; Director, Carron Holdings Ltd; Mem. Council of White Ensign Assoc. *Address:* 22 Down Street, W1; Kilncopse Farm, Kirdford, Sussex. *Clubs:* Turf, City of London; Hawks (Cambridge); RAF Yacht.

**SCRIMSHAW, Frank Herbert;** Director-General, Electronics Research and Development, Ministry of Technology, since 1967; *b* 25 Dec. 1917; *s* of late John Leonard Scrimshaw and Jessie Scrimshaw (*née* Sewell), Lincoln; *m* 1950, Joan Olive, *d* of Leslie Stephen Paskall, Felixstowe; one *s. Educ:* The City Sch., Lincoln; University Coll., Nottingham. BSc London. Joined Scientific Civil Service, 1939; various posts at RAE, Farnborough, and Blind Landing Experimental Unit, RAF Martlesham Heath, 1939-58; Dir of Scientific Research (Electronics), Min. of Aviation, 1959-61; RRE, Malvern: Head of Guided Weapons Group, 1961-65; Head of Mil. and Civil Systems Dept, 1965-67. *Address:* 81 Bullescroft Road, Edgware, Middlesex. *T:* 01-958 6741.

**SCRIVENER, Ronald Stratford,** CMG 1965; Ambassador to Panama, since 1969; *b* 29 Dec. 1919; *s* of Sir Patrick Scrivener, KCMG; *m* 1st, 1947, Elizabeth Drake-Brockman (marr. diss., 1952); 2nd, 1962, Mary Alice Olga Sofia Jane Hohler, *d* of late Squadron-Leader Robert Charlton Lane; two step-*s* two step-*d. Educ:* Westminster School; St Catharine's College, Cambridge. Served with Royal Air Force Volunteer Reserve, 1940-45. Appointed HM Diplomatic Service, Dec. 1945. Served in Berlin, Buenos Aires, Vienna, Caracas, Berne, Bangkok. *Recreations:* travel, fishing. *Address:* British Embassy, Panama City, Panama; 72 Bedford Gardens, W8. *T:* 01-727 9069. *Clubs:* White's, Travellers'.

**SCRIVENOR, Sir Thomas (Vaisey),** Kt 1960; CMG 1956; Secretary to the Executive Council of the Commonwealth Agricultural Bureaux, since 1961; *b* 28 Aug. 1908; *e s* of late John Brooke Scrivenor, ISO, formerly Dir of Geological Survey, Malaya; *m* 1934, Mary Elizabeth Neatby; one *s* three *d. Educ:* King's School, Canterbury; Oriel College, Oxford (MA). Temp. Assistant Principal, Colonial Office, 1930-33; Assistant District Officer, Tanganyika, 1934-37; Assistant District Commissioner, Palestine, 1937-43; Assistant Lt-Governor, Malta, 1943-44; Principal, Colonial Office, 1944-46; Principal Asst Sec., Palestine, 1946-48; Civil Service Comr, Nigeria, 1948-53; Deputy High Commissioner for Basutoland, the Bechuanaland Protectorate, and Swaziland, 1953-60. *Address:* Farnham House, Farnham Royal, Bucks. *T:* Farnham Common 3816. *Club:* Oxford and Cambridge University.

**SCROGGIE, Alan Ure Reith,** OBE 1961; one of HM's Inspectors of Constabulary since 1963; *b* 1912; *s* of late Col W. R. J. Scroggie, CIE, IMS, Abbotsford Lodge, Callander, Perthshire; *m* 1940, Shiela Catherine, *d* of late Finlay Mackenzie, Gowanlea, Elgin, Morayshire; two *s. Educ:* Cargilfield Preparatory Sch.; Fettes Coll.; Edinburgh

Univ. (BL). Joined Edinburgh City Police, 1930; Asst Chief Constable of Bucks, 1947-53; Chief Constable of Northumberland, 1953-63. QPM, 1968. OStJ. *Recreations:* golf, fishing, shooting, sailing. *Address:* 11 Westfield Grove, Gosforth, Newcastle upon Tyne. *T:* Gosforth 852821. *Clubs:* Caledonian; Northumberland Golf.

**SCRUBY, Ven. Ronald Victor,** MA; Archdeacon of the Isle of Wight since 1965; *b* 23 Dec. 1919; 6th *s* of late Thomas Henry Scruby and late Florence Jane Scruby, Norwood Green, Southall, Middx; *m* 1955, Sylvia Tremayne Miles, *e d* of late Rear-Adm. Roderic B. T. Miles, Trotton, Sussex; two *s* one *d*. *Educ:* Southall Technical Coll.; Trinity Hall, Cambridge. Engineering Apprentice, London Transport, 1936-39. Royal Engineers, 1939-45; Capt. 1943. Trinity Hall, Cambridge, 1945-48; Cuddesdon Coll., Oxford, 1948-50. Asst Curate, Rogate, Sussex, 1950-53; Chaplain, King Edward VII Hosp., Midhurst, 1950-53; Chaplain, Saunders-Roe, Osborne, E Cowes, 1953-58; Vicar of Eastney, Portsmouth, 1958-65; Rural Dean of Portsmouth, 1960-65. *Recreations:* rowing, walking. *Address:* Quarr Hill House, Binstead, Ryde, Isle of Wight. *T:* Ryde 2186. *Club:* Royal Commonwealth Society.

**SCRUTTON, Thomas Hugh,** CBE 1967; Director, National Galleries of Scotland, Edinburgh, 1971; *b* 8 June 1917; *s* of Rev. Canon Tom Burton Scrutton and Lesley Hay; *m* 1st, 1941, Helen Greeves (who obtd a divorce, 1952); one *d*; 2nd, 1960, Elizabeth Quayle. *Educ:* Charterhouse; King's Coll., Cambridge (MA). Temporary Asst Keeper, Print Room, British Museum, 1946; Asst, 1947, and Director, 1948, Whitechapel Art Gallery; Director, Walker Art Gallery, Liverpool, 1952-70. *Address:* 21 Braid Avenue, Edinburgh. *Club:* Savile.

**SCRYMGEOUR, Lord; Alexander Henry Scrymgeour-Wedderburn;** *b* 5 June 1949; *s* and *heir* of 11th Earl of Dundee, *qv*. *Educ:* Eton. Page of Honour to the Queen, 1964-65. *Address:* Birkhill, Cupar, Fife. *T:* Gauldry 209.

**SCRYMGEOUR-WEDDERBURN,** family name of **Earl of Dundee.**

**SCULLARD, Howard Hayes,** FBA 1955; FSA; Professor Emeritus of Ancient History in the University of London; *b* 9 Feb. 1903; *s* of late Rev. Professor Herbert H. Scullard and Barbara Louise Scullard (*née* Dodds). *Educ:* Highgate School; St John's Coll., Cambridge (Scholar). First Class Classical Tripos Part II, 1926; Thirlwall Prize, Cambridge, 1929; MA Cambridge, PhD London, 1930. Classical Tutor, New College, London, 1926-35; Reader, 1926-35, and Professor, 1935-70, of Ancient History, King's College, London. A Governor of New College, London; Vice-Pres., Soc. for the Promotion of Roman Studies; former Mem. Council, British Acad. and of Royal Numismatic Soc.; Actg Dir, Inst. of Classical Studies, London, 1964. FKC, 1970. *Publications:* Scipio Africanus in the Second Punic War, 1930; A History of the Roman World from 753 to 146 BC, 1935, 3rd edition 1961; (edited with H. E. Butler) Livy book XXX, 1939, 6th edition 1953; (Joint Editor of and contrib. to) The Oxford Classical Dictionary, 1949, Editor (with N. G. L. Hammond) of new edn, 1970; Roman Politics, 220-150 BC, 1951; From the 1962 (Dutch, French and Spanish translations); TO Nero, 1959, 3rd edn 1970; (ed) Atlas of the Classical World, 1959 and Shorter Atlas of the Classical World, 1962; The Etruscan Cities and Rome, 1967 (Italian translation, 1969); Scipio Africanus: Soldier and Politician, 1970. (Gen. Editor of series) Aspects of Greek and Roman Life. Annual Survey of Roman history in The Year's Work in Classical Studies, 1937-48, and of ancient history in Annual Bulletin of Historical Literature, 1949-69. Articles and reviews in Journal of Roman Studies, Classical Review, Encyclopædia Britannica, etc. *Recreation:* golf. *Address:* 6 Foscote Road, Hendon, NW4. *Club:* Athenæum.

**SCULLY, Vincent William Thomas,** CMG 1946; United States Medal of Freedom (Bronze Palm); FCA; Chairman of the Board, The Steel Company of Canada Ltd, since 1966; *b* 9 Jan. 1900; *s* of James Scully, Dist. Inspector, RIC, and Katherine Scully, New Ross, County Wexford, Ireland; *m* 1930, Sylvia, *d* of late Sir Wyly Grier; one *s*. *Educ:* Christian Brothers School, New Ross and Thurles, Ireland; Trinity Coll., Dublin. Chartered Accountant, Ontario, 1929; Practised as Chartered Acct with Clarkson, Gordon, Dilworth and Nash, 1925-32; Director and Sec.-Treas., J. D. Woods & Co. Ltd, 1932-45; Controller and Sec. Treas., York Knitting Mills Ltd, 1932-45; Sec.-Treas, Plateau Co. Ltd (Crown Co.), 1940-41; Treas. and subsequently Pres. War Supplies, Ltd (Crown Co.), 1941-44; Pres. Victory Aircraft Ltd (Crown Co.), 1944-45; Deputy Minister of Reconstruction and Supply and Vice-Pres., Nat. Research Council, 1945-47; Deputy Minister of National Revenue (Taxation), 1948-51; Comptroller, The Steel Company of Canada Ltd, 1951, President, 1957, Chief Executive Officer, 1960. *Recreation:* golf. *Address:* (Home) 50 Prince Arthur Avenue, Toronto 180, Ontario, Canada; (office) The Steel Co. of Canada Ltd, PO Box 205, Toronto-Dominion Centre, Toronto 111, Ontario. *Clubs:* Rideau, Royal Ottawa Golf (Ottawa); Toronto, York, Toronto Golf (Toronto); Mount Royal (Montreal); Hamilton (Hamilton).

**SCUPHAM, John,** OBE 1961; retired as Controller of Educational Broadcasting, British Broadcasting Corporation, 1963-65; *b* 7 Sept. 1904; *s* of Roger Scupham and Kate Whittingham; *m* 1932, Dorothy Lacey Clark; one *s* one *d*. *Educ:* Market Rasen Gram. Sch.; Emmanuel Coll., Cambridge (Scholar). BA 1st Cl., History, 1926, 1st Cl. English, 1927 (Cantab). Various teaching posts, 1927-46. Joined staff of BBC as Educn. Officer, 1946; Head of School Broadcasting, 1951, of Educational Broadcasting, 1954. Member, Central Advisory Council for Education (England), 1961-63; Member, Church of England Board of Education, 1960-. President, Educational Section of British Association, 1965-66. Mem. Council, Open Univ., 1969-. *Publications:* Broadcasting and the Community, 1967; The Revolution in Communications, 1970. *Recreations:* reading, gardening. *Address:* 26 Crabtree Lane, Harpenden, Herts. *T:* Harpenden 3223.

**SCUTT, Robin Hugh;** Controller, BBC 2, since 1969; *b* Sandgate, Kent, 24 Oct. 1920; *s* of late Rev. A. O. Scutt, MA and Freda M. Scutt (*née* Palmer); *m* 1st, 1943, Judy Watson (marriage dissolved, 1960); two *s*; 2nd, 1961, Patricia A. M. Smith. *Educ:* Fonthill; Bryanston; Jesus Coll., Cambridge (BA Mod. Lang.). Served Intell. Corps, 1941-42 (invalided out). BBC Eur. Service (French Section), 1942; Senior Programme Asst., 1945; BBC TV Outside Broadcasts Producer, 1955; BBC Paris Rep., 1958; Gen. Man., Trans Europe Television, 1962; rejoined BBC TV Outside Broadcasts, 1963; Asst Head of BBC TV Presentation (BBC1), 1966; Controller: BBC Light Programme, 1967; BBC Radio 1 and 2, 1967-68. *Recreations:* music, theatre, travel.

*Address:* 23 Broom Road, Teddington, Mddx. *T:* 01-977 6788; The Abbey Cottage, Cockfield, Suffolk.

**SEABORG, Glenn Theodore;** Chairman, US Atomic Energy Commission, since 1961; Professor of Chemistry, Department of Chemistry, University of California, Berkeley, since 1945 (on leave of absence, 1961-); Member, Scientific Advisory Board, Robert A. Welch Foundation, Houston, Texas, since 1957; Chairman of Steering Committee, Chem. Education Material Study, US National Science Foundation, since 1959; Member: National Council on Marine Resources and Engineering Development, since 1966; Board of Directors National Educational Television and Radio Center since 1967 (and 1958-64); *b* 19 April 1912; *s* of Herman Theodore and Selma Erickson Seaborg; *m* 1942, Helen Lucille Griggs; four *s* two *d*. *Educ:* Univ. of California, Los Angeles (BA); Univ. of California, Berkeley (PhD). Res. Associate (with Prof. Gilbert N. Lewis), Coll. of Chem., Univ. of Calif, Berkeley, 1937-39; Instr, Dept of Chem., Univ. of Calif, 1939-41; Asst Prof. of Chem., Dept of Chem., Univ. of Calif, Berkeley, 1941-45; Research Chemist at Metallurg. Lab., Univ. of Chicago, 1942-46; Dir of Nuclear Chem. Research, Radiation Lab. of Univ. of Calif, Berkeley, 1946-58, Chancellor of the Univ., 1958-61; also Associate Dir, Lawrence Radiation Lab., 1954-61, and Mem. Bd of Dirs, Nuclear Science and Engrg Corp., Pittsburgh, Pa, 1954-61. Member: Nat. Aeronautics and Space Council, 1961-; Federal Council for Science and Technology, 1961-; Nat. Sci. Planning Bd, Century 21 Exposition, Seattle (1961), 1958-61; President's Sci. Adv. Cttee, 1959-61; Nat. Sci. Bd of Nat. Sci. Foundn, 1960-61; Bd of Trustees, Educl Services Inc., Watertown, Mass, 1961-67; Nat. Cttee on America's Goals and Resources, Nat. Planning Assoc., Wash., DC, 1962-64; Adv. Coun. on Coll. Chem., Nat. Sci. Foundn, 1962-67; Mem. and Trustee, Pacific Sci. Center Foundn, Seattle, 1962-; Trustee, Amer.-Scandinavian Foundn, 1968-; Mem. Commn on Humanities, New York, 1962-65; Mem. Coun. on Educn of Teachers in Science (Nat. Sci. Teachers Assoc.), 1963-; Trustee, Sci. Service, 1965- (Pres. 1966-); Member: Nat. Adv. Bd, Dunsmuir House Educl and Res. Center, Oakland, Calif, 1965-; Coun. on Foreign Rel., NY, 1965-; Sci. Adv. Gp, Nat. Selective Service, Wash., DC, 1965-70; Corp., Educn Develt Center, Newton, Mass, 1967-; Adv. Bd, Nova Univ., Fla, 1968-; Electoral Coll., Hall of Fame for Great Americans, NY Univ., 1969-; Bd of Governors, Internat. Platform Assoc., 1967-(Pres., 1968-69). US Delegn to USSR: (Chm.) for signing of "Memorandum on Cooperation in the Field of Utilization of Atomic Energy for Peaceful Purposes", May 1963; (Mem.) for signing of Limited Nuclear Test Ban Treaty, Aug. 1963; US Rep. to Third UN Internat. Conf. on Peaceful Uses of Atomic Energy, Geneva, 1964; US Rep., 5th-14th annual Gen. Confs of Internat. Atomic Energy Agency, 1961-69. Member and Hon. Member, Fellow and Hon. Fellow, of numerous scientific and professional societies and institutions in USA, UK, Argentine, Sweden, Germany and Spain. Holds numerous hon. doctorates from univs and colls. Awards (1947-) include: Nobel Prize in Chemistry, 1951 (joint); Perkin Medal (Am. Sect. Soc. Chem. Ind.), 1957; USAEC Enrico Fermi Award, 1959; Franklin Medal (Franklin Inst. of Phila), 1963; Charles Lathrop Parsons Award (Am. Chem. Soc.), 1964; Chem. Pioneer Award (Am. Inst. of Chemists), 1968; Arches of Science Award (Pacific Science Center, Seattle), 1968; Mugunghwa Medal, Order of Civil Merit (Korea), 1970. Co-discoverer of elements (1940-58): 94, plutonium; nuclear energy source isotope Pu-239 and U-233; 95, americium; 96, curium; 97, berkelium; 98, californium; 99, einsteinium; 100, fermium; 101, mendelevium; 102, nobelium. *Publications:* The Chemistry of the Actinide Elements (jt), 1958; The Transuranium Elements, 1958 (Silliman Lectures); Elements of the Universe (jt), 1958; Man-made Transuranium Elements, 1963; Education and the Atom (jt), 1964; The Nuclear Properties of the Heavy Elements (jt), 1964; Oppenheimer (jt), 1969; also, since 1936: numerous papers on nuclear chem. and nuclear physics, transuranium elements, high energy nuclear reactions and educn in: Physical Review, Jl Am. Chem. Soc., Annual Review of Nuclear Science, etc. *Recreations:* golf, reading, hiking. *Address:* (business) US Atomic Energy Commission, Washington, DC 20545, USA; (home) 3825 Harrison Street, NW, Washington, DC 20015, USA. *Clubs:* Faculty (Univ. Calif, Berkeley); Commonwealth Club of California, Bohemian (San Francisco); Swedish (Los Angeles); Chemists (New York); Cosmos, University, Metropolitan, Chevy Chase (Washington).

**SEABORN, Rt. Rev. Robert Lowder;** *see* Newfoundland, Bishop of.

**SEABORNE DAVIES, David Richard;** *see* Davies, D. R. S.

**SEABROOK, Air Vice-Marshal Geoffrey Leonard,** CB 1965; Construction Industry Training Board, since 1966; *b* 25 Aug. 1909; *s* of late Robert Leonard Seabrook and of Mrs H. M. Seabrook, Battle, Sussex; *m* 1949, Beryl Mary (*née* Hughes); one *s* one *d*. *Educ:* King's Sch., Canterbury. Commissioned in RAF (Accountant Branch), 1933; served in: Middle East, 1935-43; Bomber Command, 1943-45; Transport Command, 1945-47; Iraq, 1947-49; Signals Command, 1949-51; Air Ministry Organisation and Methods, 1951-53; Home Command Group Captain Organisation, 1953-56; Far East Air Force, 1957-59; idc 1960; Director of Personnel, Air Ministry, 1961-63; Air Officer Administration, HQ, RAF Tech. Trg Comd, 1963-66; retired June 1966. Air Cdre 1961; Air Vice-Marshal, 1964. Head of Secretarial Branch, Royal Air Force, 1963-66. FCA 1957 (Associate, 1932). *Recreations:* sailing, tennis, golf. *Address:* Smugglers, Crowborough, Sussex. *T:* Crowborough 2923. *Clubs:* Royal Air Force; Walton and Frinton Yacht.

**SEABROOK, John,** CMG 1970; AFC 1918; ED 1947; JP; Founder Chairman, Seabrook Fowlds Ltd, Auckland, NZ, 1919-70; Chairman, Amalgamated Pacific Industries Ltd, since 1970; *b* 6 Jan. 1896; *e s* of Albert David Seabrook and Marion May Seabrook; *m* 1926, Doreen Mary Alexina Carr, *d* of Charles Edward and Rose Louise McKenzie Carr, Auckland; one *s* one *d*. *Educ:* Auckland Grammar School. Served RFC, France, 1916-17; RAF, Middle East, 1918 (Captain). Returned to NZ, 1919, and founded Seabrook Fowlds Ltd. Served RNZAF, 1940-44 (Group Captain). Mem. Board of Trustees, NZ Inst. for Blind for 24 years; Dir, NZ National Airways, 1952-61; Dep. Chm., Blinded Servicemen's Trust Board; Mem., Nature Conservation Council, Wellington; Mem., Hauraki Gulf Maritime Park Board; Pres., Auckland Inst. and Museum, 1961-63. *Recreations:* yachting, gardening. *Address:* 146 Orakei Road, Remuera, Auckland 5, NZ. *T:* 52735. *Club:* Royal Air Force.

**SEABY, Wilfred Arthur;** Director, Ulster Museum (previously Belfast Museum and Art

Gallery), 1953-70; now in charge of Numismatic Section, in Department of Technology and Local History; *b* 16 Sept. 1910; *y s* of late Allen W. Seaby, sometime Prof. of Art, Univ. of Reading; *m* 1937, Nora, *d* of late A. E. Pecover, Reading; two *s* one *d*. *Educ:* Wycliffe College; Reading University, College of Art. Dip. Museums Assoc., 1939. Served War of 1939-45, Royal Air Force, 1940-46 (Flt-Lt). B. A. Seaby Ltd, 1927-30; Reading, Birmingham, and Taunton Museums, 1931-53. *Address:* Ulster Museum, Stranmillis, Belfast BT9 5AB. *T:* Belfast 668259; 7 Mount Pleasant, Belfast 9.

**SEAFIELD,** 13th Earl of, *cr* 1901; **Ian Derek Francis Ogilvie-Grant-Studley-Herbert;** Viscount Seafield, Baron Ogilvy of Cullen, 1698; Viscount Reidhaven, Baron Ogilvy of Deskford and Cullen, 1701; *b* 20 March 1939; *s* of Countess of Seafield (12th in line), and Derek Studley-Herbert (who assumed by deed poll, 1939, the additional surnames of Ogilvie-Grant; he *d* 1960); *S* mother, 1969; *m* 1960, Mary Dawn Mackenzie, *er d* of Henry Illingworth; two *s*. *Educ:* Eton. *Recreations:* shooting, fishing, tennis. *Heir: s* Viscount Reidhaven, *qv*. *Address:* Cullen House, Cullen, Banffshire. *T:* Cullen 594; Kinveachy Forest, Boat of Garten, Inverness-shire. *T:* Boat of Garten 232. *Clubs:* Turf, St James'.

**SEAGER,** family name of **Baron Leighton of Saint Mellons.**

**SEAGER, Basil William,** CMG 1949; OBE 1939; HM Immigration Service, retired 1970; *b* 1898; *s* of late E. J. P. Seager, Constantinople, and I. D. Seager (*née* Sellar); *m* 1944, Heather Mildred Carmichael, *d* of late Lt-Col R. C. Bell, DSO, OBE, late Central India Horse. *Educ:* abroad. Communications Department, FO, 1926; British Agency and Consulate (now HM Embassy), Jedda, Saudi Arabia, 1926-34; seconded to Aden Govt as Political Officer, 1933-34; Colonial Administrative Service as PO (Frontier Officer), 1934; Acting Political Secretary on various occasions, 1935-40; Political Officer in charge W Aden Protectorate, 1940; British Agent, Western Aden Protectorate, 1942; Chairman (ex-officio) Abyan (Cotton) Board, 1947-54; retired Colonial Administrative Service, 1954. Served European War 1914-18, 1916-22 (Captain); War of 1939-45, 1941-42 (Major). *Address:* 16 Broadwater Down, Tunbridge Wells, Kent.

**SEAGER, Ven. Edward Leslie;** Archdeacon of Dorset since 1955; Prebendary of Gillingham Major since 1968; Vicar of Gillingham, Dorset, since 1946 and of Fifehead Magdalen since 1966; *b* 5 Oct. 1904; *s* of William Seager, Chaddesley Corbett, Worcs; unmarried. *Educ:* Bromsgrove Sch.; Hatfield College, Durham Foundation Scholar, Hatfield College, 1923; BA, Jenkyn's Scholar, 1926; Diploma in Theology, 1928; MA, 1931. Deacon, 1928, priest, 1929, Newcastle upon Tyne; Chaplain, Wellington School, 1931-39. War of 1939-45, CF, 1937-46; SCF, 1942-45; DACG, 1945-46; HCF, 1946-. Rural Dean of Shaftesbury, 1951-56; Canon and Prebendary of Shipton in Salisbury Cathedral, 1954-68; Examining Chaplain to Bishop of Salisbury, 1968. Governor of Milton Abbey School, 1956-; Chairman of Governors, Gillingham School, 1959-. *Publication:* Day unto Day, 1932. *Recreations:* scouting, golf. *Address:* The Vicarage, Gillingham, Dorset. *T:* Gillingham 2435. *Club:* Public Schools.

**SEAGER, Major Ronald Frank,** RA, retired; Secretary, RSPCA, since 1966; *b* 27 May 1918; *s* of Frank Seager and Lilias K. (*née* Parr); *m* 1941, Josephine, *d* of Rev. R. M. Chadwick; one *s* one *d*. *Educ:* St Albans School. Royal Artillery (HAC), 1939; commnd, 1941; Italy, 1944-45; seconded Royal Pakistan Artillery, 1949-50; served Korean War, 1953-54; Perm. Pres. Courts Martial, Eastern Command, 1960-63. Joined RSPCA, 1963. *Recreations:* golf, gardening. *Address:* The Timbers, Thursley Road, Elstead, Surrey. *T:* Elstead 2134. *Club:* Army and Navy.

**SEAGO, Edward Brian,** RWS 1959 (ARWS 1957); RBA 1946; FIAL 1957; Painter; *b* 31 March 1910; *s* of Francis Brian Seago and Mabel Reeve Woodroffe. One-man exhibitions: London, Glasgow, New York, San Francisco, Toronto, Montreal, Los Angeles, Chicago, Johannesburg, Oslo, Bergen, Brussels, Melbourne. Loan Exhibition: in Norwich City Art Gallery, 1944 and 1962; of Italian War pictures in Norwich and Bristol Municipal Galleries, 1946; Loan exhibition, King's Lynn Festival, 1954; of pictures painted during the Duke of Edinburgh's world tour, at St James's Palace, 1957. Served with Royal Engineers, 1939-45. *Publications:* Circus Company, 1933; Sons of Sawdust, 1934; Caravan, 1936; Peace in War, 1943; High Endeavour, 1944; With the Allied Armies in Italy, 1945; A Canvas to Cover, 1947; Tideline, 1948; With Capricorn to Paris, 1956. with John Masefield: Country Scene, 1936; Tribute to Ballet, 1937; A Generation Risen, 1942. *Recreations:* reading, gardening, and "messing about with boats". *Address:* The Dutch House, Ludham, Norfolk. *T:* Potter Heigham 225. *Clubs:* Athenæum, Garrick, Beefsteak.

**SEA-LION;** *see* Bennett, Capt. G. M.

**SEAL, Sir Eric (Arthur),** KBE, *cr* 1955; CB 1941; Deputy Secretary, Ministry of Works, 1951-59, retired; *b* 16 Sept. 1898; *s* of Arthur John Todd Seal; *m* 1926, Gladys Mary, *d* of Frank Leadbitter, Sutton, Surrey; three *s*. RAF 1918-19; entered Patent Office, 1921; Admiralty, 1925; Principal Private Sec. to First Lord, 1938-40; Principal Private Sec. to Mr Winston Churchill, as Prime Minister, 1940-41; Deputy Secretary of the Admiralty (North America), 1941-43; Member of British Supply Council, Washington, 1943; Under-Secretary of Admiralty (London), 1943-45; Chief, Trade and Industry Div., CCG, 1946-47; Dir-Gen. Building Materials, Min. of Works, 1947-48; Deputy Under-Secretary of State, Foreign Office (German Section), 1948-51. *Address:* Seaforth, Spinney Lane, Chichester, Sussex. *Club:* Royal Thames Yacht.

**SEAL, Richard Godfrey,** FRCO; Organist of Salisbury Cathedral since 1968; *b* 4 Dec. 1935; *s* of William Godfrey Seal and Shelagh Seal (*née* Bagshaw). *Educ:* New Coll. Choir Sch., Oxford; Cranleigh Sch., Surrey; Christ's Coll., Cambridge (MA). FRCO 1958. Asst Organist: St Bartholomews the Great, London, 1960-61; Chichester Cathedral (and Dir of Music, Prebendal Sch.) Sussex, 1961-68. *Recreations:* squash, tennis, climbing (small-time). *Address:* 5 The Close, Salisbury, Wilts. *T:* Salisbury 6828. *Club:* Crudgemens (Chichester and Godalming).

**SEALE, Douglas (Robert);** Producer (Stage); *b* 28 Oct. 1913; *s* of Robert Henry Seale and Margaret Seale (*née* Law); *m* 1st, 1939, Daisy Elaine Wodson (marr. diss., 1948); 2nd, 1950, Joan Barbara Grattan Geary (marr. diss., 1964); two *s*; 3rd, 1964, Zenaide Alma Trigg. *Educ:* Rutlish. Studied for stage at Royal Academy of Dramatic Art and became an actor. First appeared as Starling in The Drums Begin, Embassy, 1934; subseq. in Repertory.

Served in Army, 1940-46, commissioned in Royal Signals. Joined Shakespeare Memorial Theatre Company, Stratford-on-Avon season's 1946 and 1947. From 1948 produced at Birmingham Repertory Theatre, at The Bedford, Camden Town (under Donald Wolfit), and again at Birmingham where he became Director of Productions, 1950. Later Productions include: Figaro and Fidelio, Sadler's Wells; Shaw's Caesar and Cleopatra at Birmingham Rep. Theatre, 1956 (later presented at Théâtre Sarah Bernhardt, Paris, and Old Vic). Season 1957: The Tempest, at Univ. of BC, Vancouver; King John, Stratford-on-Avon; Richard III, Old Vic; Trilogy of Henry VI, Old Vic; Season 1958; The World of the Wonderful Dark, for first Vancouver Festival; King Lear, Old Vic; Much Ado about Nothing, Stratford-on-Avon. *Old Vic productions as Associate Director,* 1958: Julius Caesar; Macbeth; 1959: Molière's Tartuffe; Pinero's The Magistrate; Dryden-Davenant-Purcell version of Shakespeare's The Tempest; St Joan; She Stoops to Conquer, 1960, Landscape with Figures, by Cecil Beaton, Dublin Festival, 1960: King John, Festival Theatre, Stratford, Ontario, 1960; Director of tours in Russia and Poland for Old Vic Theatre Co., 1961: prod. The Importance of Being Earnest, New York, 1962; The Comdedy of Errors, Henry V, Stratford, Connecticut, 1963; Regent's Prof., Univ. of Calif. at Santa Barbara, Jan.-June 1965; Artistic Director, Center Stage, Baltimore, Maryland, USA, 1965-. Has also produced for TV. *Recreation:* riding. *Address:* c/o William Morris, Inc., 1350 Avenue of the Americas, New York, NY 10019, USA.

**SEALE, Sir John Henry,** 5th Bt, *cr* 1838; ARIBA; *b* 3 March 1921; *s* of 4th Bt; *S* father, 1964; *m* 1953, Ray Josephine, *d* of Robert Gordon Charters, MC, Christchurch, New Zealand; one *s* one *d*. *Educ:* Eton; Christ Church, Oxford. Served War of 1939-45: Royal Artillery, North Africa and Italy; Captain, 1945. ARIBA 1951. *Heir: s* John Robert Charters Seale, *b* 17 Aug. 1954. *Address:* Slade, near Kingsbridge, South Devon. *T:* Loddiswell 226. *Club:* Junior Carlton.

**SEAMAN, Clarence Milton Edwards,** MA Oxon; Headmaster of Christ's Hospital, 1955-70; *b* 1908; *s* of Rev. H. W. Seaman; *m* 1936, Kathleen M. G. Askew; one *s* one *d*. *Educ:* Christ's Hosp.; St John's Coll., Oxford. Assistant Master, Bedford School, 1932-39; Assistant Master, Rugby School, 1939-45; Rector of The Edinburgh Academy, 1945-51; Headmaster of Bedford School, 1951-55. *Address:* c/o Christ's Hospital, Horsham, Sussex.

**SEAMAN, Gilbert Frederick,** CMG 1967; Under Treasurer for South Australia, since 1960; *b* 7 Sept. 1912; *s* of Eli S. Seaman, McLaren Vale, South Australia; *m* 1935, Avenal Essie Fong; one *s* one *d*. *Educ:* University of Adelaide. BEc, Associate of University of Adelaide, 1935, High School Teacher, Port Pirie and Unley, 1932-35; South Australian Public Service, 1936-41; Seconded to Commonwealth of Australia as Assistant Director of Manpower for SA, 1941-46; Economist, SA Treasury, 1946-60. Chairman, State Bank of SA, 1963-. *Address:* 27 William Street, Hawthorn, South Australia 5062. *T:* 7-4271.

**SEARCY, Philip Roy,** OBE 1966; Australian Consul-General, Los Angeles, since 1970; *b* Adelaide, South Australia, 15 April 1914; *s* of Herbert Leslie Searcy and Mary Ellen MacGregor; *m* 1946, Mary Elizabeth Gavan Duffy; four *d*. *Educ:* Collegiate School of St Peter, Adelaide; Adelaide University. Royal Australian Air Force, 1940; Air Operations, Europe, 1941; Prisoner of War, Germany, Nov. 1941-45. Joined Australian Govt Trade Commissioner Service, 1955; Australian Govt Trade Commissioner, Calcutta, 1956; Commercial Counsellor, Singapore, 1957; Australian Govt Senior Trade Commissioner: London, 1958-62; Tokyo, 1962-65; Hong Kong, 1966-70. *Address:* c/o Department of External Affairs, Canberra, ACT, Australia. *Clubs:* Naval and Military (Melbourne); Tokyo; Hong Kong.

**SEARLE, Humphrey,** CBE 1968; Composer; *b* Oxford, 26 Aug. 1915; *e s* of late Humphrey Frederic Searle and of Charlotte Mathilde Mary (*née* Schlich); *m* 1st, 1949, Margaret (Lesley) Gillen Gray (*d* 1957); 2nd, 1960, Fiona Elizabeth Anne Nicholson. *Educ:* Winchester Coll.; New Coll., Oxford. Composition study at RCM, Vienna Conservatorium, and privately with Dr Anton Webern, 1937-38. Member, BBC Music Department, 1938-40. Served Gloucestershire Regiment, Intelligence Corps and General List, 1940-46. Programme producer, BBC Music Dept, 1946-48. General Secretary, International Soc. for Contemporary Music, 1947-49. Hon. Secretary, Liszt Society, 1950-62. Member Sadler's Wells Ballet Advisory Panel, 1951-57; Resident Composer, Stanford University, California, 1964-65; Prof. of Composition, Royal Coll. of Music, 1965-; Guest composer, Aspen Music Festival, Colorado, 1967; Guest Prof., Badische Hochschule für Musik, Karlsruhe, 1968-. Hon. ARCM, 1966, FRCM 1969. *Principal Compositions:* Gold Coast Customs (Edith Sitwell), 1949; Poem for 22 Strings, 1950; The River-run (James Joyce), 1951; Piano sonata, 1951; The Shadow of Cain (Edith Sitwell), 1952; Symphony No 1, 1953; Piano Concerto No 2, 1955; Noctambules, ballet, 1956; Symphony No 2, 1958; The Great Peacock, ballet, 1958; The Diary of a Madman, opera, 1958; Symphony No 3, 1960; Symphony No 4, 1962; Dualities, ballet, 1963; The Photo of the Colonel, Opera, 1964; Song of the Birds, Song of the Sun, 1964; Symphony No 5, 1964; Scherzi for Orchestra, 1964; The Canticle of the Rose (Edith Sitwell) 1965; Oxus, scena, 1967; Hamlet, opera, 1968; Sinfonietta, 1968-69; Jerusalem (Blake), choral work, 1970; Zodiac Variations, 1970; also chamber music, theatre, radio, televison, and film scores. Orchestration of Liszt, Sonata in B minor, 1962. *Publications:* The Music of Liszt, 1954 (rev. edn, 1967); Twentieth Century Counterpoint, 1954; Ballet Music, an Introduction, 1958; (ed) Arnold Schoenberg, Structural Functions of Harmony, 1954; (ed) Hector Berlioz: Selected Letters, 1966; *translated:* Josef Rufer, Composition with Twelve notes, 1954; H. H. Stuckenschmidt, Arnold Schoenberg, 1959; Friedrich Wildgans, Anton Webern, 1966; Walter Koineder, Anton Webern, 1967; has made contributions to: Encyclopædia Britannica; Dictionary of National Biography; Grove's Dictionary of Music and Musicians; Chambers's Encyclopædia; Proceedings of the Royal Musical Association; and to various other musical publications. *Address:* 44 Ordnance Hill, NW8. *T:* 01-722 5182.

**SEARLE, Rear-Adm. (retd) Malcolm Walter St Leger,** CB 1955; CBE 1945; *b* 23 Dec. 1900; *s* of late Sir Malcolm W. Searle, Wynberg, S Africa; *m* 1930, Betty Margaret, *d* of late Dr H. R. Crampton; one *s* two *d*. *Educ:* RN Colleges Osborne and Dartmouth. Entered RN 1914; served European War, 1914-19; Comdr 1936; served War of 1939-45; Capt. 1943; Commodore, RN Barracks, Portsmouth, 1951; Rear-Adm. 1952; Deputy Chief of Naval Personnel, 1953-55; retired, 1956. *Address:*

Lindens, Kithurst Park, Storrington, Pulborough, Sussex.

**SEARLE, Ronald William Fordham,** FSIA; AGI; Artist; *b* Cambridge, 3 March 1920; *s* of late William James Searle and of Nellie Hunt; *m* 1st, Kaye Webb (marr. diss. 1967); one *s* one *d*; 2nd, 1967, Monica Koenig. *Educ:* Central Sch., Cambridge; Cambridge School of Art. Humorous work first published in Cambridge Daily News and Granta, 1935-39. Served with 287 Field Co. RE, 1939-46; captured by the Japanese at fall of Singapore, 1942; Prisoner of War in Siam and Malaya, 1942-45. Began contributing widely to nat. publications from 1946; creator of the schoolgirls of St Trinians, 1941 (abandoned them in 1953); Cartoonist to Tribune, 1949-51; to Sunday Express, 1950-51; Special feature artist, News Chronicle, 1951-53; Weekly Cartoonist, News Chronicle, 1954; Punch Theatre artist, 1949-62; joined staff of Punch 1956; Contributor: New Yorker, TV Guide, and Holiday Mags (USA). *Awards:* Art Directors Club of Philadelphia, Medal, 1959; National Cartoonists Society of America, Awards, 1959, 1960, 1966; Art Directors Club of Los Angeles, Medal, 1959; Gold Medal, III Biennale Tolentino, 1965; Prix de la Critique Belge, 1968. *One-Man Exhibitions:* Batsford Gallery, 1947; Leicester Galleries, 1948, 1950, 1954, and 1957; Kraushaar Gallery, New York, 1959; Bianchini Gallery, New York, 1963; Künstehalle, Bremen, 1965; Wilhelm Busch Museum, Hanover, 1965; 3rd Biennale, Tolentino (Italy) 1965; Künsthalle, Stuttgart, 1965; Haus am Lützowplatz, Berlin, 1965; Galerie Pro Arte, Delmenhorst, 1966; Kunstverein, Bremerhaven, 1966; Galerie Münsterberg, Basle, 1966; Pribaut Gallery, Amsterdam, 1966; Wolfgang Gurlitt Museum, Linz, 1966; Galerie La Pochade, Paris, 1966, 1967, 1968, 1969; Art Alliance Gallery, Philadelphia, 1967; Galerie Gurlitt, Munich, 1967, 1968, 1969, 1970; Grosvenor Gall., London, 1968; Galerie Obere Zaüne, Zürich, 1968; Galerie La Taille Douce, Brussels, 1968; Galerie Brumme, Frankfurt, 1969; Konsthallen, Södertälje, 1969; Rizzoli Gall., NY, 1969; Kunstverein, Konstanz, 1970; Kunsthalle, Würzburg, 1970; Galerie Ariadne, Vienna, 1970. *Works in permanent collections:* V&A, BM, London; Bibliothèque Nat., Paris; Kunsthalle, Bremen; Wilhelm-Busch Museum, Hanover; Stadtmuseum, Munich; Art Museum, Dallas, Texas. *Films based on the characters of St Trinian's:* The Belles of St Trinian's, 1954; Blue Murder at St Trinian's, 1957; The Pure Hell of St Trinian's, 1960; The Great St Trinian's Train Robbery, 1966 (Launder and Gilliat). *Film designed:* John Gilpin (for Brit. Film Inst.), 1951; On the Twelfth Day (with Wendy Toye), 1954 (Acad. Award Nomination); Energetically Yours (USA), 1957; Germany, 1960 (for Suddeutschen RTV); The King's Breakfast (Dir Wendy Toye), 1962; Those Magnificent Men in their Flying Machines (Animation Sequence), 1965; Monte Carlo or Bust (Animation Sequence), 1969; Scrooge (Animation Sequence), 1970. *Publications:* Forty Drawings, 1946; Le Nouveau Ballet Anglais, 1947; Hurrah for St Trinian's!, 1948; The Female Approach, 1949; Back to the Slaughterhouse, 1951; John Gilpin, 1952; Souls in Torment, 1953; Rake's Progress, 1955; Merry England, etc, 1956; A Christmas Carol, 1961; Which Way Did He Go, 1961; Searle in the Sixties, 1964; From Frozen North to Filthy Lucre, 1964; Pardong M'sieur, 1965; Searle's Cats, 1967; The Square Egg, 1968; Take one Toad, 1968; Baron Munchausen, 1960; Filles de Hamburg, 1969; Hello–where did all the people go?, 1969; Hommage à Toulouse-Lautrec, 1969; Secret Sketchbook, 1970. *In Collaboration:* (with D. B. Wyndham Lewis) The Terror of St Trinian's, 1952; (with Geoffrey Willans) Down with Skool, 1953; How to be Topp, 1954; Whizz for Atomms, 1956; The Compleet Molesworth, 1958; The Dog's Ear Book, 1958; Back in the Jug Agane, 1959; (with Kaye Webb) Paris Sketchbook, 1950 and 1957; Looking at London, 1953; The St Trinian's Story, 1959; Refugees 1960, 1960; (with Alex Atkinson) The Big City, 1958; USA for Beginners, 1959; Russia for Beginners, 1960; Escape from the Amazon!, 1964; (with A. Andrews & B. Richardson) Those Magnificent Men in their Flying Machines, 1965; (with Heinz Huber) Haven't We Met Before Somewhere?, 1966; (with Kildare Dobbs) The Great Fur Opera, 1970. *Address:* c/o Hope Leresche & Steele, 11 Jubilee Place, SW3. *T:* 01-352 4311. *Club:* Garrick.

**SEATON, Prof. Michael John,** FRS 1967; Professor of Physics, University College, London, since 1963; *b* 16 Jan. 1923; *s* of Arthur William Robert Seaton and Helen Amelia Seaton; *m* 1st, 1943, Olive May (*d* 1959), *d* of Charles Edward Singleton; one *s* one *d*; 2nd, 1960, Joy Clarice, *d* of Harry Albert Balchin; one *s*. *Educ:* Wallington Co. Sch., Surrey; University Coll., London. BSc 1948, PhD 1951, London. Dept of Physics, UCL: Asst Lectr, 1950; Lectr, 1953; Reader, 1959; Prof., 1963. Chargé de Recherche, Institut d'Astrophysique, Paris, 1954-55; Univ. of Colorado, 1961. *Publications:* papers on atomic physics and astrophysics in various jls. *Address:* 51 Hall Drive, Sydenham, SE6. *T:* 01-778 7121.

**SEATON, Reginald Ethelbert;** Chairman, Greater London Area Sessions (inner area), 1965-69 (Chairman, London Sessions, 1959-65); retired; Deputy Chairman, East Sussex Quarter Sessions, 1950; *b* 27 Dec. 1899; 2nd *s* of Albert Edward and Edith Gertrude Seaton; *m* 1930, Vera Wilson Barnett; one *s* three *d*. *Educ:* Epsom College; Downing College, Cambridge. BA Cantab. 1923; called to Bar, Middle Temple, 1924, Bencher, 1951; Counsel to Post Office at Central Criminal Court, 1942-43; Third Junior Prosecuting Counsel to the Crown, Central Criminal Court, 1943; Recorder of Maidstone, 1951-59; Second Senior Prosecuting Counsel to the Crown Central Criminal Court, 1954-59. *Publication:* (with R. H. Blundell) Trial of Jean Pierre Vacquier. *Recreations:* golf, gardening. *Address:* Queen Elizabeth Building, Temple, EC4. *T:* 01-353 2576.

**SEAVER, Very Rev. George,** MA (Oxon); BD (London); LittD (Dublin); FRGS; MRIA; Fellow Royal Society Antiquaries, Ireland; *b* Cheltenham, Gloucestershire, 23 July 1890. *Educ:* St Edmund Hall, Oxford. Lieutenant 40th Divisional Train, transf. Connaught Rangers, attd RAF, 1914-18; Asst Native Commissioner, Northern Rhodesia, 1919-24; ordained, 1925; first Warden of Devon Home for Wayfarers and Public Preacher Diocese of Exeter, 1930; Senior Tutor and Lecturer, St Aidan's College, Birkenhead, 1933-42; War of 1939-45, member Royal Observer Corps; Bishop's Vicar, Kilkenny Cathedral, 1946; Dean of Ossory and Rector of Kilkenny, 1950-57; Canon of St Patrick's Cathedral, Dublin, 1951-57. *Publications:* Bam: The Story of an African Boy, 1925; Edward Wilson of the Antarctic, 1933; Edward Wilson: Nature Lover, 1937; Faith of Edward Wilson, 1948; Birdie Bowers of the Antarctic, 1938; Scott of the Antarctic, 1939; Sir James Cantlie (with Col N. Cantlie), 1939; Albert Schweitzer: Christian Revolutionary, 1944; Albert Schweitzer, the Man and his Mind, 1947; Albert Schweitzer: A Vindication, 1949; Berdyaev: an Introduction to his Thought,

1950; Sir Francis Younghusband, 1952; Icelandic Yesterdays, 1957; David Livingstone: his Life and Letters, 1957; Tales of Brother Douglas (with Coleman Jennings), 1960; John Allen Fitzgerald Gregg: Archbishop, 1963; Richard Archer Houblon: a memoir, 1970; Introd. to new edition of The Worst Journey in the World, 1965. *Address:* St Ernan's, Donegal.

**SEBASTIAN, Rear-Admiral (Retired) Brian Leonard Geoffrey,** CB 1948; *b* 7 Feb. 1891; *s* of late Lewis Boyd Sebastian, Barrister-at-Law, and late Harriet M. Lennartson, Karlstad, Sweden; *m* 1927, Cicely Grace, *e d* of Dr F. W. Andrew, Hendon; one *d. Educ:* Osborne, Dartmouth and Greenwich Colleges; RN Engineering College, Keyham. Joined RN Coll., Osborne, with first term of new scheme, 1903; various appts at sea as junior officer; qualified in Engineering, 1914. Served in various ships during European War; Comdr (E) 1925; various appointments till 1936; Capt. (E) 1937; Squadron EO Home Fleet, in charge of RN Aircraft Training establishment, Newcastle-under-Lyme, and RN Eng. Coll., Keyham; Rear-Adm. (E) 1944; Deputy Head of British Admiralty Technical Mission, Ottawa; Staffs of C-in-C Rosyth and Plymouth, 1948; retired, 1948. *Address:* 58 Lynch Road, Farnham, Surrey. *T:* Farnham 5565.

**SEBASTIAN, Erroll Graham,** CBE 1946; DSO 1917; *b* 2 August 1892; *s* of Lewis Boyd Sebastian and Henrietta Maria Lennartson; *m* 1959, Mrs Hilda Reynolds Gardner. *Educ:* Winchester; University Coll., Oxford. Served European War, 2nd Buffs in France, Salonica, and Constantinople, 1914-19 (DSO); served in Consular Service in Siam, Roumania, Belgium, Greece; Consul-General at Athens, 1940-41; attached Minister of State's Office, Cairo, 1941-42; Consul-General at Gothenburg, 1942-44; at Antwerp, 1944-50; Consul-General at Milan, 1950-52; retired 1952. *Recreations:* photography, needlework, music. *Address:* Bridge House, Coggeshall, Colchester, Essex. *Club:* Oxford and Cambridge University.

**SEBRIGHT, Sir Hugo Giles Edmund,** 14th Bt, *cr* 1626; *b* 2 March 1931; *s* of Lieutenant-Colonel Sir Giles Edward Sebright, 13th Bt, CBE, and of Margery Hilda, *d* of late Admiral Sir Sydney Robert Fremantle, GCB, MVO; *S* father 1954; *m* 1st, 1952, Deirdre Ann (marr. diss. 1964), *d* of Major Vivian Lionel Slingsby Bethell, late Royal Artillery; one *s*; 2nd, 1965, Mrs Sheila Mary Howard Hervey. *Heir: s* Peter Giles Vivian Sebright, *b* 1953. *Address:* PO Box M7223, Umtali, Rhodesia. *Club:* St James'.

**SECKER, Martin;** publisher; formerly proprietor of The Unicorn Press and director of the Richards Press Ltd; *b* Kensington, 6 April 1882; *m* 1921 (marriage dissolved, 1938); one *s*; *m* 1955, Sylvia Hope Gisbone. Entered publishing trade, 1908, in office of Eveleigh Nash; started in business on his own account in the Adelphi, 1910, and published early work of Sir Compton Mackenzie, Sir Hugh Walpole, Norman Douglas, Frank Swinnerton, Gilbert Cannan, Francis Brett Young, Ivor Brown, Arthur Ransome, Viola Meynell, Oliver Onions, and all the work of D. H. Lawrence from 1921 until his death in 1930; business reconstructed under style of Martin Secker and Warburg Ltd, 1935; severed his connection therewith in 1937. *Recreations:* cultivates his garden, once actively, now metaphorically; has collected modern first editions, and is an authority on the literature of the 1890's. *Address:* Bridgefoot, Iver, Bucks. *Clubs:* none.

**SECOMBE, Harry (Donald),** CBE 1963; Actor, Comedian and Singer; *b* 8 Sept. 1921; *m* 1948, Myra Joan Atherton, Swansea; two *s* two *d. Educ:* Dynevor School, Swansea. Served with Royal Artillery, 1939-46. Windmill Theatre, 1947-48: General Variety since 1948. Appearances include: at London Palladium, 1956, 1958, 1959, 1961, 1966; in Roy. Command Perfs, 1955, 1957, 1958, 1963, 1966, 1969; (musical) Pickwick, Saville, 1963; (musical) The Four Musketeers!, Drury Lane, 1967. Radio: Goon Show, 1949-. Television: BBC, ITV, CBS (New York), 1950-. Films: Davy, for Ealing Films, 1957; Jet Stream, 1959; Bed-Sitting Room, 1968; Mr Bumble in Oliver!, 1968; Bjornsen in Song of Norway, 1969; Rhubard, 1969; Doctor in Trouble, 1970. Has made recordings for HMV, 1953-54, and Philips Records, 1955-. *Recreations:* film photography, literature, travel, golf, cricket. *Address:* Chatsworth, 129 Cheam Road, Sutton, Surrey. *T:* 01-642 7166. *Clubs:* Savage, Royal Automobile, Lord's Taverners, Variety Club of Great Britain.

**SECONDE, Reginald Louis,** CVO 1968 (MVO 1957); Counsellor, Foreign and Commonwealth Office; *b* 28 July 1922; *s* of late Lt-Col Emile Charles Secondé, Hove, Sussex; *m* 1951, Catherine Penelope Sneyd-Kynnersley; one *s* two *d. Educ:* Beaumont; King's Coll., Cambridge. Served, 1941-47, in Coldstream Guards: N Africa and Italy (despatches); Major. Entered Diplomatic Service, 1949; UK Delegn to the UN, New York, 1951-55; British Embassy: Lisbon, 1955-57; Cambodia, 1957-59; FO, 1959-62; British Embassy: Warsaw, 1962-64; Brazil, 1964-69. Comdr, Order of the Southern Cross (Brazil), 1968. *Recreation:* shooting. *Address:* c/o Foreign and Commonwealth Office, SW1; 21 Old Church Street, SW3. *T:* 01-352 8967; Fairmeadow, Mayfield, Sussex. *T:* Mayfield 2132. *Club:* Guards.

**SEDDON, Sir Herbert (John),** Kt 1964; CMG 1951; DM, MA Oxon, MB, BS (London University Gold Medal); FRCS; Hon. FACS; Dr *hc* Grenoble University; Hon. MD Malta; Hon. LLD Glasgow; retired; Hon. Consulting Surgeon, Royal National Orthopædic Hospital; Member MRC, 1956-59; *b* 13 July 1903; *s* of late John Seddon and Ellen Thornton, Sutton, Surrey; *m* 1931, Mary Lorene Lytle, Marquette, Mich., USA; one *s* one *d. Educ:* William Hulme Gram. Sch., Manchester; St Bartholomew's Hospital, London. Instructor in Surgery at the Hospital of the Univ. of Michigan, Ann Arbor, Michigan, USA, 1930, Carl Badgley Lecturer, 1963; Resident Surgeon, Country Branch of Royal National Orthopædic Hospital, London, 1931-39; Nuffield Professor of Orthopædic Surgery, University of Oxford, 1940-48; Fellow of Worcester College, 1940-48 (Hon. Fellow 1966); Director of Studies, Inst. of Orthopædics, 1948-65; Prof. of Orthopædics, Univ. of London, 1965-67; Fellow, Hon. Sec. 1940-44, Pres., 1960-61, of British Orthopædic Association; Robert Jones Medal and Association Prize, 1933; Robert Jones Lecturer, 1960 and Watson-Jones Lecturer, 1962, Royal College of Surgeons; other eponymous lectures. Hon. Mem. Brit. Pædiatric Assoc.; Corr. or Hon. Mem. of a number of foreign professional socs; Fellow Association of Surgeons Gt Britain and Ireland; FRSM (Pres., Orthopædic Section, 1948-49); Worked abroad, mainly in Africa and for HM Govt; visited East Africa as Mem. of Cttee on (EA) Univ. Needs and Priorities, 1962; formerly Mem. Colonial Advisory Med. Cttee, Tropical Med. Res. Bd, and of panel of colonial medical visitors. Lawrence Poole Prize, University of Edinburgh, 1962. Officer,

Order of the Cedar of Lebanon. *Publications:* Surgical Disorders of the Peripheral Nerves, 1971; papers in medical journals on tuberculous disease of joints, infantile paralysis and on peripheral nerve injuries. Editor and contributor MRC special report on peripheral nerve injuries. *Recreations:* gardening, photography, painting. *Address:* Lake House, Gordon Avenue, Stanmore, Mddx HA7 3QD. *T:* 01-954 0827. *Club:* Athenæum.

**SEDDON, Dr John;** Director-General Scientific Research (Air), Ministry of Technology, since Nov. 1968; *b* 29 Sept. 1915; *m* 1940, Barbara Mary Mackintosh; one *s* two *d. Educ:* Leeds Modern Sch.; Univ. of Leeds. BSc 1937, PhD 1939. Scientific Officer, RAE, Farnborough, 1939-55; Harkness Fund Fellow, California Inst. of Technology, 1955-56; Head of Experimental Supersonics, RAE, Farnborough, 1957-59; Supt, Tunnels II Div., RAE, Bedford, 1959-66; Dir, Scientific Research (Air), Min. of Technology, 1966-68. *Publications:* papers on air intakes and other aerodynamic subjects, in ARC Reports and Memoranda Series and other scientific media. *Recreations:* music, cricket. *Address:* 3 Vicarage Hill, The Bourne, Farnham, Surrey. *T:* Farnham 23680; St Giles Court, 1-13 St Giles High Street, WC2. *T:* 01-636 3644 (Ext. 1182).

**SEDDON, Richard Harding,** PhD, ARCA (London); FMA; Director of Art History and Liberal Studies in the School of Design and Furniture at High Wycombe College of Technology and Art, since 1963; painter and writer; *b* 1 May 1915; *s* of Cyril Harding Seddon; *m* 1946, Audrey Madeline Wareham. *Educ:* King Edward VII School; Roy. Coll. of Art; Univ. of Reading. Demonstrator in Fine Art, Univ. of Reading, 1944; Extra-Mural Staff Tutor in Fine Art, Univ. of Birmingham, 1947; Director, Sheffield City Art Galleries, 1948-63; Curator, Ruskin Collection, 1945-63. Hon. Advisory Panel, Hereford Art Galls, 1948; Arts Council Selection Bd (Art Students Exhib.), 1947; Sheffield Dio. Adv. Cttee; Pres. Ludlow Art Soc., 1947-67; Hon. Member: Sheffield Soc. of Artists; Oxford Folk Art Soc.; Sheffield Photographic Soc.; Mem., Oxford Bureau for Artists in War-time, 1940; Chm. Selection Cttee, Nottingham Artists Exhibition, 1953; Guest Speaker Educational Centres Association Annual Conference, 1951; West Riding Artists Exhibition Selection Committee, 1956; Northern Young Artists Exhibition Selection Committee, 1958; Member Sheffield Univ. Court; Sheffield Diocesan Advisory Cttee, 1948. Exhibitor at: RA; NEAC; RI; RBA; Internat. Artists; Architectural Assoc.; RIBA; National Gallery (War Artists) 1943; Leicester Galleries; Redfern Galleries. Official acquisitions: V. & A. Museum, 1939; Pilgrim Trust, 1942; Imperial War Museum (War Artists), 1943, 1956 (ten paintings); Graves Gall., Sheffield, 1943 and 1956; Atkinson Gall., Southport, 1953; Reading Art Gall., 1956; Leeds Education Cttee Collection, 1956. Extra Mural and Univ. Extension lectr on art to Univs of Oxford, Birmingham, London and Sheffield, 1948-; initiated Sheffield Conference on Nation's Art Treasures, 1958; Fellow of Museums Assoc., 1951; Mem. Yorkshire Fed. Museums and Art Galls, 1948 (Committee 1952 and 1957, President, 1954-55, Vice-President, 1955-56); Secretary Yorks Regional Fact Finding Committee, 1959; National Art Collections Fund Rep. for Yorks, 1954-63; Dep. Chm., Sheffield Design Council for Gold, Silver and Jewelry Trades, 1960; Mem. BBC '51 Soc., 1960; Mem. Govg Coun., Design and Res. Centre, 1960; Mem. Art Adv. Cttee Yorks Area Scheme for Museums and Art Galleries, 1963; Birmingham Post Art Critic, 1963-; Mem. Recognised Panel of London Univ. Extension Lectrs, 1964-; War Service with RAOC Field Park, France, 1940 (King's Badge); facilities by War Office Order to make war drawings in Maginot Line, 1940. *Publications:* The Technical Methods of Paul Nash (Memorial Vol.), 1949; The Artist's Vision, 1949; The Academic Technique of Oil Painting, 1960; A Hand Uplifted (war memoirs), 1962; Art Collecting for Amateurs, 1964. Articles on fine art for Jl of Aesthetics (USA), Burlington Magazine, Apollo, The Studio, The Connoisseur, Arch. Review, The Artist, The Antique Collector and daily press; lectures on art in England and abroad; criticisms; book reviews; broadcasts. *Recreations:* the theatre and photography. *Address:* 9 Ralston Street, Chelsea, SW3. *T:* 01-352 4343; College of Technology and Art, High Wycombe, Bucks. *T:* High Wycombe 22141.

**SEDDON-BROWN, Lt-Col Sir Norman Seddon,** Kt 1936; TD; *b* 27 Aug. 1880; *s* of James Brown and Helena Elizabeth Seddon; name altered by deed poll to Seddon-Brown; *m* 1904, Gertrude Mary (*d* 1969), *d* of William Martin Martin; two *s* (and one *s* killed in action, May 1944) two *d. Educ:* Privately. *Address:* Crossways, Woodspeen, Newbury. *Club:* Carlton.

**SEDGMAN, Francis Arthur;** Lawn tennis Champion; Australia, 1949, 1950; America, 1951, 1952; Wimbledon, 1952; Professional Tennis Player since 1953; Proprietor of Modern Gymnasium; Director of Flex-Straw (A/Asia) Pty Ltd; Man. dir of Isle of Wight Hotel, Cowes, Victoria, Australia; *b* Victoria, Australia, 29 Oct. 1927; *m* 1952, Jean Margaret Spence; four *d. Educ:* Box Hill High School, Vic, Australia. First played in the Australian Davis Cup team, 1949. With Kenneth McGregor, won the Australian, French, English and American doubles titles in the same year (1951), the only pair ever to do so. *Publication:* Winning Tennis, 1955. *Recreations:* swimming, golfing. *Address:* 28 Bolton Avenue, Hampton, Victoria 3188, Australia. *T:* 98 6341. *Clubs:* Melbourne Cricket (Melbourne); Kooyong Tennis; Grace Park Tennis; Yarra Yarra Golf; Cowes Golf.

**SEDGWICK, Mrs A. R. M.;** *see* Milkina, Nina.

**SEDGWICK, Patrick Cardinall Mason,** CMG 1965; *b* 8 March 1911; 2nd *s* of late William Francis Mason Sedgwick, Goudhurst, Kent; *m* 1943, Beth Mannering, Thompson, *e d* of late Frederick Mannering Thompson, St Kilda, Victoria, Australia; three *s* one *d. Educ:* St Lawrence Coll., Ramsgate; Brasenose Coll., Oxford (BA Hon.); Queens' College, Cambridge. Colonial Admin. Service: Cadet Officer, Hong Kong, 1935; seconded Malayan Civil Service, Dec. 1941-Feb. 1942; Attaché, British Embassy, Chungking, 1942-43; Hong Kong Planning Unit, CO, London, 1944-45; Various Govt Posts in Hong Kong; including Principal Assistant Colonial Secretary, Estabt Officer, Chm. Urban Council, and Dir of Commerce and Industry; Comr of Labour and Mines, 1955-65; MEC and MLC, of Hong Kong up to June 1965; Dir, Hong Kong Govt Office, London, 1965-69. *Recreations:* sailing, gardening. *Address:* Whites Cottage, Goudhurst, Kent. *T:* Goudhurst 484. *Clubs:* Hong Kong, Royal Hong Kong Yacht (Hong Kong).

**SEDGWICK, Richard Romney,** CMG 1945; *b* 29 May 1894; *er s* of late Prof. Adam Sedgwick; *m* 1936, Mana, *yr d* of late Prof. T. C. Hodson; one *s* one *d. Educ:* Westminster; Trinity

College, Cambridge. Fellow of Trinity Coll., 1919; Asst Under-Secretary of State, Commonwealth Relations Office, 1949-54; retired 1954. *Publications:* Lord Hervey's Memoirs, 1931; Letters from George III to Lord Bute, 1939; (ed) History of Parliament, 1715-1754, 1970. *Address:* 75 Flask Walk, NW3. *T:* 01-435 7288. *Club:* Travellers'.

**SEDOV, Leonid I.;** Order of Lenin, USSR; Professor, Moscow University, since 1937; Member, USSR Academy of Sciences; *b* 14 Nov. 1907; *m* 1931, Galia Tolstova; one *s* one *d*. *Educ:* Moscow University. Chief Engineer, Associate Chief lab., N.E. Yukovsky Aerohydrodynamic Inst., Moscow, 1930-47; Chief of Dept of Hydrodynamics, Moscow University, 1957; President, International Astronautical Federation. Hon. Member: American Academy of Arts and Sciences; Internat. Astronautical Acad.; Serbian Academy, Belgrade; Tech. Academy, Finland; Correspondent, Acad. of Sciences, Paris; Accademia Leopoldina. Medal of Obert; State Prize; Chapligin Prize; Lomonosov Prize. *Publications:* Theory of Plane Flow of Liquids, 1939; Plane Problems of Hydrodynamics and Aerodynamics, 1950, 1966; Similarity and Dimensional Methods in Mechanics, 1944, 1951, 1953, 1957, 1960, 1965; Introduction into the Mechanics of Continua, 1962; Mechanics of Continua Media, 4 vols; numerous articles. *Address:* Moscow University, Zone 1F, 84 Leninskie Gory, Moscow, USSR.

**SEEBOHM, Sir Frederic,** Kt 1970; TD; Lt-Col (Retd); Director of Barclays Bank Ltd since 1947 (Deputy Chairman, since 1968); Chairman of Barclays Bank, DCO, since 1965 (Vice-Chairman, 1955-59, Deputy Chairman, 1959-65); Deputy Chairman, Intercontinental Banking Services, since 1968; Director: Barclays Overseas Development Corporation Ltd, since 1963; Barclays Bank SA, since 1968; Credit Congolais, SCRL; Gillett Bros Discount Co. Ltd; Friends' Provident & Century Life Office (Chairman, 1962-68); Industrial and Commercial Finance Corporation; Chairman, Export Guarantees Advisory Council since 1967 (Deputy Chairman, 1966-67); *b* 18 Jan. 1909; *s* of late H. E. Seebohm, Poynders End, Hitchin, Herts; *m* 1932, Evangeline, *d* of late Sir Gerald Hurst, QC; one *s* two *d*. *Educ:* Leighton Park School; Trinity Coll., Cambridge. Joined Staff of Barclays Bank Ltd, 1929. Chairman: Joseph Rowntree Memorial Trust; National Institute for Social Work Training; Seebohm Cttee on Local Authority and Allied Personal Social Services. Governor, London School of Economics; Trustee, Plunkett Foundation for Co-operative Studies; Fellow, Inst. of Bankers (Pres., 1966-68). Served with Royal Artillery, 1939-45 (despatches). Bronze Star of America, 1945. Hon. LLD Nottingham, 1970. *Recreations:* shooting, painting. *Address:* 5 Lowndes Lodge, Cadogan Place, SW1. *T:* 01-235 3076; Gannet House, Chapmore End, near Ware, Herts. *T:* Ware 3453. *Clubs:* Carlton, Brooks's.

**SEEDS, Sir William,** KCMG, *cr* 1930; *b* 27 June 1882; *s* of late Robert Seeds, Queen's Advocate-General, and Lady Kaye, of 11 Fitzwilliam Square, Dublin; *m* 1911, Arabella, *d* of Theobald Butler, of Indian Civil Service; two *s* one *d* (and one *s* killed in action, 1940). *Educ:* Rugby. Entered Diplomatic Service, 1904; served at Washington, Peking, Athens, Lisbon, Berlin and Munich; HM Minister, Bogota (Colombia), 1923-25; Caracas, 1925-26; Durazzo (Albania), 1926-28; British High Commissioner in the Rhineland, 1928-30; British Ambassador to Brazil, 1930-35; to Soviet Union, 1939-40. *Address:* 99 North Gate, NW8. *T:* 01-722 7408. *Clubs:* Travellers', St James'.

*See also Sir John Dilke, Bt.*

**SEEFRIED, Irmgard Maria Theresia;** Austrian opera and concert singer; Kammersängerin at Vienna State Opera since 1943; *b* Koengetried, Bavaria; *m* 1948, Wolfgang Schneiderhan; two *d*. *Educ:* Augsburg Conservatory, Germany. First engagement under von Karajan, at Aachen, Germany, 1940. Concert tours all over the world; appeared: Metropolitan Opera, New York; Covent Garden, London; La Scala, Milan; also festivals at Salzburg, Lucerne, Edinburgh. Recipient various Mozart Medals; Lilly-Lehmann Medal; Golden Cross of merit for Culture and Science; Decoration of Chevalier I, Denmark. Hon. Mem. Boston Symphony Orch.; Vienna Philharmonic Orch. Grosses Verdienstkrenz des Verdienstordens der Bundesrepublik Deutschland, 1968. *Publications:* Articles on Mozart, Bartók, Hindemith, Hugo Wolf. *Address:* Vienna State Opera, Austria.

**SEEL, Sir George Frederick,** KCMG 1950 (CMG 1944); *b* 8 Oct. 1895; *s* of Henry Seel, Macclesfield; *m* 1923, Phyllis, *d* of Edward Eaton, JP, Macclesfield; one *s* one *d*. *Educ:* King's School, Macclesfield; Corpus Christi College, Oxford. Served European War, 1914-18, with 7th Bn Cheshire Regt, TF; Secretary, Rhodesia-Nyasaland Royal Commission, 1938; Asst Under-Sec. of State, Colonial Office, 1946-50; Comptroller for Development and Welfare in the West Indies 1950-53; Senior Crown Agent for Oversea Governments and Administrations, 1953-59; Chairman, British Leprosy Relief Assoc., 1962-. *Address:* Rosemount, Esher Place Avenue, Esher, Surrey. *T:* Esher 63401. *Club:* Athenæum.

**SEELY,** family name of **Baron Mottistone.**

**SEELY, Sir Victor Basil John,** 4th Bt *cr* 1896; *b* 18 May 1900; *s* of Sir Charles H. Seely, 2nd Bt; *S* to Baronetcy of brother, 1st Baron Sherwood, 1970; *m* 1st, 1922, Sybil Helen (divorced, 1931), *widow* of Sir John Shiffner, 6th Bt; one *s*; 2nd, 1931, Hon. Patience (*d* 1935), *er d* of 1st Baron Rochdale, CB, and sister of 1st Viscount Rochdale, *qv*; one *d*; 3rd, 1937, Mary Frances Margaret, *er d* of W. R. Collins, 31 Lennox Gardens, SW1; one *s* one *d*. *Educ:* Eton; Trinity College, Cambridge. Late Lt S Notts Yeomanry; contested (Nat L) Pontefract, 1935, (C) Derby North, 1950; War of 1939-45 Major 9th Queen's Royal Lancers DAAG 2nd Armoured Division 1940; prisoner, 1941-43, escaped; HM Legation, Berne, 1944. Dir of Investment Trusts of 117 Old Broad Street Group of Cos. Master of Gunmakers' Co., 1957 and 1965. *Heir: s* Nigel Edward Seely [*b* 28 July 1923; *m* 1949, Loraine, *d* of late W. W. Lindley-Travis; three *d*]. *Address:* 42 Orchard Court, Portman Square, W1. *T:* 01-935 1311. *Clubs:* White's, Beefsteak, City.

**SEERS, Dudley;** Director, Institute of Development Studies, University of Sussex, since 1967; *b* 11 April 1920; *s* of late George Clarence Seers and of Mabel Edith Seers (*née* Hallett); *m* 1943, Patricia Hindell; one *s* three *d*. *Educ:* Rugby Sch.; Pembroke Coll., Cambridge. Served Royal Navy, 1941-45. PM's Office, New Zealand Govt, 1945-46; Res. Off. (later Lectr and Sen. Lectr in Economic Statistics) Oxford Univ., 1946-53 and 1954-55; Mem. Min. of Health Cttee on Housebuilding Costs, 1949-50; Economist, UN Headqrs, 1953-54; Statistical Adviser to Barbados, Leeward and Windward Isles, 1955-57; Chief, Survey Section, UN Econ. Commn for Latin America, 1957-61; Vis. Prof., Yale

Univ., 1961-63; Dir, Economic Develt Div., UN Econ. Commn for Africa, 1963-64; Leader, UN Economic Mission to Zambia, 1964; Director-General, Economic Planning Staff, Ministry of Overseas Development, 1964-67. Also consultant for Govts of Burma, Ceylon, Ghana, Jamaica, Malta, Trinidad, for Internat. Bank, and for Univ. of Guyana. Member: Adv. Tech. Cttee, Univ. of West Indies; Editorial Bd, Jl of Develt Studies; Council of ODI. Leader, ILO Mission to Columbia, 1970; Order of Boyacá, Columbia, 1970. *Publications:* (ed) Cuba: The Economic and Social Revolution, 1964; contrib.: The Theory and Design of Economic Development (ed Adelman and Thorbecke), 1967; The Teaching of Development Economics (ed Martin and Knapp), 1967; Crisis in the Civil Service (ed Thomas), 1968; Africa and the World, 1969; Unfashionable Economics: essays in honour of Lord Balogh, 1970; (ed) Development in a Divided World, 1971; Econ. Jl; Oxford Econ. Papers; Social and Econ. Studies; Bulletin of the Oxford Inst. of Economics and Statistics; Jl of Polit. Economy, etc. *Recreations:* tennis, ski-ing. *Address:* 15 Hobury Street, SW10. *T:* 01-352 4394; (office) Brighton 66261.

**SEFERIADES, George;** Ambassador (Greece); Poet (pen-name George Seferis); Grand Cross Order of Phœnix; Ambassador of Greece to the Court of St James's, June 1957-August 1962; *b* Smyrna, 29 February 1900; *e s* of Stelio Seferiades, Professor of International Law, and Despo Tenekides; family settled Athens, 1914; *m* 1941, Maria Zannos. *Educ:* Athens and Paris. Entered Greek Foreign Service, 1926; Acting Consul-General, London, 1931-34; Consul, Koritza (Albania), 1936; Head, Foreign Press Service, Athens, 1938-41; with Free Greek Govt in Crete, S Africa, the Middle East and Italy; Principal, Private Sec. of Regent Archbishop Damaskinos, 1945-46; Counsellor of Embassy, Ankara, 1948-50; Minister Counsellor, London, 1951-52; Ambassador to Lebanon and Minister to Syria, Iraq and Jordan, 1953-56. Hon. LittD Camb., 1960; Nobel Prize for Literature, 1963; Hon. DPhi Thess., 1964; Hon. DLitt: Oxon, 1964; Princeton, 1965. For. Hon. Mem., Amer. Acad. of Arts and Sciences. Holds foreign orders. *Publications:* Strophi, 1931; Sterna, 1932; Mythistorema, 1935; Book of Exercises, 1940; Log Book I, 1940; Log Book II, 1944; Log Book III, 1955; Collected Poems, 1963; Essays, 1944 and 1962. *Translations:* in English: The King of Asine and other poems (London), 1948; Poems (London and Boston), 1961; Collected Poems (Princeton), 1967; Collected Poems 1924-1955, 1969; in French: Seferis (Athens), 1945; Poèmes (Paris), 1963; in Italian: Poesie (Milan), 1963; in German: Poesie (Frankfurt am Main), 1962; in Swedish: Dikter, 1963, etc. *Address:* Agras 20, Athens (501), Greece.

**SEFERIS, George;** *see* Seferiades, George.

**SEFTON,** 7th Earl of, *cr* 1771; **Hugh William Osbert Molyneux,** Viscount Molyneux, 1628; Baron Sefton (UK), 1831; DL, JP; Constable of Lancaster Castle since 1942; *b* 22 Dec. 1898; *o surv. s* of 6th Earl and Lady Helena Mary Bridgeman (*d* 1947), *d* of 4th Earl of Bradford; *S* father, 1930; *m* 1941, Josephine, OSTJ, *d* of George Armstrong, of Virginia, USA. *Educ:* Harrow; Sandhurst. Joined Royal Horse Guards, 1917, retd 1930, rejoined 1939; ADC to Governor-General of Canada, 1919; ADC to GOC Madras District, 1925-26; ADC to the Viceroy of India, 1926; Lord in Waiting to the King, 1936-37. Lord Mayor of Liverpool, 1944-45. CStJ. *Address:* Croxteth Hall, Liverpool; Grosvenor Cottage, Culross Street, W1; Abbeystead, Lancaster. *Clubs:* Buck's, White's; Jockey (Newmarket).

**SEFTON-COHEN, Arthur,** CB 1935; barrister-at-law; *b* 20 May 1879; *s* of George Sefton-Cohen and Eliza Steavenson; *m* 1922, Leonora Carlow; no *c*. Called to Bar, 1901; Assistant Director of Public Prosecutions, 1931; retired, 1944. Served European War, 1914-17. *Recreations:* fishing, rowing, swimming.

**SEGAL,** family name of **Baron Segal.**

**SEGAL,** Baron *cr* 1964, of Wytham (Life Peer); **Samuel Segal,** MRCS, LRCP; MA Oxon; retired as Regional Medical Officer, Ministry of Health, SW1 (1951-62); *b* 2 April 1902; *e s* of late Professor M. H. Segal, MA; *m* 1934, Molly, *o d* of Robert J. Rolo, OBE, Alexandria, Egypt; two *d* (one *s* decd). *Educ:* Royal Grammar Sch., Newcastle upon Tyne (Scholar); Jesus Coll., Oxford (Exhibitioner); Westminster Hosp. (Scholar). Casualty Surgeon and HP Westminster Hospital; Senior Clinical Assistant, Great Ormond Street Children's Hospital. Served on various LCC Hospital Committees. Contested (Lab) Tynemouth, 1935, Aston (Birmingham) By-Election, May 1939. Joined RAFVR Medical Branch, Oct. 1939; served in Aden 1940, Western Desert 1941, Syrian Campaign 1941; attached Greek Air Force, 1941; Squadron Leader, 1942; Sen. Med. Officer RAF Naval Co-operation Group in Mediterranean, 1942; on Headquarters Staff RAF Middle East, 1943-44; on Air Min. Med. Staff, 1944-45; has travelled extensively on RAF Medical duties throughout North and East Africa, Iraq, Persian Gulf, India, etc. MP (Lab) for Preston, 1945-50; Member Parly Delegations: to Austria, 1946; to Nigeria, Cameroons, Gold Coast, Sierra Leone and Gambia, 1947; to Egypt, 1947; Hungary, 1965; Cyprus, 1965; Bahrain, Aden, 1966; Hong Kong, Singapore and S Vietnam, 1968; Leader, Parly Delegation to Malawi, 1966. Mem. FO Mission to Persia, 1947. Chairman: Nat. Soc. for Mentally Handicapped Children; Council, Anglo-Israel Assoc.; Member: Home Office Adv. Cttee on Service Parly Candidate; Council, Oxford Society; Pres., Oxford-Paddington Passenger Assoc.; Vice-Pres., Music Therapy Charity Ltd; co-opted Mem., Wytham Conservation Cttee, Berks CC; Patron, Oxford Diocesan Assoc. for the Deaf. Hon. Fellow, Jesus College, Oxford, 1966. *Recreations:* walking, motoring, photography, travel in foreign parts. *Address:* Wytham Abbey, Oxford. *T:* Oxford 47200; 27 Chester Street, Belgrave Square, SW1. *T:* 01-235 6778. *Clubs:* Royal Air Force, Oxford and Cambridge University, United University.

**SEGAL, Prof. Judah Benzion,** MC 1942; FBA 1968; Professor of Semitic Languages in the University of London, School of Oriental and African Studies, since 1961; *b* 21 June 1912; *s* of Prof. Moses H. Segal and Hannah Leah Segal; *m* 1946, Leah (*née* Seidemann); two *d*. *Educ:* Magdalen College School, Oxford; St Catharine's College, Cambridge. Jarrett Schol., 1932; John Stewart of Rannoch Schol., in Hebrew, 1933; 1st Cl. Oriental Langs Tripos, 1935; Tyrwhitt Schol. and Mason Prizeman, 1936; BA (Cambridge), 1935; MA 1938. Mansel Research Exhibitioner, St John's Coll., Oxford, 1936-39; James Mew Schol., 1937; DPhil (Oxon.), 1939. Deputy Assistant Director, Public Security, Sudan Government, 1939-41; served War of 1939-45, GHQ, MEF, 1942-44, Captain; Education Officer, British Military Administration, Tripolitania, 1945-46. Head of Dept of Near and Middle East, Sch. of Oriental and African Studies, 1961-68. *Publications:* The Diacritical

Point and the Accents in Syriac, 1953; The Hebrew Passover, 1963; Edessa, 1970; articles in learned periodicals. *Recreation:* walking. *Address:* 17 Hillersdon Avenue, Edgware, Middlesex. *T:* 01-958 4993.

**SEGONZAC, André D. de;** *see* Dunoyer de Segonzac.

**SEGOVIA, Andres;** Spanish concert-guitarist; *b* Spain 18 Feb. 1894; *m* 1962, Emilia; one *s* (and one *s* one *d* by former marr.). Brought up in Granada; has been playing the guitar since the age of ten; first came to England as a young man; has often returned on concert tours since 1952; has had many pupils and has taught at Santiago de Compostela and Academy Chigi, Siena, and other schools; has adapted works of Bach, Haydn, Mozart and other classical composers for the guitar; has had many works composed especially for him by Casella, Castelnuovo-Tedesco, De Falla, Ponce, Roussel, Tansman, Turina, Villa-Lobos and others. Gold Medal for Meritorious Work (Spain), 1967. *Address:* c/o Ibbs & Tillett, 124 Wigmore Street, W1.

**SEGRAVE, Edmond;** Editor, Journalist-Reviewer; *b* 4 Oct. 1904; *y s* of late Michael Segrave; *m* 1936, Désirée, *o d* of Dr D. G. Macleod Munro; two *d. Educ:* St Edwards; Upholland College; Continent. Editor of The Bookseller since 1933. *Address:* 13 Bedford Square, WC1. *T:* 01-636 4748. *Club:* Savile.

**SEGRÈ, Prof. Emilio;** Grande Ufficiale, Merito della Repubblica (Italy); Professor of Physics, University of California, Berkeley, since 1946; *b* 1 Feb. 1905; *s* of Giuseppe Segrè and Amelia Segrè-Treves; *m* 1936, Elfriede Spiro; one *s* two *d. Educ:* University of Rome, Italy. Asst Prof. of Physics, Rome, 1929-35; Dir, Physics Inst., Univ. of Palermo, Italy, 1936-38; Research Associate and Lectr, Univ. of Calif., Berkeley, 1938-42; Group Leader, Los Alamos Scientific Lab., 1942-46. Hon. Prof. S Marcos Univ., Lima, 1954; Hon. DSc Palermo, 1958, etc. Nobel laureate (joint) for physics, 1959. Member: Nat. Acad. Sciences, USA, 1952; Accad. Nazionale Lincei, Roma, 1959; Heidelberg Akad. der Wissenschaften; Amer. Phil. Soc., etc. *Publications:* contrib. to Physical Review, Proc. Roy. Soc. London, Nature, Nuovo Cimento, etc. *Recreations:* mountaineering and fishing. *Address:* 36 Crest Road, Lafayette, Calif 94549, USA; University of California, Berkeley, Calif, 94720. *Club:* Univ. of California Faculty (Berkeley).

**SEIDEL, Toscha;** Violinist; *b* Odessa, 17 Nov. 1899; *s* of Samuel Seidel and Tatiana Beerman; *m* 1929, Estelle Manheim, San Francisco, Studied under Max and Alexander Fiedelmann and Auer. Debut Christiania, 1914; America, 1918; enlisted US Navy, 1942, as Musician i/c. Honourably discharged Nov. 1944. *Address:* 259 Veteran Avenue, Los Angeles 24, California. *T:* Brighton 0-4788. *Club:* Bohemians (Los Angeles).

**SEIFERT, Robin** (also known as **Richard**); JP; DipArch; FRIBA; Principal R. Seifert and Partners, Architects, since 1934; *b* 25 Nov. 1910; *s* of William Seifert; *m* 1939, Josephine Jeanette Harding; two *s* one *d. Educ:* Central Foundation Sch., City of London; University College, London (DipArch). Commenced architectural practice, 1934. Corps of Royal Engineers, 1940-44; Indian Army, 1944-46; Hon. Lt-Col, 1946. Returned to private practice, 1948. Designed: Centre Point, St Giles Circus; Drapers Gardens; HQ of the National Provincial Bank; The Royal Garden Hotel, Kensington; Tolworth Towers, Surbiton; Woolworth House, Marylebone Road; HQ of ICT, Putney; Kellogg House, Baker Street. Mem., cttee of Management, Housing Assoc. for Discharged Offenders; part-time Mem., British Waterways Bd. Liveryman, City of London. JP Barnet, 1969. Certif. for Meritorious Service, 1943. *Recreations:* chess, violin. *Address:* Eleventrees, Milespit Hill, Mill Hill, NW7. *T:* 01-959 3397. *Clubs:* Army and Navy, City Livery, Arts.

**SEKERS, Sir Nicholas (Thomas), (Miki Sekers),** Kt 1965; MBE 1955; Managing Director, West Cumberland Silk Mills, Ltd, Whitehaven, since 1938; Chairman, Sekers Fabrics Ltd; Director, Sekers Mills Ltd; *b* 15 Dec. 1910; *s* of Paul L. Szekeres and Jolan Szekeres; *m* 1941, Agota Anna Balkanyi; two *s* one *d. Educ:* Marko Real School, Budapest; Academy of Commerce, Budapest; Textile Technological College, Krefeld, Germany. Director, Adria Silk Mills Ltd, Budapest, 1931-37. Trustee: Glyndebourne Arts Trust Ltd, 1954-; Rosehill Arts Trust Ltd, 1959-; Chichester Festival Theatre, 1962-; Vice-Pres., RSA, 1968-; Vice-Chairman: London Mozart Players, 1967- (Chm., 1962-67); London Philharmonic Orchestra Council, 1967- (Chm., 1965-66); London Mozart Players; Gov., Yehudi Menuhin School, 1965-; Member of Council: Soc. of Royal Opera House, 1962-; Shakespeare Theatre Trust, 1967-; Member, Council of Industrial Design, 1966-. Duke of Edinburgh's Prize for Elegant Design, 1962; Hon. Associate Manchester College of Art and Design, 1963; Hon. MA, Univ. Manchester, 1963. FSIA; FRSA 1967-. Freeman, Worshipful Co. of Musicians, 1966-. *Recreations:* music, the theatre, reading, travel. *Address:* West Cumberland Silk Mills Ltd, Whitehaven, Cumberland. *T:* Whitehaven 2691; Rosehill, Moresby, Whitehaven, Cumberland. *T:* Whitehaven 2673; 1 Harriet Walk, Lowndes Square, SW1. *T:* 01-235 3410. *Club:* Garrick.

**SELBORNE,** 3rd Earl of, *cr* 1882; **Roundell Cecil Palmer,** PC 1929; CH 1945; Viscount Wolmer, 1883; Baron Selborne, 1872; Major (retired) 3rd Bn Hampshire Regt; President of the Church Army, 1949-61; Chairman of House of Laity, Church Assembly, 1955-59; *b* 15 April, 1887; *e s* of 2nd Earl of Selborne and Lady Beatrix Maud Cecil (*d* 1950), *d* of 3rd Marquis of Salisbury, KG; *S* father, 1942; *m* 1st, 1910, Grace (*d* 1959), *y d* of 1st Viscount Ridley; two *s* three *d*; 2nd, 1966, Valerie Irene de Thomka de Tomkahaza et Folkusfalva (*d* 1968). *Educ:* Winchester College; University Coll., Oxford. Contested (C) Newton Division, Lancs, 1910; represented Newton Div. of Lancashire, Dec. 1910-18, and Aldershot Div. of Hampshire, Dec. 1918-40; called up to House of Lords, Oct. 1940; Assistant Director War Trade, 1916-18; Parliamentary Secretary, Board of Trade, 1922-24; Asst Postmaster-General, 1924-29; Director of Cement, Ministry of Works and Buildings, 1940-42; Minister of Economic Warfare, 1942-45; JP 1911; Member of Sea Fish Commission, 1934-36; Chm. Cement Makers' Federation, 1934-42, 1945-51; Member of House of Laymen, Province of Canterbury, 1913; Master of the Mercers' Company, 1948; Chm., National Provincial Bank, 1951-54; Dep. Chm., Boots Pure Drug Co., 1936-63. *Publication:* Post Office Reform, 1932. *Heir: g s* Viscount Wolmer, *qv. Address:* Blackmoor House, Liss, Hants. *Club:* Turf.

*See also Rev. J. S. Brewis, Baroness Lucas and Dingwall, Baron O'Hagan, Hon. Lewis Palmer, Bishop of Peterborough.*

**SELBY,** 4th Viscount, *cr* 1905; **Michael Guy John Gully;** Controller for Scotland, Cayzer

Irvine & Partners Ltd, since 1969; *b* 15 Aug. 1942; *s* of 3rd Viscount and of Veronica, *er d* of late J. George and of Mrs Briscoe-George; *S* father, 1959; *m* 1965, Mary Theresa, *d* of Capt. Thomas Powell, London, SW7; one *s*. *Educ:* Harrow. ACA, ATII. *Recreations:* shooting, fishing, sailing, agriculture. *Heir:* *s* Hon. Edward Thomas William Gully, *b* 21 Sept. 1967. *Address:* Ardfern House, by Lochgilphead, Argyll.

**SELBY, Bishop Suffragan of,** since 1962; **Rt. Rev. Douglas Noel Sargent;** *b* 19 Dec. 1907; *s* of Edwin Dowdeswell Sargent, Watford, and Charlotte Elizabeth (*née* Taylor), St Albans; *m* 1942, Imogene Grace Ward; three *s* (one *d* decd). *Educ:* Watford Grammar School; King's College, Cambridge; London College of Divinity; Union Theological Seminary, New York. Deacon, 1931; Priest, 1932; Curate of Willian, 1931-34; Missionary with CMS at Chengtu, 1934-48, and at Lingling, 1949-51; Principal of CMS Men's Training College, Blackheath, 1951-52, Chislehurst, 1952-62. *Publications:* The Making of a Missionary, 1960; jointly, The Churchman's Companion, 1964. *Recreation:* tennis. *Address:* Tollgarth, 100 Tadcaster Road, Dringhouses, York.

**SELBY, Major-Gen. Arthur Roland,** CB 1943; CBE 1941; *b* 16 March 1893. Served European War, Gallipoli, 1915 (wounded); served War of 1939-45 (despatches, CBE, CB); retired pay, 1946. *Address:* Newington Old House, New Hanover, Natal, South Africa.

**SELBY, Sir Kenneth,** Kt 1970; Chairman, Bath & Portland Group Ltd, since 1969; *b* 16 Feb. 1914; *s* of Thomas William Selby; *m* 1937, Elma Gertrude, *d* of Johnstone Sleator; two *s*. *Educ:* High School for Boys, Worthing. Managing Director, Bath & Portland Group Ltd, 1963. FCWA 1969; AACCA 1946. *Address:* Hartham Park, Corsham, Wilts. *T:* Corsham 3176. *Clubs:* Reform; Savages (Bristol).

**SELBY, Ralph Walford,** CMG 1961; HM Diplomatic Service; Minister, British Embassy, Rome, since 1969; *b* 20 March 1915; *e s* of late Sir Walford Selby, KCMG, CB, CVO; *m* 1947, Julianna Snell; three *d*. *Educ:* Eton; Christ Church, Oxford. Entered HM Diplomatic Service, Sept. 1938; served in Foreign Office until Oct. 1939. Enlisted in Army and served with Grenadier Guards, March 1940-Feb. 1945, when returned to Foreign Office; seconded to Treasury for service in India as First Secretary in Office of High Commissioner for UK, Sept. 1947; transferred to The Hague, 1950; returned to FO, 1953-56; transf. to Tokyo as Counsellor, 1956, to Copenhagen in 1958, to Djakarta in 1961, to Warsaw in 1964; Chargé d'Affaires in 1952, 1958, 1959, 1960, 1961, 1962, 1964, 1965, 1969, 1970; Consul-Gen., Boston, 1966-69. *Recreation:* sports as available. *Address:* c/o Lloyds Bank Ltd, 16 St James's Street, SW1. *Club:* Turf.

**SELBY, Rear-Adm. William Halford,** CB 1955; DSC 1942; *b* 29 April 1902; *s* of E. H. Selby; *m* 1926, Hilary Elizabeth Salter (*d* 1960); two *d*; *m* 1961, Mrs R. Milne. *Educ:* Royal Naval Colleges, Osborne and Dartmouth. Entered Royal Navy, 1916; Midshipman, HMS Royal Oak, Black Sea and Dardanelles, 1920; Sub.-Lt HMS Vendetta and HMY Victoria and Albert, 1924. Destroyers, Medit and China Station between 1927 and 1936; Naval Staff Coll., 1939; War of 1939-45: in comd HMS Wren, Mashona (despatches), Onslaught (despatches). Capt. 1943; Chief of Staff, Londonderry, 1944-45; Capt. 'D' Third Flotilla in comd HMS Saumarez, 1946-47; Dep. Dir Ops Div., Admty, 1948-50; Capt-in-Charge, Simonstown, 1950-52; Rear-Adm. 1953; Head of British Naval Mission to Greece, 1953-55; retired, 1956. *Address:* The Old Cottage, Chittoe, Chippenham, Wilts.

**SELBY-BIGGE, Sir John (Amherst),** 2nd Bt, *cr* 1919; OBE 1946; Artist; *b* 20 June 1892; *s* of Sir Amherst Selby-Bigge, 1st Bt, KCB and Edith Lindsay (*d* 1939), *d* of late Rt Hon. J. R. Davison, MP; *S* father 1951; *m* 1st, 1914, Ruth (marriage dissolved, 1944), *d* of E. W. Humphries, Bradford; three *d*; 2nd, 1946, Marija (*d* 1955), *d* of Judge Martin Bacik, Vienna. *Educ:* Winchester; Christ Church, Oxford. Studied art at Slade School and became professional artist. Served European War, 1914-19, Lt RASC, Macedonian Mule Corps, Salonica, BEF; Intelligence Service, Adviser to Greek Govt on censorship. Sub-editor BBC European News Service, 1942-43; British Red Cross (Civilian Relief Overseas) Superviser with 8th Army in Italy, Asst Comr in Austria, 1943-45 (Order of Italian Red Cross, 1945). Travelled in most of Europe and resided since 1936 in Austria, France, and Spain. Exhibited in London, Provinces, and Paris. *Recreations:* gardening, travelling. *Heir:* none. *Address:* Limeuil, Dordogne, France.

**SELBY-LOWNDES, Brigadier Montacute William Worrall,** DSO 1940; Regular Army (Retired); *b* 25 June 1896; *o s* of late Henry William Selby-Lowndes, MFH; *m* 1943, Helena Olivia (who *m* 1922, 7th Earl of Radnor, marriage dissolved 1943), *y d* of C. R. W. Adeane, CB, Babraham, Cambridge. *Educ:* Oundle. Commissioned 1914, Royal Artillery; BEF, France, 1915-17; BEF, Italy, 1918 (despatches, Italian Croce di Guerra); since served Egypt, Palestine, Syria, India; BEF, France, 1940 (DSO); Acting Brigadier CRA 61 Division, 1943-45; retired pay, 1947. *Recreations:* Master and Huntsman: Sarona Vale Hounds, Palestine, 1919-22; Mhow Hounds, India, 1925-28; RA Bordon Hounds, 1929-33; Amateur Huntsman: Tedworth Foxhounds, 1933-36; Wilton Foxhounds, 1936-39; Master Newmarket and Thurlow Foxhounds, 1946; Deputy Master and huntsman Hampshire Hunt, 1947-52; Joint Master and huntsman VWH (Earl Bathurst) Foxhounds, 1952-55; Master and huntsman North Staffs Foxhounds, 1955-58. *Address:* The Beacon, Mundesley, Norfolk. *T:* Mundesley 344.

**SELDON TRUSS, Leslie;** Author; *b* 1892; *s* of George Marquand Truss and Ann Blanche, *d* of Samuel Seldon, CB; *m* 1st, 1918, Gwendolen, *d* of Charles Kershaw, Cooden Mount, Sussex; one *d*; 2nd, 1925, Kathleen Mary, *d* of Charles Hornung, of Oaklands, Hookwood, Surrey; one *s* one *d*. Lieut Scots Guards, Special Reserve, 1915-19; Major Home Guard, 1940-44. *Publications:* Gallows Bait, 1928; The Stolen Millionaire, 1929; The Man Without Pity, 1930; The Hunterstone Outrage, 1931; Turmoil at Brede, 1932; Mr Coroner Presides, 1932; They Came by Night, 1933; The Daughters of Belial, 1934; Murder Paves the Way; Escort to Danger, 1935; Draw the Blinds; Rooksmiths, 1936; The Man who Played Patience; She Could Take Care; Footsteps Behind Them, 1937; Foreign Bodies, 1938; The Disappearance of Julie Hints, 1940; Sweeter for his Going, Where's Mr Chumley?, 1949; Ladies Always Talk, 1950; Never Fight a Lady, 1951; Death of No Lady, 1952; Always Ask a Policeman, 1953; Put Out The Light, The High Wall, 1954; The Long Night, The Barberton Intrigue, 1956; The Truth About Claire Veryan, 1957; In Secret Places, 1958; The Hidden Men, 1959; One Man's Death, 1960; Seven Years Dead, 1961; A Time to Hate, 1962; Technique for Treachery,

1963; Walk a Crooked Mile, 1964; The Town That Went Sick, 1965; Eyes at the Window, 1966; The Bride That Got Away, 1967; The Hands of the Shadow, 1968; The Corpse That Got Away, 1969; under *pseudonym* of Georege Selmark, Murder in Silence, 1939; various short stories and serials. *Recreations:* anything but writing. *Address:* Dale Hill House, Ticehurst, Sussex. *T:* Ticehurst 251.

**SELF, Sir (Albert) Henry,** KCB 1947 (CB 1938); KCMG 1942; KBE 1939; retired as Chairman Electricity Council (1957-59); *b* 18 Jan. 1890; *s* of late S. A. T. Self, London; *m* 1918, Rosalind Audrey, *d* of late Sir John Lonsdale Otter, Brighton; two *s*. *Educ:* Bancrofts School, Woodford; University of London. BSc (Gen.), 1911; BSc(Maths), 1913; BA (Classics), 1929; BD (Gen.), 1932; BD (Philosophy), 1934; MSc (Philosophy of Science), 1951; PhD (Philosophy), 1956; Hon. Fellow of Birkbeck Coll.; Comp. IEE; Barrister-at-law, Lincoln's Inn (Certificate of Honour, 1922); entered Civil Service, 1907; served in Board of Trade, Post Office, Foreign Office, War Office, and Local Government Board; seconded to War Office and Ministry of Munitions, 1914-19; Air Ministry, 1919; Principal Assistant Secretary, 1936; Deputy Under-Secretary of State, 1937; served on special Air Mission to Middle East, Africa in connection with Empire Air Mail Scheme, 1935; served on two Air Missions to USA and Canada in Spring and Autumn of 1938, in connection with placing of aircraft orders for the RAF; Head of Mission to USA and Canada in Spring of 1940, from which emerged British Air Commission in Washington; Director-General British Air Commission, Washington, USA, 1940-41; attached for special duties with the British Joint Staff Mission in Washington concurrently with establishment of the Combined Chiefs of Staff Organization, Jan.-June 1942; Permanent Secretary to Ministry of Production, 1942-43; Deputy for Minister of Production on Combined Production and Resources Board, Washington, 1943-45; Deputy-Chairman British Supply Council in Washington, 1945; UK Member Combined Raw Materials Board, 1944-45; Permanent Secretary, Ministry of Civil Aviation, 1946-47; Deputy Chairman Central Electricity Authority, 1947-57. President British Electrical Development Assoc., 1953-54; Pres. British Electrical and Allied Research Assoc., 1959. Pres. Modern Churchmen's Union, 1947-57. *Recreation:* golf. *Address:* 16 Vernon Terrace, Brighton, Sussex. *T:* Hove 731842.
*See also Prof. P. J. O. Self.*

**SELF, Prof. Peter John Otter;** Professor of Public Administration, University of London, since 1963; Vice-Chairman of Executive, Town and Country Planning Association; *b* 7 June 1919; *s* of Sir (Albert) Henry Self, *qv*; *m* 1st, 1950, Diana Mary Pitt (marriage dissolved); 2nd, 1959, Elaine Rosenbloom Adams; two *s*. *Educ:* Lancing Coll.; Balliol Coll., Oxford (MA). Editorial staff of The Economist, 1944-62; Extra-mural Lectr, London Univ., 1944-49; Lectr in Public Administration, LSE, 1948-61; Reader in Political Science, LSE, 1961-63. Dir of Studies (Administration), Civil Service Dept, 1969-70. Mem. Exec. and Coun., 1954, Vice-Chm. Exec., 1955, Chm. Exec., 1961-69, Town and Country Planning Assoc.; Mem., SE Regional Economic Planning Coun., 1966-. *Publications:* Regionalism, 1949; Cities in Flood: The Problems of Urban Growth, 1957; (with H. Storing) The State and the Farmer, 1962; numerous articles on administration, politics and planning. *Recreations:* walking, golf, story-telling. *Address:* 43 Brim Hill, N2. *T:* 01-458 1046. *Club:* Reform.

**SELIGMAN, Henry,** OBE 1958; PhD; Scientific Consultant to Director General, International Atomic Energy Agency, Vienna, since 1969; Scientific Adviser, Nucleonic Data Systems Inc., since 1969; *b* Frankfurt am Main, 25 Feb. 1909; *s* of Milton Seligman and Marie (*née* Gans); *m* 1941, Lesley Bradley; two *s*. *Educ:* Liebigschule Frankfurt; Sorbonne; Universities of Lausanne and of Zürich. Staff, DSIR, Cavendish Lab., Cambridge, 1942-43. Joined British-Canadian Research Project at Montreal, 1943, Chalk River, Ontario, 1944-; Staff, Brit. Atomic Energy Project, 1946; Head of Isotope Div., Atomic Energy Research Establishment, Harwell, UK, 1947-58; Dep. Dir Gen., Dept of Research and Isotopes, Internat. Atomic Energy Agency, Vienna, 1958-69. *Publications:* papers on: physical constants necessary for reactor development; waste disposal; production and uses of radioisotopes; contrib. scientific journals. *Address:* Nucleonic Data Systems, Inc., European Office, Opernring 1/E/628, 1010 Vienna, Austria. *T:* Vienna 576624.

**SELIGMAN, Peter Wendel,** CBE 1969; Chairman, APV Holdings Ltd, since 1965; *b* 16 Jan. 1913; *s* of Richard Joseph Simon Seligman and Hilda Mary Seligman; *m* 1937, Elizabeth Lavinia Mary Wheatley; two *s* four *d*. *Educ:* King's Coll. Sch., Wimbledon; Harrow Sch.; Caius Coll., Cambridge. Joined APV Co. Ltd, as Asst to Man. Dir, 1936; appointed Dir, 1939; Man. Dir, 1947; Dep. Chm., 1961. *Recreations:* sailing, ski-ing. *Address:* 2 The Mount, Ifield, Sussex. *T:* Rusper 363. *Clubs:* Athenæum, Cruising Association; Hawks (Cambridge), Island Sailing (Cowes).

**SELKIRK,** 10th Earl of, *cr* 1646; **George Nigel Douglas-Hamilton,** PC 1955; GCMG 1959; GBE 1963 (OBE 1941); AFC; QC(Scot.), 1959; late Gp Capt. Auxiliary Air Force; Scottish Representative Peer, 1945-63; Chairman, Conservative Commonwealth Council, since 1965; *b* Merly, Wimborne, Dorset, 4 Jan. 1906; 2nd *s* of 13th Duke of Hamilton and Brandon; *S* to earldom of father under terms of special destination, 1940; *m* 1949, Audrey Durell, *o d* of late Maurice Drummon-Sale-Barker and of Mrs H. S. Brooks. *Educ:* Eton; Balliol College, Oxford, MA; Edinburgh University, LLB. Admitted to Faculty of Advocates, 1935; Commanded 603 Squadron AAF, 1934-38; Member of Edinburgh Town Council, 1935-40; Commisssioner of General Board of Control (Scotland), 1936-39; Commissioner for Special Areas in Scotland, 1937-39. Served War of 1939-45 (despatches twice). A Lord-in-Waiting to the Queen, 1952-53 (to King George VI, 1951-52); Paymaster-General, Nov. 1953-Dec. 1955; Chancellor of the Duchy of Lancaster, Dec. 1955-Jan. 1957; First Lord of the Admiralty, 1957-Oct. 1959; UK Commissioner for Singapore and Comr Gen. for SE Asia, 1959-63; also UK Council Representative to the South-East Asia Treaty Organisation, 1960-63. Freeman of Hamilton, President: National Ski Fedn of Great Britain, 1964-68; Anglo-Swiss Society, 1965; Building Societies Assoc., 1965; Royal Central Asian Society. Hon. Chief, Saulteaux Indians, 1967. *Address:* Rose Lawn Coppice, Wimborne, Dorset. *T:* Wimborne 3160; 60 Eaton Place, SW1. *Clubs:* Athenæum, Carlton; New (Edinburgh).

**SELLECK, Sir Francis Palmer,** KBE 1957; Kt 1956; MC 1918; Lord Mayor, City of Melbourne, 1954-57; *b* 20 Aug. 1895; *s* of late Christopher and Emily Selleck; *m* 1923, Mollie Constance Maud Miller; one *s* one *d*. *Educ:* High School, Shepparton, Australia. Chartered Accountant; Director of Companies; Lord Mayor of Melbourne, 1954-57; Lord Mayor, Olympic Games, Melb., 1956.

Served Australian Imperial Forces, Gallipoli, France, 1915-18 (despatches, MC). Served with Board of Business Administration, Australian Defence HQ, 1940-45. *Address:* Suite 26, 67 Queens Road, Melbourne, Australia. *T:* 51-5362; (home) 24-6780. *Club:* Naval and Military (Melbourne).

**SELLERS, Rt. Hon. Sir Frederic Aked,** PC 1957; Kt 1946; MC; a Lord Justice of Appeal, 1957-68; *b* 14 Jan. 1893; 3rd *s* of John Shuttleworth Sellers and Elizabeth Stuart; *m* 1917, Grace, *y d* of William Malin, JP, Derby; four *s* one *d*. *Educ:* Silcoates Sch.; Univ. of Liverpool. Served with King's (Liverpool) Regt 13th Battn 1914-18 (Capt.; MC 1916, 2 Bars 1918); HG, 1940-45; called to Bar, Gray's Inn, 1919; KC 1935; sometime Mem. Bar Council; Bencher, Gray's Inn, 1938; Treasurer, 1952; Vice-Treasurer, 1953; Northern Circuit; Recorder of Bolton, 1938-46; Judge, Queen's Bench Division, 1946-57. Mem., Standing Committee on Criminal Law Revision (Chm., 1959-69). Liberal Candidate Waterloo Div. of Lancashire, General Election, 1929, Hendon North, 1945. Chairman of Governors: Mill Hill School, 1951-68; Silcoates Sch., 1953-58. Hon. LLD Liverpool, 1956. *Address:* Highwood Lodge, Mill Hill, NW7. *T:* 01-959 3066. *Club:* Reform.

**SELLERS, Peter (Richard Henry),** CBE 1966; Actor; *b* 8 Sept. 1925; *s* of late William Sellers and late Agnes Marks; *m* 1951, Anne Howe (marr. diss. 1964); one *s* one *d*; *m* 1964, Britt Ekland (marr. diss. 1969); one *d*; *m* 1970, Miranda, *d* of Richard St John Quarry, and of Lady Mancroft. *Educ:* St Aloysius Coll., Highgate. War of 1939-45 (Burma Star, etc). Began career at the Windmill Theatre, 1948. *Radio:* Ray's A Laugh (5 years); The Goon Show (9 years); *television:* Idiots Weekly; A Show Called Fred; Son of Fred; *variety:* touring, 1949-54; appeared at Palladium, 4 times; *films:* The Ladykillers, The Smallest Show on Earth, The Naked Truth, Tom Thumb, Carleton Browne of the FO, The Mouse That Roared, I'm Alright Jack, Up The Creek, Two Way Stretch, Battle of the Sexes, Never Let Go, The Millionairess, Mr Topaze (also Dir), The Running, Jumping and Standing Still Film (Prod), Only Two Can Play, The Waltz of the Toreadors, The Dock Brief, Lolita, The Wrong Arm of the Law; Heavens Above!; Dr Strangelove or How I Learned to Stop Worrying and Love the Bomb; The World of Henry Orient; The Pink Panther; Shot in the Dark; What's New, Pussycat?; The Wrong Box; After the Fox; Casino Royale; The Bobo; The Party; I Love You, Alice B. Toklas; The Magic Christian; Hoffman; There's a Girl in my Soup; *stage:* Brouhaha, 1958. Has made some recordings. Awards: Best Actor for 1959 (British Film Academy Award); Golden Gate Award, 1959; San Sebastian Film Award for Best British Actor, 1962. *Recreations:* photography, cars, cricket, judo. *Address:* Barclays Bank Ltd, 119 Waterloo Road, SE1. *Club:* Royal Automobile.

**SELLERS, Rev. Dr Robert Victor;** Prebendary of Wiveliscombe in Wells Cathedral, since 1955 (Chancellor, 1956-61; Treasurer, 1955); Fellow of King's College, London, since 1954; *b* 18 Oct. 1894; *s* of late Richard and Martha Ann Sellers, Scholes, Cleckheaton, Yorks; *m* 1931, Irene, *d* of late Rev. Preb. W. O. E. Oesterley, DD; two *d*. *Educ:* Bradford Grammar School; St Catharine's College, Cambridge (Scholar); Wells Theological College. BA, 1916, MA 1920, BD 1927, DD 1939. Assistant Master King's School, Bruton, Som., 1917-19; Deacon, 1919; Priest, 1920; Asst Curate, Ossett Parish Church (Dioc. Wakefield), 1919-24; Vicar of Mytholmroyd (Yorks), 1924-31; Warden of St Augustine's House, Reading, 1931-49; Professor of Biblical and Historical Theology, Univ. of London (King's College), 1948-54; Exam. Chap. to Bishop of Oxford, 1941-54; Lecturer Bishops' Coll., Cheshunt, 1940-43; Select Preacher, Cambridge, 1942, 1958; Hon. Lectr, Christ Church, Reading, 1931-49; Boyle Lectr, 1950-52; Proctor in Convocation, Univ. of London, 1950-55. *Publications:* Eustathius of Antioch, 1928; Two Ancient Christologies, 1939; The Council of Chalcedon: a historical and doctrinal survey, 1952; contrib. Chambers's Encyclopædia. *Address:* Slade Cottage, Maddocks Slade, Burnham-on-Sea, Somerset.

**SELLON, Hugh Gilbert Rene,** MA Oxon; Professor of International Politics, University of Exeter, since 1949; *b* 1901; *s* of Anthony Gilbert and Hortense Sellon. *Educ:* University College, Oxford, BA, 1st Cl. Hons School of History, 1924; Bryce Historical Student, 1925; MA, 1934. Assistant Lecturer, later Lecturer in History, St Andrews University, 1927-35; lectured at Bonar Law College, Ashridge, on Foreign Affairs and International Relations, 1930-39; Lecturer in History and International Relations to Oxford University Delegacy for Extra-Mural Studies, and Director of Studies at Summer meetings and Vacation Courses for Foreign Students, 1935-39; Visiting Lecturer in several American and Canadian Universities, 1938; Director of British Institute in Paris, 1939-49; Prof. of French Civilization, Univ. of Reading, 1940. *Publications:* Whither England?, 1932; Democracy and Dictatorship, 1934; Europe at the Crossroads, 1937, revised ed. 1938; Articles and reviews, mainly on subjects dealing with history and international affairs. *Recreations:* walking, hill-climbing, swimming, riding, gardening. *Address:* The University, Exeter. *Clubs:* Carlton; Royal Scottish Automobile (Glasgow); Union Interalliée (Paris).

**SELLORS, Sir Thomas Holmes,** Kt 1963; DM, MCh; FRCP; PRCS; Consultant Surgeon, London Chest Hospital, since 1934; Emeritus Thoracic Surgeon, Middlesex Hospital, since 1947; Consultant surgeon, National Heart Hospital, since 1957; Consulting Surgeon, Aylesbury Group of Hospitals; *b* 7 April 1902; *s* of Dr T. B. Sellors; *m* 1st, Brenda Lyell (*d* 1928); 2nd, 1932, Dorothy Elizabeth Chesshire (*d* 1953); one *s* one *d*; 3rd, 1955, Marie Hobson. *Educ:* Loretto School; Oriel Coll., Oxford. BA Oxon 1923, MA 1927; MRCS, LRCP 1926; BM, BCh Oxon 1926; G. H. Hunt Travelling Scholarship, Univ. of Oxford, 1928; MCh 1931, DM 1933. Held various appts in London hosps; FRCS 1930; Member of Council, RCS, 1957, Vice-Pres., 1968-69, President 1969-; FRCP 1963; Chairman of Joint Consultants Committee, 1958-67; President, Thoracic Society, 1960; Pres. Soc. of Thoracic Surgeons of Great Britain and Ireland, 1961-62; Vice-Pres., Internat. Soc. Surg., 1967. Surgeon to Queen Mary's Hospital, Stratford; Regional Adviser in Thoracic Surgery, 1940-45. Hunterian Prof. RCS, 1944; Lectures: Carey Coombs, Univ. of Bristol, 1956; G. A. Gibson, RCPE, 1959; Strickland Goodall, Society Apothecaries, 1960; Entwhistle Meml and W. W. Hamburger, Chicago, 1961; St Cyre's, 1965; Grey-Turner, Internat. Soc. Surg., 1967; Gordon-Taylor, RCS, 1968; Tudor Edwards Meml, RCS, 1968; Bradshaw, RCS, 1969. Examiner in Surgery, Univ. of Oxford. Member: Acad. of Medicine, Rome; Royal Acad. of Medicine, Belgium; Hon. Mem., Europe Cardiol. Soc.; MD (*hc*), Groningen, 1964. Médaille de la Reconnaissance Française. Officer of the Order of Carlos Finlay, Cuba. *Publications:* Surgery of the Thorax, 1933.

Editor and contributor in current text books. Articles in English and foreign medical publications. *Recreations:* water-colour painting, gardening. *Address:* 16 Park Village East, Regent's Park, NW1. *T:* 01-387 7550; Spring Coppice Farm, Speen, Aylesbury, Bucks. *T:* Hampden Row 379.

**SELLS, Arthur Lytton L.;** *see* Lytton Sells.

**SELOUS, Gerald Holgate,** CBE 1946 (OBE 1929; MBE 1920); *b* 14 July 1887; *o s* of late Edmund Selous, barrister-at-law and ornithologist, and late Fanny Margaret, *d* of John Maxwell, publisher, and Mary Elizabeth Braddon, novelist; *m* Camilla, *er d* of late Jay B. Lippincott and Camilla Hare, Philadelphia, Pa; one *s. Educ:* Cheltenham College; Pembroke College, Cambridge. Student Interpreter Levant Consular Service, 1908; Vice-Consul, Saffi, Morocco, 1914-24; Consul at Casablanca, Morocco, 1924-28; Consul at Basra, Iraq, 1929-32; Commercial Counsellor at Cairo, 1933-38, and at Brussels, 1938-40; served in Dept of Overseas Trade, 1940-42; Home Guard (St James's LDV Section), 1940-42; Trade Comr at Vancouver, BC, 1942-45; Counsellor (Commercial) at Berne, 1945-47. Silver Jubilee Medal, 1935; Coronation Medal, 1937. *Publications:* Appointment to Fez, 1956; various (published) economic reports. *Recreations:* archæology, natural history. *Address:* Château d'Hauteville, 1806 St Légier-s-Vevey, Switzerland. *T:* 021/54.11.95. *Clubs:* Travellers', Lansdowne, Royal Automobile; Grande Société (Berne).

**SELSDON,** 3rd Baron, *cr* 1932, of Croydon; **Malcolm McEacharn Mitchell-Thomson;** Bt 1900; *b* 27 Oct. 1937; *s* of 2nd Baron Selsdon (3rd Bt, *cr* 1900), DSC; *S* father, 1963; *m* 1965, Patricia Anne, *d* of Donald Smith; one *s. Educ:* Winchester College. Sub-Lieut, RNVR. *Recreations:* rackets, squash, tennis, lawn tennis, cricket, ski-ing. *Heir: s* Callum Malcolm McEacharn Mitchell-Thomson, *b* 7 Nov. 1969. *Address:* 33 Cadogan Lane, SW1. *T:* 01-235 8692. *Club:* MCC.

**SELVON, Samuel Dickson;** author since 1954; *b* Trinidad, West Indies, 20 May 1923; *m* 1st, 1947, Draupadi Persaud; one *d*; 2nd, 1963, Althea Nesta Daroux; two *s. Educ:* Naparima College, Trinidad. Wireless Operator, 1940-45; Journalist, 1946-50; Civil Servant, 1950-53. Fellow, John Simon Guggenheim Memorial Foundn (USA), 1954 and 1968; Travelling Schol., Soc. of Authors (London), 1958; Trinidad Govt Schol., 1962. Humming Bird Medal (Trinidad), 1969. *Publications:* A Brighter Sun, 1952; An Island is a World, 1954; The Lonely Londoners, 1956; Ways of Sunlight, 1957; Turn Again Tiger, 1959; I Hear Thunder, 1963; The Housing Lark, 1965; The Plains of Caroni, 1970; contribs to London Magazine, New Statesman and Nation, Sunday Times, also Evergreen Review (USA). *Recreations:* tennis, swimming, gardening, cooking. *Address:* 36 Woodside Avenue, SE25.

**SELWAY, Air Marshal Sir Anthony (Dunkerton),** KCB 1961 (CB 1952); DFC 1940; Registrar and Secretary of the Order of the Bath, since 1968 (Gentleman Usher of the Scarlet Rod, 1964-68); *b* 20 Feb. 1909; *s* of C. J. Selway, CVO, CBE, TD; *m* 1936, Patricia Graham, *d* of Col. P. C. MacFarlane, Ballagan, Strathblane, Stirlingshire; one *s* one *d. Educ:* Highgate School; Cranwell. No. 1 Squadron, Tangmere, 1929; Central Flying School, 1932-34; Middle East Command, 1936-42 (despatches); Flying Trg Comd, 1942-44; Fighter Comd, 1944-45; Burma and Far East, 1945-48; Joint Services Staff Coll., 1948; Air Ministry, 1948-51; Commandant, Central Flying School, 1951-53; Air Attaché, Paris, 1953-Nov. 1955; Comdr, RAF Staff, British Joint Services Mission (USA), 1955-58; AOC No. 18 Group Coastal Command, and Air Officer, Scotland 1958-60; C-in-C FEAF, 1960-62; AOC-in-C, RAF Coastal Command, 1962-65; Group Capt. 1942; Air Cdre 1951; Air Vice-Marshal, 1955; Air Marshal, 1961; retired, 1965. *Address:* The Dower House, Burchetts Green, Berks. *T:* Littlewick Green 2797. *Clubs:* Royal Air Force, White's.

**SELWYN, John Sidney Augustus,** OBE 1962 (MBE 1939); HM Diplomatic Service, retired; HM Vice-Consul at Calais, since 1969; *b* 17 Oct. 1908; *s* of Rev. A. L. H. Selwyn; *m* 1932, Cicely Georgina Armour (marriage dissolved); one *s* one *d* (and one *d* decd); *m* 1952, Janette Bruce Mullin (*d* 1968); one *s. Educ:* St Lawrence College, Ramsgate; Royal Military Coll., Sandhurst. Entered the Indian Police, 1928. Served in NWF Campaigns, 1930, 1937 and 1941. Major, 12th Frontier Force Regt, active service in Burma, 1942-46, Allied Control Commission, Germany, 1946-48. Entered Foreign Service, 1948. Served in Bucharest, Lisbon, London, Lima, Santos, Beirut; Consul-General: Berlin, 1963; Strasbourg, 1964-68. *Recreation:* fishing. *Address:* c/o National & Grindlay's Bank Ltd, 13 St James's Square, SW1. *Clubs:* Royal Automobile, Civil Service.

**SELWYN-CLARKE, Sir Selwyn,** KBE 1951; CMG 1945; MC 1918; MD, BS London, FRCP, MRCS; DPH Cambridge, DTM&H London; Barrister-at-Law, Gray's Inn; *b* 17 Dec. 1893; *m* 1935; one *d. Educ:* Bedales; St Bartholomew's Hospital Med. Sch.; Univ. of London. RMO and Assistant Anæsthetist, St Bartholomew's Hospital; Lieutenant RAMC, Medical Officer i/c 285th Brigade, RFA, 1916; Medical Officer i/c Queen Victoria Rifles, Capt. RAMC, 1918; MOH, Colonial Medical Service, Gold Coast, 1919; Senior Health Officer, Gold Coast, Langley Memorial Prizeman, 1924; Médaille en Argent des Epidémies, 1928; Gold Coast delegate to Yellow Fever Conference, Dakar, 1928; Chief Health Officer, FMS, delegate Congress, Bangkok, 1930; ADMS Gold Coast, Director, Gold Coast Central Council Branch, BRCS, 1932; Dep. Director, Health Service, Gold Coast, 1933; Gold Coast delegate Pan-African Health Conference, Johannesburg, 1935; Dep. Director, Health Service, Nigeria, 1936; Director of Medical Services, Hong-Kong, 1937-47; MLC, 1938; Hong-Kong delegate Congress, Hanoi, French Indo-China, 1938; MEC, Pres. Hong-Kong and South China Branch, BMA, 1939; Governor and C-in-C of the Seychelles, 1947-51; Principal Medical Officer, Ministry of Health, 1951-56; Med. Sec., The Society of Medical Officers of Health, 1956-61; CMO, The King's Troop, RHA, 1962-69; Chm. Hampstead Div., BMA, 1959-60; Consultant Adviser, MRC, S Pacific Commission, 1960. Pres., Camden (formerly Hampstead) Div., BRCS, 1960-; Hon. Life Member: BRCS and Ghana Red Cross; Trustee: Chadwick Trust, 1961; Queen Elizabeth Hosp. for Children Research Appeal Fund, 1962; Prison Visitor, 1969-. CStJ 1947. *Publications:* Smallpox in Negro and Negroid Tribes of the Gold Coast, 1921; Vaccination and Smallpox, 1921; Exhibition of Acetylarsinic Acid in Treatment of Framboesia, 1926; Influence of Rainfall on Incidence of Malaria in Federated Malay States, 1931; The Bight of Benin and Beyond, 1953; Housing and Health in the Tropics and Sub-tropics, 1955; Family Doctor and Health Visitor, 1955; The British Rehabilitation Service, 1955; An ABC for Housing, 1955; Medical History of the Second World War,

Civilian Health and Medical Services, Hong Kong, 1955; Old Folks at Home, 1956; Our Duty to Old Folks and the Importance of Voluntary Effort, 1956; Housing and Health in Tropical Countries, 1957; Children in Hospital, 1958; Personal Health in the Tropics, 1959; Multiple Sclerosis, 1960; Public Health Education in the South Pacific, 1961; Team Work, 1961; Round the World in Twenty-eight Days, 1961; The Seychelles, 1961; Report on Ghana Medical, Health and Research Services, 1962; History of the Seychelles, 1962; various Colonial Reports on tropical diseases, town planning, water supplies, medical education, colonial administration, etc. *Recreation:* Commonwealth problems and social welfare. *Address:* 3 Stirling Mansions, Canfield Gardens, NW6. *Clubs:* Athenæum, Arts Theatre.

**SEMENOV, Professor Nikolai Nikolaevitch;** Orders of Lenin; State awards; Director, Institute of Chemical Physics of the USSR Academy of Sciences since 1931; Professor, Moscow State University; *b* 16 April 1896; *s* of a state employee; *m* Natalya Nikolaevna Semenova; one *s* one *d. Educ:* Leningrad State University. Chief of Electronic Phenomena Laboratory of Physio-Technical Institute in Leningrad, 1920; Assistant Professor and then Professor, Leningrad Polytechnic Institute, 1920-41. (Jointly) Nobel Prize for Chemistry, 1956. Mem. USSR Academy of Sciences, 1932-; Mem. Chem. Soc. of England, 1949-; Foreign Mem. Roy. Soc., England, 1958-; Mem. Naturalists' Soc., Leopoldina (Halle DDR), 1959; Hon. Fellow: Indian Academy of Sciences, 1959; Hungarian Academy of Sciences, 1961; New York Academy of Sciences, 1962; Roumanian Acad. Sci., 1965; Czechoslovakian Acad. Sci., 1965; Roy. Soc. of Edinburgh, 1966; For. Associate, Nat. Acad. of Sciences (USA), 1963; Corresp. Member: Akademie der Wissenschaften, Berlin, DDR, 1966; Bulgarian Acad. of Sciences, 1969; Hon. DSc: (Oxford), 1960, (Bruxelles), 1962, and (London), 1965; Hon. DrSci: Milan, 1964; Prague, 1965; Budapest, 1965. *Publications:* several textbooks and scientific monographs, notably: Chain reactions, 1934 (Russia), 1935 (Oxford); Some Problems on Chemical Kinetics and Reactivity, 1954 (Russia), enlarged 2nd edn 1958 (Russia), (Eng. trans. 1959). Numerous articles in the field of chemical physics. *Address:* Vorobyevskoye chaussée 2-B, Institute of Chemical Physics, Moscow V-334, USSR.

**SEMON, Dr Henry,** MA, DM, FRCP; retired; consulting dermatologist, Royal Northern and Hampstead General Hospitals; Medical Referee Industrial Dermatitis to Ministry of National Insurance; Vice-President Xth International Congress of Dermatology, London, 1952; *b* 9 March 1881; *e s* of late Sir Felix Semon, KCVO; *m* 1935, Marjorie, *e d* of late Captain C. F. Pilcher. *Educ:* Clifton College; Magdalen Coll., Oxford. Scholarship at University College Hospital, London, WC, 1903; qualified MRCS, LRCP 1906; took first place Indian Medical Service, 1909-10; service in England and France, Sept. 1914 to March 1919, both with Indian and British Troops; Temp. Capt. IMS, RAMC, Med. d'Honneur de la Service publique (French Republic). Pres., Dermatological Section, Royal Society of Medicine, 1941-43. *Publications:* On Diseases of the Skin; The Autobiography of Sir Felix Semon, KCVO, etc. *Recreation:* gardening. *Address:* Little White House, Penn, Bucks. *T:* Penn 2341.

**SEMPER, Dudley Henry;** Puisne Judge, Jamaica, 1954-70, retired; *b* St Kitts, BWI, 14 Nov. 1905; *s* of late D. H. Semper, ISO, and Helen Semper; *m* 1937, Aileen Malone. *Educ:* Antigua Grammar School; West Buckland School, North Devon. Called to Bar, Gray's Inn, 1927; practised at Bar of Leeward Islands, 1928-32; Colonial Service, 1933; Actg District Magistrate, Registrar Supreme Court, St Kitts-Nevis, 1934; District Magistrate, St Kitts-Nevis, 1935; Crown Attorney, St Kitts-Nevis, 1939; Actg Attorney General, Leeward Islands, 1943-44; Resident Magistrate, Jamaica, 1944. *Recreations:* shooting, fishing. *Address:* Bracebridge, Cliff Road, Worlebury, Weston-super-Mare, Somerset. *Club:* Royal Commonwealth Society.

**SEMPILL,** family name of **Lady Sempill** (*née* Forbes-Sempill).

**SEMPILL, Lady** (20th in line, of the Lordship *cr* 1489); **Ann Moira Sempill** (*née* Forbes-Sempill); *b* 19 March 1920; *d* of 19th Lord Sempill, AFC; *S* father, 1965; *m* 1st, 1941, Captain Eric Holt (marr. diss., 1945); one *d*; 2nd, 1948, Lt-Col Stuart Whitemore Chant, OBE, MC (who assumed by decree of Lyon Court, 1966, the additional surname of Sempill), now Chant-Sempill; two *s. Educ:* Austrian, German and English Convents. Served War, 1939-42 (Petty Officer, WRNS). *Heir: s* The Master of Sempill, *qv. Address:* Pibworth House, Aldworth, Berks. *T:* Compton 202; Druminnor Castle, Rhynie, Aberdeenshire.

*See also Hon. Sir Ewan Forbes of Brux, Bt.*

**SEMPILL, Master of; Hon. James William Stuart Whitemore Sempill;** *b* 25 Feb. 1949; *s* and *heir* of Lady Sempill, *qv,* and of Lt-Col Stuart Whitemore Chant-Sempill. *Educ:* The Oratory School; St Clare's Hall, Oxford.

**SEMPLE, Prof. Andrew Best,** CBE 1966; VRD 1953; QHP 1962; Medical Officer of Health, City and Port of Liverpool, and Principal School Medical Officer, also Professor of Public Health, University of Liverpool, since 1953; Hon. Treasurer, Royal Society of Health, 1963; *b* 3 May 1912; *m* 1941, Jean (*née* Sweet); one *d. Educ:* Allan Glen's School, Glasgow; Glasgow Univ. MB, ChB 1934, MD 1947, DPH 1936, Glasgow. Various hospital appointments, 1934-38; Asst MOH and Deputy Medical Superintendent, Infectious Diseases Hosp., Portsmouth, 1938-39; Asst MOH and Asst School Medical Officer, Blackburn, 1939-47 (interrupted by War Service); Senior Asst MOH, Manchester, 1947-48; Deputy MOH, City and Port of Liverpool, 1948-53. Served War of 1939-46; Surgeon Commander, RNVR; Naval MOH, Western Approaches, Malta and Central Mediterranean. Chm., Council, RSH, 1963. *Publications:* various regarding infectious disease, port health, hygiene, etc. *Address:* Kelvin, 433 Woolton Road, Gateacre, Liverpool. *T:* 051-428 2081; Health Department, Hatton Garden, Liverpool 3. *T:* 051-227 3911.

**SEMPLE, John Greenlees,** MA, PhD, MRIA; University Professor of Mathematics, King's College, London, 1936-69, now Emeritus; *b* 10 June 1904; *s* of James Semple, 240 Ravenhill Road, Belfast; *m* 1936, Daphne Caroline, *d* of Professor F. H. Hummel, Queen's University, Belfast; one *s* one *d. Educ:* Royal Belfast Academical Institution; Queen's University, Belfast, MA; St John's College, Cambridge (Philip Bayliss Student); Wrangler b star, Rayleigh Prize, 1929, Fellowship of St John's College, 1931; lecturer Edinburgh University, 1929; Professor of Pure Mathematics at Queen's University, Belfast, 1930-36. *Publications:* (with L. Roth) Introduction to

Algebraic Geometry, 1949; (with G. T. Kneebone) Algebraic Projective Geometry, 1952; Algebraic Curves, 1959; various papers in Cambridge Philosophical Society, London Mathematical Society, Royal Irish Academy, Royal Society, London, etc. *Recreations:* reading, gardening, golf. *Address:* 3 Elm Road, Redhill, Surrey. *T:* Redhill 61142.

**SEMPLE, Professor William Hugh,** MA (Belfast and Manchester), PhD (Cambridge); Professor Emeritus, University of Manchester, since 1967; Governor of John Rylands Library, since 1947; Governor of Sedbergh School, since 1943; Member of Board of Governors of United Manchester Hospitals since 1953, Vice-Chairman, since 1968; *b* 25 Feb. 1900; *s* of late James Semple, Belfast, Northern Ireland; *m* 1932, Hilda Madeline, *d* of late E. H. Wood, Malvern, Worcs; one *s*. *Educ:* Royal Belfast Academical Institution; Queen's University, Belfast; St John's College, Cambridge. Queen's University, Belfast: Assistant in Department of Greek, 1921-22; Senior Assistant in Department of English Literature, 1922-25; Research in Classics, St John's College, Cambridge, 1925-27. University of Reading: Lecturer in Classics, 1927-31; Reader in Latin, 1931-37; Univ. of Manchester, Professor of Latin, 1937-67. *Publications:* various articles in Classical Review; Classical Quarterly; Transactions of Cambridge Philological Soc.; Bulletin of John Rylands Library; Jl of Ecclesiastical History; (with Prof. C. R. Cheney) Selected Letters of Pope Innocent III concerning England. *Recreations:* walking, gardening. *Address:* 3 Linden Road, Didsbury, Manchester 20. *T:* 061-445 2558.

**SEN, Shri Binay Ranjan,** Padmabibhusan 1970; CIE 1944; ICS; Director-General of the United Nations Food and Agriculture Organisation, Rome, 1956-67; *b* 1 Jan. 1898; *s* of Dr K. M. Sen; *m* 1931, Chiroprova Chatterjee. *Educ:* Calcutta and Oxford Universities. Secretary to Govt of Bengal, Political and Appointment Departments, and Press Officer, 1931-34; District Magistrate, Midnapore, 1937-40; Revenue Secretary to Government of Bengal, 1940-43; Director of Civil Evacuation, Bengal, 1942-43; Relief Commissioner, 1942-43; Director-General of Food, Government of India, 1943-46; Sec. to Food Dept, Govt of India, 1946; Minister of the Embassy of India, at Washington, 1947-50; Indian Ambassador to: Italy and Yugoslavia, 1950-51; US and Mexico, 1951-52; Italy and Yugoslavia, 1952-55; Japan, 1955-56. Member Indian Delegation to General Assembly of United Nations, 1947; India's Rep. to United Nations Security Council, 1947; Agriculture Sec. to Govt of India, 1948; Head of Jt Mission of FAO and ECAFE (Economic Commn for Asia and the Far East) in Far East to study Agricultural Development plans; Head of Ind. Deleg. to: ECOSOC (Economic and Social Council of the UN), 1949 and 1953; Annual Conf. of FAO, 1949, and FAO Coun., 1950, 1951, 1953. Hon. Fellow, St Catherine's Coll., Oxford. Several Hon. degrees and decorations, incl. Kt Comdr Piani Ordinis, and Kt Grand Cross Ordinis Sancti Silvetri Papae. *Address:* 14/2 Palm Avenue, Calcutta 19, India.

**SEN, K. Chandra;** late Indian CS; *b* 5 Oct. 1888; *s* of Durgadas Sen and Mokshada Sundari Devi; *m* 1916, Lilavati Das-Gupta; one *s* two *d*. *Educ:* Hindu Sch., Calcutta; Presidency College, Calcutta; Trinity Hall, Cambridge (BA in Moral Sciences Tripos, 1913). Joined Indian Civil Service, 1913; Assistant Collector, Bombay Presidency, 1913-21; service in Judicial department of Government of Bombay since 1921; acted as a puisne judge of Bombay High Court, various times 1934-38; Secretary to Government of Bombay, Legal Department and Remembrancer of Legal Affairs, 1935-37; Additional Judge of High Court, 1939-41; Judge, High Court of Bombay, 1941-48; Pres. Industrial Court, Bombay, 1948-53; Pres. Bombay Co-op, Revenue, and Sales Tax Tribunals, between 1953 and 1959; Constitutional Adviser to Govt of West Bengal and Chm., State Law Commn, 1959-64; Chm., Police Commn, W Bengal, and Mem. Hindu Religious Endowments Commn, 1960-62. *Address:* 12-A, Mafatlal Park, Bombay 26, India. *T:* 36-4368. *Club:* Willingdon (Bombay).

**SENANAYAKE, Hon. Dudley Shelton;** Prime Minister, Minister of Defence and External Affairs of Ceylon, 1965-70; also Minister of Planning and Economic Affairs, and Minister of Information and Broadcasting, to 1970; President of the United National Party, Ceylon; Barrister-at-Law and Advocate; *b* 19 June 1911; *s* of late Right Honourable Don Stephen Senanayake, Prime Minister of Ceylon, and late Emily Maud Senanayake; unmarried. *Educ:* St Thomas' College, Mt Lavinia, Ceylon; Corpus Christi College, Cambridge. Elected to State Council under Donoughmore Constitution to represent Dedigama Constituency, 1936; Minister of Agriculture and Lands in Ceylon's first Cabinet after grant of Independence, 1947; Prime Minister and Minister of Defence and External Affairs, 1952-53; Prime Minister, March-April 1960. MA (Cantab); Fellow, Corpus Christi College, Cambridge. *Recreations:* golf, photography. *Address:* Woodlands, D. S. Senanayake Mawatha, Colombo 8, Ceylon. *T:* 95605.

**SENDALL, Bernard Charles,** CBE 1952; Deputy Director-General, Independent Television Authority, since 1955; *b* 30 April 1913; *s* of late William Sendall, Malvern, Worcestershire; *m* 1963, Barbara Mary, *d* of late Ambrose Coviello, DCM, FRCM. *Educ:* Magdalen College, Oxford; Harvard University. Entered Civil Service in the Admiralty, 1935; Principal Private Secretary to Minister of Information 1941-45; Controller (Home), Central Office of Information, 1946-49; Controller, Festival of Britain Office, 1949-51; Assistant Secretary, Admiralty, 1951-55. *Address:* 50 Farley Court, Allsop Place, NW1. *T:* 01-486 4030.

**SENDER, Ramòn Josè;** Medal of Morocco, 1924; Spanish Military Cross of Merit, 1924; Writer; *b* 1902; *s* of Josè Sender and Andrea Garcès Sender; *m* 1st, 1934, Amparo Barayòn (*d* 1936); one *s* one *d*; 2nd, 1943, Florence Hall (marriage dissolved, 1963). *Educ:* Colegio de la Sagrada Familia, Reus (Catalonia); Inst. de Zaragoza; Inst. de Teruel; Univ. of Madrid. Infantry Officer, Morocco, 1923-24; Editor El Sol, Madrid, 1924-31; free-lance writer, 1931-36. Major on General Staff, Spanish Republican Army, 1936-39. Prof. Spanish Lit., Amherst Coll., Mass, 1943-44; Denver Univ., 1944; Prof. of Spanish Lit., Univ. of New Mexico, 1947 (Emer. 1963). Mem. Bd of Advs, Hispanic Soc. of America; Spanish Nat. Prize of Lit., 1935; Guggenheim Fell., 1942. Speaking tour as rep. Spanish Republic, 1938; member: Ateneo governing board, sec. Ibero-American section, 1926-34; Nat. Council of Culture, Spain, 1936-39; Alliance of Intellectuals for Defense of Democracy, Spain, 1936-39. Visiting Prof., Ohio State Univ., summer 1951; Writers' Workshop, Inter Amer. Univ., San Germàn, Puerto Rico, summer 1961; Vis. Prof., Univ. of Calif in Los Angeles, semester II, 1961-62; Prof., Univ. of S Calif in Los Angeles, 1964. Life FIAL, Switzerland. *Publications:* Pro Patria, 1934;

Seven Red Sundays, 1935; Mr Witt among the Rebels, 1936; Counter-Attack in Spain, 1938; A Man's Place, 1940; Dark Wedding, 1943; Chronicle of Dawn, 1944; The King and the Queen, 1948; The Sphere, 1949; The Affable Hangman, 1954; Before Noon, 1957; Requiem for a Spanish Peasant, 1960; The Exemplary Novels of Cibola, 1963; contrib. to literary and popular journals. *Recreations:* chess, tennis. *Address:* American Literary Agency, 11 Riverside Drive, New York, NY 10023, USA.

**SENIOR, Sir Edward (Walters),** Kt 1970; CMG 1955; Chairman, Ransome Hoffman Pollard Ltd; Deputy Chairman, Tarmac Derby Ltd; *b* 29 March 1902; *s* of Albert Senior; *m* 1928, Stephanie Vera Heald; one *s* one *d. Educ:* Repton School; Sheffield University. Managing Director, George Senior & Sons Ltd, 1929; Vice-Consul for Sweden, in Sheffield, 1930; RA, TA, Major, 1938; General Director of Alloy and Special Steels, Iron and Steel Control, 1941; Director, Steel Division of Raw Materials Mission, Washington, DC, 1942; Controller of Ball and Roller Bearings, 1944; British Iron and Steel Federation: Commercial Dir, 1949-61; Dir, 1961-62; Dir-Gen., 1962-66; retd, Dec. 1966. Master of Cutlers' Company of Hallamshire in County of York, 1947; Vice-President of the Sheffield Chamber of Commerce, 1948; Chairman of Steel Re-Armament Panel, 1951. JP Sheffield, 1937-50. *Recreations:* normal country activities. *Address:* Beech Oast Grange, Wadhurst, Sussex. *T:* Wadhurst 2449. *Clubs:* United Service; Sheffield (Sheffield).

**SENIOR, Ronald Henry,** DSO 1940, Bar 1943; TD; A Deputy Chairman, Cunard Steam Ship Co.; *b* 3 July 1904; *e s* of Lawrence Henry Senior and Emmadonna Shuttleworth, *d* of Reverend J. S. Holden, Aston-on-Trent, Derbyshire; *m* 1932, Hon. Norah Marguerite Joicey, *e d* of 2nd Baron Joicey; two *d. Educ:* Cheltenham College. Chairman, Nat. Assoc. of Port Employers, 1954-59. Joined TA 1924; served France, 1940; Middle East; Sicily, NW Europe. Hon. Rank Brigadier. *Recreations:* golf, shooting. *Address:* 110 Eaton Square, SW1. *Club:* Carlton.

**SENIOR, William Hirst,** CB 1964; Deputy Secretary (Agriculture), Dept of Agriculture and Fisheries for Scotland, 1958-66; *b* 24 August 1904; *o s* of Capt. Arthur Senior, Batley, Yorks; *m* 1930, Olive Kathleen, *e d* of William Henry Killick, Shawford, Hampshire; two *s* three *d. Educ:* Bradford Grammar School; Reading University. BSc London 1926; MSc Reading 1929. Research Scholar, Reading Univ., 1926-28. Joined Dept of Agriculture for Scotland, 1929; Advisory Officer on Farm Economics, 1933; Principal, 1941; Secretary of Balfour of Burleigh Cttee on Hill Sheep Farming in Scotland, 1941-44; Asst Secretary, 1946; FRSE 1947; Under-Secretary, 1958. Mem., Agricultural Research Council, 1959-66. Chairman, Scottish Agricultural Improvement Council, 1960-66; Mem., Small Industries Council for Scotland. *Recreations:* varied. *Address:* Manse Wood, Innerwick, Dunbar, East Lothian. *Club:* Royal Commonwealth Society.

**SENSI, Most Rev. Dr Giuseppe M.;** Nuncio Apostolic to Portugal, since 1967; *b* 27 May 1907. Ordained, 1929; Sec. of Apostolic Nunciature in Roumania, 1934-38; Secretary and Auditor of Apostolic Nunciature in Switzerland, 1938-46; Councillor of Apostolic Nunciature in Belgium, 1946-47; Chargé d'Affaires of the Holy See in Prague, 1948-49; Councillor in the Secretariat of State of His Holiness, 1949-53; Permanent Observer of the Holy See at UNESCO in Paris, 1953-55; apptd Nuncio Apostolic to Costa Rica, May 1955, and consecrated Titular Archbishop of Sardi, July, 1955; Apostolic Delegate to Jerusalem, 1957; Apostolic Nuncio to Ireland, 1962-67. *Address:* Apostolic Nunciature, 18 Avenida Bivar, Lisbon, Portugal.

**SEOUL, (Korea), Bishop of,** since 1965; **Rt. Rev. Paul Chun Hwan Lee;** *b* 5 April 1922; unmarried. *Educ:* St Michael's Theological Seminary, Seoul; St Augustine's College, Canterbury. Deacon, 1952 (Pusan Parish); Priest, 1953 (Sangju and Choungju Parish). Director of Yonsei University, Seoul, 1960-; Chairman: Christian Council of Korea, 1966-67; Christian Literature Soc. of Korea, 1968-; Vice-Pres., Korean Bible Soc., 1969-. *Recreation:* reading. *Address:* 3 Chong Dong, Seoul, Korea (CPO Box 5129, Seoul, Korea). *T:* 75-6157. *Club:* Seoul Rotary (Seoul).

**SEPHTON, Ven. Arthur;** Archdeacon of Craven since 1956; *b* 25 March 1894; *s* of Thomas G. and Laura Sephton, Newport Pagnell; *m* 1924, Unita Catherine, *d* of E. Brookhouse Richards, JP; one *d. Educ:* Christ Church, Oxford (MA); Cuddesdon Theological College. Assistant Curate: St Mary Redcliffe, Bristol, 1921; St John, Hove, 1924; Christ Church, Harrogate, 1928; Vicar: Holmfirth, Yorks, 1929; Kirkburton, Yorks, 1933; Rector and Rural Dean of Skipton, 1943-64; Hon. Canon of Bradford, 1944. Proctor in Convocation, 1945-56. *Recreations:* golf and walking. *Address:* 17 Riversway, Gargrave, Skipton, Yorks. *T:* Gargrave 266.

**SERBY, John Edward,** CB 1958; CBE 1951; FRAeS; Consultant; *b* 15 March 1902; *m* 1933, Clarice Lilian (*née* Hawes); one *d. Educ:* Haberdashers' Aske's School; Emmanuel College, Cambridge (BA). Junior Scientific Officer, Admiralty, 1927-30; Scientific Officer, RAE, 1930-38; Headquarters, MAP, 1938-50; Deputy Director, Royal Aircraft Establishment, Farnborough, 1950-54; Dir-Gen. of Guided Weapons, Min. of Aviation, 1954-61. Dep. Controller Guided Weapons, Ministry of Aviation, 1961-63. *Recreation:* gardening. *Address:* Overwey, Bishopsmead, Farnham, Surrey. *T:* Farnham 3526.

**SERENA, Clara;** dramatic contralto vocalist; *b* near Adelaide, South Australia; *m* Roy Mellish, conductor and accompanist; no *c. Educ:* Elder Conservatorium of Music, Adelaide; Elder Scholar at Royal College of Music, London (ARCM); Germany and Italy. Debut in London, 1923; in January, 1924, created the title-rôle in Alkestis (Rutland Boughton) at Covent Garden; appeared in Vienna, Berlin, and Paris in 1926; sang at Royal Opera, Covent Garden, 1927, in Rheingold and Götterdämmerung, and in 1928 as Amneris in Aïda; also appeared on several occasions as Guest Artist with British National Opera Company in Samson et Dalila and Aïda; Sang the rôle of Solomon in the Royal Philharmonic Society's production of Handel's Solomon, at Queen's Hall, conducted by Sir Thomas Beecham, 1928, in the presence of the King and Queen; has sung at principal concerts Gt Britain, India and the East. *Recreations:* riding and lawn tennis. *Address:* c/o National Bank of Australasia, Ltd, 26 King William Street, Adelaide, South Australia.

**SERGEANT, Maj.-Gen. Frederick Cavendish, H.;** *see* Hilton-Sergeant.

**SERGENT, René Edmond,** Officier de la Légion d'Honneur, 1952; Président, Groupement des Industries de la Construction Electrique, since 1969; Societé Bancaire de Paris, since 1970; *b* 16 January 1904; *s* of Charles Sergent and

Emma Duvernet; *m* 1931, Monique Schweisguth; three *s* three *d. Educ:* Lycée Janson-de-Sailly, Paris, France; Ecole Polytechnique. Sub-Lieut, Artillery, 1925; Assistant, Inspection Générale des Finances, 1929; Financial Controller, Nat. Socs of Aeronautical Construction, 1937; Direction du Commerce Extérieur, 1940; Pres., French Economic and Financial Deleg. to Control Commission, Berlin, 1945; Financial Attaché, French Embassy, London, 1947; Asst Sec.-Gen. for Economics and Finance, NATO, 1952; Secretary-Gen. of OEEC, Paris, 1955; Vice-Prés. Délégué, Syndicat Général de la Construction Électrique, 1960. *Address:* 1 Boulevard de Beauséjour, Paris XVIe, France. *T:* Auteuil 3031.

**SERJEANT, Robert Bertram;** Sir Thomas Adams's Professor of Arabic since 1970, and Director, Middle East Centre, since 1965, University of Cambridge; *b* 23 March 1915; *er s* of R. T. R. and A. B. Serjeant; *m* Marion Keith Serjeant (*née* Robertson), MB, ChB; one *s* one *d. Educ:* Edinburgh; Trinity Coll., Cambridge. Vans Dunlop Schol. 1935; Visit to Syria, 1935; MA 1st Cl. Hons Semitic Langs, Edinburgh Univ., 1936; PhD Cambridge 1939; Tweedie Fellow Edinburgh, 1939; Studentship, SOAS, for research in S Arabia, 1940; Governor's Commn in Aden Prot. G Guards, 1940-41. Attached Mission 106. Lectr, SOAS, 1941; Seconded to BBC Eastern Service, 1942; Editor, Arabic Listener, 1943-45; Min. of Inf., Editor Arabic pubns, 1944. Colonial Research Fell., in Hadramawt, 1947-48; Reader in Arabic, 1948; Research in S Arabia and Persian Gulf, 1953-54; in N Nigeria, Minister of Education's mission to examine instruction in Arabic, 1956; Sec. of State for Colonies' mission to examine Muslim Education in E Africa, 1957; Inter-University Council's Advisory Delegation on University of N Nigeria, 1961; Research in Trucial States, Yemen, Aden, 1963-64 and 1966; Professor of Arabic, 1955-64, Middle East Department, SOAS, University of London; Lectr in Islamic History, ME Centre, Univ. of Cambridge, 1964-66, Reader in Arabic Studies, 1966-70. Mem., ME Comd Expedition to Socotra, 1967. *Publications:* Cat. Arabic, Persian & Hindustani MSS in New College, Edinburgh, 1942; Materials for a History of Islamic Textiles, 1942-51; Prose and Poetry from Hadramawt, I, 1950; Saiyids of Hadramawt, 1957; Portuguese off the South Arabian Coast, 1961. Articles in BSOAS, JRAS, Le Muséon, Rivista d. Studi Orientali, Islamic Culture, etc. *Address:* Faculty of Oriental Studies, Sidgwick Avenue, Cambridge. *Clubs:* Royal Central Asian Society, Royal Asiatic Society.

**SERKIN, Rudolf,** Presidential Medal of Freedom, 1963; Director, Curtis Institute of Music, Philadelphia, Pa, since 1968, Head of Piano Department, 1939; *b* 28 March 1903; *s* of Mordko Serkin and Augusta Schargel; *m* 1935, Irene Busch; two *s* four *d. Educ:* Vienna, Austria. Concert Pianist: Début, Vienna, 1915; USA since 1933; New York Philharmonic with Arturo Toscanini, 1935. President of Marlboro School of Music, Marlboro, Vermont. Mem., Nat. Council on the Arts, USA. Dr *hc*: Curtis Inst., Philadelphia; Temple Univ., Philadelphia; Univ. of Vermont; Williams Coll., Williamstown, Mass; Oberlin Coll. *Address:* RFD 3, Brattleboro, Vermont, USA.

**SEROTA,** family name of **Baroness Serota.**

**SEROTA, Baroness,** *cr* 1967 (Life Peer), of Hampstead in Greater London; **Beatrice Serota,** JP; *b* 15 Oct. 1919; *m* 1942, Stanley Serota, BSc (Eng), FICE; one *s* one *d. Educ:* LCC elementary schools; John Howard School; London School of Economics (BSc (Econ)). Ministry of Fuel and Power, 1941-46. Member: Hampstead Borough Council, 1945-49; LCC for Brixton (Lambeth), 1954-65 (Chm., Children's Cttee, 1958-65); GLC for Lambeth, 1964-67 (Chief Whip, Vice-Chm. ILEC). Baroness in Waiting, 1968-69; Minister of State (Health), Dept of Health and Social Security, 1969-70. Chm., Health Education Council, 1967-68; Member: Adv. Council in Child Care, and Central Training Council in Child Care, 1958-68; Labour Party Youth Commn, 1959; Adv. Council on Treatment of Offenders, 1960-64; Longford Cttee on "Crime–a Challenge to us all", 1964; Royal Commn on Penal System, 1964-66; Latey Cttee on Age of Majority, 1965-67; Adv. Missions (Colonial Office) on Treatment of Offenders to Pacific Territories, Bahamas and British Honduras, 1966; Adv. Council on Penal System, 1966-68; Seebohm Cttee on Organization of Local Authority Personal Social Services, 1966-68. JP Inner London (West Central Division). Peerage conferred for services to children. *Recreations:* dressmaking, gardening, collecting shells. *Address:* 78 Fitzjohns Avenue, Hampstead, NW3. *T:* 01-435 3207.

**SERPELL, Sir David Radford,** KCB 1968 (CB 1962); CMG 1952; OBE 1944; Permanent Secretary, Department of the Environment, since Oct. 1970; *b* 10 Nov. 1911; 2nd *s* of Charles Robert and Elsie Leila Serpell, Plymouth; *m*; three *s. Educ:* Plymouth Coll.; Exeter Coll., Oxford; Univ. of Toulouse (DèsL); Syracuse University, USA; Fletcher School of Law and Diplomacy, USA. (Fell.) Imp. Economic Cttee, 1937-39; Ministry of Food, 1939-42; Ministry of Fuel and Power, 1942-45; HM Treasury, 1945 (Under-Secretary, 1954-60); Dep. Sec. Min. of Transport, 1960-63; Second Secretary, Board of Trade, 1963-66; Second Permanent Secretary, 1966-68; Second Secretary, Treasury, 1968; Permanent Secretary, Min. of Transport, 1968-70. Private Secretary to Parly Sec., Ministry of Food, 1941-42; Principal Private Secretary to Minister of Fuel and Power, 1942-45. *Recreations:* fishing, golf. *Address:* Dolphin Cottage, Lamberhurst, Kent. *T:* Lamberhurst 422. *Club:* United University.

**SERVAES, Vice-Adm. Reginald Maxwell,** CB 1947; CBE 1940; *b* 25 July 1893; *s* of late J. M. Servaes; *m* 1st, 1919, Hilda Edith Johnson (*d* 1956); one *s*; 2nd, 1959, Mansel, *widow* of H. V. Bond. *Educ:* Royal Naval Colleges, Osborne and Dartmouth. Sub-Lieutenant, 1914; Lieut, 1915; European War, served in HM ships Exe, Comus and Phaeton; specialised in Gunnery, 1917; RN Staff College, 1922-23; Commander, 1928; Captain, 1935; HMS Resource, 1937; Dir of Local Defence, Admiralty, 1938-40; HMS London, 1940-42; an Assistant Chief of Naval Staff, 1943-45; ADC to King George VI, 1944-45; Rear-Adm. 1945; Rear-Admiral Commanding Second Cruiser Squadron, British Pacific Fleet, 1945-46; Flag Officer Commanding Reserve Fleet, 1947-48; retired list, 1948, Vice-Admiral. *Address:* Crocker Hill House, near Chichester, Sussex. *T:* Halnaker 220.

**SERVAN-SCHREIBER, Jean-Jacques;** economist, author and journalist; Deputy for Lorraine, French National Assembly; since 1970; Secretary-General, Parti-Radical Socialiste, France, since 1969; President, Groupe-Express (parent company of Presse-Union, Liste-Union, Société Didot-Bottin, publishing the magazines L'Express, L'Expansion, Le Management and all the annuaires in France); *b* Paris, 13 Feb. 1924; *s* of late Emile Servan-Schreiber, journalist, and of Denise Bressard; *m* 1960, Sabine de Fouquières; four *s*. *Educ:* Lycée Janson-de-Sailly, Paris; Lycée de Grenoble; Ecole Polytechnique. Served as fighter pilot, Free French Air Force, World War II. Diplomatic Editor of Le Monde, 1948-53; Founder and Director of weekly news-magazine, L'Express, 1953-69. Pres. (Founder) Fedn-nationale des anciens d'Algérie, 1958-65. Holds military cross for valour. *Publications:* Lieutenant en Algérie, 1957 (Lieutenant in Algeria, 1957); Le défi américain, 1967 (The American Challenge, 1968); Le réveil de la France, 1968 (The Spirit of May, 1968); Le Manifeste, 1970 (The Radical Manifesto, 1970). *Address:* 25 rue de Berri, Paris 8e, France.

**SESHADRI, Prof. Tiruvenkata Rajendra,** MA; PhD; DSc (*hc*); FRS 1960 (London); Padmabhushan, 1963 (India); Emeritus Professor, Department of Chemistry, University of Delhi, since 1965; *b* 3 Feb. 1900; *s* of R. T. and N. Iyengar; *m* 1924, Kamala; three *d*. *Educ:* Srirangam, Tiruchi, Madras; Manchester; London; Edinburgh. Chemist, Agricultural Research Inst., Coimbatore, 1930-33; Reader and later Prof. and Head of Chem. Dept, Andhra Univ., Waltair, 1933-49; Prof. and Head of the Chem. Dept, Delhi Univ., 1949-65. Mem., German Acad., 1961. *Publications:* The Chemistry of Vitamins and Hormones (Andhra University, Waltair), 1st edn, 1946, 2nd edn, 1951; over 800 papers in chemical jls in India and Gt Britain. *Address:* Department of Chemistry, Delhi University, Delhi 7, India. *T:* 228348.

**SETCHELL, Herbert Leonard,** CBE 1946; *b* 4 June 1892; *m* 1920, Winifred Susan, *d* of late W. Parkinson Bennett, JP, late of Bothe Hall, Sawley, Derby; two *s*. *Educ:* Bancroft Sch., Woodford; King's Coll., London. European War, 1914-18, Lt in 3rd Essex Regt; attached 2nd Essex Regt in France (Wounded); Intelligence Officer in Dept of Overseas Trade, 1918-26; HM Trade Commissioner for Victoria and South Australia, 1926-34; Commercial Secretary at HM Legation, Berne, 1934-41; Commercial Counsellor HM Embassy, Madrid, 1941-44. Commercial Counsellor HM Embassy, Stockholm, 1944-49; Minister (Commercial) as UK Commercial Representative, Cologne, 1949-52; retired July 1952. *Recreations:* yachting, golf, ski-ing. *Address:* 51 Kennedy Rise, Walesby, Newark, Notts. *T:* New Ollerton 437. *Club:* Devonshire.

**SETH, Prof. George;** Professor of Psychology (1958), Head of Department of Psychology (1946), The Queen's University, Belfast; *b* 23 April 1905; *s* of George Seth and Jane Steven Loudon; *m* 1936, May, *er d* of John Dods, Edinburgh, and Lily Anderson; three *s* one *d*. *Educ:* Royal High School and University of Edinburgh. MA (Edin.) 1928; BEd (Edin.) 1930; PhD (Edin.) 1933. Assistant in Psychology, Edinburgh University and University Psychological Clinic, 1930-34; Research Fellow, Yale Univ., USA, 1934-35; Lecturer in Education, University College, Cardiff, and Psychologist, Cardiff Child Guidance Clinic, 1935-46; Senior Psychologist, Welsh Board of Health, (Evacuation Service), 1941-45. Vans Dunlop Scholar (Psychology), Edinburgh, 1930-33; Rockefeller Fellow, USA, 1935-36. Fellow, British Psychological Soc., President, 1967, Vice-Pres., 1968; President, Psychology Section, British Association, 1961. *Publications:* (with Douglas Guthrie) Speech in Childhood, 1934; articles in various psychological and educational jls. *Address:* Queen's University, Belfast, N Ireland.

**SETON, Lady, (Alice Ida),** CBE 1949; Group Officer, WRAF, retired; *d* of late P. C. Hodge, Port Elizabeth, South Africa; *m* 1923, Capt. Sir John Hastings Seton, 10th Bt (from whom she obtained a divorce, 1950); one *s* (*see* Sir Robert Seton, 11th Bt) one *d*. *Educ:* private tuition in S Africa and England. Joined WAAF as Assistant Section Officer, 1939. *Address:* 6 Barnwell, Peterborough, Northants.

**SETON, Anya (Anya Seton Chase);** Author; *b* as British subject, New York City, USA; *d* of late Ernest Thompson Seton and late Grace Gallatin Thompson Seton. *Educ:* Spence Sch., NY; private tutors in England. *Publications:* (in USA, England and 8 foreign countries) My Theodosia, 1941; Dragonwyck, 1944; The Turquoise, 1946; The Hearth and Eagle, 1948; Foxfire, 1951; Katherine, 1954; The Mistletoe and Sword (Juvenile), 1956; The Winthrop Woman, 1958; Washington Irving (Juvenile), 1960; Devil Water, 1962; Avalon, 1966. *Recreations:* swimming, croquet, bridge, cooking. *Address:* Binney Lane, Old Greenwich, Conn 06870, USA. *Clubs:* (Hon.) Pen and Brush (New York); PEN.

**SETON, Sir Bruce;** *see* Seton, Sir C. B.

**SETON, Sir (Christopher) Bruce,** 12th Bt *cr* 1663, of Abercorn; farmer; *b* 3 Oct. 1909; *s* of Charles Henry Seton (*d* 1917), and of Mrs V. A. Neilson, Greys, Kelvedon, Essex; *S* cousin, 1969; *m* 1939, Joyce Vivian, *e d* of late O. G. Barnard, Stowmarket; two *s* two *d*. *Educ:* Marlborough; Univ. of Cambridge (BA Agric. 1931). Farming since 1931. *Heir: s* Iain Bruce Seton [*b* 27 Aug. 1942; *m* 1963, Margaret Ann, *o d* of Walter Charles Faulkner; one *s*]. *Address:* Ballast Quay Farm, Fingringhoe, Colchester, Essex. *T:* Rowhedge 335.

**SETON, Sir Claud Ramsay Wilmot,** Kt, *cr* 1944; MC; *b* 1888; *e s* of Rev. Andrew Ramsay Wilmot Seton and Emily Georgina, *e d* of Rev. George Edmund Walker; *m* 1933, Mary Eleanor (*d* 1965), *yr d* of Sir Francis Bennett; no *c*. *Educ:* Framlingham Coll.; Laleham, Margate; University College, London. Solicitor, 1910; Member of firm of Shelton and Co. London and Wolverhampton until outbreak of War; served European War, 1914-20 (wounded, despatches twice, MC); President of District Court, Jaffa, Palestine, 1920-26; Judicial Adviser Transjordan, 1926-31 (Order of Istiqlal second class); President District Court of Haifa, Palestine, 1931-35; Puisne Judge, Jamaica, 1935-41; Chief Justice, Nyasaland, 1941-45; Chief Justice of Fiji and Chief Judicial Commissioner for the Western Pacific, 1945-49; retired from Colonial Service, 1950. Various part-time appointments in Kenya, 1950-60. Called to Bar, Gray's Inn, 1928. *Publication:* Legislation of Transjordan, 1918-30. *Address:* 15 Eaton Mansions, Cliveden Place, SW1. *T:* 01-730 5807.

**SETON, Lady, (Julia);** (Julia Clements, professionally); author, speaker, international floral art judge; flower arrangement judge for RHS and National Association of Flower Arrangement Societies; *b* 10 April 1906; *d* of late Frank Clements; *m* 1962, Sir Alexander Hay Seton, 10th Bt, of Abercorn (*d* 1963); no *c*. *Educ:* Isle of Wight; Zwicker College, Belgium. Organised and conducted first Judges' School in England at Royal Horticultural Society Halls; has since conducted many other courses for judges all over Britain. *Publications:* Fun with Flowers; Fun without Flowers; 101 Ideas for Flower Arrangement; Party Pieces; First Steps with Flowers; The Julia Clements Colour Book of Flower Arrangements; Flower Arrangements in Stately Homes; Julia Clements' Gift Book of Flower Arranging, etc. *Address:* 122 Swan Court, SW3. *T:* 01-352 9039. *Clubs:* Women's Press, Anglo-Belge.

**SETON, Sir Robert (James),** 11th Bt, *cr* 1683; *b* 20 April 1926; *s* of Captain Sir John Hastings Seton, 10th Bt and Alice (*see* Lady Seton), *d* of Percy Hodge, Cape Civil Service; *S* father 1956; unmarried. *Educ:* HMS Worcester (Thames Nautical Training College). Midshipman RNVR (invalided), 1943-44. Banker, with Hong Kong and Shanghai Banking Corpn, 1946-61 (retd). *Heir: kinsman* Christall Dougal Seton [*b* 24 Sept. 1883; *m* 1909, Sara Moore; three *s* one *d*]. *Address:* 35 Collingham Road, SW5. *Club:* Tanglin (Singapore).

**SETON PRINGLE, John;** *see* Pringle, J. S. M.

**SETON-WATSON, Prof. George Hugh Nicholas,** FBA 1969; Professor of Russian History, School of Slavonic and East European Studies, University of London, since 1951; *b* 15 Feb. 1916; *er s* of late Prof. Robert William Seton-Watson and late Mrs Seton-Watson; *m* 1947, Mary Hope, *d* of G. D. Rokeling, lately of Ministry of Education; three *d*. *Educ:* Winchester; New College, Oxford. Was attached to British Legations in Roumania and Yugoslavia, 1940-41; served Special Forces GHQ, Middle East, 1941-44. Fellow and Praelector in Politics, University Coll., Oxford, 1946-51. Mem. Council, RIIA, 1952. Vis. Prof., Columbia Univ., 1957-58; Fell., Center for Advanced Study in the Behavioural Sciences, Stanford, Calif., 1963-64; Vis. Fell., Austr. Nat. Univ., Canberra, 1964. *Publications:* Eastern Europe between the Wars, 1945; The East European Revolution, 1950; The Decline of Imperial Russia, 1952; The Pattern of Communist Revolution, 1953; Neither War Nor Peace, 1960; The New Imperialism, 1961; Nationalism and Communism (Essays, 1946-63); The Russian Empire, 1801-1917, 1967. *Recreations:* travel, ornithology. *Address:* 8 Burghley Road, Wimbledon Common, SW19. *T:* 01-946 0861. *Club:* Athenæum.

**SETTLE, Alison,** OBE 1961; *m* A. Towers Settle, barrister-at-law; one *s* one *d*. Formerly Editor of Vogue; for 22 years fashion editor of The Observer and Fashion Consultant to leading firms; regular contributor to The Lady. Member of Council of Industrial Design, 1953-58; Silver Medallist, RSA. Pres. Women's Press Club, 1952-54. *Publications:* Clothes Line, 1937 (republished 1941); English Fashion (Britain in Pictures Series), 1948; Fashion as a Career, 1963. *Address:* 6 Church Street, Steyning, Sussex.

**SETTLE, Charles Arthur,** QC 1960; *b* 26 April 1905; *s* of Theodore Settle; *m* 1st, 1936, Pamela (*d* 1938), *d* of F. N. Marcy; one *d*; 2nd, 1947, Jane Anne, *d* of Huw Jones. *Educ:* Marlborough College; Trinity College, Cambridge. Called to Bar by Middle Temple, 1928; Master of Bench, 1966. Served War of 1939-45 (despatches, 1944). Vice-Chm., Bar Council, 1968-70. *Recreation:* fishing. *Address:* 3 Thurloe Close, SW7. *T:* 01-589 8932. *Clubs:* St James', Flyfishers'.

**SETTRINGTON, Lord; Charles Henry Gordon-Lennox;** *b* 8 Jan. 1955; *s* and *heir* of Earl of March and Kinrara, *qv*.

**SEUFFERT, Stanislaus,** QC 1965; Special Divorce Commissioner, since 1967; Barrister-at-Law; *b* Johannesburg, 17 May 1899; *e s* of late Philip Seuffert and Marie Winefride Seuffert (*née* Brennan); *m* 1st, Alice, *widow* of George Jackson (*née* McCarthy); 2nd, Norma (*née* Klerck), *widow* of Maj.-Gen. Pienaar, CB, DSO; one *s* one *d*. *Educ:* Marist Brothers, Johannesburg; Stonyhurst Coll., Lancashire. Served World War, Middx Regt, 1917. Barrister, Middle Temple, 1925, Bencher, 1970. First Chm., Guild of Catholic Artists, 1929; Chm. Catholic Prisoners' Aid Soc., 1938-60; Hon. Treas. and Sec., Soc. of Our Lady of Good Counsel, 1935-58. Contested (Lab) East Grinstead, 1935; Borough Councillor, Fulham, 1934-49; Dep. Civil Def. Controller, Fulham, and Leader of Council, 1939-44; Chm. Fulham Food Control Committee, 1939-46; Mayor of Fulham 1944-45. Knight Commander of Order of Holy Sepulchre of Jerusalem, 1955; Kt of Order of St Gregory (Papal), 1962. *Publications:* annotations: Matrimonial Causes Act, 1937; Local Govt Act, 1949; Adoption Act, 1950. Handbook of Matrimonial Causes. *Recreations:* playgoing, reading. *Address:* Lamb Building, Temple, EC4. *T:* 01-353 0774; Orchard End, Yester Park, Chislehurst, Kent. *T:* 01-467 1435. *Clubs:* Garrick; Norfolk (Norwich).

**SEVERN, David;** *see* Unwin, David Storr.

**SEVERSKY, Major Alexander P. de;** aeronautical consultant (USA); *b* Tiflis, Russia, 7 June 1894; *s* of Nicholas de Seversky and Vera (*née* Vasilieff); *m* 1925, Evelyn Olliphant. Grad. Imperial Naval Acad. of Russia, 1914; post Grad. student, Mil. Sch. Aeronautics, Russia. Served Russian Naval Air Service; lost right leg, 1915; returned to Air Service; Insp.-Gen. and Officer i/c Aircraft Prod. for Navy, Petrograd, 1915-16; Comdr Bombing Sqdn, Baltic Sea, 1916, later Chief of Pursuit Aviation. Came to US, 1918 (naturalized, 1927). Apptd Vice-Chm. Russian Naval Aviation Mission to US; Asst to Naval Attaché, Russian Embassy, Washington, in charge of aviation matters, 1918; when office closed, offered services to US; US Govt aeronautical engr test pilot, Inspr etc; Cons. Engr US Air Service, 1921. Founder, Pres., Gen. Man., and Dir: Seversky Aero Corp., 1922-35; Seversky Aircraft Corp. (now Republic Aviation Corp.), 1931-39; Dir, Republic Aviation Corp., 1939-40; Consultant, Chrysler Corp., 1933; Founder, Aviation Development Corp., 1940; Founder and Pres., Rotoflight Corp., 1940; Special Consultant Sec. of War, 1945; personal rep. Sec. of War at atom bomb tests, Bikini, 1946. Invented and designed bombsight, 1921; universal landing gear for sea-planes (Naval Prize), 1916; first fully automatic synchronous bombsight (purchased by US and Brit. Govts), 1921; designed and built all-metal amphibious aircraft, etc. World's record for amphibians (230.03 mph), Detroit, 1935, etc. Has won many trophies. FRSA. Mem. numerous societies and associations. Holds hon. doctorates in science. Hon. Member: Air Force Assoc., Air Forces of the Republics of Argentina, Chile, and Uruguay. Knight of St George (Russia); Medal for Merit (US), 1946; Medal d'officier d'Académie et de l'Instruction Publique (France), 1947; Officer of Legion of Honour (Fr.), 1948; Cross of Lorraine (Fr.), 1951. *Publications:* Victory Through Air Power, 1942 (also Walt Disney-Seversky adaptation for screen, 1943); Air Power: Key to Survival, 1950; America, Too Young to Die!, 1961. Contrib. United Press, 1941-43; McNaught Syndicate column on air power, 1943-44; King Features, 1950; articles to Amer. Mercury, Cosmopolitan, Reader's Digest, etc. *Address:* (home) Asharoken Beach, Northport, LI, USA; (office) 30 Rockefeller Plaza, New York 20, NY, USA. *Clubs:* Adventurers, Circus Saints and Sinners, Engineers, National Press, Wings.

**SEWARD, Sir Eric (John),** KBE 1960 (CBE 1954); Chairman: La Forestal, Argentina, SA, since 1957; Compania Financiera de Londres, since 1961; Quebrachales Fusionados Sociedad Anonima, 1964; Londres y Rio de la Plata, Cia Argentina de Seguros; Director: Las Cabezas Estancia Co. Ltd; Mellor Goodwin SAC; Richard Thomas & Baldwins (Argentina), SA; La Republica, SA; La Cantabrica, SA; *b* 18 May 1899; *s* of William Edwards Seward and Florence Lloyd; *m* 1924, Ella Maud, *d* of Frederick L'Estrange Wallace and Gwendoline Gilling-Lax; three *s*. *Educ:* Parkstone Sch. Served European War 1914-18 with 5th Cavalry Reserve Regt in UK. Local Director (in Argentina): Australian Mercantile, Land & Finance Co. Ltd; Liebig's Extract of Meat Co. Ltd. Mem. Local Cttee (in Argentina), Northern Assurance Co. Ltd. Chm. British Chamber of Commerce in the Argentine Republic, 1951-62, now Hon. Vice-President. Liveryman Worshipful Company of Butchers. *Recreations:* golf, tennis. *Address:* c/o Forestal Land, Timber & Railways Co. Ltd, The Adelphi, John Adam Street, WC2; Paseo Colon 221, Buenos Aires, Argentina. *Clubs:* Royal Automobile, Canning (London); Jockey, Circulo de Armas, Hurlingham, English (all in Argentina).

**SEWARD, Air Vice-Marshal Walter John,** CB 1950; CBE 1944; Director, Auxiliaries, Reserves and Air Cadets, Air Ministry, since 1954; Hon. Air Commodore, 661 Air Observation Post Squadron, RAAF, since 1955; AOA, BAFO, 1949-51; *b* 17 Oct. 1898; *m* 1934, Josephine Margaret Mary O'Neill; one *s*. Commissioned RFC, 1917. Comd as Air Cdre: No 12 OT Group, Canada, 1943-44; No 54 Group, 1944-46; No 27 Group, 1948-49. Air Vice-Marshal, 1950; AOC, No 61 (Eastern) Group, Home Command, RAF, 1951-54. *Recreations:* cricket, golf, shooting. *Address:* 11 Victoria Square, Lee-on-Solent, Hampshire. *Club:* Royal Air Force.

**SEWELL, Thomas Robert McKie;** Assistant Secretary, External Relations Division, Ministry of Agriculture, Fisheries and Food, since 1970; *b* 18 Aug. 1921; *s* of O. B. Fane Sewell and late Frances M. Sewell (*née* Sharp); *m* 1955, Jennifer Mary Sandeman; two *d*. *Educ:* Eastbourne Coll.; Trinity Coll., Oxford (Schol., Heath Harrison Prize, MA); Lausanne and Stockholm Univs (Schol.). HM Forces, 1940-45 (despatches); Major. Entered Foreign Service, 1949; Second Sec., Moscow, 1950-52; FO, 1952-55; First Sec., 1954; Madrid, 1955-59; Lima, 1959-61; Chargé d'Affaires, 1960; FO, 1961-63; Counsellor and Head of Chancery, Moscow, 1964-66; Diplomatic Service Rep. at IDC, 1966; Head of Associated States, West Indies and Swaziland Depts, Commonwealth Office, 1967-68; Head of N American and Caribbean Dept, FCO, 1968-70. *Recreations:* ski-ing, inland waterways cruising. *Address:* c/o Ministry of Agriculture, Fisheries and Food, Whitehall Place, SW1. *Clubs:* Travellers', Airborne.

**SEXTON, Most Rev. Harold Eustace,** DD; *b* 14 May 1888; *s* of late Richard James Sexton, Adelaide; *m* 1922, Mary Hodgman, *d* of Mrs H. A. Tyree, Toorak, Victoria. *Educ:* St Peter's College, Adelaide; Keble College, Oxford; Trinity College, Toronto. Deacon, 1911; Priest, 1912; Curate of St Paul's, Port Adelaide, 1911-14; All Saints, Hindmarsh, 1915-16; Chaplain with the British Expeditionary Forces, 1916-18; Vicar of St Martin's, Hawksburn, Melbourne, 1920-23; SPG Preacher, 1923-24; Curate of St Margaret's, Westminster, 1925-27; Vicar of All Saints, Upper Norwood, 1927-35; Bishop Coadjutor of British Columbia, 1935-36; Bishop, 1936-69; Archbishop of British Columbia, 1952-69. *Address:* 3905 Scolton Road, Victoria, BC, Canada.

**SEYLER, Athene,** CBE 1959; Actress on the London stage; *b* London, 31 May 1889; *d* of Clara Thies and Clarence H. Seyler; *m* 1st James Bury Sterndale-Bennett; one *d*; 2nd, Nicholas James Hannen, *qv*. *Educ:* Coombe Hill School; Bedford College. Gold Medallist, Royal Academy of Dramatic Art, 1908; first appearance on the stage at Kingsway Theatre, 1909; specialised in comedy acting; served on the Drama Panel of CEMA, 1943 and subsequently of the Arts Council of Great Britain. Pres. of RADA, 1950; Pres. of Theatrical Ladies Guild. Principal successes as Madame Ranevska in The Cherry Orchard, Fanny Farrelli in Watch on the Rhine, the Duchess of Berwick in Lady Windermere's Fan, Vita Louise in Harvey, Mrs Malaprop in The Rivals, The Nurse in Romeo and Juliet. Has appeared in films, 1932-. Hon. Treasurer of British Actors Equity Association, 1944. *Publication:* The Craft of Comedy, 1944. *Recreations:* walking, talking. *Address:* Lambs Cottage, Ludham, Norfolk.

**SEYMOUR,** family name of **Marquess of Hertford** and **Duke of Somerset.**

**SEYMOUR, Lord; John Michael Edward Seymour;** *b* 30 Dec. 1952; *s* and *heir* of 18th Duke of Somerset, *qv*.

**SEYMOUR, Derek Robert Gurth,** MA; Headmaster of Bloxham School since Sept. 1965; *b* 4 Sept. 1917; *s* of G. Haco Seymour; *m* 1940, Betty, *d* of late Lt-Col S. H. Little; two *s*. *Educ:* Trinity Coll., Cambridge. BA 1939; MA 1943. Head of Chemistry, Junior Housemaster, St John's School, Leatherhead, 1939-44; Asst Master, Head of Science, i/c RAF Section, CCF; Housemaster, Marlborough College, 1944-65. Seconded as Head of Chemistry and House Tutor, Cranbrook Sch., Sydney, 1951-52. Examr and Chief Examr in A and S Level Chemistry, Southern Univs Jt Bd, 1955-63. *Address:* Park Close, Bloxham, Banbury, Oxon. *T:* Bloxham 321.

**SEYMOUR, Sir Horace James,** GCMG 1946 (KCMG 1939; CMG 1927); CVO 1936; *b* 26 Feb. 1885; *e s* of late Hugh F. Seymour; *m* 1917, Violet, *d* of late Thomas Erskine; one *s* two *d*. *Educ:* Eton; Trinity College, Cambridge. Foreign Office and Diplomatic Service, 1908; British Minister, Tehran, 1936-39; Assistant Under-Secretary of State at Foreign Office, 1939-42; Ambassador to China, 1942-46; retired, 1947. *Address:* Bratton House, Westbury, Wilts. *T:* Bratton 231.

*See also Sir Ivo Stourton.*

**SEYMOUR, Lady Katharine,** DCVO 1961 (CVO 1939); Extra Woman of the Bedchamber to Queen Elizabeth the Queen Mother since 1960 (Woman of the Bedchamber to the Queen (now Queen Elizabeth the Queen Mother), 1937-60); First Woman of the Bedchamber to Queen Mary, 1927-30 (on marriage became Extra Woman of the Bedchamber, 1930-53); *b* 25 Feb. 1900; 3rd *d* of 3rd Duke of Abercorn; *m* 1930, Sir R. H. Seymour, KCVO (*d* 1938); one *s* one *d* (and one *d* decd). *Address:* Strettington House, Chichester, Sussex. *T:* Halnaker 265.

**SEYMOUR, Leslie (George),** JP; Managing Director: Improved Metallic Appliances Limited; George E. Seymour Limited; Elseemore (Caravans) Ltd; *b* 1 November 1900; *s* of late George Seymour, Birmingham; *m* 1941, Dorothy, *d* of late J. Murdoch,

Redditch, Worcestershire; two *s*. *Educ:* King's Norton Secondary School; Solihull Grammar School. Started work at 14, in a Tech. School Laboratory. Served European War, 1914-18. Sergeant, Home Guard, 1941-44. Mem. Birmingham CC, 1937-46, 1947-53; Chm. Civil Defence Cttee, 1944; Chm. Rating and Valuation Cttee, 1949; Past Chm. No 8 Hosp. Group, Regional Hosp. Bd; Mem. Regional Hosp. Bd (Past Chm. Finance Cttee); Gov., Birmingham United Hosps. Chairman Coleshill Hall Hosp. Group. JP, Birmingham, 1951. Chm. Old Yardley Div. Unionist Assoc., 1945-46; contested (U) Ladywood Div. of Birmingham, 1951; MP (C) Sparkbrook Div. of Birmingham, 1959-64. Life Vice-Chm. Birmingham Young Conservatives. Past Pres. UK Commercial Travellers' Assoc. (Birmingham branch). Fell. Inst. of Engineers. Member: National Assoc. of British Manufacturers; Birmingham Rotary Club; Birmingham Chamber of Commerce; Institute of Directors; Engineering Industries Association. Hon. Mem. Council, City of Birmingham, 1967. Civil Defence Medal; Coronation Medal, 1953. *Recreations:* golf and gardening. *Address:* 514 Warwick Road, Solihull, Warwicks. *T:* 0523; The Woodlands, Llanon, Cards; (business) 80 Cheapside, Birmingham, 12. *T:* 021-772 1221-2. *Club:* St Stephen's.

**SEYMOUR, Lynn;** Ballerina, Deutsche Oper, Berlin, since 1966; *b* Wainwright, Alberta, 8 March 1939; *d* of E. V. Springbett; *m* 1963, Colin Jones, photo-journalist. *Educ:* Vancouver; Sadler's Wells Ballet School. Joined Sadler's Wells Ballet Company, 1957. *Roles created:* Adolescent, in The Burrow, Royal Opera House, 1958; Bride, in Le Baiser de la Fée, 1960; Girl, in The Invitation, 1960; Young Girl, in Les Deux Pigeons, 1961; Principal, in Symphony, 1963; Principal, in Images of Love, 1964; Juliet, in Romeo and Juliet, 1964; Albertine, BBC TV, 1966; Concerto, 1966; Anastasia, 1966. *Other appearances include:* Danses Concertantes; Solitaire; La Fête Etrange; Sleeping Beauty; Swan Lake, Australasia, 1958-59, London, 1959; Giselle (title-role), 1960; Cinderella, London, 1961; Das Lied von der Erde, 1966. *Address:* Deutsche Oper, 1, Berlin 10, West Germany.

**SEYMOUR, Commander Sir Michael Culme-,** 5th Bt, *cr* 1809; Royal Navy (retired); *b* 26 April 1909; *o s* of Vice-Admiral Sir M. Culme-Seymour, 4th Bt, and Florence Agnes Louisa (*d* 1956), *y d* of late A. L. Nugent; *S* father, 1925; *m* 1948, Lady (Mary) Faith Nesbitt, *er d* of 9th Earl of Sandwich; one *step-d* (two *s* decd). Succeeded Rev. Wentworth Watson to the Rockingham estates, 1925; is a Farmer and a Landowner. ADC to Governor-General of Canada, 1933-35; served War of 1939-45 (despatches); served Imperial Defence College, 1946-47; retired from RN 1947. JP Northants, 1949; Mem. Northants CC 1948-55; DL Northants, 1958; High Sheriff of Northants, 1966. *Heir to baronetcy: cousin* John Dennis Culme-Seymour [*b* 3 December 1923; *m* 1957, (Elizabeth) Jane Mackessack; one *d*]. *Address:* Rockingham Castle, Market Harborough, Leics. *T:* Rockingham 326, (Office) 240. *Club:* Brooks's.

**SEYMOUR, Richard,** CMG 1966; CBE 1946; *b* 16 Sept. 1903; *s* of late Richard Seymour and Edith, *d* of William Hales; *m* 1940, Charlotte, *d* of Ernest Leigh; two *d*. *Educ:* Highgate Sch.; Christ Church, Oxford (Scholar, MA). Admitted a Solicitor, 1927; partner in firm of Rhys Roberts & Co. until 1940. Secretary, Books Commission of Conference of Allied Ministers of Education, 1942-45. Deputy Secretary-General, British Council, 1940-47, Secretary, 1947-53; Controller, Commonwealth Div., 1953-57, European Div., 1957-59; Representative in Germany, 1959-66. *Address:* The Old Manse, Staplecross, Robertsbridge, Sussex.

**SEYMOUR, Air Commodore Roland George,** CB 1961; CBE 1945; RAF, retired; *b* 16 May 1905; *s* of William and Jeannie Seymour; *m* 1942, Dorothy Beatrice Hutchings; two *s*. *Educ:* Christ's Hospital. Pilot Officer, RAF, Jan. 1929, psc 1942; Actg Air Commodore, 1945, as Dep. to Air Officer i/c Administration, Mediterranean Allied Air Forces; Air Commodore, 1958; served in: Iraq, 1930-32; N Africa and Italy, 1942-45; Singapore, 1952-54; Deputy Assistant Chief of Staff (Logistics), Supreme HQ Allied Powers Europe, 1961-63. Legion of Merit (USA), 1946. *Address:* c/o Glyn, Mills & Co., Whitehall, SW1.

**SEYMOUR, Rosalind;** *see* Wade, R. (H.).

**SEYMOUR, William Kean,** FRSL; Poet, Novelist and Journalist; a Vice-President of the Poetry Society, since 1947 (Chairman, General Council, Dec. 1961-May 1964); Vice-President, Charles Lamb Society; Member, Committee of West Country Writers' Association; *b* 1887; *s* of William Seymour and Jane Kean; *m* 1st, Beatrice Mary Stapleton; 2nd, Rosalind Herschel Wade (*see* Rosalind Wade); two *s*. *Educ:* Lawrence School, London; served in RNAS and RAF, 1917-18. Conductor (with Rosalind Wade) of Writer's Craft courses, Moor Park Coll., Farnham, 1962-. DLitt hc Free Univ., Asia, 1968. Philippines Presidential Gold Medal for Poetry, Jan. 1968. *Publications:* Poems: The Street of Dreams, 1914; To Verhaeren, 1917; Twenty-four Poems, 1918; Swords and Flutes, 1919; Cæsar Remembers, 1929; Time Stands, 1935; Chinese Crackers, 1938; Collected Poems, 1946; Burns into English (translations), 1954; The First Childermas (verse play), 1959; The Cats of Rome, 1970. Parodies: A Jackdaw in Georgia, 1925; Parrot Pie, 1927. Fiction: The Little Cages, 1944; Friends of the Swallow, 1953; The Secret Kingdom, 1954; Names and Faces, 1956. Biography: Jonathan Swift: The Enigma of a Genius, 1967. Ed. of Anthologies: A Miscellany of Poetry, 1919; ditto, 1920-22; (with John Smith) The Pattern of Poetry, 1963; (with John Smith) Happy Christmas, 1968; contribs to Poetry Review, Contemporary Review, Books and Bookmen. *Recreations:* writing, gardening. *Address:* White Cottage, Old Alresford, Alresford, Hants. *T:* Alresford 2870. *Clubs:* PEN, National Liberal.

**SEZNEC, Prof. Jean J.,** FBA 1960; Marshal Foch Professor of French Literature, Oxford, since 1950; *b* 18 March 1905; *s* of Jean Seznec and Pauline Le Férec. *Educ:* Ecole Normale Supérieure, Paris. Fellow, French School of Archaeology, Rome, 1929-31; Univ. Lecturer, Cambridge, 1931-33; Prof., Lycée of Marseilles, 1933-34; Prof., French Inst., Florence, 1934-39, Asst Director, 1939; Assoc. Professor, Harvard University, 1941-46, Professor, 1946, Smith Professor of the French and Spanish Languages, 1947-50; Mary Flexner Lecturer, Bryn Mawr, 1955; Lord Northcliffe Lecturer, London, 1958; Dillon Visiting Prof., Harvard University, 1958. Hon. DLitt, Harvard, 1961. Officier de la Légion d'Honneur, 1957. *Publications:* La Survivance des Dieux Antiques, 1940; L'Episode des Dieux dans la Tentation de Saint Antoine, 1940; Nouvelles Etudes sur la Tentation de Saint Antoine, 1949; Essais sur Diderot et l'Antiquité, 1958; John Martin en France,

1964; (joint) Fragonard, Drawings for Ariosto, 1945; Diderot, Salons, Vol. I, 1957; Vol. II, 1960; Vol. III, 1963; Vol. IV, 1967; contributions to: French Studies, Jl of Warburg and Courtauld Institutes, Romanic Review, Gazette des Beaux Arts, etc. *Address:* All Souls College, Oxford.

**SHACKLE, Prof. George Lennox Sharman,** FBA 1967; Brunner Professor of Economic Science in the University of Liverpool, 1951-69, now Professor Emeritus; *b* 14 July 1903; *s* of Robert Walker Shackle, MA (Cambridge) and of Fanny Shackle (*née* Sharman); *m* 1939, Gertrude Courtney Susan Rowe; two *s* one *d* (and one *d* decd). *Educ:* The Perse School, Cambridge; The London School of Economics; New College, Oxford. BA (London) 1931; Leverhulme Research Schol., 1934; PhD (Econ) (London), 1937; DPhil (Oxford), 1940. Oxford University Institute of Statistics, 1937; University of St Andrews, 1939; Admiralty and Cabinet Office; Sir Winston Churchill's Statistical Branch, 1939; Economic Section of Cabinet Secretariat, 1945; Reader in Economic Theory, Univ. of Leeds, 1950. Member Council of Royal Economic Society, 1955-69. F. de Vries Lecturer, Amsterdam, 1957; Visiting Professor, Columbia University, 1957-58; Pres., Section F, British Association for the Adv. of Science, 1966; Visiting Prof. of Economics and Visiting Prof. of Philosophy, Univ. of Pittsburgh, 1967. Fellow of Econometric Society, 1960. *Publications:* Expectations, Investment, and Income, 1938, 2nd edn 1968; Expectation in Economics, 1949, 2nd edn, 1952; Mathematics at the Fireside, 1952 (French edn 1967); Uncertainty in Economics and Other Reflections, 1955; Time in Economics, 1957; Economics for Pleasure, 1959, 2nd edn 1968 (paperback, 1962; also foreign editions); Decision, Order and Time in Human Affairs, 1961 (2nd edn 1969; also foreign editions); A Scheme of Economic Theory, 1965; The Nature of Economic Thought, 1966; The Years of High Theory, 1967; Expectation, Enterprise and Profit, 1970. (ed and contrib.) Uncertainty and Business Decisions, 1954, 2nd edn, 1957; The Theory of General Static Equilibrium, 1957; A New Prospect of Economics, 1958; On the Nature of Business Success, 1968. Articles in Chambers's Encyclopædia, 1950, 1967, Internat. Encyclopedia of the Social Sciences, 1968, and in other books; sixty or more main articles in learned jls. *Address:* The University, Liverpool L69 3BX.

**SHACKLETON,** family name of **Baron Shackleton.**

**SHACKLETON,** Baron *cr* 1958 (Life Peer), of Burley, **Edward Arthur Alexander Shackleton,** PC 1966; OBE 1945; Opposition Leader of the House of Lords, since 1970; *b* 15 July 1911; *s* of late Sir Ernest Shackleton, CVO, OBE; *m* 1938, Betty Homan; one *s* one *d*. *Educ:* Radley College, Magdalen College, Oxford (MA). Surveyor, Oxford University Expedition to Sarawak, 1932; Organiser and Surveyor, Oxford University Expedition to Ellesmereland, 1934-35; Lecture tours in Europe and America; BBC talks producer, MOI. Served War of 1939-45, 1940-45; RAF Station Intelligence Officer, St Eval; Anti-U-Boat Planner and Intelligence Officer, Coastal Command; Naval and Military Intelligence, Air Ministry; Wing Cdr (despatches twice, OBE). Contested (Lab) Epsom, General Election, and Bournemouth by-election, 1945; MP (Lab), Preston (by-election), 1946-50, Preston South, 1950-55, Parliamentary Private Secretary to Minister of Supply, 1949-50; Parliamentary Private Sec. to Foreign Sec., March-Oct. 1951 (to Lord President of the Council, 1950-51); Minister of Defence for the RAF, 1964-67. Minister Without Portfolio and Deputy Leader, House of Lords, 1967-68; Lord Privy Seal, Jan.-April, 1968; Paymaster-General, April-Oct. 1968; Leader of the House of Lords, April 1968-70; Lord Privy Seal, Oct. 1968-1970; Min. in charge, Civil Service Dept, Nov. 1968-70. Sen. Executive and Director, J. Lewis Partnership, 1955-64; Director: RTZ Development Enterprises; Mercury Insurance Holdings; Woodrow Wyatt Holdings, etc. Chairman, Cttee on Oil Pollution, 1962-64; Pres., Brit. Assoc. of Industrial Editors, 1960-64; Mem. Council, Industrial Soc. Special Mission to South Arabia, 1967. Pres., ASLIB, 1963-65; Vice-President, Royal Geographical Society; Cuthbert Peek Award (Royal Geographical Society), 1933; Ludwig Medallist (Munich Geog. Soc.), 1938. Pres., Arctic Club, 1960. Hon. LLD, Univ. of Newfoundland. *Publications:* Arctic Journeys; Nansen, the Explorer; (part-author) Borneo Jungle; articles, broadcasts, etc. on geographical and political subjects and personnel and general administration. *Address:* Long Coppice, Canford Magna, Dorset. *T:* Broadstone 3635. *Club:* Savile.

**SHACKLETON, Edith;** *see* Heald, E. S.

**SHACKLETON, Robert,** FBA 1966; MA, DLitt Oxon, FSA; FRSL; Bodley's Librarian, Oxford, since 1966; Fellow of Brasenose Coll. since 1946 (Professorial Fellow since 1966); *b* 25 Nov. 1919; *e s* of Albert Shackleton and Emily (*née* Sunderland); unmarried. *Educ:* Todmorden Grammar School; Oriel College, Oxford (Scholar). 1st class, Hon. School of Modern Languages, 1940. Military Service, Royal Signals, 1940-45. Candidate (L), Blackburn, Gen. Elec., 1945. Lectr, Trinity Coll., Oxford, 1946-49; Fellow, Brasenose Coll., 1946-. (Librarian, 1948-66, Sen. Dean, 1954-61, Vice-Principal, 1963-66); Lectr in French, Oxford Univ., 1949-65; Reader in French literature, Oxford Univ., 1965-66; Chm., Cttee on Oxford Univ. Libraries, 1965-66; Vis. Prof, Dept of French and Italian, Univ. of Wisconsin, 1968; Zaharoff Lectr, Oxford Univ., 1970. Corresp. Member: Acad. de Bordeaux, 1954; Acad. Montesquieu (Bordeaux), 1956; Prix Montesquieu, 1956; President, Society for French Studies, 1959-60; Member, Editorial Board: French Studies, 1960- (Gen. Ed., 1965-67); Archives internationales d'histoire des idées, 1962-. Pres., Internat. Comparative Liter. Assoc., 1964-67. Hon. Mem., Assoc. Internat. de Bibliophilie; Hon. For. Corresp. Mem., Grolier Club, NY. Hon. Dr Univ. Bordeaux, 1966; Hon. LittD Univ. of Dublin, 1967. *Publications:* Editor: Fontenelle, Entretiens sur la pluralité des mondes, 1955; Montesquieu, a critical biography, 1961; The Encyclopédie and the Clerks, 1970. Articles in learned jls, Encyclopædia Britannica, etc. *Recreations:* book-collecting, foreign travel. *Address:* Bodleian Library, Oxford. *T:* 44675; Brasenose College, Oxford. *T:* 48641. *Clubs:* Athenæum, National Liberal; Grolier (New York).

**SHACKLETON, Prof. Robert Millner,** BSc, PhD; FGS; Professor of Geology, University of Leeds, since 1962; Director, Research Institute of African Geology, University of Leeds, since 1966; *b* 30 Dec. 1909; *m* 1st, 1934, Gwen Isabel Harland; one *s* two *d*; 2nd, 1949, Judith Wyndham Jeffreys; one *s* one *d*. *Educ:* Sidcot School; University of Liverpool. BSc (Hons) 1931, PhD 1934, Liverpool; Beit Fellow, Imperial College, 1932-34; Chief Geologist to Whitehall Explorations Ltd in Fiji, 1935-36; on teaching staff, Imperial

College, 1936-40 and 1945-48; Geologist, Mining and Geological Dept, Kenya, 1940-45; Herdman Professor of Geology, University of Liverpool, 1948-62. Royal Society Leverhulme Vis. Prof., Haile Sellassie I Univ., 1970-71. Vice-Pres., Geolog. Soc. of London, 1966. Murchison Medal, 1970. *Publications:* Mining and Geological Dept of Kenya Reports 10, 11, 12; papers in geological journals, etc. *Address:* 14a Wood Lane, Leeds 6. *T:* Leeds 58402.

**SHACKLETON BAILEY, D. R.;** *see* Bailey.

**SHACKLOCK, Constance,** LRAM, FRAM; International Opera and Concert Singer; Professor, Royal Academy of Music, since 1968; *b* 16 April 1913; *e d* of Randolph and Hilda Shacklock, Nottingham; *m* 1947, Eric Mitchell (*d* 1965). *Educ:* Huntingdon Street Secondary School, Nottingham; RAM. Principal mezzo-soprano, Covent Garden, 1946-56. Outstanding rôles: Carmen, Amneris (Aida), Octavian (Der Rosenkavalier), Brangaene (Tristan und Isolde). Guest artist: Wagner Society, Holland, 1949; Berlin State Opera, 1951; Teatro Colon, Buenos Aires, 1956; Bolshoi Theatre, Moscow, 1957; Kirov Theatre, Leningrad, 1957; Elizabethan Theatre Trust, Sydney, 1958. Edinburgh Festival, 1954; Berlin Festival, 1956; Liège Opera, 1960; London production of The Sound of Music, 1961-. *Recreations:* gardening, reading, tapestry. *Address:* Royal Academy of Music, Marylebone Road, NW1.

**SHACKMAN, Prof. Ralph;** Professor of Urology, University of London, at Post-graduate Medical School, since 1961; *b* 29 March 1910; *s* of David and Sophia Shackman; *m* 1940, Ida Mary Seal; no *c. Educ:* Grocers' Company School; St Bartholomew's Hospital Medical School. MB, BS (London) 1934; FRCS 1936. Resident Surgical Officer, Royal Infirmary, Sheffield, 1937. Served War of 1939-45, Wing-Commander Surgical Specialist, RAF. Brit. Post-Grad. Travelling Fellowship in USA, 1947-48. Sen. Lectr, Post-grad. Med. Sch., 1949; Reader in Surgery, Univ. of London, 1955; Mem. Court of Examiners, RCS, England, 1962; Member of Council: Experimental Med. and Therapeutics, Roy. Soc. Med., 1962; Sect. of Urology, Roy. Soc. Med., 1963; Brit. Assoc. of Urological Surgeons, 1964; Brit. Assoc. of Surgeons, 1965; Member, International Society of Urology, 1964. *Publications:* contrib. to medical and scientific jls. *Recreations:* gardening, carpentry. *Address:* 25 Aylestone Avenue, Brondesbury Park, NW6. *T:* 01-459 2542. *Club:* South Hampstead Cricket.

**SHAFFER, Peter Levin;** Playwright; Critic; *b* 15 May 1926; *s* of Jack Shaffer and Reka Shaffer (*née* Fredman). *Educ:* St Paul's School, London; Trinity College, Cambridge. Literary Critic, Truth, 1956-57; Music Critic, Time and Tide, 1961-62. Awards: Evening Standard Drama Award, 1958; New York Drama Critics Circle Award (best foreign play), 1959-60. *Stage Plays:* Five Finger Exercise, prod. Comedy, London, 1958-60, and Music Box Theatre, New York, 1960-61; (double bill) The Private Ear (filmed, as The Pad, 1966) and The Public Eye, produced, Globe, London, 1962, Morosco Theater, New York 1963; The Merry Roosters Panto (with Joan Littlewood and Theatre Workshop) prod. Wyndham's Theatre, Christmas, 1963; The Royal Hunt of the Sun, Nat. Theatre, Chichester Festival, 1964, The Old Vic, and Queen's Theatres, 1964-67, Broadway, 1965-66 (filmed 1969); Black Comedy, Nat. Theatre, Chichester Fest., 1965; The Old Vic and Queen's Theatres, 1965-67; as double bill with White Lies, Broadway, 1967, The White Liars, Lyric, 1968; The Battle of Shrivings, Lyric, 1970. Plays produced on television and sound include: Salt Land (ITV), 1955; Balance of Terror (BBC TV), 1957; The Prodigal Father (Radio), etc. *Recreations:* music, architecture, peering about. *Address:* 18 Earls Terrace, Kensington High Street, W8. *T:* 01-937 7972.

**SHAFTESBURY,** 10th Earl of, *cr* 1672; **Anthony Ashley-Cooper;** Bt 1622; Baron Ashley 1661; Baron Cooper of Paulet, 1672; *b* 22 May 1938; *o s* of Major Lord Ashley (*d* 1947; *e s* of 9th Earl of Shaftesbury, KP, PC, GCVO, CBE) and of Françoise Soulier; *S* grandfather, 1961; *m* 1966, Bianca Maria, *o d* of late Gino de Paolis. *Educ:* Eton; Christchurch, Oxford. Chm., London Philharmonic Orchestra Council. Hon. Citizen, South Carolina, USA, 1967. Patron of seven livings. *Recreations:* ski-ing, music, shooting. *Heir: uncle* Major Hon. (Anthony) John Percy Hugh Michael Ashley-Cooper [*b* 5 Oct. 1915; *m* 1946, Julian, *d* of late Capt. George Gerald Petherick; four *d*]. *Address:* St Giles, Wimborne, Dorset. *T:* Cranborne 312. *Clubs:* Turf, White's.
*See also Viscount Head.*

**SHAFTESLEY, John Maurice,** OBE 1956; Editor of publications, Jewish Historical Society of England; A Director of The Jewish Chronicle, London, 1958-60; *b* 25 June 1901; *s* of late David Shaftesley and Nellie Rosenblum; *m* 1926, Evelyn Adler; one *d. Educ:* Salford Grammar Sch.; Manchester Sch. of Art; London University (BA Hons). Allied Newspapers, technical staff, 1924-26; Manchester Guardian staff, 1926-36; Lecturer, Department of Printing Technology, Manchester College of Technology, 1933-36; Assistant Editor, The Jewish Chronicle, 1937-46 (Editor 1946-58). Fellow Royal Society of Arts, 1938; President, Wingate Services Club, High Wycombe, War of 1939-45; Mem. Council, Friends of the Hebrew Univ. of Jerusalem; Chm., Zangwill Centenary Cttee, 1964, and of Israel Zangwill Fellowship; Hon. Sec., Soc. of Indexers, 1967-68. Works include: Cumulative Index to the *Jewish Chronicle* 1841-1880 (and in continuation, 1881-90); Cumulative Index to the *Voice of Jacob* 1841-1846; Remember the Days (Ed. and contributor), 1966; Lodge of Israel No 205: A History 1793-1968, 1968, etc. *Address:* 33 The Grove, Edgware, Middx. *T:* 01-958 9006. *Clubs:* Reform, Press.

**SHAKERLEY, Sir Geoffrey (Adam),** 6th Bt *cr* 1838; Director, Photographic Records Ltd, since 1970; *b* 9 Dec. 1932; *s* of Sir Cyril Holland Shakerley, 5th Bt, and of Elizabeth Averil (MBE 1955), *d* of late Edward Gwynne Eardley-Wilmot; *S* father, 1970; *m* 1962, Virginia Elizabeth (*d* 1968), *d* of W. E. Maskell; two *s. Educ:* Harrow; Trinity College, Oxford. *Heir: s* Nicholas Simon Adam Shakerley, *b* 20 Dec. 1963. *Address:* 23 Woodsford Square, W14.

**SHAKERLEY, Col Geoffrey Peter,** CBE 1964; MC 1945; TD; DL; Vice-Lieutenant of Gloucestershire, since 1969; *b* 11 April 1906; *s* of Lieutenant-Colonel G. C. Shakerley, DSO (killed in action, 1915) and of late Mrs G. C. Shakerley (*née* Harvey); *m* 1932, Barbara Storrs Howard; two *s* two *d. Educ:* Wellington College; Christ Church, Oxford (MA). Served War of 1939-45, with KRRC (TA), UK, Egypt, Italy; comdg R Gloucestershire Hussars (TA), 1951-53; Dep. Comdr, 129 Inf. Bde (TA), 1954-55. Chm., Gloucestershire CC, 1955-67; Vice-Chm., County Councils Assoc., 1965, Chm. 1969. DL Glos 1953; High Sheriff of Gloucestershire, 1961. *Recreation:* golf. *Address:* Wells Folly, Moreton-in-Marsh,

Glos. *T:* Moreton in Marsh 336. *Club:* Boodle's.

**SHAKESPEARE, Rt. Hon. Sir Geoffrey Hithersay,** PC 1945; 1st Bt, *cr* 1942; Barrister; Deputy Chairman, Abbey National Building Society, 1965-69, Director since 1970; *b* 1893; 2nd *s* of late Rev. J. H. Shakespeare; *m* 1st, 1926, Lady Fisher (*d* 1950), of 103 Sloane St, *widow* of Comdr Sir Thomas Fisher, RN; one *s* (one *d* decd); 2nd, 1952, Elizabeth, *er d* of late Brig.-Gen. R. W. Hare, CMG, DSO. *Educ:* Highgate School; Emmanuel, Cambridge. MA, LLB; President of the Union; served European War; Private Secretary to Rt Hon. D. Lloyd George, 1921-23; MP (NL) Wellingborough Division of Northants, 1922-23; MP (L) Norwich, 1929-31 (L Nat.), 1931-45; Lord Commissioner of the Treasury and Chief Whip Liberal Nationals, Nov. 1931-Oct. 1932; Parliamentary Secretary, Ministry of Health, 1932-36; Parliamentary Secretary to Board of Education, 1936-37; Parliamentary and Financial Secretary to the Admiralty, 1937-40; Parliamentary Secretary to Dept of Overseas Trade, April to May 1940; Parliamentary Under-Secretary of State, Dominions Office and Chairman Children's Overseas Reception Board, 1940-42; called to Bar, 1922; political journalist, 1924; Vice-Chairman, Board of Governors Westminster Hosp., 1948-63; Pres. Soc. of British Gas Industries, 1953-54; Chm. Industrial Co-Partnership Assoc., 1958-68; Chm. Nat. Liberal Exec., 1950-51. *Publication:* Let Candles be brought in (Memoirs), 1949. *Recreation:* golf. *Heir:* *s* William Geoffrey Shakespeare [*b* 12 Oct. 1927; *m* 1964, Susan Mary, *d* of A. D. Raffel, Colombo, Ceylon, and of Mrs S. G. Sproule, Hove, Sussex; one *s*]. *Address:* Flat 6, Great Ash, Lubbock Road, Chislehurst, Kent. *T:* 01-467 5898. *Clubs:* Reform, Garrick.

*See also N. T. L. Fisher.*

**SHANKER SHAMSHER JANG BAHADUR RANA, Gen.,** Hon. GBE 1949 (Hon. KBE 1946); Star of Nepal (1st Class) 1946; Om Ram Patta (1st Class) 1948; Trishakti Patta (1st Class) 1948; Dakshina Bahu (1st Class) 1941; General, Nepalese Army; *b* 1909; *s* of HH the late Maharaja Chandra Shamsher Jang Bahadur Rana, GCB, GCSI, GCMG, GCVO and HH Badamaharani Balkumari Devi; *m* 1924, Rani K. Rajya Laxmi, *e d* of Colonel Tej Bahadur Malla, of Nepal; one *s* one *d*. Acting Head of Shrestha Kousal, 1930; Head of Madesh Report Nixari and Kathmahal (Whole Terai), 1931-34; PWD, 1936-43; Head of Rail and Road Dept, 1946-47; Chief of Police, 1947-49; again Head of Madesh Report Nixari, 1947-49; Chief of Staff to HH The Maharaja, 1948-49; visited UK with Special Mission to present Nepalese honours, to HM King George VI and HM Queen Elizabeth, 1946; presented, on behalf of Govt of Nepal, Insignia of Ojaswi Rajana to HRH Princess Elizabeth, 1949, to HM Queen Juliana of the Netherlands, 1949, to President Vincent Auriol of France, 1949; Nepalese Ambassador at the Court of St James's, also, concurrently, the first Nepalese Ambassador to France and Nepalese Ambassador to the USA, 1949-54. Holds Grand Cross of Order of Orange-Nassau, 1949; Grand Officer of Legion of Honour (France), 1949. *Recreations:* big game shooting, lawn tennis, golf, riding, chess. *Address:* Harihar Bhavan, Kathmandu, Nepal. *Clubs:* St James', Royal Automobile; Royal Mid-Surrey Golf.

**SHANKLAND, Sir Thomas (Murray),** Kt 1960; CMG 1955; JP; Deputy-Governor, Western Region, Nigeria, 1954-57; retired; Chairman, London Board of Public Service Commission, Western Region, Nigeria, 1957-61; *b* 25 Aug. 1905; *y s* of late W. C. Shankland, MBE, Barrister-at-Law, and late E. B. Shankland; *m* 1931, Margaret Crawford Goudie; one *d*. *Educ:* Felsted School; Queens' College, Cambridge (BA). Administrative Officer, Class IV, Nigeria, 1929; Food and Price Controller, Nigeria, 1944-45; Director of Supplies, Nigeria, 1946-47; Secretary, Western Provinces, Nigeria, 1949; Civil Secretary, Western Region, Nigeria, 1951; Chairman, Constituency Delimitation Commn, WR Nigeria, 1959. Mem. Jt CC, Moray and Nairn, 1958-70. JP Morayshire 1960. *Recreations:* golf, curling. *Address:* Ardlarig, Grantown-on-Spey, Morayshire. *T:* Grantown-on-Spey 160. *Club:* East India and Sports.

**SHANKS, S(eymour) Cochrane,** CBE 1958; MD, ChB; FRCP; FFR; Consulting Radiologist to University College Hospital; late Lecturer in Radiology, University College Hospital Medical School (Dean of the Medical School, 1943-49); late Radiologist, Goldie Leigh Hosp.; late Hon. Radiologist: University College, London; Lord Mayor Treloar's Hosp., Alton; Past Adviser in Radiology to the Ministry of Health; Past Warden of Fellowship, Past President, and Skinner and Knox lecturer, Faculty of Radiologists; Member, Spens Committee on remuneration of Consultants and Specialists, 1947; Examiner in Radiology to Universities of Durham and Liverpool; Examiner in X-ray Diagnosis, 1942, and in Medicine, 1952, Faculty of Radiologists; Examiner in Radiology, RCP, 1940-44; Fellow (Past Hon. Treas.) RSM (PP and Hon. Mem., Section of Radiology); Fellow and Lettsomian Lecturer, Medical Society of London; Hon. Fellow, Royal Inst. of Public Health and Hygiene; Hon. Mem., British Assoc. of Dermatologists; Senior Vice-President, 6th International Congress of Radiology, 1950; Vice-Pres. Emeritus, 7th International Congress of Radiology, Copenhagen, 1953; (Immediate) Past Pres., Medical Defence Union; Chm. Institute of Dermatology, British Post-Graduate Medical Federation; Member: British Institute of Radiology; BMA (Chm. Medico-legal Sub-Cttee); Grand Council, British Empire Cancer Campaign; Distribution Cttee King Edward's Hosp. Fund, 1949-59; *b* 1893; 5th *s* of late William Shanks, JP, Barrhead, Renfrewshire, and late Catherine Cook McCallum, Leeds; *m* 1st, Edith Margaret Govan (*d* 1955); no *c*; 2nd, 1956, Chrisma Elsie Clara Govan. *Educ:* Glasgow Academy; Glasgow University (Burns and Asher-Asher Gold Medals); Western Infirmary, Glasgow; St Thomas's Hospital. House-Surgeon, Western Infirmary, Glasgow, 1915; Temp. Capt. RAMC, 1915-18; served with BEF in Egypt and France; late Medical Assessor, Ministry of Pensions; late Visiting Radiologist, Ministry of Pensions Hospital, Orpington; late Hon. Radiologist, St Mark's Hospital; Physician with charge of out-patients, Radiological Department, Charing Cross Hosp.; Radiologist, The Prince of Wales's Gen. Hosp. Hon. Member: Dutch Soc. of Radiology; Toronto Radiological Soc. Bose Gold Medal, Indian Radiological Soc. *Publications:* Jt Ed., Textbook of X-ray Diagnosis by British Authors; papers on Radiology in Med. Jls. *Recreations:* golf, motoring. *Address:* 11 Wimpole Street, W1. *T:* 01-580 1660, 01-580 4356; 11 Heath Rise, SW15. *T:* 01-789 3682. *Club:* Royal Wimbledon.

**SHANNON,** 9th Earl of, *cr* 1756; **Richard Bentinck Boyle;** Viscount Boyle, Baron of Castle-Martyr, 1756; Baron Carleton (GB), 1786; late Captain Irish Guards; Director, Conference of Industrial Research Associations and Committee of Directors of

Research Associations; Director of companies; *b* 23 Oct. 1924; *o s* of 8th Earl of Shannon; *S* father, 1963; *m* 1st, 1947, Catherine Irene Helen (marriage dissolved, 1955; she *m* 1955, Greville P. Baylis), *d* of the Marquis Demetrio Imperiali di Francavilla; 2nd, 1957, Susan Margaret, *d* of late J. P. R. Hogg; one *s* two *d*. *Educ:* Eton College. Pres., Architectural Metal Craftsmen's Assoc., 1966-69. *Heir: s* Viscount Boyle *qv*. *Address:* Old Loose Court, Loose, Maidstone, Kent. *T:* Maidstone 43139. *Club:* White's.

**SHANNON, Alastair;** journalist; Foreign News department, Daily Telegraph and Morning Post, since 1937; *b* Hawick, 1894; *o s* of late Rev. J. W. Shannon and Agnes, *d* of Rev. Alexander Renton; *m* 1920, Betty, *d* of Rev. A. Russell; one *s* one *d*. *Educ:* George Watson's College and University, Edinburgh. Served Flanders, 1915; Commission, Nov. 1915; Mesopotamia Relieving Force; Prisoner of War in Turkey, Apr. 1916 to Nov. 1918; joined Staff of Morning Post, 1919; Editor Madras Mail, 1921-23; rejoined Morning Post, 1924; Foreign Editor, Morning Post, 1928-37. *Publications:* Morning Knowledge, 1920; The Black Scorpion, 1926. *Address:* 1 Highpoint, Lyonsdown Road, New Barnet, Herts. *T:* 01-440 3593.

**SHANNON, Godfrey Eccleston Boyd,** CMG 1951; Assistant Under-Secretary of State, in the Commonwealth Office, 1956-68, retired 1968; *b* 14 Dec. 1907; *s* of late W. B. Shannon. *Educ:* Wellington; St John's College, Cambridge. Appointed to Dominions Office, 1930; visited Australia and New Zealand, as Private Sec., with 10th Duke of Devonshire, 1936; Official Sec., UK High Commissioner's Office, New Zealand, 1939-41; served on UK Delegation to various international conferences in London, Geneva, New York, Chicago and Moscow, 1944-48, to UNCTAD, 1964, and to Commonwealth Finance Ministers' meetings, Jamaica, Montreal and Trinidad, 1965-67; Deputy United Kingdom High Commissioner in Canada, 1948-50, in Calcutta, 1952-56. Member, Cttee for Exports: to Canada, 1964-68; to Australia, 1965-68. Renter Warden, Dyers' Co., 1967-68, Prime Warden, 1968-69. *Address:* 47D Lennox Gardens, SW1. *T:* 01-584 2515. *Clubs:* Travellers'; Bengal (Calcutta).

**SHANNON, Howard Huntley,** CMG 1961; Member of House of Assembly, South Australia, since 1933; Member of Parliamentary Standing Committee on Public Works since 1941, and Chairman since 1954; *b* 1892; *s* of John Wallace Shannon and Alice Jane Shannon (*née* Moody); *m* 1915, Phoebe Madeline Watson; two *s* two *d*. *Educ:* Prince Alfred College, Australia. Chairman of Directors: SA Farmers' Co-operative Union Ltd; Farmers' Co-operative Executors and Trustees Ltd; Co-operative Insce Co. of Australia Ltd. House of Assembly for dist of Murray, 1933-38, dist of Onkaparinga, 1938-62. Govt Whip, 1938-41. *Address:* Bridgewater, South Australia. *T:* 39.100.

**SHAPCOTT, Sidney Edward;** Deputy Director, Admiralty Surface Weapons Establishment, since 1968; *b* 20 June 1920; *s* of late Percy Thomas Shapcott and of Beatrice Shapcott; *m* 1943, Betty Jean Richens; two *s* one *d*. *Educ:* Hele's School, Exeter; King's College, London. Joined Air Defence Experimental Establishment, 1941; various appointments in Min. of Supply and Min. of Aviation, 1941-62; DCSO, 1963; Dir of Projects, ESRO, 1963-65; Min. of Defence, Navy Dept, 1965-68; CSO, 1968. *Recreations:* travel, cinephotography. *Address:* 10 Christchurch Gardens, Widley, Portsmouth, Hants. *T:* Cosham 71417.

**SHAPLAND, Cyril Dee,** MB, BS London, MRCP, FRCS; Ophthalmic Surgeon, 1931-67, retired; Senior Ophthalmic Surgeon, University College Hospital, London, 1933-65 (Hon. Cons. Ophth. Surg., since 1965); Hon. Cons. Surg.: Moorfields Eye Hospital since 1964 (Ophth. Surg., 1938-64); Royal Marsden Hosp., since 1959 (Ophth. Surg., 1932-59); Cons. Ophth. Surg., Queen Mary's Hosp., Roehampton, 1946-61; Teacher in Ophthalmology, University of London (University Coll. Hosp. Med. Sch. and Inst. of Ophthalmology). Vice-Pres., Ophthalmological Soc. of the UK, 1965-68 (Mem. Council, 1945-48); FRSM; Mem. Irish Ophth. Soc.; Membre Titulaire de la Société Française d'Ophtalmologie; Vice-President Section of Ophthalmology, RSM, 1952-55; Vice-President Section of Ophthalmology, BMA, Glasgow, 1954; *b* 22 Nov. 1899; *s* of John Dee Shapland, MD, Exmouth, Devon, and Gertrude Emma Bond, Axminster, Devon; *m* 1927, Elizabeth Stratton. *Educ:* Univ. Coll.; Univ. Coll. Hospital, London. House Phys. and House Surg., UCH, 1922-23; Res. Phys., Ruthin Castle, N Wales, 1924-26; Jun. and Clin. Asst Moorfields Eye Hosp., 1927-29; 3rd, 2nd and 1st House Surg., and Sen. Res. Officer, Moorfields Eye Hosp., 1929-31; Registrar and Chief Clin. Asst, Moorfields, 1931-36; Ophth. Surg. to Willesden Gen. Hosp., 1932-37; Hon. Sec., Section of Ophthalmology, BMA Oxford, 1936; Pathologist and Curator, Moorfields Eye Hosp., 1936-39; Ophth. Surg., Middlesex CC, 1931-42; Hon. Secretary, Section of Ophthalmology, RSM, 1938-42. War Service: part-time Ophth. Surg., EMS, 1939-42; RAMC Ophth. Specialist, Royal Victoria Hospital, Netley, 1942-44; Comd Ophthalmologist, Southern Command, Jan.-Nov. 1944; Comd Ophth., London Dist, and Ophthalmic Specialist, Millbank, 1944-46; Adviser in Ophthalmology, United Kingdom, 1945-46 (rank of Lieutenant-Colonel). Pres. UCH Old Students' Assoc., 1967-68. Liveryman of Worshipful Society of Apothecaries of London, and Freeman of City of London; Hon. Member Instituto Barraquer, Barcelona, Spain; Membre d'Honneur, Club Jules Gonin, Lausanne, 1966. *Publications:* contrib. to Modern Trends in Ophthalmology, 3rd Series (Ed. A. Sorsby), 1955, to Operative Surgery, Vol. 8 (Ed. Rob and Smith), 1957, to Surgical Progress, 1960; and to The Operations of Surgery, vol. 2 (ed A. Gardham and D. R. Davies), 1969; various in British Medical Jl, Lancet, Brit. Jl Ophth., Trans. Ophth. Soc., Proc. Roy. Soc. Med., Jl of RAMC, Medical World, Medical Press, etc, since 1923. *Recreations:* fishing, photography, contract bridge. *Address:* (home) Cornerways, Orley Farm Road, Harrow-on-the-Hill, Middlesex. *T:* 01-422 2450. *Club:* Flyfishers'.

**SHAPLAND, Maj.-Gen. John Dee,** CB 1948; DSO 1944; MC 1918; *b* 31 July 1897; *e s* of Dr J. Dee Shapland and G. E. Bond, Exmouth, S Devon; *m* 1920, Lily Cardew Wood; one *s* twin *d*. *Educ:* Dulwich College; Royal Military Academy, Woolwich. 2nd Lieut RGA, April 1915; served European War, 1914-18, overseas with BEF and BSF (despatches twice, MC). TA Adjt 1923-25; Instructor in Gunnery, School of Artillery, 1927-29; psc 1931; Bde Major 3 Inf. Bde, India, 1934-36; Chitral Relief Column, 1932; Mohmand Operations, 1935 (despatches twice). DAAG, War Office, 1937-39; Chief Instructor in Gunnery, School of Artillery, 1941; CRA 2 Div. 1942-43; Comd 6 Inf. Bde, 1943-44 (wounded); BRA 12 Army, 1945; Maj.-Gen. 1946; Commandant Military

Coll. of Science, 1946-48; Major-General i/c Administration, BAOR, 1948-51; retired, 1952. Resident Manager, Willoughbys Consolidated Co. Ltd Rhodesia (Ranching), 1952-62. *Address:* c/o National Westminster Bank Ltd, Woking, Surrey; 42 Lawley Road, Bulawayo, Rhodesia. *Clubs:* United Service; Bulawayo.

**SHAPLEY, Harlow;** Director of the Harvard College Observatory, 1921-52, Emeritus, 1952; *b* 2 Nov. 1885; *s* of Willis Harlow Shapley and Sarah Stowell; *m* 1914, Martha Betz; four *s* one *d*. *Educ:* Univ. of Missouri, AB, AM, LLD; Princeton Univ., PhD, ScD. Astronomer, Mount Wilson Observatory, 1914-21; Lecturer, Lowell Institute, Boston, 1922; Exchange Lecturer, Belgian Universities, 1926; Halley Lecturer, Oxford, 1928; Darwin Lecturer (Royal Astronomical Society, London) 1934; Arthur Lecturer, New York University, 1934; Harris Lecturer, Northwestern University, 1935; LLD, Oglethorpe; ScD: Univs of Pittsburgh, Pennsylvania, Brown, Harvard, Toronto, New York, Copenhagen, Delhi, Ireland, Hawaii, St Lawrence; D *hc* Mexico, Nat. Michoacan (Mexico); LittD, Bates. Medals: Draper, Univ. of Brussels, Rumford, Society of Arts and Sciences, Royal Astronomical, Bruce, Astronomical Society of Pacific, Janssen (Paris), Pope Pius XI Prize, Aguila Azteca (Mexico), Calcutta Science Soc.; Hon. Foreign Member French, Mexican, Indian, Swedish, Austrian, Portuguese, Norwegian, Belgian, Lombard and Italian National Academies, and Royal Irish Academy. Past President: Science Clubs of America; Science Service; American Acad. of Arts and Sciences; American Astronomical Society; American Association for Advancement of Science; Research Soc. of America; Worcester Foundation for Experimental Biology; World Wide Broadcasting Foundation; Trustee: Massachusetts Inst. of Tech.; Woods Hole Oceanographic Inst., etc. Pres., Inst. of Religion in an Age of Science, 1959-62. *Publications:* Star Clusters, 1930; Source Book in Astronomy, 1929; Flights From Chaos, 1930; Galaxies, 1943; Treasury of Science, 1943; Of Stars and Men (in seven languages); Climatic Changes, 1952; The Inner Metagalaxy, 1957; Reading in Phys Sciences; Source book in Astronomy, 1900-1950, 1960; Science Ponders Religion, 1960; The View from a Distant Star; 500 tech. papers. *Address:* Peterboro, NH, USA. *Clubs:* Century (New York); St Botolph, Saturday, Examiner (Boston).

**SHARMAN, Thomas Charles,** OBE 1960; HM Diplomatic Service, retired; *b* 12 April 1912; *s* of Thomas Sharman and Mary Ward; *m* 1935, Paulette Elisabeth Padioleau; one *d*. *Educ:* Long Eaton County Secondary Sch.; Clare Coll., Cambridge. HM Consular Service, 1934; Paris, 1935; Saigon, 1937; Milan, 1939; British Embassy, Lisbon, 1940, and Moscow, 1945; HM Foreign Service, 1945; Batavia, 1946; Sao Paulo, 1947; Superintending Trade Consul, New Orleans, 1949; HM Consul, Luanda, 1952, Consul (Commercial) Hamburg, 1953; Counsellor (Commercial) Lisbon, 1960; Consul-General, Atlanta, Georgia, USA, 1965-68; Consul-General, Oporto, 1968-70. *Recreations:* fell- and particularly ben-walking; foreign languages. *Clubs:* Royal Automobile; Cosmopolitan (Hamburg).

**SHARP,** family name of **Baroness Sharp.**

**SHARP,** Baroness (Life Peeress) *cr* 1966, of Hornsey; **Evelyn (Adelaide) Sharp,** GBE 1961 (DBE 1948); Permanent Secretary, Ministry of Housing and Local Government, 1955-66; Member, Independent Television Authority, since 1966; Director, Bovis Holdings, since 1968; *b* 25 May 1903; *d* of Reverend Charles James Sharp, Vicar of Ealing, Middlesex, to 1935. *Educ:* St Paul's Girls' School; Somerville College, Oxford. Entered Administrative Class of Home Civil Service, 1926. Hon. DCL Oxon, 1960; Hon. LLD: Cantab, 1962; Manchester, 1967; Sussex, 1969. *Recreation:* pottering. *Address:* The Small House, Dinton, Salisbury, Wilts. *T:* Teffont 209. *Club:* University Women's.

**SHARP, Alastair George,** MBE 1945; QC 1961; **His Honour Judge Sharp;** Judge of County Courts, since 1962; Chairman, Durham County Quarter Sessions, since 1970 (Deputy Chairman, 1965-70); Chairman, Washington New Town Licensed Premises Committee, 1966; *b* 25 May 1911; *s* of late Alexander Sharp, Advocate in Aberdeen, and of late Mrs Isabella Sharp, OBE; *m* 1940, Daphne Sybil, *d* of late Maj. Harold Smithers, RGA , and of Mrs Connor; one *s* two *d*. *Educ:* Aberdeen Grammar School; Fettes; Clare College, Cambridge (Archdeacon Johnson Exhibitioner in Classics). BA 1933, 1st Class Hons Classical Tripos Part II, Aegrotat Part I. On staff of Bonar Law College, Ashridge, 1934-35; Barrister, Middle Temple, 1935; Harmsworth Law Scholar; North Eastern Circuit, 1936. Dep. Chm. of Agricultural Land Tribunal, Northern Area, 1958-62; Recorder of Rotherham, 1960-62. Commissioned, The Gordon Highlanders, Feb. 1939; served War of 1939-45: Staff Coll., 1943; 2nd Bn The London Scottish, 1943, Temp. Major. *Recreations:* golf, gardening, music, Scottish dancing, sailing. *Address:* 49 South Street, Durham. *T:* Durham 3706; 5 King's Bench Walk, Temple, EC4. *Club:* Durham County; Bar Yacht, Derwent Reservoir Sailing, Brancepeth Castle Golf.

*See also R. L. Sharp.*

**SHARP, Sir Edward Herbert,** 3rd Bt *cr* 1922; *b* 3 Dec. 1927; *s* of Sir Herbert Edward Sharp, 2nd Bt, and Ray Alice Mary, *d* of Frederick George Bloomfield, Ealing; *S* father 1936; *m* 1949, Beryl Kathleen, *d* of L. Simmons-Green, Shirley, Warwicks; one *s* one *d*. *Educ:* Haileybury. *Heir:* *s* Adrian Sharp, *b* 17 Sept. 1951. *Address:* PO Box 292, Castries, St Lucia, West Indies.

**SHARP, Francis Everard,** CIE 1942; Indian Police (retired); *b* 4 April 1890; *s* of late Benjamin Sharp, MA (Oxon); *m* 1947, Doris Mabel, *widow* of Col C. W. Stevens, RIASC, and *d* of late Ernest Hugo Robinson. *Educ:* Felsted School. Joined Indian Police, 1909; King's Police Medal, 1921. *Address:* c/o Standard Bank of SA, Adderley St, Cape Town, South Africa. *Club:* East India and Sports.

**SHARP, Geoffrey Newton;** Founder, editor and proprietor of The Music Review, 1940; Director of Newton Sharp Estates Ltd, 1951, Chairman, 1951, 1956, 1961, 1968; *b* 14 June 1914; *m* 1940, Mary Houghton. *Educ:* Uppingham; Trinity College, Cambridge. Post-graduate course with Pye Radio, Ltd, giving special attention to LF amplification and acoustics, 1935; Royal College of Music, 1937; Fellow of Royal Philharmonic Society, 1938-41; studied operatic production under Carl Ebert at Glyndebourne, 1939. Commissioned RA, Nov. 1943; resigned commission, April 1944. Life member Royal Musical Assoc., elected to Council, 1945; Music section Critics' Circle, 1945, Hon. Secretary, 1948, Chairman 1950, Vice-Pres. of Circle, 1953, Pres. 1954; LCMC Committee, 1946. *Publications:* various essays for weekly, monthly and quarterly periodicals. *Recreation:* photography. *Address:* Herons, Barnston, Dunmow, Essex. *T:* Felsted 268. *Club:* Kennel.

**SHARP, Lt-Col Granville Maynard,** MA (Cantab); *b* 5 Jan. 1906; *s* of Walter Sharp, Cleckheaton, Yorks; *m* 1935, Margaret, *d* of Dr J. H. Vincent, Wembley Hill; two *d*. *Educ:* Cleckheaton Grammar School; Ashville College, Harrogate; St John's College, Cambridge, MA (Hons) (Economics). Lecturer in Economics at West Riding Technical Institutes, 1929-34; Chairman, Spenborough Housing and Town Planning Committee, 1935-40; Hon. Secretary, Spen Valley Divisional Labour Party, 1936-39; Battery Capt. 68 Anti-Tank Regt RA, 1939-42; Staff Capt. and DAQMG Belfast Area, 1942-43; Senior British Staff Officer, Economics Section, Allied Control Commission, Italy, 1943-44; Chief Economics and Supply Officer, Military Govt, Austria, 1944-45. MP (Lab) for Spen Valley Div. of West Riding of Yorks, 1945-50; PPS Min. of Civil Aviation, 1946; Chairman, Select Cttee of Estimates Sub-Cttee, 1946-48; Parliamentary Private Sec. to Minister of Works, 1947-50. Keymer Parish Councillor; CC East Sussex. *Recreations:* swimming, singing, scything, Sussex Downs. *Address:* 31 Wilmington Close, Hassocks, Sussex. *T:* Hassocks 2294.

**SHARP, Harold Gregory,** FIA, FFA; Former Manager and Actuary Scottish Widows' Fund and Life Assurance Soc., Edinburgh; *b* 18 Aug. 1886; *s* of late Isaac Sharp, formerly Secretary and Recording Clerk of the Society of Friends, and Isabella Gregory; *m* 1917, Hilda May (*d* 1966), 3rd *d* of late Arthur Harrison Clapham; no *c*. *Educ:* Quaker Schools at Ackworth, Yorks, and Sidcot, Somerset. Assistant Actuary, National Mutual Life Assurance Society, 1919-23; Secretary, Scottish Widows' Fund Society, 1924-29; Chairman of Associated Scottish Life Offices, 1936-38. *Address:* 40 Pentland Avenue, Edinburgh EH13 0HY. *T:* 031-441 2994. *Club:* New (Edinburgh).

**SHARP, Henry Sutcliffe,** FRCS; Surgeon, Ear, Nose and Throat Department: Hospital for Sick Children, Great Ormond Street; Charing Cross Hospital; Putney Hospital; *b* 23 June 1910; *s* of late Alexander Sharp, CB, CMG; *m* 1st, 1948, Muiriel Oliver; two *s*; 2nd, 1964, Elizabeth Plant; one *s*. *Educ:* Haileybury College; Caius Coll., Cambridge; St Thomas's Hosp. BA, MB, ChB (Cantab); FRCS. House Surgeon and Chief Asst, Ear, Nose and Throat Dept, St Thomas's Hosp., 1935. Major RAMC, 1940-45. FRSocMed; Member and past Hon. Sec. of Sections of Laryngology and Otology; Corresp. Mem., Excerpta Medica, Amsterdam. *Publications:* various articles concerning otolaryngology in Jl of Laryngology, Lancet, and Brit. Jl of Surgery. *Recreations:* golf, squash rackets. *Address:* 149 Harley Street, W1. *T:* 01-935 4444; 1 Linnell Close, Hampstead, NW11. *T:* 01-458 3937. *Clubs:* United University, Kensington Close; Sandy Lodge Golf (Moor Park).

**SHARP, Lt-Gen. Sir John (Aubrey Taylor),** KCB 1970 (CB 1969); MC 1942 and Bar 1943; GOC 1 (British) Corps, since 1970; *b* 6 Sept. 1917; *s* of A. T. Sharp, Nether Hall, Scraptoft, Leicestershire; *m* 1946, Wendy Ward; one *s* three *d*. *Educ:* Bilton Grange Prep. Sch.; Repton Sch.; Jesus Coll., Cambridge. MA Cantab, 2nd Class Hons, 1939. Served War of 1939-45: 5th Medium Regt, RA, BEF, 1939-40; 4th Regt RHA, 1941-43; Staff Coll., Quetta, 1944; Personal Liaison Officer to Field-Marshal Montgomery, 1945; Battery Comdr, 4th Regt RHA, 1945-46; Instructor, RMA, Sandhurst, 1947-50; War Office, 1951-52; Battery Comdr, 2nd Regt, RHA, 1953-55; Mil. Asst: to C-in-C, FARELF, 1955-56; Adj.-Gen. 1956-57; CO, 1st Regt, RHA, 1959-60; Comdr, 11th Infty Bde Gp, 1961-62; Student, IDC, 1963; Comdt, School of Artillery, Larkhill, 1964-66; GOC, 2nd Div., 1966-67; Comdt, Staff College, Camberley, 1967-69. Colonel Commandant: Royal Regt of Artillery, 1969-; RAEC, 1970-. *Recreations:* most games and field sports. *Address:* c/o Lloyds Bank Ltd, 6 Pall Mall, SW1. *Clubs:* Army and Navy, MCC; I Zingari; Free Foresters; Hawks, etc.

**SHARP, Brig. Mainwaring Cato Ensor,** CBE 1945; *b* 1 March 1897; *s* of late Rev. Cato Ensor Sharp; *m* 1949, Betty Yolande Constance, *o d* of late Col M. H. Knaggs, CMG. *Educ:* Trinity College School, Port Hope; RMC, Kingston, Canada. Commissioned, 1915, 5th RI Lancers; transfd Leinster Regt 1916; S Lanc. Regt 1922. Staff College, Camberley, 1928-29; retired, 1935; Insurance Broker, 1937-39; rejoined, 1939; Lt-Col 1941; Brig. 1944. Served European War and War of 1939-45 (despatches twice). Director of Maintenance, Control Commission, Germany, 1946-51; employed by War Office, 1951-58. Croix de Guerre (France); Officer, Legion of Merit (USA). *Recreations:* golf, ornithology. *Address:* The Old Malt House, Walberton, Arundel, Sussex. *T:* Yapton 274.

**SHARP, Margery;** novelist and playwright; *m* 1938, Major G. L. Castle, RA. *Educ:* Streatham Hill High School; London University. French Honours BA. *Publications:* Rhododendron Pie; Fanfare for Tin Trumpets; The Flowering Thorn; Four Gardens; The Nymph and the Nobleman; Sophy Cassmajor; Meeting at Night (play); The Nutmeg Tree, 1937 (play: USA 1940, England 1941, filmed as Julia Misbehaves, 1948); The Stone of Chastity, 1940; Cluny Brown, 1944 (filmed 1946); Britannia Mews, 1946 (filmed 1949); The Foolish Gentlewoman, 1948 (Play, London, 1949); Lise Lillywhite, 1951; The Gipsy in the Parlour, 1953; The Tigress on the Hearth, 1955; The Eye of Love, 1957; The Rescuers, 1959; Something Light, 1960; Martha in Paris, 1962; Martha, Eric and George, 1964; The Sun in Scorpio, 1965; In Pious Memory, 1968; Rosa, 1969; *books for children:* Miss Bianca, 1962; The Turret, 1964 (USA 1963); Miss Bianca in the Salt Mines, 1966; Lost at the Fair, 1967; Miss Bianca in the Orient, 1970. *Address:* c/o The Westminster Bank Ltd, St James's Square, SW1.

**SHARP, Sir Milton Reginald,** 3rd Bt, *cr* 1920; Capt. REME, TA; *b* 21 Nov. 1909; *s* of Sir Milton Sharp, 2nd Bt, and Gertrude (*d* 1940), *d* of John Earl, of London; *S* father, 1941; *m* 1951, Marie-Louise de Vignon, Paris. *Educ:* Shrewsbury; Trinity Hall, Cambridge.

**SHARP, Hon. Mitchell William,** PC (Can.); MP for Eglinton; Secretary of State for External Affairs, Canada, since 1968; *b* 11 May 1911; *s* of Thomas Sharp and Elizabeth (*née* Little); *m* 1938, Daisy Boyd; one *s*. *Educ:* University of Manitoba; London School of Economics. Statistician, Sanford Evans Statistical Service, 1926-36; Economist, James Richardson & Sons Ltd, 1937-42; Officer, Canadian Dept of Finance, Ottawa, 1942-51; Director Economic Policy Division, 1947-51; Associate Deputy Minister, Canadian Dept Trade and Commerce, 1951-57; Dep. Minister, 1957-58; Minister, 1963-65; elected to Canadian House of Commons, 1963; Minister of Finance, 1965-68. Vice-Pres., Brazilian Traction, Light & Power Co., Toronto, 1958-62. Hon. LLD

Univ. of Manitoba, 1965. *Recreations:* music, walking, skating. *Address:* Parliament Buildings, Ottawa, Ont, Canada. *T:* 992-1518. *Club:* Toronto (Toronto).

**SHARP, Noel Farquharson;** Keeper, Department of Printed Books, British Museum, 1959-66; *b* 22 Dec. 1905; *o s* of Robert Farquharson Sharp, sometime Keeper, Department of Printed Books, British Museum; *m* 1945, Rosemarie Helen, *d* of Commander E. F. Fanning, RN; one *s* one *d*. *Educ:* Haileybury College; New College, Oxford. Assistant Keeper, Department of Printed Books, British Museum, 1929-52; Deputy Keeper also Superintendent of Reading Room, British Museum, 1952-59. Hon. FLA, 1968. *Address:* 1 Tudor Cottages, Hall Street, Long Melford, Sussex.

**SHARP, Rear-Adm. Philip Graham,** CB 1967; DSC 1942; Director, The National Society for Clean Air; Chairman, Executive Committee of British Reserve Forces Association, since 1969; *b* 23 Nov. 1913; *e s* of late Rev. Douglas Simmonds Sharp; *m* 1940, Dilys Mary Adwyth, *er d* of David Roberts, Welford-on-Avon, Warwicks; one *s*. *Educ:* Northampton Sch.; Tynemouth High Sch. Sub-Lt, RNVR, 1937; Lt RNVR, HMS Sikh, 1939-42; Lt-Comdr RNVR comdg HMS Broadway, Badsworth, Cattistock and Forester, 1943-46; Lt-Comdr RN, 1947; HMS Eskimo, 1946-47; HMS King Alfred, 1947; HMS Raleigh, 1947-48; Naval Staff, Admty, 1948-50; Comdr 1949; NATO, 1950-52; HMS Gambia, 1952-54; HMS Dolphin, 1954-56; Capt. 1956; comdg HMS Defender, 1956-58; NATO, 1958-60; Capt. of Fleet, Home Fleet, 1960-62; comdg HMS Centaur 1962-63; Cdre RN Barracks, Portsmouth, 1963-65; Rear-Adm. 1965; Flag Officer Sea Training, Portland, 1965-67; retired 1967. ADC to the Queen, 1965. *Recreations:* golf, fishing, music, model-making. *Address:* The Spain House, Petersfield, Hants. *T:* Petersfield 3941. *Club:* Naval and Military.

**SHARP, Richard Lyall;** Under-Secretary, HM Treasury, since 1968; *b* 27 March 1915; *s* of late Alexander Sharp, Advocate, Aberdeen, and late Mrs Isabella Sharp, OBE; *m* 1950, Jean Helen, *er d* of late Sir James Crombie, KCB, KBE, CMG, and of Lady Crombie; two *s* two *d* (and one *d* decd). *Educ:* Fettes Coll.; Aberdeen Univ.; Clare Coll., Cambridge. MA with 1st Class Hons Classics, Aberdeen 1937; BA with 1st Class in Classical Tripos, Cambridge 1939. Served Royal Northumberland Fusiliers, 1939-46 (POW, Singapore and Siam, 1942-45). Principal, HM Treasury, 1946; Private Sec. to Chancellor of Exchequer, 1948-50 and to Minister of State for Economic Affairs, 1950; UK Treasury and Supply Delegn, Washington, 1952-56; Asst Sec., 1954; IDC, 1961; Under-Sec., Nat. Bd for Prices and Incomes, 1966-68. *Recreations:* playing the viola, gardening. *Address:* 15 Richmond Road, New Barnet, Herts. *T:* 01-449 6552.

*See also A. G. Sharp.*

**SHARP, Thomas,** CBE 1951; MA, DLitt; FRIBA, MTPI, FILA; town and country planning consultant, architect, landscape architect, writer; *b* 12 April 1901; *s* of Francis Sharp and Margaret Beresford; *m* Rachel, *d* of Cameron Morrison. *Educ:* Council Schools. Worked in local govt offices, 1917-37; Lecturer then Reader, in Town and Country Planning, Univ. of Durham, 1937-45; Senior Research Officer, Ministry of Town and Country Planning, 1941-43; since 1945 in private practice; designer of plans for Durham, Exeter, Oxford, Salisbury, Chichester, King's Lynn, Taunton, St Andrews, Kensington, Todmorden, Minehead, Stockport, Rugby and other towns, new villages in Northumberland for Forestry Commission, new seaside village, Port-Eynon, S Wales; re-landscaping of St John's Backs, Cambridge; planning adviser, Vienna, 1955; Mellon Vis. Prof. Univ. of Illinois, 1965. President of Town Planning Institute, 1945-46; President of Institute of Landscape Architects, 1949-51; Mem. Council RIBA, 1958-60. *Publications:* Future Development of South-West Lancashire, 1930; Town and Countryside, 1932; A Derelict Area, 1935; English Panorama, 1937; Town Planning, 1940; Cathedral City, 1945; Anatomy of the Village, 1946; Exeter Phoenix, 1946; Oxford Replanned, 1948; Georgian City, 1949; Newer Sarum, 1949; Oxford Observed, 1952; Design in Town and Village (jointly), 1953; Northumberland, 1954; Dreaming Spires and Teeming Towers, 1963; Town and Townscape, 1968. *Address:* 1 Farndon Road, Oxford.

**SHARPE, Sir Reginald (Taaffe),** Kt 1947; QC; Chairman of National Health Service Tribunal for England and Wales since 1948; Chairman, East Sussex Quarter Sessions, since 1969; Deputy Chairman: Quarter Sessions, Middlesex area of Greater London since 1965; Justices for Hailsham Petty Sessional Division, 1950-57 and since 1959 (Chairman, 1957-58); Member, Governing Body of Westminster School, since 1955; *b* 20 November 1898; *o s* of late Herbert Sharpe, Lindfield, Sussex. *Educ:* Westminster. Served European War: enlisted in Army, 1916; 2nd Lieut Grenadier Guards (SR), Jan. 1917; Lt, 1918; served with 2nd Bn in France (wounded). Called to Bar at Gray's Inn, Easter, 1920. Went South-Eastern Circuit and Sussex Sessions. Judge of High Court, Rangoon, 1937-48; Director of Supply, Burma (at Calcutta), 1942-44; Trustee of Rangoon University Endowment Fund, 1946-48; KC Feb. 1949; HM Comr of Assize: Western and Northern Circuits, 1949; Midland and Western Circuits, 1950; South-Eastern Circuit, 1952; North-Eastern Circuit, 1954; Birmingham October Assize, 1954; Midland Circuit, 1960. Special Comr for Divorce Causes, 1948-67. Deputy Chairman QS: E Sussex, 1949-69; W Kent, 1949-62; Kent, 1962-69; Mddx, 1963-65 (Asst Chm. 1951-63); Asst Chm., W Sussex QS, 1950-70. Mem. Standing Jt Cttee for E Sussex, 1958-65, for W Sussex, 1953-65. Mem., Nat. Arbitration Tribunal, 1951, and of Industrial Disputes Tribunal, 1951; Chairman, 1951-54, of Joint Council, and Independent Chairman, 1955-57, of Conciliation Board set up by Assoc. of Health and Pleasure Resorts and the Musicians' Union; Sole Commissioner to hold British Honduras Inquiry at Belize, March 1954; Chm., Departmental Cttee on Summary Trial of Minor Offences in Magistrates' Courts, 1954-55. JP for Sussex, Kent and Mddx. *Address:* 4 King's Bench Walk, Temple, EC4. *T:* 01-353 1696 and 1401; Northfield House, Boreham Street, nr Hailsham, Sussex. *T:* Herstmonceux 2147. *Club:* East India and Sports.

**SHARPE, William James,** CBE 1967 (OBE 1950); Director of Communications, Foreign and Commonwealth Office (formerly Foreign Office), 1965-69, retired; *b* 3 Jan. 1908; *s* of James Sharpe; *m* 1940, Doreen Winifred Cockell; three *s*. *Educ:* Aldershot Grammar School, 1927-39: Merchant Navy; Marconi International; Marine Communications Company. Commissioned Royal Corps of Signals, 1940; Served in France and South East Asia; Lt-Col 1945. Diplomatic Wireless Service, 1947; Deputy Director of Communications, 1959. *Address:* The Mount,

Tingewick, Buckingham. *T:* Finmere 291. *Club:* Naval and Military.

**SHARPLES, Richard Christopher,** OBE 1953; MC 1940; MP (C) Sutton and Cheam since November 1954; Minister of State, Home Office, since 1970; *b* 6 August 1916; *s* of Richard William Sharples, OBE; *m* 1946, Pamela Newall; two *s* two *d*. *Educ:* Eton; Royal Military College, Sandhurst. 2nd Lt Welsh Guards, 1936; served War of 1939-45 with Welsh Guards and on staff, France, Italy, Far East (wounded, despatches); Major, 1948; Military Assistant to Field Marshal Viscount Montgomery of Alamein, 1951-53. Parliamentary Private Secretary to: Minister of State for Foreign Affairs, 1955-56; Home Secretary, Rt Hon. R. A. Butler, CH, MP, 1957-59; Assistant Government Whip, 1959-60; Joint Parliamentary Secretary, Ministry of Pensions and National Insurance, 1961-62; Parliamentary Secretary, Ministry of Public Building and Works, July 1962-Oct. 1964. Vice-Chm., Conservative Party, 1968-. Silver Star Medal (USA). *Address:* 19 Great College Street, SW1. *T:* 01-930 4919; Southfield Farm, Chawton, Alton, Hants. *T:* Alton 3318. *Clubs:* Carlton, Turf, Pratt's.

**SHARWOOD-SMITH, Sir Bryan (Evers),** KCMG 1955 (CMG 1950); KCVO 1956; KBE 1953; ED; Governor, Northern Nigeria, 1954-57 (Lieut-Governor, and President Northern House of Chiefs, 1952-54); retd 1957; *b* 5 Jan. 1899; *s* of late Edward Sharwood Smith; *m* 1st, 1926; one *d*; 2nd, 1939, Winifred Joan, *d* of late Thomas and Winifred Mitchell; two *s* one *d*. *Educ:* Newbury School; Aldenham School, Herts (Platt Schol.). Elected to Open Classical Schol., Emmanuel College, Cambridge, 1916, but entered army (RFC), 1917; served France, Rhine and North West Frontier India, 1917-20. Assistant Master St Cuthbert's Preparatory School, Malvern, 1920. Entered Colonial Administrative Service, 1920; served in British Cameroons, 1920-27, Nigeria, 1927-57. Military Service, 1940-42; Resident, 1942; Resident, Kano, Nigeria, 1950-52; and President of Northern Region House of Assembly, 1950-52. Acting Chief Commissioner, Northern Provinces, Sept.-Dec. 1950. *Publication:* But Always as Friends, 1969. *Address:* 47 Cooden Drive, Bexhill, Sussex. *Club:* Royal Air Force.

**SHATTOCK, Rear-Adm. Ernest Henry,** CB 1955; OBE 1943; Managing Director, European Export and Investment Service Ltd; *b* 22 October 1904; *s* of late Ernest Mark Shattock and late Evelyn Mabel (*née* Bryde); *m* 1958, Oz Armstrong; one *s* three *d* (of previous *m*). *Educ:* Osborne; Dartmouth. Entered Osborne, 1918; specialised in flying, 1927; Commander, 1938; Captain, 1943; Rear-Admiral, 1953. Served War of 1939-45; Chief of Staff to Flag Officer Naval Air Pacific, 1944-46; Director Naval Air Warfare Division, 1946-49; commanded HMS Glory, 1949-50. Directing Captain, Senior Officers' War College, 1951; Flag Officer, Malaya, Nov. 1953-April 1956; retired list, 1956. Naval ADC to the Queen, 1953. *Publication:* An Experiment in Mindfulness, 1958. *Recreations:* music, magic. *Address:* The Mill House, Newark, Ripley, Surrey. *T:* Ripley 3020. *Club:* Royal Automobile.

**SHATTOCK, John Swithun Harvey,** CMG 1952; OBE 1946; HM Diplomatic Service, 1947-67; *b* 21 Nov. 1907; *s* of late Rev. E. A. Shattock, Kingston St Mary, Nr Taunton; unmarried. *Educ:* Westminster School; Christ Church, Oxford. Entered ICS, 1931; served in Bengal, 1931-36; Under Sec., Govt of India (Defence Dept), 1936-39; joined Indian Political Service, 1939; served in Kathiawar, Baroda, and Kashmir Residencies, 1939-44; Dep. Sec. to Crown Representative (Political Dept), New Delhi, 1944-46; Chief Minister, Chamba State, 1946-47; apptd HM Diplomatic Service, 1947; served in UK High Commission, New Delhi, 1947-49; Head of Far Eastern Dept, Foreign Office, London, 1950-51; Head of China and Korea Dept, FO 1951; FO Rep. at Imperial Defence Coll., London, 1952; Head of China and Korea Dept, FO, 1953; Counsellor, British Embassy, Belgrade, Dec. 1953-Nov. 1955; Political Representative, Middle East Forces, Cyprus, Jan. 1956-Nov. 1958. Deputy to UK Permanent Representative on North Atlantic Council, Paris, 1959-61; Minister, UK Delegation to Disarmament Conference, Geneva, 1961-63; FO, 1963-67. *Recreation:* travel. *Address:* St Mary's Cottage, Kingston St Mary, Nr Taunton, Somerset; National and Grindlay's Bank Ltd, 13 St James's Square, SW1. *Club:* Travellers'.

**SHATWELL, Prof. Kenneth Owen;** Challis Professor of Law and Dean of the Faculty of Law, in the University of Sydney, since 1947; *b* 16 Oct. 1909; *m* 1936, Betty, *d* of Thomas Rae Hogarth, Tasmania; one *s* one *d* (and one *d* decd). *Educ:* Lincoln College, Oxford. Served War of 1939-45: Lieut RANVR, on active service in Atlantic and Pacific. Prof. of Law and Dean of the Faculty of Law, Univ. of Tasmania, 1934-47; Vis. Prof., The Queen's Univ., Belfast, 1951; Australian Comr, S Pacific Commn, 1950-52; Sen. Research Fellow, Yale Univ., 1958-59, 1962; Visiting Professor: New York Univ. Law School Summer Workshop on Contracts, 1962; Temple Univ. Law School, 1968. Aust. Mem., Permanent Court of Arbitration under the Hague Convention, 1960-. *Publications:* various articles in legal jls. *Recreation:* criminology. *Address:* 36 Chilton Parade, Turramurra, NSW 2074, Australia. *T:* Sydney 48-1189. *Clubs:* Athenæum; Tasmanian (Hobart); Imperial Services (Sydney).

**SHAUGHNESSY,** family name of **Baron Shaughnessy.**

**SHAUGHNESSY,** 3rd Baron, *cr* 1916, of Montreal; **William Graham Shaughnessy;** Major Canadian Grenadier Guards (R of O); *b* 28 March 1922; *s* of 2nd Baron and Marion (*d* 1936), *d* of late R. K. Graham, Montreal; *S* father, 1938; *m* 1944, Mary Whitley, *o d* of John Whitley, Copthorne House, Letchworth; two *s* two *d*. *Heir:* *s* Hon. Patrick John Shaughnessy, *b* 23 Oct. 1944. *Address:* 1227 Sherbrooke Street W, Montreal, Canada.

**SHAVE, Kenneth George,** CEng, FIMechE; Member, London Transport Executive, since 1967; *b* 25 June 1908; *s* of George Shave and Frances Larkin; *m* 1935, Doris May Stone; one *s* one *d*. *Educ:* St Pauls School. Apprenticed London General Omnibus Company, 1925; Rolling Stock Engineer, East Surrey Traction Company, 1930; London Transport: Asst Divisional Engineer, 1935; Divisional Engineer, 1948; Rolling Stock Engineer, 1956; Chief Mechanical Engineer, 1965. OStJ 1963. *Recreations:* golf, bridge, gardening. *Address:* 37 Kinnaird Avenue, Chiswick, W4. *T:* 01-994 3020.

**SHAW;** *see* Byam Shaw.

**SHAW;** *see* Knox-Shaw.

**SHAW,** family name of **Baron Craigmyle.**

**SHAW, Alexander Malcolm,** CMG 1946; BSA; retired as Chairman, Agricultural Prices Support Board, Department of Agriculture,

Canada; *b* Woodburn, Ont., 12 June 1885; *s* of Robert Shaw and Annie Brown; *m* 1918, Winkona Wheelock (*d* 1948), *d* of Frederic Frank, Orangeville, Ontario; one *s* one *d*. *Educ:* Niagara Falls Collegiate Inst.; Ont. Agric. Coll.; Univ. of Toronto. *Address:* PO Box 518, Aylmer East, PQ, Canada.

**SHAW, Anne Gillespie, (Mrs J. H. Pirie),** CBE 1954; Chairman and Managing Director of: The Anne Shaw Organisation Ltd, since 1945; Anne Shaw Data Processing Ltd since 1960; Office Reorganisation Ltd since 1960; Director, Wescot Ltd, since 1964; *b* Uddingston, Scotland, 28 May 1904; *d* of late Major David P. Shaw, Cameronians (killed in action, 1915), and late Mrs Helen B. Shaw; *m* 1937, John Henderson Pirie; one *s* two *d*. *Educ:* St Leonards School, St Andrews, Fife; Edinburgh University; Bryn Mawr College, Philadelphia, USA. MA (Edinburgh) 1927; Post-Graduate Diploma, Social Economy (Bryn Mawr), 1928. Metropolitan-Vickers Electrical Co. Ltd, 1930-45; Production Efficiency Board, advising Sir Stafford Cripps at MAP, 1942-45; Independent Member of Cotton Working Party, 1945-46. Member: National Advisory Council on Education for Industry and Commerce, 1948-60, Management, 1963; Committee of Enquiry on Training of Teachers for Technical Colleges (set up by Minister of Education); Milk Marketing Bd, 1964-; NEDC for Post Office; Ct of Inquiry into Ford dispute, 1968. Chm. Management Consultants Assoc., 1967. Fellow, Inst. of Personnel Management (Pres. 1949-51); FBIM (Mem. Council, 1968-); CEng; FIProdE. Gilbreth Medal for contribution to scientific management (Soc. for Advancement of Management), 1948. *Publications:* Introduction to the Theory and Application of Motion Study, 1944; Purpose and Practice of Motion Study, 1952. *Recreations:* cine-photography, ski-ing, camping, gardening. *Address:* Elmhurst, Biddulph, Staffordshire. *T:* Biddulph 2243. *Clubs:* University Women's, Women's Press, Ladies Caledonian; Royal Scottish Automobile (Glasgow).

**SHAW, Arnold John;** *b* 12 July 1909; *s* of Solomon and Rachel Shaw; *m* 1935, Elizabeth Solomons; one *d*. *Educ:* Trafalgar Sq. (LCC) Primary Sch.; Coopers' Company's Sch.; Univ. of Southampton. BA (Hons) London, 1930. Entered teaching profession, 1932. Member: Stepney Borough Coun., 1934-48; Ilford Borough Coun., 1952-64 (Alderman, 1963-64); Redbridge, London Borough Coun., 1964-68. Contested (Lab) Ilford South, 1964; MP (Lab) Ilford South, 1966-70. *Recreation:* gardening. *Address:* 2a Claybury Broadway, Ilford, Essex.

**SHAW, Sir Bernard (Vidal),** Kt 1957; *b* 28 April 1891; *s* of late Bernard Vidal Shaw; *m* 1929, Katharine Ceceley, *d* of Arthur Stanley Colls. *Educ:* St Paul's School. Indian Police, 1910-23; called to Bar, Gray's Inn, 1923; entered Colonial Service (Kenya), 1925; Resident Magistrate, 1928; Relieving President, District Court, Palestine, 1936; President, 1941; Chairman, Awqaf Commission, 1939-40; Puisne Judge, Supreme Court of Palestine, 1945-48. Chairman, North Midland District Valuation Board, 1950-55; Chm., Medical Appeal Tribunals, 1952-64; Sen. Puisne Judge, Cyprus, 1955-57. *Publications:* Kenya Law Reports, 1927-30 (Collator and Editor), and 1931-32 (Editor). *Recreation:* tennis. *Address:* 45 Rivermead Court, SW6. *T:* 01-736 1644. *Clubs:* Athenæum; Hurlingham.

**SHAW, Charles James Dalrymple;** *see* Kilbrandon, Hon. Lord.

**SHAW, Sir Evelyn Campbell,** KCVO, *cr* 1947 (CVO 1930; MVO 1919); LLD (Hon.) St Andrews; Fellow of the Imperial College of Science and Technology; Hon. Associate, Royal Inst. of British Architects; Hon. Member, Royal College of Music; Hon. Fellow, British School, Rome; *b* 1882; *m* 1911, Freda, *d* of late Lieutenant-Colonel J. H. C. Whipple, MD, Coldstream Guards; two *d*. *Educ:* abroad. Dulwich College, Trinity College, Oxford. Asst Secretary, 1904-10, Secretary, 1910-47, of Royal Commission of 1851; Hon. Gen. Sec. British School at Rome, 1912-47; elected member of both bodies on retirement in 1947. Hon. Treasurer Roy. Agricultural Benevolent Inst., 1925-65. *Address:* Little Morcote, Shalford, Surrey. *Club:* Athenæum.

**SHAW, Frank Howard,** MBE 1945; TD; MA; JP; Headmaster, King's College School, Wimbledon, since 1960; *b* 13 June 1913; *s* of E. H. Shaw; *m* 1950, Harriette Alice, *d* of late His Honour Robert Peel; one *s* two *d*. *Educ:* Altrincham Grammar School; Hertford College, Oxford. Asst master: King's Coll. School, 1935-39; Marlborough College (and Housemaster), 1939-52; first Headmaster of Pakistan Air Force Public School, Murree Hills, 1952-58; Principal, Aden Coll., Aden, 1958-60. Served War of 1939-45 in Devonshire Regt; Jt Planning Staff, 1943-45. Lt-Col. JP, SW London, 1966-. *Publications:* textbooks for teaching of English in Pakistan. *Recreation:* golf. *Address:* 12 Belvedere Drive, Wimbledon, SW19. *T:* 01-946 9504. *Clubs:* Athenæum; MCC.

**SHAW, George Anthony Theodore,** CBE 1965; Secretary, Milton Keynes Development Corporation, since 1967; *b* 25 Oct. 1917; *s* of late G. E. Shaw, CMG, OBE, LLB; *m* 1st, Suzanne Alexandra Barber (marr. diss.), *d* of late H. C. Barber; one *s* one *d*; 2nd, Joan Margaret, *d* of late Rev. N. M. Livingstone, DCL, RN; two *d*. *Educ:* Marlborough Coll.; Clare Coll., Cambridge (MA). Served in Intell. Corps, Army, 1941-46, Indian Civil Service, 1944-45; HM Overseas Civil Service, 1940-67: Malaya, Singapore, Sarawak, Brunei, Malaysia; State Sec., Sarawak, 1963-67. Order of Star of Sarawak (PNBS), 1966. *Recreations:* wide. *Address:* Larchfield, Aspley Guise, Bletchley, Bucks. *Clubs:* East India and Sports; Royal Lymington Yacht.

**SHAW, Air Commodore Gerald Stanley,** CB 1952; RAF (retired); *b* 28 Oct. 1898; *s* of John Charles Shaw, JP; *m* 1935, Dorothy Margaret Dew; two *d*. *Educ:* King Edward VI School, Birmingham; University of Birmingham. Joined RNAS, 1917; transferred to RAF on formation, with commn as Lieut (Flying), 1918; graduated RAF Staff Coll., Andover, 1933; OC, No 18 (B) Sqdn, 1935; OC, RAF Station, Nairobi, E Africa, 1939; AO i/c Admin, Air HQ, E Africa, 1942-43; Director of Manning, Air Ministry, 1944-46; AOC, RAF Burma, 1947; Senior Air Liaison Officer and Air Adviser to High Commissioner, South Africa, 1948-50; Director of Personal Services, Air Ministry, 1950-52; retired, 1952. Liaison Officer Hunting Group of Companies, 1952-54. *Recreations:* tennis, swimming. *Address:* PO Box 20, Southbroom, Natal Coast, South Africa. *Club:* Royal Air Force.

**SHAW, Harry Balmforth,** MBE 1951; MA, MEd, FRGS; FRSA; retired as Headmaster, The Hulme Grammar School, Oldham (1931-65); *b* 28 November 1899; *s* of Rev. Harry Shaw and Mary Balmforth; *m* 1932, Joyce M. S. de la Rue, Guernsey, Channel Islands; no *c*. *Educ:* Nottingham High School; Manchester Grammar School (Scholar); King's College,

University of Durham, BA (Hons History), 1922, MA (Hons) 1925; Leeds Univ. MEd 1924; Hanson Sch., Bradford, 1924-26; Roundhay Sch., Leeds, 1926-31; Fellow, RGS, 1925; AmGS, 1927; RSA 1950; Member IAHM, 1931; HMC, 1932; Lt Loyal (N Lancs) Regt, 1917-19; Durham LI, TA, 1920-25, Capt.; Sen. Inspector, City of Leeds Special Constabulary, 1925-31; Commandant, Oldham Borough Special Constabulary; Chm. No 1 Police District, Commandants' Conf., 1945-52; Pres. Rotary Club of Oldham, 1947-48; Chairman, No 5 District, RIBI, 1950-52; Vice-Pres., RIBI, 1958-59; Pres., RIBI, 1959-60; Member, European Cttee Rotary Internat., 1960-61. *Publications:* numerous articles on education and current affairs. *Recreations:* motoring, foreign travel. *Address:* Saranac, Barrington Avenue, Cheadle Hulme, Cheshire. *T:* 061-485 3206.

**SHAW, Irwin;** writer (US); *b* New York, 27 Feb. 1913; *s* of William Shaw and Rose (*née* Tompkins); *m* 1939, Marian Edwards; one *s*. *Educ:* Brooklyn College (AB). Served War of 1939-45 in US Army. *Publications: plays:* Bury the Dead, 1936; Siege, 1937; The Gentle People, 1939; Quiet City, 1939; Retreat to Pleasure, 1941; Sons and Soldiers, 1943; The Assassin, 1945; Children From Their Games, 1963; *other works:* Sailor Off the Bremen, 1940; Welcome to the City, 1942; Act of Faith, 1946; The Young Lions, 1949; The Troubled Air, 1951; Mixed Company, 1952; Lucy Crown, 1956; Tip on a Dead Jockey, 1957; Two Weeks in Another Town (novel), 1960; Voices of a Summer Day, 1965; Love on a Dark Street, 1965; Rich Man, Poor Man, 1970. *Address:* c/o Weidenfeld & Nicholson, 20 New Bond Street, London, W1.

**SHAW, James John Sutherland,** CB 1970; Deputy Secretary, Civil Service Department, since 1969; *b* 5 Jan. 1912; *s* of Robert Shaw and Christina Macallum Sutherland; *m* 1947, Rosamond Chisholm Sharman; *no c*. *Educ:* Ardrossan Academy, Ayrshire; Glasgow and London Universities. Glasgow University: MA 1st Class Hons History, 1932, PhD 1935; Lecturer in History, 1936-40. Served War with RAF, 1940-45, Navigator, AC2 to Sqdn Leader (despatches). Senior Lecturer in History, Glasgow Univ., 1945-46; HM Treasury, 1946-68: Principal, Asst Secretary, Under-Secretary; Under-Secretary, Civil Service Dept, 1968-69. *Recreations:* talking, walking and gardening. *Address:* Halfpenny Corner, Halfpenny Lane, Chilworth, near Guildford, Surrey. *T:* Guildford 2534.

**SHAW, Sir John J. K. B.;** *see* Best-Shaw.

**SHAW, Rev. John Mackintosh,** MA; DD; Professor Emeritus of Systematic Theology and Philosophy of Religion, Queen's Theological College, Kingston; *b* Insh, Kingussie, Inverness-shire, 10 Aug. 1879; *er s* of John and Jessie Mackintosh Shaw; *m* Devena Frances, *yr d* of W. J. Rhind, Edinburgh; one *s* two *d*. *Educ:* Raining's School, Inverness; Edinburgh University; New College, Edinburgh; Universities of Marburg and Tübingen. MA (Edinburgh) with 1st Class Honours in Philosophy, 1898; John Edward Baxter and Sir David Baxter Scholar in Philosophy, Edinburgh University, 1898-1903; entered Ministry of United Free Church of Scotland, 1906; Assistant to Rev. Alexander Whyte, DD, of United Free St George's Church, Edinburgh, 1906-09; Minister at Logiepert, Forfarshire, 1909-14; Professor of Apologetics and Systematic Theology, Presbyterian College, Halifax, NS (United Church of Canada), 1914-27; Professor of Christian Theology, Auburn Theological Seminary, Auburn, NY, 1927-29. *Publications:* Christianity as Religion and Life, 1914; The Resurrection of Christ, 1920; The Christian Gospel of the Fatherhood of God, 1924; Essentials and Non-Essentials of the Christian Faith, 1928; The Belief in the Holy Spirit, 1936; The Christian Doctrine of the Trinity, 1937; Life after Death, 1945; Christian Doctrine, 1953 (paperback edn 1966); The Wonder of the Christian Gospel, 1958. *Recreations:* walking, golf. *Address:* 74 Barrie Street, Kingston, Ontario, Canada. *T:* 548.4092.

**SHAW, John Michael,** MC 1940; QC 1967; Barrister-at-law; *b* 14 Nov. 1914; *yr s* of late M. J. Shaw (killed in action, 1916); *m* 1940, Margaret L. *yr d* of Robert T. D. Stoneham, CBE; two *s* two *d*. *Educ:* Rugby; Worcester Coll., Oxford. Called to the Bar, Gray's Inn, 1937. Served War of 1939-45 (Major): commissioned Royal Fusiliers, 1940. *Recreations:* fishing, gardening. *Address:* South Knighton House, South Knighton, near Newton Abbot, Devon.

**SHAW, Sir John Valentine Wistar,** KCMG 1947 (CMG 1942); Kt 1946; *b* 1894; *m* 1926, Josephine Mary, *yr d* of Joseph Simpson, Horsehay, Shropshire; two *s*. *Educ:* Repton School. Served with Royal Engineers, 1914-19, in France and Palestine (despatches). Colonial Administrative Service, Gold Coast, 1921-35; Palestine, 1935-40; Colonial Sec. Cyprus, 1940-43 (despatches, CMG); Chief Sec. Palestine, 1943-46; Governor and C-in-C Trinidad and Tobago, 1947-50; retired, 1950. Attached War Office, 1950-54; Chairman, Commission of Inquiry into Industrial dispute and riots, Sierra Leone, 1955. *Address:* 2 White Close, Winchelsea, Sussex. *T:* Winchelsea 283.

**SHAW, Maurice Elgie,** DM (Oxon); FRCP; Hon. Consulting Medical Officer, Canada Life Assurance Co.; Senior Member Association of Physicians and British Society of Gastroenterologists; late: Physician and Dean of Medical School, West London Hospital; President International Committee for Life Assurance Medicine; Medical Chairman, Pensions Appeal Tribunal; *b* 1 July 1894; *yr s* of Lauriston Elgie Shaw, MD, FRCP, and Maria Howard Spalding; *m* 1927, Christine, *d* of Conrad Beck, CBE; two *s* two *d*. *Educ:* Bradfield Coll.; New Coll., Oxford; Guy's Hospital. Served European War, Gloucestershire Regt, 1914-18, Gallipoli and France. Radcliffe Travelling Fellow, Univ. of Oxford, 1923-25 (Paris, Canada and US). Fellow (late member of Council) Roy. Soc. Med. Late Examiner in medicine, RCP, London Conjoint Bd and Univ. of Oxford. *Publications:* contributions to books and medical journals. *Address:* Morton House, Chiswick Mall, W4. *T:* 01-994 2230. *Clubs:* Savile, Leander.

**SHAW, Max S.;** *see* Stuart-Shaw.

**SHAW, Michael Norman,** JP; MP (C) Scarborough and Whitby, since 1966; *b* 9 Oct. 1920; *e s* of late Norman Shaw; *m* 1951, Joan Mary Louise, *o d* of Sir Alfred L. Mowat, 2nd Bt; three *s*. *Educ:* Sedbergh. Chartered Accountant; Partner, Blackburns Robson Coates & Co., and W. H. Shaw & Sons; MP (L and C) Brighouse and Spenborough, March 1960-Oct. 1964; PPS to Minister of Labour, 1962-63. FCA. *Recreation:* sailing. *Address:* Duxbury Hall, Liversedge, Yorkshire. *T:* Heckmondwike 2270. *Club:* Junior Carlton.

**SHAW, Sir Robert,** 7th Bt *cr* 1821; Design Engineer, T. Lamb, McManus & Associates Ltd, Calgary, Alberta; *b* Nairobi, Kenya, 31

Jan. 1925; *s* of Sir Robert de Vere Shaw, 6th Bt, MC, and Joan (*d* 1967), *d* of Thomas Cross; *S* father, 1969; *m* 1954, Jocelyn, *d* of late Andrew McGuffie, Swaziland; two *d*. *Educ:* Harrow; Univs of Oklahoma and Missouri, USA. RN, 1943-47 (Lieut RN retd). BS Civil Eng. Oklahoma, 1962; MS Civil Eng. Missouri, 1964; Professional Engineer, Alberta; Mem. Engineering Inst. of Canada. *Recreation:* sailing. *Heir: n* Charles de Vere Shaw, *b* 1 March 1957. *Address:* 234 40th Avenue SW, Calgary 6, Alberta, Canada. *Club:* Alberta United Services Inst. (Calgary, Alberta).

**SHAW, Robert;** Author and Actor; *b* 9 Aug. 1927; *s* of a doctor; *m* 1st, 1952, Jennifer Bourke; four *d*; 2nd, 1963, Mary Ure, *qv*; two *s* two *d*. *Educ:* Truro Sch.; RADA. Shakespeare Memorial Theatre Co., 1949 and 1950; Rosenkrantz in Hamlet, 1951; Old Vic Co., 1951-52; Shakespeare Memorial Theatre Co., 1953. Subsequent West End plays: Tiger at the Gates; Caro William; Live Like Pigs; The Long and the Short and the Tall; One More River; A Lodging for the Bride; The Changeling; The Caretaker (Broadway); The Physicists (Broadway); Cato Street. *Films:* The Dambusters; Hill in Korea; Sea Fury; The Valiant; Tomorrow at Ten; The Caretaker; From Russia with Love; The Luck of Ginger Coffey; The Battle of the Bulge; A Man for all Seasons; Custer of the West; The Birthday Party, 1968; Battle of Britain, 1968; Royal Hunt of the Sun, 1969; Figures in a Landscape, 1969; A Town Like Bastard, 1970. *Television:* The Buccaneers (series); Luther, 1968; many television plays. *Plays:* Off the Mainland (perf. Arts Theatre, 1957); The Man in the Glass Booth (perf. St Martin's Theatre, 1967, Broadway, 1968). *Publications: novels:* The Hiding Place, 1959; The Sun Doctor, 1961 (Hawthornden Prize, 1962); The Flag, 1965; The Man in the Glass Booth, 1967; A Card from Morocco, 1969; *play:* Cato Street, 1970. *Recreations:* tennis, golf, squash. *Address:* 17a Curzon Street, W1. *Club:* Savage.

**SHAW, Mrs Robert;** *see* Ure, Mary.

**SHAW, Dr Robert Macdonald,** CB 1968; Deputy Chief Medical Officer, Department of Health and Social Security (formerly Ministry of Health), since 1965; *b* 16 Sept. 1912; *s* of Peter Macdonald and Ellen Shaw; *m* 1941, Grace Helen Stringfellow; two *s* one *d*. *Educ:* Mill Hill School; Victoria Univ. of Manchester. Miscellaneous hospital appointments, etc, 1936-39. Emergency Commission, RAMC, 1939-45. Asst County MOH, Essex, 1945-48; Department of Health and Social Security (formerly Ministry of Health), 1948-. *Address:* 42 Chelmsford Road, Shenfield, Brentwood, Essex.

**SHAW, Hon. Sir Sebag,** Kt 1968; QC 1962; **Hon. Mr Justice Shaw;** Judge of the High Court of Justice (Queen's Bench Division), since 1968; *b* 28 Dec. 1906; 2nd *s* of Henry and Marie Shaw; *m* 1928; one *s*. Called to Bar, Gray's Inn, 1931, Bencher 1967. Acting Deputy Chairman, County of London Sessions, 1949; Recorder of Ipswich, 1958-68; Prosecuting Counsel, Board of Trade, 1959-62. Member: Interdepartmental Cttee on Court of Criminal Appeal, 1964-65; Bar Council, 1964-68. Fellow UCL, 1970-. *Publication:* Law of Meetings, 1947. *Address:* Royal Courts of Justice, Strand, WC2; 69 Wynnstay Gardens, W8. *T:* 01-937 4907.

**SHAW, Sinclair,** QC (Scotland) 1950; Sheriff of Edinburgh, the Lothians and Peeblesshire and Sheriff of Chancery since 1966; *b* South Africa; *m* 1948, Denise Fanny (Mem. French Resistance, 1941-45, Médaille de la Résistance; Croix de Guerre avec Palme; Chevalier Légion d'Honneur), *e d* of Dr Charles Mantoux and Dr Dora Mantoux; no *c*. Called to Scots Bar, 1936. Chairman Scottish Council of Labour Party, 1947. Member New Towns Committee (Chm. Lord Reith) apptd by Govt to work out principles to be followed in building new towns, 1945-46. Contested (Lab): Moray and Nairn, 1945, S Aberdeen, 1951. Advocate-Depute, 1945-51; Sheriff Substitute of Fife, 1959-66. *Address:* 5 Great Stuart Street, Edinburgh EH3 6AP. *T:* 031-225 4445; Ecublé 28, France.

**SHAW, Sydney Herbert,** CMG 1963; OBE 1958; *b* 6 Nov. 1903; 2nd *s* of John Beaumont and Gertrude Shaw; *m* 1930, Mary Louise, *e d* of Ernest Lewin Chapman; one *s* one *d*. *Educ:* King's College School; Royal School of Mines, London University. BSc Hons 1st cl. Mining Engineering, 1925 and Mining Geology, 1926; MSc (Birm.) 1937; PhD (Lond.) 1949. Geophys. prospecting N and S Rhodesia, 1926-28; Imperial Geophys. Experimental Survey, Aust., 1928-30; geophys. prospecting, Cyprus, 1930. Demonstrator, Geolog. Dept, Roy. Sch. of Mines, 1931; Lectr in Geology, Birmingham Univ., 1932-37; Govt Geologist, Palestine, 1937-48 (seconded as Dep. Controller Heavy Industries, Palestine, 1942-45); Colonial (later Overseas) Geological Surveys, London, 1949, Deputy Director, 1950, Dir, 1959-65; Head, Overseas Div., Inst. of Geological Sciences, 1965-68. Geological Adviser, Colonial Office (subseq. Dept of Tech. Co-op., then Min. of Overseas Develt), 1959-68. Retd, 1968. MIMM (Pres., 1968-69); FGS. *Publications:* scientific papers in various jls. *Recreation:* gardening. *Address:* Bisham Edge, Stoney Ware, Marlow, Bucks. *T:* Marlow 4951.

**SHAW, Thomas Richard,** CMG 1960; Ambassador to Morocco, since 1969; *b* 5 Sept. 1912; *s* of Colin R. and Ida L. Shaw, Bolton, Lancs; *m* 1939, Evelyn Frances Young; four *s*. *Educ:* Repton; Clare Coll., Cambridge. Appointed probationer vice-consul at Istanbul, Nov. 1934; transferred to Bushire, December 1937; acting Consul, Grade 2, Tientsin, 1938-39; transferred to Trieste, Jan. 1940, to Leopoldville, Oct. 1940, to Elisabethville, 1942; served at Casablanca, 1943; vice-consul, Rabat, Dec. 1943; appointed one of HM vice-consuls serving in Foreign Office, 1944; promoted to consul, 1945; transferred to Bremen as consul, 1949; Deputy Consul-General, New York, 1953; actg Consul-General, 1953; Consul-General, Izmir, 1955; Inspector of Foreign Service Establishments, 1957, Senior Inspector, 1961; Ambassador to the Republics of Niger, Upper Volta and the Ivory Coast, 1964-67 (also to the Republic of Dahomey, 1964-65); Minister, Tokyo, 1967-69. *Address:* c/o Foreign and Commonwealth Office, SW1; Upton, Harrow Road West, Dorking, Surrey.

**SHAW, William Boyd Kennedy,** OBE 1943 (MBE 1941); *b* 26 Oct. 1901; *s* of late Col. F. S. K. Shaw, CBE; *m* 1936, Eleanor, *yr d* of Maj. R. A. Dyott, Freeford, Lichfield; one *s* three *d*. *Educ:* Radley Coll.; University Coll., Oxford. Sudan Forest Service, 1924-29; later employed on archæological excavations in Near East; explorations in Libyan Desert, 1927, 1930, 1932, and 1935; awarded Gill Memorial of Royal Geographical Society, 1934; Department of Antiquities, Palestine Government, 1936-40; Land Agent, 1946-53. military service, 1940-45 (despatches, MBE, OBE, Belgian Croix Militaire de 1ere Classe and Croix de Guerre 1940, avec palme); Officer Order of Orange Nassau, with swords. *Publications:* Long Range Desert Group, 1945; articles in periodicals on Libyan Desert.

*Address:* Reed Field, Eversley Cross, Hants. *T:* Yateley 3217.

**SHAW SCOTT, Gilbert;** *see* Scott, G. S.

**SHAW-STEWART, Lieut-Col Sir (Walter) Guy,** 9th Bt, *cr* 1667; MC; Lord Lieutenant of Renfrewshire, 1950-67; *b* 10 Aug. 1892; *e s* of Capt. Walter Richard Shaw-Stewart, MBE (3rd *s* of 7th Bt) and Mary Sibell, *d* of S. L. Lane and Viscountess Downe; *S* uncle, 1942; *m* 1st, 1915, Diana (*d* 1931), *d* of late George Bulteel, Pamflete, Devon; two *s* one *d*; 2nd, 1949, Elizabeth (*d* 1968), *widow* of Maj.-Gen. A. Dawnay, CBE, DSO and *yr d* of late George Bulteel, Pamflete, Devon. *Educ:* Eton. Joined Coldstream Guards, 1911, with whom he served European War of 1914-18 (wounded twice, MC); retired, 1931; commanded 5th/6th Bn Argyll and Sutherland Highldrs, 1934-41; Member TA Assoc. (Renfrewshire). JP Renfrewshire; late Convener of Renfrew County Council. *Recreations:* hunting and shooting. *Heir: s* Euan Guy Shaw-Stewart [*b* 11 Oct. 1928; *m* 1st, 1953, Mary Louise (who obtained a divorce, 1956), *d* of late Lieut-Colonel Geoffrey Reginald Devereux Shaw; one *d*; 2nd, 1962, Victoria Anne, *d* of W. Fryer]. *Address:* Ardgowan, Inverkip, Renfrewshire. *T:* Inverkip 226. *Clubs:* Guards, White's.

**SHAW-ZAMBRA, William Warren,** CVO 1956; CBE 1943; TD; MA; *b* London, 1898; *s* of late J. J. G. Zambra and Florence Beatrice Shaw; assumed by deed poll the addtl surname Shaw-; *m* 1st, 1925, Marjorie Anderson (marriage dissolved, 1950), *d* of late Sir John Mann, KBE, CA; two *d*; 2nd, 1958, Barbara Mary Price (*d* 1968), MA, ARIBA; 3rd, 1970, Monica M. Wingate. *Educ:* Chatham House School; Christ's Coll., Cambridge. Served War of 1914-18, 1st Battalion London Scottish; 2/1 Yorkshire Hussars; TARO, 1919; Captain, 1932. War of 1939-45, General List, spec. emp., local Maj. 1939, Lt-Colonel, 1941, Colonel, 1944-58. Grants Secretary National Playing Fields Association, 1934; Assistant Sec. 1935; Dep. Sec. 1936; Vice-Pres., 1969; Editor of Playing Fields, 1938-39; Sec. King George's Fields Foundation (King George V National Memorial), 1936-50, Trustee and Treasurer, 1951-65; Secretary Imperial Communications Advisory Committee, 1938-44; Joint-Secretary Imperial Communications Committee of the War Cabinet, 1940-44; Secretary, Commonwealth Communications Council, 1944-49; Sec. Gen. Commonwealth Telecommunications Board, 1949-61; Sec. Commonwealth Telegraph Conf., Australia, 1942; Sec. Bermuda Telecommunications Conf., 1945; Sec. UK Deleg. Moscow Telecomm. Conf., 1946; Sec. USA-Commonwealth Govts Telecomm. Meeting, London, 1949; Sec. Commonwealth Telecomm. Conf., 1958. A Governor, Royal Ballet, 1956-67, and of Royal Ballet School, 1955-67. *Address:* 18 East Hill Road, Oxted, Surrey. *Club:* Athenæum.

**SHAWCROSS,** family name of **Baron Shawcross.**

**SHAWCROSS,** Baron, *cr* 1959 (Life Peer), of Friston; **Hartley William Shawcross,** PC 1946; Kt 1945; QC 1939; Chairman: Panel on Take-overs and Mergers, since 1969; Thames Television, since 1969; Upjohn & Co. Ltd (Director since 1967); Dominion Lincoln Assurance Co. Ltd; Chancellor, University of Sussex, since 1965; *b* 4 Feb. 1902; *s* of John Shawcross, MA, and Hilda Shawcross; *m* 1st, 1924, Rosita Alberta Shyvers (*d* 1943); 2nd, 1944, Joan Winifred Mather; two *s* one *d*. *Educ:* Dulwich Coll.; abroad. Certificate of Honour for 1st place in Bar Final; called to Bar, Gray's Inn, 1925 (Bencher, 1939); practised on Northern Circuit. Sen. Law Lectr, Liverpool Univ., 1927-34. Chm., Enemy Aliens Tribunal, 1939-40; left practice at Bar for War Service, 1940; Chief Prosecutor for UK before Internat. Military Tribunal at Nuremberg. Asst Chm. of E Sussex QS, 1941; Recorder of Salford, 1941-45; Dep. Regional Comr, South-Eastern Region, 1941; Regional Comr, North-Western Region, 1942-45; Recorder of Kingston-upon-Thames, 1946-61; retired from practice at Bar, 1958. MP (Lab) St Helens, 1945-58; Attorney-General, 1945-51; Pres., BoT, April-Oct. 1951. A Principal Deleg. for UK to Assemblies of UN, 1945-49; a UK Mem., Permanent Court of Arbitration at The Hague, 1950-67. Independent Chm., Kent District Coal Mining Board, 1940; Chairman: Catering Wages Commn, 1943-45; Bar Council, 1952-57; Royal Commn on the Press, 1961-62; MRC, 1961-65; Internat. Law Section of British Inst. of Internat. and Comparative Law; Justice (British Br. of Internat. Commn of Jurists). President: Rainer Foundn (formerly London Police Court Mission), 1951-; British Hotels and Restaurants Assoc., 1959-. Member: Home Secretary's Adv. Council on Treatment of Offenders, 1944-45; Council, Internat. Law Assoc., 1958-; Exec. Cttee, Internat. Commn of Jurists, 1959. Hon. Member: Bar Council; Amer. and New York Bar Assoc.; Fellow, Amer. Bar Foundn. Director: Shell Transport and Trading Co., 1961-; EMI Ltd, Rank-Hovis-McDougall Ltd, and Caffyns Motors Ltd, 1965-; Morgan et Cie International SA, 1966-; Morgan et Cie SA, 1967-; Times Newspapers Ltd, 1967-; Hawker Siddeley Group Ltd, and Birmingham Small Arms Co. Ltd, 1968-; European Enterprises Development Co. SA, 1970-; Special Adviser, Morgan Guaranty Trust Co. of New York (Chm., Internat. Adv. Council). Chm. Bd of Governors, Dulwich Coll.; Member: Court, London Univ., 1958-; Council and Exec. Cttee, Sussex Univ., 1959- (Pro-Chancellor, 1960-65); Council, Eastbourne Coll. Hon. LLM Liverpool, 1932; Hon. LLD: Columbia, 1954; Liverpool, 1969; Hull 1970. JP Sussex, 1941-68. Chm., Soc. of Sussex Downsmen. *Recreations:* sailing, riding. *Address:* Friston Place, Sussex. *Clubs:* White's, Buck's, United Hunts; Travellers' (Paris); Royal Cornwall Yacht (Falmouth); Royal Yacht Squadron (Cowes); New York Yacht (US).

**SHAWCROSS, Christopher Nyholm,** QC; Barrister-at-Law; *b* 20 June 1905; *y s* of John Shawcross, MA; *m* 1st, 1932, Doreen Adeline (who obtained a divorce), *o d* of R. A. Burrows; no *c*; 2nd, 1949, Maridel, *o d* of Dr Maxwell Chance; one *s* one *d*. *Educ:* Dulwich College; University College, Oxford. Arden Scholar of Gray's Inn and Holker (Senior) Scholar, 1929; Bar Studentship and Certificate of Honour, also special prize in Examination for Barstow Scholarship, 1930; called to Bar, 1931; Lecturer Mercantile and Shipping Law, City of London College, 1932; Practised Common Law Bar, London and Midland Circuit; Bencher of Gray's Inn, 1954. Served War of 1939-45, in RNVR (Special Br.). Comdr 1944. Temp. Legal Adviser to Chm., BOAC, 1944-45. MP (Lab) for Widnes (Lancs), 1945-50; Chm., all-party Parl. Cttee for Channel Tunnel, Sec., all-party Group for European Union, 1947-49; Member Executive, British Council of European Movement; Mem. Brit. Delegation, Hague Conf., 1948. KC, 1949; QC, 1952. Retired from politics, 1950. Recorder of Nottingham, 1950-61; retired from Bar, 1960; Company Director. Travelled Europe, Canada, USA, Africa and Far East. *Publications:* The Law of Motor Insurance, 2nd ed. 1948; Air Law (with K. M. Beaumont),

2nd ed. 1950. *Address:* Bunkers Hill Farm, Streat Lane, Ditchling, Sussex. *T:* Plumpton 494. *Clubs:* Oxford and Cambridge University; Royal Naval Sailing; Bar Tennis.
*See also Baron Shawcross.*

**SHAWE-TAYLOR, Desmond (Christopher),** CBE 1965; Music Critic, The Sunday Times, since 1958; *b* 29 May 1907; *s* of Frank Shawe-Taylor and Agnes Ussher. *Educ:* Shrewsbury Sch.; Oriel Coll., Oxford. Literary and occasional musical criticism, New Statesman, etc until 1939. Served War of 1939-45 with the Royal Artillery. Music Critic, New Statesman, 1945-58. *Publications:* Covent Garden, 1948; (with Edward Sackville-West, later Lord Sackville), The Record Guide (with supplements and revisions, 1951-56). *Recreations:* travel, croquet, gramophone. *Address:* Long Crichel House, Wimborne, Dorset. *T:* Tarrant Hinton 250; 10 St Andrew's Place, NW1. *T:* 01-935 1066. *Club:* Brooks's.

**SHAWYER, Robert Cort,** MA, PhD; HM Consul-General, Argentina, 1967-69; *b* 9 Oct. 1913; *e s* of late Arthur Frederic Shawyer, sometime Gen. Manager, Martins Bank; *m* 1939, Isabel Jessie Rogers; two *d*. *Educ:* Charterhouse; Corpus Christi Coll., Oxford; Birkbeck Coll., Univ. of London. Bank of England, 1835-37. Commissioned RAEC, 1938 (Lt-Col 1945). Princ., Min. of Nat. Insce, 1948; Admty, 1951; Asst Sec., 1957; seconded to NATO, 1960; Nat. Def. Coll., Canada, 1961-62; Commonwealth Office, 1967. FRGS. *Publications:* various articles. *Address:* c/o Foreign and Commonwealth Office, King Charles Street, SW1; Keepers Corner, East Wretham, Norfolk. *Clubs:* Reform, Royal Automobile, Hurlingham.

**SHEARBURN, Rt. Rev. Victor George;** Assistant Bishop of Wakefield, since 1967; Member of Community of Resurrection, Mirfield, since 1934; *b* 28 Oct. 1900; *s* of George Shearburn, Architect, and Rebecca Millicent (*née* Jerome). *Educ:* Felsted School; Hertford College, Oxford; Ely Theological College. Curate, All Souls, Clapton Park, London, 1924-28; S Barnabas', Pimlico, 1928-31; CR Mirfield, 1932. CF, 1939; SCF, 6th Armoured Div., 1940-42; DACG, Gibraltar, 1942-43; ACG, Eastern Command, India, 1944-45; DCG, South-East Asia, 1946-47. Bishop of Rangoon, 1955-66. *Address:* House of the Resurrection, Mirfield, Yorks.

**SHEARER, Sir Bruce,** Kt 1967; CMG 1962; Chairman, James Campbell & Sons Pty Ltd and Carricks Ltd 1942-49; Chairman, Queensland Division, Australian Red Cross Society, 1959-66; *b* 3 April 1888; *m* 1952, Edith Barlow. *Educ:* Maclean High School. Man. Dir, ACF & Shirleys Fertilizers Ltd, 1916-54 (Chm., 1934-54). *Recreation:* bowls. *Address:* 8 Sector Street, Coorparoo, Queensland, Australia. *Club:* Queensland.

**SHEARER, Brigadier Eric James,** CB 1942; CBE 1941; MC; Underwriting Member of Lloyd's; *b* 23 Nov. 1892; *s* of late Colonel Johnston Shearer, CB, DSO; *m* 1919; one *s*; *m* 1945, Mary, *d* of late Sir O. G. Holmden, KBE, JP, DL. *Educ:* Wellington; RMC, Sandhurst; Staff College. Indian Army, 1911; European War (MC, Brevet Major, despatches); Iraq Rebellion, 1919 (despatches); Malabar Rebellion, 1922; psc, 1922; General Staff, War Office, 1924-29; retired and joined Fortnum & Mason Ltd, Joint Managing Director, 1933-38; returned to Army on outbreak of war, 1939; DMI, MEF, 1940-42; retd; a Managing Director United Kingdom Commercial Corporation Ltd, 1942-45; Todd Shipyards Corporation, USA, 1945-50; Chm. Overseas Tankship (UK) Ltd, 1950-60; a Managing Director, Caltex Trading & Transport Co. Ltd, 1950-60; Director: London and Overseas Freighters Ltd, 1961-66. Member of Queen's Body Guard for Scotland (Royal Company of Archers); Livery Worshipful Company of Shipwrights, 1946; Freeman City of London, 1946. Coronation Medal, 1937; Special Constabulary Medal, 1938. *Address:* Trehivin, Madron, near Penzance, Cornwall. *T:* Penzance 4158.

**SHEARER, Rt. Hon. Hugh Lawson,** PC 1969; Prime Minister of Jamaica since 1967; Minister of Defence, since 1967; Minister of External Affairs, since 1967; *b* 18 May 1923. *Educ:* St Simons Coll., Jamaica. Journalist on weekly newspaper, Jamaica Worker, 1941-44, subseq. Editor. Apptd Asst Gen. Sec., Bustamante Industrial TU, 1947, Island Supervisor, 1953-67, Vice-Pres., 1960-. Mem. Kingston and St Andrew Corp. Council, 1947; MHR for West Kingston, 1955-59; MLC (now Senator), 1962-66. Hon. Dr of Laws, Howard Univ., Washington, DC, 1968. *Address:* Prime Minister's Office, Jamaica; (home) Jamaica House, Jamaica. *T:* 25185.

**SHEARER, Rt. Hon. Ian Hamilton;** *see* Avonside, Rt. Hon. Lord.

**SHEARER, Moira; (Mrs L. Kennedy);** actress; *b* Dunfermline, Fifeshire, 17 Jan. 1926; *d* of Harold King; *m* 1950, Ludovic Kennedy, *qv*; one *s* three *d*. *Educ:* Dunfermline High School; Ndola, N Rhodesia; Bearsden, Scotland. Professional training: Mayfair Sch.; Legat Sch.; Sadler's Wells School. Début with International Ballet, 1941; joined Sadler's Wells Ballet, 1942, and in same year danced a leading rôle in Les Sylphides; first ballerina rôle in Sleeping Beauty, 1946; created rôle of Cinderella, 1948; Titania in Old Vic production of A Midsummer Night's Dream (Edin. Festival, 1954, and tour of US and Canada); American tours with Sadler's Wells Ballet, 1949, 1950-51, with Old Vic, 1954. Toured as Sally Bowles in I am a Camera, 1955; joined Bristol Old Vic, 1955. Played in Man of Distinction, Edin. Fest., 1957. *Films:* Ballerina in The Red Shoes (première, 1948); Tales of Hoffmann, 1950; Story of Three Loves, 1952; The Man Who Loved Redheads, 1954; Peeping Tom, 1960; Black Tights, 1961. *Address:* c/o MCA, 139 Piccadilly, W1.

**SHEARER, Thomas Hamilton;** Director of Establishments, Ministry of Public Building and Works, since 1967; *b* 7 Nov. 1923; *o s* of Thomas Appleby Shearer; *m* 1945, Sybil Mary Robinson, Stratford-on-Avon; one *s* one *d*. *Educ:* Haberdashers' Aske's, Hatcham; Emmanuel Coll., Cambridge (open exhibition in English). Served RAF, 1942-45 (despatches). Entered Air Ministry, as Asst Principal, 1948; Principal, 1951; Sec. to Grigg Cttee on Recruitment to Armed Forces, 1958; Asst Sec., 1959; transf. Min. of Public Building and Works, 1963; student, IDC, 1965. *Recreations:* opera, claret. *Address:* 9 Denny Crescent, SE11. *T:* 01-735 0921.

**SHEARER, Rev. W(illiam) Russell;** *b* 12 Oct. 1898; *s* of Henry S. and Jessie A. Shearer; *m* 1934, Phyllis Mary Wigfield. *Educ:* Harrogate Grammar School; Leeds University; Wesley House, Cambridge. Served European War, 1914-18, in Tank Corps. Since 1923 has been Methodist Minister at: Tunstall, Staffs; Manchester; Muswell Hill; Sutton, Surrey; Hanley. Chairman, Stoke-on-Trent Methodist District, 1943-50; Chairman, Birmingham Methodist District, 1950-63. Pres. of Methodist Conference, 1954-55; Moderator,

National Free Church Federal Council, 1959-60. *Address:* Greenways, Wincombe Lane, Shaftesbury, Dorset. *T:* Shaftesbury 3431. *Club:* National Liberal.

**SHEARMAN, Rt. Rev. Donald Norman;** *see* Rockhampton, Bishop of.

**SHEARMAN, Sir Harold (Charles),** Kt 1965; DL; MA; Chairman, Greater London Council, 1964-66; Member for Lewisham, 1964-67; Chairman: Inner London Education Cttee, 1964-65; Further and Higher Educn Sub-Cttee, 1964-67; *b* 14 March 1896; *e s* of late Rev. C. E. P. Shearman and late Mary Charlotte Shearman; *m* 1924, Frances Mary, *d* of late Henry Jameson, Hamsterley, Co. Durham; one *s*. *Educ:* Sulgrave National School; Magdalen College School, Brackley; Wolsingham Grammar School; St Edmund Hall, Oxford (1st Class, Modern History, 1922). Elementary Teacher, Durham, 1912-15. Served European War, 1914-18, Private RAMC, and Flying Officer (Observer) RAF, 1916-19. Contested (Lab) Isle of Wight, 1922. Tutor-organiser in Bedfordshire, WEA and Cambridge Extra Mural Board, 1927-35; Education Officer, WEA, 1935-45; Academic Adviser Tutorial Classes, Univ. of London, 1946-61. Member (Deptford) LCC 1946-65 (Chairman Education Cttee, 1955-61); Chairman: LCC, 1961-62; SE Gas Consultative Council, 1963-66; Member: UK delegation, UNESCO Conf., New Delhi, 1956; Committee on Higher Education (1961-63) and other Govt and Educational Cttees; Mem., Commonwealth Scholarships Commn, 1964-68; Pres. School Journey Assoc. of London, 1962-. Chairman: SE Reg. Exam. Bd (Cert. of Sec. Educn); Gov. Body, Kidbrooke Sch.; Rachel Macmillan Coll. of Educn; Garnett College; Mem., court, Brunel Univ. Hon. Treas., Council for Educn in World Citizenship. DL Greater London, 1967. *Address:* 4 Selborne Road, New Malden, Surrey. *T:* 01-942 2581.

**SHEARS, Maj.-Gen. Philip James,** CB 1943; *b* 5 April 1887. *Educ:* Oundle School. Commissioned Royal Dublin Fusiliers; transferred 1922 to Border Regiment; Adjutant, 1924-27. Served European War, 1915-18, in France and Belgium (wounded twice, despatches, French Croix de Guerre); Commandant Army Technical School (Boys), Chepstow, 1935-39. War of 1939-45: Maj.-Gen. 1941; Dist Comdr, 1942-44; retd 1945. Col The Border Regt, 1947-52.

**SHEDDEN, Sir Frederick (Geoffrey),** KCMG 1943 (CMG 1941); OBE; Former Australian Civil Servant (retired 1958); *b* 8 Aug. 1893; *s* of George Shedden, Kyneton, Victoria; *m* 1927, Anne, *d* of George Edward. *Educ:* Melbourne Univ. (BComm); London Univ. Secretary to War Cabinet, 1939-46; Secretary to Advisory War Council, 1940-45; Secretary, Department of Defence, Commonwealth of Australia, 1937-56; Member of Council of Defence, 1946-56; Chm., Defence Cttee, 1948-56; Member National Security Resources Bd, 1950-56. *Address:* 448 Barker's Road, Hawthorn, Vic. 3123, Australia.

**SHEEAN, (James) Vincent;** Writer; *b* Pana, Illinois, USA, 5 Dec. 1899; *s* of William Charles Sheean and Susan MacDermot; *m* 1935, Diana (who obtained a divorce, 1946), *y d* of late Sir Johnston Forbes-Robertson; two *d*. *Educ:* University of Chicago. Foreign correspondent, 1922-27, and at intervals since then in Europe and Asia; frequent contributor to magazines and reviews in England and America. *Publications:* The Tide, 1933; Personal History, 1935; Sanfelice, 1937; The Pieces of a Fan, 1937; A Day of Battle, 1938; The Eleventh Hour, 1939 (in America, Not Peace But A Sword); Bird of the Wilderness, 1941; Between the Thunder and the Sun, 1943; This House Against This House, 1946; A Certain Rich Man, 1949; Lead Kindly Light, 1950; The Indigo Bunting, 1951; Rage of the Soul, 1952; Lily, 1955; The Amazing Oscar Hammerstein, 1956; First and Last Love (autobiography), 1957; Orpheus at Eighty, 1959; Nehru: The Years of Power, 1959 (Eng. 1960); Dorothy and Red, 1963 (Eng. 1964). *Address:* Twin Farms, South Pomfret, Vermont, USA.

**SHEEHAN, Harold Leeming,** MD, DSc, FRCP, FRCOG; Professor of Pathology, University of Liverpool, 1946-65 (Professor Emeritus since 1965); *b* 4 Aug. 1900; *s* of Dr P. Sheehan, Carlisle; *m* 1934, E. S. G. Potter; no *c*. *Educ:* University of Manchester. Demonstrator and Lecturer in Pathology, University of Manchester, 1927-34; Rockefeller Medical Fellow in USA, 1934-35; Director of Research, Glasgow Royal Maternity Hosp., 1935-46; Hon. Lecturer in Pathology, Univ. of Glasgow, 1943-46. Served in RAMC, 1939-45; Colonel, Deputy Director of Pathology, AFHQ, Italy, 1945 (despatches, TD). Hon. Member: Fac. Med., Univ. of Chile; Fac. Med., Univ. of Concepcion; Hon. Fellow, Amer. Assoc. Obst. Gyn.; Hon. Member: Soc. Roy. Belge Gyn. Obst.; Soc. Chil. Obst. Gyn.; Soc. Argent. Neurol.; Soc. Med. Hop. Paris; Socs Endocrinology: Chile, Argentine, Roumania, Hungary. *Publications:* papers on pathology, endocrinology and renal physiology in various med. jls. *Address:* 18 Knowsley Road, Liverpool 19. *T:* 051-427 2936.

**SHEEHY, Hon. Sir Joseph Aloysius,** KBE 1970; **Hon. Mr Justice Sheehy;** Senior Puisne Judge of the Supreme Court, Queensland, since 1965; *b* Gympie, 15 April 1900; *m* 1927, Elizabeth, *d of C. Groves; one s. Educ:* Christian Brothers Colls, Gympie and Gregory Terrace, Brisbane. Clerk, Dept of Justice, Qld, 1916; Barrister-at-law, Supreme Court, Qld, 1921; Actg Crown Prosecutor, Supreme Ct, 1924; Crown Prosecutor, 1928; Judge, Supreme Ct, Qld, 1947. *Recreations:* golf, gardening, motoring. *Address:* Supreme Court, George Street, Brisbane, Queensland 4000, Australia.

**SHEEN, Barry Cross,** QC 1966; *b* 31 Aug. 1918; 2nd *s* of Ronald Sheen, FCA, St John's Wood; *m* 1946, Diane, *d* of late C. L. Donne, MD; three *s*. *Educ:* Haileybury College, Hill School (USA); Trinity Hall, Cambridge (MA). Served in RNVR, 1939-46; Commanding Officer, HMS Kilkenzie, 1943-45. Called to Bar, Middle Temple, 1947; Member Bar Council, 1959-63; Junior Counsel to Admiralty, 1961-66. On Panel of Wreck Comrs (Eng.) under Merchant Shipping Acts, 1966-; Mem., Panel of Lloyd's Arbitrators in Salvage Cases, 1966-. *Recreations:* swimming, golf. *Address:* 16 Parkside Gardens, Wimbledon Common, SW19. *T:* 01-946 8534. *Club:* Royal Wimbledon.

**SHEEN, Most Rev. Fulton John,** PhD, DD; Bishop of Rochester, New York (RC), 1966-69; Titular Archbishop of Newport, Mon, since 1969; *b* 8 May 1895; *s* of Newton Morris and Delia Fulton Sheen. *Educ:* St Viator Coll.; St Paul Seminary; Catholic University of America; University of Louvain, Belgium; Sorbonne, Paris; Collegio Angelico, Rome. STB and JCB, Catholic Univ. of America, 1920; Univ. of Louvain: PhD 1923; Agrégé en Philosophie, 1925; Cardinal Mercier Internat. Prize for Philosophy, 1925; STD Rome, 1924. Ordained, 1919; Papal Chamberlain, 1934; Domestic Prelate, 1935; Auxiliary Bishop of

New York (RC), 1951-66; National Director, Society for the Propagation of the Faith, 1950-66. Lectured in Westminster Cathedral, Cambridge Univ., and Santa Suzanna (Rome); Catholic Hour radio broadcasts for 25 years; started television series, Life Is Worth Living, 1952; taught in Cath. Univ. of Amer. for 25 years. Hon. LLD, LittD, LHD from various Universities and Colleges. *Publications:* about 60 books including: Freedom under God, 1940; Philosophies at War, 1943; Communism and Conscience of the West, 1948; Philosophy of Religion, 1948; Peace of Soul, 1949; Lift Up Your Heart, 1950; Three To Get Married, 1951; World's First Love, 1952; Way to Happiness, 1954; Thinking Life Through, 1955; Life is Worth Living, 1956; Life of Christ, 1958; This is the Mass (with D. Rops), 1958; This is Rome (with H. Morton), 1960; Go To Heaven, 1960; This Is The Holy Land, 1961; These Are the Sacraments, 1962; The Priest Is Not His Own, 1963; Missions and the World Crisis, 1964; The Power of Love, 1964; Walk with God, 1965; Christmas Inspirations, 1966; Footsteps in a Darkened Forest, 1967; The Quotable Fulton J. Sheen, 1967; Guide to Contentment, 1967; Children and Parents, 1970. Weekly column in secular press. *Address:* 205 East 78th Street, New York, NY 10021, USA.

**SHEEN, Air Vice-Marshal Walter Charles,** CB 1955; DSO 1940; OBE 1946; Adviser, Military Products, etc, British Aircraft Corporation (USA) Inc. and Vice-President, RACAL Communications Inc.; *b* 13 May 1907; *s* of late Charles William Sheen and of Beatrice Anne Sheen, Enfield; *m* 1932, Lilian E. Ashton Bailey (marr. diss., 1947); *m* 1947, Nellie Mae Nordwall, College Park, Washington, DC, USA; two *s. Educ:* Enfield Technical Coll. Aircraft apprentice, RAF, 1923; Pilot Officer, RAF, 1930; commanded 49, 61 and 106 sqdns, RAF, 1939-; Deputy Chief of Air Staff, RNZAF, 1947-49; idc 1952; Asst Commandant RAF Staff College, 1953-54; Director-General of Manning, Air Ministry, 1955-58; Commander of RAF Staff, British Joint Services Mission, Washington, 1958-60; Air Attaché, Washington, 1960-61. *Address:* 419 West Grove Boulevard, Alexandria, Virginia, USA. *T:* 768-4232. *Clubs:* Royal Air Force, Royal Automobile; Aviation (Washington, DC).

**SHEFFIELD,** 4th Baron, *cr* 1783, of Roscommon (Ire.); **Edward John Stanley;** Bt 1660; Baron Stanley of Alderley (UK) 1839 (known under this title until May 1957 when assumed the style of his senior barony); Baron Eddisbury, 1848; Lieutenant-Commander RNVR; *b* 9 Oct. 1907; *er s* of 5th Baron and Margaret Evelyn (*d* 1964), *d* of H. Evans Gordon; *S* father 1931; *m* 1932, Lady Victoria Audrey Chetwynd-Talbot (who obtained a divorce, 1936), 2nd *d* of late Captain Viscount Ingestre and Lady Winifred Pennoyer; one *d*; *m* 1944, Mrs Sylvia Fairbanks, *widow* of Douglas Fairbanks, and formerly Lady Ashley (marriage dissolved, 1948; she *m* 1949, Clark Gable, marriage dissolved; he *d* 1960); *m* 1951, Thérèse (marriage dissolved, 1957), *d* of Gen. Husson, Toulon; *m* 1961, Lady Crane, *widow* of Sir Edmund Crane. *Educ:* Eton; Balliol Coll., Oxford. *Publications:* Sea Peace, articles in journals. *Recreations:* cruising under sail, physical and chemical research. *Heir:* *b* Hon. Lyulph Henry Victor Owen Stanley, late Lieut-Comdr RNVR, *b* 22 Oct. 1915. *Clubs:* White's, Pratt's, Beefsteak, Brooks's, Royal Cruising, RNVR.

*See also Hon. Pamela M. Stanley.*

**SHEFFIELD, Bishop of,** since 1962; **Rt. Rev. Francis John Taylor,** MA Oxford; *b* 13 Nov. 1912; *er s* of late F. W. Taylor and Mrs Taylor, Hull, Yorks; *m* 1940, Margaret Esmé, *o d* of late W. H. Chapman and late Mrs Chapman, Bath; one *d* (one *s* decd). *Educ:* Hymers Coll., Hull; Queen's Coll., Oxford; Wycliffe Hall, Oxford. Scholar of Queen's Coll. Oxford; Holwell Student, Liddon Student. Deacon, 1936, priest, 1937; Curate of Walcot, Bath, 1936-38; Tutor and Lectr, 1938-42. Chaplain, 1939-42, Wycliffe Hall, Oxford; Chaplain, Corpus Christi Coll., Oxford, 1939; Actg Principal, Clifton Theol. Coll., 1942; Vicar of Christ Church, Claughton, Birkenhead, 1942-54; Vicar of St Andrew, Oxford, 1954-55. Proctor in Convocation and Member National Church Assembly: Dio. Chester, 1945-54, Dio. Oxford, 1955-62. Lectr William Temple Coll., 1947-53; Lectr St Aidan's Theol. Coll., 1950-54; WEA Lectr, 1947-54; Principal, Wycliffe Hall, Oxford, 1955-62. Exam. Chap. to Bp of Oxford, 1955-56; Select Preacher: Univ. of Edinburgh, 1951; Univ. of Aberdeen, 1952; Univ. of Oxford, 1960-61. Governor: Dean Close School; Wrekin College; Headington School; Mem. C of E Bd of Educn. *Publications:* The Church of God, 1946; Into Thy Courts, 1947; (contrib. to) Theological Word Book of the Bible, 1950; The People of God, 1951; Becoming a Christian, 1954; The Doctrine of Justification by Faith, 1954; Scripture and Tradition, 1955; Anglo-Russian Theological Conference, 1958; Die Kirche von England, 1966. Contributor to: The Churchman, Theology, Church Quarterly Review. Editor of Parish and People, 1953-60. *Recreations:* literature, walking, ecclesiastical architecture. *Address:* Ranmoor Grange, Sheffield 10. *T:* Sheffield 32170.

**SHEFFIELD, Asst Bishop of;** *see* Gerard, Rt Rev. G. V.

**SHEFFIELD, Provost of;** *see* Neill, Very Rev. I. D.

**SHEFFIELD, Archdeacon of;** *see* Johnson, Ven. Hayman.

**SHEFFIELD, Edmund Charles Reginald,** DL, JP; *b* 24 Oct. 1908; *s* of Sir Berkeley Sheffield, 6th Bt, and *b* and *heir-pres* of Sir Robert Arthur Sheffield, 7th Bt, *qv*; *m* 1931, Nancie Kidston, *d* of E. R. Soames, London; one *s* two *d. Educ:* Eton. Served War of 1939-45: Northants Yeomanry; North Africa, Italy (despatches); Captain 1941. DL 1951, JP 1954; High Sheriff of Lincolnshire, 1959. *Address:* Sutton Park, Sutton-on-the-Forest, York. *T:* Stillington 249; 4 Montagu Mews North, W1. *T:* 01-935 2709. *Club:* White's.

**SHEFFIELD, Maj.-Gen. John,** CB 1967; CBE 1961; Secretary of the Star and Garter Home, Richmond, since 1968; *b* 28 April 1910; *s* of late Major W. G. F. Sheffield, DSO, and of Mrs C. G. A. Sheffield (*née* Wing); *m* 1936, Mary Patience Vere (*née* Nicoll); two *s* one *d. Educ:* Winchester; RMA, Woolwich. Commd, 1930; served RA and RHA; transferred RAOC, 1939. Served War of 1939-45: BEF, 1939-40; MEF, 1944-48. Egypt, 1954-56; Cyprus, 1959-62; Comdr Base Organization, RAOC, 1964-67. Col Comdt, RAOC, 1970-. *Recreations:* athletics (British Olympic Team, 1936), golf, sailing. *Address:* 11 Pitt Street, W8. *T:* 01-937 3096. *Clubs:* Royal Automobile, MCC.

**SHEFFIELD, John V.;** *b* 11 Nov. 1913; *y s* of Sir Berkeley Sheffield, 6th Bt; *m* 1936, Anne (*d* 1969), *d* of Sir Lionel Faudel-Phillips, 3rd Bt; one *s* three *d. Educ:* Eton; Magdalene College, Cambridge (MA). Chairman: Norcros Ltd; Portals Ltd. Private Secretary to Minister of Works, 1943-44; High Sheriff of Lincolnshire, 1944-45. *Address:* Laverstoke House,

Whitchurch, Hants. *T:* Overton 245. *Club:* White's.

**SHEFFIELD, Sir Robert Arthur,** 7th Bt, *cr* 1756; *b* 18 Oct. 1905; *s* of Sir Berkeley Sheffield, 6th Bt, and Julia (*d* 1952), *e d* of Baron de Tuyll; *S* father 1946. *Heir: b* Edmund Charles Reginald Sheffield, *qv. Address:* Laverstoke Rectory, Whitchurch, Hants.

*See also Duke of Beaufort, J. V. Sheffield.*

**SHELBURNE, Earl of; Charles Maurice Petty-Fitzmaurice;** *b* 21 Feb. 1941; *s* of 8th Marquess of Lansdowne, *qv*; *m* 1965, Lady Frances Eliot, *o d* of 9th Earl of St Germans, *qv*; two *d. Educ:* Eton. Page of Honour to The Queen, 1956-57. Served with Kenya Regt, 1961; joined Royal Wiltshire Yeomanry, 1962. *Address:* Bremhill House, Calne, Wiltshire. *T:* Hilmartin 235; 19 Walton Street, London, SW3. *T:* 01-584 9180. *Clubs:* Turf, Buck's.

**SHELDON, John Gervase Kensington; His Honour Judge Sheldon;** County Court Judge since 1968; *b* 4 Oct. 1913; *s* of John Henry Sheldon, MD, DPH, and Eleanor Gladys Sheldon, MB, BS; *m* 1st, 1940, Patricia Mary Mardon; one *s*; 2nd, 1960, Janet Marguerite Seager; two *s* one *d. Educ:* Winchester Coll.; Trinity Coll., Cambridge (MA; 1st Cl. Hons Law). Barrister-at-Law, called Lincoln's Inn, 1939 (Cert. of Honour, Cholmeley Schol.). Served RA (TA), 1939-45 (despatches twice): Egypt, N Africa, Italy; Major, RA, 1943. *Recreation:* family and home. *Address:* 49 Elystan Place, Chelsea, SW3. *T:* 01-584 4983; Hopton, Churt, Surrey. *T:* Frensham 2035. *Club:* United Service.

**SHELDON, Robert Edward;** MP (Lab) Ashton-under-Lyne since 1964; Member, Public Accounts Committee; Company Director; *b* 13 Sept. 1923; widower; one *s* one *d. Educ:* Elementary and Grammar Schools; Engineering Apprenticeship; Technical Colleges in Stockport, Burnley and Salford. Engineering diplomas; external degree, London University. Contested Withington, Manchester, 1959; Chm., Labour Parly Economic Affairs and Finance Group, 1967-68. Director, Manchester Chamber of Commerce. Mem. Civil Service Cttee, 1966-68. *Recreations:* hill walking; various arts and crafts. *Address:* 27 Darley Avenue, Manchester 20; 2 Ryder Street, SW1.

**SHELDON, Sir Wilfrid (Percy Henry),** KCVO 1959 (CVO 1954); Physician-Pædiatrician to the Queen since 1952; Consulting Pædiatrician, King's College Hospital; Consulting Physician, Hospital for Sick Children, Great Ormond Street; Adviser in Child Health, Ministry of Health; Fellow of Royal Society of Medicine; *b* 23 Nov. 1901; *s* of John Joseph Sheldon, FLS; *m* 1927, Mabel Winifred Netherway; three *d. Educ:* King's College, London; King's College Hospital. MB, BS (Honours Anatomy and Medicine), 1921; MD London 1925; FRCP 1933. *Publications:* Acute Rheumatism following Tonsillitis, 1931; Amyoplasia Congenita, 1932; Congenital Pancreatic Lipace Deficiency, 1964; Text Book of Diseases of Infancy and Childhood, 8th edn, 1962. *Recreations:* golf, gardening. *Address:* Private Consulting Rooms, The Hospital for Sick Children, 34 Great Ormond Street, WC1. *T:* 01-405 2943.

**SHELFORD, Cornelius William;** DL; retired; *b* 6 July 1908; *s* of William Heard Shelford and Maud Ethel Shelford, Horncastle, Sharpthorne, Sussex, and Singapore; *m* 1934, Helen Beatrice Hilda Schuster; one *s* two *d. Educ:* private tutor and Trinity College, Cambridge. Chartered Accountant, 1934; Partner, Rowley Pemberton & Co., 1940 (retd 1960); Chm., Mills & Allen Ltd, 1964 (retd 1969); Chm., London County Freehold & Leasehold Properties Ltd, 1964 (retd 1970). East Sussex CC, 1952 (CA, 1957; Chm., 1964-67; Chm., Finance Cttee, 1970-); High Sheriff of Sussex, 1954; DL Sussex, 1968-. *Recreations:* travelling, walking, gardening. *Address:* Chailey Place, near Lewes, Sussex. *T:* Newick 2881. *Clubs:* Carlton, Travellers', City of London.

**SHELLEY, Charles William Evans;** Charity Commissioner since 1968; *b* 15 Aug. 1912; *s* of George Shelley and Frances Mary Anne Shelley (*née* Dain); *m* 1939, Patricia May Dolby; three *d* (and one *d* decd). *Educ:* Alleyn's Sch., Dulwich; Fitzwilliam House, Cambridge. Called to Bar, Inner Temple, 1937; practised at the Bar, to 1940. Served in Army: first in RAPC and later in Dept of Judge Advocate-General, rank Major, 1940-47. Joined Charity Commn as Legal Asst, 1947; Sen. Legal Asst, 1958; Dep. Comr, 1964. *Recreations:* English literature, listening to music, mountaineering. *Address:* Pen y Bryn, Llansilin, Oswestry, Salop. *T:* Llansilin 273. *Clubs:* Oxford and Cambridge University; Camping.

**SHELLEY, Herbert John,** CB 1953; OBE 1944; retired as Chief Inspector for Technical, Commercial and Art Education, Ministry of Education (1945-58); *b* 28 Feb. 1895; *s* of James Shelley; *m* 1921, Josephine Lamb; one *s* one *d. Educ:* Bablake School, Coventry; Victoria Univ., Manchester (BSc). Served European War, Royal Engineers, 1916-19. Senior Lecturer in Elec. Engrg, Loughborough College, 1919-20; Asst Lecturer, Faculty of Technology, Univ. of Manchester, 1920-27; HM Inspector of Technical Schools, 1927-40, Staff Inspector, 1940-45, Board of Education. CEng, MIEE. *Publication:* (with A. E. Clayton) Elementary Electrical Engineering, 1927, fifth edn, 1966. *Recreations:* drama, gardening. *Address:* Lake View, The Downs, Standlake, Witney, Oxon OX8 7SH. *T:* Standlake 447. *Club:* English-Speaking Union.

**SHELLEY, Sir John Frederick,** 10th Bt, *cr* 1611; JP; *b* 14 Oct. 1884; *er s* of 9th Bt and Marion (*d* 1948), *d* of Richard Benyon, Englefield House, Berks; *S* father, 1931; *m* 1st, 1912, Nora (*d* 1953), *d* of F. J. Coleridge Boles, Rackenford Manor, Morchard Bishop, Devon; two *s* three *d*; 2nd, 1953, Mariamne Mee. *Educ:* Winchester; Cambridge University. Sheriff of Devonshire, 1938. Chairman, Devon County Coun., 1946-55. *Heir: s* John Shelley [*b* 31 Dec. 1915; *m* 1940, Dorothy Irvine Ingram; two *s*]. *Address:* Shobrooke House, Crediton, Devon. *TA* and *T:* Crediton 15. *Club:* Naval and Military.

**SHELLEY, Ursula,** MD, FRCP; Physician to Royal Free Hospital's Children's Department, to Princess Louise (Kensington) Hospital for Children, and to Queen Elizabeth Hospital for Children; *b* 11 Apr. 1906; *d* of Frederick Farey Shelley, FIC, and Rachel Hicks Shelley, MB, BS. *Educ:* St Paul's Girls' School; Royal Free Hospital School of Medicine. MB, BS Lond., Univ. Gold Medal, 1930; MD Lond., 1932; FRCP 1948. Member: Worshipful Society of Apothecaries; British Pædiatric Assoc., 1946; Liveryman, Soc. of Apothecaries; Freeman of City of London. *Publications:* numerous articles in medical journals. *Recreations:* gardening, lion dogs. *Address:* 15 Hyde Park Gate, SW7. *T:* 01-584 7941.

**SHELTON, William Jeremy Masefield,** MP (C) Clapham since 1970; Managing Director: CPV (International) Ltd since 1967 (Dir, 1964); Grosvenor Advertising Ltd since 1969 (Dir,

1964); Director, Saracen Industrial Design Ltd, since 1966; *b* 30 Oct. 1929; *s* of Lt-Col R. C. M. Shelton, MBE, St Saviour's, Guernsey, and Mrs R. E. P. Shelton (*née* Coode), London Place, Oxford; *m* 1960, Anne Patricia, *o d* of John Arthur Warder, *qv*; one *d* (adopted). *Educ:* Radley Coll.; Tabor Academy, Marion, Mass; Worcester Coll., Oxford; Univ. of Texas, Austin, Texas. Colman, Prentis & Varley Ltd, 1952-55; Corpa, Caracas, Venezuela, 1955-60; Man. Dir, DPV (Colombiana) Ltd, Bogota, Colombia, 1960-64. Member for Wandsworth, GLC, 1967-70; Chief Whip, on ILEA, 1968-70. *Recreations:* golf, reading, painting. *Address:* 19 Bywater Street, SW3. *T:* 01-584 3159.

**SHENSTONE, Prof. Allen Goodrich,** OBE 1943; MC 1918; FRS 1950; Professor-Emeritus of Physics, Princeton University, USA, Professor 1938; *b* 27 July 1893; British; *s* of Joseph Newton Shenstone and Eliza Hara; *m* 1st, 1923, Mildred Madeline Chadwick (*d* 1967); one *s* (and one *s* one *d* decd); 2nd, 1969, Locke Tiffin Harper. *Educ:* Princeton Univ.; Cambridge Univ. Instructor in Physics, Toronto University, 1922-25; Princeton Univ.: Asst Prof., 1925-28, Assoc. Prof., 1928-38, Actg Chm. Dept of Physics, 1949-50, Chm., 1950-60, Prof. Emeritus, 1962; leave of absence, 1940-45. Special Assistant to President of National Research Council of Canada for scientific liaison, 1940-45. Served European War, Royal Engineers (2nd Lt to Capt.), 1915-19 (despatches). *Publications:* many papers on physics in various scientific journals, (mainly in spectroscopy). *Recreation:* sailing. *Address:* 111 Mercer St, Princeton, NJ 08590, USA. *T:* 924-2389. *Club:* Athenæum.

**SHEPARD, Ernest Howard,** MC; artist; *b* St John's Wood, 10 Dec. 1879; *s* of Henry Dunkin Shepard, architect, and Harriet Jessie, *d* of William Lee, RWS, water-colour painter; *m* 1904, Florence Eleanor Chaplin (*d* 1927); one *d*; *m* 1944, Norah, *e d* of J. C. Carroll. *Educ:* St Paul's School. Studied at Heatherleys and Royal Academy Schools, 1897-1902; Studio, Glebe Place, Chelsea, 1901-3; first picture exhibited Royal Academy, 1901; moved to Shamley Green, Guildford, 1904; black and white drawings for illustrated papers and book illustrations, also oil paintings; exhibited in Royal Academy and Salon, Paris; started drawing for Punch, 1907; Commission in Royal Artillery, 1915; served in France with 105th Siege Battery, May 1916-Nov. 1917, Somme, Arras, Third Ypres (Captain and MC); served in Italy, Nov. 1917-April 1919, Montello, Asiago (Major); elected to Punch Table, 1921. *Publications:* Illustrations for: When We were very Young, 1924; Playtime and Company, 1925; Holly Tree, etc, 1925; Winnie-the-Pooh, 1926; Everybody's Pepys, 1926; Jeremy, 1927; Litte Ones Log, 1927; Let's Pretend, 1927; Now we are Six, 1927; Fun and Fantasy, 1927; The House at Pooh Corner, 1928; The Golden Age, 1928; Everybody's Boswell, 1930; Dream Days, 1930; Wind in the Willows, 1931; Christmas Poems, 1931; Bevis, 1931; Sycamore Square, 1932; Everybody's Lamb, 1933; The Cricket in the Cage, 1933; Victoria Regina (Laurence Housman), 1934; Modern Struwwelpeter, 1936; Golden Sovereign (Laurence Housman), 1937; Cheddar Gorge, 1937; As the Bee Sucks (E. V. Lucas), 1937; The Reluctant Dragon, 1939; Gracious Majesty (Laurence Housman), 1941; Golden Age, and Dream Days (Kenneth Grahame) for Book of the Month Club, New York, 1948-49; Bertie's Escapade (Kenneth Grahame), 1948-49; Enter David Garrick (Anna B. Stewart), (USA) 1951; Silver Curlew (Eleanor Farjeon), 1953; Cuckoo Clock (Mrs Molesworth), 1954; Glass Slipper (Eleanor Farjeon), 1955; Operation Wild Goose (Roland Pertwee), 1955; The Islanders (Roland Pertwee), 1956, Crystal Mountain (B. D. Rugh), 1955 (USA); Susan Bills the Wolfdog (Malcolm Saville), 1954; Frogmarton (Susan Colling), 1955; The Brownies (Mrs Ewing), 1955; The Pancake (Child's Reader), 1956; Briar Rose (Child's Reader), 1957-58; Drawn from Memory, an autobiography of early boyhood written and illustrated, 1957; Old Greek Fairy Tales, 1958; Tom Brown's School Days, 1959; Noble Company (Child's Reader), 1960; Hans Andersen's Fairy Tales, 1961; Drawn from Life, a further Autobiography, 1961; Ben and Brock (for children) written and illustrated, 1965; Betsy and Jo (for children) written and illustrated, 1966; illustrations in colour for new edns of Wind in the Willows, 1969, Winnie the Pooh, 1970, House at Pooh Corner, 1970. *Recreation:* gardening. *Address:* Woodmancote, Lodsworth, Sussex. *T:* Lodsworth 212. *Clubs:* Savage, Lansdowne.

*See also E. G. V. Knox.*

**SHEPHARD, George Clifford;** NCB Board Member for Industrial Relations since 1969; *b* 2 Aug. 1915; British; *m* 1942, Mollie Dorothy Mansfield; one *s* (one *d* decd). *Educ:* Chesterfield Grammar School. Bolsover Colliery Co. Ltd, Head Office, 1933-40. Served in Army, N Africa, various Comd HQs, 1940-45. Official, National Union of Mineworkers, 1945-69. Editor, COSA Bulletin. FCIS, ACWA. *Recreations:* golf, music. *Address:* Russett Lodge, 35 The Avenue, Hatch End, Pinner, Mddx. *T:* 01-428 6444. *Club:* Grimsdyke Golf.

**SHEPHEARD, Major-General Joseph Kenneth,** CB 1962; DSO 1943, and Bar, 1945; OBE 1949; *b* 15 Nov. 1908; *s* of late J. D. Shepheard, Poole and Bournemouth; *m* 1939, Maureen, *d* of late Capt. R. McG. Bowen-Colthurst, Oak Grove, County Cork; three *d*. *Educ:* Monmouth School; RMA Woolwich; Christ's Coll., Cambridge (BA Hons). Commissioned RE, 1928; served in India with King George V's Own Royal Sappers and Miners, 1933-38; served in France with BEF as Adjt 4 Div. RE, 1939-40; Staff College, Camberley, 1940; Bde Major 161 (Essex) Inf. Bde in UK, Sierra Leone and Western Desert, 1940-41; Bde Major 18 Indian Inf. Bde in Iraq, 1941; GSO1 4 Indian Div. in N Africa and Italy, 1942-44; Comd 6 Assault Regt RE, Normandy to Baltic, 1944-46; JSSC, Latimer, Bucks, 1947; GSO1, FarELF, 1948-49; Staff Officer to Dir of Operations, Malaya, 1950; Comd 27 Fd Engrs Regt and CRE 6 Armd Div., 1951-53; Defence Research Policy Staff, 1953-56; Imperial Defence Coll., 1957; CCRE 1 (Br.) Corps in Germany, 1958-60; Chief of Staff, Northern Comd, 1960-62; Chief Engineer, Northern Army Group and BAOR, 1962-64, retd. Col Comdt, RE, 1967-; Gen. Sec., The Officers' Assoc., 1966-. *Address:* 68 Rivermead Court, Ranelagh Gardens, SW6. *Club:* United Service.

**SHEPHEARD, Peter Faulkner,** FRIBA, AMTPI, FILA; Architect, town planner and landscape architect in private practice since 1948 (Shepheard and Epstein); *b* 11 Nov. 1913; *s* of Thomas Faulkner Shepheard, FRIBA, Liverpool; *m* 1943, Mary Bailey; one *s* one *d*. *Educ:* Birkenhead Sch.; Liverpool Sch. of Architecture. BArch. (1st Cl. Hons) Liverpool, 1936; Univ. Grad. Scholar in Civic Design, 1936-37. Asst to Derek Bridgwater, 1937-40; Min. of Supply, Royal Ordnance Factories, 1940-43; Min. of Town and Country Planning: technical officer, first on Greater London Plan (Sir Patrick Abercrombie's staff), later on research and master plan for

Stevenage New Town, 1943-47. Dep. Chief Architect and Planner, Stevenage Develt Corp., 1947-48. Vis. Prof., Landscape Architecture, Univ. of Pennsylvania, 1959 and 1962-. Member: Nat. Parks Commn, 1966-68; Countryside Commn, 1968-; Royal Fine Art Commn, 1968-. Works include: housing and schools for LCC and other authorities; Landscape of part of Festival of Britain South Bank Exhibition, London, 1951; Master plan and buildings for University of Lancaster; work for the Universities of Keele, Liverpool, Oxford, and Ghana, and for Winchester College. Mem. Council of RIBA, 1950-56, 1957-62, 1963-, Pres., RIBA, 1969-71; President, Architectural Association, 1954-55; RIBA Distinction in Town Planning, 1956. Pres. Inst. of Landscape Architects, 1965-66. *Publications:* Modern Gardens, 1953; Gardens, 1969; various articles, lectures and broadcasts on architecture and landscape; drawings and illustrations of architecture and other things; illustr. A Book of Ducks, and Woodlands Birds (King Penguins). *Recreations:* music and poetry; drawing, gardening and the study of natural science. *Address:* 60 Kingly St, W1. *T:* 01-734 8577. *Club:* Savile.

**SHEPHEARD, Rex Beaumont,** CBE 1949; Director of The Shipbuilding Conference, 1952-68, now Shipbuilders & Repairers National Association; *b* 9 Aug. 1902; *s* of Harold Beaumont Shepheard, MA, solicitor; *m* 1928, Helen H. Simmers; two *s* one *d*. *Educ:* Gresham's School; Glasgow University (BSc, Naval Architecture). Apprenticed with Fairfield Shipbuilding & Engineering Co. Ltd, and with J. Samuel White & Co. Ltd; Ship Surveyor, Lloyd's Register: London, 1928; Glasgow, 1930; Hamburg, 1935; Liverpool, 1939; USA, 1941. Seconded to Admiralty, and appointed Superintendent of Welding Development (Merchant Shipbuilding), 1942; Chief Ship Surveyor, Lloyd's Register of Shipping, 1944-52. Hon. Vice-Pres. Royal Inst. of Naval Architects; Hon. Fellow, NE Coast Instn of Engineers and Shipbuilders; Member: Inst. of Engineers and Shipbuilders in Scotland; Inst. of Marine Engineers; Amer. Soc. of Naval Architects and Marine Engineers. Past Prime Warden, Worshipful Company of Shipwrights. *Publications:* papers to professional institutions. *Address:* 7b South Cliff Tower, Eastbourne, Sussex. *T:* Eastbourne 23430.

**SHEPHEARD, Sir Victor (George),** KCB 1954 (CB 1950); Director: William Denny & Brothers Ltd, Shipbuilders and Engineers, Dumbarton, 1959-63; Marinite Ltd; Director of Research, British Ship Research Association, 1959-63; *b* 21 March 1893; *e s* of late V. G. Shepheard, Shortlands, Kent; *m* 1924, Florence, *d* of late Capt. James Wood, Bridgwater. *Educ:* HM Dockyard School, Devonport; Royal Naval Coll., Greenwich. Royal Corps of Naval Constructors, 1915; Constructor Lieut, Grand Fleet, 1915-17. Professor of Naval Architecture, RN College, Greenwich, 1934-39; Chief Constructor, 1939-42; Asst Director of Naval Construction, 1942-47; Deputy Director 1947-51; Director of Naval Construction, Admiralty, 1951-58. Member Council Royal Inst. of Naval Architects, 1944-, Vice-Pres. 1952-, Hon. Vice-Pres., 1961, Treasurer, 1960-69; Vice-Pres., Soc. for Nautical Research; Member: Admty Adv. Cttee on Structural Steel; Cttee on application of Nuclear Power to Marine Purposes, 1961-63; HMS Victory Advisory Technical Cttee. Hon. Fell., NEC Inst.; Mem., Smeatonian Soc.; Liveryman of Worshipful Company of Shipwrights; Board of Governors Cutty Sark Society; formerly Trustee, Nat. Maritime Museum. Froude Gold Medal for services to Naval Architecture and Shipbuilding, 1963. Chev. de la Légion d'Honneur, 1947. *Publications:* various papers to Professional Institutions. *Recreations:* gardening, music. *Address:* Manor Place, Manor Park, Chislehurst, Kent. *T:* 01-467 5455. *Club:* Athenæum.

**SHEPHERD,** family name of **Baron Shepherd.**

**SHEPHERD,** 2nd Baron, *cr* 1946, of Spalding; **Malcolm Newton Shepherd,** PC 1965; Opposition Deputy Leader of the House of Lords, since 1970; *b* 27 Sept. 1918; *s* of 1st Baron Shepherd, PC, and Ada Newton; *S* father, 1954; *m* 1941, Allison Wilson Redmond; two *s*. *Educ:* Lower Sch. of John Lyon; Friends' Sch., Saffron Walden. War of 1939-45: commissioned RASC, 1941; served in Desert, N Africa, Sicily, Italy. Deputy Opposition Chief Whip, House of Lords, 1960. Member Parly Labour Party Exec., 1964; Deputy Speaker, House of Lords, subseq. Opposition Chief Whip, 1964. Capt. of the Hon. Corps of Gentlemen-at-Arms and Government Chief Whip, House of Lords, 1964-67. Minister of State, FCO, 1967-70; Deputy Leader of the House of Lords, 1968-70. *Recreation:* golf. *Heir: s* Hon. Graeme George Shepherd, *b* 6 January 1949. *Address:* Greensands, Brassey Road, Limpsfield, Surrey. *T:* Oxted 2583. *Clubs:* Singapore, Tanglin, Royal Singapore Golf (Singapore).

**SHEPHERD, Rear-Adm. Charles William Haimes,** CBE 1968 (OBE 1958); Assistant Controller (Polaris), Ministry of Defence, since 1971; *b* 10 Dec. 1917; *s* of William Henry Haimes Shepherd and Florence (*née* Hayter); *m* 1940, Myra Betty Joan Major; one *s*. *Educ:* Public Central Sch., Plymouth; HMS Fisgard and RNC Greenwich. Entered RN as Artificer Apprentice, 1933; specialised Engrg Officer, 1940; served War of 1939-45 in HMS: Repulse; Hero; Royal Soveriegn; Gambia (RNZN); Staff of C-in-C Pacific (Sydney); R&D, Guided Weapons, 1946-49 and 1954-58 incl. Flotilla Eng Officer 3rd Trng Flotilla (HMS Crispin), 1949-51; Sen. Officers War Course, 1961-62; Tech. Dir, UK Polaris Weapon System, 1962-68; Dir Project Teams (Submarines), and Dep. Asst Controller (Polaris), MoD (Navy), 1968-71. Sub-Lt 1940; Lieut 1941; Lt-Comdr 1949; Comdr 1952; Captain 1960; Rear-Adm. 1970. *Recreation:* Do-it-yourself. *Address:* 28 Minster Way, Bath, Somerset. *T:* Bath 5493.

**SHEPHERD, Colston;** *see* Shepherd, E. C.

**SHEPHERD, E(dwin) Colston,** BA, BLitt (Oxon); Air Correspondent The New Scientist since 1957; *b* 13 Nov. 1891; *e s* of Edwin Shepherd, Bristol; *m* 1st, 1915, Edith Julia (*d* 1959), *d* of Christopher Holloway Wootton, Oxfordshire; no *c*; 2nd, 1960, Edith Hilda Mechem. *Educ:* Merchant Venturers', Bristol; Queen's Coll., Oxford. Before European war, worked as reporter Bristol Mercury, Yorkshire Herald, Yorkshire Observer, Leeds Mercury; served four years Royal Field Artillery; joined staff of The Times, 1923; Aeronautical Correspondent and leader writer, 1929-39; Editor, The Aeroplane, 1939-43; Secretary-General of the Air League of the British Empire, 1944-50 (seconded for duty to BBC as war corr. with RAF, 1944-45). Air Correspondent, Sunday Times, 1943-61. *Publications:* Fixing of Wages in Government Employment, 1923; Great Flights, 1939; The Air Force To-day, 1939. *Address:* St Cuthman's Cottage, King's Barn Lane, Steyning, Sussex BN4 3YR. *T:* Steyning 2289.

**SHEPHERD, Eric William,** CB 1967; Senior Director, Post Office, since 1967; *b* London, 17 May 1913; *s* of late Charles Thomas Shepherd; *m* 1938, Marie Noele Carpenter; two *d. Educ:* Hackney Downs School; The Polytechnic, Regent Street. BSc 1st Class Hons (Maths and Physics) London 1932. Entered Post Office as Executive Officer, 1932. Served War of 1939-45, with Royal Engineers (Postal Section), 1940-46. Principal, Post Office, 1948; Treasury, 1949-52; Asst Accountant General, Post Office, 1952; Dep. Comptroller and Accountant General, 1953; Assistant Secretary, 1956; Director of Finance and Accounts, 1960. *Recreations:* music, especially choral singing, golf. *Address:* 2 Arkley View, Arkley, Barnet, Herts. *T:* 01-449 9316.

**SHEPHERD, His Honour Harold Richard Bowman A.;** *see* Adie-Shepherd.

**SHEPHERD, Henry Bryan,** TD; HM Diplomatic Service, retired; *b* 9 July 1917; *o s* of late George Edward Shepherd and late Anna Dixon; *m* 1957, Elizabeth June Streatfeild; one *s* one *d. Educ:* Winchester; King's College, Cambridge. 2nd Lieut Tower Hamlets Rifles (Rifle Bde), 1939; war service, 1939-46, UK, N Africa, Italy and Austria. 2nd Sec., HM Foreign Service, 1947; 2nd Sec. and First Sec., New Delhi, 1948-50; First Sec., UK Delegn to OEEC, Paris, 1950-53; First Sec. (Economic), UK Comr-Gen.'s Office, Singapore, and UK Liaison Officer with United Organisations in Far East, 1953-55; transferred to Foreign Office, 1955; First Sec. and Head of Chancery, Sofia, 1958-60; Counsellor, Dec. 1964; British Consul-General, Hanoi, Dec. 1965-Oct. 1966; Counsellor, British Embassy, Copenhagen, 1967-68. *Recreations:* walking, reading, lawn tennis, bridge, chess. *Address:* The Cottage, Shipley, Sussex. *T:* Coolham 227. *Clubs:* Travellers', MCC, Chanctonbury Ring.

**SHEPHERD, Joseph Wilfrid,** CBE 1920; *b* 1885; *s* of Richard Shepherd; *m* 1910, Gertrude Mary, *d* of F. Ainsworth. Rendered services in connection with War Refugees during European War. *Address:* Rosemary, Llandudno Road, Rhos-on-Sea, North Wales.

**SHEPHERD, Dame Margaret (Alice),** DBE 1964 (CBE 1962); a Director, Haigh Engineering Co. Ltd, Ross-on-Wye; *b* 1910; *d* of Percy S. Turner, Redcourt, Pyrford; *m* 1935, Thomas Cropper Ryley Shepherd; three *s* one *d. Educ:* Wimbledon, Lausanne and London Univ. Chairman: Conservative and Unionist Women's National Advisory Cttee, 1960-63; National Union of Conservative and Unionist Assocs, 1963-64; Conservative Political Centre National Advisory Cttee, 1966-69. *Recreations:* swimming, golf, music, dreaming. *Address:* Moraston House, Bridstow, Ross-on-Wye, Herefordshire. *T:* Ross-on-Wye 2370.

**SHEPHERD, Very Rev. Robert Henry Wishart,** DD; DLitt; retired, 1968; *b* 25 May 1888; *s* of Matthew Moncrieff Shepherd and Isabella MacEwen; *m* 1918, Mary Shearer Goodfellow; two *d. Educ:* St Andrews and Edinburgh Universities; New College Divinity Hall, Edinburgh. Missionary of United Free Church of Scotland to South Africa, 1918 (came under Church of Scotland at union, 1929); in Tembuland, Cape Province, 1920-26; Lovedale Missionary Institution, 1927-58: Chaplain, 1927-42; Director of Lovedale Press, 1927-58; Principal of Lovedale, 1942-55. President of Christian Council of S Africa, 1956-60. Moderator of the General Assembly of the Church of Scotland, May 1959-May 1960. Member, Advisory Commission on Central African Federation (Monckton Commission). Editor of South African Outlook, 1932-63. Hon. DD Edinburgh Univ. 1947; Hon. DD Rhodes Univ., S Africa, 1965; DLitt Witwatersrand University, Johannesburg, South Africa. Coronation Medal, 1953. *Publications:* Humanism of Jesus, 1926; Under the Oaks, 1934; Lovedale: The Story of a Century, 1940; Lovedale and Literature for the Bantu, 1943; Children of the Veld, 1937; A South African Medical Pioneer, 1950; (ed with Mrs M. M. S. Ballantyne) Forerunners of Modern Malawi; The Story of Lovedale, 1824-1955, 1970; contributions to journals dealing with missionary and African affairs. *Recreation:* walking. *Address:* Hutchinson Road, Reeston, (PO Box 3061), Cambridge, CP, South Africa.

**SHEPHERD, Professor William Morgan,** DSc (London); Professor of Theoretical Mechanics in Faculty of Engineering, University of Bristol, since 1959; *b* 19 Dec. 1905; *s* of Charles Henry and Elizabeth Shepherd; *m* 1932, Brenda Coulson; two *d. Educ:* Wellington School; University College of the South West, Exeter; University College, London. Asst lecturer and lecturer in mathematics, University College of North Wales, Bangor, 1928-35; Lecturer in mathematics in Faculty of Engineering, University of Bristol, 1935-44; Reader in Elasticity, University of Bristol, 1944-59; Head of Department of Theoretical Mechanics, 1951-. *Publications:* various publications, mainly on applied mathematics, in Proceedings of the Royal Society and other scientific journals. *Recreations:* gardening, cricket. *Address:* Yew Tree House, Portbury, Bristol. *T:* Pill 2206.

**SHEPHERD, William Stanley;** *b* 1918; *s* of W. D. Shepherd; *m* 1942, Betty, *d* of late T. F. Howard, MP for Islington South, 1931-35; two *s.* Served in Army, War of 1939-45. A managing director of businesses which he has established; MP (C) for Cheadle Division of Cheshire, 1950-66 (Bucklow Division of Cheshire, 1945-50); Member of the Select Committee on Estimates; Joint Hon. Sec. Conservative Parliamentary Committee in Trade and Industry, 1945-51. Director, Manchester Chamber of Commerce; Hon. Pres., Chair Frame Manufacturers Assoc.; Hon. Mem., Valuers Institution; Government Mem., Scientific Films Assoc. FREconS. *Address:* (office) 77 George Street, W1. *T:* 01-935 0753; (home) 33 Queens Grove, St John's Wood, NW8. *T:* 01-722 7526. *Club:* Carlton.

**SHEPHERD-BARRON, Wilfrid Philip,** MC, TD; LLD; FICE, FIMechE; *b* 2 May 1888; *s* of late James Barron, MInstCE, Aberdeen; *m* 1921, Dorothy Cunliffe (*d* 1953), *e d* of A. C. Shepherd; two *s. Educ:* Aberdeen Grammar School. Chief Engineer, Chittagong Port Commissioners; Chief Engineer, Karachi Port Trust. Served European War, 1914-18, France and Belgium, Royal Engineers, TF (despatches, MC); Past President, Institution of Civil Engineers; Colonel, Engineer and Railway Staff Corps, RE (TA); Chief Engineer, Port of London Authority, retired 1953. Hon. LLD Aberdeen, 1954. *Address:* 22 Ormonde Gate, Chelsea, SW3. *T:* 01-352 0170.

**SHEPPARD, Rt. Rev. David Stuart;** *see* Woolwich, Bishop Suffragan of.

**SHEPPARD, Leslie Alfred,** MA; FSA; Deputy Keeper of Printed Books, British Museum, 1945-53; *b* 9 Jan. 1890; *o s* of late Alfred Sheppard, Keynsham; *m* 1918, Dorothy, *y d* of late Rev. H. Ewbank, St John's, Ryde; two *s. Educ:* Merrywood School, Bristol; St Catharine's College, Cambridge. Served with 1st British Red Cross Unit attached to Italian

Army, 1915-19; entered British Museum, 1919. Member of Council of Bibliographical Society, 1936-46. *Publications:* A Fifteenth-Century Humanist, Francesco Filelfo, The Printers of the Coverdale Bible, Printing at Deventer in the XVth Century, A New Light on William Caxton and Colard Mansion, and other articles and reviews in Transactions of Bibliographical Society, Gutenberg Jahrbuch, and elsewhere. Translated Memoirs of Lorenzo da Ponte, 1929. *Address:* 55 Park Town, Oxford.

**SHEPPARD, Tan Sri Mervyn Cecil ffrank,** PSM (Malaysia) 1969; JMN (Malaysia), 1963; CMG 1957; MBE 1946; ED 1947; Hon. Treasurer, Board of Trustees, National Art Gallery, Malaya; *b* 1905; *s* of late Canon J. W. ff. Sheppard; *m* 1940, Rosemary, *d* of late Major Edward Oakeley; one *d. Educ:* Marlborough; Magdalene Coll., Cambridge. Cadet, Federated Malay States, 1928; Private Sec. to Chief Sec., 1928. Interned by Japanese, 1942-45. Director of Public Relations, 1946; District Officer, Klang, 1947-50; British Adviser, Negri Sembilan, 1952; Head of the Emergency Food Denial Organisation, Federation of Malaya, 1956. First Keeper of Public Records, 1957-62, and Director of Museums, 1958-63, Federation of Malaya. Panglima Setia Mahkota, 1969; Dato Jasa Purba Di-Raja, Negri Sembilan, 1967. *Address:* c/o National Art Gallery, 109 Ampang Road, Kuala Lumpur, Malaysia. *Club:* Oxford and Cambridge University.

**SHEPPARD, Prof. Norman,** FRS 1967; Professor of Chemistry, University of East Anglia, Norwich, since 1964; Dean of the School of Chemical Sciences, since 1970; *b* 16 May 1921; *s* of Walter Sheppard and Anne Clarges Sheppard (*née* Finding); *m* 1949, Kathleen Margery McLean; two *s* one *d* (and one *s* decd). *Educ:* Hymers Coll., Hull; St Catharine's Coll., Cambridge. BA Cantab 1st cl. hons 1943; PhD and MA Cantab 1947. Vis. Asst Prof., Pennsylvania State Univ., 1947-48; Ramsay Memorial Fellow, 1948-49; Senior 1851 Exhibn, 1949-51; Fellow of Trinity Coll., Cambridge and Asst Dir of Research in Spectroscopy, Cambridge Univ., 1957-64. *Publications:* scientific papers on spectroscopy in Proc. Roy. Soc., Trans. Faraday Soc., Jl Chem. Soc., Spectrochimica Acta, etc. *Recreations:* architecture, classical music, cricket. *Address:* 5 Hornor Close, Norwich NOR 63D, Norfolk. *T:* Norwich 53052.

**SHEPPARD, Prof. Percival Albert,** CBE 1963; FRS 1964; Professor of Meteorology, University of London (at Imperial College) since 1952; *b* 12 May 1907; *s* of Albert Edward Sheppard, Box, Wiltshire, and Flora Sheppard (*née* Archard); *m* 1933, Phyllis Blanche Foster, Bath; two *s*. *Educ:* City of Bath Boys' School; University of Bristol. First Class Hons Physics, 1927; Demonstrator, H. H. Wills Physical Laboratory, University of Bristol, 1927-29; Resident Observer, Kew Observatory, 1929-32; British Polar Year Expedition, NWT, Canada, 1932-33; Meteorologist, Chemical Defence Research Establishment, Porton, 1934-39; Reader in Meteorology, Imperial Coll., Univ. of London, 1939-52. Served Meteorological Office, Air Min., 1939-45. Vis. Prof., Univ. of California, Los Angeles, 1963. Royal Meteorological Society: Editor and Hon. Sec., 1950-53; Pres., 1957-59; Symons Gold Medal, 1963; Chairman, Meteorological Research Cttee, 1958-68; Mem. Science Res. Council, 1967- (Chm., Space Policy and Grants Cttee, 1965-); Vice-Chm. of Council, ESRO, 1966-68 (Chm., Scientific and Technical Cttee, 1968-). FInstP; Fellow, Amer. Meteorological Soc., 1967; Hon. ARCS. Hon. DSc Leningrad, 1969. *Publications:* papers on atmospheric electricity and meteorology in various journals. *Recreation:* life. *Address:* Seer Green House, near Beaconsfield, Bucks. *T:* Beaconsfield 6578. *Club:* Athenæum.

**SHEPPARD, Prof. Philip Macdonald,** FRS 1965; DPhil; Professor of Genetics, University of Liverpool, since 1963; *b* 27 July 1921; *s* of late George Sheppard and of Alison (*née* Macdonald); *m* 1948, Patricia Beatrice, *d* of R. H. Lee; three *s*. *Educ:* Marlborough; Worcester Coll., Oxford. RAFVR, 1940-46 (POW, 1942-45). Hons Degree in Zoology, 1948; Christopher Welch Research Schol., 1948; DPhil, Oxon, 1951. Junior Res. Officer, Dept of Zoology, Oxford, 1951-56; Rockefeller Fellow, 1954. Liverpool University: Sen. Lectr in Genetics, Dept of Zoology, 1956; Reader in Genetics, 1959. *Publications:* Natural Selection and Heredity, 1958; many articles in scientific jls. *Recreations:* fishing, rifle shooting (Capt. OU Rifle Club, 1948), breeding butterflies. *Address:* 25 Derwent Road, Meols, Hoylake, Cheshire. *T:* 051-632 4404.

**SHEPPARD, Richard,** CBE 1964; ARA 1966; FRIBA 1944 (ARIBA 1936); Architect in private practice (Richard Sheppard, Robson & Partners); work includes universities, schools and technical colleges, industrial and commercial buildings; *b* 2 July 1910; *e s* of William Sheppard and Hilda (*née* Kirby-Evans); *m* 1938, Jean Shufflebotham, ARIBA, AMTPI, *o d* of Dr Frank Shufflebotham; one *s* one *d. Educ:* Bristol Grammar School; Architectural Association School of Architecture, Bedford Square. Hons Diploma, Architectural Assoc. 1935; foreign travel, 1935-37. Principal commissions include: City Univ., London; Brunel Univ., Uxbridge; Churchill College, Cambridge (competition), 1959; and other educnl and commercial bldgs. Vice-Pres. RIBA, 1969-70. *Publications:* Building for the People, 1945; Prefabrication and Building, 1946, etc; also technical articles. *Recreation:* looking at the work of others. *Address:* The Old Rectory, Little Berkhamsted, Herts. *T:* Essendon 366. *Club:* Garrick.

**SHEPPARD, William Vincent,** CBE 1963; Member, National Coal Board, since 1967; *b* 15 Nov. 1909; *s* of late Dr H. P. Sheppard; *m* 1938, Nancy F. Watson; two *s* one *d. Educ:* Cheltenham College; Birmingham University (BSc (Hons) Min.). Mining Student with Bolsover Colliery Co. Ltd, 1931-35, Safety Officer to Co., 1935-37; Under Manager, Creswell Colliery, 1937; Manager, Rufford Colliery, 1938; Mining Devel. Engr, No 4 Area, East Midlands Div., NCB, 1947; Area Gen. Man., No 1 Area, East Midlands Div., NCB, 1948; Dir-Gen. of Reconstruction, NCB, 1957-60; Dir-Gen. of Production, NCB, 1960-67. Past-Pres., Southern Counties Inst. of Instn of Mining Engineers; MIME. CStJ 1957. *Recreations:* gardening, model-making, Rugby football (County Cap, Glos). *Address:* Langshott Manor, Horley, Surrey. *T:* Horley 2282.

**SHEPPARD FIDLER, Alwyn G.;** *see* Fidler.

**SHERA, Arthur Geoffrey,** MD, MA, BCh Cantab; MRCS, LRCP; FRCPath; Hon. Consultant Pathologist to Eastbourne Hospitals; *b* Sheffield, 7 Nov. 1889; *s* of H. A. Shera, MRCS and Fanny Louisa Wild; *m* 1915, Annie Louisa Davies; one *s*. *Educ:* Oakham School; Emmanuel Coll., Cambridge, University College Hospital, London. Fellowes Gold Medal Clinical Medicine,

University of London, 1913; British Red Cross War Medal; Hon. Capt. RAMC 1915-19; Pathologist, No 1 Red Cross Hospital, Netley; RMO Fulham Hospital, 1914; Clinical Assistant Evelina Hospital for Children, 1914; Member of Council, Association of Clinical Pathologists, 1927-28, 1932-33, and 1935-36; Pres. Channel Coast and South-East Branch Association of Clinical Pathologists, 1948-49, 1949-50. Vice-Pres. Sect. of Pathology and Bacteriology, BMA, 1931, also Chm. Museum Cttee, 1931, 1956; Chm. Eastbourne Div. BMA, 1933-34; Mem. Consulting Pathologists' Group Cttee, BMA, 1939, 1942-45; Pres. Eastbourne Medical Soc., 1934. *Publications:* Vaccines and Sera, 1918; papers on medical science in the British Medical Journal, Lancet, British Journal of Surgery (last contribs, 1963), Journal of Mental Science, Practitioner, Medical World. *Recreations:* motoring, fishing. *Address:* Holme, 24 Le Brun Road, Eastbourne, Sussex. *Club:* Devonshire (Eastbourne).

**SHERBORNE,** 7th Baron, *cr* 1784; **Charles Dutton;** *b* 13 May 1911; *e s* of 6th Baron, DSO and Ethel Mary (*d* 1969), *e d* of late William Baird; *S* father, 1949; *m* 1943, Joan Molesworth, *d* of Sir James Dunn, 1st Bt, and *widow* of John Anthony Jenkinson. *Educ:* Stowe. *Heir: b* Hon. George Edward Dutton [*b* 23 Sept. 1912; *m* 1959, Mrs Pauline Stewart Shephard, *d* of late Stewart Robinson]. *Address:* Lodge Park, Aldsworth, Cheltenham, Glos. *T:* 215. *Clubs:* St James', White's; Travellers' (Paris).

*See also Sir John Dutton Clerk.*

**SHERBORNE, Bishop Suffragan of,** since 1960; **Rt. Rev. Victor Joseph Pike,** CB 1953; CBE 1950; DD (*hc*) 1955; Prebend of Fordington with Writhlington in Salisbury Cathedral since 1960; *b* 1 July 1907; *s* of late Canon William Pike, Thurles, Co. Tipperary, and Mrs William Pike (*née* Surridge); *m* 1937, Dorothea Elizabeth Frend, *d* of late Capt. W. R. Frend, Sherwood Foresters; one *s* two *d*. *Educ:* Bishop Foy School, Waterford; Trinity College, Dublin, BA 1930; MA 1935 (Hon. DD 1955). Curate, Dundrum, Co. Dublin, 1930-32; Chaplain to the Forces, 4th Class, Aldershot, Gibraltar, RMA Woolwich, 1932-39; Senior Chaplain, 43rd Div., 11th Armoured Div., 1940-42; Deputy Assistant Chaplain-General, 5th Corps, CMF, 1942-44; OBE 1944; Assistant Chaplain-General, 8th Army, 1945 (despatches); Deputy Chaplain-General, MELF, 1946; Assistant Chaplain-General, Western Command, 1947-49; Assistant Chaplain-General, BAOR, 1950-51; Chaplain-General to the Forces, 1951-60 (with title of Archdeacon, 1958-60); Hon. Canon of Canterbury, 1951-60; QHC, 1948-53; Chaplain to the Queen, Nov. 1953-June 1960. *Recreation:* Rugby. *Address:* The Walton Canonry, 69 The Close, Salisbury, Wilts. *T:* Salisbury 5766. *Club:* Cavalry.

**SHERBORNE, Archdeacon of;** *see* Ward, Ven. E. J. G.

**SHERBROOKE, Archbishop of, (RC),** since 1968; **Most Rev. John Mary Fortier;** *b* 1 July 1920. *Educ:* Laval University, Quebec. Bishop Auxiliary, La Pocatière, PQ, 1961-65; Bishop of Gaspé, PQ, 1965-68. *Publication:* contrib. to Dictionnaire d'Histoire et de Géographie. *Address:* 130 rue de la Cathédrale, Sherbrooke, PQ, Canada. *T:* 569-6070.

**SHERBROOKE, Rear-Adm. Robert St Vincent,** VC 1942; CB 1953; DSO 1940; RN; Lord Lieutenant, County of Nottingham, since 1968; JP; Registrar and Secretary of the Order of the Bath, 1964-68; *b* 8 Jan. 1901; *s* of late Capt. Henry Graham Sherbrooke, DSO, RN, Oxton Hall, Newark, Notts; *m* 1929, Rosemary Neville, *d* of late Lt-Col P. N. Buckley, CBE; two *d*. *Educ:* RN Colleges, Osborne and Dartmouth. High Sheriff of Notts, 1958; DL Notts, 1958; JP Notts, 1960; Vice-Lieutenant Notts, 1964. KStJ 1970. *Address:* Oxton, Newark, Notts. *Clubs:* Naval and Military, White's.

*See also Baron Digby.*

**SHERBROOKE-WALKER, Col Ronald Draycott,** CBE 1961; TD 1945; TA (retired); Director of Securicor (Southern) Ltd since 1965 (of Securicor Ltd, 1945-65); *b* 1 April 1897; *s* of Rev. George Sherbrooke Walker, sometime Rector of March, Cambs; *m* 1925, Ruth Bindley, *d* of William Allen Bindley, Edgbaston. *Educ:* Sherborne. Chartered Accountant, 1923. Served European War, 1914-19; Lieut Dorset Regt and RFC. Lieut to Major 8th Bn Middx Regt TA, 1925-31. Served War of 1939-45: Lieut-Col, Middx Regt and attached RAF Regt. Mem. Middx T&AFA, 1930-63 (Vice-Chm. 1951-56); Comdt Middx Army Cadet Force, 1948-54; Vice-Chm. Army Cadet Force Assoc., 1956-66 (Vice-Pres., 1966-); Mem. Amery Cttee, 1956-57; Mem. TA Advisory Cttee, 1956-64; Governor Cadet Training Centre, Frimley Park, 1959-. FCA. DL Middx, 1947-65; Vice-Lieutenant, Middx, 1963-65; Deputy Lieutenant, Greater London, 1965-. *Publications:* Khaki and Blue, 1952; contrib. to various jls. *Recreation:* gardening. *Address:* Brookhampton House, North Cadbury, Somerset. *T:* North Cadbury 225. *Club:* United Service.

**SHERFIELD,** 1st Baron, *cr* 1964; **Roger Mellor Makins,** GCB 1960 (KCB 1953); GCMG 1955 (KCMG 1949; CMG 1944); Chancellor of Reading University since 1970; Chairman: Industrial and Commercial Finance Corporation, since 1964; Estate Duties Investment Trust since 1966; Ship Mortgage Finance Company since 1966; Technical Development Capital since 1966; A. C. Cossor, since 1968; Chairman of Governing Body and Fellow of Imperial College of Science and Technology; Chairman, Marshall Aid Commemoration Commission. Trustee: Kennedy Memorial Fund; The Times Trust; Vice-Chairman, The Ditchley Foundation; President, Parliamentary and Scientific Committee, since 1969; *b* 3 Feb. 1904; *e s* of late Brigadier-General Sir Ernest Makins, KBE, CB, DSO; *m* 1934, Alice, *e d* of late Hon. Dwight F. Davis; two *s* four *d*. *Educ:* Winchester; Christ Church, Oxford. First Class Honours in History, 1925; Fellow of All Souls College, 1925-39 and 1957-; called to Bar, Inner Temple, 1927; Foreign Office, 1928; served Washington, 1931-34, Oslo, 1934; Foreign Office, 1934; Assistant Adviser on League of Nations Affairs, 1937; Sec. Intergovernmental Cttee on Refugees from Germany, 1938-39; Adviser on League of Nations Affairs, 1939; Acting First Secretary, 1939; Acting Counsellor, 1940; Adviser to British Delegation, International Labour Conference, New York, 1941; served on Staff of Resident Minister in West Africa, 1942; Counsellor, 1942; Asst to Resident Minister at Allied Force Headquarters, Mediterranean, 1943-44; Minister at British Embassy, Washington, 1945-47; UK rep. on United Nations Interim Commission for Food and Agriculture, 1945; Asst Under-Sec. of State, FO, 1947-48, Dep. Under-Sec. of State, 1948-52; British Ambassador to the United States, 1953-56; Joint Permanent Secretary of the Treasury, 1956-59; Chairman, UK Atomic Energy Authority, 1960-64; Hill, Samuel Group, 1966-70; Dir, Times Publishing Co. Ltd, 1964-67. Mem. Council, The Royal

Albert Hall; Fellow of Winchester College; Hon. FICE; Hon. DCL Oxford; Hon. Doctor of Laws: Univs of Sheffield, New Hampshire, S Carolina, Pittsburgh, and Bowdoin Coll. *Recreations:* shooting, gardening. *Heir: s* Hon. Christopher James Makins, *b* 23 July 1942. *Address:* 8 Southwick Place, W2. *T:* 01-723 9583; Sherfield Court, near Basingstoke, Hants. *Clubs:* Athenæum, Pratt's, MCC.
*See also Baron Milford.*

**SHERGOLD, Harold Taplin,** CMG 1963; OBE 1958 (MBE 1945); serving in Foreign Office since 1954; *b* 5 Dec. 1915; *s* of late Ernest Henry Shergold; *m* 1949, Bevis Anael, *d* of late William Bernard Reid; no *c. Educ:* Peter Symonds' School, Winchester; St Edmund Hall, Oxford; Corpus Christi Coll., Cambridge. Asst Master, Cheltenham Grammar Sch., 1937-40. Joined Hampshire Regt, 1940; transferred to Intelligence Corps, 1941; served in Middle East and Italy, 1941-46 (despatches). Joined Foreign Office, 1947; served in Germany, 1947-54. *Address:* Flat B, The Corner House, Vicarage Road, East Sheen, SW14. *T:* 01-876 0634.

**SHERIDAN, Cecil Majella,** CMG 1961; *b* 9 Dec. 1911; *s* of late J. P. Sheridan, Liverpool, and Mrs Sheridan (*née* Myerscough), Preston, Lancs; *m* 1949, Monica, *d* of H. F. Ereaut, MBE, Jersey, CI; two *s* one *d. Educ:* Ampleforth College, York. Admitted Solicitor, England, 1934; called to Bar, Innner Temple, 1952. Practised as solicitor in Liverpool (Messrs Yates, Sheridan & Co.), 1934-40. Served in RAFVR, General Duties Pilot, 1940-46; resigned with hon. rank of Squadron Leader. Joined Colonial Legal Service, 1946; Crown Counsel and Dep. Public Prosecutor, Malayan Union, 1946-48; Legal Adviser, Malay States of Pahang, Kelantan, Trengganu and Selangor and Settlement of Penang, 1948-55; Legal Draftsman, Fedn of Malaya, 1955-57; Solicitor-General, Fedn of Malaya, 1957-59; Attorney-General, Fedn of Malaya, 1959-63; Attorney-General, Malaysia, retd. Mem. (Fedn of Malaya) Inter-Governmental Cttees for Borneo Territories and Singapore, 1962-63; Chm. Traffic Comrs, E Midland Traffic Area, 1965-; Pres., British Assoc. of Malaysia 1964-65. Chm., Malaysia Housing Soc., 1964-65. Hon. PMN (Malaysia), 1963. Associate Mem., Commonwealth Parly Assoc. (UK Branch). *Address:* 18 Private Road, Sherwood, Nottingham. *Clubs:* East India and Sports; Nottinghamshire.

**SHERIDAN, Hon. Sir Dermot Joseph,** Kt 1970; CMG 1965; **Hon. Mr Justice Sheridan;** Chief Justice, High Court, Uganda, since 1970; *b* 3 Oct. 1914; *s* of late Sir Joseph Sheridan. *Educ:* Downside Sch.; Pembroke Coll., Cambridge (BA, 1st Cl. Hons Law Tripos); Harmsworth Scholar, Middle Temple. Called to Bar, 1933; practised at Bar, 1933-42; Colonial Legal Service, Resident Magistrate, Uganda, 1942-48; Crown Counsel, Uganda, 1948-51; Director of Public Prosecutions, Gold Coast, 1951-55; Acting Chief Justice, Uganda, Jan.-June 1963, and 1968-70; Puisne Judge, High Court, Uganda, 1955-70. *Recreations:* music, cricket, bridge, reading. *Address:* The High Court, Kampala, Uganda. *Clubs:* MCC, East India and Sports; Kampala (Uganda).

**SHERLOCK, Sir Philip (Manderson),** KBE 1967 (CBE 1953); Secretary-General, Association of Caribbean Universities & Research Institutes, since 1969; *b* Jamaica, 25 Feb. 1902; *s* of Rev. Terence Sherlock, Methodist Minister, and Adina Sherlock; *m* 1942, Grace Marjorye Verity; two *s* one *d. Educ:* Calabar High Sch., Jamaica. Headmaster, Wolmer's Boys' Sch., Jamaica, 1933-38; Sec., Inst. of Jamaica, 1939-44; Educn Officer, Jamaica Welfare, 1944-47; Dir, Extra-Mural Dept, University Coll. of West Indies, 1947-60, also Vice-Principal, University Coll. of W Indies, 1952-62; Pro-Vice-Chancellor, Univ. of West Indies, 1962, Vice-Chancellor, 1963-69. Hon. LLD: Leeds, 1959; Carleton, 1967; St Andrews, 1968; Hon. DCL, New Brunswick, 1966; Hon. DLitt, Acadia, 1966. *Publications:* Anansi the Spider Man, 1956; (with John Parry) Short History of the West Indies, 1956; Caribbean Citizen, 1957; West Indian Story, 1960; Three Finger Jack, 1961; Jamaica, A Junior History, 1966; West Indian Folk Tales, 1966; West Indies, 1966; Land and People of the West Indies, 1967; Belize, a Junior History, 1969; The Iguana's Tail, 1969; educational books and articles. *Recreations:* reading, writing, cooking. *Address:* Association of Caribbean Universities & Research Institutes, 25 Hope Road, Kingston 10, Jamaica, West Indies. *Clubs:* National Liberal, English-Speaking Union, West Indian.

**SHERLOCK, Prof. Sheila Patricia Violet,** MD; FRCP; FRCPEd; Professor of Medicine, University of London, at the Royal Free Hospital School of Medicine, since 1959; *b* 31 March 1918; *d* of Samuel Philip Sherlock and late Violet Mary Catherine Beckett; *m* 1951, David Geraint James; two *d. Educ:* Folkestone County Sch.; Edinburgh Univ. Ettles Scholar, 1941; Beit Memorial Research Fellow, 1942-47; Rockefeller Fellow, Yale University, USA, 1948. Physician and Lecturer in Medicine, Postgraduate Medical School of London, 1948-59; Bradshaw Lecturer, RCP, 1961; Rolleston Lecturer, RCP, 1968. Councillor, RCP, 1964-68, Censor, 1970-. Hon. Member: American Gastro-enterological Soc., 1963; Australasian Gastro-enterological Soc., 1965; Mexican Gastro-enterological Soc., 1968; Czechoslovak Gastro-enterological Soc., 1968. Hon. FACP. William Cullen Prize, 1962 (shared). *Publications:* Diseases of the Liver and Biliary System, 4th edn 1968; papers on liver structure and function in various medical journals, since 1943. *Recreations:* cricket, travel. *Address:* 12 Sidmouth Road, NW2. *T:* 01-459 3069.

**SHERMAN, Mrs Alec;** *see* Bachauer, Gina.

**SHERRARD, Michael David,** QC 1968; *b* 23 June 1928; *er s* of late Morris Sherrard and Ethel Sherrard; *m* 1952, Shirley, *d* of Maurice and Lucy Bagrit; two *s. Educ:* King's Coll., London. LLB 1949. Called to Bar, Middle Temple, 1949; Mem., SE Circuit, 1950; Mem., Winn Cttee on Personal Injury Litigation, 1966. *Recreations:* oil painting, listening to opera. *Address:* 2 Crown Office Row, Temple, EC4. *T:* 01-583 2681; 14 Burgess Hill, Hampstead, NW2. *T:* 01-435 7828. *Club:* Reform.

**SHERRIFF, Robert Cedric,** FSA; FRSL; author; *b* 6 June 1896; *s* of late Herbert Hankin Sherriff, Aylesbury, Bucks, and Constance, *d* of Charles Winder, Iver, Bucks. *Educ:* Kingston Grammar School; New College, Oxford. Entered Sun Insurance Office, 1914; Captain, East Surrey Regiment, 1917; wrote first play for performance in aid of School Chapel Restoration Fund, 1921; first London Production 1929, when Journey's End was produced at Savoy Theatre. *Publications: plays:* Journey's End, 1929; Badger's Green, 1930; Windfall, 1933; St Helena (with Jeanne de Casalis), 1934; Miss Mabel, 1948; Home at Seven, 1950; The White Carnation, 1953; The Long Sunset, 1955; The Telescope 1957; Cards, with Uncle Tom (for radio), 1958; A Shred of Evidence, 1960; The Ogburn Story (television), 1963; *novels:* The Fortnight in September, 1931; Greengates, 1936; The Hopkins Manuscript, 1939; Chedworth, 1944; Another Year, 1946; King John's Treasure, 1954; The Wells of St Mary's, 1961; *motion picture screen plays* include: Invisible Man, 1933; Goodbye Mr Chips, 1936; The Four Feathers, 1938; Lady Hamilton, 1941; This Above All, 1942; Odd Man Out, 1945; Quartet, 1948; No Highway, 1950; The Dam Busters, 1955; *autobiography:* No Leading Lady, 1968. *Recreations:* archæology, farming, rowing. *Address:* Rosebriars, Esher, Surrey. *Clubs:* Athenæum, Leander.

**SHERRILL, Rt. Rev. Henry Knox,** DD; retired Bishop; Presiding Bishop of Protestant Episcopal Church in USA, 1947-58; a President, World Council of Churches, since 1954; *b* Brooklyn, New York, 6 Nov. 1890; *s* of Henry Williams Sherrill, and Maria Knox Mills; *m* 1921, Barbara Harris, Brookline, Mass; three *s* one *d*. *Educ:* Hotchkiss School; Yale University; Episcopal Theological School, Cambridge, Mass. Deacon, 1914; Priest, 1915; Assistant Minister, Trinity Church, Boston, 1914-17; Rector, Church of Our Saviour, Brookline, 1919-23; Rector, Trinity Church, Boston, 1923-30; Bishop of Massachusetts, 1930-47; Red Cross and US Army Chaplain, AEF, France, July 1917-Jan. 1919; Pres. Nat. Council of Churches of Christ in USA, 1950-52; Board of Trustees: Massachusetts General Hospital, 1928-46 (Chairman of Board, 1934-46); Fellow Corporation of Yale University; Fellow American Academy of Arts and Sciences. Hon. DD Edinburgh, Oxford; numerous doctorates in Divinity, Law, Sacred Theology, Literature and Canon Law from American Universities and Colleges. *Publications:* William Lawrence: Later Years of a Happy Life, 1943; The Church's Ministry in Our Times (Lyman Beecher Lectures, Yale Univ.), 1949. *Address:* Boxford, Mass, USA. *Clubs:* Graduates (New Haven); Union (Boston).

**SHERRIN, Ned, (Edward George Sherrin);** film, theatre and television producer, director and writer; *b* Low Ham, Som, 18 Feb. 1931; *s* of late T. A. Sherrin and D. F. Sherrin (*née* Drewett). *Educ:* Sexey's Sch., Bruton; Exeter Coll., Oxford; Gray's Inn. Producer: ATV, Birmingham, 1955-57; BBC TV, 1957-66 (prod. and dir. That Was The Week That Was). Produced films: The Virgin Soldiers, (with Leslie Gilliat) 1968; Every Home Should Have One, 1969; TV plays (with Caryl Brahms) include: Little Beggars; Benbow was his Name; Take a Sapphire; The Great Inimitable Mr Dickens; plays (with Caryl Brahms): No Bed for Bacon; Cindy-Ella or I Gotta Shoe, 1962-63; The Spoils, 1968; Nicholas Nickleby, 1969; Sing a Rude Song, 1970; directed Come Spy with Me, Whitehall, 1967. Guild of TV Producers and Directors' Awards; Ivor Novello Award, 1966. *Publications:* (with Caryl Brahms) Cindy-Ella or I Gotta Shoe, 1962; Rappell 1910, 1964; Benbow was his Name, 1967; many songs. *Address:* 3 Bywater Street, SW3. *T:* 01-589 3319.

**SHERRY, Mrs Vincent;** *see* Robinson, Kathleen M.

**SHERSTON, Brigadier John Reginald Vivian,** DSO 1917; OBE 1941; MC 1915; *b* 2 Oct. 1888; *s* of Col John Sherston, Rifle Brigade; *m* 1914, Edith Adelaide, *d* of John Lockington Impey, ICS; one *d*. *Educ:* Wellington; RMC. Served European War of 1914-18, 4th Hussars, staff; Afghanistan, 1919; psc Camberley, 1920; retired 1926; re-employed 1939-44, Brigadier 1942. Sheep farmer, New Zealand, 1926-46, now Gloucestershire. Order of Leopold II; Croix de Guerre with Palm (Belgium). *Address:* Kitebrook, Morton in Marsh, Glos.

**SHERSTON-BAKER, Sir Humphrey Dodington Benedict,** 6th Bt, *cr* 1796; *b* 13 Oct. 1907; *s* of Lt-Col Sir Dodington Sherston-Baker, 5th Bt, and Irene Roper (*d* 1950), *yr d* of Sir Roper Parkington; *S* father, 1944; *m* 1938, Margaret Alice (Bobby) (marriage dissolved, 1953), *o d* of H. W. Binns, 9 Campden Street, W, Blythburgh, Suffolk; one *s* three *d*. *Educ:* Downside; Christ's College, Cambridge. *Heir:* *s* Robert George Humphrey Sherston-Baker, *b* 3 April 1951. *Club:* Carlton.

**SHERWIN, Frederick George James,** CB 1967; Chief Inspector, Board of HM Customs and Excise, 1963-69, retired; *b* 3 Sept. 1909; *s* of J. F. Sherwin and H. E. Sherwin, Woolston, Hants; *m* 1966, Margaret Dorothea Snow, *d* of Thomas L. H. Snow, Gidea Park, Essex; one *s*. *Educ:* Gosport Secondary Sch.; HM Dockyard Sch., Portsmouth. Civil Servant; entered Customs and Excise, 17 Feb. 1930. *Recreations:* gardening, walking. *Address:* Crimond, Strathwhillan, Brodick, Isle of Arran. *T:* Brodick 198. *Club:* Civil Service.

**SHERWIN-WHITE, Adrian Nicholas,** MA; FBA 1956; Reader in Ancient History, University of Oxford, since 1966; Fellow and Tutor of St John's College, Oxford, since 1936; Keeper of the Groves, 1970; *b* 1911; *s* of H. N. Sherwin-White, Solicitors' Dept of LCC. *Educ:* Merchant Taylors' School; St John's College, Oxford (Derby Scholar, 1935; Arnold Historical Essay Prize, 1935; MA, 1937). War Service in RN and Admiralty, 1942-45. Conington Prize, 1947. Sarum Lecturer, Oxford Univ., 1960-61; Gray Lecturer, Cambridge Univ., 1965-66. *Publications:* Roman Citizenship, 1939; Ancient Rome (Then and There Series), 1959; Roman Law and Roman Society in the New Testament, 1963; Historical Commentary on the Letters of Pliny the Younger, 1966; Racial Prejudice in Imperial Rome, 1967; ed Geographical Handbook Series, Admiralty; contrib. Jl Roman Studies. *Recreations:* watching horses and growing Alpine plants. *Address:* St John's College, Oxford. *T:* Frilford Heath 496.

**SHERWOOD, Bishop Suffragan of,** since 1965; **Rt. Rev. Kenneth George Thompson;** *b* 7 Aug. 1909; *s* of George William Thompson, Doncaster, and Edith Thompson (*née* Pearson), Manningham Bradford; *m* 1935, Doreen May Latchford, Cambridge; one *s* two *d*. *Educ:* The Perse, Cambridge; Christ's Coll., Cambridge; Lincoln Theological College. BA 1932 (2nd cl. English, 3rd cl. Theology), Cambridge. Curate, S Mary's, Stoke Newington, 1933-37; Vicar, S Mark, Ford, Devonport, 1937-46. Chaplain RNVR, 1940-44; 13th Destroyer Flotilla, 1940-41; HMS Rodney, 1942-44 (despatches). Vicar of Hucknall Torkard, Notts, 1946-62; Hon. Canon of Southwell, 1954-62; Chm., Exec. Cttee, Southwell Diocesan Day Schools Board, 1966-. Proctor in Convocation, 1958-65. Hon. Chaplain to the Queen, 1962-65; Archdeacon of Newark, 1962-65. *Publication:* HMS Rodney at War, 1944. *Recreations:* reading, travel. *Address:* The Vicarage, Kneesall, Newark, Notts. *T:* Wellow Park 239. *Club:* RNVR.

**SHERWOOD, Leslie Robert,** CMG 1947; OBE 1924; *b* 1889; *m* 1911, Ella Edith Staples; one *s* one *d*. *Educ:* King's College Sch., London. Foreign Office, 1908; Staff Officer, Chief Clerk's Dept, 1919; also 1st Class Establishment and Accounts Officer, 1919; Senior Establishment and Accounts Officer, 1922; Deputy Finance Officer, 1938 (title changed to Financial Assistant from Dec. 1940); Head of Finance Department, Foreign Office, 1946-49, retired. *Address:* Honey Tye, Dry Sandford, Abingdon, Berks.

**SHEWAN, Henry Alexander,** OBE 1946; QC (Scotland) 1949; Commissioner of National Insurance, since 1966 (Deputy Commissioner, 1955-66); *b* 7 November 1906; *s* of late James Smith Shewan, Advocate in Aberdeen; *m* 1937, Ann Fraser Thomson, Aberdeen; two *s. Educ:* Robert Gordon's Coll., Aberdeen; Aberdeen Univ.; Emmanuel College, Cambridge. Advocate, 1933. Served War of 1939-45, RAF, 1940-45; RAF selected member, City of Edinburgh TA and AFA, 1947-50. Standing Junior Counsel in Scotland: to Board of Trade, Customs and Excise, and Ministry of Labour, 1945-47; to Board of Inland Revenue, 1947-49. External Examiner in Law: University of Aberdeen, 1946-49; University of Edinburgh, 1948-51. Member Scottish Medical Practices Cttee, 1948-55; Member Court of Session Rules Council, 1948-55; Dep. Chm. Panel of Arbiters and Referee under Coal Industry Nationalisation Act, 1949-55; Chm., Medical Appeal Tribunal National Insurance (Industrial Injuries) Act, 1950-55; Chairman General Nursing Council for Scot., 1960-62. *Address:* St Aubyns, Kinnear Road, Edinburgh 3. *T:* 031-552 4001. *Clubs:* Honourable Company of Edinburgh Golfers (Muirfield); Royal Scottish Automobile (Glasgow).

**SHEWELL-COOPER, Wilfred Edward,** MBE 1946; NDH; Dip. Hort. (Wye); Director, International Horticultural Advisory Bureau, since 1960; Hon. Director, Good Gardens Institute, since 1961; Chairman of Council, The Good Gardeners' Association since 1964; *b* 15 September; *s* of Col E. Shewell-Cooper, RA, and Mabel Alice Read; *m* 1925, Irene Ramsay; two *s. Educ:* Diocesan College, Rondebosch, S Africa; Monkton Combe; Wye College, Univ. London. East Malling Research Station, 1922; Horticultural Adviser, Warwick CC, 1923; Head of Hort. Dept, Cheshire School Agric., 1925; Hort. Supt, Swanley Hort. Coll., 1932, and Garden Editor, BBC (North Region); Director, Hort. Advisory Bureau, 1938; Command Hort. Officer, Eastern and S Eastern Commands, 1940-49; Lt-Col 1945; Adviser, BAOR, 1946-47; Principal, Thaxted Hort. Coll., 1950-60. Liveryman, Worshipful Company of Gardeners. Mem., Roy. Soc. of Teachers, 1923; FLS 1930; Fell. and Hon. Dr, Hort. Coll., Vienna, 1952; Chevalier du Mérite Agricole, France, 1952, Commandeur, 1964; Fell. Roy. Danish Hort. Soc., 1964. FRSL 1954; Hon. DLitt 1961. President: Internat. Mission to Miners; Protestant Reformation Soc.; Mem. of the House of Laity, 1960-; International Clans' Chief, The Campaigners, 1966-; Chm., British Assoc. of Consultants in Agric. and Hortic. 1966. Knight of the Order of Merit (Italy), 1966. *Publications:* over 66 books on horticulture beginning with The Garden, 1932, and including The Royal Gardeners, 22 Titles in the ABC series, The Complete Gardener, Mini-Work Gardening, The Complete Vegetable Gardener, Weekend Gardening, The Complete Greenhouse Gardener, Cut Flowers for the Home, and other standard works. *Recreations:* gardening, Campaigners, swimming. *Address:* Arkley Manor, Arkley, Herts. *T:* 01-449 3031/2177. *Club:* Army and Navy.

**SHIELDS, John Sinclair;** *b* 4 Feb. 1903; *s* of Rev. W. H. Shields and Margaret Louisa (*née* Sinclair); *m* 1st, 1924, Norah Fane Smith; three *d*; 2nd, 1963, Mrs Noreen Moultrie, *widow* of Comdr John Moultrie. *Educ:* Charterhouse; Lincoln Coll., Oxford (MA). Headmaster: Wem Grammar School, 1934-47; Queen Mary's School, Basingstoke, 1947-56; Headmaster, Peter Symonds' School, Winchester, 1957-63; Vice-Pres. Classical Assoc., 1958; Member: Broadcasting Cttee, 1960; Oxford Soc. (Sec. Hampshire Branch). *Recreation:* golf. *Address:* North End House, Hursley, Winchester, Hants. *Club:* Hampshire (Winchester).

**SHIELDS, (Leslie) Stuart,** QC 1970; *b* 15 May 1919; *m* 1941, Maureen Margaret McKirstry; three *s* two *d. Educ:* St Paul's School; Corpus Christi College, Oxford. Paid Local Serjeant, Oxford and Buckinghamshire Light Infantry, 1945-47. Called to the Bar, Middle Temple, 1948. *Recreation:* music. *Address:* 10 King's Bench Walk, Temple, EC4. *T:* 01-353 7534.

**SHIELDS, Sir Neil (Stanley),** Kt 1964; MC 1946; Management Consultant and company director; Managing Director, Chesham Amalgamations and Investments Ltd; Director: Anglo-Continental Investment and Finance Company Ltd; Central and Sheerwood Trust Ltd; Continental Bankers' Agents Ltd; *b* 7 September 1919; *o s* of late Archie Shields and of Mrs Hannah Shields; *m* 1970, Gloria Dawn Wilson. Member of Honourable Artillery Company 1939-. Served in Royal Artillery, 1939-46; commnd 1940; Major 1943. Prospective candidate (C) North St Pancras 1947 and contested by-election, 1949. Chairman: Camden Conservative Cttee, 1965-67; Hampstead Conservative Assoc., 1954-65 (Vice-Chm., 1951-54); Hon. Treas. 1965-67; National Union of Conservative and Unionist Assocs: Chm. of London Area, 1961-63 (Vice-Chm., 1959-61); Mem. of National Executive, 1955-59, 1961-67, 1968-69; Hampstead Borough Council: Mem. 1947-65; Deputy Leader, 1952-61; Chm. of Works Cttee, 1951-55; Chm. of Finance Cttee, 1955-59. *Recreations:* reading, walking, motoring, wining and dining. *Address:* 12 London House, Avenue Road, NW8. *T:* 01-586 4155. *Clubs:* Carlton, HAC.

**SHIELDS, Maj.-Gen. Ronald Frederick,** OBE 1943; BSc (Eng); CEng; FIEE; *b* 4 November 1912; *s* of late John Benjamin Frederic Shields, Chichester; *m* 1944, Lorna, *d* of late Frederick Murgatroyd, Manchester; one *s* one *d. Educ:* Portsmouth Grammar School. Lieut RAOC 1936. Served War of 1939-45 in Middle East and NW Europe; transferred to REME, 1942; Staff College Camberley, 1945; MELF, 1948-51; AQMG, HQ Northern Comd, 1952-55; War Office, 1956-59; REME Training Centre, 1959-62; DEME, HQ, BAOR, 1962-65; Comdt, Technical Group, REME, 1965-68; retd 1968. Col, 1955; Brig. 1962; Maj.-Gen. 1965. Col Comdt, REME, 1968-. *Address:* 16 Lavant Road, Chichester, Sussex.

**SHIELDS, Stuart;** *see* Shields, L. S.

**SHIELL, James Wyllie,** BSc, FICE, FIWE, MIMunE; Chief Engineer, Scottish Development Department, since 1968; *b* 20 Aug. 1912; *yr s* of late George Douglas Shiell, farmer, Rennieston, Jedburgh and Janet Gladstone Wyllie; *m* 1941, Maureen Cameron Macpherson Hunter, *d* of late Thomas Hunter, Leeds; two *s. Educ:* Jedburgh Grammar and Kelso High Schools; Edinburgh Univ. Municipal Engrg posts in Edinburgh, Southampton, Sunderland and Leeds, 1934-39; Sen. Engr on Staff of J. D. & D. M. Watson, Consulting Engrs, Westminster, 1939-43 and 1945-47; Civil Engr on wartime service with Admty, 1943-45; Sen. Engr, Min. of Agriculture, 1947-49; Engrg Inspector, Dept of Health for Scotland, 1949-62; Dep. Chief Engr, Scottish Development Dept, 1962-68.

Hon. FInstWPC. *Recreations:* golf, photography. *Address:* 25 Mortonhall Road, Edinburgh EH9 2HS. *T:* 031-667 8528. *Clubs:* St Stephen's; Caledonian (Edinburgh).

**SHIFFNER, Sir Henry David,** 8th Bt, *cr* 1818; Company Director; *b* 2 Feb. 1930; *s* of Major Sir Henry Shiffner, 7th Bt, and Margaret Mary, *er d* of late Sir Ernest Gowers, GCB, GBE; *S* father, 1941; *m* 1st, 1949, Dorothy Jackson (marriage dissolved, 1956); one *d* (and one *d* decd); 2nd, 1957, Beryl, *d* of George Milburn, Saltdean, Sussex; one *d*. *Educ:* Rugby; Trinity Hall, Cambridge. *Heir: cousin* George Frederick Shiffner [*b* 3 August 1936; *m* 1961, Dorothea Helena Cynthia, *d* of late T. H. McLean; one *s* one *d*]. *Address:* Old School House, Offham, Lewes, Sussex. *Club:* Royal Automobile.

**SHILLINGTON, Courtenay Alexander Rives,** CB 1953; VRD 1941; DL; Commodore, RNVR, retired 1954; *b* 18 Mar. 1902; *s* of Thomas Courtenay Shillington, Glenmachan Tower, Belfast, and Bertha Wydown Hall, Charlottesville, Virginia, USA; one *d*. *Educ:* Bilston Grange; Rugby. Entered RNVR, Sub-Lt, 1924; ADC to: Duke of Abercorn, Northern Ireland, 1927-45; Earl Granville, Governor of Northern Ireland, 1945-52; Lord Wakehurst, Governor of Northern Ireland, 1952-64; Lord Erskine of Rerrick, Governor of NI, 1964-67; Lord Grey of Naunton, Governor of NI, 1967-. Served War of 1939-45, in RN as Capt. RNVR, 1939-46; Comdr, Auxiliary Patrol, Scapa, 1939; Dep. Chief of Staff and Naval Liaison Officer to Field Marshal Lord Gort, Governor of Malta, 1942; Chief of Staff to Sen. Naval Officer, Persian Gulf, 1942; Naval Officer in Charge, Bahrain, 1943-45. DL County Down, 1956. *Recreation:* motor racing. *Address:* Balloo House, Bangor, County Down, Northern Ireland. *Clubs:* Royal Aero, Royal Automobile; Ulster, Ulster Automobile (Belfast); Royal Ulster Yacht (Bangor).

**SHILLINGTON, (Robert Edward) Graham,** CBE 1970 (OBE 1959; MBE 1951); Chief Constable, Royal Ulster Constabulary, since Nov. 1970; *b* 2 April 1911; *s* of Major D. Graham Shillington, DL, MP, and Mrs Louisa Shillington (*née* Collen); *m* 1935, Mary E. R. Bulloch, Holywood, Co. Down; two *s* one *d*. *Educ:* Sedbergh Sch., Yorks; Clare Coll., Cambridge. Royal Ulster Constabulary: Officer Cadet, 1933; 3rd Class District Inspector, 1934; 2nd Class District Inspector, 1936; 1st Class District Inspector, 1944; County Inspector, 1953; Commissioner, Belfast, 1961; Deputy Inspector General (Deputy Chief Constable), 1969-70. King's Coronation Medal, 1937; Queen's Coronation Medal, 1953; Police Long Service and Good Conduct Medal, 1955. *Recreations:* golf, gardening. *Address:* Orchard Hill, Craigavad, Co. Down. *T:* Holywood 3471. *Clubs:* Ulster (Belfast); Royal Belfast Golf.

**SHILLITO, Edward Alan,** CB 1964; Director of Greenwich Hospital, since 1969; *b* 13 May 1910; *s* of late Rev. Edward and Mrs Annie Shillito, Buckhurst Hill, Essex; *m* 1934, Dorothy Jean, *d* of late Robert J. Davies, Buckhurst Hill, Essex; two *s* three *d*. *Educ:* Chigwell School; Oriel College, Oxford (Exhibitioner). Litt Hum 2nd Class, 1933. Customs and Excise, 1934-36; HM Treas., 1936-57; Under-Secretary, 1951; Admiralty, and MoD, 1957-69; Imperial Defence College course, 1953. *Recreations:* music, lacrosse (Oxford Univ., 1931-33, now spectator only). *Address:* 8 Baldwins Hill, Loughton, Essex. *T:* 01-508 1988.

**SHIMA, Shigenobu;** Grand Master of the Ceremonies, Imperial Japanese Court, since 1968; *b* 1907; *m* 1935, Sanaye Shimasuye; two *d*. *Educ:* Tokyo Imperial University. Joined Diplomatic Service, 1930. Attaché, London, 1931-35; Private Secretary to Foreign Minister, 1936-37; 3rd Secretary and Consul in Pekin, Tientsin and Tsingtao, 1937-41; Foreign Ministry, 1942-47; Director, Osaka Liaison Office, 1948-51; Counsellor (European Affairs), 1951-53; Minister, Washington, 1954-57; Ambassador, Stockholm, 1957-60; Deputy Vice-Minister for Foreign Affairs, 1960-62; Vice-Minister for Foreign Affairs, 1963-64; Ambassador, London, 1964-68. Grand Cross: Northern Star (Sweden); St Olav (Norway); Homayun (Iran); Verdienstkreuz (Germany); Couronne (Belgium); Mayo (Argentina); Star (Afghanistan). Grand Officer: Cruzeiro do Sul (Brazil); José Matias Delgado (El Salvador). *Recreation:* music. *Address:* Shirogane 4-10-11, Minato-ku, Tokyo, Japan. *Club:* St James'.

**SHINDLER, George John,** QC 1970; *b* 27 Oct. 1922; *yr s* of late Dr Bruno and Mrs Alma Schindler; *m* 1955, Eva Muller; three *s*. *Educ:* University Coll. Sch., Hampstead, and privately. Served in Royal Tank Regt, France, Belgium, Holland and Germany, 1942-47. Called to Bar, Inner Temple, 1952. Standing Counsel to Inland Revenue at Central Criminal Court and all London sessions, 1965-70. *Recreations:* theatre, music, reading, watching soccer and cricket, stamps, walking, swimming, travel. *Address:* 3 Temple Gardens, Temple, EC4. *T:* 01-353 7855; 9 River Grove Park, Beckenham, Kent. *T:* 01-650 0542.

**SHINNIE, Prof. Peter Lewis;** Professor of Archæology, in the University of Khartoum, since 1966; *b* 1915, *s* of late Andrew James Shinnie, OBE; *m* 1940, Margaret Blanche Elizabeth Cloake; two *s* one *d*. *Educ:* Westminster Sch.; Christ Church, Oxford. Served War with RAF, 1939-45. Temp. Asst Keeper, Ashmolean Museum, 1945; Asst Commissioner for Archæology, Sudan Government, 1946; Commissioner for Archæology, Sudan Govt, 1948; Director of Antiquities, Uganda, 1966; Prof. of Archæology, Univ. of Ghana, 1958-66. FSA; AMA. *Publications:* Excavation at Soba, 1955; Medieval Nubia, 1954; Ghazali: A Monastery in Northern Sudan, 1960; Meroe–Civilization of the Sudan, 1967; articles in Journal of Egyptian Archæology, Sudan Notes and Records, Kush. *Recreations:* reading, photography, travelling in Greece. *Address:* University of Khartoum, Sudan. *Club:* Athenæum.

**SHINWELL,** family name of **Baron Shinwell.**

**SHINWELL,** Baron *cr* 1970 (Life Peer), of Easington, Durham; **Emanuel Shinwell;** PC 1945; CH 1965; *b* London, 18 October 1884. MP (Lab) Linlithgow, 1922-24 and 1928-31, Seaham Div. of Durham, 1935-50, Easington Div. of Durham, 1950-70; Financial Secretary, War Office, 1929-30; Parliamentary Secretary to Department of Mines, 1924 and 1930-31; Minister of Fuel and Power, 1945-47; Secretary of State for War, 1947-50; Minister of Defence, 1950-51. Was Chairman and Member, National Executive Labour Party; Chairman, Parly Labour Party, 1964-67. *Publications:* The Britain I Want, 1943; When the Men Come Home, 1944; Conflict without Malice, 1955; The Labour Story, 1963. *Address:* House of Lords, SW1.

**SHIPTON, Eric Earle,** CBE 1955; *b* 1 Aug. 1907; *s* of Cecil Shipton and Alice Lilian Earle; *m* 1942, Diana Kendall (marr. diss., 1955), *yr d* of

F. F. R. Channer, late Indian Forest Service; two *s.* Consul-Gen. at Kashgar, 1940-42 and 1946-48; at Kunming, 1949-51; Five expeditions to the mountains of East and Central Africa, 1929-32; climbed Kamet (25,447 ft), 1931; Member of Mount Everest Expedition, 1933; led exploratory expedition to Central Himalayas, 1934; led Mount Everest Reconnaissance Expedition, 1935; member Mount Everest Expedition, 1936; led Shaksgam Expedition, 1937; member Mount Everest Expedition, 1938; led Karakoram Expedn, 1939; led Mt Everest Reconnaissance Expedition, 1951, and British Himalaya Expedition, 1952; Expedition to Karakoram, 1957, six expeditions to Patagonia (1958-64). President, Alpine Club, 1964-67. Patron's Medal, RGS 1938. *Publications:* Nanda Devi, 1936; Blank on the Map, 1938; Upon that Mountain, 1948; Mountains of Tartary, 1951; Mount Everest Reconnaissance Expedition, 1951, 1952; Land of Tempest, 1963; (autobiography) That Untravelled World, 1969. *Address:* c/o Royal Geographical Society, SW7.

**SHIPWRIGHT, Sqdn Ldr Denis E. B. K.,** FRSA; psa; RAFRO (retired); Established Civil Servant (Telecomm. PO); Production and Administration, Gaumont British Picture Corporation, and Gainsborough Pictures; Director Cinephonic Music Co. Ltd; KStJ; *b* London, 20 May 1898; *y s* of late T. J. Shipwright and Adelina de Lara, OBE; *m* 1918, Kate (marriage dissolved, 1926; she *d* 1954), *o d* of late Sir Edward Hain, St Ives, Cornwall; one *s* two *d*; *m* 1947, Margaret, *o d* of late Robert Edgar Haynes, Woking, Surrey. *Educ:* France; University College, Oxford. Joined the Army as a private at the age of 16, 1914; despatch rider, 1915; wounded and crashed whilst flying in France in RFC; Flight Comdr, 1918; Capt. Royal 1st Devon Yeomanry, and North Devon Hussars; Capt. R of O RE, TA, to Apr. 1939; then Pilot Officer RAFVR; Flt Lt Nov. 1939; Sqdn Ldr 1940; passed out of RAF Staff College, 1940; served in France, 1940 (despatches, 1939-43 Star); Special Mission to Gibraltar, 1942. Air ED 1944. Middle Temple, 1920; MP (C) Penryn and Falmouth, 1922-23; Representative on the Film Producers Group, Federation of British Industries; Adviser to the British Films Advancement Council; Member of the Kinematograph Advisory Committee; Life Member of the Commonwealth Parliamentary Association. Member: Surrey Special Constabulary, 1950; Company of Veteran Motorists, 1953; Order of Knights of Road, 1953; Civil Service Motoring Assoc.; British Unidentified Flying Object Research Assoc.; Chm. NE Surrey Gp, Contact UFO Research Investigation Assoc. Voluntary Driver, Surrey County Council Hospitals Car and Ambulance Service. British Motor Racing Driver: Brooklands (winner 24th 100 mph Long Handicap); Speed Trials; Hill Climbs. Major, 11th (HG) Battalion, Queen's Royal Regt, 1953. Officer, Ministry of Agriculture and Food, Guildford, 1954. *Address:* Plym Lea, Triggs Lane, Woking, Surrey. *T:* Woking 61736. *Clubs:* British Racing Drivers, Royal Automobile; Oxford University Yacht (Oxford).

**SHIRER, William Lawrence;** broadcaster, journalist; author; *b* Chicago, 23 Feb. 1904; *s* of Seward Smith Shirer; *m* 1931, Theresa Stiberitz; two *d. Educ:* Coe College. Foreign Correspondent. DLitt (Hon.). Légion d'Honneur. *Publications:* Berlin Diary, 1941; End of a Berlin Diary, 1947; The Traitor, 1950; Mid-Century Journey, 1953; Stranger Come Home, 1954; The Challenge of Scandinavia, 1955; The Consul's Wife, 1956; The Rise and Fall of The Third Reich, 1960; The Rise and Fall of Adolf Hitler, 1961; The Sinking of the Bismarck, 1962; The Collapse of the Third Republic, 1970. *Recreations:* walking, sailing. *Address:* 7 West 43 Street, New York, USA. *Club:* Century (New York).

**SHIRES, Sir Frank,** Kt, *cr* 1953; *b* 10 Aug. 1899; *s* of John Shires; *m* 1929, Mabel Tidds; one *s* one *d. Educ:* West Leeds High School. Joined H. J. Heinz Co. Ltd, 1925; Director of Manufacturing and Research, 1940; Director of Sales, 1950; Deputy Managing Director, 1950-55; Director: Marsh & Baxter Co. Ltd, 1958-64; C. & T. Harris (Calne) Ltd, 1958-64. Member of Exec. Cttee of Canners' (War Time) Assoc., 1942-49; Pres. Food Manufacturers' Federation, Inc., 1950-52; Member Council of British Food Manufacturing Industries Research Assoc., 1947-55; Chm. Governing Body of Nat. Coll. of Food Technology, 1950-66; Member of Food Hygiene Advisory Council, 1955; Member of Monopolies Commission, 1957-61; Member of Council, Univ. of Reading, 1965-. Fellow, Inst. of Science Technology, 1965. *Recreations:* cricket, and golf; Rugby (Derbys, 1926-28, and Notts, Lincs and Derbys, 1926-28). *Address:* Redholt, Linksway, Northwood, Middlesex. *T:* Northwood 22493.

**SHIRLAW, John Fenton;** *b* 31 Aug. 1896; *s* of late Dr M. Shirlaw; *m* 1937, Leslie Hamilton, *d* of late Henry E. Wilkes, Linden House, Stowmarket, Suffolk; *m* 1967, Muriel Tait, *d* of late William D. Robinson, Corbridge, Northumberland. *Educ:* George Heriot's Sch. and University, Edinburgh. Professor of Pathology, Punjab Veterinary College, Lahore, 1927; Pathologist, Imperial Institute of Veterinary Research, Muktesar-Kumaon, UP, India, 1936; retired (from this), 1949; bacteriologist, veterinary research laboratory, Kabete, Kenya, E Africa, retired, 1963. *Address:* 31 Kingscroft Avenue, Dunstable, Beds.

**SHIRLEY,** family name of **Earl Ferrers.**

**SHIRLEY, Evelyn Philip Sewallis,** CMG 1952; OBE 1927; *b* 2 March 1900; *s* of late Ven. Archdeacon Shirley; *m* 1930, Marian Hamilton Bowen Powell; one *s. Educ:* Saint Columba's College, Dublin; Royal Military College, Sandhurst. Commissioned Royal Irish Fusiliers, 1918; served NW Persia and Iraq, 1920. Entered Somaliland Administrative Service, 1929; Chief Secretary and Commissioner for native affairs, Somaliland Protectorate, 1951-Nov. 1954; retd 1955. Military Service, 1940-45. *Address:* The Vicarage, Hempstead, Holt, Norfolk. *T:* Holt 3281.

**SHIRLEY, Philip Hammond;** Deputy Chairman, Cunard Steamship Company, since 1968; *b* 4 Oct. 1912; *s* of Frank Shillito Shirley and Annie Lucy (*née* Hammond); *m* 1936, Marie Edna Walsh; one *s* one *d. Educ:* Sydney Church of England Grammar School (Shore). Qualified in Australia as Chartered Accountant, 1934; with Peat Marwick Mitchell & Co., Chartered Accountants, London, 1937-49; Personal Asst to Managing Director, J. Arthur Rank Organisation Ltd, 1949-51; with Unilever from 1951; Dep. Chief Accountant, 1951-52; Chief Accountant, 1952-58; Chm. Batchelors Foods Ltd 1958-61; Mem. BTC (Oct. 1961-Nov. 1962); Mem. BR Bd, 1962-67 (Vice-Chm. Bd, 1964-67). *Recreation:* golf. *Address:* 30 Rutland Gate, SW7. *T:* 01-584 0478. *Club:* Royal Automobile.

**SHIRLEY, Air Vice-Marshal Sir Thomas (Ulric Curzon),** KBE, 1966 (CBE 1946); CB 1961; CEng; FIEE; FRAeS; DL; RAF (Retired); *b* 4

June 1908; *s* of late Capt. T. Shirley, late 60 Rifles, Bournemouth; *m* 1935, Vera, *y d* of late George S. Overton, The Grange, Navenby, Lincolnshire; one *s* one *d*. *Educ:* Reading School. Royal Air Force Aircraft Apprentice, 1925-28; cadet RAF College, Cranwell, 1928-30; served in Army Co-operation Squadrons as pilot, 1930-36; in Far East and Middle East on Signals duties, 1936-41; Officer Commanding Signals Wings, 1941-45; RAF Staff College, 1945-46; Deputy Director of Signals, Air Ministry, 1946-47; Command Signals Officer, Transport Command, 1947-48; Joint Services Staff College, 1948-49; Deputy Director Technical Plans, Air Ministry, 1949-50; Director of Radio Engineering, 1950-53; Command Signals Officer, Fighter Command, 1953-55; Imperial Defence College, 1956; Air Officer Commanding and Commandant, Royal Air Force Technical College, Henlow, Beds 1957-59; Senior Technical Staff Officer, RAF Fighter Command, 1959-60; Deputy Controller of Electronics, Ministry of Aviation, 1960-64; Air Officer C-in-C Signals Command, 1964-66. ADC to King George VI, 1950-52, to the Queen, 1952-53. DL Leicester, 1967. *Address:* 210 Seagrave Road, Sileby, Loughborough, Leics. *T:* Sileby 2309. *Club:* Royal Air Force.

**SHIRLEY-QUIRK, John Stanton;** bass-baritone singer; *b* 28 Aug. 1931; *s* of Joseph Stanley and Amelia Shirley-Quirk; *m* 1955, Patricia Hastie; one *s* one *d*. *Educ:* Holt School, Liverpool; Liverpool University. Violin Scholarship, 1945; read Chemistry, Liverpool Univ., 1948-53; BSc (Hons), 1952; Dipl. in Educn 1953; became professional singer, 1961. Officer in Education Br., RAF, 1953-57. Asst Lectr in Chemistry, Acton Technical Coll., 1957-61; Lay-clerk in St Paul's Cathedral, 1961-62. First Appearance Glyndebourne Opera in Elegy for Young Lovers, 1961; subseq. 1962, 1963. Sang in first performance of Curlew River, 1964, The Burning Fiery Furnace, 1966, The Prodigal Son, 1968, Owen Wingrove, 1970. Has sung in Europe, Israel, Australia, etc. First American tour, 1966; Australian tour, 1967. Has made numerous recordings: operas, songs, cantatas, etc. Liverpool Univ. Chem. Soc. Medal, 1965; Sir Charles Santley Meml Gift, Worshipful Co. of Musicians, 1969. *Recreations:* gardening, sailing, clocks. *Address:* The White House, Flackwell Heath, Bucks. *T:* Bourne End 21325.

**SHIRLEY-SMITH, Sir Hubert,** Kt 1969; CBE 1965; Consulting Engineer with private practice, since 1967; Consultant to W. V. Zinn & Associates, since 1969; *b* 13 Oct. 1901; *s* of E. Shirley-Smith; *m* 1927, Joan Elizabeth Powell (*d* 1963); two *d* (and one *d* decd). *Educ:* City and Guilds Coll., London. BSc (Engrg) London, 1922; MICE 1936; FCGI 1965; FIC 1966. Assisted in design of Sydney Harbour Bridge, NSW, and Birchenough and Otto Beit Bridges, Rhodesia, 1923-36; worked on construction of Howrah Bridge, Calcutta, 1936-42. Dir, Cleveland Bridge & Engrg Co., 1951-60; Mem. Bd, of Cleveland Bridge, Dorman Long (Auckland) and ACD Bridge Co.; Agent i/c construction of Forth Road Bridge, 1960-65. Mem. Council, ICE, 1952- (Pres., 1967); Mem. Council, Fedn of Civil Engrg Contractors, 1958-65; Vice-Pres., Internat. Assoc. for Bridge and Structural Engrg, 1963-69. Member, Smeatonian Soc. of Civil Engrs. *Publications:* The World's Great Bridges, 1953 (revised, 1964); article on Bridges in Encyclopædia Britannica; papers in Proc. ICE, etc. *Recreations:* travel, writing. *Address:* 70 Broxbourne Road, Orpington, Kent. *T:* Orpington 32673. *Club:* Athenæum.

**SHOAIB, Mohammad,** HPk, MA, LLB; Vice President, International Bank for Reconstruction and Development, since 1966; *b* 5 Sept. 1905; *m* 1959, Hamida Fatima Shoaib; four *s* two *d* (and one step *s* two step *d*). *Educ:* Allahabad Univ. BA 1924 (Gold Medal for distinction in economics); MA, LLB, 1926. Joined Provincial Administrative Services, 1926; Indian Military Accounts Department, 1929; Chief Controller, Army Factory Accounts, 1942; Financial Adviser for Military Finance, Pakistan, 1947; Special Delegate to Sterling Accounts Settlement Conferences; Executive Director, IBRD, 1952-58 and Feb. 1962; Minister for Finance, 1958-66. minister of Economic Co-ordination, Feb.-Dec. 1962. Fellow: Institute of Cost and Works Accountants (London); Institute of Cost and Works Accountants (Pakistan); Institute of Industrial Accountants (Pakistan); Institute of Cost and Works Accountants (India); Mem., National Association of Accountants, New York. Hilal-e-Pakistan, 1962. *Address:* 2920 Northampton Street NW, Washington, DC 20015; (office) 1818 H Street NW, Washington, DC 20433, USA. *Clubs:* Metropolitan (Washington); Sind, Karachi, Karachi Gymkhana, Jockey Club of Pakistan, Karachi Race (Karachi).

**SHOCKLEY, Dr William (Bradford);** Medal of Merit (US) 1946; Alexander M. Poniatoff Professor of Engineering Science, Stanford University, since 1963; Executive Consultant, Bell Telephone Laboratories, since 1965; *b* 13 Feb. 1910; *s* of William Hillman Shockley and May (*née* Bradford); *m* 1933, Jean Alberta Bailey; two *s* one *d*; *m* 1955, Emmy I. Lanning. *Educ:* Calif. Inst. of Technology (BS); Mass Inst. Tech. (PhD). Teaching Fellow, Mass. Inst. Tech., 1932-36; Mem. Technical Staff, Bell Teleph. Laboratories, 1936-42 and 1945-54; Director Transistor Physics Department, 1954-55. Dir of Research, Anti-submarine Warfare Ops Research Gp, US Navy, 1942-44; Expert Consultant, Office of Secretary of War, 1944-45. Visiting Lectr, Princeton Univ., 1946; Scientific Advisor, Policy Council, Jt Research and Development Bd, 1947-49; Visiting Prof., Calif. Inst. Tech., 1954; Dep. Dir and Dir of Research, Weapons Systems Evaluation Gp, Dept of Defense, 1954-55; Dir, Shockley Semi-conductor Lab. of Beckman Instruments, Inc., 1955-58; Pres. Shockley Transistor Corp., 1958-60; Director, Shockley Transistor, Unit of Clevite Transistor, 1960-63; Consultant, 1963-65. Member: US Army Science Advisory Panel, 1951-63, 1964-; USAF Science Advisory Board, 1959-63; National Academy of Science, 1951-. Hon. DSc: Pennsylvania, 1955; Rutgers 1956; Gustavus Adolphus Coll., 1963. Morris Liebmann Prize (Inst. of Radio Engineers), 1951; Air Force Citation of Honour, 1951; O. E. Buckley Prize (Amer. Physical Soc.), 1953; Comstock Prize (Nat. Acad. of Science), 1954; Wilhelm Exner Medal (Oesterreichischer Gewerberein), 1963; Holley Medal (Amer. Soc. Mech. Engrs), 1963. (Jt) Nobel Prize in Physics, 1956; Caltech Alumni Distinguished Service Award, 1966; NASA Certificate of Appreciation (Apollo 8), 1969; Public Service Group Achievement Award, NASA, 1969. *Publications:* Electrons and Holes in Semiconductors, 1950; Mechanics (with W. A. Gong), 1966. Approx 100 articles. *Recreations:* mountain climbing, swimming, sailing. *Address:* Stanford University, Stanford, Calif 94305, USA. *T:* 321-2300. *Clubs:* Cosmos, University (Washington, DC); Bohemian (San Francisco); Stanford Faculty; Palo Alto Yacht.

**SHOENBERG, Dr David,** MBE 1944; FRS 1953; Reader in Physics, Cambridge University, 1952; Fellow of Gonville and Caius College,

1947; *b* 4 Jan. 1911; *s* of Isaac and Esther Shoenberg; *m* 1940, Catherine Felicitée Fischmann; one *s* two *d*. *Educ:* Latymer Upper School, W6; Trinity College, Cambridge (Scholar). PhD 1935; Exhibition of 1851 Senior Student, 1936-39; Research at Royal Soc. Mond Laboratory, 1932-, in charge of Laboratory, 1947-. Univ. Lectr in Physics, 1944-52; UNESCO Adviser on Low Temperature Physics, NPL of India, 1953-54. Mellon Vis. Prof., Univ. of Pittsburgh, 1962; Gauss Prof., Univ. of Göttingen, 1964; Vis. Prof. Univ. of Maryland, 1968. Fritz London Award for Low Temperature Physics, 1964. *Publications:* Superconductivity, 1938, revised edn, 1952; Magnetism, 1949; scientific papers on low temperature physics and magnetism. *Address:* Royal Society Mond Laboratory, Free School Lane, Cambridge. *T:* Cambridge 54481.

**SHOLL, Hon. Sir Reginald (Richard),** Kt 1962; MA, BCL, Oxon; MA Melbourne; Legal consultant and company director, Melbourne; *b* 8 Oct. 1902; *e s* of late Reginald Frank and Maud Sholl (*née* Mumby), Melbourne; *m* 1st, 1927, Hazel Ethel (*d* 1962), *yr d* of late Alfred L. and Fanny Bradshaw, Melbourne; two *s* two *d*; 2nd, 1964, Anna Campbell, *widow* of Alister Bruce McLean, Melbourne, and *e d* of Edith and late Campbell Colin Carpenter, Indiana, USA. *Educ:* Melbourne Church of England Grammar Sch.; Trinity Coll., Univ. of Melbourne; New Coll., Oxford. 1st Cl. Final Hons and exhibn, Sch. of Classical Philology, and Wyselaskie Schol. in Classical and Comparative Philology and Logic, Melbourne Univ., 1922; Rhodes Schol., Victoria, 1924; 1st Cl. Final Hons, School of Jurisprudence, Oxford, 1926, Bar Finals, London, 1926 and BCL, Oxford, 1927; Official Law Fellow, Brasenose Coll., Oxford, 1927. Called to Bar, Middle Temple, 1927; journalist, London, 1927; Tutor in Classics, Melbourne Univ., 1928-29; Lectr, Law affecting journalism, 1928-38; Barrister, Melbourne, 1929-49; admitted to Bars of NSW and Tasmania, 1935. Served Aust. Army, 1940-44; Capt. retd. Chm. various Commonwealth Bds of Inquiry into Army contracts, 1941-42; KC Vic. and Tas., 1947, NSW 1948; Justice of the Supreme Court of Victoria, 1950-66; Australian Consul-Gen. in New York, 1966-69. Consultant to Russell, Kennedy & Cook, solicitors, Melbourne; Gen. Consultant in Australia to Sperry Rand Corp. (New York) and Pan American World Airways Incorp.; Chm., JLW Pty Ltd; Director: Nat. Trustees Executors and Agency Co. of Australasia Ltd; Ecclesiastical Property Insurance Co. Pty Ltd; Mem. Victorian State Bd, City Mutual Life Assurance Soc. Ltd. Trustee, Nat. Gall. of Vic., 1950-63, Dep. Chm. 1958; Pres. ESU (Vic. Br.) 1961-66; Fed. Chm., ESU in Aust., 1961-63, 1969-; Member: Victorian Council, Australian–Amer. Assoc.; Aust. Bd of Trustees, Northcote Children's Emigration Fund for Aust., 1950-; Bd US Educnl Foundn in Aust., 1961-64; Archbishop-in-Council, Dio. Melbourne, 1958-66, 1969-; Advocate of Diocese of Melbourne, 1969-; Mem. Councils: Trinity Coll., Melbourne, 1939-66; C of E Grammar Schs, Melbourne, 1960-66; Peninsula Sch., Mt Eliza, 1960-63; Toorak Coll., 1969-; C of E Girls' Grammar Sch., Melbourne, 1969-. Pres. Somers CC, Boy Scouts Assoc. (Vic. Br.), 1955-64; Member: State Exec. Boy Scouts Assoc., 1958-66, (Vice-Pres., 1964-66); Nat. Council Australian Boy Scouts Assoc., 1959-69, Vice-Chm., Nat. Bd; Cttee, Overseas Service Bureau (Australia), 1970-; Chairman: Nat. Fellowship Cttee; Victorian Selection Cttee; Winston Churchill Memorial Trust in Australia, 1965-66, 1969-; Victoria Cttee, Duke of Edinburgh's Award in Australia, 1964-66; Chairman, Vict. Supreme Court Rules Cttee, 1960-66. Stowell Orator, 1970-. *Publications:* contrib. to legal periodicals. *Recreations:* golf, lawn tennis, gardening; formerly football (Melbourne Univ. blue) and lacrosse (Oxford half-blue). *Address:* 401 Collins Street, Melbourne, Vic 3000, Australia. *Clubs:* Melbourne, Australian, Beefsteak (Melbourne); Peninsula Country (Victoria).

**SHOLOKHOV, Mikhail Aleksandrovich;** Order of Lenin (thrice); novelist; Deputy to Supreme Soviet of USSR since 1946; Member: Communist Party of Soviet Union, 1932; CPSU Central Committee, 1961; Academy of Sciences, USSR, 1939; Praesidium, Union of Soviet Writers, 1954; Nobel Prize for Literature, 1965; Hon. LLD, St Andrews; *b* 24 May 1905; *m* Maria Petrovna Sholokhova. First published in 1923. *Publications:* The Don Stories, 1926 (including: Woman with Two Husbands; The Heart of Alyoshka; Dry Rot; The Mortal Enemy; The Family Man; The Colt; Harvest on the Don, etc); And Quiet Flows the Don (4 vols, 1928-40, State Prize, 1940); Virgin Soil Upturned (2 vols, 1932-59, Lenin Prize, 1960); They Fought for their Country, 1954; The Destiny of Man, 1957; Collected Works, Vols I-VIII, 1959-62, etc. *Address:* Stanitsa Veshenskaya, Rostov Region, USSR; Union of Soviet Writers, Ul. Vorovskogo 52, Moscow.

**SHONE, Sir Robert Minshull,** Kt 1955; CBE 1949; Visiting Professor, The City University, since 1967; Director: The Rank Organisation Ltd; White Drummond & Co. Ltd; A.P.V. Holdings Ltd; *b* 27 May 1906; *s* of Robert Harold Shone. *Educ:* Sedbergh School; Liverpool University (MEng, 1st Cl. Hons); Chicago Univ. (MA Economics). Commonwealth Fellow, USA, 1932-34; Lecturer, London School of Economics, 1935-36; British Iron and Steel Federation, 1936-39 and 1946-53, Director 1950-53; Iron and Steel Control, 1940-45, Gen. Dir, 1943-45; Executive Member, Iron and Steel Board, 1953-62; Joint Chairman, UK and ECSC Steel Committee, 1954-62; Dir-Gen. of Staff, and Mem. NEDC, 1962-66; Research Fellow, Nuffield Coll., Oxford, 1966-67; Hon. Fellow: LSE; Pres., Soc. of Business Economists, 1963-68. *Publications:* contributions to: Some Modern Business Problems, 1937; The Industrial Future of Great Britain, 1948; Large Scale Organisation, 1950; Britain and the Common Market, 1967; The Value-Added Tax, 1969; articles in journals. *Recreation:* golf. *Address:* 7 Windmill Hill, Hampstead, NW3. *T:* 01-435 1930. *Club:* Reform.

**SHONFIELD, Andrew Akiba;** Chairman, Social Science Research Council, since 1969; *b* 10 Aug. 1917; *s* of late Victor and of Rachel Lea Schonfeld; *m* 1942, Zuzanna Maria Przeworska; one *s* one *d*. *Educ:* St Paul's; Magdalen Coll., Oxford. Hons BA (Oxon) Modern Greats, 1939. Served War of 1939-45, in RA, 1940-46; attached to AFHQ, Caserta, Italy, 1945 (despatches), Major. On Staff of Financial Times, 1947-57, Foreign Editor, 1950-57; Economic Editor, The Observer, 1958-61; Director of Studies, RIIA, 1961-68, now Research Fellow. Member: Royal Commn on Trade Unions, 1965-68; FCO Review Cttee on Overseas Representation, 1968-69. Broadcaster on sound radio and television. *Publications:* British Economic Policy since the War, 1958; Attack on World Poverty, 1960; A Man Beside Himself, 1964; Modern Capitalism, 1965. *Address:* 21 Paultons Square, SW3. *T:* 01-352 7364. *Club:* Reform.

**SHOOTER, Professor Reginald Arthur;** Professor of Bacteriology, London University, and Bacteriologist to St Bartholomew's Hospital, since 1961; *b* 1916; *s* of Rev. A. E. Shooter, TD and M. K. Shooter; *m* 1946, Jean Wallace, MB, ChB; one *s* three *d*. *Educ:* Mill Hill Sch.; Caius Coll., Cambridge; St Bartholomew's Hosp. BA 1937; MB, BChir 1940; MRCS, LRCP 1940; MA 1941; MD 1945; MRCP 1961; FRCP 1968; FRCPath 1963. After various Hosp. appts became Surgeon Lieut, RNVR. Appointments at St Bartholomew's Hospital from 1946; Rockefeller Travelling Fellow in Medicine, 1950-51; Reader in Bacteriology, University of London, 1953. *Publications:* books, and articles in medical journals. *Recreations:* squash, gardening, fishing. *Address;* 91 The Green, Ewell, Epsom, Surrey. *T:* 01-393 3530.

**SHOPPEE, Prof. Charles William,** FRS 1956; FAA 1958; Welch Professor of Chemistry, Texas Technological University, Lubbock, Texas, since 1970; *b* London, 24 Feb. 1904; *er s* of J. W. and Elizabeth Shoppee, Totteridge; *m* 1929, Eileen Alice West; one *d*. *Educ:* Stationers' Company's Sch.; Univs of London and Leeds. PhD, DSc (London); DPhil (Basle). Sen. Student of Royal Commn for Exhibition of 1851, 1926-28; Asst Lecturer and Lecturer in Organic Chemistry, Univ. of Leeds, 1929-39; Rockefeller Research Fellow, Univ. of Basle, 1939-45; Reader in Chemistry, Univ. of London, at Royal Cancer Hosp., 1945-48; Prof. of Chemistry, Univ. of Wales, at University Coll., Swansea, 1948-56; Prof. of Organic Chemistry, Univ. of Sydney, 1956-70. Visiting Professor of Chemistry: Duke Univ., N Carolina, USA, 1963; Univ. of Georgia, USA, 1966; Univ. of Mississippi, USA, 1968. *Publications:* Scientific papers in Jl Chem. Soc. and Helvetica Chimica Acta. *Recreations:* bowls, music, golf. *Address:* Department of Chemistry, Texas Technological University, Lubbock, Texas 79409, USA. *T:* 806-7470909; 41 Kenthurst Road, St Ives, NSW 2075, Australia. *T:* 449 1176. *Club:* Royal Automobile.

**SHORE,** family name of **Baron Teignmouth.**

**SHORE, Bernard Alexander Royle,** CBE 1955; FRCM, FTCL, Hon. RAM, ARCM; retired as HM Inspector of Schools, Staff Inspector for Music (1948-59); viola player; Professor of the Viola at RCM; Director of Music, Rural Music Schools Association; *b* 17 March 1896; *s* of Arthur Miers Shore and Ada Alice (*née* Clark); *m* 1922, Olive Livett Udale; two *d*. *Educ:* St Paul's School, Hammersmith; Royal College of Music (studied organ under Sir Walter Alcock). Served European War, 1914-18: enlisted in Artists Rifles, 1915, France; commissioned, 2nd Rifle Bde (wounded); seconded to RFC. Returned to RCM: studied viola under Arthur Bent and later with Lionel Tertis. Joined Queen's Hall Orchestra, 1922; first appearance as Soloist, Promenade Concert, 1925; Principal Viola, BBC Symphony Orchestra, 1930-40. War of 1939-45: RAF, 1940; Squadron Leader, 1942; demobilised, 1946. Adviser on Instrumental Music in Schools, Min. of Educn, 1946-47. *Publications:* The Orchestra Speaks, 1937; Sixteen Symphonies, 1947. *Recreations:* sketching, the viola. *Address:* 110 Castelnau, SW13. *T:* 01-748 4408.

**SHORE, Rt. Hon. Peter (David),** PC 1967; MP (Lab) Stepney since 1964; *b* 20 May 1924; *m* 1948, Elizabeth Catherine (*née* Wrong); two *s* two *d*. *Educ:* Quarry Bank High Sch., Liverpool; King's Coll., Cambridge. Political economist. Joined Labour Party, 1948; Head of Research Dept, Labour Party, 1959-64. Member of Fabian Society. Contested (Lab) St Ives, Cornwall, 1950, Halifax, 1959. PPS to the Prime Minister, 1965-66; Jt Parly Sec.: Min. of Technology, 1966-67; Dept of Economic Affairs, 1967; Sec. of State for Economic Affairs, 1967-69; Minister without Portfolio, 1969-70; Dep. Leader of House of Commons, 1969-70. *Publication:* Entitled to Know, 1966. *Recreation:* swimming. *Address:* 23 Dryburgh Road, SW15.

**SHORROCK, James Godby;** Barrister-at-Law; Recorder of Barrow-in-Furness since 1963; Deputy Chairman, Westmorland County Quarter Sessions, since 1955; *b* 10 Dec. 1910; *s* of late William Gordon Shorrock, JP, Morland, Westmorland; *m* 1936, Mary Patricia, *d* of late George Herbert Lings, Burnage, Manchester; two *s* two *d*. *Educ:* Clifton; Hertford College, Oxford. Called to Bar, Inner Temple, 1934. Served War of 1939-45: Major RA (TA) and Judge Advocate General's Department. Legal Member, Mental Health Review Tribunal, 1960-63; Legal Chm., Manchester City Licensing Planning Cttee, 1964. *Recreations:* walking, fishing, gardening. *Address:* Flat 2, Oaklands, Wilmslow Park, Wilmslow, Cheshire. *T:* Wilmslow 25775.

**SHORT, Rt. Hon. Edward Watson,** PC 1964; MP (Lab) Newcastle upon Tyne Central since 1951; *b* 17 Dec. 1912; *s* of Charles and Mary Short, Warcop, Westmorland; *m* 1941, Jennie, *d* of Thomas Sewell, Newcastle upon Tyne; one *s* one *d*. *Educ:* Bede College, Durham (LLB). Served War of 1939-45 and became Capt. in DLI. Headmaster of Princess Louise County Secondary School, Blyth, Northumberland, 1947; Leader of Labour Group on Newcastle City Council, 1950; Opposition Whip (Northern Area), 1955-62; Dep. Chief Opposition Whip, 1962-64; Parly Sec. to the Treasury and Government Chief Whip, 1964-66; Postmaster General, 1966-68; Secretary of State for Education and Science, 1968-70. Hon. Fellow, College of Preceptors, 1965. *Publications:* The Story of The Durham Light Infantry, 1944; The Infantry Instructor, 1946. *Recreation:* painting. *Address:* 4 Patterdale Gardens, Newcastle upon Tyne 7. *T:* Newcastle 661991.

**SHORT, Rev. Frank;** Minister, Congregational Church, Sherborne, Dorset; General Secretary (1957-Aug. 1965), Asia Secretary (1953-Aug. 1965) Conference of Missionary Societies in Great Britain and Ireland; *b* 6 July 1895; 3rd *s* of John Richard and Louisa M. Short; *m* 1926, Irene Alice McCalla (*d* 1967); no *c*. *Educ:* Latymer Sch., Hammersmith; Hackney Coll., Divinity School, University of London. Ordained to the Congregational Ministry, 1923. Minister, Kingsbridge, Devon, Congregational Church, 1923-26; Missionary, London Missionary Society, 1926-53; Hong Kong, 1926-49; Sec. of China Council (LMS), Shanghai, 1949-51; Representative of Board of LMS in SE Asia, 1951-53; Mem. Board of Educn of Govt of Hong Kong, 1928-48. *Publications:* occasional articles in International Review of Missions. *Recreation:* gardening. *Address:* Heathcot, South Street, Sherborne, Dorset. *T:* 2268.

**SHORT, Rev. Harry Lismer;** Principal, Manchester College, Oxford, since 1965; Tutor since 1952; Librarian, since 1956; *b* 12 July 1906; *s* of Rev. H. F. Short; *m* 1930, Agatha, *d* of Rev. L. Short; three *s* one *d*. *Educ:* Peterhouse, Cambridge; Manchester College, Oxford; Harvard Divinity School; London University. Unitarian Minister: Rochdale, 1930-35; Brixton, London, 1935-39; Macclesfield, 1939-54; Banbury, 1954-. Visiting Professor of Church History at

Meadville Theological School, Chicago, 1963. Editor, The Hibbert Journal, 1962-68. *Publications:* Dissent and the community (Essex Hall lecture, 1962); contrib. to: Essays in Unitarian Theology, 1959; The Beginnings of Nonconformity, 1964; The English Presbyterians, 1968; to Transactions of Unitarian Hist. Soc. and other jls. *Address:* 62 Rose Hill, Oxford. *T:* 77564.

**SHORT, Rev. John,** MA (Edinburgh); PhD (Edinburgh); Hon. DD (St Andrews); Minister of St George's United Church, Toronto, Canada, 1951-64; *b* Berwickshire, 27 March 1896; *m* 1st; one *s* one *d*; 2nd, 1939, Anneliese, 2nd *d* of Dr C. J. F. Bechler, Danzig; two *s*. *Educ:* Edinburgh University. Trained for a business career but attracted by religious convictions to the Christian ministry; began to study for same just before the war of 1914-18, joined army and served for 3 years and 6 months; commenced studies at Edinburgh; graduated MA. First class honours in Philosophy; awarded John Edward Baxter Scholarship in Philosophy for 3 years; received University Diploma in Education and Medal; trained for Teacher's Certificate; awarded Doctorate in Philosophy for a thesis on the Philosophic Character of English XIVth Century Mysticism; medallist in class of Moral Philosophy, and in Metaphysics; Prizeman in Psychology; trained in Scottish Congregational College for Ministry under Principal T. Hywel Hughes, DLitt, DD; called to Bathgate E. U. Congregational Church, 1924; Minister of Lyndhurst Road Congregational Church, Hampstead, 1930-37. Minister of Richmond Hill Congregational Church, Bournemouth, 1937-51; Chairman of the Congregational Union of England and Wales, 1949-50. Mason: 3° Home Lodge Amity, Poole, Dorset, 1951; 18° Downend Chapter Rose Croix, Gloucester, 1953; affiliated Ashlar Lodge, 247 GRC, Toronto, 1952; 32° Moore Sovereign Consistory, Hamilton, Ont, 1964; 33 Supreme Council A&ASR, Dominion of Canada (Hon. Inspector Gen.), 1967. DD (hc): St Andrews Univ., 1950; McMaster Univ., Hamilton, Ontario, 1964. *Publications:* Can I Find Faith?, 1937; All Things are Yours (book of sermons), 1939; The Interpreter's Bible Exposition of I Corinthians; Triumphant Believing, 1952. *Recreations:* golf, reading, and travel. *Address:* 162 Coldstream Avenue, Toronto 12, Canada. *T:* 489-8614.

**SHORT, Brig. Noel Edward Vivian,** MBE 1951; MC 1945; Secretary to Mr Speaker, House of Commons, since 1970; *b* 19 Jan. 1916; *s* of late Vivian A. Short, CIE, Indian Police, and late Annie W. Short; *m* 1st, 1949, Diana Hester Morison (*d* 1951); one *s*; 2nd, 1957, Karin Margarete Anders; one *s* one *d*. *Educ:* Radley College; RMA Sandhurst. Commissioned Indian Army, 1936; joined 6th Gurkha Rifles, 1937. Active service: NW Frontier of India, 1937, 1940-41; Assam and Burma, 1942, 1944-45; New Guinea, 1943-44; Malaysia, 1950-51, 1952-53, 1956-57. Staff College, 1946-47; jssc, 1953; Comdr, 63 Gurkha Bde, Malaysia, 1960-61; Comdr, 51 Infty Bde, Tidworth, 1962-63. Principal, Home Office, 1964-70. *Publications:* contribs: Jl of RUSI; Army Quarterly. *Recreations:* ski-ing, photography. *Address:* Cage Green Farm, Tonbridge, Kent. *T:* Tonbridge 3011. *Club:* Albemarle.

**SHORT, Mrs Renee;** MP (Lab) Wolverhampton (North-East) since 1964; *b* April 1919; *m*; two *d*. *Educ:* Nottingham County Grammar Sch.; Manchester Univ. Freelance journalist. Member: Herts County Council, 1952-67; Watford RDC, 1952-64; West Herts Group Hosp. Management Cttee; former Chm. Shrodell's Hosp., Watford. Governor: Watford Coll. of Technology; Watford Grammar Sch. Contested (Lab) St Albans, 1955, Watford, 1959. Member: Delegation to Council of Europe, 1964-68; Estimates Cttee (Chm. Social Sub-Cttee Estimates); Vice-Chm., Parly East-West Trade Gp, 1968 and 1969. Mem., Nat. Exec. Cttee of Labour Party, 1970-. National President: Nursery Schools Assoc.; Campaign for Nursery Educn. *Address:* 117 Chambersbury Lane, Nash Mills, Hemel Hempstead, Herts.

**SHORTT, Maj.-Gen. Arthur Charles,** CB 1951; OBE 1945; retired; *b* 2 April 1899; *s* of Charles William Shortt and Grace Evelyn Mary (*née* Skey); *m* 1st, 1927, Loraine (*née* Thomas), one *d*; 2nd, 1945, Nella (*née* Exelby). *Educ:* St Lawrence, Ramsgate; King's College, Cambridge; RMA Woolwich, 2nd Lt, RE, 1916. Served European War, 1914-18, in France and Belgium; Staff College, Minley, 1939. War of 1939-45: Personal Assistant to C-in-C, BEF 1940; Director of Technical Training, 1943. Military Attaché, Athens, 1947-49; formerly Director of Military Intelligence. Chief Liaison Officer on UK Service Liaison Staff, Australia, 1953-56; Retired pay, 1956; Director of Public Relations, War Office, 1956-61; Col Comdt, Intelligence Corps, 1960-64. Mem. Governing Body, St Lawrence, Ramsgate. Officer, Legion of Honour (France), 1950. *Recreation:* numismatics. *Address:* Bolnore, Hayward's Heath, Sussex. *T:* 51386. *Club:* United Service.

**SHORTT, Colonel Henry Edward,** CIE 1941; FRS 1950; LLD 1952; Colonel IMS, retired; formerly Professor of Medical Protozoology, University of London, and Head of Department of Parasitology, London School of Hygiene and Tropical Medicine; *b* 15 April 1887; *m* 1921, Eleanor M. Hobson; one *s* one *d*. *Educ:* Univ. of Aberdeen. MB, ChB 1910; MD 1936; DSc 1938; KHP 1941-44; Inspector-Gen. of Civil Hospitals and Prisons, Assam, 1941-44; retired, 1944. President, Royal Society of Tropical Medicine and Hygiene, 1949-51; Technical Expert under Colombo Plan in E Pakistan, 1952-55. Straits Settlements Gold Medal, 1938; Kaisar-i-Hind Gold Medal, 1945; Laveran Prize, 1948; Mary Kingsley medal, 1949; Darling medal and prize, 1951; Stewart prize, 1954; Manson Medal, 1959; Gaspar Vianna Medal, 1962. *Publications:* over 130 scientific papers. *Recreations:* shooting and fishing. *Address:* Castelmere, Digswell, near Welwyn, Herts.

**SHOSTAKOVICH, Dmitry Dmitrievich;** Order of Lenin; Composer; People's Artist of the USSR; First Secretary of the Soviet Union of Composers, 1960-68; *b* Leningrad, 25 Sept. 1906; *m* Nina Vasilievna (*née* Varzar) (*d* 1954); one *s* one *d*. *Educ:* Leningrad Conservatory of Music. Graduated pianoforte, 1924, composition, 1925. Laureate of International Peace Prize; Stalin and State Prizes (6 times); Lenin Prize, for 11th Symphony, 1958. Hon. Mem. St Cecilia Acad. of Music, Rome (Dip. of Hon.), 1958; Hon. DMus Oxford, 1958; Gold Medal, RPS, 1966; Hero of Socialist Labour, 1966. *Works:* 13 symphonies (first, 1925, while student); 3 ballets; 3 operas; 4 concertos; 1 oratorio; 1 cantata; 4 suites for symphony orchestra; 8 quartets; 2 pieces for octet; 24 preludes; 24 preludes and fugues; 11 song cycles; 2 symphonic poems; music for: 28 films, 12 theatrical productions, etc. *Address:* Mozhalski Chaussée d.37/45 kv.87, Moscow G-151, USSR.

**SHOTTON, Prof. Edward;** Professor of Pharmaceutics, University of London, since Oct. 1956; *b* 15 July 1910; *s* of Ernest Richard and Maud Shotton; *m* 1943, Mary Constance Louise Marchant; one *d*. *Educ:* Smethwick (Junior) Technical School; Birkbeck College, University of London. Pharmaceutical Chemist (PhC), 1933; BSc (London), 1939; PhD (London), 1955; Hon. ACT (Birmingham), 1961. FRIC 1949. Pharmaceutical research and development work at Burroughs, Wellcome & Co., Dartford, 1939-48. Sen. Lecturer in Pharmaceutics, Univ. of London, 1948-56. Chairman, British Pharmaceutical Conference, 1966. *Publications:* research papers, mainly in Jl of Pharmacy and Pharmacology. *Recreations:* gardening, cricket. *Address:* 10 Winston Gardens, Berkhamsted, Herts. *T:* 6402; (Office) 01-837 7651. *Club:* Athenæum.

**SHOTTON, Prof. Frederick William,** MBE 1946; FRS 1956; MA, ScD; FGS, FIMinE; Pro-Vice-Chancellor and Vice-Principal, University of Birmingham, since 1965; Professor of Geology since 1949; *b* 8 Oct. 1906; *s* of F. J. and Ada Shotton, Coventry; *m* 1930, Alice L. Linnett; two *d*. *Educ:* Bablake, Coventry; Sidney Sussex College, Cambridge. Wiltshire Prizeman and Harkness Scholar, Cambridge, 1926-27. Assistant Lecturer and Lecturer, University of Birmingham, 1928-36; Lecturer, Cambridge University, 1936-45. Served War of 1939-45, MEF and 21 Army Group, 1940-45. Prof. of Geology, Sheffield Univ., 1945-49. Mem., NERC, 1969-. Pres., Geological Soc., 1964-66, Vice-Pres., 1966-68. Hon. Mem., Royal Irish Acad., 1970. Prestwich Medal, Geological Soc. of London, 1954; Stopes Medal, Geologists' Assoc., 1967. *Publications:* numerous scientific. *Recreations:* archæology and natural history; gardening. *Address:* 35 Park Avenue, Solihull, Warwickshire. *T:* 021-705 3360.

**SHOVELTON, Walter Patrick;** Member, UK Negotiating Team for Entry into EEC; *b* 18 Aug. 1919; *s* of late S. T. Shovelton, CBE, and M. C. Kelly, cousin of Patrick and Willie Pearse, Irish patriots; *m* 1st, 1942, Marjorie Lucy Joan Manners (marr. diss. 1967); one *d*; 2nd, Helena Richards, 3rd *d* of D. G. Richards, *qv*. *Educ:* Charterhouse; Keble Coll., Oxford (scholar of both). Rep. Oxford Univ. at Eton fives. Served in RA and RHA, 1940-46; DAAG, War Office, 1945-46. Entered Administrative Civil Service as Asst Principal, Min. of Transport, 1946; Principal 1947; Admin. Staff College, 1951; Private Sec. to Secretary of State for Co-ordination of Transport, Fuel and Power, 1951-53; Asst Sec., 1957; transferred to Min. of Aviation, 1959; IDC, 1962; Under Secretary, 1966; transferred to Min. of Technology, 1966, and to Dept of Trade and Industry, 1970. Member: Council, RUSI, 1968-70; Council, Blackheath Soc., 1951-65; Hon. Educn Adviser, RAF Benevolent Fund, 1950-65. *Recreations:* travel, golf. *Address:* 74 Southwood Park, N6. *T:* 01-348 1961. *Clubs:* Royal Automobile; Hampstead Golf.

**SHOWERING, Keith Stanley;** Vice-Chairman, Allied Breweries Ltd, since 1969; Chairman and Chief Executive, Allied International Breweries Ltd, since 1970; *b* 6 Aug. 1930; *o s* of Herbert and Ada Showering; *m* 1954, Marie Sadie (*née* Golden); three *s* two *d*. *Educ:* Wells Cathedral School. Joined family business of Showerings Ltd, cider makers, 1947; Dir, 1951; Founder Dir, Showerings, Vine Products & Whiteways Ltd on merger of those companies, 1961; Dep. Chm., 1964; Man. Dir, John Harvey & Sons Ltd and Harveys of Bristol Ltd, 1966; Dir of Allied Breweries Ltd, 1968, also Dir of other allied subsidiary cos; Director: Guardian Assurance Co. Ltd, 1969; Licences & General Insurance Co. Ltd, 1961-69; Société Civile du Vignoble de Château Latour, 1966; Parkdale Wines Ltd (Toronto). *Recreation:* shooting. *Address:* Sharcombe Park, Dinder, Wells, Somerset BA5 3PG. *T:* Wells 72162. *Clubs:* Bath, Arts, Buck's.

**SHRAPNEL, Norman;** Parliamentary Correspondent of the Guardian since 1958; *b* 5 Oct. 1912; *yr s* of Arthur Edward Scrope Shrapnel and Rosa Brosy; *m* 1940, Mary Lilian Myfanwy Edwards; two *s*. *Educ:* King's School, Grantham. Various weekly, evening and morning newspapers from 1930; Manchester Guardian (later the Guardian) from 1947, as reporter, theatre critic and reviewer; contributor to various journals. Political Writer of the Year Award (the Political Companion), 1969. Regular broadcasts, home and overseas. *Recreations:* walking, music. *Address:* 27 Shooters Hill Road, Blackheath, SE3. *T:* 01-858 7123.

**SHREWSBURY and WATERFORD,** 21st Earl of, *cr* 1442 and 1446, **John George Charles Henry Alton Alexander Chetwynd Chetwynd-Talbot;** Baron of Dungarvan, 1446; Baron Talbot, 1733; Earl Talbot, Viscount Ingestre, 1784; Premier Earl of England, Hereditary Great Seneschal or Lord High Steward of Ireland; *b* 1 Dec. 1914; *s* of Viscount Ingestre, MVO (*d* 1915) and Lady Winifred Constance Hester Paget, *e d* of Lord Alexander (Victor) Paget (she *m* 1917, R. E. Pennoyer, and *d* 1965); *S* grandfather, 1921; *m* 1st, 1936, Nadine (marr. diss., 1963), *yr d* of late Brig.-Gen. C. R. Crofton, CBE; two *s* four *d*; 2nd, 1963, Aileen Mortlock. *Educ:* Eton. A godson of King George V and Queen Mary. Served War of 1939-45; Staff Officer to Duke of Gloucester, 1940-42; Middle Eastern and Italian Theatres of Operations, 1942-45. Late CC and JP Staffs. *Heir:* *s* Viscount Ingestre, *qv*.

*See also G. R. F. Morris.*

**SHREWSBURY, Bishop Suffragan of,** since 1970; **Rt. Rev. Francis William Cocks,** CB 1959; *b* 5 Nov. 1913; *o s* of late Canon W. Cocks, OBE, St John's Vicarage, Felixstowe; *m* 1940, Irene May (Barbara), 2nd *d* of H. Thompson, Bridlington; one *s* one *d*. *Educ:* Haileybury; St Catharine's Coll., Cambridge; Westcott House. Played Rugby Football for Cambridge Univ., Hampshire and Eastern Counties, 1935-38. Ordained, 1937. Chaplain RAFVR, 1939; Chaplain RAF, 1945; Asst Chaplain-in-Chief, 1950; Chaplain-in-Chief, and Archdeacon, Royal Air Force, 1959-65; Rector and Rural Dean of Wolverhampton, 1965-70. Mem. of Council, Haileybury and Imperial Service Coll., 1949-. Hon. Chaplain to HM the Queen, 1959-65. Prebendary of S Botolph in Lincoln Cathedral, 1959; Canon Emeritus, 1965-70; Prebendary of Lichfield Cathedral, 1968-70; Select Preacher, Univ. of Cambridge, 1960; Hon. Canon of Lichfield Cathedral, 1970-; Fellow, Woodard Schools, 1969-; Mem. Council, Denstone School, 1970-. Pres. Buccaneers CC, 1965-. *Recreations:* cricket, tennis, golf. *Address:* Athlone House, London Road, Shrewsbury. *T:* Shrewsbury 6410. *Clubs:* MCC, Royal Air Force; Hawks (Cambridge).

**SHREWSBURY, Bishop of, (RC),** since 1962; **Rt. Rev. William Eric Grasar,** DCL, STL; *b* 18 May 1913. *Educ:* Brigg Grammar School; Panton; English College, Rome. Priest 1937; Vice-Rector, English College, Rome, 1942-46; Chancellor, Nottingham Diocese, 1948-52; Rector of St Hugh's College, Tollerton, 1952-56; Vicar-General, Nottingham Diocese, 1956-62. *Address:* The Council House, Shrewsbury SY1 2AY. *T:* Shrewsbury 3513.

**SHREWSBURY, Dr J. F. D.,** DSM, MD, ChB, DPH, FRSA, Hon. FChS; retired; Professor of Bacteriology, University of Birmingham, 1937-63; Emeritus Professor, 1963; *b* 10 May 1898; *er s* of Rev. J. S. W. Shrewsbury, BA; *m* 1920, Alys Mary (*d* 1955), *yr d* of H. R. Danford, Daintree House, Upminster, Essex; three *d*; *m* Georgina, 2nd *d* of Mrs C. M. B. Hooper, Saffron Walden, Essex; one *s*. *Educ:* Woodhouse Grove School, Yorks; Liverpool University. RN, 1916-19 (DSM for services at Zeebrugge); University of Liverpool, 1919-22; MB, ChB, 1923; Gee Prize, 1922; DPH, 1924; MD, 1933; House Surgeon, VD Dept Liverpool Royal Infirmary, 1923-25; Lecturer in Public Health Bacteriology, 1924-25; Lecturer in Bacteriology, University of Birmingham, and Bacteriologist to the Queen's Hospital, Birmingham, 1925-33; Reader in Bacteriology, University of Birmingham, 1933-37; Mem. British Medical Association, Pathological Soc. of Gt Britain and Ireland and Soc. Applied Bact. *Publications:* The Plague of the Philistines and other Medical-Historical Essays, 1964; A History of the Bubonic Plague in the British Isles, 1970; The Genus Willia (Journal Pathology and Bacteriology, 1930, 33, 393-416); The Genus Monilia, (ibid 1934, 38, 313-354); numerous papers on medical and public health bacteriology, and medical biochemistry in medical journals. *Recreations:* gardening, photography. *Address:* Denstone, Ripple, Tewkesbury, Glos. *T:* Upton-on-Severn 2302.

**SHRIVER, (Robert) Sargent;** US Ambassador to France, 1968-70; *b* Westminster, Md, 9 Nov. 1915; *s* of Robert Sargent and Hilda Shriver; *m* 1953, Eunice Mary Kennedy; four *s* one *d*. *Educ:* parochial schools, Baltimore; Canterbury School, New Milford, Conn.; Yale College; Yale University. BA (*cum laude*) 1938; LLB 1941; LLD 1964. Apprentice Seaman, USNR, 1940; Ensign, 1941. Served War of 1941-45: Atlantic and Pacific Ocean Areas aboard battleships and submarines; Lt-Comdr, USNR. Admitted to: New York Bar, 1941; Illinois Bar, (retd) 1959. With legal firm of Winthrop, Stimson, Putnam & Roberts, NYC, 1940-41; Asst Editor, Newsweek, 1945-46; associated with Joseph P. Kennedy Enterprises, 1946-48; Asst Gen. Man., Merchandise Mart, 1948-61; Dir, Peace Corps, Washington, 1961-66; Dir, Office of Economic Opportunity and Special Asst to Pres. Johnson, 1964-68. Exec. Dir, Joseph P. Kennedy Jr Foundn. Democrat; Roman Catholic. *Address:* Timberlawn, Edson Lane, Rockville, Md, USA.

**SHUARD, Amy, (Mrs Peter Asher),** CBE 1966; Principal Soprano, Covent Garden; *b* 19 July 1924; British; *m* 1954, Dr Peter Asher. *Educ:* Morden, Surrey. Has sung at Sadler's Wells Theatre, 1949-54; Covent Garden, 1954. Sang, Vienna State Opera, 1961; La Scala, Milan, 1962; San Francisco, 1963; Stuttgart, 1965. Hon. FTCL, 1957. *Address:* 23 Wood Lane, Highgate, N6. *T:* 01-883 1591.

**SHUCKBURGH, Sir (Charles Arthur) Evelyn,** GCMG 1967 (KCMG 1959; CMG 1949); CB 1954; HM Diplomatic Service, retired; Chairman, Executive Committee, British Red Cross Society, since 1970; *b* 26 May 1909; *e s* of late Sir John Shuckburgh, KCMG, CB; *m* 1937, Nancy Brett, 2nd *d* of 3rd Viscount Esher, GBE; two *s* one *d*. *Educ:* Winchester; King's College, Cambridge. Entered Diplomatic Service, 1933; served at HM Embassy, Cairo, 1937-39; seconded for service on staff of UK High Comr in Ottawa, 1940; transferred to Buenos Aires, 1942; Chargé d'Affaires there in 1944; First Secretary at HM Embassy, Prague, 1945-47. Head of South American Department, FO, 1947-48; Western Dept, 1949-50; Western Organizations Dept, 1950-51; Principal Private Secretary to Secretary of State for Foreign Affairs, 1951-54; Assistant Under-Secretary, Foreign Office, 1954-56; Senior Civilian Instructor, IDC, 1956-58; Asst Sec.-Gen. (Polit.) of NATO, Paris, 1958-60; Dep. Under-Sec., FO, 1960-62; Perm. Brit. Rep. to N Atlantic Council, in Paris, 1962-66; Ambassador to Italy, 1966-69. *Address:* High Wood, Watlington, Oxon. *Club:* Turf.

**SHUCKBURGH, Sir Charles Gerald Stewkley,** 12th Bt, *cr* 1660; TD; DL; JP; Major, late 11th (City of London Yeomanry) LAA; *b* 28 Feb. 1911; *s* of 11th Bt and Honour Zoë, OBE, *d* of Neville Thursby, of Harlestone, Northamptonshire; *S* father, 1939; *m* 1st, 1935, Remony (*d* 1936), *o d* of late F. N. Bell, Buenos Aires; 2nd, 1937, Nancy Diana Mary (OBE 1970), *o d* of late Capt. Rupert Lubbock, RN; one *s* two *d*. *Educ:* Harrow; Trinity College, Oxford. JP 1946, DL 1965, Warwickshire; High Sheriff, Warwickshire, 1965. *Heir:* *s* Rupert Charles Gerald Shuckburgh, *b* 12 Feb. 1949. *Address:* Shuckburgh, Daventry. *TA:* Daventry. *T:* Daventry 2523. *Club:* Bath.

**SHUCKBURGH, Sir Evelyn;** *see* Shuckburgh, Sir C. A. E.

**SHULMAN, Milton;** writer, journalist, critic; *b* Toronto, 1 Sept. 1913; *s* of late Samuel Shulman, merchant, and of Ethel Shulman; *m* 1956, Drusilla Beyfus; one *s* two *d*. *Educ:* Univ. of Toronto (BA); Osgoode Hall, Toronto. Barrister, Toronto, 1937-40. Armoured Corps and Intelligence, Canadian Army, 1940-46 (despatches, Normandy, 1945); Major. Film critic, Evening Standard and Sunday Express, 1948-58; book critic, Sunday Express, 1957-58; theatre critic, Evening Standard, 1953-; TV Critic, Evening Standard, 1964-; executive producer and producer, Granada TV, 1958-62; Asst Controller of Programmes, Rediffusion TV, 1962-64. Hannen Swaffer Award, Critic of the Year, 1966. *Publications:* Defeat in the West, 1948; How To Be a Celebrity, 1950; The Ravenous Eye, 1971; *children's books:* Preep, 1964; Preep in Paris, 1967; Preep and The Queen, 1970; *novel:* Kill Three, 1967; *novel and film story:* (with Herbert Kretzmer) Every Home Should Have One, 1970. *Recreations:* modern art, history, tennis. *Address:* 51 Eaton Square, SW1. *T:* 01-235 7162. *Clubs:* Savile, Hurlingham.

**SHUTE, Prof. Charles Cameron Donald,** MD; Professor of Histology, Cambridge University, since 1969; Fellow of Christ's College, Cambridge, since 1957; *b* 23 May 1917; *s* of late Cameron Deane Shute; *m* 1st, 1947, Patricia Cameron (*d* 1952), *d* of F. H. Doran; 2nd, 1954, Lydia May (Wendy) (*née* Harwood); one *s* three *d*. *Educ:* Eton; King's Coll., Cambridge; Middlesex Hosp., London. MA, MB, BChir Cambridge, 1945; MD Cambridge 1958. Resident posts at Middlesex Hosp., 1945-47; RAMC (otologist), 1947-49; Demonstrator and Lectr in Anatomy, London Hosp. Med. Coll., 1951; Univ. Demonstrator and Lectr, Cambridge, 1952-69; Univ. Reader in Neuroanatomy, Cambridge, 1969. *Publications:* papers in biological jls. *Recreations:* gardening, tennis, educating and being educated by my family. *Address:* Eversden House, Great Eversden, Cambridge. *T:* Comberton 2371.

**SHUTE, John Lawson,** CMG 1970; OBE 1959; Member: Council of Egg Marketing Authorities of Australia, since 1970; Egg Marketing Board of New South Wales, since

1970; NSW Rural Reconstruction Board, since 1942; *b* Mudgee, NSW, 31 Jan. 1901; *s* of J. Shute, Mudgee; *m* 1937, Constance W. M., *d* of J. Douglas; two *s*. *Educ:* Parramatta High Sch. Asst Sec., Primary Producers' Union, NSW, 1923-33; Gen.-Sec., 1933-43; Sec., Federated Co-operative Bacon Factories, 1927-43; Member: NSW Dairy Products Bd, 1934-46; Commonwealth Air Beef Panel, 1942; Dir, Commonwealth Dairy Produce Equalisation Cttee, 1941-46; 1st Sec. Aust. Dairy Farmers' Fedn, 1942; Mem. Exec. and Asst Sec., Empire Producers' Conf., 1938; Mem. Special Dairy Industry Cttee apptd by Commonwealth Govt, 1942; Dep. Controller, Meat Supplies, NSW, 1942-46. Chairman: Aust. Meat Bd, 1946-70; Aust. Cttee of Animal Production, 1947-70; Aust. Cattle and Beef Research Cttee, 1960-66; Aust. Meat Research Cttee, 1966-70; Aust. Frozen Cargo Shippers' Cttee, 1967-70; Member: Export Development Council, 1958-66; Overseas Trade Publicity Cttee, 1955-70; Australia Japan Business Co-operation Cttee, 1962-70. *Recreations:* Rugby Union (former Internat. rep.), cricket. *Address:* 64/650 Pacific Highway, Killara, NSW 2071, Australia. *Clubs:* Australian, Commercial Travellers' (NSW).

**SHUTTLEWORTH;** *see* Kay-Shuttleworth.

**SHUTTLEWORTH,** 4th Baron, *cr* 1902, of Gawthorpe; **Charles Ughtred John Kay-Shuttleworth,** MC; Bt, *cr* 1850; JP; Capt. (retd) RHA; *b* 24 June 1917; *s* of late Capt. Hon. Edward James Kay-Shuttleworth (2nd *s* of 1st Baron) and Mrs Roger Fulford; *S* cousin, 1942; *m* 1947, Anne Elizabeth, *er d* of late Col Geoffrey Phillips, CBE, DSO; three *s* one *d*. *Educ:* Eton; Magdalene Coll., Cambridge. Served War of 1939-45 in HM's Armed Forces, 1940-42, in France and Middle East. *Heir: s* Hon. Charles Geoffrey Nicholas Kay-Shuttleworth, *b* 2 Aug. 1948. *Address:* Leck Hall, via Carnforth. *T:* Kirkby Lonsdale 375; 73 Cranmer Court, SW3. *T:* 01-589 3983.

**SHVERNIK, Nikolai Mikhailovich;** Order of Lenin, 1938 and 1946; Soviet politician and trade union leader; Chairman of All-Union Central Council of Trade Unions since 1953; Member of Supreme Soviet of USSR since 1937 (Chairman, Soviet of Nationalities, 1938-46; President, Presidium of Supreme Soviet, 1946-53); Member Central Committee of Communist Party of Soviet Union since 1925 and alternate member of its Presidium since 1953; *b* 1888. Joined Bolshevik Party, 1905; Chm. Central Cttee, Metal Workers' Union, 1929; First Sec., All-Union Central Council of Trade Unions, 1930-44. Alternate Mem., Political Bureau, 1939; led Soviet Trade Union Delegation to Great Britain, 1942; attended TUC Congress, 1943; First Vice-Pres. Presidium of USSR Supreme Soviet, and Pres. Presidium of RSFSR Supreme Soviet, 1944. *Address:* All-Union Central Council of Trade Unions, Kaluzhskoe Chaussée 66, Moscow, USSR.

**SIBERRY, John William Morgan;** Assistant Under-Secretary of State, Welsh Office, since 1964; *b* 26 Feb. 1913; *s* of late John William and Martha (*née* Morgan) Siberry; *m* 1949, Florence Jane Davies; one *s* one *d*. *Educ:* Porth County School, Rhondda; Univ. Coll. of South Wales and Monmouthshire, Cardiff. Entered Civil Service as Asst Principal, Unemployment Assistance Board (later Nat. Assistance Board), 1935; Principal, 1941; Asst Sec., 1947; transferred to Min. of Housing and Local Govt as Under-Sec., 1963; Welsh Secretary, Welsh Office and Office for Wales of the Ministry of Housing and Local Government, 1963-64. *Recreations:* gardening, walking, occasional golf. *Address:* Northgates, Pwllmelin Road, Llandaff, Cardiff. *T:* Cardiff 564666. *Club:* Cardiff and County.

**SIBLEY, Antoinette;** Senior Principal, The Royal Ballet, Covent Garden, since 1960; *b* 27 Feb. 1939; *d* of Edward G. Sibley and Winifred M. Sibley (*née* Smith). *Educ:* Arts Educational Sch. and Royal Ballet Sch. 1st performance on stage as Student with Royal Ballet at Covent Garden, a swan, Jan. 1956; joined company, July 1956. Leading role in: Swan Lake, Sleeping Beauty, Giselle, Coppelia, Cinderella, The Nutcracker, La Fille Mal Gardée, Romeo & Juliet, Harlequin in April, Les Rendezvous, Jabez & the Devil (created the role of Mary), La Fête Etrange, The Rakes Progress, Hamlet, Ballet Imperial, Two Pigeons, La Bayadère, Symphonic Variations, Scènes de Ballet, Lilac Garden, Daphnis & Chloe, The Dream (created Titania), Laurentia, Good Humoured Ladies, Blue Bird pas de deux in Sleeping Beauty, Peasant pas de deux in Giselle, Aristocrat in Mam'zelle Angot, Façade, Song of the Earth, Monotones, Jazz Calendar (created Friday's Child), Enigma Variations (created Dorabella). *Recreations:* doing nothing; opera and books. *Address:* Royal Opera House, WC2.

**SICH, Sir Rupert (Leigh),** Kt 1968; CB 1953; Registrar of Restrictive Trading Agreements since 1956; *b* 3 Aug. 1908; *s* of late A. E. Sich, Caterham, Surrey; *m* 1933, Elizabeth Mary, *d* of late R. W. Hutchison, Gerrards Cross; one *s* two *d*. *Educ:* Radley College; Merton College, Oxford. Called to Bar, Inner Temple, 1930. Board of Trade Solicitor's Dept, 1932-48; Treasury Solicitor's Dept, 1948-56. *Recreations:* J. S. Bach; gardening. *Address:* Norfolk House, The Mall, Chiswick, W4. *T:* 01-994 2133. *Clubs:* Oxford and Cambridge University, MCC.

**SICOT, Marcel Jean;** Commandeur, Légion d'Honneur, 1954; Croix de Guerre, 1945; Médaille de la Résistance française, 1945; Médaille d'Honneur de la Police, etc.; Hon. Secretary General of ICPO (Interpol); *b* 19 Feb. 1898; *m* 1923, Agnès Demy; one *s*. *Educ:* in France (Brittany and Paris). Comr of French Sûreté, 1920; Divisional Comr, 1938; Sec. Gen. for Police, 1944; Under-Secretary, Police Judiciary, 1945; Director-Inspector Gen., Nat. Sûreté, 1949; retired and appd Hon. Director-Inspector General, 1958; Sec. Gen. of Interpol, 1951; Hon. Sec. Gen., 1963. President of Honour of Assoc. Amicale des Cadres de la Sûreté Nationale; Mem. Council, Order of Civil Merit of Ministry of the Interior. Mem. jury of literary prize "Quai des Orfèvres". Comdr, Order of Vasa (Sweden); Comdr (Palm) Royal Order (Greece); Comdr, Order of Cedar (Lebanon); Comdr, Order of Dannebrog (Denmark). *Publications:* (jointly) Encyclopédie nationale de la police française, 1955; Servitude et grandeur policières–40 ans à la Sûreté, 1960; A la barre de l'Interpol, 1961; La Prostitution dans le Monde, 1964; Fausses et vraies identités, 1967. *Recreations:* fond of Association football and Breton folklore. *Address:* 4 rue Léon Delagrange, Paris XV. *T:* Blomet 91.95.

**SIDDALL, Norman;** Director General of Production, National Coal Board, since 1967; *b* 4 May 1918; *m* 1943; two *s* one *d*. *Educ:* King Edward VII School, Sheffield; Sheffield Univ. (BEng). National Coal Board: Production Manager, No. 5 Area, East Midlands Div., 1951-56; General Manager, No. 5 Area, East Midlands Div. 1956-57; General Manager, No. 1 Area, East Midlands Div., 1957-66; Chief Mining Engineer, 1966-67. Chartered Engineer; MIMinE; Member, Midland

Counties Institution of Engineers (Silver Medal, 1951; Past President). National Association of Colliery Managers: Silver Medal, 1955; Bronze Medal, 1960. Colliery Managers Certificate. *Publications:* articles in professional journals. *Address:* National Coal Board, Hobart House, Grosvenor Place, SW1. *T:* 01-235 2020; Brentwood, High Oakham Road, Mansfield, Notts. *T:* Mansfield 23479; 704 Hood House, Dolphin Square, SW1.

**SIDDELEY,** family name of **Baron Kenilworth.**

**SIDDELEY, Hon. John (Tennant Davenport);** Interior Designer; *b* 24 Jan. 1924; *o s* of 2nd Baron Kenilworth, *qv; m* 1948, Jacqueline, *d* of late Robert Gelpi, Lyon, France; one *s* one *d*. *Educ:* Marlborough; Magdalene College, Cambridge (BA). Chm. and Man. Dir, Siddeley (of Sloane Street) Ltd. Design Consultant to A.E.P. Mem. of American Inst. of Interior Designers. Lectr for INFAB. Contributor to Sydney Morning Herald. *Recreations:* opera, travel, good food. *Address:* 17 Alexandra Court, Queen's Gate, SW7; The Deans, Newton Green, Sudbury, Suffolk.

**SIDDIQUI, Dr Salimuzzaman,** MBE 1946; Tamgha-i-Pakistan 1958; Sitara-i-Imtiaz (Pakistan) 1962; FRS 1961; DPhil; DMed; Professor of Chemistry, University of Karachi; *b* 19 Oct. 1897. *Educ:* Lucknow; MAO College, Aligarh, UP; University College, London; Univ. of Frankfurt-on-Main. Returned to India, 1928; planned and directed Research Inst. at Ayurvedic and Unani Tibbi Coll., Delhi, 1928-40. Joined Council of Scientific and Industrial Research (India): Organic Chemist, 1940; Actg Dir of Chemical Laboratories, 1944. Director of Scientific and Industrial Research, Pakistan, 1951; Director and Chairman of Pakistan Council of Scientific and Industrial Research, 1953-66; Chairman, Nat. Science Council, 1962-66; Pres., Pakistan Acad. of Sciences, 1968. A chemist, working on the chemistry of natural products; has led the promotion of scientific and industrial research in Pakistan; has rep. Pakistan at internat. scientific confs, etc. Gold Medal, Russian Acad.; President's Pride of Performance Medal (Pakistan), 1966. Elected Mem., Vatican Acad. of Sciences, 1964. Hon. DSc. *Address:* Postgraduate Institute of Chemistry, University of Karachi, Karachi, Pakistan. *T:* 413414.

**SIDDONS, Arthur Harold Makins,** MChir Cantab; FRCS; FRCP; Consultant Thoracic and General Surgeon, St George's Hospital, etc., since 1948; *b* 17 Jan. 1911; *s* of late A. W. Siddons, Housemaster, Harrow School; *m* 1st, 1939, Joan Richardson Anderson (*née* McConnell) (*d* 1949); one *s* one *d*; 2nd, 1956, Eleanor Mary Oliver (*née* Hunter) (*d* 1970). *Educ:* Harrow; Jesus College, Cambridge; St George's Hospital. MB, BCh Cantab 1935. Surgeon, St George's Hospital, 1941. Served RAF Medical Branch, 1942-46. Member of Court of Examiners, Royal College of Surgeons of England, 1958-63. *Publications:* Cardiac Pacemakers, 1967; sections on lung surgery in various textbooks. *Recreations:* sailing, travel. *Address:* 29 Old Church Street, SW3. *T:* 01-352 5251.

**SIDEBOTHAM, John Biddulph,** CMG 1946; MA Cantab; retired as Assistant Secretary, Colonial Office (1941-54); *b* 23 Nov. 1891; *er s* of late Rev. Frederick William Gilbert Sidebotham, MA, Rector of Weeting, Norfolk; *m* 1st, 1917, Hilda, *d* of late F. Haviland; one *d*; 2nd, 1941, Mary, *d* of late A. Blascheck. *Educ:* King's School, Canterbury; Gonville and Caius Coll., Cambridge (Stanhope Exhibitioner, Open Class Exhibitioner, Scholar). 1st cl. theolog. tripos, pt 1, 1914; BA 1914, MA 1920; 2nd Lieut Home Counties RE (TF), 1914; Lieut 1916; served in France, 1914-15 (wounded); Inland Revenue, Somerset House, 1920; transferred to Colonial Office as asst prin. under reconstruction scheme, Dec. 1922; sec. managing cttee, Bureau of Hygiene and Tropical Diseases, 1925; sec., East African guaranteed loan advisory cttee, 1927; pte sec. to Parliamentary Under-Sec. of State for Dominion Affairs, 1928; pte sec. Permt Under-Sec. for the Colonies, 1929, principal, 1930; accompanied Permt Under-Secretary of State for the Colonies (Sir J. Maffey) to W Indies, 1936. Visited St Helena, 1939 and 1955; also visited Ceylon, Borneo, Sarawak, Hong Kong, Fiji and Mauritius. Mem. managing cttee of Bureau of Hygiene and Tropical Diseases, 1941. *Address:* Lingen Way, Aymestrey, Nr Leominster, Herefordshire. *T:* Wigmore 358.

**SIDEBOTTOM, Edward John;** Divisional Inspector, Department of Education and Science, since 1969; *b* 1918; *s* of Ernest Sidebottom, Wylam, Northumberland; *m* 1949, Brenda Millicent, *d* of late Alec H. Sadler, Wandsworth. *Educ:* Queen Elizabeth Grammar School, Hexham; Hatfield College, Durham (BSc). Entered Iraq Government education service, 1939; lecturer, Leavesden Green Emergency Training College, 1946; County Youth Organiser for Hampshire, 1947; HM Inspector of Schools, 1949-. Sec. to Albemarle Cttee on the Youth Service in England and Wales, 1958-59; seconded as Principal, Nat. Coll. for the Training of Youth Leaders, 1960-64; Member, Unesco Internat. Adv. Cttee for Out-of-School Educn, 1968-. *Address:* 6 Tennis Mews, The Park, Nottingham.

**SIDEY, Air Marshal Ernest Shaw,** CB 1965; MD, ChB, DPH; Director-General, RAF Medical Services, since 1971; *b* 2 Jan. 1913; *s* of Thomas Sidey, Alyth, Perthshire; *m* 1946, Doreen Florence Lurring; one *d* (and one *d* decd). *Educ:* Morgan Acad., Dundee; St Andrews Univ. Commissioned in RAF, 1937. Served in Burma Campaign during War of 1939-45. Recent appts include: Chief, Med. Adv. Staff, Allied Air Forces Central Europe, 1957-59; PMO: Flying Trg Comd, 1961-63; Middle East Comd, 1963-65; Transport Command, 1965-66; DDGMS, RAF, 1966-68. PMO, Strike Command, 1968-70. QHS 1966-. *Recreations:* tennis, golf, bridge. *Address:* c/o Glyn, Mills & Co., Whitehall, SW1. *Club:* Royal Air Force.

**SIDEY, John MacNaughton,** DSO 1945; Chairman: Ferrymasters Ltd; Anglo Overseas Transport Co. Ltd and associated companies; Transport Committee of CBI, since 1967; Director, P&O Steam Navigation Co., since 1970; *b* 11 July 1914; *e c* of John and Florence Sidey; *m* 1941, Eileen, *o d* of Sir George Wilkinson, 1st Bt, KCVO; one *s* (one *d* decd). *Educ:* Exeter School. Served War, 1939-45, with Royal Tank Regiment and Westminster Dragoons, finishing as Lt-Col commanding 22nd Dragoons. Member Southern Area Board, BTC, 1955-61 (Chm. Jan.-Dec. 1962); part-time Mem., British Railways Bd, 1962-68; Chm., Eastern Region Bd, British Railways, 1963-65. Pres., London Chapter, Nat. Defence Transportation Assoc. of America, 1961-62. *Recreations:* fishing, golf, gardening. *Address:* Robinswood, Effingham, Leatherhead, Surrey. *T:* Bookham 5249.

**SIDEY, Thomas Kay Stuart,** CMG 1968; Managing Director, Wickliffe Press Ltd, since 1962; Barrister and Solicitor, NZ, since 1932; *b* 8 Oct. 1908; *s* of Sir Thomas Kay Sidey; *m* 1933, Beryl, *d* of Harvey Richardson Thomas,

Wellington, NZ; one *s* one *d*. *Educ:* Otago Boys' High School; Univ. of Otago (LLM). Served War of 1939-45 (despatches): 2nd NZEF; 4 years, Middle East and Italy, rank of Major. Dunedin City Council, 1947-50, 1953-65; Dep. Mayor, 1956-59, 1968-; Mayor, 1959-65; Univ. of Otago Council, 1947-, Pro-Chancellor, 1959-70, Chancellor, 1970-; Pres., Automobile Assoc. of Otago, 1967-; Chairman: Dunedin Metropol. Reg. Planning Authority; Otago Develt Council. Past President: Dunedin Chamber of Commerce; Automobile Assoc., Otago; Otago Trustee Savings Bank; NZ Library Assoc.; Otago Old People's Welfare Council; Otago Boys' High Sch. Old Boys' Soc. *Recreations:* fishing, boating, ski-ing. *Address:* 16 Tolcarne Avenue, Dunedin, New Zealand. *T:* 60,068. *Club:* Dunedin (Dunedin, NZ).

**SIDGWICK, Rear-Admiral John Benson,** CB 1945; RN retd; late Deputy Engineer-in-Chief, Admiralty. Served European War, 1914-18; Engineer Captain, 1936; Engineer Rear-Admiral, 1942. *Address:* c/o Ministry of Defence (Navy), SW1.

**SIDMOUTH,** 6th Viscount, *cr* 1805; **Raymond Anthony Addington;** Major late 26th (KGO) Light Cavalry; *b* 24 Jan. 1887; 2nd *s* of 4th Viscount Sidmouth and Ethel Mary (*d* 1954), *o d* of late Capt. Louis Charles Henry Tonge, RN, Highway Manor, Calne; *S* brother 1953; *m* 1913, Gladys Mary Dever, *d* of late Thomas Hughes, Commissioner of Chinese Customs; six *s* three *d*. *Educ:* Cheltenham; RMC Sandhurst. Served France, 1914-16 (3 medals); S Persia, 1918-19 (medal and bar); Waziristan, NW Frontier, India, 1920-21 (Medal and bar); retired, 1928. Served as Company Comdr, 1st Wilts Home Guard, 1940-44. *Heir: s* Hon. John Tonge Anthony Pellew Addington [*b* 3 Oct. 1914; *m* 1940, Barbara Mary Angela, *d* of Bernard Rochford; two *s* five *d*]. *Address:* Highway Manor, Calne, Wilts.

**SIDNEY,** family name of **Viscount De L'Isle.**

**SIDWELL, Martindale,** FRCO; FRAM; Organist and Choirmaster, Hampstead Parish Church, since 1946; Organist and Director of Music, St Clement Danes (Church of the RAF), since 1957; Conductor, Hampstead Choral Society, since 1946; Conductor, Martindale Sidwell Choir, since 1956; Professor of Organ, Trinity College of Music, since 1955; Professor of Organ, Royal Academy of Music, since 1963; Professor, Royal School of Church Music, 1958-66; Conductor, London Bach Orchestra, since 1967; *b* 23 Feb. 1916; *s* of John William Sidwell, Little Packington, Warwicks, and Mary Martindale, Liverpool; *m* 1944, Barbara Anne (*née* Hill) (Professional Pianist under the name Barbara Hill); two *s*. *Educ:* Wells Cathedral Sch., Somerset; Royal Academy of Music. Sub-Organist, Wells Cathedral, 1932. Served War of 1939-45, Royal Engineers, 1939. Organist, Holy Trinity Church, Leamington Spa, and Director of Music, Warwick School, 1943, also at same time Conductor of Royal Leamington Spa Bach Choir. Mem. Council, Royal Coll. of Organists, 1966-. Harriet Cohen Bach Medal, 1967. Frequent broadcasts as Conductor and as Organ Recitalist, 1944-. *Address:* 1 Frognal Gardens, Hampstead, NW3. *T:* 01-435 9210.

**SIE, Hon. Banja T.;** *see* Tejan-Sie.

**SIEFF,** family name of **Baron Sieff.**

**SIEFF,** Baron, *cr* 1966 (Life Peer), of Brimpton; **Israel Moses Sieff;** BCom; President, Marks & Spencer Ltd since 1967 (Chairman and Joint Managing Director, 1964, Vice-Chairman and Joint Managing Director, 1926); Farmer; Vice-President, World Jewish Congress and Chairman European Executive; Member, Executive, Jewish Agency; Hon. President, Zionist Federation of Great Britain and Ireland; *b* 4 May 1889; *s* of Ephraim Sieff, Manchester; *m* 1910, Rebecca Doro (*d* 1966), *d* of Michael Marks; two *s* one *d* (and one *s* decd). *Educ:* Manchester Grammar School; Manchester University. Joined Marks and Spencer, Ltd, 1915. Secretary, Zionist Commission, 1918; Vice-Pres., Multiple Shops Federation, 1946-61; Pres., Anglo-Israel Chamber of Commerce (Chm. 1950-65); Hon. Pres., Joint Palestine Appeal; Hon. Fellow and Mem. Bd of Govs, Weizmann Inst. of Science, Rehovoth (established Daniel Sieff Research Inst., Rehovoth, 1934); President, PEP (Chm., 1931-39, Vice-Chairman, 1939-64). Mem. Court of Patrons, RCS England; Chm. Bd of Governors, Carmel College; FRAI; FRGS; FBIM; Hon. FRCS 1968; Hon. LLD Manchester, 1969. *Publication:* The Memoirs of Israel Sieff, 1970. *Address:* Michael House, Baker Street, W1. *T:* 01-935 4422.

*See also J. E. Sieff, Hon. Marcus Sieff.*

**SIEFF, Joseph Edward;** Chairman, Marks & Spencer Ltd, since 1967 (Deputy Chairman, 1965, Vice-Chairman, 1963), and Joint Managing Director, since 1963 (Assistant Managing Director, 1946); *b* 28 Nov. 1905; *s* of Ephraim Sieff, Manchester; *m* 1929, Maisie, *d* of Dr Sidney Marsh; two *d*; *m* 1952, Lois, *d* of William Ross; one *s* one *d*. *Educ:* Manchester Grammar School; Manchester University. Joined Marks & Spencer Ltd, 1933. Chairman Joint Palestine Appeal, 1961-65, President 1965. Hon. Vice-President, Zionist Federation of Great Britain and Ireland, 1965. *Address:* Michael House, Baker St, W1. *T:* 01-935 4422. *Club:* Savile.

*See also Baron Sieff.*

**SIEFF, Hon. Marcus Joseph;** OBE 1944; Vice-Chairman, Marks and Spencer Ltd, since 1965, Joint Managing Director, since 1967; *b* 2 July 1913; *yr s* of Baron Sieff, *qv*; *m* 1st, 1937, Rosalie Fromson (marr. diss., 1947); one *s*; 2nd, 1951, Elsie Florence Gosen (marr. diss., 1953); 3rd 1956, Brenda Mary Beith (marr. diss., 1962); one *d*; 4th, 1963, Mrs Pauline Lily Moretzki (*née* Spatz); one *d*. *Educ:* Manchester Grammar School; St Paul's; Corpus Christi College, Cambridge (BA). Served War 1939-45, Royal Artillery. Joined Marks & Spencer Ltd, 1935; Dir, 1954; Asst Man. Dir, 1963. Mem., BNEC (Chm., Export Cttee for Israel, 1965-68). Vice-Pres., Joint Palestine Appeal. *Address:* Michael House, Baker Street, W1.

**SIEGBAHN, (Karl) Manne (Georg),** DrPhil; Professor at the Royal Academy of Sciences, Director Nobel Institute for Physics, Stockholm; *b* Örebro, Sweden, 3 Dec. 1886; *m* 1914, Karin Högbom; two *s*. *Educ:* Hudiksvall, Stockholm. Studied mathematics, physics, chemistry, astronomy for the Master degree at the University of Lund; further work in physics for the DrSc (1911); Lecturer in Physics at Lund, 1911-20; Professor of Physics, Lund, 1920-23; Upsala, 1923-36; Member of the Royal Acad. of Science, Sweden 1922; For. Mem., Royal Society, London; Member of the Academies in Paris, Moscow, Edinburgh, Copenhagen, Oslo, and Helsinki; Nobel Laureate, 1925; Hughes Medal of Royal Society, 1934; Rumford Medal of Royal Society, 1940; Duddel Medal of the Physical Society, London, 1948. Dr (hc) Univs in Paris, Oslo, Freiburg and Bucharest. *Publications:* The Spectroscopy of X-Rays, 1925; a number of scientific papers, especially on X-Rays. *Address:* Nobel Institute for Physics, 10405 Stockholm 50, Sweden.

**SIEPMANN, Charles Arthur,** MC; BA; Professor Emeritus, New York University, since 1967; *b* 10 Mar. 1899; *s* of Otto and Grace Florence Siepmann; *m* 1940, Charlotte Tyler; one *s* two *d*. *Educ:* Clifton Coll. (scholar); Keble Coll. Oxford (scholar). Served European War, 1917-18; Oxford, 1919-21; Brown Shipley and Co., 1922-24; housemaster and education officer, HM Borstal Instns, Feltham and Rochester, 1924-27; joined BBC, 1927; Dir of Talks, 1932-35, of Regional Relations, 1935-36, of Programme Planning, 1936-39; University Lecturer, Harvard University, 1939-42. Office of War Information, 1942-45, as Consultant, and, latterly, Deputy Director of its San Francisco Office; New York University: Professor of Education, then Professor of Communications, 1946-67. *Publications:* Radio in Wartime; Radio's Second Chance; Radio, TV and Society; TV and our School Crisis; Educational TV in the United States. *Recreations:* walking, reading. *Address:* 267 Main Street, New Canaan, Conn 06840, USA.

**SIERRA LEONE, Bishop of;** *see under* West Africa, Archbishop of.

**SIEVEKING, Captain Lancelot de Giberne,** DSC; (**Lance Sieveking**); Author, Playwright, Producer, British Broadcasting Corporation, retired from BBC, 1956; Freeman: The Merchant Taylors' Company; The City of London; *b* Harrow, 1896; 3rd *s* of late Edward G. Sieveking and late Isabel de Giberne Sieveking (writer, suffragist, cousin of Gerard Manley Hopkins); *m* 1st, 1924, April, 5th *d* of late Harry Quilter; one *s*; 2nd, 1929, Natalie, *e d* of Court Denny; two *d*; 3rd, 1949, Maisie, 3rd *d* of late Max John Christian Meiklejohn; one *s*. *Educ:* Switzerland; St Catharine's Coll., Cambridge. Began writing at age of six; aged 13 began novel illustrated by G. K. Chesterton which was published in 1924; between ages of 16 and 18 took part in Suffragist Movement, and followed development in science of flying at Hendon; reached normal university age, but joined Artists' Rifles, 1914; was taught to fly by Claude Graham-White; commissioned RN; served in HMS Riviera, seaplane carrier, North Sea, 1915; Royal Naval Air Service under General Smuts in East Africa, 1916; France, night bombing, Jan.-Oct. 1917; shot down over Rhine, Oct. 1917; prisoner of war in Germany, 1917-18; assisted in flying arrangements for Peace Conference at Versailles; resigned commission; owned and edited The New Cambridge, co-founded The Oxford and Cambridge Miscellany, toured as actor 1919-22; Assistant Inspector of Taxes, Sussex, 1922, resigned; commnd RAF, India, 1923-24; illustrated books, wrote; joined British Broadcasting Co. as assistant to Director of Education, 1924-26; started first Running Commentaries; successfully translated colour into sound; began producing plays; produced first television play in world, 1927-31; composed music, 1932; seconded to Canadian Broadcasting Corporation, 1938-39; West Regional Programme Director, 1942-44; Drama Script Editor, 1946-50; Radio and Stage Plays: Silence in Heaven, Kaleidoscope, The Pursuit of Pleasure (with Harold Scott), The Prophetic Camera, The End of Savoy Hill, Wings of the Morning, Arrest in Africa, Seven Ages of Mechanical Music, new English version of Ibsen's Ghosts; Radio Serial plays based on Stevenson's Dr Jekyll and Mr Hyde, H. G. Wells' The Wheels of Chance, Kipps, and Mr Polly, and F. Anstey's Vice Versa, etc., 1925-46; new English version of Ibsen's The Wild Duck, based on new translation by Arthur Vivian Burbury, 1947; An Echo from the Moon, 1948-49; Tono-Bungay, based on novel by H. G. Wells; The Longest Journey, and A Passage to India, by E. M. Forster, 1957; Christmas Pudding by Nancy Mitford; Decline and Fall by Evelyn Waugh; The Polyglots, by William Gerhardi, 1960; Radio serial plays based on The First Men in the Moon, and The War in the Air by H. G. Wells, The Purple Jewel; The Shadow of the Shark based on stories by G. K. Chesterton, 1953; Around The World in Eighty Days, and Twenty Thousand Leagues Under The Sea, by Jules Verne, 1961; Eng. version of Un Carnet de Bal, 1954; A Journey to the Centre of the Earth by Jules Verne: Howards End and A Room With A View, by E. M. Forster; Scoop by Evelyn Waugh; Fertility Rite; Survival Comes First. Films: The History of Mr Polly, by H. G. Wells, 1942; The Other Side of Silence, 1948; Soul of a Heel, 1954. *Publications:* The Psychology of Flying, Dressing-Gowns and Glue, 1919; Gladstone Bags and Marmalade, 1920; The Cud, 1922; Stampede (illustrated by G. K. Chesterton), 1924; The Ultimate Island, 1925; Bats in the Belfry (with John Nash), 1926; All Children Must be Paid For, 1927; Beyond This Point (with Francis Bruguiere), 1929; Smite and Spare Not, 1933; The Woman She Was, 1934; The Stuff of Radio, 1934; The Perfect Witch, 1935; Silence in Heaven, 1936; North American Binocular, 1948; A Tomb With a view, 1950; Soul of a Heel, 1952; The Ear and the Ice-cold Seat, 1953; The Double Who Wouldn't Quit, 1954; A Private Volcano, 1955; The Eye of The Beholder, 1957; Autobiography, 1971. *Recreations:* reading old letters, and looking at the pictures of Paul Nash. *Address:* The White House, Snape, Saxmundham, Suffolk. *T:* Snape 214. *Club:* Union (Cambridge).

**SIGNORET, Simone** (pseudonym of **Simone Henriette Charlotte Montand**); actress; *b* Wiesbaden, 25 March 1921; *d* of Jean Kaminker and Louise (*née* Signoret); *m* 1947, Yves Allegret (marriage dissolved, 1950), motion picture director; one *d*; *m* 1950, Yves Montand, actor and singer. *Educ:* Cours Sicard, Paris. Worked as a teacher and typist before becoming actress. Films include: Dédée d'Anvers, La Ronde, Casque d'Or, Thérèse Raquin, La Mort en ce Jardin, Room at the Top (Oscar), Adua e le Compagne, Term of Trial, Ship of Fools, The Deadly Affair, Games, The Seagull. Has also appeared on the stage (including Lady Macbeth, Royal Ct, London 1966), and on television. Has won many awards in France, USA, England, etc, including Oscar of Acad. of Motion Picture Arts and Sciences for best actress, 1960. *Address:* 15 Place Dauphine, Paris 1, France.

**SIKORSKY, Igor Ivan;** retired as Engineering Manager Sikorsky Aircraft Division of United Aircraft Corporation, Stratford, Connecticut, 1957, now Engineering Consultant; *b* Kiev, Russia, 25 May 1889; *s* of Ivan Sikorsky, Professor of Psychology at Univ. of St Vladimir, Kiev, Russia; *m* 1924, Elizabeth Semion; four *s* one *d*. *Educ:* Naval Academy, St Petersburg; Polytechnic Institute, Kiev. Started to work in aviation by constructing a helicopter, 1909; constructed several successful airplanes, 1910-12; produced and tested in flight the first successful 4-engined airplane, 1913; produced several 4-engined bombers for Russian Govt, 1914-17; organized Sikorsky Aero Engineering Corp. in US, 1923; successful twin-engined amphibian S-38 (used extensively for pioneering several of American airlines), 1928; ship also used by Govt; trans-oceanic clipper S-42, 1934, used for pioneering of trans-Pacific and trans-Atlantic air service; first successful and practical helicopter in Western Hemisphere, 1939; during later years, until 1957, designed several other types of successful helicopters which were used by Govt and private organizations and were first and only helicopters used by US during War of 1942-45. Several Hon. Degrees from Universities. Member following Societies: Quiet Birdmen; Early Birds; Aircraft Owners and Pilots Assoc.; American Soc. of Mech. Engineers; Soc. of Automotive Engineers; Aerospace Industries Assoc. of America; Nat. Aeronautic Assoc.; OX-5 Club of America; Benjamin Franklin Fellow, RSA (England); Amer. Inst. Aeronautics and Astronautics, Inc. (Hon. Fellow); Amer. Helicopter Soc.; Hon. FRAeS, 1955. Numerous awards (over 80) including Presidential Certificate of Merit, 1948; Silver Medal from Royal Aeronautical Society of England, 1949; James Watt International Medal (London), 1955; Chevalier, Légion d'Honneur, 1960. *Publications:* The Story of the Winged S, 1938; The Message of the Lord's Prayer, 1942; The Invisible Encounter, 1947. *Recreations:* travel, photography, astronomy. *Address:* Sikorsky Aircraft, Stratford, Conn 06602, USA. *Club:* Wings (NY).

**SILBERSTON, (Zangwill) Aubrey;** University Lecturer in Economics since 1953 and Fellow of St John's College since 1958, Cambridge; *b* 26 Jan. 1922; *s* of Louis and Polly Silberston; *m* 1945, Dorothy Marion, *d* of A. S. Nicholls; one *s* one *d*. *Educ:* Hackney Downs Sch., London; Jesus Coll., Cambridge. Econs Tripos Pt II, Cambridge, 1946. Courtaulds Ltd, 1946-50; Kenward Res. Fellow in Industrial Admin., St Catharine's Coll., Cambridge, 1950-53; Tutorial Bursar, St John's Coll., 1963-66; Dir of Studies in Econs, St John's Coll., 1965-; Chairman: Faculty Bd of Econs and Politics, 1966-70; Cttee of Management, Dept of Applied Economics, 1966; Member: Monopolies Commn, 1965-68; British Steel Corp., 1967-; Departmental Cttee on Patent System, 1967-70; Indep. Mem., Econ. Develt Cttee for Motor Manufacturing Industry, 1968-70. *Publications:* Education and Training for Industrial Management, 1955; (with George Maxcy) The Motor Industry, 1959; (in collaboration with C. Pratten and R. M. Dean) Economies of Large-scale Production in British Industry, 1965; (in collaboration with K. H. Boehm) The Patent System, 1967; articles in Econ. Jl, Bulletin of Oxford Inst. of Statistics, Jl of Royal Statistical Society. *Recreations:* music, ballet. *Address:* Field House, Conduit Head Road, Cambridge. *T:* 52583. *Club:* Royal Automobile.

**SILCOX, Albert Henry;** retired; Editor of British Trade Journal and Export World, and of Industria Britanica, 1957-61; Editor, Directory of British Exporters, 1957-61; Editor Directorio de Industrias Britanicas, 1957-61; Director, The Press at Coombelands Ltd, 1942-61; *b* 27 July 1895; *s* of late Henry Silcox, Bath, and Clara, *d* of late Samuel Cox, Bath; *m* 1924, Violet Lucy, *d* of Matthew J. Cooke; one *d*. *Educ:* Bath. Journalist since 1913; Bath Chronicle, Bath Herald; editor Enfield Weekly Herald, 1922-30; Editor: The Hardware Trade Jl, 1932-34; The Gas World, 1934-57. Mem., Institute of Fuel, since 1935; Freeman of Worshipful Co. of Gold and Silver Wyre Drawers; Freeman of City of London; Fellow, Ancient Monuments Soc., 1959; served with Somerset LI European War in India, Mesopotamia, Afghanistan and Egypt, 1914-19; commissioned to 3rd Surrey Bn Home Guard, 1941. *Publications:* Specialist writer on iron and steel, export trade, etc. *Address:* Whytecotte, 21 Melrose Road, Weybridge, Surrey. *T:* Weybridge 47016. *Clubs:* Press, City Livery.

**SILK, Dennis Raoul Whitehall;** Warden of Radley College since 1968; *b* 8 Oct. 1931; 2nd *s* of Rev. Dr Claude Whitehall Silk and Mrs Louise Silk; *m* 1963, Diana Merilyn, 2nd *d* of W. F. Milton, Pitminster, Somerset; two *s* two *d*. *Educ:* Christ's Hosp.; Sidney Sussex Coll., Cambridge (Exhibr). BA (History) Cantab. Asst Master, Marlborough Coll., 1955-68 (Housemaster, 1957-68). *Publications:* Cricket for Schools, 1964; Attacking Cricket, 1965. *Recreations:* antiquarian, literary, sporting (Blues in cricket (Capt. Cambridge Univ. CC, 1955) and Rugby football). *Address:* The Warden's House, Radley College, Abingdon, Berks. *T:* Abingdon 585. *Club:* Hawks (Cambridge).

**SILKIN,** family name of **Baron Silkin.**

**SILKIN,** 1st Baron, *cr* 1950, of Dulwich; **Lewis Silkin,** PC 1945; CH 1965; a partner in the firm of Lewis Silkin & Partners, Solicitors; *b* 1889; *m* 1st, 1915, Rosa Neft (*d* 1947); three *s*; 2nd, 1948, Mrs Frieda M. Johnson (*d* 1963); 3rd, 1964, Marguerite Schlageter. *Educ:* Elementary and secondary schools; London University. Solicitor. MP (Lab) Peckham Division of Camberwell, 1936-50; Minister of Town and Country Planning, 1945-50; Deputy Leader of the Official Opposition, House of Lords, 1955-64. Chairman of Town Planning Cttee of LCC, 1940-45. *Heir: s* (Hon.) Arthur Silkin, *qv*. *Address:* 24 Victoria Road, W8. *T:* 01-937 4322; Green Shadows, Chase Lane, Haslemere. *T:* Haslemere 2285; (Office) 7 Storey's Gate, SW1. *T:* 01-839 4223.

*See also Rt Hon. J. E. Silkin, Hon. S. C. Silkin.*

**SILKIN, Arthur;** serving in Commission on Industrial Relations; *b* 20 Oct. 1916; *e s* and *heir* of 1st Baron Silkin, *qv*; *m* 1969, Audrey Bennett. *Educ:* Dulwich College; Peterhouse, Cambridge. BA 1938; Diploma in Govt Administration, 1959. Served 1940-45, Royal Air Force (A and SD Branch), Pilot Officer, 1941, subsequently Flying Officer. Entered Ministry of Labour and National Service, 1939; formerly 2nd Secretary, British Embassy, Paris. First Secretary: High Commissioner's Office, Calcutta, 1960-61; British Embassy, Dakar, May 1962-Mar. 1964; British Embassy, Kinshasa, 1964-66. *Address:* Cuzco, 33 Woodnook Road, SW16. *T:* 01-677 8733.

*See also Rt Hon. J. E. Silkin, Hon. S. C. Silkin.*

**SILKIN, Rt. Hon. John Ernest,** PC 1966; MP (Lab) Deptford since July 1963; *b* 18 March 1923; *y s* of 1st Baron Silkin, *qv*; *m* 1950, Rosamund John (actress), *d* of Frederick Jones; one *s*. *Educ:* Dulwich College; University of Wales; Trinity Hall, Cambridge. BA 1944; LLB 1946; MA 1949. Joined Royal Navy, 1941, Lieutenant-Commander RNVR, served in HMS King George V and HMS Formidable. Admitted a Solicitor, 1950. contested (Lab): St Marylebone, 1950; West Woolwich, 1951; South Nottingham, 1959. Government Pairing Whip, 1964-Jan. 1966; Lord Commissioner of the Treasury, Jan.-April 1966; Treasurer of the Household and Government Deputy Chief Whip, April-July 1966; Parly Sec. to the Treasury, and Govt Chief Whip, 1966-69; Minister of Public Building and Works, 1969-70. *Address:* 7 Storey's Gate, SW1. *T:* 01-839 4222. *Clubs:* Garrick, Royal Automobile.

*See also Arthur Silkin, Hon. S. C. Silkin.*

**SILKIN, Hon. Samuel Charles,** QC 1963; MP (Lab) Camberwell, Dulwich, since October 1964; Recorder of Bedford since 1966; *b* 6 March 1918; 2nd *s* of 1st Baron Silkin, *qv*; *m* 1941, Elaine Violet (*née* Stamp); two *s* two *d*. *Educ:* Dulwich College; Trinity Hall, Cambridge (BA). Called to Bar, Middle

Temple, 1941, Bencher 1969. Served War of 1939-45, Lt-Col RA (despatches). Member, Royal Commission on the Penal System for England and Wales, 1965-66. Chairman: Parly Labour Party's Group on Common Market and European Affairs, 1966-; Select Cttee on Parly Privilege, 1967; Soc. of Labour Lawyers, 1964-. Leader, UK Delegn to Assembly of Council of Europe, 1968-70; Chm. Council of Europe Legal Cttee, 1966-70. *Recreation:* politics. *Address:* Lamb Building, Temple, EC4.

*See also Arthur Silkin, Rt. Hon. J. E. Silkin.*

**SILLARS, James;** MP (Lab) South Ayrshire since March 1970; Head of Organization and Social Services Department, Scottish TUC, since 1968; *b* Ayr, 4 Oct. 1937; *s* of Matthew Sillars; *m* 1957, Anne O'Farrell; one *s* one *d.* *Educ:* Newton Park Sch., Ayr; Ayr Academy. Former official, Fire Brigades Union; Past Member Ayr Town Council and Ayr County Council Educn Cttee; Mem., T&GWU. Full-time Labour Party agent, 1964 and 1966 elections. Especially interested in education, social services, industrial relations, development policies. *Publication:* Labour Party pamphlet on Scottish Nationalism. *Recreations:* reading, camping, tennis, swimming. *Address:* House of Commons, SW1.

**SILLERY, Anthony,** CVO 1947; MA, DPhil; *b* 19 April 1903; *s* of late Lt-Col C. C. A. Sillery, Indian Army, and Edith Charlotte Sillery, Scalby, Scarborough, Yorkshire; *m* 1941, Valentine Mary Kennerly, *d* of late A. H. Goddard; two *d.* *Educ:* Perse School; St John's College, Oxford. Provincial Administration, Tanganyika Territory, 1925-42; Deputy Provincial Comr, 1944; seconded for service in Occupied Territories Administration, Madagascar, 1942; served War of 1939-45 with MEF, 1943-46, with rank of Lt-Col in British Military Administrations, Tripolitania and Cyrenaica, and in Civil Affairs Branch, GHQ Middle East; Resident Commissioner, Bechuanaland Protectorate, 1947-50; retired, 1951. Secretary Taylor Institution, Oxford, 1951-70. FRHistSoc. *Publications:* The Bechuanaland Protectorate, 1952; Sechele, 1954; Africa, 1961; Founding a Protectorate, 1965; articles connected with Africa, in various periodicals. *Recreations:* winter sports, fishing, African studies. *Address:* 24 Walton St, Oxford. *T:* 58261. *Club:* Ski Club of Great Britain.

**SILLINCE, William Augustus,** RWS; FSIA; RBA; Lecturer in Graphic Design, Hull Regional College of Art, since 1952; *b* 16 Nov. 1906; *er s* of Commander W. P. Sillince, RN, and of Lucy May Sillince; *m* 1938, Muriel Theresa Wynne; one *s.* *Educ:* Osborne House, Romsey. Studied at Polytechnic School of Art, and Central School of Arts and Crafts. Designer for advertising, 1928-36. Free-lance illustrator, contributor to Punch, 1936-. Part-time teacher, Brighton College of Art, 1949-52. Designed Alice in Wonderland Room at Burton Constable Hall, 1967. Work in public collections: British Museum, Science Museum, Imperial War Museum, National Gallery of New Zealand, and in municipal galleries of Sunderland, Worthing and Hull; one-man exhibn of water-colour drawings, Senior Common Room, Hull Univ., 1966. *Publications:* Comic Drawing, 1950; contrib. poems to Yorkshire Life, 1966; *collections of drawings:* We're all in it, 1941; We're still all in it, 1942; United Notions, 1943; Combined Observations, 1944; Minor Relaxations, 1945; *illustrated books include:* Wine, Water and Song, 1943; Even the Parrot, 1944; My Friend Serafin, 1949; This Merrie English, 1954; It don't cost you a Penny, 1955; Basic British, 1956; The Saint and the Boy, 1957; David John hears about Jesus, 1960; The Jet Beads, 1961; Before Jesus Came, 1963. Illustrator of: Pray Silence, 1964. Creator of BBC (North) Television series John Bull's Other Region, 1965. Contributor to Yorkshire Post, 1964-. *Recreations:* looking about, archery. *Address:* 6 Hymers Avenue, Hull; College of Art, Hull, Yorks. *Clubs:* Toby, Cartoonists; Archer-Antiquaries; Literary (Hull).

**SILLITOE, Alan;** Writer since 1948; *b* 4 March 1928; *s* of Christopher Archibald Sillitoe and Sylvina (*née* Burton); *m* 1952, Ruth Esther Fainlight; one *s.* *Educ:* various elementary schoools in Nottingham. Raleigh Bicycle Factory, 1942; wireless operator, RAF, 1946. Travelled in France, Italy, and Spain, 1952-58. Literary Adviser to W. H. Allen, 1970-. *Publications:* Saturday Night and Sunday Morning (Authors' Club Award for best first novel of 1958; filmed, 1960, play, 1964); The Loneliness of the Long Distance Runner, 1959 (Hawthornden Prize; filmed, 1962); The General, 1960 (filmed 1967 as Counterpoint); The Rats and Other Poems, 1960; Key to the Door, 1961; The Ragman's Daughter, 1963; Road to Volgograd (travel), 1964; A Falling Out of Love (poems), 1964; The Death of William Posters (novel), 1965; A Tree on Fire (novel), 1967; The City Adventures of Marmalade Jim (children), 1967; Love in the Environs of Voronezh (poems), 1968; Guzman, Go Home (stories), 1968; (with Ruth Fainlight) All Citizens are Soldiers (play), 1969 (based on Lope de Vega, Fuente Ovejuna; first perf. Theatre Royal, Stratford, 1967); This Foreign Field (first perf. Roundhouse, 1970); A Start in Life (novel), 1970. *Recreation:* travel. *Address:* 21 The Street, Wittersham, Kent.

**SILONE, Ignazio;** Writer and Politician; *b* Pescina dei Marsi, Abruzzi, Italy, 1 May 1900; *s* of Paolo and Annamaria Delli Quadri; *m* 1944, Darina Laracy, Dublin. *Educ:* various Catholic private and public schools. One of the leaders of the Italian Socialist Youth Movement, 1917-21; member Central Committee of Italian Communist Party and editor of various newspapers, 1921-29; in 1930 left Communist Party and has since been active mainly as an independent writer; with three warrants for arrest for underground political activity issued against him by the Fascist Special Tribunal, he was forced to go into exile in Switzerland, where he lived until the autumn of 1944; Member Executive Committee of Italian Socialist Party, 1941-47; Member of Italian Constituent Assembly, 1946-48; is now non-party independent Socialist. Pres. Italian Pen Club, 1945-59; Chm. Italian Cttee for Cultural Freedom; Co-Editor of Tempo Presente. *Publications:* Fontamara (novel), 1933; Fascism: its Origins and Growth (history), 1934; Mr Aristotle (short stories), 1935; Bread and Wine (novel), 1937; The School for Dictators (dialogues), 1938; Mazzini (essay and selected pages), 1939; The Seed beneath the Snow (novel), 1941; And He did Hide Himself (play), 1944; The God that failed (essay), 1950; A Handful of Blackberries (novel), 1953; The Secret of Luca (novel), 1959; The Fox and the Camellias (novel), 1961; Emergency Exit (essays), 1965; The Story of a Humble Christian (play), 1969. *Recreation:* watching football matches. *Address:* Via di Villa Ricotti 36, Rome, Italy.

**SILSOE,** 1st Baron, *cr* 1963; **Arthur Malcolm Trustram Eve;** 1st Bt, *cr* 1943 (as Sir Malcolm Trustram Eve); GBE 1950; MC, TD; QC 1935; Gentleman Usher of the Purple Rod in the Order of the British Empire, 1960-69; Independent Chairman Cement Makers'

Federation, 1951-70; President Cembureau (International Cement Makers' Association), 1952-70; Director: Yorkshire Insurance Co. Ltd, 1949-66; New River Co. Ltd, 1954-70; Governor Peabody Trust, 1957-65; Director, St Martin's Property Corp. Ltd, 1961-70; Hon. Treasurer, Royal College of Nursing, 1964-70; *b* 8 April 1894; *e s* of late Sir Herbert Trustram Eve, KBE, and late Fanny Jean Turing; *m* 1st, 1927, Marguerite (*d* 1945), *d* of late Sir Augustus Meredith Nanton, Winnipeg; twin *s*; 2nd, 1946, Margaret Elizabeth, *d* of late Henry Wallace Robertson, Ayton, Berwickshire. *Educ:* Winchester; Christ Church, Oxford, MA. Served European War, 1914-19; Gallipoli, 1915 and Egypt and Palestine, 1916-19; Capt. Royal Welch Fusiliers; GSO3 53rd Division, 1917; Brigade Major 159th Infantry Brigade, 1918-19; called to Bar, Inner Temple, 1919, Bencher, 1942, Treasurer, 1966; commanded 6th Bn Royal Welch Fusiliers, 1927-31; Col (TA) 1931; Chm. Air Transport Licensing Authority, 1938-39; AA and QMG, 1939; Brigadier, 1940; Chairman: War Damage (1941), War Works (1945), and Local Govt Boundary (1945) Commissions until 1949; Building Apprenticeship and Training Council, 1943-47; Central Land Board, 1947-49; Burnham Cttees on Teachers' Salaries, 1950-53; Police Council on Police Salaries, 1951; St George's Hosp. Medical School, 1948-54; Governors of St George's Hosp., 1952-54; Road Haulage Disposal Board, 1953-56; Lord Mayor's National Flood and Tempest Distress Fund, 1953; Prime Minister's Cttee on Administration of Crown Lands, 1955; First Crown Estate Commissioner, 1954-62; First Church Estates Commissioner, 1954-69 (Third Church Estates Commissioner, 1952-54). Electoral Boundaries Commission, Mauritius, 1957; Chairman, Fiji, Sugar Inquiry Commission, 1961; President, Ski Club of Great Britain, 1950-54; Member General Council of King Edward's Hospital Fund for London, 1953; Member Church Assembly, 1952-57; Commissioner, Fiji Coconut Industry Inquiry, 1963; Hon. Member: Royal Institution Chartered Surveyors; Chartered Auctioneers' and Estate Agents' Institute; Hon. Vice-Pres. Town Planning Institute; Hon. Fellow Inst. of Municipal Treasurers and Accountants: Hon. FIOB. *Recreations:* ski-ing (Pres. Kandahar Ski Club, 1963-) and golf. *Heir:* *s* Hon. David Malcolm Trustram Eve, *qv*. *Address:* Lower Ballacottier, Kirk Onchan, Isle of Man. *T:* Douglas 5687. *Club:* Oxford and Cambridge University.

**SILVER, Prof. Peter H. S.;** *see* Spencer-Silver.

**SILVER, Prof. Robert Simpson;** CBE 1967; FRSE; FIMechE; FInstP. james Watt Professor of Mechanical Engineering, University of Glasgow, since 1967; *b* Montrose, Angus, 13 March 1913; *s* of Alexander Clark Silver and Isabella Simpson; *m* 1937, Jean McIntyre Bruce, *er d* of Alexander and Elizabeth Bruce (*née* Livingstone); two *s*. *Educ:* Montrose Academy; University of Glasgow. MA, 1932; BSc (1st Class Hons Nat. Phil) 1934; PhD 1938; DSc 1945. Research Physicist, ICI (Explosives), 1936-39; Head of Research, G. & J. Weir Ltd, 1939-46; Asst Director, Gas Research Board, 1947-48; Director of Research, Federated Founderies Ltd, 1948-54; Chief Designer, John Brown Land Boilers Ltd, 1954-56; Chief of Development and Research, G. & J. Weir Ltd, 1956-62 (Director 1958-); Prof. of Mech. Engrng, Heriot-Watt Coll. (now Univ.), 1962-66. FInstP 1942; MIMechE 1953; FRSE 1963. Unesco Prize for Science, 1968. *Publications:* Papers on physics and engineering, with special emphasis on thermodynamics, desalination, combustion, phase-change, and heat transfer; also on philosophy of science and education; a few poems, as Robert Simpson. *Recreations:* fishing, music, theatre, Scottish history and affairs. *Address:* 14 Beech Avenue, Glasgow, S1. *T:* 041-427 1322; Oakbank, Tobermory, Isle of Mull. *T:* Tobermory 24. *Clubs:* Royal Over-Seas League; Royal Scottish Automobile (Glasgow).

**SILVERMAN, Herbert A.;** Industrial Consultant; *b* Leeds; *m* Margaret Pennington; two *d*. *Educ:* City of Leeds School; Univ. of Leeds (Senior City Scholar). Formerly Lecturer in Economics and Senior Tutor for Adult Education, University of Birmingham; Head of Department of Adult Education, University College, and Director of Vaughan College, Leicester; Director of Industrial Surveys, Nuffield College, Oxford. *Publications:* The Substance of Economics; The Economics of Social Problems; The Groundwork of Economics; Taxation: its Incidence and Effects; Economics of the Industrial System; Studies in Industrial Organisation (Nuffield College). Contributor to Adult Education in Practice, Consumer's Co-operation in Great Britain, Chambers's Encyclopædia, etc., and on industrial and financial subjects to various journals. *Address:* Sidmouth House, Sidmouth, Devon. *T:* Sidmouth 3963.

**SILVERMAN, Julius;** MP (Lab) Aston Division of Birmingham since 1955 (Erdington Division of Birmingham, 1945-55); Barrister-at-law; *b* Leeds, 8 Dec. 1905; *s* of Nathan Silverman; *m* 1959, Eva Price. *Educ:* Central High School, Leeds (Matriculated). Entered Gray's Inn as student in 1928; called to Bar, 1931; joined Midland Circuit, 1933, practised in Birmingham since; Birmingham City Councillor, 1934-45; contested Moseley Division, 1935. *Address:* 31 Wheatsheaf Road, Birmingham 16.

**SILVERSTONE, Sir Arnold,** Kt 1964; Director of Companies; *b* 28 Sept. 1911; *y s* of late Henry and Rebecca Silverstone; *m* 1937, Lillian King; no *c*. *Educ:* Llanelly County Intermediate School; University College, Swansea. Served with HM Forces, 1940-45; Major, 1944. Called to the Bar, Middle Temple, 1953. Contested (C) East Ham North, 1955; Jt Treas., Greater London Area, Cons. Central Office. Governor, Queen Charlotte's and Chelsea Hosps; Member: Cttee of Management Inst of Obstetrics and Gynæcology; Roy. Homeopathic Hosp. Management Cttee, 1964-65; Rep. Council, Family Welfare Assoc., 1961-65. Freeman of City of London; Member of Court of Worshipful Company of Needlemakers. *Address:* Gale, Chelwood Gate, Haywards Heath, Sussex. *T:* Chelwood Gate 208; 45 Lowndes Sq., SW1. *T:* 01-235 3097. *Clubs:* Junior Carlton, Carlton.

**SILVERWOOD-COPE, Maclachlan Alan Carl,** CBE 1959; Counsellor, Foreign and Commonwealth Office; *b* 15 Dec. 1915; *s* of late Alan Lachlan Silverwood-Cope and late Elizabeth Masters; *m* 1940, Hilkka (*née* Halme); one *s* one *d*. *Educ:* Malvern College. FCA 1938. HM Forces, 1939-45 (Major, RA). Foreign (later Diplomatic) Service, 1939-: served as 3rd Sec., Stockholm, 1945-50; 1st Sec., Washington, 1951 and 1956-57; Tokyo, 1952-55; Copenhagen, 1960-64; Counsellor, Buenos Aires, 1966-68. Home Front Medal (Finland), 1940; Freedom Cross (Norway), 1945. *Recreations:* tennis, bridge, music. *Address:* 20 Radnor Walk, SW3. *T:* 01-352 5213. *Club:* Hurlingham.

**SILVESTER, Frederick John;** Account Executive, J. Walter Thompson, since 1960; *b* 20 Sept. 1933; *s* of William Thomas Silvester and Kathleen Gertrude (*née* Jones); unmarried. *Educ:* Sir George Monoux Grammar Sch.; Sidney Sussex Coll., Cambridge. Called to the Bar, Gray's Inn, 1957. Teacher, Wolstanton Grammar School, 1955-57; Political Education Officer, Conservative Political Centre, 1957-60. Member, Walthamstow Borough Council, 1961-64; Chairman, Walthamstow West Conservative Association, 1961-64; MP (C) Walthamstow West, Sept. 1967-70. *Address:* 18 Aberdeen Gardens, Leigh-on-Sea, Essex.

**SILVESTER, Norman Langton,** MSc, FRMetS, FRSA; FMA; Curator Russell-Cotes Art Gallery and Museum, Bournemouth, 1932-58, retired; *b* 28 Sept. 1894; *s* of Samuel Joseph Silvester; *m* 1922, Dora Ellwood; three *d*. *Educ:* King's College, London. Graduated with 1st Class Honours London University, BSc 1920, MSc 1922; Lieut RNVR attached to RNAS, European War, 1914-18; formerly Curator Public Art Gallery and Museum, Doncaster; Pioneer of idea of Borrowing Pictures from Public Art Galleries for the Home, inaugurated Bournemouth, 1933; Vice-President, Medical Art Society; "Beggar extraordinary" for Geological Terrace, Bournemouth, 1951. *Publications:* Bulletin and Critical and Explanatory Catalogues of the above; Papers on Meteorology and Airship Navigation and Geology in Proceedings of Meteorological, Aeronautical and Geological Societies. *Recreations:* wood carving, skating. *Address:* 17 Braidley Rd, Bournemouth, Hants. *T:* Bournemouth 24277.

**SILVESTER, Victor Marlborough,** OBE 1961; *b* 25 Feb. 1900; 2nd *s* of Rev. J. W. P. Silvester, sometime Vicar of Wembley, Middlesex; *m* 1922, Dorothy Francis Newton; one *s*. *Educ:* Ardingly College, Sussex; St John's, Leatherhead, Surrey; John Lyons, Harrow, Middlesex. Served European War, 1914-18, London Scottish and Argyll and Sutherland Highlanders, 1915-18. Started as a dancer, 1918; Winner of the World's Professional Ballroom Championship, 1922. Formed orchestra, 1935; has broadcast for the BBC, made records and televised ever since. Pres. Imperial Soc. of Teachers of Dancing Incorporated. Italian Bronze Medal for Military Valour, 1917. *Publications:* Modern Ballroom Dancing, 1927 (56th edn, 1964); Theory and Technique of Ballroom Dancing, 1933; The Art of the Ballroom, 1936; Dancing is my Life, 1959. *Recreation:* physical culture. *Address:* 19 Boydell Court, St John's Wood Park, NW8. *T:* 01-586 1234.

**SILYN ROBERTS, Air Vice-Marshal (retired) Glynn,** CB 1959; CBE 1949; AFC 1939; *b* 2 April 1906; *s* of late R. Silyn Roberts, MA, and Mrs M. Silyn Roberts, MBE, BA. *Educ:* Bangor. Permanent Commission, RAF, 1930; No. 2 Squadron, 1930-32; Home Aircraft Depot 1932; Experimental Flying Dept, RAE, 1935; Aircraft Depot, Iraq, 1939; Chief Technical Officer, Empire Central Flying Sch., 1942; Dep. Dir Technical Development, MAP, 1943 (despatches); Director of Aircraft Research and Development, MAP, 1945; Commanding Officer, Experimental Flying Dept, RAE, 1947; Sen. Technical Staff Officer, No. 2 Group, Jan. 1949; Dep. Dir Military Aircraft Research and Development, Min. of Supply, Dec. 1949; Principal Dir of Aircraft Research and Development, Min. of Supply, 1955; Sen. Technical Staff Officer, Bomber Command, 1956; Dir-Gen. of Engineering, Air Min., 1958-61; retd, Nov. 1961. MSc, CEng, FRAeS. *Recreations:* fishing, shooting (Hon. Life Vice-Pres. RAF Small Arms Assoc.). *Address:* c/o Glyn, Mills & Co., Kirkland House, 22 Whitehall, SW1. *Clubs:* Royal Air Force, Royal Aero.

**SIM, Alastair,** CBE 1953; Hon. LLD Edin. 1951; Actor-Producer; *b* 9 October 1900; *s* of Alexander Sim, JP, and Isabella McIntyre; *m* 1932, Naomi Plaskitt; one *d*. *Educ:* Edinburgh. Fulton Lecturer in Elocution at New College, Edinburgh, 1925-30. Rector of Edinburgh University, 1948-51. First Stage appearance as Messenger in Othello, Savoy, 1930; Cardinal in The Venetian, Little and Apollo, 1931; played same in New York Old Vic Season, 1932-33. Produced and/or played in the following plays by James Bridie in London: Holy Isle, Mr Bolfry, It Depends What You Mean, Forrigan Reel, Dr Angelus, The Anatomist, Mr Gillie; produced and played in The Brass Butterfly by William Golding, London; produced A Clean Kill by Michael Gilbert, London; produced (with George Cole) and played in The Bargain, by Michael Gilbert, London; played Prospero in The Tempest, Old Vic; Shylock in The Merchant of Venice, Nottingham Playhouse; produced and played in Windfall, by Michael Gilbert, played in: Too True to be Good, London; The Clandestine Marriage, Chichester, 1966; Number 10, Strand, 1967; The Magistrate, Chichester and London, 1969; The Jockey Club Stakes, Vaudeville, 1970; appeared several times as Captain Hook in Peter Pan. Appeared in films since 1934. *Recreations:* tennis, swimming, chess. *Address:* Forrigan, Newnham Hill, Henley-on-Thames, Oxon. *Club:* Garrick.

**SIM, Sir Alexander;** *see* Sim, Sir G. A. S.

**SIM, David,** CMG 1946; retired; Deputy Minister of National Revenue for Customs and Excise, Canada, 1943-65; *b* Glasgow, Scotland, 4 May 1899; *s* of David Sim, and Cora Lilian Angus; *m* 1924, Ada Helen Inrig (*d* 1958); one *s* one *d*; *m* 1960, Winnifred Emily Blois. *Educ:* Haghill Public School, Glasgow; Kitchener-Waterloo Collegiate. Served European War, Canadian Army in Canada and Overseas with the 1st Canadian Infantry Battalion (wounded at Passchendaele). Bank of Nova Scotia, 1919-25; Waterloo Trust & Savings Co., 1926; Secretary to Minister of National Revenue, 1927-33; Commissioner of Excise, 1933-43; Administrator of Alcoholic Beverages, 1942-45; Administrator of Tobacco, 1942-46; Dir Commodity Prices Stabilization Corporation; Member of External Trade Advisory Cttee and Nat. Joint Council of the Public Service of Canada; Member, Board of Broadcast Governors, 1966-. Past President: Rotary Club; Canadian Club. Mem. Canadian delegation to: 1st Session of Preparatory Cttee for Internat. Conf. on Trade and Employment, London, 1946; 2nd Session of Preparatory Cttee for UN Conf. on Trade and Employment, Geneva, 1947. General Service, Victory, Jubilee and Coronation Medals. *Recreations:* golf, fishing, curling, reading. *Address:* 1833 Riverside Drive, Apt 616, Ottawa, Ontario, Canada. *Clubs:* Rideau, Canadian, Royal Ottawa Golf, Curling, Five Lakes Fishing (Ottawa).

**SIM, Sir (George) Alexander (Strachan),** Kt 1956; Director: Yule Catto & Co. Ltd 1956; Tote Investors Ltd, 1963; Director, The Cementation Co. Ltd, 1961, Deputy Chairman, 1963; *b* 18 Dec. 1905; *s* of late George Gall Sim, CSI, CIE and of Margaret Byers Sim; *m* 1938, Florence May, *d* of late Jesse James Smith; one *d*. *Educ:* Winchester College. CA (Edinburgh), 1930. Director, Andrew Yule and Co. Ltd (Calcutta), 1939, Dep. Chm., 1948, Chm., 1953-56;

Commissioner for the Port of Calcutta, 1950-55; Vice-Pres., Bengal Chamber of Commerce and Industry, 1954-55, Pres., 1955-56; Pres., Associated Chambers of Commerce of India, 1955-56; Director: W. T. Henleys Telegraph Works Co. Ltd, 1957-59 (Chm., 1958-59); Peirce Leslie & Co. Ltd, 1964-68. Chm., Horserace Totalisator Board, 1961-70. *Recreation:* golf. *Address:* Lashenden, Biddenden, Kent. *T:* Biddenden 239. *Clubs:* Oriental; Bengal, Royal Calcutta Golf, Royal Calcutta Turf, Tollygunge (Calcutta).

**SIM, Sir Wilfrid (Joseph),** KBE 1951; MC 1918; QC (New Zealand), 1939; *b* 3 Nov. 1890; *s* of William Alexander Sim, a Judge of Supreme Court and Court of Appeal of New Zealand; *m* 1921, Hazel Dashwood Hill (*d* 1950), Christchurch, NZ; one *s* one *d*. *Educ:* Otago Boys' High School, Dunedin, NZ; Collegiate School, Wanganui, NZ; Victoria College University, NZ. Admitted to Bar, NZ, 1913. President NZ National Party, 1944-51. Served European War, 1914-18. NZ Expeditionary Force, Samoa, 1914; Argyll and Sutherland Highlanders, 1915-18 (Salonika), Médaille d'Honneur (France). Practised in Christchurch, NZ (Duncan, Cotterill and Co.), 1919-39, and, after taking silk, subsequently in Wellington. Member, Christchurch City Council, 1925-27, and Chairman, Citizens' Association, 1927-29. Trustee of Wanganui Collegiate School, 1939-; NZ Adv. Cttee for Doctor Barnardo's Homes. Director, Mount Cook Tourist Co. Member, Law Revision Cttee (now Law Revision Commission), 1936-69. *Publications:* Sim's Practice of Supreme Court and Court of Appeal, NZ, 1966; Sim on Divorce, 1965. *Recreations:* golf, gardening. *Address:* 74 Upland Road, Wellington, NZ. *Clubs:* Wellington (Wellington, NZ); Christchurch (Christchurch, NZ).

**SIMCOCK, Rev. Canon James Alexander;** Canon Residentiary and Treasurer of Truro Cathedral since 1951; *b* 19 Dec. 1897; *m* 1923, Mary Dorothy, *d* of Rev. T. R. Pennington; one *s*. *Educ:* Egerton Hall, Manchester. Deacon, 1922; Priest, 1923; Curate of: St Luke, Weaste, 1922-24; Milnrow, 1924-27; Incumbent of St Mark, Chadderton, 1927-31; Rector of St Mark, Newton Heath, 1931-33; Organising Secretary, Church of England Children's Soc., for Dioceses of Bath and Wells, Exeter and Truro, and Curate of St Martin, Exminster, 1933-36; Rector of Calstock, 1936-43; Surrogate, 1939-; Vicar of St Gluvias with Penryn, 1943-51. Rural Dean of S Carnmath, 1946-49; Hon. Canon of St Germoe in Truro Cathedral, 1948-51. *Address:* The Mission House, 21 Old Bridge Street, Truro, Cornwall. *T:* Truro 2059. *Club:* Royal Over-Seas League.

**SIME, William Arnold,** MBE 1946; QC 1957; Recorder of Great Grimsby since 1963; *b* 8 Feb. 1909; *s* of William Sime, Wepener, OFS, South Africa, and Bedford, and Charlotte Edith Sime; *m* 1938, Rosemary Constance, *d* of Dr Cleaton Roberts, West Byfleet, Surrey; two *d*. *Educ:* Grahamstown, CP; Bedford School; Balliol College, Oxford. Called to the Bar, Inner Temple, 1932 (Master of the Bench, 1964); Recorder of Grantham, 1954-57, 1958-63; a Senior Puisne Judge, Cyprus, 1957-58; Senior Judge (non-resident) of the Sovereign Base Areas, Cyprus, 1960-. Served War of 1939-45 with RAF; Wing Comdr. *Recreations:* golf, cricket (captained Bedfordshire CCC, 1931-33, and Nottinghamshire CCC, 1947-50); Rugby (captained Bedford RUFC, 1932-37); racing. *Address:* Witsend, Wymeswold, Leicestershire. *T:* Wymeswold 880254; 6 King's Bench Walk, Temple, EC4. *Clubs:* Carlton, MCC; Nottinghamshire (Nottingham).

**SIMENON, Georges;** Novelist; *b* Liège, Belgium, 13 February 1903; *s* of Désiré Simenon and Henriette Brull; *m* Denise Ouimet; three *s* one *d*. *Educ:* Collège St Servais, Liège, Belgium. His books are translated into 43 languages and have been published in 31 countries. *Publications:* 205 novels, including the 77 titles of the Maigret series. *Recreation:* golf. *Address:* 1066 Epalinges, Canton de Vaud, Switzerland.

**SIMEON, Sir John Edmund Barrington,** 7th Bt, *cr* 1815; Civil Servant in Department of Social Welfare, Provincial Government, British Columbia; lately in Real Estate business; *b* 1 March 1911; *s* of Sir John Walter Barrington Simeon, 6th Bt, and Adelaide Emily (*d* 1934), *e d* of late Col Hon. E. A. Holmes-à-Court; *S* father 1957; *m* 1937, Anne Robina Mary Dean; one *s* two *d*. *Educ:* Eton; Christ Church, Oxford. Motor business, 1931-39. Served with RAF, 1939-43; invalided, rank of Flight Lt, 1943. Civil Servant, Ministry of Agriculture, 1943-51. Took up residence in Vancouver, Canada, 1951. *Recreations:* sailing, painting. *Heir:* *s* Richard Edmund Barrington Simeon, Asst Professor of Political Science, Queen's Univ., Kingston, Ont [*b* 2 March 1943; *m* 1966, Agnes Joan, *d* of George Frederick Weld]. *Address:* RR1, Cowichan Station, BC, Canada. *T:* 748-9600.

**SIMEONS, Charles Fitzmaurice Creighton,** MA; JP; MP (C) Luton since 1970; *b* 22 Sept. 1921; *s* of Charles Albert Simeons and Vera Hildegarde Simeons; *m* 1945, Rosemary (*née* Tabrum); one *s* one *d*. *Educ:* Oundle; Queens' Coll., Cambridge. Royal Artillery with 8th Indian Div., 1942-45. Man. Dir, supplier to photographic industry, 1957-70. Pres., Luton, Dunstable and District Chamber of Commerce, 1967-68; District Gov., Rotary International, 1967-68; Chm. of cttees raising funds for disabled and cancer research. JP Luton, 1959. *Recreations:* watching football, cricket, gardening. *Address:* 21 Ludlow Avenue, Luton, Beds. *T:* Luton 30965. *Clubs:* Public Schools, St Stephen's; Conservative (Luton).

**SIMES, Charles Erskine Woollard,** QC 1945; MA Oxon; *b* 1893; *s* of Frederick Albert Woollard Simes, Worcester; *m* 1923, Catherine Harriet (*d* 1964), *d* of W. M. Hayes, Vancouver, BC. *Educ:* Royal Grammar School, Worcester; St John's College, Oxford. Lieut 1/7th Batt. Worcestershire Regt, 1914-17; France, 1915; Hd Qr Staff W Midland Region, Ministry of National Service, 1917-18; Barrister-at-Law, Inner Temple, 1921; Bencher, 1961; Recorder of Banbury, 1938-51; Chm. Interdepartmental Cttee on Rating of Site Values, 1947-51; Dep. Chairman, Boundary Commission for England, 1950-56; Member, Lands Tribunal, 1951-67; Chairman Harlow New Town Licensing Cttee; a Dep. Chm. Surrey QS, 1956-66; Mem. Boundary Commission for England, 1950-66. JP Surrey, 1953. Grand Registrar, United Grand Lodge of England. *Publications:* Joint Editor Lumley's Public Health (10th, 11th and 12th Edns), Local Government Law and Administration. *Address:* 1a Queen's Gate, SW7. *T:* 01-584 7836.

**SIMKINS, Charles Anthony Goodall,** CB 1968; CBE 1963; attached Ministry of Defence; *b* 2 March 1912; *s* of Charles Wyckens Simkins; *m* 1938, Sylvia, *d* of Thomas Hartley, Silchester, Hants; two *s* one *d*. *Educ:* Marlborough; New Coll., Oxford. Barrister, Lincoln's Inn, 1936; served 1939-45 as Capt., Rifle Bde (POW); attached War Office (now Min. of Defence),

1945-. *Address:* The Cottage, 94 Broad Street, near Guildford, Surrey. *T:* Guildford 2456. *Clubs:* United Service, MCC.

**SIMMONDS, Kenneth Willison,** CMG 1956; *b* Carmacoup, Douglas, Lanarkshire, 13 May 1912; *s* of late William Henry Simmonds, Civil Servant, and late Ida, *d* of John Willison, Acharn, Killin, Perthshire; *m* 1939, Ruth Constance Sargant; two *s*. *Educ:* Bedford Sch.; Humberstone Sch.; St Catharine's Coll., Cambridge (MA). District Officer, Colonial Administrative Service, Kenya, 1935-48; Deputy Financial Secretary, Uganda, 1948-51; Financial Secretary, Nyasaland Protectorate, 1951-57; Chief Secretary, Aden, 1957-63. *Address:* 5 Porchester Road, Newbury, Berks.

**SIMMONDS, Sir Oliver Edwin,** Kt 1944; CEng; FRAeS; President: Simmonds Aerocessories of Canada Ltd; Simmonds Products of Canada Ltd (Executive Vice-President, 1966-68); 21st Century Corporation, Nassau, Bahamas; *b* 1897; *e s* of Rev. F. T. Simmonds; *m* 1922, Gladys Evelyn Hewitt; one *s* two *d*. *Educ:* Taunton; Magdalene College, Cambridge (Exhibnr; Mech. Sci. Tripos). Aerodynamic research, RAE; gave over 1000 lectures on future of civil aviation, 1922-35; joined Supermarine Aviation Works, 1924; responsible (jointly) for design Supermarine S5 (Schneider Trophy Winner, 1926; from which Spitfire was subseq. developed); invented and patented interchangeable wings for aircraft (Simmonds Spartan biplane); formed Simmonds Aircraft Ltd, 1928 (produced Spartan landplane and seaplane), Simmonds Aerocessories Ltd, 1931, Simmonds Aerocessories, NY and Paris, 1936, Melbourne 1937. Chm., Air Transport Cttee, FBI. MP (U) Birmingham Duddeston, 1931-45. Founder-Pres. ARP Inst.; Chm., Parly ARP Cttee; led delegn to Berlin to study German ARP. Mem. Exec., 1922 Cttee, 1938-45; Chm. Govt Cttee on Brick Industry, 1941-42. Developed and patented electronic fuel gauge Pacitron. Moved to Bahamas, 1948; built Balmoral Club (now Balmoral Beach Hotel); Founder Pres., Bahamas Employers Confdn, 1966-68. Vice-Pres., Bahamas Employers Confdn, 1966-68. Vice-Pres., RAeS, 1945-47. *Address:* PO Box 1480, Nassau, Bahamas. *Clubs:* Carlton, Royal Aero, Royal Thames Yacht.

**SIMMONDS, Sidney,** CBE 1957 (OBE 1945); FIL; retired as British Ambassador to Hayti (1955-59); *b* 31 Dec. 1899; 2nd *s* of John Simmonds, Bulwell, Nottingham; *m* 1st, 1928, Stella Sue (*d* 1948), *d* of Donald MacLean, St Paul, Minn., USA; one *s* one *d*; 2nd, 1951, Magda Elisabeth Kinch, *d* of late Civilingenior Niels Rasmussen, Copenhagen, Denmark; (one step *s*). *Educ:* High Pavement Secondary School and University College, Nottingham; King's College, Cambridge. Entered Levant Consular Service, 1922, and served in Morocco, 1924-28, and Roumania, 1928-29; Commercial Secretary, Moscow, 1930-31; Vice-Consul, Hamburg, 1932; Commercial Secretary, Tehran, 1933-37, Moscow, 1937-38. Athens, 1938-41; Counsellor (Commercial) at Rome, 1944-47; Counsellor (Commercial) and Consul-General at Copenhagen, 1948-52; Counsellor (Commercial), Bagdad, 1952-55. *Address:* Greystones, 16 Coppice Avenue, Great Shelford, Cambridge. *T:* Shelford 2507. *Club:* Royal Automobile.

**SIMMONS, Charles James;** *b* Moseley, Birmingham, 9 April 1893; *s* of James Henry and Mary Jane Simmons; *m* 1915, Beatrice, *d* of Matthew and Ellen Roberts; four *s*. *Educ:* Elementary. Served with Worcestershire Regt, 1914-17, France, Egypt, Gallipoli (lost leg Vimy Ridge); Editor, Birmingham Town Crier, 1940-45; mem. of Birmingham City Council, 1921-31 and 1942-45; Chairman Public Libraries Committee, Birmingham, 1929-31; Secretary Birmingham Borough Labour Party, 1942-45; Secretary Birmingham City Council Labour Group, 1942-45; MP (Lab) Erdington Division of Birmingham, 1929-31, West Birmingham, 1945-50; Brierley Hill Division of Staffordshire, 1950-Sept. 1959; Lord Commissioner of HM Treasury, 1946-49; Parliamentary Secretary, Ministry of Pensions, 1949-51; Chairman Birmingham Group of Labour MPs, 1945-50; Vice-Chm. West Midlands Group of Labour MPs, 1952, Chm., 1954-59; Opposition Whip, 1956-59. Chairman, House of Commons Branch, British Legion, 1955; Pres. Birmingham Temperance Soc., 1961, Hon. Sec., 1962; Pres., Birmingham Christian Socialist Movement, 1962. Hon. Mem., Birmingham City Council, 1967. *Address:* 20 Slack Lane, Handsworth, Birmingham 20. *T:* 021-554 5980.

**SIMMONS, Ernest Bernard,** QC (Seychelles) 1949; *b* 7 Sept. 1913; *o s* of Bernard Simmons and Ethel (*née* Booth); *m* 1940, Edna Muriel Tomlinson; one *s* three *d*. *Educ:* Highgate School; London University (Slade School). Barrister-at-Law, Gray's Inn, 1936; Assistant Principal, HM Treasury, 1940; Private Secretary to Paymaster-General (Lord Hankey), 1941, to Minister of Supply, 1942; Principal, Min. of Supply, 1942; Asst Attorney-Gen., Gibraltar, 1946; Attorney-Gen., Seychelles, 1949; Judge of the Supreme Court, Mauritius, 1952-58; Judge of the High Court, Tanganyika, 1958-61. retired. *Publications:* A Decimal System of Legal Classification, and articles. *Address:* The Gate House, 27 Middleton Road, Brentwood, Essex.

**SIMMONS, Prof. Ernest J.;** Author, Lecturer; *b* Lawrence, Mass, 8 Dec. 1903; *s* of Mark Simmons and Annie (*née* McKinnon); *m* 1940, Winifred McNamara (*d* 1970); one *s*. *Educ:* Harvard (AB, AM, PhD). Research work in Russia, 1928-29, 1932, 1935, 1937, 1947, 1958, 1965. Instr, Harvard, 1929-36; asst prof. and chairman of Board of English Tutors, Harvard, 1936-39; associate professor of English and Russian literature, Cornell Univ., 1941-46; Chm., Dept Slavic Languages and Literatures, Cornell, 1942-46; Executive Officer (Chairman), Department Slavic Languages, Columbia, 1946-58; Member, Department of Slavic Languages and Professor of Russian Literature, Russian Institute, Columbia University, 1946-59. Editor American Slavic and East European Review, 1947-50. Member: Exec. Council, Mod. Language Assoc., 1953-54; Joint Slavic Cttee of American Council of Learned Socs and Social Science Res. Council, 1947-59; Pres. Cttee on Educl Future of Columbia Univ., 1956-57; Trustee, Sarah Lawrence Coll., 1954-58; Academic Freedom Cttee, Amer. Civil Liberties Union, 1955-58; Phi Beta Kappa Vis. Schol., 1959-60, 1962-63, 1964-65; Danforth Vis. Lectr, 1961-62, 1964-65; Sen. Fellow, Center for Advanced Studies, Wesleyan Univ., 1963-64, 1965-66, Actg Dir, 1967. Patten Foundn Lectr, Indiana Univ., 1964. Editorial Bd Slavonic Review (Eng.); Amer. Slavic and E European Review. General editor of series Columbia Slavic Studies, 1955-59. Hon. LHD, Northwestern Univ., 1968; Hon. LLD Middlebury Coll., 1969. *Publications:* English Literature and Culture in Russia, 1935; Pushkin, 1937; Dostoevski: The Making of a Novelist, 1940; Outline of Modern Russian Literature 1880-1940, 1943; Leo Tolstoy, 1946; Russian Fiction and Soviet Ideology: Introduction to Fedin, Leonov and

Sholokhov, 1958; Chekhov, 1962; Introduction to Russian Realism, 1965; Introduction to Tolstoy's writings, 1968; (ed) USSR, A Concise Handbook, 1947; Through the Glass of Soviet Literature, 1953; Continuity and Change in Russian and Soviet Thought, 1955. Many articles and reviews in learned and literary journals. *Address:* Dublin, NH 03444, USA. *T:* Locust 3-3451. *Clubs:* Harvard, Century (New York).

**SIMMONS, Rev. F(rederic) P(earson) Copland,** MA; Minister, Monzie and Fowlis Wester Church, Church of Scotland, since 1969; *b* 7 July 1902; 7th *c* of Rev. Arthur Simmons, Kingskettle, Fife, Scotland; *m* 1933, Kathleen (*d* 1968), *d* of Rev. Henry Norwell, Helensburgh. *Educ:* Gateshead Secondary School; King's College, Newcastle; Westminster College, Cambridge. BA Dunelm 1922, MA 1926. Ordained to Ministry, Ashington, Northumberland, 1925; Rutherford Church of Scotland, Glasgow, 1929; Egremont Presbyterian Church, Wallasey, 1938; St Andrew's Presbyterian Church Frognal, London, NW3, 1946; St Andrew's Presbyterian Church, Bournemouth, 1963-68; Chaplain at Scots Kirk, Nice, 1936-37. Moderator of the Free Church Federal Council of England and Wales, 1955-56; Moderator, Presbyterian Church of England, 1959-60. Visiting Preacher and Lectr in USA and Canada on nine occasions. *Recreations:* music, colour photography, horse-riding, golf. *Address:* Callum's View, Hope Place, Crieff, Scotland. *T:* Crieff 2353.

**SIMMONS, Guy Lintorn,** MVO 1961; Counsellor (Commercial), British Embassy, Cairo, since 1968; *b* 27 Feb. 1925; *s* of Captain Geoffrey Larpent Simmons, RN and late Frances Gladys Simmons (*née* Wright); *m* 1951, Sheila Jacob; three *d. Educ:* Bradfield Coll.; Oriel Coll., Oxford. RAF, 1943-46; CRO, 1949; 2nd Sec., British High Commn: Lahore, 1950; Dacca, 1952; CRO, 1954-58 and 1964-66; 1st Sec.: Bombay, 1958; New Delhi, 1961; Commercial Counsellor, New Delhi, 1966-68. *Recreations:* fishing, riding, amateur dramatics. *Address:* c/o Foreign and Commonwealth Office, King Charles Street, SW1. *Club:* Turf (Cairo).

**SIMMONS, Jack;** Professor of History, University of Leicester, since 1947; Pro-Vice-Chancellor, 1960-63; Public Orator, 1965-68; *b* 30 Aug. 1915; *o c* of Seymour Francis Simmons and Katharine Lillias, *d* of Thomas Finch, MB, Babbacombe, Devon. *Educ:* Westminster Sch.; Christ Church, Oxford. Beit Lectr in the History of the British Empire, Oxford Univ., 1943-47. FRSL; FRHistS; Assoc.InstT. Mem., Adv. Council, Science Museum, 1970-; Pres., Leicester Soc. of Artists, 1969-; Leicestershire Archæological and Historical Society: Hon. Editor, 1948-61; President 1966-. Chm., Leicester Local Broadcasting Council, 1967-70. Jt Editor, The Journal of Transport History, since 1953. Editor, A Visual History of Modern Britain. *Publications:* African Discovery: An Anthology of Exploration (edited with Margery Perham), 1942; Southey, 1945; Edition of Southey's Letters from England, 1951; Journeys in England: an Anthology, 1951; Parish and Empire, 1952; Livingstone and Africa, 1955; New University, 1958; The Railways of Britain: an Historical Introduction, 1961; Transport, 1962; Britain and the World, 1965; St Pancras Station, 1968; Transport Museums, 1970; A Devon Anthology, 1970; Life in Victorian Leicester, 1970. *Address:* Department of History, The University, Leicester. *T:* 50000.

**SIMMONS, Jean, (Mrs Richard Brooks),** film actress; *b* London, 31 Jan. 1929; *m* 1950, Stewart Granger, *qv* (marriage dissolved, Arizona, 1960); one *d*; *m* 1960, at Salinas, Calif, Richard Brooks; one *d. Educ:* Orange Hill Sch.; Aida Foster School of Dancing. First film appearance in Give Us the Moon, 1942; minor parts in Cæsar and Cleopatra, The Way to the Stars, etc., 1942-44; since then has appeared in numerous British films, including: Great Expectations, Black Narcissus, Hungry Hill, Uncle Silas, Hamlet, So Long at the Fair, The Blue Lagoon, Trio, Adam and Evalyn, Clouded Yellow; The Grass is Greener; Life at the Top; began American film career, 1950; American films include: Androcles and the Lion, Ivanhoe, The Actress, Desirée, Footsteps in the Fog, Guys and Dolls, This Could Be the Night, Spartacus, Elmer Gantry, All the Way Home; Divorce, American Style, 1967; The Happy Ending, 1970. *Address:* c/o A. Morgan Maree, Jr & Assoc., Inc., 6363 Wilshire Boulevard, Los Angeles 48, California, USA.

**SIMMONS, Robert,** CMG 1954; CBE 1943; MRCVS; *b* 10 Dec. 1894; *m* 1923, Mary Dickinson Waugh; one *d. Educ:* Dunfermline High School; Royal Dick Veterinary College, Edinburgh. Served European War, 1914-19; Fife and Forfar Yeomanry, King's Own Scottish Borderers, Royal Scots. Entered Colonial Service, 1923; Director of Veterinary Services: Uganda, 1938; Nigeria, 1944. Adviser to Secretary of State, Colonial Office, 1948-55, retired. *Publications:* contributions to scientific journals. *Recreation:* golf. *Address:* Lindores, Summerfield, Dunbar, Scotland. *T:* Dunbar 3781.

**SIMMONS, William Foster,** CMG 1963; MB, ChM; FRACGP 1969; General Practitioner, 1919-64, retired; *b* 9 May 1888; *s* of William Alfred Simmons, JP, Vaucluse, NSW; *m* 1919, Edna Kathleen Millicent Goode; two *d* (and two *s* decd). *Educ:* Sydney Boys' High School; Sydney University. Served European War, Australian Imperial Force, AAMC, 1914-19 (Major). Asst Hon. Physician, 1925, Hon. Consultant Physician, 1954, St George Hospital; Hon. Treasurer, Federal Council of BMA in Australia, 1946-62; Mem. Nat. Health and Medical Research Council, 1943-63. Chm. Medical Research Adv. Cttee, 1957-64; Dir Australasian Medical Publishing Co., 1946-. Mem. Council, Aust. Coll. General Practitioners, 1964, Foundation Fellow, Oct. 1965. Awarded Gold Medal, BMA in Australia, 1961. *Recreations:* football and rowing (retired many years); gardening. *Address:* 78 Wentworth Road, Vaucluse, NSW, Australia. *T:* 337-1770.

**SIMMS, Most Rev. George Otto;** *see* Armagh, Archbishop of, and Primate of All Ireland.

**SIMON,** family name of **Viscount Simon** and of **Baron Simon of Wythenshawe.**

**SIMON,** 2nd Viscount, *cr* 1940, of Stackpole Elidor; **John Gilbert Simon,** CMG 1947; Chairman, Port of London Authority, since 1958; Member, National Ports Council, since 1967; *b* 2 Sept. 1902; *o s* of 1st Viscount Simon, PC, GCSI, GCVO, and of Ethel Mary (*d* 1902), *d* of Gilbert Venables; *S* father, 1954; *m* 1930, James Christie, *d* of William Stanley Hunt; one *s* one *d. Educ:* Winchester; Balliol College, Oxford (Scholar). With Ministry of War Transport, 1940-47. Formerly a Man. Dir and Dep. Chm. of Peninsular and Oriental Steam Navigation Co. President: Chamber of Shipping of UK, 1957-58; Inst. of Marine Engineers, 1960-61; RINA, 1961-; British Hydromechanics Res. Assoc. Officer Order of

Orange Nassau, Netherlands. *Heir: s* Hon. Jan David Simon, *b* 20 July 1940. *Address:* New Park, Buckfastleigh, Devon. *T:* Buckfastleigh 2260.

**SIMON OF WYTHENSHAWE,** 2nd Baron, *cr* 1947, of Didsbury; **Roger Simon;** *b* 16 Oct. 1913; *S* father, 1960 (but does not use the title and wishes to be known as Roger Simon); *m* 1951 (Anthea) Daphne May; one *s* one *d*. *Educ:* Gresham's School; Gonville and Caius College, Cambridge. *Heir: s* Hon. Matthew Simon, *b* 10 April 1955. *Address:* Oakhill, Chester Avenue, Richmond, Surrey. *See also Lady Simon of Wythenshawe.*

**SIMON OF WYTHENSHAWE, Lady; Shena D. Simon;** *b* 21 Oct. 1883; *d* of late John Wilson Potter and Jane Boyd Potter; *m* 1912, E. D. Simon (later 1st Baron Simon of Wythenshawe; *d* 1960); two *s*. *Educ:* home; Newnham Coll., Cambridge; London Sch. of Economics. Mem. Manchester City Council, 1924-33; Co-opted Member Education Cttee; formerly Member Board of Education Consultative Cttee; Member Royal Commission on Licensing, 1929; Member Departmental Cttee on Valuation of Dwelling Houses, 1938. Hon. Freeman, Manchester, 1964; Hon. Fellow, LSE, 1965. *Publications:* A Hundred Years of City Government (Manchester, 1838-1938), 1939; various pamphlets on Education and Rating questions. *Recreations:* reading detective novels; going to the cinema. *Address:* Broomcroft, Didsbury, Manchester 20. *Club:* University Women's. *See also Baron Simon of Wythenshawe.*

**SIMON, (Ernest Julius) Walter,** CBE 1961; DrPhil, DLit; FBA 1956; Professor of Chinese, University of London, 1947-60, Emeritus Professor, 1960; Visiting Professor: University of Toronto, 1961-62; Australian National University, Canberra, 1962; Tokyo, Canberra and Melbourne, 1970; *b* Berlin, 10 June 1893; *m* 1921, Kate (*née* Jungmann); two *s*. *Educ:* Univ. of Berlin. Higher Library Service, Berlin Univ. Library, 1919-35; Exchange Librarian, Nat. Library of Peking, 1932-33; Lecturer in Chinese, Univ. of Berlin, 1926-32; Extraordinary Prof. of Chinese, Univ. of Berlin, 1932-34; Lecturer, School of Oriental Studies, 1936; Reader in Chinese, University of London, 1938. Editor, Asia Major, 1964-. Hon. Fellow School of Oriental and African Studies, University of London; Toyo Bunko, Tokyo. Pres. Philological Soc., 1967-70. *Publications:* Reconstruction of Archaic Chinese Final Consonants, 2 Parts, 1928-29 (in German); Tibetan Chinese Word Equations, 1930 (in German); Chinese Sentence Series, 3 volumes, 1942-44; New Official Chinese Latin Script, 1942; Chinese National Language (Gwoyeu) Reader, 1943 (2nd edn 1954, repr. 1967); 1200 Chinese Basic Characters (3rd edn 1956); How to Study and Write Chinese Characters, 1944 (2nd edn 1959); Structure Drill through Speech Patterns, I. Structure Drill in Chinese, 1945 (2nd edn 1959); Beginners' Chinese-English Dictionary, 1947 (3rd edn 1964); Introduction to: K. P. K. Whitaker's 1200 Basic Chinese Characters for Students of Cantonese, 1953 (3rd edn 1965); Y. C. Liu's Fifty Chinese Stories, 1960. Contribs to: Mitteilungen des Seminars für Orientalische Sprachen, Orientalistische Literaturzeitung, Bulletin of School of Oriental and African Studies, Harvard Journal of Oriental Studies, Asia Major, etc. *Address:* 13 Lisbon Avenue, Twickenham. *T:* 01-894 3860.

**SIMON, Rt. Hon. Sir Jocelyn Edward Salis,** PC 1961; Kt 1959; President of the Probate, Divorce and Admiralty Division of the High Court of Justice since 1962; *b* 15 Jan. 1911; *s* of Frank Cecil and Claire Evelyn Simon, 51 Belsize Pk, NW3; *m* 1st, 1934, Gwendolen Helen (*d* 1937), *d* of E. J. Evans; 2nd, 1948, Fay Elizabeth Leicester, JP, *d* of Brig. H. G. A. Pearson; three *s*. *Educ:* Gresham's School, Holt; Trinity Hall, Cambridge (Exhibitioner). Called to Bar, Middle Temple, 1934 (Blackstone Prizeman). Served War of 1939-45; commissioned RTR, 1939; comd Spec. Service Sqn, RAC, Madagascar, 1942; Burma Campaign, 1944; Lieut-Col, 1945. Resumed practice at Bar, 1946; QC 1951. MP (C) Middlesbrough West, 1951-62; Mem. of the Royal Commission on the Law relating to Mental Illness and Mental Deficiency, 1954-57. Jt Parly Under-Sec. of State, Home Office, 1957-58; Financial Sec. to the Treasury, 1958-59; Solicitor-General, 1959-62. Hon. Fellow, Trinity Hall, Cambridge, 1963. *Publications:* Change is Our Ally, 1954 (part); Rule of Law, 1955 (part); The Church and the Law of Nullity, 1955 (part). *Address:* Midge Hall, Glaisdale Head, Whitby, Yorks; Carpmael Building, Temple, EC4.

**SIMON, Roger;** *see* Simon of Wythenshawe barony.

**SIMON, Walter;** *see* Simon, (E. J.) W.

**SIMON, Most Rev. (W.) G. (H.);** *see* Wales, Archbishop of.

**SIMONDS,** family name of **Viscount Simonds.**

**SIMONDS,** 1st Viscount, *cr* 1954, 1st Baron, *cr* 1952, of Sparsholt; (Life Peer), *cr* 1944, **Gavin Turnbull Simonds,** PC 1944; Kt, *cr* 1937; High Steward of Winchester (City) since 1951; *b* 28 Nov. 1881; 2nd *s* of late L. de L. Simonds of Audley's Wood, Basingstoke; *m* 1912, Mary Hope, *d* of late Judge F. H. Mellor, KC; (twin *s*; one decd, 1951, one killed in action, 1944). *Educ:* Winchester College (Scholar, Fellow of Winchester, 1933, Warden, 1946-51); New Coll., Oxford (Exhibitioner, Hon. Fellow, 1944). 1st class Mods, 1902; 1st cl. Lit. Hum., 1904. Called to Bar, 1906; KC 1924; Bencher, Lincoln's Inn, 1929, Treas., 1951; Judge of Chancery Div., High Ct of Justice, 1937-44; Chairman, Nat. Arbitration Tribunal, 1940-44; a Lord of Appeal in Ordinary, 1944-51; Lord High Chancellor of Great Britain, 1951-54; a Lord of Appeal in Ordinary, 1954-62, retd. Professor of Law, Roy. Acad. of Arts, 1951. High Steward, Oxford Univ., 1954-67. Hon. FRCOG, 1954. DLitt (Reading University) 1947; Docteur en droit (Laval Univ.), 1953; Hon. DCL (Oxford Univ.), 1954. *Heir:* none. *Address:* Flat 7, 64 Rutland Gate, SW7. *T:* 01-584 4000. *Clubs:* Brooks's, Athenæum.

**SIMONDS, Lt-Gen. Guy Granville,** CB 1944; CBE 1943; DSO 1943; CD 1951; Canadian Army, retired; now President and Director of companies; Vice-Chairman, Commercial Life Insurance Co. Ltd; Halifax Insurance Co. Ltd; Director of Charterhouse Investments (Canada) Ltd; *b* Ixworth Abbey, Bury St Edmunds, 23 April 1903; *s* of Lieutenant-Colonel Cecil Barrow Simonds, DSO, late RA; *m* 1st, 1932, Katherine Lockhart, *d* of C. M. Taylor, Winnipeg, Canada; one *s* one *d*; 2nd, 1960, Dorothy Flavelle Sinclair (*née* Harding). *Educ:* Ashbury Coll., Ottawa; Roy. Mil. Coll., Kingston. Lt Royal Canadian Horse Artillery, 1925; gunnery staff course in England, 1932; also at Staff College, Camberley; Brig., Gen. Staff Canadian Corps HQ, 1941-42; commanded Canadian Infantry Bde 1942-43; Brig., Gen. Staff HQ 1st Canadian Army, 1943; commanded a Canadian Division in Sicily and Italy, 1943-44; Comd 2nd Canadian Corps,

Western Europe, 1944; Lt-Gen. 1944; Chief Instructor, Imp. Defence Coll., 1948-49; Chief of the General Staff, Canadian Army, 1951-55, retired 1955; late Comdt National Defence College, Kingston, Canada, and Canadian Army Staff College. Virtuti Militari (Poland), 1945; Commandeur Légion d'Honneur and Croix de Guerre avec Palme (France), 1945; Commander Legion of Merit (US); Commandeur de l'ordre Léopold and Croix de Guerre avec Palme (Belgium); Grand Officer Order of Orange Nassau (Netherlands). *Address:* c/o Bank of Montreal, 9 Waterloo Place, Pall Mall, SW1; Apartment 304, 10 Benvenuto Place, Toronto 190, Ontario, Canada.

**SIMPSON, Alan,** MA, DPhil Oxon, LHD, LLD; President of Vassar College, Poughkeepsie, NY, since 1964; *b* Gateshead, Durham, England, 23 July 1912; *s* of George Hardwick Simpson and Isabella Simpson (*née* Graham); *m* 1938, Mary McQueen McEldowney, Chicago Heights, Ill; one *s* two *d*. *Educ:* Worcester Coll., Oxford (BA); Merton Coll., Oxford (MA, DPhil); Harvard Univ. (Commonwealth Fellow). Served War of 1939-45, RA, Major. Sen. Lectr in Modern British History and American History, Univ. of St Andrews, and Lectr in Constitutional Law, Law Sch., University Coll., Dundee, 1938-46; Asst Prof. of History, Univ. of Chicago, 1946-54; Associate Prof., 1954-59; Thomas E. Donnelley Prof. of History and Dean of the College, Univ. of Chicago, 1959-64. Member: Commn on Academic Affairs, and Bd of Directors, Amer. Council on Education; Commn on Liberal Learning, Assoc. of Amer. Colls; Bd of Trustees, Colonial Williamsburg; Amer. Hist. Assoc.; Conf. on British Studies; Amer. Antiquarian Soc.; Hudson River Valley Commn; Committee on the Second Regional Plan. Former Member, Council of the Inst. of Early Amer. History and Culture, Williamsburg, Va, 1957-60; Midwest Conf. of British Historians (Co-Founder, 1954; Sec., 1954-61). *Publications:* (Co-Editor) The People Shall Judge: Readings in the Formation of American Policy, 1949; Puritanism in Old and New England, 1955; The Wealth of the Gentry, 1540-1660: East Anglian Studies, 1961. *Address:* Vassar College, Poughkeepsie, New York, NY 12601, USA.

**SIMPSON, Alfred Henry; Hon. Mr Justice Simpson;** Puisne Judge, High Court of Kenya, since 1967; *b* 29 Oct. 1914; *s* of John Robertson Simpson, Dundee; *m* 1941, Hilda Corson Rodgers; one *d*. *Educ:* Grove Academy; St Andrews University; Edinburgh University. MA St Andrews, 1935; LLB Edinburgh, 1938 and Solicitor. Served in RASC, 1940-46, Middle East and Italy; Military Mission to the Italian Army and Allied Commission, Austria. Legal Officer, BMA, Cyrenaica, 1946-48. Member of the Faculty of Advocates, 1952. Crown Counsel, Singapore, 1948-56; Legal Draftsman, Gold Coast, 1956; Solicitor-General, Ghana, 1957, then Puisne Judge, Supreme Court, 1957-61; Puisne Judge, Combined Judiciary of Sarawak, North Borneo and Brunei, 1962; Senior Puisne Judge, Fedn of Malaysia High Court in Borneo, 1964; Reader, Faculty of Law, ANU, Canberra, 1965; Barrister-at-Law, NSW, 1967. *Publication:* (with others) The Laws of Singapore, revised edn, 1955. *Recreation:* golf. *Address:* PO Box 30041, Nairobi, Kenya. *Clubs:* Royal Commonwealth Society; Royal Canberra Golf.

**SIMPSON, Alfred Moxon,** CMG 1959; *b* 17 Nov. 1910; *s* of late A. A. Simpson, CMG, CBE; *m* 1938, Elizabeth Robson Cleland; one *s*. *Educ:* St Peter's College; University of Adelaide, (BSc). Associate (Commerce) of Univ. of Adelaide, 1940. Pres. Adelaide Chamber of Commerce, 1950-52; Sen. Vice-Pres. Associated Chambers of Commerce of Aust., 1953-55; Pres. SA Chamber of Manufrs, 1956-58; Pres. Associated Chambers of Manufrs of Aust., 1957-58. Mem. Hulme Cttee on Rates of Depreciation, 1956. *Recreations:* carpentry, ski-ing. *Address:* 31 Heatherbank Terrace, Stonyfell, SA 5066, Australia. *T:* 31 12 85. *Clubs:* Adelaide, Mt Lofty Ski (Adelaide); Melbourne (Melbourne); Union (Sydney).

**SIMPSON, Bertie Soutar,** OBE 1954; MB; FRCSE; Vice-Lieutenant of Sutherland since 1963; *b* 17 May 1896; *s* of James Bertie Simpson, CBE, MD, DL; *m* 1924, Margaret, *d* of James Menzies; two *s* one *d*. *Educ:* Merchiston Castle; Edinburgh University. MB, ChB, 1919; FRCSE 1922. Consultant Surgeon, County of Sutherland, 1933-61; retd 1961. County Director, BRCS, 1961. DL, Sutherland, 1958. *Publications:* contrib. to surgical jls. *Recreations:* golf, reading. *Address:* Blar Mhor, Golspie, Sutherland. *T:* Golspie 220.

**SIMPSON, Rt. Rev. Bertram Fitzgerald,** MC; DD (hon.) Durham; MA Durham; BD London; Fellow, King's College, London, 1960; *b* 25 Sept. 1883; *s* of William and Mary Ann Simpson; *m* 1912, Ethel Mary Penistan (*d* 1952); one *s* one *d*. *Educ:* University College, Durham; Theological Scholar, Hebrew Scholar, Barry Scholar, Gabbett prize. Deacon, 1907; priest, 1908; Curate of St Anne, Soho, 1907-11; London Diocesan Home Missioner at St Peter's, Harrow, 1911-13; TCF 1916-18; Vicar of St Peter's, Harrow, 1913-20; Boyle Lecturer, 1923, 1924, and 1925; Golden Lecturer, 1925; Rector and Rural Dean of Stepney, 1920-26; Vicar of St Peter's, Cranley Gardens, 1926-32; Suffragan Bishop of Kensington, 1932-42; Hon. Chaplain to the King, 1919-32; Rector of St Botolph, Bishopsgate, 1935-42; Bishop of Southwark, 1942-58; Preacher at Lincoln's Inn, 1959. *Publication:* The Prayer of Sonship. *Recreation:* gardening. *Address:* 62 Half Moon Lane, SE24. *T:* 01-274 8828.

**SIMPSON, Prof. (Cedric) Keith,** MA Oxon, MD London (Path.), FRCP; FRCPath; DMJ; Professor of Forensic Medicine to University of London since 1962 (Reader, 1946-62); Head of Department of Forensic Medicine, Guy's Hospital Medical School; *b* 20 July 1907; *s* of Dr George Herbert Simpson, Brighton, Sussex; *m* 1st, Mary McCartney Buchanan (*d* 1955); one *s* two *d*; 2nd, 1956, Jean Anderson Scott Dunn. *Educ:* Brighton and Hove Grammar School, Sussex; University of London. Guy's Hospital Medical School: Gold Medallist (Golding-Bird) in Bacteriology, 1927; Beaney Prizeman, 1927; Gull Scholar and Astley Cooper Student, 1932; Lecturer in Pathology, 1932-37; Lecturer in Forensic Medicine, 1937-47; Lecturer in Forensic Med., Oxford Univ., 1961. Examiner in Forensic Medicine to Univs: London, 1945; St Andrews, 1948; Leeds, 1950; NUI, 1952-64; Wales, 1954; Oxford, 1957; Glasgow, 1964. Member, Home Office Scientific Advisory Council. Harvard Associate in Police Science, 1952; Medallist, Strasbourg University, 1954; President: Medico-Legal Society, 1961; British Assoc. in Forensic Medicine, 1966; British Council Lecturer, France 1954, Denmark 1961. Corresponding Member Société de Médicine Légale and Amer. Acad. of Forensic Sciences. *Publications:* Forensic Medicine, 1947 (6th edn, 1969; awarded RSA Swiney Prize, 1958); Modern Trends in Forensic Medicine, 1953 (2nd edn 1967); Doctor's Guide to Court, 1962 (2nd edn 1966); (ed)

Taylor's Principles and Practice of Medical Jurisprudence, 12th edn, 1965; contrib. to medical and scientific journals. *Address:* Department of Forensic Medicine, Guy's Hospital, SE1. *T:* 01-407 0378; 146 Harley Street, W1. *T:* 01-935 2378; Dancers End Lodge, Tring, Herts. *Club:* Athenæum.

**SIMPSON, Alderman Charles Valentine George;** Director, Walker, Moate, Simpson & Co. Ltd, Birmingham, since 1960; *b* 14 Feb. 1900; 2nd *s* of Alexander Simpson, Ayrshire; *m*; two *s* one *d*; 2nd, Muriel Edwina, *e d* of Rev. Edwin Jones, Montgomeryshire; one *s*. *Educ:* Tindal Street Elementary Sch., Birmingham. RMLI, 1915-19; RNVR, 1939-45, rank of Lt-Comdr; served China, Med., Iceland, Germany. Councillor, Birmingham, 1935, Alderman 1949; Chairman, Airports Cttee, 1950, Public Works Cttee, 1966-68; Lord Mayor, City of Birmingham, 1968-69. President: RN Assoc., City of Birmingham; Handsworth Wood Residents Assoc.; Birmingham Br., RNLI; County Pres., Birmingham British Legion; Vice-Pres., Birmingham Bn, Boys' Brigade; Governor, Birmingham Univ. Successfully inaugurated appeal, 1969, for £40,000, for a new lifeboat to be called City of Birmingham. *Recreations:* bowls, foreign travel (preferably by caravan). *Address:* 16 Knowle Wood Road, Dorridge, Warwickshire. *T:* Knowle 2427; (business) 021-643 7501/2/3/4. *Club:* Caravan.

**SIMPSON, Charles Walter,** RI; *b* 1885; *s* of late Maj.-Gen. C. R. Simpson, CB; *m* 1913, Ruth (*d* 1964), *d* of Alister Alison; one *d*. Pictures in permanent collections in public galleries at Newcastle upon Tyne, Gateshead, Blackpool, Plymouth, Doncaster, Derby, Sheffield, Bournemouth, etc. Painter of famous horses and their riders; Exhibitor, Royal Academy. Exhibition of his pictures toured Municipal Galleries, 1956-58. Awarded Gold Medal at the Panama Internat. Exposition at San Francisco, 1915, and Silver Medal, Salon, 1923; also Olympic Medal at Exhibition of sporting pictures in connection with Olympic Games, Paris, 1924. *Publications:* author and illustrator of A Pastorale, 1923, El Rodeo, 1924; Leicestershire and its Hunts, 1926; The Harborough Country, 1926; Trencher and Kennel, 1927; Emily Brontë, 1929; Composition for Photographers, 1937; Photography of the Figure in Colour and Monochrome, 1938; Animal and Bird Painting, 1939; The Fields of Home, 1948. *Address:* Stanley House, Alverton, Penzance, Cornwall.

**SIMPSON, Commander Cortlandt James Woore,** CBE 1956; DSC 1945; Retired 1961; *b* 2 Sept. 1911; *s* of late Rear-Admiral C. H. Simpson, CBE, and, Edith Octavia (*née* Busby); *m* 1st, 1932, Lettice Mary Johnstone; 2nd, 1955, Ann Margaret Cubitt (*née* Tooth). *Educ:* St Ronans, Worthing; RN College, Dartmouth; London Univ. (BSc Engineering, Hons). Joined RN (Dartmouth), 1925; Lieut, 1934. Served War of 1939-45 in Home and Mediterranean Fleets; Commander, 1948. Summer expeditions to Greenland, 1950, 1951; Leader of British North Greenland Expedition, 1952-54. Polar Medal, 1954; Royal Geographical Society, Founder's Medal, 1955. *Recreations:* mountaineering, fishing, walking. *Publication:* North Ice, 1957. *Address:* Glyn Mills Bank, Kirkland House, Whitehall, SW1. *Club:* Alpine.

**SIMPSON, Sir Cyril;** *see* Simpson, Sir J. C. F.

**SIMPSON, Edward Hugh;** Under-Secretary, Civil Service Department, since 1968; *b* 10 Dec. 1922; *o s* of Hugh and Mary Simpson, of Brookfield, Ballymena, Co. Antrim; *m* 1947, Gladys Rebecca, *er d* of Samuel and Elizabeth Gibson, Ernevale, Kesh, Co. Fermanagh; one *s* one *d*. *Educ:* Coleraine Academical Institution; Queen's Univ., Belfast; Christ's Coll., Cambridge (Scholar). Dept of the Foreign Office, 1942-45; Min. of Education, 1947-50 and 1952-56; HM Treasury, 1950-52; Commonwealth Fund Fellow, USA, 1956-57; Private Sec. to Lord President of Council and Lord Privy Seal, 1957-60; Dep. Dir, Commonwealth Educn Liaison Unit, 1960-62; Sec., Commonwealth Educn Conf., New Delhi, 1962; Asst Sec. Dept of Educn and Science, 1962-68. *Address:* 40 Frays Avenue, West Drayton, Mddx. *T:* West Drayton 3417.

**SIMPSON, Ffreebairn Liddon,** CMG 1967; Secretary to the Cabinet, Mauritius, since 1967; *b* 11 July 1916; *s* of late James Liddon Simpson and of Dorothy (*née* Blyth); *m* 1947, Dorina Laura Magda (*née* Ilieva); one *s*. *Educ:* Westminster School; Trinity College, Cambridge. HM Diplomatic/Foreign Service, 1939-48; HM Treasury, 1948-50; Administrative Officer, Gold Coast, 1950-55; Dep. Colonial Sec., Mauritius, 1955; Perm. Secretary: Min. of Works and Internal Communications, 1961; Premier's Office, 1966. *Recreations:* reading, philately. *Address:* Floreal, Mauritius. *Clubs:* Oxford and Cambridge University; Stella Clavisque; Mauritius Naval and Military Gymkhana; Grand' Baie Yacht (Mauritius).

**SIMPSON, General Sir Frank (Ernest Wallace),** GBE 1953 (KBE 1947); KCB 1951 (CB 1944); DSO 1940; Chief Royal Engineer, 1961-67; Governor of Royal Hospital, Chelsea, 1961-69; *b* 21 March 1899; *s* of late Major Robert Wallace Simpson, MC; *m* 1934, Charlotte Dulcie Margaret Cooke; two *d*. *Educ:* Bedford School; Royal Military Academy, Woolwich; Trinity Hall, Cambridge. Commissioned in Royal Engineers, 1916; Lt-Col 1939; Col 1942; Maj.-Gen. 1944; Lt-Gen. 1946; Gen. 1950; served European War of 1914-18, France and Belgium (despatches, British War Medal, Victory Medal); Afghanistan and NW Frontier, 1919 (Medal with clasp); France, 1939-40 (DSO, 1939-45 Star, Defence Medal); Vice CIGS, 1946-48; GOC-in-C, Western Command, UK, 1948-51; Commandant, Imperial Defence College, 1952-54. ADC General to the King, 1951-52, to the Queen, 1952-54; retired pay, 1954; Mem. Eastern Electricity Board, 1954-63; Colonel Commandant: Royal Pioneer Corps, 1950-61; RE, 1954-67. Adviser to West Africa Cttee, 1956-66; Dir, United Services Trustee, 1961-69. JP Essex, 1955-61; DL Essex, 1956-65. Kt Gr Officer, Order of Orange-Nassau (with Swords), 1947. *Address:* 5 Northfields Close, Bath, Somerset. *Clubs:* United Service, MCC; Bath and County (Bath).

**SIMPSON, Rev. Frederick Arthur;** Fellow of Trinity College, Cambridge, since 1911; *b* 22 Nov. 1883; *s* of William Frederick Simpson, Rector of Caldbeck, Cumberland, and Frances, *d* of Edward Fidler, JP, of Standing Stone, Wigton, Cumberland. *Educ:* Rossall; Queen's College, Oxford; 1st Class Modern History, 1906. Curate of Ambleside, 1909-11; CF, 1915-18 (despatches); Hon. CF, 1919. Senior Dean, Trinity Coll., Cambridge, 1919-22, Dean of Chapel, 1922-32; Univ. Lectr in History, 1926-49; Select Preacher, Univ. of Oxford, 1932, 1935, Univ. of Cambridge, 1913, 1914, 1921, 1932. Silver Medal, Royal Soc. of Literature, 1927. *Publications:* The Rise of Louis Napoleon, 6th edn, 1968; Louis Napoleon and the Recovery of France, 5th edn. 1965. *Recreation:* gardening. *Address:* Trinity College, Cambridge.

**SIMPSON, Colonel George Selden,** CBE 1942; DSO 1916; TD; DL; *b* 1878; *s* of late R. Kirk Simpson, JP, Glasgow; *m* 1906, Jane Ethel (*d* 1937), *d* of late Andrew J. Kirkpatrick, JP, of Lagbuie, Shandon, and 5 Park Terr., Glasgow; two *s. Educ:* Kelvinside Academy, Glasgow. Was Secretary for Scotland to United Kingdom Provident Institution, 1902-27; thereafter Agency Manager, Scottish T and G Assurance Co. Ltd; retired, 1943. FCII; President, Insurance and Actuarial Society of Glasgow, 1921-22; served European War, 1914-18, commanding RFA Brigades, Gallipoli, Egypt, Palestine, and France (severely wounded, despatches thrice, DSO, Serbian Order of White Eagle with Swords, 1914-15 Star); organised and commanded 80th Lowland Field Regt RA (TA) (City of Glasgow Artillery), 1920; Supt Maryhill Div. of Special Constables, 1926-39; rep. Scottish Command on WO Committee for reconstruction of TA, 1943-47; Chairman, County of Glasgow TA and AFA, 1943-45; Vice-President, West Stirlingshire Unionist Association; Chairman Glasgow Branch National Association for Employment of Regular Sailors, Soldiers, and Airmen, 1922-45; was on Executive Committees of Erskine Hospital, Western Infirmary and Glasgow Branch, Brit. Red Cross Soc.; Commissioner of Income Tax; JP, Stirlingshire, 1936-50; Colonel and Zone Commander, 1940-44, City of Glasgow Home Guard. Deacon of the Incorporation of Weavers, Glasgow, 1941-42. *Recreations:* shooting, yachting, golf. *Address:* Kirktonshade, Kirriemuir, Angus. *Club:* Conservative (Glasgow).

**SIMPSON, Rear-Adm. George Walter Gillow,** CB 1950; CBE 1942; retired; *b* 6 June 1901; 2nd *s* of late Rev. R. H. B. Simpson, of Guildford, Surrey; *m* 1945, Alison, er d of late Capt. L. J. Hall, CBE, RNR; two *s* one *d. Educ:* RN Colleges, Osborne and Dartmouth. Served in Grand Fleet, Sept. 1917, until end of hostilities; served in submarines, 1921-54; commanded submarines, based at Malta, 1941 and 1942; Commodore "D" Western Approaches, 1943-45; First Naval Member and Chief of New Zealand Naval Staff, 1947-50; Flag Officer, Germany, and Chief British Naval Representative on Allied Control Commission, 1951; Flag Officer, Submarines, 1952-54, retired 1954. Virtuti Militari (Poland), 1942; despatches, 1943. *Recreations:* wild fowling and fishing. *Address:* 70 Kiripaka Road, Whangarei, Northland, New Zealand.

**SIMPSON, Gerald Gordon,** CMG 1967; HM Diplomatic Service; HM Consul-General, Düsseldorf, since 1970; *b* 1 Sept. 1918; *s* of Major Gerald Gordon Simpson; *m* 1943, Peggy Ena Williams; one *d. Educ:* Royal Grammar Sch., Newcastle upon Tyne. Served in British and Indian Armies, 1938-46; (retd as Lt-Col). Ministry of Labour (seconded to Control Commission for Germany), 1947-48. Joined HM Foreign Service, 1948; served in: Ankara, 1950-52; Budapest, 1952-54; Foreign Office, 1954-58; Santiago de Chile, 1958-61; Washington, 1961-62; New York, 1962-65; Consul-Gen., Houston, 1965-68; seconded to Overseas Cttee of Unilever, 1969. *Recreations:* all mountain sports; golf and painting. *Address:* Cecilien Allee 16, Dusseldorf, West Germany. *T:* Dusseldorf 434281.

**SIMPSON, Maj.-Gen. Hamilton Wilkie,** CB 1945; DSO 1940; late Royal Marines; *b* 1895. 2nd Lt Royal Marines, 1913; served European War, 1914-18; War of 1939-45 (DSO); retired list, 1946. *Club:* United Service.

**SIMPSON, Prof. Harold,** MA, DSc Oxon; Professor of Mathematics, University of London, 1912-44, Professor Emeritus, 1945-; Head of Mathematical Department, Bedford College, 1907-44; *b* 22 Oct. 1876; *e s* of Rev. H. G. Hilton; took name of Harold Simpson (in lieu of Harold Hilton), 1939; *m* 1st, Edith Marsley, *d* of Rev. J. Skinner Jones; no *c*; 2nd, Dorothy Mary, *d* of C. F. Elliott; no *c. Educ:* Lancing Coll.; Hertford Coll., Oxford (Scholar). Junior Mathematical Exhibitioner and Senior Mathematical Scholar, University of Oxford; Prize Fellow of Magdalen College, Oxford, 1898-1905; MA 1902, DSc 1913; Assistant Lecturer in Mathematics, University College, Bangor, N Wales, 1902-7; member of the Councils of the London Mathematical Society, 1915-44, and the Mineralogical Society, 1908-11, 1913-16, 1918-21, 1923-30, 1939-42. *Publications:* Mathematical Crystallography, 1903; reprinted 1963; Theory of Finite Groups, 1907; Homogeneous Linear Substitutions, 1914; Plane Algebraic Curves, 1920, 2nd edn 1932; various papers on Mathematical and Crystallographic subjects. *Recreation:* chess. *Address:* 11 Staverton Road, Oxford OX2 6XH. *T:* Oxford 58793.

**SIMPSON, Sir James Dyer,** Kt 1946; *b* 21 Aug. 1888; *m* Lucy Beavan; one *s.* Chief General Manager Royal Insurance Co. and The Liverpool & London & Globe Insurance Co.; retired 1949; Director General Administrative Services, Ministry of Supply, 1942. Past Chairman, British Insurance Assoc.; Insurance Institute of Liverpool; Liverpool Caledonian Assoc.; JP (Liverpool) 1944-50. *Publications:* pamphlets on insurance. *Recreations:* golf, fishing. *Address:* Carlton House, East Cliff, Bournemouth, Hants. *Club:* Pilgrims.

**SIMPSON, James Joseph Trevor,** KBE (Hon.) 1965 (CBE 1957); (forename James added by deed poll, 1965); Chairman and Managing Director, James Simpson & Co. Ltd; retired as Chairman, Uganda Development Corporation, Ltd (1952-64); *b* 9 Jan. 1908; 2nd *s* of late Lieut-Colonel Herbert Simpson, OBE, MC, and of Mrs Henrietta Augusta Simpson; *m* 1940, Enid Florence (*née* Danzelman). *Educ:* Ardingly College, Sussex. Branch Manager, Vacuum Oil Co., Nakuru, Nairobi, Dar es Salaam, Mombasa, Kampala, 1932-46; General Manager, The Uganda Company Ltd, 1947-52; President, Uganda Chamber of Commerce, 1941, 1946-50. Member: Uganda Executive Council, 1952-55; Uganda Legislative Council, 1950-58 (Chm. Representative Members Organization 1951-58); E African Legislative Assembly, 1957-60, 1962-63; E African Railways and Harbours, Transport Advisory Council, 1948-61; E African Industrial Council, 1947-61; Uganda Electricity Bd, 1955-60; East African Airways Corporation, 1958-; Minister of Economic Affairs, Uganda, 1962-63. *Recreations:* golf, bridge. *Address:* c/o PO Box 4343, Kampala, Uganda; PO Box 8816, Nairobi, Kenya. *Clubs:* East India and Sports; Muthaiga, Nairobi (Kenya); Kampala (Uganda).

**SIMPSON, John Alexander,** CIE 1945; MA; *b* 25 Nov. 1892; *s* of John and Christina Simpson, Aberdeen; *m* 1925, Mary W. U. Robertson (*d* 1970); no *c. Educ:* Robert Gordon's College, Aberdeen. MA 1st Cl. Hons in Classics, Aberdeen University, 1913; served European War, 1915-19; junior clerk, India Office, 1919; Joint Sec., Military Dept, India Office (now Commonwealth Relations Office), 1934-48. *Address:* 21 Falcon Gardens, Edinburgh 10. *T:* 031-447 3483.

**SIMPSON, Sir (John) Cyril Finucane,** 3rd Bt, *cr* 1935; retired; *b* 10 Feb. 1899; *s* of Sir Frank Robert Simpson, 1st Bt, CB, and Alice

Matilda (*d* 1950), *d* of late James Finucane Draper; *S* brother, 1968; *m* 1st, 1936, Betty (marriage dissolved, 1944), *d* of Frank J. Lambert; 2nd, 1945, Maria Teresa, *d* of Captain John Sutherland Harvey, Romerillo, Biarritz; no *c. Educ:* Rugby; Queen's College, Oxford. Stockbroker, 1922-63. Served European War, 1914-18, Pilot in RNAS; served abroad, 1917-18. Won Rackets Amateur Championship three years in succession and Open Championship two years, Doubles Championship four years; US Doubles Championship, 1928; Canadian Doubles Championship, 1924. *Recreation:* shooting. *Heir:* none. *Address:* Bradley Hall, Wylam, Northumberland. *T:* Wylam 2246. *Clubs:* White's, Buck's; Northern Counties (Newcastle upon Tyne); Vincent's (Oxford).

**SIMPSON, John Ferguson,** FRCS; Consulting Surgeon to Ear, Nose and Throat Department, St Mary's Hospital, retired; formerly, Lecturer in Diseases of the Ear, Nose and Throat, University of London; *b* 10 Oct. 1902; *s* of late Col P. J. Simpson, DSO, FRCVS, Maidenhead; *m* 1947, Winifred Beatrice Rood; one *s* one *d. Educ:* Reading Sch.; St Mary's Hosp. FRCS 1929; MRCS, LRCP 1926. Formerly: Surgeon to Ear, Nose and Throat Dept, Wembley Hosp.; Specialist in Otorhino-laryngology, RAF; Hon. Surg. Roy. Nat. Throat, Nose and Ear Hosp.; Hon. Asst Aural Surg. Princess Louise Kensington Hospital for Children. FRSocMed (ex-President Section of Otology). *Publications:* A Synopsis of Otorhinolaryngology (jointly), 1957. Chapters: Essentials of Modern Surgery, 1957; Operative Surgery, 1958. *Recreations:* entomology; formerly Rugby football. *Address:* Long Barn, Waverley Abbey, Farnham, Surrey. *T:* Runfold 2555.

**SIMPSON, John Liddle,** CMG 1958; TD 1950; Deputy Legal Adviser, Foreign and Commonwealth Office, since 1968; *b* 9 Oct. 1912; *s* of late James Simpson; *m* 1st, 1939, Nellie Lavender Mussett (*d* 1944); 2nd, 1959, Ursula Vaughan Washington (*née* Rigby). *Educ:* George Watson's Coll.; Edinburgh Univ. (MA, DLitt). Barrister, Middle Temple, 1937. Served War of 1939-45; GSO1, 1945. Principal, Control Office for Germany and Austria, 1946; Senior legal assistant, FO (German Section), 1948; transferred to Foreign (now Diplomatic) Service and promoted Counsellor, 1954; Legal Counsellor, FO, 1954-59 and 1961-68; Legal Adviser, United Kingdom Mission to the United Nations, New York, 1959-61. *Publications:* Germany and the North Atlantic Community: A Legal Survey (with M. E. Bathurst), 1956; International Arbitration; Law and Practice (with Hazel Fox), 1959; articles and notes in legal journals. *Address:* 52 Ashley Gardens, SW1. *T:* 01-834 4814.

**SIMPSON, Sir John (Roughton),** Kt 1957; CB 1948; Chairman, Timber Trade Federation of the United Kingdom, 1961-65; *b* 19 April 1899; *m* 1923, Margaret Statham; one *s* one *d.* Inland Revenue, 1916-40; Postal and Telegraph Censorship, 1940-44; Under Secretary and Director of Organisation and Methods, HM Treasury, 1944-53; Controller of HM Stationery Office and Queen's Printer of Acts, 1954-61. Served European War, Army, 1917-19. *Address:* 35 Downs Side, Belmont, Sutton, Surrey. *T:* 01-643 1501.

**SIMPSON, Keith;** *see* Simpson, Cedric K.

**SIMPSON, Kenneth John,** CMG 1961; Foreign and Commonwealth Office (formerly Foreign Office), since 1965; *b* 5 Feb. 1914; *s* of Bernard and Ann Simpson, Millhouses, Sheffield; *m* 1939, Harriet (Shan) Hughes; three *s. Educ:* Downing College, Cambridge. Entered HM Foreign (now Diplomatic) Service, 1937; Second Secretary, 1941; First Secretary, 1945; Counsellor, 1956. *Address:* Foreign and Commonwealth Office, Riverwalk House, Millbank, SW1; 76 Wood Ride, Petts Wood, Kent. *T:* Orpington 24710.

**SIMPSON, Maj.-Gen. Noel William,** CB 1963; CBE 1956; DSO 1942 (Bar 1944); ED 1945; *b* 22 Feb. 1907; *s* of late Harry Simpson, Rossneath, Goulburn, NSW and late Annie Simpson (*née* Thomas); unmarried. *Educ:* North Sydney High Sch. Second-in-Command, 2nd/13th Bn AIF, 1940; DAAG 7th Aust. Div. 1940-41, CO 2nd/17th Bn AIF, Middle East, New Guinea, 1942-44; CO 2nd/43rd Bn AIF, 1944-45; Brigadier, 1945; Bde Comd 23rd Inf. Bde, Bougainville, 1945; Bde Comd 6th Inf. Bde, 1953-58; GOC 3rd Aust. Div., 1959-60; CMF Member, Military Bd, 1960-62; R of O 1962. Joined National Bank of Australasia Ltd, 1922; various staff and managerial appointments, NSW and Victoria; retired, 1966. *Recreations:* walking, swimming. *Address:* 7 Chastleton Ave, Toorak, Victoria 3142, Australia. *T:* 242947. *Clubs:* Imperial Service (Sydney); Naval and Military (Melbourne).

**SIMPSON, Oliver,** MA, PhD, FInstP; Chief Scientific Officer, Cabinet Office, since 1969; *b* 28 Oct. 1924; *y s* of late Sir George C. Simpson, KCB, FRS, and Dorothy (*née* Stephen); *m* 1946, Joan, *d* of late Walter and Maud Morgan; two *s. Educ:* Highgate Sch.; Trinity Coll., Cambridge. War Service: Admiralty Research Laboratory, Teddington, on submarine detection, 1944-46. Research Scholar, 1946-49, Fellow of Trinity Coll., Cambridge, 1949-53; Asst Prof. of Physics, Univ. of Michigan, USA, 1949-52; Imperial Chemical Industries Fellow in Dept. of Theoretical Chemistry, Cambridge, 1952-53; joined Services Electronics Research Laboratory, Admty, 1953, Head of Solid State Physics, 1956-63; Supt, Basic Physics Div., Nat. Physical Laboratory, 1964-66; Dep. Dir, Nat. Physical Laboratory, 1966-69. *Publications:* articles in scientific jls on infra-red detectors, semiconductors, fluorescence and standards of measurement. *Address:* 16 Hood Road, Wimbledon, SW20. *T:* 01-946 3871. *Club:* Athenæum.

**SIMPSON, Rayene Stewart,** VC 1969, DCM 1964; Sales Representative for Caldbeck-Macgregor & Co. Ltd, Tokyo, since 1970; *b* Sydney, Australia, 16 Feb. 1926; Australian parents (British stock); *m* 1952, Shoko Simpson (*née* Sakai); no *c. Educ:* Carlingford Public Sch., Sydney, Australia. Served War of 1939-45 (Pacific theatre): enlisted in AIF, 1944; discharged, 1947. Seasonal worker and merchant seaman, 1947-50; enlisted in Aust. Regular Army, 1951; served in Korea, 1951-54, with 3rd Bn, The Royal Australian Regt; served in Malaya, Oct. 1955-57, 2nd Bn, The Royal Australian Regt; 1st SAS, 1957-62; Aust. Army Trg Team, Vietnam (AATTV), July 1962-63; 1st SAS, July 1963-64; Aust. Army Trg Team, Vietnam (AATTV) July-Sept. 1964 (wounded in action, DCM, in hosp. 8 mths); 1st Bn City of Sydney Regt (Commando), 1965-66 (discharged 1966); re-enlisted Aust. Regular Army in Saigon, 1967, and served with AATTV (VC), in S Vietnam, 1970 (discharged from Service, 1970, after 21 years). *Recreations:* walking, reading (military history), watching boxing. *Address:* (home) No 5-30-1 Chome, Yayoicho, Nakano-ku, Tokyo 164, Japan. *T:* 373 1066; (office) Caldbeck-Macgregor & Co. Ltd, GPO Box No 864, Tokyo. *Clubs:* Returned Services League

(RSL), Paddington-Woollahra Sub-Branch (Sydney).

**SIMPSON, Rev. Rennie,** MA Lambeth 1970; Precentor of Westminster Abbey since 1963; *b* 13 Jan. 1920; *o s* of late Doctor Taylor Simpson and late May Simpson, Rishton; *m* 1949, Margaret, *er d* of late Herbert Hardy and Olive Hardy, South Kirkby; one *s* one *d*. *Educ:* Blackburn Tech. Coll.; Kelham Theol College. Curate of S Elmsall, Yorks, 1945-49; Succentor of Blackburn Cath., 1949-52; Sacrist and Minor Canon of St Paul's Cath., 1952-58, Hon. Minor Canon, 1958-, Jun. Cardinal, 1954-55, Sen. Cardinal, 1955-58; Vicar of John Keble Church, Mill Hill, 1958-63. Chaplain, RNVR, 1953-55; Dep. Chaplain, Gt Ormond St Hosp., 1954-58; Asst Chaplain, 1956-64, Officiating Chaplain, 1964-, Order of St John of Jerusalem; Deputy Priest to the Queen, 1956-67; Priest-in-Ordinary to the Queen, 1967-. Life Governor, Imperial Cancer Research Fund, 1963. Liveryman of Waxchandlers' Co. and Freeman of City of London, 1955. Jt Hon. Treas., Corp. Sons of the Clergy, 1967; *Recreations:* football, cricket, theatre. *Address:* 7 Little Cloister, Westminster Abbey, SW1. *T:* 01-222 1386.

**SIMPSON, Rev. Robert,** MA, MSc; DPhil; FCP; *b* 10 November 1900; *s* of William Robert Simpson, Dungannon, Co. Tyrone, and Mary Jackson; unmarried. *Educ:* London University; Manchester University; New College, Oxford; Buckle Research Scholar in Agricultural Zoology, 1927; Egerton Hall, Manchester (Theological Coll.). Deacon, 1924; Priest, 1925; Chaplain and Science Master at Cranleigh, 1928-32; Principal, Lawrence Memorial Roy. Mil. School, Lovedale, Nilgiri Hills, 1933-37; Headmaster Ashburton School, 1937-38; Rector of Mellis, 1939-43; Head of Dept of Zoology, Achimota College (Univ. Coll. of the Gold Coast), 1943-48; Charterhouse, 1949; Headmaster of Wolmer's School, Kingston, Jamaica, 1949-53. *Publications:* Papers on Zoological and Educational subjects. *Recreations:* swimming, rowing. *Address:* Rostrevor, Southwold, Suffolk. *T:* Southwold 2559. *Clubs:* Royal Commonwealth Society, National Liberal.

**SIMPSON, Rt. Hon. Dr Robert,** PC (N Ireland) 1970; MP (U) Mid-Antrim, Parliament of Northern Ireland, since 1953; Minister of Community Relations, Government of Northern Ireland since 1969; *b* 3 July 1923; *er s* of Samuel and Agnes Simpson, Craigbilly, Ballymena; *m* 1954, Dorothy Isobel, 2nd *d* of Dr Robert Strawbridge, MA, DD, and Anne Strawbridge; two *s* one *d*. *Educ:* Ballymena Academy; Queen's University, Belfast. MB, BCh, BAO, 1946. House Surgeon, Belfast City Hosp., 1947; Resident Anaesthetist, Royal Infirmary, Leicester, 1948; GP, Ballymena, Co. Antrim, 1949-. Founder Chm., Ballymena Round Table, 1951. NI Deleg. to CPA Conf. in NZ and Australia, 1965. Director: Shamrock Sea Foods Ltd; T. B. Croft & Co. (Marketing), Isle of Man. *Publications:* contribs to medical and farming jls. *Recreations:* the country, writing, France, food. *Address:* Random Cottage, Craigbilly, Ballymena, Co. Antrim. *T:* Ballymena 6484. *Club:* Royal Over-Seas League.

**SIMPSON, S(amuel) Leonard,** MA, MD (Cambridge); FRCP; Chairman: S. Simpson, Ltd; Simpson (Piccadilly) Ltd; Daks-Simpson Ltd; Consultant in Industrial Psychology; Hon. Consulting Endocrinologist, St Mary's Hospital, London, W2; President: Simpson Imports Inc.; Daks USA Inc., New York; Daks (Canada) Ltd, Montreal; Member Council, CBI (Past Member Grand Council of FBI); Member Council, National Institute of Industrial Psychology; Member, British National Council for Rehabilitation; Member, Commonwealth Migration Council; Founder Member and Member Council, British Society of Endocrinology; Member Academic Committee of Institute of Social Psychiatry; Member Council, Institute Scientific Study of Delinquency; Hon. Member Endocrinological Societies of Argentine, Chile, France; Past President Endocrine Section Royal Society of Medicine *s* of late Simeon Simpson; *m* 1940, Heddy Monique, Baroness de Podmaniczky; one *d*. *Educ:* Westminster City School; Downing Coll., Cambridge. 1st Class Hons, Nat. Sci. Tripos, Pts I and II Physiology. Post-grad. research in America, Germany and Lister Institute, London. Life Mem., Brit. Horse Soc. Jt Founder, Walter Hagen Annual Award Trophy (in collab. with Golf Writers' Assoc. of USA). *Publications:* Major Endocrine Disorders, 1938, 1948, 1959 (3rd edn). Contrib. Hutchison's Index of Therapeutics, Rollestone's Encyclopædia of Medical practice, Endocrine Section of Price's Medicine, 1956, Endocrine Section of Medical Annual and Chambers's Encyclopædia; papers in Proc. Roy. Soc. Med., etc. *Recreations:* golf, painting, boxing (Capt. Cambridge Univ. 1922). *Address:* 28 Hyde Park Gate, SW7; Grouselands, Colgate, Sussex. *T:* Faygate 228. *Clubs:* Carlton, Simpson Services (Pres. and Founder); Machine Gun Corps Officers (Hon. Mem.); Sunningdale Golf (Sunningdale); Cowdray Park Polo.

**SIMPSON, Prof. Scott,** MA Cantab, Dr rer nat (Frankfurt-am-Main); Professor of Geology, University of Exeter, since 1959; *b* 15 September 1915; *e s* of late Sir George C. Simpson, KCB, CBE, FRS; *m* 1940, Elisabeth, *er d* of late Dr Imre Szabo, Vienna; two *s* one *d*. *Educ:* Highgate School; Clare College, Cambridge. Research at University of Frankfurt-am-Main, 1937-39. Assistant Lecturer in Geology, 1939-46 (seconded to Department of Natural Philosophy, 1941-45) and Lecturer in Geology, 1946-49, University of Aberdeen; Lecturer, 1949-59, and Reader, 1959, in Geology, University of Bristol. Awarded E. J. Garwood Fund of Geological Society, 1956. *Publications:* various papers on Pleistocene geology and geomorphology, and Devonian stratigraphy and fossils; (jt Editor) Lexique Stratigraphique International, volumes for England, Scotland and Wales. *Address:* Department of Geology, North Park Road, Exeter.

**SIMPSON, Rev. William Wynn,** OBE 1967; MA; General Secretary, Council of Christians and Jews, since 1942; *b* 11 July 1907; *m* 1933, Winifred Marjorie Povey; one *s* one *d*. *Educ:* King Edward VI Grammar School, Camp Hill, Birmingham; Birmingham University; Wesley House and Fitzwilliam House, Cambridge. Asst Minister, Leysian Mission, London, 1929-32; Oxford Methodist Circuit, 1932-33; External Student, Jews' College, London and research into contemp. Jewish problems, 1933-35; Minister Amhurst Park Methodist Church, N London, 1935-38; General Sec., Christian Council for Refugees, 1938-42. Advisory Secretary, Central Churches Gp, Nat. Council of Social Service; Chairman: Greater London Assoc. for the Disabled; Pestalozzi Children's Village Trust. Mem., Soc. for Old Testament Study. *Publications:* Readings in the Old Testament, 1932; Youth and Antisemitism, 1938; Christians and Jews Today (Beckly Social Service Lecture), 1942; (with A. I. Polack) Jesus in the Background of History, 1957; Jewish Prayer and Worship, 1965; Mini-Commentary on Pentateuch (Jerusalem Bible), 1969; pamphlets and articles on various aspects Jewish-Christian relations. *Recreations:* travel and the Arts. *Address:* 11 Old Rectory Close, Harpenden, Herts; 41 Cadogan Gardens, SW3. *T:* 01-730 5010. *Clubs:* Athenæum, English-Speaking Union.

**SIMS, Sir Alfred (John),** KCB 1960; OBE 1943; Director-General Ships, Admiralty, later Ministry of Defence, 1958-68; *b* 11 Oct. 1907; *s* of John Thomas Sims and Jessie Sims; British; *m* 1933, Barbara Mary Hunking Paul; one *s* one *d*. *Educ:* Regent St Higher Elementary Sch., Plymouth; HM Dockyard School, Devonport; RN Coll., Greenwich. Assistant Constructor, 1931; Mediterranean Fleet, 1932; Chatham Dockyard i/c successively of welding, submarine construction and the Constructive Drawing Office, 1933-37; Naval Construction Dept, Admiralty, 1937-38. Staff of Flag Officer Submarines, 1938-43, as Asst Constructor (Constr Lieut-Comdr) and later as Constructor (Constructor Commander). Naval Construction Dept, Admiralty, 1943-44, i/c of salvage vessels, slipways, habitability, etc; Chief Constructor in charge of submarine design, 1944-47. Professor of Naval Architecture, Royal Naval College, Greenwich, 1947-52. Naval Construction Department, Admiralty, 1952-54; i/c aircraft carrier design; Asst Dir of Naval Construction in charge of aircraft carrier and of submarine design, Oct. 1954-58, Dep. Dir, April-Sept. 1958. Ct of Assts Worshipful Co. of Shipwrights; Vice-President, RINA; FICE; Member NE Coast Instn of Engineers and Shipbuilders. FRSA. *Publications:* Thomas Gray Memorial Lecture to RSA, 1952; Andrew Laing Lecture, NE Coast, Instn of Engrs and Shipbuilders, 1960-61; James Forrest Lecture, Instn CE, 1965; Amos Ayre Lecture, RINA, 1968; rev. Attwood and Pengelly's Theoretical Naval Architecture. Papers before RINA, etc. *Recreations:* music, reading. *Address:* Crosslands, Bannerdown Road, Batheaston, Bath. *T:* Bath 88848. *Clubs:* Royal Commonwealth Society, Royal Automobile.

**SIMS, Arthur Mitford,** CIE 1943; Chief Engineer, North Western Railway, Lahore, retired; *b* 31 March 1889; 2nd *s* of late Sir Thomas Sims, CB; *m* 1st, 1915, Isabella May Jeffrey (*d* 1937); one *s* two *d*; 2nd, 1940, Mary Jeffrey. *Educ:* St Paul's School; Dulwich College; University Coll., London (BScEng, 1st cl. hons); MICE. Asst Engineer, Eastern Bengal Railway, 1911-16; Military Service, 1916-18, in East Africa, Capt. RE; Asst Engineer, 1918, subsequently Executive Engineer, Deputy Chief Engineer, Deputy General Manager, North Western Railway. *Publications:* railway technical papers. *Recreation:* cricket. *Address:* Whapple House, Berry Lane, Littlehampton, Sussex. *T:* Littlehampton 3308.

**SIMS, Prof. Geoffrey Donald;** Professor and Head of Department of Electronics, University of Southampton, since 1963; Dean, Faculty of Engineering, 1967-70; Deputy Vice-Chancellor, since 1970; *b* 13 Dec. 1926; *s* of Albert Edward Hope Sims and Jessie Elizabeth Sims; *m* 1949, Pamela Audrey Richings; one *s* two *d*. *Educ:* Wembley County Grammar School; Imperial College of Science and Technology, London. Research scientist, GEC, 1948-54; Sen. Scientific Officer, UKAEA, 1954-56; Lecturer/Senior Lecturer, University College, London, 1956-63. Consultant to various companies and to Department of Education and Science, 1957-; Consulting Editor, Chapman & Hall Ltd. Member Council, British Association for the Advancement of Science, 1964-; Member, EDC for Electronics Industry, 1967-. Chairman of Governors, Southampton College of Technology, 1967-69; FIEE 1963; FIERE 1966. *Publications:* Microwave Tubes and Semiconductor Devices (with I. M. Stephenson), 1963; Variational Techniques in Electromagnetism (trans.), 1965; numerous papers on microwaves, electronics and education in learned jls. *Recreations:* golf, sailing, camping, music. *Address:* Glen House, Glen Eyre Rd, Bassett, Southampton. *T:* Southampton 68561. *Club:* Stoneham Golf.

**SIMS, Monica Louie,** MA, LRAM, LGSM; Head of Children's Programmes, BBC Television, since 1967; *b* 27 October 1925; *d* of late Albert Charles Sims and Eva Elizabeth Preen, both of Gloucester. *Educ:* Girls' High School, Gloucester; St Hugh's College, Oxford. Tutor in Literature and Drama, Department of Adult Education, Hull University, 1947-50; Educn Tutor, Nat. Fedn of Women's Institutes, 1950-53; BBC Sound Talks Producer, 1953-55; BBC Television Producer, 1955-64; Editor of Woman's Hour, BBC, 1964-67. *Recreations:* cinema and theatre. *Address:* 97 Gloucester Terrace, W2.

**SIMSON, Michael Ronald Fraser,** OBE 1966; Secretary of the National Corporation for the Care of Old People since 1948; *b* 9 Oct. 1913; *er s* of Ronald Stuart Fraser Simson and Ethel Alice Henderson; *m* 1939, Elizabeth Joan Wilkinson; one *s*. *Educ:* Winchester Coll.; Christ Church, Oxford. Asst Master, West Downs Sch., 1938-40; RNVR, 1941-46; Asst Sec., Nat. Fedn of Housing Socs, 1946-48. Member: Min. of Labour Cttee on Employment of Older Men and Women, 1953-55; Cttee on Local Authority and Allied Personal Social Services (Seebohm Cttee), 1966-68; Supplementary Benefits Commn, 1967-. *Recreations:* gardening, interested in all forms of sport. *Address:* Hedley, Longhurst Road, East Horsley, Leatherhead, Surrey. *T:* East Horsley 2292.

**SINATRA, Francis Albert, (Frank);** singer, actor, film producer, publisher; *b* Hoboken, New Jersey, USA, 12 Dec. 1917; *s* of Natalie and Martin Sinatra; *m* 1st, 1939, Nancy Barbato (marr. diss.); one *s* two *d*; 2nd 1951, Ava Gardner (marr. diss.); 3rd, 1966, Mia Farrow (marr. diss.). *Educ:* Demarest High School, New Jersey. Started in radio, 1936; then became band singer with orchestras. First appearance in films, 1943. *Films include:* From Here to Eternity (Oscar for best supporting actor, 1953), Anchors Aweigh, On the Town, The Tender Trap, High Society, Guys and Dolls, The Man with the Golden Arm, Johnny Concho, The Joker is Wild, Kings Go Forth, Some Came Running, A Hole in the Head, Ocean's 11, The Devil at Four O'Clock, Sergeants Three, Manchurian Candidate, Come Blow Your Horn, Four for Texas, Robin and the Seven Hoods, None But the Brave, Marriage on the Rocks, Von Ryan's Express, Assault on a Queen, The Naked Runner, Tony Rome, The Detective, Lady in Cement. Owner music publishing companies, etc. *Publications:* composed numerous popular songs. *Address:* 4000 Warner Boulevard, Burbank, Calif, USA. *T:* 849-7177.

**SINCLAIR,** family name of **Earl of Caithness, Viscount Thurso, Baron Pentland,** and **Baron Sinclair of Cleeve.**

**SINCLAIR,** 17th Baron, *cr* 1449 (Scotland); **Charles Murray Kennedy St Clair,** MVO 1953; DL; Major, late Coldstream Guards; Extra Equerry to Queen Elizabeth the Queen Mother since 1953; Member Queen's Body Guard for Scotland (Royal Company of

Archers); *b* 21 June 1914; *o s* of 16th Baron Sinclair, MVO, and Violet (*d* 1953), *d* of Col J. Murray Kennedy, MVO; *S* father, 1957; *m* 1968, Anne Lettice, *yr d* of Sir Richard Cotterell, *qv*; one *s*. *Educ:* Eton; Magdalene Coll., Cambridge. Served War of 1939-45, Palestine, 1939 (wounded, despatches). Retired as Major Coldstream Guards, 1947. Portcullis Pursuivant of Arms, 1949-57; York Herald, 1957-68, retired. A Representative Peer for Scotland, 1959-63. DL Kirkcudbrightshire, 1969. *Heir: s* Master of Sinclair, *qv*. *Address:* Knocknalling, Dalry, Kirkcudbrightshire, Scotland. *T:* 221. *Club:* New (Edinburgh).

**SINCLAIR, Master of; Matthew Murray Kennedy St Clair;** *b* 9 Dec. 1968; *s* and *heir* of 17th Baron Sinclair, *qv*.

**SINCLAIR OF CLEEVE,** 1st Baron, *cr* 1957, of Cleeve, Co. Somerset; **Robert John Sinclair,** KCB 1946; KBE 1941 (MBE 1919); MA; United States Medal of Freedom with Gold Palm, 1947; Chairman, Bristol Waterworks Company, since 1960; Director: General Accident Assurance Corp. Ltd; Debenture Corp. Ltd; *b* 1893; *s* of late R. H. Sinclair; *m* 1917, Mary Shearer Barclay; one *s* (and one killed in action, Middle East, 1942). *Educ:* Glasgow Acad.; Oriel College, Oxford (Hon. Fellow, 1959). Commnd Aug. 1914, 5th Bn KOSB; served Gallipoli (wounded, despatches); seconded to Ministry of Munitions, 1916, Deputy Director of Munitions Inspection, 1917-19; Member of Prime Minister's Advisory Panel of Industrialists, January 1939; Director-General of Army Requirements, War Office, 1939-42; Member: Supply Council, 1939-42; Army Council, 1940-42. Deputy for Minister of Production on Combined Production and Resources Board, Washington, 1942-43; Chief Executive, Ministry of Production, 1943, and subsequently with Board of Trade until Nov. 1945; President, Imperial Tobacco Company, Ltd, 1959-67 (Chairman, 1947-59). Chairman, Committee to enquire into Financial Structure of Colonial Development Corporation, 1959; Member, UK Permanent Security Commission, 1965-; Dir, Finance Corp. for Industry, 1946-69 (Chm., 1960-64). Pro-Chancellor, Bristol Univ.; Pres., Federation of British Industries, 1949-51; High Sheriff of Somerset, 1951-52. Hon. LLD (Bristol), 1959. *Recreations:* fishing, shooting, golf. *Heir: s* Lt-Col The Hon. John Robert Kilgour Sinclair, OBE 1963, Queen's Own Cameron Highlanders [*b* 3 Nov. 1919; *m* 1950, Patricia, *d* of Lawrence Hellyer, Lockerbie, Dumfriesshire; one *s* two *d*]. *Address:* Cleeve Court, Cleeve, near Bristol. *TA* and *T:* Yatton 2124. *Clubs:* Athenæum, United University, Flyfishers'.

**SINCLAIR, Allan Fergus Wilson;** Journalist and publicist; *b* Edinburgh, 1900; *o s* of Allan Wilson Sinclair; *m* 1st, one *s* one *d*; *m* 2nd; one *d*; 3rd, 1945, Naomi Sevilla, Cairo. *Educ:* George Heriot's, Edinburgh. Studied for Ministry (United Free Church of Scotland), then entered journalism, Edinburgh Evening Despatch, 1916; on staff, Daily Record, Glasgow, 1918; sent to London Office, 1919; went to The Times, 1921; Asst Editor, Sunday Chronicle, 1922; joined staff of The People, 1925, leaving as news editor, 1931; Editor Sunday Graphic until 1936; Editor Daily Sketch, 1936-39; Assistant Director News Division, Ministry of Information, 1939-41; Press Relations Officer until 1943, then Director, British Information Services Middle East; Officer-in-Charge UN Photographic and Newsreel Pool, Cairo, Teheran, Fayoum, etc., Statesmen's Conferences, 1943 and 1945; Specialist Radio Photographic Adviser, India and Ceylon, 1945; Middle East Official Observer UN Assembly, London, 1946; joined Daily Herald, 1946; Scottish Editor, Daily Herald, 1950-53; rejoined London Staff, 1953, remaining when the paper became The Sun until May 1967; Production Editor, Club and Institute Journal, 1967-70. *Recreations:* walking, photography, painting (exhibited London, New York, Switzerland, etc.). *Address:* 41 Stoneham Road, Hove, Sussex.

**SINCLAIR, Andrew Annandale;** author; Managing Director, Lorrimer Publishing, since 1967; *b* 21 Jan. 1935; *m* Marianne Alexandre. *Educ:* Eton Coll.; Trinity Coll., Cambridge (BA, PhD); Harvard. Harkness Fellow of the Commonwealth Fund, 1959-61; Dir of Historical Studies, Churchill Coll., Cambridge, 1961-63; Fellow of American Council of Learned Societies, 1963-64; Lectr in American History, University Coll., London, 1965-67. Dir/Writer Mem., ACTT and Screenwriters' Guild. *Publications:* The Breaking of Bumbo, 1958; My Friend Judas, 1959; The Project, 1960; Prohibition, 1962; The Hallelujah Bum, 1963; The Available Man: Warren E. Harding, 1964; The Better Half, 1964; The Raker, 1965; Concise History of the United States, 1966; Gog, 1967; The Greek Anthology, 1967; Adventures in the Skin Trade, 1968; The Last of the Best, 1969; Guevara, 1970. *Recreations:* vagrancy, old movies. *Address:* 47 Dean Street, W1. *T:* 01-734 1495/6/7.

**SINCLAIR, Prof. David Cecil;** Regius Professor of Anatomy, University of Aberdeen, since 1965; *b* 28 Aug. 1915; *s* of Norman James Sinclair and Annie Smart Sinclair; *m* 1945, Grace Elizabeth Simondson, Melbourne, Vic.; one *s* one *d*. *Educ:* Merchiston Castle Sch.; St Andrews University. MB, ChB (Commendation) St Andrews, 1937; MD (Hons and Rutherford Gold Medal) St Andrews, 1947; MA Oxon, 1948; DSc Western Australia, 1965. Served in RAMC, 1940-46: AMF, 1943-45; Head of Physiology Sect., Aust. Chem. Warfare Research and Experimental Stn, 1943-44; Dep. Chief Supt, Aust. Field Experimental Stn, 1944-45. Sen. Res. Off., Dept of Human Anatomy, Oxford, 1946-49; Univ. Demonstrator in Anatomy, Oxford, 1949-56; Lectr in Anatomy, Pembroke Coll., Oxford, 1950-56; Lectr in Anatomy, Ruskin Sch. of Fine Art, 1950-56; first Prof. of Anatomy, Univ. of W Australia, 1957-64, Dean of Med. Sch., 1964. FRCSE 1966. *Publications:* Medical Students and Medical Sciences, 1955; An Introduction to Functional Anatomy, 1957 (4th edn 1970); A Student's Guide to Anatomy, 1961; Cutaneous Sensation, 1967, Japanese edn 1969; Human Growth after Birth, 1969; Muscles and Fascia (section in Cunningham's Anatomy, 11th edn), 1971; papers on chemical warfare, neurological anatomy, experimental psychology, and medical education; Editor, Jl of Anatomy. *Recreations:* reading, writing, photography, golf. *Address:* Department of Anatomy, Marischal College, Aberdeen. *T:* Aberdeen 4021, ext. M233.

**SINCLAIR, Ernest Keith,** CMG 1966; OBE 1946; DFC 1943; FRGS; Consultant to Prime Minister of Australia and Prime Minister's Department; Deputy Chairman, Australian Tourist Commission, since 1969 (Member since 1966); Director: Australian Paper Manufacturers Ltd; Hecla (Australia) Ltd; *b* 13 November 1914; 2nd *s* of Ernest and Florence Sinclair, Victoria, Australia; *m* 1949, Jill, *d* of John and Muriel Nelder, Pangbourne; one *s*. *Educ:* Melbourne High School, Australia. Literary staff, The Age, 1932-38;

Associate Editor The Age, Melbourne, 1946-69, Editor, 1959-66. Served War of 1939-45, RAF, 1940-45 (despatches, 1944). Director: Australian Assoc. Press, 1959-66 (Chm., 1965-66); Gen. Television Corp. (Melbourne), 1959-66; Member: Australian Council, Internat. Press Inst., 1959-66; Schools Bd for the Humanities, Victoria Inst. of Colleges, 1969- (Chm.); Library Council of Victoria, 1966- (Dep. Pres., 1969-); Observer, Nat. Planning Cttee. *Recreation:* swimming. *Address:* 138 Toorak Road West, South Yarra, Victoria 3141, Australia. *T:* 26-4331. *Clubs:* Press (London); Melbourne, Naval and Military (Melbourne); Commonwealth (Canberra).

**SINCLAIR, Rear-Adm. Erroll Norman,** CB 1963; DSC 1944; retired; *b* 6 Mar. 1909; *s* of late Col John Norman Sinclair, RHA; *m* 1940, Frances Elinor Knox-Gore; two *s*. *Educ:* RNC Dartmouth. Served HMS Cairo, 1936-38; HMS Gallant, 1938-40 (Dunkirk); in comd HMS Fortune, 1940, HMS Antelope, 1941-43, N African Landings; in comd HMS Eskimo, 10th Destroyer Flotilla, 1943-45 (DSC); First Lieut, RN Barracks, Chatham, 1946, Comdr 1946; Exec. Officer, RN Air Station, Eglinton, 1947; Staff Officer Ops to C-in-C, S Atlantic Station, Simonstown, and UK Liaison Officer to S Af. Naval Forces, until 1951. In comd HMS St Kitts, 5th Destroyer Sqdn, Home Fleet, 1951-53; Capt. 1952; Pres. Second Admiralty Interview Board, 1953-54; Naval Attaché at Ankara, Teheran and Tel Aviv, 1955; Capt. (D) 4th Destroyer Sqdn, HMS Agincourt, 1957-59; in comd HMS Sea Eagle and Sen. Naval Officer N Ireland, and Naval Director, Joint A/S School, Londonderry, 1959-61; Flag Officer, Gibraltar, and Admiral Superintendent, HM Dockyard, Gibraltar, also NATO Commander of Gibraltar sub areas, 1962-64; retd list, 1964; Naval Regional Officer (North), 1964-68. *Address:* Island Cottage, Wittersham, Kent. *T:* Wittersham 354.

**SINCLAIR, Sir George (Evelyn),** Kt 1960; CMG 1956; OBE 1950; MP (C) Dorking Division of Surrey, since October 1964; engaged in political work in United Kingdom and overseas, since 1960; *b* Cornwall, 6 November 1912; 2nd *s* of late F. Sinclair, Chynance, St Buryan, Cornwall; *m* 1941, Katharine Jane Burdekin; one *s* three *d*. *Educ:* Abingdon School; Pembroke College, Oxford. MA (Oxon). Entered Colonial Administrative Service, 1936; appointed to Gold Coast Administration; Asst District Comr, 1937. Military service, 1940-43. District Commissioner, Gold Coast, 1943; seconded to Colonial Office, 1943-45; Sec. to Commn on Higher Education in West Africa, 1943-45; returned to Gold Coast, 1945; Senior Assistant Colonial Secretary, 1947; Principal Assistant Secretary, 1950; Regional Officer, Trans-Volta Togoland Region, 1952; Deputy Governor, Cyprus, 1955-60; retired, 1961. Member, Parly Select Committees on: Procedure, 1965-66; Race Relations, 1969-70; Overseas Aid, 1969-70; Jt Sec., Cons. Parly Commonwealth Affairs Cttee, 1966-68. Member: Wimbledon Borough Council, 1962-65; Nat. Exec. Cttee, UNA (UK Branch), 1968-70; Council, Overseas Services Resettlement Bureau; Council of Peoples' Dispensary for Sick Animals (PDSA). Trustee, Runnymede Trust. *Recreation:* lawn tennis. *Address:* South Minack, Porthcurno, Cornwall; 113 Arthur Road, Wimbledon, SW19. *Club:* Royal Commonwealth Society.

**SINCLAIR, Hugh Macdonald,** DM, MA, BSc, FRCP, LMSSA; Fellow and Lecturer in Physiology and Biochemistry, Magdalen College, Oxford, since 1937, and Vice-President, 1956-58; *b* Duddingston House, Edinburgh, 4 Feb. 1910; 2nd *s* of late Col H. M. Sinclair, CB, CMG, CBE, RE, and Rosalie, *d* of late Sir John Jackson, CVO, LLD; unmarried. *Educ:* Winchester (Senior Science Prize); Oriel College, Oxford. First Cl. Hons Animal Physiology, 1932; Gotch Prize, 1933; Senior Demy, Magdalen College, 1932-34; University Coll. Hosp. 1933-36 (Gold and Silver Medals for Clinical Medicine); Radcliffe Schol. in Pharmacology, 1934; Radcliffe Travelling Fellow, 1937-38; Rolleston Prize, 1938; Cutter Lecturer, Harvard, 1951; Schuman Lecturer, Los Angeles, 1962; Golden Acres Lecturer, Dallas, 1963; US Medal of Freedom with Silver Palm; Officer of Order of Orange-Nassau (Holland); FCS; Member Physiological Society, Biochemical Society, Faraday Society, Medical Research Society, Soc. for Experimental Biology, Soc. Philomathique; University Demonstrator and Lecturer in Biochemistry, Oxford, until 1947; Director, Oxford Nutrition Survey, until 1947; Hon. Nutrition Consultant (with rank of Brig.), CCG, until 1947. Reader in Human Nutrition and Director of the Laboratory of Human Nutrition, Oxford, 1951-58. Master, Worshipful Soc. of Apothecaries, 1967-68. Hon. DSc Baldwin-Wallace, USA, 1968. *Publications:* papers on Human Nutrition and on Brain Metabolism in scientific and med. jls; Use of Vitamins in Medicine, in Whitla's Pharmacy, Materia Medica and Therapeutics (13th edn), 1939; Vitamins in Treatment, in Modern Therapeutics (Practitioner Handbooks), 1941; Nutrition, in Aspects of Modern Science, 1951; A Short History of Anatomical Teaching in Oxford (with A. H. T. Robb-Smith), 1950; (ed) The Work of Sir Robert McCarrison, 1953; (with McCarrison) Nutrition and Health, 1953 and 1961; (with Prof. Jelliffe) Nicholl's Tropical Nutrition, 1961; (with F. C. Rodger) Metabolic and Nutritional Eye Diseases, 1968; (with D. Hollingsworth) Hutchison's Food and Principles of Nutrition, 1969; articles on med. educn. *Recreations:* tennis, cricket, and gardening. *Address:* Magdalen College, Oxford. *T:* Oxford 41781; Lady Place, Sutton Courtenay, Berks. *T:* Sutton Courtenay 246. *Clubs:* Athenæum, MCC.

**SINCLAIR, Ian McTaggart;** Legal Counsellor, Foreign and Commonwealth Office, since 1967; *b* 14 Jan. 1926; *s* of late John Sinclair, company director; *m* 1954, Barbara Elizabeth (*née* Lenton); two *s* one *d*. *Educ:* Merchiston Castle Sch.; King's Coll., Cambridge. Asst Legal Adviser, Foreign Office, 1950-56; Legal Adviser, HM Embassy, Bonn, 1957-60; Asst Legal Adviser, FO, 1960-64; Legal Adviser, UK Mission to the UN, New York, and HM Embassy, Washington, 1964-67. Has been Legal Adviser to UK delegn at numerous internat. confs, incl. Geneva Conf. on Korea and Indo-China, 1954, and Brussels negotiations for UK entry into the EEC, 1961-63; Dep. Chm., UK delegn to Law of Treaties Conf., Vienna, 1968-69; Legal Adviser to UK delegn on negotiations for UK entry into EEC, 1970-. *Publications:* articles in British Yearbook of International Law and International and Comparative Law Quarterly. *Recreations:* golf, theatre. *Address:* 24 Vineyard Hill Road, Wimbledon, SW19. *T:* 01-946 4269. *Clubs:* Hurlingham; Royal Scottish Automobile.

**SINCLAIR, Isabel Lillias, (Mrs J. G. MacDonald),** QC (Scotland) 1964; Sheriff-Substitute of Roxburgh, Berwick, and Selkirk, at Selkirk, since 1968; *d* of William Sinclair, Glasgow, and Isabella (*née* Thomson), Glasgow; *m* 1938, J. Gordon MacDonald, BL, Solicitor, Glasgow. *Educ:* Shawlands

Academy; Glasgow Univ.; Edinburgh Univ. MA 1932; BL 1946. Worked as a newspaper-woman from 1932. Admitted to Faculty of Advocates, Edinburgh, 1949. Sheriff-Substitute of Lanarkshire at Airdrie, 1966-68. *Address:* 6 St Vincent Street, Edinburgh 3. *T:* 031-556 4806. *Club:* Ladies' Caledonian (Edinburgh).

**SINCLAIR, John,** MBE 1958; JP; Lord Lieutenant of Caithness, 1965; *b* 24 March 1898; *s* of John Sinclair and Margaret Gray Sinclair; unmarried. *Educ:* Miller Academy, Thurso. Member of Thurso Town Council, 1929-63; Bailie (Magistrate), 1932-48; Provost, 1948-61; Free Burgess of the Burgh of Thurso, 1966. Hon. Sheriff Substitute, 1948; JP 1941, Caithness. *Recreations:* music, fishing. *Address:* 20 Millers Lane, Thurso. *T:* Thurso 2481.

**SINCLAIR, Maj.-Gen. Sir John (Alexander),** KCMG 1953; CB 1945; OBE 1940; Colonel Commandant Royal Artillery, 1952-62; Director, Chinnor Industries Ltd; *b* 29 May 1897; *s* of Ven. Archdeacon J. S. Sinclair; *m* 1927, Esme Beatrice Sopwich; two *s* two *d.* *Educ:* West Downs, Winchester; RN Colleges; RMA Woolwich. Midshipman RN, 1914-16; RMA Woolwich, 1918; commissioned RFA 1919; Adjutant HAC, 1929-31; Staff Coll., 1932-33; Bt Maj., 1936; Instructor Staff Coll., 1938-39; Bt Lt-Col 1939; Deputy Director Military Operations, 1941; BGS South-Eastern Command, 1941; CRA 1st Division 1942; DCGS Home Forces, 1942; MGGS Home Forces, 1943; Director of Military Intelligence, War Office, 1944-45. Commander, Legion of Merit (US), 1945; Commander, Order of the Crown (Belgium), 1945. *Recreations:* cricket and reading. *Address:* East Ashling Grange, Chichester. *T:* West Ashling 292. *Club:* Army and Navy.

**SINCLAIR, John Alexis Clifford Cerda A.;** *see* Alexander-Sinclair.

**SINCLAIR, Sir John (Rollo Norman Blair),** 9th Bt, *cr* 1631; *b* 4 Nov. 1928; *s* of Sir Ronald Norman John Charles Udny Sinclair, 8th Bt, TD, and Reba Blair (Company Comdt, Auxiliary Territorial Service, 1938-41), *d* of Anthony Inglis, MS, Lismore, Ayrshire; *S* father 1952; *heir-pres* to 20th Earl of Caithness, *qv.* *Educ:* Wellington College. Lt Intelligence Corps 1948-49. Director, The Lucis Trust, 1957-61. *Publication:* The Mystical Ladder, 1968. *Heir: uncle* Alexander Robert Sinclair [*b* 26 Sept. 1901; *m* 1928, Vera Mabel, *d* of late Walter Stephings Baxendale, Bradbourne, Sevenoaks, Kent; one *s* one *d*]. *Address:* (Seat) Barrock House, Wick, Caithness.

*See also Baroness Masham of Ilton.*

**SINCLAIR, Capt. Sir Kenneth (Duncan Lecky),** Kt, *cr* 1954; DL; RNR; Member, Belfast Harbour Board since 1934 (Chm., 1948-67); *b* 13 June 1889; 3rd *s* of late Right Honourable Thomas Sinclair, PC, DLitt, MA, DL, Hopefield House, Belfast; *m* 1914, Eleanor Laura, *d* of late Lieut-Col J. Jackson Clark, HM Lieutenant, Largantogher, Maghera, Co. Derry; one *s* one *d.* *Educ:* Rugby School; Trinity College, Cambridge. *Address:* 44 Windsor Park, Belfast. *T:* Belfast 666698. *Club:* Ulster (Belfast).

**SINCLAIR, Air Vice-Marshal Sir Laurence (Frank),** GC 1941; KCB 1957 (CB 1946); CBE 1943; DSO 1940 (and Bar, 1943); Controller, National Air Traffic Control Services, Ministry of Aviation, and Ministry of Defence, 1962-66; *b* 1908; *m* 1941, Valerie, *d* of Lt-Col Joseph Dalton White; one *s* one *d.* Comd No 110 Sqdn in 1940; Comd RAF Watton, 1941; Comd Tactical Light Bomber Force in North Africa and Italy, 1943-44; subsequently Sen. Air Staff Officer, Balkan Air Force; commanded No 2 Light Bomber Group (Germany), 1948-49; Assistant Commandant RAF Staff College, 1949-50; Commandant, Royal Air Force College Cranwell, 1950-52; Commandant, School of Land/Air Warfare, Old Sarum, Wiltshire, 1952-53; Asst Chief of the Air Staff (Operations), 1953-55; Comdr British Forces, Arabian Peninsula, 1955-57; Commandant Joint Services Staff College, 1958-60, retired from RAF. Controller of Ground Services, Min. of Aviation, 1960-61. Legion of Merit (American), 1943; Legion of Honour, 1944; Partisan Star (Yugoslavia). *Address:* Fosseys, Great Brickhill, Bletchley, Bucks.

**SINCLAIR, Sir Leonard,** Kt 1955; Company Chairman and Director; *b* 9 June 1895; *s* of John and Mary Sinclair, Broughton, Salford, Lancs; *m* 1926, Mary Levine; one *d.* *Educ:* Higher Grade School, Broughton, Salford, Lancs. Director: Eagle Star Insurance Co. Ltd, 1958-70; Fleming and Brit. American Optical Industries Ltd, 1959-70; Pirelli Ltd, 1960-70; Ship Mortgage Finance Co. Ltd; Past Chm. Esso Petroleum Co. Ltd, 1951-58 (Dir, 1943-58). *Recreations:* golf, gardening. *Address:* Deans Croft, Deans Lane, Walton-on-the-Hill, Surrey. *T:* Tadworth 3629. *Clubs:* American, Royal Automobile.

**SINCLAIR, Sir Ronald Ormiston,** KBE 1963; Kt 1956; President, Court of Appeal: for the Bahamas and for Bermuda, 1965-70; for British Honduras, 1968-70; Chairman, Industrial Tribunals (England and Wales), 1966-69; *b* 2 May 1903; *yr s* of Rev. W. A. Sinclair, Auckland, NZ; *m* 1935, Ellen Isabel Entrican; two *s.* *Educ:* New Plymouth Boys' High School, NZ; Auckland University College, NZ; Balliol College, Oxford. Barrister and Solicitor of Supreme Court of New Zealand, 1924; LLM (NZ) (Hons) 1925; Administrative Service, Nigeria, 1931; Magistrate, Nigeria, 1936; Resident Magistrate, Northern Rhodesia, 1938; Barrister-at-Law, Middle Temple, 1939; Puisne Judge, Tanganyika, 1946; Chief Justice, Nyasaland, 1953-55; Vice-President, East African Court of Appeal, 1956-57, Pres., 1962-64; Chief Justice of Kenya, 1957-62. *Address:* c/o The Guardian Trust, PO Box 1934, Auckland, New Zealand.

**SINCLAIR, Sir William,** Kt 1957; CBE 1955; JP; retired as Director and Chief Executive, Dunlop Rubber Co. (Scotland) Ltd and as General Commissioner of Inland Revenue; *b* 17 Jan. 1895; *s* of Rev. James Steven Sinclair and Jessie Sutherland; *m* 1919, Stephanie Patricia Laline Hunte Taylour Daniel, MB, BS, MRCS, LRCP (*d* 1966); one *s* two *d.* *Educ:* Wick and Glasgow. On active service, European War, 1914-18, Vice-Pres., Scottish Motor Trade Assoc., 1941-45, 1946-47, 1948-50. FIMI (Lord Wakefield Gold Medallist, 1943). Pres. Ye Jovial Tramps, Glasgow, 1941-42 (Hon. Pres., 1957-); JP, County of City of Glasgow, 1951; Member of Merchants House of City of Glasgow, 1953, Director, 1964. Contested (C and U). Glasgow Central Div., 1951; President, Scottish Unionist Association, 1956-57; Member: Livingstone New Town Develt Corp., 1961-67; Nat. Health Service Exec. Council for Glasgow, 1960-67. Patron, Hutchesons Trust, Glasgow, 1968-. Hon. President, Scottish Commercial Travellers Association Ltd, 1960-61. *Recreation:* public service. *Address:* 58 Dalziel Drive, Glasgow, S1. *T:* 041-427 1602. *Clubs:*

Glasgow Conservative, RNVR (Glasgow); Clydesdale Cricket.

**SINCLAIR-LOCKHART, Sir Muir (Edward),** 14th Bt *cr* 1636 (NS); sheep farmer; *b* 23 July 1906; 3rd *s* of Sir Robert Duncan Sinclair-Lockhart, 11th Bt and Flora Louisa Jane Beresford Nation (*d* 1937), *d* of Captain Edward Henry Power; *S* brother, 1970; *m* 1940, Olga Ann, *d* of Claude Victor White-Parsons; one *s* one *d*. *Recreation:* hunting (harrier). *Heir: s* Simon John Edward Francis Sinclair-Lockhart, *b* 22 July 1941. *Address:* Onga Onga, Waipawa, Hawkes Bay, New Zealand.

**SINDEN, Donald Alfred;** actor; *b* 9 Oct. 1923; *s* of Alfred Edward Sinden and Mabel Agnes (*née* Fuller), Sussex; *m* 1948, Diana Mahony; two *s*. *Educ:* Webber-Douglas Sch. of Dramatic Art. First appearance on stage, 1941, in Charles F. Smith's Co., Mobile Entertainments Southern Area; Leicester Repertory Co., 1945; Memorial Theatre Co., Stratford, 1946 and 1947; Old Vic and Bristol Old Vic, 1948; The Heiress, Haymarket, 1949-50; Bristol Old Vic, 1950; Red Letter Day, Garrick, 1951. Under contract to Rank Organisation, 1952-60, appearing in 23 films including Cruel Sea, Doctor in the House, etc. Odd Man In, St Martin's, 1957; Peter Pan, Scala, 1960; Guilty Party, St Martin's, 1961; Royal Shakespeare Co., 1963 and 1964 playing Richard Plantaganet in Henry VI (The Wars of the Roses), Price in Eh!, etc; British Council tour of S America, 1965; There's a Girl in my Soup, Globe, 1966; Lord Foppington in The Relapse, Aldwych, 1967; Not Now Darling, Strand, 1968; Royal Shakespeare Co., 1969 and 1970 playing Malvolio; Henry VIII; Sir Harcourt Courtly in London Assurance. Numerous TV appearances include Our Man from St Marks series. Assoc. Artist, Royal Shakespeare Co.; Mem. Council, British Actors Equity Assoc., 1966-; Pres., Repertory Playgoers Soc.; Vice-Pres., London Appreciation Soc.; Mem. Cttee, British Theatre Museum Assoc.; FRSA. *Recreations:* theatrical history, French history, architecture, ecclesiology, numismatology, serendipity, London. *Address:* 60 Temple Fortune Lane, NW11; Rats Castle, Isle of Oxney, Kent. *Clubs:* Garrick, MCC.

**SINDERSON, Sir Harry Chapman, Pasha,** KBE, *cr* 1946 (OBE 1932); CMG 1942; MVO 1933; KStJ; Knight Commander, Order of the North Star (Sweden); Order of Istiqlal (Jordan), 2nd class; Orders of Faisal I and Rafidain (Iraq), 2nd class; Order of Nahda (Hedjaz), 2nd class; Order of Taj (Iran) 3rd class; Officer of the Order of Leopold, Belgium; Coronation and Red Crescent Medals of Iraq; Order of Polonia Restituta, 3rd Class; MB, ChB, MD, FRCPE; DTM&H (England); FRGS; late Adviser and Inspector-General of Health Services, Min. of Social Affairs, Iraq; Emeritus Professor, late Dean and Prof. of Medicine, Royal Coll. of Medicine of Iraq; Physician to HM the King and Royal Family of Iraq, 1921-46; Major, late RAMC (Militia); *b* 9 June 1891; *s* of late William Sinderson; *m* 1920, Maude Elsie Hyde (*d* 1967), *d* of late George Walter MunGavin, MBE. Served European War, 1914-18: OC Hospital Ships Stad Antwerpen and Wandilla; accompanied TM King Faisal I and II and the Prince Regent of Iraq on many official and private visits to various countries. Fellow, Roy. Soc. of Tropical Medicine and Hygiene; Vice-Patron, formerly hon. Warden, Sackville Coll., East Grinstead (Historic Building); a Vice-President, Brighton College; Council, Royal Society of St George; Representative Governor, Imperial Cancer Research Fund; Chapter-Gen. Order of St John; RIIA; Royal Central Asian Society; Guild of Freemen, City of London; Fauna Preservation Society. *Publications:* numerous articles in various medical and other jls. *Recreations:* travel, outdoor sports and country pursuits, represented Edinburgh University at Association Football, 1909-14 (Captain, 1911-12) and cricket, 1913-14. *Address:* Little Steddings, Forest Row, Sussex. *T:* Forest Row 2143. *Club:* East India and Sports.

**SINGH, St Nihal;** author, journalist, broadcaster, lecturer, globe-girdler, photographer; since early years of this century, Correspondent-at-large of numerous papers in USA, Canada, Britain, India, Ceylon, etc.; near end of Asian tour (300,000 miles) since 1930; *b* 30 May 1884; *s* of Sardar Nihal Singh Surya, Rawal Pindi, Punjab (now Pakistan), India; *m* 1907, Cathleyne Brookes (*d* 1958), Chicago. *Educ:* Punjab Univ. Began writing for the press, 1897. Lectures before universities, learned societies, and political, sociological, and religious associations; especially interested in cultural research and in movements of an International character and for promotion of peace. Coronation Medal, 1911. Accompanied HRH the Prince of Wales's Party in India, 1921-22. *Publications:* Essays on India, 1907; Messages of Uplift for India, 1909; Glimpses of the Orient To-day, 1910; Making Bad Children Good, 1910; Urge Divine, 1912; Progressive British India, 1914; Japan's Modernisation, 1914; India's Fighting Troops, 1914; The Rally of the Empire (first part), 1914; India's Fighters, 1914; The King's Indian Allies: the Rajas and their India, 1916; India and the War, 1918; Dry America: An Object Lesson to India, 1921; Dry America: Its Significance to Ceylon, 1921; The Nizam and the British Empire 1922 (privately printed); India: New and Old, 1924; The Road to India's Past, 1924; India Beckons, 1924; The Changing Scene in India, 1925; Along an Indian Railroad, 1925; Belgium Old and New, 1926; Opportunity in Canada, 1927; On the Doorstep of Prosperity in Canada, 1927; Ceylon: New and Old, 1929; Ceylon's Scenic Splendour, 1929; Relics of Old Ceylon, 1929; Shree Bhagvat Sinhjee, The Maker of Modern Gondal, 1934; Hyderabad To-Day, 1947; Dharmapala: the Man and the Missioner (Centennial year, 1964); A Crusader of Humanist Causes (Bhawanidas N. Motwala), 1965; They Brought India Freedom (6-8 vols), 1964 and succeeding years; India's Composite Culture (4-6 vols); Movements in Modern India (articles and notes contemporaneously published in papers and reviews, etc). Has ed and/or contrib. to vols presented to eminent persons, incl. Dr Rajendra Prasad, and to critiques of Indian literature. *Recreations:* delving in archæology and folklore, radio, travel, photography, theatre, walking, reading. *Address:* Suryasthanam, 16 Nemi Road, Dehra Dun, UP, India; c/o Midland Bank Ltd, Loughborough Junction Branch, 226 Coldharbour Lane, SW9.

**SINGH, Sardar Swaran;** Foreign Minister, Government of India, since 1970; *b* 19 Aug. 1907. *Educ:* Government College, Lahore; Lahore Law College. MSc (Physics) 1930; LLB 1932. Elected to Punjab Legislative Assembly, 1946; Punjab State Government: Minister for Development, Food and Civil Supplies, 1946-47; Member, Security Council, 1947; Member, Partition Committee, 1947; Minister of Home, General Administration, Revenue, Irrigation and Electricity, 1947-49; Minister of Capital Projects and Electricity, 1952; Government of India: Minister for Works, Housing and Supply, 1952-57; Member, Upper House of Indian Legislature, 1952-57; Member, Lower House of Indian Legislature,

1957-; Minister for Steel, Mines and Fuel, 1957-62; Minister for Railways, 1962-63; Minister for Food and Agriculture, 1963-64; Minister for Industry and Supply, 1964; Minister for External Affairs, 1964-66; Minister of Defence, 1966-70. Has led many Indian delegations to the United Nations, its agencies, foreign countries and international conferences. *Address:* (office) Ministry of Foreign Affairs, New Delhi, India; (home) 7 Hastings Road, New Delhi, India.

**SINGHANIA, Sir Padampat,** Kt, *cr* 1943; President of the JK Organisation, India; *b* 1905; *s* of late Lala Kamlapat Singhania; *m* Srimati Anusiya Devi; four *s* one *d*. *Educ:* Home. A pioneer of Cotton, Rayon, Nylon, Jute, Woollen Textiles, Sugar, Aluminium, Steel and Engineering, Plastic, Strawboard, Paper, Chemicals, Oil Industries, Banking, Insurance; Patron, large number of social, educational, political, and literary institutions. Founder of the Merchants' Chamber of UP: ex-Pres. of Federation of Indian Chambers of Commerce and Industry; ex-Pres., Employers' Assoc. of Northern India; Member 1st Indian Parliament, 1947-52, and many government and semi-govt bodies; Chairman, Board of Governors, IIT Kampur. Dr of Letters, Kanpur Univ., 1968. *Recreations:* riding, music, buildings, and studies. *Address:* Kamla Tower, Kanpur, India. *TA:* Laljuggi, Kanpur. *T:* 32454, 32532 and 32488. *Telex* KP215.

**SINGHATEH, Alhaji Sir Farimang (Mohamadu),** GCMG 1966; JP; Governor-General of The Gambia since 1965; *b* 30 Nov. 1912; *m* 1939; three *s* six *d* (and two *s* one *d* decd). *Educ:* Armitage Secondary School, Georgetown, The Gambia. Career as Druggist and Chemist. *Address:* Government House, Bathurst, The Gambia.

**SINGLETON, Norman,** CB 1966; Secretary, Commission on Industrial Relations, since 1969; *b* 21 March 1913; *s* of Charles and Alice Singleton, Bolton, Lancs; *m* 1936, Cicely Margaret Lucas, Claverdon, Warwick; one *s* two *d*. *Educ:* Bolton School; Emmanuel College, Cambridge. Min. of Labour, 1935; Under-Secretary: Civil Service Pay Research Unit, 1956-60; Min. of Labour (now Dept of Employment and Productivity), 1960-69. *Address:* 34 Willoughby Road, Hampstead, NW3. *T:* 01-435 4358. *Club:* Reform.

**SINHA,** 3rd Baron *cr* 1919, of Raipur; **Sudhindro Prosanno Sinha;** Chairman and Managing Director, MacNeill and Barry Ltd, Calcutta; *b* 29 Oct. 1920; *s* of Aroon Kumar, 2nd Baron Sinha (*s* of Satyendra Prasanna, 1st Baron Sinha, the first Indian to be created a peer) and Nirupama, *yr d* of Rai Bahadur Lalit Mohan Chatterjee; *S* father, 1967; *m* 1945, Madhabi, *d* of late Monoranjan Chatterjee, Calcutta; one *s* two *d* (and one *s* decd). *Educ:* Bryanston School, Blandford. *Heir: s* Sushanto Sinha, *b* 1953. *Address:* 7 Lord Sinha Road, Calcutta.

**SINHA, Hon. Mr Justice Bhuvaneshwar Prasad;** Chief Justice of India, 1959-64, retired; *b* 1 Feb. 1899; *s* of B. Kashi Nath Sinha and Sm. Sheila Devi; *m* 1914, Sm. Phulkesar Devi; three *s* three *d*. *Educ:* Arrah Zila School; Government College, Patna. BA (Patna) 1st Class Hons; 1st in History 1919 (Gold Medal); Post-Graduate Scholar, 1919-21; 1st in History, MA, 1921. Vakil, High Court, Patna, 1922; Advocate, High Court, Patna, 1927; Lecturer, Govt Law College, Patna, 1926-35; Govt Pleader, High Court, Patna, 1935-39; Asst Govt Advocate, High Court, Patna, 1940-43; Senior Advocate, Federal Court of India, 1942; Judge, High Court of Patna, 1943; Chief Justice, High Court, Nagpur, 1951-54; Judge, Supreme Court of India, Dec. 1954-Sept. 1959. *Recreations:* hiking and indoor games. *Address:* 20 Mathura Road, New Delhi, India.

**SINHA, Rajandhari,** CIE 1943; Mayor, Patna Municipal Corporation, 1954-57; Resident Representative of Patna, Tata Iron & Steel Co. Ltd, 1954-57; *b* 3 Oct. 1893; *s* of Rai Bahadur Chandradhari Sinha, Village Dharhara, PO Paliganj (District Patna); *m* 1915, *d* of late Babu Ambikanandan Sinha, Deputy Collector, UP; one *s* one *d*. *Educ:* Patna (BA, BL). Sec. of Bihar Landholders' Assoc., 1937-38; Manager of Hathwa Wards Estate, Saran, Member of Dist War Committee, Saran, and Dist Leader, National War Front, 1938-44; a Governor of Patna Arts Coll.; Member of Secondary Board of Education, Bihar and Orissa; Chairman of Dist Board, Patna, 1924-33; MLC Bihar and Orissa, 1924-37 (President, 1933-37); Member of Joint Public Service Commn of Bihar, Central Provinces and Berar and Orissa, 1947-49, and Chairman of Public Service Commn for Bihar, 1949-53; Liaison Officer, Bihar, Tata Iron & Steel Co. Ltd, 1953-54; Chairman, Bihar State Financial Corporation, 1954-57. *Address:* Dharhara House, Bankipore, Patna-4, India.

**SINKER, Sir (Algernon) Paul,** KCMG, *cr* 1954; CB 1950; Chairman, Council for Small Industries in Rural Areas, since 1968; *b* 13 April 1905; *s* of late Rev. Robert Sinker; *m* 1929, Ruth Longland; two *s* two *d*. *Educ:* Haileybury Coll.; Jesus College, Cambridge. University of Vienna, 1927-28; Prince Consort Prize; Fellow of Jesus College, Cambridge, 1927-49; Tutor, 1929-40; University Lecturer. Civil servant at Admiralty, 1940-45 (Washington, 1941-42); Treasury, 1945-50; adviser to Egyptian Government on Civil Service questions, 1950; First Civil Service Commissioner, 1951-54; Dir-Gen., British Council, 1954-68. Dep. Chm., Bd of Governors, Atlantic Coll.; Mem. Council, Voluntary Service Overseas; Mem., Governing Body, Shrewsbury Sch. Hon. Fellow, Jesus College, Cambridge, 1955. Hon. LLD: Exeter, 1961; Southampton, 1967. *Publication:* Introduction to Lucretius, 1937. *Recreations:* climbing, walking, sailing. *Address:* 11 Cowley Street, SW1; 39 Berwick Road, Shrewsbury. *Club:* Athenæum.

**SINKER, Rt. Rev. George;** Provost of Birmingham Cathedral since 1962, and Assistant Bishop of Birmingham; *b* 5 May 1900; *s* of Rev. R. Sinker; *m* 1924, Eva Margaret Madden; two *s* two *d*. *Educ:* Rossall School; Brasenose College, Oxford. CMS Missionary, Kandy, Ceylon, 1921; ordained, 1924; Bannu, NWFP, India, 1924; Peshawar, 1932; Headmaster, Bishop Cotton School, Simla 1935; Canon of Lahore Cathedral, 1944; Gen. Sec. Bible Society, India and Ceylon, 1947; Bishop of Nagpur, 1949-54; Asst Bp of Derby, 1954-62; Vicar of Bakewell, 1955-62. *Publications:* Jesus Loved Martha, 1949; What was Jesus doing on the Cross?, 1952; His Very Words, 1953. *Recreation:* Shakespeare studies. *Address:* Provost's Lodge, St Philip's Place, Birmingham 3. *T:* 021-236 1626.

**SINKER, Rev. Canon Michael Roy;** Rector of St Matthew, Ipswich, since 1967; Canon Emeritus of Lincoln Cathedral, since 1969; *b* 28 Sept. 1908; 3rd *s* of late Rev. Francis Sinker, sometime Vicar of Ilkley; *m* 1939, Edith Watt Applegate; one *s* two *d*. *Educ:* Haileybury; Clare College, Cambridge (MA); Cuddesdon College, Oxford. Curate of Dalston, Cumberland, 1932-34; Chaplain to South African Church Railway Mission, 1935-38;

Curate of Bishop's Hatfield 1938-39; Vicar of Dalton-in-Furness, 1939-46; Vicar of Saffron Walden, 1946-63; Hon. Canon of Chelmsford Cathedral, 1955-63; Rural Dean of Saffron Walden, 1948-63; Archdeacon of Stow, 1963-67. *Address:* St Matthew's Rectory, Ipswich. *T:* Ipswich 51630.

**SINKER, Sir Paul;** *see* Sinker, Sir A. P.

**SINNOTT, Ernest;** Chairman, South Eastern Electricity Board, since 1966; *b* 10 March 1909; *s* of John Sinnott and Emily (*née*) Currie; *m* 1934, Simone Marie (*née* Petitjean); two *s*. *Educ:* Salford Grammar School. City Treasurer's Dept, Salford, 1924-31; City Accountant's Dept, Chester, 1931; Borough Treasurer's Dept, Warrington, 1931-32; Dep. Borough Treasurer, Middleton 1932-35, Worthing 1935-37; Borough Treasurer, Worthing, 1937-48; Chief Accountant, SE Electricity Bd, 1948-62, Dep. Chairman, 1962-66. Chartered Accountant (hons) 1935; FIMTA (Collins gold medal), 1932; Pres. 1956-57. *Publications:* (jointly) Brown's Municipal Book-keeping and Accounts; contribs to learned journals on local government finance. *Recreations:* golf, music, reading and walking. *Address:* Litte Court, West Parade, Worthing, Sussex. *Club:* Worthing Golf.

**SISAM, Kenneth,** MA (New Zealand University); MA, BLitt Oxon; FBA 1941; Hon. DLitt Reading, 1948; Grand Kt of the Icelandic Falcon, 1948; *b* 1887; *m* 1915, Naomi (*d* 1958), *d* of R. P. Gibbons; one *s* one *d*. *Educ:* Auckland Grammar School; Auckland University College, NZ; Merton College, Oxford. Rhodes Scholar, 1910; Ministry of Food, 1917-22; Secretary to the Delegates of the Oxford University Press, 1942-48; formerly Fellow of Merton College, and Hon. Fellow, 1964-. *Publications:* Fourteenth Century Verse and Prose, 1921; Studies in the History of Old English Literature, 1953; (joint editor), The Salisbury Psalter, 1959; The Structure of Beowulf, 1965, etc. *Address:* Middle Carn, St Mary's, Isles of Scilly.

**SISSON, Charles Hubert;** Assistant Under-Secretary of State, Department of Employment and Productivity; *b* 22 April 1914; *s* of late Richard Percy Sisson and Ellen Minnie Sisson (*née* Worlock); *m* 1937, Nora Gilbertson; two *d*. *Educ:* University of Bristol, and in France and Germany. Entered Ministry of Labour as Assistant Principal, 1936; Principal, 1942. HM Forces, in the ranks, mainly in India, 1942-45. Assistant Secretary, 1953; Simon Senior Research Fell., 1956-57; Under-Sec. (Dir of Establishments), 1962-68. *Publications:* An Asiatic Romance, 1953; Versions and Perversions of Heine, 1955; The Spirit of British Administration, 1959; The London Zoo (poems), 1961; Numbers (poems); Christopher Homm, 1965; Art and Action, 1965; Catullus (translation), 1966; The Discarnation (poem), 1967; Essays, 1967; Metamorphoses (poems), 1968; English Poetry 1900-1950, 1971. *Address:* Flat 14, 92 Westbourne Terrace, W2. *T:* 01-402 4742; Moorfield Cottage, The Hill, Langport, Somerset. *T:* Langport 8845.

**SISSON, Marshall Arnott,** CBE 1959; RA 1963 (ARA 1956); FSA, FRIBA; Architect in private practice since 1928; *b* 14 Feb. 1897; *o s* of Arthur White Sisson, MIMechE, Hucclecote, Gloucestershire; *m* 1933, Marjorie, *o d* of Harold Matthews, Portishead, Somerset. *Educ:* Bartlett School of Architecture, University of London. BA (Arch.) London 1923; Jarvis Rome Scholar in Architecture, 1924; Duveen Fellow, 1927. Architectural practice has included civic, collegiate, ecclesiastical, scholastic, commercial and other buildings. Treasurer of the Royal Academy, 1965-; Member: Ancient Monuments Board for England; Diocesan Adv. Cttees of Ely and Southwark; Council, Architectural Panel of National Trust; Cathedrals Advisory Cttee; Hon. Technical Adviser to the Georgian Group. Hon. D Fine Arts, Westminster Coll., Missouri, 1969. *Publications:* Country Cottages, 1949; various papers in technical and archæological journals. *Address:* Farm Hall, Godmanchester, Huntingdon. *T:* Huntingdon 3363. *Clubs:* Athenæum, Arts.

**SITA RAM, Rai Bahadur Sir,** Kt, *cr* 1931; MA, LLB, DLitt; a member of the Upper House of the Provincial legislature in United Provinces (President, 1937-48); *b* 12 Jan. 1885; *m*; two *s* six *d* (and one *s* decd). *Educ:* Meerut; Allahabad (Honours in Sanskrit). Member Meerut Municipal Board, 1910-20; Hon. Sec. All-India Vaish Maha Sabba, 1911-25; Hon. Managing Director, Meerut District Co-operative Bank, 1918-25; Member, Indian National Congress, 1906-19; Member, United Provinces Legislative Council, 1921-37, first elected Indian non-official President, 1925-37; High Commissioner for India in Pakistan, at Karachi, March 1949-Nov. 1950. Rai Sahib, 1919; Rai Bahadur, 1923; raised a Middle English School called Deva Nagri School to the High School Standard, serving as its Hon. Secretary, 1913-36; connected with the Meerut College since 1907 as a member of its Executive Committee and as Hon. Sec., 1923-34 and 1940-46; Pres. of two Girls' Colleges at Meerut; actively associated with Executive of the Allahabad and Benares (Hindu) Universities; served on a number of Committees and Boards appointed by Government. Patron-President UP Sports Control Board; Pres. Shiri Badrinath Temple Committee, 1941-43; Patron Sangit Samaj, Meerut; ex-Chm. Universities Grants Cttee, UP; Pres. UP Ethnographical Soc.; ex-Chm. UP Police Reorganisation Cttee; ex-Chm. UP Gosamvardhan Cttee. *Address:* Champa, Meerut, UP, India.

**SITWELL, Rev. Francis Gerard,** OSB, MA; Parish Priest of St Benedict's Ampleforth, since 1969; *b* 22 Dec. 1906; *s* of late Major Francis Sitwell and Margaret Elizabeth, *d* of late Matthew Culley, Coupland Castle, Northumberland. *Educ:* Ampleforth; St Benet's Hall, Oxford. Received Benedictine Habit, 1924; Professed, 1925; Priest, 1933; Assistant Master at Ampleforth, 1933-39; Assistant Procurator at Ampleforth, 1939-47; Subprior of Ampleforth, 1946-47; Master of St Benet's Hall, Oxford, 1947-64; Priest of Our Lady and St Wilfrid, Warwick Bridge, Carlisle, 1966-69. *Publications:* Walter Hilton, Scale of Perfection, (trans. and ed); St Odo of Cluny; Medieval Spirituality; articles in Ampleforth Journal, Downside Review, Clergy Review, Month, etc. *Address:* Ampleforth Abbey, York YO6 4EN.

**SITWELL, Maj.-Gen. Hervey Degge Wilmot,** CB 1946; CVO 1967; MC 1917; FSA 1957; Keeper of The Jewel House, HM Tower of London, 1952-68, retired; *b* 25 Oct. 1896; *s* of Hervey Wheler Sitwell, Manor House, Leamington Hastings, Warwicks, and Alice Mary, *d* of Charles Schwind, Broomfield, Co. Derby; *m* 1919, Catherine Florence Parke, *d* of Dr Eustace Olive, FRCS, LRCP, Leamington Spa; one *d*. *Educ:* Wellington Coll., RMA Woolwich. Commissioned RFA, 1914; Lt 1915; Capt. 1917; Major, 1933; actg Lt-Col 1939; Brig., 1941; Maj.-Gen. (local), 1942; served European War, 1914-18 (despatches, MC); served War of 1939-45 (despatches, CB);

GOC Brit. Troops, Java, 1942; prisoner of war, Japanese hands, 1942-45; Dist Comdr, Canal North District, Egypt, 1946-49; Dep. Dist Comdr, East Anglian District, 1949-51; retired 1951. Hon. Major-General. Fellow, Society of Antiquaries, 1957. *Publication:* The Crown Jewels, 1953. *Recreations:* research on crown jewels, genealogy. *Address:* Camerton, Gate Lane, Freshwater Bay, Isle of Wight. *T:* Freshwater 2395. *Clubs:* Army and Navy; Royal Solent Yacht.

**SITWELL, Sir Sacheverell,** 6th Bt *cr* 1808; *b* Scarborough, 15 Nov. 1897; *s* of Sir George Sitwell, 4th Bt, and Lady Ida Emily Augusta Denison (*d* 1937), *d* of 1st Earl of Londesborough; *S* brother, 1969; *m* 1925, Georgia, *yr d* of Arthur Doble, Montreal; two *s*. *Educ:* Eton College. High Sheriff of Northamptonshire, 1948-49. Freedom of City of Lima (Peru), 1960. *Publications:* Southern Baroque Art, 1924; All Summer in a Day, 1926; The Gothick North, 1929; Life of Liszt, 1936; Dance of the Quick and the Dead, 1936; Conversation Pieces, 1936; La Vie Parisienne, 1937; Narrative Pictures, 1937; Roumanian Journey, 1938; Old Fashioned Flowers, 1939; Mauretania, 1939; Poltergeists, 1940; Sacred and Profane Love, 1940; Valse des Fleurs, 1941; Primitive Scenes and Festivals, 1942; The Homing of the Winds, 1942; Splendours and Miseries, 1943; British Architects and Craftsmen, 1945; The Hunters and the Hunted, 1947; The Netherlands, 1948; Selected Poems, 1948; Morning, Noon, and Night in London, 1948; Spain, 1950; Cupid and the Jacaranda, 1952; Truffle Hunt with Sacheverell Sitwell, 1953: Portugal and Madeira, 1954; Denmark, 1956; Arabesque and Honeycomb, 1957; Malta, 1958; Bridge of the Brocade Sash, 1959; Journey to the Ends of Time; Vol. I, Lost in the Dark Wood, 1959; Golden Wall and Mirador, 1961; The Red Chapels of Banteai Srei, 1962; Monks, Nuns and Monasteries, 1965; Forty-eight Poems (in Poetry Review), 1967; Southern Baroque Revisited, 1968; Gothic Europe, 1969; and 15 vols of Poetry. *Recreation:* 'Westerns'. *Heir: s* Sacheverell Reresby Sitwell [*b* 15 April 1927; *m* 1952, Penelope, *yr d* of late Col Hon. Donald Alexander Forbes, DSO, MVO; one *d*]. *Address:* Weston Hall, Towcester, Northants. *Club:* White's.

**SIXSMITH, Major-General (retd) Eric Keir Gilborne,** CB 1951; CBE 1946; *b* 15 Oct. 1904; 2nd *s* of Charles Frederick Gilborne Sixsmith, Barry; *m* 1941, Rosemary Aileen, 4th *d* of Rev. Frederick Ernest Godden; two *s* one *d*. *Educ:* Harrow; RMC, Sandhurst. Commissioned The Cameronians (Scottish Rifles), 1924; Adjutant 1st Battalion, 1933-34; Staff College, Quetta, 1935-36. Served War of 1939-45; Bde Maj. 2 Inf. Bde, 1939-40; GSO1, 51st Highland Division, 1941-42; Commander 2nd Bn Royal Scots Fusiliers, Italy (wounded), 1944; commanded 2nd Bn Cameronians (Scottish Rifles), 1944; Deputy Director Staff Duties, War Office, 1945-46; Brigade Commander, India, 1946-47; Deputy Director Personnel Administration, War Office, 1947-50; idc 1951; Chief of Staff, Hong Kong, 1952; Chief of Staff, Far East Land Forces, 1952-54; Commanding 43 (Wessex) Infantry Division (TA) 1954-57; Assistant Chief of Staff (Organisation and Training) Supreme Headquarters, Allied Powers Europe, 1957-61, retired. *Publication:* British Generalship in the Twentieth Century, 1970. *Recreations:* gardening, music. *Address:* Riversleigh, Langport, Somerset. *T:* Langport 435. *Club:* Army and Navy.

*See also P. G. D. Sixsmith.*

**SIXSMITH, (Philip) Guy (Dudley);** Stipendiary Magistrate at Pontypridd since 1966; Deputy Chairman, Glamorgan Quarter Sessions, since 1966; *b* 5 Nov. 1902; *e s* of late C. F. G. Sixsmith, Barry, Glam; *m* 1933, Alice Mary (JP Glam), *d* of C. J. Birch; one *d* (one *s* decd). *Educ:* Barry County Sch.; Harrow; Lincoln Coll., Oxford. Assistant master, Shanghai Cathedral School for Boys, 1929-35; called to the Bar, Inner Temple, 1936; Wales and Chester Circuit. Served War of 1939-45, gazetted 2nd Lt Cameronians (Scottish Rifles), 1940; Middle East and Paiforce, 1940-45. Deputy Judge Advocate (Major), 1942-45 and at War Crime Trials in Germany, 1946-48; Stipendiary Magistrate, Cardiff, 1948-66. Chairman: Cardiff Rent Tribunal, 1947-48; E Glam and Mon Br., Oxford Soc.; Glamorgan Branch, Council for Protection of Rural Wales, 1967-69; Monmouth Diocesan Schools Cttee; D. C. Jones Challenge Cup for Best Kept Village in Vale of Glamorgan. Pres., Cardiff E District Scout Council. Vice-Pres., E Glam and Mon Br., Magistrates' Assoc. (Chm., 1954-66). Member: Monmouth Diocesan Board of Finance; Governing Body, Church in Wales; Court of Governors, University Coll. of S Wales and Monmouthshire; Court, University of Wales; Council, Magistrates Assoc. Exec. Cttee, Council for Protection of Rural Wales; *Recreation:* procrastination. *Address:* St Julian's Cottage, Llanedeyrn, Cardiff CF3 9YJ. *T:* Cardiff 77846. *Club:* National Liberal.

*See also Maj.-Gen. E. K. G. Sixsmith.*

**SKAE, Sheriff Victor Delvine Burnham;** Sheriff Substitute of the Lothians at Edinburgh since 1968; *b* 25 Oct. 1914; *o s* of late Ernest Traill Skae, SSC and late Elsie Burnham; *m* 1939, Barbara Landale Melville; three *d*. *Educ:* Edinburgh Acad.; Bruges; Clifton Coll.; Peterhouse, Cambridge (BA); Edinburgh Univ. (LLB). RA, 1940-42, 652 (AOP) Sqdn; invalided out. Advocate, 1945; Advocate Depute, 1953-60; Sheriff Substitute: Falkirk, 1960-64; Linlithgow, 1964-68. *Recreations:* shooting, fishing. *Address:* 23 Royal Circus, Edinburgh 3. *T:* 031-225 1939. *Club:* New (Edinburgh).

**SKAN, Peter Henry O.;** *see* Ogle-Skan.

**SKAUG, Arne;** GCVO (Hon.); Knight Commander with Star of Order of St Olav, Norway; Ambassador of Norway to Denmark, since 1968; *b* 6 Nov. 1906. *Educ:* (Economics) Univ. of Oslo. Manager, Norwegian Social Insurance Scheme, New York, and then in Norwegian Ministry of Supply, London, 1939-44; Commercial Counsellor to Norwegian Embassy, Washington, 1944-46; Director, Central Bureau of Statistics, Oslo, 1946-48; Under-Sec. of State, Foreign Ministry, 1948; Permanent Delegate for Norway (with rank of minister), to OEEC, Paris, 1949-55, with rank of Ambassador, also concurrently Permanent Representative of Norway to NATO Council, Paris, 1953-55; Minister of Commerce and Shipping, Norway, 1955-62; Ambassador to the Court of St James's and to Ireland, 1962-68. *Address:* Royal Norwegian Embassy, Borgergade 16, 1300 Kæbenhavn K, Denmark.

**SKEAPING, John (Rattenbury),** RA 1959 (ARA 1950); sculptor; Professor of Sculpture, Royal College of Art, 1953-59; *b* 9 June 1901; *m* 1st, 1923, Barbara Hepworth (*see* Dame Barbara Hepworth) (marr. diss. 1933); one *s* (killed in action, RAF, 1953); 2nd, 1934, Morwenna Ward (marr. diss. 1969); three *s*; 3rd, 1969, Margery Scott. *Educ:* Royal Academy Schools. Rome Scholar, 1924. Exhibited Royal Academy, 1922, 1947, 1948, 1951 and 1952. *Publications:* Animal Drawing, 1934; How to

Draw Horses, 1938; The Big Tree of Mexico, 1952; Les Animaux dans l'Art, 1969 (Paris). *Recreations:* fishing and riding. *Address:* Moulin de la Taillade, Castries, Hérault, France.

**SKEAT, Theodore Cressy,** FBA 1963; BA; Keeper of Manuscripts and Egerton Librarian, British Museum, since 1961; *b* 15 Feb. 1907; *s* of Walter William Skeat, MA; *m* 1942, Olive Martin; one *s. Educ:* Whitgift School, Croydon; Christ's College, Cambridge. Student at British School of Archaeology, Athens, 1929-31; Asst Keeper, Dept. of Manuscripts, British Musuem, 1931; Deputy Keeper, 1948. *Publications:* (with H. I. Bell) Fragments of an Unknown Gospel, 1935; (with H. J. M. Milne) Scribes and Correctors of the Codex Sinaiticus, 1938; The Reigns of the Ptolemies, 1954; Papyri from Panopolis, 1964; articles in papyrological journals. *Address:* 63 Ashbourne Rd, W5. *T:* 01-998 1246.

**SKEEN, Brig. Andrew,** OBE 1945; psc; MP for Arundel (Rhodesian Parliament) since Dec. 1965; *b* 1906; *s* of late Gen. Sir Andrew Skeen, KCB, KCIE, CMG; *m* 1939, Honor St Quintin Beasley; one *s* one *d. Educ:* Wellington College; Sandhurst. 2nd Lt R Berkshire Regt, 1926; Bde Maj., 1939; Lt-Col 1941; Brig., 1943. Served, 1939-45: France, N Africa, Middle East, India and Burma (despatches); retd 1947. Chairman, Industrial Boards; Member, Rhodesian Tourist Board. Life Vice-President, Manicaland Development and Publicity Assoc. Commissioner, Rhodesian Forestry Commission. Mem., Umtali-Odzi Road Council; Chm., Vumba Town Planning Authority. High Comr for Rhodesia in London, July-Nov. 1965. *Publication:* Prelude to Independence, 1966. *Address:* Las Anod, PO Box 277, Umtali, Rhodesia. *T:* Umtali 2283-13; 19 Granta Road, Vainona, PO Borrowdale, Salisbury, Rhodesia. *T:* 882097.

**SKEET, Trevor Herbert Harry;** MP (C) Bedford since 1970; Barrister, Writer and Consultant; *b* 28 Jan. 1918; British; *m* 1958, Elizabeth Margaret Gilling; two *s. Educ:* King's College, Auckland; University of New Zealand, Auckland (LLB). Served War of 1939-45, with NZ Engineers (sergeant); 2nd Lieut, NZ Anti-Aircraft (Heavy); Sub-Lieutenant, NZ Roy. Naval Volunteer Reserve; demobilised, 1945. Formerly Barrister and Solicitor of Supreme Court of New Zealand; Barrister, Inner Temple, 1947. Has considerable experience in public speaking. Contested (C): Stoke Newington and Hackney, North, Gen. Election, 1951; Llanelly Div. of Carmarthenshire, Gen. Election, 1955; MP (C) Willesden East, 1959-64. Formerly associated with Commonwealth and Emire Industries Assoc.; Mem. council, Royal Commonwealth Soc., 1952-55, and 1956-69. A Vice-Chm. Conservative Party Power Cttee, House of Commons; Chm., Oil Sub-Cttee; Mem., Econ. Cttee, Machine Tool Trades Association for several years; Member Technical Legislation Cttee, CBI. *Publications:* contrib. to numerous journals including New Commonwealth and Mining World, on oil, atomic energy, metals, commodities, finance, and Imperial and Commonwealth development. *Address:* 1 Harcourt Buildings, Temple, EC4. *T:* 01-353 2214; 38 Ossulton Way, Hampstead Garden Suburb, N2. *T:* 01-455 3365. *Clubs:* Junior Carlton, Royal Commonwealth Society.

**SKEFFINGTON,** family name of **Viscount Massereene and Ferrard.**

**SKEFFINGTON, Arthur Massey,** BSc Econ. (Hons); FRGS; FREconS; MRST; MP (Lab) Hayes and Harlington (Middx), since March 1953; Chairman of the Labour Party, since 1969; Economist and Barrister-at-law; *b* 4 Sept. 1909; *s* of Arthur James and Edith Skeffington; *m* 1952, Sheila, *d* of Thomas MacKenzie, Birmingham; two *s. Educ:* Streatham Grammar School; London Univ. Lecturer in Economics and Teacher. Member: National Executive of Labour Party; Political Purposes Committee, Royal Arsenal Co-op. Society; late member Civil Service Arbitration Tribunal. Travelled widely in Europe. Visited the Soviet Union, 1938. Winner of Scholarship to Prague University. Reformed the Battersea Parliament, 1937, contested Streatham, 1935, By-Election West Lewisham, 1938. Mem. Fabian Soc., 1933, on the Exec. from 1943, Chm., 1957. Went to Bd of Trade to assist in the Concentration of Industry, 1941; transf., 1943, to Ministry of Supply, Assistant Director in charge of production of Medical Supplies. MP (Lab) Lewisham W, 1945-50; PPS to Minister of Pensions, 1947-48; Jt Parly Sec., Min. of Land and Natural Resources, 1964-67, Min. of Housing, 1967-70. Member, LCC (Peckham), 1950-58. Initiated Law Reform (Enforcement of Contracts) Act, 1954; Member of Commonwealth Parly Society's Delegn to E Africa, 1948, 1957; visited US, Oct. 1949, 1958, 1968, India, 1961, Australia, 1966. Jt President: Brit. Sect. Council of European Municipalities; Commonwealth Assoc. of Municipalities; Pres., Arboricultural Association; Chm. Cttee on Public Participation and Planning (convened 10 Woodlands confs to safeguard future live amenity); Life Member: National Trust; Council for Nature; Ramblers Assoc. *Publications:* Leasehold Enfranchisement; American Diary; Tanganyika in Transition. *Recreations:* cricket, the theatre, bee-keeping. *Address:* 2 Harcourt Buildings, Middle Temple, EC4. *T:* 01-353 7202; The Old Vicarage, Meopham, Kent. *Club:* Irish, Chelsea Arts, Surrey County Cricket.

**SKEFFINGTON-LODGE, Thomas Cecil;** *b* 15 Jan. 1905; *s* of late Thomas Robert Lodge and late Winifred Marian Skeffington; unmarried. *Educ:* privately; Giggleswick and Westminster Schools. For some years engaged in Advertising and Publicity both in London and the North of England; later did Public Relations and administrative work in the Coal Trade as Northern Area Organiser for the Coal Utilisation Council, in which he served Cttees of Coal Trade in North-East, North-West and Yorkshire; on the outbreak of war, became a Mines Dept official; then volunteered for the Navy; from early 1941 a Naval Officer. Lecture tour in USA under auspices of Anglo-American Parly Gp, 1949. MP (Lab) Bedford, 1945-50; contested (Lab) York, 1951, Mid-Bedfordshire, 1955; Grantham, 1959; Brighton (Pavilion), March 1969; Personal Asst to Chm., Colonial Development Corp., 1950-52. Mem. of post-war Parly Ddelegns to Eire, Belgium, Luxembourg and USA. Past-Pres. and Chm., Pudsey Divisional Labour Party; Chm., Brighton and Hove Fabian Soc.; Member: Labour Party many years, Exec. Cttee, Socialist Christian Movement; Parly Socialist Christian Group (past Chm.); German-British Christian Fellowship (past Chm.); Union of Shop, Distributive and Allied Workers; Wine and Food Society; Council for the Preservation of Rural England; Royal Society for the Protection of Birds; Georgian Group. *Recreations:* fishing, walking and climbing, travelling. *Address:* 5 Powis Grove, Brighton, Sussex. *T:* Brighton 25472. *Clubs:* Savile; Royal Commonwealth Society (Hove).

**SKELHORN, Sir Norman John,** KBE 1966; QC 1954; Director of Public Prosecutions, since 1964; *b* Glossop, Derbyshire, 10 Sept. 1909; *s* of late Rev. Samuel and late Bertha Skelhorn; *m* 1937, Rosamund, *d* of late Prof. James Swain, CB, CBE; no *c*. *Educ:* Shrewsbury School. Called to Bar, Middle Temple, 1931, Master of the Bench, 1962. Member of Western Circuit; employed in Trading with the Enemy Dept (Treasury and Board of Trade), 1940-42; in Admiralty, 1942-45, latterly as head of Naval Law Branch. Recorder, Bridgwater, 1945-54; Plymouth, 1954-62; Portsmouth, 1962-64. Chairman, Isle of Wight County Quarter Sessions, 1951-64. Member, Departmental Cttee on Probation Service, 1959-61; Appointed Member of Home Secretary's Advisory Council on Treatment of Offenders, 1962; Member Home Secretary's: Probation Advisory and Training Board, 1962; Criminal Law Revision Cttee, 1964. *Address:* Woodside, Hewshott Lane, Liphook, Hants. *Club:* Royal Automobile.

**SKELMERSDALE,** 6th Baron *cr* 1828, of Skelmersdale; **Lionel Bootle-Wilbraham,** DSO 1940; MC 1917; late Coldstream Guards; *b* 23 Sept. 1896, *s* of Major Lionel Bootle-Wilbraham, 87th Royal Irish Fusiliers (*gs* of 1st Baron) (*d* 1914), and Lavinia (*d* 1930), *d* of Abraham Wilson; *S* cousin, 1969; *m* 1936, Ann Quilter; one *s* three *d*. *Educ:* Wellington College; Cheltenham College. Served European War, 1914-18 (MC); 3 Bn Hampshire Regt, Aug. 1914, Coldstream Guards, 1915; ADC to Governor of Madras, 1924-26; Military Secretary to Governor of Madras, 1929-32; service in Turkey, 1922; China, 1927; Sudan and Egypt, 1932; Comd 126 Inf. Bde 1940, 215 Inf. Bde, 1941, 32 Gds Bde, 1941; Staff College, 1942, BGS Eastern Command, 1943; Comd 137 Inf. Bde 1945; Regtl Lt-Col Coldstream Guards, 1946-49 (DSO, despatches); retired, with rank of Brig., 1949. Dir, Brush Export Ltd and their rep. in Caribbean and Latin America, 1949-59. *Recreations:* fishing, shooting, gardening. *Heir:* *s* Hon. Roger Bootle-Wilbraham, *b* 2 April 1945. *Address:* Trunk House, Cove, Farnborough, Hants.. *T:* Farnborough 44051.

**SKELTON, Rt. Rev. Kenneth John Fraser;** Assistant Bishop of Durham, Rural Dean of Wearmouth and Rector of Bishopwearmouth, since 1970; *b* 16 May 1918; *s* of Henry Edmund and Kate Elizabeth Skelton; *m* 1945, Phyllis Barbara, *y d* of James Emerton; two *s* one *d*. *Educ:* Dulwich Coll.; Corpus Christi Coll., Cambridge; Wells Theological Coll. 1st Cl. Class. Tripos, Pt 1, 1939; 1st Cl. Theol. Tripos, Pt 1, 1940; BA 1940, MA 1944. Deacon, 1941; Priest, 1942; Curate: Normanton-by-Derby, 1941-43; Bakewell, 1943-45; Bolsover, 1945-46; Tutor, Wells Theol. Coll. and Priest-Vicar, Wells Cathedral, 1946-50; Vicar of Howe Bridge, Atherton, 1950-55; Rector, Walton-on-the-Hill, Liverpool, 1955-62; Exam. Chap. to Bp of Liverpool, 1957-62; Bishop of Matabeleland, 1962-70. *Recreation:* music. *Address:* 1 Abbotsford Grove, Sunderland, County Durham. *T:* Sunderland 56756.

**SKELTON, Rear-Adm. Peter,** CB 1956; *b* 27 Dec. 1901; *s* of Peter John and Selina Frances Skelton; *m* 1928, Ethel Janice Brown Clark; two *d*. *Educ:* RN Colleges, Osborne and Dartmouth; Trinity Hall, Cambridge. Cadet, 1915; Midshipman, HMS Valiant, 1918; Commander, 1936; Capt. 1944; Rear-Adm., 1953. Served War of 1939-45, as Staff Officer in HMS Aurora, later at Admiralty in Torpedo Division; Commander and Actg Capt. in HMS Royal Sovereign, 1942; Director of Trade Div., Admiralty, 1944; Supt of Torpedo Experimental Establishment, 1946; Sen. Naval Officer, Persian Gulf, 1949; Captain of Dockyard, Portsmouth, 1951; Admiral Superintendent, Rosyth, 1953-56; retired. Bucks CC, 1958. *Recreations:* golf, tennis, shooting. *Address:* Greythorpe, Gregories Rd, Beaconsfield, Bucks. *Club:* Royal Automobile.

**SKEMP, Frank Whittingham;** *b* 13 Dec. 1880; *s* of Rev. Thomas Rowland Skemp and Jennie, *d* of Samuel Clewis; *m* 1914, Dorothy (*d* 1965), *d* of Rev. George Frazer; two *s* one *d*. *Educ:* private school; Douglas Gram. Sch., IOM; University of Manchester; Peterhouse, Cambridge. Entered Indian Civil Service (Punjab Commission) 1904; 1st class Magistrate and JP 1906; Deputy Commissioner 1910-13; District and Sessions Judge, 1918-27; Additional Judge, Lahore High Court, 1927-33; Puisne Judge, High Court, Lahore, 1933-41; retired, 1941. *Publication:* Multani Stories, 1917. *Recreation:* reading. *Address:* Fairfield, 115 Banbury Road, Oxford.

**SKEMP, Prof. Joseph Bright,** MA Cantab, PhD Edinburgh; Professor of Greek, in the University of Durham, since 1950; *b* 10 May 1910; *s* of late Thomas William Widlake Skemp, solicitor and local government officer, and Caroline (*née* Southall); *m* 1941, Ruby James; no *c*. *Educ:* Wolverhampton Grammar School; Gonville and Caius College, Cambridge. Unofficial Drosier Fellow, Gonville and Caius College, Cambridge, 1936-47; Asst Lecturer in Latin, Univ. of Leeds, 1939; Warden of Refugee Club and Asst Sec. to Refugee Cttee, Cambridge, 1940-46; Sec., Soc. for the Protection of Science and Learning, 1944-46; Lecturer in Greek and Latin, Univ. of Manchester, 1946-49; Reader in Greek, Univ. of Durham (Newcastle Div.), 1949-50; Editor of Durham University Journal, 1953-57; Joint Editor, Phronesis, 1955-64. *Publications:* The Theory of Motion in Plato's Later Dialogues, 1942 (rep. and enl. 1967); Plato's Statesman, 1952; The Greeks and the Gospel, 1964. *Recreation:* walking. *Address:* 9 St Nicholas Drive, Whitesmocks, Durham. *T:* Durham 3630; 4 Heol y Dwr, Abergynolwyn, Tywyn, Merioneth.

**SKEMPTON, Prof. Alec Westley,** DSc London 1949; FRS 1961; FICE; Professor of Civil Engineering in the University of London (Imperial College) since 1957; *b* 4 June 1914; *o c* of late A. W. Skempton, Northampton, and Beatrice Edridge Payne; *m* 1940, Mary, *d* of E. R. Wood, Brighouse, Yorks; two *d*. *Educ:* Northampton Grammar School; Imperial College, University of London (Goldsmiths' Bursar). Building Research Station, 1936-46; University Reader in Soil Mechanics, Imperial College, 1946-54; Professor of Soil Mechanics, Imperial College, 1955-57. Member Council, Institute Civil Engineers, 1949-54; Pres., Internat. Soc. Soil Mechanics and Foundn Eng, 1957-61; Chm. Jt Cttee on Soils, Min. of Supply and Road Research Bd, 1954-59; Mem., Cathedrals Advisory Cttee, 1964-70; Lectures: Copenhagen, Paris, Harvard, Univ. of Illinois, Oslo, Stockholm, Madrid, Florence, Sydney, Quebec, Mexico City; Special Lectr, Architectural Assoc. 1948-57; Vis. Lectr Cambridge Univ. School of Architecture, 1962-66; Consultant to Binnie & Partners, John Mowlem & Co., etc. Hon. DSc Durham. *Publications:* numerous papers on soil mechanics, engineering geology and history of construction; contributor to A History of Technology (ed Dr Charles Singer). *Recreations:* architectural travel, croquet. *Address:* Imperial College, SW7. *T:* 01-589 5111; 16 The Boltons, SW10. *T:* 01-370 3457. *Clubs:* Athenæum, Hurlingham.

**SKENE, Macgregor,** DSc, FLS; formerly Professor of Botany, Bristol University; Professor Emeritus, 1955; *b* 20 Oct. 1889; *s* of Alexander and Margaret Skene; *m* 1915, Agnes Wallace Hamilton; two *s*. *Educ:* Robert Gordon's College, Aberdeen; Universities of Aberdeen, Berlin, Strasbourg and Montpellier. *Publications:* Biology of Flowering Plants; Flower Book for the Pocket; other books and memoirs on botanical subjects. *Address:* 6 Dover Court, Abdon Avenue, Birmingham 29.

**SKIKNE, L. M.;** *see* Harvey, Laurence.

**SKILBECK, Dunstan,** CBE 1957; MA Oxon; Principal, Wye College, University of London, 1945-68; Hon. Fellow, Wye College; *b* 13 June 1904; 2nd *s* of late Clement Oswald Skilbeck, FSA, and Elizabeth Bertha Skilbeck; *m* 1934, Elspeth Irene Jomini, *d* of late Edward Carruthers, MD, and Mary Carruthers; two *s* one *d*. *Educ:* University College School, London; St John's College, Oxford. Agricultural Economics Res. Inst., University of Oxford, 1927-30; Univ. Demonstrator in School of Rural Economy, University of Oxford; Director of St John's College Farm; Lecturer and Tutor in Rural Economy, St John's College, Oxford, 1930-40. Served with RAF Home and Middle East, Air Staff HQ, Middle East, 1940-45; as Wing Comdr, appointed Asst Director, Middle East Supply Centre (Food Production), 1942-45 (despatches). Vice-Chm. Imperial Coll. of Tropical Agric., 1958-60; Liaison Officer to Minister of Agriculture, for SE England, 1952-60; Chairman, Collegiate Council, 1962-65, Mem. of Senate, 1959-68, Univ. of London. Member Council: Voluntary Service Overseas, 1964-68; England and Wales Nature Conservancy, 1968-. Trustee, Ernest Cook Trust, 1966-. Hon. Freeman Worshipful Co. of Fruiterers, 1960. *Publications:* contribs to scientific and agricultural jls. *Address:* Mount Bottom, Elham, near Canterbury, Kent. *T:* Elham 258. *Clubs:* Athenæum, Farmers'.

**SKILLICORN, Alice Havergal,** CBE 1952; MSc; Principal of Homerton College, Cambridge, 1935-60, retired; *d* of Edward Skillicorn, Ramsey, Isle of Man. *Educ:* privately; London Sch. of Economics. Teaching posts, London and St Hild's Coll., Durham, 1920-28; HM Inspector of Schools, 1929-35. *Recreations:* walking, foreign travel. *Clubs:* Women Graduates', English-Speaking Union (Cambridge).

**SKILLINGTON, William Patrick Denny,** CB 1964; a Deputy Secretary, Ministry of Public Building and Works, since 1966; *b* 13 Feb. 1913; *s* of late S. J. Skillington, Leicester; *m* 1941, Dorin Kahn, Sydney, Australia; two *d*. *Educ:* Malvern College; Exeter College, Oxford. BA 1935, MA 1939, Oxford. Articled to Clerk of Leicestershire CC, 1936-39. Commissioned in R Welch Fusiliers (SR), 1933; served War of 1939-45 (despatches); regimental officer in France and Belgium, and on staff in Sicily, Italy and Greece; AA and QMG; Major (Hon. Lieut-Col) R of O. Entered Min. of Works as Principal, 1946; Asst Sec., 1952; Under-Sec. (Dir of Establishments), Min. of Public Building and Works, 1956-64; Asst Under-Sec. of State, Home Office, 1964-66. *Address:* 95a S Mark's Road, Henley-on-Thames, Oxon. *T:* Henley 3756. *Club:* United University.

**SKIMMING, Ian Edward Bowring;** Chairman, C. T. Bowring & Co. Ltd; *b* 28 Aug. 1920; *s* of Edward Hugh Bowring and Audrey Skimming; *m* 1949, Anne Miriam Barbara Maude; one *d*. *Educ:* Eton. Commnd Coldstream Guards, Feb. 1939; demobilized 1945 (despatches, 1944). Member of Lloyd's, 1942. C. T. Bowring & Co.: joined 1945; Asst Dir, 1952; Dir, 1954; Chairman and Chief Executive, 1965. FRSA. *Recreations:* shooting, ski-ing. *Address:* Shotters Farm, Newton Valence, near Alton, Hampshire. *T:* Tisted 222; 87 Dovehouse Street, SW3. *T:* 01-352 4220. *Club:* Guards.

**SKINNARD, Frederick William;** Retired as Registrar and External Director of Examinations, the Institute of Optical Science (1951-59); *b* 8 March 1902; *s* of late F. W. Skinnard, bookplate designer and engraver, Plymouth; *m* 1st, 1931, Muriel M. Lightfoot (*d* 1959); 2nd, 1960, Greta Cory Anthony. *Educ:* Devonport High School; Borough Road Training College, Isleworth. Taught under LCC Education Authority, 1922-24; from 1924 to 1945 served in Willesden schools where his pioneer work in citizenship training and local survey work attracted much attention. Lecturer to teachers' courses in England and abroad. Invited to tour the USA in 1937, and while there and in Canada made a special study of labour problems. Earliest political experience gained in the Union of Democratic Control under the late E. D. Morel. A member of the Labour Party since 1924; served on Harrow and Hendon Divisional Executives and as Vice-Pres.; MP (Lab) Harrow East, 1945-50; member of the Executive of Middlesex Federation of Labour Parties; Chairman Middlesex Labour Joint Consultative Committee. Visited Jamaica, 1946; Member Parliamentary Delegn to W Africa, 1947; Member Labour Party's Advisory Cttee on Imperial Affairs; Lecturer and writer on Colonial Problems; Mem. of Fabian Soc., NUT, Roy. Soc. of Teachers. Hon. Fell. Inst. Optical Science, 1957. *Publications:* Willesden Memorandum, in The Extra School Year; Leaving Papers for Senior Schools (privately printed, 1934 and 1935); Co-editor of Education for Citizenship in the Elementary School, 1935; The Juvenile Delinquent and the Community (The World's Children), 1946; Training and Function of the Ophthalmic Optician, 1950. *Recreations:* gardening and youth club work. *Address:* 1 Oakfield Avenue, Kenton, Harrow. *T:* 01-907 3855.

**SKINNER, Prof. Andrew Forrester,** MA, BSc, PhD (St Andrews); MA (Columbia); FEIS; Professor of Education, Ontario College of Education, University of Toronto, 1954-70, now Emeritus Professor; *b* 21 May 1902; *s* of Alexander H. and Jessie F. Skinner, Kingskettle, Scotland; *m* 1932, Elizabeth Balmer Lockhart, Manchester. *Educ:* Bell-Baxter School, Cupar, Fife; University of St Andrews. MA, BSc, 1st Cl. Hons Maths and Phys Sci., 1925; Carnegie Research Fellow in Chemistry, PhD, 1928; Commonwealth Fund Fellow, Columbia, New York, 1929-31 (Educ. MA); Teacher in various schools, 1931-37; Asst Dir of Education, Co. of Aberdeen, 1937-39; Principal Lecturer in Methods, Dundee Trg Coll., 1939-41; Prof. of Education, Univ. of St Andrews, and Principal, Dundee Trg Coll., 1941-54. Vis. Prof. Ontario Coll. of Educ., Univ. of Toronto, 1950 and 1954; Visiting Professor: E. Tennessee State Coll., 1951, State Univ. of Iowa, 1951-52; Univ. of British Columbia, 1962; Univ. of Victoria, 1964. Former Member: Scottish Council for Research in Education; Scottish Universities Entrance Bd; School Broadcasting Council for Scotland; Mem., Bd of Directors, Comparative Educn Soc. of USA; Mem. Exec., Comparative and Internat. Educn Soc. of Canada, Vice-Pres., 1968-69, Pres., 1969-70. *Publications:* (Booklet) Scottish Education in Schools, 1942; (Booklet) Introductory Course on Education in Scotland, 1944; Citizenship in the Training of Teachers, 1948. Articles in Jl of Amer. Chem. Soc.; Trans. Chem. Soc.; Scottish Educnal Jl; The Year Book of Education; Educnal Forum: Educational Record of Quebec; The American People's Encyclopedia; Canadian Education and Research Digest. *Recreations:* golf, gardening and walking. *Address:* University of Toronto, Toronto 5, Ontario, Canada. *Club:* English-Speaking Union (Toronto).

**SKINNER, C(harles) William,** OBE 1963; Barrister-at-Law; DL; JP; Chairman of Edmonton Petty Sessional Division and of Enfield, Tottenham and Wood Green Courts, 1949-65; Chairman of Westminster, Chelsea and Holborn Rent Tribunal since constituted, 1946, and of West London Tribunal, 1958-62; *b* 5 February 1895; *s* of Harry Skinner and Lizzie, *d* of Charles Sheldon, Freeman of City of London; *m* 1923, Jennie, *g d* of Rev. John Taylor, Wolverhampton; one *s* (and one *d* decd). *Educ:* St Olave's; College of Estate Management. Assoc. RICS; formerly Legal MTPI; FAI (Silver Medallist, Final Prizeman) and MRSanI. Called to Bar, Lincoln's Inn, 1937. JP 1942, DL: Middx, 1953, Greater London, 1965; Mayor of Southgate, 1942-43, Member Borough Council, 1938-46, Chm. Civil Defence Committee, 1942; Chm. MOI Committee, 1940-45; Hon. Freeman: Southgate, 1964, Enfield, 1965; member Middlesex CC, 1945-48; member Magistrate's Courts Committee (Middlesex), 1952-62. High Sheriff of Middlesex, 1955-56. Served European War, 1914-18, France and Belgium, 1st Bn HAC, 1915-19; War of 1939-45, FO, RAFVR, 1941-44; Flight Commander and Welfare Officer, ATC; Founder-President British Legion, Palmers Green Branch and Vice-Pres. Southgate Br., 1942 and RAF Assoc.; Vice-Pres. Nat. Assoc. of Probation Officers (Middlesex Branch), 1953-; President and Founder of various organisations connected with youth and with wartime activities. *Publications:* Editor of Yearly Digest of Land and Property Cases, 1939-58; Law of Compulsory Acquisition of Land, 1939; Rent and Mortgage Emergency Legislation, 1939, 1941; Landlord and Tenant (War Damage) Cases, 1942; (joint) Merlin and Skinner's War Damage Precedents, 1941; legal columnist Estates Gazette, 1937-45. *Address:* Southgate, The Clump, Chorleywood, Herts. *T:* Rickmansworth 77822; 25 Mariners Walk, Rustington, Sussex. *T:* 4327.

**SKINNER, Cornelia Otis; (Mrs A. S. Blodget);** actress, authoress, monologist; radio and motion picture actress; *d* of Otis Skinner and Maud Durbin; *m* 1928, Alden S. Blodget; one *s*. *Educ:* Baldwin School, Bryn Mawr, Pa; Bryn Mawr College; Sorbonne, Paris; Sociétaire of Comédie Française and School of Jacques Copeau. Appeared in: Blood and Sand; Will Shakespeare; Tweedles; In the Next Room; The Wild Westcotts; In His Arms; White Collars. Starred in: Candida; Theatre; The Searching Wind; Lady Windermere's Fan; Major Barbara; The Pleasure of His Company (which she wrote, with Samuel Taylor; it was filmed, 1961). Author and Producer of mono-dramas: The Wives of Henry VIII; The Empress Eugénie; The Loves of Charles II; Mansion on the Hudson; and original character sketches played in America and London; dramatized and produced mono-dramas of Margaret Ayer Barnes', Edna, His Wife, and full-length solo revue, Paris '90, with music by Kay Swift. Created and prepared scripts for radio series, William and Mary; also many other radio engagements including innumerable appearances on Information Please. Officier de l'Académie, 1953. *Publications:* Tiny Garments, 1931; Excuse It, Please, 1936; Dither and Jitters, 1937; Soap Behind the Ears (published in Eng. under title of Popcorn), 1941; Our Hearts Were Young and Gay (with Emily Kimbrough), 1942; Family Circle, 1948; omnibus publication of some of previous works, That's Me All Over, 1948; Nuts in May, 1950; Happy Family, 1950; Bottoms Up!, 1955; The Ape in Me, 1959; Elegant Wits and Grand Horizontals, 1962; Madame Sarah, 1967. *Recreation:* country. *Address:* 22 East 60th St, New York City. *TA:* Courtesy. *T:* Murray Hill 8-6110. *Clubs:* Colony, Cosmopolitan (NY).

**SKINNER, Dennis Edward;** MP (Lab) Bolsover since 1970; Miner at Glapwell Colliery; *b* 11 Feb. 1932; good working-class mining stock; *m* 1960; one *s* two *d*. *Educ:* Tupton Hall Grammar Sch.; Ruskin Coll., Oxford. Miner, 1949-. Pres., Derbyshire Miners (NUM), 1966-; Pres., NE Derbs Constituency Labour Party, 1968; Derbyshire CC, 1964-70; Clay Cross UDC, 1960-70. *Recreations:* tennis, cricket. *Address:* 61 Wheatcroft Close, Danesmoor, Clay Cross, Chesterfield, Derbs. *T:* Clay Cross 863429. *Clubs:* Miners' Welfares in Derbyshire; Bestwood Working Men's.

**SKINNER, Ernest Harry Dudley,** CBE 1957; Member, Colonial Development Corporation, 1958-60; *b* 1892; *m* 1921, Edith Lilian Stretton; one *s* one *d*. *Educ:* private school. Entered service of Bank of England, 1911; for several years acted as Private Secretary to Governor, Rt Hon. M. C. Norman, DSO (later Lord Norman); Deputy Secretary, 1932; Asst to Governors, 1935-45; General Manager to Finance Corporation for Industry from its formation in 1945 until 1948. Chm., Northern Div., NCB, 1948-50; Chairman, Durham Division, National Coal Board, 1950-57. Mem. of Council, OStJ for County Durham, 1951-57. Member, Newcastle Regional Hospital Board, 1958-59. Vice-Pres., NE Div., Northern Counties ABA, 1954-59. JP Durham County, 1957-59. *Recreations:* golf and fishing. *Address:* 4 Garden Court, Hastings Road, Bexhill-on-Sea, Sussex. *T:* Bexhill 4837. *Club:* Reform.

**SKINNER, Maj.-Gen. Frank Hollamby,** CB 1947; CIE 1945; OBE 1942; Indian Army (retired); *b* 24 March 1897. *Address:* Lime Park, Herstmonceux, Sussex. *T:* Herstmonceux 2292. *Club:* United Service.

**SKINNER, Lt-Col Harry Crawley R.;** *see* Ross Skinner.

**SKINNER, Henry Albert,** QC 1965; *b* 20 May 1926; *s* of Albert and Emma Mary Skinner; *m* 1949, Joan Weston Cassin; two *d*. *Educ:* Wyggeston Grammar Sch., Leicester; St John's Coll., Oxford. Called to Bar, Lincoln's Inn, 1950. Dep. Chm., Notts QS, 1966-69. Recorder of Leicester, 1966-; Chm., Lincolnshire (Lindsey) QS, 1968- (Dep. Chm., 1963-67). Mem. Parole Bd, 1970-. *Recreations:* gardening, walking. *Address:* 18 Pendene Road, Leicester. *T:* Leicester 704092. *Club:* Reform.

**SKINNER, James John,** QC; Chief Justice of Malawi, since 1970; *b* 24 July 1923; *o s* of late William Skinner, Solicitor, Clonmel, Ireland; *m* 1950, Regina Brigitte Reiss; three *s* two *d*. *Educ:* Clongowes Wood Coll.; Trinity Coll., Dublin; King's Inns, Dublin. Called to Irish Bar, 1946; joined Leinster Circuit; called to English Bar, Gray's Inn, 1950; called to Bar of Northern Rhodesia, 1951; QC (Northern Rhodesia) 1964; MP (UNIP) Lusaka East, 1964-68; Minister of Justice, 1964-65; Attorney-General, 1965-69 (in addition,

Minister of Legal Affairs, 1967-68); Chief Justice of Zambia, March-Sept. 1969. Grand Comdr, Order of Menelik II of Ethiopia, 1965. *Recreation:* reading. *Address:* c/o The High Court, PO Box 954, Blantyre, Malawi.

**SKINNER, Martyn;** *b* 1906; *s* of late Sir Sydney Skinner; *m* 1938, Pauline Giles; three *s* one *d* (and one *s* one *d* decd). *Educ:* two well-known Public Schools; Magdalen College, Oxford (no degree taken). Hawthornden prize, 1943; Heinemann Award, 1947; Runner-up, Barley Championship, Brewers' Exhibition, 1949. *Publications:* Sir Elfadore and Mabyna, 1935; Letters to Malaya I and II, 1941; III and IV, 1943; V 1947; Two Colloquies, 1949; The Return of Arthur, 1966. *Address:* Fitzhead, Taunton, Somerset. *T:* Milverton 337.

**SKINNER, Most Rev. Patrick James;** *see* St John's (Newfoundland), Archbishop of (RC).

**SKINNER, Sir (Thomas) Gordon,** 3rd Bt *cr* 1912; *b* 29 Dec. 1899; *er* and *o surv s* of Sir Thomas Hewitt Skinner, 2nd Bt, and Nellie Constance (*d* 1955), *d* of James Hay Hall, Highgate; *S* father, 1968; *m* 1st, 1926, Mollie Barbara (marr. diss., 1953; she *d* 1965), *e d* of Herbert William Girling, Frostenden, Suffolk; three *s*; 2nd, 1953, Jeanne, *o d* of François de Launoit, Brussels. *Educ:* Charterhouse; Exeter College, Oxford. Partner in Thomas Skinner & Co., 1926-37; Director and Manager, Thomas Skinner & Co. (Publishers) Ltd, 1937-51, retired. Served European War, 1914-18; France, 1918; War of 1939-45, RAF Intelligence Officer; 12 Sqdn Advanced Air Striking Force, France, 1940 (despatches); HQ 1st Corps; HQ Southern Command, 1940-41; HQ 9th American Air Force, 1941-45. Freeman, City of London; Liveryman, Worshipful Company of Merchant Taylors. *Recreations:* gardening and love of the sea. *Heir: e s* Thomas Keith Hewitt Skinner [*b* 6 Dec. 1927; *m* 1959, Jill, *d* of C. I. Tuckett; two *s*]. *Address:* Larchmont, 55 Hill Brow, Hove, Sussex BN3 6DD. *T:* Brighton 553114. *Clubs:* City of London, Little Ship; Royal Corinthian Yacht (Burnham-on-Crouch).

**SKINNER, Thomas Monier,** CMG 1958; MBE; MA Oxon; Company Chairman; *b* 2 Feb. 1913; *s* of Lt-Col and Mrs T. B. Skinner; *m* 1935, Margaret Adeline (*née* Pope) (*d* 1969); two *s*. *Educ:* Cheltenham Coll.; Lincoln Coll., Oxford. Asst District Officer (Cadet), Tanganyika, 1935; Asst District Officer, 1937; District Officer, 1947; Senior Asst Secretary, East Africa High Commission, 1952; Director of Establishments (Kenya), 1955-62, retired 1962. Member, Civil Service Commission, East Caribbean Territories, 1962-63; Chairman, Nyasaland Local Civil Service Commission, 1963; Salaries Commissioner, Basutoland, The Bechuanaland Protectorate and Swaziland, 1964. Reports on Localisation of Civil Service, Gilbert and Ellice Islands Colony and of British National Service, New Hebrides, 1968. *Recreation:* fishing. *Address:* 3 Barnfield Road, Exeter, Devon; Trapstile, Lustleigh, near Newton Abbot, Devon.

**SKIPWITH, Sir Patrick Alexander d'Estoteville,** 12th Bt, *cr* 1622; Marine Geologist, Ministry of Petroleum and Mineral Resources, Jeddah, Saudi Arabia, since 1970; *b* 1 Sept. 1938; *o s* of Grey d'Estoteville Townsend Skipwith (killed in action, 1942), Flying Officer, RAFVR, and Sofka, *d* of late Prince Peter Dolgorouky; *S* grandfather, 1950; *m* 1964, Gillian Patricia (marr. diss. 1970); *d* of late Charles F. Harwood and of Mrs Harwood; one *s one d*. *Educ:* Harrow; Paris; Oxford; Dublin (MA); London (DIC, PhD). With Ocean Mining Inc., in Tasmania, 1966-67, Malaysia, 1967-69, W Africa, 1969-70. *Heir: s* Alexander Grey Sebastian d'Estoteville Skipwith, *b* 9 April 1969. *Address:* Pigeon Hill, Tilford Road, Hindhead, Surrey.

**SKIRA, Albert;** Publisher; *b* Geneva, 10 Aug. 1904; *o s* of Pierre Skira and Adélaide Skira; *m* 1937, Rosabianca Venturi; three *s* one *d*. Bank clerk, Crédit Suisse, 1922-24; organizer of hotel entertainments, 1924-26; bookseller, 1926-31. Published Ovid's Metamorphoses in 1931, with etchings by Picasso; since then over 300 books on works of art and the history of art. *Address:* Editions Skira, 4 Place du Molard, Geneva, Switzerland; Dully, Vaud, Switzerland.

**SKOURAS, Spyros Panayiotis;** Chairman, Twentieth Century Fox Film Corporation, since 1962; *b* Skourohorion, Greece, 28 March 1893; *m* Saroula Bruiglia; two *s* two *d* (and one *s* one *d* decd). *Educ:* Public Schools, Greece; Jones Commercial Coll.; Benton Law School, St Louis. Owned 37 theatres by 1926; sold to Warner Bros; joined Warner Bros as General Manager of theatre circuit, 1929; Pres. subsidiary formed to operate all Paramount Theatres, 1931; appointed head of Fox Metropolitan Theatres; with brothers Charles and George also headed Wesco Corp., 1932, which became National Theatres, 1942; Pres. Twentieth Century-Fox, 1942-62. *Recreation:* golf. *Address:* 2 Shore Road, Rye, NY, USA. *T:* Owens 8-1170. *Clubs:* Westchester Country (Rye, NY); Metropolitan (NY); Athletic (NY).

**SKRIMSHIRE, Mrs John F. P.;** *see* Harvie Anderson, (Margaret) Betty.

**SKRINE, Sir Clarmont (Percival),** Kt 1946; OBE 1935; *b* London, 1888; *o s* of late Francis Henry Skrine; *m* 1920, Doris Forbes, 2nd *d* of James Whitelaw of Nungate, North Berwick. *Educ:* Winchester; New College, Oxford. Entered Indian Civil Service, 1912; served in South Persia, 1916-19; Political Agent, Quetta, 1921; Consul-General in Chinese Turkestan, 1922-24; Consul in Seistan and Kain, 1927-29; Political Agent, Sibi, Baluchistan, 1929-31; Kalat and Chagai, 1932-35; Revenue and Judicial Commissioner, Baluchistan, 1935-36; Resident for the Madras States, 1936-39; Resident for the Punjab States, 1939-41; Consul-General at Meshed, 1942-46; Counsellor for Indian Affairs, British Embassy, Tehran, 1946-48; retired, 1948; representative at Jerusalem of the Board, Jerusalem Electric Corporation, 1949-50; awarded OBE for services connected with Quetta Earthquake, 1935; awarded Gill Memorial by Royal Geographical Society for explorations in the Chinese Pamirs in 1922-24; Chm., Permanent Cttee on Geographical Names, 1960-64. *Publications:* Chinese Central Asia, 1926; World War in Iran, 1962; papers on Chinese Turkestan, Persia, Baluchistan and Israel in the Geographical and Central Asian Journals. *Recreation:* photography. *Address:* Rysa Lodge, Melsetter, Orkney. *Clubs:* Athenæum, Alpine.

**SKUTSCH, Prof. Otto;** Professor of Latin, University College London, since 1951; *b* 6 Dec. 1906; *yr s* of Latinist Franz Skutsch and Selma Dorff; *m* 1938, Gillian Mary, *e d* of late Sir Findlater Stewart, GCB, GCIE, CSI; one *s* three *d*. *Educ:* Friedrichs-Gymnasium, Breslau; Univs of Breslau, Kiel, Berlin, Göttingen. DrPhil, Göttingen, 1934; Assistant Thesaurus Linguae Latinae, 1932; Senior Assistant, Latin Dept, Queen's University, Belfast, 1938; Assistant Lecturer, Lecturer, Senior Lecturer, Univ. of Manchester, 1939, 1946, 1949; Guest Lectr,

Harvard Univ., 1958; Guest Member, Inst. for Advanced Study, Princeton, 1963, 1968; For. Mem., Kungl. Vetenskaps- och Vitterhets-Samhället i Göteborg. *Publications:* Prosodische und metrische Gesetze der Iambenkürzung, 1934; Studia Enniana, 1968. Articles in classical journals, etc. *Address:* 3 Wild Hatch, NW11. *T:* 01-455 4876.

**SKYRME, William Thomas Charles,** CB 1966; CBE 1953; TD 1949; JP; Secretary of Commissions since 1948; *b* 20 March 1913; *s* of Charles G. Skyrme, Hereford, and of Katherine Smith, Maryland, USA; *m* 1st, 1938, Hon. Barbara Suzanne Lyle (marriage dissolved 1953), *yr d* of 1st Baron Lyle of Westbourne; one *s* two *d*; 2nd, 1957, Mary, *d* of Dr R. C. Leaning. *Educ:* Rugby School; New College, Oxford (MA); Universities of Dresden and Paris. Called to the Bar, Inner Temple, 1935. Practised in London and on Western Circuit. Served War of 1939-45 in Royal Artillery in Middle East, North Africa and Italy (wounded twice). Secretary to the Lord Chancellor, 1944. Governor and Member of Committee of Management of Queen Mary's Hosp., London, 1938-48. FRGS. Pres., Commonwealth Magistrates' Assoc., 1970. JP (Oxfordshire), 1948, (London), 1952. *Recreations:* travel; rifle shooting (captained Oxford University, 1934). *Address:* 6 Montrose Court, Princes Gate, SW7; Villa Tomara, Porto Valtravaglia, Lake Maggiore, Italy. *Clubs:* Garrick; Royal Solent Yacht.
*See also Sir T. G. Waterlow, Bt.*

**SLACK, Prof. Geoffrey Layton,** OBE 1944; TD 1946; Professor of Dental Surgery (Preventive and Children's Dentistry), University of London at the London Hospital Medical College, since 1959; *b* 27 March 1912; *er s* of late Charles Garrett Slack and Gertrude Wild, Southport; *m* Doreen Percival Ball, *d* of late Walter Knight Ball and Mary Percival, Birkdale; two *d*. *Educ:* Preparatory school, Croxton and Terra Nova; Leys School, Cambridge. LDS (with distinction) Univ. of Liverpool, 1934; DDS Northwestern Univ., Chicago, 1947; FDSRCS, 1948; Nuffield Fellow, 1949; Dipl. in Bacteriology, Manchester Univ. 1950. Private practice, 1934-39; House Surg., Liverpool Dental Hosp. 1934. TA, RASC, 1934-39; served in RASC, 1939-45; Major, DADST (T) Eastern Comd HQ, 1941-43; Lieut-Col ADST (T) HQ Second Army, 1943-44; Lieut-Col ADST (T) HQ 21 Army Gp, 1944-45; demobilized 1945. Lecturer in Preventive Dentistry, Univ. of Liverpool, 1948-51; Sen. Lecturer, 1951-59; Head of Dept of Preventive and Children's Dentistry, 1948-59; Consultant Dental Surgeon 1948-59, United Liverpool Hosps; Dean of Dental Studies, The London Hosp. Med. Coll. Dental Sch., 1965-69. Member: Standing (Dental) Advisory Cttee to Central Health Services Council, 1956-; Central Health Services Council, 1969-; Vice-Chm. Dental Health Committee, British Dental Association, 1959. Hon. Adviser, Editorial Board, International Dental Journal; Mem. Editorial Board, British Dental Journal; Mem. Board of Faculty of Dental Surgery, RCS, 1961- (Vice-Dean, 1968-69); Governor: The London Hospital Medical College, 1963-69; The London Hospital, 1963-. WHO Consultant, 1963-. Fellow Am. College of Dentists, 1963; Guest Mem., Académie Dentaire, 1968-. RCS John Tomes Prize, 1960-62; RCS Charles Tomes Lectr, 1965. *Publications:* (part-author) Dental Health, 1957; World Survey of Teaching Methods in Children's Dentistry, 1958; (with T. H. Melville) Bacteriology for Dental Students, 1960; (part-author) Demand and Need for Dental Care (Report to Nuffield Foundation), 1968; (part-author) Child Dental Health, 1969; many contribs to medical and dental journals. *Recreations:* golf, sailing, the theatre and travel; formerly hockey (played Lancashire 1933-39, 1945-52 (57 Caps), North of England, 1935-39, 1945-52, England XI 1938-39). *Address:* Westerly, Carrick Drive, Sevenoaks, Kent. *Clubs:* National Liberal, Medway Yacht.

**SLACK, George Granville; His Honour Judge Granville Slack;** County Court Judge, since 1966; *b* 11 July 1906; *s* of George Edwin and Amy Beatrice Slack; *m* 1st, 1935, Ella Kathleen (*d* 1957), *d* of Henry Alexander Eason; one *d*; 2nd, 1958, Vera Gertrude, *d* of Reginald Ackland Spencer; one *s* one *d*. *Educ:* Accrington Grammar School; London University. BA (Hons History) 1926; LLB 1929; LLM 1932. Called to Bar, Gray's Inn, 1929. Served RAFVR, 1943-46. Contested (L): Twickenham, 1945; Dewsbury, 1950; Chairman: London Liberal Party, 1947-48, 1950-53; Liberal Party Organisation, 1956-57. *Publications:* Slack on War Damage, 1941; Liabilities (War Time Adjustment) Act, 1941; Liability for National Service, 1942. *Address:* 10 Baronsmede, Ealing, W5. *T:* 01-567 8164. *Club:* National Liberal.

**SLACK, Rev. Kenneth,** MBE 1946; Minister of the City Temple, London, since 1967; *b* 20 July 1917; *s* of Reginald Slack and late Nellie (*née* Bennett); *m* 1941, Barbara Millicent Blake; two *s* one *d*. *Educ:* Wallasey Grammar School; Liverpool Univ., BA Liverpool, 1937; Westminster College, Cambridge. Ordained to ministry of Presbyterian Church of England, 1941. Minister, St Nicholas', Shrewsbury, 1941-45. Chaplain, RAFVR, 1942-46, serving Air Command, South East Asia, 1943-46 (MBE). Minister, St James's, Edgware, 1946-55. General Secretary, 1955-65, British Council of Churches. Minister, St Andrew's Church, Cheam, 1965-67. Mem., Adv. Cttee, Conf. of European Churches, 1960-67. Vice-President, Toc H. Chairman: Editorial Board, New Christian, 1965-70; European Editorial Board, Christian Century. Select Preacher, Cambridge, 1961. *Publications:* The Christian Conflict, 1960; The British Churches Today, 1961; Despatch from New Delhi, 1962; Is Sacrifice Outmoded?, 1966; Uppsala Report, 1968; Martin Luther King, 1970. *Recreations:* reading, fell-walking. *Address:* The City Temple, Holborn Viaduct, EC1A 2DE. *T:* 01-583 5532, 5876; 3 High Busk, Blue Hill Road, Ambleside.

**SLACK, Timothy Willatt,** MA; Headmaster of Bedales School since 1962; *b* 18 April 1928; *yr s* of Cecil Moorhouse Slack, MC, and Dora Willatt, Beverley, Yorks; *m* 1957, Katharine, 2nd *d* of Walter Norman Hughes, MA, and Jean Sorsbie, Chepstow, Mon.; one *s* three *d*. *Educ:* Winchester Coll.; New Coll., Oxford. Hons. PPE, 1951. Asst, Lycée de Rennes, France, 1951; Asst master, the Salem School, Baden, Germany, 1952; Assistant master, Repton School, 1953-59; Headmaster of Kambawsa College, Taunggyi, Shan State, Burma, 1959-62. Chairman, Society of Headmasters of Independent Schools, 1968-70. *Address:* Bedales School, Petersfield, Hants. *T:* Petersfield 2970.

**SLADE, Sir Benjamin (Julian Alfred),** 7th Bt, *cr* 1831; *b* 22 May 1946; *s* of Sir Michael Slade, 6th Bt and Angela (*d* 1959), *d* of Captain Orlando Chichester; *S* father, 1962. *Educ:* Millfield School. *Recreations:* hunting, shooting. *Heir: kinsman* Marcus George Savill Slade [*b* 30 Sept. 1906; *m* 1944 (marr. diss., 1953); one *d*]. *Address:* Nower's Farm, Rockwell Green, Wellington, Somerset. *T:* Wellington 2682.

**SLADE, Col Cecil Townley S.**; *see* Mitford-Slade.

**SLADE, Christopher John,** QC 1965; *b* 2 June 1927; *s* of late George Penkivil Slade, KC, and Mary Albinia Alice Slade; *m* 1958, Jane Gwenllian Armstrong Buckley; one *s* three *d*. *Educ:* Eton (Scholar); New Coll., Oxford (Scholar). Eldon Law Scholar, 1950. Called to Bar, Inner Temple, 1951; in practice at Chancery Bar, 1951-. Member: Gen. Council of the Bar, 1958-62, 1965-69; Senate of Four Inns of Court, 1966-69; Lord Chancellor's Legal Educn Cttee, 1969-. Term Time Dep. for Vice-Chancellor, County Palatine of Lancaster, 1969-. *Address:* 12 Harley Gardens, SW10. *T:* 01-373 7695. *Clubs:* Oxford and Cambridge, Beefsteak.

**SLADE, Julian Penkivil;** Author and Composer since 1951; *b* 28 May 1930; *s* of G. P. Slade, KC. *Educ:* Eton College; Trinity College, Cambridge (BA). Went to Bristol Old Vic Theatre School, 1951; wrote incidental music for Bristol Old Vic production of Two Gentlemen of Verona, 1952; joined Bristol Old Vic Co. as musical director, 1952. Wrote and composed Christmas in King St (with Dorothy Reynolds and James Cairncross) Bristol, 1952; composed music for Sheridan's The Duenna, Bristol, 1953; transferred to Westminster Theatre, London, 1954; wrote and composed The Merry Gentleman (with Dorothy Reynolds), Bristol, 1953; composed incidental music for The Merchant of Venice (1953 Stratford season). Wrote musical version of The Comedy of Errors for TV, 1954, and for Arts Theatre, London, 1956; wrote (with Dorothy Reynolds) Salad Days, Bristol, 1954, then Vaudeville, London, and Free as Air, Savoy, London, 1957; Hooray for Daisy!, Bristol, 1959, Lyric, Hammersmith, 1960; Follow that Girl, Vaudeville, London, 1960; Wildest Dreams, 1960; Vanity Fair (with Alan Pryce-Jones and Robin Miller), Queen's Theatre, London, 1962; Nutmeg and Ginger, Cheltenham, 1963; Sixty Thousand Nights (with George Rowell), Bristol, 1966; The Pursuit of Love, Bristol, 1967. *Publications:* Nibble the Squirrel (children's book), 1946; music of: The Duenna, 1954; Salad Days, 1954; Free as Air, 1957; Follow That Girl, 1967; As You Like It, Bristol, 1970; A Midsummer Night's Dream and Much Ado About Nothing, Regent's Park, 1970. *Recreations:* drawing, going to theatres and cinemas, listening to music. *Address:* 3 Priory Walk, SW10. *T:* 01-370 4859.

**SLADE, Richard Gordon,** OBE 1957; FRAeS; Managing Director, Fairey Hydraulics Ltd; Director: Fairey Air Surveys Ltd, since 1959; Fairey Industrial Holdings Ltd, since 1970; *b* 10 Sept. 1912; *yr s* of late William Slade and late Helen Blanche Slade; *m* 1948, Eileen Frances, 2nd *d* of late Dr W. F. Cooper; two *s* two *d* (and one *s* decd). *Educ:* Dulwich College. Commissioned in RAF 1933. Served in Egypt and 30 Squadron, Iraq, 1933-37; with Aeroplane and Armament Experimental Establishment, Martlesham Heath, 1937-39; Boscombe Down, 1939-41. Commanded: 157 Sqdn, Fighter Command, 1942; Handling Sqdn Empire Central Flying School, 1943; 169 Sqdn and RAF Station, Swannington, Bomber Comd 1944-45; 148 and 138 Wings, British Air Forces of Occupation, 1945-46; Chief Test Pilot and Supt of Flying, Fairey Aviation Co., 1946-59. Director, Fairey Aviation Ltd, 1959-60. American Silver Star, 1946. Liveryman, Guild of Air Pilots and Air Navigators. *Recreations:* sailing, riding, ski-ing. *Address:* Mickledore, Maidenhead Thicket, Berks. *T:* Maidenhead 20052. *Clubs:* Royal Air Force, Royal Aero.

**SLANE, Viscount; Henry Vivian Pierpoint Conyngham;** *b* 23 May 1951; *s* and *heir* of Earl of Mount Charles, *qv*.

**SLANEY, George Wilson,** (*Pseudonym:* **George Woden**); Novelist; *b* Wednesbury, Staffs, 1 Sept. 1884; *m* 1914, Edith Margaret Tomkinson, *g d* of John Tomkinson, Manchester; one *d*; *m* 1970, Dorothy Clare Sheppard. *Educ:* Queen Mary's Grammar School, Walsall; London University; France; Germany. Abandoned career as engineer; became a journalist, artist, musician; settled in Glasgow as a schoolmaster in 1909; retired. *Publications:* Sowing Clover, 1913; Paul Moorhouse, 1914; The New Dawn, 1915; Little Houses, 1919; The Money's The Thing (three-act play) Scottish National Theatre, Glasgow, 1921; The Wrenfield Mystery, 1923; Thistledown (three-act play) Play Actors, London, 1923; The Great Cornelius, 1926; The Gates of Delight, 1927; This Way to Fortune, 1929; The Parson and Clerk, 1930; Mungo, 1932; Love and Let Love, 1933; Our Peter, 1934; Upside-Turvydown, 1934; Tannenbrae, 1935; Othersmith, 1936; Perhaps Young Man, 1936; The Bailie's Tale, 1937; The Cathkin Mystery, 1937; Happiness Has No Story, 1938; Holiday Adventure, 1939; Voyage Through Life, 1940; Dusk for Dreams, 1941; The Queer Folk Next Door, 1942; The Golden Lion, 1944; Ruffy & Sons, 1945; Messenger-at-Arms, 1946; The Lover's Tale, 1948; The Puzzled Policeman, 1949; Helen Enchanted, 1950; Mystery of the Amorous Music Master, 1951; Simonetta, 1952. *Recreation:* music. *Address:* 91 Marlborough Avenue, Glasgow W1. *Club:* Scottish PEN (President, 1944-47).

**SLATER,** family name of **Baron Slater.**

**SLATER,** Baron *cr* 1970 (Life Peer), of Ferryhill, Durham; **Joseph Slater,** BEM 1949; *b* 13 June 1904; *s* of William and Elizabeth Slater; *m* 1928, Hilda Clement; one *s* one *d*. (and one *d* decd). *Educ:* Chilton Lane Council School. Miner; Lodge Official of Miners' Union since 1930; member Durham Miners' Union Executive, 1940 and 1947. Joined Labour Party, 1928; MP (Lab) Sedgefield Div. of Durham, 1950-70. Member of Durham County Council, 1944-50 (Vice-Chairman of Highways and Bridges Committee); member of Parish and District Councils, 1930. Chairman Education Divisional Executive Committee; member of Estimates Cttee, 1955, 1956, 1957, 1958, 1959, 1960; Mem. Council of Europe and Western European Union, 1958. PPS to Leader of Opposition, 1960-64; Asst Postmaster-General, 1964-69. Governor of several secondary schools; member of two hospital management committees. Methodist preacher since 1932. *Address:* House of Lords, SW1.

**SLATER, Arthur Edward,** CBE 1949; *b* 27 Nov. 1895; *s* of Harry Slater; *m* 1917, Kathleen Slater (*née* Spicer); one *s*. *Educ:* Beckenham County School; King's College, London. Served European War, 1914-18 (wounded), Devonshire Regt and Machine-Gun Corps; invalided, 1919. Appointed to Air Ministry as Asst Principal, 1919. Assistant Under-Secretary (Personnel), Air Ministry, 1951; Asst Under-Sec. (General), 1955; retired, 1956. *Recreation:* chess. *Address:* 3 The Homestead, Southwold, Suffolk. *T:* Southwold 3238.

**SLATER, Eliot Trevor Oakeshott,** CBE 1966; MA, MD Cantab; FRCP; *b* 28 Aug. 1904; 2nd *s* of Gilbert Slater, MA, DSc; *m* 1935, Lydia (marriage dissolved), *d* of Leonid Pasternak; two *s* two *d*; *m* 2nd, 1946, Jeanie Fyfe Foster. *Educ:* Leighton Park; Cambridge University;

St George's Hospital. Medical Officer, Maudsley Hospital, 1931-39; with Rockefeller Fellowship studied in Munich and Berlin, 1934-35; MRC Research grant, 1935-37; Clinical Director, Sutton Emergency Hosp., 1939-45; Physician in Psychological Medicine, National Hosp., Queen Sq., WC1, 1946-64; Dir, MRC Psychiatric Genetics Unit, 1959-69. Mem. Royal Commn on Capital Punishment, 1949. Litchfield Lectr (Oxon.), 1959. Mem. Genetical Soc. Editor-in-chief, British Journal of Psychiatry, 1963-. *Publications:* Introduction to Physical Methods of Treatment in Psychiatry (with W. Sargant), 1946; Patterns of Marriage (with M. Woodside), 1951; Psychotic and Neurotic Illness in Twins, 1953; Clinical Psychiatry (with W. Mayer-Gross and M. Roth), 1969; The Ebbless Sea (poems), 1968. Papers on genetical and psychiatric subjects. *Recreations:* Shakespeare studies, music. *Address:* Institute of Psychiatry, SE5. *T:* 01-703 5411.

**SLATER, Gordon Archbold,** MusD (Dunelm); FRCO; JP; retired as Organist of Lincoln Cathedral (1930-66); Adjudicator at Music Festivals throughout UK since 1920; Organ Recitalist (including radio and TV, since 1920; Lecturer in Music, Extra-Mural Depts, Nottingham Univ. and Hull University, since 1932; *b* Harrogate, 1 Mar. 1896; *s* of late William Henry Slater, West Park, Harrogate; *m* 1920, Mary Hanson Thistlethwaite, *d* of late Samuel Newton, London; one *s* one *d*. *Educ:* privately; studied under Sir Edward C. Bairstow at York Minster, 1914-16. Served in HM Forces, 1916-19; Organist of Boston Parish Church, 1919-27; Conductor of Boston Choral Society, 1919-27; Billingborough Choral Society, 1924-27; Musical Director Holland Choirs' Triennial Festival, 1920-27; Gate Burton Players, 1925-27; Organist and Master of the Choir, Leicester Cathedral, 1927-30; Founder and Conductor Leicester Bach Choir, 1927-30; Melton Mowbray Choral Society, 1928-29; Lecturer in Singing, Leicester Univ. Coll. also in Music, Extra-Mural Dept, 1929-30; Conductor: Lincoln Musical Society, 1931-66; Symph. Orch., 1932-66. Ferens Fine Art Lecturer, 1946-47; Adjudicated Canadian Musical Festivals, 1935, 1948. *Publications:* solo songs, choral songs, piano pieces, Church and Organ Music. *Recreation:* travelling. *Address:* 3 Pottergate, Lincoln. *T:* Lincoln 26320.

**SLATER, Gordon Charles Henry,** CMG 1964; CBE 1956; Director, Branch Office in London of International Labour Office, 1964-70; Under-Secretary, Ministry of Labour, in the Overseas Department, 1960-64, retired; *b* 14 Dec. 1903; *s* of Matthew and Florence Slater; *m* 1928, Doris Primrose Hammond; one *s* one *d*. Entered Ministry of Labour, 1928, as Third Class Officer; Assistant Secretary, Organisation and Establishments, 1945, Disabled Persons Branch, 1949; Secretary of National Advisory Council on Employment of Disabled Persons, 1949-56; Sec. of Piercy Committee on Rehabilitation of Disabled, 1953-56; Under-Sec., Ministry of Labour, 1958. Member Governing Body, ILO, 1961-64; UK Govt delegate, IL Conf., 1961-64. Mem. Berkshire CC, 1970-. *Address:* White House, Altwood Road, Maidenhead, Berks. *T:* Maidenhead 27463. *Club:* Reform.

**SLATER, Alderman Mrs Harriet,** CBE 1965; *b* Tunstall, Staffordshire. *Educ:* Chell and Park Rd Council Schools; Hanley High School; Dudley Teachers' Training College. Taught at Middleport Senior Girls School. MP (Lab and Co-op) Stoke-on-Trent North, March 1953-66; a Lord Commissioner of the Treasury (Area Whip), Oct. 1964-March 1966; Member: Burslem Co-operative Management Cttee; Burslem Co-op. Soc., 1933-46; Anglesey Health Executive, 1966; Anglesey Employment Cttee, 1966. National Organiser Co-op. Party, 1942-53; City Council, Stoke-on-Trent, 1933-; Alderman, 1949-65, Hon. Alderman, 1965-; Chm. City Educ. Cttee. *Address:* Hebor, Rutland Road, Bull Bay, Amlwch, Anglesey.

**SLATER, James Derrick,** FCA; Chairman and Managing Director, Slater Walker Securities Ltd, since 1964; Director, British Leyland Motor Corporation, since 1969; *b* 13 March 1929; *o s* of Hubert and Jessica Slater; *m* 1965, Helen Wyndham Goodwyn; two *s* one *d*. *Educ:* Preston Manor County Sch. Accountant and then Gen. Man. to a gp of metal finishing cos, 1953-55; Sec., Park Royal Vehicles Ltd, 1955-58; Dep. Sales Dir, Leyland Motor Corp. Ltd, 1963. FCA 1963 (ACA 1953). *Recreations:* chess, golf, table tennis. *Address:* High Beeches, Blackhills, Esher, Surrey. *T:* Esher 64312.

**SLATER, Leonard,** MA, JP; The Master, University College, Durham, since 1953; *b* 23 July 1908; *s* of S. M. Slater, Oldham, and Heysham, Lancs; *m* 1943, Olga Patricia George; two *s*. *Educ:* Hulme Grammar School, Oldham; St Catharine's College, Cambridge. British Guiana Exped. 1929; Research at Cambridge, 1930-32; MA 1932. Lecturer in Geography, Univ. of Rangoon, 1932-37; Geography Master, Repton School, 1937. Served War, 1940-45; RE (Survey) in UK, India and SE Asia; Lieut-Col, 1944 and Hon. Lieut-Col, 1946. Durham Colleges, Univ. of Durham Geography Dept; Lectr 1939; Reader, 1948; Pro-Vice-Chancellor, Durham Univ., 1969. Mem. Peterlee Devclt Corp., 1956-63; JP, Durham, 1961; Chm., Durham Hosp. Management Cttee, 1961; Mem., Newcastle Regional Hosp. Bd, 1965-69. *Publications:* articles in geographical periodicals. *Recreations:* golf and travel. *Address:* The Master's House, Durham Castle, Durham. *T:* Durham 5481. *Club:* Pathfinders'.

**SLATER, Colonel Owen,** CIE 1947; MC 1917; *b* 19 June 1890; *o s* of late Edward Murray Slater; *m* 1935, Genevieve Felicia, *o d* of late Rear-Adm. G. H. Hewett, CIE; no *c*. *Educ:* Rugby School; RMA Woolwich. Commissioned RE, 1910; served in Mesopotamia, 1915-18; Transcaspia and East Persia, 1918-20; joined Survey of India, 1920; remainder of service in India and Burma; Colonel, 1939; retired, 1947. *Address:* Ardogeena Grange, Durrus, Co. Cork, Eire. *Club:* United Service.

**SLATER, Richard Mercer Keene,** CMG 1962; British High Commissioner in Uganda since 1970; Ambassador to Rwanda (non-resident) since 1970; *b* 27 May 1915; *s* of late Samuel Henry Slater, CMG, CIE; *m* 1939, Barbara Janet Murdoch; four *s*. *Educ:* Eton; Magdalene Coll., Cambridge. Indian Civil Service (Punjab Commission), 1939-47; joined HM Diplomatic Service, 1947; served in Karachi (on secondment to Commonwealth Relations Office), Lima, Moscow, Rangoon and Foreign Office; Ambassador to Cuba, 1966-70. *Address:* c/o Foreign and Commonwealth Office, SW1. *Club:* Oxford and Cambridge University.

**SLATER, Admiral Sir Robin L. F. D.;** *see* Durnford-Slater.

**SLATTERY, Rear-Adm. Sir Matthew (Sausse),** KBE 1960; Kt 1955; CB 1946; FRAeS 1946; Chairman, R. & W. Hawthorn, Leslie & Co.; Director: Williams & Glyn's Bank Ltd; National Bank, since Dec. 1963 (Advisory Director, 1960-63); Vice-Chairman, Air

Registration Board; *b* 12 May 1902; 3rd *s* of late H. F. Slattery, one-time Chairman of National Bank Ltd; *m* 1925, Mica Mary, *d* of Col G. D. Swain, CMG; two *s* one *d*. *Educ:* Stonyhurst Coll.; RN Colls, Osborne and Dartmouth. Joined RN, 1916; Director Air Material, Admiralty, 1939-41; commanded HMS Cleopatra, 1941-42; appointed Director-General of Naval Aircraft Development and Production, Ministry of Aircraft Production, 1941, and Chief Naval Representative, 1943; Vice-Controller (Air) and Chief of Naval Air Equipment at Admiralty, and Chief Naval Representative on Supply Council, Ministry of Supply, 1945-48; retd list. Royal Navy, 1948. Man. Dir, Short Brothers & Harland, Ltd, 1948-52, Chm. and Man. Dir, 1952-60; Chm.: (SB Realisations) Ltd, 1952-60; Bristol Aircraft Ltd, 1957-60; Dir Bristol Aeroplane Co. Ltd, 1957-60. Special Adviser to Prime Minister on Transport of Middle East Oil, 1957-59; Dir National Bank Ltd, 1959-60; Chairman: BOAC, 1960-63; BOAC-Cunard Ltd, 1962-63. Commander Legion of Merit (USA). DSc(*hc*) Queen's Univ., Belfast, 1954. *Recreations:* country pursuits. *Address:* Harvey's Farm, Warninglid, Sussex. *Clubs:* United Service, Royal Aero.

**SLAUGHTER, James Cameron,** CMG 1963; Executive Adviser, Brisbane City Council, since 1967 (Town Clerk and City Administrator, 1940-67); *b* 16 Aug. 1902; *s* of late Ernest E. Slaughter; *m* 1927, Ida M. Taylor; one *s* one *d*. *Educ:* Normal School, Brisbane. Trustee, City Debt Redemption Fund, 1940; Chm., Lang Park Trust, 1962; Town Clerk: Bundaberg City Coun., 1936-40; Coolangatta Town Coun., 1927-36; Shire Clerk: Gatton Shire Coun.; Inglewood Shire Coun.; Chief Clerk, Ithaca Town Council; Mem. Greater Brisbane Town Planning Committee. AASA; FIMA. *Recreations:* bowls, fishing. *Address:* 142 Seventh Avenue, St Lucia, Brisbane, Australia. *T:* 7-6522 Brisbane. *Clubs:* Johnsonian and Tattersalls; Rugby League, booroodabin Bowling.

**SLAYTER, Adm. Sir William Rudolph,** KCB *cr* 1952 (CB 1945); DSO 1944; DSC 1918; *b* 13 Feb. 1896; *er s* of John Howard Slayter, MBE, MB, CM, Halifax, Nova Scotia, and Dunsfold, Surrey; *m* 1925, Helen Justine (*d* 1969), *d* of Major Russell Hale; one *s*. *Educ:* RN Colleges, Osborne and Dartmouth. NOD Admiralty, 1938-41; Commanding Officer HMS Liverpool, 1941; Commanding Officer HMS Newfoundland, 1942; Chief of Staff Home Fleet, 1943; Captain HMS Excellent, 1945; Naval Representative of UK on Military Staff Committee of UN, 1947; Flag Officer Commanding, Second Cruiser Squadron, 1949-50; Admiral Commanding Reserves, 1950-52; Commander-in-Chief, East Indies Station, 1952-Aug. 1954, retired. Mem. of Cttee of Management: Royal Nat. Lifeboat Instn. Naval Vice-Pres., Combined Cadet Force Association. Served European War, 1914-18 (despatches, DSC); War of 1939-45 (despatches twice, DSO, CB). *Recreations:* gardening, golf, music. *Address:* 5 Egerton Place, SW3. *Clubs:* United Service, MCC.

**SLEEMAN, Cyril Montagu,** MA; Fellow of Queens' College, Cambridge; *b* 5 July 1883; 2nd *s* of Rev. P. R. Sleeman, Clifton, Bristol; *m* 1946, Rose Ellen, *d* of M. Paget Baxter, Hove. *Educ:* Clifton College; Christ's College, Cambridge (Scholar). Fellow Queens' College, Cambridge, 1912; Tutor and Senior Tutor, 1919-31; Lt RNVR; Wireless Officer, HM Signal School, Portsmouth, during War. *Recreations:* mountaineering, travel, swimming. *Address:* Queens' College, Cambridge; Ellergarth, Great Langdale, Westmorland. *Club:* Alpine.

**SLEIGH, Sir Hamilton (Morton Howard),** Kt 1970; Chairman and Managing Director of H. C. Sleigh Ltd since 1947; *b* 20 March 1896; *s* of Howard Crofton Sleigh and Marion Elizabeth Sleigh; *m* 1926, Doris Margherita Halbert; two *s*. *Educ:* Sherborne Sch., Dorset. Kt Cross, Order of White Rose of Finland. *Recreation:* farming. *Address:* 42 Wallace Avenue, Toorak, Victoria 3142, Australia. *Clubs:* Australian (Melbourne and Sydney).

**SLEIGHT, Sir John Frederick,** 3rd Bt, *cr* 1920; *b* 13 April 1909; *s* of Major Sir Ernest Sleight, 2nd Bt and Margaret, *d* of C. F. Carter, JP, The Limes, Grimsby; *S* father 1946; *m* 1942, Jacqueline Margaret Mundell, *widow* of Ronald Mundell and *o d* of late Major H. R. Carter of Brisbane, Queensland; one *s*. *Heir: s* Richard Sleight, *b* 27 May 1946. *Address:* 15 High Street, Thame, Oxon.

**SLEMON, Air Marshal Charles Roy,** CB 1946; CBE 1943; retired from RCAF, 1964; Executive Vice-President, US Air Force Academy Foundation Inc., since 1964; *b* Winnipeg, Manitoba, Canada, 7 November 1904; *s* of Samuel Slemon and Mary Bonser; *m* 1935, Marion Pamela Slemon, Bowmanville, Ont; one *s* two *d*. *Educ:* University of Manitoba (BSc). Lieut COTC (Army), Canada, 1923; Cadet Royal Canadian Air Force, 1923; Royal Air Force Staff College Course, England, 1938; Senior Air Staff Officer at Western Air Command Headquarters, Canada, 1939-41; commanded Western Air Command, Canada, for 5 months in 1941; Director of Operations at RCAF HQ Ottawa, 1941-42; Senior Air Staff Officer, No. 6 (RCAF) Bomber Group, England, 1942-44; Air Vice-Marshal, 1945; Deputy AOC-in-C, RCAF Overseas, March 1945; Commanded Canadian Air Forces preparing for the Pacific, 1945; Air Council Member for Supply and Organization, 1946; Air Council Member for Operations and Training, 1947-48; AOC Trg Comd, RCAF, 1949-53; Chief of the Air Staff, Canada, 1953-57; Dep. C-in-C, N American Defence Comd (Canada-USA), 1957-64, retd. Hon. LLD (Univ. of Manitoba), 1953; Hon. DMSc (RMC), Kingston, Ont, 1965. USA Legion of Merit, 1946; French Legion of Honour and Croix de Guerre with Palm, 1947. *Recreations:* golf, swimming. *Address:* (business) Air Force Academy Foundation Inc., PO Box 1838, Colorado Springs, Colorado, USA; (home) 8 Thayer Road, Broadmoor Heights, Colorado Springs, Colorado 80906, USA.

**SLESINGER, Edward G.,** OBE 1918; MS, FRCS, MB, BSc; late Chairman, Board of Governors and Consulting Surgeon Emeritus, Guy's Hospital; Hon. Consulting Surgeon N Hertfordshire and S Bedfordshire Hospital, and Surgical Home for Boys, Banstead; *b* London; *m* Gladys Eleanor Trench; two *s*. *Educ:* Dulwich College; Guy's Hosp. (Junior Science Scholar, Michael Harris Prize in Anatomy). Late Surgeon and Surgeon i/c fracture dept Guy's Hospital; Surgical Adviser EMS; BMA Research Scholar 1914 and 1919-20; Hunterian Professor, Royal College of Surgeons; Examiner in Surgery for LDS, RCS; BSc London 1st Class Hons Physiology, 1908; MB, BS (honours Medicine) 1911; MS London (University Gold Medal) 1919; President Clinical Section, Royal Society of Medicine; Temp. Surgeon-Lt RN 1914-18 (despatches, Croix de Guerre avec Palme). *Publications:* Articles–Appendicitis, Peritonitis, Intestinal Obstruction, Price's Text-book of Medicine; (joint) Surgery for Dental Students; War

Wounds and Injuries; Prevention of Operative Mortality in Ex-ophthalmic Goitre, Guy's Hospital Reports 1923, and contributions to Medical Journals on abdominal and goitre surgery and on fractures. *Recreation:* reading. *Address:* Holly House, Hedgehog Lane, Haslemere, Surrey.

**SLESSER, Rt. Hon. Sir Henry,** PC 1929; Kt 1924; JP Devon; a Lord Justice of Appeal, 1929-40; *b* London, 1883; *y s* of Ernest Slesser, Gerrards Cross, Bucks; *m* Margaret, *e d* of late Corrie Grant, KC. *Educ:* Oundle and St Paul's Schools; London Univ. Called to Bar, 1906, Bencher of the Inner Temple, 1924; KC, 1924; MP (Lab.) SE Leeds, 1924-29; HM Solicitor-General, 1924. Devon CC, 1946-68; Alderman, 1956; Chairman of Dartmoor Nat. Park Cttee, 1948-64. OSB (oblate); Hon. LLD Exeter, 1963. *Publications:* Trade Union Law, 1922 (3rd ed. 1928); Religio Laici, 1929; The Pastured Shire and Other Verses, 1935; Law (Heritage Series), 1936; Judgment Reserved, 1941; The Judicial Office and other matters, 1943; History of the Liberal Party, 1944; Order and Disorder, 1945; Administration of the Law, 1948; Middle Ages in the West, 1949 (2nd edn 1951); The Anglican Dilemma, 1952; The Art of Judgment and other legal studies, 1962. *Address:* Postbridge, Dartmoor, S Devon. *T:* Postbridge 218.

**SLESSOR, Marshal of the Royal Air Force Sir John Cotesworth,** GCB, *cr* 1948 (KCB 1943; CB 1942); DSO 1937; MC 1916; DL; *b* Rhanikhet, India, 3 June 1897; *s* of late Major Arthur Kerr Slessor, Sherwood Foresters; *m* 1923, Hermione Grace (*d* 1970), *d* of Gerald Seymour Guiness, and *widow* of Lt-Col Herbert Carter; one *s* one *d*. *Educ:* Dragon School; Haileybury. Served European War, RFC, 1915-18: London Air Defence, France, Egypt, and Sudan (despatches, wounded, MC); served RAF India, 1921-23; RAF Staff College, 1924-25; commanded No. 4 Squadron, 1925-28; Air Staff, Air Ministry, 1928-30; Instructor, Staff College, Camberley, 1931-34; India, 1935-37: commanded No. 3 Indian Wing, Quetta, 1935; Waziristan Operations, 1936-37 (despatches, DSO); Director of Plans, Air Ministry, 1937-41; ADC to the King, 1938; Air rep., Anglo-French Conversations, 1939 and Anglo-American (ABC) Staff Conversations, 1941; AOC 5 (Bomber) Group, 1941; ACAS, (Policy) Casablanca Conf., 1942-43; AOC-in-C Coastal Command, 1943; C-in-C, RAF, Mediterranean and Middle East, 1944-45; Member of Air Council for Personnel, 1945-47; Commandant Imperial Defence College, 1948-49; Principal Air ADC to the King, 1948-50; Air Commodore, 1939, Air Vice-Marshal, 1941, Air Marshal, 1943; Air Chief Marshal, 1946; Marshal of the RAF, 1950. Chief of the Air Staff, 1950-52; Rep. British Chief of Staffs, NATO Confs, Brussels, Rome, Lisbon, Paris, Washington; Mem. UK Delegations, Commonwealth Relations Confs, 1954, 1959. Order of Leopold, Belgium; Légion d'Honneur, France, Order of Phœnix, Greece; Order of St Olaf, Norway; Legion of Merit, USA; Order of the Sword, Sweden. Pres. the Victory (ex-Services) Club; Chairman, Star and Garter Home, 1953-67; Vice-Pres., Inst. of Strategic Studies; Gov.: Haileybury, Sherborne, King's (Bruton). JP and CC Somerset; High Sheriff, Somerset, 1965; DL, Somerset, 1969 *Publications:* Air Power and Armies, 1936; Strategy for the West, 1954; The Central Blue, 1956; The Great Deterrent, 1959; What Price Co-existence, 1961; These Remain, 1969. RUSI gold medal, 1936; Chesney Memorial Award, 1965. *Address:* Rimpton Manor, Yeovil, Somerset. *T:* Marston Magna 223.

*Clubs:* Royal Air Force, Naval and Military (Hon. Life); Somerset County.

**SLIGO,** 10th Marquess of, *cr* 1800; **Denis Edward Browne;** Baron Mount Eagle, 1760; Viscount Westport, 1768; Earl of Altamont, 1771; Earl of Clanricarde, 1543 and 1800 (special remainder); Baron Monteagle (UK), 1806; *b* 13 Dec. 1908; *er s* of late Lt-Col Lord Alfred Eden Browne, DSO (5th *s* of 5th Marquess) and late Cicely, *d* of Edward Wormald, 15 Berkeley Square, W; *S* uncle, 1952; *m* 1930, José Gauche; one *s*. *Educ:* Eton. *Heir:* *s* Earl of Altamont, *qv*. *Address:* c/o Messrs Trower, Still and Keeling, 5 New Square, Lincoln's Inn, WC2.
*See also Baron Brabourne.*

**SLIM,** family name of **Viscount Slim.**

**SLIM,** 1st Viscount, *cr* 1960; **Field-Marshal William Joseph Slim,** KG 1959; GCB 1950 (KCB 1944; CB 1944); GCMG 1952; GCVO 1954; GBE 1946 (CBE 1942); DSO 1943; MC; LLD (Hon.) Leeds, Birmingham, Cantab, Sydney, Adelaide, Melbourne; DCL (Hon.) Oxon; DLit (Hon.) New England, NSW; DSc (Hon.) NSW; FRACP (Hon.); FRCS Edinburgh (Hon.); late IA; Constable and Governor of Windsor Castle 1964-70 (Lt-Gov., 1963-64); *b* 6 Aug. 1891; *s* of John Slim, Bristol; *m* 1926, Aileen, *d* of Rev. J. A. Robertson, MA, Edinburgh; one *s* one *d*. *Educ:* King Edward's Sch., Birmingham. Served European War, R. Warwickshire Regt, Gallipoli (wounded), France, Mesopotamia (wounded, MC); joined 6th Gurkha Rifles, Indian Army; Instructor Staff College, Camberley, 1934-36; Imperial Defence College; Commandant 2nd Bn 7th Gurkha Rifles; Commandant Senior Officers School, India; War of 1939-45 commanded 10th Infantry Brigade, Sudan, Eritrea (wounded); 10th Indian Division Syria-Persia-Iraq (DSO); commanded 1st Burma Corps, Burma (CBE); commanded 15 Indian Corps (CB); commanded Fourteenth Army (KCB); C-in-C Allied Land Forces, SE Asia, 1945-46; Commandant Imperial Defence College, 1946-47; Chief of Imperial General Staff, 1948-52; Governor-General and Commander in Chief of Australia, 1953-60. Colonel: 7th Gurkha Rifles, 1944-56; The West Yorkshire Regt, 1947-56; 1st Gurkha Rifles (Indian Army), 1949-56. Deputy Chairman, Railway Executive, 1948; Director: London Assurance; Dalgety and New Zealand Loan Ltd (President, 1965); Edger Investments (Dep. Chm.); Imperial Chemical Industries, 1960-66; Mem., London Board of Advice, National Bank of Australasia, 1960; *Publications:* Defeat into Victory, 1956; Courage and Other Broadcasts, 1957; Unofficial History, 1959. *Relevant publication:* Sir G. C. Evans, Slim as Military Commander, 1969. *Heir:* Lt-Col Hon. John Douglas Slim [*b* 20 July 1927; *m* 1958, Elizabeth, *d* of Rawdon Spinney; two *s* one *d*]. *Address:* c/o Lloyds Bank Ltd, 6 Pall Mall, SW1. *Clubs:* Athenæum, Naval and Military.

**SLIMMINGS, Sir William Kenneth MacLeod,** Kt 1966; CBE 1960; *b* 15 Dec. 1912; *s* of George and Robina Slimmings; *m* 1943, Lilian Ellen Willis; one *s* one *d*. *Educ:* Dunfermline High School. Chartered Accountant: Partner in Thomson McLintock & Co., Chartered Accountants, London, etc., 1946-. Member: Committee of Inquiry on the Cost of Housebuilding, 1947-53; Committee on Tax-paid Stocks, 1952-53; Committee on Cheque Endorsement, 1955-56; Performing Right Tribunal, 1963-; Chairman Board of Trade Advisory Committee, 1957-66. Mem. Council, Inst. Chartered Accountants of Scotland, 1962-66, Pres., 1969-70; Mem., Scottish

Tourist Bd, 1969-. Hon. DLitt, Heriot-Watt, 1970. *Recreation:* gardening. *Address:* (business) 33 King William Street, EC4. *T:* 01-626 3232; (home) 62 The Avenue, Worcester Park, Surrey. *T:* 01-337 2579. *Club:* Caledonian.

**SLOAN, Norman Alexander,** QC (Scot.) 1953; Director, Shipbuilders and Repairers National Association; *b* 27 Jan. 1914; *s* of George Scott Sloan and Margaret Hutcheson Smith; *m* 1944, Peggy Perry; two *s* one *d*. *Educ:* Glasgow Academy; Glasgow University (BL). Solicitor, 1935; Admitted to Faculty of Advocates, 1939; Served in RNVR 1940-46. Lecturer in Industrial Law, Edinburgh University, 1946-51; Standing Counsel to Department of Health for Scotland, 1946-51; Advocate-Depute, 1951-53. Dir., The Shipbuilding Employers' Federation, 1955-68. *Recreation:* golf. *Address:* Ardyne, 53 The Mount, Fetcham, Leatherhead, Surrey. *T:* Leatherhead 6577; 21 Grosvenor Place, SW1. *T:* 01-235 5131. *Clubs:* Caledonian, City Livery; Burhill Golf.

**SLOAN, Sir Tennant,** KCIE, *cr* 1942 (CIE 1930); CSI 1936; *b* 9 Nov. 1884; *s* of Alexander Sloan, CA, Glasgow; *m* Gladys Hope, *d* of R. Hope Robertson, CA, Glasgow; one *d*. *Educ:* Glasgow Academy; Glasgow University; Christ Church, Oxford. Assistant Magistrate, 1909-13; Assistant Settlement Officer, 1913-14; Under-Secretary to Government, UP and to Government of India, 1914-19; Magistrate and Collector, 1920-21; Deputy Secretary to Government, UP and Government of India, 1921-26; Special Reforms Officer, and Secretary to Government, UP, 1927-31; Joint Secretary, Home Dept, Government of India, 1932-36; Settlement Commissioner and Commissioner, UP, 1936-39; Adviser to the Governor, United Provinces, 1939-45. *Recreations:* golf, fishing. *Address:* 6 Greenhill Park, Edinburgh 10. *T:* 031-447 3688. *Club:* Western (Glasgow).

**SLOANE, Maj.-Gen. John Bramley Malet,** CB 1967; CBE 1962 (OBE 1951); Director of Manning (Army), Ministry of Defence, 1964-67; retired; *b* 17 Sept. 1912; *m* 1939, Marjorie (*née* Crowley); three *s*. *Recreations:* golf, walking. *Address:* Jordans, Newton Blossomville, near Turvey, Beds. *T:* Turvey 392. *Club:* Army and Navy.

**SLOCUM, Captain Frank Alexander,** CMG 1953; OBE 1935; RN (retd); *b* 30 Sept. 1897; 2nd *s* of late Henry Slocum, Micheldever, Hampshire, and of Emily (*née* Clarke), *e d* of Capt. William Clarke, Roy. Fusiliers; *m* 1922, Vera, *e d* of late John Metherell Gard, Stoke, Devonport; two *d*. *Educ:* Royal Naval Establishments; Gonville and Caius College, Cambridge. Entered RN, 1914; served European War, 1914-18, in Grand Fleet; Lieut, 1918; 2nd Destroyer Flotilla, Home Fleet, 1920; qualified in (N) duties, 1921. Served in Persian Gulf, Mediterranean, and Home Fleets; psc RN Staff Coll., 1931; Mediterranean Fleet (Revenge and Resolution); staff of Tactical School, 1935; Actg Comdr, 1939; Actg Capt., 1940. Served War of 1939-45 as Dep. Dir Ops Div., Admiralty, and in charge of Auxiliary Patrol Flotillas; retd list, 1947, in war service rank of Captain. Temp. 1st Sec., British Embassy, Oslo, 1954-56. Trials Capt. for contract-built HM Ships, 1956. Croix de Guerre avec Palme (France), 1946; Comdr Legion of Merit (USA), 1946; King Haakon VII Liberty Cross (Norway), 1947; King Christian X's Freedom Medal (Denmark), 1947. *Publications:* naval and seafaring articles and short stories. *Recreations:* sailing, naval history, marine surveying. *Address:* Stone Cottage, 3a Camden Park, Tunbridge Wells, Kent. *T:* Tunbridge Wells 27395. *Clubs:* United Service, Pratt's.

**SLOMAN, Albert Edward,** DPhil; Vice-Chancellor of University of Essex, since 1962; *b* Launceston, Cornwall, 14 Feb. 1921; *y s* of Albert Sloman; *m* 1948, Marie Bernadette, *d* of Leo Bergeron, Cognac, France; three *d*. *Educ:* Launceston Coll., Cornwall; Wadham Coll., Oxford (Pope Exhibitioner, 1939). Mediæval and Mod. Langs (War Degree), 1941; MA (Oxon and Dublin); DPhil (Oxon). Served War of 1939-45 (despatches): night-fighter pilot with 219 and 68 squadrons; Flight-Lieut. Lecturer in Spanish, Univ. of California, Berkeley, USA, 1946-47; Reader in Spanish, in charge of Spanish studies, Univ. of Dublin, 1947-53; Fellow TCD, 1950-53; Gilmour Professor of Spanish, University of Liverpool, 1953-62; Dean, Faculty of Arts, 1961-62. Editor of Bulletin of Hispanic Studies, 1953-62. Reith Lecturer, 1963. Chairman, Dept of Education State Studentship Cttee (Humanities), 1965-; Pres., Conf. of European Rectors and Vice-Chancellors, 1969-; Member: Standing Conf. of European Rectors and Vice-Chancellors, 1965-; Adm. Bd, Internat. Assoc., of Univs, 1965-; Bd of Governors, Univ. of Guyana, 1966-. *Publications:* The Sources of Calderón's El Prncipe constante, 1950; The Dramatic Craftsmanship of Calderón, 1958; A University in the Making, 1964. Articles and reviews in Modern Language Review, Bulletin of Hispanic Studies, Hispanic Review, Romance Philology and other journals. *Recreation:* travel. *Address:* The University of Essex, Colchester. *Club:* Savile.

**SLOMAN, Peter;** Under-Secretary, Department of Education and Science, since 1968; *b* Oct. 1919; *s* of H. N. P. Sloman and Mary Sloman (*née* Trinder); *m* 1950, Margaret Barbara Pilkington-Rogers; one *s* one *d*. *Educ:* Winchester Coll.; New Coll., Oxford. War Service (RA), 1939-46. Home Civil Service, 1946-: Min. (later Dept) of Education; Treasury; Ministries of Defence, Land and Natural Resources, Housing and Local Govt. IDC 1960. *Address:* 26 Glebe Road, Barnes, SW13.

**SLOT, Gerald Maurice Joseph;** late Lt-Col RAMC; Consulting Physician: Royal Waterloo Hospital; St. Thomas' Hospital Group; Emeritus Consulting Physician, LCC, St Alfege's Hospital, Teddington Hospital and Hampton Hospital; Emeritus Consultant: Brook Hospital; Dulwich Hospital; King's College Hospital Group; Physician in charge of Rheumatism Supervisory Centre, LCC; late Physician Buchanan Hospital, and Royal Hospital, Richmond; Physician i/c Rheumatism Borough of Chiswick and Brentford; Physician NW Metropolitan and SW Metropolitan Boards; Paediatrician SE Metropolitan Board; *b* Johannesburg; *m* 1936, Mary, *d* of late J. A. Munton, Bradford. *Educ:* St Paul's School (Schol.); St John's Coll., Oxford (Exhibitioner); St Bartholomew's Hospital; Mercer's Scholar, Skynner Prizeman, MD (University of London Gold Medal), MRCP, DPH. Mem. Inner Temple; late Editor of Transactions Medico-legal Society; Editor of Medico-legal Journal and Criminological Review; late Medical Tutor Charing Cross Hospital and London Hospital; Harmsworth Research Fellow; late Chief Assistant St Bartholomew's Hospital and House Physician; Chadwick lecturer, 1930. *Publications:* Rheumatism in Childhood; Fume Diseases; Heart Disease in Childhood; Calcium Therapy; Pain in its Medico-Legal Relations; Deaths under Anæsthetics; Obesity; Treatment of Rheumatism with Gold; The

Treatment of Sciatica; Medico legal aspects of Drunkenness; Street Accidents, numerous articles, etc. *Recreations:* tennis, motoring, sailing, music. *Address:* 148 Harley Street, W1. *T:* 01-935 1207; Comeragh House, 42 Marine Crescent, Worthing, Sussex. *T:* Worthing 48022.

**SLOTKI, Israel Wolf,** MBE 1962; MRST, MA, LittD (Vic.); FRSL; Emeritus Director of Education, Manchester Central Board for Hebrew Education; Hon. Minister, Manchester Great Synagogue; Principal, Manchester Talmud Torah Schools, 1911-50; Hon. Superintendent of Hebrew in Manchester and Salford County Schools, 1912-50; Chaplain to: HM Prisons: Strangeways, Manchester; The Castle, Lancaster; Bela River, Westmorland; Styal, Cheshire; Calderstones, Brockhall, Lancaster Moor, Manchester Royal Infirmary, Royal Eye, St Mary's and Hope Hospitals, and Langho Epileptic Colony; *b* Jerusalem, 26 Dec. 1884; *s* of late Rabbi Moses and Sarah Slotki; *m* Sarah (*d* 1960), *y d* of Rabbi Hertz and Bessie Lowenstein; one *s* two *d*. *Educ:* High Schools in Jerusalem; privately; Univ. of Manchester. Editor of the Hayehudi, 1908; Manchester Editor Jewish Guardian, 1919-31; Member of various committees of London social, religious and philanthropic organisations, and Hon. Sec. LCC Care Committees, 1910; Founder and Hon. Sec. Manchester Society for Hebraic Studies, 1917; Hon. Sec. Mizrachi Centre of the United Kingdom, 1926-28; of Manchester and District Hebrew Visitation Board since 1941 and Hon. Director since 1949; Examiner in Hebrew and Cognate subjects in Jewish Congregational Schools in many Lancashire towns; Hon. Sec., 1922-40, Vice-Pres. 1941, and Hon. Educational Adviser, 1942-46, of joint Jewish Education Board; Vice-Pres., 1939-41, of Jewish Ecclesiastical Council for Manchester and Salford; Hon. Life Mem. Council, Manchester and Salford Jews, 1964-; Mem. Exec. National Savings Committee, for Salford, 1939-, Dep. Chm. 1962, and Chm. 1964-; Mem. Manchester and Salford and District Cttee of Roy. National Lifeboat Instn, 1937-61; Mem. of Council of Manchester Univ. Egyptian and Oriental Soc., 1925- (Pres. 1952-54); Speaker for Ministry of Information, 1940-45. *Publications:* Stichometry and Text of the Great Hallel, 1928; Jewish Education in Manchester and Salford, 1928; Forms and Features of Ancient Hebrew Poetry, 1931; Typographic Arrangement of Ancient Hebrew Poetry, 1931; Song of Deborah, 1932; Longer and Shorter Versions of Ancient Hebrew Poems, 1933; Antiphony in Ancient Hebrew Poetry, 1936; Translations and Commentaries in the First Unabridged English Edition of the Babylonian Talmud Tractates Baba Bathra (Joint) and Horayoth, (1935), Yebamoth and (Joint) Kethuboth, (1936), Erubin and Sukkah, (1938), Niddah, Kelim, Negaim, Parah and Tohoroth (1948); Soferim, Sefer Torah, Zizith, Tefillin and Mezuzah, 1965; Grammatical Guide to the Hebrew Text of the Jewish Prayer Book (1946, 2nd edn 1947); Commentaries on Isaiah, 1949; on Kings, 1950, on the Books of Chronicles, 1952; Seventy Years of Hebrew Education, 1950; Moses Maimonidas, 1952; History of the Manchester Shechita Board, 1954; contrib. to learned journals. *Recreations:* walking, reading. *Address:* 3 Bellott Street, Manchester M8 7PQ. *T:* 061-205 4906.

**SLYTH, Arthur Roy,** CB 1966; OBE 1957; Secretary, Exchequer and Audit Department, since 1963 (Deputy Secretary 1961-63); *b* 30 May 1910; *s* of Thomas Slyth; *m* 1938, Anne Mary Muir Grieve. *Educ:* Lincoln School. Entered Exchequer and Audit Department, 1929. *Recreation:* golf. *Address:* 28 Shepherd's Hill, N6. *T:* 01-340 0818.

**SMAIL, William Mitchell,** MA Edinburgh and Oxon; FEIS; *b* Edinburgh, 1885; 3rd *s* of Adam Smail, Edinburgh; *m* Nora Maunsell (*d* 1968), 3rd *d* of Colonel W. D. Gordon, Kingston, Ontario; two *d*. *Educ:* Stewart's College, Edinburgh; Edinburgh University; Oriel College, Oxford (Bible Clerk, 1907-10); First Class in Literae Humaniores, 1910; Pitt Club Scholar, Edinburgh University, 1910; Assistant Master at Oundle School, 1910-11; Assistant Professor of Classics, Queen's University, Kingston, Ont., 1911-13; Professor of Latin, Rhodes University College, Grahamstown, South Africa, 1913-29; Warden of College House, Grahamstown, 1914; Rector of Perth Academy, 1929-50. *Publication:* Quintilian on Education, 1938.

**SMAILES, Prof. Arthur Eltringham,** MA, DLit London, FRGS; Professor of Geography, University of London, at Queen Mary College, since 1955; *b* Haltwhistle, Northumberland, 23 March 1911; *o s* of John Robert and Mary Elizabeth Smailes; *m* 1937, Dorothy Forster; one *d*. *Educ:* Grammar School of Queen Elizabeth, Hexham; University College, London. BA (London) with First Cl. Hons in Geography, 1930, MA 1933, DLit 1965. Lecturer, University College, London, from 1931 and Reader in Geography, 1950-53; Head of Department of Geography, Queen Mary College, University of London, 1953-. Geographer Consultant, Middlesbrough Survey and Plan, 1944-45. Hon. Secretary, Inst of British Geographers, 1951-62, Pres., 1970. Circuit Steward, West London Mission, Kingsway Hall, 1965-69. Research Medal, RSGS, 1964. *Publications:* The Geography of Towns, 1953; North England, 1960. Various articles in geographical and town planning journals. *Recreations:* gardening, travel. *Address:* 20 Marlborough Crescent, Sevenoaks, Kent. *T:* 55742.

**SMALDON, Catherine Agnes,** CBE 1964; Chairman, General Nursing Council for England and Wales, 1960-65; retired as Chief Nursing Officer and Principal, Queen Elizabeth School of Nursing, United Birmingham Hospitals (1955-63); *b* 23 April 1903; *d* of William Ernest Smaldon and Catherine Smaldon (*née* Fairley). *Educ:* The Old Palace School, Croydon; Charing Cross Hospital. Ward Sister, Princess Mary's Hosp., Margate, 1928-29; Charing Cross Hospital: Ward Sister, Theatre Sister, Out Patient Dept Sister, Night Supt, Asst Matron, 1930-36. Matron: Brompton Hosp., London, 1936-40; Queen Elizabeth Hosp., Birmingham, 1940-55. Chm. Birmingham Area Nurse Training Cttee; Mem., Herefordshire Hospitals Management Cttee. *Recreations:* gardening, walking. *Address:* Checkley Fold, Mordiford, Hereford. *T:* Bartestree Cross 215. *Club:* Woolhope Naturalists.

**SMALE, John Arthur,** CBE 1953; AFC 1919; Technical consultant, Marconi's Wireless Telegraph Co. Ltd, 1957-62, retd; *b* 16 Feb. 1895; *s* of Charles Blackwell and Ann Smale; *m* 1920, Hilda Marguerita Watts; one *d* (one *s* killed on active service, RAF, 1941). *Educ:* Wycliffe Coll., Stonehouse; Bristol Univ. (BSc). Apprentice British Thompson Houston, Rugby, 1914; served European War, 1914-18, in RNAS; RAF, 1918-19. Engineer, Marconi's Wireless Telegraph Co. Ltd, 1919-29; Cable & Wireless Ltd, 1929-57, retired (Asst Engineer-in-Chief, 1935-48; Engineer-in-Chief, 1948-57). Chairman Cyprus Inland Telecommunications Authority, 1955-60, retired. FIEE 1941; Chairman, Radio Section of Inst. Electrical Engineers, 1953; FIEEE 1958. *Recreations:* sport, music. *Address:* Cotswold, Ilex Way, Goring-By-Sea, Sussex.

**SMALL, Sir Frank (Augustus),** Kt 1967; CBE 1962; DL; JP; Director, National Building Agency, since 1964; *b* 3 July 1903; *s* of Austin and Sarah Small; *m* 1928, Sarah Ann Foster; no *c. Educ:* Woods Foundn C of E Sch., Woodborough, Notts. Nottinghamshire County Council: Member, 1946; Chm., County Finance Cttee, 1951-63; Chairman, 1963-67; Vice-Chm., 1967-. Member: County Councils Assoc., 1952- (Chm., Parly. and Gen. Purposes Cttee, 1965); Land Commission, 1968-. JP 1952, Alderman, 1957, DL 1963, Nottinghamshire. *Recreations:* football, cricket. *Address:* The Homestead, Woodborough, Notts. *T:* 2252.

**SMALL, Very Rev. Robert Leonard,** OBE 1958; DD; Minister of St Cuthbert's Parish Church, Edinburgh, since 1956; Chaplain to the Queen in Scotland, since 1967; *b* N Berwick, 12 May 1905; *s* of Rev. Robert Small, MA, and Marion C. McEwen; *m* 1931, Jane Hay McGregor; three *s* one *d. Educ:* N Berwick High Sch.; Edinburgh Univ.; New Coll., Edinburgh. MA 1st cl. hons Classics; Sen. Cunningham Fellowship; studied in Rome, Berlin and Zurich; DD 1957. Ordained, 1931, to St John's, Bathgate; W High Church, Kilmarnock, 1935-44; Cramond Church, Edinburgh 1944-56. Convener: C of S Cttee on Huts and Canteens for HM Forces, 1946-58; Cttee on Temperance and Morals, 1958-63; Social and Moral Welfare Bd, 1963-64; Stewardship and Budget Cttee, 1964-69. Mem., Scottish Adv. Cttee on Treatment of Offenders; Regional Chaplain (Scotland), Air Trng Corps; Hon. Vice-Pres., Boys' Brigade. Warrack Lectr on Preaching, 1959. Guest Preacher: Knox Church, Dunedin, 1950; Fifth Ave., Presbyterian Church, NY, 1960; St Stephen's Presbyterian Church, Sydney, 1962. Moderator of the General Assembly of the Church of Scotland, 1966-67; First Chm., Scottish Parole Bd, 1967-. *Publications:* With Ardour and Accuracy (Warrack Lectures), 1959; No Uncertain Sound (Scholar as Preacher Series), 1964; No Other Name, 1966; contribs to The Expository Times. *Recreations:* boating, walking; formerly Association football (Edinburgh Univ. Blue, captained team, 1927-28; played as amateur for St Bernard's FC, 1928-29; capped *v* England (Amateur), 1929). *Address:* 1 Wester Coates Road, Edinburgh 12. *T:* 031-337 5002. *Club:* Royal Over-Seas League.

**SMALL, Ronald Hugh; Hon. Mr Justice Small;** Puisne Judge, Jamaica, since 1956; *b* Kingston, Jamaica, 3 July 1907; *s* of I. P. Small; *m* 1939, Annie Louise (*née* Kerr); three *s* two *d. Educ:* Kingston, Jamaica; King's College, University of London. Called to the Bar, Middle Temple, 1934; in private practice, Jamaica, 1934-37; Deputy Clerk of the Courts, Jamaica, 1937; Clerk of the Courts, 1939; Resident Magistrate, Jamaica, 1948-56. *Address:* c/o The High Court, Kingston, Jamaica.

**SMALL, William Watson,** JP; MP (Lab) Scotstoun Division of Glasgow since Oct. 1959; Parliamentary Private Secretary to Chancellor of the Duchy of Lancaster, since 1966; *b* 19 Oct. 1909; *s* of Edward Small of Lochee, Dundee; *m* 1941, Isabella Scott, *d* of Matthew Murphy of Stevenston, Ayrshire; two *d. Educ:* Calder School, Motherwell, JP, Ayrshire, 1948. PPS to Min. of Power, 1964-65; PPS to Sec. of State for Colonies, 1965. *Address:* Belle Mara, 2 Diddup Drive, Stevenston, Ayrshire. *T:* Stevenston 3474.

**SMALLBONES, Robert Townsend,** CMG 1943; MBE; a Director of Panambra, SA; *b* 19 March 1884; 2nd *s* of Paul Smallbones, Schloss Velm, Austria; *m* Inga Gjertson, Kinn, Norway; one *d. Educ:* Trinity Coll., Oxford, MA. Consular Service, 1910; Vice-Consul, Portuguese West Africa, Stavanger; Consul, Munich, 1920; Bratislava, 1922; Monrovia, 1926; Loanda, 1927; Zagreb, 1931; Consul-General at Frankfort-on-Main, 1932-Sept. 1939; and at São Paulo; retired, 1945. *Address:* CP 7205, São Paulo, Brazil. *Club:* St James'.

**SMALLEY, Beryl,** FBA 1963; MA Oxon; PhD Manchester; History Tutor, 1943-69, Vice-Principal, 1957-69, Emeritus Fellow, St Hilda's College, Oxford; *b* 3 June 1905; *d* of Edgar Smalley. *Educ:* Cheltenham Ladies' College; St Hilda's College, Oxford. Assistant Lecturer, Royal Holloway College, 1931-35; Research Fellow, Girton College, 1935-40; Temporary Assistant in Dept of Western MSS, Bodleian Library, 1940-43. Ford's Lecturer, Oxford, 1966-67. *Publications:* The Study of the Bible in the Middle Ages, 1952; English Friars and Antiquity, 1960; in Recherches de théologie ancienne et médiévale; Mediaeval and Renaissance Studies, etc. *Recreations:* walking, swimming, travel. *Address:* 5c Rawlinson Road, Oxford. *T:* Oxford 59525. *Club:* University Women's.

**SMALLEY-BAKER, Charles Ernest,** QC (Ont); MA, LLB, LLM, (Hon.) DCL; Dean Emeritus of Osgoode Hall Law School, Ont, since 1958 (Dean, 1949-58); *b* Randolph, St John, New Brunswick, 1891; *o s* of late Charles Frederick Baker of Randolph; *m* 1921, Mary (*d* 1966), *y d* of late Samuel Hadland. *Educ:* Acadia Univ., NS (BA); Harvard University (LLB); St John's College, Oxford (Overseas Scholar and College Exhibitioner, BA 1920 MA 1924). Lieut, in Canadian Overseas Military Forces, 1915-19; organised and was Dean of Law Department of Khaki University of Canada, London, 1918-19; called to Bar, Inner Temple (Yarborough Anderson Scholarship, Certificate of Honour, 1920); practised, 1920-24; Barber Prof. of Law, 1924-49, and first Dean of Faculty of Law, 1928-49. Univ. of Birmingham; founder and now Patron of Holdsworth Club of University of Birmingham; sometime Examiner in Law to Universities of Sheffield, Liverpool, Oxford (BCL) and London (LLM); Member of Lord Chancellor's Committee on Advanced Legal Studies, 1938; Pres. Soc. of Public Teachers of Law, 1946-47; called to Bar: Ontario, 1949 (QC 1950), New Brunswick, 1953; a President-Adjoint of IVth Internat. Congress of Comparative Law, Paris, 1954. Maj. H. G. and Capt. Gen. List, TA in last war. Freedom of City of London, 1956. Hon. DCL Acadia Univ., 1962. *Publications:* (ed) Constitutional Law, English and Empire Digest; Assistant Editor, seventh edition, Grant's Law of Banking; various legal articles. *Address:* Osgoode Hall, Toronto 1; 49 St Clair Avenue West, Toronto 7, Canada. *Clubs:* English-Speaking Union; Granite (Toronto).

**SMALLMAN, Barry Granger;** Head of Commonwealth Co-ordination Department, Foreign and Commonwealth Office, since 1969; *b* 22 Feb. 1924; *s* of C. Stanley Smallman, CBE, ARCM, and Ruby Marian Granger; *m* 1952, Sheila Knight; two *s* one *d. Educ:* St Paul's School; Trinity College, Cambridge (Major Scholar, MA). Served War of 1939-45, Intelligence Corps, Australia 1944-46 (Lieutenant). Joined Colonial Office, 1947; Assistant Private Secretary to Secretary of State, 1951-52; Principal, 1953; attached to United Kingdom Delegation to United Nations, New York, 1956-57, 1958, 1961, 1962; seconded to Government of Western

Nigeria, Senior Assistant Secretary, Governor's Office, Ibadan, 1959-60; transferred to CRO, 1961; British Deputy High Comr in Sierra Leone, 1963-64; Asst Sec., 1964; British Dep. High Comr in NZ, 1964-67; Imp. Defence Coll., 1968. *Recreations:* tennis, golf, making and listening to music, light verse. *Address:* Golford House, Cranbrook, Kent. *T:* Sissinghurst 295.

**SMALLPEICE, Sir Basil,** KCVO 1961; Chairman: The Cunard Steam-Ship Co. and Cunard Line since 1965 (Director 1964; a Deputy Chairman, 1965); Cunard Cargo Shipping, since 1970; Associated Container Transportation; ACT (Australia)/Australian National Line Partnership Board, since 1969; Administrative Adviser in HM Household since 1964; Director: Local London Board, Barclays Bank; Rugby Portland Cement Co.; *b* 18 Sept. 1906; *s* of late Herbert Charles Smallpeice, Banker; *m* 1931, Kathleen Ivey Singleton Brame, *d* of late Edwin Singleton Brame. *Educ:* Shrewsbury. Chartered Accountant, 1930. Accountant of Hoover, Ltd, 1930-37; Chief Accountant and later Sec. of Doulton & Co. Ltd, 1937-48; Dir of Costs and Statistics, British Transport Commission, 1948-50; BOAC: Financial Comptroller, 1950-56; Member of Board, 1953-63; Deputy Chief Executive, 1954-56; Managing Director, 1956-63. Managing Director, BOAC-Cunard Ltd, from its inception in 1962 till end of 1963; Chm. Cunard-Brocklebank, 1967-70; Mem., Council: Inst. of Chartered Accountants, 1948-57; Inst. of Transport, 1958-61; Brit. Inst. of Management, 1959-64 and 1965- (Chm., 1970-). Mem., Cttee for Exports to the US, 1964-66. Chairman: Nat. Jt Council for Civil Air Transport, 1960-61; The English Speaking Union of the Commonwealth, 1965-68. *Recreations:* gardening, golf. *Address:* Reed Thatch, Clare Hill, Esher, Surrey. *Clubs:* Athenæum; St George's Hill Golf (Weybridge, Surrey).

**SMALLWOOD, Air Marshal Sir Denis (Graham),** KCB 1969 (CB 1966); CBE 1961 (MBE 1951); DSO 1944; DFC 1942; idc; jws; jssc; psa; Vice-Chief of the Air Staff, since 1970; *b* 13 Aug. 1918; *s* of Frederick William Smallwood, Moseley, Birmingham; *m* 1940, Frances Jeanne, *d* of Walter Needham; one *s* one *d*. *Educ:* King Edward VI School, Birmingham. Joined Royal Air Force, 1938. Served War of 1939-45, Fighter Command. Group Captain, 1957; commanded RAF Guided Missiles Station, Lincs, 1959-61; AOC and Commandant, RAF Coll. of Air Warfare, Manby, 1961-62; ACAS (Ops), 1962-65; AOC No. 3 Gp, RAF Bomber Comd, 1965-67; SASO, Bomber Comd, 1967-68, Strike Comd, 1968-69; AOC-in-C, NEAF, Comdr, British Forces Near East, and Administrator, Sovereign Base Area, Cyprus, 1969-70. ADC to the Queen, 1959-64. Chm., RAF Equitation Assoc. *Address:* c/o Glyn, Mills & Co., Whitehall, SW1. *Club:* Royal Air Force.

**SMALLWOOD, Geoffrey Arthur John;** Deputy-Chairman, Leicestershire Quarter Sessions, since 1947; Stipendiary Magistrate, Staffordshire Potteries, since 1960; *b* 27 June 1900; *o s* of Arthur and Margaret Smallwood; *m* 1931, Violet Cecil Turnour Berens (*d* 1970), Kevington, St Mary Cray, Kent; no *c*. *Educ:* Lancing; Christ Church, Oxford. Called to Bar, Inner Temple, 1924. Served War of 1939-45: 2nd Lt, RA, 1940; Captain 1941, Major 1944, Dept of JAG; Lines of Communication, Brussels, June-Sept. 1945. *Recreations:* shooting; travelling in France. *Address:* Chapel Leasowe, Milford, nr Stafford. *T:* Stafford 61078. *Clubs:* Army and Navy; British Potteries Manufacturers Assoc. (Stoke-on-Trent).

**SMALLWOOD, Maj.-Gen. Gerald Russell,** CB 1943; DSO 1941; MC; *b* 18 Feb. 1889. 2nd Lt East Yorks Regt, 1912; served European War, 1914-18, France and Belgium (despatches twice, MC); GSO 1st Grade, British Military Mission to the Egyptian Army, 1937-39; specially employed, 1939; commanding troops in Madagascar, 1942; retired pay, 1946. *Address:* Kichaka, PO Box 24747, Karen, Kenya.

**SMART, D. I.,** RE; Studied etching and engraving under Sir F. Short, RA, PRE; exhibitor at RA and International Exhibitions; has works in print rooms of National collections at London, Oxford and Cambridge. *Address:* 13 Clifton Road, Lee-on-the-Solent, Hants.

**SMART, Sir Eric (Fleming),** Kt 1966; OBE 1955; farmer and grazier; *b* 12 Oct. 1911; *s* of late Percival Horace Smart, Spalding, S Australia, and Lillian Lois Rogers; *m* 1938, Jean Constance, *d* of late Hubert Arthur Oliver Davis, Adelaide, S Australia; one *s* two *d*. *Educ:* Prince Alfred Coll., Adelaide. Mem., Wongan Hills Road Bd, 1946-49; Pres., Wongan Hills Hosp. Bd, 1947-49; Mingenew Shire Councillor, 1949-67; Councillor, Royal Agricultural Society of Western Australia. Vice-Pres., British Boys Movement; Governor of Fairbridge Farm Society, 1959-. Farms 100,000 acres; properties: Erregulla Plains, Mingenew, WA; Broadview, Mount Kokeby, WA; Wingarra, Gnowangerup, WA. *Publication:* Wastelands Transformed, 1952, rev. edn (as Western Australia's Waste Land Transformed), 1962. *Recreation:* golf. *Address:* Erregulla Plains Station, Mingenew, Western Australia. *Clubs:* Royal Aero, Perth (Perth, WA); Lake Karrinyup Country.

**SMART, Professor George Algernon,** FRCP; Professor of Medicine since 1956 and Dean, Faculty of Medicine, University of Newcastle upon Tyne since 1968 (Post-graduate Sub-Dean, 1956-68); Censor, Royal College of Physicians of London, 1965-67; *b* 16 Dec. 1913; *er s* of A. Smart, Alnwick, Northumb; *m* 1939, Monica Helen Carrick; two *s* one *d*. *Educ:* Uppingham; Durham Univ., BSc 1935, MB, BS 1937, MD 1939 (Durham); MRCP 1940, FRCP 1952. Commonwealth Fund Fell., 1948-49. Lectr in Med., Univ. of Bristol 1946-50; Reader in Medicine, Univ. of Durham, 1950-56. *Publications:* contrib. to Price's Textbook of Medicine, and Progress in Clinical Medicine (Daley and Miller); (ed) Metabolic Disturbances in Clinical Medicine, 1958; (co-author) Fundamentals of Clinical Endocrinology, 1969. *Recreation:* photography. *Address:* 9 Lindisfarne Road, Jesmond, Newcastle upon Tyne 2. *T:* Newcastle 810398. *Club:* Savile.

**SMART, Henry Walter,** CB 1966; formerly Director of Savings, GPO (1958-68); *b* 7 Sept. 1908; *m*; two *s*. *Educ:* Sir Thomas Rich's School, Gloucester. *Address:* Knapp Cottage, Sheepscombe, Glos. *T:* Painswick 2091.

**SMART, Leslie Masson,** CBE 1936; *b* 22 March 1889; *s* of William Smart; *m* 1928, Annie Smith; no *c*. *Educ:* Glenbervie, Kincardineshire, Scotland. Kenya and Uganda Railway, 1913-27; Tanganyika Railways, 1927-33; General Manager Gold Coast Railway, 1933-37; General Manager Federated Malay States Railways, 1937-46, retired. *Address:* Bahati, PO Borrowdale, Salisbury, Rhodesia.

**SMART, Maj.-Gen. Robert Arthur,** CBE 1958; QHS 1968; Director of Medical Services, British Army of the Rhine, since 1970; *b* 29 April 1914; *s* of Arthur Francis Smart and Roberta Teresa Farquhar; *m* 1947, Josephine Von Oepen; one *d*. *Educ:* Aberdeen Gram. Sch.; Aberdeen University. MB, ChB 1936; DPH (Eng.) 1948; MRCP 1965. Lt, RAMC, 1936; Capt. 1937; Maj. 1946; Lt-Col 1951; Col 1960; Brig. 1964; Maj.-Gen. 1967. Served in Palestine, Egypt, Western Desert, Eritrea, France and Germany, 1939-45; N Africa and E Africa, 1951-55; Asst Dir of Army Health, E Africa, 1952-55; Leader, Royal Society's Internat. Geophysical Year Expedn to Antarctica, 1956-57; Dep. Chief Med. Off., Supreme HQ Allied Powers Europe, 1960-62; Dep. Dir of Army Health, BAOR, 1962-64; Dir of Army Health, MoD, 1964-68; DMS, FARELF, 1968-70. Polar Medal, 1958. *Recreations:* swimming, ski-ing. *Address:* c/o Glyn, Mills & Co., Kirkland House, Whitehall, SW1. *Club:* Army and Navy.

**SMART, Prof. Roderick Ninian;** Professor of Religious Studies University of Lancaster, since 1967; Pro-Vice-Chancellor, University of Lancaster, 1969; *b* 6 May 1927; *s* of Prof. W. M. Smart, *qv*; *m* 1954, Libushka Clementina Baruffaldi; one *s* two *d*. *Educ:* Glasgow Academy; The Queen's College, Oxford. Army service with Intelligence Corps, 1945-48, 2nd Lt, Captain, 1947; overseas service in Ceylon. Oxford: Mods (shortened), Class II, 1949; Lit. Hum. Class I, 1951; BPhil 1954; LHD Loyola. Asst Lecturer in Philosophy, Univ. Coll. of Wales, Aberystwyth, 1952-55, Lecturer, 1955; Vis. Lecturer in Philosophy, Yale Univ., 1955-56; Lecturer in History and Philosophy of Religion, Univ. of London, King's College, 1956-61; H. G. Wood Professor of Theology, University of Birmingham, 1961-66. Visiting Lecturer, Banaras Hindu Univ., Summer, 1960; Teape Lectr, Univ. Delhi, 1964; Vis. Prof., Univ. Wisconsin, 1965. *Publications:* Reasons and Faiths, 1958; A Dialogue of Religions, 1960; Historical Selections in the Philosophy of Religion, 1962; Philosophers and Religious Truth, 1964; Doctrine and Argument in Indian Philosophy, 1964; The Teacher and Christian Belief, 1966; The Yogi and the Devotee, 1968; Secular Education and the Logic of Religion, 1968; The Religious Experience of Mankind, 1969; Myth, Ritual and Logic, 1970; Philosophy of Religion, 1970; contrib. to Mind, Philosophy, Philosophical Quarterly, Review of Metaphysics, Scottish Journal of Theology, etc. *Recreations:* cricket, tennis. *Address:* Department of Religious Studies, University of Lancaster, Bailrigg, Lancaster. *Club:* Athenæum.

**SMART, William Marshall,** MA, DSc, LLD, FRSE; FRAS; Regius Professor of Astronomy, University of Glasgow, 1937-59; *b* Doune, Perthshire, 9 March 1889; *s* of P. F. Smart; *m* 1919, Isabel, *d* of Dr John Carswell; three *s*. *Educ:* McLaren High School, Callander; Glasgow Univ. (Cunninghame Medal, Breadalbane Scholar and Ferguson Scholar); Trinity Coll., Cambridge (Sheepshanks Exhibitioner, Scholar); Mathematical Tripos, Pt I, First Class; Pt II, Wrangler, Distinction, and Tyson medal; Rayleigh Prize, 1916; Instructor Lieutenant, RN, 1915-19; served in Grand Fleet in HMS Emperor of India; John Couch Adams Astronomer and Lecturer in Mathematics, Univ. of Cambridge, 1919-37; Thomson Lecturer, Aberdeen, 1934; Elder Lecturer, Glasgow; Sec. of the Royal Astronomical Soc., 1931-37; Vice-Pres., 1937-38, 1951-53; Pres., 1949-51; Halley Lecturer, Oxford, 1941; Dean of the Faculty of Science, Glasgow, 1946-49; Vice-Pres. Royal Soc. of Edinburgh, 1952-55; Fison Memorial Lectr, Guy's Hosp., 1961. Lorimer Medal, Edinburgh Astronomical Soc. *Publications:* Admiralty Manual of Navigation, 1922 (with Com. F. N. Shearme); Position Line Tables, 1924; The Sun, the Stars and the Universe, 1928; Astrophysics, 1928; Spherical Astronomy, 1931; Astronomy, 1937; Stellar Dynamics, 1938; Sea and Air Navigation, 1941; The Foundations of Astronomy, 1942; Introduction to Sea and Air Navigation, 1942; Astronomical Navigation, 1942; Handbook of Sea Navigation, 1943; John Couch Adams and the Discovery of Neptune, 1946; The Origin of the Earth, 1950; Some Famous Stars, 1950; Celestial Mechanics, 1953; Foundations of Analytical Geometry, 1956; Combination of Observations, 1958; Stellar Kinematics, 1968; The Riddle of the Universe, 1968. Papers in Memoirs and Monthly Notices of RAS and Cambridge Observations; Encyclopædia Britannica (1919 ed.). *Recreations:* walking, watching and talking cricket. *Address:* Westbourne House, Westbourne Road, Lancaster. *T:* 64742.

*See also Prof. R. N. Smart.*

**SMEALL, James Leathley,** MA, JP; Principal Saint Luke's College, Exeter, since 1945; *b* 16 June 1907; *s* of late William Francis Smeall, MB, BCh (Edin.), and Ethel Mary Leathley; *m* 1936, Joan Rachel Harris; one *d*. *Educ:* Sorbonne; Queens' College, Cambridge (Scholar). Class I English Tripos, Class II Division 1 Anthropological and Archæological Tripos; Assistant Master, Merchiston, 1929-30; Staff, Royal Naval College, Dartmouth, 1930-34; Housemaster, Bradfield College, 1934-36; Head of the English Department, Epsom College, 1936-39; Headmaster, Chesterfield Grammar School, 1939-45; Commissioned RAFVR, 1941-44. Mayor of Exeter, 1965-66. *Publication:* English Satire, Parody and Burlesque, 1952. *Recreations:* gardening and travel. *Address:* Saint Luke's College, Exeter. *T:* 59384; 7 Baring Crescent, Exeter. *T:* 54567. *Clubs:* English-Speaking Union; Exeter and Devon (Exeter).

**SMEDDLES, Thomas Henry;** Chief General Manager, Royal Insurance Group, 1963-69; *b* 18 Dec. 1904; *s* of late T. H. Smeddles; *m* 1931, Dorothy Boardman; one *s*. Joined The Liverpool & London & Globe Insurance Co. Ltd, 1924. *Recreations:* gardening, sailing, golf. *Address:* Tinkers Revel, Burwood Park, Walton-on-Thames, Surrey. *T:* Walton-on-Thames 20706. *Club:* Junior Carlton.

**SMEDLEY, Harold,** CMG 1965; MBE 1946; Assistant Under-Secretary of State, Foreign and Commonwealth Office, since 1970; *b* 19 June 1920; *s* of late Dr R. D. Smedley, MA, MD, DPH, Worthing; *m* 1950, Beryl Mary Harley Brown, Wellington, New Zealand; two *s* two *d*. *Educ:* Aldenham School; Pembroke College, Cambridge. Served War of 1939-45, Royal Marines. Entered Dominions Office (later Commonwealth Relations Office), 1946; Private Secretary to Permanent Under-Secretary of State, 1947-48; British High Commissioner's Office: Wellington, NZ, 1948-50; Salisbury, Southern Rhodesia, 1951-53; Principal Private Sec. to Sec. of State for Commonwealth Relations, 1954-57; Counsellor, British High Comr's Office: Calcutta, 1957; New Delhi, 1958-60; British High Comr in Ghana, 1964-67; Ambassador to Laos, 1967-70. *Address:* Oak End Way, Woodham, Weybridge, Surrey. *Club:* Oxford and Cambridge University.

**SMEED, Reuben Jacob,** CBE 1966; Professor of Traffic Studies, University College London, since 1966; *b* 1 Sept. 1909; *m* 1938, Dorothy Antrich; one *s* one *d* (and one *d* decd). *Educ:*

Central Foundation School and Queen Mary College, London. BSc London, 1st cl. Hons Maths; PhD (Eng.) 1933. Aircraft design, 1933; Demonstrator and Lectr in Mathematics, Imperial Coll., London, 1933-40; RAE, Farnborough, Telecommunications Research Estabt, Swanage, Operational Research Sections, Bomber Comd, RAF, 1940-47; Dep. Director (Traffic and Safety), Road Research Laboratory, 1947-65; Chief Scientist, Min. of Land and Natural Resources, 1965-66. *Publications:* scientific papers. *Address:* Brookmead, 65 Windsor Road, Bray, Berks. *T:* Maidenhead 23982. *Club:* Athenæum.

**SMEETON, Vice-Adm. Sir Richard Michael,** KCB 1964 (CB 1961); MBE 1942; Director and Chief Executive, Society of British Aerospace Companies, since 1966; *b* 24 Sept. 1912; *s* of Edward Leaf Smeeton and Charlotte Mildred Leighton; *m* 1940, Maria Elizabeth Hawkins; no *c*. *Educ:* RNC, Dartmouth. 800 Squadron i/c HMS Ark Royal, 1940-41; Assistant Naval Attaché (Air), Washington, DC, 1941-43; staff of Admiral Nimitz, USN 1943-44; Air Plans Officer, British Pacific Fleet, 1944-45; Dep. Director Air Warfare, Admiralty, 1950-52; Capt. (Air) Med., 1952-54; Imperial Defence College, 1955; Captain, HMS Albion, 1956-57; Director of Plans, Admiralty, 1958-59; Flag Officer Aircraft Carriers, 1960-62; NATO Deputy Supreme Allied Commander, Atlantic, 1962-64; Flag Officer, Naval Air Command, 1964-65. Rear-Admiral, 1959; Vice-Admiral, 1962. Retired Nov. 1965, at own request. *Address:* St Mary's Cottage, Shamley Green, Surrey. *T:* Bramley 3478. *Clubs:* United Service, Royal Aero.

**SMELE, William Samuel George;** Chief Information Officer, Ministry of Public Building and Works, since 1966; *b* 9 June 1912; *o s* of late C. W. Smele and of Etta Smele, Bristol; *m* 1947, Edith Stella Pascoe; one *s*. *Educ:* Cotham School, Bristol. Journalist, special writer on industry and politics, Bristol newspapers, 1929-40. War service, 1940-46. Chief reporter, Bristol Evening World, 1946; Press Officer, SW Region, Central Office of Information, 1948; Sen. Information Officer, N Region, COI, 1951; Press Officer, HM Treasury, 1954; Chief Press and Broadcast Officer, GPO, 1957; Commonwealth Relations Office, 1958; Regional Information Officer (British Information Services), Montreal, 1958; Counsellor and Director, British Information Services, S Africa, 1960, Malaysia, 1962; Head of News Dept, CRO, 1964. Member, Inst. of Public Relations. *Recreations:* motoring, reading, writing. *Address:* 40 Pymers Mead, Dulwich, SE21.

**SMELLIE, Kingsley Bryce Speakman;** Professor Emeritus of Political Science, London School of Economics, since 1965; Professor, 1949-65; *b* 22 Nov. 1897; *o s* of late John and Elizabeth Smellie; *m* 1931, Stephanie, *o d* of late A. E. Narlian. *Educ:* Mrs Bolwell, 15 Mall Road, Hammersmith; Latymer Upper School, Hammersmith; St John's College, Cambridge. Served European War, 1914-18, as private in London Scottish. Staff of London School of Economics, 1921-65. Laura Spelman Rockefeller Student in USA (Harvard Law School), 1925-26; Research Assistant, propaganda research unit of BBC, 1940; temp. principal: Ministry of Home Security, 1940-42, Board of Trade, 1942-45. *Publications:* The American Federal System, 1928; A Hundred Years of English Government, 1937; Civics, 1939; Reason in Politics, 1939; Our Two Democracies at Work, 1944; A History of Local Government, 1946; Why We Read History, 1948; British Way of Life, 1955; Great Britain since 1688, 1962. *Address:* 15 Spencer Hill, SW19. *T:* 01-946 7869.

**SMIETON, Dame Mary Guillan,** DBE 1949; MA Oxon; Permanent Secretary, Ministry of Education, 1959-63, retired; *b* 5 Dec. 1902; *d* of John Guillan Smieton, late librarian and bursar Westminster Coll., Cambridge, and of Maria Judith Toop. *Educ:* Perse Sch., Cambridge; Wimbledon High Sch.; Bedford Coll., London (1 year); Lady Margaret Hall. Assistant Keeper, Public Record Office, 1925-28; Ministry of Labour and National Service, 1928-46; on loan to Home Office as General Secretary, Women's Voluntary Services, 1938-40, and to UN as Director of Personnel, 1946-48; Deputy Secretary, Ministry of Labour and National Service, 1955-59 (Under-Secretary, 1946-55). UK representative, Unesco Executive Board, 1962-68. Trustee, British Museum, 1963-; Chm., Bedford Coll. Council, 1964-70. Member: Advisory Council on Public Records, 1965-; Standing Commn on Museums and Galleries, 1970-. Hon. Fell., Lady Margaret Hall, Oxford, 1959. *Address:* 14 St George's Road, St Margaret's on Thames, Middlesex. *T:* 01-892 9279. *Club:* Oxford and Cambridge University.

**SMIJTH-WINDHAM, Brig. William Russell,** CBE 1946; DSO 1942; *b* 21 Oct. 1907; *s* of late Arthur Russell Smijth-Windham; *m* 1934, Helen Teresa, *d* of late Brig. H. Clementi Smith, DSO; one *s* three *d*. *Educ:* Wellington College; Royal Military Academy, Woolwich. Commissioned Royal Corps of Signals, 1927; Mount Everest Expedition, 1933 and 1936; Mohmand Ops, 1935; Army Revolver VIII, 1937-39; British Pistol VIII, 1939. Served War of 1939-45, Greece and Crete, 1941; Western Desert and Tunisia, 1942-43; France and Germany, 1944-45 (despatches); British Mil. Mission to Greece during Greek Civil War, 1948-49; Chief Signal Officer, Eastern Command, 1957-60, retd 1960; ADC to the Queen, 1957-60. FIEE. *Recreations:* shooting, sailing. *Address:* Icentown House, Pitney, Langport, Somerset. *T:* Langport 525. *Club:* United Service.

**SMILEY, Sir Hugh Houston,** 3rd Bt, *cr* 1903; late Grenadier Guards; DL, JP; *b* 14 Nov. 1905; *s* of 2nd Bt and Valerie, *y d* of late Sir Claud Champion de Crespigny, 4th Bt; *S* father, 1930; *m* 1933, Nancy, *er d* of E. W. H. Beaton; one *s*. *Educ:* Eton; RMC, Sandhurst. Served with 1st Bn Grenadier Guards NW Europe, 1944-45. JP 1952. DL 1962, Hampshire; High Sheriff, 1959. Hon. Secretary Jane Austen Society, 1953-. *Heir:* *s* John Philip Smiley [*b* 24 Feb. 1934; *m* 1963, Davina Elizabeth, *e d* of late Denis Griffiths; one *s* one *d*. *Educ:* Eton; RMA, Sandhurst; Major Grenadier Grds]. *Address:* Ivalls, Bentworth, Alton, Hants. *T:* Medstead 3193. *Club:* Guards.

**SMIRK, Sir Frederick Horace,** KBE 1958; engaged in full-time research; Emeritus Research Professor of Medicine, University of Otago, Dunedin, New Zealand (Professor of Medicine, 1940-61); Director, Wellcome Research Institute, 1962; *b* 12 December 1902; *s* of Thomas Smirk and Betsy Ann (*née* Cunliffe); *m* 1931, Aileen Winifrede, *d* of Rev. Arthur Bamforth and Martha Bamforth; three *s* one *d*. *Educ:* Haslingden Gram. Sch.; Univ. of Manchester. Gaskill mathematical schol., 1919; MB, ChB 1st Cl. Hons 1925; MD Gold Medallist, 1927; FRCP 1940; FRACP (Hon.) 1940. DSc (Hon.) 1961. Med. Registrar, Manchester Royal Infirmary, 1926-29; RMO 1929; Dickenson Travelling Scholar, University of Vienna, 1930; Beit Memorial Fell., successively Asst Depts of Pharmacology, and Medicine, Univ. Coll.

London, 1930-34; Prof. of Pharmacology and Physician Postgrad. Dept, Egyptian Univ., 1935-39. Visiting Prof., Brit. Postgrad. Med. Sch., London, 1949; McIlraith Visiting Prof., Roy. Prince Alfred Hosp., Sydney, 1953; Holme Lectr Univ. Coll. Hosp. Med. Sch., 1949; Alexander Gibson Lectr, Edinburgh Coll. of Physicians, 1956; Dr N. D. Patel Inaugural lecture, Bombay, 1959; Member Board of Censors, later Senior Censor, 1940-58; Vice-President RACP, 1958-60; Chairman Clinical Reseach Committee, 1942-, Psychiatric Research Cttee, 1957-60; Mem. Council Med. Research Council of NZ, 1944-60; Mem. Expert Cttee on Hypertension and Ischaemic Heart Disease, of WHO; Life Member, New York Acad. of Science, 1961; formerly Councillor, International Society of Cardiology (Mem. Hypertension Research Sub-Cttee); Hon. overseas Mem. Assoc. of Physicians of GB, 1967. Gairdner Foundn International Award for Research in Medicine, 1965. *Publications:* Hypotensive Drugs, 1956; Arterial Hypertension, 1957; Antihypertensive Agents, 1967; jointly: Modern Trends in Geriatrics, 1956, Current Therapy, 1956, Annual Reviews of Medicine, 1955; contrib. to med. jls, mainly on disorders of the heart. *Recreations:* reading, writing, travel. *Address:* 68 Cannington Road, Dunedin, New Zealand. *T:* 86961. *Club:* Fernhill (Dunedin).

**SMIRNOVSKY, Mikhail Nikolaevich;** Soviet Ambassador to the Court of St James's since 1966; *b* 1921; *m* Liudmila A.; one *s* two *d. Educ:* Moscow Aviation Institute. Mem. Soviet Foreign Service, 1948; Assistant, 1955, Deputy Head of American Div., Ministry for Foreign Affairs, 1957-58; Counsellor, 1958, Minister-Counsellor, Soviet Embassy in Washington, 1960-62; Head of US Div., Ministry for Foreign Affairs, 1962-66. Member of Soviet Delegations to several International Conferences. *Address:* Soviet Embassy, 13 Kensington Palace Gardens, W8.

**SMITH,** family name of **Earl of Birkenhead, Viscount Hambleden, Barons Bicester, Colwyn,** and **Delacourt-Smith.**

**SMITH;** *see* Abel Smith and Abel-Smith.

**SMITH;** *see* Buchanan-Smith.

**SMITH;** *see* Spencer-Smith.

**SMITH;** *see* Stewart-Smith.

**SMITH;** *see* Walker-Smith.

**SMITH, Alan Guy E.;** *see* Elliot-Smith.

**SMITH, Alastair Macleod M.;** *see* Macleod-Smith.

**SMITH, Prof. Alexander Crampton (Alex. Crampton Smith);** Nuffield Professor of Anaesthetics, Oxford University, since 1965; *b* 15 June 1917; *s* of William and Mary Elizabeth Crampton Smith; *m* 1953, Marjorie (*née* Mason); three *s* two *d* by a former marriage. *Educ:* Inverness Royal Acad.; Edinburgh University. Edinburgh Univ., 1935-41. Served War of 1939-45 (Croix de Guerre, despatches), RNVR, 1942-46. Consultant Anaesthetist, United Oxford Hospitals, 1951; Clinical Lectr in Anaesthetics, Oxford Univ., 1961. FFA RCS 1953; MA Oxon. 1961. Civilian Consultant Anaesthetist to Royal Navy, 1968. *Publications:* Clinical Practice and Physiology of Artificial Respiration (with J. M. K. Spalding), 1963; contribs to anaesthetic, medical and physiological jls. *Recreation:* fishing. *Address:* 31 Croft Road, Thame, Oxfordshire. *T:* Thame 2338.

**SMITH, Sir (Alexander) Rowland,** Kt 1944; formerly Chairman and Managing Director, Ford Motor Co. Ltd; Director: National Provincial Bank Ltd; British Board of Reference, Zürich Insurance Co.; Ex-Member, UK Atomic Energy Authority and National Research Corp.; *b* Gillingham, Kent, 25 Jan. 1888; *s* of late Alexander James Frederick Smith, Gillingham, Kent; *m* 1913, Janet Lucretia, *d* of late George Henry Baker, Gillingham, Kent; one *s* one *d. Educ:* Mathematical School, Rochester. Freeman, City of London; Livery Cos.–Glaziers (Past Master); Coachmakers and Coach Harness Makers; Member: Ministry of Aircraft Production Mission to USA, 1941; Ministry of Pensions Standing Advisory Cttee on Artificial Limbs, 1948; Cttee on Procedure for ordering Civil Aircraft, 1948. FIB; FRSA; MIMechE; Fell. Inst. of Bankers. *Recreation:* sailing. *Address:* The Manor House, Maresfield, Sussex. *Clubs:* Athenæum, Travellers', Oriental; Royal Southern Yacht.

**SMITH, Sir Allan Chalmers,** Kt, *cr* 1953; MC 1918; *b* 22 Feb. 1893; *e s* of late Allan Frith Smith, Colonial Treasurer, Bermuda; *m* 1920, Elsie Joyce Martin; three *s* three *d. Educ:* Warwick Academy, Bermuda; Rossall School, Lancs, England; St John's College, Oxford. Rhodes Scholarship, Bermuda, 1912. Served European War, 1914-18 (despatches thrice), Temp. Capt. RFA. Called to Bar, Gray's Inn, 1920; law practice in Bermuda, 1920-34. Police Magistrate: Western District, 1928, Central District, 1931, Bermuda; Lagos, Nigeria, 1935. Puisne Judge: Trinidad, 1938, Gold Coast, 1944; Chief Justice, Sierra Leone, 1951-55; Assistant Justice, Bermuda, 1955-65. Judicial Comr of Plan for a British Caribbean Fedn, 1955. *Recreations:* golf, sailing. *Address:* Hilton, Paget, Bermuda.

**SMITH, Anthony (John Francis);** Science journalist and writer; *b* 30 March 1926; 2nd *s* of Hubert Smith (formerly Chief Agent, National Trust) and Diana Watkin; *m* 1956, Barbara Dorothy Newman; one *s* two *d. Educ:* Dragon School, Oxford; Blundell's School, Devon; Balliol College, Oxford. MA Oxon., 1951. Served with RAF, 1944-48. Oxford University, 1948-51. Manchester Guardian, 1953 and 1956-57; Drum, Africa, 1954-55; Science Correspondent, Daily Telegraph, 1957-63. Scientific Fellow of Zoological Society. *Publications:* Blind White Fish in Persia, 1953; Sea Never Dry, 1958; High Street Africa, 1961; Throw Out Two Hands, 1963; The Body, 1968; The Seasons, 1970; The Dangerous Sort, 1970. *Recreations:* travel, lighter-than-air flying. *Address;* 7 Elsworthy Terrace, NW3. *T:* 01-722 6397.

**SMITH, Arnold Cantwell;** Secretary-General of the Commonwealth since 1965; *b* 18 Jan. 1915; *m* 1938, Evelyn Hardwick Stewart; two *s* one *d. Educ:* Upper Canada Coll., Toronto; Lycée Champoléon, Grenoble; Univ. of Toronto; Christ Church, Oxford (Rhodes Scholar for Ont), BA Toronto, 1935; BA (Juris) Oxon 1937 (MA 1968); BCL 1938. Editor, The Baltic Times, Tallinn, Estonia, and Assoc. Prof. of Polit. Econ., Univ. of Tartu, Estonia, 1939-40; Attaché, British Legation, Tallinn, 1940; Attaché, British Embassy, Cairo, 1940-43; part-time Lectr in Polit. Sci. and Econs, Egyptian State Univ., Cairo, 1940-42; transf. to Canadian Diplomatic Service, 1943; Sec., Canadian Legation, Kuibyshev, USSR, 1943; Sec., Canadian Embassy, Moscow, 1943-45; Dept of External Affairs, Ottawa, 1946-47; Assoc. Dir, Nat. Def. Coll. of Canada,

Kingston, Ont, 1947-49; Mem. Canadian Delegns to various UN Confs, 1947-51; Alternate Perm. Deleg. of Canada to UN Security Coun. and Atomic Energy Commn, 1949-50; Counsellor, Canadian Embassy, Brussels, and Head of Canadian Delegn to Inter-Allied Reparations Agency, 1950-53; Special Asst to Sec. of State for External Affairs, 1953-55; Internat. Truce Comr in Indochina, 1955-56; Canadian Minister to UK, 1956-58; Canadian Ambassador to UAR, 1958-61; Canadian Ambassador to USSR, 1961-63; Asst Under-Sec. of State for External Affairs, Ottawa, 1963-65. DCL, University of Michigan, 1965; Hon. LLD: Ricker Coll., 1964; Queen's Univ., Kingston, Ont, 1966; Univ. of New Brunswick, 1968; Univ. of BC, 1969; Univ. of Toronto, 1969. *Recreations:* fishing, reading, perforce travelling. *Address:* Marlborough House, Pall Mall, SW1; 5 Carlton Gardens, SW1. *Clubs:* Athenæum, Travellers'; Rideau (Ottawa).

**SMITH, Ven. Arthur Cyril,** VRD 1955; MA; Archdeacon of Lincoln since 1960; Rector of Algarkirk since 1960; *b* 26 Jan. 1909; *s* of late Arthur Smith and of Margaret Ryde, Manchester; *m* 1940, Patricia Marion Greenwood, *d* of Lt-Col Ranolf Nelson Greenwood, *qv*; two *s* two *d*. *Educ:* St John's College, Winnipeg, Canada; Sheffield University; Westcott House, Cambridge. Curate of: Keighley, 1934-36; Bishop's Hatfield, 1936-40. Chaplain RNVR, 1940; HMS Hawkins, 1940-41; 13th Destroyer Flotilla Gibraltar, 1941-43; HMS Eaglet, 1943-44; Senior Chaplain, Liverpool 1945-46. Rector, South Ormsby Group of Parishes, 1946-60; Rural Dean, Hill North, 1955; Canon and Prebendary of Centum Solidorum, 1960. Member: Standing Cttee, House of Clergy, Church Assembly, 1966-; Inspections Cttee, Adv. Council for Churches Ministry, 1967. Church Comr, 1968. Dir, Ecclesiastical Insurance Office Ltd. *Publications:* The South Ormsby Experiment, 1960; Deaneries: Dead or Alive, 1963; Team and Group Ministry, 1965; contributor: to Mission and Communication, 1963; to Theology; to the Caring Church, 1964. *Address:* Algarkirk Rectory, Boston, Lincolnshire. *T:* Sutterton 297. *Club:* United Service.

**SMITH, Lt-Gen. Sir Arthur (Francis),** KCB 1946 (CB 1941); KBE 1942; DSO 1918; MC; *b* 9 Dec 1890; *s* of late Col Granville R. F. Smith, CVO, CB, and late Lady Blanche Smith; *m* 1918, Hon. Monica Crossley, *y d* of 1st Baron Somerleyton; three *d* (and one *s* decd). *Educ:* Eton; Sandhurst. Hon. LLD (Aberdeen), 1948. Joined Coldstream Guards, 1910; Adjt 3rd Batt. Coldstream Guards, Sept. 1914-Nov. 1915; Staff Nov. 1915-Aug. 1917; served European War, 1914-18 (wounded thrice, DSO, MC, Croix de Guerre); Adjutant RMC, Sandhurst, 1921-24; Comdt of Guards Depot, 1924-27; Staff of GOC London District, 1927-30; commanded 2nd Battalion Coldstream Guards, 1930-34; commanded Coldstream Guards Regiment and 4th Guards Brigade, 1934-38; Brigadier, General Staff, British Troops in Egypt, 1938-39; Maj.-Gen. General Staff, 1939; CGS, Middle East, 1940; GOC London District and Major-General commanding Brigade of Guards, 1942-44; GOC-in-C Persia and Iraq Command, 1944-45; GOC-in-C Eastern Command, India, 1945-46; Chief of General Staff, India, 1946; Dep. C-in-C 1947; Comdr British Forces in India and Pakistan, Nov. 1947; retired 1948; Lieutenant of the Tower of London, 1948-51. *Address:* Pirbright Lodge, Pirbright, Surrey. *T:* Brookwood 2171. *Clubs:* Guards, National.

**SMITH, Sir Arthur (Henry),** Kt 1968; Chairman, United Africa Co. Ltd, 1955-69; Director of Unilever Ltd, 1948-69; retired; *b* 18 Jan. 1905; *s* of Frederick Smith; *m* 1930, Dorothy Percy; two *s*. *Educ:* Bolton School. Specialised in Company's interests in French and Belgian Africa, incl. several years' residence in those territories. Econ. Adviser to Brit. Govt's Econ. Mission to French W Africa, 1943. Gov., St Mary's Hosp., Paddington, 1956; Chm., Africa Cttee of Brit. Nat. Export Coun., 1965. Officer, Legion of Honour, 1957 (Cross 1951); Commander, National Order of the Ivory Coast, 1969. *Recreations:* reading, theatre, walking. *Address:* 30a Orchard Court, Portman Square, W1; Varndean Lodge, London Road, Brighton, Sussex. *Club:* East India and Sports.

**SMITH, Arthur Lionel Forster,** CBE 1927; MVO 1914; Iraqi Order of Al Rafidhain; Hon. LLD Edin. and St Andrews; late 9th Batt. Hants Regt; *b* 19 Aug. 1880; *s* of late Arthur Lionel Smith, Master of Balliol. *Educ:* Rugby; Balliol College, Oxford. Fellow and Tutor of Magdalen College, Oxford, 1908-20; Fellow of All Souls, 1904-8; Director of Education, Mesopotamia, 1920-21; Adviser of Education, Iraq, 1921-31; Rector of Edinburgh Academy, 1931-45. *Address:* 84 Inverleith Place, Edinburgh.

**SMITH, Arthur Llewellyn,** MBE 1945; MA Oxon; FSA 1964; FRIBA; Architect in private practice since 1937 (Partner, Llewellyn Smith and Waters, SW7); *b* 25 July 1903; *e s* of late Sir Hubert Llewellyn Smith, GCB, and of Edith (Maud Sophia) (*née* Weekley); unmarried. *Educ:* St Edmund's Sch., Hindhead; Winchester Coll. (Scholar); New Coll., Oxford; Bartlett Sch. of Architecture, London University. 1st cl. Hon. Mods Oxon., 1924; 1st cl. Litt Hum Oxon., 1926. Asst in office of Troup & Steele, 1928-37. War service as Inspector in Passive Air Defence Div., Min. of Supply, 1939-45; seconded to Office of Chief Adviser, Factory ARP, Govt of India, 1941-45. Is mainly engaged on housing and domestic work, social and recreational buildings, churches and vicarages, and the restoration of historic buildings in Oxford and elsewhere. Jt Founder, Crown Club Hoxton (now Crown and Manor Boys' Club), 1926; Cons. Architect to Nat. Assoc. of Boys' Clubs, 1937-; Hon. Sec. and Treas., Crown and Manor Boys' Club, Hoxton; Vice-Pres., Winchester Coll. Mission; Dep. Chm., Devas Inst. Boys' Club, Battersea. Sec., Brit. Inst. of Industrial Art, 1927-33; Member, Art Workers Guild, 1946, Hon. Secretary, 1954-62, Master, 1964. Member Council RSA, 1966-. *Publications:* Buildings for Boys' Clubs, 1937; chapter in New Survey of London Life and Labour, Vol. VI, 1934; various articles and reviews in RIBA Jl, The Builder, etc. *Recreation:* sketching. *Address:* 1 Ockley Road, Streatham, SW16; (office) 103 Old Brompton Road, SW7. *T:* 01-589 4477-9. *Club:* Oxford and Cambridge University.

**SMITH, Prof. Austin Geoffrey;** Hives Professor of Thermodynamics, University of Nottingham, and Head of Department of Mechanical Engineering, since 1960; *b* 22 Aug. 1918; *s* of James Austin Smith and Olive Smith; *m* 1960, Vera Margaret Kennard; no *c*. *Educ:* Gillingham County School for Boys. Royal Scholar, Imperial College, London, 1937-40. Research engineer, Blackburn Aircraft Co., 1940-42; Engineer, Power Jets Ltd, 1942-46; Senior Scientific Officer and Principal Scientific Officer, National Gas Turbine Establishment, 1946-52; Reader in Gas Turbines, Imperial College, London, 1952-57; Professor of Aircraft Propulsion, The College of Aeronautics, 1957-60. *Publications:* many papers in the field of thermodynamics, heat transfer and aerodynamics. *Address:* The Manse, Church St, Bramcote, Nottingham. *T:* Nottingham 258397.

**SMITH, Basil Gerald P.**; *see* Parsons-Smith.

**SMITH, Basil Gerrard,** TD 1950; Treasury Solicitor's Office, since 1969; *b* 29 January 1911; *m* 1938, Marjorie Elizabeth Artz; one *s* two *d*. *Educ:* Epsom College, Surrey; Merton College, Oxford (MA). Solicitor (England), 1938. War Service, 1939-46; Hon. Lt-Col. District Judge, Pahang, 1946; joined Colonial Legal Service, 1946; District Judge: Selangor, 1947; Perak, 1948; President, Sessions Court: Ipoh, 1949; Georgetown, Penang, 1950; Barrister (Gray's Inn), 1950; Federal Counsel and Deputy Public Prosecutor, 1953; Asst Legal Draftsman, 1954; Actg Legal Draftsman, 1955; Judge, Supreme Court, Federation of Malaya, 1956-60; Attorney-General, Southern Cameroons, 1960-61; Legal Adviser to the UK Commissioner, Malta, 1962-64; Legal Asst, Solicitor's Dept, Post Office, 1964, Senior Legal Assistant, 1967-69. *Address:* 17 Burdon Lane, Cheam, Surrey.

**SMITH, Bernard Joseph Gilliat**; *see* Gilliat-Smith.

**SMITH, Sir Bryan Evers S.**; *see* Sharwood Smith.

**SMITH, Campbell (Sherston)**; Managing Director, Campbell Williams Ltd, 1960; *b* 24 April 1906; *s* of Herbert Smith and Carlotta Amelia Smith (*née* Newbury); *m* 1st, 1936, Leonora Florence Beeney (marr. diss., 1948); one *s*; 2nd, 1948, Gwenllian Elizabeth Anne Williams (marr. diss., 1963); one *s*; 3rd, 1964, Barbara Irene Winstone. *Educ:* City of London School. General Departmental Manager, Keith Prowse & Co. Ltd, 1932, Director and General Manager, 1936. Squadron Leader, RAF, 1939-45 (Defence Medal). Assistant Managing Director, Keith Prowse & Co. Ltd, 1945, Managing Director, 1951-54. Director, Performing Rights Society, 1951-54; Managing Director, Mechanical Copyright Protection Society, 1945-57; Director of MEEC Productions Ltd, 1953-62; Administrator of the Arts Theatre Club, 1954-62. *Recreation:* theatre. *Address:* Mayfair Hotel, Heene Terrace, Worthing, Sussex. *Clubs:* Garrick, Arts Theatre.

**SMITH, Sir Carl (Victor),** Kt 1964; CBE 1946; Cadbury Fry Hudson (New Zealand): Man. Dir, 1932-63; Chm., 1939-63; retd 1964; Director, several NZ companies; *b* 19 April 1897; *s* of Dr James Smith, Edinburgh; *m* 1919, Catherine Elizabeth Gettings Johnston; two *s* one *d*. *Educ:* George Watson's College, Edinburgh. Served European War, 1914-18: 4th Royal Scots, Captain. Pres. NZ Manufrs Fedn, 1940-43; Member: Armed Services Appeal Board, 1940-45; Economic Stabilisation Commn, 1941; Coun. and Hon. Treas., Univ. of Otago, 1946-68; Roy. Commn on Parly Salaries, 1955, 1957, 1958; Roy. Commn on NZ Rlys, 1952; NZ Univ. Grants Cttee (3 years). Hon. LLD Otago. *Publication:* From N to Z, 1947. *Address:* Rowheath, Dudley Place, Dunedin, New Zealand. *T:* Dunedin 60076. *Club:* Dunedin.

**SMITH, Catharine Mary S.**; *see* Scott-Smith.

**SMITH, Sir Cecil Furness**; *see* Furness-Smith.

**SMITH, Maj.-Gen. Sir Cecil (Miller),** KBE 1951 (CBE 1944; OBE 1941); CB 1947; MC; AMIMechE; psc; late RASC; *b* 17 June 1896; *s* of John Smith, Dromore, Co. Down; *m* 1930, Isabel Buswell; two *d*. *Educ:* Royal Belfast Academical Institution; Royal Military College, Sandhurst; Staff College, Camberley. Served European War, 1914-19, ASC and Royal Inniskilling Fusiliers. France and Belgium, 1916-18 (wounded, MC, two medals); War of 1939-45, Middle East, and NW Europe, 1940-44 (despatches, OBE, CBE). Lt-Col 1944; Col 1945; Maj.-Gen. 1944; Maj.-Gen. in charge of Administration, Northern Command, 1945-47; Chief of Staff, Northern Command, 1947-48; Director of Supplies and Transport, War Office, 1948-51; retired pay, 1951. Col Comdt, RASC, 1950-60. Chm. Ulster Society in London, 1964. Commander, Legion of Merit, US; Officier de la Légion d'Honneur (France). *Recreation:* golf. *Address:* Crosh, Southfield Place, Weybridge, Surrey. *T:* Weybridge 42199.

**SMITH, Mrs Cecil W.**; *see* Woodham-Smith.

**SMITH, Charles Edward Gordon,** CB 1970; MD, FRCP, FRCPath; Dean, London School of Hygiene and Tropical Medicine, since 1971; *b* 12 May 1924; *s* of late John A. and Margaret Smith, Lundin Links, Fife; *m* 1948, Elsie, *d* of S. S. McClellan, Lorton, Cumberland; one *s* two *d*. *Educ:* Forfar Academy; St Andrews University. MB, ChB (with commendation) 1947; MD (with hons and Singapore Gold Medal) 1956. House Surgeon and Physician, Cumberland Infirmary, Carlisle, 1947-48; HM Colonial Medical Service, 1948-57; Clinical appts Malacca, Kuala Lumpur, 1949-51; Virologist, Inst. for Med. Research, Kuala Lumpur, 1952-57; Sen. Lectr in Bacteriology, London Sch. of Hygiene and Trop. Med., 1957-61; Reader in Virology, London Sch. of Hygiene and Trop. Med., 1961-64; Director, Microbiological Research Estab., MoD, 1964-70. Chalmers Medal, Royal Soc. of Trop. Med. and Hygiene, 1961. *Publications:* papers mainly on arthropod-borne animal viruses and leptospirosis. *Recreations:* gardening, golf. *Address:* Langat House, Woodgreen, Fordingbridge, Hants. *T:* Breamore 246. *Club:* Athenæum.

**SMITH, Charles H. G.**; *see* Gibbs-Smith.

**SMITH, Prof. C(harles) Holt,** CBE 1955; MSc; MIEE; Professor of Instrument Technology, Royal Military College of Science, Shrivenham, 1949-68, now Emeritus; (seconded to the Indian Government for four years from 1st January, 1956, as Dean of the Institute of Armament Studies); *b* 27 Aug. 1903; *s* of Charles Smith and Emily (*née* Holt); *m* 1928, Gracie Alexandra Macdonald (*née* Livingstone); one *s* one *d*. *Educ:* Bolton Grammar School; Manchester University. Peel Connor Telephone Works, 1924-26; Royal Aircraft Establishment, Farnborough, 1926-30 and 1938-40. British Broadcasting Corporation, 1930-38. Telecommunications Research Establishment: Malvern, 1940-42; Defford, 1944-46; Malvern, 1946-49. Assistant Director of Directorate of Communications Development, Ministry of Supply, 1942-44. *Recreations:* bridge, fishing, shooting. *Address:* 37 Queens Park Avenue, Bournemouth, Hants.

**SMITH, Christopher Patrick Crawford,** MA; *b* Edinburgh, 9 May 1902; *s* of late George Smith; unmarried. *Educ:* Dulwich College; Trinity College, Oxford (Scholar, First in Classical Moderations, and First in Literae Humaniores). Assistant Master, Rugby School, 1926-38; Warden of Trinity College, Glenalmond, 1938-48; Headmaster of Haileybury, 1948-63. Chairman, Headmasters' Conference, 1961-62. *Address:* Windrush, St Andrews, Fife.

**SMITH, Sir Christopher Sydney Winwood,** 5th Bt, *cr* 1809; *b* 20 Sept. 1906; *s* of Sir William Sydney Winwood Smith, 4th Bt, and Caroline, *o d* of James Harris, County Cork; *S* father 1953; *m* 1932, Phyllis Berenice, *y d* of late Thomas Robert O'Grady, Grafton, New South Wales, and County Waterford, Ireland; three *s* two *d*. *Heir: s* Robert Sydney Winwood Smith, *b* 1939. *Address:* Junction Road, via Grafton, New South Wales, Australia.

**SMITH, Claude C.;** *see* Croxton-Smith.

**SMITH, Clifford Bertram Bruce H.;** *see* Heathcote-Smith.

**SMITH, Vice-Adm. Sir Conolly A.;** *see* Abel Smith, Vice-Adm. Sir E. M. C.

**SMITH, Cyril,** FRCM; Professor of Pianoforte at Royal College of Music, since 1934; *b* 11 Aug. 1909; *s* of Charles Ernest Smith and Eva Mary Smith; *m* 1937, Phyllis Sellick; one *s* one *d*. *Educ:* Middlesbrough High School; Royal College of Music. Worshipful Company of Musicians' Medal, Royal Coll. of Music, 1928; 1st Prize Daily Express Piano Contest, 1928. First Promenade Concert at age of 20; first broadcast, 1929. Toured Central Europe for British Council, 1936. Two pianos with Phyllis Sellick, Promenade season, 1941. During war toured abroad with Phyllis Sellick, for British Council, 1944, for ENSA, 1945. Also visited Europe for ENSA, 1945; went to Germany for Foreign Office to give concerts and recitals, 1949; returned to Berlin by invitation, 1950, to play with Berlin Philharmonic Orchestra; toured USSR with Phyllis Sellick, as part of Foreign Office Cultural Mission headed by Sir Arthur Bliss, 1956; toured New Zealand, 1965; Adjudicated Internat. Piano Comp., Munich, 1965, 1967. Recorded many concertos, solo works, and two-piano works. Works written for Cyril Smith and Phyllis Sellick by Vaughan Williams, Lennox Berkeley, Gordon Jacob and Malcolm Arnold. TV Biographies, 1960, 1967. Hon. FRCM, 1958; Hon. RAM, 1962. *Publication:* Duet for Three Hands (autobiography), 1958. *Recreations:* own children; photography; formerly yachting, golf. *Address:* Oak Lodge, 33 Fife Road, East Sheen, SW14. *T:* 01-876 5143.

**SMITH, Cyril Robert,** OBE 1945; consultant and lecturer; *b* 28 Dec. 1907; *s* of late Robert Smith and late Rose Smith (*née* Sommerville); *m* 1933, Margaret Jane Kathleen Gwladys Hughes; two *s*. *Educ:* Whitgift; Queen Mary's Coll., Univ. of London. Served in Army, Europe, N Africa, 1939-45 (despatches, OBE; Col). Entered PO as Asst Traffic Supt Telephones, 1927; Asst Inspector, Telephone Traffic PO Headquarters, 1930; Asst Surveyor, Postal Services, 1935; Asst Principal, PO Headquarters, 1936; Asst Postal Controller, 1941; Instructor, PO Management Training Centre, 1954; Postal Controller, 1955; Asst Sec. i/c of Central Organisation and Methods Br., PO Headquarters, 1958; Director, Computer Development, 1965-67; Dir, National Data Processing, GPO, 1967-68. FBCS; FBIM. *Publications:* various papers on computer matters in Computer Jl, etc. *Address:* 64 Copse Avenue, West Wickham, Kent. *T:* 01-777 1100.

**SMITH, Dan;** *see* Smith, T. D.

**SMITH, David Gerard G.;** *see* Gordon-Smith.

**SMITH, Hon. David John,** CBE 1964; JP Berkshire; Lord Lieutenant of Berkshire, since 1959; Chairman W. H. Smith & Son (Holdings) Ltd; Director: W. H. Smith & Son Ltd; Lloyds Bank Ltd; Union Discount Company of London Ltd; *b* 20 May 1907; 3rd *s* of 2nd Viscount Hambleden; *m* 1931, Lady Helen Pleydell-Bouverie, *d* of 6th Earl of Radnor; four *s* one *d*. *Educ:* Eton; Oxford. Member of Council, Bradfield College, Berkshire; High Steward of Wallingford. Chm., Delegacy, King's College, London. *Recreations:* shooting, tennis. *Address:* King's Copse House, Bucklebury, Berkshire. *T:* Bradfield 366. *Club:* White's.

**SMITH, David MacLeish,** FRS 1952; DSc; Consulting Mechanical Engineer; *b* 1900; *s* of David T. Smith, Elgin, Scotland; *m* 1941, Doris Kendrick; no *c*. *Educ:* Blairgowrie High School; Glasgow University. College Apprentice with Metropolitan Vickers Elect. Co. Ltd, Trafford Park, Manchester, 1920, and remained with that co. and its successor AEI Ltd, until 1966. DSc (Glasgow) 1932; LLD, Glasgow, 1967. MIMechE 1938; FRAeS 1949. *Publications:* Journal Bearings in Turbomachinery, 1969; various technical papers. *Address:* Flowermead, Winton Road, Bowdon, Cheshire.

**SMITH, The Hon. Sir David (Stanley),** Kt, *cr* 1948; **Hon. Mr Justice Smith;** *b* 11 Feb. 1888; *s* of Rev. J. Gibson Smith; *m* 1st, 1915, Eva Jane (*d* 1917), *d* of late Duncan Cumming; one *d*; 2nd, 1923, Margaret Elizabeth (*d* 1954), *d* of Richard Wayne Gibbs; one *s*. *Educ:* Wellington Coll.; Victoria Univ. Coll., Wellington (LLM). Barrister, Solicitor and Notary Public; American non-national member of the Permanent Commission under the Treaty of Conciliation between the United States of America and Peru, 11 Feb. 1933; Chairman of Commission on Native Affairs, New Zealand, 1934; Member of Council of Victoria University College, 1939-45; Chairman of Royal Commission on Licensing of Alcoholic Liquors, 1945-46; Chancellor, Univ. of NZ, 1945-61; Judge of Supreme Court of NZ, 1928-48 (temp. Judge, 1949-50); retired 1948; Mem. Bd Dirs, US Educl Foundn in NZ, 1948-70. Chm. NZ Bd of Trade, 1950-59. Ex-Mem. Council of Internat. Bar Assoc. Hon. DCL Oxford, 1948; Hon. LLD Univ. of New Zealand, 1961. *Recreation:* golf. *Address:* 10 Sefton Street, Wellington N1, NZ. *Club:* Wellington (Wellington).

**SMITH, Maj.-Gen. Desmond;** *see* Smith, Maj.-Gen. J. D. B.

**SMITH, Dodie,** (wrote under the name of C. L. Anthony up to 1935); Dramatist and Novelist; *d* of Ernest Walter Smith and Ella Furber; *m* 1939, Alec Macbeth Beesley. *Educ:* St Paul's School for Girls. Studied at Royal Academy of Dramatic Art; on the stage for several years; gave up the stage and became a buyer at Heal and Son, Tottenham Court Road; wrote Autumn Crocus in 1930; produced Lyric Theatre, 1931; gave up business, 1931; wrote Service, 1932; produced Wyndham's Theatre, 1932; wrote Touch Wood, 1933; produced Theatre Royal, Haymarket, 1934; wrote Call It A Day, 1935; produced Globe Theatre, 1935; Bonnet Over the Windmill; produced New Theatre, 1937; wrote Dear Octopus, 1938; produced Queen's Theatre, 1938, revived Theatre Royal, Haymarket, 1967; wrote Lovers and Friends, 1942; prod. Plymouth Theatre, New York, 1943; Letter from Paris (adapted from novel, The Reverberator, by Henry James), Aldwych, 1952; wrote I Capture the Castle, 1952 (adapted from own novel of same name), prod. Aldwych Theatre, 1953; wrote These People—Those Books, 1957; prod. Leeds, 1958; wrote Amateur Means Lover, 1956; prod. Liverpool, 1961. *Publications: Plays by C. L. Anthony:* Autumn Crocus; Service; Touch Wood; *Plays by Dodie*

*Smith:* Call It A Day; Bonnet Over the Windmill; Dear Octopus; Lovers and Friends; Letter from Paris; I Capture the Castle; *novels:* I Capture the Castle, 1949 (US 1948); The New Moon with the Old, 1963 (US 1963); The Town in Bloom, 1965 (US 1965); It Ends with Revelations, 1967 (US 1967); A Tale of Two Families, 1970 (US 1970); *children's books:* The Hundred and One Dalmatians, 1956 (US 1957); The Starlight Barking, 1967 (US 1968). *Recreations:* reading, music, dogs, donkeys. *Address:* The Barretts, Finchingfield, Essex. *T:* Gt Bardfield 260.

**SMITH, Donald Charles;** a Master of the Supreme Court of Judicature (Chancery Division), since 1969; *b* 23 Jan. 1910; *o s* of Charles Frederic Smith and Cecilia Anastasia Smith (*née* Toomey); *m* 1941, Joan Rowsell, twin *d* of Richard Norman Rowsell Blaker, MC. *Educ:* Stonyhurst College. Articled, Peacock & Goddard, Gray's Inn, 1927-31; admitted Solicitor, 1932; Solicitor with Thorold, Brodie & Bonham-Carter, Westminster, 1931-34; Legal Staff of Public Trustee Office, 1934-39; joined Chancery Registrars' Office, 1939; Chancery Registrar, 1952; Chief Registrar, 1963; first Chancery Registrar to be appointed a Master. Pres., Stonyhurst Assoc., 1969. Served in RNVR, Fleet Air Arm, 1943-46; Lieut, 1944-46. *Publications:* (Revising Editor) Atkin's Encyclopaedia of Court Forms, 1st edn, (Advisory Editor) 2nd edn; contribs to Law Jl. *Recreations:* cricket, walking, theatre, philately. *Address:* 5 Lindisfarne Road, SW20. *T:* 01-946 8212. *Club:* MCC.

**SMITH, Douglas Alexander;** Commissioner of Inland Revenue since 1968; *b* 15 June 1915; *m* 1941, Mary Eileen Lyon; one *s* one *d*. *Educ:* Glasgow High Sch.; Glasgow Univ. MA, BSc 1937. Entered Inland Revenue, 1938; Asst Secretary: Inland Revenue, 1952-59; Office of Minister for Science, 1959-61; Under-Sec., Medical Research Council, 1964-67. *Recreations:* hockey, golf, bridge, gardening. *Address:* 66 Eastwick Drive, Great Bookham, Surrey. *T:* Bookham 4274. *Club:* Civil Service.

**SMITH, Dudley Gordon;** MP (C) Warwick and Leamington, since 1968 (Brentford and Chiswick, 1959-66); Parliamentary Under-Secretary of State, Department of Employment, since 1970; *b* 14 Nov. 1926; *o s* of Hugh William and late Florence Elizabeth Smith, Cambridge; *m* 1958, Anthea Maureen Higgins; one *s* two *d*. *Educ:* Chichester High Sch., Sussex. Worked for various provincial and national newspapers, 1943-66; Asst News Editor, Sunday Express, 1953-59. Vice-Chm. Southgate Conservative Assoc., 1958-59; CC Middlesex, 1958-65. Chief Whip of Majority Group, 1961-63. Governor, mill Hill and North London Collegiate Schools; a Vice-Pres., Rural District Councils' Assoc.; a Divl Dir and Senior Exec., Beecham Group, 1966-70. Contested (C) Camberwell-Peckham, General Election, 1955. Parliamentary Private Secretary to Secretary for Tech. Co-operation, 1963-64; an Opposition Whip, 1965-66; an Opposition Spokesman on Industrial Affairs, 1969-70. *Publications:* Harold Wilson: A Critical Biography, 1964; etc. *Address:* Hunningham Hill, Hunningham, Warwicks. *T:* Marton 515; 59 Cheyne Court, Royal Hospital Road, Chelsea, SW3. *T:* 01-352 7973.

**SMITH, Dr Edgar Charles B.;** *see* Bate-Smith.

**SMITH, Edgar Dennis;** Metropolitan Magistrate (South-Western Court, SW11), since 1963; *b* 29 Jan. 1911; *yr s* of late George Henry Smith; *m* 1950, Mary, *yr d* of late Captain T. Drewery; two *s*. *Educ:* Queen Mary's School, Walsall; Birmingham University (LLM). Lord Justice Holker (Holt) Scholar, Gray's Inn, 1933. Called to Bar, Gray's Inn, 1935. Practised in London and on Oxford Circuit. Served War of 1939-45: Special Investigation Branch, Royal Military Police, 1940-46; Assistant Provost-Marshal, Special Investigation Branch, 1945. Headquarters Commissioner The Scout Association, 1947-58 (Silver Wolf, 1956); Mem. Council, The Scout Association, 1964- (Chm., Cttee of the Council, 1968-). Dep. Chm., Agricultural Land Tribunal, S Eastern Region, 1959-63; Deputy Chairman, Staffordshire Quarter Sessions, 1961-63. *Publications:* (Ed.) The County Court Pleader; (Sen. Asst Ed.) Foa's Law of Landlord and Tenant (8th Edn); various other legal works. *Recreations:* walking, music, scouting. *Address:* 20 Furze Lane, Purley, Surrey CR2 3EG. *T:* 01-660 7292. *Club:* Reform.

**SMITH, Maj.-Gen. Edmund Hakewill;** *see* Hakewill Smith.

**SMITH, Emma;** Author; *b* 1923; *m* 1951, Richard Stewart-Jones (*d* 1957); one *s* one *d*. *Publications:* Maiden's Trip, 1948 (awarded John Llewellyn Rhys Memorial Prize 1948); The Far Cry, 1949 (awarded James Tait Black Memorial Prize, 1949); Emily, 1959; Out of Hand, 1963; Emily's Voyage, 1966. *Address:* c/o Janson-Smith, 42 Great Russell Street, WC1.

**SMITH, Dame Enid Mary R. R.;** *see* Russell-Smith.

**SMITH, Eric John R.;** *see* Radley-Smith.

**SMITH, Erik (John),** ARWS 1960; RE 1959 (ARE 1948); RBA 1950; Lecturer in Art History, School of Art, High Wycombe College of Technology and Art, since 1948; *b* 6 Dec. 1914; *s* of James Frederick and Lily Gertrude Smith, Birmingham; *m* 1948, Lilian Mary Novello Williams, BA; one *s*. *Educ:* King Edward VI, Birmingham; Royal College of Art. Served War, 1940-46, Capt. Worcestershire Regt; with 1st Army in N Africa and 21 AG in Germany, Battalion Mines Officer. Associate of the Royal College of Art with 4th year scholarship, 1947, and Engraving School Prize. Designed and wrote Book of Remembrance, High Wycombe; work includes stained glass windows: Wouldham, Kent; Turville and Long Marston, Bucks. Exhibits regularly with RA, NEAC, RWS, RBA, RE and has exhibited in South Africa, USA, Brazil and Australia; also has Etchings in Ottawa Museum, Art Gallery, Canada, VA Museum, South London Art Gallery, water colours in Sheffield Art Gallery, and works in private collections. *Publications:* Articles on art in: Discovering Art; New Knowledge; The Artist; Canvas, the Old Water-Colour Society's Club Annual Vol. *Recreations:* chess, bridge, books, especially 18th century English History. *Address:* 5 Chiltern Close, Princes Risborough, Bucks. *T:* Princes Risborough 4953.

**SMITH, E(rnest) Lester,** DSc; FRS 1957; formerly Consultant, Glaxo Laboratories, Greenford; *b* 7 August 1904; *s* of Lester and Rose Smith; *m* 1931, Winifred R. Fitch; n *c*. *Educ:* Wood Green County School; Chelsea Polytechnic. Joined Glaxo Laboratories, 1926, as first post after graduation. Various posts in development, Fine Chemical Production (Head), then Biochemical Research. Shared responsibility for production of penicillin during War of 1939-45; isolation of vitamin B 12 accomplished, 1948. *Publications:* Vitamin B 12 (in series of Biochemical Monographs),

1960, 3rd edn 1965. Numerous research papers in various scientific journals, 1927-. *Recreation:* horticulture. *Address:* Amberheath, Three Oaks, Guestling, Hastings, Sussex. *T:* Hastings 51062.

**SMITH, Ernest T.**; *see* Thornton-Smith.

**SMITH, Brigadier Ernest Thomas Cobley,** CB 1955; CBE 1952; retired as Brigadier and Chief Paymaster, Royal Army Pay Corps; *b* 1895; *s* of late Herbert Smith; *m* 1920, Marie Anne, *d* of late John Hruby; one *s* one *d*. Served European War, 1915-19: France, Belgium and the Balkans (despatches, two medals, 1914-15 star); served war of 1939-45, Middle East and South-East Asia (despatches); Command Paymaster, Malta, 1942, Egypt and Sudan, 1943; Deputy Paymaster-in-Chief, SEAC, 1944; Middle East, 1948; Command Paymaster, Eastern Comd, 1951; Deputy Paymaster-in-Chief, BAOR, 1954. *Address:* Derry Gariff, Seaton Road, Camberley, Surrey. *T:* Camberley 4221. *Club:* Junior Army and Navy.

**SMITH, Col Sir Eustace;** *see* Smith, Col Sir Thomas Eustace.

**SMITH, Sir Ewart;** *see* Smith, Sir Frank Ewart.

**SMITH, Florence Margaret;** *see* Smith, Stevie.

**SMITH, Maj.-Gen. Francis Brian W.;** *see* Wyldbore-Smith.

**SMITH, Francis Edward Viney,** CMG 1942; BSc; *b* 1902; *m* 1st, 1926, Winifred Nellie Nicholson (*d* 1951), Salisbury, Wilts; three *s* one *d*; 2nd, 1956, Annie McLaren, London. *Educ:* Colston's School, Bristol; Bristol University, Department of Scientific and Industrial Research, 1921; Senior Assistant Mycologist, Ministry of Agriculture and Fisheries, 1924; Government Microbiologist, Jamaica, 1927; Comr of Commerce and Industry, Jamaica, to 1944; Devel. Sec. in charge of post-war planning and reconstruction, Nigerian Govt Secretariat, 1944-46; Commissioner on Special Duty, Nigeria, 1947-53; Chm. Cameroons Development Corp., 1947-52. Services made available, by HM Govt, to Ghana, to establish National Research Council, 1958-61. *Address:* Milbourne Cottage, Malmesbury, Wilts. *T:* Malmesbury 2306.

**SMITH, Prof. Francis Graham,** FRS 1970; Professor of Radio Astronomy, University of Manchester, since 1964; *b* 25 April 1923; *s* of Claud Henry and Cicely Winifred Smith; *m* 1945, Dorothy Elizabeth (*née* Palmer); three *s* one *d*. *Educ:* Epsom Coll.; Rossall Sch.; Downing Coll., Cambridge. Nat. Sci. Tripos, Downing Coll., 1941-43 and 1946-47; PhD Cantab 1952. Telecommunications Research Estab., Malvern, 1943-46; Cavendish Lab., 1947-64; 1851 Exhibr 1951-52; Warren Research Fellow of Royal Soc., 1959-64; Fellow of Downing Coll., 1953-64, Hon. Fellow 1970. Sec., Royal Astronomical Soc., 1964-. *Publications:* Radio Astronomy, 1960; papers in Monthly Notices of RAS, Nature and other scientific jls. *Recreations:* sailing, walking. *Address:* Parkfield, 47 Racecourse Road, Wilmslow, Cheshire. *T:* Wilmslow 27605.

**SMITH, (Francis) Raymond (Stanley);** retired as Librarian and Curator, Corporation of London (1943-56); *b* Fenny Stratford, Bucks, 12 Dec. 1890; *o s* of Rev. H. S. Smith, Baptist Minister, and Lina F. Smith. *Educ:* privately; Mercers' School. Junior Clerk, Guildhall Library, 1908. Served European War, 1916-19, Lt RAPC. Librarian and Curator, Guildhall Library and Museum, 1943; Director, Guildhall Art Gallery, 1945; Member Council of Library Assoc., 1951. Chm. Reference and Special Libraries Section, 1951-54; Chm. Exec. Cttee, Roman and Mediaeval London Excavation Council, 1952-56. Liveryman of Clockmakers Company; Hon. Librarian, Clockmakers and Gardeners Companies, 1943-56; Guild Master, Civic Guild of Old Mercers, 1952-53. Member: Soc. of Archivists; London Topographical Soc.; Cons. Librarian and Archivist, French Protestant Church of London, 1965. FLA, 1929; FSA 1944. *Publications:* Classification of London literature, 1926; The City of London: a Select Book List, 1951; (with P. E. Jones) Guide to the Records at Guildhall, London, 1951; ed Guildhall Miscellany, 1952-56; The pictorial history of the City of Lodon, 1953; The Living City, a new view of the City of London, 1957, 2nd edn 1966; The Worshipful Company of Masons, 1960; Sea Coal for London, 1961; Ceremonials of the Corporation of London, 1962; The Irish Society 1613-1963, 1966; contrib. to professional journals and books on libraries, archives, etc. *Recreations:* book-hunting, gardening, music. *Address:* 61 Sutton Rd, Seaford, Sussex.

**SMITH, Sir Frank Edwin N.;** *see* Newson-Smith.

**SMITH, Sir (Frank) Ewart,** Kt 1946; FRS 1957; MA; CEng; Hon. FIMechE; MIChemE; a past Deputy Chairman, Imperial Chemical Industries, Ltd; *b* 31 May 1897; *s* of late Richard Sidney Smith; *m* 1924, Kathleen Winifred, *d* of late H. Rudd Dawes; one *s* one *d*. *Educ:* Christ's Hospital; Sidney Sussex College, Cambridge (Scholar, 1st Class Mech. Science Tripos, John Winbolt Prizeman). War service, 1916-19, RA; ICI Ltd, Billingham Works in various engineering and managerial posts, 1923-42; chief engineer, 1932-42; Chief Engineer and Supt of Armament Design, Ministry of Supply, 1942-45; Formerly Member: Advisory Council on Scientific Policy; Scientific Advisory Council of Ministry of Works and Ministry of Fuel and Power; British Productivity Council, Cttee on Scientific Manpower; Chairman, National Health Service Advisory Council for Management Efficiency (England and Wales), etc. Hon. Fellow Sidney Sussex College; Hon. Member, City and Guilds of London Institute; Hon. Associate, Univ. of Aston. James Clayton Prize, IMechE. American Medal of Freedom with Palm, 1946. *Publications:* various technical papers. *Recreations:* sailing and gardening. *Address:* Manesty, Weydown Road, Haslemere, Surrey. *T:* Haslemere 2167. *Club:* Athenæum.

**SMITH, Frank William G.;** *see* Glaves-Smith.

**SMITH, Lieut-Col Frederick L. C.;** *see* Coldwell-Smith.

**SMITH, Frederick Llewellyn,** CBE 1964; MSc, DPhil, CEng, FIMechE; Director and Group Executive, Rolls-Royce Ltd; *b* 25 July 1909; *s* of late James Brooksbank Smith; *m* 1943, Alice Mary McMurdo; one *s* two *d*. *Educ:* Rochdale High Sch.; Univ. of Manchester; Balliol Coll., Oxford. Joined Rolls-Royce Ltd as Tech. Assistant, 1933, and has held various positions in the company; appointed to Board, 1947. Director, various Rolls-Royce subsid. and associate cos. Pres. Soc. of Motor Manufacturers & Traders Ltd, 1955-56. Mem. Nat. Research Development Corp., 1959. Pres., Motor Industry Research Assoc., 1963-65. *Address:* Whitelands, Barthomley, Crewe, Cheshire.

**SMITH, Professor Frederick Viggers;** Professor of Psychology, University of Durham, since 1950; *b* Hamilton, New South Wales, 24 Jan. 1912; *s* of Frederick Thomas Smith and Agnes (*née* Viggers); unmarried. *Educ:* Newcastle (NSW) High School; Sydney and London Universities. BA 1938, MA 1941, Lithgow Schol., Sydney; PhD London 1948. FBPsS, 1950. Pres., British Psychological Society, 1959-60. Research Office, Dept of Educ., NSW, 1936; Lecturer in Psychology, The Teachers' Coll., Sydney, 1938; Lectr, Birkbeck Coll., Univ. of London, 1946; Lectr, Univ. of Aberdeen, 1948. Visiting Prof., Cornell Univ., USA, 1957, Christchurch and Wellington Univs, NZ, 1960. *Publications:* The Child's Point of View (Sydney), 1946 (under pseudonym Victor Southward); The Explanation of Human Behaviour (London), 1951, 1960; Attachment of the Young: Imprinting and Other Developments, 1969; Papers to psychol and philosophical journals. *Recreations:* mountain walking, ski-ing, photography, music, squash, motoring. *Address:* Winslea, Deyncourt, Lowes' Barns, Durham. *T:* Durham 4971.

**SMITH, Frederick William,** CMG 1947; MC 1917; retired as Chief Contracts Officer to the Central Electricity Authority (1950-56); and as Contracts Adviser to Central Electricity Authority (1957-Dec. 1959); *b* 7 March 1896; *m* 1921, Emma Sarah Sharman; one *s*. *Educ:* Haberdashers' Aske's Hampstead School. European War, 1914-18, army service, concluded as DAAG 51st Highland Division 1914-19; Croix de Chevalier de l'Ordre de Leopold, 1917; Belgian Croix de Guerre, 1917. Civil Service: Inland Revenue Dept, Air Ministry, Ministry of Aircraft Production, Viceroy of India, Ministry of Works, Cabinet Office, Treasury, Ministry of Fuel and Power, 1920-; Deputy Secretary, Ministry of Fuel and Power, 1948-50. *Address:* Barton, Wickhurst Lane, Broadbridge Heath, Sussex. *T:* Horsham 4632.

**SMITH, Sir Gengoult;** *see* Smith, Sir Harold G.

**SMITH, Geoffrey Ellrington Fane,** CMG 1955; Senior Provincial Commissioner, Northern Rhodesia, 1951-55, retired; Colonial Office, from 1956; *b* 1903. *Educ:* King Edward VI Grammar School, Louth; Lincoln College, Oxford. Cadet, Northern Rhodesia, 1926-29; District Officer, 1929; Provincial Commissioner, Northern Rhodesia, 1947-51. *Address:* 26 Vincent Road, Stoke D'Abernon, Cobham, Surrey.

**SMITH, Geoffrey J.;** *see* Johnson Smith.

**SMITH, Vice-Adm. Sir Geoffrey T.;** *see* Thistleton-Smith.

**SMITH, Prof. George,** MBE 1945; Regius Professor of Surgery, University of Aberdeen, since 1962; *b* 4 June 1919; *s* of John Shand Smith and Lilimina Myles Mathers Smith; *m* 1951, Vivienne Marie Tuck, BA, Wooster, Ohio, USA; two *s* one *d*. *Educ:* Grove Academy; Queen's College, Univ. of St Andrews. MB, ChB (St Andrews) 1942; MD (Hons) 1957, ChM (Hons) 1959; DSc (Glasgow) 1964; FRFP&S (Glasgow) 1949; FRCS (Edinburgh) 1949; FACS 1958; FACCP 1963; FInstBiol 1963. Commonwealth Fund Fellow, 1949-51 (Johns Hopkins and Western Reserve Medical Schools). Formerly Reader in Cardiovascular Surgery, Univ. of Glasgow. *Publications:* sections in books and various papers, mainly on cardio-vascular and respiratory topics. *Recreations:* sailing, gardening, golf. *Address:* 22 Rubislaw Den North, Aberdeen. *T:* Aberdeen 36627. *Clubs:* Naval; RNVR (Glasgow).

**SMITH, Sir George Bracewell,** 2nd Bt *cr* 1947; (known as **Sir Guy Bracewell Smith**), MBE 1946; *b* 5 Nov. 1912; *s* of Sir Bracewell Smith, 1st Bt, KCVO; *S* father, 1966; *m* 1951, Helene Marie Hydock, Pennsylvania; two *s*. *Educ:* Wrekin Coll., Shropshire; Emmanuel Coll., Cambridge (MA). Chairman: Park Lane Hotel Ltd; The Ritz Hotel (London) Ltd; The Ritz Hotels Development Co. Ltd; Practical Press Ltd. Director: Arsenal Football Club Ltd; Carpac Ltd; Eagle Star Insurance Co. Ltd (West End Br.); Earls Court Ltd; Earls Court Standfitting Co. Ltd; Eurocard Ltd; The Ritz Hotel Ltd (Paris); Wembley Stadium Ltd. Chm., The Hotel & Catering Exhibitions (London) Ltd. Warden, Haberdashers' Co., 1957-58 and 1964-65. *Recreations:* golf, riding. *Heir:* *s* Guy Bracewell Smith, *b* 12 Dec. 1952. *Address:* Park Lane Hotel, Piccadilly, W1Y 8AS. *T:* 01-499 6321. *Clubs:* City Livery, Royal Automobile; Royal and Ancient (St Andrews); Highgate Golf, Sunningdale Golf, Royal Ashdown Forest Golf.

**SMITH, George Brown;** Assistant Director, Prison Department, Home Office; *b* 22 March 1905; *m* 1936; one *s* one *d*. *Educ:* Kintore, Aberdeenshire. Assistant Governor, and Governor, of various Borstals and Prisons: Nottingham, Rochester, Usk, Reading, Portland, Dartmoor, Wormwood Scrubs, etc. *Recreations:* music, golf. *Address:* Home Office, Prison Department, Horseferry House, Dean Ryle Street, Westminster, SW1.

**SMITH, George Fenwick,** CBE 1969; General Secretary, Amalgamated Society of Woodworkers and Painters, since 1959; *b* 24 June 1914; *s* of James Guthrie Smith and Agnes Pearson Fenwick; *m* 1937, Doris Ferguson Drever; two *s* one *d*. *Educ:* Inverbrothock and Downfield Schs. Amalgamated Society of Woodworkers: National Organizer, 1945-48; Asst Gen. Sec., 1949-59. Member: TUC Gen. Council, 1959; Commonwealth Development Corp, 1967. *Recreations:* photography, handcrafts. *Address:* 72 Maryland Road, Thornton Heath, Surrey. *T:* 01-764 1149.

**SMITH, George William Q.;** *see* Quick Smith.

**SMITH, Gerard Gustave L.;** *see* Lind-Smith.

**SMITH, Gerard Thomas Corley,** CMG 1952; HM Diplomatic Service, retired; *b* 30 July 1909; *s* of late Thomas and Nina Smith; *m* 1937, Joan Haggard; one *s* three *d*. *Educ:* Bolton Sch.; Emmanuel Coll., Camb. Gen. Consular Service, 1931; has served in Paris, Oran, Detroit, La Paz, Milan, St Louis, New York, Brussels, and at various times in the Foreign Office. Became 1st Sec. and Consul, on appt as Labour Attaché to Embassy in Brussels 1945; Counsellor UK Deleg. to UNO at New York and UK Alternate Rep. on UN Economic and Social Council, 1949-52; Press Counsellor, Brit. Embassy, Paris, 1952-54; Labour Counsellor, Brit. Embassy, Madrid, 1954-59; British Ambassador: to Haiti, 1960-62; to Ecuador, 1962-67. *Recreations:* music, mountains, birds. *Address:* Greensted Hall, Chipping Ongar, Essex. *Club:* Travellers'.

**SMITH, Sir Gordon;** *see* Smith, Sir W. G.

**SMITH, Gordon E.;** *see* Etherington-Smith.

**SMITH, Graham Burrell;** *b* 1880; *s* of H. Arthur Smith, Barrister-at-law. *Educ:* City of London School; King's College, Cambridge. RN College, Osborne, 1906-15; Repton School, 1919-26; Eton College, 1941-48; Headmaster,

Sedbergh School, 1927-36. Cornwall Education Committee. *Publications:* Scenes from European History; Outlines of European History, etc. *Recreations;* motoring, photography, music. *Address:* Trenadlyn, Mawnan Smith, Cornwall.

**SMITH, Sir Guy Bracewell;** *see* Smith, Sir George B.

**SMITH, Colonel Sir (Harold) Gengoult,** Kt, *cr* 1934; VD; JP; FRCPE, LRCP and SE, LRFP and SG; Chairman of Royal Visit (1949) Committee of Melbourne; *b* 25 July 1890; *s* of Hon. Louis Laurence Smith and Marion Higgins; *m* 1933, Cynthia Mary, *d* of Sir Norman E. Brookes; one *s* one *d*. *Educ:* Melbourne Church of England Gram. Sch.; Melbourne and Edinburgh Univs; Royal College of Surgeons, Edinburgh. Australian Military Forces, 1907-47; Lt-Col Brighton Rifles (seconded), 2nd Dragoon Guard (Res. Regt), 1915, 2nd Lt; Served France, 1915-16; Qualified Royal College of Surgeons, 1917; House Surgeon, Royal Edinburgh Infirmary, 1917; Medical Clinical Asst, 1923-24; Comd Balcombe Casualty Clearing Station, 1941; CO 111th Australian General Hospital, 1944; elected Melbourne City Council, 1921; Lord Mayor, 1931-32, 1932-33 and 1933-34; Chairman Victorian and Melbourne Centenary Celebrations Council, 1934-35; President Children's Cinema Council; Patron, Partially Blinded Soldiers' Assoc.; Chm. Exhibition Trustees; Zoological Board of Victoria; Board of Eye and Ear Hospital; Board of Infectious Diseases Hospital; Council of Old Colonists' Homes; Chairman of Public Works Cttee. *Recreations:* fox-hunting (Oaklands Hounds), golf, fishing, shooting, travelling. *Address:* 110 Collins Street, Melbourne, Victoria, Australia. *T:* Windsor 2083. *Clubs:* Athenæum, Peninsula Country (Melbourne); Victoria Racing.

**SMITH, Admiral Harold Page;** Legion of Merit (twice); US Navy; Commander-in-Chief, Atlantic and US Atlantic Fleet and Supreme Allied Commander, Atlantic, 1963-65; *b* Mobile, Alabama, 17 Feb. 1904; *s* of Harvey Samuel and Elizabeth Warren Smith; *m* Helen Dee Rogers, Oklahoma, USA; no *c*. *Educ:* University Military School, Mobile; US Naval Academy. Instructor: Naval Acad.; Naval Gun Factory, Washington, DC. Served War (Navy Cross, 1942; Netherlands Order of the Bronze Lion, 1942; campaign and service medals); CO, USS Stewart, 1940; on Staff of C-in-C, US Fleet (War Plans Section); commanded Destroyer Division 7, later Destroyer Squadron Four, 1943-45. Chief of Staff, Commander Destroyer Force, Atlantic Fleet, 1949-50; Deputy Chief of Information, Navy Dept, 1950-51; Director, Office of Foreign Military Affairs, Office of the Secretary of Defense, 1951; Chief of Staff to Supreme Allied Commander, Atlantic, 1956-58; Chief of Navy Personnel, 1958-60; C-in-C, US Naval Forces, Europe, 1960-63. Capt. 1943; Rear-Adm. 1952; Vice-Adm. 1956; Adm. 1960. *Address:* 13 North Monterey Street, Mobile, Alabama, USA.

**SMITH, Lt-Col Harry Cyril,** CBE 1945 (OBE 1919); MC 1917; Russian Order of St Anne (2nd Class) 1920; *b* 1888; *s* of late Arthur B. Smith, Birmingham; *m* 1st, 1920, Catherine Koulikoff, Petrograd (marr. diss.), *d* of late Baroness v. Breugel-Douglas, The Hague; one *s*; *m* 2nd, Ida Eleanor, *widow* of Capt. Lawder B. S. Smith, MC, and *e d* of late William Raymond FitzMaurice Clark, Kilballyskea, Shinrone, Offaly, Eire. *Educ:* Royal Grammar School, Worcester and Birmingham. Joined RE (TA), 1908; Engineering, S America, 1909-14; served European War, 1914-18, RE (despatches twice); CRE 28th Division, 1919; Assistant Railway Adviser, British Military Mission with Denekin, S Russia, 1919-20; Asst Director of Railways, GHQ Constantinople and simultaneously Mil. Director, Anatolian and Baghdad Rly and Pres. Inter-Allied Rly Commission in Turkey, 1920-23; Manager and Dir Anatolian Rly Co., rep. interests of Anglo-Turkish Trust Co., and Dir Port of Haidar Pasha and Mersina, Tarsus, Adana Rly Co. 1923-27; reported on transport conditions in Italy, 1928; organised Indian Roads and Transport Devel. Assoc., 1929-39; Member, Bombay Leg. Council and Indian Central Leg. Assembly (Delhi and Simla); served on various Govt Transport cttees and confs; served with Transportation Directorate, GHQ Middle East, Cairo, 1940-41. Dir-Gen, Iraqi State Railways, Baghdad, 1941-50; temp. Amir Al Liwa' (Maj.-Gen.) Iraq Army. *Address:* 5 Hickman's Close, Lindfield, Sussex. *Club:* (life member) Royal Bombay Yacht (Bombay).

**SMITH, Harry Theodore;** *b* 20 Feb. 1909. *Educ:* Pocklington Grammar School, Yorkshire; London University (BA History Hons); Kelham Theological College. Deacon, 1932; Priest, 1933. Curate, St Andrew's, Porthill, Stoke-on-Trent, 1932-36; Theological Travelling Secretary for SCM, 1936-38; Tutor, Kelham Theological College, 1938-42; Licensed Preacher, Diocese of Liverpool, 1942-44; Tutor and Chaplain, Kelham Theological Coll., 1944-45; Warden, Kelham Theological College, 1945-62. Examining Chaplain to Bishop of Manchester, 1947-50; Prior, Mother House of Soc. of Sacred Mission, 1954-62; Visiting Lecturer, General Theological Seminary, New York, 1957. Pro-Provincial, Soc. of Sacred Mission, Kelham, 1957; Vicar-General, English Province of Society of Sacred Mission, Kelham, 1958-59, 1960-61. Co-opted: Mem. Notts CC Educn Cttee, 1958-62; Governor: Notts County Trg Coll. (Eaton Hall), 1958-62; Newark County Secondary Schools, 1962; English Instr and Educl Adviser to Imperial Ethiopian Air Force, 1964. Released as Mem. SSM to become RC layman, 1965. *Recreations:* tennis, study.

**SMITH, Hedworth Cunningham; Hon. Mr Justice Smith;** Judge of the Supreme Court of the Bahama Islands since 1965; *b* 12 May 1912; *s* of James Smith and Elizabeth (*née* Brown); unmarried. *Educ:* George Watson's Coll., Edinburgh; Edinburgh University. MA 1933; LLB 1936. Solicitor, Scotland, 1937-40; Barrister-at-Law, Gray's Inn, London, 1950. Served War of 1939-45: commnd 1940; Staff Officer, GHQ India Command, 1943-46 (Major). District Magistrate, 1946, Senior District Magistrate, 1950, Gold Coast; Judge of Supreme Court of Ghana, 1957; retd from Ghana Govt service, 1961; Legal Adviser, Unilever Ltd Gp of Cos in Ghana, 1962-64. *Recreation:* golf. *Address:* Supreme Court, Nassau, Bahamas. *T:* (office) 2-2427, (home) 5433. *Clubs:* East India and Sports; (Hon. Mem.) Lyford Cay (Nassau, Bahamas).

**SMITH, Brigadier Henry Gilbertson,** CB 1945; OBE 1943; MC; TD; DL; Frihitskors Kongen Haakon VII; Partner in firm of Miller & Smiths, Solicitors; *b* 15 Nov. 1896; *e s* of late Sir Gilbertson Smith, TD; *m* 1st, Dorothea Joy (*d* 1931), *d* of Major N. L. Garrett; one *s* one *d*; 2nd, Marjorie Beatrice, *d* of George Relf, Brentwood, Essex. *Educ:* Lancing College. Served European War, 1914-18, 2/25 Bn London Regt, TA, seconded Machine Gun Corps, France; War of 1939-45, Royal Artillery, TA, England and Norway; Comdr 41 AA Bde, 27 AA Bde and 303 Infantry Bde.

FRMS; FLS; FRMetS; DL for Co. Essex, 1952; Pres. Royal Microscopical Soc., 1952, 1953. *Recreations:* microscopy, photography and science. *Address:* 26 Lime Street, EC3. *T:* 01-626 6889; Ravenscourt, Sawyers Hall, Hall Lane, Brentwood, Essex. *T:* Brentwood 270. *Clubs:* Junior Carlton; Norwegian.

**SMITH, Henry Martin,** CBE 1952 (OBE 1943; MBE 1941); HM Chief Inspector of Fire Services since 1948; *b* 10 Feb. 1907; *s* of William and Helen Smith; *m* 1937, Anita Marie Sullivan; no *c*. *Educ:* Roan School, Greenwich, London. Chief Regional Fire Officer, Southern Region, National Fire Service, 1941-46; Acting Chief of Fire Staff and Inspector-in-Chief, 1947-48. *Address:* 203 Upper Woodcote Road, Mapledurham, near Reading, Berks. *T:* Reading 73932.

**SMITH, Henry Roy William,** MA, PhD; Professor of Latin and of Classical Archaeology, the University of California, 1931-58, Professor Emeritus since 1958; *b* 13 June 1891; *o s* of Henry Joseph Smith and Gertrude Martha Swears; *m* 1926, Mary Adele Macdonald; one *s*. *Educ:* Wimbledon College; St Paul's School (Scholar); Pembroke College, Oxford (Scholar); Princeton University. Associate Professor of Classics, Saint Francis Xavier's College, Antigonish, Nova Scotia, 1914-21 (subaltern in Manchester Regiment, 1916-19); Professor of Classics, Saint Francis Xavier's College, 1921-22; Instructor in Classics, Princeton University, 1925-26; Assistant Professor of Classics, Princeton University, 1926-28; Assistant Professor of Latin, University of California, 1928-30; Associate Professor of Latin, University of California, 1930-31; Corr. Member of German Archæological Inst., 1935, Member, 1953; Travelling Fellow of John Simon Guggenheim Memorial Foundation, 1936; Member of Advisory Bd, Am. Jour. of Archaeology, 1947. Research Fell. of Bollingen Foundation, 1962. *Publications:* New Aspects of the Menon Painter, 1929; The Origin of Chalcidian Ware, 1932; Corpus Vasorum Antiquorum, United States, V (University of California, 1), 1936 and X (San Francisco Museums), 1943; Der Lewismaler, 1939; The Hearst Hydria, 1944; Problems (Historical and Numismatic) in The Reign of Augustus, 1951; (jointly) Votive Religion at Caere, 1959. *Address:* Faculty Club, University of California, Berkeley, California, USA. *T:* Thornwall 85678. *Clubs:* Oxford and Cambridge University; Faculty (Berkeley).

**SMITH, Sir Henry (Thompson),** KBE 1962; CB 1957; *b* 25 Feb. 1905; *y s* of late Ralph Smith, Gateshead; *m* 1929, Jane Harrison, *y d* of late Robert Wilson, Seahouses; three *d*. *Educ:* Sunderland Road School, Gateshead; London School of Economics. Post Office: Boy messenger, 1918; Sorting-clerk and telegraphist, 1922; Customs and Excise: Clerical officer, 1928; Officer, 1932; Asst Principal, 1934; Air Ministry: Principal, 1940; Asst Secretary, 1944; Assistant Under-Secretary of State, 1953-58; Deputy Under-Secretary of State, 1958-64; Dep. Under-Sec. of State (Air Force Dept), Min. of Defence, 1964-65, retd. *Recreations:* woodwork, gardening. *Address:* 130 Wantage Road, Wallingford, Berks. *T:* Wallingford 2330.

**SMITH, Sir Henry Wilson;** *see* Wilson Smith.

**SMITH, Herbert Alexander,** CBE 1958; Deputy Chief Inspector of Taxes, (retired); *b* 6 July 1896; *s* of late Robert Maxwell Smith, Edinburgh; *m* 1922, Jean Murray Weir. *Educ:* Boroughmuir School, Edinburgh. Entered Inland Revenue Department, 1920; Principal Inspector of Taxes, 1948; Senior Principal Inspector of Taxes, 1953. Fellow, Inst. of Chartered Accountants of England and Wales. Served European War, 1916-19 (wounded); Artists' Rifles, King's Own Royal Lancaster Regt, Lieutenant. *Recreations:* painting, music, gardening. *Address:* 91 Canford Cliffs Road, Canford Cliffs, Dorset. *T:* Canford Cliffs 77834. *Club:* Civil Service.

**SMITH, Herbert Cecil,** CBE 1945; BSc; MBOU; *b* Tunbridge Wells, Kent, 27 Jan. 1893; *m* 1925, Jane Bell Blair; one *s* one *d*. *Educ:* Eastbourne College; Edinburgh University. Joined Indian Forest Service in Burma, 1915; Served with 1/70th Burma Rifles in India, Egypt and Palestine, 1917-19. Continued as a Forest Officer in Burma until May 1942; on Reconstruction with Govt of Burma in Simla till June 1945; returned to Burma as Chief Forest Officer in the Civil Affairs Service (Burma); retired from Indian Forest Service, 1946. *Address:* Hazel Cottage, Maypole, Rockfield, Monmouth.

**SMITH, Howard Frank Trayton,** CMG 1966; British Ambassador to Czechoslovakia, since 1968; *b* 15 Oct. 1919; *m* 1943, Winifred Mary Cropper; one *d*. *Educ:* Sidney Sussex Coll., Cambridge. Employed in FO, 1939; apptd Foreign Service, 1946. Served Oslo; transf. Washington, 2nd Sec. (Inf.) 1950; 1st Sec., Dec. 1950; 1st Sec. and Consul, Caracas, 1953; FO, 1956; Counsellor: Moscow, 1961-63; Foreign Office, 1964-68. *Address:* c/o Foreign and Commonwealth Office, SW1. *Club:* Travellers'.

**SMITH, Sir Hubert S.;** *see* Shirley-Smith.

**SMITH, Hon. Hugh Adeane Vivian,** MBE; Chairman, Charter Consolidated Ltd, since 1969 (Dep. Chm. 1966); Executive Director, British South Africa Co., 1962-66; Director, Anglo American Corp. of South Africa since 1947 (Managing Dir, 1948-52); *b* 25 April 1910; *s* of 1st Baron Bicester and Lady Sybil McDonnell; *m* 1933, Lady Helen Primrose, *d* of 6th Earl of Rosebery, *qv* and of his 1st wife, Lady Dorothy Grosvenor; one *s* one *d*. Partner, Messrs Rowe & Pitman (stockbrokers), 1935-46. Served War of 1939-45 (despatches): in Hertfordshire Regt, then Irish Guards. *Recreation:* golf. *Address:* Souldern Manor, Bicester, Oxon. *T:* Fritwell 374. *Clubs:* Brooks's, Pratt's, White's.

**SMITH, Captain Hugh D.;** *see* Dalrymple-Smith.

**SMITH, Hugh W. H.;** *see* Heckstall-Smith.

**SMITH, Captain Humphry Gilbert B.;** *see* Boys-Smith.

**SMITH, Ian Douglas;** Prime Minister of Rhodesia, April 1964-11 Nov. 1965, and Leader of the Rhodesia Front regime, since 11 Nov. 1965; *b* Selukwe, S Rhodesia, 8 April 1919; *m* Janet Watt; two *s* one *d*. *Educ:* Selukwe Sch.; Chaplin Sch., Gwelo, S Rhodesia; Rhodes Univ., Grahamstown, S Africa (B Com.). Served War of 1939-45: 130 Sqdn RAF, and 237 (Rhodesia) Sqdn Western Desert and Europe, 1941-45 (Flight-Lieut). Farmer. MLA (Rhodesia Party), Southern Rhodesia, 1948; Mem. Federal Parliament (United Federal Party) 1953; Chief Govt Whip, 1958; resigned from United Federal Party, 1961; Foundn Mem., Rhodesian Front, President, 1965-; MLA (Rhodesian Front), and appointed Minister of the Treasury, S Rhodesia, Dec. 1962; Minister of Defence, April 1964-May 1965; Minister of External Affairs, April-Aug. 1964. *Address:* 8 Chancellor Avenue, Salisbury, Rhodesia; Gwenoro Farm, Selukwe,

Rhodesia. *Clubs:* Salisbury, Salisbury Sports (Rhodesia).

**SMITH, Ida Phyllis B.;** *see* Barclay-Smith.

**SMITH, Ivor Otterbein,** CMG 1963; OBE 1952; Chairman of Public Service and Police Service Commissions and Member of Judicial Service Commission, British Guiana, 1961-66; *b* Georgetown, British Guiana, 13 Dec. 1907; *s* of Bryce Otterbein Smith and late Florette Maud Smith (*née* Chapman); *m* 1936, Leila Muriel Fowler; one *s* two *d. Educ:* Queen's Coll., British Guiana; Pitman's Commercial Coll., London. Joined Brit. Guiana CS, as Clerical Asst, Treas., 1925; Sec. Commissioners of Currency, 1933; Asst Dist. Comr, 1941; Private Sec. to Gov., 1943; Dist Comr, 1945; Comr, Cayman Is, 1946-52; Dep. Comr of Local Govt, Brit. Guiana, 1953; Governor's Sec., and Clerk Exec. Coun., 1956; Dep. Chief Sec., 1960; Acted as Chief Sec. on several occasions and was Officer Administering the Govt, Sept.-Oct. 1960. Served with S Caribbean Force, 1941-43; Major, Staff Officer, Brit. Guiana Garrison. Hon. Col, British Guiana Volunteer Force, 1962-66. Chm., Nat. Sports Coun, 1962-66. *Recreations:* tennis; interested in sports of all kinds; rep. Brit. Guiana at Association and Rugby football, cricket, hockey. *Address:* Suite No 54, 2020 Comox Street, Vancouver, BC, Canada.

**SMITH, Jack,** ARCA 1952; artist; *b* 18 June 1928; *s* of John Edward and Laura Smith; *m* 1956, Susan Craigie Halkett. *Educ:* Sheffield College of Art; St Martin's School of Art; Royal College of Art. Exhibitions: Whitechapel Art Gallery, 1959; Beaux Arts Gallery, 1952-58; Matthiesen Gallery, 1960, 1963; Catherine Viviano Gallery, New York, 1958, 1961; Pittsburgh International, 1955, 1957, 1964; Grosvenor Gallery, 1965; Marlborough Gallery, 1968; Konsthallen, Gothenburg, Sweden, 1968. Guggenheim Award (Nat.), 1960. Work in permanent collections: Tate Gallery; Arts Council of Great Britain; Contemporary Art Society; British Council. *Address:* 1 Ashbridge Road, Leytonstone, E11. *T:* 01-989 5919.

**SMITH, Jack Stanley,** CMG 1970; Managing Director, P. A. Management Consultants Pty Ltd, since 1964; *b* 13 July 1916; *s* of C. P. T. Smith, Avoca, Victoria; *m* 1940, Nancy, *d* of J. C. Beckley, Melbourne; one *s* two *d. Educ:* Ballarat Grammar Sch.; Melbourne Univ. Construction Engineer, Australasian Petroleum Co., 1938-41. Served in Australian Imperial Forces, 1942-45, Lieut. Project Engineer, Melbourne & Metropolitan Bd of Works, 1946-48. P.A. Management Consultants, UK and Australia, 1949-. *Recreations:* golf, tennis. *Address:* 15 Glyndebourne Avenue, Toorak, Victoria 3142, Australia. *T:* 20 4581. *Clubs:* Melbourne (Melbourne); Lawn Tennis Association of Victoria, Metropolitan Golf (Vic.).

**SMITH, James Aikman;** TD; Sheriff-Substitute of the Lothians and Peebles at Edinburgh, since 1968; *b* 13 June 1914; *s* of Rev. W. J. Smith, DD; *m* 1947, Ann, *d* of Norman A. Millar, FRICS, Glasgow; three *d. Educ:* Glasgow Academy; The Queen's Coll., Oxford; Edinburgh Univ. BA (Oxford) 1936; LLB (Edinburgh) 1939; Mem. of Faculty of Advocates, 1939. Served War of 1939-45 (despatches): Royal Artillery, 1939-46; Lt-Col 1944. Sheriff-Substitute: of Renfrew and Argyll, 1948-52; of Roxburgh, Berwick and Selkirk, 1952-57; of Aberdeen, Kincardine and Banff, 1957-68. Pres., Sheriffs-Substitute Assoc., 1969. Member Departmental Cttee on Probation Service, 1959-62. Bronze Star (US), 1945. *Publications:* occasional articles in legal journals. *Address:* 10 India Street, Edinburgh 3. *Club:* New (Edinburgh).

**SMITH, James Alfred,** CBE 1964; TD; **Hon. Mr Justice Smith;** Puisne Judge, Supreme Court of the Bahamas since 1965; retired as Senior Puisne Judge, High Court, Northern Nigeria (1960-65); *b* Llandyssul, Cardiganshire, May 1913; *s* of late Charles Silas and Elizabeth Smith (*née* Williams), Timberdine, Lampeter, Cardiganshire. *Educ:* Christ Coll., Brecon. Solicitor of the Supreme Court, 1937; called to the Bar, Lincoln's Inn, 1949. Served War of 1939-45: various Army Staff appointments; on staff of Supreme Allied Commander, South-East Asia, with rank of Major, 1944-45. Appointed to Colonial Legal Service, as Resident Magistrate, Nigeria, 1946; Chief Magistrate, 1951; Chief Registrar of the Supreme Court, Nigeria, 1953; Puisne Judge, Nigeria, 1955; Judge, High Court, Northern Nigeria, 1955. *Address:* Supreme Court of the Bahamas, Nassau, Bahamas. *Clubs:* Naval and Military, Royal Commonwealth Society.

**SMITH, James Andrew Buchan,** CBE 1959; DSc; retired as Director of the Hannah Dairy Research Institute, Ayr, Scotland, 1951-70 (Acting Director, 1948-51); *b* 26 May 1906; *yr s* of late Dr James Fleming Smith, JP, MB, CM, Whithorn, Wigtownshire; *m* 1933, Elizabeth Marion, *d* of James Kerr, Wallasey, Cheshire; four *d. Educ:* Leamington College, Warwicks; Univ. of Birmingham. PhD (Birmingham) 1929; DSc (London) 1940. Graduate Research Asst: at UCL, 1929-30; at Imperial College, London, 1930-32; Lectr in Biochemistry, Univ. of Liverpool, 1932-36; Biochemist, Hannah Dairy Research Inst., 1936-46; Lectr in Biochemistry, Univ. of Glasgow, 1946-47. President: Society of Dairy Technology, 1951-52; Nutrition Society, 1968-; Treasurer, Internat. Union of Nutritional Sciences. Member, Food Research Advisory Committee and of committees concerned with agricultural research. Joint Editor: British Journal of Nutrition; Journal of Dairy Research, FRIC; FRSE. *Publications:* scientific papers in Biochemical Jl, Jl of Dairy Research, Proc. Nutrition Soc., etc. *Recreation:* gardening. *Address:* Hazelwood, 9 St Leonard's Road, Ayr. *T:* Ayr 64865. *Club:* Farmers'.

**SMITH, Maj.-Gen. (James) Desmond (Blaise),** CBE 1944; DSO 1944; CD 1948; Director: Pillar RTZ Ltd; E. G. Herbert Ltd; Vice-Chairman and Managing Director, Pillar Engineering Ltd; Chairman: Blaise Investments Ltd; Pneumatic Components Ltd; Welding Rods Ltd; Peak Engineering Ltd; Geerpres Europe Ltd; Mellowes-Orb Engineering Ltd; Andrew Chalmers and Mitchell; Phoenix Electrical Ltd, and subsidiary cos; Strebor Diecasting Ltd, and subsidiary cos; Hants & Sussex Aviation Ltd; Air Engine Services Ltd; B. Attewell & Sons Ltd; B. Attewell & Sons (Engineering) Ltd; Hartle-Stedall Ltd; Aeroparts Engineering Ltd; Westland Motors Ltd; *b* 7 Oct. 1911; *s* of William George Smith, Ottawa, Canada; *m* 1937, Miriam Irene Blackburn (*d* 1969); two *s. Educ:* Ottawa University, Canada; Royal Military College, Canada. Joined Canadian Army, Royal Canadian Dragoons, 1933; National Defence HQ, Ottawa, as Assistant Field Officer in Bde Waiting to Governor-General of Canada, 1939. Served War of 1939-45, in England, Italy and N W Europe holding following commands and appts: CO Roy. Canadian Dragoons; Comdr: 4th Cdn Armoured Bde; 5th Cdn Armoured Bde; 1st Cdn Inf. Bde: 5th Cdn Armoured Div.; 1st Cdn Inf. Div.; Chief of Staff, 1st Cdn Corps.

Comdt Canadian Army Staff Coll., 1946; Imp. Defence Coll., 1947; Sec. Chiefs of Staff Cttee, 1948-50; Military Sec. Cdn Cabinet Defence Cttee, 1948-50; QMG, Canadian Army, 1951; Chairman, Canadian Joint Staff, London, 1951-54; Commandant, National Defence College of Canada, 1954-58; Adjutant-General of the Canadian Army, 1958-62. Colonel, HM Regt of Canadian Guards, 1961-66. Croix de Guerre, 1944, Chevalier, Legion of Honour, 1944 (France); Comdr Military Order of Italy, 1944; Officer Legion of Merit (USA), 1944; Order of Valour (Greece), 1945. KGStJ 1961 (CStJ 1952). *Recreations:* shooting, tennis, ski-ing, painting. *Address:* 20 Eaton Place, Belgravia, SW1. *Clubs:* Carlton, Guards, Cavalry, Hurlingham.

**SMITH, James D. H.;** *see* Hindley-Smith.

**SMITH, Prof. James Eric,** FRS 1958; Secretary, Marine Biological Association of the UK, and Director Plymouth Laboratory; *b* 23 Feb. 1909; *er s* of Walter Smith and Elsie Kate Smith (*née* Pickett); *m* 1934, Thelma Audrey Cornish; one *s* one *d*. *Educ:* Hull Grammar School; King's College, London. Student Probat., Plymouth Marine Biol Lab., 1930-32; Asst Lecturer: Univ. of Manchester, 1932-35; Univ. of Sheffield, 1935-38; Univ. of Cambridge, 1938-50; Prof. of Zoology, Queen Mary Coll., Univ. of London, 1950-65 (Vice-Principal, 1963-65). Trustee, British Museum (Natural History), 1963-, Chm. Trustees, 1969-. Formerly Vice-President, Zoological Society; Member: Senate, Univ. of London, 1963-65; Scientific Advisory Committee, British Council; Science Research Council, 1965-67; Nature Conservancy, 1969-; Royal Commn, Barrier Reef, 1970. FKC 1964; Fellow, Queen Mary College, 1967. Hon. Prof., Madurai Univ., India, 1969. Hon. ScD Exeter, 1968. *Publications:* various on marine biology, embryology, nervous anatomy and behaviour. *Recreations:* walking, gardening. *Address:* The Laboratory, Citadel Hill, Plymouth. *Clubs:* Athenæum; Royal Western Yacht.

**SMITH, James Ian;** Under-Secretary, Department of Agriculture and Fisheries for Scotland, since 1967; *b* 22 April 1924; *s* of James Smith, Ballater, Aberdeenshire, and Agnes Michie; *m* 1947, Pearl Myra Fraser; one *s*. *Educ:* Alderman Newton's Sch., Leicester; St Andrews Univ. Served War of 1939-45: India and Burma; RA (attached Indian Mountain Artillery), Lieut, 1943-46. Entered Dept of Agriculture for Scotland, 1949; Private Sec. to Parly Under-Sec. of State, Scottish Office, 1953; Dept of Agriculture for Scotland: Principal, 1953; Asst Sec., 1959; Asst Sec., Scottish Development Dept, 1965-67. Mem. ARC, 1967-. *Recreation:* golf. *Address:* 15 Yewlands Crescent, Edinburgh 9. *T:* 031-664 1864. *Club:* Royal Commonwealth Society.

**SMITH, James Stewart,** CMG 1955; Nigerian Administrative Service, retired; *b* 15 Aug. 1900; 4th *s* of late Charles Stewart Smith, HM Consul-General at Odessa; *m* 1955, Rosemary Stella Middlemore, *er d* of late Dr and Mrs P. T. Hughes, Bromsgrove, Worcs. *Educ:* Marlborough; King's College, Cambridge. Entered Nigerian Administrative Service, 1924; Senior District Officer 1943; Resident 1945; Senior Resident 1951; retired 1955. Papal Order of Knight Commander of Order of St Gregory the Great, 1953. *Recreations:* gardening, fly-fishing, watching cricket, chess. *Address:* Wyre House, Wyre Piddle, Pershore, Worcs. *T:* Pershore 2516. *Club:* Oxford and Cambridge.

**SMITH, Janet (B.) A.;** *see* Adam Smith.

**SMITH, John,** OBE 1945; TD 1950; Deputy Chief Medical Officer, Scottish Home and Health Department, since 1963; *b* 13 July 1913; *e s* of late John Smith, DL, JP, Glasgow and Symington, and Agnes Smith; *m* 1942, Elizabeth Fleming, twin *d* of late A. F. Wylie, Giffnock; three *s* one *d* (and one *s* decd). *Educ:* High Sch., Glasgow; Sedbergh Sch.; Christ's Coll., Cambridge; Glasgow Univ. BA 1935; MA 1943; MB, BChir Cantab 1938; MB, ChB Glasgow 1938; MRCPG 1965; FRCPG 1967; FRCPE 1969. TA (RA) from 1935 (RAMC from 1940); War Service, 1939-46; ADMS Second Army, DDMS (Ops and Plans) 21 Army Group (despatches); OC 155 (Lowland) Fd Amb., 1950-53; ADMS 52 (Lowland) Div., 1953-56; Hon. Col 52 Div. Medical Service, 1961-67. House appts Glasgow Victoria and Western Infirmaries; joined Dept of Health for Scotland, 1947; Medical Supt, Glasgow Victoria Hosp., 1955-58; rejoined Dept of Health for Scotland, 1958; specialised in hospital planning. Officier, Ordre de Leopold I (Belgium), 1947. *Publications:* articles on medical administration and hospital services in various medical jls. *Recreations:* rifle shooting (shot in Scottish and TA representative teams); hill walking, gardening. *Address:* Murrayfield, Biggar, Lanarkshire. *T:* Biggar 36. *Clubs:* Naval and Military; Western (Glasgow), New (Edinburgh).

**SMITH, John;** MP (Lab) Lanarkshire (North) since 1970; *b* 13 Sept. 1938; *s* of Archibald Leitch Smith and Sarah Cameron Smith; *m* 1967, Elizabeth Margaret Bennett; one *d*. *Educ:* Dunoon Grammar Sch.; Glasgow Univ. (MA, LLB). Solicitor in Glasgow, 1963-66; admitted to Faculty of Advocates, 1967. *Recreations:* reading, theatre. *Address:* 1/2 Chessel's Court, Canongate, Edinburgh. *T:* 031-556 6068.

**SMITH, Professor John Cyril;** Professor of Law in the University of Nottingham since 1958; *b* 15 Jan. 1922; 2nd *s* of Bernard and Madeline Smith; *m* 1957, Shirley Ann Walters; two *s* one *d*. *Educ:* St Mary's Grammar Sch., Darlington; Downing Coll., Cambridge. Served Royal Artillery, 1942-47 (Captain). BA 1949, LLB, 1950, MA 1954 Cantab. Called to Bar, Lincoln's Inn, 1950. Assistant Lecturer in Law, Nottingham University, 1950-52. Commonwealth Fund Fellow, Harvard Law School, 1952-53. Lecturer, 1952-56, Reader, 1956-57, Nottingham University. *Publications:* (with Professor J. A. C. Thomas) A Casebook on Contract, 1957; (with Brian Hogan) Criminal Law, 1965; Law of Theft, 1968; articles in legal periodicals. *Recreations:* walking, gardening. *Address:* 445 Derby Rd, Lenton, Nottingham. *T:* Nottingham 72323.

**SMITH, Rear-Adm. John Edward D.;** *see* Dyer-Smith.

**SMITH, (John) Edward (McKenzie) L.;** *see* Lucie-Smith.

**SMITH, John Forest;** *see* Forest Smith.

**SMITH, John Gerald,** CB 1966; *b* 2 Jan. 1907; *s* of Frederick and Mary Smith; *m* 1934, Christine Mary Till; no *c*. Joined Min. of Transport, 1935, after experience and training with Consulting Engineers and local authority. Commissioned RE, 1939; served in France, Middle East and Italy (despatches) attained rank of Major. Returned to Min. of Transport, Senior Engineer, 1948; Asst Chief Engineer at HQ of Min. of Transport, 1957; Deputy Chief Engineer, 1958; Chief Highway Engineer, 1964; retired 1966. CEng, FICE. *Address:* 4 Hillfield Court, Esher, Surrey. *T:* Esher 63009.

**SMITH, John (Lindsay Eric)**; Director: Coutts & Co.; Rolls-Royce Ltd; Pearson Longman Ltd; Royal Exchange Assurance (Deputy Governor 1961-66); *b* 3 April 1923; *s* of Capt. E. C. E. Smith, MC, LLD; *m* 1952, Christian, *d* of Col U. E. C. Carnegy of Lour, *qv*; two *s* three *d*. *Educ:* Eton; New Coll., Oxford (MA). Served RNVR 1942-46 (Lieut). Chm., National Trust General Purposes Cttee, 1960-64. MP (C) Cities of London and Westminster, Nov. 1965-1970; Mem., Public Accounts Cttee, 1968-69. Member: Standing Commission on Museums and Galleries, 1958-66; Inland Waterways Redevelopment Cttee, 1959-62; Historic Buildings Cttee, National Trust, 1952-61. Director, Financial Times Ltd, 1959-68. High Steward of Maidenhead, 1966-. FSA. *Address:* Shottesbrooke Park, White Waltham, Berks; 1 Smith Square, SW1. *Clubs:* Pratt's, Beefsteak, Brooks's; Leander.

**SMITH, John Mitchell Aitken**, CBE 1968; TD 1939; Scottish Council, London Committee, 1966; *b* 18 Nov. 1902; *s* of William Smith, Calcutta and Aberdeen, and Barbara Gordon Smith, Aberdeen; *m* 1935, Nota Eleanor Buckland Cooper, *d* of Buckland Cooper, Montevideo and London: one *s* one *d*. *Educ:* Morrisons Academy, Crieff. Chartered Accountant, 1925; joined Ford Motor Co. Ltd, 1930: Secretary, 1939; Asst Man. Dir, 1953-61. President, Soc. of Motor Manufacturers, 1959-60. Member: Committee of Enquiry on Decimal Currency, 1961; Monopolies Commn, 1963-69; Chm., Nat. Computing Centre, 1966-70. Territorial Army, 1921-45. Served War of 1939-45; retired as Lt-Col Royal Fusiliers. *Recreations:* golf and chess. *Address:* 18 Eaton Square, SW1. *T:* 01-245 9063. *Clubs:* Caledonian, Hurlingham.

**SMITH, John Roger B.**; *see* Bickford Smith.

**SMITH, Rev. John Sandwith B.**; *see* Boys Smith.

**SMITH, Colonel Kenneth**, CMG 1918; Australian AMC Reserve; *b* 13 April 1885; *m* 1914, Kate, *d* of T. W. Wise. *Educ:* Brisbane Grammar School; Sydney University, MB, ChM. Served European War, 1915-19 (despatches, CMG); ADMS 4th Australian Division, 1918. Principal Medical Officer, Commonwealth Repatriation Dept, 1935-50. *Address:* Redrith, Harwood Avenue, Chatswood, Sydney, Australia.

**SMITH, Kenneth Graeme Stewart**, CMG 1958; JP; retired as Civil Secretary, The Gambia, West Africa, 1962; *b* 26 July 1918; 3rd *s* of late Prof. H. A. Smith, DCL; unmarried. *Educ:* Bradfield; Magdalen College, Oxford. Cadet, Colonial Administrative Service, Tanganyika, 1940; appointments in Colonial Service, 1945-62. JP Dorset, 1967. *Address:* The Old House, Newland, Sherborne, Dorset. *T:* Sherborne 2754.

**SMITH, Kenneth Manley**, CBE 1956; FRS 1938; DSc, PhD; formerly Director Virus Research Unit, Agricultural Research Council, Cambridge; Hon. Fellow, Downing College, Cambridge; *b* Helensburgh, Scotland; *m* 1923, Germaine Marie Noël (French); one *s*. *Educ:* Dulwich College; Royal College of Science. Served European War; Senior Lecturer and Adviser in Agricultural Entomology, University of Manchester. Vis. Prof., Dept of Botany, Univ. of Texas, Austin, 1964-69. *Publications:* A Textbook of Agricultural Entomology; Recent Advances in the Study of Plant Viruses; Plant Viruses; A Textbook of Plant Virus Diseases; The Virus; Life's Enemy; Beyond the Microscope; contributions to Scientific Journals. *Recreation:* gardening. *Address:* Hedingham House, 3 Sedley-Taylor Road, Cambridge; Downing College, Cambridge. *T:* Cambridge 47238.

**SMITH, Kenneth Shirley**, MD, BSc London, FRCP; Lieutenant-Colonel RAMC 1942; Hon. Physician and Cardiologist, Charing Cross Hospital and to the London Chest Hospital; Chief Medical Officer Marine and General Mutual Life Assurance Society; formerly Consulting Physician, Samaritan Free Hospital for Women; Staff Examiner in Medicine, University of London; Examiner in Medicine, Conjoint Board; *b* 23 Jan. 1900; *s* of E. Shirley Smith; *m* 1929, Alice Mary Hoogewerf; one *s* two *d*. *Educ:* London University; Middlesex Hospital (Senior Scholar). BSc, 1st Class Hons in Physiology, London, 1923; formerly House Physician, Casualty Medical Officer and Medical Registrar Middlesex Hospital; also Resident Medical Officer, Nat. Hosp. for Diseases of the Heart, 1927; Pres., British Cardiac Soc. Member, Assoc. of Physicians of Great Britain. Editor, British Heart Journal. Organizing Secretary, First European Congress of Cardiology, London, 1952. Served with 1st Army in N Africa, later with CMF in Italy, Greece and Austria. Gold Staff Officer, Coronation of King George VI. *Publications:* Contributor to British Encyclopædia of Medical Practice, 1937; Papers on cardiological and pulmonary subjects in British Heart Journal, American Heart Journal, Quarterly Journal of Medicine, Lancet, British Medical Journal, Practitioner, etc. *Recreation:* sketching. *Address:* 86 Harley Street, W1. *T:* 01-935 7202.

**SMITH, Sir Laurence Barton G.**; *see* Grafftey-Smith.

**SMITH, Lawrence Delpré**; Senior Puisne Judge of the Supreme Court of Sarawak, North Borneo and Brunei, 1951-64, retired; *b* 29 October 1905; *m*; one *s* three *d*. *Educ:* Christ's Hospital; Hertford College, Oxford; Gray's Inn. Colonial Administrative Service, 1929; Colonial Legal Service, 1934; Tanganyika, 1929; Palestine, 1946; Gambia, 1948. *Address:* 34 The Avenue, Muswell Hill, N10. *T:* 01-883 7198.

**SMITH, Leslie Charles**, OBE 1968; Founder and Joint Managing Director, Lesney Products, since 1947; *b* 6 March 1918; *s* of Edward A. Smith and Elizabeth Smith; *m* 1948, Nancy Smith; two *s* one *d*. *Educ:* Enfield Central School. Export Buyer, 1938-40; Lieut, RNVR, 1940-46. *Recreations:* ski-ing, sailing, golf. *Address:* White Timbers, 9a Broad Walk, N21. *T:* 01-886 1656. *Clubs:* RNVR; RNVR Sailing, Royal Ocean Racing, Little Ship Sailing, Royal Motor Yacht, Parkstone Yacht; North Middlesex Golf, South Hertfordshire Golf.

**SMITH, Maggie, (Mrs Margaret Natalie Stephens)**, CBE 1970; Actress; *b* 28 Dec. 1934; *d* of Nathaniel Smith and Margaret Little (*née* Hutton); *m* 1967, Robert Stephens; two *s*. *Educ:* Oxford High School for Girls. Studied at Oxford Playhouse School under Isabel van Beers. Variety Club of Gt Britain Award, Actress of the Year, 1963. First appearance, June 1952, as Viola in OUDS Twelfth Night; 1st New York appearance, Ethel Barrymore Theatre, June 1956, as comedienne in New Faces. Played in Share My Lettuce, Lyric, Hammersmith, 1957; Veredane in The Stepmother, St Martin's, 1958. Old Vic Co., 1959-60 season: Lady Plyant in The Double Dealer; Celia in As You Like It; Queen in Richard II; Mistress Ford in The Merry Wives of Windsor; Maggie Wylie in What Every Woman Knows. Daisy in Rhinoceros, Strand, 1960; Kathy in Strip the Willow, Cambridge,

1960; Lucille in The Rehearsal, Globe, 1961; The Private Ear and The Public Eye (Evening Standard Drama Award, best actress of 1962), Globe, 1962; Mary, Mary, Queen's, 1963 (Variety Club of Gt Britain, best actress of the year); The Country Wife, Chichester, 1969. National Theatre: 1963: Silvia in The Recruiting Officer; 1964: Desdemona in Othello, Hilda Wangel in The Master Builder, Myra Arundel in Hay Fever; 1965: Beatrice in Much Ado About Nothing, Miss Julie in Miss Julie; A Bond Honoured, 1966; The Beaux' Stratagem, 1970 (also USA); Hedda in Hedda Gabler, 1970. *Films:* The VIP's, 1963; The Pumpkin Eater, 1964; Young Cassidy, 1965; Othello, 1966; The Honey Pot, 1967; Hot Millions, 1968 (Variety Club of GB Award); The Prime of Miss Jean Brodie, 1968 (Oscar); Oh! What a Lovely War, 1968. *Recreation:* reading. *Address:* c/o Fraser and Dunlop, 91 Regent Street, W1R 8RU. *T:* 01-734 7311.

**SMITH, Rt. Hon. Dame (Margaret) Patricia H.;** *see* Hornsby-Smith.

**SMITH, Maurice George;** Under-Secretary and Principal Finance Officer, Ministry of Overseas Development, since 1968; *b* 4 Sept. 1915; *s* of Alfred Graham and Laura Maria Smith; *m* 1940, Eva Margaret Vanstone; two *s*. *Educ:* Sir Walter St John's School, Battersea. Examiner, Estate Duty Office, 1939. Flt Lieut RAF, 1942-46. Asst Principal, Min. of Civil Aviation, 1947; Principal, 1948; transferred to Colonial Office, 1950; seconded Commonwealth Office, 1954-55; Asst Secretary, Colonial Office, 1959; transferred to Dept of Technical Co-operation, 1961; Min. of Overseas Development, 1964. Hon. Secretary, Knights' Assoc. of Christian Youth Clubs, Lambeth, 1950-; Member, Scripture Union Council, 1969. *Recreations:* voluntary work in youth service, travel. *Address:* 52 Woodfield Avenue, SW16. *T:* 01-769 5356.

**SMITH, Michael J. B.;** *see* Babington Smith.

**SMITH, Murray S.;** *see* Stuart-Smith.

**SMITH, Noel James Gillies,** MA; BSc, PhD; formerly Plant Pathologist, South African Government Division of Botany; *b* 25 Dec. 1899; *e s* of late Dr W. G. Smith, Edinburgh, and Elizabeth M. Gillies; *m* 1934, Frances Isabel (*d* 1960), *o d* of late F. C. Church, Blackheath. *Educ:* George Watson's Coll., Edinburgh; Univs of Edinburgh and Cambridge. Temporary 2/Lieutenant RFA 1918; Sibbald Bursar, Vans Dunlop Scholar, and J. H. Balfour gold medallist, University of Edinburgh; Carnegie research scholar and Demonstrator in Botany School, University of Cambridge, PhD (Cambridge) 1926; was assistant in Botany, University of Aberdeen, 1925-26; Professor of Botany, Rhodes University College, Grahamstown, Cape, 1926-48; has acted as examiner in the Universities of Cape Town, Pretoria, Stellenbosch, and S Africa; has been chairman of the botanical studies committee of the University of S Africa; was president (1931) of the botanical section of the S African Association for the Advancement of Science; has taken part in expeditions for botanical exploration, the longest being (1933) into little-known parts of the Namib Desert; served with South African Artillery, 1940-41, and South African Medical Corps, 1941-42, in Africa. FLS 1934-41; FRSSA 1936. *Publications:* Has published, from 1924 onwards, in various botanical and agricultural periodicals, a series of articles on diseases of cereals and grasses caused by fungi of the genus Helminthosporium, the most important being Leaf-Stripe disease of Barley and Foot-rot of Wheat, and the longest papers being in the Annals of Applied Biology, and the South African Journal of Science; has also, from 1934 onwards, published a series on S African Gasteromycetous fungi; has also reported more general botanical results of explorations *eg* some results of Namib Desert expedition in Proceedings Linnean Soc. (1934).

**SMITH, Capt. Norman Wesley,** CBE 1960; retired as Commodore Orient Steam Navigation Co. Ltd, 1961; *b* 27 Feb. 1900; *s* of Joseph and Margaret Anne Smith; *m* 1946, Nancy Phyllis, *d* of Engineer Capt. F. J. Pedrick, RN (Retd); two *s*. *Address:* 115 Alleyn Park, West Dulwich, SE21. *T:* 01-693 1140.

**SMITH, Lt-Col Osbert Walter Dudley,** JP; Vice-Lieutenant, County of Worcester, since 1959; *b* 1 August 1898; *s* of G. D. Smith and Lady Barbara Smith, *d* of 9th Earl of Coventry. *Educ:* Eton; RMC, Sandhurst. Grenadier Guards, Dec. 1917. Served War of 1939-45; Major 3rd Bn Grenadier Guards (despatches); Lt-Colonel 4th Bn, 1940. DL and JP Worcs, 1946. High Sheriff, Worcs, 1957. *Address:* Levant Lodge, Earls Croome, Worcester. *T:* Upton-upon-Severn 2628. *Club:* Guards.

**SMITH, Prof. Patrick Horace N.;** *see* Nowell-Smith.

**SMITH, Patrick Wykeham M.;** *see* Montague-Smith.

**SMITH, Mrs Peter;** *see* Gillie, Dame A. C.

**SMITH, Rear-Adm. P(hilip) Sydney,** CB 1952; DSO 1945; retired; *b* 25 Feb. 1899; *s* of Rev. Sydney Edward Smith; *m* 1928, Edna Vere Herbert; two *d*. *Educ:* Hill House, St Leonards on Sea; Osborne; Dartmouth. Midshipman, 1914; Lieut, 1920; Comdr, 1935; Captain, 1941; Rear-Adm., 1950. Served European War, 1914-18; served War of 1939-45 (despatches, DSO); Head of British Naval Mission to Greece, 1951-53; retired Sept. 1953. *Recreations:* mainly gardening; formerly all games: especially tennis, golf, cricket. *Address:* Forge Lodge, Bredhurst, Kent.

**SMITH, Phyllis B.;** *see* Barclay-Smith.

**SMITH, Ralph G.;** *see* Gordon-Smith.

**SMITH, Ralph Henry T.;** *see* Tottenham-Smith.

**SMITH, Raymond;** *see* Smith, (Francis) Raymond (Stanley).

**SMITH, (Raymond) Gordon (Antony);** *see* Etherington-Smith.

**SMITH, Sir Raymond (Horace),** KBE 1967 (CBE 1960); Chairman of Hawker Siddeley Brush and other British cos in Venezuela; Representative, Rolls-Royce and British Aircraft Corporation; Economist; *b* 1917; *s* of Horace P. Smith and Mabelle (*née* Osborne-Couzens); *m* 1943, Dorothy, *d* of Robert Cheney Hart. *Educ:* Salesian College, London; Barcelona University. Served War of 1939-45, with British Security Co-ordination, NY, and with Intelligence Corps, in France, India, Burma, Malaya and Indonesia. Civil Attaché British Embassy, Caracas, 1941-43; Negotiator, sale of British Railway Cos to Venezuelan Govt, 1946-50; Pres. British Commonwealth Assoc. of Venezuela, 1955-57; Companion of Royal Aeronautical Society. Venezuelan Air Force Cross. *Address:* Edificio las Américas, Calle Real de Sabana Grande, Caracas, Venezuela. *Clubs:* Royal Aero; Caracas Country (Venezuela).

**SMITH, Reginald Arthur;** Journalist and author; writer on education, religion, politics and social relations; *b* 23 July 1904; *e surv s* of late Arthur and late Clara Smith, Burton-on-Trent; *m* 1931, Doris Fletcher Lean; one *s* one *d*. *Educ:* Victoria Road and Guild Street elementary schools, Burton-on-Trent. Junior Asst, Burton-on-Trent public library, 1918-21; reporter, Burton Daily Mail, Burton-on-Trent, 1921-30; sub-editor, Sheffield Mail, 1930-31; editor Westmorland Gazette, Kendal, 1931-34; reporter and special correspt Manchester Guardian, 1934-43; editor: Manchester Guardian Weekly, 1943-47; British Weekly, 1947-50; managing editor, Liberal Party publications, 1951-60; Sec., Friends' Temperance and Moral League Union, 1960-70; Chm. of the Religious Weekly Press Group, 1950-51. Mem. of Soc. of Friends. *Publications:* Can Conscience be Measured?, 1940; Towards a Living Encyclopaedia, 1942; King of Little Everywhere, 1942; A Liberal Window on the World, 1946; Industrial Implications of Christian Equality, 1949; (joint editor with A. R. J. Wise) Voices on the Green, 1945. *Address:* Walnut, Albury Heath, Guildford, Surrey. *Club:* National Liberal.

**SMITH, Mrs Reginald Donald;** *see* Manning, Olivia.

**SMITH, Col Rt. Hon. Sir Reginald Hugh D.;** *see* Dorman-Smith.

**SMITH, Reginald John,** CVO 1954; *b* 21 Aug. 1895; *o s* of late John Smith, Hardwicke, Gloucestershire; *m* 1921, Irene Victoria Hauser; two *d*. *Educ:* Sir Thomas Rich's School, Gloucester. Joined Metropolitan Police, 1915; served Royal Artillery, France and Flanders, 1917-19; rejoined Met. Police, 1919; Sergt, 1920; Inspector, 1932; Supt 1940; Assistant Chief, British Police Mission to Greece, 1945-46; Deputy Commander, 1946; Commander, 1947-58. King's Police Medal, 1945 for distinguished service during Flying Bomb attack. Chevalier, The Order of Dannebrog, 1951; OStJ. *Recreations:* cricket, bowls. *Address:* Foxwold, East Dean, Sussex. *T:* East Dean 3229. *Club:* Royal Commonwealth Society.

**SMITH, Reginald N. M.;** *see* Marsh Smith.

**SMITH, Sir Reginald Verdon;** *see* Verdon-Smith.

**SMITH, Professor Richard Edwin;** Professor of Ancient History, University of Manchester, since 1953; *b* Moscow, 15 June 1910; *s* of James Ford Smith and Katherine Louise Smith (*née* Lunn); unmarried. *Educ:* Market Bosworth and Emmanuel Coll., Cambridge. Charles Oldham Classical Scholar, University of Cambridge, 1934. Assistant Lecturer in Classics, University College, Nottingham, 1935-38; Lecturer in Ancient History, Trinity College, University of Toronto, 1938-41, Assistant Professor, 1941. Served War of 1939-45, with RCAF, 1941-45. Classical Tutor, Queens' Coll., Cambridge, 1945-46; Professor of Latin, University of Sydney, 1946-53. *Publications:* The Failure of the Roman Republic, 1955; Service in the post-Marian Roman Army, 1959; Cicero the Statesman, 1966; articles in Classical Quarterly, Classical Philology, Historia, Greece and Rome. *Recreations:* squash, tennis, motoring. *Address:* Beech Mount Hotel, Barrington Road, Altrincham, Cheshire. *T:* 061-928 4523. *Club:* Oxford and Cambridge.

**SMITH, Richard H. S.;** *see* Sandford Smith.

**SMITH, Sir Richard P.;** *see* Prince-Smith, Sir (William) Richard.

**SMITH, R(ichard) Selby,** MA (Oxon), MA (Harvard); Foundation Professor of Education, Monash University, since 1964; Dean, Faculty of Education, since 1965; *b* 1914; *s* of Selby Smith, Hall Place, Barming, Maidstone, Kent, and Annie Rachel Smith (*née* Rawlins); *m* 1940, Rachel Hebe Philippa Pease, Rounton, Northallerton, Yorks; two *s*. *Educ:* Rugby Sch.; Magdalen Coll., Oxford; Harvard Univ. Asst Master, Milton Acad., Milton, Mass, USA, 1938-39; House Tutor and Sixth Form Master, Sedbergh Sch., 1939-40; War of 1939-45: Royal Navy, 1940-46; final rank of Lt-Comdr, RNVR. Administrative Asst, Kent Education Cttee, 1946-48; Asst Education Officer, Kent, 1948-50; Dep. Chief Education Officer, Warwickshire, 1950-53; Principal, Scotch Coll., Melbourne, 1953-64. Chm., Victorian Univs and Schools Examinations Bd; Member: La Trobe Univ. Council; Commonwealth Govt's Cttee on Standards for Science Facilities in Independent Schools. *Recreations:* fishing, shooting and ornithology. *Address:* 11a The Avenue, East Malvern, Victoria 3145, Australia; Monash University, Clayton, Victoria 3168, Australia. *Clubs:* RNVR Officers'; Melbourne (Melbourne).

**SMITH, Prof. Robert Allan,** CBE 1960; PhD; FRS 1962; FRSE 1969; Principal and Vice-Chancellor, Heriot-Watt University, since 1968; *b* Kelso, Scotland, 14 May 1909; *s* of G. J. T. Smith; *m* 1934, Doris M. L. Ward; one *s* two *d*. *Educ:* Edinburgh Univ.; Cambridge University. Carnegie Research Fellow, St Andrews Univ., 1935-38; Lecturer, Reading Univ., 1939; Royal Radar Establishment, 1939-61 (Head of Physics Dept, 1947-61); Professor of Physics, Sheffield Univ., 1961-62; Professor of Physics, and First Director of Centre of Materials, Science and Engineering, Mass Inst. of Technology, 1962-68. *Publications:* Radio Aids to Navigation, 1947; Aerials for Meter and Decimeter Wave-lengths, 1949; The Physical Principles of Thermodynamics, 1952; The Detection and Measurement of Infra-Red Radiation, 1957; Semiconductors, 1959; The Wave Mechanics of Crystalline Solids, 1961. *Address:* Heriot-Watt University, Chambers Street, Edinburgh EH1 1HX. *Clubs:* Caledonian; New (Edinburgh).

**SMITH, Robert Paterson;** Chairman, The Burmah Oil Company Ltd, since 1965 (Managing Director, 1957-68); *b* 29 Jan. 1903; *s* of Thomas Smith; *m* 1935, Joyce Mary Whinney, *d* of F. T. Whinney; two *d*. *Educ:* The Ewart, Newton Stewart. Qualified Chartered Accountant, 1925; joined Asiatic Petroleum Co., Calcutta, 1926; Burmah-Shell, India, 1928-52; joined the Burmah Oil Company Ltd, London, 1952; appointed to Board of Directors, 1955; Asst Managing Director, 1956; Managing Director, 1957; Chairman, 1965. *Recreations:* fishing, gardening. *Address:* The Pound, East Blatchington, Seaford, Sussex. *T:* Seaford 3726. *Clubs:* City of London, Oriental.

**SMITH, Roderick Philip,** QC 1966; *b* 29 April 1926; Recorder of Sunderland since 1967; Deputy Chairman, Durham Quarter Sessions, since 1967; *s* of John Philip Smith and Hettie Smith (*née* Mayall); *m* 1957, Jean Rodham Hudspith; two *s* two *d*. *Educ:* Newcastle upon Tyne Royal Grammar Sch.; Merton Coll., Oxford. BA 1950. Served Royal Navy, 1945-47. Called to the Bar, Middle Temple, 1951. *Recreations:* cricket, gardening. *Address:* Oaklands Manor, Riding Mill,

Northumberland. *T:* Riding Mill 245. *Clubs:* MCC; Yorkshire (York).

**SMITH, Rodney,** MS, FRCS; Surgeon, St George's Hospital, London; Hon. Consulting Surgeon: Royal Prince Alfred Hospital, Sydney, NSW; Wimbledon Hospital; Examiner in Surgery, University of London; External Examiner in Surgery, Universities of Birmingham and Hong Kong; Member Council and formerly Chairman, Court of Examiners, Royal College of Surgeons; Dean, Institute of Basic Medical Sciences, Royal College of Surgeons; Advisor in Surgery to Department of Health and Social Security. *b* 10 May 1914; *o s* of Dr Edwin Smith and Edith Catherine (*née* Dyer); *m* 1938, Mary Rodwell; three *s* one *d*. *Educ:* Westminster Sch.; London Univ. (St Thomas's Hospital). MB, BS London, MRCS, LRCP, 1937; FRCS 1939; MS London, 1941. Surgical Registrar, Middlesex Hospital, 1939-41; Surgeon RAMC, 1941-45; appointed Surgeon, St George's Hospital, 1946. Hunterian Professor, RCS, 1947 and 1952; Arris and Gale Lecturer, 1959; Jacksonian Prize-winner, 1951; Visiting Lecturer to South Africa Assoc. of Surgeons, 1957; Penrose May Tutor in Surgery, Royal College of Surgeons, 1957-63. McIlrath Guest Professor in Surgery, Royal Prince Alfred Hospital, Sydney, NSW, 1966. *Publications:* Acute Intestinal Obstruction, 1947; Surgery of Pancreatic Neoplasms, 1951; Progress in Clinical Surgery, 1953, 1961, 1969; Operative Surgery (8 Vols), 1956-57 (14 Vols), 1968-69; Surgery of the Gallbladder and Bile Ducts, 1965; Clinical Surgery (Vols 1-14), 1965-67; papers in learned journals on pancreatic surgery, general abdominal surgery, intestinal obstruction. *Recreations:* music, cricket, golf, bridge. *Address:* 149 Harley Street, W1. *T:* 01-935 4444. *Clubs:* MCC, Crockford's; Surrey County Cricket, Royal Wimbledon Golf.

**SMITH, Ron;** Member, and Managing Director (Personnel and Social Policy), British Steel Corporation, since 1967 (Member, Organising Committee for National Steel Corporation, 1966); *b* 15 July 1915; *s* of Henry Sidney Smith and Bertha Clara (*née* Barnwell); *m* 1940, Daisy Hope, *d* of Herbert Leggatt Nicholson; one *d*. *Educ:* Workers' Education Association. Post Office Messenger, 1929; Postman, 1934; Postal and Telegraph Officer, 1951; Treasurer, Union of Post Office Workers, 1953; Gen. Sec., Union of Post Office Workers, 1957-66. General Council, TUC, 1957-66; Civil Service National Whitley Council, 1957-66; Exec. Cttee, Postal, Telegraph and Telephone International, 1957-66; Vice-Chairman, Post Office Dept, Whitley Council, 1959-66. Member: Cttee on Grants to Students, 1958-60; Development Areas, Treasury Advisory Cttee, 1959-60; Cttee on Company Law, 1960-62; National Economic Development Council, 1962-66; Court of Enquiry into Ford Motor Co. Dispute, 1963; Cttee of Enquiry into Pay, etc, of London Transport Bus Staff, 1963-64; President, Postal, Telegraph and Telephone Internat., 1966. Director, BOAC, 1964-70. *Recreations:* photography, golf. *Address:* 33 Grosvenor Place, SW1. *T:* 01-235 1212. *Club:* Royal Automobile.

**SMITH, Ronald A. D.;** *see* Dingwall-Smith.

**SMITH, Sir Ross G.;** *see* Grey-Smith.

**SMITH, Sir Rowland;** *see* Smith, Sir Alexander R.

**SMITH, Rupert R. R.;** *see* Rawden-Smith.

**SMITH, Samuel Harold,** OBE 1943; MC 1917; Deputy-Chairman, Bucks Quarter Sessions, 1959-63; *b* 1888; 5th *s* of J. R. Smith, JP, The Priory, Windermere; *m* 1918, Gladys Leonora Smith; one *s* two *d*. *Educ:* The Leys Sch., Cambridge; Caius Coll., Cambridge. Scholar of Caius Coll., 1907 and Ramadge Research Student, 1911; LLB Cambridge, 1911. Called to the Bar, Inner Temple, 1913. Served European War, 1914-19 (despatches twice, MC); Major, 5th Bn Cheshire Regt; Staff Captain, 52nd Inf. Bde, 1916; DAAG XIII Corps, 1918. Lieut-Colonel, Deputy Director Army Welfare Services, 1940-44 (OBE). Rushcliffe Cttee on Legal Aid, 1943; Member of Lord Chancellor's Advisory Cttee on Legal Aid, 1950-64. Director, Legal Division, Allied Commission for Austria, 1947-48. JP Bucks, 1950; Chairman, Appeals Cttee, Bucks Quarter Sessions, 1955. Chairman, British Tin Investment Corp. Ltd, and subsidiary companies, 1953-63. French Croix de Guerre, 1917. *Address:* Highfield, Chalfont St Giles, Bucks. *T:* Chalfont St Giles 2019.

**SMITH, Sidney,** LittD, FBA 1941; Professor Emeritus, University of London; *b* Aug. 1889; *m* Mary, *d* of H. W. Parker; one *s* one *d*. *Educ:* City of London Sch.; Queen's Coll., Cambridge (Scholar, Hon. Fellow, 1935). Director of Antiquities, Iraq, 1929-30; Hon. Fellow, School of Oriental and African Studies, University of London. Foreign Member Royal Flemish Acad. of Belgium. *Address:* Cawthorne, Barcombe, Lewes, Sussex.

**SMITH, Simon H. N.;** *see* Nowell-Smith.

**SMITH, Professor Stanley Alexander de;** *see* de Smith.

**SMITH, Stanley G.;** *see* Graham Smith.

**SMITH, Stevie; (Florence Margaret Smith);** author; *b* Hull; has lived in London since the age of three; *yr d* of Charles Ward Smith and Ethel Rahel Spear. *Educ:* Palmers Green High Sch.; North London Collegiate Sch. Marchioness of Cholmondeley Poetry Award, 1966; Queen's Gold Medal for Poetry, 1969. *Publications: novels:* Novel on Yellow Paper, 1936, repr. 1969 (Penguin, 1951); Over the Frontier, 1938; The Holiday, 1949; *poems and drawings:* A Good Time Was Had By All, 1937; Tender Only to One, 1938; Mother, What is Man?, 1942; Harold's Leap, 1950; Not Waving But Drowning, 1957; Some Are More Human Than Others (Sketch-Book), 1958; Selected Poems, 1962; The Frog Prince and Other Poems, 1966; Penguin Modern Poets, No 8 (one of three poets), 1966; The Best Beast, 1969 (USA). Cats in Colour (captions and introd.), 1959; Poems for Children (anthology), 1970. Contrib. to Observer, Sunday Times, Times Literary Supplement, New Statesman, The Listener, various anthologies. Broadcasts poems on radio and TV. LP record (reading and singing her own poems), 1966; record with other poets, 1965. *Address:* 1 Avondale Road, Palmers Green, N13. *T:* 01-886 4262.

**SMITH, Stuart Hayne Granville;** *see* Granville-Smith.

**SMITH, Sydney,** CBE 1957; Chairman: Engineering and Management Consultants (Scotland) Ltd, since 1965; Natural Gas Services, since 1967; *b* 2 Nov. 1900; *s* of John Ickringill Smith and Annie Shields Smith (*née* Hutton); *m* 1st, 1926, Claudia Jane Warburton (*d* 1947); two *s*; 2nd, 1948, Sheina Baird Wright. *Educ:* Belle Vue Sch., Bradford, Yorkshire; Bradford Technical Coll. Dep. Engineer and Manager, Gas Dept, Dunfermline, Fife, 1928-35; Chief Asst

Engineer and Works Manager, Bristol Gas Co., 1935-39; Engineer and Manager, Gas Dept, Paisley, Renfrewshire, 1939-45; General Manager and Chief Engineer, Romford Gas Co., Essex, 1945-49; Dep. Chairman, East Midlands Gas Board, 1949-52; Chairman: East Midlands Gas Board, 1952-56; The Scottish Gas Board, 1956-65. Member, Scottish Tourist Board, 1965-69. *Publications:* contrib. to technical journals. *Recreations:* motoring, photography, golf, fishing. *Address:* Eastfield, Erskine Road, Gullane, East Lothian. *T:* Gullane 2287.

**SMITH, Alderman Sydney Herbert,** MA; Director, National Newsagent Ltd; *s* of late Charles Edward and Emma Hedges, of London, Woodbridge, Suffolk, and Aylesbury, Bucks. *Educ:* Ruskin Coll.; St Catherine's, Oxford Univ. (Hons graduate). Member Hull City Council, 1923-70; Hon. Alderman; Lord Mayor, 1940-41; Hon. Freeman of Hull, 1968. MP (Lab) Hull, South-West, 1945-50. Life Mem., Court of Hull University. Former Chairman, Hull Education Cttee and Hull Housing and Town Planning Cttee. Hon. LLD Hull, 1967. Queen Marie of Roumania's Cross for Services, 1917. *Address:* 16 Southfield, Hessle, East Yorkshire. *T:* 641979; c/o National Newsagent Ltd, Lennox House, Norfolk Street, WC2.

**SMITH, Sydney M.;** *see* Macdonald-Smith.

**SMITH, Prof. Thomas Broun,** QC Scotland 1956; DCL, 1956; LLD (Edinburgh) 1963; FBA 1958; Professor of Scots Law, Edinburgh University, since 1968; *b* 3 Dec. 1915; 2nd *s* of late J. Smith, DL, JP, and Agnes Smith, Symington, Lanarkshire; *m* 1940, Ann Dorothea, *d* of late Christian Tindall, CIE, ICS, Exmouth, Devon; two *d* (one *s* decd). *Educ:* High Sch. of Glasgow; Sedbergh Sch.; Christ Church, Oxford (MA). Boulter Exhibitioner, 1st Class Hons School of Jurisprudence, 1937; Eldon Scholar, 1937; Edinburgh Univ.; 1st Class and Certificate of Honour English Bar Final, Called to English Bar by Grays Inn, 1938. Served TA from 1937; War Service, 1939-46; BEF, Home Forces, Middle East and Central Mediterranean; London Scottish (Gordon Highlanders) and RA (Fd.); variously employed on regimental and Intelligence duties and at School of Infantry; Lieut-Colonel (despatches); Lieut-Colonel (TA) Gordon Highlanders, 1950; OC Aberdeen University Contingent, Officers Training Corps, 1950-55; Hon. Colonel, 1964; TARO 1955. Attached to Foreign Office, 1946-47. Examined by and admitted to Faculty of Advocates in Scotland, 1947. Professor of Scots Law, University of Aberdeen, 1949-58; Dean of Faculty of Law, 1950-53 and 1956-58; Prof. of Civil Law, University of Edinburgh, 1958-68. Hon. Sheriff-Substitute of Aberdeen, 1950 and of Lothian and Peebles, 1964; Member Scottish Law Reform Cttee, 1954. Chairman Aberdeen Valuation Appeal Cttee, 1957-58; Member Scottish Cttee on Prescribing Costs, 1957; Trustee, National Library of Scotland, 1958; Director Scottish Universities Law Inst., 1960; Hon. Member Council Louisiana State Law Inst., 1960; Mem., Academic Advisory Cttee, Universities of St Andrews and Dundee, 1964-; Law Commissioner for Scotland, 1965. Ford Visiting Professor, Tulane Univ. (Louisiana), 1957-58; Visiting Lecturer, Cape Town and Witwatersrand Universities, 1958; Visiting Prof., Harvard Law Sch., 1962-63. Hon. Foreign Mem., Amer. Acad. of Arts and Sciences, 1969. Hon. LLD: Cape Town, 1959; Aberdeen, 1969. *Publications:* Doctrines of Judicial Precedent in Scots Law, 1952; Scotland: The Development of its Laws and Constitution, 1955; British Justice: The Scottish Contribution, 1961; Studies Critical and Comparative, 1962; A Short Commentary on the Law of Scotland, 1962; articles in the Encyclopædia of the Laws of Scotland and in various legal journals published in Britain and abroad. *Recreations:* hill-walking, foreign travel. *Address:* 11 India Street, Edinburgh 3. *T:* 031-225 8030. *Clubs:* Naval and Military; New (Edinburgh).

**SMITH, T(homas) Dan;** Chairman: Northern Economic Planning Council, since 1965; Peterlee and Aycliffe Development Corporation, since 1968; *b* 11 May 1915; *m* 1939; one *s* two *d*. Company Director. City Councillor, Newcastle upon Tyne, 1950-66 (Chairman, Finance Cttee); Member, Royal Commission on Local Government, 1966-69. Hon. DCL Newcastle University, 1966. *Recreations:* painting, music, swimming, sport. *Address:* 13 Belle Grove Terrace, Spital Tongues, Newcastle upon Tyne.

**SMITH, Colonel Sir (Thomas) Eustace,** Kt 1962; CBE 1956; TD 1943; DL 1955; JP 1946; Chairman, 1956-70 (Managing Director, 1952-65) of Smith's Dock Co. Ltd; *b* 8 Sept. 1900; *s* of Eustace Smith, Benton, Newcastle upon Tyne; *m* 1925, Sylvia May, *d* of late Captain W. E. Rogerson; three *d*. *Educ:* Eton. Served his time with R. and W. Hawthorn Leslie & Co. Ltd; joined Smith's Dock Co. Ltd, 1922, Director, 1928, Asst Managing Director, 1945, Joint Managing Director, 1948. Joined Northumberland Hussars, 1922, and in 1940 went with them to N. Africa. Later commanded 15th (Isle of Man) Light AA Regt in N. Africa and Italy and returned with them to England, 1944. Comd Northumberland Hussars for 3 years after cessation of hostilities (Hon. Colonel, 1957-62). President: NE Coast Instn of Engineers and Shipbuilders, 1952-53, and 1953-54; Shipbuilding Employers Fedn, 1953-54; Chairman, NE Coast Ship-repairers' Assoc., 1955-56 and 1956-57; Chairman, Dry Dock Owners & Repairers' Central Council, 1956-57; Chairman Tyne Shipbuilders Assoc., 1953-54 and 1954-55; Chairman, Tees Conservancy Commission, 1957-67; President, Shipbuilding Conf., 1959-61; Chairman, British Ship Research Assoc., 1962-65; Chairman, Tees and Hartlepools Port Authority, 1966-. Is also Director: Cleveland Trust Ltd; North-Eastern Improved Dwellings Co. Ltd; Lloyds Bank Ltd (Newcastle upon Tyne Cttee); Lloyds British Testing Co. Ltd. *Recreations:* shooting, fishing. *Address:* Barton Lodge, Barton, Richmond, Yorks. *T:* Barton 206. *Club:* Northern Counties (Newcastle upon Tyne).

**SMITH, Rev. Canon Thomas G.;** *see* Grigg-Smith.

**SMITH, Rt. Rev. Thomas Geoffrey Stuart;** Assistant Bishop of Leicester since 1966; Hon. Canon of Leicester since 1966; Rector of Swithland since 1966; *b* 28 Feb. 1901; *s* of late Rev. Albert James Smith and late Amy Florence Smith; *m* 1930, Barbara Agnes Read; two *s* one *d*. *Educ:* Felsted Sch.; Jesus Coll., Cambridge; Ridley Hall, Cambridge. BA 1924; Carus Prize, 1924; MA 1927. Deacon 1925, Priest 1926, Southwark; Curate of St Mary Magdalene, Bermondsey, 1925-28; Chaplain of Ridley Hall, Cambridge, 1928-30; Examining Chaplain to Bishop of Chelmsford, 1929-30 and 1960-62. Vice-Principal, Diocesan Theological Instn, and Missionary, Kottayam, S India, 1930-39; Archdeacon of Mavelikkara, 1939-47; consecrated Bishop of North Kerala (Church of S India), 1947; resigned, 1953. Vicar of Burwell, 1954-60; Rector of Danbury, 1960-66; Assistant Bishop of Chelmsford,

1961-66; Hon. Canon of Chelmsford, 1961-66; Select Preacher, University of Cambridge, 1957. *Publication:* (in Malayalam) The Prison Epistles of St Paul, A Commentary, 1938. *Address:* The Rectory, Swithland, Loughborough, Leics. *T:* Woodhouse Eaves 357.

**SMITH, Sir Thomas Gilbert,** 4th Bt, *cr* 1897; engineer; *b* 2 July 1937; *er s* of Sir Thomas Turner Smith, 3rd Bt, and Agnes, *o d* of Bernard Page, Wellington, New Zealand; *S* father, 1961; *m* 1962, Patricia Christine Cooper; one *s* one *d*. *Educ:* Huntley Sch.; Nelson Coll. *Recreation:* saloon car racing. *Heir: s* Andrew Thomas Smith, *b* 17 Oct. 1965. *Address:* 4 Kitchener Street, Lansdowne, Masterton, New Zealand.

**SMITH, Trafford,** CMG 1952; HM Diplomatic Service, retired; *b* 1 Jan. 1912; *s* of John Frank Smith, Leicester; *m* 1937, Mary Isabel, *d* of A. Graham Smith, Cheltenham; two *d*. *Educ:* City of Leicester Sch.; Trinity Coll., Cambridge. Senior Scholar, State Scholar, Jeston Exhibitioner; BA 1933 (1st Class Parts I and II Mod. and Med. Langs. Trip.); MA 1936. Asst Principal, Colonial Office, 1935; Asst Private Secretary to Mr Ormsby Gore (later Lord Harlech), 1937, to Mr Malcolm MacDonald, 1938; seconded to Fiji, 1938; Asst British Resident Commissioner, New Hebrides, 1940; served in British Solomon Islands, 1940, and Gilbert and Ellice Islands, 1941; Secretary, Soulbury Commn on Constitutional Reform, Ceylon, 1944-45; Asst Secretary, Colonial Office, 1945. Attached to UK Delegation to UN, New York, for Special General Assembly on Palestine, 1948; idc 1950; Lieutenant-Governor of Malta, 1953-59; Acting Governor, Malta, May-Sept., 1953, July-Sept. 1954; Assistant Under-Secretary of State, Commonwealth Office (previously Colonial Office), 1959-67; Ambassador to Burma, 1967-70. CStJ 1956. *Recreations:* chamber music, building, travel. *Address:* c/o National Westminster Bank, 66 Trafalgar Square, WC2.

**SMITH, Vice-Adm. Sir Victor Alfred Trumper,** KBE 1969 (CBE 1963); CB 1968; DSC 1941; Chief of Naval Staff and First Naval Member of Australian Commonwealth Naval Board since 1968; *b* 9 May 1913; *s* of George Smith; *m* 1944, Nanette Suzanne Harrison; three *s*. *Educ:* Royal Australian Naval College. Sub-Lieut, 1935; Lieut, 1936; Lieut-Commander, 1944; Commander, 1947; Captain, 1953; Rear-Admiral, 1963; Vice-Admiral, 1968. *Recreation:* walking. *Address:* Navy Office, Canberra, ACT 2600, Australia. *T:* Canberra 653251.

**SMITH, Walter Campbell,** CBE 1949; MC; TD; MA, ScD; *b* 30 Nov. 1887; 2nd *s* of late George Hamilton Smith, Solihull, Warwickshire; *m* 1936, Susan, *y d* of late John Finnegan, Belfast; one *s* one *d*. *Educ:* Solihull; Corpus Christi, Cambridge. Wiltshire Prize, Cambridge Univ., 1909; Assistant, Dept of Minerals, British Museum, 1910; Deputy Keeper, 1931-37; Deputy Chief Scientific Officer, British Museum (Natural History), 1948-52; also Keeper of Minerals, 1937-52; Non-resident Fellow Corpus Christi, Cambridge, 1921-24; Honorary Secretary, Geological Society of London, 1921-33 (Murchison Medallist, 1945), President, 1955-56; General Secretary, Mineralogical Society, 1927-38, President, 1945-48; President, geological section, British Assoc., 1950; Governor, Royal Holloway Coll., 1922-43, representing Cambridge University; served in the Artists' Rifles, 1910-35 and 1939-42; European War, France, 1914-18 (MC, despatches twice, 1914 Star); Acting Lieut-Colonel, 1918; Brevet Lieut-Colonel, 1935; Second-in-Command, 163 OCTU (The Artists' Rifles), 1939-41. *Publications:* numerous papers on minerals, rocks and meteorites. *Address:* Cranfield, Plymouth Drive, Sevenoaks, Kent. *T:* Sevenoaks 54955.

**SMITH, Walter Riddell;** a Deputy Director-General, Agricultural Development and Advisory Service, since 1971; *b* 18 Sept. 1914; *s* of John Riddell Smith and Ethel Smith (*née* Liddell); *m* 1942, Janet Henderson Mitchell; one *s* one *d*. *Educ:* Lamesley C. of E. Sch., Co. Durham; Johnston Techn. Sch., Durham City. NDA 1936; BSc(Agric.) 1936. Record Keeper: Cockle Park, Northumberland, 1936-37; School of Agriculture, Durham, 1937-39; Asst Agricultural Organiser, Northumberland CC, 1939-42; Animal Husbandry Officer, Northumberland War Agric. Exec. Cttee, 1942-47; Nat. Agric. Adv. Service, 1948-; Livestock Adviser: WR, 1948-52; Eastern Region, 1952-55; Wales, 1955-61; Dep. Regional Director, Yorks and Lancs, 1961-64; Regional Director, Northern Region, 1964-66; Dir, Nat. Agricultural Adv. Service, 1967-71. *Publications:* contributions to press, popular agric. and technical journals. *Recreations:* gardening, sport, theatre. *Address:* 6 Inner Park Road, Wimbledon Common, SW19. *T:* 01-788 2684. *Club:* Farmers'.

**SMITH, William Frederick Bottrill,** CBE 1964; Accountant and Comptroller General of Inland Revenue, 1958-68; *b* 29 Oct. 1903; *s* of late Arthur and Harriet Frances Smith; *m* 1926, Edyth Kilbourne (*d* 1970); no *c*. *Educ:* Newton's, Leicester. Entered the Inland Revenue Dept, Civil Service, 1934. President, Inland Revenue Staff Federation, 1945-47. Member, Sussex Naturalists Trust; Treasurer, Chailey Commons Society; Chairman, Management Cttee, Chailey Nature Reserve. *Address:* c/o National Provincial Bank Ltd, 96-97 Strand, WC2.

**SMITH, Sir (William) Gordon,** 2nd Bt *cr* 1945; VRD; Lieut-Commander, RNR, retired; *b* 30 Jan. 1916; *s* of Sir Robert Workman Smith, 1st Bt, and Jessie Hill, *yr d* of late William Workman, Belfast; *S* father, 1957; *m* 1st, 1941, Diana Gundreda, *d* of late Major C. H. Malden, Aberdeenshire; 2nd, 1958, Diana Goodchild; two *s*. *Educ:* Westminster; Trinity Coll., Cambridge (BA). Called to Bar, Inner Temple, 1939. Served War of 1939-45 as Lieut, RNVR (despatches). *Recreation:* yachting (Winner, International Dragon Gold Cup, 1961). *Heir: s* Robert Hill Smith, *b* 15 April 1958. *Address:* 44 Walton Street, SW3; (Seat) Crowmallie, Pitcaple, Aberdeenshire. *Clubs:* Carlton, Bath; New (Edinburgh).

**SMITH, William McGregor,** OBE 1970; HM Inspector of Constabulary for Scotland, since 1970; *b* 14 April 1910; *s* of John Smith, Milngavie and Agnes Smith (*née* Haldane); *m* 1939, Alice Mary Ewen, Montrose; one *s* one *d*. *Educ:* Bearsden Academy and Glasgow University (MA 1930). Joined City of Glasgow Police, 1933; Deputy Commandant, Scottish Police College, 1951; Chief Constable of Aberdeen, 1963. *Recreations:* golf, bridge. *Address:* Scottish Home and Health Department, North St David Street, Edinburgh. *T:* 031-226 6762. *Clubs:* University (Aberdeen); Royal Aberdeen Golf.

**SMITH, William Owen Lester,** CBE 1947; *b* Llanbrynmair, Montgomeryshire, 4 Sept. 1888; *s* of late Henry Lester Smith, Halkyn Old Hall, Flintshire; *m* Rose, *d* of J. Lloyd Evans, Warwick; no *c*. *Educ:* King's School, Chester; Merton Coll., Oxford (History Scholar); MA; Hon. LLD: Manchester, 1949; Wales, 1967. Assistant Director of Education,

Warwickshire; Chief Organiser Elementary Education, Lancashire; Director of Education. Essex, 1924-31; Chief Education Officer, Manchester, 1931-49; Professor of Sociology of Education, University of London, 1949-53. *Publications:* Contributions to Encyclopædia Britannica; To Whom do Schools Belong?, 1942; Education in Great Britain, 1949; Impact of Education on Society, 1949; Education: An Introductory Survey, 1957; Government of Education, 1965. *Address:* Bryn Gwern, Dolgellau, North Wales.

**SMITH, Sir William Reardon Reardon-,** 3rd Bt, *cr* 1920; Major, RA (TA); *b* 12 March 1911; *e s* of Sir Willie Reardon-Smith, 2nd Bt, and Elizabeth Ann, *d* of John and Mary Wakely; *S* father, 1950; *m* 1st, 1935, Nesta (marr. diss., 1954; she *d* 1959), *d* of late Frederick J. Phillips; three *s* one *d*; 2nd, 1954, Beryl, *d* of William H. Powell; one *s* three *d. Educ:* Blundell's Sch., Tiverton. Served War of 1939-45. *Heir: s* William Antony John Reardon-Smith [*b* 20 June 1937; *m* 1962, Susan, *d* of H. W. Gibson, Cardiff; two *s* one *d. Educ:* Wycliffe Coll., Glos.] *Address:* Rhode, Romansleigh, Devon. *T:* Bishops Nympton 371. *Club:* Cardiff and County (Cardiff).

**SMITH, Sir William Reginald Verdon;** *see* Verdon-Smith.

**SMITH, William W.;** *see* Wenban-Smith.

**SMITH-DODSWORTH, Sir John (Christopher),** 8th Bt, *cr* 1784; *b* 4 March 1935; *s* of Sir Claude Smith-Dodsworth, 7th Bt, and Cyrilla Marie Louise von Sobbe, 3rd *d* of William Ernest Taylor, Linnet Lane, Liverpool; *S* father, 1940; *m* 1961, Margaret Anne (*née* Jones); one *s* one *d. Educ:* Ampleforth Coll., Yorks. *Heir: s* David John Smith-Dodsworth, *b* 23 Oct. 1963. *Address:* Thornton Watlass Hall, Ripon, Yorks.

**SMITH-GORDON, Sir Lionel Eldred Pottinger,** 4th Bt, *cr* 1838; Chairman, Jencons (Scientific) Ltd; *b* 25 Nov. 1889; *o c* of 3rd Bt and Sophia Annie (*d* 1943), *o d* of Robert James Scott, BCS; *S* father, 1933; *m* 1st, 1913, Ellen, *e d* of late Senator Fletcher, USA (marr. diss.); no *c*; 2nd, 1933, Eileen Laura, *o c* of late Captain H. G. Adams-Connor, CVO, DL; one *s. Educ:* Eton (KS); Trinity Coll., Oxford (MA). Served River Emergency Service (London), 1939-40; Temp. Lieut, RNVR, 1940-43. Commandeur du Tastevin, 1956. *Publications:* Rural Reconstruction in Ireland; Co-operation in Many Lands; Co-operation for Farmers; That Basilisk (novel); translations from the French: George Villiers, Duke of Buckingam (Erlanger); Mysterious Courier (Aulen). *Recreations:* travel, wine and food. *Heir: s* Lionel Eldred Peter Smith-Gordon [*b* 7 May 1935; *m* 1962, Sandra, *yr d* of late Wing Comdr W. R. Farley, DFC, and of Mrs Dennis Poore; one *s* one *d*]. *Address:* 9 Zetland House, Marloes Road, W8. *T:* 01-937 5655. *Clubs:* Naval; Vincent's (Oxford).

**SMITH-MARRIOTT, Sir Ralph George Cavendish,** 10th Bt, *cr* 1774; Bank Official; *b* 16 Dec. 1900; *s* of late George Rudolph Wyldbore Smith-Marriott and of Dorothy Magdalene, *d* of Rev. John Parry; *S* uncle, 1944; *m* 1st, Phyllis Elizabeth (*d* 1932), *d* of Richard Kemp (late Governor HM Prison, Bristol); two *s* one *d*; 2nd, 1933, Doris Mary (*d* 1951), *d* of R. L. C. Morrison, Tenby, Pembs; 3rd, 1966, Mrs Barbara Mary Cantlay. *Educ:* Cranleigh Sch., Surrey. Bristol Univ. OTC, 1918. *Recreations:* tennis, golf, cricket. *Heir: s* Hugh Cavendish Smith-Marriott [*b* 1925; *m* 1953, Pauline Anne, *d* of F. F. Holt, Bristol]. *Address:* 28a Westover Road, Westbury-on-Trym, Bristol. *T:* Bristol 628827.

**SMITH-PEARSE, Thomas Lawrence,** CIE 1944; MA; Indian Education Service; Principal Rajkumar College, Raipur, 1931-46; *b* 15 July 1893; *s* of late Rev. T. N. H. Smith-Pearse, MA, and late Mrs E. I. Smith-Pearse, JP, Launceston; *m* 1923, Katharine, *d* of late Brig.-General Sir Danvers Waghorn, CB, CMG, RE; one *s. Educ:* Marlborough Coll.; St John's Coll., Oxford. *Address:* White Hill, Wildhern, Andover, Hants. *T:* Hatherden 230.

**SMITH-ROSE, Reginald Leslie,** CBE 1952; DSc, PhD, FCGI, FIEE, FIRE; FIC; Director of Radio Research, Department of Scientific and Industrial Research, 1948-Sept. 1960; *b* 2 April 1894; *m* 1919, Elsie Masters; two *d. Educ:* Latymer Upper Sch., Hammersmith; Imperial College of Science, London Univ. Board of Education, Royal Schol. (1st Place) 1912; Imperial College, Governor's Prize in Physics (1st Place) 1914; London Univ.: BSc, Hons Physics, Cl. 1, 1914; PhD, Science, 1923; DSc, Science, 1926. Assistant Engineer, Siemens Bros Ltd, Woolwich, 1915-19. National Physical Laboratory: Scientific Officer, Electricity Div., 1919-33; Principal Scientific Officer, Radio Div., 1933-39; Supt Radio Div., 1939-47; acting Director, 1950 and 1956. Institution of Electrical Engineers: Chairman, Radio Section, 1942-43; Member Council, 1953-56, 1960-61; Vice-President, 1961-64; Fellow, Institute of Electrical and Electronics Engineers (USA) (Vice-President, 1948); FIEEE. Member, various scientific and technical committees of Government Departments and other Institutions; delegate to various international scientific radio conferences in various countries; President, Internat. Scientific Radio Union, 1960-63; Chairman, Study Group V, Internat. Radio Consultative Cttee, 1951-70; Secretary-General, Inter-Union Cttee on Frequency Allocations for Radio Astronomy and Space Research, 1961-. Chairman, PMG's Frequency Advisory Cttee, 1960-; Member PMG's Cttee on Broadcasting, 1960. Coronation Medals, 1937, 1953; US Medal of Freedom with Silver Palm, 1947. *Publications:* many original papers published in Proc. of Royal and Phys. Societies, Instn Elect. Engrs, and elsewhere. *Address:* 21 Tumblewood Road, Banstead, Surrey. *Club:* Athenæum.

**SMITH-RYLAND, Charles Mortimer Tollemache;** Lord Lieutenant of Warwickshire since 1968; *b* 24 May 1927; *s* of Charles Ivor Phipson Smith-Ryland and Leila Mary Tollemache; *m* 1952, Hon. Jeryl Marcia Sarah Gurdon, *d* of Hon. Robin Gurdon; two *s* three *d. Educ:* Eton. Lt, Coldstream Guards, 1945-48; Reserve, Warwickshire Yeomanry. Mem., W Midland Adv. Cttee Land Commn; Warwickshire: CC, 1949; DL, 1955; Alderman, 1958; Vice-Chm. CC, 1963; Chm. CC, 1964-67; Vice-Chm. Police Authority, 1966-68; Chm., Warwickshire and Coventry Police Authority, 1969-; High Sheriff, 1967-68. KStJ 1968. *Recreations:* hunting, shooting, golf. *Address:* Sherbourne Park, Warwick. *T:* Barford 255. *Clubs:* Buck's, Turf, White's; Leamington Tennis.

*See also Baron Cranworth.*

**SMITHERMAN, Frank,** MBE 1951; HM Diplomatic Service; Ambassador to Togo and Dahomey, since 1970; *b* 13 Oct. 1913; *s* of Lt-Col H. C. Smitherman and Mildred E. Holten; *m* 1937, Frances Ellen Rivers Calvert; one *s* one *d. Educ:* Sir Joseph Williamson's Mathematical Sch., Rochester. Indian Police, Burma, 1933; served in: Yenangyaung; Rangoon; Myitkyina; Sagaing; Thayetmyo;

Thaton. Served War of 1939-45 (despatches, 1945), Burma Army Reserve of Officers; Maj. 1945. Joined Civil Affairs Service; Foreign Office, 1949; subseq. service in: Amoy; Cairo; Rome; Khartoum; Miami; Consul-General, Bordeaux, 1967-69; Counsellor, Moscow, 1969-70. *Recreations:* fishing, gardening. *Address:* c/o Foreign and Commonwealth Office, SW1; Pickwick Cottage, New Buckenham, Norfolk.

**SMITHERS, Sir Arthur Tennyson,** Kt 1959; CBE 1949; company director; *b* 30 June 1894; *s* of late Frederick Smithers; *m* 1920, Constance Helen Wise, *d* of Andrew McIntosh Wise; two *d. Educ:* Eastleigh College, Prahran. Joined Victoria Treasury, 1911; proceeded through various positions till 1937, when appointed Permanent Head. Dir of Finance, Victoria, 1937-59, retd. Pres., Marine Board, 1964-69; Mem. Cttee of Management, Royal Melbourne Hosp., 1941-; Trustee, National Gallery of Victoria, 1945-; Director of the Elizabethan Theatre Trust, 1954-; Commissioner State Savings Bank of Victoria, 1955-. AASA. *Recreations:* music, golf. *Address:* 21 Sylverley Grove, Caulfield, Melbourne, Australia. *T:* 53.2177. *Clubs:* Melbourne Cricket, Lawn Tennis Association of Victoria, Victoria Amateur Turf.

**SMITHERS, Prof. Sir David (Waldron),** Kt 1969; MD, FRCP, FRCS, FFR; Professor of Radiotherapy in the University of London; Director of the Radiotherapy Department at the Royal Marsden Hospital since 1943; Hon. Consultant Radiotherapist: Brompton Hospital for Diseases of the Chest; to Royal Navy; *b* 17 Jan. 1908; *s* of late Sir Waldron Smithers, MP; *m* 1933, Gwladys Margaret (Marjorie), *d* of Harry Reeve Angel, Officer (1st class) Order of White Rose of Finland; one *s* one *d. Educ:* Boxgrove School, Guildford; Charterhouse; Clare College, Cambridge; St Thomas's Hospital. MRCS, LRCP 1933; MB, BChir (Cantab) 1934; MD (Cantab) 1937; DMR (London) 1937; MRCP 1946; FRCP 1952; FFR 1953; FRCS 1963. Clin. Asst Children's Ear, Nose and Throat, and Skin Depts, St Thomas's Hosp., 1933; Civilian Med. Practitioner, Queen Alexandra Mil. Hosp., 1933-35; out-patient MO, Nat. Hosp. for Diseases of the Heart, 1935; Asst Radiologist, Royal Cancer Hosp., 1937-38; X-ray Therapist, Royal Cancer Hosp., 1938-39; Actg Director Radiological Dept, Royal Cancer Hosp., 1939-43; Hon. Director Radiotherapy Dept, St Thomas's Hosp., 1942-43; Pres. British Inst. of Radiology, 1946-47; President, Faculty of Radiologists, 1959-61; Member: Central Health Services Council; Standing Med. Adv. Cttee and Chm. Cancer Sub-Cttee; Grand Council, British Empire Cancer Campaign; Nat. Rose Soc. *Publications:* General Editor, Monographs on Neoplastic Disease at Various Sites; papers on cancer and radiotherapy. *Recreation:* growing roses. *Address:* The Royal Marsden Hospital, Fulham Road, SW3. *T:* 01-352 8171 (and Surrey Branch, Downs Rd, Sutton. *T:* 01-642 6011); Ringfield, Knockholt, Kent. *T:* Knockholt 2122. *Club:* Athenæum.

**SMITHERS, Donald William,** CB 1967; retired; *b* 21 Aug. 1905; *s* of William John and Mary Smithers, Portsmouth, Hants; *m* 1929, Kathleen Margery Gibbons; three *s* one *d. Educ:* Portsmouth; Royal Naval Coll., Greenwich. Asst Constructor until 1937, then Constructor, Chatham; Principal Ship Overseer, 1939-44; Constructor Captain to C-in-C Mediterranean, 1944-47; Chief Constructor: Admiralty, 1947-52; Portsmouth, 1952-54; Singapore, 1954-56; Asst Dir of Dockyards, 1956-58; Manager HM Dockyard, Chatham, 1958-61; Director of Dockyards, 1961-67; retd 1967. CEng; MRINA; RCNC. *Address:* Chevithorne, Greenway Lane, Bath. *T:* Bath 4093.

**SMITHERS, Professor Geoffrey Victor;** Professor of English Language, University of Durham, since 1960; *b* 5 May 1909; *s* of William Henry and Agnes Madeline Smithers; *m* 1953, Jean Buglass Hay McDonald; three *s* one *d. Educ:* Durban High School; Natal University College; Hertford College, Oxford. Rhodes Schol. for Natal, 1930; 1st Cl. in Final Hon. School of English, Oxford, 1933. Asst Lecturer: King's Coll., London, 1936; University Coll., London, 1938; Lectr in English Language, 1940, Senior Lecturer in English Language, 1950, Reader in Medieval English, 1954, Univ. of Oxford, and professorial Fellow of Merton Coll., 1954. *Publications:* 2nd edn of C. Brown's Religious Lyrics of the Fourteenth Century, 1952; Kyng Alisaunder, Vol. I 1952, Vol. II 1957; (with J. A. W. Bennett and N. Davis) Early Middle English Verse and Prose, 1966 (2nd edn 1968); papers in Med. Æv., English and Germanic Studies, Archivum Linguisticum, Rev. Eng. Studies. *Recreation:* music. *Address:* 20 Crossgate Peth, Durham. *T:* 3940.

**SMITHERS, Sir Peter (Henry Berry Otway),** Kt 1970; VRD with clasp; DPhil Oxon; Lt-Comdr RNR, retired; Senior Research Fellow, United Nations Institute for Training and Research, since 1969; *b* 9 Dec. 1913; *o s* of late Lt-Col H. O. Smithers, JP, Hants, and Ethel Berry; *m* 1943, Dojean, *d* of late T. M. Sayman, St Louis, Mo; two *d. Educ:* Hawtrey's; Harrow Sch.; Magdalen Coll., Oxford. Demyship in History, 1931; 1st cl. Hons Modern History, 1934. Called to Bar, Inner Temple, 1936; joined Lincoln's Inn, 1937. Commn, London Div. RNVR, 1939; British Staff, Paris, 1940; Naval Intelligence Div., Admiralty; Asst Naval Attaché, British Embassy, Washington; Actg Naval Attaché, Mexico, Central Amer. Republics and Panama. RD Councillor, Winchester, 1946-49. MP (C) Winchester Div. of Hampshire, 1950-64; PPS to Minister of State for Colonies, 1952-56 and to Sec. of State for Colonies, 1956-59; Deleg., Consultative Assembly of Council of Europe, 1952-56 and 1960; UK Deleg. to UN Gen. Assembly, 1960-62; Parly Under-Sec. of State, FO, 1962-64; Sec.-Gen., Council of Europe, 1964-69. Chairman: British-Mexican Soc., 1952-55; Conservative Overseas Bureau, 1956-59; Vice-Chm., Conservative Parly Foreign Affairs Cttee, 1958-62; Vice-Pres., European Assembly of Local Authorities, 1959-62. Master, Turners' Co., 1955; Liveryman, Goldsmiths' Co. Dr of Law *hc* Zürich, 1969. Chevalier de la Légion d'Honneur. Orden Mexicana del Aguila Azteca. Alexander von Humboldt Gold Medal, 1969. *Publication:* Life of Joseph Addison, 1954. *Recreations:* historical research, gardening. *Address:* c/o Credito Svizzero, Casella Postale, CH 6901 Lugano, Switzerland. *Clubs:* Carlton; Metropolitan (New York).

**SMITHSON, Peter Denham;** architect in private practice since 1950; *b* 18 Sept. 1923; *s* of William Blenkiron Smithson and Elizabeth Smithson; *m* 1949, Alison Margaret (*née* Gill); one *s* two *d. Educ:* The Grammar School, Stockton-on-Tees; King's College, Univ. of Durham. Served War of 1939-45: Queen Victoria's Own Madras Sappers and Miners, India and Burma, 1942-45. Asst in Schools Div. LCC, 1949-50; subseq. in private practice with wife. *Buildings:* Hunstanton School, 1950-54; Economist Building, St James's, 1959-64; Robin Hood Gardens, Tower Hamlets, 1963-70; Garden Bldg, St Hilda's Coll., Oxford,

1968-70. *Publications:* Uppercase 3, 1960; (with A. Smithson) The Heroic Period of Modern Architecture, 1965; Urban Structuring Studies of Alison and Peter Smithson, 1967; Team 10 Primer, 1968; The Euston Arch, 1968; Ordinariness and Light, 1970; theoretical work on town structuring in Architectural Review, Architectural Design and most foreign periodicals (most with A. Smithson). *Relevant publication:* synopsis of professional life in Arena, Feb. 1966. *Address:* 2 Priory Walk, SW10. *T:* 01-373 7423.

**SMOLKA, H. P.;** *see* Smollett, H. P.

**SMOLLETT, Harry Peter,** OBE 1944; author and journalist; *b* Vienna, 17 Sept. 1912; *s* of Albert V. Smolka and Vilma Wottitz; naturalised British subject since 1938; changed name to Smollett by deed poll in 1938, but continues to use Smolka as writer's name; *m* 1933, Lotte Jaeckl; two *s*. *Educ:* Vienna Gymnasium; University of Vienna; London School of Economics. London Correspondent Central European Newspapers and Central European Adviser to Exchange Telegraph Co. Ltd, 1934-38; Head of Foreign Dept, Exchange Telegraph Co., 1938-39; War Service, Min. of Information, 1939-45; Vienna Correspondent of The Times, 1947-49. Chairman and Managing Director: Vienna Metal Goods Manufacturing Co.; Vienna Metal Goods Trading Co.; Chm. Tyrolia Sporting Goods Ltd London; Jt Man. Dir·Tyrolia Metal and Sporting Goods Trading Co., Munich, Germany. Travels: all European countries, USA, Mexico, USSR, Israel. *Publication:* 40,000 Against the Arctic. *Recreation:* chess. *Address:* Lindauergasse 9, A.1238 Vienna, Austria.

**SMOUT, Professor Charles Frederick Victor;** Professor of Anatomy, University of Birmingham, 1948-61, retired; *b* 23 Oct. 1895; *s* of Thomas and Mary Elizabeth Smout; *m* 1923, Ethel May Butterworth; no *c*. *Educ:* King Edward's School, Birmingham, MB, ChB 1923; MRCS, LRCP 1923. MD (Birmingham) 1943. *Publications:* Anatomy for Students of Physiotherapy, 1943 (rev. 5th edn, Gynaecological and Obstetrical Anatomy, Descriptive and Applied, 1968); Basic Anatomy and Physiology, 1961; An Introduction to Midwifery, 1962; The Story of the Progress of Medicine, 1964; A Layman looks at life in general and at the Bible in particular, 1966. *Address:* The Spinney, 7 Nairn Road, Canford Cliffs, Poole, Dorset. *T:* Canford Cliffs 78914. *Club:* University Staff (Birmingham).

**SMYLY, Col Dennis Douglas Pilkington,** DSO 1945; *b* 1913; *s* of late Major R. J. Smyly, OBE, Sweethay Court, Trull, Somerset; *m* 1939, Hon. Dorothy Margaret Berry, 3rd *d* of 1st and last Baron Buckland; three *s* one *d*. *Educ:* Sherborne; RMC Sandhurst. 2 Lt 16/5 Lancers, 1933; served War of 1939-45, North Africa, 1942-43; Italy (despatches), 1944-45; commanded 16/5 Lancers, 1944-47. Colonel 16/5 Queens Royal Lancers, 1959-69. JP Northants, 1955-67; High Sheriff Northants, 1961; DL Northants, 1965-68; JP Glos, 1969. *Address:* Hill House, Hartpury, Glos. *T:* Hartpury 235; 120 Marsham Court, Marsham Street, SW1. *T:* 01-834 5276. *Club:* Cavalry.

**SMYTH, Rev. Canon Charles Hugh Egerton,** MA, FRHistS; Fellow of Corpus Christi College, Cambridge, 1925-32 and since 1937; *b* Ningpo, China, 31 March 1903; *s* of Richard Smyth, MD; *m* 1934, Violet, *e d* of Rev. Canon Alexander Copland, Forfar. *Educ:* Repton; Corpus Christi College, Cambridge (Scholar); Wells Theological Coll. 1st class, Historical Tripos, Part 1, 1923, and Part 2, 1924; Thirlwall Medal and Gladstone Prize, 1925. Tutor and Lectr in History, Harvard Univ., USA, 1926-27; Deacon, 1929; Priest, 1930; University Lecturer in History, Cambridge, 1929-32 and 1944-46; Curate of St Clement's, Barnsbury, Islington, 1933-34; of St Saviour's, Upper Chelsea, 1934-36; of St Giles', Cambridge, 1936-37. Birkbeck Lecturer in Ecclesiastical History, Trinity College, Cambridge, 1937-38; Dean of Chapel, Corpus Christi College, 1937-46; Hon. Canon of Derby and Chaplain to Bishop of Derby at the University of Cambridge, 1938-46; Select Preacher, Oxford, 1941-43 and 1965; Canon of Westminster and Rector of St Margaret's, Westminster, 1946-56; Hon. Canon and Prebendary of Nassington in Lincoln Cathedral, 1965-. Editor of the Cambridge Review, 1925 and 1940-41. *Publications:* Cranmer and the Reformation under Edward VI, 1926; The Art of Preaching (747-1939), 1940; Simeon and Church Order (Birkbeck Lectures), 1940; Religion and Politics, 1943; The Friendship of Christ, 1945; Dean Milman, 1949; Church and Parish (Bishop Paddock Lectures), 1955; Good Friday at St Margaret's, 1957; Cyril Forster Garbett, Archbishop of York, 1959; The Two Families, 1962; The Church and the Nation, 1962. *Address:* 12 Manor Court, Pinehurst, Cambridge; Corpus Christi College, Cambridge. *Club:* Athenæum.

**SMYTH, David Henry,** FRS 1967; Professor of Physiology, Sheffield University, since 1946; Pro-Vice-Chancellor, 1962-66; *b* 9 Feb. 1908; *s* of late Joseph Smyth, Lisburn, Co. Antrim; *m* 1942, Edith Mary Hoyle; no *c*. *Educ:* Royal Belfast Academical Institution; Queen's Univ., Belfast. QUB: BSc 1929; MB, BCh 1932; MSc 1934; MD 1935; PhD London, 1940. RMO Royal Victoria Hospital, Belfast, 1932; Demonstrator in Physiology, Belfast, 1933; Musgrave Student in Physiology at Göttingen, Germany, 1936; Lectr in Physiology, University Coll., London, 1937. Mem. Editorial Bd, Journal of Physiology, 1961-68 (Chm., 1966-68). Chm. Keeshond Club, 1960-. Robert Campbell Memorial Orator, Ulster Med. Soc., 1968. *Publications:* papers in Journal of Physiology, Quarterly Journal of Experimental Physiology, Biochemical Journal, British Medical Journal, 1934-68. *Recreations:* pedigree dogs, music. *Address:* The Swevic, Foolow, Derbyshire. *T:* Tideswell 330. *Club:* Kennel.

**SMYTH, John Andrew,** MD, BSc, DPH; Hon. Consultant Physician, formerly Physician, Royal Victoria Hospital, Belfast; *b* 27 Jan. 1893; *s* of Rev. James and Mary Frances Dill Smyth; *m* Viola May Millar; one *s* two *d*. *Educ:* Royal School, Dungannon; Queen's Univ., Belfast. BSc Engineering, with first place, 1914; MB, BCh, BAO with first class hons, first place, and specially awarded Exhibition, QUB, 1921; DPH first place; MD with gold medal, 1923; served European War, France, 1915-16; Life Fellow Ulster Medical Society (Pres., 1954-55); Pres. Irish Br., Assoc. of Clinical Pathologists, 1954-55; Chm. Belfast Br., Diabetic Assoc., 1954-55; Mem., Assoc. of Clinical Pathologists. *Publications:* Serum Diagnosis of Syphilis (jointly), Medical Research Council Report Series No 78; Diabetes: Past, Present and Future, Ulster Medical Journal, 1954, etc. *Address:* 23 University Square, Belfast BT7 1PB, Northern Ireland. *T:* Belfast 24061; Trench House, Ballyaughlis, Lisburn, N Ireland. *T:* Drumbo 207.

**SMYTH, Brig. Rt. Hon. Sir John (George),** 1st Bt *cr* 1955; VC 1915; PC 1962; MC 1920; *b* 24 Oct.

1893; *e s* of W. J. Smyth, Indian Civil Service; *m* 1920, Margaret, *d* of late Charles Dundas, ICS, Sialkot; two *s* (and *e s* killed in action 1944) one *d*; *m* 1940, Frances Read, *d* of late Lieut-Colonel R. A. Chambers, OBE, IMS. *Educ:* Repton; Sandhurst. Entered army, 1912; served European War, 1914-15 (despatches, VC, Russian Order of St George); Senussi Campaign, Western Egypt, 1915-16; Mohmand Expedition, India, 1916; Afghan War, 1919; Waziristan Frontier Expedition, 1919-20 (despatches, MC); Mesopotamia Insurrection, 1920-21 (despatches); Operations on NW Frontier, 1930 (despatches); Mohmand Operations, 1935 (despatches); Brevet-Major, 1928; Brevet Lieut-Colonel, 1933; Colonel, 1936; Instructor, Staff College, Camberley, 1931-34; Comdt 45th Rattrays Sikhs, 1936-39; GSO1, 2nd London Division, 1939-40; Commander 127 Inf. Bde in operations with BEF in France and Belgium (despatches); Acting Maj.-Gen. 1941; raised 19th Division in India; Comd 17th Division in Burma at time of Japanese invasion; retired, Nov. 1942; Hon. Brig. 1943. Military Correspondent: Kemsley newspapers, 1943-44; Daily Sketch and Sunday Times, 1945-46; Lawn Tennis Correspondent: Sunday Times, 1946-51; News of the World, 1956-57. Author, Wimbledon Programme articles, 1947-. Comptroller Royal Alexandra and Albert School, 1948-63; Governor: Gypsy Road and West Norwood Secondary Schs, 1947-49; Strand and West Norwood Secondary Schools, 1949-51; St Martin's High School for Girls, 1950-52; Dragon School, Oxford, 1953-66; Queen Mary's Hosp., Roehampton, 1956-62. Exec., Returned Brit. POW Assoc., 1946-51. First Chm. Victoria Cross Assoc., 1956-71 (Centenary of the Victoria Cross), Life Pres. 1966; Vice-Pres. Not Forgotten Assoc., 1956; Pres. S London Branch Burma Star Assoc., 1957-; Vice-Pres. Distinguished Conduct Medal League, 1957, Pres. 1958-70; Director Creative Journals Ltd, 1957-63. Govt Apptd Trustee, Far East POW and Internee Fund, 1959-61; Hon. Vice-Pres. Far Eastern POW Federation, 1960; President Old Reptonian Society, 1960 and 1961; Vice-President: Dunkirk Veterans Assoc., 1963-; Internat. Lawn Tennis Club of GB, 1966. Contested (C) Wandsworth Central, 1945. MP (C) Norwood Div. of Lambeth, 1950-56. Parly Sec., Min. of Pensions, 1951-53; Jt Parly Sec., Min. of Pensions and Nat. Insce, 1953-65. Freeman of City of London in Worshipful Co. of Farriers, 1951; Master of Farriers' Co., 1961-62. *Publications:* Defence Is Our Business, 1945; The Western Defences (ed and introd), 1951; Lawn Tennis, 1953; The Game's the Same, 1956; Before the Dawn (story of two heroic retreats), 1957; Paradise Island (children's adventure story), 1958; The Only Enemy (autobiography), 1959; Trouble in Paradise, 1959; Ann Goes Hunting (children's book), 1960; Sandhurst (A History of the Military Cadet Colleges), 1961; The Story of the Victoria Cross, 1962; Beloved Cats, 1963; Blue Magnolia, 1964; Ming (the story of a cat family), 1966; The Rebellious Rani (a story of the Indian Mutiny), 1966; Bolo Whistler (biography), 1967; The Story of the George Cross, 1968; In This Sign Conquer (The Story of the Army Chaplains), 1968; The Valiant, 1969; Will to Live: the story of Dame Margot Turner, 1970; *plays:* Burma Road (with Ian Hay), 1945; Until the Morning (with Ian Hay), 1950. *Heir: s* Julian Smyth [*b* 16 Oct. 1923; *m* 1952, Philomena Mary, *d* of John Francis Cannon; five *s* two *d*]. *Address:* 807 Nelson House, Dolphin Square, SW1. *Clubs:* Queen's, All England Lawn Tennis, Carlton; International Lawn Tennis Clubs of Britain, USA and France.

**SMYTH, Margaret Jane,** CBE 1959 (OBE 1955); *b* 23 Sept. 1897; *d* of late Colonel John Smyth, IMS. *Educ:* Uplands School (Church Education Corporation); Clifton High School. Trained at Univ. Settlement, Bristol; Health Visitors Certificate. Roy. Sanitary Inst., 1918; Central Midwives Board, SCM, 1920; Maternity and Child Welfare Certificate, RSI, 1921; SRN, 1925, trained in Nightingale Trg School, St Thomas's Hosp.; Sister, St Thomas's, Hosp., 1926-34; Matron, St Thomas's Babies' Hostel, 1934-37; Warden, St Christopher's Nursery Trg College, 1937-39; Dep. Matron, St Thomas's Hosp., 1939-45, Supt, Nightingale Trg School and Matron, St Thomas's Hospital, 1945-55; Chairman of the General Nursing Council for England and Wales, 1955-60; President Royal College of Nursing, 1960-62; Chairman, South West Metropolitan Area, Nurse Training Cttee, 1952-64, Mem., 1964-66; Vice-Chm., Long Grove Hospital Management Cttee, 1964-67; Mem., Kingston and Long Grove Hosp. Management Cttee, 1967-69. *Address:* 9 Stockbridge Gardens, Chichester, Sussex. *Club:* Cowdray.

**SMYTH, Captain Sir Philip Weyland Bowyer-,** 14th Bt, *cr* 1661; RN retired; *b* 4 Feb. 1894; *s* of late Clement Weyland Bowyer-Smijth, *b* of 13th Bt, and Maud, *d* of W. Gray, Sydney, NSW; *S* uncle, 1927; *m* 1922, Margaret Joan, OBE 1952, TD (marr. diss. 1951), *o d* of late S. McCall-McCowan, Sydney; no *c*; *m* 1951, Veronica Mary, 2nd *d* of Capt. C. W. Bower, DSC, RN retd, Fordwich, Kent; one *s* one *d*. Naval Attaché at Rome, 1939-40; ADC to the King, 1946; retired list, 1946. *Heir: s* Thomas Weyland Bowyer-Smyth, *b* 25 June 1960. *Address:* La Provençale, Plascassier, France, AM. *Clubs:* United Service; Royal Yacht Squadron.

**SMYTH-PIGOTT, Group Captain (Joseph) Ruscombe (Wadham),** CBE 1942; DSO 1915; late RAF; *b* 1889; *y s* of late Cecil Hugh Smyth-Pigott, Brockley Court, Somerset; *m* 1919, Lady Clare Feilding (*d* 1966), 5th *d* of 9th Earl of Denbigh; one *d*. *Educ:* Oratory School; Dartmouth. Entered RN 1905; served European War (despatches, DSO and bar, Croix de Guerre); retired list, RAF 1934; served with RAF again, 1939. *Address:* c/o Westminster Bank, Farnborough, Hants.

**SMYTHE, Clifford Anthony, (Tony);** General Secretary of the National Council for Civil Liberties since 1966; *b* 2 Aug. 1938; *s* of Clifford John and Florence May Smythe; *m*; four *d*. *Educ:* University College School. Conscientious Objector, 1958; General Secretary, War Resisters' International, 1959-64; Council Member, Internat. Confederation for Disarmament and Peace, 1963-. Personnel Manager, Scott Bader & Co., 1964-65. *Publication:* Conscription–a World Survey, 1968. *Address:* 68 Hewitt Road, N8.

**SMYTHE, George Quentin Murray,** VC 1942; farming in Natal; *b* 6 Aug. 1916; *s* of Edric Murray Smythe and *g s* of 1st Administrator of Natal (Hon. Charles Smythe, Methven Castle, Perthshire, Scotland); *m* 1945, Dale Griffiths, Capetown; three *s* one *d*. *Educ:* Estcourt High Sch. Went through Abyssinian Campaign with Regt, Natal Carabineers; Sgt at Alem Hanza, Egypt (VC). *Recreations:* cricket, tennis, fishing. *Address:* Murraydale, Nels Rust, Natal, S Africa.

**SMYTHE, Henry James Drew,** MC, TD; MS, MD (London); FRCS; MMSA; FRCOG; late Hon. Consulting Gynæcologist United Bristol Hospitals and Southmead General Hospital; late Gynæcologist, Weston-super-Mare and

Burnham Hospitals; Colonel RAMCT; *b* 1 June 1891; *s* of Frank Thompson Smythe and Ada Josephine Drew; *m* 1914, Enid Audrey Cloutman; two *s*. *Educ:* Taunton School; Bristol Medical School; London Hospital. Qualified 1913; House Surgeon and House Physician Bristol Children's Hospital, 1913-14; House Surgeon Bristol General Hospital, 1914; served European War, 1914-19; also served War of 1939-45; House Surgeon Royal Infirmary, 1919; Demonstrator of Anatomy, Royal Free Hospital for Women, 1921; Post-Graduate Course London Hospital, 1921-22; Surgical Registrar, Bristol General Hospital, 1923; Asst Gynæcologist, 1925; Professor of Obstetrics, University of Bristol, 1934-51. Liveryman Society of Apothecaries; Freeman of City of London. *Publications:* various in Practitioner, Bristol Med. Chir. Jl, Jl of Obst. of British Empire, etc; Operative Obstetrics (Butterworth's Modern Trends), 1949. *Recreations:* Rugby football, hockey, tennis. *Address:* 17 Withyholt Park, Charlton Kings, Cheltenham, Glos. *T:* Cheltenham 25117.

**SMYTHE, Patricia Rosemary;** *see* Koechlin, P. R.

**SMYTHE, Tony;** *see* Smythe, C. A.

**SMYTHIES, Evelyn Arthur,** CIE 1939; *b* 19 March 1885; *s* of Arthur Smythies, IFS, and Gertrude Aston; *m* 1911, Olive Muriel Cripps (*d* 1961); two *s*. *Educ:* Cheltenham College; Balliol College, Oxford. Indian Forest Service, 1908; Chief Conservator of Forests, United Provinces, India, 1937-40; Forest Adviser to the Nepal Govt, 1940-46. *Publications:* books and articles on technical forestry, sport, philately. *Recreations:* gardening, bridge, philately. *Address:* Castle Morris, Tralee, Eire.

**SNAGGE, John Derrick Mordaunt,** OBE 1944; *b* 1904; 2nd *s* of late Judge Sir Mordaunt Snagge; *m* 1936, Eileen Mary, *e d* of H. P. Joscelyne, Alvechurch, Worcestershire. *Educ:* Winchester College; Pembroke College, Oxford. Assistant Station Director BBC, Stoke-on-Trent, 1924; Announcer London (Savoy Hill), 1928; Assistant Outside Broadcast Department 1933; Commentator Oxford and Cambridge Boat Race, 1931-; Assistant Director Outside Broadcasts, 1939; Presentation Director BBC, 1939-45; Head of Presentation (Home Service), 1945-57; Head of Presentation (Sound) BBC, 1957-63; Special Duties, BBC, 1963-65. Retired from BBC 1965. Chairman of the Lord's Taverners, 1956, 1960, 1961; President, 1952, 1964; Secretary, 1965-67. *Recreation:* fishing. *Address:* Willow Tree Cottage, West End Lane, Stoke Poges, Bucks. *T:* Farnham Common 4400. *Clubs:* MCC, Leander, Lord's Taverners.

**SNAGGE, Dame Nancy (Marion),** DBE 1955 (OBE 1945); *b* 2 May 1906; *d* of late Henry Thomas Salmon; *m* 1962, Thomas Geoffrey Mordaunt Snagge, DSC, *e s* of late His Hon. Sir Mordaunt Snagge. *Educ:* Notting Hill, High Sch. Joined the WAAF on its inception, March 1939; served as a commnd officer in the WAAF and WRAF from Sept. 1939. ADC to King George VI, 1950-52; ADC to the Queen, 1952-56; Director Women's Royal Air Force, 1950-56, retired as Air Commandant. *Address:* Test Lodge, Longstock, Stockbridge, Hampshire. *T:* Stockbridge 558.

**SNAITH, Group Captain Leonard Somerville,** CB 1952; AFC 1933; retired; *b* 30 June 1902; *s* of David Somerville Snaith; *m* 1931, Joyce Edith Taylor; two *s*. *Educ:* Carlisle Cathedral Sch. Commnd, 1927; Comd 83 Sqdn, 1937-40; service in: Iraq, 1934-36; USA (Test flying), 1940-41; Egypt, Italy, Palestine, Aden, 1945-47. Schneider Trophy Team, 1931; Commandant Empire Test Pilot School, 1948-50; Comdg Officer, Experimental Flying, Royal Aircraft Establishment, Farnborough, 1950-52; retired from RAF, 1952. DL Beds, 1961-69. *Address:* Woodlands, Lions River, Natal, S Africa. *Clubs:* Royal Air Force; Victoria (Natal).

**SNAITH, Rev. Norman Henry,** DD; *b* 21 April 1898; *s* of John Allen Snaith and Mary Ann (*née* Bunn); *m* 1925, Winifred Howson Graham; one *s* two *d*. *Educ:* Paston Sch., North Walsham; Duke's Sch., Alnwick; Manchester Grammar Sch.; Corpus Christi and Mansfield Colls, Oxford. Open Mathematical Schol., Corpus Christi, Oxon, 1917; BA Hons Maths 1920, MA 1924, DD 1948, Oxford. Junior Kennicott Hebrew Schol., 1924, Senior Kennicott Hebrew Schol., 1925. Entered Methodist Ministry, 1921. Tutor in Hebrew and Old Testament subjects, Wesley College, Headingley, Leeds, 1936-61; Principal, 1954-61. Pres., Soc. for Old Testament Study, 1957; Vis. Prof. United Theol. Coll., Bangalore, 1957. Pres., Methodist Conf., 1958-59. Speaker's Lectr in Biblical Studies, Oxford, 1961-65. Hon. DD Glasgow, 1952; Hon. LittD Leeds, 1961. *Publications:* Studies in the Psalter, 1934; Have Faith in God, 1935; The Distinctive Ideas of the Old Testament, 1944; Study Notes on Bible Books, 1945-54; The Jewish New Year Festival, 1948; The Jews from Cyrus to Herod, 1949; I believe in . . ., 1949; Hymns of the Temple, 1951; New Men in Christ Jesus, 1952; Mercy and Sacrifice, 1953; Commentary on Amos, Hosea and Micah, 1956; Authority and Inspiration of the Bible, 1956; Editor: Hebrew Bible (for British and Foreign Bible Society), 1958; Leviticus and Numbers; New Century Bible, 1966; The Book of Job, 1968. *Address:* Greenacres, Castle Lane, Thetford, Norfolk. *T:* Thetford 2848.

**SNAITH, Stanley,** FLA; author and librarian; Borough Librarian, Bethnal Green Public Libraries, 1950-65; *b* Kendal, 16 Dec. 1903; *e s* of J. W. Snaith, JP, and Margaret Tebay. Held senior posts in the Kendal, Kingston-upon-Thames and Islington public libraries. Local Secretary, Ministry of Information, 1940-42; HM Forces (Heavy Anti-Aircraft Batteries), 1942-46. *Publications:* April Morning, 1926; A Flying Scroll, 1928; The Silver Scythe, 1933; North, 1934; Fieldfaring, 1935; London Pageant, 1935; Men Against Peril, 1936; Green Legacy, 1937; Modern Poetry (A Bibliography), 1937; At Grips with Everest, 1937; Alpine Adventure, 1944; Stormy Harvest, 1944 (chosen as an Ambassador Book to the USA); The Inn of Night, 1946; The Flowering Thorn, 1946; (with George F. Vale) Bygone Bethnal Green, 1948; The Naked Mountain, 1949; The Common Festival, 1950; The Mountain Challenge, 1952; The Siege of the Matterhorn, 1956; The Books in My Life, 1957; The Special Shelf, 1958; The Lost Road, 1968; *poems:* Nanga Parbat, awarded Shirley Carter Greenwood Prize, 1949; Homage to Rilke and The Hawthorn in the Bombed Church, awarded 1st Prize, Nat. Shakespearian Sonnets Competition, 1964; scripts for BBC, and numerous papers and pamphlets on antiquarian matters; texts for two pageants; contributor to Oxford Junior Encyclopædia, Encyclopædia Britannica, and to many anthologies and periodicals. *Recreations:* reading, music. *Address:* 17 Newton Rise, Swanage, Dorset.

**SNEDDON, Prof. Ian Naismith,** OBE 1969; MA Cantab, DSc Glasgow; FRSE; FIMA; Member of the Polish Academy of Sciences; Simson Professor of Mathematics in the University of Glasgow since 1956; *b* 8 Dec. 1919; *o s* of

Naismith Sneddon and Mary Ann Cameron; *m* 1943, Mary Campbell Macgregor; two *s* one *d.* *Educ:* Hyndland School, Glasgow; The University of Glasgow; Trinity College, Cambridge (Senior Scholar, 1941). Scientific Officer, Ministry of Supply, 1942-45; Research Worker, H. H. Wills Physical Lab., Univ. of Bristol, 1945-46; Lecturer in Natural Philosophy, Univ. of Glasgow, 1946-50; Professor of Mathematics in University Coll. of N Staffordshire, 1950-56 (Senior Tutor of the College, 1954-56); Visiting Prof.: Duke Univ., North Carolina, 1959 and 1960; Michigan State Univ., 1967; Adjunct Prof., North Carolina State Univ., 1965-70; Visiting Lecturer: Univ. of Palermo, 1953; Serbian Acad. of Sciences, 1958; Univ. of Warsaw, 1959; Canadian Mathematical Congress, 1961; Polish Acad. of Sciences, 1962; US Midwest Mechanics Research Seminar, 1963; Univ. of Zagreb, 1964; Univ. of Calgary, 1968; Indiana Univ., 1970; NSF Distinguished Vis. Scientist, State Univ., New York, 1969. Member: various govt scientific cttees, 1950-; Adv. Council on Scientific Research and Tech. Development, Min. of Supply, 1953-56, Min. of Defence, 1965-68; Mem., univs Science and Technology Bd (SRC), 1965-69; Vice-Pres., RSE, 1966-69. Kelvin Medal, Univ. of Glasgow, 1948; Makdougall-Brisbane Prize, RSE, 1956-58. Comdr's Cross, Order of Polonia Restituta, 1969. *Publications:* (with N. F. Mott) Wave Mechanics and Its Applications, 1948; Fourier Transforms, 1951; Special Functions of Mathematical Physics and Chemistry, 1956; The Elements of Partial Differential Equations, 1956; Introduction to the Mathematics of Biology and Medicine (with J. G. Defares), 1960; Fourier Series, 1961; Mixed Boundary Value Problems in Potential Theory, 1966; Crack Problems in the Mathematical Theory of Elasticity (with M. Lowengrub), 1969; An Introduction to the Use of Integral Transforms, 1970; articles in Handbuch der Physik, 1956-58; scientific papers on quantum theory of nuclei, theory of elasticity, and boundary value problems in jls. *Recreations:* music, painting and photography. *Address:* 15 Victoria Park Gardens South, Glasgow W1. *T:* 041-339 4114. *Club:* Authors'.

**SNELL, Ven. Basil Clark;** Archdeacon of St Albans since 1962; *b* 2 Feb. 1907; *s* of Charles Clark Snell, Vicar of Littlehampton; *m* 1933, Isobel Eills Nedeham Browne; two *d.* *Educ:* King's School, Canterbury; Queens' College, Cambridge. Curate of Crosthwaite, Keswick, 1933-35; Chaplain of Aldenham School, 1935-40; Chaplain, Loretto Sch. and Army Chaplain, 1940-47; Rector of Tattingstone, Suffolk, 1947-55; Residentiary Canon of St Edmundsbury, 1955-58; Dir of Religious Education: Dio. of St Edmundsbury and Ipswich, 1947-58; Dio. of St Albans, 1958-68. Archdeacon of Bedford, 1958-62. *Recreations:* golf, gardening. *Address:* Holywell Close, St Albans, Herts.

**SNELL, Frederick Rowlandson,** MA, BSc; Provincial Officer, Anglican Church in Central Africa, since 1968; *b* 18 Sept. 1903; *s* of Rev. C. D. Snell; *m* 1928, Margaret Lucy Sidebottom; one *s* three *d.* *Educ:* Winchester College (Scholar); Oriel College, Oxford (Scholar). BA, 1925; BSc, 1927; Lecturer in Chemistry, St John's College, Agra, UP, India, 1927-32; Senior Science Master, Eastbourne College, 1932-38; Rector of Michaelhouse, Natal, SA, 1939-52; Founder and first Rector of Peterhouse, Rhodesia, 1953-67. *Recreations:* walking and music. *Address:* 54 1st Street, Marandellas, Rhodesia. *Club:* Royal Commonwealth Society.

**SNELL, Rt. Rev. George Boyd;** *see* Toronto, Bishop of.

**SNELL, Henry William,** CMG 1964; Chairman of Directors Quarrying & Concrete Companies, since 1962; *b* 17 Aug. 1919; *s* of Charles and Grace Jessie Snell; *m* 1943, Margaret Edith White; two *s* one *d.* *Educ:* Scotch College, Melbourne. Served War of 1939-45: Tobruk, 1941 (Captain); Alamein, 1942 (Major); New Guinea, 1943-44. Lt-Col, 1952. Mayor of City of Bendigo, 1955, 1958 and 1959; President, Liberal and Country Party, Victoria, 1962-65. *Address:* 36 Ellis St, Bendigo, Victoria, Australia. *T:* 30559. *Clubs:* Naval and Military (Melbourne); Sandhurst (Bendigo).

**SNELL, William Edward,** MD; FRCP; Consultant Physician Superintendent, Colindale Chest Hospital, 1938-67; Demonstrator in Tuberculosis, St Bartholomews Hospital Medical College, 1948-67; Consultant Chest Physician, Napsbury and Shenley Hospitals, 1963-67; *b* 16 Aug. 1902; *er s* of late S. H. Snell, MD; *m* 1934, Yvonne Creagh Brown; two *s* one *d.* *Educ:* Stubbington House; Bradfield College; Corpus Christi College, Cambridge (Exhibitioner and Prizeman); University College Hospital. MA Cambridge; BSc Hons London; MD; FRCP; DPH. Tuberculosis Scholarship Tour, Canada and USA, 1930. Formerly: Pres. Brit. Tuberculosis Assoc., 1955-57; Chairman: NW Metropolitan Thoracic Soc.; Metropolitan Branch, Soc. of Med. Supts; Editorial Cttee TB Index; Member: Management Cttees, Hendon and Chelsea Groups of Hosps; Brit. Tuberculosis Research Cttee; Examiner to Gen. Nursing Council. Mem. Council (twice Vice-Pres.), History of Medicine Section, RSM. *Publications:* articles in medical press relating to tuberculosis and chest disease, accidents to patients and history of medicine. *Recreations:* gardening, sailing, collecting ship models and prints; late part owner 15 ton ketch Craignair. *Address:* Yewden Manor, Hambleden, Henley-on-Thames, Oxon. *T:* Hambleden 351. *Clubs:* Athenæum; Keyhaven Yacht; Cambridge University Cruising, etc.

**SNELLGROVE, David Llewellyn,** LittD, PhD; FBA 1969; Reader in Tibetan in the University of London since 1960 (Lecturer, 1950-60); Director of Institute of Tibetan Studies, Tring, since its foundation in 1966; *b* Portsmouth, 29 June 1920; *s* of Lt-Comdr Clifford Snellgrove, RN, and Eleanor Maud Snellgrove. *Educ:* Christ's Hospital, Horsham; Southampton Univ.; Queens' Coll., Cambridge. Served War of 1939-45: commissioned in Infantry, 1942; Intell. Officer in India until 1946. Then started seriously on oriental studies at Cambridge, 1946, cont. Rome, 1949-50. BA Cantab 1949, MA Cantab 1953; PhD London 1954; LittD Cantab 1969. Made expedns to India and the Himalayas, 1953-54, 1956, 1960, 1964 and 1967; founded with Mr Hugh E. Richardson an Inst. of Tibetan Studies, 1966. Apptd Consultant to Vatican in new Secretariat for non-Christian Religions, 1967. *Publications:* Buddhist Himalaya, 1957; The Hevajra Tantra, 1959; Himalayan Pilgrimage, 1961; Four Lamas of Dolpo, 1967; The Nine Ways of Bon, 1967; A Cultural History of Tibet (with H. E. Richardson), 1968; articles in Arts Asiatiques (Paris), Bulletin of the Secretariat for non-Christian Religions (Rome), etc. *Recreations:* travel: involving photography, filming, recording (esp. in India and the Himalayas), personal and professional visits to W Europe (fluent in several languages). *Address:* c/o Institute of Tibetan Studies, Tring, Herts; Rest-harrow, Cross Oak Road, Berkhamsted,

Herts. *T:* Berkhamsted 4782; Scolasticato Internazionale, Via Pineta Sacchetti 78a, Rome.

**SNELLING, Sir Arthur (Wendell),** KCMG 1960 (CMG 1954); KCVO 1962; HM Diplomatic Service; Ambassador to South Africa, since 1970; *b* 7 May 1914; *s* of Arthur and Ellen Snelling; *m* 1939, Frieda, *d* of late Lt-Col F. C. Barnes; one *s*. *Educ:* Ackworth Sch., Yorks; University Coll., London (BSc Econ.). Study Gp Sec., Royal Inst. of Internat. Affairs, 1934-36; Dominions Office, 1936; Private Sec. to Parl. Under-Sec., 1939; Joint Sec. to UK Delegn to Internat. Monetary Conference, Bretton Woods, USA, 1944; accompanied Lord Keynes on missions to USA and Canada, 1943 and 1944; Dep. High Comr for UK in New Zealand, 1947-50, in S Africa, 1953-55; Assistant Under-Secretary of State, Commonwealth Relations Office, 1956-59; British High Comr in Ghana, 1959-61; Dep. Under-Sec. of State, FCO (formerly CRO), 1961-69. Hon. Fellow, UCL, 1970-. *Address:* British Embassy, Pretoria, South Africa. *Club:* Reform.

**SNELSON, Sir Edward Alec Abbott,** KBE 1954 (OBE 1946); Justice, Supreme Restitution Court, Herford, German Federal Republic, since 1962; Judge, Arbitral Tribunal for Agreement on German External Debts and Mixed Commission, Koblenz, since 1969; *b* 31 Oct. 1904; *er s* of Thomas Edward and Alice Martha Snelson; *m* 1956, Prof. Jean Johnston Mackay, MA, 3rd *d* of Donald and Isabella Mackay; two *s*. *Educ:* St Olave's; Gonville and Caius Coll., Cambridge. Called to Bar, Gray's Inn, 1929; entered ICS 1929; served in Central Provinces, District and Sessions Judge, 1936; Registrar, High Court, 1941; Legal Secretary, 1946; Joint Secretary, Govt of India, 1947; retired, 1947; Official Draftsman, Govt of Pakistan, 1948; Sec. Min. of Law, 1951-61, also of Parliamentary Affairs, 1952-58. Mem. Exec. Cttee, Arts Council of Pakistan, 1953-61. *Publication:* Father Damien, 1938. *Recreations:* sailing, music, theatre. *Address:* c/o Barclays Bank, Piccadilly Circus, W1; c/o Supreme Restitution Court, Herford, BFPO 15. *Clubs:* Oxford and Cambridge University; Challoner.

**SNELUS, Alan Roe,** CMG 1960; retired as Deputy Chief Secretary, Sarawak (1955-64); *b* 19 May 1911; *s* of John Ernest Snelus, late of Ennerdale Hall, Cumberland; *m* 1947, Margaret Bird Deacon-Elliott; one *s* one *d*. *Educ:* Haileybury Coll.; St Catharine's Coll., Cambridge. Barrister, Gray's Inn, 1934. Joined Sarawak Civil Service as an Administrative Officer, 1934; Actg Chief Sec., 1958-59; Officer Administering the Government of Sarawak, March-April 1959. *Recreations:* gardening and contemplation. *Address:* Crouchers Farmhouse, Crowhurst, Nr Battle, Sussex. *T:* Crowhurst 308. *Club:* Royal Over-Seas League.

**SNOW,** family name of **Baron Burntwood** and **Baron Snow.**

**SNOW,** Baron *cr* 1964 (Life Peer); **Charles Percy Snow,** Kt 1957; CBE 1943; writer; Parliamentary Secretary, Ministry of Technology, 1964-66; Extraordinary Fellow, Churchill College, Cambridge; *b* 15 Oct. 1905; *m* 1950, Pamela Hansford Johnson, *qv*; one *s*. *Educ:* Alderman Newton's Sch., Leicester; Univ. Coll., Leicester; Christ's Coll., Cambridge. Hon. doctorates, and other academic awards, from American, Canadian, English, Scottish and Soviet universities and colleges. *Publications:* Death Under Sail, 1932; New Lives for Old, 1933; The Search, 1934 (revised and republished, 1958); since 1935, occupied with novel-sequence of eleven volumes (general title, Strangers and Brothers): Strangers and Brothers, 1940; The Light and the Dark, 1947; Time of Hope, 1949; The Masters, 1951; The New Men, 1954 (James Tait Black Memorial Prize, awarded in conjunction with The Masters); Homecomings, 1956; The Conscience of the Rich, 1958; The Affair, 1960; Corridors of Power, 1964; The Sleep of Reason, 1968; Last Things, 1970. The Two Cultures and the Scientific Revolution (Rede Lecture), 1959; Science and Government (Godkin Lectures), 1961; Appendix to Science and Government, 1962; The Two Cultures and a Second Look, 1964; Variety of Men, 1967; *plays:* View over the Park, produced Lyric Theatre, Hammersmith, 1950; The Affair (adapted by Ronald Millar), Strand Theatre, 1961-62; The New Men (adapted by Ronald Millar), Strand Theatre, 1962; The Masters (adapted by Ronald Millar), Savoy Theatre, Piccadilly Theatre, 1963-64; Time of Hope (adapted by Arthur and Violet Ketels), Philadelphia, 1963. *Address:* 85 Eaton Terrace, SW1. *Clubs:* Athenæum, Savile, MCC; Century (NY).

**SNOW, Rt. Hon. Lady;** *see* Johnson, Pamela Hansford.

**SNOW, Edgar Parks;** journalist, US; *b* Kansas City, Mo, 19 July 1905; *s* of James Edgar Parks Snow and Anna Katherine Fogarty Edelmann; *m* 1949, Lois Anne Wheeler; one *s* one *d*. *Educ:* Univ. of Missouri. Began as reporter, Kansas City Star; travelled as free-lance writer, worked as sailor; went to China, 1928, became Asst Editor China Weekly Review, Shanghai; correspondent Chicago Tribune, 1929-30; corr. Ch. Daily News-NY Sun, 1931-34; corr. Daily Herald (London), 1932-39; corr. Saturday Evening Post, 1933-51. Covered major Asiatic events, 1931-34; lecturer, Yenching Univ., Peking, 1933-35; accredited US and British war corr., 1942-46, assigned China-Burma-India, 1942; Britain, 1943; Russia, Poland, Rumania, 1943-44; France, Germany, Austria, 1945; interviewed Mao Tse-Tung, 1936 (first corr. to do so), and 1965; first American corr. to enter liberated Vienna, 1945. Visited India, Burma, Siam, Indo-China, Philippines, Japan, Korea, 1945-46; in Europe again, 1947. Associate Editor for Saturday Evening Post, 1943-52; Special Research Consultant, Harvard Univ., 1956-57; Special Correspondent to Mainland China for Look Magazine, 1960; revisited China, 1964-65 and 1970. *Publications:* Far Eastern Front, 1934; Living China, 1936; Red Star Over China, 1937; Scorched Earth, 1941; People On Our Side, 1943; Pattern of Soviet Power, 1945; Stalin Must Have Peace, 1947; Random Notes on Red China, 1957; Journey to the Beginning, 1958; The Other Side of the River: Red China Today, 1963. *Recreations:* swimming, tennis, ski-ing. *Address:* Mafroi 11, Nyon, Vaud, Switzerland. *Clubs:* National Press (Washington, DC); Overseas Press (NY); Nyon Tennis.

**SNOW, Sir Frederick (Sidney),** Kt 1965; CBE 1958 (OBE 1954); Principal of Frederick S. Snow & Partners since 1942; *b* 14 Feb. 1899; *s* of William Snow, London; *m* 1924, Rosetta Elizabeth, *d* of Edmund Brown, Colchester; two *s*. *Educ:* Brownhill Sch., Catford. Founded firm of Frederick S. Snow & Partners, Consulting Engineers, London, Newcastle and Norwich, 1942. Designer of International Airports, Jerusalem, Amman, Gatwick, Kuwait. Authority on industrial structures, heavy foundation and underpinning problems. Pres., IStructE, 1948; Pres., Sect. Britannique, Societé des Ingénieurs Civils de France, 1955; President, Reinforced Concrete

Assoc., 1956; 1st Pres., the Concrete Society, 1966. Member, Permanent Cttee of Internat. Assoc. for Bridge and Structural Engineering; Served on all major building and civil engineering cttees of BSI. Member: Construction Materials Group of EDC for Building and Civil Engineering Industries; The British Hospitals Export Council. Governor, Hammersmith College of Art and Building; Vice-Pres., Guild of Surveyors. Awarded Istiqlal Medal, 1968. Chevalier Legion d'Honneur, 1969. *Publications:* Foundations of London Structures, 1936; Human Needs and the Engineer, 1942; The De Havilland Airfield, Hatfield, 1949; The Development of Gatwick Airport, 1960; Formwork for Modern Structures, 1965. *Recreations:* fly-fishing, gardening. *Address:* Mulberry Cottage, The Knoll, Beckenham, Kent. *T:* 01-928 5688. *Clubs:* City Livery, United Service.

**SNOW, Rt. Rev. George D'Oyly;** *see* Whitby, Suffragan Bishop of.

**SNOW, Sir Harold (Ernest),** Kt 1961; CBE 1952 (OBE 1946); Director (later Deputy Chairman and Managing Director) British Petroleum Co. Ltd, 1952-62, retired; *b* 8 Sept. 1897; *s* of Ernest Alfred Snow and Elizabeth Hannah Snow (*née* May); *m* 1924. Nell Dagmar Goodale; one *s* one *d.* *Educ:* Merchant Ventures Sch., Bristol; Bristol Univ.; St John's Coll., Cambridge. A Wrangler in the Mathematics Tripos, 1921. Joined British Petroleum Co. Ltd, 1921; Group Manager, Shell-Mex and BP Ltd, 1932-36; Sec., Petroleum Board, 1939-45; Dep. Dir, Anglo-Iranian Oil Co. Ltd, 1946; Man. Dir, Anglo-Iranian Oil Co. Ltd (now the British Petroleum Co. Ltd), 1952. British Member of Internat. Consortium Mission which negotiated Oil Agreement with Iran, 1954. *Recreations:* gardening, music. *Address:* 29a Dene Road, Northwood, Middlesex. *T:* Northwood 21552. *Club:* United University.

**SNOW, Thomas;** Secretary to Oxford University Appointments Committee, since 1970; *b* 16 June 1929; *e s* of Thomas Maitland Snow, *qv*; *m* 1961, Elena Tidmarsh; two *s* one *d.* *Educ:* Winchester Coll.; New Coll., Oxford. Joined Crittall Manufacturing Co. Ltd as Management Trainee, 1952; Dir 1966; Director: Crittall Hope Ltd, Darlington Simpson Rolling Mills, Morex Metals Ltd, 1968. Held various positions in local govt; Marriage Councillor, 1964-70. JP 1964-69. *Address:* 157 Woodstock Road, Oxford.

**SNOW, Thomas Maitland,** CMG 1934; *b* 21 May 1890; *s* of Thomas Snow, Cleve, Exeter, and Edith Banbury; *m* 1st, 1927, Phyllis Annette Malcolmson; three *s*; 2nd, 1949, Sylvia, *d* of W. Delmar, Buda-Pest. *Educ:* Winchester; New Coll., Oxford. 1st Secretary, HM Diplomatic Service, 1923; Counsellor, 1930; Minister: to Cuba, 1935-37; to Finland, 1937-40; to Colombia, 1941-44 (Ambassador, 1944-45); to Switzerland, 1946-49. Retired, 1950. *Recreation:* fishing. *Address:* La Combe, Tartegnin, Switzerland.

*See also Thomas Snow.*

**SNOWDEN, Joseph Stanley;** Recorder of Scarborough, since 1951; Deputy Chairman, West Riding of Yorkshire Quarter Sessions since 1960; *b* 16 Oct. 1901; *e s* of late Joseph Snowden, JP, and late Fanny Ruth Snowden, Morecambe and Heysham; *m* 1938, Agnes Enid Mitchell; no *c.* *Educ:* Sedbergh; St John's Coll., Cambridge. Law Tripos (Cantab) 1923 (BA, LLB); called to the Bar, Inner Temple, 1925; joined North-Eastern Circuit, 1925. Contested (L) Bradford East Div., 1945 and 1950, Dewsbury Div., 1951 and 1955, Pudsey Div., 1959. Chairman, Yorkshire and Lancashire Agricultural Land Tribunal, 1963-. *Recreation:* politics. *Address:* Oakburn, 20 St James Road, Ilkley, Yorks. *T:* Ilkley 4113.

**SNOWDON,** 1st Earl of, *cr* 1961; **Antony Charles Robert Armstrong-Jones;** GCVO 1969; Viscount Linley, 1961; an Artistic Adviser to the Sunday Times and Sunday Times Publications Ltd, since 1962; Constable of Caernarvon Castle since 1963; *b* 7 March 1930; *s* of Ronald Owen Lloyd Armstrong-Jones, MBE, QC, DL (*d* 1966), and of the Countess of Rosse; *m* 1960, HRH The Princess Margaret; one *s* one *d.* *Educ:* Eton; Jesus Coll., Cambridge. Joined Staff of Council of Industrial Design, 1961, continuing on a consultative basis, 1962, also an Editorial Adviser of Design Magazine. Designed Snowdon Aviary, London Zoo, 1965. Mem. Council, Polio Research Fund. Hon. Fellow: Institute of British Photographers; Royal Photographic Soc.; Manchester College of Art and Design; Hon. Member: North Wales Society of Architects; South Wales Institute of Architects; Royal Welsh Yacht Club; Patron: Welsh Nat. Rowing Club; National Youth Theatre; Metropolitan Union of YMCAs; British Water Ski Federation. President: Contemp. Art Society for Wales; Welsh Assoc. of Youth Clubs; Civic Trust for Wales; British Theatre Museum; Welsh Theatre Company. *Publications:* London, 1958; Malta (in collaboration), 1958; Private View (in collaboration), 1965. *Heir: s* Viscount Linley, *qv.* *Address:* Kensington Palace, W8. *Clubs:* Leander (Henley-on-Thames); Hawks (Cambridge).

*See also under Royal Family, and Earl of Rosse.*

**SNOY ET D'OPPUERS, Baron Jean-Charles,** OBE 1948; Grand Officier de l'Ordre de la Couronne, Belgium; Commandeur de l'Ordre de Léopold, Belgium; Member of Belgian Parliament; Minister of Finance, Belgium, since 1968; Chairman Steering Board for Trade, OEEC, 1952; *b* 2 July 1907; *s* of 9th Baron and of Claire de Beughem de Houtem; *m* 1935, Nathalie, Countess d'Alcantara; two *s* five *d.* *Educ:* Collège Saint-Pierre, Uccle; University of Louvain; Harvard Univ. Secretary Société Belge de Banque, 1932; Attaché Cabinet Minister of Economic Affairs, 1934; Directeur Ministry Econ. Aff., 1936; Secrétaire Général, Ministère des Affaires Economiques, 1939-60; Président du Conseil de l'Union Benelux, 1945-60. War Service: Services de Renseignements et d'Action, 1940-44. Chairman, Four Party Supply Cttee, Belgium, 1945; Président du Conseil, Organisation Européenne de Coopération Economique, 1948-50 (OEEC in English); Chef de la délégation Belge pour le négociation des Traites de Rome, 1957; Président, Comité Intérimaire du Marché Commun et de l'Euratom, 1957-58; Representant Permanant de la Belgique, Communauté Economique Européenne, 1958-59; Administrateur-Délégué de la Compagnie Lambert pour l'Industrie et la Finance, Brussels, 1960-68. Holds several foreign decorations. *Publications:* La Commission des Douanes, 1932; L'Aristocratie de Demain, 1936; La Profession et l'Organisation de la Production, 1942; Revue Générale Belge. *Recreations:* shooting, tennis. *Heir: s* Bernard, Baron Snoy, *b* 27 March 1945. *Address:* Château de Bois-Seigneur-Isaac, Belgium. *T:* Nivelles 222.27; (business) 24 avenue Marnix, Brussels. *Clubs:* Club de la Fondation Universitaire, Cercle Gaulois (Brussels).

**SNYDER, John Wesley;** Chairman of Finance Committee and Director, The Overland

Corporation, 500 Security Building, Toledo, Ohio; *b* 21 June 1895; *s* of Jerre Hartwell Snyder and Ellen Hatcher; *m* 1920, Evlyn Cook; one *d*. *Educ:* Jonesboro Grade and High Sch.; Vanderbilt Univ. Various offices in Arkansas and Missouri banks, 1920-30; national bank receiver, office of Comptroller of the Currency, Washington, DC, 1930-37; in 1937 selected to head St Louis Loan Agency of RFC; and Exec. VP and Director of Defense Plant Corp., a subsidiary; early in 1943 resigned all Federal posts to become Exec. VP First National Bank of St louis; Federal Loan Administrator, Washington, 30 April 1945; Dir of Office War Mobilization and Reconversion, July 1945-June 1946; Secretary of the Treasury, United States, 1946-53; US Governor of International Monetary Fund and International Bank for Reconstruction and Development, 1946-53. Delegate International Financial Conferences: Mexico City, 1945-52; Rio de Janeiro, 1957; London, 1947; Paris, 1950-52; Ottawa, 1951; Rome, 1951; Lisbon, 1952. Served as Captain, Field Artillery, 57th Bde, during War, 1917-18; retired Colonel US Army. 1955. Member: Omicron Delta Kappa; American Legion; Reserve Officers' Association. Trustee, Harry S. Truman Memorial Library. Episcopalian. *Address:* 8109 Kerry Lane, Chevy Chase, Maryland 20015, USA. *Clubs:* Missouri Athletic (St Louis); Chevy Chase, Alfalfa, National Press (Washington); Toledo (Toledo, Ohio).

**SOAME, Sir Charles Burnett Buckworth-Herne-,** 11th Bt *cr* 1697; JP; late King's Shropshire Light Infantry; *b* 23 Sept. 1894; *s* of 10th Bt and Mary, *d* of John Edge and *widow* of P. B. Pring; *S* father, 1931; *m* 1924, Elsie May, *d* of Walter Alfred Lloyd, Coalbrookdale, Salop; one *s* one *d*. Served European War, 1914-16 (wounded). *Heir: s* Charles John Buckworth-Herne-Soame, *b* 28 May 1932. *Address:* Sheen Cottage, Coalbrookdale, Shropshire.

**SOAMES, Rt. Hon. (Arthur) Christopher (John),** PC 1958; CBE 1955; Ambassador to France since 1968; *b* 12 Oct. 1920; *m* 1947, Mary, *d* of late Rt Hon. Sir Winston Churchill, KG, PC, OM, CH, FRS, and of Baroness Spencer-Churchill, *qv*; three *s* two *d*. *Educ:* Eton; Royal Military Coll., Sandhurst. 2nd Lieut, Coldstream Guards, 1939; Captain, 1942; served Middle East, Italy and France. Assistant Military Attaché British Embassy, Paris, 1946-47, MP (C) Bedford Division of Bedfordshire, 1950-66. Parliamentary Private Secretary to the Prime Minister, 1952-55; Parliamentary Under-Secretary of State, Air Ministry, Dec. 1955-Jan. 1957; Parliamentary and Financial Secretary, Admiralty, 1957-58; Secretary of State for War, Jan. 1958-July 1960; Minister of Agriculture, Fisheries and Food, 1960-64. Director: Decca Ltd, 1964-68; James Hole & Co. Ltd, 1964-68. Croix de Guerre (France), 1942. *Address:* British Embassy, Paris, France. *Clubs:* White's, Carlton, Portland.

**SOAMES, Rt. Hon. Christopher;** *see* Soames, Rt Hon. A. C. J.

**SOAR, Joseph,** MBE 1947; DL; MusD Cantuar, MusB Dunelm, ARCM, FRCO, Hon. ARCM; Organist and Master of the Choristers, St David's Cathedral, 1922-54, Emeritus 1954; *b* 9 Oct. 1878; *s* of late M. Soar, MIME, Housley Park, Sheffield; *m* 1st, 1909, Mary Dulcie (*d* 1927), *e d* of late Sir Edwin Thomas Ann, JP, Derby; 2nd, 1934, Janet (*d* 1951), *d* of late Rev. David Williams, Rector of Clydey, Pembs. *Educ:* privately; Royal College of Music (twice Council Exhibitioner); Temple Church (under Sir Walford Davies). Music Master, Barnsley Grammar Sch.; Conductor: Tankersley Choral Society, Barnsley Operatic Society, and St Cecilia Choral Soc., 1904-15; Organist: Parish Church, Chapeltown, Sheffield, 1892; St John's Clapham, 1898; Derby Cathedral, 1901; Parish Church, Barnsley, 1904; Halifax, 1912; Burnham-on-Sea, 1921. Served 1915-21, Gallipoli, Western Front of Egypt, India; Lieut IARO; Officer in Charge, Supply and Transport Depôt, Poona and Trimulgherry. Examiner and Member of Council, Royal College of Organists, 1933-46; President National Eisteddfod, Abergwaun, 1936; Hon. Sec., St David's Life-Boat, 1926- (Bronze Medal, RNLBI, 1943); Hon. Life Governor, RNLI, 1960. Commandant Special Constabulary, 1940-44; County Pres., British Legion, Pembrokeshire; DL, Pembrokeshire, 1952. *Publications:* church music, songs, pianoforte pieces. *Recreations:* Life-boat and British Legion. *Address:* Swn y Mor, St David's, Pembrokeshire. *T:* 277.

**SOBHA SINGH, Hon. Sardar Bahadur Sir Sardar,** Kt, *cr* 1944; OBE 1938; landlord, millowner and contractor; Member of the Council of State, Delhi; Chairman, Nerbudda Valley Refrigeration Products Co. Ltd, Bhopal; Chairman, Sterling General Insurance Co. Ltd, New Delhi; Director: Machinery Manufacturers Corp. Ltd, Bombay, and several other leading Indian firms; *b* 1890; *m* Shrimati Wariam Kaur; four *s* one *d*. Member Indian Overseas League. *Address:* Baikunth, New Delhi 11, India. *Clubs:* Delhi Gymkhana, Chelmsford (New Delhi); Cricket Club of India (Bombay).

**SODDY, Dr Kenneth;** Physician, Department of Psychological Medicine, University College Hospital, London, since 1948; Consultant: to UK Atomic Energy Authority, since 1964; to National Spastics Society, since 1965; Chairman, Institute of Religion and Medicine, since 1964; Member, St Lawrence's Hospital, Caterham, Management Committee, since 1962; Lecturer, University of London, since 1948; *b* 27 July 1911; *s* of Rev. T. E. Soddy, BA; *m* 1936, Emmeline, *d* of H. E. Johnson; one *s* two *d*. *Educ:* Taunton Sch.; University College, London; University College Hospital Medical School. MB, BS 1934; DPM 1937; MD 1938. Commonwealth Fund Fellowship in Child Guidance, 1938; Psychiatrist, London Child Guidance Clinic, 1939. Temp. Commn, RAMC, 1940; Specialist Psychiatrist (Major), 1941; Advisor in Psychiatry (Lieut-Colonel), AG's Dept, India Comd, 1943; Dep. Director, Selection of Personnel, India Comd, (Colonel), 1944; Hon. Lieut-Colonel, RAMC, 1946. Medical Director, National Assoc. for Mental Health, 1946; Psychiatrist, Tavistock Clinic, 1947; Psychiatrist, 1948, Med. Dir, 1953-58, Child Guidance Training Centre. Scientific Adviser, World Federation for Mental Health, 1961-64 (Hon. Secretary, 1948; Assistant Director, 1949; Scientific Director, 1958); Member, Expert Panel on Mental Health, World Health Organisation: 1949-; Consultant to WHO, 1950 and 1957; Member various Study Groups, etc; Member RMPA, etc; Hon. Mem. American Psychiatric Assoc., 1953. *Publications:* Clinical Child Psychiatry, 1960; (with R. F. Tredgold) Mental Retardation, 11th edn, 1970; (with Mary C. Kidson) Men in Middle Life, 1967; Editor: Mental Health and Infant Development, 2 vols, 1955; Identity; Mental Health and Value Systems, 1961; (with R. H. Ahrenfeldt) Mental Health in a Changing World, 1965; Mental Health and Contemporary Thought, 1967; Mental Health in the Service of the Community, 1967; many articles in British, American and internat. medical and sociological jls. *Recreations:* organ playing, chamber music, travel. *Address:* Bourne House, Heathfield, Sussex. *T:* Heathfield 3336; 58a Wimpole Street, W1M 7DE. *T:* 01-935 4687.

**SODOR AND MAN, Bishop of,** since 1966; **Rt. Rev. (George) Eric Gordon;** *b* 29 July 1905; *s* of George Gordon, Dulwich; *m* 1938, Elizabeth St Charaine (*d* 1970), *d* of Lt-Comdr A. J. Parkes, OBE, RN, Squeen, Ballaugh, Isle of Man; one *d*. *Educ:* St Olave's Sch., London; St Catharine's Coll., Cambridge (MA); Wycliffe Hall, Oxford. Deacon, Leicester, 1929; Priest, Peterborough for Leicester, 1930; Vice-Principal, Bishop Wilson Coll., Isle of Man, 1931, Principal, and Domestic Chaplain to Bishop of Sodor and Man, 1935; Rector of Kersal, and Examining Chaplain to Bishop of Manchester, 1942; Rector and Rural Dean of Middleton, Manchester, 1945; Proctor in Convocation, 1948; Provost of Chelmsford Cathedral and Rector of Chelmsford, 1951-66. *Recreation:* photography. *Address:* Bishop's Court, Kirk Michael, Isle of Man. *T:* Kirk Michael 222. *Club:* United University.

**SOKHEY, Maj.-Gen. Sir Sahib Singh,** Kt 1946; Member, Panel of Scientists, Indian Planning Commission, since 1956; Adviser, Council of Scientific and Industrial Research, New Delhi, since 1961; *b* 15 Dec. 1887; *s* of Sardar Jwala Singh Sokhey; *m* 1914, Leila Roy (Menaka, celebrated Indian danseuse), *d* of P. L. Roy of East Bengal. *Educ:* Punjab Univ. (BSc 1907); Edinburgh Univ. (MB, ChB 1911, MA 1912, MD 1925); Trinity Coll., Cambridge; Johns Hopkins Univ.; Harvard Medical Sch.; Toronto Univ. Joined Indian Medical Service, 1913. Served European War, 1914-19; France, Belgium, Mesopotamia and Egypt; Rockefeller Foundation Fellow, 1923-25. Director, Haffkine Institute, Bombay, 1932-49; Asst Director-General, WHO, 1950-52; Member, Indian Parliament (Rajya Sabha), 1952-56; President, Assoc. of Scientific Workers of India, 1953-58; Founder Fellow Nat. Inst. of Sciences of India and Indian Acad. of Sciences. International Lenin Peace Prize, 1953. *Publications:* scientific papers in various journals. *Address:* Haffkine Institute, Bombay, India.

**SOKOTO, HH The Sultan of; Sir Siddiq Abubakar III,** GCON; GBE 1953 (KBE 1946); CMG 1941; *g g s* of Shehu Othman Dan Fodio, religious reformer and founder of Sokoto Empire; Sultan of Sokoto, Northern Region of Nigeria since 1938; Minister without Portfolio in dissolved civilian Executive Council of the Northern Region of Nigeria. Received the accolade from the Queen during her Nigerian tour, Feb. 1956. Hon. LLD, Ahmadu Bello Univ. (Zaria), 1965. *Address:* Sokoto, Northern Region, Nigeria.

**SOLDATOV, Aleksandr Alekseyevich;** Ambassador of the USSR in Cuba, since 1968; *b* 1915; *m* Rufina B.; two *d*. *Educ:* Moscow Teachers' Training Inst. (grad. Hist. Sciences, 1939). Member Soviet Foreign Service, 1941; Senior Counsellor of Soviet Delegation to the UN and Representative on Trusteeship Council, 1948-53; Head of UN Div., 1953-54, of American Div., 1954-60, Soviet Foreign Ministry; Soviet Ambassador to the Court of St James's, 1960-66; Deputy Foreign Minister, 1966-68. Member Soviet Delegation to Geneva Conferences: on Germany, 1959; on Laos, 1961. *Address:* USSR Ministry of Foreign Affairs, Moscow.

**SOLER, Antonio R.;** *see* Ruiz Soler, A.

**SOLOMON,** CBE 1946; pianist; *b* London, 1902; *m* 1970, Gwendoline Byrne. First public appearance at Queen's Hall at age of eight, June 1910; frequent appearances till 1916 then studied in London and Paris; reappeared in London at Wigmore Hall, Oct. 1921, and has since toured in the British Isles, America, France, Germany, Holland, Italy, Australia, and New Zealand. *Recreations:* golf, bridge, motoring. *Address:* 16 Blenheim Road, NW8.

**SOLOMON, David Arnold,** MBE 1944; Chairman, Liverpool Regional Hospital Board, since 1968; *b* 13 Nov. 1907; *s* of Richard Solomon and Sarah Annie Solomon (*née* Simpson); *m* 1935, Marjorie Miles; two *s* one *d*. *Educ:* Leys Sch., Cambridge; Liverpool Univ. Qualified a Solicitor, 1933; became Mem. Liverpool Stock Exchange, 1935. Served War of 1939-45, RAF (MBE). Practised as a Stockbroker until retirement, March 1969. *Recreation:* music. *Address:* Short Nab, Storrs Park, Windermere, Westmorland. *T:* Windermere 3434. *Club:* Athenæum (Liverpool).

**SOLOMON, Edwin,** QPM 1967; DL; Chief Constable, West Midlands Constabulary, since 1967; *b* 20 Sept. 1914; *s* of Richard and Jane Solomon, Co. Durham; *m* 1942, Susan Clarke; two *s*. *Educ:* The Grammar Sch., Chester-le-Street. Joined Metropolitan Police as Constable, 1934; served through ranks to Supt; Dep. Chief Constable, Newcastle upon Tyne, 1956; Chief Constable, Walsall County Borough, 1964. DL Staffs, 1969. *Recreations:* walking, fishing, gardening. *Address:* 109 Broadway North, Walsall, Staffs. *T:* Walsall 26881.

**SOLOMONS, Professor David;** Professor of Accounting in the University of Pennsylvania (Wharton School of Finance and Commerce), USA, since 1959, Chairman of Accounting Department since 1969; *b* London, 11 Oct. 1912; *e s* of Louis Solomons and Hannah Solomons (*née* Isaacs); *m* 1945, Kate Miriam (*née* Goldschmidt); one *s* one *d*. *Educ:* Hackney Downs Sch., London, E8; London School of Economics. BCom (London) 1932; DSc (Econ.) (London), 1966. Chartered accountant, 1936; engaged in professional accountancy until Sept. 1939. Enlisted in ranks on outbreak of war; 2nd Lieut, RASC, 1941; Temp. Captain, 1942; Petrol Supply Officer, HQ 88 Area (Tobruk), 1942; prisoner-of-war in Italy and Germany, 1942-45. Served with Economic Div., CCG, 1945. Lectr in Accounting, LSE, 1946; Reader in Accounting, Univ. of London, 1949-55; Prof. of Accounting, University of Bristol, 1955-59. Visiting Assoc. Prof., University of California, 1954; Prof. at Institut pour l'Etude des Méthodes de Direction de l'Enterprise (IMEDE), Lausanne, 1963-64; Director of Research, Amer. Accountancy Assoc., 1968-70. *Publications:* Divisional Performance: Measurement and Control, 1965; ed and contrib. to Studies in Cost Analysis, 1968; articles in Economic Jl, Economica, Jl of Business, Accounting Review, Jl of Accountancy, etc. *Address:* 205 Elm Avenue, Swarthmore, Pa 19081, USA. *T:* 215-KI 4-8193.

**SOLOVEYTCHIK, George M. de,** MA (Oxon); author, journalist, and lecturer; *b* St Petersburg, Russia; *s* of late Michael A. de Soloveytchik, Chairman and Managing Director of the Siberian Bank of Commerce, and *g s* of Founder thereof; Resident in Great Britain since 1919 and naturalised British subject, 1934; unmarried. *Educ:* St Catharine's and The Reformation Schools, Petrograd; Queen's Coll., Oxford; Paris and Berlin Universities. Has travelled extensively all over Europe since tender age of one. Escaped from

Soviet Russia to England, 1918; began to write and lecture while still at Oxford; frequent freelance contributor to leading British and overseas newspapers and periodicals chiefly on international affairs, history and biography, Editor, Economic Review, 1926-27; Foreign Editor, Financial Times, 1938-39; business in City of London, 1925-36; Director of Publicity, Internat. Colonial Exhibition, Paris, 1931; Special adviser to exiled Belgian Govt in London, 1941-45; official lectr to HM Forces, 1940-45; delivered addresses to American Academy of Political and Social Science, and at Princeton, Yale, etc, 1944; numerous lecture tours in USA, Canada and Europe since 1946; special mission to Scandinavian countries on behalf of UNESCO, 1947; Visiting Lecturer, Graduate Inst. of International Studies, Geneva Univ., 1948-56, also at School of Economics, St Gallen. MJI, member RIIA, and American Academy of Political and Social Science; Hon. member International Mark Twain Society, USA. Légion d'Honneur; Kt Comdr 1st cl. with Star, Lion of Finland; Comdr Leopold II; Comdr, White Lion; 1st cl. Kt of the Vasa; 1st cl. Kt of St Olav; 1st cl. Kt of the Dannebrog; Officier Ordre de la Couronne, Officier, Order of Orange-Nassau, Officier, White Rose of Finland, etc. *Publications:* The Naked Year (Editor), New York, 1928; Ivar Kreuger–Financier, 1933; Potemkin–A Picture of Catherine's Russia, 1938; Ships of the Allies, 1942; Peace or Chaos, 1944; Russia in Perspective, 1946; Great Britain since the War (in Swedish), 1947; Switzerland in Perspective, 1954; Leu and Co.: Two Centuries of History in the Life of a Swiss Bank, 1955; Benelux, 1957; chapter on How Switzerland is really governed, in Swiss Panorama, 1963; chapters on Russia in Universal Encyclopædia. *Recreations:* travel, theatre, music, Russian ballet, riding; also studying human eccentricities and foibles. *Address:* 26a North Audley Street, W1. *T:* 01-629 6208. *Clubs:* Savage, Danish.

**SOLTI, Georg;** CBE (Hon.) 1968; Musical Director: Covent Garden Opera Company, since 1961; Chicago Symphony Orchestra, since 1968; Orchestre de Paris, from Jan. 1972; *b* Budapest, 21 Oct. 1912. *Educ:* High School of Music, Budapest. Studied with Kodály, Bartók, and Donhnányi. Conductor and pianist, State Opera, Budapest, 1930-39; conductor and pianist, Zürich Opera, 1939; first prize, as pianist, Concours Internationale, Geneva, 1942; Musical Director, Munich State Opera, 1946; Musical Director, Frankfurt Opera, and Permanent Conductor, Museums Concerts, Frankfurt, 1952-61. Guest Conductor: Berlin, Salzburg, Paris, London (first conducted London Philharmonic Orchestra, 1947; Covent Garden début, 1959), Glyndebourne Festival, Edinburgh Festival, San Francisco, New York, Los Angeles, Chicago, etc. Has made numerous recordings (many of which have received international awards or prizes). *Address:* Chalet Haut Pré, Villars-sur-Ollons, Vaud, Switzerland.

**SOLZHENITSYN, Alexander Isayevitch;** Soviet author; *b* 11 Dec. 1918; *m. Educ:* Univ. of Rostov (degree in Maths and Physics); Moscow Inst. of History, Philosophy and Literature (correspondence course). Joined Army, 1941; grad. from artillery school, 1942; in comd artillery battery and served at front until 1945 (wounded, twice decorated); sentenced to eight years' imprisonment, 1945, released, 1953; exile in Siberia, 1953-56; officially rehabilitated, 1957, since when teaching and writing in Ryazan. Member Union of Soviet Writers, 1962, expelled 1969. Member Amer. Acad. of Arts and Sciences, 1969. Awarded Nobel Prize for Literature, 1970. *Publications:* One Day in the Life of Ivan Denisovich, 1962; An Incident at Krechetovka Station and Matryona's House (publ. US as We Never Make Mistakes), 1963; For the Good of the Cause (US), 1964; The First Circle and Cancer Ward (US, UK etc.), 1968 (Prix du Meilleur Livre Etranger, Paris); The Easter Procession (short story), The Love Girl and the Innocent (play, UK), 1969; In the Interests of the Cause, 1970.

**SOMERFIELD, Stafford William;** editorial consultant, since 1970; *b* 9 Jan. 1911; *m* 1st, 1933, Gertrude Camfield (marr. diss. 1951); two *d*; 2nd, 1951, Elizabeth Montgomery. *Educ:* Ashleigh Road School, Barnstaple. Exeter Express and Echo, Bristol Evening World, Daily Telegraph, 1934-39; News Chronicle, 1939, until outbreak of War. Rifleman, Queen's Westminsters, 1939-40; Major, Gloucestershire Regt. 1945. News of the World: Features Editor, Asst Editor, Northern Editor, Dep. Editor; Editor, 1960-70. *Publication:* John George Haigh, 1950. *Recreation:* pedigree dogs. *Address:* Panfield, Denne Park, Horsham, Sussex. *T:* Horsham 61939. *Clubs:* Reform, Kennel, Press.

**SOMERLEYTON,** 3rd Baron *cr* 1916; **Savile William Francis Crossley;** Bt 1863; DL; farmer; *b* 17 Sept. 1928; *er s* of 2nd Baron Somerleyton, MC; *S* father, 1959; *m* 1963, Belinda Maris Loyd, *d* of Vivian Loyd and Mrs Gerald Critchley; three *d. Educ:* Eton Coll. Captain Coldstream Guards, 1948; retired, 1956. Royal Agricultural Coll., Cirencester, 1958-59; farming, 1959-. DL Suffolk, 1964. *Heir: b* Captain Hon. (Richard) Nicholas Crossley, 9th Queen's Royal Lancers [*b* 24 Dec. 1932; *m* 1958, Alexandra Anne Maitland, *o d* of Charles Donald Graham Welch; one *s* two *d*]. *Address:* Somerleyton Hall, Lowestoft, Suffolk. *T:* Blundeston 308. *Club:* Guards.

**SOMERS,** 8th Baron *cr* 1784; **John Patrick Somers Cocks;** Bt 1772; *b* 30 April 1907; *o s* of 7th Baron and Mary Benita (*d* 1950), *d* of late Major Luther M. Sabin, United States Army; *S* father, 1953; *m* 1st, 1935, Barbara Marianne (*d* 1959), *d* of Charles Henry Southall, Norwich; 2nd, 1961, Dora Helen, *d* of late John Mountfort. *Educ:* privately; Royal College of Music, London. 2nd Music Master, Westonbirt School, 1935-38; Director of Music, Epsom Coll., 1949-53; Prof. of Composition and Theory, RCM, 1967-. BMus, ARCM. *Publications:* Three Sketches for Oboe and Piano; (song) New Year's Eve; The Song of the Redeemed (for chorus and orchestra); Sonatina for Oboe and Piano, Four Psalms for two-part Choir; Organ Sonata. *Heir: cousin* Philip Sebastian Somers-Cocks, *b* 4 Jan. 1948. *Address:* 35 Links Road, Epsom, Surrey.

**SOMERS, Finola, Lady,** CBE 1950; *b* 1896; *d* of late Captain Bertram Meeking, 10th Hussars, and late Mrs Herbert Johnson; *m* 1921, 6th Baron Somers, KCMG, DSO, MC (*d* 1944); one *d. Educ:* home. Chief Commissioner, Girl Guides' Association, 1943-49. *Address:* Garden Cottage, Eastnor, Herefordshire. *T:* Ledbury 2305. *Club:* Guide.

**SOMERSET,** family name of **Duke of Beaufort** and of **Baron Raglan.**

**SOMERSET,** 18th Duke of *cr* 1546; **Percy Hamilton Seymour;** Bt 1611; DL; Major, Wilts Regt, retired; *b* 27 Sept. 1910; *e surv. s* of 17th Duke of Somerset, DSO, OBE, and Edith Mary (*d* 1962), *d* of W. Parker, JP, Whittington Hall, Derbyshire; *S* father, 1954; *m* 1951, Gwendoline Collette (Jane), 2nd *d* of late Major J. C. C. Thomas and Mrs Thomas; two *s* one *d*. *Educ:* Blundell's Sch., Tiverton; Clare Coll., Cambridge. BA 1933. DL Wiltshire, 1960. *Heir:* *s* Lord Seymour, *qv*. *Address:* Maiden Bradley, Warminster, Wilts. *Clubs:* MCC, Surrey CC, British Automobile Racing.

**SOMERSET, Sir Henry Beaufort,** Kt 1966; CBE 1961; Managing Director of Associated Pulp and Paper Mills Ltd, Burnie, Tasmania, since 1948; *b* 21 May 1906; *s* of Henry St John Somerset; *m* 1930, Patricia Agnes Strickland; two *d*. *Educ:* St Peter's Coll., Adelaide; Trinity Coll., University of Melbourne. With Associated Pulp and Paper Mills Ltd, 1937-. Chairman: Humes Ltd; Australian Titan Products Pty Ltd; Goliath Portland Cement Co. Ltd. Director: Electrolytic Zinc Co. of Australasia Ltd; ICI of Aust. & NZ Ltd. Chancellor, University of Tasmania, 1964-; Member Australasian Inst. of Mining and Metallurgy (President, 1958 and 1966); Member of Exec., CIRO, 1965-. MSc, FRACI. *Address:* 10 Cunningham Street, Burnie, Tasmania. *Clubs:* Melbourne, Australian (Melbourne); Tasmanian (Hobart).

**SOMERSET, Brigadier Hon. Nigel FitzRoy,** CBE 1945; DSO; MC; *b* Cefntilla Court, Usk, Monmouthshire, 27 July 1893; 3rd *s* of 3rd Baron Raglan, GBE, CB; *m* 1922, Phyllis Marion Offley Irwin, Western Australia; one *s* one *d*. *Educ:* King William's Coll., IOM; RMC Sandhurst. Served France with 1st Bn Gloucestershire Regt, 12 Aug. 1914 till wounded at the Battle of the Aisne, 15 Sept. 1914; 3 Dec. 1914, till wounded at Cuinchy, 12 May 1915; Mesopotamia, Oct. 1916-May 1919, comdg 14th Light Armoured Motor Battery (despatches thrice, DSO, MC); Bt Majority on promotion to Subst. Captain, 1918; Afghan War, 1919, with Armoured Motor Brigade (Medal and Clasp); ADC to Governor of South Australia, 1920-22; Assistant Military Secretary, Headquarters, Southern Command, India, 1926-30; Major 1933; Lieut-Colonel Comdg 2nd Bn The Gloucestershire Regt, 1938; served War of 1939-45 comdg 145 Inf. Bde (PoW 1940-45; despatches; CBE); Comdg Kent Sub District, 1946-47; Brig. Special Appt Germany, 1947-48; retired pay, 1949. *Address:* 18 St Anne's Crescent, Lewes, Sussex.

**SOMERVELL, Theodore Howard,** OBE 1953; MA, MB, BCh; FRCS; medical missionary, retired; *b* 16 April 1890; *s* of William Henry Somervell of Brantfield, Kendal; *m* 1925, Margaret, *d* of Sir James Hope Simpson; three *s*. *Educ:* Rugby; Caius Coll., Cambridge; University College Hospital. Captain, RAMC (TF), BEF in France, 1915-18 (despatches); Kaisar-i-Hind Gold Medal, 1938; joined Mount Everest Expedition in 1922 and again in 1924; Medical Missionary, Neyyoor, Travancore, under London Missionary Society, 1923-49 and at Vellore, 1949-61; retired, 1961. *Publications:* After Everest, 1936; Knife and Life in India, 1939; The Surgery of the Stomach and Duodenum, 1948; The Good News, 1950; articles on mountaineering and surgical subjects. *Recreations:* painting, music. *Address:* Sykefold, Ambleside, Westmorland. *T:* 3303. *Club:* Alpine.

**SOMERVILLE, David;** Assistant Under-Secretary of State, Department of Health and Social Security, since 1968; *b* 27 Feb. 1917; *e s* of late Rev. David Somerville and of Euphemia Somerville; *m* 1950, Patricia Amy Johnston; two *s* two *d*. *Educ:* George Watson's Coll.; Fettes Coll.; Edinburgh Univ.; Christ Church, Oxford. Served with Army, 1940-45; Major, Royal Artillery. Entered Civil Service as Asst Principal, Ministry of Health, 1946; Principal, 1948; Cabinet Office, 1953-55; Asst Secretary, Ministry of Health, 1956; Under-Secretary, 1963. *Recreations:* golf, tennis, gardening. *Address:* Wood End, 39 Lower Road, Fetcham, Leatherhead, Surrey. *T:* Leatherhead 4556. *Club:* Effingham Golf.

**SOMERVILLE, John Arthur Fownes,** CBE 1964; an Under-Secretary, Government Communications Headquarters, since 1969; *b* 5 Dec. 1917; *s* of late Admiral of the Fleet Sir James Fownes Somerville, GCB, GBE, DSO; *m* 1945, Julia Elizabeth Payne; one *s* two *d*. *Educ:* RNC Dartmouth. Midshipman 1936; Sub-Lieut 1938; Lieut 1940; Lieut-Comdr 1945; retd 1950. Govt Communications Headquarters, 1950-. *Recreation:* walking. *Address:* Hoefield House, The Leigh, Gloucester. *T:* Coombe Hill 281. *Club:* Army and Navy.

**SOMERVILLE, Mrs (Katherine) Lilian,** OBE 1958; FMA 1962; Director, Fine Arts Department, British Council, since 1948; *b* 7 Oct. 1905; *d* of Captain Arthur George Tillard and Emily Katherine Close-Brooks; *m* 1928, Horace Somerville (*d* 1959); one *d*. *Educ:* Abbot's Hill; Slade School of Art, London. Painted until war. Joined British Council, 1941. *Address:* The Studio, 16a Hill Road, NW8. *T:* 01-286 1087. *Club:* Institute of Contemporary Arts.

**SOMERVILLE, Mrs Lilian;** *see* Somerville, Mrs K. L.

**SOMERVILLE, Sir Robert,** KCVO 1961 (CVO 1953); MA; FSA; Clerk of the Council of the Duchy of Lancaster, 1952-70; *b* 5 June 1906; *s* of late Robert Somerville, FRSE, Dunfermline; *m* 1932, Marie-Louise Cornelia Bergené; one *d*. *Educ:* Fettes; St John's Coll., Cambridge (1st cl. Class. Tripos, 1929); Edinburgh Univ. Entered Duchy of Lancaster Office, 1930; Ministry of Shipping, 1940; Chief Clerk, Duchy of Lancaster, 1945; Secretary, Departmental Cttee on Salford Hundred Court, 1951; Member, Departmental Cttee on a Central Criminal Court in S Lancs, 1953; Hon. Research Asst, History of Medicine, UCL, 1935-38; Chairman: Council, British Records Association, 1957-67 (Hon. Secretary, 1947-56); London Record Society; Member Advisory Council on Public Records, 1959-64; Member Royal Commn on Historical MSS, 1966-; Corr. Member, Indian Historical Records Commn. Alexander Medallist, Royal Historical Society, 1940. *Publications:* History of the Duchy of Lancaster, 1953; The Savoy, 1960; Handlist of Record Publications, 1951; (joint editor) John of Gaunt's Register, 1937; contribs to Chambers's Encyclopædia, historical journals, etc. *Address:* 15 Foxes Dale, Blackheath, SE3.

**SOMERVILLE, Rt. Rev. Thomas David;** Coadjutor Bishop of the Diocese of New Westminster, since 1969; *b* 11 Nov. 1915; *s* of Thomas Alexander Somerville and Martha Stephenson Scott; unmarried. *Educ:* King George High Sch., Vancouver; Univ. of British Columbia (BA 1937); Anglican Theological Coll. of BC (LTh 1939, BD 1951). Deacon, 1939; priest, 1940; Incumbent of: Princeton, 1940-44; Sardis with Rosedale, 1944-49; Curate of St. James, Vancouver, 1949-52, Rector, 1952-60; Chapter Canon, Dio. of New Westminster, 1957; Dean of Residence, Anglican Theological Coll. of BC, 1960-65; Gen. Secretary, Gen. Bd of Religious Education, Anglican Church of Canada, 1965-66; Director of Planning and Research, Anglican Church of Canada, 1966-69. Hon. DD, Anglican Theol. Coll. of BC, 1969.

*Recreations:* music, botany. *Address:* 692 Burrard Street, Vancouver 1, BC, Canada. *T:* 684 6306.

**SOMERVILLE, Walter,** MD, FRCP; Physician to Department of Cardiology, Middlesex Hospital, since 1954; to Cardiac Surgical Unit, Harefield Hospital, since 1952; Lecturer in Cardiology, Middlesex Hospital Medical School, since 1954; Consultant in Cardiology to the Army, since 1963; Hon. Civil Consultant to Royal Air Force, Board of Trade (Civil Aviation), and Royal Hospital, Chelsea, since 1963, to Association of Retired Naval Officers, since 1960; to King Edward VII Convalescent Home for Officers, Osborne, since 1970; *b* 2 Oct. 1913; *s* of late Patrick and Catherine Somerville, Dublin; *m* 1957, Jane Platnauer; two *s* one *d*. *Educ:* Belvedere Coll., Dublin; University College, Dublin. House appts, Mater Hosp., Dublin, 1937; out-patients Assistant, Brompton Hosp. and Chelsea Chest Clinic, 1938-39; served in War 1939-45, Lt-Col RAMC 1944. Fellow in Med., Mass General Hosp., Boston, 1946; Registrar, British Postgraduate Med. School, Hammersmith, 1947; studied in Paris, Stockholm and Univ. of Michigan, 1948; Fellow in Medicine, Peter Bent Brigham Hosp. and Boston and Harvard Med. Sch., 1949; Med. Registrar, Nat. Heart Hosp. and Inst. of Cardiology, 1951; Sen. Med. Registrar, Middlesex Hosp., 1951-54. Asst Editor, British Heart Journal, 1960-; Editl Bd, Postgrad. Medical Journal, 1960-; Member: British Cardiac Soc.; Assoc. of Physicians of Great Britain and Ireland and other socs; Corr. Member: Colombian Soc. of Cardiology; Chilean Soc. of Cardiology. Officer, Legion of Merit, USA, 1945. *Publications:* (ed) Paul Wood's Diseases of the Heart and Circulation (3rd edn), 1968; various articles on cardiovascular subjects in British and American journals. *Address:* 149 Harley Street, W1. *T:* 01-935 4444; 30 York House, Upper Montagu Street, W1H 1FR. *T:* 01-262 2144.

**SOMES, Michael (George),** CBE 1959; Assistant Director, Royal Ballet, Covent Garden; *b* 28 Sept. 1917; British; *m* 1956, Deirdre Annette Dixon (*d* 1959); *m* 1964, Antoinette Sibley. *Educ:* Huish's Grammar Sch., Taunton, Somerset. Started dancing at Sadler's Wells, 1934; first important rôle in Horoscope, 1938. *Recreation:* music.

**SOMMER, André D.;** *see* Dupont-Sommer.

**SONDES,** 5th Earl *cr* 1880; **Henry George Herbert Milles-Lade;** Baron Sondes, 1760; Viscount Throwley, 1880; *b* 1 May 1940; *o s* of 4th Earl Sondes, and Pamela (*d* 1967), *d* of Col H. McDougall; *S* father, 1970; *m* 1968, Primrose Creswell (marr. diss. 1969), *d* of late Lawrence Stopford Llewellyn Cotter. *Address:* Lees Court, Faversham, Kent. *T:* 2615.

**SONDHEIMER, Professor Ernst Helmut,** MA, ScD; Professor of Mathematics, Westfield College, University of London, since 1960; *b* 8 Sept. 1923; *er s* of Max and Ida Sondheimer; *m* 1950, Janet Harrington Matthews, PhD; one *s* one *d*. *Educ:* University College School; Trinity Coll., Cambridge. Smith's Prize, 1947; Fellow of Trinity Coll., 1948-52; Research Fellow, H. H. Wills Physical Lab., University of Bristol, 1948-49; Research Associate, Massachusetts Inst. of Technology, 1949-50; Lecturer in Mathematics, Imperial College of Science and Technology, 1951-54; Reader in Applied Mathematics, Queen Mary Coll., Univ. of London, 1954-60. Vis. Research Asst Prof. of Physics, Univ. of Illinois, USA, 1958-59; Vis. Prof. of Theoretical Physics, University of Cologne, 1967. Member of Council, Queen Elizabeth Coll., London. *Publications:* papers on the electron theory of metals. *Recreations:* mountaineering, music, gardening, photography, bridge. *Address:* 51 Cholmeley Crescent, Highgate, N6. *T:* 01-340 6607. *Club:* Swiss Alpine.

*See also Prof. Franz Sondheimer.*

**SONDHEIMER, Prof. Franz,** FRS 1967; PhD (London), DIC; Royal Society Research Professor, University College, London, since 1967; *b* 17 May 1926; *yr s* of Max and Ida Sondheimer; *m* 1958, Betty Jane Moss; one step *d*. *Educ:* Highgate School; Imperial College of Science, London. Research Fellow, Harvard University, 1949-52; Associate Director of Research, Syntex SA, Mexico City, 1952-56; Vice-President, Research, 1961-63; Head of Organic Chemistry Department, Weizmann Institute of Science, Rehovoth, Israel, 1956-64; Rebecca and Israel Sieff Professor of Organic Chemistry, 1960-64; Royal Soc. Research Prof., Univ. of Cambridge, 1964-67; Fellow of Churchill Coll., Cambridge, 1964-67; Vis. Prof., Ohio State Univ., 1958; Lectures: Andrews, Univ. of New South Wales, 1962; Edward Clark Lee, Univ. of Chicago, 1962; Tilden, Chem. Soc., 1965; Pacific Coast, 1969. Israel Prize in the Exact Sciences, 1960; Corday-Morgan Medal and Prize, Chem. Soc., 1961; Adolf-von-Bayer Medal, German Chem. Soc., 1965. For. Mem., German Acad. of Sciences, Leopoldina, 1966. *Publications:* scientific papers in chemical jls. *Recreations:* classical music, travel. *Address:* Chemistry Dept, University College, 20 Gordon Street, WC1H 0AJ. *T:* 01-387 7050; 8 Kensington Palace Gardens, W8. *T:* 01-229 0041.

*See also Prof. E. H. Sondheimer.*

**SONI, Rai Bahadur Capt. Sir Seth Bhagchand,** Kt, *cr* 1944; OBE 1941; Proprietor, banking and industrial firm of Seth Joharmal Gumbhirmal, Ajmer. *Address:* Firm of Seth Joharmal Gumbhirmal, Ajmer, India.

**SONNEBORN, Prof. Tracy Morton;** Distinguished Professor of Zoology, Indiana University, Bloomington, Indiana, since 1953; *b* 19 Oct. 1905; *s* of Lee and Daisy (Bamberger) Sonneborn; *m* 1929, Ruth Meyers; two *s*. *Educ:* Johns Hopkins Univ., Baltimore. Johns Hopkins University: Fellow, Nat. Research Coun., USA, 1928-30; Research Asst, 1930-31; Research Associate, 1931-33; Associate in Zoology, 1933-39; Indiana University: Associate Prof. in Zoology, 1939-42; Professor of Zoology, 1942-53; Actg Chm., Div. of Biological Sciences, 1963-64. Foreign Mem., Royal Soc., London, 1964. Hon. Mem., French Soc. of Protozoology, 1965. Hon. DSc, Johns Hopkins Univ., 1957. Cleveland Research Prize, Amer. Assoc. for Advancement of Science, 1946; Kimber Genetics Award, Nat. Acad. of Sciences, USA, 1959; Mendel Medal, Czechoslovak Acad. of Sciences, 1965. *Publications:* The Control of Human Heredity and Evolution, 1964; numerous chapters in books and articles in scientific jls on genetics, cell biology, micro-organisms. *Address:* 1305 Maxwell Lane, Bloomington, Indiana 47401, USA. *T:* Area 812-336-5796.

**SONTAG, Raymond James;** Ehrman Professor of History, University of California, since 1941; *b* 2 Oct. 1897; *s* of Anthony Charles Sontag and Mary Walsh; *m* 1927, Dorothea Agar (*d* 1965); three *s* one *d*. *Educ:* Univ. of Illinois; Univ. of Pennsylvania. BS 1920, MA 1921, Illinois; PhD Pennsylvania, 1924. Instructor to H. C. Lea Professor, and Chm., Dept of History, Princeton University, 1939-41; Chief, German War Documents Project, Department of State, US, 1946-49; Pres.,

American Catholic Historical Assoc., 1952; Pres., Pacific Coast Branch, Amer. Hist. Assoc., 1959. LittD Marquette, USA, 1959; LLD: Notre Dame, USA, 1960; California, 1966. *Publications:* The Middle Ages (with Dana C. Munro), 1928; European Diplomatic History, 1932; Germany and England, 1848-1894, 1938; (ed. with J. S. Beddie) Nazi-Soviet Relations, 1939-41, 1948; Documents on German Foreign Policy, 1918-45 (American editor-in-chief), 1949. *Address:* University of California, Berkeley, Calif 94720, USA.

**SOOTHILL, Ronald Gray;** President, Turner and Newall Ltd since 1967 (Chairman 1959-67); *b* 19 Aug. 1898; *o s* of late Rev. Alfred Soothill, BA, Headmaster of Ashville College, Harrogate, and late H. E. Soothill (*née* Gray); *m* 1926, Thelma, *e d* of late Edwin James Bird. *Educ:* Ashville College, Harrogate; Mill Hill; Jesus Coll., Cambridge (MA). Officer in Royal Artillery, 1917-18. Cadbury Bros Ltd, 1922-28; Turner and Newall Ltd since 1928: Dir, 1942-69; Jt Man. Dir, 1949; Dep. Chm., 1958. Director: District Bank Ltd, 1959-69; Royal Insurance Co. Ltd; Liverpool & London & Globe Insurance Co. Ltd; London & Lancashire Insurance Co. Ltd; Tube Investments Ltd, 1963-68; William Mallinson and Sons Ltd, 1957-70. Mem., Cttee of Inquiry into Shipping, 1967-70; Mem. Ct, Manchester Univ.; Chm. of Governors, Ashville Coll., Harrogate. *Address:* The Manor, Maids Moreton, Buckingham. *T:* Buckingham 2014. *Clubs:* Bath, United University.

**SOPER,** family name of **Baron Soper.**

**SOPER,** Baron, *cr* 1965 (Life Peer); **Rev. Donald Oliver Soper,** MA Cantab; PhD (London); Methodist Minister; President of the Methodist Conference, 1953, Superintendent West London Mission, Kingsway Hall, since 1936; *b* 31 Jan. 1903; *s* of late Ernest and Caroline Soper; *m* 1929, Marie Dean, *d* of late Arthur Dean, Norbury; four *d. Educ:* Aske's School, Hatcham; St Catharine's College, Cambridge University; Wesley House, Cambridge; London School of Economics, London University. Hon. Fellow, St Catharine's Coll., Cambridge, 1966. Minister, South London Mission, 1926-29; Central London Mission, 1929-36. President, League against Cruel Sports. *Publications:* Christianity and its Critics; Popular Fallacies about the Christian Faith; Will Christianity Work?; Practical Christianity To-day; Questions and Answers in Ceylon; All His Grace (Methodist Lent Book for 1957); It is hard to work for God; The Advocacy of the Gospel; Tower Hill 12.30; Aflame with Faith. *Recreations:* music and most games. *Address:* Kingsway Hall, WC2B 6TA.

**SOPER, Dr Frederick George,** CBE 1950; FRSNZ 1949; FRIC 1936; Hon. FNZIC 1965; PhD 1924; DSc (Wales) 1928; Vice-Chancellor, University of Otago, Dunedin, NZ, 1953-63, retired; Emeritus Professor since 1964; Professor of Chemistry, University of Otago, 1936-53; *b* 5 April 1898; *s* of late A. G. Soper, Hockwold, Norfolk; *m* 1st, 1921, Frances Mary Gwendolen, *d* of late Fryer Richardson, Swineshead, Lincs; one *s* one *d*; 2nd, 1938, Eileen Louise, *d* of late E. C. Service, Invercargill, NZ. *Educ:* St Asaph Grammar Sch.; University College of North Wales, 1920; Lecturer, 1921-36. Director NZ Woollen Mills Research Assoc., 1937-50; Pres. NZ Institute of Chemistry, 1947; Member of Council of Univ. of Otago, 1944-51, 1953-63; Dean of Faculty of Science, 1948-50; Member of Senate, Univ. of NZ, 1946-61. Served RA, 1916-19, and TA. Dep. Dir of Scientific Development (Chemical), DSIR (NZ), 1942-45; Member: Defence Science Advisory Cttee (NZ), 1942-53; NZ Science Deleg. to Roy. Soc. Empire Science Conf., London, 1946; Leader NZ Deleg. to Unesco Conf., Paris, 1951. Mem. NZ Med. Research Council, 1960-65; Vice-Pres., Roy. Soc. of NZ, 1962-63; Chm., NZ Nuffield Advisory Cttee, 1959-; Pres. Dunedin Public Art Gallery Coun., 1963-66; Mem. Exec., NZ Wool Research Organisation, 1964- (Vice-Chm., 1966-); Mem. Exec., Wool Industries Research Inst., 1957-68; Mem. Univ. Grants Research Cttee, 1965-. Hon. DSc Otago, 1967. *Publications:* a number of papers in Journal of Chemical Society, mainly on mechanism of chemical reactions. *Recreations:* walking and gardening. *Address:* 6 Howard Street, Macandrew Bay, Dunedin, NZ. *T:* 75.461. *Club:* Fernhill (Dunedin).

**SOPER, Dr J. Dewey;** naturalist, explorer; Canadian Wildlife Service, Department of Indian Affairs and Northern Development, Ottawa, retired Nov. 1952; *b* Guelph, Ont, 5 May 1893; *m* 1927, C. K. Freeman, Wetaskiwin, Alberta; one *s* one *d. Educ:* Alberta Coll. and Univ. of Alberta, Edmonton. Studied music 6 yrs; then took up science, specialising in ornithology and mammalogy, especially the latter; naturalist to the Canadian Arctic Expedition of 1923, visiting Greenland, Ellesmere, North Devon and Baffin Islands; engaged in biological research and exploration on Baffin Island for the Canadian Government, 1924-26; engaged in biological research, exploration and mapping of Foxe Land, Baffin Island, for Dept of the Interior, Canada, 1928-29, resulting among other things in the discovery of the mysterious breeding grounds of the Blue Goose, and for Dept of Interior, Lake Harbour region, Baffin Island, 1930-31, and Wood Buffalo Park, Alta, and NWT 1932-34, then transferred as Chief Federal Migratory Bird Officer for the Prairie Provinces. Hon. LLD Univ. Alberta, 1960. *Publications:* The Weasels of Canada; Bird Life in the Alberta Wilds; Mammalian and Avian Fauna of Islay, Alberta; Mammals of Wellington and Waterloo Counties, Ontario; Birds of Wellington and Waterloo Counties, Ontario; Mammals of the Ridout Region, Northern Ontario; A Biological Reconnaissance of Nipissing and Timiskaming Districts, Northern Ontario; A Faunal Investigation of Southern Baffin Island; Discovery of the Breeding Grounds of the Blue Goose; The Blue Goose; Solitudes of the Arctic; Intimate Glimpses of Eskimo Life in Baffin Island; The Lake Harbour Region, Baffin Island; Notes on the Beavers of Wood Buffalo Park; Local Distribution of Eastern Canadian Arctic Birds; History, Range and Home Life of the Northern Bison; Mammals of Wood Buffalo Park; Birds of Wood Buffalo Park and Vicinity; Life History of the Blue Goose; The Mammals of Southern Baffin Island, NWT; Ornithological Results of the Baffin Island Expeditions of 1928-29 and 1930-31, together with more Recent Records; Mammals of the Northern Great Plains along the International Boundary in Canada; Observations on Mammals and Birds in the Rocky Mountains of Alberta; Field Data on the Mammals of Southern Saskatchewan; The Mammals of Manitoba; The Mammals of Alberta; The Mammals of Jasper National Park, Alberta, etc. *Recreations:* biological research, woodworking, water-colour painting, reading, and writing. *Address:* 7115 81st Street, Edmonton 82, Alberta, Canada.

**SOPOUSHEK, Mrs Jan;** *see* Greig, Maysie.

**SOPWITH, Sir Charles (Ronald),** Kt 1966; Solicitor of Inland Revenue, 1963-70; *b* 12 Nov. 1905; *s* of Alfred Sopwith, S Shields, Co.

Durham; *m* 1946, Ivy Violet (*d* 1968), *d* of Frederick Leonard Yeates, Gidea Park, Essex. *Educ:* S Shields High School. Chartered Accountant, 1928; Solicitor, 1938. Assistant Director, Press Censorship, 1943-45; Assistant Solicitor, 1952-56, Principal Asst Solicitor, 1956-61, Board of Inland Revenue; Public Trustee, 1961-63. *Recreations:* music, reading history; golf. *Address:* Somerset House, WC2. *Club:* Reform.

**SOPWITH, Sir Thomas Octave Murdoch,** Kt 1953; CBE 1918; President Hawker Siddeley Group Ltd (Chairman, 1935-63); *s* of Thomas Sopwith, MICE; *b* 1888; *m* 1st, 1914, Hon. Beatrix Mary Leslie Hore-Ruthven (*d* 1930), *d* of 8th Baron Ruthven; no *c*; 2nd, 1932, Phyllis Brodie, 2nd *d* of late F. P. A. Gordon; one *s*. Founded the Sopwith Aviation Co. Ltd, Kingston-on-Thames, 1912; Chairman, 1925-27, Society of British Aircraft Constructors. *Recreations:* yachting, shooting, fishing. *Address:* Compton Manor, Kings Somborne, Hampshire. *Clubs:* Carlton; Royal Yacht Squadron.

**SOREF, Harold Benjamin;** MP (C) Ormskirk Division of Lancashire since 1970; Managing Director, Soref Bros Ltd; *b* 18 Dec. 1916; *o s* of late Paul and Zelma Soref, Hampstead. *Educ:* St Paul's Sch.; Queen's Coll., Oxford. Served with Royal Scots and Intell. Corps, 1940-45. Contested (C): Dudley, 1951; Rugby, 1955. Delegate, first all-British Africa Conf. held Bulawayo, 1938, to form Africa Defence Fedn; Member: Exec. Cttee, Monday Club (Chm. Africa Group); Council: Anglo-Jewish Assoc.; Anglo-Rhodesian Soc.; Anglo-Zanzibar Soc.; Founder Mem., Conservative Commonwealth Council. *Publications:* (jtly) The War of 1939, 1940; (with Ian Greig) The Puppeteers, 1965; numerous articles in press and periodicals. *Recreations:* research, reading, writing. *Address:* 125 Beaufort Mansions, Chelsea, SW3. *T:* 01-352 6461; 35/37 Chiswell Street, EC1. *T:* 01-606 3781. *Clubs:* Carlton, Reform, PEN, 1900; Royal Scots (Edinburgh).

**SOREL CAMERON, Brig. John,** CBE 1957; DSO 1943; retired as Chief of Staff, Headquarters Scottish Command (Oct. 1958-60); ADC to the Queen, 1957-60; *b* 19 July 1907; *er s* of late Lt-Col G. C. M. Sorel Cameron, CBE and Mrs Sorel Cameron, Gorthleck, Inverness-shire; *m* 1937, Catherine Nancy, *yr d* of late Frank Lee, JP, Halifax, Yorks; one *d*. *Educ:* Wellington; RMC Sandhurst. Gazetted 2nd Lieut Queen's Own Cameron Highlanders, 1927; regimental service, 1927-40; Staff Coll., 1940; Staff, 1940-42; comd: 5/7th Gordons, 1942; 5th Camerons, 1943; Staff, 1944-50; comd: 1st Camerons, 1951-53; 154 Highland Bde, 1953-55; Chief of Staff, British Commonwealth Forces in Korea, 1955-56; BGS, HQ Scottish Comd, 1957. Served War of 1939-45 in Middle East, India, Sicily, NW Europe (wounded thrice, despatches twice). *Recreations:* field sports, history. *Address:* 47 Drummond Road, Inverness, Scotland. *T:* Inverness 30029. *Club:* United Service.

**SORENSEN,** family name of **Baron Sorensen.**

**SORENSEN,** Baron, *cr* 1964 (Life Peer); **Reginald William Sorensen;** a Lord in Waiting, 1965-68; *b* Islington, 19 June 1891; *s* of William James Sorensen, silversmith (*s* of a Dane), and Alice (*née* Tester), *d* of Sussex fisherman; *m* 1916, Muriel, JP, *d* of Rev. W. Harvey Smith; one *s* one *d* (and one *s* decd). *Educ:* Elementary Sch.; later studied for four years in a religious community. Employed in factory, office, and shop; Ex-Minister Free Christian Church, Walthamstow; experimented with Essex farming community; Vice-Pres. Leyton Labour Party; Ex-Member, Walthamstow UDC and Essex CC; Ex-Chm., Walthamstow Educn Cttee; Labour candidate for Southampton, 1923 and 1924; MP (Lab) West Leyton, 1929-31; contested (Lab) Lowestoft By-Election, 1934; MP (Lab) West Leyton, 1935-50, Leyton, 1950-64. Chairman: India League; World Congress of Faiths; STRIVE. Vice-Pres., Indo-British Forum; President: Indo-British Parly Gp; International Friendship League; Josephine Butler Soc.; Treasurer, "Help the Aged"; Mem., Parly Deputation to India, Jan. 1946; toured USA and Canada, 1948, 1952, 1957, USA 1969, Nigeria, 1949 and 1960, Far East, 1954; with Commonwealth Parly Assoc.; Deputation, the Yemen, 1958; Inter-Parly Union Delegn to Venezuela, 1960; visited West Indies and Ghana, 1960, India and Malaysia, 1961, India, 1963, Israel and Jordan, 1966. Freeman of Borough of Leyton, 1958. Grand Cross of the Order of Merit of the Federal German Republic, 1963. *Publications:* God and Bread; Men or Sheep; The New Generation; Tolpuddle; India and The Atlantic Charter; For Sanity and Humanity; My Impressions of India; Earthquake, Wind and Fire; The Liberty of the Subject; Aden, the Protectorates and the Yemen, I Believe in Man, etc. *Address:* 38 Woodside Park Avenue, Whipps Cross, Walthamstow. *T:* 01-520 5324.

**SORINJ, Dr L. T.;** *see* Tončić-Sorinj.

**SORLEY, Air Marshal Sir Ralph Squire,** KCB, *cr* 1944 (CB 1942); OBE 1936; DSC 1918; DFC 1920; FRAeS; FRSA; *b* 9 Jan. 1898; *s* of late James Graham and Ellen Merson Sorley; *m* 1925, Mary Eileen Gayford; two *d*. *Educ:* University School, Hastings. Joined RNAS 1914 and served in RAF in Great Britain; No. 6 Squadron, Iraq; No. 14 Squadron, Palestine; No. 8 Squadron, Aden. Later considerably devoted to the development of aircraft. Assistant Chief of Air Staff (Technical Requirements), 1941; Controller of Research and Development, Ministry of Aircraft Production, 1943-45; Member of Air Council; Member of Aircraft Supply Council; AOC-in-C Technical Training Command, 1945-48; retd from RAF, 1948. Man. Dir, De Havilland Propellors Ltd, Hatfield, 1948-60. *Address:* Littlecott Mill, Enford, Wilts. *Club:* Royal Air Force.

**SORN, Hon. Lord; James Gordon McIntyre,** MC; Senator of College of Justice in Scotland, 1944-63, retd; *b* 21 July 1896; *s* of late T. W. McIntyre, of Sorn; *m* 1923, Madeline (*d* 1954), *d* of late Robert Scott Moncrieff, Downhill; one *s* one *d*. *Educ:* Winchester; Balliol Coll., Oxford (BA); Glasgow Univ. (LLB). Served European War, 1914-18, Ayrshire Yeomanry, Captain 1917 (MC and bar, French Croix de Guerre); called Scottish Bar, 1922; KC 1936; Dean of the Faculty of Advocates, 1939-44. Hon. LLD Glasgow University. *Recreations:* fishing, golf. *Address:* Sorn Castle, Ayrshire; 24 Moray Place, Edinburgh. *Clubs:* Caledonian; New (Edinburgh).

**SOROKOS, Lt-Gen. John A.,** Greek Gold Medal for Gallantry (3 times); Greek Military Cross (twice); Medal for Distinguished Services (3 times); Silver and Gold Cross (with swords) of Order of George I; Comdr, Order of George I and Order of Phoenix; Military Medal of Merit (1st Class); Ambassador of Greece to the Court of St James's since Nov. 1969; *b* 1917; *s* of A. and P. Sorokos; *m* 1954, Pia Madaros; one *s*. *Educ:* Mil. Acad. of Greece; Staff and Nat. Defence Colls, Greece; British Staff Coll., Camberley; US Mil. Schools. Company Comdr: in Second World War in Greece, 1940-

41; in El Alamein Campaign, N Africa, 1942-43; Div. Staff Officer and Bn Comdr, 1947-49; served as Staff Officer: in Mil. Units in Army HQ and Armed Forces HQ, 1952-63; in NATO Allied Forces Southern Europe, 1957-59; Instructor, Nat. Defence Coll., Greece, 1963-64; Regt Comdr, 1965; Mil. Attaché to Greek Embassies in Washington and Ottawa, 1966-68; Div. Comdr, 1968-69; Dep. Comdr, Greek Armed Forces, 1969. Officer, Legion of Merit (US). *Recreations:* horses, boating, fishing. *Address:* 51 Upper Brook Street, W1. *T:* 01-629 0694; Mimnermou 2, Athens 138, Greece.

**SORRELL, Alan,** RWS 1941; ARCA 1927; Chichester Diocesan Artist Craftsman, 1952; painter and designer; *b* 11 Feb. 1904; *s* of Ernest and Edith Sorrell; *m* 1947, Elizabeth Tanner; two *s* one *d*. *Educ:* Royal Coll. of Art; British School at Rome. Rome Scholarship in Painting, 1928; Senior Assistant Instructor of Drawing, RCA, 1931-39 and 1946-48. Served War in RAF, 1939-46. Works in permanent collections: Tate Gall., Imp. War Mus., Nat. Mus. of Wales, London Mus.; Manchester, Sheffield, Liverpool, Bradford, Ashmolean Mus., Magdalen College, Oxford, Southend, etc, and in many private collections. Exhibitor Royal Academy, Royal Watercolour Society; numerous one-man shows; mural decorations at Liverpool, Southend-on-Sea, Harlow (New Town), Bexhill, Cecil Rhodes Memorial Museum, Bishops Stortford (The Oxford Room), Warwick Oken Secondary Modern School (The Seasons), Roman House, London (Londinium Romanum), and for Festival of Britain. Progress Paintings of Hinkley Point Atomic Power Station. Drawings of Nubia, 1962; Drawings of Oxford, 1964. An authority on Roman Britain, and responsible for numerous important archæological reconstructions for Ministry of Works, many Museums, and various publications. Drawings extensively used in TV programmes. *Publications:* (with Aileen Fox) Roman Britain, 1961; (with J. R. C. Hamilton) Saxon England, 1964; Living History, 1965; (with Henry Loyn) Norman Britain, 1966; (with E. B. Green) Prehistoric Britain, 1967; Roman London, 1968; (with Margaret S. Drower) Nubia: a drowning land, 1970; (with Anthony Birley) Imperial Rome, 1970; illustrations to the Bible, 1970; various essays on drawing, painting and travel. *Recreations:* reading and writing. *Address:* Thors Mead, 185 Daws Heath Road, Thundersley, Benfleet, Essex SS7 2TF. *T:* Southend-on-Sea 557431.

**SORSBIE, Sir Malin,** Kt 1965; CBE 1956 (OBE 1942); Chairman, The Munitalp Foundation; *b* 25 May 1906; *s* of late Rev. William Frances Sorsbie and late Blanche Georgina Sorsbie; *m* 1955, Constantine Eugenie, *d* of late Albert Wheeler Johnston, Greenwich, Connecticut, USA; one step *d*. *Educ:* Brighton College; Manitoba University. Royal Canadian Mounted Police, 1926-29; RAF, 1930-35; Imperial Airways, 1936-39; BOAC, 1940-47; East African Airways (Gen. Manager), 1947-56. Life Fellow, RGS. OStJ. *Recreations:* yachting, big game photography. *Address:* PO Box 5337, Nairobi, Kenya. *T:* 65331 and 65367. *Clubs:* Bath, Royal Aero, Royal Air Force; RAF Yacht, Royal Southern (Hamble); Muthaiga Country, Nairobi (Nairobi).

**SORSBY, Arnold,** CBE 1966; MD, FRCS; Consultant Adviser, Ministry of Health, 1966-71; Editor, Journal of Medical Genetics, 1964-69; Research Professor in Ophthalmology, Royal College of Surgeons and Royal Eye Hospital, 1943-66; Emeritus Professor, 1966; Hon. Director, Wernher Research Unit on Ophthalmological Genetics, Medical Research Council, 1953-66; Vice-President, Internat. Organization against Trachoma, 1951-68; Member, Expert Advisory Panel on Trachoma, WHO, 1953-68; *b* 10 June 1900. *Educ:* Leeds Univ. Sir Arthur Keith Medal (RCS), 1966; Grimshaw Award (Nat. Fedn of the Blind), 1968. *Publications:* books and papers on ophthalmology, genetics and on medical history. *Address:* 19 Parham Court, Grand Avenue, Worthing, Sussex. *T:* Worthing 40607.

**SOSKICE,** family name of **Baron Stow Hill.**

**SOTERIADES, Antis Georghios;** Ambassador of Cyprus to Egypt, since 1966, concurrently accredited to Syrian Arab Republic and Lebanon, since 1967; *b* 10 Sept. 1924; *m* 1962, Mona, *yr d* of Petros Petrides, Nicosia; one *s* one *d*. *Educ:* London Univ.; Inns of Court, London. Practising lawyer until 1956; joined patriotic Organization EOKA and fought British Colonialism in Cyprus, 1956-59; President of the first political party formed in Cyprus after independence, 1959; High Commissioner for Cyprus in the UK, 1960-66. Kt Order of St Gregory the Great (Vatican), 1963. *Address:* 16 Cleopatra Road, Heliopolis, Cairo, Egypt.

**SOTHERS, Donald Bevan,** CIE 1944; Chief Conservator Forests, Bombay (retired); *b* 11 March 1889; *s* of George Henry Sothers; *m* 1922, Dorothy, *d* of A. G. Edie, CIE; one *s* one *d*. *Educ:* Reading School; St John's College, Oxford. Joined Indian Forest Service, 1911; War Service, 1915-18, IARO attached 114th Mahrattas, Mesopotamia; Conservator Forests, 1932; Chief Conservator, 1942; re-employed as Land Development Officer, Bombay, 1944-46. *Recreations:* shooting, golf. *Address:* Leyfield, The Chase, Reigate.

**SOUKOP, Wilhelm Josef,** RA 1969 (ARA 1963); RBA 1950; FRBS 1956; teacher of sculpture at Chelsea School of Art since 1947; Master of Sculpture, Royal Academy Schools, since 1969; freelance sculptor; *b* 5 Jan. 1907; *s* of Karl Soukop and Anna Soukop (*née* Vogel); *m* 1945, Simone (*née* Moser), Paris; one *s* one *d*. *Educ:* Vienna State School; apprenticed to an engraver; Academy of Fine Art, Vienna. Arrived in England, Dartington Hall, 1934; taught at Dartington Hall, Bryanston and Blundell's Schools, 1935-45; moved to London, 1945, and taught at Bromley Sch. of Art, 1945-46, Guildford Sch. of Art, 1945-47. Examr for Scotland, 1959-62. Sculptures for new schools in Herts, Leics, Derbs, Staffs, LCC. Work for housing estates. Sculptures in museums: USA; Cordova Mus., Boston; Chantry Bequest; Tate Gallery; Cheltenham Mus. and Gall.; Collection of LCC Educn Cttee. Work in many private collections England, America, Canada, Europe. Archibald McIndoe Award, 1964. *Recreation:* gardening. *Address:* 26 Greville Road, NW6. *T:* 01-624 5987.

**SOULBURY,** 1st Viscount, *cr* 1954, 1st Baron, *cr* 1941, of Soulbury; **Herwald Ramsbotham;** PC 1939; GCMG, *cr* 1949; GCVO, *cr* 1954; OBE 1919; MC; *b* 6 March 1887; *s* of late Herwald Ramsbotham, JP, 47 Hyde Park Gate, SW7, and late Ethel Margaret, *d* of T. Bevan, DL, JP, Stone Park, Greenhithe, Kent; *g s* of James Ramsbotham, JP, Crowborough Warren, Sussex (formerly of Old Hall, Stand, Lancs), and Jane, *d* of Joshua Fielden, Waterside, Todmorden; *m* 1st, 1911, Doris Violet (*d* 1954), *d* of late S. de Stein, London, W8; two *s* one *d*; 2nd, 1962, Mrs Ursula Wakeham (*d* 1964), London, W1, *widow* of Frederick Wakeham and *d* of late Armand and Helen Jerome. *Educ:* Uppingham; University Coll., Oxford (MA). Double First in Honours

School, Oxford (First Class Hon. Mods, First Class Lit. Hum.); called to Bar, 1911; served European War, 1914-18 (OBE, MC, despatches thrice); contested Lancaster Div., Dec. 1910, and by-election, 1928; MP (C) Lancaster Div., 1929-41; Parly Sec., Bd of Educn, 1931-35; Parly Sec., Min. of Agr. and Fisheries, 1935-36; Minister of Pensions, 1936-39; First Comr of Works, 1939-40; Pres., Bd of Educn, 1940-41; Chm. of Assistance Bd, 1941-48; of the Burnham Cttees, 1942-49; Governor-Gen., Ceylon, 1949-54; Chm. of Ceylon Commn, 1944; Pres. Classical Assoc. 1948. Chm., Bd of Govs of Royal Ballet School, 1956-64. Hon. LLD University of Ceylon; Hon. Fellow, University College, Oxford. KStJ. *Recreation:* fishing. *Heir:* *s* Hon. James Herwald Ramsbotham [*b* 21 March 1915; *m* 1949, Anthea Margaret Wilton (*d* 1950)]. *Address:* East Lane, Ovington, near Alresford, Hampshire. *T:* Alresford 115. *Club:* Carlton.

*See also Hon. P. E. Ramsbotham.*

**SOUROZH, Metropolitan of;** *see* Anthony, Archbishop.

**SOUSTELLE, Jacques;** Officier, Légion d'Honneur, 1955; *b* 3 Feb. 1912. *Educ:* Ecole Normale supérieure, Paris; Univ. of Lyon. Agrégé de l'Université 1932, PhD 1937. Asst Dir, Musée de l'Homme, 1937; Nat. Comr for Information in London, 1942; Head of French special services, Algiers, 1943-44; Governor of Bordeaux, 1945; Minister of Information and Colonies, 1945-46. Prof. of Sociology, Ecole des Hautes Etudes, 1951. Mem. Nat. Assembly, 1945-46, 1951-59. Gov.-Gen. of Algeria, 1955-56; Minister of Information, 1958; Minister delegate to the Prime Minister, France, 1959-60. FRAI. Order of Polonia Restituta, 1944; US Medal of Freedom, 1945; Hon. CBE, Great Britain, 1946. *Publications:* Mexique, terre indienne, 1935; Envers et contre tout, 1947; La Vie quotidienne des Aztèques, 1955 (Daily Life of the Aztecs, 1962); Aimée et souffrante Algérie, 1956; L'espérance tramie, 1962; Sur une route nouvelle, 1964; L'Art du Mexique ancien, 1966 (Arts of Ancient Mexico, 1967); Archæologia Mundi: Mexique, 1967 (Archæologia Mundi: Mexico, 1967, repr. as The Ancient Civilizations of Mexico, 1969); Les quatre soleils, 1967; La longue marche d'Israël, 1968 (The Long March of Israel, 1969); Vingt-huit ans de Gaullisme, 1968; Les Aztèques, 1970; papers and memoirs on anthropology and ethnology, in learned jls. *Address:* c/o 85 Avenue Henri-Martin, Paris 16E.

**SOUTH-WEST TANGANYIKA, Bishop of,** since 1962; Rt. Rev. John Richard Worthington Poole Hughes; *b* 8 Aug. 1916; *s* of late Canon W. W. Poole Hughes, Warden of Llandovery College and late Bertha Cecil (*née* Rhys). *Educ:* Uppingham School; Hertford College, Oxford; Wells Theological College. BA (Lit. Hum.) 1939, MA 1945. Royal Artillery, 1939-45. Deacon, 1947; Priest, 1948; Curate St Michael and All Angels, Aberystwyth, 1947-50; UMCA Missionary, 1950-57; Staff, St Michael's College, Llandaff, 1957-59; Home Secretary, Universities' Mission to Central Africa, 1959-62. *Publication:* Asomaye na Afahamu (SPCK), 1959. *Recreations:* photography, writing. *Address:* Bishop's House, Njombe, Tanzania; St Ethelbert's, Castle Hill, Hereford.

**SOUTHAM, Alexander William,** CBE 1948; President of the British Newfoundland Corporation Limited; *b* 1898. *Educ:* Oundle; Christ's College, Cambridge (MA). Served European War, 1915-19 (despatches, foreign orders). Then in industry and commerce; mainly associated with oil. Various war work between 1939 and 1945, when joined British Element of Allied Commission for Austria and was Director Economic Group, 1947-48; Director, Investigation and Research Division, International Authority for the Ruhr, 1949-52. *Address:* 484 Wood Avenue, Montreal, PQ, Canada.

**SOUTHAM, Gordon Ronald,** BSc; AInstP; Headmaster, Ashville College, since 1958; *b* 20 March 1918; *s* of G. H. Southam, Brackley; *m* 1948, Joan, *d* of W. Thompson; one *d*. *Educ:* Magdalen College School, Brackley; Westminster College, and King's College, London. BSc (Gen. Hons) 1938, BSc (Special Physics) 1st Class Hons 1939. Teacher's diploma, 1947, AInstP 1947. Served Royal Air Force, 1940-46: Bomber Comd, 1940-43; Staff Officer in HQ, ACSEA, 1943-46 (Sqdn Ldr). Senior Physics Master, Culford School, 1947-49; Lecturer, Royal Military Academy, Sandhurst, 1950-52; Head of Department of Science, Royal Military Academy, Sandhurst, 1953-57. *Recreations:* motoring, electronics; formerly Rugby football, athletics. *Address:* Ashville College, Harrogate, Yorkshire. *T:* Harrogate 4434.

**SOUTHAMPTON,** Barony of (*cr* 1780); title disclaimed by 5th Baron; *see under* FitzRoy, Charles.

**SOUTHAMPTON, Suffragan Bishop of,** since 1951; **Rt. Rev. Kenneth Edward Norman Lamplugh;** Canon, 1951, Residentiary Canon, 1951-62, Hon. Canon, 1962, Winchester Cathedral; Chaplain and Sub-Prelate of the Venerable Order of St John of Jerusalem, since 1962; *b* 9 Nov. 1901; *m* 1928, Naomi Ford; three *s* one *d*. *Educ:* King's Coll., Cambridge; Cuddesdon Coll., Oxford. Deacon 1925; Priest 1926; Curate of Lambeth, 1925-28; Curate of Pietermaritzburg Cathedral, Natal, 1928-31; Vicar of St Mary's, Durban, 1931-33; Vicar of Hartley Wintney, 1934; Commiss. to Bishop of Natal, 1937; Vicar of Lymington, 1941; Rural Dean of Lyndhurst, 1942; officiating CF, 1940-46; Archdeacon and Canon Residentiary of Lincoln, 1947-51; Prebendary of Gretton, 1947-51; Warden of Lincoln Diocesan Association of Lay Readers, 1947. Examining Chaplain to Bishop of Winchester, 1951; Fellow, Soc. of St Mary and St Nicholas, Lancing, 1952. Pres., Hants Assoc. for the Blind. Chm., Hants and IOW Assoc. for the Deaf. *Recreation:* travelling. *Address:* Butts Close Cottage, Winchester. *T:* Winchester 3535.

**SOUTHBOROUGH,** 3rd Baron *cr* 1917; **Francis John Hopwood;** Kt 1953; retired as Managing Director "Shell" Transport & Trading Co., 1951-70 (Director, 1946-70); *b* 7 March 1897; *s* of 1st Baron Southborough, PC, GCB, GCMG, GCVO, KCSI and his 2nd wife, Florence Emily, *d* of late Lieut-Gen. Samuel Black; *S* half-brother (2nd Baron), 1960; *m* 1918, Audrey Evelyn Dorothy, *d* of late Edgar George Money; one *s* one *d*. *Educ:* Westminster School. Served European War, 1914-18, Sub-Lieut, RNVR, Admiralty and Foreign Office; seconded, 1917, to staff of Irish Convention in Dublin and later was Sec. to War Trade Advisory Cttee. Joined Royal Dutch Shell Group of Companies, 1919; Pres. Asiatic Petroleum Corporation, USA, (also represented Petroleum Board), 1942-46; Managing Director The Shell Petroleum Co., and Bataafse Petroleum Maatschappij NV, 1946-57, retired. Mem., Oil Supply Adv. Cttee. Commander of the Order of Orange-Nassau. *Heir:* *s* Hon. Francis Michael Hopwood, late Lieut The Rifle Brigade [*b* 3 May 1922; *m* 1945, Moyna Kemp, *d* of Robert J. K. Chattey]. *Address:* Bingham's Melcombe, near

Dorchester, Dorset. *T:* Milton Abbas 202. *Club:* Brooks's.
*See also J. M. Rank.*

**SOUTHBY, Sir (Archibald) Richard (Charles),** 2nd Bt *cr* 1937; OBE 1945; Lt-Col (retd), Rifle Brigade; *b* 18 June 1910; *s* of Sir Archibald Richard James Southby, 1st Bt, and of Phyllis Mary, *er d* of late Charles Henry Garton, Banstead Wood, Surrey; *S* father, 1969; *m* 1st, 1935, Joan Alice (marr. diss. 1947), *o d* of Reginald Balston; 2nd, 1947, Olive Marion (marr. diss. 1964), *d* of late Sir Thomas Bilbe-Robinson; one *s*; 3rd, 1964, Hon. Ethel Peggy, *d* of 1st Baron Cunliffe and *widow* of Brig. Bernard Lorenzo de Robeck, MC, RA. *Educ:* Eton; Magdalen Coll., Oxford (MA). Medal of Freedom (US). *Heir: s* John Richard Bilbe Southby, *b* 2 April 1948. *Address:* Montgomery Farm, PB 545, Sinoia, Rhodesia.

**SOUTHBY, Sir Richard;** *see* Southby, Sir A. R. C.

**SOUTHCOTT, Rev. Canon Ernest William;** Canon Emeritus of Southwark Cathedral; Vicar of St Peter and St Paul, Rishton, since 1970; *b* 8 May 1915; *m* 1944, Margaret Jane Carpenter; one *s* three *d. Educ:* King Edward High School; Univ. of British Columbia. BA (BC) 1935. College of the Resurrection, Mirfield, Yorks, 1936-38; Curate: St John's, Shildon, Co. Durham, 1938-40; St James's, Gateshead-on-Tyne, 1940-42; Novice, Community of the Resurrection, 1942-43; Vicar of St Wilfrid's, Halton, Leeds, 1944-61; Hon. Canon of Ripon Cathedral, 1955-61; Rural Dean of Whitkirk, 1958-61; Provost of Southwark Cathedral, and Rector of St Saviour and All Hallows, Southwark, 1961-70. *Publications:* (with S. H. Evans) Unto a Full Grown Man (Series), 1942-; Receive This Child, 1951; The Parish Comes Alive, 1956; Meditations for Lent, 1957; contribs to Theology, etc. *Recreations:* music, theatre, walking. *Address:* The Vicarage, 4 Somerset Road, Rishton, Blackburn, Lancs BB1 4BP. *T:* Great Harwood 3191.

**SOUTHEND, Archdeacon of;** *see* Bradwell, Bishop Suffragan of.

**SOUTHERN, Ralph Lang,** CBE 1952; Accountant and Comptroller-General of Inland Revenue, 1949-54; *b* 14 May 1893; *s* of James Lang Southern; *m* 1919, Dora, *d* of Albert Smith, JP; one *s* two *d.* Entered Revenue Department, 1909. *Address:* 52 Sea Lane, Goring-by-Sea, Sussex.

**SOUTHERN, Richard;** Theatre Consultant (private) since 1947; *b* 5 Oct. 1903; *o s* of Harry Southern and Edith (*née* Hockney); *m* 1933, Grace Kathleen Loosemore; two *d. Educ:* St Dunstan's College; Goldsmiths' Art School; Royal Academy of Art. Designed scenery, 1928-, for over fifty shows (Everyman Theatre, Cambridge Festival Theatre and Various London theatres); also acted and stage-managed; specialized in study of stage technique and theatre architecture. Technical Lectr, Goldsmiths' College, 1932, London Theatre Studio, 1937, Royal Academy of Dramatic Art, 1945, Old Vic Theatre Centre, 1947; Theatre planning adviser to Arts Council, 1947; Director, Nuffield Theatre, Univ. of Southampton, 1964-66; Lectr, Drama Dept, Bristol Univ., 1959-60, and Special Lectr in Theatre Architecture, 1961-69, retired. Has planned various modern theatres and stages includ. Bristol Univ., 1951, Royal College of Art, 1952, Glasgow, 1953, Reading University, 1957, Nottingham, 1961, Southampton University, 1961, University Coll., London, 1967, also various reconstructions of historical theatres, Richmond, Yorkshire, 1950, King's Lynn, 1951, Williamsburg, Virginia, 1953. Hon. DLitt (Bristol), 1956. *Publications:* Stage Setting, 1937; Proscenium and Sightlines, 1939; The Georgian Playhouse, 1948; The Essentials of Stage Planning (with Stanley Bell and Norman Marshall), 1949; Changeable Scenery, 1952; The Open Stage, 1953; The Medieval Theatre in the Round, 1957; The Seven Ages of the Theatre, 1961; The Victorian Theatre, 1970; contrib. to specialist journals and encyclopædias. *Recreation:* figure drawing. *Address:* 102 High Street, Swanage, Dorset BH19 2NY. *Club:* Savage.

**SOUTHERN, Richard William,** FBA 1960; President of St John's College, Oxford, since 1969; *b* 8 Feb. 1912; 2nd *s* of Matthew Henry Southern, Newcastle upon Tyne; *m* 1944, Sheila (*née* Cobley), *widow* of Sqdn Ldr C. Crichton-Miller; two *s. Educ:* Royal Grammar Sch., Newcastle upon Tyne; Balliol College, Oxford (Domus Exhibr). 1st Class Hons Modern History, 1932. Junior Research Fellow, Exeter College, Oxford, 1933-37; studied in Paris, 1933-34 and Munich, 1935; Fellow and Tutor, Balliol Coll., Oxford, 1937-61 (Hon. Fell. 1966). Served Oxford and Bucks LI, 1940; 2nd Lt Durham LI 1941; 155th Regt RAC, 1942; Captain 1943; Major 1944; Political Intelligence Dept, Foreign Office, 1943-45. Junior Proctor, Oxford Univ., 1948-49; Birkbeck Lectr in Ecclesiastical History, Trinity College, Cambridge, 1959-60; Chichele Prof. of Modern History, Oxford, 1961-69; Pres. Royal Historical Soc., 1968-. Raleigh Lecture British Academy, 1962; David Murray Lecture, Glasgow Univ., 1963. Corr. Fellow, Medieval Academy of America, 1965. Hon. DLitt Glasgow, 1964, Durham, 1969. *Publications:* The Making of the Middle Ages, 1953 (numerous foreign translations); (ed) Eadmer's Vita Anselmi, 1963; St Anselm and his Biographer, 1963; Western Views of Islam in the Middle Ages, 1962; (ed with F. S. Schmitt) Memorials of St Anselm, 1969; Medieval Humanism and other studies, 1970; Western Society and the Church in the Middle Ages, 1970; articles in English Historical Review, Medieval and Renaissance Studies, etc. *Address:* President's Lodgings, St John's College, Oxford. *T:* Oxford 44419.

**SOUTHERN, Sir Robert,** Kt 1970; CBE 1953; General Secretary, Co-operative Union Ltd, since 1948; *b* 17 March 1907; *s* of Job Southern and Margaret (*née* Tonge); *m* 1933, Lena Chapman; one *s* one *d. Educ:* Stand Grammar Sch.; Co-operative Coll.; Manchester University. Co-operative Wholesale Soc., Bank Dept, 1925-29; Co-operative Union Ltd, 1929. *Publication:* Handbook to the Industrial and Provident Societies' Act. *Recreations:* photography, gardening. *Address:* 22 Glebelands Road, Prestwich, Manchester. *T:* 061-773 2699.

**SOUTHERTON, Thomas Henry,** CEng, MIEE; Director, Management Services Department, Post Office Telecommunications, since 1967; *b* 1 July 1917; *s* of C. H. Southerton, Birmingham; *m* 1945, Marjorie Elizabeth Sheen; one *s. Educ:* Bemrose Sch., Derby; Northampton Coll., London (BSc(Eng)). PO Apprentice, Derby, 1933-36; Engineering Workman, Derby and Nottingham, 1936-40; Inspector, Engineer-in-Chief's Office, 1940-45; Engineer, 1945-50; Sen. Exec. Engr, 1950-53; Factory Manager, PO Provinces, 1953-56; Dep. Controller, Factories Dept, 1956-64; Controller, Factories Dept, 1964-67. *Recreations:* dancing, reading, art. *Address:* 65 Greenways, Hinchley Wood, Esher, Surrey. *T:* 01-398 5463.

**SOUTHESK,** 11th Earl of *cr* 1633; **Charles Alexander Carnegie,** KCVO, *cr* 1926; DL; Major late Scots Guards; Baron Carnegie, 1616; Baron Balinhard (UK), 1869; Bt of Nova Scotia, 1663; *b* 23 Sept. 1893; *e s* of 10th Earl of Southesk and Ethel (*d* 1947), *o c* of Sir Alexander Bannerman, 9th Bt of Elsick; *S* father, 1941; *m* 1st, 1923, HH Princess Maud (*d* 1945), 2nd *d* of HRH Princess Louise, Princess Royal and late Duke of Fife; one *s*; 2nd, 1952, Evelyn, *e d* of Lieut-Colonel A. P. Williams-Freeman, and *widow* of Major Ion E. F. Campbell, DCLI. *Educ:* Eton; Sandhurst. DL Angus. *Heir: s* Duke of Fife, *qv*. *Address:* Kinnaird Castle, Brechin, Angus. *T:* Bridge of Dun 209. *Club:* Guards.

*See also Earl of Elgin, Vice-Admiral Sir E. M. C. Abel Smith.*

**SOUTHEY, Air Commodore Harold Frederic George,** CB 1954; attached Foreign and Commonwealth Office (formerly Foreign Office), since 1958; *b* 18 Feb. 1906; *s* of Rev. William George Southey and Edith Mary Roffey; *m* 1929, Joan Mary Gordon Davies; no *c*. *Educ:* Downside; RAF Coll., Cranwell. Served War of 1939-45 (despatches twice); AOC No 247 Group, and Senior British Officer, Azores, 1945; Air Attaché, Brussels, 1947; West Union Defence Organisation, 1951; SASO Transport Command, 1952; AOC, RAF Maritime HQ, Chatham, 1954; retired 1957. *Recreations:* fishing, shooting, and sailing. *Address:* 17 Knightsbridge Court, SW1. *T:* 01-235 6927. *Clubs:* Royal Air Force, Royal Thames Yacht.

**SOUTHEY, Robert John,** CMG 1970; Chairman, Wm Haughton & Co. Ltd, since 1968; Federal President, Liberal Party of Australia, since 1970; *b* 20 March 1922; *s* of Allen Hope Southey and Ethel Thorpe McComas, MBE; *m* 1946, Valerie Janet Cotton, *y d* of late Hon. Sir Francis Grenville Clarke, KBE, MLC; five *s*. *Educ:* Geelong Grammar Sch.; Magdalen Coll., Oxford (MA). Coldstream Guards, 1941-46 (Captain 1944). BA, 1st cl. PPE Oxon, 1948. Wm Haughton & Co. Ltd: Dir 1953; Man. Dir 1959; Chm. 1968; Director: British Petroleum Co. of Australia Ltd; International Computers (Australia) Pty Ltd; Port Phillip Mills Pty Ltd; Buckley & Nunn Ltd; Mem. Australian Adv. Council, General Accident Assurance Corp. Ltd. Victorian State Pres., Liberal Party, 1966-70; Chm. of Council, Geelong Grammar Sch., 1966-; Chm. Australian Adv. Cttee, Nuffield Foundn, 1970. *Recreations:* fishing, golf. *Address:* Denistoun Avenue, Mount Eliza, Victoria 3930, Australia. *T:* 7871701. *Clubs:* Guards, United Service, MCC; Melbourne, Australian (Melbourne); Union (Sydney); Leander.

**SOUTHGATE, Bernard Alfred,** CBE 1954; PhD, DSc (Aberdeen), FRIC; Director, Water Pollution Research, Ministry of Technology, 1965-66 (Department of Scientific and Industrial Research, 1943-65); *b* 28 Aug. 1904; *s* of Alfred and Edith Southgate; *m* 1929, Marion Hope Smith; one *s*. *Educ:* City of Norwich Sch.; Queens' Coll., Cambridge (Scholar, BA). With Marine Biological Assoc., engaged on survey of River Tees, 1929-33; joined Department of Scientific and Industrial Research, 1933; Officer-in-Charge, Survey of Mersey Estuary, 1933-37. *Publications:* Treatment and Disposal of Industrial Waste Waters, 1948; Water Pollution and Conservation, 1969. *Address:* Langham House, Langham, Norfolk.

**SOUTHWARD, Ralph;** Apothecary to HM Household since 1964; to the Households of Queen Elizabeth the Queen Mother, and HRH the Duke of Gloucester, since 1966; *b* 2 Jan. 1908; *s* of Henry Stalker Southward; *m* 1935, Evelyn, *d* of J. G. Tassell; four *s*. *Educ:* High School of Glasgow; Glasgow Univ. MB, ChB (Glasgow) 1930; MRCP 1939; FRCP 1970. Western Infirmary, and Royal Hospital for Sick Children, Glasgow; Postgraduate Medical School, Hammersmith, London. Served War of 1939-45: Medical Officer, 215 Field Ambulance, North Africa, 1940-41; Medical Specialist, Egypt, India and Ceylon, and Lieut-Colonel in charge Medical Division, 1942-43; Colonel Comdg Combined General Hospital, 1944-45. *Recreations:* trout and salmon fishing. *Address:* 9 Devonshire Place, W1; Amerden Priory, Taplow, Bucks. *T:* Maidenhead 23525.

**SOUTHWARK, Bishop of,** since 1959; **Rt. Rev. Arthur Mervyn Stockwood,** DD; *b* 27 May 1913; *s* of late Arthur Stockwood, solicitor, and Beatrice Ethel Stockwood; unmarried. *Educ:* Kelly Coll., Tavistock; Christ's Coll., Cambridge (MA). Curate of St Matthew, Moorfields, Bristol, 1936-41; Blundell's Sch., Missioner, 1936-41; Vicar, St Matthew, Moorfields, Bristol, 1941-55; Hon. Canon of Bristol, 1952-55; Vicar of the University Church, Cambridge, 1955-59; DD Lambeth, 1959; DLitt Sussex, 1963. *Publications:* There is a Tide, 1946; Whom They Pierced, 1948; I Went to Moscow, 1955; The Faith To-day, 1959; Cambridge Sermons, 1959; Bishop's Journal, 1965. *Recreation:* fishing. *Address:* Bishop's House, 38 Tooting Bec Gardens, SW16. *Club:* Athenæum.

**SOUTHWARK, Archbishop and Metropolitan of, (RC),** since 1965; **Most Rev. Mgr. Cyril Conrad Cowderoy,** DD; *b* 5 May 1905; *s* of Frederick Cowderoy and Anne Marie (*née* Lawless). *Educ:* Dulwich Coll.; St John's Seminary, Wonersh. Priest, 1931; after further studies at L'Institut Catholique, Paris, appointed Professor, St Joseph's Coll., Mark Cross, Tunbridge Wells, 1932; Diocesan Secretary, 1937; Chancellor of Diocese of Southwark, 1946; Judge of Matrimonial Court, 1947; appointed Privy Chamberlain to HH the Pope, Dec. 1948. Bishop of Southwark, 1949-65. Grand Prior of Lieutenancy in England and Wales of Order of Knights of Holy Sepulchre of Jerusalem, 1954, Knight Grand Cross, 1961. *Address:* Archbishop's House, St George's Road, Southwark, SE1. *T:* 01-928 5592.

**SOUTHWARK, Assistant Bishops of;** *see* Barham, Rt Rev. E. L., Boys, Rt Rev. J., and Robinson, Rt Rev. J. A. T.

**SOUTHWARK, Archdeacon of;** *see* Bazire, Ven. R. V.

**SOUTHWELL,** family name of **Viscount Southwell.**

**SOUTHWELL,** 7th Viscount, *cr* 1776; **Pyers Anthony Joseph Southwell,** Bt 1662; Baron Southwell, 1717; General Manager and Director, Chemical Company; *b* 14 Sept. 1930; *s* of Hon. Francis Joseph Southwell (2nd *s* of 5th Viscount) and Agnes Mary Annette Southwell (*née* Clifford); *S* uncle, 1960; *m* 1955, Barbara Jacqueline Raynes; two *s*. *Educ:* Beaumont Coll., Old Windsor, Berks; Royal Military Academy, Sandhurst. Commissioned into 8th King's Royal Irish Hussars, 1951; resigned commission, 1955. *Recreation:* golf. *Heir: s* Hon. Richard Andrew Pyers Southwell, *b* 15 June 1956. *Address:* 4 Rosebery Avenue, Harpenden, Herts. *T:* Harpenden 5831. *Clubs:* Army and Navy, MCC.

**SOUTHWELL, Bishop of,** since 1970; **Rt. Rev. John Denis Wakeling,** MC 1945; *b* 12 Dec. 1918; *s* of Rev. John Lucas Wakeling and Mary

Louise (*née* Glover); *m* 1941, Josephine Margaret, *d* of Dr Benjamin Charles Broomhall and Marion (*née* Aldwinckle); two *s*. *Educ:* Dean Close Sch., Cheltenham; St Catharine's Coll., Cambridge. MA Cantab 1944. Commnd Officer in Royal Marines, 1939-45 (Actg Maj.). Ridley Hall, Cambridge, 1946-47. Deacon, 1947; Priest, 1948. Asst Curate, Barwell, Leics, 1947; Chaplain of Clare Coll., Cambridge, and Chaplain to the Cambridge Pastorate, 1950-52; Vicar of Emmanuel, Plymouth, 1952-59; Prebendary of Exeter Cathedral, 1957, Prebendary Emeritus, 1959; Vicar of Barking, Essex, 1959-65; Archdeacon of West Ham, 1965-70. *Recreations:* cricket; formerly hockey (Cambridge Univ. Hockey Club, 1938, 1939, 1945, 1946, English Trials Caps, 1939, 1946, 1947, 1948, 1949). *Address:* Bishop's Manor, Southwell, Notts.

**SOUTHWELL, Assistant Bishop of;** *see* Gelsthorpe, Rt Rev. A. M.

**SOUTHWELL, Provost of;** *see* Pratt, Very Rev. J. F.

**SOUTHWELL, Sir (Charles Archibald) Philip,** Kt 1958; CBE 1953; MC 1918; Director, Kuwait Oil Co. Ltd, since 1946 (Managing Director, 1946-59); *s* of late Dr Charles Edward Southwell, Stoke-on-Trent; *m* 1926, Mary Burnett, *d* of Thomas Scarratt, Belmont Hall, Ipstones, Staffs; two *s*. *Educ:* Birmingham Univ. (BSc (Pet.)). President: Inst. of Petroleum, 1951-52; Oil Industries Club, 1953. Petroleum Technologist to Government of Trinidad, 1922-28. Served European War, 1914-18, with RA (MC); War of 1939-45; temp. Lt-Col. Govt Cttee Business Training, 1945. Royal Society of Arts: Silver Medal, 1953; Council, 1958. Cadman Memorial Medal, Inst. of Petroleum, 1954; Hon. Fellow, 1959. Chairman, Brown and Root (UK) Ltd. Liveryman, Company of Shipwrights. GCStJ; late Dir-Gen. St John Ambulance, 1968. Comdr, Order of Cedar of Lebanon, 1958. *Publications:* on petroleum technology. *Recreation:* gardening. *Address:* Manor House, Tendring, Essex. *T:* Weeley 286. *Clubs:* Garrick, Royal Thames Yacht.

**SOUTHWELL, Sir Richard Vynne,** Kt, *cr* 1948; FRS; MA, LLD (St Andrews, Glasgow), DSc (Belfast, Bristol, Brussels); DEng (Sheffield); Hon. MIMechE; Hon. FRAeS, Hon. FIAeS; Foreign Associate, US National Academy of Science; Hon. Fellow of Brasenose College, Oxford, and Trinity College, Cambridge; Fellow of Imperial College, London; *b* 2 July 1888; *s* of Edwin B. and Annie Southwell, Bracondale, Norwich; *m* 1918, Isabella Wilhelmina Warburton, *d* of W. W. Wingate, Scroope House, Cambridge; four *d*. *Educ:* Norwich Sch.; Trinity Coll., Cambridge. Fellow and Lecturer in Mechanical Sciences, Trinity Coll., Cambridge, 1912-20; served in RASC 1914-15, RNVR 1915-18, and RAF 1918-19; Superintendent of the Aerodynamics Dept, National Physical Laboratory, 1920-25; University Lecturer in Mathematics and Fellow of Trinity Coll., Cambridge, 1925-29; Prof. of Engineering Science and Fellow of Brasenose Coll., Oxford, 1929-42; Rector of Imperial College of Science and Technology, London, 1942-48; Member of Bridge Stress Cttee, 1923-28; of Aeronautical Research Cttee, 1927-30, 1931-34, 1935-38, 1940-43; Steel Structures Research Cttee, 1929-30; Cttee of Award for Commonwealth Fund Fellowships, 1930-38; Lord Privy Seal's (Hailey) Conference on Air Raid Shelters Policy, 1939; Civil Defence Research Comm., 1939-48; Scientific Advisory Council, Ministry of Supply, 1940-43; Ministry of Labour Higher Appts (Hankey) Commn, 1943-44; Colonial Office (Asquith) Commission on Higher Education in the Colonies, 1943-45; Board of Education (Percy) Cttee on Technological Education, 1944-45; Standing Commission on Museums and Galleries, 1946-50; President, Sect. G (Engineering), 1938, and a General Secretary, 1947-55, of British Assoc.; President, International Union Theoretical and Applied Mechanics, 1946-48; President VII International Congress of Applied Mechanics, 1948-52, Treasurer 1952-56; Worcester Reed Warner Medal (Amer. Soc. ME), 1941; James Alfred Ewing Medal (Inst. CE), 1946; Clayton Prize (Inst. ME) and US Medal of Freedom with Silver Palm, 1947; Timoshenko Medal (Amer. Soc. ME), 1959; Elliott Cresson Medal (Franklin Inst.), 1944. *Publications:* Introduction to the Theory of Elasticity, for Engineers and Physicists, 1936; Relaxation Methods in Engineering Science, 1940; Relaxation Methods in Theoretical Physics, Vol. I, 1946, Vol. II, 1956; papers on elasticity, theory of structures, hydrodynamics, etc, in Transactions of Royal Society, Philosophical Magazine, etc. *Address:* The Old House, 20 Church Lane, Trumpington, Cambridge. *T:* Trumpington 3289. *Club:* Athenæum.

*See also Baron Roberthall.*

**SOUTHWOOD, Albert Ray,** CMG 1947; ED; Cons. Physician to the Royal Adelaide Hospital; Lecturer in Public Health and Preventive Medicine, Faculty of Medicine, University of Adelaide, 1938-59; Milroy Lecturer, RCP, London, 1959; Director-General of Public Health and Chairman Central Board of Health of South Australia, 1931-59; *er s* of late J. A. Southwood, MP, and Mrs Southwood, Joslin, South Australia; *m* 1919, Elva Dillon, Toorak, South Australia; two *s* two *d*. *Educ:* Prince Alfred Coll., Adelaide; Adelaide Univ. MB, BS, MD, MS Adelaide; MRCP; FRACP (Foundation Fellow); Colonel, AAMC (retired). *Publications:* Heart Disease: Ways to Prevent it, 1962; medical papers in current journals, 1919-66; contrib. Lancet Milroy Lectures, 1959; Preventive Cardiology. *Address:* 170 North Terrace, Adelaide 5000, South Australia. *T:* 51.5123; 129 Swaine Avenue, Toorak Gardens, South Australia. *T:* 32.2028. *Club:* Naval, Military and Air Force (Adelaide).

**SOUTHWOOD, Captain Horace Gerald,** CBE 1966; DSC 1941; Royal Navy; General Manager, HM Dockyard, Devonport, since 1967; *b* 19 April 1912; *s* of late Horace George Southwood; *m* 1936, Ruby Edith Hayes; two *s* one *d*. *Educ:* HMS Fisgard, RN Coll., Greenwich. Joined RN, 1927; HMS Resolution, Medit. Stn, 1932-34; HMS Barham, 1934-35; RN Coll., Greenwich, 1935-36; HMS Royal Oak, Home Fleet, 1936-38; specialised in Submarines, 1938; HMS Lucia, 1938-39. HM Submarine, Regent, 1939-41; HMS Medway, China and Medit., 1941-42 (despatches, DSC); HM Submarine, Amphion (first of Class), 1943-45. HMS Dolphin, 1946-48; HMS Vengeance, 1948-49; Comdr, 1948; HMS Glory, 1949-51; HMS Forth, 1951-52; Admty, Whitehall, 1952-54; HM Dockyard, Portsmouth (Dep. Man.), 1954-58; jssc, 1958-59; Capt., 1958. Chief Engr, Singapore, 1959-62; Sen. Officers' War Course, 1962; Manager, Engrg Dept, HM Dockyard, Portsmouth, 1963-67. CEng, FIMechE, MBIM. *Recreations:* sailing, fishing, golf, caravanning. *Address:* Dolphin Cottage, Riverside, Newton Ferrers, Devon. *T:* Newton Ferrers 649. *Clubs:* Royal Naval (Portsmouth); Royal Western Yacht (Plymouth); Yealm Yacht (Newton Ferrers).

**SOUTHWOOD, Prof. Thomas Richard Edmund;** Professor of Zoology and Applied Entomology, University of London; Head of Department of Zoology and Applied Entomology and Director of Field Station, Imperial College, since 1967; *b* 20 June 1931; *s* of Edmund W. Southwood and late A. Mary, *d* of Archdeacon T. R. Regg; *m* 1955, Alison Langley, *d* of A. L. Harden, Harpenden, Herts; two *s*. *Educ:* Gravesend Grammar Sch.; Imperial Coll., London. BSc, ARCS 1952; PhD London, 1955; DSc London, 1963. ARC Research Schol., Rothamsted Experimental Station, 1952-55; Res. Asst and Lecturer, Zoology Dept, Imperial Coll., London, 1955-64; Vis. Prof., Dept. of Entomology, University of California, Berkeley, 1964-65; Reader in Insect Ecology, University of London, 1964-67. Governor, Glasshouse Crops Research Inst., 1969-. Scientific Medal, Zoolog. Soc., London, 1969. *Publications:* (with D. Leston) Land and Water Bugs of the British Isles, 1959; Life of the Wayside and Woodland, 1963; Ecological Methods, 1966; many papers in entomological and ecological jls. *Recreations:* natural history, gardening. *Address:* 8 Silwood Close, Ascot, Berks. *T:* Ascot 21676. *Club:* Athenæum.

**SOUTHWORTH, Sir Frederick,** Kt 1965; QC; Chief Justice, Malawi, 1964-70; *b* Blackburn, Lancashire, May 1910. *Educ:* Queen Elizabeth's Grammar Sch., Blackburn; Exeter Coll., Oxford. Called to the Bar, Gray's Inn, 1936. War of 1939-45; commissioned 1939; Department of the Judge Advocate General in India, 1943; Hon. Colonel, Crown Counsel, Palestine, 1946; Crown Counsel, Tanganyika, 1947; Attorney General of the Bahamas, 1951-55; QC Bahamas, 1952; Acting Governor, July-Aug. 1952; Acting Chief Justice, July-Oct. 1954; Puisne Judge, Nyasaland, 1955; Acting Governor-General, Malawi, at various times, 1964-66. *Address:* c/o Barclays Bank, Halkett Place, St Helier, Jersey.

**SOUZAY, Gerard** (*né* Gérard Marcel Tisserand), Chevalier de l'Ordre des Arts et Lettres; French baritone; *b* 8 Dec. 1921. *Educ:* Paris Conservatoire Musique. World Première, Stravinsky's Canticum Sacrum, Venice Festival, 1956; Bach B Minor Mass at Salzburg Festival; Pelléas et Mélisande, Rome Opera, Opera Comique, 1962; Don Giovanni, Paris Opera, 1963; second tour of Australia and New Zealand, 1964. Also tours in US, South America, Japan, Africa, Europe. Annual Lieder recitals, Salzburg Festival. Has made recordings; Grand Prix du Disque, for Ravel Recital, etc. *Recreations:* tennis, painting. *Address:* 26 rue Freycinet, Paris 16, France.

**SOVEREIGN, Rt. Rev. Arthur Henry,** MA, DD, FRGS; retired; *b* 1881; *e s* of Freeman and Helen Sovereign; *m* 1913, Ellen Fearnaught, *e d* of Hon. Price Ellison; one *s* three *d*. *Educ:* Toronto Univ.; Wycliffe Coll., Toronto; Post-graduate course at Oxford Univ. Ordained Curate at Christ Church Cathedral, Vancouver, BC, 1906; First Rector, St Mark's Church, Vancouver, BC, 1909; Professor and Lecturer, Anglican Theological Coll., Vancouver, BC, 1920-31; service with YMCA (Canadian); Canon of Christ Church Cathedral, Vancouver, BC, 1929; Bishop of Yukon, 1932-33; Bishop of Athabasca, 1933-50. *Recreations:* mountain-climbing, photography. *Address:* 2501 23rd Street, Vernon, BC, Canada.

**SOWBY, Rev. Cedric Walter,** MA Oxon, Hon. DD Wycliffe College, Toronto; Principal of Upper Canada College, Toronto, 1949-65, Principal Emeritus since 1965; *b* 29 Jan. 1902; *s* of Walter Edwin and Lily Sowby; *m* 1924, Mary, *d* of Dr F. Savery, Oxford; one *s* two *d*. *Educ:* King Edward VI Sch., Louth, Lincs; Keble Coll., Oxford; St Stephen's House, Oxford. Asst Curate, St John's Church, Keswick, 1925-28; Asst Master, St Edward's School, Oxford, 1928-33; Warden, St Columba's Coll., Co. Dublin, 1934-49; Member of Headmasters' Conference. Examining Chaplain to Bishop of Toronto. Member Internat. Council, United World Colleges. *Address:* 16 Chestnut Park Road, Toronto 289, Canada. *T:* 922-8611. *Clubs:* Athenæum, Public Schools; Kildare Street (Dublin).

**SOWERBY, Amy Millicent;** artist; 3rd *d* of John Sowerby. Has exhibited paintings in oil and water-colour at RI, Bruton Street Gallery, and other Exhibitions; has illustrated many books for children; worked in black and white for Windsor, Pall Mall, Tatler, Ladies' Field, Illustrated London News, etc; with her sister Githa Sowerby, Childhood, Yesterday's Children, and a long series beginning with The Wise Book, etc; Alice in Wonderland; Child's Garden of Verses, etc; a great number of picture post-cards. *Recreations:* reading, walking, and embroidery. *Address:* 28 Bina Gardens, SW5.

**SOWMAN, Air Commodore John Edward Rudkin,** CB 1959; CBE 1957; RAF, retired; *b* West Clandon, Surrey, 8 May 1902; *s* of Alfred William Rudkin Sowman and Ellen Sowman (*née* Bone); *m* 1928, Olive Rosa Trimmer; two *s* one *d*. *Educ:* Bedford Sch. Engineer Training, 1919-24; Pilot Officer, RAF, Oct. 1926; Flying Officer No. 70 Sqdn, Iraq, 1929-30; Flt Lieut, No. 33 Sqdn, Bicester, 1930-34, No. 47 Sqdn, Khartoum, 1934-36; RAF Staff Coll., 1937; Air Ministry, Sqdn Leader, Wing Comdr, Group Captain, 1938-43 (responsible for provision of radio equipment); on HQ Staff, MAAF, Algiers, 1943-45; Comdr No. 351 MU Algiers, 1945-46 (clearance of N Africa); Staff appts at HQ No. 40 Group and Flying Training Comd, 1946-51; Air Cdre and SESO, MEAF, 1951-53; SASO, HQ No. 40 Group, 1953-56; Director of Mechanical Transport and Marine Craft, Air Ministry, Sept. 1956-Nov. 1959. *Recreations:* rifle shooting (RAF Team, 7 times, once as Captain), won Alexandra Cup at Bisley, 1949. *Address:* 58 St Michaels Road, Bedford. *T:* Bedford 66415. *Club:* Royal Air Force.

**SOWREY, Air Vice-Marshal Frederick Beresford,** CB 1968; CBE 1965; AFC 1954; Senior Air Staff Officer, RAF Training Command, since 1970; *b* 14 Sept. 1922; *s* of late Group Captain Frederick Sowrey, DSO, MC, AFC; *m* 1946, Anne Margaret, *d* of late Captain C. T. A. Bunbury, OBE, RN; one *s* one *d*. *Educ:* Charterhouse. Joined RAF 1940; flying training in Canada, 1941; Fighter-reconnaissance Squadron, European theatre, 1942-44; Flying Instructors Sch., 1944; Airborne Forces, 1945; No. 615 (Co. of Surrey) Squadron, RAuxAF, 1946-48; Fighter Gunnery Sch., 1949-50, comdg 615 Sqdn, 1951-54; psa 1954; Chiefs of Staff Secretariat, 1955-58; comdg No. 46 Sqdn, 1958-60; Personal Staff Officer to CAS, 1960-62; comdg RAF Abingdon, 1962-64; idc 1965; SASO, Middle East Comd (Aden), 1966-67; Dir Defence Policy, MoD, 1968-70. *Recreations:* motoring sport (internat. records 1956), mechanical devices of any kind, fishing, shooting. *Address:* 40 Adam and Eve Mews, W8. *T:* 01-937 4040. *Club:* Royal Air Force.

**SOYSA, Sir Warusahennedige Abraham Bastian,** Kt, *cr* 1954; CBE 1953 (MBE 1950); JP; Mayor of Kandy, Ceylon; Proprietor of W. B. Soysa &

Co., Ceylon. *Address:* W. B. Soysa & Co., 184 Colombo Street, Kandy, Ceylon.

**SPAAK, Paul-Henri;** Lawyer and Politician, former Prime Minister of Belgium and Secretary-General of NATO; *b* 1899; *m* 1965, Mrs Simone Dear. Socialist Deputy for Brussels, 1932-66. Minister of Transport, Posts and Telegraphs, Belgium, 1935-36; Minister of Foreign Affairs and Trade, 1936-38; Prime Minister, 1938-39; Minister of Foreign Affairs, 1939-46; President, UN Assembly, 1949; Prime Minister and Minister for Foreign Affairs, 1947-49; Chairman, Council for European Recovery, 1948; President of the Consultative Assembly of the Council of Europe, 1949-51; Chairman of the International Council of the European Movement, 1950-55; Minister of Foreign Affairs, Belgium, 1954-57; Secretary-General, NATO, May 1957-March 1961; Deputy Prime Minister, Minister of Foreign and African Affairs, Belgium, 1961-66; Minister of State, 1966. Charlemagne Prize, 1957. Companion of Honour, Great Britain (Hon. CH), 1963. *Publication:* Combats inachevés, 1969. *Address:* c/o ITT Europe Ltd, 11 Boulevard de l'Empereur, Brussels, Belgium.

**SPAATZ, General Carl,** Hon. GBE 1945 (Hon. KBE 1944); retired as Chairman, Civil Air Patrol, United States Auxiliary Air Corps; *b* 28 June 1891; *m* 1917, Ruth Harrison; three *d.* United States Military Academy at West Point, 1910. Served European War, 1914-18, American Expeditionary Force, France, 1917; Second Pursuit Group, 1918; commanded Army Plane, Question Mark, 1929; graduated Command and General Staff School, 1936. War of 1939-45; observer in Britain during Battle of Britain; Chief of the Air Staff, AAF HQ, 1941; Comdr 8th Air Force and comdg General US Army Air Forces in European theater, 1942; North-West African Air Force, 1943; Comdg General Strategic Bombing Force, operating against Germany, 1944; Comdg Gen. US Strategic Air Forces in the Pacific, 1945, and supervised final strategic bombing of Japan; Comdg General US Army Air Forces, 1946-47; Chief of Staff, US Air Force, 1947-48; retired, 1948. Distinguished Service Cross, Distinguished Service Medal (3 Oak Leaf Clusters), Legion of Merit, Distinguished Flying Cross, Bronze Star medal; Grand Officer of Legion of Honor, Croix de Guerre with Palm (France); 2nd Order of Suvorov (Russia); Polonia Restituta, Commander's Cross with Star (Poland). *Address:* 5 Grafton Street, Chevy Chase, Maryland 20015, USA.

**SPACKMAN, Air Vice-Marshal (retired) Charles Basil Slater,** CB 1950; CBE 1945; DFC and Bar; *b* Happisburgh, Norfolk, 4 July 1895; *s* of Rev. George Spackman; *m* 1966, Anna Margareta Gunster. *Educ:* Lancing. Norfolk Regt, enlisted Aug. 1914, commnd 1/4th Bn 1915; War Service, Gallipoli and Egypt; RFC, seconded Oct. 1916, War Service Salonika Front, 41 and 150 Squadrons; RAF transf. on formation, 1918. Overseas service, Egypt, Iraq, Palestine, Sudan and Aden. Served War of 1939-45, Libya, 1941; AOC Sudan and Eritrea, 1941-42; HQ Fighter comd. 1942; Air Officer i/c Administration, 1943-45; AOC No 19 Group Coastal Comd, 1945-47; SASO, British Air Forces of Occupation, Germany, 1947-50; retired, 1950. *Recreation:* painting (exhibitor Royal Scottish and Hibernian Academies, RI, etc). *Address:* Greenhill, Ballyfeard, Co. Cork, Ireland. *Club:* Royal Air Force.

**SPADE, Mark;** *see* Balchin, Brig. N. M.

**SPAGHT, Monroe E.,** MA, PhD; Director, Royal Dutch Petroleum Co., since 1970 (Managing Director, 1965-70); Director, Shell Oil Co., USA, since 1970 (Executive Vice-President, 1953-60, President, 1961-65, Chairman, 1965-70); *b* Eureka, California, 9 Dec. 1909; *s* of Fred E. and Alpha L. Spaght; *m*; two *s* one *d. Educ:* Stanford Univ.; University of Leipzig. AB 1929, MA 1930, PhD 1933, Stanford Univ. (Chemistry). Research Scientist Shell Oil Co., 1933-45; Vice-President, Shell Development Co., 1945-48, President, 1949-52; Exec. Vice-President, Shell Oil Co., 1953-60, President, 1961-65; Man. Dir, Royal Dutch/Shell Group, 1965-70; Director: Stanford Research Inst., 1953-; Inst. of International Education, 1953-; American Petroleum Inst., 1953-; Trustee, Stanford Univ., 1955-65. President, Economic Club of New York, 1964-65. Hon. DSc: Rensselaer Polytechnic Inst., 1958; Drexel Inst. of Technology, 1962; Hon. LLD: Manchester, 1964; California State Colleges, 1965; Millikin Univ., Illinois, 1967; Wesleyan Univ., Middletown, Conn., 1968. Order of Francisco de Miranda, Venezuela, 1968; Cmdr, Order of Oranje Nassau, 1970. *Publications:* contribs to scientific journals. *Address:* Shell Centre, London SE1. *T:* 01-934 1234. *Clubs:* Athenæum; Blind Brook Country, Links (New York); Pacific Union (San Francisco).

**SPAIN, Stephen William;** Under-Secretary, Ministry of Technology, since 1969; *b* 18 Oct. 1924; 2nd *s* of Peter Valentine and Ellen Gammon; assumed family name of Spain, 1954; *m* 1950, Jean Margaret Evitt; three *s* one *d. Educ:* Hendon Grammar Sch.; LSE. Lieut (A) RNVR, 1942-46. Asst Principal, Min. of Labour, 1949; Private Sec. to Harold Watkinson, 1953-55; Commonwealth Dept of Labour, Melbourne, 1957-59; UK Delegn to Council of Europe, Western European Union, ILO, 1959-61; Hon. Sec., First Division Assoc., 1961-64; Asst Sec., Min. of Technology, 1965. *Recreations:* natural history, walking, gardening, poetry. *Address:* 47 Craigweil Avenue, Radlett, Herts. *T:* Radlett 4273. *Clubs:* Athenæum; Cricket and Men's (Radlett).

**SPALDING, Professor Dudley Brian,** MA, ScD; FIMechE, FInstF; Professor of Heat Transfer in the University of London at the Imperial College of Science and Technology, since 1958; *b* New Malden, Surrey, 9 Jan. 1923; *s* of H. A. Spalding; *m* 1947, Eda Ilse Lotte (*née* Goericke); two *s* two *d. Educ:* King's College Sch., Wimbledon; The Queen's Coll., Oxford; Pembroke Coll., Cambridge. BA (Oxon) 1944; MA (Cantab) 1948, PhD (Cantab) 1951. Bataafsche Petroleum Matschapij, 1944-45; Ministry of Supply, 1945-47; National Physical Laboratory, 1947-48; ICI Research Fellow at Cambridge Univ., 1948-50; Cambridge University Demonstrator in Engineering, 1950-54; Reader in Applied Heat, Imperial College of Science and Technology, 1954-58. *Publications:* Some Fundamentals of Combustion, 1955; (with E. H. Cole) Engineering Thermodynamics, 1958; Convective Mass Transfer, 1963; (with S. V. Patankar) Heat and Mass Transfer in Boundary Layers, 1967; (co-author) Heat and Mass Transfer in Recirculating Flows, 1969; numerous scientific papers. *Recreation:* squash. *Address:* (home) 2 Vineyard Hill Road, SW19. *T:* 01-946 2514; (business) Imperial College, Exhibition Road, SW7. *T:* 01-589 5111.

**SPARK, Mrs Muriel Sarah,** OBE 1967; writer; *b* Edinburgh; *d* of Bernard Camberg and Sarah Elizabeth Maud Uezzell; *m* 1937 (marr. diss.); one *s. Educ:* James Gillespie's School for Girls,

Edinburgh. General Secretary, The Poetry Society, Editor, The Poetry Review, 1947-49. FRSL 1963. *Publications:* critical and biographical: (ed. jt) Tribute to Wordsworth, 1950; (ed) Selected Poems of Emily Brontë, 1952; Child of Light: a Reassessment of Mary Shelley, 1951; John Masefield, 1953; (joint) Emily Brontë: her Life and Work, 1953; (ed) The Brontë Letters, 1954; (ed jointly) Letters of John Henry Newman, 1957; *poems:* The Fanfarlo and Other Verse, 1952; *fiction:* The Comforters, 1957; Robinson, 1958; The Go-Away Bird, 1958; Memento Mori, 1959 (adapted for stage, 1964); The Ballad of Peckham Rye, 1960 (Italia prize, for dramatic radio, 1962); The Bachelors, 1960; Voices at Play, 1961; The Prime of Miss Jean Brodie, 1961 (adapted for stage, 1966, filmed 1968); Doctors of Philosophy (play), 1963; The Girls of Slender Means, 1963; The Mandelbaum Gate, 1965 (James Tait Black Memorial Prize); Collected Stories I, 1967; Collected Poems I, 1967; The Public Image, 1968; The Very Fine Clock (for children), 1969; The Driver's Seat, 1970. *Recreations:* poetry, friends, cats, racing. *Address:* c/o Macmillan & Co. Ltd, Little Essex Street, WC2.

**SPARKE, Archibald,** Hon. MA (Manchester); Hon. FRSL, FLA; Hon. Secretary Lancashire Parish Register Society, 1931-57; *b* 19 July 1871; *o surv. s* of late Edward Sparke, Cardiff; *m* 1896, Beatrice (*d* 1948), *e d* of James Andrews, Roath Park, Cardiff; one *d* (and one *d* decd). *Educ:* Tredegarville Sch., Cardiff; private tutors. Formerly Librarian of Kidderminster, Carlisle, Bury, and Bolton; retired, 1931. Freeman of City of Exeter, 1907; Ex-Member Council Library Assoc.; Past Pres. North-West Branch Library Assoc.; Hon. Fellow of Library Assistants' Assoc.; Lectr (extra mural), Victoria Univ., Manchester. *Publications:* The Uses of Public Libraries, 1895; Handbook to Turner's Liber Studiorum, 1902; The Index to the first 16 Vols of Transactions of the Cumberland and Westmorland Antiquarian and Archæological Society (1866-1900), 1901; John Kay, Inventor: an appreciation, 1904; The Bury Art Gallery and the Wrigley Collection of Pictures, 1904; A Bibliography of the Dialect Literature of Cumberland, Westmorland, and Lancashire North of the Sands, 1907; Bibliography of Walt Whitman, 1931; editor and transcriber of The Bury Parish Registers (1647-98), 1905; The Newchurch in Rossendale Parish Registers (1653-1723), 1913; Warrington Parish Registers (1591-1653), 1933; The Township Booke of Halliwell (1640-1762), 1911; Bibliographia Boltoniensis, 1913; The Bolton Parish Registers (1573-1660), 1914; (with A. R. Corns) A Bibliography of Unfinished Books, 1915, 2nd edn, Detroit, 1968; The Deane Parish Registers (1604-1750), 2 Vols, 1917, Vol. 3 (1751-1812), 1940; Great Harwood Parish Registers (1547-1812), 1937; How the Public Library can help the Business Man, 1917, 3rd edn, 1919; Broken Arcs, 1918; The Bowyer Bible, 1920; Town Bibliographies, 1913; (with H. Hamer) The Book of Bolton, 1930; Index to Garstang Parish Registers (1660-1734), 1932; North Meols Parish Registers (1732-1812), 1935; Guide to Iwerne Minster, 1934; 2,000 Items in Notes and Queries (1905-31); Turton Parish Register (1720-1812), 1943; Leigh Parish Registers (1626-1700), 1948; Warrington Parish Registers (1653-80), 1955, (1681-1700), 1962; Notes from my Memory Box, 1963; many pamphlets and articles on librarianship and bibliography in professional jls. *Recreation:* ergophobia even in retirement. *Address:* 11 Conyers Avenue, Birkdale, Southport, Lancs. *T:* Southport 67313.

**SPARKES, Sir James;** *see* Sparkes, Sir W. B. J. G.

**SPARKES, Prof. Stanley Robert,** MSc (Bristol); PhD (London); Hon. ACGI; FICE; FIStructE; Professor of Engineering Structures, University of London, at Imperial College, since 1958; Dean of the City and Guilds College since 1967; *b* 30 Nov. 1910; *s* of late Matthew Henry and Rosina Sparkes; *m* 1937, Gladys Muriel, *d* of late Commander James Rea, RN and Alice Maud Rea; no *c*. *Educ:* Cotham Sch.; Bristol Univ. 1851 Exhibitioner, 1932. Assistant Designer Dorman Long and Co., London, 1934-35; Imperial College, London: Demonstrator, Assistant Lecturer, Lecturer, 1935-39; Ministry of Supply, Technical Officer, later Research and Development Officer, Passive Air Defence, 1939-42, and 1943-44; Government of India, Structural Precautions Adviser, 1942-43; Imperial College, 1944-; Reader in Civil Engrg, Univ. of London, 1947; seconded to be in charge of Planning Office dealing with IC Expansion Scheme, 1953; Dir of Building Works, 1955-58. Chm., Imp. Coll. Cttee for Collaboration with Indian Inst. of Technology, Delhi; Mem., UGC Technology Sub-Cttee; Member of Council: IStructE, 1958-61; ICE, 1963-68; Univ. of Science and Technology, Kumasi, 1963-68; Mem. Court, Brunel Univ. *Publications:* papers in scientific and engineering journals and publications of professional engineering and architectural bodies. *Recreations:* Rugby, squash, cricket, tennis, gardening, motoring, music and architectural planning. *Address:* Imperial College, SW7. *T:* 01-589 5111; 499 High Road, Harrow Weald, Middlesex. *T:* 01-954 1954.

**SPARKES, Sir (Walter Beresford) James (Gordon),** Kt 1970; Governing Director, Lyndley Pastoral Co., since 1958; Stud Master, Lyndley Hereford Stud and Lyndley Poll Hereford Stud; a Director, Logan Downs Pastoral Co., since 1969; *b* 1889; *s* of James Sparkes, Barbigal Station via Dubbo, NSW; *m* 1st, 1915, Jessie (*née* Lang); one *d*; 2nd, 1920, Alice Goongarry (*née* Scott); three *s* (and one *s* decd). *Educ:* St Joseph's Coll., Sydney. Established Lyndley Hereford Stud (oldest and largest Hereford Stud still operating in Australia), 1911; estab. Lyndley Poll Hereford Stud, 1932 (a pioneer of this breed in Aust.); played a leading part in formation of Aust. Hereford Soc. (in 1918) and also at a later date Aust. Poll Hereford Soc.; Chm., Wambo Shire Council, 1922-31 and 1937-52; Pres., Local Govt Assoc. of Queensland, 1928-32; Queensland State Parlt: Mem. for Dalby, 1932-35; Mem. for Aubigny, 1941-60. Vice-Pres., Royal National Agric. and Industrial Assoc. of Queensland, 1963- (Mem. Coun. 1949-). *Recreation:* tennis. *Address:* Lyndley, via Jandowae, Queensland, Australia.

**SPARKMAN, John J.;** Senator, USA, since Nov. 1946; *b* 20 Dec. 1899; *s* of Whitten J. Sparkman and Julia Mitchell (*née* Kent); *m* 1923, Ivo Hall; one *d*. *Educ:* University of Alabama. AB 1921, LLB 1923, AM 1924. Admitted to Alabama Bar, 1925; practised as Attorney, Huntsville, Ala, 1925-36; US Commissioner, 1930-31; Member of US House of Representatives, 1937-46; Democratic Nomination for Vice-Presidency, 1952. Hon. LLD: Alabama; Spring Hill Coll., Ala; Auburn. Methodist. *Address:* Huntsville, Alabama 35801, USA; Senate Office Building, Washington, DC 20510, USA. *Clubs:* Army-Navy Country, 1925 F Street (both Washington); Huntsville Country (Alabama).

**SPARKS, Arthur Charles,** BSc (Econ); Under-Secretary, Ministry of Agriculture, Fisheries and Food, since 1959; *b* 1914; *s* of late Charles Herbert and Kate Dorothy Sparks; *m* 1939, Betty Joan, *d* of late Harry Oswald and Lilian Mary Simmons; three *d*. *Educ:* Selhurst Grammar Sch.; London School of Economics. Clerk, Ministry of Agriculture and Fisheries, 1931; Administrative Grade, 1936; National Fire Service, 1942-44; Principal Private Secretary to Minister of Agriculture and Fisheries, 1946-47; Asst Secretary, Ministry of Agriculture and Fisheries, 1947-49 and 1951-59; Asst Secretary, Treasury, 1949-51. *Recreations:* reading, walking. *Address:* 7 Cottenham Place, West Wimbledon, SW20. *T:* 01-947 1908. *Club:* Farmers'.

**SPARKS, Rev. Hedley Frederick Davis,** DD Oxon, 1949; FBA 1959; Oriel Professor of the Interpretation of Holy Scripture, University of Oxford, since 1952; *b* 14 Nov. 1908; *s* of late Rev. Frederick Sparks and late Blanche Barnes Sparks (formerly Jackson); *m* 1953, Margaret Joan, *d* of C. H. Davy; two *s* one *d*. *Educ:* St Edmund's Sch., Canterbury; BNC, Oxford; Ripon Hall, Oxford. Hon. DD (St Andrews), 1963. *Recreations:* music and railways. *Address:* Oriel College, Oxford; 48 London Road, Canterbury, Kent.

**SPARKS, Joseph Alfred;** Mayor of the Borough of Acton, 1957-58; *b* 30 Sept. 1901; *s* of late Samuel and Edith Sparks; *m* 1928, Dora Brent; two *s*. *Educ:* Uffculm School and Central Labour College. Alderman of Borough of Acton and County of Middlesex, 1958-61; retired. Clerk Western Region, British Railways; President, London District Council NUR, 1934-45; Parliamentary Labour Candidate, Taunton, 1929, Chelmsford, 1931, and Buckingham, 1935. MP (Lab) Acton, 1945-Sept. 1959. Freeman of the Borough of Acton. *Address:* 10 Emanuel Avenue, W3. *T:* 01-992 2069.

**SPARROW, (Albert) Charles,** QC 1966; *b* Kasauli, India, 16 Sept. 1925; *e s* of late Captain Charles Thomas and Antonia Sparrow; *m* 1949, Edith Rosalie Taylor; two *s* one *d*. *Educ:* Royal Grammar Sch., Colchester. Served Civil Defence, 1939-43; joined Army, 1943; posted as cadet to India, commnd into Royal Signals and served in Far East, 1944-47; OC, GHQ Signals, Simla, 1947. Admitted to Gray's Inn, 1947 (Holker Senior Scholar, Atkin Scholar, Lee Prizeman and Richards Prizeman); called to Bar, 1950; LLB London Univ., 1951; admitted to Lincoln's Inn, 1967; in practice in Chancery, 1950-. Member: Chancery Procedure Cttee, 1968-; General Council of the Bar, 1969-; Senate of the Four Inns of Court, 1970-. Hon. Legal Adviser to Council for British Archæology, 1968-. *Recreation:* Romano-British archæology. *Address:* 13 Old Square, Lincoln's Inn, WC2. *T:* 01-405 3871; Croyde Lodge, Stock, Essex.

**SPARROW, Charles;** *see* Sparrow, A. C.

**SPARROW, John Hanbury Angus;** Warden of All Souls College, Oxford; *b* New Oxley, near Wolverhampton, 13 Nov. 1906; *e s* of I. S. Sparrow and Margaret Macgregor; unmarried. *Educ:* Winchester (Scholar); New Coll., Oxford (Scholar). 1st Class, Hon. Mods, 1927; 1st Class, Lit Hum, 1929; Fellow of All Souls Coll., 1929 (re-elected 1937, 1946); Chancellor's Prize for Latin Verse, 1929; Eldon Scholar, 1929; called to Bar, Middle Temple, 1931; practised in Chancery Division, 1931-39; enlisted in Oxford and Bucks LI, 1939; Commnd Coldstream Guards, 1940; Military Asst to Lt-Gen. Sir H. C. B. Wemyss in War Office and on Military Mission in Washington, Feb.-Dec. 1941; rejoined regt in England, 1942; DAAG and AAG, War Office, 1942-45; OBE 1946; resumed practice at Bar, 1946; ceased to practice on appointment as Warden of All Souls Coll., 1952; Hon. Bencher, Middle Temple, 1952; Fellow of Winchester Coll., 1951; Hon. Fellow, New Coll., 1956. Hon. DLitt, Univ. of Warwick, 1967. *Publications:* various; mostly reviews and essays in periodicals, some of which were collected in Independent Essays, 1963, and Controversial Essays, 1966; Mark Pattison and the Idea of a University, 1967; After the Assassination, 1968; Visible Words, 1969. *Address:* All Souls College, Oxford. *Clubs:* Garrick, Reform, Beefsteak.

**SPATER, Ernest George;** Chairman: Jas. Thompson & Co. Ltd, Brewers, 1952-69; Hotel Metropole (Llandrindod) Ltd, 1966; President, Lombard Banking Ltd, since 1965 (Chairman, 1951-65); *b* 29 Aug. 1886; British; *m* 1912, Florence Mary (*née* Holland) (*d* 1951); one *d*; *m* 1952, Pamela May (*née* Oliver Crofts); one *d*. *Educ:* Charterhouse Foundation Trust; St Saviour's Grammar Sch. Clerk, Sun Fire Office, 1907; Chief Clerk, British Dominions Insurance Co., 1915. Military service, 1916-19. Eagle Star Insurance Co.: Branch Manager, Cardiff, 1925; Branch Manager, Leeds, 1927; Deputy Agency Manager, 1937; Assistant General Manager, 1940; Joint General Manager, 1948; retired, 1951. Fellow Chartered Insurance Institute (by Examination). *Publication:* Box 1299 (documentary review of insurance documents), 1947. *Recreations:* photography, antiques, travel. *Address:* Daymer, Hervines Road, Amersham, Bucks. *T:* Amersham 7614.

**SPAUL, Eric A.,** DSc, PhD (London); FZS; FIBiol; Professor of Zoology, The University, Leeds, 1933-60; Professor Emeritus, 1960; *b* 27 Aug. 1895. *Educ:* Owen's School, London; Birkbeck Coll., Univ. of London. War Service, 1915-19, Commissioned Rank, London Regt and RE; graduated BSc (London), 1921, PhD 1924, DSc, 1930; Assistant Lecturer, 1921; Lecturer, 1924; Reader in Zoology, University of London, 1930-33. *Publications:* contributed to: The Natural History of the Scarborough District, Vols I & II, 1956; Van Nostrand's Scientific Encyclopedia, 3rd edn, 1958; and to Journal of Experimental Biology, Proceedings of the Zoological Soc., etc. *Recreations:* sports, travel. *Address:* 6 Churchdown Road, Poolbrook, Malvern, Worcs.

**SPEAIGHT, Richard Langford,** CMG 1949; Director of East-West Contacts, Foreign Office, 1960-66; *b* 12 July 1906; *s* of Richard Neville and Alice Langford Speaight; *m* 1934, Margaret Ida Hall; one *s* two *d*. *Educ:* Oundle Sch.; Merton Coll., Oxford. Entered HM Diplomatic Service, 1929; 3rd Secretary, Budapest, 1931; Foreign Office, 1933-35; 2nd Secretary, Warsaw, 1935-38; Foreign Office, 1938-45; 1st Secretary and later Counsellor, Cairo, 1945-48; transferred to Foreign Office, 1948, Head of Information Policy Dept, 1948-50; HM Ambassador at Rangoon, 1950-53; an Asst Under-Secretary of State, FO, 1953-56; HM Minister at Sofia, 1956-58. *Address:* Churches, Monks Eleigh, Ipswich, Suffolk.

**SPEAIGHT, Robert William,** CBE 1958; MA (Oxon); FRSL; actor and author; *b* 14 Jan. 1904; *e s* of late Frederick William Speaight; *m* 1935, Esther Evelyn Bowen; one *s*; *m* 1951, Bridget Laura Bramwell; one *s* (adopted). *Educ:* Haileybury; Lincoln Coll., Oxford. Officer, Legion of Honour, 1969. Hon. Sec., OUDS, 1925; played Peer Gynt and Falstaff for the Society, 1925 and 1926; Liverpool Repertory Theatre, 1926-27; toured Egypt in Shakespeare with Robert Atkins, 1927; Hibbert in Journey's End, at the Savoy and

Prince of Wales, 1929-30; First Player and Osric at the Haymarket in "All Star" Hamlet, Edmund in King Lear, at the Old Vic, Herod in Salome, Gate, 1931; Hamlet, Malvolio, Fluellen, Cassius, King John, etc, Old Vic Season, 1931-32; Becket in Murder in the Cathedral, Canterbury Festival and Mercury, 1935, Duchess, 1936, Provincial Tours, 1937, Tewkesbury Festival, 1937, USA, 1938, Lyric and Mercury, and at Edinburgh Festival, 1947. Played Shakespeare's Coriolanus and Chapman's Biron for William Poel's Elizabethan Stage Circle, 1930 and 1931; Antony in This Way to the Tomb!, Mercury, 1945-46; producer Antony and Cleopatra for Les Rencontres Internationales, Geneva, 1947; Christian in Pilgrim's Progress, Covent Garden, 1948; Seti in The First Born, Edinburgh Festival, 1948; adjudicator, Canadian Dominion Drama Finals Festival, 1948; prod., French versions of Murder in the Cathedral and Romeo and Juliet, Théâtre des Compagnons, Montreal, 1950; producer: The Madwoman of Chaillot, St James'; The Four Men, Festival of Sussex; Gerontius in The Dream of Gerontius, Scala, 1951; St Peter, in Out of the Whirlwind, Westminster Abbey; Pole, in His Eminence of England, Canterbury Festival, 1953; Hardlip and Prime Minister, The Burning Glass, Apollo and tour, 1954; Sir Claude Mulhammer, The Confidential Clerk, Paris Festival, and tour, 1954; Dom Diogo in The Hidden King, Edinburgh Festival, 1957; Guest Artist, Australian Broadcasting Commission, 1953; King Lear, Los Angeles; Becket in Murder in the Cathedral, Adelaide Festival, 1960; Bassa Selim in Die Entführung, Glyndebourne, 1961; More in A Man for All Seasons, Australia, 1962-63; Voice of Christ in The Man Born to be King; King Lear, Kansas City, 1965; Moulton-Barrett in Robert and Elizabeth, 1967. *Publications:* Mutinous Wind, 1932; The Lost Hero, 1934; The Angel in the Mist, 1936; Thomas Becket, 1938; The Unbroken Heart, 1939; Acting, 1939; Drama since 1939, 1948; George Eliot, 1954; William Poel, 1954; Nature in Shakespearian Tragedy, 1955; Hilaire Belloc, 1957; (ed) Letters from Hilaire Belloc, 1958; The Christian Theatre, 1960; William Rothenstein, 1962; Ronald Knox the Writer, 1966; The Life of Eric Gill, 1966; Teilhard de Chardin, 1967; The Property Basket: recollections of a divided life, 1970; Vanier, 1970; frequent articles in the weekly press. *Recreations:* walking and riding. *Address:* Campion House, Benenden, Kent. *T:* Benenden 617. *Clubs:* Garrick, Beefsteak; Stephens Green (Dublin).

**SPEAKMAN, Sergeant William,** VC 1951; HM Army; *b* 21 Sept. 1927; *m* 1956, Rachel Snitch; one *s. Educ:* Wellington Road Senior Boys' Sch., Altrincham. Entered Army as Private. Served Korean War, 1950-53 (VC), King's Own Scottish Borderers. *Recreations:* swimming, and ski-ing. *Address:* 27 Moss Lane, Altrincham, Cheshire.

**SPEAR, Ruskin,** RA 1954 (ARA 1944); artist; visiting teacher, Royal College of Art, South Kensington; *b* 30 June 1911; *s* of Augustus and Jane Spear; *m* 1935, Mary Hill; one *s. Educ:* Brook Green School; Hammersmith School of Art; Royal College of Art, Kensington, under Sir William Rothenstein. Diploma, 1934; first exhibited Royal Academy, 1932; elected London Group, 1942; President London Group, 1949-50; Visiting teacher, Royal College of Art. Pictures purchased by Chantrey Bequest, Contemporary Art Society, Arts Council of Great Britain, and British Council. Exhibited work in Pushkin Museum, Moscow, 1957; has also exhibited in Paris, USA, Belgium, S Africa, Australia, NZ. Commissions include: Altar Piece for RAF Memorial Church, St Clement Danes, 1959; four mural panels for P&O Liner Canberra. Recent portraits include: Lord Adrian (Trinity Coll., Cambridge); Herbert Butterfield (Vice-Chancellor, Cambridge Univ.); Sir Stewart Duke-Elder (Faculty of Ophthalmologists); Sir Laurence Olivier as Macbeth (Stratford Memorial Theatre); Lord Chandos (British Metals Corp.); Sir Ian Jacob (Past Dir-Gen. BBC); Sir Robin Darwin (Principal of Royal Coll. of Art); Miss Ruth Cohen (Principal of Newnham Coll., Cambridge); Sir Eric Ashby (Master of Queen's Univ., Belfast); S. S. Eriks, KBE (Dir of Mullard Ltd); Dr Ramsey, Archbishop of Canterbury (Magdalen Coll., Cambridge); Sir Aubrey Lewis (Maudsley Hospital); Arthur Armitage (Vice-Chancellor, Cambridge Univ.); Harold Wilson (Jesus Coll., Oxford); 5th Duke of Westminster. *Address:* 20 Fielding Road, Chiswick, W4. *T:* 01-995 9736; (Studio) 11a Bath Road, Chiswick, W4.

**SPEARING, Nigel John;** MP (Lab) Acton, since 1970; *b* 8 Oct. 1930; *s* of Austen and May Spearing; *m* 1956, Wendy, *d* of Percy and Molly Newman, Newport, Mon; one *s* two *d. Educ:* Latymer Upper School, Hammersmith. Ranks and commission, Royal Signals, 1950-52; St Catharine's Coll., Cambridge, 1953-56. Tutor and later Sen. Geography Master, Wandsworth School, 1956-68; Director, Thameside Research and Development Group, Inst. of Community Studies, 1968-69; Housemaster, Elliott School, Putney, 1969-70. Chairman: Barons Court Labour Party, 1961-63; Hammersmith Local Govt Cttee of the Labour Party, 1966-68. Contested (Lab) Warwick and Leamington, 1964. Chairman, Broadway Congregational Friendly Soc.; Vice-Chairman, River Thames Soc. Co-opted Mem. GLC Cttees from 1966, now Mem. Environmental Planning Cttee. *Publication:* The Thames Barrier-Barrage Controversy, (Inst. of Community Studies), 1969. *Recreations:* rowing, sailing, reading. *Address:* House of Commons, SW1. *T:* 01-930 6240.

**SPEARMAN, Sir Alexander (Bowyer),** 4th Bt, *cr* 1840; Hon. Captain late 10th Bn 7th Rajputs; Director, Delta Insurance Brokers (Pty) Ltd, Cape Town; *b* 15 Feb. 1917; *S* father, 1959; *m* 1950, Martha, *d* of John Green, Naauwpoort, SA; one *s* three *d. Educ:* Westminster. War of 1939-45, Staff Capt., Delhi, 1941-43, Paiforce, 1943-45. FCII. *Recreation:* philately. *Heir: s* Alexander Young Richard Mainwaring Spearman, *b* 3 Feb. 1969. *Address:* 88 Camps Bay Drive, Camps Bay, Cape Town, CP, South Africa.

**SPEARMAN, Sir Alexander Cadwallader Mainwaring,** Kt 1956; *b* 1901; *s* of late Commander A. C. M. Spearman, Royal Navy; *m* 1928, Diana (marriage dissolved, 1951), *d* of Colonel Sir Arthur Doyle, 4th Bt; *m* 1951, Diana Josephine, *d* of Colonel Sir Lambert Ward, 1st Bt, CVO, DSO, TD; four *s* one *d. Educ:* Repton; Hertford College, Oxford. Contested Mansfield Div., Gen. Election, 1935, Gorton Div. of Manchester, By-Election, 1937; MP (C) Scarborough and Whitby, 1941-66, retd. PPS to President of the Board of Trade, 1951-52. *Address:* The Old Rectory, Sarratt, Herts. *T:* King's Langley 4733; 32 Queen Anne's Gate, SW1. *T:* 01-930 5355; Fealar, Enochdhu, Blairgowrie, Perthshire. *Club:* Beefsteak.

**SPEARS, Maj.-Gen. Sir Edward (Louis),** 1st Bt *cr* 1953; KBE 1942 (CBE 1919); CB 1921; MC; FInstD; *b* 7 Aug. 1886; *o s* of Charles McCarthy Spears and Marguerite Melicent Hack; *m* 1918, Mary Borden, (*d* 1968) (one *s* decd); *m* 1969, Nancy, *e d* of late Maj.-Gen. Sir Frederick and Lady Maurice. *Educ:* privately.

Kildare Militia, 1903; gazetted 8th Hussars, 1906; transferred 11th Hussars, 1910; temporary Captain 1914; Brevet Major; Brevet Lt-Col; Hon. Brig.-Gen.; Head of British Military Mission, Paris, 1917-20; retired, 1920 (despatches 5 times, 4 times wounded, 3 times cited in French Army Orders, CB, CBE, MC, Commander Legion of Honour, Croix de Guerre with 3 palms, Etoile Noire, Grand Cross of White Eagle of Serbia, Czecho-Slovak Croix de Guerre; mentioned in Polish despatches); MP (NL) Loughborough Div. of Leicester, 1922-24; MP (U) Carlisle, 1931-45; Maj.-Gen. 1940; Prime Minister's Personal Rep. with French Prime Minister and Minister of Defence, May-June 1940; Head of British Mission to General de Gaulle, June 1940; Head of Spears Mission, Syria and the Lebanon, July 1941; First Minister to Republics of Syria and the Lebanon, 1942-44; Hon. Maj.-Gen. 1945; Chm. of Council, Inst. of Directors until 1965 (past Chm. of Institute, and Pres., 1953-54, Chancellor, 1966); Founder and first Chm., House of Commons Motor Club. Chm., Ashanti Goldfields Ltd; Director: Lonrho Ltd; West End Bd, Commercial Union Assurance Co. Ltd. *Publications:* Lessons of the Russo-Japanese War; Cavalry Tactical Schemes; Liaison, 1914, 1931, repr. 1968; Prelude to Victory, 1939; Assignment to Catastrophe, 1954; Two Men Who Saved France, 1966; The Picnic Basket, 1967. *Address:* 12 Strathearn Place, W2. *T:* 01-723 8849; 164 St Stephens House, SW1. *T:* 01-930 3781; St Michael's Grange, Warfield, Berks. *T:* Bracknell 66. *Clubs:* Cavalry, Carlton.

**SPECTOR, Professor Walter Graham;** Professor of Pathology in the University of London at St Bartholomew's Hospital Medical College, since 1962; Consultant Pathologist, St Bartholomew's Hospital; Secretary, Beit Memorial Fellowships Advisory Board; *b* 20 Dec. 1924; *o s* of H. Spector, London; *m* 1957, June, *o d* of Col W. F. Routley, OBE, Melbourne, Australia; two *s*. *Educ:* City of London School; Queens' Coll., Cambridge; UCH Med. School (Graham Sch.). MB 1947, MA 1949, Cambridge; MRCP 1948; FRCP 1966. Beit Memorial Fellow in Medical Research, 1951; Lecturer in Pathology, University College Hospital Med. School, 1953; Rockefeller Trav. Fell., 1956; Litchfield Lectr, Univ. of Oxford, 1957; Sen. Lectr in Pathology, Univ. Coll. Hosp. Med. School, 1960. *Publications:* Chemistry of the Injured Cell (jtly), 1960; numerous scientific papers and review articles in Pathology. *Recreations:* Australiana, amateur sociology. *Address:* Department of Pathology, St Bartholomew's Hospital, West Smithfield, EC1. *T:* 01-606 7777; 99 Kingsley Way, N2. *T:* 01-458 4720.

**SPEED, Sir Eric Bourne Bentinck,** KCB, *cr* 1945; KBE, *cr* 1943; MC; *b* 26 Jan. 1895; *s* of late Rev. Francis Bentinck Speed and Martha Ellen Chambers; *m* 1st, Rosa Dorothy Giles (marriage dissolved); one *s*; 2nd, Ursula, *d* of Alwyn Rashleigh Phipps; one *s* one *d*. *Educ:* Christ's Hospital; Scholar-elect of St John's College, Oxford, 1914. Served European War with KOYLI, 1914-18 (MC, French Croix de Guerre avec Etoile en Vermeil, despatches). Appointed to War Office, 1920; transferred to Treasury, 1934; Private Sec. to Rt Hon. Stanley Baldwin, Prime Minister and First Lord of the Treasury, 1936-37; rejoined War Office, 1940; Permanent Under-Sec. of State for War, 1942-48; retired, Dec. 1948. *Clubs:* Constitutional, MCC.

**SPEED, (Herbert) Keith,** RD 1967; MP (C) Meriden since March 1968; an Assistant Government Whip since 1970; *b* 11 March 1934; *s* of Herbert Victor Speed and Dorothy Barbara (*née* Mumford); *m* 1961, Peggy Voss Clarke; two *s* one *d* (and one *s* decd). *Educ:* Greenhill Sch., Evesham; Bedford Modern Sch.; RNC, Dartmouth and Greenwich. Officer, RN, 1947-56; Sales Man., Amos (Electronics) Ltd, 1957-60; Marketing Man., Plysu Products Ltd, 1960-65; Officer, Conservative Res. Dept, 1965-68. *Publications:* Blue Print for Britain, 1965; contribs to various political jls. *Recreations;* classical music, motor cycling, reading. *Address:* Hollyoak, 102 Kenilworth Road, Coventry, Warwickshire. *T:* Coventry 67403. *Clubs:* Atherstone Unionist, Hartshill Conservative (Warwicks).

**SPEED, Keith;** *see* Speed, H. K.

**SPEED, Sir Robert (William Arney),** Kt 1954; CB 1946; QC 1963; Counsel to the Speaker since 1960; *b* 1905; *s* of late Sir Edwin Arney Speed; *m* 1929, Phyllis, *d* of Rev. P. Armitage; one *s* one *d*. *Educ:* Rugby; Trinity College, Cambridge. Called to Bar, Inner Temple, 1928; Bencher, 1961; Principal Assistant Solicitor, Office of HM Procurator-General and Treasury Solicitor, 1945-48; Solicitor to the Board of Trade, 1948-60. *Address:* Upper Culham, Wargrave, Berks. *T:* Henley-on-Thames 4271. *Club:* Oxford and Cambridge University.

**SPEELMAN, Sir Cornelis Jacob,** 8th Bt *cr* 1686; BA; *b* 17 March 1917; *s* of Sir Cornelis Jacob Speelman, 7th Bt and Maria Catharina Helena, Castendijk; *S* father, 1949. Education Dept, Royal Dutch Army, 1947-49; with The Shell Company (Marketing Service Dept), 1950. Student, Univ. of Western Australia, 1952; formerly Master of Modern Languages at Clifton Coll. and at Geelong Grammar Sch. *Address:* 82 Ramplaan, Harlem, Netherlands.

**SPEIDEL, General Hans,** Dr phil; Knight, Württemberg Order of Merit (1914-18); Kt, Iron Cross, 1943; President, Foundation of Science and Politics, since 1964; *b* Metzingen/Württemberg, 28 Oct. 1897; *m* 1925, Ruth Stahl; one *s* two *d*. *Educ:* Eberhard-Ludwig-Gymnasium of the Humanities, Stuttgart; Univs of Berlin and Tübingen, Technische Hochschule, Stuttgart. Ensign, Grenadier Regt, König Karl (5. Württ.) Nr 123, 1914; Regimental Adjutant, Western Front, 1915-18; entered Reichswehr (3 years at Military Academy); during War of 1939-45 was successively Chief of Staff of Army Corps and Army (8) (Eastern Front), and of Field Marshal Rommel's Army Group (Western Front); arrested on Himmler's orders, 1944; released from Gestapo imprisonment at end of the War. Lecturer, Tübingen Univ. and Leibnitz University Coll.; Military Adviser, Federal Govt, 1951; Military Delegate-in-Chief to EDC (European Defence Community) and NATO negotiations, 1951-55; Commander-in-Chief of Combined German Forces, 1955-57; Commander Allied Land Forces, Central Europe, 1957-63; Special Counsellor to Federal Government, W Germany, 1963-64. Commander, US Legion of Merit, 1961; Grosses Verdienstkreuz BRII mit Stern und Schulterband. *Publications:* Invasion 1944 (a contribution to the fate of Rommel and the Reich), 1949; Zeitbetrachtungen, 1969; Editor and commentator on Vol. of Essays by Gen. Ludwig Beck, 1955; essays on Ernst Jünger, Theodor Heuss, Eugen Bircher, Gneisenau and Beck, etc. *Recreation:* study of history and literature. *Address:* Am Spitzenbach 21, Bad Honnef, Germany.

**SPEIGHT, Harold Edwin Balme;** retired college dean, United States; *b* Bradford, 1887; *s* of Edwin Speight and Charlotte Hall; *m* 1911, Mabel Grant, Ballater; two *d*; *m* 1967, Victoria Mary Tapp, Montreal, Canada. *Educ:* Univ. of Aberdeen; Exeter College, Oxford. Asst, Dept of Logic and Metaphysics, Univ. of Aberdeen, 1909-10; Fellow Manchester Coll., Oxford, 1910-12; served in the ministry, 1912-27; Chaplain with US Army in France, 1918-19; DD Tufts Univ., 1925; resigned from ministry and joined Soc. of Friends, 1928. Prof. of Philosophy, Dartmouth, 1927-29 (Hon. MA 1927); Prof. of Biography and Chm. of Dept, Dartmouth, 1929-33; Dean of Men, Swarthmore Coll., 1933-38; Dean of Coll., 1938-40; Exec. Sec., Assoc. of Colls and Univs of State of NY, 1940-42; Dean of Coll., St Lawrence Univ., 1942-45, and Actg President, 1944-45; Dean of Students, Cornell University, 1945-46; Dean of the College, Elmira College, Elmira, NY, 1946-49. Pres., Scottish Club of Twin States (NH and Vt). *Publications:* Life and Writings of John Bunyan, 1928; Editor, Creative Lives Series, 1930-33; Literary Editor, Christian Leader, 1927-38, etc. *Recreations:* gardening, photography. *Address:* 2544 Cedar Hill Rd, Victoria, BC, Canada.

**SPEIR, Sir Rupert (Malise),** Kt 1964; Chairman, Crossley Building Products Ltd; Chairman, Smith's Food Group Ltd; Director of other companies; *b* 10 Sept. 1910; *y s* of late Guy Thomas Speir and late Mary Lucy Fletcher, of Saltoun. *Educ:* Eton Coll.; Pembroke Coll., Cambridge (BA). Admitted Solicitor, 1936. Special Mem., Hops Marketing Board, 1958. Served in Army throughout War of 1939-45; commissioned in Intelligence Corps, Sept. 1939; retired with rank of Lt-Col, 1945. Contested (C) Linlithgow, 1945, Leek, 1950; MP (C) Hexham Div. of Northumberland, 1951-66, retired. Sponsor of: Litter Act, 1958; Noise Abatement Act, 1960; Local Government (Financial Provisions) Act, 1963; Parliamentary Private Secretary: to Minister of State for Foreign Affairs and to Parly Sec., CRO, 1956-59; to Parly and Fin. Sec., Admty and to Civil Lord of Admty, 1952-56. Hon. Fellow, Inst. of Public Cleansing; Vice-Pres., Keep Britain Tidy Group. *Recreations:* golf, shooting, fishing. *Address:* 120 Cheapside, EC2. *T:* 01-588 4000; 240 Cranmer Court, Sloane Avenue, SW3. *T:* 01-589 2057; Birtley Hall, Hexham, Northumberland. *T:* Wark 275. *Clubs:* Brooks's; Northern Counties (Newcastle); New (North Berwick).

**SPENCE, Allan William,** MA, MD Cantab; FRCP; in practice as Consultant Physician; Medical Referee to the Civil Service Commission since 1952; Physician on Medical Appeal Tribunal, Department of Health and Social Security, since 1969 (Ministry of Social Security, 1965-69); Hon. Consultant Physician: St Bartholomew's Hospital, since 1965; Luton and Dunstable Hospital, since 1965; King George Hospital, Ilford, since 1967; Governor, St Bartholomew's Hospital Medical College, since 1965; *b* 4 Aug. 1900; *s* of late William Ritchie Spence and Emma (*née* Allan), Bath; *m* 1930, Martha Lena, *d* of late Hugh Hamilton Hutchison, JP, Girvan, Ayrshire; two *s*. *Educ:* King Edward's VI School, Bath; Gonville and Caius College, Cambridge; St Bartholomew's Hospital, London. Brackenbury Schol. in Medicine, 1926, Lawrence Research Schol. and Gold Medal, 1929-30, Cattlin Research Fell., 1938, St Bartholomew's Hosp.; Rockefeller Foundation Fellow, USA, 1931-32. House Phys., 1927, Demonstrator of Physiology, 1928-30, of Pathology, 1930-31, First Asst, 1933-36, Asst Dir of Med. Unit, 1936-37, St Bartholomew's Hospital; Physician St Bartholomew's Hosp., London, 1937-65; King George Hospital, Ilford, 1938-67; Luton and Dunstable Hospital, 1946-65; Hon. Consultant in Endocrinology to Army at Home, 1954-65; Member Medical Research Coun. Adv. Cttee: on Iodine Deficiency and Thyroid Disease, 1933-39; and on Hormones, 1937-41. Hon. Lt-Col, RAMC; service in North Africa and Greece as OC Med. Div., 97th Gen. Hosp., 1943-45. Mem. Assoc. of Physicians of Gt Brit.; Foundation Mem. Soc. for Endocrinology, to 1965; Fellow RSM (Vice-Pres., Section of Med., 1949, Pres. Section of Endocrinology, 1951-52, Councillor, 1958-61); Foundn Mem. Internat. Soc. of Internal Medicine; Fellow Medical Soc. of London (Councillor, 1957-60); Foundn Mem., London Thyroid Club; Mem., Physiological Soc., 1935-52; Emeritus Mem., Endocrine Society, USA, 1966. Examr in Medicine: Univ. of Cambridge, 1946-50; to Society of Apothecaries of London, 1947-52; in Therapeutics to University of London, 1953-57; to the Conjoint Examining Bd in England, 1955-59; to Fellowship of Faculty of Anæsthetists, RCS, 1964-66. Mem. of Editorial Bd, Jl of Endocrinology, 1956-63. Freeman of City of London; Member of Livery, Society of Apothecaries of London. *Publications:* Clinical Endocrinology, 1953 (translated into Spanish); articles to medical and scientific journals on endocrinological and general medical subjects. *Recreations:* gardening; formerly rowing (Pres. Caius Boat Club, 1922-23). *Address:* 149 Harley Street, W1. *T:* 01-935 4444; 23 Brockley Avenue, Stanmore, Mddx HA7 4LX. *T:* 01-958 7719. *Club:* Hawks (Cambridge).

**SPENCE, Col Sir Basil H. H. N.;** *see* Neven-Spence.

**SPENCE, Sir Basil (Urwin),** OM 1962; Kt 1960; OBE 1948; TD 1957; RA 1960 (ARA 1953); ARSA 1952; RDI 1960; Professor of Architecture, Royal Academy, 1961-68; Treasurer of Royal Academy, 1962-64; RIBA Council Member from 1952 (Vice-President, 1954-55; Hon. Secretary, 1956; President, 1958-60); Member Board of Trustees, Civic Trust; Hon. Fellow Royal College of Art, 1962; Hon. Fellow American Institute of Architects, 1962; *b* 13 Aug. 1907; *s* of Urwin Spence, ICS, and Daisy Crisp; *m* 1934, Mary Joan Ferris; one *s* one *d*. *Educ:* George Watson's College, Edinburgh; Schools of Architecture, London and Edinburgh Univs. RIBA Silver Medallist, 1931; Arthur Cates Prizeman (Town Planning), 1932; Pugin Student, 1933; assisted Sir Edwin Lutyens, OM, in preparation of drawings for the Viceroy's House at Delhi. Served War in Army, 1939-45 (despatches twice). First Hoffman Wood Professor of Architecture, Leeds Univ., 1955-56. Mem. Fine Art Commn, 1956-70. Has built large country houses before War of 1939-45 and, since then, housing estates, theatres, schools, university buildings, churches and factories. Festival of Britain, 1951, award (by Council for Architecture, Town Planning and Building Research) for Housing Estate at Sunbury-on-Thames; won competition for design of new Coventry Cathedral, 1951; Saltire Award for Fishermen's Houses at Dunbar, East Lothian, 1952; Newhaven, 1960. Parish Churches: Manchester, Sheffield, Leicester, Coventry, Edinburgh, 1955-60; apptd Architectural Cons. Trawsfynydd Nuc. Power Stn, 1960; Undergrad. Rooms, Queens' College, Cambridge; Planning Cons. Southampton Univ., 1955 (Arts, Chemistry, Physics, Engrg Bldgs, Women's Hall of Residence, Sen. Common Room); apptd architect for Brit.

Embassy, Rome, 1960; Household Cavalry Barracks, Knightsbridge; Glasgow Air Terminal, Abbotsinch; Physics Buildings, Liverpool and Durham Univs; apptd Architect for Master Plan, Univ. of Sussex (Physics, Arts, Library, Biology, Chemistry, Engrg Sciences Bldgs, College House, Vice-Chancellor's House); Physics and Chemistry Bldgs, Exeter Univ.; Hampstead Civic Centre. Adviser to Bd of Trade for Brit. Industries Fair, 1947, 1948, 1949. Chief Architect: Britain Can Make It Exhibition; Enterprise Scotland, 1947 Exhibition; Scottish Industries Exhibition, 1949; Heavy Industries Exhibition, Festival of Britain, 1951; Architect, Sea and Ships Pavilion, Festival of Britain, 1951; apptd Architect for British Pavilion, 1967 World Exhbn, Montreal; Architectural Consultant: (with Prof. Nervi) for extension to Palais des Nations, Geneva; for Internat. Airport, Baghdad. Hon. DLitt: Leicester, 1963; Southampton, 1965; Hon. LLD Manitoba, 1963. Bronze Medal, RIBA, for Falmer House, Univ. of Sussex, 1963; Coventry Award of Merit, 1970. *Publication:* Phœnix at Coventry, 1962. *Recreations:* painting and sailing. *Address:* 1 Canonbury Place, N1. *T:* 01-226 7175. *Club:* Travellers'.

**SPENCE, Henry Reginald,** OBE; *b* 22 June 1897; *s* of James Henry Easton Spence and Gertrude Mary Hawke; *m* 1939, Eileen Beryl Walter; one *s* one *d.* Was Area Commandant of ATC for North-East Scotland. MP (C) Central Division, County of Aberdeen and Kincardine, 1945-50, West Aberdeenshire, 1950-59. *Recreations:* ski-ing, sailing, golf, shooting. *Address:* 11 Wynnstay Gardens, Allen Street, W8. *Club:* Caledonian.

**SPENCE, John Deane;** MP (C) Heeley Division of Sheffield since 1970; civil engineering and building contractor; director of various companies connected with construction industry; *b* 7 Dec. 1920; *s* of George Spence, Belfast; *m* 1944, Hester Nicholson; one *s* one *d.* *Educ:* Queen's Univ. of Belfast. Mem., Public Relations and Organization Cttee, Building Industry, 1967; Nat. Pres., UK Commercial Travellers' Assoc., 1965-66. *Recreations:* golf, travel. *Address:* House of Commons, SW1.

**SPENCE, Robert,** CB 1953; FRS 1959; Professor of Applied Chemistry, and Master of Keynes College, University of Kent at Canterbury, since 1968; *b* 7 Oct. 1905; British; *m* 1936, Kate Lockwood; two *s* one *d.* *Educ:* King's Coll., Univ. of Durham. Commonwealth Fund Fellow at Princeton Univ., USA, 1928-31; Lecturer in Physical Chemistry, Leeds Univ., 1931-46. War of 1939-45: OC Leeds Univ. STC, Lt-Col until 1942; Chemical Warfare Adviser, HQ RAF Middle East, 1942-43 and at HQ, MAAF, Caserta, 1943-44. Member of Anglo-Canadian Atomic Energy Laboratory, Montreal, 1945; Head of Chemistry Division, Atomic Energy Research Establishment, Harwell, 1946; Chief Chemist, 1948; Dep. Director, 1960-64; Director, 1964-68. *Publications:* scientific papers in Jl of Chemical Soc., etc. *Address:* Keynes College, The University of Kent at Canterbury, Canterbury, Kent. *T:* Canterbury 66822.

**SPENCER,** family name of **Viscount Churchill** and of **Earl Spencer.**

**SPENCER,** 7th Earl *cr* 1765; **Albert Edward John Spencer,** TD 1944; FSA; FRSA; Baron and Viscount Spencer, 1761; Viscount Althorp, 1765; Viscount Althorp (UK), 1905; Lord Lieutenant and Custos Rotulorum for Northamptonshire, 1952-67; Trustee of Wallace Collection, 1945-66; Member Standing Commission on Museums and Galleries, 1948-66; Chairman Sulgrave Manor Board; Chairman Area Management Hospital Committee for Northampton, 1948-66; President Roxburghe Club; President Walpole Society; Chairman Advisory Council of the Victoria and Albert Museum, 1961-69; *b* 23 May 1892; *e s* of 6th Earl Spencer and Hon. Margaret Baring (*d* 1906), *d* of 1st Baron Revelstoke; *S* father, 1922; *m* 1919, Lady Cynthia Ellinor Beatrix Hamilton (*see* Countess Spencer), *d* of 3rd Duke of Abercorn; one *s* one *d.* *Educ:* Harrow; Trinity Coll., Cambridge (MA). Captain 1st Life Guards; served European War (wounded); ADC Personal Staff, 1917-19; retd 1924; Hon. Colonel: 4 Bn Northants Regt (TA), 1924-37; Northants Searchlight Regt (TA), 1937-55; 438th LAA Regt, RA (TA), 1955-61; 4/5 Bn Northants Regt (TA), 1961-67; President: Hunts and Northants Territorial Assoc., to 1967; Old Contemptibles, Northants Br. Patron: E Midlands Area, Brit. Legion; Northants Br. Brit. Legion; Kettering Div. Cons. Assoc., 1924-43; Northants Rural Community Council; Northampton & County Trustee Savings Bank; Northampton Town and County Assoc. for the Blind; St John's Ambulance Coun. for Northants; Northants Antiquarian Soc.; Northants Assoc. of Boy Scouts; CPRE (Northants Br.); Roadmender Boys and Girls Club, Northampton (Jt Founder); Putney Hosp., 1938-48. Chairman: Governors of Wellington Sch., 1946-; Northants area Nat. Health Service; Northampton and County Police Authy; Governor, St Andrew's hosp., Northampton, 1920-67 (Pres. 1952-67); Mem. Church Assembly House of Laity, 1930-35; Trustee: Pytchley Hunt; Nicolls Charity; Sec., Soc. of Dilettanti; Northamptonshire: JP, 1916-67; DL 1935-52; CC 1925; CA 1952. Hon. DLitt Leicester, 1968. KStJ. *Heir: s* Viscount Althorp, *qv.* *Address:* Althorp, Northampton. *T:* East Haddon 200; 37 St James's Place, SW1. *T:* 01-499 2280. *Clubs:* Brooks's, St James', Turf.

*See also Lady Delia Peel.*

**SPENCER, Rt. Hon. Countess, (Cynthia Ellinor Beatrix),** DCVO 1953; OBE 1943; Lady of the Bedchamber to Queen Elizabeth the Queen Mother since 1937; *b* 16 Aug. 1897; 2nd *d* of 3rd Duke of Abercorn, KG, PC, KP; *m* 1919, 7th Earl Spencer, *qv*; one *s* one *d.* *Address:* Althorp, Northampton. *T:* East Haddon 200.

**SPENCER, Lt-Col Aubrey Vere,** DSO 1914; MA Oxford, 1928; DL, JP Oxfordshire; Bursar of Corpus Christi College, Oxford, 1925-46; Land Agent for Oxford University, 1939-51; late 3rd Bn Oxfordshire and Buckinghamshire Light Infantry; *b* 4 April 1886; *o s* of late Aubrey J. Spencer, JP, of Wheatfield Park, Oxfordshire, and Florence Mary, *d* of Frederick H. Janson; *m* 1926, Gwendoline Esther Hall (*d* 1968), *widow* of Capt. Claude Holdsworth Hunt, RFA and *d* of G. N. Murton, Petleys, Downe, Kent. *Educ:* Marlborough; Wye Agricultural College, Kent. Served European War, 1914 (despatches, DSO); Lieut-Col Commanding a Bn Oxfordshire Home Guard. FRICS. High Sheriff of Oxfordshire, 1959. *Address:* Wheatfield Park, Tetsworth, Oxon. *T:* Tetsworth 225.

**SPENCER, Cyril Charles,** CMG 1951; First Deputy Executive Director, International Coffee Organisation, London, 1964-68; *b* 1 Feb. 1912; *s* of Albert Edward Spencer, CBE, and late Elsie Maud Spencer; *m* 1st, 1938; one *d*; 2nd, 1949, Catherine Dewar Robertson. *Educ:* Royal Grammar Sch., Worcester; St John's Coll., Cambridge (BA 1934). Uganda: Asst Treas., 1935; Asst District Officer, 1937;

Asst Financial Sec., 1946; Economic Sec., E Africa High Commission, 1948; Financial Sec., 1948; Acting Chief Sec. at various dates; Acting Governor, July 1951; Chairman: Uganda Lint Marketing Bd; Uganda Coffee Marketing Board; Member: Uganda Electricity Board; Uganda Development Corp.; Comr on Special Duty, Uganda, 1953-61; Sec.-Gen., Inter-African Coffee Organisation, Paris, 1961-64. *Recreations:* golf, fishing and bridge. *Address:* The Lower House, Payhembury, Honiton, Devon.

**SPENCER, Brig. Francis Elmhirst,** DSO 1918; MC; late RA; *s* of late Lieut-Col C. F. H. Spencer, Royal Inniskilling Fusiliers, and late Emily, *d* of William Ball; *b* 25 July 1881; *m* 1916, Augusta (Vera) (*d* 1956), *y d* of late Col Arthur Tracey, late RA; one *s* one *d. Educ:* Dover College; RMA, Woolwich. RGA, 1900; psc; served China Expeditionary Force, 1900-01 (medal); Hong-Kong, Straits Settlements, 1901-02; Mountain Artillery, India, 1903-11; Tibet Field Force (advance to Lhasa), 1904 (medal and clasp); Mekran Field Force, 1911; Malay States Guides Mountain Battery, 1911-14; served with RFA European War, 1914-18, in France and Belgium (despatches 5 times, MC, DSO); Commandant (local Lt-Col) Straits Settlements Volunteer Force, 1921-25; Lt-Col 1927; Col 1931; Commander Royal Artillery, 55th (West Lancs) Division TA Liverpool, 1932-34; Brigadier i/c Administration, Western Comd, 1934-38; retired pay, 1938; Comdt AA Practice Camp, Bude, AA&QMG, 45th (West Country) Div. (RARO), 1939-40; Comdr 12th Devon Bn HG, 1940-41; Regional Officer London Civil Defence Region, 1941-43; Admiralty Service SVP, 1944-46. *Recreations:* shooting, yachting. *Address:* Underhill House, Lympstone, Devon. *Club:* United Service.

**SPENCER, Gilbert,** RWS 1949 (ARWS 1943); Hon. ARCA; ARA 1950, RA 1959-68; Member: NEAC; Society of Mural Painters; Faculty of Prix de Rome; Head of Department of Painting and Drawing of the Camberwell School of Arts and Crafts, 1950-57; *b* 1892; *s* of late William and Anna Spencer; *m* 1930, Margaret Ursula Bradshaw (*d* 1959); one *d. Educ:* privately and Slade School. Professor of Painting, Royal Coll. of Art, 1932-48; Head of Department of Painting and Drawing, Glasgow School of Art, 1948-50. Exhibitions: Goupil Gall., 1922, 1926 (with Mark Gertler and John Nash, RA), 1928, 1931; Leicester Galls, 1933, 1937, 1943, 1946, 1948; work rep. in many public galleries, including: Tate Gallery, Victoria and Albert Museum, Imperial War Museum, Aberdeen, Belfast, Capetown and Durban Art Galls. Commissioned by Imperial War Museum, 1919, and War Artists' Advisory Council, 1940 and 1943. Murals, Foundation Legend of Balliol Coll.; The Scholar Gipsy Students Union, Univ. of London; An Artist's Progress, Royal Academy. *Publication:* Stanley Spencer, 1961. *Address:* Tree Cottage, Upper Basildon, Reading, Berks. *T:* Upper Basildon 247.

**SPENCER, Air Vice-Marshal Ian James,** CB 1963; DFC 1941 (Bar 1943); *b* 6 June 1916; *s* of late Percival James Spencer, Pevensey, Sussex; *m* 1940, Kathleen Jeune Follis, *d* of late Canon Charles Follis, Carbury, Kildare; two *s. Educ:* King's College, London. Commissioned 1937. War of 1939-45: operated from England and in Europe with No. 2 Group (despatches). RAF Staff College, 1948; Air Attaché, Berne, 1950-53; CO, Univ. of London Air Sqdn, 1954-56; Director of Plans Second Allied TAF, 1956-59; Commanded RAF Benson, 1959-61; Air Officer, Administration, Transport Command, 1961-64; Air Secretary's Dept, Ministry of Defence, 1964-65; AOA, Far East Air Force, 1965-67. Croix de Guerre, 1944; Légion d'Honneur 1945. *Recreations:* shooting, sailing. *Address:* Rossals, Rotherfield, Sussex. *T:* Rotherfield 219. *Clubs:* Royal Air Force, Lansdowne.

**SPENCER, Mrs Joanna Miriam,** CBE 1961; Governor, Administrative Staff College, since 1969; *b* 26 July 1910; *d* of late Rev. R. S. Franks; *m* 1954, Frank Woolley Sim Spencer. *Educ:* Redland High School for Girls, Bristol; Girton College, Cambridge (MA). Asst, Lancs County Library, 1934-35; Asst Librarian: Hull Univ. Coll., 1936-37; Regent Street Polytechnic, 1938; Librarian, Selly Oak Colls, 1938-42. Temp. Civil Servant, Min. of Aircraft Production, 1942-45. Principal, Min. of Supply, 1946; Assistant Secretary, Min. of Supply, 1949-55, Board of Trade, 1955-56, Min. of Power, 1957-64; Under-Sec., Min. of Power, 1964-69. *Address:* 10 Gainsborough Mansions, Queen's Club Gardens, W14. *T:* 01-385 6911.

**SPENCER, Sir Kelvin (Tallent),** Kt 1959; CBE 1950; MC 1918; Chief Scientist, Ministry of Power, 1954-59, retired; *b* 7 July 1898; *s* of Charles Tallent and Edith Ælfrida Spencer; *m* 1927, Phœbe Mary Wills; one *s. Educ:* University College School, Hampstead; City and Guilds Engineering Coll., London Univ. Mem. Bd, Nat. Carbonising Co. Mem. Council, Exeter Univ. FCGI 1959. *Address:* Wootans, Branscombe, Seaton, Devon EX12 3DN. *T:* Branscombe 242. *Club:* Farmers'.

**SPENCER, Noël,** ARCA (London); retired as Principal, Norwich School of Art (1946-64); *b* 29 Dec. 1900; *s* of late John William Spencer; *m* 1929, Vera K. Wheeler; no *c. Educ:* Ashton-under-Lyne School of Art; Manchester School of Art; Royal College of Art. Art Teacher, Central School of Arts and Crafts, Birmingham, 1926-32; Headmaster, Moseley School of Art, Birmingham, 1929-32; Second Master, Sheffield College of Arts and Crafts, 1932-34; Headmaster, Huddersfield Art School, 1934-46. *Exhibitions:* Royal Academy, New English Art Club, Royal Birmingham Society of Artists, Sheffield Society of Artists, Liverpool, Bradford, Wakefield and Doncaster Art Galleries, Norwich Art Circle and Twenty Group, Chicago Art Institute and Los Angeles Art Museum, USA, etc. *Publication:* A Scrap Book of Huddersfield, Book I, 1944, Book II, 1948. *Recreations:* drawing and painting. *Address:* 18 Upton Close, Norwich, Norfolk. *T:* Norwich 51683.

**SPENCER, Oscar Alan,** CMG 1957; Financial Adviser to Government of Ethiopia since 1966; *b* Eastleigh, Hants, 12 Dec. 1913; *m* 1952, Diana Mary, *d* of late Edmund Walker, Henley-on-Thames; two *s* one *d. Educ:* Mayfield Coll., Sussex; London Sch. of Economics. BCom (Hons) 1936. Premchand Prize in Banking and Currency, 1936; John Coleman Postgraduate Scholar, 1936-37. Served War of 1939-45, Lt-Col (despatches twice). Economic Adviser and Development Comr, British Guiana, 1945; also Comr, Interior, 1949; Economic Sec., Malaya, 1950; Member, 1951, Minister, 1955, for Economic Affairs, Economic Adviser, and Head of Economic Secretariat, Fedn of Malaya, 1956-60. Joined UN Tech. Assistance Service, 1960: Econ. Adviser to Govt of Sudan, 1960-64; Sen. Regl Adviser on Public Finance and Head of Fiscal Sect., UN Econ. Commn for Africa, 1964-66. Chm., Central Electricity Board, Malaya, 1952-55, 1956-60; British Guiana Delegate, Caribbean Commn, 1948; Malayan Adviser to Sec. of State. Commonwealth Finance Ministers' Conf.,

1951; Leader of Malayan Reps, Internat. Rubber Study Gp, London, 1952, Copenhagen, 1953; Malayan Deleg., Internat. Tin Conf., Geneva, 1953; Adviser to Malayan Delegation, London Constitutional and Financial Confs, 1956 and 1957. Knight of the Order of Defenders of the Realm (PMN), Malaya, 1958. *Publications:* The Finances of British Guiana, 1920-45, 1946; The Development Plan of British Guiana, 1947. *Recreation:* tennis. *Address:* Gatehurst, Pett, near Hastings, Sussex. *T:* Pett 2197; Ministry of Finance, Addis Ababa. *Club:* East India and Sports.

**SPENCER, Terence John Bew;** Professor of English Language and Literature, Birmingham University, since 1958; Director of the Shakespeare Institute, since 1961; Member Board, National Theatre, since 1968; *b* 21 May 1915; *s* of Frederick John and Dorothy Emmie Spencer, Harrow; *m* 1948, Katharine Margaret, *d* of Francis William Walpole, Limpsfield, Surrey; three *d*. *Educ:* Lower School of John Lyon, Harrow; University of London (King's Coll. and University Coll.); British School at Rome. Assistant, English Department, King's Coll., London, 1938-40; Brit. Council Lectr, Brit. Inst., Rome, and Inst. of English Studies, Athens, 1939-41. Served War, 1941-46 (despatches); Cyprus Regt and Royal Pioneer Corps; commissioned 1941; Maj. 1943; actg Lt-Col 1945. Asst Lectr and Lectr in English, 1946-55, University Coll., London; Prof. of English, Queen's Univ., Belfast, 1955-58. Hon. Sec., The Shakespeare Association, 1950-; Gov., Royal Shakespeare Theatre, 1968-. General Editor: New Penguin Shakespeare; Penguin Shakespeare Library; Modern Language Review, 1960- (English Editor, 1956-). Turnbull Prof. of Poetry, Johns Hopkins University, 1968. *Publications:* Fair Greece, Sad Relic: Literary Philhellenism from Shakespeare to Byron, 1954; (ed with James Sutherland) On Modern Literature by W. P. Ker, 1955; From Gibbon to Darwin, 1959; The Tyranny of Shakespeare, 1959; Byron and the Greek Tradition, 1960; Shakespeare: The Roman Plays, 1963; ed, Shakespeare's Plutarch, 1964; ed, Shakespeare: A Celebration, 1964; ed, Romeo and Juliet, 1967; ed, A Book of Masques, 1967; Elizabethan Love Stories, 1968; contribs to other books, and to journals. *Address:* The Shakespeare Institute, The University, Birmingham 15.

**SPENCER, Sir Thomas George,** Kt 1946; CEng., FIEE; MIPE; Hon. President and Director, Standard Telephones and Cables Ltd; Chairman: Kolster Brandes Ltd; International Marine Radio Co. Ltd; Standard Telecommunication Laboratories Ltd; Vice-President, International Standard Electric Corporation; Director: Woolwich Equitable Building Society (Chairman, 1958-68); Creed & Co. Ltd; *b* 1888; *s* of Thomas and Mary Spencer, Beds; *m* 1st, 1914, Grace Adelaide (*d* 1949), *y d* of Joseph Player; one *s*; 2nd, 1953, Ethel Bailey (Ethel Bilsland, FRAM), *y d* of James Bilsland. *Educ:* Polytechnic; Royal Ordnance School, Woolwich. Joined engineering staff of Western Electric Co. Ltd, 1907, later became Chief Cable Engineer, Director of Cable Manufacture. In 1930 became European Director of Manufacture for International Standard Electric Corp.; Man. Dir of Standard Telephone & Cables Ltd, 1932-57; Chairman, 1951-65. Founder and Chm., 1943, Chm., 1956, Hon. Life Pres., 1964, Telecommunication Engineering and Manufacturing Assoc.; Mem. Governing Body, Woolwich Polytechnic, 1939-, Chm., 1949-52; Pres., Eltham and Mottingham Hosp., 1946-48. KCSG 1958. *Recreations:* fishing, golf. *Address:* STC, 190 Strand, WC2. *T:* 01-836 8055.

**SPENCER CHAPMAN, Lt-Col Frederick,** DSO 1944 (and Bar, 1946); TD 1960; MA; Warden of Wantage Hall, University of Reading, since 1966; *b* 10 May 1907; *s* of Frank Spencer Chapman, Solicitor, and Winifred Ormond; *m* 1946, Faith Mary, Flt Officer, WAAF, *d* of late Major George Harrison Townson and Violet Beatrice Birkin; three *s*. *Educ:* Sedbergh School (Kitchener Scholar); St John's College, Cambridge (Hons English and History). Member of British Arctic Air Route Expedition to Greenland, 1930-31; Member of Pan-American Arctic Airways Expedition to Greenland, 1931-32; Master at Aysgarth School, Bedale, Yorks, 1933-35; Member of Marco Pallis' Himalayan Expedition, 1935; Private Secretary to Political Officer of Sikkim and accompanied Diplomatic Mission to Lhasa, Tibet, 1936-37; made first ascent of Chomolhari (24,000 ft), 1937; Housemaster at Gordonstoun School, Elgin, Morayshire, 1938-39. Served, 1939-46, 5th Bn The Seaforth Highlanders; trained Commando troops in Scotland, 1939, in Australia, 1940, in Singapore, 1941; entered Malayan jungle Jan. 1942 in charge of Stay-behind Parties; emerged by submarine May 1945; returned by parachute Aug. 1945 to become Civil Affairs Officer, Pahang; demobilised March 1946. First Organising Secretary of Outward Bound Trust, Dec. 1946-Dec. 1947; First Headmaster King Alfred School, Plön, BAOR 6 (Germany), 1948-52; undertook Caravan Tour of Africa from Cape Town to Uganda on behalf of Outward Bound Trust, Jan.-Dec. 1953; Headmaster, St Andrew's Coll., Grahamstown, SA, 1956-62; Warden of Pestalozzi Children's Village, Sedlescombe, 1962-66. Arctic Medal 1931, Gill Memorial Medal (RGS), 1941; Mungo Park Medal (RSGS), 1948; Sunday Times Special Award and Gold Medal, 1949; Lawrence of Arabia Memorial Medal (RCAS), 1950. *Publications:* Northern Lights, 1932; Watkins' Last Expedition, 1934; Lhasa: The Holy City, 1938; Helvellyn to Himalaya, 1940; Memoirs of a Mountaineer (reprint) 1945; The Jungle is Neutral, 1948; Living Dangerously, 1952; Lightest Africa, 1955. *Recreations:* mountaineering, ski-ing, birdwatching, photography. *Address:* Wantage Hall, The University, Reading, Berks. *Clubs:* Alpine (Vice-Pres. 1967-68), Special Forces (Dep. Chm.); Harvaard Travellers' (Hon. Mem.).

**SPENCER-CHURCHILL,** family name of **Duke of Marlborough** and of **Baroness Spencer-Churchill.**

**SPENCER-CHURCHILL,** Baroness *cr* 1965 (Life Peeress), of Chartwell; **Clementine Ogilvy Spencer-Churchill,** GBE 1946 (CBE 1918); *b* 1885; *d* of late Sir Henry Hozier and late Lady Blanche Hozier, *d* of 9th Earl of Airlie; *m* 1908, Rt Hon. Sir Winston Churchill, KG, PC, OM, CH, FRS (*d* 1965); two *d* (one *s* and two *d* decd). *Educ:* at home; Berkhampsted Girls' Sch.; Sorbonne, Paris. Organised Canteens for munition workers on behalf of YMCA in NE Metropolitan Area, 1914-18; Chairman of the Red Cross Aid to Russia Fund, 1939-46; President of YWCA War Time Appeal; Chairman of Fulmer Chase Maternity Hospital for Wives of Junior Officers, 1940-46; Chairman of National Hostels Committee of YWCA, 1948-51. Freedom of Wanstead and Woodford, 1945. Hon. LLD Glasgow University, 1946; Hon. DCL Oxford University, 1946. CStJ. *Address:* 7 Princes Gate, SW7.

*See also W. S. Churchill, Rt Hon. Duncan Sandys, Rt Hon. A. C. J. Soames.*

**SPENCER-NAIRN, Sir Douglas Leslie;** *see* Nairn.

**SPENCER PATERSON, Arthur;** *see* Paterson, A. S.

**SPENCER-SILVER, Prof. Peter Hele;** Professor of Embryology in the University of London, at the Middlesex Hospital Medical School, since 1964; *b* 29 Oct. 1922; 2nd *s* of Lt-Col J. H. Spencer Silver; *m* 1948, Patricia Anne, *e d* of late Col J. A. F. Cuffe, CMG, DSO, Wyke Mark, Winchester; two *s* one *d*. *Educ:* Harrow School; Middlesex Hosp. Med. School, Univ. of London. MRCS, LRCP; MB, BS London 1945; PhD London 1952. Res., Middlesex Hosp., 1945-46. RAF, 1946-48. Demonstrator in Anatomy, Middlesex Hosp. Med. Sch., 1948-57; Mem. 2nd Internat. Team in Embryology, Hübrecht Laboratory, Utrecht, Netherlands Govt Fellowship, 1956; Reader in Anatomy, Univ. of London, 1957; US Nat. Inst. of Health Post-doctoral Travelling Fellowship, 1961; Carnegie Inst. of Washington, Dept of Embryology, Baltimore, 1961-62. FRSM. *Publications:* contribs to Jl Embryology and Experimental Morphology, Jl Physiol., Jl Anat., Lancet, etc. *Recreation:* music. *Address:* 7 More's Garden, Cheyne Walk, SW3. *T:* 01-352 2990.

**SPENCER-SMITH, Maj.-Gen. Jeremy Michael,** OBE 1959; MC 1945; Director of Manning (Army), Ministry of Defence, since 1970; *b* 28 July 1917; *s* of Michael Spencer-Smith, DSO, MC, and Penelope (*née* Delmé-Radcliffe) (she *m* 2nd, 1934, Elliot Francis Montague Butler). *Educ:* Eton; New Coll., Oxford. Welsh Guards, 1940; Adjutant, 1st Bn, 1944-46; Staff, 1st Guards Brigade, MELF, 1950-51; comd 3 KAR, Kenya, 1959-60; Staff, HQ BAOR, 1960-63; comd 148 Infantry Bde (TA), 1964-67; Dep. Dir of Manning, Ministry of Defence (Army), 1967-68; GOC Wales, 1968-70. *Recreations:* shooting, racing, travel. *Address:* St Ippolyt's End, Hitchin, Herts. *Clubs:* White's, Pratt's, Guards.

**SPENCER-SMITH, Sir John Hamilton-,** 7th Bt, *cr* 1804; *b* 18 March 1947; *s* of Sir Thomas Cospatric Hamilton-Spencer-Smith, 6th Bt, and Lucy Ashton, *o d* of late Thomas Ashton Ingram, Hopes, Norton-sub-Hamdon, Somerset; *S* father, 1959. *Educ:* Milton Abbey; Lackham College of Agriculture, Wilts. *Heir: cousin* Peter Compton Hamilton-Spencer-Smith [*b* 12 Nov. 1912; *m* 1950, Philippa Mary, *yr d* of late Captain Richard Ford; two *s*]. *Address:* Priory Orchard, Easebourne Lane, Midhurst, Sussex. *T:* Midhurst 2936.

**SPENCER WILLS, Sir John;** *see* Wills.

**SPENDER, Hon. Sir Percy Claude,** KCVO 1957; KBE 1952; QC (NSW), 1935; BA; LLB; President of the International Court of Justice at The Hague, 1964-67 (Judge, 1958-64); Australian lawyer; *b* Sydney, 5 Oct. 1897; *s* of late Frank Henry Spender, Sydney, and Mary Hanson (*née* Murray); *m* 1925, Jean Maude (*d* 1970), *d* of Samuel B. Henderson; two *s*. *Educ:* Fort Street High Sch., Sydney; Sydney Univ. BA 1918 (distinction in economics); LLB 1922, with 1st class Honours and University Medal; George and Matilda Harris Scholar, 1920; Special Wigram Allen Prize for proficiency in Roman and Constitutional Law, 1918; Morven K. Nolan Memorial Prize for Political Science, 1920; Member of Sydney Univ. Senate, 1939-44; called to NSW Bar, 1923. Member of Menzies Ministry, 1939-41; Vice-President, Fed. Exec. Council, 1940 (Member 1939); Minister without portfolio assisting Treas., and Ministerial Secretary to Cabinet, 1939; Acting Treas. 1939, Treas. 1940; Member of Economic Cabinet, 1939-40; Chairman Australian Loan Council, 1939-40; Chairman of Nat. Debt Commn, 1940; Minister for the Army, Chairman of Mil. Board, and Member War Cabinet, 1940-41; Government, then Opposition Member of Advisory War Council, 1940-45; Minister for External Affairs and of External Territories, Australia, 1949-51; MHR for Warringah, 1937-51; Australian Ambassador to the United States, 1951-58. Chairman: Australian Delegn at Conference of British Commonwealth Foreign Ministers, Colombo, 1950 (at which he put forward a plan for economic aid to S and SE Asia, subseq. known as the Colombo Plan); Conf. of British Commonwealth Consultative Cttee on Economic Aid to S and SE Asia, Sydney, 1950; Australian delegate at British Commonwealth Consultative Cttee Meeting, London, 1950; Vice-Pres., 5th General Assembly, UN, 1950-51, and Chm. and Vice-Chm., Australian Delegn UN General Assembly, 1952-56; Australian Representative at negotiation Canberra and subsequently at signing Regional Security Treaty between USA, NZ, and Australia, San Francisco, 1951; Vice-President Jap. Peace Treaty Conf., San Francisco, 1951 (Chm., Australian Delegn); Australian Governor of Internat. Monetary Fund and Internat. Bank, 1951-53; alternate Governor, Internat. Monetary Fund, 1954; Chm. Australian Delegn to UN Commemorative Session, San Francisco, 1955; Special Envoy on goodwill mission to South and Central America, July-Aug. 1955; Chairman, Australian Delegation Internat. Sugar Conf., May-June 1956 and Conf. to establish Atomic Energy Internat. Agency, Sept.-Oct. 1956; Chairman, Australian Delegation to 2nd Suez Conf., London, Sept. 1956, and to Commonwealth Finance Ministers' meeting, Washington, Oct. 1956. Mem. Gen. Council, Assicurazioni Generali (Italy), 1969-. European War, 1914-18, enlisted AIF, 1918; War of 1939-45, Lieut-Colonel on Active List AMF part-time special duties, 1942-45; now on retired list with hon. rank of Lieut-Colonel. Member: Board of Directors of USA Educational Foundation in Australia, 1950-51; US Cttee of Study and Training in Australia, 1950-51; Member of Council (1949-51) and Life Member Convocation Australian Nat. Univ.; Econ. Society of Australia and NZ; Vice-President, Royal Commonwealth Society (President, NSW Br., 1949-51); President: Sydney Club, 1967-; NSW Br. of Overseas League. Hon. LLD: Univ. of British Columbia, Hamilton Coll., NY, 1952; Univ. of Colorado, 1953; Hon. DCL Union Univ., Schnectady, 1955; Hon. Chancellor, Union Univ., Schnectady, 1955; LittD Springfield Coll., Mass, 1955; LLD Trinity Coll., Hartford, Conn, 1955; Yale, 1957; California, 1965; University of the East (Philippines), 1966. Coronation Medal, 1937 and 1953. KStJ 1958. C of E. *Publications:* Company Law and Practice, 1939; Australia's Foreign Policy, the Next Phase, 1944; Exercises in Diplomacy, 1969. *Recreations:* reading, surfing, golf. *Address:* Headingley House, Wellington Street, Woollahra, NSW 2025, Australia. *Clubs:* Elanora Country, Australasian Pioneers (Sydney); Athenæum (Melbourne).

**SPENDER, Stephen (Harold),** CBE 1962; poet and critic; Professor of English, University College, London University, since 1970; *b* 28 Feb. 1909; *s* of Edward Harold Spender and Violet Hilda Schuster; *m* 1st, 1936, Agnes Marie (Inez), *o d* of late William Henry Pearn; 2nd, 1941, Natasha Litvin; one *s* one *d*. *Educ:* University College Sch.; University College, Oxford. Co-editor Horizon Magazine, 1939-41; Counsellor, Section of Letters, Unesco,

1947; Co-Editor, Encounter, 1953-67. Fireman in NFS, 1941-44. Hon. DLitt, Univ. of Montpelier; Hon. Mem. Phi Beta Kappa (Harvard Univ.); Elliston Chair of Poetry, Univ. of Cincinnati, 1953; Beckman Prof., Univ. of California, 1959; Visiting Lecturer, Northwestern Univ., Illinois, 1963; Consultant in Poetry in English, Library of Congress, Washington, 1965; Clark Lectures (Cambridge), 1966; Mellon Lectures, Washington, DC, 1968; Northcliffe Lectures (London Univ.), 1969. Fellow, Inst. of Advanced Studies, Wesleyan Univ., 1967. Vis. Prof., Univ. of Connecticut, 1969. Hon. Mem. Amer. Acad. of Arts and Letters and Nat. Inst. of Arts and Letters, 1969. *Publications:* 20 Poems; Poems: The Destructive Element; Vienna; The Burning Cactus, 1936; Forward from Liberalism, 1937; Trial of a Judge; Poems for Spain, 1939; The Still Centre, 1939; Ruins and Visions, 1941; Life and the Poet, 1942; Citizens in War and After, 1945; Poems of Dedication, 1946; European Witness, 1946; The Edge of Being, 1949; World Within World (autobiog.), 1951; Learning Laughter (travels in Israel), 1952; The Creative Element, 1953; Collected Poems, 1954; Essay in The God that Failed; The Making of a Poem, 1955; Engaged in Writing (stories), 1958; Schiller's Mary Stuart (trans.), 1958; The Struggle of the Modern, 1963; Selected Poems, 1965; The Year of the Young Rebels, 1969. *Address:* 15 Loudoun Road, NW8. *Clubs:* Savile, Garrick.

**SPENS,** family name of **Baron Spens.**

**SPENS,** 1st Baron *cr* 1959; **William Patrick Spens,** PC 1953; KBE 1948 (OBE 1918); Kt 1943; QC 1925; *o surv. s* of late Nathaniel Spens; *m* 1st, 1913, Hilda Mary (*d* 1962), *e d* of Lieut-Colonel Wentworth Grenville Bowyer of Weston Manor, Olney, Bucks; one *s* (*yr s* died on active service, 1942) two *d*; 2nd, 1963, Kathleen Annie Fedden, *o d* of late Roger Dodds, Northumberland and Bath. *Educ:* Rugby; New Coll., Oxford. Barrister of the Inner Temple, 1910; Master of the Bench, Inner Temple, 1934; Treas., 1958; served European War, 1914-19; India, 1914-15; Mesopotamia, 1915-18 (despatches thrice, OBE); Captain and Adjt 5th Bn The Queen's Royal Regt, 1914-18; MP (C) Ashford Div. of Kent, 1933-43; Chief Justice of India, 1943-47; Chairman Arbitration Tribunal in India, 1947-48. A Comr of the Imperial War Graves Commission, 1931-43 and 1949-65. MP (C) South Kensington, 1950-59. Co-opted Member of Bacon Marketing Board, 1935; Director Southern Railway, 1941-43; Chief Comr in India of St John's Brigade Overseas, 1945-48. Director, Prudential Assurance Co. Ltd, 1949-61; Member of the London Cttee of The Bank of Scotland, 1949. KGStJ 1945. *Heir: s* Hon. William George Michael Spens [*b* 18 Sept. 1914; *m* 1941, Joan Elizabeth, *d* of late Josiah Montague Goodall; two *s* one *d*]. *Address:* Beacon Cottage, Benenden, Kent. *T:* Benenden 434. *Club:* Carlton.

*See also A. M. Grier.*

**SPENS, Colin Hope,** CB 1962; FICE, MIWE, FInstWPC, Hon. FInstPHE, FGS; Senior Consultant, Rofe, Kennard and Lapworth, consulting civil engineers, Chandos Court, Caxton Street, SW1; *b* 22 May 1906; *er s* of late Archibald Hope Spens, Lathallan, Fifeshire and Hilda Constance Hooper; *m* 1941, Josephine, *d* of late Septimus Simond; two *s* one *d*. *Educ:* Lancing Coll.; Imperial College of Science and Technology. Consulting engineering experience, 1928-39. Served War of 1939-45 with Royal Signals, 1939-41; PA to Director of Works in Ministry of Works, 1941-44; Engineering Inspectorate of Min. of Health, 1944-51, Min. of Housing and Local Govt, 1951-60; Chief Engineer, Min. of Housing and Local Govt, 1960-67. *Address:* 16 Maybourne Grange, Turnpike Link, Croydon CRO 5NH. *T:* 01-680 3276. *Club:* St Stephens.

**SPENSER-WILKINSON, Sir Thomas Crowe,** Kt 1959; Chairman, Medical Appeals Liverpool Tribunal, since 1962; *b* 28 Sept. 1899; *o surv. s* of late Henry Spenser Wilkinson and Victoria Amy Eveline Crowe; *m* 1930, Betty Margaret, *o d* of late David Aitken Horner; one *s* one *d*. *Educ:* RN Colleges Osborne and Dartmouth; Balliol Coll., Oxford. Served as Midshipman and Sub-Lieut in Grand Fleet, 1915-18; in Destroyers in Baltic, 1918-19. Barrister-at-Law, Gray's Inn, 1925; Advocate and Solicitor, Singapore, 1928; practising in Singapore, 1928-38; President, District Court, Nicosia, Cyprus, 1938, and Famagusta, 1940; Naval Control Service in Cyprus and Port Said, 1940-42; on staff of C-in-C, S Atlantic, Capetown, 1942-44; Malaya Planning Unit in London, 1945; Chief Legal Adviser, British Mil. Administration, Malaya, Sept. 1945-April 1946; Judge, Supreme Court, Malaya, 1946; Chief Justice, Nyasaland, 1956-62. *Publication:* Merchant Shipping Law of the Straits Settlements, 1946. *Recreation:* gardening. *Address:* Whitecroft, Pentre Close, Ashton, Chester. *T:* Kelsall 531. *Clubs:* Royal Commonwealth Society, English-Speaking Union.

*See also L. J. H. Horner.*

**SPENSLEY, Philip Calvert,** DPhil, FRIC; Director, Tropical Products Institute, Ministry of Overseas Development, since 1966; *b* 7 May 1920; *s* of late Kent and Mary Spensley, Ealing; *m* 1957, Sheila Ross Fraser, *d* of Alexander and late Annie Fraser, Forres, Scotland; one *s* three *d*. *Educ:* St Paul's Sch., London; Keble Coll., Oxford (MA, BSc). Technical Officer, Royal Ordnance Factories, Ministry of Supply, 1940-45; Research Chemist, Nat. Inst. for Medical Research, MRC, 1950-54; Scientific Secretary, Colonial Products Council, Colonial Office, 1954-58; Asst Director, Tropical Products Inst., DSIR, 1958-61, Dep. Director, 1961-66. Chairman, Cttee of Visitors, Royal Institution, 1959. Mem. FAO/WHO/Unicef Protein Adv. Gp. Received MRC/NRDC Inventors Award, 1963. *Publications:* various research and review papers, particularly in the fields of chemotherapeutic substances, plant sources of drugs, and aflatoxin; patents on extraction of hecogenin from sisal. *Recreations:* gardening, lawn tennis. *Address:* 96 Laurel Way, Totteridge, N20. *T:* 01-445 7895. *Clubs:* Athenæum, Royal Automobile.

**SPICER, Clive Colquhoun;** Director, Medical Research Council Computer Unit, since 1967; *b* 5 Nov. 1917; *s* of John Bishop Spicer and Marion Isobel Spicer; *m* 1941, Faith Haughton James, MB; one *s* two *d*. *Educ:* Charterhouse Sch.; Guy's Hospital. Operational research on war casualties, 1941-46; Hon. Sqdn Leader, RAF; Staff, Imperial Cancer Research Fund, 1946-49; Dept of Biometry, University Coll., London, 1946-47; Public Health Laboratory Service, 1949-59; WHO Fellow, Univ. of Wisconsin, 1952-53; Vis. Scientist, US Nat. Insts of Health, 1959-60; Statistician, Imperial Cancer Research Fund, 1960-62; Chief Medical Statistician, General Register Office, 1962-66. Main interest has been in application of mathematical methods to medical problems. *Publications:* papers in scientific journals on epidemiology and medical statistics. *Recreations:* sailing, reading. *Address:* 8 St Anne's Close, N6. *T:* 01-340 6254.

**SPICER, Hon. Sir John Armstrong,** Kt 1963; Chief Judge, Commonwealth Industrial Court, 1956; *b* Armadale, Victoria, 5 March 1899; *m* 1924, Lavinia M., *d* of Robert S. Webster; one *s*. *Educ:* Torquay (England); Hawksburn (Victoria); University of Melbourne. Admitted as Barrister and Solicitor, 1921; KC 1948; Attorney-General, Commonwealth of Australia, 1949-56. Senator in Commonwealth Parliament, 1940-44 and 1949-56. Chairman, Senate Cttee on Regulations and Ordinances, 1940-43. *Address:* 153 Glen Iris Road, Glen Iris, Victoria, Australia. *T:* 25.2882. *Clubs:* Australian, Constitutional (Melbourne).

**SPICER, Lancelot Dykes,** DSO, MC; *b* 22 March 1893; *y s* of Rt Hon. Sir Albert Spicer, 1st Bt; *m* 1920, Iris Cox (who obtained a divorce, 1935); (one *s* killed in action, 31 May 1944); *m* 1951, Dorothy Beverley, *d* of late Frank Edwin Gwyther, CIE. *Educ:* Rugby Sch.; Trinity Coll., Cambridge. Granted temp. Commn in Army, Sept. 1914; T/Capt., July 1916; Bde-Major, April 1918; served European War (MC Oct. 1917; bar to MC May 1918; DSO Sept. 1918). Chairman, Spicers Ltd, 1950-59. *Address:* 85 Onslow Square, SW7; Idbury House, Idbury, Oxford. *Clubs:* United University, Hurlingham.

*See also P. J. Spicer.*

**SPICER, (Sir) Peter James,** 4th Bt *cr* 1906 (but does not use the title); Assistant Secretary to Delegates of Oxford University Press; *b* 20 May 1921; *s* of Captain Sir Stewart Dykes Spicer, 3rd Bt, RN, and Margaret Grace (*née* Gillespie) (*d* 1967); *S* father, 1968; *m* 1949, Margaret, *e d* of Sir Steuart Wilson (*d* 1966), and Ann Mary Grace, now Lady Boult; one *s* three *d* (and one *d* decd). *Educ:* Winchester Coll. (Schol.); Trinity Coll., Cambridge (Exhibr); Christ Church, Oxford (MA). Served War of 1939-45 (despatches, 1944); Royal Sussex Regt, then RN (Temp. Lieut, RNVR). Trinity Coll., Cambridge, 1939-40; Christ Church, Oxford, 1945-47. Joined Staff of Oxford University Press, 1947; Head of Educn Dept, 1960-. Co-opted Member, Educn Cttee of Oxfordshire CC, 1959- (Chairman, Libraries Sub-Cttee, 1961-). Rep. of Congregational Church in England and Wales on British Council of Churches, 1964-. *Recreations:* gardening, walking, sailing, bird-watching, music, reading. *Heir: s* Nicholas Adrian Albert Spicer, *b* 28 Oct. 1953. *Address:* The Manor Farm House, Kidlington, Oxford. *T:* Kidlington 2316. *Club:* RNVR.

*See also L. D. Spicer.*

**SPIERS, Prof. Frederick William,** CBE 1962; Professor of Medical Physics, University of Leeds, since 1950; *b* 29 July 1907; *er s* of Charles Edward and Annie Spiers; *m* 1936, Kathleen M. Brown; one *d*. *Educ:* Prince Henry's Grammar Sch., Evesham; University of Birmingham. 1st Class Hons Physics, 1929; PhD 1932; DSc 1952. Anglo-German Exchange Scholar, Univ. of Munich, 1930. Demonstrator in Physics, University of Leeds, 1931; Senior Physicist, General Infirmary, Leeds, 1935; Vis. Lecturer, Washington Univ., St Louis, USA, 1950. Hon. Director: MRC Environmental Radiation Research Unit, 1959; MRC Regional Radiological Protection Service, Leeds, 1963; Senior Scientific Adviser for Civil Defence, NE Region, 1952; President, British Inst. of Radiology, 1955-56; Chairman, Hospital Physicists Assoc., 1944-45; Hon. Mem., Faculty of Radiologists; Member: MRC Protection Cttee; Radio-active Substances Adv. Cttee; Internat. Commn on Radiation Units and Measurements. FInstP 1970. *Publications:* Radioisotopes in the Human Body, 1968; articles on radiation physics and radiobiology in scientific journals; contribs in: British Practice in Radiotherapy, 1955; Radiation Dosimetry, 1956. *Recreations:* photography, music, gardening. *Address:* Lanesfield House, Old Lane, Bramhope, near Leeds. *T:* Arthington 2680.

**SPINK, Prof. John Stephenson;** Professor of French Language and Literature in the University of London (Bedford College) since 1952; *b* 22 Aug. 1909; *s* of William Spink and Rosetta Spink (*née* Williamson); *m* 1940, Dorothy Knowles, MA, DèsL, LRAM. *Educ:* Pickering Grammar Sch.; Universities of Leeds and Paris. BA (Leeds), 1930; MA (Leeds), 1932; Docteur de l'Université de Paris, 1934; Lauréat de l'Académie Française, 1936. Assistant at Lycée Henri IV, Paris, 1930-33; Lecteur at the Sorbonne, 1931; Asst Lectr in Univ. of Leeds, 1933-36; Lectr in Univ. of London, King's Coll., 1937-50; Prof. of French at University College, Southampton, 1950-52. *Publications:* J.-J. Rousseau et Genève, 1934 (Paris); critical edition of J.-J. Rousseau, Les Rêveries du Promeneur solitaire, 1948; Literature and the sciences in the age of Molière, 1953; French Free-Thought from Gassendi to Voltaire, 1960; critical edn of Rousseau's educational writings in Pléiade Œuvres complètes, t. IV, 1969; articles in Annales J.-J. Rousseau, Mercure de France, Revue d'Histoire littéraire, Modern Language Review, French Studies, Bulletin des Historiens du théâtre, Horizon, Europe, Revue de Litérature Comparée, Problèmes des Genres Littéraires, Cahiers de l'Association Internat. des études Françaises; trans. of Krimov, The Tanker Derbent, 1944 (Penguin). *Address:* Bedford College, Regent's Park, NW1.

**SPINKS, Rev. Dr G(eorge) Stephens;** Vicar, St Paul's, Scouthead, Oldham, 1966-69; Examining Chaplain to Bishop of Manchester, 1967-70; *b* Cambridge, 1903; *m* 1968, Mrs Annie Nightingale. *Educ:* Cathedral Choir Sch., Rochester; Manchester College and St Catherine's Society, Oxford; University College and King's Coll., London. MA (London), PhD (London); Hibbert Research Student, 1944-45; Upton Lecturer, Manchester Coll., Oxford, 1947-48 and 1949-50. Minister of All Souls' Church, Golders Green, London, 1937-47. Editor of the Hibbert Journal, 1948-51. Rector of Great Lever, Bolton, 1952-55; Rector of Clovelly, 1955-59; Priest-in-Charge, St Swithun's, Littleham by Bideford, 1962-64. Frequent broadcast talks on BBC European Service. Exeter University Extension Lecturer; Joyce Lecturer, Dio. Exeter, 1961; Tele-Lecture (from England to W Virginia, USA), 1968. *Publications:* (with E. L. Allen and James Parkes) Religion in Britain since 1900, 1952; The Fundamentals of Religious Belief, 1961; Psychology and Religion, 1963; articles in periodicals. *Address:* 35 Greenmount Drive, Greenmount, Tottington, near Bury, Lancs. *T:* Tottington 2677.

**SPITZER, Professor Lyman (Jr),** BA; PhD; Professor of Astronomy (Charles A. Young Professor since 1952), Chairman of Astrophysical Sciences Department, and Director of Observatory, Princeton University, since 1947; Chairman, Research Board, since 1967; *b* 26 June 1914; *s* of Lyman Spitzer and Blanche B. (*née* Brumback); *m* 1940, Doreen D. Canaday; one *s* three *d*. *Educ:* Phillips Academy, Andover; Yale Univ. (BA); Cambridge Univ., England; Princeton Univ. (PhD). Instructor in Physics and Astronomy, Yale Univ., 1939-42; Scientist, Special Studies Group, Columbia Univ. Div. of War Research,

1942-44; Dir, Sonar Analysis Group, Columbia Univ. Div. of War Research, 1944-46; Assoc. Prof. of Astrophysics, Yale Univ., 1946-47. Dir Project Matterhorn, Princeton Univ., 1953-61; Chm. Exec. Cttee, Plasma Physics Lab., Princeton Univ., 1961-66. Member: Nat. Acad. of Sciences; American Academy of Arts and Sciences; American Philosophical Society; Internat. Acad. of Astronautics; Corr. Member, Société Royale des Sciences, Liège; Pres., American Astronomical Soc., 1959-61. Hon. Dr of Science: Yale Univ., 1958; Case Inst. of Technology, 1961; Hon. Dr of Laws, Toledo Univ., 1963. *Publications:* (ed) Physics of Sound in the Sea, 1946; Physics of Fully Ionized Gases, 1956 (2nd edn 1962); Diffuse Matter in Space, 1968; papers in Astrophysical Jl, Monthly Notices of Royal Astronomical Soc., Physical Review, Physics of Fluids, on interstellar matter, plasma physics, etc. *Recreations:* ski-ing, mountain climbing. *Address:* 659 Lake Drive, Princeton, NJ 08540, USA. *T:* 609-924 3007. *Club:* American Alpine.

**SPOCK, Dr Benjamin McLane;** Professor of Child Development, Western Reserve University, USA, 1955-67, now writing and working for peace; *b* New Haven, Connecticut, 2 May 1903; *s* of Benjamin Ives Spock and Mildred Louise (*née* Stoughton); *m* 1927, Jane Davenport Cheney; two *s*. *Educ:* Yale Univ. (BA); Yale Medical Sch.; Coll. Physicians and Surgeons, Columbia Univ. (MD). In practice (Pediatrics) from 1933; Cornell Med. Coll.; NY Hospital; NYC Health Dept. Served, 1944-46 in US Navy. Subseq. on Staff of: Rochester (Minn) Child Health Inst., Mayo Clinic, University of Minnesota; Prof. of Child Development, University of Pittsburgh, 1951-55. *Publications:* Common Sense Book of Baby and Child Care, 1946 (repr. as Pocket Book, 1957); (with John Reinhart and Wayne Miller) A Baby's First Year, 1955; (with Miriam E. Lowenberg) Feeding Your Baby and Child, 1955; Dr Spock Talks with Mothers, 1961; Problems of Parents, 1962; (with Marion Lerrigo) Caring for Your Disabled Child, 1964; (with Mitchell Zimmerman) Dr Spock on Vietnam, 1968; Decent and Indecent: our personal and political behaviour, 1970. *Relevant publication:* The Trial of Doctor Spock, by Jessica Mitford, 1969. *Address:* 538 Madison Avenue, New York, NY 10022, USA.

**SPOFFORD, Charles Merville,** CBE (Hon.) 1945; DSM and Purple Heart (US), 1945; Lawyer (US); Trustee: Carnegie Corporation of New York; Juillard Musical Foundation; Alumni Fellow, Yale University, until 1963; Director: Council on Foreign Relations; American University in Beirut until 1963; National Council, The English-Speaking Union until 1963; Metropolitan Opera Association (Chairman Exec. Cttee, 1956-, President, 1946-50); Vice-Chairman and Director, Lincoln Center for the Performing Arts, Inc.; Trustee, Institute for Defense Analyses; Member Exec. Cttee, American Branch, International Law Association; Member Exec. Council, American Society International Law, etc.; Carnegie Lecturer, Hague Academy of International Law, 1964; Trustee, The Mutual Life Insurance Co. of New York; Director: The Distillers Co. Ltd, and subsid. CIBA Corporation; *b* 17 Nov. 1902; *s* of Charles W. and Beulah Merville Spofford; *m* 1930; two *s* two *d*; *m* 1960, Carolyn Storrs Andre. *Educ:* Northwest Univ.; University of Grenoble; Yale Univ.; Harvard Law Sch. AB 1924; JD 1928; MA (Hon.) 1956. Instructor, European History, Yale Univ., 1924-25; practised Law, Chicago, 1929-30, New York (Davis Polk & Wardwell), 1930-40; member of firm, 1940-50 and 1952-. Lieut-Colonel 1942, AFHQ Algiers; adv. on econ. and supply, French N Africa and French W Africa, 1942-43; Chief of Planning Staff (for AMG Sicily and Italy); Dep. Chief Civil Affairs Officer for Sicily and S Italy, 1943-44; AFHQ, Asst Chief of Staff, Med. Theatre, 1944-45; War Dept as Military Adv. to State Dept, 1945; Colonel, 1943; Brig-General, 1944. Asst to President and Special Counsel to American National Red Cross, 1946-50; also other former civic activities. Deputy US Representative, North Atlantic Council, and Chairman, North Atlantic Council Deputies, 1950-52; Member European Co-ordinating Cttee (US); resigned 1952, to rejoin law firm. Hon. LLD Northwestern Univ., 1959. Comdr, Order of Nishan Iftikhar, Tunisia, 1943; Croix de Guerre with palm and Commander Legion of Honour, France, 1945; Comdr, Order of SS Maurice and Lazarus, Italy, 1945; Officer, Legion of Honour, France, 1952; Commander with Star, Order of the Falcon, Iceland, 1953; Grand Officer, Order of the Crown, Belgium. *Recreation:* golf. *Publications:* articles in journals. *Address:* (business) 1 Chase Manhattan Plaza, New York, NY 10005, USA; (residence) 120 East 78 Street, New York, NY 10021; Windmill Lane, East Hampton, New York, NY 11937. *Clubs:* Century Association, Links (New York); Metropolitan (Washington); Maidstone (East Hampton); Travellers' (Paris).

**SPOONER, Edgar Clynton Ross,** DSc, BE, DPhil, FRACI, MIChemE; Consulting Engineer, since 1970; *b* 25 May 1908; British; *m* 1937; two *d*. *Educ:* Hutchins Sch., Hobart; University of Tasmania; Oxford Univ. Academic and industrial research in various countries, 1930-35; Technical Asst to Works Director, National Smelting Co., Avonmouth, 1935-37; Technical Supt, Magnesium Metal Corp., Swansea, 1937-44; Director of Research and Development, Sutcliffe, Speakman & Co., Leigh, Lancs., 1944-47; Consultant, S. G. Warburg & Co., 1944-47; Professor of Mining, Metallurgical and Chemical Engineering, and Director of Bonython Labs, University of Adelaide, 1947-62. Dir, davy Ashmore (Australasia) and other companies; Consulting Engineer, 1963-68; Chief of Project, UN Develt Project, Madras, 1969-70. Rhodes Scholar, 1931 (Tasmania); Nuffield Travelling Fellowship, 1951; Colombo Plan Adviser to Ceylon Govt, 1954. *Publications:* (Co-author) The Electrode Potential Behaviour of Corroding Metals in Aqueous Solutions, Oxford, 1938. *Address:* Stangate House, Edgeware Road, Aldgate, SA 5154, Australia. *T:* 391489.

**SPOONER, Edward Tenney Casswell,** CMG 1966; MD, MA, MRCS, LRCP; FRCP; Dean of London School of Hygiene and Tropical Medicine, 1960-70; Chairman, Public Health Laboratory Service Board, since 1963; *b* 22 May 1904; *s* of William Casswell Spooner, MB, and Edith Maud Spooner, Blandford, Dorset; *m* 1948, Colin Mary Stewart. *Educ:* Epsom Coll.; Clare Coll., Cambridge; St Bartholomew's Hospital. Foundation Scholar of Clare Coll., 1923; House Physician, St Bartholomew's Hospital, 1927-28; Commonwealth Fellow, Harvard Medical Sch., 1929-31; Fellow of Clare Coll., 1929-47; Tutor of Clare Coll., 1939-47; University Demonstrator and Lecturer, Dept of Pathology, University of Cambridge, 1931-46; Professor of Bacteriology and Immunology, London School of Hygiene and Tropical Medicine, 1947-Sept. 1960. Temporary Major, RAMC, in No 1 Medical Research Section, 1942-43; Director, Emergency Public Health Laboratory, Cambridge, 1943-44; Editor, Journal of Hygiene, 1949-55; Member Medical Research Council, 1953-57; Member Council

Epsom Coll., 1955-65. *Publications:* papers on tetanus, certain virus diseases and wound infection. *Address:* Wolverley, Burnhams Road, Little Bookham, Surrey. *Club:* Athenæum.

**SPOONER, Edwin George,** CIE 1946; Director and General Manager, Whitehead Iron & Steel Co. Ltd, Newport, Mon, 1954-63; *b* 1898; *s* of George Henry Spooner, Birmingham; *m* Thelma Marie, *d* of Eric Albert Bibra, Melbourne, Australia. *Educ:* Secondary Sch., Birmingham. Served in France with Coldstream Guards, European War, 1914-19. Iron and Steel Controller, Dept of Supply, India, 1944-47. *Address:* Thornfield, Dudsbury Avenue, Ferndown, Dorset. *T:* Ferndown 3568.

**SPORBORG, Henry Nathan,** CMG 1945; a Director of Hambros; Chairman: Skefko Ball Bearing Co.; Bewac Motor Corporation; Stirling-Astaldi; Gomme Holdings; Bishopsgate Property and General Investments; Berkeley Property & Investment Co.; Western Credit; Vice-Chairman: Sun Alliance & London Insurance Ltd; Director of Other companies; Member, Port of London Authority; Commissioner to Earl Fitzwilliam; *b* 17 Sept. 1905; *e c* of late H. N. and M. A. Sporborg; *m* 1935, Mary Rowlands; one *s* three *d*. *Educ:* Rugby Sch.; Emmanuel Coll., Cambridge. Admitted Solicitor, 1930; partner in firm of Slaughter & May, 1935; joined Ministry of Economic Warfare, 1939; Director and later Vice-Chief, Special Operations Executive, 1940-46. Chairman, Board of Governors, St Mary's Hospital, 1964-. JP Herts, 1957; Chevalier, Legion of Honour, Croix de Guerre, Order of St Olav (Norway), etc. *Recreation:* fox-hunting. *Address:* Culver, Much Hadham, Herts. *T:* Much Hadham 2506. *Club:* Boodle's.

**SPOTSWOOD, Air Chief Marshal Sir Denis (Frank),** KCB 1966 (CB 1961); CBE 1946; DSO 1943; DFC 1942; Chief of the Air Staff since April 1971; *b* 26 Sept. 1916; *s* of late F. H. Spotswood and M. C. Spotswood; *m* 1942, Ann (*née* Child); one *s*. Commissioned in RAF, 1936; UK Service in Squadrons, 1937-41; No 209 Squadron, 1939-41. Served War of 1939-45 (despatches twice, DSO). Chief Instructor, Operation Training Unit, 1941-42; Officer Commanding No 500 (County of Kent) Squadron, RAuxAF, 1942-43; Director of Plans, HQ Supreme Allied Commander, South-East Asia, 1944-46; Directing Staff, RAF Staff Coll., 1946-48; Officer Commanding RAF (Fighter) Stations, Horsham St Faith and Coltishall, 1948-50; Directing Staff, Imperial Defence Coll., 1950-52; Exchange Duties, HQUSAF in USA, 1952-54; Officer Commanding RAF (Fighter) Station, Linton-on-Ouse, 1954-56; Deputy Director of Plans, Air Ministry, 1956-58; AOC and Commandant, RAF Coll., Cranwell, 1958-61; Assistant Chief of Staff (Air Defence), SHAPE, 1961-63. AOC No 3 Group, RAF Bomber Command, 1964-65; C-in-C RAF Germany, 1965-68; Commander, 2nd Allied Tactical Air Force, 1966-68; AOC-in-C, RAF Strike Command, 1968-71; Comdr, UK Air Defence Region, 1968-70. group Captain, 1954; Air Commodore, 1958; Air Vice-Marshal, 1961; Air Marshal, 1965; Air Chief Marshal, 1968. ADC to The Queen, 1957-61, 1970-. Officer of the Legion of Merit (USA). *Recreations:* golf, sailing, shooting, bridge. *Address:* c/o Glyn Mills, Whitehall, SW1. *Club:* Royal Air Force.

**SPRAGG, Cyril Douglas,** CBE 1949; Hon. ARIBA 1959; Secretary, Royal Institute of British Architects, 1945-59; *b* 22 July 1894; *y s* of late Charles and Emily Spragg; unmarried. *Educ:* Christ's Hospital. Served European War, Queen's Westminster Rifles, 1914-19. Asst Secretary, RIBA, 1926-44. Governor of Christ's Hospital; Thames Conservancy, 1966-70; Hon. Member American Institute of Architects, 1955; Hon. Corresp. Member, Royal Architectural Inst. of Canada, 1956; Hon. Associate Royal Australian Inst. of Architects, 1957; Hon. Fellow, New Zealand Institute of Architects, 1957; Hon. Member Inst. South African Architects; Hon. Member, Institute N Rhodesian Architects, 1959; Hon. Member Ghana Society of Architects, 1959; Hon. Fellow Royal Incorporation of Architects in Scotland, 1960; Hon. Member Ceylon Inst. of Architects, 1960; Hon. Member Fedn of Malaya Society Architects, 1961. Hon. MA Durham Univ., 1958. Member: Middlesex CC, 1961; Surrey CC, 1965, Alderman, 1967-70. *Address:* 76 Ford Bridge Road, Ashford, Middlesex. *T:* Ashford, Middlesex, 52037. *Club:* Reform.

**SPRAGGETT, Colonel Richard William,** CMG 1956; CVO 1954; CBE 1948; MC; Colonel Royal Marines, retired; *s* of late G. W. Spraggett; *m* 1930, Mary Lois Cecil, *d* of Sir John Cecil Power, 1st Bt. *Educ:* privately. Served with Royal Marines, European War, 1914-18 (MC) and War of 1939-45. Private Secretary and Comptroller to the Governor of the State of Victoria, Australia, 1949-62. *Club:* United Service.

**SPREULL, Professor James (Spreull Andrew);** William Dick Professor of Veterinary Surgery, at the University of Edinburgh, since 1959; *b* 2 May 1908; *s* of late Lt-Col Andrew Spreull, DSO, TD, MRCVS, and Effie Andrew Spreull; *m* 1951, Kirsten Brummerstedt-Hansen; three *s*. *Educ:* Dundee High Sch.; Edinburgh Univ. (PhD); Royal Dick Veterinary Coll. (MRCVS). Royal Dick Veterinary College: Demonstrator of Anatomy, 1930-34, Lecturer in Applied Anatomy, 1931-34. Engaged in general practice in Dundee, 1934-59. FRSE 1965. *Publications:* various contributions to Veterinary Journals. *Recreations:* agriculture, fishing, badminton, antiques. *Address:* Spencerfield Farm House, Hillend, Dunfermline, Fife. *T:* Inverkeithing 4255. *Club:* University (Edinburgh).

**SPRIGGE, Elizabeth Miriam Squire;** writer, translator, lecturer and producer; *b* 19 June 1900; *er d* of late Sir Squire Sprigge (Editor of the Lancet), and Mary Moss, *d* of Sir Charles Moss (sometime Chief Justice of Ontario); *m* 1921, Mark Napier (marr. diss., 1946); two *d*. *Educ:* St Paul's Girls' Sch., London; Havergal Coll., Toronto; Bedford Coll., London. Lived in Sweden, 1923-25. Wrote Novels, children's books, lectured, translated from the Scandivanian languages with Claude Napier, 1927-40. Swedish Specialist at Ministry of Information, 1941-44. Director of the Watergate Theatre, 1949-52. *Publications:* novels: A Shadowy Third, 1929; Faint Amorist, 1930; The Old Man Dies, 1933; Castle in Andalusia, 1935; The Son of the House, 1937; The Raven's Wing, 1940; play: (with Katriona Sprigge) Elizabeth of Austria (produced at Garrick Theatre), 1939; children's books: Children Alone, 1935; Pony Tracks, 1936; Two Lost on Dartmoor, 1940; (with Elizabeth Muntz) The Dolphin Bottle, 1965; biographies: The Strange Life of August Strindberg, 1949; Gertrude Stein, Her Life and Work, 1957; Jean Cocteau, The Man and the Mirror, 1968 (with Jean-Jacques Kihm); translations include: Six Plays of Strindberg, 1955; Five Plays of Strindberg, 1960; Mary Stuart in Scotland, Bjørnsterne Bjørnson (Edinburgh Festival), 1960; Twelve Plays of

Strindberg, 1963; The Difficulty of Being, by Jean Cocteau, 1966; The Red Room, by August Strindberg, 1967. *Recreations:* country living, travel. *Address:* 75 Ladbroke Grove, W11. *T:* 01-727 9630.

**SPRIGGS, Leslie,** JP 1955; MP (Lab) St Helens since June 1958; *b* 22 April 1910; British; *m* 1931, Elfrida Mary Brindle Parkinson. *Educ:* Council Sch.; Trade Union Adult Schools. TU Scholarship to Belgium, 1951. Merchant Service, then Railway man until 1958. President, NW (NUR) District Council, Political Section, 1954; Vice-President, Industrial Section, 1955. Served as Auditor to Lancs and Cheshire Region of the Labour Party. Lecturer, National Council of Labour Colleges on Industrial Law; Economics; English; Foreign Affairs; Local Government; Trade Union History. *Recreations:* Rugby league; athletics; water polo. *Address:* 38 Knowle Avenue, Cleveleys, near Blackpool, Lancs. *T:* Cleveleys 2746. *Club:* Windle Labour (St Helens).

**SPRING, Frank Stuart,** FRS 1952; DSc (Manchester), PhD (Liverpool), FRIC; Director, Laporte Industries Ltd, London, W1, since 1959; *b* 5 Sept. 1907; 3rd *s* of Captain John Spring and Isabella Spring, Crosby, Liverpool; *m* 1932, Mary, 2nd *d* of Rev. John Mackintosh, MA, Heswall; one *s* one *d*. *Educ:* Waterloo Grammar Sch.; University of Liverpool. United Alkali Research Scholar, University of Liverpool, 1928-29; University Fellow, Liverpool, 1929-30. Assistant Lecturer, Lecturer and Senior Lecturer in Chemistry, University of Manchester, 1930-46; Freeland Professor of Chemistry, The Royal College of Science and Technology, Glasgow, 1946-59. Chemical Society, Tilden, Lecturer, 1950. Hon. DSc, University of Salford, 1967. *Publications:* scientific papers in chemical journals. *Address:* Flat 26, 1 Hyde Park Square, W2. *T:* 01-262 8174. *Club:* Royal Automobile.

**SPRING RICE,** family name of **Baron Monteagle of Brandon.**

**SPRINGALL, Harold Douglas;** Professor of Chemistry, University of Keele, since 1950; *b* 24 June 1910; *o s* of Harold Springall and Margaret Springall (*née* Wright); *m* 1940, Jean Helen McArthur Gordon, *d* of L. McArthur Gordon and H. Violet Gordon (*née* Holbeche); two *s* one *d*. *Educ:* Colfe's Grammar School, London; Lincoln College, Oxford (Scholar). BA (1st cl.) 1934; BSc 1934; Magdalen College, Oxford (Senior Demy), 1934-36; DPhil 1936; MA Oxon 1938. Commonwealth Fund Fellowship, Calif Tech., Pasadena, Calif, Cornell Univ., 1936-38; Rockefeller Research Grant, Oxford, 1938-39. Min. of Supply: Sci. Officer (Armament Res. Br.), 1939-44; Sen. Sci. Officer, 1944-45. Univ. of Manchester: Lectr in Chemistry, 1945-48, Sen. Lectr, 1948-50; Asst Tutor to Faculty of Science, 1949-50; Tutor in Chemistry, Dalton Hall, 1945-50; Univ. Coll. of North Staffs: Dir of Studies, 1951-52; Vice-Principal, 1957-59; Actg Vice-Principal, 1960-61. Mem. Council Chem. Soc., 1954-57; Mem. Publication Cttee, Faraday Soc., 1957-. *Publications:* The Structural Chemistry of Proteins, 1954; Sidgwick's Organic Chemistry of Nitrogen, 1966; A Shorter Sidgwick's Organic Chemistry of Nitrogen, 1969; articles in Jl Chem. Soc., Jl Amer. Chem. Soc., Trans. Faraday Soc., Nature, etc. *Recreations:* music; hill and mountain walking and climbing. *Address:* 21 Springpool, The University, Keele, Staffordshire. *T:* Keele Park 395; Cae'r Waen, Waenfawr, Caernarvonshire. *T:* Waenfawr 279. *Club:* Climbers'.

**SPRINGER, Tobias;** a Metropolitan Stipendiary Magistrate, since 1963; Barrister-at-law; *b* 3 April 1907; *o c* of late Samuel Springer, MBE; *m* 1937, Stella Rauchwerger. *Educ:* Mill Hill Sch.; Caius Coll., Cambridge. Law Tripos 1928; called to Bar, Gray's Inn, 1929. Practised London and SE Circuit. Served War of 1939-45: 60th Rifles, 1940-45; Lt-Col GSO1, GHQ, H Forces, 1944. Returned to practise at Bar, 1945. Actg Dep. Chm., Co. Lond. Sess., periods 1962, 1963. Life Gov.: Mill Hill School; Metropolitan Hosp. *Recreations:* travel, golf, reading. *Address:* 82 Cholmley Gardens NW6. *T:* 01-435 0817. *Clubs:* Royal Automobile; Porters Park Golf.

**SPROAT, Iain Mac Donald;** MP (C) Aberdeen (South) since 1970; *b* 8 Nov. 1938. *Educ:* St Mary's Sch., Melrose; Winchester; Magdalen Coll., Oxford. General Manager, Special Projects Unit, BPC Publishing, 1970-. *Publications:* (with A. Sykes): The Wit of Sir Winston, 1965, etc. *Recreation:* travel. *Address:* 12 Hans Crescent, SW1; 23 Crown Terrace, Aberdeen. *Clubs:* United University; Conservative, Constitutional (Aberdeen).

**SPROTT, Rt. Rev. John Chappell;** *see* Brechin, Bishop of.

**SPROTT, Professor Walter John Herbert;** Emeritus Professor of Psychology, Nottingham University, since 1965 (Professor, 1960-64); *b* 1897; *s* of Herbert and Mary Elizabeth Sprott. *Educ:* Felstead; Clare College, Cambridge. Demonstrator, Psychological Laboratory, Cambridge, 1922-25; Lecturer in Psychology, University College, Nottingham, 1925, Reader in Philosophy, 1928; Professor of Philosophy, Nottingham Univ., 1948-60. Public Orator to Nottingham Univ., 1948-64; Josiah Mason Lecturer, Birmingham, 1953; Charles Russell Memorial Lecture, 1955; James Seth Memorial Lecture, 1960; Hobhouse Memorial Lecture, 1962. *Publications:* Kretschmer's Physique and Character (trans.), 1925; Freud's New Introductory Lectures (trans.), 1933; General Psychology, 1937; Sociology, 1949; Philosophy and Common Sense, 1949; (with A. H. Stewart) Living in Crowds, 1949; Social Psychology, 1952; Science and Social Action, 1954; Human Groups, 1958; Sociology at the Seven Dials, 1962; Miniatures, 1964. Sundry articles. *Address:* 116 Portland Road, Nottingham. *T:* Nottingham 72871; Blakeney, Holt, Norfolk. *T:* Cley 237.

**SPROUL, Robert Gordon;** President Emeritus, University of California, since 1958 (President, 1930-58); *b* 22 May 1891; *s* of Robert Sproul and Sarah Elizabeth (Moore) Sproul; *m* 1916, Ida Amelia Wittschen; two *s* one *d*. *Educ:* Univ. of California (BS 1913). Efficiency Dept, City of Oakland, 1913; Univ. of California, 1914-30: as cashier, asst comptroller, asst sec. of Regents, Comptroller, Sec. of Regents and Land Agent, and Vice-President. Fellow, Amer. Assoc. for Advancement of Science; Hon. Mem., Calif Academy of Sciences; Director: Internat. House, Berkeley; Belgian Amer. Educl Foundn; Founder and Treas., Save-the-Redwoods League, Calif, 1921-; Vice-Chm., Trustees, Amer. Heritage Foundn; Carnegie Foundn for Advancement of Teaching, 1939-58; Cttee for Economic Development; Gen. Educ. Bd, 1939-56; Chm. of Bd and Pres. of the Corp., Pacific Sch. of Religion, 1959-. Rockefeller Foundn, 1939-56. President's Ambassador to Inauguration of Syngman Rhee, 1956. Member: Coll. of Electors, Hall of Fame, 1949; (Sponsor) Save the Children Fedn, 1948-; Advis. Cttee, Meals for Millions, 1949-; Bd of Dirs E Bay Reg. Parks, Calif,

1958- (Pres. 1963-67); Nat. Cttee for Support of Public Schools, 1962-; (Sponsor) The Atlantic Council, 1964-; US Dept of Interior Adv. Bd on Nat. Parks, Historic Sites, Bldgs and Monuments, 1959-65; Trustee: National Fund for Graduate Nursing Education, 1960-; California Alumni Foundation, 1963. Director YMCA, California, 1943-. Hon. degrees: LLD: Occidental Coll., 1926; Univ. of Southern Calif, Univ. of San Francisco, 1930; Pomona Coll., 1931; Univ. of Oregon, 1932; Univ. of Nebraska, Yale Univ., 1935; Univ. of Maine, 1938; Univ. of New Mexico, Harvard Univ., 1940; Mills Coll., 1943; Princeton Univ., 1947; Tulane Univ., St Mary's Coll., 1949; Univ. of California, 1958; Univ. of British Columbia, 1958; Rensselaer Polytechnic Inst., 1958; Brigham Young Univ., 1959; LittD, Columbia Univ., 1938; LHD, Univ. of California, 1958; Hon. Fellow: Stanford Univ., 1941; Amer. Coll. of Dentists, 1955; Internat. Coll. of Dentists, 1964. Comdr Order of Crown of Roumania, 1936; Kt of Order of Iron Crown of Italy, 1938; Officier Légion d'Honneur (France), 1939; Roy. Order of North Star (Sweden), 1950; Commander of the Order of St Olav (Norway), 1952. *Address:* 31 Tamalpais Road, Berkeley, California, USA. *Clubs:* Faculty, Rotary (Berkeley); Bohemian, University, Family (San Francisco); Sunset, Lincoln (Los Angeles); Burlingame Country (Burlingame); Athenian-Nile (Oakland).

**SPRULES, Dorothy Winifred;** *b* 3 Dec. 1883; *d* of Alfred and Mercy Sprules. *Educ:* Sutton High School; S Hugh's College, Oxford, BA, and MA 1922; Student Lincoln's Inn. Assistant Mistress Ware Grammar School, 1907-16; Travelling Investigation Officer, Ministry of Munitions, 1916; Headmistress, Tonbridge County School, 1917-19; Headmistress Haberdashers' Aske's Acton School, 1920-43. *Publications:* Victoria County History–contributions to Surrey Volumes. *Recreations:* country pursuits. *Address:* c/o Westminster Bank, Wareham, Dorset.

**SPRY, Brig. Sir Charles Chambers Fowell,** Kt 1964; CBE 1956; DSO 1943; retired as Director-General, Australian Security Intelligence Organization, 1950-70; *b* 26 June 1910; *s* of A. F. Spry, Brisbane; *m* 1939, Kathleen Edith Hull, *d* of Rev. Godfrey Smith; one *s* two *d*. *Educ:* Brisbane Grammar School. Graduated Royal Military College, Duntroon. Served War of 1939-45 as Col, Australian Imperial Force in SW Pacific (DSO) and Middle East. Director of Military Intelligence, 1946-50. *Recreation:* golf. *Address:* c/o Attorney-General's Department, Canberra, Australia. *Clubs:* Melbourne; Royal Melbourne Golf.

**SPRY, Maj.-Gen. Daniel Charles,** CBE 1945; DSO 1944; CD; President, Glenland Ltd, Montreal; Consultant, Canadian International Development Agency; *b* Winnipeg, Man, 4 Feb. 1913; *s* of Major-General Daniel William Bigelow Spry and Ethelyn Alma (*née* Rich); *m* 1939, Elisabeth, *d* of Roy Fletcher Forbes, Halifax, NS; one *s* one *d*. *Educ:* Public Schools, Calgary and Halifax; Ashford School, England; Dalhousie University. Served with Canadian Militia; 2nd Lt, Princess Louise Fusiliers, 1932; Royal Canadian Regt (permanent force), 1934. Served War, 1939-46 (CBE, DSO, CD, despatches twice); Captain 1939, Major 1940, Lt-Col 1943, Brig. 1943, Maj.-Gen. 1944; retired as Vice-Chief of Gen. Staff, 1946. Col, The Royal Canadian Regt, 1965. Chief Exec. Comr, The Boy Scouts' Assoc. of Canada, 1946-51; Dep. Dir, Boy Scouts World Bureau, 1951-53, Dir, 1953-65. Commander, Order of the Crown of Belgium, 1945; Croix de Guerre, Belgium, 1945. *Recreations:* sailing, philately, fishing. *Address:* 4 Rock Avenue, Ottawa 2, Ontario, Canada. *Clubs:* Rideau (Ottawa); Denholm Angling (Quebec).
*See also Graham Spry.*

**SPRY, Graham;** Agent General for Saskatchewan in the United Kingdom and Europe, 1947-67, retired 1968; *b* St Thomas, Ontario, 20 Feb. 1900; *e s* of Maj.-Gen. D. W. B. Spry, OBE, ED, and Ethelyn Alma Rich; *m* 1938, Professor Irene Mary Biss; two *s* one *d*. *Educ:* public schools, Toronto, Montreal and Winnipeg; University of Manitoba (BA, Rhodes Scholar); University College, Oxford (MA); Sorbonne, Paris. Served Canadian Army, Gunner, 1918. Editorial Staff, Winnipeg Free Press, 1919-22 (while at University); Internat. Labour Office, Geneva, 1925-26; Nat. Sec., Assoc. of Canadian Clubs, 1926-32. Organized and chm. of Canadian Radio League (voluntary group which advocated and secured, by unanimous vote of House of Commons, establishment of public service broadcasting), 1929-33; Canadian Politics, 1933-37. California Standard Oil Co. Ltd, London, Eng., 1938-39, Dir, and Manager, 1940-46; Director: Associated Ethyl Co., Ceylon Petroleum Co., 1940-47; British Ethyl Corp., 1944-47; Personal Asst to Rt Hon. Sir Stafford Cripps, Lord Privy Seal and Minister of Aircraft Production, 1942-45, Member of Mission to India, 1942; duties in USA for Sir Stafford Cripps, 1942, and for Rt Hon. R. K. Law, 1943. Member Inter-deptl Cttee on Internat. Civil Aviation, War Corresp., Canadian Army, Italy, Aug.-Sept., 1944, and Germany, April-May, 1945. XXth Century Fund Survey of Turkey, 1947; FRAI. Hon. LLD Brock and Saskatchewan, 1968. *Publications:* (joint) Social Planning for Canada, 1934; Canada 1941; Canada, 1946; (joint) Turkey: An Economic Appraisal, 1949. *Recreations:* books, history, ski-ing, and Tuscany. *Address:* 446 Cloverdale Road, Rockcliffe Park, Ottawa 2, Ontario, Canada; Shield's Edge, Kingsmere, Quebec. *Clubs:* Brooks's; Travellers'; Leander (Hon. Mem.); Rideau (Ottawa).
*See also D. C. Spry.*

**SPURLING, Antony Cuthbert,** QC (Sierra Leone); *b* 12 Oct. 1906; 3rd *s* of late Cuthbert Spurling; *m* 1935, Elizabeth Frances, *d* of late J. C. Stobart; two *s* one *d*. *Educ:* Berkhamsted; St Paul's; Hertford College, Oxford. Called to Bar, Inner Temple, 1931; Temp. Legal Asst, Ministry of Health, 1934; Resident Magistrate, Kenya, 1935; Crown Counsel, Kenya, 1939; Solicitor-General, Trinidad, 1946; Attorney-General, Gambia, 1951. Attorney-General, Sierra Leone, 1955-61. Retired, 1961. *Publication:* Digest and Guide to the Criminal Law of Kenya, 1946. *Recreation:* gardening. *Address:* Wheelwright Cottage, Bodle Street Green, Nr Herstmonceux, Sussex. *T:* Herstmonceux 2308.

**SPURLING, Maj.-Gen. John Michael Kane,** CB 1957; CBE 1953; DSO 1944; Lecturer in Military History and Tactics, London and Southampton Universities; *b* 9 May 1906; *s* of late Dr Clement and Mrs Spurling, Oundle, Northants; *m* 1930, Penelope, *d* of Rt Rev. Neville Lovett, CBE, DD, sometime Bishop of Portsmouth and subsequently of Salisbury; one *s* one *d* (and one *s* decd). *Educ:* Oundle. Commissioned Roy. Leics Regt, 1927; served India, UK and Palestine, 1927-38; Staff College, Camberley, 1938-39; served UK and Burma, 1940-43; North-West Europe, 1944-45, including command of 131 Bde, 7th Armoured Division, War Office, and command of a Parachute Bde, 1945-50; Commandant, Senior Officers' School, 1950-53; Chief of

Staff, West Africa, 1953-55; Chief of Staff, HQ Northern Command, 1955-58, retired. Col, 4th (Leics) Battn, The Royal Anglian Regt, 1965-68; Dep. Col, The Royal Anglian Regiment (Leicestershire and Rutland), 1968-. Governor, Milton Abbey Public School, 1961. *Recreation:* shooting. *Address:* The Manor, Fifehead Neville, Dorset. *T:* Sturminster Newton 3228. *Club:* United Service.

**SPURRIER, John Marston;** *b* 30 March 1886; *s* of late Henry Spurrier, JP, Marston-on-Dove; *m* 1909, Margery (*d* 1966), *d* of Samuel Marsden, Buxton, Derbyshire; one *s*. *Educ:* Uppingham; Royal Agricultural College, Cirencester. Served European War, 1914-18, with 4th North Midland Brigade RFA(T); JP Derbyshire, 1927; High Sheriff, Derbyshire, 1944-45; Chairman: Hilton Gravel Ltd; Hilcrete Ltd; Lord of the Manor and patron of livings of Marston-on-Dove and of Scropton and Foston. *Recreations:* racing, breeding blood stock. *Address:* The Hall, Marston-on-Dove, Hilton, Derby. *TA:* Tutbury. *T:* Tutbury 2121. *Club:* Boodle's.

**SPURRIER, Mabel Annie,** HRI; Freelance Artist; Royal Birmingham Society of Artists, 1930; *b* Moseley, Birmingham; *y d* of late William James and Caroline Spurrier, Moseley, Birmingham; unmarried. *Educ:* The Woodroughs, Moseley; College of Arts and Crafts, Birmingham, and London. *Address:* Flat 15, 11 Belsize Park Gardens, NW3. *T:* 01-722 9984.

**SQUIBB, George Drewry,** QC 1956; President Transport Tribunal, since 1962; Chairman Dorset Quarter Sessions since 1953; Norfolk Herald Extraordinary since 1959; *b* 1 Dec. 1906; *o s* of Reginald Augustus Hodder Squibb, Chester; *m* 1st, 1936, Bessie (*d* 1954), *d* of George Whittaker, Burley, Hants; one *d*; 2nd, 1955, Evelyn May, *d* of Frederick Richard Higgins, of Overleigh Manor, Chester. *Educ:* King's School, Chester; Queen's College, Oxford (BCL, MA). Barrister-at-Law, Inner Temple, 1930; Bencher, 1951; Army Officers' Emergency Reserve, 1938. Deputy Chairman Dorset Quarter Sessions, 1950-53; Junior Counsel to the Crown in Peerage and Baronetcy Cases, 1954-56; Hon. Historical Adviser in Peerage Cases to the Attorney-General, 1965-. Member: Cttee on Rating of Charities, 1958-59; Adv. Council on Public Records, 1964-; Selden Soc. (Vice-Pres., 1969-). FSA, 1946. *Publications:* The Law of Arms in England, 1953; Wiltshire Visitation Pedigrees, 1623, 1955; Reports of Heraldic Cases in the Court of Chivalry, 1956; The High Court of Chivalry, 1959; Visitation Pedigrees and the Genealogist, 1964; papers in legal and antiquarian journals. *Recreation:* genealogical and heraldic research. *Address:* 5 Paper Buildings, Temple, EC4. *T:* 01-353 3436; The Old House, Cerne Abbas, Dorset. *T:* Cerne Abbas 272. *Clubs:* Athenæum, Oxford and Cambridge University.

**SQUIRE, Raglan,** FRIBA, MSIA; Senior Partner Raglan Squire & Partners, Consultants in Architecture, Engineering, Town Planning, etc; *b* 30 Jan. 1912; *e s* of late Sir John Squire, Kt; *m* 1st, 1938, Rachel, (*d* 1968), *d* of James Atkey, Oxshott, Surrey; two *s*; 2nd, 1968, Bridget Lawless. *Educ:* Blundell's; St John's Coll., Cambridge. Private practice in London, 1935-. War service with Royal Engineers, 1942-45. Founded firm of Raglan Squire & Partners, 1948. Principal projects: housing, educational and industrial work, 1935-41; pre-fabricated bldgs and industrial design, 1945-48; Eaton Sq. Conversion Scheme, 1945-56; Rangoon Univ. Engineering Coll., 1953-56; Associated Architect, Transport Pavilion, Festival of Britain Exhib., 1951; Town Planning Scheme for Mosul, Iraq, 1955; Bagdad airport report, 1955; factories at Weybridge, Huddersfield, etc.; office buildings London, Eastbourne, Bournemouth, etc.; gen. practice at home and over-seas incl. major hotels at Teheran, Tunis, Nicosia, Malta and Singapore, 1955-65. Sec. RIBA Reconstruction Cttee, 1941-42; Council of Architectural Assoc., 1951-52; Guest Editor Architects' Journal, 1947. *Publications:* articles in technical press on organisation of Building Industry, Architectural Education, etc. *Recreations:* ocean racing and designing small yachts. *Address:* 73 Elizabeth Street, SW1. *T:* 01-730 7225. *Clubs:* Royal Thames Yacht, Royal Ocean Racing; Royal Southern Yacht (Hamble).

**SQUIRES, James Duane;** Professor of History, Colby Junior College, New London, New Hampshire, USA, since 1933; Historical Consultant to NH War Records Committee, since 1944; *b* Grand Forks, North Dakota, 9 Nov. 1904; *s* of Vernon Purinton Squires and Ethel Claire Wood; *m* 1928, Catherine Emily Tuttle, Grand Forks, North Dakota; two *s*. *Educ:* Public Schools, Grand Forks, North Dakota. BA University of North Dakota, 1925; MA, University of Minnesota, 1927; PhD, Harvard Univ., 1933; Professor of History, State College, Mayville, North Dakota, 1927-31; Graduate Student, Harvard University, 1931-33; Lecturer and writer; Official Delegate to the Harvard Tercentenary, 1936; Member: US Constitution Sesquicentennial Commission for New Hampshire, 1938; NH State Council of Defense, 1942-45; Special Consultant to USAAF, War Dept, 1943; Chm. of USO in NH, 1944. President: NH Council of Religious Educn, 1944-45; NH Library Trustees Assoc., 1957; Old Number Four Associates, 1957; Amer. Baptist Historical Soc., 1969-. Member: NH Historical Soc.; Cttee of 1000 for World Congress of Religion in 1948; Lincoln Soc.; Peabody Award Cttee for Radio; Citizens Cttee for UN Reform; Hoover Cttee for Govtl Reorganization in US, 1949; Citizens' Adv. Cttee for US Commn on Govt Security, 1957; Chairman UN Day Cttee in NH, 1949-57; Pres. NH Sons of the American Revolution, 1949; Chm. NH American Revolution Bicentennial Cttee, 1970-; Deleg.-at-large to nat. Republican Convention, Chicago, 1952; San Francisco, 1956, 1964 (Mem. Platform Cttee of Convention, 1964); Official Deleg. Second Assembly of World Council of Churches, Evanston, Ill, 1954. Director of NH Victory Speakers' Bureau, 1943; Newcomen Soc. in N America; Trustee: NH Baptist Convention; NH YMCA; NH Christian Civic League, etc; Mem., NH Commn on Historical Sites, 1950; Chm. NH Centennial Commn on the Civil War, 1958-. Judge, New London District Court, 1969-. George Washington Honor Medal of Freedoms' Foundation, 1954. LLD Univ. of N Dakota, 1958. Granite State Award, Univ. of New Hampshire, 1970. *Publications:* A History of the University of North Dakota, 1931; British Propaganda at Home and in the United States, 1914-17, 1935; Ballooning in the American Civil War, 1937; editor, The Centennial of Colby Junior College, 1937; editor, The Sesquicentennial of the Baptist Church of New London, New Hampshire, 1939; co-author, Western Civilization, 2 vols, 1942; The Founding of the Northern RR, 1948; Abraham Lincoln and the Civil War, 1949; A History of New London, New Hampshire since 1900, 1952; Experiment in Cooperation, 1953; Community Witness, 1954; A History of New Hampshire since 1623, 1956; The Story of New Hampshire, 1964.

Contributor to Journal of Modern History, American Historical Review, Christian Century, Dictionary of American Biography and Dictionary of American History. *Recreations:* fishing, numismatics. *Address:* New London, New Hampshire 03257, USA. *T:* 68. *Clubs:* Forum (New London); Boys.

**SQUIRRELL, Leonard Russell,** RE 1919 (ARE 1917); RWS 1941 (ARWS 1935); Artist (Painter and Etcher); *b* 30 Oct. 1893; *s* of Frank Squirrell and Henrietta Clements (both British); *m* 1923, Hilda Victoria Bird; one *d* (one *s* decd). *Educ:* British School, Ipswich; Ipswich School of Art; Slade School, London. Gold and Silver Medals, Nat. Competitions of Schools of Art, 1911-15; British Institution Scholarship in Engraving, 1915; Internat. Print-Makers' Exhibs at Los Angeles: silver medal, 1923; Gold medals, 1925 and 1930. Exhibitor Roy. Acad., 1912-59; official purchases by Toronto, British Museum, Victoria and Albert Museum, Fitzwilliam Museum, Cambridge, Brighton, Derby, Rochdale, etc. and Permanent Collection, Ipswich. *Publications:* Landscape Painting in Pastel, 1938; Practice in Water-Colour, 1950. *Address:* Merrydown, Witnesham, Suffolk. *T:* Witnesham 354.

**SRAFFA, Piero,** FBA 1954; MA; Fellow of Trinity College, Cambridge, since 1939; Emeritus Reader in Economics, University of Cambridge; *b* Turin, Italy, 1898. *Educ:* Univ. of Turin. *Publications:* (ed) The Works and Correspondence of David Ricardo, vols 1-10, 1951-55; Production of Commodities by Means of Commodities, 1960. *Address:* Trinity College, Cambridge.

**STABB, William Walter,** QC 1968; Official Referee, Supreme Court of Judicature, since 1969; Deputy Chairman, Bedfordshire Quarter Sessions, since 1969 (Chairman, 1961-69); *b* 6 Oct. 1913; 2nd *s* of late Sir Newton Stabb, OBE and late Lady E. M. Stabb; *m* 1940, Dorothy Margaret Leckie; four *d. Educ:* Rugby; University Coll., Oxford. Called to the Bar, 1936; Master of the Bench, Inner Temple, 1964. Served with RAF, 1940-46, attaining rank of Sqdn Ldr. Junior Counsel to Ministry of Labour, 1960; Prosecuting Counsel to BoT, 1962-68. *Recreations:* fishing, golf. *Address:* The Pale Farm, Chipperfield, Kings Langley, Herts. *T:* Kings Langley 63124; 1 King's Bench Walk, Temple, EC4. *T:* 01-353 8436.

**STABLE, Maj.-Gen. Hugh Huntington,** CB 1947; CIE 1938; Major-General, IA (retired) *b* 1896; *s* of late Alfred Henry Stable, MA and Ada Huntington; *m* 1923, Cyrille Helen Dorothy, *d* of late Rev. M. A. Bayfield, MA. *Educ:* Malvern College. First Commission 2/4th Dorset Regt 1914; served Palestine, 1917-18 (despatches); Central India Horse, 1919; Bt Lt-Col 1935; Staff Coll., Camberley, 1929-30; Army Headquarters, India, Staff Officer to Major-General Cavalry, 1932; Assistant Military Secretary (Personal) to Commander-in-Chief, 1933-36; Military Secretary to the Viceroy of India, 1936-38; Comdt, 8th KGO Cavalry, 1939-40; Bde Comdr, 1941-43; DQMG, GHQ, India, 1943-44; Comdr Lucknow Sub Area, 1945-46; Comdr Bihar and Orissa Area, 1947; QMG India, Dec. 1947; retd 1950. *Address:* 810 Rapallo, Sea Point, Cape Town, SA. *Clubs:* Army and Navy; Civil Service (Cape Town).

**STABLE, Owen;** *see* Stable, R. O. C.

**STABLE, (Rondle) Owen (Charles),** QC 1963; JP; Deputy Chairman of Quarter Sessions, Herts, since 1963; *b* 1923; *yr s* of Rt Hon. Sir Wintringham Norton Stable, *qv*; *m* 1949, Yvonne Brook, *y d* of late Maj. L. B. Holliday, OBE; two *d. Educ:* Winchester. Served with Rifle Bde, 1940-46 (Capt.). Barrister, Middle Temple, 1948; Bencher, 1969. Sec. National Reference Tribunal for the Coal Mining Industry, 1953-64; Chancellor of Diocese of Bangor, 1959-; Member, Governing Body of the Church in Wales, 1960-; Licensed Parochial Lay Reader, Diocese of St Albans, 1961-; Member, General Council of the Bar, 1962-66. Chm., Horserace Betting Levy Appeal Tribunal, 1969-. JP Hertfordshire, 1963-. *Recreations:* shooting, listening to music. *Address:* Buckler's Hall, Much Hadham, Hertfordshire. *T:* Much Hadham 2604. *Club:* Boodle's.

*See also P. L. W. Owen.*

**STABLE, Rt. Hon. Sir Wintringham (Norton),** PC 1965; Kt 1938; MC; a Judge of the High Court of Justice, Queen's Bench Division, 1938-68; *b* 19 March 1888; *s* of Daniel Wintringham Stable and Gertrude Mary Law; *m* 1916, Lucie Haden, *widow* of Richard Bayly Murphy and *d* of late F. F. Freeman, Tavistock; two *s. Educ:* Winchester; Christ Church, Oxford (MA). 2nd Class Honours School History; Bar, Middle Temple, 1913; served with the Montgomeryshire Yeomanry and 25th Battalion Royal Welch Fusiliers, 1914-18, Egypt, Palestine and France (MC, despatches); QC 1935; Chairman of Quarter Sessions for the Counties of Shropshire, 1947-67, and Merioneth, 1944-; Chancellor of Diocese of Portsmouth, 1937-38. Hon. Student of Christ Church, Oxford, 1960. *Recreation:* country life. *Address:* Plas Llwyn Owen, Llanbrynmair, Montgomeryshire. *Clubs:* Boodle's; Shropshire.

*See also P. L. W. Owen, R. O. C. Stable.*

**STABLEFORTH, Dr Arthur Wallace,** CB 1962; retired as Project Manager, UN Special Fund Sheep Diseases Research Laboratories, Pendik, Turkey, 1964-70; *b* 15 March 1902; *s* of W. Parkinson and Florence Kate Stableforth; *m* 1926, Hilda Dorothy Allen; one *s* one *d. Educ:* Allhallows School; Royal Veterinary College; London University. Demonstrator, Asst, Research Institute of Animal Pathology, 1926-33; in charge of Preventive Medicine, Royal Veterinary College, 1933-39. Veterinary Laboratory, Ministry of Agriculture and Fisheries: Senior Research Officer, 1939-49, Deputy Director, 1949-50. Director of Veterinary Laboratories and Investigation Service, 1951-63; Animal Health Officer, Food and Agriculture Organisation of the UN, 1963. Hon. FRCVS, 1968. John Henry Steele Medal, 1956; Thomas Baxter Prize, 1957. *Publications:* contributions to scientific jls and books in this and other countries; Co-editor, Infectious Diseases of Animals. *Recreations:* gardening and music. *Address:* 11 The Paddock, Merrow, Guildford, Surrey. *Clubs:* Athenæum, Royal Society of Medicine, Farmers', Royal Over-Seas League.

**STACEY, Sir Ernest,** Kt 1958; Stockbroker since 1919; *b* 1896; *s* of W. E. Stacey and Flora Stacey, Blundellsands, Lancs; *m* 1926, Mary Kathleen Taylor; one *s* one *d. Educ:* Oundle School; Liverpool University. Served in Army, 1914-17 (despatches 1916); invalided, result of wounds. Engineering training. Member Liverpool Stock Exchange, 1919-. Director of various Companies, 1930-44. Breeder of Shorthorns, 1941-53. Chm., Oundelian Memorial Trust. *Recreations:* gardening, stock and plant breeding, fishing. *Address:* Stone Hey, Thurstaston Road, Heswall, Cheshire. *T:* 051-342 3487. *Club:* Palatine (Liverpool).

**STACEY, Professor Maurice,** CBE 1966; FRS 1950; Mason Professor of Chemistry and Head of Department, University of Birmingham, since 1956; Dean of Faculty of Science, 1963-66; *b* 8 April 1907; *s* of J. H. Stacey, Bromstead, Newport, Shropshire; *m* 1937, Constance Mary, *d* of Wm Pugh, Birmingham; two *s* two *d*. *Educ:* Adam's School, Newport, Shropshire; Universities of Birmingham, London and Columbia (New York). BSc (Hons) Birmingham Univ., 1929; Demonstrator, Chemistry, Birmingham Univ., 1929-32; PhD 1932; Meldola Medal, 1933; Beit Memorial Fellow for Medical Research, School of Tropical Medicine, London Univ., 1933-37 (DSc 1939); Travelling Scholarship, Columbia Univ., New York, 1937; Lecturer in Chemistry, Univ. of Birmingham, 1937-44, Reader in Biological Chemistry, 1944-46. Tilden Lecturer of Chemical Society, 1946; P. F. Frankland Lectr, Roy. Inst. of Chemistry, 1955; Ivan Levinstein Lectr, Soc. Chem. Industry, 1956; Vice-Pres. Chemical Society, 1950-53, 1955-58, 1960-63, 1968-; Associate Editor, Advances in Carbohydrate Chem., 1950-; Editor, Advances in Fluorine Chem., 1960-; Editor-in-Chief, European Polymer Jl. Chief Scientific Adviser for Civil Defence, Midland Region, 1957-; Governor, National Vegetable Research Institute, 1961-. Member, Court of Governors: Univ. of Keele; Univ. of Warwick; Univ. of Loughborough; Gov., Adam's Sch., 1956-; Mem. Council, Edgbaston High Sch. for Girls, 1963-; Mem., Home Office Science Council, 1966-. Sugar Research Prize of National Academy of Science, New York, 1950; John Scott Medal and Award, 1969; Haworth Meml Medal, 1970. Captain, 2nd in Command Birmingham Home Guard, Chemical Warfare School, 1942-44. Defence Medal, 1945. Visiting Lecturer, Universities of Oslo, Stockholm, Uppsala and Lund, 1949, Helsinki, 1955. Has foreign Hon. doctorate and medals. John Scott Medal and Award, 1969; Haworth Meml Medal, 1970. *Publications:* (with S. A. Barker) Polysaccharides of Micro-organisms, 1961, and Carbohydates of Living Tissues; about 350 scientific contribs to Jl of Chem. Soc., Proc. Royal Soc., etc., on organic and biological chemistry subjects. *Recreations:* foreign travel, athletics (Hon. Life Mem. AAA), horticulture, alpines. *Address:* 12 Bryony Road, Weoley Hill, Birmingham 29. *T:* 021-475 2065; The University, Birmingham. *T:* 021-472 1301. *Club:* Athenæum.

**STACEY, Prof. Reginald Stephen,** MA, MD (Cambridge); Professor of Pharmacology and Therapeutics, University of London (St Thomas's Hospital Medical School) since 1958; *b* 1 May 1905; *s* of Stephen Sutton Stacey and Agnes May Measures; *m* 1st, 1933, Margery North; one *d*; 2nd, 1951, Helen Norman Duke; one *s*. *Educ:* Aske's Haberdashers' School; Trinity Coll., Cambridge; St Thomas's Hosp. Med. School; Univ. of Vienna. BA 1927, BChir 1930, MD 1935, MA 1937. First Asst, Med. Unit, St Thomas's Hosp. Med. Sch., 1932-35; Prof. of Pharmacology and Therapeutics, Roy. Coll. of Medicine, Baghdad, Iraq, 1935-47; Reader in Therapeutics, St Thomas's Hosp. Med. Sch., 1948-58. *Publications:* Recent Advances in Pharmacology, (with J. M. Robson); papers in Brit. Jl Pharmacology, Jl Physiology, Lancet, etc. *Address:* 21 Chepstow Villas, W11. *T:* 01-229 5815.

**STACK, (Ann) Prunella; (Mrs Brian St Quentin Power);** Director of The Women's League of Health and Beauty; *b* 28 July 1914; *d* of Capt. Hugh Bagot Stack, 8th Ghurka Rifles, and Mary Meta Bagot Stack, Founder of The Women's League of Health and Beauty; *m* 1st, 1938, Lord David Douglas-Hamilton (*d* 1944); two *s*; 2nd, 1950, Alfred G. Albers, FRCS (*d* 1951), Cape Town, S Africa; 3rd, 1964, Brian St Quentin Power. *Educ:* The Abbey, Malvern Wells. Mem. of the National Fitness Council, 1937-39. Mem. of Council and Exec. Cttee, Outward Bound Trust. *Publications:* Movement is Life (joint), 1937; The Way to Health and Beauty, 1938. *Recreations:* poetry, music, mountaineering, travel. *Address:* 24 Carlyle Square, SW3.

**STACK, Air Marshal Thomas (Neville),** CB 1969; CVO 1963; CBE 1965; AFC 1957; UK Permanent Military Delegate, Central Treaty Organisation, Ankara, since 1970; *b* 19 Oct. 1919; *s* of late T. Neville Stack, AFC, Pioneer Airman and Edythe Neville Stack; *m* 1955, Diana Virginia, *d* of late Oliver Stuart Todd, MBE; one *s* one *d*. *Educ:* St Edmund's College, Ware; RAF College, Cranwell. Served in Coastal Command, on Flying boats, 1939-45; Coastal Command, 1945-52; Staff Coll., 1950; Flying Coll., 1953; Transport Support duties in Far East and UK, 1954-59; Dep. Captain of The Queen's Flight, 1960-62; Transport Support duties in Far East, 1963-64; HQ, Flying Trng Comd, 1965-67; Comdt, RAF Coll., Cranwell, 1967-70. Fellow, Royal Meteorological Society. Order of Leopold (Belgium), 1945; Croix de Guerre (Belgium), 1945. *Recreations:* various outdoor sports; undergardening. *Address:* British Embassy, Ankara, Turkey. *Clubs:* Royal Air Force, Boodle's.

**STACY, Lt-Col Bertie Vandeleur,** CMG 1919; DSO 1917; retired District Court Judge, Sydney, NSW; *b* 7 Dec. 1886. Served European War, Australian Imperial Force, 1914-18 (despatches, CMG, DSO and bar). *Address:* 26 Salisbury Road, Rose Bay, Sydney, NSW, Australia.

**STACY, Reginald Joseph William,** CB 1955; *b* 1 Jan. 1904; *e s* of late Frank Dixon Stacy and Alice Summers; *m* 1932, Nina Grace Holder; one *s* one *d*. *Educ:* Wirtemburg (now Stonhouse) Street Elementary School; Sir Walter St John's School, London; Trinity College, Cambridge (Sen. Schol.). BA 1925 (Double First, Mod. Lang. Tripos). Entered Board of Trade, Commercial Relations and Treaties Department, 1927; Ottawa Imperial Conference, 1932; Commercial Mission to Colombia, 1938; led UK Trade Delegation to Warsaw, 1948-49; accompanied Minister of State, Board of Trade to South America, 1954; Insurance and Companies Department, 1956; Internat. Conferences on Insurance; Under-Sec., Bd of Trade, 1949-64, retd; French and Latin Master, Parkside Preparatory School, 1967-69. *Address:* 2 Beech Court, Easington Place, Guildford, Surrey.

**STAFFORD,** 14th Baron *cr* 1640, *confirmed* 1825; **Basil Francis Nicholas Fitzherbert;** *b* 7 April 1926; *s* of late Capt. Hon. Thomas Charles Fitzherbert, AM 1917, and Beryl (*d* 1959), 2nd *d* of John Waters and *widow* of Major Henry Brougham, RA; *S* uncle, 1941; *m* 1952, Morag Nada, *yr d* of Lt-Col Alastair Campbell, Altries, Milltimber, Aberdeenshire; three *s* three *d*. *Educ:* Avisford, Arundel; Ampleforth College, York. Lieut Scots Guards, 1945-48. Local Director, Barclays Bank Ltd (Birmingham); Dir, Stenhouse Midlands. President: North Staffs Br. Inst. of Marketing and Sales Management; Stafford Rugby FC; City of Stoke-upon-Trent Amateur Operatic Society; Staffs Assoc. of Boys' Clubs; Staffs Playing Fields Assoc.; Member Cttee of Staffs: County Cricket Club; Agric. Exec.; CLA; Show Dir, Staffs Agric. Soc.; Chm., Old Amplefordian Cricket Club. *Recreations:* cricket, shooting, yachting, fishing, tennis. *Heir:* *s* Hon. Francis Melfort

William Fitzherbert, *b* 13 March 1954. *Address:* Swynnerton Park, Stone, Staffordshire. *TA* and *T:* Swynnerton 228; Salt Winds, West Wittering, Chichester, Sussex. *T:* West Wittering 2181. *Clubs:* Guards, Army and Navy; IZ; Free Foresters; MCC.

**STAFFOkD, Bishop Suffragan of,** since 1958; **Rt. Rev. Richard George Clitherow,** MA Cantab; *b* 1 Oct. 1909; *s* of H. G. Clitherow, MRCS, and Elizabeth Willis Clitherow; *m* 1941, Diana, *d* of H. St J. Durston; two *s* one *d*. *Educ:* Dulwich College; Corpus Christi College, Cambridge; Wells Theological College. Asst Curate, St Augustine, Bermondsey, 1936-40. Chaplain to the Forces, 1940-46 (despatches). Canon Residentiary, Guildford Cathedral, 1946-58. *Recreations:* fishing and gardening. *Address:* Eversley, Uttoxeter, Staffs. *T:* Uttoxeter 81. *Club:* Army and Navy.

**STAFFORD, Archdeacon of;** *see* Stratton, Ven. Basil.

**STAFFORD, Frank Edmund,** CMG 1951; CBE 1946 (OBE 1931); FRGS; Malayan CS, retired 1951; *b* 24 Aug. 1895; *s* of late Frank Stafford and Marie Stafford; *m* 1943, Ida Wadham (marr. diss., 1950), *d* of late Conway Burton-Durham; one *s*; *m* 1953, Catherine Rolfe. *Educ:* Royal Gram. School, Guildford. Served European War, 1914-18, "Queen's" Regt. Joined staff of Civil Commissioner, Iraq, 1919; appointed to High Commission, Iraq, 1921; Financial Secretary, 1924; Financial Adviser, British Embassy, Baghdad, 1931; Colonial Service, Nigeria, 1936 (Asst Treasurer, Principal Asst Sec., Actg Financial Sec.). War of 1939-45, commissioned in Army (Lt-Col) for service with Occupied Enemy Territory Administration, 1941; Financial Adviser, Ethiopian Govt, 1942; attached LHQ Australia, 1944; Col, Military Administration, British Borneo, 1945; demobilized, 1946 (Brig.); seconded to Foreign Office, 1946; Member UK Delegn Italian Peace Conference and Council of Foreign Ministers; Head UK Delegn Four Power Commission, 1947; Member UK Delegn to UN, 1948, 1949, 1950, 1952; Foreign Office Adviser (Minister) to Chief Administrator, Eritrea, 1951-53; Adviser to Ethiopian Govt, 1953-60. Order Star of Ethiopia, 1944; Grand Officer, Star of Honour, 1955. *Publications:* contributions to Encyc. Britannica and to International Affairs. *Recreations:* astronomy, horticulture, walking. *Address:* 3 Holbrook Park, Horsham, Sussex. *T:* Horsham 2497. *Clubs:* Travellers', National Liberal.

**STAFFORD, Godfrey Harry,** PhD; Director, Rutherford High Energy Laboratory, Chilton, Didcot, Berks, since Sept. 1969; *b* 15 April 1920; *s* of Henry and Sarah Stafford; *m* 1950, Helen Goldthorp (*née* Clark); one *s* twin *d*. *Educ:* Rondebosch Boys High Sch., S Africa; Univ. of Cape Town; Gonville and Caius Coll., Cambridge. MSc Cape Town, 1941; South African Naval Forces, 1941-46; Ebden Scholar of Univ. of Cape Town at Cambridge Univ., PhD Cantab 1950; Harwell, 1949-51; Head of Biophysics Subdiv., CSIR, Pretoria, 1951-54; Cyclotron Gp, AERE, 1954-57; Rutherford High Energy Laboratory: Head of Proton Linear Accelator Gp, 1957; Head of High Energy Physics Div., 1963; Dep. Dir, 1966. *Publications:* papers and articles in learned jls on: biophysics, nuclear physics, high energy physics. *Recreations:* foreign parts, particularly Italy; camping. *Address:* 16 Boxhill Walk, Abingdon, Berkshire. *T:* (home) Abingdon 1197, (office) Abingdon 1900.

**STAFFORD, Jack,** CB 1953; Director of Statistics, Board of Trade, since 1948; *b* 1909; *s* of late John William and Ruth Stafford; *m* 1932, Miriam Claire Holt; two *s*. *Educ:* Baines' Grammar School; Manchester Univ. Asst Lecturer in Economics, Manchester Univ., 1930; Lecturer in Economics, Manchester Univ., 1934; Rockefeller Fellow, 1938; Statistician, Central Statistical Office, 1941, Acting Director, 1946. *Publications:* Essays on Monetary Management, 1933; articles and papers in Jl of Roy. Statistical Soc., Trans. Manchester Statistical Soc., Economic Jl, Manchester School. *Recreation:* gardening. *Address:* The Ivels, Headley Grove, Headley, Epsom, Surrey. *T:* Headley 227. *Club:* Royal Automobile.

**STAFFORD, John;** HM Diplomatic Service; Consul, British Consulate-General, Houston, Texas, since 1969; *b* 15 June 1920; *s* of late Frank Stafford and Gertrude Stafford, Sheffield; *m* 1949, Mary Jocelyn Goodwin, *d* of late Capt. J. G. Budge, RN. *Educ:* High Storrs Grammar Sch. Exchequer and Audit Dept, 1939. Joined RAF, 1940; Reconnaissance Pilot, Western Desert; invalided out as Warrant Officer/Pilot, 1945. Board of Trade, 1946; Assistant Trade Commissioner, Delhi, 1946-49; Karachi, 1950-54; Bulawayo, 1954-56; Trade Commissioner, Karachi, 1956; Lahore, 1957; Bombay, 1958-60; Lahore, 1963-65; Dep. High Comr in Lahore, 1965-69. *Recreations:* cricket, tennis, music. *Address:* British Consulate-General, 1005 World Trade Center, 1520 Texas Avenue, Houston, Texas 77002, USA. *Clubs:* East India and Sports; Punjab (Lahore); and various in India and Pakistan.

**STAFFORD-CLARK, David,** MD; FRCP; DPM; Physician in Charge, Department of Psychological Medicine, and Director of The York Clinic, Guy's Hospital, 1954; Consultant Physician, Bethlem Royal and Maudsley Hospitals and the Institute of Psychiatry, since 1954; *b* 17 March 1916; *s* of Francis and Cordelia Susan Stafford Clark; *m* 1941, Dorothy Stewart (*née* Oldfield); three *s* one *d*. *Educ:* Felsted; University of London. Guy's Hospital. MRCS, LRCP, 1939; MB, BS, 1939. Served War of 1939-45, RAFVR; trained as Medical Parachutist (despatches twice); demobilised 1945. Guy's Hosp., MRCP, Nuffield Med. Fellow, 1946; 3 years postgrad. trg appts, Inst. of Psychiatry, Maudsley Hosp.; MD London, 1947, DPM London, 1948; Registrar, Nat. Hosp., Queen Sq., 1948. Resident Massachusetts Gen. Hosp., Dept of Psychiatry, and Teaching Clinical Fellow, Harvard Med. School, 1949; First Asst, Professorial Unit, Maudsley Hosp., 1950; Mem. Assoc. for Research in Mental and Nervous Disorders, NY, 1950-53; Consultant Staff, Guy's Hosp., 1950; Lectureship, Psychology (Faculty of Letters), Reading Univ., 1950-54. Member: Archbishop of Canterbury's Commn on Divine Healing; Council, Royal Medico-Psychological Assoc.; Council, Medico-Legal Soc.; Examr, RCP Edtl Bd, Guy's Hosp. Reports, and Mod. Med. of Gt Britain. Acted as adviser to various motion picture companies (Universal International etc) on medical aspects of their productions; has also acted as adviser and director on a large number of medical programmes on sound radio, and both BBC and Independent Television, including the "Lifeline" series of programmes for the BBC, and documentary programmes for ITV on the emotional and intellectual growth of normal children, and the life and work of Freud; Author of Brain and Behaviour Series in Adult Education Television Programmes on BBC Channel 2; Mind and Motive Series, 1966. FRCP, 1958; Mem., NY Acad. of Sciences; FRSA (Silver Medal), 1959; Hon. RCM, 1966. *Publications:* poetry: Autumn Shadow, 1941; Sound in the

Sky, 1944. Psychiatry Today (Pelican), 1951; Psychiatry for Students, 1964, 3rd edn, 1967; What Freud Really Said, 1965. Chapts in: Emergencies in Medical Practice, 1st, 2nd and 3rd edns, 1948, 1950, 1952; Compendium of Emergencies, 1st and 2nd edns; Case Histories in Psychosomatic Medicine, 1952; Taylor's Medical Jurisprudence, 12th edn, 1965; Schizophrenia: Somatic Aspects, 1st edn, 1957; Frontiers in General Hospital Psychiatry, 1961; A Short Textbook of Medicine, 1963; The Pathology and Treatment of Sexual Deviation, 1964; Psychiatry for Students, 1964; contributions to various medical textbooks and to medical and scientific jls. *Recreations:* travel, reading, writing, making and watching films, theatre; people, sleep.

**STAFFORD-KING-HARMAN, Sir Cecil William Francis,** 2nd Bt, *cr* 1913; *b* 6 Jan. 1895; *s* of late Rt Hon. Sir Thomas Stafford, Bt, CB, and Frances Agnes King-Harman; *S* father, 1935; assumed additional surname of King-Harman, 1932; *m* 1917, Sarah Beatrice, *y d* of late Col A. D. Acland, CBE, and Hon. Mrs Acland, Feniton Court, Honiton, Devon; (one *s* killed in action) two *d. Educ:* RN Colleges, Osborne and Dartmouth; RMC Sandhurst; Christ Church, Oxford. Formerly Midshipman, Royal Navy, retired, 1912; commissioned 2nd Lt, The King's Royal Rifle Corps, 1914; Captain, 1917; served throughout European War in France and Italy (despatches); after war went to Christ Church, Oxford, MA (Hons) Agriculture; Steward, Irish Turf Club, 1938-40, 1943-46, 1948-51, 1952-55, 1959-62; Mem. of Racing Board, 1945-50. Appointed Member, Council of State for Ireland, 1956. War substantive Captain, 1940; Temporary Major, 1941; Temporary Lt-Col 1942; retired, 1943. *Recreations:* shooting, racing, fishing. *Address:* St Catherines Park, Leixlip, Co. Kildare, Ireland. *T:* Celbridge 280421. *Clubs:* Boodle's; Kildare Street, Irish Turf (Dublin).

**STAGG, Prof. Geoffrey Leonard,** MBE 1945; Professor, Department of Italian and Hispanic Studies, University of Toronto, since 1956, Chairman, 1956-66, and since 1969; *b* 10 May 1913; *s* of Henry Percy Stagg and Maude Emily Bradbury; *m* 1948, Amy Southwell, Wellesley Hills, Mass, USA; two *s* one *d. Educ:* King Edward's School, Birmingham (Scholar); Trinity Hall, Cambridge (Scholar). BA 1st cl. Hons Modern and Medieval Languages Tripos, 1934; MA 1946; Joseph Hodges Choate Mem. Fellow, Harvard Univ., 1934-36; AM (Harvard), 1935; Modern Languages Master, King Edward's School, Birmingham, 1938-40, 1946-47; served in Intelligence Corps, 1940-46; Lecturer in Spanish and Italian, Nottingham Univ., 1947-53, and Head of Dept of Spanish, 1954-56. Vice-Pres., Assoc. of Teachers of Spanish and Portuguese of GB and Ireland, 1948-; Pres., Canadian Assoc. of Hispanists, 1964-66. Fellow, New Coll., Univ. of Toronto, 1962; Senior Fellow, Massey Coll., Univ. of Toronto, 1965; Canada Council Senior Fellowship, 1967-68. *Publications:* articles on Spanish literature in learned jls. *Address:* Department of Italian and Hispanic Studies, University of Toronto, Toronto 5, Canada.

**STAGG, James Martin,** CB 1954; OBE 1937; Director of Services, Meteorological Office, till 1960; *b* 30 June 1900; *er s* of Alex. C. and Ellen Stagg, Dalkeith, Midlothian; *m* 1940, Elizabeth Nancy Kidner; two *s. Educ:* Broughton Secondary Sch., Edinburgh; Edinburgh Univ. Science Master, George Heriot's Sch., Edinburgh, 1921-23; Professional Asst, Meteorological Office, 1924; Leader, British Polar Year Exped. to Arctic Canada, 1932-33; Superintendent, Kew Observatory, 1939; Chief Meteorological Adviser to Supreme Commander, Allied Forces, Europe, 1943-45. President Royal Meteorological Society, 1959. Officer Legion of Merit (US), 1945. Gauss-Weber medal (Göttingen), 1955. *Publications:* miscellaneous publications on geomagnetism, aurora and meteorology. *Recreations:* gardening and walking. *Address:* 33 Carlton Road, Seaford, Sussex. *T:* Seaford 4760.

**STAGG, Air Commodore (retired) Walter Allan,** CB 1958; CBE 1953 (OBE 1950); *b* 2 April 1903; *s* of late Frederick Edward and late Emma Jane Stagg; *m* 1943, Olive Georgina Legg; no *c. Educ:* privately. Commnd in RAF, 1926; served India, 1928-33 (India General Service Medal, NW Frontier Clasp, 1930-31). Air Ministry (Directorate of Equipment), 1935-37. Joined HMS Glorious in Mediterranean, 1937-39. On staff of HQ Training, Flying Training and Maintenance Comds, 1940-43; Dep. Director of Equipment (2) in Air Ministry, 1943-45; Senior Equipment Staff Officer, No 214 Group, Italy, 1945; Comd No 25 Maintenance Unit, 1945-46. In Ministry of Civil Aviation, 1946-47; on staffs of HQ Maintenance Comd, 40 Group and Flying Training Comd, 1947-51; Dep. Asst Chief of Staff (Logistics) at SHAPE, 1951-53; Director of Equipment (A) Air Ministry, 1954-55; Director of Movements, Air Ministry, 1955-58; Director, Supply Services Division, NATO. Maintenance Supply Services Agency, 1958-60, retired. *Address:* High Wall, Wotton Lane, Lympstone, Devon. *T:* Exmouth 5088. *Club:* Royal Air Force.

**STAHL, Professor Ernest Ludwig;** Taylor Professor of the German Language and Literature and Fellow of The Queen's College, Oxford, 1959-69, Supernumerary Fellow, since 1969; *b* Senekal, OFS, S Africa, 10 Dec. 1902; *s* of Philip and Theresa Stahl; *m* 1942, Kathleen Mary Hudson; no *c. Educ:* Capetown, Oxford, Heidelberg abd Berne Universities. MA Capetown, 1925; First Class Hons, Oxford, 1927; PhD Berne *magna cum laude* 1931. Assistant Lecturer in German, Birmingham, 1932; Lecturer in German, Oxford, 1935; Reader in German Literature, Oxford, 1945; Student of Christ Church, Oxford, 1945, Student Emeritus, 1960. Vis. Professor: Cornell, 1956; Princeton, 1958; Yale, 1964; Kansas, 1968; Calif (Davis), 1969-70. Gold Medal, Goethe Gesellschaft, 1966. *Publications:* Die religiöse und die philosophische Bildungsidee und die Entstehung des Bildungsromans, 1934; Hölderlin's Symbolism, 1944; The Dramas of Heinrich von Kleist, 1948 (revised edn, 1961); Schiller's Drama: Theory and Practice, 1954; Goethe's Iphigenie auf Tauris, 1962. Editions of Goethe's Werther, 1942, Lessing's Emilia Galotti, 1946, Goethe's Torquato Tasso, 1962, and R. M. Rilke's Duino Elegies, 1965; revised edn, Oxford Book of German Verse, 1967; (with W. E. Yuill) Introduction to German Literature, vol. III, 1970; Co-Editor, Anglica Germanica and Oxford German Studies. Articles in Modern Language Review, Germanic Review, German Life and Letters, Journal of English and Germanic Philology. *Address:* 43 Plantation Road, Oxford.

**STAINFORTH, Maj.-Gen. Charles Herbert,** CB 1969; OBE 1955; General Officer Commanding Aldershot District, 1966-69, retired; *b* 12 Dec. 1914; *s* of Lieut-Colonel Stainforth, CMG, 4th Cavalry, IA, and Georgina Helen, *d* of Maj.-Gen. H. Pipon, CB; *m* Elizabeth, *d* of late John Tait, Easdale; one *s* one *d. Educ:* Wellington Coll.; RMC, Sandhurst. Commnd into 2nd Royal Lancers, IA; transferred British Army, 1947; Chief of Staff, Southern Comd, 1965-66.

Col Comdt, RCT, 1970-. *Address:* Lane End, Camberley, Surrey. *Clubs:* United Service, MCC.

**STAINFORTH, Graham Henry;** *b* 3 Oct. 1906; *s* of Lieut-Colonel H. G. Stainforth, CMG, Indian Cavalry, and Georgina Helen, *d* of Maj.-Gen. H. Pipon, CB; *m* 1943, Ruth Ellen Douglas-Cooper; one *s* two *d*. *Educ:* Wellington Coll., Berks; Emmanuel Coll., Cambridge. Assistant Master at Merchant Taylors' Sch., 1928-35, and Assistant Housemaster, 1933-35; Assistant Master and Tutor at Wellington Coll., 1935-45, Head of the English Department; Hon. Secretary of Wellington College Clubs at Walworth. Headmaster of Oundle and Laxton Grammar Schools, 1945-56; Master of Wellington, 1956-66. Governor: Ardingly College, 1966-, Portsmouth Grammar School, 1966-. *Address:* The Cottage, Winterbrook, Wallingford, Berkshire. *T:* Wallingford 2414.

**STAINTON, Anthony Nathaniel,** CB 1967; Parliamentary Counsel to HM Treasury; *b* 8 Jan. 1913; *s* of Evelyn Stainton, Barham Court, Canterbury; *m* 1st, 1947, Barbara Russen; three *d*; 2nd, 1966, Rachel Frances, *d* of late Col C. E. Coghill, CMG. *Educ:* Eton; Christ Church, Oxford. Called to the Bar, Lincoln's Inn, 1937.

**STAINTON, John Ross;** Deputy Managing Director of BOAC, since 1969; Member, Board, BOAC, since 1968, and BOAC (AC) Ltd, since 1961; *b* 27 May 1914; *s* of late George Stainton and of Helen Ross; *m* 1939, Doreen Werner; three *d*. *Educ:* Glengorse, Eastbourne; Malvern Coll., Worcestershire. Joined Imperial Airways as Trainee, 1933; served in Italy, Egypt, Sudan. Served with RAF in England and West Indies, 1940-42. BOAC in USA, 1942; Man. N America, 1949-53; General Sales Man. BOAC, 1954-55; General Man. Stations and Traffic, 1956; Chief of Ground Services, 1957; General Man. Eastern Routes, 1958; General Man. Western Routes, 1960; Commercial Director, 1964. MInstT (Pres., 1970-71). *Address:* Tees Green, Heatherside, Camberley, Surrey. *T:* Camberley 21338. *Clubs:* Royal Aero; Sunningdale Golf.

**STAINTON, Keith;** MP (C) Sudbury and Woodbridge since Dec. 1963; *b* 8 Nov. 1921; *m* 1946, Vanessa Ann Heald; three *s* three *d*. *Educ:* Kendal Sch.; Manchester Univ. (BA (Com.) Dist. in Economics). Insurance clerk, 1936-39. Served War of 1939-45: Lieut, RNVR, 1940-46. Manchester Univ., 1946-49; Leader Writer, Financial Times, 1949-52; Industrial Consultant, 1952-57; joined Burton, Son & Sanders, Ltd, 1957, Man. Dir 1961-69, Chm. 1962-69. Croix de Guerre avec Palmes, Ordre de l'Armée, 1943. *Address:* Little Bealings House, Woodbridge, Suffolk. *T:* Kesgrave 4205.

**STAIR,** 13th Earl of, *cr* 1703; **John Aymer Dalrymple,** CVO 1964; MBE 1941; Bt 1664 and (Scot.) 1698; Viscount Stair, Lord Glenluce and Stranraer, 1690; Viscount Dalrymple, Lord Newliston, 1703; Baron Oxenfoord (UK) 1841; Colonel (retired) Scots Guards; Lord Lieutenant of Wigtownshire, since 1961; *b* 9 Oct. 1906; *e s* of 12th Earl of Stair, KT, DSO, and Violet Evelyn (*née* Harford) (*d* 1968); *S* father, 1961; *m* 1960, Davina, *d* of late Hon. Sir David Bowes-Lyon, KCVO; three *s*. *Educ:* Eton; Sandhurst. Bde Major, 3rd (London) Infantry Bde and Regimental Adjt Scots Guards, 1935-38; served Middle East, 1941; Bde Major, 16th Inf. Bde (despatches, MBE); Lieut-Colonel 1942; commanded 1st Scots Guards, 1942-43; AMS Headquarters AAI, 1944; Comd Trg Bn Scots Guards, 1945; Comd 2nd Scots Guards, 1946-49; Comd Scots Guards, Temp. Colonel, 1949-52; retired, 1953; retired as Hon. Colonel Scots Guards, 1953. *Heir: s* Viscount Dalrymple, *qv*. *Address:* Lochinch Castle, Stranraer, Wigtownshire. *Clubs:* Guards, Turf, Pratt's.

*See also Hon. R. H. Philipps, Lady Jean Rankin.*

**STALLARD, Albert William;** MP (Lab) St Pancras (North) since 1970; *b* 5 Nov. 1921; *m* 1944; one *s* one *d*. *Educ:* Low Waters Public School; Hamilton Academy, Scotland. Engineer, 1937-65; Technical Training Officer, 1965-70. Councillor, St Pancras, 1953-59, Alderman, 1962-65; Councillor, Camden, 1965-70. AEU Order of Merit, 1968. *Address:* 8 Leybourne Street, NW1. *T:* 01-485 4707.

**STALLARD, Colonel Hon. Charles Frampton,** QC 1910; DSO 1918; MC; Minister of Mines, South Africa, 1939-45; Colonel (SA); retired; Hon. Colonel, Witwatersrand Rifles; *s* of late William Henry Stallard and late Mary Tucker; *b* London, 1871. *Educ:* St Edward's Sch. and Merton Coll., Oxford. Called to Bar, Gray's Inn (Holt Scholar); served S African War, CIV, and Paget's Horse; Member Provincial Council, Transvaal, 1910; MP Roodepoort, 1929-38; MP Maritzburg District, 1939-48 (retired); served European War, South West Africa Staff, 1914; APM 41st Division, Flanders, 1916; Captain and acting Lieut-Colonel, various battalions, Flanders, 1917-18 (wounded Messines, MC, DSO, despatches thrice). *Recreation:* farming. *Address:* PO Box 5156, Johannesburg, S Africa; Hope Woolith, Misgund, near Johannesburg. *Clubs:* Rand (Johannesburg); City (Cape Town).

**STALLARD, Hyla Bristow,** MBE 1942; TD; MD, MChir, FRCS, Hon. LLD (St Andrews); Eye Surgeon; *b* 28 April 1901; *s* of Hyla Holden Stallard and Evelyn Walsh; *m* Gwynneth Constance Page. *Educ:* Sherborne Sch.; Cambridge Univ. (MA); St Bartholomew's Hospital (Shuter Entrance Scholarship). BCh Cantab 1925; MRCS, LRCP 1926; MB Cantab 1928; FRCS 1928; MD (Cantab), Honourable mention, 1933; MChir (Cantab), 1967; Consulting Surgeon, Moorfields Eye Hospital; Consulting Eye Surgeon, St Bartholomew's Hospital. Major RAMC TA; served War of 1939-45, Middle East (despatches, MBE); in France and in Belgium. Late House Surgeon, and Eye House Surgeon, and Chief Assistant, St Bartholomew's Hospital; late Pathologist and Curator, Moorfields Eye Hospital; formerly Eye Surgeon, Radium Inst., and Mount Vernon Hospital; formerly Consulting Eye Surgeon to: Alexandra Hosp.; Royal Sch. for Deaf Children, at Margate. Formerly Editor Trans Ophthalmological Society of UK; Assistant Editor, British Journal of Ophthalmology; President, RSM, Eye Section, 1967-69; Vice-President, Ophthalmological Society, UK, 1957-60; Bentley Prize, 1927; Gifford Edmonds Prize, 1932; Nettleship Medal, 1936; Wm Mackenzie Medal, 1951. Charles H. May Memorial Lecturer, New York, 1953; Hunterian Prof. RCS, 1954-55, 1960-61, 1967-68. Doyne Memorial Lecturer, Oxford, 1962; Middlemore Lecturer, Birmingham, 1963; Craig Lecturer, Queen's Univ., Belfast, 1965. OStJ. Order of the Southern Cross (Brazil). *Publications:* Eye Surgery, 1946 (edns 1946, 1950, 1958, 1965); ed Modern Practice in Ophthalmology, 1949; Radiant energy, as a pathogenic and therapeutic agent in Ophthalmic disorders, Monograph, 1933; War Surgery of the Eye, British Journal of Ophthalmology, 1944, etc. *Recreations:* athletics, hockey, represented England in athletics, 1921-27, Great Britain at the Olympic Games, 1924, and the British Empire against the USA, 1924. *Address:* 112 Harley Street, W1. *T:* 01-935 8840.

**STALLARD, Sir Peter (Hyla Gawne),** KCMG 1961 (CMG 1960); CVO 1956; MBE 1945; Lieutenant Governor of the Isle of Man since 1966; *b* 6 March 1915; *y c* of Rev. L. B. Stallard and Eleanor, *e d* of Colonel J. M. Gawne; *m* 1941, Mary Elizabeth Kirke, CStJ; one *s* one *d*. *Educ:* Bromsgrove Sch.; Corpus Christi Coll., Oxford (MA). Cadet, Colonial Administrative Service, Northern Nigeria, 1937. Military Service; Nigeria, Gold Coast, Burma, 1939-45. Secretary to the Prime Minister of the Federation of Nigeria, 1958-61; Governor and Commander-in-Chief of British Honduras, 1961-66. KStJ 1961. *Recreation:* golf. *Address:* Government House, Douglas, Isle of Man. *T:* Douglas 5349; 18 Henley Road, Taunton, Somerset. *T:* Taunton 81505. *Club:* Athenæum.

**STALLIBRASS, Geoffrey Ward,** OBE 1952; Controller, National Air Traffic Control Services, Board of Trade/MoD (Air) since 1969 (Joint Field Commander, 1966-69); *b* 17 Dec. 1911; *s* of Thomas and Ivy Stallibrass, Midhurst; *m* 1940, Alison, *e d* of late James and Rita Scott, Norwich; two *s* three *d*. *Educ:* Wellingborough Sch. Air Service Training, Hamble (Commercial Pilot/Instrument Rating Course), 1948. Dep. Director, Civil Aviation Ops, Ministry of Civil Aviation, 1946; attached to BOAC, 1949; Dep. Director of Control and Navigation (Development), 1950; Director of Aerodromes (Tech.), Ministry of Transport and Civil Aviation, 1953; Director of Flight Safety, Min. of Aviation, 1961. Pilot's Licence, 1936-; AFRAeS. *Publications:* articles on aviation subjects. *Recreations:* walking, birdwatching, photography, flying, music. *Address:* The Adelphi, John Adam Street, WC2. *T:* 01-836 1207; 6 Birdhurst Gardens, South Croydon, Surrey CR2 7DT. *T:* 01-688 8094.

**STALLWOOD, Frank,** CMG 1967; OBE 1955; *b* 5 Sept. 1910; *s* of late Henry Robert Stallwood and late Ethel (*née* Cheeseman); *m* 1935, Cora Cécile Frances (*née* Brady); one *s* one *d*. *Educ:* Owen's Sch.; St Luke's Coll., Exeter. BA Hons London. Schoolmaster, 1932-40. Army, Captain, Intelligence Corps, Service in ME, 1940-46. Diplomatic Service, 1946-68, retired. *Recreations:* fly-fishing, conversation. *Address:* The Nook, Kintbury, Berks. *T:* Kintbury 341. *Club:* Flyfishers'.

**STALLWORTHY, John Arthur;** Nuffield Professor of Obstetrics and Gynæcology, University of Oxford, since 1967; *b* 26 July 1906; *s* of Arthur John Stallworthy; *m* 1934, Margaret Wright Howie; one *s* twin *d*. *Educ:* Auckland Grammar Sch.; Universities of Auckland and Otago, NZ. Distinction and gold medal in surgery, gynæcology and obstetrics, 1930; travelling med. schol., 1931; obstetrical travelling schol., 1932; postgrad. experience in Melbourne, London and Vienna. MRCOG 1935; FRCS 1936; FRCOG 1951. Joseph Price Orator, US, 1950; McIlrath Guest Prof., Sydney, 1952; Sommer Mem. Lecturer, US, 1958; Sims Black Prof. S Africa, 1964. Sometime Examiner in Obstetrics and Gynæcology for RCOG, RCS of S Africa, Universities of Oxford, Birmingham, Leeds, E Africa and Singapore. Hon. Cons., Royal Prince Alfred Hospital, Sydney, 1952; Assoc. Obstetrician, National Maternity Hospital, Dublin, 1959. Member Council: RCOG (Senior Vice-Pres., 1969); RSM. Pres., Medical Protection Soc., 1970; Pres.-elect, Inst. of Religion and Medicine. Hon. Fellow, Surgical, Obstetrical and Gynæcological Societies in US, Wales, Canada, S Africa, Spain and Turkey. Victor Bonney Prize, RCS, 1967-69. Member, Honourable Order of Kentucky Colonels, 1968. *Publications:* (jointly) Problems of Fertility in General Practice, 1948; (jointly) Recent Advances in Obstetrics and Gynæcology, 1966; joint contrib. to British Obstetric Practice and British Gynæcological Practice, 1959, and 1963. *Recreations:* formerly Rugby football, tennis, swimming, driving fast cars; now gardening, driving fast cars. *Address:* Shotover Edge, Headington, Oxford. *T:* Oxford 62481.

**STAMER, Sir (Lovelace) Anthony,** 5th Bt, *cr* 1809; MA; AMIMI; *b* 28 Feb. 1917; *s* of Sir Lovelace Stamer, 4th Bt, and Eva Mary, *e d* of R. C. Otter; *S* father, 1941; *m* 1st, 1948, Stella Huguette (marr. diss., 1953), *d* of Paul Burnell Binnie, Brussels; one *s* one *d*; 2nd, 1955, Margaret Lucy (marr. diss., 1959), *d* of late Major Belben and Mrs Stewart, Marandellas, S Rhodesia; 3rd, 1960, Marjorie June (marr. diss. 1968), *d* of T. C. Noakes, St James, Cape. *Educ:* Harrow; Trinity Coll., Cambridge; Royal Agricultural Coll., Cirencester. BA 1947; MA 1963; AMIMI 1963. Served RAF 1939-41; Officer in ATA 1941-45. Exec. Dir, Bentley Drivers Club Ltd. *Heir:* *s* Peter Tomlinson Stamer, *b* 19 Nov. 1951. *Address:* 76a High Street, Long Crendon, near Aylesbury, Bucks.

**STAMFORD,** 10th Earl of, *cr* 1628; **Roger Grey;** Baron Grey of Groby, 1603; *b* 27 Oct. 1896; *s* of 9th Earl and Elizabeth Louisa Penelope (*d* 1959), 3rd *d* of late Rev. Canon Charles Theobald; *S* father, 1910. 2nd Lieut, Territorial Force Reserve, 1916; Honorary Attaché, British Legation, Berne, Oct. 1918, Feb. 1919; Parliamentary Private Secretary to Viscount Peel, Secretary of State for India, 1922; JP (1918) Cheshire; DL (1937) Cheshire; Charter Mayor of Altrincham, 1937, Mayor, 1937-38; Hon. Freeman of Altrincham, 1939; is a Trustee of the John Rylands Library, Manchester. *Heir:* none. *Address:* Dunham Massey Hall, Altrincham, Cheshire. *Clubs:* Travellers'; Yorkshire.

**STAMM, Temple Theodore,** FRCS; Orthopædic Surgeon Emeritus, Guy's Hospital; *b* 22 Dec. 1905; *s* of Dr Louis Edward Stamm, Streatham, and Louisa Ethel (*née* Perry), Caterham, Surrey; *m* 1945, Pamela, *d* of Charles Russell, Chislehurst, Kent. *Educ:* Rose Hill Sch., Surrey; Haileybury Coll.; Guy's Hospital Medical School. MB, BS (London), 1930, MRCS, LRCP 1928, FRCS 1934. Fellow Royal Society of Medicine; Fellow British Orthopædic Assoc.; Member British Med. Assoc. Formerly: Orthopædic Surgeon, Bromley Hospital, 1941-66; Asst Orthopædic Surgeon and Orthopædic Registrar, Royal Nat. Orthopædic Hospital; Asst Orthopædic Surgeon, Orthopædic Registrar, Asst Anæsthetist and Demonstrator of Anatomy, Guy's Hospital. Major RAMC. *Publications:* Foot Troubles, 1957; Guide to Orthopædics, 1958; Surgery of the Foot, British Surgical Practice, Vol. 4. Contributions to Blackburn and Lawrie's Textbook of Surgery, 1958. Articles in: Lancet, Guy's Hospital Reports, Journal of Bone and Joint Surgery, Medical Press, etc. *Recreations:* farming, sailing, music. *Address:* Bosloggas, St Mawes, Cornwall.

*See also Air Vice-Marshal W. P. Stamm.*

**STAMM, Air Vice-Marshal William Percivale,** CBE 1960; Co-director, amœbiasis research project, Royal Free Pathology Unit; Senior RAF Consultant in Pathology and Tropical Medicine and Officer Commanding RAF Institute of Pathology and Tropical Medicine,

1951-69, retired; *b* 27 Aug. 1909; *s* of Dr L. E. Stamm and L. E. (*née* Perry); *m* 1939, Mary Magdalene Van Zeller; two *s* one *d*. *Educ:* Haileybury Coll.; Guy's Hospital. MRCS, LRCP, 1932; MB, BS (London) 1933; DCP (London) 1946; DTM&H 1947; MRCP 1951; FRCP 1956; FCPath 1964. House appointments, anatomy demonstrator, Guy's Hospital. Commissioned RAF, 1934; specialised in pathology and tropical medicine, 1938; comd RAF Hospital, Takoradi, 1942-43; Member Council: Royal Society Trop. Med. and Hygiene, 1951-57 and 1959-69 (Vice-President, 1957-59, and 1969-71); Assoc. of Clinical Pathologists, 1958-61 (President, 1966-67); United Services Sect., Royal Society Med., 1952-62 and 1966-69. Pres., British Div., Internat. Acad. Pathology, 1966; Hon. lectr, tropical pathology, Royal Free Med. Sch.; Hon. Cons., Royal Free Hospital. QHS 1959-69. *Publications:* contrib. to Symposium, The Pathology of Parasitic Diseases; papers in Lancet, BMJ, Journal Clin. Pathology, Trans. Royal Society Tropical Med. and Hygiene, and Proc. Royal Society of Medicine. *Recreations:* building and decorating houses and boats; sailing and sea-fishing. *Address:* Crownick Woods, Restronguet, Mylor, Cornwall. *T:* Flushing 285. *Club:* Royal Air Force.
*See also T. T. Stamm.*

**STAMMERS, Arthur Dighton;** retired; *b* 5 May 1889; *s* of late Rev. Frederick Dighton Stammers and Charlotte Christina Noble; *m* Phyllis May, *o d* of Richard George Merrifield and Beatrice Lilian Bourke. *Educ:* Dean Close Sch., Cheltenham; The London Hospital; St John's Coll., Cambridge. BA, Hons, Cambridge, 1920; MA 1934; DSc, S Africa, 1925; war service with 7th Essex Regt, 1914-18; with SA Corps of Signals, 1942-44. Demonstrator in Physiology, Cambridge, 1920; in charge of research department in Animal Nutrition, Lever Bros Ltd, Port Sunlight, 1920-21; University of the Witwatersrand, Johannesburg; Senior Lecturer in Physiology, 1921-27; Professor of Physiology, 1927-49; Dean of the Faculty of Medicine, 1948-49; Dean of the Faculty of Science, 1937-38; Member University Council, 1938-42; Professor Emeritus, 1956; Member of Government Advisory Cttee on Broadcasting, 1932-36. Organist, Anglican Cathedral, Salisbury, S Rhodesia, 1950-51; Organising Secretary, Rhodesia Univ. Assoc., 1951-53; Temp. Lecturer in Physiology, University of Cape Town, 1956-58; University of Natal, 1959-60. Acting Head of the Department of Physiology, University of Cape Town, 1961; Temp. Lecturer in Physiology, University of Natal, 1962-63; Organist, St Mark's Cathedral, George, 1965-68. *Publications:* Editor, South African Journal of Medical Sciences, 1935-42; numerous articles and papers on physiological subjects in Journal of Physiology; Biochemical Journal; Physiological Reviews; British Journal of Experimental Pathology; Proceedings of Royal Society of S Africa; S African Journal of Science, etc; (joint) The History of The Lady Margaret Boat Club. *Recreations:* rowing, fishing, music. *Address:* c/o Standard Bank, Hillbrow, Johannesburg, South Africa. *Club:* Leander.

**STAMMERS, Professor Francis Alan Roland,** CBE 1945; TD (with clasp) 1949; Emeritus Professor of Surgery, University of Birmingham (Professor, 1946-63); Hon. Cons. Surgeon, United Birmingham Hospitals; Hon. Cons.-Adviser in Surgery to Birmingham Regional Hospital Board; *b* 31 Jan. 1898; *s* of Charles Roland Stammers and Eliza Nellie Pettitt; *m* 1933, Lois Mildred Marris; one *s* two *d*. *Educ:* Dudley Grammar School; Birmingham Univ.; London Hospital; Mayo Clinic, USA. Served European War, 1914-18, 2nd Lieut, Lieut RGA, 1916-18; BSc (Birmingham) 1920; MB, ChB (Birmingham), MRCS, LRCP 1923; FRCS 1925; ChM (Birmingham), 1936. Late Surgeon: General, Children's and Queen Elizabeth Hospitals, 1929; Rockefeller Fellowship Mayo Clinic, USA, 1929; served War of 1939-45: surgical specialist and OC Surgical Division, RAMC, 1939-42; Cons. Surgeon, Brigadier AMS, W Command and Italy, 1942-45 (despatches); Hon. Colonel, AMS; Late Member Council (late Member Court of Examiners), Royal College of Surgeons, 1957-65; late External Examiner: University of London; University of Durham. Visiting Surgeon to Harvard University Medical School, Boston, Mass, USA, 1950; President, Surgical Section of Royal Society of Med. (now Hon. Member), 1952-53; British Council and BMA Lecturer in Cyprus, Baghdad and Khartoum, 1952; Australasian Postgrad. Federation in Medicine Lecturer, 1958. President: Assoc. of Surgeons of Great Britain and Ireland, 1960-61; Midland Med. Society, 1960-61; Moynihan Chirurgical Club, 1962-63; Vice-President Medical Protection Society. *Publications:* Partial Gastrectomy Complications with Metabolic Consequences (with J. Alexander Williams), 1963; numerous articles in medical and surgical journals and textbooks. *Recreations:* gardening, reading. *Address:* 56 Middle Park Road, Weoley Hill, Birmingham 29. *Club:* University Staff (Birmingham).

**STAMP,** family name of **Baron Stamp.**

**STAMP,** 3rd Baron, *cr* 1938, of Shortlands; **Trevor Charles Stamp,** MA, MD, FRCPath; Emeritus professor of Bacteriology, Royal Postgraduate Medical School, University of London (Reader, 1937-48, Professor, 1948-70); *b* 13 Feb. 1907; *s* of 1st Baron Stamp, GCB, GBE; *S* brother, 1941; *m* 1932, Frances Dawes, *d* of late Charles Henry Bosworth, Evanston, Illinois, USA; two *s*. *Educ:* Leys Sch., Cambridge; Gonville and Caius Coll., Cambridge; St Bartholomew's Hospital. MRCS, LRCP, BCh Cambridge, MA Cambridge, 1931; MB Cambridge, 1937. MD 1966. Demonstrator in Bacteriology, 1932-34, Lecturer in Bacteriology, 1934-37, London School of Hygiene and Tropical Medicine; attached to the Ministry of Supply, 1941-45; Governor of Imperial College of Science and Technology; Governor of Leys School; Governor of Queenswood School. Founder Fellow, College of Pathologists, 1963 (now RCPath). US Medal of Freedom with Silver Palm, 1947. Hon. Freedom, Barbers' Company, 1958. *Publications:* Various papers on bacteriological subjects. *Recreation:* gardening. *Heir:* *s* Dr the Hon. Trevor Charles Bosworth Stamp, MB, BCh, MRCP [*b* 18 Sept. 1935; *m* 1963, Anne Carolynn Churchill, *o d* of Mrs Eric Grey Dudley and step *d* of Eric Grey Dudley, Great Alne, Warwicks; two *d*]. *Address:* Middle House, 7 Hyde Park Street, W2. *T:* 01-723 8363; Pennyroyal, Hedgerley, Bucks. *T:* Farnham Common 2737. *Clubs:* Athenæum, Savage.

**STAMP, Hon. Arthur Maxwell;** Director: Hill Samuel & Co. Ltd, 1958; The De La Rue Co. Ltd, 1960; Triplex Holdings Ltd, 1963; Economics International Inc.; Chairman: Maxwell Stamp Associates Ltd; Maxwell Stamp (Africa) Ltd; Maxeast Ltd; Member: Council International Chamber of Commerce, 1961; Executive Committee, National Institute of Economic and Social Research, 1962; Executive Committee, European League for Economic Co-operation, 1962; *b* 20 Sept. 1915; 3rd *s* of 1st Baron Stamp, GCB, GBE; *m*

1944, Alice Mary Richards; one *s* two *d*. *Educ:* Leys Sch., Cambridge; Clare Coll., Cambridge. Called to the Bar, Inner Temple, 1939; War of 1939-45, 2nd Lieut Intelligence Corps, 1940; Major 1943; Lieut-Colonel 1944. Financial Adviser, John Lewis Partnership Ltd; 1947-49; Acting Adviser, Bank of England, 1950-53. Alternate Executive Director for the UK, International Monetary Fund, Washington, DC, USA, 1951-53; Director, European Department, International Monetary Fund, 1953-54. Adviser to the Governors, the Bank of England, 1954-57. Member Council of Foreign Bondholders, 1950-53, 1955-57; Chairman, Home Office Cttee on London Taxi-Cab Trade, 1967. Governor, LSE, 1968. *Recreations:* music, photography. *Address:* 5 Loudoun Road, NW8. *T:* 01-286 4274; Annestown, Co. Waterford, Eire. *Clubs:* Athenæum, Overseas Bankers.

**STAMP, Hon. Sir Blanshard;** *see* Stamp, Hon. Sir E. B.

**STAMP, Hon. Sir (Edward) Blanshard,** Kt 1964; **Hon. Mr Justice Stamp;** Judge of the High Court of Justice (Chancery Division) since 1964; *b* 21 March 1905; *s* of late Alfred Edward Stamp, CB, and Edith Florence Guthrie; *m* 1934, Mildred Evelyn, *d* of John Marcus Poer O'Shee; no *c*. *Educ:* Gresham's Sch., Holt; Trinity Coll., Cambridge. Called to Bar, Inner Temple, 1929; Bencher of Lincoln's Inn, 1956. Served War of 1939-45 as civilian attached General Staff, War Office. Junior Counsel to Commissioners of Inland Revenue (Chancery), 1954; Junior Counsel to Treasury (Chancery), 1960-64. Mem., Restrictive Practices Court, 1970-. *Recreations:* walking, travelling. *Address:* 30 Hanover House, St John's Wood, NW8. *Clubs:* United University, Garrick, Lansdowne.

**STAMPER, Thomas Henry Gilborn,** CIE 1938; MC; FRICS; *b* 27 Oct. 1884; *m* 1923, Edith, *d* of late Rev. Stephen Edward Gladstone; two *s* one *d*. Served European War, 1914-18 (despatches, MC, with two Bars, French Croix de Guerre). *Address:* Wath Cottage, Damerham, Fordingbridge, Hants. *T:* Rockbourne 250.

**STANBRIDGE, Air Vice-Marshal (retired) Reginald Horace,** CB 1956; OBE 1944; MRCS, LRCP, DPM, DIH; *b* 24 Nov. 1897; *s* of Horace John Stanbridge; *m* 1945, Inez Valerie, *d* of Arthur Holland; one *s*. *Educ:* Eastbourne; St Mary Coll., London Univ.; London Hospital Medical College. Principal Medical Officer in following RAF Commands: Aden, 1938-41; Transport, 1948-49; Bomber, 1950-53; KHP, 1952, QHP, 1952-56; Principal Medical Officer, Middle East Air Force, 1953-56; retired, 1956. Board of Trade Med. Dept, 1966-. Liveryman, Soc. of Apothecaries; Freeman, City of London. CStJ. *Publications:* various articles in The Lancet, RAF Quarterly, Wine and Food. *Recreations:* sailing, tennis. *Address:* The Dial House, Birdshill Road, Oxshott, Surrey. *T:* Oxshott 2175. *Club:* United Hunts.

**STANBROOK, Ivor Robert;** MP (C) Orpington since 1970; *b* 13 Jan. 1924; *y s* of Arthur William and Lilian Stanbrook; *m* 1946, Joan (*née* Clement); two *s*. *Educ:* State Schools and London and Oxford Universities. Colonial Administrative Service, Nigeria, 1949-60. Called to the Bar, Inner Temple, 1960; practising barrister, 1960-. *Address:* Hookwood House, Rushmore Hill, Orpington, Kent.

**STANBURY, Richard Vivian Macaulay;** Counsellor, British Embassy, Buenos Aires, since 1968; *b* 5 Feb. 1916; *s* of Gilbert Vivian Stanbury and Doris Marguerite (*née* Smythe); *m* 1953, Geraldine Anne Grant; one *s* one *d*. *Educ:* Shrewsbury Sch. (Exhibr); Magdalene Coll., Cambridge (Exhibr). Sudan Political Service, 1937-50 (District Comr and Magistrate); HM Foreign Service, 1951-. *Recreations:* cricket, polo, tennis, golf, squash; playing bridge; reading memoirs, biography and the classics. *Address:* Silver Birches, Sunset Lane, West Chiltington, Sussex. *T:* Pulborough 2283. *Clubs:* Bath; Hawks (Cambridge); Hurlingham (Buenos Aires).

**STANCLIFFE, Very Rev. Michael Staffurth,** MA; Dean of Winchester, since 1969; *b* 8 April 1916; *s* of late Rev. Canon Harold Emmet Stancliffe, Lincoln; *m* 1940, Barbara Elizabeth, *yr d* of late Rev. Canon Tissington Tatlow; two *s* one *d*. *Educ:* Haileybury; Trinity Coll., Oxford. Curate of St James, Southbroom, Devizes, 1940-43; priest-in-charge, Ramsbury, 1943-44; curate of Cirencester and priest-in-charge of Holy Trinity, Watermoor, 1944-49; Chaplain and Master, Westminster School, 1949-57; Canon of Westminster and Rector of St Margaret's, Westminster, 1957-69; Speaker's Chaplain, 1961-69; Preacher to Lincoln's Inn, 1954-57. *Publication:* contrib. to A House of Kings, 1966. *Address:* The Deanery, Winchester, Hants. *Club:* Athenæum.

**STANDING, John;** *see* Leon, Sir J. R.

**STANDING, Michael Frederick Cecil,** CBE 1959; retired as Controller of Programme Organisation (sound), BBC, 1957-70; *b* 28 Feb. 1910; *s* of late Sir Guy Standing, KBE, and of late Lady Standing; *m* 1947, Helen Jean Dawson, *widow* of Flying Officer Michael Hope Lumley and *d* of Lt-Comdr Dawson Miller, CBE, RN, retired; one *s* two *d* (one *s* decd). *Educ:* Charterhouse. Baring Brothers & Co. Ltd, 1927-35; BBC, 1935; Director of Outside Broadcasting, 1940-45; Head of Variety, 1945-52; Controller of Sound Entertainment, BBC, 1952-57. *Recreations:* painting, gardening, cricket. *Address:* Trottiscliffe House, near West Malling, Kent. *T:* Fairseat 293.

**STANFIELD, Hon. Robert Lorne,** PC (Canada) 1967; MP (Progressive C) Halifax, NS, since 1968 (Colchester-Hants, NS, 1967); Leader of Opposition and National Leader of Progressive Conservative Party of Canada, since 1967; *b* Truro, NS, 11 April 1914; *s* of late Frank Stanfield, sometime MLA and Lieutenant-Governor of NS, and Sarah (*née* Thomas); *m* 1st, 1940, N. Joyce (*d* 1954), *d* of C. V. Frazee, Vancouver; one *s* three *d*; 2nd, 1957, Mary Margaret, *d* of late Hon. W. L. Hall, Judge of Supreme Court and formerly Attorney-Gen. of NS. *Educ:* Colchester County Academy, Truro; Ashbury Coll., Ottawa; Dalhousie Univ.; Harvard Law Sch. Southam Cup, Ashbury Coll.; BA Political Science and Economics 1936, Governor-General's Gold Medal, Dalhousie Univ.; LLB Harvard, 1939. War of 1939-45: attached Halifax Office of Wartime Prices and Trade Bd as Regional Rentals Officer, later as Enforcement Counsel. Admitted Bar of NS, 1940. Practised law, McInnes and Stanfield, Halifax, 1945-56. President, Nova Scotia Progressive Cons. Assoc., 1947-; Leader, Nova Scotia Progressive Cons. Party, 1948-67; elected to Legislature of NS, 1949, Mem. for Colchester Co.; re-elected Mem., 1953, 1960, 1963, 1967; Premier and Minister of Education, NS, 1956; resigned as Premier of NS, 1967. Hon. LLD: University of New Brunswick, 1958; St Dunstan's Univ., PEI, 1964; McGill Univ., PQ, 1967; St Mary's Univ., NS, 1969. Anglican. *Address:* The House of Commons, Ottawa, Canada; Stornoway, 541 Acacia Avenue, Rockcliffe Park, Ottawa, Ontario.

**STANFORD, John Keith,** OBE 1932; MC 1919; author and journalist; *b* 29 April 1892; 2nd *s* of late Edward Stanford, Aldringham, Suffolk, and Caroline Fraser; *m* 1st, 1919, Evelyn Lushington; one *s*; 2nd, 1927, Eleanor, *y d* of late J. D. Davies, Ryde, Isle of Wight; one *s* two *d*. *Educ:* Rugby (Scholar); St John's Coll., Oxford (Scholar, MA). Served European War, 1914-19, Suffolk Regt and Tank Corps (wounded, despatches, MC). Entered ICS Burma, 1919; Dep. Comr, 1924; Burma Rebellion, 1930-31 (OBE); Dep. Comr, Myitkyina, 1932-36; retired, 1938. With Vernay-Cutting expedition to North-East Burma Hills, 1938-39; did much ornithological research, Burma, 1927-39. Rejoined Army, 1939, and served France, 1939-40, Middle East, 1941-43; and with 21 Army Group, 1944-45; Lieut-Colonel, 1941. Chairman Edward Stanford Ltd, 1944-50. Explored bird life of Cyrenaica for British Museum, 1952. Vice-President, British Ornithologists Union, 1951-52. *Publications:* The Birds of Northern Burma, 1938; The Twelfth, 1944; Far Ridges, 1946; Mixed Bagmen, 1949; Guns Wanted, 1949; The Awlbirds, 1949; Bledgrave Hall, 1950; Last Chukker, 1951; Reverie of a Qu'hai, 1952; No Sportsman At All, 1952; Full Moon at Sweatenham, 1953; A Bewilderment of Birds, 1954; Survey of the Ornithology of Libya, 1954; British Friesians, a History of the Breed, 1956; Fox Me, 1958; Jimmy Bundobust, 1958; The Wandering Gun, 1960; Death of a Vulpicide, 1960; Broken Lanterns, 1962; Ladies in the Sun, 1962; Grouse Shooting, 1963; Partridge Shooting, 1963; The Twelfth and After, 1964; And Some in Horses, 1965; Tail of an Army, 1966; The Complex Gun, 1968; A Keeper's Country, 1968; also papers in birds in Ibis and Journal Bombay Natural History Society; The Changing Year, 1952-61 (Field); articles on sport, travel, etc. in Blackwood's Magazine, Shooting Times, etc. *Address:* c/o Lloyds Bank, 6 Pall Mall, SW1. *Club:* East India and Sports.

**STANFORD, William Bedell,** MA, LittD; Regius Professor of Greek in University of Dublin, since 1940; Fellow of Trinity College, Dublin, since 1934 (Senior Fellow since 1962); Tutor, 1938-54; Public Orator, since 1970 (Deputy Public Orator, 1958-60); Senior Master, Non-regent, 1960-62; *b* 1910; *s* of Rev. Bedell Stanford, then Rector of Trinity Church, Belfast, and Susan Stanford; *m* 1935, Dorothy Isobel Wright; two *s* two *d*. *Educ:* Bishop Foy Sch., Waterford; Trinity Coll., Dublin (Scholar). Formerly External Examiner in Greek for National Univ., Queen's Univ., University of Wales, University of Leeds and Royal Colleges of Physicians and Surgeons, Ireland. MIRA. Sather Professor of Classical Literature, University of California, Berkeley, 1966; Visiting Prof., McGill Univ., Montreal, 1968. Editor of Hermathena, 1942-62. Rep. of Dublin Univ. in the Irish Senate, 1948-69. Irish Rep., Council of Europe, Strasbourg, 1951, European Parliamentary Conf., Vienna, 1956 and Inter-parliamentary Conf., Warsaw, 1959. Member Irish Radio Advisory Council until 1952. Governor, Erasmus Smith's and Incorporated Society's schools. Member of General Synod and Dublin Diocesan Synod of Church of Ireland; Dublin Diocesan Nominator. Secretary, Appointments Cttee, TCD, 1936-37, Hon. Secretary, TCD Assoc., 1950-55. Member Council, Hellenic Society, 1965-68; President, Birmingham Branch, Classical Association, 1968; Chairman, Irish Nat. Cttee for Greek and Latin Studies. *Publications:* Greek Metaphor, 1936; Ambiguity in Greek Literature, 1939; Livy XXIV edited for schools, 1942; Aeschylus in His Style, 1942; Homer's Odyssey, edited, 1947-48 (2nd edn, 1961-62); The Ulysses Theme, 1954 (2nd edn, 1963); Aristophanes' Frogs, edited, 1957 (2nd edn, 1963); Sophocles' Ajax, edited, 1963; The Sound of Greek, 1967; also various shorter publications on literary, linguistic, ecclesiastical and historical subjects. *Address:* 40 Trinity College, Dublin; 2 Mount Salus, Dalkey, Co. Dublin. *T:* Dublin 803329. *Club:* Royal Irish Yacht (Dun Laoghaire).

**STANFORD-TUCK, Wing Commander Robert Roland,** DSO 1940; DFC (2 bars); *b* 1 July 1916; *s* of Stanley Lewis Tuck and Ethel Constance Tuck; *m* 1945; two *s*. *Educ:* St Dunstan's Preparatory School and College, Reading. Left school, 1932, and went to sea as a cadet with Lamport and Holt; joined Royal Air Force, Sept. 1935; posted to No 65 Fighter Sqdn, Aug. 1936, and served with them until outbreak of war; posted to 92 (F) Sqdn, and went through air fighting at Dunkirk, shooting down 8 enemy aircraft (DFC); posted to Comd No 257 Burma Fighter Sqdn, Sept. 1940, till July 1941, when given command of Wing; comd Duxford and Biggin Hill Wings; prisoner 1942, escaped 1945. Record to end July 1941: 27 confirmed victories, 8 probably destroyed, 6 damaged; wounded twice, baled out 4 times. Retired list, 1948. *Relevant publication:* Fly For Your Life (by L. Forrester). *Recreations:* fencing, riding, shooting. *Address:* The Lynch, Eastry, near Sandwich, Kent.

**STANHOPE,** family name of **Earl of Harrington.**

**STANIER, Brigadier Sir Alexander Beville Gibbons,** 2nd Bt, *cr* 1917; DSO 1940 (and Bar, 1945); MC; DL, JP; CStJ; *b* 31 Jan. 1899; *s* of 1st Bart, and Constance (*d* 1948), *d* of late Rev. B. Gibbons; *S* father, 1921; *m* 1927, Dorothy Gladys, *e d* of late Brig.-Gen. Alfred Douglas Miller, CBE, DSO; one *s* one *d*. *Educ:* Eton; RMC, Sandhurst. Served European War in France, 1918 (MC); served War of 1939-45, in France 1940 and 1944 (despatches, DSO and Bar, American Silver Star, Comdr Order of Leopold of Belgium with palm, Belgian Croix de Guerre with palm). Adjutant 1st Bn Welsh Guards, 1923-26; Military Secretary, Gibraltar, 1927-30; commanded 2nd Battalion Welsh Guards, 1939-40; temp. Brigadier, 1940-45; Lieut-Colonel Commanding Welsh Guards, 1945-48. CC Salop, 1950-58. High Sheriff of Shropshire, 1951. County President of the St John Ambulance Bde, 1950-60. *Heir: s* Beville Douglas Stanier [*b* 20 April 1934; *m* 1963, Shelagh, *er d* of late Major and Mrs J. S. Sinnott, Tetbury, Glos; one *s* two *d*]. *Address:* East Farndon Manor, Market Harborough, Leics. *T:* 2104; Park Cottage, Ludford, Ludlow. *T:* Ludlow 2675.

**STANIER, Robert Spenser;** Master of Magdalen College School, Oxford, 1944-67; *b* 9 Aug. 1907; *s* of C. E. Stanier, Civil Engineer to the Underground Railways; *m* 1935, Maida Euphemia Kerr Burnett; two *s*. *Educ:* Berkhamsted School; Wadham Coll., Oxford. Assistant Master at King's School, Canterbury, 1929-35; Usher at Magdalen College School, Oxford, 1935-44. *Publications:* Selections from the Greek Lyric Poets, 1935; Magdalen School, 1940 (republished by Oxford Historical Society, 1941; augmented edition, 1958); articles in 'Journal of Hellenic Society' and 'Greece and Rome'. *Address:* 211 Morrell Avenue, Oxford. *T:* Oxford 40269.

**STANIFORTH, John Arthur Reginald,** CBE 1969; Chief Executive, CJB Group, and Managing Director of Constructors John Brown, since 1958; Director, John Brown & Co. Ltd; *b* 19 Sept. 1912; *o s* of Captain Staniforth, MC, Anston House, Anston, Yorks; *m* 1936, Penelope Cecile, *y d* of Maj.-Gen. Sir Henry Freeland; one *s* one *d*. *Educ:* Marlborough Coll. Joined John Brown Group 1929-. Chairman of governing body, Cranborne Chase Sch.; Governor, Bryanston Sch. *Recreations:* golf, fishing, sailing. *Address:* 3 Stream Close, Old Bosham, Sussex. *T:* Bosham 2419. *Clubs:* Flyfishers', MCC.

**STANISTREET, Rt. Rev. Henry Arthur;** *see* Killaloe, Bishop of.

**STANLEY,** family name of **Earl of Derby** and **Baron Sheffield.**

**STANLEY OF ALDERLEY,** 6th Baron (known by style of his senior barony since May 1957); *see* Sheffield, 4th Baron.

**STANLEY, Brian Taylor,** MA; Director of the Institute of Education, University of Newcastle upon Tyne, since 1963; *b* 1907; *s* of T. T. and Ada A. Stanley, Birmingham; *m* 1938, Audrey, *d* of H. and E. C. Topsfield, Sunbury on Thames; one *s* one *d*. *Educ:* King Edward's Sch., Birmingham; Christ Church, Oxford; London Day Trng Coll., Columbia Univ., New York; Pädagogische Akademie, Hanover. Teacher under the Warwickshire County Council and Resident Tutor, Fircroft Working Men's College, 1931; Lecturer in Education, Manchester University, 1932; Professor of Education, King's College, Newcastle upon Tyne, 1936-48; Director Institute of Education, University of Durham, 1948-63. *Publications:* The Education of Junior Citizens, 1945; contributions to various educational jls, at home and abroad. *Address:* 5 Corchester Avenue, Corbridge, Northumberland. *T:* Corbridge 2075.

**STANLEY, Carleton Wellesley,** MA Oxon, LLD Toronto and Maine, LittD Colorado, FRSC; Professor of English Literature, United College, Winnipeg, 1946-53; *b* 6 July 1886; *m* Isabel, *d* of Prof. W. J. Alexander, Toronto; one *s* one *d*. *Educ:* West Toronto High School; University of Toronto (matriculated 1st place Classics, Mathematics, grad. 1st place Classics, 1st General Proficiency); New College, Oxford (1st Lit. Hum.). Lecturer, English Literature, Victoria College, Toronto, 1913-16; engaged business, 1916-25; joined staff, McGill University, 1925, Professor of Greek; Assistant to the Principal, McGill University, 1930-31; President of Dalhousie University, Halifax, NS, 1931-45; Secretary, Canadian Universities Conference, 1928-32; Vice-President, 1932-34; Pres. 1934-37. *Publications:* Roots of the Tree, 1936; Matthew Arnold, 1938, reprinted 1939; many articles European and Canadian reviews; Canadian correspondent, Manchester Guardian, 1913-16. *Address:* 31 Mark Street, Aurora, Ont, Canada. *T:* 416-727-9972.

**STANLEY, Charles Orr,** CBE 1945 (OBE 1943); Chairman: Pye (Ireland) Ltd; Director: Sunbeam Wolsey Ltd, Seafield Gentex Ltd, Blackwater Cottons, Ltd, Associated Television Ltd, Arts Theatre Cambridge Ltd, Arts Theatre Trust, Stanley Foundation Ltd, Orr Investments Ltd, Independent Medical Services; Chairman Radio Industry Council, 1962-65; Pres., British Radio Equipment Manufacturers' Association, 1962-64; *b* 15 April 1899; *s* of John and Louisa A. Stanley; *m* 1st, Elsie Florence Gibbs; one *s*; 2nd, Velma Dardis Price. *Educ:* Bishop Foy School, Waterford; City and Guilds, Finsbury. Served European War, RFC, 1917-18; Civil Engineer, 1922. Hon. LLD Trinity College, Dublin, 1960. FCGI 1961. *Address:* 3 Lowndes Place, SW1; Sainsfoins, Little Shelford, Cambs; Lisselan, Clonakilty, County Cork, Ireland. *T:* Bandon 43249. *Clubs:* Royal Thames Yacht; Royal Cork Yacht.

**STANLEY, Henry Sydney Herbert Cloete,** CMG 1968; High Commissioner in Ghana, since 1970; *b* 5 March 1920; *er s* of late Sir Herbert Stanley, GCMG and Reniera (*née* Cloete), DBE; *m* 1941, Margaret, *d* of late Professor H. B. Dixon, CBE, FRS; three *s*. *Educ:* Eton; Balliol College, Oxford. Served with King's Royal Rifle Corps, 1940-46 (Capt.); N-W Europe, 1944-46, also HQ, CCG. Appointed to Commonwealth Relations Office, 1947. Served in Pakistan, 1950-52; Swaziland and South Africa, 1954-57; USA, 1959-61; Tanganyika, 1961-63; Kenya, 1963-65; Inspector, HM Diplomatic Service, 1966-68, Chief Inspector, 1968-70. *Address:* c/o Foreign and Commonwealth Office, SW1. *Club:* Travellers'.

**STANLEY, Dr Herbert Muggleton,** FRS 1966; Chemicals Adviser to BP Chemicals Ltd; *b* Stratford-on-Avon, 20 July 1903; *m* 1930, Marjorie Mary (*née* Johnson); two *s* two *d*. *Educ:* King Edward VI Grammar School, Stratford-on-Avon; Birmingham University (1919-29). BSc 1923; MSc 1925; PhD 1930, FRIC; Mem. Council, Royal Soc., 1968. *Publications:* articles in numerous journals, including Jl Chem. Soc., Soc. Chem. Ind. *Recreations:* archæology, gardening. *Address:* West Halse, Bow, Crediton, Devon. *T:* Bow 262.

**STANLEY, Rev. Howard Spencer,** MA; General Secretary of the Congregational Union of England and Wales, 1956-64; *b* 25 Jan. 1901; *s* of Noah and Florence Stanley, St George's, Shropshire; *m* 1950, Olive Kenyon Crowther, MA. *Educ:* Edinburgh University; Yorkshire United Theological College. Minister: Southsea, 1925-27; Basingstoke, 1927-32; Bolton, 1932-45; Hassocks, 1964-66. Sec. and Moderator, Lancashire Congregational Union, 1945-56; Chairman Congregational Union of England and Wales, 1951-52. *Recreation;* gardening. *Address:* 24 Dukes Rd, Lindfield, Sussex.

**STANLEY, Michael Charles,** MBE 1945; Director of The Proprietors of Hay's Wharf Ltd, and various subsidiary Companies; *b* 11 Aug. 1921; *s* of late Col Rt Hon. O. F. G. Stanley, PC, MC, MP, and Lady Maureen Stanley (*née* Vane-Tempest-Stewart); *m* 1951, Ailleen Fortune Hugh Smith, *d* of Owen Hugh Smith, Old Hall, Langham, Rutland; two *s*. *Educ:* Eton; Trinity College, Cambridge. Served 1939-46 with Royal Signals (Capt. 1943); N Africa, Sicily and Italy with 78th Infantry Div. Trinity, 1946-49 (Nat. Science and Engineering, MA). Served Engineering Apprenticeship with Metropolitan Vickers Electrical Co. Ltd, 1949-52. CEng 1966; MIEE 1966 (AMIEE 1952). High Sheriff for Westmorland, 1959; Westmorland County Councillor, 1961; DL 1964, Vice-Lieutenant, 1965-, Westmorland. *Recreations:* idleness, walking, wine. *Address:* Halecat, Witherslack, Grange-over-Sands, Lancs. *T:* Witherslack 229. *Clubs:* Turf, White's, Beefsteak, Brooks's; St James's (Manchester); Puffins (Edinburgh).

**STANLEY, Hon. Pamela Margaret;** *b* 6 Sept. 1909; *d* of 5th Lord Stanley of Alderley and Margaret Evans Gordon; *m* 1941, Sir David Cunynghame, *qv*; three *s*. *Educ:* Switzerland;

France. Studied at Webber-Douglas School of Acting and Singing; first appearance Lyric, Hammersmith, 1932, in Derby Day; six months at Oxford Repertory, 1933; with Martin Harvey in The Bells, Savoy, 1933; Sydney Carroll's Open Air Theatre, 1934; Wendy in Peter Pan, 1934; Queen Victoria in Victoria Regina, Gate Theatre, 1935; went to USA with Leslie Howard in Hamlet, 1936; Queen Victoria in Victoria Regina, Lyric, 1937-38; Open Air Theatre, 1938; Queen Victoria in The Queen's Highland Servant, Savoy, 1968. *Address:* 15 Madeline Road, SE20. *T:* 01-778 7740.

**STANLEY, Captain Hon. Richard Oliver;** Grenadier Guards; *b* 29 Jan. 1920; 2nd *s* of Colonel Rt Hon. Lord Stanley, PC, MC (*d* 1938), and Sibyl Louise Beatrix Cadogan (*d* 1969), *e d* of Henry Arthur, late Viscount Chelsea, and Lady Meux; *g s* of 17th Earl of Derby, KG, PC, GCB, GCVO; *b* and *heir-pres* to 18th Earl of Derby, *qv*; *m* 1965, Susan, *o d* of Sir John Aubrey-Fletcher, *qv*. *Educ:* Eton. Served War of 1939-45; 2nd Lieutenant, Grenadier Guards, 1940, later Captain. Joined staff of Conservative Central Office after the war. Parliamentary Private Secretary to First Lord of the Admiralty, 1951-55. MP (C) N Fylde Div. of Lancashire, 1950-66, retired. Joint Treasurer, Conservative Party, 1962-66. Mem., Gaming Bd, 1968-. *Address:* 26a North Audley Street, W1. *T:* 01-493 0813; New England House, Newmarket, Suffolk. *T:* Bottisham 394.

**STANLEY, Sir Robert (Christopher Stafford),** KBE 1954 (OBE 1942); CMG 1944; *b* 12 May 1899; *o s* of Frederic Arthur and Mary Stanley; *m* 1927, Ursula Cracknell; one *d*. *Educ:* Westminster; RMA, Woolwich. RGA, 1918-21; war service in Palestine; Reuter's editorial staff, 1923-24; entered Nigerian Administrative Service, 1925; transferred Cyprus, 1935; Commissioner, Larnaca, 1936-37; Chief Assistant Secretary to Govt of Cyprus, 1938-41; Colonial Secretary, Barbados, 1942; Colonial Secretary, Gibraltar, 1945; Chief Secretary, Northern Rhodesia, 1947-52; High Commissioner for Western Pacific, 1952-56, retd. Speaker of Mauritius Legislative Council, 1957-59. *Address:* 80 Aberdeen Park, N5. *Club:* Royal Commonwealth Society.

*See also Sir C. D. P. T. Haskard.*

**STANLEY, Wendell M.;** Professor of Molecular Biology and Professor of Biochemistry, University of California, since 1948 (Director of Virus Laboratory, 1948-69); *b* 16 Aug. 1904; *s* of James G. Stanley and Claire Plessinger; *m* 1929, Marian Staples Jay; one *s* three *d*. *Educ:* Earlham Coll.; Univ. of Illinois. PhD Ill, 1929; ScD (Hon.): Harvard, Yale, Earlham, 1938; Princeton, 1947; Illinois, 1959; Pennsylvania, 1964; DSc (Hon.): Pittsburgh, 1962; Gustavus Adolphus Coll., 1963; Toledo, 1968; Butler, 1968; LLD (Hon.); Univ. of California, 1946; Indiana, 1951; Jewish Theol. Seminary of America, 1953; Mills Coll., 1960; Dr (*hon. causa*) Univ. of Paris, 1947; awarded many prizes and medals for work on viruses; Nobel prize for Chemistry, 1946. Sigma Xi Nat. Lectr, 1938; Harvey Lectr, Harvey Society, 1938; Hitchcock Prof., Univ. of California, 1940; Visiting Prof. of Chemistry, Earlham College, 1941. Lectures: Messenger, Cornell, 1942; Vanuxem, Princeton, 1942; Bergen, Yale, 1944; Edgar Fahs Smith, Univ. of Pennsylvania, 1947; Silliman, Yale, 1947; Lower, Cleveland Acad. of Med., 1948; Biology Colloquium, Oregon State Coll., 1950; Hanau W. Loeb, St Louis Univ., 1956; Walter R. Bloor, Univ. of Rochester, 1956; Meyer Bodansky Meml, Univ. of Texas, 1957; R. A. F. Penrose Jr Meml, Amer. Philosophical Soc., 1957; John Wesley Powell Meml, Univ. of Arizona, 1957; American-Swiss Fdn for Scientific Exchange, 1957; E. C. Franklin Meml, Univ. of Kansas, 1958; Frank Billings, Amer. Med. Asssoc., 1958; Shannon, in Medicine, San Angelo, Texas, 1959; Stanley P. Black Meml, Los Angeles Acad. of Medicine, 1960; Martin Meml, Amer. Coll. of Surgeons, 1960; Annual Distinguished Lectr, Amer. Soc. of Hematology, 1962; Arthur Holly Compton Meml, Univ. of California, 1963; Mike Hogg, Univ. of Texas, 1963; Reynolds Distinguished Lectr, Davidson Coll., 1963; Christian Herter, New York Univ. School of Medicine, 1964; James Ewing, James Ewing Soc., 1964; Donald Johnson, in Cancer Research, Univ. of Michigan, 1964. Mem., Rockefeller Inst. for Med. Research, Dept of Animal and Plant Pathology, Princeton, 1940-48; Univ. of California: Chm. Dept of Biochem., 1948-53, Chm. Dept Virology, 1958-64; Member: Nat. Acad. of Sciences; Amer. Phil. Soc.; WHO Expert Advisory Panel on Virus Diseases; Adv. Cttee, Nat. Inst. Health; Adv. Cttee, Dept of Health, Educn and Welfare. Pres., 10th Internat. Cancer Congress, Houston, 1970. Hon. Mem., Japan Acad.; Associate For. Mem., French Acad. of Sciences; Hon. For. Mem., Academia Nacional de Medicine de Buenos Aires. *Publications:* (ed with F. M. Burnet) The Viruses, 3 vols, 1959; (with E. G. Valens) Viruses and the Nature of Life, 1961; numerous, on viruses, in scientific journals. *Address:* Virus Laboratory, University, of California, Berkeley, Calif 94720, USA. *Club:* Bohemian (San Francisco).

**STANLEY-CLARKE, Brig. Arthur Christopher Lancelot,** CBE 1940; DSO 1918; *b* 1886; *s* of late Ronald Stanley Clarke and late Mabel Octavia Shadwell; *m* 1931, Olive, 3rd *d* of late Thomas Carroll-Leahy of Woodfort, Mallow, Co. Cork; no *c*. *Educ:* Winchester; Oxford. Capt. OUAFC, 1908-9; gazetted The Cameronians (Scottish Rifles), 1909; commanded 1st Royal Scots Fusiliers, 1931-34; Assist Comdt and Chief Instructor, Netheravon Wing, Small Arms School, 1934-37, Comdr 154th (Argyll and Sutherland) Infantry Brigade TA, 1937; Commander Lothian and Border District, 1941-44; retired pay, 1944. Served European War, 1914-18 (despatches, DSO, and bar, Legion of Honour, Croix de Guerre); War of 1939-45 (CBE). *Address:* Shiel, Baily, Co. Dublin, Ireland.

**STANLEY PRICE, Peter,** QC 1956; **His Honour Judge Stanley Price;** a Judge of the Central Criminal Court, since 1969; President, National Reference Tribunal, Conciliation Scheme for Deputies employed in Coal-Mining Industry, since 1967; Judge of the Chancery Court of York, since 1967; Deputy Chairman, North Riding Quarter Sessions, since 1970; *b* 27 Nov. 1911; *s* of late Herbert Stanley Price and late Gertrude Rangeley S. P. (*née* Wightman); *m* 1st, 1946, Harriett Ella Theresa (*d* 1948), *o d* of late Rev. R. E. Pownall; two *s*; 2nd, 1950, Margaret Jane, *o d* of late Samuel Milkins (she *m* 1937, William Hebditch, RAF; he *d* 1941); one *d* one step *s*. *Educ:* Cheltenham; Exeter College, Oxford (1st cl. Final Hons Sch. of Jurisprudence, 1933). Barrister, Inner Temple, 1936, Master of the Bench, 1963. Served War of 1939-45, Lieut (S) RNVR. Recorder of Pontefract, 1954, of York, 1955, of Kingston-upon-Hull, 1958, of Sheffield, 1955-69. Dep. Chm., N Riding QS, 1955-58, Chm., 1958-70; Judge of Appeal, Jersey and Guernsey, 1964-69; Solicitor-General, County Palatine of Durham, 1965-69. *Recreations:* birds and trees; gardening, shooting. *Address:* 5 Paper Buildings, Temple, EC4. *T:* 01-353 7510; Church Hill, Great Ouseburn, York. *T:*

Green Hammerton 252. *Clubs:* Bath; Yorkshire (York).

**STANNARD, Captain Richard Been,** VC 1940; DSO 1943; RD 1942; RNR, retired; Marine Superintendent for P&O-Orient Lines, Sydney, 1955-64, retd; *b* 21 Aug. 1902; *s* of late Captain George Davis Stannard, Master Mariner, and Elizabeth Jane Knowles; *m* 1928, Phyllis May Tomkin; two *d*. *Educ:* Royal Merchant Navy School. Cadet, C and D line, 1918-21; 2nd Officer, 1924-28; entered RNR, 1929, as Sub-Lieut; joined Orient Line; Lieut RNR, 1932; 2nd Officer, 1937. Orient Line: Command HMS Arab, 1939; Lieut-Comdr RNR, 1940; Comdr RNR, 1947; Capt. RNR, 1952, retired 1954. Staff Commander, Orient Line, 1949-55. Hon. Company Master Mariners. Norwegian War Cross, 1942. *Recreation:* sailing. *Address:* 12a Burran Avenue, Mosman, NSW 2088, Australia. *T:* 969-9725.

**STANNARD, Rt. Rev. Robert William,** MA; *b* 20 Oct. 1895; *s* of late Robert John and Fanny Rebecca Stannard; *m* 1922, Muriel Rose Sylvia Knight; one *s* (elder son killed in action April 1945). *Educ:* Westminster; Christ Ch., Oxford; Cuddesdon Theological College. Served army, 1915-19, Lieut Middlesex Regiment. Oxford: Distinction in Lit. Hum., First in Theology, Liddon Student; Ordained, 1922; Curate Bermondsey Parish Church, 1922-24; Curate-in-Charge S Mary's, Putney, 1924-27; Vicar of St James, Barrow-in-Furness, 1927-34; Rural Dean of Dalton, 1934; Rector of Bishopwearmouth (Sunderland), 1934-41; Rural Dean of Sunderland, 1937-41; Archdeacon of Doncaster, 1941-47; Chaplain to the King, 1944-47; Bishop Suffragan of Woolwich, 1947-59; Dean of Rochester, 1959-66. *Recreations:* gardening and music. *Address:* Dendron, Reading Road North, Fleet, Hants. *T:* Fleet 4059.

**STANSFIELD, James Warden; His Honour Judge Stansfield;** County Court Judge, since 1963 (Circuit No 14, 1963-64; No 4, 1964-66; No 9, since 1967); *b* 7 April 1906; *s* of James Hampson Stansfield, Sunny Lea, Wilmslow, Cheshire; *m* 1937, Florence Evelyn, *d* of Arthur Harry Holdcroft, Congleton, Cheshire; two *s* one *d*. *Educ:* King's School, Macclesfield; Sidney Sussex College, University of Cambridge. BA 1927; LLB 1928; MA 1935. Called to the Bar, Inner Temple, 1929; practised Northern Circuit. Contested (C) Platting Division of Manchester, 1935. Served War of 1939-45: Royal Air Force, Middle East, and Staff of Judge Advocate-General; formerly RAFVR (Squadron Leader). *Recreations:* golf, walking. *Address:* Fairoaks, Alderley Road, Wilmslow, Cheshire. *T:* Wilmslow 23915. *Clubs:* Oxford and Cambridge University; St James's (Manchester).

**STANSGATE, Viscountcy of** (*cr* 1942, of Stansgate); title disclaimed by 2nd Viscount; *see under* Benn, A. N. W.

**STANTON, Maj.-Gen. Anthony Francis,** OBE 1955; Chief of Staff, HQ Northern Command, 1967-70, retired; *b* 6 Aug. 1915; *s* of Brig.-Gen. F. H. G. Stanton and Hilda Margaret (*née* Parkin); *m* 1943, Elizabeth Mary, *d* of John Reginald Blackett-Ord, Whitfield Hall, Hexham; one *s* two *d*. *Educ:* Eton Coll.; RMA Woolwich. Commissioned RA, 1936. Served in: India, 1936-41; ME, 1941-43; NW Europe, 1944-45; subseq. in Germany, Far East and UK; Imp. Def. Coll., 1962. *Recreation:* country sporting pursuits. *Address:* Wooperton Hall, Alnwick, Northumberland. *T:* Wooperton 241. *Club:* Army and Navy.

**STANTON, Blair R. H.;** *see* Hughes-Stanton.

**STANTON, Rev. John Maurice,** MA; Headmaster, Blundell's School, Tiverton, Devon, since Sept. 1959; *b* 29 Aug. 1918; *s* of Frederick William Stanton, MInstCE and Maude Lozel (*née* Cole); *m* 1947, Helen Winifred (*née* Bowden); one *s* two *d*. *Educ:* King's School, Rochester (King's Scholar); University College, Oxford (Gunsley Scholar in Science). 2nd Class Hons, Final Hon. Sch. of Nat. Science, 1947; MA 1947. Fellow of Chemical Society, 1947. Commissioned Royal Artillery, 1940, 92nd Field Regt, RA, 1940-43. ISLD, CMF, 1943-46 Assistant Master, Tonbridge School, 1947-59. Ordained Deacon, 1952; Priest, 1953. *Recreations:* water colour painting, gardening. *Address:* Blundell House, Tiverton, Devon. *T:* Tiverton 2543.

**STANTON, Lt-Col John Percy,** DL; JP; *b* 1899; *s* of late Henry and Angelica Florence Stanton, Snelston. *Educ:* Harrow; Sandhurst. 2nd Lt, Roy. Scots Greys, 1919; seconded Sudan Defence Force, 1930; Palestine, 1938 (despatches); Middle East, 1939-45 (despatches). Retired, 1945. JP 1952, DL 1957, Derbyshire; High Sheriff of Derbyshire, 1954. *Address:* Snelston Hall, Ashbourne, Derbyshire. *Club:* Cavalry.

**STANTON, Walter Kendall,** MA, DMus Oxon; Emeritus Professor of Music, University of Bristol, 1958; *b* 29 Sept. 1891; *s* of W. B. Stanton; *m* 1931, Edith Monica Leslie Wood (*d* 1956). *Educ:* Choristers' Sch., Salisbury; Lancing Coll. Organ Scholar, Merton Coll., Oxford, 1909-13; Director of Music, St Edward's Sch., Oxford, 1915-24, Wellington Coll., Berks, 1924-37; Reading Univ., 1927-37; Music Dir, Midland Region, BBC, 1937-45; Prof. of Music, Univ. of Bristol, 1947-58. President: Incorporated Society of Musicians, 1953; Union of Graduates in Music, 1953-57. City Organist, Bristol, 1956-58. Examiner in Music at Oxford, Durham and Edinburgh Universities and the University of Wales. Mem., Management Board, Bournemouth Symph. Orch., 1967 (Chm., 1967-68). Editor-in-Chief, BBC Hymn Book. *Recreation:* philately. *Address:* Barley Close, Kingston Deverill, Warminster, Wilts.

**STANWAY, Rt. Rev. Alfred;** *see* Central Tanganyika, Bishop of.

**STAPLEDON, Sir Robert (de Stapledon),** KCMG 1956 (CMG 1955); CBE 1953 (OBE 1944); retired as Governor and C-in-C of the Bahamas (1960-64); *b* 6 Feb. 1909; *s* of Ernest Allen Stapledon and Vivien Stapledon (*née* Garvice); *m* 1933, Marjorie Winifred Radford. *Educ:* Marlborough; Trinity Coll., Cambridge. Provincial Administration, Nigeria, 1931; Sec., West African Governors Conf., 1940; Resident Minister's Office, West Africa, 1942; Financial Secretary, Western Pacific High Commission, 1946; Economic Secretary, East Africa High Commission, 1948: Chief Secretary, Tanganyika, 1954-56; Governor, Eastern Region, Nigeria, 1956-60. KStJ 1958. *Address:* Old Rectory, Littleham, Nr Bideford, N Devon. *T:* Bideford 3752. *Club:* East India and Sports.

**STAPLES, Sir Robert George Alexander,** 13th Bt, *cr* 1628; *b* 21 Sept. 1894; *o s* of Sir Robert Ponsonby Staples, 12th Bt, and Ada Louise, *d* of H. Stammers, London; *S* father 1943; *m* 1922, Vera Lilian, *y d* of John Jenkins, Dulwich Wood Park, London; two *d*. *Educ:* Campbell College, Belfast; Trinity College, Dublin. Served European War, Lt RASC, 1916-19; service in German East Africa. Entered business, 1926, and has been entirely employed in Sales Promotion and Management; joined staff of Kelvinator Ltd, 1923; Sales Manager, Kelvinator Ltd, 1940-43; Director, Peter Marsh & Sons (NI) Ltd, 1961. *Recreations:* contract bridge, poker, and a good argument. *Address:* Lissan, Cookstown, Co. Tyrone, Ireland. *T:* Cookstown, 2315. *Club:* Killymoon Golf.

**STAPLETON, Air Vice-Marshal Deryck Cameron,** CB 1960; CBE 1948; DFC; AFC; psa; British Aircraft Corporation Area Manager, Libya; *b* 1918; *s* of John Rouse Stapleton, OBE, Sarnia, Natal; *m* 1942, Ethleen Joan Clifford, *d* of Sir Cuthbert William Whiteside, *qv. Educ:* King Edward VI Sch., Totnes. Joined RAF, 1936; served Transjordan and Palestine (AFC), 1937-39; War of 1939-45 (DFC). Middle East, N Africa, Italy. Asst Sec. (Air), War Cabinet Offices, 1945-46; Secretary, Chiefs of Staff Cttee, Ministry of Defence, 1947-49; OC RAF, Odiham, 1949-51; subsequently, Plans, Fighter Comd HQ; OC, RAF, Oldenburg (Germany); Plans, Bomber Comd HQ, 1957-60; Air Ministry, 1960-62; Dir, Defence Plans, Min. of Defence, 1963-64; AOC No 1 Group, RAF Bomber Command, 1964-66; Comdt, RAF Staff Coll., Bracknell, 1966-68. Assoc. Fellow, British Interplanetary Soc., 1960. *Recreations:* most sports. *Address:* c/o Westminster Bank, Haymarket, SW1. *Clubs:* Royal Air Force, White's.

**STAPLETON, Air Vice-Marshal Frederick Snowden,** CB 1961; DSO 1941; DFC 1941; FAIM; retired from the Royal Air Force, 1966; *b* 4 Feb. 1912; *s* of John Gillard Stapleton; *m* 1950, Marion Wendy Thomas; two *s. Educ:* Eastbourne College; Downing College, Cambridge. BA 1933. Awarded University Commn, 1936; Navigation Specialist, 1939; Hornchurch Wing Leader, 1941; In Command No 42 Navigation School, S Africa, 1943; Dep. Dir Operational Requirements, Air Min., 1945; Staff Coll., 1947; Gp Capt. Ops Fighter Comd, 1948; Sector Comr Fighter Comd, 1949; Station Comr RAF Wunsdorf, 2nd TAF, 1951; Gp Capt Ops, 2nd TAF, HQ, 1952; Chief Instructor, Royal Air Force Flying College, Manby, 1953; idc 1955; Northern Sector Comr, Fighter Comd, 1956-58; SASO No 13 Group, 1958; Head of British Defence Liaison Staff, Australia, 1959-60; Senior Air Staff Officer, RAF Transport Command, 1961-64; Dir-Gen. of Manning, Min. of Defence (RAF), 1964-66. FAIM 1967. *Recreations:* ski-ing, squash. *Address:* c/o Glyn Mills & Co., Whitehall, SW1; No 4, 23 Glyndon Avenue, Brighton, Melbourne, Australia. *Clubs:* Royal Society of St George, Royal Commonwealth Society; Naval and Military (Melbourne).

**STAPLETON, Major Sir Miles Talbot,** 9th Bt, *cr* 1679; *b* 26 May 1893; *o s* of Richard Talbot Plantagenet Stapleton, 2nd *s* of 7th Bt, and Emma, *d* of late Rev. J. Duncombe Shafto; *S* uncle, 1899; *m* 1st, 1913, Doris (*d* 1933), *g d* of Capt. David Fender; one *d*; 2nd, 1935, Miriam Edna, *d* of late H. Ludford, S Wales; two *d*. Owns about 2000 acres. *Heir: kinsman,* Henry Alfred Stapleton [*b* 2 May 1913; *m* 1961, Rosslyne Murray, *d* of late Capt. H. S. Warren, RN, Parkstone, Dorset]. *Address:* Rotherfield, Cold Ash, Newbury, Berks.

**STAPLETON-COTTON,** family name of **Viscount Combermere.**

**STAREY, Captain Stephen Helps,** MA Cantab; DL and JP Beds; *b* 26 Jan. 1896; *s* of John Helps Starey and Grace Catherine Dingwall; *m* 1927, Anne Ashworth Drew; three *s* one *d. Educ:* Bradfield Coll.; Trinity Coll., Cambridge. Served European War; KSLI 1914; RFC, 1916; RAF, 1918 (wounded twice). Interested in all youth work; British and Tropical Agriculture. High Sheriff for Bedfordshire, 1948-49. *Recreations:* shooting (formerly most outdoor sports). *Address:* Milton Ernest, Bedford. *TA* and *T:* Oakley (Beds) 2260. *Club:* Royal Air Force.

**STARK, Andrew Alexander Steel,** CMG 1964; CVO 1965; seconded to United Nations Organization, New York, as Under-Secretary-General, since Oct. 1968; *b* 30 Dec. 1916; *yr s* of late Thomas Bow Stark and of late Barbara Black Stark (*née* Steel), Fauldhouse, West Lothian; *m* 1944, Helen Rosemary, *er d* of Lt-Col J. Oxley Parker, *qv*; two *s* (and one *s* decd). *Educ:* Bathgate Acad.; Edinburgh Univ. MA (Hons), Eng. Lit, Edinburgh, 1938. Served War of 1939-45, 2nd Lieut Green Howards, 1940; Capt. 1942; Major 1945. Entered Foreign Service, 1948, and served in Foreign Office until 1950; 1st Secretary, Vienna, 1951-53; Asst Private Sec. to Foreign Secretary, 1953-55; Head of Chancery: Belgrade, 1956-58 (Chargé d'Affaires, 1957); Rome, 1958-60; Counsellor: FO, 1960-64; Bonn, 1964-68; attached to Mission to UN with rank of Ambassador, Jan. 1968. *Recreations:* ski-ing, tennis. *Address:* 41 Eaton Place, SW1. *T:* 01-235 7624. *Clubs:* Travellers', MCC.

**STARK, Freya Madeline,** CBE 1953; *d* of late Robert Stark, sculptor, Ford Park, Chagford, Devon; *m* 1947, Stewart Perowne, *qv. Educ:* privately in Italy; Bedford College, London University; School of Oriental Studies, London. Engaged on Govt service in Middle East and elsewhere, 1939-45. Awarded Back Grant, 1933, for travel in Luristan; Triennial Burton Memorial Medal from Royal Asiatic Society, 1934; Mungo Park Medal from Royal Scottish Geographical Society, 1936; Founder's Medal from Royal Geographical Society, 1942; Percy Sykes Memorial Medal from R Central Asian Soc., 1951. Sister of the Order of St John of Jerusalem, 1949. LLD Glasgow Univ., 1951. *Publications:* Bagdad Sketches, 1933; enlarged edition, 1937; The Valleys of the Assassins, 1934; The Southern Gates of Arabia, 1936; Seen in the Hadhramaut, 1938; A Winter in Arabia, 1940; Letters from Syria, 1942; East is West, 1945; Perseus in the Wind, 1948; Traveller's Prelude, 1950; Beyond Euphrates, 1951; The Coast of Incense, 1953; Ionia: a Quest, 1954; The Lycian Shore, 1956; Alexander's Path, 1958; Riding to the Tigris, 1959; Dust in the Lion's Paw, 1961; The Journey's Echo, 1963; Rome on the Euphrates, 1966; The Zodiac Arch, 1968; Space, Time and Movement in Landscape, 1969; The Minaret of Djam, 1970. *Recreations:* travel, mountaineering and embroidery. *Address:* Montoria, San Zenone degli Ezzelini (Treviso), Italy; c/o John Murray, 50 Albemarle Street, W1.

**STARK, Admiral Harold Raynsford,** GBE (Hon.) 1945; US Navy, retired; *b* Wilkes-Barre, Pa, 12 Nov. 1880; *s* of Benjamin Franklin Stark and Mary Frances Warner; *m* 1907, Katharine Adele Rhoads, Wilkes-Barre, Pa; two *d. Educ:* Naval Academy, Annapolis, Md (graduated in Class of 1903). Commissioned ensign, 1905, promoted through grades to Rear-Admiral, 1934; served on various ships and stations, 1903-7; aide on staff of Adm. Sims, comdg US Naval Forces operating in European waters, 1917-19; inspector in charge of ordnance, Naval Proving Ground, Dahlgren, Va, and Naval Powder Factory, Indian Head, Md, 1925-28; aide on staff and chief of staff, Destroyer Squadrons, Battle Fleet, 1928-30; aide to Sec. of Navy, Washington, DC, 1930-33; comdg USS West Virginia, 1933-34; chief of Bureau of Ordnance, Navy Dept, Washington, DC, 1934-37; comdg Cruiser div. US Fleet, 1937-38; Comdg Cruisers, Battle Force, 1938-39; chief of naval operations, 1939-42; Commander, US Naval Forces in Europe, 1942-45; European Campaign Ribbon; Mexican Campaign, World War, Defense, Dominican Campaign and World War II medals (US); Expeditionary Medal, DSM (USN); Order of Crown of Italy; Gold Star Citation to DSM (USN); Gold Star in lieu of third DSM (USN); National Order of the Southern Cross (Brazilian); DSM (US Army); Commander French Legion of Honour; French Croix de Guerre with Palm; Norwegian Grand Cross of the Order of St Olaf; Knight Grand Cross Order of Orange Nassau with Swords; Belgian Croix-de-Guerre with Palm; Grand Officer Belgian Order of Leopold, with Palm; Chevalier Order of Polonia Restituta, 1st Class. *Address:* 4900 Glenbrook Road NW, Washington, DC 20016, USA. *Clubs:* Army and Navy, Athenæum; Army and Navy (Washington, DC); Chevy Chase (Md); New York Yacht (New York); Westmorland, Wilkes-Barre (Pa); Sachem's Head Yacht (Conn).

**STARKE, Leslie Gordon Knowles,** CBE 1953; *b* 23 May 1898; *s* of William and Martha Starke; *m* 1929, Joan Mary Davidson; no *c*. *Educ:* Andover Grammar School; University College, Southampton; Queen's College, Oxford. Served European War, 1914-18, RE (Signal Service), 1918. Entered Government Actuary's Dept, 1919; Ministry of Food, 1939-46 (Director of Statistics and Intelligence, 1943-46); Principal Actuary and Establishment Officer, Government Actuary's Dept, 1946-58; Deputy Government Actuary, 1958-63. *Recreations:* gardening, walking. *Address:* Brack Mound House, Castle Precincts, Lewes, Sussex. *T:* Lewes 4139.

**STARKER, Janos;** Concert cellist, recording artist; Distinguished Professor of Music, Indiana University, since 1958; *b* 5 July 1924; *s* of F. Sandor and M. Margit; *m* 1944, Eva Uranyi; one *d*; *m* 1960, Rae D. Busch. *Educ:* Franz Liszt Academy of Music, Budapest; Zrinyi Gymnasium, Budapest. Solo cellist: Budapest Opera and Philh., 1945-46; Dallas Symphony, 1948-49; Metropolitan Opera, 1949-53; Chicago Symphony, 1953-58; numerous recordings. Grand Prix du Disque, 1948. Holds an Hon. Doctorate of Music, 1961. *Publications:* Cello Method, 1963; articles in: Hi-Fi Stereo, Music, Mademoiselle. *Recreations:* writing, swimming, ping-pong. *Address:* Indiana University Music Department, Bloomington, Ind 47401, USA.

**STARKEY, Lieut-Col Sir William Randle,** 2nd Bt, *cr* 1935; *b* 11 Dec. 1899; *o s* of Sir John Starkey, 1st Bt, and Emily, 2nd *d* of Sir Charles Seely, 1st Bt; *S* father, 1940; *m* 1935, Irene Myrtle Francklin (*d* 1965); two *s* one *d*. *Educ:* Eton; Sandhurst. Rifle Bde, 1919-35; called to Bar (Middle Temple), 1938. Served in London Irish Rifles and Reconnaiss. Corps, 1939-45. JP, DL Notts; High Sheriff of Nottinghamshire, 1954. *Heir: s* John Philip Starkey [*b* 1938; *m* 1966, Victoria Henrietta Fleetwood, *y d* of Lt-Col Christopher Fuller, Jaggards, Corsham, Wilts; one *d*]. *Address:* Norwood Park, Southwell, Notts. *T:* Southwell 3117. *Clubs:* Army and Navy, MCC; Notts County (Nottingham).

*See also Maj.-Gen. B. T. Wilson, Sir F. P. M. H. Bathurst, Bt.*

**STARKIE, Walter Fitzwilliam,** CMG 1954; CBE 1948; MA, LittD; MRIA; FRSA; FRSL; Hon. FTCD; Director British Institiute, Madrid, and British Council Representative in Spain, 1940-54; Special Lecturer, English Literature, Madrid University, 1948-56; FTCD, 1924-47; Professor of Spanish in Dublin University; Lecturer in Italian Literature in Dublin University, 1926-47; a Director Irish National (Abbey) Theatre, 1927-42; Member Irish Academy of Letters; Corresponding Member Spanish Academy, and of Academy of History; Knight of Order of Alfonso XII; Knight of Order of the Crown of Italy; Chevalier de la Légion d'Honneur; Commander, Order of Isabel the Catholic; LittD (Hon.) Trinity College, Hartford, USA; *b* 9 Aug. 1894; *o s* of late Rt Hon. W. J. M. Starkie, LittD, and May, *d* of late Cornelius Walsh, Dublin; *m* Itaia Augusta, 2nd *d* of Cav. Alberto Porchietti of Genoa and Buenos Aires, and Delfina, *d* of Generale Landi conte Vincenzo; one *s* one *d*. *Educ:* Shrewsbury; Trinity College, Dublin. Classical Foundation Scholarship; Senior Moderator and gold medallist in Classics; also in History and Political Science; Brooke Prizeman; received musical education at Royal Irish Academy of Music (winner of Vandeleur Academy Violin Scholarship, 1913), and abroad; served in the YMCA during War and attached to BEF Italy; Lecturer in Romance Languages, Trinity College, 1920; course of lectures on Modern Spanish Drama at King's College, London, 1923; course of lectures in Spanish on Modern Drama at Residencia de Estudiantes, Madrid, 1924, under auspices of Anglo-Spanish Society, and 1928; at British Institute, Florence, April 1926; on Spanish Literature at Stockholm and other cities in Sweden; Olaus Petri Foundation Lectures at University of Upsala, Sept. 1926; Lecture tours in USA and Canada, 1929, 1930, and 1931; Lectures at American and Canadian Universities; Lecture tours in France, Dec. 1931 and 1932; Visiting Professor in Romance Languages at University of Chicago, 1930; Lord Northcliffe Lectureship in Literature at University College, London, 1936; Lecture Tour: Central and South America, 1950; in USA 1956-57; Visiting Professorship in Romance Langs, Univ. of Texas, 1958; visiting Prof.: Univ. of New York, 1959; University of Kansas, 1960; University of Colorado, 1961; Sloan Professor, Menninger Foundation of Psychiatric Research, Topeka, Kansas, 1961; Professor in Residence, University of California, Los Angeles, 1961-70. *Publications:* Jacinto Benavente, 1924; Il Teatro Contemporaneo Inglese, 1926; Writers, Modern Spain, 1929; Raggle Taggle, 1933; Translation of Tiger Juan by Ramon Pérez de Ayala, 1933; Spanish Raggle-Taggle, 1934; Don Gypsy, 1936; Luigi Pirandello, 1937 (3rd edn 1965); The Waveless Plain, 1938; Grand Inquisitor, 1940; In Sara's Tents, 1953; abridgement of Don Quixote (with Prelude), 1954, complete translation, 1964; The Road to Santiago, 1957; Spain: A Musician's Journey through Time and Space, 1958; Scholars and Gypsies, 1963; Six Exemplary Novels of Cervantes; Eight Plays of the Spanish Golden Age, 1964; The Dukes of Alba, 1970; Translation of The Spaniards in their History, by Menendez Pidal (with Introduction); contributions to Enciclopedia Italiana; Enciclopedia Americana; Chambers's, Grove's Dictionary of Music, etc. *Recreations:* violin playing, wandering. *Address:* 10782 Wellworth Avenue, Los Angeles, California 90024, USA. *T:* 474-8137. *Clubs:* Athenæum; University (Dublin).

**STARLEY, Hubert Granville,** CBE 1946; FIMI; Managing Director: Champion Sparking Plug Co. Ltd, Feltham, Middlesex; Champion Sparking Plug Co. (Ireland) Ltd; Bougie Champion, Paris; Chairman, Starleys Estates Ltd, Bournemouth; *b* Skipton, 16 April 1909; *s* of late Hubert Ernest and Fanny Starley,

Teddington, Middlesex; *m* 1933, Lilian Amy Heron; one *s* one *d*. *Educ:* Ermysteds; Skipton, Yorks. Assistant to Lord Beaverbrook, Minister of Supply, 1941; Advisor to War Office and Air Ministry on Stores Packaging, 1943; Chairman Anglo-American Packaging Exhibition Committee, 1944; Member Barlow Mission to the USA, 1944; Chairman Motor Industry Jubilee Committee, 1946; Chairman Accessory and Component Manufacturers' Cttee, Society of Motor Manufacturers and Traders, Ltd, 1945-46, 1953-55, 1961-62 (Mem. Council Management Cttees, 1953-68, Mem., General Purposes Cttee, 1968); Pres., Cycle and Motor Cycle Assoc., 1970 (Vice-Pres., 1969-70); Chm. Inter-Services Packaging Cttee, 1958-65; Founder, Mem. Council and Dir, Aims of Industry, Ltd, 1942-68. Vice-Pres., Inst. of Motor Industry, 1970; Mem. Council, CBI, 1970; Councillor, Aeronautical Educn Trust. Past Chm., Home Office Mobile Crime Prevention Cttee. Patron, Twickenham Conservative Assoc., 1966-70. Master, Livery Company of Coachmakers and Coach Harness Makers, 1966-67; Pres., Pickwick Bicycle Club, 1954. Hon. Pageant Master and Organiser, History of British Motoring Cavalcade, Lord Mayor's Show, 1964; Hon. Organiser, 6 day Cycle Race, Earl's Court, 1967. *Address:* Champion Sparking Plug Co. Ltd, Feltham, Middlesex. *T:* 01-759 6442. *Clubs:* Carlton, Junior Carlton, Royal Automobile, Royal Thames, Yacht; Royal Mid-Surrey Golf (Richmond).

**STARLING, Brigadier John Sieveking,** CBE 1945; retired; *b* 18 Jan. 1898; *o s* of late Prof. Ernest H. Starling, CMG, MD, FRS, and Florence, *d* of late Sir Edward Sieveking; *m* 1st, 1934, Vivian Barbara, *d* of late Henry J. Wagg, OBE (marriage dissolved 1948); one *s*; 2nd, 1948, Marion, *d* of late A. G. Pool, and *widow* of C. A. Morell-Miller. *Educ:* University College School; Royal Military Academy; Trinity College, Cambridge. Commissioned 2nd Lt RA, 1916; served European War, France and Flanders, 1916-18 (wounded twice); normal career of a Regimental Officer in UK, Egypt and India. Attached French Army, 1939; served France and Flanders, Middle East and Italy, 1939-46 (despatches, wounded, CBE); retired from Regular Army as Hon. Brig., 1948. *Recreations:* fishing, shooting, sailing. *Address:* Le Hurel, Trinity, Jersey, CI. *T:* North 66. *Club:* Army and Navy.

**STARR, Kenneth William,** CMG 1956; OBE 1941; ED 1946; FRCS, FACS, FRACS; MS; Hon. Consulting Surgeon, Sydney Hospital, New South Wales, since 1958; Medical Director, NSW State Cancer Council; President, Medical Board of NSW (Member since 1962); Member, National Health and Medical Research Council of Australia, since 1963; *b* 9 Jan. 1908; *s* of Edward Starr, Cowra, NSW; *m* 1940, Alison Neville, *d* of Sir Neville Howse, VC, KCB, KCMG, FRCS; two *s* three *d*. *Educ:* Fort St Boys' High School; Sydney University. MB (Sydney) 1930; FRCS 1936; MS (Melbourne) 1940; FACS 1936; FRACS 1940. Hallett Prize, Jacksonian Prize, 1944, Hunterian Prof., 1952, Royal Coll. of Surgeons; Hons Award American College of Surgeons, 1937; Mayo Foundation Lecturer (Rochester, Minn), 1952; Examr and President, Royal Australian Coll. Surgeons; Examr, RCS, 1950; Mem. Bd of Governors of Amer. Coll. of Surgeons, 1953; Mem. James IV Assoc. Surgeons, 1961; Corresp. Mem., Assoc. of Surgeons of Great Britain and Ireland. Hon. Mem. Soc. Med. Consultants of Armed Forces of USA; FACS (Hon.), 1954. *Publications:* Delayed Union of Fractures (Jacksonian Prize), 1944; Choledochotomy (Mayo Foundation Lecture), 1952; Surgical Technique (British Encyclopædia of Surgery), 1949; articles in internat. surgical jls. *Recreations:* golf, gardening. *Address:* 36 Dudley Street, Coogee, NSW 2034, Australia. *T:* 27 4563. *Clubs:* Australian, Australian Jockey (Sydney); Elanora Country.

**STASSEN, Harold Edward;** lawyer, politician, educator, United States; Partner in law firm Stassen, Kephart, Sarkis and Scullin, 1958; Chief Consultant to Middle East Technical University, Ankara, 1958; *b* W St Paul, Minn, 13 April 1907; *s* of William Andrew Stassen and Elsie Emma Mueller; *m* 1929, Esther G. Glewwe; one *s* one *d*. *Educ:* Univ. of Minnesota Coll. (BA 1927; LLB 1929); Law School. Has several hon. degrees. Admitted to Minnesota Bar, 1929; practised South St Paul; County Attorney, Dakota County, 1930-38; thrice elected Governor of Minnesota, 1939-43; resigned for service with Navy; Lt Comdr, USN; Comdr on staff of Admiral Halsey in South Pacific, 1943-44; asst Chief of Staff, 1944; Capt., USN; released to inactive duty, 1945. One of US delegates to San Francisco Conference of UN, 1945. Pres., Minnesota Young Republicans; Delegate to Republican Convention, 1936; Temporary Chairman and Keynoter of Republican National Convention and floor manager for Wendell Wilkie, 1940; twice elected National Chairman National Governors' Conference, and of Council of State Governments, 1940-41. President, University of Pennsylvania, 1948-53. President International Council of Religious Education, 1942, 1950; Vice-Pres. Nat. Council of Churches, 1951-52; President, Div. of Christian Educ. of Nat. Council of Churches, 1953-. Director Foreign Operations Admin., 1953-55; Special Assistant to the President for Disarmament, 1955-58; Dep. US Rep. on Disarmament Commn, UN, 1955-58. Delivered Godkind Lectures on Human Rights, Harvard Univ., 1946; candidate for Republican nomination for President of US, 1948 and 1952. Legion of Merit (Western Pacific campaign), 1945, Bronze Star, 1945. Baptist. Mason. *Publications:* Where I Stand, 1947; Man was meant to be Free, 1951. *Address:* (Office) Fidelity-Philadelphia Trust Building, Philadelphia 9, Pa, USA; (Home) Penn Towers, Philadelphia, Pa, USA.

**STATHAM, Heathcote Dicken,** CBE 1967; MusDoc Cantab; FRCO; Hon. ARCM; retired as Organist and Choirmaster, Norwich Cathedral (1938-66); Organist Emeritus, 1967; *b* 7 Dec. 1889; *e s* of H. Heathcote Statham, FRIBA; *m* 1928, Mary Claudine, *d* of Rev. Bourchier Wrey; one *s*. *Educ:* St Michael's College, Tenbury (Scholar); Gresham's Sch., Holt (Scholar); Caius College, Cambridge (Scholar); Royal College of Music. Organist Calcutta Cathedral, 1913; S Michael's Coll., Tenbury, 1920; Parish Church, Southampton, 1926; Conductor Southampton Philharmonic 1927; Norwich Philharmonic, 1928-61; Norwich Triennial Festival, 1936-61; Symphony Concerts, Queen's Hall, 1943-46; conducted London Symphony Orchestra in various concerts in London and Provinces; Examiner to Associated Board of the Royal Schools of Music, 1942. FRSCM, 1963. *Publications:* organ music, songs, part-songs, operetta; Ed. Dr John Blow's Church Music (17th Cent.). *Recreation:* walking. *Address:* 11 The Close, Norwich, Norfolk. *T:* Norwich 26746.

**STATHAM, Norman,** CMG 1967; CVO 1968; Head of European Integration Department, Foreign and Commonwealth Office, since 1970; *b* Stretford, Lancs, 15 Aug. 1922; *s* of Frederick William and Maud Statham; *m* 1948, Hedwig Gerlich; two *s* one *d*. *Educ:* Seymour

Park Council School, Stretford; Manchester Grammar School; Gonville and Caius College, Cambridge (MA). Intelligence Corps, 1943-47; Manchester Oil Refinery Ltd and Petrochemicals Ltd, 1948-50; Foreign Service, 1951: Foreign Office, 1951; Consul (Commercial), New York, 1954-58; First Secretary (Commercial), Bonn, 1958-63; Administrative Staff College, Henley, 1963; Foreign Office, 1964; Counsellor, Head of European Economic Integration Dept, 1965-68; Consul-General, São Paulo, 1968-70. *Recreations:* gardening, hill-walking, star-gazing, reading. *Address:* Underhill House, Underhill Park Road, Reigate, Surrey. *Club:* Travellers'.

**STATON, Air Vice-Marshal William Ernest,** CB 1947; DSO and Bar, 1940; MC 1918; DFC and Bar, 1918; *b* 1898; *m* 1919, Norah Carina Workman (*d* 1969); two *s*. Served European War, 1914-19 (despatches); War of 1939-45 (despatches); Wing Comdr, 1939; Group Capt., 1940; Actg Air Commodore, 1941; Air Vice-Marshal, 1950; SASO Singapore, 1942; prisoner of war, Japan, 1942-45 (despatches); ADC to the King, 1940-46; AOC No. 46 Group, 1945-47; Commandant Central Bomber Establishment, 1947-49; Air Officer-in-Charge of Administration, Technical Training Command, 1949-52; retired 1952. Chm. RAF Small Arms Assoc., 1947-52; Capt. British Shooting Teams, Olympic Games, 1948 and 1952. Ex-Mem. of Councils; Internat. Shooting Union, Stockholm; Nat. Rifle Assoc.; Nat. Small Bore Rifle Assoc.; Brit. Olympic Assoc. (1952-57). *Address:* Wildhern, Creek End, Emsworth, Hants. *Club:* Emsworth Sailing (Flag Officer, 1968-).

**STAUGHTON, Christopher Stephen Thomas Jonathan Thayer,** QC 1970; *b* 24 May 1933; *yr s* of late Simon Thomas Samuel Staughton and Edith Madeline Jones; *m* 1960, Joanna Susan Elizabeth, *er d* of late George Frederick Arthur Burgess; two *d*. *Educ:* Eton Coll. (Scholar); Magdalene Coll., Cambridge (Scholar). 2nd Lieut, 11th Hussars PAO, 1952-53; Lieut, Derbyshire Yeomanry TA, 1954-56. George Long Prize for Roman Law, Cambridge, 1955; BA 1956; MA 1961. Called to Bar, Inner Temple, 1957. *Publication:* (Jt Editor) The Law of General Average (British Shipping Laws vol. 7), 1964. *Recreations:* bridge, growing dahlias. *Address:* 11 Wilton Street, SW1. *T:* 01-235 5791; Sarratt Hall, Sarratt, Herts. *T:* King's Langley 62698.

**STAVELEY, Martin Samuel,** CMG 1966; CVO 1966; CBE 1962 (MBE 1955); First Secretary, Kaduna, Nigeria, since 1969; *b* 3 Oct. 1921; fourth *s* of late Herbert Samuel Staveley and Edith Emma Staveley (*née* Shepherd); *m* 1942, Edith Eileen Baker; one *s* two *d*. *Educ:* Stamford School; Trinity College, Oxford. Appointed Cadet, Colonial Administrative Service, Nigeria, 1942; Secretary, Development and Welfare Organisation in the West Indies, 1946-57; Secretary to Governor-General, Federation of the West Indies, 1958-62; Administrator, British Virgin Islands, 1962-67; First Sec., FCO, 1967-69. *Recreations:* golf, music. *Address:* Windover, Tangley Lane, Worplesdon, Surrey. *T:* Worplesdon 2641. *Club:* West Indian.

**STAWELL, Maj.-Gen. (retd) William Arthur Macdonald,** CB 1945; CBE 1944; MC 1917; *b* 22 Jan. 1895; *s* of G. C. Stawell, ICS; *m* 1926, Amy, *d* of C. W. Bowring, New York; one *s*. *Educ:* Clifton College; RMA, Woolwich. Served European War, 1914-21, France, Greek Macedonia, Serbia, Bulgaria, Turkey (wounded, MC); 2nd Lieut 1914; Temp. Captain, 1916-17; Acting Major, Mar.-April 1917 and 1918-19; Captain, 1917; Major 1929; Lieut-Col 1937; Col 1940; Brig. 1940. GSO3 War Office, 1931-32; Brigade Maj., Aldershot, 1932-35; DAAG India, 1935-37; CRE 1937-40; AA and QMG Feb.-July 1940; GSO1 July-Nov. 1940; DDMI War Office, 1940-42; Brig., Comdr Home Forces, Feb.-Nov. 1942; Brig. General Staff, Home Forces, 1942-43; MEF and CMF, 1943-45 (CBE, CB); Temp. Maj.-Gen. 1943-45; Deputy Chief of Operations UNRRA, Nov. 1945-Aug. 1946; Deputy Chief Intelligence Division, CCG, 1947-48. *Recreations:* yachting, golf. *Address:* Park Hill, Oulton, nr Lowestoft, Suffolk. *T:* Blundeston 322. *Clubs:* Army and Navy; Royal Norfolk and Suffolk Yacht.

**STAYNER, Brig. Gerrard Francis Hood,** CB 1945; CBE 1943 (OBE 1941); psc; retired; late Inf.; *b* 29 July 1900; 2nd *s* of Hewlett James Stayner and Mabel Palmer, Llanstephan, Teignmouth, Devon; *m* 1927, Leslie Edna, 2nd *d* of Horace and Diana Imber; no *c*. *Educ:* Cheltenham College; RMC Sandhurst. 2nd Lieut Leicestershire Regiment, 1919; served with Sudan Defence Force, 1925-35; Eritrean Campaign (OBE); Malta 1942-43 (CBE); Italy 1944-45 (CB, Legion of Merit Degree of Officer, USA); seconded to UNRRA Oct. 1945; Dep. Chief of Mission for Supply and Distrib., UNRRA Greece, 1945-46. OC Troops and Brigadier i/c Administration, Fortress HQ Gibraltar, 1950-53; retd 1953. Controller, Airborne Forces Security Fund, 1962-66. *Address:* 6 Lansdowne House, Lansdowne Road, W11. *T:* 01-727 4829.

**STEAD, Christina Ellen;** Fellow in Creative Arts, Australian National University, Canberra, since 1969; *b* 17 July 1902; *d* of Ellen Butters and David George Stead; *m* William J. Blake (*d* 1968). *Educ:* Sydney Univ., NSW. In business: London, 1928-29, Paris, 1930-35. Cinema: Senior Writer, MGM, Hollywood, Calif, 1943. Instructor, Workshop in the Novel, New York Univ., 1943-44. *Publications:* Short Story Collection: Salzburg Tales, London, 1934, NY, 1935, Melbourne, 1966. Novels: Seven Poor Men of Sydney, London and NY, 1935, Sydney and London, 1966 (new edn, 1970); The Beauties and Furies, London and NY, 1936; House of All Nations, London and NY, 1938; The Man who Loved Children, London, 1941, NY, 1940, 1965, London 1966; For Love Alone, NY, 1944, London, 1945, New York, 1965, London, 1966, Sydney, 1969; Letty Fox, Her Luck, NY, 1946, London, 1947; A Little Tea, A Little Chat, NY, 1948; The People with the Dogs, Boston, 1951; Dark Places of the Heart, New York, 1966; The Puzzleheaded Girl, novellas, 1967; short stories: in Southerly, 1963; in Kenyon Review, Saturday Evening Post, 1965; in Meanjin, 1968, 1970; in Hemisphere, 1970; in New Yorker, 1970. *Address:* c/o Laurence Pollinger, Ltd, 18 Maddox Street, W1.

**STEAD, Gilbert;** Professor Emeritus of Physics in the University of London since 1953; Consulting Physicist Emeritus to Guy's Hospital since 1953; *b* 3 Feb. 1888; *s* of late Richard Stead, Folkestone; *m* 1916, Margaret, *d* of late Thomas Gallimore, Leamington; one *s* two *d*. *Educ:* Bradford Grammar School; Clare College, Cambridge (Scholar). 1st Class Nat. Sci. Tripos, Pt I, 1908, Pt II, 1909; BA 1909; MA 1913; DSc (London), 1940; Assistant Demonstrator, Cavendish Laboratory, 1910; attached to HM Signal School, Portsmouth, 1915-19; Reader in Physics, Guy's Hospital Medical School, University of London, 1923-38, Professor of Physics, 1939-53; Honorary Consulting Physicist to Guy's Hospital, 1948-53; Governor of Guy's Hospital Medical School, 1948-53; University Lecturer in

Physics as applied to Medical Radiology, Cambridge, 1925-38; Sec. for Cambridge Diploma in Medical Radiology, 1927-42; FInstP; Fellow of Physical Society; FRSA; Hon. Member of Indian Radiological Assoc.; Member British Institute of Radiology, Pres., 1947-48. Hon. Member of the Faculty of Radiologists; Fellow of Cambridge Philosophiocal Society; Member Hospital Physicists' Association (President, 1951-52; Hon. Member 1960). *Publications:* Elementary Physics, 1924; Notes on Practical Physics, 1939; various original papers in Proc. Roy. Soc., Philosophical Magazine, Journ. Institution of Electrical Engineers, Proc. Cambridge Philosophical Soc. *Address:* Flat 8, Coombe Court, The Avenue, Tadworth, Surrey. *T:* Tadworth 2466.

**STEAD, Robert,** CBE 1965; retired as Controller, BBC North Region, 1958-69; *b* 10 Aug. 1909; *s* of Charles Fearnley Stead and Mary Ellen Taylor; *m* 1932, Constance Ann Sharpley; two *s. Educ:* Morley Gram. Sch. In Journalism, 1926-40; served in RN, 1940-45. Talks Producer, BBC North Region, 1946-48; Head of North Region Programmes, 1948-53; BBC Australian Representative, 1953-57. *Recreations:* golf, gardening, theatre. *Address:* The Dingle, Chapel Lane, Wilmslow, Cheshire. *T:* Wilmslow 25536.

**STEAVENSON, Dr William Herbert;** *b* 26 April 1894; *s* of late Rev. Frederick Robert Steavenson, Rector of Quenington, Glos. *Educ:* Cheltenham College; Guy's Hospital. LMSSA London, 1918; Civil Surgeon, Queen Alexandra Military Hospital, Millbank, 1918-19; Captain RAMC, 1919-21; served in Egypt. President: British Astronomical Assoc., 1926-28 (Goodacre Medallist, 1961); Royal Astronomical Soc., 1957-59 (Jackson-Gwilt Medallist, 1928); Member of National Committee for Astronomy, 1927-59. Gresham Professor in Astronomy, 1946-64; Astronomical corr., The Times, 1938-69. *Publications:* A Catalogue of the Instruments of Sir William Herschel (Optical Society); Note on Egyptian Mirage (R Met. Society's Journal); Joint Editor and part author of Splendour of the Heavens, 1923; Physical Observations of Mars, 1924 (Greenwich Observations); edited and revised Proctor's Half Hours with the Telescope; Suns and Worlds, 1933; numerous papers in the Monthly Notices of the Royal Astronomical Society and the Journal of the British Astronomical Association. *Address:* Gordon Cottage, South Marston, Swindon, Wilts. *T:* Stratton St Margaret 3478.

**STEDEFORD, Sir Ivan (Arthur Rice),** GBE 1961 (KBE 1954); Life President, Tube Investments Ltd, since 1963, after nineteen years as Chairman and Managing Director; Director: Tube Investments of India; The Rank Organisation and subsidiary cos; *b* Exeter, 28 Jan. 1897; *s* of late Rev. Charles Stedeford, ex-Pres. United Methodist Church; *m* 1923, Gwendoline Edith Aston; three *d. Educ:* Shebbear Coll., N Devon; King Edward VI Grammar School, Birmingham. Engineer Apprentice Wolseley Motors Ltd; served European War, RNAS, 1918-19. A Deputy Chairman, National Provincial Bank, 1964-68, and National Westminster Bank, 1968-69. Member: Television Advisory Cttee, 1949-50; Committee of Enquiry into British Broadcasting Corporation 1949-50; a Governor of the BBC, 1951-55. Member: Advisory Council, Department of Scientific and Industrial Research, 1950-52; UK Atomic Energy Authority, 1954-59; Chairman, Advisory Group on British Transport Commission, 1960. Hon. Kentucky Colonel. *Recreations:* country pursuits. *Address:* Clifford Hill Court, Clifford Chambers, Stratford-on-Avon, Warwicks. *T:* Stratford-on-Avon 2758. *Club:* Athenæum.

**STEDMAN, Edgar,** FRS 1938; DSc, PhD; Reader (Emeritus) in Biochemistry in the University of Edinburgh; *b* 12 July 1890; *m* 1920, Ellen Field (*d* 1962); no *c*; *m* 1964, Martha Jefferson Taylor. *Educ:* University of London. *Publications:* Author and Joint Author of various Scientific Memoirs published chiefly in Journal of the Chemical Society, Biochemical Journal and Philosophical Transactions and Proceedings of the Royal Society. *Recreation:* gardening. *Address:* 13 Kline Boulevard, Frederick, Maryland 21701, USA. *T:* 301-663-5330.

**STEDMAN, Sir George (Foster),** KBE 1957; CB 1948; MC 1919; Civil Service, retired; *b* 1895; *s* of James Mathew and Marguerite Adele Stedman, Leytonstone, Essex; *m* 1925, Olive May Scrivener; one *d* (one *s* decd). *Educ:* Mercers' School, London; Trinity Coll., Camb. Served European War, 1914-18, with York and Lancaster Regt, France and Macedonia (MC, despatches twice). Entered Civil Service, Ministry of Transport, 1920; Private Secretary to Minister, 1926-30; Under-Sec., 1946. Deputy Secretary, Ministry of Transport and Civil Aviation, 1954-57. *Address:* 57 Westhorpe, Southwell, Notts.

**STEEDMAN, Air Vice-Marshal Alexander McKay Sinclair,** CBE 1965; DFC 1944; Assistant Chief of the Air Staff (Policy), Ministry of Defence, since 1969; *b* 29 Jan. 1922; *s* of late James Steedman, Hampton-on-Thames, Middx and Anna McKay Steedman (*née* Sinclair), Fulford, York; *m* 1945, Dorothy Isobel, *d* of Col Walter Todd, Knockbrex, Kirkcudbright; one *s* two *d Educ:* Hampton Gram. School. Entered RAF, 1941; Flt Comdr, 241 Sqdn, 1942-44, 2 Sqdn, 1945; Air Min., 1945-48; comd 39 Sqdn, Khartoum, 1948-49; comd 8 Sqdn, Aden, 1949-50; CFS Course, 1951; Trng Sqdn Comdr, 201 AFS, 1951-53; Syndicate Ldr, Aircrew Selection Centre, Hornchurch, 1953-54; psa 1955; Chief Instructor, CFS (B), 1955-57; Comdr Royal Ceylon Air Force, Katanyake, 1957-59; jssc 1959-60; Directing Staff, Jt Services Staff Coll., 1960-62; Comdr RAF Lyneham, 1962-65; Gp Capt. (Ops), HQ Transport Comd, 1965; CAS, Royal Malaysian Air Force, 1965-67; Dir of Defence Plans (Air), MoD, 1967-68. Dir, Defence Ops Staff, MoD, 1968-69. ARAeS 1960; MBIM 1968. Johan Mangku Negara (Malaysia), 1967. *Recreations:* golf, tennis, squash, motoring. *Address:* The Lodge, North Weald, Epping, Essex. *T:* North Weald 2682. *Clubs:* Royal Air Force; Royal Selangor (Kuala Lumpur).

**STEEDMAN, Maj.-Gen. John Francis Dawes,** CMG 1963; CBE 1945; MC 1918; *b* 30 Nov. 1897; *s* of John Francis Steedman, FRCS, Streatham; *m* 1931, Olive Ursula (Kaisar-i-Hind Medal), *d* of Earl Oliver Besant, Reading; one *d. Educ:* Bradfield; RMA, Woolwich. 2nd Lt, RE, 1916; Served European War, 1914-18, Salonika (MC, despatches twice); Afghanistan, 1919; Waziristan (MBE, despatches), 1920-21; Khajuri (despatches), 1930-31; Malaya, as CRE 11 Ind. Div. (Despatches), 1941-42; Comdt QVO Madras Sappers and Miners, 1942-43; Burma, as CE 33 Ind. Corps and XII Army (CBE, despatches), 1944-46; Chief Engineer, Southern Command, India, 1946; Engineer-in-Chief, Dominion of India, 1947; Chief Engineer, Southern Command, UK, 1948-51; ADC to HM King George VI, 1949-51; retired as Hon. Maj.-Gen., 1951; Director of Works,

Commonwealth War Graves Commission, 1951-63. *Address:* Valley Farm House, East Knoyle, Salisbury, Wiltshire. *T:* East Knoyle 329.

**STEEGMULLER, Francis;** writer; *b* New Haven, Conn, 3 July 1906; *s* of Joseph Francis Steegmuller and Bertha Tierney; *m* 1st, 1935, Beatrice Stein (decd); 2nd, 1963, Shirley Hazzard. *Educ:* Columbia University, New York. Member, Nat. Inst. of Arts and Letters, 1966. Chevalier de la Légion d'Honneur, 1957. *Publications:* O Rare Ben Jonson (under pseudonym Byron Steel), 1928; Flaubert and Madame Bovary, 1939, reprinted 1947, 1958, 1968; States of Grace, 1947; Maupassant, 1950; Blue Harpsichord (under pseudonym David Keith), 1950; The Two Lives of James Jackson Jarves, 1953; (trans. and ed) The Selected Letters of Gustave Flaubert, 1954; La Grande Mademoiselle, 1955; The Christening Party, 1961; Le Hibou et la Poussiquette, 1961; Apollinaire, 1963; Papillot, Clignot et Dodo (with Norbert Guterman), 1965; (trans.) Gustave Flaubert, Intimate Notebook, 1967; Cocteau, 1970. Articles in The Cornhill Magazine, etc. Works published abroad include a translation of Madame Bovary (1957) and many short stories and articles in The New Yorker. *Address:* 200 East 66th Street, New York, NY 10021, USA. *Clubs:* Athenæum; Century (New York).

**STEEL, Anthony Bedford,** OBE 1946; MA; LittD, LLD; JP; Principal, University College, Cardiff, 1949-66; Vice-Chancellor, University of Wales, 1956-58, 1959-61; *b* 24 Feb. 1900; *s* of Major Edwin Bedford Steel, RAMC; *m* 1924, Eileen M. Johnson; one *s*; *m* 1956, Elizabeth Tesni, *yr d* of Sir Wynne Cemlyn-Jones. *Educ:* Rugby; New College, Oxford (1st Class Lit. Hum.). 2nd Lt RASC, MT, 1918-19, France and Germany; Fellow, Christ's College, Cambridge, 1924-, University Lecturer in History, 1930-49; Senior Proctor, 1937-38; Steward of Christ's College, 1937-39; Tutor, 1945-49; Ministry of Information, 1939-40; British Council, 1940-45. Assistant Director-General (Overseas), St John Ambulance Association, 1952-54; CStJ. *Publications:* Jorrock's England, 1932; Richard II, 1941; The Custom of the Room (Early Winebooks of Christ's College, Cambridge), 1951; The Receipt of the Exchequer, 1377-1485, 1954; contrib.: Cambridge History of the British Empire; Studies presented to Sir Hilary Jenkinson, 1957. *Recreations:* fishing, bridge. *Address:* Wrangbrook, Lisvane Road, Llanishen, Cardiff. *T:* Cardiff 752498. *Clubs:* United Service; Cardiff and County, Cardiff Bridge (Cardiff).

**STEEL, Byron;** *see* Steegmuller, Francis.

**STEEL, Brig. Charles Deane,** CMG 1957; OBE 1941; *b* 29 May 1901; *s* of Dr Gerard Steel, JP, Leominster, Herefs; *m* 1932, Elizabeth Chenevix-Trench; two *s*. *Educ:* Bedford; Royal Military Academy, Woolwich. Prize Cadetship, Woolwich, 1919. Armstrong Memorial Prize, 1921. Commissioned 2nd Lieut RE, 1921; served in India (Bengal Sappers and Miners), 1924-29; Staff College, Camberley, 1936-37; War of 1939-45; E Africa and Abyssinia, 1941; Western Desert, 1942; POW, 1942; Switzerland, 1943; Dep. Head, British Mil. Mission to Greece, 1945-49; Dep. Mil Sec., 1949-52; retd Feb. 1952; Head of Conference and Supply Dept, Foreign Office, 1952-64; Head of Accommodation Department Diplomatic Service, 1965-67. *Recreations:* golf, and gardening. *Address:* Little Hill, Nettlebed, Oxfordshire. *T:* Nettlebed 287. *Clubs:* United Service, Shikar.

**STEEL, Sir Christopher Eden,** GCMG 1960 (KCMG 1951; CMG 1945); MVO 1936; HM Ambassador to Bonn, 1957-63, retired; *b* 12 Feb. 1903; *er s* of late Col Richard Steel and Adine, *d* of W. Acton-Adams, Tipapa, Canterbury, NZ; *m* 1932, Catherine, *er d* of late Lieut-Gen. Sir Sidney Clive, GCVO, KCB, CMG, DSO; two *s* one *d*. *Educ:* Wellington College (Scholar); Hertford College, Oxford (Scholar). Entered Diplomatic Service, 1927; has served at Rio de Janeiro, Paris, The Hague, Berlin and Cairo. Assistant Private Sec. to the Prince of Wales, 1935-36; British Political Officer, SHAEF, 1945; Political adviser to Commander-in-Chief, Germany, 1947, Dep. High Commissioner, 1949; Minister, British Embassy, Washington, 1950-53; UK Permanent Representative on the North Atlantic Council, 1953-57. Chairman, Anglo-German Association, 1966-. *Address:* Southrop Lodge, Nr Lechlade, Glos. *Club:* Travellers'.

**STEEL, David Edward Charles,** DSO 1940; MC 1945; TD; Managing Director, British Petroleum Company since 1965; *b* 29 Nov. 1916; *s* of late Gerald Arthur Steel, CB; *m* 1956, Ann Wynne, *d* of Maj.-Gen. C. B. Price, *qv*; one *s* two *d*. *Educ:* Rugby School; University Coll., Oxford, BA. Joined Inns of Court Regt, 1938; Commissioned 9 QR Lancers, 1940; served 1940-45 France, Middle East, North Africa, Italy (DSO, MC, despatches thrice). Admitted a Solicitor, June 1948; on Staff of Linklaters and Paines, 1948-50; with Legal Dept of The British Petroleum Co. Ltd, 1950-56; posted to New York, 1958; Pres. BP (N Amer.) Ltd, 1959-61; Man. Dir, Kuwait Oil Co. Ltd, 1962-65. *Address:* 37 Ormonde Gate, SW3; Queen Wood Farm, Christmas Common, near Watlington, Oxon. *Clubs:* Cavalry; Links (New York).

**STEEL, David Martin Scott;** MP (L) Roxburgh, Selkirk and Peebles since 1965; journalist and broadcaster; Liberal Chief Whip, since 1970; *b* 31 March 1938; *s* of Rev. Dr David Steel, Linlithgow; *m* 1962, Judith Mary, *d* of W. D. MacGregor, CBE, Dunblane; one *s* one *d*. *Educ:* Prince of Wales School, Nairobi, Kenya; George Watson's College and Edinburgh University. MA 1960; LLB 1962. President: Edinburgh University Liberals, 1959; Students' Representative Council, 1960. Visited Soviet Union, 1961. Asst Secretary, Scottish Liberal Party, 1962-64; Scottish Liberal Whip, 1967-70; Pres., Nat. League of Young Liberals, 1967-; Mem. Parly Delegn to UN Gen. Assembly, 1967; Liberal Spokesman on Commonwealth affairs; Sponsor, Private Member's Bill to reform law on abortion, 1966-67; Pres., Anti-Apartheid Movement of GB, 1966-69; Chm., Shelter, Scotland, 1969-. BBC television interviewer in Scotland, 1964-65; Presenter of STV weekly religious programme, 1966-67, and for Granada, 1969. Foundn Oration, University Coll., London, 1970. *Publications:* Boost for the Borders, 1964; Out of Control, 1968; No Entry, 1969; contrib. to The Guardian, other newspapers and political weeklies. *Recreations:* angling, riding, motoring, gardening. *Address:* Cherry Dene, Ettrick Bridge, Selkirkshire. *T:* Ettrick Bridge 213. *Clubs:* National Liberal; Scottish Liberal (Edinburgh).

**STEEL, Edward,** JP; **His Honour Judge Steel;** County Court Judge, Circuit No 8 (Manchester), since 1961; *b* 9 May 1906; *er s* of Thomas S. Steel, Solicitor, Warrington; *m* 1936, Mary Evelyn Griffith Roberts, *er d* of late Alderman R. G. Roberts, JP; two *d*. *Educ:* Boteler Grammar School, Warrington; Hutton Grammar School, Preston; Liverpool University (LLB). Solicitor, Nov. 1928; called to Bar, Gray's Inn, 1937; served War of 1939-45, Judge Advocate-General's Dept, (Lt-Col); Judge Advocate, Trial of War Criminals, Germany and Norway; Assistant Recorder, Liverpool City Quarter Sessions, 1948-56; Chancellor, Diocese of Liverpool, 1957; County Court Judge, Circuit 12 (Yorkshire), Jan. 1958, Circuit 10 (Oldham, etc), 1958-61, Circuit 5 (Salford, etc), Jan.-May, 1961; Circuit 8 (Manchester), May 1961-; Commissioner, Crown Court, Manchester, 1961-; Deputy Chm. Lancashire County Quarter Sessions, 1959; Cheshire County Quarter Sessions, 1961; Vice-President Manchester Meeting, British Association for the Advancement of Science, 1962. JP Cheshire, 1958. *Recreation:* cinematography. *Address:* Woodlands, Walton, Cheshire. *T:* Warrington 62383. *Club:* University (Liverpool).

**STEEL, Major Sir (Fiennes) William Strang,** 2nd Bt, *cr* 1938; DL; JP; Major (retired), 17/21st Lancers; Forestry Commissioner since 1958; *b* 24 July 1912; *e s* of Sir Samuel Steel, 1st Bt and of Hon. Vere Mabel (*d* 1964), *d* of 1st Baron Cornwallis; *S* father, 1961; *m* 1941, Joan, *d* of late Brig.-Gen. Sir Brodie Haldane Henderson, KCMG, CB, Braughing, Ware; two *s* one *d*. *Educ:* Eton; RMC, Sandhurst; joined 17/21st Lancers, 1933; Major, 1941; retired, 1947. Convener, Selkirk CC, 1967. DL Selkirkshire, 1955, JP 1965. *Heir: s* Fiennes Michael Strang Steel, *b* 22 Feb. 1943. *Address:* Philiphaugh, Selkirk. *T:* Selkirk 3216. *Clubs:* Cavalry; New (Edinburgh).

**STEEL, Henry,** OBE 1965; HM Diplomatic Service; Legal Counsellor, Foreign and Commonwealth Office (formerly Commonwealth Office), since 1967; *b* 13 Jan. 1926; *yr s* of late Raphael Steel; *m* 1960, Jennifer Isobel Margaret, *d* of Brig. M. M. Simpson, MBE; two *s* two *d*. *Educ:* Christ's Coll., Finchley; New Coll., Oxford. BA Oxon 1950. Called to Bar, Lincoln's Inn, 1951; Legal Asst, Colonial Office, 1955; Senior Legal Asst, CO, 1960; Asst Legal Adviser, CRO, 1965. Military Service, RASC and Intelligence Corps, 1944-47. *Address:* Wentways, Priestwood, Meopham, Kent. *T:* Meopham 2183.

**STEEL, Sir James,** Kt 1967; CBE 1964; JP, DL; Hon. Life President, Steel Group Ltd, 1966; President, Northern Group, Royal Institute of Public Administration; Member, Commission on the Constitution, since 1969; Chairman: Washington Development Corporation; Textile Council; Director: Geo. Angus & Co. Ltd; Northern Shipbuilding & Industrial Holdings Ltd; Hall Russell & Co. Ltd; Hocroft Trust Ltd; Rea Brothers Ltd; Stag Line Ltd; Westool Ltd; Westforth Electrical and Automation Ltd; North of England Building Society; Newcastle upon Tyne Local Board, Barclays Bank; *b* 19 May 1909; *s* of Alfred Steel and Katharine (*née* Meikle); *m* 1935, Margaret Jean MacLauchlan; two *s* two *d*. *Educ:* Trent College. Steel & Co. Ltd: Apprentice, 1927; Employee, 1931; Director, 1935; Dep. Man. Dir, 1942; Chm. and Man. Dir, 1956. Trustee, Sir John Priestman Charity Trust; Member: Northern Gas Bd; Board, National Research Dev. Corp.; Council, Durham University; Northern Region Council, CBI; Northern Regional Cttee, United Europe Assoc. Chairman: British Productivity Council, 1966-67; North-East Regional Coun., British Inst. of Management; Pres., YMCA, Sunderland; Vice-President: Young Enterprise Nat. Council; NE Div., Nat. Council of YMCAs. Liveryman, Worshipful Co. of Founders. FBIM. JP Sunderland; DL Durham, 1969. *Recreations:* ornithology, photography, horse-riding. *Address:* Fawnlees Hall, Wolsingham, County Durham. *T:* 307. *Clubs:* Junior Carlton; St James's (Manchester).

**STEEL, Sir (Joseph) Lincoln (Spedding),** Kt 1965; JP; Director Charterhouse Investment Trust; Chairman, Triplex Holdings Ltd, 1961-66 (Deputy Chairman, 1960-61); *b* 24 March 1900; *s* of late Comdr Joseph Steel, RD, RNR, and Esther Alice (*née* Spedding); *m* 1st, 1928, Cynthia Smith (*d* 1929); one *s*; 2nd, 1938, Barbara I. T., *y d* of late Colonel S. G. Goldschmidt; one *s*. *Educ:* Christ's Hospital; St John's College, Oxford (Open Scholar, MA). Served RE, 1918-19. Joined Brunner Mond & Co. Ltd, 1922; Delegate Dir, ICI (Alkali) Ltd, 1932; Man. Dir, Alkali Div. of ICI Ltd, 1942; Chm. Alkali Div. of ICI Ltd, 1943; Dir, Imperial Chemical Industries Ltd, 1945-60, retd. Chm. British Nat. Cttee of International Chamber of Commerce, 1951-63; Pres. Internat. Chamber of Commerce, 1963-65; Vice-Pres. 1951-63; Hon. Pres. 1965-; Chairman Overseas Cttee of FBI, 1950-65; Member: Council of CBI, 1965-68; EFTA Consultative Cttee, 1960-69. Leader, UK Industrial Mission to W Indies, 1962. Member Cheshire County Council, 1937-45; JP Cheshire, 1939; JP Bucks, 1960; Gen. Comr for Income Tax, Burnham District, 1968-. FRSA 1963. *Recreations:* gardening, walking, travel. *Address:* The Warren, Chesham Bois, Bucks. *T:* Amersham 406. *Clubs:* Carlton, Garrick, Beefsteak.

**STEEL, Sir Lincoln;** *see* Steel, Sir J. L. S.

**STEEL, Robert;** Secretary, Royal Institution of Chartered Surveyors, since 1968; *b* 7 April 1920; *e s* of late John Thomas Steel, Wooler, Northumberland; *m* 1943, Averal Frances, *d* of Arthur Pettitt; one *s* one *d*. *Educ:* Duke's Sch., Alnwick, Northumb.; Univ. of London (BSc 1945); Gray's Inn (Barrister, 1956). Surveyor, 1937-46; Asst Sec., Under Sec., Royal Instn of Surveyors, 1946-61; Dir of Town Development, Basingstoke, 1962-67. Sec.-Gen., Internat. Fedn of Surveyors, 1967-69; Sec., Commonwealth Assoc. of Surveying and Land Economy, 1969-. FRICS. *Publications:* on Property Law; contrib. professional jls. *Recreations:* squash, mountain walking, travel. *Address:* 22 Sefton Road, Petts Wood, Kent. *T:* Orpington 22309. *Clubs:* United Service, Royal Commonwealth Society.

**STEEL, Prof. Robert Walter,** BSc, MA Oxon; John Rankin Professor of Geography, University of Liverpool, since 1957; Dean, Faculty of Arts, 1965-68, Pro-Vice-Chancellor, since 1971; *b* 31 July 1915; *er s* of late Frederick Grabham Steel; *m* 1940, Eileen Margaret, *er d* of late Arthur Ernest Page, Bournemouth; one *s* two *d*. *Educ:* Great Yarmouth Grammar Sch.; Cambridge and County High School for Boys; Jesus College, Oxford (Open Exhibitioner in Geography). RGS Essay Prize, 1936. Drapers' Co. Research Scholarship for Geography, 1937-39, for work in Sierra Leone; Departmental Lectr in Geography, Univ. of Oxford, 1939-47; Naval Intelligence Div., Admiralty, 1940-45; attached to Sociological Dept of W African Inst. of Arts, Industry and Social Science as geographer to Ashanti Social Survey, Gold Coast, 1945-46; Univ. Lectr in Colonial Geography, Univ. of Oxford, 1947-56. Murchison Grant (RGS), 1948; Council RGS, 1949-53, 1968-; Inst. of Brit. Geographers: Council, 1947-60; Actg Sec., 1948, Asst Sec., 1949-50; Hon. Editor of Publications, 1950-60; Vice-President, 1966-67, Pres. 1968; Pres., Section E (Geography), British Association for the Adv. of Science, 1966; Pres., African

Studies Assoc. of the UK, 1970-71 (Vice-Pres., 1969-70). Visiting Prof., Harvard Univ. Summer Sch., 1952; delegate to Internat. Geog. Congress, Washington, DC, 1952, Stockholm, Sweden, 1960, and New Delhi, India, 1968; Vis. Prof., Univ. of Ghana, 1964; Canadian Commonwealth Vis. Fellow, Carleton Univ., 1970. Lecturer in Geography, St Peter's Hall, Oxford, 1951-56; Official Fellow and Tutor in Geography, Jesus College, Oxford, 1954-56. *Publications:* ed (with A. F. Martin), and contrib. to, The Oxford Region: a Scientific and Historical Survey, 1954; ed (with C. A. Fisher), and contrib. to Geographical Essays on British Tropical Lands, 1956; ed (with R. M. Prothero), and contrib. to Geographers and the Tropics: Liverpool Essays, 1964; ed (with R. Lawton), and contrib. to Liverpool Essays on Geography: a Jubilee Collection, 1967; articles, mainly on tropical Africa, in Geographical Jl and other geog. jls. *Address:* Gatesgarth, 52 Graham Road, West Kirby, Wirral, Cheshire L48 5DW. *T:* 051-632 1928.

**STEEL, Major Sir William Strang;** *see* Steel, Major Sir F. W. S.

**STEELE, Prof. Alan John;** Professor of French Literature, University of Edinburgh, since 1961; *b* Bellshill, Lanark, 11 April 1916; *s* of John Steele, MA, BD, and Anne (*née* Lawson); *m* 1947, Claire Alice Louise Belet; one *s* one *d*. *Educ:* Royal Grammar School, Newcastle upon Tyne; Blyth Secondary School, Northumberland; Universities of Edinburgh, Grenoble and Paris. MA 1st Cl. Hons in French Language and Literature, Vans Dunlop Schol., Univ. of Edinburgh, 1938. Served War of 1939-45, at sea with 4th Maritime AA Regt, RA, 1941-42; commissioned, 1942, with 64th LAA Regt RA in Algeria, Italy and Greece. Lecturer in French, University of Edinburgh, 1946. *Publications:* (with R. A. Leigh) Contemporary French Translation Passages, 1956; Three Centuries of French Verse, 1956, new edn, 1961; contrib. to Cahiers de l'Assoc. Internat. des Etudes françaises, Modern Language Review. *Recreation:* golf. *Address:* 17 Polwarth Grove, Edinburgh 11. *T:* 031-337 5092.

**STEELE, Mrs Alfred N.;** *see* Crawford, Joan.

**STEELE, Air Marshal Sir Charles Ronald,** KCB 1951 (CB 1944); DFC 1918; DL; *b* 9 November 1897; *s* of late Rev. Canon Steele, Lincoln; *m* 1920, Joan Evelyn, *d* of late H. M. R. Hopkins, CSI; one *s* one *d*. *Educ:* Oundle; Royal Military College, Sandhurst. Gazetted to Green Howards 1916 and seconded to RFC; served in France 1916-18 with Nos 15, 20, and 48 Squadrons RFC and RAF (DFC); India with 28 Squadron, 1919-23; served on Indian Frontier, 1921-23, in Wana and Razmak Campaigns; RAF Staff College, 1926-27; No 1 Air Defence Group (HQ Auxiliary Air Force), 1927-29; No 47 Squadron, Khartoum, 1930-31; HQ, RAF, Jerusalem, 1932-33; Staff College, Camberley, 1934-35; commanded No 18 Squadron RAF, 1936-37; HQ BAFF (France), 1940 (despatches); Rhodesian Air Training Group, S Rhodesia, 1941-42; HQ No 9 Group as SASO, 1942; AOC No 10 Group RAF, 1943-44; AOC No 85 Group RAF, 1944-45; SASO, British Air Forces of Occupation (Germany), 1945-47; AOC, RAF, Malta, 1947-49; AOC-in-C, Coastal Command, 1950-51; invalided out of RAF, 1952. DL Cambridge, 1962. Order of George I of Greece, 1942; Commander Legion of Honour, Croix de Guerre (France), 1946; Commander Order of Crown of Belgium, Croix de Guerre (Belgium), 1946. *Address:* 17 Rutherford Road, Cambridge. *Club:* MCC.

**STEELE, (Francis) Howard,** ACGI, BSc(Eng), CEng, FIEE; Director of Engineering, The Independent Television Authority, since 1969; *b* Gt Bookham, Surrey, 23 Sept. 1929; *s* of Arnold Francis Steele, MBE, and Florence Anne Winifred Steele; *m* 1953, Elaine Barnes Steele (*née* Mason); two *s*. *Educ:* Mill Hill School; Imperial College of Science and Technology. Engineer, Marconi Company, Chelmsford, 1952-57; Asst Engineer in Charge, Alpha Television Services, Birmingham, 1957-58; Head of Planning and Installation Dept, 1958-61, Chief Engineer, 1961-66, ABC Television Ltd; Chief Engineer, ITA, 1966-69. *Recreations:* motoring and sailing. *Address:* Silverdale, Beech Drive, Kingswood, Surrey. *T:* Mogador 2232.

**STEELE, Commander Gordon Charles,** VC, RN, retired; Hon. Captain, RNR, 1949; Captain Superintendent of Thames Nautical Training College, HMS Worcester, off Greenhithe, 1929-57; Fellow of Institute of Navigation, 1951; *b* Exeter, 1892; *s* of late Captain H. W. Steele, RN, and S. M., *d* of Major-General J. C. Symonds, RMLI. *Educ:* Vale College, Ramsgate; HMS Worcester. Midshipman, Royal Navy Reserve; joined P & OSN Co. as cadet and served in RNR and P & O till outbreak of war; served in HM Submarines D8 and E22 and in Q ships; transferred to Royal Navy as Sub-Lieutenant for distinguished service in action, Aug. 1915; served in HMS Royal Oak as Lieut RN in Jutland, and in Iron Duke; commanded HM ships P63 and Cornflower, 1917-18; served in coastal motor boat raid on Kronstadt Harbour, Aug. 1919 (VC); specialised in anti-submarine duties; Naval Interpreter in Russian; retired list, 1931; served in HMS Osprey as Anti-Submarine Commander, and Inspector of Anti-Submarine Equipment, in War, 1939-45; a Younger Brother of Trinity House; Member Worshipful Company of Shipwrights; Freeman City of London; a Lay-Reader. *Publications:* Electrical Knowledge for Ships' Officers; The Story of the Worcester. *Address:* 3 Avereng Road, Folkestone, Kent. *T:* 53404. *Club:* Public Schools.

**STEELE, Lt-Col Harwood (Robert Elmes),** MC; FRGS; Author and Journalist; *b* Fort Macleod, Alberta, Canada, 5 May 1897; *o s* of late Maj.-Gen. Sir S. B. Steele, KCMG, and Lady Steele (*née* de Lotbiniere Harwood), *d* of co-seigneur of Vaudreuil, Quebec. *Educ:* England, Canada and South Africa. Served European War, 1914-18 (Capt., MC, despatches); Capt. Winnipeg Grenadiers, 1915-26; Capt. 17th DYRC Hussars 1926; Major, 1929; Lieut-Colonel and OC 1938. Historian, Canadian Govt Arctic Expedition. CGS Arctic, 1925, to Far North; Asst Press Representative, CPR, 1923-25; lectured, with Govt endorsement, on RCM Police through Canada and Eastern US, 1928-30. Served War of 1939-45 in England, Northern Ireland, NW Frontier, India, 14th Army, East of Brahmaputra and GHQ, India Command; War Subst. Major 17/21 Lancers, 1939; Temp. Lt-Col 1944 (despatches). Lectured in England and Canada on India, Canada and RCM Police, 1945-63. *Publications:* Cleared for Action (Naval Poems), 1914; The Canadians in France, 1915-18, 1920; Spirit of Iron, novel, 1923; I Shall Arise, novel, 1926; The Ninth Circle, novel, 1927; Policing the Arctic, history of RCM Police in Far North, 1936; India: Friend or Foe? a political study, 1947; To Effect An Arrest, short stories of RCMP, 1947; Ghosts Returning (novel), 1950; The Marching Call, early life of Sir S. B. Steele, 1955; The Red Serge, short stories of RCMP, 1961; short history of RCMP, 1968; poems, short stories, broadcasts, articles. *Address:*

Warrene Lodge, Pulborough, Sussex. *Club:* Savage.

**STEELE, Howard;** *see* Steele, F. H.

**STEELE, General Sir James Stuart,** GCB, *cr* 1950 (KCB, *cr* 1949; CB 1943); KBE, *cr* 1946; DSO 1940; MC 1917; LLD (QUB) 1947; *b* 26 Oct. 1894; *s* of late Samuel Steele, Ballycarry, Co. Antrim; *m* 1923, Janet Gibson Gordon; two *d. Educ:* Royal Belfast Academical Instn; Queen's Univ., Belfast. 2nd Lt Royal Irish Rifles, Sept. 1914; served France and Belgium, 1915-17 (MC, despatches); NW Frontier, 1920 (despatches); commanded 1st Bn Sherwood Foresters, 1937-39; Palestine, 1939; AAG War Office, 1939; Colonel, 1939; Bde Comdr, 1939-41; France and Belgium, 1940 (DSO); Divisional Comdr 1941-42; Corps Commander 1942; DCGS and CGS, Middle East, 1942-43; DSD War Office, 1943-45; Maj.-Gen. 1944; C-in-C British Troops and High Commissioner, Austria, 1946-47; Lt-Gen. 1946; General, 1947. Col The Royal Ulster Rifles, 1947-57. Adj.-Gen. to Forces, 1947-50. ADC General to the King, 1950; retired pay, 1950. Chm. Legal Aid Cttee, N Ireland, 1958-60. Col Comdt, Royal Army Educational Corps, 1950-59; Hon. Colonel QUB Contingent OTC, 1951-59. Pres., Army Benevolent Fund, 1954-64. *Recreation:* gardening. *Address:* Churchills, Stourpaine, Blandford, Dorset. *Club:* Army and Navy.

**STEELE, Thomas;** *b* 15 Nov. 1905; *s* of late James Steele, miner; *m* 1939, Helen Thomson; two *s.* Stationmaster to 1945; MP (Lab) Lanark Division of Lanarkshire, 1945-50, West Dunbartonshire, 1950-70; Parliamentary Secretary, Ministry of National Insurance, 1946-50. Member GMC. *Address:* Windyridge, Lesmahagow, Lanark.

**STEELE, Tommy, (Thomas Hicks);** Actor; *b* Bermondsey London, 17 Dec. 1936; *s* of Thomas Walter Hicks and Elizabeth Ellen (*née* Bennett); *m* 1960, Ann Donoghue; one *d. Educ:* Bacon's Sch. for Boys, Bermondsey. First appearance on stage in variety, Empire Theatre, Sunderland, Nov. 1956; first London appearance, variety, Dominion Theatre, 1957; Buttons in Rodgers and Hammerstein's Cinderella, Coliseum, 1958; Tony Lumpkin in She Stoops to Conquer, Old Vic, 1960; Arthur Kipps in Half a Sixpence, Cambridge Theatre, London, 1963-64 and Broadhurst Theatre (first NY appearance), 1965; Truffaldino in The Servant of Two Masters, Queen's, 1969; Dick Whittington, London Palladium, 1969. Entered films in Kill Me Tomorrow, 1956; subseq. films include: The Tommy Steele Story; The Duke Wore Jeans; Tommy the Toreador; Touch It Light; It's All Happening; The Happiest Millionaire; Half a Sixpence; Finian's Rainbow; Where's Jack? *Recreation:* football. *Address:* c/o Talent Artists Ltd, 13 Bruton Street, W1. *T:* 01-493 0343.

**STEELE-PERKINS, Surgeon Vice-Admiral Sir Derek (Duncombe),** KCB 1966 (CB 1963); KCVO 1964 (CVO 1954); FRCS; FRACS; *b* 19 June 1908; *s* of late Dr Duncombe Steele-Perkins, Honiton, Devon, and Sybil Mary Hill-Jones, Edinburgh; *m* 1937, Joan Boddan, Birkdale, Lancashire; three *d. Educ:* Allhallows School, Rousdon; Edinburgh University and College of Surgeons (Edin.). Entered RN, 1932; RN Hosp., Haslar, 1932; HMS Mantis, China, 1934-36; HMS Ganges, Shotley, 1936-38; HMS Vindictive, 1938-39; RN Hospitals: Haslar, 1939-40; Chatham, 1940-44; Sydney, Australia, 1944-46; Malta, 1946-50; RY Gothic, 1951-52; Chatham, 1952-59; Senior Surgical Specialist, RN Hosp., Bighi, Malta, Oct. 1959-61; Medical Officer-in-Charge, Royal Naval Hospital, Haslar, 1961; Command MO to C-in-C, Portsmouth, 1962-63; Medical Director of the Navy, 1963-66. FRSocMed Royal Commonwealth Tours, 1953-54, 1959. QHS 1961. CStJ. *Recreations:* sailing, fly-fishing, shooting. *Address:* c/o National Westminster Bank, Haven Road, Canford Cliffs, Dorset. *Club:* Army and Navy.

**STEEN, Marguerite;** FRSL; novelist and playwright; *b* 1894; *d* of Captain George Conolly Benson, KSLI, and Margaret Jones; adopted *d* of Joseph and Margaret Jane Steen. *Educ:* privately. Taught in private sch. during war; became a dancing mistress, and left this profession for the stage; three years with Fred Terry–Julia Neilson Co.; left stage and started career as novelist, 1926. *Publications:* Gilt Cage, 1927; Duel in the Dark, 1928; The Reluctant Madonna, 1929; They That Go Down, 1930; When the Wind Blows, 1931; Unicorn, 1931; The Wise and the Foolish Virgins, 1932; Oakfield Plays, 1932; Stallion, 1933; Spider, 1933; Hugh Walpole, a study 1933; The Spanish Trilogy: Matador, 1934 (Book Society Choice England and Book of the Month, USA); The Tavern, 1935; The One-Eyed Moon, 1935; Return of a Heroine, 1936; The Lost One, 1937; Who Would Have Daughters?, 1937; The Marriage Will Not Take Place, 1938; Family Ties, 1939; The Sun is My Undoing, 1941 (Book Society Choice, England, Literary Guild, USA); William Nicholson, a biography, 1943; Rose Timpson, 1946; Granada Window, 1949; Twilight on the Floods, 1949; The Swan, 1951; Phoenix Rising, 1952; Anna Fitzalan, 1953; Bulls of Parral, 1954; The Unquiet Spirit, 1955; Little White King, 1956; The Woman in the Back Seat, 1959; The Tower, 1959; A Pride of Terrys (biography), 1962; A Candle in the Sun, 1964; Looking Glass I (autobiography), 1966; Pier Glass (autobiography), 1968. *Plays:* Matador (with Matheson Lang), prod. 1936; French for Love (with Derek Patmore), prod. 1939. *Recreation:* writing. *Address:* Little Triton, Blewbury, Berks. *T:* 294.

**STEEN, Robert Elsworth,** MD, Past President RCPI; FRCP Glasgow (Hon.); Hon. Visiting Physician, National Children's Hospital, Dublin, and Sunshine Home, Stillorgan; Consulting Pædiatrician Royal Victoria Eye and Ear Hospital, Dublin, St Kevin's Hospital, Dublin, Monkstown Hospital, Dublin, Stewart's Hospital, Palmerstown, and Cottage Home, Dun Laoghaire; Professor of Pædiatrics, Dublin University; *b* 11 April 1902; *s* of David Miller Steen and Jane Elsworth (*née* Orr); *m* 1939, Elizabeth Margaret Cochrane; one *s* one *d. Educ:* St Andrew's College and Trinity College, Dublin. Graduated 1924; held following posts: Demonstrator in Biochemistry and Pathology, Dublin University; House Surgeon and House Physician, Monkstown Hospital, Dublin, and French Hospital, London; House Physician, Hospital for Sick Children, Great Ormond Street, London; Assistant Physician, Royal City of Dublin Hospital and Meath Hospital, Dublin; Physician, Dr Steeven's Hospital, Dublin, and Meath Hospital, Dublin; Medical Director, St Patrick's Infant Hosp. and Nursery Training Coll., Temple Hill, Blackrock; formerly Lecturer in Hygiene, Metropolitan School of Nursing, Dublin, and Pædiatrician to the Rotunda Hospital, Dublin. Fellow and late President Section of Pædiatrics, Royal Academy of Medicine in Ireland; late President: Irish Cardiac Soc.; Irish Pædiatric Assoc.; Dublin University Biological Assoc.; British Pædiatric Assoc.; Hon. Member, Assoc. of European Pædiatric Cardiologists; Sen. Member, Assoc. of Physicians of GB and Ireland; Extra Ordinary

Member, British Cardiac Soc. *Publications:* Infants in Health and Sickness; numerous publications in medical journals. *Recreations:* hunting, ski-ing, croquet, bridge. *Address:* Department of Pædiatrics, University of Dublin, National Children's Hospital, Harcourt Street, Dublin 2. *T:* Dublin 752355; Mountsandel, Carrickmines, Co. Dublin. *T:* 893184. *Clubs:* Kildare Street, Friendly Brother House (Dublin), Ireland.

**STEEN, Stephen Nicholas;** Chairman: Smith & Nephew Associated Companies Ltd, since 1968; Jeyes Group Ltd, since 1966; British Tissues Ltd, 1967-69; *b* 19 July 1907; *m* 1934; one *s* one *d.* Arthur Berton & Co. Ltd, 1943; Director, Smith & Nephew Associated Companies Ltd, 1958, Dep. Chm. 1962. Underwriting Member, Matthews Wrightson Pulbrook Ltd; Called to the Bar, Grays Inn, 1949. *Recreation:* golf. *Address:* (office) 2 Temple Place, WC2. *T:* 01-836 7922. *Club:* Devonshire.

**STEER, Kenneth Arthur,** MA, PhD, FRSE, FSA; Secretary, Royal Commission on the Ancient and Historical Monuments of Scotland, since 1957; *b* 12 Nov. 1913; *o s* of Harold Steer and Emily Florence Thompson; *m* 1941, Rona Mary Mitchell; one *d. Educ:* Wath Grammar School; Durham University. Research Fellowship, 1936-38. Joined staff of Royal Commission on Ancient and Historical Monuments of Scotland, 1938. Intelligence Officer in Army, 1941-45 (despatches twice). Monuments, Fine Arts and Archives Officer, North Rhine Region, 1945-46. Corresponding Member, German Archæological Inst.; Horsley Memorial Lecturer, Durham University, 1963; Rhind Lectr, 1968. Mem., Ancient Monuments Board for Scotland. *Publications:* numerous articles in archæological journals. *Address:* 18 Esslemont Road, Edinburgh. *T:* 031-667 5167.

**STEER, Rt. Rev. Stanley Charles;** *see* Saskatoon, Bishop of.

**STEER, William Reed Hornby,** DL, MA, LLB, Barrister-at-Law; Recorder of South Molton, 1936-51; Deputy Chairman, London County Council, 1948-49; Lt-Col in the Army (released); *b* 5 April 1899; *s* of late Rev. W. H. Hornby Steer, TD MA, JP; unmarried. *Educ:* Eton; Trinity College, Cambridge. Commissioned in Royal Field Artillery; served European War, France and Belgium; called to Bar, Inner Temple, 1922; joined Western Circuit; Standing Counsel to Commons, Open Spaces, and Footpaths Preservation Society; to Council for Preservation of Rural England; to National Smoke Abatement Society and to Pure Rivers Society; an Examiner in Law to Chartered Institute of Secretaries; Legal Member of Town Planning Inst.; Fellow of Royal Soc. of Health; Associate of Royal Institution of Chartered Surveyors; a representative for Hampstead on London County Council, 1931-52; a representative of London County Council on International Union of Local Authorities; Master of Worshipful Company of Turners, 1949-50; a Governor of Haberdashers' Aske's Schools and of Royal Free Hospital; a Governor and an Almoner of Christ's Hospital, Dep. Chm. Council of Almoners, 1970-; Chairman Children's Hospital, Hampstead; Vice-Chairman London Old Age Pensions Committee; Treasurer, London Soc.; Kt of Justice, Order of St John; Joint Hon. Secretary of League of Mercy; Gold Staff Officer at Coronation of King George VI; Inspector of Metropolitan Special Constabulary; Army Officers Emergency Reserve, 1938; Extra Regimentally Employed, Military Dept, Judge Advocate-General's Office, 1939; Deputy Judge Advocate-General, Malta, 1941-43; graded Assistant Adjutant-General, War Office, 1944; Staff Officer (I), Control Commission for Germany, 1945; Captain, 1939; Major, 1941; Lt-Col 1943; Member of Territorial Army and Air Force Association of the County of London. *Publications:* articles on the law relating to Highways; Assistant Editor of Glen's Public Health Act, 1936; Steer's Law of Smoke Nuisances, 1938, 2nd edn 1948; contributions to Lord Macmillan's Local Government Law and Administration. *Recreation:* sailing. *Address:* 71A Whitehall Court, SW1. *T:* 01-930 3160. *Clubs:* Oxford and Cambridge University, Carlton, Pratt's, MCC; Royal Corinthian Yacht (Burnham-on-Crouch); Hampshire (Winchester).

**STEERS, James Alfred,** MA; Professor Emeritus of Geography and Emeritus Fellow of St Catharine's College, Cambridge; Chairman, National Committee of Geography, since 1967; Coastal Consultant to Conservation Committee of Council of Europe, 1968; Chairman: Coastal Conferences, 1966-67; *b* 8 Aug. 1899; *s* of J. A. Steers, Bedford; *m* 1942, Harriet, *d* of J. A. Wanklyn, Cambridge; one *s* one *d. Educ:* Elstow (Private) School, Bedford; St Catharine's Coll., Cambridge. Senior Geography Master, Framlingham Coll., 1921-22; elected Fellow of St Catharine's, 1925, subsequently Dean, Tutor and President, Univ. Demonstrator, 1926-27; Univ. Lecturer, 1927-49; Member of the British Expedition to the Great Barrier Reefs, 1928; Leader of Geographical Expedition to the Reefs, 1936; Expedition to the Jamaica Cays, 1939; War Service, 1917-18; Vice-Pres., Royal Geog. Soc., 1959-63, 1967-; Pres. Norfolk and Norwich Naturalists Soc., 1940-41; Pres., Section E British Association (Oxford), 1954; President, Inst. Brit. Geographers (Reading), 1956; President, Geographical Assoc., 1959; Member: Council of Senate, Cambridge, 1941-48; Wild Life Conservation Cttee; Nature Conservancy, 1949-54, 1957-66; Scientific Policy Cttee, 1949-66; Cttee for England, 1949-68, 1970-; Nat. Parks Commn, 1960-66. Hon. Adviser on Coastal Preservation to Ministry of Town and Country Planning and to Department of Health, Scotland; Departmental Cttee on Coastal Flooding, 1953; Advisory Committee. . . to improve Sea Defences, 1954-; Hydraulics Research Board, DSIR, 1957-61; Visiting Prof., Berkeley, Calif, 1959; Visiting Fellow, Aust. Nat. Univ., 1967. Victoria Medal, RGS, 1960; Scottish Geographical Medal, 1969. *Publications:* Introduction to the Study of Map Projections; The Unstable Earth; Scolt Head Island (Editor and Contributor, 2nd rev. edition, 1960); The Coastline of England and Wales (2nd enl. edn, 1969); A Picture Book of the Whole Coast of England and Wales; The Coast of England and Wales in Pictures; The Sea Coast; Editor: new edns of P. Lake's Physical Geography; Vol. on Field Studies in the British Isles, Internat. Geog. Union. London meeting, 1964; Brit. Assoc. Advancement of Science, The Cambridge Region, 1965; Engl. edn of V. P. Zenkovitch, Processes of Coastal Development, 1967; papers on Coastal Physiography, Coral Islands, etc., in various scientific publications. *Recreations:* walking, philately, travel. *Address:* 3 Thornton Close, Girton, Cambridge. *T:* Cambridge 76007. *Clubs:* Travellers', Geographical.

**STEIL, John Wellesley,** CMG 1951; MBE 1937; *b* 15 Aug. 1899; *s* of late Lt W. J. Steil, RN; *m* Annetta Elise (*d* 1961), 2nd *d* of late S. Fichat, Nairobi, Kenya; one *s* one *d. Educ:* Christ's Hospital, Horsham; Portsmouth Grammar

School; Cadet Ship HMS Conway. Served European War, 1917-19, Harwich Force, HMTB 85, HMS Dragon, Malayan American Rubber Co., Malaya and Sumatra, 1920-24; Colonial Administrative Service, Cadet, Uganda, 1925; Asst District Officer, 1927; District Officer, 1936; Provincial Comr, 1947, Senior Provincial Commissioner, 1949; Secretary for African Affairs, Uganda, MEC and MLC, 1950-51. Farming in WA, 1957-62. *Address:* The Weld Club, GPO Box B54, Perth, WA 6001, Australia. *Clubs:* Royal Commonwealth Society; Weld (Perth, WA).

**STEIN, John Alan,** CIE 1943; *b* 31 Oct. 1888; *s* of late Hamilton Stein; *m* 1st, 1920, Phyllis (*d* 1949), *d* of Lindsay Horne, Aberdeen; one *d*; 2nd, Vera Craig, *d* of T. H. Patterson, Sunderland. *Educ:* Bedford School; City and Guilds College, London Univ. Joined Indian Service of Engineers, 1912, apptd to Bengal; served with Indian Sappers and Miners in Mesopotamia, Palestine, and Syria, 1916-19 (wounded); Executive Engineer, 1919; Under Secretary, Govt of Bengal, 1926; Superintending Engineer, 1931-41; Chief Engineer, Communications and Works Dept, Bengal, 1941-43; Chief Engineer, Civil Supplies Dept, Bengal, 1945-47. Handicapper, Royal Calcutta Turf Club, 1947-52. *Address:* 26 North End House, Fitzjames Avenue, W14. *Clubs:* East India and Sports; Royal Calcutta Turf.

**STEIN, Leonard Jacques;** OBE 1953; Vice-President: Anglo-Jewish Association (President, 1939-49); Jewish Historical Society of England (President, 1964-65); *b* London, 12 Dec. 1887; *s* of Philip Stein and Matilda, *d* of Louis Beaver, Manchester; *m* 1928, Sarah, *d* of H. B. Kitay, Paterson, NJ, USA; two *s*. *Educ:* St Paul's School; Balliol College, Oxford; President of the Oxford Union, 1910. Called to Bar, Inner Temple, 1912; served in Army, 1914-20 (Staff-Captain, Palestine Military Administration and subsequently on Political Staff, EEF, in Jerusalem and at GHQ, Cairo, 1918-20); Political Sec., World Zionist Organisation, 1920-29; Honorary Legal Adviser, Jewish Agency for Palestine, 1929-39; contested (L) Dover, 1922, North Kensington, 1923, West Bermondsey, 1929. *Publications:* Edition of the Vicar of Wakefield, 1912; Zionism, 1925, republished in new edition, 1932; Syria, 1926; (Joint) Tax Avoidance, 1936, The National Defence Contribution, 1937, The Excess Profits Tax, 1940; Tax, 1940: The Balfour Declaration, 1961; Weizmann and England, 1965; (Jt Editor) Letters and Papers of Chaim Weizmann, Vol. I, 1968. *Address:* 1 Temple Gardens, Temple, EC4. *T:* 01-353 1672. *Club:* Reform.

**STEIN, Professor Peter Gonville,** JP; Regius Professor of Civil Law in the University of Cambridge, and Fellow of Queens' College, since 1968; *b* 29 May 1926; *o s* of late Walter Stein, MA, Solicitor, and Effie Stein (*née* Walker); *m* 1953, Janet Mary, PhD, *yr d* of late Clifford Chamberlain, Desborough, Northants; three *d*. *Educ:* Liverpool Coll.; Gonville and Caius Coll., Camb. (Classical Exhibitioner); University of Pavia. Served in RN, Sub-lieut (Sp) RNVR, 1944-47. Admitted a Solicitor, 1951; Italian Govt Scholar, 1951-52; Asst Lecturer in Law, Nottingham Univ., 1952-53; Lecturer in Jurisprudence, 1953-56, Prof. of Jurisprudence, 1956-68, Dean of Faculty of Law, 1961-64, Aberdeen Univ. PhD (Aberdeen), 1955. Visiting Prof. of Law: Univ. of Virginia, 1965-66; Univ. of Colorado, Summer 1966. Member: Council of Max Planck Inst. for European Legal History, Frankfurt; Sec. of State for Scotland's Working Party on Hospital Endowments, 1966-69; Chm., Bd of Management, Royal Cornhill and Assoc. (Mental) Hospitals, Aberdeen, 1967-68. JP Cambridge, 1970-. *Publications:* Fault in the formation of Contract in Roman Law and Scots Law, 1958; editor, Buckland's Textbook of Roman Law, 3rd edn, 1963; Regulae Iuris: from juristic rules to legal maxims, 1966; Roman Law in Scotland in Ius Romanum Medii Aevi, 1968; Roman Law and English Jurisprudence, 1969; articles in legal periodicals mainly on Roman Law and legal history. *Recreation:* hill walking. *Address:* 29 Millington Road, Cambridge. *T:* Cambridge 53137.

**STEINBERG, Jack;** Chairman, Steinberg & Sons (London & South Wales) Ltd, since 1966; *b* 23 May 1913; *s* of Alexander and Sophie Steinberg; *m* 1938, Hannah Anne, *d* of late Solomon Wolfson, JP; two *d*. *Educ:* privately, London. Underwriting Member of Lloyd's. Chairman: Horrockses Fashions Ltd; Butte-Knit (London) Ltd; Texifused Ltd; Clothing Export Council; Member, NEDC; Vice-Pres., British Mantle Manufacturers' Assoc.; Chm., Central Maccabi Fund Youth Clubs. Member of Plumbers' Livery Co.; Freeman, City of London. *Recreation:* farming. *Address:* 74 Portland Place, W1. *T:* 01-580 5908; Chartners Farm, Hartfield, Sussex. *T:* Hartfield 248.

**STEINBERG, William;** Conductor and Musical Director of the Pittsburgh Symphony Orchestra, Pennsylvania, USA, since 1952; simultaneously, Music Director of the Boston Symphony Orchestra, since 1969; *b* Cologne, 1 Aug. 1899; *s* of Julius Steinberg and Bertha Matzdorf; *m* 1934, Lotti Stern; one *s* one *d*. *Educ:* School of Higher Musical Studies, Cologne University. Studied piano with Uzielli, composition with Boelsche and conducting with Abendroth. Conductor Cologne Opera House, 1920; Opera Director, German Theatre, Prague, 1925-29; subseq. General Music Director, Frankfort Opera House, Guest Conductor, Berlin State Opera House, Conductor, Ceska Philharmonie, Prague, Museum Gesellschaft, Frankfort, and Palestine Orchestra. Went to USA, 1938; Guest Conductor with orchestras of many US cities; Conductor, San Francisco Opera, 1944-; Musical Director: Buffalo Philharmonic Orch., 1945-52; London Philharmonic Orch., 1958-60. Has made many gramophone records. *Address:* 11c Gateway Towers, Pittsburgh, PA 15222, USA; (Manager) Ronald A. Wilford, Columbia Artists, 165 West 57th Street, New York, NY 10019, USA.

**STEINER, Rear-Adm. Ottokar Harold Mojmir St John,** CB 1967; Asst Chief of Defence Staff, 1966-68, retired; *b* 8 July 1916; *e s* of late O. F. Steiner; *m* 1940, Evelyn Mary Young; one *s* one *d*. *Educ:* St Paul's School. Special entry cadet, RN, 1935. Served War of 1939-45 (despatches twice), HMS Ilex, Havelock, Frobisher, Superb. Naval Staff Course, 1947; Staff of C-in-C, Far East Fleet, 1948-50; Comdr 1950; jssc 1953; HMS Ceylon, 1953-54; NATO Defence Coll., 1955; HMS Daedalus, 1955-56; Capt. 1956; Admiralty, 1956-58; in comd HMS Saintes and Capt. (D) 3rd Destroyer Squdn, 1958-60; Naval Adviser to UK High Commission, Canada, 1960-62; Senior Offrs War Course, 1962; In Comd HMS Centaur, 1963-65; Rear-Adm., 1966. Chm., Cttee of Management, Shipwrecked Fishermen and Mariners Royal Benevolent Soc. Freeman, City of London; Liveryman, Coachmakers and Coach Harness Makers. *Recreations:* sailing, golf. *Address:* St Mary's, Sidlesham, Sussex. *T:* Sidlesham 450; 5 Belvedere Court, St Julians, Malta. *Clubs:* United Service, Royal Ocean

Racing, Royal Cruising; Royal Yacht Squadron, Itchenor Sailing, Goodwood Golf.

**STEINER, Professor Robert Emil;** Professor of Diagnostic Radiology, University of London, Postgraduate Medical School, since 1961; *b* 1 Feb. 1918; *s* of Rudolf Steiner and Clary (*née* Nordlinger); *m* 1945, Gertrude Margaret Konirsch; two *d*. *Educ:* University of Vienna; University College, Dublin. Dep. Director, Dept of Radiology, Hammersmith Hosp.; Lecturer Diagnostic Radiology, Postgraduate Med. School of London, 1950, Sen. Lecturer, 1955, Director, 1955-. Hon. Fellow, Amer. Coll. of Radiology. Barclay Medal British Inst. of Radiology. Former Editor, British Jl of Radiology. *Publications:* Clinical Disorders of the Pulmonary Circulation, 1960; contrib. to British Journal of Radiology, Clinical Radiology, British Heart Jl, Lancet, BMJ, etc. *Address:* 12 Stonehill Road, East Sheen, SW14. *T:* 01-876 4038.

**STENGEL, Prof. Erwin;** retired as Professor of Psychiatry (now Emeritus), University of Sheffield; Visiting Psychotherapist, HM Prison, Wakefield; *b* 25 March 1902; *s* of late Markus Stengel and of Franziska Stengel; *m* 1935, Anna Kohl. *Educ:* University of Vienna. MD (Vienna), 1926. Senior Lecturer in Neurology and Psychiatry, Univ. of Vienna, 1937; Research Fellow in Psychiatry, Edinburgh, 1942; Director of Research, Graylingwell Hosp., Chichester, 1947; Reader in Psychiatry Univ. of London, 1949. Cons. Physician, The Bethlem Royal and The Maudsley Hosp., 1949; Chm. Med. Section, British Psychol. Soc., 1954, now Hon. Fellow. President: Sect. of Psychiatry, Roy. Soc. Med., 1957-58; Roy. Med.-Psychol Assoc., 1966-67; Internat. Assoc. for Suicide Prevention. *Publications:* (with N. G. Cook) Attempted Suicide: Its Social Significance and Effects, 1958; Suicide and Attempted Suicide, 1966; articles in medical and psychological journals. *Recreations:* music, travelling. *Address:* 7 Montrose Court, Hill Turrets Close, Sheffield S11 9RF. *T:* 360267.

**STENHOUSE, Sir Nicol,** Kt 1962; *b* 14 Feb. 1911; 2nd *s* of late John Stenhouse, Shanghai, China, and Tring, Hertfordshire; *m* 1951, Barbara Heath Wilson; two *s* one *d*. *Educ:* Repton. Joined Andrew Yule & Co. Ltd, Calcutta, India, 1937; Managing Director, 1953-59; Chairman and Senior Managing Director, 1959-62; Director: Lead Industries Group Ltd; S & K Holdings Ltd; President: Bengal Chamber of Commerce and Industry, Calcutta, 1961-62; Associated Chambers of Commerce of India, Calcutta, 1961-62. *Recreations:* golf, gardening. *Address:* Harvieston, Holly Bank Road, Hook Heath, Woking, Surrey. *Clubs:* Oriental; Bengal, Tollygunge (Calcutta).

**STENING, Sir George (Grafton Lees),** Kt 1968; ED; Hon. Consultant Gynæcological Surgeon, Royal Prince Alfred Hosp., Sydney; Chancellor, Order of St John, in Australia; *b* 16 Feb. 1904; *s* of George Smith Stening and Muriel Grafton Lees; *m* 1935, Kathleen Mary Packer; one *s* one *d*. *Educ:* Sydney High Sch.; Univ. of Sydney. MB, BS (Syd.) 1927 (Hons Cl. II); FRCS (Ed.) 1931; FRACS 1935; FRCOG 1947; Carnegie Trav. Fellow, 1948. Served War of 1939-45: Middle East, New Guinea, Australia; OC, 3rd Aust. Surgical Team, Libyan Desert, 1941; CO, 2/11 Aust. Gen. Hosp., 1941-44; CO, 113 Aust. Gen. Hosp., 1945. Hon. Col, RAAMC; KStJ 1951. *Publication:* A Text Book of Gynæcology (co-author), 1948. *Recreations:* golf, yachting. *Address:* 87 Victoria Road, Bellevue Hill, NSW 2023, Australia. *T:* 363227. *Clubs:* Australian, Royal Sydney Golf (Sydney).

**STENTON, Lady (Doris Mary),** FBA 1953; University Reader, retired; *b* 27 Aug. 1894; *d* of Joseph and Amelia Parsons; *m* 1919, Prof. Sir Frank M. Stenton (*d* 1967), FBA. *Educ:* Abbey Sch., Reading; Univ. Coll., Reading. 1st cl. hons History (Lond.) 1916. Lectr, Univ. Coll., Reading, 1917; Reader, Reading Univ., 1955; Raleigh Lectr, 1958. Hon. Sec. and Gen. Ed., Pipe Roll Soc., 1925-62. Hon. LLD, Glasgow; Hon. DLitt, Oxford, 1968. *Publications:* The Pipe Rolls beginning with New Series, vol. I, 1925; Cambridge Medieval History, Henry II, 1926; The Earliest Lincolnshire Assize Rolls, 1926 (Lincoln Record Soc. vol. 22); The Earliest Northamptonshire Assize Rolls, 1930; Rolls of the Justices in Eyre for Lincolnshire 1218-19 and Worcestershire 1221, Selden Soc. vol. 53; Rolls of the Justices in Eyre for Yorkshire 1218-19; Rolls of the Justices in Eyre for Gloucestershire, Warwickshire and Shropshire, Selden Soc. vols 56 and 59; (with Lewis C. Loyd) Sir Christopher Hatton's Book of Seals (presented to F. M. Stenton), 1950; English Society in the Early Middle Ages, 1951; Pleas before the King or his Justices 1198-1202 (2 vols), Selden Soc. vols 67 and 68, 1952 and 1953; The English Woman in History, 1957; King John and the Courts of Justice, Pleas before the King or his Justices, vols 3 and 4, Selden Soc. vols 83 and 84, 1967; English Justice 1066-1215; The Free Peasantry of the Northern Danelaw, 1969. *Address:* Whitley Park Farm, Reading, Berks. *T:* Reading 81585.

**STEPHEN, Sir Alexander Murray,** Kt 1946; MC; DL; JP; BA; Lord Lieutenant of Lanarkshire, 1955-59; *b* 1892; *e s* of late F. J. Stephen; *m* 1922, Kathrene Paton Mitchell; two *s* one *d*. *Educ:* Cargilfield; Fettes College; King's Coll., Cambridge (1st Class Hons Mechanical Science Tripos). Served European war, RGA, 1914-18, Major (despatches, MC); Ex-Pres.: Institution of Engineers and Shipbuilders in Scotland; Shipbuilding Employers Federation; Shipbuilding Conference; British Shipbuilding Research Assoc. JP 1955, DL 1960, Lanarkshire. LLD (Hon.) Glasgow 1957. *Recreation:* shooting. *Address:* Craigmarloch, Kilmacolm, Renfrewshire. *Club:* Western (Glasgow).

**STEPHEN, Derek Ronald James;** Under Secretary, Civil Service Department, since 1969; *b* 22 June 1922; *s* of Ronald James Stephen; *m* 1948, Gwendolen Margaret, *d* of William James Heasman; three *s* one *d*. *Educ:* Bec Sch.; Christ's Coll., Cambridge (Scholar). 1st cl. Class. Tripos, Pt I, 1941; Royal Armoured Corps, 1941-45 (Captain); 1st cl. Class. Tripos, Pt II, 1946. Entered Civil Service and joined War Office, Dec. 1946; Asst Private Sec. to Sec. of State for War, 1949-50; Principal, 1951; Private Sec. to Sec. of Cabinet, 1958-60; Asst Sec., WO (later Ministry of Defence), 1960; HM Treasury, 1968; Civil Service Dept (on its formation), 1968. *Recreations:* golf, tennis, travel. *Address:* 30 Oaken Lane, Claygate, Surrey. *T:* Esher 63383.

**STEPHEN, George,** CBE 1960; DL; Hon. LLD (Aberdeen) 1959; Lord Provost of Aberdeen, 1955-61; Lord Lieutenant of County of City of Aberdeen, 1955-61; *b* 12 Sept. 1886; *s* of George Stephen and Helen Peters; *m* 1917, Mary Annand Turner; one *d*. *Educ:* Skene Square School, and Central Secondary School, Aberdeen. Postal Service, Aberdeen, 1900-47. Served with 89th Field Ambulance RAMC in Gallipoli and France, 1914-18 (despatches).

Aberdeen Town Council, 1947-61; First Patron of Aberdeen Burns Club. Member: Executive Committee British Waterworks Association, 1948-51; Scottish Gas Consultative Council, 1952-57. DL Aberdeenshire, 1964. *Publications:* When the Nichts are comin' doon and other poems, 1955; A Breath o' the North-East–A Second Book of Verse, 1958; Poems at Eventide, 1969; hymn in Church of Scotland Hymn Book for Special Services, 1923. *Recreation:* gardening. *Address:* 25 Bonnymuir Place, Aberdeen. *T:* Aberdeen 20414.

**STEPHEN, Harbourne Mackay,** DSO 1941; DFC and bar 1940; Managing Director, Daily Telegraph and Sunday Telegraph, since 1963; *b* 18 April 1916; *s* of Thomas Milne Stephen, JP, and Kathleen Vincent Park; *m* 1947, Sybil Erica Palmer; two *d. Educ:* Shrewsbury. Staff of Allied Newspapers, London, 1931; Evening Standard, 1936-39. RAFVR, 1937; served RAF, 1939-45 (destroyed numerous enemy aircraft): 605 and 74 Sqdns, 1939-40; at MAP, 1941, then formed 130 Sqdn and comd 234 Sqdn; served Far East, 1942-45; Wing Comdr (Flying) Dum Dum; RAF Jessore, Bengal; comd 166 Fighter Wing; then to Fighter Ops, 224 Gp Arakan; Ops "A" Air Comd SEA. Was OC 602 City of Glasgow (F) Sqdn RAuxAF, 1950-52. Returned to Beaverbrook Newspapers, Oct. 1945; worked on Scottish Daily Express, Scottish Sunday Express, and Evening Citizen in Glasgow, 1945-55. General Manager, Sunday Express, 1958; General Manager, Sunday Graphic, 1960, and thereafter General Manager, Thomson Papers, London; Asst Man. Dir, Daily Telegraph and Sunday Telegraph, 1963; Dir, Internat. Newspaper Colour Assoc., Darmstadt, 1964-69. *Recreations:* normal, occasionally. *Address:* Donnington Holt, Newbury, Berks. *T:* Newbury 105. *Clubs:* Bath, Royal Automobile.

**STEPHEN, Sir James Alexander,** 4th Bt, *cr* 1891; *b* 25 Feb. 1908; *s* of Sir Harry Lushington Stephen, 3rd Bt, and Barbara (*d* 1945), *y d* of late W. Shore Nightingale of Embley, Romsey and Lea Hurst, Derbyshire; *S* father, 1945; unmarried. *Educ:* Eton; Trinity College, Cambridge. *Heir:* none. *Recreations:* lawn tennis, billiards. *Address:* The Cottage, Landor House, St Cross, Winchester, Hants. *T:* Winchester 3887.

**STEPHEN, John Low,** ChM (Aberdeen), FRCS (Edinburgh), FRCS (England); Surgeon St Mary's Hospital, W2 since 1958; Senior Surgeon, St Mary's Hospital, W9 (formerly Paddington General Hospital), since 1948; *b* 13 May 1912; 2nd *s* of late Dr J. H. Stephen, Aberdeen; *m* 1938, Mary Milne, MA, BSc; one *s* one *d. Educ:* Aberdeen Grammar School; Aberdeen and Edinburgh Universities. MA 1931, MB 1935, Aberd.; FRCSEd, 1937; ChM Aberd., 1945. Various university and hospital appointments in Scotland and England. Associate Teacher in Surgery, St Mary's Hosp. Med. School, 1950-. FRSocMed. *Publications:* chapters in Operative Surgery (Smith and Rob); various articles on abdominal surgery in Brit. Jl of Surgery. *Recreations:* golf, motoring. *Address:* 148 Harley St, W1. *T:* 01-935 1207; 6 Alleyn Park, SE21. *T:* 01-670 0547.

**STEPHEN, Maj.-Gen. Robert Alexander,** CB 1965; CBE 1958 (OBE 1954); MD, ChM; FRCS; QHS 1960-67; Director of Army Surgery and Consulting Surgeon to the Army, Royal Army Medical College, 1959-67; Consultant in Surgery, Royal Hospital, Chelsea; *b* 20 June 1907; *s* of late James Alexander Stephen, MB, ChB, DPH; *m* 1935, Audrey Vivien, *d* of late George William Royce, Cambridge; one *d. Educ:* Aberdeen Grammar School; Aberdeen University. MD 1933, ChM 1960, Aberdeen. FRCS 1947. MS Malaya, 1959. Lieut, RAMC, 1934. Served War of 1939-45, in France, Egypt, Libya, Greece, Crete, Belgium, Holland and Germany; Lt-Col 1941. Formerly Asst Prof. of Military Surgery, Royal Army Medical College, London; Consulting Surgeon, FARELF, 1956-59; Hon. Consulting Surgeon, General Hospital, Singapore, 1956; Brigadier, 1958; Major-General, 1961. Hunterian Prof., RCS, 1958. Fellow: Royal Society of Medicine; Assoc. of Surgeons of Great Britain and Ireland. OStJ. *Recreations:* golf and gardening. *Address:* Cornerways, Shortheath, Farnham, Surrey. *T:* Farnham 5814.

**STEPHENS, Air Commandant Dame Anne,** DBE 1961 (MBE 1946); Hon. ADC to the Queen, 1960-63; Director, Women's Royal Air Force, 1960-63; *b* 4 Nov. 1912; *d* of late General Sir Reginald Byng Stephens, KCB, CMG and late Lady Stephens. *Educ:* privately. Joined WAAF, 1939; served in UK, Belgium and Germany, 1939-45. Command WRAF Depot, Hawkinge, 1950-52; promoted Group Officer, 1951; Inspector WRAF, 1952-54; Deputy Director, 1954-57; Staff Officer, HQ 2nd TAF, 1957-59; promoted Air Commandant, 1960. *Address:* The Forge, Sibford Ferris, Banbury, Oxfordshire. *T:* Swalcliffe 452.

**STEPHENS, Arthur Veryan,** MA Cantab; CEng; FRAeS; Professor of Aeronautical Engineering, The Queen's University, Belfast, since 1956; *b* 9 July 1908; *s* of Arthur John Stephens and Mildred, *d* of Robert Fowler Sturge; *m* 1938, Jane Dows, *d* of F. W. Lester; three *s* one *d. Educ:* Clifton College; St John's College, Cambridge (Mechanical Sciences Tripos, John Bernard Seely Prize). Scientific Officer, Royal Aircraft Establishment, 1930-34; Fellow of St John's College, Cambridge, 1934-39; Lawrence Hargrave Professor of Aeronautics, 1939-56, Dean of the Faculty of Engineering, 1947-56, University of Sydney, NSW. Edward Busk Memorial Prize of RAeS, 1934; Member: Australian Flying Personnel Research Cttee, 1940-45; Australian Council for Aeronautics, 1941-46; Chairman, Aeronautical Research Consultative Cttee, 1947-54; Chairman, Australian Aeronautical Research Committee, 1954-56; Member Australian Defence Research and Development Policy Committee, 1953-56; Chairman, Australian Division of Royal Aeronautical Society, 1947-56. Dean of Faculty of Applied Science and Technology, 1961-64; Vice-President (Buildings), 1964-67. *Publications:* numerous papers on applied aerodynamics published by Aeronautical Research Council, Australian Dept of Supply and in Jl of RAeS. *Address:* 14 Deramore Park South, Belfast 9. *T:* 660236. *Club:* Athenæum.

**STEPHENS, Cedric John;** Director General of Research, Chief Scientist, Home Office, since 1969; *b* 13 Feb. 1921; *s* of Col J. E. Stephens, Truro, Cornwall. *Educ:* London University. Entered Scientific Civil Service, 1951; Dir, Space Activities, Min. of Aviation, 1961; Mem. Coun., European Launcher Development Organisation, Paris, 1962; Chm. Technical Cttee, European Coun. on Satellite Communications, 1964; Imperial Defence Coll., 1965; Director, Signals Research and Develt Estab, Min. of Technology, 1966-67; Chief Scientific Adviser, Home Office, 1968. *Address:* c/o Coutts & Co., Strand, WC2. *Club:* Athenæum.

**STEPHENS, Christopher Wilson T.;** *see* Stephens, Wilson T.

**STEPHENS, Sir David,** KCB 1964; CVO 1960; Clerk of the Parliaments, House of Lords, since 1963; *b* 25 April 1910; *s* of late Berkeley John Byng Stephens, CIE, and Gwendolen Elizabeth (*née* Cripps), Cirencester; *m* 1st, 1941, Mary Clemency, JP (*d* 1966), *er d* of late Colonel Sir Eric Gore Browne, DSO, OBE, TD; three *s* one *d*; 2nd, 1967, Charlotte Evelyn, *widow* of Henry Manisty, *d* of late Rev. A. M. Baird-Smith; three step *s*. *Educ:* Winchester College; Christ Church, Oxford (2nd cl. Lit. Hum.). Laming Travelling Fellow, the Queen's College, Oxford, 1932-34; Clerk in the Parliament Office, House of Lords, 1935-38; Member Runciman Mission to Czechoslovakia, 1938; Transf. HM Treasury, 1938; Political Warfare Executive, 1941-43; Prin. Priv. Sec. to the Lord Pres. of the Council (Mr Herbert Morrison), 1947-49; Asst Sec., HM Treasury, 1949; Secretary for Appointments to two Prime Ministers (Sir Anthony Eden and Mr Harold Macmillan), 1955-61; Reading Clerk and Clerk of the Journals, House of Lords, 1961-63. *Recreations:* gardening, cricket and outdoor sports. *Address:* 19 Bedford Gdns, W8. *T:* 01-727 5265; The Old Rectory, Coates, near Cirencester, Glos. *T:* Kemble 258. *Clubs:* Brooks's, MCC.

**STEPHENS, Sir Edgar;** *see* Stephens, Sir L. E.

**STEPHENS, Frederick James;** Managing Director, The "Shell" Transport and Trading Co. Ltd, since 1957 (Director since 1951; Chairman, 1961-67); Chairman, The Shell Petroleum Co. Ltd, since 1961 (Managing Director, 1951-61); Managing Director, Shell International Petroleum Co. Ltd, 1959-61; Director, Bataafse Petroleum Maatschappij NV (Principal Director, 1956-61, Delegate Member of Board from 1951); *b* 30 July 1903; *er s* of late Canon John Frederick Douglas Stephens and Frances Mary (*née* Mirrlees); *m* 1948, Sara Clark (*d* 1954), Dallas, Texas; no *c*. *Educ:* Marlborough Coll.; Grenoble Univ., France; Pembroke Coll., Cambridge. BA 1926, MA 1956, Cambridge. Joined Royal Dutch Shell Group of Companies, 1926, and served in Venezuela, London and US; Director and Exec. Vice-Pres. of Asiatic Petroleum Corp., New York, 1946; returned to London, 1948. Hon. Fellow, University Coll., London, 1958; Visiting Fellow Nuffield Coll., Oxford, 1961; Member of Court, University of Reading, 1962. Comdr, Order of Orange-Nassau, 1968. *Recreations:* gardening, golf, photography. *Address:* Crossacres, Pyrford Woods, Woking, Surrey. *T:* Byfleet 43525. *Clubs:* Junior Carlton; New Zealand Golf (Byfleet).

**STEPHENS, Mrs George Arbour;** *see* Williams, Mary.

**STEPHENS, Engineer Rear-Admiral George Leslie,** CB 1946; CBE 1943; Royal Canadian Navy, retired; *b* 2 Jan. 1889; *s* of George Selleck and Ernestine Stephens; *m* 1913, Edna Louise Woodill; one *s* two *d*. *Educ:* Plympton Public School, Plympton; Stoke Public School, Devonport. Naval Engineering training, HM Dockyard, Devonport, England, 1903-10; joined Royal Canadian Navy as Engine-room Artificer, 1910. Warrant Rank, 1912; Engineer Lieut 1915; Engineer Comdr 1929; Engineer Capt. 1940; Engineer-in-Chief, Naval Service HQ, Ottawa, 1941; Engineer Rear-Adm. 1943. *Recreations:* curling and golf. *Address:* Apt. 301 The Croydon, 201 McLeod Street, Ottawa 4, Ontario, Canada. *Club:* Royal Ottawa Golf (Ottawa).

**STEPHENS, Ian Melville,** CIE 1935; MA Cantab; *b* 1903; *e s* of J. A. Melville Stephens, Fleet, Hants; unmarried; hon. adopted son, Dr Arthur Kwok Cheung Li. *Educ:* Winchester; King's Coll., Cambridge (foundn scholar, R. J. Smith research student); 1st class hons, Natural Sciences Tripos, Pt I, 1924, and Historical Tripos, Pt II, 1925. Business appts, 1927-30; Deputy Dir, Bureau of Public Information, Govt of India, 1930-32; wrote the M & MP Reports for 1929-30 and 1930-31; was Indian corresp., The Round Table; Publicity Officer, Indian Franchise (Lothian) Cttee, 1932; Dir, Bureau of Public Information, 1932-37; Asst Editor, The Statesman newspaper, Calcutta and Delhi, 1937; also on the Board, 1939; Editor, 1942-51 (also aeronautical corresp., and a staff photographer). War Corresp., SEAC and SHAEF, 1943-45. Member: Standing Cttee, All-India Newspaper Editors' Conf., 1942-51; Indian Delegn to Commonwealth Press Conf., Canada, 1950; Brit. Group, Inst. of Pacific Relations Conf., Lucknow, 1950. Retired from India, 1951. Fellow, King's Coll., Cambridge, 1952-58; also Mem. Council, and Hon. Treasurer Appeals Cttee, New Hall, Cambridge. Chm., Mount Vernon (Ceylon) Tea Co., 1953-57. Historian, Pakistan Govt, GHQ, Rawalpindi, 1957-60. Has travelled in South Asia, Australia, NZ, Canada, USA. *Publications:* Horned Moon, illus. with own photographs, 1953 (3rd edn 1966); Pakistan, 1963 (paperback edn 1964, 3rd edn 1967); Monsoon Morning, 1966; (ed) Sir R. Reid's Years of Change, 1966; The Pakistanis, 1968; A Curiosity, 1970; contribs to Chambers's Encyclopaedia (1966 edn); articles, lectures, broadcasts, reviews. *Address:* c/o The Manager, Lloyds Bank, 6 Pall Mall, SW1. *Club:* Oriental.

**STEPHENS, Maj.-Gen. Keith Fielding,** CB 1970; OBE 1957; *b* Taplow, Bucks, 28 July 1910; *s* of late Edgar Percy and Mary Louise Stephens; *m* 1937, Margaret Ann, *d* of late Alexander MacGregor; two *s*. *Educ:* Eastbourne College; St Bartholomew's Hospital. MB, BS London 1934; FFARCS 1953; DA 1945. Commissioned into RAMC, 1937; served in India, 1937-43; France and Germany, 1944-46; Cyprus, 1954-56; Adviser in Anæsthetics to the Army, 1949-53 and 1957-66; Commandant and Director of Studies, Royal Army Medical College, 1966-68; DDMS, Southern Command, 1968-70, retired. Pres., Sect. of Anæsthetics, Roy. Soc. Med., 1970-71 (Hon. Sec., 1963-65); Member, Assoc. of Anæsthetists of Gt Brit. and Ireland. Fellow: Royal Soc. of Tropical Medicine and Hygiene; Med. Soc. of London. Hon. FFARCS (Ireland), 1970; QHS, 1964-70. Mitchiner Medal, 1962. CStJ 1967. *Publications:* numerous articles in medical journals. *Address:* 3 Carnegie Place, Parkside, Wimbledon, SW19. *Club:* United Service.

**STEPHENS, Sir (Leon) Edgar,** Kt 1960; CBE 1945; formerly Clerk of the Peace and of County Council of Warwickshire, Clerk to the Lieutenancy, Registration Officer, Acting Returning Officer (1927-67); *b* 7 Jan. 1901; *s* of late W. Edgar Stephens, OBE, FSA, The Greylands, Gorleston; *m* 1st, 1928, Joan Beeching (*d* 1946), *yr d* of late Edwin H. Johnson, JP, Flixton House, Nr Lowestoft; three *d*; 2nd, 1947, Joan, 2nd *d* of late Captain J. G. Miles, Gorleston, Suffolk. *Educ:* Felsted; Trinity Hall, Cambridge (MA, LLB). Barrister, Middle Temple, 1924; County Controller for Civil Def., Warwicks, 1939-45, 1964-67; Clerk of War Zone Court, Midland Region, 1939-45. Hon. Sec., Soc. of Clerks of the Peace of Counties and of Clerks of County Councils, 1947-53, Chairman, 1953-56; Hon. Treas. 1956-67; Mem. Master of the Rolls Archives Cttee, 1946-56; Mem. Historical Manuscripts Commn, 1959-; Chm. Centenary (1969) Committee; FSA, 1943; DL

Warwickshire, 1950; JP 1967. *Publications:* contrib. to Macmillan's Local Government Law and Administration; The Warwickshire County Book, 1933, 1939 and 1959 Editions; The Clerks of the Counties, 1360-1960. *Recreations:* golf, gardening and reading; coxed Cambridge University Boat 1921 and 1922. *Address:* Flixton House, Rowington, Warwick. *T:* Lapworth 2019. *Clubs:* United University; Leander; Stratford-on-Avon Golf; Tennis Court (Leamington).

**STEPHENS, Peter Scott,** CMG 1962; *b* 25 Nov. 1910; *s* of Major John August Stephens, TD, and Elsie Evelyn Stephens (*née* Watson). *Educ:* Sherborne School; Oriel Coll., Oxford. HM Consular Service, 1933; served New York and Manila; transferred to Foreign Office, 1941; Leopoldville and Elizabethville, Belgian Congo, 1942-45; in charge of Consular Section, British Embassy, Brussels, 1945-47; transf. to Foreign Office, 1947; First Secretary, Washington, 1949; First Secretary and First Secretary (Commercial), British Embassy, Havana, 1951-54; acted as Chargé d'Affaires, there, in 1951, 1952, 1953 and 1954; Counsellor (Commercial) British Embassy, Caracas, April 1955-Nov. 1958; acted as Chargé d'Affaires, there, in 1955, 1956, 1957 and 1958; Commercial Counsellor, Madrid, 1959-62; HM Consul-General, Milan, 1962-68. *Address:* The Garden House, Thornhill, Stalbridge, Dorset. *T:* Stalbridge 366. *Club:* Travellers'.

**STEPHENS, Major Robert,** CVO 1964; ERD; Private Secretary to Governor of Northern Ireland since 1955; *b* 1909; *s* of late John Samuel Stephens; *m* 1939, Kathleen, *d* of late R. I. Trelford, Helen's Bay, Belfast. *Educ:* Campbell Coll., Belfast. Ulster Bank, 1929-39. Served War of 1939-45: RA, Middle East, 1941-45. Commercial Manager, Newforge Ltd, 1946-55; Comptroller to: Lord Wakehurst, 1955-64; Lord Erskine of Rerrick, 1964-68; Lord Grey of Naunton, 1968-. *Recreation:* golf. *Address:* Government House, Hillsborough, Co. Down, Northern Ireland. *T:* Hillsborough 244.

**STEPHENS, William Henry,** CB 1961; MSc, CEng, FRAeS; Minister, Defence Research and Development, British Embassy, Washington, since 1969; *b* Kilkenny, Ireland, 18 March 1913; *s* of William Henry Stephens, MBE, and Helena Read Stephens (*née* Cantley); *m* 1938, Elizabeth Margaret Brown, BSc; one *s* one *d*. *Educ:* Methodist College and Queen's University, Belfast. Air Ministry, Royal Aircraft Establishment (Aerodynamic Research), 1935-38; War Office, Woolwich (Rocket Research), 1938-39; Ministry of Aircraft Prod., London (Air Defence Research), 1939-44; Asst Scientific Attaché and Asst Director, UK Scientific Mission, British Commonwealth Scientific Office, Washington, USA, 1944-47; Min. of Supply, RAE, Head of Guided Weapons Dept and later Dep. Director, 1947-58; Dir-Gen. Ballistic Missiles, Ministry of Aviation, 1959-62; Technical Dir, European Space Launcher Develt Organisation, Paris, 1962-69. *Publications:* contrib. to Jl Royal Aeronautical Soc.; Proc. Brit. Assoc.; Proc. Internat. Congress of Aeronautical Sciences. *Recreations:* travel, music, art, theatre. *Address:* British Embassy, 3100 Massachusetts Avenue, NW, Washington, DC 20008, USA. *Clubs:* Athenæum; Cosmos (Washington).

**STEPHENS, Wilson (Treeve);** Editor of The Field since 1950; *b* 2 June 1912; *s* of Rev. Arthur Treeve Stephens, Shepton Beauchamp, Somerset, and Margaret Wilson; *m* 1st, 1934, Nina, *d* of Arthur Frederick Curzon, Derby; two *d*; 2nd, 1960, Marygold Anne, *o d* of Major-General G. O. Crawford, *qv*; two *d*. *Educ:* Christ's Hosp. Formerly on editorial staffs of several provincial newspapers, and of The Star and Daily Express. Served War of 1939-45, Royal Artillery; special operations, Far East and Italy, 1944-46. *Publications:* is a contributor to numerous journals. *Recreation:* fly-fishing. *Address:* c/o 8 Stratton Street, W1. *T:* 01-499 7881. *Club:* Kennel.

**STEPHENS SPINKS, Rev. Dr G.;** *see* Spinks.

**STEPHENSON, Basil Ernest,** CBE 1963; *b* 11 Dec. 1901; *o s* of late Basil Stephenson; *m* 1927, Edna (*née* Broderick); one *s*. *Educ:* Woking Co. Sch. Gen. engineering, 1918-27; aircraft engineering at Vickers, Weybridge, 1927; appointed Asst Chief Designer, 1945; Chief Designer, 1953; Chief Engineer, 1957; appointed a Director, Vickers-Armstrongs (Aircraft) Ltd, 1957; Dir of Engineering, 1959; Director of Engineering, British Aircraft Corporation, Weybridge Division, 1963-64. FRAeS 1953. British Gold Medal for Aeronautics, 1960. *Address:* Cedar Ridge, St John's Hill Road, Woking, Surrey. *T:* Woking 2307.

**STEPHENSON, Donald,** CBE 1957 (OBE 1943); Controller, Overseas and Foreign Relations, BBC; *b* 18 May 1909; *yr s* of J. V. G. Stephenson; *m* 1940, Alison (*d* 1965), *yr d* of late Wynn ap H. Thomas, OBE, LLB, and of Mrs Wynn Thomas; one *s* three *d*. *Educ:* Denstone College (Scholar); Paris; Baghdad. Banking business, 1925-31; permanent commission. RAF, 1932; Flt Lt, 1936; served France and Middle East, 1935-37; language specialist (interpreter, French and Arabic); Special Duty List, 1938; Arabic Editor, BBC, 1939; Director, BBC, New Delhi, 1944-45; Director, Eastern Services, 1946-47; Asst Controller in Overseas Div., 1948; Controller, North Region, 1948-56; Controller, Overseas Services, BBC, 1956-58; Chief Executive, Anglia Television Ltd, 1959; Head of Overseas and Foreign Relations, BBC, Dec. 1960. A Governor of Manchester Univ., 1950-58. A delegate to 5th Commonwealth Broadcasting Conf., Canada, 1963, to 7th Conf., NZ, 1968, and 8th Conf., Jamaica, 1970. *Recreation:* family life. *Address:* Trevereux Manor, Oxted, Surrey. *T:* Limpsfield Chart 3151; Broadcasting House, W1. *T:* 01-580 4468. *Club:* Athenæum.

**STEPHENSON, Ven. Edgar,** MM 1918; TD 1950; Archdeacon Emeritus of Rochdale, since 1962, Archdeacon, 1951-62; Director of Religious Education in Diocese of Manchester, 1955-62; *b* 24 Sept. 1894; *y s* of late T. J. Stephenson, Tamworth, Staffs; *m* 1926, Kathleen, *d* of late William Taws, Macclesfield, Cheshire; no *c*. *Educ:* Manchester University. BA 1922; BD 1925; MA 1929. CF(TA), 1933-50. Vicar of St Mary's, Oldham, 1947-55. *Recreations:* reading, walking, gardening. *Address:* Gwelfryn, Francis Avenue, Rhos-on-Sea, Denbighshire. *T:* Colwyn Bay 48793.

**STEPHENSON, Colonel Eric Lechmere,** DSO 1940; MC and two bars; *b* 18 April 1892; *s* of late Dr O. T. and Jane Marriott Stephenson; *m* 1934, Helen Joyce Marples; one *s*. *Educ:* King Alfred's School, Wantage. Regular Commission in Army, 1912; retired pay, 1946. *Recreations:* cricket and polo. *Address:* 2 Comptons Lea, Comptons Lane, Horsham, Sussex. *Club:* Army and Navy.

**STEPHENSON, Lieut-Col Sir Francis;** *see* Stephenson, Lt-Col Sir (Henry) F. (B).

**STEPHENSON, Vice-Admiral Sir Gilbert Owen,** KBE, *cr* 1943; CB 1930; CMG 1919; retired; Hon. Commodore Sea Cadet Corps, 1949-58; *b* 1878; *s* of R. M. Stephenson; *m* 1903, Helen Chesney (*d* 1954), *d* of late Col Robert Frederic Williamson, CB; two *s* one *d*. Served European War, commanded Otranto Mobile Barrage Force, 1914-19 (CMG, Order of St Maurice and St Lazarus, of Crown of Italy, of Redeemer of Greece, Distinguished Service Medal, USA, Valore Militare (silver), Italy); Chief of Staff, Portsmouth, 1924; commanded Royal Naval Barracks, Portsmouth, 1926-28; Rear-Adm. and retired list, 1929; Vice-Adm., retired, 1934; General Sec. of the Navy League, 1932-35; returned to Active Service, Sept. 1939. Commanded HMS Western Isles, at Tobermory, 1940-45 (despatches). Commander, with Star, of the Royal Order of St Olaf (Norway), 1948; Officer, Legion of Honour, 1948. *Address:* 27 Gold Street, Saffron Walden, Essex. *Club:* United Service.

**STEPHENSON, Prof. Gordon,** CBE 1967; FRIBA, MTPI, FRAIA, FAPI, FILA; Consultant Architect, University of Western Australia, 1960-69, and Dean, School of Architecture; Member, National Capital Planning Committee, Canberra; *b* 6 June 1908; *s* of Francis E. and Eva E. Stephenson, Liverpool; *m* 1938, Flora Bartlett Crockett, Boston, USA; three *d*. *Educ:* Liverpool Institute; University of Liverpool; University of Paris; Massachusetts Institute of Technology. Elmes Scholar, Univ. of Liverpool, 1925-30; Holt Scholar, 1928; First Cl. Hons in Architecture, 1930; Chadwick Scholar at Brit. Inst. in Paris and Univ. of Paris, 1930-32; BArch; MCP(MIT). Lecturer and Studio Instructor in Architecture, University of Liverpool, 1932-36; Commonwealth Fellow and Medallist, Massachusetts Inst. of Technology, 1936-38; Studio Master, Architectural Assoc., School of Architecture, 1939-40; Lever Professor of Civic Design, School of Architecture, University of Liverpool, 1948-53; Professor of Town and Regional Planning in the University of Toronto, Canada, 1955-60. Architectural and Planning practice: asst to Corbett, Harrison and McMurray, NY City, 1929; asst to Le Corbusier and Pierre Jeanneret, Paris, 1930-32; Div. Architect, with W. G. Holford, on Royal Ordnance Factory work, 1940-42; Research Officer, Sen. Research Officer, and Chief Planning Officer, Min. of Works and Planning, and Min. of Town and Country Planning, 1942-47; seconded to assist Sir Patrick Abercrombie on Greater London Plan, 1943-44; in private practice, houses, militia camp, university bldgs, community centre, housing schemes, town and regional planning studies. Editor, Town Planning Review, 1949-54. Hon. MTPIC 1960. *Publications:* (with Flora Stephenson) Community Centres, 1941; (with F. R. S. Yorke) Planning for Reconstruction, 1944; (with J. A. Hepburn) Plan for the Metropolitan Region of Perth and Fremantle, 1955; a Redevelopment Study of Halifax, Nova Scotia, 1957; (with G. G. Muirhead) A Planning Study of Kingston, Ontario, 1959. Articles and papers in British and Foreign Technical Professional Jls. *Recreations:* architectural practice, drawing and travel. *Address:* The University of Western Australia, Nedlands, WA 6005, Australia. *Club:* Weld (Perth).

**STEPHENSON, Lt-Col Sir (Henry) Francis (Blake),** 2nd Bt, *cr* 1936; OBE 1941; DL Derbyshire, 1948; TD; *b* 3 Dec. 1895; *e s* of late Lieut-Colonel Sir Henry Kenyon Stephenson, DSO, and Frances, *e d* of late Major W. G. Blake, DL, JP; *S* father, 1947; *m* 1925, Joan, *d* of Maj. John Herbert Upton (formerly Upton Cottrell-Dormer), JP; one *s*. *Educ:* Eton. Lt Col (QO) Yorks Dragoons; served European War, 1914-18, BEF, 1915-18 (1914-15 Star, two medals); War of 1939-45. Middle East, 1939-42 (OBE); JP City of Sheffield; High Sheriff of Derbyshire, 1948-49. Hon. LLD, Sheffield, 1955. *Heir:* *s* Henry Upton Stephenson [*b* 26 Nov. 1926; *m* 1962, Susan, *o d* of Major J. E. Clowes, Ashbourne, Derbyshire, and of Mrs Kingscote; three *d*]. *Address:* Hassop Hall, Bakewell, Derbyshire. *T:* Great Longstone 210.

**STEPHENSON, Henry Shepherd,** MIMinE; HM Chief Inspector of Mines and Quarries, 1962-70; Chairman, Mining Qualifications Board, since 1970; *b* 11 Oct. 1905; *m* 1934, Faith Estelle, 3rd *d* of Tom Edward Arnold, Bolton Old Hall, Bradford; two *d*. *Educ:* Whitehaven Grammar School; Armstrong College, Durham University (BSc). Articled apprentice Mining Engineer, Whitehaven Colliery Co., 1924-28; official posts, Whitehaven Colliery Co., 1928-35; HM Junior Inspector of Mines Northern Div., 1935-39; Mining Agent, Cumberland Coal Co., 1939-41; HM Junior Inspector of Mines (Yorkshire), 1941-44; Senior Inspector (Scotland), 1944-47; Senior Dist Inspector (Durham), 1948-52; Senior Dist Inspector (West Midland), 1952-58; Divisional Inspector (East Midland), 1958-62; Deputy Chief Inspector, Jan. 1962. *Recreations:* gardening, golf. *Address:* 51 Mospey Crescent, Burgh Heath Road, Epsom, Surrey.

**STEPHENSON, Sir Hugh (Southern),** GBE 1966 (OBE 1944); KCMG 1956 (CMG 1954); CIE 1947; CVO 1957; *b* 29 Nov. 1906; *s* of late Sir Hugh Stephenson, GCIE, KCSI; *m* 1936, Patricia Elizabeth, *d* of late Maj.-Gen. Sir Arthur Mills, CB, DSO; three *s*. *Educ:* Winchester Coll.; Christ Church, Oxford. 1st cl. hons, Jurisprudence. Barrister-at-Law (Inner Temple). Entered Indian Civil Service, 1931; Under-Secretary to Govt of India, 1935-38; Secretary to Governor of United Provinces, 1940-44; Collector and Dist Magistrate, Cawnpore, 1944-47. HM Foreign Service since 1947; Dep. High Comr, Lahore, 1947-49; IDC 1951; Counsellor, British Middle East Office, Faiyid, 1952-54; HM Ambassador to Viet Nam, 1954-57; Consul-General in New York, 1957-60; Deputy Under-Secretary of State, Foreign Office, 1960-63; Ambassador to South Africa, 1963-66 (High Comr of Basutoland, the Bechuanaland Protectorate and Swaziland until the abolition of this office in August 1964). (First) Chancellor of the University of Basutoland, Bechuanaland Protectorate and Swaziland, 1964-66. Retired from the Foreign Service, Nov. 1966. A Director, Ernest Benn Ltd. Dir-Gen., St John Ambulance Brigade; KStJ 1970. *Address:* 2 Sloane Terrace Mansions, SW1. *Club:* Oriental.

**STEPHENSON, Hon. Sir John (Frederick Eustace),** Kt 1962; **Hon. Mr Justice John Stephenson;** Judge of Queen's Bench Division, High Court of Justice, since 1962; *b* 28 March 1910; 2nd *s* of late Sir Guy Stephenson, CB, and of late Gwendolen, *d* of Rt Hon. J. G. Talbot; *m* 1951, Frances Rose, *yr d* of late Lord Asquith of Bishopstone, PC; two *s* two *d*. *Educ:* Winchester College (Schol.); New Coll., Oxford (Schol.). 1st Cl. Hon. Mods. 1930, 1st Cl. Litt Hum. 1932, BA 1932, MA 1956. Called to Bar, Inner Temple (Entrance Scholarship), 1934. Sapper RE (TA), 1938; War Office, 1940; Intelligence Corps, Captain 1943, Major 1944 and Lieut-Col 1946; Middle East and NW Europe; Regional Intelligence Officer, Hamburg, 1946; Recorder of Bridgwater, 1954-59; Recorder of Winchester, 1959-62;

Chancellor of the Diocese: of Peterborough, 1956-62; of Winchester, 1958-62; QC 1960; Deputy Chairman, Dorset Quarter Sessions, 1962. *Publication:* A Royal Correspondence, 1938. *Address:* Royal Courts of Justice, Strand, WC2; 30 Drayton Gardens, SW10. *T:* 01-373 8289. *Clubs:* Boodles', MCC.

**STEPHENSON, Air Vice-Marshal John Noel Tracy,** CB 1956; CBE 1954; Retired; Member Directing Staff, Administrative Staff College, since 1960, Director of Studies, 1968-69; *b* Nov. 1907; *m* 1959, Jill Sheila Fitzgerald, *d* of William Fitzgerald Hervey. *Educ:* Whitgift; RAF College. Served War of 1939-45: in UK and in Burma and on loan to Australian Defence Ministry. Berlin Airlift, 1948. Comdt, RAF Staff Coll., 1949-52; Dir of Organisation (Air Ministry), 1952-54; Sen. Air Staff Officer, Middle East Air Forces, 1954-57; Suez Operations, 1957 (despatches); Asst Chief of Air Staff, 1957-59. Officer, American Legion of Merit. *Address:* 10 St Andrews Road, Henley-on-Thames, Oxon. *Club:* Royal Air Force.

**STEPHENSON, Prof. Patrick Hay,** MA, CEng, FIMechE; Director of Institute of Advanced Machine Tool and Control Technology, Ministry of Technology and University of Strathclyde, since 1967; Director, Joint Services Unit Ltd; *b* 31 March 1916; *e s* of late Stanley George Stephenson; *m* 1947, Pauline Coupland; two *s* one *d*. *Educ:* Wyggeston Sch., Leicester; Cambridge Univ. (MA). Apprenticeship and Research Engr, Brit. United Shoe Machinery Co., 1932-39. War Service as Ordnance Mechanical Engr and REME, India and Far East, 1939-45. Chief Mechanical Engr, Pye Ltd, 1949-67. Mem. Council, IMechE, 1960-68; Mem. Bd, UKAC, 1964-. *Publications:* papers and articles in technical press. *Recreations:* music, vintage motoring. *Address:* 69 East Kilbride Road, Busby, Glasgow. *T:* 041-644 1043. *Club:* St Stephen's.

**STEPHENSON, Philip Robert,** CMG 1962; OBE 1951; *b* 29 May 1914; *s* of Robert Barnard Stephenson and Lilian Stephenson (*née* Sharp); *m* 1947, Marianne Hurst Wraith; two *s*. *Educ:* Berkhamsted School; Imperial College, London; Downing College, Cambridge; Imperial College of Tropical Agriculture, Trinidad. Colonial Agricultural Service, Entomologist, Uganda, 1938. Military Service, 1940-43. East African Anti-Locust Directorate, 1943-47, Director, Desert Locust Survey, 1948-62, HM Overseas Service. Member, British Advisory Mission on Tropical Agriculture in Bolivia, Dept of Technical Co-operation, 1963-64. *Address:* c/o Lloyds Bank, Berkhamsted, Herts. *Club:* MCC.

**STEPHENSON, Thomas,** CBE 1943; retired as Clerk of the Peace, Clerk of the County Council, Clerk of Lieutenancy, for the East Riding of Yorks. (1940-61); *b* 17 Oct. 1889; *e s* of G. A. Stephenson, Beverley; *m* 1917, Madge, *d* of A. P. Bannister, Branley, Yorks. *Address:* Flat 1, The Expanse, Bridlington, Yorks. *T:* Bridlington 2015.

**STEPHENSON, Sir William Samuel,** Kt 1945; MC; DFC; *b* 11 Jan. 1896; *s* of Victor Stephenson, Canada; *m* 1924, Mary French, *d* of William Simmons, of Tennessee. *Educ:* Canada. Served European War, Capt. RFC, 1914-18. Formerly: Director of British Security Co-ordination in the Western Hemisphere, 1940-46; Chairman Caribbean Development Corporation. Croix de Guerre avec Palmes, 1918; French Légion d'Honneur; US Medal for Merit. *Relevant publications:* (biography by H. M. Hyde) The Quiet Canadian, 1962 (as Room 3603, in USA); Heroes of the Sunlit Sky, by Arch Whitehouse, USA, 1968; Canadians at War, vol. II, 1969. *Address:* Camden House, Camden North, Paget, Bermuda. *TA:* Intrepid, Bermuda. *Clubs:* Junior Carlton; Royal Aero; Royal Yacht (Bermuda).

**STEPNEY, Suffragan Bishop of,** since 1968; **Rt. Rev. Trevor Huddleston,** DD; *b* 15 June 1913; *s* of late Capt. Sir Ernest Huddleston, CIE, CBE; unmarried. *Educ:* Lancing; Christ Church, Oxford; Wells Theological College. 2nd class Hon. Mod. Hist., Oxford, 1934 (BA), MA 1937. Deacon, 1936; Priest, 1937. Joined Community of the Resurrection; Professed, 1941. Apptd Priest-in-charge Sophiatown and Orlando Anglican Missions, diocese Johannesburg, Nov. 1943; Provincial in S Africa, CR, 1949-55; Guardian of Novices, CR, Mirfield, 1956-58; Prior of the London House, Community of the Resurrection, 1958-60; Bishop of Masasi, 1960-68. A Vice-Pres., Anti-Apartheid Movement, 1969-. Hon. DD (Aberdeen Univ.), 1956. *Publications:* Naught for Your Comfort, 1956; The True and Living God, 1964; God's World, 1966. *Recreation:* fishing. *Address:* 400 Commercial Road, E1. *T:* 01-790 4382.

**STERLING, Thomas Smith,** MBE; MA Cantab; *b* 13 April 1883; *e s* of late John and Mrs Sarah J. Sterling. *Educ:* Downing Coll., Cambridge (Mediaeval and Modern Languages Tripos); Geneva. First Charles Oldham Shakespeare Scholar in University of Cambridge; Pres., Mermaid Literary Club (Undergraduate), Cambridge; Lectr, in English, University College, Southampton; Indian Educational Service, Professor of English Language and Literature, Presidency College, Calcutta, 1909-27; Principal, Presidency College, 1926; Fellow of University of Calcutta, 1914-27; Adviser, Students' Information Bureau, Calcutta, 1923-27; during European War, 1914-18, raised and for a time commanded the first OTC in India, the Calcutta Univ. Training Corps; retired, 1928; Asst Secretary and Secretary, Universities Bureau of the British Empire, London, 1927-29; Professor of English Literature and for some time Dean of the Faculty of Arts, Egyptian University, Cairo, 1929-33; tours in America, Australia and New Zealand in connection with Empire Migration, 1934-37; held a post as a principal in Information Department of India Office, April 1940-Sept. 1941; Secretary, School of Oriental and African Studies, Univ. of London, Sept. 1941-Oct. 1945. *Publications:* text-books for students. *Recreations:* travelling, tennis, walking. *TA:* c/o Ejus London. *T:* 01-930 1000. *Clubs:* East India and Sports, Authors' (Life Mem.; Chm., 1948-51).

**STERN,** family name of **Baron Michelham.**

**STERN, Gladys Bertha;** author; *b* London, 17 June 1890; 2nd *d* of Albert and Elizabeth Stern; *m* 1919, Geoffrey Lisle Holdsworth. *Educ:* Notting Hill High School. Travelled in Europe; trained at the Academy of Dramatic Art for nearly two years; wrote first novel in her twentieth year–having written plays since the age of eight; has done free-lance journalism and reviewing, and published many short stories; also worked for Studios in Hollywood and Denham. *Publications:* Pantomime, 1914; See-Saw, Twos and Threes, Grand Chain, A Marrying Man, Children of No Man's Land, Larry Munro, The Room; Smoke Rings; The Back Seat, 1923; Tents of Israel, 1924; Thunderstorm, 1925; A Deputy was King, 1926; The Dark Gentleman; Bouquet; Jack a'Manory; Debonair, 1938; Petruchio, 1929;

Mosaic, 1930; The Shortest Night, 1932; Long-lost Father, 1932; Little Red Horses, 1932; The Augs, 1933; Shining and Free, 1935; Monogram, 1936; Oleander River, 1937; The Ugly Dachshund, 1938; The Woman in the Hall, 1939; A Lion in the Garden, 1940; Another Part of the Forest, 1941; The Young Matriarch, 1942; Talking of Jane Austen (with Sheila Kaye-Smith), 1943; Trumpet Voluntary, 1944; The Reasonable Shores, 1946; No Son of Mine, 1948; Benefits Forgot, 1949; A Duck to Water, 1949; More Talk of Jane Austen (with Sheila Kaye-Smith), 1950; Ten Days of Christmas, 1950; The Donkey Shoe, 1952; A Name to Conjure With, 1953; Johnny Forsaken, 1954; All in Good Time, 1954; For All We Know, 1955; The Way It Worked Out, 1956; Seventy Times Seven, 1957; The Patience of a Saint, 1958; And Did He Stop and Speak to You?, 1958; Unless I Marry, 1959; Bernadette, 1960; Dolphin Cottage, 1962; Promise Not to Tell, 1964; *plays:* The Matriarch, 1929; (with Frank Vosper) Debonair, 1930; The Man Who Pays the Piper, St Martin's Theatre, 1931. *Address:* c/o A. D. Peters, 10 Buckingham Street, Adelphi, WC2. *T:* Blewbury 256.

**STERN, Isaac;** violinist; *b* Kreminiecz, Russia, 21 July 1920; *s* of Solomon and Clara Stern; *m* 1948, Nora Kaye; *m* 1951, Vera Lindenblit; three *c.* Studied San Francisco Conservatory, 1930-37. First public concert as guest artist San Francisco Symphony Orchestra, 1931; played with Los Angeles Philharmonic Orchestra and in concerts in Pacific Coast cities; New York debut, 1937. Has since played in concerts throughout USA, in Europe, Israel, Australia, South America, Japan, India, The Philippines, Soviet Union and Iceland; has played with major American and European orchestras. Took part in Prades Festivals, 1950-52; Edinburgh and other major festivals in Europe and US. President, Carnegie Hall, NY. *Address:* c/o Hurok Attractions, 730 Fifth Avenue, New York City, NY 10022, USA.

**STERNBERG, Sir Rudy,** Kt 1970; Chairman, Sterling Group of Companies; Chairman, British Agricultural Export Council, since 1968; *b* 17 April 1917; *s* of George Sternberg, Germany, and Paula (*née* Michel); *m* 1951, Dorothée Monica, *d* of Major Robert Bateman Prust, OBE, Vancouver; two *d. Educ:* in Germany. Freeman, City of London, 1960; Liveryman, Worshipful Company: of Farmers, 1963; of Horners, 1960. *Recreations:* farming, yachting. *Address:* 79b Elizabeth Street, SW1; Plurenden Manor, High Halden, Kent; Skiathos, Greece. *Club:* City Livery.

**STEVAS, Norman Antony Francis St J.;** *see* St John-Stevas.

**STEVEN, Guy Savile,** MBE 1945; Chairman of Allied Ironfounders Ltd since 1960; *b* 24 Nov. 1906; *s* of John Hugh Steven and Ernestine May Shepherd; *m* 1937, Marion Grace Mackenzie-Kennedy; one *s. Educ:* Preparatory School; Marlborough College. Joined McDowall, Steven & Co., Ltd, Ironfounders, Falkirk, April 1925; this company became a member of Allied Ironfounders Ltd on the Group's formation, 1929. Director, Allied Ironfounders, 1947; Dep. Man. Dir, 1954; Man. Dir, 1956-67. Served War of 1939-45 (despatches): RASC in Middle East, Italy and North West Europe (Lieut-Col). *Recreations:* shooting and tennis. *Address:* Pickhurst, Chiddingfold, Surrey. *T:* Wormley 2919. *Club:* Hurlingham.

**STEVENS, Air Marshal Sir Alick (Charles),** KBE, *cr* 1952; CB 1944; retired; *b* 31 July 1898; *s* of late Charles Edward Russell Stevens, Jersey; *m* 1927, Beryl, *d* of B. J. Gates, Wing, Bucks; one *s. Educ:* Victoria College, Jersey. Joined RNAS 1916; transferred to RAF on formation, 1918; Wing Comdr, 1937; Air Commodore, 1942. Dep. Director, 1940-42, and then Director of Operations (Naval Co-operation) at Air Ministry, 1942-43; SASO, No 18 Group, 1943-44 (despatches); AOC, RAF, Gibraltar, 1944-45; AOC No 47 Group, 1945; AOC No 4 Group, Transport Command, 1946; Air Vice-Marshal, 1947; AOC No 22 Group, Technical Training Comd, 1946-48; AOC British Forces, Aden, 1948-50; SASO, Coastal Comd, 1950-51; AOC-in-C, Coastal Comd, 1951-53; Air C-in-C, Eastern Atlantic Area, Atlantic Comd, 1952-53; Allied Maritime Air C-in-C Channel and Southern North Sea, Channel Comd, 1952-53; retd Dec. 1953; Vice-Chairman, Gloucestershire T&AFA, 1955-63. *Address:* Cherry Tree Cottage, Cadmore End, nr High Wycombe, Bucks. *T:* Lane End 569. *Club:* Royal Air Force.

**STEVENS, Hon. Sir Bertram Sydney Barnsdale,** KCMG, *cr* 1941; Consulting Accountant, Sydney; *b* 2 Jan. 1889; *m* 1914 (wife *d.* 1966); one *s* two *d. Educ:* Fort Street High School, Sydney. Inspector of Public Service Board; Under Secretary and Director of Finance, NSW; MLA for Croydon, New South Wales, 1927-40; Assistant Treasurer, 1927-29; Treasurer and Minister for Railways, 1929-30; Deputy Leader of Opposition, 1930-32, Leader, 1932, Premier and Treasurer, 1932-39. Australian Representative, Empire Eastern Group Supply Council, New Delhi, 1941-42. *Publications:* Planning for War and Peace; The Next Year in the Pacific; New Horizon—a study of Indo-Australian relationships. *Address:* 19 Julia Street, Ashfield, NSW 2131, Australia.

**STEVENS, Denis William;** Professor of Music, Columbia University, New York, since 1964; *b* 2 March 1922; *s* of William J. Stevens and Edith Driver; *m* 1949, Sheila Elizabeth Holloway; two *s* one *d. Educ:* Jesus College, Oxford. Served War of 1939-45, RAF Intelligence, India and Burma, 1942-46. Producer, BBC Music Div., 1949-54; Assoc. Founder and Conductor, Ambrosian Singers, 1952; Vis. Professor of Musicology, Cornell Univ., 1955, Columbia Univ., 1956; Secretary, Plainsong and Mediaeval Music Soc., 1958; Editor, Grove's Dictionary of Music and Musicians, 1959-63. Professor, Royal Acad. of Music, 1960. Artistic Dir, Accademia Monteverdiana, 1961; Vis. Prof. Univ. of California (Berkeley), 1962; Distinguished Visiting Professor, Pennsylvania State University, 1962-63. Lectures on music, especially British, in England, France, Germany, Italy, USA. FSA; Member Worshipful Company of Musicians. Hon. RAM, 1960. Hon.D, Humane Letters, Fairfield Univ., Connecticut, 1967. *Publications:* The Mulliner Book, 1952; Thomas Tomkins, 1957, rev. edn 1966; A History of Song, 1960; Tudor Church Music, 1966; A Treasury of English Church Music (I), 1965; many edns of early music, including Monteverdi Vespers and Orfeo; articles in English and foreign journals; also many LP and Stereo recordings. *Recreations:* travel, photography. *Address:* 41 Blenheim Park Road, Croydon, Surrey. *Club:* Garrick.

**STEVENS, E. S.;** *see* Drower, Lady.

**STEVENS, Frank Leonard;** formerly Editor, FBI Review and Publicity Officer, Federation of British Industries; *b* Mexborough, 8 Jan. 1898; *s* of late Frederick Thomas Stevens; *m* 1925, Winifred, 2nd *d* of Alexander Bruce, JP; two *s. Educ:* Mexborough Grammar School;

University College, London. After a year as teacher, three years in the Army (1916-19), entered journalism, South Yorkshire Times, Allied Newspapers, Manchester; Manchester Evening News; assistant editor, John O' London's Weekly; Daily News sub-editorial staff; associate editor, Everyman; joint editor, monthly Clarion. *Publications:* Under London, 1939; On Going to Press, 1928; Through Merrie England, 1926. *Recreations:* reading and sketching. *Address:* Barn Cottage, Singleton, Chichester, Sussex. *T:* Singleton 653.

**STEVENS, Geoffrey Paul;** Chartered Accountant, 1926; *b* 10 Nov. 1902; *yr s* of late Alfred Stevens and Maria Ennriquetta Stevens, both of London. *Educ:* Westminster School. Partner with Pannell Fitzpatrick & Co., 1930-70. Contested (C) Park Division of Sheffield, general election, 1945; MP (C) Portsmouth, Langstone, 1950-64. *Recreation:* gardening. *Address:* Littlewick Place, Littlewick Green, near Maidenhead, Berks. *T:* Littlewick Green 2813. *Clubs:* Royal Thames Yacht, United and Cecil.

**STEVENS, George (Cooper);** American film director and producer; *b* Oakland, California, 1905; *s* of Landers Stevens, actor, and Georgia (*née* Cooper), actress. *Educ:* Sonoma High School, California. Cameraman, Hollywood, 1921; Director, 1930. Served War, 1943-45; Major, Lt-Col; Head of special film unit, US Army Signal Corps, assigned to 6th Army; served in Africa, Middle East, Europe. President, Screen Directors' Guild, 1946; Member of Board, 1950. Films include: Alice Adams, Vivacious Lady, Gunga Din, Penny Serenade, Woman of the Year, The Talk of the Town, The More the Merrier, I Remember Mama, A Place in the Sun, Shane, Giant, The Diary of Anne Frank, The Greatest Story Ever Told; The Only Game in Town. Has received high awards for films. *Address:* c/o Desilu Studio, 9336 W Washington Boulevard, Culver City, California, USA.

**STEVENS, Hon. Henry Herbert,** LLD; broker and accountant; Chairman of Board, C. Gardiner-Johnson Co. Ltd, Vancouver Shipping Agents; *b* Bristol, England, 8 Dec. 1878; *s* of Richard Harvey and Jane Anne Stevens, Cornwall; *m* 1905, Gertrude M., *d* of George Glover, Vancouver, BC, formerly of Grimsby; two *s* two *d*. *Educ:* Bristol; Peterboro, Ontario; British Columbia. Came to Canada, 1887; Alderman City Vancouver, 1910-11; Chairman of the Greater Vancouver Sewage Scheme, also Chairman of Greater Vancouver Annexation Committee; MP Vancouver, Centre, BC, 1911-30; MP East Kootenay, 1930-40; Minister of Customs and Excise in Meighen Government, 1926; Minister of Trade and Commerce, Canada, 1921, and 1930-34; Chairman of Royal Commission on Price Spreads, 1934. resigned portfolio in Government and Chairmanship of Commission, 1934. Leader of Reconstruction Party, Canada, 1935-38; realigned himself with Conservative Party, 1938; candidate (C), Vancouver Centre, Gen. Elec., 1949. Member and President of Citizens Rehabilitation Council, Vancouver, 1941-49; President of Vancouver, BC, Board of Trade, 1952. Has travelled extensively, Europe, China, Japan, and South Sea Islands; Pres. of British and Foreign Bible Soc. (BC Auxiliary), 1948-. United Church of Canada. *Address:* 1676 Pine Crescent, Vancouver 9, BC. *Clubs:* Canadian, Vancouver (Mem. for over 50 years), Kiwanis (Vancouver); Rideau (Ottawa).

**STEVENS, Herbert Lawrence,** CBE 1952 (OBE 1936); Consulting Engineer with Messrs Sandberg, 40 Grosvenor Gardens, SW1, since 1954; *b* 26 April 1892; *s* of Thomas Waghorn Stevens and Louisa Cecillia (*née* Davis); *m* 1st, 1917, Beryl Marjorie Gentry (*d* 1949); one *s* two *d* (and one *s* killed in action); 2nd, 1950, Amelia Beatrice Paice. *Educ:* Bradfield College, Berks; Downing College, Cambridge. Schriner Schol., Downing Coll., 1911; 2nd Cl. hons, Part I Maths Trip., 1912; 2nd Cl. hons, Mech. Sci. Trip., 1914; BA Cantab, 1914. Joined Royal Aircraft Estabt, Farnborough, 1914 (became head of full-scale flying sect.); Chief Tech. Officer, Aeroplane and Armament Exper. Estab., RAF Martlesham Heath, 1927; Head of Structures Dept, RAE, 1931; Supt of Scientific Research. RAE, 1937; Dep. Dir, Brit. Air Commn, Washington, 1940; Dep. Dir, RAE, 1941; Prin. Dir Equipment Research and Develt (Air), Min. of Supply, 1950; retd from Govt service, 1953. Fellow Roy. Aeronautical Soc.; MIMechE. *Publications:* various papers to Aeronautical Research Council. *Recreations:* photography and gardening. *Address:* Kariba, Copse Avenue, Weybourne, Farnham, Surrey.

**STEVENS, Jocelyn Edward Greville;** Managing Director, Evening Standard Co. Ltd, since 1969; *b* 14 Feb. 1932; *s* of Major C. G. B. Stewart-Stevens and of Mrs Greville Stevens; *m* 1956, Jane Armyne Sheffield; two *s* one *d*. *Educ:* Eton; Cambridge. Military service in Rifle Bde, 1950-52; Journalist, Hulton Press Ltd, 1955-56; Chairman and Managing Dir, Stevens Press Ltd, and Editor of Queen Magazine, 1957-68; Personal Asst to Chairman of Beaverbrook Newspapers, May-Dec. 1968. *Recreation:* shooting. *Address:* 48 Chelsea Park Gardens, SW3. *T:* 01-352 6276; Testbourne, Longparish, near Andover, Hants. *T:* Longparish 232. *Clubs:* Buck's, Beefsteak; Lyford Cay (Bahamas).

**STEVENS, Vice-Adm. Sir John (Felgate),** KBE, *cr* 1955 (CBE 1945); CB 1951; *b* 1 June 1900; *o surv. s* of late Henry Marshall Stevens, Droveway Corner, Hove; *m* 1928, Mary, *o d* of J. Harry Gilkes, JP, Wychcote, Patcham, Sussex; one *s* two *d*. Midshipman, 1918; King's Coll., Cambridge, 1922, specialised in Navigation, 1924; Staff College, 1930; Commander, 1933; Captain, 1940. Served War of 1939-45 (despatches, CBE); Director of Plans, Admiralty, 1946-47; commanded HMS Implacable, 1948-49; Rear-Admiral, 1949; Director of Naval Training, 1949-50; Chief of Staff to Head of British Joint Services Mission. Washington, 1950-52; Flag Officer, Home Fleet Training Squadron, 1952-53; Commander-in-Chief, America and West Indies Station, and Deputy Supreme Allied Commander, Atlantic, 1953-55; retired list, 1956. *Recreations:* sailing and golf. *Address:* Ashurst, Fernhurst, Sussex. *T:* Fernhurst 352. *Club:* United Service.

**STEVENS, Sir John (Melior),** KCMG 1967; DSO, 1945; OBE 1944; TD 1950; a Managing Director, Morgan Grenfell & Co. Ltd, since 1967; Director: Suez Finance Company, since 1967; Bank of England, since 1968; Investment Trust Corp., since 1968; Metropolitan Trust Co., since 1968; British Bank of Middle East, since 1968; Merchants Trust Ltd, since 1969; British Petroleum Ltd, since 1969; *b* 7 Nov. 1913; *s* of late Courtenay Stevens and Melior Frances Barker; *m* 1940, Frances Anne, *d* of late Christopher Douglas Hely Hutchinson, MC; one *s* two *d*. *Educ:* Winchester. Admitted a Solicitor, 1937. Served War of 1939-45, with HM Forces in France, Middle East, Greece and Italy (despatches thrice, DSO, OBE); demobilised with rank of hon. Col. Entered service of Bank of England as an Adviser, 1946; Director of European Department of

International Monetary Fund, Washington, DC, 1954-56; Executive Director, Bank of England, 1957-64; Head of Treasury Delegation and Economic Minister in Washington, 1965-67; UK Exec. Dir, IMF and IBRD, 1965-67. Chm., E European Trade Council, 1970-; Member: Council of Foreign Bondholders, 1957-64; BBC General Advisory Council, 1963-64; High Sheriff of County of London, 1964. Fellow, University Coll., London, 1968-. *Recreations:* fishing and shooting. *Address:* 62 Bedford Gardens, W8. *T:* 01-727 6206; East Worlington House, Crediton, Devon. *T:* Witheridge 332. *Clubs:* Carlton, Beefsteak, MCC.

**STEVENS, Kenneth Henry;** Chief Executive Commissioner, The Scout Association, since 1970; *b* 8 Oct. 1922; *s* of Horace J. Stevens, CBE, sometime Senior Principal Inspector of Taxes, and Nora Stevens (*née* Kauntze); *m* 1947, Yvonne Grace Ruth (*née* Mitchell); one *s* one *d. Educ:* Brighton Coll.; Brighton Technical Coll. South Coast Civil Defence, 1941-44. Alliance Assurance Co., 1944-47; Asst Dir of Adult Leader Training, Internat. Scout Training Centre, Gilwell Park, Chingford, 1947-56; Organising Comr, World Scout Jamboree, Indaba and Rover Moot, Sutton Coldfield, 1956-58; Dep. Dir of Adult Leader Training, Internat. Scout Training Centre, 1958-61; Asst Chief Exec. Comr, The Scout Assoc., 1961-63; Dep. Chief Exec. Comr, 1963-70. *Publication:* Ceremonies of The Scout Movement, 1958. *Recreations:* motoring, cricket, gardening. *Address:* 37 Pine Hill, Epsom, Surrey. *T:* Epsom 25031. *Club:* MCC.

**STEVENS, Professor Kenneth William Harry;** Professor of Theoretical Physics, University of Nottingham since 1958; *b* 17 Sept. 1922; *s* of Harry and Rose Stevens; *m* 1949, Audrey A. Gawthrop; one *s* one *d. Educ:* Magdalen College School, Oxford; Jesus and Merton Colleges, Oxford. MA 1947, DPhil 1949. Pressed Steel Company Ltd Research Fellow, Oxford University, 1949-53; Research Fellow, Harvard University, 1953-54; Reader in Theoretical Physics, University of Nottingham 1953-58. (Jointly) Maxwell Medal and Prize, 1968. *Publications:* contrib. to learned journals. *Recreations:* music, tennis, squash. *Address:* The University, Nottingham.

**STEVENS, Philip Theodore;** Professor of Greek in the University of London (Bedford College) since 1950; *b* 11 Nov. 1906; *s* of late Rev. Herbert Stevens, Vicar of Milwich; *m* 1939, Evelyn Grace, 2nd *d* of late G. L. Crickmay, FRIBA, Oatlands Park, Weybridge, Surrey; one *s. Educ:* Wolverhampton Grammar School; New Coll., Oxford (Scholar). 1st Cl. Hon. Mods, 1927; 2nd Cl. Lit. Hum., 1929; Asst Master, Liverpool Institute, 1929-30; Tutor at Univ. Corresp. Coll., Cambridge, 1930-32; Asst Lecturer in Greek, Univ. of Aberdeen, 1933-38; PhD Aberdeen 1939. Lectr in Classics, Univ. of Cape Town, 1938-41. War Service, S African Mil. Intelligence, 1941-45. Lecturer in Latin and Greek, University of Liverpool, 1945-50. *Publications:* Euripides, Andromache, 1971; contribs to English and foreign classical periodicals. *Recreations:* music, tennis. *Address:* Department of Greek, Bedford College, Regent's Park, NW1. *T:* 01-486 4400. *Club:* Reform.

**STEVENS, Sir Roger Bentham,** GCMG 1964 (KCMG 1954; CMG 1947); retired as Vice-Chancellor, Leeds University, 1963-70; Director, British Bank of the Middle East, since 1964; Chairman, Yorkshire and Humberside Economic Planning Council, 1965-70; *b* 8 June 1906; *s* of F. Bentham Stevens, JP, and Cordelia Wheeler; *m* 1931, Constance Hallam Hipwell; one *s. Educ:* Wellington; Queen's Coll., Oxford; Hon. Fellow 1966. Entered Consular Service, 1928; served in Buenos Aires, New York, Antwerp, Denver and FO; Secretary of British Civil Secretariat, Washington, 1944-46; Foreign Office, 1946-48; Assistant Under-Secretary of State, Foreign Office, 1948-51; British Ambassador to Sweden, 1951-54; British Ambassador to Persia, 1954-58. Adviser to First Secretary of State on Central Africa, 1962; Deputy Under-Secretary of State, Foreign Office, 1958-63. *Publication:* The Land of the Great Sophy, 1962. *Recreations:* aquatic, equestrian, pedestrian. *Address:* Hill Farm, Thursley, Surrey; Parsons Close, Giggleswick, W Riding. *Club:* Travellers'.

**STEVENS, Hon. Dr Siaka (Probyn);** Prime Minister of Sierra Leone since 1968 (sworn in 1967; re-appointed 1968, after Army interventions); *b* 24 Aug. 1905; *m* 1940, Rebecca Stevens; seven *s* five *d. Educ:* Albert Academy, Freetown; Ruskin Coll., Oxford. Joined Sierra Leone Police Force, 1923, and became 1st Cl. Sergt and Musketry Instr; worked for Sierra Leone Development Co., and became first Gen. Sec. of United Mine Workers Union (co-founder), 1931-46. Member: Moyamba Dist Council; Freetown City Council (rep. Protectorate Assembly); several Govt Cttees, 1946-48; Sec., Sierra Leone TUC, 1948-50; MLC (elec. by Assembly), 1951, and became first Minister of Lands, Mines and Labour; Dep. Leader of (the now dissolved) Peoples' National Party, 1958-60; formed Election before Independence Movement (which later became the All Peoples' Congress), 1960; became Leader of the Opposition, All Peoples' Congress, 1962; apptd Mayor of Freetown, 1964. Hon. DCL Univ. of Sierra Leone, 1969. *Recreation:* walking. *Address:* Prime Minister's Office, Tower Hill, Freetown, Sierra Leone. *T:* 2757.

**STEVENS, Lt-Col Thomas Harry Goldsworthy,** OBE 1919; *b* 27 Jan. 1883; *s* of late Marshall Stevens, MP, promoter of Manchester Ship Canal and Trafford Park Estates Ltd. *Educ:* King William's College; Royal Indian Engineering College, Coopers Hill. Public Works Dept, Burma, 1903-21; Lt-Col Indian Army Reserve of Officers (retd); Active Service RE's, Mesopotamia (OBE, despatches thrice); Master of Worshipful Company of Glaziers, 1939; *Publications:* Trees and Shrubs in My Garden, 1939; Manchester of Yesterday, 1959. *Recreation:* gardening. *Address:* Dingle Bank, Bowdon, Cheshire. *T:* Altrincham 1441.

**STEVENS, Professor Thomas Stevens,** FRS 1963; FRSE 1964; Emeritus Professor of Chemistry, University of Sheffield; *b* 8 Oct. 1900; *o c* of John Stevens and Jane E. Stevens (*née* Irving); *m* 1949, Janet Wilson Forsyth; no *c. Educ:* Paisley Grammar School; Glasgow Academy; Universities of Glasgow and Oxford. DPhil 1925. Assistant in Chemistry, Univ. of Glasgow, 1921-23, Lecturer, 1925-47; Ramsay Memorial Fellow, Oxford, 1923-25; Sen. Lectr in Organic Chemistry, Univ. of Sheffield, 1947-49, Reader, 1949-63, Prof., 1963-66; Visiting Prof. of Chemistry, Univ. of Strathclyde, Oct. 1966-Sept. 1967. *Publications:* contrib. to Elsevier-Rodd, Chemistry of Carbon Compounds, 1957-60. Papers in scientific jls. *Recreation:* unsophisticated bridge. *Address:* 313 Albert Drive, Glasgow, S1.

**STEVENS, Thomas Terry Hoar;** *see* Terry-Thomas.

**STEVENS, Thomas Wilson,** CBE 1962; RD 1942; Commodore, Royal Mail Line Fleet, 1961-63, retired; *b* 16 Oct. 1901; *s* of John Wilson Stevens and Susan Eliza Smith; *m* 1939, Mary Doreen Whitington; one *s* one *d*. *Educ:* Sir Walter St John's, Battersea. Joined Royal Mail Steam Packet Co. as a Cadet, 1917; joined Royal Naval Reserve as Sub-Lieut 1927. Active service, Royal Navy, 1939-47. Younger Brother of Trinity House, 1944. Captain Royal Mail Lines, 1947; Captain Royal Naval Reserve, 1950. *Recreation:* golf. *Address:* 79 Offington Lane, Worthing, Sussex. *T:* Swandean 1100.

**STEVENS, William Charles,** FCA; *b* 20 Jan. 1900; *s* of late Joseph William Stevens, Woodford, Essex, and late Alice Mary Eagland; *m* 1923, Ida Grace Bullivant; two *s*. With Deloitte, Plender, Griffiths & Co., Chartered Accountants, 1915-29; qualified as Incorporated Accountant, 1927; Fellow, 1947; The Exchange Telegraph Co. Ltd: Secretary, 1929-49; Director, 1946; General Manager, 1949; Chairman, 1954-61. Served War, 1918-19, in HAC. *Recreations:* golf, cricket. *Address:* Clinton Brier, 38 Roslin Road South, Bournemouth, Hants.

**STEVENS, Maj.-Gen. William George,** CB 1944; CBE 1941; *b* London, 11 Dec. 1893; *m* 1916, Gladys Barker (*d* 1967); three *s*. *Educ:* Auckland Grammar Sch.; Royal Military Coll., Australia, 1912-14; served European War, 1915-19; various positions NZ Military Forces, 1920-37; Staff Coll., 1926-27; Imperial Defence Coll., 1928; Prime Minister's Dept, New Zealand, 1937-39 (Sec. of Organisation for National Security); Officer in Charge administration, Second New Zealand Expeditionary Force in Mediterranean, 1940-45; GOC NZEF, 1945-46; Official Secretary to High Commissioner for New Zealand, London, 1946-53; retd 1953. *Publications:* Problems of 2 NZEF; Bardia to Enfidaville; Freyberg, the Man. *Address:* 159a Queen Street, Richmond, Nelson, New Zealand.

**STEVENS, William George,** CB 1943; late Principal Assistant Secretary, Ministry of Aircraft Production (retired 1943); *b* 11 Aug. 1883; *e s* of William Henry and Elizabeth Stevens, Cambridge; *m* 1926, Edith Constance Stevens (*d* 1962), *d* of late W. J. Stevens Tout, Winkleigh, Devon; one *s*. *Educ:* Perse Sch.; St Catharine's College, Cambridge. Various appointments in War Office, National Insurance Audit Dept, Air Board, Air Ministry, and Ministry of Aircraft Production. *Address:* Corner House, Raleigh Drive, Claygate, Esher. *T:* Esher 63974. *Club:* Oxford and Cambridge University.

**STEVENS, William Oswald,** CMG 1949; Ceylon Civil Service (retired); *b* 27 Feb. 1891; *s* of late George William Stevens; *m* 1st, 1916, Joyce Garrett; two *d* (one *s* killed in action, 1940); 2nd, 1945, Gertrude Mary Langford. *Educ:* Dulwich Coll.; Trinity Coll. Oxford. Entered Ceylon Civil Service, 1914; retired 1949. *Address:* Sussex Barn, Brockhill Rd, Hythe, Kent. *T:* 67159.

**STEVENSON, Alan;** *see* Stevenson, D(avid) Alan.

**STEVENSON, Dr Alan Carruth;** Director, Population Genetics Research Unit, Medical Research Council, Oxford, since 1958; *b* 27 Jan. 1909; *s* of Allan Stevenson, CBE, and Christina Kennedy Lawson; *m* 1937, Annie Gordon Sheila Steven; two *s* one *d*. *Educ:* Glasgow Academy; Glasgow University. BSc 1930, MB, ChB 1933, MD 1946, Glasgow; MRCP 1935; FRCP 1955. Appointments: Royal Infirmary, Glasgow; Highgate Hospital, London; London Hospital. Served RAMC 1939-45 (despatches); retired with hon. rank of Lieutenant-Colonel, 1946-48. Professor of Social and Preventive Medicine, The Queen's University, Belfast, 1948-58. Reader in Public Health, London University. *Publications:* Recent Advances in Social Medicine, 1948; Build your own Enlarger, 1943. Articles on Tropical and Preventive Medicine and human genetics in appropriate scientific journals. *Recreation:* fishing. *Address:* Newlands Street, Eynsham, Oxon. *T:* Eynsham 298.

**STEVENSON, Alan Leslie;** Metropolitan Magistrate since Oct. 1951; *b* 1 Apr. 1901; *yr s* of late James Stevenson, London and Calcutta. *Educ:* Bradfield College; Christ Church, Oxford (BA). Called to the Bar, Inner Temple, 1926; South Eastern Circuit, Kent and London Sessions. Part time Ministry of Food, London Divisional Food Office, Licensing (Revocations) Officer, 1942-49; Chairman Milk Marketing Board Disciplinary Committee, 1950-51. *Recreations:* golf and tennis. *Address:* 48 Lincoln House, Basil Street, SW3. *T:* 01-589 9026. *Clubs:* Bath; Royal St George's Golf (Sandwich); Royal Cinque Ports Golf (Deal).

**STEVENSON, Hon. Sir (Aubrey) Melford (Steed),** Kt 1957; **Hon. Mr Justice Melford Stevenson;** Justice of the High Court since 1957 (Queen's Bench Division since 1961; Probate, Divorce and Admiralty Division, 1957-61); Presiding Judge, South-Eastern Circuit, since 1970; *b* 17 October 1902; *o s* of late Rev. J. G. Stevenson; one *d* (by 1st marriage); *m* 2nd, Rosalind Monica, *d* of late Orlando H. Wagner; one *s* one *d*. *Educ:* Dulwich Coll. LLB (London). Called to Bar, Inner Temple, 1925; Major and Dep. Judge Advocate, 1940-45; KC 1943; Bencher, 1950. Recorder of Rye, 1944-51, of City of Cambridge, 1952-57; Dep. Chairman, West Kent Quarter Sessions, 1949-55; mem. Inter-Departmental Committee on Human Artificial Insemination, 1958-60. *Recreation:* golf. *Address:* Royal Courts of Justice, WC2; 94 Old Church Street, SW3. *T:* 01-352 6230; Truncheons, Winchelsea, Sussex. *T:* Winchelsea 223. *Club:* Garrick.

**STEVENSON, D(avid) Alan,** BSc (Edinburgh); FRSE; FICE; technical historian; *b* Edinburgh, 7 Feb. 1891; *s* of Charles A. Stevenson; *m* 1923, J. L. M. MacLellan; one *s* two *d*. *Educ:* Edinburgh Academy and privately. In 1912 joined family business of civil engineering and was engaged principally with lighthouses, harbours and rivers, until retiring in 1952 to study technical history. In 1914-18 carried out lighthouse work round Scottish Coast and Eastern Mediterranean and served as Captain, RME. In 1925-26 surveyed lighthouses from Siam to Aden for a report to Govt of India; has lectured on lighthouses in Canada and USA. Member Queen's Body Guard for Scotland, Royal Company of Archers. *Publications:* Lighthouse Tours of Robert Stevenson, 1946; Triangular Stamps of Cape of Good Hope, 1950 (Crawford medal, internat. award for research of Roy. Philatelic Soc.); The World's Lighthouses before 1820, 1959; and technical papers. *Recreations:* skating, golf, philately, study of Scottish sea-charts and exploring Portugal. *Address:* 22 Glencairn Crescent, Edinburgh EH12 5BT. *T:* 031-337 2832. *Clubs:* Athenæum; New (Edinburgh), Hon. Company of Edinburgh Golfers.

**STEVENSON, D. E.;** Author; Novels, Children's Verse, Lectures and Belles-lettres; *b* 1892; *d* of D. A. Stevenson, CE, Edinburgh; *cousin* of Robert Louis Stevenson; *m* 1916,

Major J. R. Peploe, Highland LI (*d* 1969); two *s* one *d*. *Educ:* home. *Publications:* Miss Buncle's Book, 1934; Miss Buncle Married; Mrs Tim of the Regiment; Miss Bun the Baker's Daughter; The English Air, 1941; Spring Magic, 1942; Celia's House; Listening Valley; The Two Mrs Abbotts; The Four Graces, 1944; Rosabelle Shaw; Green Money; Rochester's Wife; The Empty World; Smouldering Fire; Divorced from Reality; Mrs Tim Carries On; Mrs Tim Gets a Job; Kate Hardy, 1947; Young Mrs Savage, 1948; Vittoria Cottage, 1949; Music in the Hills, 1950; Winter, and Rough Weather, 1951; Mrs Tim Flies Home, 1952; Five Windows, 1953; Charlotte Fairlie, 1954; Amberwell, 1955; Summerhills, 1956; The Tall Stranger, 1957; Anna and Her Daughters, 1958; Still Glides the Stream, 1959; The Musgraves, 1960; Bel Lamington, 1961; Fletchers End, 1962; The Blue Sapphire, 1963; Katherine Wentworth, 1964; Katherine's Marriage, 1965; The House on the Cliff, 1966; Sarah Morris Remembers, 1967; Sarah's Cottage, 1968; The English Air, 1968; Crooked Adam, 1969; Gerald and Elizabeth, 1969; The House of the Deer, 1970; also various publications in America. Works translated into Dutch, Danish, German and Spanish. Collection of papers, MSS, letters etc in Meml Lib., Boston Univ., Mass. *Address:* North Park, Moffat, Dumfriesshire. *TA:* Moffat. *T:* Moffat 44.

**STEVENSON, Dr Derek Paul,** MRCS, LRCP; Secretary, British Medical Association, since Nov. 1958; *b* 11 July 1911; *s* of late Frederick Stevenson and Maud Coucher; *m* 1941, Pamela Mary, *d* of late Col C. N. Jervelund, OBE; two *s* one *d*. *Educ:* Epsom College; Guy's Hospital. Lieut RAMC, 1935; Capt. RAMC 1936; Maj. 1942; Lt-Col 1943; service in China and Malaya. Asst Director-General Army Medical Service, War Office, 1942-46; Sec. Army Medical Advisory Bd 1943-46. War Office rep. on Central Med., War Cttee, 1943-46. Asst Sec., BMA 1946-48; Dep. Sec. BMA 1948-58. Sec. Jt Consultants Cttee, 1958-. Vice-Pres. British Medical Students Assoc.; Hon. Sec./Treas. British Commonwealth Med. Conf.; Delegate, Gen. Assembly World Medical Assoc., Sydney, 1968, Paris, 1969, Chm. Council, 1969 (Mem. Council, 1967-). Medical Sec. to Nat. Ophthalmic Treatment Board Assoc.; Mem. Council of London Hospital Service Plan; Mem. Cttee of Management, Medical Insurance Agency. Hon. Sec. and Treas., British Commonwealth Medical Assoc., 1964. Liaison Officer, MoD, 1964. Mem. Bd of Governors, Epsom College. Fellow, Royal Commonwealth Soc., 1968. Hon. LLD, Manchester, 1964. *Publications:* contrib. Irish Medical Jl; BMA Lecture delivered to Irish Medical Assoc.; contrib. Canadian Med. Assoc. Jl, and address at Centennial meeting, Montreal. *Recreations:* golf, sailing, gardening. *Address:* Greenway, Linkside West, Hindhead, Surrey. *T:* Hindhead 667; BMA House, Tavistock Square, WC1. *T:* 01-387 4499. *Clubs:* Athenæum, Royal Commonwealth Society; Hindhead Golf.

**STEVENSON, Dame Hilda (Mabel),** DBE 1967 (CBE 1963; OBE 1960); Vice-President, Royal Children's Hospital, Melbourne, Victoria, Australia, 1938; *b* 1895; *d* of H. V. McKay, CBE, Sunshine, Vic; *m* 1st, Cleveland Kidd (*d* 1925); one *d*; 2nd, Col G. I. Stevenson (*d* 1958), CMG, DSO, VD. *Educ:* Presbyterian Ladies' College. *Address:* 17 St George's Road, Toorak, Victoria, Australia. *T:* 24-4628. *Clubs:* International Sportsmen's; Sunningdale Golf; Alexandra (Melbourne).

**STEVENSON, Sir Hubert Craddock,** KCMG 1942 (CMG 1938); Kt 1941; OBE 1934; MC; *b* January 1888; 2nd *s* of late Henry Thomas Stevenson; unmarried. *Educ:* Harrow. Served European War with RFA, 1915-19; appointed to Nigerian Administrative Service, 1920; Resident, 1934; Chief Commissioner Ashanti, 1936; Governor and C-in-C, Sierra Leone, 1941-47. *Recreations:* shooting, fishing. *Address:* Vorder, Bishopsteignton, S Devon. *Clubs:* Athenæum, Travellers'.

**STEVENSON, James Arthur Radford;** formerly craftsman in wrought ironwork and writer and lecturer on this subject; *m* 1st, 1954, Enid Bannister (*d* 1969); 2nd, 1970, Feodora Joanna Winifred Eaton. *Educ:* Harrow; Trinity College, Cambridge. Short Service Commission, RAF, 1922; Commn RAFVR, 1940-43. Air Ministry "A" Licence 777; fitter in aircraft factory; free-lance journalist; reporter on London daily newspaper. Became interested in wrought ironwork, and founded the Devon Smithy, 1926, which has specialised in decorative ironwork. *Publications:* Crafty Smiths; The Din of a Smithy; Sonnets; More Sonnets. *Recreations:* reading, fishing, swimming. *Address:* Windmill Farm, Kelvedon, Essex.

**STEVENSON, Air Vice-Marshal Leigh Forbes,** CB 1944; Director of various Canadian companies; *b* 24 May 1895; *s* of John Henry Stevenson and Mary Ann Irving; *m* 1926, Lillian Myrtle Comber; two *d*. *Educ:* Richibucto Grammar School, Richibucto, NB, Canada. Canadian Expeditionary Force, 1914-17; Commissioned, 1916; RFC 1917-18; RAF 1918-19; RCAF 1920-45. Air Vice-Marshal, 1942; Graduate Royal Naval Staff College, Greenwich, 1930; AOC, RCAF Overseas, 1940-41; retired, Oct. 1945. MLA of BC, 1946-53. US Commander of Legion of Merit, 1945. *Recreations:* shooting, fishing. *Address:* 1163 Balfour Avenue, Vancouver, BC, Canada. *Club:* Vancouver (BC).

**STEVENSON, Sir Matthew,** KCB 1966 (CB 1961); CMG 1953; Permanent Secretary, Ministry of Housing and Local Government, 1966-70; *b* 1910; *s* of James Stevenson; *m* 1937, Mary Sturrock Campbell White. Under-Secretary, HM Treasury, Oct. 1955-61; Permanent Secretary, Ministry of Power, 1965-66 (Deputy Secretary, 1961-65). *Address:* c/o Ministry of Housing and Local Government, Whitehall, SW1; Arden, Towncourt Crescent, Petts Wood, Kent. *T:* Orpington 22626. *Club:* Travellers'.

**STEVENSON, Hon. Sir Melford;** *see* Stevenson, Hon. Sir A. M. S.

**STEVENSON, Sir Ralph Clarmont Skrine,** GCMG 1949 (KCMG 1946; CMG 1938); JP; *b* 16 May 1895; *s* of late Surg.-Gen. H. W. Stevenson, CSI; *m* 1st, 1921, Helen Barbara Izabel (marriage dissolved 1944), *d* of Jonkheer R. J. R. Boreel; one *s*; 2nd, 1946, Marjorie Josephine Wernham Bentley, (formerly wife of 8th Viscount Portman) *d* of late G. B. Gerrard, Montreal, Canada. *Educ:* Wellington College, Berks; University College, Oxford. Served European War, Rifle Brigade; 2nd Lt 1914; Lt 1915; Captain, 1917; Third Secretary in HM Diplomatic Service and Foreign Office, 1919; Second Secretary, 1921; First Secretary, 1928; Acting Counsellor, 1937; Counsellor, 1938; Minister, 1941; served in Foreign Office and HM Missions at Copenhagen, Berlin, Sofia, The Hague, Cairo and Barcelona; Chargé d'Affaires with local rank of Minister Plenipotentiary, at Barcelona, Oct. 1938; mission terminated Feb. 1939; Principal Private Secretary to Secretary of State for Foreign Affairs, 1939-41; Minister at Montevideo, 1941-43; Ambassador to

Yugoslavia, 1943-46; Ambassador to China, 1946-50; Ambassador to Egypt, 1950-55; retired, 1955. Mem., Legislative Council, IOM, 1955-70; Mem., Exec. Council, 1962-69. Chairman: Palace Group of Companies; Prospect Holdings Ltd; Captain of the Parish of Arbory, IOM. *Address:* Balladoole, near Castletown, Isle of Man. *T:* Castletown 2550. *Clubs:* St James', Curzon House.

**STEVENSON, Robert,** MA; Writer and Motion Picture Director, Walt Disney Productions Inc., California; *b* 1905; *s* of late Hugh Hunter Stevenson, Buxton; *m* Ursula Henderson, MB, BS (London). *Educ:* Shrewsbury School; St John's College, Cambridge (Scholar), 1st Class Mechanical Sciences Tripos and John Bernard Seely Prize for Aeronautics, 1926; Editor of Granta 1927; President of Cambridge Union Society, and research in psychology, 1928. Entered motion picture industry 1929. Motion Picture Producer for US War Dept, 1942, Capt, 1943-46; Maj. US Army Res., 1946-53. Films directed include Tudor Rose (in America, Nine Days a Queen), King Solomon's Mines, Owd Bob (in America, To the Victor), The Ware Case, Young Man's Fancy, Tom Brown's Schooldays, Back Street, Joan of Paris, Jane Eyre, To the Ends of the Earth, Walk Softly Stranger, The Las Vegas Story, Old Yeller, Darby O'Gill and the Little People, Kidnapped, The Absent-minded Professor, The Castaways, Son of Flubber, Mary Poppins, That Darn Cat, The Gnome-Mobile, Blackbeard's Ghost, The Love Bug. Has also written and directed very many television films. Film stories which he has written include Tudor Rose and Young Man's Fancy. *Publication:* Darkness in the Land, 1938. *Address:* c/o Walt Disney Productions, 500 South Buena Vista Street, Burbank, Calif 91503, USA.

**STEVENSON, Robert Barron Kerr,** MA; FSA; Keeper, National Museum of Antiquities of Scotland, since 1946; *b* 16 July 1913; *s* of late Professor William B. Stevenson; *m* 1950, Elizabeth M. Begg; twin *s*. Member, Ancient Monuments Board for Scotland, 1961. *Address:* 8 Cobden Crescent, Edinburgh 9. *T:* 031-667 3164.

**STEVENSON, Sir William Alfred,** KBE 1965 (OBE 1954); JP (NZ); civil engineering contractor; Managing Director: W. Stevenson and Sons Ltd; The Roose Shipping Co. Ltd; Director, Dillingham Corporation of NZ Ltd; Formerly Mayor of Howick for 9 years. Manager and Coach, rowing section, Empire Games team, Vancouver, BC, 1954; Manager, NZ Olympic team, Tokyo, 1964. KStJ 1968. *Recreation:* NZ Champion: single sculls, 1923, 1924, 1926. 1927; double sculls, 1925, 1926. *Address:* W. Stevenson and Sons Ltd, Otahuhu, Auckland, New Zealand; Cockle Bay Road, Howick, Auckland.

**STEWARD, Prof. Frederick Campion,** FRS 1957; Charles A. Alexander Professor of Biological Sciences and Director of Laboratory for Cell Physiology and Growth, Cornell University, Ithaca, NY, since 1965 (Professor of Botany in the University, 1950-65); *b* 16 June 1904; *s* of Fredk Walter and Mary Daglish Steward; *m* 1929, Anne Temple Gordon, Richmond, Va, USA; one *s*. *Educ:* Heckmondwike Gram. Sch., Yorks; Leeds Univ. Demonstrator in Botany, Leeds Univ., 1926; Rockefeller Fellow: Cornell Univ., 1927, Univ. of California, 1928; Asst Lecturer, Univ. of Leeds (Botany), 1929; Rockefeller Foundation Fellow, 1933-34; Reader in Botany, Univ. of London (Birkbeck Coll.), 1934; War Service with MAP (Dir of Aircraft Equipment), 1940-45; Prof. of Botany and Chm. of Dept, Univ. of Rochester, Rochester, NY, 1946-50; John Simon Guggenheim Fell., 1963-64. Fellow American Academy of Arts and Sciences, 1956; Merit Award, Botanical Society of America, 1961. *Publications:* Plants at Work, 1964; Growth and Organisation in Plants, 1968; (ed) Treatise on Plant Physiology, 1959; papers in scientific journals and proceedings of learned societies. *Recreations:* gardening, swimming. *Address:* 621 Highland Road, Ithaca, NY 14850, USA. *T:* Ithaca AR2-2353.

**STEWARD, George Coton,** MA, ScD, DSc; Professor of Mathematics, The University, Hull, 1930-61, Emeritus Professor, since 1961; *b* 6 April 1896; *o c* of Joseph Steward and Minnie, *d* of William Coton, Wolverhampton; unmarried. *Educ:* The Grammar School, Wolverhampton; Gonville and Caius College, Cambridge (Senior Scholar). Wrangler, with distinction, Mathematical Tripos, 1920; ScD, 1937; First Class Honours in Mathematics in BSc (Honours), Univ. of London, 1917; MSc, 1919; DSc, 1926; Smith's Prize, Univ. of Cambridge, 1922, for contributions on Geometrical and Physical Optics; Member of Scientific Staff of Optics Department of National Physical Laboratory, 1918; Assistant Lecturer in Applied Mathematics, University of Leeds, 1920; Fellow of Gonville and Caius College, Cambridge, 1922; Fellow and Mathematical Lecturer, Emmanuel College, Cambridge, 1923. *Publications:* The Symmetrical Optical System, Cambridge Mathematical and Physical Tracts, No 25, 1928, 1958; papers on Geometrical and Physical Optics, and Plane Kinematics, in Transactions of Royal Society, of Cambridge Philosophical Society, etc. *Address:* 42 South Street, Cottingham, E Yorks. *T:* Hull 847654.

**STEWARD, Harold MacDonald;** *b* 8 Sept. 1904; *s* of late John Steward, Rainhill, Lancs; *m* 1941, Joyce Mary, *d* of late Thomas Nevison, Liverpool; one *s* three *d*. *Educ:* Rainhill School; Municipal Technical College, St Helen's. Consulting Engineer. Member of Liverpool City Council, 1953; Alderman, City of Liverpool, 1961; Leader of the City Council, 1967. JP Lancashire, 1951. Contested (C) Liverpool, Edge Hill, 1951; MP (C) Stockport South, 1955-64. During War of 1939-45, was engaged in radar industrial research. Formerly Member of Inter-Services Mission to Ex-enemy Countries. *Address:* Crawfordsburn, Glenrose Rd, Woolton, Liverpool 25.

**STEWARD, Nigel Oliver Willoughby,** OBE 1946; MA Oxon, BA Cantab; Consul-General, Haifa, 1955-59, retired; *b* 16 October 1899; *s* of Arthur Bennett Steward, ICS, and Alice Willoughby; *m* 1933, Raquel Wyneken, of Viña del Mar, Chile; three *d*. *Educ:* Winchester (Scholar); Trinity College, Oxford. Entered Consular Service, 1924. Vice-Consul at San Francisco, Valparaiso, Guatemala (Second Secretary), and Paris; Consul and First Secretary at Montevideo; Minister (local rank) to Paraguay; First Secretary, Bucharest, 1946; Deputy Consul-Gen., New York, 1946-48; Minister to Nicaragua, 1948-52; Consul-General, Nice and Monaco, 1952-55. *Recreation:* gardening. *Address:* Middle Park Farmhouse, Beckley, Oxford. *Club:* United University.

**STEWARD, Maj.-Gen. Reginald Herbert Ryrie,** CB 1946; CBE 1945 (OBE 1938); DSO 1943; MC 1918; Maj.-Gen., retired; *b* 8 June 1898; *s* of Col R. H. Steward, OBE, and A. R. Steward, OBE; *m* 1934, Vera Beatrice, *d* of Wilson Stuckey; two *d*. *Educ:* Cheltenham College. First Royal Engineers, then Royal Signals. Served European War, 1917-18 (MC); Palestine, 1936-39 (despatches, OBE); War of

1939-45 (despatches, DSO and Bar, CBE, CB). ADC to King George VI, 1947, and to the Queen, 1952. *Recreations:* fishing and shooting. *Address:* The Red House, Middle Winterslow, Wiltshire.

**STEWARD, Stanley Feargus,** CBE 1947; CEng; FIProdE, FIBM; Director, British Electrical and Allied Manufacturers Association, 1959-70; Chairman: William Steward (Holdings) Ltd; William Steward & Co. Ltd; George Thurlow and Sons Ltd; Thurlow Nunn & Sons Ltd; *b* 9 July 1904; *s* of late Arthur Robert and late Minnie Elizabeth Steward, Mundesley, Norfolk; *m* 1929, Phyllis Winifred, *d* of late J. Thurlow, Stowmarket, Suffolk; one *s* one *d*. *Educ:* The Paston Sch., North Walsham, Norfolk. Was apprenticed to East Anglian Engineering Co. (subseq. Bull Motors Ltd) and subseq. held positions of Chief Designer, Sales Manager and Dir, Min. of Supply: Electrical Adviser to Machine Tool Control, 1940; Director of Industrial Electrical Equipment, 1941-44; Dir Gen. of Machine Tools, 1944-45; Chm. Machine Tool Advisory Council, 1946-47; Chm. Gauge & Tool Advisory Council, 1946-47. Director: E. R. & F. Turner, Ltd, Ipswich, 1944-48. Chm., South Western Electricity Board, 1948-55. Member: British Electricity Authority, 1952-53; Elect. Engineering EDC, 1962-; Chm., British Electrical Development Assoc., 1954; President: Ipswich and District Electrical Assoc., 1964-67; Electrical Industries Club, 1966-67; Assoc. of Supervisory and Exec. Engineers, 1970-. Man. Dir Lancashire Dynamo Holdings Ltd, 1956-59 (Chm. 1957-58), retired. Formerly Chairman: Lancashire Dynamo and Crypto Ltd; Lancashire Dynamo Electronic Products Ltd; Lancashire Dynamo Group Sales; Pres., Exec. Cttee, Organisme de Liaison des Industries Metalliques Europeénes, 1963-67. Freeman of City of London; Master, Worshipful Company of Glaziers and Painters of Glass, 1964. *Recreations:* reading, music, theatre. *Address:* 41 Fairacres, Roehampton Lane, SW15. *T:* 01-876 2457. *Club:* Athenæum.

**STEWARD, Sir William Arthur,** Kt, *cr* 1955; Director of restaurant and property companies; gentleman farmer; *b* 20 Apr. 1901; *s* of late W. A. Steward and of Mrs C. E. Steward, Norwich; *m* 1939. *Educ:* Norwich Model Sch., and privately. Freeman of City of London; Master, Worshipful Co. of Distillers, 1964-65; Liveryman, Worshipful Co. of Fruiterers. Served RAF, 1938-45; Sen. Catering Officer at Air Min., 1943-45; retired with rank of Squadron Leader. MP (C) Woolwich West, 1950-59; Chm. Kitchen Cttee, House of Commons, Nov. 1951-Sept. 1959. Mem. of London County Council for Woolwich West, 1949-52. Chm., London Conservative Union, 1953-55. *Address:* Sulgrave Manor, Nassau, Bahamas. *Clubs:* Carlton; Royal Thames Yacht.

**STEWARDSON, Prof. Edward Alfred;** Professor of Physics, University of Leicester, 1947-69; *b* 27 Aug. 1904; *s* of Alexander and Frances Margaret Stewardson; *m* 1937, Winefred Muriel Jones. *Educ:* Hawarden County School; Liverpool University (State Scholar and Flintshire County Exhibitioner). BSc 1st Cl. Hons Physics Liverpool, 1924, MSc 1925. Research Student, Cambridge, 1926-28; PhD Cantab 1930; Oliver Lodge Fellow, Liverpool University, 1928-30. Professor of Physics, Nat. Central Univ., Nanking, China, 1934-39; Lecturer in Charge of Physics Dept, Univ. College of Leicester, 1940-46. *Publications:* papers in scientific journals. *Recreations:* music and mountaineering. *Address:* Clatterbrune, Presteigne, Radnorshire. *T:* Presteigne 216. *Club:* Athenæum.

**STEWART,** family name of **Earl of Galloway.**

**STEWART;** *see* Vane-Tempest-Stewart, family name of Marquess of Londonderry.

**STEWART, Dr Alan;** Vice-Chancellor of Massey University since 1964; *b* 8 Dec. 1917; *s* of Kenneth and Vera Mary Stewart; *m* 1950, Joan Cecily Sisam; one *s* three *d*. *Educ:* Massey Agricultural College; University College, Oxford. Sen. Lectr, Massey Agric. Coll., 1950-54; Chief Consulting Officer, Milk Marketing Board, England and Wales, 1954-58; Principal, Massey Agric. Coll., 1959-63. *Address:* Massey University, Palmerston North, New Zealand.

**STEWART, Alexander Bernard,** MD; MRCPE; FRCP; Medical Adviser to the Greater London Council since 1965 (apptd 1964); *b* 15 June 1908; *s* of late Alexander Murray Stewart and Helen Howie Edmonds; *m* 1937, Isabelle Webster; one *s*. *Educ:* Grove Academy, Broughty Ferry; Univ. of St Andrews. MB, ChB 1931; DPH 1934; MD 1936. Hospital appointments, 1931-33; Asst in Bacteriology, Univ. of St Andrews, 1933-35; Lectr in Bacteriology, Univ. of St Andrews, 1935-37; Asst MOH, Tynemouth, 1937-40; Dep. MOH, Finsbury, 1940-46; MOH, Paddington, 1946-52; Deputy MOH, LCC, 1952-64, MOH, LCC, 1964-65. Trustee, The Chadwick Trust. Fellow: Soc. MOH; RSH (Mem. Council); RIPH&H. Liveryman, Soc. of Apothecaries. *Publications:* various papers in professional journals, and annual reports, on medical and public health subjects. *Recreations:* reading, the arts. *Address:* The County Hall, SE1. *T:* 01-928 5000; Fernwood, Onslow Road, Burwood Park, Walton-on-Thames, Surrey. *T:* 24655. *Club:* Athenæum.

**STEWART, Alexander Boyd,** CBE 1962; Director of Macaulay Institute for Soil Research, Aberdeen, 1958-68, retired; *b* 3 Nov. 1904; *s* of late Donald Stewart, Farmer, Tarland, Aberdeenshire; *m* 1939, Alice F., 3rd *d* of late Robert Bowman, Aberdeen; one *s*. *Educ:* Aberdeen University; Zürich Polytechnic. Aberdeen: MA 1925; BSc (1st Cl. Hons) 1928; PhD 1932. Macaulay Inst. for Soil Research, Craigiebuckler, Aberdeen: Head of Dept of Soil Fertility, 1932; Asst Dir, 1943; Dep. Dir, 1945; seconded as Agronomist to Ind. Council of Agric. Research, 1945-46; part-time mem., Develt Commn team to survey agric., forestry and fishery products in UK, 1949-51; Strathcona-Fordyce Professor of Agriculture, University of Aberdeen, 1954-58. Mem. various tech. cttees of Dept of Agric. for Scotland, Agric. Res. Council, Colonial Office and Forestry Commn. Has visited most West European Countries, India, USA, and Canada. *Publications:* papers on soils and agriculture in agric. jls. *Recreations:* bowls, golf. *Address:* 14 Woodburn Avenue, Aberdeen. *T:* Aberdeen 34348. *Club:* Farmers'.

**STEWART, Andrew;** Professor, University of Ibadan, since 1970; *b* 17 Jan. 1904; *s* of Andrew Stewart, Edinburgh, Scotland, and Marcia Sabina (*née* Sprot); *m* 1931, Jessie Christobel Borland; four *s* two *d*. *Educ:* Daniel Stewart's College, Edinburgh, Scotland; East of Scotland College of Agriculture (CDA); University of Manitoba. BSA 1931, MA 1932 (Univ. of Manitoba). Lecturer in Agricultural Economics, Univ. of Manitoba, 1932-33; Lecturer, 1935, Prof. 1946, of Political Economy, Dean of Business Affairs, 1949, President, 1950-59, Univ. of Alberta; Chm. Bd of Broadcast Governors, Ottawa, 1958-68; Chm. Alberta Univs Commn, 1968-70.

Member of Royal Commissions: Province of Alberta (Natural Gas), 1948; Canada (Economic Prospects), 1955-57; Canada (Price Spreads of Food Products) (Chairman), 1958-59; Pres. Nat. Conf. of Canadian Univs, 1958; Chm. Assoc. of Univs of British Commonwealth, 1958. Hon. LLD Manitoba, New Brunswick, Melbourne, Alberta; Hon. DEcon Laval; FRSC; Fellow, Agricultural Inst. of Canada. *Address:* University of Ibadan, Ibadan, Nigeria.

**STEWART, Andrew,** CBE 1954; *b* 23 June 1907; *s* of James Stewart; *m* 1937, Agnes Isabella Burnet, *d* of James McKechnie, JP. *Educ:* Glasgow University (MA). Joined BBC at Glasgow, 1926; Glasgow Representative, 1931-35; Scottish Programme Director, 1935-48; Controller (N Ire.), 1948-52; Controller (Home Service), 1953-57; Controller, Scotland, 1957-68. Min. of Information, 1939-41. Director, Scottish Television. Member: Films of Scotland Committee; Scottish Advisory Council of British Council. *Recreations:* reading, the theatre, mountaineering. *Address:* 36 Sherbrooke Avenue, Glasgow, S1.

**STEWART, Andrew,** CBE 1962; President, since 1968, and Director, since 1931, Huddersfield Building Society (General Manager, 1928-67; Vice-President, 1958-68); *b* Cramond, Midlothian, 30 June 1895; *s* of late David Stewart and Jessie Peebles, Edinburgh; *m* 1933, Norah Lucy, *d* of late David Plaistowe, Highgate, N6; one *s*. *Educ:* Broughton and Edinburgh University. Member, Institute of Chartered Accountants in Scotland, 1918; Fell. Institute of Cost and Works Accountants, 1923 (Member Council, 1924-26); FCIS 1934. Founder Member, Council of Building Societies Institute, 1934-46 (Vice-Pres., 1946-); Member Council, Building Socs Assoc., 1932-66 (Chm. of Coun., 1946-48; Chm. Taxation Cttee, 1938-66; Vice-President, 1966-); Vice-Pres., Yorkshire County Assoc. of Building Socs, 1968- (Chm., 1937-42 and 1956-59); Mem. Coun., Internat. Union of Building Socs and Savings Assocs, 1960-66; Founder Mem., Nat. House-Builders Registration Council, 1935- (Chm. 1948-54; Vice-Pres., 1954-); Trustee, Housing Centre Trust, 1953-; Sea Cadet Council, 1958-61; Pres., St John Ambulance Brigade, SW Yorks; Mem. Council, OStJ, W Riding, Yorks. European War, 1914-18: HM Forces (invalided 1915); on staff of Accountant Gen. of the Navy, 1917-21; War of 1939-45: nominee of Min. of Supply on Board of Rendan (Great Britain) Ltd (Chm.) and John Fowler & Co. Ltd, Leeds (Dir) and Associated Companies. *Publication:* Costing for Light Castings, Ironfounders, 1923. *Recreations:* golf, fishing. *Address:* Broomfield, Fixby, Huddersfield, Yorks. *T:* Huddersfield 20276. *Clubs:* Huddersfield; Huddersfield Golf.

**STEWART, Andrew Charles,** CMG 1955; OBE 1942; Ambassador to Libya, 1962-63; *b* 22 April 1907; *s* of Frederick Naylor F. Stewart; *m* 1935, Emily Caroline Martin; two *s* one *d*. *Educ:* Scarborough Coll.; RMC Sandhurst. Commissioned Indian Army, 1927; transferred to Indian Political Service, 1933; appointed to Foreign Service, 1947; British Minister to Korea, 1954-56; Consul-General at Jerusalem, 1957-59; Ambassador and Consul-General, Iceland, 1959-61. *Recreation:* golf. *Address:* Uiginish Lodge, Dunvegan, Skye. *T:* Dunvegan 213. *Club:* East India and Sports.

**STEWART, Brian Thomas Webster,** CMG 1969; Assistant Secretary, Cabinet Office, since 1968; *b* 27 Apr. 1922; *s* of Redvers Buller Stewart and Mabel Banks Sparks, Broich, Crieff; *m* 1946, Millicent Peggy Pollock; two *d*. *Educ:* Trinity Coll., Glenalmond; Worcester Coll., Oxford (MA). Commnd The Black Watch (RHR), 1942; served Europe and Far East (Capt.). Joined Malayan Civil Service, 1946; studying Chinese Macau, 1947; Asst Sec., Chinese Affairs, Singapore, 1949; Devonshire Course, Oxford, 1950; Asst Comr for Labour, Kuala Lumpur, 1951; Sec. for Chinese Affairs, Supt of Chinese Schs, Malacca and Penang, 1952-57; joined HM Diplomatic Service, 1957; served Rangoon, Peking, Shanghai, Manila, Kuala Lumpur, Hanoi. *Publication:* All Men's Wisdom (anthology of Chinese Proverbs), 1957. *Recreations:* climbing, sailing, ski-ing, chamber music, orientalia particularly chinoiserie. *Address:* The Broich, Crieff, Perthshire. *T:* Crieff 2544. *Club:* Royal Commonwealth Society.

**STEWART, Sir Bruce Fraser,** 2nd Bt, *cr* 1920, Chairman, Pigeon Bay Road Board; ex-Flying Officer, New Zealand Air Force; *b* Sept. 1904; *s* of 1st Bt; *S* father, 1924; *m* 1925, Constance, *d* of W. S. Gray, Cambridge; two *d*. *Educ:* Eton; Cambridge. Past-President, Canterbury Aero Club. *Recreations:* polo, flying, boating, and golf. *Address:* Strathmore, Pigeon Bay, Banks Peninsula, Canterbury, NZ.

**STEWART, Charles Cosmo Bruce,** CMG 1962; serving in the Foreign and Commonwealth Office (formerly Foreign Office), since 1968; *b* 29 July 1912; *o s* of late Brig.-Gen. Cosmo Gordon Stewart, CB, CMG, DSO, and Mrs Gladys Berry Stewart (*née* Honeyman). *Educ:* Eton; King's Coll., Cambridge. Barrister-at-law, Middle Temple, 1938. Served War, 1939-46. Foreign Service Officer, 1946; First Sec., Rome, 1949; First Secretary (Commercial), Cologne, 1951; transf. to Foreign Office, 1954; Head of Information Policy Dept, 1955-58; Counsellor and Consul-General, Saigon, Vietnam, 1958-61; Counsellor and Head of Chancery, Copenhagen, 1961-63; Consul-General at Luanda, 1963-68. *Address:* c/o Foreign and Commonwealth Office, Downing Street, SW1. *Club:* Travellers'.

**STEWART, Air Vice-Marshal Colin Murray,** CB 1962; CBE 1952 (OBE 1945); CEng, FIEE, MBIM; RAF, retired; Controller, Computing Services, University of London, since 1968; *b* 17 June 1910; *s* of Archie Stewart, Sherborne, Dorset; *m* 1940, Anthea, *d* of Maynard Loveless, Stockbridge, Hants; four *s*. *Educ:* Wycliffe College, Stonehouse, Glos. Joined RAF, 1932; served in 5 Sqdn, NWF, India, and 16 Sqdn at home; specialised in Signals, 1937. Served War of 1939-45 (despatches, OBE): CSO various formations at home and in Europe. Chairman: British Joint Communications Board, 1952-55; Communications Electronics Cttee of Standing Group, Washington, 1955-57; AOC, No. 27 Gp, 1957-58; Comd Electronics Officer, Fighter Comd, 1958-61; Dir-Gen. of Signals, Air Ministry, 1961-64; STSO, Fighter Comd, 1964-67; SASO, Technical Training Comd, 1967-68, retired. *Recreations:* fishing, gardening, sailing, etc. *Address:* 37 Petersham Road, Richmond, Surrey. *Club:* Royal Air Force.

**STEWART, Sir David James H.;** *see* Henderson-Stewart.

**STEWART, Desmond Stirling;** *b* 20 April 1924; *e s* of late R. M. Stewart, MD, FRCP and of Agnes Maud Stewart (*née* Stirling of Muiravonside); unmarried. *Educ:* Haileybury College (classical scholar); Trinity College, Oxford (classical scholar). MA Hons; BLitt. Asst Prof. of English, Baghdad Univ., 1948-56;

Inspector of English in Islamic Maqāsid Schs of Beirut, 1956-58; thereafter chiefly resident in Egypt, writing fiction and non-fiction with a Middle Eastern background. *Publications:* Fiction: Leopard in the Grass, 1951; Memoirs of Alcibiades, 1952; The Unsuitable Englishman, 1955; A Woman Besieged, 1959; The Men of Friday, 1961; The Sequence of Roles, a trilogy (The Round Mosaic, 1965; The Pyramid Inch, 1966; The Mamelukes, 1968); Non-fiction: (with J. Haylock) New Babylon: a portrait of Iraq, 1956; Young Egypt, 1958; Turmoil in Beirut: a personal account, 1958; The Arab World (with Editors of 'Life'), 1962; Turkey (with Editors of 'Life'), 1965; Early Islam (with Editors of 'Life'), 1967; Orphan with a Hoop, 1967; Great Cairo, Mother of the World, 1968; Translations: A. R. Sharkawi, Egyptian Earth, 1962; F. Ghanem, The Man who lost his Shadow, 1966. *Recreations:* swimming, walking. *Address:* Ilex House, Wells-next-the-Sea, Norfolk. *T:* Wells (Norfolk) 264.

**STEWART, Donald,** CIE 1944; OBE 1937; MA, BSc; *b* 14 March 1894. Joined Indian Forest Service, 1921; Dep. Dir Gen., Directorate-General of Supply, New Delhi, India, 1943-45; President Forest Research Institute and Colleges, Dehra Dun, India, 1945-47; retired, 1949. *Address:* Melrose, Silverburn, Ballasalla, Isle of Man.

**STEWART, Donald James;** MP (Scottish Nat. Party) Western Isles, since 1970; *b* 17 Oct. 1920; *m* 1955, Christina Macaulay. *Educ:* Nicolson Institute, Stornoway. Provost of Stornoway, 1958-64 and 1968-70; Hon. Sheriff Substitute, 1960. *Recreations:* fishing, photography, gardening. *Address:* Heatherlea, 30 Goathill Road, Stornoway, Isle of Lewis. *T:* Stornoway 2672.

**STEWART of Appin, Dugald Leslie Lorn,** CMG 1969; HM Diplomatic Service; Counsellor, since 1962; Inspector of Diplomatic Missions since 1965; *b* 10 Sept. 1921; *m* 1947, Sibyl Anne Sturrock, MBE; three *s*. one *d*. *Educ:* Eton; Magdalen College, Oxford. Foreign Office, 1942. Served HM Embassies: Belgrade, 1945; Berlin, 1948; Iraq, 1950; Cairo, 1951; Moscow, 1962; Cairo, 1968. *Recreations:* shooting, fishing, golf, tennis, squash. *Address:* c/o Foreign and Commonwealth Office, SW1; Braevallich, by Dalmally, Argyll. *T:* Ford 243.

**STEWART, Edith Anne;** *see* Robertson, E. A. S.

**STEWART, Ewan George Francis,** MC 1945; QC (Scotland) 1960; *b* 9 May 1923; *s* of late George Duncan Stewart, CA, Edinburgh, and late Catherine Wilson Stewart; *m* 1953, Sheila Margaret, *er d* of Major K. G. Richman, East Lancs Regt (retd); one *s* one *d*. *Educ:* George Watson's Coll., Edinburgh; Edinburgh Univ. Served War of 1939-45 with 7/9 (Highlanders) Bn, The Royal Scots, in 52 (L) Division. Mem. of Faculty of Advocates, 1949; standing junior counsel to Min. of Civil Aviation in Scotland, 1955-60; Hon. Sheriff-Substitute of the Lothians and Peebles, 1961-64; practised at New Zealand Bar, 1962-64; resumed practice at Scottish Bar, 1964; Home Advocate-Depute, 1965-67; Solicitor-General for Scotland, 1967-70. Governor, St Denis School, Edinburgh, 1967. Contested (Lab) Edinburgh Pentlands, 1970. *Address:* 5 Munro Drive, Edinburgh 13; Canty Bay, East Lothian. *Club:* Caledonian.

**STEWART, Ewen;** Sheriff-Substitute at Wick since 1962; *b* 22 April 1926; *o s* of late Duncan Stewart and Kate Blunt, and *gs* of late Ewen Stewart, Kinlocheil; *m* 1959, Norma Porteous Hollands, *d* of late William Charteris Hollands, Earlston; one *d*. *Educ:* Edinburgh University. BSc (Agric.) 1946; MA (Econ.) 1950; LLB 1952. Asst Agricultural Economist, East of Scotland Coll. of Agriculture, 1946-49; practised at Scottish Bar, 1952-62. *Address:* Strath, Watten, Caithness. *T:* Watten 210.

**STEWART, Prof. Frederick Henry,** FRS 1964; PhD Cantab; FRSE; FGS; Regius Professor of Geology, since 1956, Dean of Science Faculty, 1966-68, and Member, University Court, since 1969, Edinburgh University; *b* 16 Jan. 1916; *o s* of Frederick Robert Stewart and Hester Alexander, Aberdeen; *m* 1945, Mary Florence Elinor Rainbow (*see* Mary Stewart); no *c*. *Educ:* Fettes Coll.; Univ. of Aberdeen (BSc); Emmanuel Coll., Cambridge. Mineralogist in Research Dept of ICI Ltd (Billingham Div.), 1941-43; Lectr in Geology, Durham Colls in the Univ. of Durham, 1943-56. Lyell Fund Award, 1951, J. B. Tyrrell Fund, 1952, Geological Soc. of London; Mineralogical Soc. of America Award, 1952; Lyell Medal, 1970. Vice-Pres., Geological Soc. of London, 1965-66; Member: Council for Scientific Policy, 1967-; Geol. Physics Cttee, NERC, 1967-70. *Publications:* papers in Mineralogical Magazine, Journal of Geological Society of London, etc., dealing with igneous and metamorphic petrology and salt deposits. *Address:* King's Buildings, West Mains Road, Edinburgh. *T:* 031-667 1011.

**STEWART, George Girdwood,** MC, TD; Commissioner for Forest and Estate Management, Forestry Commission, since 1969; *b* 12 Dec. 1919; *o s* of late Herbert A. Stewart, BSc, and of Janetta Dunlop Girdwood; *m* 1950, Shelagh Jean Morven Murray; one *s* one *d*. *Educ:* Kelvinside Academy, Glasgow; Glasgow Univ.; Edinburgh Univ. (BSc). Dist. Officer, Forestry Commn, 1949; Asst Conservator, 1961; Conservator, West Scotland, 1966. Comdg Officer, 278 (Lowland) Field Regt RA (TA), 1957-60. *Recreations:* ski-ing, (Vice-Pres. Scottish Ski Club, 1969), gardening. *Address:* Laverockbrae, Balmore, Torrance, Glasgow. *T:* Balmore 204. *Club:* Ski Club of Great Britain.

**STEWART, Gordon William,** CVO 1964; Chairman and General Manager, Scottish Region, British Railways, since 1967; Chairman and Managing Director, British Transport Ship Management (Scotland) Ltd, since 1967; Director, British Transport Hotels Ltd, since 1968; *b* 13 April 1906; *s* of James E. Stewart and Margaret Stewart; *m* 1935, Dorothy Swan Taylor. *Educ:* Daniel Stewart's Coll.; George Heriot Sch., Edinburgh. L & NER: Traffic Apprentice, 1929; appts in London, Lincoln and Manchester, 1942-52; Prin. Asst to Gen. Man., Eastern Region, 1952; Asst Gen. Man., Scottish Region, 1956. *Recreations:* golf, shooting. *Address:* Creag Mor, Blairforkie Drive, Bridge of Allan, Stirlingshire. *T:* Bridge of Allan 2266.

**STEWART, Prof. Harold Charles;** FRCP; DL; Head of Pharmacology Department, St Mary's Hospital Medical School, since 1950; Professor of Pharmacology in the University of London since 1965 (Reader, 1949-64); Gresham Professor in Physic, City University, 1968-69; Consultant in Pharmacology to St Mary's Hospital, 1946; *b* 23 Nov. 1906; *s* of Bernard Halley Stewart, MA, MD, FRSE, FKC, Pres. of Sir Halley Stewart Trust, and Mabel Florence Wyatt. *Educ:* Mill Hill Sch.; University Coll. London; Jesus Coll., Cambridge; University Coll. Hospital. Cambridge Univ.: BA 1928, MA 1934; MB, BCh 1931, MD 1935. London Univ.: PhD 1941, MRCP 1949. Gen. practice, Barnet,

Herts, 1932-36. Sub-Dean, St Mary's Hospital Med. Sch., 1950-52. Examr now or formerly, Univs of London, Cambridge, Birmingham, Bristol and Wales, RCS, Soc. of Apothecaries. Research work, mainly on fat absorption and transport in the human subject, and on problems of pain and analgesia. Cons. in Pharmacology to Army; Med. Adviser and Mem. Commonwealth Council, Brit. Commonwealth Ex-Services League; Trustee Sir Halley Stewart Trust for Research and Buttle Trust for Children; Mem. Asthma Research Council; Prin. MO, St John Ambulance Assoc. (Dist Surg. for London, SJAB, 1950-64); Mem. Chapter-Gen., Order of St John (KStJ); Mem. Council, Stewart Soc.; Liveryman, Soc. of Apothecaries of London; Freeman, City of London: Mem. Physiolog., Brit. Pharmacolog., Nutrition and Genealog. Socs. RAMC, T, 1935; Mem. LDV, later Major and Med. Adviser, HG; comd and reformed Med. Unit, Univ. of London STC as Major RAMC, 1942-46. Defence Medal; Gen. Serv. Medal, 1939-46; Coronation Medal, 1953. DL Greater London, 1967. *Publications:* Drugs in Anæsthetic Practice (with F. G. Wood-Smith), 1962; contribs to jls. *Recreations:* voluntary service; sport (lacrosse: Cambridge Half-Blue 1928; lawn tennis); genealogy and heraldry. *Address:* Wilson House, 38-76 Sussex Gardens, W2. *T:* 01-723 1252. *Club:* Athenæum.

**STEWART, Sir Herbert (Ray),** Kt 1946; CIE 1939; FRCScI, DIC, NDA, MSc; *b* 10 July 1890; *s* of Hugh Stewart, Ballyward, Co. Down; *m* 1917, Eva (*d* 1955), *d* of William Rea, JP, Ballygawley, Co. Tyrone; one *d*; *m* 1957, Elsie, *d* of Walter J. Pyne, London. *Educ:* Excelsior Academy, Banbridge; Royal College of Science, Dublin; Imperial College of Science and Technology, London. Military Service, 1915-19; entered the Indian Agricultural Service as Deputy Director of Agriculture, 1920; Professor of Agriculture, Punjab, 1921-27; Assistant Director of Agriculture, 1928-32; Agricultural Expert, Imperial Council of Agricultural Research, Government of India, 1938; Director of Agriculture, Punjab, 1932-43; Member of the Punjab Legislative Council from time to time, 1927-36; Fellow of the University of the Punjab, 1929-43; Dean of the Faculty of Agriculture, 1933-43; Agriculture Commissioner with Government of India, 1943-46; Vice-Chairman, Imperial Council of Agricultural Research, 1944-46; Agricultural Adviser to British Middle East Office, Cairo, 1946-51; Principal Consultant, Agriculture, to UN Economic Survey Mission for Middle East, 1949; Agricultural Adviser to UN Relief and Works Agency for Palestine Refugees, 1950-51; Chief, Agricultural Mission to Colombia of Internat. Bank for Reconstruction and Development, 1955-56; Agricultural Consultant to Bank Missions to Pakistan, 1956, 1958, Italy, 1957, Yugoslavia and Uganda, 1960 and Kenya, 1961-62. *Publications:* various pamphlets and reports on agriculture and farm accounts in India, and on agriculture in Middle East. *Address:* 29 Alyth Road, Bournemouth, Hants. *T:* Westbourne 64782.

**STEWART, Maj.-Gen. Herbert William Vansittart,** CBE 1940; DSO 1914; *b* 15 Aug. 1886; 4th *s* of late Lieut-General J. M. Stewart; *m* 1919, Doreen Evelyn, *y d* of late J. G. Ohlenschlager, Ashurst, Fernhurst, Sussex; one *s* one *d*. Joined Royal Scots Fusiliers, 1906; Captain, 1914; Major, The Seaforth Highlanders, 1924; Lt-Col 1930; Col 1933; Temp. Maj.-Gen. 1943; served European War, 1914-18 (despatches, DSO); commanded 1st Batt. The Seaforth Highlanders, 1930-33; Instructor Senior Officers' School, Sheerness, 1934-36; Commander 152nd (Seaforth and Cameron) Infantry Brigade, 1936-40; ADC 1941-44; France, 1940 (wounded); Middle East, 1943-44; retired, 1944. Hon. Sheriff Substitute for Moray and Nairn, Inverness and Ross and Cromarty, 1948. *Address:* Minerva, Nairn, Scotland. *Club:* Naval and Military.

**STEWART, Sir Hugh Charlie Godfray,** 6th Bt, *cr* 1803, of Athenree; Major; High Sheriff, Co. Tyrone, 1955; *b* 13 April 1897; *s* of Colonel Sir George Powell Stewart, 5th Bt, and Florence Maria Georgina, *d* of Sir James Godfray; *S* father, 1945; *m* 1st, 1929 (marriage dissolved, 1942); one *s* one *d*; *m* 2nd, 1948, Diana Margaret, *d* of late Capt. J. E. Hibbert, MC, DFC, and late Mrs R. B. Bannon, Jersey; one *s* one *d*. *Educ:* Bradfield Coll., Berkshire; RMC, Sandhurst. Served European War, Royal Inniskilling Fusiliers, 1916; Arras, 1917 (wounded); France, 1939-40. Foreign Service has included India, Iraq, China, Malaya, South Africa and Syria; retired. *Heir:* *s* David John Christopher Stewart [*b* 19 June 1935; *m* 1959, Bridget Anne, *er d* of late Patrick W. Sim and of Mrs Leslie Parkhouse]. *Address:* Lough Macrory Lodge, Co. Tyrone, N Ireland. *Club:* Tyrone County.

**STEWART, Sir Iain (Maxwell),** Kt 1968; FIMechE, MRINA, MIMarE; Chairman: Hall-Thermotank Ltd; Higher Productivity (Organisation and Bargaining) Ltd; Director: Babcock & Wilcox Ltd; Beaverbrook Newspapers Ltd; British European Airways; Design & Industrial Styling Consultants Ltd; Dorchester Hotel Ltd; Dunbar & Co. Ltd; Eagle Star Insurance Co. Ltd; Glasgow and West of Scotland Housing Association Ltd; Heatherset Management and Advisory Services Ltd; Lyle Shipping Co. Ltd; Royal Bank of Scotland Ltd; Scottish Television Ltd (Deputy Chairman, since 1969); Select Vending Machines Ltd; West of Scotland Football Co. Ltd; Industrial Communications Ltd; *b* 16 June 1916; *s* of William Maxwell Stewart and Jessie Naismith Brown; *m* 1941, Margaret Jean Walker; two *s* two *d*. *Educ:* Loretto Sch.; Glasgow Univ. (BSc Mech. Eng.). Apprenticeship at Thermotank Ltd, 1935-39. Served War of 1939-45, Technical Adjutant, Fife and Forfar Yeomanry, 1939-41. Dir, Thermotank Ltd, 1941, Man. Dir, 1946, Chairman, 1950-65; Chm., Fairfields (Glasgow) Ltd, 1966-68; Dep. Chm., Upper Clyde Shipbuilders Ltd, 1967-68. Pres., Inst. of Engineers & Shipbuilders in Scotland, 1961-63; Second Warden, Worshipful Co. of Shipwrights; Mem. Chamber of Commerce, Glasgow. *Recreation:* golf. *Address:* Lochbrae House, Bearsden, Glasgow. *T:* 041-942 0202. *Clubs:* Carlton, Bath, Caledonian; Western (Glasgow).

**STEWART, Jackie;** *see* Stewart, John Young.

**STEWART, James Cecil Campbell,** CBE 1960; Deputy Chairman, British Nuclear Design and Construction, since 1969; *b* 1916; *s* of late James Stewart and Mary Campbell Stewart; *m* 1946, Pamela Rouselle, *d* of William King-Smith; one *d*. *Educ:* Armstrong College and King's College, Durham University (BSc Physics). Telecommunications Research Establishment, 1939-46; Atomic Energy Research Establishment, Harwell, 1946-49; Industrial Group, UKAEA, 1949-63; Member: UKAEA, 1963-69; Central Electricity Generating Bd, 1965-69. *Recreation:* gardening. *Address:* Whitethorns, Higher Whitley, Cheshire. *T:* Norcott Brook 377. *Club:* East India and Sports.

**STEWART, Brig. James Crossley,** CBE 1944; DSO 1918; CD with clasp, 1951; Retired Canadian Army, 1947; *b* Kingston, Ontario, 17 Feb. 1891, Scotch Canadian; *m* 1915, Florence Bemrose Valleau (*d* 1951); two *s* two *d*; *m* 1953, Nancy Barbara Alleyn. *Educ:* Kingston Public Schools; Kingston Collegiate; Royal Military College. Lt 4th Hussars, 1911; Capt. Canadian Field Artillery, 1914; served European War, 1914-18 (wounded, despatches thrice, DSO, 1914-15 Star, General Service and Victory Medals). Brig. and District Officer Commanding MD 1, London, Ontario, 1936-38; District Officer Commanding MD 11 1938-39; served War of 1939-45 (Canadian Volunteer Service Medal with Maple Leaf, Italy Star, France and Germany Star, War Medal): CRA 1st Canadian Division, Dec. 1939, and proceeded overseas; CCRA 7th British Corps 1940; CCRA 1st Cdn Corps June 1941; Served Italy and NW Europe; District Officer Commanding MD6, Halifax, 1945; retired, 1947; retd as Manager, Industrial Assoc. of BC (1947-60). Jubilee Medal, 1935; Coronation Medals, 1937, 1953. *Address:* 501 Hampton House, 2155 West 38th Avenue, Vancouver 13, BC. *Club:* Vancouver.

**STEWART, James Gill,** CB 1958; CBE 1952; Hon. FITO; *b* 13 March 1907; *s* of John Stewart (builder) and Isabella Stewart, late of Edinburgh; *m* 1936, Jessie Dodd; one *s* one *d*. *Educ:* George Watson's College, Edinburgh; Edinburgh University. Passed Home Civil Service Administrative Class Competition, 1929; entered Min. of Labour, Asst Principal, 1930; Private Sec. to Permanent Sec., 1934; Principal, 1936; Asst Sec., 1941; on loan to Min. of Works, 1941-43; on loan to UN (Bureau of Personnel), 1946-47; on loan to Cabinet Office, 1947-49; Industrial Relations Dept, 1950-53; Under-Sec., Employment Dept, 1953; Training Dept, 1960, retired, 1967. Trustee, Industrial Training Foundn, 1967. *Recreations:* choral singing, hill walking. *Address:* 104 Highgate West Hill, N6. *T:* 01-340 2014. *Club:* English-Speaking Union.

**STEWART, James Lablache;** *see* Granger, Stewart.

**STEWART, James (Maitland),** DFC with 2 oak leaf clusters (US); Air Medal with 3 oak leaf clusters; DSM (US); actor, stage and film; *b* Indiana, Pa, 20 May 1908; *s* of Alexander Maitland Stewart and Elizabeth Ruth (*née* Jackson); *m* 1949, Gloria McLean; two *s* twin *d*. *Educ:* Mercersburg Academy, Pa; Princeton University (BS Arch.). War Service, 1942-45: Lt-Col Air Corps; Europe, 1943-45 (Air Medal, DFC); Colonel, 1945. USAF Reserve; Brig.-Gen. 1959. Dir, Air Force Assoc. First New York appearance, Carry Nation, 1932; subseq. played in Goodbye Again, Spring in Autumn, All Good Americans, Yellow Jack, Divided by Three, Page Miss Glory, A Journey by Night. Entered films, 1935; films include: Murder Man, Next Time We Love, Seventh Heaven, You Can't Take It With You, Made for Each Other, Vivacious Lady, The Shopworn Angel, Mr Smith Goes to Washington, Destry Rides Again, No Time for Comedy, Philadelphia Story, The Shop around the Corner, Pot o' Gold, Ziegfeld Girl, Come Live with Me, It's a Wonderful Life, Magic Town, On Our Merry Way, You Gotta Stay Happy, Call Northside 777, Rope, The Stratton Story, Malaya, The Jackpot, Harvey, Winchester '73, Broken Arrow, No Highway in the Sky, Bend of the River, Carbine Williams, The Greatest Show on Earth, Thunder Bay, Naked Spur, The Glen Miller Story, Rear Window, The Man from Laramie, The Far Country, Strategic Air Command, The Man Who Knew Too Much, Night Passage, Spirit of St louis, Midnight Story, Vertigo, Bell, Book and Candle, Anatomy of a Murder, The FBI Story, The Mountain Road, The Man Who Shot Liberty Valance, Mr Hobbs Takes a Vacation, Take her, She's Mine, Cheyenne Autumn, Shenandoah, The Rare Breed, Firecreek, Bandalero; The Cheyenne Social Club; Fool's Parade. *Play:* Harvey (Broadway), 1970. Holds many awards, from Amer. Motion Picture Academy, Venice Film Festival, etc. *Address:* PO Box 550, Beverly Hills, Calif., USA.

**STEWART, James Robertson,** OBE 1964; Clerk of the University Court, University of London, since 1950 (Deputy Clerk, 1946-49); *b* 1917; *s* of James and Isabella Stewart; *m* 1941, Grace Margaret Kirsop; two *s* one *d*. *Educ:* Perth Acad.; Whitley and Monkseaton High Sch.; Armstrong Coll. (later King's Coll.), Newcastle, Univ. of Durham. BA Dunelm (1st cl. hons Mod. History) 1937; DThPT (1st cl.) 1938; research in Canada (Canada Co.), 1938-39; awarded Holland Rose Studentship, Cambridge, and William Black Noble Fellowship, Durham, 1939; MA Dunelm 1941. Served Army, 1939-46: Royal Artillery (BEF); Combined Ops HQ; Directorate of Combined Ops, India; Major (Actg Lt-Col); Certif. of Good Service. *Recreations:* golf, stamp collecting, gardening, watching (now) soccer and cricket. *Address:* 84 Fir Tree Road, Banstead, Surrey. *T:* Burgh Heath 54370. *Clubs:* Athenæum; Cuddington (Banstead) Golf.

**STEWART, Very Rev. James Stuart,** MA, Hon. DD; Professor Emeritus of New Testament Language, Literature and Theology, University of Edinburgh, New College (retired 1966); Extra Chaplain to the Queen in Scotland (Chaplain, 1952-66); *b* 21 July 1896; *s* of William Stewart, Dundee, and Katharine Jane Stuart Duke; *m* 1931, Rosamund Anne Barron, Berkeley Lodge, Blandford, Dorset; two *s*. *Educ:* High School, Dundee; St Andrews University (MA, BD); New College, Edinburgh; University of Bonn, Germany. Minister of following Church of Scotland Congregations: St Andrews, Auchterarder, 1924-28; Beechgrove, Aberdeen, 1928-35; North Morningside, Edinburgh, 1935-46. Hon. DD, St Andrews Univ., 1945. Held following special lectureships: Cunningham Lectures, New Coll., Edinburgh, 1934; Warrack Lectures, Edinburgh and St Andrews Univs, 1944; Hoyt Lectures, Union Seminary, New York, 1949; Lyman Beecher Lectures, Yale University, USA, 1952; Duff Missionary Lectures, 1953; Turnbull Trust Preacher, Scots Church, Melbourne, 1959; Stone Lectures, Princeton, 1962; Earl Lectures, Berkeley, California, 1967; Moderator of General Assembly of Church of Scotland, May 1963-64. *Publications:* The Life and Teaching of Jesus Christ, 1932; A Man in Christ: St Paul's Theology, 1935; The Gates of New Life, 1937; The Strong Name, 1941; Heralds of God, 1945; A Faith To Proclaim, 1953; Thine Is The Kingdom, 1956; The Wind of the Spirit, 1968. Joint Editor, English Trans. of Schleiermacher, The Christian Faith, 1928. *Address:* 6 Crawfurd Road, Edinburgh EH16 5PQ. *T:* 031-667 1810.

**STEWART, Sir James (Watson),** 4th Bt, *cr* 1920; *b* 8 Nov. 1922; *s* of Sir James Watson Stewart, 3rd Bt and Janie Steuart Stewart (*née* Sim) (she *m* 2nd, 1961, Neil Charteris Riddell); *S* father 1955; *m* 1946, Anne Elizabeth Glaister; no *c*. *Educ:* Uppingham; Aberdeen University. Served 1940-47: Royal Artillery; 1st Special Air Service: Parachute Regiment. *Heir: brother* John Keith Watson Stewart [*b* 25 Feb. 1929; *m* 1954, Mary Elizabeth, *d* of John Francis

Moxon; two *s* one *d*]. *Address:* Cruachan, Kilmacolm, Renfrewshire, Scotland. *T:* Kilmacolm 3265.

**STEWART, Sir Jocelyn Harry,** 12th Bt, *cr* 1623; *b* 24 Jan. 1903; *s* of Sir Harry Jocelyn Urquhart Stewart, 11th Bt, and Isabel Mary (*d* 1956), 2nd *d* of Col Mansfield, DL, Castle Wray, Co. Donegal; *S* father, 1945; *m* 1st, Constance Shillaber (*d* 1940); one *s*; 2nd, 1946, Katherine Christina Sweeney, Tamney, Co. Donegal; three *s* two *d*. *Heir: s* Alan D'Arcy Stewart [*b* 29 Nov. 1932; *m* 1952, Patricia, *d* of Lawrence Turner, Ramelton, Co. Donegal; two *s* two *d*].

**STEWART, John Alexander;** Partner, Kerr MacLeod and Macfarlan, CA, Glasgow, since 1953; *b* 4 Oct. 1915; *s* of John Stewart and Mary Cruickshanks; *m* 1944, Mary Scott Welsh; one *s*. *Educ:* Paisley. Inst. of Chartered Accountants of Scotland: admitted, 1949; member, General Examining Board, 1960-65; Vice-President, 1967-68; President, 1968-69. *Recreations:* gardening, walking, fishing. *Address:* (home) Lagnaha, Lochwinnoch Road, Kilmacolm, Renfrewshire. *T:* Kilmacolm 2666; (office) 100 Wellington Street, Glasgow C2. *T:* 041-221 6933. *Club:* Conservative (Glasgow).

**STEWART, Captain John Christie,** CBE 1947; DL; JP; Lord Lieutenant of Lanarkshire, 1959-63; Chairman Red Cross Council for Scotland, 1956-59; *b* 1 Aug. 1888; *o surv s* of late Sir Robert King Stewart, KBE; *m* 1928, Agnes Violet Averil, JP Lanarks, *d* of Brig.-Gen. Douglas Campbell Douglas, CB, and Hon. Mrs Douglas. *Educ:* Eton; University Coll., Oxford. MA Oxon, 1912. Served 1914-19 with HLI, and on general staff as Captain. Member of Royal Company of Archers (Queen's Body Guard for Scotland). Chairman Red Cross Exec. Cttee for Scotland, 1942-56. Grand Master Mason of Scotland, 1942-46. DL 1933, JP 1926, VL, 1957-59, Lanarkshire. *Recreations:* shooting and travelling. *Address:* Murdostoun Castle, Newmains, Lanarkshire. *T:* Wishaw 4757. *Clubs:* Oxford and Cambridge University; New (Edinburgh).

**STEWART, John Innes Mackintosh;** Reader in English Literature, Oxford University, since 1969; Student of Christ Church, Oxford, since 1949; *b* 30 Sept. 1906; *s* of late John Stewart, Director of Education in the City of Edinburgh, and Eliza Jane, *d* of James Clark, Golford, Nairn; *m* 1932, Margaret Hardwick; three *s* two *d*. *Educ:* Edinburgh Academy; Oriel College, Oxford. Bishop Fraser's Scholar, 1930; 1st class Eng. Lang. and Lit. 1928; Matthew Arnold Memorial Prize, 1929; Lectr in English in Univ. of Leeds, 1930-35; Jury Professor of English in Univ. of Adelaide, 1935-45; Lectr in Queen's Univ., Belfast, 1946-48; Walker-Ames Prof., Univ. of Washington, 1961. Hon. DLitt New Brunswick, 1962. *Publications:* Montaigne's Essays: John Florio's Translation, 1931; Character and Motive in Shakespeare, 1949; Eight Modern Writers, 1963; Rudyard Kipling, 1966; Joseph Conrad, 1968; Thomas Hardy, 1971; Shakespeare's Lofty Scene (Shakespearean Lectr, British Acad.), 1971. Detective novels and broadcast scripts (under pseudonym of Michael Innes) Hamlet, Revenge!, 1937; The Hawk and the Handsaw, 1948; The Journeying Boy, 1949; The New Sonia Wayward, 1960; Silence Observed, 1961; A Connoisseur's Case, 1962; A Family Affair, 1969; Death at the Chase, 1970; and others; (*novels* as J. I. M. Stewart) Mark Lambert's Supper, 1954; The Guardians, 1955; A Use of Riches, 1957; The Man Who Won the Pools, 1961; The Last Tresilians, 1963; An Acre of Grass, 1965; The Aylwins, 1966; Vanderlyn's Kingdom, 1967; Cucumber Sandwiches, 1969; Avery's Mission, 1971. *Recreation:* walking. *Address:* Fawler Copse, Kingston Lisle, Wantage, Berks.

*See also M. J. Stewart.*

**STEWART, John Philip,** MD, FRCSE, FSA Scotland; Consulting Surgeon, Deaconess Hospital; Hon. Consulting Surgeon, Royal Infirmary, Edinburgh; former Hon. Senior Lecturer and Head of Department of Otorhinolaryngology, member, Faculty of Medicine and Senatus Academicus, University of Edinburgh; *b* 1 Feb. 1900; *s* of late George Stewart, SSC, JP, and Flora Philip, MA; *m* 1928, Elizabeth Josephine Forbes Wedderburn. *Educ:* Daniel Stewart's College and University, Edinburgh; Paris and Vienna. 2nd Lieut RFA 1918; MB, ChB Edinburgh Univ. 1923; MD 1925; FRCSE 1926; Lt-Col RAMC, Adviser in Oto-Rhino-Laryngology, BLA; served France, 1940; Egypt and Persia, 1942-43; North-West Europe, 1944-45 (despatches). *Publication:* Turner's Diseases of Ear, Nose and Throat. *Recreation:* golf. *Address:* 18 Chester Street, Edinburgh. *T:* 031-225 1750.

**STEWART, John Young, (Jackie Stewart);** racing driver; *b* 11 June 1939; *s* of Robert Paul Stewart and Jean Clark Young; *m* 1962, Helen McGregor; two *s*. *Educ:* Dumbarton Academy. First raced, 1961; competed in 4 meetings, 1961-62, driving for Barry Filer, Glasgow; drove for Ecurie Ecosse and Barry Filer, winning 14 out of 23 starts, 1963; 28 wins out of 53 starts (incl. 11 wins in Formula 3), 1964; drove Formula 1 for BRM, 1965-67 and for Ken Tyrrell, 1968-70; by May 1970 had won 12 World Championship Grands Prix, also Australian and New Zealand, Swedish, Mediterranean, Japanese and many other non-championship, major internat. motor races; led Indianapolis, 1966, until retiring with engine failure with less than 10 miles to finish. 3rd in World Championship, 1965; 2nd in 1968; World Champion, 1969. *Recreations:* golf, fishing; shooting (Mem. British Team for Clay Pigeon shooting; former Scottish, English, Irish, Welsh and British Champion; won Coupe des Nations, 1959 and 1960; reserve for two-man team, 1960 Olympics). *Address:* Clayton House, 1268 Begnins, Vaud, Switzerland. *T:* Geneva 66-14-15. *Clubs:* British Racing Drivers', Annabells, Burkes; (Hon.) Royal Scottish Automobile; (Pres.) Scottish Motor Racing (Duns).

**STEWART, Maj.-Gen. Sir Keith (Lindsay),** KBE 1958 (CBE 1945; OBE 1935; MBE 1919); CB 1947; DSO 1941; retired list of the New Zealand Army; *b* 30 Dec. 1896; *m* 1922, Rita Moss; one *s* one *d*. *Educ:* Wanganui Collegiate School, NZ. Served European War, 1914-18, Wellington Mounted Rifles and DAAG, NZEF; War of 1939-45, GSO 1, NZ Div.; BGS Creforce, Crete; DCGS, New Zealand; Commander: 4 NZ Armoured Bde; 5 NZ Infantry Bde; NZEF in British Commonwealth Occupation Force, Japan; Adjutant-General, 1946-49; Chief of General Staff, 1949-52. Greek Military Cross, 1941; Officer, Legion of Merit, USA, 1943. *Recreations:* golf, sea fishing. *Address:* Kerikeri, Bay of Islands, NZ.

**STEWART, Sir Kenneth (Dugald),** 1st Bt *cr* 1960; GBE 1950 (KBE 1927); *b* 29 March 1882; 4th and *y s* of late H. D. Stewart, Strathgarry, Blair Atholl; *m* Noel (*d* 1946), *y d* of Kenric Brodribb, Melbourne, Australia; two *s* two *d*. *Educ:* Trinity Coll., Glenalmond. In the service of Maitland & Co., Ltd, in Shanghai, 1903-19; President Trustee Savings Banks Association, 1966 (Chairman, 1946-66); Vice-Pres. National Savings Cttee, 1958; Delegate to the Special China Tariff Conference of

1925-26; *Heir: s* David Brodribb Stewart [*b* 20 Dec. 1913; *m*; no *c*]. *Address:* Newton House, Alderley Edge, Cheshire. *T:* Alderley Edge 2117. *Club:* St James's (Manchester).

**STEWART, Mary (Florence Elinor), (Mrs Frederick H. Stewart);** *b* 17 Sept. 1916; *d* of Rev. Frederick A. Rainbow, Durham Diocese, and Mary Edith (*née* Matthews), NZ; *m* 1945, Frederick Henry Stewart, *qv*; no *c*. *Educ:* Eden Hall, Penrith, Cumberland; Skellfield School, Ripon, Yorks; St Hild's Coll., Durham Univ. BA 1938; MA 1941. Asst Lectr in English, Durham Univ., 1941-45; Part-time Lectr in English, St Hild's Training Coll., Durham, and Durham Univ., 1948-56. FRSA 1968. *Publications: novels:* Madam, Will You Talk?, 1954; Wildfire at Midnight, 1956; Thunder on the Right, 1957; Nine Coaches Waiting, 1958; My Brother Michael, 1959; The Ivy Tree, 1961; The Moonspinners, 1962; This Rough Magic, 1964; Airs Above the Ground, 1965; The Gabriel Hounds, 1967; The Wind Off The Small Isles, 1968; The Crystal Cave, 1970; also articles, poems, radio plays. *Recreations:* riding, gardening, music, painting, theatre. *Address:* 79 Morningside Park, Edinburgh 10. *T:* 031-447 2620.

**STEWART, Rt. Hon. Michael,** PC 1964; CH 1969; MP (Lab) Fulham since 1955 (East Fulham, 1945-55); *b* 6 Nov. 1906; *s* of Robert Wallace Stewart, DSc and Eva Stewart; *m* 1941, Mary Elizabeth (JP, Chm., Bd of Governors, Charing Cross Hosp.), *d* of Herbert Birkinshaw; no *c*. *Educ:* Christ's Hosp.; St John's Coll., Oxford. Pres. Oxford Union, 1929; Asst Master, Merchant Taylors' Sch., 1930-31; Asst Master, Coopers' Company's School, and Lectr for Workers' Educational Assoc., 1931-42. Joined Army Intelligence Corps, 1942. Trans. to Army Educational Corps, 1943; commissioned and promoted to Capt., 1944. Contested (Lab) West Lewisham, 1931 and 1935; Vice-Chamberlain of HM Household, 1946-47; Comptroller of HH Household, 1946-47; Under-Sec. of State for War, 1947-51; Parly Sec., Min. of Supply, May-Oct. 1951; Sec. of State for Education and Science, Oct. 1964-Jan. 1965; Sec. of State for Foreign Affairs, Jan. 1965-Aug. 1966; First Sec. of State, 1966-68; Sec. of State for Economic Affairs, 1966-67; Secretary of State for Foreign and Commonwealth Affairs, 1968-70. Freeman of Hammersmith, 1967. Hon. Fellow, St John's Coll. Oxford, 1965; Hon. LLD, Leeds, 1966. *Publications:* The Forty Hour Week (Fabian Soc.), 1936; Bias and Education for Democracy, 1937; The British Approach to Politics, 1938; Modern Forms of Government, 1959. *Recreations:* chess, painting. *Address:* 158 Walton Street, SW3.

**STEWART, Michael James;** Reader in Political Economy, University College, London University, since 1969; *b* 6 Feb. 1933; *s* of John Innes Mackintosh Stewart, *qv*; *m* 1962, Frances Kaldor, *d* of Nicholas Kaldor, *qv*; two *d*. *Educ:* Campbell Coll., Belfast; St Edward's Sch., Oxford; Magdalen Coll., Oxford. 1st cl. PPE (Oxon), 1955. Asst Res. Off., Oxford Univ. Inst. of Statistics, 1955-56; Barnett Fellow, Cornell Univ., 1956-57; Econ. Asst, HM Treasury, 1957-60; Sec. to Council on Prices, Productivity and Incomes, 1960-61; Econ. Adviser, HM Treasury, 1961-62, Cabinet Office, 1964-67 (Senior Econ. Advr, 1967), Kenya Treasury, 1967-69; Economic Adviser to Malta Labour Party, 1970-. Contested (Lab); Folkestone and Hythe, 1964; Croydon North-West, 1966. Asst Editor, Nat. Inst. Econ. Review, 1962-64. *Publication:* Keynes and After, 1967. *Recreation:* walking. *Address:* 39 Upper Park Road, NW3. *T:* 01-722 0177. *Club:* Reform.

**STEWART, Sir Michael (Norman Francis),** KCMG 1966 (CMG 1957); OBE 1948; Ambassador to Greece, since 1967; *b* 18 Jan. 1911; *s* of late Sir Francis Stewart, CIE, and of Lady Stewart; *m* 1951, Katharine Damaris Houssemayne du Boulay; one *s* two *d*. *Educ:* Shrewsbury; Trinity College, Cambridge. Assistant Keeper, Victoria and Albert Museum, 1935-39; Ministry of Information, 1939-41; Press Attaché: HM Embassy, Lisbon, 1941-44; HM Embassy, Rome, 1944-48; employed in Foreign Office, 1948-51; Counsellor, Office of Comr-Gen. for UK in SE Asia, 1951-54; Counsellor, HM Embassy, Ankara, 1954-59; HM Chargé d'Affaires, Peking, 1959-62; Senior Civilian Instructor, IDC, 1962-64; HM Minister, British Embassy, Washington, 1964-67. *Recreation:* country life. *Address:* British Embassy, Athens, Greece. *Club:* Brooks's.

**STEWART, Dame Muriel (Acadia),** DBE 1968; Headmistress, Northumberland LEA, since 1940; *b* 22 Oct. 1905; *d* of late James Edmund Stewart. *Educ:* Gateshead Grammar Sch.; Durham Univ. BA Hons 1926; MA 1929. Teacher: Newcastle upon Tyne, 1927-29; Northumberland, 1929-; Shiremoor Middle School, 1969-70. Nat. Pres., Nat. Union of Teachers, 1964-65; Chairman, Schools Council, 1969-. Hon. MEd, Newcastle Univ., 1965. *Recreation:* music. *Address:* 44 Coldwell Road, Gosforth, Newcastle upon Tyne NE3 2AX. *T:* Newcastle upon Tyne 853400.

**STEWART, Major Oliver,** MC, AFC; CompRAeS; writer and broadcaster; *b* 26 Nov. 1895; *m* 1921, Odette Suzanne Le Lay; one *d*. *Educ:* Copthorne Sch.; Bradfield; Royal Coll. of Music. 2nd Lt 9th Mddx, Oct. 1914; Flying Officer, RFC, 1915; Ferry Pilot, 1916; No. 54 Squadron (single-seat fighters), 1917; Major (Technical), April, 1918; Major (Flying), June 1918; permanent commission, Capt. 1919; gazetted out, Major, 1921; test pilot Orfordness and Martlesham Heath; aeronautical correspondent, Morning Post, 1924-37; The Times, 1939; Evening Standard, 1940; The Manchester Guardian, 1941-58; Editor, Aeronautics, 1939-62. *Publications:* Aerobatics, 1928; Aeolus, or the Future of the Flying Machine; Cross-Country Flying, 1931; Air Power and the Expanding Community, 1944; First Flights, 1957; Danger in the Air, 1958; of Flight and Flyers, 1964; Aviation: The Creative Ideas, 1966; Words and Music for a Mechanical Man, 1967. *Address:* Osborne, Seaview, Isle of Wight. *Clubs:* Royal Aero, Lansdowne; Seaview Yacht.

**STEWART, Potter;** Associate Justice of the Supreme Court of the United States, since 1958; *b* 23 Jan. 1915; *s* of James Garfield Stewart and Harriet Loomis Stewart (*née* Potter); *m* 1943, Mary Ann Bertles; two *s* one *d*. *Educ:* Hotchkiss School, Lakeville, Connecticut; Yale College; Yale Law School. One-year fellowship, Cambridge, Eng. General practice of law as associate with Debevoise, Stevenson, Plimpton and Page, New York City, 1941-42, 1945-47; associate with Dinsmore, Shohl, Sawyer and Dinsmore, Cincinnati, O, 1947; partner of that firm, 1951-54; Judge, US Court of Appeals for 6th Circuit, 1954-58. Member, Cincinnati City Council, 1950-53 (Vice-Mayor, 1952-53). Hon. LLD: Yale Univ., 1959; Kenyon Coll., 1960; Wilmington Coll., 1962; Univ. of Cincinnati, 1963; Ohio Univ., 1964; Univ. of Michigan, 1966. *Address:* Supreme Court Building, Washington, DC 20543, USA. *Clubs:* Camargo

(Cincinnati, Ohio); Chevy Chase (Chevy Chase, Md).

**STEWART, Lt-Col Robert Christie,** TD 1962; Lord Lieutenant of Kinross-shire since 1966; *b* 3 Aug. 1926; *m* 1953, Ann Grizel Cochrane; three *s* two *d*. *Educ:* Eton; University College, Oxford. Lt Scots Guards, 1945-49. Oxford Univ., 1949-51 (BA Agric.). TA, 7 Argyll and Sutherland Highlanders, 1948-66; Lt-Col Comdg 7 A & SH, 1963-66. DL Kinross 1956, VL 1958; Chairman Kinross County Council, 1963-. Dir Coltness Industries 1964. *Address:* Arndean, By Dollar, Kinross-shire. *T:* Dollar 2527. *Club:* New (Edinburgh).

**STEWART, Rt. Hon. Robert Maitland Michael;** *see* Stewart, Rt Hon. Michael.

**STEWART, Sir Ronald (Compton),** 2nd Bt, *cr* 1937; Chairman, London Brick Co. Ltd; *b* 14 Aug. 1903; *s* of Sir (Percy) Malcolm Stewart, 1st Bt, OBE, and Cordelia (*d* 1906,) *d* of late Rt Hon. Sir Joseph Compton Rickett, DL, MP; *S* father, 1951; *m* 1936, Cynthia, OBE, JP, *d* of Harold Farmiloe. *Educ:* Rugby; Jesus College, Cambridge. High Sheriff of Bedfordshire, 1954. *Heir: half-b* Malcolm Stewart [*b* 20 Dec. 1909; *m* 1935 Mary Stephanie (marr. diss. 1957), *d* of Frederick Ramon de Bertodano, 8th Marquis del Moral (Spain)]. *Address:* Maulden Grange, Maulden, Bedfordshire.

**STEWART, Stanley Toft;** Singapore High Commissioner in Australia since 1966; *b* 13 June 1910; *s* of Charles Campbell Stewart and Jeanette Matilda Doral; *m* 1935, Therese Zelie de Souza; seven *d*. *Educ:* St Xavier's Instn, Penang; Raffles Coll., Singapore. Straits Settlements CS, 1934-46; Overseas Civil Service, 1946-. District Officer, Butterworth, Province Wellesley, 1947-52; Dep. Chm., Rural Board, Singapore, 1952-54; Chm., Rural Board, Singapore, 1954; Dep. Sec., Ministry of Local Government, Lands and Housing, Singapore, 1955, Actg Permanent Sec., 1955; Actg Chief Sec., Singapore, Oct. 1957-Jan. 1958; Permanent Secretary: Home Affairs, 1959-63; to Prime Minister, 1961-66. *Recreations:* cricket, tennis, gardening. *Address:* 8 Mugga Way, Canberra, ACT, Australia. *Clubs:* Singapore Recreation; Wanderers' Cricket (Canberra).

**STEWART, Brigadier Thomas G.;** *see* Grainger-Stewart.

**STEWART, Sir Walter Guy Shaw;** *see* Shaw-Stewart.

**STEWART, William,** MC; MA; Master of Haileybury, since 1963; *b* 5 April 1916; *er s* of late Mr and Mrs W. A. Stewart, Allerton, Liverpool; *m* 1942, Betty Hele Sandeman, *er d* of late Colonel and Mrs J. Sandeman Allen, Birkenhead, Cheshire; three *s* one *d*. *Educ:* Liverpool College; Trinity College, Cambridge (Choral Schol.). Sixth Form History Master, Brighton College, 1937-39. Commissioned in 96th (Royal Devon Yeomanry) Field Regiment RA, 1940; Battery Commander in 61st Field Regiment RA, 1944; fought in NW Europe, 1944-45. Returned to Brighton College as Housemaster, 1945; Headmaster of Brighton College, 1950-63. *Recreations:* reading, music, all games. *Address:* The Master's Lodge, Haileybury, Hertford. *T:* Hoddesdon 62352. *Clubs:* Public Schools; Union (Cambridge).

**STEWART, Prof. William Alexander Campbell,** MA, PhD; Vice-Chancellor, University of Keele, since 1967; *b* Glasgow, 17 Dec. 1915; *s* of late Thomas Stewart, Glasgow, and Helen Fraser, Elgin, Morayshire; *m* 1947, Ella Elizabeth Burnett, of Edinburgh; one *s* one *d*. *Educ:* Colfe's Grammar Sch., London; University Coll., and Inst. of Education, Univ. of London. Exhibitioner, University Coll., London., 1934-37; BA 1937; MA 1941; PhD 1947; Diploma in Education, 1938. Sen. English Master: (and Housemaster), Friends' School, Saffron Walden, Essex, 1938-43; Abbotsholme School, Derbyshire, 1943-44 (Member of Governing Body, 1960-); Asst Lectr and Lectr in Education, University Coll., Nottingham, 1944-47; Lectr in Education, Univ. of Wales (Cardiff), 1947-50; Prof. of Education, Univ. of Keele, 1950-67. Vis. Prof., McGill Univ., 1957, Univ. of Calif., Los Angeles 1959; Simon Vis. Prof., Univ. of Manchester, 1962-63; Chairman: Nat. Adv. Council for Child Care, 1968-; Univs Council for Adult Educn, 1969-; Mem., Inter-Univ. Council for Higher Education Overseas; Mem., Commonwealth Univ. Interchange Council; Fellow, Internat. Inst. of Art and Letters. *Publications:* Quakers and Education, 1953; (ed with J. Eros) Systematic Sociology of Karl Mannheim, 1957; (with K. Mannheim) An Introduction to the Sociology of Education, 1962; contrib. to The American College (ed Sanford), 1962; The Educational Innovators (Vol. 1, with W. P. McCann), 1967; The Educational Innovators (Vol. 2), 1968. *Recreations:* formerly most games; travelling, talking, theatre, music. *Address:* The Clock House, The University, Keele, Staffs. *T:* Keele Park 394. *Clubs:* Athenæum, Oriental; Federation House (Stoke on Trent).

**STEWART, William Ian,** QC 1965; *b* 8 Nov. 1925; *s* of late John Stewart, FRIBA, and Mrs Maysie Shepherd Service or Stewart, Drimfearn, Bridge of Allan; *m* 1955, Naomi Joan Douglas, *d* of late Sir James Boyd Douglas, CBE, and of Lady Douglas, Barstibly, Castle Douglas; one *s* one *d*. *Educ:* Loretto; Glasgow and Edinburgh Univs. Sub-Lt, RNVR, 1944-46. Called to the Bar, 1951; Advocate-Depute, 1959-64. mem., Criminal Injuries Compensation Bd, 1969-70. *Address:* 60 Northumberland Street, Edinburgh 3. *T:* 031-556 2823. *Clubs:* New (Edinburgh); RNVR (Glasgow).

**STEWART, William McCausland;** Professor of French, University of Bristol, 1945-66; Emeritus, 1966; *b* 17 Sept. 1900; *yr s* of late Abraham McCausland Stewart, Londonderry, and Alexandrina Catherine Margaret Elsner, Dublin; *m* 1933, Ann Cecilia Selo (*d* 1969); two *d*. *Educ:* Foyle Coll., Londonderry; Trinity Coll., Dublin (Sizar, Schol. and Sen. Moderator in Mod. Literature–French and German; Prizeman in Old and Middle English; Vice-Chancellor's Prizeman in English Verse). BA 1922; MA 1926; Lecteur d'Anglais, Univ. of Montpellier, 1922-23 (Certificat de Licence en Phonétique, 1923). Resident Lecteur d'Anglais at Ecole Normale Supérieure, Paris, 1923-26; also studied Sorbonne (Diplôme d'Etudes Supérieures de Lettres; Langues Classiques, 1925) and Ecole des Hautes Etudes, Paris, and taught Collège Sainte-Barbe, Paris; Lectr in French, Univ. of Sheffield, 1927 and 1928; Lectr in French and Joint Head of French Dept, Univ. of St Andrews and University College, Dundee, from 1928 onwards. Seconded for War Service in Foreign Research and Press Service (Chatham House), Balliol College, Oxford, Sept. 1939; Head of French Section of same, 1940-43; Head of French Section, Research Dept of Foreign Office, 1943-45. Chairman, University of Bristol Art Lectures Committee, 1946-66; Dean of Faculty of Arts, 1960-62; Visiting Professor, Univ. of Auckland, 1967. Member Council, RWA;

Governor, Bath Academy of Art, Corsham Court; Chairman, Bristol-Bordeaux Assoc.; Corr Mem. Acad. des Sciences, Belles Lettres et Arts de Bordeaux and of Acad. Montesquieu. Chevalier de la Légion d'Honneur, 1950. Officier des Palmes Académiques, 1957, Commandeur, 1966. DLitt (*hc*), Nat. Univ. of Ireland, 1963. *Publications:* Les Etudes Françaises en Grand Bretagne, Paris, 1929 (with G. T. Clapton); translation of Paul Valéry's Eupalinos, with Preface, Oxford, 1932, and of his Dialogues, Bollingen Series XLV, New York, 1956 and London, 1958; Aspects of the French Classical Ideal, 1967; Tokens in Time (poems), 1968. Contribs to literary reviews and learned periodicals, English, French and American, mainly connected with 17th Century Literature and contemporary France. *Address:* 5 Cotham Park, Bristol. *T:* Bristol 48156.

**STEWART-CLARK, Sir Stewart,** 2nd Bt, *cr* 1918; JP; *b* 4 July 1904; *s* of 1st Bt and Marie Gertrude (*d* 1937), *d* of Major Marcell Conran of Brondyffryn, Denbigh; *S* father, 1924; *m* 1927, Jane, *d* of late Major Arundell Clarke, Fremington House, North Devon; one *s* one *d*. *Educ:* Eton. Served War of 1939-45 (Lieutenant, RA). A Member of the Royal Company of Archers (HM Body Guard for Scotland). *Recreations:* squash-rackets (represented Scotland *v* England and Ireland, 1937-38, and against Ireland in 1946, twice runner-up in Scottish Squash Rackets Championships), lawn tennis (has played for East of Scotland), shooting, and fishing, golf and billiards. *Heir: s* John Stewart-Clark [*b* 17 Sept. 1929; *m* 1958, Lydia F., *d* of W. Loudon, Valkenhorst, Valkenswaard, Holland; one *s* three *d*]. *Address:* Dundas Castle, South Queensferry, West Lothian. *T:* S Queensferry 364. *Clubs:* MCC, Queen's; Hon. Company of Edinburgh Golfers (Muirfield); Royal Burgess Golfing Society (Edinburgh); North Berwick Golf.

**STEWART-JONES, Mrs Richard;** *see* Smith, Emma.

**STEWART-RICHARDSON, Sir Simon (Alaisdair),** 17th Bt *cr* 1630; student; *b* 9 June 1947; *s* of Sir Ian Rorie Hay Stewart-Richardson, 16th Bt, and of Audrey Meryl, *e d* of Claude Odlum; *S* father, 1969. *Educ:* Trinity College, Glenalmond. *Heir: b* Ninian Rorie Stewart-Richardson, *b* 20 Jan. 1949. *Address:* Lynedale House, Longcross, near Chertsey, Surrey. *T:* Longcross 248.

**STEWART-ROBERTS, Walter Stewart,** CBE 1948; *b* 24 March 1889; *s* of late Rev. Ernest Stewart Roberts, Master of Gonville and Caius College, Cambridge; *m* 1928, Elizabeth Marie Errol, CStJ, *d* of late Errol Kerr, New York City, USA; one *s* one *d*. *Educ:* Eton College; Gonville and Caius College, Cambridge, 1912-24. Egyptian Civil Service: Ministry of the Interior, Inspector of Interior, and ultimately Director of Personnel of the Ministry; retired 1924. 1924-40 and 1951-, member of the London Stock Exchange. 1940-48, Foreign Office: Director of Finance and Admin., 1940-46, Dep. Director-Gen., 1946, Political Intelligence Dept.; Asst Sec., Head of Estab. and Finance Dept (Information), 1946-48; retired 1948. Order of the Nile, 4th Class, 1919. *Recreation:* gardening. *Address:* Pond House, South Chailey, near Lewes, Sussex. *T:* Barcombe 240; 7 Birchin Lane, EC3. *T:* 01-626 5644. *Club:* Leander (Henley-on-Thames).

**STEWART-SMITH, Ven. David Cree,** MA; Archdeacon of Rochester and a Canon Residentiary of Rochester Cathedral, since 1969; *b* 22 May 1913; 3rd *s* of late Thomas Stewart Stewart-Smith, JP, Heathlands, Kinver, Staffs, and Mabel (*née* McDougall); *m* 1943, Kathleen Georgiana Maule Ffinch, *d* of Rev. K. M. Ffinch, Ifield, Kent. *Educ:* Marlborough; King's Coll., Cambridge; Cuddesdon Theol. College. BA 1939, MA 1943. Vicar-Choral and Sacrist, York Minster, 1944-49; Vicar of Shadwell, Leeds, 1949-52; Warden, Brasted Place Coll., 1952-63; Dean of St George's Cath., Jerusalem, and Administrator of St George's Coll., 1964-67; Commissary for Archbishop in Jerusalem, 1968-; Archdeacon of Bromley and Hon. Canon of Rochester, 1968-69; Director of Ordinands, dio. Rochester, 1968-; Fellow of Woodard Corp.: Northern Div., 1949-52; Southern Div., 1959-64. *Recreations:* architecture, music, travel, gardening. *Address:* The Archdeaconry, Rochester, Kent. *T:* Medway 42527. *Club:* United University.

**STEWART-SMITH, Dudley Geoffrey;** MP (C) Belper Division of Derbyshire since 1970; financial public relations consultant since 1968; *b* 28 Dec. 1933; *s* of Dudley Cautley Stewart-Smith; *m* 1956, Kay Mary; three *s*. *Educ:* Winchester; RMA Sandhurst. Regular Officer, The Black Watch, 1952-60. Sec., Foreign Affairs Circle; Editor, East-West Digest; Dir, Foreign Affairs Publishing Co.; Financial Times, 1968. *Publications:* The Defeat of Communism, 1964; No Vision Here: Non-Military Warfare in Britain, 1966; contribs to various foreign, defence and communist affairs jls at home and overseas. *Recreations:* walking, swimming, shooting and stalking. *Address:* Church House, Petersham, Surrey. *T:* 01-940 2885. *Clubs:* Carlton; Church Gresley Memorial.

**STEWARTSON, Keith,** FRS 1965; Goldsmid Professor of Mathematics, University College, London, since 1964; *b* 20 Sept. 1925; *s* of late G. C. Stewartson and M. Stewartson (*née* Hyde); *m* 1953, Elizabeth Jean Forrester; two *s* one *d*. *Educ:* Stockton Secondary Sch.; St Catharine's Coll., Cambridge. Lectr in Applied Mathematics at Bristol Univ., 1949-53; Research Fellow in Aeronautics, California Inst. of Technology, 1953-54; Reader in Applied Mathematics at Bristol Univ., 1954-58; Prof. of Applied Mathematics, Durham Univ. (late Durham Colls), 1958-64. FIMA, 1964. *Publications:* Laminar Compressible Boundary Layers, 1964; papers in Mathematical and Aeronautical Journals. *Recreations:* coaching boats, music. *Address:* 51 Dunstan Road, NW11. *T:* 01-455 1702.

**STEYN, Hon. Lucas Cornelius; Hon. Mr Justice Steyn,** LLD; Chief Justice of Union of South Africa since 1959; *b* Geluksdam, Orange Free State, 21 Dec. 1903; *s* of late Christiaan Louwrens Steyn; *m* 1928, Huibrecht Magdalena, *d* of C. B. van Schoor; one *s* one *d*. *Educ:* Kroonstad Secondary School; Stellenbosch University. Lecturer in Roman Dutch Law at Stellenbosch University, 1926-28; Attorney-General, South-West Africa, 1931; Senior Law Adviser, Union Government, 1944; Judge of Transvaal Provincial Division, 1951-55; Judge of Appeal, 1955-59. *Publication:* Uitleg van Wette. *Address:* Supreme Court, Appellate Division, Bloemfontein, South Africa; 33 Waverley Road, Bloemfontein. *Club:* Constantia (Pretoria).

**STIBBS, Prof. Douglas Walter Noble,** MSc Sydney, DPhil Oxon; FRAS, FRSE; Napier Professor of Astronomy and Director of the University Observatory, University of St Andrews, since 1959; *b* 17 Feb. 1919; 2nd *s* of Edward John Stibbs, Sydney, NSW; *m* 1949, Margaret Lilian Calvert, BSc, DipEd

(Sydney), AID, *er d* of Rev. John Calvert, Sydney, NSW; two *d. Educ:* Sydney High Sch.; Univ. of Sydney; New College, Oxford. Deas Thomson Scholar, Sch. of Physics, Univ. of Sydney, 1940; BSc (Sydney), 1st Class Hons, Univ. Medal in Physics, 1942; MSc (Sydney), 1943; DPhil (Oxon), 1954. Johnson Memorial Prize and Gold Medal for Advancement of Astronomy and Meteorology, Oxford Univ., 1956. Asst Lectr, Dept of Mathematics and Physics, New England University Coll., Armidale, NSW (now the Univ. of New England), 1942-45; Scientific Officer and Sen. Scientific Officer, Commonwealth Observatory, Canberra, ACT, 1945-51; Radcliffe Travelling Fellow in Astronomy, Radcliffe Observatory, Pretoria, S Africa, and Univ. Observatory, Oxford, 1951-54; PSO, UKAEA, 1955-59; Vis. Prof. of Astrophysics, Yale Univ. Observatory, 1966-67; British Council Vis. Prof., Univ. of Utrecht, 1968. Member: Internat. Astronomical Union, 1951- (Chm. Finance Cttee, 1964-67); Amer. Astronomical Soc., 1956-; Adv. Cttee on Meteorology for Scotland, 1960-69; Board of Visitors, Royal Greenwich Observatory, 1963-65; Council RAS, 1964-67, 1970-; Council, RSE, 1970-; National Cttee for Astronomy, 1964-; SRC Cttees for Royal Greenwich Observatory, and Royal Observatory, Edinburgh, 1966-; SRC Astronomy, Space and Radio Bd, 1970-. *Publications:* The Outer Layers of a Star (with Sir Richard Woolley), 1953; contrib. Theoretical Astrophysics and Astronomy in Monthly Notices of RAS and other Jls. *Recreations:* music, photography. *Address:* University Observatory, Buchanan Gardens, St Andrews, Fife. *T:* St Andrews 2643.

**STIEBEL, Victor Frank;** formerly Couturier; now writer and journalist; *b* South Africa, 14 March 1907; *s* of late Frank Stiebel, Durban, Natal, S Africa. *Educ:* South Africa; Jesus College, Cambridge. Opened own couture business, 1932. Army, 1940-45. Has designed clothes: for the Princess Margaret, the Countess of Snowdon; for the Duchess of Gloucester; for the late Princess Marina; for the Princess Alexandra, the Hon. Mrs Angus Ogilvy. Chm. and Vice-Chm., Incorporated Society of London Fashion Designers for many years. Retd, 1963. *Publication:* South African Childhood (vol. 1 of autobiography), 1968. *Recreation:* music. *Address:* 22 Hyde Park Gardens, W2.

**STIFF, Rt. Rev. Hugh Vernon;** *see* Keewatin, Bishop of.

**STIKKER, Dirk Uipko;** Hon. GCVO 1958; Hon. GBE 1951; Grand Cross, Order of Orange Nassau; Knight, Order of Netherlands Lion; Director: Friesch-Groningsche Hypotheekbank; Wm H. Müller & Co.; Deli-Maatschappij; *b* 5 Feb. 1897; *s* of Uipko Obbo Stikker and Ida Meursing; *m* 1922, Catherina Paulina van der Scheer; two *s. Educ:* Latin-grammar school; University of Groningen (Doctor of Law, 1922). Manager, Lissense Bank Vereniging, Lisse, 1931; Man. Dir, Heinekens Bierbrouwerijen, 1935; Bd of Directors, Nederlandse Bank en Nederlandse Handel Maatschappij; Organiser and Pres., Netherlands Labour Foundation, 1945; Organiser and Chm., Party of Freedom, later known as People's Party for Freedom and Democracy (liberal), 1946. Member Netherlands Govt Delegation to Round Table Conf. on political status of Netherlands West-Indies, 1946; Round Table Conf. with reps of Indonesia and preparation for Independence of Indonesia, 1948; Netherlands Minister of Foreign Affairs, 1948-52; Member Political Purging Council, 1945; Netherlands rep., Council, OEEC, 1950; Chairman OEEC, 1950-52; Netherlands Envoy Extraordinary and Minister Plenipotentiary to Icelandic Republic, 1954-56; Netherlands Ambassador at the Court of St James, 1952-58; Netherlands Ambassador to the Icelandic Republic, 1956-58. Chairman Netherlands Delegation to Economic and Social Council, UN, 1955-56. Netherlands Permanent Representative on the North Atlantic Council and to the Council of OEEC in Paris, 1958-61; Secretary-General of NATO, 1961-64; Consultant to Unctad, 1966. Holds Grand Cross of several orders in Europe, South America, etc. *Publications:* Men of Responsibility, 1966; (for UNCTAD) The role of private enterprise in investment and promotion of exports in developing countries, 1967; many articles. *Recreation:* golf. *Address:* Villa Belfaggio, Menaggio-Loveno, Lago di Como, Italy. *T:* Menaggio 2361.

**STILES, Walter Stanley,** OBE 1946; FRS 1957; PhD, DSc; formerly Deputy Chief Scientific Officer, The National Physical Laboratory, Teddington, retired 1961; *b* 15 June 1901; *s* of Walter Stiles and Elizabeth Catherine (*née* Smith); *m* 1928, Pauline Frida Octavia, *d* of Judge Henrik Brendstrup, Hillerōd, Denmark; no *c. Educ:* University College, London; St John's College, Cambridge. Andrews Scholar, University Coll., London, 1918. Demonstrator in Physics, 1920-22; PhD London 1929, DSc London 1939; Carpenter Medallist, London Univ., 1944. Technical Officer, RN Signal School, 1923-25; Scientific Officer, Nat. Physical Lab., 1925-61. Gen. Sec. Internat. Commn on Illumination, 1928-31; Vice-President Physical Soc., 1948-49; President, Illuminating Engineering Soc., 1960, Gold Medallist, 1967; Chm. Colour Group of Physical Soc., 1949-51, Newton Lectr, 1967; Thomas Young Orator (Physical Soc.), 1955; Regents' Lectr (UCLA), 1964; Tillyer Medallist (Optical Society of America), 1965; Finsen Medallist (Congr. Internat. de Photobiologie), 1968. *Publications:* Thermionic Emission, 1932; Color Science (with G. Wyszecki), 1967; many papers on illuminating engineering and physiological optics in Proc. Royal Soc., Trans Illum. Eng Soc., etc. *Recreation:* painting. *Address:* 89 Richmond Hill Court, Richmond, Surrey. *T:* 01-940 4334.

**STINSON, David John; His Honour Judge Stinson;** County Court Judge since 1969; *b* 22 Feb. 1921; *s* of late Henry John Edwin Stinson, MC, MA, LLB, Beckenham, Kent (sometime Chief Commoner of City of London, solicitor), and late Margaret Stinson (*née* Little); *m* 1950, Eleanor Judith (*née* Chance); two *s* two *d* (and one *s* decd). *Educ:* Eastbourne Coll.; Emmanuel Coll., Cambridge. MA 1946; Jesters Club, 1949 (Rugby Fives). Served War of 1939-45: Essex Yeomanry, Capt. RA, and Air OP, 1941-46 (despatches). Called to Bar, Middle Temple, 1947; Dep. Chm., Herts QS, 1965. Liveryman, Worshipful Co. of Needlemakers. *Recreations:* bird-watching, carpentry, growing vegetables. *Address:* Hoop House, Little Hadham, Herts. *T:* Bishops Stortford 51673.

**STIRLING, Alfred,** CBE 1953 (OBE 1941); *b* Melbourne, Victoria, Australia, 8 Sept. 1902; *s* of Robert Andrew and Isabel Stirling. *Educ:* Scotch College, Melbourne; Melbourne Univ.; University Coll., Oxford (MA, LLB). Victorian Bar, 1927-33. Private Secretary to Attorney-General of Commonwealth (Rt Hon. R. G. Menzies), 1934-35; Assistant External Affairs Officer, London, 1936; head of Political Section, Dept of External Affairs, Canberra, 1936-37; External Affairs Officer,

London, 1937-45; Counsellor, Australian Legation to Netherlands, 1942-45; High Commissioner for Australia in Canada, 1945-46; Australian Minister in Washington, 1946-48; Australian High Comr in S Africa, 1948-50; Australian Ambassador: to the Netherlands, 1950-55; to France, 1955-59; to the Philippines, 1959-62; to Greece, 1964-65; to Italy, 1962-67. Grand Cross of St Gregory; Grand Cordon of Royal George (Greece). *Publication:* (part author) Victorian, 1934; Joseph Bosisto, 1970. *Address:* Flat 30, St Ives, 166 Toorak Road West, South Yarra, Victoria 3141, Australia. *Clubs:* Melbourne (Melbourne); Caledonian (London).

**STIRLING, (Archibald) David,** DSO 1942; OBE 1946; Chairman, Television International Enterprises Ltd; *b* 15 Nov. 1915; *s* of late Brigadier-General Archibald Stirling of Keir, and of Hon. Mrs Margaret Stirling, OBE, 4th *d* of 13th Baron Lovat. *Educ:* Ampleforth College, Yorks; (for a brief period) Cambridge University. In Sept. 1939 was Mem. SRO, Scots Guards and served with that Regt for first six months of War when he was transferred to No. 3 Commando (Brigade of Guards) and went out with this unit to Middle East; subseq. served with First SAS Regt (POW, 1943-45). President, Capricorn Africa Society, 1947-59, living at that time in Africa based on Salisbury and Nairobi. Officer, Légion d'Honneur. *Address:* 21 Sloane Street, SW1. *T:* 01-235 4604. *Clubs:* White's, Turf, Pratt's, Beefsteak.

**STIRLING, Carl Ludwig,** CBE 1943; *b* 10 Nov. 1890; *yr s* of late Professor William Stirling, Victoria University of Manchester; *m* 1915, Fenna Kemp Fenn-Smith; one *s* one *d. Educ:* Norman House School; Victoria University of Manchester (LLB). Called to Bar, Middle Temple, 1913; Western Circuit, 1915-18, in the Forces (Capt.); entered office of the Judge Advocate-General, 1924; KC 1946; Deputy Judge Advocate-General of the Forces, 1938-52; retired, 1952. *Address:* The Old Ground, Halse, Nr Taunton, Somerset. *T:* Bishop's Lydeard 392.

**STIRLING, Sir Charles (Norman),** KCMG 1955 (CMG 1941); KCVO 1957; *b* 19 Nov. 1901; *er s* of late F. H. Stirling Victoria, British Columbia; *m* 1950, Ann, *o d* of J. H. Moore; one *s* two *d. Educ:* Wellington College; Corpus Christi College, Oxford. Third Secretary, Diplomatic Service, 1925; Second Secretary, 1930; First Secretary, 1937; Head of a Department in Ministry of Economic Warfare, 1939-42; Acting Counsellor in the Foreign Office, 1942; Counsellor, British Embassy, Lisbon, 1946; Consul-General, Tangier, 1949-51; Ambassador to Chile, 1951-54; Ambassador to Portugal, 1955-60. *Recreation:* fishing. *Address:* Borovere, Alton, Hants. *Club:* Travellers'.

**STIRLING, David;** *see* Stirling, Archibald D.

**STIRLING, Duncan Alexander;** JP; DL; Director: National Westminster Bank Ltd, since 1969 (Chairman, Westminster Bank, 1962-68, National Westminster Bank, 1968-69); London Life Association (President, 1951-65); Mercantile Investment Trust; Baring Foundation; *b* 6 Oct. 1899; 4th *s* of late Major William Stirling, of Fairburn, Ross-shire, and Charlotte Eva, *d* of late Æneas Mackintosh, Daviot, Inverness-shire; *m* 1926, Lady Marjorie Murray, *e d* of 8th Earl of Dunmore, VC, DSO, MVO; two *s. Educ:* Harrow; New College, Oxford. Coldstream Guards, 1918 and again 1940-43. Partner, H. S. Lefevre & Co., Merchant Bankers, 1929-49; Director, Westminster Bank, 1935-69. Pres., Inst. of Bankers, 1964-66; Chm., Cttee of London Clearing Bankers and Pres., British Bankers' Assoc., 1966-68. Prime Warden Fishmongers Co., 1954-55. *Address:* 28 St James's Place, SW1; Hinton Ampner Place, Alresford, Hants. *Club:* Brooks's.

**STIRLING, Hon. Sir James;** *see* Stirling, Hon. Sir R. J. L.

**STIRLING, Sir John,** Kt 1956; MBE 1919; Lord Lieutenant of Ross and Cromarty, 1964-68; Member, County Council of Ross and Cromarty, 1919-70 (Convener, 1935-61); Forestry Commissioner, 1948-62; Chairman, Scottish National Committee of Forestry Commission, 1950-59; Freeman, Royal Burgh of Dingwall; *b* Sept. 1893; *e s* of William Stirling, Fairburn; *m* 1915, Marjory Kythe, *d* of Sir Kenneth Mackenzie, 7th Bt of Gairloch; one *s* three *d* (and one *s* decd). *Educ:* Harrow; Magdalen College, Oxford. Served with Lovat Scouts, 1914-35. *Address:* Fairburn, Muir of Ord, Ross-shire. *T:* Urray 208. *Club:* New (Edinburgh).

*See also Maj.-Gen. S. M. O'H. Abraham.*

**STIRLING, John Bertram;** Chairman of Board E. G. M. Cape & Co. Ltd since 1960; Chancellor, Queen's University, Kingston, Ontario, since 1960; *b* 29 Nov. 1888; *s* of Dr James A. Stirling and Jessie Bertram, Picton, Ont; *m* 1928, Emily P., *d* of Col and Mrs E. T. Sturdee, Saint John, NB; one *d. Educ:* Queen's University, Kingston, Canada. BA 1909, BSc 1911, Queen's Univ., Kingston. Resident Engineer, Chipman and Power, Cons. Engineers, Toronto, 1911-15; with E. G. M. Cape and Co. Ltd from 1915; Field Engineer, 1915; Supt 1924; Gen. Supt, 1930; Vice-Pres., 1940. President: Canadian Construction Assoc., 1942; Montreal Board of Trade, 1950; Engineering Inst. of Canada, 1952. Hon. LLD: Queen's, Kingston, 1951; Toronto, 1961; Hon. DSc: Royal Mil. Coll., Canada, 1962; McGill, 1963. Hon. Col 3rd Field Regt Royal Can. Engrs. Sir John Kennedy Medal of Eng. Inst. of Canada, 1954; Montreal Medal, Queen's Univ. Alumni Assoc., 1955; Julian Smith Medal, Eng. Inst. of Canada, 1963. *Recreations:* sailing, country life, music. *Address:* Lacolle, PQ, Canada. *Clubs:* Saint James's, Forest and Stream (Montreal); Halifax.

**STIRLING, Rear-Adm. Michael Grote;** Agent-General for British Columbia in the United Kingdom and Europe, since 1968; *b* 29 June 1915; *s* of late Hon. Grote Stirling and late Mabel Katherine (*née* Brigstocke), Kelowna, British Columbia; *m* 1942, Sheelagh Kathleen Russell; two *s* one *d. Educ:* Shawnigan Lake School, BC; RNC Greenwich. Cadet, RCN, 1933; HMS Frobisher for training till 1934, then as Midshipman and Sub-Lt in RN, returning Canada Jan. 1938; Ships of RCN until 1941; specialized in Signals at HM Signal School, Portsmouth, then Home Fleet; Deputy Director, Signal Div., Naval Service HQ, Ottawa, 1942-43; SSO to C-in-C, Canadian North-West Atlantic, 1943-44; Commanded destroyers, 1944-46; Director Naval Communications, rank of Commander, 1949-51; promoted Captain and staff of Supreme Allied Commander Atlantic, Norfolk, Va, 1953-55; Commanded HMCS Cornwallis, 1955-57; 2nd Cdn Escort Sqdn, 1957-58; Naval Member of Directing Staff, Nat. Defence College as Commodore, 1958-61; Senior Canadian Officer Afloat, 1961-62; Chief of Naval Personnel and Rear-Admiral, 1962-64; Flag Officer Pacific Coast and Maritime Commander, Pacific, 1964-66; Director, Univ. of Victoria Foundation, 1967-68. *Recreations:* golf, ski-ing. *Address:* British Columbia House,

1 Regent Street, SW1. *Clubs:* East India and Sports, Royal Automobile; Union Club of British Columbia, Victoria Golf (Victoria, BC).

**STIRLING, Hon. Sir (Robert) James (Lindsay),** Kt 1964; **Hon. Mr Justice Stirling;** Judge of the High Court of Justice, Probate, Divorce and Admiralty Division, since 1964; *b* 18 Oct. 1907; *s* of Robert Stirling, MD, FRCSE, and Mary Elizabeth Martin. *Educ:* Fettes Coll.; Worcester Coll., Oxford (Hon. Fellow, 1969). Called to Bar 1931; QC 1955. Served War of 1939-45 with RA; commissioned, Dec. 1939; served in Middle East, 1941-June 1945; Staff of Judge Advocate General, 1942-Dec. 1945; Lt-Col, 1945. Vice-Pres. and Chm. Council, Worcester Coll. Soc.; Chm. Council, London Acad. of Music and Dramatic Art. Hon. Fellow, Worcester Coll., Oxford, 1969-. *Recreations:* golf, music. *Address:* 5 Lecky Street, SW3. *T:* 01-373 1264; Whiteacre, Cold Harbour, Cray's Pond, Near Reading, Berks. *T:* Pangbourne 2318. *Club:* Garrick.

**STIRLING, Viola Henrietta Christian,** CBE 1947; TD 1951; DL; *b* 3 June 1907; *d* of late Charles Stirling of Gargunnock. *Educ:* Queen Ethelburga's Sch., Harrogate; Lady Margaret Hall, Oxford (BA). Joined Auxiliary Territorial Service, 1939; Deputy Director ATS Scottish Command, 1945; released with Hon. Rank of Controller, 1949. Member: Finance Committee, ATS Benevolent Fund, 1948-64; of Stirling and Clackmannan Hospitals Board of Management, 1948-64; selected military member TA & AFA, County of Stirling, 1948-68; Hon. Colonel 317 (Sc. Comd) Bn WRAC/TA, 1959-62. Member of Stirling County Council, 1958-67; DL Co. of Stirling, 1965. *Address:* Gargunnock, Stirlingshire. *T:* Gargunnock 202. *Club:* Ladies' Caledonian (Edinburgh).

**STIRLING, Brig. Walter Andrew,** DSO 1918; MC; DL; late RFA; *b* 5 Aug. 1883; 3rd *s* of late Gen. Sir William Stirling, KCB, Col Comdt, Royal Artillery; *m* 1914, Louie, 2nd *d* of late J. V. Faber, KCD, Consul-General for Denmark; one *s* two *d*. *Educ:* Wellington College; RMA, Woolwich. Received Commission in RFA, 1902; France, Feb. 1915; Brigade-Major RA 18th Div. Feb. 1917-March 1919; RA Mid. Div. Army of Rhine, March-April 1919; Brigade Major 4th Division, Colchester, 1919-22; retired pay, 1923; recalled, 1939; raised 119th AA Battery; Comd 30th LAA Regt, 1939-40; 40th AA Bde, 1941; Worcester Sub-Area, 1942-43; retired for age, 1943. Director Red Cross and St John Civilian Relief, France and Belgium, 1944: Red Cross HQ 1945. Hon. Commissioner, Boy Scouts, Suffolk; DL Suffolk 1958. *Address:* Nussteads, Polstead, Suffolk. *T:* Boxford 255. *Club:* Army and Navy.

**STIRLING, Gen. Sir William (Gurdon),** GCB 1965 (KCB 1961; CB 1957); CBE 1952; DSO 1945; psc; idc; Gentleman Usher to the Sword of State since 1967; ADC General to the Queen, 1964-66; Commander-in-Chief, British Army of the Rhine and Commander NATO Northern Army Group, 1963-66, retired; late Royal Artillery; *b* 25 May 1907; *s* of Major Charles Stirling and Hon Mrs Stirling; *m* 1941, Frances Marguerite, OStJ, *d* of J. Wedderburn Wilson, Burley Bushes, Ascot; three *d*. *Educ:* Wellington College; RMA Woolwich. Commissioned, 1926; CRA 1 Div., Palestine, 1947-48; Chief of Staff, AA Comd, 1950-52; Comd 27 Inf. Bde, 1952-55; Principal Staff Officer to Chairman of Chiefs of Staffs, 1956-58; GOC 6th Armoured Div., 1958; General Officer Commanding 2 Division, 1958-60; General Officer Commanding-in-Chief, Western Command, 1960-61; Military Secretary to the Sec. of State for War, 1961-63. Colonel Commandant, Royal Artillery, 1962-66. Officer, Legion of Merit (USA). *Recreation:* shooting. *Address:* Saxham Hall, Bury St Edmunds, Suffolk. *T:* Barrow 259. *Clubs:* Army and Navy, Boodle's.

**STIRLING-HAMILTON, Sir Robert William;** *see* Hamilton.

**STOBART, Patrick Desmond,** MBE 1950; Counsellor, HM Diplomatic Service; Head of Export Promotion Department, Foreign and Commonwealth Office, since 1970; *b* 14 Feb. 1920; *s* of late Reginald and Eva Stobart; *m* 1951, Sheila, *d* of late A. W. Brown, Belfast; three *s* one *d*. *Educ:* Cathedral and Cleveland House Schools, Salisbury; St Edmund Hall, Oxford. Served Royal Artillery and Wilts Regiment, 1940-46. Tübingen University, 1946; Political Officer, Trucial Oman, 1947; Chancery, Bonn, 1951-53; FO, 1953-54; Consul, Benghazi, 1954-58; FO, 1958-60; Commercial Counsellor, British Embassy, Helsinki, 1960-64, Copenhagen, 1964-66; Consul-General, Gothenburg, 1966-68; seconded to Aero-Engine Div., Rolls-Royce Ltd, 1968-68; Gwilym Gibbon Research Fellow, Nuffield College, Oxford, 1969-70. *Recreations:* history, sailing, fishing. *Address:* 12 Beech Lane, Guildford, Surrey. *T:* Guildford 69281. *Club:* Travellers'.

**STOBY, Sir Kenneth Sievewright,** Kt 1961; Director, Demerara Bauxite Co. Ltd, Georgetown; Chancellor of the Judiciary, Guyana, 1966-68; *b* 19 Oct. 1903; *s* of late Mr and Mrs W. S. Stoby; *m* 1935, Eunice Badley; one *s* one *d*. *Educ:* Christ Church Sch., Georgetown; Queen's Coll., Georgetown. Called to Bar, Lincoln's Inn, 1930; private practice until 1940; Magistrate, 1940; seconded Dep. Controller of Prices, 1944; seconded again, 1947, Controller Supplies and Prices; acted Legal Draftsman; Chairman several Boards and Committees; Magistrate Nigeria, 1948; Registrar of Deeds and Supreme Court, British Guiana, 1950; Puisne Judge, 1953; Chief Justice, Barbados, 1958. *Address:* Demerara, Guyana.

**STOCK, Allen Lievesley;** Chairman, The Morgan Crucible Co. Ltd, 1959-69; *b* 24 September 1906; 2nd *s* of late Cyril Lievesley and Irene Mary Stock; *m* 1933, Rosemary Nancy Hopps; two *s* one *d*. *Educ:* Charterhouse; Faraday House; Christ's College, Cambridge. Belliss & Morcom, 1926-27; The British Thomson-Houston Co. Ltd, Rugby, 1928-32; The Morgan Crucible Company Ltd, 1932-69. Chairman, London Chamber of Commerce, 1958-62, Vice-Pres., 1962-; Mem. Post Office Users' Council, 1966-69. Hon. Treasurer, The Sail Training Assoc., 1969-. *Recreations:* boats, gardening, bird-watching. *Address:* Furzefield Cottage, Bosham Hoe, W Sussex. *T:* Bosham 3231. *Clubs:* Junior Carlton; Hawks (Cambridge).

**STOCK, Keith L(ievesley),** CB 1957; Under Secretary, Department of Economic Affairs, 1965-68, retired; *b* 24 Oct. 1911; *s* of late Cyril Lievesley Stock and Irene Mary Stock (*née* Tomkins); *m* 1937, Joan Katherine Stock (*née* Milne); two *s* one *d*. *Educ:* Charterhouse; New College, Oxford. Petroleum Department, Board of Trade, 1935; Ministry of Fuel and Power, 1942; Imperial Defence College, 1951; Cabinet Office, 1954; Ministry of Fuel and Power, 1955; UK Delegn to the Brussels and ECSC Conferences, 1962; UK Delegn to the European Communities, Brussels, 1963. Min. of Technology, 1964. *Address:* c/o Barclays Bank, Millbank, SW1.

**STOCK, Col Philip Graham,** CB 1918; CMG 1947; CBE 1919; FRCP. Hon. FRCSE; formerly: Medical Consultant, World Health Organisation; Senior Medical Officer and Medical Adviser, Ministry of Health; Director of Medical Services, Union of South Africa; *y s* of Granger Stock, Clifton, Glos; *m* 1934, Frances, *o d* of Hugh Feuchelle, Piazza Di Spagna, Rome. *Educ:* Clifton; Bristol University. Formerly Captain RAMC; served South African War, 1900-02 (Queen's medal three clasps, King's medal two clasps); DDMS South African Contingent to Europe; DMS German S West African Campaign (despatches, CB, CBE). Médaille (d'Argent) de la Reconnaissance Française. *Publications:* various scientific papers. *Address:* Tankard Cottage, Ramsbury, Wilts. *T:* Ramsbury 273. *Clubs:* Athenæum; Rand (Johannesburg).

**STOCK, Raymond,** QC 1964; Recorder of Southampton since 1966; Deputy Chairman, Dorset Quarter Sessions, since 1964; *b* 1913; *s* of late A. E. and M. E. Stock; *m* 1969, E. Dorothy Thorpe. *Educ:* West Monmouth School; Balliol College, Oxford. Barrister-at-law, Gray's Inn, 1936, Bencher, 1969. Royal Artillery, 1939-45. Recorder: of Penzance, 1962-64; of Exeter, 1964-66. *Address:* Shellwood Manor, Leigh, Surrey; 2 King's Bench Walk, Temple, EC4. *Clubs:* United Service; Hampshire.

**STOCKDALE, Sir Edmund (Villiers Minshull),** 1st Bt *cr* 1960; Kt 1955; JP; *b* 16 April 1903; 2nd *s* of late Major H. M. Stockdale, JP, and Mrs Stockdale, Mears Ashby Hall, Northants; *m* 1937, Hon. Louise Fermor-Hesketh, *er d* of 1st Lord Hesketh; two *s* one *d. Educ:* Wellington College. Entered Bank of England, 1921; Assistant to Governors, Reserve Bank of India, 1935; Asst Principal, Bank of England, 1937, Dep. Principal, 1941; pensioned, 1945. Elected Court of Common Council, City of London, 1946, Alderman, Ward of Cornhill, 1948; one of HM Lieuts, City of London, Comdr of Assize, 1948-63; Sheriff, City of London 1953; Lord Mayor of London, 1959-60; Chm., Lord Mayor's Appeal Fund, King George's Jubilee Trust, 1960; Mem., Adv. Bd, etc., Holloway Prison, 1948-60. Chairman 1951-53; Member, Holloway Discharged Prisoners Aid Society Cttee, 1964; Vice-President, The Griffins (formerly Holloway DPAS), 1965; Member, Boards: Bridewell, Christ's, Royal Bethlem and Maudsley Hosps, 1948-63; Mem., Emerg. Bed Service Cttee, King Edward Hosp. Fund, 1963-69; Vice-Pres. King Edward's School, Witley, 1960-63; Governor, United Westminster Schools, 1948-54; Wellington College. Director, Embankment Trust Ltd and other Cos. A Church Comr for England, 1962; Mem. Winchester Dioc. Bd of Finance (Exec. Cttee), 1963. Junior Grand Warden (Acting), Grand Lodge of England, 1960-61. Partner, Read Hurst-Brown and Co.; Member: London Stock Exchange, 1946-60; Court of Assistants, Carpenters' Co. (Master, 1970), Glaziers' Co. JP London (Inner London Sessions), 1968. Grand Officer, Legion of Honour, France; Grand Cross, Order of Merit, Peru; Grand Official, Order of Mayo, Argentina; Knight Comdr, Order of Crown, Thailand; Order of Triple Power, Nepal; Comdr, Royal Order of North Star, Sweden; KStJ. Gold Medal, Madrid. *Recreations:* shooting, drawing. *Heir: er s* Thomas Minshull Stockdale [*b* 7 Jan. 1940; *m* 1965, Jacqueline Ha-Van-Vuong; one *s* one *d*]. *Address:* Hoddington House, Upton Grey, Basingstoke. *T:* Long Sutton 437; Delnadamph, Strathdon, Aberdeenshire. *T:* Corgarff 253. *Clubs:* Buck's, MCC.

**STOCKDALE, Frank Alleyne,** MA; JP; **His Honour Judge Stockdale;** County Court Judge, Circuit No 58 (Ilford), since 1965 (Circuit No 39, 1964); Deputy Chairman, Greater London Quarter Sessions, since 1966; *b* 16 Oct. 1910; *er s* of late Sir Frank Stockdale, GCMG, CBE, MA, FLS; *m* 1942, Frances Jean, *er d* of late Sir FitzRoy Anstruther-Gough-Calthorpe, Bt; one *s* two *d. Educ:* Repton; Magdalene College, Cambridge. Called to Bar, Gray's Inn, 1934; Bencher, 1964. Served War of 1939-45: 5th Royal Inniskilling Dragoon Guards, BEF, 1939-40; North Africa, 1942-43 (despatches); psc; Lt-Col. Dep. Chm., Hampshire QS, 1954-66. Chm. of Hampshire County British Legion, 1960-63; Member: Deptl Cttee on Adoption Law, 1969; British Legion Poppy Factory Council, 1965-. JP Hants, 1952. *Address:* 4 Verulam Buildings, Gray's Inn, WC1. *T:* 01-242 3916. *Club:* Cavalry.

**STOCKDALE, Maj.-Gen. Reginald Booth,** CB 1963; OBE 1945; BSc (Eng); FIMechE; MBIM; retired; an international official with Western European Union, in Paris, since 1963; *b* 12 Jan. 1908; *s* of late Reginald Hind Stockdale, Preston, Lancs; *m* 1940, Betty Celia, *d* of late William Alexander Tucker, Bromley, Kent; two *s* one *d. Educ:* Bedford Modern School. psc. Lieut, RAOC, 1931. Served War of 1939-45: BEF, 1939-40; UK, 1940-42; transferred to REME as Major, 1942; MEF, 1942-43; CMF, 1943-45. MELF, 1945-46; East Africa, 1946-48; Lt-Col, 1948; BAOR, 1948-50; Colonel, 1951; BAOR, 1952-53; DDME, Southern Command, 1953-56; DEME, BAOR, 1956-59; Commandant, Technical Group, REME, 1960-63. Brigadier, 1958; Major-General, 1960. Col Comdt, REME, 1963-68. *Address:* c/o Glyn Mills & Co., Kirkland House, Whitehall, SW1; 106 rue de la Tour, Paris 16e, France. *T:* Trocadero 0182; (office) 43 Avenue du Président Wilson, Paris 16e, France. *Club:* Army and Navy.

**STOCKER, Prof. Bruce Arnold Dunbar,** FRS 1966; MD; Professor of Medical Microbiology in Stanford University, since 1966; *b* 26 May 1917. *Educ:* King's College, London; Westminster Hospital, MB, BS, 1940; MRCS, LRCP, 1940; MD 1947. Guinness Prof. of Microbiology, Univ. of London, and Dir of Guinness-Lister Microbiological Research Unit, Lister Inst. of Preventive Med., until Dec. 1965. *Publications:* articles in scientific jls. *Address:* Dept of Medical Microbiology, Stanford University, Stanford, Calif. 94305, USA.

**STOCKER, John Dexter,** MC, TD; QC 1965; *b* 7 Oct. 1918; *s* of late John Augustus Stocker and Emma Eyre Stocker (*née* Kettle), Hampstead; *m* 1956, Margaret Mary Hegarty; no *c. Educ:* Westminster Sch.; London University. 2nd Lt, QO Royal West Kent Regt, 1939; France, 1940; Middle East, 1942-43; Italy, 1943-46; Maj. 1943; Lt-Col 1945. LLB London 1947. Called to Bar, Middle Temple, 1948. *Recreations:* golf, cricket. *Address:* 24 Wallgrave Road, SW5. *T:* 01-373 1295. *Clubs:* Bath, MCC, Royal Wimbledon Golf.

**STOCKIL, Sir Raymond (Osborne),** KBE 1964 (OBE 1958); Farmer and Director of Companies; *b* 15 April 1907; *s* of Francis Robert Stockil and Ruth (*née* Coventry); *m* 1929, Virginia Fortner; one *s* three *d* (and one *s* decd). *Educ:* Heldeberg College, Cape Province; Washington University, USA (BA). Took up Civil Aviation and Manufacturing in USA, 1929-33 (5 USA Patents); returned to Natal, 1934; commenced farming in Fort Victoria, 1936. Served War of 1939-45 with SR Signal Corps. MP for Victoria, 1946-62; Leader of Opposition, 1948-53 and 1956-59;

resigned from Parliament, 1962. Chairman, Hippo Valley Estates Ltd, 1956. *Recreation:* owner and trainer of racehorses. *Address:* Rugare, Addington Lane, Highlands, Salisbury, Rhodesia. *T:* 882501. *Club:* Salisbury (Salisbury, Rhodesia).

**STOCKLEY, David Dudgeon,** BSc (Engineering, London 1st Class Hons 1921); CEng, FIMechE; Principal, Aston Technical College, 1936-60; *b* 2 July 1900; *s* of Charles Rennie Stockley and L. Dudgeon; *m* 1928, Elizabeth Nina Baty; no *c. Educ:* Sunderland Technical College. Various industrial posts, 1921-25; Lecturer Huddersfield Technical College, 1925-27; Sunderland Technical College, 1927-30; Head of Engineering Department, School of Engineering and Navigation, Poplar, 1930-32; Head of Dept of Engineering and Building, Borough Polytechnic, SE1, 1932-36. *Publications:* Papers on technical and educational subjects. *Recreation:* fishing. *Address:* 15 South Grange Road, Ripon, Yorks.

**STOCKLEY, Gerald Ernest,** CBE 1957; *b* Simla, India, 15 Dec. 1900; *s* of late Brig.-Gen. E. N. Stockley, DSO, late RE, and Elsie Shewell Cooper; *m* 1st, Phillipina Mary Prendergast (marr. diss.); two *d*; 2nd, Katharine Noel Parker. *Educ:* Wellington Coll.; Christ's Coll., Cambridge, BA Hons, English and Mod. Langs. China Consular Service, 1925, and served at numerous posts in China: Consul (Grade II) 1935, Consul, Foochow, 1936-38, and Tengyüeh, 1938-40; Consul (Grade I) 1939, Acting Consul-Gen., Kunming, 1939; served with British Military Mission in China, 1941-43; Acting Consul-General, Kweilin, 1943-44; Consul, Seattle (USA), 1944-45; Consul-Gen., Hankow, 1946-48; Counsellor, FO, 1948-49; Minister to Republic of Honduras, 1950-54; Consul-General, Naples, 1954-59; retired, Dec. 1959; Consul and Consul-General (personal rank), Nice, 1960-66. *Address:* 6 Harrogate House, 29 Sloane Square, SW1. *Club:* Unione (Naples).

**STOCKMAN, Henry Watson,** CBE 1949; *b* London, 20 April 1894; *s* of late Henry Stockman; *m* 1921, Margaret Reid Robertson; one *s* one *d. Educ:* Battersea Polytechnic. National Health Insurance Commn (England), 1912-19; Ministry of Health, 1919-44; Ministry of National Insurance (later Min. of Pensions and Nat. Insurance), 1945-55; Asst Secretary, 1945-50; Chief Insurance Officer, 1950-53; Under-Secretary, 1953-55; International Labour Office, Geneva, Social Security Division, 1957-59; Technical Adviser, International Social Security Association, Geneva, 1959-64. *Publications:* History and Development of Social Security in Great Britain, 1957; Development and Trends in Social Security in Great Britain, 1962. *Recreation:* gardening. *Address:* Christmas Cottage, 22 Grove Road, Beaconsfield, Bucks. *T:* Beaconsfield 3722. *Club:* National Liberal.
*See also H. Bondi.*

**STOCKPORT, Suffragan Bishop of,** since 1965; **Rt. Rev. Rupert Gordon Strutt,** BD; *b* 15 Jan. 1912; *s* of Rupert Henry and Maude Mortlock Strutt; *m* 1st, 1936, Eva Gertrude Rabbitts; one *s* one *d*; 2nd, 1949, Constance Mary Fergusson Foden; one *s* two *d. Educ:* University of London; London College of Divinity; Wycliffe Hall, Oxford. Deacon, 1942; Priest, 1943. Curate of Carlton-in-the-Willows, 1942-43; Chaplain to the Forces (Emergency Commission), 1943-45; Rector of Normanton-on-Soar, 1945-48; Vicar of Holy Trinity, Leicester, 1948-52; Curate-in-Charge, St John the Divine, Leicester, 1949-52; Vicar of Addiscombe, Diocese of Canterbury, 1952-59. Chaplain to HM Prison, Leicester, 1948-52. Commissary to the Bishop of Saskatoon, 1958-. Archdeacon of Maidstone and Canon Residentiary of Canterbury Cathedral; also Prior of St John's Hospital, Canterbury, 1959-65. *Address:* Bishop's Lodge, Macclesfield Road, Alderley Edge, Cheshire. *T:* Alderley Edge 2074.

**STOCKS,** family name of **Baroness Stocks.**

**STOCKS,** Baroness *cr* 1966 (Life Peeress), of the Royal Borough of Kensington and Chelsea; **Mary Danvers Stocks,** BSc (Econ.); LLD, LittD; Member of Cassel Trust; *b* 1891; *d* of Dr R. D. Brinton; *m* 1913, J. L. Stocks (*d* 1937), Fellow of St John's College, Oxford, Vice-Chancellor of Liverpool University; one *s* two *d. Educ:* St Paul's Girls' Sch.; London School of Economics. Asst Lecturer, London School of Economics, 1916-19; Lecturer on Economics, King's Coll. for Women, 1918-19; Extension Lecturer and Extra-Mural tutor, Manchester Univ., 1924-37; JP Manchester City, 1930-36; General Sec. London Council of Social Service, 1938-39; Principal of Westfield College, University of London, 1939-51. Member of the Unemployment Insurance Statutory Committee and various other Government committees. *Publications:* Fifty Years in Every Street, 1945; Eleanor Rathbone, 1948; History of the Workers' Educational Association, 1953; A Hundred Years of District Nursing, 1960; Ernest Simon of Manchester, 1963; Unread Best-Seller, 1967; Where is Liberty?, 1968; My Commonplace Book, 1970; *plays:* Everyman of Every Street; King Herod; Hail Nero!; Dr Scholefield. *Recreations:* reading, attending the House of Lords. *Address:* Aubrey Lodge, Aubrey Road, W8. *Club:* BBC.

**STOCKS, Charles Lancelot,** CB 1936; Headmaster of Betteshanger School, Kent, 1941-67; *b* 6 March 1878; *s* of late John Edward Stocks, Archdeacon of Leicester, and Emily Jane Mallam; *m* 1926, Olive Gwendolen Law, of Hawksworth Hall, Bradford; (one *s* decd). *Educ:* Rossall School (Schol.); Wadham Coll., Oxford (Schol.). Master at Eton; Treasury, Whitehall; Secretary of the Royal Commission on Oxford and Cambridge Universities, Crown Estate Comr, 1934-41. *Publications:* Future Evolution, 1969; People and Places (prose and verse), 1970. *Recreations:* played football for the Casuals, and hockey for Oxford University and England; sang for many years in Oriana Madrigal Soc. and Philharmonic Choir. *Address:* Old Rectory, Betteshanger, near Deal, Kent. *T:* Eastry 287. *Club:* Athenæum.

**STOCKS, Percy,** CMG 1948; MA, MD, BCh, FRCP, DPH; *b* 5 Nov. 1889; *s* of John and Margaret Ann Stocks; *m* 1914, Augusta Griffiths; no *c. Educ:* Manchester Grammar Sch.; King's Coll., Cambridge (Foundation Scholar); Victoria Univ., Manchester; Sch. of Tropical Medicine, Liverpool. Nat. Sci. Tripos, Cambridge, 1st Cl. hons, 1910; MB, ChB (2nd Cl. hons, distinctions in Medicine and Surgery), Manchester, 1913; MB, BCh Cambridge, 1914; MD 1917, DPH 1918, MA 1920, Cambridge; FRCP 1948; Jenner medal, Royal Society of Medicine, 1956; Bisset Hawkins medal, Royal College of Physicians, 1959. House Physician, Manchester Royal Infirmary, 1913; House Surgeon, Oldham Royal Infirmary, 1914; Temp. Lt RAMC, Asst in General Practice and Bacteriologist, 1914-18. Asst School Medical Officer, Bristol, 1918-21; Reader in Medical Statistics, Galton Laboratory, University Coll., London, 1921-33; Chief Medical Statistician, General Register Office, London, 1933-50; Sen.

Research Fellow, Brit. Empire Cancer Campaign, 1951-57. Chm., Expert Cttee on International Classification of Diseases, World Health Organisation, 1946-48; Member, Expert Cttee on Health Statistics, World Health Organisation, 1949-50; Member: Statistical and Medical Committees, Royal Commission on Population, 1945. Hon. Fellow Amer. Public Health Association. *Publications:* Blood Pressure in Early Life, 1924; Hereditary Disorders of Bone Development, 1925; Biometric investigation of Twins and their brothers and sisters, Annals of Eugenics, 1930 and 1933; (with N. East and H. P. Young) The Adolescent Criminal, 1942; numerous papers on Cancer, Tuberculosis, Measles, Whooping Cough, Diphtheria, Vital Statistics. *Recreations:* music, philately, foreign travel. *Address:* Arrochar, 34 Brompton Avenue, Rhos-on-Sea, Denbighshire. *T:* Colwyn Bay 48477.

**STOCKWELL, Air Cdre Edmund Arthur,** CB 1967; MA; FRAeS; Command Education Officer, Training Command, since 1968 (Flying Training Command, 1964-68); *b* 15 Dec. 1911; *e s* of Arthur Davenport Stockwell, Dewsbury; *m* 1937, Pearl Arber; one *s* two *d*; *m* 1955, Lillian Gertrude Moore (*d* 1965), OBE, MRCP; two *s*; *m* 1970, Mrs Kathleen (Betty) Clarke, Chesham. *Educ:* Wheelwright Grammar School; Balliol Coll., Oxford. Entered RAF Educational Service, Cranwell, 1935; RAF Educn in India, 1936; Punjab and NW Frontier, 1936-38; RAFVR (Admin and Special Duties), 1939; Lahore, Simla, Delhi, 1939-44; Group Educn Office, No 6 (RCAF) Group, 1944; Air Min., 1944-48; OC, RAF Sch. of Educn, 1948-51; Comd Educn Officer, Coastal Comd, 1951-53; Comd Educn Officer, FEAF, 1953-55; Principal Educn Officer, Halton, 1956-59; Comd Educn Officer, Maintenance Comd, 1959-62; Dep. Dir of Educational Services, Air Min., 1962-64. Group Captain, 1954; Air Commodore, 1964. *Recreations:* golf, gardening. *Address:* 31 Park Lane, Brampton, Huntingdon. *Club:* Royal Air Force.

**STOCKWELL, Gen. Sir Hugh Charles,** GCB 1959 (KCB 1954; CB 1946); KBE 1949 (CBE 1945); DSO 1940 and Bar 1957; late Infantry; retired; *b* 16 June 1903; *s* of late Lt-Col H. C. Stockwell, OBE, late Highland Light Infantry, Chief Constable of Colchester, and Gertrude Forrest; *m* 1931, Joan Rickman Garrard, *d* of Charles and Marion Garrard, Kingston Lisle, Berkshire; two *d*. *Educ:* Cothill House, Abingdon; Marlborough; Royal Military Coll., Sandhurst. Joined 2/Royal Welch Fusiliers, 1923; served West Africa, 1929-35; Instructor, Small Arms School, Netheravon, 1935-38; Brigade-Major, Royal Welch Brigade, 1938-40; served in Norway (DSO); 30 East African Bde, 1942-43; 29th Independent Bde, 1943-45; Burma (CB); Commander 82 (WA) Division, Jan. 1945-June 1946; Commander, Home Counties District, UK, July 1946-47; Commander Sixth Airborne Division, Palestine, 1947-48; Commandant, RMA, Sandhurst, 1948-50; Comdr, 3rd Inf. Div., and Comdr, East Anglian Dist, 1951-52; General Officer Commanding: Malaya, 1952-54; 1 Corps, BAOR, 1954-56; Ground Forces, Suez Operation, 1956; Military Secretary to the Secretary of State for War, 1957-59; Adjutant-General to the Forces, 1959-60; Deputy Supreme Allied Commander, Europe, 1960-64, retired. Gen., 1957. Col, The Royal Welch Fusiliers, 1952-65; Col, The Royal Malay Regt 1954-59; Col Commandant, Army Air Corps, 1957-63; Col Commandant, Royal Army Educational Corps October 1959-64. ADC General to the Queen, 1959-62. Governor, Felsted School, 1954. Grand Officier, Légion d'Honneur (France), 1958. *Recreations:* shooting, painting, travel. *Address:* Westminster Bank, Ltd, 36 St James's Street, SW1. *Clubs:* MCC, Army and Navy.

**STOCKWOOD, Rt. Rev. Arthur Mervyn;** *see* Southwark, Bishop of.

**STODART, James Anthony;** MP (C) Edinburgh West since Oct. 1959; Parliamentary Secretary, Ministry of Agriculture, Fisheries and Food, since 1970; *b* 6 June 1916; *yr s* of late Col Thomas Stodart, CIE, IMS, and of Mary Alice Coullie; *m* 1940, Hazel Jean Usher. *Educ:* Wellington. Farming at Kingston, North Berwick, 1934-58, and now at Leaston, Humbie, East Lothian. Hon. Pres., Edinburgh Univ. Agricultural Soc., 1952; Pres. East Lothian Boy Scouts' Assoc., 1960-63. Vice-Chm., Conservative Agric. Cttee, House of Commons, 1962-63, 1964-65, 1966-70. Contested: (L) Berwick and East Lothian, 1950; (C) Midlothian and Peebles, 1951; Midlothian, 1955; Jt Parly Under-Sec., of State, Scottish Office, Sept. 1963-Oct. 1964. An Opposition spokesman on Agriculture, 1966-69, on Scottish Affairs, 1966-69. *Publications:* (jt author) Land of Abundance, a study of Scottish Agriculture in the 20th Century, 1962; contrib. on farming topics to agricultural journals and newspapers. *Recreations:* music, playing golf and preserving a sense of humour. *Address:* Lorimers, North Berwick, East Lothian. *T:* North Berwick 2457. *Clubs:* Carlton, Caledonian; New (Edinburgh).

**STODDART, Alexander Frederick Richard,** CMG 1952; *b* 25 Aug. 1904; *s* of Alexander Reid Stoddart and Agnes Ferguson McBain. *Educ:* St Peter's, York; Loretto; Trinity College, Oxford. Colonial Administrative Service: Nigeria, 1927-42; Chief Assistant Colonial Secretary, Sierra Leone, 1942-49; Colonial Secretary, Fiji, 1949-57. *Address:* Mount Lodge, Nightingale Lane, Storrington, Sussex.

**STODDART, David Leonard;** MP (Lab) Swindon, since 1970; Power Station Clerical Worker, since 1951; *b* 4 May 1926; *s* of Arthur Leonard Stoddart, coal miner, and Queenie Victoria Stoddart (*née* Price); *m* 1961, Jennifer Percival-Alwyn; two *s* one *d*. *Educ:* elementary; St Clement Danes and Henley Grammar Schools. Youth in training, PO Telephones, 1942-44; business on own account, 1944-46; Railway Clerk, 1947-49; Hospital Clerk, 1949-51. Joined Labour Party, 1947; Member Reading County Borough Council, 1954-; served at various times as Chairman of Housing, Transport and Finance Cttees; Leader of the Reading Labour Group of Councillors, 1962-. Contested (Lab) Newbury, 1959 and 1964, Swindon, 1969. Member of Thames Valley Water Board and Thames Valley Police Authority since their foundation; Member of the Court and Council, Reading University. *Recreations:* gardening, boating, music. *Address:* 15 Trelleck Road, Reading, Berks. *T:* Reading 56726.

**STODDART-SCOTT, Colonel Sir Malcolm,** Kt 1957; OBE 1945; TD 1943; DL; MD; ChB; MP (C) Ripon Division of West Riding since 1950 (Pudsey and Otley, 1945-50); *b* 23 Sept. 1901; *o s* of John and Jemima Stoddart-Scott, Friarwood House, Pontefract; *m* 1940, Elsie Mary, JP, *o d* of late B. Parkinson, JP, Creskeld Hall, Arthington, nr Leeds; one *s* one *d*. *Educ:* Elmfield College, York; Ashville College, Harrogate; University of Leeds. On Medical Staff of Leeds General Infirmary 1926-39; in RAMC, 1939-45; ADMS 48th

Division, 1943-45; Hon. Col 18th (West Riding) Bn Mobile Defence Corps, 1957-60. Past Chairman British Rheumatic Asssoc. Chairman: British Group of the Inter-Parly Union, 1951-59; Yorkshire Conservative Assoc., 1957-65; Parly Medical Cttee, 1959-62. Member of the Church Assembly. Chairman of Governors of Charterhouse Rheumatism Clinic; Chairman, Hospital Saturday Fund, 1964; Vice-Chairman, Yorkshire Cancer Campaign, 1963. DL, W Riding, Yorks, 1967. *Address:* Creskeld Hall, Arthington, nr Leeds, Yorks. *T:* Arthington 2222.

**STOKER, Prof. Michael George Parke;** FRS 1968, FRSE 1960; Director, Imperial Cancer Research Fund Laboratories, London, since 1968; Visiting Professor, University College, London, since 1968; *b* 4 July 1918; *e s* of Dr S. P. Stoker, Maypole, Monmouth; *m* 1942, Veronica Mary English; three *s* two *d. Educ:* Oakham Sch.; Sidney Sussex Coll., Cambridge; St Thomas' Hosp., London, MRCS, LRCP 1942; MB, BChir 1943; MD 1947. RAMC, 1942-47; Demonstrator in Pathology, Cambridge Univ., 1947-48; Univ. Lecturer in Pathology, 1948-50; Huddersfield Lecturer in Special Pathology, 1950-58; Fellow of Clare Coll., 1948-58; Asst Tutor and Dir of Medical Studies, Clare Coll., 1949-58; Prof. of Virology, Glasgow Univ., and Hon. Dir, MRC Experimental Virus Research Unit, 1959-68. WHO Travel Fellow, 1951. Mem., European Molecular Biology Organisation. *Publications:* various articles on cell biology and virology. *Address:* Oxley House, Lenham, Kent. *Club:* Athenæum.

**STOKES,** family name of **Baron Stokes.**

**STOKES,** Baron *cr* 1969 (Life Peer), of Leyland; **Donald Gresham Stokes,** Kt 1965; TD; DL; Chairman and Managing Director, British Leyland Motor Corporation Ltd, since 1968; *b* 22 March 1914; *o s* of Harry Potts Stokes; *m* 1939, Laura Elizabeth Courteney Lamb; one *s*. *Educ:* Blundell's School; Harris Institute of Technology, Preston. Started Student Apprenticeship, Leyland Motors Ltd, 1933. Served War of 1939-45: REME, 1939-46 (Lt-Col). Re-joined Leyland as Exports Manager, 1946; General Sales and Service Manager, 1950; Director, 1954; Managing Director, and Deputy Chairman, Leyland Motor Corp., 1963, Chm. 1967. Executive Chairman of Standard-Triumph International Ltd, 1964; Director: Albion Motors Ltd, 1964; Scammell Lorries Ltd, 1967; Aveling-Barford Ltd, 1968; Associated Commercial Vehicles Ltd, 1962; Rover, 1967; Jaguar Cars Ltd, 1968; Pressed Steel Fisher Ltd, 1968; British Leyland (Austin-Morris) Ltd, 1969; National Westminster Bank, 1969; London Weekend Television Ltd; Vice-President, Empresa Nacional de Autocamiones SA, Spain. President, Society of Motor Manufacturers and Traders Ltd, 1961-62; Pres. Motor Industry Res. Assoc., 1965-66; Mem., NW Economic Planning Council, 1965-70; Mem. (part-time), Industrial Re-organisation Corp., 1966-71, Dep. Chm. 1969; Chairman, EDC for Electronics Industry, 1966-67; Mem. EDC for the Motor Manufacturing Industry, 1967-. Member: Council, Public Transport Assoc.; Worshipful Co. of Carmen. Hon. Fellow, Keble Coll., Oxford, 1968. Hon. LLD Lancaster, 1967; Hon. DTech Loughborough, 1968; Hon. DSc Southampton, 1969. Officier de l'Ordre de la Couronne (Belgium), 1964. *Recreations:* shooting, golf. *Address:* 25 St James's Place, SW1. *T:* 01-493 7450. *Clubs:* Royal Automobile; Royal Western Yacht.

**STOKES, Adrian Durham;** writer; *b* 27 Oct. 1902; *m* 1947, Ann Mellis, *d* of Rev. David Mellis Mellis; two *s* one *d. Educ:* Rugby School; Magdalen College, Oxford. Trustee, Tate Gallery, 1960-67. *Publications:* The Thread of Ariadne, 1925; Sunrise in the West, 1926; The Quattro Cento, 1932; Stones of Rimini, 1934; Tonight the Ballet, 1934; Russian Ballets, 1935; Colour and Form, 1937; Venice, an Aspect of Art, 1945; Inside Out, 1947; Cezanne, 1947; Art and Science, 1949; Smooth and Rough, 1951; Michelangelo: A Study in the Nature of Art, 1955; Raphael, 1956; Monet, 1958; Greek Culture and the Ego, 1958; Three Essays on the Painting of our Time, 1961; Painting and the Inner World, 1963; The Invitation in Art, 1965; Venice, 1965; Reflections on the Nude 1967. *Address:* 20 Church Row, NW3. *T:* 01-435 4640.

**STOKES, Prof. Eric Thomas,** MA, PhD; Smuts Professor of the History of the British Commonwealth, Cambridge, since 1970; *b* 10 July 1924; *s* of Walter John Stokes; *m* 1949, Florence Mary Lee; four *d. Educ:* Holloway Sch.; Christ's Coll., Cambridge. MA 1949; PhD 1953. War Service, 1943-46: Lieut, RA; Royal Indian Mountain Artillery. Lecturer in: History, Univ. of Malaya, Singapore, 1950-55; Colonial History and Administration, Univ. of Bristol, 1955-56; Prof. of History, Univ. Coll. of Rhodesia and Nyasaland, 1956-63; Lecturer in History (Colonial Studies), Univ. of Cambridge, and Fellow and Tutor, St Catharine's Coll., 1963-70; Reader in Commonwealth History, 1970. *Publications:* The English Utilitarians and India, 1959; The Political Ideas of English Imperialism, an inaugural lecture, 1960; (ed with Richard Brown) The Zambesian Past, 1966; contributed to: Historians of India, Pakistan and Ceylon (ed C. H. Philips), 1961; Elites in South Asia (ed E. R. Leach and S. N. Mukherjee), 1970; articles in Historical Jl, Past and Present, etc. *Recreations:* walking, swimming, soliloquising, and balladmongering. *Address:* St Catharine's College, Cambridge. *T:* Cambridge 59445. *Club:* Royal Commonwealth Society.

**STOKES, John Fisher,** MA, MD, FRCP; Physician, University College Hospital, since 1947; *b* 19 Sept. 1912; *e s* of Dr Kenneth Stokes and Mary (*née* Fisher); *m* 1940, Elizabeth Joan Rooke; one *s* one *d. Educ:* Haileybury (exhibitioner); Gonville and Caius Coll., Cambridge (exhibitioner); University Coll. Hosp. (Fellowes Silver Medal for clinical medicine). MB BChir (Cambridge) 1937; MRCP 1939; MD (Cambridge) 1947 (proxime accessit, Horton Smith prize); FRCP 1947; Thruston Medal, Gonville and Caius Coll., 1948. Appointments on junior staff University Coll. Hosp. and Victoria Hosp. for Children, Tite St, 1937-42; RAMC 1942-46; served in Far East, 1943-46, Lt-Col (despatches). Examiner in Medicine, various Univs, 1949-70. Member of Council, Royal Soc. of Med., 1951-54, 1967-69. Vice-Pres., RCP, 1968-69. Amateur Squash Rackets Champion of Surrey, 1935, of East of England, 1936, Runner-up of British Isles, 1937; English International, 1938; Technical Adviser to Squash Rackets Assoc., 1948-52; Chm. Jesters Club, 1953-59. *Publications:* contrib. on liver disease and general medicine in medical journals. *Recreations:* music, lawn tennis, painting. *Address:* Flat 4, 68 Wimpole Street, W1. *T:* 01-935 2345; Private Consulting Rooms, University College Hospital, Grafton Way, WC1. *T:* 01-387 2160. *Clubs:* Athenæum, Savile.

**STOKES, John Heydon Romaine;** MP (C) Oldbury and Halesowen since 1970; *b* 23 July 1917; *o surv. s* of late Victor Romaine Stokes, Hitchin; *m* 1939, Barbara Esmée, *y d* of late R.

E. Yorke, Wellingborough; one *s* two *d*. *Educ:* Temple Grove; Haileybury Coll.; Queen's Coll., Oxford. BA 1938; MA 1946. Hon. Agent and Treas., Oxford Univ. Conservative Assoc., 1937; Pres., Monarchist Soc., 1937; Pres., Mermaid Club, 1937. Served War, 1939-46: Dakar Expedn, 1940; wounded in N Africa, 1943; Mil. Asst to HM Minister Beirut and Damascus, 1944-46; Major. Contested (C): Gloucester, 1964; Hitchin, 1966. Personnel Officer, Imperial Chemical Industries, 1946-51; Personnel Manager, British Celanese, 1951-59; Dep. Personnel Manager, Courtaulds, 1957-59; Partner, Clive & Stokes, Personnel Consultants, 1959-. Mem. Exec. Cttee, Oxford Soc.; Mem. Gen. Cttee, Haileybury Society. Order of Merit (Syria), 1946. *Publications:* several articles on personnel management. *Recreations:* gardening, tennis, travel, English history. *Address:* Tempsford, Grove Road, Beaconsfield, Bucks. *T:* Beaconsfield 4077. *Club:* Carlton.

**STOKES, (Hon.) Brig. Ralph Shelton Griffin,** CBE 1942 (OBE 1919); DSO, 1917; MC 1916; *b* 31 July 1882; *s* of Francis Griffin Stokes, BA Oxon; *m* 1921, Lora Mary Bradford; four *d*. *Educ:* St Mark's, Windsor and privately. Served Anglo-Boer War, Paget's Horse, 1901-02; European War, 1914-18 (DSO, MC, despatches thrice); Field Company, RE; Tunnelling Companies; Lieut-Col, Controller of Mines, First Army; Colonel, Chief Engineer on Staff of Gen. Ironside, Archangel, North Russia, 1918-19 (OBE, despatches twice); War of 1939-45 (CBE): with RE; France, 1939-40; Narvik 1940 (despatches); CE Xth Corps, 1940; Brig. CE Airfields, Middle East, 1941-43 (despatches twice); War Office, 1943-44. Field Engineer, International Nickel Co., New York, 1912-14; Superintendent of Mines, De Beers Consolidated, Kimberley, 1920-28; Consulting Engineer, and Manager, Central Mining & Investment Corporation, 1928-44, Director, 1944-59. Chairman of Trinidad Leaseholds Ltd, 1944-47. Past President: Geological Soc. of S Africa; SA Inst. of Mining and Metallurgy; Instn of Mining and Metallurgy, London; Past Vice-Pres., Royal African Soc. *Publication:* Mines and Minerals of the British Empire, 1908. *Address:* Highfield, Leweston, Sherborne, Dorset. *T:* Holnest 425. *Clubs:* Army and Navy; Rand (Johannesburg).

**STOKES, William Henry,** CBE 1950; JP 1950; Personnel Manager, Armstrong Siddeley Motors Ltd, Coventry, 1954-59; Chairman, Coventry Pre-Retirement Committee, since 1968; *b* 18 Nov. 1894; *s* of William Henry Stokes, Coventry, and Annie Maria (*née* Jenkins); *m* 1918, Frances Emily Beckett; no *c*. *Educ:* Coventry. Chm. Midland Regional Bd for Industry, 1945-50; Vice-Chm. Midland Regional Production Bd, 1940-45; Member: Nat. Production Advisory Council, 1940-50; BBC Advisory Cttee, Midland Region; Divisional Organiser, Amalgamated Engineering Union (Coventry area), 1937-50; Iron and Steel Corporation of Great Britain, 1950-53; (part-time), East Midlands Electricity Board, 1959-65. *Recreations:* interest in Rugby football (a Vice-Pres. Coventry RFC); golf. *Address:* 57 Rochester Road, Coventry. *T:* Coventry 72860.

**STOKOWSKI, Leopold (Boleslawowicz Stanislaw Antoni),** FRCM; BMus Oxon; DMus University of Pennsylvania; LLD University of California; Hon. Fellow Queen's College, Oxford; Conductor-Founder, American Symphony Orchestra, New York, since 1962; *b* London, April 1887; *s* of Boleslaw Stokowski, Lublin, Poland; *gs* of Leopold Stokowski. *Educ:* Royal Coll. of Music, London; France; Germany. Conductor Cincinnati Orchestra, 1909-12; Conductor Philadelphia Orchestra, 1912-36; later Conductor San Francisco and Hollywood Orchestras; Music Director of Hollywood Bowl Symphony Orchestra, 1944-46; conducted, with Artur Rodzinski, concerts in New York with the New York Philharmonic and on tour with same orchestra, 1946; conducted New York Philharmonic Orchestra, 1947-50; Houston Symphony Orchestra, Texas, 1955-60. Organiser of All American Youth Orchestra. Starred with Deanna Durbin in film, A Hundred Men and a Girl, 1937; appeared in: Great Broadcast of 1937; Fantasia, a feature picture with music in conjunction with Walt Disney, 1940; Carnegie Hall, 1946. Has made many symphonic transcriptions of the works of Bach. Makes records for: RCA Victor Co., His Master's Voice, Columbia Recording Co., Capitol Records, Everest Records, United Artists Records, London Records (Decca). *Publication:* Music for All of US, 1943. *Address:* 1067 Fifth Avenue, New York, NY 10028, USA.

**STONE, Alan Reynolds;** *see* Stone, Reynolds.

**STONE, Bertram Gilchrist,** OBE 1955; *b* 3 June 1903; *s* of late Reverend William Arthur Stone, Warden of St Thomas' Coll., Colombo, and of Clare Frances Stone; *m* 1933, Dorothy Kneale, *y d* of late D. E. McCracken, OBE, Liverpool; two *s*. *Educ:* Bromsgrove School; Sidney Sussex College, Cambridge (Scholar), Classical Tripos, BA 1925, MA 1929. District Officer, Colonial Administrative Service, Nigeria, 1925-36; Administrative Officer, Nat. Council of Social Service, 1937-43, Midland Regional Officer, 1944-47; Colonial Office, 1947; official visits to Nigeria, 1955 and 1959, Aden and Somaliland, 1957; Head of Students Branch, Colonial Office and Ministry of Overseas Development, 1956-65. *Publications:* contrib. to educational journals. *Recreations:* photography, gardening, reading. *Address:* Manor Barn, Kingston-near-Lewes, Sussex. *T:* Lewes 4569. *Club:* Royal Commonwealth Society.

**STONE, Prof. Francis Gordon Albert;** Head of Department of Inorganic Chemistry, and Professor since 1963, Bristol University; *b* 19 May 1925; *s* of Sidney Charles and Florence Stone; *m* 1956, Judith M. Hislop, Sydney, Australia; three *s*. *Educ:* Exeter Sch.; Christ's Coll., Cambridge. BA 1948, MA and PhD 1952, ScD 1963, Cambridge. Fulbright Schol., Univ. of Southern Calif., 1952-54; Instructor and Asst Prof., Harvard Univ., 1954-62; Reader, Queen Mary Coll., London, 1962-63. Vis. Professor: Monash Univ., 1966; Princeton Univ., 1967; Univ. of Arizona, 1970; Guggenheim Fellow, 1961; Boomer Lectr, Univ. of Alberta, 1965; Sen. Vis. Fellow, Australian Acad. of Sciences, 1966; Firestone Lectr, Univ. of Wisconsin, 1970. Mem. Council, Chem. Soc., 1968-70. *Publications:* (Editor) Inorganic Polymers, 1962; Hydrogen Compounds of the Group IV Elements, 1962; (Editor) Advances in Organometallic Chemistry, vols 1-8, 1964-70; numerous papers in Jl Chem. Soc., Jl Amer. Chem. Soc., etc. *Recreation:* world travel. *Address:* 6 Rylestone Grove, Bristol BS9 3UT. *T:* Bristol 627408.

**STONE, Sir (John) Leonard,** Kt, *cr* 1943; OBE 1943; QC 1948; *b* 6 Nov. 1896; *s* of late John Morris Stone, Blackheath and Lincoln's Inn, and late Edith Emily Stone, *d* of Alderman Edward Hart; *m* 1923, Madeleine Marie, *d* of late Frederick Scheffler, New York; one *s*. *Educ:* Malvern College. Served European War, 1914-22, commissioned Worcester Regt, Oct.

1914, Gallipoli, Army of the Black Sea, Control Officer Eskishehir, 1919-20; Inter-Allied Commission of Inquiry Turco-Greek War, 1921 (despatches, thrice). Called to Bar, Gray's Inn, 1923; joined Lincoln's Inn, 1931; Bencher, Gray's Inn, 1942, Treas., 1956. Pres., Commission of Inquiry, Bombay Explosions, 1944; Chief Justice High Court, Bombay, 1943-47; Vice-Chancellor, County Palatine of Lancaster, 1948-63. Chairman of Departmental Committee on Hallmarking, 1956-58. Mem. Council, Imp. Soc. of Knights Bachelor. *Address:* 2 Gray's Inn Square, WC1.
*See also R. F. Stone.*

**STONE, (John) Richard (Nicholas),** CBE 1946; MA; P. D. Leake Professor of Finance and Accounting, University of Cambridge, since 1955; Fellow of King's College, Cambridge, since 1945; *b* 30 Aug. 1913; *o c* of late Sir Gilbert Stone; *m* 1941, Feodora Leontinoff (*d* 1956); one *d*; *m* 1960, Mrs Giovanna Croft-Murray, *d* of Count Aurelio Saffi. *Educ:* Westminster School; Gonville and Caius College, Cambridge. With C. E. Heath and Co., Lloyd's Brokers, 1936-39; Ministry of Economic Warfare, 1939-40; Offices of the War Cabinet, Central Statistical Office, 1940-45; Dir Dept of Applied Economics, Cambridge, 1945-55. Member of the Internat. Statistical Inst. Pres., Econometric Soc., 1955; Hon. Mem., Soc. of Incorp. Accountants, 1954; For. Hon. Mem., Amer. Acad. of Arts and Sciences, 1968. FBA 1956. ScD 1957. Hon. doctorates, Univs of Oslo and Brussels, 1965. *Publications:* The Role of Measurement in Economics, 1951; (with others) The Measurement of Consumers' Expenditure and Behaviour in the United Kingdom 1920-1938, 1954; Quantity and Price Indexes in National Accounts, 1956; Input-Output and National Accounts, 1961; National Income and Expenditure (7th edn with G. Stone), 1964; Mathematics in the Social Sciences, and Other Essays, 1966; gen. editor and pt author series A Programme for Growth, 1962-; numerous articles in learned journals, particularly on social accounting and econometrics, 1936-. *Recreation:* staying at home. *Address:* 13 Millington Road, Cambridge; King's College, Cambridge. *Club:* Reform.

**STONE, Sir Joseph Ellis,** Kt 1970; Medical Practitioner; *m* 27 May 1903; 2nd *s* of late Henry Silverstone and Rebecca Silverstone (*née* Ellis); *m* 1932, Beryl, *y d* of late Alexander and Jane Bernstein; one *s* one *d*. *Educ:* Llanelli County Intermediate Sch.; Cardiff Univ.; Westminster Hosp., SW1. MB, BS London 1927; MRCS, LRCP 1925. Casualty Officer and Ho. Surg., Westminster Hosp., 1925-26; Sen. Ho. Surg., N Staffs Royal Infirmary, 1926-28; MO, St George in the East Hosp., 1928-32; gen. med. practice, 1932-. Served RAMC, 1940-45, Captain; graded med. specialist. Mem. Med. Soc. of London; Mem. Hampstead Med. Soc. Yeoman of Worshipful Soc. of Apothecaries. *Recreation:* golf. *Address:* 615 Finchley Road, Hampstead, NW3. *T:* 01-435 7333.

**STONE, Prof. Julius;** Challis Professor of International Law and Jurisprudence, University of Sydney, since 1942; Academic Director, Truman Center for the Advancement of Peace, Jerusalem, since 1968; Member of New Zealand and Victorian Bars; Solicitor, Supreme Court, England; *b* 7 July 1907; *s* of Israel and Ellen Stone, Leeds, Yorkshire; *m* 1934, Reca Lieberman, BSc, LDS; two *s* one *d*. *Educ:* Univs of Oxford, Leeds, Harvard. BA, BCL, DCL (Oxford); LLM (Leeds); SJD (Harvard). Asst Lectr, University Coll., Hull, 1928-30; Rockefeller Fellow in Social Sciences, 1931; Asst Prof. of Law, Harvard Univ., 1933-36; Prof. of Internat. Law and Organisation, Fletcher Sch. of Law and Diplomacy, USA, 1933-36; Lectr in Law, Univ. of Leeds, 1936-38; Prof. and Dean Faculty of Law, Auckland University Coll., NZ, 1938-42; Vis. Prof., New York Univ. and Fletcher Sch. of Law and Diplomacy, 1949; Acting Dean, Sydney Faculty of Law, 1954-55, 1958-59; Visiting Professor: Columbia Univ., 1956; Harvard Univ., 1956-57; Hague Academy of Internat. Law, 1956; Charles Inglis Thomson Guest Prof., Univ. of Colorado, 1956; Award of Amer. Soc. of Internat. Law, 1956; Prize of Legatum Visserianum, Leyden Univ., 1956; Roscoe Pound Lectr, Univ. of Nebraska, 1957; John Field Sims Memorial Lectr, Univ. of New Mexico, 1959; first Pres., Internat. Law Assoc., Aust., Br., 1959; Council, Internat. Commn of Jurists, Aust. Section, 1959; Vis. Prof., Indian Sch. of Internat. Affairs, Delhi, 1960. Mem. Titulaire, Inst. of Internat. Law; Associate, Internat. Acad. of Comparative Law. Chm., NSW Research Group, Aust. Inst. of Internat. Affairs, 1942-45; Vice-Chm., Prime Minister's Cttee on National Morale, and with Directorate of Research, LHQ, War of 1939-45 (Lt-Col). Founding and Exec. Mem., Aust. Social Science Research Council; Chm. Aust. Unesco Cttee for Social Sciences; Aust. Deleg., 6th Unesco Gen. Conf., Paris, 1951; Aust. rep., Second Corning Conf. on The Individual in the Modern World, 1961; Official Observer of Internat. Commn of Jurists, Eichmann Trial, 1961; General Editor, Sydney Law Review, 1953-60; cont. on Editorial Cttee; Hon. Life Member: Amer. Soc. Internat. Law, 1962; Indian Soc. Internat. Law, 1964. Joint Swiney Prize, RSA, 1964; Fellow: Centre for Study of the Behavioral Sciences, 1964; World Acad. of Arts and Sciences, 1964. Patron, Amnesty International, 1963. Mem., Advisory Cttee, Internat. League for Rights of Man, 1964; Regular Broadcaster on Internat. Affairs (Australian Broadcasting Commn), 1945-. *Publications:* International Guarantees of Minority Rights, 1932; Regional Guarantees of Minority Rights, 1933; The Atlantic Charter–New Worlds for Old, 1943; Stand Up and Be Counted, 1944; The Province and Function of Law, Law as Logic, Justice and Social Control (Aust., Eng. and Amer. edns), 1946, 1947, 1950, 1961; (with the late S. P. Simpson) Law and Society (3 vols), 1949-50; Legal Controls of International Conflict, A Treatise on the Dynamics of Disputes- and War- Law, 1954 (Aust., Eng. and Amer. Edns; revised impression, 1958); Sociological Inquiries concerning International Law, 1956; Aggression and World Order, 1958 (Aust., Eng. and Amer. edns); Legal Education and Public Responsibility, 1959; Quest for Survival, 1961 (German, Portuguese and Arabic trans); The International Court and World Crisis, 1962; Legal System and Lawyers' Reasonings, 1964; Human Law and Human Justice, 1965; Social Dimensions of Law and Justice, 1966; Law and the Social Sciences in the 2nd Half-Century, 1966; The Middle East Under Cease-Fire, 1967; No Peace - No War in The Middle East, 1969; Approaches to International Justice, 1970; numerous articles in Anglo-American legal journals. *Recreations:* swimming, gardening, landscape gardening. *Address:* 1 Holland Road, Double Bay, NSW 2028, Australia. *T:* 36.6927.

**STONE, Lawrence,** MA Oxon; Director, Shelby Cullom Davis Center for Historical Studies, since 1968; *b* 4 Dec. 1919; *s* of Lawrence Frederick Stone and Mabel Julia Annie Stone; *m* 1943, Jeanne Caecilia, *d* of Prof. Robert Fawtier, Membre de l'Institut, Paris; one *s* one *d*. *Educ:* Charterhouse School, 1933-38;

Sorbonne, Paris, 1938; Christ Church, Oxford, 1938-40, 1945-46. Lieut RNVR 1940-45. Bryce Research Student, Oxford Univ., 1946-47; Lectr, University Coll. Oxford, 1947-50; Fellow, Wadham Coll., Oxford, 1950-63; Mem. Inst. for Advanced Study, Princeton, 1960-61; Dodge Prof. of History, 1963-; Chm., Dept of History, 1967-70. Mem., Amer. Philosophical Soc., 1970. Fellow, Amer. Acad. of Arts and Sciences, 1968. *Publications:* Sculpture in Britain: The Middle Ages, 1955; An Elizabethan: Sir Horatio Palavicino, 1956; The Crisis of the Aristocracy, 1558-1641, 1965; numerous articles in History, Economic History Review, Past and Present, Archæological Jl, English Historical Review, Bulletin of the Inst. for Historical Research, Malone Soc., Comparative Studies in Society and History, History Today, etc. *Address:* 71 College Road West, Princeton, NJ 08540, USA. *T:* Princeton 921.2717; 231 Woodstock Road, Oxford. *T:* Oxford 59174.

**STONE, Sir Leonard;** *see* Stone, Sir J. L.

**STONE, Reynolds,** CBE 1953; RDI 1956; FRSA 1964; Designer and Engraver; *b* 13 March 1909; *s* of Edward Wellington and Laura Neville Stone; *m* 1938, Janet Woods; two *s* two *d*. *Educ:* Eton; Magdalene College, Cambridge. Studied printing at the University Press, Cambridge, after taking degree in History Tripos, 1930. Worked in a printing house, Barnicott & Pearce of Taunton, for two years, then as a free-lance designer and engraver. Served in RAF (photo interpretation), 1941-45. Designs for printers and publishers chiefly, and has decorated a number of books and produced many devices and book labels with an emphasis on lettering. Also designs and executes memorial tablets and engraves glass. Designed 3d Victory Stamp 1946, seal and device for The Arts Council, book-labels for National Trust and The British Council and an engraving of the Royal Arms for HM Stationery Office, 1956, Five Pound and Ten Pound Notes. Designed and executed the Winston Churchill Memorial for Westminster Abbey, 1965. *Publications:* Among the books decorated are: A Shakespeare Anthology, 1935; Rousseau's Confessions, 1938; Old English Wines and Cordials, 1938; The Praise and Happiness of the Countrie Life, Guevara, 1938; Apostate, Forrest Reid, 1946; The Open Air, Adrian Bell, 1949. *Recreations:* hunting in second-hand bookshops; interest in trees and 19th century wood-engraving. *Address:* Litton Cheney Old Rectory, Dorchester, Dorset. *T:* Long Bredy 230.

**STONE, Richard Evelyn,** CMG 1962; HM Overseas Civil Service, retired; Administrator, Agricultural Economics Institute, Oxford University, since 1967; *b* 20 Dec. 1914; 2nd *s* of late R. G. and late A. L. Stone, Yetminster, Dorset; *m* 1948, Mavis Betty Leanor Malet, 2nd *d* of late E. D. Tongue, OBE, and late E. E. Tongue. *Educ:* Blundell's School; Wadham College, Oxford. MA (Hons jurisprudence). Served War of 1939-45 (despatches): Adjt 34th Bn KAR; Staff Capt. and Bde Major 21st (EA) Inf. Bde; qualified Staff Coll., Quetta, 1945. Dist Comr, Uganda, 1948-55; Permanent Sec. of Various Mins; Dep. Resident, Buganda, 1959, Resident, 1960-62. Retd 1963, on Independence of Uganda. Farmed in Devon, 1963-67. *Recreations:* fishing, cricket. *Address:* Brackenhurst, Boar's Hill, Oxford. *Club:* MCC.

**STONE, Richard Frederick,** QC 1968; *b* 11 March 1928; *s* of Sir Leonard Stone, *qv*; *m* 1st, 1957, Georgina Maxwell Morris (decd); two *d*; 2nd, 1964, Susan van Heel; two *d*. *Educ:* Lakefield College Sch., Canada; Rugby; Trinity Hall, Cambridge (MA). Lt, Worcs Regt, 1946-48. Called to Bar, Gray's Inn, 1952; Mem., Bar Council, 1957-61; Mem., Panel of Lloyd's Arbitrators in Salvage Cases. *Recreation:* sailing. *Address:* 5 Raymond Buildings, Gray's Inn, WC1. *T:* 01-242 2697; Seascape, Wittering Road, Hayling Island, Hants.

**STONE, Riversdale Garland,** CMG 1956; OBE 1946; HM Consul-General, Los Angeles, 1957-59; *b* 19 Jan. 1903; *m* 1927, Cassie Gaisford; no *c*. Information Officer, Rio de Janeiro, Brazil, 1946; transf. to Singapore, 1948; First Secretary (Economic), Staff of Commissioner-General for the UK in SE Asia, 1948; Transf. to Batavia, 1949; Counsellor (Commercial), Mexico City, 1952; Counsellor, HM Diplomatic Service, retired. *Address:* c/o National Westminster Bank Ltd, Piccadilly Circus Branch, Glasshouse Street, W1.

**STONE, Lt-Gen. Robert Graham William Hawkins,** CB 1942; DSO 1919; MC; FRGS; *b* Dover, 16 Jan. 1890; *o s* of late Brig.-Gen. F. G. Stone, CMG; *m* 1928, Ena, *yr d* of late W. H. Rowe. *Educ:* Wellington Coll.; RM Academy, Woolwich. Served in District Mounted Troop, Aliwal North, during last six months of South African War, 1902; passed into RMA, Woolwich, 1908; awarded Pollock Medal on passing out 1st; 2nd Lieut in RE 1909; served at Chatham and Aldershot; throughout European War in France as a regimental officer and on the staff (DSO, MC, despatches five times); Brigade Major to 32nd Infantry Brigade, 1917; Staff Coll., 1922-23; GSO2, War Office, 1930-33; Bt Lt-Col 1931; Lt-Col 1933; CRE Deccan District, India, 1934-35; Col 1935; Military Attaché, Rome, 1935-38; Brigadier, 1938; Assistant Commandant and Chief of Staff, Sudan, 1938-40; Chief of British Mission to Egyptian Army, 1940-42; GOC British Troops in Egypt, 1942-44 (CB, despatches four times). Temp. Maj.-Gen. 1941; Acting Lt-Gen. 1942; Maj.-Gen. 1943; Temp. Lt-Gen. 1943-44; retired with rank of Lt-Gen., 1947. *Recreations:* lawn tennis, golf. *Address:* 14 Mallord Street, Chelsea, SW3. *Clubs:* United Service; All England Lawn Tennis; Royal Mid-Surrey Golf.

**STONEHAVEN,** 2nd Viscount, *cr* 1938, of Ury; **James Ian Baird,** 2nd Baron, *cr* 1925; 3rd Bt, *cr* 1897; Master of Kintore; AIStructE; Major, RM, Royal Marine Engineers; Vice-Lieutenant of Kincardineshire since 1965; Vice-Convenor, Kincardine County Council, since 1967; Member Royal Company of Archers; *b* 25 July 1908; *er s* of 1st Viscount Stonehaven, PC, GCMG, DSO and Lady Ethel Keith-Falconer (*see* Countess of Kintore, 12th in line, to whom he is *heir*), *e d* of 10th Earl of Kintore; *S* father, 1941; *m* 1935, Delia Virginia, *d* of William Loyd; two *s* one *d*. *Educ:* Eton; Royal School of Mines, London. UK Delegate to Council of Europe and Western European Union, 1954-64. DL Kincardineshire, 1959. *Heir:* *s* Hon. Michael Canning William John Keith, Master of Inverurie, *b* 1939. *Address:* Rickarton House, Stonehaven, Kincardineshire AB3 2SU. *T:* Stonehaven 2756. *Clubs:* Beefsteak; New (Edinburgh); Rand (Johannesburg).

**STONEHEWER BIRD, Sir Hugh,** KCMG 1945 (CMG 1939); OBE 1929; *b* 13 Nov. 1891; *s* of late Frank Stonehewer Bird; *m* 1918, Françoise, *d* of Jean Laczynski; one *s* one *d*. *Educ:* Berkhamsted School; Pembroke College, Cambridge. Student Interpreter, Levant Consular Service, 1913; HM Vice-Consul, 1917; served at Skoplje, Jassy, Bucarest, Belgrade, Mogador, Rabat; HM Agent and Consul at Jedda, 1927; Consul, Casablanca, 1930-36; acting Consul-General,

Rabat, 1936-37; Consul-General, Addis Ababa, 1937-39; Minister at Jedda, 1939-43; Consul-General for French Zone of Morocco, 1943-45; HM Ambassador to Iraq, 1945-48; retired 1948. UK rep. on UNO Council for Libya, 1950. *Recreations:* television, bridge. *Address:* Marks Danes, Bruton, Som. *T:* Bruton 3329.

*See also M. W. Errock.*

**STONEHOUSE, Rt. Hon. John Thomson,** PC 1968; MP (Lab Co-op) Wednesbury since Feb. 1957; Chairman, Export Promotion and Consultancy Services Ltd, since 1970; *b* 28 July 1925; *m* 1948, Barbara Joan Smith; one *s* two *d.* *Educ:* Elementary Sch. and Tauntons Sch., Southampton; Univ. of London (London Sch. of Econs and Political Science). Asst to Senior Probation Officer, Southampton, 1941-44. Served in RAF as pilot and education officer, 1944-47. Studied at LSE, 1947-51 (Chm., Labour Soc., 1950-51); BSc (Econ.) Hons, 1951. Dir of London Co-operative Soc. Ltd, 1956-62 (Pres., 1962-64); Mem. until 1962 of Development Cttee of the Co-operative Union; Dir of Society Footwear Ltd until 1963. Contested Norwood, London CC Election, 1949; contested (Lab): Twickenham in General Election, 1950, and Burton in General Election, 1951. Man. for African Co-operative Socs in Uganda, 1952-54; Sec. Kampala Mutual Co-operative Soc. Ltd (Uganda), 1953-54. United Kingdom Delegate to the Council of Europe and the Western European Union, 1962-64. Parly Sec., Min. of Aviation, 1964-66; Parly Under-Sec. of State for the Colonies, 1966-67; Minister of Aviation, 1967; Minister of State, Technology, 1967-68; Postmaster-General, 1968-69; Minister of Posts and Telecommunications, 1969-70. Leader, UK Govt Delegns, Independence Ceremonies in Botswana and Lesotho, 1966; attended Independence Ceremonies in Uganda, 1962, Kenya, 1963, Zambia, 1964, and Mauritius, 1968, as special guest of Independence Governments. Councillor, Islington Borough Council, 1956-59. Member, Royal Inst. of Internat. Affairs, 1955-65. *Publications:* Prohibited Immigrant, 1960; (part author) Gangrene 1959. *Recreations:* music, learning to ski, desmology. *Address:* House of Commons, SW1. *Clubs:* Royal Aero (Hon. Mem.); Royal Automobile.

**STONELEY, Robert,** FRS 1935; MA, ScD Cantab; Emeritus Reader in Theoretical Geophysics, formerly Stokes Lecturer in Mathematics, University of Cambridge; Fellow of Pembroke College; *b* 14 May 1894; *s* of Robert Stoneley and Fanny Bradley; *m* 1927, Dorothy, *d* of Gayford Duge Minn and Annie Okey; two *s* (one *d* decd). *Educ:* Parmiter's School; City of London School; St John's Coll., Cambridge (Foundation Scholar; Taylor Research Studentship). Asst Lecturer in Mathematics, Sheffield University, 1920-23; Curator of University Observatory, 1922-23; at The University of Leeds, 1923-34: Assistant Lecturer in Applied Mathematics, 1923; Astronomical Observer, 1924; Lecturer in Applied Mathematics, 1927; Hon. Reader in Geophysics, 1933; Lecturer in Mathematics, Univ. of Cambridge, 1934; Lecturer and Dir of Studies in Mathematics, Pembroke Coll., Cambridge, 1935-61. Pres., Internat. Assoc. of Seismology, 1946-51; Visiting Professor: Institute of Geophysics, Univ. of Calif., 1948; Amer. Univ. Washington, DC, 1955-56. Research Fellow in Geophysics, Calif. Inst. of Technol., 1956. Geophysicist (Seismology), Office of R&D, US Coast and Geodetic Survey, 1961-63; Prof. of Geophysics, Univ. of Pittsburgh, Pa, 1964-68. Pres., Section A, British Association, 1960-61. Chairman: British Nat. Cttee for Geodesy and Geophysics, 1949-54; British Assoc. Cttee on Seismological Investigations, 1946-. Hon. Dir, Internat. Seisomological Summary, 1957-63. Chm., Cttee for Internat. Seismological Summary, 1948-67. Nat. Corresp. for Seismology and Geodesy, UK Cttees: for Internat. Geophysical Year, 1953-60; on Antarctic Research, 1958-; on Co-operation in Geophysics, 1961-68. UNESCO Senior Consultant, Internat. Inst. of Seismology and Earthquake Engineering, Tokyo, 1963-67; Mem., UNESCO Consultative Cttee on Seismology and Earthquake Engineering, 1965-. Fellow, Amer. Geophysical Union, 1967; Mem., Pontifical Acad. of Sciences, 1970. *Publications:* Papers on geophysical subjects, mainly on earthquake waves. *Address:* Pembroke College, Cambridge.

**STONES, Prof. Edward Lionel Gregory,** MA, PhD; Professor of Mediæval History, University of Glasgow, since Oct. 1956; *b* Croydon, 4 March 1914; *s* of Edward Edison Stones, Elland, Yorks, and Eleanor Gregory; *m* 1947, Jeanne Marie Beatrice, *d* of A. J. Fradin and Florence B. Timbury; one *s* one *d.* *Educ:* Glasgow High Sch.; Glasgow Univ.; Balliol Coll., Oxford. 1st Cl. English Lang. and Lit. (Glasgow), 1936; 1st Class Modern History (Oxford), 1939; PhD (Glasgow), 1950; FRHistS, 1950; FSA, 1962. Asst Lectr in History, Glasgow Univ., 1939. War of 1939-45: joined Royal Signals, 1940; Major 1943; GSO2, GHQ, New Delhi (Signals Directorate), 1943-45. Lectr in History, Glasgow, from 1945. Lay Mem., Provincial Synod, Episcopal Church of Scotland, 1963-66. Pres., Glasgow Archaeological Soc., 1969-; Member: Ancient Monuments Board for Scotland, 1964- (Chm. 1968-); Council, Royal Hist. Soc., 1968-. *Publications:* Anglo-Scottish Relations, 1174-1328, 1965; and in various historical journals. *Recreations:* books, music, photography. *Address:* 70 Oakfield Avenue, Glasgow, W2. *T:* 041-339 3333.

**STONEY, Brigadier Ralph Francis Ewart,** CBE 1952 (OBE, 1943); Director-General, The Royal Society for the Prevention of Accidents, 1959-68; *b* 28 June 1903; *o s* of late Col R. D. S. Stoney, The Downs, Delgany, Co. Wicklow and of Mrs E. M. M. Stoney; *m* 1939, Kathleen Nina (*née* Kirkland); one *d.* *Educ:* Royal Naval Colleges, Osborne and Dartmouth; Royal Military Academy, Woolwich. Commissioned Royal Engineers, 1923; Staff College, Camberley, 1937-38. Served War of 1939-45 as GSO, 1939-43 (OBE) and as CRE, 82 Div., 1943-46, in Burma (despatches twice). CRE 5th Div. and 2nd Div., 1947-48; Col GS (Intelligence), War Office, 1949-51; Brig. GS (Intelligence), Middle East, 1952-54. Retired, 1954. *Recreations:* sailing; workshop practice. *Address:* Keystones, Kingfield Road, Woking, Surrey. *T:* Woking 61852.

**STONHAM,** Baron, *cr* 1958 (Life Peer); **Victor John Collins,** PC 1969; OBE 1946; *b* 1 July 1903; *s* of Victor and Eliza Sarah Collins; *m* 1929, Violet Mary Savage; one *s.* *Educ:* Regent St Polytechnic; London Univ. Entered family business of J. Collins & Sons, Ltd, London, E1, 1923, subseq. Gov. Dir until 1964, when in office. Joint Parly Under-Sec. of State, Home Office, 1964-67, Minister of State, 1967-69. Pres. Employers Fedn of Cane and Willow Workers Assocs, 1932; Pres. National Willow Growers Assoc., 1945; Chairman: National Basket and Willow Trades Advisory Cttee, 1942-64; National Council on Inland Transport, 1962-64; National Soc. for Mentally Handicapped Children, 1963-64; Youth Ventures, 1959-64; Advisory Council on Probation and After-Care, 1970-. mp (Lab) for Taunton Div. of Somerset, 1945-50, for

Shoreditch and Finsbury, 1954-58; Minister of State, Home Office, 1967-69. *Address:* House of Lords, SW1. *T:* 01-930 8100.

**STONHOUSE, Sir Philip (Allan),** 18th Bt, *cr* 1628, and 14th Bt *cr* 1670; Assessor and Land Appraiser, Government of Alberta; *b* 24 Oct. 1916; *s* of Sir Arthur Allan Stonhouse, 17th Bt, and Beatrice C. Féron; *S* father, 1967; *m* 1946, Winnifred Emily Shield; two *s*. *Educ:* Western Canada Coll.; Queen's Univ., Kingston, Ontario. Gold Mining, 1936-40; General Construction, 1940-42; Ranching, 1942-54; Assessing, 1954-68. Is a Freemason. *Recreations:* water-fowl and upland game hunting, tennis, ski-ing. *Heir: s* Michael Philip Stonhouse, *b* 4 Sept. 1948. *Address:* 521-12 Street SW, Medicine Hat, Alberta, Canada. *T:* 526-5832. *Club:* Medicine Hat Ski.

[*But his name does not, at the time of going to press, appear on the Official Roll of Baronets.*

**STONHOUSE-GOSTLING, Maj.-Gen. Philip Le Marchant Stonhouse,** CB 1955; CBE 1953; retired; *b* 28 August 1899, *s* of Colonel Charles Henry Stonhouse-Gostling and Alice Seton (*née* Fraser-Tytler); *m* 1946, Helen Rimington Myra (*née* Pereira), Ottawa, Ontario, Canada. *Educ:* Cheltenham College; RMA Woolwich. Entered RA, 1919; served India with RA, 1920-26; Mil. Coll. of Science, 1927-29; i/c Technical Intelligence, WO, 1930; Woolwich Arsenal: Asst Inspector Guns and Carriages, 1931-38; Supt Carriage Design, 1939; Technical Adviser to Canadian Govt and British Purchasing Commn for Armaments, 1939-40; Dep. Dir of Supply, British Supply Mission, Washington, 1941-44; Director of Supply (Armaments), 1944-46; Dep. Dir Technical Services, British Jt Staff Mission, 1942-46; Director, 1946-50; Dep. Chief Engineer, Armaments Design Establishment in UK, 1951; President, Ordnance Board, Feb. 1954-Feb. 1955; Retired from Army, March 1955. Legion of Merit (Officer), USA 1944. *Recreations:* sailing, photography. *Address:* Island House West, Tequesta, Florida 33458, USA; c/o Lloyds Bank, Cox's and King's Branch, 6 Pall Mall, SW1.

**STONIER, George Walter,** MA; author; critic; journalist; *b* Sydney, Australia, 1903; *m* 1951, Patricia, *d* of James Nelson Dover. *Educ:* Westminster School; Christ Church, Oxford. Assistant Literary Editor of the New Stateman and Nation, 1928-45. Has written plays for BBC: Robert Tasker Deceased, Squeaky Shoes, Chap in a Bowler Hat, etc. *Publications:* Gog Magog, 1933; The Shadow Across the Page, 1937; Shaving Through the Blitz, 1943; My Dear Bunny, 1946; The Memoirs of a Ghost, 1947; Round London with the Unicorn, 1951; Pictures on the Pavement, 1954; English Countryside in Colour, 1956; Off the Rails, 1967; Rhodesian Spring, 1968; (ed) International Film Annual, vols 2 and 3. Contributions to Observer, New Statesman and Nation, Punch, Sunday Telegraph, Sight and Sound. *Address:* 1 Riebeeck, Acton Road, Rondebosch, Cape Town, South Africa.

**STONOR,** family name of **Baron Camoys.**

**STOOKE, Sir George Beresford-,** KCMG 1948 (CMG 1943); Gentleman Usher of the Blue Rod in the Order of St Michael and St George since 1959; *b* 3 Jan. 1897; *m* 1931, Creenagh, *y d* of late Sir Henry Richards; one *s* one *d*. Royal Navy, 1914-19; Colonial Service, 1920-48; Governor and C-in-C, Sierra Leone, 1948-53; Second Crown Agent for Oversea Governments and Administrations, 1953-55. Member, Kenya Camps Inquiry, 1959. President, Anglo-Sierra Leone Society, 1962. 2nd Class Order of Brilliant Star of Zanzibar, 1942. KStJ, 1951. *Address:* Hillfarrance House, Hillfarrance, Taunton, Somerset. *Clubs:* Athenæum, Royal Societies.

*See also W. F. Page.*

**STOPFORD,** family name of **Earl of Courtown.**

**STOPFORD, Viscount; James Patrick Montagu Burgoyne Winthrop Stopford;** *b* 19 March 1954; *s* and *heir* of 8th Earl of Courtown, *qv*.

**STOPFORD, Edward Kennedy,** CB 1955; Assistant Under-Secretary of State, Ministry of Defence, since 1964; *b* 10 Oct. 1911; *yr s* of late Major Heneage Frank Stopford, Royal Field Artillery, and Margaret, *d* of late Edward Briggs Kennedy; *m* 1952, Patricia Iona Mary, *widow* of Duncan Stewart, CMG, and *d* of late Howard Carrick; one *s*. *Educ:* Winchester; New College, Oxford. 1st Class, Lit. Hum., 1933. Entered War Office, 1936; Under-Secretary, 1954-64. *Address:* Ryestead Common, Chiddingfold, Surrey. *T:* Wormley 3335.

**STOPFORD, Rear-Admiral Frederick Victor,** CBE 1952; retired; *b* 6 July 1900; *yr s* of late Rear-Admiral Hon. W. G. Stopford; *m* 1924, Mary Guise, *d* of late Captain F. C. U. Vernon-Wentworth; three *s* one *d*. *Educ:* Osborne; Dartmouth. Served European War, 1916-18; Commander, 1933; War of 1939-45; Captain, 1943; Rear-Admiral, 1950. ADC, 1948-50. *Address:* Ash Farm House, Grenofen, Tavistock, S Devon.

**STOPFORD, Gen. Sir Montagu George North,** GCB 1948 (KCB 1947; CB 1943); KBE 1944; DSO 1940; MC 1917; DL; Vice-President Army Cadet Force Association, since 1961 (Chairman, 1951-61); *b* 16 Nov. 1892; *m* 1921, Dorothy, *d* of late Lt-Col H. F. Deare. *Educ:* Wellington College; RMC, Sandhurst. 2nd Lt Rifle Brigade, 1911; Maj.-Gen. 1941; Lt-Gen. 1944; Gen. 1946; served European War, France and Belgium, 1914-18 (despatches twice, MC); War of 1939-45 (despatches, DSO, CB, KBE); Comd 17 Inf. Bde, BEF, 1939-40; GOC 56 (London) Div. 1941; Comdt Staff College, 1942; GOC 33rd Ind. Corps, Burma, 1943-45; GOC-in-C 12th Army, Burma Command and Allied Forces, Netherlands East Indies, 1945-46; C-in-C Allied Land Forces, SE Asia, 1946-47; GOC-in-C, Northern Command, 1947-49; ADC General to King George VI, 1947-49; retired, 1949; Col Comdt The Rifle Bde, 1951-58. DL Oxford, 1962. Commander Legion of Merit (USA), 1946. *Address:* Rockhill House, Chipping Norton, Oxon. *Club:* United Service.

**STOPFORD, Robert Jemmett,** CMG 1946; Commander of the Order of Orange Nassau; US Medal of Freedom; Vice-Chairman, Imperial War Museum, 1954-68; *b* 19 May 1895; *s* of late Jemmett J. Stopford, Dublin; unmarried. *Educ:* St Paul's Sch.; Magdalene Coll., Cambridge. Served European War, 1914-18; Banking, 1921-38. Private Sec. to Chm., Indian Statutory Commission, 1928-30; Member of Runciman Mission to Czechoslovakia, 1938; Liaison Officer for Refugees with the Czechoslovakian Govt, 1938-39; Financial Counsellor, British Embassy, Washington, 1940-43; War Office, 1943-45. Formerly Chairman National Film Finance Corporation. *Address:* Oyles Mill Cottage, Iwerne Minster, Blandford, Dorset. *Club:* Athenæum.

**STOPFORD, Rt. Rev. and Rt. Hon. Robert Wright;** *see* London, Bishop of.

**STOPFORD SACKVILLE, Colonel Nigel Victor,** CBE 1963 (OBE 1945); TD 1945; DL; JP; CA;

*b* 27 Jan. 1901; *s* of late Col Lionel Stopford Sackville, Rifle Brigade; *m* 1st, 1929, Beatrix, *d* of late Col H. A. Pakenham, CMG; one *s* one *d*; 2nd, 1946, Lilah, *d* of Capt. Percy Hare. *Educ:* Repton; Royal Military College, Sandhurst. Lieut 14th/20th Hussars 1921; Northamptonshire Yeomanry: Capt. 1930; Lt-Col 1940; Hon. Col 1952-67. Col comdg RAC Tactical School, 1942; Col 2nd i/c 9th Armoured Bde, 1943; served in Middle East and Italy (despatches). Chm. Northants Agric. Exec. Cttee, 1953-68; Personal Liaison Officer to Minister of Agriculture, 1955. Chm., Northants. T & AFA, 1952-66. JP 1933, CC 1931, CA 1945, Northants; DL County of Northampton, 1965. *Publication:* (privately) Drayton, History of Drayton House, 1939. *Recreation:* shooting. *Address:* Drayton House, Lowick, Kettering, Northants. *T:* Lowick 202. *Club:* White's.

**STOPPARD, Tom;** playwright and novelist; *b* 3 July 1937; *yr s* of Eugene and Martha Straussler; *m* 1965, Jose, *yr d* of John and Alice Ingle; two *s*. *Educ:* abroad; Dolphin Sch., Notts; Pocklington, Yorks. Journalist: Western Daily Press, Bristol, 1954-58; Bristol Evening World, 1958-60; freelance, 1960-63. *Plays:* Enter a Free Man, London, 1968 (TV play, A Walk on the Water, 1963); Rosencrantz and Guildenstern are Dead, Nat. Theatre, 1967 (subseq. NY, etc); The Real Inspector Hound, London, 1968; After Magritte, Ambiance Theatre, 1970; *radio:* The Dissolution of Dominic Boot, 1964; M is for Moon Among Other Things, 1964; If You're Glad I'll Be Frank, 1965; Albert's Bridge, 1967; Where Are They Now?, 1970; *television:* A Separate Peace, 1966; Teeth, 1967; Another Moon Called Earth, 1967; Neutral Ground, 1968. John Whiting Award, Arts Council, 1967; Evening Standard Award for Most Promising Playwright, 1968; Tony Award for Best Play, NY, 1968; NY Drama Critics Circle Award for Best Play, 1968. *Publications:* (short stories) Introduction 2, 1964; (novel) Lord Malquist and Mr Moon, 1965; *plays:* Rosencrantz and Guildenstern are Dead, 1967; The Real Inspector Hound, 1968; Albert's Bridge (Prix Italia), Enter a Free Man, etc, 1968. *Recreations:* conversation, cricket, croquet. *Address:* River Thatch, Abbotsbrook, Bourne End, Bucks. *T:* Bourne End 21077.

**STOPPELMAN, Mrs J. W. F.;** *see* Klinghoffer, C.

**STOREY,** family name of **Baron Buckton.**

**STOREY, Christopher,** MA, PhD; Headmaster, Culford School, Bury St Edmunds, since 1951; *b* 23 July 1908; *s* of William Storey and Margaret T. B. Cowan, Newcastle upon Tyne; *m* 1937, Gertrude Appleby, Scarborough; four *s*. *Educ:* Rutherford Coll., Newcastle upon Tyne; King's Coll., Univ. of Durham (BA Hons French, cl. I); Univ. of Strasbourg (PhD). Modern Languages Master, Mundella Sch., Nottingham, 1931-34; French Master: Scarborough High Sch. for Boys, 1934-36; City of London Sch., 1936-42. Headmaster, Johnston Grammar Sch., Durham, 1942-51. Officier d'Académie, 1947. *Publications:* Etude critique de la vie de St Alexis, 1934; Apprenons le mot juste!, 1939; La Vie de St Alexis, 1946; Sprechen und Schreiben (with C. E. Bond), 1950; articles in Modern Language Review. *Address:* Headmaster's Lodge, Culford School, Bury St Edmunds, Suffolk. *T:* Culford 262.

**STOREY, David Malcolm;** Writer and dramatist; *b* 13 July 1933; *s* of Frank Richmond Storey and Lily (*née* Cartwright); *m* 1956, Barbara Rudd Hamilton; two *s* two *d*. *Educ:* Queen Elizabeth Grammar Sch., Wakefield, Yorks; Slade School of Fine Art, London. *Plays:* The Restoration of Arnold Middleton, 1967; In Celebration, 1969; The Contractor, 1969; Home, 1970. *Publications:* This Sporting Life, 1960; Flight into Camden, 1960; Radcliffe, 1963. *Address:* 2 Lyndhurst Gardens, NW3.

**STOREY, (M.) Gladys,** OBE 1919; authoress; *b* Hampstead; *d* of Prof. G. A. Storey, RA, and Emily Hayward, London. *Educ:* Allen-Olney Sch., Hampstead. On stage, ingénue parts with Sir George Alexander, gave up stage for war-work; pioneer of Women's Services; commenced recruiting on own initiative, gaining approval of Lord Roberts; became only female recruiter at HQ Recruiting Depot, Whitehall, 1914; ran fund (under own name) for providing Bovril to soldiers in trenches in every theatre of War, 1914-18; donations, King George V; grant from the Army Council; supplied British Military Mission in N and S Russia (by special request of GOC), 1919-20; transferred from Recruiting HQ to supervise staff at HQ National Registration, London, 1915-17; Sept. 1939, re-inauguration of Great War Fund (under own name) providing Bovril for HM Forces in all war and other areas; continuation of supplies after European War by request of Field-Marshal Montgomery to British Army of the Rhine, 1945-47, and British Troops, Jerusalem, 1946-47. Fund supported by King George VI and War Office. *Publications:* Humorous Stories of Famous People, 1916; All Sorts of People, 1929; Dickens and Daughter (at her request), 1939; made drawing (1925) of Mrs Perugini (Kate Dickens) bound in at beginning of vol. containing Charles Dickens' letters to his wife, Br. Museum, 1934. *Recreations:* gardening, odd jobs. *Address:* 10 Wellington Road, St John's Wood, NW8. *T:* 01-722 5177.

**STORK, Herbert Cecil,** CIE 1945; *b* 28 June 1890; *s* of Herbert William and Florence Stork; *m* 1919, Marjorie (*née* Cosens); two *d*. *Educ:* Merchant Taylors' School; Queen's College, Oxford (BA). Appointed to ICS, Dec. 1913; served Bengal and Assam, various posts, concluding with Legal Remembrancer and Secretary to Government of Assam; retired from ICS, 1947. Served European War, 1914-18; GSO III, 9th (Secunderabad) Division, and Staff Captain, Dunsterforce, MEF. *Recreations:* cricket, tennis. *Address:* 127 Cumnor Hill, Oxford. *T:* Cumnor 2692. *Club:* Oxford Union Society.

**STORK, Joseph Whiteley,** CB 1959; CBE 1949; retired as Director of Studies, Britannia Royal Naval College, Dartmouth (1955-59) (Headmaster, 1942-55); *b* Huddersfield, 9 Aug. 1902; *s* of John Arthur Stork, Huddersfield; *m* 1927, Kathleen, *d* of Alderman J. H. Waddington, JP, Halifax; one *s* three *d*. *Educ:* Uppingham; Downing Coll., Cambridge (scholar). 1st Class Nat. Sci. Tripos Pt 1, 2nd Class Nat. Sci. Tripos Pt II (Zoology); Senior Biology Master, Cambridge and County School, 1926; Head of Biological Dept, Charterhouse School, 1926-36; Headmaster, Portsmouth Grammar School, 1936-42. Mem., Devon Educn Cttee. *Publications:* Joint Author of: Fundamentals of Biology, 1932, Junior Biology, 1933, Plant and Animal Ecology, 1933. *Address:* 1 The White House, 5 Trefusis Terrace, Exmouth, Devon.

**STORM, Lesley;** Playwright; (*née* Margaret Cowie), *d* of Rev. William Cowie, MA, and Christian Ewen; *m* James Doran Clark, MB, ChB, DPM (*d* 1955); two *s* two *d*. *Educ:* Peterhead Academy; Aberdeen University (MA). *Publications:* Plays: Tony Draws a

Horse, 1939; Great Day, 1942; Black Chiffon, 1949; The Day's Mischief, 1952; The Long Echo, 1956; Roar Like a Dove, 1957; The Paper Hat, 1965; Three Goose-quills and a Knife, 1967. *Recreation:* travel. *Address:* 3 St Simon's Avenue, SW15. *T:* 01-788 6028.

**STORMONT, Viscount; William David Mungo James Murray;** Barrister-at-law, 1958; Lieutenant The Scots Guards (RARO); *b* 7 July 1930; *o s* of 7th Earl of Mansfield and Mansfield, *qv*; *m* 1955, Pamela Joan, *o d* of W. N. Foster, CBE; two *s* one *d*. *Educ:* Eton; Christ Church, Oxford. *Heir: s* Master of Stormont, *qv*. *Address:* 10 Ormonde Gate, SW3; (Seat) Scone Palace, Perthshire. *Clubs:* Turf, Pratt's, Garrick, MCC.

**STORMONT, Master of; Hon. Alexander David Mungo Murray;** *b* 17 Oct. 1956; *s* and *heir* of Viscount Stormont, *qv*.

**STORMONTH DARLING, James Carlisle,** MC 1945; TD; Secretary, The National Trust for Scotland, since 1949; *b* 18 July 1918; *s* of late Robert Stormonth Darling, Writer to the Signet, Rosebank, Kelso, Roxburghshire, and late Beryl Madeleine Sayer, Battle, Sussex; *m* 1948, Mary Finella, BEM 1945, *d* of Lt-Gen. Sir James Gammell, *qv*; one *s* two *d*. *Educ:* Winchester Coll.; Christ Church, Oxford; Edinburgh Univ. 2nd Lt KOSB (TA), 1938; War Service, 1939-46, in KOSB and 52nd (L) Reconnaissance Regt, RAC, of which Lt-Col comdg in 1945 (TD). BA Oxon 1939; LLB Edinburgh; admitted Writer to the Signet, 1949. Member, Queen's Body Guard for Scotland (Royal Company of Archers), 1958. *Address:* The Harestanes, Longniddry, East Lothian. *T:* Aberlady 203; 6 Buckingham Terrace, Edinburgh 4. *T:* 031-332 5414; National Trust for Scotland, 5 Charlotte Square, Edinburgh. *Club:* New (Edinburgh).

**STORR, Norman,** OBE 1947; with Charity Commission, since 1968; *b* 9 Dec. 1907; *s* of Herbert Storr and Beatrice Emily Storr, Barnsley; *m* 1937, Kathleen Mary Ward; two *s* one *d*. *Educ:* Holgate's Grammar School, Barnsley; Keble College, Oxford. Open schol. in Mod. History, Keble Coll., Oxford, 1926; BA Hons Mod. History, 1929. Entered Indian Civil Service, 1930; Session Judge, 1935; Registrar, Allahabad High Court, 1939; Registrar, Federal Court of India, 1943-47. Principal, Home Office, 1947; Principal, 1952, Establishment Officer, 1958, Comr and Sec., 1962, Prison Commission; Asst Sec., Estab. Div. Home Office, 1966-67, retired. *Recreation:* painting. *Address:* 19 St John's Avenue, Ewell, Surrey. *Club:* Royal Over-Seas League.

**STORRAR, Sir John,** Kt, *cr* 1953; CBE 1949; MC 1917; Town Clerk of Edinburgh, 1941-56; *b* 8 Dec. 1891; *s* of late Rev. Wm Storrar, Hardgate, Dalbeattie, Kirkcudbrightshire; *m* Agnes Drennan, *d* of late James Cameron, Hollos, Lenzie; one *d*. *Educ:* Castle Douglas Academy; Edinburgh Univ. Solicitor, 1914. Served European War, Royal Scots, 1914-19 (despatches, MC). Local Government service, 1923; Depute Town Clerk, Edinburgh, 1934. Member of various government committees. Hon. LLD Edinburgh, 1957. *Address:* 13 Cadogan Road, Edinburgh. *T:* 031-664 3503.

**STORRAR, Air Vice-Marshal Ronald Charles,** CB 1957; OBE 1945; Senior Air Staff Officer, RAF Maintenance Command; *b* 4 Sept. 1904; *m* 1932, Vera Winifred Butler; one *s*; psa; Royal Air Force; serving in the Equipment Branch. Air Commodore, 1954; Air Vice-Marshal, 1959; retired, 1963. *Address:* The Mill Leat, Bishopswood, near Chard, Somerset. *T:* Buckland St Mary 212. *Club:* Royal Air Force.

**STORRS, Rt. Rev. Christopher E.,** MA, ThDoc (Australia); *b* 4 Feb. 1889; *s* of John Storrs, Dean of Rochester; *m* 1939 Joan Williams, Perth, Western Australia; two *s* two *d*. *Educ:* Malvern College (Senior Scholar); Pembroke College, Cambridge (Senior Scholar, 1st Class Classical Tripos); Leeds Clergy School. Boxed Cambridge v Oxford, 1908; Deacon, 1912; Priest, 1915; Leeds Parish Church, 1912-15; CF 1916-19; Macedonia, Palestine, Egypt; Chaplain and Assistant Master, Malvern College, 1915-30; St George's College, Perth, Western Australia, 1930-39; Archdeacon of Northam, W Australia, 1939-46; Bishop of Grafton, New South Wales, 1946-55; Warden of St John's Theological College, Morpeth, NSW, 1955-60; Rector of Hazelbury Bryan, Dorset, 1960-64. *Publications:* edited pamphlets The Christian and the War Series by Australian authors, 1941; Mr Valiant for Truth: an Anthology, 1942; Many Creeds One Cross (Moorhouse Lectures 1943, USA, 1944). *Recreations:* chess, golf, music, reading, talking. *Address:* 37 Westgate, Chichester, Sussex.

**STORY, A. M. Sommerville** (former pen-name, **Frankfort Sommerville**); journalist and author; *b* Frankfort-on-Main; *s* of late A. T. Story; *m* 1st, 1903, Alice Loughton (*d* 1919); one *s* one *d*; 2nd, 1924, Thelma Thomas. *Educ:* Brussels; Lancashire; London; Bonn. Former editor Belgian Times and News; Continental Daily Mail, Paris Evening Telegram and other publications; President of Anglo-American Press Association of Paris, 1915; frequent contributor to English, American, and French journals and magazines. *Publications:* The Face of Pan, 1907; A Parisian Princess, 1911; The Spirit of Paris, 1913; Paris in Ten Days, a Little Guide for Tommy and the Yank, 1919; The Battlefields of France, 1919-20; Paris à la Carte, 1922; Twenty Years in Paris (with a Pen), 1927; The Tales of My Study, 1928; Tales of France, 1931; Auguste Rodin, 1939; France and the French, 1951; edited The Memoirs of Ismail Kemal Bey, 1920. *Address:* 92 Talbot Road, W2.

**STOTESBURY, Herbert Wentworth;** Assistant Under-Secretary of State, Home Office, since 1966; Probation and Aftercare Department, since 1969; *b* 22 Jan. 1916; *s* of Charles and Ada Stotesbury; *m* 1944, Berenice Mary Simpson; one *s* two *d*. *Educ:* Christ's Hospital; Emmanuel College, Cambridge. Home Office, 1939; Army, 1940-45. Lecturer, Military Coll. of Science, 1941-45. Home Office, 1945-; Asst Secretary, 1953. *Recreations:* music, camping. *Address:* 65 Woodside, Wimbledon, SW19. *T:* 01-946 9523.

**STOTT, Rt. Hon. Lord; George Gordon Stott,** PC 1964; QC (Scotland) 1950; Senator of College of Justice in Scotland since 1967; *b* 22 Dec. 1909; *s* of Rev. Dr G. Gordon Stott; *m* 1947, Nancy, *d* of A. D. Braggins; one *s* one *d*. *Educ:* Cramond Sch.; Edinburgh Acad.; Edinburgh Univ. Advocate 1936; Advocate-Depute, 1947-51; Editor, Edinburgh Clarion, 1939-44; Member, Monopolies Commission, 1949-56; Sheriff of Roxburgh, Berwick and Selkirk, 1961-64; Lord Advocate, 1964-67. *Address:* 12 Midmar Gardens, Edinburgh. *T:* 031-447 4251.

**STOTT, Rt. Hon. George Gordon;** *see* Stott, Rt Hon. Lord.

**STOTT, Rev. John Robert Walmsley,** MA Cantab; Rector of All Souls Church, Langham Place, W1, since 1950; Hon. Chaplain to the Queen, since 1959; *b* 27 April 1921; *s* of late Sir

Arnold W. Stott, KBE, physician, and late Emily Caroline Holland. *Educ:* Rugby Sch.; Trinity Coll., Cambridge; Ridley Hall, Cambridge. Curate of All Souls, Langham Place, 1945; Rector of All Souls, 1950, with St Peter's, Vere Street, 1952. Chm., C of E Evangelical Council, 1967. *Publications:* Men with a Message, 1954; What Christ Thinks of the Church, 1958; Basic Christianity, 1958; Your Confirmation, 1958; Fundamentalism and Evangelism, 1959; The Preacher's Portrait, 1961; Confess Your Sins, 1964; The Epistles of John, 1964; Canticles and Selected Psalms, 1966; Men Made New, 1966; Our Guilty Silence, 1967; The Message of Galatians, 1968; One People, 1969; Christ The Controversialist, 1970. *Recreations:* bird watching and photography. *Address:* 12 Weymouth Street, W1. *T:* 01-580 1867; (from May 1971) 13 Bridford Mews, W1.

**STOTT, May, Lady, (May B. Lee)**; RMS; *b* Lahore, India; *e d* of late John Bridges Lee, MA Cantab, Barrister-at-Law, Inner Temple, Advocate of High Courts of Calcutta, Allahabad and Lahore; *m* Sir Philip Stott, 1st Bt, as his second wife. *Educ:* in England; studied Art at Lambeth School of Art. Exhibited Royal Academy 34 years (46 portraits), Salon Artistes Français 32 times, also occasionally Royal Scottish Academy, Walker Art Gallery, Liverpool. Mem. of Soc. of Women Artists, Royal Soc. of Miniature Painters, Sculptors and Gravers, Society of Miniaturists and Ridley Art Club; Portrait Painter in oils, water colours and miniatures. Has painted numerous portraits of well-known people (including sons of the Princess Royal) and been commissioned to paint many presentation large portraits and miniatures. Mention honorable, Salon 1950 (Section de Peinture), Société des Artistes Français. *Recreations:* reading, dancing, travelling, friends. *Address:* 162 Cromwell Road, Kensington, SW5. *T:* 01-373 3516.

**STOTT, Peter Frank**, MA, FICE, FIHE, MIEAust; Joint Director of Planning and Transportation, Greater London Council, since 1969; *b* 8 Aug. 1927; *s* of Clarence Stott and Mabel Sutcliffe; *m* 1953, Vera Watkins; two *s*. *Educ:* Bradford Grammar Sch.; Clare Coll., Cambridge. Partner, G. Maunsell & Partners, Consulting Engineers, 1955-63; Deputy Chief Engineer (Roads) and later Chief Engineer, London County Council, 1963-65; Dir of Highways and Transportation, GLC, 1964-67; Traffic Comr and Dir of Transportation, GLC, 1967-69. President: Reinforced Concrete Assoc., 1964; Concrete Soc., 1967; Vice-Pres., Instn of Highway Engineers. *Address:* 7 Frank Dixon Way, SE21. *T:* 01-693 5121.

**STOTT, Sir Philip Sidney**, 3rd Bt *cr* 1920; ARIBA, AIAA; Senior Architect in private practice; *b* 23 Dec. 1914; *e s* of Sir George Edward Stott, 2nd Bt, and Kate (*d* 1955), *o d* of late George Swailes, Oldham; *S* father 1957; *m* 1947, Cicely Florence, *widow* of V. C. W. Trowbridge and *o d* of Bertram Ellingham; two *s*. *Educ:* Rossall; Trinity Hall, Cambridge. Registered Chartered and Incorporate Architect; ARIBA 1947; AIAA 1950. *Recreations:* astronomy, chess, music and tennis. *Heir:* *s* Adrian George Ellingham Stott, *b* 7 Oct. 1948. *Address:* 144 West Osborne, North Vancouver, BC, Canada.

**STOUGHTON, Raymond Henry**, ARCS; DSc (London); LLD (Toronto); retired as principal, University College of Ghana, 1957-61; *b* 8 Jan. 1903; *yr s* of Arnold Stoughton-Harris and Mary Townsend Jefferis; *m* 1925, Audrey Milne Rennie (*d* 1950); three *s*. *Educ:* St Peter's Sch., York; Imperial Coll. of Science and Technology, ARCS, 1923; BSc London 1924; DSc London 1932; Mycologist, Rubber Research scheme, Ceylon 1924-26; Assistant Mycologist, Rothamsted Experimental Station, 1926-33. Professor of Horticulture, University of Reading, 1933-57. Victoria Medal of Honour (RHS), 1955. *Publications:* various on plant pathology and bacterial cytology in Proceedings of the Royal Society, Annals of Applied Biology, etc., and on physiology and horticulture in various journals. *Recreations:* philately and art history. *Address:* The Flat, Roseneath, Hook, Hants. *T:* Hook 2318.

**STOURTON**, family name of **Baron Mowbray, Segrave and Stourton.**

**STOURTON, Sir Ivo (Herbert Evelyn Joseph)**, Kt 1961; CMG 1951; OBE 1939; KPM 1949; Inspector General of Colonial Police 1957-66; *b* 18 July 1901; *s* of late Major H. M. Stourton, OBE, and late Hon. Mrs H. Stourton; *m* 1st, 1926, Lilian (*d* 1942), *d* of late G. Dickson; two *s* one *d*; 2nd, 1945, Virginia, *d* of Sir Horace Seymour, *qv*; one *d*. *Educ:* Stonyhurst College, Lancs. Joined Colonial Police Service, 1921; Asst Supt of Police; served Mauritius, 1921-33; Commissioner of Police: Bermuda, 1933-39; Zanzibar, 1939-40; Aden, 1940-45; Uganda, 1945-50; Nigeria, 1950; Inspector-Gen. of Police, Nigeria, 1951, retd 1953. Re-appointed as Deputy Inspector General of Colonial Police, 1953-57. King's Police Medal, 1949. *Address:* The Old Bakery, Kimpton, Andover, Hants. *T:* Weyhill 446.

**STOURTON, Hon. John Joseph**, TD; *b* 5 March 1899; *yr s* of 24th Lord Mowbray; *m* 1st, 1923, Kathleen Alice (who obtained a divorce 1933), *d* of late Robert Louis George Gunther, of 8 Princes Gardens and Park Wood, Englefield Green, Surrey; two *s* two *d*; 2nd, 1934, Gladys Leila *d* of late Col Sir W. J. Waldron. *Educ:* Downside School. MP (C) South Salford, 1931-45. Served N Russian Relief Force at Archangel, 1919; and in European War, 1939-43; late Lt 10th Royal Hussars; Major The Royal Norfolk Regiment. *Address:* Miniature Hall, Wadhurst, Sussex.

*See also Earl of Gainsborough.*

**STOUT, Alan Ker**, MA; Professor of Philosophy, University of Sydney, 1939-65, now Emeritus Professor; *s* of late Professor G. F. Stout and Ella Ker; *m* Evelyn Roberts, BA; one *s* one *d*. *Educ:* Fettes College, Edinburgh; Oriel College, Oxford. First Class Hon. Mods Oxford; Second Class Lit Hum Oxford; Bishop Fraser Research Scholar, Oriel Coll., 1922; Lecturer in Philosophy, Univ. College of North Wales, Bangor, 1924-34, Univ. of Edinburgh, 1934-39. Visiting Prof., Univ. of Wisconsin, 1966. Pres., Council for Civil Liberties, 1964-67; Member: Aust. Social Sciences Research Council; Aust. National Film Board, 1945-47; Aust. Nat. Adv. Cttee for UNESCO and Aust. Govt Delegn to 4th Session, Paris, 1949. Chm., Aust. Film Institute. Exec. Member: Aust. Consumers' Assoc.; Nat. Theatre and Fine Arts Soc., Tasmania. Fellow: Univ. Senate, Univ. of Sydney, 1954-69; Aust. Acad. of the Humanities. Editor, Australasian Jl of Philosophy, 1950-67. *Publications:* Articles and Reviews (especially on the Philosophy of Descartes and on Moral Theory) in Mind, Proceedings of Aristotelian Soc., Philosophy, Australasian Journal of Philosophy, Australian Quarterly, etc., from 1926; Editor God and Nature (posthumously published Gifford lectures of G. F. Stout), 1952. *Recreation:* the theatre. *Address:* 12 Lambert Avenue, Sandy Bay, Hobart, Tasmania 7005,

Australia. *Club:* Royal Commonwealth Society (Tasmania).

**STOUT, Sir Duncan,** *see* Stout, Sir T. D. M.

**STOUT, Samuel Coredon;** Deputy High Commissioner and Minister (Commercial), Karachi, Foreign and Commonwealth Office, since Aug. 1968; *b* 17 Feb. 1913; *m* 1st, Mary Finn (*d* 1965); two *s* one *d*; 2nd, 1966, Jill Emery. Ministry of National Insurance, 1937-40; Admiralty, 1940-46; Board of Trade, 1946-65 (Trade Commissioner, Singapore, Bombay and Melbourne); Counsellor (Commercial), Canberra, 1966-68. *Address:* c/o Foreign and Commonwealth Office, SW1.

**STOUT, Sir (Thomas) Duncan (Macgregor),** Kt 1962; CBE 1943 (OBE 1919); DSO 1917; ED; MB, MS London; FRCS; FRACS; FACS; Hon. LLD, New Zealand; Hon. Cons. Surgeon, Wellington Hospital; Past Member Council and past Chancellor, Victoria University of Wellington; Past Member Council, Massey Agricultural College; Trustee, NZ Cancer Societies; Past President, Wellington Branch (NZ) British Empire Cancer Campaign; *b* 25 July 1885; *s* of late Rt Hon. Sir R. Stout, KCMG; *m* 1919, Agnes I. Pearce; three *s* one *d*. *Educ:* Wellington College, NZ; Guy's College and Hospital. Consultant Surgeon, Wellington Hospital (NZ); served European War, 1914-18, Samoan Force (OBE, DSO); attached to No. 1 NZ Stationary Hospital at Port Said, Salonica, and France; Divisional Surgeon at Brockenhurst (NZ Hospital in England); War of 1939-45 (England, Middle East and Italy); Consultant Surgeon 2nd NZEF (CBE). Editor NZ Medical War History, 1939-45; President, NZ Branch BMA, 1937-38. *Recreations:* golf and bowls. *Address:* 1 Katherine Avenue, Wellington N1, New Zealand. *T:* 44.968. *Club:* Wellington (Wellington, NZ).

**STOUT, William Ferguson,** CB 1964; Permanent Secretary, Ministry of Development, Northern Ireland, since 1965; *b* Holywood, Co. Down, 22 Feb. 1907; *s* of late Robert and Amelia Stout; *m* 1938, Muriel Kilner; one *s* one *d*. *Educ:* Sullivan Upper Sch., Holywood; Queen's Univ., Belfast. Ministry of Home Affairs: Principal, 1943; Asst Sec., 1954; Senior Asst Sec., 1959; Permanent Sec., 1961-64; Permanent Sec., Min. of Health and Local Govt, 1964. *Recreation:* golf. *Address:* 259 Belmont Road, Belfast 4. *T:* 654425.

**STOW, Archdeacon of;** *see* Clark, Ven. S. H.

**STOW, Sir Frederic Lawrence Philipson-,** 3rd Bt, *cr* 1907; *b* 19 Sept. 1905; *e s* of Sir Elliot Philipson Philipson-Stow, 2nd Bt and Edith (*d* 1943), *y d* of late E. H. Pery-Knox-Gore, DL, JP, of Coolcronan, Ballina, Co. Mayo; *S* father 1954; *m* 1st, 1932, Daphne Morriss (marr. diss.; she *d* 1960), *e d* of late W. G. Daffarn; 2nd, 1951, Cynthia Yvette, *d* of late W. R. Jecks, Johannesburg. *Educ:* Eton. *Heir: b* Edmond Cecil Philipson-Stow, MBE 1946, *b* 25 Aug. 1912. *Address:* Apartado 211, Mahon, Menorca, Spain.

**STOW, Sir John Montague,** GCMG 1966 (KCMG 1959; CMG 1950); KCVO 1966; Governor-General of Barbados, 1966-67; retired, 1967; since employed as consultant by Stewart, Smith & Co. Ltd; *b* 3 Oct. 1911; *s* of late Sir Alexander Stow, KCIE; *m* 1939, Beatrice Tryhorne; two *s*. *Educ:* Harrow School; Pembroke College, Cambridge. Administrative Officer, Nigeria, 1934; Secretariat, Gambia, 1938; Chief Sec., Windward Islands, 1944; Administrator, St Lucia, BWI, 1947; Dir of Establishments, Kenya, 1952-55; Chief Sec., Jamaica, 1955-59; Governor and C-in-C Barbados, 1959-66. KStJ 1959, Mem., Chapter General. *Recreations:* cricket, tennis. *Address:* 26a Tregunter Road, SW10. *T:* 01-370 1921. *Clubs:* Royal Automobile, MCC.

**STOW, (Julian) Randolph;** writer; *b* Geraldton, W Australia, 28 Nov. 1935; *s* of Cedric Ernest Stow and Mary Stow (*née* Sewell). *Educ:* Guildford Grammar Sch., W Australia; Univ. of Western Australia. Lecturer in English Literature: Univ. of Leeds, 1962; Univ. of Western Australia, 1963-64; Harkness Fellow, United States, 1964-66; Lectr in English and Commonwealth Lit., Univ. of Leeds, 1968-69. Miles Franklin Award, 1958; Britannica Australia Award, 1966. *Publications: poems:* Outrider, 1962; A Counterfeit Silence, 1969; *novels:* To The Islands, 1958; Tourmaline, 1963; The Merry-go-round in the Sea, 1965; *for children:* Midnite, 1967. *Address:* c/o Curtis Brown Ltd, 13 King Street, WC2.

**STOW, Randolph;** *see* Stow, J. R.

**STOW HILL,** Baron *cr* 1966 (Life Peer), of Newport; **Frank Soskice;** PC 1948; Kt, *cr* 1945; QC 1945; *b* 23 July 1902; *m* 1940, Susan Isabella Cloudesley Hunter; two *s*. *Educ:* St Paul's School; Balliol College, Oxford. Called to Bar, Inner Temple, 1926; Bencher, 1945. MP (Lab) for Birkenhead East, 1945-50, for Neepsend Div. of Sheffield, (April) 1950-55, for Newport (Monmouthshire), (July) 1956-66; Solicitor-General, 1945-51; Attorney-General, April-Oct. 1951; Home Secretary, 1964-65; Lord Privy Seal, 1965-66. UK Delegate to UN General Assembly, 1950. Treasurer, Inner Temple, 1968. *Address:* House of Lords, SW1.

**STOWELL, Gordon William,** ARCA; journalist and encyclopedist; *b* 6 September 1898; *yr s* of Rev. Arthur Knight Stowell, Leeds, and Elizabeth Ann Finlinson; *m* 1st, 1921, May Fairbrother (*d* 1926); 2nd, 1929, Milicent Louise Dods. *Educ:* Leeds Modern School; Leeds School of Art; Royal College of Art (Diploma of Associateship in Decorative Painting). Principal, Weston-Super-Mare School of Science and Art, 1923-26. Joined British Broadcasting Corporation on Staff of Radio Times, 1932; Deputy Editor, 1933; Editor, 1941-44. With Fleetway Publications 1944-64, edited New Universal Encyclopedia, The Book of Knowledge, Practical Knowledge for All, Children's Encyclopedia (30th edn), etc; Founder-Editor: Waverley Encyclopedia, 1952; The Book of Words, 1962; Junior Year Book, 1964. Served in ranks of London Territorials, 1916-18, France (wounded). *Publications:* The History of Button Hill (novel) 1929; many articles and reviews. *Address:* 113 Howard's Lane, Putney, SW15. *T:* 01-788 4754.

**STOWELL, Thomas Edmund Alex,** CBE 1949; MD, FRCS, FRSM, FRIPHH, etc; Consulting Surgeon, Emergency Medical Service; Diploma, Industrial Diseases (hc), Buenos Aires; Diploma in Industrial Health (hc), Society of Apothecaries; Hon. Surgeon, Victoria Infirmary, Northwich; Senior Hon. Surgeon and Radiologist Mid-Cheshire Orthopædic Clinic, Northwich; Traumatic Surgeon Messrs Brunner Mond & Co. Ltd; formerly Surgeon, Queen Mary's Hospital, Sidcup; Chairman of British Committee of International Congresses on Industrial Health and Safety; Lecturer and Examiner, St John Ambulance Association and British Red Cross Society; Member British Social Hygiene Council; Member of House of Laity National Church Assembly; Member of Ministry of Pensions Committee on rates of compensation for specific injuries sustained by members of HM Forces; *m* 1913, Lilian, *er d* of W. Wagner, Hayle, Cornwall; one *s* (one *d* decd). *Educ:* St Paul's; St Thomas' Hospital, (Tite Scholar); Leeds, Manchester, Liverpool, Newcastle, Zürich, Vienna and Harvard. Held appointments at St Thomas' Hospital, Royal Southern Hospital, Liverpool, etc.; formerly Lecturer London School of Economics, University of London; formerly Asst Ophthalmic Surgeon: St Andrews Hosp., Bromley-by-Bow; Battersea Gen. Hosp.; formerly Chief Medical Officer to Imperial Chemical Industries, Ltd. A Founder of Assoc. of Industrial Medical Officers; Chm. of Council of Industrial Medicine, and of Medical Advisory Cttee of Industrial Welfare Soc.; Hon. Member of American Union of Industrial Medicine; Member of Court of Examiners for Diploma of Industrial Health; Surgeon Specialist, BEF; Surgeon, The Ley and Numsmere Red Cross Hospitals; Member Ross Institute Cttee on Tropical Diseases; Medical Referee Standard and other Assurance Cos; Member of Industrial Diseases Sub-Committee, Chemical Employers Federation; Senior Vice-Pres. Congrès International de Sauvetage et de Premier Secours en Cas d' Accidents; Chairman of Children's Committee of London Diocesan Council of Moral Welfare; Chm. British Organising Council for IX International Council Industrial Health, 1948; President Commission Internationale Permanente (Malades de Travail); Vice-President Casualties Union. *Publications:* Some Thoughts and Doubts on the Etiology of Dupuytren's Contracture (Proceedings of XIII International Congress on Occupational Health, New York), 1960; (co-editor) Archiv für Gewerbepathologie und Gewerbehygiene; chapters on injuries to the elbow and injuries to lower extremity in Injuries in Sport; papers to BMJ, etc, and Proc. of the National Safety First Congress, 1935. *Address:* B3 Archers, Archers Road, Southampton SO1 2ND. *T:* Southampton 26000. *Club:* Athenæum.

**STOWERS, Arthur,** BSc (Eng), London; ACGI, FIMechE, MICE, FMA; retired; *b* 24 Jan. 1897; *yr s* of James H. Stowers, MD; *m* 1929, Freda, *d* of Richard Hall, FRIBA; two *s*. *Educ:* Haileybury; City and Guilds (Engineering) College, South Kensington. Contracts Engr, after 3 yrs pupilage, at W. H. Allen, Sons & Co., Bedford, 1923; Asst Keeper, Science Museum, South Kensington, 1930. Min. of Aircraft Production, 1940; Keeper, Science Museum, Department of Mechanical and Civil Engineering, 1950-62. Jt Hon. Sec. Newcomen Soc., 1933-48, Pres., 1955-57; Dickinson Memorial Medal, 1962. *Address:* 15 The Highway, Sutton, Surrey.

**STOY, Prof. Philip Joseph;** Professor of Dentistry, Queen's University of Belfast, since 1948; *b* 19 Jan. 1906; *m* 1945, Isabella Mary Beatrice Crispin; two *s*. *Educ:* Wolverhampton School. Queen's Scholar, Birmingham Univ., 1929; LDS, RCS, 1931; BDS (Hons), Birmingham 1932; FDS, RCS, 1947; Fellow of the Faculty of Dentistry, RCSI, 1963 (FFDRCSI). Lectr in Dental Mechanics, Univ. of Bristol, 1934; Lectr in Dental Surgery, Univ. of Bristol, 1940. Dean, Faculty of Dentistry, RCSI; Dental Dean, Faculty of Medicine, QUB. *Publications:* articles in British Dental Journal, Dental Record. *Recreations:* reading, walking, painting; dental history. *Address:* 8 Kensington Park, Belfast 5, Northern Ireland. *T:* Belfast 655881.

**STRABANE, Viscount; James Harold Charles Hamilton;** *b* 19 Aug. 1969; *s* and *heir* of Marquess of Hamilton, *qv*.

**STRABOLGI,** 11th Baron of England, *cr* 1318; **David Montague de Burgh Kenworthy;** Assistant Opposition Whip, House of Lords, since 1970; *b* 1 Nov. 1914; *e s* of 10th Baron Strabolgi and Doris, *o c* of late Sir Frederick Whitley-Thomson, JP, MP; *S* father, 1953; *m* 1961, Doreen, *e d* of late Alexander Morgan, Ashton-under-Lyne. *Educ:* Gresham's School, Holt; Chelsea Sch. of Art. Served with HM Forces, BEF, 1939-40; MEF, 1940-45, as Lt-Col RAOC. Mem. Parly Delegations to USSR, 1954, SHAPE, 1955. PPS to Minister of State, Home Office, 1968-69; PPS to Leader of the House of Lords and Lord Privy Seal, 1969-70. Dir, Bolton Building Soc.; FInstD; Member: Inst. Journalists; Inst. Public Relations; Labour Party; Fabian Soc. Jt Vice-Chm., Labour Parly Films Gp., 1968-. First Pres., AEGIS, 1965-. *Heir-pres:* *b* Rev. Hon. Jonathan Malcolm Atholl Kenworthy, MA, Vicar of Christ Church, Penge, Kent; Chaplain HM's Forces [*b* 15 Sept. 1916; *m* 1st, 1943, Joan Gaster (*d* 1963); two *d*; 2nd, 1963, Victoria Hewitt; one *s* one *d*]. *Address:* c/o House of Lords, SW1.

*See also Sir Harold Hood, Bt.*

**STRACEY, Sir Michael (George Motley),** 8th Bt, *cr* 1818; *b* 7 July 1911; *s* of Sir Edward Stracey, 7th Bt, and Mary Elizabeth Brinsley, *e d* of late Algernon Sheridan, Frampton Court, Dorchester; *S* father, 1949. *Educ:* Harrow; Queen's College, Oxford. *Heir: cousin* John Simon Stracey, *b* 30 Nov. 1938. *Address:* c/o Barclays Bank DCO, Corner Smith and Field Streets, Durban, Natal, South Africa.

**STRACHAN, Hon. Lord; James Frederick Strachan;** Senator, College of Justice in Scotland, 1948-67; *b* 11 October 1894; *s* of James K. Strachan, Glasgow; *m* 1926, Irene Louise, *d* of Timothy Warren, LLD, Glasgow; two *s* one *d*. *Educ:* Glasgow Academy; Glasgow Univ. MA, LLB; admitted Faculty of Advocates, 1921; Advocate Depute, 1936-38; KC 1938; Vice-Dean Faculty of Advocates, 1941-48; Procurator Church of Scotland, 1938-48. Sheriff of Argyll, 1942-45; Sheriff of Perth and Angus, 1945-48. Hon. LLD Glasgow, 1961. *Address:* Woodville, Canaan Lane, Edinburgh. *Club:* New (Edinburgh).

**STRACHAN, Sir Andrew (Henry),** Kt, *cr* 1953; CBE 1947; FCA; Director of Companies; *b* 28 August 1895; *s* of late A. Strachan, Co. Antrim, N Ireland; *m* 1929, Barbara Marian Celia, *d* of Sir Bourchier Wrey, 12th Bt, CBE; one *s* one *d*. *Educ:* mainly at Rathmines College, Dublin. Articled clerk to John Mackie & Co. (now Craig, Gardner & Co.), Chartered Accountants, Dublin and Belfast; qualified as Chartered Accountant. Served European War, 1914-18, throughout with Royal Dublin Fusiliers, Gallipoli and France. Joined British South Africa Company's Administration, 1921; Commissioner of Taxes, 1933; Secretary to the Treasury, S Rhodesia, 1941-53, Federation of Rhodesia and Nyasaland, 1953-55. Chm., Rhodesia Railways Board, 1954-59; Chm., Rhodesia Television, Ltd, 1960-64. *Address:* 20 Hurworth Road, Highlands, Salisbury, Rhodesia. *T:* Salisbury 42662. *Club:* Salisbury (Rhodesia).

**STRACHAN, Lt-Col Henry,** VC 1917; MC; Fort Garry Horse; retired; Hon. ADC to Governor General of Canada since 1935; Field Representative, The Canadian Bank of Commerce, since 1928; *b* Bo'ness, Scotland, 1889; *m*; one *d*. *Educ:* Royal High School, Edinburgh; Edinburgh University. Ranches in Alberta, Canada; joined FGH, 1914;

Commission July 1916; served European War, 1914-18 (MC, wounded, VC); War of 1939-45, Lt-col Cmdg 1st Bn Edmonton Fusiliers. *Recreations:* badminton, golf. *Address:* 3008 West 31st Avenue, Vancouver 8, British Columbia, Canada. *Clubs:* Alberta Golf, Country (Calgary).

**STRACHAN, James Frederick;** *see* Strachan, Hon. Lord.

**STRACHEY,** family name of **Barons O'Hagan** and **Strachie.**

**STRACHIE,** 2nd Baron, *cr* 1911; **Edward Strachey,** Bt, *cr* 1801; *b* 13 Jan. 1882; *o s* of 1st Baron and Constance (*d* 1936), *o c* of late C. B. Braham; *S* father, 1936; *m* 1933, Mrs William Ethelred Jennings (*d* 1962). *Educ:* Harrow. JP Somerset; late Lt-Col 4th Somerset Light Infantry; late Lt Grenadier Guards; served European War, 1914-20. *Heir:* (to Barony) none; (to Baronetcy) *cousin* Charles Strachey, *b* 20 June 1934. *Address:* Sutton Court, Pensford, Somerset. *TA:* Bishop-Sutton, Somerset. *T:* Chew Magna 407.

**STRADBROKE,** 4th Earl of, *cr* 1821; **John Anthony Alexander Rous;** Bt 1660; Baron Rous, 1796; Viscount Dunwich, 1821; Lord Lieutenant and Custos Rotulorum for the County of Suffolk since 1948; Commander Royal Navy, retired list; *b* 1 April 1903; *e s* of 3rd Earl of Stradbroke, KCMG, CB, CVO, CBE, and Helena Violet Alice, DBE, *cr* 1927, Lady of Grace of St John (*d* 1949), *d* of Gen. Keith Fraser; *S* father, 1947; *m* 1929, Barbara, *yr d* of late Lord Arthur Grosvenor; two *d.* *Educ:* RN Colleges, Osborne and Dartmouth; Christ Church (Hon. MA), Oxford. Member E Suffolk CC 1931-45, Alderman 1953-64. Private Sec. to Governor of Victoria, Australia, 1946-47. Estate Owner, Agriculturist and Forester. National Vice-Pres. (Pres. Eastern Area), Brit. Legion; Vice-Pres., Assoc. of (Land) Drainage Authorities. Chm., Daejan Holdings Ltd; Chm., Ipswich Bd, Eagle Star Insurance Co.; Served Royal Navy, 1917-28, and on Naval Staff, Admiralty 1939-46. Lately Hon. Colonel 660 HAA Regiment (TA); Pres., TA & VRA for E Anglia. Dep. Grand Master, Grand Lodge of Mark Master Masons; Provincial Grand Master, Freemasons, Province of Suffolk, and Mark Masons Province of E Anglia, 1948-. KStJ. *Heir: b* Hon. (William) Keith Rous [*b* 10 Mar. 1907; *m* 1st, 1935, Pamela Catherine Mabell (marriage dissolved, 1941), *d* of late Capt. Hon. Edward James Kay-Shuttleworth; two *s*; 2nd, 1943, April Mary, *d* of late Brig.-General Hon. Arthur Melland Asquith, DSO; one *s* three *d*]. *Address:* Henham, Wangford, Beccles, Suffolk. *T:* Wangford 212 and 214. *Clubs:* Travellers'; Jockey Club Rooms (Newmarket); Ipswich and Suffolk County (Ipswich); Royal Norfolk and Suffolk Yacht.

**STRADLING, Rt. Rev. Leslie E.;** *see* Johannesburg, Bishop of.

**STRADLING THOMAS, John;** MP (C) Monmouth, since 1970; farmer; *b* 10 June 1925; *s* of Thomas Roger Thomas and Catherine Thomas (*née* Delahay); *m* 1957, Freda Rhys Evans; one *s* two *d.* *Educ:* Rugby School. Contested (C) Aberavon, 1964; Cardigan, 1966. Member Council, NFU, 1963-70. *Address:* Brynglas, Rhydargaeau, Carmarthen. *T:* Llanpumpsaint 206.

**STRAFFORD,** 7th Earl of, *cr* 1847; **Robert Cecil Byng,** Baron Strafford (UK), 1935; Viscount Enfield, 1847; *b* 29 July 1904; *o surv s* of late Hon. Ivo Francis Byng (4th *s* of 5th Earl) and late Agnes Constance, *d* of S. Smith Travers, Hobart, Tasmania; *S* uncle 1951; *m* 1st, 1934, Maria Magdalena Elizabeth (marriage dissolved, 1947), *d* of late Henry Cloete, CMG, Alphen, S Africa; two *s*; 2nd, 1948, Clara Evelyn, *d* of late Sir Ness Nowrosjee Wadia, KBE, CIE. *Heir: s* Viscount Enfield, *qv.* *Address:* 98 Cheyne Walk, SW10.
*See also Maj.-Gen. R. F. B. Naylor.*

**STRAHAN, Frank,** CVO 1934; CBE 1928; resigned from Commonwealth Government Service, 1949; late Secretary to Cabinet; *b* 2 July 1886; *s* of late Richard Strahan; *m* 1914, Ella, *d* of William Moore, Bendigo. *Educ:* Melbourne University, BA, LLB. Assistant Secretary Prime Ministers' Dept 1921-35; Director Amalgamated Wireless (Australasia) Ltd, 1930-62. Secretary Prime Minister's Department, 1935-49; Secretary to Australian Delegation to Imperial Conferences, 1923 and 1937; Secretary, British, Australian and New Zealand Antarctic Research Expedition; Secretary of Australian tour of Duke of Gloucester (CVO). *Address:* c/o Amalgamated Wireless (Australasia) Ltd, 167 Queen Street, Melbourne, Vic 3000, Australia.

**STRAHAN, Lt-Col Geoffrey Carteret,** CIE 1944; OBE 1920; *b* 17 Sept. 1886; *y s* of H. Strahan, MA, JP, Hythe, Kent; *m* 1916, Eileen Olivia, *e d* of Col St G. L. Steele, CB; two *d.* *Educ:* King's School, Canterbury; Keble College, Oxford. 1st commission, 1909, Indian Army; Recruiting Officer for Gurkhas, 1937-45; retired to IRRO, 1940; re-employed, 1940. Served European War (despatches twice, OBE, Bt Major); War of 1939-45 (CIE). *Address:* Kelston, Graffham, Petworth, Sussex.

**STRAIGHT, Whitney Willard,** CBE 1944; MC; DFC; Legion of Merit (USA); Norwegian War Cross; Deputy Chairman, Rolls-Royce Ltd, since 1957 (Executive Vice-Chairman, 1956-57); Joint Deputy Chairman, Post Office Corporation, since 1969; Chairman: Arran Trust Ltd; Director, Midland Bank Ltd; Chairman, Contemporary Art Society; Companion, Royal Aeronautical Society; *b* 6 Nov. 1912; *e s* of late Maj. W. D. Straight and late Mrs Dorothy Whitney Elmhirst; *m* 1935, Lady Daphne Finch-Hatton, *d* of 14th Earl of Winchilsea and Nottingham; two *d.* *Educ:* Lincoln Sch., USA; Dartington Hall; Trinity Coll., Cambridge. Became professional motor car driver and won many International races and held speed records. Gave up motor racing in 1934 to enter Civil Aviation. Started a number of Companies and was appointed to Govt and other National Cttees. Served War of 1939-45, in RAF; Fighter Comd, Transport Comd, Air Cdre 1942 (despatches, MC, DFC, CBE, Norwegian War Cross, American Legion of Merit). Air ADC 1944. Chm., Straight Corp. and subsidiary cos, 1935-39; Dep. Chm. BEA, 1946-47; Man. Dir (Chief Exec.), BOAC, 1947-49, Dep. Chm., 1949-55. Member: Aerodrome Owners Assoc., 1936; Air Registration Bd, 1939-42, 1947-54; Council, RCA, 1955-58; Council, Business Aircraft Users Assoc., 1962; CoID, 1957-66; Council, UK S African Trade Assoc., 1969; Nat. Adv. Council on Art Educn, 1959-65; Cttee, RGS; Vice-Pres., British Light Aircraft Centre; Pres., PO Art Club of GB, 1969; Vice-Pres. and Chm., Geoffrey de Havilland Flying Foundn, 1966; Chairman: Govt Adv. Cttee on Private Flying, 1947; Exec. Cttee, Alexandra Day, 1957. Royal Air Forces Assoc.: Pres., Ealing Br., 1965; Mem., Central Council, 1966; Vice-Pres., 1967. Member: Inst. Transport; Inst. Directors; Inst. of Navigation; British Air Line Pilots Assoc.; Fellow: Royal Soc. for Protection of Birds; Brit. Inst. of Management; FRSA; FRGS; FZS. Liveryman:

Guild of Air Pilots and Navigators; Worshipful Co. of Goldsmiths; Worshipful Co. of Coachmakers and Coachharnessmakers. *Publications:* numerous articles on aviation subjects. *Recreations:* flying, under-water fishing, ski-ing, music, art, industrial design. *Address:* The Aviary, Windmill Lane, Southall, Middlesex. *T:* 01-574 2711. *Clubs:* White's, Buck's, Royal Aero (Chm. 1946-51, Vice-Pres. 1951-68); Royal Yacht Squadron, Cruising Association; Racquet and Tennis (New York); Corviglia Ski (St Moritz).

**STRANDERS, Michael O'Connell,** QC 1960; *b* 25 March 1911; *s* of late Vivian Stranders, MA and late Patricia O'Connell Stranders; *m* 1944, Anne Mary, *d* of late Col Richard L. Winton-Wiener and of Marguerite Winton-Wiener, Montreal, Canada; two *s* one *d*. *Educ:* Henry Thornton Sch.; University Coll., London; Schol. 1930, Joseph Hume Schol. (Jurisprudence), 1934, University Coll., London; LLB (London) (1st Cl. Hons and Univ. Schol.), 1934; Barrister, Lincoln's Inn, 1934 (Tancred and George V Coronation Studentships, Buchanan Prize); Bencher, 1969. *Recreations:* foreign travel, languages, the theatre. *Address:* 5 New Square, Lincoln's Inn, WC2. *T:* 01-405 6171, 01-242 3436; 27 Park Drive, East Sheen, SW14. *T:* 01-876 2021.

**STRANG,** family name of **Baron Strang.**

**STRANG,** 1st Baron, *cr* 1954, of Stonesfield; **William Strang,** GCB 1953 (KCB 1948; CB 1939); GCMG 1950 (KCMG 1943; CMG 1932); MBE 1918; Chairman, National Parks Commission, 1954-66; Member Nature Conservancy, 1954-66; Chairman Food Hygiene Advisory Council, 1955; Chairman, Royal Institute of International Affairs, 1958-65; a Deputy Speaker and Deputy Chairman of Committees, House of Lords, 1962; *b* 1893; *e s* of late James Strang, Englefield, Berks; *m* 1920, Elsie Wynne, *y d* of late J. E. Jones; one *s* one *d*. *Educ:* Palmer's School; University Coll., London; Sorbonne. BA (London), 1912; Quain Essay, 1913; served European War with 4th Bn Worcestershire Regt, and HQ, 29th Div. (MBE); entered Foreign Office, 1919; 3rd Sec., Belgrade, 1919; 2nd Sec., 1920; Foreign Office, 1923; 1st Sec., 1925; acting Counsellor of Embassy at Moscow, 1930; Counsellor, 1932; Asst Under-Sec. of State in Foreign Office, 1939-43; UK Representative on European Advisory Commission, with rank of Ambassador, 1943-45; Political Adviser to C-in-C, British Forces of Occupation in Germany, 1945-47; Permanent Under-Sec., FO (German Section), 1947-49; Permanent Under-Sec. of State, Foreign Office, 1949-53; retired 1953. Fellow University College, London, 1946; Chairman College Committee, 1963; Hon. LLD (London), 1954. *Publications:* The Foreign Office, 1955; Home and Abroad, 1956; Britain in World Affairs, 1961; The Diplomatic Career, 1962. *Heir: s* Hon. Colin Strang [*b* 12 June 1922; *m* 1955, Barbara Mary Hope, *o d* of F. A. Carr; one *d*]. *Address:* 41a Ennismore Gardens, SW7. *Club:* Travellers'.

**STRANG, Gavin Steel;** MP (Lab) Edinburgh East since 1970; *b* 10 July 1943; *s* of James Steel Strang and Marie Strang (*née* Finkle); unmarried. *Educ:* Univs of Edinburgh and Cambridge. BSc Hons Edinburgh, 1964; DipAgricSci Cambridge, 1965; PhD Edinburgh, 1968. Mem., Tayside Econ. Planning Consultative Group, 1966-68; Scientist with ARC, 1968-70. *Publications:* articles in Animal Production. *Recreations:* golf, swimming, films. *Address:* 22 Southfield Place, Edinburgh. *T:* 031-669 5999. *Club:* New Craighall Miners' Welfare (Edinburgh).

**STRANG STEEL, Major Sir F. W.;** *see* Steel, Major Sir F. W. S.

**STRANGE,** 15th Baron *cr* 1628 (title abeyant, 1957-65); **John Drummond;** *s* of late Capt. Malcolm Drummond of Megginch, Grenadier Guards, and late Geraldine Margaret, *d* of 1st Baron Amherst of Hackney; *m* Violet Margaret, *d* of Sir R. B. Jardine, 2nd Bt of Castlemilk; three *d* (*co-heiresses* to *Barony*). *Educ:* Eton. *Publications:* The Bride Wore Black, 1942; Pocket Show Book, 1943; Charter for the Soil, 1944; Playing to the Gods, 1944; Inheritance of Dreams, 1945; A Candle in England, 1946; Behind Dark Shutters, 1948; Gold over the Hill, 1950; The Naughty Mrs Thornton, 1952; Proof Positive, 1956. *Address:* Tholt-E-Will, Sulby Glen, Isle of Man. *Club:* Bath.

**STRANGE OF KNOKIN, Baroness;** *see* St Davids, Elizabeth, Viscountess.

**STRANGER-JONES, Leonard Ivan;** Probate Registrar since 1967; *b* 8 May 1913; *s* of Walter Stranger-Jones; *m* 1st, 1935, Elizabeth Evelyn Williams (marr. diss., 1942); 2nd, 1943, Iris Christine Truscott; one *s* one *d*. *Educ:* Lancing; Oriel Coll., Oxford (MA). Called to the Bar, 1938. Served War of 1939-45: RAF, Sept. 1939; Pilot, 1942. Returned to the Bar, Sept. 1945; Bencher, Middle Temple, Nov. 1967. *Publication:* Eversley on Domestic Relations, 1951. *Recreations:* photography, history. *Address:* 21 Springfield Road, St John's Wood, NW8. *T:* 01-624 8660.

**STRANGMAN, James Gonville,** QC 1950; *b* 1 Dec. 1902; *s* of Sir Thomas Strangman, *qv*; *m* 1935, Eileen, *d* of J. S. Mallam, FCA; one *s* two *d*. *Educ:* Charterhouse; Trinity Hall, Cambridge. Called to Bar by Middle Temple, Jan. 1927. Elected Bencher, Middle Temple, 1958. *Recreation:* horticulture. *Address:* 13 Old Square, Lincoln's Inn, WC2; Brook House, Crowborough, Sussex.

**STRANGMAN, Sir Thomas (Joseph),** Kt, *cr* 1920; QC 1938; Bencher, Lincoln's Inn, 1944; *b* 7 Jan. 1873; *s* of Joseph Strangman; *m* 1896, Winifred (*d* 1955), *d* of Capt. W. J. J. Warneford; two *s* two *d*. *Educ:* Charterhouse; Trinity Hall, Cambridge. Called to Bar, Middle Temple, 1896; Advocate-General and Member of the Legislative Council, Bombay, 1908-15, and 1916-22; contested (C) Crewe Division of Cheshire, Dec. 1923, and East Wolverhampton, Oct. 1924. *Address:* 24 Hans Court, Hans Road, SW3. *T:* 01-589 8336. *Clubs:* Brooks's, City of London.

**STRANGWAYS;** *see* Fox-Strangways, **family name of Earl of Ilchester.**

**STRANKS, Ven. Charles James;** Archdeacon of Auckland, since 1958; 10th Canon of Durham since 1958; *b* 10 May 1901; *s* of Joseph and Elizabeth Stranks; *m* 1930, Elsie Lilian, *d* of John and Anne Buckley; two *s*. *Educ:* St Chad's Coll., Durham; St Boniface Coll., Warminster. BA, 1925; MA and Diploma in Theology, 1928; MLitt, 1937. Curate of All Saints, Leeds, 1926-28; Missionary, Dio. Kobe, Japan, 1928-40; Examining Chaplain to Bishop in Kobe, 1938-40; SPG Organizing Sec., 1940-41; Vicar of St Barnabas, Morecambe, 1941-47; Warden of Whalley Abbey, Canon of Blackburn, and Dir of Relig. Educ., 1947-54; Proctor in Convocation for Archdeaconry of Blackburn, 1949-54; Sixth Canon of Durham Cathedral, 1954. Chm., Lord Crewe's Trustees, 1963. *Publications:* The Apostle of the Indies, 1933; Japan in the World Crisis, 1941; The Approach to Belief, 1947; Our Task To-day, 1950; The Life and Writings of Jeremy Taylor, 1952;

Dean Hook, 1954; Anglican Devotion, 1961; Country Boy: The Autobiography of Richard Hillyer, 1966; (ed) The Path of Glory: The Autobiography of John Shipp, 1969. Contributed to Encyclopædia Britannica. *Recreations:* walking, gardening. *Address:* The College, Durham. *T:* 1069. *Club:* Royal Commonwealth Society.

**STRATFORD, Esme C. W.;** *see* Wingfield-Stratford.

**STRATH, Sir William,** KCB 1959 (CB 1951); MA; Chairman, British Aluminium Co. Ltd, since 1962; Deputy Chairman, Tube Investments Ltd, since 1968 (Joint Managing Director, since 1961); Director, Legal and General Assurance Society Ltd; *b* 16 Nov. 1906; *s* of J. G. and Elizabeth Strath; *m* 1938, Vera Lucy Brown; no *c. Educ:* Girvan High Sch.; Glasgow University. Served in following Government Departments: Inland Revenue, 1929-38; Air Ministry, 1938-40; Ministry of Aircraft Production, 1940-45; Ministry of Supply, 1945-47; Central Economic Planning staff, 1947-55; Treasury, 1948-55; Member, Economic Planning Board, 1949-55; Full-time Member Atomic Energy Authority, 1955-59; Permanent Sec.: Min. of Supply, 1959; Min. of Aviation, 1959-60. Hon. LLD Strathclyde, 1969. *Recreation:* mountaineering. *Address:* C6, Albany, Piccadilly, W1. *T:* 01-734 2452. *Clubs:* United Service, Alpine.

**STRATHALLAN, Viscount; John Eric Drummond;** *b* 7 July 1935; *e s* of 17th Earl of Perth, *qv*; *m* 1963, Margaret Ann, *o d* of Robin Gordon; two *s. Heir: s* Hon. James David Drummond, *b* 24 Oct. 1965. *Address:* 40 Addison Road, W14. *T:* 01-603 3139; Stobhall, by Perth.

**STRATHALMOND,** 2nd Baron *cr* 1955, of Pumpherston, Co. Midlothian; **William Fraser,** CMG 1967; OBE 1945; TD 1955; a Managing Director of British Petroleum Co. Ltd, since 1962; *b* 8 May 1916; *o s* of 1st Baron Strathalmond, CBE, and Mary (*d* 1963), *d* of Thomson McLintock, Glasgow; *S* father, 1970; *m* 1945, Letitia, *d* of late Walter Krementz, New Jersey, USA; one *s* two *d. Educ:* Loretto; Clare Coll., Cambridge. Barrister-at-Law, 1946-50; British Petroleum Co. Ltd, 1950-59; Managing Dir, Kuwait Oil Co. Ltd, 1959-62. KStJ 1961. Bronze Star, USA, 1945. *Recreations:* golf, fishing. *Heir: s* Hon. William Robertson Fraser, *b* 22 July 1947. *Address:* 19 Cumberland Terrace, Regent's Park, NW1. *T:* 01-486 2075. *Clubs:* Boodle's; Links, River (New York).

**STRATHCARRON,** 2nd Baron, *cr* 1936; of Banchor; **David William Anthony Blyth Macpherson;** Bt, *cr* 1933; Director: Strath Air Charter Ltd; First National Fine Metals Ltd; Kirchhoff (East Africa) Ltd; Kirchhoff (London) Ltd; Partner, Strathcarron & Co.; Chairman: Seabourne Shipping Co.; The Austin Hall Group Ltd; *b* 23 Jan. 1924; *s* of 1st Baron and Jill (*d* 1956), *o d* of Sir George Rhodes, 1st Bt; *S* father, 1937; *m* 1st, 1947, Valerie Cole (marr. annulled on his petition, 1947); 2nd, 1948, Mrs Diana Hawtrey Curle, *o d* of Comdr R. H. Deane; two *s Educ:* Eton; Jesus College, Cambridge. Served War of 1939-45, RAFVR, 1942-47. Motoring Correspondent of The Field. Member, British Parly Delegn to Austria, 1964. *Publication:* Motoring for Pleasure, 1963. *Recreations:* motor-racing, flying, golf. *Heir: s* Hon. Ian David Patrick Macpherson, *b* 31 March 1949. *Address:* 55 Cumberland Terrace, Regents Park, NW1. *T:* 01-935 5913; Otterwood, Beaulieu, Hants. *Club:* Boodle's.

*See also Sir D. C. F. Lowson, Bt.*

**STRATHCLYDE,** 1st Baron, *cr* 1955, of Barskimming; **Thomas Dunlop Galbraith,** PC 1953; Commander, Royal Navy, retired; *b* 20 March 1891; 2nd *s* of William Brodie Galbraith, JP, CA, Glasgow, and Annie Dunlop; *m* 1915, Ida, *e d* of Thomas Galloway, Auchendrane, Ayrshire; four *s* (and one killed in action, 1940), two *d. Educ:* Glasgow Academy; RN Colleges, Osborne and Dartmouth. Entered Royal Navy, 1903; served throughout European War, 1914-18, in HMS Audacious and HMS Queen Elizabeth; RN Staff College, Greenwich, 1920-22; retired 1922; War of 1939-45, on Staff of C-in-C Coast of Scotland, 1939-40; Deputy British Admiralty Supply Representative in USA, 1940-42. MP (Nat. C) for Pollok Div. of Glasgow, 1940-April 1955; Jt Parly Under-Sec. of State for Scotland, 1945 and 1951-55; Minister of State, Scottish Office, 1955-58, resigned; Chm., North of Scotland Hydro-Electric Board, 1959-67; Mem., South of Scotland Electricity Board, 1965-67. Chartered Accountant, 1925; Partner Galbraith, Dunlop & Co., CA, Glasgow; Member of Corporation of Glasgow, 1933-40; Magistrate, 1938-40. President, Electrical Research Association, 1965-66. Hon. FRCPE; Hon. FRCPSGlas; a Governor of Wellington College, 1948-61; Hon. Governor, Glasgow Academy. Freedom of Dingwall, 1965; Freedom of Aberdeen, 1966. *Heir: s* Hon. Thomas Galloway Dunlop Galbraith, *qv. Address:* Barskimming, Mauchline, Ayrshire. *Clubs:* Carlton, United Service; New (Edinburgh); Conservative, Western (Glasgow).

**STRATHCONA and MOUNT ROYAL,** 4th Baron, *cr* 1900, **Donald Euan Palmer Howard;** late Lieutenant RNVR; *b* 26 Nov. 1923; *s* of 3rd Baron Strathcona and Mount Royal and Diana Evelyn, twin *d* of 1st Baron Wakehurst; *S* father 1959; *m* 1954, Lady Jane Mary Waldegrave, 2nd *d* of Earl Waldegrave, *qv*; two *s* four *d. Educ:* King's Mead, Seaford; Eton; Trinity Coll., Cambridge; McGill University, Montreal (1947-50). Served War of 1939-45: RN, 1942-47: Midshipman, RNVR, 1943; Lieutenant, 1945. With Urwick, Orr and Partners (Industrial Consultants), 1950-56. Chairman, Bath Festival Society, 1966-70. Dep. Chm., SS Great Britain Project, 1970. *Recreations:* gardening, sailing, motor sport. *Heir: s* Hon. Donald Alexander Smith Howard, *b* 24 June 1961. *Address:* 20 Lansdown Crescent, Bath, Somerset; Kiloran, Isle of Colonsay, Scotland. *T:* Colonsay 1. *Club:* Brooks's.

*See also Hon. Sir Arthur Howard.*

**STRATHEDEN,** 4th Baron, *cr* 1836, **and CAMPBELL,** 4th Baron, *cr* 1841; **Alastair Campbell,** CBE 1964; Vice-Lieutenant of Roxburgh since 1962; *b* 21 Nov. 1899; *s* of late Hon. John Beresford Campbell and Hon. Alice Susan Hamilton (*d* 1949), *d* of 1st Baron Hamilton of Dalzell; *S* grandfather, 1918; *m* 1st, 1923, Jean, CBE 1954 (*d* 1956), *o d* of late Col W. Anstruther-Gray; three *d*; 2nd, 1964, Mrs Noël Vincent. *Educ:* Eton; Sandhurst. Joined Coldstream Guards, 1919; Regimental Adjutant, 1931-34; Staff Officer Local Forces, Kenya and Uganda, 1936-39; Lt-Col, 1941; served War of 1939-45 (wounded, despatches); Regtl Lt-Col, 1945-46; Brig., 1946; Comd 32nd Guards Bde, 1946, 4th Inf. Bde, 1947-49; Deputy Director Personal Services, War Office, 1949; retired 1950. Ensign, Royal Company of Archers, Queen's Body Guard for Scotland. Chm. Roxburgh, Berwick and Selkirk-shires T&AFA, 1958-63; Chm.

Edinburgh and E of Scotland Coll. of Agriculture, 1956-70; Chm. Hill Farming Research Organisation, 1958-69; Convener Roxburgh County Council, 1960-68; Pres., Assoc. of County Councils in Scotland, 1966-68. Chm., Historic Buildings Council for Scotland, 1969-. DL Roxburgh, 1946. Hon. LLD Edinburgh Univ. *Heir: b* Major Hon. Gavin Campbell, late KRRC [*b* 28 Aug. 1901; *m* 1933, Evelyn, *d* of late Col H. A. Smith, CIE; one *s*]. *Address:* Hunthill, Jedburgh, Scotland. *T:* Jedburgh 2413. *Clubs:* Guards, Turf; New (Edinburgh).

*See also Hon. Nicholas Ridley.*

**STRATHMORE and KINGHORNE,** 16th Earl of, *cr* 1677; Earl (UK), *cr* 1937; **Timothy Patrick Bowes-Lyon,** Baron Glamis (Scotland), 1445; Earl of Kinghorne, Lord Lyon, Baron Glamis, 1606; Earl of Strathmore and Kinghorne, Viscount Lyon, Lord Glamis, Tannadyce, Sydlaw, and Strathdichtie, 1677; Baron Bowes (UK), 1887; late 2nd Lieutenant Black Watch; *b* 18 March 1918; *o surv s* of 15th Earl of Strathmore and Lady Dorothy Osborne (*d* 1946), 3rd *d* of 10th Duke of Leeds; *S* father, 1949; *m* 1958, Mary (Bridget) Brennan, Leix, Eire (*d* 1967); one *d* decd. *Educ:* Stowe. Served War of 1939-45, Black Watch; retired (ill-health), 1944. *Recreation:* shooting. *Heir-pres: cousin,* Fergus Michael Claude Bowes-Lyon [*b* 31 December 1928; *m* 1956, Mary Pamela, *yr d* of Brig. N. D. McCorquodale, MC; one *s* two *d*]. *Address:* Glamis Castle, Angus, Scotland. *T:* Glamis 244; Holwick Hall, Middleton-in-Teesdale, Barnard Castle, Co. Durham. *T:* Middleton-in-Teesdale 212. *Clubs:* Bath, Turf.

*See also Lord Elphinstone.*

**STRATHNAVER, Lord; Alistair Charles St Clair Sutherland;** Master of Sutherland; *b* 7 Jan. 1947; *e s* of Charles Noel Janson, DL, and the Countess of Sutherland, *qv*; *heir* to mother's titles; *m* 1968, Eileen Elizabeth, *o d* of Richard Wheeler Baker, Jr, Princeton, NJ; one *d*. *Educ:* Eton; Christ Church, Oxford. Police Constable, Metropolitan Police, 1970-. *Address:* Uppat House, Brora, Sutherland. *T:* 202; 39 Edwardes Square, W8. *T:* 01-603 0659.

**STRATHSPEY,** 5th Baron, *cr* 1884; **Donald Patrick Trevor Grant of Grant,** 17th Bt, of Nova Scotia, *cr* 1625; 32nd Chief of Grant; Lieutenant-Colonel retired; *b* 18 March 1912; *s* of 4th Baron and Alice Louisa (*d* 1945), *d* of T. M. Hardy-Johnston, MICE London, of Christchurch, NZ; *S* father, 1948; *m* 1st, 1938, Alice (marr. diss. 1951), *o c* of late Francis Bowe, Timaru, NZ; one *s* two *d*; 2nd, 1951, Olive, *d* of W. H. Grant, Norwich; one *s* one *d*. *Educ:* Stowe Sch.; South Eastern Agricultural Coll. War Dept Land Agent and Valuer, Portsmouth, 1944-48; Command Land Agent, HQ Scottish Command, 1948-60; Asst Chief Land Agent and Valuer, War Office, 1960-63; Command Land Agent, HQ Cyprus District, 1963-64; Asst Director of Lands, NW Europe, 1964-66; Asst Chief Land Agent, MoD HQ, 1966-. Associate, Land Agents' Soc. Fellow, Royal Institution of Chartered Surveyors. Defence Medal; 1939-45 medal; Coronation medal. *Recreation:* yachting. *Heir: s* Hon. James Patrick Grant of Grant, *b* 9 Sept. 1943. *Address:* 111 Elms Ride, West Wittering, Sussex.

**STRATTEN, Thomas Price;** Chairman, Union Corporation Limited, since 1962 (Managing Director, 1954-67); *b* Kimberley, Cape Province, S Africa, 4 June 1904; *m* 1930, Mary A. Morris, New York, USA; two *s* one *d*. *Educ:* University of Cape Town; Balliol College, Oxford (Rhodes Scholar). Dir of War Supplies, S Africa, 1940-45. Chairman: South African Pulp and Paper Industries Ltd; African Wire Ropes Ltd; Director: Bay Hall Trust Ltd; Charter Consolidated Ltd; South African Reserve Bank; Tsumeb Corp. Ltd; Comr, Electricity Supply Commission, 1954-69. Past President, Associated Scientific and Technical Societies of South Africa; Past President and Hon. Member, S African Inst. of Electrical Engrs. Hon. LLD, Univ. of Witwatersrand, 1966. *Recreation:* golf. *Address:* (home) 16 Pallinghurst Road, Westcliff, Johannesburg, South Africa; (office) 74-78 Marshall Street, Johannesburg. *Clubs:* Rand, Johannesburg Country, Royal Johannesburg Golf (Johannesburg).

**STRATTON, Andrew,** MSc, FInstP, CEng, FIEE, FInstNav, FIMA; Director, Defence Operational Establishment, since 1968; *b* 5 Sept. 1918; *m* 1949, Ruth Deutsch; one *s* one *d*. *Educ:* Skinners' Company Sch., Tunbridge Wells; University Coll. of the South West, Exeter; Univ. of London (BSc 1st cl. Hons Physics). RAE Farnborough: Air Defence and Armament Depts, 1939-54; Supt, Instruments and Inertial Navigation Div., 1954-62; Head of Weapon Research and Assessment Group, 1962-66; Prof. and Head of Maths Dept, Coll. of Aeronautics, Cranfield, 1966-68. Chm. and Mem. of Cttees, Aeronautical and Electronics Research Councils; Pres., Inst. of Navigation, 1967-70; Chm. of Convocation, Univ. of Exeter. Hodgson Prize, RAeS, 1969. US Medal of Freedom with Bronze Palm, 1947. *Publications:* contrib. to Unless Peace Comes, 1968; to The Future of Aeronautics, 1970; papers on aircraft instruments, navigation, air traffic, operational analysis in Jl IEE, Jl IMechE, Jl RAeS, Jl Inst. Navigation. *Recreations:* painting, hill-walking. *Address:* Chartley, 39 Salisbury Road, Farnborough, Hants. *T:* Farnborough 42514.

**STRATTON, Ven. Basil,** Archdeacon of Stafford and Canon Residentiary of Lichfield Cathedral, since 1959; Chaplain to the Queen, 1965, *b* 1906; *s* of Reverend Samuel Henry Stratton and Kate Mabel Stratton; *m* 1934, Euphemia Frances Stuart; one *s* three *d*. *Educ:* Lincoln School; Hatfield College, Durham University. Deacon 1931; Priest 1932; Curate, St Stephen's, Grimsby, 1931-32; SPG Missionary, India, 1932-34; Indian Ecclesiastical Establishment, 1935-47. Chaplain to the Forces on service in Iraq, India, Burma and Malaya, 1941-46 (despatches); officiated as Chaplain-General in India, 1946. Vicar of Figheldean with Milston, Wilts, 1948-53; Vicar of Market Drayton, Shropshire, 1953-59. *Address:* 24 The Close, Lichfield, Staffs. *T:* Lichfield 3535. *Club:* United Service.

**STRATTON, Sir (Francis) John,** Kt 1968; CBE 1948; Chairman: 1952-57 (Managing Director, 1947-57), Dolcis Ltd and its Associated Companies; Dolcis (Canada) Ltd, 1947-57; FMC Ltd; FMC (Meat) Ltd; NFU Development Trust Ltd; FMC Products Ltd; Marsh & Baxter Ltd; C & T. Harris (Calne) Ltd; Director, Fatstock Finance Ltd; *b* 18 Jan. 1906; *o s* of Ernest William Stratton, Great Stukeley, Hunts; *m* 1936, Christine, *d* of Edward Harrison; one *d*. *Educ:* Fitzwilliam House, Cambridge. MA Cantab (BA Honours English Tripos, Part I, Archæological and Anthropological Tripos). Eastern Associated Telegraph Co., Ltd; Lewis's Ltd. Served War of 1939-45, Royal Artillery (TA), Major, 1939-47; Dir of Service Footwear and Leather Equipment; Controller of Service and Civilian Footwear and finally Controller of Leather and Footwear. Chairman Stratton Mission to Germany, on Hides, Skins, Leather, Footwear, Leather Substitutes and Ancillary machinery, 1945. Fellow, Royal Soc. of Arts (Mem., Council, 1963-); Fellow, National Instn of Boot and Shoe Industry; Fellow, British Inst. of Management (Mem. Council, 1954-60); Independent Mem., National Advisory Council for Motor Manufacturing Industry, 1947-59; Member: Council of Industrial Design, 1947-59; Inst. of Personnel Management; Staff Management Assoc.; Footwear Distributors' Fedn (Chm. 1951-56, Pres., 1956-57); Multiple Shoe Retailers' Assoc. (Chm. Exec. Council, 1953-56); Council of Multiple Shops Fedn, 1947-57; Exec. Cttee of Dollar Exports Board, 1950-51; Exec. Cttee British Productivity Council (Chm., Retail Section); Distribution Cttee, and Pigs Cttee, Meat and Livestock Commn; Guild of Cordwainers, Master, 1956, 1957. Amer. Medal of Freedom with Palm, 1947. *Recreation:* farming. *Address:* Rotherwood, Fittleworth, Sussex. *T:* Fittleworth 396. *Clubs:* United University, Brooks's.

**STRATTON, Sir John;** *see* Stratton, Sir F. J.

**STRATTON, Julius Adams,** ScD; Chairman of Board, The Ford Foundation, since 1966; *b* Seattle, 18 May 1901; *s* of Julius A. Stratton and Laura (*née* Adams); *m* 1935, Catherine N. Coffman; three *d. Educ:* Univ. of Washington; Mass Inst. of Technology (SB, SM); Eidgenössische Technische Hochschule, Zurich (ScD). Expert Consultant, Sec. of War, 1942-46. MIT: Res. Assoc. in Communications, 1924-26; Asst Prof., Electrical Engrg, 1928-31; Asst Prof., Physics, 1931-35; Assoc. Prof., Physics, 1935-41; Prof., Physics, 1941-51; Mem. Staff, Radiation Lab., 1940-45; Dir, Res. Lab. of Electronics, 1945-49; Provost, 1949-56; Vice-Pres., 1951-56; Chancellor, 1956-59; Actg Pres., 1957-59; Pres., 1959-66; Pres. Emer., 1966-. Chm., Commn on Marine Science, Engrg and Resources, 1967-69. Director: American-Swiss Association, Inc.; Westinghouse Electric Corp.; Life Mem. Corp., MIT; Trustee: John F. Kennedy Meml Library; Pine Manor Jun. Coll.; FIEEE; Fellow: Amer. Acad. of Arts and Scis; Amer. Phys. Soc.; Member: Amer. Philos. Soc.; Council on For. Relations, Center for Inter-American Relations; Nat. Acad. of Engrg; Nat. Acad. of Scis; Pilgrims of US; Sigma Xi; Tau Beta Pi; Zeta Psi; Eminent Mem., Eta Kappa Nu. Hon. Fellow, Coll. of Science and Technology, Manchester, England, 1963; Hon. Mem. Senate, Technical Univ. of Berlin, 1966. Holds numerous hon. doctorates of Engrg, Humane Letters, Laws and Science. Medal for Merit, 1946; Certif. of Award, US Navy, 1957; Medal of Honor, Inst. Radio Engrs, 1957; Faraday Medal, IEE (England), 1961; Boston Medal for Distinguished Achievement, 1966. Officer, Legion of Honour, France, 1961; Orden de Boyacá, Colombia, 1964; Kt Comdr, Order of Merit, Germany, 1966. *Publications:* Electromagnetic Theory, 1941; Science and the Educated Man, 1966; numerous papers in scientific and professional jls. *Address:* (home) 800 Park Avenue, New York, NY 10021, USA; (office) 320 East 43rd Street, New York, NY 10017, USA. *Clubs:* Century Association, University (New York); St Botolph (Boston).

**STRATTON, Richard James;** a Member of HM Diplomatic Service; Imperial Defence College, 1970; *b* 16 July 1924; *s* of William Henry and Cicely Muriel Stratton. *Educ:* The King's Sch., Rochester; Merton Coll., Oxford. Served in Coldstream Guards, 1943-46. Joined Foreign Service, Oct. 1947; British Embassy, Rio de Janeiro, 1948-50; FO, 1951-53; British Embassy, Tokyo, March-Aug. 1953; British Legation, Seoul, 1953-55; Private Sec. to Parly Under-Sec. of State, FO, Nov. 1955-Feb. 1958; NATO Defence Coll., Paris, Feb.-Aug. 1958; British Embassy, Bonn, Sept. 1958-July 1960; British Embassy, Abidjan, Ivory Coast, Aug.-1960-Feb. 1962; Private Sec. to Lord Carrington, as Minister without Portfolio, FO, 1963-64; to Minister of State for Foreign Affairs, 1964-66; Counsellor, British High Commn, Rawalpindi, 1966-69. *Recreations:* tennis, bridge. *Address:* c/o Foreign and Commonwealth Office, SW1. *Club:* Travellers'.

**STRATTON, Mrs Roy Olin;** *see* Dickens, Monica Enid.

**STRATTON, Air Vice-Marshal William Hector,** CB 1970; CBE 1963; DFC 1939 and Bar 1944; Chief of the Air Staff, RNZAF, since 1969; *b* 22 July 1916; *s* of V. J. Stratton; *m* 1954, Dorothy M., *d* of J. D. Whyte; one *s* two *d. Educ:* Hawera Tech. High School, and privately. RAF, 1937-44. Appointments include: in comd RNZAF, Ohakea; Air Member for Personnel; assistant chief of Air Staff; Head NZ Defence Staff, Canberra; Head NZ Defence Staff, London. *Address:* Air Staff, Defence HQ, Private Bag, Wellington, NZ. *T:* 49-800.

**STRATTON, Lt-Gen. Sir William (Henry),** KCB 1957 (CB 1948); CVO 1944; CBE 1943; DSO 1945; *b* 1903; *o s* of late Lt-Col H. W. Stratton, OBE; *m* 1930, Noreen Mabel Brabazon, *d* of late Dr and Mrs F. H. B. Noble, Sittingbourne, Kent; no *c. Educ:* Dulwich Coll.; RMA, Woolwich. 2nd Lieut RE 1924; psc; Lt-Col (temp.), 1940; Brig. (temp.), 1941; Col 1945; idc 1946; Maj.-Gen. 1947; Chief of Staff, BAOR, 1947-49; Comdt Joint Services Staff Coll., 1949-52; Commander British Army Staff, and Military Member British Joint Services Mission, Washington, 1952-53; Comdr 42 (Lancs) Inf. Div. (TA), 1953-55; Lt-Gen. 1955; Commander, British Forces, Hong Kong, 1955-57; Vice-Chief of the Imperial General Staff, 1957-60, retired. Col Comdt RE, 1960-68; Inspector-General of Civil Defence, Home Office, 1960-62. Chairman: Edwin Danks (Oldbury) Ltd; Penman & Co. Ltd; Babcock-Moxey Ltd. *Club:* United Service.

**STRAUSS,** family name of **Baron Conesford.**

**STRAUSS, Claude L.;** *see* Levi-Strauss.

**STRAUSS, Franz Josef;** Grand Cross, Order of Merit, Federal Republic of Germany; Member of Bundestag, Federal Republic of Germany, since 1949; President, Christian Social Union (CSU), since 1961; *b* Munich, 6 Sept. 1915; *s* of Franz Josef Strauss and Walburga (*née* Schiessl); *m* 1957, Marianne (*née* Zwicknagl); two *s* one *d. Educ:* Gymnasium, Munich; Munich Univ. Served in War of 1939-45, Lieut. In Bavarian State Govt, 1946-49; Pres., Govt Cttee on Youth in Bavaria, 1946-49; Minister for Special Tasks, 1953-55; Minister for Atomic Questions, 1955-56; Minister of Defence, 1956-62; Minister of Finance, 1966-69. President: Landrat (County Commissioner) of Schongau, 1946-49; Committee on Questions of European Security. Dr *hc*: Detroit University, USA, 1956; Kalamazoo College, 1962; Case Institute of Technology, Cleveland (Ohio), 1962; De Paul University, Chicago, 1964. Holds decorations from other European countries. *Publications:* The Grand Design, 1965; Herausforderung und Antwort, 1968; Challenge and Response: A programme for Europe, 1969; Finanzpolitik: Theorie und Wirklichkeit, 1969; many articles on political affairs in newspapers and periodicals. *Address:* Rott/Inn, Bayern, Germany

**STRAUSS, Rt. Hon. George Russell,** PC 1947; MP (Lab) for Vauxhall Division of Lambeth since 1950 (North Lambeth, 1929-31 and 1934-50); LCC Representative North Lambeth, 1925-31; for South East Southwark, 1932-46; *s* of Arthur Strauss, formerly MP (C) Camborne Div. of Cornwall and N Paddington; *m* 1932, Patricia O'Flynn (*see* P. F. Strauss); two *s* one *d*. *Educ:* Rugby. PPS to Minister of Transport, 1929-31, to Lord Privy Seal, and later Minister of Aircraft Production, 1942-45; Parly Sec., Min. of Transport, 1945-47; Minister of Supply, 1947-51; LCC Chm. Highways Cttee, 1934-37; Vice-Chm. Finance Cttee, 1934-37; Chm. Supplies Cttee, 1937-39; Mem. London and Home Counties Traffic Advisory Cttee, 1934-39. Introduced Theatres Bill for the abolition of stage censorship, 1968. *Recreations:* painting and chess. *Address:* 1 Palace Green, W8. *T:* 01-937 1630; Naylands, Slaugham, Sussex. *T:* Handcross 270.

**STRAUSS, Hon. Jacobus Gideon Nel,** QC (South Africa) 1944; Leader of the South African United Party, 1950-56; MP for Germiston District since 1932; *b* Calvinia CP, 17 Dec. 1900; *s* of late H. J. Strauss; *m* 1928, Joy Carpenter; two *s* two *d* (and one *s* decd). *Educ:* Calvinia High Sch.; Univ. of Cape Town; Univ. of South Africa. Private Sec. to the Prime Minister (General J. C. Smuts), 1923-24; commenced practice at Johannesburg Bar, 1926; Minister of Agriculture and Forestry in Smuts Cabinet, 1944; succeeded Field Marshal J. C. Smuts as Leader of the Opposition. *Recreations:* riding, mountaineering and golf. *Address:* PO Box 398, Bryanston, Transvaal, South Africa. *Clubs:* Rand, Royal Johannesburg Golf (Johannesburg); Bryanston Country. City, Civil Service (Cape Town); Pretoria (Pretoria).

**STRAUSS, Lewis L.,** DSM, (US) 1952; Legion of Merit, 1943; Medal of Freedom (US); Secretary of Commerce (US), 1958-59; Special Assistant to President (US), 1953; *b* Charleston, West Virginia, 1896; *s* of Lewis Strauss and Rosa (*née* Lichtenstein); *m* 1923, Alice Hanauer; one *s* (and one *s* decd). *Educ:* Public schools, Richmond, Virginia. Private Secretary to Herbert Hoover, 1917-19; Kuhn Loeb & Co., 1919-46. Served War of 1939-45, Rear-Adm., USNR. Past Pres., Institute for Advanced Study. Chairman of the United States Atomic Energy Commission, 1953-58 (Mem., 1946-50). Various hon. degrees and foreign decorations. *Publication:* Men and Decisions, 1963. *Address:* Brandy Station, Virginia 2274, USA.

**STRAUSS, Patricia Frances; (Mrs George Strauss);** Governor: the Old Vic since 1951; Sadler's Wells Theatre since 1951; the Royal (Sadler's Wells) Ballet School since 1951; the Royal Ballet since 1957; Whitechapel Art Gallery since 1957; *b* 1909; *m* 1932, Rt Hon. George Russell Strauss, *qv*; two *s* one *d*. Member of London County Council, 1946-58; Chairman: Parks Cttee (LCC), 1947-49; Supplies Cttee (LCC), 1949-52. Contested (Lab) South Kensington, Parliamentary General Election, 1945. *Publications:* Bevin and Co., 1941; Cripps, Advocate and Rebel, 1942. *Recreations:* painting, chess, foreign travel. *Address:* 1 Palace Green, W8. *T:* 01-937 1630; Naylands, Slaugham, Sussex. *T:* Handcross 270.

**STRAVINSKY, Igor;** composer; *b* Oranienbaum, near St Petersburg, 5 (18) June 1882; American citizen, 1945; *m* 1940, Vera de Bosset. *Works:* L'Oiseau de Feu, 1910; Petrouchka, 1911; Le sacre du Printemps, 1913; Rossignol, 1914; Renard, 1916; Les Noces, 1917-23; L'Histoire du Soldat, 1918; Pulcinella, 1919; Symphonies d'Instruments à vent, 1920; Mavra, 1922; Octuor, 1923; Concerto pour piano et orchestre, 1924; Oedipus-Rex, 1927; Apollon Musagete, 1928; Le Baiser de la Fée, 1928; Capriccio pour piano et orchestre, 1929; Symphonie de Psaumes, 1930; Concerto pour violin et orchestre, 1931; Duo Concertant pour violin et piano, 1932; Persēphone, 1934; Concerto pour deux pianos-solo, 1935; Jeu de Cartes, 1937; Symphony in C, 1940; Danses Concertantes, 1942; Scènes de Ballet, 1944; Symphony in 3 movements, 1945; Orpheus, 1947; Mass, 1948; The Rake's Progress (opera), 1951; Cantata, 1952; Septet, 1953; Three Songs from Shakespeare, 1953-54; In Memoriam Dylan Thomas, 1954; Canticum sacrum ad honorem Sancti Marcis nominis, 1956; Agon, ballet for twelve dancers, 1957; Threni, 1958; Movements, 1959; Gesualdo Monumentum, 1960; A Sermon, A Narrative, and A Prayer, 1961; The Dove Descending, 1962; The Flood, 1962; Abraham and Isaac, 1964; Elegy for J. F. K., 1964; Variations in Memory of Aldous Huxley, 1965; Requiem Canticles, 1966; Fanfare for a New Theatre, 1964. Awards: Gold Medal, Royal Philharmonic Society, 1954; Sibelius Gold Medal, 1955; Sibelius Prize, Wihuri International Prize Foundation, 1963. *Relevant Publications:* Stravinsky, by Roman Vlad, 1958 (English trans. 1960); Conversations with Igor Stravinsky, Vol. I, 1959, Vol. 2, 1960, Vol. 3, 1962, Vol. 4, 1968. *Address:* 1218 North Wetherly Drive, Hollywood, California 90069, USA.

**STRAWSON, Peter Frederick,** FBA 1960; Fellow of University College, Oxford, 1948-Aug. 1968, subsequently Fellow of Magdalen College; Waynflete Professor of Metaphysical Philosophy in the University of Oxford, since Aug. 1968 (Reader 1966-68); *b* 23 November 1919; *s* of late Cyril Walter and Nellie Dora Strawson; *m* 1945, Grace Hall Martin; two *s* two *d*. *Educ:* Christ's College, Finchley; St John's College, Oxford (scholar). Served War of 1939-45, RA, REME, Capt. Asst Lecturer in Philosophy, University Coll. of N. Wales, 1946; John Locke Schol., Univ. of Oxford, 1946; Lecturer in Philosophy, 1947, Fellow and Praelector, 1948, University Coll., Oxford. Vis. Prof., Duke Univ., N Carolina, 1955-56; Fellow of Humanities Council and Vis. Associate Prof., Princeton Univ., New Jersey, 1960-61. *Publications:* Introduction to Logical Theory, 1952; Individuals, 1959; The Bounds of Sense, 1966; (ed) Philosophical Logic, 1968; (ed) Studies in the Philosophy of Thought and Action, 1968; contrib. to Mind, Philosophy, Proc. Aristotelian Soc., Philosophical Review, etc. *Address:* 25 Farndon Road, Oxford. *T:* Oxford 55026.

**STREAT, Sir (Edward) Raymond,** KBE 1957 (CBE 1930); Kt 1942; Member of Council, Manchester University (Chairman, 1957-65, Treasurer, 1951-57); Hon. Fellow, Nuffield College, Oxford (Visiting Fellow, 1944-59); Vice-President, Lancashire and Merseyside Industrial Development Association; Trustee, John Rylands Library; *b* 7 Feb. 1897; *s* of late Edward Streat, Prestwich; *m* Doris, *d* of late Amos Davies, JP; two *s* (and one *s* died of wounds, 1944). *Educ:* Manchester Grammar School. Lt 10th Manchester Regiment (TA), 1915-18; Assistant Secretary, Manchester Chamber of Commerce, 1919; Director and Secretary, 1920-40; Hon. Director, Lancashire Industrial Development Council, 1931-40; Chairman, The Cotton Board, Manchester, 1940-57; President, Manchester Statistical Soc., 1936-38; President, Association of Technical Institutions, 1944-45; Secretary, Export Council, Board of Trade, Jan.-June

1940; Member, Advisory Council, DSIR, 1942-47; President, Manchester Luncheon Club, 1946-47; Pres., the Textile Institute, 1946-48; Chairman: Manchester Joint Research Council, 1948-51; N-Western Electricity Consultative Council, 1960-68; Member, Gen. Advisory Council, BBC, 1947-52. Hon. LLD, Manchester University, 1963. Commander of Order of Orange Nassau (Netherlands). *Recreation:* golf. *Address:* 2 Avenue Lodge, Alderley Edge, Cheshire. *T:* Alderley Edge 4212. *Club:* St James's (Manchester).

**STREATFEILD, Sir Geoffrey Hugh Benbow,** Kt 1947; MC; Judge of the High Court of Justice, Queen's Bench Division, 1947-66; *b* 28 July 1897; *yr s* of late Maj. H. S. Streatfeild, Ryhope, Co. Durham, and Barlay, Balmaclellan, Kirkcudbrightshire; *m* 1918, Marjorie, *yr d* of late Charles Booth, Sunderland; three *d. Educ:* Rugby School. Served with 4th Batt. Durham Light Infantry and Royal Flying Corps and RAF, 1914-19, Capt. 1917 (MC); called to Bar, Inner Temple, 1921; KC 1938. Joined North Eastern Circuit, 1922; Recorder of Rotherham, 1932-34; Huddersfield, 1934-43; Kingston-upon-Hull, 1943-47; Solicitor-General and Attorney General of the County Palatine of Durham, 1939-47; Bencher of the Inner Temple, 1945; Major (Deputy Judge Advocate), 1940; Lt-Col Asst Judge Advocate-General, 1942-43; Comr of Assize, Western Circuit, 1946. Chairman, Inter-Departmental Cttee on the Business of the Criminal Courts, 1958-60; Deputy Chairman, Somerset Quarter Sessions. Hon. DCL Durham Univ., 1957. *Address:* Cheddon Corner, Cheddon Fitzpaine, Taunton, Somerset. *T:* Kingston St Mary 277.

**STREATFEILD, Noel;** Novelist; *d* of late William Champion Streatfeild, Bishop of Lewes and late Janet Mary Venn; unmarried. *Educ:* Laleham; Eastbourne. *Publications:* The Whicharts; Parson's Nine; Tops and Bottoms; Shepherdess of Sheep; It Pays to be Good; Caroline England; Luke; The Winter is Past; I Ordered a Table for Six; Myra Carroll; Saplings; Grass in Piccadilly; Mothering Sunday; Aunt Clara; Judith; The Silent Speaker; Magic and The Magician: a biography of E. Nesbit; *autobiography:* A Vicarage Family; Away from the Vicarage; *for children:* Ballet Shoes; The Circus is Coming (Carnegie Gold Medal); The Children of Primrose Lane; Curtain Up; Party Frock; The Painted Garden; (ed) The Years of Grace; Growing Up Gracefully; White Boots; The Fearless Treasure; The Bell Family; Wintle's Wonders; The Royal Ballet School; New Town; Apple Bough; The Children on the Top Floor; The Growing Summer; Caldicott Place; Thursday's Child. *Recreation:* wild flower collecting. *Address:* 51 Elizabeth Street, Eaton Square, SW1. *T:* 01-730 5673.

**STREDDER, James Cecil;** Headmaster Wellington School, Somerset, since 1957; *b* 22 Sept. 1912; 4th *s* of late Rev. J. Clifton Stredder and late Mrs Stredder; *m* 1938, Catherine Jane, *er d* of late Rev. A. R. Price, RN (Retd), Paignton, Devon; one *d. Educ:* King Edward VI School, Stratford-on-Avon; Jesus College, Oxford. Senior Chemistry Master at: Victoria College, Alexandria, Egypt, 1935; St Lawrence Coll., Ramsgate, 1936; Fettes Coll., Edinburgh, 1940; Tonbridge School, 1942-57. BA (Hons) Natural Science (Chemistry) Oxon 1935, MA 1943. *Recreations:* rowing and walking. *Address:* Wellington School, Somerset. *Club:* Somerset County (Taunton).

**STREET, Prof. Harry,** LLM, PhD; FBA 1968; Professor of English Law, Manchester University, since 1960; Member, Commission on the Constitution, since 1969; *b* 17 June 1919; *s* of Alfred and Lilian Street; *m* 1947, Muriel Hélène Swain; two *s* one *d. Educ:* Farnworth Grammar School; Manchester Univ. LLB 1938, LLM 1948; PhD 1951. Qualified as Solicitor, 1940. Flt-Lt, RAF, 1942-46. Lectr in Law, Manchester Univ., 1946-47; Commonwealth Fund Fellow at Columbia Univ., USA, 1947-48; Lectr in Law, 1948-51, Senior Lectr in Law, 1951-52, Manchester Univ.; Prof. of Law, Nottingham Univ., 1952-56; Prof. of Public Law and Common Law, Manchester Univ., 1956-60. Visiting Prof. of Law, Harvard Univ., USA, 1957-58. Chm., Cttee on Racial Discrimination, 1967. *Publications:* Principles of Administrative Law (with J. A. G. Griffith), 4th edn 1967; A Comparative Study of Governmental Liability, 1953; Law of Torts, 4th edn 1968; Law of Damages, 1961; Freedom, the Individual and the Law, 2nd edn 1968; Law relating to Nuclear Energy (with F. R. Frame), 1966; Road Accidents (with D. W. Elliott), 1968; Justice in the Welfare State (Hamlyn Lectures), 1968. Articles in numerous English, Canadian and American Jls of law and public administration. *Recreations:* mountain walking, cricket. *Address:* Faculty of Law, Manchester University, Manchester M13 9PL; 1 Queen's Gate, Bramhall, Cheshire. *T:* 061-439 4922.

**STREET, John Edmund Dudley,** CMG 1966; Assistant Secretary, Ministry of Defence, since 1967; *b* 21 April 1918; *er s* of Philip Edmund Wells Street and Elinor Gladys Whittington-Ince; *m* 1940, Noreen Mary, *o d* of Edward John Griffin Comerford and Mary Elizabeth Winstone; three *s* one *d. Educ:* Tonbridge School; Exeter College, Oxford. Served War of 1939-45, HM Forces, 1940-46. Entered Foreign Service, 1947; First Secretary: British Embassy, Oslo, 1950; British Embassy, Lisbon, 1952; Foreign Office, 1954; First Secretary and Head of Chancery, British Legation, Budapest, 1957-60; HM Ambassador to Malagasy Republic, 1961-62, also Consul-General for the Island of Réunion and the Comoro Islands, 1961-62. *Recreations:* reading, golf, bridge. *Address:* 162 Oatlands Drive, Weybridge, Surrey. *T:* Weybridge 46205.

**STREET, John Hugh,** CB 1965; Under-Secretary, Ministry of Housing and Local Government, since 1956; *b* 24 Aug. 1914; *s* of Hugh W. Street and Augusta Street; *m* 1938, Alicia, *d* of Oscar Kumpula, Wakefield, Mich., USA; two *d. Educ:* Aldenham School; Pembroke College, Cambridge. Home Office, 1937-46; Ministry of Town and Country Planning, 1946-47; Central Land Board, 1947-53; Treasury, 1953-54; Ministry of Housing and Local Government, 1955-. *Recreations:* looking at pictures, gardening, travel. *Address:* 43 Teignmouth Road, NW2. *T:* 01-452 5337.

**STREET, Hon. Sir Kenneth (Whistler),** KCMG 1956; Lieutenant-Governor of New South Wales since 1950; Chief Justice of New South Wales, 1950-60; *b* Sydney, NSW, 28 Jan. 1890; *e s* of late Hon. Sir Philip Street, KCMG; *m* 1916, Jessie Mary Grey (*d* 1970), *e d* of C. A. G. Lillingston, Yulgilbar, Clarence River, NSW; two *s* two *d. Educ:* Sydney Grammar School; Sydney University (BA, LLB (honours), Harris Scholarship, Wigram Allen Scholarship, Pitt Cobbett Prize). Called to Bar, 1915; held position as lecturer, Sydney University Law School in Legal Interpretation; Contracts, Mercantile Law and Torts, Legal Ethics; a member of the industrial Commission of NSW with the rank and title of a Supreme Court Judge, 1927; Puisne Judge of Supreme Court, 1931-50; held Commission in 1914 in Duke of Cornwall's Light Infantry, discharged medically unfit active service; served in Australia, 1915-19, at German Concentration Camps, NSW District HQ Staff, and General Staff, Army HQ, Melbourne; Hon. LLD, Sydney Univ. KStJ 1952. *Address:* 2 Greenoaks Avenue, Darling Point, Edgecliff, Sydney, NSW 2027, Australia. *T:* 32-2203. *Clubs:* Union, Royal Sydney Golf (Sydney).

**STREETEN, Paul Patrick;** Warden of Queen Elizabeth House, Director, Institute of Commonwealth Studies, and Fellow of Balliol College, Oxford, since Oct. 1968; *b* 18 July 1917; *e s* of Wilhelm Hornig, Vienna; changed name to Streeten under Army Council Instruction, 1943; *m* 1951, Ann Hilary Palmer, *d* of Edgar Higgins, Woodstock, Vermont; two *d* (and one step *s*). *Educ:* Vienna; Aberdeen Univ.; Balliol Coll., Oxford (Hon. Schol.). Mil. service in Commandos, 1941-43; wounded in Sicily, 1943. Fellow, Balliol Coll., Oxford, 1948-66; Associate, Oxford Univ. Inst. of Econs and Statistics, 1960-64; Dep. Dir-Gen., Econ. Planning Staff, Min. of Overseas Develt, 1964-66; Prof. of Econs, Fellow and Dep. Dir of Inst. of Develt Studies, Sussex Univ., 1966-68. Rockefeller Fellow, USA, 1950-51; Fellow, Johns Hopkins Univ., Baltimore, 1955-56; Fellow, Center for Advanced Studies, Wesleyan Univ., Conn.; Sec., Oxford Econ. Papers, until 1961 and Editor, Bulletin of Oxford Univ. Inst. of Econs and Statistics, 1961-64; Mem. Council: Walloon Inst. of Econ. Develt; UK Nat. Commn of Unesco, 1966; Commonwealth Develt Corp., 1967; Member, Governing Body: Queen Elizabeth House, Oxford, 1966-68; Inst. of Develt Studies, Univ. of Sussex, 1968-. *Publications:* (ed) Value in Social Theory, 1958; Economic Integration, 1961; contrib. to Economic Growth in Britain, 1966; The Teaching of Development Economics, 1967; (ed with M. Lipton) Crisis in Indian Planning, 1968; (contrib. to) Gunnar Myrdal, Asian Drama, 1968; (ed) Unfashionable Economics, 1970; contribs to Quarterly Jl of Econs, Review of Econ. Studies, Oxford Econ. Papers, Bulletin of Inst. of Econs and Statistics, Manchester Sch., Jl of Develt. Studies, etc. *Address:* Queen Elizabeth House, 20 St Giles, Oxford. *T:* Oxford 52952 (office); Oxford 59000 (home). *Club:* United University.

**STREETER, John Stuart; His Honour Judge Streeter;** Deputy Chairman, Kent Quarter Sessions, since 1967; *b* 20 May 1920; *yr s* of late Wilfrid A. Streeter, osteopath, and of Mrs R. L. Streeter; *m* 1956, Margaret Nancy Richardson; one *s* two *d*. *Educ:* Sherborne. Served War of 1939-45 (despatches): Captain, Royal Scots Fusiliers, 1940-46. Called to Bar, Gray's Inn, Nov. 1947. Post Office Counsel SE Circuit, 1957; Treasury Counsel, London Sessions, 1959; Part-time Dep. Chm., Kent Quarter Sessions, 1963. *Recreation:* fishing. *Address:* Robin Hill, 12 Wood Drive, Chislehurst, Kent BR7 5EU. *T:* 01-467 3031. *Club:* Kent County (Maidstone).

**STREIT, Clarence Kirshman;** President, International Movement for Atlantic Union, since 1958, and Federal Union, Inc., USA, since 1939; author; lecturer since 1939; Editor, Freedom & Union, since 1946; *b* 21 Jan. 1896; *s* of Louis L. Streit and Emma Kirshman, California, Mo, USA; *m* 1921, Jeanne Defrance, of Paris, France; one *s* two *d*. *Educ:* Missouri and Montana public schs; State Univ. of Montana; Sorbonne; University Coll., Oxford (Rhodes Schol.), Hon. LLD, LittD, DHL. US public land surveyor in Montana and Alaska, 1912-16; served as volunteer in American Expeditionary Force, France, 1917-19, first as private, 18th Engineers Railway, then as sergeant in Intelligence Service, attached to American Delegation, Paris Peace Conference; then Rhodes Scholar, Oxford; correspondent Philadelphia Public Ledger, 1920-24, Greco-Turk War, Rome, Istanbul, Paris; correspondent, New York Times, 1925-39, Carthage excavations, Riff war, Vienna, New York, Latin America, Geneva, 1929-38, Washington, DC, 1938-39. 1st Kefauver Union of the Free Award, 1968. *Publications:* Where Iron is, There is the Fatherland, 1920; Hafiz: The Tongue of the Hidden (rubaiyat), 1928; Report on How to Combat False News, League of Nations, 1932; Union Now, 1939; Union Now with Britain, 1941; Chapter on Briand in Dictators and Democrats, 1941; (joint) The New Federalist, 1950; Freedom Against Itself, 1954; Freedom's Frontier–Atlantic Union Now, 1960. *Address:* Ontario Apartments, Washington, DC 20009, USA. *T:* (202) 234-3232 (Washington, DC).

**STRETTON, Eric Hugh Alexander;** Under-Secretary, Ministry of Public Building and Works, since 1962; *b* 22 June 1916; *y s* of Major S. G. Stretton, Wigston, Leicester; *m* 1946, Sheila Woodroffe Anderson, MB, BS, *d* of Dr A. W. Anderson, Cardiff (formerly of Ogmore Vale); one *s* one *d*. *Educ:* Wyggeston School; Pembroke College, Oxford. BA 1939, MA 1942. Leicestershire Regt and 2/4 PWO Gurkha Rifles (Major), 1939-46. Asst Sec., Birmingham Univ. Appointments Board, 1946. Entered Ministry of Works, 1947; Principal Private Secretary to Minister of Works, 1952-54; Assistant Secretary, 1954. *Address:* The Hop House, Churt, Surrey. *T:* Headley Down 3242. *Club:* United University.

**STRICKLAND;** *see* Hornyold-Strickland.

**STRICKLAND, Lady; (Barbara),** DBE 1923; *b* 2 April 1884; *d* of Martin W. B. and Wilhelmine M. E. ffolkes; *m* 1st, 1911, Francis Joseph Cresswell, Norfolk Regt (*d* 1914); two *d*; 2nd, 1918, General Sir E. P. Strickland, KCB, KBE, CMG, DSO (*d* 1951); one *d*. *Address:* The Old Hall, Snettisham, Norfolk. *T:* Snettisham 213.
*See also Sir Roy Harrod.*

**STRICKLAND, Maj.-Gen. Eugene Vincent Michael,** CMG 1960; DSO 1944; OBE 1955; MM 1940; Chief of Joint Services Liaison Organization, British Forces, Germany, 1966-69, retired; *b* 25 Aug. 1913; *s* of Capt. V. N. Strickland (*d* of wounds, 1917) and of Mary Erina Strickland (*née* O'Sullivan); *m* 1939, Barbara Mary Farquharson Meares Lamb; four *s* one *d*. *Educ:* Mayfield College; RMC Sandhurst. Commissioned, 1934; served in India, 1935; War of 1939-45, in France and Belgium, 1940; N Africa, 1942-43; Italy, 1943-45; Greece, 1945-46; Egypt, 1948; WO, (MI), 1948-50; Min. of Defence, 1952-54; Arab Legion, 1955-56; Sen. British Officer, Jordan, 1956-57; Min. of Defence, on staff of Chief of Defence Staff, 1957-58; Mil. Adviser to King Hussein of Jordan, 1958-59; Director of Plans, War Office, 1960-63; psc 1947; jssc 1952; idc 1960; NATO Defence College, 1963; DAQMG 1st Corps, 1963-66. Star of Jordan, 1959. CStJ 1960. *Recreations:* shooting, cricket, etc. *Address:* Greenacre, Elham, Canterbury, Kent.

**STRICKLAND, Hon. Mabel Edeline,** OBE 1944; Leader of the Progressive Constitutional Party in Malta, since 1953; *b* Malta, 8 Jan. 1899; 3rd *d* of 1st and last Baron Strickland, of Sizergh Castle, Kendal (and 6th Count della Catena in the Island of Malta) and of late Lady Edeline Sackville. *Educ:* privately in Australia.

Attached Naval HQ, Malta, 1917-18; War Correspondent, attached 21st Army Group, BAOR, Aug. 1945. Asst Sec., Constitutional Party, 1921-45; Editor: Times of Malta, 1935-50; Sunday Times of Malta, 1935-56; Member: Malta Legislative Assembly, 1950, 1951-53, 1962-66; Malta Chamber of Commerce; Man. Dir, Allied Malta Newspapers Ltd, 1940-55; Chairman: Xara Palace Hotel Co. Ltd, 1949-61, 1966-; Allied Malta Newspapers Ltd, 1950-55, 1966-; Director, Progress Press Co. Ltd, 1957-61, 1966-. Life Member: Commonwealth Parliamentary Assoc.; Air League; RSA; Mem. Royal Horticultural Soc.; Hon. Corresp. Sec. (Malta), Royal Commonwealth Soc. CStJ 1969. Coronation medal, 1953. *Publications:* A Collection of Essays on Malta, 1923-54; Maltese Constitutional and Economic Issue, 1955-59. *Recreations:* swimming, gardening. *Address:* Villa Parisio, Lija, Malta. *T:* 41286. *Clubs:* Lansdowne; United Services Sports (Malta).

**STRICKLAND-CONSTABLE, Sir Henry Marmaduke,** 10th Bt, *cr* 1641; *b* 4 Dec. 1900; *s* of late Lt-Col Frederick Charles Strickland-Constable and Margaret Elizabeth (*d* 1961), *d* of late Rear-Adm. Hon. Thomas Alexander Pakenham; *S* cousin 1938; *m* 1929, Countess Ernestine, *d* of late Count Rex. *Educ:* Eton; Magdalen Coll., Oxford. BA, BMus. *Heir: b* Robert Frederick Strickland-Constable [*b* 22 Oct. 1903; *m* 1st, 1929 (marriage annulled, 1931), Rosaline Mary, *d* of Arthur Webster; 2nd, 1936, Lettice, *y d* of late Major Frederick Strickland; two *s* two *d*]. *Address:* Wassand Hall, Seaton, Near Hull, Yorks. *T:* Hornsea 3767.

**STRINGER, John Daniel,** CMG 1960; *b* 2 May 1914; *s* of late Harold Stringer, MA, AMICE; *m* 1939, Elizabeth, *d* of Colonel S. C. Layzell, MC, Kenya; one *s* two *d*. *Educ:* Uppingham; Peterhouse, Cambridge (MA). District Officer and District Commissioner, Kenya, 1936-52; Senior District Commissioner, Zanzibar, 1953; Senior Commissioner, Zanzibar, 1956. Order of the Brilliant Star of Zanzibar, 1960. *Recreations:* squash racquets, sailing, fishing. *Address:* North House, Aldeburgh, Suffolk. *Clubs:* Lansdowne; Mombasa (Mombasa).

**STRINGER, Pamela Mary;** Headmistress, Clifton High School for Girls, since 1965; *b* 30 Aug. 1928; *e d* of late E. Allen Stringer. *Educ:* Worcester Grammar Sch. for Girls; St Hugh's Coll., Oxford. MA (Hons Lit Hum). Asst Classics Mistress, Sherborne Sch. for Girls, 1950-59; Head of Classics Dept, Pate's Grammar Sch. for Girls, Cheltenham, 1959-64 (Dep. Head, 1963-64). *Recreations:* travel in Tuscany and Umbria, reading, theatre, cooking. *Address:* Glendower House, Clifton Park, Clifton, Bristol 8. *Club:* Public Schools.

**STROBL, Kisfalud Sigismund de;** Sculptor; Professor Royal Academy of Art, Budapest, since 1924; *b* Alsōrajk, Hungary, 1884; *m* 1916, Maria Mellinger; one *d*. *Educ:* Royal Academy, Budapest; Vienna; Paris; Italy. At the age of 24 completed his first great monument; several museums own his works; worked in his vacations in London, where he completed the busts of the Duke of Kent, Earl of Athlone, G. B. Shaw, Sir Austen Chamberlain, Sir John Simon, Field Marshal Allenby, Lady Astor, etc; and later completed the busts of Princess Elizabeth, Lord and Lady Londonderry, etc.; won several gold medals; has a one-man show in London in the White Allom Gallery, 1935; exhibited several times at Royal Academy in London; historical monuments for Budapest: The Liberation, Lajos, Kossuth, Ference Rākōczi. Kossuth Prize, 1950, 1953. Order of Merit (Hungary), 1954. *Recreations:* shooting, fishing. *Address:* XIV. Stefānia-ut 20, Budapest. *T:* Budapest 296-445. *Club:* Rotary.

**STRODE, Warren C.;** *see* Chetham-Strode.

**STRODE-JACKSON, Colonel Arnold Nugent Strode,** CBE 1920; DSO 1917 and 3 Bars (July 1917, May and Dec. 1918); late KRRC; *s* of late Morton Strode Jackson, ISO and Diana Martin, miniaturist; *m* 1918, Dora Berryman, *d* of late W. A. Mooney, USA, and Winifred Hunter Tewson; one *s*. *Educ:* Malvern Coll.; Brasenose Coll., Oxford (BA). Called to Bar, Middle Temple. Pres. OUAC; 1500 metres record at Olympic Games, Stockholm, 1912. Capt. and Adjt 13th (S) Bn Rifles Bde and Bt Maj., Temp. Lt-Col comdg 13th (S) Bn KRRC, Actg Brig. 111th Inf. Bde, 37th Div.; served on Western Front (despatches 6 times, wounded thrice). Mem. Olympic Council, 1920. Mem. Brit. Delegn to Peace Conf., Paris, 1919-20. Directed first Kentucky Derby Festival, 1935; Colonel on Staff of Governor of Kentucky. War of 1939-45: Admin. Officer of Inspection Bd of UK and Canada in New York and Ottawa, in charge of Inspectors and Anti-Sabotage precautions. *Publication:* Kentucky Heyday, a biographical novel 1787-1827, 1956 (New York). *Recreations:* fishing, horticulture. *Clubs:* Pendennis (Louisville, Ky); Canadian (New York).

**STRONG, Air Cdre David Malcolm,** CB 1964; AFC 1941; *b* 30 Sept. 1913; *s* of Theo Strong; *m* 1941, Daphne Irene Warren-Brown; two *s* one *d*. *Educ:* Cardiff High School. Pilot, under trng, 1936; Bomber Sqdn, 1937-41; POW, 1941-45. Station Commander, RAF Jurby, RAF Driffield, 1946-48; Staff Coll. (psa), 1949; Staff Officer, Rhodesian Air Trng Grp, 1949-51; Directing Staff, Staff Coll., 1952-55; Air Warfare Coll. (pfc), 1956; Station Comdr, RAF Coningsby, 1957-59; Dir of Personnel, Air Min., 1959-61; Senior Air Staff Officer, RAF Germany, 1962-63; Officer Commanding, RAF Halton, 1964-66. Retired, 1966. *Recreation:* golf. *Address:* Clematis Cottage, Great Kimble, Bucks. *T:* Princes Risborough 3985. *Club:* Royal Air Force.

**STRONG, Maj.-Gen. Sir Kenneth William Dobson,** KBE 1966 (OBE 1942); Kt 1952; CB 1945; Director: Philip Hill Investment Trust; Eagle Star Insurance Co.; *o s* of late Prof. John Strong, CBE, LLD, and of late Mrs Strong, Eastbourne; unmarried. *Educ:* Montrose Academy; Glenalmond; RMC, Sandhurst. 2nd Lt 1st Bn Royal Scots Fusiliers, 1920. Military career (which included command of 4/5 Bn Royal Scots Fusiliers), 1920-45; attendance at the Camberley Staff College Course; Defence Security Officer, Malta and Gibraltar; staff appts at WO; a tour of duty as Military Attaché, Berlin, and residence in Germany, France, Italy and Spain prior to qualifying as an interpreter in the languages of these countries. In Feb. 1943 appointed to be head of General Eisenhower's Intelligence Staff. In this capacity remained with the Supreme Commander during his campaigns in Africa, Sicily, Italy, France and Germany, leaving him at the dissolution of Supreme HQ in July 1945 (despatches). Member, delegns for conducting Armistice negotiations with Italy, in Lisbon and Sicily, 1943; and with Germany in Rheims and Berlin, 1945. Director General of Political Intelligence Dept of Foreign Office, 1945-47; retired pay, 1947. First Director of Joint Intelligence Bureau, Ministry of Defence, 1948-64; first Director-General of Intelligence, Min. of Defence, 1964-66. Distinguished Service Medal (USA), Legion of Merit (USA). Chevalier and Officer of Legion of Honour, Croix de Guerre with Palms (France); Order of the Red Banner (Russia).

*Publications:* Intelligence at the Top, 1968; Men of Intelligence, 1970; various newspaper articles. *Recreation:* golf. *Address:* 25 Kepplestone, Eastbourne, Sussex. *Club:* Army and Navy.

**STRONG, Most Rev. Philip Nigel Warrington,** KBE 1970; CMG 1958; MA Cantab; ThD ACT; DD Lambeth, 1968; *b* Sutton-on-the-Hill, Etwall, 11 July 1899; *s* of late Rev. John Warrington Strong, Oxford, formerly Vicar of Dodford with Brockhall, and late Rosamond Maria, *d* of late John Digby Wingfield Digby, Sherborne Castle, Dorset. *Educ:* King's School, Worcester; Selwyn Coll., Cambridge; Bishops' College, Cheshunt. Served European War with RE (Signal Service), 1918-19; BA Cambridge, 1921; MA 1924; Deacon, 1922; Priest, 1923; Curate of St Mary's, Tyne Dock, 1922-26; Vicar of Christ Church, Leeds, 1926-31; Vicar of St Ignatius the Martyr, Sunderland, 1931-36; Proctor of Convocation of York and Member of Church Assembly for Archdeaconry of Durham, 1936; Bishop of New Guinea, 1936-62; MLC, Territory of Papua and New Guinea, 1955-63; Archbishop of Brisbane and Metropolitan of Queensland, 1962-70; Primate of Australia, 1966-70. Senior CF (Australian Army), 1943-45. Hon. Fellow, Selwyn College, Cambridge, 1966. Sub-Prelate, Order of St John of Jerusalem, 1967. **Publication:** Out of Great Tribulation, 1957. *Clubs:* Queensland (Brisbane); University (Sydney).

**STRONG, Roy Colin,** PhD, FSA; Director, Keeper and Secretary of the National Portrait Gallery since 1967 (Assistant Keeper, 1959); *b* 23 Aug. 1935; *s* of G. E. C. Strong. *Educ:* Edmonton Co. Grammar Sch.; Queen Mary Coll., London; Warburg Inst., London. *Publications:* Portraits of Queen Elizabeth I, 1963; (with J. A. van Dorsten) Leicester's Triumph, 1964; Holbein and Henry VIII, 1967; Tudor and Jacobean Portraits, 1969; The English Icon: Elizabethan and Jacobean Portraiture, 1969; contributor to learned jls and organiser of exhibitions. *Address:* 2E Morpeth Terrace, SW1.

**STRONGE, Captain Rt. Hon. Sir (Charles) Norman (Lockhart),** PC N Ireland, 1946; 8th Bt, *cr* 1803; HM Lieutenant for Co. Armagh; MP Mid-Armagh, Northern Ireland Parliament, 1938-69; Speaker House of Commons, Northern Ireland, 1945-69; President British Legion, Northern Ireland Area, since 1946; *b* 23 July 1894; *s* of Sir Charles Edmond Sinclair Stronge, 7th Bt, and Marian (*d* 1948), *d* of Samuel Bostock, The Hermitage, Epsom; *S* father 1939; *m* 1921, Gladys Olive Hall, OBE 1943, OStJ, of Knockbrack, Athenry, Co. Galway, *o d* of Major H. T. Hall, late 18th Hussars; one *s* two *d*. *Educ:* Eton. Served European War, 1914-19, R Inniskilling Fusiliers and R Irish Rifles (MC, despatches twice, Belgian Croix-de-Guerre); Asst Parliamentary Sec., Ministry of Finance, Northern Ireland, 1941-42; Parliamentary Sec., Ministry of Finance (Chief Whip), 1942-44; JP Co. Londonderry; JP Co. Armagh; High Sheriff Co. Londonderry, 1934; Director Commercial Insurance Company of Ireland Ltd; Chairman Armagh County Council, 1944-55; North Irish Horse (Royal Armoured Corps), invalided. Hon. Col 5th Bn Royal Irish Fusiliers (TA), 1949-63. KStJ; Comdr of the Order of Leopold (Belgium), 1946. *Recreations:* shooting, fishing. *Heir:* *s* James Matthew Stronge [*b* 21 June 1932. *Educ:* Eton; Christ Church, Oxford (MA). Captain, Grenadier Guards, RARO. MP (N Ireland), Mid-Armagh, 1969-. JP Co. Armagh]. *Address:* Tynan Abbey, Tynan, Co. Armagh, Northern Ireland. *TA:* Tynan. *T:* Middletown 205. *Club:* Ulster (Belfast).

**STRONGE, Brig. Humphrey Cecil Travell,** CBE 1945; DSO 1919; MC; *b* London, 24 Feb. 1891; *e s* of late W. Cecil Stronge; *m* 1923, Elsie Margaret, *e d* of late Canon W. F. Burnside; one *d*. *Educ:* The Oratory School; RMC Sandhurst. Commissioned the Buffs, 1910; seconded W African Frontier Force, 1914; served European War, 1914-18, in Cameroons, German East Africa and France (DSO, MC, despatches twice); Staff College, 1926-27; Bt Lt-Col, 1937; Mil. Attaché Belgrade and Prague, 1936-39; Col 1939; Asst Comdt Nigeria Regt 1939; served War of 1939-45; Comdr, Southern Bde, Nigeria, 1939; GSO 1, War Office, 1940; Comdr, Blackdown Sub-Area, 1940-41; Brig. 1940; Comdr L of C Area, N Africa, Sicily, 1942-43; Head of Mil. Mission to Corsica, and Personal Representative of C-in-C, 1943-44; Comdr, Area in France and Holland, 1944-45 (CBE, despatches twice). Retd 1946. Rep., British Council: Sweden, 1946-48, Portugal, 1948-52. FRGS. *Address:* Milton Rill Cottage, Watledge, Nailsworth, Glos.

**STRONGE, Rt. Hon. Sir Norman;** *see* Stronge, Rt Hon. Sir C. N. L.

**STROWGER, Gaston Jack;** Managing Director, Thorn Electrical Industries, since 1970; *b* 8 Feb. 1916; *s* of Alfred Henry Strowger, Lowestoft boat-owner, and Lily Ellen Tripp; *m* 1939, Katherine Ellen Gilbert; two *s* one *d*. *Educ:* Lowestoft Grammar School. Joined London Electrical Supply Co., 1934; HM Forces, 1939-43. Joined TEI, as an Accountant, 1943; Group Chief Accountant, 1952; Exec. Dir 1961; full Dir 1966; Financial Dir 1967. *Recreations:* gardening, fishing. *Address:* Dormers, 27 Beech Hill Avenue, Hadley Wood, Barnet, Herts. *T:* Barnet 6289.

**STRUTT,** family name of **Barons Belper** and **Rayleigh.**

**STRUTT, Vice-Adm. Hon. Arthur Charles,** CBE 1928; *b* 2 Oct. 1878; 2nd *s* of 3rd Baron Rayleigh and Evelyn, *d* of J. M. Balfour of Whittingehame, and Blanche, *d* of 2nd Marquis of Salisbury; *m* 1934, Hon. Mrs Cyril Ward. *Educ:* HMS Britannia, etc. Served as Master of the Fleet in HMS Queen Elizabeth under the Flag of Earl Beatty, 1916-18; Director of Navigation, Admiralty, 1923-25; Lieut, 1900; Comdr, 1913; Capt. 1917; Rear-Adm., 1929; retired, 1929; Vice-Adm., retired, 1933. *Recreations:* fishing and golf. *Address:* 3 Whitehall Court, SW1. *T:* 01-930 3160.

**STRUTT, Sir Austin;** *see* Strutt, Sir Henry Austin.

**STRUTT, Hon. Charles Richard;** *b* 25 May 1910; *s* of 4th Baron Rayleigh and Lady Mary Hilda Strutt, *d* of 4th Earl of Leitrim; *b* and *heir-pres* of 5th Baron Rayleigh, *qv*; *m* 1952, Jean Elizabeth, *d* of 1st Viscount Davidson, *qv*; one *s* two *d*. *Educ:* Eton; Trinity College, Cambridge. Governor of Felsted School, 1936. Member, Church Army Bd, 1950 (Vice-Pres. 1963). Hon. Treas., Soc. for Psychical Research, 1954. Director of various companies including Australian Estates Co. Ltd, 1949, and Lord Rayleigh's Farms Inc. (Chairman), 1957. King Christian IX Liberation Order (Denmark). *Recreation:* gardening. *Address:* Berwick Place, Hatfield Peverel, Chelmsford, Essex. *T:* Hatfield Peverel 321. *Club:* Brooks's.

**STRUTT, Geoffrey St John,** CBE 1920; JP; *b* 28 March 1888; 2nd *s* of late Hon. Richard Strutt and Augusta, *o c* of 5th Baron Braybrooke; *m*

1912, Sybil Eyre, *d* of Sir Walpole Greenwell, 1st Bt; two *s* (and one killed in action). *Educ:* Winchester; Magdalen College, Oxford, BA. Member of the Stock Exchange, 1912-17; enlisted Sept. 1914; obtained a commission in the 2/5th Essex Regiment; served in France with 2/5th Glosters (wounded, 1917); became Private Secretary to Sir Laming Worthington Evans at the Ministry of Munitions, and went with him to the Foreign Office and Ministry of Pensions; retired to stand as a Tory for the Harwich Division, 1922; worked for the League of Nations Union, and later became first News Editor of the BBC. *Address:* St Catharine's Court, Bath, Somerset BA1 SHA. *T:* Batheaston 88159. *Club:* Bath and County.

**STRUTT, Sir (Henry) Austin,** KCVO *cr* 1953 (CVO 1943; MVO 1937); CB 1949; JP; Extra Gentleman Usher to the Queen since 1961; Chairman: Council of Voluntary Welfare Work, 1962; Church of England Pensions Board, 1965; *b* 23 Jan. 1903; *er s* of late Henry Strutt and Elizabeth Maher, Rathkeale, Co. Limerick; *m* 1927, Gladys May, *o d* of late Arthur Salter Holt; two *d. Educ:* Roan School; Magdalen College, Oxford. 1st Class Modern History, 1924; Senior Demy, 1925-26; Home Office, 1925-61; Principal Private Secretary to Mr Herbert Morrison, 1940-43; Assistant Under-Secretary of State, Home Office, 1943-57; Principal Establishment and Organisation Officer, Home Office, 1945-57; subseq. Dep. Under-Sec. of State, Home Office. Registrar of the Baronetage, 1945-61; Director, John Lewis Partnership Ltd, 1962-67. JP Bucks. KStJ. *Address:* 51 Sussex Place, Slough, Bucks. *T:* Slough 21008.

**STRUTT, Nigel Edward,** TD; DL; Chairman and Managing Director, Strutt & Parker (Farms) Ltd; Managing Director, Lord Rayleigh's Farms Inc.; *b* 18 Jan. 1916; *yr s* of late Edward Jolliffe Strutt. *Educ:* Winchester; Wye Agricultural College (Fellow, 1970). Essex Yeomanry (Major), 1937-56. Part-time Mem., Eastern Electricity Bd, 1964-; Mem., Agricultural Advisory Council, 1963- (Chm. 1969-); Mem., NEDC for Agriculture, 1967-; President, Country Landowners' Associaton, 1967-69. DL Essex 1954; High Sheriff of Essex, 1966. *Recreations:* shooting, ski-ing. *Address:* Sparrows, Terling, Essex. *T:* Terling 213. *Clubs:* Brooks's, Farmers'.

**STRUTT, Rt. Rev. Rupert Gordon;** *see* Stockport, Suffragan Bishop of.

**STUART,** family name of **Earl Castle Stewart, Earl of Moray** and **Viscount Stuart of Findhorn.**

**STUART;** *see* Crichton-Stuart, **family name of Marquess of Bute.**

**STUART OF FINDHORN,** 1st Viscount *cr* 1959; **James Gray Stuart,** PC 1939; CH 1957; MVO 1921; MC; DL; Member, Royal Commission on Working of the Tribunals of Inquiry (Evidence) Act, 1921, since 1966; *b* 9 Feb. 1897; 3rd *s* of 17th Earl of Moray; *m* 1923, Lady Rachel Cavendish, OBE, 4th *d* of 9th Duke of Devonshire; two *s* one *d. Educ:* Eton. Capt. 3rd Bn the Royal Scots; served European War, 1914-18 (MC and bar); Brigade-Major, 1918; Equerry to Duke of York, 1920-21. MP (U) Moray and Nairn, 1923-59; a Lord Commissioner of the Treasury, 1935-41; Joint Parliamentary Secretary to the Treasury and Government Chief Whip, 1941-45; Chief Opposition Whip, 1945-48; Secretary of State for Scotland, 1951-57. *Publication:* Within the Fringe; an autobiography, 1967. *Heir: er s* Hon. David Randolph Moray Stuart [*b* 20 June 1924; *m* 1st, 1945, Grizel Mary Wilfreda (*d* 1948), *d* of D. T. Fyfe and *widow* of Michael Gillilan; one *s*; 2nd, 1951, Marian, *d* of Gerald Wilson; one *s* three *d. Educ:* Eton. DL Caernarvon, 1963-68]. *Address:* Harthill House, Redlynch, Salisbury, Wilts. *Clubs:* White's, Buck's; New (Edinburgh).

**STUART, Viscount; Andrew Richard Charles Stuart;** *b* 7 Oct. 1953; *s* and *heir* of 8th Earl Castle Stewart, *qv*.

**STUART, Prof. Alan;** Professor Emeritus, University of Exeter, 1959 (Professor, and Head Department of Geology, 1957-59); *b* 25 April 1894; *s* of James Anderson Stuart and Elizabeth (*née* Gladwell); *m* 1921, Ruth May Hugill; one *s* two *d. Educ:* Gateshead Secondary Sch.; Armstrong Coll. (now University of Newcastle upon Tyne). BSc Hons Geology, 1921; MSc 1923. Asst Lectr, Lectr and First Lectr, Dept of Geology, University Coll. of Swansea, 1921-47; Indep. Head of Dept of Geology, University Coll., Exeter, 1947-57. War Service: RAMC Dardanelles and Egypt, 1915-16; India, 1916-18; Indian Army, (TC), 2/27 Punjabis (Adjutant), Afghan War, 1919. Civil Defence, 1939-45; at University Coll., Swansea, during War, worked on crystallography of explosives for Ministry of Supply. *Publications:* (with N. H. Hartshorne): Crystals and the Polarising Microscope, 4th edn, 1970; Practical Optical Crystallography, 2nd edn 1969. Contribs to jls mainly concerned with sedimentary petrology and applications of microscopy to chemical problems. *Recreations:* photography, study of landscape, microscopy, problems of water supply. *Address:* Bridge House, Neopardy, Crediton, Devon. *T:* Crediton 2992.

**STUART, Alexander John Mackenzie,** QC (Scotland) 1963; *b* 18 Nov. 1924; *s* of late Prof. A. Mackenzie Stuart, KC, and Amy Margaret Dean, Aberdeen; *m* 1952, Anne Burtholme Millar, *d* of late J. S. L. Millar, WS, Edinburgh; four *d. Educ:* Fettes Coll., Edinburgh (open Schol.); Sidney Sussex Coll., Cambridge (schol. 1949, 1st cl. Pt II Law Tripos, BA 1949); Edinburgh Univ. (LLB (dist.) 1951). Royal Engineers (Temp. Capt. 1946), 1942-47. Admitted Faculty of Advocates, 1951; Standing Junior Counsel: to Scottish Home Dept, 1956-57; to Inland Revenue in Scotland, 1957-63. *Publications:* articles in legal publications. *Recreation:* collecting. *Address:* 7 Doune Terrace, Edinburgh. *T:* 031-225 1089. *Club:* New (Edinburgh).

**STUART, Sir Alexander M.;** *see* Moody-Stuart.

**STUART, Sir Campbell,** GCMG 1939; KBE 1918; one of HM's Lieutenants for the City of London. *Educ:* private schools; LLD College of William and Mary, Va, and Melbourne University. Represented HQ Staff of Canadian Army on visit to Ireland of the Duchess of Connaught's Own Irish Canadian Rangers, Jan. 1917, which batt. he recruited in the Province of Quebec for service in the European War (Lt-Col Canadian Army, despatches); Assistant Military Attaché, British Embassy, Washington, 1917; Military Secretary to the British War Mission to the United States of America, 1917; Vice-Chairman of the London Headquarters of the British War Mission to the USA 1918; Deputy Director of Propaganda in Enemy Countries, 1918; Managing Editor of the Daily Mail, 1921; represented The Times at the Imperial Press Conference Canada, 1920, London, 1930, and at Conference of Press Experts of the League of Nations, Geneva, 1927; Mem. Council of Empire Press Union, 1920-54; Representative of Govt of Canada on the Pacific Cable Board, 1923-28; Representative of the Government of

Canada at the Imperial Wireless and Cables Conference, 1928; Chairman: Quebec House Cttee, Westerham, 1926-50; Wolfe Memorial Cttee, Greenwich, 1930; Admiral Saunders Memorial Cttee, Westminster Abbey, 1930; Representative at different periods of Govts of Gt Britain, N Ireland, Canada, Australia and Southern Rhodesia on the Imperial Communications Advisory Committee; Chairman of the Imperial Communications Advisory Committee, and its successor, the Commonwealth Communications Council, 1933-45; Treasurer King George's Jubilee Trust, 1935-47; Chm. of the Commonwealth Telegraph Conference (Australia), 1942. Chairman Advisory Cttee of Ministry of Information, 1939; Director of Propaganda in Enemy Countries, 1939-40; Chm. and Treas. King George's Fields Foundation (National Memorial to King George V), 1936-54; Treas. Franklin Roosevelt Memorial Cttee, 1946-48; Vice-Pres. The Pilgrims (Chm. 1948-58); Chm. Beit Cttee for Scientific Research; Chm. Hudson's Bay Record Soc., 1938-59; Governor of Imperial College of Science and Technology. Dir of The Times, 1919-60 (Man. Dir, 1920-24); Director of Times Book Company, 1920-60. KStJ, 1951. *Publications:* Secrets of Crewe House (the official record of enemy propaganda in the War of 1914-18); Opportunity Knocks Once; Memorial to a King. *Recreation:* gardening. *Address:* 4 The Grove, Highgate Village, N6. *T:* 01-340 2266. *Clubs:* Brooks's, Pratt's; Century (New York).

**STUART, Charles Russell;** *b* 20 April 1895; *yr s* of late John David Stuart, advocate and solicitor, Straits Settlements; *m* 1925, Margaret, *e d* of Robert Vere Bogle, New South Wales; one *d*. *Educ:* Cranleigh School. Rifle Brigade, 1915-19 (despatches); Capt. 1917. Barrister-at-law, Gray's Inn, 1921; Advocate and Solicitor, Straits Settlements, 1922; Magistrate, Uganda, 1937; Chancellor, Diocese of Uganda, 1941-53; Puisne Judge, Nigeria, 1953-55; Judge of High Court, Western Region, Nigeria, 1955-57. *Address:* Hilltop, Windlesham, Surrey. *Club:* Royal Commonwealth Society.

**STUART, Rt. Rev. Cyril Edgar;** *s* of Canon E. A. Stuart, Canterbury, and Emily Ada Guy; *m* 1924, Mary Summerhayes; two *s*. *Educ:* Repton; St John's College, Cambridge; MA. Public School Brigade, 1914; 3rd N Staffs, 1915; Salonica, 1916-19; ordained as Curate of St Mary's, Hornsey Rise, 1920; Chaplain and Lecturer, Ridley Hall, Cambridge, 1921-24; Chaplain and Librarian Achimota College, Gold Coast, 1925-30; CMS Missionary, Uganda, 1931; Asst Bishop of Uganda, 1932-34; Bishop of Uganda, 1934-53; Assistant Bishop of Worcester and Rector of St Andrew's and All Saints with St Helen's, St Alban's and St Michael's, Worcester, 1953-56; Residentiary Canon of Worcester Cathedral, 1956-65. *Address:* Liberty Cottage, Gorran Haven, St Austell, Cornwall.

**STUART, Francis;** *b* Queensland, Australia, 1902; *s* of Henry and Elizabeth Stuart, Co. Antrim, Ireland; *m* 1st, 1920, Iseult Gonne; one *s* one *d*; 2nd, 1954, Gertrude Meiszner. *Educ:* Rugby. First book, poems, which received an American prize and also award of the Royal Irish Academy, published at age of twenty-one; first novel published in 1931 at age of 29; contributor to various newspapers and periodicals. *Publications: novels:* Women and God, 1930; Pigeon Irish, 1932; The Coloured Dome, 1933; Try the Sky, 1933; Glory, 1934; The Pillar of Cloud, 1948; Redemption, 1949; The Flowering Cross, 1950; Good Friday's Daughter, 1951; The Chariot, 1953; The Pilgrimage, 1955; Victors and Vanquished, 1958; Angels of Providence, 1959; We the Condemned, 1971; *poetry:* We Have Kept the Faith; *autobiography:* Things to Live For, 1936. *Recreations:* horse-racing, golf. *Address:* The Reask, Dunshaughlin, Co. Meath, Ireland.

**STUART, Hilda Violet;** Headmistress, Sherborne School for Girls, Dorset, 1930-Dec. 1949; Chairman of the Governors Foster School and Lord Digby's School, Sherborne, 1934; Central Council of School Broadcasting; Chairman English Sub-Committee, 1931; *b* Highbury, London; 4th *d* of late Canon E. A. Stuart, Canterbury. *Educ:* Notting Hill High School; Girton College, Cambridge. Assistant Classical Mistress St Leonards School, St Andrews, 1913; Assistant LCC Elementary Schools, 1917; Assistant, Darlington North Road Elementary School, 1918; Headmistress, Arthur Pease School, Darlington, 1919; Travelling scholarship, English-Speaking Union, 1925; Head of Classical Side, St Leonards School, St Andrews, 1926; Housemistress, St Leonards School, St Andrews, 1927. Retired, 1949. Nat. Council of Women: British Educational Rep., Internat. Council of Women, Athens, 1951, Montreal, 1957; Chm. Education Cttee, 1954-63; Vice-President, Women's Liberal Federation. Hon. Vice-Pres. Nat. Council of Women. *Address:* 23 Rusthall Avenue, Bedford Park, W4. *T:* 01-994 6749. *Clubs:* Oxford and Cambridge University, National Liberal.

**STUART, Malcolm Moncrieff,** CIE 1947; OBE 1944, ICS retired; Recorder to Council of Lord High Commissioners; *b* 21 May 1903; *s* of George Malcolm Stuart and Mary Elizabeth Scott Moncrieff; *m* 1928, Grizel Graham Balfour Paul; one *s* one *d*. *Educ:* Sedbergh; St John's College, Cambridge; Queen's Coll., Oxford. Entered ICS 1927; served as Dist Magistrate of various districts and was on special duty for Govt Estates, 1938; during War of 1939-45 was mostly Dist Magistrate of Chittagong and also Comr there. Served in Pakistan until 1950, as additional Member, Board of Revenue. *Publications:* Bob Potts at Murshedabad (Bengal Past and Present), 1933; Handbook to Bengal Records, 1948; and other stories. *Recreations:* golf, shooting, bridge. *Address:* Old Manse, Pilmuir, Haddington, East Lothian. *Clubs:* New (Edinburgh); Muirfield Golf.

**STUART, Sir Phillip (Luttrell),** 9th Bt *cr* 1660; late F/O RCAF; *b* 7 September 1937; *s* of late Luttrell Hamilton Stuart and late Irene Ethel Jackman; *S* uncle, Sir Houlton John Stuart, 8th Bt, 1959; *m* 1st, 1962, Marlene Rose Muth (marr. diss. 1968); two *d*; 2nd, 1969, Beverley Clare Pieri. *Educ:* Vancouver. Enlisted RCAF, Nov. 1955; commnd FO (1957-62). *Heir: kinsman* Arthur Ernest Stuart, *b* 1896. *Address:* 1401 Mars Drive, Winnipeg 19, Manitoba, Canada.

[*But his name does not, at the time of going to press, appear on the official Roll of Baronets.*

**STUART-CLARK, Arthur Campbell,** MA; Registrar, Huntingdon Research Centre, since 1970; *b* 23 Feb. 1906; *s* of late Canon Stuart H. Clark; *m* 1935, Peggy Annette, *o d* of A. Anthony; two *s*. *Educ:* Tonbridge School; Clare College, Cambridge. Assistant Master, Chillon College, Villeneuve (Vaud), Switzerland, 1927-31; Housemaster, Weymouth College, Dorset, 1931-37; Hon. Organising Sec. National Association of Boys' Clubs for Dorset, 1933-37; Headmaster, Steyning Grammar School, Steyning, Sussex, 1937-44; Headmaster of Brighton College, 1944-50; Senior Tutor, Hospital Administrative Staff Coll. (King Edward's

Hosp. Fund for London), 1950-63; Fellow and Bursar, Darwin Coll., Cambridge, 1964-69, Emeritus Fellow, 1970. Vice-Chm., Church of England Schools Council, 1946-51; Chairman: Wandsworth Hosp. Management Cttee, 1954-57; Papworth-Huntingdon Hosp. Management Cttee, 1967; Mem. E Anglian Regional Hosp. Bd, 1968. Citizen and Skinner. *Publication:* Administering the Hospital Group, 1956. *Recreations:* reading, gardening. *Address:* Riverside, Earith, Huntingdon. *T:* Earith 313; Huntingdon Research Centre, Huntingdon. *T:* Woolley 431. *Club:* Queen's.

**STUART-FORBES, Sir Charles Edward;** *see* Forbes.

**STUART-HARRIS, Sir Charles (Herbert),** Kt 1970; CBE 1961; MD; FRCP; Professor of Medicine, University of Sheffield and Physician United Sheffield Hospitals, since 1946; Member, Public Health Laboratory Service Board, since 1961; *b* 12 July 1909; *s* of late Dr and Mrs Herbert Harris, Birmingham; *m* 1937, Marjorie, *y d* of late Mr and Mrs F. Robinson, Dulwich; two *s* one *d*. *Educ:* King Edward's High School, Birmingham; St Bartholomew's Hospital Medical School. MB, BS London 1931 (Gold Medal); MD 1933 (Gold Medal); FRCP 1944. House-Physician and Demonstrator in Pathology, St Bartholomew's Hosp.; First Asst, Dept of Medicine, Brit. Postgrad. Medical Sch., 1935; Sir Henry Royce Research Fellow. Univ. of London, 1935; Foulerton Research Fellow, Royal Society, 1938. War Service, 1939-46; Specialist Pathologist Comdg Mobile Bacteriological, Command and Field Laboratories; Colonel RAMC, 1945; Goulstonian Lectr Royal College of Physicians, 1945; Visiting Prof. of Medicine, Albany Medical Coll., New York, 1953; Sir Arthur Sims Commonwealth Travelling Prof., 1962. Vis. Professor of Medicine: Vanderbilt Univ., Tennessee, 1961; Univ. of Southern California, Los Angeles, 1962; Croonian Lectr, Royal Coll. of Physicians, 1962; Henry Cohen Lectr, Hebrew Univ. of Jerusalem, 1966; Waring Prof., Univ. of Colorado and Stanford Univ., Calif., 1967. Member: MRC, 1957-61; UGC 1968-. Hon. Member: Assoc. of Amer. Physicians; Infectious Diseases Soc. of Amer. *Publications:* Influenza and other virus infections of the respiratory tract, 1965; (co-author) Virus and Rickettsial Diseases, 1967; (co-author) Chronic bronchitis emphysema and cor pulmonale, 1957; papers in med. and scientific jls on influenza, typhus and bronchitis. *Recreation:* music. *Address:* 28 Whitworth Road, Sheffield 10, Yorks. *T:* Sheffield 31200.

**STUART-MENTETH, Sir James;** *see* Menteth.

**STUART-SHAW, Max,** CBE 1963; Executive Director, Olympic Airways; *b* 20 Dec. 1912; *e s* of Hermon and Anne Louise Stuart-Shaw; *m* 1967, Janna Job. *Educ:* Belmont School, Sussex; St Paul's, London. Imperial Airways/BOAC, 1931-46; Aer Lingus Irish Airlines; Traffic Manager, Commercial Manager, Asst Gen. Manager, 1947-57; Chief Exec. and Gen. Manager, Central African Airways, Salisbury, Rhodesia, 1958-65; Man. Dir, BUA, 1966-67; Vice-Chairman, British United Airways, 1967-68. MInstT. *Recreations:* air transport, racing. *Address:* c/o Olympic Airways, Athens, Greece. *Clubs:* Royal Aero, Institute of Directors; Salisbury (Rhodesia).

**STUART-SMITH, Murray,** QC 1970; Barrister-at-Law; *b* 18 Nov. 1927; *s* of Edward Stuart-Smith and Doris Mary Laughland; *m* 1953, Joan Elizabeth Mary Motion, BA, JP; three *s* three *d*. *Educ:* Radley; Corpus Christi Coll., Cambridge (MA, LLB). Called to the Bar, Gray's Inn, 1952. *Recreations:* playing 'cello, shooting. *Address:* Serge Hill, Abbots Langley, Herts. *T:* Kings Langley 62116. *Club:* Bath.

**STUART TAYLOR, Sir Eric;** *see* Taylor.

**STUBBLEFIELD, Sir (Cyril) James,** Kt 1965; FRS 1944; FGS; FZS; DSc (London), ARCS; lately Director, Geological Survey of Great Britain and Museum of Practical Geology, 1960-66; Director, Geological Survey in Northern Ireland, 1960-66; *b* 6 Sept. 1901; *s* of late James Stubblefield; *m* 1932, Muriel Elizabeth, *d* of late L. R. Yakchee; two *s*. *Educ:* Perse Sch.; Chelsea Polytechnic; Royal College of Science, London (Royal Scholar); London Univ. Geology Scholar, 1921. Demonstrator in Geology, Imperial College of Science and Technology, 1923-28; first Warden of Imperial Coll. Hostel, 1926-28. Apptd Geological Survey as Geologist, 1928; Chief Palæontologist, 1947-53; Asst Director, 1953-60. Pres. Geological Soc. of London, 1958-60; Bigsby Medallist, 1941; Murchison Medallist, 1955. Sec. of Palæontographical Soc., 1934-48; Pres., 1966-. Member Council Brit. Assoc. for Advancement of Science, 1946-52, 1958-63; Pres. Section C (Geology), Oxford, 1954; Pres. Internat. Congress Carboniferous Stratigraphy and Geology, 6th Session, Sheffield, 1967. Vice-Pres. International Paleontological Union, 1948-56. Corresp. Paleont. Soc. (USA), 1950-; Corresp. Mem. Geol Soc. Stockholm, 1952-; Senckenbergische Naturforschende Gesellschaft, 1957-; Mem. Gov. Body, Chelsea Coll. of Science and Technology, 1958-; Mem. Council, Royal Soc., 1960-62. Hon. Fellow Pal. Soc. India, 1961-; Fellow Imperial Coll. of Science and Technology, 1962-; For. Corr. Geol Soc., France, 1963-, For. Vice-Pres., 1966. Hon. DSc Southampton, 1965. *Publications:* papers on Palæozoic fossils and rocks and contributions to Geological Survey Memoirs. Joint Editor of the Handbook of the Geology of Great Britain, 1929. *Address:* 35 Kent Avenue, Ealing, W13. *T:* 01-997 5051. *Club:* Athenæum.

**STUBBS, John F. A. H.;** *see* Heath-Stubbs.

**STUBBS, Stanley;** Headmaster, The Perse School, Cambridge, 1945-69; *b* 19 Feb. 1906; *o s* of late James Bloor Stubbs, Smallthorne, Stoke-on-Trent; *m* 1934, Margaret Eleanor, *er d* of late William Harley Grocott, Stoke-on-Trent; one *d*. *Educ:* Newcastle High School, Staffordshire; Emmanuel College, Cambridge. BA 2nd Cl. Hons Mod. and Med. Languages Tripos, 1933; MA 1937; Cambridge University Certificate in Education, 1934; Manager at Royal Doulton Potteries, Stoke-on-Trent, 1924-29; Assistant Master and Housemaster of Day Boys at Gresham's School, Holt, Norfolk, 1934-39; Headmaster, Soham Grammar School, Cambs, 1939-45; Officer Commanding ATC Squadron, 1941-45. *Recreations:* cricket, football, reading. College AFC Captain. *Address:* 264 Hills Road, Cambridge. *T:* Cambridge 48369. *Clubs:* Public Schools; Hawks (Cambridge).

**STUBBS, William Frederick,** CMG 1955; CBE 1952 (OBE 1941); HMOCS (Retired); *b* 19 June 1902; *e s* of late Lawrence Morley Stubbs, CSI, CIE, ICS (retd); *m* 1929, Eileen Mary (*d* 1963), *y d* of late Sir W. E. Stanford, KBE, CB, CMG, Rondebosch, S Africa; one *d*. *Educ:* Winchester. Joined British S Africa Police, S Rhodesia, 1921; N Rhodesia Police on transfer, 1924; Colonial Administrative Service, Northern Rhodesia, 1926; District Officer, 1928; District Comr of various districts; seconded to Labour Department, 1940; Labour Comr, 1944-48; Provincial Comr, 1949; acted as Secretary for Native Affairs, 1951 and 1953; Secretary for Native Affairs, 1954-57; *Ex-officio* member of Executive and Legislative Councils (Speaker, Legislative Council, and Chm. Public Service Commn Somaliland Protectorate, 1960, until Union with Somalia). Associate Commonwealth Parliamentary Association. *Recreations:* shooting and fishing. *Address:* Littleworth End, Benson, Oxon. *Club:* Royal Commonwealth Society.

**STUCLEY, Major Sir Dennis Frederic Bankes,** 5th Bt, *cr* 1859; DL; JP; *b* 29 Oct. 1907; *s* of Sir Hugh Nicholas Granville Stucley, 4th Bt, and Gladys (*d* 1950), *d* of W. A. Bankes, Wolfeton House, Dorchester; *S* father, 1956; *m* 1932, Hon. Sheila Bampfylde, *o d* of 4th Baron Poltimore; one *s* four *d* (and one *s* decd). *Educ:* Harrow; RMC Sandhurst. 2nd Lt Grenadier Guards, 1927; retired, 1932. Devon CC, 1934, CA, 1955. Capt. Royal Devon Yeomanry, 1937, Major, 1944. JP Devon, 1936; Deputy Lieutenant, Devon, 1955; Mayor of Bideford, 1954-56; High Sheriff of Devon, 1956, County Alderman, Devon, 1956. Joint Master, Dulverton Foxhounds, 1952-54. Chairman: SW Advisory Cttee, Forestry Commn, 1958; Timber Growers Organization, 1966-69; Exmoor Nat. Park (Devon) Cttee, 1968. *Recreations:* hunting, shooting and fishing. *Heir: s* Lieut Hugh George Coplestone Bampfylde Stucley, Royal Horse Guards [*b* 8 Jan. 1945; *m* 1969, Angela Caroline, *er d* of Richard Toller, Theale, Berks]. *Address:* Hartland Abbey, Bideford, Devon. *T:* Hartland 234; Affeton Castle, Crediton, Devon. *T:* Witheridge 225; 13 Kensington Gate, W8. *T:* 01-584 9063. *Clubs:* Guards, Turf, Beefsteak.
*See also Baron Cobbold.*

**STUDD, Sir Eric,** 2nd Bt, *cr* 1929; OBE 1946; formerly Senior Partner, J. Thomas & Co., Calcutta; *b* 10 June 1887; *e s* of Sir Kynaston Studd, 1st Bt, and Hilda (*d* 1921), *d* of Sir Thomas Beauchamp, 4th Bt; *S* father, 1944; *m* 1923, Stephana Langmead, *o d* of L. J. Langmead, London; three *s* one *d*. *Educ:* Winchester. Went to India, 1906; MLA, India, 1930-34; MLC, Bengal, 1936; MLA Bengal, 1937; retd from India, 1938. *Recreation:* shooting. *Heir: s* Robert Kynaston Studd, formerly Captain Coldstream Guards [*b* 9 July 1926; *m* 1958, Anastasia, *d* of Lt-Col Harold Leveson-Gower, The Green, Cotherstone, Barnard Castle; three *d*]. *Address:* Tenchleys Park, Limpsfield Common, Surrey. *T:* Limpsfield Chart 2208. *Club:* Oriental.

**STUDD, Brig. Malden Augustus,** DSO 1919; MC; Royal Tank Corps; *b* 29 Sept. 1887; *m* two *s* one *d*. Joined RA 1907; Captain, 1914; Major, 1917; Bt Lt-Col 1927; Lt-Col 1928; Col 1931; served European War (DSO; despatches); Assistant Director of Mechanisation War Office, 1932-36; Brigadier i/c Administration, Malaya, 1937-40; Commanded Salisbury Plain Area, 1940-42; ADC to King George VI, 1941-43; retired pay, 1943. *Address:* c/o National Westminster Bank, 1 Stratford Place, W1.
*See also Sir P. M. Studd.*

**STUDD, Sir Peter Malden,** Kt 1969; Lord Mayor of London for 1970-71; Director: De La Rue & Co. Ltd; Beaver Housing Society; *b* 15 Sept. 1916; *s* of Brig. Malden Augustus Studd, *qv*; *m* 1943, Angela Mary Hamilton (*née* Garnier); two *s*. *Educ:* Harrow; Clare Coll., Cambridge (MA). Served War of 1939-45: commnd into RA, 1939; served at War Office and in Middle East; Adjt, 153 (Leics Yeo.) Field Regt, Guards Armoured Div., European Campaign. Member, Merchant Taylors' Co. (Mem. Ct, 1959). Chm., Florence Nightingale Hosp., NW1; Governor: Lady Eleanor Holles Sch., Hampton; Polytechnic of Central London; Cripplegate Foundation. Hon. Liveryman, Worshipful Co. of Fruiterers. Surrey County Pres., St John Ambulance. City of London: Alderman, 1960; Sheriff, 1967-68. *Recreations:* gardening, fishing, sailing, golf. *Address:* Arbourne, Copsem Lane, Esher, Surrey. *T:* Esher 65252. *Clubs:* City Livery, MCC.

**STUDDERT, Ven. Augustine John de Clare,** MA; Archdeacon of Surrey, 1957-68, Archdeacon Emeritus since 1968; Rector of Busbridge, 1939-69; *b* 31 Jan. 1901; *s* of Thomas de Clare Studdert; *m* 1936, Marjorie Joyce Chettle; one *s*. *Educ:* Trinity Coll., Dublin. BA 1924, MA 1936. Curate of Glendermott, Londonderry, 1925-29; St Martin-in-the-Fields, London, 1929-32; Assistant Chaplain, British Embassy Church in Paris, 1932-34; Curate of Cranleigh, Surrey, 1934-39. Rural Dean of Godalming, 1950-57; Hon. Canon of Guildford Cathedral, 1956-57, 1968-69. Examining Chaplain to Bishop of Guildford, 1961-69. *Address:* Southlands, Churt Road, Hindhead, Surrey. *T:* Hindhead 20.

**STUDDY, Sir Henry,** Kt 1951; CBE 1947; KPM 1954; retired; *b* 20 April 1894; *e s* of late Major H. E. M. Studdy; *m* 1924, Marion Stonor, *o d* of H. T. S. Forrest, ICS; one *d*. *Educ:* St Paul's School, London. W Indian Police, 1914-35. Served European War, 1917-19, with Indian Cavalry, Capt. 1918 (despatches). Chief Constable: of Northumberland, 1935-43; of County Durham, 1943-44; of West Riding of Yorkshire, 1944-Oct. 1959. Mem. Police Recruiting Mission to Palestine, 1948; Mem. Advisory Council on the Treatment of Offenders, 1945-59; Mem. Board of Governors of Police College, 1948-59; Mem. Singapore Riots Inquiry Commn, 1951; Chm. Cyprus Police Commn, 1956. Vice-Pres. Royal Life Saving Society, 1956-, Dep. Grand Pres., 1968- (Dep. Pres., UK Branch, 1960, Pres., 1963-69); Member Road Research Board, 1959-63. Chairman, St Loye's College for Training and Rehabilitation of Disabled, 1963-69, Pres., 1969-. *Publication:* (ed jtly) A Police Constable's Guide to his Daily Work, 1961. *Recreation:* golf. *Address:* Little Westcott, Northview Road, Budleigh Salterton, Devon. *T:* Budleigh Salterton 3264. *Club:* Royal Automobile.

**STUDHOLME, Sir Henry (Gray),** 1st Bt, *cr* 1956; CVO 1953; DL; *b* 13 June 1899; *s* of late William Paul Studholme, Perridge House, Exeter; *m* 1929, Judith, *d* of Henry William Whitbread, Norton Bavant Manor, Warminster; two *s* one *d*. *Educ:* Eton; Magdalen Coll., Oxford (MA). Served European War with Scots Guards, 1917-19; Member LCC, 1931-45; rejoined Scots Guards, 1940; Staff appointments, 1941-44. MP (C) Tavistock Division, 1942-66. PPS to late Comdr R. Brabner, Under-Sec. of State for Air, Nov. 1944-March 1945; Conservative Whip, 1945-56; Joint Treas. of the Conservative Party, 1956-62. Vice-Chamberlain of King George VI's Household, 1951-52, of the Queen's Household, 1952-56. DL Devon, 1969. *Heir: s* Paul Henry William Studholme, late Capt. Coldstream Guards [*b* 16 Jan. 1930; *m* 1957, Virginia Katherine, *yr d* of late Sir Richmond Palmer, KCMG; two *s* one *d*]. *Address:* Wembury House, Wembury, Plymouth. *T:* Wembury 210. *Club:* Carlton.

**STURDEE, Rear-Adm. Arthur Rodney Barry,** DSC 1945; Flag-Officer, Gibraltar, since 1969; *b* 6 Dec. 1919, *s* of Comdr Barry V. Sturdee, RN, and Barbara (*née* Sturdee); *m* 1953,

Marie-Claire Amstoutz, Mulhouse, France; one *s* one *d. Educ:* Canford Sch. Entered Royal Navy as Special Entry Cadet, 1937. Served War of 1939-45: Midshipman in HMS Exeter at Battle of the River Plate, 1939; Lieut, 1941; specialised in Navigation, 1944; minesweeping in Mediterranean, 1944-45 (DSC). Lt-Comdr, 1949; RN Staff Coll., 1950-51; Staff of Navigation Sch., 1951-52; Comdr, 1952; JSSC, 1953; BJSM, Washington, 1953-55; Fleet Navigating Officer, Medit., 1955-57; Exec. Officer, RNAS, Culdrose, 1958-59; Captain 1960; NATO Defence Coll., 1960-63; Queen's Harbour-Master, Singapore, 1963-65; Staff of Chief of Defence Staff, 1965-67; Chief of Staff to C-in-C, Portsmouth (as Cdre), 1967-69; Rear-Adm. 1969. *Address:* The Mount, Gibraltar. *Club:* United Service.

**STURDEE, Rear-Admiral Sir Lionel (Arthur Doveton),** 2nd Bt, *cr* 1916, of the Falkland Isles; CBE 1946; *b* 3 Sept. 1884; *o s* of Admiral of the Fleet Sir Doveton Sturdee, GCB, KCMG, CVO, LLD, 1st Bt, and Marion Adela, *d* of W. J. Andrews; *S* father 1925; *m* 1910, Dorothy Mary Mowbray (*d* 1966), *d* of W. F. Sayer; one *d. Educ:* Stanmore Park; HMS Britannia. Lieut RN 1906; Lt-Comdr 1914; Comdr 1919; Captain, 1926; Rear-Admiral, 1938; served European War, 1914-19; in command of HM Ships Forth and Hazard of Dover Patrol (was present in latter when HM Hospital Ship Anglia was mined, and received thanks of Army Council for saving life) and later in Grand Fleet; comd HM Ships Calliope, Assistance and Defiance, 1927-32; Flag Captain and Chief Staff Officer, Malta, 1932-34 (Member of Governor's Nominated Council, 1933-34); commanded HM Ships Dauntless, 1936, and Resolution, in Home Fleet, 1936-38; Naval ADC to King, 1936-38; retired, 1938; Hon. Wing Comdr, General Duties Branch and Commandant, RAFVR Cambridge District, 1939; Rear-Admiral (retired) HMS President for special service under the War Office and later under the Ministry of Information as Chief Telecommunications Censor, 1940-45. King Haakon VII Liberty Cross (Norway), 1947. *Heir:* none. *Address:* Brendon Park Road, Winchester, Hants. *T:* Winchester 4731. *Clubs:* United Service; Hampshire (Winchester).
*See also Vice-Adm. E. B. Ashmore.*

**STURGE, Arthur Collwyn,** MC 1945; a Deputy Chairman of Lloyd's, 1969, 1970; *b* 27 Sept. 1912; *yr s* of Arthur Lloyd Sturge and Jessie Katherine Howard; *m* 1938, Beryl Gwenllian, *yr d* of Thomas Arthur, Hong Kong; two *s* two *d. Educ:* Harrow; Brasenose Coll., Oxford (BA). Member of Lloyd's, 1933; elected to Cttee of Lloyd's, 1967. Partner, R. W. Sturge & Co. Commissioned 64 Field Regt RA (TA), 1937; served War of 1939-45, Middle East, Italy. *Recreations:* golf, shooting. *Address:* 38 Lennox Gardens, SW1; Faircrouch, Wadhurst, Sussex. *T:* Wadhurst 2281. *Clubs:* City of London; Rye Golf.
*See also R. W. Sturge.*

**STURGE, Harold Francis Ralph;** Metropolitan Magistrate, 1947-68; *b* 15 May 1902; *y s* of Ernest Harold Sturge; *m* 1936, Doreen, *e d* of Sir Percy Greenaway, 1st Bt; two *s* (and one *s* decd). *Educ:* Highgate Sch.; Oriel Coll., Oxford. Called to Bar, Inner Temple, 1925; Midland Circuit. War of 1939-45, served on staff of Judge Advocate-General. Member Departmental Cttee on the Probation Service, 1959; President, Old Cholmelian Society, 1962-63. *Publications:* The Road Haulage Wages Act, 1938; (jointly with T. D. Corpe, OBE) Road Haulage Law and Compensation, 1947. *Recreation:* painting. *Address:* Burdore, 85 Woodlands Road, Surbiton, Surrey. *Club:* Royal Automobile.

**STURGE, Raymond Wilson;** Chairman of Lloyd's, 1964, 1965 and 1966; *b* 10 June 1904; *er s* of late Arthur Lloyd Sturge and late Jessie Katharine (*née* Howard); *m* 1929, Margaret, *y d* of late Walter J. Keep, Sydney, NSW; one *s* four *d. Educ:* Harrow; Brasenose Coll., Oxford (BA). Mem. of Lloyd's, 1926; first elected to Committee, 1953; Dep. Chm., 1963. Served War of 1939-45, Royal Scots Fusiliers, Staff Duties. Pres., Insurance Institute of London, 1967-68 (Dep. Pres., 1966-67). Hon. Treas., King George's Fund for Sailors. *Address:* Ashmore, near Salisbury, Wilts. *T:* Fontmell Magna 261. *Clubs:* Brooks's, City of London.
*See also A. C. Sturge.*

**STUTTAFORD, Dr Thomas;** MP (C) Norwich (South), since 1970; medical practitioner; *b* 4 May 1931; 2nd *s* of late Dr W. J. E. Stuttaford, MC, Horning, Norfolk; *m* 1957, Pamela, *d* of Col Richard Ropner, TD, DL, Tain; three *s. Educ:* Gresham's Sch.; Brasenose Coll., Oxford; West London Hosp. 2nd Lieut, 10th Royal Hussars (PWO), 1953-55; Lieut, Scottish Horse (TA), 1955-59. Qualif. MRCS, LRCP, 1959; junior hosp. appts, 1959 and 1960. Gen. Med. practice, 1960-70. Mem. Blofield and Flegg RDC, 1964-66; Mem., Norwich City Council, 1969-. *Recreations:* country life, collecting the work of East Anglian Artists. *Address:* Bramerton House, Bramerton, Norwich. *T:* Surlingham 261. *Clubs:* Cavalry; Norfolk (Norwich).

**STYLE, Sir William Montague,** 12th Bt, *cr* 1627; *b* 21 July 1916; *s* of Sir William Frederick Style, 11th Bt, and Florence (*d* 1918), *d* of J. Timm; *S* father, 1943; *m* 1941, La Verne, *d* of T. M. Comstock; two *s. Heir: s* William Frederick Style, *b* 13 May 1945. *Address:* 9516 Harding Boulevard, Wauwatosa 13, Wisconsin, USA.

**SUÁREZ, Dr Eduardo;** Mexican Ambassador to Great Britain 1965-70; *b* Texcoco, Mexico, 3 Jan. 1895; *s* of Eduardo Suárez and Antonia Aránsolo de Suárez; *m* 1935, Maria de la Luz Dávila; four *s* one *d.* (and one *s* decd). *Educ:* Col. Municipal, Texcoco; Col. Inglés, Tacubaya; Nat. Univ. of Mexico. Supt Under Sec., State of Hidalgo; Pres., Central Conciliation and Arbitration Bd of City of Mexico; Prof. of Jurisprudence, Nat. Univ. of Mexico, at different times, 1916-48. Counsel for Mexico, in Claims between: Mexico and the US, June 1926-Aug. 1927; Mexico and Gt Britain, Aug.-Dec. 1928; Member, Arbitration Tribunal between Mexico and France. Head of Legal Dept, Min. of For. Affairs, 1929-31, 1931-34, Jan.-June 1935; Minister of Finance and Public Credit, 1935-46. Dr (*hc*); holds foreign decorations. *Publications:* pamphlets, articles. *Clubs:* White's, St James', Clermont; Club de Banqueros (Mexico).

**SUAREZ, Juan L.;** *see* Lechin-Suarez.

**SUBAK-SHARPE, Prof. John Herbert;** FRSE 1970; Professor of Virology, University of Glasgow, since 1968; Hon. Director, Medical Research Council Virology Unit, since 1968; *b* 14 Feb. 1924; *s* of late Robert Subak and late Nelly (*née* Bruell), Vienna, Austria; *m* 1953, Barbara Naomi Morris; two *s* one *d. Educ:* Humanistic Gymnasium, Vienna; Univ. of Birmingham. BSc (Genetics) (1st Cl. Hons) 1952; PhD 1956. Refugee from Nazi oppression, 1939; farm pupil, 1939-44; HM Forces (Parachute Regt), 1944-47. Asst Lectr in Genetics, Glasgow Univ., 1954-56; Mem. scientific staff, ARC Animal Virus Research Inst., Pirbright, 1956-60; Nat. Foundn Fellow, California Inst. of Technology, 1961; Mem.

Scientific staff of MRC, in Experimental Virus Research Unit, Glasgow, 1961-68. Vis. Prof., US Nat. Insts of Health, Bethesda, Md, 1967; Sec., Genetical Soc., 1966-. Member: European Molecular Biology Orgn, 1969-; British Nat. Cttee of Biophysics, 1970-. *Publications:* articles in scientific jls on genetic studies with viruses and cells. *Recreations:* mountain walking and bridge. *Address:* 17 Kingsborough Gardens, Glasgow, W2. *T:* 041-334 1863.

**SUCKSMITH, W.,** FRS 1940; DSc Leeds; Professor of Physics, Sheffield University, 1940-63, Emeritus since 1963. Formerly Reader in Magnetism, Bristol University. *Address:* 27 Endcliffe Grove Avenue, Sheffield 10.

**SUDAN, Bishop in the,** since 1953; **Rt. Rev. Oliver Claude Allison;** *b* Stafford, 1908; *s* of Rev. W. S. Allison. *Educ:* Dean Close School, Cheltenham; Queen's College and Ridley Hall, Cambridge. BA 1930, MA 1934, Deacon, 1932; Priest, 1933; Curate of Fulwood, 1932-36; of St John, Boscombe, and Jt Sec. Win. Dioc. Council of Youth, 1936-38; CMS Miss. at Juba, Dio. Sudan, 1938-47; Asst Bp in the Sudan, 1948-53. *Address:* The Clergy House, PO Box 135, Khartoum, Sudan.

**SUDBURY, Col Frederick Arthur,** OBE 1942; ERD 1951; JP; Managing Director, Shipping, Chartering and Lighterage Companies of Tate & Lyle Group, 1951-69; *b* 14 Sept. 1904; *m* 1929, Florence Joan Egan (marr. diss. 1951); one *s* two *d*; *m* 1952, Pauline Adela, *d* of late Walter Widdop, Halifax, Yorks. *Educ:* Colfe Grammar School, Lewisham; London School of Economics. Joined Tate & Lyle, 1925. Served War of 1939-45, Army Officers Emergency Reserve; Col, Dir of Inland Water Transport, Iraq, 1941-43; Col, Movements and Transportation, 14th Army, 1944-45; Lt-Col Supplementary Reserve, 1947-51; Col, Army Emergency Reserve, 1951-62; Hon. Col., RE (AER), 1951-66. Mem. Thames Conservancy, 1958-65 (Vice-Chm., 1960-65). Underwriting Mem. of Lloyd's. Liveryman and Mem. Court Shipwrights' Co.; Freeman and Mem. Court, Co. of Watermen and Lightermen (Master, 1960-61-62). JP County of London, 1962-. *Recreation:* yachting. *Address:* 1 Abbotsbury Close, W14. *T:* 01-603 2880. *Clubs:* Royal Thames Yacht, City Livery.

**SUDDABY, Arthur,** PhD, MSc, ARIC, AMIChemE; Provost, City of London Polytechnic, since 1970; *b* 26 Feb. 1919; *e s* of George Suddaby, Kingston-upon-Hull, Yorks; *m* 1944, Elizabeth Bullin Vyse (decd), *d* of Charles Vyse; two *s*. *Educ:* Riley High Sch., Kingston-upon-Hull; Hull Technical Coll.; Chelsea Polytechnic; Queen Mary Coll. London. Chemist and Chemical Engr, in industry, 1937-47; Lectr in Physical Chemistry, and later Sen. Lectr in Chem. Engrg, West Ham Coll. of Technology, 1947-50; Sir John Cass Coll.: Sen. Lectr in Physics, 1950-61; Head of Dept of Physics, 1961-66; Principal, 1966-70. Member: Chem. Engrg Cttee, London and Home Counties Regional Adv. Council, 1948-51; Bd of Examrs and Educn Cttee, Inst. of Chem. Engrs, 1948-51; CNAA Chem. Engrg Bd, 1969-; Exec. Cttee of Assoc. of Navigation Schs, 1969-; Court of the City University, 1967-. Scientific consultant on physical and chemical problems of carriage of goods by sea, 1955-; Editorial consultant to Chemical Processing, 1955-. *Publications:* various original research papers in theoretical physics, in scientific jls; review articles. *Recreation:* hunting. *Address:* Flat 3, 16 Elm Park Gardens, Chelsea, SW10. *T:* 01-352 9164; Bothkerran House, Dengie, Essex. *T:* Tillingham 340.

**SUDDARDS, (Henry) Gaunt; His Honour Judge Suddards;** Judge of County Courts, since 1963; Deputy Chairman, West Riding Quarter Sessions, since 1961; *b* 30 July 1910; *s* of Fred Suddards and Agnes Suddards (*née* Gaunt); unmarried. *Educ:* Cheltenham College; Trinity College, Cambridge (MA). Barrister, Inner Temple, 1932; joined NE Circuit, 1933. Served War of 1939-45, RAFVR, 1940-46. Recorder of Pontefract, 1960-61; Recorder of Middlesbrough, 1961-63; Chairman, Agricultural Land Tribunal, Northern Area, 1961-63, Dep. Chairman 1960. *Recreations:* fishing, shooting, sailing. *Address:* Rockville, Frizinghall, Shipley, Yorkshire. *Clubs:* Royal Automobile; Union (Bradford).

**SUDELEY,** 7th Baron *cr* 1838; **Merlin Charles Sainthill Hanbury-Tracy,** *b* 17 June 1939; *o c* of late Captain Michael David Charles Hanbury-Tracy, Scots Guards, and Colline Ammabel, *d* of late Lt-Col C. G. H. St Hill and *widow* of Lt-Col Frank King, DSO, OBE; *S* cousin, 1941. *Educ:* at Eton and in the ranks of the Scots Guards. *Publications:* contribs to Quarterly Review and trans of Bristol and Gloucestershire Archaeol. Soc. *Recreations:* Ancestor worship; cultivating his sensibility. *Heir:* *u* (Ninian) John Frederick Hanbury-Tracy [*b* 7 Dec. 1910; *m* 1st, 1935, Hon. Blanche Mary (marr. diss., 1954), *er d* of 15th Baron Arundell of Wardour; one *d*; 2nd, 1954, Daphne, *d* of late Col Vivian Henry, CB]. *Address:* c/o The National Bank Ltd, 21 Grosvenor Gardens, SW1. *Club:* Brooks's.

**SUDLEY, Viscount; Arthur Desmond Colquhoun Gore;** *b* 14 July 1938; *e s* of 8th Earl of Arran, *qv*. *Educ:* Eton; Balliol College, Oxford. 2nd Lieutenant, 1st Bn Grenadier Guards (National Service). *Recreations:* tennis, shooting, fruit-picking, bird-watching. *Address:* Pimlico House, Hemel Hempstead, Herts. *T:* Kings Langley 2240. *Club:* Turf.

**SUENSON-TAYLOR,** family name of **Baron Grantchester.**

**SUFFIELD,** 11th Baron *cr* 1786; **Anthony Philip Harbord-Hamond,** Bt, *cr* 1745; MC 1950; Major, retired, 1961; *b* 19 June 1922; *o s* of 10th Baron and Nina Annette Mary Crawfuird (*d* 1955), *e d* of John Hutchison of Laurieston and Edingham, Stewartry of Kirkcudbright; *S* father 1951; *m* 1952, Elizabeth Eve, *er d* of late Judge Edgedale; three *s* one *d*. *Educ:* Eton. Commission, Coldstream Guards, 1942; served War of 1939-45, in North African and Italian campaigns, 1942-45; Malaya, 1948-50. Officer of the Order of Orange Nassau, 1950. *Recreations:* normal. *Heir:* *s* Hon. Charles Anthony Assheton Harbord-Hamond, *b* 3 Dec. 1953. *Address:* Langham Lodge, Holt, Norfolk. *T:* Binham 373. *Club:* Guards.

**SUFFIELD, (Henry John) Lester;** Head of Defence Sales, Ministry of Defence/Ministry of Technology, since 1969; *b* 28 April 1911; *m* 1940, Elizabeth Mary White; one *s* one *d*. *Educ:* Camberwell Central, LCC. Served with RASC, 1939-45 (Major). LNER, 1926-35; Morris Motors, 1935-38 and 1945-52; Pres., British Motor Corp., Canada and USA, 1952-64; Dep. Man. and Dir, British Motor Corp., Birmingham, 1964-68; Sales Dir, British Leyland Motor Corp., 1968-69. *Recreation:* golf. *Address:* 38 Maitland Court, Hyde Park, W2. *T:* 01-723 0892. *Club:* Royal Automobile.

**SUFFOLK and BERKSHIRE,** 21st Earl of, *cr* 1603; **Michael John James George Robert Howard;** Viscount Andover and Baron

Howard, 1622; Earl of Berkshire, 1626; *b* 27 March 1935; *s* of 20th Earl (killed by enemy action, 1941) and Mimi (*d* 1966), *yr d* of late A. G. Forde Pigott; *S* father 1941; *m* 1960, Mme Simone Paulmier (marr. diss. 1967), *d* of late Georges Litman, Paris; one *d* (decd). Owns 10,000 acres, celebrated picture-gallery and well-known collection of Old Masters. *Heir: b* Hon. Maurice David Henry Howard, *b* 1936. *Address:* Charlton Park, Malmesbury, Wilts.
*See also Hon. G. R. Howard.*

**SUFFOLK, Archdeacon of;** *see* Scott, Ven. Claud Syms.

**SUGDEN,** family name of **Baron St Leonards.**

**SUGDEN, Maj.-Gen. Sir Henry (Haskins Clapham),** KBE 1960 (CBE 1945; OBE 1941); CB 1954; DSO 1943; Member, House of Keys; *b* 15 April 1904; *s* of Dr H. C. Sugden, West House, Ramsey, IOM; *m* 1934, Joan Morgan, *d* of J. M. R. Francis, The Firs, Kingston-on-Thames; two *s*. *Educ:* King William's College, Isle of Man; RMA Woolwich. Commissioned in Royal Engineers, 1924; Captain, 1935. Served War of 1939-45 (despatches twice); Major 1940; Temp. Lt-Col 1941; Temp. Brig. 1943; Col 1948; Temp. Major-General, 1952; Major-General, 1953. Col Comdt RE, 1961-69. Engineer-in-Chief, War Office, 1957-60, retd. Mem., House of Keys, IoM, 1962-. Grand Officer, Order of Orange Nassau, Holland. FICE. *Recreations:* sailing, shooting, gardening. *Address:* River House, Ramsey, Isle of Man. *T:* 2260. *Club:* Naval and Military.

**SUGDEN, John Goldthorp,** MA; ARCM; Headmaster, Wellingborough School, since 1965; *b* 22 July 1921; *s* of A. G. Sugden, Brighouse, Yorkshire; *m* 1954, Jane Machin; two *s*. *Educ:* Radley; Magdalene College, Cambridge. War Service, Royal Signals, 1941-46. Asst Master, Bilton Grange Prep. School, 1948-52; Asst Master, The King's School, Canterbury, 1952-59; Headmaster, Foster's School, Sherborne, 1959-64. *Recreations:* music, golf, tennis. *Address:* The School, Wellingborough, Northants.

**SUGDEN, Group Capt. Ronald Scott,** CBE 1945; AFC 1918; DL; *b* 25 May 1896; *s* of Edward Scott Sugden, MD, Aintree, Liverpool; *m* 1928, Helen Mary, *d* of William Henry Brain, Cwrt-yr-Ala, Nr Cardiff; one *d*. *Educ:* Eastmans, Southsea; RN Colleges, Osborne and Dartmouth. Royal Navy 1909-19 (despatches); attached RNAS, 1915-18; transferred to RAF on its formation; retd as Group Capt., 1946. Served in Iraq, 1925-27 (medal); Palestine, 1936 (medal); War of 1939-45 (despatches). ADC to Governor of Trinidad and Tobago, 1920-21. High Sheriff of Glamorgan, 1957; DL Glamorgan, 1958. *Recreations:* golf, shooting, fishing, racing, bowls. *Address:* Merevale, Dinas Powis, Glam. *T:* Dinas Powis 2106. *Club:* Army and Navy.

**SUGDEN, Theodore Morris,** MA, ScD; FRS 1963; Director, Thornton Research Centre, Shell Research Ltd, Chester, since 1967; Associate Professor in Molecular Sciences, University of Warwick, since 1965; *b* 31 December 1919; *s* of Frederick Morris Sugden and Florence Sugden (*née* Chadwick); *m* 1945, Marian Florence Cotton; one *s*. *Educ:* Sowerby Bridge Grammar School; Jesus College, Cambridge. Stokes Student, Pembroke Coll., Cambridge, 1945-46; H. O. Jones Lecturer in Physical Chemistry, Univ. of Cambridge, 1950-60; Reader in Physical Chemistry, Univ. of Cambridge, 1960-63; Fell. Queen's Coll., Cambridge, 1957-63. Hon. DTech Univ. of Bradford, 1967. Medallist of the Combustion Inst., 1960. *Publications:* (with C. N. Kenney) Microwave Spectroscopy of Gases, 1965; articles in Proc. Roy. Soc., Transactions of Faraday Soc., Nature, etc. *Recreations:* pianoforte, film, travel, talk. *Address:* The Tithe Barn, Great Barrow, Tarvin, Cheshire. *Club:* Savage.

**SUGERMAN, Hon. Sir Bernard,** Kt 1970; President, Court of Appeal, Supreme Court of New South Wales, since 1970; *b* 5 July 1904; *s* of Solomon Reuben Sugerman and Florence Sugerman; *m* 1928, Sarah Rosenblum; two *s*. *Educ:* Sydney High Sch.; Univ. of Sydney. Admitted to Bar, 1926; Lecturer in Law, Univ. of Sydney, 1926-43; KC 1943; Judge: Commonwealth Court of Conciliation and Arbitration, 1946-47; Land and Valuation Court, 1947-61; Supreme Court of New South Wales, 1947-; Judge of Appeal, 1966-70. *Publications:* The Australian Digest (ed), 1934-46; The Australian Law Journal (ed), 1927-46; Commonwealth Law Reports (ed), 1941-46; numerous articles in legal periodicals. *Recreations:* bowls, reading. *Address:* 9 Yamba Road, Bellevue Hill, Sydney, NSW 2023, Australia. *T:* 36-3175. *Club:* University (Sydney).

**SUGG, Aldhelm St John,** CMG 1963; retired as Provincial Commissioner, Southern Provinces of Northern Rhodesia, Aug. 1963; *b* 21 Oct. 1909; *s* of H. G. St J. Sugg; *m* 1935, Jessie May Parker; one *s* one *d*. *Educ:* Colchester Royal Grammar School. Palestine Police, 1930-31; Northern Rhodesia Police, 1932-43; Colonial Administrative Service, in N Rhodesia, 1943-63. Retired to England, 1963. *Recreations:* sailing, field sports, tennis. *Address:* Bushbury, Blackboys, Uckfield, Sussex. *T:* Framfield 282. *Club:* Royal Commonwealth.

**SUIRDALE, Viscount; Richard Michael John Hely-Hutchinson;** *b* 8 Aug. 1927; *er s* of 7th Earl of Donoughmore, *qv*; *m* 1951, Sheila, *o c* of late Frank Frederick Parsons, and of Mrs John McCulloch; four *s*. *Educ:* Winchester; New College, Oxford (MA; BM, ChB). Employed W. R. Grace & Co. *Heir: s* Hon. John Michael James Hely-Hutchinson, *b* 7 Aug. 1952. *Clubs:* MCC, Hurlingham; Vincent's (Oxford).

**SUKET, Major HH Bharat Dharam Bhushan Raja Lakshman Sen Bahadur, Raja of;** *b* 1894; *m* 1917; five *s* two *d*; crowned 1919. *Educ:* Lahore Aitchison Chiefs College. Belongs to Rajput family of the Chandravanshi race and Sena Dynasty of Nadiya Gaur Bengal. The State has an area of 420 square miles and a population of 80,000, the Ruling Prince's salute being 11 guns; past Mem. the Chamber of Princes; State merged in Himachal Pradesh (India), 1948. Has received many medals, FRGS; MRAS. *Publication:* Shiv Swarodaya (in Hindi), 1955 (a Science of Inhaling). *Recreations:* tennis and cricket. *Heir:* Yuvraj Lalit Sen Bahadur, MA [*b* 21 April 1932; *m* 1950, *d* of HH Maharawal Dungarpur, *qv*; one *s*, (*b* 10 Aug. 1955); one *d*]. *Address:* Rangmahal, Sundarnagar, Himachal Pradesh, India.

**SULLIVAN, Albert Patrick Loisol,** CBE 1944 (MBE 1941); MM; MIFireE; *b* 19 October 1898; *s* of late William Sullivan, Cobh, Eire; *m* 1st, 1920, Margaret Elizabeth Mary Andrews (*d* 1951); one *s*; 2nd, 1964, Rose Mabel, *d* of late Richard John Dance. Served European War (France), 1915-19. London Fire Brigade 1919-41; Chief Supt LFB 1940-41; Deputy Chief of Fire Staff, National Fire Service, 1941-47; Chief of Fire Staff and Inspector in Chief, NFS, Mar.-Nov. 1947; Chief Fire Officer to the Ministry of Civil Aviation, 1948-50. President Institution of Fire Engineers, 1946-47; OStJ; King's Police and Fire Services

Medal, 1948. *Address:* 9 Lake Close, Wimbledon, SW19. *T:* 01-946 6271. *Club:* Royal Over-Seas League.

**SULLIVAN, Prof. (Donovan) Michael;** Professor of Oriental Art, Stanford University, California, since 1966; *b* 29 Oct. 1916; *s* of Alan Sullivan and Elisabeth Hees; *m* 1943, Khoan, *d* of Ngo Eng-lim, Kulangsu, Amoy, China; no *c*. *Educ:* Rugby School; Corpus Christi College, Cambridge (MA); Univ. of London (BA Hons); Harvard Univ. (PhD); LittD Cambridge, 1966. Chinese Govt Scholarship, Univ. of London, 1947-50; Rockefeller Foundn Travelling Fellowship in USA, 1950-51; Bollingen Foundn Research Fellowship, 1952-54; Curator of Art Museum and Lectr in the History of Art, Univ. of Malaya (now Univ. of Singapore), Singapore, 1954-60; Lectr in Asian Art, Sch. of Oriental and African Studies, Univ. of London, 1960-66. Vis. Prof. of Far Eastern Art, Univ. of Michigan (Spring Semester), 1964. *Publications:* Chinese Art in the Twentieth Century, 1959; A Introduction to Chinese Art, 1961; The Birth of Landscape Painting in China, 1962; Chinese Ceramics, Bronzes and Jades in the Collection of Sir Alan and Lady Barlow, 1963; Chinese and Japanese Art, 1965; A Short History of Chinese Art, 1968; The Cave Temples of Maichishan, 1969; contrib. to Apollo, Artibus Asiæ, Archives of Ancient Art, Art Bulletin, Harvard Jl of Asiatic Studies, Trans. of Oriental Ceramic Soc., Chambers's Encyclopædia. *Address:* Department of Art, Stanford University, Stanford, Calif 94305, USA. *Club:* Athenæum.

**SULLIVAN, Very Rev. Martin Gloster;** Dean of St Paul's since 1967; Dean of the Order of the British Empire since 1967, of the Order of St Michael and St George since 1968; *b* Auckland, 30 March 1910; *s* of Denis Sullivan; *m* 1934, Doris, *d* of Canon C. H. Grant Cowen. *Educ:* Auckland Grammar School; St John's (Theological) College, Auckland University College. MA (NZ). Deacon 1932; Priest 1934; Asst Curate, St Matthew's, Auckland, 1932; Vicar, St Columba, Grey Lynn, 1934; Te Awamutu, 1936-46; Exam. Chap. to Bp of Waikato, 1937-46; on staff, St Martin-in-the-Fields, London, 1945-46; Chaplain to SCM Wellington, 1946-49; CF, 1941-46; Principal, College House, Christchurch, 1950-58; Dean of Christchurch, 1951-62; Vicar-General, 1952-62. Commissary to Bp of Christchurch, 1962. Council of Univ. of Canterbury, 1953-62; Senate of Univ. of NZ, 1961-62; Court of Directors, Royal Humane Soc. of NZ, 1956-62; Rep. of Vice-Chancellor of Univ. of Canterbury on Assoc. of Univs of Brit. Commonwealth, 1962. Archdeacon of London and Canon Residentiary of St Paul's, 1963-67. Member Central Council, Royal Over-Seas League; Mem., Guild of Freemen of City of London. Hon. DLitt, 1970. Chaplain and Sub-Prelate, Order of St John, 1968. *Publications:* Children Listen, 1955; Listen Again, 1956; A Word for Everyman, 1956; Draw Near with Faith, 1956; On Calvary's Tree, 1957; Approach With Joy, 1961; A Dean Speaks to New Zealand, 1962; A Funny Thing Happened to me on the way to St Paul's, 1968. *Recreations:* reading, theatre. *Address:* The Deanery, St Paul's, EC4. *T:* 01-248 4227. *Club:* Travellers'.

**SULLIVAN, Prof. Michael;** *see* Sullivan, D. M.

**SULLIVAN, Sir Richard (Benjamin Magniac),** 8th Bt, *cr* 1804; *b* 26 Oct. 1906; *s* of Capt. Richard Sullivan, RN (*d* 1928; 2nd *s* of 6th Bt) and Beatrix Evelyn (*d* 1936), *d* of Arthur Magniac, The Hermitage, Ascot; *S* uncle (Rev. Sir Frederick Sullivan, 7th Bt) 1954; *m* 1928, Muriel Mary Paget, *y d* of Francis Charles Trayler Pineo; two *s*. *Educ:* St Andrew's Coll., Grahamstown, South Africa. Colonial Administrative Service; Bechuanaland and Nigeria; retired 1957. *Heir: s* Richard Arthur Sullivan, BSc (Univ. Cape Town), SM (Mass. Inst. Tech.) [*b* 9 Aug. 1931; *m* 1962, Elenor Mary, *e d* of K. M. Thorpe; one *s* two *d*]. *Address:* PO Ruwa, Rhodesia. *T:* Salisbury 2640320. *Clubs:* Royal Commonwealth Society; Salisbury (Rhodesia).

**SULLIVAN, Sir William (John),** KBE 1956 (CBE 1938); CMG 1950; HM Foreign Service, retired; *b* London, 11 Oct. 1895; *o s* of late William Charles Sullivan, MD (RUI); *m* 1922, Catherine Mary (*d* 1963), *y d* of late Hugo Meynell; one *s*. *Educ:* St Augustine's College, Ramsgate; St Paul's School; Trinity College, Dublin (BA). Served in European War, 1915-16 (invalided); Administrative Officer Central Control Board (Liquor Traffic) 1916-20; entered Consular Service, 1920; Vice-Consul at Tallinn, 1922, Bogota, 1924; Chargé d'Affaires and Acting Consul General there, 1925-26, Chicago, 1927, Marseilles, 1930, and Genoa, 1934; Acting Consul General in Marseilles and Genoa in each year from 1930 to 1935; temporarily attached to Commercial Secretariat at Rome, in 1935, 1939 and 1940, and to Consulate General, Marseilles, 1936; Consul at Madrid, 1936, Valencia 1936; First Secretary (temp. local rank) in HM Diplomatic Service, 1936-38; attached Imperial Defence College, 1939; Acting Consul at Trieste, 1939; attached to the Spears Mission, 1940-41; Commercial Secretary and Counsellor (local rank), Berne, 1941-45; attached UK Delegn to Paris Conf. and Council of Foreign Ministers, New York, 1946; British Political Adviser, Trieste, 1945-50; British Minister to Roumania, 1951-54; British Ambassador to Mexico, 1954-56; UK Delegation to United Nations, 1956-57; to Conf. on Law of the Sea, Geneva, 1958. Called to Bar, Inner Temple, 1921. *Address:* c/o 25 Banstead Road, Purley, Surrey.

**SULLY, Air Vice-Marshal John Alfred,** CB 1944; AFC 1918; Chairman, Dominion Road Machinery Co. Ltd, 1962; *b* 1892; *s* of J. A. Sully, Metcalfe, Ont.; *m* 1912, Elodie Marguerite, *d* of R. K. Milks, Ottawa; two *s* one *d*. Joined RCAF 1934; Air Vice-Marshal, 1941. Commander, Legion of Merit (USA), 1944. OStJ 1965. *Address:* Goderich, Ont., Canada.

**SULLY, Leonard Thomas George,** CBE 1963; Assistant General Manager, Covent Garden Market Authority, since 1967; *b* 25 June 1909; British; *m* 1935, Phyllis Emily Phipps, Bristol; one *d*. *Educ:* elementary schs; Fairfield Grammar Sch., Bristol. Public Health Dept, Bristol Corp., 1927; Assistance Officer, Unemployment Assistance Board, Bristol District, 1934; subseq. served in Bath, Weston-super-Mare, etc.; Staff Officer, Air Ministry, London, 1943; Principal, and allocated to Air Ministry, 1949; Asst Sec., 1954, Dir of Contracts, 1960; Dir of Contracts (Air) MoD, 1964. *Recreation:* gardening. *Address:* Coppins, Brackendale Close, Camberley, Surrey. *T:* Camberley 63604.

**SULZBERGER, Arthur Ochs;** President and Publisher of The New York Times since 1963; *b* 5 Feb. 1926; *s* of late Arthur Hays Sulzberger; *m* 1st, 1948, Barbara Grant (marr. diss. 1956); one *s* one *d*; 2nd, 1956, Carol Fox Fuhrman; one *d* (and one adopted *d*). *Educ:* Browning School, New York City; Loomis School, Windsor, Conn.; Columbia University, NYC. Reporter, Milwaukee Journal, 1953-54; Foreign Correspondent, New York Times, 1954-55; Asst to the Publisher, New York

Times, 1956-57; Asst Treasurer, New York Times, 1957-63. Hon. LLD: Dartmouth, 1964; Bard, 1967. *Recreation:* golf. *Address:* 229 West 43rd Street, New York, NY 10036, USA. *T:* 556-1771. *Clubs:* Overseas Press, Century Country, Explorers (New York); Metropolitan, Federal City (Washington, DC).

**SUMMERFIELD, Prof. Arthur,** BSc Tech; BSc; FBPsS; Professor of Psychology, University of London, and Head of the Department of Psychology at Birkbeck College since 1961; *b* 31 March 1923; *s* of late Arthur and Dora Gertrude Summerfield; *m* 1946, Aline, *d* of late Herbert Thomas and Ethel May Whalley; one *s* one *d*. *Educ:* Manchester Grammar Sch.; Manchester Univ.; University Coll. London (1st cl. hons Psychology). Served War of 1939-45, Electrical Officer, RNVR, 1943-46. Asst Lectr in Psychology, University Coll. London, 1949-51, Lectr, 1951-61, Hon. Research Associate, 1961-; Mem. Council, British Psychological Soc., 1953-65, 1967- (Hon. Gen. Sec., 1954-59; Pres., 1963-64); Mem. Exec. Cttee, International Union of Psychological Science, 1963-, Assembly, 1957-; Chm., Dept of Education and Science Working Party on Psychologists in Educn Services, 1965-68. Vis. Prof., Univ. of California (at Dept of Psychobiology, Irvine Campus), 1968. Governor, Enfield Coll. of Technology, 1968-. Editor, British Journal of Psychology, 1964-67; Scientific Editor, British Med. Bulletin issues on Experimental Psychology, 1964, Cognitive Psychology, 1971. *Publications:* articles on perception, memory, statistical methods and psycho-pharmacology in scientific periodicals. *Address:* Birkbeck College, Malet Street, WC1E 7HX.

**SUMMERHAYES, Sir Christopher (Henry),** KBE, *cr* 1955 (MBE 1929); CMG 1949; *b* 8 March 1896; *s* of late Rev. H. Summerhayes; *m* 1921, Anna (Johnson); two *s* two *d*. Served HM Forces, 1914-19 and 1940-45, Gloucestershire Regt (despatches). HM Foreign Service; Consul-General at Alexandria, 1946-51; Ambassador to Nepal, 1951-55. *Address:* Limpsfield, Surrey.

*See also D. M. Summerhayes.*

**SUMMERHAYES, David Michael;** Head of Disarmament Department, Foreign and Commonwealth Office, since 1970; *b* 29 Sept. 1922; *s* of Sir Christopher Summerhayes, *qv*; *m* 1959, June van der Hardt Aberson; two *s* one *d*. *Educ:* Marlborough; Emmanuel Coll., Cambridge. Served War of 1939-45 in Royal Artillery (Capt.) N Africa and Italy. 3rd Sec., FO, 1948; Baghdad, 1949; Brussels, 1950-53; 2nd Sec., FO, 1953-56; 1st Sec. (Commercial), The Hague, 1956-59; 1st Sec. and Consul, Reykjavik, 1959-61; FO, 1961-65; Consul-General, 1965-67, Counsellor, 1967-70, Buenos Aires. Hon. Officer, Order of Orange Nassau. *Recreations:* sailing, travel, wildlife. *Address:* 6 Kingsmere Road, Wimbledon, SW19. *Clubs:* United University; Itchenor Sailing.

**SUMMERHAYS, Reginald Sherriff;** Solicitor (retired); Author; *b* 5 April 1881, British; *m* 1st, 1906, Annie May, *d* of Arthur Owen; one *s* two *d*; 2nd, Winifred Edna (*d* 1963), *d* of Walter Varley, Doncaster, Yorks. *Educ:* Westminster Sch. Judge of light horses and other types; on the Council of a number of societies connected with horses. Apptd Civilian Remount Purchasing Officer and subsequently commissioned in European War, 1914-18, and became Dep. Controller of Aircraft Contracts. *Publications:* Here's Horse Sense; From Saddle and Fireside; Elements of Riding; Elements of Hunting; Riding for All; The Observer's Book of Horses and Ponies; The Problem Horse; Summerhays' Encyclopaedia for Horsemen; It's a Good Life with Horses; Riding on a Small Income; The Story of the International; The Young Rider's Guide to the Horse World; A Lifetime with Horses; The Arabian Horse in Great Britain; (with Stella A. Walker) The Controversial Horse; The Country Life Horseman's Pocket Book; (with Lt-Col C. E. G. Hope) Horse Shows; The Donkey Owner's Guide. *Recreations:* judging horses, donkeys and ponies, writing of and for them. *Address:* 30a Arterberry Road, Wimbledon, SW20. *T:* 01-946 1445.

**SUMMERS, Sir Geoffrey,** 1st Bt *cr* 1952; CBE 1942; CStJ 1956; *b* Greenfield, Yorks, 2 Sept. 1891; *s* of Henry Hall Summers; *m* 1st, 1915, Doris M. (marr. diss. 1930), *d* of G. R. Edgecombe, Brenchley, Kent; one *s* one *d* (and one *s* (of twin *s*) decd); 2nd, 1931, Margaret A., *d* of H. P. Stace, Brackley, Northants; two *d*. *Educ:* Uppingham; Cambridge (MA). Joined firm of John Summers and Sons, Ltd, Steel Manufacturers, Shotton, Chester, 1912; served in HM forces, 1914-18; returned to firm, 1919; a director of the firm, 1921-67; DL, County of Flint, 1938; High Sheriff, 1939; Chairman: Flintshire County Council, 1940-42; formerly Dee and Clwyd River Authority; Steel Sheet Trade Wages Bd, 1933 now retd; Member Development Corp. for Wales, 1958-67. *Recreations:* mountaineering, golf, music. *Heir: s* Felix Roland Brattan Summers [*b* 1 Oct. 1918; *m* 1945, Anna Marie Louise, *d* of late Gustave Demaegd, Brussels; one *d*]. *Address:* Craig-y-Castell, Dyserth, Flintshire. *T:* Dyserth 281. *Club:* Alpine.

**SUMMERS, Sir (Gerard) Spencer,** Kt 1956; *b* 27 Oct. 1902; *s* of late Frank Bright Summers, Froyle Place, Alton, Hants, and late Constance Taylor; *m* 1930, Jean, adopted *d* of John Pickering; one *s* one *d* (and one *s decd*). *Educ:* Wellington; Trinity College, Cambridge. Chm. of Sheet Makers' Conference, 1936-39; Dir-Gen. of Regional Organisation, Min. of Supply, 1941-44; MP (U) Northampton, 1940-45; MP (C) Aylesbury Div. of Bucks, 1950-70; Mem. Parly Delegn to Australia and NZ, 1944; Sec. Dept of Overseas Trade, 1945. Pres. International Sheet Comptoir, 1936-39; Chm. Exec. Cttee, Outward Bound Trust, 1947-; Pres. British Direct Mail Advertising Assoc., 1956-64. *Recreations:* hunting, shooting, golf. *Address:* Thenford House, Banbury, Oxon. *Club:* Boodle's.

**SUMMERS, Henry Forbes,** CB 1961; Under-Secretary, Ministry of Housing and Local Government, since 1955; *b* 18 August 1911; *s* of late Rev. H. H. Summers, Harrogate, Yorks; *m* 1937, Rosemary, *d* of late Robert L. Roberts, CBE; two *s* one *d*. *Educ:* Fettes Coll., Edinburgh; Trinity College, Oxford. Sixth form master, Marlborough Coll., 1934; entered Min. of Health, 1935; Principal, 1940; Minister's Principal Private Secretary, 1945; Assistant Secretary, 1947; Ministry of Housing and Local Govt, 1951-. *Address:* Folly Fields, Tunbridge Wells, Kent. *T:* 27671. *Club:* United University.

**SUMMERS, Sir Richard (Felix),** Kt 1962; Chairman, John Summers & Sons Ltd, since 1938; Director: National Westminster Bank Ltd (Chairman, North Region Board); Steetley Co. Ltd, Royal Insurance Co. Ltd, Liverpool & London & Globe Insurance Co. Ltd; Member, London Midland Railway Board (past Member Midland Area Board, BTC); Governor of Shrewsbury School; *b* 10 Dec. 1902; *y s* of Henry Hall Summers; *m* 1925, Evelyn, *d* of W. F. Irvine, FSA, Bryn Llwyn,

Corwen; four *s*. *Educ:* Shrewsbury; Clare College, Cambridge. Entered John Summers & Sons Ltd, 1925, Dir, 1931, Man. Dir, 1936, Chairman, 1938. Dir-in-Charge, Summers Div., Scottish and NW Gp, BSC, 1967-68. High Sheriff for County of Flint, 1944-45. Pres., British Iron and Steel Fedn, 1960. *Address:* Denna Hall, Burton Point, Wirral, Cheshire. *T:* 051-336 2117.

**SUMMERS, Sir Spencer;** *see* Summers, Sir G. S.

**SUMMERSCALE, Sir John (Percival),** KBE 1960 (CBE 1951); Retired 1960, as Minister (Commercial), British Embassy, Rio de Janeiro; Editor, Penguin Books, 1961; *b* 23 Nov. 1901; *s* of Annie and Percy Summerscale; *m* 1931, Nelle Blossom Stogsdall; two *s* two *d*. *Educ:* Latymers' School, Edmonton; Cambridge University. Levant Consular Service, 1926; served in Beirut, Hamadan, Shiraz, Tehran, Bagdad. Commercial Secretary (Grade II), Washington, 1938; Counsellor (Commercial) there, 1945; transferred to Board of Trade, 1946, and to Warsaw, 1948 as Commercial Counsellor; Consul-Gen., Munich, 1951; Minister (Commercial), Rio de Janeiro, 1954-60. *Recreation:* tennis. *Address:* 27 Church Row, Hampstead, NW3; Tarrant Hinton, Dorset.

**SUMMERSKILL,** Baroness (Life Peeress), *cr* 1961, of Ken Wood, **(Edith),** PC 1949; CH 1966; *b* Doughty St, London, 1901; *d* of William and Edith Summerskill; *m* 1925, Dr E. Jeffrey Samuel; one *s* one *d*. *Educ:* King's Coll., London; Charing Cross Hosp. Qualified as a doctor, 1924. Member of Middlesex County Council for Green Lanes division of Tottenham, 1934-41. Contested Parly by-election in Putney, 1934, and Bury div. General Election, 1935; MP (Lab) for West Fulham, 1938-55, for Warrington, 1955-61. Parly Sec., Min. of Food, 1945-50; Minister of National Insurance, 1950-51. Chm. of Labour Party, 1954-55. Hon. LLD Newfoundland, 1968. *Publications:* Babies without Tears, 1941; The Ignoble Art, 1956; Letters to my Daughter, 1957; A Woman's World, 1967. *Address:* Pond House, Millfield Lane, Highgate, N6.

*See also Dr the Hon. S. C. W. Summerskill.*

**SUMMERSKILL, Dr the Hon. Shirley Catherine Wynne;** MP (Lab) Halifax since 1964; Medical Practitioner since 1960; *b* London, 9 Sept. 1931; *d* of Dr E. J. Samuel and of Baroness Summerskill, *qv*; *m* 1957, John Ryman. *Educ:* St Paul's Girls' Sch.; Somerville Coll., Oxford; St Thomas' Hospital. MA, BM, BCh., 1958. Treas., Oxford Univ. Labour Club, 1952. Resident House Surgeon, later House Physician, St Helier Hosp., Carshalton, 1959. Contested (Lab) Blackpool North by-election, 1962. UK delegate, UN Status of Women Commn, 1968 and 1969; Mem. British delegn, Council of Europe and WEU, 1968. Vice-Chm., Parly Labour Party Health Group, 1964-69, Chm., 1969-70. hon. Vice-Pres., Socialist Medical Assoc. *Publication:* A Surgical Affair (novel), 1963. *Address:* House of Commons, SW1.

**SUMMERSON, Sir John (Newenham),** Kt 1958; CBE 1952; FBA 1954; BA(Arch); FSA; ARIBA; Fellow, University College, London; Curator of Sir John Soane's Museum since 1945; *b* 25 Nov. 1904; *o s* of late Samuel James Summerson of Darlington and Dorothea Worth Newenham; *m* 1938, Elizabeth Alison, *d* of H. R. Hepworth, CBE, Leeds; three *s*. *Educ:* Harrow; University College, London. From 1926 worked in architects' offices, including those of late W. D. Caröe and Sir Giles Gilbert Scott, OM. Instructor in Sch. of Architecture, Edinburgh Coll. of Art, 1929-30. Asst Editor, Architect and Building News, 1934-41; Dep. Dir, National Buildings Record, 1941-45. Lectr in History of Architecture, Birkbeck Coll. and Institute of Archæology, London; Slade Prof. of Fine Art Oxford, 1958-59; Ferens Prof. of Fine Art, Hull, 1960-61 and 1970-71; Slade Prof. of Fine Art, Cambridge, 1966-67; Bampton Lectr, Columbia Univ., 1968. Silver Medallist (Essay), RIBA, 1937. Member of: Royal Fine Art Commn, 1947-54; Royal Commn on Historical Monuments (England), 1953-; Historic Buildings Council, Min. of Works, 1953-; Arts Council Art Panel, 1953-56; Historical Manuscripts Commn, 1959-; Listed Buildings Cttee Min. of Housing and Local Govt, 1944-66 (Chm., 1960-62); Adv. Council on Public Records, 1968-; Mem. of Council, Architectural Assoc., 1940-45; Trustee, National Portrait Gallery, 1966-. Hon. Fellow, Trinity Hall, Cambridge, 1968. Foreign Hon. Mem., Amer. Acad. of Arts and Sciences, 1967; Chairman, National Council for Diplomas in Art and Design, 1961-70. Hon. DLitt: Leicester, 1959; Oxford, 1963; Hon. DSc Edinburgh, 1968. *Publications:* Architecture Here and Now (with C. Williams-Ellis), 1934; John Nash, Architect to George IV, 1935; The Bombed Buildings of Britain (with J. M. Richards), 1942 and 1945; Georgian London, 1946; The Architectural Association (Centenary History), 1947; Ben Nicholson (Penguin Modern Painters), 1948; Heavenly Mansions (essays), 1949; Sir John Soane, 1952; Sir Christopher Wren, 1953; Architecture in Britain, 1530-1830 (Pelican History of Art), 1953, 5th edn 1969; New Description of Sir J. Soane's Museum, 1955; The Classical Language of Architecture, 1964; The Book of John Thorpe (Walpole Soc., vol. 40), 1966; Inigo Jones, 1966; Victorian Architecture (four studies in evaluation), 1969; (ed) Concerning Architecture, 1969. *Recreation:* music. *Address:* 1 Eton Villas, NW3. *T:* 01-722 6247. *Clubs:* Athenæum, Beefsteak.

**SUMMERSON, Thomas Hawksley,** DL; JP; Director of various public companies; *b* 22 April 1903; *s* of late Robert Bradley Summerson, Coatham Mundeville, Co. Durham; *m* 1943, Joan, *d* of Walter Rogers, Ashington, Sussex; three *s* one *d*. *Educ:* Harrow. Dir for Steel Castings, Iron and Steel Control, Ministry of Supply, 1940-43; Chairman and Joint Man. Dir, Summerson Holdings Ltd, 1944-65; Chairman: British Steel Founders' Association, 1951-54; NE Industrial and Development Association, 1952-55; Home Affairs and Transport Division. Association of British Chambers of Commerce, 1952-59 (Vice-President, 1954, Deputy President, 1960-62, President, 1962-64); Darlington and District Local Employment Cttee, 1953-; Design Panel, British Transport Commn, 1956-63; Dep. Chairman, Peterlee Development Corp., 1954-55. Chairman, North Eastern Area Board, British Transport Commission, 1955, and Part-time Member of the Commission, until 1962; Part-time Member, British Railways Board, Jan. 1963-Oct. 1963, and Chm. North Eastern Railway Bd, Jan.-Oct. 1963. Member: Aycliffe New Town Development Corp., 1947-61; Development Areas Treasury Advisory Cttee, 1951-55; President: Tees-side and S-W Durham Chamber of Commerce, 1948-50; Tees-side Industrial Development Board, 1954-57; Member, Independent Television Authority, 1957-60; Mem., North East Development Council, 1965-. Mem. Darlington RDC, 1937- (Chm. 1949-52); Chm., Sedgefield Div. Conservative and Unionist Assoc. JP Co. Durham, 1946; Chm. Darlington County Bench, 1951-53 and 1955-

61; High Sheriff, County Durham, 1953-54; DL County Durham, 1958. Chm. South Durham Hunt. *Recreations:* shooting, fishing. *Address:* Hall Garth, Coatham Mundeville, Darlington, Durham. *T:* Aycliffe 2818; 68 Barnsbury Road, Islington, N1. *Clubs:* Brooks's, MCC.

**SUMMERVILLE, Sir Alan;** *see* Summerville, Sir W. A. T.

**SUMMERVILLE, Sir (William) Alan (Thompson),** Kt 1968; DSc, FAIAS; Agent-General for Queensland in London, 1964-70; Chairman, Queensland Sugar Board, since 1970; *b* 6 Feb. 1904; *s* of W. H. Summerville, Ipswich, Queensland; *m* 1930, Ethel, *d* of T. F. Barker; two *d. Educ:* Ipswich Grammar School; University of Queensland. Entomological Investigations, 1930-36; Plant Physiology Research, 1937-45. Studied Agricultural Research Methods in Ceylon, Egypt, Palestine, GB, USA, Canada, Hawaii and NZ, 1936-37 and 1955. Dir, Div. of Plant Industry, Dept of Agric. and Stock, Qld, 1955-58; Dir-Gen. and Under-Sec., Dept of Agric. and Stock, Qld, 1958-64. Hon. LLD (Qld), 1963. *Publications:* various, on entomological and physiological subjects. *Recreations:* golf and gardening. *Address:* c/o Queensland Sugar Board, Queen Street, Brisbane, Queensland, Australia. *Clubs:* East India and Sports, Royal Automobile; Johnsonian (Brisbane).

**SUMNER, Donald;** *see* Sumner, W. D. M.

**SUMNER, John Richard Hugh,** CBE 1945; DL; JP; *b* 1886; *s* of late Sir John Sumner, FSA, Ham Hill, Powick; *m* 1914, Beatrice Mary, *d* of Henry Severn Black, Frisby-on-the-Wreake, Leics; one *s* one *d. Educ:* privately. Pres., Typhoo Tea Ltd; Chm. of a number of charitable trusts created by his father and himself; Jt Master and Master Worcs Hounds, 1934-45; late Chm. Worcs Agric. Committee for 19 years. High Sheriff of Worcs, 1944-45; DL 1953. Mem. National Hunt Cttee, and Council of the Hunter and Light Horse Improvement Society. *Recreation:* racing. *Address:* Rashwood Lodge, Droitwich. *T:* Wychbold 251. *Club:* Worcestershire (Worcester).

**SUMNER, (William) Donald (Massey),** OBE 1945; QC 1960; **His Honour Judge Sumner;** Judge of County Courts, Circuit 49 (Kent) since Oct. 1961; *b* 13 Aug. 1913; *s* of Harold Sumner, OBE, Standish, Lancs. *Educ:* Charterhouse; Sidney Sussex Coll., Cambridge. Called to the Bar, Lincoln's Inn, 1937. Member Orpington Urban District Council, 1950-53. Served War of 1939-45 with Royal Artillery; Lt-Col and Asst Adjutant-General, 21st Army Group. Acted as Asst Recorder of Plymouth frequently, 1954-61. MP (C) Orpington Div. of Kent, Jan. 1955-Oct. 1961; PPS to Solicitor-General, Nov. 1959-Oct. 1961. Officier, Ordre de la Couronne and Croix de Guerre (Belgian); Bronze Star Medal (American). *Address:* 2 Harcourt Buildings, Temple, EC4; Brissenden House, Bethersden, Kent. *Club:* Carlton.

**SUMSION, Herbert Whitton,** CBE 1961; DMus, Cantuar; MusBac, Dunelm; FRCM, Hon. RAM, FRCO, ARCM, FRSCM; Organist of Gloucester Cathedral, 1928-67; Director of Music, Ladies' Coll., Cheltenham, 1935-68; *b* Gloucester, 19 Jan. 1899; *m* 1927, Alice Hartley Garlichs, BA; three *s*. Organist and Choirmaster at Christ Church, Lancaster Gate; Director of Music, Bishop's Stortford College; Asst Instructor in Music at Morley Coll., London; Teacher of Harmony and Counterpoint, Curtis Institute, Philadelphia, 1926-28; Conductor Three Choirs Fest., 1928, 1931, 1934, 1937, 1947, 1950, 1953, 1956, 1959, 1962, 1965. *Publications:* Introduction and Theme for Organ, 1935; Morning and Evening Service in G, 1935; Two pieces for Cello and Piano, 1939 (No. 1 arranged for String Orchestra); Magnificat and Nunc Dimittis in G for Boys' Voices, 1953, for Men's Voices, 1953; Cradle Song for Organ, 1953; Benedicite in B flat, 1955; Four Carol Preludes for Organ, 1956. *Address:* Hartley, Private Road, Rodborough Common, Stroud, Glos. *T:* Amberley 3528.

**SUNARIO, Dr;** Indonesian diplomat and scholar; Professor of Political science and International law and relations, President of Diponegoro State University, Semarang, Java, since 1963; *b* Madiun, E Java, 28 Aug. 1902; *m* 1930; one *s* four *d. Educ:* Univ. of Leyden (Grad.). Solicitor and Barrister, 1927-41; Chief Editor, daily newspaper Sedya-Tama, Jogjakarta, 1941-42; Sen. Official, Dept for Justice, Djakarta, 1942-45; Co-founder and later Dean of Faculty of Law and concurrently Lectr in polit. sciences, Gadjah Mada Univ., Jogjakarta, 1946-47; Polit. Sec. to Delegn of Republic of Indonesia for Indonesian-Dutch negotiations, 1947-48; Mem. Provisional Parlt (DPR), Djakarta (several times Chm. Foreign Affairs Cttee), 1950-53; Chm. Parly mission to Gt Britain, 1951; Chm. Indonesian UN Assoc., Djakarta, 1951-53; Chm. Indonesian Nat. Gp of Interparly Union, 1951-53; Foreign Minister, Republic of Indonesia, 1953-55, and in that capacity: Leader, Delegn of Indonesia to Gen. Assembly of UN, New York, 1953 and 1954, also Chm. Indonesian Delegn to Colombo-plan Conf., Ottawa, 1954, and Dep. Chm. of same to Asian-African Conf., Bandung, 1955; Indonesian Ambassador to the Court of St James's, Nov. 1956-Aug. 1961. Mem. Indonesian Delegn, UN Gen. Assembly, 1959; Chm. Indonesian Delegn to UN Conf. on Prevention of Crime, London, 1960. Extraord. Prof. of Constitutional and Diplomatic History, Faculty of Lit. and Philos., Univ. of Indonesia, Djakarta, 1955-56. Mem.-founder Indonesian Nationalist Party (PNI), 1927; participated in re-establishing PNI after the war. *Publications:* books and articles on political subjects, human rights, etc. *Address:* Universitas Diponegoro, Djalan Hajam Wuruk, Semirang, Java, Indonesia.

**SUNDERLAND, Earl of; Charles James Spencer-Churchill;** *b* 24 Nov. 1955; *o surv. s* and *heir* of Marquess of Blandford, *qv*.

**SUNDERLAND, (George Frederick) Irvon;** DL; **His Honour Judge Sunderland;** Judge of County Courts Circuit No. 21 (Birmingham), since 1966; *b* 8 May 1905; *o s* of Frederick and Mary Jane Sunderland; *m* 1929, Mary Katharine, *d* of Arthur John Bowen; four *s*. *Educ:* privately. Called to Bar, Gray's Inn, 1932 (H. C. Richards Prizeman); joined Midland Circuit; Assistant Recorder: Birmingham Quarter Sessions, 1960-63; Coventry Quarter Sessions, 1962-63; County Court Judge, Derbyshire, 1964-66; Chairman, Warwick County QS, 1967-. Deputy Chairman: East Midlands Agricultural Land Tribunal, 1959-63; Birmingham Mental Health Review Tribunal, 1959-63; Chm., Birmingham Local Bar Cttee, 1959-63. DL Warwicks, 1967. *Recreations:* gardening, the theatre. *Address:* The Old Vicarage, Rose Hill, Rednal, Birmingham. *T:* 021-453 3155.

**SUNDERLAND, Prof. Sydney,** CMG 1961; FAA 1954; Professor of Experimental Neurology since 1961, and Dean of the Faculty of Medicine since 1953, University of Melbourne; *b* Brisbane, Aust., 31 Dec. 1910; *s* of Harry and

Anne Sunderland; *m* 1939, Nina Gwendoline Johnston, LLB; one *s*. *Educ:* University of Melbourne. BM, BS 1935, DSc 1945, DMed 1946, Melbourne. FRACP 1941; FRACS 1952. Sen. Lectr in Anatomy, Univ. of Melbourne, 1936-37; Demonstrator in Human Anatomy, Oxford, 1938-39; Prof. of Anatomy, Univ. of Melbourne, 1940-61. Mem. Zool. Bd of Vict., 1944-65 (Chm. Scientific Cttee, 1958-62); Dep. Chm., Adv. Cttee to Mental Hygiene Dept, Vict., 1952-63; Mem. Nat. Health and MRC, 1953-69; Chm., Med. Research Adv. Cttee of Nat. Health and MRC, 1964-69. Visiting Prof. of Anatomy, Johns Hopkins Univ., 1953-54; Sec., Div. of Biol Sciences, Aust. Acad. Sci., 1955-58; Mem. Nat. Radiation Adv. Cttee, 1957-64 (Chm. 1958-64); Mem. Defence Research and Development Policy Cttee, 1957-; Mem., Med. Services Cttee, Dept of Defence, 1957-; Mem. Council, AMA, Victorian Branch, 1960-68; Chm. Safety Review Cttee, Aust. Atomic Energy Commn, 1961-; Mem. Aust. Univs Commn, 1962-; Mem. Cttee of Management, Royal Melbourne Hosp., 1963-; Chm. Protective Chemistry Research Adv. Cttee, Dept of Supply, 1964-. Trustee, National Museum, 1954-. *Publications:* Nerves and Nerve Injuries, 1968; about 100 articles in scientific jls in Gt Britain, Europe, US and Australia. *Address:* 11 Scotsburn Grove, Toorak, Victoria 3142, Australia. *T:* 203431. *Club:* Melbourne.

**SUNLIGHT, Joseph;** Architect; *b* 2 Jan. 1889; *s* of Israel and Minnie Sunlight. *Educ:* Private School, Kingston-on-Thames. MP (L) Shrewsbury, 1923-24. *Address:* 14 Victoria Square, SW1. *T:* 01-834 4734; Hallside, Knutsford, Cheshire. *T:* Knutsford 3339; Sunlight House, Manchester. *T:* 061-834 7113.

**SUPHAMONGKHON, Dr Konthi,** Kt Comdr of Order of Chula Chom Klao, Thailand; Special Grand Cordon Order of the White Elephant, Thailand; Special Grand Cordon, Order of the Crown of Thailand; Ambassador of Thailand to the Court of St James's since 1970; *b* 3 Aug. 1916; *m* 1951, Dootsdi Atthakravi; two *s* one *d*. *Educ:* Univ. of Moral and Political Sciences, Bangkok (LLB); Univ. of Paris (Dr-en-Droit). Joined Min. of Foreign Affairs, 1940; Second Sec., Tokyo, 1942-44; Chief of Polit. Div., 1944-48; Dir-Gen., Western Affairs Dept, 1948-50; UN Affairs Dept, 1950-52; Minister to Australia, 1952-56, Ambassador, June 1956-59, and to New Zealand, Oct. 1956-59; Dir-Gen. of Internat. Organizations, 1959-63; Adviser on Foreign Affairs to the Prime Minister, 1962-64; Sec.-Gen., SEATO, 1964-65; Ambassador to Federal Republic of Germany, 1965-70, and to Finland, 1967-70. Frequent Lecturer, 1944-; notably at Thammasat Univ., 1944-52, at National Defence Coll., 1960-62, and at Army War Coll., Bangkok, 1960-63. Holds foreign decorations. *Publication:* Thailand and her relations with France, 1940 (in French). *Recreations:* tennis, golf, swimming. *Address:* Royal Thai Embassy, 29 Queen's Gate, SW7. *T:* 01-589 2853. *Clubs:* Travellers', Hurlingham; Royal Wimbledon Golf.

**SURPLICE, Reginald Alwyn,** BMus (Dunelm), FRCO, LRAM; Organist and Master of the Choristers, Winchester Cathedral, since 1949; Tutor in Music, King Alfred's College, Winchester; *b* 20 Aug. 1906; *s* of Reginald Frank and Ethel Mary Surplice; *m* 1933, Mary Florence Coxeter; two *s* one *d*. *Educ:* Reading Collegiate and Reading University. Organist, Pangbourne Parish Church, 1922-24, Easthampstead Parish Church, 1924-26; Holy Trinity, Windsor, 1928-40; Asst Organist St George's Chapel, Windsor, 1932-45; Organist and Master of the Choristers, Bristol Cathedral, 1946-49. War of 1939-45, served 1940-45. *Address:* 6 The Close, Winchester, Hants. *T:* Winchester 4392.

**SURREY, Archdeacon of;** *see* Evans, Ven. J. M.

**SURRIDGE, Brewster Joseph,** CMG 1950; OBE 1941; Adviser on Co-operatives to Minister of Overseas Development, 1964-67 (to Secretary of State for Colonies, 1947-64); retired 1967; *b* 12 Feb. 1894; *e s* of E. E. Surridge; *m* 1922, Winifred Bywater-Ward (*née* Lawford). *Educ:* Felsted School; Downing College, Cambridge. Served European War, Army, 1914-17. Colonial Administrative Service, Cyprus, 1918-33; Registrar of Co-operative Societies, Cyprus, 1934-43; Financial Secretary, Gold Coast, 1943-45; retired, 1946. Adviser on Co-operation to the Government of Iraq, 1946-47. *Publications:* A Survey of Rural Life, Cyprus, 1931; A Manual of Co-operative Law and Practice, 1948. *Address:* 2 Furze Croft, Hove 2, Sussex. *T:* Brighton 70027. *Club:* Farmers'.

**SURRIDGE, Sir (Ernest) Rex (Edward),** Kt, *cr* 1951; CMG 1946; retired; *b* 21 Feb. 1899; *s* of late E. E. Surridge, Coggeshall, Essex; *m* Roy, *d* of late Major F. E. Bradstock, DSO, MC; two *s*. *Educ:* Felsted; St John's College, Oxford. European War, 1917-20, Lieut 7th Bn DCLI; St John's College, Oxford, 1920-22, Mod. Hist. (Hons); Colonial Admin. Service, 1924, Tanganyika; Assistant Chief Secretary, Tanganyika, 1936; Deputy Chief Secretary, Kenya, 1940; Chief Secretary to Govt of Tanganyika, 1946-51; Salaries Comr, Cyprus, 1953-54; Financial Comr, Seychelles, 1957-58; Salaries Comr, High Commn Territories (South Africa), 1958-59; Salaries Comr, Gibraltar, 1959-60. *Address:* Flat 4, Wytham Abbey, Oxford. *T:* Oxford 44733.

**SURTEES, Maj.-Gen. George,** CB 1943; CBE 1941; MC; Colonel, The Lancashire Fusiliers, since 1945; *b* 17 Dec. 1895. Served European War, 1914-18 (wounded, despatches, MC and Bar); War of 1939-45 in ME and NW Europe (despatches five times, CBE, CB) Grand Officer of Order of White Lion of Czechoslovakia, and Czechoslovak Military Cross; Comdr of Order of Crown of Belgium; Officer Legion of Honour, and Croix de Guerre with palm (France); American Bronze Star Medal. Retired pay, 1949. *Address:* Teedleham Grove, near Canterbury, Kent.

**SURTEES, John,** MBE 1961; motor racing since 1961; also controlling companies involved in automobile construction and development, and property; *b* 11 Feb. 1934; *s* of John Norman and Dorothy Surtees; *m* 1962, Patricia Phyllis Burke; no *c*. *Educ:* Ashburton School, Croydon. 5 year engineering apprenticeship, Vincent Engrs, Stevenage, Herts. Motorcycle racing, 1952-60; British Champion, 1954, 1955; World 500 cc Motorcycle Champion, 1956; World 350 and 500 cc Motorcycle Champion, 1958, 1959, 1960. At end of 1960 he retd from motorcycling and subseq. began motor racing. With Ferrari Co., won World Motor Racing title, 1964; 5th in World Championship, 1965 (following accident in Canada due to suspension failure); in 1966 left Ferrari in mid-season and joined Cooper, finishing 2nd in World Championship; in 1967 with Honda Motor Co. as first driver and develt engr (1967-68); 3rd in World Championship; with BRM as No 1 driver, 1969; designed and built own Formula 1 car, 1970. *Publications:* Motorcycle Racing and Preparation, 1958; John Surtees Book of Motorcycling, 1960; Speed, 1963; Six Days in August, 1968. *Recreations:* music, architecture; interested in most sports. *Address:* c/o Surtees Racing

Organisation, Station Road, Edenbridge, Kent. *T:* Edenbridge 3773.

**SUSMAN, Maurice Philip,** MB, ChM Sydney; FRCS; FRACS; AAMC; Hon. Consulting Surgeon, Sydney Hospital, 1958; Hon. Consulting Thoracic Surgeon, Royal North Shore Hospital, Sydney, 1958; *b* 4 Aug. 1898; *s* of Philip Tasman Susman and Gertrude Lehane; *m* 1934, Ina May Shanahan; one *d.* *Educ:* Sydney Church of England Grammar School; University of Sydney. *Publications:* various papers on surgical subjects. *Recreations:* chess, being idle, flying. *Address:* 22 Bathurst Street, Woollahra, Sydney, Australia. *T:* 38 6053. *Club:* Royal Aero (NSW).

**SUSSKIND, (Jan) Walter;** conductor, composer and concert pianist; Music Director and Principal Conductor, St Louis Symphony Orchestra, since 1968; *b* 1 May 1913; of Czech parents; *m* 1970, Jane Seymour; (one *s* by former marr.). *Educ:* Prague State Conservatorium. Conductor Prague Opera, 1934-37; Principal Conductor Royal Carl Rosa Opera Co., 1943-45; Principal Conductor Sadler's Wells Opera Co., 1946; Conductor of the Scottish National Orchestra, 1946-52; Principal Conductor Glyndebourne Opera Co. (at 1st Edinburgh Festival), 1947; Resident Conductor, Victorian Symphony Orch., Melbourne (8 mths each yr), 1954-56; Principal Conductor, Toronto Symphony Orch., 1956-65; Records for HMV and Columbia since 1945 (over two hundred records so far). Regular Guest Conductor, NYC Center Opera, 1961-; Guest Conductor of most leading orchestras in Europe, 1952-; many world tours as guest conductor of the world's leading orchestras; has conducted in over thirty countries on all five continents. Music Director of: Mendelssohn Choir, 1958-64; National Youth Orchestra of Canada, 1960-; Music Festival, Aspen, Colorado, 1961-68; Mississippi River Festival (St Louis Symphony's summer festival). Conductor and Mem. Adv. Cttee, Internat. Festival of Youth Orchestras, St Moritz, Switzerland. Dir, Amer. Inst. of Orchestral Conducting. Orchestrator of many piano works. Hon. Dr of Humanities, Univ. of Southern Illinois, 1969. *Address:* c/o W. Van Wyck, 80 Wigmore Street, London, W1.

**SUSSKIND, Walter;** *see* Susskind, (Jan) W.

**SUTCH, Ven. Ronald Huntley;** Archdeacon Emeritus of Cheltenham since 1965 (Archdeacon 1951-65); Hon. Canon of Gloucester, 1944-69, Canon Emeritus since 1969; *b* 5 March 1890; *s* of W. F. J. Sutch; *m* 1st, 1916, Elizabeth Lang Jones (*d* 1969); two *s*; 2nd, 1970, Mrs Betty Hibbett, *widow* of Basil Hibbett, Cirencester. *Educ:* Batley Grammar School; Merton College, Oxford. Deacon, 1914; Priest, 1915; Curate of Christ Church, Glasgow, 1914-16; Rector of St Mungo, Alexandria, Scotland, 1916-17; Vicar of Ravensthorpe, 1917-25; CF, 1918-19; Rector of Slymbridge, 1925-36; Vicar of St Stephen, Cheltenham, 1936-41. Surrogate, 1941-68; Rural Dean of Cirencester, 1941-51; Vicar of Cirencester, 1941-62; Proctor in Convocation, 1943-51. *Address:* The Plough Cottage, South Cerney, Cirencester, Glos. *T:* South Cerney 326.

**SUTCLIFF, Rosemary;** writer of historical novels for adults and children; *b* 14 Dec. 1920; *d* of George Ernest Sutcliff and Elizabeth Sutcliff (*née* Lawton). *Educ:* privately. *Publications:* Chronicles of Robin Hood, 1950; The Queen Elizabeth Story, 1950; The Armourer's House, 1951; Brother Dusty-feet, 1952; Simon, 1953; The Eagle of the Ninth, 1954; Outcast, 1955; Lady in Waiting, 1956; The Shield Ring, 1956; The Silver Branch, 1957; Warrior Scarlet, 1958; Rider of the White Horse, 1959; Lantern Bearers, 1959; Houses and History, 1960; Knights Fee, 1960; Rudyard Kipling, 1960; Beowulf, 1961; Dawn Wind, 1961; Sword at Sunset, 1963; The Hound of Ulster, 1963; The Mark of the Horse Lord, 1965; Heroes and History, 1965; The Chief's Daughter, 1967; The High Deeds of Finn McCool, 1967; A Circlet of Oak Leaves, 1968; The Flowers of Adonis, 1969; The Witches' Brat, 1970. *Recreations:* painting, needlework, dogs, travel. *Address:* Swallowshaw, Walberton, Arundel, Sussex. *T:* Yapton 316.

**SUTCLIFFE, Edward Davis,** QC 1959; **His Honour Judge Sutcliffe;** a Judge of the Central Criminal Court, since 1969; *b* 25 Aug. 1917; 3rd *s* of late Richard Joseph and of Anne Sutcliffe; *m* 1939, Elsie Eileen Brooks; two *d.* *Educ:* University College School, Hampstead; Wadham College, Oxford (MA). Served Royal Artillery, 1939-46 (despatches). Called to Bar, Inner Temple, 1946; Bencher, 1966. Recorder of Canterbury 1968-69. Mem., Criminal Injuries Compensation Board, 1964-69. *Address:* Central Criminal Court, Old Bailey, EC4. *Club:* United University.

**SUTCLIFFE, Professor Frank Edmund;** Professor of Classical French Literature, University of Manchester, 1966; Directeur de recherches, Institut Collégial Européen; *b* 8 Aug. 1918; *er s* of Charles Edmund Taylor Sutcliffe and of Ellen Sutcliffe; *m* 1966 Jane Ceridwen Bevan. *Educ:* Huddersfield College; University of Manchester. BA 1940, MA 1948, PhD 1958. Served War of 1939-45, with Royal Artillery and Hong Kong and Singapore Royal Artillery, 1940-46. Asst lectr in French, 1946-49. Lecturer in French, 1949-55, Senior Lecturer in French, 1955-61. Professor of Modern French Literature, 1961-66, Univ. of Manchester. Visiting Professor: Univ. of Kiel, 1968; Université Laval, Québec, 1968-69. Chevalier de l'Ordre National du Mérite, 1965. *Publications:* La Pensée de Paul Valéry, 1955; Guez de Balzac et son temps; littérature et politique, 1960; Le réalisme de Charles Sorel: problèmes humains du XVIIe siècle, 1965; (ed) Discours politiques et militaires by Fr de la Noue, 1967; (trans.) Descartes, Discours de la Méthode, 1968; book reviews; contrib. to French Studies, Le Bayou (Houston, Texas), Jahrbuch (Univ. of Hamburg), Bulletin of the John Rylands Library. *Address:* 61 Daisy Bank Road, Victoria Park, Manchester 14. *T:* 061-224 1864.

**SUTCLIFFE, Geoffrey Scott,** OBE 1944; TD 1952; Deputy Chairman, Turner & Newall Ltd, since 1967; Chairman, Ferodo Italiana SpA; *b* 12 June 1912; *o s* of late John Walton Sutcliffe and late Alice Mary Sutcliffe (*née* Scott); *m* 1946, Mary Sylvia, *d* of late George Herbert Kay; two *s* one *d.* *Educ:* Repton. TA 2nd Lieut, 1939; Lt-Col, 1943; GSO1, AFHQ, N Africa and Italy; served France and Belgium, 1940; N Africa and Italy, 1943-45 (despatches, OBE). Ferodo Ltd, 1932: Works Dir, 1947; Home Sales Dir, 1952; Man. Dir, 1955; Chm., 1956-67; Turner & Newall Ltd: Dir, 1957; Jt Man. Dir, 1963. Director: Bell Asbestos Mines Ltd, Canada; Certain-teed Products Corp., USA; Hardie-Ferodo Ltd, Australia; Société Anonyme Française du Ferodo; Turners Asbestos Fibres Ltd. *Recreations:* tennis, gardening, swimming. *Address:* Brierwood House, Disley, Cheshire. *T:* Disley 2292. *Clubs:* Army and Navy, Royal Automobile.

**SUTCLIFFE, John Harold Vick;** MP (C) Middlesbrough West since 1970; *b* 30 April

1931; *o s* of late Sir Harold Sutcliffe and Emily Theodora Cochrane; *m* 1959, Cecilia Mary, *e d* of Ralph Meredyth Turton; three *s* one *d*. *Educ:* Winchester Coll.; New Coll., Oxford (Scholar; MA). 2nd Lieut RA, 1950-51. Called to Bar, Inner Temple; practised until 1960, Midland Circuit. Company Director. Contested (C): Oldham West, 1959; Chorley, Lancs, 1964; Middlesbrough West, 1966. *Recreations:* gardening, travel, reading. *Address:* Chapelgarth, Great Broughton, Middlesbrough, Teesside. *T:* Wainstone 228. *Clubs:* St Stephen's; Leander (Henley).

**SUTCLIFFE, Joseph Richard,** ED, BSc; Member the Stock Exchange of Melbourne since 1950; *b* 25 Jan. 1897; *s* of late A. H. Sutcliffe and Kate Elizabeth Haybittle; *m* 1923, Aileen, *d* of Henry H. Batchelor, NZ; one *s* one *d*. *Educ:* Palmerston North Boys' High School; Victoria University College, New Zealand. War Service, 1916-19, with NZ Machine Gun Corps and Royal Air Force; Major retd; Headmaster Scots College, Wellington, NZ, 1930-38; Melbourne Church of England Grammar School, 1938-49. *Address:* 35 York Avenue, Ivanhoe, Melbourne, Victoria 3079, Australia. *Club:* Melbourne (Melbourne).

**SUTCLIFFE, Kenneth Edward;** Headmaster, Latymer Upper School, Hammersmith, W6, since 1958; *b* 24 March 1911; *s* of late Rev. James Sutcliffe; *m* 1937, Nora, *d* of late Charles Herbert Burcham; two *d*. *Educ:* Manchester Grammar School; King's College, Cambridge (Scholar). BA Modern and Medieval Languages Tripos 1932; MA 1936. Assistant Master, Stockport Grammar School, 1933-38; Assistant Master, Liverpool Institute High School, 1938-46; Headmaster, Cockburn High School, Leeds, 1946-57. Served with Royal Armoured Corps and Intelligence Corps, 1940-46, Captain (General Staff). *Publications:* German Translation and Composition, 1948; French Translation and Composition, 1951; Fahrt ins Blaue (a German course for schools), 1960. *Address:* 34 Grove Way, Esher, Surrey. *T:* 01-398 4348.

**SUTCLIFFE, Prof. Reginald Cockcroft,** CB 1961; OBE 1942; FRS 1957; BSc, PhD Leeds; Professor of Meteorology, Reading University, 1965-70, now Emeritus Professor; President, International Association of Meteorology, since 1967; *b* 16 Nov. 1904; 2nd *s* of late O. G. Sutcliffe and late Jessie Sutcliffe (*née* Cockcroft), Cleckheaton, Yorkshire; *m* 1929, Evelyn, *d* of late Rev. William Williams, Halkyn; two *d*. *Educ:* Whitcliffe Mount Grammar Sch., Cleckheaton; Leeds Univ.; University Coll., Bangor. Professional Asst, Meteorological Office, 1927; Meteorological Office appointments: Malta, 1928-32, Felixstowe, 1932-35; Air Ministry, 1935-37; Thorney Island, 1937-39. Squadron Leader RAFVR, France, 1939-40; Sen. Meteorological Officer, No. 3 Bomber Group RAF, 1941-44; Group Capt., Chief Meteorological Officer AEAF, later BAFO, Germany, 1944-46. Research in Meteorological Office, 1946-; Director of Research, 1957-65. President, Commission for Aerology of World Meteorological Organization, 1957-61; Mem. Adv. Cttee, World Meteorological Organization, 1964-68; Mem. Council, Royal Soc., 1968-; Pres. Royal Meteorological Soc., 1955-57 (Buchan Prize, 1950, Symons Gold Medal, 1955); Charles Chree Medal, Physical Soc., 1959; Internat. Meteorological Organization Prize, 1963. *Publications:* Meteorology for Aviators, 1938; Weather and Climate, 1966; meteorological papers in jls. *Address:* Lanreath, 14 Llanvair Close, South Ascot, Berks. *T:* Ascot 23682. *Club:* Athenæum.

**SUTCLIFFE, Air Commodore Walter Philip,** CB 1958; DFC 1940; *b* 15 Aug. 1910; *s* of late W. Sutcliffe, Brampton, Cumberland; *m* 1947, Margery Anne Taylor, *d* of W. L. Taylor, Tulse Hill, SW2; one *s*. *Educ:* Durham School; Royal Air Force Coll., Cranwell. Fleet Air Arm, 1933-35 and 1937-39; Central Flying Sch., 1936. War of 1939-45; Bomber Command, 1939-42, India and Burma, 1942-45 (despatches). RAF Staff College, 1946; Director of Operational Training, Air Ministry, 1948-50; Standing Group, NATO, 1950-51; RAF Station, Wittering, 1953-55; SHAPE, 1955-56; Atomic Weapon Trials, Australia, 1957; Director of Intelligence, Air Ministry, 1958-61; retd April 1961; now employed Officers' Association. Officer, Legion of Merit (USA), 1945. *Address:* The Pond House, Pluckley, Kent. *T:* Pluckley 209; Officers' Association, 28 Belgrave Square, W1. *Club:* Royal Air Force.

**SUTHERLAND,** family name of **Countess of Sutherland.**

**SUTHERLAND,** 6th Duke of, *cr* 1833; **John Sutherland Egerton;** Bt 1620; Baron Gower, 1703; Earl Gower, Viscount Trentham, 1746; Marquis of Stafford (county), 1786; Viscount Brackley and Earl of Ellesmere, 1846; TD; DL; *b* 10 May 1915; *o s* of 4th Earl of Ellesmere and Violet, *e d* of 4th Earl of Durham; *S* father, 1944; *S* kinsman as Duke of Sutherland, 1963; *m* 1939, Lady Diana Percy, *yr d* of 8th Duke of Northumberland. Served War of 1939-45 (prisoner). DL Berwickshire, 1955. *Heir:* *c* Cyril Reginald Egerton [*b* 7 Sept. 1905; *m* 1st, 1934, Mary (*d* 1949), *d* of late Rt Hon. Sir Ronald Hugh Campbell, PC, GCMG; one *s* three *d*; 2nd, 1954, Mary, *d* of late Sir Sydney Lea, Dunley Hall, Worcestershire]. *Address:* Mertoun, St Boswell's, Roxburghshire; Stetchworth Park, Newmarket. *Clubs:* White's Turf; Jockey (Newmarket).

*See also J. M. E. Askew, Lady M. Colville, Rt Hon. Sir A. Douglas-Home, Lady A. Egerton, Viscount Rochdale.*

**SUTHERLAND,** Countess of (24th in line) *cr* (*c*) 1235; **Elizabeth Millicent Sutherland;** Lady Strathnaver (*c*) 1235; Chief of Clan Sutherland; *b* 30 March 1921; *o c* of Lord Alastair St Clair Sutherland-Leveson-Gower, MC (*d* 1921; 2nd *s* of 4th Duke), and Baroness Osten Driesen (*d* 1931); *niece* of 5th Duke of Sutherland, KT, PC; *S* (to uncle's Earldom of Sutherland and Lordship of Strathnaver), 1963; *m* 1946, Charles Noel Janson, DL, late Welsh Guards; two *s* one *d* (and one *s* decd). *Educ:* Queen's College, Harley Street, W1, and abroad. Land Army, 1939-41; Laboratory Technician: Raigmore Hospital, Inverness, 1941-43; St Thomas' Hospital, SE1, 1943-45. Chairman: Dunrobin School (Sutherland) Ltd; Trentham Gardens Ltd; The Northern Times Ltd. *Recreations:* reading, swimming, sunbathing. *Heir:* *e s* Lord Strathnaver, *qv*. *Address:* Dunrobin Castle, Sutherland; Uppat House, Brora, Sutherland. *T:* 202; 39 Edwardes Square, W8. *T:* 01-603 0659.

**SUTHERLAND, Anthony (Frederic Arthur);** Assistant Under-Secretary of State and Accountant-General, Department of Employment and Productivity; *b* 19 Oct. 1916; *e s* of Bertram and Grace Sutherland; *m* 1940, Betty Josephine Glass; one *s* two *d*. *Educ:* Christ's Hosp.; Gonville and Caius Coll., Cambridge (Classical Schol.). 1st cl. hons Classics, 1938; MA 1944. HM Forces, 1940-45 (Major, Mddx Regt). Asst Prin., Min. of Labour, 1938; Prin., 1943; Prin. Private Sec. to Ministers of Labour, 1948-53; Counsellor (Labour), British Embassy, Rome, 1953-55; Asst Sec., 1955; Imp. Def. Coll., 1960; Under-

Sec., 1967. *Address:* 159 Francklyn Gardens, Edgware, Mddx. *T:* 01-958 5821. *Club:* Army and Navy.

**SUTHERLAND, Sir (Benjamin) Ivan,** 2nd Bt, *cr* 1921; *b* 16 May 1901; *er surv s* of Sir Arthur Munro Sutherland, 1st Bt, KBE, and Fanny Linda (*d* 1937), 2nd *d* of Robert Hood Haggie; *S* father 1953; *m* 1st, 1927, Marjorie Constance Daniel (marriage dissolved, 1944), *yr d* of late Frederic William Brewer, OBE, MA, Newcastle upon Tyne; two *s*; 2nd, 1944, Margaret, *d* of Albert Owen, Chalfont St Giles, Bucks; three *s*. *Heir: s* John Brewer Sutherland [*b* 19 Oct. 1931; *m* 1958, Alice Muireall, *d* of late W. Stanford Henderson, Kelso; two *s* one *d*]. *Address:* Dunstan Steads, Embleton, Northumberland.

**SUTHERLAND, Carol Humphrey Vivian,** CBE 1970; FBA 1970; Keeper of the Heberden Coin Room, Ashmolean Museum, Oxford, since 1957; Student of Christ Church, Oxford, since 1945; *b* 5 May 1908; *s* of late George Humphreys Vivian and Elsie Sutherland; *m* 1933, Monica La Fontaine Porter (*see* Monica La F. Sutherland); no *c*. *Educ:* Westminster Sch.; Christ Church, Oxford. Barclay Head Prize for Ancient Numismatics, 1934; Asst Keeper of Coins, Ashmolean Museum, Oxford, 1932-52; Deputy Keeper, 1952-57; University Lecturer in Numismatics, 1939-; DLitt, 1945. Curator of Pictures, Christ Church, 1947-55, 1970-; President, Royal Numismatic Society, 1948-53; Winslow Lectr, Hamilton Coll., Clinton, NY, 1949 and 1957; Huntington Medallist of the American Numismatic Soc., 1950; Royal Numismatic Soc. Medallist, 1954; Silver Medallist, Royal Soc. of Arts, 1955; ed Numismatic Chronicle, 1953-66; Pres., Commn Internationale de Numismatique, 1960-; Pres., Centro Internazionale di Studi Numismatici, Naples, 1966-; Visiting Mem. Inst. for Advanced Study, Princeton, 1962-63, 1968; Mem. Royal Mint Advisory Cttee, 1963-; Hon. Member: Société française de numismatique; Société royale de numismatique de Belgique; Corresp. Mem., German Archaeol Inst. Governor, Westminster Sch. and Wallingford Grammar Sch. Officier, Palmes Académiques (France), 1965. *Publications:* Coinage and Currency in Roman Britain, 1937; (with H. Mattingly, E. A. Sydenham and R. A. G. Carson) The Roman Imperial Coinage, 1939-; The Romans in Spain, 1939; Anglo-Saxon Gold Coinage in the Light of the Crondall Hoard, 1948; (with J. G. Milne and J. D. A. Thompson) Coin Collecting, 1950; Coinage in Roman Imperial Policy, 1951; Art in Coinage, 1955; Gold, 1959; articles in Numismatic Chronicle, Jl Roman Studies, etc. *Recreations:* music, gardening. *Address:* Westfield House, Cumnor, Oxford. *T:* Cumnor 2178.

**SUTHERLAND, David M.,** MC; RSA 1936 (ARSA 1923); Principal, Gray's School of Art, Gordon's Colleges, Aberdeen, retired, 1948; *b* Wick, Caithness-shire, 1883; *m* 1924, Dorothy Johnstone; one *s* one *d*. *Educ:* Pulteneytown Academy, Wick. Studied Art at Royal Institution (Mound) Edinburgh School of Art and Life Class of Royal Scottish Academy; awarded Carnegie Travelling Scholarship, and studied in Paris and Madrid; appointed to staff of Edinburgh Coll. of Art; served European War, Capt. Royal Scots Regt (despatches, MC); retired, 1948. Hon. LLD Aberdeen, 1953. *Exhibited works:* portrait, figure subjects and landscape in principal Scottish Exhibitions of Art. *Address:* Woodhouselee, Cults, Aberdeenshire.

*See also I. J. M. Sutherland.*

**SUTHERLAND, Sir (Frederick) Neil,** Kt 1969; CBE 1955; MA; Chairman, The Marconi Co. (formerly Marconi's Wireless Telegraph Co. Ltd), and of Marconi Instruments, 1965-69; Director, English Electric Co. Ltd, 1965; *b* 4 March 1900; *s* of late Neil Hugh Sutherland; *m* 1931, Naruna d'Amorim Jordan (*d* 1970); one *s*. *Educ:* St Catharine's College, Cambridge. MA 1922. Served apprenticeship with English Electric Co. Ltd; Gen. Manager, English Electric Co. in Brazil, 1928; Man. Dir, English Electric (South Africa) Ltd, 1937; Gen. Manager, Marconi's Wireless Telegraph Co. Ltd, 1948; Man. Dir, Marconi Co. Ltd, 1958-65; Dep. Chm., 1962-65. *Recreation:* golf. *Address:* 44 Springfield Green, Chelmsford, Essex. *T:* Chelmsford 53980.

**SUTHERLAND, Sir Gordon (Brims Black McIvor),** Kt 1960; FRS 1949; Hon. LLD St Andrews, 1958; Hon. DSc, Strathclyde, 1966; Master of Emmanuel College, Cambridge, since 1964; *b* Watten, Caithness, 8 April 1907; *y s* of late Peter Sutherland and late Eliza Hope Sutherland, Dundee, Scotland; *m* 1936, Gunborg Elisabeth, *er d* of Konstnar Filip and Anna Wahlström, Gothenburg, Sweden; three *d*. *Educ:* Morgan Academy, Dundee; St Andrews Univ. (MA, BSc); Cambridge Univ. (PhD, ScD). Commonwealth Fund Fellow, 1931-33; Stokes Studentship, Pembroke Coll., 1934-35; Fellow and Lectr, Pembroke Coll., Cambridge, 1935-49. Leverhulme Fellow 1939, for study in US; Asst to Director of Scientific Research, Min. of Supply, 1940-41; Head of group carrying out extra-mural research in Cambridge Univ. for Min. of Aircraft Prodn, Min. of Supply and Admiralty, 1941-45; Asst Dir of Research in Dept of Colloid Science, Cambridge, 1944-47; Foster Lecturer, Univ. of Buffalo, 1948; Univ. Proctor, Cambridge, 1943-44; Member of Council of Senate 1946-49; Reader in Spectroscopy, Cambridge, 1947-49; Prof. of Physics in the Univ. of Michigan, 1949-56; Dir, National Physical Laboratory, 1956-64; Reilly Lectr, Univ. of Notre Dame, 1954-55; Guggenheim Fellow, 1956; Governor: Coll. of Aeronautics, Cranfield, 1957-63; London Sch. of Economics, 1957-65; Northampton Coll. of Advanced Technology, 1960-65. Hon. Fellow, Pembroke Coll., Cambridge, 1959. Vice-Pres., royal Soc., 1961-63; Internat. Organisation for Pure and Applied Biophysics, 1961-64; Internat. Cttee on Data for Science and Technology, 1968-; Pres., Triple Commn for Spectroscopy, 1962-63; Vice-Pres., Internat. Union of Pure and Applied Physics, 1963-69; President: Inst. of Physics and the Physical Soc., 1964-66; Section X, British Assoc., 1968; Mem., Council for Scientific Policy, 1965-68. For. Hon. Member: Amer. Acad. of Arts and Sciences, 1968; Société Royale des Sciences de Liège, 1960. *Publications:* Infra-Red and Raman Spectra, 1935. Scientific papers and articles on Infra-red Spectroscopy, Molecular Structure and Science Policy. *Recreation:* golf. *Address:* The Master's Lodge, Emmanuel College, Cambridge. *T:* Cambridge 58356. *Club:* Athenæum.

**SUTHERLAND, Graham (Vivian),** OM 1960; Painter; Designer; *b* London, 24 Aug. 1903; *e s* of late G. H. V. Sutherland, Civil Servant, and E. Sutherland; *m* 1928, Kathleen Frances Barry; no *c*. *Educ:* Epsom Coll.; Goldsmiths' College School of Art, Univ. of London. Retrospective Exhibitions: XXVI Biennale Venice, 1952; Musée Nationale d'Art Moderne, Paris, 1952; Stedelijk Museum, Amsterdam, 1953; Kunsthaus, Zürich, 1953; Tate Gallery, London, 1953; New London Gallery, 1962; Galleria d'Arte Moderna, Turin, 1965; Basel, Munich, The Hague and Cologne, 1966-68; Marlborough Fine Art

Gallery, 1968. Rep. permanent collection: Tate Gallery; British Museum; Victoria and Albert Museum; Museum of Modern Art, New York; Musée de l'Art Moderne, Paris; Musée des Beaux-Arts, Brussels; The Albertina, Vienna; Museum des 20 Jahrhunderts Künstmuseum, Basel; New Pinaleotok, Munich. Trustee of Tate Gallery, 1948-54. Designed tapestry, "Christ in Majesty", hung in Coventry Cathedral, 1962. Hon. DLitt: Oxford, 1962; Leicester, 1965. Museum of Modern Art, São Paulo, Prize; Foreign Secretary's Prize, Tokyo. *Relevant publication:* The Work of Graham Sutherland, by Douglas Cooper, 1961. *Address:* La Villa Blanche, Route de Castellar, 06 Menton, France.

**SUTHERLAND, Iain Johnstone Macbeth;** Head of South Asian Department, Foreign and Commonwealth Office, since 1969; *b* Edinburgh, 15 June 1925; *s* of Dr D. M. Sutherland, *qv*; *m* 1955, Jeanne Edith Nutt; one *s* two *d*. *Educ:* Aberdeen Grammar School; Aberdeen Univ.; Balliol College, Oxford. Served in HM Forces (Lieut, RA), 1944-47. Entered Foreign (now Diplomatic) Service, 1950; Third Secretary, Moscow, 1951; Foreign Office, 1953; First Secretary, Belgrade, 1956; Head of Chancery, Havana, 1959; transf. Washington, 1962; Asst, Northern Dept, FO, 1965; Counsellor and Consul-Gen., Djakarta, 1967-69. *Address:* c/o DSAO, SW1; 24 Cholmeley Park, Highgate, N6. *Club:* Travellers'.

**SUTHERLAND, Ian,** MA; Director of Education to the Health Education Council, since 1970; *b* 7 July 1926; *s* of A. J. Sutherland, Hunstanton, Norfolk; *m* 1951, Virginia Scovil Bliss; one *s* one *d*. *Educ:* Wyggeston Grammar School, Leicester; Sidney Sussex College, Cambridge. Assistant Professor of Classics, Univ. of New Brunswick, NB, Canada, 1949-50; Asst Master: Christ's Hospital, 1951-52; Harrow School, 1952-60; Head Master, St John's School, Leatherhead, 1960-70. FRSA 1969. *Publication:* From Pericles to Cleophon, 1954. *Recreations:* painting, cricket. *Address:* 57 Burntwood Grange, Handsworth Common Road, SW18. *Clubs:* MCC, Free Foresters'.

**SUTHERLAND, Sir Ivan;** *see* Sutherland, Sir Benjamin Ivan.

**SUTHERLAND, Prof. James Runcieman,** FBA 1953; MA, BLitt; Emeritus Professor of Modern English Literature, University College, London (Lord Northcliffe Professor, 1951-67); *b* Aberdeen, 26 April 1900; *s* of Henry Edward Sutherland, Stockbroker; *m* 1931, Helen, *d* of Will H. Dircks. *Educ:* Aberdeen Grammar Sch.; Univ. of Aberdeen; Oxford Univ. Lecturer in English, Univ. of Saskatchewan, 1921-23; Merton Coll., Oxford, 1923-25; Chancellor's English Essay Prize, Oxford, 1925; Lecturer in English, University College, Southampton, 1925; BLitt, Oxford, 1927; Lecturer in English, University of Glasgow, 1925-30; Senior Lecturer in English, University College, London, 1930-36; Professor of English Literature, Birkbeck College, London, 1936-44; Prof. of English Language and Literature, Queen Mary College, London, 1944-51; Warton lecturer on English Poetry to the British Academy, 1944; editor of The Review of English Studies, 1940-47. Visiting Professor: Harvard Univ., 1947; Indiana Univ., 1950-51; Univ. California, Los Angeles, 1967-68; Mellon Prof., Univ. of Pittsburgh, 1965; Berg Prof., NY Univ., 1969-70. Sir Walter Scott Lectures, Edinburgh University, 1952; Clark Lectures, Cambridge University, 1956; Alexander Lectures, Toronto University, 1956; Public Orator, University of London, 1957-62; W. P. Ker Memorial Lecture, Glasgow Univ., 1962; Clark Library Fellow, Univ. of California, Los Angeles, 1962-63. Hon. Mem. Modern Language Assoc. of America, 1960. Hon. LLD Aberdeen, 1955; Hon. DLitt Edinburgh, 1968. *Publications:* Leucocholy (Poems), 1926; Jasper Weeple, 1930; The Medium of Poetry, 1934; Defoe, 1937; Background for Queen Anne, 1939; The Dunciad, 1943; English in the Universities, 1945; A Preface to Eighteenth Century Poetry, 1948; The English Critic, 1952; The Oxford Book of English Talk, 1953; On English Prose, 1957; English Satire, 1958; English Literature of the late Seventeenth Century, 1969; editions of plays by Nicholas Rowe, Thomas Dekker, John Dryden, William Shakespeare; contributions to various literary journals. *Recreations:* fishing, second-hand book catalogues. *Address:* Courtenay Pitts, Sutton Courtenay, Berks. *T:* Sutton Courtenay 237.

**SUTHERLAND, Joan,** CBE 1961; Prima Donna, Royal Opera House, Covent Garden, since 1952; *b* 7 Nov. 1926; *d* of McDonald Sutherland, Sydney, NSW; *m* 1954, Richard Bonynge; one *s*. *Educ:* St Catherine's, Waverley, Sydney. Début as Dido in Purcell's Dido and Aeneas, Sydney, 1947; subsequently concerts, oratorios and broadcasts throughout Australia. Came to London, 1951; joined Covent Garden, 1952; début as First Lady in The Magic Flute. Rôles at Covent Garden include: Countess, in Figaro; Agathe, in Der Freischütz; Olympia, Antonia and Giulietta, in The Tales of Hoffman; Pamina, in The Magic Flute; Gilda, in Rigoletto; Desdemona, in Otello; Lucia, in Lucia di Lammermoor; Violetta, in La Traviata; Amina, in La Sonnambula, by Bellini (opening Covent Garden season, 1960-61); Queen of the Night in The Magic Flute; Marie in La Fille du Regiment. Countess, in Figaro, in bicentenary celebration of Mozart's birth, Glyndebourne. Donna Anna, in Don Giovanni, Sept. 1959, Desdemona and Donna Anna, Dec. 1959, Vienna State Opera; Italian début, Feb. 1960 (Alcina); French début April 1960 (Lucia); US début, Nov. 1960, followed by tour, 1961; appeared at the Metropolitan Opera, New York, in season 1961-62; début, La Scala, Milan, April 1961 (Lucia); then sang Bellini's Beatrice di Tenda there (first time in over 100 years); re-engaged for La Scala, 1962 and 1963; opened 1961-62 Season, San Francisco; opened 1961-62 Season, Chicago. Has made many recordings in G Brit. and France. *Recreations:* collecting autographed opera scores, 19th century operatic lithographs and 19th century books on singers of that period. *Address:* c/o Royal Opera House, Covent Garden, WC2.

**SUTHERLAND, Dame Lucy Stuart,** DBE 1969 (CBE 1947); DLitt Oxon 1955; Principal, Lady Margaret Hall, Oxford, 1945-71; Pro-Vice-Chancellor, Univ. of Oxford, 1960-69; *b* 21 June 1903; *d* of Alexander Charles Sutherland, MA, MCE, and Margaret Mabel Goddard. *Educ:* Roedean School, South Africa; University of the Witwatersrand, S Africa (Herbert Ainsworth Scholar, MA (Distinction), 1925); Somerville College, Oxford (BA (Hons) Modern History Cl. I, 1927; MA 1931). Fellow and Tutor of Somerville College, Oxford, 1928-45; first Temp. Principal, then Temp. Assistant Secretary, Board of Trade, 1941-45; Chm. Lace Working Party, 1946; Pres. GPDST; Member: Cttee of Enquiry into Distribution and Exhibition of Cinematograph Films, 1949; Royal Commission on Taxation of Profits and Income, 1951; Committee of Enquiry into Grants for Students, 1958; Hebdomadal Council, Oxford Univ., 1953-71; Sponsoring

Body, Univ. of Kent, Canterbury; UGC, 1964-69; Editorial Bd, The History of Parliament Trust. Governor, Administrative Staff Coll., Henley, 1964-69. FRSA 1950; FBA 1954. Hon. LittD: Cantab, 1963; Kent, 1967; Hon. LLD Smith College, Northampton, Mass, 1964; Hon. DLitt: Glasgow, 1966; Keele, 1968; Hon. DLit Belfast, 1970. Foreign Hon. Member, Amer. Acad. of Arts and Sciences, 1965. *Publications:* A London Merchant (1695-1774), 1933; edited (with M. McKisack) Mediaeval Representation and Consent, by M. V. Clarke, 1936, and Fourteenth Century Studies, by M. V. Clarke, 1937; edited (with H. Cam and M. Coate) Studies in Manorial History, by A. E. Levett, 1938; (joint) Report of the Lace Working Party, 1947; The East India Company in Eighteenth Century Politics, 1952; edited The Correspondence of Edmund Burke, Vol. II, 1960; contributions to English Historical Review, Economic History Review, Economic History, Transactions of the Royal Historical Society, etc. *Address:* Lady Margaret Hall, Oxford. *T:* Oxford 54353; 59 Park Town, Oxford. *Clubs:* Oxford and Cambridge University, University Women's.

**SUTHERLAND, Mary Elizabeth,** CBE 1949; MA; Chief Woman Officer, Labour Party, 1932-60. *Educ:* elementary and secondary schools; Aberdeen University. MA Hons History, Aberdeen. Trade Union Organiser, 1920-22; Labour Party Women's Organiser, Scotland, 1924-32; Member, Women's Consultative Cttee, Ministry of Labour, 1941-65; Director National Institute of Houseworkers, 1946-66; UK representative, United Nations Commission on Status of Women, 1947-52; Secretary, National Joint Cttee of Working Women's Organisations, 1932-61. Chairman, International Council of Social Democratic Women, 1959-61. *Address:* 63 Dunlop Tower, East Kilbride, Glasgow.

**SUTHERLAND, Monica La Fontaine;** author; *d* of C. M. McAnally, Hon. Canon of Norwich, and Mabel Adelaide McAnally (*née* La Fontaine); *m* 1st, R. W. Porter, Hon. Canon of Chelmsford, Vicar of East Ham; two *d* (one *s* killed in action); 2nd, C. H. V. Sutherland, *qv*; no *c*. *Educ:* Eastbourne; Paris. Formerly: served in National Fire Service and Red Cross Prisoner-of-War Books Section, 1941-45. Vice-Chm., Oxford Diocesan Council for Moral Welfare. *Publications:* La Fontaine, 1953; Louis XIV and Marie Mancini, 1956; The San Francisco Disaster, 1959; various newspaper and magazine articles. *Recreations:* travel, languages. *Address:* Westfield House, Cumnor, Oxford. *T:* Cumnor 2178.

**SUTHERLAND, Sir Neil;** *see* Sutherland, Sir F. N.

**SUTHERLAND, Ranald Iain,** QC (Scot) 1969; *b* 23 Jan. 1932; *s* of J. W. and A. K. Sutherland, Edinburgh; *m* 1964, Janice Mary, *d* of W. S. Miller, Edinburgh; two *s*. *Educ:* Edinburgh Academy; Edinburgh University. MA 1951, LLB 1953. Admitted to Faculty of Advocates, 1956; Advocate Depute, 1962-64; Standing Junior Counsel to Min. of Defence (Army Dept), 1964-69. *Recreations:* sailing, shooting. *Address:* 38 Lauder Road, Edinburgh. *T:* 031-667 5280. *Clubs:* New (Edinburgh); Royal Forth Yacht.

**SUTHERLAND, Scott,** RSA 1970; Head of Sculpture Department, Duncan of Jordanstone College of Art, Dundee, since 1947; *b* 15 May 1910; *s* of Major David Sutherland, MC, TD; *m* 1942; one *s* two *d*. *Educ:* Wick Academy; Wick High Sch.; Edinburgh Coll. of Art; Ecole des Beaux Arts, Paris. Works include: Commando Memorial, Spean Bridge, 1952; Black Watch Memorial, 1959. *Address:* 17 Norwood, Newport-on-Tay, Fife. *T:* Newport-on-Tay 3336.

**SUTHERLAND-HARRIS, Sir Jack (Alexander),** KCVO 1968; CB 1959; Second Crown Estate Commissioner, 1960-68; *b* 8 May 1908; *s* of late Lieut-Colonel A. S. Sutherland-Harris, DL, JP, Burwash, Sussex; *m* 1934, Rachel Owen Jones, *yr d* of late Capt. Owen Jones, CBE, Worplesdon, Surrey; two *s* two *d*. *Educ:* Winchester Coll.; New Coll., Oxford. Entered Min. of Agriculture and Fisheries as Asst Principal, 1932; Principal Private Secretary to Minister of Agriculture and Fisheries, 1941-43; Asst Sec., 1943-50; Under-Sec., 1950-60. *Recreation:* lawn tennis. *Address:* Wychanger, Shere, Surrey. *T:* Shere 2300. *Clubs:* Royal Commonwealth Society, MCC.

**SUTTIE, Sir (George) Philip Grant-,** 8th Bt, *cr* 1702; *b* 20 Dec. 1938; *o s* of late Maj. George Donald Grant-Suttie and Marjorie Neville, *d* of Capt. C. E. Carter, RN, of Newfoundland; *S* cousin, 1947; *m* 1962, Elspeth Mary (marr. diss. 1969), *e d* of Maj.-Gen. R. E. Urquhart, *qv*; one *s*. *Educ:* Sussex Composite High School, NB, Canada; Macdonald College, McGill University, Montreal. *Heir: s* James Edward Grant-Suttie, *b* 29 May 1965. *Address:* (seat) Balgone, North Berwick; Sheriff Hall, North Berwick, East Lothian. *T:* 2569. *Club:* New (Edin.).

**SUTTIE, Col Hubert Francis Grant-,** CBE 1940; DSO 1918; MC; RA; *b* 15 Dec. 1884; *e s* of late Robert Grant-Suttie and Hon. Edith Mary Dawnay, *d* of 7th Viscount Downe; *m* 1920, Torfrida Alianore, *er d* of Sir Wroth Lethbridge, 5th Bt, and Hon. Mrs Walter Yarde-Buller of Marchington Hall, Staffs; one *s* one *d*. Served European War, 1914-18 (despatches four times, DSO, MC); Lt-Col 1933; Col 1936; AQMG War Office, 1936-39; retired pay, 1939; served War of 1939-45 (CBE); Command Welfare Officer, Scotland, 1943-47; CStJ, 1953 (OStJ, 1948). Member Royal Co. of Archers, Queen's Body Guard in Scotland. *Address:* 31 Whitelands House, Chelsea, SW3. *Club:* Caledonian.

**SUTTIE, Sir Philip Grant-;** *see* Suttie, Sir G. P. G.

**SUTTON, Denys;** Editor of Apollo since 1962; Art critic to Financial Times; *b* 10 Aug. 1917; *s* of Edmund Sutton and Dulcie Laura Wheeler; *m* 1940, Sonja Kilbansky (marr. diss.); 1952, Gertrud Kœbke-Knudson (marr. diss.); 1960, Cynthia Sassoon; one *s* one *d*. *Educ:* Uppingham School; Exeter Coll., Oxford (BA, BLitt). Foreign Office Research Dept, 1940-46; Sec., Internat. Commn for Restitution of Cultural Material, 1946; Fine Arts Specialist as UNESCO 1948; Visiting lectr at Yale Univ., 1949. Organiser, Bonnard Exhibition, RA, 1966, France in the 18th Century, RA, 1968. Formerly: Art Critic to Country Life; Saleroom Correspondent of Daily Telegraph. *Publications:* Watteau's Les Charmes de la Vie, 1946; Matisse, 1946; Picasso, Blue and Pink Periods, 1948; French Drawings of the 18th Century, 1949; American Painting, 1949; Flemish Painting, 1950; Bonnard, 1957; Christie's since the War, 1959; André Derain, 1959; Nicholas de Staël, 1960; Gaspard Dughet, 1962; Toulouse-Lautrec, 1962; Titian, 1963; Nocturne; The Art of Whistler, 1964; Sergio de Castro, 1965; Triumphant Satyr, 1966; Whistler: Paintings, Drawings, Etchings and Water-colours, 1966; An Italian Sketchbook by Richard Wilson RA, 1968; Letters of Roger Fry, 1971; *introductions:* Vlaminck, Dangerous Corner, 1961; R. A. M. Stevenson, Velasquez, 1962; *jointly:* Artists in

17th Century Rome (with Denis Mahon), 1955; Catalogue of French, Spanish and German schools in Fitzwilliam Museum, Cambridge (with J. W. Goodison), 1960; Painting in Florence and Siena (with St John Gore), 1965. Contribs to magazines, etc. *Recreations:* theatre, swimming. *Address:* 22 Chelsea Park Gardens, SW3. *T:* 01-352 5141; Westwood Manor, Bradford-on-Avon, Wilts. *Club:* Travellers'.

**SUTTON, Brigadier George William,** CBE 1939; DSO 1918; TD; *b* 10 Jan. 1893; *y s* of late Charles William Sutton; unmarried. *Educ:* Kersal School, 2nd Lt 8th Lancashire Fusiliers (TF) from Manchester Univ. OTC, Aug. 1914; Lt 1915; Capt. 1916; served European War, Egypt, 1914-15; Gallipoli; 1915 (wounded); Sinai Peninsula, 1916; France, 1917-18 (severely wounded, DSO, despatches); attached General Staff Adjutant OTC Universities of Manchester, Leeds, Sheffield, Liverpool, and University College, Nottingham, 1919-20; Adjutant 8th Lancashire Fusiliers 1920-23 and commanded that unit, 1932-38; Col (TA), 1938; commanded 125th Infantry Brigade, 1938-40 (France, etc.), GSO 1 (HG) Canadian Corps and Sussex and Surrey District, 1941-44; Personnel Director, Cook's of St Paul's, 1948-52. *Address:* c/o Lloyds Bank Ltd, 6 Pall Mall, SW1.

**SUTTON, Sir Graham;** *see* Sutton, Sir O. G.

**SUTTON, Prof. John,** FRS 1966; FGS; DSc, PhD; ARCS; Professor of Geology, Imperial College of Science and Technology, London, since 1958 and Head of Geology Department, since 1964; *b* 8 July 1919; *s* of Gerald John Sutton; *m* 1949, Janet Vida, *d* of Professor D. M. S. Watson, *qv*. *Educ:* King's School, Worcester; Royal College of Science, London. Service with RAOC and REME, 1941-46. Research, Imperial College, 1946-48; Lecturer in Geology, Imperial College, 1948; Reader in Geology, Imperial College, 1956. Dean, Royal Sch. of Mines, 1965-68. President, Geologists' Association, 1966-68. Bigsby Medal, Geological Society of London, 1965 (jointly with Mrs Sutton). *Publications:* papers dealing with the Geology of the Scottish Highlands. *Recreation:* gardening. *Address:* Imperial College of Science and Technology, SW7; Hartfield, Sandy Drive, Cobham, Surrey. *T:* Oxshott 3129.

**SUTTON, Leslie Ernest,** FRS 1950; MA, DPhil Oxon; Fellow and Lecturer in Chemistry, Magdalen College, Oxford since 1936; Reader in Physical Chemistry since Oct. 1962 (University Demonstrator and Lecturer in Chemistry since 1945); *b* 22 June 1906; *o c* of Edgar William Sutton; *m* 1st, 1932, Catharine Virginia Stock (*d* 1962), *er d* of Wallace Teall Stock, Maplewood, NY, USA; two *s* one *d*; 2nd, 1963, Rachel Ann Long, *er d* of Lt-Col J. F. Batten, Swyncombe, Henley-on-Thames; two *s*. *Educ:* Watford Gram. Sch.; Lincoln Coll., Oxford (Scholar). 1st Class Hon. School Chemistry, 1928; research at Leipzig Univ., 1928-29, and at Oxford University; Meldola Medal (R Inst. of Chemistry), 1932; Fellow by Examination, Magdalen College, 1932-36; Rockefeller Fellow, California Inst. of Technology, 1933-34; Harrison Prize (Chemical Soc.), 1935; Tilden Lecturer (Chemical Soc.), 1940. Vice-Pres., Magdalen College, 1947-48. Hon. Sec. Chemical Society, 1951-57; a Vice-Pres., 1957-60. Visiting Prof., Heidelberg Univ., 1960, 1964, 1967. *Publications:* papers in scientific jls; (as scientific Editor) Tables of Interatomic Distances and Configuration in Molecules and Ions, 1958, 1964; Chemische Bindung und Molekülstruktur, 1961. *Address:* Magdalen College, Oxford. *T:* Oxford 41781.

**SUTTON, Sir (Oliver) Graham,** Kt 1955; CBE 1950; FRS 1949; BSc, Oxon, DSc Wales; JP; Vice-President, University College of Wales, Aberystwyth, since 1967; *b* 4 Feb. 1903; *s* of Oliver Sutton, late of Cwmcarn, Mon, and Rachel, *d* of William Rhydderch, Brynmawr, Brecon; *m* 1931, Doris, *e d* of T. O. Morgan, Porthcawl; two *s*. *Educ:* Pontywaun Grammar School; University College of Wales, Aberystwyth (Scholar); Jesus Coll., Oxford (Scholar); Hon. Fellow, 1958. Lectr, University College of Wales, Aberystwyth, 1926-28; Professional Assistant, Meteorological Office, 1928-41; Superintendent of Research, CDEE, Porton, 1942-43; Superintendent, Tank Armament Research, 1943-45; Chief Superintendent, Radar Research and Development Estab., Malvern, 1945-47; Bashforth Prof. of Mathematical Physics, 1947-53 and Dean, 1952-53, RMCS; Dir-Gen., Meteorological Office, 1953-65. Chm., Atmospheric Pollution Research Cttee, 1950-55; Scientific Adviser to the Army Council, 1951; President: Royal Meteorological Soc., 1953-55; IPCS, 1957-61; Chm., NERC, 1965-68; Member: Nature Conservancy, 1956-59; Council of University Coll. of Wales, Aberystwyth, 1958-64. Hon. Mem., Amer. Met. Soc.; Hon. FSE. Hon. DSc Leeds; Hon. LLD Wales. President's Gold Medal, Soc. of Engineers, 1957; Symons Gold Medal, RMetS, 1959; Internat. Met. Organization Prize, 1968; Frank A. Chambers Award, Air Pollution Control Assoc., 1968. *Publications:* Atmospheric Turbulence, 1949; The Science of Flight, 1950; Micrometeorology, 1953; Mathematics in Action, 1953; (with D. S. Meyler) Compendium of Mathematics and Physics, 1957; Understanding Weather, 1960; The Challenge of the Atmosphere, 1961; Mastery of the Air, 1965; scientific papers in various journals. *Address:* Hafod, 4 The Bryn, Sketty Green, Swansea, Glam.

**SUTTON, Rt. Rev. Peter (Eves);** *see* Nelson, NZ, Bishop of.

**SUTTON, Sir Robert Lexington,** 8th Bt, *cr* 1772; *b* 18 Jan. 1897; *s* of Sir Arthur Sutton, 7th Bt, and Cecil (Blanche) (*d* 1948), *d* of W. D. Dumbleton, Cape Colony; *S* father, 1948; *m* 1936, Gwladys, *d* of Maj. A. C. Gover, MC; two *s*. *Educ:* Wellington; RMC, Sandhurst. Served European War, 1915-19. *Heir: s* Richard Lexington Sutton [*b* 27 April 1937; *m* 1959, Fiamma Ferrari; one *s* one *d*]. *Address:* Clinger Farm, Wincanton, Somerset.

**SUTTON, Robert William,** CB 1962; OBE 1946; retired as Superintendent and Chief Scientific Officer, Services Electronics Research Laboratories, Baldock, Herts, 1946-70; *b* 13 Nov. 1905; *s* of late William Sutton; *m* 1951, Elizabeth Mary, *d* of George Maurice Wright, CBE, Chelmsford; one *s* two *d*. *Educ:* Brighton College; Royal College of Science, London University. Formerly with Ferranti Ltd, and then with E. K. Cole Ltd until 1938. Admiralty from 1939. *Address:* 33 Hitchin Street, Baldock, Herts. *T:* Baldock 3373.

**SUTTON, Sir Stafford William Powell F.;** *see* Foster-Sutton.

**SUTTON, Stanley Cecil,** CBE 1961; Librarian, India Office Library, since 1949, and Keeper, India Office Records, since 1954; *b* 23 Sept. 1907; *s* of John Archibald and Margaret Sutton; *m* 1935, Elizabeth, *y d* of Bruce and Bessie Sinclair; two *s* two *d*. *Educ:* County Sch., Tottenham; London Sch. of Economics;

University Coll., London. BSc Econ, Graham Wallas Prizeman LSE 1930, MSc Econ 1937; DipLibr 1931, Sir John MacAlister Medallist UCL. Joined Staff of British Library of Political and Economic Science, 1931; Sub-librarian, India Office Library, 1935; Asst Keeper 1937; Keeper 1946; Chm., British South Asia Library Group, 1967-. Sir Percy Sykes Memorial Medallist, RCAS, 1969. FSA 1970. *Publications:* Guide to the India Office Library, 1952 (2nd edn 1967); articles and reviews in librarianship jls. *Recreations:* music, walking. *Address:* 24 Stanley Hill Avenue, Amersham, Bucks. *T:* Amersham 3516.

**SUTTON, Thomas Francis;** Director, J. Walter Thompson Co. Ltd, since 1960 (Managing Director, 1960-66); Director and Executive Vice-President, J. Walter Thompson Co., New York, since 1966; *b* 9 Feb. 1923; *m* 1950, Anne Fleming; one *s* two *d*. *Educ:* King's School, Worcester; St Peter's College, Oxford. Research Officer, British Market Research Bureau Ltd, 1949-51; Advertising Manager, Pasolds Ltd, 1951-52; Managing Director, J. Walter Thompson GmbH, Frankfurt, Germany, 1952-59. FIPA; FIS; Fellow, Royal Statistical Soc. Mem. Adv. Bd, Sch. of Internat. Business, Rutgers Univ. Internat. Advertising Man of the Year Award, 1970. *Recreations:* chess, skiing, tennis, riding. *Address:* Coldharbour, Warninglid, Sussex; 45 E 89th Street, New York, NY 10028, USA.

**SUTTON, Professor William Godfrey;** Principal and Vice-Chancellor, University of the Witwatersrand, Johannesburg, 1954-62; *b* 28 March 1894; *s* of late William Godfrey Sutton, and late Mary Sutton (*née* Bennett); *m* 1954, Aletta McMenamin (*née* Wilson). *Educ:* King Edward VII School, Johannesburg; University of Cape Town. Served European War, 1916-18, in German East African Campaign; Asst Engineer, Union Irrigation Dept, 1918-26; attached to US Reclamation Service, 1921-22; Professor of Civil Engineering, Univ. of the Witwatersrand, Johannesburg, 1926-54; War of 1939-45 Gen. Manager Central Organisation of Tech. Trg, Dept of Defence, 1941-44; Chief Technical Advisor, Dept of Commerce and Industries, 1944-45. President: South African Institute of Engineers, 1936; SA Society of Civil Engrs, 1945; Associated Scientific and Tech. Socs of SA, 1951. Member: Universities Advisory Council; National Film Board; Smuts Meml Cttee; US-S Africa Leader Exchange Program; Trustee, S Africa Foundn. *Recreation:* bowls. *Address:* 48 Eastwood Road, Dunkeld, Johannesburg, South Africa. *T:* 42-1680. *Clubs:* Rand, Country (Johannesburg).

**SUTTON CURTIS, John;** Chairman: Thames Board Mills Ltd, since 1969; Workington Saw Mills Ltd, since 1966; *b* 2 July 1913; *s* of Harold Ernest Curtis; *m* 1936, Muriel Rose Hastwell; one *s*. *Educ:* Watford Grammar School. Served War of 1939-45, Royal Artillery. Thames Board Mills Ltd: Director, 1958; Vice-Chm., 1965; Dep. Chm. and Man. Dir, 1966-69. Chm., Assoc. of Board Makers, 1965-. *Recreations:* golf, motoring. *Address:* Covertside, Priests Lane, Shenfield, Essex. *T:* Brentwood 98.

**SUVA, Archbishop of, (RC),** since 1967; **Most Rev. George Pearce;** *b* 9 Jan. 1921; *s* of George H. Pearce and Marie Louise Duval. *Educ:* Marist Coll. and Seminary, Framingham Center, Mass, USA. Entered Seminary, 1940; Priest, 1947; taught in secondary sch. in New England, USA, 1948-49; assigned as missionary to Samoa, 1949; consecrated Vicar Apostolic of Samoa, 1956. *Address:* Archbishop's House, Box 393, Suva, Fiji. *T:* 28426.

**SUYIN;** *see* Han Suyin.

**SVENNINGSEN, Nils Thomas;** Grand Cross, Order of Dannebrog, Denmark; *b* 28 March 1894; *s* of Anders Svenningsen (Norwegian), Average Adjuster, and Anna Svenningsen (*née* Bennet, Swede); *m* 1922, Eva (*née* Larsen) (*d* 1960); one *d*. *Educ:* University of Copenhagen. Candidatus juris, 1917; practised as Assistant to a Danish Advocate in Copenhagen; entered Min. of Justice, Copenhagen, 1918. Joined Danish Foreign Service, 1920; Secretary to Danish Legation in Berlin, 1924-30; then different posts in Danish Foreign Ministry. Permanent Under-Secretary of State for Foreign Affairs, 1941-45; and 1951-61; Danish Ambassador to: Stockholm, 1945-50; Paris, 1950-51; the Court of St James's, 1961-64; retd. Chm., Swedish-Norwegian Commn on reindeer grazing, 1964. Hon. GBE 1957. *Recreation:* riding. *Address:* Overgaden oven Vandet 50, Copenhagen K. *T:* Asta 1566.

**SVENSON, Mrs Sven G.;** *see* Grey, Beryl.

**SWABEY, Christopher,** CMG 1962; Director, Commonwealth Forestry Bureau, since 1965; *b* 6 April 1906; *s* of late Reverend M. R. Swabey and Mrs Swabey; *m* 1947, Gabrielle Patricia (*née* Markham); one *d*. *Educ:* Winchester College; Edinburgh University (BSc). MA Oxon 1966. Assistant Conservator of Forests, Trinidad, 1928; Conservator of Forests, Jamaica, 1937; Conservator of Forests, British Guiana, 1946; Chief Conservator of Forests, Uganda, 1951; Forestry Adviser: Colonial Office, 1957-64; Ministry of Overseas Development, 1964-65. *Publications:* bulletins, reports and papers on tropical forestry problems. *Address:* Commonwealth Forestry Bureau, South Parks Road, Oxford. *T:* Oxford 57185. *Club:* Royal Commonwealth Society.

**SWABY, Rt. Rev. John Cyril Emerson;** *see* Jamaica, Bishop of.

**SWAIN, Air Commodore (Francis) Ronald Downs,** CB 1954; CBE 1946 (OBE 1941); AFC 1937; psa; retired; *b* 1903; *s* of late Major Charles Sanchez de Pina Swain, TD, Southsea, Hants; *m* 1938, Sarah Mitchell, *d* of Charles H. Le Fèvre, Washington, DC; three *d*. *Educ:* Stonyhurst Coll. Joined Royal Air Force, 1922; Wing Comdr, 1939; Air Commodore, 1949. Commanded Cairo-Rhodesia Flight, 1933; gained World High Altitude Record, 1936 (AFC); served War of 1939-45 (despatches, OBE, CBE); Air Officer Commanding No. 28 Group, RAF, 1949-50; Senior Air Staff Officer and Deputy Head of Air Force Staff, British Joint Services Mission, Washington, 1950-54, retired 1954. *Address:* c/o Westminster Bank Ltd, 133 Westbourne Grove, W2; St Martins, Emsworth, Hants; British Joint Services Mission (Air Force Staff), 1910 K Street, NW, Washington, DC, USA.

**SWAIN, Freda Mary;** composer and pianist; *b* Portsmouth, Hants; *d* of Thomas Swain and Gertrude Mary Allen; *m* Arthur Alexander (pianist, Prof. at RCM) (*d* 1969). *Educ:* St John's Southsea (private sch.); Matthay Pianoforte Sch. (under Dora Matthay); RCM. Won Associated Board Exhibition for piano at early age; Ada Lewis Scholarship for piano (RAM); Portsmouth-Whitcombe Scholarship for Composition (RCM); chose latter and studied under Sir Charles Villiers Stanford at RCM and (during last year) under Arthur Alexander (piano); Sullivan Prize for composition and Ellen Shaw Williams Prize for piano; Prof. of piano, RCM, for 14 years; founded British Music Movement, later NEMO concerts, with which former is now incorporated; extensive tours of S Africa and Australia (lecturing and piano), mainly on behalf of British music. FRCM. *Works in manuscript* include: orchestral; concertos (two piano, one clarinet); chamber music (two string quartets, one pianoforte quartet, violin and piano sonata, poem for violin and piano, sonata for violin solo, Summer Rhapsody for viola and piano, Rhapsody No. 2 for viola and piano, sonata for left hand (piano), Three Movements for violin and piano); anthems and wedding anthems; hymns, various; a one-act opera; Perceptions (for two pianos); Flourish (for two pianos); over ninety songs. *Publications* include; *Piano:* Humoresque; Mountain Ash; An English Idyll; Two S African Impressions; Autumn Landscape; Wayward Waltz; Marionette on Holiday; Croon of the Sea; Musical Box; Windmill; Two Sonatas; Prelude and Toccata; Ballet-Scherzo for Three Pianos; *Clarinet:* The Willow Tree; Two Contrasts; Waving Grass; Laburnum Tree; Three Whimsies (solo); Rhapsody (with piano); *Oboe and Piano:* Paspy; Fantasy-Suite; *Violin or Flute:* Tambourin Gai (with piano); *Organ:* English Pastoral. *Songs:* Winter Field; Experience; Blessing; Country Love; The Lark on Portsdown Hill; The Green Lad from Donegal; Song for Scouts and Guides; Climbing The Terraces (Chinese); *Choral:* A Chinnor Carol; Sweet Content; Two Christmas Carols; A Gaelic Prayer; Carol of the Seasons; Te Deum; Jubilate; Cantata in Memoriam; Bird of the Wilderness (Song Cycle); Hymns. *Recreations:* reading, the English countryside. *Address:* High Woods, Chinnor Hill, Oxfordshire. *T:* Kingston Blount 285.

**SWAIN, Thomas Henry;** MP (Lab) Derbyshire North-East since Oct. 1959; *b* 29 Oct. 1911; *s* of late Thomas Henry Swain, Burton-on-Trent; *m* 1931, Ruth Hannah (*d* 1969), *d* of Frank Wootton, Staveley, Derbyshire; six *s* four *d*; *m* 1969, Rosemary Fischer. *Educ:* Broadway School, Burton-on-Trent. Miner. Member: Staveley UDC, 1944-56; Derbyshire CC, 1946- . Vice-Pres., Derbyshire Area Exec., and Branch Sec., National Union of Mineworkers. *Address:* Hotel Cecil, 13 Belgrave Road, SW1; 3 Markham Crescent, Staveley, Derbyshire.

**SWAINE, Edward Thomas William,** CMG 1968; MBE 1952; Director, Exhibitions Division, Central Office of Information, since 1961; *b* 17 July 1907; *s* of Edward James Swaine; *m* 1942, Ruby Louise (*née* Ticehurst). Entered Govt Service, Min. of Information, 1940; Festival of Britain, 1948-52; Dir of Exhibns, British Pavilion, Montreal World Exhibn, 1967 and Tokyo World Exhibn, 1970. *Recreation:* photography. *Address:* 6/12 Northwood Hall, Highgate, N6. *T:* 01-340 4392.

**SWALLOW, John Crossley,** PhD; FRS 1968; Physical Oceanographer, National Institute of Oceanography, since 1954; *b* 11 Oct. 1923; *s* of Alfred Swallow and Elizabeth (*née* Crossley); *m* 1958, Mary Morgan (*née* McKenzie); one *step d*. *Educ:* Holme Valley Gram. Sch.; St John's Coll., Cambridge. Admty Signal Estabt, 1943-47; research in marine geophysics, at Cambridge and in HMS Challenger, 1948-54; work on ocean circulation, in RRS Discovery II, and in RRS Discovery, and other vessels, 1954-. Murchison Grant of RGS, 1965. Holds American awards in oceanography. *Publications:* papers on physical oceanography. *Address:* Crossways, Witley, Surrey. *T:* Wormley 2819.

**SWALLOW, Sir William,** Kt 1967; FIMechE; Chairman: Shipbuilding Industry Board, since 1966; Economic Development Council for Hotel and Catering Industry, since 1966; *b* 2 Jan. 1905; *s* of William Swallow, Gomersal, Yorks; *m* 1929, Kathleen Lucy Smith; no *c*. *Educ:* Batley and Huddersfield Technical Colleges. Draughtsman, Karrier Motors Ltd, 1923; senior draughtsman, chief body designer, Short Bros, 1926; Gilford Motors Ltd, 1930; development engineer, Pressed Steel Co., 1932; chief production engineer, Short Bros, 1943; development engineer, General Motors Overseas Operations, New York, 1947; i/c manufacturing staff, General Motors Ltd, 1948; gen. man., A. C. Sphinx Spark Plug Div. of Gen. Motors Ltd, 1950; Managing Director, General Motors Ltd, 1953, Chairman, 1958; Chm., Vauxhall Motors Ltd, Luton, Beds, 1961-66 (Man. Dir, 1961-65). Mem., Advisory Council on Technology, 1968-; Chm., NPL Adv. Bd, 1969-. ARAeS; MSAE. President: SMMT, 1964-65 (Dep. Pres. 1966-67); Inst. Road Tspt Engrs, 1966-68. *Address:* Alderton Lodge, Ashridge Park, Berkhamsted, Herts. *T:* Little Gaddesden 2284. *Club:* Royal Automobile.

**SWAN, Conrad Marshall John Fisher,** PhD; York Herald of Arms since 1968; *b* 13 May 1924; *yr s* of late Dr Henry Peter Swan, Major RAMC and RCAMC, of BC, Canada and Colchester, Essex, and of Edna Hanson Magdalen (*née* Green); *m* 1957, Lady Hilda Susan Mary Northcote, *yr d* of 3rd Earl of Iddesleigh; one *s* four *d*. *Educ:* St George's Coll., Weybridge; Sch. of Oriental and African Studies, Univ. of London; Univ. of Western Ontario; Peterhouse, Cambridge. BA 1949, MA 1951, Univ. of W Ont; PhD 1955, Cambridge. Served Europe and India (Capt. Madras Regt, IA), 1942-47. Assumption Univ. of Windsor, Ont.: Lectr in History, 1955-57; Asst Prof. of Hist., 1957-60; Univ. Beadle, 1957-60. Rouge Dragon Pursuivant of Arms, 1962-68. On Earl Marshal's staff for Investiture of HRH Prince of Wales, 1969. Woodward Lectr, Yale, 1964; Centennial Lectr, St Thomas More Coll., Univ. of Saskatchewan, 1967; Inaugural Sir William Scott Meml lectr, Ulster-Scotland Hist. Foundn, 1968; first Herald to execute transatlantic duties in Tabard, Bermuda, 1969. World lecture tour, 1970. Hon. Citizen, State of Texas; Freemanships in USA; Freeman, St George's, Bermuda, 1969; Fellow, Amer. Heraldry Soc.; Hon. Vice-Pres. and a Founder, Heraldry Soc. of Canada. Kt of Grace and Devotion, SMO of Malta, 1964 (Dep. Dir, Ceremonies, 1969-). *Recreation:* hunting. *Address:* College of Arms, Queen Victoria Street, EC4. *T:* 01-248 1850; Boxford House, Boxford, near Colchester. *T:* Boxford (Suffolk) 208.

**SWAN, Major-General Dennis Charles Tarrant,** CB 1953; CBE 1948; *b* 2 Sept. 1900; *s* of late Lt-Col C. T. Swan, IA; *m* 1930, Patricia Ethel Mary Thorne (*d* 1960); one *s* one *d*. *Educ:* Wellington Coll., Berks; Royal Military Academy, Woolwich. Commissioned as 2nd Lt RE, 1919; served War of 1939-45 (despatches twice): with BEF France, Feb.-May 1940; CRE 1 Burma Div., 1941; Comdt No. 6 Mech. Eqpt Group, IE 1944; Chief Engineer, 15 Ind. Corps 1945; District Chief Engineer, BAOR, 1946, Chief Engineer, 1948; Capt 1930; Adjutant, 36 (Mx) AA Bn, 1935; Major, 1938; Lt-Col, 1945; Colonel 1947; Brig. 1948; Maj.-Gen., 1952; Director of Fortification and Works, War Office, 1952-55, retired. Pres., Instn of Royal Engineers, 1961-65. *Address:* 15 Lancastrian Grange, Tower Street, Chichester, Sussex. *T:* Chichester 86899.

**SWAN, Harold Couch,** CMG 1948; OBE 1934; *b* 1 April 1890; *s* of late Henry Edwin Swan and Mary Westcott Couch; *m* 1916, May Augusta, *d* of late Henry James Hollier; two *d*. *Educ:*

Swansea Grammar School; German High School, Genoa. British Pro-Consul at Venice, 1913; Temp. British Vice-Consul, 1916-20; transferred to Milan and granted a Civil Service Certificate as HM Vice-Consul in the Consular Service; transferred to Savona, 1922; to New Orleans, 1924; HM Chargé d'Affaires at San Salvador, 1925; HM Consul at Havre, 1928, HM Consul-General at Leopoldville (Belgian Congo), 1932; British Sub-Agent, Malaga, Spain, 1938-39; Consul-General for the Republic of San Marino and Consul at Florence, Italy, 1939; Consul at Trieste, 1939-40; Consul at Seattle, 1940-44; Consul-General at Naples, 1944-45; HM Consul-General at Genoa (Italy), 1945-50; retired, 1951. Member Caterham and Warlingham UDC, 1954-63. Coronation Medal, 1937. *Recreations:* golf, shooting, motoring. *Address:* 7 Clareville Road, Caterham, Surrey. *T:* Caterham 43734.

**SWAN, Lt-Comdr Sir Kenneth Raydon,** Kt 1949; OBE 1919; QC 1936; RNVR; *b* Lowfell, Gateshead-on-Tyne, 13 March 1877; 3rd *s* of Sir Joseph Wilson Swan, FRS; *m* 1919, Emily Louisa, *o d* of Edward Robert Tatchell; (one *d* decd). *Educ:* Rugby School; Balliol College, Oxford. 2nd Hon. Mods, 2nd Hon. Law; called to Bar, 1902; served European War in RNVR, 1914-19, in HMS Cyclops and at Naval Barracks, Buncrana; Board of Education (O Branch), 1919-20; resumed practice at Bar, 1920; Bencher, Middle Temple, 1943. Chairman: Board of Trade Patents Cttee, 1944; Dep. Chairman of Royal Commission on Awards to Inventors, 1946; Chairman of Special Cttee Southern Province under Reorganization Areas Measure (1944), 1947; President of British Sailors' Soc., 1959 (Chairman, 1940-59); President, Royal Skating Club, 1955. *Publications:* Patents, Designs and Trade Marks; Memoir of Sir Joseph W. Swan, FRS. *Recreations:* lawn tennis, golf, skating, ski-ing, music, chess. *Address:* Cobwood, Woolton Hill, Newbury. *T:* Highclere 436. *Clubs:* Athenæum, Ski Club of Great Britain (Pres., 1911-13).

**SWAN, Sheriton Clements;** Director of: Swan, Hunter (Shipbuilders) Ltd; The Wallsend Slipway and Engineering Co. Ltd 1957; M. W. Swinburne & Sons, Ltd; Barclay Curle & Co. Ltd; Glasgow Iron & Steel Co. Ltd; Brims & Co., Ltd; Henry Hall (Gateshead) Ltd; *b* 15 Jan. 1909; *s* of late Sir Charles Sheriton Swan, Stocksfield-on-Tyne; *m* 1936, Rosalind Maitland, *d* of late D. S. Waterlow; two *s* one *d*. *Educ:* Cambridge Univ. Went to Architectural Assoc. in London to complete architectural training; joined firm of Swan, Hunter and Wigham Richardson, Ltd, in 1935. *Address:* Milestone Cottage, Wall, Northumberland. *T:* Humshaugh 319.

**SWAN, Thomas,** MA, LLB; Partner in Warren Murton & Co., Solicitors, 1927-67; Chairman of Smith's Group of cos, 1963-67, and a director of other public cos; *b* 11 Aug. 1899; *s* of Thomas David Swan; *m* 1922, Iola Blanche Winfield Roll; two *s* two *d*. *Educ:* Royal Grammar School, Newcastle upon Tyne; Emmanuel College, Cambridge. Served European War, 1914-18: Lt, The Black Watch, 1918-19; served War of 1939-45: Major, RA, 1940-45. Emmanuel College, 1919-21. Admitted Solicitor, 1923. Director: Walt Disney Productions; Vernon Packaging Ltd, etc. Member of Worshipful Company of Fan Makers (Master, 1956-57). *Recreations:* golf and bridge. *Address:* 20 Amhurst Court, Grange Road, Cambridge. *T:* Cambridge 63194. *Club:* United Service.

**SWAN, Lt-Col William Bertram,** CBE 1968; TD 1955; JP; farmer since 1933; Lord Lieutenant of Berwickshire since 1969; *b* 19 Sept. 1914; *er s* of late N. A. Swan, Duns, Berwickshire; *m* 1948, Ann Gilroy, *d* of late G. G. Hogarth, Ayton, Berwickshire; four *s*. *Educ:* St Mary's Sch., Melrose; Edinburgh Academy. Served 1939-42 with 4 Bn KOSB (UK and France) and 1942-45 with IA. Pres., Nat. Farmers Union of Scotland, 1961-62; Pres., Scottish Agric. Organisation Society Ltd, 1966-68; Mem., Development Commn. County Comdt, Army Cadet Force, Roxburgh, Berwick and Selkirk. JP 1964. *Recreation:* sport. *Address:* Blackhouse, Reston, Eyemouth, Berwickshire. *T:* Cumleage 242.

**SWANBOROUGH,** Baroness (Life Peeress); *see under* Reading, Dowager Marchioness of.

**SWANN, Sir Anthony (Charles Christopher),** 3rd Bt *cr* 1906; CMG 1958; OBE 1950; Minister for Defence and Internal Security, Kenya, 1959-63; *b* 29 June 1913; *s* of Sir (Charles) Duncan Swann, 2nd Bt,; *m* 1940, Jean Margaret Niblock-Stuart; one *s*. *Educ:* Eton College; New College, Oxford. Joined Colonial Service, Kenya, 1936. Served, 1940-43, with King's African Rifles (Major). District Commissioner, Kenya, 1946-54; Provincial Commissioner, Kenya, 1955-59. Chairman East African Land Forces Organisation, 1959-60. *Recreations:* music, reading, fishing, shooting. *Heir: s* Michael Christopher Swann [*b* 23 Sept. 1941; *m* 1965, Hon. Lydia Mary Hewitt, *e d* of Viscount Lifford, *qv*; one *s* one *d*]. *Address:* 23 Montpelier Square, SW7. *Clubs:* Carlton, Pratt's.

**SWANN, Donald Ibrahim,** MA; Composer and performer, free-lance since 1948; *b* 30 Sept. 1923; *s* of late Dr Herbert William Swann, Richmond, Surrey and Naguimé Sultan; *m* 1955, Janet Mary (*née* Oxborrow), Ipswich, Suffolk; two *d*. *Educ:* Westminster School; Christ Church, Oxford. Hons Degree Mod. Lang. (Russian and Mod. Greek). Contributed music to London revues, including Airs on a Shoestring, 1953-54, as joint leader writer with Michael Flanders; Wild Thyme, musical play, with Philip Guard, 1955; in At the Drop of a Hat, 1957, appeared for first time (with Michael Flanders) as singer and accompanist of own songs (this show ran over 2 yrs in London, was part of Edinburgh Festival, 1959; Broadway, 1959-60; American and Canadian tour, 1960-61; tour of Great Britain and Ireland, 1962-63). At the Drop of Another Hat (with Michael Flanders), Haymarket, 1963-64, Globe, 1965; Aust. and NZ tour, 1964; US Tour, 1966-67. Compositions include: satirical music to Third Programme series by Henry Reed, ghosting for Hilda Tablet. London Sketches with Sebastian Shaw, 1958; Festival Matins, 1962; Perelandra, music drama with David Marsh based on the novel of C. S. Lewis, 1961-62; Settings of John Betjeman Poems, 1964; Sing Round The Year (Book of New Carols for Children), 1965; The Road Goes Ever On, book of songs with J. R. R. Tolkien; Requiem for the Living, to words of C. Day Lewis, 1969. Arranged concerts of own settings: Set by Swann, An Evening in Crete, Soundings by Swann, 1967-68; Between the Bars: an autobiography in music (theatrical sequence), 1970. Member of several Christian pacifist groups and has given lectures. *Publications:* The Space Between the Bars, 1968; many works are published and recorded. *Recreation:* going to the launderette. *Address:* 13 Albert Bridge Road, SW11. *T:* 01-622 4281.

**SWANN, Professor Michael Meredith,** MA, PhD; FRS 1962; FRSE 1952; Principal and Vice-Chancellor of the University of Edinburgh, since 1965; *b* 1 March 1920; *er s* of late M. B. R. Swann, MD, Fellow of Gonville and Caius

Coll., Cambridge, and of Marjorie (she *m* 2nd, Sir Sydney Roberts, he *d* 1966); *m* 1942, Tess, ARCM, ARCO, *d* of late Prof. R. M. Y. Gleadowe, CVO, Winchester; two *s* two *d*. *Educ:* Winchester; Gonville and Caius College, Cambridge. Served War, 1940-46, in various capacities, mainly scientific (despatches, 1944). Fellow of Gonville and Caius College, Cambridge, 1946-52; University Demonstrator in Zoology, Cambridge, 1946-52; Professor of Natural History, University of Edinburgh, 1952-65. Member: Adv. Council on Educn in Scotland, 1957-61; Fisheries Adv. Cttee, Develt Commn, 1957-65. Council St George's School for Girls, 1959-; Edinburgh Univ. Court, 1959-62; MRC, 1962-65; Cttee on Manpower Resources, 1963-68; Council for Scientific Policy, 1965-69; SRC, 1969-; Chairman: Nuffield Foundation Biology Project, 1962-65; Jt Cttee on Use of Antibiotics in Animal Husbandry and Veterinary Medicine, 1967-68; Dean of the Faculty of Science, Edinburgh University, 1963-65. Hon. FRCSE 1967. Hon. LLD Aberdeen, 1967; Hon.D Univ. York, 1968; Hon. DSc Leicester, 1968. *Publications:* papers in scientific journals. *Recreations:* gardening, sailing, golf. *Address:* Ormsacre, 41 Barnton Avenue, Edinburgh 4. *T:* 031-336 1325; The Old College, Edinburgh 8. *T:* 031-667 1011. *Clubs:* Athenæum; New (Edinburgh).
*See also Bishop Suffragan of Willesden.*

**SWANN, Robert Swinney,** MBE 1947; Inspector, HM Diplomatic Service; *b* 17 Nov. 1915; *s* of R. N. and F. Swann. *Educ:* George Watson's Boys' College, Edinburgh; Edinburgh University. Indian Civil Service, 1938-47; Diplomatic Service, 1947-. *Recreations:* music; theatre. *Address:* 6 Collingham Gardens, SW5. *Club:* Travellers'.

**SWANN, Rev. Canon Sidney Ernest;** Hon. Canon of Bristol Cathedral, 1938, Canon Emeritus since 1951; *b* 24 June 1890; *s* of late Rev. Sidney Swann and Josephine Anderson; *m* 1917, Marjorie, *e d* of late Rt Rev. C. T. Abraham; one *s* one *d*. *Educ:* Rugby; Trinity Hall, Cambridge. Rowed in Cambridge crews of 1911, 1912, 1913 and 1914, being president in the last year; coached the Cambridge crews of 1920, 1921, 1922, 1924, and 1946; was a member of the Leander crew which won the Eights at the Olympic Games of 1912 and was second in 1920; twice won the Goblets at Henley, with his brother, Alfred Swann; a member of the Leander crew which won the Grand, in record time, at Henley in 1913; won the Colquhoun Sculls at Cambridge, at his first attempt, in 1910, and the Visitors and Wyfolds, at Henley the same year; President National Amateur Rowing Assoc. 1938-56; Hon. Life Mem. Amateur Rowing Assoc., 1956. Served European War, 1914-18, Chaplain to the forces, 1916-19; Chaplain of Trinity Hall, Cambridge, 1920-24; Archdeacon of Nairobi, Kenya Colony, 1926; Archdeacon in Egypt and subdean of the pro Cathedral at Cairo, 1928-33; Vicar of Leighton Buzzard, 1933-36; Vicar of St Mary Redcliffe, Bristol, 1937-51; Vicar of Timberscombe, Minehead, 1951-59. A mem. of the Mission of Help to India in 1922 and 1923; Select Preacher, Cambridge University, 1939; Rural Dean of Bedminster, 1940-49; Chaplain to the Queen, 1952-65 (to King George VI, 1941-52); Archbishop's Visitor to RAF, 1943-44. *Address:* Manor Cottage, Burghfield, Reading, Berks.

**SWANSEA,** 4th Baron *cr* 1893; **John Hussey Hamilton Vivian,** Bt 1882; DL; *b* 1 Jan. 1925; *s* of 3rd Baron and Hon. Winifred Hamilton (*d* 1944), 4th *d* of 1st Baron Holm Patrick; *S* father, 1934; *m* 1956, Miriam Antoinette, 2nd *d* of A. W. F. Caccia-Birch, MC, of Guernsey Lodge, Marton, NZ; one *s* two *d*. *Educ:* Eton; Trinity Coll., Cambridge. DL, County of Brecknock, 1962. *Recreations:* shooting, fishing, rifle shooting. *Heir: s* Hon. Richard Anthony Hussey Vivian, *b* 24 Jan. 1957. *Address:* Glanyrafon, Erwood, Breconshire. *T:* Erwood 662; 37 Bark Place, W2. *T:* 01-727 2268. *Club:* Junior Carlton.
*See also Hon. C. B. A. Bernard.*

**SWANSEA and BRECON, Bishop of,** since 1958; **Rt. Rev. John James Absalom Thomas,** DD Lambeth 1958; *b* 17 May 1908; *s* of William David and Martha Thomas; *m* 1941, Elizabeth Louise, *d* of Very Rev. H. L. James, DD, former Dean of Bangor; one *s*. *Educ:* University College of Wales, Aberystwyth; Keble College, Oxford. Curate of Llanguicke, 1931-34; Curate of Sketty, 1934-36; Bishop's Messenger and Examining Chaplain, 1936-40; Warden of Church Hostel, Bangor, and Lecturer in University Coll. of N Wales, 1940-44; Vicar of Swansea, 1945-58, also Chaplain to Bishop of Swansea and Brecon; Canon of Brecon Cathedral, 1946; Precentor, 1952; Rural Dean of Swansea, 1952-54; Archdeacon of Gower, 1954-58; Chm. of Governors, Christ Coll., Brecon, 1961-. Chaplain and Sub-Prelate, Order of St John of Jerusalem, 1965. *Address:* Ely Tower, Brecon.

**SWANSON, Gloria, (Gloria May Josephine Swanson);** American film actress; *b* Chicago; *d* of Joseph and Adelaide Swanson; *m* 1st, Wallace Beery (marr. diss.); 2nd, Herbert K. Somborn (marr. diss.); one *d*; 3rd, Marquis de la Falaise de la Coudraye (marr. diss.); 4th, Michael Farmer (marr. diss.); one *d*; 5th, William N. Davey (marr. diss.). Began film career in Mack Sennett comedies; later formed Gloria Swanson Productions; recently starred in Sunset Boulevard. Has also appeared in various theatrical rôles. Produced and played in own television show, The Gloria Swanson Hour, 1948. Cross of Honour and Merit, SMO Malta; OStJ 1963. *Address:* Gloria Swanson Enterprises Inc., 920 5th Avenue, New York, NY 10021, USA.

**SWANSON, John Leslie;** Director of The Wolverhampton and Dudley Breweries, Ltd, and of Associated Companies; *b* 29 Nov. 1892; *s* of late John Swanson, Edinburgh; *m* 1915, Frances Mary, *e d* of late Edwin John Thompson, Dudley, Worcs; one *s* (and a son killed on active service) one *d*. *Educ:* Edinburgh Academy. Member of the Inst. of Chartered Accountants of Scotland; Lieut 2/7th Battalion Worcestershire Regiment, 1915-19, France, 1916-17; President, Wolverhampton Chamber of Commerce, 1929-31; Chairman, Tettenhall Urban District Council, 1932-40 and 1943-45; High Sheriff of Staffordshire, 1941. *Recreation:* fishing. *Address:* The Orchard, Compton, Wolverhampton, Staffs. *T:* Wolverhampton 751640.

**SWANSTON, Commander David,** DSO 1945; DSC 1941, and Bar, 1942; RN; Assistant Serjeant at Arms, House of Commons, since 1957; *b* 13 Feb. 1919; *s* of late Capt. D. S. Swanston, OBE RN; *m* 1st, 1942, Sheila Anne Lang (marr. diss.); 2nd, 1953, Joan Margaret Nest Stockwood, *d* of I. H. Stockwood and late Mrs Stockwood; three *s* one *d*. *Educ:* Royal Naval College, Dartmouth. Joined Royal Navy, 1932; served in submarines at Home, Mediterranean, and East Indies Stations, from 1939. Comd Shakespeare, 1944-45; Alaric, 1948; Tudor, 1949; Naval Liaison Officer, RMA Sandhurst, 1951-53; passed RN Staff course, 1953; Commander, 1953; invalided from Royal Navy, 1955. Industrial employment, 1955-56. *Recreations:* golf, rifle shooting. *Address:* High Meadow, Linchmere, Haslemere, Surrey.

**SWANTON, Ernest William,** OBE 1965; Cricket and formerly Rugby football Correspondent to the Daily Telegraph; BBC Commentator; *b* 11 Feb. 1907; *s* of late William Swanton; *m* 1958, Ann, *d* of late R. H. de Montmorency and widow of G. H. Carbutt. *Educ:* Cranleigh. Evening Standard, Sporting Correspondent, 1927-39; Illustrated Sporting and Dramatic News Correspondent, and BBC Commentator, 1934-39. Played Cricket for Middlesex, 1937-38. Served 1939-46; captured at Singapore, 1942; POW Siam, 1942-45; Actg Maj. Bedfordshire Yeomanry (RA). Joined Daily Telegraph staff, 1946. Toured S Africa, 1938-1939, 1948-49, 1949-50, 1956-57; Australia, 1946-47, 1950-51, 1954-55, 1958-59, 1962-63, 1965-66; W Indies, 1948, 1954, 1960, 1968, with MCC; managed own XI to West Indies, 1956 and 1961 and to Malaya and Far East, 1964. Editorial Director, The Cricketer. *Publications:* (with H. S. Altham) A History of Cricket, editions 1938, 1946, 1948, 1962 (in 2 vols); Denis Compton, A Cricket Sketch, 1948; Elusive Victory (with F. R. Brown's Team in Australia), 1951; Cricket and The Clock, 1952; Best Cricket Stories (An Anthology), 1953; The Test Matches of 1953, 1953; West Indian Adventure, 1954; Victory in Australia, 1954/5, 1955; The Test Matches of 1956, 1956; Report from South Africa (with P. B. H. May's MCC Team, 1956-1957), 1957; West Indies Revisited, 1960; The Ahes in Suspense, 1963. General Editor of The World of Cricket, 1966; Cricket from all Angles, 1968. *Recreations:* cricket, golf. *Address:* Delf House, Sandwich, Kent. *Club:* MCC, Bath.

**SWANWICK, Hon. Sir Graham Russell,** Kt 1966; MBE 1944; **Hon. Mr Justice Swanwick;** Judge of the High Court of Justice (Queen's Bench Division), since 1966; Chairman, Derbyshire Quarter Sessions, 1963-66, Deputy Chairman, since 1966; Master of the Bench, Inner Temple, 1962; *b* 24 August 1906; *s* of Eric Drayton Swanwick and Margery Eleanor (*née* Norton), Whittington House, Chesterfield; *m* 1st, 1933, Helen Barbara Reid (marr. diss., 1945; she *d* 1970); two *s*; 2nd, 1952, Audrey Celia Parkinson. *Educ:* Winchester Coll.; University Coll., Oxford (BA). Called to Bar, Inner Temple, 1930; QC 1956; Leader Midland Circuit, 1961-65. Wing Comdr RAFVR, 1940-45 (MBE). Recorder: City of Lincoln, 1957-59; City of Leicester, 1959-66; Judge of Appeal, Channel Islands, 1964-66. *Recreations:* tennis, shooting. *Address:* 35 Wynnstay Gardens, W8. *T:* 01-937 2883; Sweethill, Ashurst, Steyning, Sussex. *T:* Partridge Green 241.

**SWART, Hon. Charles Robberts,** BA, LLB; State President, Republic of South Africa, May 1961-May 1967, retired; *b* 5 Dec. 1894; *m* 1924, Nellie de Klerk; one *s* one *d*. *Educ:* University Coll. of OFS, South Africa (BA, LLB); Columbia University, New York. Practised as Advocate, Supreme Court, S Africa, 1919-48; MP (Nat) for Ladybrand, OFS, 1923-38 and for Winburg, OFS, 1941-59; Minister of Justice, 1948-59; also Minister of Education Arts and Science, 1949-50; Deputy Prime Minister and Leader of the House, 1954-59; Acting Prime Minister, 1958; Governor-General of the Union of South Africa, 1960-61. Hon. Col, Regt, Oos-Vrystaat, 1953-; Hon. Col Regt Univ. Oranje-Vrystaat, 1963-. Chancellor, Univ. of OFS, 1951-. Hon. LLD, Univ. of OFS, 1955, Rhodes Univ., 1962, and Potchefstroom Univ., 1963; Hon. Fellow, Coll. of Physicians, Surgeons and Gynaecologists of SA, 1963-; Hon. Mem. SA Acad. of Science and Art; Life Mem. Federn of Afrikaans Cultural Socs; Hon. Fellow, SA Inst. of Architects; Life Patron-in-Chief, SA Voortrekker Youth Movement. *Publications:* (both in Afrikaans Language) Kinders van Suid-Africa, 1933; Die Agterryer, 1939. *Address:* De Aap, Brandfort, OFS, Republic of South Africa.

**SWASH, Stanley Victor,** MC 1917 and Bar 1918; *b* 29 February 1896; British; *s* of A. W. Swash, JP and Sylvia Swash; *m* 1924; *m* 1955, Jane Henderson. *Educ:* Llandovery College; St John's College, Oxford; Lincoln's Inn. Served European War, 1915-19, RFA. MA (Mathematics); short period in Ministry of Pensions; served Royal Navy as Lieut Inst., 1921-24; worked in Woolworth Company, 1924-55; Director, 1939, Chairman, 1951-55; retired 1955. Called to Bar, Lincoln's Inn, 1938. OC 57 County of London Home Guard Battalion, Lieut-Colonel, 1940-45. Chairman, Horticultural Marketing Advisory Council, 1958; Member Milk Marketing Board, 1957-63; Chm. BOAC/MEA Cttee of Enquiry, 1963-64. *Recreations:* golf, bridge. *Address:* Park Avenue, St Andrews, Malta. *Club:* Oxford and Cambridge.

**SWAYTHLING,** 3rd Baron, *cr* 1907; **Stuart Albert Samuel Montagu,** Bt, *cr* 1894; OBE 1947; late Grenadier Guards; formerly director, Messrs Samuel Montagu and Co. Ltd; *b* 19 Dec. 1898; *e s* of 2nd Baron and Gladys Helen Rachel, OBE, (*d* 1965), *d* of late Col A. E. Goldsmid; *S* father, 1927; *m* 1925, Mary Violet (from whom he obtained a divorce, 1942), *e d* of late Major Levy, DSO, and late Hon. Mrs Ionides; two *s* one *d*; *m* 1945, Mrs Jean Knox, Director ATS (*see* Lady Swaythling). *Educ:* Clifton; Westminster; Trinity College, Cambridge. JP Surrey. President, English Guernsey Cattle Society, 1950-51. Master of The Company of Farmers, 1962-63. *Heir: s* Hon. David Charles Samuel Montagu [*b* 6 Aug. 1928; *m* 1951, Françoise Christianne (Ninette), *d* of Edgar Dreyfus, Paris; one *s* two *d*]. *Address:* Crastock Manor, Crastock, Woking, Surrey. *T:* Worplesdon 2265. *Club:* Bath.

*See also Hon. E. E. S. Montagu, Ivor Montagu.*

**SWAYTHLING, Lady, (Jean M.),** CBE 1943; Chief Controller and Director, Auxilliary Territorial Service, 1941-43 (as Mrs Jean Knox); *b* 14 Aug. 1908; *m* Squadron Leader G. R. M. Knox; one *d*; *m* 1945, 3rd Baron Swaythling, *qv*. *Address:* Crastock Manor, Crastock, Woking, Surrey. *T:* Worplesdon 2265.

**SWAZILAND, Bishop of,** since 1968; **Rt. Rev. Anthony George Weaver Hunter;** *b* 3 June 1916; *s* of Herbert George Hunter and Ethel Frances Weaver; *m* 1948, Joan Isobel Marshall. *Educ:* Wanstead; Leeds Univ. (BA); Coll. of the Resurrection, Mirfield. Deacon, 1941; Priest, 1942; Curate of St George's, Jesmond, 1941-43; Orlando Mission Dist, 1943-47; Johannesburg Coloured Mission, 1947-48; Curate of St George's, Jesmond, 1948-49; Vicar of Ashington, 1949-60; Proctor in Convocation, 1959-60; Vicar of Huddersfield, 1960-68; Rural Dean of Huddersfield, 1960-68; Hon. Canon of Wakefield, 1962-68; Proctor in Convocation, 1962-68. OStJ. *Recreations:* walking, gardening, travel. *Address:* Bishop's House, PO Box 118, Mbabane, Swaziland, Southern Africa. *T:* 2333. *Club:* St John's.

**SWEANEY, William Douglas,** CMG 1965; Assistant Secretary, Ministry of Overseas Development, since 1964; *b* 12 Nov. 1912; *s* of late Lt-Comdr William Sweaney, MBE, RN, and late Elizabeth Bridson; *m* 1939, Dorothy Beatrice Parsons; one *s*. *Educ:* Gillingham

Gram. Sch.; London Sch. of Economics. Clerical Officer, Inland Revenue (Special Comrs of Income Tax), 1929; Officer of Customs and Excise, 1932; seconded to Colonial Office, 1943 (promoted Surveyor of Customs and Excise *in absentia*); transferred to Colonial Office, 1948; Principal, 1948; Private Secretary to Minister of State for Colonial Affairs, 1953; Asst Secretary, 1955; seconded to Dept of Technical Co-operation, 1961. *Recreations:* walking, ornithology. *Address:* Crowlink, Borde Hill Lane, Haywards Heath, Sussex. *T:* Haywards Heath 50341.

**SWEENEY, Maj.-Gen. Joseph A.;** *b* Burton Port, 13 June 1897; *s* of John and Margaret Sweeney Burton Port; two *s* one *d.* MP (SF) West Donegal, 1918-22; Member, of Dail for County Donegal, 1922-23; GOC Donegal Command, 1923-24; GOC Curragh Command, 1924-26; GOC Athlone Command, 1926-28; Adjutant General, 1928-30; Quartermaster-General, 1930-31; Chief of Staff, General Headquarters, Dublin, 1930-31; GOC Curragh Command, 1931-38; GOC Athlone Command, 1938-40; retired, 1940. Area Officer, Irish Red Cross Society, 1950-54; Dep. Sec. Gen., 1954-56; Gen. Sec., 1956-62. Retd Dec. 1962. Mem. Board of Governors, Michael Collins Memorial Foundation, 1965. *Address:* 26 Orchardstown Park, Dublin 14.

**SWEET, Prof. Peter Alan,** MA, PhD; Regius Professor of Astronomy in the University of Glasgow, since Oct. 1959; *b* 15 May 1921; *s* of David Frank Sweet; *m* 1947, Myrtle Vera Parnell; two *s. Educ:* Kingsbury County Grammar School, London; Sidney Sussex College, Cambridge. Open Maj. Schol. in Maths, Sidney Sussex Coll., 1940-42, Wrangler, 1942, BA Cantab 1943. Junior Scientific Officer, Min. of Aircraft Prod., 1942-45; BA Scholar, at Sidney Sussex Coll., 1945-47; MA Cantab 1946; Mayhew Prizeman, 1946, PhD Cantab 1950. Lectr in Astronomy, Univ. of Glasgow, 1947-52; Lectr in Astronomy and Asst Director of the Observatory, Univ. of London, 1952-59. Visiting Asst Professor of Astronomy, Univ. of California, Berkeley, 1957-58; Vis. Res. Fellow, NASA Inst. for Space Studies, NY, 1965-66. *Publications:* papers on Stellar Evolution, Cosmic Magnetism, and Solar Flares in Monthly Notices of Royal Astronomical Soc., etc. *Recreations:* music, gardening. *Address:* 17 Westbourne Crescent, Bearsden, Glasgow. *T:* 041-942 4425.

**SWEETING, William Hart,** CMG 1969; CBE 1961; Deputy Governor, Bahamas, since 1969; *b* 18 Dec. 1909; *s* of late Charles Cecil Sweeting, Nassau, Bahamas; *m* 1950, Isabel Jean (*née* Woodall). *Educ:* Queen's Coll., Nassau; London Univ. Entered Bahamas Public Service as Cadet, 1927; served in Colonial Secretary's Office, 1927-37; acted as Asst Colonial Sec. for short periods in 1928 amd 1936; transferred to Treasury, 1937; Cashier, Public Treasury, 1941; Asst Treasurer and Receiver of Crown Dues, 1946; seconded as Financial Sec., Dominica, 1950-52; Receiver-Gen. and Treasurer, Bahamas, 1955; MLC, Bahamas, 1960-64; Chm., Bahamas Currency Comrs, 1955-63; Chm., Bahamas Broadcasting and Television Commn, 1956-62. Acted as Governor various periods 1959, 1964, 1965, 1966, 1968, 1969; acted as Colonial Secretary various periods, 1962-63; Chief Secretary, Bahamas 1964. *Recreations:* tennis, swimming, painting, music, bird watching. *Address:* Prospect Ridge, PO Box 573, Nassau, Bahamas. *T:* 3-4057. *Clubs:* Corona; Rotary (Nassau, Bahamas).

**SWEETMAN, Mrs Ronald Andrew;** *see* Dickson, Jennifer J.

**SWEETT, Cyril,** FRICS; Senior Partner, Cyril Sweett & Partners, Chartered Quantity Surveyors; *b* 7 April 1903; *s* of William Thomas Sweett; *m* 1931, Barbara Mary, *d* of late Henry Thomas Loft, Canterbury and London; one *d. Educ:* Whitgift Sch.; Coll. of Estate Management. Artists Rifles, TA, 1923-27. Army Service: RE, 1939-43, France, N Africa and Italy; demob. as Lt-Col. Mem. Council, RICS, 1959-61 (Founder Chm., Cost Research Panel, 1956-60); Chm., Nat. Jt Consultative Cttee of Architects, Quantity Surveyors and Builders, 1962-63. Master, Worshipful Co. of Painter Stainers, 1964-65, 1966-67; Sheriff of City of London, 1965-66. *Address:* 22 Raynham Norfolk Crescent, W2. *T:* 01-262 8600; 26 Warnham Court, Grand Avenue, Hove, Sussex. *T:* Brighton 777292. *Clubs:* Garrick, Reform, Royal Thames Yacht, Royal Ocean Racing, Royal Burnham Yacht (Cdre, 1963-65).

**SWIFT, Reginald Stanley,** CB 1969; Assistant Under-Secretary of State, Department of Health and Social Security, since 1968; *b* 2 Nov. 1914; *e s* of Stanley John and Annie Swift; *m* 1940, Mildred Joan Easter; no *c. Educ:* Watford Grammar School; Christ's College, Cambridge. BA Cantab (1st Cl. Hons in Classics) 1936; MA Cantab 1940; BSc (Econ.) London 1944. Entered Civil Service as Asst Comr, National Savings Cttee, 1938; transferred to Min. of National Insurance as Principal, 1947; Principal Private Secretary to Minister, 1953-54; Assistant Secretary, 1954; Under-Secretary, 1962. *Recreations:* gardening, golf, sailing. *Address:* Woodpeckers, The Chase, Kingswood, Tadworth, Surrey. *T:* Mogador 2951. *Clubs:* Oxford and Cambridge; Kingswood Golf.

**SWINBURN, Maj.-Gen. Henry Robinson,** CB 1947; OBE 1945; MC 1922; *b* 8 May 1897; *e s* of late Henry Swinburn; *m* 1932, Naomi Barbara, *yr d* of late Major-General Sir C. P. Amyatt Hull, KCB; two *s.* Entered Indian Army, 1918; Royal Ludhiana Sikhs: served European War, 1914-18, Operations, NWF India, 1919, Iraq, 1920, Kurdistan, 1922-23 (wounded, MC); BEF France, 1940 (despatches, OBE). Staff College, Quetta, 1929-30; psc†; GSO II, GHQ India, 1932-36; Instructor Staff Coll., Camberley, 1937-38; Instructor Senior Staff College, Minley, 1939; Chief Instructor School of Military Intelligence, 1939-40; GSO I, 51 Highland Div., 1940; Director of Morale, India, 1945; Deputy Mil. Sec., GHQ India, 1946; Military Secretary, GHQ India, 1946-47; retired, 1948. Bt Major, 1934; Bt Lt-Col, 1939; Temp. Maj.-Gen., 1946; Subs Col, 1947; Counsellor, UK High Commission in India, 1948-49. Schools Liaison Officer, 1952-60. *Recreation:* fishing. *Address:* Stoney Close, Nunton, Salisbury, Wilts. *T:* Bodenham 241. *Club:* Naval and Military.

*See also Field Marshal Sir R. A. Hull.*

**SWINBURNE, Nora;** actress; *b* Bath, 24 July 1902; *d* of H. Swinburne Johnson; *m* 1st, Francis Lister (marriage dissolved); one *s*; 2nd, Edward Ashley-Cooper (marriage dissolved); 3rd, 1946, Esmond Knight, *qv. Educ:* Rossholme College, Weston-super-Mare; Royal Academy of Dramatic Art. First West End appearance, 1916; went to America, 1923; returned to London stage, 1924; New York, again, 1930; continuous successes in London, from 1931; went into management, 1938, in addition to acting. Played as Diana Wentworth in The Years Between (which ran for more than a year), Wyndhams, 1945; Red Letter Day, Garrick; A Woman of No Importance,

Savoy, 1953; The Lost Generation, Garrick, 1955; Fool's Paradise, Apollo, 1959; Music at Midnight, Westminster, 1962. *Films include:* Jassy, Good Time Girl, The Blind Goddess, Fanny by Gaslight, They Knew Mr Knight, Quartet, Christopher Columbus, My Daughter Joy, The River (made in India), Quo Vadis, also Helen of Troy (made in Italy), Third Man on the Mountain, Conspiracy of Hearts, Music at Midnight, Interlude, Anne of the Thousand Days. Has appeared on television (incl. Forsyte Saga, Post Mortem). *Address:* 35 Bywater Street, Chelsea, SW3.

**SWINDELL, Rev. Frank Guthrie,** MA Oxon; Permission to Officiate, diocese of Exeter and diocese of Truro; *b* 18 Dec. 1874; *s* of Rev. T. G. Swindell; *m* 1910, Gladys Dorothy, *d* of S. Wells Page, Penn House, Wolverhampton. *Educ:* Pocklington Sch., Yorks; St Catherine's Society, Oxford University. Deacon, 1898; Priest, 1899; Curate of Boxley, Maidstone, 1898-1902; Chaplain of Selangor (St Mary's Church, Kuala Lumpur), FMS 1902-06; Colonial Chaplain of Malacca and Negri Sembilan, 1906-16; acting in Singapore, 1907 and 1911, and in Penang, 1912; Colonial Chaplain of St Andrew's Cathedral, Singapore, 1914-29; Archdeacon of Singapore, 1916-29 (retired); Rector of Isfield, diocese of Chichester, 1930-50 (resigned). *Publication:* A Short History of St Andrew's Cathedral, Singapore. *Address:* Rhylla, Townlake, Tavistock, S Devon. *T:* Milton Abbot 263.

**SWINDELLS, Rev. Bernard Guy,** SJ; BSc (London), BSc (Liverpool), ARCSc; *b* 24 May 1887. *Educ:* Stonyhurst College. Rector of Stonyhurst College, 1945-52; Rector of St Ignatius' College, 1953-59; Spiritual Father at Beaumont College, 1959-61; Rector of Manresa College, Roehampton, 1961-62; Rector of Harlaxton Manor, 1962-65. *Address:* St Ignatius' Presbytery, South Tottenham, N15. *T:* 01-800 2121.

**SWINDLEHURST, Joseph Eric,** OBE 1951; CEng, FInstCE, FIStructE; Borough Engineer and Surveyor, Hampstead, 1924-55; *b* 2 Aug. 1890; *s* of late Joseph Eaves Swindlehurst, MInstCE, and E.I. Artis; *m* 1928, Gwendolen (*d* 1964), *d* of late Ernest Spencer Warne; no *c*. *Educ:* King Henry VIIIth School, Coventry; Gonville and Caius College, Cambridge, MA. Articled to J. E. Swindlehurst, MInstCE, City and Water Engineer, Coventry; served in various capacities the Municipalities of Coventry, Eastbourne, and Preston; served with commission in RE 1914-19. President Association of Metropolitan Borough Engineers and Surveyors, 1936 and 1949; Pres. Inst. of Highway Engineers, 1937 and 1938; Pres. Incorporated Association of Architects and Surveyors, 1939-40; Vice-Pres. Royal Soc. of Health, 1945-; Pres. Instn Struct. E, 1950-51; Pres. Brit. Sect., Soc. des Ingénieurs Civils de France, 1952 and 1953; Member of Building Technical Advisory Cttee of Min. of Home Security; Mem. of Architecture and Public Utilities Committee and of Civil Engineering Committee of Ministry of Labour and Nat. Service Central Register Advisory Council, 1939; Director, Bituminous Roads Development Group, 1957. Freeman of City of London; Freeman and Liveryman of Worshipful Company of Painter Stainers; Registered Architect; James Forrest Medallist and Miller Prizeman, InstCE. *Publications:* various papers. *Recreations:* motoring, foreign travel. *Address:* The Moorings, The Avenue, Bushey, Herts. *Club:* Oxford and Cambridge.

**SWINDON, Archdeacon of;** *see* Temple, Ven. F. S.

**SWINFEN,** 2nd Baron, *cr* 1919, of Chertsey; **Charles Swinfen Eady;** Barrister-at-Law, Inner Temple; *b* 2 Feb. 1904; *s* of 1st Baron and Blanche, (*d* 1946), *y d* of S. W. Lee; *S* father, 1919; *m* 1st, 1937, Mary Aline (from whom he obtained a divorce, 1945), *yr d* of late Col H. Mynors Farmar, CMG, DSO; two *s*; 2nd, 1950, Averil Kathleen Suzanne Knowles, *er d* of late Maj. W. M. H. Humphreys, Eire. *Educ:* Eton; Christ Church, Oxford. *Heir: s* Hon. Roger Mynors Swinfen Eady [*b* 14 Dec. 1938; *m* 1962, Patricia Anne, *o d* of F. D. Blackmore, Doone, Highfield Park, Dundrum, Co. Dublin; three *d*]. *Clubs:* St James', Carlton. *See also H. W. Farmar.*

**SWINLEY, Captain Casper Silas Balfour,** DSO 1941; DSC 1940; Royal Navy; *b* 28 Oct. 1898; *y s* of late Gordon Herbert Swinley, Assam, India, and Margaret Eliza, *d* of late Prof. J. H. Balfour, Edin.; *m* 1928, Sylvia Jocosa, 4th *d* of late Canon W. H. Carnegie, Rector of St Margaret's, Westminster, and Sub-Dean of Westminster Abbey; two *s* twin *d*. *Educ:* Epsom College. Entered Royal Navy with Special Entry Cadetship, 1916; served European War, 1916-18, as Midshipman and Sub-Lieut in HMS New Zealand; HMS Ceres, evacuation of Odessa, 1919-20; Queen's Coll., Cambridge, 1920; ADC and Private Sec. to Sir Charles O'Brien, Governor of Barbados, 1921-22; HMS Curacoa, evacuation of Smyrna, 1922-23; HMS Calcutta, Flagship West Indies Station, 1924-26; HMS Ganges, Boys' Training Establishment, Shotley, 1926-28; Flag-Lieut to Adm. Sir E. Alexander-Sinclair, C-in-C the Nore, 1928-30; HMS Repulse, 1930-32; HMS Carlisle, Africa Station, under Adm. Sir Edward Evans, 1932-34; Comdr 1934; commanded HMS Express, 5th Destroyer Flotilla, Abyssinian crisis, Spanish War, Jubilee Review, 1935-37; NID, Admiralty Naval Staff, 1937-39; commanded HMS Impregnable, Boys' Training Establishment, Devonport, 1939; commanded HMS Codrington and Dover Patrol Destroyers, taking the King to France also Mr Winston Churchill, 1939-40; French Destroyer Brestois for Liaison duties; evacuation of Namsos, Norway; commanded demolition party at Calais (DSC). 1940; commanded HMS Isis, North Sea, Genoa, Greece, Crete (DSO); Syrian campaign, 1940-41; commanded HMS Miranda and Minesweepers, Great Yarmouth; Capt. 1942; Chief Staff Officer to Vice-Adm. Sir Ralph Leatham, Malta, 1942; Director of Service Conditions, Admiralty, 1943-45; Commanded HMS Arethusa, 1945-46; Chief Staff Officer to Vice-Adm. Sir F. Dalrymple Hamilton, Malta, 1946; commanded HMS Flamingo and Senior Officer Reserve Fleet, Devonport, 1946-47; Chief Naval Information, Admiralty, 1947-48; Captain in Charge, Captain Superintendent and King's Harbour Master, Portland, 1949-51. Naval ADC to the King, 1951; Commodore and Chief of Staff, Royal Pakistan Navy, 1953-54. Senior Whale Fishery Inspector, South Georgia, 1959-60. Appeals Organiser, BRCS, Gloucestershire, 1963-67. *Recreations:* painting, scrap-book collecting. *Address:* Broughtons, near Newnham, Glos. *T:* Westbury-on-Severn 328. *Club:* Royal Naval (Portsmouth).

**SWINNERTON, Frank Arthur;** novelist and critic; President, Royal Literary Fund, 1962-66; *b* Wood Green, 12 Aug. 1884; *y s* of Charles Swinnerton and Rose Cottam; *m* 1924, Mary Dorothy Bennett; one *d*. *Publications:* The Merry Heart, 1909; The Young Idea, 1910; The Casement, 1911; The Happy Family, 1912; George Gissing: a Critical Study, 1912; On the Staircase, 1914; R. L. Stevenson: a Critical Study, 1914; The Chaste Wife, 1916;

Nocturne, 1917; Shops and Houses, 1918; September, 1919; Coquette, 1921; The Three Lovers, 1922; Young Felix, 1923; The Elder Sister, 1925; Summer Storm, 1926; Tokefield Papers, 1927; A London Bookman, 1928; A Brood of Ducklings, 1928; Sketch of a Sinner, 1929; Authors and the Book Trade, 1932; The Georgian House, 1932; Elizabeth, 1934; The Georgian Literary Scene, 1935; Swinnerton: an Autobiography, 1937; Harvest Comedy, 1937; The Two Wives, 1939; The Reviewing and Criticism of Books, 1939; The Fortunate Lady, 1941; Thankless Child, 1942; A Woman in Sunshine, 1944; English Maiden, 1946; The Cats and Rosemary, (US) 1948, (England) 1950; Faithful Company, 1948; The Doctor's Wife Comes to Stay, 1949; A Flower for Catherine, 1950; The Bookman's London, 1951; Master Jim Probity, 1952; Londonder's Post, 1952; A Month in Gordon Square, 1953; The Sumner Intrigue, 1955; Authors I Never Met, 1956; Background with Chorus, 1956; The Woman from Sicily, 1957; A Tigress in Prothero, 1959; The Grace Divorce, 1960; Death of a Highbrow, 1961; Figures in the Foreground, 1963; Quadrille, 1965; A Galaxy of Fathers, 1966; Sanctuary, 1966; The Bright Lights, 1968; Reflections from a Village, 1969; On the Shady Side, 1970. *Address:* Old Tokefield, Cranleigh, Surrey. *Club:* Reform.

**SWINNERTON-DYER, (Henry) Peter (Francis);** FRS 1967; Lecturer in Faculty of Mathematics, University of Cambridge, since 1960; Fellow and Director of Studies in Mathematics, Trinity College, since 1955, Dean since 1963; *b* 2 Aug. 1927; *s* of Sir Leonard S. S. Dyer, 15th Bt, *qv. Educ:* Eton; Trinity College, Cambridge. Research Fellow, Trinity College, 1950-54; Commonwealth Fund Fellow, Univ. of Chicago, 1954-55; University Lecturer, Mathematical Laboratory, 1960-67. *Publications:* numerous papers in mathematical journals. *Recreation:* tennis. *Address:* Trinity College, Cambridge.

**SWINTON,** 1st Earl of, *cr* 1955; **Philip Cunliffe-Lister,** PC 1922; GBE, *cr* 1929 (KBE, *cr* 1920); CH 1943; MC; DL; Viscount Swinton, 1935; Baron Masham, 1955; *b* 1 May 1884; *y s* of late Colonel Y. G. Lloyd-Greame of Sewerby House, Bridlington; *m* 1912, Mary Constance, *o d* of late Rev. Ingram Boynton, Barmston, Yorks; (one *s* decd) and *er s* died of wounds, received in action, 1943); assumed name of Cunliffe-Lister, 1924. *Educ:* Winchester; University Coll., Oxford. Called to Bar, 1908; served in Army, 1914-17; Joint Secretary of Ministry of National Service, 1917-18; MP (U) Hendon Division of Middlesex, 1918-35; Parliamentary Secretary to Board of Trade, 1920-21; Secretary of Overseas Trade Department, 1921-22; President of the Board of Trade, 1922-23, 1924-29 and in 1931; Secretary of State for the Colonies, 1931-35; Secretary of State for Air, 1935-38; Chairman UK Commercial Corp., 1940-42; Cabinet Minister Resident in West Africa, 1942-44; Minister for Civil Aviation, 1944-45; Chancellor of the Duchy of Lancaster, and Minister of Materials, 1951-52; Secretary of State for Commonwealth Relations, Dec. 1952-Apr. 1955. Deputy Leader of the House of Lords, 1951-55; Chairman of Permanent Labour Committee of War Cabinet War Priorities Committee, 1918; Member of Select Committee on National Expenditure and Select Committee on High Prices and Profits, 1919; Chairman Imperial Economic Conference, 1923. Pres. Nat. Union of Conservative and Unionist Associations, 1949; Chairman of Governors of Swinton Conservative College, 1958-. DL North Riding, Yorkshire. Hon. Fellow University College, Oxford. Hon. LLD Liverpool University. Grand Officier, Order of Leopold. Hon. Air Commodore 608 Squadron RAF. *Publications:* I Remember, 1948; Sixty Years of Power: Some Memories of the Men Who Wielded it, 1966. *Recreations:* shooting and fishing. *Heir: gs* Lord Masham, *qv. Address:* 16 Kingston House, SW7. *T:* 01-589 0994; Swinton, Masham, Yorks. *T:* Masham 310. *Club:* Carlton.

**SWINTON, Brig. Alan Henry Campbell,** MC; FSA (Scotland) 1956; late Scots Guards; *b* 15 March 1896; *s* of late Capt. G. S. C. Swinton; *m* 1923, Mariora Hankey (who obtained a divorce, 1944); one *s*; *m* 1945, Mrs J. E. A. Best, *d* of Charles Baker, Southampton; one *s* one *d. Educ:* University College School; RMC, Sandhurst. A Member of the Queen's Body Guard for Scotland. The Royal Company of Archers (retd list). Hon. Sheriff Substitute, Berwickshire, 1954; County Councillor, 1949-. *Address:* Kimmerghame, Duns, Berwickshire. *T:* Duns 3277. *Clubs:* Pratt's; New (Edinburgh).

**SWIRE, John Kidston;** Director, John Swire & Sons, Ltd, 1920-68 (Chairman, 1946-66); Hon. President, Cathay Pacific Airways Ltd; Member, General Committee, Lloyd's Register of Shipping, 1940-68; *b* 19 Feb. 1893; *er s* of late John Swire, Hillingdon House, Harlow, Essex; *m* 1923, Juliet Richenda, *d* of Theodore Barclay, Fanshaws, Hertford; two *s* two *d. Educ:* Eton Coll.; University Coll., Oxford. Major Essex Yeomanry, with whom he served in European War 1914-19. DL Essex, 1928-68; High Sheriff, Essex, 1941-42. Min. of Shipping Rep. at Min. of Economic Warfare and on the Contraband Cttee, 1939-40; Chm. Port Employers in London and Port Labour Exec. Cttee, 1941-45. Chm. China Association, 1951-55. *Address:* Hubbards Hall, Harlow, Essex. *TA* and *T:* Harlow 29470. *Clubs:* Turf, Cavalry, City of London.
*See also Brig. E. J. Todhunter.*

**SWYER, Dr Gerald Isaac Macdonald;** Consultant Endocrinologist, Department of Obstetrics and Gynæcology, University College Hospital, London, WC1, since 1951; *b* 17 Nov. 1917; *s* of Nathan Swyer; *m* 1945, Lynda Irene (*née* Nash); one *s* one *d. Educ:* St Paul's School; Magdalen College and St John's College, Oxford; University of California; Middlesex Hospital Medical School. Foundation Schol. and Leaving Exhib., St Paul's School, 1931-36; Open Exhib. and Casberd Schol., St John's Coll., Oxford, 1936-39; Welsh Memorial Prize, 1937; Theodore Williams Schol. in Anatomy, 1938; 1st Cl. Final Honour School of Animal Physiology, 1939; Senior Demy, Magdalen Coll., 1940; Rockefeller Medical Student, Univ. of Calif, 1941. MA, DPhil, BM Oxon 1943; MD Calif, 1943; DM Oxon 1948; MRCP 1945; FRCP 1964. Mem. of Scientific Staff, Nat. Inst. for Med. Res., 1946-47; Endocrinologist, UCH Med. Sch., 1947. 1st Sec., formerly Chm., Soc. for the Study of Fertility; formerly, Mem. Council, Soc. for Endocrinology; formerly Pres., Sect. of Endocrinology, Roy. Soc. Med.; Sec.-Gen., Internat. Fedn of Fertility Societies; Mem. Exec. Sub-Cttee Internat. Endocrine Soc. *Publications:* Reproduction and Sex, 1954; papers in medical and scientific journals. *Recreations:* music, sailing. *Address:* 34 Chester Close North, Regent's Park, NW1. *T:* 01-935 5232.

**SWYNNERTON, Maj.-Gen. (Hon.) Charles Roger Alan,** CB 1950; DSO 1945; retired; *b* 12 February 1901; *s* of F. Swynnerton, Isle of Man; *m* 1926, Clare Inès, *d* of T. R. Stevenson, Moor Court, Amberley, Glos.; two *s. Educ:* RMC, Sandhurst. Commissioned The North

Staffordshire Regt. 1920; Capt. 1933; Major, 1938; Lt-Col 1947; Colonel, 1947; Brigadier, 1947; Temp. Maj.-Gen. 1947-49; ADC 1949-54. Served in Ireland, Mediterranean, India, West Africa and Burma; Military Attaché, HBM Embassy, Ankara, Turkey, 1950-54; ADC to King George VI and subsequently to Queen Elizabeth II, 1950-54; retd, 1954. Col Comdt, Royal West African Frontier Force, 1954-58; Col The North Staffordshire Regt, 1955-58. *Address:* Finca Las Chumberas, Alhaurin de la Torre, Málaga, Spain. *Club:* Army and Navy.

**SWYNNERTON, Roger John Massy,** CMG 1959; OBE 1951; MC 1941; Agricultural Adviser, Commonwealth Development Corporation, since 1962; *b* S Rhodesia, 16 Jan. 1911; *s* of late C. F. M. Swynnerton, CMG, formerly Dir Tsetse Research, Tanganyika, and Mrs N. A. G. Swynnerton (*née* Watt Smyth); *m* Grizel Beryl Miller, *d* of late R. W. R. Miller, CMG, formerly Member for Natural Resources, Tanganyika; two *s*. *Educ:* Lancing College; Cambridge University; Imperial College of Tropical Agriculture, Trinidad. BA (Hons) Cantab 1932; DipAgric Cantab 1933. AICTA, 1934. Entered Colonial Agricultural Service as Agric. Asst, 1934; Agric. Officer, 1935, and Sen. Agric. Officer, 1949, in Tanganyika Territory. Served War, 1939-42, with 1/6 Bn King's African Rifles (Temp. Capt.), Abyssinian Campaign; TARO, 1933-60; seconded to Malta on Agric. duty, 1942-43. Transferred to Kenya on promotion, Asst Director of Agric., 1951, Dep. Dir, 1954, Director, 1956. Nominated Member of Kenya Legislative Council, 1956-60; Permanent Sec., Min. of Agriculture, 1960-61, retd 1963; Mem. Advisory Cttee on Development of Economic Resources of S Rhodesia, 1961-62. *Publications:* All About KNCU Coffee, 1948; A Plan to Intensify the Development of African Agriculture in Kenya, 1954. Various Agricultural and scientific papers. *Address:* 35 Lower Road, Fetcham, Surrey. *Clubs:* Royal Commonwealth Society, Royal Over-Seas League; Nairobi (Kenya).

**SYCAMORE, Thomas Andrew Harding,** CBE 1949; retired; a Managing Director, Liebig's Extract of Meat Co. Ltd, 1963-66; Chairman, Chipmunk Ltd, 1962-66; Director: Beefex Products Ltd, 1954-66; Bellamy's Wharf & Dock Ltd, 1958-66; Oxo Ltd, 1954-66 (Managing Director 1954-63); Oxo (Canada) Ltd, 1954-66; Oxo (Ireland) Ltd, 1954-66; Oxo (USA) Ltd, 1954-66; Thames Side Properties Ltd, 1955-66; Produits Liebig SA, Basle, 1965-66; Euro-Liebig SC, Antwerp, 1964-66; Compagnie Française des Produits Liebig SA, Paris, 1963-66; Compagnie Liebig SA, Antwerp, 1963-66; Compagnia Italiana Liebig SpA, Milan, 1963-66; Nederlandse Oxo Maatschappij NV, Rotterdam, 1963-66; Liebig GmbH, Cologne, 1963-66; Beefco Corp., New York, 1963-66 (Chairman, 1964-66); London Philharmonic Society Ltd, 1960-66; *b* 31 Aug. 1907; *s* of late Henry Andrew and Caroline Helen Sycamore; *m* 1932, Winifred Clara Pellett; one *s* two *d*. *Educ:* privately. At Oxford Univ. Press, 1924-35; Manufacturing Confectioners' Alliance, 1936-40 (Asst Sec. 1940); Food Manufacturers' Federation Inc., 1936-54; Asst Sec., 1940; Sec., 1945; Director and Gen. Sec., 1947. Secretary, Bacon Marketing Bd, and many other food manufacturers' associations, etc; Mem., Food Research Adv. Cttee, 1960-66; Vice-Pres., Assoc. Internat. de l'Industrie des Bouillons et Potages (Paris), 1963-65. Member Council: British Food Manufacturing Industries Research Association (formerly Sec.); Food Manufacturers' Federation, Inc.; Grocers' Institute (a Vice-Pres. 1958-66, Hon. Treas. 1961-66); English Stage Soc.; Mem. Grand Council, FBI (member many committees); Deputy Leader and Sec. of two productivity teams which went to the US; helped to create Food Industries Council (Sec. for many years); helped in formation of National College of Food Technology, and to establish British Food Fair at Olympia (Sec. for many years). Served on Councils or Committees of various other bodies; a Governor of several schools. President of Appeal, Royal Commercial Travellers' Schools, 1960-61; Life Hon. Vice-President, Huddersfield Branch, United Commercial Travellers' Assoc., 1962; Chm., Nat. Music Council of Gt Brit., 1963-64. Freeman, City of London. Liveryman, Worshipful Company of Loriners; Life Mem., Guild of Freemen of City of London; FREconS; Hon. Fellow, Grocers' Institute; Officier de l'Ordre de la Couronne (Belgium), 1965. *Recreations:* music, theatre, reading, tennis, cricket. *Address:* Gainsborough, Warren Lane, Friston, near Eastbourne, Sussex. *T:* East Dean 2127.

**SYDNEY, Archbishop of,** since 1966; (Metropolitan of the Province of New South Wales); **Most Rev. Marcus Lawrence Loane,** DD; *b* 14 Oct. 1911; *s* of K. O. A. Loane; *m* 1937, Patricia Evelyn Jane Simpson Knox; two *s* two *d*. *Educ:* The King's School, Parramatta, NSW; Sydney University (MA). Moore Theological College, 1932-33; Australian College of Theology (ThL, 1st Class, 1933; Fellow, 1955). Ordained Deacon, 1935, Priest, 1936; Resident Tutor and Chaplain, Moore Theological College, 1935-38; Vice-Principal, 1939-53; Principal, 1954-59. Chaplain AIF, 1942-44. Canon, St Andrew's Cathedral, 1949-58; Bishop-Coadjutor, diocese of Sydney, 1958-66. Hon. DD Wycliffe College, Toronto, 1958. *Publications:* Oxford and the Evangelical Succession, 1950; Cambridge and the Evangelical Succession, 1952; Masters of the English Reformation, 1955; Life of Archbishop Mowll, 1960; Makers of Religious Freedom, 1961; Pioneers of the Reformation in England, 1964; Makers of Our Heritage, 1966; The Hope of Glory, 1968; The Surpassing Excellence, 1969; They Were Pilgrims, 1970. *Address:* Diocesan Church House, George Street, Sydney, NSW 2000, Australia. *TA:* Epistralia.

**SYDNEY, Archbishop of, (RC),** since 1940; **His Eminence Sir Norman Thomas Cardinal Gilroy,** KBE 1969; DD; *b* Sydney, NSW, 22 Jan. 1896; *s* of William James Gilroy and Catherine Slattery. *Educ:* Convent Schools of Sisters of the Good Samaritan and Sisters of Charity; Marist Brothers' School. Entered Postal Department, 1909; Wireless Operator on Commonwealth Transport Steamer Bulla carrying Australian troops to Egypt and Indian troops to the Dardanelles, 1915; present at landing of Troops on Gallipoli, 25 April 1915; entered St Columba's College, Springwood, 1917; Urban College of Propaganda, Rome, 1919; Priest for the Diocese of Lismore, NSW, 1923; Doctor of Theology, 1924; Secretary to the Apostolic Delegate, 1924-31; Secretary to Bishop and Chancellor of the Diocese of Lismore, 1931-34; Bishop of Port Augusta, South Australia, 1935-37; Titular Archbishop of Cypsela and Coadjutor to RC Archbishop of Sydney, 1937-40; Cardinal, 1946. *Address:* St Mary's Cathedral, Sydney, NSW 2000, Australia.

**SYDNEY, Coadjutor Bishops of;** *see* Begbie, Rt. Rev. H. G. S., Dain, Rt. Rev. A. J., Dilbridge, Rt. Rev. G. R., Hulme-Moir, Rt. Rev. Francis Oag.

**SYER, William George,** CVO 1961; CBE 1957; Secretary, West Africa Committee, since

1970; *b* 22 June 1913; *s* of late William Robert Syer and late Beatrice Alice Theresa Syer, Alton, Hants; *m* 1948, Marjorie Leila, *d* of late S. G. Pike, Essex. *Educ:* Kent College, Canterbury. Joined Colonial Police Service, 1933; Gibraltar, 1933-35; Jamaica, 1935-40; Nigeria, 1940-51; Comr of Police, Sierra Leone, 1951; retired, 1962; Comr of Police, Swaziland, 1964-68. Formerly Comr St John Ambulance Brigade, Sierra Leone. CStJ 1969. *Recreations:* gardening, golf. *Address:* South Grays, Highercombe Road, Haslemere, Surrey. *Club:* East India and Sports.

**SYERS, Sir Cecil George Lewis,** KCMG 1949 (CMG 1947); CVO 1941; JP; *b* 29 March 1903; *s* of late G. W. Syers; *m* Yvonne, *d* of late Inglis Allen; one *s*. *Educ:* St Paul's; Balliol Coll., Oxford (Scholar). 1st Class Honour Mods 1922, and Lit. Hum. 1925; MA 1929. Entered Dominions Office, 1925; Asst Private Secretary to Secretary of State for Dominion Affairs, 1930-34; Private Secretary to Prime Minister, 1937-40; Assistant Secretary, Treasury, 1940; Deputy UK High Commissioner in the Union of South Africa, 1942-46; an Assistant Under-Secretary of State, Commonwealth Relations Office, 1946-48, Deputy Under-Secretary of State, 1948-51; High Commissioner for the United Kingdom in Ceylon, 1951-57; Doyen of Diplomatic Corps, Ceylon, 1953-57. Pres., Ceylon Branch, Oxford Soc., 1954-57; Pres., Classical Assoc. of Ceylon, 1956, 1957. Secretary of the University Grants Committee, 1958-63. Mem. Governing Body, School of Oriental and African Studies, Univ. of London, 1963-; Director, Foundation Fund Appeal, Univ. of Kent at Canterbury 1964-66. JP Hove, 1967. *Address:* 25, One Grand Avenue, Hove, Sussex BN3 2LA. *T:* Brighton 732545. *Club:* United University.

**SYFRET, Adm. Sir (Edward) Neville,** GCB, *cr* 1948 (KCB, *cr* 1942; CB 1941); KBE, *cr* 1945; *b* 20 June 1889; *s* of Edward Ridge Syfret, Cape Town, SA; *m* 1913, Hildegarde Warner; one *s* one *d*. *Educ:* Diocesan College, SA; HMS Britannia. Entered RN 1904; Lieut 1909; Commander, 1922; Captain, 1929; Rear-Adm. 1940; Vice-Adm. 1943; Adm. 1946; Naval Secretary to 1st Lord, 1939-41; commanded Force "H" Sea Command, 1941-43; Vice-Chief of Naval Staff, 1943-45; Commander-in-Chief Home Fleet, 1945-48. *Address:* c/o Standard Bank, 10 Clements Lane, EC4.

**SYKES, (Arthur) Frank (Seton),** CVO 1962; DL; Agricultural Adviser to the Queen at Windsor, since 1950; *b* 4 July 1903; *e s* of late Sir Percy Sykes, KCIE, CB, CMG; *m* Barbara Godolphin, *e d* of W. H. Yeatman Biggs; one *s*. *Educ:* Rugby. Chairman: Frank Sykes Ltd; Central Line Sisal Estates Ltd. Mem. Royal Commission on East Africa, 1953. Alderman, Wilts CC, 1952; High Sheriff of Wilts, 1964; DL Wilts, 1968. *Publications:* This Farming Business, 1944; Living from the Land, 1957. *Recreations:* travel, hunting, fishing. *Address:* Stockton, Warminster, Wilts.

**SYKES, Lt-Col Arthur Patrick,** MBE 1945; JP; DL; *b* 1 Sept. 1906; *e s* of late Herbert R. Sykes, JP; *m* 1936, Prudence Margaret, *d* of late Maj.-Gen. D. E. Robertson, CB, DSO, Indian Army; one *s* one *d*. *Educ:* Eton; Magdalene College, Cambridge. 2nd Lt 60th Rifles, 1929; served India, Burma, Palestine; ADC to Governor of Bengal, 1933-35; War of 1939-45, Middle East (wounded); Lt-Col 1944. JP 1950, DL 1951, High Sheriff, 1961, Shropshire. *Address:* Lydham Manor, Bishop's Castle, Salop. *T:* Bishop's Castle 86.

**SYKES, Sir (Benjamin) Hugh,** 2nd Bt, *cr* 1921; *b* 8 June 1893; *e s* of Sir Charles Sykes, 1st Bt, and Mary (*d* 1944), *y d* of late Benjamin Newsome; *S* father, 1950; *m* 1935, Audrey Winifred, *o d* of late F. C. Thompson, Cricklewood, NW2; no *c*. *Educ:* Leys School, Cambridge. *Heir:* *n* John Charles Anthony Le Gallais Sykes, *b* 19 April 1928. *Address:* 19 Bouverie Gardens, Harrow HA3 0RQ. *T:* 01-907 3884. *Club:* Royal Automobile.

**SYKES, Bonar Hugh Charles;** Counsellor, Foreign and Commonwealth Office, since 1968; *b* 20 Dec. 1922; *s* of late Sir Frederick Sykes and of Isabel, *d* of Andrew Bonar Law; *m* 1949, Mary, *d* of late Sir Eric Phipps and of Frances Phipps; four *s*. *Educ:* Eton; The Queen's Coll., Oxford. War service in Navy (Lieut RNVR), 1942-46. Trainee with Ford Motor Co. (Tractor Div.), 1948-49. Joined Foreign Service, 1949: served in Prague, Bonn, Tehran, Ottawa. *Address:* Conock Manor, Devizes, Wiltshire. *T:* Chirton 227.

**SYKES, Sir Charles,** Kt 1964; CBE 1956; FRS 1943; FInstP; DSc, PhD; JP; Director, Thos Firth and John Brown Ltd, Sheffield, since 1944 (Managing Director, 1951-57; Deputy Chairman, 1962-64); Chairman: Firth Brown Ltd, 1962-67; Firth-Vickers Stainless Steel Ltd; Member, East Midlands Gas Board; *b* 27 Feb. 1905; *m* 1930, Norah Staton. *Educ:* Staveley; Netherthorpe Grammar School; Sheffield Univ. Superintendent, Metallurgy Dept, National Physical Laboratory, 1940-44; Superintendent Terminal Ballistics Branch, Armament Research Dept, 1943-44; Director of Research, Brown-Firth Research Laboratories, 1944-51. Pres., Inst. of Physics, 1952-54; Member, Council for Scientific and Industrial Research, 1962-65; Chairman, Adv. Councils on Research and Development, Min. of Power: Fuel and Power, 1965-70; Iron and Steel, 1967-70. Pro-Chancellor, Sheffield University, 1967-. Iron and Steel Inst. Bessemer Gold Medal, 1956; Glazebrook Medal and Prize (IPPS), 1967. *Address:* Atlas Works, Sheffield 1.

**SYKES, Christopher Hugh,** FRSL; Author; Script-writer and Producer, BBC, 1949-68; Member, London Library Committee, since 1965; *b* 17 Nov. 1907; 2nd *s* of late Sir Mark Sykes, Bart, Sledmere; *m* 1936, Camilla Georgiana, *d* of El Lewa Sir Thomas Russell Pasha, CMG; one *s*. *Educ:* Downside; Christ Church, Oxford. Hon. Attaché to HM Embassy, Berlin, 1928-29, and to HM Legation, Tehran, 1930-31. Served War of 1939-45: 7 Battalion The Green Howards, 1939; GHQ, Cairo, 1940-41; HM Legation, Tehran, 1941-43; seconded to SAS Bde (despatches, Croix de Guerre). Special correspondent of the Daily Mail for the Persian Azerbaijan Campaign, 1946; Deputy Controller, Third Programme, BBC, 1948. *Publications:* Wassmuss, 1936; (with late R. Byron), Innocence and Design, 1936; Stranger Wonders, 1937; High Minded Murder, 1943; Four Studies in Loyalty, 1946; The Answer to Question 33, 1948; Character and Situation, 1949; Two Studies in Virtue, 1953; A Song of A Shirt, 1953; Dates and Parties, 1955; Orde Wingate, 1959; Cross Roads to Israel, 1965; Troubled Loyalty: a Biography of Adam von Trott, 1968. *Recreation:* music. *Address:* The Old Rectory, Swyre, Dorchester, Dorset. *Club:* White's.

**SYKES, Edwin Leonard,** CMG 1966; Secretary, Office of the Parliamentary Commissioner for Administration, since 1967; *b* 1 May 1914; *m* 1946, Margaret Elizabeth McCulloch. *Educ:* Leys School, Cambridge (Schol.); Trinity Coll., Cambridge (Senior Schol.). Entered

Dominions Office, 1937; Asst Priv. Sec. to Secretary of State, 1939. Served War, 1939-45 (despatches). Served in British High Commissions, Canada, 1945-47, India, 1952-54; idc 1955; Dep. UK High Commissioner in Federation of Rhodesia and Nyasaland, 1956-59; Asst Under-Sec. of State, CRO, 1964-65; Dep. UK High Commissioner in Pakistan, 1965-66. *Address:* Highwood, Woodland Drive, East Horsley, Surrey. *Club:* United University.

**SYKES, Sir Francis (Godfrey),** 9th Bt, *cr* 1781, of Basildon; Regional Secretary to Country Landowners' Association since 1957; *b* 27 Aug. 1907; *s* of Francis William Sykes (*d* 1945) (*ggs* of 2nd Bt) and Beatrice Agnes Sykes (*née* Webb) (*d* 1953); *S* cousin, Rev. Sir Frederic John Sykes, 8th Bt, 1956; *m* 1934, Eira Betty (*d* 1970), *d* of G. W. Badcock; one *s* one *d*. *Educ:* Blundell's School, Devon; Nelson College, New Zealand. Tea planting, 1930; Air Ministry, 1939; fruit farming and estate management, 1945-57. FCIS. *Heir: s* Francis John Badcock Sykes [*b* 7 June 1942; *m* 1966, Susan Alexandra, *er d* of Vice-Admiral E. B. Ashmore, *qv*; two *s*]. *Address:* Gubbals House, Preston Gubbals, near Shrewsbury, Salop. *T:* Bomere Heath 272. *Clubs:* Royal Over-Seas League; Shropshire (Shrewsbury).

**SYKES, Frank;** *see* Sykes, A. F. S.

**SYKES, Sir Hugh;** *see* Sykes, Sir B. H.

**SYKES, Joseph Walter,** CMG 1962; CVO 1953; Chief Secretary, Bermuda, since June 1968; *b* 10 July 1915; *s* of Samuel Sykes and Lucy M. Womack; *m* 1940, Elima Petrie, *d* of late Sir Hugh Hall Ragg; three *s* two *d*. *Educ:* De La Salle Coll., Sheffield; Rotherham Gram. Sch.; Jesus Coll., Oxford. Colonial Administrative Service, Fiji; Cadet, 1938; Dist Officer, 1940; District Commissioner, 1950; Deputy Secretary for Fijian Affairs, 1952; Assistant Colonial Secretary, 1953; transferred to Cyprus as Dep. Colonial Sec., Nov. 1954; Admin. Sec., Cyprus. 1955-56; Colonial Sec., Bermuda, 1956-68. *Publication:* The Royal Visit to Fiji 1953, 1954. *Recreations:* photography, tennis. *Address:* Colonial Secretariat, Hamilton, Bermuda. *Club:* Oxford and Cambridge.

**SYKES, Professor Keble Watson;** Head of Chemistry Department, since 1959, and Professor of Physical Chemistry, Queen Mary College, University of London, since 1956; *b* 7 Jan. 1921; *s* of Watson and Victoria May Sykes; *m* 1950, Elizabeth Margaret Ewing Forsyth; three *d* (and one *s* decd). *Educ:* Seascale Preparatory Sch.; St Bees Sch.; The Queen's Coll., Oxford, MA, BSc, DPhil (Oxon.). ICI Research Fellow, Physical Chemistry Lab., Oxford, 1945-48; Lecturer, 1948-51, and Senior Lecturer in Chemistry, 1951-56, University Coll. of Swansea, Univ. of Wales. Hon. Sec. Chemical Soc. of London, 1960-66, Vice-Pres., 1966-69. Member Council, Westfield College, University of London. *Publications:* scientific papers in journals of Royal Society, Faraday Soc. and Chem. Soc. *Address:* 58 Wood Vale, Muswell Hill, N10. *T:* 01-883 1502.

**SYKES, Sir (Mark Tatton) Richard,** 7th Bt, *cr* 1783; JP; DL; High Sheriff, Yorkshire, 1948-49; *b* 24 Aug. 1905; *s* of 6th Bt and late Edith Violet, 3rd *d* of Rt. Hon. Sir J. E. Gorst; *S* father, 1919; *m* 1942, Virginia (*d* 1970), *o d* of John Gilliat and Lillian (*widow* of 5th Marquess of Anglesey and *d* of Sir George Chetwynd, 4th Bt); four *s* two *d*. *Educ:* Downside; Trinity Coll., Cambridge. Member East Riding County Council, Alderman 1946-; President: Bridlington Div. Conservative Assoc.; East Riding Georgian Soc.; E Yorkshire Local History Soc.; Northern Counties Musical Soc. Lieutenant 5th Bn The Green Howards, 1925-27; Lt 7th Bn The Green Howards, 1939; served France, 1940; Captain, 1940. Lt-Col comdg 6th E R Yorks Home Guard, 1952-54. Jt Master, E Middleton Foxhounds, 1931-39; Member, Jockey Club. *Recreations:* horse breeding, coursing, organist. *Heir: s* Tatton Christopher Mark Sykes, *b* 24 Dec. 1943. *Address:* Sledmere, Driffield, Yorks. *Club:* White's.
*See also Earl of Antrim.*

**SYKES, Lt-Col Peter Thomas Wellesley,** OBE 1942; DL; farming at Chitterne since 1948; *b* 21 Dec. 1903; *s* of late Lt-Col H. P. Sykes and Winifred Charlotte Jane (*née* Wellesley); *m* 1st, 1931, Nina Violet Eyre Coote (*d* 1935); two *s*; 2nd, 1937, Violet Lavender Christie-Miller; one *s* one *d*. *Educ:* Rugby; Sandhurst. Joined The Queens Bays, 1924; Adjutant, 1935-38. Served War of 1939-45 (wounded twice); i/c Royal Wiltshire Yeomanry, 1942; GSO1, War Office, 1943; i/c 54th training regt, 1944; i/c The Queens Bays 1945. Retired from Army, 1947. Mem. Wilts TAA, 1950; CC 1949, DL 1963, High Sheriff 1963; CA 1964, Wilts. *Recreations:* shooting, fishing. *Address:* Chitterne House, Chitterne, Warminster, Wilts. *T:* Codford St Mary 209. *Club:* Cavalry.

**SYKES, Sir Richard;** *see* Sykes, Sir (M. T.) R.

**SYKES, Richard Adam,** CMG 1965; MC 1945; Ambassador to Cuba, since 1970; *b* 8 May 1920; *s* of late Brig. A. C. Sykes, CBE, DSO; *m* 1953, Ann Georgina, *d* of Brig. A. F. Fisher, *qv*; two *s* one *d*. *Educ:* Wellington Coll.; Christ Church, Oxford. Served Army, 1940-46; Major, Royal Signals. Joined HM Foreign Service, 1947; served: Foreign Office, 1947-48; Nanking, 1948-50; Peking, 1950-52; Foreign Office, 1952-56; Brussels, 1956-59; Santiago, 1959-62; Athens, 1963-66; Foreign and Commonwealth Office, 1967-69. Croix de Guerre (France), 1945. *Address:* c/o Westminster Bank Ltd, Warminster, Wilts. *Clubs:* Travellers', Army and Navy.

**SYLVESTER, Albert James,** CBE, 1920; JP, Wilts; *b* Harleston, Staffs, 24 Nov. 1889; *s* of late Albert and Edith Sylvester; *m* Evelyn (*d* 1962), *d* of late Rev. W. Welman, Reading; one *d*. *Educ:* Guild Street School, Burton-on-Trent; privately. Private Secretary to Sec. of Cttee of Imperial Defence, 1914-21; Private Sec. to Sec., War Cabinet and Cabinet, 1916-21; Private Secretary to Secretary, Imperial War Cabinet, 1917; Private Secretary to British Secretary, Peace Conference, 1919; Private Secretary to successive Prime Ministers, 1921-23; Principal Secretary to late Earl Lloyd George of Dwyfor; Commander of the Order of the Crown of Italy, and Sacred Treasure of Japan. *Publication:* The Real Lloyd George, 1947. *Recreations:* riding and golf. *Address:* Rudloe Cottage, Corsham, Wilts. *T:* Hawthorn 375. *Club:* National Liberal.
*See also A. Sylvester-Evans.*

**SYLVESTER, George Harold,** CBE 1967; retired 1967 as Chief Education Officer for Bristol; *b* 26 May 1907; *s* of late George Henry and Martha Sylvester; *m* 1936, Elsie Emmett; one *s*. *Educ:* Stretford Grammar School; Manchester University. BA Manchester 1928; MA Bristol 1944. Teaching, Manchester, 1929-32; Administrative posts (Education) in Wolverhampton and Bradford, 1932-39; Assistant Education Officer, Bristol, 1939-42; Chief Education Officer, Bristol, 1942-67. Hon. MEd Bristol, 1967. *Recreations:* golf, music. *Address:* 43 Hill View, Henleaze, Bristol. *T:* Bristol 62-8144.

**SYLVESTER-BRADLEY, Professor Peter Colley;** Professor of Geology, University of Leicester, since 1959; *b* 21 May 1913; 2nd *s* of Lt-Col C. R. Sylvester-Bradley; *m* 1945, Joan Eveleen Mary Campbell; three *s* one *d. Educ:* Haileybury College; University of Reading. Lecturer, Seale Hayne Agricultural College, 1937-39. Served War of 1939-45, Royal Navy. Assistant Lecturer, Lecturer, and Senior Lecturer, University of Sheffield, 1946-59; Rose Morgan Professor, University of Kansas, 1955-56; Internat. Commissioner of Zoological Nomenclature, 1953-58. *Publications:* (ed) The Species Concept in Paleontology, 1956; (ed) The Geology of the East Midlands, 1968; papers on palæontology, stratigraphy, taxonomy, evolution and the origin of life. *Recreations:* natural history, travel, landscape gardening, photography, the gramophone, country wines. *Address:* Department of Geology, University of Leicester. *T:* Leicester 50000; Noon's Close, Stoughton, Leicester. *T:* Oadby 3764.

**SYLVESTER-EVANS, Alun;** Under-Secretary, Ministry of Housing and Local Government, since 1966; *b* 21 April 1918; *o c* of Daniel Elias Evans and Esther Evans, Rhymney, Mon.; *m* 1945, Joan Maureen, *o c* of A. J. Sylvester, *qv*; two *s. Educ:* Lewis' School, Pengam; University of Wales, Aberystwyth. Armed services, 1940-46 (Capt.-Adjt RA, Major RAEC). Asst Research Officer, Min. of Town and Country Planning, 1946-47; Asst Principal, 1947-48; Principal Private Sec. to Minister of Housing and Local Govt, 1954-57; Asst Secretary, 1957-66. *Recreation:* golf. *Address:* 2 Enmore Road, Putney, SW15. *T:* 01-788 3043. *Club:* Arts Theatre.

**SYME, Sir Colin (York),** Kt 1963; LLB; Company Director; Chairman, Broken Hill Pty Co. Ltd, 1952-71 (Director, since 1937); *b* 22 April 1903; *s* of Francis Mark Syme; *m* 1933, Patricia Baird; three *s* one *d. Educ:* Scotch College, Claremont, WA; Universities of Perth and Melbourne, Australia. Partner, Hedderwick, Fookes & Alston, Solicitors, 1928-66. Pres., The Walter & Eliza Hall Inst. of Medical Research; Director of: Elder Smith Goldsbrough Mort Ltd; Australian Iron & Steel Pty Ltd (Chairman); Commonwealth Aircraft Corporation Pty Ltd; Imperial Chemical Industries of Australia and New Zealand Ltd; Tubemakers of Australia Ltd (Chm.). Mem., Internat. Adv. Cttee, Chase Manhattan Bank; a Vice-Chm., Private Investment Co. for Asia; Hon. Mem., Aust. Inst. of Mining and Metallurgy. Hon. DSc, Univ. of NSW, 1960. *Recreation:* fishing. *Address:* 22 Stonnington Place, Toorak, Victoria 3142, Australia. *Clubs:* Melbourne, Australian (Melbourne); Adelaide (Adelaide); Newcastle (Newcastle); Links (New York).

**SYME, Sir Ronald,** Kt 1959; FBA 1944; retired as Camden Professor of Ancient History, Oxford, 1949-70; *b* 11 March 1903; *e s* of David and Florence Syme, Eltham, New Zealand. *Educ:* NZ; Oriel College, Oxford (Classical Prizes and First Class Hons, Lit Hum, 1927). Fellow of Trinity College, 1929-49; Conington Prize, 1939. Press Attaché with rank of First Secretary, HM Legation, Belgrade, 1940-41; HM Embassy, Ankara, 1941-42; Professor of Classical Philology, University of Istanbul, 1942-45; President, Society for the Promotion of Roman Studies, 1948-52; President, International Federation of Classical Societies, 1951-54; Secretary-General, Internat. Council for Philosophy and Humanistic Studies, 1952; Vice-President: Prize Cttee of Balzan Foundation, 1963; Assoc. Internat. pour l'Etude du Sud-Est Européen, 1967. Hon. Fellow, Oriel College, Oxford, 1958. Hon. LittD NZ, 1949; Hon. DLitt: Durham, 1952; Belfast, 1961; Graz, 1963; Emory, US, 1963; D ès L: Paris, 1963; Lyon, 1967; Ohio, 1970; Membre Associé de l'Institut de France (Académie des Inscriptions et Belles-Lettres), 1967; Corresp. Member, German Archæological Institute, 1931, Member, 1953; Member, Royal Danish Acad. of Letters and Sciences, 1951; For. Mem. Lund Society of Letters, 1948. Corresponding Member Bavarian Academy, 1955; For. Member: American Philosophical Soc., 1959; Amer. Acad. of Arts and Sciences, 1959; Massachusetts Historical Society, 1960; Istituto di Studi Romani, 1960; Amer. Historical Soc., 1963; Real Academia de la Historia, 1963; Istituto Lombardo, 1964; Corresponding Member Austrian Academy, 1960. *Publications:* The Roman Revolution, 1939; Tacitus (2 vols), 1958; Colonial Elites, 1958; Sallust, 1964; Ammianus and the Historia Augusta, 1968; Ten Studies in Tacitus, 1970; Emperors and Biography, 1970; articles in learned jls; chaps in Cambridge Ancient History. *Address:* Wolfson College, Oxford.

**SYMES, Maj.-Gen. George William,** CB 1946; MC; *b* 12 Jan. 1896; *o s* of late George and Eliza Symes; *m* 1st, 1939, Katherine Bellairs Lucas (*d* 1961); 2nd, 1967, Kathleen Champion de Crespigny. *Educ:* Bridport Gram. Sch. Commissioned 1915, York and Lancaster Regt; served with MG Corps, 1915-19 (MC and bar); Staff College, Camberley, 1930-31; Bt Major, 1932; Major, 1938; Bt Lt-Col, 1939; Col, 1942; Acting Maj.-Gen. 1942; Temp. 1943; Subst. Maj.-Gen., 1944. Comd 8th Inf. Bde, 1940-41; Brig.-Gen. Staff, Eastern Comd, 1941-42; Comd 70th Division, 1942-43; Deputy Commander Special Force, India, 1943-44; Deputy Commander L of C 21st Army Group, May-Nov. 1944 (despatches); Comd L of C Comd, SEAC, 1944-45; Comd South Burma District, June-Dec. 1945 (despatches); Commander South-Western District, Taunton, Som., 1946-48, and 43rd (Wessex) Division TA, 1947-48; retired April 1949. Colonel, York and Lancaster Regt, 1946-48. *Recreation:* golf. *Address:* 81 Esplanade, Tennyson, SA 5022, Australia. *T:* 56-8568. *Clubs:* United Service; Adelaide (Adelaide).

**SYMES, (Lilian) Mary;** Clerk to Justices, 6 Divisions in Suffolk, since 1970; *b* 18 Oct. 1912; *d* of Walter Ernest and Lilian May Hollowell; *m* 1953, Thomas Alban Symes; one *s. Educ:* St Mary's Convent, Lowestoft; Great Yarmouth High School. Articled in Solicitor's Office; qualified as Solicitor, 1936. Became first woman Clerk to Justices (Stowmarket), 1942; first woman Deputy Coroner, 1945; Clerk to the Justices, Woodbridge, 1948, Bosmere and Claydon, 1951; first woman Coroner, 1951; Deputy Coroner, Eastern District, Suffolk, 1951-70. *Recreations:* Worcester porcelain, gardening. *Address:* Little Orchard, Westerfield, Ipswich, Suffolk. *T:* Ipswich 54634.

**SYMINGTON, David,** CSI 1947; CIE 1943; *b* 4 July 1904; 2nd *s* of James Halliday Symington, merchant, Bombay, India, and Maud McGrigor (*née* Aitken); *m* 1929, Anne Ellen Harker; one *s* one *d. Educ:* Cheltenham College; Oriel College, Oxford (Scholar). Entered Indian Civil Service, 1926; held various appointments including Backward Classes Officer, Bombay Province, 1934-37; Municipal Commissioner, City of Bombay, 1938; ARP Controller, Bombay, 1941; Secretary to Government of Bombay, Home

Dept, 1942, Secretary to Governor, 1943-47; retired from ICS, 1948; Member, John Lewis Partnership, 1948-52; Director, N Rhodesia Chamber of Mines, 1953-60; Chairman Copperbelt Technical Foundation, 1955-60. Councillor, Royal Borough of Kensington, 1950. Member of Council, Cheltenham College, 1961-. *Publications:* Report on Aboriginal Tribes of the Bombay Province, 1938; (as James Halliday): I Speak of Africa, 1965; A Special India, 1968; also short stories; (TV play) The Brahmin Widow, 1968. *Recreations:* writing, bridge. *Address:* 5 Paragon Terrace, Cheltenham, Glos.

**SYMINGTON, Stuart;** United States Senator for Missouri since 1952; *b* Amherst, Massachusetts, 26 June 1901; *s* of William Stuart and Emily Haxall Symington; *m* 1924, Evelyn Wadsworth; two *s*. *Educ:* Yale University; International Correspondence School. Joined Symington Companies, Rochester, New York, 1923; President Colonial Radio Co., Rochester, 1930-35; President, Rustless Iron & Steel Co., Baltimore, 1935-37; President and Chairman, Emerson Electric Manufacturing Co., St Louis, 1938-45; Surplus Property Administrator, Washington, 1945-46; Assistant Secretary of War for Air, 1946-47; Secretary of Air Force, National Defense, 1947-50; Chairman, National Security Resources Board, 1950-51; Administrator, Reconstruction Finance Corporation, 1951-52. Is a Democrat. *Address:* Senate Office Building, Washington, DC 20510, USA; 230 S Brentwood, St Louis, Mo 63105, USA.

**SYMINGTON, Professor Thomas,** MD; FRSE; Director, Institute of Cancer Research, Royal Cancer Hospital, since 1970; *b* 1 April 1915; *m* 1943, Esther Margaret Forsyth, MB, ChB; two *s* one *d*. *Educ:* Cumnock Academy. BSc (Hons Biochemistry), 1936; MB ChB, 1941; MD (Hons), 1950. St Mungo (Notman) Prof. of Pathology, Univ. of Glasgow, 1954-70. Visiting Prof. of Pathology, Stanford Univ., Calif., 1965-66. Member, Medical Research Council, 1968-. FRSE, 1956; FRIC, 1958 (ARIC, 1951); FRCP(G), 1963; FRFPS (G), 1958; FRCPath, 1964; FIBiol, 1970. *Publications:* Functional Pathology of the Human Adrenal Gland, 1969; numerous papers on problems of adrenal glands in Journals of Endocrinology and Pathology. *Recreation:* golf. *Address:* 130 Northey Avenue, Cheam, Surrey. *T:* 01-642 7628. *Clubs:* Athenæum, Royal Commonwealth Society.

**SYMMERS, Professor William St Clair;** Professor of Histopathology (formerly Morbid Anatomy), in the University of London, Charing Cross Hospital Medical School, and Hon. Consultant Pathologist and Lecturer in Morbid Anatomy and Histology, Charing Cross Hospital Group, since 1953; *b* 16 Aug. 1917; *s* of William St Clair Symmers (Professor of Pathology and Bacteriology, QUB) and Marion Latimer (*née* Macredie); *m* 1941, Jean Noble Wright; one *s*. *Educ:* Royal Belfast Academical Institution; Queen's University of Belfast; Guy's Hospital Medical School. MB, BCh, BAO (QUB), 1939; MD (QUB), 1946; PhD (Birmingham), 1953; MRCP (Lond.), 1946; FRCP (Lond.), 1959; MRCP (Edin.), 1965; MCPA 1967; FRCPath, 1963. Extern Surgeon, Royal Victoria Hospital, Belfast, 1940. Served War of 1939-45, Surgeon Lieutenant, RNVR, 1940-46. Demonstrator in Pathology and pupil of Prof. G. Payling Wright, Guy's Hosp. Med. Sch., 1946-47; Registrar in Clinical Pathology, Guy's Hospital, 1946-47; Deptl Demonstrator of Pathology, University of Oxford, 1947; Senior Assistant Pathologist, Radcliffe Infirmary, Oxford, 1947-48; Senior Lecturer in Pathology, Univ. of Birmingham, 1948-53; Hon. Cons Pathologist: United Birmingham Hosps, 1948-53; Birmingham Regional Hosp. Bd, 1949-53. Visiting Prof. of Pathology: Univ. of Heidelberg, 1962; Univ. of Cincinnati, 1962; New York Univ., 1963; Vargas Hosp. School of Medicine, Univ. of Caracas, Venezuela, 1963; Univ. of São Paulo, 1969; Med. Univ. of S Carolina, 1969. Visiting Scholar, Louisiana State Univ., 1962; Guest Speaker, Mayo Clinic, 1962. Visiting Lecturer, 1961 onwards, in Universities of Europe, Asia, Africa, North and South America and Australasia, inc. Ehrlich Lectr, Frankfurt, 1962; Dr Dhayagude Meml Lectr, Seth GS Med. Sch., Univ. of Bombay, 1967; Pasteur Lectr, Dakar, 1969; Examiner, Universities of: Birmingham, 1948-53; Cambridge, 1956-67; London, 1953-61, 1966-70; the West Indies, 1963, 1965; Cairo, 1966; East Africa, 1966; Ceylon, 1966; Malaysia, 1967-69; Lagos, 1967-69; Bristol, 1967-69; Dublin, Cork and Galway, 1970-; Malta, 1970; Examining Bd in England, 1962-66; Royal Coll. of Physicians, 1966-; RCS, 1968-; Inst. of Medical Laboratory Technology, 1949-55. Pres., Section of Pathology, RSM, 1969-70. Fellow, Ulster Med. Soc. Yamagiwa Medal, Univ. of Tokyo, 1969. *Publications:* contrib. Brit. and foreign medical works; jt ed (with late Prof. G. Payling Wright), Systemic Pathology, 1966; Curiosa, 1971. *Address:* Whitefriars, 30 Sandy Lodge Way, Northwood, Middlesex. *T:* Northwood 25688; Department of Histopathology, Charing Cross Hospital Medical School, Chandos Place, WC2N 4HH. *T:* 01-836 7788 (ext. 224); (personal) 01-240 0604.

**SYMON, Sir Alexander (Colin Burlington),** KCMG 1955 (CMG 1948); KCVO 1961; OBE 1944; retired; British High Commissioner in Pakistan, 1954-61; *b* 13 May 1902; 2nd *s* of late J. M. Symon, Hull, Yorks; *m* 1930, Doris (Dodo) Olive, *o d* of late E. J. Comfort, Harrow, Middlesex and Meopham, Kent; no *c*. *Educ:* Technical College, Hull. Appointed to India Office, 1921; Assistant Secretary, Indian Delegation to Disarmament Conf., Geneva, 1932-33; Sec. to Indian Delegation to London Naval Conf., 1935; Sec. to Indian Supply Mission in USA, 1941-46; Deputy High Commissioner for the United Kingdom in India, 1946-49; visited Nepal, 1947, to negotiate Agreement for British Gurkha Brigade; Asst Under-Secretary of State, Commonwealth Relations Office, 1949-52; Deputy Under-Secretary of State, Commonwealth Relations Office, 1952-54. Member, UK Deleg. to Consultative Cttee of Colombo Plan, Karachi, 1952, Delhi, 1953, Ottawa, 1954; Member UK delegation to SEATO Council meeting, Karachi, 1956; Member UK delegation to Bagdad Pact Council meeting, Karachi, 1957, London, 1958 and Karachi, 1959-61. President, Jockey Club of Pakistan, 1959-61; Director of Companies. *Recreation:* golf. *Address:* Runnymede, Links Road, Worthing, Sussex. *Club:* Oriental.

**SYMON, Mrs David;** *see* Moore, Miss Jocelyn A. M.

**SYMON, Harold,** CB 1949; *b* 1896; *s* of Harris Zaiman, Sheffield; *m* 1st, 1917, Winifred Lilian Ashwell; one *s* one *d*; 2nd, 1968, Edith Celia Napier Boreham. *Educ:* Central School, Sheffield; King's College, Cambridge. Entrance Scholar, King's College, Cambridge, 1913; Wrangler with special distinction, 1916. Assistant Principal, Dept of Scientific and Industrial Research, 1919; Assistant to Director of Building Research, and Secretary, Building Research Bd, 1925-34; Ministry of

Health: Sec., Cttee on Constructing Flats, 1934-36, Principal, 1936, Asst Sec., 1941, Principal Asst Sec., 1945, Under-Sec., 1946; Under-Secretary, Ministry of Housing and Local Govt (formerly Min. of Local Govt and Planning), 1951-55; Director and Consultant to Assoc. of Land and Property Owners, 1955-68. *Recreation:* golf. *Address:* Knowle Holt, Tilford Road, Hindhead, Surrey. *Clubs:* Reform; Hindhead Golf.

**SYMONDS, Sir Charles Putnam,** KBE 1946; CB 1944; MA, DM Oxon; FRCP, Hon. FRCPEd; Air Vice-Marshal RAFVR; Consulting Physician Emeritus for Nervous Diseases, Guy's Hospital; Consulting Physician Emeritus, The National Hospital, Queen Square; Hon. Consulting Neurologist, RAF; *b* 1890; *s* of Sir Charters Symonds; *m* 1st, 1915, Janet Palmer Poulton (*d* 1919); 2nd, 1920, Edythe Dorton; four *s*. *Educ:* Rugby; New Coll., Oxford; Guy's Hospital; Entrance Scholarships Rugby and Guy's Hospital. Served European War, 1914-18 (Médaille Militaire); Medical Registrar Guy's Hospital; Radcliffe Travelling Fellow, Oxford University, 1920; FRSM (Ex-Pres. Sections of Psychiatry and Neurology); Ex-Pres., Assoc. of British Neurologists, 1956. Hon. Visiting Neurologist, Johns Hopkins Hosp.; Sims Commonwealth Travelling Professor for 1953; Harveian Orator, RCP, 1954. Hon. Member, Amer. Neurological Assoc.; Member Correspondant de la Société de Neurologie de Paris; Hon. Member, New York Neurological Soc. Hon. Fellow RSM 1964. *Publications:* Studies in Neurology, 1970; Section on Nervous Diseases in Taylor's Textbook of Medicine; papers on neurological subjects in scientific journals. *Recreations:* photography, bird-watching, fly-fishing. *Address:* Field House, Ham, near Marlborough, Wilts. *T:* Inkpen 348. *Club:* Royal Air Force.

**SYMONDS, Joseph Bede,** OBE 1957; *b* 17 Jan. 1900; *m* 1921; four *s* six *d* (three *s* decd). *Educ:* St Bede's Secondary School, Jarrow. Councillor, Jarrow, 1929; Alderman 1935; Mayor 1945; County Councillor, Durham, 1946; Freeman, Borough of Jarrow, 1955. Past Chairman National Housing Town Planning Council, 1948-50 (Exec. Member, 1938-); Chairman Jarrow Housing Cttee, 1935-. MP (Lab) Whitehaven, June 1959-70. *Recreations:* cricket; welfare work (old people); Air Training Corps. *Address:* 11 Hedworth View, Jarrow, Durham. *T:* Jarrow 897246.

**SYMONDS-TAYLER, Admiral Sir Richard Victor,** KBE 1951; CB 1948; DSC 1915; *b* 27 Oct. 1897; *s* of late Lt-Col R. H. Symonds-Tayler, Hereford; *m* 1925, Letitia Mary, *d* of late E. J. Gunner, IW; one *s* one *d*. *Educ:* Hereford Cathedral School; RNC, Osborne and Dartmouth. Joined RN as cadet, 1910; served Wars, 1914-18, 1939-45. Comdr, 1931; Capt., 1936; Rear-Adm., 1946; Vice-Adm., 1949; Adm. (retd), 1953. Graduated Naval Staff Coll., 1928; Imperial Defence College, 1938; British Naval Mission to Greece, 1929-31; commanded HMS Centurion, 1938-39; HMS Sussex, 1940; HMS London, 1942-44; Director of Training and Staff duties, Admiralty, 1940-42; Chief of Staff to C-in-C Portsmouth, 1945-46; Chief of Staff to Naval Representative of British Chiefs of Staff, Military Staff Committee, United Nations, 1946-47; Flag Officer commanding First Cruiser Squadron, 1947-48; C-in-C America and West Indies Station, 1949-51. Iraq Petroleum Company Ltd, 1952-58. *Recreations:* fishing, golf. *Address:* Copper Beeches, Worplesdon, Surrey. *Clubs:* Army and Navy.

**SYMONETTE, Sir Roland Theodore,** Kt 1959; Premier of the Bahamas, 1964-67; Member of HM Executive Council, Bahamas, since 1949; Leader of Government in the House of Assembly, 1955-67; MHA since 1925; shipyard owner, Bahamas; Contractor for the Construction of roads, wharfs, and harbours; *b* 16 Dec. 1898; *m* 1945, Margaret Frances Thurlew; four *s* one *d* (and one *d* decd). *Educ:* day school at Current Eleuthera, Bahama Islands. *Recreation:* yachting. *Address:* 601 Bay Street, Nassau, Bahamas. *Clubs:* Nassau Yacht (Bahamas); North American Yacht Racing Association (New York).

**SYMONS, Hubert Wallace,** FRCS; Emeritus Professor of Clinical Surgery, University of Leeds; Honorary Surgeon, General Infirmary, Leeds; Honorary Consulting Surgeon: Bartholomew Hospital, Goole; District Hospital, Castleford; Selby War Memorial Hospital; *b* 24 Nov. 1890; *s* of William Wallace Symons and Mary Helen Symons (*née* Lilly); *m* 1925, Charlotta Dolores Naomi de Wilde, MRCS, LRCP; one *s* one *d*. *Educ:* Bradford Grammar School; Leeds University. MB, ChB Leeds, 1912; FRCS 1924. Formerly: Demonstrator in Anatomy and Surgical Tutor, University of Leeds; Resident Surg. Officer, Leeds General Infirmary; Lieutenant-Colonel, RAMC (T). *Address:* 120 Grove End Gardens, St John's Wood, NW8. *T:* 01-286 8996.

**SYMONS, Julian Gustave;** Author; *b* 30 May 1912; *y s* of M. A. Symons; *m* 1941, Kathleen Clark; one *s* one *d*. Editor, Twentieth Century Verse, 1937-39. Chairman, Crime Writers Association, 1958-59; Sunday Times Reviewer, 1958-. *Publications:* Confusions About X, 1938; (ed) Anthology of War Poetry, 1942; The Second Man, 1944; The Immaterial Murder Case, 1945; A Man Called, Jones, 1947; Bland Beginning, 1949; The Thirty First of February, 1950; A. J. A. Symons, 1950; Charles Dickens, 1951; Thomas Carlyle, 1952; The Broken Penny, 1952; The Narrowing Circle, 1954; Horatio Bottomley, 1955; The Paper Chase, 1956; The General Strike, 1957; The Colour of Murder, 1957 (CWA Critics' Award); The Gigantic Shadow, 1958; The Progess of a Crime, 1960 (MWA Edgar Allan Poe Award); A Reasonable Doubt, 1960; The Thirties, 1960; The Killing of Francis Lake, 1962; The Detective Story in Britain, 1962; Buller's Campaign, 1963; The End of Solomon Grundy, 1964; The Belting Inheritance, 1965; England's Pride, 1965; Critical Occasions, 1966; A Picture History of Crime and Detection, 1966; The Man Who Killed Himself, 1967; The Man Whose Dreams Came True, 1968; The Man Who Lost His Wife, 1970; (ed) Essays and Biographies by A. J. A. Symons, 1969; several plays for television. *Recreations:* watching cricket and Association football. *Address:* 37 Albert Bridge Road, SW11. *T:* 01-622 3981. *Club:* Garrick.

**SYMONS, Noel Victor Housman,** CIE 1941; MC 1916; JP; Major, Army in India Reserve of Officers, 1934; *b* 27 Nov. 1894; *s* of late Edward William Symons, MA (Oxon.), Headmaster King Edward VI's School, Bath, and Katharine Elizabeth, *sister* of A. E. and Laurence Housman; *m* 1924, Cicely Dorothea Richards; no *c*. *Educ:* King Edward VI's School, Bath. British Army, 1914-19, Lt Worcestershire Regt; Indian Civil Service, 1920; District work till 1931; Secretary, Board of Revenue, 1931-34; Private Secretary to Governor of Bengal, 1934-35; Revenue Secretary, Govt of Bengal, 1938-40; Commissioner, Presidency Division, and ARP Controller, Bengal, 1940; Commissioner, Rajshahi Division, and Additional Secretary, Civil Defence, Bengal, 1941; Joint Secretary,

Civil Defence Dept, Govt of India, 1942; Director-General, Civil Defence, and Additional Secretary, Defence Dept, Govt of India, 1943; retired from ICS Aug. 1946. JP Hampshire, 1951. Appionted to Appeal Cttee, Quarter Sessions, 1959; Dep. Chm., Lymington Petty Sessions and Mem. Council, Magistrates' Assoc., 1964. Chm., Lymington Petty Sessions, 1966. *Publication:* The Story of Government House (Calcutta) 1935. *Recreations:* yachting, beagling, fell walking. *Address:* Bucklands, Lymington, Hants. *T:* Lymington 2719. *Clubs:* Royal Over-Seas League; Royal Lymington Yacht.

**SYMONS, Ronald Stuart,** CMG 1960; CIE 1945; HM Treasury; *b* 24 July 1904; *s* of William John and Margaret Lilian Symons, Maresfield, Sussex; *m* 1st, 1930, Joan Alice (marr. diss. 1942), *d* of John Robertson, Wormley, Surrey; one *s*; 2nd, 1944, Phyllis Jane (*d* 1955), *d* of Henry Wingfield King, Reigate, Surrey; one *d*; 3rd, 1958, Christine Mary Vivienne Gresty, *d* of Canon H. H. Coley, Holne Vicarage, Devon. *Educ:* Christ's Hospital, Horsham; King's College, Cambridge. Joined Indian Civil Service, 1927; Magistrate and Collector, district Pilibhit, UP, 1933-34; Revenue and Finance Minister, Rampur State, UP, 1935-37; Deputy Secretary in Finance Dept, Govt of India, 1938-40; various appointments in Military and Supply Finance Depts of Govt of India, 1940-45; Joint Secretary to Govt of India in Finance Dept, 1945-47; retired from ICS and joined Home Civil Service, 1947; Assistant Secretary, HM Treasury, 1949. Minister in UK Delegn to OECD, Paris, 1961-65; retired 1965. Re-employed by HM Treasury. *Recreations:* golf, photography, ornithology, gardening. *Address:* Chantry Cottage, High Street, Lindfield, Sussex. *T:* Lindfield 3509. *Club:* Royal Commonwealth Society (Fellow).

**SYMS, John Grenville St George,** QC 1962; Barrister-at-Law; Deputy Chairman, Court of Quarter Sessions, Co. of Huntingdon and Peterborough since 1965; *b* 6 Jan. 1913; *s* of late Harold St George Syms and Margaret (*née* Wordley); *m* 1951, Yvonne Yolande (*née* Rigby); one *s*. *Educ:* Harrow; Magdalen College, Oxford (BA). Called to the Bar, 1936. Served in RAFVR, 1940-45 (despatches); Wing Commander, 1944. *Recreations:* hunting, shooting and fishing. *Address:* Willinghurst, Shamley Green, Surrey. *T:* Cranleigh 2828. *Club:* Flyfishers'.

**SYNGE, John Lighton,** FRS 1943; MA, ScD Dublin; MRIA, FRSC (Tory Medal, 1943); Senior Professor, School of Theoretical Physics, Dublin Institute for Advanced Studies, since 1948; *b* Dublin, 1897; *y s* of Edward Synge; *m* 1918, Elizabeth Allen; three *d*. *Educ:* St Andrew's Coll., Dublin; Trinity Coll., Dublin. Senior Moderator and Gold Medallist in Mathematics and Experimental Science, 1919; Lecturer in Mathematics, Trinity College, Dublin, 1920; Assistant Professor of Mathematics, University of Toronto, 1920-25; Secretary to the International Mathematical Congress, Toronto, 1924; Fellow of Trinity College, Dublin, and University Professor of Natural Philosophy, 1925-30; Treas., Royal Irish Academy, 1929-30. Sec., 1949-52. Pres., 1961-64; Professor of Applied Mathematics, Univ. of Toronto, 1930-43; Professor of Mathematics and Chm. of Dept, Ohio State Univ., 1943-46; Prof. of Mathematics and Head of Dept, Carnegie Inst. of Technology, 1946-48; Visiting Lecturer, Princeton Univ., 1939; Vis. Prof.: Brown Univ., 1941-42; Inst. for Fluid Dynamics and Applied Maths, University of Maryland, 1951. Ballistics Mathematician, United States Army Air Force, 1944-45. Hon. FTCD. Hon. LLD St Andrews; Hon. ScD: QUB; NUI. *Publications:* Geometrical Optics, 1937; (with B. A. Griffith) Principles of Mechanics, 1942; (with A. E. Schild) Tensor Calculus, 1949; Science: Sense and Nonsense, 1951; Geometrical Mechanics and de Broglie Waves, 1954; Relativity: the Special Theory, 1956; The Hypercircle in Mathematical Physics, 1957; The Relativistic Gas, 1957; Kandelman's Krim, 1957; Relativity: the General Theory, 1960; papers on geometry and applied mathematics; Ed. Sir W. R. Hamilton's Mathematical Papers, Vol. I. *Address:* Torfan, Stillorgan Park, Blackrock, Co. Dublin. *T:* 881251.

**SYNGE, Richard Laurence Millington,** FRS 1950; Biochemist at Food Research Institute, Norwich, since 1967; Hon. Professor, School of Biological Sciences, University of East Anglia, since 1968; *b* 28 Oct. 1914; *s* of late Laurence M. Synge and of Katharine C. Synge (*née* Swan), Great Barrow, Chester; *m* 1943, Ann, *d* of late Adrian L. Stephen and Karin Stephen (*née* Costelloe), both of London; three *s* four *d*. *Educ:* Winchester College; Trinity College, Cambridge. International Wool Secretariat Research Student, University of Cambridge, 1938; Biochemist, Wool Industries Research Assoc., Leeds, 1941; Biochemist, Lister Institute of Preventive Medicine, London, 1943; Biochemist, Rowett Research Institute, Bucksburn, Aberdeen, 1948. Editorial Board, Biochemical Journal, 1949-55; (jtly) Nobel Prize for Chemistry, 1952. *Publications:* papers in biochemical and chemical journals, etc, 1937-. *Address:* ARC Food Research Institute, Colney Lane, Norwich NOR 70F; 19 Meadow Rise Road, Norwich NOR 97F. *T:* Norwich 53503.

**SYNGE, Sir Robert Carson,** 8th Bt, *cr* 1801; Manager and Owner, Rob's Furniture; *b* 4 May 1922; *s* of late Neale Hutchinson Synge (2nd *s* of 6th Bt) and Edith Elizabeth Thurlow (*d* 1933), Great Parndon, Essex; *m* 1944, Dorothy Jean Johnson, *d* of T. Johnson, Cloverdale; two *d*. *S* uncle, 1942. *Heir: u* Edward Synge [*b* 3 July 1882; *m* 1901, Agnes Emily, *d* of James Jelley; one *s* one *d*]. *Address:* 19364 Fraser Highway, RR4, Langley, British Columbia, Canada.

**SYNGE, Victor Millington,** MD, DPH, FRCPI; FRCP; Regius Professor of Physic, Trinity College, Dublin; Visiting Physician, Royal City of Dublin Hospital; *b* 1893; *s* of Edward Synge; *m* 1919, Edith Allen; two *s*. *Educ:* Trinity College, Dublin (Foundation Scholar in Experimental Science, Medical Travelling Prizeman); Paris. Formerly Professor of Preventive Medicine and Medical Jurisprudence, and later Professor of Medicine in the Royal College of Surgeons, Ireland. *Publications:* Contributions on medical subjects to Irish Journal of Medical Science, and Lancet. *Recreations:* walking, travel. *Address:* Killakee Cottage, Rockbrook, Dublin 14. *T:* Dublin 909797.

**SYNNOT, R. V. O. H.-;** *see* Hart-Synnot.

**SYNNOTT, Pierce Nicholas Netterville,** CB 1952; Deputy Under-Secretary of State, Ministry of Defence, 1964-65; *b* 6 Sept. 1904; *e s* of Nicholas J. Synnott, JP, Furness, Naas, and Barbara (*née* Netterville); *m* 1939, Ann (from whom he obtained a divorce, 1948), *d* of Sir Abe Bailey, 1st Bt, KCMG; one *s*. *Educ:* Oratory School; Balliol College, Oxford. 1st Class Mods and 1st Class Litterae Humaniores, Oxford. Asst Principal,

Admiralty, 1928; Principal, 1936. Served War of 1939-45 in Army (60th Rifles), in African and Italian campaigns. Returned to Admiralty, 1945; Under-Secretary, 1947; Deputy Secretary, 1958. JP County of London, 1961. Order of St Olav, Norway (1st Class), 1947; Knight of Malta, 1961. *Address:* Furness, Naas, Co. Kildare. *Club:* Kildare Street (Dublin).

**SYSONBY,** 3rd Baron, *cr* 1935, of Wonersh; **John Frederick Ponsonby;** *b* 5 Aug. 1945; *s* of 2nd Baron Sysonby, DSO and Sallie Monkland, *d* of Dr Leonard Sanford, New York; *S* father 1956. *Address:* PO Box 349, Kitale, Kenya.

**SZEMERÉNYI, Professor Oswald John Louis,** DrPhil (Budapest); Professor of Indo-European and General Linguistics, University of Freiburg-im-Breisgau, since 1965; *b* 7 Sept. 1913; *m* 1940, Elizabeth Kövér; one *s. Educ:* Madách Imre Gimnazium; University of Budapest. Classics Master in Beregszász and Mátyásföld, 1939-41; Lecturer in Greek, 1942-45, Reader, 1946, Professor of Comparative Indo-European Philology in University of Budapest, 1947-48. Came to England, Oct. 1948; employed in industry, 1949-52; research fellow, Bedford Coll., London, 1952-53; asst lecturer, 1953-54, lecturer, 1954-58, reader, 1958-60, in Greek at Bedford College; Professor of Comparative Philology, University College, London, 1960-65. *Publications:* The Indo-European liquid sonants in Latin, 1941; Studies in the Indo-European System of Numerals, 1960; Syncope in Greek and Indo-European, 1964; contrib. to British and foreign learned journals. *Recreations:* calculus, chess. *Address:* Albert-Ludwigs-Universität, Freiburg-im-Breisgau, W Germany.

**SZENT-GYORGYI, Albert,** MD, PhD Cantab, Dhc; Director of Research, Institute of Muscle Research, Massachusetts, USA, since 1947; *b* Budapest, 16 Sept. 1893; *s* of Nicholas Szent-Györgyi and Josephine, *d* of Joseph Lenhossék, Professor of Anatomy; *m* 1941, Marta Borbiro; one *d. Educ:* Budapest University; Cambridge University. Matriculated Medical Faculty, Budapest, 1911; war service, 1914-18 (wounded); Assistant, University Pozsony, 1918; working at Prague and Berlin, 1919; in Hamburg in scientific research, 1919-20; Assistant at Univ. Leiden, Holland, 1920-22; privaat dozent at Groningen, 1922-26; working at Cambridge, England, with the interrruption of one year spent in USA, 1926-30; Prof. of Medical Chemistry, Szeged Univ., 1931-45; Professor of Biochemistry Univ. of Budapest, Hungary, 1945-47. Formerly: Pres. Acad. of Sciences, Budapest; Vice-Pres. Nat. Acad., Budapest. Prix Nobel of Medicine, 1937; Visiting Prof., Harvard Univ., 1936; Franchi Prof., Univ. of Liége, Belgium, 1938. Cameron Prize (Edinburgh), 1946. Lasker Award, 1954. Hon. ScD Cantab, 1963. Hon. Fellow, Fitzwilliam Coll., Cambridge, 1967. *Publications:* Oxidation, Fermentation, Vitamins, Health and Disease, 1939; Muscular Contraction, 1947; The Nature of Life, 1947; Contraction in Body and Heart Muscle, 1953; Bioenergetics, 1957; Submolecular Biology, 1960; Science, Ethics and Politics, 1962; Bioelectronics, 1968; many scientific papers. *Recreations:* sport of all kinds, chiefly sailing, swimming and fishing. *Address:* Laboratory of the Institute for Muscle Research, Woods Hole, Mass 02543, USA; Penzance, Mass, USA.

**SZERYNG, Henryk;** Hon. Professor, Faculty of Music, Mexican National University, Mexico City; Concert Violinist; *b* Warsaw, 22 Sept. 1921; Mexican Citizen since 1946. *Educ:* Warsaw, Berlin, Paris. Graduated violin class of Carl Flesch, Berlin, 1933; 1st Prize special mention, Paris Conservatoire, 1937; Composition study with Nadia Boulanger, 1934-39. War of 1939-45: played over 300 concerts for Allied Armed Forces, Red Cross and other welfare institutions in Scotland, England, Canada, USA, Caribbean area, Middle East, North Africa, Brazil and Mexico. Has covered the four continents in recitals, also soloist with major orchestras, 1953-. Hon. Music Counsellor to Mexican delegn, UNESCO, Paris. Numerous recordings; Grand Prix du Disque, 1955, 1957, 1960, 1961, 1967. Officer of Cultural Merit, Roumania, 1935; Kt Comdr, Order of Polonia Restituta (Poland), 1956; Silver Medal of City of Paris, 1963; Officer, Order of Arts and Letters (France), 1964; Commander, Order of the Lion (Finland), 1966. *Publications:* several chamber music works, also for piano and violin. Revised violin concertos by Nardini, Vivaldi and others. *Recreations:* climbing, golf, motoring, reading. *Address:* c/o Wilfred Van Wyck, 80 Wigmore Street, W1. *T:* 01-935 0218.

**SZIGETI, Joseph;** violinist; *b* Budapest, 5 Sept. 1892. *Educ:* Budapest. Pupil of Hubay; made his debut at the age of 13 years; toured England several times with Busoni, McCormack, Melba, etc., between 1907 and 1914; from 1919 concertized on the Continent. Professor of the classe de virtuosité at the Geneva Conservatory, 1917-24; first American Tour, 1925-26; since then every season in USA in recital and as soloist with every major orchestra, and extensive tours in the Far East, Australia, NZ, South America, and South Africa, 1931-38; led Edinburgh Festival Quartet (Schnabel, Primrose, Fournier), 1947 and 1952; toured Japan, 1953, South America, 1954. Cross of Chevalier of the Légion d'Honneur, 1930; Officer of Légion d'Honneur, 1939; Hungarian Order of Merit, 1931; Commander of Belgian Order of Leopold, 1937; has published several violin transcriptions of contemporary works, among others by Bela Bartok and Sir Edward Elgar (Serenade and Adieu; Elgar's last completed compositions); also transcribed works by Peter Warlock, Scriabin, de Falla, Bach, Weber, Lie, Rameau, etc. Bach Seminar (the Six Solo Sonatas), Northwestern Univ., Evanston, Ill., 1955, Cycle of 20th Century Masterpieces (3 programmes) in Zürich, and USA, 1956-57. Hon. RAM London; Hon. Member, Guildhall School of Music. Film debut in Warner Bros film Hollywood Canteen. *Publications:* With Strings Attached (a volume of memoirs), (London), 1949; A Violinist's Note Book (London), 1964; The Violin Sonatas of Beethoven (Illinois), 1965; Szigeti on the Violin, 1970. *Address:* Le Crepon, Baugy sur Clarens (Vaud), Switzerland.

**SZWARC, Michael M.,** FRS 1966; Distinguished Professor of Chemistry of the State University of New York; *b* 9 June 1909; Polish; *m* 1933, Marja Frenkel; one *s* two *d. Educ:* Warsaw Inst. of Technology (Chem. Eng. 1933); Hebrew Univ., Jerusalem (PhD 1942). University of Manchester (Lecturer), 1945-52; PhD (Phys. Chem.) 1947; DSc 1949; State University Coll. of Forestry at Syracuse Univ., 1952-; Prof. of Physical and Polymer Chemistry; Research Prof.; Distinguished Prof. of Chemistry; Dir, Polymer Research Inst. Amer. Chem. Soc. Award for Outstanding Achievements in Polymer Chemistry, 1969. *Publications:* Carbanions, Living Polymers and Electron Transfer Processes, 1968; numerous contribs to Jl Chem. Soc., Trans. Faraday Soc., Proc. Royal Soc., Jl Am. Chem. Soc., Jl Chem. Phys., Jl

Phys. Chem., Jl Polymer Sci., Nature, Chem. Rev., Quarterly Reviews, etc. *Address:* 406 Hillsboro Parkway, Syracuse, New York 13214, USA. *T:* Gibson 6-2448.

# T

**TABOR, Dr David,** FRS 1963; PhD, ScD; Reader in Physics in the University of Cambridge and Acting Head of Surface Physics, Cavendish Laboratory; Fellow of Gonville and Caius College, Cambridge, since 1957; *b* 23 Oct. 1913; *s* of Charles Tabor and Rebecca Weinstein; *m* 1943, Hannalene Stillschweig; two *s*. *Educ:* Regent St Polytechnic; Universities of London and Cambridge. BSc London 1934; PhD Cambridge 1939; ScD Cambridge 1956. *Publications:* The Hardness of Metals, 1951; Gases, Liquids and Solids, 1969; (with F. P. Bowden) Friction and Lubrication of Solids, Part I, 1950 (rev. edn, 1954); Part II, 1964; contributions to learned jls on friction, adhesion, lubrication and hardness. *Recreations:* Judaica. *Address:* Cavendish Laboratory, Free School Lane, Cambridge; Gonville and Caius College, Cambridge; 8 Rutherford Road, Cambridge. *T:* Trumpington 3336.

**TABOUIS, Geneviève;** Officier, Légion d'Honneur, 1959; Rédacteur Diplomatique quotidien à Paris Jour, à Radio-Luxembourg, La Dépêche du Midi, Juvénal; *d* du peintre Le Quesne; niêce de Jules Cambon et du Général Tabouis; *m* 1916, Robert Tabouis, Président-Directeur Général de la Cie Générale de Télégraphie sans Fil; one *s* one *d*. *Educ:* Couvent de l'Assomption; Faculté des lettres, Paris, Ecole archéologique du Louvre. Journaliste diplomatique; débuta en 1924 à la SDN comme correspondante de La Petite Gironde, du Petit Marseillais; chargée de 1924 à 1932 de toutes les grandes enquêtes diplomatiques, de tous les grands reportages politiques et de nombreuses conférences diplomatiques; diplomatic Leader à La Petite Gironde et Le Petit Marseillais, 1932-37, à L'Œuvre 1932-40; fonda et dirigea l'hebdomadaire français, Pour La Victoire, New York, 1939-45; retour à Paris, 1946-56; diplomatic leader à La France Libre, L'Information, L'Espoir. Correspondant diplomatique du Sunday Dispatch de Londres, de La Critica de Buenos-Ayres; collaboratrice à de nombreux journaux et revues; déploié une grande activité dans les meetings politiques et les conférences politiques et diplomatiques; nombreuses hautes décorations étrangeres. Vice-Présidente de l'Association de la Presse Diplomatique. *Publications:* 4 livres historiques couronnés par l'Académie Française: Tout Ank Amon, Nabuchodonosor, Salomon, Sybaris; une biographie: Jules Cambon par l'un des siens (couronné par l'Académie Française): un livre de politique: Le Chantage à la Guerre; Albion Perfide ou Loyale; tous ces ouvrages ont paru également en Angleterre; Ils l'ont appellée Cassandre (New York); Grandeurs et Servitudes américaines (Paris); Quand Paris Résiste; 20 Ans de Suspense Diplomatique. *Recreations:* Aucune récréation; travaille tout le temps, même le dimanche, ne connact pas le week-end; comme seule distraction joue avec ses chats. *Address:* 24 Place Malesherbes, Paris 17e, France. *Club:* Soroptimist Interallié.

**TACON, Air Cdre Ernest William,** CBE 1958; DSO 1944; MVO 1950; DFC 1940 (Bar 1944); AFC 1942 (Bar 1953); *b* 6 Dec. 1917; *s* of Ernest Richard Tacon, Hastings, New Zealand; *m* 1st, 1949, Clare Keating (*d* 1956), *d* of late Michael Keating, Greymouth, NZ; one *s* two *d*; 2nd, 1960, Bernardine, *d* of Thomas Leamy, Wellington, NZ; three *s*. *Educ:* St Patrick's College, Silverstream, New Zealand. Joined RNZAF, 1938. Served with RAF, 1939-46. Transferred to RAF, 1946. CO, King's Flight, Benson, 1946-49. Overseas Services since War: Canal Zone, 1951-53; Cyprus, 1956-58; Persian Gulf, 1961-63; Commandant, Central Fighter Establishment, 1963-65; Air Cdre, Tactics, HQ Fighter Comd, 1966-67; AOC Military Air Traffic Ops, 1968-71. *Address:* c/o Bank of New Zealand, 1 Queen Victoria Street, EC1. *Club:* Royal Air Force.

**TAEJON (Korea), Bishop of,** since 1968; **Rt. Rev. Cecil Richard Rutt,** MA; *b* 27 Aug. 1925; *s* of Cecil Rutt and Mary Hare Turner; *m* 1969, Joan Mary Ford. *Educ:* Huntingdon Grammar School; Kelham Theol. Coll.; Pembroke Coll., Cambridge. RNVR, 1943-46. Deacon, 1951; Priest, 1952. Asst Curate, St George's, Cambridge, 1951-54; Dio. of Korea, 1954; Parish Priest of Anjung, 1956-58; Warden of St Bede's House Univ. Centre, Seoul, 1959-64; Rector of St Michael's Seminary, Oryu Dong, Seoul, 1964-66; Archdeacon, West Kyonggi (Dio. Seoul), 1965-66; Asst Bishop of Taejon, 1966-68. Associate Gen. Sec., Korean Bible Soc., 1964-. Tasan Cultural Award (for writings on Korea), 1964. *Publications:* (ed) Songgonghoe Songga (Korean Anglican Hymnal), 1961; Korean Works and Days, 1964; P'ungnyu Han'guk (in Korean), 1965; The Bamboo Grove, an introduction to Korean Sijo poetry, 1970; (trans.) An Anthology of Korean Sijo, 1970; (ed) Gale's History of the Korean People, 1971; (trans.) The Nine Cloud Dream, 1971; contribs on Korean classical poetry and history to Trans. Royal Asiatic Soc. (Korea Br.) and various Korean publications. *Recreation:* Chinese calligraphy. *Address:* PO Box 22, Taejon, Korea.

**TAFT, Charles Phelps;** Attorney at Law; Mayor of Cincinnati, USA, 1955-57; Chairman US Advisory Committee on Voluntary Foreign Aid (Agency for International Development); General Counsel, Committee for a National Trade Policy; *b* 20 Sept. 1897; *s* of William H. Taft (27th President of the US and Chief Justice) and Helen Herron; *m* 1917, Eleanor Kellogg (*d* 1961), *d* of Irving H. Chase of Ingersoll-Waterbury Co.; two *s* three *d* (and two *d* decd). *Educ:* The Taft School, Watertown, Connecticut; Yale University. BA 1918, LLB 1921; Hon. LLD (Yale), 1952, etc.; Doctor of Hebrew Letters, Hebrew Union College, 1948. Enlisted 12 FA 2nd Div., AEF, 1917 (Fr., Jan.-Dec. 1918), discharged as 1st Lt 1919. Prosecuting Attorney Hamilton County, 1927-28; Partner Taft: Stettinius & Hollister, 1924-37; Headley, Sibbald & Taft, 1946-59; Taft & Lavercombe, 1959-66; Taft & Luken, 1967-; Chm. Fed. Steel Mediation Bd, 1937; Dir, Community War Services, Fed. Security Agency, 1941-43; Dir, Wartime Economic Affairs, Department of State, 1944-45; City Councilman of Cincinnati, 1938-42, 1948-51, 1955-. Trustee, Twentieth Century Fund, Carnegie Institution of Washington, Committee for Economic Development; Senior Warden, Christ Episcopal Church, Cincinnati; Pres. Fed. Council of Churches of Christ in America, 1947-48. Medal for Merit, 1946. *Publications:* City Management: The Cincinnati Experiment, 1933; You and I–and Roosevelt, 1936; Why I am for the Church, 1947; Democracy in Politics and Economics, 1950. *Recreations:* fishing, local politics, topical daily broadcasting. *Address:* (office)

1003 First National Bank Building, Cincinnati, Ohio 45202, USA; (home) 6 Burton Woods, Cincinnati, Ohio 45229, USA.

**TAGGART, John S.**; *see* Scott-Taggart.

**TAHOURDIN, John Gabriel,** CMG 1961; HM Ambassador to Senegal since 1966, and concurrently HM Ambassador to Mauritania since 1968, to Mali since 1969, and to Guinea since 1970; *b* 15 Nov. 1913; *s* of late John St Clair Tahourdin; *m* 1957, Margaret Michie; one *s* one *d*. *Educ:* Merchant Taylors' School; St John's College, Oxford. Served HM Embassy, Peking, 1936-37; Private Secretary to HM Ambassador at Shanghai, 1937-40; Vice-Consul, Baltimore, 1941; Foreign Office, 1942; Private Secretary to Parliamentary Under-Secretary of State, 1943, and to Minister of State, 1945; Athens, 1946; returned to Foreign Office, 1949; Counsellor, British Embassy, The Hague, 1955; Foreign Office, 1957; Minister, UK Delegn to 18 Nation Disarmament Conf., Geneva, 1963-66. *Address:* c/o Foreign and Commonwealth Office, SW1; Stone Street Farm, Aldington, Kent. *Club:* Travellers'.

**TAILYOUR, General Sir Norman (Hastings),** KCB 1966 (CB 1964); DSO 1945, and Bar to DSO 1956; *b* 12 Dec. 1914; *s* of late Lt-Col G. H. F. Tailyour and Mrs Tailyour (*née* Hutcheson); *m* 1941, Priscilla June Southby; one *s* one *d*. *Educ:* Nautical College, Pangbourne. 2nd Lieutenant, RM 1933; seconded to Royal West African Frontier Force (Nigeria Regiment), Captain RM, 1939; 5th Battalion RM, RM Div., 1941; Staff College, Camberley, 1943; G2, HQs RM Div., 1943; OCRM, HMS Robertson, then Exec. Officer, HMS St Mathew (Landing Craft Base), 1943-44; CO 27th Bn RM, NW Europe, 1945 (despatches, DSO); OC Training Cadre, Inf. Sch., RM, 1946; Sen. Course, US Marine Corps, Quantico, USA, Major RM, 1947; Chief Instr Amphibious Sch., RM, 1948; GI Plans and Ops RN Rhine Flotilla, 1949; JSSC, Latimer, 1951; GI Amphibious Warfare HQ, London, 1952; Lieut-Col Comdg Officer 45 Commando, RM, Cyprus (Bar to DSO), Port Said (wounded, despatches), 1954; NATO Defence Coll., Paris, 1957; CO RM Barracks, Plymouth, 1957; Chief of Amphibious Warfare's Rep., BJSM, Washington, 1958; Asst Naval Mem., Mil. Staff Cttee, UN, Col RM; Comdr 3rd Commando Bde, RM, Brig. RM, 1960; Comdr Plymouth Gp, RM, Maj.-Gen., 1962; Lt-Gen. 1965; General 1967. Comdt-Gen., Royal Marines, 1965-68. *Recreation:* sailing. *Address:* Ale Farm, Sutton-by-Dover, Kent. *Clubs:* Army and Navy; Royal Yacht Squadron; Royal Cinque Ports Yacht; (Life Vice-Cdre) Royal Marines Sailing; Royal Naval Sailing Association.

*See also Col Sir O. W. Williams-Wynn, Bt.*

**TAIT, Sir James (Blair),** Kt 1963; QC (Australia); Barrister; *b* 15 October 1890; *s* of John Tait; *m* 1st, 1922, Annie Frances (*d* 1962), *d* of Dr George Howard; one *s* one *d*; 2nd, 1964, Sophie, *widow* of Dr J. Thomson-Tait. *Educ:* Geelong College; Melbourne University. War, 1914-18: Lt Aust. Flying Corps; Pilot Officer in France. Called to Bar in Victoria, 1919; KC 1945. Hon. Treas., Victorian Bar Council; Pres., Graduate Union, Melbourne Univ.; Chairman: Equity Trustees Co, Ltd; Alliance Investment Co. Ltd; Barristers' Chambers Ltd; Millbank Investment Fund (Aust.) Inc.; Pres., Management International Australia Ltd (Bermuda). Chairman, Cttee of Inquiry into Stevedoring Industry in Australia, 1955-57. *Recreations:* golf and bowls. *Address:* Owen Dixon Chambers, 205 William Street, Melbourne, Victoria 3000, Australia. *T:* Melbourne 60.0791. *Clubs:* Australian (Melbourne); Peninsula Country Golf (Frankston).

**TAIT, Prof. James Francis,** PhD; FRS 1959; Joel Professor of Physics Applied to Medicine, University of London, since 1970; *b* 1 December 1925; *s* of Herbert Tait and Constance Levinia Brotherton; *m* 1956, Sylvia Agnes Simpson (*née* Wardropper) (*see* S. A. Tait). *Educ:* Darlington Grammar Sch.; Leeds Univ. Lectr in Medical Physics, Middlesex Hospital Medical School, 1948-55; External Scientific Staff, Medical Research Council, Middlesex Hospital Medical School, 1955-58; Senior Scientist, Worcester Foundation for Experimental Biology, USA, 1958-70. *Publications:* Papers on medical uses of isotopes and on endocrinology. *Recreations:* squash rackets, tennis, gardening. *Address:* Department of Physics Applied to Medicine, Middlesex Hospital, Medical School, Cleveland Street, W1P 6DB.

**TAIT, Sir James (Sharp),** Kt 1969; LLD, PhD, BSc(Eng), CEng, FIEE, FIMechE; Vice-Chancellor and Principal, The City University since 1966 (formerly Northampton College of Advanced Technology, London, of which he was Principal, 1957-66); *b* 13 June 1912; *s* of William Blyth Tait and Helen Sharp; *m* 1939, Mary C. Linton; two *s* one *d*. *Educ:* Royal Technical College, Glasgow; Glasgow Univ. (BSc (Eng.)). Lecturer, Royal Technical Coll., Glasgow, 1935-46; Head of Electrical Engineering Department: Portsmouth Municipal Coll., 1946-47; Northampton Polytechnic, EC1, 1947-51; Principal, Woolwich Polytechnic, SE18, 1951-56. Member: Adv. Council on Scientific Policy, 1959-62; National Electronics Council; Academic Cttee of the Further Education Staff College, Blagdon, Somerset; Advisory Board for the Royal Air Force College, Cranwell. Hon. LLD, Univ. of Strathclyde, 1967. *Recreation:* open-air pursuits. *Address:* 23 Trowlock Avenue, Teddington, Mddx. *T:* 01-977 6541.

**TAIT, Sir John,** Kt, *cr* 1943; Director, Eastern Tractors Ltd and Subsidiaries; *s* of Robert Tait, Girvan, Ayrshire; *m* 1919, Sarah Turner (*d* 1946), *d* of R. Montgomery; one *d*; *m* 1950, Nancy, *widow* of W. R. Glen, and *d* of J. Purdie, Glasgow. MLA India, 1931-32; Member of the Senate, Burma; Chairman, Burma Chamber of Commerce. *Address:* 113 Rivermead Court, SW6. *T:* 01-736 2976. *Clubs:* Oriental, Hurlingham, City of London; Mid-Surrey Golf.

**TAIT, Mrs Sylvia Agnes Sophia, (Mrs James F. Tait),** FRS 1959; biochemist; distinguished for her work on the hormones controlling the distribution of salts in the body; *m* 1956, James Francis Tait, *qv*. *Address:* Department of Physics Applied to Medicine, Middlesex Hospital Medical School, W1P 6DB.

**TAIT, Air Vice-Marshal Sir Victor Hubert,** KBE 1944 (OBE 1938); CB 1943; Director: Ultra Electronics Ltd; Ultra Electronics (Holdings) Ltd (Chairman, 1963-67); *b* 8 July 1892; *s* of Samuel Tait, Winnipeg; *m* 1st, 1917; one *d*; 2nd, 1929; one *s*; 3rd, 1957, Nancy Margaret, *d* of late Andrew Muecke, Adelaide, Australia. *Educ:* University of Manitoba (BSc). Canadian Army, 1914-17; RFC and RAF, 1917-45. Director of Radar and Director-General of Signals, Air Ministry, 1942-45; Operations Director, BOAC, 1945-56. Chairman: International Aeradio Ltd, 1946-63; Lindley Thompson Transformer Co., 1959-66. Air Transport Electronic Council, UK, 1958. Dir,

Flight Safety Foundn of America, 1959-69. President, British Ice Hockey Association. Mem. Council, Royal Geographical Society. Order of the Nile (Egypt), 1936; Order of Merit (USA), 1945. *Address:* 81 Swan Court, SW3. *T:* 01-352 6864. *Clubs:* United Service; Hurlingham.

**TALBOT,** family name of **Baron Talbot de Malahide.**

**TALBOT DE MALAHIDE,** 7th Baron *cr* 1831; **Milo John Reginald Talbot;** CMG 1957; Baron Talbot of Malahide, Baron Malahide of Malahide (I), 1831; Baron Talbot de Malahide (UK), 1856; Hereditary Lord Admiral of Malahide and adjacent seas (15 Edward IV); *b* 1 Dec. 1912; *o s* of Colonel Hon. Milo George Talbot, CB, RE (4th *s* of 4th Baron), and Eva, *d* of Col John Joicey, MP; *S* cousin, 1948; unmarried. *Educ:* Winchester; Trinity Coll., Cambridge. Entered Diplomatic Service, 1937; Foreign Office, 1937-39; Min. of Economic Warfare, 1939-40; Foreign Office, 1940-43 and 1947-54; Ankara Embassy, 1943-45; Beirut Legation, 1945-47; HM Ambassador to Laos, 1955-56 (Minister Sept. 1954-July 1955); resigned from HM Diplomatic Service, 1958. Director, The Irish Investment Co. Ltd. FLS 1968. *Recreations:* music, gardening and travel. *Heir:* (*to Irish Barony only*): *cousin,* Reginald Stanislaus Victor Talbot, MC [*b* 7 May 1897; *m* 1924, Cecily Elizabeth, *d* of Major Garstang Hodgson, Clevedon, Som.; one *d*]. *Address:* Malahide Castle, Co. Dublin. *Clubs:* Brooks's; Kildare Street (Dublin).

**TALBOT, Vice-Adm. Sir (Arthur Allison) FitzRoy,** KBE 1964; CB 1961; DSO 1940 and Bar 1942; Commander-in-Chief, Plymouth, 1965-67; retired; *b* 22 October 1909; *s* of late Henry FitzRoy George Talbot, Captain Royal Navy, and of Susan Blair Athol Allison; *m* 1940, Joyce Gertrude Linley; two *d. Educ:* RN College, Dartmouth. Served War of 1939-45: Comd 10th A/S Striking Force, North Sea, 1939, and 3rd MGB Flotilla, Channel, 1940-41 (DSO); Comd HMS Whitshed, East Coast, 1942 (Bar to DSO); Comd HMS Teazer, Mediterranean, 1943-44. Comdr 1945; Chief Staff Officer, Commodore Western Isles, 1945; Staff Officer Ops to C-in-C Brit. Pacific Fleet and Far East Station, 1947-48; Comd HMS Alert, 1949. Capt. 1950; Naval Attaché, Moscow and Helsinki, 1951-53. Imperial Defence College, 1954. Capt. (D) 3rd Destroyer Squadron, 1955-57; Commodore RN Barracks Portsmouth, 1957-59; Rear-Adm. 1960; Flag Officer: Arabian Seas and Persian Gulf, 1960-61; Middle East, 1961-62; Vice-Adm. 1962; Commander-in-Chief, S Atlantic and S America, 1963-65. *Recreations:* riding, shooting. *Address:* Thickthorn Manor, Ilminster, Somerset. *T:* Ilminster 2738. *Club:* United Service.

**TALBOT, Bridget Elizabeth,** OBE 1920; Croce di Guerra; National Labour Council; *d* of late Hon. Alfred Chetwynd-Talbot, *y s* of 18th Earl of Shrewsbury and Emily Louisa Augusta, *e d* of 5th Baron Walsingham. Belgian refugee committee, 1914; Anglo-Italian Red Cross, 1916-19 (Italian Medal for Valour); 1920-22, in Turkey started committee to deal with Russian refugees and later co-operative farm colony in Asia Minor; went to Russia, 1932, with Lady Muriel Paget's Mission. Sailed on 4-masted sailing ship Pamir to Finland, 1937. Started National Labour enquiry into state of Merchant Navy, 1939. Invented a watertight electric torch for lifebelts and was instrumental in getting these made compulsory by Parliament for all MN, RAF and RN personnel, and so saved hundreds of lives. In 1914 started the cultivation of co-operative gardens on waste land; Ministry of Agriculture later adopted the scheme all over the country. Was instrumental in securing Ashridge Estate to National Trust. Contested Bermondsey (L), 1950. Lord of the Manor of Scorton; hereditary Gov. Scorton Gram. Sch. Vice-Pres. Red Ensign Club; Vice-Pres. Watch Ashore Assoc. Hon. Mem., St Dunstan's Governing Cttee. Hon. Officer, Roman Grenadier Guards (apptd following battle of Monte Santo, 1917). *Publication:* treatise on co-ordinating Empire sea and air Transport. *Address:* Little Gaddesden House, Berkhamsted, Herts; Kiplin Hall, Scorton, Yorks.

**TALBOT, Maj.-Gen. Dennis Edmund Blacquière,** CB 1960; CBE 1955; DSO 1945; MC 1944; DL; *b* 23 Sept. 1908; *s* of late Walter Blacquière Talbot, St John, Jersey; *m* 1939, Barbara Anne, *o d* of late Rev. R. B. Pyper, Rector of Pluckley, Kent; three *s* two *d. Educ:* Tonbridge; RMC Sandhurst. 2nd Lieut Roy. West Kent Regt, 1928. Served War of 1939-45 (despatches, DSO, MC); Brigade Major, 30th Infantry, Bde, BEF; GSO 2, HQ 1st Corps; GSO 2 and 1, Combined Ops; 2nd i/c 5th Bn Dorset Regt; in command, 7th Bn Hampshire Regt, NW Europe, 1944-45. I/c 2nd Bn Royal W Kent Regt, 1945-46; GSO 1, HQ, Far ELF, 1947-48; Senior UK Army Liaison Officer, NZ, 1948-51; Lt-Col 1949; Col 1952; i/c 18th Inf. Bde and 99th Gurkha Inf. Bde, Malaya, 1953-55; Brig. 1956; BGS, HQ, BAOR, 1957-58; Maj.-Gen. 1958; GOC, E Anglian Dist and 54th Inf. Div. (TA), 1958-61; Dep. Comdr, BAOR, and Comdr British Army Group Troops, 1961-63; Chief of Staff, BAOR, and GOC Rhine Army Troops, 1963-64, retired; Civil Service, 1964-. Graduate of: Staff Coll., Camberley; RN Staff Coll., Greenwich; Joint Services Staff Coll., Latimer; Imperial Defence College, London; Civil Defence Staff Coll., Sunningdale. Col, The Queen's Own Royal West Kent Regt, 1959-61; Dep. Colonel, The Queen's Own Buffs, The Royal Kent Regt, 1961-65; Hon. Col, 8 Queen's Cadre (formerly 8 Bn The Queen's Regt (West Kent)), 1968. DL Kent, 1964. Knight Commander 1962, Grand Cross 1965, Order of the Dannebrog (Denmark). *Recreations:* shooting, gardening. *Address:* Oast Court, Barham, near Canterbury, Kent.

**TALBOT, Vice-Adm. Sir FitzRoy,** *see* Talbot, Vice-Adm. Sir A. A. F.

**TALBOT, Frank Heyworth,** QC 1949; LLB (London) 1929; Barrister; *b* 4 June 1895; *s* of Edward John Talbot and Susan (*née* Heyworth); *m* 1st, 1922, Mabel (*d* 1956), *d* of John Williams, Brecon; two *s*; 2nd, 1969, Heather, *d* of J. F. Williams, Great Missenden, Bucks. *Educ:* Tottenham Grammar School; London Univ. Civil Service, 1912-31. Inns of Court Regt, 1918. Called to the Bar, Middle Temple, 1931; practice at the Bar, 1931-. Bencher, Middle Temple, 1958. *Recreation:* music. *Address:* Flat no 11, 24 Old Buildings, Lincoln's Inn, WC2; *T:* 01-242 0494; 11 New Square, Lincoln's Inn, WC2. *T:* 01-242 4017.

**TALBOT, Godfrey Walker,** MVO 1960; OBE 1946; broadcaster, lecturer, journalist; Senior News Reporter and Commentator on staff of British Broadcasting Corporation, 1946-69; official BBC observer accredited to Buckingham Palace, 1948-69; *b* 8 Oct. 1908; *s* of Frank Talbot and Kate Bertha Talbot (*née* Walker); *m* 1933, Bessie, *d* of Robert and Clara Owen, Bradford House, Wigan; two *s. Educ:* Leeds Grammar School. Joined editorial staff on The Yorkshire Post, 1928; Editor of The Manchester City News, 1932-34; Editorial Staff, Daily Dispatch, 1934-37. Joined BBC,

1937; War of 1939-45: BBC war correspondent overseas, 1941-45 (despatches, OBE); organised BBC Home Reporting Unit, as Chief Reporter, after the war. BBC Commentator, Royal Commonwealth Tour, 1953-54, and other overseas visits by HM the Queen. *Publications:* Speaking from the Desert, 1944; Royalty Annual, 1952, 1953, 1954, 1955, 1956. *Recreations:* keeping quiet and walking. *Address:* 28 Onslow Gardens, Sanderstead, Surrey. *T:* 01-657 3476.

**TALBOT, Sir Hilary Gwynne,** Kt 1968; **Hon. Mr Justice Talbot;** a Judge of the High Court of Justice, Queen's Bench Division, since 1968; a Presiding Judge, Wales and Chester Circuit, since 1970; Deputy Chairman Hants Quarter Sessions, since 1964; *b* 22 Jan. 1912; *s* of late Rev. Prebendary A. T. S. Talbot, RD, and Mrs Talbot; *m* 1963, Jean Whitworth, *o d* of late Kenneth Fisher and of Mrs Fisher, Cranford. *Educ:* Haileybury Coll.; Worcester Coll., Oxford. BA Oxon (Hons). Called to Bar by Middle Temple Jan. 1935. Dep. Chm., Northants QS, 1948-62; Chm., Derbyshire QS, 1958-63; Judge of County Courts, 1962-68. Formerly Dep. Chm., Agricultural Land Tribunals. *Recreations:* angling, walking. *Address:* Greystones, Denmead, Portsmouth, Hampshire. *Club:* Athenæum.

**TALBOT, Very Rev. Maurice John;** Dean of Limerick since 1954; *b* 29 March 1912; 2nd *s* of late Very Rev. Joseph Talbot, sometime Dean of Cashel; *m* 1942, Elisabeth Enid Westropp; four *s. Educ:* St Columba's College; Trinity College, Dublin (MA). Curate of Nantenan, 1935; Rector of Rathkeale, 1942; Rector of Killarney, 1952; Prebendary of Taney, St Patrick's Nat. Cathedral, Dublin. *Publications:* Pictorial Guide to St Mary's Cathedral, Limerick; contrib. to North Munster Studies. *Recreations:* tennis, shooting, fishing. *Address:* The Deanery, Limerick, Ireland.

**TALBOT, Lt-Gen. Sir Norman (Graham Guy),** KBE 1969 (OBE 1945); TD 1950; Director-General, Army Medical Services, since April 1969; *b* Hastings, 16 Feb. 1914; *s* of late Rev. Richard Talbot, MA, and late Ethel Maude Talbot (*née* Stuart); *m* 1939, Laura Winifred, *d* of late William Kilby, Donington, Lincs; two *s* one *d. Educ:* Reigate Grammar Sch.; King's Coll., London; King's Coll. Hosp. MRCS, LRCP 1937; MB, BS London 1938; DA England 1939; MRCOG 1951; MD London 1953; FRCOG 1960. Commission into RAMC from RAMC (TA), Aug. 1939. Served War of 1939-45 (despatches, twice, OBE): in BEF, 1939-40; Egypt, Palestine and Syria, 1941-43; Sicily and Italy, 1943-46. Adviser in Obstetrics and Gynæcology to Army, 1951-58 and 1963-66. Served in Malta, 1958-61, and in Germany, 1961-63; DDMS, 1 (Br.) Corps, 1967-68; Comdt and Dir of Studies, Roy. Army Med. Coll., 1968-69. Brig. 1967; Maj.-Gen. 1968; Lt-Gen. 1969. FRSM; Mem. Council, Section of Obstetrics of RSM; Vice-Pres., United Svcs Section, RSM; Examiner: RCOG; Central Midwives Board. Fellow, Med. Soc. London; Mem., Anglo-German Med. Soc. QHS 1968. CStJ 1970 (OStJ 1966). *Recreations:* gardening, caravaning. *Address:* The Beeches, Church Road, Fleet, Hants. *T:* Fleet 7727; 503 Beatty House, Dolphin Square, SW1. *T:* 01-834 3800. *Clubs:* United Services, United Hunts.

**TALBOT, Richard Michael Arthur Chetwynd;** Recorder of Banbury since Nov. 1955; Chairman, Shropshire Quarter Sessions, since 1967 (Deputy Chairman, 1950-67); Barrister-at-Law; *b* 28 Sept. 1911; 3rd *s* of late Reverend Prebendary A. H. Talbot and late Mrs E. M. Talbot; unmarried. *Educ:* Harrow; Magdalene College, Cambridge (MA). Called to Bar by Middle Temple, 1936, Bencher, 1962. Mem. Bar Council, 1957-61. Served War of 1939-45, in Army. Major, King's Shropshire Light Infantry. *Address:* 4 Brick Court, Temple, EC4. *T:* 01-353 7744.

**TALBOT, Thomas George,** CB 1960; QC 1954; Counsel to the Chairman of Committees, House of Lords, since 1953. *b* 21 Dec. 1904; *s* of late Rt Hon. Sir George John Talbot and late Gertrude Harriet, *d* of late Albemarle Cator, Woodbastwick Hall, Norfolk; *m* 1933, Hon. Cynthia Edith Guest; one *s* three *d. Educ:* Winchester; New Coll., Oxford. Called to Bar, Inner Temple, 1929; Bencher, 1960. RE (TA), 1938; Scots Guards, 1940-44 (Hon. Captain). Assistant, subsequently Deputy, Parliamentary Counsel to Treasury, 1944-53. *Address:* Falconhurst, Edenbridge, Kent. *T:* Cowden 641; House of Lords, SW1. *Club:* Brooks's.

**TALLACK, Sir Hugh M.;** *see* Mackay-Tallack.

**TALLERMAN, Dr Kenneth H.,** MC; MA, MD, FRCP; Consulting Physician, Paediatric Department, The London Hospital; Consulting Paediatrician, St Margaret's Hospital, Epping; Hon. Lieutenant-Colonel RAMC; *b* London, 1894; *s* of late P. Tallerman and late Mrs C. G. L. Wolf; *m* 1st, 1929, Alice Campbell (*d* 1960), *yr d* of late D. C. Rose, Otago, NZ; 2nd, 1961, Florence M., *widow* of Frank Keeble and *d* of late Canon Small. *Educ:* Charterhouse School; Caius College, Cambridge University. Served in the Royal Field Artillery during European War, 1914-1919, and in the RAMC during War of 1939-45; graduated Medicine from St Thomas's Hosp., and obtained the degree MD (Cantab.); FRCP (London); late Cons. Pædiatrician, North-East Metropolitan Regional Board and Dr Barnardo's Home, and Physician to The Infants, and Paddington Green Children's Hospitals, Asst to the Medical Unit St Thomas's Hospital, Fellow and Instructor in Pediatrics, Washington University School of Medicine, USA, etc. Hon. Member (Past Pres.) Brit. Pædiatric Assoc.; Past Pres. Pædiatric Section, RSM. *Publications:* The Principles of Infant Nutrition (with Hamilton), 1928; numerous scientific and medical papers, 1920-58. *Recreation:* gardening. *Address:* Brantham Lodge, Brantham, near Manningtree, Essex. *T:* Holbrook 385. *Club:* Savile.

**TALLEY, Marion Nevada;** opera singer; *b* Nevada, Missouri, 20 Dec. 1906; *d* of Charles Marion Talley and Helen H. Brown. *Educ:* Grammar and High Schools of Kansas City. Sang leading rôles in operas Mignon and Bohemian Girl, with Kansas City Civic Opera Company, 1922; first audition at Metropolitan Opera House, New York, 1922; second Metropolitan audition, 1924; one year study in Italy, 1924-25; third audition in Lyric Theatre, Milan, 1925; debut as Gilda in Rigoletto, at the Metropolitan Opera House of New York, 1926; leading rôles, Rigoletto, Lucia, Tales of Hoffman, Nightingale, Magic Flute, Mignon, Coq d'Or; retired from Opera, 1929; re-entered opera and concert field, 1933; signed contract with Republic Pictures of California, 1936. *Address:* Beverly Hills, California, USA.

**TAME, William Charles,** CB 1963; Deputy Secretary, Ministry of Agriculture, Fisheries and Food, since 1967; *b* 25 June 1909; *s* of late Charles Henry Tame, Wimbledon, Surrey; *m* 1935, Alice Margaret, *o d* of late G. B. Forrest, Witherslack, Westmorland; one *s* one *d. Educ:* King's College School, Wimbledon; Hertford College, Oxford. Entered Ministry of

Agriculture as Assistant Principal, 1933. Chairman, International Whaling Commission, 1966-68. *Recreation:* music. *Address:* Windrush, Walton Lane, Bosham, Chichester. *T:* Bosham 3217. *Club:* United University.

**TAMM, Igor Evgenievich;** Soviet physicist; Head of Theoretical Department of the Lebedev Institute of Physics under USSR Academy of Sciences; *b* 1895. *Educ:* Moscow University. Worked at Moscow University from 1924; produced quantum theory of acoustical vibrations and scattering of light in solid bodies, developed theory of interaction of light with electrons (1930); indicated existence of surface states (Tamm's Levels) of electrons in crystals, 1933; developed theory of nuclear forces due to exchange of electrons and neutrinos ($\beta$-forces), 1934, produced jointly Cherenkov Radiation theory 1937. Institute of Physics, Academy of Sciences of USSR, 1934-. Suggested, with others, a method of obtaining controlled thermonuclear reaction, 1950. Mem. Acad. of Sciences, USSR, 1953; For. Mem., Polish Acad. of Sciences, 1961; For. Mem. Amer. Acad. of Arts and Sciences, 1961. Awarded Nobel Prize for Physics (jointly with P. A. Cherenkov and I. M. Frank) for discovery and interpretation of Cherenkov effect, 1958. Hero of Socialist Labour; State Prize. *Publications:* Foundations of the Theory of Electricity, 1929, 8th edn 1966; Exchange Forces Between Neutrons and Protons, 1937; Relativistic Interaction of Elementary Particles, 1945. *Address:* Lebedev Institute of Physics, Academy of Sciences of the USSR, Leninski Prospekt 53, Moscow, B-17, USSR.

**TAMMADGE, Alan Richard;** Master, Magdalen College School, Oxford, since Sept. 1967; *b* 9 July 1921; *m* 1950, Rosemary Anne Broadribb; two *s* one *d*. *Educ:* Bromley County Sch.; Dulwich Coll.; Emmanuel Coll., Cambridge. BA (Maths) 1950; MA 1957. Royal Navy Special Entry, 1940; resigned, 1947 (Lt); Cambridge, 1947-50; Lectr, RMA Sandhurst, 1950-55; Asst Master, Dulwich College, 1956-58; Head of Mathematics Dept, Abingdon School, 1958-67. FIMA 1965. *Publications:* Complex Numbers, 1965; (jtly) School Mathematics Project Books 1-5, 1965-69; (jtly General Education, 1969; articles in Mathemat. Gazette, Mathematics Teacher (USA), Aspects of Education (Hull Univ.). *Recreations:* music, coarse hockey, etc, educational TV. *Address:* Magdalen College School, Oxford. *T:* Oxford 42191.

**TAMWORTH, Viscount; Robert William Saswalo Shirley;** *b* 29 Dec. 1952; *s* and *heir* of 13th Earl Ferrers, *qv*.

**TANCRED, Sir H. L.;** *see* Lawson-Tancred.

**TANDY, Jessica;** actress, stage and screen; *b* London, 7 June 1909; *d* of Harry Tandy and Jessie Helen (*née* Horspool); *m* 1st, 1932, Jack Hawkins (marr. diss.); one *d*; 2nd, 1942, Hume Cronyn (Young); one *s* one *d*. *Educ:* Dame Owen's Girls' Sch.; Ben Greet Acad. of Acting. Birmingham Repertory Theatre, 1928; first London appearance, 1929; first New York appearance, 1930; subsequently alternated between London and New York. *New York plays include:* The Matriarch, 1930; The Last Enemy, 1930; Time and the Conways, 1937; The White Steed, 1939; Geneva, 1940; Jupiter Laughs, 1940; Anne of England, 1941; Yesterday's Magic, 1942; A Streetcar Named Desire, 1947-49 (Antoinette Perry Award, 1948); Hilda Crane, 1950; The Fourposter, 1951-53 (Comœdia Matinee Club Bronze Medallion, 1952); Madame Will You Walk?, 1953; Face to Face, 1954; the Honeys, 1955; A Day by the Sea, 1955; The Man in the Dog Suit, 1957-58; Triple Play, 1959; Five Finger Excrcise, 1959- (New York League's Delia Austria Medal, 1960); The Physicists, 1964; A Delicate Balance, 1966-67. *London plays include:* The Rumour, 1929; Autumn Crocus, Lyric, 1931; Children in Uniform, Duchess, 1932; Hamlet, New, 1934; French without Tears, Criterion, 1936; Anthony and Anna, Whitehall, 1935. Open-Air Theatre, London, 1933 and 1939; Old Vic, 1937 and 1940, leading Shakespearian rôles, etc. Toured Canada, 1939; tour of US with husband, (poetry and prose readings), 1954; they also toured Summer Theatres (in plays), 1957. Opening Season of the Tyrone Guthrie Theatre Minneapolis, USA: 1963: Hamlet; Three Sisters; Death of A Salesman; 1965; The Way of the World, The Cherry Orchard and the Caucasian Chalk Circle. The Miser, Los Angeles, 1968; Heartbreak House, Shaw Festival, Niagara-on-the-Lake, Ontario, 1968. *Films include:* The Indiscretions of Eve, The Seventh Cross, The Valley of Decision, Dragonwyck, The Green Years, A Woman's Vengeance, Forever Amber, September Affair, Rommel–Desert Fox, A Light in the Forest, Adventures of a Young Man, The Birds. Television: all major American dramatic programs. *Address:* 120 East 75th Street, New York, NY 10021, USA. *Club:* Cosmopolitan (New York).

**TANG, Sir Shiu-kin,** Kt 1964; CBE 1957 (OBE 1949; MBE 1934); JP; Chairman and Managing Director of Knowloon Motor Bus Co. (1933) Ltd since its inception; *b* 21 Mar. 1901; *s* of late Tang Chi-Ngong, JP; *m* May Fung. *Educ:* Queen's Coll., Hong Kong; St Stephen's Coll., Hong Kong. Dir, Tung Wah Hosp., 1924 (Chm. Bd of Dirs, 1928); Life Mem., Court of Univ. of Hong Kong; Member: Urban Coun., 1938-41; St John Coun. for Hong Kong, St John Ambulance Assoc. and Bde; Grantham Scholarships Fund Cttee; Cttee of Aberdeen Tech. Sch.; Chinese Temples Cttee, 1934-64; Bd of Chinese Perm. Cemetery; Tung Wah Gp of Hosps Adv. Bd; Po Leung Kuk Perm. Bd of Dirs (Chm. 1932); Exec. Cttee, Nethersole, Alice and Ho Miu Ling Hosp.; Trustee, Street Sleepers' Shelter Soc.; Vice-Pres. and Trustee of Hong Kong Br., Brit. Red Cross Soc.; Vice-President: The Boy Scouts' Assoc.; S China Athletic Assoc.; Adviser: Hongkong Juvenile Care Centre; Chinese Chamber of Commerce. Hon. LLD, Hong Kong, 1961. JP Hong Kong, 1929. Certificate of Honour Class I, and Life Mem., British Red Cross Soc., 1967. KStJ 1962. *Address:* 5 Broom Road, Hong Kong.

**TANGANYIKA;** *see* Central Tanganyika, and South-West Tanganyika.

**TANGE, Sir Arthur (Harold),** Kt 1959; CBE 1955 (OBE 1953); Secretary, Department of Defence, since 1970; *b* 18 August 1914; 2nd *s* of late Charles L. Tange, Solicitor, Gosford, New South Wales; *m* 1940, Marjorie Florence, 2nd *d* of late Professor Edward O. G. Shann; one *s* one *d*. *Educ:* Gosford High School; Western Australia University (BA; 1st Cl. Hons Economics). Joined Bank of NSW, 1931; Economist, Bank of NSW, 1938; Economic Research in Commonwealth Depts, Canberra, 1942-46. Entered Australian Diplomatic Service, 1946; First Secretary, Australian Mission to United Nations, 1946-48; Counsellor, United Nations Division, Canberra, 1948-50; Assistant Secretary, Department of External Affairs, Canberra, 1950-53; Minister at Australian Embassy, Washington, 1953-54; Secretary of Dept of External Affairs, Canberra, 1954-65; High Comr in India and Ambassador to Nepal, 1965-70. Represented Australia at many international economic and trade conferences, 1944-63. *Publication:* (jointly) Australia Foots the Bill, 1942. *Recreation:* fishing. *Address:* 32 La Perouse Street, Canberra, ACT 2603, Australia. *Club:* Commonwealth (Canberra).

**TANGLEY,** Baron *cr* 1963 (Life Peer), of Blackheath, Co. Surrey; **Edwin Savory Herbert,** KBE 1956; Kt 1943; LLB; Hon. LLD: Montreal 1956; Leeds 1960; Solicitor; *b* 29 June 1899; *s* of Henry William Herbert; *m* 1932, Gwendolen Hilda, *d* of late Thomas Langley Judd, CBE; one *s* three *d. Educ:* Queen's College, Taunton; Law Society's Law School. Solicitor, Senior Partner Sydney Morse & Co.; Chairman, Ultramar Co. Ltd, 1946-70, Consultant 1970-; Chairman: The Industrial and General Trust Ltd; Trustees Corporation Ltd; Imperial Continental Gas Association, and other companies. Director: Rediffusion Ltd (Deputy Chairman); National and Commercial Banking Group; Rediffusion TV Ltd (Dep. Chm.) and other companies. Served at sea as Signalman RNVR, 1917-19; LLB London, 1919 (University Law Scholar); Solicitor, 1920; Member of Council of Law Society, 1935-58 (President, 1956); Member various Departmental Committees; Aliens Tribunal, 1939; Chairman London Regional Price Regulation Cttee, 1939-40; Director-General of Postal and Telegraph Censorship Department, 1940-45; Member of Inter-dept Cttee on Matrimonial Causes, 1947; Member of Inter-dept Cttee on Leaseholds, 1948; Chairman: Committee on Intermediaries, 1949; Cttee of Inquiry into Electricity Supply Industry, 1954; Roy. Commn: on Local Govt in Greater London, 1957; on Trade Unions and Employers' Assocs, 1965-68. Pres., Court of Arbitration, Internat. Chamber of Commerce, 1970-. Pres. Alpine Club, 1953-55 (Hon. Sec. 1935-40); Chm. Finance Committee, Trans-Antarctic Expedition. Hon. Fellow, 1969, and Hon. LLD, 1969, Darwin Coll., Cambridge. Medal for Merit, USA; King Haakon's Liberty Cross, 1947. *Recreations:* mountaineering, ski-ing, sailing. *Address:* Tangley Way, Blackheath, near Guildford, Surrey. *T:* Bramley 3072. *Clubs:* Athenæum, Reform, Alpine; RYS (Cowes); Royal Corinthian Yacht (Burnham-on-Crouch).
*See also Baron Brain.*

**TANGNEY, Senator Dame Dorothy Margaret,** DBE 1968; Senator for West Australia since 1943; *b* 13 March 1911; *d* of E. Tangney, Claremont, West Australia. *Educ:* St Joseph's Convent, Fremantle, University of West Australia. Teaching staff, Education Department, West Australia. First woman to be elected to Commonwealth Senate. Mem., Standing Cttee, Convocation, University of West Australia. *Recreations:* tennis, motoring, badminton, reading. *Address:* 12 Mary Street, Claremont, West Australia.

**TANKERVILLE,** 8th Earl of, *cr* 1714; **Charles Augustus Ker Bennet,** FZS; ARAeS; Baron Ossulston, 1682; JP Northumberland; Flight-Lieutenant RAFVR; late Captain RAF; *b* 16 Aug. 1897; *s* of 7th Earl and Leonora Sophie (*d* 1949), *d* of J. G. Van Marter, of New York; *S* father, 1931; *m* 1st, 1920, Roberta (marriage dissolved, 1930), *e d* of Mrs Percy Mitchell; two *s*; 2nd, 1930, Violet, *d* of Erik Pallin, Stockholm; one *s* one *d. Heir: s* Lord Ossulston, *qv. Address:* Estate House, Chillingham, Alnwick, Northumberland. *T:* Chatton 213.

**TANN, Florence Mary,** CBE 1952; MA Cantab; *b* 12 Aug. 1892; *d* of William Robert Baldwin Tann, organist and choirmaster. *Educ:* Norwich High School; Girton Coll., Cambridge. Teaching in schools in S Africa, 1915-18; English Lecturer, University of Witwatersrand, Johannesburg, 1918-19; Organiser, National Union of Societies for Equal Citizenship, 1920-21; HM Inspector of Schools, 1921; Divisional Inspector, Board of Education, 1940-45; Chief Inspector, Primary Schools, Ministry of Education, 1945-52. Member National Book League. *Recreations:* gardening and needlework. *Address:* East Martyns, Henfield, Sussex. *T:* Henfield 2866. *Club:* University Women's.

**TANNER, Sir Edgar (Stephen),** Kt 1968; CBE 1957; ED; Member for Ripponlea, then for Caulfield, Victoria, in Victorian Legislative Assembly, since 1955; Hon. Secretary and Treasurer, Australian Olympic Federation; *b* 1912; *s* of late Edgar Tanner; *m* 1938, Edna, *d* of late Miles de H. Ponsonby; one *s* one *d. Educ:* All Saints' Gram. Sch., Melbourne; Melbourne Univ. Served War of 1939-45 as Captain AIF (prisoner). Hon. Sec. Organising Cttee, Olympic Games, Melbourne, 1956; President: Olympians International; Australian Amateur Boxing Union. *Address:* 14 Vautier Street, Elwood, Victoria, Australia. *Clubs:* Naval and Military, Amateur Sports, Melbourne Cricket (Melbourne).

**TANNER, Herbert George,** LLD; JP; Managing Director, E. S. & A. Robinson, Ltd and its subsidiary companies, until retirement in 1945; Director of Friends Provident and Century Life Office and Century Insurance Co. Ltd, 1940-58, retired (Chairman, 1945-55; Deputy Chairman, 1955-58); *b* 19 Nov. 1882; 2nd *s* of S. T. Tanner, JP, Bath; *m* 1906, Agatha Mary (*d* 1957), *d* of Edwin L. Gales, Bath; one *d* (two *s* decd). *Educ:* privately. Sheriff of Bristol, 1930-31; Treasurer of Bristol Univ., 1939-57, Pro-Chancellor, Nov. 1957-; JP Bristol since 1934; formerly Chairman of Justices, Bristol, and of Bristol Licensing Justices; JP Somerset, 1940; Chairman SW Reg. Hospital Board, 1947-53. Hon. LLD (Bristol), 1954. *Address:* Trinmore, Clifton Down, Bristol 8. *T:* Bristol 36409.

**TANNER, Dr John Ian;** Director, Royal Air Force Museum, since 1963; *b* London, 2 Jan. 1927; *o s* of R. A. and I. D. M. Tanner; *m* 1953, April Rothery; one *d. Educ:* Salisbury; City of London Library Sch.; Universities of London and Nottingham. MA, PhD Nottingham. Reading Public Library, 1950; Archivist-Librarian, Kensington Library, 1950-51; Leighton House Art Gall. and Museum, 1951-53; Curator, Librarian and Tutor, RAF Coll., 1953-63; Hon. Sec., Old Cranwellian Assoc., 1956-64; Extra-mural Lectr in History of Art, Univ. of Nottingham, 1959-63. Freeman, City of London, 1966; Liveryman, Worshipful Co. of Gold and Silver Wyre Drawers, 1966. Hon. Mem. Collegio Araldico of Rome, 1963; OStJ. 1964. Holds foreign Orders and awards. *Publications:* (Ed.) List of Cranwell Graduates, 2nd edn, 1963; (jtly) Encyclopedic Dictionary of Heraldry, 1968; Gen. Ed., Museums and Libraries (Internat. Series); reviews and articles in professional and other jls. *Recreations:* cricket, fishing, reading. *Address:* Flat One, 57 Drayton Gardens, SW10. *Clubs:* Hurlingham, MCC, Royal Air Force.

**TANNER, Lawrence Edward,** CVO 1953 (MVO 1932, 5th cl. 1932 4th cl. 1948); MA, FSA; Librarian, Westminster Abbey, since 1956 (Keeper of the Muniments, 1926-66), and Secretary HM's Royal Almonry, 1921-64; *b* 12 Feb. 1890; *y s* of Ralph Tanner, Senior Assistant Master, Westminster School, and Lucy L. le G., *d* of G. L. Phipps Eyre; *m* 1945, Joan Doreen, *e d* of Hon. Assheton N Curzon. *Educ:* Westminster; Pembroke College,

Cambridge. Hist. Tripos Pts I and II; Winchester Reading Prize, Cambridge University, 1912; BA, 1912; MA, 1919; Lieutenant (Gen. List), European War; Master, History Form, Westminster School, 1919-32; Clerk to Worshipful Company of Weavers, 1919-60 (Member Court, 1960); Upper Bailiff, Weavers Company, 1963-64. FSA 1926 (Vice-President, 1951-55); FRHistS, 1929 (Council, 1936-39); Vice-President, Society of Genealogists, 1939; Hon. Vice-Pres., R Arch. Inst. 1952. President, Brit. Archæological Association, 1951-56. OStJ, 1931. Gold Staff Officer, Coronations 1937 and 1953. Hon. DLitt Southampton, 1967. *Publications:* Westminster School, its Buildings and their Associations, 1923; Story of Westminster Abbey, 1932; Westminster School: A History, 1934 (2nd ed 1951); Recent Investigations regarding the fate of the Princes in the Tower, 1935; Unknown Westminster Abbey (King Penguin), 1948; The History of the Coronation, 1952; The History and Treasures of Westminster Abbey, 1953; Recollections of a Westminster Antiquary, 1969; articles and lectures on Westminster Abbey, etc. *Recreation:* fishing. *Address:* 59 Warwick Square, SW1. *T:* 01-834 8641. *Clubs:* Athenæum, Oxford and Cambridge.

**TANNER, Norman Cecil,** FRCS; Consulting Surgeon, Charing Cross Hospital, since 1953; Senior Surgeon, St James's Hospital, London, since 1948; *b* 13 June 1906; *s* of late Henry John Tanner and of Mrs Annie Tanner, Bristol; *m* 1940, Dr Evelyn Winifred Glennie, Aberdeen; two *s* one *d. Educ:* Merchant Venturers School, Bristol; Bristol University; Guy's Hospital. MB, ChB 1929, MD 1954, Bristol; MRCS, LRCP 1929; FRCS 1931. Resident hosp. appts, many Bristol and London hosps. Inaugurated gastro-enterological dept at St James's Hosp., 1939; Jacksonian Prize, 1948; Lectures: First Simpson-Smith Memorial, 1949; Macarthur, Edinburgh, 1951; Lettsomian, London, 1954; Price, Univ. of Utah, 1966; Gallie, Univ. of Toronto, 1968; Moynihan, Leeds, 1969; Visiting Prof. of Surgery: Ein Shams Univ., Cairo, 1954; Royal North Shore Hosp., Sydney, Australia, 1960; Hunterian Prof. RCS 1960; Mem. Council, RCS. Vice-Chm., British Journal of Surgery; Asst Editor, Gut, Editorial Board, and The Indian Journal of Cancer. Visitor for King Edward VII Hosp. Fund for London. Examr in Surgery to Univs of Cambridge and London. President: Clinical Sect, RSM, 1961-63, Sect of Surgery, 1965-66; British Soc. Gastro-enterology, 1967-68; W London Med. Chirurgical Soc., 1968-69. Hon. FACS 1966; Hon. FRCSI, 1969. Grand Cross, Patriarchal Order, St Mark, Alexandria; Grand Band of Star of Africa (Liberia). *Publications:* (ed) Tumours of the Oesophagus, 1961; chapters in: Techniques in British Surgery, 1950; Recent Advances in Surgery, 1959; Modern Operative Surgery, 1956; Operative Surgery, 1956; Management for Abdominal Operations, 1953, 1957; Abdominal Operations, 1952; Modern Trends in Gastroenterology, 1958; Demonstrations of Operative Surgery for Nurses; Cancer, Vol. 4 1958; many publications in The Medical Annual, Brit. Jl of Surg., Lancet, BMJ, etc. *Recreations:* ski-ing, music. *Address:* 149 Harley Street, W1. *T:* 01-935 4444. *Clubs:* Athenæum, Hurlingham, Coombe Wood Golf.

**TANSLEY, Sir Eric (Crawford),** Kt 1953; CMG 1946; Chairman, Pacol; Director: Bank of West Africa; Standard Bank Ltd; Standard & Chartered Banking Group Ltd; *b* 25 May 1901; *o s* of William and Margaret Tansley; *m* 1931, Iris, *yr d* of Thomas Richards; one *s* one *d. Educ:* Mercers' Sch. Formerly: Mem., Colonial, now Commonwealth, Development Corporation, 1948-51, 1961-68; Chairman: London Cocoa Terminal Market Assoc., 1932; Cocoa Assoc. of London, 1936-37; Marketing Director, West African Produce Control Board (Colonial Office), 1940-47. Retired, 1961 as Managing Director, Ghana Cocoa Marketing Co. and Adviser, Nigerian Produce Marketing Co. *Address:* 11 Cadogan Square, SW1. *T:* 01-235 2752.

**TAPLIN, Walter;** Editor of Accountancy, the Journal of the Institute of Chartered Accountants in England and Wales, since 1961; *b* Southampton, 4 Aug. 1910; *m*; three *s* two *d. Educ:* University College, Southampton (Foundation Scholar); The Queen's Coll., Oxford (Southampton Exhibitioner). Tutor-Organiser for Adult Education, W Hants and E Dorset, 1936-38; Editorial Staff of The Economist, 1938-40; Ministry of Food, 1940-42; Offices of the War Cabinet (Central Statistical Office), 1942-45; joined the Spectator as Asst Editor, 1946; Editor, 1953-54; Senior Economist, Iron and Steel Board, 1955-56; Research Fellow in Advertising and Promotional Activity, London School of Economics and Political Science, 1957-61. *Publications:* Advertising: A New Approach, 1960; Origin of Television Advertising, 1961; History of the British Steel Industry (with J. C. Carr), 1962. *Recreation:* reading. *Address:* Kent Hatch Lodge, Crockham Hill, Edenbridge, Kent. *T:* Crockham Hill 356. *Club:* Reform.

**TAPP, Maj.-Gen. Sir Nigel (Prior Hanson),** KBE 1960 (CBE 1954); CB 1956; DSO 1945; Lieutenant-Governor and Secretary, Royal Hospital, Chelsea, since 1967; *b* 11 June 1904; *y s* of late Lt-Col J. Hanson Tapp, DSO, and of late Mrs Hanson Tapp (*née* Molesworth), Duns, Berwickshire; *m* 1948, Dorothy, *y d* of late Alexander Harvey. *Educ:* Cheltenham College; Royal Military Academy, Woolwich. 2nd Lieutenant RA, 1924; Sudan Defence Force, 1932-38; ADC to Governor-General, Sudan, 1935-36; Staff College, Camberley, 1939; GSO 3, 1 Corps BEF, 1940; GSO 2, War Office, 1940-41; GSO 1 Staff College, Camberley, 1941-42; CO, 7 Field Regt, RA, UK, Normandy, Belgium, and Holland, 1942-45; Comd RA 25 Div., SEAC, 1945; District Commander, Eritrea, 1946-47; Dep. Dir Land/Air Warfare, 1948; Dep. Dir RA, 1949; idc, 1950; Commander 1 Corps Royal Artillery, BAOR, 1951-53; General Officer Commanding 2 AA Group, 1954; Director of Military Training, War Office, 1955-57; GOC East Africa Command, 1957-60; retd 1961. Col Comdt, Royal Regt of Artillery, 1963-68. *Recreations:* riding and fishing. *Address:* Royal Hospital, Chelsea, SW3; 9 Cadogan Square, SW1. *Club:* Army and Navy.

**TAPP, Norman Charles,** QC 1967; *b* 22 May 1925; *e s* of C. Charles and Dorothea Tapp; *m* 1951, Patricia Rose Whatmoor; three *s. Educ:* Lydgate House, Hunstanton; Bootham Sch.; Corpus Christi, Cambridge. RNVR, 1943-46. Called to Bar, 1948. *Recreations:* sailing, gardening, music. *Address:* Hamptons Farm House, Shipbourne, Tonbridge, Kent. *T:* Plaxtol 547. *Clubs:* United Service, Naval.

**TAPPER-JONES, Sydney,** LLB (London); Town Clerk and Clerk of the Peace, Cardiff, 1942-70; *b* 12 March 1904; *s* of David and Frances Caroline Mary Jones; *m* 1947, Florence Mary (Joan) Hellyer; one *d. Educ:* Pentre (Rhondda) Secondary School. Articled Cousins, Botsford & Co., Solicitors, Cardiff. LLB Lond. (External) (Hons), 1924. Solicitors' Final Exam. (Hons), 1925; Admitted Solicitor, 1925. Managing Clerk with Allen Pratt & Geldard (with whom were amalgamated Vachell & Co.), Solicitors, Cardiff, 1925-27; Cardiff Corporation: Conveyancing Solicitor, 1927-29, Prosecuting Solicitor, 1929-33; Deputy Town Clerk and Deputy Clerk of the Peace, 1933-42; Commissioner for Oaths. Member of Convocation, 1925. Member, Order of St John, 1966. *Address:* Maes-y-Coed, 59 Heath Park Avenue, Cardiff. *T:* Cardiff 751306.

**TAPPS-GERVIS-MEYRICK, Lieutenant-Colonel Sir George David Elliot;** *see* Meyrick.

**TAPSELL, Peter Hannay Bailey;** MP (C) Horncastle (Lincs) since 1966 (Nottingham (West), 1959-64); *b* 1 Feb. 1930; *s* of Eustace Tapsell; *m* 1963, Hon. Cecilia Hawke, 3rd *d* of 9th Baron Hawke, *qv*; one *s*. *Educ:* Tonbridge; Merton Coll., Oxford (MA). Served Royal Sussex Regt, 1948-50 (Middle East). 1st Cl. Hons Mod. Hist., 1953; Hon. Postmaster of Merton Coll., 1953; Librarian of Oxford Union, 1953; Rep. Oxford Union on debating tour of United States, 1954. Personal Asst to Prime Minister (Sir Anthony Eden) during 1955 General Election Campaign. Conservative Research Department, 1954-57. Member of London Stock Exchange; Partner, James Capel & Co. (Stockbrokers); Chairman, Coningsby Club, 1957-58; Jt Chm., British-Caribbean Assoc., 1963-64. Contested (C) Wednesbury, 1957. Court Mem., Univs of Nottingham and Hull. *Address:* Albany, Piccadilly, W1. *T:* 01-734 6641; Roughton Hall, near Woodhall Spa, Lincolnshire. *T:* Horncastle 2572. *Clubs:* Carlton, Hurlingham.

**TARBAT, Viscount; John Ruaridh Blunt Grant MacKenzie;** *b* 12 June 1948; *s* and *heir* of 4th Earl of Cromartie, *qv*. *Educ:* Rannock School, Perthshire; Strathclyde University. *Address:* Castle Leod, Strathpeffer, Ross-shire.

**TARBAT, Sir John Allan,** Kt 1937; *b* 1891; *s* of late John Allan Tarbat, Arbroath, Angus, Scotland; *m* 1960, Rita Grace, *er d* of late Herbert Wallis Marsh, Beckenham, Kent. *Educ:* Queen's Park School, Glasgow. Fellow: Chartered Institute of Secretaries; Certified and Corporate Accountants; Royal Society of Arts. Is a JP and Unofficial Magistrate for Judicial District of Colombo; Member of Senate, Ceylon, 1947-55. Formerly General Manager of James Finlay & Co. Ltd, Colombo; Chairman of Ceylon Chamber of Commerce, 1932-40 and 1945-47. *Address:* Galle Face Hotel, Colombo, Ceylon. *Clubs:* Caledonian; Queen's (Colombo, Ceylon).

**TARRANT, Dorothy,** MA Cantab, MA, PhD London; Professor Emeritus of Greek, University of London; *b* 7 May 1885; *d* of late Rev. William George Tarrant, Wandsworth, and Alice, *d* of Henry Stanley of Manchester. *Educ:* Clapham High School (LCC Scholar); Girton College, Cambridge (Scholar). Classical Tripos, Cambridge, Part I 1907, Part II (Ancient Philosophy), 1908; London BA Hons Classics, 1906; MA 1909, PhD 1930; at Girton, Agnata Butler and Thérèse Montefiore Prizes, and Gilchrist Fellowship for research, 1908-9; Assistant Lecturer in Classics, Bedford College, 1909; in Greek, 1915; Lecturer, 1921; University Reader, 1929; University Professor and Head of Greek Department, 1936-50. Hon. Fellow: Girton Coll., 1955; Bedford Coll., 1969; Manchester Coll., Oxford, 1969. President: Unitarian Assembly, 1952-53, Hellenic Society, 1953-56, Classical Association, 1957-58. *Publications:* The Hippias Major attributed to Plato, 1928; contributions to Year's Work in Classical Studies, and to various classical and other periodicals. *Address:* 3 Alcon Court, 20 Earlsfield Road, Wandsworth, SW18. *T:* 01-870 3785. *Club:* University Women's.

**TARRY, Frederick Thomas,** CB 1962; CBE 1946 (OBE 1937); MM; HM Inspector of Constabulary, 1946-62; *b* 19 Dec. 1896; *m* 1922, Frances Winter (*d* 1967); two *s*. *Educ:* Hartfield, Sussex. Served European War, 1914-19 (despatches, MM and Bar) in Queen's Own (Royal West Kent) Regiment. Served in Brighton police force, 1919-30; chief constable, Exeter, 1930-40; chief constable, Southampton, 1941-46. Serving Brother, Ven. Order of St John, 1933. King's Gold Medal, 1932; King's Police Medal, 1941. Trustee, Police Coll. and Chm., Coll. Adv. Cttee, 1948-62; Mem., Southampton Group Hosp. Management Cttee, 1955-; Chairman: General Hospital; Knowle Group Hosp. Management Cttee. *Address:* Beechcroft, King's Close, Chandlers Ford, Hants.

**TARVER, Major-General Charles Herbert,** CB 1961; CBE 1958; DSO 1945; DL; jssc; psc; late Infantry; retired Feb. 1964; *b* 6 Oct. 1908; *s* of Major-General A. L. Tarver, CB, CIE, DSO; *m* 1932, Margaret Poad; three *s*. *Educ:* King's School, Bruton; RMC, Sandhurst. Deputy Director of Military Intelligence, War Office, 1956-58; Assistant Chief of Staff (Intelligence) at Supreme Headquarters, Allied Powers Europe, 1958-61; Chief of Staff to C-in-C Allied Forces Northern Europe, 1961-64. Colonel 1953; Brigadier, 1957; Major-General, 1958. Dep. Col, The Queen's Regt, 1967-; Hon. Col., 7th Bn, The Queen's Regt (E Kent), 1970-. DL, Kent, 1968. *Recreations:* golf, fishing. *Address:* Flat 2, 23 Clifton Crescent, Folkestone, Kent. *Club:* Army and Navy.

**TASKER, Antony Greaves,** CBE 1966 (OBE 1945; MBE 1943); Director, Overseas Development Institute, since 1968; *b* 27 March 1916; *o s* of late Captain R. G. Tasker, Worcestershire Regt, and of Mrs Harold Raymond (*see* H. Raymond); *m* 1940, Elizabeth Gilmor, *e d* of late Maj. Harold Carter, TD. *Educ:* Bradfield Coll.; Christ Church, Oxford. Served War of 1939-45 (despatches twice); Western Desert, Sicily, Italy, NW Europe, SE Asia; Col GS(I). Org. Dir, Internat. Tea Market Expansion Bd, 1948-52; Dir Public Rel., Booker Gp of Cos in Guyana, 1954-62 (Chm., 1962-67). Member: Br. Guiana Senate, 1961-64 (MLC, 1957-61); Governor: Inst. of Develt Studies, Sussex; Oversea Service Coll.; Member: UK Nat. Commn for Unesco; Exec. Cttee, British Council; Council, Royal Commonwealth Soc. for the Blind; Voluntary Cttee on Overseas Aid and Develt; British Volunteer Programme; Consultant: Bd of Christian Aid. US Bronze Star, 1944; Officer, US Legion of Merit, 1945. *Address:* 104 Ashley Gardens, SW1. *T:* 01-828 0184. *Club:* Reform.

**TASKER, Rev. Canon Derek Morris Phipps;** Canon Residentiary and Treasurer of Southwark Cathedral since 1962; Director of Post-ordination Training for Diocese of Southwark, since 1965; Director of Ordinands, since 1968; *b* 15 Nov. 1916; *er s* of Morris Bennet and Geraldine Emily Tasker. *Educ:* Sherborne Sch.; Exeter Coll., Oxf. (BA, DipTheol); Westcott House, Cambridge. Curate, St Mary Redcliffe, Bristol, 1939-47; Vicar, St Stephen, Southmead, Bristol, 1947-55; King George VI Training Officer, Church of England Youth Council, 1955-62. *Publications:* The Parish and Young People, 1957; Letters to an Apprentice, 1958; Vocation and Work, 1960; Training the Youth Group, 1960. *Recreations:* English literature, contemporary theatre, cricket. *Address:* 195 New Kent Road, SE1. *T:* 01-407 5735.

**TASKER, Rev. Randolph Vincent Greenwood,** MA, BD Cantab; DD Lambeth; Professor of New Testament Exegesis, King's College, London, 1936-61, Professor Emeritus since 1961; *b* 31 Aug. 1895; *s* of William Henry and Evelyn Tasker; *m* 1928, Helen, *d* of Robert Wilkinson, MD; one *s* one *d*. *Educ:* Rossall; Corpus Christi College, Cambridge; Westcott House, Cambridge. Curate of Christ Church, Purley, 1922-24; Domestic Chaplain to Bishop Burge, Bishop of Oxford, 1924-25; Lecturer at King's College, London, 1926; Rector of Chenies, Bucks, 1928-34; Head of Department of New Testament, King's College, London, 1934; Chaplain of Lincoln's Inn, 1936-39; Rector of Lambourne with Abridge, 1942-46; Exam. Chap. to Bp of Ripon, 1938-46, to Bp of Salisbury, 1946-58; Dean of Faculty of Theology, University of London, 1948-52, and 1956-59. DD Lambeth, 1961. *Publications:* The Nature and Purpose of the Gospels, 1944; The Old Testament in the New Testament, 1945; The Gospel in the Epistle to the Hebrews, 1950; The Biblical Doctrine of the Wrath of God, 1951; The Narrow Way, 1952; The Epistle of James, 1956; The Second Epistle of Paul to the Corinthians, 1958; The Gospel according to John, 1960; The Gospel according to Matthew, 1961; Greek New Testament, 1964; Editor Augustine. City of God (Everyman's Library), 1945; articles in Church Quarterly Review, Journal of Theological Studies, Harvard Theological Review, etc. *Address:* 42 Stafford Way, Hassocks, Sussex.

**TASKER, Sir Theodore James,** Kt 1937; CIE 1932; OBE 1919; Indian Civil Service; retired; County Councillor, Dorset (Swanage-East), 1946; County Alderman, 1955-70; *b* 20 Jan. 1884; *s* of late Rev. John Greenwood Tasker, DD; *m* 1915, Jessie Helen Mellis-Smith (Kaisar-i-Hind Gold Medal); three *s* one *d*. *Educ:* King Edward's School, Birmingham; Trinity Coll., Cambridge (Major Scholar in Classics, First Class Honours Classical Tripos). Entered ICS 1908; Under-Secretary to Madras Govt, 1913-15; District Magistrate, Civil and Military Station, Bangalore, 1917-22; Commissioner of Coorg, 1923-26; services lent to Government of Nizam of Hyderabad as Director-General of Revenue and Revenue Secretary, 1927-35, and Member of Council, 1935-42; Supervisor, ICS. Probationers' Training, Dehra Dun, 1942-44; retired, 1944. *Address:* Southover, Swanage, Dorset BH19 2JF. *T:* Swanage 2033.

**TASMANIA, Bishop of,** since 1963; **Rt. Rev. Robert Edward Davies,** MA, ThD; *b* Birkenhead, England, 30 July 1913; *s* of late R. A. Davies, Canberra; *m* 1953, Helen M., *d* of H. M. Boucher; two *d*. *Educ:* Cessnock High School; Queensland University; St John's Theological College, Morpeth, NSW. Assistant Priest, Christ Church Cathedral, Newcastle, NSW, 1937-41. War of 1939-45: Toc H Army Chaplain, 1941-42; Chaplain, Royal Australian Air Force, Middle East and Mediterranean, 1942-46. Vice-Warden, St John's College, University of Queensland, Brisbane, 1946-48; Archdeacon of Canberra and Rector of Canberra, 1949-53; Archdeacon of Wagga Wagga, NSW, 1953-60; Assistant Bishop of Newcastle and Warden of St John's Theological College, Morpeth, NSW, 1960-63. *Recreations:* golf, tennis. *Address:* Bishopscourt, 30 Margaret Street, Sandy Bay, Tasmania 7005, Australia. *Clubs:* Tasmanian, Naval Military and Air Force of Tas. (Tas.).

**TATE, Ellalice;** *see* Hibbert, Eleanor.

**TATE, Francis Herbert;** Vice-Chairman, Tate & Lyle Ltd, since 1962; Chairman of Central Council, Royal Commonwealth Society, since 1969; *b* 3 April 1913; 2nd *s* of late Alfred Herbert Tate and late Elsie Tate (*née* Jelf Petit); *g g s* of Sir Henry Tate, Bt, founder of Henry Tate & Sons (now Tate & Lyle, Ltd) and donor of the Tate Gallery; *m* 1937, Esther, *d* of late Sir John Bromhead-Matthews, KC, JP, and late Lady Matthews, JP; one *s* two *d*. *Educ:* Private Tutor; Christ Church Oxford (BA 1934, MA 1963). Called to the Bar, Inner Temple, 1937. War Service, 1940-46, Royal Corps of Military Police (Lt-Col). Joined Tate & Lyle Ltd, 1946; Man. Dir, 1949. Chairman: British Sugar Bureau, 1966-; Council, London Chamber of Commerce, 1962-64 (Vice-Pres., 1964-); Federation of Commonwealth Chambers of Commerce, 1964-69. Member: Council, Friends of the Tate Gallery, 1963-; Council, Industrial Management Research Assoc.; Council of Foreign Bondholders, 1967-. Chairman, Wakefield (Tower Hill) Trust. Master of Mercers' Company, 1967-68. *Recreations:* golf (played for Oxford, 1934-35); motoring. *Address:* High Housen, Hook Heath, Woking, Surrey. *T:* Woking 60532.

**TATE, Lt-Col Sir Henry,** 4th Bt, *cr* 1898; TD; DL; late Royal Welch Fusiliers TA; *b* 29 June 1902; *s* of Sir Ernest Tate, 3rd Bt and Mildred Mary, 2nd *d* of F. H. Gossage of Camp Hill, Woolton, Liverpool; *S* father, 1939; *m* 1927, Nairne, *d* of late Saxon Gregson-Ellis, JP; two *s*. Sometime Lt Grenadier Guards. Joint Master Cottesmore Hounds, 1946-58. Councillor Rutland CC, 1958-70; High Sheriff of Rutland, 1949-50. Commanding 1st Bn Rutland Home Guard, 1954-57. DL, Co. of Rutland, 1964. *Heir:* *s* Henry Saxon Tate [*b* 28 Nov. 1931; *m* 1953, Sheila Ann, *e d* of Duncan Robertson; four *s*, including twin *s*]. *Address:* Preston Lodge, Withcote, Oakham, Rutland; Galltfaenan, Trefnant, Denbighshire. *Clubs:* Buck's, Turf.

**TATE, Phyllis (Margaret Duncan), (Mrs Alan Frank);** composer (free-lance); *b* 6 April 1911; *d* of Duncan Tate, FRIBA, and Annie S. Holl; *m* 1935, Alan Frank; one *s* one *d*. *Educ:* Royal Academy of Music, London. FRAM 1964. *Works:* (some commissioned by the BBC, and for festivals, etc, and several commercially recorded): Saxophone Concerto, 1944; Nocturne for Four Voices, 1945; Sonata for Clarinet and Cello, 1947; String Quartet, 1952; Choral Scene from The Bacchae, 1953; The Lady of Shalott, for Tenor and Instruments, 1956; Air and Variations for Violin, Clarinet and Piano, 1958; London Fields, 1958; Two Piano Sonatina, 1959; Witches and Spells, Choral Suite, 1959; Opera: The Lodger, 1960; Television Opera: Dark Pilgrimage, 1963; A Victorian Garland, for Two Voices and Instruments, 1965; Gravestones, for Cleo Laine, 1966; Seven Lincolnshire Folk Songs, for Chorus and Instruments, 1966; A Secular Requiem, for Chorus and Orchestra, 1967; Christmas Ale, for Soloist, Chorus and Orchestra, 1967; Apparitions, for Tenor and Instruments, 1968; Coastal Ballads, for Baritone and Instruments, 1969; Illustrations, for Brass Band, 1969; To Words by Joseph Beaumont, for women's chorus, 1970; Variegations, for solo viola, 1970; and many small choral pieces, songs and works for young people, including: Street Sounds, The Story of Lieutenant Cockatoo, Twice in a Blue Moon; A Pride of Lions. *Address:* 12 Heath Hurst Road, NW3. *T:* 01-435 0607.

**TATHAM, Francis Hugh Currer;** Editor of Whitaker's Almanack since 1950; Director, Sporting Handbooks Ltd; *b* 29 May 1916; *s* of late Harold Lewis Tatham, Gravesend, Kent, and late Frances Eva (*née* Crook); *m* 1945, Nancy Margaret, *d* of John Robins, Newton Abbot; two *s*. *Educ:* Charterhouse; Christ

Church, Oxford. Missioner, Shrewsbury School Mission, Liverpool, 1939-42; Sub-Warden, Mary Ward Settlement, 1942-45; Army Cadet Force, 1943-45; Editor, Church of England Newspaper, 1945-47; Vice-Pres., London Fedn of Boys' Clubs, 1960-; Vice-Pres. and Mem. Council, London Youth Football Association; Vice-Chm. and Mem. Council, Soc. of Indexers. *Recreations:* cricket, walking. *Address:* 35 Little Common, Stanmore, Middlesex. *T:* 01-954 4760. *Clubs:* National Liberal, MCC.

**TATI, Jacques, (Jacques Tatischeff)**; French film actor and Director; *b* Pecq, Seine et Oise, 9 Oct. 1908. Stage début as Music Hall artist; subsequently, 1933-, Actor, Director and Script-writer, Gérant de Cady Films. *Films* (many of which have received international awards or prizes) include: Gai Dimanche; L'Ecole des Facteurs; Soigne ton gauche; Jour de Fête; Les Vacances de Monsieur Hulot; Mon Oncle; Play Time, 1968; Yes Monsieur Hulot. Has won several awards for films. *Address:* 12 rue du Château, 92 La Garenne-Colombes, France.

**TATISCHEFF, Jacques;** *see* Tati, Jacques.

**TATLOW, Professor John Colin,** FRIC; PhD, DSc (Birmingham); Professor of Organic Chemistry in the University of Birmingham, since 1959; *b* 19 Jan. 1923; *s* of Thomas George and Florence Annie Tatlow, Cannock, Staffs; *m* 1946, Clarice Evelyn Mabel, *d* of Eric Millward and Mabel Evelyn Joiner, Sutton Coldfield; two *d*. *Educ:* Rugeley Grammar School, Staffs; University of Birmingham. Scientific Officer, Min. of Supply, 1946-48; Lectr in Chemistry, Univ. of Birmingham, 1948-56; Sen. Lectr, Univ. of Birmingham, 1956-57; Reader in Organic Chemistry, Univ. of Birmingham, 1957-59. Council of Chemical Society, 1957-60. Examiner, Royal Inst. of Chemistry, 1963-67. *Publications:* scientific papers mainly in Jl of Chem. Soc., and Tetrahedron. Editor, Advances in Fluorine Chemistry. *Address:* 30 Grassmoor Road, King's Norton, Birmingham 30. *T:* 021-458 1260.

**TATTON BROWN, William Eden,** CB 1965; ARIBA; Hospital Planning Consultant; *b* 13 Oct. 1910; *m* 1936, Aileen Hope Johnston Sparrow; two *s* one *d* (and one *d* decd). *Educ:* Wellington Coll.; King's Coll., Cambridge (MA); Architectural Association School, London; School of Planning, London. Special Final Examination of Town Planning Institute. Chief Design Asst, Messrs Tecton, Architects, 1934-38; private practice, 1938-40; Finsbury Borough Council, 1940-41. Served in HM Forces, Major, Royal Engineers, 1941-46. Asst Regional Planning Officer, Min. of Town and Country Planning, 1946-48; Dep. County Architect, Herts CC, 1948-59; Chief Architect, Min. of Health, later Dept of Health and Social Security, 1959-70. Steuben-Corning Research Fellowship, Travelling Scholarship to USA, 1957. Guest Lectr, Internat. Hosp. Confs: Finland, 1966; Holland, 1967; Australia, 1967; Düsseldorf, 1969; Tunisia, 1969; Sweden, 1970; Canada, 1970; WHO Commn to Madrid, 1968. Lecturer and broadcaster. *Publications:* contributor to technical and national press. *Address:* The Wall House, Little Berkhamsted, near Hertford, Herts. *T:* Essendon 536.

**TATUM, Dr E(dward) L(awrie);** Member and Professor, Rockefeller University, New York, NY, since 1957; *b* 14 Dec. 1909; *s* of Arthur L. and Mabel W. Tatum; *m* 1st, 1934, June Alton; two *d*; *m* 1956, Viola Kantor. *Educ:* University of Wisconsin. Asst Prof. of Biology, Stanford Univ., 1941-45; Assoc. Prof. of botany, 1945-46, Prof. of microbiology, 1946-48, Yale Univ.; Prof. of biology, 1948-56, Prof. of biochemistry, 1956-57, Stanford Univ. (jointly) Nobel prize for physiology and medicine, 1958. *Publications:* more than 100 papers in learned journals. *Recreations:* music (French horn); sports (swimming, skiing, etc). *Address:* 450 East 63rd Street, New York, NY 10021, USA. *T:* TE 8-5645.

**TAUNTON, Suffragan Bishop of,** since 1962; **Rt. Rev. Francis Horner West,** MA; also Prebendary of Wells and Rector of Dinder since 1962; *b* 9 Jan. 1909; *o s* of Sydney Hague and Mary West, St Albans, Herts; *m* 1947, Beryl Elaine, 2nd *d* of late Rev. W. A. Renwick, Smallbridge, Rochdale; one *s* one *d*. *Educ:* Berkhamsted School; Magdalene Coll. and Ridley Hall, Cambridge. Exhibitioner, Magdalene, Cambridge; MA 1934; Curate St Agnes, Leeds, 1933-36; Chaplain, Ridley Hall, Cambridge, 1936-38; Vicar of Starbeck, Yorks, 1938-42. Served War of 1939-45, as CF with BEF, MEF, CMF and SEAC, 1939-46 (despatches, 1945); Director of Service Ordination Candidates, 1946-47; Vicar of Upton, Notts, 1947-51; Archdeacon of Newark, 1947-62; Vicar of East Retford, 1951-55. Select Preacher, Cambridge Univ., 1962. *Publications:* Rude Forefathers, The Story of an English Village, 1600-1666, 1949; The Great North Road in Nottinghamshire, 1956; Sparrows of the Spirit, 1957; The Country Parish Today and Tomorrow, 1960. *Recreations:* gardening, local history. *Address:* The Rectory, Dinder, Wells, Somerset. *T:* Wells 2384.

**TAUNTON, Archdeacon of;** *see* Hilder, Ven. G. F.

**TAUNTON, Doidge Estcourt,** CB 1951; DSO and bar 1945; DL; Secretary, Northamptonshire TA and AFA, 1952-68; *b* 9 Nov. 1902; *s* of late J. G. C. Taunton, Launceston, Cornwall; *m* 1930, Rhona Caroline Wetherall (*d* 1951); one *s* (and one *s* decd). *Educ:* Cheltenham College; RMC Sandhurst; 2nd Lt Northamptonshire Regt, 1923; Lt 1925; Capt. 1935, and Adjt TA, 1932-36; Major 1940; Lt-Col 1941; Col 1948; Temp. Brig. 1945-47 and 1948-52. Served NWF India, 1936-38 (Medal and 2 clasps); War of 1939-45, India and Burma, 1936-45; French Indo-China and Netherlands East Indies, 1945-46 (Medal and clasp); Comd Somaliland Area, 1948-50; Comd 2nd Inf. Brigade, 1950-51; retired pay, 1951. DL Northants, 1969. *Address:* Great Hayne, Duston, Northampton.

**TAUSKY, Vilem;** FGSM 1968; Director of Opera, Guildhall School of Music, since 1966; Artistic Director, Phoenix Opera Co., since 1967; BBC Conductor since 1950; *b* 20 July 1910; *s* of Emil Tausky, MD, Prerov, Czechoslovakia, and Josefine Ascher, opera singer; *m* 1948, Margaret Helen Powell. *Educ:* Univ. of Brno; Janáček Conservatoire, Brno; Meisterschule, Prague. Military Service in France and England, 1939-45. National Opera House, Brno, Czechoslovakia, 1929-39; Musical Director, Carl Rosa Opera, 1945-49. Guest Conductor: Royal Opera House, Covent Garden, 1951-; Sadler's Wells Opera, 1953-. FGSM 1968. Czechoslovak Military Cross, 1944; Czechoslovak Order of Merit, 1945. *Publications:* Czechoslovak Christmas Carols, 1942; Oboe Concerto, 1957; Concertino for harmonica and orchestra, 1963; Divertimento for strings, 1966; Soho: Scherzo for orchestra, 1966; Concert Overture for Brass Band, 1969. *Recreation:* country life. *Address:* 44 Haven Green Court, W5. *T:* 01-997 6512; Rose Cottage, Towersey, near Thame, Oxon. *T:* Thame 2192.

**TAVERNE, Dick,** QC 1965; MP (Lab) Lincoln, since March 1962; *b* 18 Oct. 1928; *s* of Dr N. J. M. and Mrs L. V. Taverne; *m* 1955, Janice Hennessey; two *d. Educ:* Charterhouse School; Balliol College, Oxford (First in Greats). Oxford Union Debating tour of USA, 1951. Called to Bar, 1954. Parliamentary Under-Secretary of State, Home Office, 1966-68; Minister of State, Treasury, 1968-69; Financial Secretary to the Treasury, 1969-70. *Recreations:* squash, sailing. *Address:* 34 Emperor's Gate, SW7. *T:* 01-373 0377.

**TAVISTOCK, Marquess of; Henry Robin Ian Russell;** *b* 21 Jan. 1940; *s* and *heir* of 13th Duke of Bedford, *qv*; *m* 1961, Henrietta Joan, *d* of Henry F. Tiarks, *qv*; two *s. Educ:* Le Rosey, Switzerland; Harvard University. *Heir: s* Lord Howland, *qv. Address:* 3 Clarendon Place, W2. *T:* 01-262 5588; Chevington Russell, Chevington, Bury St Edmunds, Suffolk. *T:* Chevington 215. *Clubs:* Buck's; Jockey Club Rooms; Harvard, The Brook (New York).

**TAYLER, Admiral (retired) Sir R. V. S.;** *see* Symonds-Tayler.

**TAYLOR;** *see* Suenson-Taylor.

**TAYLOR,** family name of Barons **Taylor, Taylor of Gryfe** and **Taylor of Mansfield.**

**TAYLOR,** Baron *cr* 1958 (Life Peer), of Harlow; **Stephen James Lake Taylor,** MD, BSc, FRCP; President and Vice-Chancellor, Memorial University of Newfoundland, since 1967; *b* 30 Dec. 1910; *s* of John Reginald Taylor, MInstCE, and Beatrice Violet Lake Taylor; *m* 1939, Dr May Doris Charity Clifford (*see* Lady Taylor); two *s* one *d. Educ:* Stowe Sch.; St Thomas's Hosp. Med. Sch., Univ. of London. BSc 1st cl. Hons; MB, BS (Hons Hygiene and Forensic Medicine); MD. FRCP 1960. Served War of 1939-45: Surg. Lt-Comdr (Neuro-psychiatric Specialist), RNVR; Dir of Home Intelligence and Wartime Social Survey, MOI, 1941-45. Formerly: Casualty Officer and HP, St Thomas' Hosp.; Grocers' Co. Research Scholar, Med. Unit, St Thomas' Hosp.; Sen. Resident Med. Officer, Royal Free Hosp.; HP, Bethlem Royal Hosp.; Asst Med. Officer, Maudsley Hosp. MP (Lab) Barnet Div. of Herts, 1945-50; PPS to Dep. Prime Minister and Lord President of Council, 1947-50; Under-Sec. of State for Commonwealth Relations and Colonies, 1964-65. Consultant in Occupational Health, Richard Costain Ltd, 1951-64 and 1966-67; Med. Dir, Harlow Industrial Health Service, 1955-64 and 1965-67. Visiting Research Fellow, Nuffield Provincial Hospitals Trust, 1953-55; Chadwick Lectr, RSH, 1963. Mem., Harlow New Town Develt Corp., 1950-64 and 1966-67. Chm., Labour Party Study Group on Higher Educn; Vice-Chm., British Film Inst.; Member: N-W Metropolitan Regional Hosp. Bd; Health Adv. Cttee of Labour Party; Cohen Cttee on Gen. Practice, Beveridge Cttee on BBC; Bd of Governors, UCH. *Publications:* Scurvy and Carditis, 1937; The Suburban Neurosis, 1938; Mental Illness as a Clue to Normality, 1940; The Psychopathic Tenth, 1941; The Study of Public Opinion, 1943; Battle for Health, 1944; The Psychopath in our Midst, 1949; Shadows in the Sun, 1949; Good General Practice, 1954; The Health Centres of Harlow, 1955; The Survey of Sickness, 1958; First Aid in the Factory, 1960; Mental Health and Environment, 1964; articles in Lancet, etc. *Address:* Mount Scio House, Memorial University of Newfoundland, St John's, Newfoundland, Canada.

**TAYLOR, Lady, (Charity),** MB, BS, MRCS, LRCP; retired as Assistant Director and Inspector of Prisons (Women), (1959-66); Member, BBC General Advisory Council, 1964-67; President, Newfoundland and Labrador Social Welfare Council, since 1968; *b* Sept. 1914; *d* of W. George and Emma Clifford; *m* 1939, Stephen J. L. Taylor (*see* Lord Taylor); two *s* one *d. Educ:* The Grammar School, Huntingdon; London (Royal Free Hospital) School of Medicine for Women. HS Royal Free Hospital; HS Elizabeth Garrett Anderson Hospital; Assistant Medical Officer HM Prison, Holloway; Medical Officer, HM Prison Holloway; Governor, HM Prison, Holloway, 1945-59. *Recreations:* reading, conversation. *Address:* c/o The Lord Taylor, Memorial University of Newfoundland, St John's, Newfoundland, Canada.

**TAYLOR OF GRYFE,** Baron *cr* 1968 (Life Peer), of Bridge of Weir; **Thomas Johnston Taylor; Chairman, Forestry Commission, since 1970 (Commissioner since 1963);** *b* 27 April 1912; *m* 1943, Isobel Wands; two *d. Educ:* Bellahouston Acad., Glasgow. Mem.: British Railways Bd; Board of Scottish Television Ltd, 1968-. President, Scottish CWS, 1965-70. Dir, Scottish Civic Trust. DL Renfrewshire, 1970. *Recreations:* theatre, golf, walking. *Address:* Tigh-an-Rhu, Bridge of Weir, Renfrewshire. *T:* Bridge of Weir 2649. *Clubs:* National Liberal, Caledonian.

**TAYLOR OF MANSFIELD,** Baron *cr* 1966 (Life Peer), of Mansfield; **Harry Bernard Taylor,** CBE 1966; *b* 18 Sept. 1895; *s* of Henry Taylor, Mansfield Woodhouse; *m* 1921, Clara, *d* of John Ashley. *Educ:* Council Schools. A Coal Miner. MP (Lab.) Mansfield Div. of Nottinghamshire, 1941-66; Parliamentary Private Secretary to Parliamentary Secretary, Ministry of Aircraft Production, 1942; to Minister of National Insurance, 1945; Parliamentary Secretary, Ministry of National Insurance, 1950-51. *Address:* 47 Shakespeare Avenue, Mansfield Woodhouse, Nottinghamshire.

**TAYLOR, Professor Alan Carey,** BA Sydney, DUP, DèsL, Lauréat de l'Académie Française; Professor of French, Birkbeck College, University of London, since 1948; *b* Goulburn, NSW, 11 Feb. 1905; *s* of late W. Carey Taylor; *m* Yvonne Albertine Antoinette, *d* of Ernest Le Gal, Conseiller à la Cour d'appel, Caen; two *s* one *d. Educ:* North Sydney High School; Univ. of Sydney, Sydney Teachers' College; University of Paris. BA 1926, Dip. Mod. Lang. 1927; French Govt Travelling Schol., 1927; DUP, 1929. Taught at North Sydney and Goulburn High Schools; Lecturer, Univ. of Sydney, 1933; Rep. Sydney Univ. at Internat. Phonetics Congress, 1935; DèsL, 1938; Lecturer and Senior Lecturer, Melbourne Univ., 1938-48. French Translator and Announcer, Radio Australia, 1941-48; Vice-Pres. French Australian Assoc. of Victoria, 1944-48; Hon. Sec. of Assoc. of Heads of French Departments, 1950-; Mem. Mixed Commission under Franco-British Cultural Convention, 1957-. Exchange Professor, University of Paris, 1959, Univ. of Moscow, 1969. Mem. Senate, Univ. of London, 1963-, Dean of Faculty of Arts, 1968-. Croix des Forces Françaises Libres (hon.), 1947. Médaille de la Langue Française (French Acad.), 1948; Chevalier, Légion d'Honneur, 1961. *Publications:* Carlyle: sa première fortune littéraire en France, 1929; Carlyle et la pensée latine, 1937; Le Président de Brosses et l'Australie, 1938. Annotated Edns Th Gautier: Jean et Jeannette, 1934; A Book of French Verse, 1939; Contes et nouvelles, 1942; Vingt et un Contes, 1949. Contributions to learned periodicals, mainly on 19th Century Literature. *Recreations:* walking, swimming, reading. *Address:* 29 Menelik Road, Hampstead, NW2. *T:* 01-435 6264.

**TAYLOR, Alan John Percivale;** historian and journalist; FBA 1956; Fellow of Magdalen College, Oxford; Hon. Director, The Beaverbrook Library; *b* Birkdale, Lancs, 25 March 1906; *o s* of Percy Lees and Constance Sumner Taylor; four *s* two *d. Educ:* Bootham School, York; Oriel Coll., Oxford. Formerly Lectr in Modern History, University of Manchester. Lecturer in International History, Oxford University, 1953-63; Tutor in Modern History, Magdalen College, 1938-63; Ford's Lecturer in English History, Oxford University, 1955-56; Leslie Stephen Lecturer, Cambridge University, 1960-61. Hon. DCL, New Brunswick, 1961; DUniv York, 1970. *Publications:* (many of them translated into other languages): The Italian Problem in European Diplomacy 1847-49, 1934; Germany's First Bid for Colonies 1884-85, 1938; The Habsburg Monarchy 1815-1918, 1941, rewritten 1948; The Course of German History, 1945; From Napoleon to Stalin, 1950; Rumours of Wars, 1952; The Struggle for Mastery in Europe, 1848-1918, 1954; Bismarck, 1955; Englishmen and Others, 1956; The Trouble Makers: Dissent over Foreign Policy, 1792-1939, 1957; The Russian Revolution of 1917, 1958 (script of first lectures ever given on television); The Origins of the Second World War, 1961; The First World War: an Illustrated History, 1963; Politics in Wartime and Other Essays, 1964; English History, 1914-1945, 1965; From Sarajevo to Potsdam, 1966; Europe: Grandeur and Decline, 1967; War by Timetable, 1969; (ed) Lloyd George: twelve essays, 1970. *Address:* Beaverbrook Library, 33 St Bride Street, EC4. *T:* 01-353 2444.

**TAYLOR, Rt. Hon. Sir Alan Russell,** PC 1963; KBE 1955; **Hon. Mr Justice Taylor;** Justice of the High Court of Australia since 1952; *b* 25 Nov. 1901; *m* 1933, Ceinwen Gertrude Williams; one *s* one *d. Educ:* University of Sydney, NSW. Admitted to NSW Bar, 1926; Challis Lecturer, Sydney University Law School; Equity and Company Law, 1933-34; Legal Interpretation, 1935-38. KC 1943 (QC 1952). President NSW Bar Association, 1948-49; Justice of the Supreme Court of NSW, 1952-. *Recreations:* golf, bowls. *Address:* 7 Wentworth Road, Vaucluse, Sydney, NSW, Australia. *T:* FU 2369. *Clubs:* Australian, Royal Sydney Golf, Elanora Country (Sydney); Athenæum (Melb.).

**TAYLOR, Albert Booth,** MA Oxon; Professor of English Language and Literature, University of Tasmania, 1925-57, Professor Emeritus since 1957; *b* Manchester, 1896; *s* of A. Taylor, Auckland, NZ; *m* 1931, Molly, *o d* of Douglas Fitzgerald, Hobart; three *s. Educ:* Auckland Grammar School; Auckland University College; Merton College, Oxford (First Class Honours in English). University Scholar, University of New Zealand, 1914; Overseas Scholarship from Rhodes Trust, 1918; served in New Zealand Expeditionary Force, 1915-18; Lecturer in English, Leeds University, 1920-21; Armstrong College, Durham University, 1921-25. *Publications:* An Introduction to Mediæval Romance, 1930; The History of Long Diphthongs in Middle Kentish, Modern Language Review, Jan. 1924; edit. Floris and Blanchefleur, 1927; edit. Shakespeare's Macbeth, 1936 and Merchant of Venice, 1937. *Recreation:* bowling. *Address:* 316 Davey Street, Hobart, Tasmania. *T:* Hobart 2-2203.

**TAYLOR, Alexander Burt,** CBE 1961; *b* 6 June 1904; *s* of Rev. A. B. Taylor; *m* 1st, 1935, Jean Allardice (*d* 1959); two *s* one *d*; 2nd, 1965, Elizabeth Gordon (*née* Hogg). *Educ:* Hamilton Academy; Kirkwall Grammar School; Edinburgh University; Columbia University. MA Edinburgh 1925; DLitt Edinburgh 1935. Inspector of Schools, Scottish Education Dept, 1933; Principal, Dept of Health for Scotland, 1939; Asst Sec., 1947; Registrar General for Scotland, 1959-66. Member of interdepartmental cttees on medical auxiliaries, 1949-51, on rehabilitation, 1953-56, and on number of doctors, 1955-57. FRSE 1961. *Publications:* Orkneyinga Saga, A New Translation with Introduction and Notes, 1938; articles on educational, historical and linguistic topics. *Recreations:* gardening, woodwork, studies in Scandinavian influences on Scottish History, study of early Scottish maps. *Address:* 35 Balgreen Road, Edinburgh 12. *T:* 031-337 3681. *Club:* Royal Commonwealth Society.

**TAYLOR, Rear-Admiral Alfred Hugh,** CB 1942; OBE 1919; retired; *b* 24 Oct. 1886; 3rd *s* of late Alfred Taylor, JP, of Starston Place, Norfolk; *m* 1911, Maud Violet (*d* 1959), *e d* of late Col Sir William Bisset, KCIE; three *s* one *d. Educ:* HMS Britannia. Entered Navy, 1901; Rear-Adm. and retired, 1936; rejoined, 1939-45; JP, Norfolk, 1937, DL 1951. *Address:* The Manor House, Diss, Norfolk. *T:* Diss 2096. *Clubs:* United Service; Norfolk (Norwich).

**TAYLOR, Professor (Alfred) Maurice,** PhD, MA; FInstP; Professor of Physics, University of Southampton, 1945-68, now Emeritus Professor; *b* 6 Feb. 1903; *o s* of Alfred Ernest Taylor, MA, Clerk in Holy Orders, and Helen Caroline Georgiana (*née* Adams); *m* 1938, Sarah Margaret Alston, *yr d* of Edward Judge; one *s* one *d. Educ:* Reigate Grammar School; Trinity College, Cambridge. Sen. Schol., Alhusen and Coutts-Trotter Research Student, etc, Trinity Coll., Cambridge, 1921-27; PhD Cambridge 1927, MA 1928. Madden Prizeman, TCD, 1928; Ramsay Memorial Fellow, 1927-29. Asst Prof. of Physical Optics, Univ. of Rochester, NY, USA, 1929-34; Lectr in Natural Philosophy, Univ. of St Andrews, Scotland, 1934-45 (seconded to Southampton in 1941); Dep. Prof. of Physics, University Coll., Southampton, 1941-45: Professor of Physics, University College, Southampton (now Univ. of Southampton), 1945-68; Vis. Lectr on the Tallman Foundation, Bowdoin Coll., Brunswick, Maine, USA, 1964-65; Vis. Professor: Hollins Coll., Virginia, USA, 1965-66; Bowdoin Coll., Brunswick, Maine, USA, 1968-69, 1969-70. *Publications:* (with F. I. G. Rawlins) Infra-red Analysis of Molecular Structure, 1929. Imagination and the Growth of Science (Tallman Lectures, 1964-65, given at Bowdoin College, USA), 1966. Papers in Proceedings Royal Society, Philosophical Magazine, Trans Faraday Soc., Proc. Physical Soc., Jl of Scientific Instruments, Jl of Optical Soc. of Amer., etc. *Recreations:* gardening, caravanning. *Address:* Randal's, Chilworth, Southampton. *T:* Southampton 68114.

**TAYLOR, Maj.-Gen. Allan Macnab,** MC 1944; Commandant, Staff College, Camberley, since 1969; *b* 26 March 1919; *s* of Alexander Lawrence Taylor and Winifred Ethel (*née* Nisbet); *m* 1945, Madeleine Turpin (marr. diss. 1963); two *d. Educ:* Fyling Hall School, Robin Hood's Bay. Joined TA, 1938; Troop Leader, 10th R Tank Regt, 1940; Squadron Leader, 7th R Tank Regt, 1942; 6th R Tank Regt, 1946; Staff College, 1948; GSO, 2, 56 London Armoured Div., 1949; Bde Major 20 Armoured Bde, 1952; Instructor, Staff College, 1954; Squadron Leader, 1st R Tank Regt, 1957; Second in Comd 5th RTR, 1959; Comdg Officer: 5th RTR, 1960 and 3rd, 1961; AA & QMG, 1st Div., 1962; Commandant, RAC

Gunnery School, 1963; Comd Berlin Brigade, 1964; Imperial Defence College, 1967; Comdr, 1st Div., 1968. *Recreation:* golf. *Address:* Staff College, Camberley, Surrey.

**TAYLOR, Andrew James,** CBE 1965; Chairman, British Manufacturing and Research Co., Grantham, Lincs, since 1968; *b* 1902; *s* of late Alfred George Ralph Meston Taylor, Broughty Ferry, Dundee; *m* 1925, Mary Ann Symmers, *d* of George Cowie, Aberdeen; three *s* one *d*. *Educ:* Robert Gordon's Coll., Aberdeen. Dir of Manufacture and Exec. Dir, Ford Motor Co. Ltd, 1962-65; Deputy Managing Director, 1965-67. *Recreations:* photography, fishing. *Address:* 45 Hall Lane, Upminster, Essex. *T:* Upminster 23916. *Club:* Royal Automobile.

**TAYLOR, Arnold Joseph,** MA Oxon; FSA, FRHistS; Chief Inspector of Ancient Monuments, Ministry of Public Building and Works, since 1961; Director, Society of Antiquaries, since 1970 (Vice-President, 1963-64; Secretary, 1964-70); *b* 24 July 1911; *y s* of late John George Taylor, Headmaster of Sir Walter St John's School, Battersea; *m* 1940, Patricia Katharine, *d* of late S. A. Guilbride, Victoria, BC; one *s* one *d*. *Educ:* Merchant Taylor's School; St John's College, Oxford. Assistant master, Chard School, Somerset, 1934; Assistant Inspector of Ancient Monuments, Ministry of Works, 1935. Served War of 1939-45, Intelligence Officer, RAF, 1942-46. Inspector of Ancient Monuments for Wales, Min. of Works, 1946-54, Asst Chief Inspector, 1954-61. Commissioner: Royal Commissions on Ancient and Historical Monuments (Wales and Monmouthshire), 1956-; Historical Monuments (England), 1963- . Member, Cathedrals Advisory Cttee, 1964; Vice-Pres., Royal Archaeol. Inst., 1968; Pres., Cambrian Archaeolog. Assoc., 1969. Mem., Sir Walter St John's Schools Trust, 1970. Hon. DLitt Wales. *Publications:* Records of the Barony and Honour of the Rape of Lewes, 1940; official guides to: Minster Lovell, 1939; Basingwerk Abbey, 1946; Rhuddlan Castle, 1949; Raglan Castle, 1950; Monmouth Castle, 1951; Caernarvon Castle, 1953; Conway Castle and Westminster Jewel Tower, 1956; chapter on Military Architecture, in vol. Medieval England, 1958; (part author) History of the King's Works, 1963; contrib. on medieval architectural history in Eng. Hist. Rev., Antiquaries Jl, Archaeologia Cambrensis, etc. *Recreation:* music. *Address:* 56 Langham Road, Teddington, Middlesex. *T:* 01-977 5030. *Club:* Athenæum.

**TAYLOR, Prof. Arthur John;** Professor of Modern History, Leeds University, since 1961; *b* 29 Aug. 1919; *s* of Victor Henry and Mary Lydia Taylor, Manchester; *m* 1955, Elizabeth Ann Jeffries; one *s* two *d*. *Educ:* Manchester Grammar School; Manchester University. Assistant Lecturer in History, University Coll., London, 1948; Lecturer, 1950. *Publications:* contrib. to books and learned journals. *Recreations:* cricket, gardening, music. *Address:* Redgarth, Leeds Road, Collingham, Wetherby, Yorks. *T:* Collingham Bridge 2930.

**TAYLOR, Arthur Wood,** CB 1953; Chairman, Horserace Totalisator Board, since 1970; *b* 23 June 1909; *s* of late Richard Wood and Ann Taylor; *m* 1936, Mary Beatrice Forster; one *d*. *Educ:* Royal School, Wolverhampton; Wolverhampton Grammar School; Sidney Sussex College, Cambridge. Wrangler (Tyson Medal), 1930; joined HM Customs and Excise, 1931; Principal, 1936; Asst Secretary, 1943. Comr of Customs and Excise, 1949; Under-Secretary, HM Treasury, 1957-63; Comr of Customs and Excise, 1964-65, Dep. Chm., 1965-70. *Address:* Tote House, New Bridge Street, EC4. *Club:* Reform.

**TAYLOR, Maj.-Gen. Sir Brian;** *see* Taylor, Maj.-Gen. Sir G. B. O.

**TAYLOR, Dr Charity;** *see* Taylor, Lady.

**TAYLOR, Sir Charles (Stuart),** Kt 1954; TD; MA Cantab; DL (Sussex); MP (C) Eastbourne since March 1935; *b* 10 April 1910; *s* of Alfred George and Mary Taylor; *m* 1936, Constance Ada Shotter; three *s* one *d*. *Educ:* Epsom College; Trinity College, Cambridge. Hons Degree Law Tripos. President of Grosvenor House (Park Lane) Ltd; Director: Onyx Property Investment Co. Ltd; Brightstone Estates Ltd, and other cos; President, Residential Hotels Association of Great Britain, until 1948 and Vice-Chairman of Coun. of British Hotels and Restaurants Association until 1951; Vice-President Building Societies Association; member of Council of the British Travel and Holidays Assoc. Leader of Parly Delegns to Germany and Ethiopia. Joined TA 1937 (Royal Artillery), Capt., August 1939; DAAG and Temp. Major, Jan. 1941; attended Staff College, June 1941 (war course), graduated sc. Hon. Colonel. Serving Brother, Order of St John. *Recreations:* yachting (rep. Gt Britain *v* USA and Old World *v* New World in six-metre yacht races, 1955), shooting, fishing. *Address:* 4 Reeves House, Reeves Mews, W1. *T:* 01-499 3730. *Clubs:* Royal Thames Yacht, 1900, MCC; Travellers' (Paris).

**TAYLOR, Dr Daniel Brumhall Cochrane;** Vice-Chancellor, Victoria University of Wellington, New Zealand; *b* 13 May 1921; *s* of Daniel Brumhall Taylor, Coleraine, NI and Anna Martha Taylor (*née* Rice); *m* 1955, Elizabeth Page, Christchurch, NZ; one *s* one *d*. *Educ:* Coleraine Academical Instn, NI; Queen's Univ., Belfast. BSc (Mech. Engrg) 1942, BSc (Elec. Engrg) 1943, MSc 1946, PhD 1948, QUB; MA Cantab 1956; FIMechE 1968. Lecturer in Engineering: Liverpool Univ., 1948-50; Nottingham Univ., 1950-53; ICI Fellow, Cambridge Univ., 1953-56; Lectr in Mechanical Sciences, Cambridge Univ., 1956-68; Fellow of Peterhouse, 1958-68, Fellow Emer. 1968-; Tutor of Peterhouse, 1958-65, Senior Tutor 1965-68. *Publications:* numerous engrg and metallurgical papers. *Recreations:* golf; formerly rowing (Ireland VIII, Olympic Games, 1948). *Address:* Victoria University of Wellington, PO Box 196, Wellington, New Zealand. *T:* Wellington 46040. *Clubs:* Leander (Henley-on-Thames); Wellington (NZ).

**TAYLOR, Desmond S.;** *see* Shawe-Taylor.

**TAYLOR, Dorothy Mary,** CBE 1960; MD, DPH; late Senior Medical Officer, for Maternity and Child Welfare, Ministry of Health; *b* 17 August 1902; *d* of late Thomas Taylor, Highfield, Dreghorn Loan, Colinton, Edinburgh 13; unmarried. *Educ:* George Watson's Ladies' Coll., Edinburgh; Edinburgh Univ. House Surgeon Female VD Department, Edinburgh Royal Infirmary, 1925-26; Clinical Assistant, Maternity and Child Welfare Department, Edinburgh, Apr.-Oct. 1926; House Physician, Royal Hospital for Sick Children, Edinburgh, 1926-27; Resident Medical Officer, Sick Children's Hospital, Newcastle on Tyne, 1927-28; Senior Clinical Assistant, Female VD Department, Royal Infirmary, Edinburgh, 1928-30; Medical Officer, Maternity and Child Welfare Department, Edinburgh, 1930-31; Assistant MOH, Maternity and Child Welfare Department, Sunderland, 1932-35. *Address:* 4

Clerk's Acre, Keymer, Hassocks, Sussex. *T:* Hassocks 2143. *Club:* University Women's.

**TAYLOR, Douglas,** CMG 1960; Deputy Director General, Confederation of British Industry since 1966; *b* 22 May 1915; *s* of George Taylor, Oldham, Lancs; *m* 1947, Margaret Bryant; one *s* two *d.* *Educ:* Manchester Grammar School; Oriel College, Oxford. Entered Ministry of Labour, 1939. Served War of 1939-45, RAF, Middle East, 1941-45. Seconded Commonwealth Department of Labour and National Service, Australia, 1948-51; Labour Attaché; British Embassy: Athens, 1954-55; Rome, 1955-59; Asst Sec., Min. of Labour, 1959-62, resigned from CS to become Internat. Sec., Brit. Employers' Confedn, 1962; Dep. Dir, 1963. Mem., SW Metropolitan Regional Hosp. Bd, 1970. *Address:* 14 Corkran Road, Surbiton, Surrey. *T:* 01-399 1554. *Club:* Reform.

**TAYLOR, Edward Macmillan;** MP (C) Cathcart Division of Glasgow since 1964; journalist and author; Parliamentary Under-Secretary of State, Scottish Office, since 1970; *b* 18 April 1937; *s* of late Edward Taylor and of Minnie Hamilton Taylor. *Educ:* Glasgow High School and University (MA (Hons) Econ. and Politics). Commercial Editorial Staff of Glasgow Herald, 1958-59; Industrial Relations Officer on Staff of Clyde Shipbuilders' Assoc., 1959-64. *Publications:* (novel) Hearts of Stone, 1968; formerly, contributions to the press. *Address:* 74 Craig Road, Glasgow S4. *T:* 041-637 1704.

**TAYLOR, Edward Plunket,** CMG 1946; Chairman: Argus Corporation Ltd; Lyford Cay Co. Ltd; Windfields Farm Ltd; New Providence Development Co., Nassau; Roy West Banking Corporation Ltd, Nassau; Jockey Club Ltd; Trust Corp. of the Bahamas Ltd; Royal Bank of Canada International Ltd, Nassau; Executive Committee, Massey-Ferguson Ltd; Director: The Royal Bank of Canada Trust Corp. Ltd, London; Bass Charrington Ltd, London; and other companies; *b* Ottawa, Ontario, 29 January 1901; *s* of late Lieut-Colonel Plunket Bourchier Taylor and Florence Gertrude Magee; *m* 1927, Winifred Thornton, *d* of late Charles F. M. Duguid, Ottawa, Ontario; one *s* two *d.* *Educ:* Ashbury College; Ottawa Collegiate Institute, Ottawa; McGill University, Montreal (BSc in Mechanical Engineering, 1922). Director Brading Breweries Limited, 1923, also entered the investment house of McLeod, Young, Weir & Co., Limited, Ottawa, 1923, a Director 1929, resigned to become Pres. Canadian Breweries Ltd, 1930 (Chm. of Board, 1944). Member, Thoroughbred Racing Assoc. Inc.; Mem. Bd of Governors: Trinity Coll. Sch.; Ashbury College. Wartime appointments held: member, Executive Committee, Dept of Munitions and Supply, Ottawa, April 1940; Joint Director-General of Munitions Production, Nov. 1940; Executive Assistant to the Minister of Munitions and Supply, Feb. 1941; President War Supplies Limited, Washington, DC, April 1941; by Prime Minister Churchill appointed President and Vice-Chairman, British Supply Council in North America, Sept. 1941; Director-General British Ministry of Supply Mission, Feb. 1942; Canadian Deputy Member on the Combined Production and Resources Board, Nov. 1942; also Canadian Chairman, Joint War Aid Committee, US-Canada, Sept. 1943. Member, Delta Upsilon Fraternity. Anglican. *Recreation:* riding. *Address:* Lyford Cay, New Providence, Bahamas; Birch Hall, Windlesham, Surrey, England. *Clubs:* Buck's, Turf; Royal Yacht Squadron (Cowes); Toronto, York (Toronto); University, Montreal (Montreal); Rideau (Ottawa); Metropolitan, Twenty Nine (New York).

**TAYLOR, Edward Wilfred,** CBE 1946; FRS 1952; Hon. DSc Leeds, 1957; FRMS; *b* 29 April 1891; *s* of Harold Dennis Taylor and Charlotte Fernandes Barff; *m* 1921, Winifred Mary, *d* of Edward George Hunter, Hastings; one *s.* *Educ:* Oundle School. Joined Messrs Cooke Troughton & Simms, 1908; served European War, 1914-19, Lieut RNVR Admiralty War Staff; Optical Manager, 1923; Technical Manager, 1932; Joint Managing Director, 1937-56; Director, 1956-61. Govt sponsored missions, US, 1943; Jena, 1945; Delegate, Commission Internationale d'Optique, 1948, 1950, 1953, 1956 and 1959. President Yorkshire Naturalists' Trust, 1952-. *Publications:* Design and Construction of Surveying Instruments, 1938; contributions to technical and scientific journals, including Proceedings of the Royal Society, on microscopy and surveying. *Recreations:* fishing and ornithology. *Address:* 11 The Avenue, York. *T:* 22621.

**TAYLOR, Alderman Edwin,** JP; *b* 1905; *s* of Lawrence Taylor and Elizabeth (*née* Waterhouse); *m* Sarah Elizabeth Rostron; one *s* one *d.* *Educ:* St John's School, Wingates; Bolton Technical College. Member Bolton Town Council, 1940-44 and 1947-, Alderman, 1955, JP Bolton, 1952; Mayor, 1959-60, Dep. Mayor, 1960-61; Founder Chairman, Bolton and District Master Bakers' Assoc.; Master Baker; President Bolton Master Bakers, 1961. MP (C) Bolton East, Nov. 1960-Sept. 1964. Mem. Trade Union Gp attached to Conservative Party. Past Pres. Bolton Chamber of Trade. Chm. Fire Service Cttee, Assoc. of Municipal Corpns. *Recreations:* cricket and music. *Address:* 602 Tonge Moor Road, Bolton, Lancs. *T:* Bolton 51571. *Clubs:* Constitutional; Rotary (Bolton).

**TAYLOR, Edwin,** CMG 1936; *b* 10 Nov. 1881; *m* 1912, E. M. Messom (*d* 1955); two *c.* *Educ:* Nottingham School; King's College, London. Colonial Office, 1901; served South African War, 1901; Board of Trade, 1902-05; Nyasaland, 1906-08; Asst Treasurer Uganda, 1909-16; Civil Administration German East Africa Occupied Territory, 1917-19; Treasurer, etc., Seychelles, 1919-23; Deputy Treasurer Uganda, 1923-25; President, Freetown Municipal Council, 1928; Deputy Treasurer, Sierra Leone, 1925-30; Treasurer, Hong Kong, 1931; Chairman Exchange Fund Advisory Committee, 1936; Assessor, Estate Duty Commissioner; retired, 1937. Temp. Administrative Officer Ministry Economic Warfare, 1940-42; Colonial Office, 1942-45. *Address:* 3 Cavendish Road, Bognor Regis, Sussex.

**TAYLOR, Elizabeth, (Mrs J. W. K. Taylor);** Author; *b* 3 July 1912; *d* of Oliver Coles and Elsie (*née* Fewtrell); *m* 1936, John William Kendall Taylor; one *s* one *d.* *Educ:* The Abbey School, Reading. *Publications:* At Mrs Lippincote's, 1946; Palladian, 1947; A View of the Harbour, 1949; A Wreath of Roses, 1950; A Game of Hide-and-Seek, 1951; The Sleeping Beauty, 1953. Hester Lilly and Other Stories, 1954. Angel, 1957; The Blush and Other Stories, 1958; In a Summer Season, 1961; The Soul of Kindness, 1964; A Dedicated Man, 1965; Mossy Trotter (for children), 1967; The Wedding Group, 1968; The Excursion to the Source, 1970. *Address:* Grove's Barn, Penn, Buckinghamshire. *T:* Penn 3270.

**TAYLOR, Elizabeth;** film actress; *b* London, 27 Feb. 1932; *d* of Francis Taylor and Sara (*née*

Sothern); *m* 1st, 1950, Conrad Nicholas Hilton, Jr (marr. diss.; he *d* 1969); 2nd, 1952, Michael Wilding (marr. diss.); two *s*; 3rd, 1957, Mike Todd (*d* 1958); one *d*; 4th, 1959, Eddie Fisher (marr. diss.); 5th, 1964, Richard Burton, *qv*. *Educ:* Byron House, Hampstead; Hawthorne School, Beverly Hills; Metro-Goldwyn-Mayer School; University High School, Hollywood. *Films include:* Lassie Come Home, 1942; National Velvet, 1944; Courage of Lassie, 1946; Little Women, 1948; The Conspirator, 1949; Father of the Bride, 1950; A Place in the Sun, 1950; Ivanhoe, 1951; Beau Brummel, 1954; Giant, 1956; Raintree County, 1957; Suddenly Last Summer, 1959; Butterfield 8 (Academy Award for Best Actress), 1960; Cleopatra, 1963; the VIPs, 1963; The Sandpiper, 1965; Who's Afraid of Virginia Woolf?, 1966; The Taming of the Shrew, 1967; Boom, 1968; The Comedians, 1968; Reflections in a Golden Eye, 1968; Secret Ceremony, 1968; The Only Game in Town, 1970. *Publication:* Elizabeth Taylor, 1966. *Address:* c/o World Film Services, 72 Brook Street, W1.

**TAYLOR, Sir Eric Stuart,** 2nd Bt, *cr* 1917; OBE; MA, MD Cantab; MRCP; Médaille des Epidémies; *b* 28 June 1889; *s* of 1st Bt and Helen Mary (*d* 1917), *d* of Frederic Manby of East Rudham, Norfolk; *S* father, 1920; *m* 1st, 1920, Evelyn Thérèse (*d* 1946), MA Oxon., JP County Gloucester, *er d* of late James Calvert, CBE, MD, FRCP; one *s* one *d*; 2nd, 1949, Lilian Rosamond (*d* 1958), *widow* of Mr Justice P. A. Farrer Manby, and *e d* of late E. H. Leeder, Swansea; 3rd 1959, Hope, *widow* of Norman Alfred Yarrow, Victoria, BC. *Educ:* Clifton; King's Coll., Cambridge (Exhibitioner), Guy's Hospital; Capt. RAMC, TF, 1914-19. Medical practice in Hong Kong, 1919-28; Cheltenham, 1928-46; City of London, 1947-53. Retired, 1953. Member Council Cheltenham Ladies' College. *Heir: s* Richard Laurence Stuart Taylor, MA Cantab. [*b* 27 Sept. 1925; *m* 1950, Iris Mary, *d* of Rev. E. J. Gargery. one *s* one *d*]. *Address:* 2875 Lansdowne Road, Victoria, BC, Canada. *Clubs:* Oxford and Cambridge University; Union (BC).

**TAYLOR, Eric W.,** RE 1948 (ARE 1935); ARCA 1934; ASIA (Ed) 1965; printmaker, painter and sculptor; Head of Faculty of Art and Design, Leeds Polytechnic, since 1969 (Principal, Leeds College of Art, 1956-69); *b* 6 Aug. 1909; *s* of Thomas John and Ethel Annie Taylor; *m* 1939, Alfreda Marjorie Hurren; one *s* one *d*. *Educ:* William Ellis School, Hampstead; Royal College of Art, South Kensington. Worked for 3 years in London Studio; then as a free-lance illustrator; won British Inst. Scholarship, 1932; runner-up in Prix de Rome, 1934, while at Royal College of Art. Exhibited: Royal Academy; Royal Scottish Academy; Doncaster Art Gallery; New York; Brooklyn; Chicago; London Group; New English Art Club. Pictures in permanent Collections of Stockholm Art Gallery, Art Inst. of Chicago, Washington Art Gallery, War Museum, London. Logan Prize for best Etching in International Exhibition of Etching and Engraving at Art Institute of Chicago, 1937. Selected by British Council to exhibit in Scandinavian Exhibition, 1940, S America, 1942-44, Spain and Portugal, 1942-44, Turkey, 1943-45, Iceland, 1943, Mexico, 1943-45, China, 1945, Czechoslovakia, 1948, and Rotterdam, 1948. Associate Chicago Society of Etchers, 1937. War pictures bought by National Gallery Advisory Committee for Imperial War Museum, 1945. Volunteered for RA, Nov. 1939. Instructor at Northern Command Camouflage School, 1941-43; Royal Engineers, France and Germany, 1943-45; instructing for Educational Corps Germany, 1946; Art Instructor Camberwell School of Art, 1936-39; Willesden School of Art, 1936-49; Central School of Art, 1948-49; Examiner: Bristol Univ., 1948-51; Min. of Education NDD Pictorial Subjects, 1957-59. Designer and Supervisor of Lubeck School of Art for the Services, 1946. Head of the Design School, Leeds Coll. of Art, 1949-56. Leverhulme Research Awards, 1958-59, visiting Colleges of Art in Austria, Germany, Holland, Denmark and Italy. Study of Mosaics, Italy, 1965. Representative Exhibition, Wakefield Art Gall., 1960. British Representative Speaker, International Design Conference, Karachi, 1962. Print selected by Royal Soc. of Painter Etchers for Presentation to Print Collections Club, 1947. Mem. of Senefelder Club, 1947. Picture purchased by British Council, 1948. *Publications:* Etching Published in Fine Prints of the Year, 1935. 1936, 1937, and in 1939 and 1940 issues of Print Collectors Quarterly. *Address:* Gordale, 13 Tredgold Avenue, Bramhope, near Leeds, Yorks.

**TAYLOR, Vice-Adm. Sir Ernest Augustus,** Kt, *cr* 1952; CMG 1920; CVO 1919; *b* 1876; *s* of late Lt-Col F. H. Taylor, RHA; *m* 1st, 1898, Rose Isabel (*d* 1956), *d* of Louis Alexander Campbell; one *s* two *d*; 2nd, 1957, Hilda (Jill), *widow* of Major Horace Gough Turner. *Educ:* Stubbington. Commanded HMS Renown during Prince of Wales' tours in Canada, 1919, and Australia and New Zealand, 1920; Retired List, 1924. Served in the War, 1940-46. MP (Empire Crusade) South Paddington, 1930-31. (U), 1931-50. Member of London County Council for 3 years. Silver Medal, 1909, certificate, 1913, Royal Humane Society. Commander Crown of Italy, 1917. *Address:* Old Way House, Stogumber, Taunton, Somerset. *Club:* Royal Yacht Squadron (Cowes).

**TAYLOR, Ernest Edward,** CBE 1956; *b* 10 Dec. 1897; *s* of late Alfred George Taylor and Mary Taylor; *m* 1920, Dorothy Eileen (*d* 1969), *d* of Charles Henry Hardy; one *s* four *d*. *Educ:* Epsom Coll. Dir, Onyx Property Investment Co. Ltd. Chm. Brit. Sailors' Soc. *Address:* Hazelmere, 1 Chelwood Avenue, Goring by Sea, Worthing, Sussex. *Clubs:* Farmers', City Livery, Royal Commonwealth Society.

**TAYLOR, Ernest Richard;** Headmaster of Wolverhampton Grammar School, since 1956; *b* Oldham, 9 Aug. 1910; *e s* of late Louis Whitfield and Annie Taylor; *m* 1936, Muriel Hardill; twin *s*. *Educ:* Hulme Grammar School, Oldham; Trinity College, Cambridge. Hist. Tripos, Class I, 1931; Sen. Schol. and Earl of Derby Research Student (Trinity), 1931-32; Thirlwall and Gladstone Prizes, 1933; MA 1935. Asst Master, Culford School, 1932-36; Moseley Gram. Sch., Birmingham, 1936-39; Manchester Gram. Sch., 1939-47. War Service in RA and AEC, 1940-46. Headmaster of Quarry Bank High School, Liverpool, 1947-56; Member, Schools Council for Curriculum and Examinations (formerly Secondary Schools Examinations Council), 1962-. Walter Hines Page Scholar, HMC, 1964. Pres. Incorporated Assoc. of Head Masters, 1965; Chm. Central Exec., Jt Four Secondary Assocs, 1970. *Publications:* Methodism and Politics, (1791-1851), 1935; Padre Brown of Gibraltar, 1955; Religious Education of pupils from 16 to 19 years, 1962. *Recreations:* cricket, fell walking. *Address:* Western Lodge, Compton Road, Wolverhampton, Staffs. *T:* Wolverhampton 20174. *Club:* English-Speaking Union.

**TAYLOR, Lt-Col Eustace Trevor Neave,** CIE 1943; MB, ChB; IMS, retired; *b* 8 Nov. 1894. *Educ:* Edinburgh University (MB, ChB 1917).

IMS 1918-47; Lt-Col 1937; Served in France, Iraq and Burma; late Dep. Dir Gen. *Address:* c/o Barclays Bank, Hermanus, Cape Province, South Africa.

**TAYLOR, Francis, (Frank Taylor)**; Founder, Chairman and Managing Director, Taylor Woodrow Ltd since 1935; Director: Taylor Woodrow of Canada Ltd since 1953; Monarch Investments Ltd, Canada, since 1954; Vice-President Taylor Woodrow Blitman, since 1962; *b* 7 Jan. 1905; *s* of late Francis Taylor and late Sarah Ann Earnshaw; *m* 1st, 1929 (marriage dissolved); two *d*; 2nd, 1956, Christine Enid Hughes; one *d*. Founded, 1922, Taylor Woodrow, Building and Civil Engineering Contractors, which became Public Company, in 1935. Member of Advisory Council to Minister of State, 1954-55; Chm. Export Group for Constructional Industries, 1954-55; International Road Federation, 1954-; President Provident Institution of Builders' Foremen and Clerks of Works, 1950; Member Advisory Council on Middle East Trade. Dir, BOAC, 1958-60. Governor, Queenswood School for Girls, 1948-. Fellow Inst. of Builders. *Recreations:* tennis, swimming, riding. *Address:* (office) 10 Park Street, W1Y 4DD; (home) 8 Park Street, W1Y 3WE. *Clubs:* Royal Automobile, Queen's, Hurlingham.

**TAYLOR, Rt. Rev. Francis John**; *see* Sheffield, Bishop of.

**TAYLOR, Frank**; *see* Taylor, Francis.

**TAYLOR, Frank**, CBE 1969; Chief Fire Officer, Liverpool Fire Brigade, since 1962; *b* 6 April 1915; *s* of Percy and Beatrice Taylor; *m* 1940, Nancy (*née* Hefford); two *s* two *d*. *Educ:* Council Sch., Sheffield. Fireman, Sheffield Fire Bde, 1935-41; Instr, NFS West Riding, 1941-42; Company Officer up to Station Officer (ops), NFS in Yorkshire, 1942-49; Chief Officer, Western Fire Authority, N Ire., 1949-51; Divl Officer N Ire. Fire Authority, 1951-57; Belfast: Dep. Chief Officer, 1958-60; Chief Officer, 1960-62. Queen's Fire Service Medal, 1965. *Recreations:* football, gardening. *Address:* 22 Allerton Drive, Liverpool 18. *T:* 051-724 1352.

**TAYLOR, Frank Henry**, MP (C) Moss Side Division of Manchester since Nov. 1961; Principal of two firms of Chartered Accountants: Frank H. Taylor & Co., City of London; W. T. Flower & Co., Wimbledon; *b* 10 Oct. 1907; 2nd, *s* of George Henry Taylor, Cambridgeshire; *m* 1936, Margaret Dora Mackay (*d* 1944), Invernesshire; one *d*; *m* 1948, Mabel Hills, Hertfordshire; two *s*. *Educ:* Rutlish School, Merton, Surrey, FCIS 1929; FCA 1930. Commenced in practice as Chartered Accountant, 1930; Ministry of Food Finance Director of Tea, Coffee and Cocoa, 1942; Min. of War Transport Finance Rep. overseas, 1944; visited over 30 countries on financial missions. Lt-Colonel comdg 1st Caernarvonshire Bn Home Guard, 1943. Contested (C) Newcastle under Lyme, 1955, Chorley, 1959. Governor of Rutlish School, 1946-. Liveryman, City of London. Member: Worshipful Co. of Bakers, 1947; Guild of Air Pilots. *Recreations:* numerous including Rugby (for Surrey County), Sculling (Thames Championship), punting (several Thames championships), golf (Captain RAC 1962). *Address:* 25 Craven St, WC2. *T:* 01-930 5033; Tinker Taylor, Sennen Cove, Cornwall. *T:* Sennen 220. *Clubs:* City Livery, Royal Automobile, British Sportsman's.

**TAYLOR, Frank Herbert Graham**, CIE 1941; *b* 17 Jan. 1890; *s* of late E. Taylor, HBM Consul, Dunkirk; unmarried. *Educ:* Haileybury College. Joined Indian Police, 1910; Director-General of Police and Jails, Hyderabad State, 1942-45; Managing Director, Sassoon J. David & Co. Ltd, Bombay, 1945-54; retired 1954. King's Police Medal, 1933. *Address:* c/o National and Grindlay's Bank Ltd, 13 St James's Square, SW1. *Clubs:* Oriental, Devonshire.

**TAYLOR, Frederick William**, MA Cantab, LLM Wales; Barrister; Professor of Law, University of Hull, since 1956 (Dean of Faculty of Arts, 1954-57); *b* 8 March 1909; *o s* of late James Edward Taylor, Solicitor, and of Emily Price; *m* 1938, Muriel Vera Markreed, *d* of Onek Vosguerchian; two *d*. *Educ:* Twynyrodyn Elementary and Cyfarthfa Secondary Schools, Merthyr Tydfil; University College of Wales, Aberystwyth; St John's College, Cambridge. Solicitor, 1931; LLB Wales, Sir Samuel Evans Prize 1933, BA Cantab, Scholar of St John's Coll., 1935; Asst Lecturer in Law, University Coll., Hull, 1935; Acting Head, Dept of Law: University Coll., Southampton, 1940; Hull, 1941; called to Bar, Cert. of Honour, Middle Temple Prize, 1943; Head of Dept of Law, University Coll., Hull, 1949; LLM Wales 1954. Examiner in Laws, Univ. of London; formerly Mem. of Bd of Studies in Laws of Univ. of London. Equity draftsman and conveyancer, 1944-, formerly at Leeds and later at Hull. *Publications:* articles in Law Journal, The Conveyancer, Jl of Soc. of Public Teachers of Law, Solicitors' Journal, The Solicitor, Secretaries Chronicle. *Recreations:* natural history, etc. *Address:* The University of Hull, Hull. *T:* 408960; Victoria Chambers, Bowlalley Lane, Hull. *T:* Hull 23264; 1 Hurn View, Beverley, Yorks. *T:* 883561.

**TAYLOR, Prof. Sir Geoffrey Ingram**, OM 1969; Kt 1944; FRS 1919; formerly Yarrow Research Professor of the Royal Society; *b* 7 March 1886; *s* of Edward Ingram Taylor and Margaret, *d* of Dr George Boole; *m* 1925, Grace Stephanie Francis Ravenhill (*d* 1967). *Educ:* University Coll. School; Cambridge University. Elected to Fellowship at Trinity College, Cambridge, 1910; Meteorologist to Scotia Expedition to the North Atlantic, 1913; engaged in experimental aeronautics and meteorology during war of 1914-18; pilot's certificate at Brooklands, July 1915. Worked in Los Alamos, New Mexico, with group making first nuclear explosion, 1944-45. Dr (*hc*): Univ. of Paris (Fac. des Sciences), Oxford, Cambridge, London, Birmingham, Liverpool, Bristol, Edinburgh, Vancouver, Aachen, Oslo, Rice, Michigan. Royal Medal, 1933, Copley Medal, 1944, Royal Society; American Medal for Merit, 1947; gold Medal, Roy. Aeronautical Soc., 1954; Exner Medal, Oesterreichischer Gewerbeverein, 1954; de Morgan Medal, Lond. Math. Society, 1956; Internat. Panetti Prize and Medal, accad. delle Scienze di Torino (1st Award) 1958; Timoshenko Medal, Amer. Soc. of Mech. Engineers, 1958; Kelvin Gold Medal, Instn of Civil Engineers, 1959; Franklin Medal, Franklin Inst., US, 1962; Platinum Medal, Inst. of Metals, 1964; James Watt International Gold Medal, 1965. Foreign corresponding or hon. member of numerous societies. *Publications:* papers on mathematics, meteorology, aeronautics and engineering in proceedings of learned societies. *Address:* Trinity College, Cambridge.

**TAYLOR, Sir George**, Kt 1962; FRS 1968; DSc, FRSE, FLS; Director of the Royal Botanic Gardens, Kew, since October 1956; Visiting Professor, Reading University, since 1969; Director, Stanley Smith Horticultural Trust, 1970; *b* 15 February 1904; *o s* of George William Taylor and Jane Sloan; *m* 1st, 1929,

Alice Helen Pendrich; two *s*; 2nd, Norah English (*d* 1967); 3rd, Beryl, Lady Colwyn. *Educ:* George Heriot's Sch., Edinburgh; Edinburgh Univ. BSc (1st class hons Botany), 1926; Vans Dunlop Scholar. Member of Botanical Expedition to South Africa and Rhodesia, 1927-28; Joint Leader of British Museum Expedition to Ruwenzori and mountains of East Africa, 1934-35; Expedition to SE Tibet and Bhutan, 1938. Principal in Air Ministry, 1940-45. Deputy Keeper of Botany, British Museum (Natural History), 1945-50; Keeper of Botany, 1950-56. Botanical Sec. Linnean Soc., 1950-56; Vice-Pres. 1956. Percy Sladen Trustee, 1951-. Mem. Council: Royal Horticultural Soc., 1951; National Trust (Chm. Gardens Cttee); RGS 1957-61 (Vice-Pres. 1964); Mem. Min. of Transport Adv. Cttee on Landscaping Treatment of Trunk Roads, 1956- (Chm. 1969-). Editor, Curtis's Botanical Magazine, 1962-. Gen. Sec., Brit. Assoc. for the Advancement of Science, 1951-58. President: Botanical Society of British Isles, 1955; Division of Botany, Internat. Union Biol Sci., 1964-69; Internat. Assoc. for Plant Taxonomy, 1969-. Member Royal Society Science, Uppsala, 1956; Corr. Member Royal Botanical Soc. Netherlands. Hon. Freeman, Worshipful Co. of Gardeners, 1967. VMH 1956; Veitch Gold Medal, Royal Horticultural Soc., 1963; Bradford Washburn Award, Museum of Science, Boston, USA, 1969. Hon. DrPhil Gothenburg, 1958. *Publications:* An Account of the Genus Meconopsis, 1934; contributions on flowering plants to various periodicals. *Recreations:* angling, gardening, music. *Address:* Royal Botanic Gardens, Kew, Surrey; Belhaven House, Dunbar, East Lothian. *Club:* Athenæum.

**TAYLOR, Maj.-Gen. Sir (George) Brian (Ogilvie),** KBE, *cr* 1942 (CBE 1919); CB 1940; RE; *s* of late Edward Taylor and Mary Alexander; *m* Cecilia Maria Julia, *d* of late Col D. ffrench Mullen, retired IMS; one *s*. *Educ:* Cheltenham College; RMA, Woolwich. Served European War, 1914-19 (despatches, CBE); Asst Director of Works, BEF, Salonica, 1917-18; Dep. Director, 1918-19; Staff Officer to Chief Engineer, Aldershot, 1922-24; Deputy Assistant-Director of Fortifications and Works, War Office, 1924-26; Chief Instructor SME, Chatham, 1926-29; Chief Engineer to RAF Iraq, 1929-31. Assistant Director of Works, War Office, 1935-37; Chief Engineer, Northern Command, 1937-39; Director of Fortifications and Works, War Office, 1939-40; an Inspector-General, 1940; Director Bomb Disposal, 1941-42; Engineer-in-Chief, Persia and Iraq, 1942-43, retired pay, 1943. *Recreations:* golf, tennis, croquet, squash, badminton. *Address:* Tresillian, Durley Road, Seaton, Devon.

**TAYLOR, George Francis,** CBE 1943; Chairman, The Forestal Land, Timber & Railways Co. Ltd, since 1962 (Director, 1948); Deputy Chairman, Bank of London and South America, since 1966 (Director, 1950); *b* 13 Jan. 1903; *s* of George Arthur Taylor and Anna Maria (*née* Ryan); *m* 1937, Vivian Judith Elizabeth, *d* of late Lt-Comdr Vivian Rose Price, RN; one *s* two *d*. *Educ:* Xavier Coll., Melbourne; Melbourne Univ. (MA, LLB). Served 1939-45 with Special Ops, (SOE), Middle East, Greece, Yugoslavia, India, SE Asia and SW Pacific; Chief of Staff, HQ, 1940-42; Colonel. TARO, 1945-53. Director: Cia Financiera de Londres SA, 1960; Ashmole Investment Trust Ltd, 1955. FRSA 1967. *Recreations:* fishing, sailing, riding, tennis. *Address:* 99 Abbotsbury Road, W14. *T:* 01-602 1605. *Clubs:* Boodle's, United Hunts.

**TAYLOR, Prof. Gerard William,** MS, FRCS; Professor of Surgery, University of London, since 1960; Surgeon and Director Surgical Professorial Unit, St Bartholomew's Hospital, London; Honorary Consultant in Vascular Surgery to the Army since 1962; *b* 23 September 1920; *s* of William Ivan Taylor; *m* 1951, Olivia Gay; one *s* one *d*. *Educ:* Bemrose School, Derby; St Bartholomew's Hospital Medical College. Served War of 1939-45, Capt. RAMC, 1944-47. Fellow in Surgery, Asst Resident, Fulbright Schol., Stanford Univ. Hosp., San Francisco, Calif., 1950-51; Surgeon, St Bartholomew's Hosp., London, Reader in Surgery, Univ. of London, 1955; Hunterian Prof., RCS, 1962; Vis. Prof. of Surgery: Univ. of Calif., Los Angeles, 1965; Univ. of Melbourne, 1969. Examiner in Surgery: Univ. of London, 1960; NUI, 1966; Univ. of Cambridge, 1966; Trinity Coll., Dublin, 1969. *Publications:* contrib. to Recent Advances in Surgery, 1960, and on surgical subjects to med. jls. *Recreation:* motoring. *Address:* Mark Oak House, Cobham Road, Fetcham, Surrey. *T:* Bookham 3008.

**TAYLOR, Greville Laughton;** Puisne Judge, Windward Islands and Leeward Islands, 1957-64; *b* 23 Oct. 1902; *s* of Rowland Henry and Edith Louise Taylor; *m* 1947, Mary Eileen Reece Mahon; one *s* one *d*. *Educ:* Lodge School, Barbados; St John's College, Oxford. Called to the Bar, Lincoln's Inn, 1927. Clerk to the House of Assembly, Barbados, 1930-36. Police Magistrate, Barbados, 1936-44; Army 1940-44 (UK, N Africa, Italy); Registrar, Barbados, 1944-46; Judge of the Assistant Court of Appeal, Barbados, 1947-57. *Recreations:* reading, shooting, fishing. *Address:* Highgate House, St Michael, Barbados, West Indies. *T:* 207. *Clubs:* Royal Barbados Yacht; Bridgetown (Bridgetown).

**TAYLOR, Harold George K.;** *see* Kirwan-Taylor.

**TAYLOR, Harold Joseph,** CBE 1966; Chief Director, Prison Department, Home Office, 1965-68; *b* 7 May 1904; *s* of Herbert Taylor and Gertrude Mary Taylor; *m* 1940, Olive Alice Slade, *d* of Harry Slade, Honor Oak Park, SE; one *s* (adopted). *Educ:* Blandford Sec. Gram. Sch.; Southampton University. Teacher, Brighton Education Authority, 1924-28; Asst Housemaster, Prison Commission, HM Borstal, Portland, 1928; Housemaster, Portland Borstal, 1930; Superintendent, Borstal Training School, Thayetmyo, Burma, 1933-37; Governor, HM Borstal: Feltham, Middx, 1938-41; Lowdham Grange, 1941-46; Governor, HM Prison: Camp Hill, IoW, 1946-49; Sudbury, Derby, 1949-51; Asst Comr, HM Prison Commission, 1951-57; Comr and Director of Borstal Administration, 1958-65. *Recreations:* fishing, country lore, tinkering. *Address:* 45 Church Way, Pagham, Bognor Regis, Sussex. *T:* Pagham 3750.

**TAYLOR, Harold McCarter,** CBE 1955; TD 1945; retired, 1967; *b* Dunedin, New Zealand, 13 May 1907; *s* of late James Taylor, and late Louisa Urquhart Taylor; *m* 1st, 1933, Joan (*d* 1965), *d* of late George Reginald Sills, Lincoln; two *s* two *d*; 2nd, 1966, Dorothy Judith, *d* of Charles Samuel, Liverpool. *Educ:* Otago Boys' High School and Univ. of Otago, NZ; Clare Coll., Cambridge. MSc New Zealand, 1928; MA, PhD Cambridge, 1933. Allen Scholar and Smith's Prizeman, 1932. Fellow of Clare College, Cambridge, 1933-61; Hon. Fellow, 1961-; Lecturer in Mathematics, University of Cambridge, 1934-45; Treasurer of the University, 1945-53; Secretary General of the Faculties, 1953-61; Vice-Chancellor, University of Keele, 1962-67 (Principal, University College of North Staffordshire,

1961-62); Rede Lecturer, Cambridge University, 1966. Hon. LLD Cambridge, 1967; Hon. DLitt Keele, 1968. Commissioned in TA, NZ, 1925; served War of 1939-45 as Major and Lieut-Col RA; Instructor and Senior Instructor in Gunnery at School of Artillery, Larkhill. *Publication:* (with Joan Taylor) Anglo-Saxon Architecture, 1965. *Recreations:* mountaineering and ski-ing; Anglo-Saxon art and architecture; photography. *Address:* 192 Huntingdon Road, Cambridge. *T:* 76324.

**TAYLOR, Henry Archibald;** CBE 1952; journalist; *s* of George Taylor and Ellen E. Collins; *m* Mollie Little (Capt., WRAC, Retd); two *s.* After provincial experience, joined staff of Daily Chronicle; served European War, Western Front; Royal Fusiliers and Staff. Chm. Newspaper Features, Ltd, 1923-64; Editor, Empire Review, 1943-44; special political contributor, Evening Standard, 1945-46, Yorkshire Post, 1949-60; leader writer, Country Life 1956-; President Institute of Journalists, 1938; Member: Court of Bristol Univ., 1936-68. Lord Chancellor's Cttee on Law of Defamation, 1939-48. Chairman Restoration Cttee St Bride's Church, Fleet Street, 1951-57. Parliamentary Candidate (C) Doncaster, 1939-45, NE Leicester, 1949, contesting that division at General Election and subsequent by-election, 1950. *Publications:* Goodbye to the Battlefields, 1930; Smith of Birkenhead; The Strange Case of Andrew Bonar Law; Jix, Viscount Brentford; Robert Donald, Will You Be Left? (in collaboration), 1945; The British Press: a Critical Survey, 1961; (with Sir Linton Andrews), Lords and Labourers of the Press, 1970. *Address:* Oldwell House, Dummer, Basingstoke, Hants. *T:* Dummer 227. *Clubs:* Press, Whitefriars.

**TAYLOR, Henry George,** DSc(Eng); Director of Electrical Research Association 1957-69; *b* 4 Nov. 1904; *m* 1931, Gwendolyn Hilda Adams; one *s* two *d. Educ:* Taunton School; Battersea Polytechnic Inst., City and Guilds Engineering College. Metropolitan Vickers, 1929-30; Electrical Research Assoc., 1930-38; Copper Development Assoc., 1938-42; Philips Lamps Ltd, 1942-47; British Welding Research Assoc., 1947-57. *Publications:* contribs to: Inst. of Electrical Engineers Jl, Jl of Inst. of Physics, etc. *Recreation:* walking. *Address:* 9 La Valette Court, Qawra Point, St Paul's Bay, Malta GC.

**TAYLOR, Herbert,** CMG 1959; Chartered Accountant; now retired; *b* 11 May 1885; *s* of R. H. W. Taylor; *m* 1919, Doris Madeline Brock; three *s. Educ:* Caulfield Grammar School, Victoria. Clerk, W. J. Bush & Co. Melbourne, 1904-07; clerk, Flack & Flack, Melb. & Perth, 1907; admitted 1918. Life Governor, Roy. Victorian Inst. for the Blind and of Freemasons Hosp.; President: Assoc. Chambers of Commerce of Australia, 1945-47; Melbourne Chamber of Commerce, 1943-44. Past Member: Melbourne University Council (Chairman of Finance Cttee); Council, Institute of Public Affairs; Past Coun. and Finance Committee, Victorian Red Cross Soc. *Publications:* The Organisation of a Chartered Accountants Office, 1933; The Audit of Sharebrokers Accounts, 1937; The Businessman and His Investments, 1945. *Address:* (private) 10 Glenbrook Avenue, East Malvern, Victoria 3145, Australia. *T:* 25-3429. *Clubs:* Royal Automobile of Victoria (Past Pres., Life Member), Portsea Golf (Portsea, Vic.) (Life Mem.); Metropolitan Golf (Oakleigh, Vic.) (Capt., Pres., Life Mem.); Melbourne Cricket.

**TAYLOR, Hermon,** MA, MD, MChir, FRCS; Surgeon, London Hospital, E1; Surgeon, King George Hospital, Ilford; *b* 11 May 1905; *s* of Enoch Oliver Taylor and L. M. Taylor (*née* Harrison); *m* 1932, Mēarie Amēlie Pearson; three *s* two *d. Educ:* Latymer School, Edmonton; St John's Coll., Cambridge (scholar); St Bartholomew's Hospital (Entrance Scholar). BA 1926; MRCS, LRCP 1929; MB, ChB Cantab. 1930; FRCS Eng. 1930. House Surgeon, Demonstr of Pathology, St Bart's Hosp.; Res. Surgical Officer: Hertford Co. Hosp., Lincoln Co. Hosp.; Surgical Registrar, Prince of Wales' Hosp., Tottenham. MChir Cantab 1932; MD Cantab 1934; Horton Smith Prize, Univ. Cantab; Luther Holden Research Scholar, St Bartholomew's Hospital; BMA Research Scholar, Surgical First Assistant London Hospital. Moynihan Fellow, Assoc. of Surgeons of GB and Ireland; Hunterian Professor, RCS. Past President, British Society of Gastro-enterology; Hon. Member Amer. Gastro-enterological Assoc. *Publications:* Carcinoma of the Stomach, in Modern Trends in Gastro-Enterology, 1952; contrib. to BMJ, Lancet, etc., 1942-. *Address:* 9 Cambridge Gate, Regent's Park, NW1. *T:* 01-935 5212. *Club:* Athenæum.

**TAYLOR, Sir Hugh (Stott),** KBE 1953; FRS 1932; DSc Liverpool, 1914; President Emeritus, Woodrow Wilson Fellowship Foundation; David B. Jones Professor of Chemistry Emeritus, Princeton University; Chairman of Chemistry Department, 1926-51; Dean of the Graduate School, 1945-58, retired; *b* St Helens, Lancashire, 6 Feb. 1890; *s* of James Taylor and Ellen Stott; *m* 1919, Elizabeth (*d* 1958), *d* of James Sawyer, Southport, Lancs; two *d. Educ:* Cowley School, St Helens; Liverpool University; Nobel Institute, Stockholm; Technische Hochschule, Hannover. From 1914 with Princeton University, Department of Chemistry; Munitions Inventions Department, London, 1917-19; Nichols medallist, American Chemial Society, 1928; Mendel Medallist, Villanova Coll., 1933; Franklin medallist, Amer. Philos. Soc., 1941; Longstaff Medallist, Chem. Soc. London, 1942; Franklin medallist, Franklin Inst., 1957; Proctor Prize, Research Soc. of Am., 1964. Francqui Professor, University of Louvain, Belgium, 1937. Member various scientific societies of USA and Europe; holds numerous Hon. degrees. Commander of Order of Leopold II of Belgium, 1938; Kt Comdr, Order of St Gregory (Papal), 1953. *Publications:* (with E. K. Rideal) Catalysis in Theory and Practice; Industrial Hydrogen; Treatise of Physical Chemistry (Editor and Part Author); Elementary Physical Chemistry; Fuel Production and Utilization; numerous articles on Physical Chemistry in various scientific journals. *Recreation:* photography. *Address:* 191 Library Place, Princeton, NJ 08540, USA. *TA:* Princeton, New Jersey. *T:* 924-2211. *Clubs:* Century, Princeton, Chemists (New York); Nassau (Princeton).

**TAYLOR, Prof. Ian Galbraith;** Ellis Llwyd Jones Professor of Audiology and Education of the Deaf, University of Manchester, since Oct. 1964; *b* 24 Apr. 1924; *s* of David Oswald Taylor, MD, and Margaret Ballantine Taylor; *m* 1954, Audrey Wolstenholme; two *d. Educ:* Manchester Grammar Sch.; Univ. of Manchester. MB, ChB, DPH Manchester; MD (Gold Medal) Manchester 1963. Ho. Surg., Manchester Royal Infirm., 1948; DAD, Army Health of N Regional Canal Zone, and OC Army Sch. of Hygiene, ME, 1949-51; Asst MO, City of Manchester, 1951-54. Univ. of Manchester: Hon. Special Lectr and Ewing

Foundn Fellow, Dept of Education of the Deaf, 1956-60; Lectr in Clinical Audiology, 1963-64. Consultant in Audiology, United Manchester Hosps, 1968. FCST (Hon.) 1966. *Publication:* Neurological Mechanisms of Hearing and Speech in Children, 1964. *Recreations:* gardening, fishing. *Address:* Carlton House, 45 High Grove Road, Cheadle, Cheshire. *T:* 061-428 6894.

**TAYLOR, Sir James,** Kt 1966; MBE 1945; DSc, FRIC, FInstP, Hon. MIMinE; Deputy Chairman, Royal Ordnance Factories Board, since 1959 (Member, 1952-); Director: Fulmer Research Institute Ltd; Oldham & Son Ltd; *b* 16 Aug. 1902; *s* of James and Alice Taylor; *m* 1929, Margaret Lennox Stewart; two *s* one *d.* *Educ:* Bede College, Sunderland; Rutherford College, Newcastle upon Tyne; Universities of Durham, Sorbonne, Utrecht, Cambridge. BSc (1st cl. Hons Physics) 1923; PhD 1925; Dr of Physics and Maths (*cum laude*) Utrecht, 1927; DSc Dunelm, 1931. ICI Ltd; joined Nobel Div. 1928; Research Dir, 1946; Jt Man. Dir, 1951; Director, 1952-64. Chairman: Yorkshire Imperial Metals Ltd, 1958-64; Imperial Aluminium Co. Ltd, 1959-64; Imperial Metal Industries Ltd, 1962-64. Director: Nuclear Developments Ltd, 1961-64; European Plumbing Materials Ltd, 1962-64; BDH Group Ltd, 1965-67. Member: Adv. Coun. on Scientific Research and Tech. Develt, MoD, 1965-68; NPL Steering Committee, 1966; Adv. Coun. on Calibration and Measurement, 1966; Chm., Glazebrook Cttee, NPL, 1966. Member: Court, Brunel Univ., 1967; Council, British Non-Ferrous Metals Research Assoc., 1954-67 (Vice-Chm. 1961-67); Council, City and Guilds of London, 1969-; Court, RCA, 1969-; Pres. Section B British Assoc. 1960, Council 1965; Pres. Inst. of Physics and Physical Society, 1966-68 (Hon. Treas. 1957-66); FRIC 1945; MIMinE 1947 (Hon. Member, 1960); FInstP 1948; FRSA 1962 (Member Council 1964-, Chm., 1969-71, Silver Medal, 1969); Hon. Pres., Research and Development Soc., 1970; Hon. Mem., Newcomen Soc. in N America, 1970. Hon. DSc Bradford, 1968; Hon. DCL Newcastle, 1969. Medal, Society Chemical Industry, 1965. *Publications:* On the Sparking Potentials of Electric Discharge Tubes, 1927; Detonation in Condensed Explosives, 1952; British Coal Mining Explosives, 1958; Solid Propellent and Exothermic Compositions, 1959; The Modern Chemical Industry in Great Britain (Cantor Lectures, Jl of Roy. Soc. Arts), 1961; Restrictive Practices (Soc. of Chm. Ind. Lecture), 1965; Monopolies and Restrictive Practices (RSA), 1967; The Scientist and The Technologist in Britain today (Pres. Address, IPPS), 1967; Britain's Technological Future (IPPSs Jubilee Address), 1968; Arts, Crafts and Technology (RSA), 1969; Cobalt, Madder and Computers (RSA), 1969; numerous contribs to Proc. Roy. Soc., Phil. Mag., Trans Inst. Min. Eng., Advancement of Science, ICI Magazine. *Recreations:* gardening and writing. *Address:* Culvers, Seale, near Farnham, Surrey. *T:* Runfold 2210. *Clubs:* Royal Scottish Automobile, RNVR Carrick (Hon.) (Glasgow).

**TAYLOR, Air Vice-Marshal James Clarke,** CB 1970; OBE 1953; Deputy Director General, RAF Medical Services, 1968-70, retired; *b* 6 July 1910; *s* of William and Agnes Taylor; *m* 1961, Moira Jane, *d* of late Sir Hector Macneal, KBE; no *c.* *Educ:* Glasgow Acad.; Glasgow Univ. Commissioned RAF, 1937; various appts; PMO, Arabian Peninsula, 1957-59; PMO, Near East Air Force, 1961-64; Officer Commanding Central Medical Estab., RAF, London, 1965-66; PMO, Bomber Command, 1967-68, Strike Command, 1968-69. QHP 1967-70. *Recreation:* golf. *Address:* Dormer Cottage, Aston Clinton, Bucks. *T:* Aston Clinton 217. *Clubs:* Royal Air Force; Royal and Ancient (St Andrews).

**TAYLOR, Sir John,** Kt, *cr* 1937; Solicitor; Senior Partner in Firm of John Taylor and Co., Manchester and Blackburn; *b* 28 March 1876; *s* of Joseph and Mary Berry Taylor; *m* 1904, Helen Louisa Anne (*d* 1944), *d* of John Jackson; one *s* one *d.* *Educ:* Whalley Grammar School; privately. Formerly Chm. and Leader of the Conservative Party in Blackburn and Leader of the Town Council; at time of resignation in 1936 Alderman of the Borough; for six years Chairman of the Finance Committee. *Publications:* many papers in connection with Factory Legislation, Yarn and Cloth Contracts-International Arbitration in the Cotton Trade and other Cotton Trade matters. *Club:* District and Union (Blackburn).

**TAYLOR, Brigadier John Alexander Chisholm,** DSO 1918; MC, TD; DL; FRIBA; RA; Chartered Architect; *s* of late Tom Taylor; *m* 1927, Jean Bell, *d* of late Dr Johnstone. *Educ:* Sedbergh Sch. Served European War, 1914-18 (despatches, DSO, MC with bar). War of 1939-45. DL Lancs 1946. *Address:* Torbeckhill, Waterbeck, Dumfriesshire.

**TAYLOR, Dr John Bryan,** FRS 1970; Head of Theoretical Physics Division, Culham Laboratory, since 1963; *b* 26 Dec. 1928; *s* of Frank and Ada Taylor, Birmingham; *m* 1951, Joan M. Hargest; one *s* one *d.* *Educ:* Oldbury Grammar Sch.; Birmingham Univ. Atomic Weapons Research Establishment, Aldermaston, 1955-59 and 1960-62; Univ. of California (Berkeley), 1959-60; Culham Laboratory (UKAEA), 1962-69 and 1970-; Inst. for Advanced Study, Princeton, 1969. FInstP 1969. *Publications:* contribs to scientific learned jls. *Address:* Culham Laboratory, Abingdon, Berks. *T:* Oxford 41721.

**TAYLOR, John Debenham,** CMG 1967; OBE 1959; TD 1967; Counsellor, Washington, since 1969; *b* 25 April 1920; *s* of John Francis Taylor and Harriett Beatrice (*née* Williams); *m* 1966, Gillian May James. *Educ:* Aldenham School. Eastern Counties Farmers Assoc. Ltd, Ipswich and Great Yarmouth, 1936-39. Commd in RA (TA), Feb. 1939; served War of 1939-46 in Finland, Middle East, UK and SE Asia (despatches, 1946). Foreign Office, 1946; Control Commn for Germany, 1947-49; 2nd Sec., Bangkok, 1950; Actg Consul, Songkhia, 1951-52; Vice-Consul, Hanoi, 1952-53; FO, 1953-54; 1st Sec., Bangkok, 1954-56; FO, 1956-58; Singapore, 1958-59; FO, 1960-64; Counsellor, 1964; Counsellor: Kuala Lumpur, 1964-66; FCO (formerly FO), 1966-69. *Recreations:* walking, reading, history. *Address:* Bulls Hall, Witnesham, Suffolk. *T:* Witnesham 297. *Clubs:* Travellers', Royal Aero; Royal Singapore Flying.

**TAYLOR, John Hugh;** Deputy Principal, Civil Service College, since 1970; *b* 1 Dec. 1916; *yr s* of Arthur and Etna Taylor, Steeton, Yorks; *m* 1954, Romayne F. E. Good, *d* of I. E. Good, Fulmer; two *s.* *Educ:* Boys' Grammar Sch., Keighley; Peterhouse, Cambridge (Scholar). 1st Cl. Historical Tripos Part I, 1938, 1st Cl. Part II, 1939. Administrative Class, Civil Service, 1939, Asst Principal, Admiralty; Private Secretary to Civil Lord 1941-1942; Private Secretary to Civil Lord and also to Parliamentary Secretary, 1942-43; Principal Private Secretary to First Lord, 1950-51; Assistant Secretary, 1951-61; Under-Secretary, Admiralty, 1961-64; Asst Under-

Sec. of State, MoD, 1964-69; Under-Sec., Civil Service Dept, 1969-70. *Recreations:* ornithology and photography. *Address:* 14 Duke's Wood Drive, Gerrards Cross, Bucks. *T:* Gerrards Cross 84241. *Club:* Oxford and Cambridge.

**TAYLOR, John Idowu Conrad; Hon. Mr Justice Taylor;** Chief Justice of the High Court, Lagos, Nigeria, since July 1964; Justice of the Supreme Court of Nigeria since 1960; *b* 24 Aug. 1917; *s* of E. J. Alex. Taylor and Mrs R. A. Taylor; *m* 1st 1943, Josephine Luke (*d* 1947); no *c*; 2nd, 1949, Ivy Pratt; one *s* two *d*. *Educ:* Culford Sch., Bury St Edmunds; King's College, London; Brasenose College, Oxford. MA Oxford, 1944. Legal Practitioner, Dec. 1941-March 1956; Judge of High Court, W Reg. Nigeria, 1956-60. Pro-Chancellor, Univ. of Lagos, 1967-. *Recreations:* cricket, tennis, motor sport, golf, fishing; formerly boxing (Blue for Oxford, 1936-40). *Address:* Chief Justices' Chambers, High Court, Lagos, Nigeria. *Club:* British Automobile Racing.

**TAYLOR, John Lang;** Minister (Commercial), British Embassy, Buenos Aires, since 1969; *b* 3 Aug. 1924; *y s* of Sir John William Taylor, *qv*; *m* 1952, Molly, *o d* of James Rushworth; five *s* three *d*. *Educ:* Prague; Vienna; Imperial Services Coll., Windsor; Baltimore Polytechnic Inst., Md; Cornell Univ.; Trinity Coll., Cambridge. RAFVR, 1944-47 (Flt-Lt 1946). Joined HM Foreign (now Diplomatic) Service, 1949; served in: FO, 1949-50 and 1957-60; Saigon, 1950-52; Hanoi, 1951; Beirut, 1952-55; Prague, 1955-57; Montevideo, 1960-64; Bonn, 1964-69. *Address:* c/o Foreign and Commonwealth Office, King Charles Street, SW1. *Club:* Travellers'.

**TAYLOR, John Ralph Carlisle,** CIE 1943; Past Director, Davy-Ashmore International Co. Ltd; *b* Sydney, NSW, Australia, 18 Aug. 1902; *o s* of Charles Carlisle Taylor and Jean Sawers; *m* 1933, Nancy (Ann) Marguerite Sorel-Cameron; one *s*. *Educ:* Winchester. Shaw Wallace & Co., London, Calcutta, Karachi, 1921-28; Burmah-Shell, 1928-39 and 1945-54; General Manager in India, 1951-54. Service in RIASC (Lt-Col) 1941-42, GHQ India (Lt-Col) 1942; Petroleum Officer; *ex-officio* Dep. Sec., Defence Dept, Govt of India, 1942-45. Chairman, Shell Group of Companies in Australia, 1955-60; retired from Shell, 1960. *Recreations:* walking, reading, racing. *Address:* 166 Oakwood Court, W14. *Clubs:* Oriental; Melbourne, Hurlingham, Victoria Racing (Melbourne).

**TAYLOR, Rev. Canon John Vernon;** General Secretary, Church Missionary Society, since Sept. 1963; Hon. Canon of Namirembe Cathedral since 1963; *b* 11 Sept. 1914; *s* of late Bishop J. R. S. Taylor and Margaret Irene Taylor (*née* Garrett); *m* 1940, Margaret Wright; one *s* two *d*. *Educ:* St Lawrence Coll., Ramsgate; Trinity Coll., Cambridge; St Catherine's Soc., Oxford; Wycliffe Hall, Oxford; Institute of Education, London. Curate, All Souls, Langham Place, W1, 1938-40; Curate in Charge, St Andrew's Church, St Helens, Lancs, 1940-43; Warden, Bishop Tucker College, Mukono, Uganda, 1945-54; Research Worker, Internat. Missionary Council, 1955-59; Africa Sec., CMS, 1959-63. Hon. DD (Wycliffe Coll., Toronto), 1964. *Publications:* Man in the Midst, 1955; Christianity and Politics in Africa, 1957; The Growth of the Church in Buganda, 1958; African Passion, 1958; Christians of the Copperbelt, 1961; The Primal Vision, 1963; For All the World, 1966; Change of Address, 1968. *Recreations:* theatre, music. *Address:* 4 The Orchard, Blackheath, SE3. *T:* 01-852 4177. *Club:* Royal Commonwealth Society.

**TAYLOR, Sir John (William),** KBE 1954 (MBE 1929); CMG 1947; Director, Electrical & Industrial Securities; *b* 1 Mar. 1895; *e s* of late John S. Taylor, Aberdeen; *m* 1st, Rachel (*d* 1925), *d* of late Rev. James Thomason Lang, Fellow of Corpus Christi; four *s*; 2nd, Margaret (*d* 1961), *d* of James B. Simpson, CBE, MD Edinburgh; two *d*; 3rd, 1961, Joan Maria Cecilia, *d* of late Bernard Hickman, Wolverhampton. *Educ:* Aberdeen University (MA). Served European War, 1914-18, in Gordon Highlanders; Captain 1916; entered HM Foreign Service, 1919; consular posts in France, Czechoslovakia, Austria, USA and Commercial Secretary for Central America; Dep. British Delegate on International Danube Commission, 1934-38; Commercial Counsellor, Prague, 1945-46; Minister (Commercial), Cairo, 1946; Minister (Commercial) British Embassy, Washington, 1948-50; British Ambassador to Mexico, 1950-54; Chm., British Mexican Soc., 1954-64; Dir Gen. Hispanic and Luso-Brazilian Councils, 1954-62. Council, Royal Geographical Soc., 1958-61; Council, Royal Soc. of Arts, 1959-65. Silver Medallist, Royal Soc. of Arts, 1958; Coronation Medal, 1953. Mexican Order of Aztec Eagle, First Class, 1958; Grand Cross, Order of Merit of Chile, 1959. *Address:* 25 Park Mansions, 141 Knightsbridge, SW1. *T:* 01-589 5648.

*See also J. L. Taylor.*

**TAYLOR, Mrs John William Kendell;** *see* Taylor, Elizabeth.

**TAYLOR, Joseph Charlton,** TD; Chairman, Mersey Docks and Harbour Board, since 1969 (Member since 1950); Vice-President, Docks and Harbours Authorities Association, 1969; Director, Cunard Steam-Ship Co. Ltd, and other companies; *b* 13 Aug. 1913; *er s* of late Percy James Taylor and Nancy Skelton Charlton; *m* 1948, Kathleen Margaret Williams; two *d*. *Educ:* Charterhouse. Served War of 1939-45, RASC (despatches 1944). Pres., Liverpool Cotton Assoc. Ltd, 1948-49. High Sheriff of Cheshire, 1971. *Recreations:* tennis, golf, gardening. *Address:* Fiddlestone Wood, Burton-in-Wirral, Cheshire. *T:* 051-336 2109. *Clubs:* Royal Thames Yacht; Racquet (Liverpool).

**TAYLOR, Kenneth;** Under-Secretary, Board of Trade, since 1969; *b* 10 Oct. 1923; *s* of William and May Taylor; *m* 1952, Mary Matilda Jacobs; one *s* one *d*. *Educ:* Merchant Taylors' Sch., Crosby; University Coll., Oxford (MA). Commnd RAF, 1943; Flt-Lt 212 Sqdn, 1944-45. Entered Min. of Civil Aviation as Asst Principal, 1947; BoT, 1948-56, 1959-; Treasury, 1957-59; Asst Sec. 1963; idc 1967. *Recreations:* squash, tennis, chess. *Address:* High Trees, West Hill Way, Totteridge, N20. *T:* 01-445 7173. *Clubs:* Terenure Country; Union Society (Oxford).

**TAYLOR, Kenneth Roy Eldin,** CVO 1955; *b* 27 Sept. 1902; *s* of late Thomas Taylor, Welbourn, Lincoln; *m* 1926, Katharine Mary, *er d* of late Frederick Ernest Taylor, FRCS, LRCP, Brancaster, Norfolk; three *s*. *Educ:* Lincoln School; Selwyn College, Cambridge (BA, LLM, Exhibitioner and Univ. Squire Law Schol.). Chm., Industrial Appeals Tribunals, 1967-; Sec., Diocesan Conf., 1966-68; Solicitor for Affairs of HM Duchy of Lancaster, 1942-67; former Member of Council, British Records Association; Member, Portsmouth Diocesan Board of Finance. *Recreations:* rowing, gardening. *Address:* Lancaster House, 108 High Street,

Old Portsmouth, Hants. *T:* 26293. *Clubs:* Leander; Royal Albert Yacht, Royal Naval (Portsmouth).

**TAYLOR, Len Clive;** Director, Nuffield Foundation 'Resources for Learning' project, since 1966; *b* 4 Aug. 1922; *s* of late S. R. Taylor, Calcutta, India; *m* 1951, Suzanne Dufault, Mamaroneck, New York, USA; one *s* two *d*. *Educ:* Sevenoaks School; New College, Oxford; Chicago University. New College, Oxford; 1st Cl. Hons Mod. Hist.; Commonwealth Fund Fellowship. Assistant Master, St Paul's School, Darjeeling, India, 1940-42 and 1945-46; Indian Army Intelligence Corps, 1942-45; New College, Oxford, 1946-49; Chicago University, 1949-50; Senior History Master, Repton School, 1950-54; Headmaster, Sevenoaks School, 1954-68. *Publication:* Experiments in Education at Sevenoaks, 1965. *Address:* 43 The Drive, Sevenoaks, Kent. *T:* Sevenoaks 51448.

**TAYLOR, Leon Eric Manners;** Economic Counsellor, British High Commission, Kuala Lumpur, Malaysia, since 1966; *b* 28 Oct. 1917; *s* of late Leon Eric Taylor and of Veronica (*née* Rogers; now Mrs Veronica Dalmahoy); *m* 1963, Margaret Betty Thompson; no *c*. *Educ:* Fettes Coll., Edinburgh; Oriel Coll., Oxford. Captain RA (Service, 1939-46). Asst Principal, 1945, Principal, 1948, in Bd of Trade until 1963. First Sec., UK Delegn to the European Communities, 1963-66. Called to Bar, Inner Temple, 1951. Attended Joint Services Staff College, 1952. *Recreations:* walking, amateur theatre, golf. *Address:* Sam's Hill Cottage, Middle Barton, Oxford. *T:* Steeple Aston 540. *Clubs:* Selangor, Royal Selangor Golf, Lake (all at Kuala Lumpur).

**TAYLOR, Leonard Whitworth,** OBE 1947; MA Oxon; retired; *b* 29 March 1880; *s* of Thomas Taylor, JP, CA; *m* 1904, Madeline Hills; no *c*. *Educ:* Warwick School; New College, Oxford. Assistant Master Stratford-on-Avon; Second Master, Bournemouth School; Headmaster Darlington Grammar School, 1913-33; Captain OTC and 5th Battalion DLI; served European War in France, 1916-18 (wounded, prisoner); Pres. IAHM, 1931; Secretary IAHM and HMC, 1934-55. *Address:* 8 Inman's Lane, Sheet, Petersfield, Hants. *Club:* National Liberal.

**TAYLOR, Lionel Robert Stewart;** Civilian Consultant in Otolaryngology to Royal Navy, since 1962; Cons. ENT Surgeon: Charing Cross Hospital since 1950; Royal Masonic Hospital since 1962; King Edward VII Hospital for Officers, since 1963; *b* 4 Nov. 1915; *s* of Rev. Reginald Charles Taylor and Mildred Eleanor Taylor (*née* Stewart); *m* 1945, Gillian Bridget (*née* Baily); one *s* two *d*. *Educ:* Monkton Combe School; Emmanuel College, Cambridge; St Thomas's Hospital. BA Camb. 1937; MB, BChir 1940; FRCS Eng. 1946. Served RNVR, 1941-45. Chief Asst, ENT Dept, St Thomas's Hosp., 1948-50; Temp. Fellow in Otolaryngology, Yale Univ., USA, 1948. Assistant Editor, Journal of Laryngology and Otology. *Recreations:* lawn tennis, gardening, philately, motor sport. *Address:* 55 Harley Street, W1. *T:* 01-580 3456. *Club:* Royal Automobile.

**TAYLOR, Air Vice-Marshal Malcolm Lincoln,** CBE 1943; AFC 1918; *b* 15 Nov. 1893; 2nd *s* of late Leo Taylor, OBE, FIC, Kingswood, Surrey; *m* 1st, 1917, Gwendolen Dewberry; one *d*; 2nd, 1946, Pamela Susan Mary, *o c* of late Major D. R. Ewing, Cameronians. *Educ:* Churchfields, Margate; Louth School. Served European War, 1914-18, in France in RE, RFC, and RAF (AFC); commanded No. 29 Squadron, 1927-29; Chief Instructor, School of Photography, 1930; commanded No 40 Squadron, 1931-34; Wing Comdr, 1934; commanded School of Photography and RAF Station, Farnborough, 1934-36; commanded RAF Station Hal Far, Malta, 1936-38; Group Capt, 1938; Organisation Staff HQ Bomber Command, 1938-39; commanded RAF Station, Bassingbourne, 1939-41 (despatches); Acting Air Commodore and Air Officer i/c Administration, Malta, 1941-42 (despatches twice, CBE); Air Commodore, 1942; AOC East Africa, 1942 (despatches); Levant, 1943; Acting Air Vice-Marshal, 1943-45, and again, 1945-46; AOC No 203 Group, Middle East, 1943-45; SASO Flying Training Command, 1945-46; retired list, 1946. Hon. Freeman City of London, 1918. *Recreations:* tennis, golf. *Address:* Oldner House, Chipping Norton, Oxon. *T:* Chipping Norton 2696.

**TAYLOR, Martin,** lawyer; *b* Hereford, England, 15 Dec. 1885; *s* of James Durham and Mary Taylor (*née* Preece); *m* 1915, Caroline Strong Reboul (decd); one *d*. *Educ:* Trinity Coll.; Columbia Univ., USA. Admitted New York Bar, 1913. Practice, New York: Strong & Mellen, 1915; De Forest Bros., 1917; thereafter McKinstry, Taylor & Patterson and successor firms. Former Counsel: New York State Tax Commission; Reed, Hoyt Taylor & Washburn. Rep. numerous British interests in USA; Mem., Internat. Law Assoc.; Chm. Cttee on Constitutional Law, New York Bar Assoc.; Mem. Assoc. of The Bar of City of New York. Formerly: Director of Consolidated RR of Cuba, The Cuba Company, Relief for Americans in the Philippines; Common Law Foundation; Library of Sei-Kiu-Do Common Law Inst., Tokyo; National Jail Assoc.; New York Post Graduate Med. Sch. and Hospital. Founder, Village of Nissequogue; Co-Founder, Tilney-Taylor Prize. Episcopalian. *Publications:* Reorganization of the Federal Judiciary (Supreme Court Controversy), 1937; The Common Law Foundation, 1963; A Footnote to History, 1970. *Recreations:* book collecting, bridge and tennis. *Address:* (office) 52 Wall Street, New York, NY 10005, USA; (residence) 163 E 81st Street, New York, NY 10028. *Clubs:* Beefsteak, Portland; Union, Down Town Assoc., University, River (NYC).

**TAYLOR, Maurice;** *see* Taylor, A. M.

**TAYLOR, General Maxwell Davenport,** DSC (US) 1944; DSM (US) 1945 (3 Oak Leaf Clusters, 1954, 1959, 1964); Silver Star 1943 (Oak Leaf Cluster, 1944); Legion of Merit; Bronze Star; Purple Heart; Consultant to President of US; President, Institute of Defense Analyses; Member, Foreign Intelligence Advisory Board, since 1965; *b* 26 Aug. 1901; *s* of John Earle Maxwell Taylor and Pearle Davenport; *m* 1925, Lydia Gardner (*née* Happer); two *s*. *Educ:* US Milit. Academy (BS). Became artillery commander of 82nd Airborne Division by Dec. 1942; served in Sicilian and Italian Campaigns; in 1944 became Commanding Gen. of 101st Airborne Div., which he led in the airborne invasion of Normandy, the airborne invasion of Holland, and in the Ardennes and Central Europe Campaigns; supt US Mil. Acad., 1945; Chief of Staff, European Comd HQ, Heidelberg, Jan. 1949; first US Comdr, Berlin, Sept. 1949; Asst Chief of Staff for Ops, G3, Dept of Army, Feb. 1951; Dep. Chief of Staff for Ops and Admin. of Army, Aug. 1951; Comdg Gen., 8th US Army in Korea, 1953; Comdr of all ground forces in Japan, Okinawa and Korea, at Camp Zama, Japan, Nov. 1954; C-in-C of Far East Comd and UN Comd, 1955; Chief of Staff, US Army, 1955-59; Mil. Representative of the

President of the USA, 1961-62; Chairman, Joint Chiefs of Staff, US, Oct. 1962-June 1964; American Ambassador to South Vietnam, 1964-65; Special Consultant to President, 1965-69. Formerly Director of companies (including Chairman Board, Mexican Light & Power Co); was also President, Lincoln Center for the Performing Arts. Holds fifteen Honorary doctorates. Many foreign decorations. *Publications:* The Uncertain Trumpet, 1960; Responsibility and Response, 1967. *Recreations:* tennis, handball and squash. *Address:* 3505 Chevy Chase Lake Drive, Chevy Chase, Maryland 20015, USA. *Clubs:* University (NYC); Army and Navy, International, Chevy Chase (Washington); Cercle Sportif (Saigon).

**TAYLOR, Nicholas George Frederick,** CMG 1970; Commissioner for the Eastern Caribbean Governments in the United Kingdom since 1967; *b* 14 Feb. 1917; 3rd *s* of Louis Joseph Taylor and Philipsie (*née* Phillip); *m* 1952, Morella Agnes, *e d* of George Duncan Pitcairn and Florence (*née* La Guerre); two *s* two *d*. *Educ:* St Mary's Coll., St Lucia; LSE, London; Gonville and Caius Coll., Cambridge. Clerk, various Depts, St Lucia, 1937-46; Asst Social Welfare Officer, 1948-49; Public Relations and Social Welfare Officer, 1949-54; District Officer, and Authorised Officer, Ordnance Area, St Lucia, 1954-57; Dep. Dir St Lucia Br., Red Cross Soc., 1956-57; Perm. Sec., Min. of Trade and Production, 1957-58 (acted Harbour Master in conjunction with substantive duties); Commn for W Indies in UK: Administrative Asst, 1959; Asst Sec.-Chief Community Development Officer, Migrants Services Div., 1961; Commn in UK for Eastern Caribbean Govts: Officer-in-Charge, 1962-63; Actg Comr, 1964-66. Vice-Chm. Commonwealth Assoc., Bexley, Crayford and Erith, 1965-67; a Patron, British-Caribbean Assoc., 1962-. Member: West India Committee Executive, 1968-; Bd of Governors, Commonwealth Inst., 1968-. Assoc. Mem. 1951, Mem. 1962, (British) Inst. of Public Relations. JP 1948. Coronation Medal, 1953; British Red Cross Medal, 1949-59. *Recreations:* cricket, lawn tennis, reading. *Address:* King's House, 10 Haymarket, SW1. *T:* 01-930 7902/4. *Club:* West Indian.

**TAYLOR, Peter Murray,** QC 1967; Recorder of Huddersfield, since 1969; Deputy Chairman, Northumberland Quarter Sessions, since 1970; *b* 1 May 1930; *s* of Herman Louis Taylor, medical practioner and Raie Helena Taylor (*née* Shockett); *m* 1956, Irene Shirley, *d* of Lionel and Mary Harris; one *s* three *d*. *Educ:* Newcastle upon Tyne Royal Gram. Sch.; Pembroke Coll., Cambridge (Exhibr). Called to Bar, Inner Temple, 1954. *Recreation:* music. *Address:* 21 Graham Park Road, Gosforth, Northumberland. *T:* Gosforth 54506; 11 King's Bench Walk, EC4. *T:* 01-353 3337.

**TAYLOR, Sir Reginald (William),** Kt 1958; CMG 1951; MICE; Engineer-in-Chief, Crown Agents for Overseas Governments and Administrations, 1954-61; *b* 1 Dec. 1895; *y s* of John Edward Taylor, Dunkirk, France, and Mary Houldsworth (*née* Alexander); *m* 1928, Ruth du Boulay, *y d* of Dr W. J. Tyson, MD, FRCP, FRCS; two *s*. *Educ:* St Lawrence College, Ramsgate; University College, London (BSc). Served European War, 1914-18, France. Public Works Department: Uganda, 1921-37; Nigeria, 1938-51; Director of Public Works, Nigeria, 1947-51, Kenya, 1951-54. Fellow, UCL, 1963. *Publications:* Aerodrome Construction, 1945; Nigerian Highways, 1951. *Recreation:* sketching. *Address:* The Crown House, Great Haseley, Oxfordshire. *T:* Great Milton 226.

**TAYLOR, Robert George;** MP (C) Croydon North West since 1970; *b* 7 Dec. 1932; 2nd *s* of Frederick and Grace Taylor, Eastbourne; *m* 1964, Rosemary (*née* Box); one *s* one *d*. *Educ:* Cranleigh School. Exec. Dir, G. & S. Allgood Ltd; Chm., (South African subsidiary) G. & S. Allgood (Pty) Ltd; Dir, G. Harrison & Sons Ltd. Contested (C) North Battersea, 1959 and 1964. *Recreations:* bridge; formerly Rugby football (played for Sussex). *Address:* Amberleaf, West Clandon, Surrey. *T:* Clandon 363. *Clubs:* Junior Carlton, Public Schools.

**TAYLOR, Sir Robert (Mackinlay),** Kt 1963; CBE 1956; Chairman, Richard Costain Ltd, Group since 1969 (Group Chief Executive, 1965-69; Director, Richard Costain Ltd, 1962); Director: Standard Bank Ltd; Standard Bank of West Africa; Thomas Tilling; *b* 29 Sept. 1912; *s* of late Commander R. M. Taylor, DSC, Royal Navy, and late Mrs Taylor; *m* 1944, Alda Cecilia Ignesti; one *d*. *Educ:* Plymouth College; Hele's School, Exeter; University Coll. of the SW, Exeter (MSc(Econ.) London). Entered Home CS, 1937; transf. Colonial Service, 1948. Dep. Comr, Nat. Savings Cttee, 1939. War Service, 1939-46; Commnd 2 Lieut, RA, 1940; Occupied Enemy Territory Admin., Eritrea, 1941-43, Finance Officer (Major); Dep. Controller Finance and Accounts (Lt-Col), Brit. Somaliland, Reserved Areas of Ethiopia, Italian Somaliland, 1943-45; Controller, Finance and Accounts (Col) E Africa Comd, 1945, Middle East Comd, 1945-46. Economic Adviser, Govt of Fiji, 1947; Fin. Sec., Fiji, 1948-52; Fin. Sec., N Rhodesia, 1952-58; seconded to Govt of Fedn of Rhodesia and Nyasaland, 1953; Sec. for Transport until end 1954; thereafter Sec. to Federal Treasury; retd from HMOCS, Dec. 1958. Mem. Adv. Commn on Review of Constitution of Rhodesia and Nyasaland (Monckton Commn), 1960. *Publication:* A Social Survey of Plymouth, 1937. *Recreation:* golf. *Address:* c/o Richard Costain Ltd, 111 Westminster Bridge Road, SE1. *Clubs:* Naval and Military; MCC; Salisbury (Rhodesia).

**TAYLOR, Robert Richardson,** QC (Scotland) 1959; MA, LLB, PhD; *b* 16 Sept. 1919; *m* 1949, Märtha Birgitta Björkling; two *s* one *d*. *Educ:* Glasgow High School; Glasgow University. Called to Bar, Scotland, 1944; called to Bar, Middle Temple, 1948. Lectr in Internat. Private Law, Edinburgh Univ., 1947-69. Contested (U and NL): Dundee East, 1955; Dundee West, 1959 and Nov. 1963. Chm., Central and Southern Region, Scottish Cons. Assoc. *Recreations:* fishing, ski-ing. *Address:* 51 Northumberland Street, Edinburgh. *T:* 031-556 1722.

**TAYLOR, Most Rev. Robert Selby;** *see* Cape Town, Archbishop of.

**TAYLOR, Robert Walter,** CMG 1933, CBE 1928 (OBE 1919); Controller of Exchange, Bahamas, 1947-56, retired; *b* 30 Nov. 1883; *y s* of late Joseph Needham Taylor; *m* 1930, Irene (*d* 1968), *er d* of Allister Macmillan, FRGS, FRSA. *Educ:* Emanuel Sch.; King's Coll., London. Somaliland, 1906-10; Uganda, 1910-14; Somaliland, 1914-20; Tanganyika, 1920-33; Treasury in each Territory; retired from post of Treasurer of Tanganyika in 1933; Receiver-General and Treasurer, Bahamas, 1936-42; Financial Secretary, Jamaica, 1942-47; retd, 1947. *Address:* Barclays Bank, 160 Piccadilly, W1.

**TAYLOR, Rupert Sutton,** OBE 1945; TD (three bars) 1943; FDS, RCS; MRCS, LRCP; Hon. Consulting Dental Surgeon, Westminster Hospital Teaching Group and Seamen's

Hospital Group, 1970; Consultant Dental Surgeon, Westminster Hospital, 1937-70, Seamen's Hospital, 1930-70; Recognised Teacher, University of London, since 1948; *b* 18 July 1905; *s* of G. W. and M. F. Taylor; *m* 1951, Mary Angela Tebbs. *Educ:* Newtown School, Waterford; Middlesex Hospital; Royal Dental Hospital. LDS 1928; commissioned RAMC, TA (Hygiene Coys), 1928; Dental Ho. Surg., Middlesex Hosp., 1928; Clin. Asst, Dental Dept, Westminster Hosp., 1929-31; Sen. Clin. Asst. to Dental Surgeon, Nose, Ear, and Throat Hosp., Golden Square, 1931-32; Hon. Dental Surgeon, Nat. Hosp., Queen's Square, 1933-37. External Examr Dental Surgery and Materia Medica, Queen's Univ., Belfast, 1938-39 and 1945-48. Dental Member, London Exec. Council (National Health Service), 1948-62; Chm. London Executive Council, 1953 and 1954-Mar. 1956 (Vice-Chm., 1951-53); FDS, RCS (by election), 1948. Served with RAMC War of 1939-45; Major, 1938-42, Lt-Col, 1942-45; commanded 127 Light Field Amb. and 146 Field Amb.; 161 Field Ambulance, TA, 1957-58; Hon. Col Medical Units 54 (EA) Infantry division, 1959-66. OStJ 1959; CStJ 1961. *Publications:* various articles on oral surgery. *Recreations:* sailing, fishing. *Address:* Thie-ny-Chibbyr, Lezayre Road, Ramsey, Isle of Man. *T:* Ramsey, IoM 2585. *Club:* Savage.

**TAYLOR, Selwyn Francis;** Dean of the Royal Postgraduate Medical School, London; Senior Lecturer in Surgery, and Surgeon, Hammersmith Hospital; Examiner in Surgery, Universities of Oxford, London, Manchester, Leeds, National University of Ireland, and Society of Apothecaries; *b* Sale, Cheshire, 16 Sept. 1913; *s* of late Alfred Petre Taylor and Emily Taylor, Salcombe, Devon; *m* 1939, Ruth Margaret, 2nd *d* of late Sir Alfred Howitt, CVO; one *s* one *d*. *Educ:* Peter Symonds, Winchester; Keble College, Oxford; King's College Hospital. BA (Hons) Oxford, 1936; Burney Yeo Schol., King's Coll. Hosp., 1936; MA Oxon; MRCS, LRCP, 1939; FRCS 1940; MCh, 1946; DM 1959. Surgical Registrar, King's Coll. Hosp., 1946-47; Oxford Univ. George Herbert Hunt Travelling Schol., Stockholm, 1947; Rockefeller Travelling Fellow in Surgery, 1948-49; Research Fellow, Harvard Univ., and Fellow in Clin. Surgery, Massachusetts Gen. Hosp., Boston, Mass, USA, 1948-49. RNVR, 1940-46; Surgeon Lt-Comdr; Surgeon Specialist, Kintyre, East Indies, Australia; Surgeon: Belgrave Hosp. for Children, 1946-65; King's Coll., Hospital, 1951-65. Pres., Harveian Soc.; Member: Council, RCS, 1966-; Surgical Research Soc.; Internat. Soc. for Surgery; Fellow Assoc. Surgeons of Gt Brit.; FRSM; Corresp. Fellow Amer. Thyroid Assoc.; Pres., London Thyroid Club and Sec., Fourth Internat. Goitre Conference. Director Heinemannn Medical Books. *Publications:* books and papers on surgical subjects and thyroid physiology. *Recreations:* sailing, tennis, wine. *Address:* 5 Addisland Court, W14. *T:* 01-603 5533; Trippets, Bosham, Sussex. *T:* Bosham 3387. *Clubs:* Garrick, Hurlingham.

**TAYLOR, Stanley Grisewood,** CIE 1946; Indian Police (retired); *b* 19 May 1893; *s* of Edmund Judkin Taylor, Solicitor, Bristol; *m* 1919, Coralie May, *d* of Robert Elphinstone Bradley, Indian Police; one *d* (one *s* decd). *Educ:* Clifton Coll. Appointed to Indian Police, 1913; seconded to Indian Army, 1916-19, serving in Mesopotamia, 1917-18; Principal, Police Training College, Bengal and Assam, 1936-39; Dep. Inspector-General of Police, Bengal, 1939; Inspector-General of Police, Bengal, 1945; retired 1947. Intelligence Officer, Ministry of Food, Tunbridge Wells, 1948; Deputy Chief Constable, Ministry of Civil Aviation Police, London, 1949; Commandant, Police College, Federation of Malaya, 1951-53. King's Police Medal, 1934; Indian Police Medal, 1944. *Address:* The Mount, St Michael's, Tenterden, Kent. *T:* Tenterden 2176.

**TAYLOR, Thomas Whiting,** MA PhD Cantab; BD London; Headmaster, Haberdashers' Aske's School, Elstree, Hertfordshire, since 1946; *b* 29 Nov. 1907; *m* 1937, Margaret, *y d* of late Prof. H. H. Swinnerton, CBE; one *s* five *d*. *Educ:* Liverpool Collegiate School; Christ's College, Cambridge, 1926-30 (Classical Scholar, Classical Tripos Pt I 1st class honours, Pt II 2nd class honours, Burney Prize); Frankfurt-am-Main University, 1931-32; Christ's College, Cambridge, 1932-34. Senior Classical Master at Worksop College, Notts, 1930-31; Assistant Tutor in Classics at Handsworth College, Birmingham, 1934-36; Sixth Form Classical Master at Bradford Grammar School, Yorks, 1936-39; Headmaster, City of Bath School, 1940-46. Chairman: Governors, Henrietta Barnett Schools; Exec. Cttee, Nat. Youth Orchestra; Nat. Council, Amer. Field Service, UK; Vice-Chairman: ESU Brit.-Amer. Schoolboy Scholarships Cttee; Member: Coun., Royal Holloway College, Univ. of London; Coun., Sch. of Slavonic Studies, Univ. of London; Hispanic Council; Educl Interchange Council. Governor: North London Collegiate Sch.; Camden Sch. *Recreations:* drama, music, foreign travel. *Address:* Haberdashers' Aske's School, Elstree, Herts. *T:* 01-953 4141.

**TAYLOR, William,** CB 1947; retired; Under-Secretary, Ministry of Labour and National Service, 1946-52; *b* 1 May 1892; *s* of late Alexander Taylor, Cullen, Banffshire; *m* 1st, 1919, Gaynor Yseult Brockbank; one *d*; 2nd, 1963, Mildred Hartley, Somerville College, Oxford. *Educ:* Fordyce Academy; Aberdeen University. MA 1st Class Hons Mental Philosophy, 1913; Hutton Prize; Bain Gold Medal. Served European War, 1914-18, 4th Battalion Gordon Highlanders (despatches, 1916; Captain). Asst Principal, Ministry of Labour, 1919; Chief Insurance Officer, 1937; Director of Services and Establishments, 1938; Vice-Chm. Civil Service Selection Board, 1945; UK Govt Deleg., Internat. Lab. Conf., Geneva, 1949; Chm. Rehabilitation Cttee, Brussels Treaty Powers, 1950; Chm. Working Party on Employment of Blind Persons, 1950-51; Mem. Bd of Management, Aberdeen Gen. Hosps, 1953-63; Chm., Jute and Bespoke Tailoring Wages Councils, 1954-59; Chancellor's Assessor, Aberdeen Univ., 1955-63; Mem., Indust. Injuries Adv. Council, 1960-64. Hon. LLD Aberdeen, 1962. *Address:* Old Post Office, Kirtlington, Oxford.

**TAYLOR, Sir William (Johnson),** 1st Bt *cr* 1963; CBE 1951 (OBE 1943); DL; JP; is a Civil Engineer; Member of Lloyds; Director, Building, Insurance and Engineering Companies; Liveryman, Fishmongers Company; Freeman of London; Member, Air Cadet Council, Ministry of Defence; Chairman, Sheffield Diocesan Board of Finance; Commander, West Riding St John Ambulance; *b* 23 Oct. 1902; *s* of Frank and Margaret Elizabeth Taylor; *m* 1930, Mary Hall; two *d*. *Educ:* Archbishop Holgate's Grammar School, Barnsley; Sheffield Univ. Member, Barnsley County Borough Council, 1933-45. Major TA, R of O; raised and commanded 1st Cadet Bn, The York and Lancaster Regt, 1943-45; Capt., 72nd Bn WR Home Guard, 1941-44. Parly Sec., Min. of Supply, 1957-Oct. 1959. Chm.: Yorks ATC Assoc., 1940-46; ATC Central Council of Welfare, 1958; Member:

ATC Consultative Cttee, Air Ministry, 1946-51; Air Cadet Council, 1951-; Exec. Council, Air League of British Empire, 1940-57; Air Cadet League of Canada (hon.); Exec. Council, Assoc. of British Chambers of Commerce. 1947-50; Vice-Chm., West Riding, T&AFA Air Cttee, 1946-56; Chm. Wentworth Conservative Assoc., 1940-46; Pres., Penistone Cons. and Unionist Assoc., 1965-; Pres., Mid-Yorks Cons. Fedn, 1965-; Pres., N Bradford Cons. Assoc.; Chm. Yorkshire Provincial Area Cons. and Unionist Assoc., 1956-57. Contested East Bradford (C) 1945; MP (C and Nat. L) Bradford North, 1950-64. Parliamentary Under-Secretary of State for Air, 1959-62, and Vice-Pres of The Air Council. Hon. Air Commodore, RAFVR, 1963. Mayor, Hon. Co. of Merchants of the Staple of England, 1965-66; Fellow, Inst. of Builders. DL, 1943, W Riding of Yorkshire and City and County of City of York; JP Barnsley County Borough. 1943; High Sheriff of Hallamshire, 1968-69. CStJ. *Recreations:* music, fishing. *Heir:* none. *Address:* Bentwood, Cawthorne, near Barnsley, Yorks. *T:* Silkstone 266; Flat 19b, 36 Buckingham Gate, SW1. *T:* 01-834 7959. *Clubs:* Carlton, Royal Air Force.

**TAYLOUR,** family name of **Marquess of Headfort.**

**TAYSIDE,** Baron, *cr* 1967 (Life Peer); **David Lauchlan Urquhart,** OBE 1966; JP; Chairman, Don Brothers Buist & Co. Ltd Group, since 1966, Managing Director since 1952; Chairman, Tayside Economic Planning Consultative Group, 1969-70 (Vice-Chairman, 1966-69); *b* 13 Sept. 1912; *s* of David Urquhart, Kirriemuir; *m* 1939, Hilda Gwendoline Harris, BSc (Hons), St Andrews Univ., *d* of John Thomson Harris, Dundee; two *s* one *d*. *Educ:* Harris Academy, Dundee; St Andrews Univ. Member, Inst. of Chartered Accountants of Scotland (distinction), 1936. Member: Forfar Town Council, 1951-59 (Provost, 1956-59); Angus County Council, 1953-59; Chairman, Forfar Local Labour Party, 1959-65; Vice-Chm., S Angus Constituency Labour Party, 1959-. Member: Parliamentary Labour Party, 1967-; Local Cttee Forfar Air Training Corps Sqdn, 1945- (Chm. 1955-); Scottish Air Cadet Council, 1962-68; Valuation Appeal Cttee for Angus, 1957-; Scottish Economic Planning Council, 1968-70. General Commissioner for Income Tax, 1966-; Pres. Dundee Chamber of Commerce, 1967-68; Mem., North of Scotland Hydro-Electric Bd, 1966-. Chairman: Strathmore Woollen Co. Ltd, Forfar; Don & Low Ltd, Arbroath; Director: Daniel Buchanan & Sons Ltd, Prestonpans; J. & J. Smart (Brechin) Ltd, Brechin; Low Brothers & Co. (Dundee) Ltd, Dundee; Grampian Television Ltd, Aberdeen, etc. Member: Inst. of Taxation, 1945; Inst. of Directors, 1953; Licenciate, Textile Inst., 1954. Chancellor's Assessor, Court of Univ. of Dundee, 1967-. *Address:* The Manor, Forfar, Angus. *T:* Forfar 3338. *Club:* Eastern (Dundee).

**TEAGUE, Colonel John,** CMG 1958; CBE 1946 (OBE 1925); MC 1916; Retired; *b* 16 Nov. 1896; *y s* of William and Helen Teague; *m* 1926, Heather Fairley (*d* 1966), *d* of late Capt. James William Fairley, Tunbridge Wells; two *s* one *d*. *Educ:* Portsmouth Grammar School. Studied music under Dr A. K. Blackall, FRAM, and was his Assistant Organist at St Mary's, Warwick, 1913. Commissioned Royal Warwickshire Regt, 1914; served in France, 1915-17 (wounded twice, despatches, MC). Transf. Indian Army (Baluch Regt). With Sykes' Mission in South Persia and Staff Capt., Shiraz Brigade, 1918. Attached Indian Political Service as Vice-Consul Shiraz, 1919. Iraq Insurrection (despatches) 1920. General Staff (intelligence), GHQ Baghdad, 1920, later with RAF, Iraq, Kurdistan Operations (severely wounded), 1922. NW Frontier, India, 1930. Language student in Persia (Interpreter), 1933. Liaison Officer, RAF Palestine during Arab Revolt, 1936-39. GHQ, Middle East, 1942. Transferred to Foreign Office, 1945. Director, Passport Control, 1953-58. Polonia Restituta, 1945; Legion of Merit (USA), 1946; White Lion (Czechoslovakia), 1947. *Publications:* occasional articles for press about Middle East. *Recreations:* music, reading and walking. *Address:* 5 Hungershall Park, Tunbridge Wells, Kent. *T:* Tunbridge Wells 26959. *Club:* Royal Air Force.

**TEAKLE, Prof. Laurence John Hartley,** CMG 1970; Deputy Vice-Chancellor, University of Queensland, 1963-70, retired; *b* 2 Aug. 1901; *s* of David John and Bertha Teakle; *m* 1927, Beatrice Elizabeth Inch; three *s* one *d*. *Educ:* Perth Modern Sch., WA; Univ. of Western Australia; Univ. of California (Berkeley). Dept of Agriculture, WA: Agricultural Adviser, 1923; Research Officer, 1928-46; Comr for Soil Conservation, 1946-47; Univ. of Queensland: Prof. of Agriculture, 1947-62; Dep. Vice-Chancellor, 1963-70; Acting Vice-Chancellor, 1968-70. Hon. LLD Queensland, 1969. *Publication:* Fertilizers for the Farm and Garden (Teakle and Boyle), 1958. *Address:* 51 Goldieslie Road, Indooroopilly, Queensland 4068, Australia. *T:* 78.1502. *Clubs:* Rotary of Brisbane, University of Queensland Staff (Brisbane).

**TEALE, Sir Edmund Oswald,** Kt 1936; DSc, FGS, FRGS, MIMM; *b* Melbourne, Victoria, of British parentage, 29 Nov. 1874; *m* 1909, Charlotte W. Stalker; one *s* one *d*. *Educ:* Victorian State School, New College, Box Hill; Victorian Schools of Mines; Melbourne University. Science teacher at Victorian Schools of Mines; Caroline Kay Scholarship, Melbourne University; Field Geologist, Geological Survey, Victoria; Geological work in Africa, Nigeria, P E Africa, Gold Coast, Tanganyika Territory, starting in 1908; Director Geological Survey, Tanganyika Territory, 1926-35; Mining Consultant to Government of Tanganyika Territory, 1935-40. *Publications:* Geological and Geographical Papers on Australian and African Regions. *Recreations:* gardening, photography. *Address:* The Bungalow, Pirbright, near Woking, Surrey; *T:* Brookwood 2119.

**TEALE, Rear-Adm. Godfrey Benjamin,** CB 1962; CBE 1953; retired as Chief Staff Officer (Administration) on staff of C-in-C, Portsmouth (1960-63); *b* 27 Oct. 1908; *s* of Captain G. C. Teale; *m* 1933, Frances Evelyn Turreff; one *s* one *d*. *Educ:* Radley. Entered Royal Navy, 1926; Sec. to Admiral of the Fleet Sir Rhoderick McGrigor, GCB, DSO, 1938-55; Director of Manning, Admiralty, 1957-60. *Recreations:* cricket, tennis. *Address:* Apartado 92, Marbella, Malaga, Spain. *Club:* Royal Naval (Portsmouth).

**TEARE, R(obert) Donald,** MD, FRCP, FRCPath; Professor of Forensic Medicine, University of London, since 1967 (Reader, 1963-67); Consultant Pathologist, St George's Hospital; Lecturer in Forensic Medicine, St Bartholomew's Hospital Medical College; *b* 1 July 1911; *s* of late A. H. Teare, JP, and Margaret Green; *m* 1937, Kathleen Agnes Gracey, JP; three *s* one *d*. *Educ:* King William's College, Isle of Man; Gonville and Caius College, Cambridge; St George's Hospital. BA 1933; MRCS 1936; MB, BCh 1937; MRCP 1937; MA, MD 1948; FRCP 1962; DMJ,

FRCPath 1963. Examr in Forensic Medicine at various times in Univs of Oxford, London, Bristol, Nat. Univ. of Ireland and Soc. of Apothecaries, and in Pathology in Univ. of Cambridge. Past Pres., Med. Defence Union; Past Pres., Medico-Legal Soc.; Treasurer, RCPath; Past Sec. and Pres., Brit. Assoc. in Forensic Medicine; Brit. Coun. Lectr, Denmark, 1964. *Publications:* scientific papers in Lancet, BMJ, JL of Bone and Joint Surgery, Thorax, and many forensic jls. *Recreations:* golf, gardening. *Address:* 8 Highdown Road, Putney, SW15. *T:* 01-788 6663; St George's Hospital, SW1. *T:* 01-235 6303; Ripple Cottage, Castletown, Isle of Man. *T:* Castletown 3353. *Clubs:* Bath, MCC; Woking Golf.

**TE ATAIRANGIKAAHU, Arikinui,** DBE 1970; Arikinui and Head of Maori Kingship, since 1966; *b* 23 July 1932; *o d* of King Koroki V; *m* 1952, Whatumoana; two *s* five *d*. *Educ:* Waikato Diocesan School, Hamilton, NZ. Elected by the Maori people as Head of the Maori Kingship on the death of King Koroki V, with title of Arikinui (Queen), in 1966. *Recreation:* the fostering of all aspects of Maori culture and traditions. *Heir: s* Tuheitia, *b* March 1955. *Address:* Turangawaewae Marae, Ngaruawahia, New Zealand.

**TEBALDI, Renata;** Italian Soprano; *b* Pesaro, Italy, 1 Feb. 1922; *o c* of Teobaldo and Giuseppina (Barbieri) Tebaldi. Studied at Arrigo Boito Conservatory, Parma; Gioacchino Rossini Conservatory, Pesaro; subsequently a pupil of Carmen Melis and later of Giuseppe Pais. Made professional début as Elena in Mefistofele, Rovigo, 1944. First sang at La Scala, Milan, at post-war reopening concert (conductor Toscanini), 1946. Has sung at Covent Garden and in opera houses of Naples, Rome, Venice, Pompeii, Turin, Cesana, Modena, Bologna and Florence; toured England, France, Spain and South America. American début in title rôle Aïda, San Francisco, 1950; Metropolitan Opera House Season, New York, 1955. *Address:* c/o Columbia Artists Management Inc., 165 W 57th Street, New York City 19, NY, USA; 1 Piazza Guastalla, Milan, Italy.

**TEBBIT, Donald Claude,** CMG 1965; Minister (Commercial), British Embassy, Washington, since 1970; *b* 4 May 1920; *m* 1947, Barbara Margaret Olson Matheson; one *s* three *d*. *Educ:* Perse School; Trinity Hall, Cambridge (MA). Served War of 1939-45, RNVR. Joined Foreign (now Diplomatic) Service, 1946; Second Secretary, Washington, 1948; transferred to Foreign Office, 1951; First Secretary, 1952; transferred to Bonn, 1954; Private Secretary to Minister of State, Foreign Office, 1958; Counsellor, 1962; transferred to Copenhagen, 1964; Commonwealth Office, 1967; Asst Under-Sec. of State, FCO, 1968-70. *Address:* British Embassy, 3100 Massachusetts Avenue NW, Washington, DC 20008, USA; Hill Cottage, Hill Close, Harrow-on-the-Hill, Middx.

**TEBBIT, Norman (Beresford);** MP (C) Epping since 1970; *b* 29 March 1931; 2nd *s* of Leonard and Edith Tebbit, Enfield; *m* 1956, Margaret Elizabeth Daines; two *s* one *d*. *Educ:* Edmonton County Grammar Sch. Embarked on career in journalism, 1947. Served RAF: commissioned GD Branch; qualif. Pilot, 1949-51; Reserve service RAuxAF, No 604 City of Mddx Sqdn, 1952-55. Entered and left publishing and advertising, 1951-53. Civil Airline Pilot, 1953-70 (Mem. BALPA; former holder various offices in that Assoc.). Active mem. and former holder various offices, Conservative Party, 1946-. Sec. Cons. Members Housing and Local Govt Cttee, 1970-. *Recreations:* formerly politics, now aviation. *Address:* House of Commons, SW1.

**TEBBUTT, Dame Grace,** DBE 1966 (CBE 1960); JP; Member of Sheffield City Council since 1929, Alderman since 1934; *b* 5 January 1893; *d* of Alfred and Ann Elizabeth Mellar; *m* 1913, Frank Tebbutt; two *d*. *Educ:* Coleridge Road School, Sheffield 9. Chairman: Parks Cttee, Sheffield, 1934-47 and 1950-55; Health Cttee, 1947-49; Children's Committee, 1956-; Vice-Chm., Nat. Bureau for Co-operation in Child Care, 1964-; Mem., Home Office Central Advis. Council in Child Care and Central Training Council in Child Care, 1959-. Lord Mayor of Sheffield, 1949-50; JP 1950; Hon. Freeman of Sheffield, 1959. Hon. LLD Sheffield Univ., 1965. *Address:* 56 Reney Avenue, Sheffield 8, Yorks. *T:* 364533.

**TEDDER,** family name of **Baron Tedder.**

**TEDDER,** 2nd Baron, *cr* 1946, of Glenguin; **John Michael Tedder;** Purdie Professor of Chemistry, St Salvator's College, University of St Andrews, since 1969; *b* 4 July 1926; 2nd and *er surv s* of 1st Baron Tedder, GCB, and Rosalinde (*née* Maclardy); *S* father, 1967; *m* 1952, Peggy Eileen Growcott; two *s* one *d*. *Educ:* Dauntsey's School, Wilts; Magdalene College, Cambridge (MA 1951; ScD 1965); University of Birmingham (PhD 1951; DSc 1961). Roscoe Professor of Chemistry, University of Dundee, 1964-69. FRSE. *Publications:* Valence Theory, 1966; Basic Organic Chemistry, 1966; papers in Jl of Chemical Society, Trans of Faraday Society, and other scientific jls. *Heir: s* Hon. Robin John Tedder, *b* 6 April 1955. *Address:* Little Rathmore, Kennedy Gardens, St Andrews, Fife. *T:* St Andrews 3546; Department of Chemistry, St Salvator's College, St Andrews, Fife, Scotland. *T:* St Andrews 2651.

**TEELING, Sir (Luke) William (Burke),** Kt 1962; MA; author and traveller; *b* 5 Feb. 1903; *o c* of late Luke Alexander Teeling and Margaret Mary, *o d* and *heiress* of William Burke of Ower, Co. Galway; *m* 1942, Mary Julia (*d* 1953), *e d* of late Charles H. O'Conor and *sister* of the 25th O'Conor Don. *Educ:* The Oratory School, Edgbaston; Magdalen College, Oxford. BA 1924; MA 1958. Exec. Chm., Catholic Emigration Society of Great Britain and Northern Ireland, 1929-31; represented Overseas League as Mem. Council at Melbourne Centenary, 1934; contested (C) Silvertown Division of West Ham, 1929. Served 1940-45 in RAF. MP (U) Brighton, 1944-50, Pavilion Div. of Brighton, 1950-69; Led Parliamentary Delegation to Finland, 1947; Member, Govt Parliamentary Delegation to Japan, 1947 and to Peru, 1955, and of Commonwealth Parly Delegation to British Guiana, 1965. Vice-Chairman: Parly Anglo-Norwegian and Anglo-Danish Cttees, 1963-65; Anglo-Irish Parly Cttee, 1967-69; attended Independence Celebrations of Malta as guest of Maltese Govt, Sept. 1964. Rep. European anti-Communist organisations at opening of South Korean Freedom Centre, Seoul, Dec. 1964. Hon. Secretary: Holiday Resorts Committee in House of Commons, 1944-54; House of Commons Branch, RAF Association, 1945-62; Chairman: Essex Junior Imp. League, 1928-30; Channel Tunnel Parliamentary Committee, 1954-69; Cons. Parly Mediterranean Sub-Cttee (visited Gibraltar, 1967). President: Brighton Young Conservatives, 1961-69; UK Branch, Korean Taikwan-Do Soc.; Founder, 1946, and Vice-Pres., Regency Soc.; Mem. Council: Catholic Union, 1952-59; Japan Society, 1949-61; Anglo-Korean Society; a Governor of the

Oratory School. Hon. Sec., Irish Peers Assoc., 1970-. President: Brighton Antique Dealers' Fair, 1955-69; Hove Squash Rackets Club, 1946-69; Nat. Dog Owners Assoc. Is a Director of several companies. Freeman, City of Seoul, South Korea. Commander Order of Merit (Peru), 1957; Knight of Malta (Honour and Devotion); Order of the Brilliant Star (China). Coronation Medal, 1937, 1953; Gold Staff Officer, Coronation, 1937. *Publications:* England's French Dominion?, 1932; The Near-By Thing, 1933; American Stew, 1933 (also in Tauchnitz Edition for Europe 1934); Gods of Tomorrow, 1936; The Pope in Politics, 1937; Why Britain Prospers, 1938; Crisis for Christianity, 1939; Know thy Enemy, 1939; Corridors of Frustration, 1970. Contribs to: The Times, The Sunday Times, Daily Telegraph, The Tablet, The Tatler. *Recreations:* walking, travelling. *Address:* c/o Royal Bank of Scotland, Burlington Gardens, W1. *Clubs:* Carlton, Press, St James', Royal Air Force; Kildare Street (Dublin).

**TEELOCK, Dr Leckraz,** CBE 1968; MB, ChB, DTM, LM; High Commissioner for Mauritius in UK since 1968 (Commissioner, 1964-68); *b* 1909; *m* Vinaya Kumari Prasad, BA, Barrister-at-Law, Middle Temple; one *s* one *d*. *Educ:* Royal College, Curepipe; Edinburgh University; Liverpool University, and Dublin. Medical practitioner, 1939-64. Member Legislative Assembly, 1959-63. Chairman, Mauritius Family Planning Association, 1959-62; Director, Mauritius Free Press Service Ltd, 1940-63. *Address:* (office) Grand Buildings, Northumberland Avenue, Trafalgar Square, WC2; (home) Flat 1, Chelsea House, Lowndes Street, SW1. *T:* 01-235 6299.

**TEESDALE, Edmund Brinsley,** CMG 1964; MC 1945; Director, Association of British Pharmaceutical Industry, since 1965; *b* 30 Sept. 1915; *s* of late John Herman Teesdale and late Winifred Mary (*née* Gull); *m* 1947, Joyce, *d* of late William Mills and of Mrs J. T. Murray; three *d*. *Educ:* Lancing; Trinity College, Oxford. Entered Colonial Administrative Service, Hong Kong, 1938. Active Service in Hong Kong, China, India, 1941-45. Subsequently various administrative posts in Hong Kong; Colonial Secretary, Hong Kong, 1963-65. *Recreations:* tennis, gardening, swimming, reading. *Address:* The Hogge House, Buxted, Sussex.

**TEIGNMOUTH,** 7th Baron, *cr* 1797; **Frederick Maxwell Aglionby Shore;** Bt 1792; DSC and Bar 1944; *b* 2 Dec. 1920; *yr s* of 6th Baron and Anna Adelaide Caroline, *d* of Col Marsh; *S* father, 1964; *m* 1947, Daphne Beryl (marriage annulled, 1952), *o d* of W. H. Freke-Evans, Hove. *Educ:* Wellington College. Served War of 1939-45: Lieut, RNVR (despatches twice, DSC and Bar). *Recreations:* fishing, shooting, painting. *Heir:* none. *Address:* Brownsbarn, Thomastown, Co. Kilkenny, Eire. *Club:* East India and Sports.

**TEJAN-SIE, Banja,** CMG 1967; **Hon. Chief Justice Tejan-Sie;** Chief Justice of Sierra Leone since 1967; Acting Governor-General of Sierra Leone, since 1968; *b* 7 Aug. 1917; *s* of late Alpha Ahmed Tejan-Sie; *m* 1946, Admira Stapleton; three *s* one *d*. *Educ:* Bo Sch., Freetown; Prince of Wales Sch., Freetown; LSE, London University. Called to Bar, Lincoln's Inn, 1951. Station Clerk, Sierra Leone Railway, 1938-39; Nurse, Medical Dept, 1940-46; Ed., West African Students' Union, 1948-51; Nat. Vice-Pres., Sierra Leone People's Party, 1953-56; Police Magistrate: Eastern Province, 1955; Northern Province, 1958; Sen. Police Magistrate Provinces, 1961; Speaker, Sierra Leone House of Representatives, 1962-67. Mem. Keith Lucas Commn on Electoral Reform, 1954. Hon. Sec. Sierra Leone Bar Assoc., 1957-58. Chm. Bd of Management, Cheshire Foundn, Sierra Leone, 1966. Has led delegations and paid official visits to many countries throughout the world. *Recreations:* music, reading. *Address:* 14b Syke Street, Freetown, Sierra Leone. *Club:* Royal Commonwealth Society.

**TELFER, Rev. Andrew Cecil,** MA; FRAS; *b* 1893; 2nd *s* of Rev. A. Telfer, Faversham, Kent; *m* 1928, Dorothy, *y d* of C. J. Britton, Ford End, Essex; two *d*. *Educ:* King's School, Canterbury; Selwyn College, Cambridge. Deacon, 1943; Priest, 1944; served European War, 1914-19 (wounded); Captain CUH and H, 1913-20; President CUAC, 1919-20; Assistant Master Felsted School, 1920-27; Headmaster Ludlow Grammar School, 1927-33; Housemaster, Felsted School, 1933-46; retired, 1960. Co-Founder Achilles Club. *Address:* Felsted, Essex.

**TELFORD, Robert,** CBE 1967; CEng, FIEE, FIProdE, FBIM, FRSA; Managing Director: The Marconi Co. Ltd, since 1965; GEC-Marconi Electronics Ltd, since Dec. 1968; Director, The English Electric Co. Ltd, since 1968; *b* 1 Oct. 1915; *s* of Robert and Sarah Annie Telford; *m* 1st, 1941 (marr. diss. 1950); one *s*; 2nd, 1958, Elizabeth Mary Telford (*née* Shelley); three *d*. *Educ:* Christ's Coll., Cambridge (MA). Grad. Apprentice, Marconi's W. T. Co. Ltd, 1937-40; Works Manager, Hackbridge Works, Marconi's W. T. Co. Ltd, 1940-46; Man. Dir, Companhia Marconi Brasileira, 1946-50; Personal Asst to Gen. Manager, Marconi's W. T. Co. Ltd, 1950-53; Gen. Works Manager, Marconi's W. T. Co. Ltd, 1953-61; Gen. Manager, The Marconi Co. Ltd, 1961-65. *Address:* Rettendon House, Rettendon, Chelmsford, Essex. *T:* Wickford 3131.

**TELLER, Prof. Edward;** Professor of Physics-at-Large, University of California, Berkeley, since 1960; Chairman, Department of Applied Science, University of California, 1963-66; Associate Director, Lawrence Radiation Laboratory, University of California, since 1954; *b* Budapest, Hungary, 15 January 1908; *s* of a lawyer; became US citizen, 1941; *m* 1934, Augusta Harkanyi; one *s* one *d*. *Educ:* Karlsruhe Technical Inst., Germany; Univ. of Munich; Leipzig (PhD). Research Associate, Leipzig, 1929-31; Research Associate, Göttingen, 1931-33; Rockefeller Fellow, Copenhagen, 1934; Lectr, Univ. of London, 1934-35; Prof. of Physics, George Washington Univ., Washington, DC, 1935-41; Prof. of Physics, Columbia Univ., 1941-42; Physicist, Manhattan, Engineer District, 1942-46, Univ. of Chicago, 1942-43; Los Alamos Scientific Laboratory, 1943-46; Prof. of Physics, Univ. of Chicago, 1946-52; Asst Dir, Los Alamos (on leave, Chicago), 1949-52; Consultant, Livermore Br., Univ. of Calif, Radiation Laboratory, 1952-53; Prof. of Physics, Univ. of Calif, 1953-60; Dir, Livermore Br., Lawrence Radiation Lab., Univ. of Calif, 1958-60. Mem. Nat. Acad. of Sciences, etc. Holds several hon. degrees, 1954-. Has gained awards, 1957-. *Publications:* The Structure of Matter, 1949; Our Nuclear Future, 1958; The Legacy of Hiroshima, 1962; The Reluctant Revolutionary, 1964; The Constructive Uses of Nuclear Explosives, 1968; Great Men of Physics, 1969. *Address:* 1573 Hawthorne Terrace, Berkeley, Calif 94708, USA.

**TEMPEL, Frederik Jan;** Commander, Oranje Nassau; Kt, Order of Netherlands Lion; Chairman of Unilever NV, 1955-66, and a Vice-Chairman of Unilever Ltd, 1954-66, retired; *b* 26 Dec. 1900; Dutch nationality; *s* of Jacob Tempel and Minke Tempel (*née* van der Meulen); *m* 1925, Annie Zwartsenberg; no *c*. *Educ:* Gymnasium Assen, Holland; Handels HS, Rotterdam, Holland. Joined Van den Bergh's Fabr. NV, Rotterdam, 1923; Head of local Unilever companies in France, Italy and Germany, 1929-40; in Holland during the War; Germany, 1945-47; Director, Unilever NV and Unilever Ltd, 1947-66; Advisory Director, Unilever NV, 1966-. *Recreations:* shooting, fishing, golf. *Address:* c/o Unilever House, Rotterdam. *Club:* Dutch.

**TEMPEST, Margaret (Mary), (Lady Mears);** Author and Illustrator; *d* of Charles Ernest Tempest, JP, Ipswich; *m* 1951, Sir Grimwood Mears, KCIE (*d* 1963). *Educ:* Westminster Sch. of Art; Royal Drawing Soc.; Chelsea Illustrators. *Publications:* author and illustrator of: The Lord's Prayer for Children, 1943; A Thanksgiving, 1944; A Belief, 1945; The Christchild, 1947; A Sunday Book, 1954; The Little Lamb of Bethlehem, 1956; also of The Pinkie Mouse and Curly Cobbler series, 1944. Has illustrated many books including (1929-) The Grey Rabbit series. *Recreations:* yachting; yacht-racing. *Address:* 3 St Edmund's Road, Ipswich, Suffolk. *T:* 54261. *Club:* Royal Harwich Yacht.

**TEMPEST, Prof. Norton Robert;** William Roscoe Professor of Education, Liverpool University, since 1954; *b* 29 Dec. 1904; *s* of James Henry and Veronica Tempest (*née* Fletcher); *m* 1932, Mary MacDermott (*d* 1962), Danvers, Mass, USA; one *s*. *Educ:* Liverpool Univ.; Harvard Univ. William Noble Fellow, Liverpool Univ., 1927-28; Commonwealth Fund Fellow, 1930-32. Taught in Grammar Schools; asst lecturer, later lecturer, Manchester and Sheffield Univs, 1932-45; senior lecturer in Education, Liverpool Univ., 1945-49; Director, Sheffield Univ. Inst. of Education, 1949-54. *Publications:* The Rhythm of English Prose, 1930; articles and reviews in various journals. *Address:* The University, Liverpool L69 3BX.

**TEMPLE OF STOWE,** 7th Earl, *cr* 1822; **Ronald Stephen Brydges Temple-Gore-Langton;** *b* 5 November 1910; *s* of Captain Hon. Chandos Graham Temple-Gore-Langton (*d* 1921); granted rank, title and precedence as an Earl's son, which would have been his had his father survived to succeed to the title; nephew of 5th Earl; *S* brother, 1966. Company representative. *Recreations:* sailing, swimming, bird watching. Resident in Victoria, Australia.

**TEMPLE, Maj.-Gen. Bertram;** CB 1947; CMG 1952; OBE 1941; MC and Bar; *b* 1896; *s* of Lieut-Colonel John Temple, RA; *m* 1924, Dulcibella Mary, *d* of Col F. W. Radcliffe, Dorset Regt; one *s* one *d*. *Educ:* Clifton College; Royal Military College, Sandhurst. Served European War, 1914-19, Gloucester Regiment; War of 1939-45; Bt Lt-Col, 1939; Brig. 1941 (despatches). Director of Staff Duties, General Headquarters, India, 1946 (actg Maj.-Gen.); Maj.-Gen. 1949; late Dep. Director of Quartering. ADC to the King, 1948-49; Head of British Services Mission to Burma, 1949-52. *Address:* Hayfield, Hill Crest Road, Hythe, Kent.

**TEMPLE, Ernest Sanderson,** MBE; MA; QC 1969; Chairman, Westmorland Quarter Sessions, since 1969; *b* 23 May 1921; *o s* of Ernest Temple, Oxenholme House, Kendal; *m* 1946, June Debonnaire, *o d* of W. M. Saunders, Wennington Hall, Lancaster; one *s* two *d*. *Educ:* Kendal School; Queen's Coll., Oxford. Served in Border Regt in India and Burma, attaining temp. rank of Lt-Col (despatches, 1945). Barrister-at-Law, 1943. Joined Northern Circuit, 1946. *Recreations:* farming and horses. *Address:* Yealand Hall, Yealand Redmayne, near Carnforth, Lancs. *T:* Burton (Westmorland) 200.

**TEMPLE, Frances Gertrude Acland, (Mrs William Temple);** *b* 23 Dec. 1890; *yr d* of late Frederick Henry Anson, 72 St George's Square, SW1; *m* 1916, William Temple, later Archbishop of Canterbury (*d* 1944). *Educ:* Francis Holland School for Girls, SW1; Queen's College, Harley Street, W1. JP for City of Manchester, 1926-29. Member of Care of Children Cttee (The Curtis Cttee), 1945-47. Church Commissioner, 1948-59; Mem. of Board of Visitors of Rochester Borstal Institution, 1943-60. Vice-Pres., YHA. MA (*hc*) Manchester Univ., 1954. *Address:* The Garth House, St Cross, Winchester, Hants. *Club:* Royal Commonwealth Society.

**TEMPLE, Ven. Frederick Stephen;** Archdeacon of Swindon, since 1970; *b* 24 Nov. 1916; *s* of Frederick Charles and Frances Temple; *m* 1947, Joan Catharine Webb; one *s* one *d* (and one *s* decd). *Educ:* Rugby; Balliol Coll., Oxford; Trinity Hall, Cambridge; Westcott House, Cambridge. Deacon, 1947, Priest, 1948; Curate, St Mary's, Arnold, Notts, 1947-49; Curate, Newark Parish Church, 1949-51; Rector, St Agnes, Birch, Manchester, 1951-53; Dean of Hong Kong, 1953-59; Senior Chaplain to the Archbishop of Canterbury, 1959-61; Vicar of St Mary's, Portsea, 1961-70; Proctor, Canterbury Convocation, 1964; Hon. Canon, Portsmouth Cathedral, 1965. *Publication:* Some Lambeth Letters, 1942-44, William Temple. *Recreations:* tennis, bathing, reading. *Address:* Morwena, Mill Lane, Westlecot Road, Swindon, Wilts. *T:* Swindon 5798.

**TEMPLE, George,** CBE 1955; FRS 1943; PhD, DSc, MA; Sedleian Professor of Natural Philosophy, University of Oxford, 1953-68, now Professor Emeritus; Emeritus Fellow of Queen's College, Oxford; *b* 2 Sept. 1901; *o s* of late James Temple, London; *m* 1930, Dorothy Lydia, *e d* of late Thomas Ellis Carson, Liverpool. *Educ:* Ealing County School; Birkbeck College, University of London; Trinity College, Cambridge. Research Assistant and Demonstrator, Physics Dept, Birkbeck College, 1922-24; Assistant Lecturer, Maths Dept, City and Guilds (Eng.) College, 1924-28; Keddey Fletcher Warr Studentship, 1928; 1851 Exhibition Research Student, 1928-30; Assistant Professor in Maths Dept, Royal College of Science, 1930-32; Professor of Mathematics, University of London, King's College, 1932-53. Seconded to Royal Aircraft Establishment, Farnborough, 1939-45. Chairman, Aeronautical Research Council, 1961-64. Hon. DSc: Dublin, 1961; Louvain, 1966; Hon. LLD W Ontario, 1969. *Publications:* An Introduction to Quantum Theory, 1931; Rayleigh's Principle, 1933; General Principles of Quantum Theory, 1934; An Introduction to Fluid Dynamics, 1958; Cartesian Tensors, 1960; papers on Mathematical Physics, Relativity, Quantum Theory and Aerodynamics. *Address:* 341 Woodstock Road, Oxford; The Queen's College, Oxford. *Club:* Athenæum.

**TEMPLE, John Meredith;** MP (C) City of Chester since Nov. 1956; JP; *b* 9 June 1910; *m* 1942, Nancy Violet, *d* of late Brig.-Gen. Robert Wm Hare, CMG, DSO, DL, Cobh, Eire, and Norwich; one *s* one *d*. *Educ:* Charterhouse; Clare College, Cambridge (BA). Served War of 1939-45 (despatches). ADC to Governor of S Australia, 1941. Pres.,

Fisheries Organisation Soc.; Council Mem., RASE; President: Chester Conservative and Unionist Club; National Council of Salmon Netsmen of England and Wales; Vice-President: The Salmon and Trout Assoc.; Assoc. of River Authorities; North Western British Friesian Breeders' Club; Rural District Councils Assoc.; Assoc. of Municipal Corporations; Army Benevolent Fund (Chester Branch); Member Executive Cttee: Industrial Co-Partnership Assoc.; British Group, Inter-Parliamentary Union; Chm., Anglo-Colombian Parly Gp; Mem., NW Region Bd, Abbey Nat. Building Soc. JP 1949, Cheshire. *Address:* Picton Gorse, near Chester. *T:* Mickle Trafford 239 and 393; 126 Whitehall Court, SW1. *T:* 01-930 3160, Ext. 26. *Clubs:* Carlton; Racquet (Liverpool); Grosvenor, City (Chester).

**TEMPLE, Rawden John Afamado,** CBE 1964; QC 1951; Barrister; *b* 1908; *m* 1936, Margaret Jessie Wiseman, *d* of late Sir James Gunson, CMG, CBE; two *s*. *Educ:* King Edward's School, Birmingham; The Queen's College, Oxford. BA 1930; BCL, 1931; called to Bar, 1931; Master of the Bench, Inner Temple, 1960; Vice-Chairman, General Council of the Bar, 1960-64. War Service, 1941-45. A Nat. Insurance Comr, 1969-. Liveryman Worshipful Company of Pattenmakers, 1948. *Recreations:* fishing; collecting portraits and oriental rugs. *Address:* 3 King's Bench Walk North, Temple, EC4.

**TEMPLE, Sir Richard Anthony Purbeck,** 4th Bt, *cr* 1876; MC 1941; *b* 19 Jan. 1913; *s* of Sir Richard Durand Temple, 3rd Bt, DSO; *S* father, 1962; *m* 1st, 1936, Lucy Geils (marr. diss., 1946), 2nd *d* of late Alain Joly de Lotbinière, Montreal; two *s*; 2nd, 1950, Jean, *d* of late James T. Finnie, and *widow* of Pilot Officer Oliver P., Croom-Johnson; one *d*. *Educ:* Stowe; Trinity Hall, Cambridge; Lausanne University. Served War of 1939-45 (wounded, MC). Sometime Major, KRRC. *Recreation:* sailing. *Heir:* *s* Richard Temple [*b* 17 Aug. 1937; *m* 1964, Emma Rose, 2nd *d* of late Maj.-Gen. Sir Robert Laycock, KCMG, CB, DSO; two *d*]. *Address:* Salford Manor, near Bletchley, Bucks.

**TEMPLE, Mrs William;** *see* Temple, F. G. A.

**TEMPLE-BLACKWOOD;** *see* Blackwood, Hamilton-Temple-.

**TEMPLE-GORE-LANGTON,** family name of **Earl Temple of Stowe.**

**TEMPLE-GORE-LANGTON, Comdr Hon. Evelyn Arthur Grenville,** DSO 1918; RN retired; *b* 5 April 1884; 3rd *s* of 4th Earl Temple of Stowe; *m* 1922, Irene (*d* 1967), *d* of Brig.-Gen. C. W. Gartside-Spaight, Tzonhalem Ranch, Duncan, BC; one *s* one *d*. *Educ:* Stubbington House School; HMS Britannia. Entered Royal Navy, 1900; retired, 1911; rejoined, 1914; served in minesweeping flotilla till Feb. 1919, when demobilised (DSO). Served War of 1939-45, in RN.

**TEMPLE-MORRIS, Sir O. T.;** *see* Morris.

**TEMPLEMAN, Geoffrey,** MA (London); PhD (Birmingham); FSA; Vice-Chancellor, University of Kent at Canterbury, since 1963; *b* 15 February 1914; *s* of R. C. Templeman; *m* 1939, Dorothy May Heathcote; two *s* one *d*. *Educ:* Handsworth Grammar School; Universities of Birmingham, London and Paris. University of Birmingham: teaching history from 1938, Registrar, 1955-62. Chairman: Northern Univs Jt Matric. Bd, 1961-64; Universities Central Council on Admissions, 1964-. Mem. Review Body on Doctors' and Dentists' Remuneration, 1965-70. *Publications:* Dugdale Soc. Pubs vol. XI together with articles in learned jls, incl. Trans Royal Hist. Soc. and Cambridge Hist. Jl. *Address:* The University, Canterbury, Kent. *Club:* Athenæum.

**TEMPLEMAN, Philip George,** CBE 1965; Alderman; Chairman: Wessex Regional Hospital Board, since 1959; Bournemouth and East Dorset Hospital Management Committee, since 1957; Vice-Chairman, Dorset and Bournemouth Police Authority, since 1968; *b* 2 June 1910; *s* of William James and Amelia Ruth Templeman, Bournemouth; *m* 1934, Elizabeth Kathleen, *d* of Howard Stanley Fudge, Bournemouth; three *d*. *Educ:* Taunton Sch., Somerset. Chm., Templeman & Son, Bournemouth, Masonry Contractors, 1942-. Mayor, 1956-57, Alderman, 1961, Leader of Council, 1963- (Chm. 3 Cttees), Bournemouth. Chm., Bournemouth and Christchurch Bldg Soc., 1960-. Mem. Council, Southampton Univ., 1967-; Pres., Inst. Social Welfare Southern Centre, 1967-. Past Pres. various Bournemouth organisations. Freeman, Co. Borough of Bournemouth, 1970. MInstD. *Recreations:* reading, music. *Address:* The Garden House, 22a Cavendish Road, Bournemouth, Hants. *T:* Bournemouth 25476. *Club:* Constitutional (Bournemouth).

**TEMPLEMAN, Sydney William,** MBE 1946; QC 1964; Attorney General of the Duchy of Lancaster and Attorney and Serjeant within the County Palatine of Lancaster, since 1970; *b* 3 March 1920; *s* of late Herbert William and Lilian Templeman; *m* 1946, Margaret Joan (*née* Rowles); two *s*. *Educ:* Southall Grammar School; St John's College, Cambridge (schol.). MA 1940. Served War of 1939-45: commnd 4/1st Gurkha Rifles, 1941; NW Frontier, 1942; Arakan, 1943; Imphal, 1944; Burma with 7 Ind. and 17 Ind. Divisions, 1945 (despatches; Hon. Major). Called to the Bar, 1947; Harmsworth and MacMahon schols; Mem., Middle Temple and Lincoln's Inn; Mem., Bar Council, 1961-65; Bencher, Middle Temple, 1969. *Address:* Southcote, Church Road, Horsell, Woking, Surrey. *T:* Woking 60796; 2 New Square, Lincoln's Inn, WC2. *T:* 01-405 1745. *Club:* United University.

**TEMPLEMORE,** 5th Baron *cr* 1831; **Dermot Richard Claud Chichester;** late 7th Queen's Own Hussars; one of HM Bodyguard, Honourable Corps of Gentlemen at arms, since 1966; *b* 18 April 1916; 2nd *s* of 4th Baron Templemore, PC, KCVO, DSO, and Hon. Clare Meriel Wingfield, 2nd *d* of 7th Viscount Powerscourt, PC Ireland (she *d* 1969); *heir-pres.* to 6th Marquis of Donegall, *qv*; *S* father 1953; *m* 1946, Lady Josceline Gabrielle Legge, *y d* of 7th Earl of Dartmouth, GCVO, TD; one *s* two *d*. *Educ:* Harrow; RMC, Sandhurst. 2nd Lt 7th Hussars, 1936; Lt 1939; served War of 1939-45 in Middle East and Italy (prisoner); Major, 1944; retired, 1949. *Recreations:* hunting, shooting, fishing. *Heir:* *s* Hon. Arthur Patrick Chichester, *b* 9 May 1952. *Address:* Dunbrody Park, Arthurstown, Co. Wexford, Eire. *T:* Duncannon 4. *Clubs:* Carlton, Cavalry; Kildare Street (Dublin).

**TEMPLER, Field-Marshal Sir Gerald (Walter Robert),** KG 1963; GCB 1955; GCMG 1953; KBE 1949; DSO 1936; HM Lieutenant of Greater London since 1967; *b* 11 Sept. 1898; *o s* of late Lt-Col Walter Francis Templer, CBE, DL; *m* 1926, Ethel Margery, *o d* of Charles Davie, JP, Bishops Tawton, Barnstaple; one *s* one *d*. *Educ:* Wellington Coll.; RMC, Sandhurst. Joined Royal Irish Fus, 1916; Capt. Loyals 1928; Bt Maj. 1935; Capt. Royal Irish

Fus 1937; Bt Lt-Col 1938; commanded between 1942 and 1944 2 Corps, 47th (London) Div., 1st Div., 56th (London) Div. and 6th Armd Div.; Dir of Milit. Govt 21 Army Group, 1945-46; Director of Military Intelligence, War Office, 1946-48; Vice-CIGS, 1948-50; GOC-in-C, Eastern Command, 1950-52; High Commissioner, and Director of Operations, Federation of Malaya, 1952-54; Chief of the Imperial General Staff, 1955-58; ADC General to the Queen, 1952-54 (to King George, VI, 1951-52). Colonel: The Royal Irish Fusiliers, 1946-60; Fedn Regiment of Malaya, 1954-59; 7th Gurkha Rifles, 1956-64; Royal Horse Guards (The Blues) 1963-69, The Blues and The Royals, 1969-; Gold Stick to the Queen 1963-. Constable of HM Tower of London, 1965-70. Served European War, 1914-18; operations in North-West Persia and Mesopotamia, 1919-21 (medal and two bars); operations in Palestine, 1936 (despatches, DSO); War of 1939-45 (wounded, OBE, CB). Hon. Freeman, Armourers' and Braziers' Co., 1965. Trustee: National Portrait Gall., 1958-; Imperial War Museum, 1959-66; Mem. Council and Chairman of Executive Cttee, National Army Museum. Mem. Executive Cttee: the National Trust; Voluntary Service Overseas; Trustee, Historic Churches Preservation Trust; Pres., British Horse Soc., 1968-70. Director: Royal Exch. Assce; Amalgamated Metal Corp.; Chm. British Metal Corp. Mem. Cttee of Inquiry into Security Procedures and Practices, 1961. Hon. DCL Oxon. *Address:* 12 Wilton Street, SW1. *Clubs:* Boodle's, Buck's.

**TEMPLETON, Mrs Edith;** author, since 1950; *b* 7 April 1916; *m* Edmund Ronald, MD; one *s*. *Educ:* Prague and Paris; Prague Medical University. During War of 1939-45 worked in American War Office, in office of Surgeon General. Conference (1945-46) and Law Court Interpreter for British Forces in Germany, rank of Capt. *Publications:* Summer in the Country, 1950 (USA 1951); Living on Yesterday, 1951; The Island of Desire, 1952; The Surprise of Cremona, 1954 (USA 1957); This Charming Pastime, 1955. Contributor to The New Yorker, Holiday, Atlantic Monthly, Vogue, Harper's Magazine. *Recreation:* travel, with the greatest comfort possible. *Address:* c/o Curtis Brown, 13 King Street, WC2.

**TEMPLETON, James Stanley; Hon. Mr Justice Templeton;** Puisne Judge, Supreme Court, Kenya, since 1957; *b* 24 January 1906; *m* 1932, Elizabeth Dorothy Scott; two *s* two *d*. *Educ:* Bangor Grammar Sch., N Ireland. Crown Counsel, Kenya, 1949; Sen. Crown Counsel, Kenya, 1955. *Recreation:* photography. *Address:* 8 High Trees, Beach Road, Canford Cliffs, Poole, Dorset. *T:* Canford Cliffs 79207. *Club:* Nairobi.

**TEMPLETOWN,** 5th Viscount, Ireland, *cr* 1806; **Henry Augustus George Mountjoy Heneage Upton;** *cr* Baron 1776; late Lieut Royal East Kent Mounted Rifles; *b* 12 Aug. 1894; *o surv. s* of 4th Viscount and Lady Evelyn Georgina Finch-Hatton (*d* 1932), *d* of 9th Earl of Winchilsea and Nottingham; *S* father, 1939; *m* 1916, Alleyne, *d* of late Henry Lewes Conran, RN; one *d* (one *s* decd). *Educ:* Eton; Magdalen College, Oxford. *Recreations:* shooting, fishing, ski-ing. *Heir:* none. *Address:* The Holme, Balmaclellan, Castle Douglas, Kirkcudbrightshire. *T:* New Galloway 243.

**TENBY,** 2nd Viscount, *cr* 1957, of Bulford; **David Lloyd George;** *b* 4 Nov. 1922; *s* of 1st Viscount Tenby and of Edna, Viscountess Tenby; *S* father, 1967. *Educ:* Eastbourne Coll.; Jesus Coll. (Scholar), Cambridge (MA). Served War of 1939-45, Royal Artillery. *Heir: b* Hon. William Lloyd George [*b* 7 Nov. 1927; *m* 1955, Ursula Diana Ethel Medlicott; one *s* two *d*].

**TENISON;** *see* King-Tenison.

**TENISON, Richard H.;** *see* Hanbury-Tenison.

**TENISON, Lt-Col William Percival Cosnahan,** DSO 1917; late Royal Artillery; *b* 25 June 1884; *e s* of Col William Tenison, DL, JP, of Loughbawn, Ballybay, Ireland; *m* 1915, Olive Leonora, *d* of late C. L. Mackenzie and Baroness Wesselenyi of Hadad, Hungary; two *d*. *Educ:* Marlborough; RMA, Woolwich. First commn, 1903; served European War, 1914-17 (DSO); retired pay, 1922. Guildford Borough Council, 1925-31; Hon. Associate British Museum (Natural History); FLS, FZS (Mem. Council, 1943-47), MBOU; Compiler Zoological Record-Aves; zoological artist; Field Studies Council; Worshipful Company of Farriers; Mem., Old Contemptibles Association; a Governor of Archbishop Tenison's Grammar School. Raised and commanded 54th Surrey (Wimbledon) Bn Home Guard, 1940-45. *Address:* 2 Wool Road, SW20.

**TENNANT,** family name of **Baron Glenconner.**

**TENNANT, Captain Iain Mark,** JP; Lord Lieutenant, County of Moray, since 1964; Crown Estate Commissioner, since 1970; *b* 11 March 1919; *e s* of late Col Edward Tennant, Innes, Elgin and Mrs Georgina Tennant; *m* 1946, Lady Margaret Helen Isla Marion Ogilvy, 2nd *d* of 12th Earl of Airlie, Kt, GCVO, MC; two *s* one *d*. *Educ:* Eton College; Magdalene College, Cambridge. Scots Guards, 1939-46. Caledonian Cinemas, 1947; Chm., Grampian Television Ltd, 1968-; Director, Times Publishing Co. Ltd, 1962-66; Chm., Glenlivet Glengrant Distilleries Ltd, 1964-; Chm. Bd of Governors, Gordonstoun School, 1954-. DL Moray, 1954; JP Moray, 1961. *Recreations:* shooting, fishing; formerly rowing (rowed for Eton, 1937). *Address:* Innes House, Elgin, Moray. *T:* Lhanbryde 228.

**TENNANT, Sir Mark (Dalcour),** KCMG 1964 (CMG 1951); CB 1961; Deputy Secretary, Ministry of Public Building and Works since 1965; *b* 26 December 1911; *o surv. s* of late N. R. D. Tennant, Haileybury, Hertford; *m* 1936, Clare Elisabeth Ross, *o d* of late Sir Ross Barker, KCIE, CB. *Educ:* Marlborough College; New College, Oxford (Open Classical Schol.). Entered Min. of Labour as Asst Principal, 1935; Private Secretary to Parliamentary Secretary, Ministry of Labour, 1938-39; and to Parliamentary Secretary, Ministry of Food, 1939-40. Served War of 1939-45, Royal Artillery, 1942-44. Assistant Secretary, 1945; Member of UK Delegation to International Labour Conference, 1949-53; Student Imperial Defence College, 1956; Under-Secretary, 1957; Secretary-General Monckton Commission on the Review of the Constitution of the Federation of Rhodesia and Nyasaland, 1960; Dir Organisation and Establishments, Min. of Labour, 1960; Secretary, Central African Office, 1962-64. Third Secretary, HM Treasury, 1964-65. *Address:* c/o Barclays Bank Ltd, 1 Pall Mall East, SW1. *Club:* Travellers'.

**TENNANT, Peter Frank Dalrymple,** CMG 1958; OBE 1945; Director-General, British National Export Council since 1965; *b* 29 Nov. 1910; *s* of G. F. D. Tennant and Barbara Tennant (*née* Beck); *m* 1st, 1934 (marr. diss., 1952), Hellis, *d* of Professor Fellenius, Stockholm; one *s* two *d*; 2nd, 1953, Galina Bosley, *d* of K. Grunberg, Helsinki; one *step s*. *Educ:* Marlborough;

Trinity College, Cambridge. Sen. Mod. Languages Scholar, Trinity College, Cambridge, 1929; Cholmondely Studentship, Lincoln's Inn; 1st Cl. Hons Mod. Langs Tripos, 1931; BA 1931, MA 1935, Cambridge. Cambridge Scandinavian Studentship, Oslo, Copenhagen, Stockholm, 1932-33; Fellow Queens' College, Cambridge, and University Lecturer, Scandinavian Languages, 1933; Press Attaché, British Legation, Stockholm, 1939; Information Counsellor, British Embassy, Paris, 1945-50; Deputy Commandant, British Sector, Berlin, 1950-52; resigned Foreign Service to become Overseas Director, FBI, 1952-63. Deputy Director-General, FBI, 1963-65. Special Advr, CBI, 1964-65. Member: Council of Industrial Design; Wilton Park Academic Council; Oversea Service Coll. Bd; Gabbitas Thring Educational Trust. *Publications:* Ibsen's Dramatic Technique, 1947; The Scandinavian Book, 1952. *Recreations:* writing, painting, travel, languages, sailing, country life. *Address:* Anchor House, Shottermill Ponds, Haslemere, Surrey. *T:* Haslemere 3124. *Club:* Travellers'.

**TENNYSON,** family name of **Baron Tennyson.**

**TENNYSON,** 4th Baron *cr* 1884; **Harold Christopher Tennyson;** *b* 25 March 1919; *e s* of 3rd Baron and Hon. Clarissa Tennant (*d* 1960), *o d* of 1st Baron Glenconner; *S* father 1951. *Educ:* Eton; Trinity Coll., Cambridge. BA 1940. Employed War Office, 1939-46. Hon. Freeman, City of Lincoln, 1964. *Heir: b* Hon. Mark Aubrey Tennyson, DSC 1943; RN ret. [*b* 28 March 1920. *Educ:* RN College, Dartmouth. Served War of 1939-45 (despatches, DSC); Comdr RN, 1954]. *Address:* 18 Rue Galilée, Paris 16me, France; Millwall House, Sandwich, Kent. *Clubs:* White's, Royal Automobile; Royal and Ancient.

**TENNYSON, Sir Charles Bruce Locker,** Kt, *cr* 1945; CMG 1915; MA; Secretary to the Dunlop Rubber Company, 1928-48; *b* 8 Nov. 1879; 2nd *s* of late Hon. Lionel Tennyson and late Eleanor Bertha Mary, *d* of Frederick Locker (*m* 2nd, Rt Hon. Augustine Birrell); *m* 1909, Ivy Gladys (*d* 1958), OBE, *d* of late W. J. Pretious; one *s* (two having been killed on active service, 1941 and 1945). *Educ:* Eton College (King's Scholar); King's College, Cambridge (Eton Scholarship). Whewell Scholar in International Law, Cambridge University; 1st Division 1st Class, Classical Tripos, 1902; Arden Scholar, Gray's Inn, 1904; called to Bar, 1905; Junior Equity Counsel to Office of Works, 1909-11; Asst Legal Adviser to Colonial Office, 1911-19; one of the British delegates at the New Hebrides Conf., 1914; Chairman of Board of Trade Utility Furniture Committee, 1943, and Furniture Production Committee, 1944; President Association of Technical Institutes, 1946, and of Union of Educational Instns, 1948; Chm. of Council, Bedford College, London Univ., 1946-53; Vice-Pres. Fedn Brit. Industries (late Dep. Dir); Fellow Bedford College, Hon. Fellow King's College, Cambridge, and Royal College of Art; FRSL. Hon. LLD Cambridge; Hon. DLitt Leicester Univ. *Publications:* Cambridge from Within, 1912; Alfred Tennyson, 1950; Life's all a Fragment, 1953; Six Tennyson Essays, 1953; Stars and Markets, 1957; (with H. Dyson) Dear and Honoured Lady, 1969. Edited, Shorter Poems of Frederick Tennyson, 1913, The Devil and the Lady, by Alfred Lord Tennyson, 1930; Unpublished Early Poems by Alfred Tennyson, 1931. *Recreation:* represented Cambridge University against Oxford at golf, 1902. *Address:* 23 The Park, NW11.

**TENNYSON D'EYNCOURT, Sir (Eustace) Gervais,** 2nd Bt, *cr* 1930; *b* 19 Jan. 1902; *o s* of Sir Eustace Tennyson-d'Eyncourt, 1st Bt, KCB, FRS, and Janet (*d* 1909), *widow* of John Burns, *e d* of Mathew Finlay, Langside, Glasgow; *S* father 1951; *m* 1st, 1926, Pamela (*d* 1962), *yr d* of late W. B. Gladstone; two *s* one *d*; 2nd, 1964, Vinnie Lorraine, *widow* of Robert J. O'Donnell and *yr d* of late Andrew Pearson, Minneapolis, Minnesota. *Educ:* Charterhouse. Prime Warden of the Fishmongers' Company, 1960-61. *Recreations:* golf, shooting. *Heir: s* John Jeremy Eustace Tennyson d'Eyncourt [*b* 8 July 1927; *m* 1964, Mrs Sally Fyfe-Jamieson, *e d* of Robin Stratford, QC]. *Address:* 16 Pelham Place, SW7. *T:* 01-589 1670. *Clubs:* Turf, Beefsteak, White's; Ulster (Belfast). *See also Nigel Nicolson.*

**TENZING NORGAY,** GM 1953; Sherpa Climber; Director of Field Training, Himalayan Mountaineering Institute, Darjeeling (established by Indian Government, 1954); *b* Tami, Nepal, 1914; *m* Anglahmu; two *d*; *m* 1962, Dawa Phuti; one *s*. Migrated to Bengal, 1932. High altitude Sherpa in British mountaineering expeditions, 1935, 1936 and 1938; took part in expeditions to Karakoram, 1950, and Nanda Devi, 1951, climbing to east peak; Sirdar and full Member to 2 Swiss expedns (climbing record 28,215 ft), 1952; Sirdar and Full Member to Sir John Hunt's expedition, 1953; with Sir Edmund Hilary reached summit of Mount Everest, May 1953. President of Sherpa Buddist and Climber's association. Coronation Medal, 1953; Hon. Citizen of Chamonix, 1954. Star of Nepal, 1953. Holds numerous foreign medals and awards. *Relevant publication:* Man of Everest by James Ramsay Ullman, 1955 (Amer. edn Tiger of the Snows). *Address:* Himalayan Mountaineering Institute, Birch Hill, Darjeeling, W Bengal; 1 Tonga Road, Darjeeling, W Bengal.

**TERESHKOVA, Valentina N.;** *see* Nikolayeva-Tereshkova.

**TERRAINE, John Alfred;** author; *b* 15 Jan. 1921; *s* of Charles William Terraine and Eveline Holmes; *m* 1945, Joyce Eileen Waite; one *d*. *Educ:* Stamford Sch.; Keble Coll., Oxford. Joined BBC, 1944; Pacific and S African Programme Organiser, 1953-63; resigned from BBC, 1964. Associate producer and chief scriptwriter of The Great War, BBC TV, 1963-64; part-scriptwriter The Lost Peace, BBC TV, 1965; scriptwriter, The Life and Times of Lord Mountbatten, Rediffusion/Thames TV, 1966-68. *Publications:* Mons: The Retreat to Victory, 1960; Douglas Haig: The Educated Soldier, 1963; The Western Front, 1964; The Great War: An Illustrated History, 1965 (NY); General Jack's Diary, 1964; The Life and Times of Lord Mountbatten, 1968; Impacts of War 1914 and 1918, 1970. *Recreation:* convivial and congenial conversation. *Address:* 74 Kensington Park Road, W11. *T:* 01-229 8152; Vittoria, Church Street, Amberley, Arundel, Sussex. *T:* Bury 638.

**TERRELL, Edward,** OBE 1953; QC 1955; Chairman Chevrons Club for Non-commissioned Officers of Royal Navy, Army, Royal Air Force and Commonwealth; Recorder of Newbury since 1935; *b* 12 June 1902; *s* of Thomas Terrell, KC; *m* 1928, Winifred Packard Shyvers; one *s*. *Educ:* Berkhamsted School; London University. Called to Bar, Gray's Inn, 1924; Member of Middle Temple. War Service: joined RNVR as Temp. Lieut 1940; Lieut-Comdr (acting), 1941; Comdr (acting), 1942; Capt. (acting), 1944; apptd to personal staff of First Sea Lord

(Adm. of the Fleet Sir Dudley Pound) for duties on U-Boat Warfare, 1941-45; inventor of Plastic Armour (July 1940) which was fitted to 10,000 Allied War and Merchant Ships, 1940-44 (award from Royal Commission on Awards to Inventors, 1949); inventor of first Allied Rocket Bomb for attacks on U-Boat shelters. *Publications:* The Law of Running Down Cases, Edns, 1931, 1936, 1965; Admiralty Brief (an autobiography of the War), 1958. *Recreations:* tennis, yachting, inventing. *Address:* 14 Keats Grove, Hampstead, NW3. *T:* 01-435 2402; 4 Brick Court, Temple, EC4. *TA:* 77 Temple. *T:* 01-353 2725.

**TERRELL, Captain Sir Reginald,** Kt 1959; *b* 1889; *y s* of late George Terrell; *m* 1923, Marjorie Ethel, 2nd *d* of late Mr O'Connor; two *d. Educ:* Harrow. Served his apprenticeship in sailing ships. Joined the London and North-Western Works at Crewe. Entered the Grenadier Guards, 1915; served European War, 1915-19; MP (C) Henley Division of Oxfordshire, December 1918-October 1924. *Address:* Cliff Lodge, Cliff Road, The Leas, Folkestone, Kent. *T:* Folkestone 51806. *Clubs:* Carlton, Royal Thames Yacht, Guards.

**TERRELL, Colonel Stephen,** OBE 1952; TD; QC 1965; DL. Called to the Bar, Gray's Inn, 1946; Bencher, Gray's Inn, 1970. South Eastern Circuit. DL Middlesex, 1961. *Address:* Queen Elizabeth Building, Temple, EC4. *T:* 01-353 4788.

**TERRINGTON,** 4th Baron, *cr* 1918, of Huddersfield; **James Allen David Woodhouse;** Member, Stock Exchange, London; Partner in Sheppards and Chase; Director, S. J. Carr & Co. (Gunmakers); Deputy Chairman: Wider Share Ownership Council; London Group, Oxford Committee for Famine Relief; *b* 30 December 1915; *er s* of 3rd Baron Terrington and Valerie (*née* Phillips) (*d* 1958), Leyden's House, Edenbridge, Kent; *S* father, 1961; *m* 1942, Suzanne, *y d* of Colonel T. S. Irwin, DL, JP, late Royal Dragoons, Justicetown, Carlisle, and Mill House, Holton, Suffolk; three *d. Educ:* Winchester; Royal Military College, Sandhurst. Joined Royal Norfolk Regiment, 1937. Served War of 1939-45 in India, North Africa and Middle East (wounded); ADC to GOC Madras, 1940; psc 1944; GSOII, Allied Force HQ Algiers, Ninth Army, Middle East, and War Office, Military Operations; retired as Major, 1948; joined Queen's Westminster Rifles (KRRC), TA. Joined Messrs Chase Henderson and Tennant, 1949 (now Sheppards and Chase). Deputy Chairman of Cttees, House of Lords, 1961-63. *Recreations:* shooting, racing. *Heir: b* Hon. Christopher Montague Woodhouse, *qv. Address:* Alward House, Alderbury, Salisbury, Wilts; 3 Egerton Place, SW3. *Clubs:* Boodle's, City of London, Pratt's.

**TERRY, Major Sir Edward Henry Bouhier I.;** *see* Imbert-Terry.

**TERRY, Michael,** FRGS; FRGS(A); Explorer and author; *b* Newcastle upon Tyne 3 May 1899; *s* of late Major A. M. and late Catherine Terry; *m* 1940, Ursula (marriage dissolved 1945), *yr d* of Capt. Noel Livingstone-Learmonth. *Educ:* Charters Towers School; King Edward School, Birmingham; Durham University. Served in Russia; invalided out; went to Australia upon discharge; took first motor across Northern Australia from Winton, Queensland, to Broome on the North-West Coast, in 1923; Cuthbert-Peek Grant in support of expedition undertaken, 1925, from Darwin to Broome; authorised to name Dummer Range and Mount Rosamund; third expedition started Port Hedland, 1928; proceeded Broome, Halls Creek, Tanami, Alice Springs, Melbourne. Made gold and potassium nitrate discoveries. Explored extensively in N Territory, also in S and W Australia, 1929-33; found Hidden Basin, a 40x20 mile subsided area, covered 1200 miles on camels and collected data for Waite Research Institute, Meteorological Bureau, and Lands Dept.; Sept.-Nov. 1933, Tennants Creek Goldfield; 1934-36, prospecting NW of Laverton, WA. Mem. Aust. Soc. Authors. *Publications:* Across Unknown Australia; Through a Land of Promise; Hidden Wealth and Hiding People; Untold Miles; Sand and Sun; Bulldozer; And now this!; My next skyline?, etc; and in numerous journals. *Recreations:* tennis, surfing, riding, dancing. *Address:* c/o Customers' Mail, Rural Bank, Martin Place, Sydney, NSW 2000, Australia. *T:* (Private) 92.1885.

**TERRY, Phyllis N.;** *see* Neilson-Terry.

**TERRY-THOMAS, (Thomas Terry Hoar Stevens);** Actor; *b* 14 July 1911; *s* of Ernest Frederick Stevens and Ellen Elizabeth (*née* Hoar); *m* 1938, Ida Patlanskey; *m* 1963, Belinda Cunningham; two *s. Educ:* Ardingly College, Sussex. Served War of 1939-45: in army, Royal Corps of Signals, 1941-46. Piccadilly Hayride, Prince of Wales Theatre, 1946-47; Radio Series: To Town With Terry, 1948-49; Top Of The Town, 1951-52; TV Series: How Do You View, 1951-52. *Films:* Private's Progress, Green Man, 1956; Brothers-in-Law, Blue Murder at St Trinians, Lucky Jim, Naked Truth, 1957; Tom Thumb, Happy is the Bride, 1958; Carlton Browne of the FO, I'm All Right Jack, Too Many Crooks, 1959; Make Mine Mink, School for Scoundrels, His and Hers, 1960; A Matter of Who, Bachelor Flat, Operation Snatch, The Wonderful World of the Brothers Grimm, 1961; Kill or Cure, Its a Mad, Mad, Mad, Mad World, 1962; Wild Affair, 1963; How to Murder Your Wife, 1964; Those Magnificent Men in their Flying Machines, 1965; Jules Verne's Rocket to the Moon, 1967; Don't Look Now, 1968; Where Were You When the Lights Went Out?, 1968; Monte Carlo or Bust!, 1969; Thirteen, 1970; Seven Times Seven, 1970; Arthur, Arthur, 1970. *Publication:* (as Terry-Thomas) Filling the Gap, 1959. *Recreations:* horse-riding and water ski-ing. *Address:* 81 Piccadilly, W1. *T:* 01-493 8811. *Club:* Savage.

**TERTIS, Lionel,** CBE 1950; FRAM; *b* W Hartlepool, Dec. 1876; *m* 1st, Ada (*d* 1951), *d* of Rev. Hugh Gawthrop; 2nd, 1959, Lillian Florence Margaret, *o d* of the late H. H. Warmington and Mrs Warmington, Bournemouth. Propagandist for Viola as solo instrument. Gold Medallist, Worshipful Company of Musicians; Chevalier de l'Ordre de Couronne, Belgium. Has written numerous published articles decrying lack of facilities and opportunity for English musical talent. Is responsible for design of a viola (The Tertis Model) which is being made in fifteen countries; a "Tertis Model" Violoncello (1959) and a "Tertis Model" Violin (1962), designed on the same lines. Hon. Fellow, Trinity Coll., London, 1966. Kreisler Award of Merit, 1950; Gold Medal, Royal Philharmonic Society, 1964; Eugene Ysaye Medal and Diploma of Honour, Ysaye Foundation, Brussels, 1968. *Publications:* numerous arrangements for Viola; Beauty of Tone in string playing, 1938; Cinderella No More, an Autobiography, 1953. *Address:* 42 Marryat Road, Wimbledon Common, SW19. *T:* 01-946 5541. *Club:* Sesame.

**TESH, Robert Mathieson,** CMG 1968; Foreign and Commonwealth Office, since 1970; *b* 15 Sept. 1922, *s* of E. Tesh, Hurst Green, Surrey; *m* 1950, Jean Bowker; two *s* one *d*. *Educ:* Queen Elizabeth's, Wakefield; Queen's College, Oxford (MA). Oxford, 1940-42 and 1945-47; Rifle Brigade, 1942-45; HM Foreign Service, 1947: New Delhi, 1948-50; FO, 1950-53 and 1957-60; Delegation to NATO, Paris, 1953-55; Beirut, 1955-57; Bangkok, 1960-64; Dep. High Comr, Ghana, 1965-66; Lusaka, 1966; Consul-General British Interests Section, Canadian Embassy, Cairo, 1966-67; Counsellor, British Embassy, Cairo, 1968; IDC, 1969. *Recreations:* riding, sea fishing, water ski-ing. *Address:* c/o National Westminster Bank, Tothill Street, SW1. *Club:* Travellers'.

**TESTAFERRATA, Marquis;** *see* St Vincent Ferreri, Marquis of.

**TESTER, Air Cdre John Andrews,** CB 1958; CBE 1953 (OBE 1942); BA; Royal Air Force (retired); Allied Radio Frequency Agency, NATO, since 1960; *b* Lancaster, 21 Aug. 1907; *s* of William Andrews Tester, Consultant Engineer; *m* 1932, Kathleen Blanche, *d* of Herbert Hill Parry, Heswall, Cheshire; one *d* (one *s* killed while in RAF, in an aircraft accident, 1958). *Educ:* Hastings Grammar School; Downing College, Cambridge. Entered RAF, Sept. 1930; usual varied career as General Duties Officer; retired from RAF 1958. *Recreations:* most forms of sport. *Address:* 41 Square des Latins, 1050 Brussels, Belgium. *T:* 47.13.26.

**TESTER, Leslie,** CMG 1942; MC; Brilliant Star Zanzibar; late British Member of the Allied Quadripartite Directorates for Finance, Economics, Transport and Social Administration, Austria; *b* 1891; *s* of late William George Tester, JP, County Kent; unmarried. Served European War, 1914-19. York and Lancaster Regiment Special Reserve (despatches 5 times, MC). Colonial Service, Nigeria, 1919-32, Member of Exec. and Leg. Councils, Mauritius, 1932-34, Zanzibar, 1934-40, Tanganyika, 1940-41, Kenya, 1941-45. Commissioner of Currency, Mauritius; Chairman, E African Land Bank. Deputy Chief, British Finance Division, Germany, 1946-47; Austria, 1947-50. *Address:* c/o The National Westminster Bank, Ashford, Kent.

**TETLEY, Sir Herbert,** KBE 1965; CB 1958; Government Actuary since 1958; *b* 23 April 1908; *s* of Albert Tetley, Leeds; *m* 1941, Agnes Maclean Macfarlane Macphee; one *s*. *Educ:* Leeds Grammar School; The Queen's College, Oxford. Hastings Scholar, Queen's College, 1927-30; 1st Cl. Hons Mods (Mathematics), 1928; 1st Cl. Final Hons School of Mathematics, 1930. Fellow of Institute of Actuaries, 1934; Fellow of Royal Statistical Society; served with London Life Assoc., 1930-36; Scottish Provident Instn, 1936-38; National Provident Instn, 1938-51 (Joint Actuary). Joined Government Actuary's Dept as Principal Actuary, 1951; Deputy Government Actuary, 1953; Chairman: Civil Service Insurance Soc., 1961-; Cttee on Economics Road Research Board, 1962-65; Cttee on Road Traffic Research, 1966-. Pres., Inst. of Actuaries, 1964-66. *Publications:* Actuarial Statistics, Vol. I, 1946; (jointly) Statistics, An Intermediate Text Book, Vol. I, 1949, Vol. II, 1950. *Recreations:* gardening, music, fell-walking. *Address:* 8-b Langley Avenue, Surbiton, Surrey. *T:* 01-399 3001. *Club:* Reform.

**TETLEY, Brig. James Noel,** DSO 1944; TD; DL; President, Joshua Tetley & Son Ltd; Director, Leeds Permanent Building Society; *b* 30 Dec. 1898; *s* of Frank Tetley, Leeds; *m* 1925, Joyce Carine, *d* of C. E. Grierson, Walton-le-Dale; one *s* one *d*. *Educ:* St Bees School; Pembroke College, Oxford. In Brewing Industry with Joshua Tetley & Son, 1923-. Territorial Army Service, 1918-63; Comdr of Armoured Bde, in UK, N Africa and Italy, 1941-44. ADC to King George VI, 1948, to the Queen, 1952-58. Pro-Chancellor, 1956-64, Treasurer, 1964-70, Univ. of Leeds. DL 1956. Hon. LLD Leeds. *Recreations:* shooting, fishing. *Address:* Moor House, Moortown, Leeds 17. *T:* 661329. *Club:* Leeds (Leeds).

**TETT, Sir Hugh (Charles),** Kt 1966; ARCS, BSc, DIC; *b* Exeter, Devon, 28 Oct. 1906; *e s* of late James Charles Tett and late Florence Tett (*née* Lihou); *m* 1st, 1931, Katie Sargent (*d* 1948); one *d*; 2nd, 1949, Joyce Lilian (*née* Mansell); one *d*. *Educ:* Hele's School, Exeter; University College, Exeter; Royal College of Science (Kitchener's Scholar). Joined Esso Petroleum Co. Ltd, 1928; Technical Advisory Committee, Petroleum Board, 1940-45; Lieut-Colonel, Combined Intelligence Objectives Sub-Cttee, 1944-45; Chairman of Council, Institute of Petroleum, 1947-48; Managing Director, Esso Research Ltd, 1947-49; Director, Esso Petroleum Co. Ltd, 1951, Chairman, 1959-67. Member: Council for Scientific and Industrial Research, 1961-64; Advisory Council, Ministry of Technology, 1964-67. Chairman, Economic Development Cttee for Motor Manufacturing Industry, 1967-69. Mem., London Adv. Bd, Development Finance Corporation, 1970-. Pro-Chancellor, Univ. of Southampton, 1967-. Fellow, Imperial Coll. of Science & Technology, 1964. Hon. DSc Southampton, 1965. *Recreation:* golf. *Address:* Fernwood House, Rodona Road, St George's Hill, Weybridge, Surrey. *T:* Weybridge 46999. *Clubs:* Athenæum, Royal Automobile; St George's Hill Golf (Weybridge).

**TEVERSHAM, Brigadier Mark Symonds,** CIE 1946; MC; late Indian Army; *b* 5 April 1895; *s* of late Col R. K. Teversham, DSO, OBE, IA; *m* 1918, Evelyn Mary Ross (*d* 1954); twin *s*. *Educ:* Bedford School; Cheltenham College; RMC, Sandhurst. Commissioned Aug. 1914; served European War, 1914-18, France and Flanders and Iraq with 2nd Bn Lincolnshire Regt and 32nd Sikh Pioneers; Arab Rebellion, Iraq, 1920; NWF, 1922-24 and 1941; Staff College, Quetta, 1930-31; commanded 5th Bn Rajputana Rifles, 1937-40; 1st Ind. Inf. Bde, 1940-41; 62nd Ind. Inf. Bde, 1941-43; Dir of Quartering, GHQ, India, 1944-47; retd 1947. CStJ. *Address:* c/o Lloyds Bank, Emsworth, Hampshire. *Club:* United Service.

**TEVIOT,** 2nd Baron, *cr* 1940, of Burghclere; **Charles John Kerr;** *b* 16 Dec. 1934; *s* of 1st Baron Teviot, DSO, MC, and Florence Angela, *d* of late Lt-Col Charles Walter Villiers, CBE, DSO; *S* father, 1968; *m* 1965, Patricia Mary Harris. *Educ:* Eton. Sales Representative; Bus Conductor and Driver; Salesman; Accounts Exec., C. & J. Prickett Ltd. *Recreations:* reading, walking. *Address:* 2 Eaton Gardens, Hove, Sussex. *T:* Brighton 772537.

**TEW, Professor John Hedley Brian,** PhD; Midland Bank Professor of Money and Banking, University of Nottingham, since 1967; *b* 1 Feb. 1917; *s* of Herbert and Catherine Mary Tew; *m* 1944, Marjorie Hoey Craigie; one *s* one *d*. *Educ:* Mill Hill School, Leicester; University College, Leicester; Peterhouse, Cambridge. BSc (Econ.) London; PhD Cantab. Iron and Steel Control, 1940-42; Ministry of Aircraft Production, 1942-45; Industrial and Commercial Finance Corp.,

1946; Professor of Economics, Univ. of Adelaide (Australia), 1947-49; Professor of Economics, University of Nottingham, 1950-67; Part-time Member: Iron and Steel Board, 1964-67; East Midlands Electricity Board, 1965-. *Publications:* Wealth and Income, 1950; International Monetary Co-operation 1952; (jt editor) Studies in Company Finance, 1959; Monetary Theory, 1969. *Address:* 121 Bramcote Lane, Wollaton, Notts. *Club:* United University.

**TEWKESBURY, Suffragan Bishop of,** since 1960; **Rt. Rev. Forbes Trevor Horan;** *b* 22 May 1905; *s* of Rev. Frederick Seymour Horan and Mary Katherine Horan; *m* 1939, Veronica, *d* of late Rt Rev. J. N. Bateman-Champain, sometime Bishop of Knaresborough; two *s* two *d. Educ:* Sherborne and Trinity Hall, Cambridge. RM College, Sandhurst, 1924-25; Oxford and Bucks Lt Infantry, Lieutenant, 1925-29; Trinity Hall, Cambridge, 1929-32; Westcott House, Cambridge, 1932-33; Curate, St Luke's, Newcastle upon Tyne, 1933-35; Curate, St George's, Jesmond, Newcastle upon Tyne, 1935-37; Priest-in-charge, St Peter's, Balkwell, 1937-40; RNVR, 1940-45; Vicar of St Chad's, Shrewsbury, 1945-52; Vicar of Huddersfield Parish Church, 1952-60. *Recreations:* gardening, walking. *Address:* The Old Rectory, Tibberton, near Gloucester, Gloucestershire.

**TEWSON, Sir (Harold) Vincent,** Kt 1950; CBE 1942; MC; *b* 4 Feb. 1898; *s* of late Edward Tewson, Bradford, Yorks; *m* 1929, Florence Elizabeth Moss; two *s. Educ:* Bradford. Secretary Organisation Dept, TUC, 1925-31; Asst Gen. Sec., 1931-46; Gen. Sec. 1946-60, retired. Member of the Economic Planning Board, 1947-60; Part-time Mem. London Electricity Board, 1960-68. Mem., ITA, 1964-69. *Address:* 7 Campana Court, Blenheim Road, Barnet, Herts. *T:* 01-449 0386.

**TEYNHAM,** 19th Baron, *cr* 1616; **Christopher John Henry Roper-Curzon,** DSO 1945; DSC 1944; despatches 1944; Captain, RN (retired); King Haakon Cross of Liberty; Younger Brother of Trinity House; formerly a Deputy Speaker of House of Lords and Deputy Chairman of Committees; HM Lieutenant of the City of London; a Director of British Sailors Society; a Governor and Member of Managing Committee of Royal National Lifeboat Institute; Chairman of Prince of Wales Sea Training School, Dover; Chancellor of the Primrose League, 1948; Member, Council, Navy League; Member Post Office Advisory Board; Member of Court of Directors of Royal Exchange Assurance; *b* 6 May 1896; *e s* of 18th Baron and Mabel (*d* 1937), *d* of late Col Henry Green Wilkinson, Scots Guards, Pannington Hall, Ipswich; *S* father, 1936; *m* 1927, Elspeth Grace (marr. diss., 1954; she *m* 1958, 5th Marquess of Northampton), *e d* of late William Ingham Whitaker, Pylewell Park, Lymington; two *s*; *m* 1955, Anne Rita Curzon-Howe; two *d. Educ:* Royal Naval Colleges, Osborne and Dartmouth. Served with Grand Fleet European War, 1914-18, and War of 1939-45; Naval Control Service Officer Port of London, 1939-40; commanded Destroyers HMS Campbeltown, Venomous, and Amazon and the Minesweeping Forces from HMS Ambitious in the Invasion Area North France (DSO). Chm. Automobile Association, 1953-57. Chevalier Légion d'Honneur. KStJ. A Conservative. *Heir: e s* Hon. John Christopher Ingham Roper-Curzon [*b* 25 Dec. 1928; *m* 1964, Elizabeth, *d* of late Lt-Col the Hon. David Scrymgeour Wedderburn and of the Countess of Dundee; one *s* three *d*]. *Address:* Inwood House, Sarisbury Green, Hants. *Clubs:* Carlton; Royal Yacht Squadron (Cowes).

**TEYTE, Dame Maggie, (Dame Margaret Cottingham),** DBE 1958; prima donna; *b* Wolverhampton, 17 April 1888; *m* 1921, W. S. Cottingham (from whom she obtained a divorce, 1931). *Educ:* Royal College of Music; Paris, under Jean de Reszke. Was for several years a member of the Opéra Comique, where she, at the age of nineteen, sang in June 1908 the rôle of Melisande in Debussy's Pelleas and Melisande; since then she has appeared in London at many concerts, and with the T. Beecham Opera Co. in Nozze di Figaro (Cherubino); Tales of Hoffmann (Antonia); Faust (Marguerite), and also Pelleas and Melisande; sang in Philadelphia, Chicago and New York, 1911-12-13-14; touring England with Kubelik, 1914; toured America, 1915-18; returned to England for Monsieur Beaucaire and Little Dutch Girl; joined BNOC, 1922; joined Covent Garden Opera Co., 1930; sang in Pelleas and Melisande, Covent Garden, 1930. Chevalier of the Legion of Honour, 1957. *Publication:* Star on the Door, 1958. *Recreations:* motoring, golf, tennis, and all out-of-door sports. *Address:* D II 6 Century Court, Grove End Road, NW8.

**THACKER, Charles,** CBE 1961; Director, Ford Motor Co. Ltd, 1953-64, retired; *b* 13 Feb. 1897; *m* 1927, Edith May Genese; one *d.* Joined Ford Motor Co. Ltd, 1924: General Manager (Germany, 1945; Belgium, 1946-48); Managing Director, England, 1957-62, retired. Served in Army, European War, 1914-19. *Address:* 36 Gough Way, Cambridge.

**THACKER, Prof. Thomas William,** MA Oxon; Director of School of Oriental Studies, and Professor of Semitic Philology, University of Durham, since 1951; *b* 6 Nov. 1911; *s* of Thomas William and Edith Maud Thacker; *m* 1939, Katharine E. Hawthorn; one *s. Educ:* City of Oxford School; St Catherine's, Oxford; Berlin University. Clothworkers' Exhibitioner, 1931-33; BA 1933; Goldsmiths' Research Scholar, 1933-35; University Senior Student, Oxford, 1935-37; Mark Quested Exhibitioner, Oxford, 1937-39; studied in Berlin, 1933-36. Member of Egypt Exploration Society's expedition to Tell-el-Amarna, 1935; Asst Lecturer in Semitic Languages, University Coll. of N Wales, Bangor, 1937; Reader in Hebrew, Univ. of Durham, 1938-45; Prof. of Hebrew and Oriental Languages, Univ. of Durham, 1945-51; Foreign Office, 1940-45. Examiner at Univs of Wales (Hebrew and Old Testament), Manchester, Liverpool and Leeds (Semitic Languages), Oxford (Egyptology and Hebrew). Foreign Mem., Royal Flemish Acad. *Publications:* The Relationship of the Semitic and Egyptian Verbal Systems, 1954; articles and reviews in various periodicals. *Address:* 28 Church Street, Durham. *T:* Durham 4385.

**THALBEN-BALL, George Thomas,** CBE 1967; DMus Cantuar 1935; ARCM; FRCM 1951; FRCO; Fellow of the Royal School of Church Music, 1956 (diploma 1963); Bard Ylewyth Mur; Freeman of City of London; Civic and University Organist, Birmingham, 1949; Organist, the Temple Church; Curator-Organist, The Royal Albert Hall, London; Professor and Examiner, the Royal College of Music; Examiner to the Associated Board of the Royal Academy of Music and the Royal College of Music; Member of the Council and Examiner of Royal College of Organists; Examiner on behalf of the Cape University, 1925; Adviser and Consultant to BBC, 1941; *b* Sydney, NSW; *s* of George Charles Thalben-Ball and Mary Hannah Spear, Newquay,

Cornwall; *m* Evelyn (*d* 1961), *d* of Francis Chapman, NZ; one *s* one *d*. *Educ:* private tuition. Exhibitioner and Grove Scholar, Royal College of Music; Chappell and Hopkinson Gold Medallist; Lafontaine Prize, RCO; Organist, Whitefield's Tabernacle, 1911-14; Holy Trinity Church, Casteinau, 1914-16; Paddington Parish Church, 1916-19; acting Organist, the Hon. Societies of Temple, 1919; Organist, the Hon. Societies of the Temple, 1923; studied pianoforte with Fritz Hartvigson, Franklin Taylor, and Fanny Davies; harmony and composition with Sir Frederick Bridge, Sir Charles Stanford, and Dr Charles Wood; musical history with Sir Hubert Parry; organ with Sir Walter Parratt and F. A. Sewell. Pres. London Soc. of Organists, 1936; President Royal College of Organists, 1948; President Incorporated Association of Organists, 1944-46; Member Board of Governors, Royal Normal Coll. of the Blind. Hon. Bencher, Inner Temple, 1959. Guest Organist, Les Amis de l'Orgue, Paris, 1937; Toured Australia as guest organist in connection with Jubilee of the formation of the Commonwealth, 1951, toured South Africa, 1954; Guest of honour, Amer. Guild of Organists Convention, NY, 1956. EMI Gold Disc, 1963. Has played the organ on the Continent and in America and was a regular broadcaster and performer at the Sir Henry Wood Promenade Concerts. Composer of Organ and Choral music including Sursum Corda for chorus, orchestra and trumpet fanfares (commissioned by BBC). *Recreations:* golf and riding. *Address:* 3 Paper Buildings, Inner Temple, EC4. *Club:* Athenæum.

**THANT, U;** Maha Thray Sithu, 1961 (Sithu, 1957); Thiripyanchi, 1953; Wunna Kyaw Htin, 1949; Secretary-General, United Nations, since 1962 (Acting Secretary-General, 1961-62); Burmese Statesman; *b* Jan. 1909; *m*; one *d* (one *s* decd). *Educ:* National High School, Pantanaw, Burma; University Coll., Rangoon. Sen. Master, Nat. High School, Pantanaw, 1928, Head Master, 1931, 1943-47; Sec. Education Re-organisation Cttee, Burma, 1942. Free-lance journalist. Press Director, Govt of Burma, 1947; Director of Broadcasting, 1948; Sec., Min. of Information, 1949-57; Sec. for Projects, Office of the Prime Minister, 1953. United Nations: Mem. Burmese Delegn to 7th Session of Gen. Assembly, 1952; Permanent Burmese Rep., 1957-61; Chm. Burmese Delegn, 1957-61; Chm. Asian-African Standing Cttee, on Algeria, 1957; Vice-Pres. Gen. Assembly, 1959; Chm. Cttee on a UN Development Fund, 1961; Chm. UN Congo Conciliation Commn, 1961. Hon. Mem., American Academy of Arts and Sciences, 1963. *Publications:* (in Burmese) Cities and their Stories, 1930; League of Nations, 1933; Towards a New Education, 1946; Democracy in Schools, 1952; History of Post-War Burma (3 vols), 1961; Toward World Peace. *Address:* United Nations, New York, NY, USA.

**THAPAR, Prem Nath,** CIE 1944; Vice-Chancellor, Punjab Agricultural University, Ludhiana, since 1962; Indian Civil Service; *b* 13 April 1903; *s* of Diwan Bahadur Kunj Behari Thapar, CBE; *m* 1932, Leela Dutta; one *s* two *d*. *Educ:* Govt Coll., Lahore; New Coll., Oxford. Joined ICS 1926. Dep. Commissioner, Kangra, Attock; Deputy Commissioner and Colonisation Officer, Montgomery, 1934-37; Settlement Officer, Jhelum, 1937-41; Joint Secretary, Information and Broadcasting Department, Government of India, 1941-46; Secretary, Food and Civil Supplies Department, Punjab, 1946-47; Commissioner, Lahore Division, 1947; Financial Commissioner, East Punjab, 1947-53; Chief Administrator, Chandigarh Capital Project, 1950-53; Adviser, Planning Commission, Government of India, 1953-54; Sec., Min. of Food and Agric., Govt of India, 1954-58; Member, Atomic Energy Commission and *ex officio* Secretary to Government of India, Dept of Atomic Energy, Bombay, 1958-62. Mem. Punjab Admin. Reforms Commn, 1964-65; Consultant, Review Team, FAO, UN, Rome, 1966-67. Trustee, Internat. Rice Research Inst., Manila, Philippines. *Publications:* Settlement Report, Jhelum District, 1945; Customary Law, Jhelum District, 1946. *Address:* Vice-Chancellor, Punjab Agricultural University, Ludhiana, India. *T:* (office) Chandigarh 3636, (residence) Chandigarh 4191.

**THATCHER, Mrs Margaret Hilda;** MP (C) Finchley since 1959; Secretary of State for Education and Science, since 1970; *b* 13 Oct. 1925; *d* of late Alfred Roberts, Grantham, Lincs; *m* 1951, Denis Thatcher; one *s* one *d* (twins). *Educ:* Kesteven and Grantham Girls' School; Somerville College, Oxford (MA, BSc). Research Chemist, 1947-51; Joint Parliamentary Secretary, Ministry of Pensions and National Insurance, October 1961-64. Barrister, Lincoln's Inn, 1953-. *Recreation:* music. *Address:* House of Commons, SW1; 19 Flood Street, SW3.

**THEILER, Max,** MRCS, LRCP; Director of Laboratories, The Rockefeller Foundation, since 1951; *b* 30 Jan. 1899; *s* of late Sir Arnold Theiler, KCMG, and Emma Jegge; *m* 1928, Lillian Graham; one *d*. *Educ:* University of Cape Town; St Thomas's Hospital, London. MRCS, LRCP, DTM&H London School of Tropical Medicine, 1922. Assistant and later Instructor in Department of Tropical Medicine, Harvard Medical School, Boston, Massachusetts, 1922-30; staff member, Rockefeller Foundation, 1930-. Chalmers Medal, Royal Soc. Trop. Med. and Hygiene, England, 1939; Flattery Medal, Harvard University, 1945; Lasker Award, Lasker Foundation, 1949; Nobel Prize for Physiology and Medicine, Caroline Inst., 1951. *Publications:* scientific articles. Chapter 2 of Yellow Fever (ed by G. K. Strode). *Address:* 48 Circle Drive, Hastings-on-Hudson, New York, USA. *T:* Hastings 5-2076.

**THELLUSSON,** family name of **Baron Rendlesham.**

**THEORELL, (Axel) Hugo (Teodor),** MD; Director of Nobel Medical Institute, Department of Biochemistry, Stockholm, since 1937; *b* Linköping, Sweden, 6 July 1903; *s* of Ture and Armida (Bill) Theorell; *m* 1931, Margit Alenius; three *s*. *Educ:* Linköpings Högre Allm. Läroverk; Pasteur Institute, Paris; Royal Caroline Medico-Surgical Institute, Stockholm. MD Stockholm, 1930. Asst Professor of Biochemistry, Uppsala University, 1932; with Prof. Otto Warburg, Kaiser Wilhelm Institut für Zellphysiologie, Berlin-Dahlem, 1933-35; engaged upon research into enzyme structure; awarded Nobel Prize in Physiology and Medicine, 1955, for discoveries concerning nature and effects of oxidation enzymes. Secretary, Swedish Society of Physicians and Surgeons, 1940-46 (Chm., 1946-47 and 1957-58, Hon. Mem., 1956); Chairman: Wenner-Gren Society; Wenner-Gren Center Foundation; Swedish Chemists' Assoc., 1947-49; Stockholm Symphony Soc. Pres., Internat. Union of Biochemistry, 1967; Member: Swedish Academy of Science (President, 1967-69); Swedish Academy of Engineering Science; Swedish Acad. of Music; Royal Danish Acad. Scis and Letters; Norwegian Acad. Sci. and

Letters; Royal Norwegian Soc. Arts and Scis; Amer. Acad. Arts and Scis; Nat. Acad. Scis, Washington; Amer. Philos. Soc., Philadelphia; NY Acad. of Sci.; l'Accademia Nazionale del XL of Rome; Polish Acad. Naukoznawcze; Indian Acad. Sci. For. Mem., Roy. Soc. Hon. Dr: Univ. Sorbonne, Paris; Univ. Pennsylvania USA; Univ. Louvain; Univ. Libre, Brussels, Belgium; Univ. Brasil, Rio de Janeiro; Univ. Kentucky, USA; Univ. Michigan, USA. 1st Cl. Comdr Royal Order of the Northern Star; 1st Cl. Comdr, Order of Finnish Lion; Comdr Royal Norwegian Order of St Olav; Comdr, Légion d'Honneur (France); Officer, Order of Southern Cross (Brazil). Trafvenfelt Medal, 1945; Scheele Medal, 1956; Caroline Inst. 150 years Jubilee Medal, 1960; Emanuel e Paterno Medal, 1962; Paul Karrer Medal, 1965. *Recreation:* music. *Address:* Sveavägen 166H, 11346 Stockholm, Sweden; Nobel Medical Institute, Stockholm.

**THEOTONIO PEREIRA, Pedro,** GCVO (Hon.) 1955; Grand Cross of Cristo of Portugal; *b* 7 Nov. 1902; *s* of João Theotonio Pereira and Dona Virginia Herrmann; *m* 1926, Isabel van Zeller Palha; one *s* two *d. Educ:* Univ. of Lisbon (high mathematics). Member Portuguese Cabinet (first Social Welfare and later Commerce and Industry), 1933-37; Ambassador to Madrid, then Rio de Janeiro and Washington, 1938-50; Ambassador to the Court of St James's, 1953-58; Minister of the Presidency, Portugal, 1958-61; Ambassador to Washington, 1961-63. Life Member of Portuguese Council of State. Grand Cross of Carlos III, Merito Naval, Merito Militar, Yugo y Flechas, of Spain; Cruzeiro do Sul, of Brasil; Grand Cross, Order of George I, of Greece. *Recreation:* yachting (schooner Bellatrix). *Address:* Alameda de Algés, TP, Dáfundo, Portugal. *Club:* Royal Yacht Squadron (Cowes).

**THESIGER,** family name of **Viscount Chelmsford.**

**THESIGER, Hon. Sir Gerald (Alfred),** Kt 1958; MBE 1946; **Hon. Mr Justice Thesiger;** Judge of the High Court of Justice, Queen's Bench Division, since 1958; QC 1948; *b* 25 Dec. 1902; *s* of late Maj.-Gen. George Thesiger, CB, CMG; *m* 1932, Marjorie Guille, *d* of late Raymond Guille, Long Island, NY; three *d. Educ:* Greshams School, Holt; Magdalen College, Oxford (MA). Demy, 1921; BA, 1924; called to Bar, Inner Temple, 1926, Bencher, 1956; South Eastern Circuit; Member General Council of the Bar, 1936-41, 1958; Recorder of Rye, 1937-42; Recorder of Hastings, 1943-57; Recorder of Southend, 1957-58; Chairman West Kent Quarter Sessions, 1947-58. Member Borough Council, Fulham, 1934-37, Chelsea, 1937-58, Alderman, 1945; Chief Warden, Chelsea, 1939-41; Major, Deputy Judge Advocate Staff, 1941-45; Mayor of Chelsea, 1944-46, Hon. Freeman 1964; Chairman Departmental Cttee on Licensing of Road Passenger Services, 1953-54; Chairman of Governors, United Westminster Schools, 1947-58; Dep. Chm. Boundary Commn (England), 1962. *Address:* 44 Chelsea Park Gardens, SW3. *T:* 01-352 4686. *Club:* Hurlingham.

**THESIGER, Roderic Miles Doughty;** Director, P. & D. Colnaghi and Co. Ltd, since 1955; *b* 8 Nov. 1915; *y s* of late Hon. Wilfred Thesiger, DSO, and Mrs Reginald Astley, *qv*; *m* 1st, 1940, Mary Rose (marr. diss. 1946; she *d* 1962), *d* of Hon. Guy Charteris; 2nd, 1946, Ursula, *d* of A. W. Whitworth, Woollas Hall, Pershore; one *s* one *d. Educ:* Eton; Christ Church, Oxford; Courtauld Institute. Served War of 1939-45, Welsh Guards, 1939-41; 1st Parachute Bde, 1941-44 (twice wounded, POW). Assistant, Tate Gallery, 1945-46; afterwards worked with Messrs Sotheby and privately until 1954. *Recreations:* visiting Italy and France. *Address:* 22 Bedford Gardens, W8. *T:* 01-727 7988. *Clubs:* Brooks's, Pratt's.
*See also W. P. Thesiger.*

**THESIGER, Wilfred Patrick,** CBE 1968; DSO 1941; MA Oxon; *b* 3 June 1910; *e s* of late Hon. Wilfred Thesiger, DSO, and of Mrs Reginald Astley, *qv. Educ:* Eton; Magdalen College, Oxford (MA). Repres. Oxford at boxing, 1930-33; Captain Oxford Boxing Team, 1933; Hon. Attaché Duke of Gloucester's Mission to Abyssinia, 1930; served Middle East, 1941 (DSO); explored Danakil country of Abyssinia and the Aussa Sultanate, 1933-34 (awarded Back Grant by RGS, 1935); Sudan Political Service, Darfur-Upper Nile, 1935-40; served in Ethiopian, Syrian and Western Desert campaigns with SDF and SAS regiment with rank of Major; explored in Southern Arabia, 1945-49; twice crossed the Empty Quarter. Founder's Medal, RGS, 1948; Lawrence of Arabia Medal, RCAS, 1955; Livingstone Medal, RSGS, 1962; W. H. Heinemann Award (for 1964), RSL, 1965; Burton Memorial Medal, Roy. Asiatic Soc., 1966. FRSL; Hon. DLitt Leicester. 3rd Class Star of Ethiopia. *Publications:* Arabian Sands, 1959; The Marsh Arabs, 1964. *Recreations:* travelling, photography. *Address:* 15 Shelley Court, Tite Street, SW3. *T:* 01-352 7213. *Clubs:* Brooks's, Pratt's, Travellers'.
*See also R. M. D. Thesiger.*

**THETFORD, Suffragan Bishop of,** since 1963; **Rt. Rev. Eric William Bradley Cordingly,** MBE 1946; Archdeacon of Norfolk since 1962; *b* 17 May 1911; 2nd *s* of Charles and Edith Maud Phillips; *m* 1937, Mary Eileen Mathews; three *s* one *d. Educ:* King's Coll., London, 1930-33 (AKC 1933); St Stephen's House, Oxford, 1933-34. Ordained Deacon, 1934; Priest, 1935; Curate: St Peter-le-Poer, Friern Barnet, 1934-36; Holy Trin., Minchinhampton, Dio. Gloucester, 1936-38; Rector: Stanton with Snowshill, Glos., 1938-41; Leckhampton, Cheltenham, 1941-55; Stevenage 1955-62. CF, 1940-46; France and Belgium, 1940; Malaya, Siam and Burma Rly (POW), 1942-45. Hon. CF, 1946-. Bishop's Chaplain for Youth (Glos). 1946-55. Chaplain to the Queen, 1960-63; Residentiary Canon and Librarian of Norwich Cathedral, 1962-63. Governing Body of SPCK, 1958-. Mem. Stevenage Development Corp., 1960-62. *Address:* The Rectory, Caistor St Edmunds, Norwich NOR 52W. *T:* Framingham Earl 490. *Club:* Athenæum.

**THEUNISSEN, Most Rev. John Baptist Hubert,** DD; Titular Archbishop of Skalholt, since 1968; *b* Schimmert, Holland, 3 Oct. 1905; *Educ:* Schimmert and Oirschot, Holland; Rome University. DD 1929. Professor, Major Seminary, Oirschot, Holland, 1930; Professor, Major Seminary, Portugal, 1935; Superior Regional of the Missions in Portuguese East Africa, 1937; Superior Provincial of Dutch Province of Montfort Fathers, 1947; consecrated Bishop of Blantyre, 1950; Archbishop of Blantyre, Malawi, 1959; Apostolic Administrator of Iceland, 1967; retd, 1968. Knight, Order of the Lion (Netherlands), 1960. *Recreation:* music. *Address:* Bishop's House, Langstraat 68, Schimmert (L.), The Netherlands.

**THICKNESSE, Very Rev. Cuthbert Carroll,** MA; Dean of St Albans and Rector of the Abbey Church, St Albans, 1936-55; Dean Emeritus, 1955; *b* 19 Nov. 1887; *o surv. s* of late Ven. F. N. Thicknesse and late Mary Sibylla, *d* of Rev.

Joseph Walker, sometime Vice-Principal of BNC, Oxford; *m* 1916, Rhoda Oonah Marjorie, *d* of late Rev. H. Madan Pratt, JP and G. S. M., *d* of Sir Mathew Wilson, Bt; two *s* five *d*. *Educ:* Marlborough; Keble College, Oxford. Deacon, 1913; Priest, 1914; Curate of St John-at-Hackney, 1913-15; temporary Chaplain to Forces, attached RA, 1915-17; wounded at Ypres and invalided out; Rector of Badsworth, Yorkshire, 1917-22; Rector of Wigan, 1922-36; Proctor in Convocation for Diocese of Liverpool, 1925; Hon. Canon of Liverpool Cathedral, 1926-36; Select Preacher, Cambridge, 1935; Chaplain to the King, 1935-36; Priest-in-charge of Luccombe, 1956-63. Consulting Editor of the Church Times, 1950-54. *Address:* Heatherlands, Doverhay, Porlock, Minehead, Somerset. *T:* Porlock 440.

**THIMAN, Eric Harding,** DMus; FRCO; Professor, Royal Academy of Music, London, since 1931; Dean of the Faculty of Music, London University, since 1956; Organist to the City Temple, London, since 1958; *b* 12 Sept. 1900; *s* of Israel Phoebus Thiman and Muriel Kate Harding; *m* 1928, Clare Madeline Arnold. *Educ:* Caterham. FRCO 1926, DMus (London) 1927. Member, professorial staff, Royal Acad. of Music, 1931, after musical training, largely private, and self-administered. Musical pursuits: lecturer, examiner, composer, organ recitalist, adjudicator at musical festivals. Hon. RAM. *Publications:* compositions for organ and choir; school music; instrumental and orchestral works and musical textbooks. *Recreations:* walking, motoring, foreign travel. *Address:* 7 Edmunds Walk, N2. *T:* 01-883 4718.

**THIMANN, Prof. Kenneth Vivian;** Professor of Biology, and Provost of Crown College, University of California, Santa Cruz, Calif, USA, since 1965; *b* 5 Aug. 1904; *s* of Phoebus Thimann and Muriel Kate Thimann (*née* Harding); *m* 1931, Ann Mary Bateman, Sutton Bridge, Lincs; three *d*. *Educ:* Caterham Sch., Surrey; Imperial Coll., London. BSc, ARCS 1924; DIC 1925; PhD 1928. Beit Memorial Res. Fellow, 1927-29; Demonstr in Bacteriology, King's Coll. for Women, 1926-28; Instr in Biochem., Calif Inst. of Techn., 1930-35; Harvard University: Lectr on Botany, 1935; (Biology): Asst Prof., 1936, Associate Prof., 1939, Prof., 1946, and Higgins Prof., 1962. Scientific Consultant, US Navy, 1942-45. Pres., XIth Internat. Botanical Congress, Seattle, USA, 1969. Hon. AM Harvard, 1940; PhD (Hon.) Univ. of Basle, 1959; Doctor (Hon.) Univ. of Clermont-Ferrand, 1961. Foreign Member: Royal Society (London); Accademia Nazionale dei Lincei (Rome); Leopoldina Akademie (Halle); Roumanian Academy (Bucharest); Botanical Societies of Japan and Netherlands. *Publications:* (in USA) Phytohormones (with F. W. Went), 1937; The Action of Hormones in Plants and Invertebrates, 1948; The Life of Bacteria, 1955, 2nd edn 1963 (German edn 1964); about 200 papers in biological and biochemical jls. *Recreations:* music (piano), gardening. *Address:* Provost's Residence, Crown College, Santa Cruz, California 95060, USA. *T:* 423-0437. *Clubs:* Harvard Faculty (Cambridge, Mass); Harvard (San Francisco).

**THIRKELL, Lancelot George, (Lance Thirkell);** Controller, Staff Training and Appointments, BBC, since 1964; *b* 9 Jan. 1921; *s* of George Lancelot Thirkell, engineer, and Angela Margaret Mackail (Angela Thirkell, novelist); *m* 1946, Katherine Mary Lowinsky, *d* of Thomas Esmond Lowinsky, artist, and Ruth Jeanette Hirsch; two *s* two *d*. *Educ:* Saint Paul's School (Schol.); Magdalen Coll. Oxford (Demy). HM Forces, 1942-46; active service D-day to the Rhine with Essex Yeo. and in SE Asia with RA. HM Foreign Service, 1946-50; granted Civil Service Certificate, 1946; Third Sec., Western Dept, 1946; Third Sec., Budapest, 1947; Second Sec., Eastern Dept, 1948. Joined BBC as Report Writer, Monitoring Service, 1950; Assistant, Appointments Dept, 1953; Assistant Staff Administration, 1956; Head of Secretariat, 1961. Governor, Thomson Foundn Television Coll., 1964-. Councillor, Royal Borough of Kensington, 1959-62; Chm. Notting Hill Adventure Playground, 1964-; Appeals Sec., Portobello Project for unattached youth; Mem., European Adv. Council, Salzburg Seminar in American Studies. *Publications:* A Garden Full of Weeds, 1962; (with Ruth Lowinsky) Russian Food for Pleasure, 1953. *Recreations:* ski-ing, sailing. *Address:* 31 Lansdowne Road, W11. *T:* 01-727 6046; Oxbow, Harkstead, Suffolk. *Clubs:* Leander (Henley-on-Thames); Royal Harwich Yacht.

**THIRKETTLE, William Ellis,** CBE 1959; Principal, London College of Printing, 1939-67; *b* 26 July 1904; *s* of William Edward Thirkettle; *m* 1930, Alva, *d* of Thomas Tough Watson; two *s*. *Educ:* Tiffin School. Principal, Stow College of Printing, Glasgow, 1936-39. *Address:* Clanfelde Cottage, Clanfield, Oxon.

**THIRKILL, Sir Henry,** Kt, *cr* 1951; CBE 1946; MC; Master of Clare College, Cambridge, 1939-58, retired; President of Clare College, 1930-39; Tutor, 1920-39; Lecturer, 1918-39; Fellow, 1910-39, and since 1958; *b* 8 Aug. 1886; *s* of William Thirkill and Alice, *d* of Henry Pickles. *Educ:* Clare Coll., Cambridge, MA. Late Univ. Lectr in Experimental Physics; Vice-Chancellor of Cambridge Univ., 1945-47; Deputy Vice-Chancellor of Cambridge, 1947-55, 1956-58; Member of Council of Senate, 1927-56. Served European War: RE, 1914-19. OC Wireless, East African Campaign, 1915-18. Chm., Cambridge Univ. Joint Recruiting Bd, 1940-58. *Address:* Clare College, Cambridge. *Club:* Athenæum.

**THISTLETHWAITE, Frank;** Vice-Chancellor, University of East Anglia, Norwich, since 1961; *b* 24 July 1915; *s* of Lee Thislethwaite and Florence Nightingale Thistlethwaite; *m* 1940, Jane, *d* of H. Lindley Hosford, Lyme, Connecticut, USA; one *s* three *d* (and one *s* decd). *Educ:* Bootham School; St John's College, Cambridge (Exhibitioner and Scholar). BA 1938. Editor, The Cambridge Review, 1937. Commonwealth Fund Fellow, University of Minnesota, 1938-40; British Press Service, New York, 1940-41. Served in RAF, 1941-45; seconded to Office of War Cabinet, 1942-45. Fellow, St John's College, Cambridge, 1945-61; at various times, Tutor, Praelector, Steward; University Lecturer in Faculty of Economics and Politics, 1949-61; Visiting Prof. of American Civilization, Univ. of Pennsylvania, 1956. Member: Inst. for Advanced Study, Princeton, 1954; Academic Adv. Cttee, Chelsea Coll. of Science and Technology, 1964-66; Provisional Council, Univ. of Zambia, 1965-69; Marshall Aid Commemoration Commn, 1964-; US-UK Educnl Commn, 1964-; Academic Adv. Cttee, Open Univ., 1969-; Chairman: British Assoc. for American Studies, 1955-59; Cttee of Management, Inst. of US Studies, Univ. of London; Adviser to Nat. Council of Higher Educn, Ceylon, 1967. FRHistS. *Publications:* The Great Experiment: An Introduction to the History of the American People, 1955; The Anglo-American Connection in the Early Nineteenth Century, 1958. Contrib.: New Cambridge Modern History and other historical works and journals; New

Universities in the Modern World (ed. M. G. Ross). *Recreation:* music. *Address:* University of East Anglia, Earlham Hall, Norwich NOR 88C. *Clubs:* Athenæum; Norfolk (Norwich).

**THISTLETON-SMITH, Vice-Admiral Sir Geoffrey,** KBE 1959; CB 1956; GM 1941; *b* 10 May 1905; *m* 1931, Mary Katherine Harvey; one *s* one *d.* Captain, 1944; HMS Pembroke, Royal Naval Barracks, Chatham (in Command), 1952; Chief of Staff to C-in-C Home Fleet and Eastern Atlantic, Dec. 1953; Rear-Admiral, 1954; Admiral Commanding Reserves, 1956-58; Vice-Admiral, 1957; Admiral, British Joint Services Mission, Washington, 1958-60, retd. CC West Sussex, 1964-. *Address:* Down Place, Harting, Petersfield, Hants.

**THODAY, Prof. John Marion,** FRS 1965; BSc Wales, PhD, ScD Cantab; Arthur Balfour Professor of Genetics, Cambridge University, since Oct. 1959; Fellow of Emmanuel College, 1959; *b* 30 Aug. 1916; *s* of Professor D. Thoday, FRS; *m* 1950, Doris Joan Rich, PhD; one *s* one *d. Educ:* Bootham School, York; University Coll. of N Wales, Bangor; Trinity College, Cambridge. Photographic Intelligence, Royal Air Force, 1941-46; Cytologist, Mount Vernon Hospital, 1946-47; Assistant Lecturer, and then Lecturer for Cytogenetics, Departments of Botany and Zoology, University of Sheffield, 1947-54; Head of Department of Genetics, Sheffield, 1954-59. Director, OECD Project for reform of secondary school Biology teaching 1962, 1963. *Publications:* articles on radiation cytology, experimental evolution, the genetics of continuous variables and biological progress. *Address:* 7 Clarkson Road, Cambridge.

**THODE, Dr Henry George,** CC (Canada) 1967; MBE 1946; FRS 1954; FRSC 1943; FCIC 1948; President and Vice-Chancellor since 1961 (Vice-President, 1957-61; Director of Research at Hamilton College, 1947-61), McMaster University, Canada; *b* 10 September 1910; Canadian; *m* 1935, Sadie Alicia Patrick; three *s. Educ:* University of Saskatchewan; University of Chicago; Columbia University. Research Associate, Columbia Univ., 1936-39; Research Chemist, US Rubber Co., 1939; McMaster University: Asst Prof. of Chem., 1939-42; Assoc. Prof. of Chem., 1942-44; Professor of Chemistry, 1944-; Head, Department of Chemistry, 1948-52. Nat. Science Foundn Sen. Foreign Res. Fellow, California Inst. of Technology, Pasadena, Calif, 1970. National Research Council, War Research-Atomic Energy, 1943-45. Member: Nat. Research Council, 1955-61; Defence Research Bd, 1955-61; Board of Governors, Ontario Research Foundation; Board, Royal Botanical Gardens; Dir, Atomic Energy of Canada Ltd. Hon. DSc: Universities: Toronto, 1955; BC, Acadia, 1960; Laval, 1963; RMC, 1964; McGill, 1966; Queen's, 1967; Hon. LLD Sask., 1958. Medal of Chemical Inst. of Canada, 1956; Tory Medal, Royal Society of Canada, 1959. *Publications:* Chapter for Annual Review of Physical Chemistry, 1952; numerous papers in various learned journals. *Recreations:* swimming, farming. *Address:* President's House, McMaster University, Hamilton, Ontario, Canada. *T:* Ja 7-7250. *Club:* Rotary (Hamilton, Ont.).

**THODY, Prof. Philip Malcolm Waller;** Professor of French Literature, University of Leeds, since 1965; *b* Lincoln, 21 March 1928; *s* of Thomas Edwin Thody and Florence Ethel (*née* Hart); *m* 1954, Joyce Elizabeth Woodin; two *s* two *d. Educ:* Lincoln Sch.; King's Coll., Univ. of London. Temp. Asst Lectr, Univ. of Birmingham, 1954-55; Asst Lectr, subseq. Lectr, Queen's Univ. of Belfast, 1956-65. Vis. Professor: Univ. of Western Ontario, Canada, 1963-64; Berkeley Summer Sch., 1964; Harvard Summer Sch., 1968. *Publications:* Albert Camus, a study of his work, 1957; Jean-Paul Sartre, a literary and political study, 1960; Albert Camus, 1913-1960, 1961; Jean Genet, a study of his novels and plays, 1968; Jean Anouilh, 1968; Choderlos de Laclos, 1970; contribs to French Studies, Times Literary Supplement, Modern Languages Review, London Magazine, Twentieth Century, Encounter. *Recreations:* cricket, golf, talking, bridge. *Address:* 6 The Nook, Primley Park, Alwoodley, Leeds 17. *T:* Leeds 687350.

**THOM, Alexander;** Professor of Engineering Science, Oxford University, 1945-61; *b* 26 March 1894; Scottish parents; *m* 1917, Jeanie Boyd Kirkwood; one *s* one *d* (one *s* killed 1945). *Educ:* Glasgow University. BSc 1915, PhD 1926, DSc 1929, Glasgow; MA (Oxford) 1945; Emeritus Fellow, Brasenose College, 1961. Employed by various engineering and aeronautical firms, 1913-21; Lectr, Glasgow University, 1922-39; Royal Aircraft Establishment, Farnborough, on aeronautical research, 1939-45. Hon. LLD Glasgow, 1960. *Publications:* three books; papers to various scientific Institutions. *Recreation:* sailing. *Address:* The Hill, Dunlop, Ayrshire.

**THOM, Herbert James,** CIE 1943; CBE 1962; MC; MA; *b* 24 Feb. 1895; *s* of J. MacGillivray Thom; *m* 1922, Nan Mary, *d* of J. B. Clark, CBE, LLD; one *s* one *d. Educ:* Daniel Stewart's College; Edinburgh University. Served European War, 1914-19; Captain Royal Scots (MC). Indian Police, 1921-45; Principal, Police Training College; Commandant Military Police, Deputy Inspector-General CID (CIE). Transport Commissioner, United Provinces, 1945-47; Department of Health for Scotland, 1947-48; Chairman, Traffic Commn; Licensing Authority for Goods Vehicles, S Wales Traffic Area, 1948-53; South Eastern Traffic Area, 1953-65, retired. Chairman, Motor Transport Commn, Northern Rhodesia, 1951. *Address:* Hillside, Brockham Lane, Betchworth, Surrey. *T:* Betchworth 2032.

**THOM, James Robert;** Project Manager, United Nations Forest Industries Development Survey, Guyana, since 1968; *b* 22 July 1910; *er s* of late Wm and Caroline Thom; *m* 1937, Constance Daphne, *d* of late Dr A. C. L. La Frenais, British Guiana; two *s. Educ:* George Watson's Coll., Edinburgh; Edinburgh University. BSc (Forestry) Edinburgh Univ., 1932. District Officer, Forestry Commission, 1933; Divisional Officer, 1940; Conservator, 1946; Director of Forestry for Wales, 1958-63, for England, 1963-65; Dir of Research, 1965-68, Forestry Commn. *Recreations:* Rugby football (represented Scotland, 1933), golf, shooting. *Address:* Kirkton Lodge, Little Austins, Farnham, Surrey. *T:* Farnham 4976. *Club:* Caledonian.

**THOMAS, Rt. Rev. Albert;** *see* Bathurst (NSW), Bishop of, (RC).

**THOMAS, Ambler Reginald,** CMG 1951; Under-Secretary, Ministry of Overseas Development, since Oct. 1964; *b* 12 Feb. 1913; *s* of late John Frederick Ivor Thomas, OBE, MICE, MIME and of Elizabeth Thomas; *m* 1943, Diana Beresford Gresham; two *s* three *d. Educ:* Gresham's School, Holt; Corpus Christi College, Cambridge. Entered Home Civil Service as Asst Principal and apptd to Ministry of Agriculture and Fisheries, 1935; transferred to Colonial Office, 1936. Asst Private Sec. to Sec. of State for Colonies, 1938-39; Principal,

Colonial Office, 1939; Asst Sec., 1946; Chief Sec. to Govt of Aden, 1947-49; Establishment and Organization Officer, Colonial Office, 1950-52; Assistant Under-Sec. of State, Colonial Office, 1952-64. Member, Exec. Cttee, British Council, 1965-68. *Address:* Park Farm, Langhurstwood Road, Horsham, Sussex. *Club:* Oxford and Cambridge University.

**THOMAS, Brig. Arthur Frank Friend,** CIE 1942; *b* 8 Aug. 1897; *s* of Arthur Ernest Thomas, Parkhurst, South Norwood; *m* 1928, Elizabeth Stephenson Walker, MB, BCh, DPH, *d* of Rev. S. Walker, MA, Donaghadee, Co. Down; one *s*. one *d*. *Educ:* Melbourne College. ADC, EEF, 1920-21; DADOS Waziristan District, 1928-31; Staff Capt. AHQ 1931-33; DADOS, AHQ, 1933-36; AD of C, AHQ, 1936-39; DD of C 1939-40; D of C 1940; CCPM 1940-41; Deputy Controller-General of Inspection, GHQ, India, 1941-45; Director of Civil Personnel, 1945-47; retired, 1947. Served European War, 1914-21, Egypt, 1914-16, France, 1916-17, EEF 1918 (wounded, despatches); NW Frontier, India, 1930; War of 1939-45. *Recreations:* gardening, cine-photography. *Address:* Drayton House, Loxley Road, Stratford-on-Avon, Warwicks.

**THOMAS, Arthur Hermann,** MA, LLD Cantab; Hon. DLit London; FSA, FRHistSoc; CStJ; Deputy-Keeper of the Records to the Corporation of London, 1914-45; *b* Newton Heath, Lancashire, 5 April 1877; 2nd *s* of Rev. Hallowell Thomas; *m* 1902, Marie Louise Sophie (*d* 1965), *e d* of John Charles Andreae, Champion Hill, SE; one *s* three *d* (and one *s* decd, War of 1939-45). *Educ:* St Catharine's College, Cambridge (Exhibitioner); Manchester College, Oxford; University of Berlin. Sometime lecturer in ecclesiastical history in the University of Sheffield; served as a Major, Lancashire Fusiliers, 1914-17, France and Belgium (despatches twice); and in the Historical Sect. (Military Branch), Cttee of Imperial Defence, 1917-18; Pres. Brit. Archæological Assoc., 1938-45. *Publications:* A History of the Early Church: its Orders and Institutions, 1907; A History of the Great Meeting, 1908; (joint) Descriptive Catalogue of the Jackson Collection of Charters, Rolls, etc, 1913; Court and Account Rolls of Hallamshire, 1920-23; Calendar of Early Mayor's Court Rolls (1298-1307), 1924; Calendar of Plea and Memoranda Rolls (1323-1364), 1926; Calendar of P and M Rolls (1365-1381), 1929; Calendar of Select Pleas and Mem. (1381-1412), 1932; (joint) Great Chronicle of London, 1938; Calendar of P and M Rolls (1413-1437), 1943; articles on medieval history and records in historical and archæological publications. *Recreations:* walking, swimming. *Address:* 2 West Park Lane, Worthing, Sussex. *T:* Worthing 42423.

**THOMAS, Sir A. L. U.;** *see* Ungoed-Thomas.

**THOMAS, Sir Ben Bowen,** Kt 1950; Member, Commission on the Constitution, since 1969; Permanent Secretary to the Welsh Department, Ministry of Education, 1945-63; *b* Ystrad Rhondda, 1899; *o s* of late Jonathan Thomas and Ann (*née* Bowen); *m* 1st, Rhiannon Williams (*d* 1932), 3rd *d* of late Rev. I. Jones Williams, Llandderfel, Merion.; one *d*; 2nd, Gweneth (*d* 1963), *o d* of late Alderman Ellis W. Davies, Caernarvon. *Educ:* Rhondda Grammar School, Porth; University Coll. of Wales, Aberystwyth; Jesus Coll., Oxford Univ. Tutorial Class Lectr, Univ. of Wales, 1922-27; Warden Coleg Harlech, Harlech, 1927-40; Director of Extra Mural Studies, University Coll. of Wales, Aberystwyth, 1940; seconded, 1941, to Ministry of Labour and National Service as Chairman, Swansea Man Power Board; Chairman, Cardiff Man Power Board, May 1945; Member Bd of Education Cttee on Training of Teachers and Youth Leaders, 1942-44. UK Deleg. 1946-62; Member: Exec. Bd, Unesco, 1954-62 (Chm., 1958-60); ITA, 1964-70; President: London Welsh Assoc., 1953-55; Nat. Inst. of Adult Education, 1964-; University College of Wales, Aberystwyth, 1964-; Baptist Union of Wales, 1966-67; Hon. Society of Cymmrodorion, 1969-. Chm. N Wales Assoc. for the Arts, 1967-. Dep. Chm., Christian Aid, 1967-69. Hon. Fellow, Jesus College, Oxford, 1963. Hon. LLD Wales, 1965. *Publications:* An Economic History of Wales, 1941; The Old Order, 1945; Baledi Morgannwg, 1951; Drych y Baledwr, 1958; (Editor) Harlech Studies, 1938; (Editor) Lleufer y Werin, 1965; articles on historical subjects relating to Wales. *Recreations:* strolling and travel. *Address:* Wern, Bodlondeb, Bangor, N Wales. *T:* Bangor 2971. *Club:* Reform.

**THOMAS, Brian (Dick Lauder),** OBE 1961; Mural Painter and Stained Glass Designer; *b* 19 Sept. 1912; *s* of Frank Leslie Thomas, MB, BS, and Margaret Mary (*née* Lauder). *Educ:* Bradfield College. Rome Scholarship in Mural Painting, 1934; Camouflage Directorate, Min. of Home Security, 1939-45; Principal, Byam Shaw Sch. of Art, 1946-54; Master, Art Workers Guild, 1957, Editor, Artifex, 1968-; Fellow, Brit. Soc. of Master Glass Painters, 1958; Chm. of Governors, Hurstpierpoint Coll., 1958-67; Governing Body, SPCK, 1957-; Mem. Coun., Artists' Gen. Benevolent Instn, 1964-. *Principal works:* St Paul's Cathedral (stained glass in American and OBE Chapels); Westminster Abbey (stained glass); Winchester Cathedral (shrine of St Swithun); Wellington Cathedral, NZ (War Memorial windows); St George's Chapel, Windsor (panels in altar rails); St George's Church, Stevenage New Town (stained glass); memorials to Dame Nellie Melba, John Ireland, Russell Colman, Sir Harold Graham-Hodgson and others; painted ceiling at Templewood, Norfolk; murals and mosaics in many religious and secular buildings London and the provinces. *Publications:* Vision and Technique in European Painting, 1952; Geometry in Pictorial Composition, 1969. *Address:* The Studio, 3 Hill Road, NW8. *T:* 01-286 0804. *Clubs:* Arts, Athenæum.

**THOMAS, Brinley,** OBE 1955; MA, PhD; Professor of Economics, University College, Cardiff; *b* 6 Jan. 1906; *e s* of late Thomas Thomas and Anne Walters; *m* 1943, Cynthia, *d* of late Dr Charles T. Loram, New Haven, Connecticut; one *d*. *Educ:* Port Talbot County School; University College of Wales, Aberystwyth; London School of Economics. MA (Wales) (with distinction), 1928; Fellow of the University of Wales, 1929-31; Social Science Research Training Scholar, 1929-31; PhD (London), 1931; Hutchinson Silver Medal, London School of Economics, 1931; Acland Travelling Scholar in Germany and Sweden, 1932-34; Lecturer in Economics, London School of Economics, 1931-39; War Trade Department, British Embassy, Washington, 1941-42; Political Intelligence Dept of Foreign Office, 1942-45; Member: National Assistance Bd, 1948-53; Anderson Cttee on Grants to Students, 1958-60; Min. of Labour Cost of Living Advisory Cttee. Chairman: Welsh Advisory Committee of British Council; Welsh Council; Member, Exec. Committee, British Council. *Publications:* Monetary Policy and Crises, A Study of Swedish Experience, 1936; Migration and Economic Growth, A Study of Great Britain and the Atlantic Economy, 1954; (ed)

Economics of International Migration, 1958; (ed) The Welsh Economy: Studies in Expansion, 1962; International Migration and Economic Development: A Trend Report and Bibliography, 1961; articles in various journals. *Address:* 44a Church Road, Whitchurch, Glamorgan. *T:* Cardiff 62835. *Club:* Reform.

**THOMAS, Cecil,** OBE 1953; FRBS; Sculptor; *s* of J. Thomas, Engraver; *m* 1930, Dora Margaret (*d* 1967), *yr d* of late Alderman George Pearson, JP, Wigton, Cumberland; one *s*. *Educ:* London, Central School, Heatherly's, Slade. Served War of 1914-18, service in Belgium as Lt in Middlesex Regiment; Flying Officer, RAF, 1940-45; Master, Art Workers Guild, 1946; exhibited at RA, Salon, Walker Art Gallery, Washington, etc. *Principal Works:* Relief portraits of Queen Elizabeth II for overseas coinage, Coronation Medal, the embossed stamps for UK and NZ; modelled four of the reverses of new UK coinage; decimal coinage for Ghana, 1965, with portrait of Dr Nkrumah; Recumbent memorials to Archbishop Davidson in Canterbury Cathedral; Bishop Talbot in Southwark Cathedral, Alfred Forster at Exbury and Newcastle Cathedral, Australia, the Toc H Monument; and Admiral Nelson-Ward at Boxgrove Priory, Chichester; Bronze statue, New Zealand Youth, King's College, Auckland; Peter Pan and The Darling children learning to fly, Botanical Gardens, Dunedin; Peter Pan, Wanganui, New Zealand. Lord Wakefield's portrait at Tower Hill, also two groups on The Terrace representing The Sea, children playing with porpoises; The Lees, Dundonald, Montagu, Vyner, and Prebendary Boyd memorials, etc; part of heraldic decoration of Brit. pavilion, NY World's Fair, 1939; sculpture on rebuilt Church of All Hallows by the Tower, and St John of Jerusalem, Clerkenwell. *Publications:* articles and lectures on Art and Crafts. *Address:* 108 Old Brompton Rd, SW7. *T:* 01-373 5377. *Club:* Arts.

**THOMAS, Cecil James,** CMG 1950; *b* 14 June 1902; *y s* of late Thomas Thomas, Cardiff; *m* 1946, Ruth Christabel, *o d* of late A. W. Jeffree, West Kensington Court, W14. *Educ:* privately. Entered Colonial Service, 1930, and has served in Ceylon, Cyprus, Sarawak and Malaya. Member, Advisory Development Service, World Bank, 1962-64; Ministry of Overseas Development, 1965-67. *Address:* 7 Furze Croft, Hove, Sussex BN3 1PB.

**THOMAS, Sir Clement Price;** *see* Price Thomas.

**THOMAS, David Monro;** Inspector, Legal & General Assurance Society Ltd, since 1951; *b* 31 July 1915; *s* of Henry Monro and late Winifred Thomas, East Hagbourne, Berks; *m* 1948, Ursula Mary, *d* of late H. W. Liversidge; two *s* one *d*. *Educ:* St Edward's School, Oxford; St Edmund Hall, Oxford. Oxford House, 1937; Army, 1939, Major, Royal Welch Fusiliers; Head of Oxford House, 1946-48; Secretary of Greek House, 1948-51. *Address:* Watcombe Corner, Watlington, Oxon. *T:* Watlington 403.

**THOMAS, Rev. Canon Dennis Daven-;** Vicar of St Mary-de-Lode with St Nicholas, Gloucester; since 1967; Residentiary Canon of Gloucester Cathedral, since 1968 (Hon. Canon, 1961-67); Director of Ordination Training and Chief Examining Chaplain to the Bishop of Gloucester since 1957; *b* 7 April 1913; *y s* of David and Maud Thomas, Kidwelly, Carms; *m* 1939, Joan, *d* of Greig and May Simpson, Langland Bay, Swansea; one *s* one *d*. *Educ:* Christ College, Brecon; St David's College, Lampeter; Jesus College, Oxford; St Michael's College, Llandaff. Asst Curate: St Mary, Swansea, 1936-39; Oystermouth, 1939-42. Organising Secretary Waifs and Strays Soc., 1942-44; Vicar of Falfield and Rector of Rockhampton, Dio. of Gloucester, 1944-46; Chaplain, Leyhill Prison, 1945-46; Vicar of Christ Church, Gloucester, 1946-57. Chaplain, HM Prison, Gloucester, 1946-53; Rural Dean of Gloucester, 1955-57; Rural Dean of Dursley, 1962-64; Canon Missioner, 1957-60; Rector of Dursley, 1961-65; Vicar of Maisemore, 1965-67. *Address:* 38 St Mary's Square, Gloucester. *T:* Gloucester 20864.

**THOMAS, Ebenezer Rhys,** OBE 1941; DCL, MA, MSc; retired Part-time Lecturer, Physics Department, University of Newcastle upon Tyne; *s* of late D. Thomas, Aberystwyth; *m* Mary Foster (*d* 1956), *d* of Hugh Richardson, MA, Stocksfield, Northumberland; three *s*. *Educ:* Aberystwyth School and University College; Emmanuel College, Cambridge. Late Headmaster Royal Grammar School, Newcastle upon Tyne; formerly Head of Science Dept, Rugby School; did work on high explosives during the European War; later DAQMG, GHQ, BEF, France (despatches). *Publications:* papers in Journal of Chemical Society and other scientific journals; articles in Listener; School Science Review; New Scientist; Editor of Classics of Scientific Method; joint author of Newton and the Origin of Colours. *Recreations:* research on singing sands, chamber music. *Address:* Physics Department, University, Newcastle upon Tyne 1.

**THOMAS, Prof. Edgar,** CBE 1958; BSc Wales; BLitt Oxon; Professor of Agricultural Economics, University of Reading, 1945-65, Emeritus Professor since 1965 (Dean of the Faculty of Agriculture and Horticulture, 1955-59); President, Thames Valley Rent Assessment Panel, since 1966; *b* 24 July 1900; *y s* of Henry Jones Thomas, JP, Penrhos, Llanfynydd, Carmarthenshire, and Elizabeth Lewis; *m* 1927, Eurwen Parry-Williams (*d* 1951); two *d*. *Educ:* Llandeilo County Scho.; University Coll. of Wales, Aberystwyth; Wadham College, Oxford; Royal Agricultural Coll., Copenhagen. Research Assistant, Agricultural Economics Research Institute, Oxford, 1926-27; Chief Advisory Officer and Lecturer in Agricultural Economics, Reading Univ., 1927-45; Vice-President, Internat. Conference of Agricultural Economists, 1952-64; Hon. Sec., Agricultural Economics Society, 1930-52, President, 1953-54; Chairman of Curators of Museum of English Rural Life, 1954-65; Corresponding Member: Accad. Economico-Agraria dei Georgofili, Florence, 1958; Scientific Agricultural Society of Finland, 1961; a Vice-President of Hon. Society of Cymmrodorion. *Publications:* The Economics of Smallholdings, 1927; An Introduction to Agricultural Economics, 1946. Contributions to Journal of Agricultural Economics, Proceedings International Conference of Agricultural Economists and to other economic journals and Reviews. *Address:* 81 Elm Road, Earley, Reading, Berks. *T:* 81474.

**THOMAS, Emyr,** LLB, LAMTPI; General Manager, Telford New Town Development Corporation, since 1969; *b* 25 April 1920; *s* of late Brinley Thomas, MA, Aldershot; *m* 1947, Barbara J. May; one *d*. *Educ:* Aldershot County High School. Served War of 1939-45, RASC. Admitted Solicitor, 1947. Asst Solicitor, Exeter City Council, 1947-50; Sen. Asst Solicitor, Reading County Borough Council, 1950-53; Dep. Town Clerk, West

Bromwich County Borough Council, 1953-64; Sec. and Solicitor, Dawley (later Telford) Development Corp., 1964-69. *Recreation:* gardening. *Address:* 8 Kynnersley Lane, Leighton, near Shrewsbury, Salop. *T:* Cressage 332.

**THOMAS, Rt. Rev. Eryl Stephen;** *see* Monmouth, Bishop of.

**THOMAS, Frederick Maginley,** CMG 1962; retired Civil Servant; *b* 1 July 1908; 3rd *s* of Rev. Canon F. Thomas; *m* 1941, Dorothea Mary (*d* 1969), *o d* of Edward North; two *d.* *Educ:* Truro Cathedral School; Exeter College, Oxford. Cadet, Colonial Administrative Service, 1931; District Officer, Northern Rhodesia, 1933; Asst Secretary, 1949; Provincial Commissioner, 1954; Minister of Native Affairs, Northern Rhodesia Government, 1960-63; Deputy Governor, Northern Rhodesia, 1964-65. Served 1940-47; 3rd Battalion KAR; 3 Bn NRR; GSO1 Civil Affairs, Lt-Col. *Publication:* Historical Notes on the Bisa, 1953. *Recreations:* most outdoor pursuits and water colours. *Address:* Rock House, Halse, Taunton, Somerset. *T:* Bishops Lydeard 293.

**THOMAS, Sir Frederick William,** Kt 1959; Managing Director, W. C. Thomas & Sons Pty Ltd, Flour Millers, Melbourne, Australia; Councillor, City of Melbourne, 1953-65 (Lord Mayor, 1957-59); *b* 27 June 1906; *s* of F. J. Thomas; *m* 1968, Dorothy Alexa Gordon; three *s* by former marr. *Educ:* Melbourne Grammar School. Served War of 1939-45, RAAF (Air Efficiency Award, two bars); Group Captain. Comdr Order of Orange Nassau with swords (Holland), 1943. *Recreation:* golf. *Address:* 193 Domain Road, South Yarra, Victoria 3141, Australia. *Clubs:* Naval and Military, Australian (Melbourne); Barwon Heads Golf.

**THOMAS, Air Vice-Marshal Geoffrey Percy Sansom,** CB 1970; OBE 1945; Senior Air Staff Officer, Royal Air Force Maintenance Command, since 1969; *b* 24 April 1915; *s* of Reginald Ernest Sansom Thomas, New Malden; *m* 1940, Sally, *d* of Horace Biddle, Gainsborough; one *s* one *d.* *Educ:* King's College School, Wimbledon. Commissioned RAF, 1939; served India and Ceylon, 1942-45; lent to Turkish Air Force, 1950-52; Group Captain, 1958; served with RAAF, 1960-62; Air Commodore, 1965; Director of Movements, 1965; Air Vice-Marshal, 1969. *Address:* Dancy Close, Weyhill, Hants. *T:* Weyhill 541. *Club:* Royal Air Force.

**THOMAS, Rt. Hon. George;** *see* Thomas, Rt Hon. T. G.

**THOMAS, Sir George Alan,** 7th Bt, *cr* 1766; late Lieutenant 6th Battalion Hampshire Regiment; *b* 14 June 1881; *s* of 6th Bt and Edith Margaret, *d* of Morgan Hugh Foster, CB, Brickhill, Bedfordshire; *S* father, 1918. *Educ:* Wellington. British Chess Champion, 1923 and 1934; All England Badminton Champion, Singles, 1920-23, Doubles nine times. *Publication:* The Art of Badminton, 1923. *Heir:* none. *Address:* Normandie Hotel, Knightsbridge, SW7.

**THOMAS, Maj.-Gen. George Arthur,** CB 1960; CBE 1957; retired; *b* 2 May 1906; *s* of Colonel F. H. S. Thomas, CB, and Diana Thomas; *m* 1936, Diana Zaidee Browne; one *s* one *d.* *Educ:* Cheltenham College; Royal Military Academy, Woolwich. Commissioned, Royal Artillery, 1926; served in UK and Egypt; Staff College, 1940; CO 17 Field Regt, 1st Army, 1942-43; GSO1, 4 Division, 1943-44; BGS 8th Army, 1944-45; CRA 16 Airborne Div., 1947-48; Imperial Defence Coll., 1952; BGS, MELF, 1955-57; Chief of Staff, HQ Northern Command, 1958-60; Chief of Staff, GHQ Far ELF, 1960-62. Retired, 1962. *Recreations:* games and sports of all kinds. *Address:* Cherrywell, Salisbury Road, Andover, Hants. *T:* Andover 2120. *Clubs:* Army and Navy; MCC.

**THOMAS, Gilbert Oliver;** author and journalist; *b* 1891; *s* of late J. Oliver Thomas, Leicester; *m* 1928, Dorothy Kathleen, *y d* of late Robert Dann, Hythe, Kent; one *s* one *d.* *Educ:* Wyggeston School, Leicester; Leys, Cambridge. Editorial Staff, Chapman & Hall, 1910-14; Editor, The Venturer, 1919-21. *Publications:* Birds of Passage (Poems), 1912; The Wayside Altar (Poems), 1913; The Voice of Peace, and other Poems, 1914; The Grapes and the Thorns: Thoughts in War Time, 1915; The Further Goal and other Poems, 1915; Towards the Dawn, and other Poems, 1918; Things Big and Little (Essays), 1919; Poems: 1912-1919, 1920; Sparks from the Fire (Essays), 1923; Mary of Huntingdon and other Poems, 1928; Calm Weather (Essays), 1930; John Masefield (Modern Writers Series), 1932; The Master Light; Letters to David, 1932; William Cowper and the Eighteenth Century, 1935, revised edition, 1949; The Inner Shrine: anthology of the author's devotional poems, 1943; Builders and Makers (literary essays), 1944; Times May Change (essays), 1946. Autobiography: 1891-1941, 1946; Paddington to Seagood: The Story of a Model Railway, 1947; Selected Poems Old and New, 1951; Window in the West (Essays), 1954; Later Poems, 1960; Double Headed: Two Generations of Railway Enthusiasm (in collaboration with David St John Thomas), 1963; One Man Speaks (Text of broadcast poem), 1967; Collected Poems, 1969; contributor, Observer, Sunday Times, Spectator, and many others. For some years wrote regular weekly book feature for Birmingham Post. *Recreations:* music, model railways. *Address:* Woodthorpe, Clampit Lane, Ipplepen, Devon.

**THOMAS, Sir (Godfrey) Michael (David),** 11th Bt, *cr* 1694; Member of Stock Exchange, London, since 1959; *b* 10 Oct. 1925; *o s* of Rt Hon. Sir Godfrey Thomas, PC, GCVO, KCB, CSI, 10th Bt, and Diana, *d* of late Ven. B. G. Hoskyns; *S* father 1968; *m* 1956, Margaret Greta Cleland, *yr d* of John Cleland, Stormont Court, Godden Green, Kent; one *s* two *d,* of whom one *s* one *d* are twins. *Educ:* Harrow. The Rifle Brigade, 1944-56. *Heir:* *s* David John Godfrey Thomas, *b* 11 June 1961. *Address:* 2 Napier Avenue, SW6. *T:* 01-736 6896. *Clubs:* MCC, Hurlingham.

**THOMAS, General Sir (Gwilym) Ivor,** GCB 1952 (KCB 1950; CB 1944); KBE 1947; DSO 1917; MC; psc; ns; late RA; *b* 1893; *s* of late John Thomas (Pencerdd Gwalia), Harpist to Queen Victoria and King Edward VII, and late Joan Francis, *y d* of William Denny, Tralee, Co. Kerry; *m* 1949, Elliott Ellen, *o d* of late Major van Kriekenbeek, 128th Pioneers, and late Mrs H. S. Wilding. *Educ:* Cheltenham College; Royal Military Academy, Woolwich. Commissioned, 1912; served European War, 1914-18 (DSO, MC and bar, despatches); Bt Major, 1929; Major, 1931; Bt Lt-Col, 1933; Col, 1936; Brigadier, 1939; Maj.-Gen., 1942; Acting Lt-Gen., 1945; Lt-Gen., 1946; Gen., 1949; commanded 43rd Div. in campaign in NW Europe, 1944-45 (despatches); Commander, 1st Corps District, BAOR, 1945-47; Administrator of Polish Forces under British Command, 1947; GOC-in-C Anti-Aircraft Command, 1948-50; Quarter-Master-

General to the Forces, 1950-52. Col Comdt RA, 1947-57. Officier Légion d'Honneur, 1945; Knight Grand Officer of the Order of Orange Nassau with swords, 1946; Comdr Order of Leopold with Palm, 1950; Croix de Guerre avec palme (France), 1945; Croix de Guerre avec palme (Belgium), 1950. *Recreations:* hunting, polo. *Address:* c/o Lloyds Bank, Ltd, 6 Pall Mall, SW1. *Club:* Army and Navy.

**THOMAS, Gwyn;** author; *b* 6 July 1913; *s* of Walter and Ziphorah Thomas; *m* 1938, Eiluned Thomas. *Educ:* Porth Grammar Sch.; St Edmund Hall, Oxford Univ.; Madrid Univ. BA Hons Oxon, 1934. Univ. Extension Lectr, 1934-40; Schoolmaster (Mod. Langs), 1940-62. Television appearances, 1962-. *Publications: novels:* The Dark Philosophers, 1946; Where Did I Put My Pity, 1946; The Alone To The Alone, 1947; All Things Betray Thee, 1949; The World Cannot Hear You, 1951; Now Lead Us Home, 1952; A Frost On My Frolic, 1953; The Stranger At My Side, 1954; Point Of Order, 1956; Gazooka, 1957; The Love Man, 1958; Ring Delirium 123, 1959; A Welsh Eye, 1964; A Hatful of Humours, 1965; Leaves In The Wind, 1968; *plays:* The Keep, 1961; Loud Organs, 1962; Jackie the Jumper, 1962; *autobiog.:* A Few Selected Exits, 1968. *Recreations:* opera, staring. *Address:* Cherry Trees, Wyndham Park, Peterston-super-Ely, Cardiff. *T:* Peterston-super-Ely 435. *Club:* Pontcanna Studio (Cardiff).

**THOMAS, Gwyn Edward Ward;** *see* Ward Thomas.

**THOMAS, Herbert Percival,** CIE 1933; BSc, *b* 12 Dec. 1879; *s* of John Caldwell Thomas, MD, etc, and Annie M. Calder; *m* 1907, Elsie Geard, *d* of Thos Harbottle Guenett; two *s* one *d*; *m* 1949, Esther Amelia (*d* 1956), *d* of late Alfred David Price, Melbourne. *Educ:* Melbourne Church of England Grammar School; Melbourne University; McGill University, Montreal. Erection Engineer, Allis Chalmers, Bullock, 1907; Electrical Engineer, Town of Kenora, Ontario, 1908; Manager, Public Utilities City of Nelson, British Columbia, 1912; Coates and Co., Melbourne, Australia 1920; Chief Engineer, Southland Electric Power Board, New Zealand, 1921; Superintending Engineer, Punjab PWD Hydro Electric Branch, 1926; Chief Engineer, Punjab Public Works Department Electricity Branch, 1932-39; retired, 1939. Mobilised 1942 in RANVR as Squadron Skipper Naval Auxiliary Patrol, equivalent rank Lieut RANVR; Staff Officer Coastal Craft, Jan.-July 1945; then Lieut RANVR to HMAS Moreton (additional); demobilised, 1946. *Recreations:* golf, tennis, fishing. *Address:* Rakiura, PO Box 34, Mansfield, Victoria, Australia.

**THOMAS, Howard,** CBE 1967; Managing Director, Thames Television Ltd since 1968 (of ABC Television, 1955-68); *b* 5 March 1909; *s* of W. G. Thomas and A. M. Thomas; *m* 1934, Hilda, *d* of Harrison Fogg; two *d.* Trained in advertising, journalism and broadcasting. Started Commercial Radio Department, London Press Exchange Ltd, 1938. Writer and Producer for BBC Sound Radio and during 3 years directed and produced 500 programmes. Entered film industry as Producer-in-Chief, Associated British Pathé Ltd, 1944. Director: Associated British Picture Corp. Ltd; Associated British Productions Ltd; Independent Television News Ltd; Independent Television Companies Association; Literators Ltd. Chm., Independent Television Network Programme Cttee, 1969-; Mem., Advertising Standards Authority Ltd. Radio Programmes: Showmen of England, Beauty Queen, The Brains Trust, Shipmates Ashore, etc. Films: Elizabeth is Queen (Coronation) and many documentaries. *Publications:* How to Write for Broadcasting, 1936; The Blackout Book, 1939; Britain's Brains Trust, 1941; The Truth About Television, 1962. *Address:* Thames Television House, Euston Road, NW1. *T:* 01-387 9494; 6 Eaton Place, SW1; Laburnum Cottage, Pheasants Hill, Hambleden, Bucks. *Clubs:* Lord's Taverners, Variety, Hurlingham.

**THOMAS, Hugh Swynnerton;** Writer; Professor of History, University of Reading, since 1966; *b* 21 Oct. 1931; *s* of Hugh Whitelegge Thomas, CMG, Colonial Service, Gold Coast (Ghana) and Margery Swynnerton; *m* 1962, Vanessa Jebb, *d* of 1st Baron Gladwyn, *qv*; two *s* one *d*. *Educ:* Sherborne; Queens' Coll., Cambridge (Scholar); Sorbonne, Paris. Pres. Cambridge Union, 1953. Foreign Office, 1954-57; Sec. to UK delegn to UN Disarmament Sub-Cttee, 1955-56; Lectr at RMA Sandhurst, 1957; prospective parly candidate (Lab) Ruislip-Northwood, 1957-58; worked for UNA, 1960-61, as Dir of its Disarmament Campaign. Somerset Maugham Prize, 1962. *Publications:* The World's Game, 1957; The Oxygen Age, 1958; (ed) The Establishment, 1959; The Spanish Civil War, 1961; The Story of Sandhurst, 1961; The Suez Affair, 1967; (ed) Crisis in the Civil Service, 1968; Cuba, or the Pursuit of Freedom, 1971. *Address:* 29 Ladbroke Grove, W11. *T:* 01-727 2288. *Clubs:* Reform, Beefsteak.

**THOMAS, Gen. Sir Ivor;** *see* Thomas, General Sir G. I.

**THOMAS, Ivor B.;** *see* Bulmer-Thomas.

**THOMAS, Ivor Owen;** Retired; *b* 5 Dec. 1898; *s* of late Benjamin L. and Margaret Thomas, Briton Ferry, Glamorgan; *m* 1929, Beatrice, *d* of late Councillor William Davis, Battersea; one *d. Educ:* Vernon Place Council Sch., Briton Ferry; London Labour College, 1923-25. Gwalia Tinplate Works, Briton Ferry, 1912-19; Engine Cleaner GWR, Pontypool Rd, 1919-23; NUR Head Office Staff, 1925-45. Member Battersea Borough Council, 1928-45; Chm. Housing Cttee, 1934-38. MP (Lab) the Wrekin Division of Shropshire, 1945-55. Resumed NUR Head Office Staff, 1955-58. Waterloo CCE Dept British Rlys, Southern Region, 1960-64; Westminster City Council, Land Use Survey, 1965-66. *Address:* Marobea, 26 Sumburgh Road, SW12. *T:* 01-228 2874.

**THOMAS, Sir (James William) Tudor,** Kt 1956; DSc, MD, MS, FRCS; Hon. LLD Glasgow; Hon. Ophthalmic Surgeon, United Cardiff Hospitals and Welsh Regional Hospital Board; *b* 23 May 1893; *s* of late Thomas Thomas, Ystradgynlais, Breconshire, and late Mary Thomas; *m* 1938, Bronwen Vaughan Pugh, Cardiff; two *s. Educ:* Cardiff Medical School (Alfred Sheen Prize); Middlesex Hospital (Leopold Hudson Prize). BSc Wales 1913; LRCP, MRCS 1915; MB, BCh Wales 1916; MD Wales 1929; DSc Wales 1931; MB, BS London 1916; MS London 1929; FRCS 1925. Captain RAMC (SR), 1914-18 War. Hunterian Prof. RCS, 1930-31. Assoc. Surg. i/c Corneo-plastic Dept, Central London Ophth. Hosp., 1935-40; Ophthalmic Surgeon, Cardiff Royal Infirmary, and United Cardiff Hospitals, 1921-58 and Corneo-plastic Surgeon to 1960. Member: Ophthalmological Society of UK (President, 1966-68); Master, Oxford Ophthalmological Congress, 1956-58; Vice-President, British Medical Association (President, 1953-54). President Cardiff Med. Soc., 1948-49. Hon. Pres. British Medical Students' Assoc., 1957-58. Montgomery

Lectr, TCD, 1936; Middlemore Lectr, Birmingham and Midland Eye Hosp., 1933; Doyne Memorial Lectr Oxford Ophthalmological Congress, 1955. Sheriff of Breconshire, 1956. FRSocMed. Gold Medal in Therapeutics, Worshipful Society of Apothecaries of London, 1960. *Publications:* Contrib. on Corneal Transplantation experimental and clinical, 1930-, in BMJ, Lancet, Trans Ophthalmological Soc. UK, Proc. Roy. Soc. Med., Proc. Oxford Ophthalmological Congress, etc. *Recreations:* golf and fishing. *Address:* Clifton Lodge, 16 Cathedral Road, Cardiff. *T:* Cardiff 28679. *Clubs:* Cardiff and County; Royal Porthcawl Golf.

**THOMAS, Jeffrey;** MP (Lab) Abertillery since 1970; *b* 12 Nov. 1933; *s* of John James Thomas and Phyllis Thomas (*née* Hile); *m* 1960, Margaret Jenkins, BSc(Econ). *Educ:* Abertillery Grammar Sch.; King's Coll. London; Gray's Inn. Called to the Bar, Gray's Inn, 1957. Pres., Univ. of London Union, 1955-56. Served Army (National Service): commnd in Royal Corps of Transport, 1959 (Senior Under Officer); later served in Directorate of Army Legal Services: Major, Dep. Asst Dir, HQ BAOR 1961. Contested (Lab) Barry, 1966. Member Court of Governors: University Coll. of Wales, Aberystwyth; Nat. Museum of Wales (ex officio); Nat. Library of Wales; Vice President: Western Valley Sewerage Board; North Monmouthshire Youth Rugby Union. *Recreations:* watching Rugby football, travelling. *Address:* (home) 60 Lamont Road, SW10. *T:* 01-351 1303; (chambers) 2 Pump Court, Temple, EC4. *T:* 01-583 8682. *Clubs:* Reform; Abertillery Rugby Football.

**THOMAS, Rt. Rev. John James Absalom;** *see* Swansea and Brecon, Bishop of.

**THOMAS, Lt-Gen. Sir (John) Noel,** KCB 1969 (CB 1967); DSO 1945; MC 1945; BEng; *b* 28 Feb. 1915; *s* of John Ernest Thomas; *m* 1946, Jill, *d* of Edward Gordon Cuthbert Quilter; two *s*. *Educ:* Royal Grammar School, Newcastle upon Tyne; Liverpool University. 2nd Lieut, Royal Engineers, 1936. Served War of 1939-45 (MC, DSO). Imperial Defence College, 1963; General Officer Commanding 42 (Lancashire and Cheshire) Div. (TA), North West District, 1963-65; Director, Combat Development (Army), MoD, 1965-68; Dep. Chief of Defence Staff (Operational Requirements), MoD, 1968-70. Lt-Gen. 1968. Hon. Col, Liverpool Univ. Contingent, OTC, 1965-. Colonel Commandant: Royal Pioneer Corps, 1968-; Royal Engineers, 1968-. *Address:* Little Portobello, Brenchley, Kent. *Clubs:* Royal Ocean Racing, United Hunts.

**THOMAS, Rev. Canon John Roland Lloyd;** Principal of St David's College, Lampeter, since Oct. 1953; Canon of St David's, 1956; Chancellor, 1963; *b* 22 Feb. 1908; 2nd *s* of late John Thomas, ME, and Mrs Ann Thomas; *m* 1949, Mrs Elizabeth Swaffield (*née* Rees); three *d*. *Educ:* King's Coll., Taunton; St David's Coll., Lampeter; Jesus College, Oxford. Welsh Church Scholar, St David's College, Lampeter, BA (1st Class Hons History), 1930, Senior Scholar, 1929-30; Meyricke Graduate Scholar, 1930-32, Jesus Coll., Oxford, BA (2nd Class Th. Hons), 1932; MA 1936. Deacon, 1932; priest, 1933; Curate of St John Baptist, Cardiff, 1932-40. CF (EC) 1940-44. Rector of Canton, Cardiff, 1944-49; Vicar of St Mark's, Newport, 1949-52; Dean of Monmouth and Vicar of St Woolos Parish, Newport, 1952-53. OCF, 1949-52; SCF (TA), 1950-52; Hon. CF 1952. *Recreation:* fishing. *Address:* St David's University College, Lampeter, Cards. *T:* Lampeter 335. *Club:* Athenæum.

**THOMAS, Prof. Joseph Anthony Charles;** Professor of Roman Law in the University of London, since 1964; *b* 24 Feb. 1923; *e c* of Joseph and Merle Thomas, Bridgend, Glam; *m* 1949, Margaret (marr. diss. 1970), *d* of John and Jean Hookham, Cambridge; three *s* one *d*. *Educ:* County Grammar School, Bridgend; Trinity College, Cambridge. MA, LLB Cantab 1949; Barrister, Gray's Inn, 1950. Lecturer in Law, Nottingham Univ., 1949-54; Sen. Lecturer, Univ. of Glasgow, 1954-57; Douglas Professor of Civil Law, University of Glasgow, 1957-64. Served with Intelligence Corps, Psychological Warfare Branch, and Allied Commission, Austria, 1942-46. *Publications:* Private International Law, 1955; (with J. C. Smith) A Casebook on Contract, 1957 (4th edn 1969); articles in legal periodicals. *Recreations:* walking, reading. *Address:* University College, Gower Street, WC1. *T:* 01-387 7050; 1 Hornton Street, W8. *T:* 01-937 1688.

**THOMAS, Maj.-Gen. Lechmere Cay,** CB 1948; CBE 1945 (OBE 1939); DSO 1940 and Bar 1942; MC and Bar 1917; Hon. Major-General, retired; late Royal Northumberland Fusiliers; *b* 20 Oct. 1897; *s* of late Kempson Thomas, Farnham, Surrey; *m* 1st, 1929, Kathleen Primrose (*d* 1929), 2nd *d* of late Albert White, JP, Birney Hill, Ponteland, Northumberland; 2nd, 1951, Sylvia E, *widow* of Eric Smith, Colonial Service, and *d* of late Newman Hall, Forest Hill, Jersey, CI. *Educ:* Cranleigh School, Surrey. Served European War, 1914-18, in France and Belgium (wounded, MC and Bar, two medals); Iraq, 1920 (wounded); commanded 2nd Battalion King's African Rifles, 1934-39; served War of 1939-45, in France, Malaya and Burma (despatches, DSO, and Bar, CBE); Commander: 9th Bn R Northumberland Fusiliers, 1940-42; 1st Bn, Wilts Regt, 1942; 88th Indian Inf. Bde, 1942-43; 36th Indian Inf. Bde, 1943-45; Inspector General, Burma Army, 1945-47; GOC Burma Army, 1947-48. *Address:* Forest Hill, Beaumont, Jersey, CI. *Club:* Army and Navy.

**THOMAS, Sir Leslie (Montagu),** Kt 1963; MBE 1945; TD; *b* 24 April 1906; *s* of late Rt Hon. J. H. Thomas, PC; *m* 1929, Ursula Mary, *d* of late H. B. Owen; two *s* one *d*. *Educ:* elementary, private and Dulwich College. Great Western Railway, 1923-29; Member London Stock Exchange, 1931-. Served War of 1939-45, North Africa and Italy; demobilised with rank of Major. Member: Caterham and Warlingham UDC, 1932-35; Whitstable UDC, 1950-52. Contested (Nat Lab), Leek, Staffs, 1935. MP (C) Canterbury Div. of Kent, 1953-66, retd. *Recreations:* golf, gardening. *Address:* Dene Park, Tonbridge, Kent. *Club:* Carlton.

**THOMAS, (Lewis John) Wynford V.;** *see* Vaughan-Thomas.

**THOMAS, Lowell;** Author, Producer, Radio Commentator; *b* 6 April 1892; *s* of Colonel Harry G. Thomas, MD, and Harriet Wagner; *m* 1917, Frances Ryan; one *s*. *Educ:* University of Northern Indiana (BSc); Univ. of Denver (BA, MA); Princeton Univ. (MA). Reporter Chicago Journal until 1914; Professor of Oratory, Chicago Kent College of Law, 1912-14; Instructor Dept of English, Princeton, 1914-16; Chief of Civilian Mission for historical record of First World War (Palestine Campaign and Arabian revolution). Associate-Editor, Asia Magazine, 1919-23. Studied international aviation (25,000 mile flight over 21 countries), 1926-27. Made many war broadcasts from European and Far

Eastern war points; Tibetan Expedition, 1949. Brought out Cinerama for the first time 1952; producer of This Is Cinerama, The Seven Wonders of The World, and Search for Paradise. In 1957, 1958, 1959; organised many TV expedns and prod. TV programmes in remote parts of the World. FAGS, FRGS. Member English-Speaking Union (hon. life), Life member, American Museum of Natural History. Fraternities: Kappa Sigma; Tau Kappa Alpha; Phi Delta Phi; Sigma Delta Chi; Alpha Epsilon. Mason. *Publications:* With Lawrence in Arabia, 1924; The First World Flight, 1925; Beyond Khyber Pass, 1925; Count Luckner, The Sea Devil, 1927; European Skyways, 1927; Raiders of the Deep, 1928; Adventures in Afghanistan for Boys, 1928; Woodfill of the Regulars, 1929; The Sea Devil's Fo'c's'le, 1929; The Hero of Vincennes, 1929; India, Land of the Black Pagoda, 1930; Wreck of the Dumaru, 1930; Lauterback of the China Sea, 1930; Rolling Stone, 1931; Tall Stories, 1931; Kabluk of the Eskimo, 1932; This side of Hell, 1932; Old Gimlet Eye, 1933; The Untold Story of Exploration, 1935; Adventures Among Immortals, 1937; Pageant of Adventure, 1940; Pageant of Life, 1941; Pageant of Romance, 1943; These Men Shall Never Die, 1943; Back to Mandalay, 1951; Great True Adventures, 1955; The Seven Wonders of the World, 1957; History as You Heard It, 1958; The Vital Spark, 1959; Sir Hubert Wilkins: His World of Adventure, 1961; More Great True Adventures, 1963; Book of the High Mountains, 1964. *Recreations:* ski-ing, riding, golf. *Address:* Hammersley Hill, Pawling, NY, USA; (office) 24E 51st Street, New York City. *Clubs:* Royal and Ancient (St Andrews); Princeton, Explorers, Dutch Treat, Overseas Press (New York); Bohemian (San Francisco); Pine Valley Golf (New Jersey); Assoc. of Radio and TV News Analysts; Marco Polo.

**THOMAS, Sir Lynn U.;** *see* Ungoed-Thomas.

**THOMAS, Margaret,** RBA 1947; FRSA 1951; NEAC 1950; Women's International Art Club, 1940; Contemporary Portrait Society, 1970; Practising Artist (Painter); *b* 26 Sept. 1916; *d* of Francis Stewart Thomas and Grace Whetherly. *Educ:* privately; Slade Sch.; RA Schools. Slade Scholar, 1936. Hon. Sec. Artists International Assoc., 1944-45; Group exhibitions, Wildensteins, 1946, 1949 and 1962; First one-man show at Leicester Galls, 1949, and subsequently at same gallery, 1950; one-man shows in Edinburgh (Aitken Dotts), 1952, 1955, 1966, and at Outlook Tower, Edinburgh, during Internat. Fest., 1961; RBA Galleries, London, 1953; at Canaletto Gall. (a barge, at Little Venice), 1961; Exhibition of Women Artists, Wakefield Art Gall., 1961; Howard Roberts Gallery Cardiff, 1963, The Minories, Colchester, 1964 and Queen's University, Belfast, 1967. Regular exhibitor Royal Academy and Royal Scottish Academy. Official purchases: Prince Philip, Duke of Edinburgh; Arts Council; Exeter College, Oxford; Min. of Education; Min. of Works; Wakefield, Hull, Paisley and Carlisle Art Galleries; Edinburgh City Corporation; Nuffield Foundation Trust; Steel Co. of Wales; Financial Times; GLC and county education authorities in Yorks, Bucks, Monmouth, Derbyshire, Hampshire and Wales. Coronation painting purchased by Min. of Works for British Embassy in Santiago. *Publications:* work reproduced in: Daily Telegraph, News Chronicle, Listener, Studio, Scottish Field, Music and Musicians, The Lady, Arts Review. *Recreations:* antique collecting, gardening, vintage cars. *Address:* Halfway Cottage, 11a North Road, Highgate Village, N6. *T:* 01-340 2527; 8 North Bank Street, Edinburgh 1. *T:* 031-225 3343.

**THOMAS, Meirion,** FRS 1949; MA, FRSE; Professor of Botany, King's College, Newcastle upon Tyne, 1946-60; Professor Emeritus since 1961; *b* 28 Dec. 1894; *s* of late J. Thomas, V.-P. Normal Coll., Bangor. *Educ:* Friars' School; University College of North Wales; Trinity Hall, Cambridge. 2nd Lt South Wales Borderers, 1914-15; served with Special Companies, Royal Engineers in France, 1915-19; demobilised with rank of Capt.; at Cambridge, 1919-24; subsequently at what is now called The University of Newcastle upon Tyne, as Lecturer in Botany (1924-43), Reader in Plant Physiology (1943-46). Service with Durham University Senior Training Corps, 1940-45, and Home Guard, 1941-45. President, Section K, British Association, Belfast, 1952. Vice-President RSE, 1955-58. Hon. DSc Wales, 1964. Charles Reid Barnes Hon. Life Mem. of Amer. Soc. of Plant Physiologists, 1963. *Publications:* Textbook: Plant Physiology, 4th edn (with Ranson and Richardson), 1956; several papers on Plant Physiology. *Recreations:* formerly association football (blue, 1922), cricket (elected to Crusaders Club, 1923), now golf. *Address:* Glannant, Bryn Crug, Towyn, Merioneth.

**THOMAS, Melbourne,** QPM 1953; Chief Constable, South Wales Constabulary, since 1969; *b* 1 May 1906; *s* of David and Charlotte Frances Thomas; *m* 1930, Marjorie Elizabeth Phillips; one *d. Educ:* Newport (St Julian's) High School. Metropolitan Police, 1928-29; Newport Borough Police, 1929-45 (Dep. Chief Constable, 1941-45); Chief Constable: Merthyr Borough Police, 1945-63; Glamorgan Constabulary, 1963-69. CStJ 1958. *Recreations:* Rugby, cricket, athletics. *Address:* The Old Malthouse, Llantwit Major, Glam. *T:* Llantwit Major 153.

**THOMAS, Air Vice-Marshal Meredith,** CSI 1946; CBE 1941; DFC 1922; AFC; Royal Air Force, retired; *b* 1892. Served European War, 1914-19; Flying Officer, RFC, 1917; Group Captain, 1938; SASO, No. 5 Grp, 1938; Dir of Techn. Trg, Air Min., 1940; Air Cdre, 1943; AOC, India, 1944-46; retired, 1946. *Address:* c/o Ministry of Defence (Air), Whitehall, SW1.

**THOMAS, Sir Michael,** 3rd Bt; *see* Thomas, Sir W. M. M.

**THOMAS, Sir Michael,** 11th Bt; *see* Thomas, Sir G. M. D.

**THOMAS, Sir Miles;** *see* Thomas, Sir W. M. W.

**THOMAS, Sir Noel;** *see* Thomas, Sir J. N.

**THOMAS, Rt. Hon. Peter John Mitchell,** PC 1964; QC 1965; MP (C) Hendon South, since 1970; Secretary of State for Wales, since 1970; Barrister at Law; JP; *b* 31 July 1920; *o s* of late David Thomas, Solicitor, Llanrwst, Denbighshire, and Anne Gwendoline Mitchell; *m* 1947, Frances Elizabeth Tessa, *o d* of Basil Dean, CBE and Lady Mercy Greville; two *s* two *d. Educ:* Epworth College, Rhyl; Jesus College, Oxford (MA). Served War of 1939-45, in RAF; Prisoner of War (Germany), 1941-45. Called to Bar, 1947, Middle Temple; Member of Wales and Chester Circuit. MP (C) Conway Div. of Caernarvonshire, 1951-66; Parliamentary Private Secretary to the Solicitor-General, 1954-59; Parliamentary Secretary, Ministry of Labour, 1959-61; Parliamentary Under-Secretary of State, Foreign Office, 1961-63; Minister of State for Foreign Affairs, 1963-64. Dep. Chairman:

Cheshire QS, 1966-70; Denbighshire QS, 1968-70. Member, Historic Buildings Council for Wales, 1965-. JP 1966. *Address:* 145 Kennington Road, SE11. *T:* 01-735 6047; Bath, Llanbedr-y-Cennin, Conway. *T:* Tynygroes 376. *Club:* Carlton.

**THOMAS, Ralph Philip,** MC 1942; Film Director; *b* Hull, Yorks, 10 Aug. 1915; *m* 1944, Joy Spanjer; one *s* one *d. Educ:* Tellisford School, Clifton. Entered film industry, 1932, and worked in all production depts, particularly editing, until 1939. Served War of 1939-45, as Regimental Officer 9th Lancers until 1944; thereafter Instructor Royal Military College. Returned to Film Industry, in Rank Organisation Trailer Dept, 1946; Joined Gainsborough Pictures, 1948, and directed Once Upon a Dream, Traveller's Joy. Films directed at Pinewood Studios: The Clouded Yellow, Appointment with Venus, The Venetian Bird, A Day to Remember, Doctor in the House, Mad About Men, Above Us The Waves, Doctor at Sea, The Iron Petticoat, Checkpoint, Doctor at Large, Campbell's Kingdom, A Tale of Two Cities, The Wind Cannot Read, The 39 Steps, Upstairs and Downstairs, Conspiracy of Hearts, Doctor in Love, No My Darling Daughter, No Love for Johnnie, The Wild and the Willing, Doctor in Distress, Hot enough for June, The High Bright Sun, Doctor in Clover, Deadlier than the Male, Nobody Runs Forever, Some Girls Do. *Address:* Boundary House, Beaconsfield, Bucks. *Clubs:* Cavalry, Royal Automobile.

**THOMAS, Lt-Col Sir Reginald Aneurin,** Kt 1946; CBE 1919; late RA; Chief Inspector of Explosives, Home Office, 1931-45; *b* 1879; *s* of A. H. Thomas, Gampola, Ceylon; *m* 1st, 1910, Violet Mary (*d* 1910), *d* of H. Anderson; 2nd, 1918 Kathleen Mary, *d* of late G. C. Bliss, Glen Lyon, Ceylon; three *s* one *d. Educ:* Cheltenham College; RMA Woolwich. Served S Africa, 1900-2 (Queen's medal with three clasps, King's medal with two clasps); European War, 1914-19 (despatches, CBE). *Address:* 14 Quarry High Street, Headington, Oxford. *T:* Oxford 63358.

**THOMAS, Lt-Col Reginald Silvers W.;** *see* Williams-Thomas.

**THOMAS, Richard,** MA London; MA, DSc Wales; Principal, Normal College, Bangor, 1935-58; Member: Education Committee, Caernarvonshire (Chairman); University of Wales Council, Court of Governors and Council of Music; Council and Court of Governors, University College, Aberystwyth, and University of Wales Institute of Science and Technology; Welsh Joint Education Committee; Vice-President, University College, Bangor; *b* Trefeglwys, Montgomeryshire, 1890; *s* of John Thomas; *m* 1919, Margaret (*d* 1963), *d* of David Edwards, Aberystwyth; *m* 1969, Sarah, *d* of John S. Duffy, Liverpool. *Educ:* University College of Wales, Aberystwyth. Assistant Master under London County Council Education Committee, 1913; Served in the Royal Artillery, Balkan Expeditionary Force 1915-19; Lecturer in Education, University College of Wales, Aberystwyth, 1919; Lecturer in English, 1922; Lectr in Education, University College of South Wales and Monmouthshire, Cardiff, 1923; Master of Method, 1933; Member: Exec. Cttee, Central Welsh Bd, 1936-49; Min. of Education Interim Cttee for Teachers, 1946-48; Welsh Joint Education Cttee, 1949-55; National Advisory Committee on Art Examinations, 1952-55; Univ. of Wales Board for Training Colleges and Education Board, 1935-58. *Publications:* Articles in Educational Journals. *Recreations:* golf, gardening. *Address:* 22 Kings Road, Colwyn Bay, North Wales.

**THOMAS, Robert Antony C.;** *see* Clinton-Thomas.

**THOMAS, Sir Robert (Evan),** Kt 1967; JP, DL; Trade Union Official, 1937-66, retired; *b* 8 Oct. 1901; *s* of Jesse and Anne Thomas; *m* 1924, Edna Isherwood; one *s* one *d. Educ:* St Peter's, Leigh, Lancs. Miner, 1914; served Army, 1919-21; Bus Driver, 1924-37; Member, Manchester City Council, 1944-; Lord Mayor of Manchester, 1962-63. JP Manchester, 1948; DL County Palatine of Lancaster, 1967. *Recreation:* dancing. *Address:* 29 Milwain Road, Manchester M19 2PX. *T:* 061-224 5778.

**THOMAS, Ronald Hamilton Eliot,** OBE 1946; Member National Coal Board 1955-60, retired (Chairman, Opencast Executive, 1957-60); *b* 12 June 1896; 2nd *s* of William Eliot and Emily Thomas, Torquay, Devon; *m* 1920, Ethel Mary Green; two *d. Educ:* St Winifred's School, Torquay. Founder of firm of Milner, Thomas & Co. Ltd, London, Coal Distributors, 1921; Deputy Director-General of Marketing, National Coal Board, 1947. *Recreation:* golf. *Address:* Belliver, 39 The Downs, Wimbledon, SW20. *T:* 01-946 1857. *Club:* Royal Wimbledon Golf.

**THOMAS, Rev. Ronald Stuart;** poet; Vicar of St Hywyn, Aberdaron, with St Mary, Bodferin, since 1967; *Educ:* University of Wales (BA); St Michael's College, Llandaff. Ordained deacon, 1936; priest, 1937. Curate of Chirk, 1936-40; curate of Hanmer, in charge of Talarn Green, 1940-42; Rector of Manafon, 1942-54; Vicar of Eglwysfach, 1954-67. *Publications:* poems: Stones of the Field (privately printed), 1947; Song at the Year's Turning, 1955 (Heinemann Award of the Royal Society of Literature, 1956); Poetry for Supper, 1958; Tares, 1961; Bread of Truth, 1963; Pieta, 1966; Not That He Brought Flowers, 1968; edited: A Book of Country Verse, 1961; George Herbert, A Choice of Verse, 1967. *Address:* Aberdaron Vicarage, Pwllheli, Caernarvonshire.

**THOMAS, Stephen Peter John Quao; Hon. Mr Justice Thomas;** Chief Justice of the High Court, Mid-Western Region, Nigeria, since 1964; *b* 31 March 1904; *e s* of late Peter John Claudius Thomas, Freetown, Sierra Leone, and Lagos, Nigeria; *m* 1940, Margaret Amelia, *o d* of I. K. Roberts, Barrister-at-Law; one *s* four *d. Educ:* King's College, Lagos; London School of Economics and Political Science, Univ. of London. Master, King's College, Lagos, 1925-26; Mercantile Asst, 1926-29; called to Bar, Middle Temple, 1933; Sierra Leone Bar, 1935; Nigeria Bar, 1935; Magistrate, Grade I, 1941; Acting Puisne Judge, Supreme Court, 1951; Chief Magistrate, 1951; Puisne Judge, 1953-55; Judge, High Court, Western Region, 1955-63. Coronation Medal, 1953. *Recreations:* gardening, walking. *Address:* 52 Wembley Park Drive, Wembley, Middlesex. *T:* 01-902 6965. *Club:* Royal Commonwealth Society.

**THOMAS, Terry;** *see* Terry-Thomas.

**THOMAS, Terry,** MA, LLB Cantab, BSc London and Wales, PhD London; Headmaster, Leeds Grammar School, 1923-53; *b* 19 Oct. 1888; *e s* of late David Terry Thomas, Cardiff; *m* 1915, Mair, *e d* of late Major Henry Davies, OBE, CC, Cardiff; two *d. Educ:* Howard Gardens; University College, Cardiff (Isaac Roberts' Science Scholar); St John's Coll., Cambridge (Foundation Scholar). First Class Honours in Physics, BSc Wales; Second

Class Honours in Physics BSc, London; 1st Cl. Natural Sci. Tripos, Part II, Physics; Second Class Mathematical Tripos, Part I; Third Class Law Tripos, Part II. Chief Science Master, Inverurie Academy, 1909-11; Head of Military and Engineering Side, Haileybury Coll., 1914-22; former Mem. of Headmasters' Conference Committee; Captain OTC; Pres. of the Incorporated Association of Headmasters, 1936, Hon. Treas., 1938-46; former Member Secondary School Examination Council; Member of Norwood Committee; formerly Mem. Court, Univ. of Leeds; JP, Leeds, 1937-; Chm. Visiting Magistrates, Leeds Prison, 1948-63; Dep. Chairman Leeds Group B Hospital Management Committee, 1948-54; Chm. Leeds Bench, 1950-63; Pres. W Riding Branch Magistrates' Association, 1956, 1957, and 1958; President Leeds Lit. and Philosophical Society, 1952 and 1953. Mem. Nat. Assistance Bd Tribunal; Education Adviser, RAF Benevolent Fund. Hon. LLD Leeds, 1948. *Publications:* Mathematical and Science Papers for Army Candidates; Revision Arithmetic and Mensuration; Notes on Dynamics; Outlines of the Calculus; The Leeds Intelligence Test; The Science of Marking. *Recreations:* fly-fishing, golf, painting. *Address:* Fairmount, 25 Shire Oak Road, Leeds 6. *T:* Leeds 51895.

**THOMAS, Theodore Lynam;** Headmaster, Repton School, 1944-61; *b* 17 Sept. 1900; *s* of late Canon L. W. Thomas; *m* 1931, Margaret Astbury; two *s. Educ:* Dragon School, Oxford; King William's College, Isle of Man; St John's College, Cambridge. Assistant Master Rugby School, 1923-44. *Address:* Barton End, Beaminster, Dorset. *T:* Beaminster 411.

**THOMAS, Rt. Hon. (Thomas) George,** PC 1968; MP (Lab) West Cardiff since 1950, Central Cardiff, 1945-50; Ex-Chairman, Welsh Parliamentary Labour Party. *Educ:* University Coll., Southampton. Parliamentary Private Secretary, Min. of Civil Aviation, 1951. Member, Chairman's Panel, House of Commons; Ex-President, National Brotherhood Movement. Schoolmaster. Vice-Pres. of the Methodist Conference, 1960-61. First Chm. of the Welsh Parliamentary Grand Committee. Jt Parly Under-Sec. of State, Home Office, 1964-66; Minister of State: Welsh Office, 1966-67; Commonwealth Office, 1967-68; Secretary of State for Wales, 1968-70. Freeman, Borough of Rhondda, 1970. *Publication:* The Christian Heritage in Politics. *Address:* Tilbury, 173 King George V Drive, Heath, Cardiff. *T:* Cardiff 51513.

**THOMAS, Trevor,** BA; artist, author; art editor, Gordon Fraser Gallery Ltd; *b* 8 June 1907; 2nd *s* of William Thomas and Mary Richards; *m* 1947; two *s. Educ:* Sir Alfred Jones Scholar, University Coll. of Wales, Aberystwyth. Demonstrator, Dept of Geography and Anthropology, University Coll. of Wales, Aberystwyth, 1929-30; Secretary and Lecturer-Assistant, Department of Geography, Victoria University, Manchester, 1930-31; Cartographer to Geographical Association, Manchester, 1930-31; Keeper, Departments of Ethnology and Shipping, Liverpool Public Museums, 1931-40; Rockefeller Foundation Museums Fellow, USA, 1938-39; Director, Museum and Art Gallery, Leicester, 1940-46; Surveyor, Regional Guide to Works of Art, Arts Council of Great Britain, 1946-48; Designer of Exhibitions for the British Institute of Adult Education, 1946-48; Director, Crafts Centre of Great Britain, 1947-48; Programme Specialist for Education through the Arts, UNESCO, Paris, 1949-56; Visiting Prof. of Art Education, Teachers' Coll., Columbia Univ., NY, USA, 1956; Prof. of Art, State Univ. of New York, College for Teachers, Buffalo, 1957-58; Prof. of Art Hist., University of Buffalo, and Art Critic, Buffalo Evening News, 1959-60. *Publications:* Penny Plain Twopence Coloured: the Aesthetics of Museum Display; (ed.) Education and Art: a Symposium; contrib. to Journals. *Recreations:* art, music, theatre. Research: Art. *Address:* 36 Pembroke Street, Bedford. *T:* 58879.

**THOMAS, Trevor Cawdor,** MA, LLB Cantab, LLB Wales; Vice-Chancellor, University of Liverpool, since 1970; *b* 19 April 1914; *o s* of James Elwyn Thomas and Charlotte Thomas (*née* Ivatt); *m* 1943, Mrs Marjory Molony, *widow* of John Bernard Molony, and *y d* of Samuel Harry Guteridge Higgs and Fanny Higgs, Reading. *Educ:* University College of Wales, Aberystwyth; Trinity Hall, Cambridge. LLB Wales 1936 (first class (at Aberystwyth) and Sir Samuel Evans prizeman); Foundn Schol., Trinity Hall, 1937; Trinity Hall Law Studentship, 1938; Joseph Hodges Choate Memorial Fellowship, 1938; LLB Cantab 1938 (first class, Pt II Law Tripos, 1937; first class with dist. in final LLB). Entrance Schol., Gray's Inn, 1936; Bar Final Examinations, 1940 (first class with certif. of honour); called to Bar, Gray's Inn, 1941; Lecturer in Law, Univ. of Leeds, 1939-41. RAF, Intell. Br., 1941-45. Fellow of Trinity Hall, Cambridge, 1945-60, Hon. Fellow, 1970; Univ. Lectr in Law, Univ. of Cambridge, 1945-60; Fellow and Sen. Bursar, St John's Coll., Cambridge, 1960-69. Mem. Statutory Commn for Royal Univ. of Malta, 1960-. JP, City of Cambridge, 1966-69. *Publications:* co-editor, Jenks' Digest of English Civil Law, 4th edn 1947; articles in Cambridge Law Jl. *Recreations:* gardening, travel, fishing. *Address:* The Vice-Chancellor's Lodge, Sefton Park Road, Liverpool 8. *T:* 051-727 2168. *Club:* Farmers'.

**THOMAS, Sir Tudor;** *see* Thomas, Sir J. W. T.

**THOMAS, Maj.-Gen. Vivian Davenport,** CB 1949; CBE 1946 (OBE 1942); Royal Marines, retired; *b* 31 Oct. 1897; *s* of Arnold Frederick Davenport Thomas, London; *m* 1929, Theresa, *d* of Colonel E. J. Previte, VD, TD, Burstow, Surrey; one *s. Educ:* St Paul's. Served European War, 1914-18: with Royal Marines, 1914-19; HMS Princess Royal, 1st Battle Cruiser Squadron, 1915-18. War of 1939-45, North Africa; Lieutenant-Colonel, 1942; acting Colonel Commandant (temp. Brig.) 1943; Maj.-Gen. 1946; Chief of Amphibious Warfare, 1950-54; retired, 1954. Hon. Col Comdt, Plymouth Group Royal Marines, 1957-61. Master, Armourers' and Brasiers' Company, 1962-63. *Address:* Glebe House, Framfield, Uckfield, Sussex. *Clubs:* Boodle's; Royal Yacht Squadron.

**THOMAS, Maj.-Gen. Walter Babington,** DSO 1943; MC and Bar, 1942; Commander, HQ Far East Land Forces, since Nov. 1970 (Chief of Staff, April-Oct. 1970); *b* Nelson, NZ, 29 June 1919; *s* of Walter Harington Thomas, Farmer; *m* 1947, Iredale Edith Lauchlan (*née* Trent); three *d. Educ:* Motueka Dist High Sch., Nelson, NZ. Clerk, Bank of New Zealand, 1936-39. Served War of 1939-45 (despatches, MC and Bar, DSO): 2nd NZEF, 1940-46, in Greece, Crete, Western Desert, Tunis and Italy; Comd 23 (NZ) Bn, 1944-45; Comd 22 (NZ) Bn, in Japan, 1946; transf. to Brit. Army, Royal Hampshire Regt, 1947; Bde Major, 39 Inf. Bde Gp, 1953-55 (despatches); GSO2, UK JSLS, Aust., 1958-60; AA&QMG, HQ 1 Div. BAOR, 1962-64; Comd 12 Inf. Bde Gp, 1964-66; IDC, 1967; GOC 5th Div., 1968-70. Silver Star, Medal, 1945 (USA). *Publications:* Dare to be Free, 1951; Touch of Pitch, 1956.

*Recreation:* riding. *Address:* c/o Bank of New Zealand, PO Box No 402, 1 Queen Victoria Street, EC4.

**THOMAS, William,** CB 1951; former Director of the Council of Social Service for Wales and Monmouthshire (Inc.); retired; now farming at Trefloyne; *m* Elizabeth Morgan, BSc; one *s* (and one *s* decd). *Educ:* University College of Wales, Aberystwyth; Royal University of Holland, Groningen; Emmanuel College, Cambridge (1851 Research Exhibitioner, Research Exhibitioner); MA Cantab; DSc Wales; PhD Aberdeen; Fellow of the University of Wales; Hon. LLD Wales, 1968. Principal, Tech. Inst., Wrexham. Army Rank, Captain. Chief Inspector of Schools for Wales, retired 1952. Member Court of Governors of: Univ. of Wales; Nat. Library of Wales; Nat. Museum of Wales. *Publications:* Twelve original papers in Chemical Journals; Complex Salts, 1924. *Recreation:* golf. *Address:* Trefloyne, Tenby, Pembrokeshire.

**THOMAS, William Herbert Evans,** CBE 1941; retired; *b* 28 Dec. 1886; *s* of late John Owen Thomas and Mary Elizabeth Evans, Llantwit Major, Glamorgan; *m*; two *s* one *d. Educ:* Privately; London University. Joined Chartered Bank of India, Australia and China, 1907; Manager at Peking, Tientsin and Hong Kong Branches; Inspector of Branches, 1939; British Member Stabilization Board of China, 1943. Financial Counsellor, HBM Embassy, Chungking, 1944, 1945-46. *Publication:* Vanished China. *Address:* c/o Chartered Bank, 38 Bishopsgate, EC2.

**THOMAS, Sir William James Cooper,** 2nd Bt, *cr* 1919; TD; JP; Captain RA; *b* 7 May 1919; *er s* of Sir William James Thomas, 1st Bt, and Maud Mary Cooper, Bexhill-on-Sea; *S* father 1945; *m* 1947, Freida Dunbar, *yr d* of late F. A. Whyte; two *s* one *d. Educ:* Harrow School; Cambridge Univ. Barrister, Inner Temple, 1948. Member TA, 1938. Served War of 1939-45. *Heir: s* William Michael Thomas, *b* 5 Dec. 1948. *Address:* Rockfield Park, near Monmouth. *T:* Monmouth 2757. *Club:* Army and Navy.

**THOMAS, Sir (William) Michael (Marsh),** 3rd Bt *cr* 1918; Managing Director of Goss Nurseries Ltd, 1955; *b* 4 Dec. 1930; *s* of Sir William Eustace Rhyddlad Thomas, 2nd Bt, and Enid Helena Marsh; *S* father 1957; *m* 1953, Geraldine Mary, *d* of Robert Drysdale, Anglesey; two *d. Educ:* Oundle School, Northants. *Heir: u* Robert Freeman Thomas [*b* 8 Jan. 1911; *m* 1947, Marcia, *d* of Walter Lucas]. *Address:* Belan, Rhosneigr, Anglesey.

**THOMAS, Sir (William) Miles (Webster),** Kt 1943; DFC; CEng; FIMechE; MSAE; FRAeS; President, National Savings Committee, since 1965 (also Chairman, 1965-70); Chairman: Britannia Airways Ltd; Neumo Ltd; Carbon Electric Holdings Ltd; Chesham Amalgamations and Investments Ltd; Throughways Transport Ltd; Cherry-Burrell; SSV Ltd; Deputy Chairman: P. Leiner & Sons Ltd, since 1961; Deritend Stamping Co., since 1968; Director: Sun Insurance Office, Ltd; Dowty Group Ltd; Thomson Organisation (Sunday Times, etc); Thomson Travel Holdings Ltd; Cold Precision Forgings (D. & C.) Ltd; South Wales Forgemasters Ltd; Vice-Chairman, Welsh Economic Council, 1965-66; *b* 2 March 1897; *s* of late William Henry Thomas and Mary Elizabeth Webster; *m* 1924, Hylda Nora Church, Kidlington, Oxford; one *s* one *d. Educ:* Bromsgrove School. Served as Engineering Premium Pupil at Bellis and Morcom Ltd, Birmingham; joined Armoured Car Squadron as private; served in German East African campaign as Armoured Car Driver; Commissioned to RFC in Egypt; Stunt Flying and Aerial Fighting Instructor at Heliopolis; afterwards served with RAF in Mesopotamia, Persia and Southern Russia (DFC); Demobilised, 1919; became editor on technical journals; joined Lord Nuffield (then Mr W. R. Morris) as adviser on Sales Promotion, 1924; founded Morris-Oxford Press in 1926; Director and General Sales Manager of Morris Motors Ltd, 1927; Director and General Manager of Morris Commercial Cars Ltd, Birmingham, 1934; of Wolseley Motors Ltd, Birmingham, 1935; Managing Director of Wolseley Motors Ltd in 1937; Vice-Chairman and Managing Director of Morris Motors Ltd and Subsidiary Companies, 1940-47. Chairman: Cruiser Tank Production Group and member of Advisory Panel on Tank Production, 1941; British Tank Engine Mission to US, 1942; Govt of Southern Rhodesia Development Co-ordinating Commission, 1947; Oxfordshire Council, Order of St John, 1947. President, Soc. of Motor Manufacturers, 1947-48; Director, Colonial Development Corporation, 1948-51; Chairman of BOAC, 1949-56; President: Advertising Assoc., 1949-53; International Air Transport Assoc., 1951-52. Member: BBC General Advisory Council, 1952-56; Chairman of Monsanto Chemicals Ltd, 1956-63; Brit. Productivity Council, 1957-62 (Chm., 1959); Chm., Welsh Adv. Cttee for Civil Aviation, 1961-66; Development Corp for Wales, 1958-67. Comdr of Cedar of the Lebanon. Lebanon. *Publications:* Treatise on the development and use of multi-wheel vehicles for cross-country and military purposes, 1924; numerous articles, broadcast talks and television "Brains Trust" and "Get Ahead", 1934-64. (Autobiography) Out on a Wing, 1964. *Recreations:* modest motoring and simple gardening. *Address:* Remenham Court, Henley-on-Thames. Oxon. *T:* Henley 5400. *Clubs:* Athenæum, Royal Automobile, Garrick; The Links (New York).

**THOMAS, William R.;** *see* Rees-Thomas.

**THOMAS, Wyndham;** General Manager, Peterborough New Town Development Corporation, since 1968; *b* 1 Feb. 1924; *s* of Robert John Thomas and Hannah Mary; *m* 1947, Elizabeth Terry Hopkin; one *s* three *d. Educ:* Maesteg Grammar School. Served Army (Lieut, Royal Welch Fusiliers), 1943-47. Schoolmaster, 1950-53; Director, Town and Country Planning Association, 1955-67; Member, Land Commission, 1967-68; Member, Commission for the New Towns, 1964-68. Mayor of Hemel Hempstead, 1958-59. *Publications:* many articles on town planning, housing, etc, in learned jls. *Recreations:* collecting old furniture, work. *Address:* 20 High Street, Castor, near Peterborough. *T:* Castor 409.

**THOMAS, Wynford V.;** *see* Vaughan-Thomas.

**THOMPSON, Dr Alan Eric;** *b* 16 Sept. 1924; *o c* of late Eric Joseph Thompson and of Florence Thompson; *m* 1960, Mary Heather Long; two *s* one *d. Educ:* University of Edinburgh. MA 1949, MA (Hons Class I, Economic Science), 1951, PhD 1953, Carnegie Research Scholar, 1951-52; Asst in Political Economy, 1952-53, Lectr in Political Economy, 1953-59, and 1964-, Univ. of Edinburgh. Parly Adviser to Scottish Television, 1966-. Visiting Prof. Graduate School of Business, Stanford Univ., USA, 1966, 1968. MP (Lab) Dunfermline, 1959-64. Chm., Adv. Bd on Economics Educn (Esmée Fairbairn Research Project), 1970-; Member: Scottish Cttee, Public Schools Commn, 1969-70; Cttee enquiring into conditions of service life for young servicemen, 1969. Pres., Edinburgh Amenity and Transport Assoc., 1970. Has broadcast and appeared on TV (economic and political talks and discussions) in Britain and USA. *Publications:* contribs to learned journals. *Address:* 11 Upper Gray Street, Edinburgh 9. *T:* 031-667 2140. *Club:* Scottish Arts.

**THOMPSON, Aubrey Denzil Forsyth,** CMG 1944; CVO 1947; CBE 1941; *b* 3 Oct. 1897; *s* of Ernest Alfred Thompson; *m* 1924, Kathleen Esther Murray; one *s* one *d*. *Educ:* Weenen County College, Natal; New College, Oxford. Served European War, France, RFA, Lieut 1917-19; Oxford, 1919-20 (BA); Administrative Officer, Uganda, 1921-37; Asst Resident Commissioner and Govt Secretary, Bechuanaland Protectorate, 1937-42; Resident Commissioner, 1942-46; Resident Commissioner, Basutoland, 1946-51; retired, 1951. *Recreation:* gardening. *Address:* PO Box 553, Mbabane, Swaziland, S Africa.

**THOMPSON, Aubrey Gordon D.;** *see* Denton-Thompson.

**THOMPSON, Lt-Col Cecil Henry Farrer,** DSO 1918; OBE 1919; TD 1924; *b* 16 Dec. 1882; *s* of late Geo. Rodie Thompson, JP, DL, of Lynwood, Ascot, and Alice Howard, *d* of Capt. H. H. Barber, 17th Lancers; *m* 1915, Rachel Ellen, *d* of late John Holmes, of Brooke Hall, Norwich; three *s*. *Educ:* Harrow; Trinity College, Cambridge, BA. Called to Bar, Inner Temple, 1910; 2nd Lieut London Rifle Brigade, 1909; Captain, 1913; Major, 1917; served European War, 1914-19 (DSO, OBE, despatches four times; French Croix de Guerre); Bt Lt-Col, 1922; DL, JP, Cumberland; High Sheriff of Cumberland, 1940. *Address:* Nunwick Hall, Penrith, Cumberland. *T:* Langwathby 205. *Clubs:* Brooks's, MCC.

**THOMPSON, Charles Allister;** HM Consul-General, British Consulate-General, Philadelphia, since 1970; *b* 21 July 1922; *yr s* of late Herbert Ivie Thompson and of Margaret Mary Browne-Webber, Managua, Nicaragua; *m* 1950, Jean Margaret, *er d* of late Alexander Bruce Dickson; two *s* two *d*. *Educ:* Haileybury; Hertford Coll., Oxford (MA, BLitt). War Service, 1942-46, 1st King's Dragoon Guards. Joined Foreign Service (now Diplomatic Service), 1947, and served in FO until 1949; 3rd Sec., Prague, 1949-50; 2nd Sec. (Commercial), Mexico City, 1950-53; FO 1953-56; 1st Sec., Karachi, 1956-59; Head of Chancery, Luxembourg, 1959-62; FO, 1962-65; Counsellor, 1965; Dep. Consul-Gen., New York, 1965-67; Dep. High Comr, Port of Spain, 1967-70. *Recreations:* sailing, fishing, photography. *Address:* c/o Foreign and Commonwealth Office, SW1.

**THOMPSON, Charles Paxton,** CMG 1961; OBE 1956; Bursar, University of Birmingham, since 1961; *b* 31 May 1911; *s* of W. P. Thompson; *m* 1938, Gweneth Barbara Toby; one *s* one *d*. *Educ:* Merchant Taylors' School, London; University College, London; Trinity Hall, Cambridge. Cadet, Colonial Administrative Service (Nigeria), 1933; Economic Secretary to Prime Minister of Federation of Nigeria, 1958; Permanent Secretary, Ministry of Economic Development, Lagos, 1960. *Recreations:* reading omnivorously; gardening. *Address:* The Mount, Stoke Prior, Bromsgrove, Worcs. *T:* Bromsgrove 4081. *Club:* Oriental.

**THOMPSON, Sir Cyril Ivan;** *see* Thompson, Sir Ivan.

**THOMPSON, Daniel Varney;** author and columnist; Registered Professional Engineer (Massachusetts); *b* 29 Dec. 1902; *s* of Daniel Varney and Grace Randall Thompson; *m* 1927, Cécile de Luze Simonds; one *d* (one *s* decd). *Educ:* Harvard. AB *cum laude* Harvard 1922; AM 1926; Instr and tutor, Harvard Univ., 1923-24, 1925-26 (Sheldon Fellow, 1922-23, 1924-25); Technical Adviser, Fogg Art Museum China Expedition 1924-25; Instructor and Assistant Professor of the History of Art in Yale University, 1926-33 (Sterling Fellow, 1931-32); Research Fellow of American Council of Learned Societies, 1933-34; Research and Technical Adviser Courtauld Institute of Art, 1934-36; Head of its Scientific Department, 1936-38; Professor of the History of the Technology of Art in University of London, 1938-46. Director, Daniel Varney Ltd, 1943-47. Technical Consultant, Head of Research and Development, E-Z Mills, Inc., 1948-50. Sen. Staff Consulting Engr, AVCO Corp. Res. and Advanced Develt, Missile Systems Div., Advanced Electronics Gp, 1956-68, retd. Member Royal Institution (Board of Visitors, 1946-48); Technical Consultant, Sylvania Electric Products, Electronics Division, 1951; Comstock & Wescott, Inc., 1952 and 1955-67; Chief Engineer, Jarrell-Ash Co., 1953-55; Vice-Pres. Swett & Sibley Co. 1955-57. Food and Garden Editor, North Shore Magazine, 1966-. Hon. Mem. Soc. of Painters in Tempera (London). *Publications:* Il Libro dell' Arte 1932; The Craftsman's Handbook, 1933 (rev. 1936); De Arte Illuminandi: The Technique of Manuscript Illumination, 1933; The Practice of Tempera Painting, 1936 (1962); The Materials of Medieval Painting, 1936 (repr. as The Materials and Techniques of Medieval Painting, 1957); contrib. various learned and tech. jls, magazines and newspapers. *Recreations:* greenhouses and gardening. *Address:* Barn End, Linden House, Beverly Farms, Mass 01915, USA. *T:* 617-927-0247. *Club:* Athenæum.

**THOMPSON, David Richard;** Master of the Crown Office and Queen's Coroner and Attorney Registrar of Criminal Appeals and of the Courts Martial Appeal Court since 1965; *b* 11 Feb. 1916; *s* of William George Thompson; *m* 1952, Sally Jennifer Rowntree Thompson (*née* Stockton); two *s* four *d*. *Educ:* Alleyn's Sch., Dulwich; Jesus Coll., Oxford. BA Physics 1938. Royal Corps of Signals, 1939-46 (despatches). Called to Bar, Lincoln's Inn, 1946; Office of Director of Public Prosecutions, 1948-54; Dep. Asst Registrar, then Asst Registrar, Court of Criminal Appeal, 1954-65. *Publication:* (with H. W. Wollaston) Court of Appeal Criminal Division, 1969. *Recreation:* riding. *Address:* 54 Highbury Grove, N5. *T:* 01-226 6514.

**THOMPSON, Donald Henry,** MA Oxon; JP; Headmaster, Chigwell School, Essex, since 1947; *b* 29 Aug. 1911; *s* of H. R. Thompson, solicitor, Swansea; *m* 1942, Helen Mary Wray; four *s*. *Educ:* Shrewsbury School; Merton College, Oxford. Postmaster in Classics, Merton Coll., Oxford, 1930; 1st Class Hon. Mod., 1932; 1st Class Literae Humaniores, 1934; Asst Master Haileybury Coll., Hertford, 1934-46. Served War of 1939-45, RA, 1940-45. JP Essex, 1955. *Recreations:* cricket, bird-watching, walking. *Address:* The Haylands, Chigwell, Essex. *T:* 01-500 3019.

**THOMPSON, Rev. Douglas Weddell;** President of the Methodist Conference 1966-67; *b* 4 July 1903; *s* of Nathan Ellis and Florence Thompson; *m* 1929, Gladys Wentworth; one *d*. *Educ:* Gateshead Grammar Sch.; Handsworth Coll., Birmingham. Missionary, Hunan,

China, 1925-27; Chaplain, Bengal, India, 1927-28; Hunan, China, 1929-39. Served War, 1939-45 (despatches): Chaplain, HMF, W Africa, Western Desert; POW Chaplain, Italy, Germany. Methodist Home Missions, London and Portsmouth, 1945-58. Gen. Sec. and Chm. of Officers, Methodist Overseas Mission Dept, 1958-68. *Publications:* Wisdom of the Way, 1945; About to Marry, 1945; Into Red Starlight, 1950; Captives to Freedom, 1951; The Mystery of the White Stone, 1961; The World He Loves, 1963; numerous articles in Ecumenical and Missionary jls. *Recreation:* mountain and fell-walking. *Address:* 87 Willingdon Road, Eastbourne, Sussex. *T:* 21551. *Club:* Royal Commonwealth Society.

**THOMPSON, Mrs E. Roffe;** *see* Lejeune, Miss C. A.

**THOMPSON, Lt-Col Edgar Hynes,** OBE 1944; MA, ScD; Professor of Photogrammetry and Surveying, University College, London, since 1951; *b* 13 Jan. 1910; *s* of Edgar Thompson, OBE; *m* 1934, Muriel May Smith; two *d. Educ:* Cheltenham; Royal Mil. Acad., Woolwich; Downing College, Cambridge. Commissioned, 2nd Lt Royal Engineers, 1930; Ordnance Survey, 1938-39, 1944-47, 1950-51. Served War of 1939-45: BEF France, Middle East, Italy (despatches twice); retired, 1951. FRAS, FRGS, FRICS. *Publications:* An Introduction to the Algebra of Matrices, 1969; numerous papers on geodetic and air surveying subjects. *Address:* University College, Gower Street, WC1. *T:* 01-387 7050.

**THOMPSON, Professor Edward Arthur;** FBA 1964; Professor of Classics, University of Nottingham, since 1948; *b* 22 May 1914; *s* of Robert J. Thompson and late Margaret Thompson, Rathmines, Dublin. *Educ:* Trinity Coll., Dublin. Lecturer in Classics: Dublin, 1939-41; Swansea, 1942-45; King's College, London, 1945-48. Vis. Bentley Prof. of History, Univ. of Michigan, 1969-70. *Publications:* The Historical Work of Ammianus Marcellinus, 1947; A History of Attila and The Huns, 1948; A Roman Reformer and Inventor, 1952; The Early Germans, 1965; The Visigoths in the Time of Ulfila, 1966; The Goths in Spain, 1969. *Address:* The University, Nottingham.

**THOMPSON, Sir Edward (Hugh Dudley),** Kt 1967; MBE 1945; TD; Chairman, P-E Consulting Group; Director: Allied Breweries Ltd; Sun Alliance & London Insurance Ltd; *b* 12 May 1907; *s* of Neale Dudley Thompson and Mary Gwendoline Scutt; *m* 1st, 1931, Ruth Monica, 3rd *d* of Charles Henry Wainwright, JP; two *s*; 2nd, 1947, Doreen Maud, *d* of George Tibbitt; one *s* one *d. Educ:* Uppingham; Lincoln Coll., Oxford. Served War of 1939-45 (despatches, MBE); 1st Derbyshire Yeomanry, 1939-43, in N Africa; General Staff, 1943-45, in Italy and Germany. Solicitor, 1931-36. Asst Man. Dir, Ind Coope & Allsopp Ltd, 1936-39, Managing Director, 1939; Chairman: Ind Coope Ltd, Burton on Trent, 1955-62; Allied Breweries Ltd (formerly Ind Coope Tetley Ansell Ltd), 1961-68. Chm. Brewers' Soc., 1959-61; High Sheriff of Derbyshire, 1964; Founder Member of World Security Trust; Trustee, Civic Trust; Mem., Northumberland Foot and Mouth Cttee. *Recreations:* farming, sailing, ski-ing. *Address:* Culland Hall, Brailsford, Derby. *T:* Brailsford 247. *Club:* Boodle's.

**THOMPSON, Edward Vincent,** CB 1943; *b* 1880; *s* of Reginald E. Thompson, MD, and Anne Isabella, *d* of Prof. Augustus De Morgan; *m* 1912, Jessie Forbes (*d* 1968), *d* of James Cameron, Stanley, Perthshire; two *s* one *d. Educ:* St Paul's Sch.; King's College, Cambridge (MA). Solicitor, 1907; entered Treasury Solicitor's Department, 1912; Principal Assistant Solicitor to HM Treasury, 1941-49. *Address:* 24 High Street, Southwold, Suffolk. *T:* 2046.

**THOMPSON, Sir Edward (Walter),** Kt 1957; JP; Chairman John Thompson Ltd, Wolverhampton, 1947-67, now Hon. President; Director, Barclays Bank, since 1958 (Local Director, Barclays Bank (Birmingham) since 1952); *b* 11 June 1902; *s* of late Albert E. Thompson and late Mary Thompson; *m* 1930, Ann E., *d* of Rev. George L. Amphlett, Four Ashes Hall, Stourbridge, Worcs; one *s* three *d. Educ:* Oundle; Trinity Hall, Cambridge. MA (Engineering) Cambridge. Joined family firm of John Thompson's, 1924; Dir John Thompson Watertube Boilers, 1930; Joint Man. Dir John Thompson Ltd, 1936-62. Chm. Watertube Boilermakers Assoc., 1951-54; Pres. Brit. Engineers Assoc., 1957-59 (Vice-Pres. 1956). Mem. Midland Chapter Woodard Schools and Custos (Chairman) School of St Mary and St Anne, Abbots Bromley. Chairman: Birmingham Regional Hosp. Bd, 1957-61; Redditch Development Corp., 1964-; Leader SE Asia Trade Delegation, 1961. JP Co. Salop, 1953; Dep. Chm. Bridgnorth Bench, 1956-66; High Sheriff, Staffordshire, 1955-56. *Recreations:* shooting, fishing, gardening. *Address:* Gatacre Park, Bridgnorth, Salop. *T:* Bobbington 211. *Clubs:* Brooks's; Shropshire (Shrewsbury).
*See also Viscount Bledisloe.*

**THOMPSON, Eric;** *see* Thompson, John Eric Sidney.

**THOMPSON, E(rnest) Heber,** RE 1939 (ARE 1923); Artist, Etcher, Painter; *b* 1891; *s* of John Brown Thompson and Victoria Marie Dyer; *m* 1919, Nellie Florence Gutteridge (*d* 1967); one *d. Educ:* Dunedin, New Zealand. Began as free-lance Black and White artist in Dunedin, New Zealand; served European war, 1915-17 in Egypt and France with New Zealand Expeditionary Force (wounded); after war studied at Slade School (drawing and painting) and at Royal College of Art and Central School of Arts and Crafts (etching); Finalist, Prix de Rome (engraving), 1923. Representative in London, NZ Nat. Art Gallery, 1951-66. Retrospective exhbn, Dunedin Public Art Gallery, 1970. Work represented in permanent collections of: Ashmolean Museum, Oxford, British Museum, Bradford and Harrogate Art Galleries, National Art Gallery, New Zealand, Dunedin Public Art Gallery, Hocken Library Art Gallery, Dunedin. *Publications:* The Sketcher, Nos 1-7, 1914-15; Light Diet, 1919. *Recreations:* gardening, walking. *Address:* Mount Warren, Upper Warren Avenue, Caversham, Reading, Berks.

**THOMPSON, Estelle Merle O'Brien;** *see* Oberon, Merle.

**THOMPSON, Francis L.;** *see* Longstreth-Thompson.

**THOMPSON, Frank Charles,** DMet Sheffield; MSc Manchester; BSc London; Professor of Metallurgy, University of Manchester, 1921-59, Emeritus Professor, 1959; Pro-Vice-Chancellor, 1937-41; Fellow of Institute of Metals, 1962; *b* 3 April 1890. *Educ:* Royal Grammar School, Sheffield; King Edward VII School, Sheffield; Univ. of Sheffield; Lecturer in Metallurgy of the Univ. of Sheffield; Sorby Research Fellow, 1920-21. President, Institute of Metals, 1953-54; Pres., Institution of Metallurgists, 1955-56. Hon. Curator of

Coins, Manchester Museum, 1959-. *Publications:* many papers on Metallurgical subjects, particularly relating to the effects of strain. *Address:* Appledore, 45 Moss Lane, Bramhall, Stockport, Cheshire.

**THOMPSON, Air Commodore Frederick William,** CBE 1957; DSO 1944; DFC 1942; AFC 1944; Engineering Manager, Hawker Siddeley Dynamics Co. Ltd, since 1964; *b* 9 July 1914; *s* of William Edward Thompson, Winster, Poulton-le-Fylde, Lancs; *m* 1941, Marian, *d* of Wm Bootyman, Hessle, E Yorks; two *d*. *Educ:* Baines's Grammar School; Liverpool University. BSc 2nd Cl. Hons Maths; Advanced Diploma in General Hygiene (Hons). Joined RAF, 1935, invalided 1936. S Rhodesian Education Dept, 1936-39. Served War of 1939-45 (despatches, DFC, AFC, DSO): S Rhodesian Air Force, 1940, Pilot Officer; seconded to RAFVR, 4 Gp Bomber Command, 1940; Flight Comdr 10 Sqdn Bombers, 1941; 1658 HCU, 1942; CO 44 Bomber Sqdn, 1944; Bomber Command Instructor's School, 1944; Station Commander, RAF Heany, 1945; HQ Mid Med., 1946-47; Min. of Defence, 1947-50; HQ CC, 1950-53; OC Aswdu, 1953; Group Capt., CO Luqa, 1954; Deputy Director Operational Requirements (1), Air Ministry, 1957-60. Air Cdre Imperial Defence Coll., 1960; Director of Guided Weapons (Trials), Ministry of Aviation, 1961. Retired from RAF at own request to join de Havilland Aircraft Co. Ltd as Representative of the Company on the West Coast of America. idc, jssc, psc, cfs. *Recreations:* tennis, swimming. *Address:* Westwick, Lye Green Road, Chesham, Bucks. *T:* Chesham 5413. *Club:* Royal Air Force.

**THOMPSON, Lt-Gen. Sir Geoffrey (Stuart),** KBE 1960 (MBE 1941); CB 1954; DSO 1944; late Royal Artillery; *b* 6 Jan. 1905; 3rd *s* of late Brig.-Gen. W. A. M. Thompson, CB, CMG; *m* 1934, Agnes Mary Colville, *e d* of late Captain H. D. Wakeman-Colville, RN retd; one *d*. *Educ:* Sherborne Sch.; RN Colls, Osborne and Dartmouth. Commissioned, 1925; served War of 1939-45 (North Africa and Italy); Commander 1st Field Regiment RA, Italy, 1944-45; Commander No. 2 Army Group, Royal Artillery, Egypt, 1950-52; Director Land/Air Warfare and Dir for NATO Standardisation, War Office, 1952-54; Senior Army Instructor, Imperial Defence College, 1955-57; Director of Staff Duties, War Office, 1957-59; Military Secretary to the Secretary of State for War, 1959-61. Col Comdt, RA, 1961-69. Asst Man. Dir, Arthur Guinness Son & Co., Dublin, 1961-70. Officer of Legion of Merit, USA, 1945; Commander of Order of Leopold, Belgium, 1950; Croix de Guerre, Belgium, 1950. *Recreations:* fishing, hunting. *Address:* Auburn House, Malahide, Co. Dublin. *T:* Dublin 350440. *Club:* Army and Navy.

**THOMPSON, Gertrude C.;** *see* Caton-Thompson.

**THOMPSON, Godfrey;** *see* Thompson, W. G.

**THOMPSON, Sir Harold (Warris),** Kt 1968; CBE 1959; FRS 1946; MA, DSc (Oxon); PhilD (Berlin); Professor of Chemistry, Oxford University; *b* 15 Feb. 1908; *m* 1938, Grace Penelope Stradling; one *s* one *d*. *Educ:* King Edward VII Sch., Sheffield; Trinity College, Oxford (Open Millard Scholar); Berlin University. 1st Class Hons Chemistry, Oxford, 1929; Junior Research Fellow, St John's College, Oxford; Official Fellow and Tutor, St John's College, 1930-64, Professorial Fellow, 1964-; University Reader in Infra red spectroscopy, 1954-64; Leverhulme Research Fellow (Pasadena), 1937; Tilden Lecturer, 1943; Gnehm Lecturer, Zürich, 1948; Reilly Lecturer, 1961; Cherwell Memorial Fellow, 1961. Chemical Research for Ministry of Supply and Ministry of Aircraft Production, 1939-45; Member, Chemical Research Board, DSIR, 1949-54 and Committees of Scientific Advisory Council and MRC, 1947-55; Scientific Adviser, Home Office Civil Defence, Southern Region, 1952-63; Member General Board, Oxford University, 1949-55; Hebdomadal Council, 1957-61; President: Internat. Coun. of Scientific Unions, 1963-66; Inst. Information Scientists, 1967-70; Vice-Pres., Aslib, 1969-; Chm., Commn on Molecular Spectroscopy of Internat. Union of Pure and Applied Chem., 1955-61, and of IUPAC Publications Cttee, 1957-; Member: IUPAC Bureau, 1963-; UK Unesco Commn, 1966-; Exec. Cttee, British Council, 1966-. Mem. Coun., Royal Soc., 1959-64, Vice-Pres., 1963-64, 1965-, For. Sec., 1965-. Ciamician Medal, Bologna, 1959; Davy Medal of Royal Society, 1965; John Torrance Tate Gold Medal (Am. Inst. Physics), 1966. Hon. Treasurer OUAFC, 1931-; Founder and Chairman of Pegasus FC. Secretary, 1948-54; Member, FA Coun., 1941-, Vice-Chm., 1967-; Pres., AFA. Editor, Spectrochimica Acta, 1957-. Hon. DSc Newcastle upon Tyne, 1970. Order of Aztec Eagle, Mexico, 1970. *Publications:* A Course in Chemical Spectroscopy, 1938; (ed) Advances in Spectroscopy, Vol. I 1959, II 1961; Papers in Proc. of scientific socs and journals. *Recreation:* Association football (Oxford *v* Cambridge, 1928-29). *Address:* 33 Linton Road, Oxford. *T:* Oxford 58925. *Club:* Athenæum.

**THOMPSON, Sir Herbert;** *see* Thompson, Sir (Joseph) Herbert.

**THOMPSON, Colonel Horace Cuthbert Rees,** CBE 1955; TD; JP, DL Monmouthshire; *b* 11 Jan. 1893; *s* of Cuthbert and Ada Thompson; *m* 1st, 1920, Margaret (*d* 1946), *d* of T. B. R. Wilson; one *s* two *d*; 2nd, 1956, Violet Mary, *widow* of John Watcyn Morgan, MC. Commissioned 1913, 1st (Rifle) Bn Monmouthshire Regt TA; seconded King's African Rifles, 1917; served in France, Belgium, Egypt, and East Africa; rejoined Monmouthshire Regt 1919; commanded it, 1929-32; late Hon. Colonel 603 HAA Regt RA, TA. High Sheriff of Monmouthshire, 1944; late Chairman and Military Member of Monmouthshire T&AFA. *Recreation:* salmon fishing. *Address:* Oakdene, Llantarnam, Mon. *T:* Cwmbran 2323.

**THOMPSON, Sir (Humphrey) Simon M.;** *see* Meysey-Thompson.

**THOMPSON, Hon. Sir John,** Kt 1961; **Hon. Mr Justice Thompson;** Judge of the High Court of Justice, Queen's Bench Division since 1961; *b* Glasgow, 16 Dec. 1907; *e s* of Donald Cameron Thompson and Jeanie Dunn (*née* Nisbet); *m* 1934, Agnes Baird, *o d* of John and Jeanie Drummond, Glasgow; two *s*. *Educ:* Bellahouston Academy; Glasgow University; Oriel College, Oxford. Glasgow University: MA and Arthur Jones Memorial Prize, 1928; Ewing Gold Medal, 1929; Oxford University: BA, 1930; MA 1943. Barrister-at-Law, Powell Prize, Middle Temple, 1933. QC 1954; Bencher, Middle Temple, 1961. Vice-Chm., Gen. Council of the Bar, 1960-61 (Mem. 1958-61). Commissioner of Assize (Birmingham) 1961. *Publications:* (edited with H. R. Rogers) Redgrave's Factories, Truck and Shops Acts. *Recreation:* golf. *Address:* 73 Sevenoaks Road, Orpington, Kent. *T:* Orpington 22339.

**THOMPSON, John Crighton,** CB 1965; CBE 1958; retired as Director of Electrical Engineering, Navy Department, Ministry of Defence; *b* 14 July 1902; *s* of William Thompson and Margaret Thompson (*née* Turner); *m* 1928, Jessie Walker, *née* Ashton; three *s* one *d* (and one *d* decd). *Educ:* King Edward VI School, Norwich; Faraday House Elec. Engineering Coll., London. BSc (Eng) London 1922. Pupil, Brush Elec. Engineering Co., Loughborough, 1922-23; Asst Engineer, Callenders Cable and Construction Co., 1923-26; Asst Elec. Engineer, Admiralty, 1927; after service at home and abroad, apptd Director of Electrical Engineering and Head of RNES, 1960; retd, 1964. FIEE. *Recreations:* Elder and Chairman of Board of Managers, Trinity Presbyterian Church, Bath; motoring, gardening, fishing. *Address:* 135 Bradford Road, Combe Down, Bath. *T:* Combe Down 2228. *Club:* Royal Commonwealth Society (Fellow).

**THOMPSON, J(ohn) Eric S(idney),** FBA 1959; retired from staff of Department of Archaeology, Carnegie Institution of Washington (1935-58); *b* 31 Dec. 1898; *yr s* of George W. Thompson, FRCS and Mary Thompson (*née* Cullen); *m* 1930, Florence L. Keens; one *s*. *Educ:* Winchester Coll.; Cambridge Univ. 2nd Lt Coldstream Guards, 1918. Assistant Curator, in charge of Central and South American archaeology and ethnology, Chicago Natural Hist. Mus., 1926-35. Hon. Professor, Museo Nacional de México, 1941-; Hon. curator, Middle American archæology, Chicago Nat. Hist. Mus., 1945-; President, 32nd Internat. Congress of Americanists, 1952; Consejero, Centro de Investigaciones antropológicas mexicanas, 1953-; Member, Faculty Board of Archæology and Anthropology, Cambridge Univ., 1958-; Professor, Seminario Maya, Univ. Mexico, 1960. Rivers Memorial medal, R. Anthrop. Inst., 1945; Viking Fund medal for Anthropology, New York, 1955; Huxley Meml Medal, 1966. LLD Univ. of Yucatan, 1959; DLit: Univ. of Pennsylvania, 1962; Encomienda de Isabel la Católica, 1964; Order of the Aztec Eagle, 1965. *Publications:* Excavations at San Jose, British Honduras, 1939; Maya hieroglyphic writing; introduction, 1950; The Rise and Fall of Maya Civilization, 1954; Thomas Gage's Travels in the New World, 1958; Maya History and Religion, 1970; many papers in American and Mexican anthropological publications. *Address:* Harvard, Ashdon, Saffron Walden, Essex. *T:* Ashdon 265.

**THOMPSON, John Kenneth,** CMG 1963; Director of the Commonwealth Institute, since 1969; *b* Halstead, Essex, 12 May 1913; *e s* of W. Stanton Thompson, MBE, and Evelyn Thompson; *m* 1937, Jenny More; two *s*. *Educ:* Dover County School; King's College, London; Lausanne Univ. BA, AKC, DipEd Mod. Lang. Master, Queen's Royal Coll., Trinidad, 1935-39; Censor, Trinidad, 1939-41; Chief Censor, 1941-42; Asst Sec., Postal and Tel. Censorship, London, 1943-45; Principal, Colonial Office, 1945-49; Colonial Attaché, Brit. Embassy, Washington, 1950-53; Asst Sec., Colonial Office, 1953-59; Director, Colombo Plan Bureau, SE Asia, 1959-62; Asst Sec., Dept of Technical Co-operation, 1962-64; Dir of Overseas Appointments, ODM, 1964-69. Governor, Hartwell House, Aylesbury. Chm. Exec. Cttee, Royal Commonwealth Soc. for the Blind. *Address:* 9 Grove Way, Esher, Surrey. *T:* 01-398 4461. *Club:* Royal Commonwealth Society.

**THOMPSON, John Leonard C.;** *see* Cloudsley-Thompson.

**THOMPSON, John McLean,** MA, DSc, D ès Sc; FLS; FRSE; Professor of Botany, the University, Liverpool, 1921-52; *b* Rothesay, 1887; 2nd *s* of Hugh Thompson, Rothesay; *m* 1920, Simonne Denil, MB, ChB. *Educ:* Rothesay Academy; Glasgow University. Demonstrator in Geology and Dobbie-Smith Medallist, Glasgow University, 1910-11; Robert Donaldson Research Scholar in Biology and Senior Assistant in Botany, Glasgow University, 1913-15; Protozoologist to the Military Hospitals in the West of Scotland, 1915-19; Lecturer in Plant Morphology, Glasgow University, 1918-21; Botanical Expeditions to Jamaica, 1920 and to Columbia, Dominica, Venezuela and Panama, 1930 and 1931; Neill Prize, RSE 1924. *Publications:* chiefly memoirs on Floral Structure to RSE, in Publications of Hartley Botanical Laboratories, and in Proc. Linnean Soc. *Address:* 8 Linnet Lane, Sefton Park, Liverpool. *T:* 051-727 3174.

**THOMPSON, Air Commodore John Marlow,** CBE 1954; DSO 1943; DFC 1940 (and Bar 1942); AFC 1952; RAF retired; *b* 16 Aug. 1914; *s* of late John Thompson and Florence Thompson (*née* Marlow); *m* 1938, Margaret Sylvia Rowlands; one *s* one *d* (and one *s* decd). *Educ:* Bristol Grammar School. Joined RAF 1934; comd 111 Sqdn, Battle of Britain; comd 131 and 350 Sqdns in UK, 1941-42; Spitfire Wing, Malta, 1942-43, Middle East, 1943-45; Germany, 1946-49; SASO 11 Group, 1952-54; Central Fighter Establishment, 1954-56; comd RAF Leeming, 1956-57; Dir of Air Defence, Air Ministry, 1958-60; AOC, Military Air Traffic Ops, 1962-65. Graduate Imperial Defence College, 1961. Belgian MC 1st Class, 1942; Danish Order of Dannebrog, 1951. *Recreation:* golf. *Address:* Redstone, Redstone Hill, Redhill, Surrey. *T:* Redhill 64931. *Clubs:* Royal Air Force, RAF Reserves.

**THOMPSON, Rear-Adm. John Yelverton,** CB 1960; DL; retired 1961; *b* 25 May 1909; *s* of late Sir John Perronet Thompson, KCSI, KCIE, and Ada Lucia, Lady Thompson (*née* Tyrrell); *m* 1934, Barbara Helen Mary Aston Key; two *s*. *Educ:* Mourne Grange, Kilkeel, Co. Down; RN College, Dartmouth. Midshipman: HMS Repulse and Berwick, 1926-29; Sub-Lieutenant: HMS Warspite, 1931; Lieutenant: HMS Queen Elizabeth, 1931-32, Restless 1933, Excellent 1933-34, Queen Elizabeth 1935, Glasgow 1936-39; Lieut-Commander: HMS Excellent 1939-41, Anson 1941-43; Commander: Admiralty, Naval Ordnance Dept, 1943-45; US Fifth Fleet, 1946; HMS Liverpool, 1947; HMS Newcastle, 1948; Captain: Ordnance Board, 1948-50; HMS Unicorn, 1951-52; Director, Gunnery Division, Naval Staff, 1952-54; Imperial Defence College, 1955; Commodore: Royal Naval Barracks, Portsmouth, 1956-57; Rear-Admiral: Admiralty Interview Boards, 1958; Adm. Superintendent, HM Dockyard, Chatham, 1958-61. ADC to the Queen, 1957. Governor, Aldenham Sch., 1967-. DL Hertfordshire, 1966. American Legion of Merit, 1953. *Address:* Maynes Farmhouse, Gorhambury, St Albans, Herts. *T:* St Albans 50463. *Club:* United Service.

**THOMPSON, Sir (Joseph) Herbert,** Kt 1947; CIE 1945; Rowing Correspondent, Sunday Times, 1954-68; Member, Board of Governors, St Thomas' Hospital, 1950-65; *b* 9 March 1898; *o s* of J. Arnold Thompson, JP, and Ellen Stewart Fraser, Wilmslow, Cheshire; *m* 1925, Kathleen (Kaiser-i-Hind Silver medal, 1948), *d* of J. H. Rodier; three *d*. *Educ:* Manchester Grammar School; Brasenose College, Oxford (MA). Royal Naval Air Service (Sub-Lt) 1916, RAF (Capt.) 1918 and served principally as a fighter pilot (despatches). Assistant Master, Oundle School, 1921-22; ICS 1922; served in Madras Presidency; appointed to Foreign and Political Department, Govt of India (later Indian Political Service), 1926; Dep. Sec., Political Department, 1941-43; Revenue and Divisional Commissioner NWF Province, 1943; Resident for Kolhapur and Deccan States, 1944-45; Resident for the Punjab States, 1945-47; on special duty in connection with lapse of Paramountcy, 1947. General Secretary, London Council of Social Service, 1949-50; Diocesan Secretary, Worcester, 1951-53; BBC (Appointments Dept), 1956-59; Member, SW Metropolitan Regional Hospitals Board, 1959-63. *Recreations:* walking, gardening and rowing. *Address:* Fair Acre, Haddenham, Bucks. *T:* Haddenham 212. *Clubs:* Royal Automobile; Leander; Vincent's (Oxford).

**THOMPSON, Rt. Rev. Kenneth George;** *see* Sherwood, Bishop Suffragan of.

**THOMPSON, Sir Kenneth (Pugh),** 1st Bt *cr* 1963; *b* 24 Dec. 1909; *s* of Ernest S. and Annie Thompson; *m* 1936, Nanne Broome, Walton; one *s* one *d*. *Educ:* Bootle Grammar School. Formerly newspaper reporter, and subsequently entered commercial life; lectured for the Economic League. Worked for Ministry of Information as Regional Officer during War of 1939-45. Member of Liverpool City Council, 1938-58. Director of several Liverpool companies. MP (C) Walton Div. Liverpool, 1950-64; Chairman Conservative Nat. Advisory Cttee on Local Govt, 1956-57; Assistant Postmaster-General, 1957-Oct. 1959; Parliamentary Secretary, Ministry of Education, October 1959-July 1962. *Publications:* Member's Lobby, 1966; Pattern of Conquest, 1967. *Heir:* *s* Paul Anthony Thompson, *b* 6 Oct. 1939. *Address:* Atherton Cottage, Formby, Lancs.

**THOMPSON, Sir Lionel;** *see* Thompson, Sir L. L. H. *and* Thompson, Sir T. L. T., Bt.

**THOMPSON, Llewellyn E.;** Ambassador of the United States to the Soviet Union, 1966-Jan. 1969; Foreign Affairs Consultant, since 1969; *b* 24 Aug. 1904; *m* 1948, Jane Monroe Goelet; two *d*. *Educ:* University of Colorado. Appointed Foreign Service Officer, January 1929; Vice-Consul, Colombo, March 1929; Geneva, 1933-37; Army War College, Jan. 1940; Moscow, 1940-43; London, 1944-45; Washington, 1946-47; Rome, 1950-52; US High Commissioner for Austria, 1952-55; US Ambassador to Austria, 1955-57, to USSR, 1957-62; Ambassador-at-Large, 1962-66. Medal of Freedom, 1947; Department of State distinguished service award, 1956; President's Award for Distinguished Federal Civilian Service, 1962; Rockefeller Public Service Award, 1962. *Address:* 3915 Watson Place NW, Washington, DC 20016, USA. *Clubs:* Metropolitan, Chevy Chase (Washington, DC).

**THOMPSON, Sir (Louis) Lionel (Harry),** Kt, *cr* 1953; CBE 1946; Deputy Master and Comptroller of the Royal Mint and *ex-officio* Engraver of HM's Seals, 1950-57; retired 1957; *b* 10 March 1893; *o s* of William Thompson, Eaton, Retford; *m* Mary, *d* of William White, MD, Hadfield, Derbyshire; two *s*. *Educ:* King Edward VI School, Retford; Sheffield Univ.; Exeter Coll., Oxford (scholar). First Cl. Classical Mods, 1913. Served European War, 1914-18, Cheshire Regt (Territorial), Temp. Major. Asst Principal Treasury, 1919; Asst Secretary to Commissioner for Special Areas, 1937-39; Under-Secretary, Treasury, 1947-50. *Recreations:* walking, gardening. *Address:* 61 Woodbury Avenue, Petersfield, Hants. *T:* 3277. *Club:* United University.

**THOMPSON, Oliver Frederic,** OBE 1945; Pro-Chancellor of The City University, London, EC1; *b* 26 Jan. 1905; 3rd *s* of late W. Graham Thompson and late Oliveria C. Prescott; *m* 1939, Frances Phyllida, *d* of late F. H. Bryant; one *s* three *d*. *Educ:* Tonbridge. Mem. Shell Gp of Cos, 1924-64: managerial posts in USA, Caribbean, London. Head of Oil Sect., Min. of Econ. Warfare, and Mem. War Cabinet Sub-Cttee on Oil, 1942-46; rep. UK, Suez Canal Users Assoc.; rep. UK on various UN and OECD Cttees; Mem. Parly and Sci. Cttee, 1955-65. Past Master and Mem. Ct, Worshipful Co. of Skinners. Chm. Governing Body, Northampton Coll. of Advanced Technology, 1956-66 (now City University); Governor, Tonbridge Sch. and Kingston Polytechnic; Chm., W Surrey Coll. of Art and Design. FInstP (Past Mem. Council); Chm. Qualifications Cttee, British Computor Society, 1968. County Councillor, Surrey, 1967-. Hon. DSc, City Univ., 1967. *Publications:* various papers on economics of energy and petroleum. *Recreation:* country pursuits. *Address:* Park Cottage, Downside, Cobham, Surrey. *T:* Cobham 2097.

**THOMPSON, Sir Peile Beaumont,** 4th Bt *cr* 1890; *b* 4 Feb. 1874; 2nd *s* of Sir Peile Thompson, 2nd Bt, and Jessie (*d* 1927), *d* of Joseph Beaumont, Huddersfield; *S* brother 1956; *m* 1908, Stella Mary, *d* of Arthur Harris, Heaton Grove, Bradford; one *s* one *d*. *Educ:* Sedbergh; Trinity College, Cambridge. Tomato grower, Guernsey, 1908-18. *Recreations:* travelling and gardening. *Heir:* *s* Lt-Col Peile Thompson, OBE [*b* 28 Feb. 1911; *m* 1937, Barbara Johnson, *d* of late H. J. Rampling; one *s* one *d*]. *Address:* Thames Bank, Goring-on-Thames, Oxford.

**THOMPSON, Reginald Aubrey,** CMG 1964; *b* 22 Nov. 1905; *s* of John Thompson, Mansfield; *m* 1932, Gwendoline Marian Jackson; one *s*. *Educ:* Brunts Sch., Mansfield; University Coll., Nottingham. BSc London (1st Cl. Hons Chemistry), 1927. Research, Organic Chemistry, 1927-29; Science Master, various grammar schools, 1929-41; Scientific Civil Service, Min. of Supply, 1941-46; transf. to Admin. Class (Principal), 1946; Asst Sec., 1953; Assistant Secretary, Department of Education and Science (formerly Office of Minister of Science), 1956-64; Ministry of Technology, 1964; retd, 1966. Led UK Delegn at Confs on: liability of operators of nuclear ships, Brussels Convention, 1962; liability for nuclear damage, Vienna Convention, 1963. *Recreations:* golf, gardening, music. *Address:* 19 Deepdene Avenue, Dorking, Surrey. *T:* 2650.

**THOMPSON, Reginald Stanley;** Headmaster of Bloxham School, 1952-65, retired; *b* 23 Sept. 1899; *s* of late Reverend Canon C. H. Thompson, formerly Vicar of Eastleigh, Hants, and of Newport, Isle of Wight; *m* 1938, Phyllis Barbara, *y d* of Henry White, Solicitor, Winchester, Hants; one *s* two *d*. *Educ:* Hereford Cathedral School; Lancing College; Oriel College, Oxford. Assistant Master at Sherborne School, 1922-52 (Housemaster, 1936-52). *Recreations:* music, gardening, books, cricket. *Address:* Westcott Close, Clifton-upon-Teme, Worcestershire. *T:* Shelsley Beauchamp 234.

**THOMPSON, Sir Richard (Hilton Marler),** 1st Bt *cr* 1963; MP (C) Croydon South, 1955-66 and since 1970; *b* Calcutta, India, 5 Oct. 1912; *m* 1939, Anne Christabel de Vere, *d* of late Philip de Vere Annesley, MA, and of Mrs

Annesley, BEM; one *s*. *Educ:* Malvern College. In business in India, Burma and Ceylon, 1930-40; travelled in Tibet, Persia, Iraq, Turkey, etc. Served in RNVR, 1940-46, volunteering as ordinary seaman; commissioned, 1941 (despatches, 1942); Lieut-Comdr 1944. MP (C) Croydon West, 1950-55; Assistant-Government Whip, 1952; Lord Commissioner of the Treasury, 1954; Vice-Chamberlain of HM Household, 1956; Parliamentary Secretary, Ministry of Health, 1957-59; Under-Secretary of State, CRO, 1959-60; Parliamentary Secretary, Ministry of Works, October 1960-July 1962. A Cottonian family Trustee of the British Museum, 1951-63; re-apptd as a Prime Minister's Trustee, 1963. Chm., Overseas Migration Bd, 1959; led UK delegation to ECAFE in Bangkok, 1960; signed Indus Waters Agreement with India, Pakistan and World Bank for UK, Sept. 1960. Led UK Parliamentary Delegation to Tanganyika, to present Speaker's chair, Jan. 1963. Director: Capital and Counties Property Co. (Chairman); Rediffusion Television Ltd; Rediffusion Holdings Ltd; Greenhaven Securities Ltd; Rockweld Ltd. Chm., British Museum Society, 1970-. *Recreations:* mountaineering, foreign travel, study of history. *Heir:* *s* Nicholas Annesley Marler Thompson, *b* 19 March 1947. *Address:* Rhodes House, Sellindge, Kent. *Club:* Carlton.

**THOMPSON, Sir Robert Grainger Ker,** KBE 1965; CMG 1961; DSO 1945; MC 1943; *b* 12 April 1916; *s* of late Canon W. G. Thompson; *m* 1950, Merryn Newboult; one *s* one *d*. *Educ:* Marlborough; Sidney Sussex College, Cambridge (MA). Cadet, Malayan Civil Service, 1938. Served War of 1939-45 (MC, DSO), RAF, 1941-46. Asst Commissioner of Labour, Perak, 1946; jssc 1948-49; Staff Officer (Civil) to Director of Operations, 1950; Co-ordinating Officer, Security, 1955; Dep. Sec. for Def., Fedn of Malaya, 1957; Perm. Sec. for Def., 1959-61; Head, British Advisory Mission to Vietnam, 1961-65. Johan Mangku Negara (JMN), Malaya, 1958. *Publications:* Defeating Communist Insurgency, 1966; The Royal Flying Corps, 1968; No Exit from Vietnam, 1969; Revolutionary War in World Strategy, 1945-1969, 1970. *Recreations:* all country pursuits. *Address:* Pitcott House, Winsford, Minehead, Som. *Club:* Junior Carlton.

**THOMPSON, Robert Henry Stewart,** MA, DSc, DM, BCh; FRCP; FCPath; Courtauld Professor of Biochemistry, Middlesex Hospital Medical School, University of London, since 1965; Trustee, Wellcome Trust, 1963; *b* 2 Feb. 1912; *s* of Dr Joseph Henry Thompson and Mary Eleanor Rutherford; *m* 1938, Inge Vilma Anita Gebert; one *s* two *d*. *Educ:* Epsom College; Trinity College, Oxford; Guy's Hospital Medical School. Millard Scholar, Trinity College, Oxford, 1930; Theodore Williams Scholar in Physiology, Oxford, 1932; 1st Class Animal Physiology, Oxford, 1933; Senior Demy, Magdalen College, Oxford, 1933; Univ. Scholar, Guy's Hosp. Med. School, 1933; Adrian Stokes Travelling Fellowship to Hosp. of Rockefeller Inst., New York, 1937-38; Gillson Research Scholar in Pathology, Soc. of Apothecaries of London, 1938; Fellow of University Coll., Oxford, 1938-47; Demonstrator in Biochemistry, Oxford, 1938-47; Dean of Medical School, Oxford, 1946-47; Prof. of Chemical Pathology, Guy's Hosp. Medical School, Univ. of London, 1947-65; Secretary-General International Union of Biochemistry, 1955-64; Hon. Sec. Royal Society of Medicine, 1958-64; Mem. of Medical Research Council, 1958-62. Radcliffe Prize for Medical Research, Oxford, 1943. Served War of 1939-45, Major, RAMC, 1944-46. *Publications:* (with C. W. Carter) Biochemistry in relation to Medicine, 1949; Joint Editor (with E. J. King) Biochemical Disorders in Human Disease, 1957; numerous papers on biochemical and pathological subjects in various scientific journals. *Recreation:* gardening. *Address:* Brockenhurst, Rockfield Road, Oxted, Surrey. *T:* Oxted 3526; Orchard's Almshouses, Launcells, N Cornwall. *Clubs:* Athenæum, Oxford and Cambridge University.

**THOMPSON, Sir (Thomas) Lionel Tennyson,** 5th Bt, *cr* 1806; Barrister-at-Law; *b* 19 June 1921; *s* of Lt-Col Sir Thomas Thompson, 4th Bt, MC, and of Milicent Ellen Jean, *d* of late Edmund Charles Tennyson-d'Eyncourt, Bayons Manor, Lincolnshire; *S* father, 1964; *m* 1955, Mrs Margaret van Beers (marr. diss. 1962), *d* of late Walter Herbert Browne; one *s* one *d*. *Educ:* Eton. Served War of 1939-45: Royal Air Force Volunteer Reserve, 1940; Flying Officer, 1942 (invalided, 1944); Able Seaman, Royal Fleet Auxiliary, 1944-46. Awarded 1939-45 Star, Aircrew (Europe) Star, Defence and Victory Medals. Called to the Bar, Lincoln's Inn, 1952. *Recreations:* shooting, sailing, flying and photography. *Heir:* *s* Thomas d'Eyncourt John Thompson, *b* 22 Dec. 1956. *Address:* 3 Temple Gardens, EC4. *T:* 01-353 7855; 16 Old Buildings, Lincoln's Inn, WC2. *T:* 01-405 7929; Merry Gardens, Burley, Hants. *T:* Burley 2127. *Clubs:* Royal Aero; Island Sailing (Cowes).

**THOMPSON, Maj.-Gen. (Hon. Lt-Gen.) Sir Treffry Owen,** KCSI 1947; CB 1946; CBE 1942; KHP 1944; County Patron BRCS, Devon Branch; *b* 9 Aug. 1888; *s* of late Rev. W. F. Thompson (Chaplain, India), Fyfield, Abingdon, Berks; *gs* of Sir Charles Bell, Anatomist and Surgeon; *m* 1916, Mary Emily (*d* 1958), *d* of late Rev. Canon Medd, North Cerney, Gloucester; two *s* two *d*; *m* 1959, Vera Elaine, *d* of late E. J. F. Ward; *Educ:* Dragon Sch., Oxford; Priory, Repton; St John's Coll., Oxford; St George's Hosp., London. House appointments Radcliffe, Oxford; RAMC, 1914; served European War, 1914-19, with RAMC; Lt, 1914; Capt., 1915; Major, 1926; DAD Hygiene, India, 1926-29; Lt-Col, 1935; AD Hygiene and Path., India, 1933-37; AD of Hygiene, War Office, 1938-39; DD Hygiene, and Pathology, India, 1939; Col, 1941; DDMS L of C Iraq Forces; Brig., 1942; DDMS Burma, Jan.-May 1942; Acting Maj.-Gen. 1942; DDMS Cen. Command, India; DDMS Eastern Army, 1943-44; Maj.-Gen. 1944; Medical Adviser SACSEA; DMS ALFSEA, 1944-45; DMS SACSEA, 1945; DMS in India, 1946-47; Lt-Gen. (local) 1947; retd, 1948; Col Comdt RAMC, 1950-53. Br. Red Cross Comr for relief work in India and Pakistan, 1947-49; Editor, RAMC Journal, 1950; writer for Official Medical History, Campaigns of World War, 1939-45. County Dir British Red Cross Soc. Devonshire Br., 1951-65. CStJ 1945; Special Service Cross, BRCS 1960. Italian Croce di Guerra, 1917. *Publications:* scientific (Hygiene) articles. *Recreations:* hockey (Oxford Occasionals, Oxford County, 1910-14), cricket, Rugby football, tennis, squash, fishing, bee-keeping. *Address:* Savourys, Chulmleigh, N Devon EX18 7ES. *T:* Chulmleigh 314.

*See also M. E. D. Poore.*

**THOMPSON, Vernon Cecil,** MB, BS London; FRCS; retired 1970 as Surgeon to Department of Thoracic Surgery, The London Hospital; Surgeon, London Chest Hospital; Hon. Consulting Thoracic Surgeon to: West London Hospital, Hammersmith; King Edward VII Hospital, Windsor; Harefield Hospital, Middlesex; Broomfield and Black

Notley Hospitals, Essex; *b* 17 Sept. 1905; 2nd *s* of Dr C. C. B. Thompson, Tidenham, Glos; *m* 1942, Jean, *d* of late H. J. Hilary; one *s* one *d*. *Educ:* Monmouth School; St Bartholomew's Hospital. Resident House appointments followed by First Assistant to a Surgical Unit, St Bartholomew's Hospital, 1929-37. Dorothy Temple Cross Travelling Fellowship, Vienna, and University Hosp., Ann Arbor, Michigan, USA, 1937. President, Soc. of Thoracic Surgeons of Great Britain and Ireland, 1966; Hon. Mem. Amer. Soc. for Thoracic Surgery, 1967. *Publications:* contrib. on surgical diseases of the chest to jls and text books. *Recreations:* fishing, shooting, gardening. *Address:* The Old Vicarage, Llowes, Hereford. *T:* Glasbury 323.

**THOMPSON, William Bell,** MA, PhD; Professor of Physics, University of California, since 1965; *b* N Ireland, 27 Feb. 1922; *m* 1953, Gertrud Helene Goldschmidt, PhD; one *s* one *d*. *Educ:* Universities of British Columbia and Toronto, Canada. BA 1945, MA 1947, Univ. of BC; PhD Toronto, 1950. AERE Harwell; Senior Research Fellow, 1950; Deputy Chief Scientist, 1959. Visiting Prof., Univ. of California, 1961; Head, Theoretical Physics Division, Culham Laboratory, UKAEA, 1961-63; Prof. of Theoretical Plasma Physics, Oxford Univ., 1963-65. *Publications:* Introduction to Plasma Physics, 1962; numerous papers in learned journals, on controlled thermonuclear research, plasma physics, kinetic theory, etc. *Recreations:* music, literature, and gardening (alas!). *Address:* Physics Department, University of California at San Diego, La Jolla, California, USA.

**THOMPSON, (William) Godfrey;** Guildhall Librarian and Director of Art Gallery, City of London, since 1966; *b* 28 June 1921; *s* of late A. and E. M. Thompson, Coventry; *m* 1946, Doreen Mary Cattell; one *s*. *Educ:* King Henry VIII Sch., Coventry. Served with Royal Signals, 1941-46. Entered Library Service, Coventry, 1937; Dep. Borough Librarian, Chatham, 1946; Dep. City Librarian: Kingston-upon-Hull, 1952; Manchester, 1958; City Librarian, Leeds, 1963. Hon. Librarian to Clockmakers' Co. and Gardeners' Co., 1966. Pres., Assoc. of Assistant Librarians, 1962. Member: Council, Library Assoc., 1968-; Council, Aslib, 1968- Hon. Sec. Internat. Assoc. Metropolitan Libraries. FLA 1947. *Publications:* (ed) London for Everyman, 1969; (ed) Encyclopædia of London, 1969. *Address:* Guildhall Library, EC2. *T:* 01-606 3030.

**THOMPSON, Rt. Rev. William Jameson,** CBE 1953; MA; *b* 27 Oct. 1885; *s* of late Robert Wade Thompson, JP, DL, and E. I. Jameson; *m* 1926, M. R. Carr; three *d*. *Educ:* Monkton Combe School, Nr Bath; Trinity College, Cambridge. Master on Staff of Jay Narayans' School, Benares, 1908-10; Engineer in charge of building St John's College, Agra, 1910-12; Teacher's Diploma of Education, Oxford, 1913; Lieut and Capt. Indian Army Reserve of Officers (IARO); served with the Mesopotamia Expeditionary Force, attached to RE Works Dept, 1915-19 (despatches twice); Deacon, 1920; Priest, 1921; Principal of the Stuart Memorial College, Isfahan, 1921-35; Archdeacon of Isfahan, 1933-35; Bishop in Iran, 1935-Oct. 1960. Retd, 1960. *Address:* 29 Portman Avenue, SW14. *Club:* Royal Over-Seas League.

**THOMPSON, William John,** CB 1968; Comptroller and Auditor-General, Northern Ireland. *Address:* Exchequer and Audit Department, Arnott's Buildings, 12 Bridge Street, Belfast BT1 1LZ.

**THOMPSON, Dr William Robin,** FRS 1933; Director, Commonwealth Institute of Biological Control, 1947-58 (Retired); *b* London, Canada, 29 June 1887; son of late William Thompson, Editor of Canadian Agricultural Weekly (The Farmer's Advocate), and Alice Morgan; *m* 1919, Mary, *d* of late Lieut-Commander R. E. Carmody, USN, one *s* one *d*. *Educ:* London Collegiate Institute, London, Canada; Universities of Toronto (BSc 1909), Cornell (MSc 1912), Paris (D ès Sc 1921), Cambridge (Special Research, 1914-15), St Maximin (PhD 1924). Entomologist, US Dept of Agriculture, 1909-13, 1919-28; Bacteriologist, RN 1915-19; Assistant Director, Imperial Institute of Entomology, 1928-47, and Director, Imperial Parasite Service, 1940-47; FRS Canada, 1949; Hon. Member, Prof., Institute of the Civil Service of Canada, 1949; Corresp. Mem. Nat. Acad. of Bordeaux; Lauréat Société Entomologique de France (Prix Passet); Past Pres., Aquinas Society; Editor, Canadian Entomologist, 1947-58; Pres., 10th Internat. Congress of Entomology, 1956. Distinguished Vis. Prof., Michigan State Univ., 1959. Hon. FRES, London. Hon. Fellow RIA; Hon. Mem. Entomolog. Soc. Canada. Medal: Univ. Bordeaux; Nat. Academy of Bordeaux; DUniv hc Bordeaux; DSc hc Carleton. First Harry Scott Smith Award, 1967. *Publications:* Science and Common Sense, 1937; numerous on biological subjects. *Recreations:* philosophy, fishing. *Address:* Apartment 310, 150 Driveway, Ottawa, Ontario, Canada.

**THOMPSON HANCOCK, P(ercy) E(llis);** *see* Hancock.

**THOMPSON-McCAUSLAND, Lucius Perronet,** CMG 1966; *b* 12 Dec. 1904; *e s* of late Sir John Perronet Thompson, KCSI, KCIE and Ada Lucia Tyrrell; *m* Helen Laura, *d* of late Rt Hon. M. M. McCausland, sometime Lieut of Co. Londonderry; two *s* three *d* (and one *s* decd). *Educ:* Repton; King's Coll., Cambridge (Scholar). Helbert Wagg & Co., 1928; Financial News, 1929-34; Moody's Economist Service, 1929-39; Bank of England, 1939-65, Adviser to Governor, 1949-65 (accompanied Lord Keynes to pre-Bretton Woods Conf., 1943, Havana Conf., 1948); Consultant to HM Treasury on internat. monetary problems, 1965-68. Director: Dun & Bradstreet Ltd, 1965-; Trinidad Canadian Oil Ltd, 1967- (Chm., 1970-); Moodies Services Ltd, 1968- (Chm., 1970-). Governor of Repton, 1952- (Chm., 1959-); Chm., Corp. of Working Men's Coll., 1964-69, Principal, 1969-. High Sheriff of Hertfordshire, 1965-66. *Recreations:* garden, travel. *Address:* Epcombs, Hertingfordbury, Hertford. *T:* Hertford 2580. *Clubs:* Athenæum, Gresham; Leander (Henley).

**THOMPSTONE, Sir Eric Westbury,** KBE 1950; CMG 1946; MC; *b* 21 May 1897; *s* of late S. W. Thompstone, CMG, FRCS, FRCP, Deloraine, St Saviour, Jersey, Channel Islands (sometime PMO Northern Nigeria); *m* 1963, Enid Maryon, *widow* of J. J. A. Johnson. *Educ:* Shrewsbury School. Commissioned KSLI 1915; served France and Italy, 1916-19 (MC, Italian Silver Medal for Military Valour, wounded). Joined Colonial Administrative Service, Nigeria, 1919; Resident, 1937; Senior Resident, 1942; Chief Commissioner, NP, 1947-51; Lieutenant-Governor of Northern Region, Nigeria, 1951-52; President: Northern Region House of Assembly, 1946; Northern Region House of Chiefs, 1947-52; MEC and MLC, Nigeria, 1947-52; retired, 1952. *Recreations:* various. *Address:* Deloraine, St Saviour, Jersey, CI. *Club:* Royal Commonwealth Society.

**THOMSON,** family name of **Baron Thomson of Fleet.**

**THOMSON, Hon. Lord; Alexander Thomson;** a Senator of the College of Justice, Scotland, since 1965; *b* 9 Nov. 1914; *s* of James Stuart Thomson, Dunfermline, Fife; *m* 1957, Marie Wilson, *o d* of late David G. Cowan, Milngavie. *Educ:* Dunfermline High School; Edinburgh University (MA, LLB). Served War of 1939-45, Capt., RA. Mem. Faculty of Advocates, Edinburgh, 1946 (Dean, 1964-65); QC (Scotland) 1955; Sheriff of Renfrew and Argyll, 1962-64. *Address:* 11 Moray Place, Edinburgh 3.

**THOMSON OF FLEET,** 1st Baron, *cr* 1964; **Roy Herbert Thomson,** GBE 1970; Chairman: The Thomson Organisation Ltd (and subsidiaries including The Times and The Sunday Times); The Scotsman Publications Ltd; Thomson Newspapers Ltd, Canada; Founder, The Thomson Foundation; *b* 5 June 1894; *s* of Herbert Thomson and Alice Maud Coombs; became British citizen, 1963; *m* 1916, Edna Alice (*d* 1951), *d* of John Irvine, Drayton, Ontario; one *s* one *d* (and one *d* decd). *Educ:* Jarvis Collegiate, Toronto. Director: Security Trust Co. of Birmingham Ltd; Royal Bank of Canada Trust Corp. Ltd; Imperial Life Assurance Co. of Canada, Ltd; Trustee of Reuters Ltd, 1965-. Vice-Pres., Periodical Proprietors Assoc. Ltd; Vice-Chm. of Council, Commonwealth Press Union. Vice-Pres., Publicity Club of London. Formerly: Dir, Royal Bank of Canada; Chancellor, Memorial Univ., Newfoundland. Liveryman, Worshipful Co. of Stationers and Newspaper Makers. FRSA; FBIM. Hon. DLitt St John's Memorial Univ., Newfoundland; Hon. DCL New Brunswick Univ.; Hon. LLD Northern Michigan Univ.; Hon. LHD Long Island Univ., NY. Former Hon. Col, Toronto Scottish Regt. Comdr, Royal Order of Phoenix, Greece. *Recreations:* reading Who Dunnits and balance sheets, light music. *Heir:* *s* Hon. Kenneth (Roy) Thomson, *qv.* *Address:* Alderbourne Arches, Gerrards Cross, Bucks. *T:* Fulmer 2215; Thomson House, Gray's Inn Road, WC1. *T:* 01-837 1234; 425 University Avenue, Toronto, Ont, Canada. *Clubs:* Caledonian; Albany, National, Toronto, York (Toronto).

**THOMSON, Adam;** Chairman since 1964 and Managing Director since 1960, Caledonian Airways; *b* 7 July 1926; *s* of Frank Thomson and Jemina Rodgers; *m* 1948, Dawn Elizabeth Burt; two *s.* *Educ:* Rutherglen Acad.; Coatbridge Coll.; Royal Technical Coll., Glasgow. Pilot; Fleet Air Arm, 1944-47; Flying Instructor 1947-50; BEA, West African Airways, Britavia, 1951-59. *Recreations:* squash, skin-diving. *Address:* 154 Buckswood Drive, Crawley, Sussex. *T:* Crawley 21165. *Clubs:* Caledonian, Royal Aero, Institute of Directors.

**THOMSON, A(dam) Bruce,** OBE 1963; RSA 1946 (ARSA 1937); RSW 1947, President, 1956-63, Hon. RSW 1968; President, SSA 1937; *b* 22 Feb. 1885; *m* 1918, Jessie I. Hislop; one *s* two *d.* *Address:* 65 Cluny Gardens, Edinburgh EH10 6BW. *T:* 031-447 4031. *Club:* Scottish Arts (Edinburgh).

**THOMSON, Alexander;** *see* Thomson, Hon. Lord.

**THOMSON, Alfred Reginald,** RA 1945 (ARA 1939); RP 1944; *b* Bangalore, India; father, Civil Service, India; *m*; one *s* one *d.* Farm training in Kent and Buckingham. *Murals:* Hotel, Duncannon Street; The Science Museum, London; private houses near Cannes, France; The Queen Mary; County Hall of Essex, Chelmsford; The Dental Hospital, Birmingham, etc.; official artist to Royal Air Force (portraits of the Queen and members of Royal Family for RAF Commem. Dinner); White collar Dinner of Pytchley Hunt at Althorp. *Portraits:* King George of Greece; Cardinal Godfrey; Bishop of London, 1961; Bishop of Southwark, 1961; Lord Mayors of Liverpool, Duke of Marlborough, Lord Vansittart, Lord Trenchard, etc.; *landscape:* The Houses of Parliament, The Greater London Council, The Royal Yacht Squadron; book illustrations, The XIV Olympiad Gold Medallist for painting of sports, London, 1948. FSA 1948. *Recreation:* talking nonsense. *Address:* Milton House, 2 Fernshaw Road, SW10. *Clubs:* Chelsea Arts, London Sketch.

**THOMSON, Sir (Arthur) Landsborough,** Kt, *cr* 1953; CB 1933; OBE 1919; DSc; LLD; late Second Secretary, Medical Research Council, having been second officer from 1919 (Assistant Secretary, Principal Assistant Secretary 1936, Under-Secretary 1946, Second Secretary 1949) and retiring to part-time special duties, 1957; late Chairman, Public Health Laboratory Service Board, 1950-61 (MRC), 1961-63 (statutory); President, Zoological Society of London, 1954-60 (Vice-President, 1945-48, 1950-53, 1960-64); Chairman, Home Office Advisory Committee on Protection of Birds, 1954-69; Chairman (formerly President), Council for Nature, 1964-69; Chairman of Trustees, British Museum (Natural History), 1967-69 (Trustee since 1963); *b* Edinburgh, 8 Oct. 1890; *e s* of late Professor Sir J. Arthur Thomson, LLD, Aberdeen; *m* 1920, Mary Moir (*d* 1969), 2nd *d* of late Professor J. W. H. Trail, MD, FRS, Aberdeen. *Educ:* Royal High School, Edinburgh; Aberdeen Grammar School; Univs of Heidelberg, Aberdeen, and Vienna. MA Aberdeen 1911; BSc (with distinction in Zoology) 1914; DSc 1920; Hon. LLD 1956; Asst to the Prof. of Natural History, University of Aberdeen, 1914. On active service in France and Flanders, 1915-19, with Argyll and Sutherland Highlanders and on the Staff, latterly as Assistant Quartermaster-General at GHQ (despatches twice, OBE); demobilised with rank of Lieut-Col. Secretary, Distemper Research Cttee, 1923-32; Sec., Tropical Medical Research Cttee, 1936-41; member, National Radium Commission, 1937-41; Member Colonial Medical Research Committee (CO and MRC), 1954-60; Chm., British Ornithologists' Club, 1938-43; Chm. British Trust for Ornithology, 1941-47; President, British Ornithologists' Union, 1948-55; President, XI Internat. Ornithological Congress, Basel, 1954; mem., Serengeti National Park Enquiry Cttee (Govt of Tanganyika), 1957; FRSE, FRGS, Hon. Fellow Amer. Orn. Union. Hon. Member Société Orn. de France. Buchanan Medal, Royal Society, 1962, etc. *Publications:* Problems of Bird Migration, 1926; Birds, an Introduction to Ornithology, 1927; Bird Migration, a Short Account, 1936, 3rd edn 1949; (ed) A New Dictionary of Birds, 1964; various papers on migration of birds, etc. *Recreation:* travel, formerly climbing. *Address:* 42 Girdwood Road, Southfields, SW18. *T:* 01-788 8692. *Clubs:* Athenæum, Alpine.

**THOMSON, Sir Arthur (Peregrine),** Kt 1959; MC, MD, FRCP; Consulting Physician to United Hospitals, Birmingham; *b* 1890; *s* of Arthur Henry Thomson, Colonial Civil Service; *m* Minnie Scott Lindsley (*d* 1960); one *d.* *Educ:* Dulwich College; University of Birmingham (Queen's Scholar, Ingleby Scholar and Russell Prizeman); RAMC, TF, 1915-19, retiring with rank of Major (Croix de

Guerre, 1918). Lumleian Lectr, RCP, 1949; Linacre Lectr, St John's College, Cambridge, 1959; Harveian Orator, RCP, 1961. Member Gen. Medical Council, 1953-65. Pres. BMA, 1958-59. Chm. Birmingham Reg. Hosp. Bd, 1962-63. Sen. Fellow in Med. Hist., Birmingham Univ., 1960-65. LLD (*hc*) Edinburgh, 1959; Birmingham, 1965. *Publications:* contributions to medical journals. *Address:* 74 Richmond Hill Road, Edgbaston, Birmingham. *T:* 021-454 0735. *Clubs:* National Liberal, Union (Birmingham).

**THOMSON, Bryden;** Orchestral Conductor; Principal Conductor, BBC Northern Symphony Orchestra, since Sept. 1969; *b* Ayr, Scotland. *Educ:* Ayr Academy; Royal Scottish Academy of Music; Staatliche Hochschule für Musik, Hamburg. BMus Dunelm; DipMusEd (Hons) RSAM; LRAM; ARCM. Asst Conductor, BBC Scottish Orchestra, 1958; Conductor: Royal Ballet, 1962; Den Norske Opera, Oslo, 1964; Stora Teatern, Göteborg, Sweden, 1965; Royal Opera, Stockholm, 1966. Associate Conductor, Scottish National Orch., 1966. Guest Conducting: Norway; Sweden; Denmark; Canada; Germany; S Africa. *Recreations:* golf, learning about music. *Address:* c/o BBC, Manchester.

**THOMSON, Daniel,** CB 1963; MD; FRCP; Civil Service Medical Adviser, since 1968 (Treasury Medical Adviser, 1965-68); *b* 30 May 1912; *s* of John Duncan Thomson and Janet Simpson Macfadyen, Dundee and Carradale, Argyll; *m* 1946, Dorothy Violet Coles; two *s*. *Educ:* St Andrews and Edinburgh Universities. MB, ChB 1935; DPH 1946; MD 1948; MRCP 1965. Various hospital and university appointments, 1935-39; served RAMC, 1939-46; Asst Co. MOH, Surrey CC, 1947-50; MO, Min. of Health, 1950; Dep. Chief MO, 1958-65. QHP 1962. Pres., Section of Epidemiology and Preventive Medicine, Royal Soc. of Medicine, 1964-; Milroy Lectr, 1966. *Publications:* articles on medicine and public health. *Recreations:* reading, gardening. *Address:* Langhurst, Prey Heath, Worplesdon, Surrey. *T:* Worplesdon 2078. *Club:* Athenæum.

**THOMSON, Hon. David Spence,** MC 1942; ED; MP (National) for Stratford, New Zealand since 1963; Minister of Defence since 1966; also Minister of Police, Minister in Charge of War Pensions, Minister in Charge of Rehabilitation, since Dec. 1969; *b* Stratford, 14 Nov. 1915; *s* of Percy Thomson, MBE; *m* 1942, June Grace Adams; one *s* three *d*. *Educ:* Stratford Primary and High Sch. Territorial Army, 1931-59; served Middle East, 1939-42; Prisoner of War, 1942-45; Brigadier (Reserve of Officers); Chairman Federated Farmers Sub-provincial Exec., 1959-63; Minister of Defence, Minister in charge of Tourism, Minister in charge of Publicity, 1966-Feb. 67; Minister of Defence, Minister Asst to Prime Minister, Minister in charge of War Pensions, Minister in charge of Rehabilitation, Feb.-March 1967; Minister of Defence, Minister Asst to Prime Minister, Minister in charge of Publicity, Minister in charge of War Pensions, Minister in charge of Rehabilitation, March 1967-Dec. 1969. *Recreations:* golf, gardening, classical music. *Address:* Ministry of Defence, Wellington, New Zealand.

**THOMSON, Donald F.,** OBE 1945; DSc, PhD Cantab 1950, DipAnthrop; Research Fellow in Anthropology, University of Melbourne, 1932-37 and since 1945 (Senior Research Fellow with status of Associate Professor, 1953-64, Professor, 1964-68, Professor Emeritus, 1968); *b* 26 June 1901; *s* of Harry Alexander Thomson; *m* 1925, Gladys Winifred Coleman; twin *s*; *m* 1955, Dorita Maria McColl; one *s*, three *d*. *Educ:* Scotch College, Melbourne; Universities of Melbourne, Sydney and Cambridge. Led three field expeditions to Cape York Peninsula, North Queensland, and has lived among the native tribes of this region for several years, learning the languages of the aborigines; made two subsequent journeys surveying distribution of natives and studying Papuan Hero cults, 1928-29; biologist to the Walter and Eliza Hall Institute of Research, on problems connected with Australian Snakes, 1930-31; appointed research fellow of the University of Melbourne, 1932, to resume field work among the native tribes of Northern Australia; conducted a third expedition, 1932-33; loaned by University of Melbourne to act as Special Commissioner for the Commonwealth Government in Arnhem Land, Northern Territory of Australia, among native tribes of that region, 1935-37; on return proceeded to University of Cambridge, 1937-39; Survey of Administration of N American Indians under auspices of Rockefeller Foundation, 1939; recalled to Australia for military service on outbreak of war; invalided from RAAF (1939-44), Wing Comdr, after being severely wounded in action in Dutch New Guinea while leading a patrol behind the Japanese lines (OBE). Guest lecturer (British Council and Nuffield Foundation) at invitation of Universities of Birmingham and Cambridge, 1952. Led expedition to desert area of Western Central Australia to study Bindibu Tribe, 1957; led 2nd expedition to Great Sandy Desert, WA, under auspices of RGS and Univ. of Melbourne, 1963; field expedition, 1968, to Cape York, Arnhem Land, Great Sandy and Simpson Deserts (ARGC and Nuffield Grants). Member: Aboriginal Welfare Board (Victoria), 1957-67, resigned; Interim Council, Aboriginal Studies, Commonwealth, 1962-63; Foundn Mem., Aust. Inst. Aborig. Research, 1962. Awarded Cuthbert Peek Grant for 1948 by RGS; Patron's Medal, by RGS, for geographical discovery and scientific research in Arnhem Land, 1951; John Lewis Gold Medal by RGS of Australasia (S Austr.), for geographical discovery in Arnhem Land, 1952; Rivers Memorial Medal for Field Work, RAI (London), 1953. Harbison-Higinbotham Prize by Univ. of Melbourne, 1934 and 1949, and David Syme Research Prize, 1936; Wellcome Medal, London, 1939. Two documentary films on desert tribes of Central W Australia. *Publications:* Economic Structure and the Ceremonial Exchange Cycle in Arnhem Land (London, Melbourne), 1949; The Masked Dancers of Cape York; papers in scientific journals. *Recreations:* Australian snakes and mammals, ornithology, gardening. *Address:* Worlingworth, Eltham, Victoria, Australia.

**THOMSON, Sir Douglas;** *see* Thomson, Sir J. D. W.

**THOMSON, Eric Hugh,** CEng, FICE, MIHE; Chief Engineer, Road Construction Units, Ministry of Transport, since 1967; *b* 29 Jan. 1909; *s* of late Hugh Marsh Thomson; *m* 1937, Sarah Skinner Anderson, *d* of late George Anderson, St Andrews; one *s* two *d*. *Educ:* Bradfield; London Univ. (BSc(Eng)). Joined Air Min. Works Directorate, 1935; seconded to RAF Airfield Construction Br. Served War of 1939-45: Middle East, 1942-45. Germany, 1948-50; Chief Engr, Bomber Command, 1951; Dep. Dir of Works, Air Min., 1952; Air Cdre, Chief Engr, Second TAF, 1955; Head of NATO Perm. HQ Office, Paris, 1957; Dir of Works, Air Min., 1960; Dir of Works (Civil Aviation), Min. of Aviation, 1962; Regional Dir, Germany, Min. of Public Bldg and Works, 1964. *Recreations:* domestic architecture, gardening, motoring, travel. *Address:* Brora

Croft, Broomfield Hill, Great Missenden, Bucks. *T:* Great Missenden 4375.

**THOMSON, Ewen Cameron,** CMG 1964; Temporary Project Manager, UNDP/FAO, National Food and Nutrition Programme, Zambia, 1970; *b* 12 April 1915; *s* of Francis Murphy Thomson, Woodhill, Forfar, Angus; *m* 1948, Betty, *d* of Lt-Col J. H. Preston, MBE, Far Horizons, Trearddur Bay, Anglesey; one *s* three *d. Educ:* Forfar Academy; St Andrews University. Cadet, Northern Rhodesia Provincial Admin., 1938. War Service, 1st Bn Northern Rhodesia Regt, 1939-46. District Commissioner, 1946; Dep. Prov. Comr, 1956; Prov. Comr, 1957; Senior Provincial Commissioner, 1961; Permanent Sec. for Native Affairs, 1962; Minister for Native Affairs, 1962; Permanent Secretary, Ministry of Transport and Works, Zambia, 1964; Director of Communications, Contingency Planning Organisation, Zambia, 1966; Exec. Sec., Nat. Food and Nutrition Commn, Zambia, 1967. *Recreations:* tennis, golf, cooking. *Address:* Acorns, Roundhill, Woking, Surrey. *T:* Woking 3223. *Clubs:* Royal Commonwealth Society; Lusaka (Zambia).

**THOMSON, Rt. Rev. Francis;** *see* Motherwell, Bishop of, (RC).

**THOMSON, Francis Paul,** CEng, MIERE; Consultant to Post Office National Giro Service since 1969; *b* Corstorphine, Edinburgh, 17 Dec. 1914; *y s* of late William George and Elizabeth Hannah Thomson, Goring-by-Sea; *m* 1954, E. Sylvia, *e d* of Lokförare J. Erik Nilsson, Bollnäs, Sweden. *Educ:* Friends' Sch., Sibford Ferris; Sch. of Engrg, Polytechnic, London; in Denmark and Sweden. TV and radar research, 1935-42; Special Ops Exec., 1942-44; Sen. Planning Engr, postwar reconstruction, communications industry; founded British Post Giro Campaign, 1946 and conducted Campaign to victory in Parlt, 1965; Lectr, Stockholm Univ. Extension, 1947-49; Founder, and Man. Editor, English Illustrated, 1950-61; techn. exports promotion with various firms, esp. electronic equipment, 1950-60; pioneered electronic language laboratory equipment and methods, 1930, subseq. joined consultancy-production groups; Bank Computerisation Consultant, 1967-. Governor, Watford Coll. of Technology, 1965-. *Publications:* Giro Credit Transfer Systems, 1964; Money in the Computer Age, 1968; (ed jtly) Banking Automation, 1971; Money for the Million: an investment and savings handbook for the new adult, 1971; numerous papers in European, Asian and other learned jls. *Recreations:* gardening; archaeology, holidays in Sweden and USA, genealogy, collecting old purses, money-belts and wallets. *Address:* The Cottage, 39 Church Road, Watford, Herts WD1 3PY. *T:* Watford 36673. *Club:* Special Forces.

**THOMSON, Garry;** Scientific Adviser to the Trustees and Head of the Scientific Department, National Gallery, London, since 1960; *b* 13 Sept. 1925; *s* of Robert Thomson and Mona Spence; *m* 1954, M. R. Saisvasdi Svasti; four *s. Educ:* Charterhouse; Magdalene College, Cambridge (MA). Editorial Staff of A History of Technology, 1951; Research Chemist, National Gallery, 1955; Hon. Editor, Studies in Conservation (jl of Internat. Inst. for Conservation of Historic and Artistic Works), 1959-67. *Publications:* Recent Advances in Conservation (Ed.), 1963; Museum Climatology (Ed.), 1967; reviews and articles in Nature, Museums Journal, Studies in Conservation, etc. *Recreation:* underwater swimming. *Address:* 3 The Chase, Churt, Surrey. *T:* Frensham 2910. *Club:* Athenæum.

**THOMSON, Prof. George Derwent;** Professor of Greek, University of Birmingham, 1937-70; *b* 19 Aug. 1903; *s* of William Henry and Minnie Thomson; *m* 1934, Katharine Fraser Stewart; two *d. Educ:* Dulwich College; King's College, Cambridge. Craven Student, University of Cambridge, 1926-27; Fellow of King's College, Cambridge, 1927-33 and 1934-36. Member, Czechoslovak Academy of Sciences, 1960-. *Publications:* Greek Lyric Metre, 1929 (new edn, 1960); Aeschylus, Prometheus Bound, 1932; M. O'Sullivan, Twenty Years A-Growing (trans. from the Irish), 1933 (World's Classics edition, 1953); Aeschylus, Oresteia, 2 vols, 1938 (new edn, 1966); Aeschylus and Athens, 1941 (new edn, 1966); Marxism and Poetry, 1946 (new edn, 1954); Studies in Ancient Greek Society, Vol. I, The Prehistoric Aegean, 1949 (new edn, 1961); Vol. II, The First Philosophers, 1955 (new edn, 1961); The Greek Language, 1960 (new edn, 1966); Geras: Studies Presented to G. T. on his Sixtieth Birthday, 1963; A Manual of Modern Greek, 1966; Palamas, Twelve Lays of the Gipsy, 1969; books in Irish and Greek and articles in learned and other journals; foreign editions of his books in 16 languages. *Address:* 58 Billesley Lane, Birmingham 13. *T:* 021-449 2656.

**THOMSON, George Ewart;** Director, C. E. Heath & Co. Ltd, 1941-69 (Chairman, 1959-66); *b* 7 May 1897; *s* of John and Alice Susanna Thomson; *m* 1930, Wilhelmina Marjory (*née* Morrison); three *s* one *d. Educ:* Caterham Sch., Surrey; Rastrick Grammar Sch., Yorks. Joined C. E. Heath & Co. Ltd, 1914. Served European War, 1914-18, Infantry, 1916-19. Member of Lloyd's, 1933; Director, C. E. Heath & Co. Ltd, 1941; Member Cttee of Lloyd's, 1945-63; Dep. Chairman of Lloyd's, 1956, Chairman of Lloyd's, 1961. Export Credits Guarantee Advisory Council, 1959-67. *Recreation:* golf. *Address:* Red Hatch, Ridgeway, Hutton, Brentwood, Essex. *T:* Brentwood 70.

**THOMSON, George Malcolm;** Author and Journalist; *b* Leith, Scotland, 2 Aug. 1899; *e s* of Charles Thomson, journalist, and Mary Arthur, *d* of John Eason; *m* 1926, Else (*d* 1957), *d* of Harald Ellefsen, Tænsberg, Norway; one *s* one *d*; *m* 1963, Diana Van Cortland Robertson. *Educ:* Daniel Stewart's College, Edinburgh; Edinburgh University. Journalist. *Publications:* Caledonia, or the Future of the Scots, 1927; A Short History of Scotland, 1930; Crisis in Zanat, 1942; The Twelve Days, 1964; The Robbers Passing By, 1966; The Crime of Mary Stuart, 1967; Vote of Censure, 1968; A Kind of Justice, 1970. *Address:* 46 well Walk, NW3. *T:* 01-435 5853. *Club:* Garrick.

**THOMSON, Rt. Hon. George (Morgan),** PC 1966; MP (Lab) Dundee East since July 1952; *b* 16 Jan. 1921; *s* of late James Thomson, Monifieth; *m* 1948, Grace Jenkins; two *d. Educ:* Grove Academy, Dundee. Served War of 1939-45, in Royal Air Force, 1940-45. Assistant Editor, Forward, 1946, Editor, 1948-53. Contested (Lab) Glasgow, Hillhead, 1950. Member: Fabian Commonwealth Bureau; Exec. Coun., CPA; Joint Chm., Council for Education in the Commonwealth, 1959-64; Adviser to Educational Institute of Scotland, 1960-64. Minister of State, Foreign Office, 1964-66; Chancellor of the Duchy of Lancaster, 1966-67; Joint Minister of State, Foreign Office, 1967; Secretary of State for Commonwealth Affairs, Aug. 1967-Oct. 1968; Minister Without Portfolio, 1968-69; Chancellor of the Duchy of Lancaster, 1969-

70. Hon. LLD Univ. of Dundee, 1967. *Address:* 44 Ramsay Street, Monifieth, Dundee.

**THOMSON, Sir George Paget,** Kt 1943; FRS 1930; DSc Cantab; Master of Corpus Christi, Cambridge, 1952-62, retired; Emeritus Professor of Physics, London University, since 1952; Hon. Fellow: Trinity College, Cambridge; Corpus Christi College, Cambridge; Imperial College of Science and Technology; Institute of Physics; Foreign Member: American Academy of Arts and Sciences; Lisbon Academy; Corresponding Member, Austrian Academy of Sciences; Hon. degrees: DSc Lisbon; LLD Aberdeen; ScD Dublin, Sheffield, Wales, Reading, Westminster College, Mo; Dr Humane Letters Ursinus College, Pa; *b* 1892; *s* of late Sir J. J. Thomson, OM, FRS; *m* 1924, Kathleen Buchanan (*d* 1941), *d* of late Very Rev. Sir George Adam Smith; two *s* two *d*. *Educ:* Perse School, Cambridge; Trinity Coll., Cambridge. First Cl. Math. Trip. Parts I and II, Nat. Sc. Trip. Part II, Fellow and Lecturer, Corpus Christi College, Cambridge, 1914; served in France with 1st Queen's, 1914-15; attached RFC and RAF, 1915-19; worked on various problems of aeronautical research; returned to Cambridge, 1919; Member of Aeronautical Research Committee, 1937-41; Professor of Natural Philosophy in University of Aberdeen, 1922-30; Professor of Physics, Imperial College of Science, 1930-52; Chm. first British Cttee on Atomic Energy, 1940-41; Scientific Adviser: to Air Ministry, 1943-44; to Brit. Delegation Atomic Energy Commn of UN, 1946-47. President, Institute of Physics, 1958-60; President, British Assoc. for Advancement of Science, 1960. Awarded Nobel Prize for Physics, 1937; Hughes Medal, 1939, and Royal Medal, 1949, of Royal Society; Faraday Medal of Institute of Electrical Engineers, 1960. *Publications:* Applied Aerodynamics, 1919; The Atom; Wave Mechanics of the Free Electron; The Foreseeable Future; The Inspiration of Science; J. J. Thomson, 1964; papers on Physics in Scientific Journals and on Aeronautics in Government publications; (with Sir J. J. Thomson) Conduction of Electricity through Gases, 3rd edition; (with W. Cochrane) Theory and Practice of Electron Diffraction. *Recreation:* ship models. *Address:* Little Howe, Mount Pleasant, Cambridge. *T:* 54790. *Club:* Athenæum.

**THOMSON, Very Rev. Ian;** *see* White-Thomson.

**THOMSON, Sir Ivo Wilfrid Home,** 2nd Bt, *cr* 1925; *b* 14 Oct. 1902; *s* of Sir Wilfrid Thomson, 1st Bt, and Ethel Henrietta, 2nd *d* of late Hon. Reginald Parker; *S* father 1939; *m* 1st, 1933, Sybil Marguerite (from whom he obt. a divorce), *yr d* of C. W. Thompson, The Red House, Escrick; one *s* one *d*; 2nd, 1954, Viola Mabel (who *m* 1937, Keith Home Thomson, from whom she obt. a divorce), *d* of Roland Dudley, Linkenholt Manor, Andover. *Educ:* Eton. *Heir: s* Mark Wilfrid Home Thomson, *b* 29 Dec. 1939. *Address:* Frilsham Manor, Hermitage, Newbury, Berks. *T:* Yattendon 291.

**THOMSON, Tun Sir James (Beveridge),** KBE 1966; Kt 1959; *b* 24 March 1902, *e s* of late Rev. William Archibald Thomson, Dalmellington, Ayrshire; *m* 1931, Dr Florence Adam; one *s*. *Educ:* Dalmellington Village School; George Watson's College, Edinburgh; Edinburgh University. MA, 1st Cl. Hons History, Edin. Called to English Bar, Middle Temple, 1929; admitted Advocate in Scotland, 1955. District Officer, 1926 and Resident Magistrate, 1932, N Rhodesia; Judge, Fiji, Chief Justice of Tonga and a Judicial Commissioner for Western Pacific, 1945-48; Judge, Federation of Malaya, 1948; Chief Justice 1956; (first) Lord President of the Federal Court of Malaysia, 1963-66; (last) President of the High Court of S Arabia, 1967; Chm., Delimitation Commn, Republic of Botswana, 1968. Meritorious Service Medal (Perak), 1957; Panglima Mangku Negara (Federation of Malaya), 1958; Seri Maharajah Mangku Negara (Malaysia), 1966. *Publications:* The Laws of the British Solomon Islands, 1948; The Law of Tonga, 1951. *Address:* Craig Gowan, Carr Bridge, Inverness-shire. *T:* Carr Bridge 257. *Club:* Scottish Liberal (Edinburgh).

**THOMSON, Sir (James) Douglas (Wishart),** 2nd Bt, *cr* 1929; Chairman, William Thomson & Co., Shipowners, Edinburgh; *b* 30 Oct. 1905; *s* of Sir Frederick Charles Thomson, 1st Bt, KC, MP, and Constance Margaret (*d* 1970), *yr d* of Hamilton A. Hotson, General Manager British Linen Bank, Edinburgh; *S* father 1935; *m* 1935, Bettina, *er d* of late Lt-Comdr David W. S. Douglas, RN; two *s* three *d*. *Educ:* Eton; University College, Oxford, BA. MP (U) South Aberdeen, 1935-46. *Heir: s* Frederick Douglas David Thomson [*b* 14 Feb. 1940; *m* 1967, Caroline Anne, *d* of Major Timothy S. Lewis; two *s*]. *Address:* Holylee, Walkerburn, Peeblesshire. *T:* Walkerburn 207. *Clubs:* Carlton; New (Edinburgh).

**THOMSON, James Frederick Gordon;** *see* Migdale, Hon. Lord.

**THOMSON, Prof. James Leonard,** CBE 1955; Professor Emeritus in Civil Engineering, Royal Military College of Science, Shrivenham, since 1970; *b* 9 Aug. 1905; *s* of James Thomson, Liverpool. *Educ:* University of Manchester; St John's College, Cambridge. Mather & Platt, Ltd, Manchester, 1923-26; Univ. of Manchester, 1926-30 (BSc (Tech.) 1st Cl. Hons and Stoney Prizeman); Lecturer, Technical College, Horwich, 1930-32; Whitworth Senior Scholar, 1931; St John's Coll., Cambridge, 1932-34 (BA 1934, MA 1938); Research Engineer, ICI, Billingham-on-Tees, 1934-38; Lecturer, Dept of Civil and Mechanical Engineering, Univ. of London, King's College, 1938. Seconded for War-time Service: Managing Engineer, HM Royal Ordnance Factory, Pembrey, Carms, 1940-42; Principal Technical Officer, School of Tank Technology, 1942-46. Royal Military College of Science, Shrivenham: Prof. of Mechanical Engrg and Head of Dept of Civil and Mechanical Engrg, 1946-61; Prof. of Civil Engrg and Head of Dept of Civil Engrg, 1965-70; seconded to ME Technical Univ., Ankara, Turkey, 1961-65 : Consultant Dean and Mechanical Engrg Specialist; later Chief Technical Adviser for UNESCO project in Turkey. *Publications:* various scientific papers dealing with High Pressure Techniques. *Recreations:* mountaineering, sailing. *Address:* Royal Military College of Science, Shrivenham, Berks. *T:* Shrivenham 551, Ext. 61.

**THOMSON, Maj.-Gen. James Noel,** CB 1946; DSO 1917; MC; *b* 25 Dec. 1888; *s* of James Thomson and Margaret Stuart; *m* 1929, Lorna Carmen, *d* of late Sir Edward Buck, CBE; no *c*. *Educ:* Fettes; RMA Woolwich. Senior Under Officer RMA Woolwich, 1909; Commissioned in Royal Field Artillery, 1909; European War France and Germany, 1914-19 (DSO, MC, despatches thrice, French Croix de Guerre); Adjutant Royal Military Academy, 1919-21; Staff College, Camberley, 1921; War Office, 1922-23; Brigade Major 1st Rhine Brigade, 1923-24; General Staff Rhine Army (Operations and Intelligence) 1924-26; Staff

Officer to Major-General Royal Artillery, India, 1927-30; Lieut Colonel, 1929; idc 1932; Asst Master Gen. of the Ordnance in India, 1934-37; Col, 1935; Brig. RA, N Command, India, 1938-41; Comdr 6 Ind. Div., 1941; Temp. Maj.-Gen., 1942; Dep. Master Gen. of Ord. GHQ, India, 1943. ADC to the King, 1939; retired pay, 1946, with hon. rank of Maj.-Gen. *Recreations:* horses, racing. *Address:* c/o Meerut Race Club, Meerut, UP, India. *Club:* United Service.

**THOMSON, Professor James Oliver,** OBE 1919; Professor of Latin, University of Birmingham, 1919-55; Emeritus Professor, 1956; *b* 1889; *s* of J. A. Thomson, tea-planter, Tezpore, Assam, and Isabella Watt; *m* 1935, Linda Marie Kelly, Milngavie; two *s*. *Educ:* Gordon's College, Aberdeen; Univ. of Aberdeen (MA); Trinity College, Cambridge. First Cl. Hons in Classics, Fullerton Scholar, Aberdeen; Ferguson Scholar, Scottish Universities; Senior Scholar of Trinity Coll., Cambridge; Classical Tripos, Pt I, Cl. I, Div. I, 1914, Pt II, Cl. I, 1915; Chancellor's Medal; Charles Oldham Shakespeare Scholarship. Served European War, in France, in KOYLI and Intelligence, 1915-19. Croom Robertson Fell., Aberd. Bailiff of King Edward VI Foundn, Birm., 1951-52. *Publications:* History of Ancient Geography, 1948; Dent's Everyman's Classical Atlas, 1961; articles in learned journals. *Recreations:* gardening, sketching, geology. *Address:* Overdale, Baldernock Road, Milngavie, by Glasgow. *T:* 041-956 1607.

**THOMSON, Very Rev. James Sutherland,** MA; Hon. DD, Toronto, 1936, Glasgow, 1946, Emmanuel College, Saskatoon, 1949, Pine Hill, Halifax, 1957; Hon. LLD State Coll. of Washington, 1944, Queen's Univ., Kingston, Ont., 1945, Univ. of Tor., 1945, McGill Univ., Montreal, 1946, McMaster Univ., Hamilton, Ont., 1947; Manitoba, 1948, Alta, 1949, Sask., 1951, Mount Allison Univ., Sackville, NB, 1958; FRSC 1942; *b* 1892; *s* of late John Thomson and Margaret Sutherland; *m* 1922, Margaret Stewart, *d* of late David Troup; one *s* one *d*. *Educ:* Eastbank Academy, Glasgow; Univ. of Glasgow (MA, 1st Cl. Hons Philosophy, 1914); Trin. Coll. Glasgow (Hons in Theol. 1920). John Clark (Milend) Fell., 1914-20, Univ. of Glasgow; ordained, 1920; Minister Middle Ch., Coatbridge, 1920-24; Sec. for Educ., Church of Scotland, 1924-30; Professor, Systematic Theology, Pine Hill College, Halifax, NS, 1930-37; Pres., Univ. of Saskatchewan, 1937-49; Prof. of Philosophy of Religion (Dean of Divinity) McGill Univ., 1949-59 (Emeritus Prof., 1966); Lecturer, McGill Univ., 1959-65. Served Cameron Highlanders, 1915-17; Rifle Brigade, 1917-19; Temp. Capt., later Hon. Col, Canadian OTC; Chairman, United Council Miss. Educ., 1927-29; Vice-Pres. Brit. and For. Bib. Soc. 1945; President, United Nations Soc. of Can., 1946; Pres., Sect. II, Royal Soc. of Canada, 1955-56; Swander Lecturer, Lancaster, Penn., 1934; Chancellor's Lecturer, Queen's Univ., Kingston, Ont., 1942; Nathaniel Taylor Lecturer, Yale Univ., 1943; Armstrong Lecturer, Toronto Univ., 1950; Alexander Robertson Lecturer, Univ. of Glasgow, 1952-54. Moderator, United Church of Canada, 1956-58. Canadian Centennial Medal, 1967. *Publications:* Studies in the Life of Jesus, 1927; The Way of Revelation (with others), 1928; The Hope of the Gospel, 1955; The Divine Mission, 1957; The Word of God, 1959; God and His Purpose, 1964; Yester-Years, 1969; many articles; presented with Festschrift, The Christian in the Modern World, 1967. *Address'* 4544 Kensington Avenue, NDG, Montreal 261, Canada. *Clubs:* McGill Faculty, Royal Montreal Curling.

**THOMSON, Lt-Col (Bt-Col) John,** TD 1944; MA; Lord Lieutenant of Oxfordshire since 1963; Chairman Barclays Bank Ltd since 1962; Director, Union Discount Company of London Ltd; *b* 1908; *s* of late Guy Thomson, JP, Woodperry, Oxford; *m* 1935, Elizabeth, JP, *d* of late Stanley Brotherhood, JP, Thornhaugh Hall, Peterborough; no *c*. *Educ:* Winchester; Magdalen College, Oxford. Commanded Oxfordshire Yeomanry Regt, RATA, 1942-44 and 1947-50. Deputy High Steward of Oxford University; a Curator of Oxford University Chest; Chairman: Nuffield Medical Trustees; Nuffield Orthopædic Centre Trust. President, British Bankers' Association, 1964-66 (Vice-President, 1963-64); FIB. Mem. Royal Commn on Trade Unions and Employers' Assocs, 1965-68; Mem. BNEC. Hon. Fellow St Catherine's Coll., Oxford. Hon. Colonel: 299 Fd Regt RA (TA), 1964-67; Oxfordshire Territorials, 1967-; Bt Col, 1950. DL Oxfordshire, 1947; High Sheriff of Oxfordshire, 1957; Vice-Lieut, 1957-63. Mem. Jockey Club. Hon. DCL Oxford, 1957. *Address:* Woodperry, Oxford. *T:* Stanton St John 204; Achnaba, Lochgilphead, Argyll. *T:* Lochgilphead 263. *Clubs:* Cavalry, Beefsteak.

**THOMSON, John Adam;** Chief of Assessments Staff, Cabinet Office, since 1968; *b* 27 April 1927; *m* 1953, Elizabeth Anne McClure; three *s* one *d*. Foreign Office, 1950; Third Secretary, Jedda, 1951; Damascus, 1954; Foreign Office, 1955; Private Secretary to Permanent Under-Secretary, 1958-60; First Secretary, Washington, 1960-64; Foreign Office, 1964; Acting Head of Planning Staff, 1966; Counsellor, 1967; Head of Planning Staff, Foreign Office, 1967; seconded to Cabinet Office, 1968. *Recreation:* castles. *Address:* 2 Rosemead Road, W11. *Club:* Athenæum.

**THOMSON, John (Ian) Sutherland,** CMG 1968; MBE 1944; Administrator, British Virgin Islands, since 1967; *b* 8 Jan. 1920; *s* of late William Sutherland Thomson and of Jessie McCaig Malloch; *m* 1945, Nancy Marguerite Kearsley, Suva, Fiji; seven *s* one *d*. *Educ:* High Sch. of Glasgow; Univ. of Glasgow (MA Hons). Served War of 1939-45: Black Watch, 1940; Fiji Military Forces, 1941-45; (Captain). Appointed Cadet, Colonial Administrative Service, Fiji and Western Pacific, 1941; District Administration and Secretariat, Fiji, 1946-54; Seconded to Colonial Office, 1954-56; Dep. Comr, Native Lands and Fisheries, Fiji, 1957-58; Comr of Native Reserves and Chairman, Native Lands and Fisheries Commission, Fiji, 1958-62; Divisional Commissioner, Fiji, 1963-66. *Recreation:* tennis. *Address:* Government House, Road Town, British Virgin Islands. *T:* 2400. *Club:* Fiji.

**THOMSON, Sir John Mackay,** Kt 1946; CB 1941; MA Edinburgh and Oxon; FRSE; (Hon.) FEIS, 1947; *b* Dunning, Perthshire, 21 March 1887; *er s* of late Rev. Peter Thomson, DD, and Margaret, *d* of John Mackay of Inveralmond, Cramond Bridge; unmarried. *Educ:* Trinity College, Glenalmond; Edinburgh University (Bruce of Grangehill Scholar, 1908; Guthrie Fellowship in Classics, 1911); Oriel College, Oxford (Scholar, 1st Classical Moderations, 1911; 2nd Lit Hum 1913). Assistant to Professor of Humanity, Edinburgh University, 1913-14; VIth Form Master, Fettes College, 1915-20; Rector of Aberdeen Grammar School, 1920-21; Scottish Education Department: HM Inspector of Schools, 1921-24; Junior Assistant Secretary, 1925-35; Senior Assistant Secretary, 1935-36; Second Secretary, 1936-39; Acting Secretary, 1939; Secretary of Scottish Education Department,

1940-52; retired 1952. Member of: Scottish Inter-Departmental Cttee on Road Safety among School Children, 1935; Scottish Cttee of Bd of Trade Council for Art and Industry, 1937-39. Chevalier, First Class, of the Order of St Olav, 1948. *Recreations:* fishing, motoring. *Address:* 14 Royal Circus, Edinburgh 3. *T:* 031-225 6845. *Club:* New (Edinburgh).

**THOMSON, J(ohn) Murray,** RSA 1957 (ARSA 1939); RSW; *b* 17 Dec. 1885; *m* 1917, Ellen May Frew; one *s.* *Educ:* Morrison's Academy, Crieff. Studied art in Edinburgh and Paris; specialised in painting animals and birds; ex-President, Society of Scottish Artists. *Recreations:* fly-fishing for trout and salmon. *Address:* 7 Randolph Cliff, Edinburgh 3. *T:* 031-225 6468.

**THOMSON, John Stuart,** CIE 1935; *b* 4 Aug. 1888; *s* of John Cunningham Thomson; *m* 1941, Mary Catherine Frances, *d* of late Maj.-Gen. W. V. Coppinger, CIE, DSO; two *d.* *Educ:* Charterhouse; Oriel College, Oxford. Joined Indian Civil Service, 1912; military duty, 1915-17; Civil Administration, Iraq, 1917-23; Deputy Commissioner in Punjab, 1923-31; Development Commissioner NWFP, 1931-32; Revenue Commissioner NWFP, 1932-36; retired, 1937. *Address:* Gunnels Cottage, The Avenue, Bucklebury, Reading, Berks.

**THOMSON, Hon. Kenneth (Roy);** newspaper proprietor; Chairman of the Board, Times Newspapers Ltd, since 1968 (Deputy Chairman, 1966-67); Chairman of the Board, President and Director, Thomson Newspapers Limited (owners of 40 newspapers in Canada); President and Director, Thomson Newspapers Inc. (owners of 31 newspapers in the United States); Chairman of the Board, President and Director, The Independent Inc.; Chairman of the Board and Director: Central Canada Insurance Service Limited; Scottish and York Holdings Limited; Director, Toronto Dominion Bank; President, Vice-President or Director of numerous newspapers and other communications companies in Canada and the US; *b* Toronto, Ont., 1 Sept. 1923; *s* and *heir* of 1st Baron Thomson of Fleet, *qv*; *m* 1956, Norah Marilyn, *d* of A. V. Lavis; two *s* one *d.* *Educ:* Upper Canada Coll.; Univ. of Cambridge, England (MA). Served War of 1939-45 with RCAF. Began in editorial dept of Timmins Daily Press., Timmins, Ont., 1947; Advertising Dept, Galt Reporter, Galt, 1948-50, General Manager, 1950-53; returned to Toronto Head Office of Thomson Newspapers to take over direction of Company's Canadian and American operations. Member, Baptist Church. *Recreations:* collecting antiques and old master paintings. *Address:* (home) 8 Kensington Palace Gardens, W8; (office) Times Newspapers Limited, Printing House Square, EC4. *Clubs:* National, Toronto, Granite, Toronto Hunt (Toronto).

**THOMSON, Sir Landsborough;** *see* Thomson, Sir (Arthur) Landsborough.

**THOMSON, Leslie G.;** *see* Grahame-Thomson.

**THOMSON, L. M. M.;** *see* Milne-Thomson.

**THOMSON, Nigel Ernest Drummond;** Sheriff-Substitute of Lanarkshire at Hamilton since 1966; *b* 19 June 1926; *y s* of late Rev. James Kyd Thomson, and late Joan Drummond; *m* 1964, Snjólaug Magnússon, *yr d* of Consul-General Sigursteinn Magnússon; one *s* one *d.* *Educ:* George Watson's College, Edinburgh; Univs of St Andrews and Edinburgh. Served with Scots Guards and Indian Grenadiers, 1944-47. MA (St Andrews) 1950; LLB (Edin.) 1953. Called to Scottish Bar, 1953. Pres., Speculative Soc., Edinburgh, 1960. Standing Counsel to Scottish Educn Dept, 1961-66. *Recreations:* music, woodwork, golf. *Address:* Elderslie, Newton Road, Strathaven, Lanarkshire. *T:* Strathaven 3256.

**THOMSON, Peter;** Sheriff Substitute of Lanarkshire since 1962; *b* 1914; *s* of John Thomson, SSC, and Matha Lindsay Miller; *m* 1939, Jean Laird Nicoll; two *s* one *d.* *Educ:* Royal High School, Edinburgh; Edinburgh University. Gordon Highlanders, 1941-46; Capt. 1944. Called to Scottish Bar, 1946. Founded Scottish Plebiscite Society, 1947. Sheriff Substitute of Caithness, Sutherland, Orkney and Zetland, 1955. Chairman, Thistle Prize, 1964. *Recreations:* walking, golf. *Address:* Haughhead Farm House, Uddingston, Lanarkshire. *Club:* University (Aberdeen).

**THOMSON, Robert John Stewart,** CMG 1969; MBE 1955; Ministry of Defence, since 1970; *b* 5 May 1922; *s* of late John Stewart Thomson, FRIBA, and Nellie Thomson (*née* Morris). *Educ:* Bromsgrove Sch.; Worcester Coll., Oxford. Service with Sudan Defence Force, 1943-45. Sudan Political Service, 1943-54 (District Commissioner, 1950-54). Attached Ministry of Defence, 1955-57; First Sec., British High Commission, Accra, 1957-60, 1962-64, Counsellor, 1966-69. *Recreations:* polo, singing. *Address:* 38 Greycoat Gardens, Westminster, SW1. *Clubs:* Royal Over-Seas League; Polo (Accra).

**THOMSON, Colonel Roger Gordon,** CMG 1918; DSO 1916; late RA; *b* 4 Apr. 1878; *s* of late Maj.-Gen. D. Thomson, RE; *m* 1904, Florence Lucy (*d* 1949), *y d* of late Maj.-Gen. W. E. Delves Broughton, Bengal Staff Corps; one *s* two *d.* *Educ:* Cheltenham College; RMA, Woolwich. Joined Army, 1898; Capt. 1905; Major, 1914; Temp. Lt-Col 1916; Col 1922; served European War, 1914-18 (DSO, CMG); retired pay, 1926; employed at the War Office, Oct. 1927-April 1942, and then at Ministry of Home Security (Home Office), June 1942-Sept. 1945. *Recreations:* hunting, rowing, cricket. *Address:* Quarrymead, Hillcrest Road, Hythe, Kent.

*See also Sir R. D. M. R.-Bunbury, Bt.*

**THOMSON, Air Vice-Marshal Ronald Bain,** CB 1959; DSO 1943; DFC 1943; *b* 15 April 1912; *s* of George Thomson, Aberdeen, and Christina Ann (*née* Reid); *m* 1940, Elizabeth Napier (*née* Ayling); two *d.* *Educ:* Robert Gordon's College, Aberdeen. Joined Royal Auxiliary Air Force (612 County of Aberdeen Squadron), 1937. Senior Lecturer Physical Educ. and Hygiene, Pretoria Technical College, S Africa, 1939. War of 1939-45, Coastal Command. AOC, RAF, Gibraltar, 1958-60; AOC, RAF, Scotland and Northern Ireland, 1960-63; AOA, Flying Training Command, 1963-66; retired. Member of the Queen's Body Guard for Scotland, The Royal Company of Archers. Commander Order of St Olav, 1963. *Recreations:* shooting, golf. *Club:* Royal Air Force.

**THOMSON, Sir Ronald (Jordan),** Kt 1950; Lord Lieutenant of Peeblesshire, 1956-68; *b* 13 March 1895; *s* of William Thomson, shipowner; *m* 1919, Patricia Martha Burrell Guild (*d* 1955); one *s* (one *d* decd). Commissioned Border Regiment, 1914; served European War, 1914-18; resigned commission on account of wounds, 1917. Elected Peeblesshire County Council, 1922; Convener of Peeblesshire, 1932-58; President, Association of County Councils in Scotland, 1948-50; Civil Defence Controller, Eastern

Scotland, 1954-60; Chairman, Scottish Special Housing Association, 1952-62. JP 1922-69; DL 1930, VL 1945, Peeblesshire. *Address:* Kaimes, West Linton, Peeblesshire. *T:* West Linton 413.

**THOMSON, Roy Harry Goodisson,** FCA; *b* 2 Jan. 1891; *m* 1921, Margaret Hewetson Harper, *d* of James Williamson Blacklock; two *d*. *Educ:* Merchant Taylors' School. Joined Trinity House Service as Deputy Accountant, 1922; Secretary of the Corporation, 1946-51. Retired. Younger Brother, Trinity House, 1953. *Address:* 56 Trinity Church Square, SE1.

**THOMSON, Rev. T(homas) B(entley) Stewart,** MC 1918; TD 1939; Hon. DD Aberdeen 1946; Extra Chaplain to the Queen since 1959 (Chaplain to the Queen, 1952-59, to King George VI, 1951-52); *b* 1889; *s* of Rev. William Stewart Thomson, MA, FSA, FRGS, Principal of Aberdeen CS and Business Coll.; *m* 1918, Margaret Rolland Menzies, *d* of Rev. Robert Mackenzie, MA, Alloa; one *s* two *d*. *Educ:* Robert Gordon's College; Aberdeen University (MA Hons), BD, (Lyon Prizeman, Brown Scholar). Missioner on the Canadian prairies, 1913; Asst Minister, Glasgow Cathedral, 1914; ordained to Dalziel (Motherwell), 1919; St Stephen's, Edinburgh, 1923; Govan Old, Glasgow, 1939; Dunbarney (Bridge of Earn), 1948-59. 2nd Lieut Glasgow Hldrs, 1915; Capt., 1917; Divisional Gas Officer, 19th and 62nd Divs; CF (TA), 1922; SCF, 52nd (Lowland) Div., 1928; SCF, Scottish Comd, 1934; DACG, 10th Corps, 1940; invalided out of TA, 1941. For many years Vice-pres., British Legion; Chm., Church of Scotland Young Men's Guild, 1926-29; Convener: Cttee on Socs for Young Men and Women, 1929-31; Jewish Mission Cttee, 1931-34; Home Mission Cttee, 1945-47; Home Board, 1947-52; Cttee on Ministers' War Memorial and Orphan Funds, 1953-63; Moderator of Presbytery of Edinburgh, 1938; Moderator of Synod of Perth and Stirling, 1954-55; Moderator of Presbytery of Perth, 1957-58; Senior Past Grand Chaplain, Grand Lodge of Scotland. *Publications:* Crumbs for the Children, 1923; Preparing for the Lord's Table, 1925; The Quest of Youth, 1926; Studies in the Teaching of Jesus, 1928; Bens and Glens, 1938; Job: A dramatised version, 1939; Five Hundred Texts for Special Occasions, 1945; Guide to Govan Old Parish Church, 1947; The Chaplain in the Church of Scotland (Baird Lecture), 1947. *Recreation:* journalism. *Address:* 7 Tullylumb Terrace, Perth. *T:* Perth 21797. *Clubs:* Caledonian, Royal Scots (Edinburgh); Perth Conservative.

**THOMSON, Thomas Davidson,** CMG 1962; OBE 1959; *b* 1 April 1911; *s* of J. A. Thomson, FFA, FRSE, and Barbara M. Davidson, Edinburgh; *m* 1947, Marjorie Constance, *d* of T. R. Aldred, Limbe, Nyasaland; one *s*. *Educ:* George Watson's Coll., Edinburgh; Edinburgh Univ. (MA, LLB); Magdalene Coll., Cambridge. Editor, The Student, 1932; Travel Secretary, Scottish National Union of Students, 1932; Cadet, Nyasaland Administration, 1934; Civil Demobilisation Officer, 1945; Assistant Secretary, Nyasaland, 1947; Officer in charge, Domasi Community Development Scheme, 1949; Officer in charge, School of Local Government, 1955, Social Development, 1958; retired as Commissioner for Social Development, Nyasaland, 1963. Carried out survey of Adult Education in Nyasaland, 1956-57; organised Nyasaland Council of Social Service, 1959. Served War of 1939-45, E Africa (Major). Sec., Eastern Border Development Assoc., 1962-67. Member, Bd, Scottish Rights of Way Soc., Ltd, 1966; Chm., Scottish Rural Community Development Cttee, 1968. Pres., Berwickshire Naturalists' Club, 1969-70. Brain of Britain, BBC Radio, 1969. *Publications:* A Practical Approach to Chinyanja, 1947; sundry reports and papers on Nyasaland affairs; papers in Hist. Berwickshire Naturalists' Club. *Recreations:* gardening, philately, Scouting (Chief Commissioner, Nyasaland, 1958; County Commissioner, Berwickshire, 1966). *Address:* The Hill, Coldingham, Berwickshire. *T:* Coldingham 209. *Club:* Caledonian (Edinburgh).

**THOMSON, Sir William,** Kt 1970; OBE 1960; JP; Chairman: Turner & Co. (Gibraltar) Ltd, since 1946, also of Mediterranean Bank Ltd; Hon. Consul for the Netherlands, Gibraltar, since 1946; *b* 30 Aug. 1916; *s* of William J. Thomson, and Africa Ruiz; *m* 1943, Clemencia Isola; no *c*. *Educ:* Forest Sch., Essex; Downing Coll., Cambridge (MA). Joined Gibraltar Defence Force, 1939, Major comdg AA Battery, 1943. Director (family firm), Turner & Co. (Gib.) Ltd (founded 1831), 1940. Hon. Col, Gibraltar Defence Force, later Gibraltar Regt, 1953-58; Mem., Public Service Commn, 1959-; Speaker, Legislative Council, later House of Assembly, 1964-69; Mayor of Gibraltar, Aug.-Dec. 1969. Actively engaged since 1946 in shipping matters in Gibraltar and on Boards of various companies. JP (Gibraltar). Chevalier, Order of Orange Nassau, Netherlands, 1959. *Recreations:* shooting, yachting. *Address:* 63/65 Irish Town, Gibraltar. *T:* 5794. *Clubs:* Royal Thames Yacht; Royal Gibraltar Yacht (past Vice-Commodore), Calpe Rowing (past Vice-Pres.), Mediterranean Racing (Gibraltar).

**THOMSON, William Archibald Robson,** MD; Editor of The Practitioner since 1944; Chairman: The Leprosy Study Centre; Medical Section, British Academy of Forensic Sciences; Medical Adviser, E. & S. Livingstone and J. & A. Churchill; *b* 6 Nov. 1906; 2nd *s* of late Rev. W. A. Thomson; *m* 1934, Marion Lucy Nannette, *d* of late Sir Leonard Hill, FRS; two *s*. *Educ:* University of Edinburgh. MB, ChB 1929, MD (Hons), 1933, University of Edinburgh. Clin. Asst, Ho. Phys. and Clin. Tutor, Royal Infirmary, Edinburgh; Asst, Dept of Medicine, also Davidson Research Fellow in Applied Bacteriology, Univ. of Edinburgh; Paterson Research Scholar and Chief Asst, Cardiac Dept, London Hospital; First Assistant, Medical Unit, St Thomas' Hospital. FRSocMed; FRIPHH; Founder Member, The British Academy of Forensic Sciences. *Publications:* Black's Medical Dictionary; The Searching Mind in Medicine; The Practitioner's Handbook (ed); Practical Dietetics (ed); Calling the Laboratory (ed); The Doctor's Surgery (ed); Sex and Its Problems (ed); Various articles on medical and cardiological subjects in Quarterly Journal of Medicine, British Heart Jl, Lancet, etc. *Address:* 4 Rutland Court, Queens Drive, W3. *T:* 01-992 8685; 5 Bentinck Street, W1. *T:* 01-935 1978. *Club:* Athenæum.

**THONEMANN, Peter Clive,** MSc, DPhil; FPS; Head of Department of Physics, University College, Swansea, since 1968; *b* 3 June 1917. *Educ:* Melbourne Grammar Sch., Melbourne; Sydney and Oxford Univs. BSc Melbourne, 1940; MSc Sydney, 1945; DPhil Oxford, 1949. Munition Supply Laboratories, Victoria, Australia, 1940; Amalgamated Wireless, Australia, 1942; University of Sydney, Commonwealth Research Fellow, 1944; Clarendon Laboratory, Oxford, ICI Research Fellow, 1946; United Kingdom Atomic Energy Authority, 1949; Dep. Dir, Culham Laboratory, 1965-68. FPS 1948. *Address:*

Department of Physics, University College, Swansea, Singleton Park, Swansea, Wales.

**THORBY, Hon. Harold Victor Campbell,** JP; farmer and grazier; *b* Annandale, NSW, 2 Oct. 1888; 3rd *s* of late F. J. Thorby; *m* 1st, Vera Lynda (*d* 1958), 2nd *d* of late A. F. Morley; two *d*; 2nd, 1960, Alfreda Elizabeth. *Educ:* Geurie PS; Sydney Grammar School; Technical College, Sydney. President Farmers' and Settlers' Assoc., NSW, 1923-26; Member for Wammerawa, NSW Assembly, 1922-27; Castlereagh, 1927-30; Minister for Agriculture, Sydney, NSW, 1927-30; MHR Calare, 1931-40; Assistant Minister for Repatriation and War Service Homes, 1934; Asst Minister for Commerce, 1935; Acting Minister Commerce, 1936; Acting Minister for Defence, 1937; Minister for Defence and Civil Aviation, 1938; Minister of Civil Aviation and Works, 1938-39; Postmaster-General and Minister of Health, 1940; Deputy Leader Australian Country Party, 1937-40; Chairman Water Conservation and Irrigation Commission, 1927-30; Chairman River Murray Commission, 1938-39; Member Trade Delegation, London, 1935, and International Wool Conference, Berlin, 1935; Chm. Dubbo Graziers' Assoc., 1951-53; NSW Graziers' Gen. Council, 1952-53; Exec. Cttee, 1953-54. Chm. Medical Dental Bldg Ltd, 1957-58. Trustee, Lawson and Dubbo, 1956-60. Chm. Dirs, Gibb & Beeman, Optometrists, 1957-63. Life Member: FSA, NSW; Aust. Country Party; NSW Ambulance Brigade. MEC, 1934-40. *Address:* 29 Carnarvon Road, Roseville, Sydney, NSW 2069, Australia.

**THORLEY, Charles Graham;** Under-Secretary, Department of Trade and Industry (formerly Ministry of Technology), since 1969; *b* 4 Jan. 1914; *s* of Charles Lord Thorley; *m* 1958, Peggy Percival Ellis (*née* Boor); one step *s* one step *d*. *Educ:* Manchester Grammar Sch.; King's Coll., Cambridge (Mod. Lang. Scholar). Served War of 1939-45, Eritrea and Cyrenaica (Lt-Col). Entered Civil Service as Economist, Bd of Trade, 1936; attached to British Embassy, China, 1936-38; Mem. British Economic Mission to Belgian Congo, 1940-41; HM Treasury, 1940-57; served on UK financial delegns and missions in Japan, US, Egypt, France, Switzerland, W Germany, etc; Min. of Power, 1957; Under-Secretary and Head of Coal Div., 1965-69; Acct-Gen. and Dir of Finance, 1969. Chm., NATO Petroleum Planning Cttee, 1962-65. *Recreation:* travel. *Address:* 15 Thornton Way, NW11. *T:* 01-455 2784. *Club:* Reform.

**THORN, John Leonard,** MA; Headmaster of Winchester College since 1968; *b* 28 April 1925; *s* of late Stanley L. Thorn and of Winifred M. Thorn (*née* King); *m* 1955, Veronica Laura, *d* of late Sir Robert Maconochie, OBE, QC; one *s* one *d*. *Educ:* St Paul's School, West Kensington; Corpus Christi College, Cambridge. Served War of 1939-45, Sub-Lieutenant, RNVR, 1943-46. 1st Class Historical Tripos, Parts I and II, 1948-49; Assistant Master, Clifton College, 1949-61 (Head of History Dept, 1951-58, Housemaster, 1958-61); Headmaster, Repton School, 1961-68. *Publications:* (joint) A History of England, 1961. *Address:* Headmaster's House, Winchester College, Winchester. *T:* 4328.

**THORN, Sir Jules,** Kt 1964; Chairman of Thorn Electrical Industries Limited since 1937 (Managing Director, 1937-69); other companies are included in the Thorn Group. Chairman, Radio Industry Council, 1966. Hon. Master of the Bench, Middle Temple, 1969. *Address:* Thorn Electrical Industries Limited, Thorn House, Upper St Martins Lane, WC2. *T:* 01-836 2444.

**THORNDIKE, (Arthur) Russell;** actor and author; *b* 6 Feb. 1885; *s* of Rev. Arthur J. W. Thorndike, Hon. Canon of Rochester, and Agnes Macdonald Bowers; *m* Rosemary Benvenuta Dowson (*d* 1970). *Educ:* St George's School, Windsor; King's School, Rochester; Ben Greet's Academy. First stage appearance, Theatre Royal, Cambridge, 1904; first London appearance, Marlborough Theatre, Holloway, 1905; member of Ben Greet's company in England and America, 1905-08; in Shakespeare season, Court Theatre, 1909; toured with Matheson Lang in South Africa, India and the Far East, 1911-13; Horniman repertory, Manchester, 1913; served in Egypt and Gallipoli with 1st Westminster Dragoons, 1914-16; invalided out; with Old Vic company 1916-20, as leading man and joint-producer in 1919-20; Grand Guignol, 1920; Old Vic, 1922; played name part in his own play Dr Syn, at Lyceum, on tour, and at Strand under own management, 1926-27; lead in Ben Greet's company in America, 1929-30; in Shakespeare season, Kingsway, 1932. Since 1932 has had many parts in West End productions, notably in Shakespeare, including Open Air Seasons, also made frequent appearances as Smee in Peter Pan. Has appeared in several films. *Publications:* The Tragedy of Mr Punch (with Reginald Arkell); The Slype; Herod's Peal; Jet and Ivory; Vandekkers; The Water Witch; Sybil Thorndike, a biography; Show House Sold; The House of Jeffreys; The Master of the Macabre; In the Steps of Shakespeare; The First Englishman; also the "Dr Syn" Saga. *Address:* 5 Oaklands Road, SW14.

**THORNDIKE, Dame Sybil,** CH 1970; DBE 1931; LLD Manchester and Edinburgh; DLitt: Southampton, Oxford and Surrey; actress and manager; *b* Gainsborough, 1882; *d* of Rev. A. J. W. Thorndike, Hon. Canon of Rochester; *m* 1908, Sir Lewis Casson, MC (*d* 1969); two *s* two *d*. *Educ:* Rochester High School. Shakespearian Repertory in America with Ben Greet; about 100 parts in twenty-five plays, 1903-7; Miss Horniman's Co., Manchester, 1908-9; Chas. Frohman's Repertory, Duke of York's Theatre, 1910; American tour with John Drew, 1910-11; leads with Miss Horniman's Company, 1911-13; Shakespearian leads at Old Vic, 1914-18; played in numerous London productions, 1919-20; Little Theatre, 1920-22, London's Grand Guignol; about thirty parts in as many plays including Louise (The Old Women), the Model (The Medium), Judy (The Tragedy of Mr Punch), Mrs Meldon (Progress); in management various London theatres, 1922-27, productions include Saint Joan (and revivals), The Trojan Women, Medea, The Verge, Hippolytus, Henry VIII, Macbeth, The Greater Love, also took leading parts in many; played leading parts for the Old Vic season at the Lyric, Hammersmith, 1927; Nurse Cavell in Dawn (film); produced Judith of Israel, playing the title-rôle, 1928; toured South Africa for nine months; returned in Jan. 1929, and played the name part in Major Barbara, Lily Cobb in Mariners by Clemence Dane, and revived Jane Clegg and the Medea in one bill; toured with Madam Plays Nap, playing Henriette, and played at New Theatre, 1929; played Phèdre in French; Sylvette in Fire, and Mrs Alving in Ghosts, Emilia in Othello at the Savoy, 1930; Jess Fortune in Matchmaker's Arms, Eloise in Marriage by Purchase, 1931; revived Saint Joan and toured with it, 1931; toured in Egypt, Palestine, Australia, and New Zealand, 1932-33; on return to London played Evie in The Distaff Side, Victoria Van Brett (Double Door), Z in

Shaw's Village Wooing; autumn 1934, The Distaff Side in New York; 1935, Grief Goes Over, London; Short Story; 1936, Kind Lady; My Son's my Son; Six Men of Dorset; Hippolytus (Nurse); 1937, Yes My Darling Daughter; 1938, Time and the Conways, New York; The Corn is Green, Duchess Theatre, 1940, Piccadilly Theatre; six war-time tours with the Old Vic under CEMA, 1940-42; 1942-43 in House of Jeffreys; Ibsen's Ghosts and Shaw's Captain Brassbound's Conversion, Dublin; 1943, Bristol and Liverpool Season with She Stoops to Conquer and Queen Bee; Vaudeville, London, in Lottie Dundass; Alice in Wonderland, White Queen and Queen of Hearts, Old Vic Repertory, New Theatre, 1944. Old Vic Repertory, New Theatre and ENSA tour Belgium, Germany and Paris, 1945-46; Clytemnestra in Electra, and Mrs Wilson in In Time to Come, King's, Hammersmith, 1946; Mrs Fraser in Call Home the Heart, St James's, 1946-47; Mrs Linden in The Linden Tree, Duchess, 1947-48; Mrs Jackson in The Return of the Prodigal, Globe, 1948; Isobel Brocken in The Foolish Gentlewoman, Duchess, 1949; Aunt Anna Rose in Treasure Hunt, Apollo, 1949; Lady Douglas in Douglas, Edinburgh Festival, 1950; Mrs Whyte in Waters of the Moon, Haymarket, 1951; Laura Anson in A Day by the Sea, Haymarket, 1953. Recitals in Australia, New Zealand, Far East, Africa, Turkey and Israel for the British Council, 1954-56; A Family Reunion, Phœnix Theatre, 1956; film of The Prince and the Showgirl; The Potting Shed, New York; tour, Australia, in The Chalk Garden, 1957-58; Eighty in the Shade, Globe, 1959; tour of Sea Shell, 1959; film, Big Gamble; film Hand in Hand; Waiting in the Wings, tour and Duke of York's, 1960; Teresa of Avila, Dublin and Vaudeville, 1961. Toured Australia in recitals, 1962; Chichester Festival, 1962; Vanity Fair, tour and Queen's, 1962-63; Chichester Festival, 1963; The Reluctant Peer, Duchess, 1964; Season of Goodwill, Queen's, 1964; Return Ticket, Duchess, 1965; Arsenic and Old Lace, Vaudeville, 1966; The Viaduct, Yvonne Arnaud, Guildford, 1967; There Was an Old Woman, Sybil Thorndike Theatre, 1969. Has appeared on television. Freedom of Rochester, 1929. *Publications:* Religion and the Stage; Lillian Baylis (with R. Thorndike). *Recreation:* piano. *Address:* 98 Swan Court, Chelsea, SW3. *T:* 01-352 1315.

**THORNE, Rt. Rev. Frank Oswald,** CBE 1957; DD; *b* 21 May 1892; *s* of Leonard Temple Thorne and Ada Theodosia Franklin; unmarried. *Educ:* St Paul's School; Christ Church, Oxford (Scholar). 2nd Class Hon. Mods, 1913; BA (War Degree), 1918; 2nd Class Theology, 1921; MA 1935; Served European War, 13th (S) Bn The Manchester Regt, Captain and Adjutant, 1915-17; Brigade Major, No 1 Section Tyne Garrison, 1918-19 (wounded, MC); Ordained, 1922; Curate All Souls' Clapton Park, 1922-25; joined Universities Mission to Central Africa, 1925; First Warden of S Cyprian's Theological Coll., Tunduru, Diocese of Masasi, Tanganyika Territory, 1930-34; Bishop of Nyasaland, 1936-61; Dean of Prov. of Central Africa, 1955-61. MLC Nyasaland, 1937-43, 1946-49. DD Lambeth, 1958. *Address:* PO Box 52, Lindi, Tanzania.

**THORNE, Peter Francis,** CBE 1966; Deputy Serjeant at Arms, House of Commons, since 1957; *b* 1914; *y s* of late Gen. Sir Andrew Thorne, KCB, CMG, DSO; *m* 1959, Lady Anne Pery, MA, DPhil, *d* of 5th Earl of Limerick, GBE, CH, KCB, DSO, TD; one *s* three *d. Educ:* Eton; Trinity Coll., Oxford. Served War of 1939-45; with 3rd Bn Grenadier Guards (wounded), 1939-41; HQ 2nd Div., 1941-42; Staff College, Quetta, 1942; on staff of India Command and HQ, SACSEA, 1943-45; demobilised with rank of Hon. Lieut-Col, 1946. With Imperial Chemical Industries Ltd, 1946-48. Assistant Serjeant at Arms, House of Commons, 1948-57. *Address:* Speaker's Green, House of Commons, SW1. *T:* 01-930 6240 (ext. 309). *Clubs:* Guards; Royal Yacht Squadron.

*See also Angela Countess of Limerick.*

**THORNE, Robin Horton John,** CMG 1966; OBE 1963; HM Overseas Service, retired; with Vice-Chancellors' Committee, since 1967; *b* 13 July 1917; *s* of late Sir John Anderson Thorne; *m* 1946, Joan Helen Wadman; one *s. Educ:* Dragon Sch., Oxford; Rugby (open scholar); Exeter College, Oxford (open scholar). War Service, Devonshire Regiment and King's African Rifles, 1939-46. Colonial Administrative Service (now HM Overseas Civil Service), 1946-67; Tanganyika Administration, 1946-58; Aden, 1958-67; Asst Chief Sec. (Colony), MLC and Mem. of Governor's Exec. Coun., 1959-63; Ministerial Sec. to Chief Minister, 1963-65; Assistant High Commissioner, 1966-67. Trustee of Aden Port Trust, 1959-66. *Recreations:* various. *Address:* The Old Vicarage, Old Heathfield, Sussex. *T:* Heathfield 3160. *Club:* Royal Commonwealth Society.

**THORNELY, Gervase Michael Cobham;** Headmaster of Sedbergh School since Sept. 1954; *b* 21 Oct. 1918; *er s* of Major J. E. B. Thornely, OBE, and Hon. Mrs M. H. Thornely; *m* 1954, Jennifer Margery, *d* of Sir Hilary Scott, *qv*, Knowle House, Addington, Surrey; two *s* two *d. Educ:* Rugby Sch.; Trinity Hall, Cambridge. Organ Scholar; 2nd Cl. Hons, Modern and Mediæval Languages Tripos; BA, 1940; MA, 1944. FRSA 1968. Assistant Master, Sedbergh School, 1940. *Recreations:* music, fly-fishing. *Address:* Birksholme, Sedbergh, Yorkshire. *T:* Sedbergh 491. *Club:* Public Schools.

**THORNEYCROFT,** family name of **Baron Thorneycroft.**

**THORNEYCROFT,** Baron *cr* 1967 (Life Peer), of Dunston; (**George Edward**) **Peter Thorneycroft,** PC 1951; Barrister-at-law; late RA; Chairman: Pye Holdings; Pye of Cambridge Ltd; Pirelli General Ltd; Pirelli Ltd; Director, Securicor; *b* 26 July 1909; *s* of late Major George Edward Mervyn Thorneycroft, DSO, and Dorothy Hope, *d* of Sir W. Franklyn, KCB; *m* 1st, 1938, Sheila Wells Page (who obtained a divorce, 1949); one *s*; 2nd, 1949, Countess Carla Roberti; one *d. Educ:* Eton; Roy. Mil. Acad., Woolwich. Commissioned in Royal Artillery, 1930; resigned Commission, 1933; called to Bar, Inner Temple, 1935; practised Birmingham (Oxford Circuit); MP (C) Stafford, 1938-45, Monmouth, 1945-66. Parliamentary Secretary, Ministry of War Transport, 1945. President of the Board of Trade, October 1951-January 1957; Chancellor of the Exchequer, Jan. 1957-Jan. 1958, resigned; Minister of Aviation, July 1960-July 1962; Minister of Defence, 1962-64; Secretary of State for Defence, Apr.-Oct. 1964. Exhibition of paintings, Trafford Gallery, 1961. *Address:* 42c Eaton Square, SW1. *Club:* Army and Navy.

**THORNHILL, Lt-Col Edmund Basil,** MC 1918; Vice-Lieutenant of Cambridgeshire and Isle of Ely, since 1965; *b* 27 Feb. 1898; *e s* of late E. H. Thornhill, Manor House, Boxworth, Cambridge; *m* 1934, Diana Pearl Day, *d* of late Hubert G. D. Beales, Hambleden and Cambridge; two *s* one *d. Educ:* St Bees School; Royal Military Academy. 2nd Lieut Royal

Artillery, 1916; served European War, 1914-18, France and Belgium (wounded, MC); served War of 1939-45, France, Western Desert (Eighth Army) and Italy (despatches); psc 1934; Lt-Col 1945; retd 1948. Chm., Cambs and I of Ely TA & AFA, 1957-62. DL Cambs and Isle of Ely, 1956. *Address:* Manor House, Boxworth, Cambridge. *T:* Elsworth 209. *Club:* Army and Navy.

**THORNLEY, Sir Colin (Hardwick),** KCMG 1957 (CMG 1953); CVO 1954; Director-General, Save the Children Fund, since 1965 (Deputy Director, 1963-65); *b* 1907; *s* of late Dr and Mrs J. H. Thornley; *m* 1940, Muriel Betty Hobson; one *s* two *d*. *Educ:* Bramcote School, Scarborough; Uppingham; Brasenose College, Oxford. MA (hons jurisp.). Colonial Administrative Service, The Tanganyika Territory, 1930-39, seconded to Colonial Office, 1939-45; Principal Private Secretary to Secretary of State for the Colonies, 1941-45; Admin. Secretary, Kenya, 1945-47; Dep. Chief Secretary, Kenya, 1947-52; Chief Secretary, Govt of Protectorate of Uganda, 1952-55; Governor and Commander-in-Chief, British Honduras, 1955-61; retired, 1962. Mem., Regional Boundaries Commn, Kenya, 1962; Trustee, Imp. War Museum, 1968. *Recreations:* lawn tennis, golf, cricket. *Address:* 16 Larpent Avenue, Putney, SW15. *T:* 01-789 3368. *Clubs:* East India and Sports, Hurlingham.

**THORNTON, Dr (Clara) Grace,** CBE 1965 (OBE 1959); MVO 1957; Head of Consular Department, Foreign and Commonwealth Office, since 1970; *b* 27 June 1913; *d* of late Arthur Augustus Thornton and Clara Maud Hines; unmarried. *Educ:* Kettering High School; Newnham Coll., Cambridge (MA, PhD). Research: Iceland, Cambridge, 1935-39. Min. of Information, 1940-45. Press Attaché, Copenhagen, 1945-48; Vice-Consul, Reykjavik, 1948-51 (Chargé d'Affaires during 1949 and 1950); Foreign Office, 1951-54; 1st Sec. and Consul, Copenhagen, 1954-60; 1st Sec. and Information Officer, Brussels, 1960-62; 1st Sec. and Consul, Djakarta, 1962-64 (Consul-General, 1963-64); Consul-General, Lisbon, 1965-70. FRSA 1969. Danish Freedom Medal, 1945; Order of Dannebrog, 1957. *Recreations:* music, embroidery, Scandinavica, cats. *Address:* 17 Onslow Court, Drayton Gardens, SW10. *T:* 01-373 2965. *Clubs:* Oxford and Cambridge University, University Women's.

**THORNTON, Ernest,** MBE 1951; JP; DL; *b* Burnley, Lancs, 18 May 1905; *s* of Charles Thornton and Margaret (*née* Whittaker); *m* 1930, Evelyn, *d* of Fred Ingham, Blacko, Nelson; one *s* (and one *s* decd). *Educ:* Walverden Council Sch., Nelson, Lancs. Cotton weaver, 1918-26; costing clerk, 1926-29. Rochdale Weavers and Winders' Assoc.; Asst Secretary, 1929-40, Secretary, 1940-. President, Amalgamated Weavers' Assoc., 1960-65. Secretary, United Textile Factory Workers' Assoc., 1943-53. Member: Lord President's Advisory Council for Scientific and Industrial Research, 1943-48; Council of British Cotton Industry Research Assoc., 1948-53. MP (Lab) Farnworth, 1952-70; Joint Parliamentary Secretary, Min. of Labour, 1964-66. Member: UK Trade Mission to China, 1946; Anglo-American Cotton Textile Mission to Japan, 1950; Cotton Board's Mission to India, 1950. Mayor of County Borough of Rochdale, 1942-43. JP 1944. Comp. TI 1966. DL Lancaster, 1970. *Address:* 6 Lyndhurst Avenue, Castleton, Rochdale, Lancs. *T:* Rochdale 31954.

**THORNTON, George Edwin,** CMG 1948; MBE 1932; Member of Board, Central African Building Society; *b* 1899. Served European War 1914-18, in E Africa, 1916-17; Colonial Service, Northern Rhodesia, 1918; Financial Secretary, Northern Rhodesia, 1945-51. *Address:* 37 Kew Drive, Highlands, Salisbury, Rhodesia.

**THORNTON, Sir Gerard;** *see* Thornton, Sir H. G.

**THORNTON, Dr Grace;** *see* Thornton, Dr C. G.

**THORNTON, Sir (Henry) Gerard,** Kt 1960; FRS 1941; DSc; formerly Head of Department of Soil Microbiology, Rothamsted; *b* 22 Jan. 1892; *s* of Francis Hugh Thornton, Kingsthorpe, Northampton; *m* 1924, Gerda, *d* of Kai Nærregaard, Copenhagen; one *s*. *Educ:* Radley; New Coll., Oxford. Northamptonshire Regt, 1914-19 (Seconded Royal Flying Corps and RAF), served in Egypt, Sudan and Salonika; Rothamsted Experimental Station, 1919-57, researches on nitrogen-fixing and other soil bacteria. Foreign Secretary, Royal Society, 1955-60. *Publications:* Papers on researches in Proceedings of Royal Society, Journal of Agricultural Science and other periodicals. *Recreations:* gardening and geology. *Address:* 3 Romeland Cottage, St Albans, Herts. *T:* St Albans 51333. *Clubs:* Athenæum, Savile.
*See also P. K. Thornton.*

**THORNTON, Air Vice-Marshal Henry Norman,** CBE 1946; retired; *b* 25 April 1896; *s* of Edward Thornton, Dersingham; *m* 1933, Lucie Marie Louise, *d* of A. Argod, Paris. *Educ:* Chatham House Sch. Northumberland Fusiliers, 1914-16; RFC, 1917-18; RAF, 1918-47. 601 Squadron, 1928-30; Staff Coll., Camberley, 1931-32; Air Attaché, Low Countries and Scandinavia, 1935-37; Stockholm, Helsinki, 1940-41; Washington, 1941-43; Bomber Command, 1944; AOC a group in SEAC, 1945; AOC a group in BAOR, 1946. *Recreation:* golf. *Address:* West Lavington Hill, Midhurst, Sussex. *T:* Midhurst 2593. *Clubs:* White's, Royal Air Force.

**THORNTON, Lt-Gen. Sir Leonard (Whitmore),** KCB 1967 (CB 1962); CBE 1957 (OBE 1944); Chief of Defence Staff, New Zealand, since 1965; *b* Christchurch, 15 Oct. 1916; *s* of late Cuthbert John Thornton and Frances Caverhill Thornton; *m* 1942, Gladys Janet, *d* of W. F. and E. Sloman, Wellington; three *s*. *Educ:* Christchurch Boys' High Sch.; Royal Military Coll., Duntroon, Australia. Commissioned in New Zealand Army, 1937. Served War of 1939-45 (despatches twice, OBE), Middle East and Italy in 2nd New Zealand Expeditionary Force; Commander, Royal Artillery, 2 New Zealand Division. Commander, Tokyo Sub-area, 1946; Deputy Chief of General Staff, 1948; idc 1952; Head, New Zealand Joint Service Liaison Staff, 1953 and 1954; QMG, New Zealand, 1955; AG, 1956-58; Chief, SEATO Planning Office, Thailand, 1958-59; Chief of General Staff, NZ, 1960-65. *Recreation:* fishing. *Address:* 7 Bristow Place, Karori, Wellington, NZ. *T:* 766.526. *Clubs:* Wellington, Wellesley, United Services Officers (Wellington).

**THORNTON, Peter Eustace;** Deputy Secretary, Cabinet Office, since 1970 (Under-Secretary, 1967-70); *b* 28 Aug. 1917; *s* of Douglas Oscar Thornton and Dorothy (*née* Shepherd); *m* 1946, Rosamond Hobart Myers, US Medal of Freedom, Sewanee, Tennessee; two *s* one *d*. *Educ:* Charterhouse; Gonville and Caius, Cambridge. Served with RA, mainly in Middle

East and Italy, 1940-46. Joined Board of Trade, 1946. Secretary, Company Law Cttee (Jenkins Cttee), 1959-62; Assistant Under-Secretary of State, Department of Economic Affairs, 1964-67. *Recreations:* sailing, walking. *Address:* Manor Farm House, Seale, near Farnham, Surrey. *T:* Runfold 2685. *Club:* Oxford and Cambridge.

**THORNTON, Peter Kai;** Keeper, Department of Furniture and Woodwork, Victoria and Albert Museum, London, since 1966; *b* 8 April 1925; *s* of Sir Gerard Thornton, *qv; m* 1950, Mary Ann Rosamund, *d* of E. A. P. Helps, Cregane, Rosscarbery, Co. Cork; three *d. Educ:* Bryanston Sch.; De Havilland Aeronautical Technical Sch.; Trinity Hall, Cambridge. Served with Army, Intelligence Corps, Austria, 1945-48; Cambridge, 1948-50 (Hon. Tripos, Mod. Langs); Voluntary Asst Keeper, Fitzwilliam Museum, Cambridge, 1950-52; Joint Secretary, National Art-Collections Fund, London, 1952-54; entered Victoria and Albert Museum as Asst Keeper, Dept of Textiles, 1954; transf. to Dept of Woodwork, 1962. *Publications:* Baroque and Rococo Silks, 1965; contribs to several joint works including World Furniture, 1965; articles on textiles and furniture in Burlington Magazine, Gazette des Beaux Arts and other journals. *Recreations:* various, none over-riding. *Address:* 23 Bury Walk, SW3. *T:* 01-589 5543; Carrigillihy, Union Hall, Co. Cork; Phillips Farm Cottage, Eaton Hastings, Faringdon, Berks.

**THORNTON, Sir Ronald (George),** Kt 1965; a Director, Bank of England, 1966-70; *b* 21 July 1901; *s* of late Henry George Thornton; *m* 1927, Agnes Margaret (*née* Masson); one *s* one *d. Educ:* St Dunstan's Coll., Catford. Director, Barclays Bank Ltd, 1961; General Manager, 1946; Vice-Chairman, 1962-66; Director: Friends' Provident & Century Life Office; The Century Insurance Co. Ltd; Century Insurance, Trust Ltd; United Dominions Trust Ltd, 1962-; Member: Cttee of Inquiry on Decimal Currency, 1961-62; Export Council for Europe, 1960-64; Chairman, Bank Education Service, 1965-66; Member Governing Body, St Dunstan's Educational Foundation. Fellow, Inst. of Bankers. *Address:* Little Coombe, Wildernesse Avenue, Sevenoaks, Kent. *Club:* Royal Automobile.

**THORNTON, Colonel Thomas Anson,** CVO 1939; Order of Sword of Sweden, 1935; *b* 1887; *s* of late T. W. Thornton, JP, Brockhall, Northampton; *m* 1916, Constance Maude Stuart (*d* 1964); *d* of late Sir S. Fraser, KCSI, CIE; two *d* (*er s* killed in action, 1944; *yr s* decd 1951). *Educ:* Harrow; RMC, Sandhurst. Joined 7th Hussars, 1906; served European War, 1914-19 with 7th Hussars and in Afghanistan on Staff, 1919; Lt-Col Commanding 7th Hussars, 1927-31; re-employed, 1940-44. Equerry to Prince Arthur of Connaught, 1932-38; High Sheriff of Northamptonshire for 1946-47; DL Northamptonshire, 1947; Colonel of 7th Hussars, 1948-52. *Address:* Brockhall, Northampton. *T:* Weedon 214. *Club:* Cavalry.

**THORNTON-DUESBERY, Rev. Julian Percy,** MA; Canon-Theologian at Liverpool Cathedral, since 1968; *b* 7 Sept. 1902; *s* of late Rt Rev. Charles Leonard Thornton-Duesbery (formerly Bishop of Sodor and Man) and late Ethel Nixon Baumgartner. *Educ:* Forest Sch., Snaresbrook; Rossall Sch.; Balliol Coll., Oxford (Domus Exhbn); Wycliffe Hall, Oxford. Goldsmiths' Exhibition, 1922; *prox acc* Craven Scholarship, 1922; 1st Class Hon. Moderations (Classics), 1923; 1st Class Lit Hum 1925; 1st Class Theology, 1926; Junior Canon Hall Greek Testament Prize, 1926; Senior Denyer and Johnson Scholarship, 1928; Deacon, 1926; Priest, 1927; Chaplain of Wycliffe Hall, Oxford, 1926-27; Vice-Principal, 1927-33; Chaplain, Fellow, and Librarian of Corpus Christi Coll., Oxford, 1928-33; Headmaster of St George's Sch., Jerusalem, 1933-40; Master of St Peter's Hall, 1940-45; Rector of St Peter-le-Bailey, Oxford, 1940-45, 1955-61; Acting Principal, Wycliffe Hall, 1943-44; Principal of Wycliffe Hall, Oxford, 1944-55; Master, St Peter's Coll. (formerly St Peter's Hall), Oxford, 1955-68, Hon. Fellow, 1968. Commissary to Bishop in Jerusalem, 1943-63; Member of Council: St Lawrence Coll., Ramsgate, 1941; Headington Sch., 1943; Forest Sch., Snaresbrook, 1958-68; St Stephen's Coll., Broadstairs, 1970-. Examining Chaplain to: Bishop of Blackburn, 1927-33; Bishop in Jerusalem, 1933-40; Bishop of Worcester, 1941-; Bishop of Oxford, 1955-68; Bishop of Sodor and Man, 1967-. Select Preacher, University of Oxford, 1943-45. *Publication:* The Open Secret of MRA, 1964. *Recreation:* walking. *Address:* 26 Beech Court, Allerton Road, Liverpool 18. *T:* 051-724 4958; Hillside Cottage, Corony Hill, Maughold, Isle of Man. *T:* Ramsey, IoM 3020.

**THORNTON-KEMSLEY, Colonel Sir Colin (Norman),** Kt 1958; OBE 1946; TD 1950; MA; *b* 2 Sept. 1903; *e s* of late Norman Kemsley, Woodford Green, Essex; *m* 1930, Alice Helen, *o c* of late William Thornton of Thornton; assumed additional surname Thornton by Deed Poll upon marriage; one *s* two *d. Educ:* Chigwell Sch.; Wadham Coll., Oxford. Until 1969, a partner in Kemsley, Whiteley and Ferris, Chartered Surveyors, and a Director, John Lewis Properties Ltd. A Director, Thornton Farms Ltd; Hon. Treasurer, Essex and Middlesex Provincial Area, National Union of Cons. and Unionist Associations, 1938-43. MP (U) Kincardine and West Aberdeenshire, 1939-50, North Angus and Mearns, 1950-64. Vice-Chairman Cons. Parliamentary Cttee for Agriculture and Food, 1950-53; Chairman, Scottish Unionist Members' Cttee, 1957-58; Chairman, Liberal-Unionist Parliamentary Group, 1961-62; Member Public Accounts Cttee, 1955-64. A Vice-Pres., Town and Country Planning Assoc. Trustee, Speech Therapists Union. President, Kincardineshire Scout Assoc. Dir, BRCS, Kincardineshire, 1968-. Rejoined Royal Artillery from TARO, Sept. 1939; passed Staff Coll. (Sen. Wing), and held various staff appointments including AQMG (ops), Eastern Command; Colonel comdg an Area, 1945. *Recreations:* golf, shooting, caravanning and grandchildren. *Address:* Thornton Castle, Laurencekirk, Kincardineshire. *T:* Laurencekirk 301. *Clubs:* Carlton; MCC.

**THORNTON-SMITH, Ernest T.;** Fellow of the Institute of Directors; Fellow of the Royal Society of Arts; *b* 7 March 1881. *Educ:* City of London Sch. Served with the Queen's Westminsters, 1914-16; with the Ministry of Food, 1917-19; Grand Council, Our Dumb Friends League, since 1918; Squire of Telscombe since 1933; Chairman of the National Mark Egg and Poultry Trade Cttee, 1933-36; Government Director on the National Mark Egg Central Board, 1931-36; Minister of Agriculture's representative on the Pig Marketing Board, 1935-39; London Area Officer Ministry of Food, 1939-41; Master Worshipful Company of Gardeners, 1938-39. Member Westminster City Council, 1947-53; Chairman, Hospital for Women, Soho, 1937-57; Board of Governors Middlesex Hospital, 1948-57; Hon. Treas., Blue Cross, 1962; Member Council of Educational

Television, 1961; Exec. Cttee of The Friends of St Johns, 1963. Gave historic Manor House, Telscombe Village and considerable acreage of surrounding farmlands and downs to the National Trust, 1960; gave Park Head, Cornwall with a mile of coast to the Trust in connection with Enterprise Neptune, 1966. Instituted Scholarship for Royal Gardens, Kew, for annual study of tropical and botanical growth in Caribbean and S America, 1967. Coronation Medal, 1937. *Publications:* The State and Agriculture, etc. *Recreations:* chess, riding, racing (won Oaks with Chatelaine, 1933; gave stallion Jock Scot and ten brood mares to National Stud, 1952), punting, skating, paddling-mate to the Royal Canoe Club, 1909-14. *Address:* 14 Carlos Place, W1. *T:* 01-499 4338; Telscombe Village, near Lewes, Sussex. *T:* Brighton 32167. *Club:* Bath.

**THORNYCROFT, John Ward,** CBE 1957; CEng; Hon. President, John I. Thornycroft & Co. Ltd, since 1966 (Chairman, 1960-66; Managing Director, 1942-66); Director: Southampton, Isle of Wight and South of England Royal Mail Steam Packet Co. Ltd, since Jan. 1961; Vosper Ltd; *b* 14 Oct. 1899; *s* of late Sir John E. Thornycroft; *m* 1930, Esther Katherine, *d* of J. E. Pritchard; one *s* one *d*. *Educ:* Royal Naval Colleges, Osborne, Dartmouth and Keyham; Trinity Coll., Cambridge. Served European War, 1914-18, HMS Canada, HMS Opal, HM Submarine G10, HMS Spenser (1914-15 War Service Star). Member Council, RINA. *Recreations:* golf, sailing and gardening. *Address:* Steyne, Bembridge, Isle of Wight. *T:* Bembridge 2502. *Clubs:* United Service; Bembridge Sailing (IOW); Royal Southampton Yacht.

**THOROGOOD, Kenneth Alfred Charles;** Managing Director, Tozer Kemsley & Millbourn (Holdings) Ltd, since 1965; *b* 1924; *s* of Albert Jesse and Alice Lucy Thorogood; *m* 1947, José Patricia Smith; two *d*. *Educ:* Highbury County Grammar School. Flt Lt RAF, 1942-46. Tozer Kemsley & Millbourn (South Africa) Ltd, 1947 and (Rhodesia) Ltd, 1954. Chairman, Brit. Export Houses Assoc., 1968-; Member, Committee of Invisibles, 1968-. *Publications:* contribs to financial and technical journals. *Recreations:* aviation, athletics, music. *Address:* 3 Romney Close, NW1. *Clubs:* City of London; Wanderers (Johannesburg).

**THOROLD, Captain Sir Anthony (Henry),** 15th Bt, *cr* 1642; OBE 1942; DSC 1942, and Bar 1945; DL; JP; RN Retired; *b* 7 Sept. 1903; *s* of Sir James (Ernest) Thorold, 14th Bt; *S* father, 1965; *m* 1939, Jocelyn Elaine Laura, *er d* of late Sir Clifford Heathcote-Smith, KBE, CMG; one *s* two *d*. *Educ:* Royal Naval Colleges Osborne and Dartmouth. Entered RN 1917; qualified as Navigating Officer, 1928; psc 1935; Commander, 1940; served in Mediterranean and Home Fleets, 1939-40; Staff Officer Operations to Flag Officer Commanding Force 'H', 1941-43; in command of Escort Groups in Western Approaches Comd, 1944-45; Captain, 1946; Naval Assistant Secretary in Cabinet Office and Ministry of Defence, 1945-48; Sen. Officer, Fishery Protection Flotilla, 1949-50; Captain of HMS Dryad (Navigation and Direction Sch.), 1951-52; Commodore in Charge, Hong Kong, 1953-55; ADC to the Queen, 1955-56; retired, 1956. CC Kesteven, 1958; DL Lincs, 1959. JP Lincolnshire (Parts of Kesteven), 1961; High Sheriff of Lincolnshire, 1968. Chairman: Grantham Hospital Management Cttee, 1963; Lincoln Diocesan Trust and Board of Finance, 1966. *Recreation:* shooting. *Heir:* *s* Anthony Oliver Thorold, *b* 15 April 1945. *Address:* Syston Old Hall, Grantham, Lincs. *T:* Honington 270. *Club:* Army and Navy.

**THORPE, Bernard;** Senior Partner, Bernard Thorpe & Partners, since 1922; Land Agent, Surveyor, Farmer; *b* 27 June 1895; *m* 1916, Hilda Mary, *d* of Edwin Wilkinson, Coventry; one *s* one *d* (and one *s* killed as Pilot Officer Royal Air Force). *Educ:* private tutor; Nottingham Univ. Member Godstone (Surrey) RDC and of its Board of Guardians, 1926-36; Past President, (1939) and Past Chairman, Surrey and Sussex Br. Incorp. Society of Auctioneers and Landed Property Agents; sometime Member Council, Home Grown Timber Marketing Assoc.; Director (Tile Section), Redland Holdings Ltd; Chairman, Park Investments Ltd, 1958-63; Chairman, Assoc. of Land and Property Owners, 1962-64. Past Master, Worshipful Company of Gold and Silver Wyre Drawers, 1966 (Member 1938, and Past Warden); Member Court of Assistants, Worshipful Company of Paviors (Member 1938); Freeman, City of London. Freemason. *Recreations:* hunting and shooting; formerly Rugby football. *Address:* Stanley House, Mount Ephraim, Tunbridge Wells, Kent. *T:* Tunbridge Wells 20709. *Club:* City Livery.

**THORPE, Rt. Hon. Jeremy;** *see* Thorpe, Rt Hon. John Jeremy.

**THORPE, Rt. Hon. (John) Jeremy,** PC 1967; MP (L) North Devon since Oct. 1959; Leader of the Liberal Party since 1967; *b* 29 April 1929; *s* of late J. H. Thorpe, OBE, KC, MP (C) Rusholme, and Ursula, *d* of late Sir John Norton-Griffiths, Bt, KCB, DSO, sometime MP (C); *m* 1968, Caroline (*d* 1970), *d* of Warwick Allpass, Kingswood, Surrey; one *s*. *Educ:* Rectory Sch., Connecticut, USA; Eton Coll.; Trinity Coll., Oxford. President, Oxford Union Society, Hilary, 1951; Barrister, Inner Temple, 1954. Member Devon Sessions. Contested (L) N Devon, 1955. Hon. Treasurer, Liberal Party Organisation, 1965-67. A Vice-Pres., Anti-Apartheid Movement, 1969-. *Publications:* (joint) To all who are interested in Democracy, 1951; contrib. to newspapers and periodicals. *Recreations:* music; collecting Chinese ceramics. *Address:* House of Commons, SW1. *Clubs:* Reform, National Liberal; Barnstaple and North Devon, Barnstaple and District (Barnstaple).

**THORPE, Prof. Lewis (Guy Melville),** BA, L-ès-L, PhD, D de l'U; FIAL; Professor of French, University of Nottingham, since 1958; *b* 5 Nov. 1913; *e s* of late Lewis Thorpe and Jessie Emily Thorpe, of Brighton, Sussex; *m* 1939, Barbara Reynolds, *qv*, *d* of late Alfred Charles Reynolds; one *s* one *d*. *Educ:* University College, London; University of Paris. War service with Rifle Brigade, Intelligence Corps, Army Educational Corps in Algeria, Tunisia, Italy, Greece, Austria, 1940-46; 2nd Lieut, 1942, Captain, 1942, Major, 1943, Lt-Col, 1945; despatches, 1945. Lecturer in Romance Linguistics, University College, Nottingham, 1946-54; Reader, 1955-57. Hon. Sec., British Branch, Internat. Arthurian Soc., 1951-66, Pres., 1966-, Internat. Sec., 1966-; Hon. Treas. of Assoc. of University Teachers of French, 1951-52, Hon. Sec., 1953-55, Pres., 1956; Member: Calvin Editorial Cttee, World Alliance of Reformed and Protestant Churches, 1962-; Assoc. degli Scrittori Veneti, 1964-; Cttee, British Branch, Société Rencesvals, 1964-; Cttee, Assoc. Internat. des Docteurs (Lettres) de l'Université de Paris, 1965-67; Visiting Professor, French Language and Literature, University of Munich, 1965. Editor: Nottingham Mediæval Studies since inception in 1957; Nottingham French Studies since inception in 1962; Bulletin Bibliographique de la Société Internationale Arthurienne, 1967-. *Publications:* La France Guerrière, 1945; Le roman de Laurin, fils de Marques le Sénéchal: a first contribution to the study of the Linguistics of an unpublished thirteenth-century Prose-Romance, 1950; The Study of French in a Modern University, 1958; Le roman de Laurin, fils de Marques le Sénéchal: the text of MS BN f. fr. 22548, 1960; Geoffrey of Monmouth: The History of the Kings of Britain, 1966 (limited edn, 1969); (with Barbara Reynolds), Guido Farina, Painter of Verona, 1896-1957, (and Italian edn) 1967; Two Lives of Charlemagne, 1969; Einhard the Frank: The Life of Charlemagne, 1970; contribs to Erasmus, French Studies, Modern Language Notes, Modern Language Review, Renaissance and Modern Studies, Rivista di Letterature Moderne, Romania, Scriptorium, etc. *Recreations:* travel, cricket, amateur antiquarianism. *Address:* Department of French, The University, Nottingham. *T:* Nottingham 56101. Ext. 2476. *Club:* MCC.

**THORPE, William Geoffrey,** CBE 1970; Deputy Chairman, British Railways Board, since 1969 (Vice-Chairman, 1968-69); Chief Executive (Railways), since 1970; *b* 14 Oct. 1909; *s* of Robert Smith Thorpe and Maude Elizabeth Taylor Thorpe, York; *m* 1940, Gwendoline Margaret Marriott; one *s. Educ:* Nunthorpe Grammar Sch., York. Traffic Apprentice, L&NER, 1934; series of posts in Operating Dept, 1934-39; attached to Admiralty, 1939-41; further series of posts in Operating Dept, 1942-57; Line Traffic Manager (Great Eastern), 1957-62; Asst General Manager, London Midland Region, May 1962; General Manager, Scottish Region, Oct. 1963; Chairman and General Manager: Scottish Railway Board, 1964-67; London Midland Railway Board, 1967. MInstT. *Recreations:* golf, gardening (supervisory). *Address:* 222 Marylebone Road, NW1. *T:* 01-262 2587. *Club:* United Service.

**THORPE, Prof. William Homan,** FRS 1951; MA, ScD (Cantab); Fellow since 1932, President since 1969, Jesus College, Cambridge; Emeritus Professor of Animal Ethology, Cambridge University; Joint Editor of "Behaviour: an International Journal of Comparative Ethology"; Chairman, Arthur Stanley Eddington Memorial Trust; *b* 1 April 1902; *o s* of Francis Homan and Mary Amelia Thorpe (*née* Slade), Hastings and Weston-super-Mare; *m* 1936, Winifred Mary, *o d* of Preb. G. H. Vincent; one *d. Educ:* Mill Hill Sch.; Jesus Coll., Cambridge. Research Fellow of International Education Board (Rockefeller Foundation) at University of California, 1927-29; Research Entomologist at Farnham Royal Parasite Laboratory of Imperial Bureau of Entomology, 1929-32; Tutor Jesus Coll., Cambridge, 1932-45; Lecturer in Entomology in the University, 1932-59; Leverhulme Research Fellow in East Africa, 1939; Senior Tutor, Jesus Coll., Cambridge, 1945-47. President, Association for Study of Animal Behaviour, 1948-52; President, Society British Entomology, 1951-53; Prather Lecturer in Biology, Harvard Univ., 1951-52; President of British Ornithologists Union, 1955-60; President Sect. D (Zoology) British Association (Sheffield), 1956; Visiting Prof., University of California, 1958; Eddington Lecturer, 1960; Riddell Lecturer, Durham Univ., 1961; Fremantle Lecturer, Balliol Coll., Oxford, 1962-63; Gifford Lectr, St Andrews Univ., 1970-71. *Publications:* Learning and Instinct in Animals, 1956; (ed. with O. I. Zangwill) Current Problems in Animal Behaviour, 1961; Bird Song: The Biology of Vocal Communication and Expression in Birds, 1961; Biology and the Nature of Man, 1962; Science, Man and Morals, 1965; Quakers and Humanists, 1968; (ed. with A. M. Pantin) The Relations Between the Sciences, by late C. F. A. Pantin, 1968; numerous papers on Entomology, Ornithology, Comparative Physiology and Animal Behaviour (Ethology): in Journal Society Exp. Biology, Biol. Reviews, Ibis, etc. *Recreations:* music, swimming. *Address:* Jesus College, and 9 Wilberforce Road, Cambridge. *T:* 50943.

**THORPE DAVIE, Cedric;** *see* Davie, C. T.

**THORSON, Hon. Joseph T.,** PC Canada, 1941; President of Exchequer Court, Canada, since 1942; Barrister-at-law, Winnipeg; *b* Winnipeg, 15 March 1889; *s* of Stephen Thorson who came from Iceland, 1887; *m* 1916, Alleen B. Scarth; one *s* two *d. Educ:* Manitoba Coll., Winnipeg; New Coll., Oxford. BA University of Manitoba, 1910; First Class Honours and Silver Medal in Classics. Rhodes Scholar for Manitoba, 1910; BA in Jurisprudence, University of Oxford, 1912; LLB University of Manitoba, 1921; Juris Doctor (Hon.), University of Iceland, 1930; Hon. LLD University of Manitoba, 1958; called to Bar, Middle Temple, 1913; Manitoba, 1913; enlisted CEF, 1916; served in France, rank Captain; Dean of Manitoba Law School, 1921-26; MP (L) Winnipeg South Centre, 1926-30; MP (L) Selkirk, 1935-42, Canadian House of Commons; Minister National War Services, Canada, 1941-42; KC 1930; appointed one of delegates of Canada to assembly of League of Nations, Sept. 1938; Chairman, War Expenditures Cttee, House of Commons, 1941; President, International Congress of Jurists, Berlin, 1952, Athens, 1955. Awarded the Grand Cross of the Order of the Falcon, Iceland. Religion: Anglican. *Recreations:* gardening, golf. *Address:* 20 Crescent Road, Rockcliffe, Ottawa, Canada. *Clubs:* Canadian, Rideau, Royal Ottawa Golf (Ottawa); University (Toronto).

**THOULESS, Robert Henry;** Reader Emeritus in the University of Cambridge since 1961; Fellow of Corpus Christi College, Cambridge, since 1945; *b* 15 July 1894; *s* of Henry James Thouless; *m* 1924, Priscilla Gorton; one *s* one *d. Educ:* City of Norwich Sch.; Corpus Christi Coll., Cambridge. BA (Nat. Sci.), 1915. Served European War, 2nd Lieut, RE, British Salonika Force, 1917. PhD (Cambridge) 1922; Lecturer in Psychology, Manchester Univ., 1921, Glasgow Univ., 1926, Cambridge Univ., 1938; Reader in Educational Psychology, 1945-61; Consultant NFER, 1964. President, Section J British Association, 1937; Riddell Memorial Lecturer, 1940; President, Society for Psychical Research, 1942; President, British Psycholog. Society, 1949 (Hon. Fellow 1962); Hulsean Lecturer, 1951. Lecturing in Australia, 1962, 1966; Eddington Memorial Lecturer, 1963, T. B. Davie Memorial Lecturer (Cape Town), 1964. ScD (Cambridge), 1953. *Publications:* An Introduction to the Psychology of Religion, 1923; The Lady Julian, 1924; Social Psychology, 1925; The Control of the Mind, 1927; Straight and Crooked Thinking, 1930; General and Social Psychology, 1937, 1951 and 1957; Straight Thinking in War Time, 1942; Authority and Freedom, 1954; Experimental Psychical Research, 1963; Map of Educational Research, 1969; Articles in British Journal of Psychology, Proc. of Society of Psychical Research, Journal of Parapsychology, etc. *Recreations:* camping and painting. *Address:* 2 Leys Road, Cambridge.

**THRELFALL, Richard Ian,** QC 1965; *b* 14 Jan. 1920; *s* of William Bernhard and Evelyn Alice

Threlfall; *m* 1948, Annette, *d* of George C. H. Matthey; three *s* three *d*. *Educ:* Oundle; Gonville and Caius Coll., Cambridge. War service, 1940-45 (despatches twice); Indian Armoured Corps (Probyn's Horse) and Staff appointments. Barrister, Lincoln's Inn, 1947. FSA, 1949. Mem. Court of Assistants, Worshipful Co. of Goldsmiths. *Address:* Gray's Inn Chambers, Gray's Inn, WC1. *T:* 01-405 7211; Pebble Hill House, Limpsfield, Surrey. *T:* Oxted 2452.

**THRING, Rear-Adm. George Arthur,** CB 1958; DSO 1942 and Bar 1952; DL; *b* 13 Sept. 1903; *s* of late Sir Arthur Thring, KCB; *m* 1929, Betty Mary, *er d* of Colonel Stewart William Ward Blacker, DSO; two *s* two *d*. *Educ:* Royal Naval Colleges, Osborne and Dartmouth. Commander, 1941; Captain, 1946; Rear-Admiral, 1956; retired, 1958. Commanded: HMS Deptford, 1940-41; 42nd and 20th Escort Groups, Atlantic, 1943-45; HMS Ceylon, 1951-52; Flag Officer, Malayan Area, 1956-58. Officer, Legion of Merit (USA), 1945. DL Somerset, 1968. *Recreations:* golf, tennis, shooting and fishing. *Address:* Alford House, Castle Cary, Somerset. *T:* Wheathill 329.

**THRING, Professor Meredith Wooldridge;** Professor of Mechanical Engineering, Queen Mary College, London University, since 1964; *b* 17 Dec. 1915; *s* of Captain W. H. C. S. Thring, CBE, RN, and Dorothy (*née* Wooldridge); *m* 1940, Alice Margaret Hooley; two *s* one *d*. *Educ:* Malvern Coll., Worcs; Trinity Coll., Cambridge (Senior Scholar, 1937). Hons Degree Maths and Physics, 1937; ScD, 1964. Student's Medal, Inst. of Fuel, for work on producer gas mains, 1938; British Coal Utilisation Research Assoc.: Asst Scientific Officer, 1937; Senior Scientific Officer and Head of Combustion Research Laboratory, 1944; British Iron and Steel Research Assoc.; Head of Physics Dept, 1946; Superintendent, 1950; Assistant Director, 1953; Prof. of Fuel Technology and Chemical Engineering, Sheffield Univ., 1953-64; Sir Robert Hadfield medal of Iron and Steel Inst. for studies on open hearth furnaces, 1949; Parsons Memorial Lecture on Magnetohydrodynamics, 1961; General Superintendent International Flame Radiation Research, 1951-. Visitor: Production Engineering Research Assoc., 1967; Machine Tool Industry Research Assoc., 1967. Member Clean Air Council, 1957-62; Fuel Research Board, 1957-58; Fire Research Board, 1961-64; BISRA Council, 1958-60; President, Inst. of Fuel, 1962-63 (Vice-President, 1959-62); Member: Adv. Council on Research and Development, Ministry of Power, 1960-66; Acad. Adv. Council, University of Strathclyde, 1962-67; Education Cttee, RAF, 1968-. FInstP 1944; FInstF 1951; MIChemE 1956; FIMechE 1968 (MIMechE 1964); FIEE 1968 (MIEE 1964); FRSA 1964; MRI 1965; FRAeS 1969. *Publications:* The Science of Flames and Furnaces, 1952, 2nd edn, 1960; (with J. H. Chesters) The Influence of Port Design on Open Hearth Furnace Flames (Iron and Steel Institute Special Report 37), 1946; (with R. Edgeworth Johnstone) Pilot Plants, Models and Scale-up Methods in Chemical Engineering, 1957; (ed.) Air Pollution, 1957; Nuclear Propulsion, 1961. *Recreations:* carpentry, wood-carving. *Address:* The Coach House, Powell Road, Buckhurst Hill, Essex. *Clubs:* Athenæum, Royal Automobile.

**THROCKMORTON, Geoffrey William Berkeley,** CB 1947; Clerk of the Journals, House of Commons, 1940-48, retired; *b* 3 Sept. 1883; *yr s* of Sir Richard Throckmorton, 10th Bart; unmarried. Clerk in the House of Commons since 1908. Served European War, 1914-19, Captain, Berkshire Yeomanry (wounded, despatches). *Address:* Spiney House, Coughton, Alcester, Warwicks. *Club:* Cavalry.

**THROCKMORTON, Sir Robert George Maxwell,** 11th Bt, *cr* 1642; Lieutenant (A) RNVR; *b* 15 Feb. 1908; *s* of late Lt-Col Courtenay Throckmorton and Lilian (*d* 1955), *o d* of Colonel Langford Brooke, Mere Hall, Cheshire; *S* grandfather, 1927; *m* 1st, 1942, Jean (marr. diss. 1948), (former wife of Arthur Smith-Bingham, *d* of late Charles Garland; she *m* 1959, 3rd Baron Ashcombe); 2nd, 1953, Lady Isabel Guinness, *d* of 9th Duke of Rutland. *Educ:* Downside; RMC, Sandhurst. *Heir:* *cousin* Nicholas Joseph Anthony Throckmorton [*b* 24 Nov. 1913; *m* 1955, Rosemary Anne, *o c* of Major Edward Rowland Miles Alston, MBE]. *Address:* Coughton Court, Alcester, Warwickshire; Molland Bottreaux, South Molton, N Devon. *Clubs:* Guards, White's.

**THUILLIER, Lt-Col Henry Shakespear,** DSO 1940; late Royal Artillery (Regular); *b* 10 Sept. 1895; *s* of late Maj.-Gen. Sir Henry Thuillier, KCB, CMG; *m* Beatrice Winifred, *d* of late Captain F. H. Walter, RN; two *s*. *Educ:* Dragon Sch.; Dover Coll.; RMA, Woolwich. Commissioned RA, 1915; Captain, 1917; Major, 1935; Acting Lt-Col, 1940; Lt-Col, 1942; served Gallipoli and Mesopotamia, 1915-20; BEF, France, 1939-40 (DSO); North African Campaign, 1942-43; Italian Campaign, 1944-45 (despatches twice); retired, 1946; Commissioned RCA, 1950, appointed Lt-Col (SR); retired, 1955. *Address:* 2424 Beach Drive, Victoria, BC, Canada.

**THUILLIER, Maj.-Gen. Leslie de Malapert,** CB 1958; CVO 1966; OBE 1944; Assistant Secretary, Cabinet Office, 1958-67; *b* 26 Sept. 1905; *s* of late Lt-Col L. C. Thuillier, Indian Army; *m* 1936, Barbara Leonard Rawlins; one *s* two *d*. *Educ:* Berkhamsted Sch.; Royal Military Academy, Woolwich. Commissioned as 2nd Lieut, Royal Corps of Signals, 1926; Lieut, 1929; Captain, 1937; Staff Coll., Camberley, 1939; Temp. Major, 1940; Temp. Lt-Col, 1941; Temp. Colonel, 1945; Colonel, 1949, Brigadier, 1951; Maj.-Gen., 1955. War Office, 1940-41; Middle East and Italy, 1941-45; Chief Signal Officer, Northern Ireland District, 1945-46; British Troops in Egypt, 1951-53; Northern Command, 1954-55; Director of Telecommunications, War Office, 1955-58. FRGS 1947; CEng; MIEE 1968 (AMIEE 1958). *Recreation:* gardening. *Address:* St Katharines House, Savernake, Marlborough, Wilts. *T:* Great Bedwyn 374. *Club:* United Service.

**THUMBOO CHETTY, Amatyasiromani Sir Bernard T.;** Kt, *cr* 1946; OBE 1935; *b* 18 Aug. 1877; *s* of Rajadharmapravina late T. R. A. Thumboo Chetty, CIE; *m* Gertrude, *d* of S. Rajaratna Chetty, Madras; two *d*. *Educ:* St Joseph's Coll. and Central Coll., Bangalore; BA Madras Univ. Joined Mysore Civil Service, 1904, as Assistant Commissioner; Assistant Secretary to the Maharaja, 1914; Deputy Commissioner, 1921; Huzur Secretary to the Maharaja, 1922; given status of Member of Executive Council, 1929; Private Secretary to Maharaja of Mysore, 1942-49; retired, 1949. Titles of Rajasabhabhushana, 1928, and Amatyasiromani, 1942, from the Maharaja; KSG 1938, KCSG 1946. *Publications:* articles on St Philomena and other subjects in Catholic journals. *Recreations:* tennis and photography. *Address:* Alphonsa Manor, No. 6 Cunningham Road, Bangalore, India.

**THURAISINGHAM, Dato Sir (Ernest Emmanuel) Clough,** Kt 1955; CBE 1950; JP;

LLD; Member for Racial Minorities, Federal Legislative Council, Malaysia; President of Ceylonese Federation of Malaysia; Member Malaysian Estate Owners' Associated Council and of Central Welfare Council; *b* 1899. *Educ:* St Thomas's Coll., Colombo, Ceylon; Selwyn Coll., Cambridge. Called to the Bar, Middle Temple, London, 1924. Formerly Member for Education, Federal Legislative Council, Malaya (resigned); Ex-Member of Malayan Union Advisory Council and of Council of State, Selangor. Order of Crown of Johore (2nd class). *Address:* c/o Federal House, Kuala Lumpur, Malaysia.

**THURBURN, Gwynneth Loveday,** OBE 1956; Hon. FCST; Principal, Central School of Speech and Drama, 1942-67; *b* 17 July 1899; *d* of Robert Augustus Thurburn and Bertha Loveday. *Educ:* Birklands, St Albans; Central School of Speech and Drama. Member of Council, Central Sch. of Speech and Drama. *Publications:* Voice and Speech, 1939; (with J. Compton) New Speech, 1949; contributed to Spoken English, Its Practice in Schools and Training Colleges, 1941. *Address:* Church Cottage, Darsham, Saxmundham, Suffolk.

**THURBURN, Brigadier Roy Gilbert,** CB 1950; CBE 1945 (OBE 1941); Secretary, Army Museums Ogilby Trust, since 1957; *b* 6 July 1901; *y s* of late Reginald Phibbs Thurburn; *m* 1936, Rhona Moneen Hignett; one *s*. *Educ:* St Paul's Sch.; Royal Military Coll., Sandhurst. Commissioned in the Cameronians (Scottish Rifles), 1921; took part in operations in Southern Kurdistan, 1923; attended Staff Coll., Camberley, 1933-34. Served War of 1939-45, in Middle East, North Africa and Italy (despatches twice). ADC to the Queen, 1952-53; retired, 1953. Gold Medallist, United Services Institution of India, 1932. Legion of Merit (USA), 1947. *Publications:* various in journals. *Recreations:* many. *Address:* Lindens, Lytton Road, Woking, Surrey.

**THURLOW,** 7th Baron, *cr* 1792; **Maj.-Gen. Henry Charles Hovell-Thurlow-Cumming-Bruce,** CB 1961; CBE 1956 (OBE 1948); DSO 1944 (Bar 1945); *b* 29 May 1910; *e s* of 6th Baron and Grace Catherine (*d* 1959), *d* of Canon Trotter of Christ Church, Barnet; *S* father, 1952. *Educ:* Eton; RMC, Sandhurst. Commissioned 2nd Lieut, Seaforth Highlanders, 1930; ADC to High Commissioner, Palestine, 1936-39; Assistant Military Secretary, British Troops in Palestine, 1940; served with 2nd Cameron Highlanders, Eritrea, 1941; Libyan Arab Force, Western Desert, 1942; Bde Major 152nd Inf. Bde, 1942 (despatches); Instructor Senior Officers' School, 1943; OC 1st Bn Gordon Highlanders, NW Europe, 1944 (Lt-Col); Comd 44 Lowland Bde, 1944 (Brig.); Comdt, BAOR Training Centre, 1945; OC Highland Bde Training Centre, 1947; GSO 1, GHQ, MELF, 1949; AA&QMG, 1st Infantry Div., 1950. Comd 39 Inf. Bde, East Africa Command, 1954 (despatches). Staff Coll., 1942. Joint Services Staff Coll., 1949. Imperial Defence Coll., 1953. Dep. Director of Infantry, War Office, 1956-59; GOC 50 (N) Division and Northumbrian Area, 1959-62; GOC Troops, Malta and Libya, 1962-63; retired, 1964. Bt Lt-Col 1950, Colonel 1952, Brigadier 1958, Maj.-Gen. 1959. Member Royal Company of Archers (Queen's Body Guard for Scotland). President: Missions to Seamen, 1965-; SSAFA Berks, 1969-. Chairman: Directors, Jerusalem and the East Mission, 1967-; St Christopher's Hospice, Beckenham, 1966-. CStJ 1968 (OStJ 1937). *Recreation:* gardening. *Heir: b* Hon. Sir Francis Edward Hovell-Thurlow-Cumming-Bruce, *qv* (*under* Cumming-Bruce). *Address:* The Old Vicarage, Mapledurham, near Reading, Berks. *T:* Kidmore End 3339. *Clubs:* United Service, Pratt's.

*See also Hon. Sir J. R. H.-T.-Cumming-Bruce.*

**THURLOW, Rev. Canon Alfred Gilbert Goddard,** MA; Canon Residentiary of Norwich since 1964, Vice-Dean since 1969; *b* 6 April 1911; *s* of Rev. A. R. Thurlow; *m* 1955, Thelda Mary Hook; two *s*. *Educ:* Selwyn Coll., Cambridge; Cuddesdon Coll., Oxford. MA Cantab, 1936. Curate, All Saints, Wokingham, 1934-39; Precentor of Norwich Cathedral, 1939-55; Rector of St Clement, St George Colegate and St Edmund Norwich, 1943-52; Vicar of: St Andrew and St Michael at Plea, Norwich, 1952-55; St Nicholas, Great Yarmouth, 1955-64. FSA 1948; FRHistS 1962. *Publications:* Church Bells and Ringers of Norwich, 1947; St George Colegate Norwich, a Redundant Church, 1950; The Mediæval Painted Panels of Norwich Cathedral, 1959; Norwich Cathedral, 1962; Great Yarmouth Priory and Parish Church, 1963; Cathedrals at Work, 1966; City of Norwich, 1970. *Recreations:* change ringing, travel. *Address:* 27 The Close, Norwich NOR 16P. *T:* Norwich 28506. *Clubs:* Cambridge Union; Rotary.

**THURSO,** 2nd Viscount *cr* 1952, of Ulbster; **Robin Macdonald Sinclair;** Bt 1786; JP; Vice-Lieutenant of Caithness, since 1964; Chairman, Lochdhu Hotels Ltd; Director: Caithness Glass Ltd; Stephens (Plastics) Ltd; Thurso Fisheries Ltd; *b* 24 Dec. 1922; *s* of 1st Viscount Thurso, KT, PC, CMG, and of Marigold, *d* of late Col J. S. Forbes, DSO; *S* father, 1970; *m* 1952, Margaret Beaumont Brokensha, *widow* of Lieut G. W. Brokensha, DSC, RN, and *d* of Col J. J. Robertson, DSO, DL, TD; two *s* one *d*. *Educ:* Eton; New College, Oxford; Edinburgh Univ. Served RAF, 1941-46; Flight Lieut 684 Sqdn, 540 Sqdn, commanded Edinburgh Univ. Air Sqdn, 1946; Captain of Boats, Edinburgh Univ. Boat Club, 1946-47, Green 1946, Blue, 1947. Caithness CC, 1949, 1952, 1955, 1958; Thurso Town Coundil, 1957, 1960, resigned 1961, re-elected 1965, 1968, Dean of Guild 1968, Baillie 1969. Pres. North Country Cheviot Sheep Soc., 1951-54; Chm. Caithness and Sutherland Youth Employment Cttee; Mem., Red Deer Commn, 1965-. DL 1952, JP 1959, Caithness. *Recreations:* fishing, shooting, amateur drama. *Heir: s* Hon. John Archibald Sinclair, *b* 10 Sept. 1953. *Address:* Thurso East Mains, Thurso, Caithness, Scotland. *T:* Thurso 2600. *Clubs:* Brooks's, Royal Air Force; New (Edinburgh).

**THURSTAN, Violetta,** MM, FRGS; *o d* of Edward Paget Thurstan, MD. *Educ:* Ladies' Coll., Guernsey; Germany; LLA St Andrews. Honours in Aesthetics and Fine Art. Sent to Brussels in Aug. 1914 by the Order of St John of Jerusalem; and served throughout the War in Belgium and Russia (Military Medal, 1914 Star, etc.); Officer WRNS, 1939-44. Late Director of Bedouin Industries Frontier Districts Administration, Egypt. Officer in Allied Commission, Austria, 1946-48. *Publications:* Field Hospital and Flying Column; The People Who Run, Tragedy of the Refugees in Russia; Desert Songs; The Use of Vegetable Dyes; Decorative Textiles and Tapestries, 1934; Weaving Patterns of Yesterday and To-day; History of Ancient Fabrics (republished 1954); Weaving without Tears, 1956; Stormy Petrel; The Foolish Virgin. *Recreations:* travelling, gardening, weaving. *Address:* Old Mill House, The Square, Penryn, Cornwall. *T:* Penryn 2339. *Club:* Challoner.

**THURSTON, Gavin (Leonard Bourdas),** CBE 1966; FRCP, FRCGP; HM Coroner, Inner West London, since 1965 (Western District,

County of London, 1956-65); Deputy Coroner to the Royal Household since 1964; Hon. Secretary, Coroners' Society of England and Wales since 1960; *b* 26 March 1911; 4th *s* of John Bourdas Thurston, London; *m* 1st, 1935, Ione Witham (*d* 1967), *d* of J. T. Barber, JP; one *s* one *d*; 2nd, 1969, Janet Hazell, MB, ChB, LRAM. *Educ:* Dulwich Coll.; Guy's Hosp. Med. School. MRCS, LRCP 1933; MRCP, 1937; DCH, 1937; FRCP 1969; FRCGP 1969. Barrister, Inner Temple, 1952. Treasurer's Cert. in Clinical Surgery, Guy's, 1933; Res. MO, Pembury Hosp. and Belgrave Hosp., 1933-35. Served War of 1939-45, RAMC, India and NW Europe; Specialist in Medicine, Lt-Col. Asst Dep. Coroner: South Essex, 1946-56; City of London, 1950-56; Dep. Coroner: Metropolitan Essex, 1949-56; North London, 1952-56; West Ham, 1950-56; Treasury MO, 1950-56. Hon. Treasurer, Coroners' Soc., 1958-60; Lecturer in Forensic Medicine, W London Hosp. Med. Sch., 1956-60; Sen. Lectr in Forensic Medicine, Charing Cross Hosp. Med. Sch., 1969-; Hon. Ed. Medico-Legal Journal, 1958-; Founder Member, British Acad. of Forensic Sciences, 1959; Vice-Pres., Medical Defence Union, 1960-; Pres., Medico-Legal Soc., 1969-; Examiner for DMJ, 1963-; Examiner for Milburn Prize, 1961-. Chm., Authors' Club, 1967-69. DMJ (hc) 1963. *Publications:* Coroner's Practice, 1958; contrib. to Atkin's Court Forms, 1961; contrib. to Encyclopædia of General Practice, 1963; The Great Thames Disaster, 1965; The Clerkenwell Riot, 1967; articles on medico-legal subjects. *Recreations:* reading and writing. *Address:* Coroner's Court, 65 Horseferry Road, SW1. *T:* 01-834 6515. *Club:* Authors'.

**THWAITES, Brian St George,** CMG 1958; *b* 22 April 1912; *s* of late Henry Thwaites and Ada B. Thwaites (*née* Macnutt); *m* 1938, Madeleine Elizabeth Abell; one *s* two *d*. *Educ:* Canford School; Clare Coll., Cambridge. Entered Colonial Service (now HM Overseas Civil Service), 1935; served as Administrative Officer in Eastern Nigeria, 1935-47 and 1948-57; Palestine, 1947-48; retired, 1957. *Address:* Cox Hill, Marnhull, Sturminster Newton, Dorset. *T:* Marnhull 286.

**THWAITES, Dr Bryan,** MA, PhD; FIMA; Principal of Westfield College since 1966; *b* London, 6 December 1923; *e s* of Ernest James and Dorothy Marguerite Thwaites; *m* 1948, Katharine Mary, 4th *c* of late H. R. Harries and late Mrs L. Harries, Longhope, Glos; four *s* two *d*. *Educ:* Dulwich College; Winchester College; Clare College, Cambridge. Scientific Officer, National Physical Laboratory, 1944-47; Lecturer, Imperial College, London, 1947-51; Assistant Master, Winchester College, 1951-59; Professor of Theoretical Mechanics, Southampton Univ., 1959-66. Chairman and member of various committees of Aeronautical Research Council, 1948-69. Special Lecturer, Imperial College, 1951-58. Director of the School Mathematics Project, 1961-; Member, United States Educational Commn, 1966-; Member, Acad. Advisory Committee: Univ. of Bath, 1963-; Open Univ., 1969-; Chairman: Council of C of E Colleges of Education, 1969-; Northwick Park Hosp. Management Cttee, 1970-; Gresham Prof. in Geometry, City Univ., 1969-; Hon. Sec. and Treasurer, Dulwich College Mission, 1946-57; Member of Approved School Committee, Hampshire CC, 1954-58, 1961-66; JP, Winchester City Bench, 1963-66; Governor of various schools. Pres. Institute of Mathematics and its Applications, 1966-67. *Publications:* (Ed.) Incompressible Aerodynamics, 1960; (Ed.) On Teaching Mathematics, 1961; numerous contributions to Proc. Royal Soc., Reports and Memoranda of Aeronautical Research Council, Quart. Jl of Applied Mech., Jl of Royal Aeronautical Soc., etc. *Recreation:* music. *Address:* Milnthorpe, Winchester, Hants. *T:* Winchester 2394; The Old House, Westfield College, NW3. *T:* 01-794 2090. *Clubs:* Athenæum; Hollington (SE5).

**THYNNE,** family name of **Marquess of Bath.**

**TIARKS, Rt. Rev. Geoffrey Lewis;** *see* Maidstone, Suffragan Bishop of.

**TIARKS, Henry Frederic,** FRAS; Banker; Director, Stanhope Transatlantic Fund, Luxembourg; *b* 8 Sept. 1900; *e s* of late Frank Cyril Tiarks, OBE; *m* 1st, 1930, Lady Millicent Olivia Taylour (marr. diss. 1936), *d* of 4th Marquess of Headfort; (one *s* decd); 2nd, 1936, Joan, *d* of Francis Marshman-Bell, one *d* (one *s* decd). *Educ:* Eton College. Served European War 1914-19. Midshipman RNVR 1918; Sqdn Ldr AAF, 1940; Wing Commander, 1942-43, Retd (invalided). Former directorships: J. Henry Schroder & Co., Partner 1926-57, J. Henry Schroder & Co. Ltd, 1957-62, J. Henry Schroder Wagg & Co. Ltd, 1962 (May to Sept.), Schroders Ltd, 1962-65; J. Henry Schroder Banking Corpn, NY, 1945-62; Antofagasta (Chili) and Bolivia Railway Co. Ltd, 1926-67 (Chairman 1966-67); Securicor Ltd (founder) 1939-68; Pressed Steel Co. Ltd, 1936-66; Joseph Lucas Ltd, 1946-68; Bank of London & South America Ltd, 1958-68; Bank of London & Montreal Ltd, Nassau, 1959-69; Anglo-Scottish Amalgamated Corpn Ltd, 1935-68. Vice-Pres. and Jt Hon. Treas.: European-Atlantic Group. Member: Dollar Exports Council, 1952-60; Western Hemisphere Exports Council, 1960-64; European League for Economic Co-operation (European Central Council); International EFTA Action Committee; The Wildfowl Trust. Trustee: World Wildlife Fund (International), Morges, Switzerland. *Recreations:* golf, shooting, swimming. *Address:* Casa Ina, Marbella Club, Marbella, (Malaga) Spain; 120 Cheapside, EC2. *Clubs:* Overseas Member: White's, Royal Thames Yacht; Royal and Ancient Golf (St Andrews), Swinley Forest Golf (Ascot), Royal St George's Golf (Sandwich), Berkshire Golf (Bagshot), The Brook (New York), Mid-Ocean (Bermuda), Lyford Cay (Nassau, Bahamas).

*See also Marquess of Tavistock.*

**TIARKS, Rt. Rev. John G.;** *see* Chelmsford, Bishop of.

**TIBBITS, Alderman Sir Cliff,** Kt, *cr* 1948; JP; Managing Director of Jabez Cliff & Co.; *b* 15 Sept. 1884; *s* of Frederick and Mary Tibbits, Aldridge; *m* 1914; two *d*. *Educ:* Queen Mary's School, Walsall. *Address:* Cedar Court, Aldridge, Walsall, Staffs. *T:* (home) Aldridge 52132; (business) Walsall 21676. *Club:* National Liberal.

**TIBBLE, Prof. John William,** MA, MEd; Professor of Education, University of Leicester, 1946-66; Emeritus since 1967; Academic Secretary, Universities Council for Education of Teachers, since 1967; *b* Skelton in Cleveland, Yorks, 3 April 1901; *s* of the late Henry Tibble, Redcar, Yorks; *m* 1928, Anne, *d* of F. Northgrave, Rounton, Northallerton; one *s* one *d*. *Educ:* Guisborough Grammar School; Leeds University. Assistant Master, Deacon's School, Peterborough, 1924-32; Lecturer in Education, University Coll. of the South West, Exeter, 1932-46. Visiting Asst Professor of Education, Teachers' College, Columbia Univ., New York, 1936-37. Past Dir, Univ. of Leicester Sch. of Educn. Editor,

Education for Teaching, 1963-68; Gen. Editor, Students' Library of Education, 1966-. *Publications:* (with Anne Tibble) John Clare, A Life, 1932; The Poems of John Clare, 1935; (with Anne Tibble) The Letters of John Clare, 1951; (with Anne Tibble) The Prose of John Clare, 1951; The Rôle of the Teacher in Modern Society, 1950; Physical Education and the Educative Process, 1953; (ed.) The Study of Education, 1966; W. B. Curry: A Pioneer of Education, 1967; (ed) The Extra Year; contrib. on educational topics to books and periodicals. *Address:* Clare Cottage, Guilsborough, Northants. *T:* Guilsborough 396.

**TICKELL, Maj.-Gen. Sir Eustace Francis,** KBE 1945 (CBE 1941); CB 1942; MC; Officer of Legion of Honour (France), 1944; *b* 10 Dec. 1893; *s* of late Charles Tickell, Indian Public Works Department, and late Alice Esther Francis; *m* 1921, Mary Violet, *d* of Marston Clarke Buszard, KC; two *s* one *d*. *Educ:* Bedford; RMA, Woolwich. Entered Royal Engineers, 1913; various regimental and staff appointments with 6th, 28th, 26th, 54th and 15th Divisions in France, Salonica, and Palestine, 1914-18; Chatham, 1919; Instructor at RMA, Woolwich, 1924; North China, 1928; in charge of RE officers at Cambridge University, 1932; Commander RE, York, 1936; Commander RE, 5th Division, Catterick, 1938; Chief Engineer, British Troops in Egypt, 1939; General Headquarters Middle East Forces, Director of Works 1940, Engineer-in-Chief 1944; BLA Director of Works, 1944, Chief Engineer, 1945; Engineer-in-Chief, War Office, 1945-48; retired pay, 1949. Colonel Comdt, Corps of Royal Engineers, 1950-58; Hon. Col, Resources Units, RE, Army Emergency Reserve, 1953-59. President, Institution of Royal Engineers, 1948-51; Chairman RE Assoc., 1954-56. *Address:* Wood End, Silvermere, Cobham, Surrey. *T:* Cobham 3056. *Club:* Army and Navy.

**TICKLE, Rt. Rev. Gerard William;** Titular Bishop of Bela and Bishop-in-Ordinary to HM Forces (RC), since Nov. 1963; *b* 2 Nov. 1909; 2nd *s* of William Joseph Tickle and Rosanna Kelly. *Educ:* Douai School; Venerable English College, Rome. Priest, 1934. Curate at St Joseph's Church, Sale, 1935-41; Army Chaplain, 1941-46; Vice-Rector, 1946, Rector, 1952, Venerable English College, Rome. Privy Chamberlain to Pope Pius XII, 1949; Domestic Prelate to Pope Pius XII, 1953. *Address:* 54 Ennismore Gardens, SW7. *T:* 01-589 1273.

**TIERNEY, Dom Francis Alphonsus,** OSB, MA; Headmaster of Douai School since 1952; *b* 7 March 1910; *s* of James Francis Tierney and Alice Mary Claypoole. *Educ:* Douai; St Benet's Hall, Oxford. Headmaster of Douai Junior School, Ditcham Park, 1948-52. *Address:* Douai School, Woolhampton, Berkshire. *T:* Woolhampton 3114.

**TIERNEY, Michael,** DLitt (Hon.) NUI and Queen's University Belfast; President, University College, Dublin, 1947-64; Professor of Greek, 1923-47; Vice-Chairman Seanad Eireann (representing National University), 1938-44; Member, Council of State, 1940-44; Member Royal Irish Academy; *b* 20 Sept. 1894; *s* of Michael Tierney, of Esker, Castleblakeney, Co. Galway and Bridget Finn; *m* 1923, Eibhlin, *e d* of Professor Eoin MacNeill; five *s* one *d* (and one *d* decd). *Educ:* St Joseph's College, Ballinasloe; University College, Dublin; Sorbonne, Athens, Berlin. BA degree First Class Hons. Classics, 1914; Travelling Studentship NUI 1917; Student British School of Archæology, Athens, 1919; Member of Dail Eireann for North Mayo, 1925-27; for National University, 1927-32; Member Gaeltacht Commission, 1925; Second Chamber Commission, 1936; Commission on Vocational Organisation, 1939. KSG 1955. *Publications:* (ed) A Tribute to Newman, 1945; (ed) Daniel O'Connell, 1949; (ed) Struggle With Fortune, 1954; articles in Studies, Classical Quarterly, Journal of Hellenic Studies, etc. *Address:* Alloon, Taney Road, Dundrum, Co. Dublin.

**TIFFANY, Stanley,** CBE 1967; Hotelier and Caterer; *b* 1908. *Educ:* Leeds Modern School; Technical College. Trained as electrical engineer. Lately Director Peterborough and District Co-operative Soc. Ltd and Leeds Co-operative Soc. MP (Lab) Peterborough Division of Northamptonshire, 1945-50. Councillor (Leader of Council), Wakefield County Borough, 1952-67. Has been member of several Parliamentary delegations to European countries. *Address:* Alexandra Hotel, Bridlington, Yorks.

**TIGHE, Rear-Adm. Wilfred Geoffrey Stuart,** CB 1961; *b* 29 July 1905; *yr s* of late Wilfred Tighe and of Mrs Tighe, Rossanagh, Co. Wicklow; *m* 1935, Dorothea Rosemary, *yr d* of late Julius Benedict Simpson and Mrs Simpson, Claremont, Weymouth; one *s* one *d*. *Educ:* Arnold House; Haileybury Coll. Joined Royal Navy as Paymaster Cadet, 1923; Comdr 1942; Captain 1952; Rear-Admiral 1959. Qualified as Interpreter in Italian, 1931, and in Russian 1934. Member of Institute of Patentees, 1933, and granted British Letters Patent in that year for invention and design of the electric razor. Staff of C-in-C East Indies Squadron, 1935-37; specialised in Communications Security and attached to Foreign Office, 1938-39. Served during War of 1939-45 in the Home Fleet and as Assistant Director of Signal Division, and Intelligence Division, of the Naval Staff. Assistant Director of Plans, Admiralty, 1953-55; Supply Officer, HMS Raleigh, 1955-57; Base Supply Officer at Chatham, 1957-59; Rear-Admiral (Personnel), Home Naval Air Command, Lee-on-Solent, 1959-62, retired. *Recreations:* fishing and shooting. *Address:* Haddon, The Avenue, Fareham, Hants. *T:* 3297; Bridge House, Inistioge, Co. Kilkenny. *T:* Kilkenny 29449. *Clubs:* Naval and Military; Kildare Street (Dublin).

**TILEA, Viorel Virgil,** CBE 1938; LLD; Roumanian politician, diplomat and industrialist; *b* Sibiu, 6 April 1896; *s* of O. Tilea, MSc, and Emilia Ratiu; *m* 1921, Eugenia Pop (*d* 1947); one *s* three *d*; *m* 1951, Mrs Manuela Munroe; one *s* one *d*. *Educ:* Univs of Bratislava, Vienna, and Cluj; London School of Economics. Founded in Sibiu, students' club, Britannia, for English language, literature and institutions, 1913; Secretary Roumanian National Council, 1918; Delegate Roumanian National Council for Transylvania to Bern and Paris, 1918-19; PS to Pres. Transylvanian Reg. Govt, 1919; Attaché and Secretary to Roumanian Legation in London, 1920; founded first Anglo-Roumanian Soc. (cultural) in Roumania-Cluj, 1923; entered Politics and Industry, 1923; head of timber concern and dir various industrial concerns, 1924-38; candidate for Cluj county, 1925; Leader National Peasant Youth of Transylvania, 1926; co-founder Central Anglo-Roumanian Society in Bucharest, 1927; MP, Sec. Foreign Affairs Committee, Member Delegation and Delegate to LON Assemblies, Tariff Conference and Inter-parliamentarian Conferences, 1928-33; Head of Roumanian Commercial Delegation and signatory Anglo-Roumanian Commercial Treaty, 1930, and Roumanian-Hungarian Com. Tr., 1931, 1932;

Under Sec. of State to Presidency of Council, Press and Information, 1930-33; Vice-Pres. and Acting Pres. Anglo-Roumanian Soc. in Roumania, 1931-39; Pres. Federation of Association Football Clubs, 1932-39; Roumanian Minister at Court of St James's, 1938; recalled by Hitler's order but stayed in England and started Free Roumanian Movement, July 1940 (dissolved as Roumania broke with Axis, Aug. 1944); nationality taken and property seized by Antonescu pro-Nazi govt, Jan. 1941, restored 1944, re-confiscated by Communist Regime, 1947; kept contact with opposition in Roumania; several broadcasts, articles and lectures in England and Scotland, 1940-44; against Communist domination in Roumania, but favours the more independent policy from Russia. Capt. in Reserve Roumanian Horse Guard; Grand Crosses of St Sava and Skander Beg; Grand Officer St Sylvester and Polonia Restituta; Comm. Carol I; Knight of Ferdinand; Knight Ord. of Malta, etc. *Publications:* Le Désarmement de la Haine, 1924; The New Slovakia (trans.), 1925; Roumania's Diplomatic Action, 1925; Iuliu Maniu, Der Mann und das Werk, 1927; Articles in Periodicals and Daily Papers, Roumanian and Foreign. *Address:* 28 Redcliffe Square, SW10. *T:* 01-373 8246.

**TILEY, Arthur;** Insurance Broker and Marine Underwriter; Chairman, Clarkson Tiley Ltd, Incorporated Insurance Brokers, Bradford; Director: H. Clarkson (Home) Ltd; Hargreaves Peake & Co. Ltd; *b* 17 January 1910; *m* 1936, Mary, *d* of late Craven and Mary Tankard, Great Horton; one *s* one *d.* *Educ:* Grange High School, Bradford. Treasurer, Young Women's Christian Association, Bradford, 1934-50. Contested (C and Nat. L) Bradford Central, 1951. MP (C and Nat. L) Bradford West, 1955-66. Served War of 1939-45 as Senior Company Officer, National Fire Service. Member: Council, Churchill Memorial Trust, 1965; Conciliation Cttee, NE Race Relations Bd. JP. *Address:* 10 Petersgarth, Moorhead Lane, Shipley, Yorks.

**TILL, Barry Dorn;** Principal of Morley College, London, since 1965; *b* 1 June 1923; *s* of John Johnson and Hilda Lucy Till; *m* 1st, 1954, Shirley Philipson (marr. diss. 1965); two *s*; 2nd, 1966, Antonia, *d* of Michael Clapham, *qv*; one *d.* *Educ:* Harrow; Jesus College and Westcott House, Cambridge. Lightfoot Scholar, University of Cambridge, 1949. Deacon, 1950; Priest, 1951; Asst Curate, Bury Parish Church, Lancs, 1950-53; Fellow of Jesus Coll., Cambridge, 1953-60, Chaplain, 1953-56, Dean, 1956-60, Tutor, 1957-60; Univ. Preacher, Cambridge, 1955; Examining Chaplain to Bishop of Lichfield, 1957-60; Dean of Hong Kong, 1960-64. Chm., Asia Christian Colleges Assoc., 1968-. Governor, British Inst. of Recorded Sound, Youth and Music. *Publications:* contrib. to The Historic Episcopate, 1954; Change and Exchange, 1964; Changing Frontiers in the Mission of the Church, 1965; contrib. to A Holy Week Manual, 1967. *Recreation:* travel. *Address:* 44 Canonbury Square, N1. *T:* 01-359 0708. *Club:* Travellers'.

**TILLETT, Mrs Emmie Muriel;** Managing Director, Ibbs & Tillett, since 1948; *b* 7 December 1896; *d* of Arthur and Florence Bass; *m* 1941, John Hudson Tillett; no *c.* *Educ:* privately. With Chappell & Co. Ltd (Music Publishers), 1916-22; joined the firm of Ibbs & Tillett, 1922. *Recreations:* water colour painting, walking, reading. *Address:* 11 Elm Tree Road, St John's Wood, NW8. *T:* 01-286 6161.

**TILLEY, Cecil Edgar,** FRS 1938; BSc; PhD Cantab; Hon. DSc Manchester, Sydney; Professor of Mineralogy and Petrology, Cambridge, 1931-61; Fellow of Emmanuel College, Cambridge, 1931; Vice-Master, 1952-58; *b* 14 May 1894; *m* 1928, Irene Doris Marshall; one *d.* *Educ:* Univs of Adelaide and Sydney. Demonstrator in Geology and Mineralogy, Univ. of Sydney, 1916; Chemist to Dept of Explosives Supply, Queensferry, 1917-18; 1851 Exhibition Scholar, 1920-22, and Senior 1851 Exhibition, 1922-24, University of Cambridge; Wollaston Fund, Geological Society of London, 1924; Lecturer in Petrology, Cambridge, 1928-31; Sedgwick Prize, 1931; Bigsby Medal, 1937; Roebling Medal, 1954; Wollaston Medal, 1960. Pres., Mineralogical Soc., 1948-51, 1957-60; Pres., Geological Soc. of London, 1949-50; Vice-Pres. Royal Soc., 1949; Royal Medal, Royal Soc., 1967; Hon. FRSE; Foreign Associate, Nat. Acad. of Sciences, USA; Hon. Fellow, Geological Soc. of America; Foreign Mem.: Geological Soc. of Sweden; Mineralogical Soc. of America; Roy. Swed. Acad. of Sciences, 1966; Hon. Member, Royal Society, New Zealand; Foreign Hon. Mem. Amer. Acad. of Arts and Sciences, 1966; Research Associate, Carnegie Institution of Washington, 1956-67; President International Mineralogical Association, 1964-70. Sen. Vis. Fellow in Dept of Geology, Manchester Univ., 1967-. *Publications:* Contributions to igneous and metamorphic petrology. *Address:* 30 Tenison Avenue, Cambridge; Emmanuel College, Cambridge. *T:* 52234.

**TILLOTSON, Prof. Kathleen Mary,** FBA 1965; MA, BLitt; Hildred Carlile Professor of English in the University of London, at Bedford College, since 1958; *b* 3 April 1906; *e d* of late Eric A. Constable, BLitt (Durham), journalist, and of Catherine H. Constable, Berwick-on-Tweed and Birmingham; *m* 1933, Geoffrey Tillotson, FBA (*d* 1969); two adopted *s.* *Educ:* Ackworth School; Mount School, York; Somerville College, Oxford (Exhibitioner and Shaw Lefevre Scholar). Charles Oldham Shakespeare Scholarship, 1926; BA 1927; temporary tutor, Somerville College, 1928-29; BLitt 1929; teaching at Somerville and St Hilda's Colleges, 1929-39; part-time Assistant, later Junior Lecturer, Bedford College, 1929; Lecturer, 1939; Reader in the University of London at Bedford College, 1947-58. Warton Lecture, British Academy, 1956. James Bryce Memorial Lecturer, Somerville College, Oxford, 1963, Hon. Fellow, 1965. Rose Mary Crawshay prize, British Academy, 1943. *Publications:* (with J. W. Hebel and B. H. Newdigate) Works of Michael Drayton, Vol. V, 1941; Novels of the Eighteen-Forties, 1954; Matthew Arnold and Carlyle (Warton Lecture), 1957; (with John Butt) Dickens at Work, 1957; Introduction to The Warden, 1958; The Tale and the Teller, (inaugural lecture), 1959; Introduction to Framley Parsonage, 1960, to The Small House at Allington, 1965, to The Last Chronicle, 1966, to Doctor Thorne, 1968; Vanity Fair (ed with G. Tillotson), 1963; Mid-Victorian Studies (with G. Tillotson), 1965; (Associate Editor) Letters of Charles Dickens, 1965; Oliver Twist, 1966; (ed with A. Trodd) The Woman in White, 1969; contributions to periodicals. *Address:* 23 Tanza Road, NW3. *T:* 01-435 5639. *Club:* University Women's.

**TILMAN, Harold William,** DSO 1945; MC; FRGS (Founder's Medal); LLD; late RA; *b* 14 Feb. 1898; *s* of late John Hinkes Tilman. *Educ:* Berkhamsted School; Royal Military Academy, Woolwich. Commissioned Royal Artillery, July 1915; served on Western Front with RFA and RHA until end of War (MC and bar); resigned, 1919; Reserve of Officers; Farming in Kenya, 1919-33; expeditions to Mts Kenya, Kilimanjaro, and Ruwenzori; various expeditions to Himalaya; Mt Everest Reconnaissance, 1935; Nanda Devi, 1934-36; Leader Mt Everest, 1938; two journeys to Sinkiang, 1947, 1948; two journeys to Nepal, 1949-50. Served with Royal Artillery in France (despatches), Syria, Irak, Western Desert, Tunisia, 1939-43; with Albanian partisans, 1943-44, and with Italian partisans, 1944-45 (DSO, Freeman of City of Belluno, N Italy). Hon. LLD University of St Andrews, 1954. Blue Water Medal of Cruising Club of America, 1956. *Publications:* Ascent of Nanda Devi, 1937; Snow on the Equator, 1938; When Men and Mountains Meet, 1947; Mount Everest, 1938, 1948; Two Mountains and a River, 1949, China to Chitral, 1951; Nepal Himalaya, 1952; Mischief in Patagonia, 1957; Mischief Among the Penguins, 1961; Mischief in Greenland, 1964; Mostly Mischief, 1966; Mischief goes South, 1968. *Address:* Bodowen, near Barmouth, Merioneth. *T:* Barmouth 630. *Clubs:* Alpine, United Service, Ocean Cruising, Royal Cruising.

**TILNEY, Charles Edward,** CMG 1956; Minister for Finance and Economics, Tanganyika, 1957-60; *b* 13 April 1909; *yr s* of late Lt-Col N. E. Tilney, CBE, DSO, and late Mrs Tilney; *m* 1952, Rosalind Hull, *e d* of Lt-Col E. C. de Renzy-Martin, *qv* and late Mrs de Renzy-Martin; two *s. Educ:* Rugby School; Oriel College, Oxford. Ceylon Civil Service, 1932; Tanganyika: Asst Chief Secretary (Finance), 1948; Dep. Financial Secretary, 1948; Secretary for Finance, 1950; Member for Finance and Economics, 1953. Retd from E Africa, 1960. *Address:* Woodborough House, Worton, Devizes, Wilts. *T:* Devizes 2672. *Clubs:* Oxford and Cambridge University; Royal Colombo Yacht.

**TILNEY, Guinevere, (Mrs John Tilney);** UK Representative on United Nations Commission on Status of Women since 1970; *b* 8 Sept. 1916; *y d* of Sir Hamilton Grant, 12th Bt, KCSI, KCIE, and of Margaret Lady Grant, Hampton Court Palace; *m* 1st, 1944, Captain Lionel Hunter (*d* 1947), Princess Louise Dragoon Guards; one *s*; 2nd, 1954, Col John Tilney, *qv. Educ:* Westonbirt. WRNS, 1941-45; Private Sec. to Earl of Selborne, 1949-54; Vice-Chm., SE Lancs Br., British Empire Cancer Campaign, 1957-64; Founder Mem., 1st Chm., and now 1st Pres., Merseyside Conservative Ladies Luncheon Club, 1957-; Nat. Council of Women of Great Britain: Vice-Pres., 1958-61, Pres., 1961-68, Liverpool and Birkenhead Br.; Sen. Nat. Vice-Pres., 1966-68; Nat. Pres., 1968-70; Co-Chm., Women's Nat. Commn, 1969-70; Mem., North Thames Gas Consultative Council, 1967-69; Mem., BBC Gen. Adv. Council, 1967-. *Recreations:* reading, music, theatre. *Address:* 3 Victoria Square, SW1. *T:* 01-828 8674; 25 Fulwood Park, Liverpool. *T:* 051-727 3153. *Club:* Women's United Service.

**TILNEY, Col John Dudley Robert Tarleton,** JP; TD; MP (C) Wavertree Division of Liverpool since 1950; Director, John Holt & Co. (Liverpool) Ltd; *b* 19 Dec. 1907; *yr s* of late Col R. H. Tilney, DSO; *m* 1954, Guinevere Tilney, *qv*; one step *s. Educ:* Eton; Magdalen College, Oxford. Member, Liverpool Stock Exchange, 1932-; now Mem. Northern Stock Exchange. Served during War of 1939-45 (despatches), with 59th (4th West Lancs) Medium Regt, RA, and 11th Medium Regt, RA; commanded 47/49 359 (4th West Lancs), Medium Regt RATA; Hon. Col 470 (3 W Lancs), LAA Regt, 1957-61. Governor, Liverpool Coll.; Trustee Bluecoat Sch.; Mem. of Cathedral Cttee, The Liverpool Merchants' Guild; Chairman, Liverpool Luncheon Club, 1948-49; Chm. of Liverpool Branch of Royal Commonwealth Soc., 1955-60, Pres., 1965. Parliamentary Private Sec. to the Sec. of State for War, 1951-55, to the Postmaster-General, 1957-59; Chm. Inter-Parl. Union, Brit. Gp, 1959-62; Chm. Conservative Commonwealth Council W Africa Cttee, 1954-62; Parliamentary Private Secretary to Minister of Transport, 1959-62; Parly Under-Sec. of State for Commonwealth Relations, 1962-64 and for the Colonies, 1963-64; Member, Exec. Cttee, Nat. Union of Conservative and Unionist Assocs; Chm. Merseyside Conservative MPs, 1964 (Mem. NW Area Cttee); Treasurer, UK Branch, Commonwealth Parly Assoc. Croix de Guerre with Gilt Star, 1945; Legion of Honour, 1960. *Recreations:* golf, gardening, travel, etc. *Address:* 25 Fulwood Park, Liverpool 17. *T:* 051-727 3153; 3 Victoria Square, SW1. *Clubs:* Brooks's, MCC, Carlton; Jesters; Royal Tennis Court; Liverpool Cricket, Liverpool Racquet, Liverpool University.

**TILNEY, Brig. Robert Adolphus George,** CBE 1962; DSO 1945; TD; *b* 2 November 1903; *s* of late Colonel William Arthur Tilney and late Hylda Paget, Sutton Bonington, Notts; *m* 1933, Frances Moore, *d* of late Robert Cochrane Barclay, Virginia, USA; three *d* (one *s* decd). *Educ:* Eton; Cambridge University. Joined Leics Yeo., 1924; Major 1935; Lt-Col Comdg Leics Yeo., 1940-43; Brig. Comdg 234 Bde 1943; Comdg Fortress Leros, 1943 (despatches). High Sheriff, Leics, 1953. *Address:* 13 Cottesmore Court, Stanford Road, W8.

*See also T. J. King.*

**TILSTON, Col Frederick Albert,** VC 1945; Chairman of the Board and Chief Executive Officer, Sterling Drug Ltd, Canada, since 1970; *b* Toronto, Ontario, 11 June 1906; *s* of late Fred Tilston, English birth, and late Agnes Estelle Le May, Cdn birth; *m* 1946; one *s. Educ:* De La Salle Collegiate, Toronto; Ontario College of Pharmacy (graduated 1929). Salesman for Sterling Products Ltd, Windsor, Ont., manufacturers of nationally advertised drug products, 1930-36; Canadian Sales Manager for Sterling Products Ltd, 1937-40; Vice-Pres. in charge of sales, Sterling Products Ltd, Windsor, Ontario, 1946-57; Pres., Sterling Drug Ltd, 1957-70. Canadian Army, 1941-46. Hon. Col, Essex and Kent Scottish Regt. *Recreations:* swimming, ice hockey, golf; amateur pianist. *Address:* Wellington Street West, Aurora, Ont, Canada. *T:* Aurora Area 416, 727-4617. *Clubs:* New Windsor, Press, Essex County Golf and Country (Windsor, Ont); Royal Canadian Military Institute (Toronto); Summitt Golf and Country (Oak Ridges).

**TILTMAN, H(ugh) Hessell,** OBE 1959; Author and Journalist; Contributing Editor and Senior Adviser on Japan and Asian affairs to Encyclopædia Britannica (Japan) Inc.; Adviser on Japan and Asian affairs to the Encyclopædia Britannica; *b* 2 February 1897; *s* of Frank Tiltman, Rye, Sussex, and Ada Wood Rose; *m* 1925, Marjorie (author of Quality Chase, 1940; Born a Woman, 1951, etc), *e d* of Sydney Hand; no *c. Educ:* privately. Newspaper correspondent in Europe, United States and Far East, 1934-51. War Correspondent in Sino-Japanese hostilities in China, 1937-38; in Nationalist Spain, 1938-39; and accredited to United States Forces in Japan, 1945-63; Japan Correspondent of The Guardian, 1951-63; special writer on Japanese affairs for the Washington Post, 1948-62. Japanese Order of the Sacred Treasure, 1959. *Publications:* James Ramsay MacDonald: an Authentic Life, 1929;

The Terror in Europe, 1930; Peasant Europe, 1934; The Far East comes nearer, 1936; Uncensored Far East, 1937; Nightmares must End, 1940; (with Col P. T. Etherton)–The Pacific: A Forecast, 1928; Manchuria: The Cockpit of Asia, 1932; Japan: Mistress of the Pacific?, 1933. *Recreation:* travel. *Address:* Foreign Correspondents Club of Japan, 1 Shimbun Alley, Marunouchi, Tokyo, Japan. *Club:* Savage.

**TILTMAN, Brig. John Hessell,** CMG 1954; CBE 1944 (OBE 1930); MC; late King's Own Scottish Borderers; *b* 25 May 1894; *s* of late A. Hessell Tiltman, FRIBA; *m* 1926, Tempe Monica Robinson; one *d*. *Educ:* Charterhouse. *Address:* 4740 Connecticut Avenue NW, Washington, DC 20008, USA. *Club:* Army and Navy.

**TIMMS, Dr Cecil,** DEng, CEng, FIMechE, FIProdE; Head of Machine Tools Branch, Ministry of Technology, since 1965; *b* 13 Dec. 1911; *m*; no *c*. *Educ:* Liverpool Univ. Head of Metrology, Mechanisms and Noise Control Div., 1950-61; Supt of Machinery Group, National Engrg Laboratory, 1961-65. *Publications:* contribs to Proc. IMechE, Metalworking Prod. and Prod. Engr. *Address:* Broom House, Ballsdown, Chiddingfold, Surrey. *T:* Wormley 2014.

**TIMOSHENKO, Stephen;** Professor Emeritus of Theoretical and Applied Mechanics at Stanford University since 1944; *b* 23 Dec. 1878; *s* of Prokop Timoshenko and Jezefina Sarnavskaja; *m* 1902, Alexandra Archangelskaya; one *s* two *d*. *Educ:* Institute of Engineers of Ways of Communication; St Petersburg. Laboratory of testing materials, Inst. of Engineers of Ways of Communication, 1902-3; Asst Prof., Petersburg Polytech. Inst., 1903-6; Prof. Kiew Polytechn. Inst., 1907-11; Prof. Inst. of Engrs of Ways of Communication and also Prof. Polytech. Inst. Petersburg, 1912-18; Consulting Engr, Russian Navy, 1912-18. Member Acad. of Sciences, Kiew, 1918-20; Prof. Polytechn. Inst., Zagreb, Yugoslavia, 1920-22; Research Engr Vibration Speciality Co., Philadelphia, USA, 1922-23; Research Engr Westinghouse El. and Mfg Co., Pittsburgh, USA, 1923-27; Prof. Michigan Univ., USA, 1927-36; Prof. Stanford Univ., 1936-44. Corresp. de l'Acad. des sciences, Paris, 1939-; Member Nat. Acad. of Sciences, Washington, DC, 1941; For. Mem. Royal Soc. London, 1944-; Foreign member Accademia Nationale dei Lincei, Rome, 1948-. *Publications:* books and papers published in Russian until 1920; since leaving Russia, following books published in English: Applied Elasticity, 1924; Theory of Vibrations, 1928; Strength of Materials (Vols 1 and 2), 1930; Theory of Elasticity, 1934; Theory of Elastic Stability, 1936; Theory of Plates, 1940; (with Prof. D. H. Young) Statics and Dynamics, 1936, Theory of Structures, 1945; Advanced Dynamics, 1948; History of Strength of Materials, 1953; The Collected Papers of Stephen P. Timoshenko, 1953; Engineering Education in Russia, 1959. *Address:* Böcklin Str. 35, 56 Wuppertal E, Germany.

**TINBERGEN, Dr Jan;** Officer, Order of The Lion; Commander, Order of Orange Nassau; Professor, Netherlands School of Economics, since 1933; *b* 12 April 1903; *s* of Dirk Cornelis Tinbergen and Jeannette Van Eek; *m* 1929, Tine Johanna De Wit; three *d* (and one *d* decd). *Educ:* Leiden University. On Staff, Central Bureau of Statistics, 1929-45; Staff, League of Nations, 1936-38; Director, Central Planning Bureau (Dutch Government), 1945-55; Advisor to various governments and international organisations, 1955-. Hon. Degrees from 15 Universities, 1954-. (Jointly) Prize in Economics to the memory of Alfred Nobel, 1969. *Publications:* Economic Policy, Principles and Design, 1956; Selected Papers, 1959; Shaping the World Economy, 1962; articles. *Recreations:* languages, drawing. *Address:* Haviklaan 31, The Hague, Netherlands. *T:* 070-394884.
*See also N. Tinbergen.*

**TINBERGEN, Prof. Nikolaas,** DPhil, MA; FRS 1962; Professor in Animal Behaviour, Oxford University, since 1966 (Reader, 1960-66); *b* 15 April 1907; *s* of Dirk C. Tinbergen and Jeannette Van Eek; *m* 1932, Elisabeth A. Rutten; two *s* three *d*. *Educ:* Leiden; Vienna; Yale. Lecturer, Leiden University, 1936; Professor of Experimental Zoology, Leiden, 1947; Lecturer in Animal Behaviour, Oxford Univ., 1949; Godman-Salvin Medal, British Ornithol. Union, 1969. Italia Prize (documentaries), 1969. *Publications:* Eskimoland, 1935; The Study of Instinct, 1951; The Herring Gull's World, 1953; Social Behaviour in Animals, 1953; Curious Naturalists, 1959; Animal Behaviour, 1965; Signals for Survival, 1970; contribs to German, Dutch, British and American journals. *Address:* 88 Lonsdale Road, Oxford. *T:* Oxford 58662.
*See also Dr J. Tinbergen.*

**TINDAL-CARILL-WORSLEY, Air Commodore Geoffrey Nicolas Ernest,** CB 1954; CBE 1943; Royal Air Force, retired; *b* 8 June 1908; *s* of late Philip Tindal-Carill-Worsley; *m* 1st, 1937, Berys Elizabeth Gilmour (marr. diss., 1951; she *d* 1962); one *s*; 2nd, 1951, Dorothy Mabel Murray Stanley-Turner. *Educ:* Eton; RAF Coll., Cranwell. Commanding Officer, RAF Station, Halton, Bucks, 1954-56; Sen. Technical Staff Officer, Far East Air Force, 1956-59; Director of Technical Training, Air Ministry, 1959; retired 1960. *Recreations:* fishing, shooting. *Club:* Army and Navy.

**TINDALL, Rev. Canon Frederick Cryer,** BD 1923; AKC 1922; Principal Emeritus of Salisbury Theological College since 1965; Canon and Prebendary of Salisbury Cathedral since 1950; *b* 2 July 1900; *s* of late Frederick and Frances Tindall, Hove, Sussex; *m* 1942, Rosemary Phyllis, *d* of late Frank and Katharine Alice Newman, Woking; one *s* (one *d* decd). *Educ:* Brighton Grammar Sch.; King's Coll., London (Fellow, 1951-); Ely Theological College. Curate of S Cyprian, S Marylebone, 1924-28; Lecturer and Bursar, Chichester Theological College, 1928-30, Vice-Principal, 1930-36; Warden of Connaught Hall and Lecturer in Theology, University College, Southampton, 1936-39; Vicar of St Augustine, Brighton, 1939-50; Principal, Salisbury Theological Coll., 1950-65 (Sabbatical Year 1965-66). Proctor in Convocation for Diocese of Chichester, 1936-45, 1949-50; Examining Chaplain to Bishop of Chichester, 1941-50, Canon and Prebendary of Chichester Cathedral, 1948-50; Proctor in Convocation for Diocese of Salisbury, 1951-; Member: Commn for Revision of the Catechism, 1958; Church Assembly Standing Orders Cttee, 1963; Archbishop's Commn on London and SE England, 1965; Greater London Area Liaison Cttee, 1968; Pastoral Measure Appeal Tribunal, 1969. Clerical Judge, Court of Arches, Canterbury, 1969-. Pro-Prolocutor, Lower House of Convocation of Canterbury, 1959-. *Publications:* England Expects, 1946; a History of S Augustine's Brighton, 1946; Christian Initiation, Anglican Principles and Practice, 1951; contributor to: History of Christian Thought, 1937; Encyclopædia Britannica Year Book, 1939; Baptism To-Day,

1949; Theology, Church Quarterly Review, Guardian, etc. *Recreations:* lawn tennis, golf, ski-ing. *Address:* Bemerton House, 71 Lower Road, Salisbury, Wilts. *T:* Salisbury 22373. *Clubs:* Athenæum, Royal Commonwealth Society, Ski Club of Great Britain.

**TINKER, Brian;** TD; JP; *b* 4 Apr. 1892; *s* of Charles Shaw Tinker, JP, CC, Meal Hill, Hepworth, Yorks; *m* Helen Violet Brameld, *d* of Frank Johnson, Scarborough; no *c*. *Educ:* Repton; Magdalene College, Cambridge. Studied Mining Engineering with H. St John Durnford at Doncaster; entered Tinker Bros Ltd, 1913; joined QO Yorks Dragoons, 1912; served with them during European War; retired with rank of Major, 1930; commanded the Huddersfield and Wakefield Squadron. JP WR Yorks, 1928. *Recreations:* hunting, Master, Rockwood Harriers, 1927-31, Master, Badsworth Hounds, 1931-34; Master, Grove Hounds, 1937-39. *Address:* Meal Hill, New Mill, Huddersfield, Yorks. *TA:* New Mill. *T:* Holmfirth 3170.

**TINKER, Prof. Hugh Russell;** Director, Institute of Race Relations, since 1970; *b* 20 July 1921; *s* of late Clement Hugh Tinker and of Gertrude Marian Tinker; *m* 1947, Elisabeth McKenzie (*née* Willis); three *s*. *Educ:* Taunton Sch.; Sidney Sussex Coll., Cambridge (BA Scholar). Indian Army, 1941-45; Indian civil admin, 1945-46. Lectr, Reader and Prof., Sch. of Oriental and Af. Studies, 1948-69; Vis. Prof., Univ. of London, 1969-; Prof., Univ. of Rangoon, 1954-55; Prof., Cornell Univ., USA, 1959. Mem. Research Cttee, RIIA; Mem. Council, Minority Rights Gp. Contested (L) Barnet, gen. elecs 1964 and 1966; Mem. Liberal Party Foreign Affairs Cttee. *Publications:* The Foundations of Local Self-Government in India, Pakistan and Burma, 1954; The Union of Burma, a Study of the First Years of Independence, 1957 (4th edn 1967); India and Pakistan, a Political Analysis, 1962; Ballot Box and Bayonet, People and Government in Emergent Asian Countries, 1964; Reorientations, Studies on Asia in Transition, 1965; South Asia, a Short History, 1966; Experiment with Freedom, India and Pakistan, 1947, 1967; (ed and wrote introduction) The Mission to the Court of Ava in 1855, new edn 1969. *Recreations:* writing, walking. *Address:* Holmdene Avenue, Mill Hill, NW7. *T:* 01-959 2513; Aspen Lea, Little Hampden, Bucks. *Club:* Travellers'.

**TINN, James;** MP (Lab) Cleveland since 1964; *b* 23 Aug. 1922; *s* of James Tinn and Nora (*née* Davie). *Educ:* Consett Elementary School; Ruskin College; Jesus College, Oxford. Cokeworker until 1953; Branch official, Nat. Union of Blastfurnacemen. Full-time study for BA (PPE Oxon). Teacher, secondary modern school, 1958-64. PPS to Sec. of State for Commonwealth (formerly for Commonwealth Relations), 1965-66, to Minister for Overseas Development, 1966-67. *Address:* 36 High Street, Marske by the Sea, Redcar, Yorks. *T:* Redcar 4012.

**TINNISWOOD, Maurice Owen;** Director of Personnel, BBC, since 1970; *b* 26 March 1919; *y s* of late Robert Tinniswood, OBE; *m* 1946, Anne Katharine, *yr d* of late Rev. J. Trevor Matchett; one *s* one *d*. *Educ:* Merchant Taylors' School. Served with Royal Hampshire Regt, 1939-46 (Major). Joined PO, 1938 as Executive Officer, Principal, 1949; Asst Secretary, 1958; Imperial Defence College, 1963; Director of Establishments and Organisation, 1965; Director of Reorganization, 1966; Secretary to the Post Office, 1969-70. *Address:* Little Croft, Weston Green Road, Thames Ditton, Surrey. *T:* 01-398 4561. *Club:* Royal Automobile.

**TIPPETT, Sir Michael (Kemp),** Kt 1966; CBE 1959; Composer; *b* 2 Jan. 1905; *s* of Henry William Tippett and Isabel Kemp. *Educ:* Stamford Grammar Sch.; Royal College of Music (Foley Scholar). Ran Choral and Orchestral Society, Oxted, Surrey, and taught French at Hazelwood School, till 1931. Entered Adult Education work in music (LCC and Royal Arsenal Co-operative Society Education Depts), 1932. Director of Music at Morley College, London, 1940-51. Sent to prison for 3 months as a conscientious objector, June 1943. A Child of Our Time first performed March 1944, broadcast Jan. 1945. Symphony performed Nov. 1945 by Liverpool Philharmonic Society. Cobbett Medal for Chamber Music, 1948. Artistic Dir, Bath Festival, 1969-. *Works include:* String Quartet No. 1, 1935; Piano Sonata, 1937; Concerto for Double String Orchestra, 1939; A Child of Our Time, Oratorio, 1941; Variations for Piano and Orchestra, 1942; String Quartet, No 2, 1943; Symphony No 1, 1945; String Quartet No 3, 1946; Little Music for Strings, 1946; Suite in D, 1948; Song Cycle, The Heart's Assurance, 1951; Opera, The Midsummer Marriage, 1952 (first performed 1955); Ritual Dances, excerpts from the Opera for Orchestra, 1952; Fantasia Concertante on a Theme of Corelli for String Orchestra, 1953 (commnd for Edinburgh Festival); Divertimento, 1955; Concerto for piano and orchestra, 1956 (commnd by City of Birmingham Symphony Orch.); Symphony No 2, 1957 (commnd by BBC); Crown of the Year (commnd by Badminton School), 1958; Opera, King Priam (commnd by Koussevitsky Foundation of America), 1961; Magnificat and Nunc Dimittis (commnd by St John's Coll., Cambridge), 1961; Piano Sonata No 2, 1962; Incidental music to The Tempest, 1962; Praeludium for Brass etc (commnd by BBC), 1962; Cantata, The Vision of St Augustine, 1966; The Shire Suite, 1970; Opera, The Knot Garden, 1970. Hon. MusD: Cambridge, 1964; Trinity Coll., Dublin, 1964; Leeds, 1965; Oxford, 1967; D Univ York, 1966. *Publication:* Moving into Aquarius, 1959. *Recreation:* croquet. *Address:* c/o Schott & Co., 48 Great Marlborough Street, W1. *TA:* Shotanco, London. *T:* 01-437 1246.

**TISELIUS, Professor Arne (Wilhelm Kaurin);** Head, Nobel Institute, Royal Swedish Academy of Sciences, Stockholm, since 1968; Professor of Biochemistry, University of Uppsala, Sweden, 1938-68, retired 1968; President, Nobel Foundation, 1960-64; *b* 10 Aug. 1902; *s* of Dr Hans A. Tiselius and Rosa Kaurin; *m* 1930, Greta Dalén; one *s* one *d*. *Educ:* Uppsala Univ. DSc Uppsala, 1930; Docent of Chemistry, Uppsala Univ., 1930-38; Nobel Prize in Chemistry, 1948. Hon. Degrees: Stockholm, 1948 (MD); University of Paris, 1948; University of Cambridge, 1949; University of Bologna, 1955; University of Glasgow, 1956; University of Madrid, 1957; University of Oxford, 1958 (DSc); University of Oslo, 1961; University of Lyon, 1962; Gustavus Adolphus Coll., Minnesota, 1963; University of California, 1964; University of Michigan, 1967; Charles Univ., Prague, 1968. Hon. Member: Harvey Society of New York, 1939; New York Academy of Sciences, 1943; New York Academy of Medicine, 1947; Royal Institution of Great Britain, 1947; Chem. Society, London, 1949; Real Sociedad Española de Física y Química, 1952; Consejo Superior de Investigaciones Cientificas, Madrid, 1953; Finnish Society of Science, 1953; Royal Dutch Chemical Society, 1953; Swiss Chemical Society, 1955; Nat. Acad. of

Sciences of India, Allahabad, 1956; Franklin Institute, 1956; French Chem. Society, 1957; American Society of Biol. Chemists, 1961; Acad. Republ. Populare Romine, Bucarest; Soc. for Electrophoresis, Tokyo. Hon. Foreign Member: Society of Chemical Industry, London, 1951; Royal Inst. of Chemistry, London, 1952; American Academy of Arts and Sciences, 1953; Czechoslovak Acad. of Sciences, 1965; World Acad. of Art and Science, 1965; Deutsche Akad. d. Wissenschaft, Berlin, 1969. Member: several Swedish Academies; National Academy of Sciences, Washington; Royal Danish Scientific Society; Accademia Nazionale Dei Quaranta, Rome; Corresp. Member Acad. of Sciences, Lissabon, 1953; Corresp. Member Académie des Sciences, Paris, 1955; Member Pontificia Scientiarum Academia, Vatican, 1955; Foreign Member: Royal Society, 1957; Polish Acad. of Sciences, Warsaw, 1959; Inst. Chem. of India, 1959; Hon. Member Society Swedish Physicians, 1959. Chairman, Nobel Cttee for Chemistry, 1945-; Vice-President Nobel Foundation, 1947-60. Chairman Swedish Natural Science Research Council, 1946-50; President International Union of Pure and Applied Chemistry, 1951-55; Member Science Advisory Council to the Government, 1962-68; Hon. Member, Amer. Soc. Biol. Chemists, 1962; Foreign Member, American Philosophical Society, 1964. *Publications:* various papers, mostly in scientific journals, about protein chemistry, electrophoresis and adsorption. *Recreation:* birdwatching. *Address:* Thunbergsvägen 22, 75238 Uppsala, Sweden. *T:* 135554.

**TISSERANT, His Eminence Cardinal Eugène;** Dean of Sacred College of Cardinals, since 1951; Cardinal Bishop of Ostia, 1951-66; Cardinal Bishop of Porto and Santa Rufina, 1946-66; *b* Nancy, 24 March 1884; *s* of Hippolyte Tisserant, Veterinary Surgeon and Octavie Connard. *Educ:* Collège Saint-Sigisbert; Grand Séminaire de Nancy; École Biblique Saint-Etienne de Jérusalem; École des Langues Orientales vivantes, École des Hautes Études, École du Louvre; Institut Catholique de Paris. Ordained Priest, 1907; Curator of Oriental MSS, Vatican Library, 1908; Professor of Assyrian, Apollinarian Univ., Rome, 1908-13. Served European War of 1914-18 in French Army. Asst Prefect, Vatican Library, 1919-30; Adviser of the Sacred Congregation for Eastern Church Affairs, 1926; Prelate of His Holiness, 1929; Pro-Prefect, Vatican Library, 1930-36; Protonotary Apostolic, 1936; Cardinal-Deacon, 1936; Cardinal-Priest, 1937; Sub-Dean, Sacred College of Cardinals, 1948. President, Commn Biblique, 1938; Member: Institut de France; Académie Française. Grand Croix de la Légion d'Honneur. *Publications:* Ascension d'Isaïe, 1909; Codex Zuquinensis Rescriptus Veteris Testamenti, 1911; Specimina Codicum Orientalum, 1914; Codices Armeni Bybliothecae Vaticanae, 1927; Codices Aethiopici Bybliothecae Vaticanae, 1936; Luigi Maria Grignion de Montfort: le Scuole di Carità e le Origini dei Fratelli di San Gabriele, 1949; Saint Louis Marie Grignion de Montfort, les écoles charitables et les origines des Frères de Saint Gabriel, 1960. *Address:* Via Giovanni Prati 4, Rome, Italy.

**TITCHENER, John Lanham Bradbury,** CMG 1955; OBE 1947; Adviser, Middle East; *b* 28 Nov. 1912; *s* of of late Alfred Titchener and late Alicia Marion Leonora Bradbury; *m* 1937, Catherine Law Clark (marr. diss. 1958); no *c;* *m* 1958, Rikke Marian Lehmann (*née* Bendixsen), *e d* of late Frederik Carl Bendixsen and Kammerherreinde Nina Grandjean of Vennerslund, Falster, Denmark; two step *s. Educ:* City of London Sch.; Royal College of Music. Nat. Council of Education of Canada, 1934; BBC 1938-43; War of 1939-45: served HM Forces, Jan.-Aug. 1943; Psychological Warfare Branch, Allied Force HQ, Algiers, 1943; 15th Army Group HQ, Italy, 1944-45; Asst Dep. Director, Political Warfare Div., SACSEA, 1945; Political Warfare Adviser to C-in-C, Netherlands East Indies, 1945-46; First Secretary, HM Foreign Service, 1947; served in FO until 1950, when transferred to HM Embassy, Moscow; then at HM Embassy, Ankara, 1953-54; Economic Counsellor, HM Embassy, Tehran, 1954-56, Chargé d'Affaires, 1955. Resigned HM Foreign Service, 1957. *Recreations:* music, gardening, fishing. *Address:* PO Box 1627, Tehran, Iran. *Club:* Travellers'.

**TITMAN, Sir George (Alfred),** Kt, *cr* 1954; CBE 1948 (OBE 1937); MVO (4 cl.) 1942; Secretary, Lord Chamberlain's Office, 1939-54, retired; *b* 12 July 1889; *o s* of late George Titman, Lewisham; *m* 1914, Eva Ellen, *e d* of late Charles Comfort, Cheltenham; one *s* one *d* (twins). Clerk, Duchess of Albany's Household, 1910-16; served in The King's (Liverpool) Regt, 1916; Clerk in Queen Mary's Household, 1916-19; Central Chancery of Orders of Knighthood, 1919-22; entered Lord Chamberlain's Office, 1922; First Clerk, 1932; Asst Secretary, 1936; a Sergeant-at-Arms to King George VI, 1946-52, to the Queen, 1952-54. Order of St John; Officer Legion of Honour; Chev. Order of Dannebrog (Denmark); Officer House of Orange (Netherlands); Chevalier (Cl. IV), Order of Vasa (Sweden); Cav. Crown of Italy; Order of Menelik II (Cl. IV); Star of Ethiopia (3). *Publication:* Dress and Insignia Worn at Court, 1937. *Address:* 42 Chadacre Road, Stoneleigh, Epsom, Surrey. *T:* 01-393 1683.

**TITMAS, Air Commodore John Francis,** CB 1950; CBE 1946; CEng; AFRAeS; psa; retired; *b* 20 Aug. 1898; *s* of late W. R. Titmas, Anerley, Kent; *m* 1925, Doris Maude, *d* of late Captain F. W. Young, JP; one *d. Educ:* Whitgift School. Served European War, 1914-19, Lieut, RFC, 1917. Air Commodore, RAF, 1944; AOC, RAF Station, Halton, Bucks, 1946-49; Senior Technical Staff Officer, HQ Bomber Command, 1949-50; Director of Aeronautical Inspection Services, Air Ministry, 1951-54; retired 1954. JP Kent, 1956. *Address:* St Ronans, Anerley Road, Anerley, SE20. *T:* 01-778 3065. *Club:* RAF Reserves.

**TITMUSS, Professor Richard Morris,** CBE 1966; Professor of Social Administration, University of London, London School of Economics, since 1950; Deputy Chairman, Supplementary Benefits Commission, since 1968 (Member, 1967-68); Member, Community Relations Commission, since 1968; *b* 1907; *m* 1937, Kathleen Caston Miller; one *d. Educ:* private school, to age of 15. Industrial and commercial experience, 1922-42; historian, Cabinet offices, 1942-49; Social Medicine Research Unit of Medical Research Council, 1949-50. Hon. DSc University of Wales, 1959; Hon. LLD: Edinburgh, 1962; Toronto, 1964; Chicago, 1970. *Publications:* Poverty and Population, 1938; (with F. Le Gros Clark) Our Food Problem, 1939; (with K. C. Titmuss) Parents Revolt, 1942; Birth, Poverty and Wealth, 1943; Problems of Social Policy (official War History), 1950; (with B. Abel-Smith) The Cost of the National Health Service, 1955; The Social Division of Welfare, 1956; Essays on the Welfare State, 1958; Health in Law and Opinion in England in the Twentieth Century (ed M. Ginsberg), 1959; (with B. Abel-Smith and T. Lynes) Social Policy and Population Growth in Mauritius,

1961; Income Distribution and Social Change, 1962; The Health Services of Tanganyika (ed); Choice and the Welfare State, 1967; Commitment to Welfare, 1968; The Gift Relationship, 1970. Various papers in The Lancet, British Journal of Sociology, Political Quarterly, etc. *Address:* 32 Twyford Avenue, W3.

**TITO, President (Josip Broz);** Marshal of Yugoslavia since 1943; Prime Minister and Minister of National Defence, Yugoslavia, since 1945; President of Yugoslavia, since 1953; President of the League of Communists of Yugoslavia; Supreme Commander of the Yugoslav Army; *b* 25 May 1892; *s* of Franjo and Marija Broz; a Croatian; *m* 1st, 1918 (wife decd); one *s*; 2nd, 1939 (marr. diss.); one *s*; 3rd, 1952, Jovanka Budisavljevic. Served in Austro-Hungarian Army, 1913-15; war prisoner, Russia, 1915-17; fought with Red Army, 1917-20; returned to Yugoslavia, worked as machinist and mechanic, and became Croatian Labour leader working with Metal Workers' Union; was imprisoned for five years for conspiracy after taking part in illegal Communist activities, 1928; left the country, on release, and recruited Yugoslavs for the International Brigades in Spanish Civil War, 1936-37; became Member of Central Committee, 1934; Secretary General of the Yugoslav Communist Party, 1937; returned to Yugoslavia before War of 1939-45, during which, at head of Yugoslav Communist Party, led general people's uprising and revolution in occupied Yugoslavia; Supreme Commander of Yugoslav National Liberation Army. Elected Marshal of Yugoslavia and President Nat. Liberation Cttee, 1943. Elected President of the Yugoslav Government, 1945; elected President of the Republic, 1953, re-elected 1954, 1958 and 1963. Decorations: Grand Star of Yugoslavia; Order of Liberty; National Hero; Hero of Socialist Work; National Liberation; War Flag; Great Cordon of Yugoslav Flag; Partisan Star with Golden Wreath; Merit for the People with Golden Star; Fraternity and Unity with Golden Wreath; Outstanding Courage. *Publications:* nineteen volumes of articles, speeches and other documents covering the period 1941-61. *Address:* Užička 15, Belgrade, Yugoslavia.

**TITTERTON, Prof. Sir Ernest (William),** Kt 1970; CMG 1957; FRSA; FAA; Professor of Nuclear Physics, Australian National University, since 1950; Dean of the Research School of Physical Sciences, Australian National University, 1966-68, Director of Research School of Physical Sciences, since 1968; *b* 4 March 1916; *e s* of W. A. Titterton, Tamworth, Staffs; *m* 1942, Peggy Eileen, *o d* of Captain A. Johnson, Hagley, Worcs; one *s* two *d*. *Educ:* Queen Elizabeth's Grammar Sch., Tamworth; University of Birmingham (BSc, MSc, PhD). Research Officer, Admiralty, 1939-43; Member British Scientific Mission to USA on Atomic Bomb development, 1943-47; Sen. Member of Timing Group at 1st Atomic Bomb Test, Alamagordo, 1945; Adviser on Instrumentation, Bikini Atomic Weapon Tests, 1946; Head of Electronics Div., Los Alamos Lab., USA, 1946-47; Group Leader in charge of Research team at AERE, Harwell, 1947-50. Member Australian Atomic Energy Commn Scientific Advisory Cttee, 1955-64; Dep. Chairman Australian Atomic Weapons Safety Cttee, 1954-56; Chm., Atomic Weapons Safety Cttee, 1957- (in this capacity attended all British Atom Bomb tests in Australia, 1952-); Member, Defence Research and Development Policy Cttee, 1958-; Member National Radiation Advisory Cttee, 1957-. *Publications:* Facing the Atomic Future (London, New York, Melbourne), 1956; some 145 papers mainly on nuclear physics, atomic energy and electronics in technical journals. *Recreations:* music and tennis. *Address:* 8 Somers Crescent, Forrest, Canberra, ACT 2603, Australia. *T:* Canberra 7-32280.

**TIVERTON, Viscount; Adam Edward Giffard;** *b* 3 June 1934; *o s* of 3rd Earl of Halsbury, *qv*; *m* 1963, Ellen, *d* of late Brynjolf Hovde. *Educ:* Stowe; Jesus Coll., Cambridge. *Address:* 337 West 20th Street, New York, NY 10011, USA.

**TIWANA, Lt-Col Nawab Sir Malik Khizar Hayat Khan,** KCSI 1946; OBE 1931; Member of Legislative Assembly; *b* 7 Aug. 1900. *Educ:* Aitchison Chiefs' Coll., Lahore. Minister of Public Works, Punjab, 1937-42; Premier of the Punjab, 1942-47. Attended the Jubilee Celebrations in London, 1935; as Premier, Punjab, attended Victory Celebrations, London, 1945, and Paris Peace Conf., 1945, representing India. Hon. DCL Oxford 1945. Jubilee Medal, 1935; Coronation Medal, 1937. *Address:* Kalra, District Sargodha, West Pakistan; 47 Wellington Mall, Lahore Cantonment, West Pakistan.

**TIZARD, Prof. Jack;** Professor of Child Development, University of London, Institute of Education, since 1964; *b* 25 Feb. 1919; *s* of John Marsh Tizard; *m* 1947, Barbara Patricia Parker; three *s* two *d*. *Educ:* Timaru Boys' High Sch.; Canterbury University Coll., NZ; Universities of Oxford and London. MA NZ 1940; BLitt Oxford 1948; PhD London 1951. Army Service, 2 NZEF, MEF, and CMF, 1940-45. Lecturer in Psychology, St Andrews, 1947-48; Sci. Staff, MRC, Social Psychiatry Research Unit, 1948-64. Bartholomew Lecturer, University of Keele, 1966. Kennedy International Award, 1968. Member, Social Science Research Council and Chm. of its Educational Research Board; Consultant Adv. in Mental Subnormality, Dept of Health and Social Security; Chm., Sec. of State's Adv. Cttee on Handicapped Children; Consultant on Mental Subnormality, WHO. FBPsS. *Publications:* The Social Problem of Mental Deficiency (with N. O'Connor), 1956; The Mentally Handicapped and their Families (with J. C. Grad), 1961; Community Services for the Mentally Handicapped, 1964; Education, Health and Behaviour (with M. L. Rutter and T. K. Whitmore), 1970; Patterns of Residential Care (with R. D. King and N. V. Raynes), 1971; articles on mental retardation and child development. *Address:* 83 Burbage Road, SE24. *T:* 01-274 6550.

**TIZARD, John Peter Mills;** Professor of Pædiatrics in the Institute of Child Health at the Royal Postgraduate Medical School, University of London, since 1964; Hon. Consultant Children's Physician, Hammersmith Hospital; *b* London, 1 April 1916; *e s* of late Sir Henry Thomas Tizard, GCB, AFC, FRS, and late Lady (Kathleen Eleanor) Tizard; *m* 1945, Elisabeth Joy, *yr d* of late Clifford John Taylor, FRCSE; two *s* one *d*. *Educ:* Rugby Sch.; Oriel Coll., Oxford; Middlesex Hospital. BA Oxon 1938; Oxford and Cambridge Schol. (Biochemistry and Physiology), Middlesex Hospital, 1938; MA, BM, BCh Oxon 1941; MRCP 1944; FRCP 1958; DCH England 1947. Served War of 1939-45 with RAMC, 1942-46 (Temp. Major). Med. Registrar and Pathologist, Hospital for Sick Children, Great Ormond Street, 1947; Asst Director, Pædiatric Unit, St Mary's Hospital Medical Sch., 1949; Physician, Paddington Green Children's Hospital, 1949; Nuffield Foundation Medical Fellow, 1951; Research Fellow in Pediatrics, Harvard Univ., 1951; Reader in Child Health, Institute of Child

Health, University of London, 1954-64. Blackfan Memorial Lecturer, Harvard Univ., 1963. Member: British Pædiatric Assoc., 1953; European Pædiatric Research Soc., 1959 (Pres., 1970-71); Hon. Secretary, Neonatal Society, 1964-66; Member: Assoc. Physicians of Great Britain and Ireland, 1965; Assoc. British Neurologists, 1969; corresp. Member: Société française de Pédiatrie, 1969; Pædiatric Soc. of Chile, 1968; Hon. Mem., Pædiatric Soc. of Concepcion, 1968. *Publications:* papers in scientific and medical journals. *Address:* Ickenham Manor, Ickenham, Uxbridge, Middlesex. *T:* Ruislip 32262. *Club:* Athenæum.

**TOBIAS, Rt. Rev. George Wolfe Robert;** retired; *b* 30 Sept. 1882; *s* of late Canon Charles Frederick Tobias, Cape Town; *m* 1933, Edith Anne Perkins; one *s* one *d*. *Educ:* University of Cape of Good Hope, BA 1902; Sidney Sussex Coll., Cambridge (Scholar), BA 1906, MA; Cuddesdon Coll., 1906-07. Deacon, 1907; priest, 1908; Curate, King Cross, Halifax, 1907-10; Priest-in-Charge, All Saints, Roodebloem, Cape, 1910-23; served in South African Medical Corps, 1915-17; Temp. CF, 1917-19 (MC); priest-in-charge of St Mary's Mission, Ovamboland, 1924-39; Bishop of Damaraland, 1939-49, resigned, 1949; Rector of Simonstown, 1949-54; Priest-in-Charge, Hout Bay, Cape, 1954-56, retired. *Address:* 8 Rubicon Road, Rondebosch, Cape, South Africa.

**TOBIAS, Prof. Stephen Albert,** DSc, PhD Edinburgh, MA Cantab, DiplEng Budapest; MIMechE; MIProdMechE; Chance Professor of Mechanical Engineering and Head of Department, University of Birmingham, since 1959; *b* Vienna, 10 July 1920; *s* of Bela and Zelma; *m* 1945, Stephanie Paula Garzo; two *s*. *Educ:* Josef Eotvos Gymnasium, Budapest; Technological Univ., Budapest; Edinburgh Univ. DiplEng Technological Univ., Budapest, 1943. Machine Tool Design Engineer, 1943-47; British Council Scholarship, 1947; ICI Research Fellow, 1951-54; Assistant Director of Research, Department of Engineering, Cambridge Univ., 1956. T. Bernard Hall Prize, 1957, and Whitworth Prize, 1959, of Instn of Mechanical Engineers; Blackall Machine Tool Award, 1958, of American Society of Mech. Engineers. *Publications:* Schwingungen an Werkzeugmaschinen, 1961; Machine-Tool Vibration, 1965 (Japanese edn, 1969); contributions to engineering journals and proceedings of learned societies dealing with linear and non-linear vibrations, dynamic stability of metal cutting process, high energy rate forming and design. *Recreations:* colour photography, music, cultivation of cactus plants. *Address:* Department of Mechanical Engineering, PO Box 363, University of Birmingham, Birmingham 15. *T:* 021-472 1301. *Club:* Athenæum.

**TOCHER, Rev. Forbes Scott,** CBE 1928; MC; DD (Aberdeen University, 1934); *b* 9 Feb. 1885; *s* of James Tocher, Whitehills, Banffshire; *m* 1917, Johanna, MA (*d* 1957), *d* of John Forbes, Cullen, Banffshire; one *d*; *m* 1965, Helen Dickie Wilson. *Educ:* Fordyce Academy; Aberdeen Univ.; Edinburgh Univ. Ordained Missionary of the Church of Scotland at Ichang, China, 1909-15 and 1920-48; in the Army, Royal Field Artillery, at first as gunner and after as Commissioned Officer, 1916-19. Held by Japanese in Shanghai from Sept. 1940; Relief Work among destitute Britons in Shanghai from Dec. 1941; interned in Lunghwa Civilian Assembly Centre near Shanghai, June 1943; released from internment Aug. 1945; retured direct to work at Ichang; retired, 1948. Minister of the Parish of Botriphnie, Banffshire, 1948-55. *Recreation:* gardening. *Address:* 10 Scotstown, Banff. *T:* Banff 2163.

**TOD, Air Vice-Marshal John Hunter H.;** *see* Hunter-Tod.

**TOD, Marcus Niebuhr,** OBE, MA; FBA 1929; Hon. LittD Dublin, 1938; Hon. LLD Edinburgh, 1948; Hon. DLitt Birmingham, 1953, Oxford, 1967. Fellow of Oriel College, Oxford, 1903-47, Hon. Fellow, since 1947; Tutor, 1914-40; Vice-Provost, 1934-45; Hon. Member of Staff, Birmingham University, 1952; *b* Highgate, 24 Nov. 1878; 2nd *s* of John Tod, Highgate, and Gertrude von Niebuhr; *m* 1909, Mabel Bowker, 3rd *d* of George F. Byrom, Manchester; one *s* one *d*. *Educ:* Merchant Taylors' Sch., London; St John's Coll., Oxford (Scholar); First Class Classical Mods, 1899, First Class Lit Hum 1901; Senior Student of British School at Athens, 1901; Senior Scholar of St John's Coll., Oxford, 1902; Craven Travelling Fellow, 1902; Assistant Director and Librarian of British School at Athens, 1902; Fellow of Oriel Coll., 1903; Corresponding Member of Imperial German Archæological Institute, 1906; University Lecturer in Greek Epigraphy at Oxford, 1907; University Reader, 1927-49; Secretary to Cttee for Classical Archæology, Oxford, 1907; Conington Prize, 1912; Captain, Intelligence Corps (Croix de Guerre, despatches thrice); Secretary to Oxford Cttee of the Royal Commission on Oxford and Cambridge Universities, 1919; Hon. Fellow St John's Coll., Oxford, 1946. Hon. Life Governor of British and Foreign Bible Society, 1945. *Publications:* Catalogue of the Sparta Museum (with Mr A. J. B. Wace), 1906; International Arbitration amongst the Greeks, 1913; Sidelights on Greek History, 1932 (German trans. 1968); A Selection of Greek Historical Inscriptions, 1933 (2nd edition, 1946), Vol. 2, 1948; assistant editor of Supplementum Epigraphicum Græcum, vols I-XXIV; numerous articles on Greek Epigraphy, Archæology and History in The British School Annual, Journal of Hellenic Studies, Classical Quarterly, etc. *Address:* 64 Elizabeth Road, Moseley, Birmingham 13. *T:* 021-449 0763.

**TOD, Murray Macpherson,** RSW 1953; Artist; *b* 15 Jan. 1909; 2nd *s* of William Tod, Glasgow; *m* 1938, Marjorie A. Lucas, ARCA, *d* of Stanley B. Lucas, London; one *s* two *d* (and one *er s* decd). *Educ:* Kelvinside Academy, Glasgow, Glasgow School of Art, 1927-31; Royal College of Art, London, 1932-35; Rome Schol. in Engraving, 1935-37; Teacher of Art, Dalbeattie High Sch., 1940-47; Part-time Assistant (etching), School of Drawing and Painting, Edinburgh College of Art, 1949-59. RE 1953, retired 1966. Member: Society of Scottish Artists; Royal Glasgow Institute of Fine Arts; FRSA. Chairman, Edinburgh Branch of Muscular Dystrophy Group, 1957-69, Hon. Pres. 1969. *Recreations:* music (listening), watching sport, reading. *Address:* 3 Seton Place, Edinburgh EH9 2JT. *T:* 031-667 5930.

**TODD,** Baron, *cr* 1962, of Trumpington (Life Peer); **Alexander Robertus Todd,** Kt 1954; FRS 1942; DSc Glasgow; Dr Phil nat Frankfurt; DPhil Oxon; MA Cantab; FRIC; Professor of Organic Chemistry, University of Cambridge, since 1944; Fellow of Christ's College, Cambridge, Master since 1963; Hon. Fellow, Oriel College, Oxford; (first) Chancellor, University of Strathclyde, Glasgow; Director, Fisons Ltd; Member, National Research Development Corporation, since 1968; *b* Glasgow, 2 Oct. 1907; *e s* of Alexander Todd, JP, Glasgow; *m* 1937, Alison Sarah, *e d* of Sir H. H. Dale, OM, GBE, FRS; one *s* two *d*. *Educ:*

Allan Glen's Sch.; University of Glasgow. Carnegie Research Scholar, University of Glasgow, 1928-29; Univ. of Frankfurt a M, 1929-31; 1851 Exhibition Senior Student, Univ. of Oxford, 1931-34; Assistant in Medical Chemistry, 1934-35, and Beit Memorial Research Fellow, 1935-36, University of Edinburgh; Member of Staff, Lister Institute of Preventive Medicine, London, 1936-38; Reader in Biochemistry, University of London, 1937-38; Visiting Lecturer, California Institute of Technology, USA, 1938; Sir Samuel Hall Professor of Chemistry and Director of Chemical Laboratories, University of Manchester, 1938-44. Chairman, Advisory Council on Scientific Policy, 1952-64. Visiting Professor: University of Chicago, 1948; University of Sydney, 1950; Mass. Inst. Tech., 1954. Chemical Society, Tilden Lecturer, 1941, Pedler Lecturer, 1946; Meldola Medal, 1936; Leverhulme Lecturer, Society of Chemical Industry, 1948; President: Chemical Soc., 1960-62; Internat. Union of Pure and Applied Chemistry, 1963-65; British Assoc. Advancement of Science, 1969-70. Chairman: Royal Commn on Medical Education, 1965-68; Board of Governors, United Cambridge Hospitals. Member Council, Royal Society, 1967-; Hon. Member French, German, Spanish, Belgian Chemical Societies; Foreign Member: Nat. Acad. Sciences, USA; American Acad. of Arts and Sciences; Austrian Acad. of Science; Akad. Naturf. Halle; Australian Acad. Science; Ghana Acad. Science; American Phil. Soc.; New York Acad. Science. Hon. Fellow: Australian Chem. Institute; Manchester College Technology; Royal Society Edinburgh. Managing Trustee, Nuffield Foundation; Lavoisier Medallist, French Chemical Society, 1948; Davy Medal of Royal Society, 1949; Bakerian Lecturer, 1954; Royal Medal of Royal Society, 1955; Nobel Prize for Chemistry, 1957; Cannizzaro Medal, Italian Chemical Society, 1958. Paul Karrer Medal, Univ. Zürich, 1962; Stas Medal, Belgian Chemical Society, 1962; Longstaff Medal, Chemical Society, 1963. Hon. LLD: Glasgow, Melbourne, Edinburgh, California; Hon. Dr rer nat Kiel; Hon. DSc: London, Madrid, Exeter, Leicester, Aligarh, Sheffield, Wales, Yale, Strasbourg, Harvard, Liverpool, Adelaide, Strathclyde, Oxford, ANU, Paris, Warwick, Durham; Hon. DLitt Sydney. Pour le Mérite, German Federal Republic, 1966. Master, Salters' Company, 1961. *Publications:* numerous scientific papers in chemical and biochemical journals. *Recreations:* fishing, golf. *Address:* Master's Lodge, Christ's College, Cambridge. *T:* Cambridge 56688. *Club:* Athenæum.

**TODD, Alan Livesey Stuart,** CBE 1958; MA Oxon; JP; Barrister-at-Law; Executive Director, National Association of Drop Forgers and Stampers, 1948-69; Member of Worcestershire County Council since 1938; Alderman since 1953; *b* 3 June 1900; *s* of late Richard Stuart Todd of Eastcliffe, Budleigh Salterton, Devon; *m* Cynthia, *d* of H. Sanders, Paignton, Devon; one *s. Educ:* Wellington Coll.; Magdalen Coll., Oxford. MP (U) Kingswinford Division of Staffordshire, 1931-35; Regional Commissioners Staff, Midland Civil Defence Region, 1940-45; Asst Regional Controller, Board of Trade Midland Region, 1945; Chairman, Brierley Hill Petty Sessional Div. (Staffs), 1958-67; Dep. Chm. Seisdon Div. (Staffs), 1967-; President, Bromsgrove Div. Cons. Assoc., 1962-67. JP Staffordshire. *Publication:* Indian Constitutional Reform, 1934. *Recreation:* gardening. *Address:* Clent House Farm, Clent, Stourbridge, Worcs. *T:* Hagley 2633. *Clubs:* Carlton, Royal Automobile.

**TODD, (Alfred) Norman,** FCA; CompIEE; Chairman, National Bus Company; *b* 18 Oct. 1904; *s* of late Alfred and Rachel Todd; *m* 1935, Mary Watson; one *s* one *d. Educ:* Bishops Stortford College. With Deloitte Plender Griffiths & Co., 1929-48; Assistant, then Deputy Chief Accountant, Merseyside and North Wales Electricity Board, 1948-51; Assistant Chief Accountant, British Electricity Authority, 1951-54; Chief Accountant, London Electricity Board, 1954-56; Dep. Chairman, London Electricity Board, 1956-61; Chairman, East Midlands Electricity Board, 1962-64. Member, Central Electricity Generating Board, 1965-68. *Recreation:* golf. *Address:* Ranworth, 74 Croham Manor Road, South Croydon CR2 7BF. *T:* 01-688 6254. *Club:* East India and Sports.

**TODD, Ann;** Actress; *m* 1933, Victor Malcolm; one *s*; *m* 1939, Nigel Tangye; one *d*; *m* 1949, David Lean, *qv* (marr. diss.). Stage plays and films include: *Plays:* Peter, in Peter Pan, Winter Garden, 1942-43; Lottie, in Lottie Dundass, Vaudeville, 1943; Madeleine Smith, in The Rest is Silence, Prince of Wales, 1944; Francesca Cunningham in The Seventh Veil, Princes, 1951; Foreign Field, 1953; Old Vic Season, 1954-55; Macbeth; Love's Labour's Lost; Taming of the Shrew; Henry IV, Parts I and II; Jennifer Dubedat in The Doctor's Dilemma, Saville, 1956; Four Winds, New York, 1957; Duel of Angels, London, 1958. *Films:* The Seventh Veil, 1945; Daybreak, 1948; The Paradine Case, 1948; So Evil My Love, 1948; The Passionate Friends, 1949; Madeleine, 1950; The Sound Barrier, 1952; The Green Scarf, 1954; Time Without Pity, 1956; Taste of Fear, 1960; Son of Captain Blood, 1961; 90 Degrees in the Shade, 1964; The Vortex, 1965; Produced Travelogues: Thunder in Heaven (Kathmandu); Thunder of the Gods (Delphi); Thunder of the Kings (Egypt); Persian Fairy Tale. Appears frequently on radio and television both in US and Great Britain. *Address:* 1 Ilchester Place, W14.

**TODD, Arthur James Stewart;** retired; *b* 12 Feb. 1895; *s* of George Todd, ISO, and Emily Mary Ellerman; *m* 1927, Marjorie Elizabeth Moughton; one *d. Educ:* St Paul's Sch.; University of Lausanne. Served at home and abroad during the European War in the Army from the outbreak to end 1916 and the Naval Auxiliary Services during 1918 (Mons medal, Army medal, Allied medal, Naval medal). Home Guard, 1940-44; Staff Captain, 1943-44. *Recreations:* rugby commentator, philately. *Address:* Flat 42, 4 Grand Avenue, Hove, Sussex. *Clubs:* Sussex County Cricket, Sussex Rugby, Brighton Rugby.

**TODD, Hon. Garfield;** *see* Todd, Hon. R. S. G.

**TODD, Sir Geoffrey Sydney,** KCVO 1951 (CVO 1947); OBE 1946; DL; MB, ChM, FRCP; FRACP; Medical Superintendent, King Edward VII Hospital, Midhurst, 1934-70; *b* 2 Nov. 1900; *s* of late George William Todd, and Amy Louisa Webb; *m* 1955, Margaret Alan Sheen, *o d* of late F. A. Sheen, MC, and of Mrs Sheen, Tudor Cottage, Midhurst. *Educ:* King's Sch., Parramatta, Australia; Sydney Univ., Australia. Resident MO, 1925-26, Medical Superintendent, 1926-27, Wagga District Hospital; House Physician 1929, House Surgeon 1930, Resident MO 1930-34, Brompton Hospital for Chest Diseases, London. Vice-Chm., SW Met. RHB, 1968-; Mem., Board of Governors, Brompton Hospital. President, Hospital Caterers' Association. DL Sussex, 1968. CStJ. *Publications:* various, in medical journals, 1936-56. *Recreations:* sailing, golf, photography. *Address:* Friars Gate, 1 Priory Road, Chichester, Sussex. *T:* Chichester 82798. *Clubs:* Naval and Military; Sussex; Chichester Yacht (Commodore).

**TODD, Sir Herbert John,** Kt, *cr* 1947; CIE 1944; retired as Chief Representative, Iraq Petroleum Company and Associate Companies, Baghdad (1952-59); *b* 15 Oct. 1893; *m* 1919, Nancy, 2nd *d* of Colonel A. F. Pullen, RA; two *d.* Imperial Police, Burma, 1913; 11th Bengal Lancers (Probyns Horse), 1917; Civil Administration, Mesopotamia, 1919; Indian Political Service, 1921; Asst Political Agent, Sibi, 1921; Kalat, 1922; Political Agent, Gilgit, 1927; Quetta-Pishin, 1932; Political Agent, E Rajputana States, 1935; Prime Minister and Vice-President, Council of State, Jaipur, 1939; Political Agent, Mewar, 1940; Secretary, Baluchistan, 1941; Resident for the Madras States, 1943; Resident for the Eastern States. *Address:* Brentwood, Woodhurst Park, Oxted, Surrey.

**TODD, James Maclean,** MA; Secretary to the Oxford University Delegacy for the Inspection and Examination of Schools and Oxford Secretary to the Oxford and Cambridge Schools Examination Board, since 1964; Fellow and Dean of Degrees of St Cross College, Oxford; *b* 1907; *s* of late John Todd, Oxford, and Mary, *d* of late Robert Spottiswoode, Gattonside; *m* 1944, Janet, *d* of late Andrew Holmes, Glasgow; one *s* one *d.* *Educ:* City of Oxford School; The Queen's Coll., Oxford (Open Mathematical Scholar). First Class Mathematical Mods, 1928; 2nd Class Lit. Hum., 1930; 2nd Class Hon. School of Theology, 1931. Awarded Holwell Studentship in Theology. Assistant Master, Radley, Bryanston, Bromsgrove and Stowe. Headmaster, The High School, Newcastle, Staffs, 1948-63. *Publications:* The Ancient World, 1938; Hymns and Psalms for use in Newcastle High School (New Edn), 1951; Voices from the Past: a Classical Anthology (with Janet Maclean Todd), 1955 (Grey Arrow edn, 1960); Peoples of the Past (with Janet Maclean Todd), 1963. *Address:* The White House, Headington Quarry, Oxford. *T:* Oxford 63624.

**TODD, John Arthur,** FRS 1948; PhD; Reader in Geometry in the University of Cambridge, since 1960; Fellow of Downing College, 1958; *b* 23 Aug. 1908; *s* of John Arthur and Agnes Todd. *Educ:* Liverpool Collegiate School; Trinity Coll., Cambridge. Assistant Lecturer in Mathematics, University of Manchester, 1931-37; Lecturer in Mathematics in the University of Cambridge, 1937-60. *Publications:* Projective and Analytical Geometry, 1947; various mathematical papers. *Address:* Downing College, Cambridge. *T:* Cambridge 59491.

**TODD, Mary Williamson Spottiswoode,** MA; Headmistress of Harrogate College since 1952; *b* 11 June 1909; *d* of John and Mary Todd, Oxford. *Educ:* Oxford High School; Lady Margaret Hall, Oxford. MA Hons Oxon. Final Hon. Sch.: Mathematics, 1932, Nat. Science, 1933; London Diploma in Theology, 1941. Various Teaching posts: St Felix School, Southwold, 1933-37; Clifton High School, Bristol, 1937-39; Westonbirt School, Glos, 1939-46; Headmistress of Durham, 1946-52. *Address:* Harrogate College, Yorkshire. *T:* Harrogate 66012.

**TODD, Norman;** *see* Todd, A. N.

**TODD, Hon. R(eginald) S(tephen) Garfield;** *b* 13 July 1908; *s* of late Thomas and Edith C. Todd; *m* 1932, Jean Grace Wilson; three *d.* *Educ:* Otago Univ.; Glen Leith Coll.; University of Witwatersrand. Minister Oamaru Church of Christ, NZ, 1932-34; Superintendent Dadaya Mission, 1934-53. MP for Shabani, 1946-58; formed United Rhodesia Party and returned as leader and Prime Minister of S Rhodesia, 1953-58; Federal President, Central Africa Party, 1959-60; President, New Africa Party, 1961. Holds hon. doctorates. First Vice-President World Convention of Churches of Christ (Disciples), 1955-60. Managing Director of Hokonui Ranch, Belingwe District, SR. *Recreation:* cine-photography. *Address:* PO Dadaya, Rhodesia. *Club:* Bulawayo (Rhodesia).

**TODD, Richard, (Richard Andrew Palethorpe-Todd);** Actor; *b* 11 June 1919; *s* of Major A. W. Palethorpe-Todd, Castlederg, Co. Tyrone, and Marvil Agar-Daly, Ballymalis Castle, Kerry; *m* 1st, 1949, Catherine Stewart Crawford Grant-Bogle (marr. diss. 1970); one *s* one *d*; 2nd, 1970, Virginia Anne Rollo Mailer. *Educ:* Shrewsbury; privately. Entered the theatre in 1937. Served in King's Own Yorkshire Light Infantry and The Parachute Regt, 1940-46. Films since War of 1939-45 include: The Hasty Heart, 1949; Stage Fright, 1950; Robin Hood, 1952; Rob Roy, 1953; A Man Called Peter, 1954; The Dambusters, 1954; The Virgin Queen, 1955; Yangtse Incident, 1957; Chase a Crooked Shadow, 1957; The Long and the Short and the Tall, 1960; The Hellions, 1961; The Longest Day, 1962; Operation Crossbow, 1964; Coast of Skeletons, 1964; The Love-Ins (USA), 1967; Subterfuge, 1968; Dorian Grey, 1969; Stage appearances include: An Ideal Husband, Strand, 1965-66; Dear Octopus, Haymarket, 1967-68. Formed Triumph Theatre Productions, 1970. *Recreations:* shooting and farming. *Address:* 197 Albany Street, Regent's Park, NW1.

**TODD, Ronald Ruskin;** Colonial Administrative Service, retired; *b* 23 March 1902; *er s* of late A. E. Todd, Histon, Cambridge; *m* 1947, Madge, *yr d* of late Captain H. Griffiths, Wallasey; one *s.* *Educ:* Cambridge and County High School; Emmanuel Coll., Cambridge (Scholar). Colonial Administrative Service, Hong Kong, 1924; various administrative posts, 1927-41; Acting Financial Secretary, 1941; interned by Japanese, 1942-45; Secretary for Chinese Affairs, Hong Kong, 1946-55, and Member of Executive and Legislative Councils. Acting Colonial Secretary various occasions, 1946-53. *Recreation:* tennis. *Address:* Manston, Kippington Road, Sevenoaks, Kent. *T:* Sevenoaks 51582. *Club:* Royal Commonwealth Society.

**TODD, Thomas Robert Rushton,** MD, FRCPEd; *b* 23 Dec. 1895; *s* of Robert Todd; *m* 1951, Mary Isabel Johnston, Auckland, New Zealand. *Educ:* Edinburgh Institution (now Melville College); Edinburgh University. Lieut, 8th Bn, Seaforth Highlanders, France, 1916-17; graduated MB, ChB, Edinburgh Univ., 1919; gold medal for MD thesis, Edinburgh Univ., 1925. House Physician, Edinburgh City Hospital; House Physician, Clinical Tutor, Asst Pathologist, Asst Physician, Royal Infirmary, Edinburgh; Physician, Leith Hospital; Physician in Charge, Royal Infirmary, Edinburgh, 1941-61; Senior Physician, Queensberry House Hosp., Edinburgh, 1961-70. President, Edinburgh Medical Missionary Society, 1952-68. *Publications:* contributions to medical journals. *Recreations:* walking, motoring, photography. *Address:* 13 Lansdowne Crescent, Edinburgh EH12 5EH. *T:* 031-337 2966.

**TODD-JONES, Sir (George) Basil,** Kt 1957; *s* of Edgar William Todd-Jones and Theodora, *d* of Captain David Anderson; *m* 1st, 1928, Margaret Helen (*d* 1950), *d* of Sir Alexander Mackenzie, KCSI; no *c*; 2nd, 1954, Anne Elizabeth, *d* of William Scott Adie. *Educ:* Sherborne; University College, Oxford. Served European War, 1914-18; RFA, 1916-19, France 1917 and 1918. Called to Bar, 1922, Midland Circuit. Office of Solicitor of Inland Revenue, 1928-36; Special Commissioner of Income Tax, 1945-63; Presiding Commissioner, 1953-63. Retired, 1963. *Address:* 93 Rivermead Court, SW6. *T:* 01-736 1654. *Club:* Hurlingham.

**TODHUNTER, Brig. Edward Joseph,** TD 1944; JP; Farmer; *b* 4 Oct. 1900; *e s* of late Benjamin Edward Todhunter, OBE, and late Ethel Christine Todhunter, Kingsmoor, Harlow, Essex; *m* 1927, Agnes Mary, *yr d* of John Swire, Hillingdon House, Harlow, Essex; one *s* three *d*. *Educ:* Rugby. 2nd Lieut Essex Yeo., 1922; Lt-Col, 1938. Served War of 1939-45: Palestine, Western Desert, Italy, India (despatches, POW 1941-43); CRA 2nd Armd Div., 1941; Comdr Transit Command Calcutta, 1945. Colonel, 1945; Brigadier, 1946. Comdr 97 Army Group Royal Artillery (TA), 1946-50. Military Member, Essex T&AFA, 1938-65; Chairman Essex ACF Cttee, 1959-65; Chairman Essex Assoc. of Boys' Clubs, 1959-64. CC 1952-55, DL 1949-68, JP 1946-68, High Sheriff 1964, Essex; JP Wilts, 1968. *Recreation:* shooting. *Address:* The Glebe House, Great Bedwyn, near Marlborough, Wilts. *T:* Great Bedwyn 351. *Club:* Cavalry.

*See also J. K. Swire.*

**TOH CHIN CHYE,** BSc, PhD, DipSc; Member of Parliament, Singapore, since 1959; Minister of Science and Technology since 1968; Vice-Chancellor, University of Singapore, since 1968; *b* 10 Dec. 1921; *m*. *Educ:* Raffles Coll., Singapore. Reader in Physiology, 1958-64, Research Associate 1964, Univ. of Singapore. Dep. Prime Minister of Singapore, 1959-68; Chm., People's Action Party, 1954- (a Founder Mem.). Chm. Board of Governors, Singapore Polytechnic, 1959. *Publications:* papers in Jl of Physiology and other relevant jls. *Address:* 23 Greenview Crescent, Singapore 11.

**TOLANSKY, Samuel,** FRS 1952; DSc, PhD, DIC, FRAS, DThPT; Professor of Physics, Royal Holloway College (University of London), Egham, Surrey, since 1947; *b* 17 Nov. 1907; *s* of B. Tolansky; *m* 1935, Ethel Pincasovich; one *s* one *d*. *Educ:* Rutherford Coll. and King's Coll., Newcastle upon Tyne; Imperial Coll., London. Fellow of Armstrong Coll., 1929; Earl Grey Fellow, 1931; 1851 Exhibition Senior Student, 1932; Asst Lecturer, Physics, 1934, Lecturer 1937, Senior Lecturer 1945, Reader 1946, Manchester Univ. Research work conducted in Optics and in Spectroscopy; research work carried out in connection with Atomic Energy during war years; Member of Governors, Sir John Cass Coll., London. Awarded C. V. Boys Prize for contributions to optics by London Physical Society, 1948; Silver Medallist, RSA, 1961. *Publications:* Introduction to Atomic Physics (5th ed.), 1963, Spanish and Italian Translations, 1950; Hyperfine Structure in Line Spectra and Nuclear Spin (2nd ed.), 1947; High Resolution Spectroscopy, 1947 (Russian Translation, 1955); Multiplebeam Interferometry of Surfaces and Films, 1948; Introduction to Interferometry, 1955; Microstructure of Diamond Surfaces, 1955; Surface Microtopography, 1960; History and Use of Diamond, 1962; Optical Illusions, 1964; Curiosities of Light Rays and Light Waves, 1964; Interference Microscopy for the Biologist, 1968; The Strategic Diamond, 1968; Microstructures of Surfaces, 1968; Revolution in Optics, 1968; over 250 scientific papers in optics and spectroscopy. *Recreations:* gardening, music, reading in folklore and psychology. *Address:* Physics Department, Royal Holloway College, Egham, Surrey. *T:* Egham 4455. *Club:* Athenæum.

**TOLER, Maj.-Gen. David Arthur Hodges,** OBE 1963; MC 1945; GOC East Midland District since Feb. 1970; *b* 13 Sept. 1920; *s* of Major Thomas Clayton Toler, DL, JP, Swettenham Hall, Congleton; *m* 1951, Judith Mary, *d* of James William Garden, DSO, Aberdeen; one *s* one *d*. *Educ:* Stowe; Christ Church, Oxford (MA). 2nd Lieut Coldstream Guards, 1940; served War of 1939-45, N Africa and Italy; Regimental Adjt, Coldstream Guards, 1952-54; Bde Major, 4th Gds Bde, 1956-57; Adjt, RMA Sandhurst, 1958-60; Bt Lt-Col 1959; comd 2nd Bn Coldstream Guards, 1962-64; comd Coldstream Guards, 1964-65; comd 4th Guards Bde, 1965-68; Dep. Comdt, Staff Coll., Camberley, 1968-69; Dep. Comdr, Army, N Ireland, 1969-70. *Recreations:* shooting, fishing. *Address:* Woodborough Hall, Nottingham. *Club:* Guards.

**TOLER, GRAHAM-,** family name of **Earl of Norbury.**

**TOLKIEN, John Ronald Reuel,** MA Oxon, Hon. DLitt: University College, Dublin; Nottingham; Hon. Dr en Phil et Lettres Liege; FRSL; Merton Professor of English Language and Literature, 1945-59; Emeritus Fellow, Merton College; Hon. Fellow, Exeter College, Oxford; *b* 3 Jan. 1892; *e s* of late Arthur Reuel Tolkien, of Birmingham, and Bloemfontein, South Africa; *m* 1916, Edith, *d* of late F. Bratt; three *s* one *d*. *Educ:* King Edward VI School, Birmingham; Exeter Coll., Oxford. Served with Lancashire Fusiliers, 1915-18; Reader in English Language, University of Leeds, 1920; Professor of the English Language, University of Leeds, 1924-25; Rawlinson and Bosworth Professor of Anglo-Saxon, Oxford, 1925-45; Fellow of Pembroke College, 1926-45. Leverhulme Research Fellow, 1934-36; Andrew Lang Lecturer, St Andrews, 1939; W. P. Ker Lecturer, Glasgow, 1953; Vice-President Philological Society; Hon. Member of Hid Islenzka Bókmennta-félag. Benson Medal (RSL), 1966. *Publications:* A Middle-English Vocabulary, 1922; Sir Gawain and the Green Knight (edited with E. V. Gordon), 1925; Chaucer as a Philologist (Philological Society), 1934; Beowulf: the Monsters and the Critics (British Academy), 1936; On Fairy-stories, 1938; The Homecoming of Beorhtnoth (Essays and Studies, Eng. Assoc.), 1953; Ancrene Wisse (EETS), 1962; Tree and Leaf (reprint of On Fairy Stories, 1938, and Leaf by Niggle, 1945), 1964; also The Hobbit, 1937; Aotrou and Itroun (Welsh Review), 1945; Farmer Giles of Ham, 1949; The Fellowship of the Ring: The Lord of the Rings (vol. i), 1954; The Two Towers (vol. ii), 1954; The Return of the King (vol. iii), 1955; The Adventures of Tom Bombadil, 1962; Smith of Wootton Major, 1967; (with Donald Swann) The Road Goes Ever On, 1968; Sir Gawain and the Green Knight and Pearl (translation), 1969. *Address:* c/o George Allen and Unwin Ltd, 40 Museum Street, WC1.

**TOLLEMACHE,** family name of **Baron Tollemache.**

**TOLLEMACHE,** 4th Baron, *cr* 1876; **John Edward Hamilton Tollemache,** MC 1940; DL; Chairman, Tollemache's Breweries Ltd; Director: Tollemache & Cobbold Breweries

Ltd; General Reinsurance Co. Ltd; New London Reinsurance Co. Ltd; *b* 24 April 1910; *o s* of Maj.-Gen. E. D. H. Tollemache, DSO, MC (*d* 1947), *g s* of 1st Baron, late Coldstream Guards, of Devenish House, Sunningdale, Berks, and of Violet (*d* 1970), *d* of late Rt Hon. Sir (Joseph) West Ridgeway, GCB, GCMG, KCSI; *S* cousin 1955; *m* 1939, Dinah Susan, *d* of late Sir Archibald Auldjo Jamieson, KBE, MC; four *s*. *Educ:* Eton; Royal Military College, Sandhurst. 2nd Lieut, Coldstream Guards, Jan. 1930; served War of 1939-45 (wounded, MC); Major Reserve of Officers, Coldstream Guards, 1945. DL Suffolk, 1958; Cheshire, 1970. *Recreations:* shooting, ornithology. *Heir:* *s* Hon. Timothy John Edward Tollemache [*b* 13 Dec. 1939; *m* 1970, Alexandra, *yr d* of late Col Hugo Meynell and of Mrs Meynell, Hollybush Park, Burton-on-Trent. *Educ:* Eton. Lieut, Coldstream Guards, 1961]. *Address:* Helmingham Hall, Stowmarket, Suffolk. *T:* Helmingham 217; Home Farm, Peckforton, Tarporley, Cheshire. *T:* Bunbury 301; 43 Belgrave Mews North, SW1. *T:* 01-235 1767. *Clubs:* Guards, MCC.

**TOLLEMACHE, Maj.-Gen. Sir Humphry (Thomas),** 6th Bt *cr* 1793; CB 1952; CBE 1950; DL; *b* 10 Aug. 1897; *s* of Sir Lyonel Tollemache, 4th Bt (*d* 1952), and Hersilia Henrietta Diana (*d* 1953), *d* of late H. R. Oliphant; *S* brother, 1969; *m* 1926, Nora Priscilla, *d* of John Taylor, Broomhill, Eastbourne; two *s* two *d*. *Educ:* Eastbourne Coll. 2nd Lieut, Royal Marines, 1915; served European War, 1914-19; War of 1939-45 in Middle East and Far East; Bt Major, 1934; Bt Lt-Col, 1942; Actg Colonel Comdt, temp. Brigadier, 1943; Colonel, 1946; Maj.-Gen., 1949; Commanded Portsmouth Group, Royal Marines, 1949-52 and Hon. Colonel Comdt, 1958-60; Colonel Comdt, Royal Marines, 1961-62; Rep. Colonel Comdt, 1961. Member Hampshire CC, 1957; Alderman, 1969. DL, Hampshire, 1965. *Heir:* *s* Lyonel Humphry John Tollemache [*b* 10 July 1931; *m* 1960, Mary Joscelyne, *e d* of William Henry Whitbread, *qv*; two *s* two *d*]. *Address:* Sheet House, Petersfield, Hants. *Club:* United Service.

**TOLLERFIELD, Albert Edward,** CB 1963; Assistant Comptroller, Patent Office, 1959-66; retired from Civil Service; *b* 8 Dec. 1906; *s* of late Frank Tollerfield; *m* 1930, Lilian May; three *d*. *Educ:* Royal Dockyard School, Portsmouth. Examiner, Patent Office, 1930; Intelligence Department, Min. of Shipping, 1939-43; Superintending Examiner and Hearing Officer, Patent Office, 1955-59. Chairman, Patents Appointments Boards, Civil Service Commn, 1966-69. *Recreation:* do-it-yourself. *Address:* 12 Wenham Drive, Westcliff-on-Sea, Essex. *T:* Southend 40992.

**TOLLEY, Major Cyril James Hastings,** MC; Councillor (Conservative), County Borough of Eastbourne, 1958-62; *b* London, 14 Sept. 1895; *yr* and *o surv s* of late James T. Tolley and late Christiana Mary Pascall. *Educ:* University College, Oxford. Served European War, Royal Tank Corps, 1915-19 (MC); Prisoner of War, 1917-18; Royal Sussex Regt, 1940-45. Liberal Candidate South Hendon, Feb. 1950; Hon. Treasurer London Liberal Party, 1950-51. President: Eastbourne Downs Golf Club; Eastbourne Society of Artists; Vice-President Eastbourne Downs Artisans' Golf Club. British Amateur Golf Champion, 1920 and 1929; French Open Golf Champion, 1924 and 1928; Welsh Open Amateur Golf Champion, 1921 and 1923; Captain Royal and Ancient, St Andrews, 1948; Captain, Oxford and Cambridge Golfing Society, 1946-48. London Stock Exchange, 1921-29, and 1933-39. *Publication:* The Modern Golfer, 1924. *Recreations:* golf, bowls, croquet; apiarist; philately. *Address:* Pommern Lodge, Eastbourne. *Clubs:* Royal Automobile; Vincent's, Bullingdon (Oxford); Royal and Ancient (St Andrews); Oxford and Cambridge Golfing Society; Royal Eastbourne Golf; Woking; Pine Valley Golf (Pa, USA), etc.; Eastbourne (Saffrons) Bowling, Preston (Brighton) Bowling, Compton Croquet.

**TOLLEY, Rev. George;** Principal, Sheffield Polytechnic, since 1969; Curate, St Andrew's, Sharrow; *b* 24 May 1925; *s* of George and Elsie Tolley, Old Hill, Staffordshire; *m* 1947, Joan Amelia Grosvenor; two *s* one *d*. *Educ:* Halesowen Grammar Sch.; Birmingham Central Tech. Coll. (part-time); Princeton Univ., USA. BSc, MSc, PhD (London); FRIC. Rotary Foundation Fellow, Princeton Univ., 1949-50. Head, Department of Chemistry, College of Advanced Technology, Birmingham, 1954-58; Head of Research and Experimental Dept, Allied Ironfounders Ltd, 1958-61; Principal, Worcester Tech. College, 1961-65; Senior Director of Studies Royal Air Force Coll., Cranwell, 1965-66; Principal, Sheffield Coll. of Technology, 1966-69. Chairman: Council, Plastics Inst., 1959-61; City and Guilds Plastics Adv. Cttee; Member: Council for Nat. Academic Awards; Council of Assoc. of Colleges of Further and Higher Educn; Gen. Council, British Assoc. for Commercial and Industrial Education. *Publications:* many papers relating to plastics and education in British and foreign journals. *Recreations:* music, hill walking, bird watching. *Address:* 74 Furniss Avenue, Dore, Sheffield. *Clubs:* Royal Air Force; Sheffield.

**TOLLINTON, Richard Bartram Boyd,** CBE 1955 (OBE 1947); *b* London, 28 Aug. 1903; *o s* of Rev. Canon Tollinton, DD, DLitt, and Minnie Tollinton (*née* Boyd Carpenter); *m* 1931, Mary Judith Paulina, *d* of late Judge Harold Chaloner Dowdall. *Educ:* Rugby; Balliol Coll., Oxford. Levant Consular Service, 1926; Acting Vice-Consul, Tehran, 1928; Bushire, 1929; Vice-Consul, Rotterdam, 1931; Consul (local rank) and Commercial Secretary (local rank), Sofia, 1934; Vice-Consul, Casablanca, 1938; seconded to British Council, London, 1939-40; Vice-Consul and Second Secretary (local rank), Washington, 1940; Acting Consul, Boston, 1941, Consul 1944; First Secretary and Consul, Sofia, 1944; Acting Political Rep., Sofia, 1946-47; Consul, Oporto, 1947; Consul–General, 1948; Consul-General, Leopoldville, 1952; HM Ambassador to Nepal, 1955-57; HM Foreign Service, Levant Dept, Foreign Office, 1957-60, HM Ambassador to Honduras, 1960-63, retired. *Publications:* Economic Conditions in Bulgaria, 1935 and 1937. *Recreations:* hill scrambling, tennis, amateur theatricals. *Address:* 256 Rua do Molhe, Foz do Douro, Portugal. *T:* Oporto 681165. *Clubs:* Royal Automobile; Oxford Union; Himalayan; Automovel de Portugal.

**TOLSTOY, Alexandra;** Farmer, Speaker, Writer; President, Tolstoy Foundation Inc. (for Russian Welfare and Culture), New York, since 1939; *b* Yasnaia Poliana, Russia, 1 July 1884; *d* of Leo and Sophia Tolstoy. *Educ:* Moscow; Home. Secretary to Tolstoy, 1901-10; in 1911, fulfilled Tolstoy's will, edited his posthumous works; bought land of father's estate with money secured and distributed it among Yasnaia Poliana Peasants (1800 acres); 1914 went to war first as a nurse, then as representative for refugees at the Western front; worked as a chief of a sanitary detachment at the Western Front; in 1918 organised a society in Moscow to study and work on a complete edition of Tolstoy's works (91 volumes); organised Museums, several schools in Yasnaia Poliana, kindergartens, a hospital; worked in Russia till 1929; compelled to leave because the Soviets instilled anti-religious propaganda in Tolstoy's museums and schools; in 1929 went to Japan, lectured there; entered USA 1931; lectured all over America, now lives on a farm (Resettlement Center of Tolstoy Foundn; Chm. Nursing Home and Homes for the Aged, etc, of the Tolstoy Foundation Inc. of which she is President); in 1941 became an American citizen. Hon. DHL, Hobart and William Smith Colleges, USA, 1962. *Publications:* Tragedy of Tolstoy (numerous trans.); I Worked for the Soviet, 1934; Tolstoy–a Life of My Father, 1953 (numerous trans.); The Real Tolstoy, 1968; contrib. magazines. *Address:* Tolstoy Foundation Inc., 250 West 57th Street, New York, NY 10019, USA; (home) Valley Cottage, Tolstoy Foundation Resettlement Center, New York 10989, USA.

**TOLSTOY, Dimitry,** QC 1959; Barrister-at-law; *b* 8 Nov. 1912; *s* of late Michael Tolstoy-Miloslavsky and Eileen May, *d* of Harry Arthur Hamshaw, Leicester; *m* 1st, 1934, Frieda Mary Wicksteed (marr. diss.); one *s* one *d*; 2nd, 1943, Natalie Deytrikh; one *s* one *d*. *Educ:* Wellington; Trinity Coll., Cambridge. President of Cambridge Union, 1935. Called to Bar, Gray's Inn, 1937. Lecturer in Divorce to Inns of Court, 1952-68. *Publications:* Law of Divorce and Matrimonial Causes (6th edn), 1967; articles in legal periodicals. *Address:* c/o Barclays Bank, 137 Brompton Road, SW3.

**TOMBLINGS, Douglas Griffith,** CMG 1939; *b* Canterbury, Kent, 24 Sept. 1889; *y s* of late Lt-Col E. G. Tomblings; unmarried. *Educ:* King Edward VI's Sch., Stratford-on-Avon; King's Sch., Ely; Selwyn Coll., Cambridge. BA 1911, MA 1920; Asst District Commissioner Uganda, 1912; Secretariat and Private Secretary to the Governor to 1917; served European War, East Africa, 1917-19 (despatches); District Commissioner, Lango, Uganda, 1920-23; Makerere Coll., Uganda, 1924; Principal, 1924-39; Headmaster: Queen Victoria Sch., Fiji, 1940-47; Nyakasura Sch., Toro, Uganda, 1947-48; Masaba Sch., Bugisu, Uganda, 1953-56. Hon. Fellow, Makerere University College, 1964; Hon. LLD, University of East Africa, 1967. *Publications:* African Native Medical Corps in the EA Campaign (with Major Keane, CMG, DSO), 1920; Physical Training for Boys' Schools (Uganda), 1926. *Address:* Gangu, PO Box 404, Kampala, Uganda, East Africa. *Clubs:* Royal Societies, Royal Commonwealth Society, Royal Over-Seas League; Uganda (Uganda).

**TOMES, Brigadier Clement Thurstan,** CBE 1940; DSO 1918; MC; *b* 28 Aug. 1882; *s* of Lt-Col A. Tomes, IMS; *m* 1912, Edith Gladys (*d* 1947), *d* of late Lt-Col W. P. Newall, Indian Army; two *s* one *d; m* 1948, Clare, *widow* of Lt-Col Rev. T. E. H. Taylor. *Educ:* Marlborough Coll.; RMC, Sandhurst. Joined The Royal Warwickshire Regt, 1901; served in the operations on the North-West Frontier of India, 1908; France and Belgium, 1914-18 (twice wounded, DSO, MC, Legion of Honour); passed the Staff Coll., 1919; Brigadier in charge of Administration, British Troops in Egypt, 1935-39; retired pay, 1939; Colonel, The Royal Warwickshire Regt, 1935-46. *Address:* Minson's Common, Charmouth, Dorset. *T:* 323. *Club:* United Service.

**TOMKINS, Sir Edward Emile,** KCMG 1969 (CMG 1960); CVO 1957; Ambassador to the Netherlands, since 1970; *b* 16 Nov. 1915; *s* of late Lt-Col E. L. Tomkins; *m* 1955, Gillian Benson; one *s* two *d*. *Educ:* Ampleforth Coll.; Trinity Coll., Cambridge. Foreign Office, 1939. Military service, 1940-43. HM Embassy, Moscow, 1944-46; Foreign Office, 1946-51; HM Embassy, Washington, 1951-54; HM Embassy, Paris, 1954-59; Foreign Office, 1959-63; HM Embassy, Bonn, 1963-67; HM Embassy, Washington, 1967-69. *Address:* Winslow Hall, Winslow, Bucks. *T:* Winslow 2544; 17 Thurloe Place Mews, SW7. *T:* 01-589 9623. *Clubs:* St James', Garrick.

**TOMKINS, Rt. Rev. Oliver Stratford;** *see* Bristol, Bishop of.

**TOMKINSON, Charles,** CMG 1947; retired Colonial Administration, Kenya; *b* 4 Aug. 1893; 8th *s* of late Michael Tomkinson, JP, DL, Franche Hall, near Kidderminster; *m* 1922, Hyacinthe Gabrielle, *d* of M. Bally, Calais. *Educ:* Winchester Coll. Asst District Commissioner, 1915; served European War, 1914-18, Turkana Expedition, 1915 (African General Service Medal and clasp); Provincial Commissioner, Central Province, Kenya, 1938-46, and Official Member of Legislative Council. *Recreation:* fishing. *Address:* Nyeri, Kenya. *Club:* East India and Sports.

**TOMKINSON, John Stanley,** FRCS; Obstetric Surgeon, Queen Charlotte's Maternity Hospital, since 1953; Director of Department of Obstetrics and Gynæcology, Guy's Hospital, since 1967; Gynæcological Surgeon, New Cross General Hospital, since 1954; Consultant adviser in Obstetrics and Gynæcology to Ministry of Health, since 1966; *b* 8 March 1916; *o s* of Harry Stanley and Katie Mills Tomkinson, Stafford; *m* 1954, Barbara Marie Pilkington; two *s* one *d*. *Educ:* Rydal Sch.; Birmingham University Medical Sch.; St Thomas' Hospital. MRCS, LRCP 1941; MB, ChB Birmingham 1941; FRCS 1949; MRCOG 1952; FRCOG 1967. Medal in Surgery and Priestley-Smith Prize, Birmingham. Demonstrator of Anatomy, Birmingham Medical School, 1946; appointments in General Surgery, Obst. and Gynæcol., at Birmingham and Midland Hosp. for Women, Birmingham Maternity Hospital, and Queen Elizabeth Hospital, Birmingham, 1941-42 and 1947-52; Registrar, Professorial Unit in General Surgery and Professorial Unit in Obst. and Gynæcol., Birmingham; Chief Asst, Chelsea Hospital for Women, 1952-53; Resident Obstetrician and Tutor in Obstetrics (Postgrad. Inst. of Obst. and Gynæcol. of University of London), Queen Charlotte's Maternity Hospital, 1952-53; Obst. and Gynæcol. Surg., Guy's Hospital, 1953-67. Travelling Fellow (Guy's Hospital), USA and Canada, 1954. William Hawksworth Meml Lectr, 1969; Sir Winston Churchill Meml Lectr, Canterbury, 1970. Examiner for Central Midwives Board, Univ. of London, RCOG, QUB, Univ. of Oxford, Univ. of Cambridge, Univ. of East Africa, Conjoint Examng Bd, Univ. of Birmingham. FRSM. Member: Gynæcological Club of Great Britain; Birmingham and Midland Obst. and Gynæcol. Society; Central Midwives Board; Member Council: RCOG; RCS; section of Obstetrics and Gynæcology, RSM; Mem. Cttee on Maternal Mortality, Internat. Fedn of Obstetrics and Gynaecology. Foreign Member, Continental Gynæcol. Society (of America). Surgeon Lieut, RNVR, 1942-46. *Publications:* (ed) Queen Charlotte's Textbook of Midwifery; papers of General Surgical, obstetric and gynæcological interest. *Recreations:* fishing, painting and the arts generally. *Address:* 109 Harley Street, W1. *T:* 01-935 5855; 140 Priory Lane, SW15. *T:* 01-876 2006. *Club:* Athenæum.

**TOMKINSON, Vice-Adm. Wilfred,** CB 1918; MVO 1919; RN retired; *b* 1877; 4th *s* of Michael Tomkinson, Franche Hall, Kidderminster; *m* 1907, Edith Joan, *d* of Colonel G. H. Bittleston, Royal Artillery; one *s* four *d*. *Educ:* Stubbington House, Fareham. Entered HMS Britannia, 1891. Served China War, 1900; European War; took part in operations against Zeebrugge and Ostend, 1918; a Naval ADC to the King, 1926; Chief of Staff to Admiral Sir Roger Keyes, Bt, Commander-in-Chief of Mediterranean Fleet, 1927; Rear-Admiral, 1927; Assistant Chief of Naval Staff, 1929-31; in command of Battle Cruiser Squadron, 1931-32; Vice-Admiral, 1932; retired list, 1935; Flag Officer in Charge, Bristol Channel, 1940-42; officer of the Orders of St Maurice and Lazarus of Italy and Leopold of Belgium; French Croix de Guerre; awarded gold medal of Royal Humane Society, 1913. *Address:* Stert House, near Devizes, Wilts. *T:* Devizes 3713.

*See also Air Vice-Marshal H. A. V. Hogan.*

**TOMLIN, Eric Walter Frederick,** CBE 1965 (OBE 1959); British Council Representative in France and Cultural Attaché, British Embassy, Paris, since 1969; *b* 30 Jan. 1913; *s* of Edgar Herbert Tomlin and Mary (*née* Dexter); *m* 1945, Margaret Stuart (marr. diss. 1952); one *s*. *Educ:* Whitgift; Brasenose Coll., Oxford. Asst Master: Sloane Sch., Chelsea, 1936-38; Marlborough, 1939; Resident Tutor, Wilts, Bristol Univ. Bd of Extra-Mural Studies, 1939-40; joined Local Defence Volunteers, 1940; British Council Lecturer, Staff Coll. Baghdad and RMC, 1940-41; worked in Information Dept, British Embassy, Baghdad, 1941; British Council: Ankara, 1941-42; Regional Dir, S Turkey, 1942-45; Headquarters London, 1945-47 and 1952-56; Paris, 1947-51; Rep. in Turkey and Cultural Attaché British Embassy Ankara, 1956-61; Rep. in Japan and Cultural Counsellor British Embassy Tokyo, 1961-67. Bollingen Foundn Fellow and Vis. Prof., Univ. of Southern California, 1961; Leverhulme Foundn Fellow, 1967-69. FRSL 1961. *Publications:* Turkey, the Modern Miracle, 1939; Life in Modern Turkey, 1946; The Approach to Metaphysics, 1947; The Western Philosophers, 1950; The Eastern Philosophers, 1952; Simone Weil, 1954; R. G. Collingwood, 1954; Wyndham Lewis, 1955; Living and Knowing, 1955; La Vie et l'Oeuvre de Bertrand Russell, 1963; (ed) T. S. Eliot: a Tribute from Japan, 1965; Tokyo Essays, 1967; Wyndham Lewis: an Anthology of his Prose, 1969; (ed) Charles Dickens, a Centenary Volume, 1969; The Last Country, 1971; contribs to Criterion, Scrutiny, Times Literary Supplement, and many foreign reviews, etc. *Recreations:* travel, reading, music. *Address:* Tall Trees, Morwenstow, Cornwall. *T:* Morwenstow 206; 36 rue des Ecoles, Paris 5, France. *T:* 633 3535. *Clubs:* Athenæum, Reform, Public Schools, Authors'.

**TOMLINSON, David (Cecil MacAlister);** Actor; *b* 7 May 1917; *s* of C. S. Tomlinson, Solicitor, Folkestone, Kent, and F. E. Tomlinson (*née* Sinclair-Thomson); *m* Audrey Freeman, actress; four *s*. *Educ:* Tonbridge Sch. Served War of 1939-45: Flight Lieut, Pilot, RAF; demobilised, 1946. Chief roles include: Henry, in The Little Hut, Lyric, Aug. 1950-Sept. 1953; Clive, in All for Mary, Duke of York's, June 1954-May 1955; David, in Dear Delinquent, Westminster and Aldwych, June 1957-July 1958; Tom, in The Ring of Truth, Savoy, July 1959; Robert, in Boeing Boeing, Apollo, 1962; directed, and acted Nero, in Mother's Boy, Globe, 1964; A Friend Indeed, Cambridge, 1966; The Impossible Years, Cambridge, 1966; Prime Minister, in On the Rocks, Dublin Festival, 1969. First appeared in films, 1939; since then has appeared, in leading roles, in over 40 films. *Recreation:* antique collecting. *Address:* Brook Cottage, Mursley, Bucks. *T:* Mursley 213. *Club:* Travellers'.

**TOMLINSON, Sir (Frank) Stanley,** KCMG 1966 (CMG 1954); Deputy Under-Secretary of State, Foreign and Commonwealth Office, since 1969; *b* 21 March 1912; *m* 1959, Nancy, *d* of E. Gleeson-White and Mrs Gleeson-White, Kensington. *Educ:* High Pavement Sch., Nottingham; University College, Nottingham. Probationer Vice-Consul, Tokyo, 1935; Acting Consul, Kobe and Yokohama, 1936; a Vice-Consul in Japan, 1937; served at: Kobe, 1940; Saigon, 1941; Thailand, 1941; United States, 1943; Consul, Washington, 1945; Acting Consul-General, Manila, 1945, Chargé d'Affaires, 1946; Foreign Office, 1947; Washington, 1951, Counsellor; Head, SE Asia Dept, 1954; Dep. Commandant, Berlin, 1958; Minister, UK Permanent Delegation to NATO, 1961-64; Consul General, New York, 1964-66; British High Comr, Ceylon, 1966-69. *Address:* c/o Foreign and Commonwealth Office, SW1.

**TOMLINSON, Rt. Rev. Mgr George Arthur;** Domestic Prelate to HH Pope Paul VI; Canon of the Chapter of Westminster; Rector of St James's, Spanish Place, London, since 1967; *b* Hampstead, NW, 21 May 1906; *s* of late George Henry and Frances Tomlinson. *Educ:* Hastings Grammar Sch.; Keble Coll., Oxford. BA 1929; MA 1942. Ordained in Church of England, 1930; Curate of South Kirby, Yorkshire, 1930-32; received into Catholic Church, 1932; Pontifical Beda Coll., Rome, 1933-37; Priest, 1937; Chaplain to the Oratory Sch., 1937-41; Curate at Kentish Town, 1941; Brentford, 1942; Headmaster, The Oratory Sch., South Oxon, 1943-53; re-established Oratory Preparatory Sch., Branksome Park, Dorset, 1946. Senior Catholic Chaplain to University of London, 1953-64; Administrator Westminster Cathedral, 1964-67. Member: National Liturgical Commn; Westminster Diocesan Ecumenical Commn; Council, Royal Sch. of Church Music. Painter of Frescoes in chapel of Our Lady and the English Martyrs, Little Crosby, Lancs, and various smaller works. Ecclesiastical Assistant to the Union of Catholic Students. *Publications:* regular contributor to theological reviews. *Recreations:* music, painting, swimming. *Address:* 22 George Street, W1. *Club:* Royal Automobile.

**TOMLINSON, Reginald R.,** OBE 1959; RBA; ARMS; ARCA; Senior Inspector of Art to the LCC, 1925-51; *b* Overton, Hants, 10 Oct. 1885; *s* of F. C. Tomlinson; *m* 1914, Emily E., *d* of A. E. Mullins; two *s* one *d*. *Educ:* Farnham Grammar Sch. Apprentice Designer to Minton, Hollins & Co.; Pottery Painter and Designer for Bernard Moore, 1906-09; Royal College of Art; Art Director to the Crown Staffordshire China Co. Ltd, 1913-19; Principal of Cheltenham Coll. of Arts and Crafts, 1922-25; Acting Principal, Central School of Arts and Crafts, London, 1935-36 and 1939-46; President English Speaking Nations International Art Congress, Brussels, 1935; Chairman British Cttee for International Art Congress, Paris, 1937; awarded two international Gold Medals for Design and Craftsmanship, in collaboration with Bernard Moore, at Ghent and Turin; exhibited at Principal Exhibitions and Art Galleries. Chm., Bd of Examiners for ATD, Univ. of London. Hon. Fellow, Institute of British Decorators; Hon. Fellow, College of Handicrafts. Liveryman of Company of Goldsmiths; President Royal Drawing

Society; President Artists Annuity and Benevolent Fund; Master Art Workers' Guild, 1955. *Works purchased:* Pottery by Museums in this country and abroad; *Portraits:* Sir Aylmer Firebrace, J. J. Mallon, CH, Sir Arthur Middleton, Edwin Bayliss, Douglas Macmillan, etc. *Publications:* Lettering for Arts and Crafts; Memory and Imaginative Drawing; Picture Making by Children, 1934; contributed Encyclopædia Britannica, Art in General Education; Crafts for Children, 1935; Children as Artists (King Penguin), 1945; Picture and Pattern Making by Children, 1950; (with J. F. Mills) Growth of Child Art, 1966. *Recreation:* gardening. *Address:* Chestnut Cottage, The Drive, Chichester, Sussex. *T:* Chichester 7551. *Club:* Royal Commonwealth Society.

**TOMLINSON, Miss Ruth,** CBE 1960 (MBE 1928); UK representative at 12th, 13th, 14th Sessions (1958, 1959, 1960) of United Nations Status of Women Commission; Vice-President, International Federation of Business and Professional Women, 1956-62; Lecturer. *Educ:* Liverpool. Secretary, Federated Assocs of Boot and Shoe Manufacturers of Great Britain and Ireland (London), 1922-37; Secretary, Nat. Institute of Boot and Shoe Industry (Technical Education), 1927-37; Consultant Administration, 1937-39; Director Domestic Bureau for Refugees, 1939-42; Ministry of Labour and National Service, Man Power Board, 1943-48; Rep. at UN Commissions and Confs for International Federation of Business and Professional Women, 1949-58. *Recreations:* walking, reading. *Address:* Woodfield, Sparkbridge, Ulverston, Lancs.

**TOMLINSON, Sir Stanley;** *see* Tomlinson, Sir F. S.

**TOMNEY, Frank;** MP (Lab) Hammersmith North since 1950; *b* 24 May 1908; *m*; one *s* one *d.* Branch Secretary of National Union of Municipal and General Workers. Joined Labour Party, 1925; Industrial Consultant. *Address:* 27 Shepherds Way, Rickmansworth, Herts.

**TOMONAGA, Dr Sin-itiro;** Professor Emeritus, since 1969, Tokyo Kyoiku University (Tokyo University of Education); *b* 31 March 1906; *s* of Sanjuro and Hide Tomonaga; *m* 1940, Ryoko Sekiguchi; two *s* one *d. Educ:* Kyoto Imperial University. Research Student, Institute of Physical and Chemical Research, 1932-39; studied at University of Leipzig, Germany, 1937-39; Asst, Inst. of Physical and Chemical Research, 1939-40; Lecturer, Tokyo Bunrika Univ. (absorbed into Tokyo University of Education, 1949), 1940; Prof. of Physics, Tokyo Bunrika Univ., 1941; studied at Inst. for Advanced Study, Princeton, USA, 1949-50; Prof. of Physics, Tokyo Univ. of Educn, 1949-69 (President, 1956-62); Director, Inst. for Optical Research, 1963-69; Pres., Science Council of Japan, 1963-69. Japan Academy Prize, 1948; Order of Culture, Japan, 1952; Lomonosov Medal, USSR, 1964; Nobel Prize for Physics (jointly), 1965. *Publications:* Quantum Mechanics, Vol. I, 1962, Vol. II, 1966. *Recreation:* rakugo. *Address:* 3-17-12 Kyonan-cho, Musashinoshi, Tokyo, Japan.

**TOMPKINS, Prof. Frederick Clifford,** FRS 1955; Professor in Physical Chemistry, Imperial College of Science and Technology, SW7, since 1959; Editor and Secretary of The Faraday Society since 1950; *b* 29 Aug. 1910; *m* 1936, Catherine Livingstone Macdougal; one *d. Educ:* Yeovil Sch.; Bristol Univ. Asst Lectr, King's Coll., Strand, 1934-37; Lectr and Senior Lectr, Natal Univ., Natal, S Africa, 1937-46; ICI Fellow, King's College, Strand, 1946-47; Reader in Physical Chemistry, Imperial College of Science and Technology, 1947; Hon. ARCS 1964. *Publications:* contributions to Proc. Royal Society, Journal Chem. Soc., Trans Faraday Soc., Jl Chem. Physics, Zeitung Elektrochem. *Address:* 32 Grosvenor Street, W1. *T:* 01-493 9575; Cleddens, Preston Candover, Hants. *T:* Preston Candover 318.

**TOMPKINS, (Granville) Richard (Francis);** Chairman and Managing Director, Green Shield Trading Stamp Co. Ltd, since 1958; *b* 15 May 1918; *s* of Richard and Ethel May Tompkins; *m* 1942, Valerie Margaret Try; two *d. Educ:* Pakeman St LCC Sch., London, N7. Laundry delivery man and filling station attendant, 1932; van salesman, 1934; engineering draughtsman, 1938. Founded several companies in printing and advertising, 1945; also Green Shield Trading Stamp Co., 1958. *Recreations:* travel, theatre, golf. *Address:* 7 Belgrave Square, SW1.

**TOMPKINS, Richard;** *see* Tompkins, G. R. F.

**TONBRIDGE, Bishop Suffragan of,** since 1968; **Rt. Rev. Henry David Halsey;** *b* 27 Jan. 1919; *s* of George Halsey, MBE and Gladys W. Halsey, DSc; *m* 1947, Rachel Margaret Neil Smith; four *d. Educ:* King's Coll. Sch., Wimbledon; King's Coll., London (BA); Wells Theol. College. Curate, Petersfield, 1942-45; Chaplain, RNVR, 1946-47; Curate, St Andrew, Plymouth, 1947-50; Vicar of: Netheravon, 1950-53; St Stephen, Chatham, 1953-62; Bromley, and Chaplain, Bromley Hosp., 1962-68; Rural Dean of Bromley, 1965-66; Archdeacon of Bromley, 1966-68. *Recreations:* cricket, sailing, reading, gardening, walking. *Address:* Bishop's Lodge, 48 St Botolph's Road, Sevenoaks, Kent. *T:* Sevenoaks 56070.

**TONBRIDGE, Archdeacon of;** *see* Earle, Ven. E. E. M.

**TONČIĆ-SORINJ, Dr Lujo;** Secretary-General, Council of Europe, since Sept. 1969 (elected in May); Minister of Foreign Affairs, Austria, retired; *b* Vienna, 12 April 1915; *s* of Dusan Tončić-Sorinj (formerly Consul-Gen. in service of Imperial Ministry for Foreign Affairs), and Mabel (*née* Plason de la Woesthyne); *m* 1956, Renate Trenker; one *s* three *d. Educ:* Secondary sch. (Gymnasium), Salzburg. Studied law and philosophy at Univs of Vienna and Agram (Zagreb), 1934-41, also medicine and psychology (LLD Vienna); political science, Institut d'Etudes Politiques, Paris. Head of Polit. Dept of Austrian Research Inst. for Economics and Politics in Salzburg and Editor of Berichte und Informationen, 1946-49; MP for Land Salzburg, 1949-66; Chairman: Legal Cttee of Austrian Parl., 1953-56; For. Affairs Cttee, 1956-59; in charge of For. Affairs questions, Austrian People's Party, 1959-66; Austrian Parly Observer to Consultative Assembly of Council of Europe, 1953-56; Austrian Mem., Consultative Assembly, 1956-66; Vice-Pres., Council of Europe; Vice-Pres., Political Commn, 1961-62; Minister for Foreign Affairs, Austria, 1966-68. Grand Cross of several foreign orders including Order of St Michael and St George, Great Britain (Hon. GCMG). *Publications:* over 350 articles and essays on politics, economics, internat. law and history; Editor of (political weekly periodical) Berichte und Informationen (publ. by Austrian Research Inst. for Economics and Politics in Salzburg). *Recreations:* swimming, diving, history, geography. *Address:* 5020

Salzburg, Schloss Fürberg, Pausingerstrasse 11, Austria. *T:* 06222/73437; Council of Europe, Strasbourg, France.

**TONG, Sir Walter (Wharton),** Kt 1955; JP; MSc; *b* 26 February 1890; *e s* of William Tong and Bertha Tong (*née* Wharton), both of Bolton; *m* 1919, Anne, 2nd *d* of Alfred Glaister, Bolton; three *d. Educ:* Bolton School; Giggleswick Sch.; Manchester Univ. Mem. Bolton Town Council, 1925-52; Alderman 1941; Mayor of Bolton, 1940-41; Chm. Housing Cttee, 1931-41; Chm. Finance Cttee, 1941-46 and 1948-52; Leader of Conservative Party in Town Council, 1942-52. Governor: Canon Slade Grammar Sch.; Bolton School; Bolton County Grammar School. Pres. Bolton Rotary Club, 1942-43; Trustee, Bolton Trustee Savings Bank. JP, Bolton, 1935. Contested (C) Bolton West Division, 1950. *Address:* Greenleaves, Bromley Cross, Bolton, Lancs. *T:* Bolton 53892.

**TONGA,** HM the King of; **King Taufa'ahau Tupou IV;** Hon. KCMG 1968; Hon. KBE 1958 (Hon. CBE 1951); b 4 July 1918; *s* of Prince Uiliami Tupoulahi Tungi and Queen Salote Tupou of Tonga; *S* mother, 1966; *m* 1947, Halaevalu Mata'aho 'Ahome'e; three *s* one *d. Educ:* Tupou College, Tonga; Newington College, Sydney; Wesley College, Sydney University. *Heir: s* HRH Prince Taufa'ahau Manumataongo, *b* 4 May 1948. *Address:* The Palace, Nukualofa, Tonga. *T:* Nukualofa 1.

**TONGE, George Edward,** CBE 1960; JP; Managing Director, Hay's Wharf Ltd; a Director of Proprietors Hay's Wharf Ltd and associated companies; Chairman, Chambers Wharf & Cold Stores; Director: National Cold Stores (Management) Ltd; Exmouth Docks Co.; Member, National Dock Labour Board; *b* 30 April 1910; bachelor. Chairman, nat. Assoc. of Port Employers; Council Mem., CBI; Chm., Oxford and Bermondsey Boys' Clubs; Governor, St Olave's and St Saviour's Grammar School Foundation and Schools; Treasurer, Royal Society of Arts, 1958-62. *Recreations:* sailing, gardening, the arts. *Address:* Sherbrook Dene, Budleigh Salterton, Devon. *T:* Budleigh Salterton 3148. *Clubs:* Garrick, Royal Thames Yacht; Exe Sailing (Exmouth).

**TOOHEY, Mrs Joyce;** Under-Secretary, Ministry of Public Building and Works, since 1964; *b* 20 Sept. 1917; *o d* of late Louis and Lena Zinkin (*née* Daiches); *m* 1947, Monty I. Toohey, MD, MRCP, DCH (*d* 1960); two *d. Educ:* Brondesbury and Kilburn High Sch.; Girton Coll., Cambridge; London Sch. of Economics. BA 1938, MA 1945, Cambridge. Asst Principal, Min. of Supply, 1941; transferred to Min. of Works (now Min. of Public Building and Works), 1946; Principal, 1948; Asst Secretary, 1956; Under-Secretary, 1964. *Recreations:* reading, walking. *Address:* 11 Kensington Court Gardens, W8. *T:* 01-937 1559. *Club:* United University.

**TOOKER, H. C. W.;** *see* Whalley-Tooker.

**TOOKEY, Geoffrey William,** QC 1949; *b* 26 Nov. 1902; *er s* of late William Alfred Tookey, Bromley, Kent; *m* 1933, Rosemary Sherwell, *y d* of late Arthur Henry Clogg; two *s* two *d. Educ:* St Dunstan's College, Catford; City and Guilds College, Imperial College of Science and Technology. FCGI. Mem. Delegacy of C and G College. Called to Bar, Gray's Inn, 1924; Bencher, 1952; Treasurer, 1967; Vice-Treasurer, 1968. Member, Inns of Court Senate, 1966-69; Appointed, 1955-68, to exercise appellate jurisdiction of Board of Trade under Trade Marks Act; Member British Delegation, Lisbon Diplomatic Conference 1958. Chairman, Board of Trade Advisory Group on European Patents and Unification of Patent Laws, 1961-66. Membre d'Honneur, International Association for Protection of Industrial Property (President, British Group, 1954-64). Hon. Mem., Chartered Inst. of Patent Agents, 1969. General List TA, 1922-27 (Captain); War of 1939-45: Royal Air Force Volunteer Reserve, 1940-45, Squadron Ldr (despatches). *Address:* 12 Orchard Road, Bromley, Kent BR1 2PS. *T:* 01-460 4003. *Club:* Royal Air Force.

**TOOLEY, John;** General Administrator, Royal Opera House, Covent Garden, since 1970; *b* 1 June 1924; *yr s* of late H. R. Tooley; *m* 1st, 1951, Judith Craig Morris (marr. diss., 1965); three *d*; 2nd, 1968, Patricia Janet Norah Bagshawe. *Educ:* Repton; Magdalene Coll., Cambridge. Sec., Guildhall School of Music and Drama, 1952-55; Asst to Gen. Administrator, Royal Opera House, Covent Garden, 1955-60; Asst Gen. Administrator, Royal Opera House, Covent Garden, 1960-70. Chm., Nat. Music Council Executive, 1970-. *Recreations:* sailing, theatre. *Address:* 12 Earl's Court Gardens, SW5.

**TOOMEY, Ralph;** Assistant Under-Secretary of State, Department of Education and Science, since 1969; *b* 26 Dec. 1918; *s* of late James and Theresa Toomey; *m* 1951, Patricia Tizard; two *d. Educ:* Cyfarthfa Grammar Sch., Merthyr Tydfil; University Coll., London; Univ. of Caen. Served British and Indian Army, 1940-46. Teacher, Enfield Grammar Sch., 1947; Lecturer, Univ. of London, at Sch. of Oriental and African Studies, 1948. Min. of Education, 1948-60 and 1963- (seconded to Govt of Mauritius, 1960-63, Principal Asst Sec. in Colonial Secretary's Office and Min. of Local Govt and Co-operative Develt). *Address:* 8 The Close, Montreal Park, Sevenoaks, Kent. *T:* Sevenoaks 52553. *Club:* Knole Park Golf (Sevenoaks).

**TOOSEY, Philip John Denton,** CBE 1955 (OBE 1946); DSO 1945; TD 1944; DL; JP; Director, Barclays Bank Ltd (Liverpool Board); Chairman, Albany Investment Trust Ltd; *b* 12 Aug. 1904; *s* of C. D. Toosey; *m* 1932, Muriel Alexandra Eccles; two *s* one *d. Educ:* Gresham's Sch., Norfolk. Baring Brothers & Co. Ltd, 1927-64. Formerly on Boards of Cammell Laird, Ocean Steam Ship Co., Liner Holdings Ltd, Barclays Bank Trust Co. Ltd, and Coast Lines Ltd. JP Cheshire, 1947; DL Lancs 1961; High Sheriff, County Palatine of Lancaster, 1964. Hon. Col, West Lancs Regt, RA (Territorials), T&AVR, 1967-69. *Recreations:* shooting and gardening. *Address:* Heathcote, Hooton, Wirral, Cheshire. *T:* 051-339 2225. *Club:* Racquet (Liverpool).

**TOOTH, Geoffrey Cuthbert,** MD, MRCP, DPM; Visiting Scientist, National Institute of Mental Health, USA, 1968-71; *b* 1 Sept. 1908; *s* of late Howard Henry Tooth, CB, CMG, MD, FRCP, and late Helen Katherine Tooth, OBE (*née* Chilver); *m* 1st, 1934, Princess Olga Galitzine (*d* 1955), *d* of Prince Alexander Galitzine, MD; 2nd, 1958, Princess Xenia Romanoff, *d* of Prince Andrew of Russia. *Educ:* Rugby Sch.; St John's Coll., Cambridge;

St Bartholomew's Hosp.; Johns Hopkins Hosp., Baltimore, Md, USA. MRCS, LRCP 1934, MA Cantab 1935, MD Cantab 1946, DPM 1944; MRCP 1965. Asst Psychiatrist, Maudsley Hosp., 1937-39. Surg. Lt-Comdr, RNVR, Neuropsychiatric Specialist, 1939-45. Colonial Social Science Research Fellow, 1946-53; Comr, Bd of Control, 1954-60; transf. to Min. of Health, and retd as Sen. PMO, Head of Mental Health Section, Med. Div., 1960. Mem. Expert Advisory Panel (Mental Health), WHO. *Publications:* Studies in Mental Illness in the Gold Coast, 1950; various reports to learned societies; articles and papers in med. jls. *Recreations:* sailing, gardening, metal work, photography. *Address:* Prouillac, 24 Plazac, France.

**TOOTH, Sir Hugh;** *see* Munro-Lucas-Tooth.

**TOOTHILL, Sir John (Norman),** Kt 1964; CBE 1955; Director, Ferranti Ltd, Edinburgh; *b* 11 Nov. 1908; *s* of John Harold and Helena Toothill; *m* 1935, Ethel Amelia Stannard. *Educ:* Beaminster Grammar School. Apprenticed Tilling Stevens Ltd, Hoffman Manufacturing Co. Ltd, Harris Lebus Ltd. Joined Ferranti Ltd, Hollinwood, 1935, as Chief Cost Accountant; Gen. Manager, Ferranti Ltd, Edinburgh, 1943; Director: Ferranti Ltd, Hollinwood, Lancs, 1958; AI Welders Ltd, Inverness, 1963; Edinburgh Investment Trust, 1964; Caledonian Assurance Co., 1966; R. W. Toothill Ltd; Chm., EDC Vehicle Distribution and Repair. Governor, College of Aeronautics, Cranfield. CompIEE, Comp. British IRE, Hon. Comp. Royal Aeronautical Soc., FRSE. Hon. LLD Aberdeen, 1966; Hon. DSc Heriot-Watt, 1968. *Publication:* Toothill Report on the Scottish Economy, 1961. *Recreations:* fishing, golf. *Address:* St Germains, Longniddry, East Lothian. *T:* Longniddry 2106; Lennoxbrae, Ordiequish, Fochabers, Morayshire. *T:* Fochabers 268. *Club:* Caledonian.

**TOPOLSKI, Feliks;** Painter; *b* 14 Aug. 1907; *s* of Edward Topolski (actor) and Stanislawa Drutowska; *m* 1944, Marion Everall; one *s* one *d*. *Educ:* Mikolaj Rey Sch.; Acad. of Art, Warsaw; Officers' Sch. of Artillery Reserve, Wlodzimiers Wolynski; self-tutoring in Italy, Paris. Settled in England, 1935. Exhibited in London and provincial galleries, in Poland, USA, Canada, Eire, France, India, Australia, Italy, Argentine, Switzerland, Denmark, Norway, Israel, Brazil and Portugal; has contributed to numerous publications; to BBC television programmes; and designed theatrical settings and costumes; as War Artist (1940-45) pictured Battle of Britain, sea and air war, Russia, Middle East, India, Burma, China, Africa, Italy, Germany. British subject since 1947. Painted the Cavalcade of Commonwealth (60' x 20') for Festival of Britain, 1951 (now in Victoria Memorial Hall, Singapore); four murals for Finsbury Borough Council, 1952; Coronation of Elizabeth II (100' x 4') for Buckingham Palace, 1958-60; murals for Carlton Tower Hotel, London, 1960; St Regis Hotel, New York, 1965; twenty portraits of English writers for University of Texas, 1961-62. Film: Topolski's Moscow (for CBS TV), 1969. Works at British Museum, Victoria and Albert Museum, Imperial War Museum; Galleries: the Tate, Edinburgh, Glasgow, Aberdeen, Nottingham, Brooklyn, Toronto, Tel Aviv, New Delhi, Melbourne, Lisbon, Warsaw. *Publications:* The London Spectacle, 1935; Illustrator of Bernard Shaw's Geneva, 1939, In Good King Charles's Golden Days, 1939, and Pygmalion, 1941; Penguin Prints, 1941; Britain in Peace and War, 1941; Russia in War, 1942; Three Continents, 1944-45; Portrait of GBS, 1946; Confessions of a Congress Delegate, 1949; 88 Pictures, 1951; Coronation, 1953; Sketches of Gandhi, 1954; The Blue Conventions, 1956; Topolski's Chronicle for Students of World Affairs, 1958; Topolski's Legal London, 1961; Face to Face, 1964; Holy China, 1968; (with Conor Cruise O'Brien) The United Nations: Sacred Drama, 1968; Shem Ham & Japheth Inc., 1970; Topolski's Chronicle, 1953-. *Address:* 14 Hanover Terrace, NW1. *T:* 01-262 6059.

**TOPP, Brig. Charles Beresford,** CBE 1945; DSO 1919; MC; Member Canadian Pension Commission since 1956; *b* 7 December 1893; *s* of Richard Ussher Topp, MD, FRCS, and Mary Eliza Beley; *m* 1919, Constance Christine Helliwell; one *s* one *d*. *Educ:* Public Schools; Toronto University. Reporter, Toronto Globe and Toronto Mail and Empire; sent to London, England, as correspondent for Toronto Mail and Empire, 1914; resigned to enlist for war service, May 1915; served in France with 42nd Battalion Royal Highlanders of Canada (thrice wounded, despatches thrice, DSO, MC and Bar, three service medals); on discharge held rank of Major; served with the Governor-General's Foot Guards, Canadian Militia, Ottawa, since 1920; commanded the 1st Battalion with rank of Lt-Col, 1925-30; commanded 4th Canadian Inf. Bde, 2nd Canadian Division Overseas, 1940-42; Staff appts 1942-45; Hon. ADC to Lord Willingdon, Gov.-Gen. of Canada; served in various capacities in admin of Canadian Pension law since war of 1914-18; mem. special committee appointed by Canadian Government to Revise Pension Law, 1932. Past Pres. Ottawa Branch, Canadian Legion, British Empire Service League. *Publications:* History of the 42nd Battalion Royal Highlanders of Canada; various short stories and articles principally on hunting and fishing topics. *Recreations:* hunting, fishing, golf. *Address:* 635 Blair Road, Ottawa 9, Ontario, Canada. *Clubs:* Royal Commonwealth Society; (Hon. Pres.) University (Ottawa); Lake Bernard Fish and Game (Lascelles, Quebec).

**TOPP, Wilfred Bethridge,** CMG 1949; retired; formerly London Technical Advisor to Diamond Producers Association; *b* 29 Aug. 1891; *s* of Joseph Bethridge Topp, Kimberley, S Africa; *m* 1918, Beatrice Maud Matthews, Port Elizabeth, S Africa. *Educ:* Kimberley, S Africa. Joined De Beers Consolidated Mines Ltd, 1909. served with 7th S African Inf., 1914-17. Joined Consolidated Diamond Valuation Staff, 1920; one of valuators for famous Hans Merensky diamond finds at Orange River mouth, 1926; taken over by Union Govt for valuations of State Alluvial Diamonds, 1928. At amalgamation of all S African Diamond producers sent to Kimberley Central Office, until sent to England in 1934. At outbreak of War of 1939-45 joined a board of experts to control export of diamonds; after termination of hostilities examined all diamonds for export and import on two days each week (duties for the State honorary since 1939). *Recreations:* rifle shooting, golf. *Address:* Laughing Waters, Valley Road, Kenilworth, Cape, South Africa. *Club:* City (Cape Town).

**TOPPING, James,** MSc, PhD, DIC, FInstP; FIMA; Vice-Chancellor, Brunel University, since 1966; *b* 9 Dec. 1904; 3rd *s* of James and Mary A. Topping, Ince, Lancashire; *m* 1934, Muriel Phyllis Hall (*d* 1963); one *s*; *m* 1965, Phyllis Iles. *Educ:* Univ. of Manchester; Imperial Coll. of Science and Technology. BSc (Manchester), 1924; PhD (London), 1926; Beit Scientific Research Fellow, 1926-28. Asst Lectr, Imperial Coll., 1928-30; Lectr Chelsea Polytechnic, 1930-32; Lectr, Coll. of

Technology, Manchester, 1932-37; Head, Dept of Maths and Physics, Polytechnic, Regent St, 1937-53; Principal, Technical Coll., Guildford, 1953-54; Principal, Brunel College, W3, 1955-66. Member Council for National Academic Awards. Hon. DTech, Brunel, 1967; Hon. DSc, CNAA, 1969. *Publications:* Shorter Intermediate Mechanics (with D. Humphrey), 1949; Errors of Observation, 1955; papers in scientific jls. *Address:* 33 Harriotts Lane, Ashtead, Surrey. *T:* Ashtead 2168. *Club:* Athenæum.

**TOPPING, Rt. Hon. Walter William Buchanan,** PC (NI), 1957; QC (NI); Recorder of Belfast since 1960; *b* 13 Jan. 1908; *m* 1933, Maureen Gallaher; three *s*. *Educ:* Rossall School; Queen's University, Belfast. Called to Bar, NI, 1930; QC 1946. MP Larne Div. of Co. Antrim, Parliament of Northern Ireland, 1945; Chief Government Whip, Northern Ireland Parliament, 1947-56; Minister of Home Affairs, 1956-59. *Address:* Windy Ridge, Dunmurry, County Antrim, Northern Ireland.

**TORLESSE, Rear-Adm. Arthur David,** CB 1953; DSO 1946; retired; Regional Director of Civil Defence, North Midlands Region, 1955-Jan. 1967; *b* 24 Jan. 1902; *e s* of Captain A. W. Torlesse, Royal Navy, and H. M. Torlesse (*née* Jeans); *m* 1933, Sheila Mary Susan, *d* of Lt-Col Duncan Darroch of Gourock; two *s* one *d*. *Educ:* Stanmore Park; Royal Naval Colleges, Osborne and Dartmouth. Served as midshipman, Grand Fleet, 1918; specialised as observer, Fleet Air Arm, 1926; Commander, 1935; staff appointments in HMS Hood and at Singapore and Bangkok (Naval Attaché), 1936-39; Executive officer, HMS Suffolk, 1939-40; aviation staff appointments at Lee on Solent and Admiralty, 1940-44; Captain, 1942; commanded HMS Hunter, 1944-45; Director of Air Equipment, Admiralty, 1946-48; Imperial Defence College, 1949; commanded HMS Triumph, Far East, 1950, taking part in first 3 months of Korean War (despatches); Rear-Admiral, 1951; Flag Officer, Special Squadron and in command of Monte Bello atomic trial expedition, 1952; Flag Officer, Ground Training, 1953-54, retired Dec. 1954. Officer, US Legion of Merit, 1954. *Recreations:* fishing, entomology. *Address:* 1 Sway Lodge, Sway, near Lymington, Hants. *T:* Sway 550. *Club:* United Service.

**TORNARITIS, Criton George,** QC (Cyprus); LLB (Hons, Athens); Attorney-General of the Republic of Cyprus since 1960 (Attorney-General, Cyprus, 1952); seconded as Commissioner for Consolidation of the Cyprus Legislation since 1956; *b* 27 May 1902; *m* 1934, Mary (*née* Pitta); one *s*. *Educ:* Gymnasium of Limassol; Athens University; Gray's Inn. Advocate of the Supreme Court of Cyprus, 1924; District Judge, Cyprus, 1940; President District Court, Cyprus, 1942; Solicitor-General, Cyprus, 1944; Attorney-General, Cyprus, 1952. Attached to Legal Div. of the Colonial Office, 1955. Legal Adviser to Greek-Cypriot Delegation on the Mixed Constitutional Commission, 1959; Greek-Cypriot delegate to Ankara for initialling of Constitution of Republic of Cyprus, 1960. *Publications:* contributions to legal journals and periodicals; The revised edition of the Laws of Cyprus, 1959. *Recreations:* walking, reading. *Address:* 87 Archbishop Makarios Avenue, Nicosia, Cyprus. *T:* 77242. *Clubs:* Oxford and Cambridge University, Royal Commonwealth Society; Nicosia (Cyprus).

**TORNEY, Thomas William;** JP; MP (Lab) Bradford South since 1970; Derby and District area organizer, Union of Shop, Distributive and Allied Workers, since 1946; *b* London, 2 July 1915. *Educ:* elementary school. Joined Labour Party, 1930; Election Agent: Wembley North, 1945; Derbyshire West, 1964. Mem. General Management Cttee, Derby Labour Party. Member: (Past Chm.) North Midland Regional Joint Apprenticeship Council for catering industry; Local Appeals Tribunal, Min. of Social Security, 1946-68. Especially interested in education, social security, industrial relations. JP Derby, 1969. *Address:* House of Commons, SW1; 76 The Hollow, Littleover, Derby. *T:* Derby 23705.

**TORONTO, Cardinal-Archbishop of,** since 1934; **His Eminence Cardinal James Charles McGuigan,** DD; *b* Hunter River, PEI, 1894. *Educ:* Prince of Wales College and St Dunstan's Coll., Charlottetown, PEI; Grand Seminary and Laval Univ., Quebec; DD, PhD, JCD, LLD; course at Catholic Univ. of America, Washington, 1927. Priest, 1918; Prof. at St Dunstan's Coll., 1918-19; Sec. and Chancellor of Charlottetown, 1919-20; and of Edmonton, 1920-25; Vicar-Gen. of Edmonton, 1923-30; Rector of St Joseph's Cathedral, Edmonton, 1925-27; Rector St Joseph's Seminary, Edmonton, 1927-30; RC Archbishop of Regina, 1930-34; Cardinal, 1946. *Address:* Archbishop's House, Old Yonge Street, Willowdale, Ont, Canada.

**TORONTO, Coadjutor Archbishop of, (RC),** since 1961; **Most Rev. Philip F. Pocock,** LLD. *Educ:* Univ. of Western Ontario; St Peter's Seminary, London, Can.; Catholic University of America, Washington, DC; Angelicum University, Rome. Ordination to Priesthood, 1930; Angelicum University, Rome, JCD, 1934; Professor of Moral Theology, St Peter's Seminary, 1934; consecrated Bishop of Saskatoon, 1944; Apostolic Administrator of Winnipeg, June 1951; Titular Archbishop of Apro and Coadjutor Archbishop of Winnipeg, Aug. 1951; Archbishop of Winnipeg, 1952-61. Hon. LLD Univ. of Western Ontario, 1955; Univ. of Ottawa, 1958; Univ. of Manitoba, 1958; Assumption Univ. of Windsor, Ont., 1961; St Francis Xavier Univ., Antigonish, 1963; Hon. DD, Huron Coll., London, Ont., 1967. *Address:* 55 Gould Street, Toronto 2, Ontario, Canada.

**TORONTO, Bishop of,** since 1966; **Rt. Rev. George Boyd Snell,** DD, PhD; *b* Toronto, Ontario, 17 June 1907; *s* of John George Snell and Minnie Alice Boyd; *m* 1934, Esther Mary. *Educ:* Trinity College, Toronto. BA 1929, MA 1930, PhD 1937, DD 1948. Deacon, Toronto, 1931; Priest, Niagara (for Tor.), 1932; Curate of St Michael and All Angels, Tor., 1931-39; Rector, 1940-48; Private Chaplain to Bp of Tor., 1945-48; Rector of Pro-Cathedral, Calgary, and Dean of Calgary, 1948-51; Exam. Chaplain to Bp of Calgary, 1948-51; Rector of St Clem. Eglinton, Tor., 1951-56; Archdeacon of Toronto, 1953-56; Exam. Chaplain to Bp of Toronto, 1953-55. Consecrated Bp Suffragan of Toronto, 1956; elected Bp-Coadjutor of Toronto, 1959. Hon. DD: Wycliffe Coll., Toronto, 1959; Huron Coll., Ontario, 1968. *Address:* Synod House, 135 Adelaide Street East, Toronto 1, Ont, Canada. *Clubs:* Albany, National, University (Toronto).

**TORPHICHEN,** 13th Baron *cr* 1564; **John Gordon Sandilands;** *b* 8 June 1886; *s* of 12th Baron and Ellen, *d* of Lt-Gen. Charles Edward Park Gordon, CB; *S* father, 1915; *m* 1st, 1916, Grace Douglass (*d* 1948), 2nd *d* of Winslow Pierce, Bayville, Long Island, NY; one *s*; 2nd, 1950, Isabel Fernandez Phillips, 2nd *d* of Mrs Barnett, North Berwick and Monte Carlo. *Educ:* Eton; Birmingham Univ. *Heir:* *s* Master of Torphichen, *qv*. *Address:* Calder House,

Mid-Calder, Midlothian. *T:* Mid-Calder 319. *Club:* New (Edinburgh).

**TORPHICHEN, Master of; Hon. James Bruce Sandilands;** *b* 26 Oct. 1917; *o s* of 13th Baron Torphichen, *qv*; *m* 1st, 1943, Mary Thurstan Vaudrey (marriage dissolved, 1952); one *s* one *d*; 2nd, 1955, Margaret Jane, *d* of George Dawson, New York City. *Educ:* Eton; Balliol College, Oxford. *Address:* St Vincent's College, Latrobe, Pennsylvania, USA; Calder House, Mid-Calder, Midlothian.

**TORRANCE, Rev. Prof. Thomas Forsyth,** MBE 1945; DLitt, DTh, DThéol, Dr Teol, DD; Professor of Christian Dogmatics, University of Edinburgh, and New College, Edinburgh, since 1952; *b* 30 Aug. 1913; *e s* of late Rev. T. Torrance, then of Chengtu, Szechwan, China; *m* 1946, Margaret Edith, *y d* of late Mr and Mrs G. F. Spear, The Brow, Coombe Down, Bath; two *s* one *d*. *Educ:* Chengtu Canadian School; Bellshill Academy; Univs of Edinburgh, Oxford, Basel. MA Edinburgh 1934; studies in Jerusalem and Athens, 1936; BD Edinburgh 1937; post-grad. studies, Basel, 1937-38; Prof. of Theology, Auburn, NY, USA, 1938-39; post-grad. studies, Oriel Coll., Oxford, 1939-40; ordained minister of Alyth Barony Parish, 1940; Church of Scotland chaplain (with Huts and Canteens) in MEF and CMF, 1943-45; returned to Alyth; DTh Univ. of Basel, 1946; minister of Beechgrove Church, Aberdeen, 1947; Professor of Church History, Univ. of Edinburgh, and New Coll., Edinburgh, 1950-52. Hewett Lecturer, 1959 (New York and Boston). Mem., Académie Internationale des Sciences Religieuses, 1965; Hon. Pres., Soc. for Study of Theology, 1966-68; For. Mem., Société de l'Histoire du Protestantisme Français, 1968; Mem. Soc. Internat. pour l'Etude de la Philosophie Médiévale, 1969; Hon. Pres., Church Service Soc. of the Church of Scotland, 1970-71. DD (*hc*) Presbyterian Coll., Montreal, 1950; DThéol (*hc*) Geneva, 1959; DThéol (*hc*) Paris, 1959; DD (*hc*) St Andrews, 1960; Dr Teol (*hc*) Oslo, 1961; DLitt Edinburgh. Cross of St Mark (first class), 1970. *Publications:* The Modern Theological Debate, 1942; The Doctrine of Grace in the Apostolic Fathers, 1949; Calvin's Doctrine of Man, 1949; Royal Priesthood, 1955; Kingdom and Church, 1956; When Christ Comes and Comes Again, 1957; The Mystery of the Lord's Supper (Sermons on the Sacrament by Robert Bruce), 1958; ed Calvin's Tracts and Treatises, Vols I-III, 1959; The School of Faith, 1959; Conflict and Agreement in the Church, Vol. I, Order and Disorder, 1959; The Apocalypse Today, 1959; Conflict and Agreement in the Church, Vol. II, The Ministry and the Sacraments of the Gospel, 1960; Karl Barth: an Introduction to his Early Theology, 1910-1930, 1962; ed (with D. W. Torrance) Calvin's NT Commentaries, 1959-70; Theology in Reconstruction, 1965; Theological Science, 1969 (Collins Religious Book Award); Space, Time and Incarnation, 1969; God and Rationality, 1970; Jt Editor, Church Dogmatics, Vols 1, 2, 3 and 4, by Karl Barth, 1956-69; Jt Editor Scottish Jl Theology. *Recreations:* squash, golf, fishing. *Address:* 37 Braid Farm Road, Edinburgh EH10 6LE. *T:* 031-447 3050.

**TORRES BODET, Jaime;** Mexican Minister of Education, 1958-64; *b* Mexico City, 17 Apr. 1902; *m* 1929, Josefina Juarez. *Educ:* Escuela Normal; Univ. of Mexico (Faculty of Philosophy and Letters). Head of the Libraries Department, Ministry of Education, Mexico, 1922; Professor of French Literature, Univ. of Mexico, 1924-28; Sec. Mexican Legation, Spain, 1929, France, 1931; Mexican Chargé d'Affaires, Netherlands, 1932; Head of Diplomatic Dept, Min. of Foreign Affairs, Mexico, 1936; Mexican Chargé d'Affaires, Belgium, 1938-40; Under-Sec. for Foreign Affairs, Mexico, 1940-43; Minister of Education, 1943-46; Minister for Foreign Affairs, 1946-48; Director-General, Unesco, Dec. 1948-Nov. 1952; Mexican Ambassador in Paris, 1954-58. Holds numerous foreign orders. Gold Medal of Pan-American League (US). Doctor *hc* of several univs both in Mexico and abroad. *Publications:* Fervor, (Mexico) 1919; La casa, (Mexico) 1923; Los dias, (Mexico) 1923; Poemas, (Mexico) 1924; Biombo (Mexico) 1925; Poesía, (Madrid) 1926; Margarita de Niebla, (Mexico) 1927; La educación sentimental, (Madrid) 1929; Destierro, (Madrid) 1930; Proserpina rescatada, (Madrid) 1931; Estrella de dia, 1933; Primero de enero, 1934; Sombras, 1937; Cripta, (Mexico) 1937; Nacimiento de Venus y otros relatos, (Mexico) 1941; Sonetos, (Mexico) 1949; Fronteras, (Mexico) 1954; Tiempo de Arena, 1955; Essays: Contemporáneos, 1928; Educación Mexicana, 1944; Educación y concordia internacional, 1948; Balzac, 1960; Maestro venecianos, 1961; Obras escogidas, 1961; Tolstoi, 1965; Poesía de Jaime Torres Bodet, 1965; Discursos, 1965; Rubén Darío, 1966; Tiempo y Memoria en la Obra de Proust, 1967; Obra Poética, 1967. *Address:* Güemes 326, Mexico 10, DF.

**TORRIE, Malcolm,** *see* Mitchell, Gladys, M. W.

**TORRINGTON,** 11th Viscount, *cr* 1721; **Timothy Howard St George Byng;** Bt 1715; Baron Byng of Southill, 1721; *b* 13 July 1943; *o s* of Hon. George Byng, RN (*d* on active service, 1944; *o s* of 10th Viscount) and Anne Yvonne Wood (she *m* 2nd, 1951, Howard Henry Masterton Carpenter); *S* grandfather, 1961. *Educ:* Harrow; St Edmund Hall, Oxford. *Recreation:* travel. *Heir: kinsman,* John Launcelot Byng, MC [*b* 18 March 1919; *m* 1955, Margaret Ellen Hardy; one *s* two *d*]. *Address:* 34 Belgravia Court, SW1; South End House, High Ham, Nr Langport, Somerset. *T:* Langport 436.

**TORTELIER, Paul;** Conductor; *b* 21 March 1914; *s* of Joseph Tortelier, cabinet maker; *m* 1946, Maud Martin; one *s* three *d*. *Educ:* Conservatoire National de Musique, Paris; gen. educn privately. Leading Cellist, Monte Carlo, 1935-37; Cellist, Boston Symphony Orch., 1937-40; Leading Cellist, Société des Concerts du Conservatoire de Paris, 1945-47; Internat. solo career began in Concertgebouw, Amsterdam, 1946, and London, 1947 (under Sir Thomas Beecham's baton). Concert tours: Europe, N America, North Africa, Israel, etc. As a conductor: debut with Israel Philharmonic, 1956; Prof. of Violoncello: Conservatoire Nat. Supérieur de Musique, Paris, 1956-69; Folkwang Hochschule, Essen; conducts in Paris and in England. Master classes, for BBC TV, 1970. Hon. Mem., Royal Acad. of Music (England). *Publications:* Cello Sonata, Trois p'tits tours; Spirales for Cello and piano; Suite for unaccompanied cello; Elegie, Saxe, Toccata for cello and piano; Pièces en trio for oboe and 2 cellos. Edition of Sammartini Sonata; Cadenzas for classical concertos. The Great Flag (internat. anthem, written for UNO). *Recreations:* no time for these! *Address:* 14 rue Léon Cogniet, Paris 17e. *T:* Wagram 64.64.

**TORY, Sir Geofroy (William),** KCMG 1958 (CMG 1956); British High Commissioner to Malta, 1967-70; *b* 31 July 1912; *s* of William Frank Tory and Edith Wreghitt; *m* 1st, 1938, Emilia Strickland; two *s* one *d*; 2nd, 1950, Hazel Winfield. *Educ:* King Edward VII Sch., Sheffield; Queens' Coll., Cambridge. Apptd

Dominions Office, 1935; Private Sec. to Perm. Under-Sec. of State, 1938-39; served War, 1939-43, in Royal Artillery; Prin. Private Sec. to Sec. of State, 1945-46; Senior Sec., Office of UK High Comr, Ottawa, 1946-49; Prin. Sec., Office of UK Rep. to Republic of Ireland, 1949-50; Counsellor, UK Embassy, Dublin, 1950-51; idc 1952; Dep. High Comr for UK in Pakistan (Peshawar), 1953-54, in Australia, 1954-57; Asst Under-Sec. of State, CRO, 1957; High Comr for UK in Fed. of Malaya, 1957-63; Ambassador to Ireland, 1964-66. FRAS 1951. PMN (Malaysia) 1963. *Recreations:* fishing, painting, golf. *Address:* Rathclaren House, Kilbrittain, Co. Cork, Ireland. *Clubs:* Travellers'; Kildare Street (Dublin).

**TOSELAND, Charles Stephen,** CBE 1955 (MBE 1934); *b* 1 Sept. 1894; *s* of late Stephen Charles and Charlotte Toseland; *m* 1924, Kathleen Muriel (*née* Coombs); no *c. Educ:* Owen's School; King's College, London. Entered Civil Service, 1910; British Vice-Consul, Norway, 1917-19; Department of Overseas Trade, 1920-39 and 1945-47; Asst Sec. and Principal Asst Sec., Ministry of Food, 1939-45; Secretary-General, British Tourist and Holidays Board, 1948-50; Under Secretary, Board of Trade, Jan. 1949-55, retired. Mem. (Chm. 1958) Epping Urban District Council, 1956-59. *Recreation:* motoring. *Address:* The Willows, Beulah Road, Epping, Essex. *T:* Epping 2113.

**TOTNES, Archdeacon of;** *see* Newhouse, Ven. Robert John Darrell.

**TOTTENHAM,** family name of **Marquess of Ely.**

**TOTTENHAM, Rear-Adm. Edward Loftus,** CB 1952; OBE 1937; DL; *b* 12 May 1896; 3rd *s* of Rev. C. F. B. Tottenham, sometime Rector of Castletownroche, Co. Cork; *m* 1924, Florence Luise, *d* of W. Gates, Oldcastletown, Kildorrery, Co. Cork; one *s* one *d. Educ:* Bishop Foy School, Waterford; Dean Close School, Cheltenham. Entered RN, 1913. Served European War, 1914-18, various ships in Grand Fleet. Sec. to Adm. Sir Hugh D. R. Watson in various appts, 1920-28; HMS Triad, Persian Gulf, 1930-33; Naval Sec. and mem. NZ Naval Board, 1935-39; HMS Fiji, 1939-41; HMS Illustrious (despatches), 1942-44; Asst Director of Air Equipment, Admiralty, 1945-46; Captain (S) 1945; Fleet Supply Officer, E Indies Station, 1946-47; HMS Ceres, Supply Br. Trg Establishment in Command, 1948-50. Rear-Adm (S) 1950. Retired 1963. DL Hampshire, 1965. *Address:* Struan, Links Lane, Rowlands Castle, Hants. *T:* Rowlands Castle 310. *Club:* Naval and Military.

**TOTTENHAM, Sir (George) Richard (Frederick),** KCIE 1946 (CIE 1930); Kt 1937; CSI 1936; *b* 18 Nov. 1890; 2nd *s* of late Lt-Col F. St L. Tottenham, DL, JP, of Mount Callan, Inagh, Co. Clare; *m* 1917, Hazel Joyce (*d* 1955), 2nd *d* of late Major J. H. Gwynne; one *s* one *d. Educ:* Harrow; New College, Oxford. Entered ICS 1914; Sec. to the Government of India, Defence Department, 1932-37; Addtl Secretary and Secretary Home Department, 1940-46; retired, 1948. *Address:* Weston Farm House, Totland Bay, IOW. *T:* Freshwater 2722.

**TOTTENHAM, Percy Marmaduke,** CBE 1919; *b* 17 Aug. 1873; *e s* of late Capt. Francis Loftus Tottenham of Coolmore, Crowboro', and Cicell, *d* of late Colonel C. Grimston, of Grimston Garth, Yorkshire; *m* 1909, Angel, *o d* of Rt Hon. Sir Edward M. Archdale, 1st Bt; two *s* one *d. Educ:* Repton; RIEC, Coopers Hill. Entered the Egyptian Public Works Ministry, 1895; Inspector-General of Irrigation in the Sudan, 1909-14, and Member of Governor-General's Council, 1910-14; Inspector-General of Irrigation for Lower Egypt, 1914-16; Inspector-General of Public Works, 1917-19; Under-Secretary of State for Public Works, Egypt, 1919-25; Agent to Egyptian Government, London, 1925-37; Grand Cordon Nile, 2nd Ismail, 2nd Medjidie and 4th Osmania. *Address:* 4 Croft Lodge, Crowborough, Sussex.

**TOTTENHAM, Richard E.,** MD, BA, DPH, FRCPI, FRCOG; *s* of late Edward Tottenham, Mallow, County Cork, Ireland; *m* Norah Margaret (*d* 1965), *d* of late H. J. Daly, Dublin. *Educ:* Trinity College, Dublin. Late Professor of Obstetrics and Gynæcology, University of Hong Kong; Consultant to the Hong Kong Government; Assistant Master, Rotunda Hospital, Dublin; Surgeon Lieut, Royal Navy; Obstetric Physician and Gynæcologist, Steevens' Hospital; Obstetrician and Gynæcologist, City and County Hospital, Londonderry; Rockefeller Travel Grant for USA and Canada, 1924; Medical Tour, Europe, 1930. Member Royal Dublin Society. King's Jubilee Medal, 1935. *Publications:* A Handbook of Midwifery; A Handbook of Practical Midwifery (in Chinese); A Short Practice of Gynæcology (Jellet and Tottenham); Aids to Gynæcology, 6th, 7th and 8th edns; Impressions of Continental Clinics; A New Pelvimeter; Articles on Irish History, etc. *Recreations:* fishing, historical research, carpentry, golf. *Address:* Gortmore, 169 Strand Road, Merrion, Dublin 4, Ireland.

**TOTTENHAM-SMITH, Ralph Henry,** CBE 1946; FRGS; *b* 21 Sept. 1893; *o s* of Robert Tottenham-Smith, Johannesburg, South Africa; *m* 1917, Alice Geneviève Marie, *d* of René Martin, Rouen; one *s* one *d. Educ:* Johannesburg College; Clifton College; Trinity College, Dublin. Served European War, France, 1914-17 (prisoner); entered Consular Service, 1919; Vice-Consul: Valparaiso, 1919; Constanza, 1922; Cettinje, 1925; Dubrovnik, 1926; Paris, 1927; Consul and Chargé d'Affaires, Asuncion, 1931; Special Envoy there for inauguration of President, 1932; Consul, Turin, 1937; Lisbon, 1940; Commercial Secretary, Lisbon, 1944; Counsellor of Embassy and HBM Consul-General, Paris, 1944, Minister, 1948. Chairman of British Charitable Fund, Paris, 1945-48; Member, Cttee of Management of Hertford British Hosp., Paris, 1945-50; Coronation Medals, 1937, 1953. Special Ambassador for inauguration of President of El Salvador, 1950; Minister to El Salvador, 1950-53; retired 1953. *Recreations:* tennis (Pres. Paraguayan LT Assoc., 1936), motoring, golf, bridge, reading. *Address:* Clareen, 9 Marina Drive, Parkstone, Poole, Dorset. *T:* Parkstone 3255. *Clubs:* Royal Over-Seas League; Parkstone Golf.

**TOTTLE, Prof. Charles Ronald;** Professor and Head of School of Materials Science, University of Bath, since 1967; *b* 2 Sept. 1920; *m* 1944, Eileen P. Geoghegan; one *s* one *d. Educ:* Nether Edge Grammar School; University of Sheffield (MMet). English Electric Co. Ltd, 1941-45; Lecturer in Metallurgy, University of Durham, King's College, 1945-50; Ministry of Supply, Atomic Energy Division, Springfields Works, 1950-51; Culcheth Laboratories, 1951-56 (UKAEA); Head of Laboratories, Dounreay, 1956-57; Deputy Director, Dounreay, 1958-59; Prof. of Metallurgy, Univ. of Manchester, 1959-67; Resident Research Associate, Argonne Nat. Laboratory, Illinois, USA, 1964-65. Vice-Pres., Instn of Metallurgists; Jt Editor, Institution of Metallurgists Series of

Textbooks, 1962-70. FIM; FInstP, 1958. Hon. MSc Manchester. *Publications:* The Science of Engineering Materials, 1965; various contribs to metallurgical and engineering jls. *Recreations:* music, model making, gardening. *Address:* Bath University, Claverton Down, Bath. *Club:* Science (Bath).

**TOUCH, Dr Arthur Gerald,** CMG 1967; Chief Scientist, Government Communications Headquarters, since 1961; *b* 5 July 1911; *s* of A. H. Touch, Northampton; *m* 1938, Phyllis Wallbank, Birmingham; one *s*. *Educ:* Oundle; Jesus College, Oxford. MA, DPhil 1937. Bawdsey Research Station, Air Ministry, 1936; Radio Dept, RAE, Farnborough, 1940; British Air Commn, Washington, DC, 1941; Supt, Blind Landing Experimental Unit, RAE, 1947; Director: Electronic R and D (Air), Min. of Supply, 1953; Electronic R and D (Ground), Min of Supply, 1956-59; Imperial Defence College, 1957; Head, Radio Dept, RAE, 1959; Min. of Defence, 1960. *Recreations:* fly fishing, horticulture (orchids). *Address:* 26 Sandy Lane, Charlton Kings, Cheltenham, Glos. *T:* Cheltenham 59724.

**TOUCHE, Rt. Hon. Sir Gordon (Cosmo),** 1st Bt, *cr* 1962; PC 1959; Kt 1952; *b* 8 July 1895; *s* of Sir George Touche, 1st Bt; *m* 1926, Ruby Anne Hume-Purves, *d* of late Sir Duncan Macpherson, CIE; one *s* one *d*. *Educ:* Marlborough; University College, Oxford, MA. Served in Army, 1915-19; Barrister-at-Law, Inner Temple; Director: Trustees Corp. Ltd; City National Investment Trust, Ltd; Cedar Investment Trust Ltd; Chm. Surrey Conservative and Unionist Club, 1950-57; Chairman United Club, 1938-42; contested (C) Ashton-under-Lyne, 1928, and North Islington, 1929; MP (C) Reigate Division of Surrey, 1931-50, Dorking Division, 1950-64. Dep. Chm. of Ways and Means, Nov. 1956-Oct. 1959; Chm. of Ways and Means, 1959-Jan. 1962. Hon. Freeman of Reigate, 1942. *Publications:* The Law of Parliamentary Elections; The Law of Criminal Procedure. *Heir:* *s* Rodney Gordon Touche [*b* 5 Dec. 1928; *m* 1955, Ouida Ann, *er d* of F. Gerald MacLellan, Moncton, New Brunswick; one *s* three *d*]. *Address:* Gable End, Mill Road, Holmwood, near Dorking, Surrey. *T:* Dorking 6444. *Club:* Royal Automobile.

**TOUCHE, Sir Norman George,** 2nd Bt, *cr* 1920; barrister; Director of Industrial and General Trust, Ltd, 1921-67; *b* 11 May 1888; *s* of Sir George Touche, 1st Bt, and Jessie (*d* 1917), *d* of late Isaac Brown; *S* father, 1935; *m* 1923, Eva Maitland, *e d* of P. E. Cameron, Salachan, Ardgour, Argyllshire; two *d*. *Educ:* Marlborough; Univ. College, Oxford, MA, BCL. Called to Bar, Lincoln's Inn, 1914; served European War, 1915-19. *Heir:* *n* Anthony George Touche [*b* 13 Jan. 1927; *m* 1961, Hester Christina, *er d* of Dr Werner Plauger, Leek, Staffs; three *s* one *d*]. *Address:* Ivy Cottage, Westcott, near Dorking, Surrey. *Club:* Oxford and Cambridge.
*See also Rt Hon. Sir Gordon Touche, Bt.*

**TOULMIN, Stephen Edelston,** MA, PhD; Professor of Philosophy, Michigan State University, since 1969; *b* 25 March 1922; *s* of late G. E. Toulmin and of Mrs E. D. Toulmin; *m* 1st, 1945, Margaret Alison (marr. diss., 1960), *d* of late C. R. V. Coutts and Mrs H. G. Coutts; two *s* two *d*; 2nd, 1960, Gwyneth June, *d* of late R. M. Goodfield and of Mrs E. F. Goodfield. *Educ:* Oundle School; King's College, Cambridge. BA 1943; MA 1946; PhD 1948; MA (Oxon) 1948. Junior Scientific Officer, Ministry of Aircraft Production, 1942-45; Fellow of King's College, Cambridge, 1947-51; University Lecturer in the Philosophy of Science, Oxford, 1949-55; Acting Head of Department of History and Methods of Science, University of Melbourne, Australia, 1954-55; Professor of Philosophy, University of Leeds, 1955-59; Visiting Prof. of Philosophy, NY Univ. and Stanford Univ. (California) and Columbia Univ. (NY), 1959-60; Director, Nuffield Foundation Unit for History of Ideas, 1960-64; Prof. of Philosophy, Brandeis Univ., 1965-69; Counsellor, Smithsonian Institution, 1966-. *Publications:* The Place of Reason in Ethics, 1950; The Philosophy of Science: an Introduction, 1953; Metaphysical Beliefs (3 essays: author of one of them), 1957; The Uses of Argument, 1958; Foresight and Understanding, 1961; The Ancestry of Science, Vol. I (The Fabric of the Heavens) 1961, Vol. II (The Architecture of Matter), 1962, Vol. III (The Discovery of Time), 1965; Night Sky at Rhodes, 1963; also films, broadcast talks and contribs to learned jls and weeklies. *Recreations:* sailing, botanising, travel. *Address:* Department of Philosophy, Michigan State University, East Lansing, Mich 48823, USA; Tile Barn, Alfriston, Sussex. *Club:* Savile.

**TOURS, Kenneth Cecil,** CMG 1955; *b* 16 Feb. 1908; *y s* of late Berthold George Tours, CMG, HM Consul-General in China; *m* 1934, Ruth Grace, *y d* of late Hugh Lewis; two *s*. *Educ:* Aldenham School; Corpus Christi College, Cambridge (MA). Administrative Service, Gold Coast, 1931; Gambia, 1935; Palestine, 1938; Malaya, 1945; Col (Food Control) and (Supplies), Brit. Mil. Administration, Malaya, 1945-46; Chm., Jt Supply Board, 1946; Establishment Office, Singapore, 1947; Permanent Sec., Min. of Finance, Gold Coast, 1950; Financial Sec. and Minister of Finance, 1954; Economic Adviser, Ghana, 1954; retd from Colonial Service, 1957. *Recreation:* gardening. *Address:* Farriers, Tismans Common, Rudgwick, Sussex. *T:* Rudgwick 230.

**TOUT, Herbert,** CMG 1946; MA; Reader in Political Economy, University College, London, 1947-68, retired; *b* Manchester, 20 April 1904; *e s* of Professor T. F. Tout, Manchester University, and Mary Johnstone; unmarried. *Educ:* Sherborne School; Hertford College, Oxford. Instructor in Economics, University of Minnesota, USA, 1929-35; Assistant Lecturer, University College, London, 1936; Colston Research Fellow and Director of University of Bristol Social Survey, 1936-38; Lecturer, University of Bristol, 1938-47; Temp. Principal, Board of Trade, 1940-41; Assistant Secretary, 1941-45. *Recreations:* walking, farming, gardening. *Address:* Little Greeting, West Hoathly, East Grinstead, Sussex. *T:* Sharpthorne 400. *Club:* United University.

**TOVEY,** family name of **Baron Tovey.**

**TOVEY,** 1st Baron, *cr* 1946, of Langton Matravers; **Adm. of the Fleet John Cronyn Tovey,** GCB 1943 (KCB 1941; CB 1937); KBE 1941; DSO 1919; *b* 1885; *s* of late Lieutenant-Colonel Hamilton Tovey, RE; *m* 1916, Aida (*d* 1970), *d* of John Rowe. Served European War, 1914-19 (despatches, DSO); Capt. 1923; Naval Assistant to the Second Sea Lord, 1930-32; commanded HMS Rodney, 1932-34; ADC to the King, 1935; Commodore RN Barracks, Chatham, 1935-37; Rear-Adm. 1935; Rear-Admiral Destroyers, Mediterranean, 1938-40; Vice-Admiral, 1939; Vice-Admiral Second-in-Command Mediterranean Fleet, 1940; C-in-C Home Fleet, 1940-43; Admiral, 1942; Admiral of the Fleet, 1943; Commander-in-Chief, the Nore, 1943-46; First and Principal Naval ADC to the King, 1945-46. Third Church Estates

Commissioner, 1948-52. *Recreations:* golf, fishing. *Address:* House of Lords, SW1.

**TOWELL, Brig. Rowland Henry,** CBE 1940; MC; *b* 4 Feb. 1891; *o surv. s* of late H. J. Towell, Great Missenden; *m* 1940, Joan Margaret, *o d* of James S. Lacy, Burwash Place, Sussex; one *s* one *d. Educ:* Clifton Coll.; RMA, Woolwich. Served War of 1914-18, France and Flanders (MC and Bar, despatches twice, 1914 Star, wounded twice); commanded Chestnut Troop RHA, 1935-38; Brigadier, 1939; CRA, 3rd Division, France and Belgium, 1939-40 (CBE); CCRA 9 Corps, 1941-42; Commandant School of Artillery, 1942-45; retd pay, 1946. King Haakon VII Liberty Cross (Norway). *Club:* Army and Navy.

**TOWER, Maj.-Gen. Philip Thomas,** CB 1968; DSO 1944; MBE 1942; Commandant, Royal Military Academy, Sandhurst, since August 1968; *b* 1 March 1917; *s* of late Vice-Admiral Sir Thomas Tower, KBE, CB and late Mrs E. H. Tower; *m* 1943, Elizabeth, *y d* of late Thomas Ralph Sneyd-Kynnersley, OBE, MC and Alice Sneyd-Kynnersley. *Educ:* Harrow; Royal Military Acad., Woolwich. 2nd Lt Royal Artillery, 1937; served in India, 1937-40; served War of 1939-45 (despatches); Middle East, 1940-42; POW Italy, 1942-43; escaped, 1943; Arnhem, 1944; Norway, 1945; Staff Coll., 1948; Instructor at RMA Sandhurst, 1951-53; comd J (Sidi Rezegh) Bty RHA in Middle East, 1954-55; Joint Services Staff Coll., 1955-56; GSO1 Plans, BJSM Washington, DC, 1956-57; comd 3rd Regt RHA, 1957-60; Imperial Defence Coll., 1961; Comd 51 Inf. Bde Gp, 1961-62; Comd 12 Inf. Bde Gp, BAOR, 1962-64; Director of Public Relations (Army), 1965-67; GOC Middle East Land Forces, 1967 (despatches). Col Comdt, Royal Regt of Arty, 1970-. *Recreations:* sailing, shooting, under-gardening, ski-ing and polo. *Address:* Government House, RMA Sandhurst, Camberley, Surrey. *T:* Camberley 63045; Darts, Bembridge, Isle of Wight. *T:* Bembridge 2579. *Clubs:* Army and Navy; Royal Yacht Squadron.

**TOWERS, Graham Ford,** CC (Canada) 1969; CMG 1944; LLD; Chairman: Canadian Investment Fund Ltd; Canadian Fund Inc.; Director: Moore Corporation; Canada Life Assurance Co.; Governor, Bank of Canada, Ottawa, Ontario, 1934-54; *b* Montreal, Quebec, 1897; *s* of William Crawford and Caroline Towers (*née* Auldjo); *m* 1924, Mary Scott, *d* of C. H. Godfrey, Montreal. *Educ:* Montreal High Sch.; St Andrew's Coll.; McGill Univ. (BA). Joined Royal Bank of Canada, Montreal, 1920; Accountant, Havana Branch, 1922; Inspector, Foreign Dept, 1924; Chief Inspector, 1929; Asst Gen. Man., 1933; Chm., Foreign Exchange Control Bd, 1939-51; Chm., Nat. War Finance Cttee, 1943-45; President, Industrial Development Bank, 1944-54; Alternate Governor, International Monetary Fund, Washington, DC, 1946-54. Lieut, Canadian Army, 1915-19. Hon. LLD: McGill Univ., 1944, Queen's Univ., 1954; Hon. DCL Bishop's Univ., 1961. *Address:* 260 Park Road, Rockcliffe, Ontario, Canada. *Clubs:* Rideau, Country, Anglican (Ottawa).

**TOWN, Sir (Hugh) Stuart,** Kt, *cr* 1947; Director, 1925-47, of: Binny & Co. (Madras) Ltd, Madras; Buckingham & Carnatic Co. Ltd, Madras; Bangalore Woollen, Cotton & Silk Mills Ltd, Bangalore; *b* 19 April 1893; *s* of Christopher Edward and Mary Town; *m* 1920, Christine Mary, K-i-H (silver), OStJ, *d* of Richard Lewis and Mary Tucker, New Barnet; one *s. Educ:* privately. Served European War, 1914-18, with RAMC. Joined Binny & Co. (Madras), Ltd, 1920. Mem. Income Tax Bd of Referees; Trustee Madras Port Trust, 1937-47; MLA (Central), 1938; MLA Madras, 1939-47; Chm. S India Branch of European Assoc., 1939-40; Chm. Nat. Service Advisory Cttee, 1940 and 1945; Mem. Income Tax Appellate Tribunal, 1940; Chm. Employers' Federation of S India, 1940, and again, 1945; served on ARP and Governor's War Fund Cttee; Treasurer St John Ambulance, Madras, 1941-47; Chm. Madras Presidency Electric Licencees Assoc., 1944-45; Chm. Madras Chamber of Commerce, 1945 and 1946; Local Board Imperial Bank of India, 1945. Senate Madras Univ., 1945; Sheriff of Madras, 1946. OStJ. *Address:* Uplands, Innox Hill Gardens, Frome, Somerset.

**TOWNDROW, Ven. Frank Noel;** Archdeacon of Oakham since 1967; Residentiary Canon of Peterborough since 1966; *b* 25 Dec. 1911; *e s* of F. R. and H. A. Towndrow, London; *m* 1947, Olive Helen Weinberger; one *d* (one *s* decd). *Educ:* St Olave's Gram. Sch.; King's Coll., Cambridge; Coll. of Resurrection, Mirfield. Curate, Chingford E4 1937-40; Chaplain, RAFVR, 1940-47; Rector of Grangemouth, Stirlings, 1947-51; Vicar of Kirton Lindsey, Lincs, 1951-53; Rector of Greenford, Middx, 1953-62; Vicar of Ravensthorpe, E Haddon and Rector of Holdenby, 1962-66. *Recreations:* modern history, squash rackets. *Address:* 18 Minster Precincts, Peterborough. *T:* Peterborough 62762. *Club:* National Liberal.

**TOWNEND, Arnold Ernest,** JP Lancs; railway clerk (retired); *b* 10 April 1880; *m* Florrie, *d* of William Edward Parrish, Sale; one *s* one *d. Educ:* Woodhouses Church School, Ashton-under-Lyme. Contested Blackley Division, Manchester, 1918 and 1922; Stockport, 1923 and 1924; MP (Lab) Stockport, 1925-31. *Address:* 5 Milton Close, Milbourne St Andrew, Blandford Forum, Dorset.

**TOWNEND, Donald Thomas Alfred,** CBE 1952; DSc London, PhD, DIC; FRIC; MIMinE; Fellow, Imperial College of Science and Technology; *b* Hackney, London, 15 July 1897; *s* of Charles Henry Townend; *m* 1924, Lilian, *er d* of Samuel William Lewis, Bexley, Kent; one *s* one *d. Educ:* Bancroft's School, Woodford Green, Essex. East London (now Queen Mary) College, 1919-20; Imperial College of Science and Technology, 1920-38; Salters' Research Fellow, 1923-24; Rockefeller International Research Fellow, 1924-26; Livesey Prof. of Coal Gas and Fuel Industries, University of Leeds, 1938-46; Dir-Gen., British Coal Utilisation Research Assoc., 1946-62; formerly Research Fell. and Hon. Lectr in Roy. Coll. of Science. Jubilee Memorial Lectr, 1945, Brotherton Memorial Lecturer, 1946 and Hodsman Memorial Lectr, 1954, Soc. of Chemical Industry; Dalton Lecturer, Inst. of Chemistry, 1947; William Young Memorial Lectr, N Brit. Assoc. of Gas Managers, 1947; Des Vœux Memorial Lectr, Nat. Soc. for Clean Air, 1950; Melchett Lectr, Inst. of Fuel, 1952. Vice-Pres. 1957-61, Vice-Chm. 1961-64, Parly and Sci. Cttee. Gold Medallist, Institut Français des Combustibles et de l'Energie, 1958; BCURA Coal Science Medallist, 1963; Hon. FIGasE (Birmingham Medallist, IGasE); Hon. MInstF (Past Pres. and Melchett Medallist, InstF). Hon. DSc Tech Sheffield. *Publications:* (with late Professor W. A. Bone) Flame and Combustion in Gases, 1927; Gaseous Combustion at High Pressures, 1929; Papers in Proceedings of Royal Society, etc. *Recreations:* cricket, horticulture. *Address:* Uplands, Yarm Way, Leatherhead, Surrey. *T:* Leatherhead 3520. *Club:* Athenæum.

**TOWNEND, Sir Harry (Douglas),** Kt 1947; Director, 1948-70 (Chairman, 1955-61), R. G.

Shaw & Co. Ltd, 19 Leadenhall Street, London, EC3; *b* 29 Dec. 1891; *s* of late Rev. A. J. Townend, CF, and Margaret Wiseman Townend, *d* of Hon. William John Stairs, Halifax, Nova Scotia; *m* 1925, Mary Winifred Edwards, *d* of late Rev. E. Stanley Edwards and of Kathleen Mary Edwards; one *d* (one *s* decd). *Educ:* King's Sch., Canterbury; Queens' College, Cambridge (MA). Joined Shaw Wallace & Co., Eastern Merchants, 1913, Senior Partner India, 1942-47; Member Local Board, Reserve Bank of India, 1943-46; Pres. Bengal Chamber of Commerce and Associated Chambers of Commerce of India, 1946-47; Member Council of State, India, 1946-47. *Address:* Parkgrove, Lye Green, Crowborough, Sussex. *T:* Crowborough 2088. *Clubs:* Oriental, City of London, Royal Commonwealth Society; Bengal (Calcutta).

**TOWNER, Major Edgar Thomas,** VC 1918; MC; on Army retired list; grazier; *b* Glencoe, near Blackall, Central Queensland, 19 April 1890; *s* of E. T. and Greta Towner; unmarried. *Educ:* Blackall State Sch.; private tuition. Engaged in pastoral pursuits from an early age; enlisted for service in European War, 2 Jan. 1915, at Blackall, Central Queensland; served in Egypt and France (wounded, VC and MC, despatches twice); served War of 1939-45 until Jan. 1942, in Australia. Life Member Returned Soldiers', Sailors' and Airmen's Imperial League of Australia; Fellow, Royal Geog. Society of Australia (Queensland); Thompson Gold Foundation Medal, RGS, Australia. Member Royal Historical Society of Queensland. *Publication:* Lake Eyre and its Tributaries. *Recreations:* riding, shooting, tennis, literature. *Address:* Kaloola, Longreach, Central Queensland, Australia. *T:* 62K Isisford. *Clubs:* Longreach; Blackall; United Service (life Hon. Member) (Brisbane); Imperial Service (Sydney); Town and Country Cricket (Vice-President) (Longreach).

**TOWNES, Charles Hard;** Professor-at-Large, University of California, USA; *b* Greenville, South Carolina, 28 July 1915; *s* of Henry Keith Townes and Ellen Sumter (*née* Hard); *m* 1941, Frances H. Brown; four *d*. *Educ:* Furman Univ. (BA, BS); Duke Univ. (MA); California Institute of Technology (PhD). Assistant in Physics, California Inst. of Technology, 1937-39; Member Techn Staff, Bell Telephone Labs, 1939-47; Associate Prof. of Physics, Columbia Univ., 1948-50; Prof. of Physics, Columbia Univ., 1950-61; Exec. Director, Columbia Radiation Lab., 1950-52; Chairman, Dept of Physics, Columbia Univ., 1952-55; Vice-President and Director of Research, Inst. for Defense Analyses, 1959-61; Provost and Professor of Physics, MIT, 1961-66; Institute Professor, MIT, 1966-67. Guggenheim Fellow, 1955-56; Fulbright Lecturer, University of Paris, 1955-56, University of Tokyo, 1956; Lecturer, 1955, 1960, Dir, 1963, Enrico Fermi Internat. Sch. of Physics; Scott Lecturer, University of Cambridge, 1963. Centennial Lecturer, University of Toronto, 1967. Director: Perkin-Elmer Corp.; Bulletin of Atomic Scientists, 1964-69. Board of Editors: Review of Scientific Instruments, 1950-52; Physical Review, 1951-53; Journal of Molecular Spectroscopy, 1957-60; Columbia University Forum, 1957-59. Fellow: American Phys. Society (Richtmyer Lecturer, 1959; Member Council, 1959-62, 1965-; President, 1967); Optical Society of America; Inst. of Electrical and Electronics Engrs; Chairman, Sci. and Technology Adv. Commn for Manned Space Flight, NASA, 1964-; Member: President's Science Adv. Cttee, 1966-69 (Chm., 1967-69); Scientific Adv. Bd, US Air Force, 1958-61; Soc. Française de Physique (Member Council, 1956-58); Nat. Acad. Scis (Mem. Council, 1969-); Phys. Society of Japan; American Acad. Arts and Sciences; American Philos. Society; American Astron. Society; American Assoc. of Physics Teachers. Trustee: Salk Inst. for Biological Studies, 1963-68; Rand Corp., 1965-70; Carnegie Instn of Washington. Holds numerous honorary degrees. Nobel Prize for Physics (jointly), 1964. Research Corp. Annual Award, 1958; Comstock Prize, Nat. Acad. of Sciences, 1959; Stuart Ballantine Medal, Franklin Inst., 1959, 1962; Rumford Premium, Amer. Acad. of Arts and Sciences, 1961; Thomas Young Medal and Prize, Inst. of Physics and Physical Soc., England, 1963; Medal of Honor, Inst. of Electrical and Electronics Engineers, 1967; C. E. K. Mees Medal, Optical Soc. of America, 1968; Churchman of the Year Award, Southern Baptist Theological Seminary, 1967; Golden Plate Award, Amer. Acad. of Achievement, 1969; Distinguished Public Service Medal, NASA, 1969. *Publications:* (with A. L. Schawlow) Microwave Spectroscopy, 1955; (ed) Quantum Electronics, 1960; (ed with P. A. Miles) Quantum Electronics and Coherent Light, 1964; many scientific articles on microwave spectroscopy, molecular and nuclear structure, astrophysics and quantum electronics; fundamental patents on masers and lasers. *Address:* Department of Physics, University of California, Berkeley, California 94720, USA. *T:* 642-1128. *Club:* Cosmos (Washington, DC).

**TOWNESEND, Air Cdre Ernest John Dennis,** CBE 1947; BA, CEng; FRAeS; RAF (retired); *b* 21 March 1896; *e s* of late Charles John Henry Fyler Townesend, late a civil engineer in India; *m* 1929, Ethel Aiken; one *s* one *d*. *Educ:* Dulwich Coll.; University Sch., Victoria, British Columbia; RMC, Kingston, Canada; Jesus Coll., Cambridge; Imperial College of Science and Technology, London. Served European War, 1914-18, in RFA, RFC, and RAF as observer (No. 21 Sqdn) and pilot (No. 60 Sqdn); at Air Ministry, 1918-20; RAF Engineer Specialist Course, 1920-23; Assistant to Chief Technical Officer, A&AEE, Martlesham Heath, 1923-25; Iraq Aircraft Depot and AHQ, Baghdad, 1925-27; Station Engineer Officer, Upper Heyford, 1928-32; HQ Wessex Bombing Area, 1932, DDRM, Air Ministry, 1932-35; HQ Western Area, 1935; served in Iraq Aircraft Depot, 1935-37; OC No 3 School of Tech. Training, Manston, 1937-39; HQ No 41 Group, 1939-41; transferred to Tech. Branch, 1940; OC No 30 Maintenance Unit and RAF Station, Sealand, 1942-43; Air Commodore, 1944; OC 13 Maintenance Unit and RAF Station, Henlow, 1943-46; retired as Air Commodore, 1946; Engineer I, Directorate of Engine Production, Ministry of Supply, 1946-56. R. M. Groves Aeronautical Research Prize, 1926; Order of Polonia Restituta. *Address:* 30 Watcombe Road, Southbourne, Bournemouth, Hants BH6 3LU.

**TOWNLEY, Rt. Rev. George Frederick,** MA; an Assistant Bishop of Peterborough, since 1970; *b* 15 April 1891; *s* of Frederick William and Emily Louisa Townley; *m* 1915, Charlotte Catherine Whiting; no *c*. *Educ:* Lincoln Coll., Oxford (MA); Ripon Hall, Oxford. Served European War, 1914-18, Gallipoli and Egypt, in Northamptonshire and Bedfordshire Regts. Curate of Keighley, 1922-25; Curate in Charge of Harden, Bingley, 1925-27; Vicar of Lidget Green, Bradford, 1927-32. Vicar of St Barnabas, Linthorpe, Middlesbrough, 1932-44; Canon and Preb. of York, 1939-57; Vicar and Rural Dean of Scarborough, 1944-47; Archdeacon of Cleveland, 1947; Archdeacon of York and Secretary to the York Diocesan

Board of Finance, 1947-57; Suffragan Bishop of Hull, 1957-65. *Publication:* The Great Ambition, Mystery Play, 1933. *Recreation:* golf. *Address:* Orchard Gate, 16 Park Street, Earls Barton, Northampton. *T:* Earls Barton 182.

**TOWNLEY, Sir John (Barton),** Kt 1960; *b* 14 June 1914; *s* of Barton Townley and Margaret Alice, *d* of Richard Gorst; *m* 1939, Gwendoline May Ann, *d* of Arthur Simmonds; one *s* three *d. Educ:* Rydal Sch.; Downing Coll., Cambridge. BA 1936, MA 1939, Cambridge. President: Preston Conservative Assoc., N. and S. Divisions, 1954- (Chairman, Preston S. Conserv. Assoc., 1949-54); Preston Sea Cadet Corps, 1954-; Preston Circle King George's Fund for Sailors, 1949-; Preston Charities Assoc., 1949-; Preston, Chorley, Leyland Conservative Clubs Council, 1949-; Vice-Chairman, Northern Commercial Vehicle Group; Chairman and Governing Director of Alfresco Garage Group of Bradford and Keighley; Chairman: Preston YMCA Special Appeals Cttee; Preston N. Conservative Assoc., 1958-. *Recreations:* a little golf and shooting and talking about Rugger and cricket. *Clubs:* Winckley (Preston); District (Blackpool).

**TOWNLEY, Reginald Colin,** CMG 1968; retired; *b* 5 April 1904; *s* of Reginald George and Susan Townley; *m* 1930, Irene Winifred Jones; three *s* one *d. Educ:* Hobart High Sch.; University of Tasmania. Chemist, 1927-64; Army, 1939-45, Middle East and Pacific. Tasmanian Parliament, 1946-64 (Leader of Opposition, 1950-56). *Recreation:* gardening. *Address:* 1 Carlton Street, New Town, Tasmania 7008, Australia. *T:* 81291. *Club:* Naval and Military (Hobart).

**TOWNSEND, Albert Alan,** FRS 1960; PhD; Reader (Experimental Fluid Mechanics), Cavendish Laboratory, University of Cambridge, since 1961 (Assistant Director of Research, 1950-61); Fellow of Emmanuel College, Cambridge, since 1947; *b* 22 Jan. 1917; *s* of A. R. Townsend and D. Gay; *m* 1950, V. Dees; one *s* two *d. Educ:* Telopea Park IHS; Melbourne and Cambridge Universities. PhD 1947. *Publications:* The Structure of Turbulent Shear Flow, 1956; papers in technical journals. *Address:* Emmanuel College, Cambridge.

**TOWNSEND, Brigadier Edward Philip,** CBE 1957 (OBE 1951); DSO 1950; retired; *b* 24 July 1909; 2nd *s* of late Lt-Col E. C. Townsend, Indian Army; *m* 1952, Imogen Martin; two *d. Educ:* Haileybury; RMC, Sandhurst. Commissioned, 1929; joined 5th Royal Gurkha Rifles, 1930; Commanded: 2nd Bn 5th RGR, 1944-47; 1st Bn 6th Gurkha Rifles, 1948-51; 48th Gurkha Infantry Brigade, Aug. 1953-Feb. 1955; 99th Gurkha Infantry Brigade, Oct. 1955-Nov. 1957; British Gurkha L. of C. Nepal, July 1958-April 1961; retired, 1961. *Address:* Uplands Cottage, Wellington Heath, Ledbury, Herefordshire.

**TOWNSEND, Mrs Lena Moncrieff;** Leader of the Opposition, Inner London Education Authority, since 1970 (Leader, 1969-70); Alderman, GLC, since 1970; Member, Race Relations Board, since 1969; *b* 3 Nov. 1911; twin *d* of late Captain R. G. Westropp, Cairo, Egypt; *m* (twice); two *s* one *d. Educ:* Downe House, Newbury; Somerville Coll., Oxford; Heidelberg Univ., Germany. During War of 1939-45 was an Organiser in WVS and in Women's Land Army, and then taught at Downe House. Mem. for Hampstead, LCC, 1955-65; Alderman, London Borough of Camden, 1964-65; Mem. for Camden, GLC, 1967-70. Chairman: London Coll. of Fashion and Clothing Technology; Haverstock Secondary Sch.; Member: Nat. Women's Advisory Cttee of Conservative Party; executive of various Anglo-European assocs; Pres., Anglo-Egyptian Assoc. *Recreations:* foreign languages, travel, the arts, swimming, gardening, sewing. *Address:* 16 Holly Mount, NW3. *T:* 01-435 8555.

**TOWNSEND, Rear-Adm. Michael Southcote,** CB 1959; DSO 1942; OBE 1940; DSC 1940 (Bar, 1941); *b* 18 June 1908; *s* of Colonel Edward Coplestone Townsend and Gladys Hatt-Cook; *m* 1932, Joan Pendrill Charles; one *s* two *d. Educ:* Royal Naval Coll., Dartmouth. Rear-Admiral, 1956; Flag Officer, Admiralty Interview Boards and President, First Admiralty Interview Board, 1956-58; Commander Allied Naval Forces, Northern Area, Central Europe, 1958-61, retired; Admiralty Officer, Wales, 1962-68. *Address:* Tor-y-Mynydd Farm, Devauden, Chepstow, Mon. *T:* Trellech 417.

**TOWNSEND, Prof. Peter Brereton;** Professor of Sociology, University of Essex, since 1963; *b* 6 April 1928; *s* of Philip Brereton Townsend and Alice Mary Townsend (*née* Southcote); *m* 1949, Ruth (*née* Pearce); four *s. Educ:* Fleet Road Elementary Sch., London; University Coll. Sch., London; St John's Coll., Cambridge Univ.; Free Univ., Berlin. Research Sec., Political and Economic Planning, 1952-54; Research Officer, Inst. of Community Studies, 1954-57; Research Fellow and then Lectr in Social Administration, London Sch. of Economics, 1957-63; Chm., the Fabian Society, 1965-66 (Chm., Home Research Cttee, 1967-); Pres., Psychiatric Rehabilitation Assoc., 1968-; Chm., Child Poverty Action Gp, 1969-. *Publications:* The Family Life of Old People, 1957; National Superannuation (co-author), 1957; Nursing Homes in England and Wales (co-author), 1961; The Last Refuge: a survey of residential institutions and homes for the aged in England and Wales, 1962; The Aged in the Welfare State (co-author), 1965; The Poor and the Poorest (co-author), 1965; Old People in Three Industrial Societies (co-author), 1968; The Concept of Poverty, 1970. *Recreation:* athletics. *Address:* 2 Mansfield Place, NW3. *T:* 01-794 3072.

**TOWNSEND, Group Captain Peter Wooldridge,** CVO 1947; DSO 1941; DFC and Bar, 1940; *b* 22 Nov. 1914; *s* of late Lt-Col E. C. Townsend; *m* 1959, Marie Luce, *d* of Franz Jamagne, Brasschaat, near Antwerp, Belgium; one *s* two *d* (two *s* by former marriage). *Educ:* Haileybury; Royal Air Force Coll., Cranwell. Royal Air Force, 1933; served War of 1939-45, Wing Commander, 1941 (despatches, DFC and Bar, DSO). Equerry to King George VI, 1944-52; Deputy Master of HM Household, 1950; Equerry to the Queen, 1952-53; Air Attaché, Brussels, 1953-56. *Publications:* Earth, My Friend, 1959; Duel of Eagles, 1970. *Address:* La Bulliere, Levis Saint Nom, Yvelines, France.

**TOWNSHEND,** family name of **Marquess Townshend.**

**TOWNSHEND,** 7th Marquess *cr* 1787; **George John Patrick Dominic Townshend;** Bt 1617; Baron Townshend, 1661; Viscount Townshend, 1682; Chairman: Anglia Television Ltd; Anchor Enterprises Ltd; Director: Norwich Union Life Insurance Society Ltd; Norwich Union Fire Insurance Society Ltd; Scottish Union & National Insurance Co.; Maritime Insurance Co. Ltd; East Coast Grain Silos Ltd; Raynham Farm Co. Ltd; London Merchant Securities; D. E.

Longe & Co. Ltd; Invergordon Distillers (Holdings) Ltd; J. Berkmann and Co. Ltd; Napak Ltd; Companhia Agricola Portuguesa Lda; Anglia Radio Ltd; Anglia Broadcasting Ltd; Trustee, East Anglian Trustee Savings Bank; *b* 13 May 1916; *s* of 6th Marquess and Gladys Ethel Gwendolen Eugenie (*d* 1959), *e d* of late Thomas Sutherst, barrister; *S* father, 1921; *m* 1st, 1939, Elizabeth (marr. diss. 1960; she *m* 1960, Brig. Sir James Gault, *qv*) *o d* of Thomas Luby, Indian CS; one *s* two *d*; 2nd, 1960, Ann Frances, *d* of Arthur Pellew Darlow; one *s* one *d*. Norfolk Yeomanry TA, 1936-40; Scots Guards, 1940-45. Owns about 7,000 acres. DL Norfolk, 1951-61. *Heir: s* Viscount Raynham, *qv*. *Address:* Raynham Hall, Fakenham, Norfolk. *T:* Fakenham 2133. *Clubs:* White's, Pratt's, MCC; Norfolk (Norwich).

**TOWNSHEND, Hugh,** CB 1947; Assistant Secretary-General (retired), International Telecommunication Union, 1950-57; *b* 17 Nov. 1890; *s* of late Colonel G. R. Townshend, RA; *m* 1920, Winifred Dora Mary Higham; one *s* two *d*. *Educ:* King's Sch., Canterbury; Trinity Coll., Cambridge. Civil Servant (General Post Office), 1914-49. Served European War, 1914-18: Royal Engineers, 1916-18. *Publication:* (with Myra Curtis) Modern Money, 1937. *Address:* Puckaster Corner, Niton Undercliff, Ventnor, Isle of Wight.

**TOWNSVILLE, Bishop of, (RC),** since 1967; **Most Rev. Leonard Anthony Faulkner;** *b* Booleroo Centre, South Australia, 5 Dec. 1926. Ordained Propaganda Fide Coll., Rome, 1 Jan. 1950. *Address:* Bishop's House, Stanley Street, Townsville, Queensland 4810, Australia.

**TOWRY, Peter;** *see* Piper, D. T.

**TOY, Francis Carter,** CBE 1947; DSc, FInstP; *b* 5 May 1892; 2nd *s* of late Sir Henry Toy, CA, JP, Helston, Cornwall; *m* 1921, Gladys Marguerite, *d* of late James Thomas, CA, JP, Tregays, Lostwithiel, Cornwall; one *d*. *Educ:* Launceston Coll., Cornwall; University College, London. Fellow of University College, London. Served European War, 1914-18; Lieut, Cornwall Fortress Engineers, 1914-16; Lieut, First Army Field Survey Co. (Sound Ranging, Y section), BEF France, 1917-18. Physicist, British Photographic Research Association, 1919-29; Deputy Director of the Shirley Institute, Research Station of British Cotton Industry Research Association, 1930-43, Director, 1944-55. President: Manchester Fedn of Scientific Societies, 1953-55; Inst of Physics, 1948-50; Manchester Statistical Society, 1951-53; Manchester Literary and Philosophical Society, 1956-58; Past Chairman Cttee of Directors of Research Associations; Fellow of the Textile Institute; Member Court and Council, UMIST. *Publications:* numerous scientific. *Recreations:* travel, music and sport (cricket and golf). *Address:* 8 Fulshaw Court, Wilmslow, Cheshire. *T:* Wilmslow 25141. *Club:* Athenæum.

**TOYE, Wendy;** theatrical producer; film director; choreographer, actress, dancer. First professional appearance as Mustard-seed in A Midsummer Night's Dream, Old Vic, 1929; principal dancer in Hiawatha, Royal Albert Hall, 1931; Marigold, Phœbe in Toad of Toad Hall and produced dances, Royalty, Christmas, 1931-32; danced in C. B. Cochran's The Miracle, Lyceum, 1932; masked dancer in Ballerina, Gaiety, 1933; principal dancer for Ninette de Valois in The Golden Toy, Coliseum, 1934; toured with Anton Dolin's ballet (choreog. for divertissements and short ballets), 1934-35; in Tulip Time, Alhambra, then Markova-Dolin Ballet as principal dancer and choreog., 1935; in Love and How to Cure It, Globe, 1937. Arranged dances and ballets for all George Black's productions for next 7 years including Black Velvet in which also principal dancer, 1939. Shakespearean season, Open Air Theatre, 1939. *Theatre productions:* Big Ben, Bless the Bride, Tough at the Top (for C. B. Cochran), Adelphi; The Shepherd Show, Prince's; Co-Director and Choreographer, Peter Pan, New York; And So To Bed, New Theatre; Co-Director and Choreographer, Feu d'Artifice, Paris; Night of Masquerade, Q; Second Threshold, Vaudeville; Choreography for Three's Company in Joyce Grenfell Requests the Pleasure, Fortune; Wild Thyme, Duke of York's; Lady at the Wheel, Lyric, Hammersmith; Majority of One, Phœnix; Magic Lantern, Saville; As You Like It, Old Vic; Virtue in Danger, Mermaid and Strand; Robert and Elizabeth, Lyric; On the Level, Saville; Soldier's Tale, Edinburgh Festival, 1967; Boots and Strawberry Jam, Nottingham Playhouse, 1968; The Great Waltz, Drury Lane, 1970. *Opera Productions:* Bluebeard's Castle (Bartok), Sadler's Wells and Brussels; The Telephone (Menotti), Sadler's Wells; Russalka (Dvořák), Sadler's Wells; Fledermaus, Coliseum and Sadler's Wells; Orpheus in the Underworld, Sadler's Wells and Australia; La Vie Parisienne, Sadler's Wells; Seraglio, Bath Festival, 1967; The Impresario, Don Pasquale (for Phoenix Opera Group), 1968; The Italian Girl in Algiers, Coliseum, 1968. *Films directed:* The Stranger Left No Card; The Teckman Mystery; Raising a Riot; The Twelfth Day of Christmas; Three Cases of Murder; All for Mary; True as a Turtle; We Joined the Navy; The King's Breakfast; Cliff in Scotland; A Goodly Manor for a Song; Girls Wanted–Istanbul. Productions for TV, etc. Appeared with and was choreographer for Camargo Society; guest artist with Sadler's Wells Ballet and Mme Rambert's Ballet Club; went to Denmark as principal dancer with British Ballet, organised by Adeline Geneé, 1932. Tour of Latin America, 1964. Trained with Euphen MacLaren, Karsavina, Dolin, Morosoff, Legat, Rambert. *Address:* c/o London Management, 235 Regent Street, W1.

**TOYNBEE, Arnold Joseph,** CH 1956; Hon. DLitt (Oxon, Birmingham and Columbia), LittD (Cambridge), DCL (Princeton); FBA, 1937; Director of Studies in the Royal Institute of International Affairs, 1925, and Research Professor of International History in the University of London, both on the Sir Daniel Stevenson Foundation; retired, 1955; Professor Emeritus, 1955; Associate Member, Academy Moral and Political Sciences, Institut de France, 1968; *b* 14 April 1889; *m* 1913, Rosalind (marr. diss. 1946), *d* of late Professor Gilbert Murray, OM; two *s*; *m* 1946, Veronica Marjorie, *d* of Rev. Sidney Boulter. *Educ:* Winchester (Scholar); Balliol Coll., Oxford (Scholar). Fellow and Tutor, Balliol Coll., Oxford, 1912-15; various Government work in connection with the War, 1915-19; Political Intelligence Dept, Foreign Office, April 1918; Member of Middle Eastern Section, British Delegation, Peace Conference, Paris, 1919; Koraes Professor of Byzantine and Modern Greek Language, Literature, and History at London Univ., 1919-24; War Work: Director, Foreign Research and Press Service, Royal Institute of International Affairs, 1939-43; Director, Research Department, Foreign Office, 1943-46; member of British Delegation, Peace Conference, Paris, 1946. Hon. Fellow Balliol Coll., Oxford, 1957. *Publications:* Nationality and the War, 1915; The New Europe, 1915;

The Western Question in Greece and Turkey, 1922; Greek Historical Thought, 1924; Greek Civilisation and Character, 1924; The World after the Peace Conference, 1925; A Survey of International Affairs for 1920-23, 1924, 1925 (vol. i: The Islamic World since the Peace Settlement), etc, to 1938, vol. i; Joint Editor with V. M. Toynbee, of vols covering 1939-46; (with K. P. Kirkwood) Turkey, in the Nations of the Modern World Series, 1926; A Journey to China, 1931; Editor, British Commonwealth Relations, 1934; A Study of History, Vols i-iii, 1934, Vols iv-vi, 1939 (Abridgement of Vols i-vi, 1946); Vols vii-x, 1954; Vol. xi, 1958; Vol. xii, 1961; Civilisation on Trial, 1948; War and Civilisation, 1951; The World and the West (1952 Reith Lectures), 1953; An Historian's Approach to Religion (Edinburgh Gifford Lectures, 1953 and 1954); Christianity Among the Religions of the World, 1958; East to West: a Journey Round the World, 1958; Hellenism, 1959; Between Oxus and Jumna, 1961; (with T. P. Toynbee) Comparing Notes: a Dialogue across a Generation, 1963; Between Niger and Nile, 1965; Hannibal's Legacy, 1965; Change and Habit, 1966; Acquaintances, 1967; Between Maule and Amazon, 1967; (co-author) Man's Concern with Death, 1968; (ed) The Crucible of Christianity, 1968; Cities of Destiny, 1969; Experiences, 1969; Some Problems of Greek History, 1969; Cities on the Move, 1970. *Address:* 95 Oakwood Court, W14. *T:* 01-602 2238; Hall Beck, Killington, Kirkby Lonsdale, Westmorland. *T:* Sedbergh 436. *Club:* Athenæum.

*See also T. P. Toynbee.*

**TOYNBEE, Prof. Jocelyn Mary Catherine,** MA, DPhil; FSA; FBA; Laurence Professor Emerita of Classical Archæology, Cambridge University (Professor, 1951-62); Hon. Fellow of Newnham College; *b* 3 March 1897; *d* of late Harry Valpy Toynbee and late Sarah Edith (*née* Marshall). *Educ:* Winchester High School for Girls; Newnham Coll., Cambridge. Classical Tutor, St Hugh's Coll., Oxford, 1921-24; Lecturer in Classics, Reading University, 1924-27; Fellow and Director of Studies in Classics, Newnham Coll., Cambridge, and Lecturer in the Faculty of Classics, Cambridge Univ., 1927-51. Hon. Dlitt: University of Newcastle upon Tyne; University of Liverpool. *Publications:* The Hadrianic School: a Chapter in the History of Greek Art, 1934; Roman Medallions (American Numismatic Society, New York), 1944; Some Notes on Artists in the Roman World, (Brussels) 1951; The Shrine of St Peter and the Vatican Excavation (with John Ward Perkins), 1956; The Flavian Reliefs from the Palazzo della Cancelleria in Rome, 1957; Art in Roman Britain, 1962; Art in Britain under the Romans, 1964; The Art of the Romans, 1965. Contributions to Journal of Roman Studies, Papers of British School, Rome, Numismatic Chronicle, Classical Review, Classical Quarterly, Antiquaries Journal, Archæologia, Antiquity, Gnomon, etc. *Recreation:* travelling. *Address:* 22 Park Town, Oxford. *T:* 57886.

**TOYNBEE, (Theodore) Philip;** Novelist; foreign correspondent of The Observer and member of editorial staff since 1950; *b* 25 June 1916; *s* of Arnold Joseph Toynbee, *qv*; *m* 1st, 1939, Anne Barbara Denise Powell (marr. diss. 1950); two *d*; 2nd, 1950, Frances Genevieve Smith; one *s* two *d*. *Educ:* Rugby Sch.; Christ Church, Oxford. Editor of the Birmingham Town Crier, 1938-39; commission in Intelligence Corps, 1940-42; Ministry of Economic Warfare, 1942-44; on staff of SHAEF in France and Belgium, 1944-45; Literary Editor of Contact Publications, 1945-46. *Publications:* The Savage Days, 1937; School in Private, 1941; The Barricades, 1943; Tea with Mrs Goodman, 1947; The Garden to the Sea, 1953; Friends Apart, 1954; Pantaloon, 1961; (with Arnold Toynbee) Comparing Notes: a Dialogue across a Generation, 1963; (with Maurice Richardson) Thanatos: a Modern Symposium, 1963; Two Brothers, 1964; A Learned City, 1966; Views from a Lake, 1968. Contrib.: New Statesman and Nation, Horizon, New Writing, Les Temps Modernes. *Recreations:* gardening, fishing and sailing. *Address:* The Barn House, Brockweir, near Chepstow, Monmouthshire. *T:* Tintern 365. *Club:* Oxford Union Society.

**TOZER, Col William,** CBE 1938; TD; Stockbroker; *b* 11 Feb. 1894; *er s* of Major William Tozer, VD, Tapton Edge, Sheffield; *m* 1919, Eileen Nanciebel (*d* 1958), *er d* of Lt-Col Herbert Higginson Sykes, VD, Briar Court, Lindley, Huddersfield; one *s* one *d*. *Educ:* Malvern Coll.; Clare Coll., Cambridge. Now a Governor of Malvern Coll. Served The Hallamshire Battalion, The York and Lancaster Regt, 1914-38; European War, 1914-19, France and Belgium (despatches, 1914-15 Star); Lt-Col Commanding, 1931-38; Brevet Colonel, 1935; Colonel, 1939; War of 1939-45; AA and QMG; a Member of West Riding of Yorks TA Assoc., 1931-39; Master of Cutlers Company of Sheffield, 1936. Councillor of East Grinstead UDC, 1955-58. *Address:* Wye House, Courtlands Estate, Sharpthorne, Sussex; c/o Gerald Hodgson, Andreae & Co., 2 Copthall Buildings, EC2. *T:* 01-628 9991.

*See also B. A. Johnston.*

**TRACY;** *see* Hanbury-Tracy, family name of **Baron Sudeley.**

**TRACY, Rear-Adm. Hugh Gordon Henry,** CB 1965; DSC 1945; CEng; Engineering Consultant (Research and Development); Chairman, Mechanical Engineering Industry Standards Committee, BSI; *b* 15 Nov. 1912; *e s* of Comdr A. F. G. Tracy, RN; *m* 1938, Muriel, *d* of Maj.-Gen. Sir R. B. Ainsworth, CB, DSO, OBE; two *s* one *d*. *Educ:* Nautical Coll., Pangbourne. Joined RN, 1929; Lieut, 1934; served in HMS Shropshire, Hawkins and Furious, in Admiralty and attended Advanced Engineering course before promotion to Lt-Comdr, 1942; Sen. Engineer, HMS Illustrious, 1942-44; Asst to Manager, Engineering Dept, HM Dockyard Chatham, 1944-46; Comdr 1946; served in HMS Manxman, Admiralty, RN Engineering Coll. and HM Dockyard Malta; Captain, 1955; Asst Director of Marine Engineering, Admiralty, 1956-58; CO HMS Sultan, 1959-60; Imperial Defence Coll., 1961; CSO (Tech.) to Flag Officer, Sea Training, 1962-63; Rear-Admiral, 1963; Director of Marine Engineering, Ministry of Defence (Navy), 1963-66; retired, 1966. MIMechE, MIMarE, MBIM. *Recreations:* gardening, painting, fishing. *Address:* Orchard House, Claverton, near Bath, Somerset. *T:* Bath 22589. *Club:* United Service.

**TRAFFORD;** *see* de Trafford.

**TRAFFORD, Dr Anthony;** *see* Trafford, Dr J. A. P.

**TRAFFORD, Dr (Joseph) Anthony (Porteous);** MP (C) The Wrekin since 1970; Consultant Physician, Brighton and Lewes Group of Hospitals, since 1965; *b* 20 July 1932; *s* of Dr Harold Trafford, Warlingham, Surrey, and late Laura Trafford; *m* 1960, Helen Chalk; one *s* one *d*. *Educ:* St Edmund's, Hindhead; Charterhouse; Guy's Hosp., Univ. of London. MB, BS Hons 1957; MRCP 1961. Various medical appts, 1957-63; Fulbright Scholar, Johns Hopkins Univ., 1963; Dir, Artificial Kidney Unit, Brighton, 1967. *Publications:* contribs to BMJ and Lancet. *Recreations:* golf, tennis, squash. *Address:* Tarnova, 14b The Upper Drive, Hove, Sussex. *T:* Brighton 731567.

**TRAFFORD, Rt. Rev. Ralph Sigebert,** OSB; Manager Downside Settlement; 4th *s* of late E. S. and late Hon. Mrs E. S. Trafford of Wroxham Hall, Norfolk. *Educ:* Downside. Priest, 1912; Headmaster of Downside, 1918-34; Prior of Worth, 1934-38; Abbot of Downside, 1938-46; Abbot-Pres. of English Benedictine Congregation, 1939-41; Abbot of St Alban's, 1953. *Address:* Mount Benet, Gorey, Co. Wexford, Ireland. *T:* Holyfort 4.

**TRAHERNE, Sir Cennydd (George),** KG 1970; Kt 1964; TD 1950; MA; HM Lieutenant for the County of Glamorgan since 1952; *b* 14 Dec. 1910; *er s* of late Comdr L. E. Traherne, RN, of Coedarhydyglyn, near Cardiff, and Dorothy, *d* of G. F. S. Sinclair; *m* 1934, Olivera Rowena, JP, DStJ, *d* of late James Binney, and late Lady Marjory Binney, Pampisford Hall, Cambridgeshire. *Educ:* Wellington; Brasenose Coll., Oxford. Barrister, Inner Temple, 1938. 81st Field Regt RA (TA), 1934-43; 102 Provost Coy, Corps of Military Police, 1943-45 (despatches); Dep. Asst Provost Marshal, Second British Army, 1945; 53rd Div. Provost Company, Royal Military Police, 1947-49, TA; Hon. Colonel, 53 Div. Signal Regt, 1953-58; Hon. Colonel 282 (Glamorgan Yeomanry) Field Regt RA (TA), 1958-61; Hon. Colonel, 282 (Glam. and Mon.) Regt RA (TA), 1962-67. DL 1946. JP 1946, Glamorgan. Deputy Chairman Glamorgan Quarter Sessions, 1949-52; President, Welsh College of Advanced Technology, 1957-65. Chairman, Rep. Body of the Church in Wales, 1965. Director: Cardiff Building Society, 1953; Wales Gas Board, 1958; Chairman: Wales Gas Consultative Council, 1958; Advisory Local Dir, Barclays Bank Ltd; Local Adviser, S Wales area, National Provident Institution for Mutual Life Assurance. Member, Gorsedd of the Bards of Wales. Hon. LLD University of Wales. KStJ. *Address:* Coedarhydyglyn, near Cardiff, S Wales. *T:* Peterston-super-Ely 321. *Clubs:* Athenæum; Cardiff and County (Cardiff).

**TRAIL, Richard Robertson,** CBE 1953; MC, MA, MD, FRCP; late Medical Director, Papworth and Enham-Alamein Village Settlements; Hon. Consultant to the RAF (Air Commodore, RAFVR Medical Service); Past-Master, Society of Apothecaries; Member, Medical Research Council Committee on Tuberculosis in War-time; late Medical Superintendent, King Edward VII Sanatorium, Midhurst; *b* 25 May 1894; *m* 1924, Marion Dawson McAfee; one *s*. *Educ:* Robert Gordon's Coll., Aberdeen; King's College and Marischal College, Aberdeen Univ. Matriculated 1911; served European War, Captain RA (SR). MA (Hons), MB, ChB (Hons), MD Aberdeen, Simpson Gold Medallist, FRCP. Resident Officer Aberdeen Maternity Hospital; House Physician, later Assistant RMO, later RMO, Brompton Hosp., London; Mitchell Lectr, RCP, 1936; Fitzpatrick Lectr, RCP, 1964-65; Sydenham and Gideon de Laune Lectr, Faculty of History, Soc. of Apothecaries, 1964. Life Member, BRCS. Chevalier of the Legion of Honour; Officier de l'Ordre de la Santé Publique; Order of Merit, first class, of Czechoslovakia; CStJ. *Publications:* Pulmonary Tuberculosis: A report upon the experience of the Patients of King Edward VII Sanatorium, Midhurst, 1931; Inaugural Lecture of the Varrier-Jones Memorial Lectureship, The Early Diagnosis of Pulmonary Tuberculosis, 1942; Mass Miniature Radiography (with Trenchard and Kennedy), 1943; Chest Examination: Physical Signs and X-Ray Findings correlated through Pathology, 1943; numerous articles on Tuberculosis in leading medical journals. *Address:* 82b Ashley Gardens, Westminster, SW1. *T:* 01-828 8897.

**TRAILL, Air Vice-Marshal Thomas Cathcart,** CB 1948; OBE 1940; DFC 1918; Royal Air Force, retired; *b* 6 Aug. 1899; *s* of Edmund Bernard Traill, Chirn, Traill, Argentine, and Gertrude Ann (*née* Dickinson); *m* 1931, F. M. Harvey; two *d*; *m* 1945, W. B. Reeves; one *s*. *Educ:* RN Colleges, Osborne and Dartmouth; St Catharine's Coll., Cambridge (MA). Joined HMS Lord Nelson, 2nd Aug. 1914; served European War, 1914-19, Dardanelles Campaign; transferred to RFC 1917, and joined No. 20 Sqdn, France, May 1918 (temp. Captain, DFC). Asst Air Attaché, Washington, 1919-20; Cambridge, BA, MA, 1922-24. Served Iraq, Trans-Jordan and Egypt. In War of 1939-45 served in Bomber Command, N Africa and Air Ministry. Retired, 1954. US Legion of Merit, 1944, when he was serving on the Staff of General Spaatz. *Address:* Flat 4, Garrick's Villa, Hampton, Middlesex. *Club:* Royal Air Force.

**TRANTER, Professor Clement John,** CBE 1967 (OBE 1953); Bashforth Professor of Mathematical Physics, Royal Military College of Science, Shrivenham, since 1953; *b* 16 Aug. 1909; *s* of late Archibald Tranter, and Mrs Tranter, Cirencester, Glos.; *m* 1937, Joan Louise Hatton, *d* of late J. Hatton, MBE, and Mrs Hatton, Plumstead, SE18. *Educ:* Cirencester Grammar Sch.; Queen's Coll., Oxford (Open Math. Scholar; 1st Class Hons Mathematical Mods, 1929; 1st Class Hons Final Sch. of Maths, 1931; MA (Oxon) 1940; DSc (Oxon) 1953). Commissioned RA, TA, 1932; Captain, 1938. Junior Assistant Research Dept, Woolwich, 1931-34; Senior Lecturer, Gunnery and Mathematics Branch, Military College of Science, Woolwich, 1935-40; Asst Professor 1940-46; Assoc. Professor of Mathematics, Royal Military College of Science, Shrivenham, 1946-53. *Publications:* Integral Transforms in Mathematical Physics, 1951; Advanced Level Pure Mathematics, 1953; Techniques of Mathematical Analysis, 1957; (with C. G. Lambe) Differential Equations for Engineers and Scientists, 1961; Mathematics for Sixth Form Scientists, 1964; (with C. G. Lambe) Advanced Level Mathematics, 1966; Bessel Functions with some Physical Applications, 1968; mathematical papers in various journals. *Recreations:* golf, fly-fishing. *Address:* Flagstones, Stanton Fitzwarren, near Swindon, Wilts. *T:* Stratton St Margaret 2289.

**TRAPNELL, Alan Stewart; His Honour Judge Trapnell;** Chairman of Middlesex Quarter Sessions, since 1969; *b* 12 Jan. 1913; *s* of Francis C. Trapnell, MD, Beckenham, Kent. *Educ:* The Leys Sch., Cambridge; Jesus Coll., Cambridge. Served War of 1939-45, Queen Victoria's Rifles. Barrister-at-Law. Called to Bar, Inner Temple, 1936. Western Circuit, Hampshire Sessions. Member of Bar Council, 1958-62. Recorder of Barnstaple, 1962-64. Judge of: Bow County Court, 1964-66; Shoreditch County Court, 1966-67; Bromley County Court, 1968-69. *Address:* Francis Taylor Building, Temple, EC4. *T:* 01-353 2182. *Clubs:* Oxford and Cambridge University; Hampshire (Winchester).

**TRAPNELL, Barry Maurice Waller,** MA, PhD Cantab; DL; Headmaster of Oundle School, since 1968; *b* 18 May 1924; *s* of Waller Bertram and late Rachel Trapnell; *m* 1951, Dorothy Joan, *d* of late P. J. Kerr, ICS; two *d*. *Educ:* University College Sch., Hampstead; St John's Coll., Cambridge (Scholar). Research in physical chemistry in Department of Colloid Science, Cambridge, 1945-46, and Royal Institution, London, 1946-50; Commonwealth Fund Fellow, Northwestern Univ., Ill., 1950-51; Lecturer in chemistry: Worcester Coll., Oxford, 1951-54; Liverpool Univ., 1954-57; Headmaster, Denstone Coll., 1957-68. Visiting Lecturer, American Association for Advancement of Science, 1961. Council Member, Lichfield Theological Coll.; Member C. of E. Commn on Religious Education. FRSA. DL Staffs, 1967. *Publications:* Chemisorption, 1955 (Russian edition, 1958; 2nd English edition, 1964; Polish edition, 1969); Learning and Discerning, 1966; papers in British and American scientific journals. *Recreations:* several games (represented Cambridge *v* Oxford at cricket and squash rackets, and Gentlemen *v* Players at cricket; won Amateur Championships at Rugby Fives); English furniture and silver; Italian art. *Address:* Cobthorne, Oundle, Northants. *T:* Oundle 3536. *Clubs:* Public Schools; Hawks (Cambridge); Vincent's (Oxford).

**TRAPP, Rt. Rev. Eric Joseph;** *see* Bermuda, Bishop of.

**TRAPPES-LOMAX, Michael Roger;** Somerset Herald, 1951-67, retired; *b* 16 Oct. 1900; 3rd *s* of late Richard Trappes-Lomax, Allsprings, Great Harwood, Lancashire, and late Hon. Alice Mary Wilhelmina Fitzherbert, sister of 13th Baron Stafford. *Educ:* Stonyhurst; New Coll., Oxford. Major, late R. of O., Scots Guards. Rouge Dragon Pursuivant of Arms, 1946-51; Admiralty Adviser on Heraldry, 1954. Librarian, College of Arms, 1960. FSA 1960. Kt Grand Cross, Order of Malta. *Publications:* One of These Days, 1926; Pugin, 1933; Bishop Challoner, 1936. *Address:* Pamments, Great Hockham, Thetford, Norfolk. *Clubs:* Pratt's, Royal Ocean Racing.

**TRASENSTER, Michael Augustus Tulk,** CVO 1954; *b* 26 Jan. 1923; *er s* of late Major William Augustus Trasenster, MC, and Brenda de Courcy Trasenster; *m* 1950, Fay Norrie Darley, *d* of Thomas Bladworth Darley, Cantley Hall, Yorkshire; two *d*. *Educ:* Winchester. Served with 4th/7th Royal Dragoon Guards, 1942-; NW Europe, 1944; Middle East, 1946; Tripolitania, 1950; ADC to Governor of South Australia, 1947-49; School of Tank Technology, 1951; retired, 1952. Military Secretary and Comptroller to the Governor General of New Zealand, 1952-55. Chevalier of Order of Leopold II of Belgium, 1944; Belgian Croix de Guerre, 1944. *Recreations:* tennis; photographer and artist. *Address:* c/o Glyn, Mills and Co., Kirkland House, Whitehall, SW1. *Club:* Cavalry.

**TRATMAN, Edgar Kingsley,** OBE 1949; retired; *b* 23 Feb. 1899; *s* of J. F. W. and E. S. Tratman. *Educ:* Clifton Coll.; University of Bristol. Prof. of Dental Surgery: King Edward VII College of Medicine, Singapore, 1929-49; University of Malaya, 1949-50; University of London (University College Hospital Med. Sch.), 1950-51. FDS, RCS 1949; MD University of Malaya, 1950; FDS, RCSE, 1951. FSA 1938. *Publications:* many contributions to Dental and Archæological Journals. *Recreations:* cave exploring and prehistoric archæology. *Address:* Penrose Cottage, Burrington, near Bristol, Somerset. *T:* Blagdon 274.

**TRAVANCORE-COCHIN, Rajpramukh of; Major-General H. H. Sri Padmanabha Dasa Bala Rama Varma;** GCSI 1946; GCIE 1935; *b* 1912. Founder of Travancore University and sometime Chancellor. Formerly: Colonel-in-Chief of Travancore State Forces; Hon. Major-General in British Army. Has introduced many reforms. Holds Hon. Doctorates. *Address:* Kaudiar Palace, Trivandrum 3, Kerala State, S. India.

**TRAVERS, Basil Holmes,** OBE 1943; BA (Sydney); MA (Oxon); BLitt (Oxon); FACE; Headmaster of Sydney Church of England Grammar School, North Sydney, NSW, since 1959; *b* 7 July 1919; *s* of Colonel R. J. A. Travers, DSO, and late Dorothy Mabel Travers, *d* of Maj.-Gen. William Holmes, CMG, DSO; *m* 1942, Margaret Emily Marr; three *d*. *Educ:* Sydney Church of England Grammar Sch.; Sydney Univ.; New Coll., Oxford Univ. Rhodes Scholar for NSW, 1940. Served War of 1939-45 (despatches, OBE); AIF, 2/2 Australian Infantry Battalion; ADC to Maj.-Gen. Sir I. G. Mackay, 1940; Brigade Major, 15 Aust. Inf. Bde, 1943-44; psc 1944; GSO 2, HQ, 2 Aust. Corps, 1944-45. Assistant Master, Wellington Coll., Berks, England, 1948-49; Assistant Master, Cranbrook Sch., Sydney, 1950-52; Headmaster, Launceston Church Grammar Sch., Launceston, Tasmania, 1953-58. Lt-Col commanding 12 Inf. Bn (CMF), 1955-58. Member: Soldiers' Children Education Board, 1959-; NSW Cttee, Duke of Edinburgh's Award Scheme in Australia. *Publications:* Let's Talk Rugger, 1949; The Captain General, 1952. *Recreations:* cricket (Oxford Blue, 1946, 1948), swimming, rugby (Oxford Blue, 1946, 1947), athletics (Half Blue, 1947); also Sydney Blue, football, cricket; Rugby Union International for England, 1947, 1948, 1949; represented NSW, 1950. *Address:* Sydney Church of England Grammar School, North Sydney, NSW 2060, Australia. *T:* 922263. *Clubs:* University, Rugby Union (Sydney).

**TRAVERS, Ben;** dramatist and novelist; *b* 1886; *e s* of W. F. Travers; *m* 1916, Violet (*d* 1951), *o c* of D. B. W. Mouncey; two *s* one *d*. *Educ:* Abbey Sch., Beckenham; Charterhouse. Served in RNAS, 1914-18, Squadron Commander; transferred RAF as Major, 1918; received Air Force Cross, 1920; rejoined RAF for War Service, Nov. 1939; Sqdn Leader, 1940; Prime Warden of Fishmongers' Company, 1946. *Publications: Plays, Novels and Films:* The Dippers, 1922; A Cuckoo in the Nest, 1925 (revived, 1964); Rookery Nook, 1926; Mischief, 1926; Thark, 1927 (revived 1965); Plunder, 1928; The Collection To-day, 1928; A Cup of Kindness, 1929; A Night Like This, 1930; Turkey Time, 1931; The Chance of a Night-time, 1931; Dirty Work, 1932; Just My Luck, 1932; A Bit of a Test, 1933; Hyde Side Up, 1933; Up to the Neck, Lady in Danger, 1934; Fighting Stock, 1935; Stormy Weather, 1935; Foreign Affairs, 1935; Pot Luck, 1936; Dishonour Bright, 1936; O Mistress Mine, 1936; For Valour, 1937; Second Best Bed, 1937; Old Iron, 1938; Banana Ridge, 1938; Spotted Dick, 1939; She Follows Me About, 1943; Outrageous Fortune, 1947; Wild Horses, 1952; Nun's Veiling, 1956; Vale of Laughter (autobiography), 1957; Corker's End, 1969. Television Play, Potter, 1948. *Recreation:* watching cricket. *Address:* c/o Curtis Brown Ltd, 13 King Street, WC2. *Clubs:* Garrick, MCC.

**TREACHER, Rear-Adm. John Devereux;** Flag Officer Carriers and Amphibious Ships and Commander Carrier Striking Group Two since 1970; *b* Chile, 23 Sept. 1924; *s* of late Frank Charles Treacher, Bentley, Suffolk; *m* 1st,

1953, Patcie Jane (marr. diss. 1968), *d* of Dr F. L. McGrath, Evanston, Ill; one *s* one *d*; 2nd, 1969, Kirsteen Forbes, *d* of D. F. Landale, *qv*. *Educ:* St Paul's School. Entered RN, 1942; served in HM Ships Nelson, Glasgow, Keppel and Mermaid in Mediterranean, Russian convoys and Second Front; Lieut 1945; qual. Fleet Air Arm pilot, 1947; 800 Sqdn HMS Triumph, Korean War, 1949; CO: 778 Sqdn 1951, 849 Sqdn 1952-53 (Lt-Comdr); subseq. HMS Protector, HMS Victorious, Naval Asst to Controller of the Navy; CO, HMS Lowestoft, 1964-66; Dir Naval Air Warfare (Naval Staff), 1966-68; CO, HMS Eagle, 1968-70. Comdr 1956; Captain 1962; Rear-Adm. 1970. *Recreations:* water ski-ing, tennis, photography. *Address:* Reynolds Barn, Fishbourne, Sussex. *T:* Chichester 86725. *Club:* United Service.

**TREACY, Rt. Rev. Eric;** *see* Wakefield, Bishop of.

**TREADWELL, Charles James;** British Political Agent, Abu Dhabi, Persian Gulf, since 1968; *b* 10 Feb. 1920; *s* of late C. A. L. Treadwell, OBE, Barrister and Solicitor, Wellington, NZ; *m* 1946, Philippa, *d* of late W. J. Perkins, CBE, MC; three *s*. *Educ:* Wellington Coll., NZ; University of New Zealand (LLB). Served with HM Forces, 1939-45. Sudan Political Service and Sudan Judiciary, 1945-55; FO, 1955-57; British High Commn, Lahore, 1957-60; HM Embassy, Ankara, 1960-62; HM Embassy, Jedda, 1963-64; British Dep. High Comr for Eastern Nigeria, 1965-66; Head of Joint Information Services Department, Foreign Office/Commonwealth Office, 1966-68. *Recreation:* fishing. *Address:* 48 Lindfield Gardens, London Road, Guildford, Surrey. *T:* Guildford 69380; British Political Agency, Abu Dhabi, Arabian Gulf.

**TREASE, Prof. George Edward,** BPharm, Dr *hc* Strasbourg; Dr *hc* Clermont; FPS, FRIC, FLS; Professor of Pharmacognosy, Nottingham University, 1957-67, now Emeritus Professor; Head of Department of Pharmacy, University of Nottingham, 1944-67; *b* 8 July 1902; *e s* of George and Florence Trease; *m* 1928, Phyllis Thornton Wilkinson; two *d* (one *s* decd). *Educ:* Nottingham High Sch.; London College of Pharmacy. Lecturer in Pharmacognosy, University College, Nottingham, 1926. Served in Min. of Economic Warfare, 1939-40. Reader in Pharmacognosy, 1945; Examiner in Pharmacognosy to: Pharmaceutical Society, 1934-; University of London, 1937-; QUB, 1949, 1963-65; University of Glasgow, 1950-; University of Wales, 1945-; University of Nottingham, 1950-; University of Singapore, 1962; University of Bradford, 1966-; Pharmaceutical Society of Eire, 1959-. Vice-Pres., British Soc. for History of Pharmacy, 1967-70. Worshipful Society of Apothecaries of London, 1959. Dr *hc* Strasbourg University, 1954; Dr *hc* Clermont University, 1962. *Publications:* Chemistry of Crude Drugs, 1928 (with Prof. J. E. Driver); Textbook of Pharmacognosy, 1934, 10th edn 1971; Pharmacy in History, 1964; many papers and articles on pharmacognosy, pharmaceutical history and pharmaceutical education. *Recreation:* local history. *Address:* George Hill, Crediton, Devon. *T:* Crediton 2983.

**TREATT, Hon. Sir Vernon (Haddon),** KBE 1970; MM 1918; QC (Austr.) 1940; MA, BCL; private interests; *b* 15 May 1897; *s* of Frank Burford Treatt and Kate Ellen Treatt; *m* 1st, 1930, Dorothy Isobelle Henderson; one *s* one *d*; 2nd, 1960, Franki Embleton Wilson. *Educ:* Sydney C of E Grammar Sch.; St Paul's Coll., Sydney Univ.; New Coll., Oxford. Sydney Univ., 1915-16 (BA); AIF, 1916-18 (Gunner, MM); Oxford Univ., 1921-23. Called to Bar, Lincoln's Inn, 1923; Bar of NSW, 1924. NSW Legislative Assembly, 1938-62: Minister of Justice, 1939-41; Leader of Opposition, 1946-54; title of Honourable for life, 1955. Chm., Local Govt Boundaries Commn NSW, 1964-69. Chief Comr (in loco Lord Mayor), City of Sydney, 1967-69. *Publication:* Workers Compensation Law NSW. *Recreations:* swimming, reading, rural property. *Address:* 27 Waruda Street, Kirribilli, NSW 2061, Australia. *T:* 922668; Riverview, O'Connell, NSW 2795. *T:* Brewongle 37-5538. *Clubs:* University, Royal Sydney Golf, Union, Australasian Pioneers' (Sydney).

**TREDENNICK, Prof. (George) Hugh (Percival Phair);** Profesor Emeritus of Classics, University of London; *b* 30 June 1899; *yr s* of late Canon G. N. H. Tredennick, Sparkbrook, Birmingham; *m* 1924, Louella Margaret (*d* 1970), *o d* of late Canon E. E. M. Phair, Winnipeg, Canada; one *s* two *d*. *Educ:* King Edward's, Birmingham; Trinity Hall, Cambridge. War Service in France with Royal Artillery, 1918-19; Trinity Hall, Cambridge (Scholar and Prizeman), 1919-22; First Class Classical Tripos: Part I, 1921, Part II, 1922; BA, 1922; MA 1926. Assistant Master, Rossall School, 1923-24; Lecturer in Classics, University of Sheffield, 1924-36; Reader in Classics, Queen Mary College, University of London, 1936-46; Professor of Classics, Royal Holloway Coll., 1946-66. Dean of the Faculty of Arts, University of London, 1956-60; Editor (with C. J. Fordyce) The Classical Review, 1961-67. *Publications:* text and translation of Aristotle's Metaphysics, Vol. I, 1933, Vol. II, 1935; text and translation of Aristotle's Prior Analytics, 1938; The Last Days of Socrates (Penguin Classics), 1954; text and translation of Aristotle's Posterior Analytics, 1960; Memoirs of Socrates (Penguin Classics), 1970; contributions to classical journals. *Recreations:* music, indoor gardening. *Address:* 9 Wilbury Lodge, Eaton Road, Hove, Sussex BN3 3PA. *T:* Brighton 776410.

**TREDENNICK, Rev. John Nesbitt Ernest,** MA; *b* 23 Sept. 1892; *e s* of late Canon G. N. H. Tredennick; *m* 1931, Marjorie Phyllis, *y d* of Henry Currie; two *d*. *Educ:* King Edward's School, Birmingham; Trinity Hall, Cambridge (Scholar), BA 1914; MA 1921 (Hons in Classics and Theology); Ridley Hall, Cambridge, 1919-21. Served European War, 1914-19, as Captain (R War. Regiment and General List); wounded in 1st Battle of the Somme, July 1916; Deacon, 1921; Priest, 1922; Curate of St James's, Paddington, 1921-24; Principal of Bishop Wilson Theological College, Isle of Man, and Domestic Chaplain to the Bishop of Sodor and Man, 1924-31; Vicar of Emmanuel Church, Southport, 1931-52; Vicar of Crockham Hill, Kent, 1952-68. *Recreations:* fishing, sailing, motoring. *Address:* 111 Dean Court Road, Rottingdean, Sussex. *T:* Brighton 36423.

**TREDGOLD, Joan Alison,** MA Cantab; Principal, Cheltenham Ladies' College, Sept. 1953-July 1964; *b* 6 Sept. 1903; *d* of Alfred Frank Tredgold, MD, FRCP, and Zoë B. T. Tredgold. *Educ:* Cheltenham Ladies' College; Newnham College, Cambridge. Mathematical Tripos part II, Class I, 1924; Fourth Year Scholarship, Newnham, 1924-25. Assistant Mistress, Sherborne School for Girls, 1925-29; Assistant Mistress, Cheltenham Ladies' College, 1929-35. Senior Mathematical Mistress, 1935-53, Assistant House Mistress, 1938-39, Second Mistress, 1939-53, Roedean School. *Recreations:* walking, foreign travel. *Address:* 12 Newcourt Park, Charlton Kings,

Cheltenham, Glos. *T:* Cheltenham 59242. *Club:* University Women's.

**TREDGOLD, Rt. Hon. Sir Robert Clarkson,** PC 1957; KCMG 1955 (CMG 1943); Kt 1951; QC; *b* 1899; *s* of Sir Clarkson Tredgold, KC; *m* 1925, Lorna Doris Keilor; no *c. Educ:* Prince Edward School, Salisbury, Rhodesia; Rondebosch High School; Hertford College, Oxford. Hon. Fellow, Hertford College, Oxford, 1961. On Military Service, 1918; called to Bar, Inner Temple, 1923; practised in Southern Rhodesia and Northern Rhodesia with Headquarters at Bulawayo; acted Judge in N Rhodesia; MP for Insiza District, 1934-43; KC (S Rhodesia), 1936; Minister of Justice and Defence, S Rhodesia, 1936-43; also Minister of Natives, 1941, 1942-43; High Court Judge, Southern Rhodesia, 1943-50; Chief Justice, SR, 1950-55; Chief Justice, Federal Supreme Court, Federation of Rhodesia and Nyasaland 1955-60, resigned. Acted as Governor of S Rhodesia and Gov.-Gen. of Federation, on a number of occasions. LLD (Hon.) Witwatersrand Univ., 1953. *Publication:* The Rhodesia That Was My Life, 1968. *Recreations:* fishing and shooting. *Address:* Tynwald South, Salisbury, Rhodesia. *T:* Salisbury 2067782. *Clubs:* Bulawayo (Bulawayo); Salisbury (Salisbury).

**TREDGOLD, Roger Francis,** MD; Physician to Department of Psychological Medicine, University College Hospital; Hon. Consultant in Psychiatry to the Army at Home; *b* 23 Oct. 1911; *s* of late Alfred Frank Tredgold, FRCP, FRSE; *m* 1938, Verity Micheline, *d* of late Sir Gilbert Walker, CSI, FRS; one *s* one *d. Educ:* Winchester Coll.; Trinity Coll., Cambridge; Univ. Coll. Hosp. Medical School. MA (Cantab.) 1939; MD 1947; DPM 1939; MRCP 1965. Asst MO, Brentwood Mental Hosp., 1937-40. RAMC, 1940-46; served in S India and SE Asia Commands, as Adviser in Psychiatry, with rank of Lt-Col; also Reader in Psychiatry, RAM College, Millbank. Boots Lectr in Industrial Health, Roffey Park Rehabilitation Centre, 1946-48. Regional Psychiatrist, South East Metropolitan Regional Hosp. Bd, 1948-56. *Publications:* Human Relations in Modern Industry, 2nd edn 1963; (jointly with late A. F. Tredgold) Manual of Psychological Medicine, 3rd edn 1953; (jointly with K. Soddy) Mental Retardation, 11th edn 1970; (ed) Bridging the Gap, 1958. *Recreations:* fencing, chess, bird-watching. *Address:* Old Common, Cross in Hand, Sussex. *T:* Heathfield 3258. *Club:* London Fencing.

**TREE, Ronald;** *o s* of Arthur Tree and late Countess Beatty; *m* 1920, Nancy, 2nd *d* of Moncure Perkins, Richmond, Virginia, and *widow* of Henry Field, of Chicago; two *s*; *m* 1947, Mrs Mary Endicott Fitzgerald, *o d* of Rt Rev. Malcolm Peabody, Syracuse, NY; one *d. Educ:* Winchester. Served war of 1914-18, in Italy and France, 1917-18. Managing Ed. of Forum Magazine, NY, 1922-26; Joint Master Pytchley Hounds, 1927-33; MP (C) Harborough division of Leicestershire, 1933-45; Parliamentary Private Secretary to R. S. Hudson when Minister of Pensions and when Secretary to Overseas Trade Dept, 1936-38; to Sir John Reith, Minister of Information, to Rt Hon. Alfred Duff-Cooper and to Rt Hon. Brendan Bracken, 1940-43; Parliamentary Secretary, Ministry of Town and Country Planning, 1945; a Trustee of the Wallace Collection. Member of Council, Univ. of the West Indies: Pres., Barbados National Trust. *Recreations:* hunting, shooting, yachting. *Address:* Heron Bay, Barbados, WI; 123 East 79 Street, New York City, USA. *Clubs:* Turf, White's; Century (New York).

**TREE, Ven. Ronald James,** MA, BLit; Archdeacon of St David's, since 1968; Canon of Mydrim, since 1968; Diocesan Director of Religious Education, since 1966; *b* 30 March 1914; *s* of Frederick George and Susan Maud Tree, Garnant, Carms; *m* 1944, Ceredwen, *d* of G. C. Thomas, Gwaun-Cae-Gurwen, Glamorgan; one *s* one *d. Educ:* University College of Wales, Swansea; New College, Oxford; St Michael's Theological College, Llandaff. 1st Class Hons Philosophy, BA 1937, MA 1939 Wales; BLitt 1941 Oxon. Curate: of Cwmamman, 1941; of Aberystwyth, St Michael's, 1944; Lecturer in Philosophy, St David's Coll., Lampeter, 1946; Professor of Philosophy, 1950; Senior Tutor and Bursar, 1956; Warden and Headmaster, Llandovery College, 1957-66; Vicar of St Mary's, Haverfordwest, 1966-68. Member, Governing Body, Church in Wales. Canon of Mathry in St David's Cathedral, 1961-68. *Publications:* contributor: Efrydiau Athronyddol; Theology; Journal of the Historical Society of the Church in Wales. *Recreation:* carpentry. *Address:* The Archdeaconry, St David's, Pembs.

**TREFGARNE;** family name of **Baron Trefgarne.**

**TREFGARNE,** 2nd Baron, *cr* 1947, of Cleddau; **David Garro Trefgarne;** *b* 31 March 1941; *s* of 1st Baron Trefgarne and of Elizabeth (who *m* 1962, Commander A. T. Courtney, from whom she obtained a divorce, 1966, *qv*), *d* of C. E. Churchill; *S* father, 1960; *m* 1968, Rosalie, *d* of Peter Lane; one *s. Educ:* Haileybury; Princeton University, USA. Awarded Royal Aero Club Bronze Medal (jointly) for flight from England to Australia and back in light aircraft, 1963; Joint holder of Class C1d records London to New York, London to Reykjavik and Reykjavik to New York. Also Class C1 records London to Reykjavik and Reykjavik to New York, (Fedn Aeronautique Internat.), 1964. *Recreations:* flying and photography. *Heir: s* Hon. George Garro Trefgarne, *b* 4 Jan. 1970. *Address:* House of Lords, SW1. *Clubs:* Royal Aero, Public Schools.

**TREFUSIS;** *see* Fane Trefusis, family name of **Baron Clinton.**

**TREHANE, Sir (Walter) Richard,** Kt 1967; Chairman of the Milk Marketing Board since 1958; *b* 14 July 1913; *s* of James Trehane and Muriel Yeoman Cowl; *m* 1948, Elizabeth Mitchell; two *s. Educ:* Monkton Combe School, Somerset; University of Reading (BSc (Agric.)). On staff of School of Agriculture, Cambridge, 1933-36; Manager of Hampreston Manor Farm, Dorset, 1936-. Member Dorset War Agric. Exec. Cttee, 1942-47; Mem. Milk Marketing Board, 1947- (Vice-Chm., 1952-58); Dep. Chm. Dorset Agric. Exec. Cttee, 1947-52; Mem. (later Vice-Chm.) Avon and Stour Catchment Bd, subseq. Avon & Dorset Rivers Bd, 1944-53; Mem. Dorset County Council and Chm. Secondary Education Cttee, 1946-49; Chm. Dorset National Farmers' Union, 1947-48; Member, Nat. Milk Publicity Council, 1954- (1st Pres. 1954-56); Chm. English Country Cheese Council, 1955-; Pres. British Farm Produce Council, 1963 (Chm. 1960-63); Chm. Govg Body, Grassland Research Institute, Hurley, Berks, 1959-; Chm. and Pres. European Cttee on MIlk/Butterfat Recording, 1957-60; Director of British Semen Exports Ltd, 1960-; Vice-President: World Assoc. Animal Production, 1965-68; President: European Assoc. Animal Prodn, 1958-59, 1961-67; British Soc. Animal Prodn, 1961; British Friesian Cattle Soc., 1969-70; Royal Assoc. British Dairy Farmers, 1968; Internat. Dairy Fedn, 1968-; Chm., UK

Dairy Assoc., 1963-69. Dir, Southern Television, 1969-. Governor, Monkton Combe School, 1957-. Justus-von-Liebig Prize, Kiel Univ., 1968; Gold Medal, Soc. of Dairy Technology, 1969. Comdr du Mérite Agricole, 1964. *Address:* Milk Marketing Board, Thames Ditton, Surrey. *T:* 01-398 4101; Hampreston Manor Farm, Wimborne, Dorset. *Clubs:* Constitutional, Farmers', Travellers'; Royal Motor Yacht (Poole).

**TRELAWNY, Sir John Barry Salusbury-,** 13th Bt *cr* 1628; *b* 4 Sept. 1934; *s* of Sir John William Robin Maurice Salusbury-Trelawny, 12th Bt and of his 1st wife, Glenys Mary, *d* of John Cameron Kynoch; *S* father, 1956; *m* 1958, Carol Knox, *yr d* of late C. F. K. Watson, The Field, Saltwood, Kent; one *s* three *d. Educ:* HMS Worcester. Subseq. Sub-Lt RNVR (National Service); 2nd Officer, Merchant Navy. *Heir: s* John William Richard Salusbury-Trelawny, *b* 30 March 1960. *Address:* 21 Brockhill Road, Hythe, Kent. *T:* 66476. *Club:* Royal Cinque Ports Yacht.

**TREMAYNE, Air Marshal Sir John Tremayne,** KCB 1942 (CB 1939); CBE 1934; DSO 1915; DL, JP Cornwall; *b* 20 July 1891; *s* of C. H. Babington, 47 Lennox Gdns, SW1; renounced surname of Babington, 1945; *m* 1916, Cicely (*d* 1953), *y d* of Philip Beresford-Hope, Bedgebury; two *d.* Served European War, 1914-15 (DSO, Chevalier Legion of Honour); Air Representative to League of Nations, 1929-34; Air Officer Commanding RAF Halton, 1934-36; No 24 (Training) Group, 1936-38; Far East, 1938-41; Air Officer Commanding-in-Chief, Technical Training Command, 1941-43; Head of RAF Mission in Moscow, 1943; retired 1944. High Sheriff of Cornwall, 1954. *Address:* Croan, Wadebridge, Cornwall. *T:* St Mabyn 368. *Club:* United Service.

**TREMELLEN, Norman Cleverton;** FRSA; FZS; *b* 8 March 1895; *s* of Henry Josiah and Elizabeth Tremellen; *m* 1923, Lorna, *o d* of Dr John McKeague and *g d* of Judge Purcell, Dublin. *Educ:* Villa Longchamp, Lausanne, Switzerland. Served European War, 1914-18 (4 General Service Medals). Member Common Council, City of London; Founder Chm. and Hon. Treas., City of London Sheriffs Society. Insurance Broker and Underwriting Member of Lloyd's; Fellow of the Corporation of Insurance Brokers; Past President, London Cornish Association. Governor of: The Bridewell and Bethlem Royal Hospitals; Archbishop Tenison's Grammar Sch. Member Court of Assistants, Corporation of Sons of Clergy. Chairman of Insurance Debating Society. Sheriff of the City of London, 1953-54. Upper Warden Worshipful Co. of Weavers; Mem. Worshipful Co. of Shipwrights; Past Pres., City Livery Club (also Past Pres. and Past Master of other City Clubs); Vice-Pres., United Wards Club; Governor (for 18 years), Bishopsgate Foundn. Past Dep. Gov. The Hon. The Irish Soc.; Fellow, Royal Soc. for Protection of Birds; FAMS; FInstD. Mem. Anglo-Ethiopian Soc. Comdr Roy. Order of the North Star (Sweden). *Recreation:* foreign travel. *Address:* Burlington, Orchehill Avenue, Gerrards Cross, Bucks. *T:* 83047. *Clubs:* Royal Automobile, City Livery.

**TREMLETT, Rt. Rev. Anthony Paul;** *see* Dover, Suffragan Bishop of.

**TREMLETT, Col C. P.,** CBE 1919; TD; DL; *s* of late W. W. Tremlett, JP, Exeter; *m* Dorothy, *d* of late Percy Gray, MBE, Indian Civil Service; three *s* two *d. Educ:* Inverness College. *Address:* Highlands, Littleham Cross, Exmouth, Devon. *T:* Exmouth 2016.

**TREMLETT, Maj.-Gen. Erroll Arthur Edwin,** CB 1944; TD 1948; *b* 22 Dec. 1893; *s* of late Col E. J. Tremlett, RA; *m* Dorothy Mary, *d* of late H. W. Capper, 24 Suffolk St, Pall Mall; one *s* one *d.* Served in European War, 1914-19, with RA, (despatches) (awarded Regular Commn in the "Field," Sept. 1916) and in France and Belgium 1940 (despatches); Comdr 44 AA Brigade, Nov. 1940; Major-General, Commander 10 AA Division, Feb. 1942; Commander AA Defences of London, 1942-44; Comdr Flying Bomb Deployment, E Anglia, 1945. Commander 2 AA Group, 1945-46; RARO 1946. Hon. Colonel 656 Light AA Regt RA (RB), 1947-57. Gold Staff Officer, Coronation of HM Queen Elizabeth II. *Address:* Clapham Cottage, Clapham, Nr Exeter, Devon. *T:* Kennford 586. *Clubs:* Naval and Military, MCC.

**TRENAMAN, Nancy Kathleen, (Mrs M. S. Trenaman);** Principal of St Anne's College, Oxford, since 1966; Member, Commission on the Constitution, since 1969; *b* 1919; *d* of Frederick Broughton Fisher and Edith Fisher; *m* 1967, M. S. Trenaman. *Educ:* Bradford Girls' Grammar School; Somerville College, Oxford. Board of Trade, 1941-51; Assistant Secretary, Ministry of Materials, 1951-54; Counsellor, British Embassy, Washington, 1951-53; Board of Trade, 1954-66, Under-Sec. 1962-66. *Address:* 38 Gloucester Crescent, NW1. *T:* 01-485 2212; St Anne's College, Oxford. *Club:* Oxford and Cambridge University.

**TRENCH,** family name of **Baron Ashtown.**

**TRENCH,** *see* Chenevix-Trench and Le Poer Trench.

**TRENCH, Sir David (Clive Crosbie),** GCMG 1969 (KCMG 1962; CMG 1960); MC 1944; Governor and Commander-in-Chief, Hong Kong, 1964-Oct. 1971; *b* 2 June 1915; *s* of late William Launcelot Crosbie Trench, CIE, and Margaret Zephanie (*née* Huddleston); *m* 1944, Margaret Gould; one *d. Educ:* Tonbridge School; Jesus College, Cambridge (MA). Cadet, British Solomon Islands Protectorate, 1938; seconded to W Pacific High Commission, 1941. Served War of 1939-45 (MC, US Legion of Merit); British Solomon Islands Defence Force, 1942-46, Lt-Col. Secretary to the Government, British Solomon Islands Protectorate, 1947; attended Joint Services Staff Coll., 1949; Asst Sec., Deputy Defence Sec., Hong Kong, 1950; Deputy Financial Sec., 1956; Commissioner of Labour and Mines, 1957; attended Imperial Defence College, 1958; Deputy Colonial Secretary, Hong Kong, 1959; High Commissioner for The Western Pacific, 1961-63. Hon. LLD: Univ. of Hong Kong, 1968; Chinese Univ. of Hong Kong, 1968. Legion of Merit (US), 1944. *Recreation:* golf. *Address:* c/o Lloyds Bank, Cox's and King's Branch, 6 Pall Mall, SW1; Government House, Hong Kong. *Club:* Royal Commonwealth Society.

**TRENCH, Nigel Clive Cosby,** CMG 1966; Ambassador in Korea, since 1969; *b* 27 Oct. 1916; *s* of Clive Newcome Trench and Kathleen, 2nd *d* of Major Ivar MacIvor, CSI; *m* 1939, Marcelle Catherine Clotterbooke Patyn; one *s. Educ:* Eton; Univ. of Cambridge. Served in HM Forces, 1940-46 (despatches). Appointed a Member of the Foreign (subseq. Diplomatic) Service, 1946; Lisbon, 1946; First Secretary, 1948; returned Foreign Office, 1949; First Secretary (Commercial) Lima, 1952; transf. Foreign Office, 1955; Counsellor, Tokyo, 1961; Counsellor, Washington, 1963; Cabinet Office, 1967. *Address:* c/o Foreign and Commonwealth Office, SW1. *Club:* Bath.

**TRENCH, Peter Edward,** CBE 1964 (OBE 1945); TD 1949; JP; Managing Director, Peter Trench & Associates Ltd; *b* 16 June 1918; *s* of James Knights Trench and Grace Sim; *m* 1940, Mary St Clair Morford; one *s* one *d*. *Educ:* privately; London Sch. of Economics, London Univ.; St John's Coll., Cambridge Univ. BSc (Econ.) Hons. Served in The Queen's Royal Regt, 1939-46: Staff Coll., 1942; Mil. Raid Planner, Combined Ops HQ, 1943; AAG, HQ 21 Army Gp, 1944-45 (OBE). Man. Dir, Bovis Ltd, 1954-59; Dir, Nat. Fedn of Bldg Trades Employers, 1959-64; Dir, Nat. Bldg Agency, 1964-66; Part-time Mem., Nat. Bd for Prices and Incomes, 1965-68. Chairman: Crendon Timber Components Ltd; James Davies (Holdings) Ltd; Dep. Chm., Y. J. Lovell (Holdings) Ltd; Director: IBSAC Ltd; Crendon Concrete Ltd; Architectural Newsreel Ltd; Building Marketing Consultancy Ltd; Lifetime Plastics Ltd. Chm., London Bldg Centre; Vice-Pres., Modular Soc.; Hon. Mem., Architectural Assoc.; Mem. Council, City and Guilds of London Inst.; Employer Member, Industrial Court; Mem. Bd of Govs, St Mary's Hosp., London. JP Inner London, 1963. FIOB; FRSA. *Recreations:* ski-ing, swimming, tennis, golf, travelling. *Address:* 33 Elm Tree Road, St John's Wood, NW8. *T:* 01-286 5995. *Club:* Athenæum.

**TRENCHARD,** family name of **Viscount Trenchard.**

**TRENCHARD,** 2nd Viscount, *cr* 1936, of Wolfeton; **Thomas Trenchard,** Baron, *cr* 1930; Bt, *cr* 1919; MC 1944; *b* 15 Dec. 1923; *o surv. s* of 1st Viscount Trenchard, GCB, OM, GCVO, DSO, first Marshal of the RAF, and of Katherine Viscountess Trenchard (*d* 1960); *S* father 1956; *m* 1948, Patricia, *d* of late Admiral Sir Sidney Bailey, KBE, CB, DSO and of Lady Bailey; three *s*. *Educ:* Eton. Served War of 1939-45, Captain, King's Royal Rifle Corps (MC). *Heir:* *s* Hon. Hugh Trenchard, *b* 12 March 1951. *Address:* Abdale House, Warrengate Road, North Mymms, Herts. *Club:* Brooks's.

**TREND, Sir Burke St John,** GCB 1968 (KCB 1962; CB 1955); CVO 1953; Secretary of the Cabinet since 1963; *b* 2 Jan. 1914; *o s* of late Walter St John Trend and of Mrs Trend; *m* 1949, Patricia Charlotte, *o d* of Rev. Gilbert Shaw; two *s* one *d*. *Educ:* Whitgift; Merton College, Oxford (Postmaster). 1st Cl. Honour Mods, 1934; 1st Cl. Lit. Hum., 1936; Hon. Fellow, Merton College, 1964. Hon. DCL Oxford, 1969. Home Civil Service Administrative Class, 1936; Min. of Education, 1936; transferred to HM Treasury, 1937; Asst Private Sec. to Chancellor of Exchequer, 1939-41; Principal Private Sec. to Chancellor of Exchequer, 1945-49; Under Secretary, HM Treasury, 1949-55; Office of the Lord Privy Seal, 1955-56; Deputy Secretary of the Cabinet, 1956-59; Third Secretary, HM Treasury, 1959-60, Second Secretary, 1960-62. *Address:* Cabinet Office, Whitehall, SW1. *T:* 01-930 5422. *Club:* Athenæum.

**TRENDALL, Prof. Arthur Dale,** CMG 1961; MA, LittD; FSA; FBA; FAHA; Resident Fellow, Menzies College, La Trobe University; Emeritus Professor, University of Sydney, 1954; *b* Auckland, NZ, 28 March 1909; *s* of late Arthur D. Trendall and late Iza W. Uttley-Todd; unmarried. *Educ:* King's College, Auckland; Univs of Otago (MA 1929, LittD 1936) and Cambridge (MA 1937, LittD 1968). NZ Post-Graduate Scholar in Arts, 1931; Rome Scholar in Archæology, 1934-35; Fellow of Trinity Coll., Cambridge, 1936-40; Librarian British School at Rome, 1936-38; FSA 1939; Professor of Greek, Univ. of Sydney, 1939-54; Dean, Faculty of Arts, 1947-50; Chairman Professorial Board, 1949-50, 1952; Acting Vice-Chancellor, 1953; Master of Univ. House, ANU, 1954-69, retd; Hon. Fellow, 1969. Hon. Curator, Greek and Roman Section, Nicholson Museum, 1954, and Hon. Consultant, National Gallery of Victoria, 1957; Deputy Vice-Chancellor, ANU, 1958-64; Mem. Royal Commn on Univ. of Tas., 1955. Geddes-Harrower Professor of Greek Art and Archæology, Aberdeen Univ., 1966-67. Chm. Aust. Humanities Research Council, 1957-59. Mem., Nat. Capital Planning Cttee, 1958-67; Mem. Australian Universities Commission, 1959-70. FBA 1968. Hon. LittD: Melbourne, 1956; ANU 1970; Hon. DLitt Adelaide, 1960. KCSG, 1956; Commendatore, Ordine al Merito, Republic of Italy, 1965 (Cav. Uff. 1961). *Publications:* Paestan Pottery, 1936; Frühitaliotische Vasen, 1938; Guide to the Cast Collection of the Nicholson Museum, Sydney, 1941; The Shellal Mosaic, 1942, 3rd edn 1964; Handbook to the Nicholson Museum (editor), 2nd edn 1948; Paestan Pottery, Supplement, 1952; Vasi Italioti del Vaticano, vol. i, 1953; vol. ii, 1955; The Felton Greek Vases, 1958; Phlyax Vases, 1959, 2nd edn 1967; Paestan Addenda, 1960; Apulian Vase Painters of the Plain Style (with A. Cambitoglou), 1962; South Italian Vase Painting (British Museum Guide), 1966; The Red-figured Vases of Lucania, Campania and Sicily, 1967, Supplement I, 1970; Greek Vases in the Felton Collection, 1968; Greek Vases in the Logie Collection, Christchurch, NZ, 1970; several articles in learned periodicals. *Recreations:* travel, walking. *Address:* Menzies College, La Trobe University, Bundoora, Vic 3083, Australia.

**TRENT, Group Captain Leonard Henry,** VC 1946; DFC 1940; *b* 14 April 1915; *s* of Leonard Noel Trent, Nelson, New Zealand; British; *m* 1940, Ursula Elizabeth Woolhouse; one *s* two *d*. *Educ:* Nelson Coll., NZ. Entered firm of W. & R. Fletcher (New Zealand) Ltd 1935; joined RNZAF, 1937; joined RAF 1938. Arrived in England, 1938; served War, 1939-43, France and England (POW 1943); transferred to RNZAF, 1944; transferred back to RAF, 1947, Permanent Commission. Formerly: OC 214 Valiant Sqdn, RAF Marham; Trg HQ No. 3 Gp, Mildenhall, 1948-59; Comdg RAF Wittering, 1959-62; Asst Air Attaché, Washington, also SASO and Chief Intell. Officer (RAF), 1962-65. ADC to the Queen, 1962-65. *Recreations:* golf, ski-ing, tennis, bridge, shootin' an' fishin'. *Address:* 5 Macleod Road, Applecross, Perth, W Australia.

**TRESIDDER, gerald Charles,** FRCS; Surgeon, Department of Urology of The London Hospital, E1, since 1951; also Lecturer in Surgery, The London Hospital Medical College; *b* Rawalpindi, 5 Dec. 1912; *s* of late Lt-Col A. G. Tresidder, CIE, MD, FRCS; *m* 1940, Ida Marguerite Livingston Bell; one *s* two *d*. *Educ:* Haileybury College; University of London, Queen Mary College and The London Hospital Medical College. LRCP, MRCS 1937; MB, BS London 1938; FRCS 1946. Resident appointments at The London Hospital, 1937-39. Surgical Specialist, Major, Indian Medical Service, 1940-46. Postgraduate appointments at The London Hospital and Demonstrator of Anatomy at The London Hospital Medical College, 1946-48; Sen. Assistant to Surgical Unit, 1948-51. FRSM. Member of Internat. Soc. of Urology; Mem. of British Assoc. of Urological Surgeons; Member of International Fertility Association. *Publications:* contributions to: Rob and Smith's Clinical Surgery and

Operative Surgery; British Jl of Surgery; British Jl of Urology; Lancet. *Recreations:* walking and talking. *Address:* The London Hospital, E1. *T:* 01-247 5454. *Club:* Oriental.

**TRESS, Ronald Charles,** CBE 1968; BSc (Econ.) London, DSc Bristol; Master of Birkbeck College, University of London, since 1968; Development Commissioner since 1959; *b* Upchurch, Sittingbourne, Kent, 11 Jan. 1915; *er s* of S. C. Tress; *m* 1942, Josephine Kelly, *d* of H. J. Medland; one *s* two *d. Educ:* Gillingham (Kent) County School; Univ. College, Southampton. Gladstone Student, St Deiniol's Library, Hawarden, 1936-37; Drummond Fraser Research Fellow, Univ. of Manchester, 1937-38; Asst Lecturer in Economics, Univ. Coll. of the S West, Exeter, 1938-41; Economic Asst, War Cabinet Offices, 1941-45; Economic Adviser, Cabinet Secretariat, 1945-47; Reader in Public Finance, Univ. of London, 1947-51; Prof. of Political Economy, Univ. of Bristol, 1951-68. Managing Editor, London and Cambridge Economic Service, 1949-51; Member: Reorganisation Commn for Pigs and Bacon, 1955-56; Nigeria Fiscal Commn, 1957-58; Departmental Cttee on Rating of Charities, 1958; Financial Enquiry, Aden Colony, 1959; East Africa Economic and Fiscal Commn, 1960, Uganda Fiscal Commn, 1962; Kenya Fiscal Commn (Chm.), 1962-63; National Incomes Commn, 1963-65. SW Economic Planning Council (Chm.), 1965-68; Mem. Council, Royal Econ. Soc., 1960-70. *Publications:* articles and reviews in Economic Journal, Economica, LCES Bulletin, etc. *Address:* Birkbeck College, Malet Street, WC1E 7HX; 22 The Beach, Walmer, Deal, Kent. *T:* Deal 3254.

**TRETHOWAN, (James) Ian (Raley);** Managing Director Radio, BBC, since 1969; *b* 20 Oct. 1922; *s* of Major J. J. R. Trethowan, MBE and late Mrs R. Trethowan; *m* 1963, Carolyn Reynolds; three *d. Educ:* Christ's Hospital. Entered Journalism, 1939. Fleet Air Arm, 1941-46. Political Corresp., Yorkshire Post, 1947-55; News Chronicle, 1955-57; Dep. Editor Political Editor, Independent Television News, 1958-63; joined BBC, 1963, as Commentator on Politics and Current Affairs; Political Commentator: The Economist, 1953-58, 1965-67; The Times, 1967-68. *Address:* 15 Pembroke Square, W8. *T:* 01-937 4489. *Clubs:* Travellers', MCC.

**TREVASKIS, Sir (Gerald) Kennedy (Nicholas),** KCMG 1963 (CMG 1959); OBE 1948; *b* 1 Jan. 1915; *s* of late Rev. Hugh Kennedy Trevaskis; *m* 1945, Sheila James Harrington, *d* of Col F. T. Harrington; two *s* one *d. Educ:* Summer Fields, Marlborough; King's College, Cambridge. Entered Colonial Service, 1938, as Administrative Cadet, N Rhodesia. Enlisted N Rhodesia Regt 1939; captured by Italian Forces Tug Aqan, Br. Somaliland, 1940 and POW until 1941. Seconded British Military Administration, Eritrea, 1941-48 (Lt-Col) and British Administration, 1948-50; Senior Divisional Officer, Assab, 1943; Serae, 1944; Western Province, 1946; Political Secretary, 1950. Member British delegation four Power Commission ex-Italian Colonies, 1947-48 and Liaison Officer, United Nations Commission, Eritrea, 1950. N Rhodesia, 1950-51; District Commissioner, Ndola. Political Officer, Western Aden Protectorate, 1951, Deputy British Agent, 1952, Adviser and British Agent, 1954; High Commissioner for Aden and the Protectorate of South Arabia, 1963-65 (Deputy High Commissioner, Jan.-Aug. 1963). Member British Delegation, Anglo-Yemeni meeting in London, 1957. Chm. Middle East Financial Services. Governor, Summer Fields, 1966-. *Publications:* A Colony in transition: the British occupation of Eritrea, 1941-52, 1960; Shades of Amber: A South Arabian Episode, 1968. *Recreations:* beagling, gardening. *Address:* The Old Vicarage, Warnham, Sussex. *T:* Horsham 61700. *Club:* Bath.

**TREVELYAN,** family name of **Baron Trevelyan.**

**TREVELYAN,** Baron *cr* 1968 (Life Peer); **Humphrey Trevelyan,** GCMG 1965 (KCMG 1955; CMG 1951); CIE 1947; OBE 1941; *b* 27 Nov. 1905; 2nd *s* of late Rev. George Philip Trevelyan; *m* 1937, Violet Margaret, *d* of late Gen. Sir William H. Bartholomew, GCB, CMG, DSO; two *d. Educ:* Lancing; Jesus College, Cambridge Univ. (Hon. Fellow, 1968). Entered Indian Civil Service, 1929; Indian Political Service, 1932-47. Served as Political Agent in the Indian States; Washington, 1944; Joint Sec. to Govt of India in External Affairs Dept, 1946; retired from Indian Political Service and entered Foreign (later Diplomatic) Service, 1947; Counsellor in Baghdad, 1948; Economic and Financial Adviser, UK High Commission for Germany, 1951-53; HM Chargé d'Affaires in Peking, 1953-55; Ambassador to Egypt, 1955-56; Under-Sec. at UN, 1958; Ambassador to Iraq, 1958-61; Deputy Under-Secretary of State, Foreign Office, 1962; Ambassador to the USSR, 1962-65, retd. High Commissioner in South Arabia, 1967. Director: British Petroleum Company; British Bank of the Middle East; General Electric and English Electric Cos Ltd; President, Council of Foreign Bondholders. Chm. of Trustees, British Museum, 1970-; Chm., RIIA, 1970-; Chm., British Group, Anglo-Soviet Consultative Commn. Hon. LLD, Cambridge, 1970. *Publication:* The Middle East in Revolution, 1970. *Address:* 13 Wilton Street, SW1. *Club:* Brooks's.

**TREVELYAN, Sir George (Lowthian),** 4th Bt, *cr* 1874; Warden, Shropshire Adult College, Attingham Park, Shrewsbury, since 1947; *b* 5 Nov. 1906; *e s* of Rt Hon. Sir C. P. Trevelyan, 3rd Bt; *S* father 1958; *m* 1940, Editha Helen, *d* of Col John Lindsay-Smith; one adopted *d. Educ:* Sidcot School; Trinity College, Cambridge. Worked as artist-craftsman with Peter Waals workshops, fine furniture, 1930-31. Trained and worked in F. M. Alexander re-education method, 1932-36. Taught at Gordonstoun School and Abinger Hill School, 1936-41. Served in Rifle Brigade, 1941-45 (Captain). Taught No. 1 Army Coll., Newbattle Abbey, 1945-47. *Recreations:* countryside, climbing, crafts. *Heir: b* Geoffrey Washington Trevelyan [*b* 4 July 1920; *m* 1947, Gillian Isabel, *d* of late Alexander Wood; one *s* one *d*]. *Address:* Attingham Park, Shrewsbury. *T:* Upton Magna 255.

**TREVELYAN, Julian Otto;** painter and etcher; *b* 20 Feb. 1910; *s* of late R. C. Trevelyan; *m* 1934, Ursula Darwin (divorced, 1950); one *s*; *m* 1951, Mary Fedden. *Educ:* Bedales; Trinity College, Cambridge. Studied art in Paris, Atelier 17, 1930-33; has since lived and worked in Hammersmith. One man exhibns at Lefèvre Gall., 1935, 1938, 1942, 1943, 1944, 1946, 1948 and at Gimpel Fils, 1950, Redfern Gall., 1952, Zwemmer Gall., 1955, 1958, 1960, 1963, 1966, 1967, Galerie de France, Paris, 1947, St George's Gall., 1959. Pictures in public and private collections in England, America, Sweden, France, Eire and the USSR. Served War of 1939-45, as Camouflage Officer in Roy. Engineers, 1940-43. Engraving tutor at the Royal College of Art, 1955-63. *Publications:* Indigo Days, 1957; The Artist and His World, 1960; Etching (Studio Books), 1963. *Recreation:* sailing on the Thames. *Address:*

Durham Wharf, Hammersmith Terrace, W6. *T:* 01-748 2749.

**TREVELYAN, Mary,** CBE 1968 (OBE 1956); ARCM, ARCO; Founder and Governor, International Students' House, London; *e d* of late Rev. G. P. Trevelyan. *Educ:* Grovely College, Boscombe; Royal College of Music, London (Exhibitioner and George Carter Scholar). Musical posts included: organist and choirtrainer, St Barnabas, Oxford, music staff of Radley College and Marlborough College; conductor Chelsea Madrigal Society and Kensington Choral Society. Travelled from Ceylon to Kashmir, 1930-31; Warden of Student Movement House (international house for University students) London, 1932-46. Travelled to Far East, 1936-37, to study problems concerning migration of students from east to west for study and the effects on their return home; also visited USA to study work of the International Houses. Served on Programme Staff of YMCA with BLA in Belgium and France, Oct. 1944-June 1945; Head of Field Survey Bureau, Reconstruction Section, Paris, and made surveys on post-war priority needs in educn in Greece, the East and Far East, 1946-48; first Adviser to Overseas Students, Univ. of London, 1949-65; British Council Lecture Tour in W and E Africa, 1954; first Dir, Internat. Students House, London, 1965-67. Survey Tours, on Ford Foundn award, to univs and internat. centres in USA, Canada, Australia, NZ, the East, Far East and Middle East, 1967-69. Mem. Bd of Governors, Overseas Service Coll., 1966-70. *Publications:* From the Ends of the Earth, 1942; I'll Walk Beside You, 1946. *Recreation:* music. *Address:* Flat 5, 23 Embankment Gardens, Chelsea, SW3. *T:* 01-352 6773.

**TREVELYAN, Sir Willoughby John,** 9th Bt, *cr* 1662; *b* 16 April 1902; *s* of 8th Bt and Alice Edith Money, *y d* of late W. J. Money, CSI; *S* father, 1931. *Heir: kinsman* Norman Irving Trevelyan [*b* 29 Jan. 1915; *m* 1951, Jennifer Mary, *d* of Arthur E. Riddett, Burgh Heath, Surrey; two *s* one *d*]. *Address:* Old Manor House, Salisbury, Wilts.

**TREVELYAN OMAN, Julia;** *see* Oman.

**TREVETHIN,** 3rd Baron *cr* 1921 **and Oaksey,** 1st Baron, *cr* 1947; **Geoffrey Lawrence,** PC 1944; Kt 1932; DSO 1918; TD; (to be known as Lord Oaksey); Vice-Lieutenant of Wiltshire since 1954; *b* 1880; *y s* of 1st Baron Trevethin; *S* brother 1959, in Trevethin Barony, and assumed double title; *m* 1921, Marjorie, *yr d* of late Comdr Chas. N. Robinson, RN, retd; one *s* three *d*. *Educ:* Haileybury; New Coll., Oxford (Hon. Fellow, 1944). Hon. DCL 1947. Barrister, Inner Temple, 1906; KC 1925; Attorney-General to the Prince of Wales and a member of the Council, 1928-32; Recorder of Oxford, 1924-32; Judge of High Court of Justice, King's Bench Division, 1932-44; a Lord Justice of Appeal, 1944-47; a Lord of Appeal in Ordinary, 1947-57; Counsel to the Jockey Club, 1922-32; Examiner in Ecclesiastical Causes, 1927-32; JP Wilts, 1924; DL Wilts, 1945; Chairman Quarter Sessions, 1945-55; served Herts RFA European War, 1914-18 (despatches twice, DSO); commanded 86th Bde RA, TA, 1919-26; Bt Col, 1925; Col, 1926. British President of International Tribunal Nuremberg, 1945. President, British Dairy Farmers' Assoc., 1953; Treasurer, Inner Temple, 1955. *Heir: s* Hon. John Geoffrey Tristram Lawrence [*b* 21 March 1929; *m* 1959, Victoria Mary, *er d* of Major John Dennistoun, Letcombe Regis, Berkshire; one *s* one *d*]. *Address:* Hill Farm, Oaksey, Malmesbury. *T:* Crudwell 214. *Club:* Brooks's.
*See also P. G. D. Adams.*

**TREVOR,** 4th Baron *cr* 1880; **Charles Edwin Hill-Trevor,** JP; *b* 13 Aug. 1928; *e s* of 3rd Baron and Phyllis May, 2nd *d* of J. A. Sims, Ings House, Kirton-in-Lindsey, Lincolnshire; *S* father, 1950; *m* 1967, Susan Janet Elizabeth, *o d* of Dr Ronald Bence; one *s*. *Educ:* Shrewsbury. CStJ. *Heir: s* Hon. Mark Charles Hill-Trevor, *b* 8 Jan. 1970. *Address:* Brynkinalt, Chirk, Wrexham. *T:* Chirk 3425.

**TREVOR, Sir Cecil Russell,** Kt, *cr* 1950; CIE 1946; retired; *b* 20 Feb. 1899; *s* of James and Isabel Mary Trevor. *Educ:* St Xavier's College, Bruges, Belgium. Served European War, 1914-18, as Lieut King's Liverpool Regt; joined Imperial Bank of India, 1921; Chief Accountant, Reserve Bank of India, 1935; Deputy Governor, Reserve Bank of India, 1943-50. *Recreations:* golf, bridge. *Clubs:* Oriental; Bengal (Calcutta); Royal Bombay Yacht (Bombay).

**TREVOR, David;** Orthopædic Surgeon, Charing Cross Hospital; Senior Surgeon Royal National Orthopædic Hospital; late Orthopædic Surgeon, West Herts Hospital; *b* 24 July 1906; *m* 1935, Kathleen Fairfax Blyth; two *d*. *Educ:* Tregaron County School; St Bartholomew's Hospital Medical College; Charing Cross Hospital (Post Graduate). MRCS, LRCP 1931; MB, BS London 1931; FRCS 1932; MS London, University Medal, 1934. Fellow, Internat. Soc. Orthop. and Traumatology, 1951. Past Pres., Orthopædic Section, RSocMed; late Examr in Surgery, Univ. of London; Mem. Council, RCS (Hunterian Prof., 1968; late Mem. Court of Examrs); Vice-Pres., British Orthopædic Assoc. *Publications:* contributor to BMJ, Journal of Bone and Joint Surgery, Proc. RSM, Annals RCS. *Recreations:* golf, shooting. *Address:* 48 Wimpole Street, W1. *T:* 01-935 3380.

**TREVOR, Elleston;** author; *b* Bromley, Kent, 17 Feb. 1920; *m* 1947, Iris May Burgess; one *s*. *Educ:* Sevenoaks. Apprenticed as a racing driver upon leaving school, 1938. Served in Royal Air Force, War of 1939-45. Began writing professionally in 1945. Dir, Picturemakers Ltd. Member: Writers' Guild of GB; Authors' Guild of America, British Interplanetary Soc. *Publications:* Chorus of Echoes, 1950 (filmed); Tiger Street, 1950; Redfern's Miracle, 1951; The Passion and the Pity, 1951; A Blaze of Roses, 1952; The Big Pick-up, 1953 (filmed); Squadron Airborne, 1954; The Killing Ground, 1955; Gale Force, 1956 (filmed) The Pillars of Midnight, 1957 (filmed); The VIP, 1959 (filmed); The Billboard Madonna, 1960; The Burning Shore, 1961; The Flight of the Phœnix, 1964 (filmed); The Shoot, 1966; The Freebooters, 1967 (filmed); A Place for the Wicked, 1968; Bury Him Among Kings, 1970. Under pseudonym Adam Hall: Volcanoes of San Domingo, 1964; The Quiller Memorandum, 1964 (filmed); The 9th Directive, 1966; The Striker Portfolio, 1969. Under pseudonym Caesar Smith: Heatwave, 1957 (filmed); under pseudonym Roger Fitzalan: A Blaze of Arms, 1967. *Recreations:* chess, reading, travelling, astronomy. *Address:* Domaine de Chateauneuf, Valbonne (AM), France. *T:* Opio 67.63.61.

**TREVOR, Kenneth Rowland Swetenham,** CBE 1964 (OBE 1952); DSO 1945; Brigadier (retired 1966); *b* 15 April 1914; 2nd *s* of late Mr and Mrs E. S. R. Trevor, formerly of The Acres, Upton Heath, Chester; *m* 1941, Margaret Baynham, *er d* of late Reverend J. H. Baynham, ACG; two *s*. *Educ:* Rossall; RMC, Camberley. Joined 22nd (Cheshire) Regt, 1934; served in India and with RWAFF in Nigeria. War of 1939-45 (despatches and DSO): No. 1 Commando, N Africa and Burma, 1941-45, as CO, 1943-45; Staff College, Camberley, 1945-46; Bde Major, 29 Infantry Brigade Group, 1949-51; served Korea, 1950-51 (despatches, OBE); GSO1 and Chief Instructor, RMA, Sandhurst, 1954-56; Commanded 1st Bn Cheshire Regt, 1956-58; Malaya, 1957-58 (despatches); Deputy Commander, 50 Infantry Brigade Group/Central Area, Cyprus, 1959; Brigade Col Mercian Brigade, 1960-61; Commander, 2 Infantry Brigade Group and Devon/Cornwall Sub District, 1961-64; Commander, British Guiana Garrison, 1963; Inspector of Boys' Training (Army), 1964-66; Vice-Pres., The Commando Assoc. *Recreation:* golf. *Address:* Barrelwell Hill, Chester. *Club:* Army and Navy.

**TREVOR, Meriol;** Author; *b* 15 April 1919; *d* of Lt-Col Arthur Prescott Trevor and Lucy M. E. Trevor (*née* Dimmock). *Educ:* Perse Girls' Sch., Cambridge; St Hugh's Coll., Oxford. FRSL. *Publications: novels:* The Last of Britain, 1956; The New People, 1957; A Narrow Place, 1958; Shadows and Images, 1960; The City and the World, 1970; *poems:* Midsummer, Midwinter, 1957; *biography:* Newman: The Pillar of the Cloud, 1962; Newman: Light in Winter, 1962; Apostle of Rome, 1966; Pope John, 1967; Prophets and Guardians, 1969; also books for children. *Address:* 70 Pulteney Street, Bath, Somerset BA2 4DL.

**TREVOR, William, (William Trevor Cox);** Writer; *b* 24 May 1928; *er s* of J. W. Cox; *m* 1952, Jane, *yr d* of C. N. Ryan; two *s*. *Educ:* St Columba's College, Co. Dublin; Trinity College, Dublin. *Publications:* A Standard of Behaviour, 1956; The Old Boys, 1964 (Hawthornden Prize); The Boarding-House, 1965; The Love Department, 1966; The Day We Got Drunk on Cake, 1967; Mrs Eckdorf in O'Neill's Hotel, 1969. *Address:* 19 Langside Avenue, SW15; Stentwood House, Dunkeswell, Honiton, Devon.

**TREVOR COX, Major Horace Brimson,** *o s* of late C. Horace Cox, Roche Old Court, Winterslow, Wilts and formerly of Whitby Hall, nr Chester; *m* 1957, Gwenda Mary, *d* of Alfred Ellis, Woodford, Essex; one *d*. *Educ:* Eton; Germany and USA. Major late Welsh Guards (SR); served in France with BEF, 1939-40, and on General Staff, 1940-44; Major AA Comd. HQ, 1944-46, RARO, 1946-61. Studied commercial and political conditions in Germany, 1927-29, in America and Canada, 1929-30, and in Near East (Egypt and Palestine), 1934; contested (C) NE Derbyshire, 1935, Stalybridge and Hyde, 1937; MP (C) County of Chester, Stalybridge and Hyde, 1937-45; Parliamentary Private Secretary to: Rt Hon. Sir Ronald Cross when Under-Secretary Board of Trade, 1938-39, and when Minister of Economic Warfare, 1939-40; Minister of Health Rt Hon. H. U. Willink, 1945. Hon. Treasr, Russian Relief Assoc., 1945-47. Contested (C) Stalybridge and Hyde, 1945, Birkenhead, 1950; Parly Candidate (C) for Romford and Brentwood, Essex, 1953-55; contested (Ind) Salisbury by-election, 1965; later joined Labour Party; contested (Lab) RDC, Wilts, 1970. Member of Exec. County Committee, British Legion, Wilts, 1946-62; Chm., Salisbury and S Wilts Branch, English-Speaking Union, 1957-63; Mem. Exec. Cttee, CLA, for Wilts, Hants, IoW and Berks. Farmer and landowner. Lord of Manor of East Winterslow. *Address:* Roche Old Court, Winterslow, Wilts. *Clubs:* St James', Guards, English-Speaking Union.

**TREVOR JONES, Alan;** *see* Jones.

**TREVOR-ROPER, Hugh Redwald;** Regius Professor of Modern History, Oxford, since 1957; *b* 15 January 1914; *er s* of Dr B. W. E. Trevor-Roper, Glanton and Alnwick, Northumberland; *m* 1954, Lady Alexandra Howard-Johnston, *e d* of late Field-Marshal Earl Haig, KT, GCB, OM. *Educ:* Charterhouse; Christ Church, Oxford. 1st Class Hon. Mods, 1934, Mod. Hist., 1936; Craven Scholar, 1934; Hertford Scholar, 1935; Ireland Scholar, 1935; Research Fellow Merton Coll., 1937-39. Student of Christ Church, Oxford, 1946-57; Censor 1947-52. *Publications:* Archbishop Laud, 1940; The Last Days of Hitler, 1947; The Gentry, 1540-1640, 1953; (ed) Hitler's Table Talk, 1953; (ed with J. A. W. Bennett) The Poems of Richard Corbett, 1955; Historical Essays, 1957; (ed) Hitler's War Directives, 1939-45, 1964; (ed) Essays in British History Presented to Sir Keith Feiling, 1964; The Rise of Christian Europe, 1965; Religion, The Reformation and Social Change, 1967; (ed) The Age of Expansion, 1968; The Philby Affair, 1968. *Address:* Oriel College, Oxford; 8 St Aldate's, Oxford; Chiefswood, Melrose. *Clubs:* Savile, Beefsteak; New (Edinburgh).

*See also Earl Haig, P. D. Trevor-Roper.*

**TREVOR-ROPER, Patrick Dacre,** MA, MD, BChir Cantab; FRCS, DOMS England; Consultant Ophthalmic Surgeon: Westminster Hospital, since 1947; Moorfields Eye Hospital; King Edward VII Hospital for Officers; Teacher of Ophthalmology, University of London; *b* 1916; *yr s* of Dr B. W. E. Trevor-Roper, Alnwick, Northumberland; unmarried. *Educ:* Charterhouse (senior classical schol.); Clare Coll., Cambridge (exhibitioner); Westminster Hospital Medical Sch. (scholar). Served as Captain, NZ Medical Corps, 1943-46, in Central Mediterranean Forces. Held resident appointments, Westminster Hospital and Moorfields Eye Hospital. Examiner for diploma of Ophthalmology, RCS. Member: Ophth. Group Cttee, BMA; Ophth. Services Cttee, London Exec. Council; London Med. Cttee. FRSocMed; FZS; Hon. Member Brazilian Society of Ophthalmology, 1958; Hon. dipl., Peruvian and Columbian Societies of Otolaryngology and Ophthalmology, 1958; President, etc., of various clubs in connection with sports, music and drama, both hospital and county. *Publications:* (ed) Music at Court (Four 18th century studies by A. Yorke-Long), 1954; Ophthalmology, a Textbook for Diploma Students, 1955 and 1962; Lecture-notes in Ophthalmology, 1959, 1965, 1968; (ed) International Ophthalmology Clinics VIII, 1962; The World Through Blunted Sight: an inquiry into the effects of disordered vision on character and art, 1970; miscellaneous articles in medical and other journals; Editor, trans. Ophthalmological Society UK, 1949-. *Recreations:* music, travel. *Address:* 3 Park Square West, Regents Park, NW1. *T:* 01-935 5052; Long Crichel House, near Wimborne, Dorset. *Clubs:* Athenæum, Beefsteak.

*See also H. R. Trevor-Roper.*

**TREW, Peter John Edward,** MICE; MP (C) Dartford since 1970; *b* 30 April 1932; *s* of Antony Trew, DSC; *m* 1955, Angela, *d* of Kenneth Rush, CBE; two *s* one *d*. *Educ:* Diocesan Coll., Rondebosch, Cape. Royal Navy, 1950-54. Awarded Chartered Inst of Secretaries Sir Ernest Clarke Prize, 1955. Director: Rush & Tompkins Developments Ltd, 1965-; Rush & Tompkins Ltd, 1968-. Contested (C) Dartford, Gen. Elec., 1966. Admitted as AMICE, 1963. *Address:* Great Oaks, Shipbourne, Kent. *Club:* Naval and Military.

**TREWBY, Rear-Adm. George Francis Allan;** Assistant Controller (Polaris), Ministry of Defence, 1968-71; *b* Simonstown, S Africa, 8 July 1917; *s* of late Vice-Admiral G. Trewby, CMG, DSO, and of Dorothea Trewby (*née* Allan); *m* 1942, Sandra Coleridge Stedham; two *s*. *Educ:* RNC, Dartmouth; RNEC, Keyham; RNC, Greenwich. Naval Cadet, Dartmouth, 1931 (King's Dirk, 1934). Served in HMS: Frobisher, Barham, Nelson, Duke of York, Dido, Cadiz, Albion. Comdg Officer, HMS Sultan, 1963-64; IDC, 1965; Captain of Naval Base, Portland, 1966-68. Commander, 1950; Captain, 1959; Rear-Admiral, 1968. CEng; FIMechE; MIMarE; MRINA; Akroyd Stuart Award of InstMarE for 1954-55. *Recreations:* swimming; Past Captain Navy Athletics Team. *Address:* 49 St Mary Abbots Terrace, Kensington, W14. *T:* 01-602 3098. *Club:* Army and Navy.

**TREWIN, John Courtenay;** FRSL; dramatic critic and author; *b* 4 Dec. 1908; *o s* of Captain John Trewin, The Lizard, Cornwall, and Annie (*née* James); *m* 1938, Wendy Monk; two *s*. *Educ:* Plymouth Coll. Editorial Staff: Western Independent, 1926-32; The Morning Post, London, 1932-37; second dramatic critic, 1934-37. Contributor to The Observer, 1937-; editorial staff, 1942-53; Literary Editor, 1943-48; second dramatic critic, 1943-53. Dramatic critic: Punch, 1944-45; John o' London's, 1945-54; The Illustrated London News, 1946-; The Sketch, 1947-59; The Lady, 1949-; The Birmingham Post, 1955-; Radio-drama critic, of The Listener, 1951-57; Editor: The West Country Magazine, 1946-52; Plays of the Year series (39 vols), 1948-; The Year's Work in the Theatre (for the British Council), 1949-51. President, The Critics' Circle, 1964-65; Chairman, W Country Writers' Assoc., 1964-. *Publications:* The Shakespeare Memorial Theatre, 1932; The English Theatre, 1948; Up From The Lizard, 1948; We'll Hear a Play, 1949; (with H. J. Willmott) London-Bodmin, 1950; Stratford-upon-Avon, 1950; The Theatre Since 1900, 1951; The Story of Bath, 1951; Drama 1945-50, 1951; Down To The Lion, 1952; (with E. M. King) Printer to the House, 1952; A Play To-night, 1952; (with T. C. Kemp) The Stratford Festival, 1953; Dramatists of Today, 1953; Edith Evans, 1954; (ed.) Theatre Programme, 1954; Mr Macready, 1955; Sybil Thorndike, 1955; Verse Drama Since 1900, 1956; Paul Scofield, 1956; The Night Has Been Unruly, 1957; Alec Clunes, 1958; The Gay Twenties: A Decade of the Theatre, 1958; Benson and the Bensonians, 1960; The Turbulent Thirties, 1960; A Sword for A Prince, 1960; John Neville, 1961; The Birmingham Repertory Theatre, 1963; Shakespeare on the English Stage, 1900-1964, 1964; completion of Lamb's Tales, 1964; Drama in Britain, 1951-64, 1965; (with H. F. Rubinstein) The Drama Bedside Book, 1966; (ed.) Macready's Journals, 1967; Robert Donat, 1968; The Pomping Folk, 1968; Shakespeare's Country, 1970; (with Arthur Colby Sprague) Shakespeare's Plays Today, 1970; Peter Brook, 1971; ed several other books. *Recreation:* all things Cornish: a Bard of the Cornish Gorsedd (Den an Lesard). *Address:* 15 Eldon Grove, Hampstead, NW3. *T:* 01-435 0207. *Club:* Garrick.

**TRIBE, Rear-Admiral Raymond Haydn,** CB 1954; MBE 1944; *b* 9 April 1908; *s* of Thomas and Gillian Ada Tribe; *m* 1938, Alice Mary (*née* Golby); no *c*. Served War of 1939-45 (MBE, despatches twice). Commander, 1947; Captain, 1955; Rear-Admiral, 1962. Inspector-General, Fleet Maintenance, and Chief Staff Officer (Technical) to C-in-C Home Fleet, 1962-65; retired from Royal Navy, Sept. 1965. Distinguished Battle Service Medal of Soviet Union, 1943. *Recreations:* gardening, painting. *Address:* Oak Cottage, Compton, near Newbury, Berks. *T:* Compton, Berks, 253. *Clubs:* United Service; Royal Naval (Portsmouth).

**TRILLING, Lionel;** American Author; University Professor, Columbia University, USA, since 1970; *b* 4 July 1905; *s* of David W. and Fannie Cohen Trilling; *m* 1929, Diana Rubin; one *s*. *Educ:* Columbia Univ. AB, MA, PhD. Instructor: University of Wisconsin, 1926-27; Hunter Coll., 1927-32; Columbia University: Instructor, 1932-39, Asst Professor, 1939-45, Assoc. Professor, 1945-48, Professor, 1948-65, George Edward Woodberry Prof. of Literature and Criticism, 1964-70. George Eastman Vis. Prof., Oxford, 1964-65; Charles Eliot Norton Vis. Prof. of Poetry, Harvard Univ., 1969-70. Senior Fellow of School of Letters, Indiana Univ. Member: Nat. Inst. of Arts and Letters, 1951; American Acad. of Arts and Sciences, 1952. Hon. DLitt: Trinity Coll., Hartford, Conn., 1955; Harvard Univ., 1962; Case Western Reserve Univ., 1968; Hon. LHD Northwestern Univ., 1963. Creative Arts Award, Brandeis Univ., 1968. *Publications:* Matthew Arnold, 1939; E. M. Forster, 1944; The Middle of the Journey, 1948; The Liberal Imagination, 1950; The Opposing Self, 1955 (all dates of English publications); Freud and the Crisis of Our Culture, 1955 (US); A Gathering of Fugitives, 1956 (US), 1957 (England); Beyond Culture, 1965 (US), 1966 (Eng.); edited: The Portable Matthew Arnold, 1949; The Letters of John Keats, 1950; stories and essays to Partisan Review, Kenyon Review, The Nation, etc. *Address:* Hamilton Hall, Columbia University, New York, NY 10027, USA. *Clubs:* Athenæum; Century (New York).

**TRILLO, Rt. Rev. Albert John;** *see* Hertford, Bishop Suffragan of.

**TRIMBLE, Brigadier (retired) Arthur Philip,** CBE 1961; Deputy Surgeon, The Royal Hospital, Chelsea; Consultant Physician, Army Medical Services; *b* 21 Aug. 1909; *s* of Melville and Florence Trimble, Holywood, Co. Down, N. Ireland; *m* 1952, Felicia, *d* of W. H. Friend, Bures, Suffolk; two *s*. *Educ:* St Columba's Coll., Co. Dublin; Queen's Univ., Belfast. MB 1931; MD; FRCPE. Joined RAMC, 1931. Served in Syrian, Western Desert, and Italian Campaigns, 1939-45; SMO 2nd Armoured Brigade. Consultant Physician: FarELF, 1953-56; BAOR, 1957-62; Near ELF, 1963. *Publications:* various articles on tropical diseases and diseases of children in Proc. Royal Society Med., Trans. Royal Society of Tropical Med., Archives of Disease in Childhood and Journal of RAMC. *Recreation:* golf. *Address:* Light House Court, The Royal Hospital, Chelsea, SW3.

**TRIMLESTOWN,** 19th Baron *cr* 1461; **Charles Aloysius Barnewall;** *b* 2 June 1899; *o surv s* of 18th Baron and Margaret (*d* 1901), *d* of R. J. Stephens, Brisbane, Queensland; *S* father, 1937; *m* 1st, 1926, Muriel (*d* 1937), *o c* of Edward Oskar Schneider, Mansfield Lodge, Whalley Range, Manchester; two *s* one *d*; 2nd, 1952, Freda Kathleen Watkins. *Educ:* Ampleforth. Lieut, Irish Guards, 1918; served European War. *Heir:* *s* Hon. Anthony Edward Barnewall [*b* 2 Feb. 1928; *m* 1963, Lorna Margaret Marion Ramsay, *d* of late Douglas Ramsay and Mrs Richard Herbert]. *Address:* c/o Provincial Bank of Ireland, Cork.

**TRIMMER, Sir George (William Arthur),** Kt 1937; MInstCE; FIMechE; MInstT; Ministry of Supply, retired; *b* 12 Feb. 1882; *e s* of late Rev. G. J. Trimmer, Ceylon, and Caroline

Elizabeth, *d* of late Rev. W. S. Bestall; *m* 1939, Phyllis Primrose, *widow* of Colonel B. H. Beaumont-Checkland, MC, Sherwood Foresters, and *d* of Edward Hodgson, Beverley, Yorks. *Educ:* Harrogate Coll., Yorks; Kingswood Sch., Bath. Pupil of Pulsometer Engineering Co., Reading; Engineer in charge Mugra Hat. Bengal and Mon Canals Burma Irrigation construction, 1904-10; Construction of Empire Dock and reconstruction Wharves Singapore with Topham Jones and Railton, 1911-18; Assistant General Manager and Local Chairman Singapore Harbour Board, 1919; Chairman, General Manager and Chief Engineer Singapore and Penang Harbour Boards, Straits Settlements, 1923-39; Director of Building Construction, 1940-43; Controller Building Construction, 1943-47, Adviser Building Constr. (part time), 1947-56, Ministry of Supply. *Recreations:* riding, golf, and tennis. *Address:* Croft Point, Links Road, Bramley, near Guildford, Surrey. *T:* Bramley 2389. *Clubs:* Junior Carlton, East India and Sports, Royal Automobile.

**TRINDER, Sir (Arnold) Charles,** GBE 1969; Kt 1966; Chairman: Trinder Anderson & Co. Ltd, The Australind Steam Shipping Co. Ltd; *b* 12 May 1906; *s* of Arnold Anderson Trinder, Oxshott; *m* 1st, 1929, Elizabeth Cairns; one *d*; 2nd, 1937, Elaine Chaytor; two *d. Educ:* Wellington Coll.; Clare Coll., Cambridge (MA (Hons)). Entered Trinder Anderson & Co., 1927. Member, Baltic Exchange, 1928; Common Councilman, 1951; Alderman of Aldgate, 1959; Sheriff, City of London, 1964; Lord Mayor of London for 1968-69. Member: Governing Body, School of Oriental and African Studies; Board of Governors, Museum of London; Court, The City University (Chancellor, 1968-69). Member, Court of Assistants, Worshipful Company of Shipwrights, 1963; Master, Worshipful Company of Fletchers, 1966. FICS 1963. Hon. DSc, City Univ., 1968. KStJ 1969. Order of Merit, Chile, 1965; Nat. Order of Niger, 1969; Order of Merit, Italy, 1969; Order of Lion of Finland, 1969. *Publication:* O Men of Athens, 1946. *Recreations:* gardening, astronomy, ancient history, logodaedaly. *Address:* 12-20 Camomile Street, EC2. *T:* 01-283 7301. *Clubs:* Royal Automobile, City Livery, Guildhall; Royal Solent Yacht.

**TRINDER, Sir Charles;** *see* Trinder, Sir A. C.

**TRINDER, Air Vice-Marshal Frank Noel,** CB 1949; CBE 1944; psa; *b* 24 Dec. 1895; *s* of Alfred Probus Trinder, MRCS, LRCP, Parkstone, Dorset; *m* 1925, Marjorie Agnes Scott, *d* of Archie Scott Blake, Melrose, Scotland; one *s. Educ:* Epsom College. Served European War, 1914-18, with North Staffordshire Regt, 1915-17; France, 1915 (wounded); Lieut, 1916; transferred to RFC, 1917. Egypt, 1917-20; Iraq, 1920; Air Ministry, 1921-28; Staff College, 1929; Headquarters, India, 1930-35; Wing Commander, 1937; War of 1939-45 (despatches, CBE); Group Captain, 1940; Headquarters, Far East, 1938-40; USA, 1940-43; Air Commodore, 1943; Cossac Staff, 1943-44; SHAEF, 1944-45; Air Div. CCG, 1945-46; Senior Air Staff Officer, Headquarters Maintenance Command, 1947-49; Director-General of Equipment, Air Ministry, 1949-52; retired, 1952. *Address:* c/o Lloyds Bank, Ltd, 6 Pall Mall, SW1; Broom Lodge, Teddington, Middlesex. *Clubs:* Royal Air Force Yacht; British Ski.

**TRING, A. Stephen;** *see* Meynell, L. W.

**TRIPP, John Peter;** HM Diplomatic Service; Ambassador to Libya, since 1970; *b* 27 March 1921; *s* of Charles Howard and Constance Tripp; *m* 1948, Rosemary Rees Jones; one *s* one *d. Educ:* Bedford Sch.; Sutton Valence Sch.; L'Institut de Touraine. Served War of 1939-45: Royal Marines, 1941-46. Sudan Political Service, 1946-54. Foreign (subsequently Diplomatic) Service, 1954-; Political Agent, Trucial States, 1955-58; Head of Chancery, Vienna, 1958-61; Economic Secretary, Residency Bahrain, 1961-63; Counsellor 1963; Political Agent, Bahrain, 1963-65; sabbatical year at Durham Univ., 1965; Amman, 1966-68; Head of Near Eastern Dept, FCO, 1969-70. *Recreations:* theatre, reading, fishing, shooting. *Address:* Tanyffridd, Llanfechain, Montgomeryshire; 30 Ormonde Gate, SW3. *Club:* Travellers'.

**TRIPPE, Juan Terry;** Hon. Chairman, Pan American World Airways Inc. (Chairman, 1964-68); Chairman or Director of other companies; *b* Seabright, New Jersey, USA, June 1899; *s* of Charles White Trippe and Lucy Adeline (*née* Terry); *m* 1928, Betty Stettinius; three *s* one *d. Educ:* Yale Univ. (PhB). With Pan American World Airways Inc., 1927-. Member or Trustee of various organisations and societies. Holds hon. degrees and has had numerous awards. *Address:* Pan Am Building, NYC, USA.

**TRISTRAM, William John,** CBE 1965; JP; Pharmaceutical Chemist; Liverpool City Council, 1934-55 (Alderman, 1944-55); appointed Hon. Alderman, 1964; *b* 6 Oct. 1896; *s* of late Rev. W. J. Tristram and Elizabeth Critchlow; *m* 1966, Philomena Mary Moylan, Drogheda. *Educ:* Scarborough High Sch.; Leeds Central High Sch.; Liverpool College of Pharmacy. Member Council Pharmaceutical Society of Great Britain, 1944-67 (President, 1952-53, FPS, 1966, Gold Medal, 1968); Hon. Treasurer and Member Executive National Pharmaceutical Union, 1936-68 (Chairman, 1943-44); Chairman, Joint Cttee for the Pharmaceutical Service, 1946-52; Member Central Health Services Council (Min. of Health), 1948-64. Vice-Chairman, Standing Pharmaceutical Advisory Cttee (Min. of Health), 1946-48 (Chairman, 1948-59); Chairman, Liverpool Licensing Cttee, 1965-70; Dep. Chairman, South Liverpool Hospitals Management Cttee, 1965-70; Liverpool Exec. Council (Min. of Health), 1948- (Chairman, 1960-64); Chairman, Liverpool Homœopathic Hospital, 1960-70. JP, Liverpool, 1938-; Lord Mayor of Liverpool, 1953-54; Dep. Lord Mayor, 1954-55. *Recreations:* cricket-watching, walking. *Address:* (business) 718 Longmoor Lane, Liverpool 10. *T:* 051-525 2837; Childwall, Westway, Heswall, Cheshire. *T:* 051-342 1678. *Clubs:* National Liberal; Lyceum (Liverpool).

**TRITTON, Arthur Stanley,** MA, DLitt; *b* 1881; *s* of late Rev. William Tritton and Eliza Squire. *Educ:* Mansfield Coll., St Catherine's Society, Oxford; Göttingen. Teacher in the Friends' Sch., Brumana, Mt Lebanon; Assistant in Universities of Edinburgh and Glasgow; Professor of Arabic, Aligarh, UP, India; Professor of Arabic at the School of Oriental and African Studies, University of London, 1938-46; Hon. Fellow, School of Oriental and African Studies, 1946; Professor Emeritus since 1947. Hon. Vice-Pres., Royal Asiatic Soc., 1969. *Publications:* Rise of the Imams of Sanaa, 1925; Caliphs and their Non-Muslim Subjects, 1930, reprinted 1970; Arabic Self Taught; Muslim Theology, 1947; Islam, Beliefs and Practices, 1951; Materials on Muslim Education in the Middle Ages, 1957; articles in various encyclopædias and journals. *Address:* 44 Kensington Gardens Square, W2. *Club:* Athenæum.

**TRITTON, Major Sir Geoffrey Ernest,** 3rd Bt *cr* 1905; CBE 1958 (MBE 1945); DL; Rifle Brigade (TA); *b* 3 Nov. 1900; *s* of Sir Alfred Ernest Tritton, 2nd Bt, and Agneta Elspeth (*d* 1960), *d* of W. M. Campbell; *S* father, 1939; *m* 1925, Mary Patience Winifred, *y d* of late J. Kenneth Foster; one *s* one *d*. *Educ:* Eton; Trinity Coll., Cambridge. Served War of 1939-45 (MBE, French Croix de Guerre, US Bronze Star, Czech. Medal of Merit 1st Class). DL Wiltshire, 1956; High Sheriff of Wiltshire, 1958. *Heir: s* Anthony John Ernest Tritton [*b* 4 March 1927; *m* 1957, Diana, *d* of Rear-Admiral St J. A. Micklethwait, *qv*; one *s* one *d*. *Educ:* Eton. Major, 3rd KO Hussars]. *Address:* Stanton House, Highworth, Wiltshire. *T:* Stratton St Margaret's 3237.

*See also Sir Timothy Harford, Bt, Sir Robert Dent.*

**TRITTON, Julian Seymour,** FICE, FIMechE, MConsE; Consulting Engineer; retired from practice in the firm of Rendel, Palmer & Tritton (Partner, 1929-55; Consultant, 1955-65); *b* Calcutta, 31 Oct. 1889; *er s* of late Sir Seymour Tritton, KBE; *m* 1918, Theodora, *er d* of late Canon W. G. Kerr, Truro; one *s* one *d*. *Educ:* Rugby Sch.; King's Coll., University of London. Served European War, 1914-18; commissioned RE, in Transportation Branch at WO, and later in Afghanistan Campaign; War of 1939-45: Technical Adviser to India Supply Mission in Washington. Was in charge of firm's Calcutta Branch, 1929-32. President, Instn of Locomotive Engineers, 1947 and 1951; Chairman, Assoc. of Consulting Engineers, 1953-54 and 1955-56; President International Federation of Consulting Engineers (FIDIC), 1955-63 (Hon. Member, 1963); President, Diesel Engineers' and Users' Association, 1962-63; Fellow and Silver Medallist, Royal Society of Arts. *Publications:* Presidential addresses and technical papers before Instn of Locomotive Engineers, Royal Society of Arts, and British Assoc. for Advancement of Science. *Recreations:* golf, bowls. *Address:* St Aubyn's, Oakshade Road, Oxshott, Surrey. *T:* Oxshott 2490. *Clubs:* Athenæum, Royal Automobile.

**TRIVEDI, Sir Chandulal Madhavlal,** KCSI 1945 (CSI 1941); Kt 1945; CIE, 1935; OBE 1931; LLD (hon. causa) Punjab University; Hon. DLitt Andhra University, 1955; Padma Vibhushan, 1956; *b* 2 July 1893; *m* 1906, Kusum Trivedi (Kaisar-i-Hind Gold Medal). *Educ:* Elphinstone Coll., Bombay; Bombay Univ. (BA, 1913); St John's Coll., Oxford. Entered Indian Civil Service, 1917; Under Secretary to Government of CP and Berar; Deputy Secretary and Offig. Joint Secretary to Government of India, Home Dept; Commissioner in various divisions in CP and Berar; Chief Secretary to Government of CP and Berar; Addl. Secretary, Dept of Communications, Government of India, March-June 1942; Secretary, War Dept, Government of India, New Delhi, until 1946; Governor of Orissa, 1946-47; Governor of Punjab (India), 1947-53; Governor of Andhra, 1953-56; Governor of Andhra Pradesh, 1956-57; Member, Indian Planning Commission, 1957-Sept. 1963; Dep. Chairman, Planning Commission, Oct.-Dec. 1963; Arbitrator for UP and Bihar Boundary, Government of India, Jan.-Aug. 1964; Chairman, Madhya Pradesh Police Commn, 1964-65. Chancellor, Gujarat Ayurvedu Univ.; President, Bharat Scouts and Guides. *Address:* Chandra-Bhuvan, Kapadwanj, Gujarat State, India.

**TROLLOPE, Sir Anthony Owen Clavering,** 16th Bt, *cr* 1642; *b* 15 Jan. 1917; *s* of Sir Gordon Clavering Trollope, 15th Bt; *S* father, 1958; *m* 1942, Joan Mary Alexis, *d* of Alexis Robert Gibbs, Manly, New South Wales; two *s*. Served War of 1939-45: 2nd/5th Australian Field Regt, Royal Australian Artillery, Middle East and New Guinea. Director, Thomas C. Denton and Co. Pty Ltd. JP for State of NS Wales. *Heir: s* Anthony Simon Trollope, *b* 1945. *Address:* Clavering, Roseville Avenue, Roseville, New South Wales, Australia.

**TROTMAN-DICKENSON, Dr Aubrey Fiennes;** Principal, University of Wales Institute of Science and Technology, Cardiff, since 1968; Member, Wales Gas Board, since 1967; *b* 12 Feb. 1926; *s* of Edward Newton Trotman-Dickenson and Violet Murray Nicoll; *m* 1953, Danusia Irena Hewell; two *s* one *d*. *Educ:* Winchester Coll.; Balliol Coll., Oxford. MA, PhD, DSc. Fellow, National Research Council, Ottawa, 1948-50; Asst Lecturer, ICI Fellow, Manchester Univ., 1950-53; E. I. du Pont de Nemours, Wilmington, USA, 1953-54; Lecturer, Edinburgh Univ., 1954-60; Professor, University College of Wales, Aberystwyth, 1960-68. *Publications:* Gas Kinetics, 1955; Free Radicals, 1959; Tables of Bimolecular Gas Reactions, 1967; contrib. to learned journals. *Address:* Radyr Chain, Llantrisant Road, Cardiff. *T:* Cardiff 563263.

**TROTT, George Henry,** CBE 1946; Director: Blue Star Line Ltd, since 1945; Albion Insurance Co. Ltd, since 1957; *b* 7 May 1889; *m*; one *s* three *d*. *Educ:* private. Secretary, 1916-20, Manager, 1920-39, Blue Star Line Ltd; Director of Refrigerator Tonnage, Ministry of Food, Sept. 1939-March 1945. *Address:* 17 Newnham House, Loughton, Essex. *T:* 01-508 1119.

**TROTT, Hon. Sir William James Howard,** Kt 1943; CBE 1937; President of Frascati Hotel Company Ltd; *b* 1 Feb. 1883; *s* of Thaddeus Trott and Margaret Pearman; *m* 1910, Elmina Morrison Hutchings, Paget, Bermuda; two *s* (and one *s* decd), two *d*. *Educ:* Whitney Institute; Ontario Business Coll. *Recreations:* golf and tennis. *Address:* Hamilton, Bermuda. *TA:* Trottmore, Bermuda. *T:* 1-2164. *Clubs:* Royal Bermuda Yacht, Hamilton Dinghy; Mid Ocean; Riddell's Bay Golf.

**TROTTER, Alexander Cooper,** CBE 1958; JP; Editor, Scottish Daily Express, 1934-59; Chairman, Beaverbrook newspaper interests in Scotland, 1959-70; *b* 31 Dec. 1902; *s* of A. E. Trotter, Edinburgh; *m* 1925, Sarah Sherry, Portobello; one *s* two *d*. *Educ:* St Mary's Cathedral Choir School, Edinburgh. Former Vice-Chm., Scottish Tourist Board (Mem. 1946-69); Mem., Countryside Commn, 1969. JP Glasgow. *Recreation:* newspapers. *Address:* 77 Dublin Street, Edinburgh. *T:* 031-556 4630. *Clubs:* Press; Royal Scottish Automobile, Arts (Edinburgh).

**TROTTER, Richard Stanley; His Honour Judge Trotter;** County Court Judge since 1961; *b* 29 June 1903; *s* of Thomas Ashton and Alice Howe Trotter; *m* 1946, Ruth Elizabeth Pierce; three *s* one *d*. *Educ:* Shrewsbury Sch.; Magdalen Coll., Oxford. BA Oxon 1925. Called to the Bar, 1926; practised on Northern Circuit, 1927-61. *Address:* Corner House, Acre Lane, Heswall, Cheshire. *T:* 051-342 2632.

**TROUBRIDGE, Sir Peter,** 6th Bt, *cr* 1799; RN retired; Member of the Stock Exchange, since 1970; with Stirling & Co.; *b* 6 June 1927; *s* of late Vice-Admiral Sir T. H. Troubridge, KCB, DSO, and Lily Emily Kleinwort; *S* cousin, 1963; *m* 1954, Hon. Venetia Daphne Weeks; one *s* two *d*. *Educ:* Eton; Cambridge. Served Korean War, 1952-53, HMS Ocean; retired from RN (Lt-Comdr), 1967. *Recreations:* shooting, gardening, birdwatching. *Heir: s*

Thomas Richard Troubridge, *b* 23 Jan. 1955. *Address:* The Manor House, Elsted, Midhurst, Sussex. *T:* Harting 286. *Clubs:* White's, MCC.

**TROUGHTON, Charles Hugh Willis,** CBE 1966; MC 1940; TD 1959; Chairman, W. H. Smith & Son Ltd, since 1969; Director: W. H. Smith & Son (Holdings) Ltd; Equity & Law Life Assurance Society Ltd; Electric & General Investment Co. Ltd; *b* 27 Aug. 1916; *o s* of Charles Vivian and Constance Scylla Troughton; *m* 1947, Constance Gillean Mitford, *d* of Colonel Mitford, Berryfield House, Lentran, Inverness-shire; three *s* one *d*. *Educ:* Haileybury Coll.; Trinity Coll., Cambridge. BA 1938. Joined TA, 1938; served War of 1939-45, Oxford and Bucks Light Infantry; Prisoner of War, 1940-45. Called to the Bar, 1945. Member Board of Management of NAAFI. *Recreations:* reading, fishing, shooting, cricket. *Address:* Woolleys, Hambleden, Henley-on-Thames, Oxfordshire. *T:* Hambleden 244. *Clubs:* Garrick, MCC.

**TROUGHTON, John Frederick George,** CMG 1948; MBE 1936; *b* 24 May 1902; *o s* of late Charles A. J. Troughton and Ellen Troughton; *m* 1st, 1927, Margaret Walker Pike (marr. diss. 1957); three *s* one *d*; 2nd, 1957, Beryl Rose Froome. *Educ:* Rathmines, St Andrews and Trinity Colleges, Dublin. Senior Moderatorship in Mental and Moral Philosophy; Administrative Cadet, Kenya Colony, 1926; LLB (Dublin), 1929; Clerk to Executive and Legislative Councils, 1933; seconded to BBC as Empire News Editor, 1936-38; Deputy Financial Secretary, Kenya, 1939; Economic Secretary, 1944; Financial Secretary, Member for Finance, 1946-49; MLC, 1943-49; Member East Africa Central Legislative Assembly, 1948-49; Controller of Finance in E. Africa, Overseas Food Corp., 1949-50, retired; Barrister-at-law, Gray's Inn, 1952; private legal practice, Uganda, 1953-61. Magistrate, Swaziland, 1961-, Acting Chief Justice, 1965 and subsequent occasions. *Address:* c/o National and Grindlay's Bank, 23 Fenchurch Street, EC3; PO Box 229, Manzini, Swaziland. *Clubs:* East India and Sports; various E African and Swaziland.

**TROUP, Vice-Adm. Sir James Andrew Gardiner,** KBE 1943; CB 1936; *b* Broughty Ferry, Angus, 7 March 1883; 2nd *s* of late Rev. G. E. Troup; *m* 1946, Kathleen Phyllis Simpson, *d* of late William Melvin, Glasgow. *Educ:* Dundee High School; Ascham House, Bournemouth. Battles of Colenso, Spion Kop, Vaalkrantz, Tugela Heights, Relief of Ladysmith, 1899-1900; Boxer War Tientsin and Relief of Pekin, 1900; specially promoted, 1903, for services in South African War; Commander, 1916; Master of the Fleet, 1920-22; Captain, 1922; Captain HM Navigation School, 1928-30; Flag Captain, HMS Revenge, 1930-32; Director of Tactical School, 1933-35; ADC to the King, 1934; Rear-Admiral, 1935; Director of Naval Intelligence, 1935-39; Vice-Admiral, 1939; retired, 1939; Flag Officer in charge Glasgow and District Shipyard Controller, 1940-46. Order of Polonia Restituta, 2nd class, 1944; Commander Legion of Honour and Croix de Guerre with Palm, 1946. *Publication:* On the Bridge, 1934, 4th edn 1952. *Address:* Broom, Auchterarder, Perthshire. *T:* Auchterarder 2254. *Club:* United Service.

**TROUP, Rear-Adm. John Anthony Rose,** DSC and Bar; Commander Far East Fleet, since 1971; *b* 18 July 1921; *s* of late Captain H. R. Troup, RN and N. M. Troup (*née* Milne-Thompson); *m* 1st, 1943, B. M. J. Gordon-Smith (marr. diss. 1952); two *s* one *d*; 2nd, 1953, C. M. Hope; two *s* one *d*. *Educ:* RNC Dartmouth. Entered RN, 1936; served in HMS Cornwall, 1939; in submarines, 1941-45 (DSC and Bar, despatches), 1st Lieut Turbulent and i/c Strongbow; Staff Course, and Staff of Flag Officer Submarines, 1953-55; Exec. Officer Aircraft Carrier, HMS Victorious, 1956-59; Naval Asst to 1st Sea Lord, 1959-61; comd 3rd Submarine Sqdn, 1961-63; Dir of Naval Equipment, 1963-65; Captain of the Fleet (Home), 1965-66; comd HMS Intrepid, 1966-68; Flag Officer Sea Training and in comd HM Naval Base Portland, 1969-71. Comdr 1953; Captain 1959; Rear-Adm. 1969. *Recreations:* sailing, ski-ing, shooting, painting. *Address:* Bridge Gardens, Hungerford, Berks. *T:* Hungerford 2742. *Clubs:* Army and Navy; Royal Yacht Squadron.

**TROUT, Sir H(erbert) Leon,** Kt 1959; FASA; Director of several Companies; Solicitor; *b* 12 Feb. 1906; *s* of late Walter John Trout and Margaret Alice Trout; *m* 1936, Peggy Elaine Hyland. *Educ:* Brisbane Grammar Sch. Fed. President, Australian Automobile Assoc., 1946; President, Brisbane Chamber of Commerce, 1953-56; Fed. President, Associated Chambers of Commerce of Australia, 1956-59; Member of Exports Payment Insurance Corporation, 1958; Member of Manufacturers' Industries Advisory Council, 1958. President, Liberal Party of Queensland, 1953-57. President, Queensland National Art Gallery Society, 1951-54; Chairman of Trustees, Queensland Art Gallery; President, Queensland Musical Literary self-aid Society for the Blind, 1938-45. Active service overseas with RAAF, War of 1939-45; commissioned rank, Queensland Cameron Highlanders. *Recreations:* golf and bowls. *Address:* Everton House, Old Northern Road, Everton Park, Brisbane, Queensland 4053, Australia. *Clubs:* Brisbane (President, 1955, 1956); Royal Queensland Yacht; (Hon. Life Member) Royal Automobile of Queensland (President, 1946, 1947, 1948).

**TROUTBECK, Sir John Monro,** GBE 1955; KCMG 1948 (CMG 1939); *b* 2 Nov. 1894; *s* of John Troutbeck and Harriet Elizabeth Monro; *m* 1924, Katherine Morley; one *d* (and *er d* decd). *Educ:* Westminster Sch.; Christ Church, Oxford. Served European War, 1914-19; entered Foreign Office, 1920; 2nd Secretary, Stamboul, 1927; 1st Secretary, Addis Ababa, 1930; Imperial Defence College, 1932; 1st Secretary, Rio de Janeiro, 1933; 1st Secretary, Foreign Office, 1935; 1st Secretary, Prague, 1937; seconded to Ministry of Economic Warfare, 1939-43; Counsellor, Foreign Office, 1943; Assistant Under-Secretary, Foreign Office, 1946-47; Head of British Middle East Office, Cairo, 1947-50; HM Ambassador to Iraq, 1951-54, retired 1954. UK Member of Saar Referendum Commission, 1955. Chairman of Save the Children Fund, 1956-62. *Address:* 28 The Causeway, Horsham, Sussex. *T:* Horsham 5263.

**TROWBRIDGE, Rear-Adm. Richard John;** Flag Officer Royal Yachts since Aug. 1970; *b* 21 Jan. 1920; *s* of A. G. Trowbridge, Andover, Hants; *m* 1955, Anne Mildred Perceval; two *s*. *Educ:* Andover Grammar Sch.; Royal Navy. Joined RN as Boy Seaman, 1935. War of 1939-45: commissioned as Sub Lieut, Dec. 1940 (despatches Aug. 1945). Comdr, 1953; commanded Destroyer Carysfort, 1956-58; Exec. Officer, HMS Bermuda, 1958-59, and HMS Excellent, 1959-60; Captain, 1960; commanded Fishery Protection Sqdn, 1962-64; completed course IDC, 1966; commanded HMS Hampshire, 1967-69; Rear-Adm., 1970. An Extra Equerry to the Queen, 1970-. *Recreations:* fishing, sailing, golf; most outdoor pursuits. *Address:* Old Idsworth

Garden, Finchdean, Portsmouth. *T:* Rowlands Castle 714. *Club:* United Service.

**TROYAT, Henri;** Légion d'Honneur; writer; Member of the French Academy, 1959; *b* Moscow, 1 Nov. 1911; *m* 1948, Marguerite Saintagne; one *s* one *d. Educ:* Paris. *Publications:* novels: l'Araigne (Prix Goncourt, 1938); Les Semailles et les Moissons (5 vols); Tant que la Terre durera (3 vols); La Lumière des Justes (5 vols); biographies: Pushkin, Dostoievsky, Tolstoi. *Address:* Académie Française, Quai de Conti, Paris.

**TRUBSHAW, (Ernest) Brian,** CBE 1970 (OBE 1964); MVO 1948; AFRAeS; General Manager Flight Operations and Chief Test Pilot, Filton and Weybridge Divisions of British Aircraft Corporation Ltd; Director, Filton and Weybridge Divisions, BAC Ltd; Special Director, BAC Ltd; *b* 29 Jan. 1924; *s* of late Major H. E. Trubshaw and Lumly Victoria (*née* Carter). *Educ:* Winchester College. Royal Air Force, 1942-50: Bomber Command, 1944; Transport Command, 1945-46; The King's Flight, 1946-48; Empire Flying School, 1949; RAF Flying Coll., 1949-50. Joined Vickers-Armstrongs (Aircraft) Ltd as Experimental Test Pilot, 1950; Dep. Chief Test Pilot, 1953; Chief Test Pilot, 1960; Company renamed British Aircraft Corp. (Operating) Ltd, Weybridge Division, 1964. Warden, Guild of Air Pilots, 1958-61; Fellow, Society Experimental Test Pilots, USA. Derry and Richards Memorial Medal, 1961 and 1964; Richard Hansford Burroughs Memorial Trophy (USA), 1964; R. P. Alston Memorial Medal, 1964. *Recreations:* cricket, golf. *Address:* The Red House, Egerton Road, Weybridge, Surrey. *T:* Weybridge 42201. *Clubs:* Royal Aero, Royal Air Force.

**TRUDEAU, Hon. Pierre Elliott;** MP (Canada); Prime Minister of Canada and Leader of the Liberal Party of Canada, since April 1968; *b* Montreal, 8 Oct. 1919; *s* of Charles-Emile Trudeau and Grace Elliott. *Educ:* Jean-de-Brébeuf College, Montreal; University of Montreal; Harvard University; Ecole des Sciences Politiques, Paris; London School of Economics. Called to Bar, Quebec, 1943; practised law, Quebec; co-founder of review Cité Libre; Associate Professor of Law, University of Montreal, 1961-65. Elected to House of Commons, 1965; Parliamentary Secretary to Prime Minister, Jan. 1966-April 1967; Minister of Justice and Attorney General, April 1967-July 1968. Member: Bars of Provinces of Quebec and Ontario; Royal Society of Canada; Founding Member, Montreal Civil Liberties Union. Hon. Dr of Laws, University of Alberta, 1968. Hon. Fellow, LSE, 1969. *Publications:* La Grève de l'Amiante, 1956; (with Jacques Hébert) Deux Innocents en Chine Rouge, 1961 (Two Innocents in Red China, 1969); Le Fédéralisme et la Société canadienne-française, 1968 (Federalism and the French Canadians, 1968); Réponses, 1968. *Recreations:* swimming, ski-ing, flying, scuba diving, canoeing. *Address:* Prime Minister's Residence, 24 Sussex Drive, Ottawa, Canada.

**TRUETA, Joseph,** MA Oxon; MD Barcelona; DSc (*hc*) Oxford, Bogotá; MD (*hc*) Gothenburg, Buenos Aires, Rio de Janeiro; FRCS England; FRCS (Hon.) Canada; FACS (Hon.); (Hon.) FRFPS(G); Hon. Member, National Academy of Medicine, Buenos Aires; Nuffield Professor of Orthopædic Surgery, University of Oxford, 1949-66 (now Emeritus); Fellow, Worcester College, Oxford (Hon. Fellow, 1966); President Congress of International Society of Orthopædic and Traumatic Surgery; Officier de la Légion d'Honneur, 1963; Commander, Order of Southern Cross, Brazil, 1957; Hon. Surgeon, Nuffield Orthopædic Centre; *b* 27 Oct. 1897; *m* 1923, Amelia Llacuna; three *d. Educ:* Barcelona Institute and Univ. Licentiate in Medicine, 1921; Dr, 1922; Auxiliary Prof. of Surgery, University of Barcelona, 1932; Director of Surgery, General Hospital of Catalonia, University of Barcelona, 1935; Acting Surgeon-in-Charge, Accident Service, Radcliffe Infirmary, Oxford, 1942-44; Member Catalan Society of Surgery, 1928; Founder Spanish Orthopædic Assoc., 1934; Member: Association Française de Chirurgie, 1933; Vice-President, Soc. Internat. de Chirurgie Orthopédique et de Traumatologie, 1954; Hon. Member: British Orthopædic Assoc.; Società Italiana di Ortopedia e Traumatologia; Société Pathologie Renale; Soc. française d'Orthop. et de Traumat.; Deutschen Orthop. Gesellschaft; Soc. Orthop. Scandinavia; Soc. Latino-Americana de Ortop. y Traumat.; Soc. Brasileira de Orthop. e Traumat.; Soc. Argen. de Ortop. y Traumat; Soc. Portuguesa de Ortop.; Soc. Colombiana de Cirugia Ortop. y Traumat.; Soc. Venezolana de Ortop. y Traumat.; Hon. Member Section of Orthopædics, RSM. Visiting Prof. University of Pittsburgh, Ohio State Univ. Coll. of Medicine, 1958, University of Padua, 1960, Univ. of British Columbia, 1970. associé Etranger, 1949, Académie de Chirgurgie, Paris; Hon. Mem., Real Academia de Medicina, Barcelona, 1970; Corres. Member: Spanish Orthop. Soc.; Institut d'Estudis Catalans. Prix Laborie, 1948; Gold Medal, Univ. of Mérida, 1956; Prix Robert Danis, 1963. *Publications:* Els tumours malignes primitius dels ossos, Barcelona, 1933; La Hidatidosi ossia, Barcelona, 1936; Tractament de les Fractures de Guerra, 1938; Treatment of War Wounds and Fractures, London, 1939; Principles and Practice of War Surgery, London-St Louis, 1943; The Spirit of Catalonia, 1946; (in collaboration) Studies of the Renal Circulation, 1947; An Atlas of Traumatic Surgery, Oxford, 1949; (in collaboration) A Hand Book of Poliomyelitis, 1956; Studies of the Development and Decay of the Human Frame, 1968. *Recreations:* tennis, swimming. *Address:* Overmead, Jack Straw's Lane, Headington Hill, Oxford. *T:* Oxford 61178; Rambla de Cataluña 74, Barcelona, Spain.

**TRUFFAUT, François;** Director of films; *b* Paris 17ème, France, 6 Feb. 1932; *s* of Roland Truffaut and Janine Truffaut (*née* de Monferrand); *m* 1957, Madeleine Morgenstern; two *d.* Reporter, film critic, 1954-58; Director of films, 1957, Producer, 1961; *productions include:* Les Mistons, 1958; Les Quatre Cents Coups, 1959 (prize, Cannes Film Festival); Tirez sur le Pianiste, 1960; L'Amour à 20 ans, 1962; Jules et Jim, 1962; La Peau Douce, 1963; Fahrenheit 451, 1966; La Mariée était en Noir, 1967; Baisers Volés, 1968; La Sirène du Mississipi, 1969; L'Enfant Sauvage, 1970; Domicile Conjugal, 1970. *Publication:* Hitchcock, 1966. *Address:* 5 rue Robert-Estienne, Paris 8ème, France.

**TRUMAN, Harry S.;** President of USA, April 1945-Jan. 1953; *b* Lamar, Barton County, Mo., 8 May 1884; *s* of John Anderson Truman (*d* 1914) and Martha Ellen Young (*d* 1947); *m* 1919, Bess Wallace; one *d. Educ:* Public schools in Independence; Field Artillery Sch. (Ft Sill. Okla.), 1917-18; Kansas City Sch. of Law, 1923-25. Operated family farm, 1906-17. First Lieut, Battery F and Captain, Battery D, 129th Field Artillery, 35th Division, US Army, in European War and served in Vosges operations, St Mihiel and Meuse-Argonne offensives, 18 Aug. to 11 Nov. 1918; discharged with rank of Major, USARC, 1919; Colonel, USARC, since 1927; Judge, Jackson County (Mo.) Court, 1922-24, Presiding Judge, 1926-34; elected to United States Senate from Missouri, 1934, and re-elected 1940; served on Appropriations, Enrolled Bills, Military Affairs, Printing, Interstate Commerce, and Public Buildings and Grounds Cttees and as Chairman of the Special Committee to Investigate the National Defense Program; elected Vice-President, 7 Nov. 1944, and took office 20 Jan. 1945; acceded to Presidency, 12 April 1945, on death of President Roosevelt; elected for second term, Nov. 1948-Jan. 1953. Democrat. Member of the Baptist Church; Past Grand Master of Masons of Missouri. *Publications:* Autobiography: Vol. I, Year of Decisions, 1955; Vol. II, Years of Trial and Hope, 1956; Mr Citizen, 1961. *Address:* Independence, Mo., USA.

**TRURO, Bishop of,** since Dec. 1959; **Rt. Rev. John Maurice Key,** DD Lambeth, 1960; MA; *b* 4 June 1905; *s* of late Preb. Frederick John Key, Lichfield, and Winifred Mary Head, Hexham, Northumberland; *m* 1935, Agnes Joan Dence (JP 1946-), *d* of late Rev. A. T. Dence, Abbotskerswell, Devon; three *s* one *d*. *Educ:* Rossall Sch.; Pembroke Coll., Cambridge; Westcott House, Cambridge. Assistant Curate, S. Mary's, Portsea, 1928-32; Vicar of Aylesbeare, Exeter, 1932-34; Rector of Highweek with S. Mary's, Newton Abbot, 1934-40; Rector of Stoke Damerel with S. Bartholomew's and S. Luke's, Devonport, 1940-47; Rural Dean of the Three Towns (Plymouth), 1944-47; Bishop Suffragan of Sherborne, 1947-59. *Recreations:* music, gardening and country. *Address:* Lis Escop, Truro, Cornwall. *T:* Feock 657. *Clubs:* Athenæum, Royal Commonwealth Society.

**TRURO, Assistant Bishop of;** *see* Lash, Rt Rev. W. Q.

**TRURO, Dean of;** *see* Lloyd, Very Rev. Henry Morgan.

**TRUSCOTT, Sir Denis (Henry),** GBE 1958; Kt 1953; TD 1950; President of Brown Knight and Truscott Ltd; *b* 9 July 1908; *s* of Henry Dexter Truscott, JP, and Evelyn Metcalf Truscott (*née* Gibbes); *m* 1932, Ethel Margaret, *d* of late Alexander Lyell, of Gardyne Castle, Guthrie, Angus, and Mrs Lyell; four *d*. *Educ:* Bilton Grange; Rugby Sch.; Magdalene Coll., Cambridge. Joined family firm of Jas. Truscott & Son Ltd, printers, 1929; Director, 1935; Chairman, 1951-66, of Brown, Knight & Truscott Ltd (amalgamation of Jas. Truscott & Son Ltd with Wm Brown & Chas. Knight Ltd, 1936). Director: Bedford General Insurance Co. Ltd. Elected to Court of Common Council, City of London, 1938, for Ward of Dowgate; Deputy, 1943; Alderman Dowgate Ward, 1947; Sheriff of City of London, 1951-52; Lord Mayor of London, 1957-58. Master Worshipful Company of Vintners, 1955-56; Master Worshipful Company of Musicians, 1956-57; Master, Guild of Freemen of the City of London, 1957; Master of Worshipful Company of Stationers and Newspaper Makers, 1959-60. Member of Board of Governors, St Bartholomew's Hospital, Royal Hospital and Home for Incurables, Putney; Chairman Trustees Rowland Hill Benevolent Fund; Member Exec. Cttee, Automobile Assoc.; President, Printing and Allied Trades Research Assoc., 1956-64; President, Institute of Printing, 1961-63; Chairman, Squash Racquets Assoc. of England, 1961-. Grand Officer of Order of Merit, Italian Republic; Grand Cross of Merit of Order of Merit, Republic of Germany. *Recreations:* lawn tennis, squash racquets and golf. *Address:* Ivermark, 65 Burghley Road, Wimbledon, SW19. *T:* 01-946 6111. *Clubs:* United University, Royal Automobile, City Livery, All England Lawn Tennis.

**TRUSCOTT, Sir Eric Homewood Stanham,** 2nd Bt, *cr* 1909; MA; *b* 16 Feb. 1898; *o surv. s* of Sir George Wyatt Truscott, 1st Bt, Lord Mayor of London, 1908-09, and Jessie Guthrie (*d* 1921), DGStJ, *e d* of late Geo. Gordon Stanham, architect; *S* father, 1941; *m* 1st, 1924, Mary Dorcas (*d* 1948), *d* of late Rev. Canon T. H. Irving, MA; one *s* one *d*; 2nd, 1950, Marjorie Berta (*d* 1951), *y d* of late Prof. Leonard Trelawny Hobhouse, MA, LittD, and *widow* of Alfred William Sutton; 3rd, 1953, Renée Franklin, *y d* of John William Marshall, and former wife of William Archibald Redgrave (from whom she obtained a divorce, 1947). *Educ:* Rugby; Trinity Coll., Cambridge. BA 1920; MA 1925; served European War, 1916-18, and War of 1939-45. *Heir:* *s* George James Irving Truscott [*b* 24 Oct. 1929; *m* 1962, Yvonne Dora Nicholson; one *s* one *d*]. *Address:* 55 Kingsley Way, N2.

**TRUSS, Leslie S.;** *see* Seldon-Truss.

**TRUSTED, Sir Harry Herbert,** Kt, *cr* 1938; QC; *b* 27 June 1888; *s* of the Rev. Wilson Trusted; *m* Mary, *d* of Sir Marshall Warmington, KC, 1st Bt; two *s* three *d*. *Educ:* Ellesmere Coll.; Trinity Hall, Cambridge. Called to Bar, Inner Temple, 1913; served overseas (Duke of Cornwall's Light Infantry and Staff), 1914-19; Puisne Judge, Supreme Court, Leeward Islands, 1925-27; Attorney-General, Leeward Islands, 1927-29; Attorney-General, Cyprus, 1929-32; Attorney-General, Palestine, 1932-37; Chief Justice, Palestine, 1937-41; Chief Justice, FMS, 1941-45; Chairman, Malayan Union and Singapore Salaries Commission, 1947; Commissioner to inquire into disturbances at Aden, 1948; special duty with Foreign Office (FOAAT), 1951-53; sat as Divorce Commissioner, 1953-63. *Address:* 7 Garrick Close, Walton-on-Thames, Surrey. *T:* Walton-on-Thames 27986.

**TRUSTRAM EVE;** *see* Eve.

**TRUSTRAM EVE, Hon. David Malcolm;** Barrister, Inner Temple, since 1955; *b* 2 May 1930; *er twin s* and *heir* of Baron Silsoe, *qv*; *m* 1963, Bridget Min, *d* of Sir Rupert Hart-Davis, *qv*; one *s* one *d*. *Educ:* Winchester; Christ Church, Oxford (MA); Columbia Univ., New York. 2nd Lt, Royal Welch Fusiliers, 1949-50; Lieut, Queen Victoria's Rifles (TA), 1950-53. Bar Auditor, Inner Temple, 1965-70; Bencher, 1970. *Recreation:* ski-ing. *Address:* Neals Farm, Wyfold, Reading, Berks RG4 9JB. *Clubs:* Oxford and Cambridge University, Ski of Great Britain.

**TRYHORN, Frederick Gerald,** CBE 1963; *b* 1893; *s* of Frederick George Tryhorn, Salisbury; *m* 1919, Beryl, *e d* of R. V. Marwood, Ambleside. *Educ:* Liverpool Univ. BSc 1st Hons Chemistry, 1914; DSc 1928. FRIC; Sub-Lt, RNVR, 1917; Lieut, RAF, 1918; Assistant Lecturer, Liverpool Univ., 1919-20; Lecturer on Physical Chemistry, University of Sheffield, 1920-28; Professor of Chemistry, University College, Hull, 1928-46; Director, Forensic Science Laboratories: Nottingham, 1946-52; Wakefield, 1952-54; Harrogate, 1954-58; Forensic Science Adviser, Home Office, 1958-63, retired. *Publications:* contribs. to scientific journals; contribs. to police science and criminological studies. *Address:* Carr Naze, Sleights, Whitby, Yorks. *T:* Sleights 368.

**TRYON,** family name of **Baron Tryon.**

**TRYON,** 2nd Baron, *cr* 1940, of Durnford; **Charles George Vivian Tryon,** GCVO 1969 (KCVO 1953); KCB 1962; DSO 1945; Brigadier, retired, Grenadier Guards; Keeper of the Privy Purse and Treasurer to the Queen since 1952 (Assistant Keeper, 1949-52); *b* 1906; *s* of 1st Baron and Hon. Averil Vivian (*d* 1959), 2nd *d* of 1st Lord Swansea; *S* father, 1940; *m* 1939, Etheldreda Josephine, *d* of late Sir Merrik Burrell, 7th Bt, CBE; one *s* one *d*. *Educ:* Eton. ADC Governor-General of Canada, 1933-34; Commanded 5th Guards Brigade, 1945-46. Commander, Legion of Honour, 1960. *Heir: s* Hon. Anthony George Merrik Tryon, *b* 26 May 1940. *Address:* Church Farm House, Great Durnford, near Salisbury, Wilts. *T:* Middle Woodford 281; Ambassador's Court, St James's Palace, SW1. *T:* 01-930 1629. *Clubs:* Turf, White's.

**TRYPANIS, Constantine Athanasius,** MA (Oxon); DPhil (Athens); FRSL; University Professor of Classics, Chicago University, since 1968; *b* Chios, 22 Jan. 1909; *s* of Athanasius G. Trypanis and Maria Zolota; *m* 1942, Alice Macri; one *d*. *Educ:* Chios Gymnasium; Universities of Athens, Berlin and Munich. Classical Lecturer, Athens Univ., 1939-47; Bywater and Sotheby Professor of Byzantine and Modern Greek Language and Literature, and Fellow of Exeter Coll., Oxford, 1947-68; Emeritus Fellow, 1968-. FRSL, 1958; Life Fellow, International Institute of Arts and Letters, 1958; Member Institute for Advanced Study, Princeton, USA, 1959-60; Visiting Professor: Hunter Coll., New York, 1963; Harvard Univ., 1963, 1964; Univ. of Chicago, 1965-66; Univ. of Cape Town, 1969. Corresponding Member Institute for Balkan Studies (Greece). Archon Hieromnemon of the Oekumenical Patriarchate. *Publications:* Influence of Hesiod upon Homeric Hymn of Hermes, 1939; Influence of Hesiod upon Homeric Hymn on Apollo, 1940; Alexandrian Poetry, 1943; Tartessos, 1945; Medieval and Modern Greek Poetry, 1951; Pedasus, 1955; Callimachus, 1956; The Stones of Troy, 1956; The Cocks of Hades, 1958; (with P. Maas) Sancti Romani Melodi Cantica, 1963, vol. II, 1970; Pompeian Dog, 1964; The Elegies of a Glass Adonis, 1967; Fourteen Early Byzantine Cantica, 1968; articles in classical and literary periodicals. *Recreations:* walking, tennis, painting. *Address:* 5825 South Dorchester Avenue, Chicago, Ill 60637, USA.

**TRYTHALL, Rear-Adm. John Douglas,** CB 1970; OBE 1953; Assistant Chief, Personnel and Logistics, Ministry of Defence, since 1969; *b* 21 June 1914; *er s* of Alfonso Charles Trythall, Camborne, and Hilda Elizabeth (*née* Monson); *m* 1943, Elizabeth Loveday (*née* Donald); two *s* two *d*. *Educ:* Stretford Grammar Sch. Cadet, 1931; appointments in Home Fleet, America and West Indies, East Indies. Lent to RNZN, 1939; Battle of River Plate; Western Approaches; BJSM, Washington; Pacific; Hong Kong; Mediterranean. Secretary to: Second Sea Lord, C-in-C The Nore, and C-in-C Plymouth; Asst Director of Plans, 1960-62; Captain of the Fleet, Medit., 1964-65; Head of Personnel Panel, MoD, 1966-67; subseq. on MoD Cttee. JSSC, 1953; IDC, 1963. Commander, 1949; Captain, 1959; Rear-Admiral, 1968. FCIS 1956. *Recreations:* all ball games but now reduced to spectator; gardening. *Address:* 3 Kyrle Road, SW11. *T:* 01-223 5862. *Club:* MCC.

**TSIBU DARKU, Nana Sir,** Kt 1948; OBE 1945 (MBE 1941); *b* 19 March 1902; *s* of late Adrian Nicholas deHeer of Elmina, and late Effuah Tekyiwa (*née* Hagar Dadson), Cape Coast and Fanti Yankumasi; *m* 1930, Maud, *d* of late Daniel Sackey, Accountant, PWD, Gold Coast, nine *s* nine *d*. *Educ:* African Methodist Episcopal Zion Mission Sch., Cape Coast; SPG Grammar Sch. (now Adisadel Coll.), Cape Coast. Served in Junior Service Political Administration, 1923-30; elected Paramount Chief of Asin Atandaso, Gold Coast (now Ghana), West Africa, 18 Nov. 1930; abdicated 18 Nov. 1951; re-elected Paramount Chief of Asin Atandaso Traditional Area, 13 Aug. 1962. Provincial Member Gold Coast Legislative Council, 1932-51; Sen. Unofficial Member of the Legislature, 1943-51; Member Governor's Exec. Council, Gold Coast, 1943-51. Served on various Government Cttees, including University Council of the Gold Coast and Coussey Cttee on Constitutional Reforms; Member, Adisadel College Board of Governors and Mfantsipim School Board of Management; Member, Aggrey Secondary Sch. Board of Governors, Member, Cape Coast Municipal Council, 1953-55; Chairman, Tema Devel. Corp., 1954-59; Chairman, Ghana Cocoa Marketing Board, 1959-66; Chairman, Kwame Nkrumah Trust Fund (Central Collection Cttee), 1959-66 (Chairman Trustees, 1960-66). Silver Jubilee Medal, 1935; Coronation Medal, 1937; King's Medal for Africa Chiefs, 1939. *Address:* PO Box 19, Fanti Nyankumasi, via Cape Coast, Ghana.

**TS'ONG, Fou;** *see* Fou Ts'ong.

**TUAM, Archbishop of, (RC),** since 1969; **Most Rev. Joseph Cunnane;** *b* 5 Oct. 1913; *s* of William and Margaret Cunnane, Knock, Co. Mayo. *Educ:* St Jarlath's Coll., Tuam; St Patrick's Coll., Maynooth. BA 1st Hons, Ancient Classics, 1935; DD 1941; Higher Dip. Educn 1941. Priest, 1939. Prof. of Irish, St Jarlath's Coll., 1941-57; Curate, Balla, Co. Mayo, 1957-67; Curate, Clifden, Co. Galway, 1967-69. Cross of Chaplain Conventual, SMO Malta, 1970. *Publications:* Vatican II on Priests, 1967; contribs to Irish Ecclesiastical Record, Furrow, Doctrine and Life, Studies in Pastoral Liturgy, etc. *Address:* Archbishop's House, Tuam, Co. Galway, Ireland. *T:* Tuam 24166.

**TUAM, KILLALA and ACHONRY, Bishop of,** since 1970; **Rt. Rev. John Coote Duggan;** *b* 7 April 1918; *s* of Rev. Charles Coote Whittaker Duggan, BD and Ella Thackeray Duggan (*née* Stritch); *m* 1948, Mary Elizabeth Davin; one *s* one *d* (and one *d* decd). *Educ:* High School, Dublin; Trinity Coll., Dublin (Schol.). Moderator (1st cl.) Men. and Moral Sci., 1940; Bernard Prize, Div. Test. (2nd cl.); BA 1940; BD 1946. Deacon 1941; Priest 1942. Curate Asst: St Luke, Cork, 1941-43; Taney, Dublin, 1943-48; Hon. Clerical Vicar, Christ Church Cath., 1944-48; Incumbent: Portarlington Union, Kildare, 1948-55; St Paul, Glenageary, Dublin, 1955-69; Westport and Achill Union, Tuam, 1969-70; Archdeacon of Tuam, 1969-70. Exam. Chaplain to Archbp of Dublin, 1958-69; Examiner in BD Degree, Univ. of Dublin, 1960-69. Editor, Irish Churchman's Almanack, 1958-69. *Publication:* A Short History of Glenageary Parish, 1968. *Recreation:* fishing. *Address:* Bishop's House, Knockglass, Crossmolina, Co. Mayo. *T:* Crossmolina 17. *Club:* University (Dublin).

**TUBB, Carrie, (Mrs A. J. E. Oliveira);** singer; *b* London; *d* of John Tubb and Anne Bardon; *m* Alexander John Ede Oliveira (*d* 1936). *Educ:* Guildhall School of Music. Made début Covent Garden, 1910; sang Birmingham Festival, 1912. *Address:* 29 Ashburn Place, SW7.

**TUBBS, Francis Ralph,** CBE 1960; MSc, PhD, ARCS, DIC, FIBiol; Director of the East Malling Research Station, near Maidstone, 1949-69; *b* 8 Oct. 1907; *s* of William Edward and Elizabeth Clara Tubbs; *m* 1939, Helen Beatrice Alice Green; two *s* two *d*. *Educ:* Hackney Downs School; Imperial College of Science. Forbes Medallist, 1928; Research at Rothamsted, 1928-30; Plant Physiologist, Tea Research Institute of Ceylon, 1930-48. On active service, 1939-45, Lt-Col RARO, The Durham Light Infantry. Officer Order of Orange Nassau, 1946; Chevalier Order of Leopold II, avec Palme, 1946; Croix de Guerre, 1940, avec Palme, 1946. *Publications:* in scientific journals. *Recreations:* gardening and sailing. *Address:* Hayletts, Barton Turf, Norwich NOR 36Z.

**TUBBS, Oswald Sydney,** FRCS; Surgeon-in-Charge, Department of Thoracic Surgery, St Bartholomew's Hospital and Surgeon to Brompton Hospital; *b* 21 March 1908; *s* of late Sydney Walter Tubbs, The Glebe, Hadley Common, Hertfordshire; *m* 1934, Marjorie Betty Wilkins; one *s* one *d*. *Educ:* Shrewsbury School; Caius College, Cambridge; St Bartholomew's Hospital. MA, MB, BCh, FRCS. Surgical training at St Bartholomew's Hosp. and Brompton Hosp. Dorothy Temple Cross Fellowship, spent as Surgical Fellow at Lahey Clinic, Boston, USA. Served War of 1939-45, in EMS. Consulting Chest Surgeon to Royal Navy, Papworth Village Settlement and to various Local Authorities. *Publications:* papers on surgical subjects. *Recreations:* fishing and gardening. *Address:* 96 Harley Street, W1. *T:* 01-935 1972; Lyndale House, 108 Highgate Hill, N6. *T:* 01-340 2129.

**TUBBS, Ralph,** OBE 1952; FRIBA; Architect; *b* 9 Jan. 1912; *s* of late Sydney W. Tubbs and Mabel Frost; *m* 1946, Mary Taberner; two *s* one *d*. *Educ:* Mill Hill School; Architectural Assoc. School (Hons Dip.). Sec. MARS Group (Modern Architectural Research), 1939; Member: Council and Executive Committee of RIBA, 1944-50, re-elected Council, 1951; Vice-Pres. Architectural Assoc., 1945-47; Associate Institute of Landscape Architects, 1942-. Member Presentation Panel and Design Group for 1951 Festival of Britain, and architect of Dome of Discovery in London Exhibn (then the largest dome in world, 365 ft diam.). Other works include: Baden-Powell House for Boy Scouts' Assoc., London; Indian Students' Union building, Fitzroy Sq., London; TV Centre and Studios, Manchester; Cambridge Inst. Educn; Ramsay Hall for University Coll., London, Residential Areas at Harlow and Basildon New Towns; Industrial Buildings. Architect for new Charing Cross Hospital, London. *Publications:* Living in Cities, 1942; The Englishman Builds, 1945. *Recreation:* keeping five senses alert. *Address:* 46 Queen Anne Street, W1. *T:* 01-935 0694.

**TUCK, Sir Bruce (Adolph) Reginald,** 3rd Bt, *cr* 1910; *b* 29 June 1926; *o s* of Major Sir (William) Reginald Tuck, 2nd Bt, and Gladys Emily Kettle (*d* 1966), *d* of late N. Alfred Nathan, Wickford, Auckland, New Zealand, and *widow* of Desmond Fosberry Kettle, Auckland Mounted Rifles; *S* father 1954; *m* 1st 1949, Luise (marr. diss., in Jamaica, 1964), *d* of John C. Renfro, San Angelo, Texas, USA; two *s*; *m* 2nd, 1968, Pamela Dorothy Nicholson, *d* of Alfred Nicholson, London. *Educ:* Canford School, Dorset. Lieutenant, Scots Guards, 1945-47. *Heir: s* Richard Bruce Tuck, *b* 7 Oct. 1952. *Address:* Montego Bay PO Box 274, Jamaica. *Club:* Lansdowne.

**TUCK, Maj.-Gen. George Newsam,** CB 1950; OBE 1944; retired; Hon. Colonel 121 Army Engineer Regiment (TA), since 1959; *b* 18 Dec. 1901; *s* of Harry Newman Tuck, Burma Commn; *m* 1929, Nell (*née* Winter); three *s*. *Educ:* Cheltenham Coll.; RMA, Woolwich. Commissioned Royal Engineers, 1921. Egypt, 1925-30; Instructor RMA, 1930-34; Staff Coll., 1935-36; Chief Instructor (RE), RMA, 1939; GSO1, Scapa Defences, 1939-40; DDRA, 1941; CRE 46 Div., 1942; Mil. Deputy to Scientific Adviser, War Office, 1943; Comdr Army Group RE, France and Germany, 1944-45; DSP, War Office, 1946; idc, 1947; DDSD, War Office, 1948; Chief of Staff, BAOR, 1949-Dec. 1951; Engineer-in-Chief, War Office, 1952-54; Deputy Controller of Munitions, Ministry of Supply, 1954-57; retired, 1957. Col Comdt, Corps of Royal Engineers, 1958-66. *Address:* c/o Lloyds Bank, Shaftesbury, Dorset.

**TUCK, Prof. John Philip;** Professor of Education, University of Newcastle upon Tyne (formerly King's College, University of Durham) since 1948; *b* 16 April 1911; *s* of late William John and Annie Tuck, Uplyme, Lyme Regis; *m* 1936, Jane Adelaide (*née* Wall); two *s*. *Educ:* Strand School; Jesus College, Cambridge. BA Hons English and History, Class I, 1933; Cambridge certificate in Education, 1934; Adelaide Stoll Bachelor Research Scholar, Christ's College, 1935; MA 1937. English Master: Gateshead Grammar School, 1936; Manchester Central High School, 1938; Wilson's Grammar School, 1939 and 1946. Served War of 1939-45, East Surrey Regt, and Army Education Corps, N Africa, Sicily, Italy, Austria. Lecturer in Education, King's College, Newcastle upon Tyne, 1946-48. Hon. Fellow, Coll. of Speech Therapists, 1966. *Address:* 30 Montagu Avenue, Newcastle upon Tyne 3. *T:* Gosforth 852977.

**TUCK, Raphael Herman;** MP (Lab) Watford since 1964; *b* 5 April 1910; *er* and *surv s* of late David Lionel Tuck and late Olive Tuck; *m* 1957, Monica J. L. Greaves. *Educ:* St Paul's School; London School of Economics; Trinity Hall, Cambridge; Harvard University, USA. BSc Econ. London 1936; MA Cantab 1939; LLM Harvard, 1940. British Embassy, Washington, 1940; Lecturer and later Professor of Law, University of Saskatchewan, Canada, 1941-45; Constitutional Adviser to Premier of Manitoba, 1943; Special Research, Dept of Labour, Ottawa, 1944; Prof. of Political Science, McGill Univ., Montreal, 1945; Prof. of Political Science, Tulane Univ., New Orleans, La, 1947-49. Barrister-at-Law, Gray's Inn, 1951-. Member: Soc. of Labour Lawyers; "Justice"; Harvard Law Assoc. of UK; Harvard Club of London; Herts Assoc. (Vice-Pres.); Watford Soc. for Mentally Handicapped Children (Vice-Pres.). *Publications:* articles in University of Toronto Law Journal, Canadian Bar Review, Sask. Bar Review, Public Affairs, Canadian Jl of Econs and Polit. Science, Solicitor's Jl. *Recreations:* photography, music. *Address:* 10 King's Bench Walk, Temple, EC4. *T:* 01-353 3647.

**TUCK, Wing Comdr Robert Roland S.;** *see* Stanford-Tuck.

**TUCK, Prof. Ronald Humphrey;** Head of Department of Agricultural Economics, University of Reading, and Provincial Agricultural Economist (Reading Province), since Sept. 1965, now Department of Agricultural Economics and Management; *b* 28 June 1921; *s* of Francis Tuck and Edith Ann Tuck (*née* Bridgewater); *m* 1942, Margaret Sylvia Everley; one *s* two *d*. *Educ:* Harrow County Sch.; Corpus Christi Coll., Oxford. War Service, RAOC and REME, mainly N

Africa and Italy, 1941-45 (despatches). Univ. of Reading, Dept of Agric. Economics: Research Economist, 1947-49; Lecturer, 1949-62; Reader, 1962-65. *Publications:* An Essay on the Economic Theory of Rank, 1954; An Introduction to the Principles of Agricultural Economics, 1961 (Italian trans., 1970); reviews etc. in Jl of Agric. Economics and Economic Jl. *Recreations:* reading, music, drawing, travelling, walking. *Address:* 211 Kidmore Road, Caversham, Reading, Berks. *T:* Reading 73426.

**TUCKER,** family name of **Baron Tucker.**

**TUCKER,** Baron (Life Peer), *cr* 1950; **Frederick James Tucker,** PC 1945; Kt 1937; a Lord of Appeal in Ordinary, 1950-61; *b* 1888; *s* of Frederick Nugent Tucker and Alice Green; *m* 1918, Benedicta, *d* of Rev. C. P. Berryman. *Educ:* Winchester; New College, Oxford. Called to the Bar (Inner Temple), 1914; KC 1933; Treasurer of the Inner Temple, 1960. Served as Lieut (General List), European War; Member of General Council of the Bar, 1930-37; Recorder of Southampton, 1936-37; Justice of High Court of Justice, King's Bench Division, 1937-45; a Lord Justice of Appeal, 1945-50; Hon. Fellow New College, Oxford, 1946. *Address:* Fairfield House, Great Bookham, Surrey. *Club:* Athenæum.

**TUCKER, Prof. Archibald Norman;** Professor of East African Languages, School of Oriental and African Studies, University of London, since 1951; *b* Cape Town, 10 March 1904; *s* of Norman Tucker and Gertrude Sarah Tucker (*née* Matthews); *m* 1931, Elizabeth Berthe Hills; four *s* one *d. Educ:* South African College School; University of Cape Town; University of London. MA Cape Town 1926; PhD London 1929; DLit London 1949. Linguistic research in Basutoland and Transvaal for Univ. of Cape Town, 1926; Linguistic Expert to Sudan Govt for non-Arabic langs, 1929-31; joined staff of School of Oriental Studies, 1932; Linguistic Research in S Sudan and S Africa on Internat. African Inst. Fellowship, 1932-33; Dinka orthography unification for Sudan Govt, 1938. Conscientious objector during War of 1939-45; foundation member of Peace Pledge Union; served in Pacifist Service Unit in E End Hosp.; subseq. active Mem., Campaign for Nuclear Disarmament. Orthographic Research for Uganda and Kenya Govts in Luganda, Kikuyu and Nilotic langs, 1946-47; launched 1949 (and supervised, 1950-51) Bantu line expedition in Belgian Congo for Internat. African Inst.; research in Uganda, Kenya, and in Southern Sudan, 1949, 1950-51; organized and directed orthography conference, W Uganda, 1954; research expedition in Tanzania, Kenya, Uganda, 1965-66, in which discovered grammatical resemblances between Ik (North Uganda) and Ancient Egyptian; Member Executive Council of International African Institute; Chairman of Subcommisson on Place-names in Africa south of Sahara. *Publications:* Comparative Phonetics of Suto-Chuana, 1929; Primitive Tribal Music and Dancing in the Southern Sudan, 1933; The Disappointed Lion and other stories from the Bari of Central Africa, 1938; The Eastern Sudanic Languages, Vol. I, 1941; Sotho-Nguni Orthography and Tone-marking, 1950; (with Mrs E. O. Ashton) Swahili Phonetics, 1943; (with Ashton, Mulira, Ndawula) a Luganda Grammar, 1954; (with J. T. Mpaayei) a Maasai Grammar, 1955; (with M. A. Bryan) Handbook of African Languages, Vol. III, 1956, Linguistic Survey of Northern Bantu Borderland, Vol. IV, 1957; Linguistic Analyses, 1966; (with P. E. Hackett), Le groupe linguistique zande, 1959; numerous articles in Bulletin School of Oriental and African Studies, Africa, African Studies, Kongo-Overzee, Afrika und Ubersee, etc. *Recreations:* photography, African music. *Address:* 76 Granville Road, Sevenoaks, Kent. *T:* Sevenoaks 52572. *Club:* East Africa House.

**TUCKER, Brian George,** OBE 1963; Under-Secretary, Cabinet Office, since 1970; *b* 6 May 1922; *s* of late Frank Ernest Tucker and of May Tucker; *m* 1948, Marion Pollitt; three *d. Educ:* Christ's Hospital. Entered Home Civil Service, 1939, as Clerical Officer, Admty; successive postings at home, in Africa, the Middle East, Ceylon and Hong Kong till 1953; promoted Executive Officer, 1945; Higher Executive Officer, 1949. Min. of Power, Asst Principal, 1954, Principal, 1957; seconded to HMOCS, 1957-62, Asst Sec., Govt of Northern Rhodesia; returned to MOP, 1962, Principal Private Sec. to Minister, 1965-66, Asst Sec., 1966, Under-Sec., Ministry of Technology, 1969-70. *Recreations:* gardening, music. *Address:* 1 Sondes Place Drive, Dorking, Surrey. *T:* Dorking 4720.

**TUCKER, Rt. Rev. Cyril James;** *see* Argentina and Eastern South America with the Falkland Islands, Bishop in.

**TUCKER, Prof. David Gordon;** Professor and Head of Department of Electronic and Electrical Engineering, University of Birmingham, since 1955; *b* 17 June 1914; *s* of John Ferry and Frances Tucker; *m* 1945, Florence Mary Barton; three *s* one *d. Educ:* Sir George Monoux Grammar School, London; University of London. BSc, 1936; PhD, 1943; DSc, 1948. On research staff of GPO, at the PO Research Station, Dollis Hill, 1934-50; Royal Naval Scientific Service (Senior Principal Scientific Officer), 1950-55. Member: Gen. Council of Instn of Electronic and Radio Engineers, 1958-62 and 1965-66, Education Committee, 1958-65, Research Committee, 1962-; Council of British Acoustical Society, 1965- (Vice-Pres., 1967-70; Pres., 1970-); Council, Soc. for Underwater Technology, 1967-; National Electronics Research Council, 1963-66; Treasury Committee on Scientific Civil Service, 1964-65; Natural Environment Research Council, Oceanography and Fisheries Cttee, 1965-; National Inst. of Oceanography Cttee, 1966-; and of various other Univ., Government, professional and educational committees. FIERE, 1953; FIEE, 1954. Clerk Maxwell Premium of IERE, 1961. *Publications:* Modulators and Frequency-Changers, 1953; Electrical Network Theory, 1964; Circuits with Periodically-Varying Parameters, 1964; Applied Underwater Acoustics (with B. K. Gazey) 1966; Underwater Observation Using Sonar, 1966; Sonar in Fisheries: A Forward Look, 1967; papers in professional and scientific journals. *Recreation:* history of technology. *Address:* 26 Twatling Road, Barnt Green, Birmingham. *T:* 021-445 1820.

**TUCKER, Edward William,** CB 1969; Head of Royal Naval Engineering Service, 1966-70; Director of Dockyards, Ministry of Defence, at Bath, 1967-70, retired; *b* 3 Nov. 1908; *s* of Henry Tucker, Plymouth; *m* 1935, Eva, *d* of Arthur Banks, Plymouth. *Educ:* Imperial Coll. of Science and Technology, London Univ.; Royal Naval Coll., Greenwich. BSc (Eng). Electrical Engineer in Admiralty service, at Plymouth, London, Hong Kong and Bath, 1935-64; General Manager of HM Dockyard, Chatham, 1964-66. *Recreations:* gardening, golf. *Address:* Gulls Cry, Thurlestone, Kingsbridge, Devon. *T:* Thurlestone 265. *Club:* Royal Western Yacht Club of England.

**TUCKER, Hon. Sir Henry (James),** Kt 1961; CBE 1946; Government Leader, Executive Council, Bermuda, since 1968; General Manager, Bank of Bermuda Ltd, Hamilton, Bermuda, since 1938; *b* 14 March 1903; *s* of Henry James and Nella Louise Tucker; *m* 1925, Catherine Newbold Barstow; two *s* one *d*. *Educ:* Saltus Grammar School, Bermuda; Sherborne School, Dorset, England. New York Trust Co., 1924-26; Kelley, Drayton and Converse (Brokers), 1926-30; Milne Munro & Tucker (Brokers), 1930-34; joined Bank of Bermuda Ltd, 1934. Pres., Anglo Norness Shipping, 1968-. *Recreation:* golf. *Address:* The Lagoon, Paget, Bermuda. *T:* 2-1657. *Clubs:* Mid-Ocean Golf, Royal Bermuda Yacht, Royal Hamilton Dinghy, Riddells Bay Golf (all in Bermuda).

**TUCKER, Norman Walter Gwynn,** CBE 1956; a Governor of The Royal Ballet since 1957; *b* 24 April 1910; *s* of Walter Edwin and Agnes Janet Tucker. *Educ:* St Paul's School; New College, Oxford. Solo pianist, 1935-39. Civil servant, Treasury, 1939-45 (private sec. to Sir Kingsley Wood, Sir John Anderson (later *cr* Visc. Waverley) and Hugh Dalton). Director of Opera, Sadler's Wells, 1947; Director of Sadler's Wells Theatre, 1951-66. *Recreations:* playing the piano, squash racquets.

**TUCKER, Robert St John P.;** *see* Pitts-Tucker.

**TUCKER, William Eldon,** CVO 1954; MBE 1944; TD 1951; FRCS; Honorary Orthopædic Surgeon, Royal London Homœopathic Hospital; Director and Surgeon, The Clinic, Park Street, since 1936; *b* 6 Aug. 1903; *s* of late Dr W. E. Tucker, Hamilton, Bermuda; *m* 1931, Jean Stella (marr. diss. 1953), *d* of James Ferguson, Rudgwick, Sussex; two *s*; *m* 1956, Mary Beatrice Castle. *Educ:* Sherborne; Gonville and Caius Coll., Cambridge. MA 1931; FRCS 1930; MB, BCh 1946. St George's Hospital, 1925-34; Lt RAMC, TA, 1930-34; Major RAMC, Orthopædic Specialist, 1939-45; Lt-Col, RAMC, TA, 1946-51; Col and Hon. Col 17th General Hospital, TA, 1951-63. Surgeon, St John's Hosp., Lewisham, 1931-37; Registrar, Royal Nat. Orthop. Hosp. 1933-34; Orthopædic Consultant, Horsham Hosp., 1945, Dorking Hosp., 1956. Hunterian Prof., RCS, Oct. 1958. *Publications:* Active Alerted Posture, 1960; Home Treatment in Injury and Osteoarthritis, 1961, new edn, Home Treatment and Posture in Injury, Rheumatism and Osteoarthritis, 1969; (with J. R. Armstrong) Injury in Sport, 1964. *Recreations:* tennis, Rugby football exec. (formerly Cambridge XV, Captain 1925; England XV, 1926-30); ball-room dancing. *Address:* 71 Park Street, W1. *T:* 01-629 3763. *Club:* Pilgrims.

**TUCKWELL, Edward George,** MCh, FRCS; Surgeon to the Queen, since 1969, to HM Household, since 1964; Surgeon, St Bartholomew's Hospital, London, since 1947; Surgeon, Royal Masonic Hospital, since 1958; Consultant Surgeon, King Edward VII Convalescent Home, Osborne, since 1965; *b* 12 May 1910; *e s* of Edward Henry Tuckwell and Annie Clarice (*née* Sansom); *m* 1934, Phyllis Courthope Regester (*d* 1970); two *s* one *d*. *Educ:* Charterhouse; Magdalen College, Oxford; St Bartholomew's Hospital. BM, BCh Oxon. 1936; MCh 1948; FRCS 1939. War Service in EMS and RAMC, Surgical Specialist, North-West Europe and South-East Asia, Lt-Col. Examiner in Surgery to Univs of London, Manchester, Oxford, and in Pathology to Conjoint Board and Royal College of Surgeons; Dean of Medical School, St Bartholomew's Hospital, 1952-57; Surgeon, King Edward VII Hospital for Officers, 1961-. Mem., Governing Body of Charterhouse School (London University representative); Governor, St Bartholomew's Hosp., 1954-. *Publications:* articles in medical journals. *Recreations:* gardening, shooting, travelling. *Address:* Goblin Glade, Seale, Farnham, Surrey. *T:* Runfold 2421; 73 Harley Street, W1. *T:* 01-935 7288; Pensioners' Court, Charterhouse, EC1. *T:* 01-253 1177. *Clubs:* Oriental; Kennel.

**TUDOR DAVIES, William;** *see* Davies, W. T.

**TUDOR EVANS, Haydn,** QC 1962; *b* 20 June 1920; 4th *s* of John Edgar Evans and Ellen Stringer; *m* 1947, Sheilagh Isabella Pilkington; one *s*. *Educ:* West Monmouth School; Lincoln College, Oxford. RNVR, 1940-41. Open Scholar, Lincoln Coll., Oxford (Mod. History), 1940; Stewart Exhibitioner, 1942; Final Hons Sch., Mod. History, 1944; Final Hons Sch., Jurisprudence, 1945. Scholar, Lincoln's Inn, 1946; called to the Bar, Lincoln's Inn, 1947, Bencher 1970. *Address:* 30 Stanford Road, W8. *T:* 01-937 1953. *Clubs:* Garrick, MCC.

**TUDSBERY, Marmaduke Tudsbery,** CBE 1941; FCGI 1950; FICE 1932; Fellow 1953 and Governor since 1942, Imperial College of Science and Technology; Hon. Member Institution of Royal Engineers, 1937; President Smeatonian Society of Civil Engineers, 1956; *b* 4 Oct. 1892; 3rd *s* of late J. H. T. Tudsbery, DSc; unmarried. *Educ:* Westminster; Imperial College, London University; engineering training under late John J. Webster, FICE, and at works of Yarrow & Co. Ltd, Glasgow. Commissioned, Special Reserve of Officers, RE: France, 1915 (9th Field Company), Army of the Rhine, Mesopotamia Expeditionary Force; staff of RE Board, War Office, 1920-25; Member, later Chairman, War Office Cttee on Army Building, 1940-44; Member: Home Office Committee on Structural Precautions against Air-Attack, 1936-39; Science Museum Adv. Council, 1959-69. The Civil Engineer to BBC, 1926-52; Consulting Civil Engineer to BBC, 1952-60. *Address:* 49 Hallam Street, W1. *Clubs:* Athenæum, MCC, Royal Cruising, Royal Thames Yacht.

**TUFNELL-BARRETT, Hugh,** CIE 1943; K-i-H Gold Medal 1938; *b* 13 Jan. 1900; *s* of late Rev. Wilfrid Tufnell-Barrett, formerly of Court Lodge, Shorne, Kent; *m* 1929, Frances Eleanor, *d* of late Julian Claude Platts, Melbourne, Australia; one *s* two *d*. *Educ:* St John's School, Leatherhead; Cadet College, Wellington, India. 2nd Lieut 31st Punjabis, IA, 1918; Temporary Captain and Staff Captain, Bushire Field Force, South Persia, 1920-21; Offg Bde Major, 3rd Ind. Inf. Bde, Peshawar, 1922; resigned, 1922; entered ICS, 1923; District Magistrate, Dacca, Bengal, 1931, Bakarganj, Bengal, 1935; Joint Sec. Commerce and Labour Dept, Bengal, 1939; Addl Sec. Home Dept, Bengal, 1939; Dep. Sec. to Govt of India, Dept of Labour, 1939-43; Joint Secretary to Govt of India, Dept of Labour, April 1943; Offg Sec. to Govt of India, Dept of Labour, June 1943; Civil Representative of Bengal Govt with Eastern Army and Additional Home Sec., Bengal, Dec. 1943; Director-General, Food, and Addtl Commissioner for Civil Supplies, Bengal, 1945; entered service of Pakistan Govt, Sept. 1947; Commissioner, Chittagong Division, E Pakistan, 1947-49; Secretary, Ministry of Kashmir Affairs, Government of Pakistan, 1949-50. *Recreation:* reading. *Address:* 2 Queen's Gate Place, SW7.

**TUFTON,** family name of **Baron Hothfield.**

**TUGENDHAT, Christopher Samuel;** MP (C) Cities of London and Westminster since 1970; *b* 23 Feb. 1937; *er s* of Dr Georg Tugendhat, *qv*, and Mrs Maire Tugendhat; *m* 1967, Julia Lissant Dobson. *Educ:* Ampleforth Coll.; Gonville and Caius Coll., Cambridge. Financial Times leader and feature writer, 1960-70; Publisher, Longman Group, 1970. *Publication:* Oil: the biggest business, 1968. *Recreations:* reading, following football, conversation. *Address:* 47 Emperor's Gate, SW7. *T:* 01-373 7210. *Club:* Carlton.

**TUGENDHAT, Georg,** LLD, MSc (Econ.); a founder of the Manchester Oil Refinery Group of Companies, Petrocarbon Ltd and Petrochemicals Ltd; lately one of their Managing Directors; Independent Consultant on energy, chemical and industrial problems; *b* 17 February 1898; *s* of Samuel Tugendhat, Vienna, and Gabriele (*née* Schick); *m* 1934, Maire, *d* of late Major Arthur Charles Littledale, RFA; two *s* two *d*. *Educ:* Vienna University (LLD); London School of Economics (MSc). First Lt KK Schützenregiment 24, Imperial Austrian Army, 1916-18. Arrived in England, 1921. 1922-28: London representative Neue Freie Presse, Vienna; Deutscher Volkswirt, Berlin. Acting Financial Adviser to Austrian Legation in London, 1924-28; London representative of Reichskredit Gesellschaft AG of Berlin, 1930-33. A Gov. and Hon. Fell., London School of Economics and Political Science; Fell. of Royal Economic Soc.; Foreign Mem. Association Française des Techniciens du Pétrole. *Publications:* Sources of Energy; Wanted–A Policy for Fuel; Freedom for Fuel and Dilemma of the State Monopolies; contrib. to: The Times; American, French, German and Belgian economic periodicals. *Recreations:* writing, travelling, music. *Address:* 6 Rutland Court, Knightsbridge, SW7. *T:* 01-589 3015. *Clubs:* Reform, Political Economy, Hurlingham.
*See also C. S. Tugendhat.*

**TUITE, Sir Dennis (George Harmsworth),** 13th Bt *cr* 1622; MBE 1946; Major RE, retired; *b* 26 Jan. 1904; *s* of late Hugh George Spencer Tuite and late Eva Geraldine Tuite (*née* Hatton); *S* brother, 1970; *m* 1947, Margaret Essie, *o d* of late Col Walter Leslie Dundas, DSO, late 3rd QAO Gurkha Rifles; three *s*. *Educ:* St Paul's School; RMA Woolwich. Commissioned, Royal Engineers, 1925; served in India, North West Frontier, 1928-30, Burma, 1930-32 (medal). Served War, in Europe, 1939-45; Kenya, 1948-52; retired, 1959. *Recreation:* fly fishing. *Heir: s* Christopher Hugh Tuite, *b* 3 Nov. 1949. *Address:* Heathside, Crossways Road, Grayshott, Hindhead, Surrey. *T:* Hindhead 5026.

**TUKE, Anthony William;** Director: Barclays Bank Ltd (Chairman, 1951-62); Fellow of Winchester College (Warden, 1962-70); Chairman of Trustees, D'Oyly Carte Opera Trust Ltd; Trustee, Historic Churches Preservation Trust; *b* 24 Feb. 1897; *s* of William Favill Tuke (*d* 1940) and Eva Marian (*d* 1919), *d* of Martin Nockolds; *m* 1919, Agnes Edna (*d* 1966), *d* of late Henry George Gannaway; one *s* (and two *s* decd). *Educ:* Winchester. Joined Barclays Bank on demobilisation, 1919; Local Dir of Luton Dist, 1923-31; Gen. Man. 1931-46; Vice-Chm., 1946-47; Dep. Chm., 1947-51; Pres. British Bankers' Assoc. 1952-54; Hon. Treas. of St Dunstan's, 1947-57. Officer of the Order of St John of Jerusalem. *Publication:* History of Barclays Bank Ltd (with P. W. Matthews). *Recreations:* fishing, gardening. *Address:* Freelands, Wherwell, Hampshire. *Clubs:* Brooks's, Flyfishers'.

**TUKE, Comdr (retired) Seymour Charles,** DSO 1940; Royal Navy; *b* 20 May 1903; 3rd *s* of late Rear-Adm. J. A. Tuke; *m* 1928, Marjorie Alice Moller; one *s* one *d*. *Educ:* Stonyhurst; RNC, Osborne and Dartmouth. Midshipman, 1921; Lieutenant, 1926; Acting Commander, 1945; FAA, 1927-29; Local Fishery Naval Officer, English Channel, 1935-37; served War of 1939-45 (DSO, 1939-45 Medal, Atlantic Star, Italy Star, War Medal); in command of SS Hannah Boge (first prize of the war), 1939; Senior Officer Res. Fleet, Harwich, 1946; Maintenance Comdr to Senior Officer Res. Fleet, 1947-48; retired, 1948. *Address:* Henstridge House, Crudwell, Malmesbury, Wiltshire. *T:* Crudwell 283.

**TULL, Thomas Stuart,** CBE 1963 (OBE 1946); DSO 1946; High Commissioner at Zomba, since 1967; *b* 11 October 1914; *surv yr s* of late Frank Stuart Tull and of Phyllis Mary Tull (*née* Back); *m* 1946, Constance Grace Townsend; one *s* two *d* (one *step s* one *step d*). *Educ:* Rossall School; Jesus College, Oxford. Entered Indian Civil Service, 1938; served in Punjab, 1939-41; ADC to the Governor, 1941; lent to War Department, Govt of India, for service with RAF, 1941; on active service in India and SE Asia Commands, 1941-46; retired from ICS and entered HM Diplomatic Service, 1947. Foreign Office, 1947-48; First Secretary at British Legation, Berne, 1948-51; Foreign Office, 1951-53; HM Consul at San Francisco, 1953-54; HM Consul at Denver, 1954-56; Press Counsellor at British Embassy, Cairo, 1956; HM Consul-General at Gothenburg, 1958-61; at Philadelphia, 1961-66; at Durban, 1966-67. *Recreations:* sailing, riding, photography. *Address:* (when on leave) Hunter's Moon, Longworth, near Abingdon, Berks. *T:* Longworth 234. *Clubs:* Royal Air Force, Travellers', Special Forces, Royal Commonwealth Society.

**TULLOCH, Maj.-Gen. (Donald) Derek (Cuthbertson),** CB 1955; DSO 1944; MC 1940; late RA; Game Farmer; *b* 28 April 1903; *s* of late Lt-Col D. F. Tulloch, DSO, late RA, and late Diana Mary Tulloch; *m* 1927, Mary, *e d* of late Jonathan Formby, Firwood, Formby, Lancs; two *s*. *Educ:* Temple Grove, Eastbourne; Imperial Service College; Royal Military Academy, Woolwich. 2nd Lt RA 1923; ADC to GOC-in-C, Southern Command, Salisbury, 1926; GSO2, GHQ, BEF, 1939-40; evacuated Dunkirk, 1940; BGS to Maj.-Gen. Wingate, Chindit Operation Burma, 1943-44; BRA Southern Command, 1952-54; General Officer Commanding Singapore Base District, Far ELF, 1954-57, retired. ADC to The Queen, 1953-55. Commissioner, St John Ambulance Brigade, Wiltshire, 1961-66; CStJ. Testimonial of Royal Humane Society on Vellum, 1927. *Recreations:* shooting and fishing. *Address:* The Old Rectory, Rushall, Pewsey, Wiltshire. *Club:* Army and Navy.

**TUNBRIDGE, Sir Ronald (Ernest),** Kt 1967; OBE 1944; Professor of Medicine, University of Leeds, since 1946; Chairman, Standing Medical Advisory Committee, Ministry of Health, since 1963; *b* 2 June 1906; *s* of Rev. W. J. Tunbridge and Norah (*née* Young); *m* 1935, Dorothy Gregg; two *s*. *Educ:* Kingswood School, Bath; University of Leeds. Research Fellowship in Physiology, 1928; Hons degree in Physiology, BSc, 1928, MSc, 1929; MB, ChB, Hons 1931; MD 1933; MRCP 1933; FRCP 1944; numerous resident appointments in Leeds. Clinical asst for one year at St Bartholomew's Hosp., under Sir Francis Fraser; Reader in Medicine, Univ. of Leeds; Consultant to Hosps in Leeds area. Military Service, 1941-46; Adviser in Medicine, Malta

Command; Cons. in Med., BLA and BAOR, 1945-46 (despatches). FRSoc Med. Mem. of: Assoc. of Physicians of Gt Brit. and Ire.; Med. Research Soc.; Heberden Soc. (serving on Council of latter, Pres., 1954 and 1955); The Diabetic Assoc. (Banting Memorial Lectr, 1953); Chm., Bd of Science, BMA, 1968-; Governing Body of 1st and 2nd International Gerontological Congresses (Member, Governing Body of Third Internat. Congress; Chm. Brit. Organizing Cttee of Third Congress); Leeds Regional Hosp. Bd, 1947-51; Mem. Bd of United Leeds Hosps, 1952-; Chm., Educn Cttee, King Edward's Hospital Fund for London, 1967-; Mem. Central Health Services Council, 1959- (Vice-Chm., 1963-); Executive Committee, Nat. Old People's Welfare Council (Vice-Chm. Yorkshire Council); Chm., Leeds Local Broadcasting Council, 1968-. Bobst Award, Internat. Association of Gerontology, 1957; Heberden Orator, 1956; Procter Memorial Lecture, 1958; Past. Pres. Brit. Spas Federation, 1955-63. Asst Editor, Gerontolgia. *Publications:* articles in Quarterly Jl of Medicine, Lancet, BMJ, etc. *Recreation:* walking. *Address:* (home) 9 Ancaster Road, Leeds 16; Department of Medicine, Leeds University. *Clubs:* Athenæum, Authors'.

**TUNNARD, John,** ARA 1967; ARCA, NRD; Hand block printer of fabrics; Painter and Designer; teaching at Penzance School of Art; *b* Cæsar's Camp, Sandy, Beds, 7 May 1900; *s* of John Charles and late Nina Tunnard; *m* 1926, Mary May Robertson (*d* 1970); no *c*. *Educ:* Charterhouse; Royal Coll. of Art. Diploma, ARCA 1921; designer on retaining fee to Messrs Tootal, Broadhurst, Lee Co., Textile Manufacturers, 1924-27; art adviser to H. & M. Southwell, Carpet Manufacturers, 1927-29; selector to John Lewis & Co., Oxford Street, 1929-30; visiting teacher in Design to Central School of Arts and Crafts, Southampton Row, 1930. Then gave up all commercial work to paint, and retired to Cornwall; first one-man show of landscapes and still life, Redfern Gallery, 1932; one-man show of abstract painting, Guggenheim Jeune, Cork Street, W1, 1939; one-man show of non-representational painting, Redfern Gallery, 1942; one-man show of gouaches, Nierendorf Gallery, New York, 1945; one-man show, McRoberts and Tunnard Gall., Curzon St, W1, 1959, 1961 and 1964; Durlacher Gallery, New York, 1961; Galleria l'Attico, Rome, 1962; also exhibited at Leicester Galleries, Lefevre Gallery, Leger, Redfern, etc.; pictures purchased by Tate Gallery, Museum of Modern Art, NY, San Francisco, etc., also by Manchester, Glasgow, Leicester City, Hull, Birmingham, Nat. Gallery of Australia, Melbourne, etc. Member of The London Group. *Recreations:* field botany, bug hunting, bird watching, boating. *Address:* Trethinnick, Lamorna, Penzance, Cornwall.

**TUNNICLIFFE, Charles Frederick,** RA 1954 (ARA 1944); RE 1934; ARCA; *b* 1 Dec. 1901; *s* of William and Margaret Tunnicliffe; *m* 1929, Winifred Wonnacott, ARCA (*d* 1969). *Educ:* St James School, Nr Macclesfield; Macclesfield and Manchester Schools of Art; Royal Exhibition Scholarship to Royal College of Art, 1921; Diploma of RCA in Painting, 1923; occupied in painting, engraving, book illustrating. *Publications:* My Country Book, 1942; Bird Portraiture, 1945; Shorelands Summer Diary, 1952. *Address:* Shorelands, Malltraeth Bay, Bodorgan, Anglesey.

**TUOHY, John Francis, (Frank Tuohy);** Novelist; Short Story Writer; *b* 2 May 1925; *s* of late Patrick Gerald Tuohy and Dorothy Marion, (*née* Annandale). *Educ:* Stowe Sch.; King's College, Cambridge. Prof. of English Language and Literature, Univ. of São Paulo, 1950-56; Contract Prof., Jagiellonian Univ., Cracow, Poland, 1958-60; Vis. Prof., Waseda Univ., Tokyo, 1964-67. FRSL 1965. *Publications:* The Animal Game, 1957; The Warm Nights of January, 1960; The Admiral and the Nuns, short stories (Katherine Mansfield Memorial Prize), 1962; The Ice Saints (James Tait Black and Geoffrey Faber Memorial prizes), 1964; Portugal, 1970; Fingers in the Door, 1970. *Recreation:* travel. *Address:* c/o Macmillan and Co. Ltd, Little Essex Street, WC2.

**TUOHY, Thomas,** CBE 1969; Managing Director, Production Group, United Kingdom Atomic Energy Authority, since 1964; *b* 7 Nov. 1917; *s* of Michael and Isabella Tuohy, Cobh, Eire; *m* 1949, Lilian May Barnes; one *s* one *d*. *Educ:* St Cuthberts Grammar Sch., Newcastle; Reading Univ. (BSc). Chemist in various Royal Ordnance Factories, 1939-46. Manager: Health Physics, Springfields Nuclear Fuel Plant, Dept Atomic Energy, 1946; Health Physics, Windscale Plutonium Plant, 1949; Plutonium Piles and Metal Plant, Windscale, 1950; Works Manager: Springfields, 1952; Windscale, UKAEA, 1954; Windscale and Calder Hall: Dep. Gen. Manager, 1957; Gen. Manager, 1958. *Publications:* various technical papers on reactor operation and plutonium manufacture. *Recreations:* golf, gardening. *Address:* Ingleberg, Beckermet, Cumberland. *T:* Beckermet 226.

**TUOMINEN, Leo Olavi;** Finnish Ambassador to Sweden, since 1969; *b* 19 Jan. 1911; *s* of Johan Tuominen (until 1897 Seipel) and Johanna Johansson; *m* 1938, Johanna, *d* of Emil Habert; one *s* three *d*. *Educ:* Turku Univ. (MA). Joined Finnish Foreign Service, 1934; served abroad, 1934-39; Min. of For. Affairs, 1940-46; Legation in Brussels, 1946-48; Asst Under Sec., Min. of For. Affairs, 1948-50; Perm. Deleg. to Int. Orgns in Geneva, 1950-52; Envoy to Argentina, Chile and Uruguay, 1952-55. Min. of Foreign Affairs: Dep. Under Sec., 1955-56; Perm. Under-Sec. of State, 1956-57; Ambassador to Court of St James's, 1957-68, to Italy, 1968-69. Head of Delegn for econ. negotiations with many countries, incl. UK, 1945-56 (Pres. delegn at GATT Conf. Torquay, 1950). Hon. KBE, and holds other foreign decorations. *Publications:* articles and essays on economics. *Recreations:* athletics, ski-ing, reading, gardening. *Address:* v. Traedgårdsgatan 13, Stockholm, Sweden. *Clubs:* Hurlingham, Travellers'.

**TUPLIN, Prof. William Alfred,** DSc, FIMechE, AILocoE; Emeritus Professor of Applied Mechanics, Sheffield University, since 1969 (Professor of Applied Mechanics, and in charge of Post Graduate Dept of Applied Mechanics, 1951-68); formerly Chief Engineer David Brown and Sons (Huddersfield) Ltd and Head of Engineering Research and Development, David Brown Group of companies. DSc Manchester 1939. *Publications:* Torsional Vibration, 1934 (1966); Gear Design, 1962; Involute Gear Geometry, 1962; Great Western Steam, 1958; North Western Steam, 1963; Great Central Steam, 1967; British Steam since 1900, 1969; North Eastern Steam, 1970; Great Northern Steam, 1970. *Address:* Beech Dell, Collegiate Crescent, Sheffield S10 2BA.

**TUPOLEV, Andrei Nikolaevich;** Hero Socialist Labour (twice); Order of Lenin; aeronautical engineer and designer; *b* 11 Nov. 1888. *Educ:* studied Prof. Zhukovsky, Moscow. Higher Technical Institute. Became a Lieut-General in the Engineering-Technical Service. Helped to found Central Aerodynamical Institute, Moscow, 1918; Asst Director, 1918-35; Head of Designing Bureau, 1922; Chief Engineer, 1923-38; designed first aeroplane to fly from Moscow to New York, 1927; designed TU types and many other airliners. Deputy of the Supreme Soviet; Mem. Acad. of Sciences of USSR; President, Soviet-Bulgarian Friendship Soc., 1957. Honoured Worker of Science and Technology, Russian Soviet Federative Socialist Republic, 1933; State Prizes, 1943, 1948; Orders of Lenin, 1947, 1949; Lenin Prize, 1957; Gold Medal, Internat. Aviation Federation, 1959. *Address:* Academy of Sciences of the USSR, Moscow, USSR.

**TUPPER, Sir Charles Hibbert,** 5th Bt *cr* 1888, of Armdale, Halifax, Nova Scotia; *b* 4 July 1930; *o s* of Sir James Macdonald Tupper, 4th Bt, formerly Assistant Commissioner, Royal Canadian Mounted Police, and of Mary Agnes Jean Collins; *S* father, 1967; *m* 1959, Bernice Yvonne Quinn; one *s*. *Heir: s* Charles Hibbert Tupper, *b* 10 July 1964. *Address:* 955 Marine Drive, West Vancouver, British Columbia, Canada.

**TURBERVILLE, Geoffrey,** MA; Principal, Leulumoega High School, Samoa, 1959-62, (retired); *b* 31 Mar. 1899; *o s* of A. E. Turberville, FCA, Stroud Green, London; *m* Jane Campbell Lawson. *Educ:* Westminster Sch. (King's Scholar); Trinity College, Cambridge (Exhibitioner). 2nd Lieut, Queen's Royal West Surrey Regt, 1917-19; Senior Classical Master, Liverpool Collegiate School, 1921-25; Senior Classical Master, Epsom College, 1925-30; Headmaster of Eltham College, 1930-59. Chm. Dorset Congregational Assoc., 1970-71. *Publications:* Cicero and Antony; Arva Latina II; Translation into Latin. *Address:* Kingsbere, St James, Shaftesbury, Dorset.

**TURBOTT, Sir Ian (Graham),** Kt 1968; CMG 1962; CVO 1966; *b* Whangarei, New Zealand, 9 March 1922; *s* of late Thomas Turbott and late E. A. Turbott, both of New Zealand; *m* 1952, Nancy Hall Lantz, California, USA; three *d*. *Educ:* Takapuna Grammar School, Auckland, NZ; Auckland University; Jesus College, Cambridge; London University. NZ Forces (Army), 1940-46: Solomon Is area and 2 NZEF, Italy. Colonial Service (now Overseas Civil Service): Western Pacific, Gilbert and Ellice Is, 1948-56; Colonial Office, 1956-58; Administrator of Antigua, The West Indies, 1958-64; also Queen's Representative under new constitution, 1960-64; Administrator of Grenada and Queen's Representative, 1964-67; Governor of Associated State of Grenada, 1967-68. Director: Spencer Stuart and Associates, 1968-; Canterbury Frozen Meat Co. (London) Ltd, 1968-; L. A. Nichol Ltd, 1968-. Holds 1939-45 Star, Pacific Star, Italy Star, Defence Medal, War Medal, New Zealand Service Medal. CStJ 1964. *Publications:* various technical and scientific, 1948-51, in Jl of Polynesian Society (on Pacific area). *Recreations:* cricket, tennis, golf, fishing. *Address:* c/o Bank of New Zealand, 1 Queen Victoria Street, EC4.

**TURECK, Rosalyn;** concert artist (Bach specialist); conductor; writer; *b* Chicago, 14 Dec. 1914; *d* of Samuel Tureck and Monya (*née* Lipson); *m* 1964, George Wallingford Downs (*d* 1964). *Educ:* Juilliard Sch. of Music, NY. Member Faculty: Philadelphia Conservatory of Music, 1935-42; Mannes School, NYC, 1940-44; Juilliard School of Music, 1943-53; Lecturer Music, Columbia University, NY, 1953-55. Visiting Professor, Washington University, St Louis, 1963-64; Regents Professorship, University of California, San Diego, 1966; Prof. of Music, 4th Step, Univ. of California, San Diego, 1966-. Has appeared as soloist and conductor of leading orchestras in US, Europe and Israel, and toured US, Canada, South Africa, South America; since 1947 has toured extensively in Europe, and played at festivals in Edinburgh, Venice, Holland, Wexford, Schaffhausen, Bath, Brussels World Fair, Glyndebourne, etc.; 1965-66; extensive tours: Australia, New Zealand and Far East, 1971. Formed: Tureck Bach Players, 1959; Internat. Bach Soc., Inc., 1966; Inst. for Bach Studies, 1968. Hon. Member, Guildhall School of Music and Drama, London, 1961; Member: Royal Musical Assoc., London; Inc. Soc. of Musicians, London; Amer. Musicological Soc. Numerous recordings. Hon. Dr of Music, Colby Coll., USA, 1964; Hon. DMus: Roosevelt Univ., 1968; Wilson Coll., 1968. Has won several awards. *Publications:* An Introduction to the Performance of Bach, 1960; (ed) Bach-Sarabande, C minor, 1960; many articles. *Address:* c/o Tillett & Holt Ltd, 124 Wigmore Street, London W1.

**TURING, Sir John Leslie,** 11th Bt *cr* 1638; MC; *b* 13 Sept. 1895; *s* of Sir James Walter Turing, 9th Bt and Mabel Rose, *d* of Andrew Caldecott; *S* twin brother, 1970. *Educ:* Wellington College. Formerly Lieut, Seaforth Highlanders; served European War, 1914-18 (wounded, MC). *Heir: kinsman* John Ferrier Turing [*b* 1 Sept. 1908; *m* 1st, 1934, Joan (marr. diss. 1960), *d* of Robert Humphreys; three *d* (one *s* decd); 2nd, 1960, Beryl Mary Ada, *d* of late Herbert Vaughan Hann; one *s*]. *Address:* c/o Royal Oak Hotel, High Street, Sevenoaks, Kent.

**TURLE, Henry Bernard,** CBE 1958 (OBE 1954); Member Capital Issues Committee, 1946; *b* 18 Sept. 1885; *s* of Edward and Jessie Elizabeth Turle; *m* 1922, Alison Lee Rabett; three *d*. *Educ:* Wellington Coll. In business in India, 1907-16; Indian Army Reserve of Officers, 1916-19; Stockbroker in Calcutta, 1919-28; Stockbroker in London, 1929-56. *Publications:* plays: Miss Smith, 1936; The Old Master, 1938; Marie Antoinette, 1953. *Recreations:* golf, bridge. *Address:* Cedars, Sunninghill, Berks.

**TURNBULL, Brig. Douglas John Tulloch,** CBE 1945; DSO 1941; Regular Army Officer, Royal Horse Artillery; *b* 12 Dec. 1901; *s* of Lt-Col W. J. Turnbull, VD, MICE, and Margaret Stuart Tulloch; *m* 1927, Adelia Brackenbury; three *s*; *m* 1948, Mrs Andrea Warren (*d* 1966), *d* of late Admiral Sir Ernest Troubridge, and late Una, Lady Troubridge; *m* 1968, Mrs Marjorie Benge. *Educ:* Cheltenham Coll.; RMA, Woolwich. Regular Army: India, Egypt, at home, also in Ethiopia (Local Maj.-Gen.); first commission, 1921; served in War of 1939-45: France and Belgium, 1939 till Dunkirk evacuation; Egypt and Libya campaigns, 1940-43 (wounded); Aegean Sea, 1943-45; retired 1954. Kt Commander Royal Order of the Phœnix (Greece), 1945. *Recreations:* hunting, polo, shooting. *Address:* Vine Cottage, Filkins, Lechlade, Glos. *Clubs:* Cavalry, United Service, MCC.

**TURNBULL, Sir Frank (Fearon),** KBE 1964; CB 1954; CIE 1946; HM Civil Service, retired; *b* 30 April 1905; *m* 1947, Gwynnedd Celia Marian Lewis; three *s*. *Educ:* Marlborough Coll.; Trinity Hall, Cambridge. Entered India Office, 1930; Principal Private Secretary to Secretary of State, 1941-46; Secretary to Cabinet Mission to India, 1946; Under-Secretary, HM Treasury, 1949-59; Secretary, Office of the Minister for Science, 1959-64; Deputy Under-Secretary of State, Dept of Education and Science, 1964-66. Member, Board of Governors, Imperial College, 1967-. Hon. DSc Edinburgh, 1967. *Address:* 12 Aveley Lane, Farnham, Surrey. *T:* Farnham 21986.

**TURNBULL, Gilbert Learmonth,** CBE 1954; Deputy Chief Inspector of Taxes, 1952-Oct. 1960; *b* 22 Oct. 1895; *s* of late D. Lowe Turnbull, Edinburgh. *Educ:* George Watson's Coll. Entered Inland Revenue Department, 1914; retired as Dep. Chief Inspector of Taxes, Oct. 1960. *Address:* 5 Rowben Close, Totteridge, N20. *T:* 01-445 9555.

**TURNBULL, Lt-Col Sir Hugh Stephenson,** KCVO 1937; KBE 1929; Commissioner of Police for the City of London, 1925-50; *b* 25 Aug. 1882; 3rd *s* of late Maj.-Gen. P. S. Turnbull, IMS, Hon. Surgeon to the King, and late Mary Oliver of Borthaugh, Hawick; *m* 1909, Jean, *d* of late John Grant, MD, of Grantown-on-Spey, Scotland; two *s* one *d*. *Educ:* Merchiston Castle Sch., Edinburgh; Royal Military Coll., Sandhurst. Indian Army; Royal Irish Constabulary; Chief Constable of Argyllshire; Chief Constable of Cumberland and Westmorland; Major, 8th Argyll and Sutherland Highlanders, 1914-16; Lt-Col, 7th Gordon Highlanders, 1916-19; Member, Queen's Body Guard for Scotland (The Royal Company of Archers); Liveryman of Fanmakers' Company; Mem., Highland Society of London. KJStJ, Mem., Scottish Priory, Order of St John of Jerusalem; Officer, Order of House of Orange (Holland); Commander, Legion of Honour (France); Grand Cross, Order of Etoile Noire (France); 2nd class Order of Leopold II (Belgium), and other Foreign Orders. King's Police Medal, 1936. *Recreations:* shooting, golf, curling, etc. *Address:* Reidhaven, Grantown-on-Spey, Morayshire. *T:* Grantown 61. *Club:* United Service.

**TURNBULL, Ven. John William;** Archdeacon of Richmond and Canon Residentiary of Ripon Cathedral since 1962; *b* 29 Aug. 1905; 2nd *s* of William and Elizabeth Turnbull; *m* 1938, Alice Trewick Atkinson; one *s* one *d*. *Educ:* Durham Univ.; Edinburgh Theological Coll. Deacon, 1934, Priest 1935, Newcastle Cathedral. Curate of Horton, Northumberland, 1934-36; Curate of Alnwick, 1936-41; Vicar of Longbenton, 1941-48; Vicar of All Saints', Gosforth, 1948-62. *Address:* Canon's Lodge, Ripon, Yorkshire. *T:* Ripon 3270.

**TURNBULL, Sir Richard (Gordon),** GCMG 1962 (KCMG 1958, CMG 1953); *b* 7 July 1909; *s* of Richard Francis Turnbull; *m* 1939, Beatrice, *d* of John Wilson, Glasgow; two *s* one *d*. *Educ:* University College School, London; University College, London; Magdalene Coll., Cambridge. Colonial Administrative Service, Kenya: District Officer, 1931-48; Provincial Comr, 1948-53; Minister for Internal Security and Defence, 1954; Chief Secretary, Kenya, 1955-58; Governor and C-in-C, Tanganyika, 1958-61; Governor-General and Commander-in-Chief, 1961-62; Chairman, Central Land Board, Kenya, 1963-64; High Commissioner for Aden and the Protectorate of South Arabia, 1965-67. Fellow of University College, London; Hon. Fellow, Magdalene College, Cambridge, 1970-. KStJ 1958. *Address:* Wharfe House, Henley-on-Thames, Oxon.

**TURNER,** family name of **Baron Netherthorpe.**

**TURNER, Rt. Hon. Sir Alexander (Kingcome),** PC 1968; Kt 1963; **Rt. Hon. Mr Justice Turner;** QC (NZ) 1952; Judge of the Court of Appeal, New Zealand, since 1962; *b* Auckland, New Zealand, 18 Nov. 1901; *s* of J. H. Turner; *m* 1934, Dorothea F., *d* of Alan Mulgan; two *s* one *d*. *Educ:* Auckland Grammar Sch.; Auckland Univ. (Scholar). BA 1921; MA 1922; LLB 1923. Served War of 1939-45, National Military Reserve, New Zealand. Barrister and Solicitor, 1923. Carnegie Travelling Fellowship, 1949. Judge of the Supreme Court of New Zealand, 1953-62; Senior Resident Judge at Auckland, 1958-62; President, Auckland University Students' Assoc., 1928; President, Auckland District Court of Convocation, 1933; Member, Auckland Univ. Council, 1935-51; Vice-President, Auckland Univ., 1950-51; a Governor, Massey Agricultural Coll., 1944-53. Hon. LLD Auckland, 1965. *Publications:* (with George Spencer Bower) The Law of Estoppel by Representation, 1966; Res Judicata, 1969. *Recreations:* gardening, golf, Bush conservation, agriculture. *Address:* Court of Appeal, Wellington, New Zealand; 75 Messines Road, Wellington 5, New Zealand.

**TURNER, Sir Alfred Charles;** *see* Turner, Sir Victor A. C.

**TURNER, Adm. Sir (Arthur) Francis,** KCB 1970 (CB 1966); DSC 1945; Chief of Fleet Support, Ministry of Defence, since May 1967; *b* 23 June 1912; *s* of Rear-Admiral A. W. J. Turner and Mrs A. M. Turner (*née* Lochrane); *m* 1963, Elizabeth Clare de Trafford; two *s*. *Educ:* Stonyhurst Coll. Entered RN, 1931; Commander, 1947; Captain, 1956; Rear-Admiral, 1964; Vice-Admiral, 1968; Admiral, 1970. Dir.-Gen. Aircraft (Navy), MoD, 1966-67. *Recreations:* cricket, golf. *Address:* 15 West Way, Rickmansworth, Herts. *Clubs:* Army and Navy; Union (Malta).

**TURNER, Arthur James,** CBE 1950; MA, DSc, FTI; Director, 1940-56, of Linen Industry Research Association, Lambeg, Co. Antrim; retired, 1956; *b* 30 Sept. 1889; *s* of A. A. Turner, Camberwell, SE; *m* 1st, 1916, Winifred (*d* 1945), *y d* of Alfred Fisher, Streatham, SW; three *s* one *d*; 2nd, 1959, Winifred Doris (*d* 1970), *er d* of late Sir Frederick (Joseph) and Lady West, Wilmslow. *Educ:* Wilson's Grammar Sch., Camberwell, SE. Gonville and Caius Coll., Cambridge (Scholar and Research Student). Assistant at National Physical Laboratory, 1912-15; Head of Experimental Fabrics Laboratory, Royal Aircraft Establishment, 1915-19; Prof. of Textile Technology, Manchester Univ., and College of Technology, Manchester, 1919-23; Director, Technological Research Laboratory, Indian Central Cotton Cttee, Bombay, 1924-30; Head of Spinning Dept, British Cotton Industry Research Assoc., Manchester, 1931-40; Member of Flax Development Cttee, Northern Ireland, 1940-56; Member of Flax Cttee, Ministry of Supply, 1942-50; Chairman, Flax Utilisation Sub-Cttee, 1943-50; Member of Council of Textile Institute, 1941-48, Vice-President, 1948-52, President, 1952-54; Adviser to Bombay Textile Research Assoc., 1958. Hon. Assoc. College of Technology, Manchester, 1951. Hon. Liveryman, 1923, and Member of Court, Worshipful Company of

Weavers, Upper Warden, 1946, Upper Bailiff, 1962. *Publications:* Quality in Flax, 1955; Technological Reports on Standard Indian Cottons; numerous scientific and technical papers. *Recreations:* gardening, walking, cricket, chess. *Address:* Springfield, 12 Lumley Road, Kendal, Westmorland. *T:* Kendal 22324.

**TURNER, Comdr Bradwell Talbot,** CVO 1955; DSO 1940; OBE 1951; JP; RN, retired April 1957; with The Marconi Company; *b* 7 April 1907; *s* of late A. F. and A. I. Turner; *m* 1937, Mary G. B., *d* of Professor W. Nixon; three *d*. *Educ:* Christ's Hospital; RN Colleges Osborne and Dartmouth. Joined Royal Navy, 1921; Barrister-at-Law, 1956; Naval Attaché, Oslo, Norway, 1954-57. MIEE 1946. JP 1962. Officer, Legion of Merit (USA), 1945. *Recreation:* riding. *Address:* Delimara, Little Baddow, Essex.

**TURNER, Air Vice-Marshal Cameron Archer,** CB 1968; CBE 1960 (OBE 1947); Royal New Zealand Air Force, retired; Director, New Zealand Inventions Development Authority, since 1969; *b* Wanganui, NZ, 29 Aug. 1915; *s* of James Oswald Turner and Vida Cathrine Turner; *m* 1941, Josephine Mary, *d* of George Richardson; two *s*. *Educ:* New Plymouth Boys' High Sch.; Victoria University of Wellington. CEng, FIEE, FRAeS. Commn RAF, 1936-39; commn RNZ Air Force, 1940; served War of 1939-45, UK, NZ, and Pacific; comd RNZAF Station Nausori, Fiji, 1944; comd RNZAF Station, Guadalcanal, Solomon Islands, 1944; Director of Signals, 1945-47; psa 1947; RNZAF Liaison Officer, Melbourne, Australia, 1948-50; comd RNZAF Station, Taieri, NZ, 1950-52; Director of Organization, HQ, RNZAF, 1953-56; comd RNZAF Station Ohakea, NZ, 1956-58; Asst Chief of Air Staff, HQ, RNZAF, 1958; Air Member for Personnel, HQ, RNZAF, 1959; idc 1960; AOC HQ, RNZAF, London, 1961-63; Air Member for Supply, HQ, RNZAF, 1964-65; Chief of Air Staff, HQ RNZAF, 1966-69. *Recreations:* fishing, golf. *Address:* 37a Parkvale Road, Wellington 5, New Zealand. *T:* 766063. *Clubs:* Wellington, United Services Officers' (Wellington).

**TURNER, Maj.-Gen. Cecil Douglas Lovett,** CIE 1946; OBE 1943; retired; *b* 25 Feb. 1898; *s* of G. D. Pitt Turner, Bristol; *m* 1928, Frances Joan, *d* of T. W. Morcom-Harneis, Urchfont, Wilts; two *s*. *Educ:* Denstone; RMC and Staff Coll., Camberley. Joined 5th Royal Mahrattas, 1917; served European War, 1917-18, India; Afghanistan and Waziristan, 1919-22; Brig. Q Plans Ops. and Admin. Co-ordination, GHQ India Command, 1939-46; Lt-Col, 1941; Brigadier, 1943; Maj.-Gen., 1949. *Recreation:* gardening. *Address:* Herbsland House, Hurstbourne Tarrant, Andover, Hants. *T:* Hurstbourne Tarrant 295.

**TURNER, Sir Cedric Oban,** Kt 1967; CBE 1958; Chief Executive and General Manager, Qantas Empire Airways Ltd, 1955-67; *b* 13 Feb. 1907; *s* of S. Turner, Gulgong, NSW; *m* 1935, Shirley, *d* of late Sir Joseph Totterdell, sometime Lord Mayor of Perth, Western Australia; one *s* three *d*. *Educ:* Sydney High Sch. Chartered Accountant: Robert W. Nelson, 1924-29, UK and Europe, 1929-34. Joined Qantas Empire Airways, 1934; Chief Accountant; Assistant General Manager, 1949-51; General Manager, 1951-55. *Recreation:* golf. *Address:* 58 Burns Road, Wahroonga, NSW 2076, Australia.

**TURNER, Brig. Charles Edward Francis,** CBE 1944 (OBE 1941); DSO 1943; late RE; *b* 23 April 1899; *s* of late Lieut A. E. Turner, RE, and E. B., *d* of Maj.-Gen. Sir C. H. Scott, KCB; *m* 1930, Mary Victoria, *d* of H. Leeds Swift, York; one *s* two *d*. *Educ:* Twyford Sch., Winchester; Wellington Coll., Berks; Royal Military Academy, Woolwich. Regular Officer, Royal Engineers, Sept. 1917; BEF France, June-Nov. 1918; NREF Russia, July-Sept. 1919; India, 1920-23, including two years on North-West Frontier on service (despatches); Christ's Coll., Cambridge, 1923-24; Ordnance Survey, York and Edinburgh, 1925-30; Staff Coll., Camberley, 1931-32; Singapore, Egypt, Palestine, 1934-37, including service in Palestine (Bt Major, despatches); War Office, 1937-39; MEF 1940-43 (OBE, DSO, CBE, despatches twice); Malaya, 1948-50; retired pay, 1950. National Council of Social Service, 1950-58; Secretary, Iona Appeal Trust, 1958-61. *Address:* The Colleens, Cousley Wood, Wadhurst, Sussex. *T:* Wadhurst 2387.

**TURNER, Christopher Gilbert;** Headmaster, Dean Close School, since 1968; *b* 23 Dec. 1929; *s* of Theodore F. Turner, *qv*; *m* 1961, Lucia, *d* of late Prof. S. R. K. Glanville (Provost of King's Coll., Cambridge); one *s* two *d*. *Educ:* Winchester Coll. (Schol.); New Coll., Oxford (Exhibnr). Asst Master, Radley Coll., 1952-61; Senior Classics Master, Charterhouse, 1961-68. Schoolmaster Student at Christ Church, Oxford, 1967. Foundation Member of Council, Cheltenham Colleges of Educn, 1968. FRSA. Rotarian. *Publication:* chapter on History, in Comparative Study of Greek and Latin Literature, 1969. *Recreations:* music (violin-playing), walking, farming, bookbinding; OUBC 1951. *Address:* Dean Close House, Lansdown Road, Cheltenham, Glos. *T:* Cheltenham 52537 (study 22640); Meadow House, Rhossili, near Swansea, Glam. *T:* Rhossili 282. *Clubs:* Oxford and Cambridge University; Vincent's (Oxford).

**TURNER, Colin William Carstairs,** DFC 1944; *b* 4 Jan. 1922; *s* of late Colin C. W. Turner, Enfield; *m* 1949, Evelyn Mary, *d* of late Claude H. Buckard, Enfield; three *s* one *d*. *Educ:* Highgate Sch. Served War of 1939-45 with RAF, 1940-45, Air observer; S. Africa and E. Africa, 223 Squadron; Desert Air Force, N. Africa, 1942-44; commissioned, 1943; invalided out as Flying Officer, 1945, after air crash. Member Enfield Borough Council, 1956-58. Joint Managing Director, Colin Turner and W. Ager Group of Companies, International Media Representatives and Marketing Consultants. President, Overseas Press and Media Association, 1956-67 (Hon. Secretary, 1967; Editor, Overseas Media Guide, 1968, 1969, 1970). Member Nat. Exec., Cons. Party, 1946-53, 1968-69; Chm. PR Cttee, Commonwealth Press Union, 1969. Contested (C) Enfield (East), 1950 and 1951; MP (C) Woolwich West, 1959-64. *Recreations:* gardening, do-it-yourself, sailing, fishing. *Address:* 55 Rowantree Road, Enfield, Middlesex. *T:* 01-363 2403. *Clubs:* RAF Reserves, Publicity.

**TURNER, Douglas William,** JP; Director, Midland Bank Ltd; *b* 8 Dec. 1894; *m* 1922, Mary Kathleen, *d* of Alfred Rogers; one *s*. *Educ:* Repton. Served European War, 1914-18, Warwickshire Yeomanry. Governor of Birmingham Univ. *Recreation:* golf. *Address:* Home Lea, Woodbourne Road, Edgbaston, Birmingham. *T:* 021-454 3740. *Clubs:* Conservative, Edgbaston Golf, Moseley Golf (Birmingham).

**TURNER, Dudley Russell Flower;** Assistant Under-Secretary of State, Training Division, Department of Employment and Productivity, since 1968; *b* 15 Nov. 1916; *s* of Gerald Flower Turner and Dorothy May Turner (*née* Gillard), Penang; *m* 1941, Sheila

Isobel Stewart; one *s* one *d*. *Educ:* Whitgift Sch.; London Univ. (BA Hons). Served RA (Captain), 1940-46. Entered Ministry of Labour, 1935; HM Treasury, 1953-56; Principal Private Secretary to Minister of Labour, 1956-59; Assistant Secretary: Cabinet Office, 1959-62; Ministry of Labour, 1962-64, 1966; Under-Secretary, Ministry of Labour, 1967. Imperial Defence Coll., 1965. *Recreations:* tennis, music, gardening. *Address:* 10 Melville Avenue, South Croydon, Surrey. *Club:* Army and Navy.

**TURNER, Eric,** CBE 1968; FCA; Chairman since 1961 and Chief Executive since 1960, The Birmingham Small Arms Company Ltd; Chairman: BSA Guns Ltd; Ariel Motors Ltd; BSA Motor Cycles Ltd; BSA Tools Ltd; Burton, Griffiths & Co. Ltd; BSA Small Tools Ltd; BG Machinery Ltd; BSA Broach Co. Ltd; Carbodies Ltd; Idoson Motor Cylinder Co. Ltd; Churchill Machine Tool Co. Ltd; Director: The Blackburn Group Ltd; English & Scottish Investors Ltd; Triumph Engineering Co. Ltd; Jessop-Saville Ltd; Birtley Engineering Ltd; *b* 18 July 1918; *o s* of William Edmund and Elsie Turner, Staveley, Derbyshire; *m* 1943, Zena Doreen Schellenberg. *Educ:* Chesterfield Sch. Served India and Burma, War of 1939-45; demobilised, 1946, Lt-Col. Chairman (1955-59) and Managing Director (1951-59), The Blackburn Group. Member: Malta Industrial Development Board; Advisory Council, Export Credits Guarantee Dept, 1965. Treasurer and Chairman of Finance Cttee, University of Aston, 1968-. *Recreation:* golf. *Address:* Dale Cross Grange, Barnt Green, Worcestershire. *T:* Hillside 1676. *Clubs:* Royal Aero, East India and Sports.

**TURNER, Eric Gardner,** FBA; Professor of Papyrology, University College, London, since 1950; *b* 26 Feb. 1911; *s* of late William Ernest Stephen Turner; *m* 1940, Louise B. Taylor; one *s* one *d*. *Educ:* King Edward VII Sch., Sheffield; Magdalen Coll., Oxford (Demy). First Class Hons Classical Mods, 1932, and Lit Hum, 1934; Goldsmiths' Senior Scholar, 1935; Assistant in Humanity, University of Aberdeen, 1936; Lecturer in Classics, Aberdeen Univ., 1938-48; Reader in Papyrology, University of London, 1948-50; first Dir, Univ. of London Inst. of Classical Studies, 1953-63. President: Internat. Assoc. of Papyrologists; Hellenic Soc.; Vice-President, Roman Soc.; Chairman: Organising Cttee, Third Internat. Congress of Classical Studies, London, 1959; Cttee, Egypt Exploration Soc.; Jt Editor, Graeco-Roman publications. Visiting Member, Inst. for Advanced Study, Princeton, NJ, 1961, 1964, 1968. Mem., Union Académique Internationale. Hon. Dr Phil et Lettres Brussels. *Publications:* Catalogue of Greek Papyri in University of Aberdeen, 1939; (with C. H. Roberts) Catalogue of Greek Papyri in John Rylands Library, Vol. IV, 1951; The Hibeh Papyri, Part II, 1955; (with others) The Oxyrhynchus Papyri Part XXIV, 1957, Part XXV, 1959, Part XXVII, 1962, Part XXXI, 1966, Part XXXIII, 1968, Part XXXVIII, 1971; (with H. I. Bell, V. Martin, D. van Berchem) The Abinnæus Papyri, 1962; New Fragments of the Misoumenos of Menander, 1965; Greek Papyri, an Introduction, 1968; Greek Manuscripts of the Ancient World, 1970. Various papers in learned journals. *Recreations:* chamber music, playing the gramophone, walking, sailing. *Address:* Bayston, Cross Oak Road, Berkhamsted, Herts. *T:* Berkhamsted 4974. *Club:* Oxford and Cambridge.

**TURNER, Dame Eva,** DBE 1962; FRAM; Prima donna; *b* Oldham, Lancashire; unmarried. Began to sing at an early age and, whilst in her teens, spent some years at the Royal Academy of Music; joined Royal Carl Rosa Opera Company in 1916, and became the Prima donna of the Company, remaining with it until 1924, when Toscanini engaged her for La Scala, Milan. Appeared all over Europe, USA, and S. America; London, at Covent Garden in 1928 when she sang in Puccini's opera Turandot, Aida, and many others; for the Celebrations in connection with the commemoration of the Centenary of Bolivar, was specially chosen by President Gomez to be the Prima Donna. Visiting Professor of Voice to Music Faculty of University of Oklahoma, USA, 1949-59 (resigned); Professor of Voice Royal Academy of Music, London, 1959-66 (resigned). Hon. Internat. Member Sigma Alpha Iota, 1951-; Hon. Internat. Soroptomist, 1955-. Member National Assoc. of Teachers of Singing (USA). *Recreations:* swimming, riding, motoring. *Address:* 26 Palace Court, W2; Junesca, Brusino-Arsizio, Lake of Lugano, Switzerland. *Club:* Royal Over-Seas League.

**TURNER, Brig. Dame Evelyn Marguerite;** *see* Turner, Brig. Dame Margot.

**TURNER, Sir Francis;** *see* Turner, Sir Arthur Francis.

**TURNER, Francis McDougall Charlewood,** MC; DFC; MA; Emeritus Fellow of Magdalene College, Cambridge; Bye Fellow, 1923; Fellow, 1926; President, 1957-62; *b* 17 March 1897; fifth *s* of late Charles Henry Turner, DD, Bishop of Islington, and Edith Emma, *d* of late Bishop McDougall; unmarried. *Educ:* Marlborough Coll.; Magdalene Coll., Cambridge. Royal Flying Corps, 1916-19 (MC, DFC). *Publication:* The Element of Irony in English Literature, 1926. *Recreation:* music. *Address:* 1 St Martin's Square, Chichester, Sussex. *Club:* Oxford and Cambridge.

**TURNER, Vice-Admiral Sir Frederick Richard Gordon,** KCB 1943 (CB 1942); OBE 1918; *b* 29 March 1889; *e s* of R. J. Turner, Solihull, Warwickshire; *m* 1914, Emily A. Gregory; one *s* three *d*. *Educ:* RNE Coll., Keyham. Engineer-in-Chief of the Fleet, 1942-45; retired list, 1945. *Address:* The Friary, 19 St Cross Road, Winchester, Hants.

**TURNER, Sir George Wilfred,** KCB 1950 (CB 1942); KBE 1944; Director: Creed & Co. Ltd; Goodyear Tyre and Rubber Co. (Great Britain) Ltd; *b* 22 Jan. 1896; *s* of John W. Turner, Rotherham, Yorks; *m* 1921, Elizabeth, *d* of late P. T. Chirgwin, Penzance; one *s*. War Office, 1911-39; Ministry of Supply, 1939-48; Principal Asst Secretary, 1939; Under-Secretary, 1941; Second Secretary, 1942; Permanent Under-Secretary of State for War, 1949-56, retired. Member, Royal Commission on the Police. Served European War in ranks with Grenadier Guards, 1916-19. *Address:* Pentreeve, Gulval, Penzance, Cornwall. *Club:* Reform.

**TURNER, Harold Goodhew,** CMG 1960; Malayan Civil Service (retired); *b* 23 Dec. 1906; *s* of George Prior Turner and Blanche Winifred Turner; *m* 1934, Aileen Mary Mace; one *s* one *d* (and one *s* decd). *Educ:* St Olave's and St Saviour's Grammar Sch., London; Trinity Coll., Cambridge. Cadet, Malayan CS, 1929; Principal Establishment Officer, 1958; Secretary to the Treasury, 1959. CRO 1962-68; Director of Studies, Royal Institute of Public Administration, 1969- (Associate Dir, 1961-

69); *Recreations:* gardening and chess. *Address:* 54 Robson Road, West Worthing, Sussex. *T:* Worthing 41924. *Club:* Royal Commonwealth Society.

**TURNER, Harold H.;** *see* Horsfall Turner.

**TURNER, Sir Harvey,** Kt 1967; CBE 1953; Chairman of Directors of a number of Companies; *b* 11 Sept. 1889; *s* of Edward and Maude Turner; *m* 1914, Margaret Ethel Penman; three *s* two *d*. *Educ:* Huia Sch.; Giles Business College; Auckland Technical College. Served War of 1914-18, New Zealand; War of 1939-45 (Middle East, 1941-42; Major; despatches). Past President, Auckland Chamber of Commerce; Past Chairman, Auckland Harbour Board. *Publication:* (with Allan Kirk) Turners of Huia, 1966. *Recreations:* tennis, swimming, gardening. *Address:* 40 Summit Drive, Auckland 3, New Zealand. *T:* Auckland 84572.

**TURNER, Rev. Professor Henry Ernest William,** DD; Canon Residentiary, Durham Cathedral, since 1950; Treasurer since 1956; Sub-Dean since 1959; Van Mildert Professor of Divinity, Durham University, since 1958; *b* 14 Jan. 1907; *o s* of Henry Frederick Richard and Ethel Turner, Sheffield; *m* 1936, Constance Parker, *d* of Dr E. P. Haythornthwaite, Rowrah, Cumberland; two *s*. *Educ:* King Edward VII Sch., Sheffield; St John's Coll., Oxford; Wycliffe Hall, Oxford. MA 1933; BD 1940; DD 1955. Curate, Christ Church, Cockermouth, 1931-34; Curate, Holy Trinity, Wavertree, 1934-35; Fellow, Chaplain and Tutor, Lincoln Coll., Oxford, 1935-50; Chaplain, RAFVR, 1940-45; Librarian, Lincoln Coll., 1945-48; Senior Tutor, Lincoln Coll., 1948-50; Lightfoot Prof. of Divinity, Durham Univ., 1950-58. Select Preacher, Oxford Univ., 1950-51; Member: Anglican delegation to Third Conference of World Council of Churches, Lund, 1952; Anglican-Presbyterian Conversations, 1953-; Doctrine Commn of the Church of England, 1967-; Bampton Lecturer (Oxford), 1954. Theological Consultant to Anglican Roman Catholic Conversations, 1970. *Publications:* The Life and Person of Jesus Christ, 1951; The Patristic Doctrine of Redemption, 1952; Jesus Master and Lord, 1953; The Pattern of Christian Truth (Bampton Lectures), 1955; Why Bishops?, 1955; The Meaning of the Cross, 1959; (jt author with H. Montefiore) Thomas and the Evangelists, 1962; Historicity and the Gospels, 1963; Contributions to the Guardian, Theology and Church Quarterly Review. *Address:* 14 The College, Durham. *T:* Durham 4657.

**TURNER, H(enry) F(rederic) Lawrence;** *b* 30 Dec. 1908; *s* of G. F. Turner, Goring; *m* 1938, E. M. Hartley; one *s* one *d*. *Educ:* Radley; Reading Univ.; Exeter Coll., Oxford. Served War of 1939-45, at first in the ranks and later commissioned, RA; served Thailand (prisoner-of-war, Burma Road); lectured on politics during captivity. Contested (C) North Paddington, by-election, 1946, and general election, 1950; MP (C) Oxford, 1950-59; Information Officer, Central Office of Information, 1961-. General Manager, Amalgamated Developers Ltd. *Address:* 22 Pembridge Villas, Notting Hill, W11. *T:* 01-229 3597.

**TURNER, Sir Henry Samuel Edwin,** Kt, *cr* 1946; *b* 18 Aug. 1887; *s* of Samuel Turner and Lillian, *d* of Henry Thorne; *m* 1912, Edith (*d* 1948), *d* of William Rose; two *d*; *m* 1959, Louise, *d* of late Ernest Kirk, Batley, Yorks, and *widow* of Marshal Shaw Lodge. *Educ:* Lower School of John Lyon, Harrow. English Civil Service, 1907-19; Board of Education, Ministry of Food; British Economic Section, Peace Conference, Paris; London Manager, NZ Refrigerating Co. Ltd, 1919-22; NZ Manager, NZ Refrigerating Co. Ltd, 1923-39; Controller of Meat and Livestock, Ministry of Food, London, 1940-50; Chairman, Towers & Co. Ltd, 1950-66; former Dir, Express Dairy Co. Ltd; Past President, Canterbury Chamber of Commerce, NZ; Past Vice-President, Associated Chambers of Commerce of NZ. *Recreations:* reading and watching cricket. *Address:* 29 St Mary Abbots Court, W14. *Clubs:* Junior Carlton, City Livery; Christchurch (NZ).

*See also J. M. M. Fisher.*

**TURNER, Herbert Arthur;** Assistant Under-Secretary of State, Department of Health and Social Security, since 1968; *b* 9 March 1912; *s* of Thomas Stewart Turner, Rochester, Kent, and Ellen Spice, Bapchild, Kent; *m* 1937, Paule Felicia Gerardine Delecroix, Douvrin, France; two *s* one *d*. *Educ:* High Storrs Grammar Sch., Sheffield; Sidney Sussex Coll., Cambridge (Scholar). Ministry of Transport: Asst Principal, 1935, Principal, 1939; Asst Secretary, 1944; HM Treasury, 1946-49; Central Economic Planning Staff, 1949-50; Under-Secretary, 1961; Secretary, Forestry Commission, 1950-65; Under-Secretary: Ministry of Land and Natural Resources, 1965-67; Ministry of Social Security, 1967-68. *Recreations:* various. *Address:* 71 Stanley Road, SW14. *Club:* Medway Cruising.

**TURNER, Prof. Herbert Arthur (Frederick),** BSc Econ London, PhD Manchester, MA Cantab; Montague Burton Professor of Industrial Relations, University of Cambridge, since Oct. 1963; Fellow of Churchill College, Cambridge; Part-time Member, National Board for Prices and Incomes, since 1967; *b* 11 Dec. 1919; *s* of Frederick and May Turner; *Educ:* Henry Thornton Sch., Clapham; University of London BSc (Econ) London, 1939; PhD Manchester, 1960. Member Trade Union Congress Research and Economic Department, 1944; Assistant Education Secretary, TUC, 1947; Lecturer, 1950, Senior Lecturer, 1959, University of Manchester; Montague Burton Professor of Industrial Relations, University of Leeds, 1961-63. Sometime Adviser to Govts of Congo, UAR, Tanzania, Fiji, Papua-New Guinea, Zambia and other African states. *Publications:* Trade Union Growth, Structure and Policy, 1962; Wages: the Problems for Underdeveloped Countries, 1965; Prices, Wages and Incomes Policies, 1966; Labour Relations in the Motor Industry, 1967; various reports of ILO, monographs, papers and articles on labour economics and statistics, industrial relations. *Address:* Churchill College, Cambridge.

**TURNER, James Grant Smith,** CMG 1949; *b* 7 Aug. 1897; *s* of Hector and Mary Turner; *m* 1st, 1930, Jemima Cunningham (*d* 1937); one *s* one *d*; 2nd, 1947, Freda Gurling (*d* 1970); one *s*. *Educ:* Allan Glen's Sch., Glasgow; Glasgow Univ.; Liverpool Univ. MB, ChB, Glasgow, 1924; BSc, DPH, Glasgow, 1926; DTM, Liverpool, 1927. MO, Nigeria, 1927; Senior Health Officer, 1938; transferred to Sierra Leone, 1941; DDMS, Gold Coast, 1945, DMS, 1946-50; retired Jan. 1950. Military service: European War, 1915-18; War of 1939-45, 1940-41. *Recreations:* walking, fishing. *Address:* c/o Barclays Bank, St Austell, Cornwall.

**TURNER, Hon. Joanna Elizabeth,** MA; **Hon. Mrs J. F. Turner;** Headmistress, Badminton School, Bristol, 1966-69; *b* 10 Jan. 1923; 2nd *d* of 1st Baron Piercy, CBE, and Mary Louisa, *d* of Hon. Thomas Pelham; *m* 1968, James

Francis Turner, *er s* of late Rev. P. R. Turner. *Educ:* St Paul's Girls' Sch.; Somerville Coll., Oxford (Sen. Classics Schol.). Asst Classics Mistress: Downe House, Newbury, 1944-46; Gordonstoun Sch., 1947-48; Badminton Sch., Bristol, 1948-65. *Recreations:* painting, foreign travel, reading. *Address:* The Old Rectory, Wem, Shropshire. *T:* Wem 2581. *Club:* English-Speaking Union.

**TURNER, Dr J(ohn) W(illiam) Aldren,** MA, DM Oxon; FRCP; Neurologist, St Bartholomew's Hospital, since 1946; Neurologist, St Alban's City Hospital and Finchley Memorial Hospital; *b* 13 Feb. 1911; *s* of W. Aldren Turner, CB, MD, FRCP; unmarried. *Educ:* Clifton Coll.; New Coll., Oxford; St Bartholomew's Hospital Medical Coll. BA (Oxon) 1932 (1st class honours Final School of Natural Science); Theodore Williams Scholarship in Anatomy and Gotch Medal in Physiology, University Entrance Scholarship, St Bart's. Walsham Prize in Pathology and Brackenbury Scholarship in Medicine; BM, BCh (Oxon), 1935; MRCP 1937; DM 1940; FRCP 1946. Resident house appointments at St Bart's, and at National Hospital for Nervous Diseases, Queen Square. Served War of 1939-45, Temp. Lt-Col, RAMC (adviser in Neurology, Southern Command, India). Sub-dean, St Bart's Medical Coll., 1946-50. Examiner in Neurology: University of London; Manchester and Conjoint Board. *Publications:* (joint) Clinical Neurology, 1952; papers on neurological subjects in medical journals. *Recreations:* philately, travel. *Address:* 149 Harley Street, W1. *T:* 01-935 4444; (home) 23 Malvern Court, Onslow Square, SW7. *T:* 01-589 1086. *Club:* Athenæum.

**TURNER, Lawrence;** *see* Turner, H. F. L.

**TURNER, Brig. Dame Margot, (E. M. Turner),** DBE 1965 (MBE 1946); RRC 1956; QHNS 1964; Matron-in-Chief and Director Army Nursing Service, 1964-68; *b* 10 May 1910; *d* of late Thomas Frederick Turner and late Molly Cecilia (*née* Bryan). *Educ:* Finchley County Sch., Middlesex. Trained at St Bartholomew's Hospital, London, 1931-35. Joined QAIMNS, 1937 (became QARANC, 1949). Served in UK, India, Malaya, Hong Kong, Bermuda, Germany and Near East. POW Sumatra, Feb. 1942-Aug. 1945. Col Comdt, QARANC, 1969-. CStJ 1966. *Relevant Publication:* Sir John Smyth, Will to Live: the story of Dame Margot Turner, 1970. *Recreations:* reading, photography, golf, tennis. *Address:* 2 Chantry Court, Frimley, Surrey. *T:* Camberley 22030. *Club:* United Nursing Services

**TURNER, Sir Mark;** *see* Turner, Sir Ronald Mark Cunliffe.

**TURNER, Sir Michael (William),** Kt 1961; CBE 1957; Colonial Police Medal 1956; formerly Chairman and Chief Manager of The Hong-Kong and Shanghai Banking Corporation, retired 1962; *b* 25 April 1905; *s* of late Sir Skinner Turner, HBM Supreme Court at Shanghai, and late Lady Turner; *m* 1938, Wendy Spencer Stranack; three *s*. *Educ:* Marlborough Coll.; University Coll., Oxford (MA). Joined The Hong-Kong and Shanghai Banking Corporation, 1926. Served in: Hong Kong, Shanghai, Singapore. Interned at Singapore, 1942-45. Director: The British Bank of the Middle East (Chairman, 1964-67); National Westminster Bank Ltd; Member Board of Governors: The City Univ., London; Hong Kong House, London; Member, London Cttee, The Hong Kong and Shanghai Banking Corp., 1962-70. Skinner and Citizen of the City of London; Master of the Skinners Company, 1967-68. FZS (London). Hon. LLD (Hong Kong), 1959. CStJ 1960; Commander, Order of Prince Henry the Navigator (Portugal), 1963. *Recreations:* shooting, fishing, walking, formerly hockey (Oxford Univ., Hockey XI, 1925, 1926). *Address:* Flat 6, 6 Hyde Park Gardens, W2. *T:* 01-262 9565. *Clubs:* Hurlingham; Overseas Bankers; Vincent's (Oxford); Hong Kong (Hong Kong).

**TURNER, Norman Henry;** Official Solicitor to the Supreme Court of Judicature since 1970; *b* 11 May 1916; *s* of Henry James Turner, MA and late Hilda Gertrude Turner; *m* 1939, Dora Ardella (*née* Cooper); three *s* two *d*. *Educ:* Nottingham High School. Articled, Nottingham, 1933; admitted Solicitor (Hons), 1938; joined Official Solicitor's Dept, 1948; Asst Official Solicitor, 1958. *Recreation:* camping. *Address:* 48 Rushington Avenue, Maidenhead, Berks. *T:* Maidenhead 22918.

**TURNER, Philip,** LLB (London); Principal Assistant Solicitor to Post Office since 1962; *b* 1 June 1913; *er s* of late George Francis and late Daisy Louise Turner (*née* Frayn), Alverstoke, Hants; *m* 1938, Hazel Edith, *d* of late Douglas Anton and Edith Ada Benda; two *d*. *Educ:* Peter Symonds, Winchester. Admitted Solicitor, 1935. Entered General Post Office Solicitor's Dept, 1935. Served in Royal Navy, 1940-46 (Lt-Comdr). Asst Solicitor to General Post Office, 1953. Chm., Civil Service Legal Soc., 1957-58. FRSA 1955. *Recreations:* piano, golf. *Address:* Well House, The Marld, Ashtead, Surrey. *T:* Ashtead 73656. *Clubs:* Naval; RAC Country (Epsom).

**TURNER, Surgeon Rear-Admiral (D) Philip Stanley,** CB 1963; QHDS 1960-64; Director of Dental Services, RN, Admiralty, Nov. 1961-64; *b* 31 Oct. 1905; *s* of Frank Overy Turner and Ellen Mary Turner, Langton Green, Tunbridge Wells; *m* 1934, Marguerite Donnelly; one *d* (and one *s* decd). *Educ:* Cranbrook Coll.; Guy's Hospital. LDS, RCS 1927. Surgeon Lieut (D) Royal Navy, 1928; Surgeon Captain (D) 1955; Surgeon Rear-Admiral (D), 1961; Senior Specialist in Dental Surgery, 1946-61. Served in: HMS Ramillies, Vanguard, Implacable, Indomitable; HMHS Maine, Tjitjalengka; RN Hospitals Haslar, Plymouth; RN Barracks Portsmouth, etc; Naval HQ, Malta. Foundation Fellow, British Assoc. of Oral Surgeons, 1962. *Address:* Woodhurst, Warren Lane, Cross-in-Hand, Heathfield, Sussex. *T:* Heathfield (Sussex) 3532.

**TURNER, Lt-Col Ralph Beresford,** CMG 1919; DSO 1917; *b* 1879; 4th *s* of late E. J. Turner, MA, JP, Hants; *m* 1st, 1908, Ailsa (*d* 1949), *d* of late W. J. and Mrs Scudamore Smith; 2nd, 1950, Maude, *widow* of late Sir Edward Denham, GCMG, KBE. *Educ:* Winchester. Served South African War, 1899-1902, Royal Engineers (despatches, Queen's Medal 2 clasps, King's Medal 2 clasps); Asst Dir Repatriation and Farming in Transvaal, 1903-14; served European War, SW Africa and E Africa, 1914-19, DAQMG 3rd Div. and AQMG GHQ, East Africa Expeditionary Force (despatches 7 times, DSO, CMG); investigating sisal industry, E Africa and Yucatan, 1919-20; investigating inter-trade, South Africa and East Africa, 1922-23; Comr for the Union of South Africa in East African Territories, 1924-39; Kenya Information Officer, 1939-40; DAQMG L. of C. East African Comd, 1940-41; Chief Evacuation Officer, Occupied Territories Administration HQ, Civil Affairs Branch, East African Comd, 1941-47 (despatches); Nairobi Agent, Civil Affairs Directorate, War Office, 1947-49.

*Address:* Little Park House, Brimpton, Berks. *T:* Woolhampton 3236.

**TURNER, Sir Ralph Lilley,** Kt 1950; MC; FBA 1942; MA, LittD, Hon. DLitt (Benares, India); Hon. DLit: Ceylon; London, 1967; Director of the School of Oriental and African Studies, 1937-57 (Hon. Fellow, 1957); Professor of Sanskrit, University of London, 1922-54, Emeritus Professor since 1954; *b* 5 Oct. 1888; *s* of George Turner, MA, JP, OBE, Cambridge; *m* 1920, Dorothy Rivers, *d* of William Howard Goulty, Hale, Cheshire; one *s* three *d*. *Educ:* Perse Grammar Sch. and Christ's Coll., Cambridge (Senior Scholar). Classical Tripos Part I Class I, Div. 3; Oriental Languages Trip. Class I; Class. Trip. Part II Sect. E, Class I with distinction; Brotherton Memorial Sanskrit Prize; Fellow of Christ's Coll., 1912 (Hon. Fellow, 1950); Indian Educational Service, Lectr in Sanskrit at Queen's Coll., Benares, 1913; Wilson Philological Lectr, Bombay Univ., 1914; Indian Army R of O, attached 2/3rd QAO Gurkha Rifles, 1915-19; Examiner Or. Lang. Trip. and Class. Trip. Part II Cambridge; Prof. of Indian Linguistics, Benares Hindu Univ., 1920; Wilson Philological Lectr, Bombay Univ., 1922; Hon. Treasurer (Pres., 1939-43) Philological Soc.; Pres., 1952-55, Royal Asiatic Soc. (Gold Medallist, 1953, Hon. Vice-Pres., 1963); 7th International Congress of Linguists, 1952; 23rd International Congress of Orientalists, 1954; Hon. Fellow, Deccan Coll., Poona. Formerly Member: Inter-Services Cttee on Language Training; Linguists' Cttee of Min. of Labour and National Service; Colonial Social Science Research Council; Adv. Cttee on the Humanities of the British Council; Adv. Cttee on Education in the Colonies; Treasury sub-cttee for studentships in foreign languages and cultures; sub-cttee University Grants Cttee on Oriental and African Studies; Corr. Member: Czecho-Slovakian Oriental Institute of Prag, Institut de France, Acad. des Inscriptions et Belles Lettres; Hon. Member: Norwegian Acad. of Science and Letters, Ceylon Acad. of Letters, Soc. Asiatique, Paris, American Oriental Soc., Deutsche Morgenländische Gesellschaft, Bihar Research Soc., Bhandarkar Oriental Research Inst., Ceylon Branch of Royal Asiatic Soc., Nagaripracarini Sabha, Banaras, Sanskrit Vishva Parishad, Vishveshvaranand Vedic Research Inst., Ganganatha Jha Research Inst., Linguistic Soc. of America, Linguistic Soc. of India, Ceylon Linguistic Society. Campbell Gold Medallist, Asiatic Soc. of Bombay, 1967. Nepalese Order of Gorkha Dakshina Bahu, 2nd Class, 1951, 1st Class, 1960. *Publications:* Gujarati Phonology; The Position of Romani in Indo-Aryan; A Comparative and Etymological Dictionary of the Nepali Language; The Gavimath and Palkigundu Inscriptions of Asoka; ed. Indian Studies presented to Professor E. J. Rapson, Indian and Iranian Studies presented to Sir G. A. Grierson; Report to the Nuffield Foundation on a visit to Nigeria; Problems of Sound-change in Indo-Aryan; A Comparative Dictionary of the Indo-aryan Languages; articles in Encyclopædia Britannica, etc. *Address:* Haverbrack, Bishop's Stortford, Herts. *T:* 4135; Courtfield, Charmouth, Dorset. *T:* 465.

**TURNER, Raymond C.;** *see* Clifford-Turner.

**TURNER, Richard,** CMG 1956; LRIBA; Consultant architect, retired; *b* 2 May 1909; *m* 1933, Annie Elizabeth Gair; one *d*. *Educ:* Dame Alice Owen's School. Entered Min. of Works, 1929; in charge of ME Office, 1938-47, centred in Istanbul and, later, Cairo; Asst Chief Architect, Min. of Works, 1951; Dir of Works (Overseas), 1960-65; Dir, Overseas Svcs, MPBW, 1965-69. *Address:* Leigh Court Knoll, Cobham, Surrey. *T:* 3275. *Club:* Travellers'.

**TURNER, Dr Richard Wainwright Duke,** OBE 1945; Senior Physician and Physician in Charge of the Cardiac Department, Western General Hospital, Edinburgh, since 1946; Reader in Medicine, University of Edinburgh; *b* Purley, Surrey, 30 May 1909; *s* of Sydney Duke Turner, MD (General Practitioner), and Lilian Maude, *d* of Sir James Wainwright; *m* Paula, *d* of Henry Meulen, Wimbledon; three *s* one *d*. *Educ:* Epsom Coll.; Clare Coll., Cambridge; St Thomas' Hosp., London. 1st Class Hons Nat. Sci. Tripos, Cambridge, 1934. MA, MB, BChir Cantab 1934; MRCS, LRCP 1935; MRCP 1936; MD Cantab 1940; FRCP 1950; FRCPE 1952. Served in RAMC, 1939-45: UK, Egypt and Italy (Lt-Col); officer i/c Med. Div. 31st and 92nd British General Hospitals. Examiner in Medicine: Univs of Edinburgh and Leeds; RCP; RCPE. Member: Assoc. Physicians of GB; British Cardiac Soc.; Hon. Member, Cardiol Socs of India and Pakistan. *Publications:* Diseases of Cardiovascular System in Davidson's Principles and Practice of Medicine, 1952-65; Electrocardiography, 1963; Auscultation of the Heart, 1963; contribs to British Heart Jl, Lancet, BMJ, Quarterly Jl of Med., American Heart Jl, etc. *Recreations:* travel, climbing, gardening, photography. *Address:* 15 Russell Place, Edinburgh 5. *T:* 031-552 5237; Department of Medicine, 12 George Square, Edinburgh 8. *T:* 031-667 1011. *Clubs:* Royal Over-Seas League; University Staff (Edinburgh).

**TURNER, Robert Noel,** CMG 1955; retired; *b* 28 Dec. 1912; *s* of late Engr Rear-Adm. A. Turner and late Mrs V. E. Turner; *m* 1946, Evelyn Heynes Dupree; two *s*. *Educ:* Dover Coll.; Wadham Coll., Oxford. First Class Hons Modern History. Cadet, Malayan Civil Service, 1935; Third Asst Sec. to Govt, FMS, 1936; Asst District Officer, Lower Perak, FMS, 1938; Supernumerary Duty (Lower Perak), 1939; Asst Resident, Brunei, 1940 (interned by Japanese, Borneo, Dec. 1941-Sept. 1945); Asst Sec. to Governor-General, Malaya, May 1946; Prin. Asst Sec., Sarawak, Aug. 1946; First Asst Malayan Establishment Officer, 1948; Acting Dep. Malayan Establishment Officer, April 1950; Chief Sec., Barbados, 1950-56 (title changed from Colonial Sec., 1954); Acting Governor, Barbados, Nov. 1952-May 1953 and 1955, North Borneo, 1957-62; Chief Sec., North Borneo, 1956-63; State Sec., Sabah, Fedn of Malaysia, 1963-64. Hon. Mem., First Grade, Order of Kinabalu, Sabah (title: Dato; lettering: PDK), 1963. *Recreations:* tennis, watching cricket. *Address:* Kinabalu, The Rise, Brockenhurst, Hants SO4 7SJ. *T:* 3197.

**TURNER, Vice-Admiral Sir Robert Ross,** KBE, *cr* 1946; CB 1937; DSO 1916; Royal Navy, retired; *b* 13 Oct. 1885; *s* of Thomas Turner, Sheffield, and Jessie Alice Ross, Cape Town; *m* 1910, Mabel, *d* of James Fisher, Barrow-in-Furness; three *s* three *d*. *Educ:* Dulwich Coll. Joined Navy, 1900; Lieut 1906; joined Submarine service; served in HMS Argyll, 1912-14; outbreak of war commanded C 15; transferred to comd D 3, Oct. 1914; commanded E 23, Jan. 1916; Comdr 1917; Captain, 1923; comd First Flotilla, 1924-26; Captain Submarine Depot at Fort Blockhouse, 1927-29; Dep. Dir of Operations Div., 1929-31; idc 1932; Comd HMS Leander, 1933-35; Adm. Supt, Portsmouth Dockyard, 1935-40; Vice-Adm. 1939; retired list, 1939; on active service abroad, 1940; Dir-Gen. of Shipbuilding and Repairs, India, Dec. 1941-44;

Senior British Naval Officer, Greece, 1945-46. Kt Comdr Cross of King George I of Greece with crossed swords, 1946; Grand Officer of Order of Orange Nassau, 1949. *Address:* Lowgill, Worth Matravers, Swanage, Dorset.

**TURNER, Sir (Ronald) Mark (Cunliffe),** Kt 1946; Deputy Chairman: Kleinwort, Benson Ltd, 1966; Rio Tinto-Zinc Corporation, 1966; Chairman: British Home Stores Ltd; Mercantile Credit Co. Ltd; Director: The Commercial Union Assurance Co. Ltd; William Mallinson & Sons Ltd; Whitbread Investment Co. Ltd; Nuclear Developments Ltd; National Cash Register Co.; Toronto-Dominion Bank; Midland & International Banks Ltd, and other companies; Chairman, Economic Development Committee for Paper and Board Industry; *b* 29 March 1906; *s* of Christopher Rede Turner and Jill Helen Pickersgill Cunliffe; *m* 1st, 1931, Elizabeth Mary Sutton (marr. diss. 1936); one *d* decd; 2nd, 1939, Margaret Wake; three *s* two *d*. *Educ:* Wellington Coll., Berks. City, 1924, with M. Samuel & Co. Ltd, Merchant Bankers; Nov. 1934 until outbreak of war with Robert Benson & Co. Ltd, Merchant Bankers; with Ministry of Economic Warfare, 1939-44; Foreign Office, 1944-45; Under-Secretary Control Office for Germany and Austria, 1945-47. Trustee: Observer Trust; Glyndebourne Arts Trust. *Address:* 3 The Grove, Highgate, N6. *T:* 01-340 3421. *Club:* Brooks's.

**TURNER, Theodora,** OBE 1961; ARRC 1944; retired as Matron of St Thomas' Hospital and Superintendent Nightingale Training School (1955-65); *b* 5 Aug. 1907; *er d* of H. E. M. Turner. *Educ:* Godolphin School, Salisbury; Edinburgh School of Domestic Economy. Ward Sister, St Thomas' Hosp., 1935-38; Administrative Course, Florence Nightingale Internat. Foundn, 1938-39. QAIMNS Reserve, 1939-45. Administrative Sister, St Thomas' Hosp., 1946-47; Matron Royal Infirmary, Liverpool, 1948-53; Education Officer, Educn Centre, Royal College of Nursing, Birmingham, 1953-55. Pres., Royal Coll. of Nursing and National Council of Nurses of the United Kingdom, 1966-68. *Recreations:* gardening and painting. *Address:* Achraich, Clachan Seil, by Oban, Argyll.

**TURNER, Theodore Francis,** QC 1943; Barrister-at-law; *b* 19 Nov. 1900; *s* of George Lewis and Mabel Mary Turner; *m* 1st, 1925, Elizabeth Alice, *o d* of 1st Baron Schuster, GCB, CVO, QC; two *s* one *d*; 2nd, 1949, Ruth, 2nd *d* of late L. C. Ledyard, Jr, and late Mrs W. E. S. Griswold, NY. *Educ:* Downside; Balliol Coll., Oxford (Exhibitioner). Called to Bar, 1924; joined South Eastern Circuit. Regional Controller, Ministry of Fuel and Power, North Midland Region, 1944-45; Recorder of Rochester, 1946-50; Chairman Mining Subsidence Cttee, 1947-48. Admitted New York Bar, 1962. *Address:* Windswept, East Norwich, Long Island, NY 11732, USA; 570 Park Avenue, New York City, NY 10021, USA. *Clubs:* Garrick; The Brook (NY).
*See also W. H. Hughes, C. G. Turner.*

**TURNER, Sir Victor (Alfred Charles),** Kt, *cr* 1947; CSI 1946; CIE 1941; MBE; MA; JP; late ICS; assumed additional Christian name of Victor on receiving knighthood; *b* 12 March 1892; *y s* of late W. C. Turner, Kensington; *m* 1957, Winifred Bessie Howarth; one *s* one *d* (by a former marriage). *Educ:* Emmanuel Coll., Cambridge. Wrangler, 1914; War service, 1914-19, Royal Fus., and Inspector Propellant Explosives, Inspection Dept, Woolwich Arsenal, rank of Captain; arrived in India, 1920, and posted to Lucknow as Asst Comr; Settlement Officer Rae Bareli, 1926-29; Census Supt, UP, 1930-33; Revenue Sec. to UP Govt, 1935; Finance Sec., UP Govt, 1936; Additional Sec., Finance Dept, Govt of India, 1941; Financial Comr for Railways, Govt of India, 1945; Prin. Sec., Finance Dept, 1947; Sec., Min. of Finance, Govt of Pakistan, 1947-50; Financial Adviser to High Comr for Pakistan in London, 1950-54. Economic Adviser to The De La Rue Co. Ltd, 1954-64. *Publications:* Settlement Report of Rae Bareli District, UP, 1929; Census Report of the UP, 1931. *Recreations:* fishing, shooting, etc. *Address:* Gate of Derry, Wonersh, Surrey.

**TURNER, Lt-Col Victor Buller,** VC 1942; CVO 1966; late Rifle Brigade; *b* 17 Jan. 1900; *s* of late Major Charles Turner, Royal Berkshire Regt; unmarried. *Educ:* Wellington Coll., Berks; RMC Sandhurst. Commnd Rifle Bde, 1918; Iraq, 1919-20 (medal with clasp); War of 1939-45, Middle East, 1941-42 (wounded, VC); retired, 1949. Exon of the Yeomen of the Guard, 1950, Ensign, 1953, Clerk of the Cheque and Adjutant, 1955-67, Lieutenant, HM Body Guard, 1967-70. *Recreation:* shooting. *Address:* Ditchingham Cottage, Bungay, Suffolk. *T:* Bungay 2303. *Club:* Naval and Military.

**TURNER, Lt-Gen. Sir William (Francis Robert),** KBE 1962; CB 1959; DSO 1945; DL; *b* 12 Dec. 1907; *er s* of late Mr and Mrs F. R. Turner, Kelso, Roxburghshire; *m* 1938, Nancy Maude Stilwell, *er d* of late Lt-Col and Mrs J. B. L. Stilwell, Yateley, Hants; one *s*. *Educ:* Winchester College; RMC Sandhurst. 2nd Lieut, KOSB, 1928; served in Great Britain and India, 1928-39; Capt. 1938; BEF, 1939-40; Staff College, 1941; OC, 5 KOSB, 1942-45 (despatches), NW Europe; OC, 1 KOSB, 1945-46, NW Europe and Middle East; GSO1, Middle East and Great Britain, 1947-50. Colonel Brit. Military Mission to Greece, 1950-52; Comd 128 Inf. Bde (TA), 1952-54; BGS HQ Western Comd, 1954-56; GOC 44 (Home Counties) Infantry Div. (TA) and Home Counties District, and Deputy Constable of Dover Castle, 1956-59; President, Regular Commissions Board, 1959-61; GOC-in-C, Scottish Comd, and Governor of Edinburgh Castle, 1961-64; retd 1964; Colonel, King's Own Scottish Borderers, 1961-70; Brigadier Queen's Body Guard for Scotland (Royal Company of Archers). HM Comr, Queen Victoria School, Dunblane. DL, Dumfriesshire, 1970-. Comdr with Star, Order of Saint Olav, Class II (Norway), 1962; Order of the Two Niles, Class II (Republic of the Sudan), 1963. *Address:* Milnhead, Kirkton, Dumfries. *T:* Dumfries 71319. *Clubs:* Naval and Military; New (Edinburgh).

**TURNER, William Hovell,** CIE 1947; CBE 1957; MC; MA; Director of Audit, Indian Accounts in the UK, 1943-56; *b* 10 Sept. 1891; *s* of George Turner, OBE, JP, and Bertha, *d* of W. Eaden Lilley, Cambridge; *m* 1920, May Calder Scott, *d* of Mrs M. C. Turner, Godstowe Sch.; two *s* one *d*. *Educ:* Perse School and Christ's Coll., Cambridge; State Coll. of Washington, USA; Jena Univ., Germany. Served European War, 1914-19, RFA, Major (despatches twice). Junior clerk, India Office, 1919; Private Sec. to Earl of Lytton, Parly Under-Sec. of State, 1920-22; Sec. of Indian Delegn to League of Nations Assembly, 1932 and 1933; Asst Sec. Burma Office, 1940, Min. of Supply, 1943. *Address:* Cherry Brack, Barrels Down Road, Bishop's Stortford, Herts. *T:* Bishop's Stortford 51684.

**TURNER CAIN, Maj.-Gen. George Robert,** CB 1967; CBE 1963; DSO 1945; Chairman: F. & G. Smith Ltd, Maltsters; Walpole & Wright Ltd,

Hauliers; Director, Crisp Maltings Ltd; *b* 16 Feb. 1912; *s* of late Wing Comdr G. Turner Cain; *m* 1938, Lamorna Maturin, *d* of late Col G. B. Hingston; one *s* one *d*. *Educ:* Norwich Sch.; RMC Sandhurst. 2nd Lt Norfolk Regt, 1932; 1st Bn Royal Norfolk Regt, India, 1933-38; Waziristan Campaign, 1937. Served War of 1939-45 with 1st Royal Norfolk and 1st Hereford Regt, BLA, 1944-45. Comd 1st Royal Norfolk Regt, Berlin, 1947-48; Hong Kong and UK, 1953-55; Comd Tactical Wing, School of Infantry, 1955-57; Comd 1st Fed. Inf. Bde, Malaya, in operations in Malaya, 1957-59; BGS, HQ, BAOR, 1961; Maj.-Gen. Administration, GHQ FARELF, 1964-67, retired; ADC 1961-64. Croix de Guerre avec Palm, 1945; Star of Kedah (Malaya), 1959. *Recreations:* shooting, ski-ing, curling. *Address:* Holbreck, Hollow Lane, Stiffkey, near Wells-next-the-Sea, Norfolk.

**TURNER-WARWICK, Richard Trevor,** MA, BSc, DM Oxon, MCh, FRCS, MRCP, FACS; Surgeon and Senior Urologist to the Middlesex Hospital, W1; Urologist to King Edward VII Hospital for Officers, St Peter's Hospital Group and Royal National Orthopædic Hospital; Senior Lecturer, London University Institute of Urology; *b* 21 Feb. 1925; *s* of W. Turner Warwick, FRCS; *m* 1951, Margaret Elizabeth, MA, DM Oxon, PhD London, FRCP, *d* of W. Harvey Moore, QC; two *d*. *Educ:* Bedales School; Oriel Coll., Oxford; Middlesex Hosp. Medical School. Pres. OUBC, 1946; Mem. Univ. Boat Race Crew, Isis Head of River crew and Univ. fours, 1946; Winner OU Silver Sculls, 1946; BSc thesis in neuroanatomy, 1946. Sen. Broderip Schol., Lyell Gold Medallist and Freeman Schol., Middx Hosp., 1949; surgical trg at Middx Hosp. and St Paul's Hosp., London, and Columbia Presbyterian Med. Centre, NY, 1959. Hunterian Prof. of RCS, 1957; Moynihan Prize of Assoc. of Surgeons, 1957; Comyns Berkeley Travelling Fellowship to USA, 1959; FRSocMed; Fellow: Assoc. of Surgeons of Great Britain and Ireland; British Assoc. of Urological Surgeons; Mem., Internat. Soc. of Urology; Corresp. Mem., American, Australian and Belgian Urological Assocs. *Publications:* various articles on surgery and urology in scientific journals. *Recreations:* water and air. *Address:* 61 Harley House, NW1. *T:* 01-935 2550; Tirnanog, 55 Fitzroy Park, Highgate, N6. *T:* 01-340 6339. *Clubs:* Vincent's (Oxford); Leander (Henley), Royal Motor Yacht (Poole).

**TURNOUR,** family name of **Earl Winterton.**

**TURPIN, James Alexander,** CMG 1966; HM Diplomatic Service; Minister (Economic and Commercial), New Delhi, since 1967; *b* 7 Jan. 1917; *s* of late Samuel Alexander Turpin; *m* 1942, Kathleen Iris Eadie; one *d*. *Educ:* King's Hosp., Dublin; Trinity Coll., Dublin (MA). Asst Lectr, Trinity College, Dublin, 1940. Served Army (Royal Irish Fusiliers), 1942-46. Joined Foreign Service, 1947; Mem., UK Delegn to OEEC, Paris, 1948; 1st Sec., 1949; FO, 1950; Warsaw, 1953 (Chargé d'Affaires, 1953, 1954); Tokyo, 1955; Counsellor, 1960; seconded to BoT, 1960-63; Counsellor (Commercial), The Hague, 1963-67. *Recreations:* tennis, music, swimming. *Address:* c/o Foreign and Commonwealth Office, SW1; British High Commission, New Delhi, India.

**TURPIN, Kenneth Charlton;** Provost, Oriel College, Oxford, since 1957; Pro-Vice Chancellor, Oxford University, 1964-66, and since 1969 (Vice-Chancellor, 1966-69); Member, Hebdomadal Council, since 1959; *b* 13 Jan. 1915; *e s* of Henry John Turpin, Ludlow. *Educ:* Manchester Grammar Sch.; Oriel College, Oxford. Treasury, 1940-43; Asst Private Sec. to C. R. Attlee, Lord President and Dep. Prime Minister, 1943-45; 2nd Asst Registrar, University Registry, Oxford, 1945-47; Sec. of Faculties, Univ. of Oxford, 1947-57; professorial fellow, Oriel Coll., 1948; Hon. Fellow Trinity Coll., Dublin, 1968. *Recreations:* golf, walking. *Address:* Provost's Lodgings, Oriel College, Oxford. *T:* Oxford 41962; Copthorne, Knighton, Radnorshire. *T:* 687. *Club:* Athenæum.

**TURPIN, Maj.-Gen. Patrick George,** CB 1962; OBE 1943; MInstT 1961; *b* 27 April 1911; 3rd *s* of late Rev. J. J. Turpin, MA, BD, late Vicar of Misterton, Somerset; *m* 1947, Cherry Leslie Joy, *d* of late Major K. S. Grove, York and Lancaster Regiment; one *s* one *d*. *Educ:* Haileybury Coll., Hertford; Exeter College, Oxford (Sen. Classical Schol.). BA (Hons) Oxford (Lit. Hum.), 1933; MA 1963. Commd RASC, 2nd Lt, 1933; Lt 1936; Capt. 1941; Major 1946; Lt-Col 1949; Col 1953; Brig. 1959; Maj.-Gen. 1960. Served War of 1939-45 (despatches twice, OBE): Adjt, 1939-40; AQMG, 30 Corps, W Desert, 1943; AA&QMG, 5th Div., Italy, 1943-44; DA&QMG (Brig.), 1 Corps, BLA, 1945; Brig. A, 21 Army Gp, 1945-46; Comd 6 Training Bn, RASC, 1947; ADS&T, WO, 1948; AA&QMG (Plans), HQ, BTE (Egypt), 1950; GSO1 (instructor), Jt Services Staff Coll., 1951-53; ADS&T (Col), WO, 1953-54; DAG, HQ, BAOR, 1956-59; Brig. i/c Adm., 17 Gurkha Div., Malaya, 1959-60; DST, 1960-63; Dir of Movements, MoD (Army), 1963-66; psc 1941; jssc 1949; idc 1955; Col Comdt, Royal Corps of Transport, 1965-; Col Gurkha Transport Regt, 1965- (Col Gurkha Army Service Corps, 1960-65). Sec.-Gen., Assoc. of British Travel Agents, 1966-69. *Recreations:* lawn tennis (Somerset County Champion, 1948, Army Colours, 1952); squash rackets (Bucks County Colours, 1952); golf. *Address:* Cottswood, West Clandon, Guildford, Surrey. *T:* Clandon 580. *Clubs:* United Service; Oxford Union Society; All England Lawn Tennis; International Lawn Tennis; Escorts Squash Rackets.

**TURQUET, Gladys,** DLit, MA (London); Professor Emeritus of French Language and Literature, University of London, since 1952 (Professor of French Language and Literature, at Bedford College, 1934-52); *d* of late Alfred Milnes, DLit; *m* 1912, André Turquet, CBE (*d* 1940); one *s*. *Educ:* privately; University College, London. Head of French Dept, Westfield College (Univ. of London), 1916-34; Univ. Reader in French, 1921; Dep. Chm. of Convocation, 1936; Mem. Senate, 1936-46. *Publications:* The Influence of Baudelaire in France and England; Some Modern Belgian Writers; Some Modern French Writers (a study in Bergsonism); From Pascal to Proust; Introduction to Mallarmé in English Verse; Poems; Paul Valéry; The Defence and Illustration of the French Language by Joachim du Bellay; Apples I have Picked; contribs to reviews, etc. *Recreation:* music. *Address:* West Wittering, near Chichester, Sussex; 52 Bloomsbury Street, WC1. *T:* 01-636 7658.

**TURTON, Rt. Hon. Robert Hugh,** PC 1955; MC 1942; DL; JP; MP (C) Thirsk and Malton Division since 1929; Chairman, Commonwealth Industries Association, since 1963; *b* 8 Aug. 1903; *s* of late Major R. B. Turton, Kildale Hall, Kildale, York; *m* 1928, Ruby Christian, *d* of late Robert T. Scott, Beechmont, Sevenoaks; three *s* one *d*. *Educ:* Eton; Balliol Coll., Oxford. Called to Bar, Inner Temple, 1926; joined 4th Bn of Green

Howards at outbreak of war, 1939; served as DAAG 50th (N) Division, AAG GHQ MEF. Parly Sec., Min. of Nat. Insurance, 1951-53, Min. of Pensions and Nat. Insce, 1953-54; Joint Parly Under-Sec. of State for Foreign Affairs, Oct. 1954-Dec. 1955; Minister of Health, Dec. 1955-Jan. 1957; Chm., Select Cttee on Procedure, 1970-. JP, N Riding, Co. York, 1936; DL, N Riding, Co. York, 1962. Hon. Colonel, 4/5th Bn The Green Howards (TA), 1963-67. *Address:* Upsall Castle, Thirsk, Yorkshire. *T:* Upsall 202; 15 Grey Coat Gardens, SW1. *T:* 01-834 1535. *Club:* Carlton.

**TURTON-HART, Sir Francis (Edmund),** KBE 1963 (MBE 1942); Chairman, Dorman Long & Amalgamated Engineering Ltd, Nigeria and Dorman Long (Ghana) Ltd, since 1959; *b* 29 May 1908; *s* of David Edwin Hart and Zoe Evelyn Turton; *m* 1947, Margaret Greaves; one *d.* *Educ:* Uppingham. Served with Royal Engineers, 1939-46 (Hon. Major, 1946). East Africa, 1924-38; Portugal, 1939; West Africa, 1946-65; Federal House of Representatives, Nigeria, 1956-60; President, Lagos Chamber of Commerce, 1960-63. *Recreations:* shooting, fishing, golf. *Address:* Bagton, Kingsbridge, Devon. *Clubs:* East India and Sports; Royal Western Yacht (Plymouth).

**TURVEY, Ralph;** Joint Deputy Chairman, National Board for Prices and Incomes, since 1968 (Full-time Member since 1967); *b* 1 May 1927; *s* of John and Margaret Turvey; *m* 1957, Sheila Bucher; one *s* one *d.* *Educ:* Sidcot School; London School of Economics; Uppsala University. Lectr, then Reader in Economics, at London School of Economics, 1948-64, with interruptions. Vis. Lectr, Johns Hopkins Univ., 1953; Ford Foundation Vis. Res. Prof., Univ. of Chicago, 1958-59; Economic Section, HM Treasury, 1960-62; Center of Economic Research, Athens, 1963. Chief Economist, The Electricity Council, 1964-67. *Publications:* The Economics of Real Property, 1957; Interest Rates and Asset Prices, 1960; Studies in Greek Taxation (joint author), 1964; Optimal Pricing and Investment in Electricity Supply, 1968; papers on macro-economics and applied welfare economics in Economic Jl, Amer. Economic Review, etc. *Recreations:* talking Swedish, abstaining from gardening. *Address:* National Board for Prices and Incomes, Kingsgate House, 66 Victoria Street, SW1. *T:* 01-834 9444. *Club:* Reform.

**TURVILLE-PETRE, Prof. Edward Oswald Gabriel;** Vigfússon Reader in Ancient Icelandic Literature and Antiquities, Oxford University, 1941, title of Professor since 1953; Student of Christ Church, 1964; *b* 25 March 1908; *s* of late O. H. P. Turville-Petre and Margaret Lucy (*née* Cave); *m* 1943, Joan Elizabeth Blomfield; three *s.* *Educ:* Ampleforth; Christ Church, Oxford (MA, BLitt). Studied Icelandic language and literature in Iceland, Scandinavia and Germany. Lecturer, University of Iceland, 1936-38; Hon. Lectr in Modern Icelandic, Univ. of Leeds, 1935-50; Vis. Prof., Univ. of Melbourne, 1965. Corr. Mem. Icelandic Acad. of Sciences, 1959. Hon. DPh Univ. of Iceland, 1961. Kt of Falcon (Ice.), 1956, Comdr, 1963. *Publications:* Viga-Glúms Saga, 1940 (enlarged edn, 1960); The Heroic Age of Scandinavia, 1951; Origins of Icelandic Literature, 1953 (2nd edn 1967); Hervarar Saga, 1956; Myth and Religion of the North, 1964; numerous articles in learned journals. *Address:* The Court, Old Headington, Oxford. *T:* Oxford 62502.

**TUSHINGHAM, Rita;** actress; *b* 14 March 1942; *d* of John Tushingham; *m* 1962, Terence William Bicknell; one *d.* *Educ:* La Sagesse Convent, Liverpool. Student, Liverpool Playhouse, 1958-60. *Stage appearances:* Royal Court Theatre: The Changeling, 1960; The Kitchen, 1961; A Midsummer Night's Dream, 1962; Twelfth Night, 1962; The Knack, 1962; The Giveaway, 1969. *Films:* A Taste of Honey, 1961 (Brit. Film Acad. and Variety Club awards for Most Promising Newcomer, 1961; NY Critics, Cannes Film Festival and Hollywood Foreign Press Assoc. awards); The Leather Boys, 1962; A Place to Go, 1963; Girl with Green Eyes, 1963 (Variety Club award); The Knack, 1964 (Silver Goddess award, Mexican Assoc. of Film Corresps); Dr Zhivago, 1965; The Trap, 1966; Smashing Time, 1967; Diamonds For Breakfast, 1967; The Guru, 1968; The Bed-Sitting Room, 1970. *Recreation:* cooking. *Address:* c/o ALS Management Ltd, 67 Brook Street, W1. *T:* 01-629 9121.

**TUSTIN, Arnold;** Professor Emeritus, MSc, FIEE, retired; *b* 1899; *m* 1948; no *c.* *Educ:* King's Coll., Univ. of Durham. Subsequently Chief Asst Engineer, Metropolitan-Vickers Electrical Co., until 1945. Visiting Webster Prof., Massachusetts Inst. of Technology, 1953-54; Prof. of Electrical Engineering, Univ. of Birmingham, 1947-55; Prof. of Heavy Electrical Engineering, Imperial Coll., Univ. of London, 1955-64. Chm. Measurement and Control Section, IEE, 1959-60; Chm. Research Adv. Council, Transport Commn, 1960. Hon. DTech Bradford, 1968. *Publications:* Direct Current Machines for Control Systems, 1952; The Mechanism of Economic Systems, 1953; (ed) Automatic and Manual Control, 1951. *Address:* Middlepiece, Christchurch Road, Tring, Herts.

**TUTIN, Dorothy,** CBE 1967; actress (stage and films); *b* 8 April 1931; *d* of late John Tutin, DSc, and of Adie Evelyn Tutin; *m* 1963, Derek Barton-Chapple (stage name Derek Waring); one *s* one *d.* *Educ:* St Catherine's, Bramley, Surrey; RADA. Began career, 1950; Stratford Festival, 1958, 1960. *Parts include:* Rose, in The Living Room; Katherine, in Henry V; Sally Bowles, in I am a Camera; St Joan, in The Lark; Catherine, in The Gates of Summer; Hedwig, in The Wild Duck; Viola, in Twelfth Night; Juliet, in Romeo and Juliet; Ophelia, in Hamlet; during Shakespeare Memorial Theatre tour of Russia, 1958, played parts of Ophelia, Viola and Juliet; Dolly, in Once More, With Feeling (New), 1959; Portia, Viola, Cressida (S-on-A), 1960; Sister Jeanne, in The Devils (Aldwych), 1961, 1962; Juliet, Desdemona (S-on-A), 1961; Varya, in The Cherry Orchard (S-on-A, and Aldwych), 1961; Cressida, Prioress, in The Devils (Edinburgh), 1962; Polly Peachum, in The Beggar's Opera (Aldwych), 1963; The Hollow Crown (New York), 1963; Queen Victoria, in Portrait of a Queen, Vaudeville, 1965; Rosalind, As You Like It, Stratford, 1967, Los Angeles, 1968; Portrait of a Queen, NY, 1968; Play on Love, St Martin's, 1970. *Films:* Polly Peachum, in The Beggar's Opera; Cecily, in The Importance of Being Earnest; Lucie Manette, in A Tale of Two Cities; Henrietta Marie in Cromwell. Has appeared on television. *Recreations:* music; Isle of Arran. *Address:* c/o London International, 11-12 Hanover Street, W1.

**TUTIN, Prof. Thomas Gaskell;** Professor of Taxonomy, University of Leicester, since 1967; *b* 21 April 1908; *o s* of Frank and Jane Tutin; *m* 1942, Winifred Pennington; one *s* three *d.* *Educ:* Cotham Sch., Bristol; Downing Coll., Cambridge. Expedition to British Guiana, 1933; Marine Laboratory, Plymouth, 1934-37; expedition to Lake Titicaca, 1937; part-time Demonstrator, KCL, 1938-39; Asst Lectr, Univ. of Manchester, 1939-42;

Geographer, Naval Intelligence Div., 1942-44; Lectr, Univ. College of Leicester, 1944-47; Prof. of Botany, Univ. of Leicester, 1947-67. Foreign Member, Societas Scientiarum Fennica (Section for Natural Science), 1960. *Publications:* (with Clapham and Warburg) Flora of the British Isles, 1952, 2nd edn 1962; (with Clapham and Warburg) Excursion Flora of the British Isles, 1959, 2nd edn 1968; (with V. H. Heywood *et al*) Flora Europaea, Vol. I 1964 Vol. II 1968; (with A. C. Jermy) British Sedges, 1968; papers in Annals of Botany, New Phytologist, Jl of Ecology, Watsonia, etc. *Recreations:* botany, music, gardening. *Address:* Home Farm, Knighton, Leicester LE2 3WG. *T:* Leicester 707356.

**TUTTLE, Sir Geoffrey (William),** KBE 1957 (OBE 1940); CB 1945; DFC 1937; FRAeS 1960; Air Marshal retired; Director and Vice-Chairman, British Aircraft Corporation (Weybridge) Ltd; *b* 2 Oct. 1906; *s* of late Maj. E. W. Tuttle, Lowestoft. *Educ:* St Paul's School. Joined RAF, 1925; India, 1932-37; comd 105 Sqdn, 1937-39; France, 1939-40; Wing Comdr and Group Capt. Coastal and Photo Reconnaissance units in UK, 1940-43; Tunisia, Corsica, Sardinia, Italy, Greece, 1943-45; AOC RAF, Greece, 1944-46; idc 1947; Air Cdre 1948; Dir of Operational Requirements, Air Min., 1948-49; AOA, HQ Coastal Comd, 1950-51; Air Vice-Marshal 1952; Asst Chief of Air Staff (Operational Requirements), 1951-54; AOC No 19 Group, RAF, 1954-56; Deputy Chief of the Air Staff, 1956-Dec. 1959, retired. Pres. British Motor Cycle Racing Club. Order of Patriotic War, 2nd Class (Soviet), 1944; Grand Officer Royal Order of the Phœnix (Greece), 1945; Commandeur Légion d'Honneur (France); Croix de Guerre (France). *Recreation:* sailing. *Address:* Silver Waters, Kingswood Creek, Wraysbury, Bucks. *T:* Wraysbury 2346. *Clubs:* Army and Navy, Royal Air Force.

**TUZO, Maj.-Gen. Harry Craufurd,** OBE 1961; MC 1945; Director, Royal Artillery, since 1969; *b* 26 Aug. 1917; *s* of John Atkinson Tuzo and Annie Katherine (*née* Craufurd); *m* 1943, Monica Patience Salter; one *d. Educ:* Wellington Coll.; Oriel Coll., Oxford. BA Oxon 1939, MA 1970. Regimental Service, Royal Artillery, 1939-45; Staff appts, Far East, 1946-49; Royal Horse Artillery, 1950-51 and 1954-58; Staff at Sch. of Infantry, 1951-53; GSO1, War Office, 1958-60; CO, 3rd Regt, RHA, 1960-62; Asst Comdt, Sandhurst, 1962-63; Comdr, 51 Gurkha Infantry Bde, 1963-65; Imp. Def. Coll., 1966; Chief of Staff, BAOR, 1967-69. Dato Setia Negeri Brunei, 1965. *Recreations:* sailing, music, shooting. *Address:* Director's House, Royal Military Academy, Woolwich, SE18. *Club:* Army and Navy.

**TWEEDDALE,** 12th Marquis of, *cr* 1694; **David George Montagu Hay,** AM; Baron, 1488; Earl of Tweeddale, 1646; Earl of Gifford, Viscount Walden, 1694; Baron (UK), 1881; farmer and lobster fisherman since 1965; *b* Oct. 1921; *s* of Col Lord Edward Hay and Bridget Barclay; *S* kinsman, 1967; *m* 1st, 1946, Sonia Peake (marr. diss. 1958); three *s* (inc. twin *s*); 2nd, 1959, Nella Doreen Dutton; two *s* (twins). *Educ:* Eton. Merchant Service, 1939; Royal Naval Reserve, 1941; retired 1947. Worked in London various private enterprise jobs. Local Director, Martins Bank Ltd, 1955; retired, 1965. Albert Medal, 1941; Lloyd's Medal, 1942; Royal Life Saving Medal, 1943. *Recreations:* philately, entomology, ornithology; striving to exist after dynamic Socialism. *Heir: s* Earl of Gifford, *qv. Address:* Tavool, Isle of Mull. *T:* Tiroran 207. *Club:* Puffins (Edinburgh).

**TWEEDIE, Brig. John William,** CBE 1958; DSO 1944; *b* 5 June 1907; *e s* of late Col William Tweedie, CMG, CBE; *m* 1937, Sheila Mary, *d* of Brig.-Gen. Thomas Hudson, CB; one *s* one *d. Educ:* Ampleforth; Royal Military College, Sandhurst. 2/Lt Argyll and Sutherland Highldrs, 1926; Adjutant, 1935-39; OC 2nd Bn, 1942-44; Brigade Commander, 39 Inf. Bde, 1951-54; ADC to the Queen, 1959-61; retired 1961. *Address:* Woodslee House, Canonbie, Dumfriesshire. *T:* 206. *Club:* Army and Navy.

**TWEEDSMUIR,** 2nd Baron, *cr* 1935, of Elsfield; **John Norman Stuart Buchan,** CBE 1964 (OBE 1945); CD 1964; FRGS; FRSA; FZS; Lieutenant-Colonel Canadian Infantry Corps; LLD (Hon.), Aberdeen, 1949, Queen's (Canada), 1955; *b* 25 November 1911; *e s* of 1st Baron and Susan Charlotte (*see* Susan, Lady Tweedsmuir); *S* father, 1940; *m* 1948, Priscilla Jean Fortescue (*see* Baroness Tweedsmuir of Belhelvie); one *d. Educ:* Eton; Brasenose Coll., Oxford (BA). Asst District Comr, Uganda Protectorate, 1934-36; joined Hudson's Bay Company, 1937; wintered in their service at Cape Dorset, Baffin Land, Canadian Arctic, 1938-39; served War of 1939-45 in Canadian Army (wounded, despatches twice, OBE, Order of Orange-Nassau, with swords); comd Hastings and Prince Edward Regt in Sicily and Italy, 1943; Hon. Col, 1955-60. Rector of Aberdeen Univ., 1948-51; Chm., Joint East and Central African Board, 1950-52; Pres., Commonwealth and British Empire Chambers of Commerce, 1955-57; a Governor, Commonwealth Inst., 1958-; Pres., Inst. of Export, 1964-67; Mem. Board, BOAC, 1955-64. *Publications:* (part author) St Kilda papers, 1931; Hudson's Bay Trader, 1951; Always a Countryman, 1953; One Man's Happiness, 1968. *Recreations:* fishing, shooting, falconry. *Heir: b* Hon. William de l'Aigle Buchan, RAFVR [*b* 1916; *m* 1st, Nesta (marr. diss. 1946), *o d* of Lt-Col C. D. Crozier; one *d*; 2nd, 1946, Barbara (marr. diss. 1960), 2nd *d* of E. N. Ensor, late of Hong Kong; three *s* three *d*; 3rd, Sauré Cynthia Mary, *y d* of late Major G. E. Tatchell, Royal Lincolnshire Regt; one *s. Educ:* Eton; New College, Oxford]. *Address:* 40 Tufton Court, Westminster, SW1. *T:* 01-222 6997; Potterton House, Balmedie, Aberdeenshire. *T:* Balmedie 230. *Clubs:* Carlton, Travellers', Pratt's, Flyfishers'.
*See also Hon. A. F. Buchan.*

**TWEEDSMUIR OF BELHELVIE,** Baroness *cr* 1970 (Life Peeress), of Potterton, Aberdeen; **Priscilla Jean Fortescue Buchan;** Minister of State, Scottish Office, since 1970; *b* 25 Jan. 1915; *d* of late Brig. Alan F. Thomson, DSO; *m* 1934, Major Sir Arthur Lindsay Grant, 11th Bt, Grenadier Guards (killed in action, 1944); two *d*; 2nd, 1948, 2nd Baron Tweedsmuir, *qv*; one *d. Educ:* England, Germany, France. Contested (C) N Div. of Aberdeen, July 1945. Past Chm. Scottish Panel, the British Council. Delegate Council of Europe, 1950-53; Mem. Council Royal Institute of International Affairs; Mem. Commonwealth Parliamentary Delegation, West Indies, 1955; UK Delegate to UN General Assembly, 1960-61; Jt Parly Under-Sec. of State, Scottish Office, 1962-64; MP (C) South Aberdeen, 1946-66. Vice-Chm., Advisory Cttee on Juvenile Crime, 1963; Director: Factoryguards, 1966-70; Cunard Steam-ship Co., 1966-68; Cunard Line, 1968-70; Member, Cttee for Exports to Canada. Hon. Col (316 Scottish Command) Bn WRAC/TA, 1958-61. *Publications:* writes for TV and newspapers. *Recreations:* swimming, gardening, bee-keeping. *Address:* 40 Tufton Court, Westminster, SW1. *T:* 01-222 6997; Potterton House, Balmedie, Aberdeenshire. *T:* Balmedie 230.

**TWEEDSMUIR, Susan, Lady;** *d* of Hon. Norman Grosvenor; *m* 1907, John Buchan, author (1st Baron Tweedsmuir, PC, GCMG, GCVO, CH); three *s* one *d*. *Educ:* at home. George V Jubilee, George VI Coronation medals. DStJ 1936. Hon. DLitt: McGill Univ., Montreal; Univ. of Toronto. *Publications:* Sword of State; Canada (Britain in Pictures Series); John Buchan by his Wife and Friends; The Lilac and the Rose (autobiography); Winter Bouquet (essays); Cousin Harriet (novel); Dashbury Park (novel); A Stone in the Pool (novel); The Edwardian Lady (social history); *children's books:* Freedom of the Garden, etc; *one act plays:* The Vision at the Inn; The Wife of Flanders. *Recreation:* gardening. *Address:* Hill House, Burford, Oxfordshire. *T:* Burford 2218. *Club:* VAD Ladies'.

*See also Baron Tweedsmuir, Hon. A. F. Buchan.*

**TWINING, Gen. Nathan Farragut,** DSM (with two Oak Leaf Clusters), Navy DSM, Legion of Merit (with Oak Leaf Cluster), DFC; US Air Force (Retired); *b* Monroe, Wis., 11 October 1897; *s* of Clarence Walker Twining and Maize Barber; *m* 1932, Maude McKeever; two *s* one *d*. US Mil. Acad., 1918; student Inf. Sch., 1919-20, Air Corps Tactical Sch., 1935-36; Command and Gen. Staff Sch., 1936-37; rated command pilot. Served in Ore. Nat. Guard, 1916-17; comd 2nd Lt, Inf., Nov. 1918; transferred Air Corps, 1924, promoted through grades to Lt-Gen., 1945; Gen., USAF, 1950. Chief of Staff to Comdg Gen., USAFISPA, 1942-43; Comdg Gen., 13th Air Force, Solomon Is, 1943; 15th Air Force, Italy, and Mediterranean Allied Strategic Air Forces, 1943; 20th Air Force, Pacific, 1945; Air Materiel Command, Wright Field, Ohio, 1945-47; C-in-C Alaska, 1947-50; Vice-Chief of Staff, Air Force, 1950-53; Chief of Staff, Air Force, 1953-57; Chairman, Joint Chiefs of Staff, 1957-60. Has also numerous medals (US) and foreign decorations including Hon. KBE (Gt Brit.). *Recreations:* hunting, fishing, golf, carpentry. *Address:* Sea Pines Plantation, Hilton Head Island, South Carolina 29928, USA.

**TWINING, Richard Haynes,** CBE 1959; Member of Council of Foreign Bondholders; *b* 3 Nov. 1889; *s* of Herbert Haynes Twining; *m* 1915, Ellen Irene Rosalind Tweed (*d* 1961); one *s* (killed in Tunisia, 1943). *Educ:* Eton; Magdalen Coll., Oxford. Served European War, 1914-18, in Queen's Royal West Surrey Regt; served War, 1939-46, Home Guard and Civil Defence. Deputy Chairman, The Stock Exchange, London, 1949-58. Trustee of MCC, President, 1964-65, Hon. Life Vice-President, 1969. *Recreations:* cricket (Eton XI, 1907-09, Captain 1909; Oxford University XI, 1910-13, Captain 1912); golf. *Address:* 114 Gloucester Road, SW7. *T:* 01-373 2320. *Clubs:* Buck's, White's, MCC, I Zingari; Free Foresters.

**TWINN, Frank Charles George,** CMG 1943; *b* 1 Sept. 1885; *m* 1913, Lilian May Tomlinson; two *s*. *Educ:* St Olave's Grammar School, London; St John's College, Cambridge. Entered Post Office, 1910; Director of Postal Services and Director of Army Postal Services, 1939-40; Regional Director, South Western Region, GPO, 1940-46. *Recreations:* gardening and reading. *Address:* 16 Greenhill Way, Farnham, Surrey. *T:* 22249.

**TWISLETON-WYKEHAM-FIENNES;** *see* Fiennes.

**TWISLETON-WYKEHAM-FIENNES, Gerard Francis Gisborne,** OBE 1957; Chairman, Hargreaves Transport, since 1968; Director, Hargreaves Group, since 1968; *b* 7 June 1906; *s* of Gerard Yorke Twisleton-Wykeham-Fiennes, CBE, and Gwendolen; *m* 1st, 1934, Norah Davies (*d* 1960), Penymaes, Llangollen; three *s* two *d*; 2nd, 1962, Jean Kerridge. *Educ:* Horris Hill, Newbury; Winchester Coll.; Hertford Coll., Oxford. LNER 1928. Asst Yardmaster, Whitemoor, 1932; Chief Controller, Cambridge, 1934; appts at York, Liverpool Street, Edinburgh and Shenfield; District Supt; Nottingham, 1943; Stratford, 1944; Operating Supt, Eastern Region, 1956; Line Traffic Manager, King's Cross, 1957; Chief Operating Officer, BR, 1961; Chm., Western Railway Board, 1963; Lt-Col Railway Staff and Engrg Corps, 1963; Chm., Eastern Railway Board, and Gen. Manager, Eastern Region, British Railways, 1965-67. Broadcasts on radio and TV. FRSA 1966; MInstT 1955. OStJ 1967. *Publications:* I Tried to Run a Railway, 1967; various chapters and articles in railway technical press. *Recreations:* golf, sailing, fishing, railways. *Address:* Dartmouth, Aldeburgh, Suffolk. *T:* 2457. *Clubs:* United Service, MCC.

**TWISLETON-WYKEHAM-FIENNES, Sir John (Saye Wingfield),** KCB 1970 (CB 1953); First Parliamentary Counsel, since 1968; *b* 14 April 1911; *s* of Gerard Yorke Twisleton-Wykeham-Fiennes and Gwendolen (*née* Gisborne); *m* 1937, Sylvia Beatrice, *d* of Rev. C. R. L. McDowall; two *s* one *d*. *Educ:* Winchester; Balliol College, Oxford. Called to Bar, Middle Temple, 1936; Bencher, 1969. Joined parliamentary counsel office, 1939; Second Parly Coun., Treasury, 1956-68. Parliamentary Counsel, Malaya, 1962-63 (Colombo Plan). With Law Commission, 1965-66. Hon. JMN (Malaysia). *Address:* High Street, Roydon, Essex. *T:* Roydon 3130. *Club:* Athenæum.

**TWISS, Adm. Sir Frank (Roddam),** KCB 1965 (CB 1962); DSC 1945; Gentleman Usher of the Black Rod, House of Lords, since 1970; *b* 7 July 1910; *s* of Col E. K. Twiss, DSO; *m* 1936, Prudence Dorothy Hutchison; two *s* one *d*. *Educ:* RNC Dartmouth. Cadet 1924; Midshipman 1928; Lieut 1931; Comdr 1945; Captain 1950; Rear-Adm. 1960; Vice-Adm. 1963; Adm. 1967. Naval Sec., Admty, 1960-62; Flag Officer, Flotillas, Home Fleet, 1962-64; Comdr Far East Fleet, 1965-67; Second Sea Lord and Chief of Naval Personnel, 1967-70. Mem., Commonwealth War Graves Cttee, 1970-. *Recreations:* fishing, walking. *Address:* House of Lords, SW1; Chalkstone House, Broad Hinton, near Swindon, Wilts. *Club:* United Service.

**TWISS, (Lionel) Peter;** OBE 1957; DSC 1942 and Bar 1943; Test Pilot of Fairey Aviation Ltd, since 1946; Director, Fairey Marine Ltd, Hamble, since 1958; *b* 23 July 1921; *m* 1950, Mrs Vera Maguire (marr. diss.); one step *s* one step *d*. one *d* (and one *d* decd); *m* 1960, Cherry (marr. diss.), *d* of Sir John Huggins, *qv*; one *d*; *m* 1964, Mrs Heather Danby, Titchfield. *Educ:* Sherborne Sch. Joined Fleet Air Arm, 1939; served on catapult ships, aircraft-carriers, 1941-43; night fighter development, 1943-44; served in British Air Commn, America, 1944. Empire Test Pilots School, Boscombe Down, 1945; Test Pilot, Fairey Aviation Co. Ltd, 1946. Holder of World's Absolute Speed Record, 10 March 1956. *Publication:* Faster than the Sun, 1963. *Address:* Nettleworth, South Street, Titchfield, Hants. *T:* 3146. *Clubs:* Royal Southern Yacht, Island Sailing.

**TWIST, George,** QPM; LLM; Chief Constable, Bristol Constabulary, since 1964; *b* 12 March 1913; British; *m* 1947, Edith Kathleen Ibbotson; no *c*. *Educ:* Ormskirk Grammar Sch.; Liverpool University. Police Cadet,

Liverpool, 1929-34; Liverpool City Police, 1934-64 (Constable to Asst Chief Constable). Mem., Home Secretary's Adv. Council on Penal Reform; Moderator to the Police Promotion Examinations in England and Wales. OStJ 1969. *Publications:* articles on police communications and crime prevention in Police Jl and Home Office Research and Planning Bulletin. *Recreations:* amateur radio (transmitting); music (organ). *Address:* 80 Bell Barn Road, Bristol BS9 2DG. *Clubs:* Savages, British Commonwealth (Bristol).

**TWIST, Henry Aloysius,** CMG 1966; OBE 1947; HM Diplomatic Service; British Deputy High Commissioner, Rawalpindi, Pakistan, since Oct. 1966, and Minister (Commercial), since 1968; *b* 18 June 1914; *s* of John Twist, Preston; *m* 1941, Mary Monica, *yr d* of Nicholas Mulhall, Manchester; one *s* one *d*. *Educ:* Liverpool Univ. (BA). Senior Classics Master, St Chad's Coll., Wolverhampton, 1936-40; Lecturer in English, South Staffordshire High School of Commerce, 1939-40. Served War of 1939-45 with RASC and RAEC, 1940-46; released with rank of Lt-Col, 1946. Principal, Dominions Office, 1946; Offical Secretary, Office of the British High Commissioner in Ceylon, 1948-49; Office of the British High Commissioner in Australia, 1949-52; Commonwealth Relations Office, 1952-54; Secretariat, Commonwealth Economic Conference, London, 1952; Deputy High Commissioner for the United Kingdom in Bombay, 1954-57; Assistant Secretary, Commonwealth Relations Office, 1957-60; British Deputy High Commissioner, Kaduna, Northern Region, Federation of Nigeria, 1960-62; Commonwealth Service representative on the 1963 Course at Imperial Defence College; Commonwealth Office, 1964; Asst Under-Sec., 1966. *Recreation:* golf. *Address:* c/o Foreign and Commonwealth Office, SW1. *Club:* Travellers'.

**TWITCHETT, Prof. Denis Crispin,** FBA 1967; Professor of Chinese in the University of Cambridge, since 1968; *b* 23 Sept. 1925; *m* 1956, Umeko (*née* Ichikawa); two *s*. *Educ:* St Catharine's Coll., Cambridge. Lectr in Far-Eastern History, Univ. of London, 1954-56; Univ. Lectr in Classical Chinese, Univ. of Cambridge, 1956-60; Prof. of Chinese, SOAS, London Univ., 1960-68. *Publication:* The Financial Administration of the T'ang dynasty, 1963. *Address:* St Catharine's College, Cambridge; 24 Arbury Road, Cambridge.

**TWOHIG;** *see* O'Brien-Twohig.

**TYACKE, Maj.-Gen. David Noel Hugh,** CB 1970; OBE 1957; General Officer Commanding, Singapore District, 1966-70, retired; *b* 18 Nov. 1915; *s* of Capt. Charles Noel Walker Tyacke (killed in action, March 1918) and late Phoebe Mary Cicely (*née* Coulthard), Cornwall; *m* 1940, Diana, *d* of Aubrey Hare Duke; one *s*. *Educ:* Malvern Coll.; RMC Sandhurst. Commissioned DCLI, 1935; India, 1936-39; France and Belgium, 1939-40; India and Burma, 1943-46; Instructor, Staff Coll., Camberley, 1950-52; CO 1st Bn DCLI, 1957-59; Comdr 130 Inf. Bde (TA), 1961-63; Dir of Administrative Planning (Army), 1963-64; Brig. Gen. Staff (Ops), Min. of Defence, 1965-66. Dep. Col, The Light Infantry (Somerset and Cornwall), 1970-. *Recreations:* walking, motoring, bird-watching. *Address:* c/o Lloyds Bank Ltd, Cox's & King's Branch, 6 Pall Mall, SW1. *Club:* United Service.

**TYDEMAN, Col Frank William Edward,** CMG 1966; CIE 1945; Port Consultant; Consulting Engineer, Ports and Harbours, Western Australian Government since 1946; General Manager, Fremantle Port Authority, 1950-65; *b* 20 January 1901; *s* of Harvey James and Kate Mary Anne Tydeman; *m* 1924, Jessie Sarah Mann (*d* 1947); two *s*. *Educ:* London University. BSc (Eng) London 1920. Chartered Civil Engineer. FICE, FIMechE, FIStructE, FIEAust, FInstT. Served Palestine; Haifa Harbour, 1930; Jaffa Port, 1934; Singapore Harbour Board, 1937; Colonel, Deputy Director Transportation, India and Burma, 1942. *Recreation:* golf. *Address:* c/o Australia & New Zealand Bank Ltd, Perth, Western Australia. *Clubs:* Naval and Military, West Australian Golf (Perth).

**TYERMAN, Donald;** journalist; Director, United City Merchants Ltd; Editor of The Economist, 1956-65; *b* 1 March 1908; *s* of late Joseph and late Catherine Tyerman, Middlesbrough, Yorks; *m* 1934, Margaret Charteris Gray; two *s* three *d*. *Educ:* Friends' School, Great Ayton; St Mary's College, Middlesbrough; Coatham Grammar Sch., Redcar; Gateshead Secondary Sch., Gateshead-on-Tyne; Brasenose College, Oxford. Lectr, University College, Southampton, 1930-36; Assistant and then Deputy Editor, The Economist, 1937-44; Deputy Editor, The Observer, 1943-44; Asst Editor, The Times, 1944-55. Chm., Exec. Bd of International Press Inst., 1961-62; Member: Press Council, 1963-69; Council, Commonwealth Press Union; Council, Nat. Institute of Economic and Social Research; Exec. Cttee, Overseas Development Inst.; Council, Univ. of Sussex. Governor, LSE; Hon. Treasurer and Chm., finance cttee, Save the Children Fund; Life Vice-Pres., Ingatestone Cricket Club. *Recreations:* reading and watching games. *Address:* 41 Buckingham Mansions, West End Lane, NW6. *T:* 01-435 1030; Holly Cottage, Westleton, near Saxmundham, Suffolk. *T:* Saxmundham 73-261. *Club:* Reform.

**TYLECOTE, Dame Mabel,** DBE 1966; Vice-President of National Federation of Community Associations since 1961 (President, 1958-61); *b* 4 Feb. 1896; *d* of late John Ernest Phythian and Ada Prichard Phythian (*née* Crompton); *m* 1932, Frank Edward Tylecote (*d* 1965); one *s* (and one step *s* one step *d*). *Educ:* Univ. of Manchester; Univ. of Wisconsin (USA). BA, PhD (Manchester). Lectr in History, Huddersfield Techn. Coll., 1920-24; Asst Lectr in History, Univ. of Manchester, 1926-30; Warden of Elvington Settlement, 1930-32; part-time Lectr, Univ. of Manchester Joint Cttee for Adult Educn, 1935-51; Vice-Pres., WEA, 1960-68. Member: Pensions Appeal Tribunal, 1944-50; Manchester City Coun., 1940-51; (co-opted) Manchester Educn Cttee, 1951-; Stockport Borough Coun., 1956-63; Chm. of Coun., Assoc. of Art Instns, 1960-61; Chm. Exec. Cttee, Nat. Inst. of Adult Educn, 1960-63; Mem. Court, 1945-, Mem. Coun., 1960-, Univ. of Manchester; Mem. Court, Univ. of Manchester Inst. of Science and Technology, 1960-; Vice-President: Manchester and Salford Council of Social Service, 1968-; Union of Lancashire and Cheshire Institutes, 1969-. Contested (Lab): Fylde, 1938; Middleton and Prestwich, 1945; Norwich South, 1950, 1951, 1955. *Publications:* The Education of Women at Manchester University 1883-1933, 1941; The Mechanics' Institutes of Lancashire and Yorkshire before 1851, 1957; The Future of Adult Education (Fabian pamphlet), 1960; articles in various social and educnl jls. *Address:* 1 Rusholme Gardens, Wilmslow Road, Manchester M14 5LG. *T:* 061-224 9366.

**TYLER, Brig. Arthur Catchmay,** CBE 1960; MC 1945; DL; Secretary, Council of Territorial Auxiliary and Volunteer Reserve Associations, since 1967; *b* 20 Aug. 1913; 4th *s* of Hugh Griffin Tyler and Muriel Tyler (*née* Barnes); *m* 1938, Sheila, *d* of James Kinloch, Meigle, Perthshire; three *s* one *d*. *Educ:* Allhallows Sch.; RMC, Sandhurst. Commissioned, The Welch Regt, 1933. Served War of 1939-45: Africa, India and Burma (despatches). Staff Coll., 1946; JSSC, 1951; Sec., BJSM, Washington, 1952-54; Lt-Col, 1954; Comd 4th (Carms) Bn The Welch Regt, 1954-57; Col, 1957; AAG, War Office, 1957-60; Brig. 1960; Senior UK Liaison Officer and Military Adviser to High Commissioner, Canada, 1960; Asst Chief of Staff (Ops and Plans), Allied Forces Central Europe, 1963. DL Surrey, 1968. *Recreations:* all forms of sport. *Address:* 24 Sandy Lane, Cheam, Surrey. *T:* 01-642 1104. *Clubs:* Army and Navy, United Hunts.

**TYLER, Cyril,** DSc, PhD, FRIC; Professor of Physiology and Biochemistry, University of Reading, since 1958; Deputy Vice-Chancellor, since 1968; *b* 26 Jan. 1911; *er s* of John and Annie Tyler; *m* 1939, Myra Eileen, *d* of George and Rosa Batten; two *s* one *d*. *Educ:* Ossett Grammar Sch.; Univ. of Leeds. BSc 1st Class Hons 1933, PhD 1935, DSc 1959, Leeds. Lectr in Agricultural Chemistry. RAC, Cirencester, 1935-39; Univ. of Reading: Lecturer in Agricultural Chemistry, 1939-47; Professor, 1947-58; Dean of the Faculty of Agriculture, 1959-62. *Publications:* Organic Chemistry for Students of Agriculture, 1946; Animal Nutrition (2nd edn), 1964; Wilhelm von Nathusius 1821-1899 on Avian Eggshells, 1964; numerous papers on poultry metabolism and egg shells in scientific journals. *Address:* 22 Belle Avenue, Reading, Berks.

**TYLER, Froom,** OBE 1969; *b* 30 Jan. 1904; *o s* of John Frederick Tyler, Bristol; *m* 1st, 1928, Doris May (*née* Chubb) (*d* 1963); one *d*; 2nd, Diana Griffiths (*née* Kirby). Editor of the Evening World, Bristol, 1936-40; Foreign Editor, Daily Mail, 1940-43; Staff Officer (Press) to Admiral (Submarines), 1943-45. Editor of Overseas Daily Mail, 1946-50; Editor of Leicester Evening Mail, 1950-57; Editor of South Wales Evening Post, 1957-69; Pres., Royal Instn of S Wales, 1969-; Pres., Gower Soc., 1969-. *Publications:* Cripps: A Portrait and a Prospect, 1942; His Majesty's Submarines (the Admiralty Account), 1945; News in Our Time (Daily Mail Jubilee Book), 1946; The Man Who Made Music, 1947. *Address:* 26 Glanmor Park Road, Sketty, Swansea.

**TYLER, Ven. Leonard George;** Principal, William Temple College, Rugby, since 1966; Anglican Adviser to ABC Television, 1958-68; *b* 15 April 1920; *s* of Hugh Horstead Tyler and Mabel Adam Stewart Tyler; *m* 1946, Sylvia May Wilson; one *s* two *d*. *Educ:* Darwen Grammar School; Liverpool University; Christ's College, Cambridge; Westcott House. Chaplain, Trinity College, Kandy, Ceylon, 1946-48; Principal, Diocesan Divinity School, Colombo, Ceylon, 1948-50; Rector, Christ Church, Bradford, Manchester, 1950-55; Vicar of Leigh, Lancs, 1955-66 (Rural Dean, 1955-62); Chaplain, Leigh Infirmary, 1955-66; Archdeacon of Rochdale, 1962-66. *Publications:* contributor to Theology. *Address:* William Temple College, Rugby, Warwicks.

**TYLER, Maj.-Gen. Sir Leslie (Norman),** KBE 1961 (OBE 1942); CB 1955; BScEng; CEng; FIMechE; *b* 26 April 1904; *s* of late Major Norman Tyler, Addiscombe, Surrey; *m* 1st, 1930, Louie Teresa Franklin (*d* 1950); one *s* one *d*; 2nd, 1953, Sheila, *widow* of Maj.-Gen. L. H. Cox, CB, CBE, MC; two *s* two step *d*. *Educ:* RN Colleges Osborne and Dartmouth; King's College, Univ. of London. Commissioned Lieut, RAOC, 1927; served War of 1939-45, Malta and NW Europe; transferred to REME, 1942; DDME, Second Army, 1945; Comdt REME Training Centre, 1945-47; AAG, War Office, 1948-49; DME, MELF, 1949-50; DDME, War Office, 1950-53; DME, MELF, 1953-55; Commandant, Headquarters Base Workshop Group, REME, 1956-57; Director of Electrical and Mechanical Engineering, War Office, 1957-60; retd 1960. Regional Dir, MPBW, Central Mediterranean Region, 1963-69. Colonel Commandant, REME, 1962-67. Freeman, City of London; Liveryman, Worshipful Company of Turners, 1961-. Fellow, King's Coll., London, 1969. *Address:* Higher Combe East, Haslemere, Surrey. *T:* Haslemere 3900. *Clubs:* United Service; Casino Maltese (Valletta).

**TYMMS, Sir Frederick,** KCIE 1947 (CIE 1935); Kt 1941; MC; FRAeS; *b* 4 Aug. 1889; *s* of William Henry Tymms. *Educ:* Tenby; King's College, London. War Service: 4th Bn South Lancs Regt and Royal Flying Corps, France; British Aviation Mission to the USA, 1915-18 (MC, Chevalier de l'Ordre de la Couronne, Croix de Guerre, Belgium). Civil Aviation Dept, Air Min., 1920-27; Oxford Univ. Arctic Expedition to Spitsbergen, 1924; Air Min. Supt of Egypt-India air route, 1927; seconded to Govts of the Sudan, Kenya, Uganda and Tanganyika, 1928; Chief Technical Asst to Dir of Civil Aviation, Air Min., 1928-31; Air Min. Representative on the Commn to Africa, to organise the Cape to Cairo air route, 1929-30; Dir of Civil Aviation in India, 1931-42 and 1943-45; Man. Dir, Tata Aircraft Ltd, Bombay, 1942-43; Dir-Gen. of Civil Aviation in India, Sept. 1945-March 1947; UK Representative on Council of Internat. Civil Aviation Organisation, Montreal, 1947-54; retd from Civil Service, 1955. Govt of India delegate to Internat. Civil Aviation Conf., Chicago, 1944; Leader of UK Civil Aviation Mission to New Zealand, 1948. Master of Guild of Air Pilots and Air Navigators, 1957-58. Chm., Commn of Enquiry on Civil Aviation in West Indies, 1960. *Address:* High Thicket, Dockenfield, near Farnham, Surrey; c/o Lloyds Bank, Pall Mall, SW1. *Club:* Royal Aero.

**TYMMS, Prof. Ralph Vincent,** MA; Professor of German Language and Literature in the University of London (Royal Holloway College), since 1956; Head of German Department since 1948, Vice-Principal since 1969, Royal Holloway College; *b* 9 Jan. 1913; *s* of Arthur Hugh Tymms and Janet Scott Coventon. *Educ:* Bradford Grammar Sch., Yorkshire; Magdalen Coll., Oxford; Universities of Vienna and Giessen. John Doncaster Scholar in German, Magdalen Coll., Oxford, 1931-34; 1st Class Hons, Oxford, 1934. Assistant Lecturer in German, University of Manchester, 1936. Intelligence Corps, 1941-45; Major, 1945. Lecturer in German, Manchester Univ., 1945; Reader in German Language and Literature in the University of London, 1948. *Publications:* Doubles in Literary Psychology, 1949; German Romantic Literature, 1955. *Address:* Little Ormonde Lodge, Cooper's Hill, Englefield Green, Surrey. *T:* Egham 2125. *Club:* Athenæum.

**TYNAN, Kenneth Peacock,** FRSL; Literary Consultant of the National Theatre since 1969 (Literary Manager, 1963-69); *b* 2 April 1927; *s* of Sir Peter Peacock and Letitia Rose Tynan; *m* 1951, Elaine Brimberg (marr. diss. 1964);

one *d*; *m* 1967, Kathleen Halton; one *d*. *Educ:* King Edward's Sch., Birmingham; Magdalen Coll., Oxford. Dramatic Critic of: Spectator, 1951; Evening Standard, 1952-53; Daily Sketch, 1953-54; Observer, 1954-63; New Yorker, 1958-60. Script Ed., Ealing Films, 1955-57; Ed., TV programme Tempo, 1961-62; Film Critic of Observer, 1964-66. Member Drama Panel, British Council. *Co-produced:* Soldiers, New, 1968. *Devised and part-wrote review:* Oh, Calcutta!, NY, 1969, London, 1970. *Publications:* He That Plays the King, 1950; Persona Grata, 1953; Alec Guinness, 1954; Bull Fever, 1955; The Quest for Corbett, 1960; Curtains, 1961; Tynan Right and Left, 1967; edited books on National Theatre productions of The Recruiting Officer, 1965, and Othello, 1966. *Recreations:* word-games, watching bull-fights. *Address:* 20 Thurloe Square, SW7.

**TYNDALE-BISCOE, Rear-Adm. Alec Julian,** CB 1959; OBE 1946; lately Chairman of Blaw Knox Ltd; *b* 10 Aug. 1906; *s* of late Lt-Col A. A. T. Tyndale-Biscoe, Aubrey House, Keyhaven, Lymington, Hants; *m* 1939, Emma Winifred Haselden; four *d*. *Educ:* RN Colleges Osborne and Dartmouth. Entered RN, 1920. Served War, 1939-46. Captain, 1949; Rear-Adm. 1957. Retired as Flag-Officer Reserve Aircraft (July 1957-Sept. 1959). *Address:* Buckhurst Little, Horsted Keynes, Sussex. *Club:* Army and Navy.

**TYNDALL, Sir Arthur,** Kt, *cr* 1955; CMG 1939; **Hon. Mr Justice Tyndall;** MInstCE; FASCE; FNZIE; ARANZ; Solicitor of the Supreme Court; Judge, Court of Arbitration, New Zealand, 1940-65; *b* Dunedin, Otago, NZ, April 1891; *s* of late A. W. Tyndall, Dunedin; *m* 1916, Gladys Muriel, *d* of Col A. Stoneham, Gisborne, NZ. *Educ:* Blue Spur Sch.; Lawrence District High Sch.; Otago Univ., Dunedin; Massachusetts Institute of Technology. Joined New Zealand Public Works Dept, 1909; Under-Secretary, Mines Dept, 1934-40; also Director Housing Construction, 1936-40. Jubilee Medal, 1935; Coronation Medal, 1937 and 1953. *Address:* 5 Gilmer Terrace, Wellington, C1, New Zealand.

**TYNDALL, Rt. Rev. Charles John,** DD; *b* 30 May 1900; *m* 1924, Alice O., *d* of Canon R. J. Mitchell, MA, Rector of Cashel and Rathclyne; one *s* one *d*. *Educ:* King's Hospital Sch. (Blue-coat), and Trinity Coll., Dublin. Ordained, 1924; priest, 1925; Hon. Clerical Vicar, Christ Church, 1927; Asst Curate: Clontarf, 1924-29; Leeson Park, 1929; Rector: Enniscorthy, Co. Wexford, 1930-36; Drumcondra with North Strand, 1936-45; Rural Dean of Fingal, 1943; Rector of Calry, Sligo (Elphin and Ardagh), 1945; Archdeacon of Elphin and Ardagh, 1951-55; Bishop of Kilmore and Elphin and Ardagh, 1956-58; Bishop of Derry and Raphoe, 1958-69. DD (Jure Dignitatis), TCD, 1956. *Publications:* The Ancient Parish and Church of St John the Baptist, Sligo; Cavalcade of History. *Recreations:* golf, fishing, gardening, walking, reading. *Address:* c/o Diocesan Office, London Street, Londonderry, N Ireland.

**TYNDALL, Maj.-Gen. William Ernest,** CB 1946; CBE 1943; MC 1918; BA, MB, DPH England; *b* 27 May 1891; *s* of J. P. Tyndall; *m* 1918, Helen O'Connell Bianconi (*d* 1958); one *s*. *Educ:* Castleknock Coll., Dublin; Trinity Coll., Dublin. Served European War, RAMC, France, 1914-19 (MC); India; BAOR; West Africa; China. Specialist in Pathology; Instructor Anti-gas, SAS, 1929-32. Served War of 1939-45 (despatches, CBE, CB): Norway; ADMS 11th Armoured Div.; DMS, GHQ, Home Forces; Dep. Director-General, AMS War Office; DMS, GHQ, ALFSEA; DDMS, GHQ, Southern Command, UK; KHS, 1948-51; retired, Major-General, 1951. Surgeon, Furness Withy & Co., New York, 1951-56; Adviser, Public Health, GHQ Civil Affairs, 2nd Br. Corps, 1956. Dep. Dir.-Gen., St John Assoc., 1957. CStJ. *Address:* c/o Glyn Mills & Co., Kirkland House, Whitehall, SW1.

**TYRELL-KENYON;** *see* Kenyon.

**TYRONE, Earl of; Henry Nicholas de la Poer Beresford;** *b* 23 March 1958; *s* and *heir* of 8th Marquess of Waterford, *qv*.

**TYRRELL, Dr David Arthur John,** FRS 1970; FRCP; Deputy Director of Clinical Research Centre, Northwick Park, Harrow, and Head of Division of Communicable Diseases, since 1970; *b* 19 June 1925; *s* of Sydney Charles Tyrrell and Agnes Kate (*née* Blewett); *m* 1950, Betty Moyra Wylie; one *s* two *d*. *Educ:* Sheffield University. Junior hosp. appts, Sheffield, 1948-51; Asst, Rockefeller Inst., New York, 1951-54; Virus Research Lab., Sheffield, 1954-57; Common Cold Research Unit, Salisbury, 1957-70. *Publications:* Common Colds and Related Diseases, 1965; numerous papers on infectious diseases and viruses. *Recreations:* music-making, gardening, walking; various Christian organizations. *Address:* 29 The Ridgeway, Stanmore, Mddx HA7 4BE.

**TYRRELL, Gerald Fraser;** Buyer, Stewart Dry Goods Co., Louisville, USA, and London; *b* London, 7 March 1907; *s* of late Lt-Col G. E. Tyrrell, DSO, RA, and C. R. Tyrrell (*née* Fraser); *m* 1937, Virginia Lee Gettys, Louisville, Kentucky; three *s* one *d*. *Educ:* Eton; Magdalene Coll., Cambridge. Student Interpreter, China Consular Service, 1930; served in Tientsin, Chungking, Shanghai, Foochow, Canton; Vice-Consul at San Francisco, 1941; Vice-Consul, Boston, 1942, Acting Consul-General, 1944; 1st Secretary, Washington, 1945; Consul at Cincinnati, 1946; Acting Consul-General, New Orleans, 1947; Consul-General, Canton, 1948; Foreign Office, 1949, resigned, 1950. *Address:* 2333 Glenmary Avenue, Louisville, Kentucky 40204, USA.

**TYRRELL, Sir Murray (Louis),** KCVO 1968 (CVO 1954); CBE 1959; JP; Official Secretary to Governor-General of Australia, since 1947; *b* 1 Dec. 1913; *s* of late Thomas Michael and Florence Evelyn Tyrrell; *m* 1939, Ellen St Clair, *d* of late E. W. St Clair Greig; one *s* two *d*. *Educ:* Orbost and Melbourne Boys' High Schools, Victoria. Central Office, Postmaster General's Department, Melbourne, 1929-39; Asst Private Secretary to Minister for Air and Civil Aviation, 1940; Private Secretary to Minister for Air, 1940, to Minister for Munitions, 1940; Personal Asst to Secretary, Min. of Munitions, 1942; Private Secretary: Commonwealth Treas. and Min. for Post-War Reconstruction, 1943, to Prime Minister and Treasurer, 1945; Official Secretary and Comptroller to Governor-General, 1947; resigned Comptrollership, 1953. Attached, Royal Household, Buckingham Palace, May-Aug. 1962. Director, Canberra C of E Girls' Grammar Sch., 1952-65; Director, Canberra Grammar Sch., 1954-65. CStJ 1969. *Recreation:* fishing. *Address:* Government House, Canberra, ACT 2600, Australia. *T:* 81-1211.

**TYRWHITT, Brig. Dame Mary (Joan Caroline),** DBE, *cr* 1949 (OBE 1946); TD; *b* 27 Dec. 1903; *d* of Admiral of the Fleet Sir Reginald Tyrwhitt, 1st Bt, GCB, DSO; unmarried.

Senior Controller, 1946 (rank altered to Brigadier, 1950); Director, ATS, 1946-49, Women's Royal Army Corps, 1949-50, retired Dec. 1950; Hon. ADC to the King, 1949-50. *Address:* New Place, Jenkins Hill, Bagshot, Surrey.

**TYRWHITT, Sir Reginald (Thomas Newman),** 3rd Bt, *cr* 1919; *b* 21 Feb. 1947; *er s* of Admiral Sir St John Tyrwhitt, 2nd Bt, KCB, DSO, DSC and Bar (*d* 1961), and of Nancy (Veronica) Gilbey (who *m* 1965, Sir Godfrey Agnew, *qv*); *S* father, 1961. *Educ:* Downside. 2nd Lieut, RA, 1966, Lieut 1969; RARO 1969. *Recreations:* shooting, fishing. *Heir: b* John (Edward Charles) Tyrwhitt, *b* 27 July 1953. *Address:* Pinehurst, South Ascot, Berks. *T:* Ascot 20036.

*See also Dame Mary Tyrwhitt.*

**TYSER, Granville;** Director, Lazard Brothers & Co. Ltd, 1920-60; *b* 29 Nov. 1884; *m* 1st, 1913, Constance Evelyn (*d* 1922), *d* of George Wood, JP, Brandon, Suffolk; one *s* two *d*; 2nd, 1957, Elsie, *d* of late Edward and Jane Selwood. *Educ:* Highgate School; London Univ. (LLB). Solicitor, 1907-19 (John Mackrell Prizeman Solicitors' Final); Partner in Paines Blyth & Huxtable (now Linklaters & Paines). A Managing Director of Lazard Brothers & Co. Ltd, 1920-50. Director Mercantile Group of Investment Trust Companies, 1948-60; Director, Phoenix Assurance Co., 1935-61; Director, Colonial Development Corporation, 1951-57. *Address:* Winterton Lodge, Westerham, Kent. *Clubs:* City of London, Travellers'.

**TYSON, Geoffrey (William),** CIE 1941; Adviser, India, Pakistan, Burma Association, 1953-69 (Secretary, 1953-68); *b* Reigate, 14 June 1898; *s* of Thomas William Tyson and Annie Irwin Smith; *m* Kathleen Corbett; one *s*. *Educ:* Lancaster Royal Grammar Sch.; London School of Economics (University of London). RN Reserve (afloat), 1914-18; Editorial Staffs, Northern Whig, News Agencies; Editor, Capital. Chairman, Public Relations Cttee, Bengal, 1940-45; Publicity Adviser to Bengal Government, 1942-46; Member, Indian Legislative Assembly, 1944-47. Adviser on Public Relations to Indian Jute Mills Assoc., 1947-52. Editor of Capital, Calcutta, 1932-52. *Publications:* Danger in India, 1930; India Arms for Victory, 1942; Forgotten Frontier, 1945; The Bengal Chamber of Commerce, a Centenary Survey, 1953; 100 Years of Banking in Asia and Africa, 1963; Nehru: The Years of Power, 1966; contribs on India and economic topics to reviews, etc; short stories, occasional magazine articles under pseudonym Geoffrey Irwin. *Club:* Oriental.

**TYSON, George Alfred,** CMG 1952; FRICS; Consultant to Tysons Ltd, Nairobi (Land, Estate and Managing Agents); *b* 4 Sept. 1888; *m* 1942, Ann (*d* 1958), *d* of late James Macdonald and of Mrs Macdonald, Hill House, Portree, Isle of Skye; *m* 1961, Elaine Violet Pryor. Went to Kenya, 1921. Member Nairobi City Council, 1933-; Alderman, 1946; Mayor, 1947-48. Nominated MLC, Kenya, 1953-60. Pres., Associated Chambers of Commerce of Eastern Africa, 1948. Is a Director of several commercial and financial companies operating in East Africa. *Address:* Mansion House, PO Box 228, Nairobi, Kenya. *T:* (office) 22011, (house) 23675. *Club:* Nairobi (Nairobi).

**TYSON, Sir John (Dawson),** KCIE, *cr* 1947; CSI 1945; CBE 1933; *b* 25 April 1893; *s* of Rev. Henry Tyson and Eliza Baird; *m* 1930, Dorrice (*d* 1965), *d* of A. D. Yuill, Durban; two *d*. *Educ:* Aldenham; Magdalen Coll., Oxford (MA). Commissioned in Argyll and Sutherland Highlanders (Special Reserve), Aug. 1914; served in France 1915 and 1917; Captain, 1917; entered Indian Civil Service, 1920; Chief Presidency Magistrate of Calcutta, 1926-27; Secretary to Agent of Govt of India in South Africa, 1927-29, and Acting Agent, 1930; Private Sec. to Governor of Bengal, 1930-35, Sec., 1938 and 1945-47; Adviser, Cooch Behar State, 1936; represented Govt of India before West India Royal Commn, 1939; officiated as Sec. to Govt of India, Communications Dept, 1939; Sec., Govt of India, Dept of Education, Health and Lands, 1940-45; Pres., Himalayan Club, 1943-45. *Recreations:* mountain and big game photography. *Address:* Lloyds Bank, 6 Pall Mall, SW1; 462 Musgrave Road, Durban, South Africa. *Clubs:* East India and Sports; Durban Country.

**TYTLER, Christian Helen F.;** *see* Fraser-Tytler.

**TYZACK, Group Captain John Edward Valentine,** CBE 1944; Chairman: John Tyzack & Partners Ltd, since 1959; Dollar Land Holdings Ltd, since 1970; Chairman and Director, various companies; *b* 11 Jan. 1904; *s* of late Ernest and Mildred Tyzack; *m* 1935, Carol, *d* of late Alfred and Caroline Davidson; two *s* one *d*. *Educ:* Harwich High Sch. RAF, 1929-46: served in Aden and Sudan, 1932-36; DAQMG, Palestine, 1936-37; Staff Coll., psa, 1938; HQ British Air Forces in France (despatches), 1939-40; Dep. Dir of Admin. Plans, Air Min., 1940-44; Dep. Dir, of Movements (Air), Air Min., 1944-45; retd at own request, 1946. Dir of Admin. Services, BEA, 1946-52; Man. Dir, Concrete Development Co. Ltd, 1953-56. *Recreations:* work, enjoyment of all the arts, gardening. *Address:* Minster Cottage, Charlbury, Oxon; 10 Devonshire Place, W1. *Club:* Savile.

# U

**UBBELOHDE, Prof. Alfred R. J. P.,** CBE 1963; FRS 1951; MA, DSc Oxon; FRIC; FInstP; Hon. FCGI; Dr *hc* Faculty of Science, Université Libre, Brussels, 1962; Hon. Laureate, Padua University; Professor of Thermodynamics, University of London (Imperial College), since 1954; Head of Department of Chemical Engineering and Chemical Technology, since 1961; *b* 14 Dec. 1907; 3rd *s* of F. C. Ubbelohde and Angele Verspreeuwen; unmarried. *Educ:* St Paul's Sch.; Christ Church, Oxford. Dewar Fellow of Royal Instn, 1935-40; research on explosives; Min. of Supply, 1940-45; Prof. of Chemistry, Queen's Univ., Belfast, 1945-54, Dean of the Faculty of Science, 1947-51. Chairman Fire Research Board, 1956-61; President of Council Institut Solvay, 1957-64, 1965-; Director of Salters' Institute, 1959-; Past President, Faraday Society, 1963-; Past Vice-President, Society of Chemical Industry; Chairman, Science and Engineering Panel, British Council, 1964-; Member: Agricl Research Council, 1966-; Pontifical Academy of Sciences, 1968. *Publications:* Modern Thermodynamical Principles, 1937 (2nd edn 1952); Time and Thermodynamics, 1947; Man and Energy, 1954; Graphite and its crystal compounds, 1960; Melting and Crystal Structure, 1965; papers in Proceedings and Journals of scientific societies. *Address:* Imperial College, South Kensington, SW7; 48 Cottesmore Court, Stanford Road, W8; Platts Farm, Burwash, Sussex. *Clubs:* Athenæum, Royal Automobile.

**UBEE, Air Vice-Marshal Sydney Richard,** CB 1952; AFC 1939; Royal Air Force; retired as Air Officer Commanding, No. 2 Group, 2nd Tactical Air Force, Germany (1955-58); *b* 5 March 1903; *s* of late Edward Joseph Ubee, London; *m* 1942, Marjorie Doris (*d* 1954), *d* of George Clement-Parker, Newport, Mon; two step *s*. *Educ:* Beaufoy Technical Institute. Joined RAF, 1927, with short service commission; permanent commission, 1932; test pilot, Royal Aircraft Establishment, Farnborough, 1933-37; served in India, Iraq, Iran, Burma, and Ceylon, 1937-43; Airborne Forces Experimental Establishment, 1943-47; Comdg Officer, Experimental Flying, RAE Farnborough, 1946-47; Commandant Empire Test Pilots' Sch., Cranfield, Bucks, and Farnborough, 1947-48; Deputy Director Operational Requirements, Air Min., 1948-51; Commandant RAF Flying Coll., Manby, 1951-54; Director-General of Personnel (II), Air Ministry, 1954-55. Air Commodore, 1951. *Address:* Fresh Woods, Reading Road North, Fleet, Hants. *Club:* Royal Air Force.

**UDOJI, Jerome Oputa** (Chief), The Igwe Ozuloha of Ozubulu, 1964; CMG 1960; Chief Secretary and Head of Civil Service, Eastern Nigeria, 1959; *b* 31 July 1917; 3rd *s* of Udoji Ezembadogbu of Ozubulu; m 1942, Marcellina Uzo Onuchukwu; two *s* one *d*. *Educ:* King's Coll., Cambridge. MA, LLB (Cantab). Barrister, Gray's Inn. Assistant District Officer, Western Nigeria, 1948-53; District Officer, Western Nigeria, 1953-54; Assistant Secretary, Nigerian Secretariat, 1954; Permanent Secretary, Eastern Nigeria, 1955-59. Member: Universities Grants Commn, Nigeria; Nat. Savings Cttee, Nigeria; Nigerian Honours Cttee. *Recreations:* farming, youth work. *Address:* Enugu, Nigeria. *T:* 2087; (home) 3275. *Club:* Rotary (Enugu).

**UDOMA, Sir (Egbert) Udo,** Kt 1964; Justice, Supreme Court of Nigeria, Lagos, since 1969; *b* 21 June 1917; *s* of Chief Udoma Inam of Ibekwe Ntanaran Akama of Opobo, Nigeria; *m* 1950, Grace Bassey; six *s* one *d*. *Educ:* Methodist Coll., Uzuakoli, Nigeria; Trinity Coll., Dublin; St Catherine's Coll., Oxford. BA 1942; LLB 1942; PhD 1944; MA 1945. President, Dublin Univ. Philosophical Society, 1942-43. Called to Bar, Gray's Inn, 1945; practised as Barrister-at-Law in Nigeria, 1946-61; Member, House of Representatives, Nigeria, 1952-59; Judge of High Court of Federal Territory of Lagos, Nigeria, 1961. Member Nigeria Marketing Board and Director Nigeria Marketing Co. Board, 1952-54; Member Managing Cttee, West African Inst. for Oil Palm Research, 1953-63; Nat. President, Ibibio State Union, 1947-63; Vice-President, Nigeria Bar Assoc., 1957-61; Member: Internat. Commn of Jurists; World Assoc. of Judges; Chief Justice, High Court, Uganda, 1963-69; Acting Gov.-Gen., Uganda, 1963; Vice-President, Uganda Sports Union, 1964; Chairman, Board of Trustees, King George V Memorial Fund, 1964-69. LLD (*hc*) Ibadan, 1967. Awarded title of Obong Ikpa Isong Ibibio, 1961. *Publication:* The Lion and the Oil Palm and other essays, 1943. *Recreations:* billiards, tennis, gardening and walking. *Address:* Supreme Court, Lagos, Nigeria, West Africa. *T:* Lagos 21651, 55088. *Club:* Yoruba Tennis (Lagos, Nigeria).

**UDOMA, Sir Udo;** *see* Udoma, Sir E. U.

**UFFEN, Kenneth James;** Economic Counsellor, British Embassy, Washington, since 1970; *b* 29 Sept. 1925; *s* of late Percival James Uffen, MBE, former Civil Servant, and Gladys Ethel James; *m* 1954, Nancy Elizabeth Winbolt; one *s* two *d*. *Educ:* Latymer Upper Sch.; St Catharine's Coll., Cambridge. HM Forces (Flt-Lt, RAFVR), 1943-48; St Catharine's Coll., 1948-50; 3rd Sec., FO, 1950-52; Paris, 1952-55; 2nd Sec., Buenos Aires, 1955-58; 1st Sec., FO, 1958-61; 1st Sec. (Commercial), Moscow, 1961-63; seconded to HM Treasury, 1963-65; FCO, 1965-68; Counsellor, Mexico City, 1968-70. *Recreation:* music. *Address:* c/o Foreign and Commonwealth Office, King Charles Street, SW1.

**UGANDA, RWANDA and BURUNDI, Archbishop of,** since 1966; **Most Rev. Erica Sabiti;** Bishop of Ruwenzori since 1960; *b* 10 Jan. 1903; *m* 1934, Geraldine Kamuhigi; four *s* three *d*. *Educ:* Mbarara High Sch.; King's Coll., Budo; Makerere Coll. Teacher, 1920-25 and 1929-30; training in education, 1925-29; training for Ministry, 1931-32; ordained, 1933. *Address:* PO Box 37, Fort-Portal, Uganda. *T:* Fort-Portal 121; PO Box 14123, Kampala, Uganda. *T:* Kampala 64218.

**ULANOVA, Galina Sergeyevna;** Order of Lenin, 1953; People's Artist of the USSR (1951); Order of Red Banner of Labour, 1939, 1951; Badge of Honour, 1940; Prima Ballerina, Bolshoi Theatre, Moscow, 1944-61, retired; ballet-mistress at the Bolshoi Theatre since 1963; *b* 10 Jan. 1910; *d* of Sergei Nikolaevich Ulanov and Maria Feodorovna Romanova (dancers at Mariinsky Theatre, Petersburg). *Educ:* State School of Choreography, Leningrad. Début Kirov Theatre of Opera and Ballet, Leningrad, 1928; danced Odette-Odile in Swan Lake, 1929; Raimonda, 1931; Solweig in The Ice Maiden, 1931; danced Diane Mirelle in first performance of Flames of Paris, 1932; Giselle, 1933; Masha in The Nutcracker Suite, 1933; The Fountain of Bakhchisarai, as Maria, 1934; Lost Illusions, as Coralie, 1936; Romeo and Juliet, as Juliet, 1940; Cinderella, as Cinderella, 1945; Parasha in The Bronze Horseman, 1949; Tao Hua in The Red Poppy, 1950; Katerina in The Stone Flower, 1954. Visited London with the Bolshoi Theatre Ballet, 1956. Awarded Stalin Prize, 1941; for Cinderella, 1945; for Romeo and Juliet, 1947; for Red Poppy, 1950. Awarded Lenin prize for outstanding achievement in ballet, 1957. Fellow, Royal Academy of Dancing, 1963. *Address:* Bolshoi Theatre, Moscow. *Clubs:* All-Russian Theatrical Society, Central House of Workers in the Arts.

**ULLENDORFF, Prof. Edward,** FBA 1965; MA Jerusalem, DPhil Oxford; Professor of Ethiopian Studies, School of Oriental and African Studies, University of London, since 1964; *b* 25 Jan. 1920; *s* of late Frederic and Cilli Ullendorff; *m* 1943, Dina Noack. *Educ:* Gymnasium Graues Kloster; Universities of Jerusalem and Oxford. Chief Examiner, British Censorship, Eritrea, 1942-43; Editor, African Publ., British Ministry of Information, Eritrea-Ethiopia, 1943-45; Assistant Political Secretary, British Military Admin., Eritrea, 1945-46; Asst Secretary, Palestine Government, 1947-48; Research Officer and Librarian, Oxford Univ. Inst. of Colonial Studies, 1948-49; Scarbrough Senior Research Studentship in Oriental Languages, 1949-50; Reader Lectr, 1950-56) in Semitic Languages, St Andrews Univ., 1956-59; Professor of Semitic Languages and Literatures, University of Manchester, 1959-64. Carnegie Travelling Fellow to Ethiopia, 1958; Research Journeys to Ethiopia, 1964, 1966, 1969. Catalogued Ethiopian Manuscripts in Royal Library, Windsor Castle. Chairman: Assoc. of British Orientalists, 1963-64; Anglo-Ethiopian Soc., 1965-68 (Vice-Pres. 1969-); Pres., Soc. for Old Testament Study, 1970. Joint Organizer, 2nd Internat. Congress of Ethiopian Studies,

Manchester, 1963. Schweich Lectr, British Academy, 1967. FRAS. Imperial Ethiopian Gold Medallion, 1960. *Publications:* The definite article in the Semitic languages, 1941; Exploration and Study of Abyssinia, 1945; Catalogue of Ethiopian Manuscripts in the Bodleian Library, Oxford, 1951; The Semitic Languages of Ethiopia, 1955; The Ethiopians, 1959, 1965; (with Stephen Wright) Catalogue of Ethiopian MSS in Cambridge University Library, 1961; Comparative Semitics in Linguistica Semitica, 1961; (with S. Moscati and others) Introduction to Comparative Grammar of Semitic Languages, 1964; An Amharic Chrestomathy, 1965; The Challenge of Amharic, 1965; Ethiopia and the Bible, 1968; Joint Editor of Studies in honour of G. R. Driver, 1962; Joint Editor of Ethiopian Studies, 1964; articles and reviews in journals of learned societies; contribs to Encyclopaedia Britannica, Encyclopaedia of Islam, etc; Joint Editor, Journal of Semitic Studies, 1961-64. *Recreations:* music, motoring in Scotland. *Address:* School of Oriental and African Studies, London University, WC1.

**ULLMAN, Maj.-Gen. Peter Alfred,** CB 1946; OBE 1940; *b* 14 June 1897; *s* of Percy David Ullman; *m* 1929, Elinor Agnes Bradshaw (marr. diss. 1942); one *s* one *d*. *Educ:* Cheltenham Coll.; RMA Woolwich; Trinity Coll., Cambridge. First commission, 1915, in Royal Engineers; European War, 1914-18, served in France and East Africa (despatches); North-West Frontier, 1923-29 (medal and clasp); War Office, 1934-38; Palestine, 1938-39 (medal and clasp, despatches); Lt-Col 1939; Col 1942; Brigadier, 1947; MEF, 1939-41 (OBE, despatches); Home Forces, 1942-43, CE 2 Corps; Persia and Iraq Command, 1943-44, Chief Engineer; 21 Army Group, 1944-45 (despatches). War Office (Deputy Engineer-in-Chief), 1945; Chief Engineer, South East Asia, 1946-48; retired pay, 1948. *Address:* Rowan Tree Cottage, Effingham Common, Leatherhead, Surrey. *Club:* Army and Navy.

**ULLMANN, Prof. Stephen,** MA, PhD, DLitt; Professor of the Romance Languages, Oxford University, since 1968; *b* 13 June 1914; *s* of late Dr and Mrs István Ullmann; *m* 1939, Susan Gáspár; one *s* two *d*. *Educ:* Teachers' Training Coll.; Univ. of Budapest. PhD Budapest, 1936; DLitt Glasgow, 1949; MA Oxford, 1968. Employed by BBC Monitoring Service, 1940-46. Lecturer, from 1950 Senior Lecturer, in Romance Philology and General Linguistics, University of Glasgow, 1946-53; Professor of French Language and Romance Philology, University of Leeds, 1964-68 (Professor of Romance Philology, 1953-64). Joint Editor of jl Archivum Linguisticum, 1949-64; Pres., Philological Soc., 1970. *Publications:* Words and their Use, 1951; The Principles of Semantics, 1951, 2nd edn 1957; Précis de sémantique française, 1952, 4th edn 1969; Style in the French Novel, 1957; The Image in the Modern French Novel, 1960; Semantics: An Introduction to the Science of Meaning, 1962; Language and Style, 1964; articles and reviews in learned journals. *Address:* 128 Evans Lane, Kidlington, Oxford.

**ULLMANN, Walter,** MA, LittD; FBA 1968; Professor of Medieval Ecclesiastical History, University of Cambridge, since 1966; Fellow of Trinity College, Cambridge; *b* 29 Nov. 1910; *m* 1940, Mary Elizabeth Finnemore Knapp; two *s*. *Educ:* Universities of Vienna, Innsbruck (JUD), and Munich. Research at Cambridge University; Assistant Lecturer, University of Vienna, 1935-38. War service, 1940-43. History and Modern Languages Master, Ratcliffe Coll., Leicester, 1943-47; part-time Lecturer, Pol. Int. Dept, Foreign Office, 1944-46; Lecturer in Medieval History, University of Leeds, 1947-49; Maitland Mem. Lectr, Univ. of Cambridge, 1947-48; Univ. Lectr in Medieval History, Cambridge, 1949-57; Reader, 1957-65. Co-Editor Ephemerides Juris Canonici, 1951-64. Prof. of Humanities, Johns Hopkins Univ., 1964-65. Birkbeck Lectr, Cambridge, 1968-69. Pres. Ecclesiastical History Soc., 1969-70. Jubilee Medal for distinguished services, Univ. of Innsbruck, 1970. *Publications:* The Medieval Idea of Law, 1946, repr. 1969; The Origins of the Great Schism, 1948, repr. 1967; Medieval Papalism, 1949; The Growth of Papal Government in the Middle Ages, 1955 (rev. edn German: Die Machtstellung d. Papsttums im Mittelalter, 1960), 4th edn 1970; The medieval papacy, St Thomas and beyond (Aquinas lecture, 1958), 1960; Liber regie capelle, 1961; Principles of Government and Politics in the Middle Ages, 1961, 2nd edn 1966 (trans. into Spanish); Hist. Introd. to Lea's Inquisition, 1963; A History of Political Thought in The Middle Ages, 1965, rev. edn 1970; The Relevance of Medieval Eccles. History (inaug. lecture, 1966); Papst und König, 1966; The Individual and Society in the Middle Ages, 1967 (trans. into Japanese); The Carolingian Renaissance and the Idea of Kingship, 1969; contributed to English Historical Review, Journal of Ecclesiastical History, Journal of Theol. Studies, Cambridge Hist. Journal, Law Quarterly Review, Trans. Royal Hist. Society, Studi Gregoriani, Studia Gratiana, Studi Federiciani, Studi Accursio, Misc. Hist. Pont., Rev. Bénédictine, Rev. hist. droit, Europa e il Diritto Romano, Arch. storico Pugliese, Savigny Z., Studia Patristica, Bartolo da Sassoferrato: studi e documenti; Acta Iuridica; Settimana studio Spoleto; Annali storia amministrativa; Recueils Soc. Bodin; Speculum Historiale; Historische Zeitschrift; Studies in Church History, etc. *Recreations:* music and travelling. *Address:* Trinity College, Cambridge.

**ULLSWATER,** 2nd Viscount *cr* 1921, of Campsea Ashe, Suffolk; **Nicholas James Christopher Lowther;** *b* 9 Jan. 1942; *s* of Lieut John Arthur Lowther, MVO, RNVR (*d* 1942), and Priscilla Violet (*d* 1945), *yr d* of Reginald Everitt Lambert; *S* great-grandfather, 1949; *m* 1967, Susan, *d* of James Howard Weatherby; two *d*. *Educ:* Eton; Trinity Coll., Cambridge. *Address:* Knoyle Down Farm, Hindon, Salisbury, Wilts. *T:* Hindon 224.

**UMFREVILLE, William Henry,** CBE 1959; ISO 1951; retired as Accountant and Comptroller-General, Board of Inland Revenue (1954-58); *b* 7 June 1893; *e s* of William Henry Umfreville; *m* 1916, Daisy Catherine Colson; two *d*. *Educ:* Palmer's School. Post Office, 1909-12; Ministry of Agriculture and Fisheries, 1913-23; Inland Revenue, 1924-58, retired. *Address:* 2 Cumberland Avenue, Worthing, Sussex.

**UNBEGAUN, Prof. Boris Ottokar,** MA, DLitt Oxon, D ès L; Professor of Slavic Languages, New York University, since 1965; Professor Emeritus, University of Oxford; *b* 23 Aug. 1898; *s* of late Henri Unbegaun and Gabrielle Koehler; *m* 1928, Helena, *d* of late Ivan Maksouroff; one *d*. *Educ:* Reformed Church School, Moscow; Constantine Artillery School, St Petersburg; University of Ljubljana, Yugoslavia; Sorbonne; Ecole des Langues Orientales Vivantes, Paris. Served European War, Russian Artillery (twice wounded), 1917-20. Librarian, Institut d'Etudes Slaves, University of Paris, 1925-37; Chargé de Cours, 1936-45 and Professor of Slavonic Philology, 1946-53, Institut de Philologie et d'Histoire Orientales et Slaves, Univ. of Brussels; Maître de Conférences,

1937-45, and Professor of Slavonic Philology, 1946-53, University of Strasbourg; Director of the Slavonic Institute, University of Strasbourg, 1937-53; Prof. of Comparative Slavonic Philology, University of Oxford and Fellow, Brasenose Coll., 1953-65, Emeritus Fellow, 1965. Vis. Prof., Columbia Univ., NY, Yale Univ., Aust. National Univ., Canberra. Hon. Prof., Univs of Brussels and Strasbourg. Associate Mem., Royal Belgian Acad.; Corresp. Member, Akademie der Wissenschaften und der Literatur, Mainz. Chevalier de l'Ordre de Léopold (Belgium), 1948; Commandeur de l'Ordre de la Couronne (Belgium), 1955; Chevalier de la Légion d'Honneur, 1965. *Publications:* Catalogue des Périodiques Slaves des Bibliothèques de Paris, 1929; La Langue russe au XVIe siècle, 1935; Les Débuts de la langue littéraire chez les Serbes, 1935; (ed) Pushkin, Tales of the late I. P. Belkin, 1947; La Religion des anciens Slaves, 1948; Grammaire russe, 1951; A Bibliographical Guide to the Russian Language, 1953; Russian Versification, 1956; Russian Grammar, 1957; Russische Grammatik, 1969; various papers in learned journals. *Recreation:* walking. *Address:* 1 Washington Square Village, New York, NY 10012, USA.

**UNDERHILL, Herbert Stuart;** Assistant Publisher, Financial Times of Canada, since 1970; *b* 20 May 1914; *s* of Canon H. J. Underhill and Helena (*née* Ross); *m* 1937, Emma Gwendolyn MacGregor; one *s* one *d*. *Educ:* University Sch., Victoria, BC. Correspondent and Editor, The Canadian Press, Vancouver, BC, Toronto, New York and London, 1936-50; Reuters North American Editor, 1950; Asst General Manager, Reuters, 1958; Managing Editor, 1965-68; Dep. Gen. Manager, with special responsibility for North and South America and Caribbean, 1963-70. 1Recreations: travel, reading. *Address:* 1520 McGregor Avenue, Montreal 109, Canada.

**UNDERWOOD, Edgar Ashworth,** MA, BSc; MD; DPH; FRSS; FLS; FRCP; Chevalier de la Légion d'Honneur; Hon. Lecturer, Department of History and Philosophy of Science, University College, London; Examiner in the University of London and Member of Board of Studies in the History and Philosophy of Science; Hunterian Trustee, Royal College of Surgeons, since 1953; President British Society for History of Science, 1957-62; Fellow, Royal Society Medicine (President, 1948-50, and Hon. Secretary, 1942-48, Section of History of Medicine, late Hon. Secretary Section of Epidemiology and State Medicine); FRSH; Hon. Fellow, American Medical Association; Corresponding Member of numerous foreign societies for history of medicine, etc; *b* Dumfries, 9 March 1899; *s* of David Underwood and Janet Milligan Grierson; *m* 1928, Embling Halliday, MA (marr. diss.); *m* 1949, Nancy W. Singer; two *d*. *Educ:* Dumfries Acad. (Modern dux, 1917); Univs of Glasgow (Cullen Medal in materia medica, Hunter Medals in midwifery and in clinical surgery) and Leeds. Served European War (France), 1917-19, Cameron Highlanders. Hospital and public health posts in Glasgow and County of Lanark, 1925-29; Dep. MOH, Co. Borough of Rotherham, and Med. Supt of Oakwood Hall Sanatorium, 1929-31; Dep. MOH, City of Leeds, and Lectr in Public Health, Univ. of Leeds, 1932-34; MOH, Metrop. Borough of Shoreditch, 1934-37; MOH and Chief Sch. MO, Co. Borough of West Ham, 1937-45; Dir of the Wellcome Inst. of History of Medicine, 1946-64. Thomas Vicary Lectr, RCS, 1946; Guest Lectr, Centenary Meeting of Amer. Med. Assoc., 1947; Fielding H. Garrison Lectr, Amer. Assoc. for History of Medicine, 1947; 2nd John Ash Lectr, Univ. of Birmingham, 1970. Hon. DLitt Glasgow, 1970. *Publications:* A Manual of Tuberculosis, Clinical and Administrative, 3rd Edn, 1945; Science Medicine and History, Essays in honour of Charles Singer, 2 vols (ed), 1953; A Short History of Medicine (jt), 1962; memoir on Charles Creighton, the Man and his Work, 1965; (trans. and adapted) Pollak, The Healers (Die Jünger des Hippokrates), 1968; contribs to Chambers's Encyclopædia and the Encyclopædia Britannica; publications on History of Society of Apothecaries of London, 1963 and in progress; papers on historical, epidemiological and statistical subjects in Proc. RSM, Annals of Science, and in other jls. *Recreations:* books, music, mountains. *Address:* Glenmerle, 36 Burwood Park Road, Walton-on-Thames, Surrey. *T:* Walton-on-Thames 25725. *Club:* Athenæum.

**UNDERWOOD, Prof. Eric John,** CBE 1963; FRS 1970; FAA 1954; Hackett Professor of Agriculture and Director, Institute of Agriculture, University of Western Australia; *b* London, England, 7 Sept. 1905; 2nd *s* of James and Elizabeth Underwood; *m* 1934, Erica Reid Chandler; two *s* two *d*. *Educ:* Perth Modern Sch.; Univ. of Western Australia; Cambridge Univ.; Univ. of Wisconsin. Research Officer in Animal Nutrition, Dept of Agriculture, WA, 1931; Hackett Prof. of Agriculture, Dean of Faculty of Agric., and Dir, Inst. of Agric. in Univ. of Western Australia, 1946-. Part-Time Mem. of Exec., Commonwealth Scientific and Industrial Research Organization, 1966-. Hon. degrees: DRurSci Univ. of New England, 1967; DScAgric Univ. of Western Australia, 1969. *Publications:* Principles of Animal Production, 1946; Trace Elements in Human and Animal Nutrition, 1956 (1962 and 1971) (NY); The Mineral Nutrition of Livestock (FAO/CAB Pubn), 1966 (Aberdeen); about 100 pubns in Agricultural Research, Veterinary and Biological Research jls. *Recreations:* reading, gardening. *Address:* 2 Wattle Avenue, Dalkeith, Western Australia 6009, Australia.

**UNDERWOOD, Leon;** artist, sculptor, painter, engraver, writer, inventor; *b* London, 25 Dec. 1890; *m* 1917, Mary Louise Coleman; two *s* one *d*. *Educ:* Hampden Gurney School; Royal College of Art; Slade School. Studied Holland, Germany, Russia, 1914; served European War, 1914-18, Captain, RE (Camouflage Section); Civil Defence camouflage, 1939, 1942; travelled Iceland, Canada, USA; Mexico, West Africa (1945). Exhibitions: Alpine Gallery, 1923; Chenil Gallery (etchings), 1924; New York, Weyhe Gallery, 1928; Leicester Gallery, 1934; Beaux Arts Gallery, 1936, 1953; Zwemmer Gallery, 1939; Kaplan Gallery, 1961, 1963; Acquavella Galleries, New York, 1962; The Minories, Colchester, 1969. Official purchase by Chantrey Bequest, 1964. FRAI. Hon. FRBS, 1962. *Publications: written and illustrated:* Animalia, 1926; The Siamese Cat, 1927 (New York); Art for Heaven's Sake, 1934; Figures in Wood of West Africa, 1947; Masks of West Africa, 1948; Bronzes of West Africa, 1949; *illustrated:* The Music from Behind the Moon (New York), 1926; John Paul Jones (New York), 1927; Red Tiger; Travels in Yucatan and Lesser Known Mexico (New York), 1929. *Address:* 12 Girdlers Road, Brook Green, W14. *T:* 01-603 3517.

**UNGOED-THOMAS, Hon. Sir (Arwyn) Lynn,** Kt 1951; QC 1947; **Hon. Mr Justice Ungoed-Thomas;** Judge of Chancery Division, High Court of Justice, since 1962; *b* Carmarthen, 29 June 1904; *s* of late Rev. Evan Ungoed-Thomas and Katherine Howells; *m* 1933, Dorothy, *d* of

Jasper Travers Wolfe, Skibbereen, County Cork; two *s* one *d*. *Educ:* Haileybury Coll.; Magdalen Coll., Oxford (Demy). Reserve Welsh Rugby International XV, 1924. Called to Bar, Inner Temple, 1929; Profumo Prizeman and Yarborough Anderson Exhibitioner of Inner Temple; Member Lincoln's Inn (Bencher, 1951; Treasurer, 1968); Member Gen. Council of the Bar, 1946; Chairman, Chancery Bar Assoc. Served throughout War of 1939-45; Major RA. MP (Lab) Llandaff and Barry Div. of Glamorgan, 1945-Feb. 1950; contested (Lab) Carmarthen, Feb. 1950; MP (Lab) North East Leicester, 1950-62; Solicitor-General, April-Oct. 1951. Member: Cttee on Leasehold Reform (Chm. Lord Uthwatt) appointed by the Lord Chancellor, 1948, and signed Minority Report recommending Leasehold Enfranchisement; Cttee on Naval Courts Martial (Chm. Mr Justice Pilcher) appointed by the First Lord of the Admiralty, 1949; Statute Law Revision Cttee (Chm. Lord Chancellor), 1950; British delegate to Council of Europe, Strasbourg, 1949. *Address:* Royal Courts of Justice, Strand, WC2.

**UNMACK, Randall Carter,** MA, Docteur de l'Université, Sorbonne, Paris; Headmaster of King's College, Taunton, 1937-65, retired; *b* West Horsley, Surrey, 26 Aug. 1899; *s* of late Rev. E. C. Unmack, DD, formerly Rector of W Horsley, and of Emily, *d* of late Dean West, Ardagh, Ireland; *m* 1933, Anne Roberta, *d* of late Dr Robert Stuart, Durham; one *s* one *d*. *Educ:* King's College Sch., Wimbledon; Queen's Coll., Oxford; Sorbonne, Paris. Served in RNAS and RAF, 2nd Lieut; Airship Pilot on Anti-submarine Patrol, 1918-19; taught at Oakham Sch., Rutland, Ecole Normale, Laval, Bristol Grammar Sch. and Mill Hill Sch. between 1921 and 1928; Senior Modern Language Master at Lancing Coll., 1928-33; Headmaster of Doncaster Grammar Sch,, 1933-37. Member Adv. Cttee on Religious Broadcasting, Western Region, 1952-56. Member, Governing Body St Audries Sch., 1960-66. Hon. Fellow, Woodard Corp., 1966; Governor, Cathedral School, Exeter, 1969. Order of Menelik II (Ethiopia), class IV, 1953. *Publications:* Education et Décentralisation, Paris, 1927; The Family and Education, London, 1962; articles on education and religious teaching. *Recreations:* travelling, sailing. *Address:* 6 St Leonards Road, Exeter, Devon EX2 4LA. *T:* Exeter 75544.

**UNSTEAD, Robert John;** author; *b* 21 Nov. 1915; *s* of Charles and Elizabeth Unstead; *m* 1939, Florence Margaret Thomas; three *d*. *Educ:* Dover Grammar Sch.; Goldsmiths' Coll., London. Schoolmaster, 1936-40. Served in RAF, 1940-46. Headmaster, Norton Road CP Sch., Letchworth, 1947-51, Grange Sch., Letchworth, 1951-57. Member, Herts Education Cttee, 1951-57; Chairman, Letchworth Primary Schools' Cttee of Management, 1960-64. Chm., Educational Writers' Group, Soc. of Authors, 1965-68. *Publications:* Looking at History, 1953; People in History, 1955; Teaching History in the Primary School, 1956; Travel by Road, 1958; A History of Houses, 1958; Looking at Ancient History, 1959; Monasteries, 1961; Black's Children's Encyclopædia (co-author), 1961; The Medieval Scene, 1962; Crown and Parliament, 1962; Some Kings and Queens, 1962; The Rise of Great Britain, 1963; A Century of Change, 1963; Royal Adventurers, 1964; Early Times, 1964; Men and Women in History, 1965; Britain in the Twentieth Century, 1966; The Story of Britain, 1969; Houses in Australia, 1969; Castles, 1970; Transport in Australia, 1970; general editor, Black's Junior Reference series, Looking at Geography, etc; contribs and reviews to educational journals. *Recreations:* golf, gardening. *Address:* Reedlands, Thorpeness, Suffolk. *T:* Aldeburgh 2665. *Club:* Authors'.

**UNSWORTH, Sir Edgar (Ignatius Godfrey),** Kt 1963; CMG 1954; QC (N Rhodesia) 1951; Chief Justice of Gibraltar, 1965; *b* 18 April 1906; *yr s* of John William and Minnie Unsworth; *m* 1964, Eileen, *widow* of Raymond Ritzema. *Educ:* Stonyhurst Coll.; Manchester Univ. (LLB Hons). Barrister-at-Law, Gray's Inn, 1930; private practice, 1930-37. Crown Counsel: Nigeria, 1937; N Rhodesia, 1942; Solicitor-General: N Rhodesia, 1946; Fedn of Malaya, 1949; Chm. of Cttees, N Rhodesia, 1950; Attorney-General, N Rhodesia, 1951-56. Acting Chief Sec. and Dep. to Governor of N Rhodesia for periods during 1953, 1954 and 1955; Attorney-General, Fedn of Nigeria, 1956-60; Federal Justice of Federal Supreme Court of Nigeria, 1960-62; Chief Justice, Nyasaland, 1962-64; Director of a Course for Government Officers from Overseas, 1964-65. Member Rhodesia Railways Arbitration Tribunal, 1946; Chm., Commn of Enquiry into Central African Airways Corp., 1947. *Publication:* Laws of Northern Rhodesia (rev. edn), 1949. *Address:* Gibraltar. *Club:* East India and Sports.

**UNTERMEYER, Louis;** author, lecturer, editor; *b* New York City, 1 Oct. 1885; *s* of Emanuel Untermeyer and Julia Michael; *m* 1948, Bryna Ivens; no *c*; (by previous marriages: three *s*, and one *s* decd). *Educ:* privately and abroad. Contributing Editor to The Masses and The Liberator. Editor of Publications at Office of War Information and Associate Editor of The Armed Services Editions during War of 1939-45. Lectr at various Univs throughout USA, including Michigan, Amherst, Knox, etc. Editor of Decca Records, 1945-58. Consultant in Poetry at Library of Congress in Washington, 1961-63. *Publications:* by 1969 author and editor of more than ninety volumes of prose and verse, including: Challenge, 1914; Roast Leviathan, 1923; Moses, a novel, 1928; Food and Drink, 1932; The Book of Living Verse, 1932; Rainbow in the Sky, 1935; Selected Poems and Parodies, 1935; Heinrich Heine: Paradox and Poet (2 vols), 1937; Play in Poetry, 1937; Modern American Poetry (8th edn 1951); Modern British Poetry (7th edn 1951); A Treasury of Great Poems, 1942; The Wonderful Adventures of Paul Bunyan, 1945; A Treasury of Laughter, 1946; The New England Poets, 1948; The Inner Sanctum, Walt Whitman, 1949; The Best Humor of 1949-50, 1950-51, 1951-52; The Magic Circle, 1952; Makers of the Modern World, 1955; A Treasury of Ribaldry, 1956; Lives of the Poets, 1959 (USA), 1960 (Eng.); The Golden Treasury of Poetry for Young People, 1959; The Britannica Library of Great American Writing, 1960; Collins Albatross Book of Verse, 1962; Long Feud: Selected Poems, 1962; An Uninhibited Treasury of Erotic Poetry, 1963; The Letters of Robert Frost to Louis Untermeyer, 1963; The World's Great Stories, 1964; Labyrinth of Love, 1965; Bygones: An Autobiography, 1965; The Paths of Poetry: Twenty-five Poets from Chaucer to Frost, 1966; Tales of the Ballets, 1968; The Firebringer and other Stories, 1968; The Pursuit of Poetry, 1969. *Recreations:* piano-playing, gardening and cats. *Address:* Great Hill Road, Newtown, Conn 06470, USA.

**UNWIN, Ven. Christopher Philip,** TD 1963; Archdeacon of Northumberland, since 1963; *b* 27 Sept. 1917; *e s* of Rev. Philip Henry and Decima Unwin. *Educ:* Repton Sch.; Magdalene Coll., Cambridge; Queen's Theological Coll.,

Birmingham. Deacon, 1940, Priest, 1941. Asst Curate of: Benwell, 1940-43; Sugley, 1944-47; Vicar of: Horton, Northumberland, 1947-55; Benwell, 1955-63. *Recreations:* reading, walking. *Address:* 80 Moorside North, Newcastle upon Tyne 4. *T:* Newcastle upon Tyne 38245.

**UNWIN, David Storr;** author; *b* 3 Dec. 1918; *e s* of late Sir Stanley Unwin, KCMG; *m* 1945, Periwinkle, *yr d* of late Captain Sidney Herbert, RN; twin *s* and *d*. *Educ:* Abbotsholme. League of Nations Secretariat, Geneva, 1938-39; George Allen & Unwin Ltd, Publishers, 1940-44. *Publications:* The Governor's Wife, 1954; (Authors' Club First Novel Award, 1955); A View of the Heath, 1956; *for children:* (under pen name David Severn) Rick Afire!, 1942; A Cabin for Crusoe, 1943; Waggon for Five, 1944; Hermit in the Hills, 1945; Forest Holiday, 1946; Ponies and Poachers, 1947; Dream Gold, 1948; The Cruise of the Maiden Castle, 1948; Treasure for Three, 1949; My Foreign Correspondent through Africa, 1950; Crazy Castle, 1951; Burglars and Bandicoots, 1952; Drumbeats!, 1953; The Future Took Us, 1958; The Green-eyed Gryphon, 1958; Foxy-boy, 1959; Three at the Sea, 1959; Clouds over the Alberhorn, 1963; Jeff Dickson, Cowhand, 1963. *Recreations:* travel, motoring, ski-ing. *Address:* St Michael's, Helions Bumpstead, Haverhill, Suffolk. *T:* Steeple Bumpstead 316. *Club:* PEN.

*See also R. S. Unwin.*

**UNWIN, Rear-Adm. John Harold,** CB 1959; DSC 1941; retired 1961; Educational Services Ltd, Bristol, since 1969; *b* 13 Nov. 1906; *s* of G. H. Unwin and S. P. Unwin (*née* Hallowes); *m* 1939, Elizabeth Strong, *d* of late Prof. Sir David Kennedy Henderson; three *s* one *d*. *Educ:* Preparatory Sch.; RN Colleges Osborne and Dartmouth. RNC Osborne, 1920; HM Ships: Marlborough, 1924, Versatile, 1928, Queen Elizabeth, 1930, Devonshire, 1934, Douglas, 1938, Valiant, 1939-42, Dido, 1942; CO, HQ, 1942-44; HMS Indefatigable, 1946-47; Captain, 1948; HMS Mounts Bay, 1949-50; Admiralty, 1951-53; Portsmouth Dockyard, 1953-55; Commodore, Hong Kong, 1955-57; Rear-Admiral, 1957; Admiral Supt, HM Dockyard, Portsmouth, 1957-61. Jt Man. Dir, Furness Shipbuilding Co., 1961-64; Man. Dir, Product Knowledge Ltd, 1964-69. Legion of Merit (USA), 1950. *Recreations:* gardening, golf. *Address:* Barton Cottage, Langford, Cullompton, Devon. *T:* Plymtree 361. *Club:* United Service.

**UNWIN, Sir Keith,** KBE 1964 (OBE 1937); CMG 1954; MA; HM Ambassador to Uruguay, 1966-69; *b* 3 Aug. 1909; *er s* of late Edwin Ernest Unwin and Jessie Magdalen Black; *m* 1935, Linda Giersé; one *s* two *d*. *Educ:* Merchant Taylors' Sch.; Lycée Condorcet, Paris; St John's Coll., Oxford. Department of Overseas Trade, 1932; Madrid, 1934; Istanbul, 1937; San Sebastian (later Madrid), 1939; Mexico City, 1944; Paris, 1946; Prague, 1949; Buenos Aires, 1950; Rome, 1955-59; Inspector, 1959-62; UK Representative on Economic and Social Council of the United Nations, 1962-66; Mem., Human Rights Commn of UN, 1970-. *Recreations:* gardening, reading. *Address:* Wildacres, Fleet, Hants. *Clubs:* Oxford and Cambridge University, Canning.

**UNWIN, Nora Spicer,** RE 1946 (ARE 1935); ARCA; artist, painter, print-maker, book-illustrator; *b* 22 Feb. 1907; *d* of George Soundy and Eleanor Mary Unwin. *Educ:* Surbiton High Sch. Studied at Leon Underwood's; Kingston School of Art; Royal College of Art, 1928-32; Diploma in Design, 1931; wood-engravings exhibited at Royal Academy; other galleries and international exhibitions in Europe and N and S America; Near and Far East; works purchased by Contemporary Art Society for British Museum; by Boston Public Library; by Library of Congress, Washington, DC; by Fitchburg Art Museum (Mass.); by New York Public Library for permanent collection; also represented in Metropolitan Museum, NY. One-man exhibitions held in Boston and cities in Eastern US, 1948-50, 1954-56, 1957, 1960, 1964, 1965, 1966, 1967, 1969. Exhibition Member: Royal Soc. Painter-Etchers and Engravers; Soc. of Wood-engravers; American Nat. Acad.; Boston Print Makers; Print Club of Albany; Soc. of American Graphic Artists; NH Art Assoc.; Boston Watercolour Soc.; Cambridge Art Assoc. (CAA), etc. Awards: Soc. of American Graphic Artists, 1951; Boston Independent Artists, 1952; NHAA, 1952; NAWA, 1953; ANA, 1954; National Academy Design, 1958; Fitchburg Art Museum, 1965; BSWCP, 1965. CAA 1967. *Publications:* author-illustrator of: Round the Year, 1939; Lucy and the Little Red Horse, 1942; Doughnuts for Lin, 1950; Proud Pumpkin, 1953; Poquito, the Little Mexican Duck, 1959; Two Too Many, 1962; The Way of the Shepherd, 1963; Joyful the Morning, 1963; The Midsummer Witch, 1966; Sinbad the Cygnet, 1970; numerous books illustrated for English and American publishers. *Recreations:* music, swimming, walking, gardening, etc. *Address:* Pine-Apple Cottage, Old Street Road, Peterborough, NH 03458, USA.

**UNWIN, Rayner Stephens;** Chairman, George Allen & Unwin Ltd, since 1968; *b* 23 Dec. 1925; *s* of Sir Stanley Unwin and Mary Storr; *m* 1952, Carol Margaret, *d* of Harold Curwen; one *s* three *d*. *Educ:* Abbotsholme Sch.; Trinity Coll., Oxford (MA); Harvard, USA (MA). Sub-Lt, RNVR, 1944-47. Entered George Allen & Unwin Ltd, 1951. Mem. Council, Publishers' Assoc., 1965 (Treasurer, 1969); Director: The Australasian Publishing Co., 1969; Dillon's University Bookshop, 1969. *Publications:* The Rural Muse, 1954; The Defeat of John Hawkins, 1960. *Recreations:* skiing, walking up-hill. *Address:* (home) Limes Cottage, Little Missenden, near Amersham, Bucks. *T:* Great Missenden 2900; 28 Little Russell Street, WC1. *T:* 01-242 3781. *Club:* Garrick.

*See also D. S. Unwin.*

**UPDIKE, John Hoyer;** freelance writer; *b* 18 March 1932; *s* of Wesley R. and Linda G. Updike; *m* 1953, Mary E. Pennington; two *s* two *d*. *Educ:* Harvard Coll. Worked as journalist for The New Yorker magazine, 1955-57. *Publications: poems:* Hoping for a Hoopoe (in America, The Carpentered Hen), 1958; Telephone Poles, 1968; Midpoint and other poems, 1969; *novels:* The Poorhouse Fair, 1959; Rabbit Run, 1960; The Centaur, 1963; Of the Farm, 1966; Couples, 1968; *short stories:* The Same Door, 1959; Pigeon Feathers, 1962; The Music School, 1966; Bech: A Book, 1970; *miscellany:* Assorted Prose, 1965. *Address:* Labor-in-vain Road, Ipswich, Mass 01938, USA.

**UPHAM, Captain Charles Hazlitt,** VC 1941 and Bar, 1943; JP; sheep-farmer; *b* Christchurch, New Zealand, 21 Sept. 1908; *s* of John Hazlitt Upham, barrister, and Agatha Mary Upham, Christchurch, NZ; *m* 1945, Mary Eileen, *d* of James and Mary McTamney, Dunedin, New Zealand; three *d* (incl. twins). *Educ:* Waihi Prep. School, Winchester; Christ's Coll., Christchurch, NZ; Canterbury Agric. Coll., Lincoln, NZ (Diploma). Post-grad. course in valuation and farm management. Farm manager and musterer, 1930-36; govt valuer,

1937-39; farmer, 1945-. Served War of 1939-45 (VC and Bar, despatches): volunteered, Sept. 1939; 2nd NZEF (Sgt 1st echelon advance party); 2nd Lt; served Greece, Crete, W Desert (VC, Crete; Bar, Ruweisat); Captain; POW, released 1945. *Relevant Publication:* Mark of the Lion: The Story of Captain Charles Upham, VC and Bar (by Kenneth Sandford), 1962. *Recreations:* rowing, Rugby (1st XV Lincoln Coll., NZ). *Address:* Lansdowne, Hundalee, North Canterbury, NZ. *Clubs:* Canterbury, Christchurch, RSA (all NZ).

**UPJOHN,** family name of **Baron Upjohn.**

**UPJOHN,** Baron, *cr* 1963 (Life Peer), of Little Tey; **Gerald Ritchie Upjohn,** PC 1960; Kt 1951; CBE 1945; DL; a Lord of Appeal in Ordinary since 1963; Bencher of Lincoln's Inn, 1948, Treasurer, 1965; *b* 25 Feb. 1903; *y s* of late William Henry Upjohn, KC, and Lucy Upjohn; *m* 1947, Marjorie, *y d* of late Major E. M. Lucas. *Educ:* Eton; Trinity College, Cambridge. Exhibitioner, 1924; 1st Class Mechanical Sciences Tripos, 1925; 1st cl. Pt II Law Tripos, 1926; called to Bar, 1929 (Certif. of Honour); KC 1943; Attorney-General, Duchy of Lancaster, 1947-51; Deputy Chairman Board of Referees, 1946-51; member panel of Chairmen of Tribunal, Coal Industry Nationalisation Act, 1947-51; Judge of Chancery Division, High Court of Justice, 1951-60; Judge of the Restrictive Practices Court, 1956-60; a Lord Justice of Appeal, 1960-63. Member, Statute Law Committee, 1966-70. Hon. Treasurer Gen. Council of Bar, 1946-51. Joined Welsh Guards, 1939; Captain and Technical Adjt 2nd Armoured Bn Welsh Guards, 1941-43; Col 1943-44; Brig. 1944-45; Chief Legal Adviser, Allied Control Commission (Italy), 1943; Vice-Pres. Allied Control Commn, 1944-45 (despatches). Fellow of Eton; Governor of Felsted School. Chm. St George's Hosp. Med. Sch., 1954-64. Hon. Fellow, Trinity College, Cambridge. DL Essex. Officer Legion of Merit, 1946. *Recreation:* fishing. *Address:* 309 Hawkins House, Dolphin Square, SW1. *T:* 01-834 9237; The Old Rectory, Little Tey, Colchester, Essex. *T:* Marks Tey 410. *Clubs:* Athenæum, United University; Pratt's; New Forest Hunt.

**UPJOHN, Maj.-Gen. Gordon Farleigh,** CB 1966; CBE 1959 (OBE 1955); Controller of Administration, Automobile Association; *b* 9 May 1912; *e s* of late Dudley Francis Upjohn; *m* 1946, Rita Joan, *d* of late Major Clarence Walters; three *d. Educ:* Felsted School; RMC Sandhurst. 2nd Lieut, The Duke of Wellington's Regt; RWAFF, 1937; Adjt 3rd Bn The Nigeria Regt, 1940; Staff Coll., 1941; GSO2 Ops GHQ Middle East, 1941; Bde Maj. 3 WA Inf. Bde, 1942 (despatches); Lt-Col Comd 6 Bn The Nigeria Regt, 1944 (despatches); DAA&QMG Southern Comd India, 1946; GSO2 Mil. Ops Directorate WO, 1948; Lt-Col Chief Instructor RMA Sandhurst, 1951; Lt-Col Comd WA Inf. Bn, 1954; Bde Comdr 2 Inf. Bde Malaya, 1957 (despatches); Provost Marshal WO, 1960; GOC Yorkshire District, 1962-65. With Automobile Assoc., Fanum House, 1966. *Recreations:* golf, cricket, field sports. *Address:* c/o Lloyds Bank Ltd, 62 Brook Street, W1. *Club:* Army and Navy.

**UPJOHN, Sir William George Dismore,** Kt 1958; OBE 1919; MD, MS, FRCS, FRACS, LLD (Melbourne), 1962; Hon. Surgeon to Inpatients and Clinical Lecturer in Surgery, Royal Melbourne Hospital, since 1927; Consulting Surgeon Royal Children's Hospital, Melbourne and Royal Melbourne Hospital; *b* Narrabri, NSW, 16 March 1888; *s* of George Dismore Upjohn; *m* 1927, Norma S., *d* of John Withers; two *s* two *d. Educ:* Wesley College; Melbourne University; Middlesex Hospital Medical School; London Hospital Med. School. RMO, Clinical Asst and Hon. Surgeon to Outpatients, Melbourne Hospital, 1910-27; Lectr in Surgery and Stewart Lectr in Anatomy, Melbourne Univ., 1912-18. Served in both world wars: Dep. Chm. Central Coordination Cttee, War of 1939-45 (despatches). Lieutenant-Colonel Australian Army Medical Corps, R of O. Chancellor, Melbourne University, 1966-67 (Council, 1958-; Dep. Chancellor, 1962-66). President: Greenvale Village for the Aged, 1959; Royal Melbourne Hospital, 1960. *Publication:* Human Osteology, 1913. *Recreations:* art, music, literature. *Address:* 12 Collins Street, Melbourne, Australia. *Club:* Melbourne (Melbourne).

**UPTON,** family name of **Viscount Templetown.**

**UPTON, James Bryan,** MBE 1945; TD 1945; JP, DL; Major, retired, Hon. Colonel, 1964; Director of Reckitt & Colman Holdings Ltd (Chairman from firm's formation in 1953 until 1966), retired 1968; *b* 18 Dec. 1900; *e s* of Colonel E. J. Upton, DL and Mary Kathleen Upton (*née* Reckitt), Coptfold Hall, Margaretting, Essex; *m* 1931, Guendolene Price; three *s* one *d. Educ:* Harrow; Trinity College, Cambridge. Westinghouse Airbrake Co., Pittsburgh, USA, 1922; Reckitt & Sons Ltd, 1924, Director, 1930; Director, Reckitt & Colman Ltd, on formation, 1938. Served War of 1939-45, Major (Essex Yeomanry) RHA (prisoner of war 1941-45). Mem., E Riding of Yorks TA&VRA (Chm. E Riding TA&AFA, 1956-65). Member: Yorkshire Electricity Board, 1961; Council, Hull Univ., 1966-; Past Pres., Hull Chamber of Commerce. JP Kingston-upon-Hull, 1951; DL Yorks, 1953; High Sheriff, Yorks, 1960. Hon. Colonel: E Riding Yorks Army Cadet Force, 1955-; 129 Corps Engineer Regt TA, 1964-67. *Recreation:* shooting. *Address:* Hotham House, Hotham, York. *T:* North Cave 2244. *Clubs:* Cavalry, Lansdowne, MCC.

**UPTON, Leslie William Stokes,** CBE 1967 (MBE 1954); JP; retired as Registrar of the Privy Council (1963-66); Barrister-at-law, Gray's Inn, 1952; *b* 29 June 1900; *yr s* of late Alfred Charles Upton; *m* 1927, Frances, *yr d* of late Richard John Snowden Jesson; one *s. Educ:* Coopers' Company's School. Served with Hon. Artillery Company, 1918; Asst Clerk, War Office, 1918; transferred to Treasury, 1921; 3rd Clerk, 1925; 2nd Clerk, 1937, to the Judicial Cttee of the Privy Council; Chief Clerk, Judicial Cttee of the Privy Council, 1954-63. JP Kent, 1956. *Publications:* contribs to legal jls. *Recreations:* music, motoring. *Address:* 114 Copse Avenue, West Wickham, Kent. *T:* Springpark 3162. *Clubs:* Civil Service, Royal Commonwealth Society.

**URE, Mary (Eileen), (Mrs Robert Shaw);** actress; *b* Glasgow, 18 Feb. 1933; *d* of Colin McGregor Ure and Edith Hannah Eileen (*née* Willis Swinburne); *m* 1st, 1957, John James Osborne, *qv*; 2nd, 1963, Robert Shaw, *qv*; two *s* two *d. Educ:* The Mount School, York; Central School of Speech Training and Dramatic Art. First stage appearance in Simon and Laura, Opera House, Manchester, 1954; first London appearance in Time Remembered, Lyric, Hammersmith, 1954; other plays include: Hamlet (Ophelia), Brighton, 1955; View from the Bridge, New Watergate, 1956; Look Back in Anger, New York, 1958; Othello (Desdemona) and A Midsummer Night's Dream (Titania), Stratford-on-Avon, 1959; Duel of Angels, New York, 1960; The Crucible, Royal Court, 1960; The Changeling,

Royal Court, 1961. Films include: Windom's Way; Look Back in Anger; Sons and Lovers; The Mindbenders; The Luck of Ginger Coffey; Custer of the West, 1966; Where Eagles Dare, 1968. Has appeared on Television in US and England. *Recreations:* travelling, reading, sailing. *Address:* c/o Richard Hatton Ltd, 17a Curzon Street, W1.

**UREN, Reginald Harold,** FRIBA; private practice of architecture since 1933; *b* New Zealand, 5 March 1906; *s* of Richard Ellis and Christina Uren; *m* 1930, Dorothy Marion Morgan; one *d. Educ:* Hutt Valley High School, New Zealand; London University. Qualified as Architect in New Zealand, 1929; ARIBA, London, 1931; won open architectural competition for Hornsey Town Hall (281 entries), 1933; joined in partnership with J. Alan Slater and A. H. Moberly, 1936; architectural practice includes public buildings, department stores, domestic, commercial and school buildings. Works include: John Lewis Store, Oxford Street; Arthur Sanderson & Sons Building, Berners Street; Norfolk County Hall. Freeman of City of London, 1938; Master, Tylers and Bricklayers Company, 1966. War service, 1942-46, Capt. Royal Engineers. Council, RIBA, 1946-65; London Architecture Bronze Medal, 1935; Tylers and Bricklayers Company Gold Medal, 1936; Min. of Housing and Local Govt Medal for London Region, 1954; New Zealand Inst. of Architects Award of Merit, 1965. *Recreation:* debate. *Address:* 5 Gower Street, WC1. *T:* 01-636 7668. *Clubs:* Reform, Arts.

**UREY, Harold Clayton;** Emeritus Professor of Chemistry, University of California, La Jolla, California, since 1958; Eastman Professor, Oxford University, 1956-June 1957; Foreign Member of the Royal Society, 1947; *b* 29 April 1893; *s* of Samuel Clayton Urey and Cora Rebecca Reinoehl; *m* 1926, Frieda Daum; one *s* three *d. Educ:* University of Montana (BS); Univ. of California (PhD); American Scandinavian Foundation Fellow to Denmark, 1923-24. Research Chemist, Barrett Chemical Co., 1918-19; Instructor in Chemistry, University of Montana, 1919-21; Associate in Chemistry, Johns Hopkins University, 1924-29; Associate Professor of Chemistry, Columbia University, 1929-34; Professor of Chemistry, 1934-45; Distinguished Service Prof. of Chem., Univ. of Chicago, 1945-52; Martin A. Ryerson Distinguished Service Professor of Chemistry, University of Chicago, Chicago, Illinois, 1952-58; Executive Officer, Department of Chem., Columbia, 1939-42; Dir of War Research Atomic Bomb Project, Columbia, 1940-45. Editor, Jl of Chemical Physics, 1933-40; Board of Directors, Amer.-Scandinavian Foundation; Mem., many scientific and other learned socs; ARAS, 1960. Willard Gibbs Medal, 1934; Nobel Prize in Chemistry, 1934; Davy Medal, Royal Society of London, 1940; Franklin Medal, Franklin Inst., 1943; Medal for Merit, 1946; Cordoza Award, 1954; Honor Scroll, Amer. Inst. Chemists, 1954; Joseph Priestley Award, Dickinson Coll., 1955; Alexander Hamilton Award, Columbia Univ., 1961; J. Lawrence Smith Award, National Academy of Science, 1962; Remsen Memorial Award, Amer. Chem. Soc., Baltimore, 1963; Univ. Paris Medal, 1964; National Sci. Medal, 1964; Gold Medal, RAS, 1966; Chemical Pioneer Award, Amer. Inst. of Chemists, 1969; Leonard Medal, Meteoritical Soc., 1969; Arthur L. Day Award, Geological Soc. of America, 1969; Linus Pauling Award, Oregon State Univ., 1970. Hon. DSc of many universities. *Publications:* Atoms, Molecules and Quanta, with A. E. Ruark, 1930; The Planets, 1952; numerous articles in Chemical journals on the structure of atoms and molecules, discovery of heavy hydrogen and its properties, separation of isotopes, measurement of paleotemperatures, origin of the planets, origin of life. *Address:* c/o University of California, La Jolla, California 92037, USA.

**URGÜPLÜ, Ali Suat Hayri;** Turkish diplomat and lawyer; a Senator of the Presidential Contingent; Prime Minister of Turkey, Jan.-Oct. 1965; Scheik-ul-Islam of the Ottoman Empire; *b* 13 Aug. 1903; *s* of Mustafa Hayri Urgüplü; *m* 1932, Z. Nigâr Cevdet; one *s. Educ:* Galatasaray Grammar Sch., Istanbul; Faculty of Law of Istanbul Univ. Turkish Sec. to Mixed Courts of Arbitration (Treaty of Lausanne), 1926-29. Magistrate, Supreme Commercial Court, Istanbul, 1929-32; Lawyer at Courts of Istanbul and Member Administrative Council, 1932-39. Deputy for Kayseri, Grand Nat. Assembly of Turkey, 1939-46 and from 1950; Minister of Customs and Monopolies, 1943-46; Turkish rep. and Pres. of Turkish Delegn to Cons. Assembly of Council of Europe, Strasbourg and Vice-Pres. of Consultative Assembly, 1950, 1951 and 1952; rep. Turkey at Conf. of Inter-parly Union, Dublin and Istanbul, 1950 and 1951; re-elected Member 9th Legislative Period, 1950, Turkey; Ambassador of Turkey to German Federal Republic, 1952-55; Ambassador of the Turkish Republic to the Court of St James's, 1955-57; Turkish Delegate to: Tripartite Conf. on Eastern Mediterranean and Cyprus, London, 1955, Suez Canal, London, 1956; Turkish Ambassador to the United States, 1957-60, to Spain, 1960. Elected as Indep. Senator from Kayseri, then elected from all parties, as Speaker to Senate of the Republic for 2 yrs; Hon. Chm. various Parly Groups of friendship with foreign countries. Holds foreign decorations. *Publications:* articles and studies in various judicial reviews. *Recreation:* reading. *Address:* c/o Grand National Association, Ankara, Turkey.

**URLING CLARK, Sir Henry (Laurence),** Kt, *cr* 1950; *b* 2 Jan. 1883; *s* of Edward Clark, JP, Lapsewood, Sydenham Hill; *m* 1910, Norah Ferrand Hooper; one *s* three *d* (and two *s* decd); assumed by Deed Poll, 1950, the surname of Urling Clark. *Educ:* Harrow. Member Stock Exchange, 1904-67; Mem. Hatry Crisis Cttee, 1929; Chm. Stock Exchange Benevolent Fund, 1930-34; Trustee and Manager, 1933-47; Dep. Chm. of Council, 1945-47; Chairman of Council, 1947-49. *Recreation:* gardening. *Address:* Borrowdale, Blanford Road, Reigate, Surrey. *T:* Reigate 43666.

**URMSON, James Opie,** MC 1943; Fellow and Tutor in Philosophy, Corpus Christi College, Oxford, since 1959; *b* 4 March 1915; *s* of Rev. J. O. Urmson; *m* 1940, Marion Joyce Drage; one *d. Educ:* Kingswood School, Bath; Corpus Christi College, Oxford. Senior Demy, Magdalen College, 1938; Fellow by examination, Magdalen College, 1939-45. Served Army (Duke of Wellington's Regt), 1939-45. Lecturer of Christ Church, 1945-46; Student of Christ Church, 1946-55; Professor of Philosophy, Queen's College, Dundee, University of St Andrews, 1955-59; Visiting Associate Prof., Princeton Univ., 1950-51. Visiting Lectr, Univ. of Michigan, 1961-62, 1965-66, and 1969. *Publications:* Philosophical Analysis, 1956; The Emotive Theory of Ethics, 1968; articles in philosophical jls. *Recreations:* gardening, music. *Address:* Standfast, Tumbledown Dick, Cumnor, Oxford. *T:* Cumnor 2769.

**URQUHART, Sir Andrew,** KCMG 1963 (CMG 1960); MBE 1950; General Manager, The Housing Corporation, 1964-70; *b* 6 Jan. 1918; *s* of late Rev. Andrew Urquhart and of J. B. Urquhart; *m* 1956, Jessie Stanley Allison; two *s*. *Educ:* Greenock Academy; Glasgow University. Served War of 1939-45, Royal Marines, 1940-46. Cadet, Colonial Administrative Service, 1946; Senior District Officer, 1954; Admin. Officer, Class I, 1957; Permanent Sec., 1958; Deputy Governor, Eastern Region, Nigeria, 1958-63. *Recreation:* golf. *Address:* c/o British Linen Bank, Tollcross, Edinburgh.

**URQUHART, Donald John,** CBE 1970; Director, National Lending Library for Science and Technology, since 1961; *b* 27 Nov. 1909; *s* of late Roderick and Rose Catherine Urquhart, Whitley Bay; *m* 1939, Beatrice Winefride, *d* of late W. G. Parker, Sheffield; two *s*. *Educ:* Barnard Castle School; Sheffield University (BSc, PhD). Research Dept, English Steel Corp., 1934-37; Science Museum Library, 1938-39; Admiralty, 1939-40; Min. of Supply, 1940-45; Science Museum Library, 1945-58; DSIR Headquarters, 1948-61. Chm., Standing Conf. of Nat. and Univ. Libraries, 1969-. FLA. *Publications:* papers on library and scientific information questions. *Recreation:* gardening. *Address:* Wood Garth, First Avenue, Bardsey, near Leeds. *T:* Collingham Bridge 3228. *Club:* Athenæum.

**URQUHART, Maj.-Gen. (retd) Robert Elliott,** CB 1944; DSO 1943; *b* 28 Nov. 1901; *e s* of Alexander Urquhart, MD; *m* 1939, Pamela Condon; one *s* three *d*. *Educ:* St Paul's, West Kensington; RMC Sandhurst. 2nd Lt HLI 1920; Staff Coll., Camberley, 1936-37; Staff Capt., India, 1938; DAQMG, AHQ, India, 1939-40; DAAG, 3 Div., 1940; AA&QMG, 3 Div., 1940-41; commanded 2nd DCLI, 1941-42; GSO1, 51st Highland Div. N Africa, 1942-43; commanded 231 Malta Brigade, Sicily, 1943, and in landings Italy, 1943 (DSO and Bar); BGS 12 Corps, 1943; GOC 1st Airborne Div., 1944-45 (CB); Col 1945; Maj.-Gen. 1946; Director Territorial Army and Army Cadet Force, War Office, 1945-46; GOC 16th Airborne Division, TA, 1947-48; Commander, Lowland District, 1948-50; Commander Malaya District and 17th Gurkha Division, Mar.-Aug. 1950; GOC Malaya, 1950-52; GOC-in-C British Troops in Austria, 1952-55; retired, Dec. 1955. Col Highland Light Infantry, 1954-58. Netherlands Bronze Lion, 1944; Norwegian Order of St Olaf, 1945. *Publication:* Arnhem, 1958. *Recreations:* golf, ski-ing. *Address:* Gaidrew, By Drymen, Stirlingshire. *T:* Drymen 346. *Clubs:* Naval and Military; Royal Scottish Automobile.

*See also Sir G. P. Grant-Suttie, Bt, Sir John Kinloch, Bt.*

**URQUHART, Sir Robert William,** KBE, *cr* 1950 (OBE 1923); CMG 1944; *b* 14 August 1896; *s* of late Robert Urquhart and Margaret Stewart; *m* 1925, Brenda Gertrude Phillips; four *d*. *Educ:* Aberdeen; Cambridge. Entered Levant Consular Service, 1920; Consul at Tabriz, 1934; transferred to Foreign Office, 1938; Inspector-General of Consulates, 1939; seconded to the Home Office, 1940-41; Consul-General, Tabriz, 1942, transferred to New Orleans, La, USA, 1943; reappointed Inspector-General of HM Consular Establishment, 1945; HM Minister at Washington, 1947; HM Consul-General at Shanghai, 1948-50; British Ambassador to Venezuela, 1951-55; retired from Foreign Service, 1955. Chairman of the Crofters' Commission, 1955-63. Hon. LLD Aberdeen, 1954. *Address:* c/o Midland Bank, Central Hall, Westminster, SW1.

**URSELL, Prof. Fritz Joseph;** Beyer Professor of Applied Mathematics, Manchester University, since Oct. 1961; *b* 28 April 1923; *m* 1959, Katharina Renate (*née* Zander); two *d*. *Educ:* Clifton; Marlborough; Trinity College, Cambridge. BA 1943, MA 1947, ScD 1957, Cambridge. Admiralty Service, 1943-47; ICI Fellow in Applied Mathematics, Manchester Univ., 1947-50. Fellow (Title A), Trinity Coll., Cambridge, 1947-51; Univ. Lecturer in Mathematics, Cambridge, 1950-61; Stringer Fellow in Natural Sciences, King's Coll., Cambridge, 1954-60. FIMA 1964. MSc (Manchester), 1965. *Address:* 28 Old Broadway, Withington, Manchester 20. *T:* 061-445 5791.

**URTON, Sir William (Holmes Lister),** Kt 1960; MBE 1943; TD 1952; *b* 30 June 1908; *s* of late Capt. Edgar Lister Urton; *m* 1946, Kirsten Hustad, *d* of late Einar Hustad, Namsos, Norway; two *d*. *Educ:* Chesterfield Grammar Sch. Conservative Agent: Chesterfield, 1930; Howdenshire, 1935. TA, 1936; HQ 150 Inf. Bde, 1939-41. HQ 50 (Northumbrian) Division, 1941-46. Conservative Central Office Agent: Yorkshire, 1946; London, 1952. Electoral Adviser, WEU Saar Commission, 1955. General Director, Conservative and Unionist Central Office, 1957-66. *Recreations:* walking, gardening. *Address:* Namsos, The Way, Reigate, Surrey. *T:* Reigate 46343. *Clubs:* Constitutional, Junior Carlton.

**URWICK, Lyndall Fownes,** OBE, MC; MA; Hon. DSc; CIMechE, MASME, MIPE, FIIA, FRSA; Hon. Associate Manchester College of Technology and College of Technology, Birmingham; President Urwick, Orr & Partners Ltd, since 1963; Chairman Emeritus, Urwick Currie & Co. Ltd, Canada; *b* 3 March 1891; *o c* of late Sir Henry Urwick; *m* 1923, Joan Wilhelmina Bedford; one *s* one *d*; *m* 1941, Betty, *o d* of late Major H. M. Warrand; one *s* one *d*. *Educ:* Boxgrove School, Guildford; Repton School; New College, Oxford (Hist. Exhibitioner). Duke of Devonshire Prize, 1910; BA 1913; MA 1919. War Service, 1914-18 (despatches thrice); Employers' Sec., Joint Industrial Council of Glove-making Industry, 1919-20; employed by Rowntree & Co. Ltd, York, 1922-28; Hon. Sec., Management Research Groups, 1926-28; Dir Internat. Management Inst., Geneva, 1928-33; Gen. Sec., Internat. Cttee of Scientific Management, 1932-35; Consultant to HM Treasury, 1940-42; Mem., Mitcheson Cttee on Min. of Pensions, 1940-41; Lt-Col Petroleum Warfare Dept, 1942-44. Chm., Cttee on Educn for Management, 1946; Vice-Chm. Coun., BIM, 1947-52; Chm., Anglo-Amer. Productivity Team on Educn for Management in USA, 1951; Dir, American Management Assoc. Study of Management Education, 1952-53; Pres., Institutional Management Assoc., 1956-59; Colombo Plan Adviser to Indian Govt, 1956; Pres., European Fedn of Management Consultants' Assocs., 1960-61; Hon. Vis. Prof., Univ. of York, Toronto, 1967. Life Member: American Management Assoc., 1957; American Soc. Mechanical Engineers, 1952. Past Master, Company of Glovers. Hon. DSc Aston Univ., 1969. Kt, 1st Cl. Order of St Olaf (Norway); Silver Medal, RSA, 1948; Gold Medal, Internat. Cttee for Scientific Management, 1951; Wallace Clark Internat. Management Award, 1955; Henry Laurence Gantt Gold Medal, 1961; Taylor Key, 1963; Bowie Medal, 1968. *Publications:* Factory Organisation, 1928; Organising a Sales Office, 1928, 2nd edn 1937; The Meaning of Rationalisation, 1929; Problems of Distribution in Europe and the United States, 1931; Management of To-Morrow, 1933; Committees in Organisation, 1937; Papers on the Science of Administration, 1937; The Development of Scientific Management in Great Britain, 1938; Dynamic Administration, 1941; The Elements of Administration, 1943; The Making of Scientific Management, vol. i, Thirteen Pioneers, 1945, vol. ii, British Industry, 1946, vol. iii, The Hawthorne Experiments, 1948; Freedom and Coordination, 1949; Management Education in American Business, 1955; The Pattern of Management, 1956; Leadership in the XXth Century, 1957; Organisation, 1964; articles on rationalisation, and scientific management. *Address:* Poyntington, 83 Kenneth Street, Longueville, NSW 2066, Australia. *T:* Sydney 42102; Urwick House, Castle Lane, SW1. *Clubs:* Savile, Reform.

**URWIN, Thomas William;** MP (Lab) Houghton-le-Spring since 1964; *b* 9 June 1912; *s* of a miner; *m* 1934, Edith Scott, *d* of a miner; three *s* one *d. Educ:* Brandon Colliery and Easington Lane Elementary Schools and NCLC. Bricklayer, 1926-54; full-time Organiser, Amalgamated Union of Building Trade Workers, 1954-64. Minister of State, DEA, 1968-69; Minister of State, with responsibilities for regional policy, and special responsibility for the Northern Region, Oct. 1969-June 1970. Member Houghton-le-Spring Urban District Council, 1949-65, Chm. 1954-55, Chm. Planning and Housing, 1950-65. *Recreations:* football (local soccer), cricket. *Address:* 28 Stanhope Close, Houghton-le-Spring, Co. Durham. *T:* Houghton-le-Spring 3139.

**USBORNE, Henry Charles,** MA; JP; President, Nu-Way Heating Plants Ltd, Droitwich; Chairman, UA Engineering Ltd, Sheffield; Director: Oil Firing Publications Ltd, Midhurst; Best & Lloyd Ltd, Birmingham; *b* 16 Jan. 1909; *s* of Charles Frederick Usborne and Janet Lefroy; *m* 1936; two *s* two *d. Educ:* Bradfield; Corpus Christi, Cambridge. MP (Lab) Yardley Div. of Birmingham, 1950-59 (Acock's Green Div. of Birmingham, 1945-50). *Address:* Totterdown, The Parks, Evesham, Worcs.

**USHER, Col Charles Milne,** DSO 1940; OBE 1919; MA (Edinburgh); Director of Physical Education, Edinburgh University, 1946-59; *b* 6 September 1891; *s* of Robert Usher, Edinburgh; *m* 1919, Madge Elsa, *d* of F. Carbut Bell, London; two *s. Educ:* Merchiston Castle School, Edinburgh; RMC Sandhurst. Joined Gordon Highlanders, 1911; Lt-Col 1938; actg Brig. 1940; served European War, 1914-18 (OBE, Mons Star, 2 Medals); War of 1939-45 (despatches, DSO, Chevalier Legion of Honour, Croix de Guerre with Palm); Citoyen d'honneur of the town of Caen (Calvados). Captained Mother Country, Scotland, Army, and London Scottish at Rugby Football, also Captained Scotland versus USA at Fencing (Sabre and Epée), and British Empire Games, New Zealand, 1950. Hon. Pres., Scottish Amateur Fencing Union and Scottish Univs Rugby Club; Vice Patron, Army Rugby Union. Grand Prix du Dirigeant Sportif, 1958. *Publications:* The Usher Family in Scotland, 1956; The Story of Edinburgh University Athletic Club, 1966. *Recreations:* hunting and shooting. *Address:* The White House, North Berwick, East Lothian. *T:* 2694. *Clubs:* Caledonian; New (Edinburgh).

**USHER, Sir Peter Lionel,** 5th Bt *cr* 1899, of Norton, Midlothian, and of Wells, Co. Roxburgh; *b* 31 Oct. 1931; *er s* of Sir (Robert) Stuart Usher, 4th Bt, and Gertrude Martha, 2nd *d* of Lionel Barnard Sampson, Tresmontes, Villa Valeria, Prov. Cordoba, Argentina; *S* father, 1962. *Educ:* privately. *Heir: b* Robert Edward Usher, *b* 18 April 1934. *Address:* (Seat) Hallrule, Hawick, Roxburghshire. *T:* Bonchester Bridge 216.

**USHER, Brig. Thomas Clive,** CBE 1945; DSO and Bar 1943; RA, retired 1958; now farming; *b* 21 June 1907; *s* of Sir Robert Usher, 2nd Bt, of Norton and Wells; *m* 1939, Valentine Sears Stockwell; one *d. Educ:* Uppingham; RMA. Served War of 1939-45: North Africa, Sicily and Italy (DSO and Bar, CBE); Temp. Brig. 1944. Lt-Col 1950; Col 1951; Temp. Brig. 1953; ADC, 1957-58. Formerly Military Adviser to UK High Comr in India; OC 18 Trg Bde, RA, 1955-57; Brig. RA, Scottish Comd, 1958. *Recreations:* riding, sailing, fishing, shooting. *Address:* Wells Stables, Hawick, Roxburghshire. *T:* Denholm 235.

**USHER-WILSON, Rt. Rev. Lucian Charles,** CBE 1961; MA; an Assistant Bishop of Guildford and Vicar of Churt since 1964; Hon. Canon of Guildford Cathedral since 1965; *b* 10 Jan. 1903; *s* of Rev. C. Usher-Wilson; *m* 1929, Muriel Constance Wood; one *s* three *d. Educ:* Christ's Hospital; Lincoln College, Oxford; St Augustine's College, Canterbury. Asst Master, King William's College, Isle of Man; Asst Master, King's College, Budo, Kampala, Uganda; CMS Missionary at Jinja, Busoga, Uganda; Rural Dean, Busoga District, Uganda; Bishop on Upper Nile, 1936-61, Bishop of Mbale, 1961-64 (name of Dio. changed, 1961). *Recreation:* gardening. *Address:* Churt Vicarage, Farnham, Surrey. *Clubs:* Old Blues, Royal Commonwealth Society.

**USHERWOOD, Kenneth Ascough,** CBE 1964; Chairman, Prudential Assurance Co. Ltd (General Manager, 1961-67, Deputy Chairman, 1969-70); *b* 19 Aug. 1904; *s* of late H. T. Usherwood and late Lettie Ascough; *m* 1st, 1933, Molly Tidbeck (marr. diss. 1945), Johannesburg; one *d*; 2nd, 1946, Mary, *d* of T. L. Reepmaker d'Orville; one *s. Educ:* City of London School; St John's College, Cambridge (MA). Prudential Assurance Co. Ltd, 1925-: South Africa, 1932-34; Near East, 1934-37; Deputy General Manager, 1947-60. Director of Statistics, Ministry of Supply, 1941-45. Chm., Industrial Life Offices Assoc., 1966-67. Institute of Actuaries: Fellow (FIA) 1925; Pres. 1962-64. Mem. Gaming Board, 1968-. *Address:* 24 Litchfield Way, NW11. *T:* 01-455 7915. *Club:* Oxford and Cambridge University.

**USTINOV, Peter Alexander,** FRSA; actor, dramatist, film director; Rector of the University of Dundee, 1968; Goodwill Ambassador for UNICEF, 1969; *b* London, 16 April 1921; *s* of Iona Ustinov and Nadia Benois, painter; *m* 1st, 1940, Isolde Denham (marr. diss. 1950); one *d*; 2nd, 1954, Suzanne Cloutier; one *s* two *d. Educ:* Westminster School. Author of plays: House of Regrets, 1940 (prod Arts Theatre 1942); Blow Your Own Trumpet, 1941 (prod Playhouse [Old Vic] 1943); Beyond, 1942 (prod Arts Theatre, 1943); The Banbury Nose, 1943 (prod Wyndham's 1944); The Tragedy of Good Intentions, 1944 (prod Old Vic, Liverpool, 1945); The Indifferent Shepherd (prod Criterion, 1948); Frenzy (adapted from Swedish of Ingmar Bergman, (prod St Martin's, 1948); The Man in the Raincoat (Edinburgh Festival, 1949); The Love of Four Colonels (Wyndham's, 1951); The Moment of Truth (Adelphi, 1951); High Balcony, 1952 (written 1946); No Sign of the Dove (Savoy, 1953); The Empty Chair (Bristol Old Vic, 1956); Romanoff and Juliet (Piccadilly, 1956) film, 1961; Photo Finish (prod and acted in it, Saville, 1962); The Life in My Hands, 1963; The Unknown Soldier and his Wife, 1967 (prod and acted in it, Chichester, 1968); Halfway up the Tree (Queen's), 1967. Co-Author of film: The Way Ahead, 1943-44. Author and Director of films: School for Secrets, 1946; Vice-Versa, 1947. Author, director, producer and main actor in film Private Angelo, 1949; acted in films: Odette, Quo Vadis, Hotel Sahara, 1950; Beau Brummell, The Egyptian, We're No Angels, 1954; An Angel Flew Over Brooklyn, 1957; Spartacus, 1960; The Sundowners, 1961; Topkapi, 1964; John Goldfarb, Please Come Home; Blackbeard's Ghost; The Comedians, 1968; Hot Millions, 1968; Viva Max, 1969. Director, producer and actor in film Billy Budd, 1961. Produced operas at Covent Garden, 1962, and Hamburg Opera, 1968. Acted in revues: Swinging the Gate, 1940, Diversion, 1941. Served in Army: Royal Sussex Regiment and RAOC, 1942-46. Acted in plays: Crime and Punishment, New Theatre, 1946; Frenzy, St Martin's, 1948; Love in Albania, St James's, 1949; acted in own play, The Love of Four Colonels, 1951; directed Lady L, 1965. Member, British Film Academy. Benjamin Franklin Medal, Royal Society of Arts, 1957. *Publications:* House of Regrets, 1943; Beyond, 1944; The Banbury Nose, 1945; Plays About People, 1950; The Love of Four Colonels, 1951; The Moment of Truth, 1953; Romanoff and Juliet (Stage and Film); Add a Dash of Pity (short stories), 1959; The Loser (novel), 1961; The Frontiers of the Sea, 1966; Ustinov's Diplomats (a book of photographs), 1960; contributor short stories to Atlantic Monthly. *Recreations:* lawn tennis, squash, collecting old masters' drawings, music. *Address:* c/o Christopher Mann Ltd, 140 Park Lane, W1. *Clubs:* Garrick, Savage, Royal Automobile, Arts Theatre, Queen's.

**UTLEY, Clifton Maxwell;** commentator, television and radio newspaper columnist, USA; *b* 31 May 1904; *m* 1931, Frayn Garrick; three *s. Educ:* Univs of Chicago, Munich, and Algiers. Director, Chicago Council on Foreign Relations, 1931-41; commentator, NBC, USA, 1941-59; American commentator, British Broadcasting Corporation, 1945-53. Dupont award for TV and radio commentaries, 1957. Hon. DHL, Illinois Coll., 1946; Hon. LLD, Lawrence Coll., 1945. *Address:* 601 East 32 Street, Chicago, Illinois 60616, USA. *Clubs:* Quadrangle, Commonwealth, Wayfarers' (Chicago).

**UTTERSON-KELSO, Maj.-Gen. John Edward,** CB 1943; DSO 1918; OBE 1936; MC; Chairman of Ayrshire T&AFA, 1952-57; *b* 1893; *m* 1915, Florence Mary (*d* 1955), *d* of Rev. Francis Henry Payne-Gallwey; two *d* (one *s* killed 1944). RSF 1912-36; served European War, 1914-18 (DSO and bar, MC and bar, wounded, despatches); Instructor, Netheravon Wing, Small Arms School, 1928-32; Commander, Lines of Communication Troops Palestine and Transjordan, 1936; operations in Palestine, 1936 (OBE); commanded 2nd Bn The Devonshire Regt, 1937-39; Area Commander, 1939; Infantry Brigade Commander, 1939-41; Commander of a Division, 1941; retired pay, 1946. *Address:* Bryn, Clynnog Road, Caernarvon, N Wales.

**UTTLEY, Prof. Albert Maurel,** PhD; Research Professor of Experimental Psychology, University of Sussex, since 1966; *b* 14 Aug. 1906; *s* of George Uttley and Ethel Uttley (*née* Player), London; *m* 1941, Gwendoline Lucy Richens; two *d. Educ:* King's College, London University. BSc Mathematics; PhD Psychology. Dep. Chief Scientific Officer (Individual Merit Post), Royal Radar Establishment, 1940-56; Superintendent of Autonomics Div., NPL, 1956-66. Fellow, Center for Advanced Studies in Behavioral Sciences, Univ. of Stanford, Calif, 1962-63. Pres., Biological Engineering Soc., 1964-66. Kelvin Premium, IEE, 1948; Simms Gold Medal, RAeS, 1950. *Publications:* papers in various scientific journals on theory of control and of computers and on theoretical neurophysiology of brain function. *Recreations:* formerly mountaineering, now painting, travel. *Address:* Merlins, South Street, Ditchling, Sussex.

**UTTLEY, Alison;** *d* of Henry Taylor and Hannah Dickens, Castle Top Farm, Cromford, Derbyshire; *m* 1911, James A. Uttley, MSc, MInstCE (*d* 1930); one *s. Educ:* Bakewell Grammar School; Manchester University. BSc Hons Physics. Hon. LittD Manchester, 1970. *Publications:* The Country Child, 1931; Moonshine and Magic, 1932; Candlelight Tales, 1936; Ambush of Young Days, 1937; Adventures of No Ordinary Rabbit, 1937; Mustard, Pepper and Salt, 1938; High Meadows, 1938, new edn 1967; A Traveller in Time, 1939; Tales of Four Pigs and Brock the Badger, 1939; Adventures of Sam Pig, 1940; Sam Pig goes to Market, 1941; The Farm on the Hill, 1941; Sam Pig and Sally, 1942; Sam Pig at the Circus, 1943; Cuckoo Cherry-tree, 1943; Country Hoard, 1943; When all is done, 1945; The Weathercock, 1945; Country Things, 1946; The Washerwoman's Child (a play), 1947; John Barleycorn, 1948; Carts and Candlesticks, 1948; Buckinghamshire (in the County series), 1950; Sam Pig in Trouble, 1948; Macduff, 1950; The Cobbler's Shop, 1950; Yours ever, Sam Pig, 1951; Plowmen's Clocks, 1952; The Stuff of Dreams, 1953; Sam Pig and the Singing Gate, 1955; Here's a New Day, 1956; A Year in the Country, 1957; Magic in my Pocket, 1957; Tim Rabbit and Company, 1959; The Swans fly over, 1959; Snug and Serena count Twelve, 1959; Snug and Serena go to Town, 1961; Something for Nothing (Essays), 1960; John at the Old Farm, 1960; Sam Pig goes to the Seaside, 1960; The Little Knife who did all the work (Coll. fairy tales), 1962; Wild Honey (Essay), 1962; The Country Child (Penguin), 1963; Cuckoo in June (Essays), 1964; Tim Rabbit's Dozen, 1964; The Sam Pig Story Book, 1965; A Peck of Gold (Essays), 1966; Recipes from an Old Farmhouse, 1966; The Button-Box (Essays), 1968; Lavender Shoes, 1970; A Ten O'Clock Scholar and other essays, 1970. Grey Rabbit Books; Brown Mouse books; Little Red Fox books; Cowslip books, 1966. *Recreations:* reading, music. *Address:* Thackers, Beaconsfield, Bucks. *T:* 3059.

**UVEDALE OF NORTH END,** 1st Baron *cr* 1946, of North End, in the County of Middlesex; **Ambrose Edgar Woodall,** Kt 1931; Resident Surgeon Manor House Hospital, NW11, 1920-58; *b* 24 April 1885; 2nd *s* of late Rev. S. R. Woodall; *m* 1949, Joyce Eleanor, JP, 2nd *d* of late S. H. Holman, Highgate and St Margarets Bay, and *widow* of Rt Hon. H. B. Lees-Smith, PC, MP. *Educ:* Univ. of Manchester. BSc 1905; MB, ChB (Hons), 1908; MSc 1909; MD 1911; FRCS 1916; Civil Surgeon and Capt. RAMC, 1915-19; Surgical Specialist Ministry of Pensions, 1921-24; Medical Adviser, National Union of Railwaymen and other Trade Unions, 1922-58. Member Central Medical War Cttee, 1940-46. *Heir:* none. *Address:* No 1 The Park, NW11. *T:* 01-458 3636.

**UWINS, Cyril Frank,** OBE 1943; AFC 1937; FRAeS; retired as a Director; *b* 2 August 1896; *e s* of late Frank Uwins; *m* 1st, 1919, Joyce Marguerite Boucher (*d* 1950); two *d*; 2nd, 1955, Naomi Scott Short, *widow* of Capt. E. D. Short, King's Regt, and *d* of late H. A. Scott-Barrett. *Educ:* Whitgift Sch., Croydon. Served

War of 1914-18 in RFC; seconded as Test Pilot to Bristol Aeroplane Co. Ltd, 1918; demobilised 1919; joined Bristol Aeroplane Co. as Chief Test Pilot. Set up World Altitude Record of 43,976 ft in Vickers Vespa, 1932; awarded Britannia Trophy, 1932; British Silver Medal for Aeronautics; Hon. MSc Bristol Univ., 1964. President SBAC, 1956-58; Board Member, Air Registration Board, 1959-64. *Address:* 7 Bathwick Hill, Bath, Som. *Club:* Royal Aero.

**UXBRIDGE, Earl of; Charles Alexander Vaughan Paget;** *b* 13 Nov 1950; *s* and *heir* of 7th Marquess of Anglesey, *qv. Educ:* Dragon School, Oxford; Eton.

# V

**VAEA,** Baron of Houma; High Commissioner for Tonga in UK, since 1970; *b* 15 May 1921; *s* of Viliami Vilai Tupou and Tupou Seini Vaea; *m* 1952, Tuputupu Ma'afu; three *s* three *d. Educ:* Wesley College, Auckland, NZ. RNZAF, 1942-45; Tonga Civil Service, 1945-53; ADC to HM Queen Salote, 1954-59; Governor of Haapai, 1959-68; Commissioner and Consul in UK, 1969. Given the title Baron Vaea of Houma by HM The King of Tonga, 1970. *Recreations:* Rugby, cricket, fishing. *Heir: e s* Albert Tuivanuavou Vaea, *b* 19 Sept. 1957. *Address:* Greenbanks, Lyndale, NW2.

**VAILLANCOURT, Hon. Cyrille,** CBE 1944; Commandeur, St Grégoire le Grand; Eminent Chevalier, Société du Bon Parler français; Senator, Canada, since 1944; Manager: L'Union régionale des Caisses populaires de Quebec, La Caisse Centrale Desjardins de Lévis; La Féderation des Caisses Populaires Desjardins; Les Productions de Sucre d'Erable de Quebec (Co-op. Soc.); Vice-President La Société d'Assurance des Caisses Populaires; President: L'Assurance-vie Desjardins; L'Assoc. Co-op. Desjardins; Director: La Caisse populaire de Lévis; Dupius Frères, Ltée; *b* 17 January 1892; *s* of Dr C. E. and Marie-Louise Larochelle Vaillancourt, Saint-Anselme (Dorchester County), PQ, Canada; *m* 1920, Blanche Lajoie; three *s* five *d. Educ:* Lévis Coll.; Laval Univ., Quebec (DSA, Hon.). Clerk at L'Etoile du Nord, Joliette, 1914; Head of Apiculture Service, Dept of Agriculture, Quebec, 1915; Head of Apiculture and Maple Sugar Services, Quebec, 1918. MLC Quebec, 1943-44; Senator Dominion of Canada, 1944. Editor of La Revue Desjardins, 1941. Roman Catholic. *Address:* 7 St Mary, Lévis, PQ, Canada. *T:* 837-7285. *Clubs:* Garnison, Club des Journalistes, Cercle Universitaire Laval (Quebec); Saint-Denis (Montreal).

**VALANTINE, Louis Francis,** CBE 1964 (MBE 1956); High Commissioner for The Gambia in London, 1965-68; *b* 7 July 1907; *s* of late René Charles Valantine, JP, Bathurst; *m* 1940, Priscilla Ellen, *d* of late Sir John Mahoney, OBE, JP, Bathurst; three *s* two *d. Educ:* Hagan St Sch.; Boys' High Sch., Bathurst; Fourah Bay Coll., Sierra Leone. BA (Durham), 1930. Joined The Gambia Civil Service, 1933; Administrative Officer, 1949-59; Asst Postmaster General, 1959-60; Postmaster General, 1960-62; Chm. of Public Service Commn, 1962-64; Gambia Comr in London, 1964. JP, Bathurst, 1960. *Recreations:* reading, walking. *Address:* 9 Picton Street, Bathurst, The Gambia.

**VALDAR, Colin Gordon;** Consultant Editor and Chairman, Bouverie Publishing Co. Ltd, since 1964; *b* 18 Dec. 1918; 3rd *s* of Lionel and Mary Valdar; *m* 1940, Evelyn Margaret Barriff; two *s. Educ:* Haberdashers' Aske's Hampstead School. Free-lance journalist, 1936-39. Served War of 1939-45, Royal Engineers, 1939-42. Successively Production Editor, Features Editor, Asst Editor Sunday Pictorial, 1942-46; Features Editor, Daily Express, 1946-51; Asst Editor, Daily Express, 1951-53; Editor, Sunday Pictorial, 1953-59; Editor, Daily Sketch, 1959-62. Director, Sunday Pictorial Newspapers Ltd, 1957-59; Director, Daily Sketch and Daily Graphic Ltd, 1959-62. *Address:* 143 Clifford's Inn, Fleet Street, EC4. *T:* 01-583 8858.

**VALE, Brigadier Croxton Sillery,** CMG 1960; CBE 1946; MC 1918; psc; retired; *b* 23 Feb. 1896; *s* of Dr Charles Sillery Vale of Mathon, and Martha Elizabeth (*née* Crabtree); *m* 1927, Emily (*d* 1956), *d* of John Graham, Belfast; two *d. Educ:* Brighton Coll.; RMC Sandhurst. 2nd Lieut, RASC, 1914. Served European War of 1914-18: France, 1914-18; N Russia, 1919; DADST, N Russia, 1919 (despatches twice). GSO3, WO, 1932; Staff Captain, 44 Div. and HC Area, 1934; Military Attaché, Riga, 1936; DDMI, 1942; Brigadier i/c Admin. and Deputy Fortress Comdr, Gibraltar, 1944; Director of Prisoners of War and Director Graves Registration and Enquiries, War Office, 1947; retired, 1949; Regional Director, Commonwealth War Graves Commission, 1948-61. 4th Class, Order of St Anne, Russia. *Recreation:* golf. *Address:* Flat 102, Wick Hall, Furze Hill, Hove, Sussex. *T:* Brighton 731805.

**VALENTIA,** 14th Viscount (Ireland) *cr* 1621 (Dormant 1844-1959); **Francis Dighton Annesley,** Baron Mountnorris (Ireland) 1628; Bt 1620; MC 1918; MRCS, LRCP; Brigadier retired, late RAMC; *b* 12 Aug. 1888; *o s* of late George Dighton Annesley (uncle of *de jure* 13th Viscount); *S* cousin, 1951, established his succession, 1959; *m* 1925, Joan Elizabeth, 2nd *d* of late John Joseph Curtis; one *s* three *d. Educ:* St Lawrence Coll.; Guy's Hospital. Lieut, RAMC, 1914; served European War, France, Belgium, Aug. 1914-March 1919; Afghanistan, 1919; Waziristan, 1922-23; War of 1939-45, India, Iraq, Persia, Egypt, France, Germany, Lt-Col 1936; Col 1941; Brig. 1942; retd 1948. Croix de Guerre (Belge), 1918. *Heir: s* Hon. Richard John Dighton Annesley, Captain, RA, retd [*b* 15 Aug. 1929; *m* 1957, Anita Phyllis, *o d* of W. A. Joy; three *s* one *d*]. *Address:* St Michael's, Lea, Malmesbury, Wilts. *T:* Malmesbury 2312.

**VALENTINE, Sir Alec, (Alexander Balmain Bruce),** Kt 1964; MA; OStJ; *b* 22 Dec. 1899; *o s* of late Mr and Mrs Milward Valentine (and *g s* of late Prof. A. B. Bruce, DD, of Glasgow); *m* 1936, Beryl, *o c* of late Eng. Capt. F. Barter, RN, and Mrs Barter; one *s* two *d. Educ:* Highgate School; Worcester Coll., Oxford (Scholar, 1918). Dep. Editor, British Commercial Gas Assoc., 1922-27; entered service of Underground Group of Companies, 1928; transferred to London Passenger Transport Board, 1933; Personal Asst to late Frank Pick, 1928-36; Chief Supplies Officer, 1943-47; Chief Commercial Officer, 1945-47; Operating Manager (Railways), 1946-47; Member: Railway (London Plan) Cttee, 1946-48; Railway Executive Cttee, 1947; London Transport Executive, 1947-54; British Transport Commission, 1954-62, and its Southern Area Board, 1955-59; Chairman: London Transport Executive, 1959-62; London Transport Board, 1963-65. Pres., Inst. of Transport, 1951-52; Mem., Supervisory Cttee, Channel Tunnel Study Group, 1957-62;

Dir, Channel Tunnel Co., 1956-69. Colonel (Commanding) Engineer and Railway Staff Corps, RE, 1963-64. Mem., Oxford University Appointments Cttee, 1955-69. Governor of Highgate School, 1963-69. Pres., Design and Industries Assoc., 1963-64. *Publication:* Tramping Round London by "Fieldfare" (of the Evening News), 1933. *Recreations:* exploring wild country, bird watching, fishing. *Address:* Balmain, Borders Lane, Etchingham, Sussex. *T:* Etchingham 220; Chypraze House, Morvah, Pendeen, Cornwall. *Club:* United University.

**VALENTINE, Rt. Rev. Barry;** *see* Rupert's Land, Bishop of.

**VALENTINE, Professor David Henriques;** George Harrison Professor of Botany, University of Manchester, since 1966; *b* 16 Feb. 1912; *s* of Emmanuel and Dora Valentine; *m* 1938, Joan Winifred Todd; two *s* three *d*. *Educ:* Manchester Grammar Sch.; St John's Coll., Cambridge. MA 1936, PhD 1937. Curator of the Herbarium and Demonstrator in Botany, Cambridge, 1936; Research Fellow of St John's Coll., Cambridge, 1938; Ministry of Food (Dehydration Division), 1941; Reader in Botany, Durham, 1945, Prof., 1950-66. *Publications:* Flora Europaea, vol. I 1964, Vol. 2 1968; papers on experimental taxonomy in botanical journals. *Recreation:* reading novels. *Address:* 4 Pine Road, Didsbury, Manchester M20 0UY. *T:* 061-445 7224.

**VALLAT, Prof. Sir Francis Aimé,** KCMG 1962 (CMG 1955); QC 1961; Professor of International Law, King's College, University of London, since 1970 (Reader, 1969-70); Director of International Law Studies, King's College, since 1968; *b* 25 May 1912; *s* of Col Frederick W. Vallat, OBE; *m* 1939, Mary Alison Cockell; one *s* one *d*. *Educ:* University College, Toronto (BA Hons); Gonville and Caius Coll., Cambridge (LLB). Called to Bar, Gray's Inn, 1935; Assistant Lecturer, Bristol Univ., 1935-36; practice at Bar, London, 1936-39; RAFVR (Flt Lieut), 1941-45; Asst Legal Adviser, Foreign Office, 1945-50; Legal Adviser, UK Permanent Deleg. to UN, 1950-54; Deputy Legal Adviser, FO, 1954-60, Legal Adviser, 1960-68. (On leave of absence) Actg Director, Inst. of Air and Space Law, and Vis. Prof. of Law, McGill Univ., 1965-66. Dir of Studies, Internat. Law Assoc., 1969-. Associate Member, Institut de Droit international, 1965. *Publications:* articles in British Year Book of International Law and other journals. *Recreation:* sailing. *Address:* 40 Paultons Square, SW3. *T:* 01-352 2495. *Clubs:* Athenæum, Hurlingham.

**VALOIS, Dame Ninette de;** *see* de Valois.

**VALON, Maj.-Gen. Albert Robert,** CB 1943; OBE 1919; MC 1916; CEng, FIMechE; WhE; retired; *b* 9 June 1885; *s* of E. J. D. Valon; British; *m* 1st, 1909, Nellie Hildred Worke (decd); one *s* one *d*; 2nd, 1951, Muriel Irene Hope Potten. *Educ:* University College, London. Commissioned, 1906. Served European War, 1914-18, BEF, France, 1915-19 (OBE, MC); Col RAOC, 1936; Principal Ord. Mech. Engineer, War Office, 1937-40; Dir of Ord. Services (Engrg), WO, 1940; Inspector of Army Ord. Workshop Services, WO, 1940-42; transferred to REME, 1942; Inspector, REME, WO, 1942-43; Col Comdt REME, 1942-51. With British Council, 1945-49. A Director, Plint and Partners, Wargrave-on-Thames, 1955-63; Past President, Whitworth Society. *Address:* Flat 1, Gordon House, 8A Carew Road, Eastbourne, Sussex.

**VAN ALLEN, Prof. James Alfred;** Professor of Physics and Head of Department of Physics (of Physics and Astronomy since 1959), University of Iowa, USA, since 1951; *b* Iowa, 7 Sept. 1914; *s* of Alfred Morris and Alma Olney Van Allen; *m* 1945, Abigail Fithian Halsey II; five *c*. *Educ:* Public High School, and Iowa Wesleyan Coll., Mount Pleasant, Iowa (BSc); State University of Iowa, Iowa City (MSc, PhD). Research Fellow, then Physicist, Carnegie Instn of Washington, 1939-42; Physicist, Applied Physics Lab., Johns Hopkins Univ., Md, 1942. Ordnance and Gunnery Officer and Combat Observer, USN, 1942-46, Lt-Comdr 1946. Supervisor of High-Altitude Research Group and of Proximity Fuze Unit, Johns Hopkins Univ., 1946-50. Leader, various scientific expeditions to Central and S Pacific, Arctic and Antarctic, for study of cosmic rays and earth's magnetic field, using Aerobee and balloon-launched rockets, 1949-57. Took part in promotion and planning of International Geophysical Year, 1958-59; worked on radiation measuring equipment of first American satellite, Explorer I, and subseq. satellites; has continued study of earth's radiation belts, aurorae, cosmic rays, energetic particles in interplanetary space, etc. Research Fellow, Guggenheim Memorial Foundation, 1951; Research Associate (controlled thermonuclear reactions), Princeton Univ., Project Matterhorn, 1953-54. Associate Editor; Physics of Fluids, 1958-62; Jl of Geophys. Research, 1959-. Member, Space Science Board of Nat. Acad. of Sciences, 1958-; Consultant, President's Science Advisory Cttee; Mem., Rocket and Satellites Research Panel, and other technical cttees, etc. Fellow, American Phys. Society, etc; Member, Nat. Acad. of Sciences; Founder Member, International Acad. of Astronautics, etc. Holds many awards and hon. doctorates. *Publications:* numerous articles in learned journals and contribs to scientific works. *Address:* Department of Physics and Astronomy, University of Iowa, Iowa City, Iowa 52240, USA; 5 Woodland Mounds Road, RFD 5, Iowa City, Iowa 52240, USA.

**VANCOUVER, Archbishop of, (RC),** since 1969; **Most Rev. James F. Carney,** DD; *b* Vancouver, BC, 28 June 1915. *Educ:* Vancouver College; St Joseph's Seminary, Edmonton, Alta. Ordained, 1942; Vicar-General and Domestic Prelate, 1964; Auxiliary Bishop of Vancouver, 1966. *Address:* 646 Richards Street, Vancouver 3, BC, Canada. *T:* 683-0281.

**VANDEN-BEMPDE-JOHNSTONE;** *see* Johnstone.

**VAN DEN BERGH, James Philip,** CBE 1946; Director of Unilever Ltd, 1937-65, retired; Vice-Chairman of Lindustries since 1965; Deputy Chairman, William Baird & Co., since 1965; Chairman, National Cold Stores (Management Ltd), since 1965; *b* 26 April 1905; *s* of Albert Van den Bergh; *m* 1929, Betty D'Arcy Hart; one *s* one *d*. *Educ:* Harrow; Trinity Coll., Cambridge. Entered Van den Berghs Ltd, 1927; subseq. Managing Director; Chairman, 1942. Min. of Food: Director of Margarine and Cooking Fats, 1939; Director of Dehydration, 1940; Director of Fish Supplies, 1945. Government Director, British Sugar Corp., 1956-58, retired. Member Exec. Council, Food Manufacturers' Federation, 1957 (President, 1958-61); Member Food Research Advisory Cttee, 1960-65 (Chairman, 1963); Member Council, Queen Elizabeth Coll., London Univ., 1961-; Hon. Fellow, 1968. *Recreations:* shooting, gardening. *Address:* 7 Marland House, 28 Sloane Street,

SW1. *T:* 01-235 1099; Field House, Cranleigh, Surrey. *Clubs:* Bath; Leander (Henley).

**VAN DEN BOGAERDE, Derek Niven, (Dirk Bogarde);** actor; *b* 28 March 1921. *Educ:* University College School; Allan Glen's (Scotland). Served War of 1939-45: Queen's Royal Regt, 1940-46, Europe and Far East, and Air Photographic Intelligence. *Films* include (since 1947): Hunted, Appointment in London, They Who Dare, The Sleeping Tiger, Doctor in the House, Doctor at Sea, Doctor at Large, Simba, The Spanish Gardener, Cast a Dark Shadow, Ill Met by Moonlight, The Blue Lamp, So Long at the Fair, Quartet, A Tale of Two Cities (Sidney Carton), The Wind Cannot Read, The Doctor's Dilemma, Libel, Song Without End, The Angel Wore Red, The Singer Not The Song, Victim, HMS Defiant, The Password is Courage, The Lonely Stage, The Mindbenders, The Servant, Doctor in Distress, Hot Enough for June, The High Bright Sun, King and Country, Darling . . ., Modesty Blaise, Accident, Our Mother's House, Mister Sebastian, The Fixer, Oh What A Lovely War, Götterdämmerung, Justine, Death in Venice. *Theatre:* Cliff, in Power Without Glory, 1947; Orpheus, in Point of Departure, 1950; Nicky, in The Vortex, 1953; Alberto, in Summertime, 1955-56; Jezebel, Oxford Playhouse, 1958, etc. *Recreations:* gardening, painting, motoring. *Address:* c/o London International, 11/12 Hanover Street, W1.

**VANDERBILT, Cornelius;** author, lecturer, radio commentator, columnist; *b* 30 April 1898; *s* of late Cornelius Vanderbilt and late Grace Graham Wilson; *m* 1st, 1919, Rachel Littleton (div. 1927); 2nd, 1927, Mary Weir Logan (div. 1931); 3rd, 1935, Helen Varner Anderson (div. 1940); 4th, 1946, Maria Pablos (div. 1947); 5th, 1948, Patricia Murphy Wallace (div. 1953); 6th, 1957, Ann Needham (div. 1960); 7th, 1967, Mrs Gardner Bristol; no *c. Educ:* private and public schools in Europe and USA. 27th Division (USA) HQ Troop, AEF, 1917-19, private; Lieut; Captain; Major MI, US Army Reserve Corps, 1919-41; Inspector-General Army Transports, 1941-42; Croix de la Croix Rouge (France); FBI Distinguished Service Cross (US); Abdon Cauldron (Ecuador); invalided Walter Reed Army Hospital, Washington, DC, Nov. 1942-July 1943, retired US Army, Aug. 1943. Reporter NY Herald, 1918-20; political correspondent NY Times, Albany, NY, March-Oct. 1920; congressional correspondent, NY Times, Washington, DC, Nov. 1920-June 1921; Washington correspondent, Universal News Service, 1921-23; editor and publisher, Los Angeles Illustrated Daily News, 1923-27; editor and publisher, San Francisco Daily Herald and Miami, Florida, Daily Tab., 1923, 1927; associate editor, NY Daily Mirror, 1927, 1929; roving correspondent, United Press, 1929, 1930; editorial staff, Liberty Weekly, 1931-41; Washington Columnist, New York Post Syndicate, Aug. 1943-Aug. 1945; national survey chief of the Roosevelt party, April-Nov. 1932; national survey man for Democratic National Cttee, 1932-33, 1936-37 and 1940-41. Edited and published Vagabonding with Vanderbilt Inc., 1952-65. Vice-President, American Film Prod., Inc., 1960-65. *Publications:* Lines from the Front Lines, 1918; The Gas Attack, 1919; Experiences of a Cub Reporter, 1920; Experiences of a Legislative Correspondent, 1921; Experiences of a Washington Correspondent, 1922; The Far West, 1923; Symposium on Japanese-American Relations, 1925; Reno, 1927; Park Avenue, 1928; Palm Beach, 1929; Farewell to Fifth Avenue, 1935; A Woman of Washington, 1936; Filthy Rich, 1939; The Vanderbilt Feud, 1957; Man of the World, 1959. *Recreations:* horseback-riding, shooting, motoring, chess. *Address:* Box 654, Reno, USA.

**VAN DER BYL, Major Hon. Pieter Voltelyn Graham,** MC; MA Cantab; LLD; JP; farmer and landowner; Deputy Chairman, South African Mutual Life Assurance Society; Director: SAM Finance Corp. Ltd; Mortgage Investment Corp. Ltd; Fire & General Insurance Co. Ltd; Investment Corp.; Rhodesia Corp., and other companies; *b* 21 Feb. 1889; *m* 1922, Joy Clare, *d* of late Colonel and Mrs S. Fleming; two *s. Educ:* Diocesan Coll., Rondebosch; Pembroke Coll., Cambridge (Rowing "Blue" 1911). SW African Campaign, 1914-15; E African Campaign, 1916-17; GHQ Royal Air Force, 1918-19 (despatches twice, MC, Chevalier Légion d'Honneur (France), Cross of Merit of Netherlands Red Cross). Entered Parliament, 1929; Cabinet Minister, 1939-48; Minister of Native Affairs, 1943-48; retired from politics, 1966. Leader South African Delegation International Affairs Conference on Commonwealth Relationships at Sydney, 1938; Past President, Western Province Agric. Society. Hon. Colonel, UCT Regt. Hon. LLD Rhodes. *Address:* Fairfield, Caledon, South Africa. *Clubs:* Royal Air Force, Leander (England); (President) Civil Service, Olympic Sports, Western Province Sports, SA Turf, Milnerton Turf (Cape Town); Country (Johannesburg).

**VAN DER KISTE, Wing Commander Robert Edgar Guy,** DSO 1941; OBE 1957; Royal Auxiliary Air Force, retired; Secretary, Plymouth Incorporated Chamber of Trade and Commerce, since 1964; *b* 20 July 1912; *y s* of late Lt-Col F. W. Van der Kiste, DSO; *m* 1939, Nancy Kathleen, *er d* of Alec George Holman, MRCS, LRCP, and Grace Kathleen Brown; one *s* two *d* (and one *s* decd). *Educ:* Cheltenham College. Commissioned Royal Air Force, Nov. 1936. Served War of 1939-45 (despatches, DSO); retired, 1959. Commanded No 3 MHQ Unit, Royal Auxiliary Air Force. *Recreation:* sailing. *Address:* Yonder Cross, South Brent, Devon.

**VAN DER MEULEN, Daniel;** Arabist author and traveller; *b* 4 Sept. 1894; *m* 1st, 1917, A. C. E. Kelling; three *s* (and one *s* murdered in Germany) two *d*; 2nd, 1959, Dr H. M. Duhm; one *s. Educ:* Leyden Univ. Netherlands EI Civil Service, North of Sumatra in Toba-lake district of Toba Batak country, 1915-23; studied Arabic and Islam under Prof. Dr C. Snouck Hurgronje, Leyden Univ.; consular and diplomatic service, Jeddah, Sa'oudi-Arabia, 1926-31; first exploration in South Arabia, 1931; Dutch EI Civil Service, Pajakumbuh, Central Sumatra, Palembang, South Sumatra, 1932-38; second exploration in South Arabia, 1939; Netherlands EI Civil Service, Makassar, South Celebes, 1939-41; Minister in Jeddah, Sa'oudi-Arabia, 1941-45; Resident Adviser to Netherlands East India Government at Batavia, 1945-48; Chief of the Arabic Section of Radio Netherland World-broadcast at Hilversum, 1949-51. Officer, Oranje Nassau; Patron's Medal, Royal Geographical Society, London, 1947. *Publications:* Hadhramaut, some of its mysteries unveiled (with map by Prof. Dr H. von Wissmann), 1932; Aden to the Hadhramaut, 1947 (numerous trans.); Ontwakend Arabië, 1954; Mÿn weg naar Arabië en de Islaam, 1954; The Wells of Ibn Sa'ud, 1954; Ver dwijnend Arabië, 1959; Faces in Shem, 1961; Ik Stond Erbÿ, het einde van ons koloniale rÿk, 1965. *Address:* 9 Flierder Weg, Gorssel, Holland. *T:* 05759-1684.

**VAN DER POST, Laurens Jan,** CBE 1947; writer, farmer, explorer; *b* Philippolis, S Africa, 13 Dec. 1906; *s* of late C. W. H. Van Der Post, Chairman of Orange Free State Republic Volksraad, and late M. M. Lubbe, Boesmansfontein, Wolwekop, and Stilton; *m* 1928, Marjorie Wendt; one *s* one *d; m* 1949, Ingaret Giffard. Served War of 1939-45: Ethiopia; North Africa; Syria; Dutch East Indies; Java; commanded 43 Special Military Mission, Prisoner of War 1943-45, thereafter attached to British Minister, Batavia, until 1947. Since then has undertaken several missions for British Government and Colonial Development Corp. in Africa, including Government Mission to Kalahari, 1952. FRSL. Hon. DLitt, University of Natal. *Film:* Lost World of Kalahari, 1956. *Publications:* In a Province, 1934; Venture to the Interior, 1952 (Book Society choice and Amy Woolf Memorial Prize); A Bar of Shadow, 1952; The Face Beside the Fire, 1953; Flamingo Feather, 1955 (German Book Society choice); The Dark Eye in Africa, 1955; Creative Pattern in Primitive Man, 1956; The Lost World of the Kalahari, 1958; The Heart of the Hunter, 1961; The Seed and the Sower, 1963 (South African CNA Award for best work published in 1963); Journey into Russia, 1964; A Portrait of all The Russias, 1967; The Hunter and the Whale, 1967 (CNA and Yorkshire Post Fiction Awards); A Portrait of Japan, 1968; The Night of the New Moon, 1970. *Recreations:* walking, climbing, ski-ing, tennis, studying grasses and cooking in winter. *Address:* 27 Chelsea Towers, SW3; Turnstones, Aldeburgh, Suffolk; Wolwekop, Philippolis, South Africa.

**VANDRY, Rt. Rev. Mgr Ferdinand,** CMG 1946; *b* Quebec, 8 Dec. 1887; *s* of late Joseph Ulric Vandry and Caroline (*née* Fraser), Quebec City. *Educ:* Seminary of Quebec; Laval Univ. BA 1910; LPh 1911; DTh 1921. Priest of Roman Catholic Church, 1914; Prof. of Philosophy and Theology from 1916; Superior of Grand Seminary of Quebec, 1938-45; created by the Pope, Apostolic Protonotary in 1945. Formerly Vicar-General, Dio. Quebec. Rector of Laval Univ., 1945-54, then President, Vice-President. Hon. LLD: Universities of Fordham (NY), Ottawa (Canada), Toronto (Canada), 1947; University of Oxford (England), 1948; Universities of Western Ontario (Canada), Edmonton (Alberta, Canada), 1949; Queen's (Kingston, Canada), Montreal, 1951; McGill, Manitoba, 1952; St Francis-Xavier (Antigonish, NS); Bishop's Univ. (Lennoxville, PQ). Hon. PhLitD, Louvain, 1949. Fellow Unattached, RSC, 1952. Knight of the Legion of Honour (France). *Address:* c/o Laval University, Quebec, Canada.

**VANE,** family name of **Baron Barnard.**

**VANE, (FLETCHER-);** family name of **Baron Inglewood.**

**VANE-TEMPEST-STEWART,** family name of **Marquess of Londonderry.**

**van HASSELT, Marc;** Headmaster, Cranleigh School, since 1970; *b* 24 April 1924; *s* of Marc and Helen van Hasselt; *m* 1949, Geraldine Frances Sinclair; three *s* one *d. Educ:* Sherborne; Selwyn Coll., Cambridge (MA). Served War of 1939-45 (despatches): commissioned in Essex Yeomanry, RHA, 1944; served North-West Europe. Lecturer in Commonwealth Studies, RMA, Sandhurst, 1950-58; Asst Master, Oundle School, 1959-70 (Housemaster, Sanderson House, 1963-70). *Publications:* occasional articles in Yachting World. *Recreation:* cruising under sail. *Address:* Headmaster's House, Cranleigh School, Cranleigh, Surrey. *T:* Cranleigh 4640; Kilbronogue, Ballydehob, Co. Cork, Ireland. *Club:* Royal Cruising.

**van HEYNINGEN, William Edward,** MA Oxon, ScD Cantab; Master of St Cross College, Oxford, since 1965; Reader in Bacterial Chemistry, University of Oxford, since 1966; *b* 24 Dec. 1911; *s* of late George Philipus Stephanus van Heyningen and late Mabel Constance (*née* Higgs); *m* 1940, Ruth Eleanor Treverton; one *s* one *d. Educ:* Village schools in S Africa; Univs of Stellenbosch and Cambridge. Commonwealth Fund Fellow, Harvard Univ., and College of Physicians and Surgeons, Columbia Univ., 1936-38; Senior Student of Royal Commn for Exhibn of 1851, 1938-40. Staff Member, Wellcome Physiological Research Laboratories, 1943-46; Sen. Res. Officer, Sir William Dunn School of Pathology, Oxford Univ., 1947-66; Sec., Soc. for Gen. Microbiology, 1946-52; Curator of the Bodleian Library, 1961-; Mem. Hebdomadal Council, Oxford Univ., 1963-69. Vis. Prof., State Univ. of New York, 1967. Visitor of the Ashmolean Museum, 1969-. Expert Consultant, Pakistan-SEATO Cholera Research Laboratory, 1968-69. *Publications:* Bacterial Toxins, 1950; articles in various books and journals. *Address:* St Cross College, Oxford. Club: United University.

**van LENNEP, Jonkheer Emile;** Knight, Order of the Netherlands Lion; Officer, Order of Orange Nassau; Secretary-General, OECD, since Oct. 1969; *b* 20 Jan. 1915; *s* of Louis Henri van Lennep and Catharina Hillegonda Enschede; *m* 1941, Alexa Alison Labberton; two *s* two *d. Educ:* Univ. of Amsterdam. Foreign Exchange Inst., 1940-45; Netherlands Bank, 1945-48; Financial Counsellor, High Representative of the Crown, Indonesia, 1948-50; Netherlands Bank, 1950-51. Treasurer-General, Ministry of Finance, The Netherlands, 1951-69. Chairman: Monetary Cttee, EEC, 1958; Working Party No 3, OECD, 1962; Mem., Board Directors, KLM (Airline), 1951. KStJ. Grand Officer or Comdr in various foreign orders. *Address:* (office) OECD, 2 rue André Pascal, Paris 16e, France; (private) 44 rue de la Faisanderie, Paris 16e, France. *Club:* Haagsche (The Hague).

**van MEERBEKE, René Louis Joseph Marie;** Grand Officier, Orders of the Crown and of Léopold II (Belgium); Officier, Orders of: Léopold, the Crown and Léopold II (with swords); Croix de Guerre (Belgium), 1914-18 (with palms); Croix de Feu; Civil Cross (1st Class); *b* 15 Nov. 1895; *m* 1926, Léonor Restrepo del Corral; two *s* one *d. Educ:* University of Ghent (Licentiate of Faculty of Law in Commercial and Consular Sciences). Entered Diplomatic Service, 1920; Secretary, Legation, Lima, 1921; Chargé d'Affaires a.i. Bogota, 1924; Chargé d'Affaires, 1936; Minister, Bogota, 1945; Ambassador, Rio de Janeiro, 1954; Ambassador to the Court of St James's, 1957-61, and concurrently Belgian Perm. Rep. to Council of WEU. Entrusted with special missions as Representative of the Belgian Government at the investitures of new Presidents of the Republic: in Colombia, in 1946, 1950 and 1958; in Ecuador in 1948 and 1952, and in Brazil in 1956. Grand Cross Orders of Merit (Ecuador), Southern Cross (Brazil) and Boyaca (Colombia); Commander Legion of Honour; Commander, Order of the Liberator (Venezuela); Officer, Order of the Sun (Peru); Golden Medal of the French Reconnaissance, etc. *Recreation:* horse riding. *Address:* 22 Rue des Trévires, Brussels 4.

*Clubs:* Anglo-Belgian; Cercle Royal Gaulois (Brussels); (Vice-Pres.) Royal Golf Club de Belgique.

**VANNECK,** family name of **Baron Huntingfield.**

**VAN OSS, (Adam) Oliver,** MA; FSA; Headmaster of Charterhouse since Jan. 1965; *b* 28 March 1909; *s* of S. F. Van Oss, The Hague, newspaper proprietor; *m* 1945, Audrey (*d* 1960), *widow* of Capt. J. R. Allsopp; two *d*. *Educ:* Dragon Sch., Oxford; Clifton; Magdalen Coll., Oxford. Housemaster and Head of Modern Language Dept, Eton Coll.; Lower Master, and Acting Headmaster, Eton Coll., 1959-64. Formerly Hon. Editor Transactions English Ceramic Circle. Chevalier de la Légion d'Honneur. *Publications:* articles on ceramics and travel. *Recreations:* all forms of art and sport except racing; formerly Rugby football (played for Berkshire). *Address:* Charterhouse, Godalming, Surrey. *T:* Godalming 22589. *Club:* Athenæum.

**VAN PRAAGH, Dame Peggy,** DBE 1970 (OBE 1966); Artistic Director of the Australian Ballet, since 1962; director and producer of ballet in UK and many other countries; *b* London, 1 Sept. 1910; *d* of Harold John Van Praagh, MD, and Ethel Louise Shanks. *Educ:* King Alfred Sch., Hampstead. Studied and trained in the Cecchetti Method of classical ballet with Margaret Craske; passed Advanced Cecchetti Exam., 1932; danced in Tudor's Adam and Eve, Camargo Society, 1932. Joined Ballet Rambert and danced at Ballet Club, 1933-38; created rôles in Tudor's Ballets: Jardin aux Lilas, Dark Elegies, Gala Performance, Soirée Musicale, etc; joined Tudor's Co., the London Ballet, as a Principal Dancer, 1938. Examiner and Cttee member, Cecchetti Society, 1937-. Joined Sadler's Wells Ballet as dancer and teacher, 1941; danced Swanhilda in Coppelia, Blue Girl in Patineurs, etc. Producer and Asst Director to Ninette De Valois, Sadler's Wells Theatre Ballet, and worked with that company, 1946-56. Produced many TV ballets for BBC. Guest Teacher and Producer for National Ballet of Canada, 1956; Guest Producer: Munich, Bavarian Opera House, 1956; Theatre Royal, Stockholm, 1957; Director: Norsk Ballet, 1957-58; Edinburgh International Festival Ballet, 1958; Borovansky Ballet in Australia, 1960; Guest Teacher: Jacob's Pillow, USA, 1959; Ballet of Marquis de Cuevas, 1961. Brought Australian Ballet to Commonwealth Festival, London, 1965; to Expo '67 Montreal, followed by tour of S America, 1967. Queen Elizabeth II Coronation Award, Royal Academy of Dancing, 1965. *Publications:* How I Became a Ballet Dancer, 1954; The Choreographic Art (with Peter Brinson), 1963. *Recreations:* motoring, swimming. *Address:* 48 Neville Court, Abbey Road, NW8. *T:* 01-286 3400; c/o The Australian Ballet, Melbourne, Victoria, Australia.

**VAN RHYN, Albertus Johannes Roux,** MSc, PhD; *b* 7 July 1890; *s* of Gerhardus Petrus van Rhyn and Aletta (*née* Roux); *m* 1917, Miriam Hélène de Villiers; one *s* two *d*. *Educ:* Univ. of Stellenbosch, S Africa; Frankfurt A/M, Germany. Stellenbosch, 1910-20 (BA, MSc); Frankfurt A/M, 1921 (PhD). Lecturer in Chemistry, University of Stellenbosch, 1919-20; Principal, High School, Calvinia, 1921-25; Editor in Chief, Volksblad, 1925-48; Member of Parliament, 1948-51; Administrator of South West Africa, 1951-53; Minister of Mines and Economic Affairs, S Africa, 1953-58; High Comr in London, Dec. 1958-61. *Recreations:* hunting, tennis. *Address:* Troe-Troe, Dawn Street, Rondebosch, Cape Province, S Africa.

**VAN RYNEVELD, Gen. Sir Pierre,** KBE 1920; CB 1945; DSO 1919; MC; *b* Orange Free State, 2 May 1891; *s* of late D. J. Van Ryneveld, JP, Theunissen; *m* 1931, Edith S., yr d of late Rev. E. K. Graham, MA, Warwickshire. *Educ:* Grey College School and Grey Univ. Coll., South Africa; Imperial Coll., Univ. of London. BA Cape of Good Hope, 1909; BSc London, 1914. FCGI, Fellow Imperial College of Science. Commissioned Loyal North Lancashire Regt, 2 Sept. 1914; transferred RFC April 1915; served Egypt (Western Frontier and Palestine), Salonika, France, Army Occupation; SA Liaison at Air Ministry (with the RFC and RAF); Pioneer Flight from London to Cape Town via Cairo, 1920; Commandant, SA Military Coll., 1929; Officer Commanding Troops, Roberts' Heights, 1929; Chairman, Civil Air Board, 1931; Chief of the General Staff, Union Defence Forces, 1933-49; retired, 1949. *Address:* Spitzkop, Bronkhorstspruit, Transvaal, South Africa. *Clubs:* Pretoria (Pretoria); Bulawayo (Bulawayo).

**VANSITTART, Guy Nicholas;** Director, Kreglinger & Co.; *b* 8 Sept. 1893; *y s* of late Capt. Robert Arnold Vansittart and late Alice (*née* Blane). *Educ:* Eton; Trinity Coll., Oxford. BA (Oxon), Honour School of History. Captain, Indian Army, Central India Horse, 1913-22. *Recreations:* shooting, riding. *Address:* 51 South Street, Mayfair, W1.

**van STRAUBENZEE, William Radcliffe,** MBE 1954; MP (C) Wokingham since Oct. 1959; Joint Parliamentary Under-Secretary of State, Department of Education and Science, since 1970; *b* 27 Jan. 1924; *o s* of late Brig. A. B. van Straubenzee, DSO, MC and of Margaret Joan, 3rd *d* of A. N. Radcliffe, Kensington Square, W8, and Bag Park, Widecombe-in-the-Moor, Newton Abbot, S Devon. *Educ:* Westminster. Served War of 1939-45: five years with Royal Artillery (Major); Regimental and Staff Appointments, including two years in Far East. Admitted a Solicitor, 1952. Member, Conservative Overseas Bureau, 1950-66; Chairman, Young Conservative Nat. Advisory Cttee, 1951-53; contested Wandsworth (Clapham), 1955; PPS to Minister of Educn (Sir David Eccles), 1960-62. Member of Richmond (Surrey) Borough Council, 1955-58. Chairman: United and Cecil Club, 1965-68 (Hon. Sec., 1952-59); Westminster House Boys' Club, Camberwell, 1965-68 (Hon. Sec., 1952-65); Member: Council, Nat. Assoc. of Almshouses; Council of The Friends of Malta; Court of Reading Univ.; Governor, Archbishop Tenison's Grammar Sch., Kennington (Chm). Hon. Sec., Fedn of Conservative Students. A Church Comr; Mem. House of Laity, Church Assembly; Patron of Living of Rockbourne, Hants. Hon. Vice-Pres., National Union of Students. *Recreations:* walking, swimming, reading. *Address:* 199 Westminster Bridge Road, SE1. *T:* 01-928 6855; 30 Rose Street, Wokingham, Berkshire. *T:* West Forest 4464. *Club:* Carlton.

**VAN VLECK, Prof. John Hasbrouck;** Hollis Professor of Mathematics and Natural Philosophy, Harvard University, 1951-69, now Professor Emeritus; *b* 13 March 1899; *s* of Edward Burr Van Vleck and Hester Raymond Van Vleck; *m* 1927, Abigail Pearson; no *c*. *Educ:* Wisconsin Univ.; Harvard Univ. AB Wisconsin, 1920; AM 1921, PhD 1922, Harvard. Instructor, Harvard Univ., 1922-23; Asst Prof., then Prof., Minnesota Univ., 1923-28; Prof., Wisconsin Univ., 1928-34; Harvard Univ.: Assoc. Prof., 1934-35; Prof., 1935-; Head of Theory Group, Radio Res. Lab., 1943-45; Dean of Engineering and Applied Physics,

1951-57. Guggenheim Fellow, 1930; Lorentz Visiting Prof., Leiden Univ., 1960; Eastman Prof., Oxford Univ., 1961-62; Visiting Lecturer, various universities; member numerous scientific societies; President, American Phys. Soc., 1952-53; MNAS; Member: Amer. Philosoph. Soc.; Amer. Acad. of Arts and Sciences; Foreign Member: Royal Society, London; Royal Netherlands Acad. of Science; Royal Swedish Acad. of Science; Royal Uppsala Acad. of Science; Corresp., Académie des Sciences, France; Hon. Member, Phys. Soc. of France. Hon. ScD: Wesleyan, 1936; Wisconsin, 1947; Maryland, 1955; Oxford, 1958; Rockford Coll., 1962; Harvard, 1966; Chicago, 1968; Dr *hc*: Grenoble, 1950; Paris, 1960; Nancy, 1961. Michelson Prize, Case Inst. of Technology, 1963; Langmuir Award, American Phys. Society, 1965; National Medal of Science, US, 1966. Chevalier, Légion d'Honneur. *Publications:* Quantum Principles and Line Spectra, 1926; The Theory of Electric and Magnetic Susceptibilities, 1932. *Address:* Lyman Laboratory of Physics, Harvard University, Cambridge, Mass 02138, USA. *T:* 547-1427. *Clubs:* Harvard (New York and Boston).

**van ZEELAND, Paul, (Vicomte);** Croix de Guerre avec Palme; Médaille de la Victoire; Médaille Commémorative; Croix Civique; Grand Cordon de l'Ordre de la Couronne; Ministre D'Etat Belgium; Président de la Banque Belge d'Afrique; Professor Emérite at Louvain University; *b* Soignies, 11 Nov. 1893; *m* 1926, Renée, *o d* of Gen. Baron Dossin de St Georges; two *s* two *d*. *Educ:* Louvain University (Doctor at Law, Doctor in Political and Diplomatic Sciences, PhB); Princeton Univ., USA (MA Econ), Hon. LLD, Princeton and Brown; Hon. DCL Wesleyan; Hon. Doctor, Costa Rica; Docteur (*hc*) en Sciences Sociales de la Faculté de Philosophie et Lettres, Juiz de Fora, Brésil; Mem., American Philosophical Soc. of Philadelphia; Membre de l'Académie Méditerranéenne; Membre de l'Institut de France. Formerly: Prime Minister; President Assembly of the League of Nations; Minister of Foreign Affairs and Foreign Trade; Member of Cabinet; Senator. Pres. Belgian Commission pour l'Étude des Problèmes d'Après-Guerre; Director Institute of Economic Sciences of Univ. of Louvain; Vice-Governor Banque Nationale de Belgique; Deputy Director Bank for International Settlements; Belgian commissioner for Repatriation; President: Co-ordinating Foundation for Refugees; OEEC; Cttee of Ministers of Council of Europe. Council of Governors, Atlantic Institute; Founder and Hon. Pres., European League of Economic Co-operation; Conseillier Général, Administrateur de la Banque de Bruxelles. Holds numerous foreign decorations and orders. *Publications:* La Réforme bancaire aux États-Unis d'Amérique de 1913 à 1921, 1922; Réflexions sur le plan quinquennal, 1931; Regards sur l'Europe 1932, 1933; Report to the Governments of the United Kingdom and France on the Possibility of Obtaining a General Reduction of the Obstacles to International Trade, 1938; numerous articles. *Address:* La Maison Flamande, 7 Avenue Charle Albert, 1170 Brussels.

**VARAH, Rev. Edward Chad,** OBE 1969; Founder, The Samaritans (to befriend the suicidal and despairing), 1953, and Director of London Branch since 1953; Rector, Lord Mayor's Parish Church of St Stephen Walbrook, in the City of London, since 1953; *b* 12 Nov. 1911; *e s* of Canon William Edward Varah, Vicar of Barton-on-Humber, and Mary (*née* Atkinson); *m* 1940, Doris Susan Whanslaw; four *s* (three of them triplets) one *d*. *Educ:* Worksop Coll., Notts; Keble Coll., Oxford; Lincoln Theol. Coll. Exhibnr in Nat. Sci. (Keble); BA Oxon (Hons in PPE), 1933, MA 1943. Deacon, 1935, Priest, 1936. Curate of: St Giles, Lincoln, 1935-37; Putney, 1937-40; Barrow-in-Furness, 1940-42; Vicar of: Holy Trinity, Blackburn, 1942-49; St Paul, Clapham Junction, 1949-53. Staff Scriptwriter-Visualiser for Eagle and Girl, 1950-61; Sec., Orthodox Churches Aid Fund, 1952-69; Pres., Cttee for Publishing Russian Orthodox Church Music, 1960-; Chm., The Samaritans (Inc.), 1963-66; Pres., Internat. Fedn for Services of Emergency Telephonic Help, 1964-67. Roumanian Patriarchal Cross, 1968. *Publications:* Notny Sbornik Russkogo Pravoslavnogo Tserkovnaya Peniya, 1962; The Samaritans (ed.), 1965. *Recreations:* music, television, photography, growing dahlias. *Address:* St Stephen's Church, Walbrook, EC4; 39 Walbrook, EC4. *T:* 01-626 2277. *Clubs:* Sion College (EC4); Oxford Union.

**VARIN, René Louis;** Croix de Guerre, 1916; Médaille de la Résistance, 1945; Comdr, Légion d'Honneur, 1958; Inspector-General of English Teaching in State Schools, France, since 1959; *b* 13 Feb. 1896; *s* of Edouard Varin and Sophie de Vignacourt; *m* 1921, Germaine Bessé; one *s* four *d*. *Educ:* La Sorbonne (Agrégé d'Univ.); University Coll., London. Lecturer in French: Nevers, 1920; Rambouillet, 1922; Versailles, 1926; Inspector General of Education, 1946; Dep. Director of Cultural Relations, Ministry of Foreign Affairs, 1940. Served European War, 1914-18, in Infantry and French Air Force, 1915-19; Major, French Air Force, 1939-40; French Rep. at Air Executive Cttee, London, 1940; Cultural Counsellor, The French Embassy, 1945-59. CBE (Hon.) 1946; DCL (Hon.) Oxford, 1952; Knight of the Order of St Gregory The Great, 1955. *Publications:* articles in reviews, literary and linguistic magazines. *Recreations:* art, book collecting. *Address:* 25 bis, rue Alexis Fourcault, Versailles, Seine-et-Oise, France. *Club:* Athenæum.

**VARLEY, Eric Graham;** MP (Lab) Chesterfield, since 1964; *b* 11 Aug. 1932; *s* of Frank Varley, retired miner, and Eva Varley; *m* 1955, Marjorie Turner; one *s*. *Educ:* Secondary Modern and Technical Schools; Ruskin Coll., Oxford. Apprentice Engineer's Turner, 1947-52; Engineer's Turner, 1952-55; Mining Industry (Coal) Craftsman, 1955-64. National Union of Mineworkers: Branch Sec., 1955-64; Mem. Area Exec. Cttee, Derbyshire, 1956-64. Asst Govt Whip, 1967-68; PPS to the Prime Minister, 1968-69; Minister of State, Min. of Technology, 1969-70. *Recreations:* reading, motoring, sport. *Address:* 189 Middlecroft Road, Staveley, Chesterfield, Derbyshire. *T:* (London) 01-930 6240.

**VARLEY, George Copley,** MA, PhD Cantab, MA Oxon; Hope Professor of Zoology (Entomology), Oxford, since 1948; *b* 19 Nov. 1910; *s* of late George Percy Varley and Elsie Mary Varley (*née* Sanderson); *m* 1955, Dr Margaret Elizabeth Brown; one *s* one *d*. *Educ:* Manchester Grammar Sch.; Sidney Sussex Coll., Cambridge. Scholar of Sidney Sussex Coll., 1929-33; First Class in both parts of Nat. Sci. Tripos, Frank Smart Prizeman in Zoology, 1933; Research Student, 1933-35; Research Fellow, Sidney Sussex Coll., 1935-38; Hon. Research Fellow, University of California, 1937-38. Supt of Entomological Field Station, Cambridge, 1933-37; University Demonstrator in Zoology, Cambridge, and Curator of Insects in the University Museum of Zoology, 1938-45. Experimental Officer, and later Senior Experimental Officer in Army Operational Research Gp, Min. of Supply, studying centimetric radar on South Coast, 1941-45. Reader in Entomology, King's Coll., Newcastle upon Tyne, 1945-48; Fellow of Jesus Coll., Oxford, 1948-. *Publications:* various papers on insects and population dynamics in scientific periodicals. *Recreations:* games include squash racquets, tennis, etc; sedentary pastimes include sailing, gliding, ski-ing. *Address:* 18 Apsley Road, Oxford OX2 7QY. *T:* Oxford 56988.

**VARVILL, Michael Hugh,** CMG 1959; with G. Bell & Sons, publishers since 1960 (Director, 1963); *b* 29 Sept. 1909; *s* of Dr Bernard and Maud Varvill; unmarried. *Educ:* Marlborough; New Coll., Oxford (Scholar; BA). Appointed to Colonial Service, Nigeria, 1932; seconded to Colonial Office, 1943-47; Senior District Officer, 1951; Nigeria, Permanent Secretary: Ministry of Transport, 1952; Ministry of Works, 1953-54; and again (Federal) Ministry of Transport, 1955, retired 1960. *Recreations:* tennis, hockey, chess. *Address:* c/o Glyn Mills & Co., Whitehall, SW1. *Club:* Travellers'.

**VASCONCELLOS, Josephina de,** FRBS; Founder Member, Society of Portrait Sculptors; *d* of late H. H. de Vasconcellos, Brazilian Consul-General in England, and Freda Coleman; *m* 1930, Delmar Banner, painter; two *s*. *Educ:* sculpture: London, Paris, Florence; Royal Academy Schools. Works: High Altar and Statue, Varengeville, Normandy, 1925; Bronze St Hubert, National Gallery of Brazil, 1926; Music in Trees, in stone, Southampton Gallery, 1933; Ducks, in marble, Glasgow Art Gallery, 1946; Refugees, in stone, Sheffield Art Gallery, 1949; Episcopal Crozier in Perspex, for Bishop of Bristol, 1948. Exhibits Royal Academy, Leicester Galleries. Exhibn with husband, of 46 sculptures in 20 materials at RWS Gallery, 1947; Last Chimera (8 foot) Christ, Canongate Kirk, Edinburgh; (in Portland Stone), National War Memorial, Aldershot, 1950. Exhibited two works, Festival of Britain, Lambeth Palace, 1951; Second Sculpture Exhibn, with husband, RWS Galleries, 1955; War Memorial, St Bees School, 1955; two figures, St Bees Priory, 1955; commissioned to execute life-size Mary and Child and design group of 11 sculptures by 11 collaborators, for Nativity, St Paul's Cathedral, Christmas 1955; figure of Mary and Child bought for permanent possession of St Paul's, 1956; life-size Resurrection for St Mary, Westfield, Workington, 1956-57; figure of St Francis, for Church of St Francis, Ormsgill, Barrow-in-Furness, 1957; Madonna and Child, St James's, Piccadilly, 1957; Rising Christ in St Bartholomew the Great, Smithfield; Winter, carving in Perspex, Oldham Gallery, 1958; Nativity (for ruins of Coventry Cathedral), 1958; Flight into Egypt, for St Martin-in-the-Fields, 1958 (now in Cartmel Priory); War Memorial, Reredos of carved oak, Rossall School Chapel, 1959; Nativity Set, life-size figures, St Martin-in-the-Fields, 1959, 1964; Winged Victory Crucifix, Clewer Church, 1964; life-size Holy Family, Liverpool Cathedral, 1965; other sculptures at Dallas, Tulsa, Chicago, USA; Portrait in bronze of Rt Hon. Lord Denning, 1969; Portrait of Rt Rev. the Lord Bishop of Norwich. Documentary film Out of Nature (on her work), 1949; BBC programme, 1968. Founder, Outpost Emmanus (a base for young people needing mountain adventure therapy). Hon. Member, Glider Pilots Regimental Assoc. *Publications:* Woodcut illustrations for The Cup (Poems by F. Johnson), 1938; contrib. to They Became Christians (ed Dewi Morgan), 1966. *Recreation:* working on Jeu Libre (new methods of movements for blind and handicapped children); invented Braille Carpet. *Address:* Bield, Little Langdale, Ambleside, Westmorland. *T:* Langdale 254. *Club:* Reynolds.

**VASEY, Sir Ernest (Albert),** KBE 1959; CMG 1945; Financial and Economic Adviser, World Bank Development Service, 1962-66; Resident Representative, IBRD, Pakistan, 1963-66; *b* 27 Aug. 1901; *m* 1st, 1923, Norah May Mitchell; one *s*; 2nd, 1944, Hannah Strauss; one *s*. Member Shrewsbury Town Council, England. Mayor of Nairobi, 1941-42, 1944-46; Member Kenya Legislative Council for Nairobi North, 1945-50; Member for Education, Health and Local Government for Kenya, 1950; Minister for Finance and Development, Kenya, 1951-59; Minister for Finance and Economics, Tanganyika, 1959-60; Minister for Finance, Tanganyika, 1960-62. Brilliant Star of Zanzibar, 2nd Class, 1955; Hilal-i-Quaid-i-Azam (Pakistan), 1966. *Address:* Box 14235, Nairobi, Kenya.

**VASSAR-SMITH, Major Sir Richard Rathborne,** 3rd Bt, *cr* 1917; TD; RA; Headmaster of St Ronan's Preparatory School, since 1957; *b* 24 Nov. 1909; *s* of late Major Charles Martin Vassar-Smith (2nd *s* of 1st Bt); *S* uncle, 1942; *m* 1932, Mary Dawn, *d* of late Sir Raymond Woods, CBE; one *s* one *d*. *Educ:* Lancing; Pembroke College, Cambridge. Employed by Lloyds Bank Ltd, 1932-37; Schoolmaster, 1938-39. War of 1939-45, Major, RA. *Recreation:* Association football (Cambridge, 1928-31). *Heir: s* John Rathborne Vassar-Smith, *b* 23 July 1936. *Address:* Orchard House, Hawkhurst, Kent. *T:* Hawkhurst 2300. *Clubs:* Royal Automobile; Hawks (Cambridge); Rye Golf.

**VAUGHAN,** family name of **Earl of Lisburne.**

**VAUGHAN, Viscount; David John Francis Malet Vaughan;** *b* 15 June 1945; *e s* of 8th Earl of Lisburne, *qv*. *Address:* 22 York House, Kensington Church Street, W8. *T:* 01-937 3043; High Ridge, Bembridge, IOW. *T:* 220.

**VAUGHAN, Rt. Rev. Benjamin Noel Young;** *see* Honduras, British, Bishop of.

**VAUGHAN, Brig. (Charles) Hilary (Vaughan),** DSO 1944; DL; JP; late Royal Welch Fusiliers and Adjutant 60th AT Regiment RA (TA); *b* 29 Oct. 1905; *e s* of Col C. H. Pritchard, Indian Political Service; *m* 1935, Hon. Mary Patricia Monck, *yr sister* of 6th Viscount Monck, *qv*; four *d*. *Educ:* Sherborne; Trinity Hall, Cambridge (BA). Changed name by deed poll from Pritchard to Vaughan (his mother's maiden name) on inheriting the Nannau Estates in N Wales, Nov. 1956. Joined Royal Welch Fusiliers, 1927; ADC to Gov. and C-in-C, Gibraltar, 1931-32; Adjt, Depot RWF, 1933-34. Staff College, Camberley, 1939; served War of 1939-45: N Africa, Italy, S France, Greece, Palestine; MO4, War Office, 1940-42; 2nd in Comd 70th Bn RWF, Temp. Lt-Col, 1942; Comd 6th (Royal Welch) Bn The Parachute Regt, Temp. Col, 1943; Brig. 1943; Comd 2nd Indep. Parachute Bde Group, 1943-46; Comdr Airborne Establishments, 1946-48; Comdg Officer 10th Cadet Bn RWF; retd 1949. DL, JP 1950; High Sheriff, Merioneth, 1956-58. Now engaged in farming and running his estate. Commander, Royal Order of George I with Swords (Greece). *Address:* Nannau Home Farm, Dolgellau, Merioneth. *T:* 674.

**VAUGHAN, David Wyamar,** CBE 1962; Director Barclays Bank Ltd, since 1952; Local Director, Barclays Bank, Cardiff, since 1939; *b* 15 July 1906; *s* of late Dr W. W. Vaughan, MVO, DLitt and Margaret, *d* of J. Addington

Symonds; *m* 1st, 1928, Norah (*d* 1963), *d* of late J. H. Burn; two *s* one *d*; 2nd, 1966, Mrs Joy Beebee. *Educ:* Rugby. Joined Barclays Bank, 1930; Local Director: Shrewsbury, 1934; Swansea, 1945-57. Served War of 1939-45, with Welsh Guards, 1940-45, resigned with rank of Major. Treas., Univ. Coll. of S Wales and Monmouthshire, 1951-57; Mem. Court, Univ. of Wales, 1957-67; Hon. Treas., Welsh Nat. Sch. of Medicine, 1962-67. Dir and Treas., Empire and Commonwealth Games, 1958. Chm. Finance Cttee, Representative Body Church in Wales, 1955-. JP County Glamorgan, 1956-66. High Sheriff of Glamorgan, 1963. LLD Univ. of Wales, 1965. *Recreations:* shooting, fishing and all country pursuits; Rugby football. *Address:* The Old Rectory, Wherwell, Hants. *T:* Chilbolton 270. *Club:* Boodle's.

**VAUGHAN, Sir Edgar;** *see* Vaughan, Sir G. E.

**VAUGHAN, Ernest James,** CBE 1961; retired as Director of Materials Research, Royal Naval Scientific Service; *b* 19 Oct. 1901; 3rd *s* of late James and Helena Vaughan; *m* 1927, Marjorie Solly; one *s* decd. *Educ:* Brockley; London University. BSc, MSc London; ARCS; DIC. Jun. Chemist, War Dept; Chemist, 1925-27; Chemist, Chemical Dept, Portsmouth Dockyard, 1927-36; Dep. Supt, then Supt, Bragg Laboratory, 1936-49; Dep. Dir, then Dir of Materials Research, Royal Naval Scientific Service, 1949-66. Hon. Treas., Royal Inst. of Chemistry, 1963-. *Publications:* Protective Coatings for Metals, 1946; (monograph) Metallurgical Analysis; papers in learned jls. *Address:* Copse Edge, 51 Rothesay Drive, Highcliffe-on-Sea, Hants. *T:* Highcliffe 4696. *Club:* Savage.

**VAUGHAN, Sir (George) Edgar,** KBE 1963 (CBE 1956; OBE 1937); Professor of History since 1967, and Dean of Arts and Science since 1969, University of Saskatchewan, Regina Campus (Special Lecturer, 1966-67); *b* 24 Feb. 1907; *s* of late William John Vaughan, BSc, of Cardiff, and Emma Kate Caudle; *m* 1933, Elsie Winifred Deubert; one *s* two *d*. *Educ:* Cheltenham Grammar Sch.; Jesus Coll., Oxford (Exhibitioner and later Hon. Scholar; Hon. Fellow, 1966). 1st Cl. Honour School of Mod. Hist., 1928; 1st Cl. Honour School of Philosophy, Politics and Economics, 1929; Laming Travelling Fellow of the Queen's College, Oxford, 1929-31. Entered Consular Service, 1930; Vice-Consul at: Hamburg, 1931; La Paz, 1932-35; Barcelona, 1935-38; Buenos Aires, 1938-44; Chargé d'Affaires, Monrovia, 1945-46; Consul at Seattle, Washington, 1946-49; Consul-General at Lourenço Marques, 1949-53, Amsterdam, 1953-56; Minister and Consul-General at Buenos Aires, 1956-60; Ambassador, 1960-63 and Consul-General, 1963, at Panama; Ambassador to Colombia, 1964-66. Retired from Diplomatic Service, 1966. FRHistS 1965. *Recreation:* golf. *Address:* 50 Academy Park Road, Regina, Sask, Canada. *Club:* Travellers'.

**VAUGHAN, Dr Gerard Folliott,** MB, FRCP, DPM; MP (C) Reading since 1970; Physician, Guy's Hospital (i/c Bloomfield Clinic); Chairman, Strategic Planning Committee, GLC; Member, South-East Economic Planning Council (co-op. 1968) since 1969; *b* Xinavane, Portuguese E Africa, 11 June 1923; *s* of late Leonard Vaughan, DSO, DFC, and Joan Vaughan (*née* Folliott); *m* 1955, Joyce Thurle (*née* Laver); one *s* one *d*. *Educ:* privately in E Africa; London Univ.; Guy's Hosp. MB, BS 1947; MRCP 1949; Academic DPM London 1952; FRCP 1966. Consultant Staff, Guy's Hosp., 1958. Has acted as advisor to: Dr Barnardo's; Nat. Inst. for Deaf; British Epilepsy Assoc.; Nat. Soc. for Autistic Children. Member: Royal Medico-Psychological Assoc.; Paediatric Adv. Cttee, RCP; New York Acad. of Sciences. FRSM. Alderman, LCC, 1955-61; LCC Streatham, 1961-64; GLC Lambeth, 1966-70; Alderman, GLC, 1970-; Inner London Educn Authority (co-op. 1964), 1966-70. Governor: University Coll., London, 1959-68; various schools. Freeman, City of London; Liveryman, Worshipful Co. of Barbers. Contested (C) Poplar, 1955. *Publications:* various professional and general literary publications and chapters in books. *Recreations:* ski-ing, shooting, painting, farming; also interested in: journalism, medical and general TV and radio programmes, making films. *Address:* 35 Wimpole Street, W1; Polebrook Hall, near Peterborough, Northants. *Club:* Carlton.

**VAUGHAN, Brig. Hilary;** *see* Vaughan, Brig. C. H. V.

**VAUGHAN, Hilda, (Mrs Charles Morgan);** novelist; *b* Builth, Breconshire; *d* of late Hugh Vaughan Vaughan; *m* 1923, Charles Morgan, LLD, FRSL (*d* 1958); one *s* one *d*. *Educ:* privately. FRSL 1963. *Publications:* The Battle to the Weak; Here Are Lovers; The Invader; Her Father's House; The Soldier and the Gentlewoman; A Thing of Nought; The Curtain Rises; Harvest Home; Pardon and Peace; Iron and Gold; The Candle and the Light. *Plays:* She, too, was Young; Forsaking All Other (both with Laurier Lister); Introduction to Thomas Traherne's Centuries. *Address:* 16 Campden Hill Square, W8.

*See also Marchioness of Anglesey.*

**VAUGHAN, Dame Janet (Maria),** DBE 1957 (OBE 1944); DM, FRCP; Principal of Somerville College, Oxford, 1945-67, Hon. Fellow since 1967; *b* 18 October 1899; *d* of William Wyamar Vaughan and Margaret Symonds; *m* 1930, David Gourlay (*d* 1963); two *d*. *Educ:* North Foreland Lodge; Somerville College, Oxford; University College Hospital (Goldsmith Entrance Scholar). Asst Clinical Pathologist, Univ. Coll. Hosp.; Rockefeller Fellowship, 1929-30; Beit Memorial Fellowship, 1930-33; Leverhulme Fellow, RCP, 1933-34; Asst in Clinical Pathology, British Post-Graduate Medical School, 1934-39; Mem. Inter-Departmental Cttee on Medical Schools, 1942; Nuffield Trustee, 1943; late Medical Officer in charge North-West London Blood Supply Depot for Medical Research Council. Mem., Royal Commn on Equal Pay, 1944; Chm., Oxford Regional Hosp. Board, 1950-51 (Vice-Chm. 1948); Member: Cttee on Economic and Financial Problems of Provision for Old Age, 1953-54; Medical Adv. Cttee of University Grants Cttee; University Grants Cttee on Libraries; Commonwealth Scholarship Commn in the UK. Osler Meml Medal, Univ. of Oxford. Hon. DSc: Univ. of Wales; Univ. of Leeds; Hon. DCL: Oxford and London. *Publications:* The Anæmias, 1st edn 1934, 2nd edn 1936; The Physiology of Bone, 1969; numerous papers in scientific jls on blood diseases, blood transfusion and metabolism of strontium isotopes; section on leukæmias, Brit. Ency. Med. Pract.; section on blood transfusion in British Surgical Practice, 1945. *Recreations:* travel, gardening. *Address:* 1 Fairlawn End, First Turn, Wolvercote, Oxford. *T:* Oxford 54111.

**VAUGHAN, (John) Keith,** CBE 1965; painter, designer, illustrator; Tutor at Slade School of Art, London; *b* 23 Aug. 1912; *e s* of E. G. S. Vaughan, civil engineer, and Gladys Regina Marion (*née* Mackingtosh); unmarried. *Educ:*

Christ's Hospital. Mem. Faculty of Painting, British School at Rome, 1962; Advisory Cttee for Painting, Gulbenkian Foundation, 1964; Hon. Fellow Royal Coll. of Art, 1964. First exhibited at Lefevre Gallery, 1942. One-man shows at following galleries: Lefevre, 1944, 1946, 1948, 1951; Redfern, 1950, 1952; Hanover, 1951; Durlacher, New York, 1948, 1952, 1955, 1957, 1966; Inst. of Modern Art, Buenos Aires, 1950; Leicester Galls, London, 1953, 1955, 1956, 1958, 1959; Matthiesen Gall., London, 1960; Whitechapel Art Gall., 1962; Sao Paulo Bienal, 1963; Marlborough Gall., London, 1964, 1965, 1969. Works in public collections: Tate Gall., Arts Council, British Council, Contemporary Art Society; Balliol College, Oxford; Fitzwilliam Museum, Cambridge; Nat. Gall. of Scotland, Edinburgh; Municipal Galleries of Leeds, Manchester, Wakefield, Birmingham, Leicester, Newcastle, Bristol, Huddersfield; Art Inst. of Chicago; Norwich Castle Museum; Glynn Vivian Gall., Swansea; NSW Gallery; Nottingham Museum; Christ Church College, Oxford; VA Museum, London; Whitworth Museum, Manchester; Museum of Modern Art, New York; Albright Museum, Buffalo; Toronto Art Gallery; Wadsworth Athenæum, Connecticut; Tel Aviv Museum; City of Auckland Gallery, New Zealand; State University of Iowa, USA. Executed central mural in Dome of Discovery, Festival of Britain, 1951; mural for Aboyne Estate, Wandsworth, 1963 (LCC Commn). Member of Arts Panel, Arts Council of Great Britain, 1956, 1959. *Publications:* books illustrated: Tom Sawyer, 1947; Rimbaud, Une Saison en Enfer, 1949; Journal and Drawings, 1939-65, 1966. *Address:* 9 Belsize Park, NW3.

**VAUGHAN, Keith;** *see* Vaughan, John Keith.

**VAUGHAN-HUGHES, Brig. Gerald Birdwood,** MC 1918; DL; JP; retired 1948; *b* 14 April 1896; *s* of Gerald Mainwaring Vaughan-Hughes and Isabel Bridget Crawford (*née* Birdwood); *m* 1927, Violet Mary Jessie (*d* 1968), *d* of Maj.-Gen. W. H. Kay, CB, DSO; two *s*. *Educ:* Wellington College; RMA Woolwich. Served European War, 1914-18 (wounded thrice, despatches, MC); RHA and RFA, 2nd Lt, 1914; RHA, 1916; India, RFA, 1919-28; Capt. 1926; ADC to C-in-C India, 1927-28; RHA, 1930; Staff Coll., 1931-32; Maj. 1934; SO: RA Southern Comd, 1934-35; Aldershot, 1936-37; GSO2, Palestine, 1939. War of 1939-45, AAG, Palestine, Greece and Crete, 1941; GSO1 RA, ME, 1941; Comdg Northumberland Hussars and II RHA, 1941-42; CRA (Brig.) 7th Armoured Div., 1942 (despatches twice), retired. DL 1958, JP 1956, High Sheriff, 1960, Monmouthshire. *Address:* Wyelands, Chepstow, Mon. *T:* Chepstow 2127.

**VAUGHAN-JACKSON, Oliver James,** VRD 1951; FRCS; Orthopædic Surgeon to The London Hospital, 1946, to St Bartholomew's Hospital, Rochester, 1947, to Halliwick Cripples School, 1946; Consultant in Orthopædics to the Royal Navy, 1956; *b* 6 July 1907; *e s* of Surgeon Captain P. Vaughan-Jackson, RN, Carramore, Ballina, County Mayo; *m* 1939, Joan Madeline, *er d* of E. A. Bowring, CBE, St Johns, Newfoundland; two *s*. *Educ:* Berkhamsted School; Balliol Coll., Oxford; The London Hospital. Kitchener Scholar; BA, BM, BCh Oxon, 1932; MRCS, LRCP, 1932; FRCS 1936. House Physician, Demonstrator of Pathology, House Surgeon, Resident Accoucheur, and Surgical Registrar at The London Hosp. Surgeon Lieut-Comdr RNVR, Retd, Surgical specialist, Roy. Naval Hosp., Sydney, Australia. Sen. Registrar (Orthopædic), The London Hosp. Consultant Orthopædic Surgeon to Claybury Mental Hospital, 1946-64. Fellow: British Orthopædic Assoc.; RSM (Pres., Section of Orthopædics, 1968-69); Med. Soc. London; Mem., Soc. Internat. de Chirurgie Orthopédique et de Traumatologie; Associate Mem. Brit. Assoc. of Plastic Surgeons; Mem., The British Soc. for Surgery of the Hand. Former Mem., Editorial Board of Jl of Bone and Joint Surgery. *Publications:* Sections on: Arthrodesis (Maingot's Techniques in British Surgery), 1950; Arthrodesis of the Hip, and Osteotomy of the Upper End of Femur (Operative Surgery, ed Rob and Smith), 1958; Surgery of the Hand; Orthopædic Surgery in Spastic conditions; Peripheral Nerve Injuries (Textbook of British Surgery, ed Sir Henry Souttar and Prof. J. C. Goligher), 1959; The Rheumatoid Hand; Carpal Tunnel Compression of the Median Nerve (Clinical Surgery, ed Rob and Smith), 1966; contribs to Jl of Bone and Joint Surgery, etc. *Recreations:* gardening, photography. *Address:* The White Cottage, Bowesden Lane, Shorne, near Gravesend, Kent. *T:* Shorne 2321. *Clubs:* Naval and Military; Castle (Rochester).

**VAUGHAN-MORGAN,** family name of **Baron Reigate.**

**VAUGHAN-THOMAS, (Lewis John) Wynford,** MA Oxon; radio and television commentator since 1937; author, journalist; Director of Programmes, Harlech Television Ltd; Director, Television Advisors Ltd; *b* 15 Aug. 1908; *s* of Dr David Vaughan-Thomas and Morfydd Vaughan-Thomas; *m* 1946, Charlotte Rowlands, MBE; one *s*. *Educ:* Swansea Grammar Sch.; Exeter College, Oxford. Keeper of MSS and Records, National Library of Wales, 1933; Area Officer, S Wales Council of Social Service, 1934-37; joined BBC, 1937. Commentator, Royal Commonwealth Tours, BBC War Correspondent, 1942-45; Croix de Guerre, 1945. *Publications:* Royal Tour, 1953-54, 1954; Anzio, 1961; Madly in all Directions, 1967; (with Alun Llewellyn) The Shell Guide to Wales, 1969. *Recreations:* mountaineering, sailing. *Address:* (home) 51 Belsize Avenue, NW3. *T:* 01-794 3525; 25 Manchester Square, W1. *T:* 01-935 8921. *Clubs:* Authors', Climbers', Savile.

**VAUTELET, Renée G., (Mme H. E.),** CBE 1943; *b* 27 July 1897; *d* of Aimé Geoffrion, KC; *m* Lt-Col Henri Vautelet (*d* 1964), lately head of Insurance Brokerage firm of O'Halloran & Vautelet; two *d*. *Educ:* private. *Recreations:* painting, writing. *Address:* 16 Bellevue Avenue, Westmount, Montreal 6, Quebec, Canada. *T:* Hunter 8-1622.

**VAUX OF HARROWDEN,** 9th Baron, *cr* 1523; **Rev. Peter Hubert Gordon Gilbey,** OSB, MA; Rector of St Mary's Catholic Church, Warrington; *b* 28 June 1914; *e s* of William Gordon Gilbey and Grace Mary Eleanor, 8th Baroness Vaux of Harrowden; *S* mother, 1958. *Educ:* Ampleforth College; St Benet's Hall, Oxford. Became a Benedictine monk at Ampleforth, 1932; ordained at Ampleforth, 1940; Assistant Master at Ampleforth College, 1939-53; Assistant Priest at St Mary's Catholic Church, Cardiff, 1953-57; subseq. at St Alban's, Warrington. *Heir:* *b* Hon. John Hugh Philip Gilbey [*b* 4 Aug. 1915; *m* 1939, Maureen Pamela Gilbey; three *s* one *d*]. *Address:* St Mary's Priory, Buttermarket Street, Warrington, Lancs. *T:* Warrington 30928.

**VAVASOUR, Comdr Sir Geoffrey William,** 5th Bt *cr* 1828; DSC 1943; RN (retired); a Director of W. M. Still & Sons; *b* 5 September 1914; *s* of Captain Sir Leonard Vavasour, 4th Bt, RN, and Ellice Margaret Nelson; *S* father, 1961; *m* 1940, Joan Robb (marr. diss. 1947); two *d*. *Educ:* RNC Dartmouth. *Heir:* kinsman Oswald Joseph Stanislaus Vavasour [*b* 7 Feb. 1883; *m* 1915, Mary Dorothy Moore (*d* 1952); one *s* one *d*]. *Address:* 7 Blenheim, 80 Wimbledon Parkside, SW19. *Clubs:* MCC, Hurlingham, Royal Wimbledon Golf.

**VEAL, Group Captain John Bartholomew,** CBE 1956; AFC 1940; Director General of Safety and Operations, Board of Trade, since 1968; *b* 28 September 1909; *er s* of John Henry and Sarah Grace Veal; *m* 1933, Enid Marjorie Hill; two *s*. *Educ:* Christ's Hosp. Special trainee, Metropolitan-Vickers, 1926-27; commissioned in RAF as pilot officer, 1927; served in Nos 4 and 501 Squadrons and as flying Instructor at Central Flying School, transferring to RAFO, 1932; Flying-Instructor, Chief Flying Instructor, and Test Pilot, Air Service Training Ltd, 1932-39; recalled to regular RAF service, 1939; commanded navigation and flying training schools, 1939-43; Air Staff No. 46 Transport Group, 1944 and Transport Command, 1945-46 (despatches); released from RAF, 1946, to become Deputy Director of Training, Ministry of Civil Aviation; Director of Air Safety and Training, 1947; Director of Operations, Safety and Licensing, 1952; Deputy Director-General of Navigational Services, Ministry of Transport and Civil Aviation, 1958; Director-General of Navigational Services, Ministry of Aviation, 1959-62; Chief Inspector of Accidents, Civil Aviation Department, Board of Trade (formerly Min. of Aviation), 1963-68. FRAeS 1967 (AFRAeS 1958). *Recreation:* trout fishing. *Address:* 19 Ridge Park, Purley, Surrey. *T:* 01-647 6752. *Club:* Royal Aero.

**VEALE, Sir Douglas,** Kt, *cr* 1954; CBE 1929; Hon. LLD Melbourne; Hon. DCL Oxford; Registrar of University of Oxford, 1930-58, retired; Fellow of Corpus Christi College, 1930-58; Hon. Fellow of Corpus Christi College; Hon. Fellow (formerly Trustee) of St Edmund Hall, 1958; Secretary, Oxford Preservation Trust, 1958-62, Trustee, 1962; *b* 2 April 1891; 3rd *s* of Edward Woodhouse Veale and Maud Mary Rootham; *m* 1914, Evelyn Annie (*d* 1970), *d* of J. A. Henderson; one *s* two *d*. *Educ:* Bristol Grammar Sch.; Corpus Christi Coll., Oxford (1st Mods 1912, 2nd Greats, 1914, MA 1930). Second Class Clerk, Local Government Board, 1914; Private Sec. to Permanent Sec., Ministry of Health, 1920; Private Secretary to Dr Addison and successive Ministers of Health, 1921-28; Principal, 1926. Served European War, France and Belgium, with 4th Bn Gloucester Regiment (1915); subsequently Adjutant of Reserve Battalion. *Address:* 94 Lonsdale Road, Oxford. *T:* 55199. *Club:* United University.
*See also R. B. McCallum.*

**VEALE, Hon. Sir Geoffrey,** Kt 1961; **Hon. Mr Justice Veale;** Judge of the High Court of Justice (Queen's Bench Division) since 1961; *b* 12 Jan. 1906; *s* of late Dr Henry Veale, Clifford House, Ilkley; *m* 1937, Elizabeth Patricia Barrow; one *d*. *Educ:* Rugby; Oriel College, Oxford. BA, BCL Oxon. Called to the Bar, 1929; Bencher, Inner Temple, 1959; KC 1951. Chairman Ilkley UDC, 1936; Recorder of Scarborough, 1950-51; Recorder of Sunderland, 1951-54; Recorder of Kingston upon Hull, 1954-57; Recorder of Leeds, 1957-61. Dep. Chm.: NR Yorks Quarter Sessions, 1949-54; WR Yorks Quarter Sessions, 1954-61; Solicitor-General of the County Palatine of Durham, 1955-57; Attorney-General of the County Palatine of Durham, 1957-61. Served War of 1939-45, 4 years' service Middle East (despatches); Colonel, Deputy Judge Advocate General to Middle East forces, 1944. Hon. LLD Leeds, 1966. *Recreation:* shooting. *Address:* West House, Wetherby, Yorks. *T:* Wetherby 2130; 26 Montpelier Walk, SW7. *T:* 01-589 6965. *Club:* Oxford and Cambridge University.

**VEALL, Harry Truman,** CB 1963; Controller of Death Duties, Board of Inland Revenue, 1960-64, retired; *b* 19 Feb. 1901; 2nd *s* of late Wright Veall, Ewyas Harold, Herefs, and late Bertha Veall; *m* 1926, Lily Kershaw, *yr d* of Joshua E. Ryder, Alverthorpe, Wakefield, Yorks; two *d*. *Educ:* Wakefield Grammar Sch. LLB (external) London, 1926. Entered Civil Service, 1916; Asst Controller of Death Duties, 1953, Dep. Controller, 1957. *Address:* 30 Camborne Avenue, Ealing, W13. *T:* 01-567 0360.

**VEASEY, Brig. Harley Gerald,** DSO 1939; late the Queen's Royal Regiment; a Vice-President, Surrey County British Legion; *b* 29 Jan. 1896; *o s* of late H. C. Veasey, Ranchi, Bihar; *m* 1922, Iris, *o d* of late W. P. Morrison, Reigate, Surrey; two *d*. *Educ:* Haileybury College. Commissioned TA 1915, 2/5th Battalion The Queen's Royal Regiment, served European War, 1914-18, France (wounded); Regular Commission The Queen's Royal Regiment, 1916; Ireland, 1920-22; Adjt 5th Bn The Queen's Royal Regiment, 1922-25; Hong-Kong, 1927; Malta, 1929; North China, 1930-34; Palestine, 1939 (DSO, despatches); Commanding 2nd Bn Northern Rhodesia Regt, Northern Rhodesia and Madagascar, 1940-43; MEC and MLC, Mauritius (as OC Troops), 1943; Temp. Col, Temp. Brig., Comdr 28th EA Inf. Bde, Kenya and Ceylon, 1943-44; commanded 1/7th Bn The Queen's Royal Regt, 1945; 13th Infantry Training Centre, 1946-47; No. 2 PTC 1947-48; retired Sept. 1948, with Hon. rank of Brig. Organising Director of Conservative and Unionist Films Association, 1948-51; Sector Commander, Home Guard (West Surrey), 1952-57. *Address:* Woodhill Farm House, Shamley Green, Guildford, Surrey.

**VEITCH, Allan,** CBE 1960 (OBE 1953; MBE 1947); *b* 23 May 1900. Served at Hankow, 1927; Kunming, 1930; Shanghai, 1938; Chungking, 1942. Higher Executive Officer, 1943; Nanking, 1946; Actg Consul-Gen., Kunming, 1946; Consul and Actg Consul-Gen., Hankow, 1946; Consul-Gen., Chungking, 1947; Consul, Los Angeles, 1948; Consul, and Consul-General, Shanghai, 1950-54; Counsellor, HM Embassy, Bonn, 1955-57; HM Consul at Tamsui, 1958-60; retired, 1960. *Address:* c/o Lloyds Bank Ltd, Cox's & King's Branch, 6 Pall Mall, SW1.

**VEITCH, Marian; (Mrs Donald Barnie);** National Woman Officer, General and Municipal Workers Union, since 1960; *b* 8 July 1913; *d* of Arthur Edward and Elizabeth Veitch; *m* 1965, Donald Barnie, MA. *Educ:* Huntsman's Gardens Sch., Sheffield; Ruskin Coll., Oxford. Clerk up to 1956; Yorkshire Dist Official, G&MWU, 1957-60. Member: Sheffield City Council, 1945-56; Food Standards Cttee, 1965-68; Confedn Shipbuilding and Engineering Unions Exec. Cttee, 1962-; Internat. Metal Workers Fedn Women Workers' Cttee, 1962-; Internat. Union of Food and Allied Workers Assoc., 1964-; Internat. Fedn of Industrial Organisations Women's Cttee (Chairman, 1969-); Engrg Trg Bd, 1964-; Food, Drink and Tobacco Trg Bd, 1968-. *Recreation:* reading. *Address:* (office) G&MWU, Ruxley Towers, Claygate, Esher, Surrey. *T:* Esher 62081; (home) 12 Rosehill, Claygate, Esher, Surrey.

**VENABLES, Comdr Gilbert Henry,** DSO 1940; OBE 1946; AMIMechE; Royal Navy; *b* 2 June 1904; *s* of Robert Edward Stopford Venables and Baronne Juliette C. S. de Geymuller; *m* 1937, Joan Haes; one *s* one *d*. *Educ:* RN Colleges, Osborne and Dartmouth; HMS Thunderer; RNEC Keyham. Specialised in Submarines, 1927. Retired, 1954. Manager and Engineer, Crinan Canal, Argyll, 1960.

**VENABLES, Sir Peter (Percy Frederick Ronald),** Kt 1963; PhD, BSc, FRIC; Pro-Chancellor, and Chairman of Council, Open University, since 1969; University Fellow, University of Aston in Birmingham, since 1969; *b* 5 Aug. 1904; British; *m* 1932, Ethel Craig Howell, MSc (PhD 1956); two *s* two *d*. *Educ:* Liverpool University. BSc 1st Cl. Hons, 1925; Education Diploma, 1926; PhD 1928; Research Fellowship, 1928-30. Principal: Municipal Coll., Southend-on-Sea, 1941-47; Royal Technical College, Salford, 1947-56; Coll. Advanced Technology, Birmingham, 1956-66; Vice-Chancellor, Univ. of Aston in Birmingham, 1966-69. Leverhulme Research Fellowship, 1955-56. Commonwealth Senior Visiting Fellowship, Australia, 1960. President: Assoc. of Principals of Technical Instns, 1952-53; Manchester Literary and Philosophical Soc., 1954-56; Birmingham and Midland Inst., 1969-70; Vice-President: BACIE, 1969-; Nat. Inst. of Adult Educn, 1970-; Chairman: Council of Assoc. of Technical Institutions, 1953-54; ITA Adult Education Adv. Cttee, 1965-69; BBC Further Education Adv. Council for the UK, 1965-69; Open University Planning Cttee, 1967-69; Member: Central Advisory Council for Education (England), 1956-60; Adv. Council on Scientific Policy, 1962-64; Cttee on Manpower Resources, 1965-; Northern Ireland Cttee on Univ. and Higher Tech. Educn, 1963-64; West Midlands Economic Planning Council, 1965-68; Midlands Electricity Board (part-time), 1967-. Hon. Fellow, Univ. of Manchester Inst. of Science and Technology. Hon. DSc Aston, 1969. *Publications:* Technical Education, 1956; Sandwich Courses for training Technologists and Technicians, 1959; British Technical Education, 1959; The Smaller Firm and Technical Education, 1961; papers in educational jls. *Recreations:* varied. *Address:* 15 Forest Road, Moseley, Birmingham 13. *T:* 021-449 3462. *Club:* Athenæum.

**VENABLES-LLEWELYN, Brig. Sir (Charles) Michael Dillwyn-,** 3rd Bt, *cr* 1890; MVO 1937; Lord Lieutenant of Radnorshire since 1949; *b* 23 Feb. 1900; 2nd and *o surv s* of Sir Charles Leyshon Dillwyn-Venables-Llewelyn, 2nd Bt, CB; *S* father, 1951; *m* 1934, Lady Delia Mary Hicks-Beach, *o d* of Viscount Quenington (killed in action, 1916) and *sister* of 2nd Earl St Aldwyn, *qv*; one *s* one *d*. *Educ:* Eton; RMC Sandhurst. Joined Grenadier Guards, 1918; Captain, 1927; Lt-Col, comd 2nd Bn Gren. Gds, 1941; Brigadier, 1943; retired, 1946, with rank of Hon. Brig. Commanded 159 Inf. Bde TA, 1947-49. JP 1946, DL 1947, County of Radnor. *Heir: s* John Michael Dillwyn-Venables-Llewelyn [*b* 12 Aug. 1938; *m* 1963, Nina, *d* of late Lt J. S. Hallam and of Mrs E. L. Thomas; two *d*]. *Address:* Llysdinam, Newbridge-on-Wye, Llandrindod Wells, Radnorshire. *T:* Newbridge-on-Wye 200. *Clubs:* Guards, United Service.

**VENABLES-LLEWELYN, Brig. Sir Michael;** *see* Venables-Llewelyn, Brig. Sir C. M. D.

**VENKATASUBBA RAO, Sir Mutta,** Kt 1936; BA; BL; *b* 18 July 1878; *m* Andalamma (Founder-Secretary, Madras Seva Sadan, awarded Kaiser-i-Hind Silver Medal, 1931, Silver Jubilee Medal, 1935, and Padma Bhushan, Republic Day 1957). *Educ:* Free Church Institution, Madras; Christian College and the Law College, Madras. Enrolled a Vakil of the High Court, Madras, 1903; practised (1903-21) in partnership with Mr Radhakrishnaiya under the firm name of Venkatasubba Rao & Radhakrishnaiya; had a large and leading practice on the Original Side of the High Court; Election Commissioner, 1921-22; Puisne Judge, Madras High Court, 1921-38; officiating Chief Justice, Madras High Court, in 1935 and 1936; Political Agent to Nizam of Hyderabad and Berar in CP and Berar, 1939-42; Founder-President of The Madras Seva Sadan; Member, Indian Delimitation Committee, 1935-36. *Address:* Vraja, 36 Tirumalai Pillai Road, Madras 17, India.

**VENN, Air Commodore George Oswald,** CBE 1945; *b* 15 Sept. 1892; *er s* of George Venn, Warrington; *m* 1st, 1923, Betty (*d* 1953), *d* of Alderman T. Stopher, Winchester; two *s* one *d*; 2nd, 1960, Monica, *d* of Rev. J. B. Cholmeley. *Educ:* Boteler Grammar Sch., Warrington. Architecture, 1909-14 (Student RIBA); served European War, 1914-16, Royal Fusiliers (University Public Sch. Bn), 1916-45, RFC and RAF (despatches twice). War of 1939-45, Iraq, Abyssinia, Western Desert, Fighter Command; Director of Personal Services, Air Ministry, 1943-45; retired, 1945. Executive Director Remploy Ltd, 1945-61. *Address:* Great Glenham, Saxmundham, Suffolk. *Club:* Royal Air Force.

**VENTER, Maj.-Gen. Christoffel Johannes,** CB 1944; DFC; Director, English Electric Company of South Africa, since 1958; *b* 1892; *s* of Sarel Johannes Venter; *m* 1918, Catherine Josephine Clarke, Liverpool; two *d*. Reserve of Officers. Subsequently became Director of companies. *Address:* Greystones, PO Box 12013, Clubview, via Pretoria, Transvaal, S Africa.

**VENTRY,** 7th Baron, *cr* 1800; **Arthur Frederick Daubeney Olav Eveleigh-de-Moleyns;** *b* Norton Malreward, Som, 28 July 1898; *er s* of 6th Baron and Evelyn Muriel Stuart (*d* 1966), *y d* of Lansdowne Daubeney, Norton Malreward, Somerset; *S* father, 1936. *Educ:* Old Malthouse, Swanage; Wellington Coll., Berks. Served Irish Guards, 1917-18 (wounded); afterwards in RAF; served RAF, 1939-45. Certificated Aeronaut. *Publications:* on aerostation and scouting. *Recreations:* music, travelling, airship piloting. *Heir: nephew* Andrew (Harold) Wesley Daubeny De Moleyns [*b* 28 May 1943; *m* 1963, Nelly Edouard Renée, *d* of Abel Chaumillon, Torremolinos, Spain; one *s* two *d*]. *Address:* Lindsay Hall, Lindsay Road, Bournemouth. *Clubs:* Royal Aero, Norwegian, Balloon and Airship.

**VERCO, Walter John George,** CVO 1970 (MVO 1952); Chester Herald since Nov. 1960; Secretary to the Earl Marshal since 1961; Hon. Genealogist: to the Order of the British Empire, since 1959; to Royal Victorian Order, since 1968; *b* 18 January 1907; *s* of late John Walter Verco, Chelsea; *m* 1929, Ada Rose, *d* of late Bertram Leonard Bennett, Lymington, Hants; one *s* one *d*. Served War, 1940-45, with RAFVR, Flight Lt. Secretary to Garter King of Arms, 1949-60; Rouge Croix Pursuivant of Arms, 1954-60. Fellow, Royal Commonwealth Soc. OStJ. *Address:* College of Arms, Queen Victoria Street, EC4. *T:* 01-248 6185; 53 Alington Crescent, Kingsbury, Middlesex. *T:* 01-205 7553.

**VERCORS;** (pen-name of Jean Bruller); writer; designer-engraver (as Jean Bruller); Légion d'honneur; médaille de la Résistance; *b* Paris, 26 February 1902; *s* of Louis Bruller and E. Bourbon; *m* 1931, Jeanne Barusseaud (marriage dissolved); three *s*; *m* Rita Barisse. *Educ:* Ecole Alsacienne, Paris. Dessinateur-graveur: publié, 1926-39; Albums: 21 Recettes de Mort Violente, 1926; Hypothèses sur les Amateurs de Peinture, 1927; Un Homme Coupé en tranches, 1929; Nouvelle Clé des Songes, 1934; L'enfer, 1935; Visions intimes et rassurantes de la guerre, 1936; Silences, 1937. Décor et costumes pour L'Orphelin de la Chine, de Voltaire, à la Comédie Française, 1965. *Publications:* Publication périodique; Les Relevés Trimestriels, planches dont l'ensemble (160 planches) forme La Danse des Vivants, 1932-38; Nombreuses illustrations pour livres de luxe. En 1941, fondation des Editions de Minuit clandestines, publication, sous le nom de Vercors: du Silence de la Mer, 1942; depuis, sous le même nom, La Marche à l'Etoile, 1943; Le Songe, 1944; Les Armes de la Nuit, 1946; Le Sable du Temps, 1945; Les Yeux et la Lumière, 1948; Plus ou Moins Homme, 1950; La Puissance du jour, 1951; Les Animaux dénaturés (Borderline), 1952; Les Pas dans le Sable; Portrait d'une Amitié, 1954, Divagations d'un Français en Chine; Colères (The Insurgents), 1956; PPC, 1957; Sur Ce Rivage (I. Le Périple, II. Monsieur Prousthe, 1958, III. Liberté de Décembre, 1959); Sylva, 1961; Zoo (comedy) Prod. Carcassonne, 1963, Théâtre National Populaire, Paris, 1964; et dans de nombreux pays d'Europe et d'Amérique; Hamlet (trad. et illus.), 1965; Les Chemins de l'Etre (en coll. av. P. Misraki), 1965; Quota ou les Pléthoriens (en coll. av. Coronel), 1966; La Bataille du Silence, 1967; Oedipe-Roi (drame d'après Sophocle) prod. La Rochelle, 1967; Le Radeau de la Méduse (novel), 1969; Le Fer et le Velours (play), prod. Nîmes, 1969; Oedipe et Hamlet, 2 plays, 2 dossiers, 1970. Nombreux articles dans les periodiques. *Address:* Faremoutiers, Seine-et-Marne, France. *Clubs:* PEN, section française; Comité National des Ecrivains (Hon. Pres.).

**VERDIN, Lt-Col Sir Richard Bertram,** Kt 1962; OBE 1954; TD; DL; JP; Deputy Chairman, Meat and Livestock Commission, since 1967; *b* 1912; *e s* of late Lt-Col Richard Norman Harrison Verdin, DL, JP, Garnstone, Weobley, Herefordshire; *m* 1950, Helen Margaret, *e d* of Sir Watkin Williams-Wynn, 8th Bt; one *s*. *Educ:* Harrow; Magdalen Coll., Oxford. Barrister, Inner Temple 1937. Liaison Officer, Ministry of Agriculture, Fisheries and Food, 1958-; Chairman: Pig Industrial Develt Authority (PIDA), 1962-69; Lawes Trust Cttee, Rothamstead, 1964-. Served with Cheshire Yeomanry, 1931-54; Lt-Col 1952. Chm., County Agric. Exec. Cttee, 1955-; Pres., Country Landowners' Assoc., 1959-61. DL, JP, Cheshire, 1955. *Address:* Stoke Hall, Nantwich, Cheshire.

**VERDON-SMITH, Sir (William) Reginald,** Kt 1953; Chairman, British Aircraft Corporation (Holdings) Ltd, since 1969, Deputy Chairman: Lloyds Bank Ltd,; since 1967; Babcock and Wilcox Ltd, since 1960; Lloyds Bank Europe Ltd, since 1969; Partner, George White, Evans & Co., Stockbrokers; Pro-Chancellor, Bristol University, since 1965; *b* 5 Nov. 1912; *s* of late Sir William G. Verdon Smith, CBE, JP; *m* 1946, Jane Margaret, *d* of late V. W. J. Hobbs; one *s* one *d*. *Educ:* Repton School; Brasenose College, Oxford (Scholar), 1st class School of Jurisprudence, 1935; BCL 1936 and Vinerian Law Scholar; Barrister-at-law, Inner Temple. Bristol Aeroplane Co., 1938-68: Dir., 1942; Jt Asst Man. Dir., 1947; Jt Man. Dir., 1952; Chm. 1955. Vice-Chm., Rolls Royce Ltd, 1966-68. President SBAC, 1946-48; Chairman, Fatstock and Meat Marketing Committee of Enquiry, 1962-64; Mem. of Council, Univ. of Bristol (Chm., 1949-56). Mem. Cttee on the Working of the Monetary System (Radcliffe Cttee), 1957-59. Mem., Review Body on Remuneration of Doctors and Dentists, 1964-68. Master, Worshipful Co. of Coachmakers and Coach Harness Makers, 1960-61; Master, Soc. of Merchant Venturers, 1968-69. Hon. LLD Bristol, 1959; Hon. Fellow, Brasenose Coll., Oxford, 1965. *Recreations:* golf and sailing. *Address:* 13 Redcliffe Parade West, Bristol 1; Old Manor, Littlehempston, Totnes, S Devon. *T:* Staverton 631. *Clubs:* Athenæum; Royal Yacht Squadron, Royal Thames Yacht, Royal Cruising.

**VERE OF HANWORTH, Lord; Charles Francis Topham de Vere Beauclerk;** *b* 22 Feb. 1965; *s* and *heir* of Earl of Burford, *qv*.

**VERE-LAURIE, Lt-Col George Halliburton Foster Peel,** DL; JP; High Sheriff of Notts, 1957-58; *b* 22 Aug. 1906; *er s* of Lt-Col George Laurie (killed in action, 1915), and Florence, Viscountess Masserene and Ferrard; *m* 1932, Caroline Judith (from whom he obtained a divorce, 1968), *yr d* of Edward Francklin, JP, Gonalston Hall, Notts; one *s* one *d*. *Educ:* Eton; RMC Sandhurst. 2nd Lieut 9th Lancers, 1927; Captain and Adjutant, Notts Yeomanry, 1934-38; Capt. 1938; Maj. 1940; Lt-Col Royal Military Police, 1946; retired pay, 1947. Served War of 1939-45, France and Palestine. DL Notts, 1948, JP Notts 1952. Gold Staff Officer, Coronation, 1953. Chairman: Southwell RDC, 1951 and 1956; Governors of Newark Technical Coll., 1952-61; a General Commissioner of Income Tax, 1956. Freeman City of London. Court of Assistants, Saddlers' Co., 1959, Master, 1965; Lord of the Manors of Carlton-on-Trent and Willoughby-in-Norwell. *Recreations:* hunting and shooting (Hon. Sec. Rufford Foxhounds, 1949-55; Joint Master and Huntsman, South Notts Foxhounds, 1956-58, Joint Master, 1959-68). *Address:* Carlton Hall, Carlton-on-Trent, Newark, Notts. *T:* Sutton-on-Trent 288. *Club:* Cavalry.

**VEREKER,** family name of **Viscount Gort.**

**VEREKER, Sir (George) Gordon (Medlicott),** KCMG, *cr* 1948 (CMG 1942); MC; *b* 11 Dec. 1889; *s* of late George Medlicott Vereker, Sharpitor, Salcombe, South Devon; *m* 1945, Roxana Wentworth van Rensselaer, NYC, USA (*d* 1968). *Educ:* Eton; Trinity Coll., Cambridge. Amateur Epée Champion, 1913. Served European War, 1914-18; HQ 8th Div. 1914; 2nd Bn Grenadier Guards, 1915-19; entered Diplomatic Service, 1919; Cairo, 1919-23; Peking, 1923-27; Budapest, 1927-30; Foreign Office, 1930-32; Warsaw, 1932-34; Stockholm, 1934-36; Foreign Office, 1936-37; Counsellor British Embassy, Moscow, 1937-39; Minister in Finland, 1940-41, till rupture of relations; special service at Gibraltar, 1942. Minister in Uruguay, 1943; British Ambassador to Uruguay, 1944-49; retired, 1949. *Address:* Domaine de Beaumont, Valbonne, Alpes Maritimes, France. *Clubs:* Carlton, Guards, White's.

**VEREY, David Cecil Wynter;** retired as Senior Investigator, Historic Buildings, Ministry of Housing and Local Government (1946-65); architectural historian and writer; *b* 9 Sept. 1913; *o s* of Rev. Cecil Henry Verey and Constance Lindaraja Dearman Birchall; *m* 1939, Rosemary Isabel Baird, *d* of Lt-Col Prescott Sandilands, DSO; two *s* two *d*. *Educ:* Eton; Trinity Coll., Cambridge (MA). ARIBA 1940. Capt., Royal Fusiliers, 1940; seconded SOE 1943, N Africa and Italy. Chm., Gloucester Diocesan Adv. Cttee on Churches;

Chm., Buildings and Excavations Cttee of Bristol and Gloucestershire Archæological Society. High Sheriff of County of Gloucester, 1966. FSA. *Publications:* Shell Guides to six counties, England and Wales; The Buildings of England (Gloucestershire Vol.), 1970; articles on architectural history. *Recreations:* private museum, Arlington Mill, Bibury; gardening. *Address:* Barnsley House, Cirencester, Glos. *T:* Bibury 281.

**VEREY, Michael John,** TD 1945; Deputy Chairman of J. Henry Schroder Wagg & Co. Ltd since 1966; *b* 12 Oct. 1912; *yr s* of late Henry Edward and late Lucy Alice Verey; *m* 1947, Sylvia Mary, *widow* of Charles Bartlet and *d* of late Lt-Col Denis Wilson and late Mrs Mary Henrietta Wilson; two *s* one *d*. *Educ:* Eton; Trinity College, Cambridge (BA). Joined Helbert, Wagg & Co. Ltd, 1934. Served War of 1939-45, Middle East, Italy, Warwickshire Yeomanry (Lt-Col). Chm., Broadstone Investment Trust Ltd; Director: Boots Pure Drug Co. Ltd; Commercial Union Assurance Co. Ltd; NEGIT SA; Continental & Industrial Trust Ltd; Sviluppo e Gestione Investimenti Mobiliari, SpA; Schroders Ltd and other cos; Mem., Covent Garden Market Authority, 1961-66. High Sheriff of Berkshire, 1968. *Recreations:* gardening, ski-ing. *Address:* Little Bowden, Pangbourne, Berks. *T:* Pangbourne 2210; Flat 16, 1 Sloane Court East, SW5. *T:* 01-730 6946. *Club:* Boodle's.

**VERITY, Group Captain Conrad Edward Howe,** OBE 1943; JP; Engineering Consultant; *b* 18 February 1901; *s* of Edward Storr Verity and Annie Amelia Verity (*née* Howe); *m* 1931, Doreen Louise Bishop; one *s* one *d*. *Educ:* Wellingborough Sch. Engrg Trg, W. H. Allen Sons & Co. Ltd, Bedford, and Bedford Tech. Coll., 1917-22; Contracts Engr, W. H. Allen Sons & Co. Ltd, Bedford, 1922-24; Tech. Engr, Contraflo Engrg Co. Ltd, 1924-27; Tech. Engr (Mech.), London Power Co., 1927-40. Served War, 1940-45: RAF, finishing as Gp Capt.; service in England, USA, NW Africa, Pacific, India, China, etc. Chief Development and Testing Engineer, London Power Co., 1945-48; Generation Constr Engr, Brit. Elec. Authority, 1948-50; Dep. Chief Engr, Brit. Elec. Authority, and later Central Elec. Authority, 1950-55; Dir, Foster Wheeler Ltd and Manager Steam Div., 1955-59, Managing Dir, 1960-62, Chm., 1962-66; Dep. Chm., Foster Wheeler John Brown Boilers Ltd, 1966-67; Dir, Rolls-Royce and Associates, Derby, 1959-67. JP 1960. American Legion of Merit (Officer), 1945. *Publications:* technical papers to: Institution Civil Engrs; Electrical Power Engrs Assoc.; Instn of Mech. Engrs, etc. *Recreations:* rowing, and sport generally. *Address:* Farthings, Earleydene, Sunninghill, Berks. *T:* Ascot 22033. *Clubs:* United Service; Twickenham Rowing (Hon. Life Mem.); Burway Rowing (Vice-Pres.); Laleham Village Cricket (Vice-Pres.), etc.

**VERITY, Sir Edgar (William),** KBE, *cr* 1954; CB 1948; *b* 21 October 1891; *s* of late William Verity, Bradford, Yorkshire; *m* 1937, Dorothy, *d* of late William Hobson, Heysham, Lancashire; one *d*. *Educ:* Bradford Grammar School; Brasenose College, Oxford. Entered Civil Service (Inland Revenue Dept), 1914; Assistant Secretary, 1936; Commissioner of Inland Revenue, 1945; Deputy Chairman, Board of Inland Revenue, 1951-54. *Address:* Flat 2, Westfield, Raglan Road, Reigate, Surrey. *T:* Reigate 42752.

**VERNER, Sir Edward Derrick Wingfield,** 6th Bt, *cr* 1846; *b* 28 May 1907; *s* of 5th Bt, of Corke Abbey, Bray, Co. Wicklow, and Agnes Dorothy (*d* 1951). *y d* of late Henry Laming; *S* father 1936; *m* 1948, Angèle Becco, Menton. *Educ:* Greshams, Holt; Magdalen College, Oxford (BA 1928). *Address:* c/o Glyn, Mills & Co., 67 Lombard St, EC3.

**VERNEY,** family name of **Baron Willoughby de Broke.**

**VERNEY, Sir Harry (Calvert Williams),** 4th Bt, *cr* 1818; DSO 1918; MA (Oxford); Lt-Colonel; *b* 7 June 1881; *s* of 3rd Bt and Margaret, *e d* of Sir John Hay Williams and Lady Sarah, *d* of 1st Earl Amherst; *S* father, 1910; *m* 1911, Lady Rachel Bruce (*d* 1964), *d* of 9th Earl of Elgin; five *s* three *d*. *Educ:* Harrow; Balliol College, Oxford. Assistant Private Secretary to Secretary of State for the Colonies, Lord Elgin, 1907-08, Lord Crewe, 1908-1910; MP (L) North Bucks, 1910-18; Parliamentary Private Secretary to the Chief Secretary for Ireland, 1911-14; Parliamentary Secretary to the Board of Agriculture, 1914-15; served European War, 1915-18 (despatches twice, DSO). CC Anglesey, 1949-55. *Publication:* (ed) The Verneys of Claydon, 1969. *Recreation:* old letters. *Heir: s* Ralph Bruce Verney, *qv*. *Address:* Ballams, Middle Claydon, Bletchley, Bucks. *T:* Steeple Claydon 321. *Club:* St James'.

*See also R. M. Hare, Sir Ronald M. J. Harris.*

**VERNEY, Sir John,** 2nd Bt, *cr* 1946; MC 1944; Painter, Illustrator, Author; *b* 30 Sept. 1913; *s* of Sir Ralph Verney, 1st Bt (Speaker's Secretary, 1921-55); *S* father, 1959; *m* 1939, Lucinda, *d* of late Major Herbert Musgrave, DSO; one *s* five *d* (and one *s* decd). *Educ:* Eton; Christ Church, Oxford. Served War of 1939-45 with N. Somerset Yeomanry, RAC and SAS Regt in Palestine, Syria, Egypt, Italy, France and Germany (despatches twice, MC). Exhibitor: RBA; London Group; Leicester, Redfern, AIA and Zwemmer Galleries. Légion d'Honneur, 1945. *Publications:* Verney Abroad, 1954; Going to the Wars, 1955; Friday's Tunnel, 1959; Look at Houses, 1959; February's Road, 1961; Every Advantage, 1961; The Mad King of Chichiboo, 1963; ismo, 1964; A Dinner of Herbs, 1966; Fine Day for a Picnic, 1968; Seven Sunflower Seeds, 1968. Periodic contributor to Cornhill, National and English Review, The Elizabethan, etc. *Recreation:* Hon. Sec., Farnham Trust. *Heir: s* John Sebastian Verney, *b* 30 Aug. 1945. *Address:* Runwick House, Farnham, Surrey. *T:* Farnham 6323.

**VERNEY, Ralph Bruce,** JP; Landowner; Vice-Lieutenant of Buckinghamshire since 1965; *b* 18 Jan. 1915; *e s* of Sir Harry Verney, 4th Bt, *qv*; *m* 1948, Mary Vestey; one *s* three *d*. *Educ:* Canford; Balliol Coll., Oxford. 2nd Lieut Bucks Yeomanry, 1940; Major, Berks Yeomanry, 1945 and Bucks Yeomanry, 1946. Vice-President for Great Britain, Confédération Européenne de L'Agriculture, 1965; Chairman, Forestry Commn Cttee for England, 1967; Forestry Comr, 1968-; Member: Nature Conservancy, 1966; Milton Keynes New Town Corporation, 1967. Buckinghamshire County Council: Member, 1951; Chairman, Finance Cttee, 1957; Planning Cttee, 1967; CA 1961; JP Bucks, 1954; High Sheriff of Buckinghamshire, 1957-58; DL Bucks, 1960; High Steward of Buckingham, 1966. Prime Warden, Worshipful Co. of Dyers, 1969-70. *Recreation:* shooting. *Address:* Claydon House, Bletchley, Bucks. *T:* Steeple Claydon 297; Plas Rhôscolyn, Holyhead, Anglesey. *T:* Trearddwr Bay 288. *Clubs:* Brooks's, Cavalry, Farmers'.

**VERNEY, Air Commodore Reynell Henry,** CBE 1937; DL; RAF (retired); *b* Lighthorne, Warwickshire, 12 Jan. 1886; 2nd *s* of late Rev.

Hon. Walter R. Verney; *m* 1942, Hon. Dorothy Ceciley Tollemache, *er d* of 3rd Baron Tollemache. *Educ:* Seafield Park Coll.; Imperial Service Coll. 2nd Lieut, ASC, 1910; seconded RFC, 1914; transferred RAF, 1918; retired list, 1938; employed Supply Dept (Aircraft), Government of India, 1943-46. DL Warwickshire, 1952. *Address:* Stone House, Bishop's Hill, Lighthorne, Warwick. *T:* Moreton-Morrell 246. *Club:* United Service.

**VERNEY-CAVE,** family name of **Baron Braye.**

**VERNON,** family name of **Barons Lyveden** and **Vernon.**

**VERNON,** 10th Baron, *cr* 1762; **John Lawrance Vernon;** *b* 1 Feb. 1923; *s* of 9th Baron, and Violet, *d* of Colonel Clay; *S* father, 1963; *m* 1955, Sheila Jean, *d* of W. Marshall Clark, Johannesburg; two *d*. *Educ:* Eton; Magdalen Coll., Oxford. Served in Scots Guards, 1942-46, retiring with rank of Captain. Called to Bar, Lincoln's Inn, 1949. Served in various Government Departments, 1950-61; attached to Colonial Office (for service in Kenya), 1957-58. *Heir: kinsman,* 2nd Viscount Harcourt, *qv*. *Address:* Sudbury House, Derby. *Club:* Boodle's.

**VERNON, Sir James,** Kt 1965; CBE 1962 (OBE 1960); General Manager since 1958 and Director, Colonial Sugar Refining Co. Ltd; Chairman: CSR Chemicals Ltd; Pilbara Iron Ltd; Gove Alumina Ltd; Director: Australian National Power Alcohol Co. Pty Ltd; New Zealand Sugar Co. Ltd; United Telecasters Sydney Ltd; Nabalco Pty Ltd; *b* 1910; *s* of Donald Vernon, Tamworth, New South Wales; *m* 1935, Mavis, *d* of C. Lonsdale Smith; two *d*. *Educ:* Sydney Univ. (BSc); University College, London (PhD). Colonial Sugar Refining Co. Ltd: Chief Chemist, 1938-51; Senior Exec. Officer, 1951-56; Asst General Manager, 1956-57. Chairman, Commonwealth Cttee of Economic Enquiry, 1963-65. Member, Manufacturing Industries Advisory Council; Vice-President: Australian Industries Development Assoc.; Australia/Japan Business Co-operation Cttee; Member, Australian Universities Commn; Member, Australian Admin. Staff Coll. Council. Leighton Medal, Royal Australian Chemical Inst., 1965. Hon. DSc: Sydney, 1965; Newcastle, 1969. FRACI. *Address:* 27 Manning Road, Double Bay, NSW, Australia. *Clubs:* Australian, Union, Royal Sydney Golf (Sydney).

**VERNON, James William,** CMG 1964; Under-Secretary, Ministry of Housing and Local Government, since 1969; *b* 1915; *s* of late John Alfred Vernon; *m* 1941, Betty Désirée, *d* of Gordon E. Nathan; one *s* one *d*. *Educ:* Wallasey Grammar Sch.; Emmanuel Coll., Cambridge (Scholar). BA 1937, MA 1940. Entered Civil Service, Ministry of Food, 1939; Flt Lieut, RAF, 1943; Wing Comdr (despatches), 1945; Principal Scientific Officer, Ministry of Works, 1945; Principal, Colonial Office, 1948; Assistant Secretary, Colonial Office, 1954-64; Economic Adviser, British High Commission, Lusaka, 1966; Asst Under-Sec. of State, DEA, 1966-69. Queen's Commendation for Brave Conduct, 1955. *Recreations:* gardening, photography, house painting. *Address:* Department of Economic Affairs, Storey's Gate, SW1. *T:* 01-839 7848.

**VERNON, Professor Magdalen Dorothea,** MA (Cantab) 1926; ScD (Cantab) 1953; Professor of Psychology in the University of Reading, 1956-67; *b* 25 June 1901; *d* of Dr Horace Middleton Vernon and Katharine Dorothea Ewart. *Educ:* Oxford High Sch.; Newnham Coll., Cambridge. Asst Investigator to the Industrial Health Research Board, 1924-27; Research Investigator to the Medical Research Council, in the Psychological Laboratory, Cambridge, 1927-46; Lecturer in Psychology, 1946-51, Senior Lecturer in Psychology, 1951-55, Reader in Psychology, 1955-56. University of Reading. President, British Psychological Society, 1958 (Hon. Fellow, 1970); President, Psychology Section, British Assoc., 1959. *Publications:* The Experimental Study of Reading, 1931; Visual Perception, 1937; A Further Study of Visual Perception, 1952; Backwardness in Reading, 1957; The Psychology of Perception, 1962; Experiments in Visual Perception, 1966; Human Motivation, 1969; Perception through Experience, 1970; numerous papers on Perception, etc. in British Journal of Psychology and British Journal of Educational Psychology. *Recreations:* walking, gardening. *Address:* 50 Cressingham Road, Reading, Berks. *T:* Reading 81088. *Club:* University Women's.

**VERNON, Sir Nigel (John Douglas),** 4th Bt, *cr* 1914; Director, Castle Brick Co. Ltd, since 1966; *b* 2 May 1924; *s* of Sir (William) Norman Vernon, 3rd Bt, and of Janet Lady Vernon; *S* father, 1967; *m* 1947, Margaret Ellen (*née* Dobell); two *s* one *d*. *Educ:* Charterhouse. Royal Naval Volunteer Reserve (Lieutenant), 1942-45. Spillers Ltd, 1945-65. *Recreations:* golf, gardening. *Heir: s* James William Vernon, *b* 2 April 1949. *Address:* Top-y-Fron Hall, Kelsterton, near Flint, N Wales. *T:* Connah's Quay 2129. *Club:* Naval.

**VERNON, Professor Philip Ewart,** MA, PhD, DSc; Professor of Psychology and Senior Research Consultant, University of Calgary, since 1968; Emeritus Professor, University of London; *b* 6 June 1905; *e s* of late Horace Middleton Vernon; *m* 1st, 1938, Annie C. Gray; 2nd, 1947, Dorothy Anne Fairley Lawson, MA, MEd; one *s*. *Educ:* Oundle Sch.; St John's Coll., Cambridge; Yale and Harvard Universities. First Class Hons in Nat. Sci. Tripos, Part I, 1926, and Moral Sci. Tripos, Part II, 1927; John Stewart of Rannoch Scholarship in Sacred Music, 1925; Strathcona Research Studentship, 1927-29; Laura Spelman Rockefeller Fellowship in Social Sciences, 1929-31; Fellowship of St John's Coll., Cambridge, 1930-33; Pinsent-Darwin Studentship in Mental Pathology, 1933-35. Psychologist to LCC at Maudsley Hospital Child Guidance Clinic, 1933-35; Head of Psychology Dept, Jordanhill Training Centre, Glasgow, 1935-38; Head of Psychology Dept, University of Glasgow, 1938-47; Psychological Research Adviser to Admiralty and War Office, 1942-45; Prof. of Educational Psychology, Inst. of Education, University of London, 1949-64; Prof. of Psychology, 1964-68. *Publications:* (with G. W. Allport) Studies in Expressive Movement, 1933; The Measurement of Abilities, 1940, 1956; (with J. B. Parry) Personnel Selection in the British Forces, 1949; The Structure of Human Abilities, 1950, 1961; Personality Tests and Assessments, 1953; Secondary School Selection, 1957; Intelligence and Attainment Tests, 1960; Personality Assessment: A Critical Survey, 1963; Intelligence and Cultural Environment, 1969; numerous papers in British and American psychological journals. *Recreation:* music. *Address:* 6 Varview Place, Calgary, NW Alberta, Canada.

**VERNON, Sir Wilfred (Douglas),** Kt 1960; JP; President of Spillers Ltd, 1965-69 (Chairman, 1953-65); *b* 27 April 1897; 4th *s* of late William Allen and Elizabeth Vernon; *m* 1923, Nancy Elizabeth, *d* of late Tom Jackson, JP, Bolton;

one *s* (and one *s* killed on active service, 1944). *Educ:* Sedbergh; Trinity Coll., Cambridge. Served European War, 1915-18: London Regt, Royal Fusiliers, 1915; attached RFC, 1917-18. Director of Spillers Ltd, 1930. President, Nat. Assoc. of British and Irish Millers, 1947-48; JP, 1952-; High Sheriff of Surrey, 1960-61. *Recreation:* shooting. *Address:* Anningsley Park, Ottershaw, Surrey. *T:* Byfleet 45088.
*See also W. M. Vernon.*

**VERNON, Major Wilfrid Foulston;** *b* 1882; *s* of George Thomas Vernon, Islington, London, and Rebecca Clark, Nottingham; *m* 1st, 1907, Josephine Mary, *d* of Joseph Jervis, Stafford; two *s*; 2nd, 1918, Laura Gladys Adeline, *d* of Dr H. Meade, Bradford. *Educ:* Stationers Company's Sch.; City and Guilds Technical Coll. Apprenticed to Electrical Engineering Siemens, Woolwich; Assistant Engineer Siemens, Stafford, Designer and Engineer Humphrey Pump Co. European War, Lieut and Lieut-Commander, RNVR, Squadron Comdr RNAS, Major RAF, technical assistant to Comdr Porte, pioneer flying boat designer at Felixstowe Air Station. Chief draughtsman Bristol Aeroplane Co., 1923; Technical Officer Royal Aircraft Establishment, 1925-37. War of 1939-45, associated with Tom Wintringham in founding Osterley Park Home Guard Sch.; Lecturer and Demonstrator No. 1 War Office Home Guard Sch., Denbies, Dorking; Lecturer to Forces and Civil Defence Workers; Workers Educational Association Tutor and Organiser. MP (Lab.) Dulwich Division of Camberwell, 1945-51; LCC Member for Dulwich, 1952-55, Borough Councillor, Camberwell, 1953-56. *Address:* Wyngarth, Easter Compton, Bristol. *T:* Pilning 329.

**VERNON, William Michael;** Chairman and Chief Executive of Spillers Ltd, since 1968; *b* 17 April 1926; *o surv. s* of Sir Wilfred Vernon, *qv*; *m* 1952, Rosheen O'Meara; one *s*. *Educ:* Marlborough Coll.; Trinity Coll., Cambridge. MA 1948. Lieut, Royal Marines, 1944-46. Joined Spillers Ltd, 1948: Dir 1960; Jt Man. Dir 1962. Pres., Nat. Assoc. of British and Irish Millers, 1965. *Recreations:* ocean racing, shooting, ski-ing. *Address:* Ropley House, Alresford, Hants. *Clubs:* Royal Thames Yacht, Royal Ocean Racing (Cdre 1964-68); Royal Yacht Squadron.

**VERONESE, Dr Vittorino;** Cavaliere di Gran Croce della Repubblica Italiana; Gold Medal Awarded for Culture (Italian Republic); Doctor of Law (Padua, 1930); lawyer, banker, administrator; Chairman, Board of Directors, Banco di Roma, since Nov. 1961 (Auditor, 1945-53; Director, 1953-57); *b* Vicenza, 1 March 1910; *m* 1939, Maria Petrarca; four *s* three *d*. General Secretary: Catholic Movement Graduates, 1939; Italian Catholic Action, 1944-46 (President, 1946-52); Vice-President, Internat. Movement of Catholic Intellectuals of Pax Romana, 1947-55. Vice-President, Banca Cattolica del Veneto, 1952-57; President, Consorzio di Credito per le Opere Pubbliche and Istituto di Credito per le Imprese di Pubblica Utilitá, 1957-58; Italian Deleg. to General Conf. of UNESCO, Beirut, 1950, Paris, 1952-53; Member Italian Nat. Commn, 1953-58; Vice-President, Exec. Board, 1954-56; President, 1956-58. Director-General of UNESCO, 1958-61, resigned; Vice-President, Comité Consultatif International de Liaison pour l'Alphabétisation, UNESCO, 1967; Pres., Italian Consultative Cttee for Human Rights, 1965. Pres., Circolo di Roma, 1968. Lay Observer in Concilio Ecumenico Vaticano II; Member, Pontificia Commissione Justitia et Pax, 1967. Cav. di Gran Groce dell' Ordine di S. Silvestro Papa; Commendatore dell' Ordine Piano. Holds several foreign orders. *Address:* c/o Banco di Roma, Via del Corso 307, Rome, Italy; 21 Via Cadlolo, Rome, Italy.

**VERRY, Frederick William,** CMG 1958; OBE 1948; Assistant Secretary, Air Ministry, 1953-62, retired; *b* 15 Feb. 1899; *s* of late Herbert William Verry; *m* 1926, Phyllis, *d* of late William Pitt MacConochie. *Educ:* Stockport Secondary Sch.; Northern Polytechnic Sch., London. Joined Civil Service as Boy Clerk, War Office, 1914. Served in RN Airship Service and RAF, 1917-19. Air Ministry, 1920. Financial Adviser, Middle East Air Force, 1946-49. *Recreation:* painting. *Address:* Kenilworth Close, Banstead, Surrey. *T:* Burgh Heath 55550. *Club:* National Liberal.

**VERSCHOYLE, Derek Hugo;** Wing Commander, RAFO; Managing Director, Derek Verschoyle (Publishers) Ltd; *b* 24 July 1911; *e s* of late William Denham Verschoyle, Tanrago House, County Sligo, Ireland, and late Iole MacDonnell; *m* 1956, Moyra, *o d* of late James Sutherland, Knockbrex, Kirkcudbright; one *s* one *d*. *Educ:* Malvern; Trinity Coll., Dublin; Paris. Literary Editor of Spectator, 1932-40. Served in Royal Air Force, 1939-46. First Secretary HM Embassy, Rome, 1946-50. Man. Dir, Grower Pubns, and Man. Editor, The Grower, 1960-66; Man. Dir, Deben Bookshop, Woodbridge, and Ancient House Bookshop, Ipswich, 1967-69. *Publications:* XXX Poems, 1931; Spectator's gallery (with Peter Fleming), 1933; The English Novelists, 1936; The Balcony, 1949. *Recreations:* travel, reading, music. *Address:* Lower Upham, Ashfield, near Stowmarket, Suffolk. *T:* Earl Soham 200. *Club:* Garrick.

**VERSEY, Henry Cherry;** Emeritus Professor of Geology, University of Leeds, since 1959; *b* 22 Jan. 1894; *s* of Charles Versey, Welton, East Yorkshire; *m* 1923, Hypatia Ingersoll, *d* of Greevz Fysher, Leeds; two *s* two *d*. *Educ:* Hymers Coll., Hull; University of Leeds. Service with RAOC, European War, 1916-19. Lecturer in Geology, University of Leeds, 1919-49; Reader in Applied Geology, 1949-56, Professor of Geology, 1956-59, University of Leeds. Hon. LLD (Leeds), 1967. Phillips Medal, Yorkshire Geological Society, 1964. *Publications:* Geology of the Appleby District, 1941; Geology and Scenery of the Countryside round Leeds and Bradford, 1948. Many papers on Yorkshire geology. *Recreation:* philately. *Address:* 1 Stainburn Terrace, Leeds LS17 6NJ. *T:* Leeds 682244.

**VERSTONE, Philip Eason,** FJI; author and journalist; *b* 13 Nov. 1882; *s* of late Joseph Verstone, Liverpool; *m* Ethel Yathē (*d* 1947), *e d* of late Max Mandelbom; three *d*. *Educ:* Dr Tate's Laboratory, Liverpool; Liverpool Univ. Educated for analytical chemistry, but entered journalism, 1901; London correspondent of New York Dramatic Mirror, 1903-06; alternated between play writing, dramatic criticism and technical journalism from 1906; joined Fleet Street Volunteers, 1915; 2nd City of London Volunteer Regt, 1916-17; adjutant, 7th City of London Cadet Regt, The Royal Fusiliers, to 1919; Founder, and Editor until 1959, of The Paper Container, 1919; The Paper Sampler, 1929; The Fibreboard Container, 1934; Year Book of British Paper Box Industry, 1952; Councillor of the Institute of Journalists, 1924-53; Chairman, Establishment Cttee of the Institute, 1929-37; Chairman, Post-War Conditions Cttee, 1941-46; Chairman, London District, 1934; President of Institute, Jubilee Year, 1940; President, Press Golfing Society, 1958 (Hon. Treasurer, 1933-54;

Captain, 1952; Vice-President, 1955); Asst Hon. Social Secretary Press Club, London, 1935-46. Is a Freemason. Commendatore dell' Ordine Capitolare e Militare della Libertà, 1948. *Publications:* The Manufacture of Paper Containers, 1922, 2nd edn 1932, 3rd edn 1949, 4th edn 1960; How to be Natural, a three-act play, 1927; Technical articles and dramatic criticism. *Recreations:* theatre, golf. *Address:* Flat 1, Osborn Lodge, 8 West Parade, West Worthing, Sussex. *T:* Worthing 32539. *Club:* Press.

*See also M. V. S. Hunter.*

**VERULAM,** 6th Earl of, *cr* 1815; **John Grimston,** DL; Bt 1628; Baron Forrester (Scotland), 1633; Baron Dunboyne and Viscount Grimston (Ireland), 1719; Baron Verulam (Great Britain), 1790; Viscount Grimston (UK), 1815; *b* 17 July 1912; 2nd *s* of 4th Earl of Verulam (*d* 1949) and *b* of 5th Earl; *S* brother, 1960; *m* 1938, Marjorie Ray, *d* of late W. Duncan; one *s* four *d. Educ:* Oundle Sch.; Christ Church, Oxford. RAFO, 1930-36; AAF 1937; Chairman Enfield Rolling Mills, 1960, Director and General Manager, 1938, Managing Director, 1953; Chairman, Delta Metal Co. Ltd, 1968-. MP (C) St Albans and Mid Herts Div., 1943-45, 1950-Sept. 1959. Hon. Air Commodore, No 1 (County of Hertford) Maritime Headquarters Unit, RAAF, 1963. President: London Chamber of Commerce, 1963-66; International Wrought Non-Ferrous Council, 1963. DL Herts 1963. *Recreation:* shooting. *Heir: s* Viscount Grimston, *qv. Address:* Gorhambury, St Albans, Herts. *T:* St Albans 55000. *Club:* Bath.

*See also Viscount Pollington.*

**VERYKIOS, Dr Panaghiotis Andrew;** Kt Commander of Order of George I, of Greece, and of Order of the Phoenix; MM (Greece); Greek Ambassador to Spain, since 1969; *b* Athens, 1910; *m* 1939, Mary (*née* Dracoulis); three *s. Educ:* Athens and Paris. Law (Dr) and Political Sciences. Greek Diplomatic Service, 1935. Served in the Army, 1939-40. Various diplomatic posts until 1946; Secretary of Embassy, London, 1947-51; Counsellor, Dep. Representative of NATO, Paris, 1952-54; Counsellor of Embassy, Paris, 1954-56; Head of NATO Div., Min. of Foreign Affairs, Athens, 1956-60; Ambassador to: The Netherlands, 1960-64; Norway, 1961-67; Denmark, 1964-67; Iceland, 1967; Court of St James's, 1967-69. Holds foreign decorations. *Publication:* La Prescription en Droit International, 1934 (Paris). *Recreations:* music, stamps and other collections. *Address:* 29 Almagro, Madrid, Spain. *T:* Madrid 4197345. 6 Iras Street, Ekali, Athens. *T:* 8031216. *Club:* Athenian (Athens).

**VESEY,** family name of **Viscount de Vesci.**

**VESEY, Sir Henry;** *see* Vesey, Sir N. H. P.

**VESEY, General Sir Ivo Lucius Beresford,** KCB 1935 (CB 1921); KBE 1923; CMG 1919; DSO 1917; late The Queen's Regiment; *b* 11 Aug. 1876; 2nd *s* of Maj.-General George H. Vesey and Constance, 2nd *d* of George Marshall; *m* 1913, Geraldine (*d* 1963), *e d* of Vice-Admiral Francis J. Foley; one *s* (and one *s* decd). Served S. African War, 1899-1901; European War, 1914-18 (CMG, DSO); Director of Recruiting and Organisation, War Office, 1919-23; Director of Organisation and Staff Duties, Air Ministry, 1923-29; Maj.-Gen. 1928; commanded 48th South Midland Division, TA, 1930-31; Director of Staff Duties, War Office, 1931-34; Lt-Gen. 1934; GOC-in-C, Western Command, India, 1935-36; Southern Command, India, 1936-37; General, 1937; Chief of General Staff, India, 1937-39; retired pay, 1939; Colonel of Queen's Royal Regt, 1939-45; Officer Legion of Honour and of the Order of the Crown, St Michael and Lazarus, Croix de Guerre. *Address:* Gosfield Hall, Halstead, Essex.

**VESEY, Sir (Nathaniel) Henry (Peniston),** Kt 1965; CBE 1953; Chairman, H. A. & E. Smith Ltd, since 1939; Chairman, Bank of N. T. Butterfield & Son Ltd, since 1970; Member of House of Assembly, Bermuda, since 1938; *b* 1 June 1901; *s* of late Hon. Nathaniel Vesey, Devonshire, Bermuda; *m* 1920, Louise Marie, *d* of late Captain J. A. Stubbs, Shelly Bay, Bermuda; two *s. Educ:* Saltus Grammar Sch. Chairman: Food and Supplies Control Board, 1941-42; Board of Trade, 1943; Finance Cttee of House of Assembly, 1943-44; Bermuda Trade Development Board, 1945-56, 1960-69; Board of Civil Aviation, 1957-59; Board of Agriculture, 1957-59. MEC, 1948-57. Mem. Executive Council for Tourism and Trade 1968-69. *Recreations:* fishing, golf. *Address:* Windward, Shelly Bay, Bermuda. *T:* 3-0186. *Clubs:* Royal Aero; Royal Bermuda Yacht, Mid Ocean (Bermuda); Bankers (New York).

**VESEY-FITZGERALD, Brian Seymour;** Author; Member Honourable Society of Cymmrodorion; President of the British Fairground Society, 1953-63; Editor-in-Chief of The Field, 1938-46; Chairman of Preliminary Enquiry into Cause of Canine Hysteria, 1938; Chairman, Association of School Natural History Societies, 1947-48; Member of Institute for the Study of Animal Behaviour; Member of Gypsy Lore Society. Field Fare Broadcasts, 1940-45; There and Back Broadcasts, 1947-49. Editor of Country Books since 1943. *Publications:* Amateur Boxing, Professional Boxing (Lonsdale Library, Sporting Records), 1936; Badgers Funeral, 1937; A Book of British Waders, 1939; Hampshire Scene, 1940; The Noctule, 1941; Programme for Agriculture, 1941; A Country Chronicle, 1942; Farming in Britain, 1942; Hedgerow and Field, 1943; Gypsies of Britain, 1944; British Countryside, 1946; British Game, 1946; The Book of the Horse, 1946; It's My Delight, 1947; British Bats, 1947; A Child's Biology, 1948; Bird Biology for Beginners, 1948; The Book of the Dog, 1948; Background to Birds, 1949; Hampshire, 1949; Rivermouth, 1949; (co-ed) Game Fish of the World, 1950; The River Avon, 1951; Gypsy Borrow, 1953; Winchester, 1953; British Birds and their Nests, 1953; More British Birds and their Nests, 1954; Nature Recognition, 1955; Cats, 1956; A Third Book of British Birds and their Nests, 1956; The Domestic Dog, 1957; A Book of Wildflowers, 1958; Instructions to Young Naturalists, 1959; The Beauty of Cats, 1959; A Book of Garden Flowers, 1960; The Beauty of Dogs, 1960; A Book of Trees, 1962; About Dogs, 1963; The Cat Lover's Encyclopædia, 1963; Foxes in Britain, 1964; Animal Anthology, 1965; The Dog-Owners Encyclopædia, 1965; Portrait of the New Forest, 1966; Garden Alive, 1967; The World of Reptiles, 1968; The Vanishing Wild Life of Britain, 1969; The World of Ants, Bees and Wasps, 1969; The Domestic Cat, 1969. *Recreations:* bird-watching, gardening. *Address:* c/o Laurence Pollinger Ltd, 18 Maddox Street, W1.

**VESTEY,** family name of **Baron Vestey.**

**VESTEY,** 3rd Baron, *cr* 1922, of Kingswood; **Samuel George Armstrong Vestey;** Bt, *cr* 1913; *b* 19 March 1941; *s* of late Captain the Hon. William Howarth Vestey (killed in action in Italy, 1944; *o s* of 2nd Baron Vestey and Frances Sarah Howarth) and of Pamela Helen Fullerton, *d* of George Nesbitt Armstrong; *S* grandfather, 1954; *m* 1970, Kathryn Mary, *er d* of John Eccles, Moor Park, Herts. *Educ:* Eton. Lieut, Scots Guards. Director, Union International Co. Ltd, and associated companies. *Recreations:* polo, shooting. *Heir:* *b* Hon. Mark William Vestey [*b* 16 April 1943. *Educ:* Eton]. *Address:* Stowell Park, Northleach, Glos. *Clubs:* White's; Melbourne (Melbourne).

**VESTEY, Sir (John) Derek,** 2nd Bt, *cr* 1921; *b* 4 June 1914; *s* of John Joseph Vestey (*d* 1932) and Dorothy Mary (*d* 1918), *d* of John Henry Beaver, Gawthorpe Hall, Bingley, Yorkshire; *g s* of Sir Edmund Vestey, 1st Bt; *S* grandfather 1953; *m* 1938, Phyllis Irene, *o d* of H. Brewer, Banstead, Surrey; one *s* one *d*. *Educ:* Leys Sch., Cambridge. Served War of 1939-45: Flt-Lieut, RAFVR, 1940-45. *Heir:* *s* Paul Edmund Vestey [*b* 15 Feb. 1944. *Educ:* Radley]. *Address:* 5 Carlton Gardens, SW1; Harcombe House, Ropley, Hants. *Clubs:* Marylebone Cricket, Royal Automobile.

*See also R. A. Vestey.*

**VESTEY, Ronald Arthur;** DL; Chairman: Blue Star Line; Lamport & Holt Line; Booth Steamship Co.; Albion Insurance Co.; Western United Investment Co.; Director Union International Co. and Associated Companies, and other Companies; *b* 10 May 1898; 4th but *e surv s* of Sir Edmund Hoyle Vestey, 1st Bt; *m* 1923, Florence Ellen McLean (*d* 1966), *e d* of Colonel T. G. Luis, VD, Broughty Ferry, Angus; one *s* three *d*. *Educ:* Malvern Coll. Travelled extensively throughout world, with interests in many countries. Owner of Thurlow Estate, Suffolk; farms extensively in Suffolk. High Sheriff of Suffolk, 1961; DL Suffolk, 1970. *Recreations:* shooting, fishing. *Address:* Great Thurlow Hall, Suffolk. *T:* Thurlow 240. *Clubs:* Flyfishers', Carlton; Highland (Inverness).

**VEYSEY, Geoffrey Charles,** CB 1948; *b* 20 Dec. 1895; *e s* of late Charles Veysey, Exeter; *m* 1925, Eileen Agnes, *d* of late Charles Henry Byers, Gunnersbury. *Educ:* Latymer Upper Sch., Hammersmith. Served European War, 1914-18. Lieut, RGA. Entered Ministry of Labour, 1919; Private Secretary to Parliamentary Secretaries and Permanent Secretaries of Ministry, 1929-32; Assistant Secretary, 1938; Principal Assistant Secretary, 1944; Under-Secretary, Ministry of Labour and National Service, 1946-60. *Address:* 8 Stokes House, Sutherland Avenue, Bexhill-on-Sea, Sussex. *T:* Bexhill-on-Sea 4320. *Club:* Athenæum.

**VIBERT, McInroy Este;** Consular Service, retired; *b* Chiswick, 6 June 1894; *o s* of late Arthur Reginald Vibert and Margaret Eleanor Fraser; *m* 1st, Joyce Havell; one *s* one *d*; 2nd, Ellen Fiebiger-Guermanova. *Educ:* Taunton Sch.; France and Germany. Served European War, 1914-18, 10th Royal Fusiliers; Vice-Consul at Brussels, 1919, and subsequently at Philadelphia, Stettin, Koenigsberg, Memel, Frankfort-on-Main, Punta Arenas, Cologne, and Tunis; Consul at Sarajevo, 1936-39, and Split, 1939-41, Lisbon, 1941-44, Barcelona, 1944, Curacao, 1944-45; Consul-General (local rank) and Counsellor of Legation at Havana, 1945-47; Chargé d'Affaires, July 1946; Foreign Office, 1947-48; Consul at Vigo; retired, 1950, on Pension. *Recreations:* water-colour painting, philately. *Address:* Matinada, S'Arraco, Mallorca, Spain.

**VICARS-HARRIS, Noël Hedley,** CMG 1953; *b* 22 Nov. 1901; *o s* of late C. F. Harris and Evelyn C. Vicars, The Gate House, Rugby; *m* 1st, 1926, Maria Guimarães of Sao Paulo, Brazil (marr. dissolved, 1939); two *s*; 2nd, 1940, Joan Marguerite Francis; one *s*. *Educ:* Charterhouse; St John's Coll., Cambridge. BA Agric., 1924. Employed in Brazil by Brazil Plantations Syndicate Ltd, 1924-27; HM Colonial Service, Tanganyika, 1927-55; Official Member of Legislative and Executive Councils, Tanganyika, 1950-Nov. 1953; Member for Lands and Mines, Tanganyika, 1950-55. *Recreation:* gardening. *Address:* Bampfylde Cottage, Sparkford, Somerset. *T:* North Cadbury 454.

**VICARY, Col. Alexander Craven,** CB 1945; DSO and Bar, 1918; MC 1915; late Gloucestershire Regiment; *b* 1888; *m* 1919, Kathleen Hamilton (*d* 1942), *d* of late F. Hilton Green, JP; one *d* (one *s* killed in action, 1943); *m* 1947, Bridget, *widow* of Commander J. B. W. Hale, RNVR, and *d* of late John L. Hunter, Larkbeare, Talaton, Devon. *Educ:* Newton Coll.; RMA, Woolwich. Entered Army, 1908; Lieut and Adjutant, 2nd Batt., Gloucestershire Regt, 1914; Captain, 1914; acting Lt-Col, 1917-19; Major, 1925; Bt Lt-Col, 1929; Adjutant, 1919; Passed Staff Coll., Camberley, 1921; held Staff appointments GSO 3, Scottish Command, Bde Major Small Arms Sch., GSO 1, War Office; served European War, 1914-19, France, Macedonia, Russia (DSO and bar, Bt-Major, MC, Knight of Legion of Honour, despatches six times); retired pay, 1930. Served War of 1939-45: GSO 1, 51st Div. Comdg SAS Italy and Burmah (despatches, CB). Lord of the Manor of Gidleigh. *Address:* Scorhill, Gidleigh, near Chagford, Devon.

**VICARY, Rev. Canon Douglas Reginald;** Headmaster of the King's School, Rochester, since 1957; Hon. Canon of Rochester Cathedral; *b* 24 Sept. 1916; *e s* of R. W. Vicary, Walthamstow; *m* 1947, Ruth, *y d* of late F. J. L. Hickinbotham, JP, and of Mrs Hickinbotham, Edgbaston; two *s* two *d*. *Educ:* Sir George Monoux Grammar Sch., Walthamstow; Trinity Coll., Oxford (Open Scholar), Wycliffe Hall, Oxford. 1st Class Nat. Sci. 1939; BSc 1939, MA 1942; Diploma in Theology with distinction, 1940; deacon, 1940; priest, 1941. Asst Chaplain and House Master, St Lawrence Coll., Ramsgate, while evacuated at Courteenhall, Northampton, 1940-44; Chaplain, Hertford Coll., Oxford, 1945-48; Tutor at Wycliffe Hall, 1945-47, Chaplain 1947-48; Director of Religious Education, Rochester Diocese, 1948-57; Minor Canon, Rochester Cathedral, 1949-52; Exam. Chaplain to Bishop of Rochester, 1950-; Canon Residentiary and Precentor, 1952-57. Secretary, CACTM Exams Cttee and GOE, 1952-57; Director of Post-Ordination Training, 1952-57. Member: Kent Education Cttee, 1948-57; Archbishop's Liturgical Commn, 1955-62; Schools Council, C of E Board of Education; Court of the University of Kent at Canterbury. FRSA 1960. *Address:* Oriel House, Rochester, Kent. *T:* Medway 43913.

**VICK, F(rancis) Arthur,** OBE 1945; BSc, PhD; FIEE, FInstP; President and Vice-Chancellor, Queen's University of Belfast, since 1966; *b* 5 June 1911; *s* of late Wallace Devenport Vick and late Clara (*née* Taylor); *m* 1943, Elizabeth Dorothy Story; one *d*. *Educ:* Waverley Grammar School, Birmingham; Birmingham Univ. Asst Lectr in Physics, University Coll., London, 1936-39, Lectr, 1939-44; Asst Dir of Scientific Research, Min. of Supply, 1939-44; Lectr in Physics, Manchester Univ., 1944-47, Sen. Lectr, 1947-50; Prof. of Physics, University Coll. of N Staffs, 1950-59 (Vice-Principal, 1950-54, Actg Principal, 1952-53); Dep. Dir, AERE, Harwell, 1959-60, Dir, 1960-64; Dir of Research Group, UKAEA, 1961-64; Mem. for Research, 1964-66. Institute of

Physics: Mem. Bd, 1946-51; Chm., Manchester and District Branch, 1948-51; Vice-Pres., 1953-56; Hon. Sec., 1956-60. Chairman: Manchester Fedn of Scientific Societies, 1949-51; Naval Educn Adv. Cttee, 1964-; RDA Academic Adv. Council, MoD, 1969-. Pres., Assoc. of Teachers in Colls and Depts of Educn, 1964-; Vice-Pres., Arts Council of NI, 1966-. Member: Adv. Council on Bldg Research, Min. of Works, 1955-59; Scientific Adv. Council, Min. of Supply, 1956-59; UGC, 1959-66; Colonial Univ. Grants Adv. Cttee, 1960-65; Adv. Council on Research and Develt, Min. of Power, 1960-63; Nuclear Safety Adv. Cttee, Min. of Power, 1960-66; Governing Body, Nat. Inst. for Research in Nuclear Science, 1964-65. Kt Comdr, Liberian Humane Order of African Redemption, 1962. *Publications:* various scientific papers and contributions to books. *Recreations:* music, gardening, using tools. *Address:* Vice-Chancellor's Lodge, 16 Lennoxvale, Belfast BT9 5BY. *T:* Belfast 665370; Queen's University of Belfast, Belfast BT7 1NN. *T:* Belfast 45133. *Clubs:* Athenæum, Savile.

**VICK, Reginald Martin,** OBE; TD; MA; MChir, FRCS; Consulting Surgeon to St Bartholomew's Hospital, London; *s* of Richard William Vick, JP, West Hartlepool, Co. Durham; *m* 1920, Mary Kate, *d* of Sir Reginald Neville, 1st Bt; four *d. Educ:* Leys Sch., Cambridge; Jesus Coll., Cambridge; Saint Bartholomew's Hospital. Served in Territorial Army, 1912-20; European War, France and Salonika, 1914-18 (despatches four times); Warden of St Bartholomew's Hospital, 1920-36; Consulting Surgeon to several hospitals (Walton, Bexhill-on-Sea, etc); late Asst Surgeon to Metropolitan Hospital; late Officer i/c Surgical Division Friern War Emergency Hospital; late Director of Cancer Records Bureau, S Western Area of England. *Publications:* medical. *Address:* Old Schoolhouse, Baas Manor, Broxbourne, Herts. *T:* Hoddesdon 62559. *Club:* United University.

*See also Admiral Sir A. N. C. Bingley.*

**VICK, Richard (William); His Honour Judge Vick;** County Court Judge, since 1969; Deputy Chairman of Quarter Sessions for Middlesex Area of Greater London, since 1965; *b* 9 Dec. 1917; *s* of late Richard William Vick, JP, and Hilda Josephine (*née* Carlton), Windsor, Berks; *m* 1947, Judith Jean, *d* of Denis Franklin Warren, Eastry, Kent; one *s* two *d. Educ:* Stowe; Jesus Coll., Cambridge (BA). Served in RNVR, 1939-46 (Lieut). Called to Bar, Inner Temple, 1940. Dep. Chairman, W Kent QS, 1961-62; Dep. Chairman, Kent QS, 1962-65. *Publication:* The Administration of Civil Justice in England and Wales, 1967. *Recreations:* sailing, shooting, swimming, bridge. *Address:* 32 Emperor's Gate, Kensington, SW7. *T:* 01-373 0457. *Club:* Hawks (Cambridge).

**VICKERS, Sir (Charles) Geoffrey,** VC 1915; Kt, *cr* 1946; Solicitor, Administrator and Author; *b* 13 Oct. 1894; *y s* of C. H. Vickers, Nottingham; *m* 1st, 1918, Helen Tregoning (marr. diss. 1934), *y d* of A. H. Newton, Bexhill, Sussex; one *s* one *d*; 2nd, 1935, Ethel Ellen, *y d* of late H. R. B. Tweed, Laindon Frith, Billericay, Essex; one *s. Educ:* Oundle Sch.; Merton Coll., Oxford (MA). Served World War I with the Sherwood Foresters and other regts (2nd Lt-Major, 1915-18). Admitted Solicitor, 1923; Partner, Slaughter & May, 1926-45. World War II, re-commissioned (Colonel), specially employed; seconded as Deputy Dir.-Gen., Ministry of Economic Warfare, in charge of economic intelligence, and Member, Joint Intelligence Cttee of Chiefs of Staff, 1941-45. Legal adviser to National Coal Board, 1946-48, Board Member in charge of manpower, training, education, health and welfare, 1948-55; Director, Parkinson Cowan Ltd, 1955-65. Member, many public and professional bodies including: London Passenger Transport Board, 1941-46; Council of Law Society, 1944-48; Med. Research Council, 1952-60; Chairman, Research Cttee of Mental Health Research Fund, 1951-67. *Publications:* (1953-) 40 papers and 5 books on application of system theory to management, government, medicine and human ecology, including The Art of Judgement, 1965, Value Systems and Social Process, 1968, Freedom in a Rocking Boat, 1970. *Address:* Little Mead, Goring-on-Thames, Reading, Berks. *T:* Goring 2933.

**VICKERS, Dame Joan (Helen),** DBE 1964 (MBE 1946); MP (C) Devonport Division of Plymouth since 1955; *e d* of late Horace Cecil Vickers and late Lilian Monro Lambert Grose. *Educ:* St Monica's Coll., Burgh Heath, Surrey. Member of the London County Council for the Norwood Division of Lambeth, 1937-46. Contested (C) South Poplar, 1945. Served with British Red Cross in SE Asia (MBE); Colonial Service in Malaya, 1946-50. Chairman: Anglo-Indonesian Society; British Vigilance Assoc.; Status of Women Cttee; Foreign Affairs Cttee, Europe Union of Women. President: International Cttee for Suppression of Traffic in Persons; Inst. of Qualified Private Secretaries, 1968-; Member, Commonwealth Parliamentary Assoc.; UK Delegate, UN Status of Women Commission, 1960-64. UK Delegate (Cons), Council of Europe and Western European Union, 1967-. Netherlands Red Cross Medal. *Address:* House of Commons, SW1; 6 Albemarle Villas, Devonport.

**VICKERS, Jon,** CC (Canada) 1968; Canadian tenor; *b* Prince Albert, Saskatchewan, 1926; *m* 1953, Henrietta Outerbridge; three *s* two *d.* Studied under George Lambert, Royal Conservatory of Music, Toronto. Made debut with Toronto Opera Company, 1952; Stratford (Ontario) Festival, 1956. Joined Royal Opera House, Covent Garden, 1957. First sang at: Bayreuth Festival, 1958; Vienna State Opera, San Francisco Opera, and Chicago Lyric, 1959; Metropolitan, New York, and La Scala, Milan, 1960; Buenos Aires, 1962; Salzburg Festival, 1966. *Films:* Carmen; Pagliacci. Has made many recordings. Presbyterian. Hon. Dr: University of Saskatchewan, 1963; Bishop's Univ., 1965. Canada Centennial Medal, 1967. *Address:* c/o John Coast, 1 Park Close, SW1; c/o Metropolitan Opera Company, New York City, New York, USA.

**VICKERS, Thomas Douglas,** CMG 1956; *b* 25 Sept. 1916; 2nd *s* of late Ronald Vickers, Scaitcliffe, Englefield Green, Surrey; *m* 1951, Margaret Awdry, *o c* of late E. A. Headley, Wagga, NSW; one *s* one *d. Educ:* Eton; King's Coll., Cambridge (MA Hons). Cadet, Colonial Administrative Service, 1938. Served War of 1939-45; Coldstream Guards, 1940-45. Colonial Office, 1938-40 and 1945-50; Gold Coast, 1950-53; Colonial Secretary, British Honduras, 1953-60; Chief Secretary, Mauritius, 1960-67, Dep. Governor, 1967-68; retired from HMOCS, Oct. 1968. Imperial Cancer Research Fund, 1969-. *Address:* Braeside, Englefield Green, Surrey. *T:* Egham 2173. *Club:* Travellers'.

**VICKERS, William John,** CMG 1950; MRCS, LRCP, DPH Cambridge; DTM&H Cambridge; Barrister-at-Law (Inner Temple); Deputy Coroner for East Staffordshire and

County Borough of Burton-on-Trent, since 1959; *b* 21 March 1898; *s* of late William Vickers; *m* 1939, Elizabeth Rachel, *d* of late S. Vernon Jackson; one *s* one *d*. *Educ:* Privately; Birmingham Medical Sch. Served European War, 1917-19, 2nd Lieut, RFA; resident Staff, General Hospital, Birmingham, 1923-25; Colonial Medical Service, 1925-54 (retired 1954); Malaya, 1925-38; Medical Officer, Health Officer, Acting Senior Health Officer, Kedah; Palestine, 1938-44: Senior Medical Officer, Acting Dep. Director of Medical Services; British West Indies, 1944-45: Adviser on Human Nutrition to Development and Welfare Organisation. British Military Administration, Singapore (Temporary Colonel), 1945-46; gazetted Hon. Colonel. Director of Medical Services, Colony of Singapore, 1946-54; MLC, Colony of Singapore, 1948-54. CStJ, 1951. *Publications:* (Government): (jointly) Health Survey of the State of Kedah, 1936; A Nutritional Economic Review of War-Time Palestine, 1944. *Address:* 174 Ashby Road, Burton-on-Trent, Staffs. *T:* Burton-on-Trent 2899. *Clubs:* East India and Sports; various (Singapore); Burton (Abbey).

**VICKERS, Lt-Gen. Wilmot Gordon Hilton,** CB 1942; OBE 1919; *b* 8 June 1890; *s* of late Lt-Col Hilton Vickers, IA; *m* Mary Catherine (*decd*), *d* of Dr A. E. Nuttall; two *s*. *Educ:* United Services Coll., Westward Ho!, and Windsor (now Haileybury and Imperial Service Coll.). Commissioned Indian Army (Unattached List), 1910; 2nd Lieut, Indian Army, 1911; Captain, 1915; Major, 1926; Bt Lt-Col, 1931; Col, 1935; Maj.-Gen., 1940; Lt-Gen., 1943; Comdt and Chief Instructor, Equitation Sch., India, 1934-35; Dep. Dir of Staff Duties, India, 1935-37; Brigade Comdr, India, 1939-40; Dir of Supplies and Transport, India, 1940-41; Maj.-Gen. i/c Administration, Iraq-Persia, 1941-42; Quarter-master-General, India, 1942-44; retired, 1944. DL County of Gloucestershire. County Cadet Commandant, Gloucestershire, Army Cadet Force, 1946-55. County Chief Warden, Civil Defence, Gloucestershire, 1949-60. *Address:* Hadley House, Bayshill, Cheltenham. *Clubs:* Cavalry; New (Cheltenham).

**VICKERY, Sir Philip Crawford,** Kt, *cr* 1948; CIE 1939; OBE 1923; *b* 23 Feb. 1890; *s* of late John Evans Vickery and Alice Maud Mary Vickery; *m* 1920, Phyllis Field Fairweather; one *s* (*yr s*, Coldstream Guards, died of wounds in Italy, April 1945). *Educ:* Portora Royal Sch., Enniskillen; Dean Close Sch., Cheltenham; Trinity Coll., Dublin. Joined Indian Police, 1909; Coronation Durbar, Delhi, 1911; served European War, 1915-21 and War of 1939-45; Acting Lieut-Colonel, Sept. 1939, and Colonel, 1942. Commonwealth Relations Office, 1952-65. *Clubs:* East India and Sports, Royal Automobile.

**VICTORIA, Sir (Joseph Aloysius) Donatus,** Kt, *cr* 1950; CBE 1948 (OBE 1945); JP; Merchant and Landed Proprietor; *b* 15 Oct. 1893; *s* of Joseph Salvadore Victoria and Maria Nevizal Paiva; *m* 1916, Mary Louise Pancras de Rose; one *s* one *d*. *Educ:* St Benedict's Coll., Colombo; St Joseph's Coll., Trichinopoly. JP 1947. *Recreations:* riding and horse racing. *Address:* Alacoque, Skelton Road, Colombo 5, Ceylon. *T:* 8374. *Clubs:* Orient, '80' (Colombo); Cosmopolitan (Madras).

**VICTORIA NYANZA, Bishop of,** since 1963; **Rt. Rev. Maxwell Lester Wiggins;** *b* 5 Feb. 1915; *s* of Herbert Lester and Isobel Jane Wiggins; *m* 1941, Margaret Agness (*née* Evans); one *s* two *d*. *Educ:* Christchurch Boys' High Sch., NZ; Canterbury University College, NZ (BA). Asst Curate, St Mary's, Merivale, NZ, 1938; Vicar of Oxford, NZ, 1941; CMS Missionary, Diocese Central Tanganyika, 1945; Head Master, Alliance Secondary Sch., Dodoma, 1948; Provost, Cathedral of Holy Spirit, Dodoma, 1949; Principal, St Philip's Theological Coll., and Canon of Cathedral of Holy Spirit, Dodoma, 1954; Archdeacon of Lake Province, 1956; Asst Bishop of Central Tanganyika, 1959. *Address:* Box 278, Mwanza, Tanzania. *T:* Mwanza 2494.

**VIDAL, Gore;** author; *b* 3 Oct. 1925; *s* of Eugene and Nina Gore Vidal. *Educ:* Phillips Exeter Academy, New Hampshire, USA (grad. 1943). Army of the US, 1943-46: Private to Warrant Officer (jg) and First Mate, Army FS-35, Pacific Theatre Ops. Democratic-Liberal candidate for US Congress, 1960; apptd to President Kennedy's Adv. Council of the Arts, 1961-63. *Publications: novels:* Williwaw, 1946; In a Yellow Wood, 1947; The City and the Pillar, 1948; The Season of Comfort, 1949; A Search for the King, 1950; Dark Green, Bright Red, 1950; The Judgment of Paris, 1952; Messiah, 1954; Julian, 1964; Washington, DC, 1967; Myra Breckinridge, 1968; Two Sisters, 1970; *essays:* Rocking the Boat, 1962; Reflections upon a Sinking Ship, 1969; *short stories:* A Thirsty Evil, 1956; *plays:* Visit to a Small Planet (NY prod.), 1957; The Best Man (NY prod.), 1960; Romulus (adapted from F. Dürrenmatt) (NY prod.), 1962; Weekend (NY prod.), 1968; On the March to the Sea (German prod.), 1962; *screenplays,* from 1955: Wedding Breakfast, 1957; Suddenly Last Summer, 1958; The Best Man, 1964, etc; *television plays:* 1954-56: The Death of Billy the Kid (translated to screen as The Lefthanded Gun, 1959), etc; *literary and political criticism for:* NY Review of Books, Esquire, Partisan Review, TLS, etc. *Recreations:* as noted above. *Address:* Casa Willi, Klosters, Graubünden, Switzerland. *T:* 41819.

**VIDLER, Rev. Alexander Roper,** LittD; Fellow of King's College, Cambridge, 1956-67; Dean, 1956-66; *b* 1899; *s* of late Leopold Amon Vidler, JP, Rye, Sussex; unmarried. *Educ:* Sutton Valence Sch.; Selwyn Coll., Cambridge. BA 2nd Class Theol. Tripos, 1921; MA 1925; Norrisian Prize, 1933; BD 1938; LittD 1957; University of Edinburgh, DD, 1946; Hon. DD: University of Toronto, 1961; College of Emmanuel and St Chad, Saskatoon, 1966. Wells Theological Coll.; Deacon, 1922; Priest, 1923; Curate of St Philip's, Newcastle upon Tyne, 1922-24; of St Aidan's, Birmingham, 1925-31; on staff of the Oratory House, Cambridge, 1931-38; Warden of St Deiniol's Library, Hawarden, 1939-48; Hon. Canon of Derby Cathedral, 1946-48; Canon of St George's Chapel, Windsor, 1948-56; licensed by Cambridge Univ. to preach throughout England, 1957; University Lecturer in Divinity, 1959-67; Commissary for Bishop of New Guinea, 1936-62; Hale Lecturer (USA), 1947; Birkbeck Lecturer (Trinity Coll., Cambridge), 1953; Firth Lecturer (Nottingham Univ.), 1955; Robertson Lecturer (Glasgow Univ.), 1964; Sarum Lecturer (Oxford Univ.), 1968-69. Ed. of Theology, 1939-64; Secretary of the Christian Frontier Council, 1949-56; Co-editor of The Frontier, 1950-52. *Publications:* Magic and Religion, 1930; Sex, Marriage and Religion, 1932; The Modernist Movement in the Roman Church, 1934; A Plain Man's Guide to Christianity, 1936; God's Demand and Man's Response, 1938; God's Judgement on Europe, 1940; Secular Despair and Christian Faith, 1941; Christ's Strange Work, 1944; The Orb and the Cross, 1945; Good News for Mankind, 1947; The Theology of F. D. Maurice, 1949; Christian Belief, 1950; Prophecy and Papacy, 1954; Christian Belief and This World, 1956;

Essays in Liberality, 1957; Windsor Sermons, 1958; The Church in an Age of Revolution, 1961; A Century of Social Catholicism, 1964; 20th Century Defenders of the Faith, 1965; F. D. Maurice and Company, 1966; A Variety of Catholic Modernists, 1970; (jointly): The Development of Modern Catholicism, 1933; The Gospel of God and the Authority of the Church, 1937; Natural Law, 1946; Editor, Soundings: Essays concerning Christian Understanding, 1962; Objections to Christian Belief, 1963. *Recreations:* gardening, golf and beekeeping. *Address:* The Old Stone House, Rye, Sussex.

**VIDOR, King (Wallis);** Independent Film Director and Producer (US); *b* Galveston, Texas, 8 Feb. 1896; *s* of Chas S. Vidor and Kate (*née* Wallis); *m* 1st, 1919, Florence Vidor; one *d*; 2nd, 1927, Eleanor Boardman; two *d*; 3rd, 1937, Elizabeth Hill. *Educ:* Peacock Military College, Texas; Jacob Tome Institute, Maryland. Directed films when aged 19, in Texas, 1914; in film industry worked as cameraman, writer and actor; directed again from 1918. Films directed include: Turn in the Road; The Jack Knife Man; Peg O' My Heart; Wild Oranges; The Big Parade; La Bohème; The Crowd; Hallelujah; Street Scene; The Champ; Bird of Paradise; Our Daily Bread; The Texas Rangers; Stella Dallas; The Citadel; Northwest Passage; HM Pulham Esq.; American Romance; Duel in the Sun; The Fountainhead; Ruby Gentry; Man Without a Star; War and Peace; Solomon and Sheba. D. W. Griffith award by Screen Directors Guild (for outstanding contributions in film, direction over a long period of years), 1957; many awards for various films throughout America and Europe. Golden Thistle Award, Edinburgh Festival, 1964. Cavaliere Ufficiale, Italy, 1970. *Publications:* A Tree is a Tree (autobiography), 1953 (New York), also published in England; Guerra e Pace, Tree (autobiography), 1953 (New York), also published in England; Guerra e Pace, 1956 (Italy). *Recreations:* golf; plays classical Spanish Guitar; paints in oils. *Address:* 1880 Century Park East, Suite 211, Los Angeles, Calif 90067. *T:* 553-5111. *Clubs:* Academy Motion Picture Arts and Sciences, Bel Air Country, Screen Directors Guild, PEN (USA).

**VIELER, Geoffrey Herbert,** FCA; Managing Director, Posts and National Giro, and Member of Board, Post Office Corporation, since 1969; *b* 21 Aug. 1910; *s* of late Herbert Charles Stuart Vieler, Huddersfield, and Emily Mary; *m* 1934, Phyllis Violet; one *d*. *Educ:* Fairway Sch., Bexhill-on-Sea. Articled to and with Vale & West, Chartered Accountants, Reading, 1927-41 (qual. 1932); War Service, 1941-46: commnd RAOC, 1943, Major 1945; joined staff of Binder, Hamlyn & Co., Chartered Accountants, 1946, Partner 1959-69. Mem. Techn. Adv. Cttee, Inst. of Chartered Accountants in England and Wales, 1967-. *Publications:* papers on subjects of professional interest to chartered accountants. *Recreations:* Thames cruising, gardening, lecturing, stamp collecting. *Address:* Addington House, 14 Addington Road, Reading RG1 5PJ. *T:* Reading 61606; Riversmeet, Mill Lane, Lower Shiplake RG9 3LY. *T:* Wargrave 3401.

**VIERTEL, Deborah Kerr;** *see* Kerr, D. J.

**VIGARS, Robert Lewis;** Chairman, Environmental Planning (formerly Planning and Transportation) Committee, Greater London Council, since 1967; Partner in Simmons & Simmons, London, EC2, since 1951; *b* 26 May 1923; *s* of Francis Henry Vigars and Susan Laurina May Vigars (*née* Lewis); *m* 1962, Margaret Ann Christine, *y d* of late Sir John Walton, KCIE, CB, MC, and of Lady Walton; two *d*. *Educ:* Truro Cathedral Sch.; London Univ. (LLB (Hons)). Served War of 1939-45: RA and Royal Corps of Signals, 1942-47; attached Indian Army (Captain), 1944-47; Captain, Princess Louise's Kensington Regt, TA, 1951-54. Qualified as solicitor (Hons), 1948. Young Conservative deleg. to World Assembly of Youth at Dakar (W Africa), 1952. Member: Kensington Borough Council, 1953-59; London and Home Counties Traffic Adv. Cttee, 1956-58; London Roads (Nugent) Cttee, 1958-59; LCC and GLC (South Kensington), 1955-; Standing Conf. on London and SE Regional Planning and of Transport Co-ordinating Council for London. *Publication:* Let Our Cities Live (Bow Gp, jointly). *Recreation:* mountain walking. *Address:* 24 Cope Place, Kensington, W8. *Club:* Hurlingham.

**VILLIERS,** family name of **Earls of Jersey** and **Clarendon.**

**VILLIERS;** *see* De Villiers.

**VILLIERS, Viscount; George Henry Child Villiers;** *b* 29 Aug. 1948; *s* and *heir* of 9th Earl of Jersey, *qv*; *m* 1969, Verna, 2nd *d* of K. A. Stott, Aux Virages, St Mary, Jersey. *Educ:* Eton; Millfield. Late The Royal Hussars (PWO), now Army Reserve. *Address:* Radier Manor, Longueville, Jersey, CI.

**VILLIERS, Alan John,** DSC; *b* 23 Sept. 1903; *s* of Leon Joseph Villiers and Anastasia Hayes; *m* 1940, Nancie, *o d* of Alban Henry and Mabel Wills, Melbourne; two *s* one *d*. *Educ:* State Schools, Essendon High School, Melbourne. Went to sea 1919 in sail, whaling in Antarctic with Norwegian Carl Anton Larsen's first Ross Sea Expedition in whaler Sir James Clark Ross, 1923-24; joined Captain De Cloux in purchase of four-masted barque Parma, 1931; bought Danish schoolship Georg Stage June 1934, renamed her Joseph Conrad and sailed 58,000 miles round world, 1934, 1935, 1936; sailing in Kuweit dhows in Persian Gulf–Zanzibar trade, 1938-39; Lieut, RNVR, 1940-42; Lt Cdr 1943; Comdr 1944. Commanded 'A' Squadron of Landing Craft (Infantry) in the invasions of Italy and Normandy (DSC) and at the occupation of Rangoon, Malaya, and East Indies; Master, training ship Warspite, Outward Bound Sea School, Aberdovey, N Wales, 1949; sailed with Portuguese Arctic codfishing fleet in schooner Argus, 1950. Commendador of Portuguese Order of St James of the Sword. Volunteered as Master of Mayflower replica, 1956, and sailed the vessel to the USA, 1957. In command of square-rigged ships for films: Moby Dick, 1955; John Paul Jones, 1958; Billy Budd, 1961; Hawaii, 1965. President, Soc. for Nautical Research; FRGS; Trustee of National Maritime Museum; Governor Cutty Sark Preservation Soc.; Member: HMS Victory Technical Advisory Committee; Ships Cttee, Maritime Trust. *Publications:* Whaling in the Frozen South; Falmouth for Orders; By Way of Cape Horn; The Sea in Ships; Sea Dogs of To-day; Voyage of the Parma; Vanished Fleets; The Last of the Windships; Cruise of the Conrad; Stormalong; The Making of a Sailor, 1938; Sons of Sinbad, 1940; The Set of the Sails, 1949; The Coral Sea, 1950; The Quest of the Schooner Argus, 1951 (Camões Prize, Portugal); The Indian Ocean, 1952; The Way of a Ship, 1954; Posted Missing, 1956; Pioneers of the Seven Seas, 1956; The Western Ocean, 1957; Give Me a Ship to Sail, 1958; The New Mayflower, 1959; The Oceans, 1963; The Battle of Trafalgar, 1965; Captain Cook, the Seamen's Seaman, 1967; The War with Cape

Horn, 1970. *Recreations:* sailing, photography. *Address:* 1a Lucerne Road, Oxford. *T:* Oxford 55632. *Clubs:* Naval; Royal Harwich Yacht (Harwich); Royal Cruising; Circumnavigators (New York); Cosmos (Washington, DC).

**VILLIERS, Charles Hyde,** MC 1945; Chairman, Guinness Mahon & Company Ltd, since 1971; Director: Guinness Mahon Holdings Ltd; Sun Life Assurance; Bass Charrington; Banque Belge; Darling Holdings; Chairman, Theatre Royal, Windsor; *b* 14 Aug. 1912; *s* of Algernon Hyde Villiers (killed in action, 1917) and of Beatrix Paul (now Dowager Lady Aldenham); *m* 1st, 1938, Pamela Constance Flower (*d* 1943); one *s*; 2nd, 1946, Marie José, *d* of Count Henri de la Barre d'Erquelinnes, Jurbise, Belgium; two *d*. *Educ:* Eton; New Coll., Oxford. Asst to Rev. P. B. Clayton, of Toc H, 1931; Glyn Mills, Bankers, 1932. Grenadier Guards (SRO), 1936; served at Dunkirk, 1940 (wounded, 1942); Special Ops Exec., London and Italy, 1943-45; parachuted into Jugoslavia and Austria, 1944; Lt-Col and Comd 6 Special Force Staff Section, 1945 (MC). A Man. Dir, Helbert Wagg, 1948, and J. Henry Schroder Wagg, 1960-68. Man. Dir, IRC, 1968-70. Formerly Chm., Ashdown Trans-Europe and Trans-Australian Investment Trusts. Member: Inst. Internat. des Etudes Bancaires, 1959- (Pres. 1964); Minister of Labour's Resettlement Cttee for London and SE, 1958 (Chm. 1961-68). Mem., Chelsea Borough Council, 1950-53. *Recreations:* gardening and ciné. *Address:* 1 Lowndes Square, SW1. *T:* 01-235 7551; Blacknest House, Sunninghill, Berks. *T:* Ascot 22137. *Club:* Brooks's.

*See also Baron Aldenham.*

**VILLIERS, Vice-Adm. Sir (John) Michael,** KCB 1962 (CB 1960); OBE 1943; *b* 22 June 1907; 3rd *s* of late Rear-Adm. E. C. Villiers, CMG and of Mrs Villiers; *m* 1936, Rosemary, CStJ, 2nd *d* of late Lt-Col B. S. Grissell, DSO, and late Lady Astley-Cubitt; two *d*. *Educ:* Oundle School; Royal Navy. Served War of 1939-45 (despatches, OBE). Comd HMS Ursa, 1945, and HMS Snipe, 1946-47; directing staff of Joint Services Staff College, 1948-49; Assistant Director of Plans Admiralty, 1950-51; Capt. of Dockyard, Malta, 1952-54; comd HMS Bulwark, 1954-57; Chief of Naval Staff, New Zealand, 1958-60; a Lord Commissioner of the Admiralty, Fourth Sea Lord and Vice-Controller, 1960-63; Lt-Governor and C-in-C Jersey, 1964-69. KStJ 1964. *Address:* Decoy House, Melton, Woodbridge, Suffolk. *Club:* Army and Navy.

**VILLIERS, Vice-Adm. Sir Michael;** *see* Villiers, Vice-Adm. Sir J. M.

**VILLIERS, Brig. Richard Montagu,** DSO 1944 (Bar 1945); Secretary, Royal Hospital and Home for Incurables, Putney, 1951-68, retired; *b* 10 Sept. 1905; *s* of late John R. Villiers and of Grace E. Villiers; *m* 1932, Nancy Godwin; one *s* three *d*. *Educ:* Winchester; RMC Sandhurst. Commissioned, The Cameronians, 1923; retired, 1949. *Recreations:* fishing and shooting. *Address:* Nutwood, Strathpeffer, Ross-shire.

**VINAVER, Eugène,** MA, DLitt, D ès L; Emeritus Professor in the University of Manchester; *b* St Petersburg, 18 June 1899; *s* of Maxime Vinaver; *m* 1939, Alice Elisabeth Malet Vaudrey; one *s*. *Educ:* Univs of Paris and Oxford. Lectr in French Language and Literature at Lincoln College, Oxford, 1924-28; Lecturer in French, University of Oxford, 1928-31; Reader in French Literature, 1931-33; Professor of French Language and Literature, Univ. of Manchester, 1933-66; Zaharoff Lecturer, Univ. of Oxford, 1960; Alexander White Professor, Univ. of Chicago, 1960; Visiting Professor of French, Stanford Univ., 1962; Herbert F. Johnson Professor, Univ. of Wisconsin, 1964-65; Phi Beta Kappa Visiting Scholar, 1967-68; Visiting Professor: University of Wisconsin, 1966-70; Northwestern Univ., 1970-. President: Modern Language Assoc., 1961; Modern Humanities Research Association, 1966; Internat. Arthurian Soc., 1966-69 (Hon. Pres., 1969-). BLitt 1922. MA 1927, Oxford; Docteur ès Lettres at Paris, 1925; DLitt, Oxford, 1950; Hon. DHL, Chicago, 1960; Hon. DLitt: Hull, 1964; Univ. of Wales, 1969; Hon. Fellow, Lincoln College, Oxford; Foreign Mem. Belgian Roy. Acad. of French Language and Literature; Hon. Mem., Modern Language Assoc. of America; Chevalier of the Legion of Honour. *Publications:* The Love Potion in the Primitive Tristan Romance, 1924; Le Roman de Tristan et Iseut dans l'œuvre de Malory, 1925; Etudes sur le Tristan en prose, 1925; Malory, 1929, 2nd imp. 1970; Principles of Textual Emendation, 1939; Hommage à Bédier, 1942; Le Roman de Balain (Introduction) 1942; Racine et la poésie tragique, 1951 (Eng. trans. 1955; revised French edn, 1963); L'Action poétique dans le théâtre de Racine, 1960; Tristan et Iseut à travers le temps, 1961; A la Recherche d'une poétique médiévale, 1970; The Rise of Romance, 1970; critical editions of Renan, Prière sur l'Acropole, 1934; Racine, Principes de la Tragédie, 1944, 2nd edn, 1951; The Works of Sir Thomas Malory, 3 vols, 1947 (reprinted 1948; one vol. edn, 1954, 1970; 2nd rev. edn 1967); Malory's Tale of the Death of King Arthur, 1955, 1967; King Arthur and His Knights, 1956, 1968; articles in Medium Aevum, French Studies, Bulletin of the John Rylands Library, Revue d'Histoire littéraire de la France, Cahiers de Civilisation médiévale, etc.; Editor of Arthuriana, 1929-31. *Address:* 27 Palace Street, Canterbury, Kent; 4 Rue des Eaux, Paris, 16e.

**VINCENT, Maj.-Gen. Douglas,** CB 1969; OBE 1954; Head, Australian Joint Services Staff, Washington, DC, USA, since 1968; *b* Australia, 10 March 1916; *s* of William Frederick Vincent, civil engineer, and Sarah Jane Vincent; *m* 1947, Margaret Ector, *d* of N. W. Persse, Melbourne; two *s* one *d*. *Educ:* Brisbane State High School; Royal Military Coll., Duntroon. Commissioned, Dec. 1938; Middle East (7 Div.), 1940-42; BLA, 1944; NW Europe (30 Corps); Borneo Campaign, 1945; Brit. Commonwealth Forces, Korea, 1954; Dir of Signals, 1954-58; Dir of Staff Duties, 1958-60; Chief of Staff, Eastern Command, 1960-62; Commander, Aust. Army Force, 1962-63 (Singapore, Malaya); idc 1964; Commander: 1 Task Force, 1965; 1st Div., 1966; Aust. Force, Vietnam, 1967-68. *Recreations:* golf, swimming. *Address:* c/o Army Headquarters, Canberra, ACT, Australia. *Clubs:* United Services (Sydney); Singapore Island Country.

**VINCENT, Prof. Eric R. P.,** CBE 1947; LittD; DPhil; MA; Professor Emeritus of Italian, Cambridge University, since 1962 (Professor, 1935-62); Fellow of Corpus Christi College, Cambridge; President, 1954-59; *b* 10 Dec. 1894; *s* of Charles Vincent, MusDoc Oxon., and Hannah Phillips; *m* 1923, Ivy, 3rd *d* of Lt-Col W. Barrow-Simonds, JP; one *d*. *Educ:* Berkhamsted School; Christ Church, Oxford (Heath-Harrison travelling scholar. First class honours in the School of Modern and Medieval languages, 1921). Studying in Germany at outbreak of war, 1914, and interned as a civil prisoner of war in Ruhleben Camp until Nov. 1918. Lecturer in Italian at King's College, University of London, 1922; Univ. Lecturer in

Italian language and literature at Oxford, 1927-34; Assistant Dir in a Department of Foreign Office, 1939-45; Member: Anglo-Italian Government Cultural Commission. Commendatore, Order Al merito della Repubblica Italiana, 1955. *Publications:* Ardengo Soffici, Six Essays on Modern Art, Preface and Notes, 1922; The Italy of the Italians, 1927; R. B. Adam Library Publication, trans. and editing of Italian MSS in this collection, 1930; Enciclopedia Italiana, many articles, 1932-34; Machiavelli, Il Principe, Preface and revision of text 1935; Gabriele Rossetti in England, 1936; The Commemoration of the Dead (Foscolo's Sepolcri), 1936; British Academy Lecture on Dante, 1945; Byron, Hobhouse and Foscolo, 1949; Ugo Foscolo, An Italian in Regency England, 1953; Contributions to learned periodicals; translations, etc. *Recreation:* mowing lawns. *Address:* Fulford Grange, Kingston St Mary, Taunton, Somerset; Corpus Christi College, Cambridge.

**VINCENT, Prof. Ewart Albert;** Professor of Geology, and Fellow of University College, Oxford, since 1967; *b* 23 Aug. 1919; *o s* of Albert and Winifred Vincent, Aylesbury; *m* 1944, Myrtle Ablett; two *d. Educ:* Reading Sch.; Univ. of Reading. BSc (Reading) 1940; PhD 1951; MA (Oxon) 1952; MSc (Manch.) 1966. FRIC, FGS. Chemist, Min. of Supply, 1940-45; Geologist, Anglo-Iranian Oil Co., 1945-46; Lectr in Mineralogy and Crystallography, Univ. of Durham, 1946-51; Lectr in Geology, Oxford Univ., 1951-56; Reader in Mineralogy, Oxford Univ., 1956-62; Prof. of Geology, Manchester Univ., 1962-66. Vice-Pres., Internat. Assoc. of Volcanology, 1968-. Hon. Corresp. Mem., Soc. Géol. de Belgique. Awarded Wollaston Fund, Geol Soc. London, 1961. *Publications:* scientific papers in learned jls. *Recreations:* music, photography. *Address:* 10a Bardwell Road, Oxford; Department of Geology and Mineralogy, Parks Road, Oxford. *T:* Oxford 54511.

**VINCENT, Sir (Harold) Graham,** KCMG, *cr* 1953; CB 1935; CVO 1932; *b* 1891; *s* of late William Vincent; *m* 1921, Brenda, *d* of late Edward Wood-White, MD, BS; one *d. Educ:* Haileybury; Jesus College, Cambridge. First Class, Mathematical Tripos, 1914; served European War, 1914-18, in London Rifle Bde and Army Signal Service (Captain); entered HM Treasury, 1919; Private Sec. to the Parliamentary Sec. to the Treasury, 1924; Private Secretary to successive Prime Ministers, 1928-36; Principal Private Secretary, 1934-36; Principal Assistant Secretary Committee of Imperial Defence, 1936-39; Ministry: of Food, 1939-40; of Works and Buildings, and of Town and Country Planning, 1940-44; of Production, 1944-46; of Civil Aviation, 1946-49; Secretary, Government Hospitality, 1949-56. *Recreation:* golf. *Address:* 5 Poyntell Crescent, Chislehurst, Kent. *Club:* United University.

**VINCENT, Ivor Francis Sutherland,** CMG 1966; MBE 1945; HM Diplomatic Service; Ambassador at Managua, since Nov. 1970; *b* 14 Oct. 1916; *s* of late Lt-Col Frank Lloyd Vincent and Gladys Clarke; *m* 1949, Patricia Mayne; four *d. Educ:* St Peter's Coll., Radley; Christ Church, Oxford. Served Indian Army, Royal Garhwal Rifles, 1941-46. Entered HM Foreign Service, 1946; Second Secretary, Foreign Office, 1946-48; First Sec., Buenos Aires, 1948-51; UK Delegn, NATO, Paris, 1951-53; FO, 1954-57; Rabat, 1957-59; Geneva (Disarmt Delegn), 1960; Paris (UK Delegn to OECD), 1960-62; Counsellor, FO, 1962-66; Baghdad, Jan.-June, 1967; Caracas, Oct. 1967-70. *Recreations:* music, walking. *Address:* 101 Barkston Gardens, SW5. *T:* 01-373 5273. *Clubs:* Oxford and Cambridge University, Travellers'.

**VINCENT, Prof. John Joseph,** MSc, MSc Tech., FTI; Professor of Textile Technology, University of Manchester Institute of Science and Technology, since 1957; *b* 29 June 1907; 2nd *s* of J. H. Vincent, MA, DSc; *m* 1935, M. Monica Watson, MSc, PhD, of Sheffield; one *s* one *d. Educ:* County Grammar Sch., Harrow; University Coll., London. Mathematics Dept, University Coll., London, 1927-29; Shirley Inst., Manchester, 1929-42 and 1945-57. Ministry of Aircraft Production, 1942-45. Council of the Textile Institute, 1959-. President of the British Assoc. of Managers of Textile Works, 1963-64; Mem., Cotton and Allied Textiles Industry Training Bd, 1966-. *Publications:* papers on textile technology. *Recreations:* gardening, reading, listening to music. *Address:* 16 Sunny Bank, Holly Road, Wilmslow, Cheshire SK9 6DY. *T:* Wilmslow 20416.

**VINCENT, Leonard Grange,** CBE 1960; FRIBA, MTPI, DipTP, Distinction Town Planning (RIBA); Architect and Town Planner; Principal Partner, Vincent and Gorbing, Architects and Planning Consultants; *b* 13 April 1916; *s* of late Godfrey Grange Vincent; *m* 1942, Evelyn (*née* Gretton); twin *s* one *d. Educ:* Forest House School. Trained as architect in London, 1933, and subsequently as a town planner; experience in private practice and local government. Served War of 1939-45: Royal Engineers (Major); mostly overseas, in Western Desert, and Italian campaigns with 8th Army, 1940-45. Formerly Chief Architect and Planner, Stevenage Development Corporation. *Publications:* various technical and planning articles in technical press. *Recreations:* archaeology, golf and photography. *Address:* Medbury, Rectory Lane, Stevenage, Hertfordshire. *T:* Stevenage 51175.

**VINCENT, Air Vice-Marshal Stanley Flamank,** CB 1945; DFC; AFC; DL; *b* 7 April 1897; *s* of Dr Charles Vincent, MusDoc Oxon. and Hannah Phillips; *m* 1921, Elisabeth Ursula Peyton; two *s* one *d. Educ:* King's College Choir School, Cambridge; Lancing College. Commission RFC Dec. 1915; France, 60 Sqdn, 1916-17; instructing and hospital, England, to 1919; taught Prince of Wales, Croydon, early 1919 (AFC); instructor Cadet College Cranwell, 1920-23; 30 Sqdn Iraq, 1923-25; 2 Arm. Car Coy., Palestine, 1926-27; 1 Sqdn Tangmere, 1928-31; CO 41 Sqdn Northolt, 1931-33; Sqdn Ldr 1931; CO 84 Sqdn Shaibah, Iraq, 1933-35; armament course, 1936; CO Air Fighting Development Estabt, 1937; Stn Comdr Northolt, end 1937; Wing Comdr, 1937; Air Ministry, 1938; Naval Staff College, 1939; Stn Comdr Northolt and North Weald, 1940 and 1941; Group Capt., 1940 (DFC); Singapore, Sumatra, Java, Australia, NZ, USA, England, 1942-43; Air Commodore, 1941; Fighter Command and AOC 13 Group Scotland, 1943; AOC 221 Group SE Asia Air Forces, Burma, 1944-45 (CB); Actg Air Vice-Marshal, 1944; Air Vice-Marshal, 1947; SASO Fighter Command, 1945-48; AOC No. 11 (F) Group, 1948-50; retired, 1950; Commandant Eastern Area, Royal Observer Corps, 1954-65. DL, Suffolk, 1962. Comdr Legion of Merit (USA), 1945. *Address:* 10 Angel Hill, Bury St Edmunds, Suffolk. *T:* Bury St Edmunds 3110.

**VINCENT, Sir William (Percy Maxwell),** 3rd Bt, *cr* 1936; *b* 1 February 1945; *o s* of Sir Lacey Vincent, 2nd Bt, and of Helen Millicent, *d* of Field Marshal Sir William Robert Robertson,

1st Bt, GCB, GCMG, GCVO, DSO; *S* father, 1963. *Educ:* Eton College. 2nd Lieutenant, Irish Guards, 1964-67. *Recreations:* water skiing, sailing. *Heir:* none. *Address:* 17 Eresby House, Rutland Gate, SW7. *T:* 01-589 4217.

**VINCENT BROWN, Kenneth;** *see* Brown, Kenneth V.

**VINCENT-JONES, Captain Desmond,** DSC; Royal Navy; retired 1964; Director, Vendaline Ltd, and Partner in Mediterranean and Caribbean Marina Consortiums; *b* 13 Feb. 1912; *s* of late Sir Vincent Jones, KBE; *m* 1944, Jacqueline, *e d* of Col Sloggett, DSO; two *d*. *Educ:* Beacon School, Crowborough; Royal Naval College, Dartmouth. Served in Royal Navy, 1929-64; War of 1939-45, in aircraft carrier operations in Atlantic and Mediterranean (DSC and Bar); Served in Air Staff appointments and in Command of HM Ships, 1946-64. Graduate of US Armed Forces and British Services Staff Colleges. Naval and Military Attaché to Buenos Aires and Montevideo, 1958-60. On retirement from RN joined Marine Consortiums as consultant. *Recreations:* golf, tennis, fishing, cruising. *Address:* 63 Sussex Square, W2. *T:* 01-262 0449. *Clubs:* White's, MCC, Free Foresters; Sunningdale Golf.

**VINCZE, Paul,** FRBS, FRNS; *b* Hungary, 15 August 1907; *s* of Lajos Vincze; British subject, 1948; *m* 1958, Emilienne Chauzeix. *Educ:* High School of Arts and Crafts, Budapest, later under E. Telcs. Won a travelling scholarship to Rome, 1935-37; came to England, 1938. *Exhibited:* Royal Academy, Rome, Budapest, Paris, etc; *works represented in:* British Museum, London; Museum of Fine Arts, Budapest; Ashmolean Museum, Oxford; Swedish Historical Museum; Danish Nat. Museum; Museum of Amer. Numismatic Soc.; Smithsonian Instn, Washington; Cabinet des Medailles, Paris, etc. *Works include:* Aga Khan Platinum Jubilee Portrait; Sir Bernard Pares Memorial Tablet, Senate House, London Univ.; President Truman, portrait medallion; Pope Paul VI, portrait medallion; official medal to commemorate 400th Anniversary of birth of William Shakespeare; medal to commemorate Independence of Ghana; official seal of Ghana Govt; (designed) Smithsonian Instn Award Medal (1965); Nat. Commemorative Society (USA) Winston Churchill Medal; Florence Nightingale Medal for Société Commemorative de Femmes Célèbres; E. and J. De Rothschild Medal for inauguration of Knesset, 1966; Yehudi Menuhin 50th Birthday Medal, 1966; Prince Karim Aga Khan 10th Anniversary Medal, 1968; Cassandra Memorial Tablet for Internat. Publishing Corp. Bldg, 1968; Shakespeare-Garrick Medal, 1969; Medal to commemorate 100th Anniversary of birth of Sir Henry J. Wood, 1969; Dickens 100th Anniversary Medal for Dickens Fellowship, 1970; *coin designs:* obverse and reverses, Libya, 1951; obverses, Guatemala, 1954; reverses, threepence, sixpence and shilling, Cen. African Fedn, 1955; obverses, Ghana, 1958; reverses, Guernsey, 1957; threepence and florin, Nigeria, 1960; Guinea, obverse and reverses, Malawi, 1964; reverse, Uganda crown, 1968; Bustamante Portrait for obverse of Jamaican Dollar, 1969; reverses for decimal coins, Guernsey, 1970, etc. Awarded Premio Especial, Internat. Exhib., Madrid, 1951; Silver Medal, Paris Salon, 1964; first gold Medal of Amer. Numismatic Assoc., 1966. *Address:* 5 Rossetti Studios, Flood Street, Chelsea, SW3. *T:* 01-352 3975; Cantarella, 56 Avenue du 3 Septembre, 06 Cap d'Ail, France. *T:* 06 84 85. *Club:* Art Workers Guild.

**VINDEN, Frederick Hubert,** CIE 1945; *b* 3 Dec. 1898; *o s* of F. W. Vinden, Mt Radford, Exeter; *m* 1918, Eva, *y d* of T. Beynon Thomas, Newcastle Emlyn; one *s*. *Educ:* Exeter School; the Sorbonne. Commissioned, 1917, Suffolk Regt; Staff College, Camberley, 1929-30. General Staff, War Office, Malaya and China, 1931-40; AAG Infantry, 1940; Director of Selection of Personnel, India, 1943; retired, 1945; Home Dept, Govt of India, 1945-47; special appointment with UNESCO, 1951-62; Mission to Pakistan for World Veterans Federation, 1954; Consultant, OECD, 1962-64; National Foundation for Educational Research, 1964-. *Address:* 79 Wimpole Street, W1. *Club:* Army and Navy.

**VINE, Rev. Aubrey Russell,** DD, MA, BA, BSc; General Secretary, Free Church Federal Council, 1957-69, General Secretary Emeritus, since 1970; *b* 11 July 1900; *yr s* of Rev. C. H. Vine, Ilford, Essex; *m* 1924, Constance Ida Brand; one *s* one *d*. *Educ:* Cranbrook Park School, Ilford; Trinity College, Dublin (MA); New College, London (DD). Minister: Maze Hill Congregational Church, Greenwich, 1924-27; Broad Street Congregational Church, Reading, 1927-51; Professor, Yorkshire United Independent Coll., Bradford, 1951-57; Director, Independent Press Ltd, 1950-; Review Editor, Congregational Quarterly, 1951-58; Member Congregational Council, 1934-; Deleg. to Internat. Congregational Councils, 1949, 1954, 1958, 1962, 1966; Pres., Berks, Bucks and Oxon Free Church Federation, 1950-52; Chairman Yorkshire Congregational Union, 1957-58; Free Church Representative, Atlantic Congress, 1959; President, Congregational Church in England and Wales, 1967-68. *Publications:* The Nestorian Churches, 1937; An Approach to Christology, 1948; The Free Churches and the State, 1953; Thine is the Kingdom, 1954; Free Church Unity, 1957; contrib. to Expository Times, Congregational Quarterly, London Quarterly and Holborn Review. *Recreations:* foreign travel; chess. *Address:* 26 Newlands Avenue, Radlett, Herts. *Club:* Athenæum.

**VINE, Philip Mesban;** Town Clerk and Chief Executive Officer, Nottingham, since 1966; *b* 26 Oct. 1919; *s* of late Major George H. M. Vine and Elsie Mary (*née* Shephard), London; *m* 1944, Paulina, *d* of late Arthur Oyler, Great Hormead Hall, Herts; one *s* one *d*. *Educ:* Sherborne Sch.; Taft Sch., USA; Sidney Sussex Coll., Cambridge (MA, LLB). Served in Royal Artillery, 1939-45; Adjutant 90th Field Regt, RA. Articled to W. H. Bentley, Town Clerk of Paddington; admitted Solicitor, 1948; Asst Solicitor, Paddington, 1948-50; Chief Asst Solicitor, Birkenhead, 1950-53; Deputy Town Clerk: Wallasey, 1953-59; Southend-on-Sea, 1959-62; Town Clerk, Cambridge, 1963-66. Mem. Court, Nottingham Univ. Liveryman, Clockmakers' Co. *Recreations:* fishing, painting, enjoyment of music. *Address:* 23 Lucknow Drive, Mapperley Park, Nottingham NG3 5EU. *T:* Nottingham 61269; Guildhall, Nottingham. *T:* Nottingham 48571. *Club:* United Services (Nottingham).

**VINELOTT, John Evelyn,** QC 1968; *b* 15 Oct. 1923; *s* of George Frederick Vine-Lott and Vera Lilian Vine-Lott (*née* Mockford); *m* 1956, Sally Elizabeth, *d* of His Honour Sir Walker Kelly Carter, *qv*; two *s* one *d*. *Educ:* Queen Elizabeth's Gram. Sch., Faversham, Kent; Queen's Coll., Cambridge (MA). War Service, Sub-Lieut RNVR, 1942-46. Called to Bar, Gray's Inn, 1953; in practice since then at the Chancery Bar. *Publications:* articles on Revenue Law, in specialist periodicals. *Address:* 9 Campden Hill Square, W8. *T:* 01-727

4778; 7 New Square, Lincoln's Inn, WC2. *T:* 01-405 1266/8. *Club:* Royal Ocean Racing.

**VINEN, William Frank;** Third Professor of Physics, University of Birmingham, since 1962; *b* 15 Feb. 1930; *o s* of Gilbert Vinen and Olive Maud Vinen (*née* Roach); *m* 1960, Susan-Mary Audrey Master; one *s* one *d*. *Educ:* Watford Grammar Sch.; Clare College, Cambridge. Research Fellow, Clare College, 1955-58. Royal Air Force, 1948-49. Demonstrator in Physics, Univ. of Cambridge and Fellow of Pembroke Coll., 1958-62. *Recreation:* good food. *Address:* 52 Middle Park Road, Birmingham B29 4BJ.

**VINES, Prof. Howard William Copland,** MA, MD retired; *b* 10 March 1893; *yr s* of late Emer. Prof. S. H. Vines; *m* 1st, 1921, Dorothy Mary Beatrice Brindley (*d* 1951); one *s* one *d*; 2nd, 1953, Ingrid Gertrud Hedwig Apel; two *d*. *Educ:* Rugby School; Christ's Coll., Cambridge; St Bartholomew's Hosp. 1st Cl. Nat. Sci. Tripos 1 and Bachelor Schol. Christ's Coll., 1914; MB, BCh (Cantab.) 1920; MD (Cantab.) and Horton-Smith Prize, 1922; Fellow of Christ's Coll. and Director of Med. Studies, 1919-26; Beit Memorial Fellow, 1921-23; Foulerton Research Student, 1923-27. Sector Pathologist EMS, 1939-44; Professor of Pathology, University of London, 1948-53; Pathologist, Charing Cross Hospital, 1928-53; Dean, Charing Cross Hospital Medical School, 1945-50; Mem. Charing Cross Hosp. Council, 1945-48; Bd of Governors, 1948-55; Chm., Charing Cross Hosp. and Med. Sch. Planning Cttees, 1948-55; Mem. West Cornwall Hosp. Management Cttee, 1954-; Member North West Metropolitan Regional Board, 1948-50. *Publications:* The Parathyroid Glands, 1924; (jointly) The Adrenal Cortex and Intersexuality, 1938; Green's Pathology, 15th edn 1934; 16th edn 1940, 17th edn 1949; Background to Hospital Planning, 1952. Papers on endocrinology in Pathol and Med. journals; papers on Hospital Planning. *Recreation:* gardening. *Address:* Gull Rock House, St Austell, Cornwall. *T:* Par 2632.

**VINES, William Joshua,** CMG 1969; AASA; ACIS; psc; Chairman: Dalgety Australia Ltd; Wiggins Teape Australia Pty Ltd; Thorn Holdings Pty Ltd; Australian Wool Marketing Corporation Pty Ltd; Director: Lewis Berger & Sons (Aust.) Ltd; Commercial Union Assurance Co. of Australia Ltd; P&O Australia Holdings Pty Ltd; Port Phillip Mills Pty Ltd; Tubemakers of Australia Ltd; Board Member, International Wool Secretariat, since 1969; Grazier at Old Southwood, Tara, Queensland, since 1966; *b* 27 May 1916; *s* of P. V. Vines, Canterbury, Victoria, Australia; *m* 1939, Thelma J., *d* of late F. J. Ogden; one *s* two *d*. *Educ:* Haileybury College, Brighton Beach, Victoria. Managing Director, Berger, Jenson & Nicholson Ltd, 1960, Dir, 1961-69; Group Managing Director, Lewis Berger & Sons Ltd, 1955; Director: Lewis Berger & Sons (Aust.) Pty Ltd & Sherwin Williams Co. (Aust.) Pty Ltd, 1952-55; Goodlass Wall & Co. Pty Ltd, 1947-49; Man. Dir, Internat. Wool Secretariat, 1961-69. Vice-President Melbourne Legacy, 1949-51; Pres. Building Industry Congress, Vic., 1954-55. Served War of 1939-45 (despatches), 2nd AIF, 2/23 Aust. Inf. Bn, Middle East, New Guinea and Borneo, Capt. *Recreation:* golf. *Address:* 73 Yarranabbe Road, Darling Point, Sydney, NSW 2027, Australia. *T:* 32.7970. *Clubs:* Junior Carlton, Royal Automobile; Union, Royal Sydney Golf (Sydney); Australian, Naval and Military, Royal Melbourne (Melbourne).

**VINEY, Elliot (Merriam),** DSO 1945; MBE 1946; TD; DL; FSA; Director of British Printing Corporation Ltd, and of Hazell, Watson & Viney Ltd; *b* 21 Aug. 1913; *s* of Col. Oscar Viney, *qv*, and Edith Merriam; *m* 1950, Rosamund Ann Pelly; two *d*. *Educ:* Oundle; Univ. Coll., Oxford. Bucks Bn, Oxford and Bucks Light Infantry (TA), 1932-46. JP 1950, DL 1952, High Sheriff, 1964, Buckinghamshire. Master, Grocers' Company, 1970-71. *Recreations:* archæology, beagling, music, walking. *Address:* Green End House, Aylesbury, Bucks. *T:* Aylesbury 3091. *Clubs:* Army and Navy, Alpine.

**VINEY, Lt-Col Horace George,** CMG 1918; CBE 1919; DSO 1917, French Croix de Guerre (with palms); psc 1921; Australian Staff Corps (retired); journalist; *b* Parkside, S Australia, 8 June 1885; *s* of George Viney, JP; *m* 1st, 1918, Gwendoline Darragh (decd), *d* of John O'Neill, of Holywood, County Down, Ireland; one *s*; 2nd, Margaret Jane Lillian, *d* of Robert Browne of Melbourne, Australia. *Educ:* Adelaide High School; Adelaide University; Royal Staff College, Camberley. Commissioned in Australian Permanent Forces, 1912; Adjutant 3rd Light Horse Regiment (Australian Imperial Forces), Aug. 1914, and subsequently served (1914-18) war as Brigade Major, 5th Austn Inf. Brigade; AA and QMG 1st Austn Division; AQMG Australian Corps (despatches five times, DSO, CMG, CBE); returned to Australia on demobilisation, Sept. 1919; resigned from Australian Permanent Forces and posted to Citizen Forces, 1922. *Recreations:* represented Adelaide University at rowing, lacrosse and athletics. *Address:* Gracedale, 42 Bee Farm Road, Springwood, NSW 2777, Australia.

**VINEY, Col Oscar Vaughan,** TD; DL; *b* 16 March 1886; *s* of Joseph Elliott Viney; *m* 1912, Edith (*d* 1951), *d* of C. P. Merriam; three *s* (and one *s* and one *d* decd). *Educ:* Mill Hill School; Germany. Master Printer. Bucks Bn Oxford and Bucks Light Infantry, TA, 1914-33; commanded, 1930-33. High Sheriff of Buckinghamshire, 1950-51; Chm. Hazell Sun Ltd, Printers, 1950-58. Governor, Mill Hill School, 1929-65 (Vice-Chairman, 1951-61). *Recreations:* travel, books. *Address:* Green End House, Aylesbury, Bucks. *T:* Aylesbury 2186. *Club:* Garrick.

*See also E. M. Viney.*

**VINTER, (Frederick Robert) Peter,** CB 1965; a Deputy Secretary, Ministry of Technology, since 1969; *b* 27 March 1914; *m* 1938, Margaret Rake; two *s*. *Educ:* Haileybury Coll.; King's Coll., Cambridge (MA). Min. of Economic Warfare, 1939; Cabinet Office, 1943; HM Treasury, 1945-69, Third Sec., 1965-69. Nuffield Travelling Fellowship (in India), 1950-51. *Address:* 3 Sunnyside, Wimbledon, SW19. *T:* 01-946 4137.

**VINTER, Geoffrey Odell;** JP; Director of Companies; Underwriting Member of Lloyd's; *b* 29 April 1900; *s* of Harold Skelsey Vinter; *g s* of James Odell Vinter, High Sheriff Cambridgeshire and Huntingdonshire, 1921; *m* 1925, Mary Margaret Hardy (novelist: Mary Vinter); one *d*. *Educ:* Clifton; University Coll., Oxford (MA). High Sheriff of Cambridgeshire and Huntingdonshire, 1948-49; JP Cambs 1951. *Recreations:* shooting, fishing. *Address:* Thriplow Manor, Royston, Herts. *T:* Fowlmere 255.

**VINTER, Peter;** *see* Vinter, F. R. P.

**VIRTANEN, Artturi Ilmari,** PhD, MedD (*hc*) University of Lund, 1936; DTechn (*hc*) Finland Institute of Technology, Helsinki,

1949, and Tekniska Högskolan, Stockholm, 1949, University of Paris, 1952; DAgric (*hc*) University of Helsinki, 1955, Justus-Liebig University, Giessen, 1955; Nobel Laureate; Emeritus Member, Academy of Finland (President, 1943-63); Director, Biochemical Research Institute, Helsinki (Director of the Laboratory of Valio, Finnish Co-operative Dairies' Assoc., 1921-70, and Director of Laboratory of Foundation for Chemical Research since 1931); *b* Helsinki, 15 Jan. 1895; *s* of engine-driver Kaarlo Virtanen and Serafiina Isotalo; *m* 1920, Lilja Moisio, MSc; two *s*. *Educ:* Classical Lyceum in iipuri (grad 1913); Univ. of Helsinki (MSc 1916, PhD 1919); Univ. studies in Zürich, Münster and Stockholm. First assistant of the Central Laboratory of Industry, 1916-17; chemical assistant of the Government Butter and Cheese Control Station, 1919; chemist of the Laboratory of Valio, Finnish Co-operative Dairies' Assoc., 1919-20; Docent in Chemistry, Univ. of Helsinki, 1924-39; Prof. of Biochemistry at Finland Inst. of Technology, 1931-39; Professor of Biochemistry at University of Helsinki, 1939-48. Member: Finnish Chemical Soc., 1919; Finnish Acad. of Sciences, 1927; Swedish Acad. of Agriculture, 1933; British Assoc. for the Advancement of Science, 1935; Finnish Acad. of Agriculture, 1939; Royal Scientific Soc. of Uppsala, 1939; Royal Scientific Acad. of Sweden, 1939; Swedish Acad. of Engineering Sciences, 1945; Danish Acad. of Technical Sciences, 1947; Fellow: Amer. Assoc. for Advancement of Science, 1948; Royal Soc. of Arts, 1948; Royal Flemish Acad. of Sciences (Belgium), 1949; Bavarian Acad. of Sciences, 1949; Norwegian Acad. of Sciences, 1950; Pontifical Acad. of Sciences, 1955; German Acad. Leopoldina, 1963; Accad. Pugliese delle Scienze (Bari), 1964; US Nat. Acad. of Sciences, 1969. Hon. Member: European Nutritionists, 1965; Biochemical Soc. of Stockholm, 1943; Finnish Medical Soc. Duodecim, 1945; Finnish Technical Soc., 1946; Finnish Chemical Soc., 1946; Finnish Academy of Sciences, 1968; Austrian Chemical Society, 1952; Royal Society of Edinburgh, 1959; American Institute of Nutrition, 1960; American Society of Biological Chemists, 1961; Deutsche Gesellschaft für Ernährung, 1963; Hon. Councillor, Higher Council for Scientific Research (Madrid), 1964; Member: American Society of Microbiology, 1966; Finnish Acad. of Sciences, 1968; German Soc. for Quality Research, 1969. Friesland Prize, Holland, 1967; Atwater Prize, 1968; Siegfried Thannhauser Medal, 1969. *Publications:* Cattle Fodder and Human Nutrition, 1938; AIV-järjestelmä karjanruokinnan perustana (AIV-system as the basis of cattle-feeding), Helsinki, 1943 (3rd edition 1945); AIV-systemet såsom grundval för husdjurens utfodring, Stockholm, 1945; *c* 800 essays on various biochemical problems; biochemistry of bacteria, symbiotic nitrogen fixation and related agricultural problems, vitamins, antimicrobial substances in cultivated plants, amino acids, etc. *Recreation:* fishing. *Address:* Biochemical Research Institute, Helsinki 18, Kalevank 56 b, Finland. *TA:* Virtanen, Valio. *T:* 646211.

**VISCONTI, Luchino;** stage and film director; *b* 2 November 1906. Produced plays by Chekov, Shakespeare, Miller, Williams, Goldoni, Anouilh, Sartre, Beaumarchais, etc. Plays include: 'Tis a Pity She's a Whore, Paris; La Monaca di Monza, Rome. Operas by Verdi, Bellini, Donizetti, Strauss, etc. produced at: La Scala, Milan; Royal Opera House, Covent Garden; Festival, Spoleto; Rome Opera House; Vienna State Opera. Directed films: Ossessione; La Terra Trema; Bellissima; Senso; Le Notti Bianche; Rocco e i suoi Fratelli; Boccaccio 70 (Dir of 1 of 4 sequences); The Leopard; Vaghe stelle dell' orsa, (English title) Of a Thousand Delights; The Witches; The Stranger; Götterdämmerung. Prod ballets: Marathon, Berlin State Opera House; Mario e il Mago, La Scala. Director of Morelli-Stoppa Company; produced with it La LOcandiera, The Impresario from Smyrna, Figli d' Arte, at Paris International Drama Festival. *Address:* 366 via Salaria, Rome, Italy.

**VISHNEVSKAYA, Galina;** principal soprano of the Bolshoi Theatre, Moscow; *b* 25 Oct. 1926; *m* 1955, Mstislav Rostropovich, *qv*; two *d*. *Educ:* studied with Vera Garina. Toured with Leningrad Light Opera Co., 1944-48, with Leningrad Philharmonic Soc., 1948-52; joined Bolshoi Theatre, 1952. Concert appearances in Europe and USA, 1950-; first appeared at Metropolitan Opera, NY, 1961. Rôles include: Leonora in Fidelio and Tatiana in Eugene Onegin. Has sung in Britain at Festival Hall, Aldeburgh Festival, Edinburgh Festival, Covent Garden. Makes concert tours with her husband. Has made many recordings. *Address:* c/o Bolshoi Theatre, Sverdlovsk Square, Moscow, USSR.

**VISSER 't HOOFT, Willem Adolf,** DD; Commander, Order of the Lion (Netherlands); Officer, Legion of Honour (France); Grand Cross, Order of Merit, with ribbon and star (Federal Republic of Germany); Cross of Great Commander of Holy Sepulchre; Order of St Vladimir, Orthodox Church of Russia; Commander, Order of St Andrew (Ecumenical Patriarchate); Hon. KStJ; General Secretary of World Council of Churches, 1938-66, Hon. President, 1968; *b* 20 Sept. 1900; *m* 1924, Henriette Philippine Jacoba Boddaert (*d* 1968); two *s* one *d*. *Educ:* Leyden University. Secretary, World Committee of YMCA, 1924-31; General Secretary, World Student Christian Federation, 1931-38. Hon. DD, Aberdeen, 1939; Hon. Prof., Theological Faculty, Budapest, 1947; Hon. DD, Princeton Univ., USA; Trinity Coll., Toronto, Canada, 1950; Hon. DD: Geneva, 1951; Yale University and Oberlin College, 1954; Oxford University, 1955; Harvard University, Cambridge, Mass., 1958, St Paul's Univ., Tokyo, 1959; Faculté Libre de théologie, Paris, 1963; Hon. Prof.: Theolog. Acad., Moscow, 1964; Kirchliche Hochschule, Berlin, 1964; Brown Univ., Providence, RI, 1965; Theol. Faculty, Zürich, 1966; Univ. Catholique, Louvain, 1967. *Publications:* Anglo-Catholicism and Orthodoxy, 1933; None other Gods, 1937; The Church and its Function in Society (with J. H. Oldham), 1937; Wretchedness and Greatness of the Church, 1943; The Struggle of the Dutch Church, 1946; Kingship of Christ, 1948; Rembrandt et la Bible, 1947; the Meaning of Ecumenical, 1953; Rembrandt's Weg zum Evangelium, 1955; Rembrandt's Weg tot het Evangelie, 1956; Le Renouveau de l'Eglise, 1956; The Renewal of the Church (Eng. edn 1956); Rembrandt and the Gospel, 1957; The Pressure of our Common Calling, 1959; No Other Name, 1963; Hauptschriften, Bd 1 and 2, 1967. *Address:* 150, route de Ferney, 1211 Geneva 20, Switzerland. *T:* 33 34 00.

**VIVENOT, Baroness de (Hermine Hallam-Hipwell),** OBE 1967; free lance writer; *b* Buenos Aires; *d* of late Humphrey Hallam-Hipwell and Gertrude Hermine Isebrée-Moens tot Bloois; *m* 1931, Baron Raoul de Vivenot, *e s* of Baron de Vivenot and Countess Kuenburg, Vienna; one *s*. *Educ:* Northlands, Buenos Aires. Joined Min. of Information, 1941; transferred Foreign Office, 1946; appointed to Foreign (subseq. Diplomatic) Service, Jan. 1947; Vice-Consul, Bordeaux,

1949-52, Nantes, 1952-53; Foreign Office, 1953-55; First Secretary (Information), HM Embassy, Brussels, 1955-59; Foreign Office, 1959-62; First Secretary (Information), HM Embassy, The Hague, 1962-66; retired 1967. External Examiner, Univ. of London. *Publications:* The Ninas of Balcarce, a novel, 1935; Younger Argentine painters; Argentine Art Notes; Buenos Aires Vignettes; Poems, etc. *Recreations:* whippets and conversation with my Siamese. *Address:* Coppinghall, Uckfield, Sussex. *T:* Uckfield 2778.

**VIVIAN,** family name of **Barons Swansea** and **Vivian.**

**VIVIAN,** 5th Baron, *cr* 1841; **Anthony Crespigny Claude Vivian;** Bt *cr* 1828; *b* 4 March 1906; *e s* of 4th Baron and Barbara, *d* of William A. Fanning; *S* father 1940; *m* 1930, Victoria, *er d* of late Captain H. G. L. Oliphant, DSO, MVO; two *s* one *d*. *Educ:* Eton. Served RA. *Heir: s* Major Hon. Nicholas Crespigny Laurence Vivian, 3rd Carabiniers [*b* 11 Dec. 1935; *m* 1960, Catherine Joyce, *y d* of James Kenneth Hope, *qv*; one *s* one *d*]. *Address:* 154 Coleherne Court, SW5.

*See also Marquess of Bath, Earl of Glasgow, Earl Haig.*

**VIVIAN, Arthur Henry Seymour;** Clerk of the Skinners' Company, 1941-59; Hon. Freeman and Member of Court of the Company, 1959; *b* 30 June 1899; *o s* of late Henry Chester Vivian, Cardiff; *m* 1927, Elizabeth, *yr d* of late Maj. R. H. Hood-Haggie; one *d*. *Educ:* Harrow and Magdalen Coll., Oxford. (MA). RFA, 1918; called to the Bar, Inner Temple, 1923; Assistant to Clerk of Skinners' Company, 1933. Commissioned London Welsh AA Regiment, 1939-43. Hon. Secretary Governing Bodies' Association, 1953-67, Hon. Member, Committee, 1967. *Recreation:* golf (played for Oxford, 1921 and 1922). *Address:* 24 Sandy Lodge Road, Moor Park, Rickmansworth, Herts. *T:* Rickmansworth 74055. *Clubs:* Royal Automobile, MCC; Royal Porthcawl Golf; Moor Park Golf.

**VIVIAN, Graham Linsell,** CSI 1946; CIE 1944; *b* 1 Aug. 1887; *s* of late Richard Thomas Vivian; *m* 1923, Norah, *d* of late E. H. Ashworth; two *s* one *d*. *Educ:* Epsom Coll.; Selwyn Coll., Cambridge. Entered Indian Civil Service, 1911; held various administrative posts in United Provinces, rising to Commissioner, 1941; Adviser to the Governor, 1945; retired, 1946. *Address:* Middlemead, Rectory Close, Burwash, Sussex. *T:* Burwash 436.

**VIVIAN, Richard P. G.;** *see* Graham-Vivian.

**VLASTO, Michael,** MB, BS, FRCS; Officier de l'Instruction Publique; late Consulting Throat and Ear Surgeon to West London Hospital and Consulting Surgeon to Throat and Ear Departments of Queen's Hospital for Children; Fellow of Royal Society of Medicine; *b* 1888; *o s* of Ernest and Helen Vlasto; *m* 1919, Chrissy Mitchell Croil, Aberdeen; one *s* three *d*. *Educ:* Winchester Coll.; University College Hospital. Surgeon-Lieut, 1914-19; late Surgeon-in-Chief of Ear, Nose and Throat Dept of Royal Naval Hospitals of Portsmouth and Malta; Registrar Golden Square Nose and Throat Hospital. Fellow Royal Commonwealth Society. *Publications:* Diseases of the Ear, Nose, Throat, for Nurses, and various papers in medical journals. *Recreations:* croquet, chess. *Address:* Gresham Lodge, Limpsfield-Oxted, Surrey. *T:* Oxted 3961.

**VOCKLER, Rt. Rev. John Charles (Brother John Charles, N/SSF);** Hon. Assistant Bishop of Worcester, since 1970; Bishop of Polynesia, 1962-68; *b* 22 July 1924; *e s* of John Thomas Vockler and Mary Catherine Vockler (*née* Widerberg), Dee Why, New South Wales. *Educ:* Sydney Boy's High Sch.; University of Queensland; Moore Theological Coll.;St John's Theological College, Morpeth, NSW; General Theological Seminary, New York. LTheol, Australian College of Theology, 1948. Deacon, 1948; priest, 1948; Asst Deacon, Christ Church Cathedral, Newcastle, 1948; Asst Priest, 1948-50; Vice-Warden of S John's Coll., within University of Queensland, 1950-53; Acting Chaplain, C of E Grammar School for Boys, Brisbane, 1953. BA (1st Class Hons History) University of Queensland, 1953; University Gold Medal for outstanding achievement, 1953; BA University of Adelaide, aegr, 1961; Walter and Eliza Hall Foundation Travelling Scholarship, University of Queensland, 1953; Fulbright Scholar, 1953. Acting Vice-Warden, S John's Coll., Morpeth and Lecturer in Old Testament, 1953; Graduate Student, General Theological Seminary, New York, 1954. STB (General Seminary), 1954. Asst Priest, Cathedral of S John the Divine, NY and Chaplain, St Luke's Home for Aged Women and the Home for Old Men and Aged Couples, 1955; Australian Delegate to Anglican Congress, 1954; Fellow and Tutor Gen. Theol. Seminary, 1954-56; STM (Gen. Theol. Seminary), 1956. Asst Priest, St Stephen's Church, West 69th Street, NY, 1955; Priest-in-charge, St Stephen's, New York, 1956; Asst Priest, parish of Singleton, NSW, 1956-59; Lecturer in Theology, St John's Theological College, Morpeth, NSW, 1956-59; Secretary, Newcastle Diocesan Board of Education, 1958-59. Titular Bishop of Mount Gambier and Assistant Bishop of Adelaide (Coadjutor, 1959; title changed to Assistant, 1961), until 1962; also Archdeacon of Eyre Peninsula, 1959-62; Vicar-General, Examining Chaplain to Bishop of Adelaide, 1960-62. President, Harry Charman's All Races Sports and Social Club, Suva, Fiji, 1962-68, Hon. Life Vice-Pres., 1968; Chairman: S Pacific Anglican Council, 1963-68; Council of Pacific Theological Coll., 1963-68; President, Fiji Council of Social Services, 1964-68. Permission to officiate, Dio. Salisbury, 1969. ThD (*jure dig.*) Australian College of Theology, 1961; STD (*hc*) General Theological Seminary, New York, 1961; BD (*ad eund*), Melbourne College of Divinity, 1960. *Publications:* Can Anglicans Believe Anything–The Nature and Spirit of Anglicanism, 1961 (NSW); Forward Day by Day, 1962; (ed) Believing in God (by M. L. Yates), 1962 (Australian edn); contributions to: Preparatory Volume for Anglican Congress, Toronto, 1963; Mutual Responsibility: Questions and Answers, 1964; All One Body (ed T. Wilson), 1968; Australian Dictionary of Biography; St Mark's Review, Australian Church Quarterly, The Anglican, The Young Anglican, Pacific Journal of Theology, New Zealand Theological Review. *Recreations:* classical music, detective stories, tennis, theatre, films, prints and engravings. *Address:* c/o The Friary of S Francis, Hilfield, Dorchester, Dorsetshire. *Club:* Tonga (Nukualofa).

**VOGT, Dr Martha Louise,** FRS 1952; Dr med Berlin, Dr phil Berlin; PhD Cantab; *b* 1903; *d* of Oskar Vogt and Cécile Vogt (*née* Mugnier). *Educ:* Auguste Viktoria-Schule, Berlin; University of Berlin. Research Assistant, Department of Pharmacology, Berlin Univ., 1930; Research Assistant and head of chemical division, Kaiser Wilhelm Institut für Hirnforschung, Berlin, 1931-35; Rockefeller Travelling Fellow, 1935-36; Research Worker,

Dept of Pharmacology, Cambridge Univ., 1935-40; Alfred Yarrow Research Fellow, of Girton Coll., 1937-40; Member Staff of College of Pharmaceutical Society, London, 1941-46; Lecturer, later Reader, in Pharmacology, University of Edinburgh, 1947-60; Head of Pharmacology Unit, Agricultural Research Council, Institute of Animal Physiology, 1960-68. Vis. Associate Prof. in Pharmacology, Columbia Univ., New York, 1949; Vis. Prof., Sydney 1965, Montreal 1968. Supernumerary Fellow, Girton Coll., Cambridge, 1960-. *Publications:* papers in neurological, physiological and pharmacological journals. *Address:* Agricultural Research Council Institute of Animal Physiology, Babraham, Cambridge.

**VOKES, Maj.-Gen. Christopher,** CB 1945; CBE 1944; DSO 1943; retired from the Canadian Army in 1960; *b* 13 April 1904; *e s* of late Major F. P. Vokes, Kingston, Ontario, and Elizabeth Briens; *m* 1932, Constance Mary Waugh (*d* 1969), Winnipeg; two *s. Educ:* RMC, Kingston; McGill Univ., Montreal. 1st Commission Royal Canadian Engineers, 1925; Staff Coll., Camberley, 1934-35; Brigadier Comd 2 Cdn Inf. Bde, 1942-43; Maj.-Gen. GOC 1 Cdn Div., 1943-44; GOC 4 Cdn Armd Div., 1944-45. Campaigns: Sicily, Italy, NW Europe (despatches twice, DSO, CBE, CB); GOC Cdn Occupation Force, Germany, 1945; Officer of Legion of Honour (France); Croix de Guerre avec Palme (France); Order of Golden Ariston Andrias (Greece); Commander Mil. Order of Italy. *Address:* 155 Navy Street, Oakville, Ontario, Canada.

**von BITTENFELD;** *see* Herwarth von Bittenfeld.

**von BRAUN, Wernher;** Deputy Associate Administrator, National Aeronautics and Space Administration, Washington, DC, since 1970; *b* 23 March 1912; *s* of Magnus and Emmy van Braun; *m* 1947, Maria L. von Quistorp; one *s* two *d. Educ:* University of Berlin (PhD). Experimented with liquid fuel rockets from 1930; Technical Director Liquid Fuel Rocket and Guided Missile Centre at Peenemuende, 1937-45. After coming to America, worked, Sept. 1945-April 1950 as project director of R & D Svc (Sub-Ofc Rocket) and, simultaneously, advisor for V-2 test firings at White Sands Proving Ground, New Mexico; Tech. Director, Guided Missile Dev. Group, Redstone Arsenal, April 1950-Nov. 1952; Chief, Guided Missile Dev. Division there, Nov. 1952-Feb. 1956; Director, Development Ops Div. Army Ballistic Missile Agency, Redstone Arsenal, 1956-60; Director, George C. Marshall Space Flight Center, NASA, Huntsville, Alabama, 1960-70. Member: Internat. Acad. of Astronautics; Nat. Acad. of Engineering; Fellow, American Astronautical Society Inc.; Hon. Fellow: American Inst. for Aeronautics and Astronautics; various foreign interplanetary societies. Langley Medal (Smithsonian) 1967. Holds hon. degrees, awards, etc. *Publications:* The Mars Project, 1952; (Jointly) Physics and Medicine of the Upper Atmosphere, 1952; Space Medicine, 1952; Across the Space Frontier, 1952; Conquest of the Moon, 1953; The Exploration of Mars, 1956; Project Satellite, 1958; First Men to the Moon, 1960; A Journey through Space and the Atom, 1962; (with F. I. Ordway) History of Rocketry and Space Travel, 1966; Space Frontier, 1967 (rev. edn 1971); (jointly) Entdecker des Weltraums, 1967. *Recreations:* boating, scuba diving, flying. *Address:* Code A.A.D., National Aeronautics and Space Administration, Washington, DC 20546, USA. *Club:* Explorers (New York).

**VON DER HEYDE, Brigadier John Leslie,** CMG 1960; CBE 1943 (OBE 1941); MC; *b* 1 Oct. 1896; *s* of Major J. L. Von der Heyde, Brighton; *m* 1930, Sybil Marjorie Buckwell; one *d. Educ:* Trescoe House Sch., Brighton TA 1914-17; Regular Army, 1917; substantive promotions: Captain, 1929; Major, 1938; Lieut-Colonel, 1944. Adjut Regular Army twice, TA once; Temp. Colonel, 1941; Temp. Brigadier, 1943. Served European War, 1914-18 (MC, despatches); Palestine (medal); War of 1939-45 (OBE, CBE, despatches); retired pay, 1949 (Hon. Brigadier). Foreign Office, 1948-54; Chairman, Public Service Commission, Tanganyika, 1955-60. Surrey County Councillor, 1965. Coronation Medal, 1953. *Recreation:* golf. *Address:* Beechcroft, Wonersh Road, Shamley Green, near Guildford, Surrey. *T:* Bramley 2412. *Clubs:* Royal Over-seas League, Army and Navy.

**VON HAGEN, Victor Wolfgang,** FZS; FRGS; Leader, Roman Road Expeditions, 1962; Director: Inca High Expedition; American Geographical Society; History of Science Society; Latin American Adviser, Encyclopedia Americana; Research Associate Museum of the American Indian, New York; Consultant UN Guggenheim Fellowship for creative writing, 1949, renewed 1950-51; American Philosophical Society (Research Fellow); *b* Saint Louis, Mo., 29 Feb. 1908; *s* of Henry von Hagen and Eleanor Josephine Stippe-Hornbach; *m* 1933, Christine Inez Brown (divorced); one *d; m* 1951, Silvia Hofmann-Edzard (marr. dissolved, 1962); two *d. Educ:* Morgan Park Military Acad.; New York Univ.; Univ. de Quito, S America. Served US Army, War of 1941-45, 13th Inf. Regt, Texas. Explorer, naturalist, ethnographer. Expedition Mexico, 1931-33; Ecuador, Amazon, Peru, Galapagos Islands, 1934-36; Honduras, Mosquito Coast, Guatemala, 1937-38, to study quetzal bird for Zoo, Regent's Park; Panama, Costa Rica, 1940; Colombia, Peru, 1947-48; resided BWI, 1949-50; Expedition to Peru, 1952-54; studied Roman Roads, Lubeck to Africa, 1955; Expedition to Mexico, 1957; Yucatan, 1958-59; Study of Roman Roads in Italy, 1961; Exploration of Roman Roads: throughout Tunisia, Libya, Egypt, Arabia, Petra, 1963; Spain and Yugoslavia, 1965; Egyptian Eastern Desert, Sinai, Turkey, Bulgaria and Greece, 1966. Professor (*h c*) Universidad Catolica del Peru. Member, Academia de Historia de Bogota (Columbia), Centro de historia de Pasto (Columbia), Instituto Investigaciones Historicas (Peru). Discovered "extinct" tribe of Jicaque Indians in Honduras. Orden al Merito, Ecuador; Comdr, Orden al Merito, Peru. *Publications:* Off With their Heads, 1937; Ecuador the Unknown, 1939; Quetzal Quest (with Hawkins), 1940 (repr. 1968); Tsátchela Indians of Western Ecuador, 1939; The Encantadas of Herman Melville, 1940; Treasure of Tortoise Islands, 1940; Riches of South America, 1941; Riches of Central America, 1942; The Jicaque Indians of Honduras, 1943; Natural History of Termites, 1943; Paper and Civilisation, 1943; The Aztec and Maya Papermakers, 1943, 2nd edn, 1944; Jungle in the Clouds, 1945 (American edition, 1940); La Fabricación del Papel entre los aztecas y los Mayas, Mexico, 1945; South America Called Them, a biography, 1945; Maya Explorer, the life of John Lloyd Stephens, 1947; The Green World of the Naturalists (Anthology), 1948; Ecuador and the Galapagos Islands, 1949; Regional Guides to Peru, 1949; Frederick Catherwood, Architect (with Introduction by Aldous Huxley), 1950; El Dorado, The Golden Kingdoms of Colombia, 1951; The Four Seasons of Manuela (biography), 1952;

Highway of the Sun, 1956; The High Voyage, 1956; (Trans.) The Journals of J. B. Boussingault, 1957; Realm of the Incas, 1957; The Aztec: Man and Tribe, 1958; The Sun Kingdom of the Aztecs, 1958; The World of the Maya, 1960; Royal Road of the Incas, 1961; The Ancient Sun Kingdom of The Americas, 1961; The Desert Kingdoms of Peru, 1965; The Story of the Roman Roads, 1966 (for children; two book awards); F. Catherwood: Architect-Explorer of Two Worlds, 1967; The Roads that Led to Rome (in 6 languages), 1967; The Road Runner (autobiog.), 1970; (ed) The Incas (Chronicles) of Pedro de Cieza de Leon, 1959; (ed) Stephens' Incidents of Travel in Yucatan, 1961; (ed) Stephens' Incidents of Travel in Arabia Petraea, 1968. *Recreations:* miniature camera, fencing. *Address:* Via Agostino Bassi 33/9, 00191 Rome, Italy.

**von HASE, Karl-Günther,** Hon. KCMG 1965; German Ambassador to the Court of St James's, since 1970; *b* 15 Dec. 1917; *m* 1945, Renate Stumpff; five *d. Educ:* German schools. Professional Soldier, 1936-45; War Academy, 1943-44; Training College for Diplomats, 1950-51. German Foreign Service: German Embassy, Ottawa, 1953-56; Spokesman, Foreign Office Bonn, 1958-61; Head, West European Dept, 1961-62; Spokesman of German Federal Government, 1962-67; State Secretary, Min. of Defence, German Federal Govt, 1968-69. Holds German and other foreign decorations. *Recreations:* hunting, riding. *Address:* German Embassy, 23 Belgrave Square, SW1. *T:* 01-235 5033.

**VON KARAJAN, Herbert;** Conductor; Director, Salzburg Festival, since 1964; Artistic Manager of the Vienna State Opera, 1956-64; Life Director Gesellschaft der Musikfreunde, Vienna; Artistic Director, Berlin Philharmonic Orchestra; *b* Salzburg, 5 April 1908; *s* of Ernest van Karajan and Martha v. Karajan Cosmâc; *m* 1942, Anita Gütermann. *Educ:* Salzburg Hochschule and Mozarteum; Vienna Univ. Conductor: Ulm Opernhaus, 1927-33; Aachen Opernhaus, 1933-40; Berlin Staatsoper, 1938-42; Festivals: Salzburg; Bayreuth; Edinburgh, 1953-54; Lucerne, 1947-56; Conductor and régisseur, La Scala, Milan, 1948-55; Musical Director, Berlin Philharmonic Orchestra, 1955-56. First European Tour with Philharmonia Orchestra, 1952; Director, Salzburg Festival, 1957. Films directed and conducted include: Bajazzo, Carmen, Beethoven's 9th Symphony. *Recreations:* ski-ing, mountaineering, flying, yachting, motoring, theatre, acoustical research. *Address:* Festspielhaus, Salzburg, Austria.

**von WEIZSÄCKER, Freiherr Carl-Friedrich,** Dr.phil; Cross of the Federal Republic of Germany, 1959; Order Pour le Mérite, 1961; (ord.) Professor of Philosophy, University of Hamburg, since 1957, and Director of Philosophical Seminary in the University; *b* Keil, 28 June 1912; *m* 1937, Gundalena (*née* Wille); three *s* one *d. Educ:* Universities of Leipzig, Göttingen, Copenhagen. Dr.phil 1933, Dr.phil.habil, 1936, Univ. Leipzig; Dozent, Univ. of Berlin, 1937; Asst Kaiser Wilhelm Inst., Berlin, 1936-42; Prof. Theor. Physik, Univ. of Strassburg, 1942-44; Hon. Prof., Univ. Göttingen and Abt. Leiter, Max Planck Inst. für Physik, Göttingen, 1946-47. Gifford Lecturer, Glasgow Univ., 1959-61. Deutsche Akademie der Naturforscher Leopoldina, Halle (DDR); Deutsche Akademie für Sprache und Dichtung, Darmstadt; Wiss. Mitglied der Max-Planck-Gesellschaft, Göttingen. Max Planck Medal, 1957; Goethe Prize (Frankfurt) 1958; Friedenspreis des deutschen Buchhandels, 1963; Erasmus Prize (with Gabriel Marcel), 1969. *Publications:* Die Atomkerne, 1937; Zum Weltbild der Physik, 10th edition, 1963 (in France, Le Monde vu par la physique, 1956; in Holland, Het wereldbeeld in de fysica, 1959); Die Geschichte der Natur, 5th edition, 1962 (English, Chicago, 1949); Physik der Gegenwart (with J. Juilfs), 2nd edition, 1958 (Engl., 1957); Die Verantwortung der Wissenschaft im Atomzeitalter, 4th edition, 1963; Atomenergie und Atomzeitalter, 3rd edition, 1958; Die Tragweite der Wissenschaft, 1964. *Recreations:* ski, tennis, chess. *Address:* Schwarzbuchenweg 40, Hamburg 64, Germany. *T:* Hamburg 526 52 56. *Club:* PEN.

**VONWILLER, Oscar Ulrich;** Professor of Physics in the University of Sydney, 1923-46, Emeritus Professor, 1946; *b* 18 Feb. 1882; *s* of late J. U. Vonwiller, Merchant, Sydney; *m* 1st, 1907, Vera Bennett (*d* 1920); one *s*; 2nd, 1925, Elsie Taylor (*d* 1961); one *s. Educ:* Paddington Public Sch.; Sydney Boys' High Sch.; University of Sydney. Lecturer in Physics, 1903; Assoc. Professor, 1920; Dean of Faculty of Science and Fellow of Senate, 1939-41; Fellow of Institute of Physics, 1927; Vice-President, Australian Branch, 1942; President, Royal Society of New South Wales, 1930-31 (Medal 1950); Hon. Treasurer, Australian National Research Council, 1934-42; Foundation President, Science Teachers Assoc. of NSW, 1919-22, then Hon. Life Vice-President; Member of Board of Visitors, Sydney Observatory, 1930-61; Vice-President, NSW Branch of British Astronomical Association, 1928-58; Member of Board of Visitors, Commonwealth Observatory, Chairman 1944-55; Member of Commonwealth Optical Scientific Instruments and Panel; Director Optical Munitions Annex, University of Sydney, 1940-46; Fellow, Australian Inst. of Physics, 1963. Hon. Life Member, Teachers' Guild of NSW, 1960. *Publications:* Practical Physics (with late Professor J. A. Pollock); various papers in scientific journals. *Recreation:* gardening. *Address:* Rathkells, Kangaroo Valley, NSW 2577, Australia. *Clubs:* University, High (Sydney, NSW).

**VORSTER, Hon. Balthazar Johannes,** BA, LLB; MP for Nigel in the Parliament of South Africa; Prime Minister of the Republic of South Africa, since 1966; Leader of the National Party of South Africa, since 1966; *b* 13 Dec. 1915; *s* of late William Carel Vorster; *m* 1941, Martini, *d* of P. A. Malan; two *s* one *d*. *Educ:* Sterkstroom High Sch.; Stellenbosch Univ. LLB 1938. Attorney, Port Elizabeth and Brakpan, until 1953; Member, Johannesburg Bar, practising 1953-58. Contested Brakpan, 1948; MP Nigel, 1953; Deputy Minister of Education, Arts, Science, Social Welfare and Pensions, 1958-61; Minister of Justice, 1961-66; Minister of Justice, of Police and of Prisons, 1966. DPhil (*hc*) Stellenbosch Univ., 1966; LLD (*hc*); University of Pretoria; Univ. of OFS, 1967; Univ. of Potchefstroom. *Recreations:* golf, chess. *Address:* (office) Union Buildings, Pretoria, South Africa. *T:* 20851; Marks Buildings, Cape Town, South Africa. *T:* 27511; (residence) Libertas, Pretoria, South Africa; Groote Schuur, Cape Town, South Africa. *Clubs:* Zwartkops Golf; Rondebosch Golf.

**VOWDEN, Desmond Harvey Weight,** QC 1969; *b* 6 Jan. 1921; *s* of late Rev. A. W. J. Vowden, MBE, TD; *m* 1964, Iris, *d* of L. A. Stafford-Northcote. *Educ:* Clifton Coll. Served in RN and RM, 1938-50; Captain RM, retired 1950. Called to the Bar, 1950; Dep. Chm., Wiltshire Quarter Sessions, 1968-. *Recreations:* music, gardening. *Address:* 33 Chapel Street, SW1. *T:* 01-235 4596. *Club:* Garrick.

**VOYSEY, Charles C.;** *see* Cowles-Voysey.

**VULLIAMY, Colwyn Edward;** author; *b* 20 June 1886; *s* of Edwin Papendiek Vulliamy and Edith Jane Beavan; *m* 1916, Eileen (*d* 1943), *d* of Harry H. Hynes; one *s* one *d*. *Educ:* privately. Studied art under Stanhope A. Forbes at Newlyn, 1910-13; served in France, Macedonia and Turkey, European War; active interest in field archæology for many years; contributor to Spectator and other periodicals. *Publications:* Charles Kingsley (Fabian Tract), 1914; Prehistoric Forerunners, 1925; Unknown Cornwall, 1925; Immortal Man, 1926; Letters of Tsar Nicholas II, 1929; Red Archives, 1929; The White Bull (trans.), 1929; Archæology of Middlesex and London, 1930; Voltaire, 1930; Rousseau, 1931; John Wesley, 1931; The Vicar's Experiments, 1932; Lobelia Grove, 1932; James Boswell, 1932; William Penn, 1933; Family Matters, 1934; Fusilier Bluff, 1934; Scarweather, 1934; Judas Maccabeus, 1934; Aspasia (Life and Letters of Mrs Delany), 1935; Mrs Thrale of Streatham, 1936; Royal George (Life of George III), 1937; Outlanders; Imperial Expansion in South Africa, 1938; Crimea: The Campaign of 1854-55, with an Outline of Politics, etc., 1939; Calico Pie, an Autobiography, 1940; A Short History of the Montagu-Puffins, 1941; The Polderoy Papers, 1943; Doctor Philligo: His Journal and Opinions, 1944; English Letter Writers, 1945; Edwin and Eleanor, 1945; Ursa Major: Dr Johnson and his Friends, 1946; Man and the Atom, 1947; Byron, 1948; Prodwit's Guide to Writing, 1949; Henry Plumdew, 1950; The Anatomy of Satire, 1950; Rocking Horse Journey, 1952; Don among the Dead Men, 1952; The Onslow Family, 1953; Jones: A Gentleman of Wales, 1954; The Proud Walkers, 1955; Body in the Boudoir, 1956; Cakes for your Birthday, 1959; Justice for Judy, 1960; Little Arthur's Guide to Humbug, 1960; Tea at the Abbey, 1961; Floral Tribute, 1963. *Address:* c/o National Westminster Bank, Guildford, Surrey.

**VULLIAMY, Maj.-Gen. Colwyn Henry Hughes,** CB 1945; DSO 1938; Director: Standard Telephones and Cables, 1949-67; Creed & Co., 1949; *b* 22 April 1894; *s* of Colwyn Williams Vulliamy, Lieut-Colonel Her Majesty's 17th Foot, and Lilian Isobel Gosling; *m* Veronica Mary, *y d* of Rev. John Ellis; two *s* one *d*. *Educ:* Cheltenham Coll.; Royal Military Academy, Woolwich. Commissioned RE, 1913; transferred to Royal Signals in 1926; served European War, France and Flanders, 1914-18 (despatches thrice); service in India, 1921-30 and 1935-38, including Waziristan, 1922-23, 1936-37, Mohmand, 1935 (despatches twice, DSO); has held appointments on Rhine Army HQs, 1919, and in War Office, 1931-34; Chief Signal Officer, Anti-Aircraft Command, 1939-40; Signal Officer in Chief, Middle East, 1943 (despatches); at Supreme HQ, NW Europe, 1943-45 (CB, Commander US Legion of Merit, Officer Légion d'Honneur, Croix de Guerre avec palme); GHQ, India, 1945-46; Director of Signals, War Office, 1946. Retired pay, 1949. Colonel Comdt, RCS, 1949-58, Rep. 1951 and 1955. *Recreation:* golf. *Address:* Dunimarle, Dunmow Hill, Fleet, Hants. *T:* Fleet 4233.

**VYNER, Clare George,** DL; *b* 1894; 2nd *s* of late Lord Alwyne Frederick Compton and Mary Evelyn, *e d* of Robert Charles de Grey Vyner, of Newby Hall, Yorks, and Gautby, Lincs; *m* 1923, Lady Doris Gordon-Lennox, 2nd *d* of 8th Duke of Richmond and Gordon; one *s* (and one *s* one *d* decd). Formerly Lieut, RN, serving war of 1939-45, Commander. Assumed surname of Vyner, 1912. DL, W Riding of Yorkshire and City and Co. of York. *Address:* 41a Hays Mews, W1. *T:* 01-499 1431; Keanchulish, Ullapool, Ross-shire; Fountains Hall, Ripon, Yorks.

*See also Marquess of Northampton.*

**VYSE, Charles,** ARCA; sculptor and potter; *b* 16 March 1882; *s* of Charles Vyse, of Stoke-on-Trent; *m* o *d* of John Edwards, Sanderstead; one *s* one *d*. *Educ:* Royal College of Art; Italy. Double Gold Medallist; National Scholarship; Royal College of Art Scholarship; Travelling Scholar. *Address:* Cheyne Cottage, Crown Court, 14 Middle Street, Deal, Kent. *Club:* Chelsea Arts.

**VYSE, Lt-Gen. Sir Edward D. H.;** *see* Howard-Vyse.

**VYVYAN, Jennifer (Brigit),** FRAM 1955; soprano; *d* of late Major Cecil Albert Vyvyan and of late Mrs Brigit Sinclair; *m* 1962, Leon Crown, FCA; one *s*. *Educ:* Kensington High Sch.; St Paul's Girls' Sch., London; Talbot Heath, Bournemouth. Joined Royal Academy of Music as pianoforte student and gained LRAM (performer's degree), also LRAM (teacher's degree) for singing; Fred Walker Scholarship; studied singing with Roy Henderson; Boise Foundation travelling Sch. (studies with Fernando Carpi, and also in Milan, and Rome); studied with David Keren, London; 1st prize, Concours Internat. de Genève, 1951 (1st British singer to receive an award). Appeared as Donna Anna in Don Giovanni and as Constanze in Die Entführung by Mozart with Sadler's Wells Opera, 1952; appeared with Glyndebourne Opera as Electra in Mozart's Idomeneo, Edinburgh Festival, 1953. Visited Russia with group led by Sir Arthur Bliss, 1956; visited S Africa and S Rhodesia, recital and concert tour, 1958; first visit to USA for 4 perfs of Britten's Spring Symphony with New York Philharmonic Orchestra, etc., 1963. Created roles of: Lady Rich in Britten's Coronation opera, Gloriana, Covent Garden; Governess in Britten's opera, The Turn of the Screw, Venice Festival, 1954 (subseq. in European cities, Canada and London, and on TV); Miss Hargreaves in The Spur of the Moment, an opera written for TV by Guy Halahan; Tytania, in Britten's opera, A Midsummer Night's Dream, at Aldeburgh Festival and Holland Festival (subseq. in London); Countess of Serendin in The Violins of St Jacques (Malcolm Williamson), Sadler's Wells; Agnes in The Growing Castle (Malcolm Williamson), Dynevor Castle, 1968 (subseq. at Australia House and in Sweden); series of comedy cameos in Lucky Peter's Journey (Malcolm Williamson), Sadler's Wells, 1969. Other roles include: Miss Wordsworth in Britten's Albert Herring; Thérèse in Poulenc's Les Mamelles de Tirésias; Polissena in Handel's Radamisto; Armida in Handel's Rinaldo, etc. Large repertoire of works by Bach (3 visits Bethlehem Bach Festival, USA), solo cantatas, etc; has sung in Beethoven's 9th Symphony with many distinguished Conductors. Many European Concerts and Festivals, including Britten's Les Illuminations (Prague Festival, Bratislava and Budapest, 1968, with Giulini and New Philharmonia Orch.; London and Bath Festival, 1969); concert performances, Aldeburgh, Brussels and Lucerne Festivals, Purcell's Fairy Queen; Flanders Festival, 1970. Numerous recordings and appearances on TV. *Recreations:* the theatre, reading, painting. *Address:* 59 Fitzjohn's Avenue, NW3. *T:* 01-435 2342.

**VYVYAN, Major-General Ralph Ernest,** CBE 1944 (MBE 1923); MC; *b* 1891; *s* of late Captain H. R. Vyvyan, sometime Devonshire Regt and Chief Constable of Devon, 1907-31; *cousin* and *heir-pres.* to Sir Richard Philip Vyvyan, BT, *qv*; *m* 1st, 1915 Vera Grace (from whom he obtained a divorce), *er d* of late Robert Arthur Alexander, Portglenone, Co. Antrim; one *s*; 2nd, 1930, Kathleen Antonia, *o d* of Haskett Farquhar Haskett-Smith, Starcross, S Devon; one *d*. *Educ:* Stubbington; Exeter; RMC, Sandhurst. 2nd Lieut, Worcestershire Regt, 1910; served European War, 1914-19, with Regt, Army Signal Service and Staff (despatches, MC); transferred to R Signals, 1920; Lieut-Colonel, 1931; Colonel, 1934; Brig., 1941; temp. Maj.-Gen., 1942-45; Chief Signal Officer: Eastern Command, India, 1932-35; Western Command, India, 1935-39 (Quetta Earthquake, 1935, thanks of Viceroy); Northern Command, India, 1939-40; Signal Officer-in-Chief and Director of Signals, India (including for periods Burma, Ceylon and Iraq), 1941-45; retired 1946, hon. rank of Maj.-Gen. Editor Journal of RUSI, 1950-57, and Registrar of the Museum, 1948-58. *Address:* Limes Well, Streatley-on-Thames, Berks. *T:* Goring-on-Thames 2364. *Clubs:* Army and Navy, MCC.

**VYVYAN, Sir Richard Philip,** 11th Bt, *cr* 1645; *b* 21 Nov. 1891; *s* of late Major Richard Walter Comyn Vyvyan, 2nd *s* of 9th Bt; *S* uncle, 1941. *Heir: cousin,* Maj.-Gen. Ralph Ernest Vyvyan, *qv*.

# W

**WAAL, Brig. Pieter De;** *see* De Waal.

**WACE, Ernest William Cornish,** CSI 1946; CIE 1941; Indian Police (Retired); *b* 11 May 1894; *s* of late Colonel E. C. Wace, DSO, RA; *m* 1921, Irene Marguerite Sant; one *s* one *d* (*er d* killed on active service, Burma, 1945). *Educ:* Felsted Sch., Essex. Appointed to Indian Police, 1914; served in Indian Army, 1915-17, till invalided; held charge of the Police in several Punjab districts and in the Delhi Province; Deputy Inspector-General, 1936; Deputy Inspector-General CID, 1941-45; Inspector-General, Police, Punjab, 1945; Indian Police Medal, 1933. Security Officer, Ministry of Supply, 1948, retired. *Recreation:* gardening. *Address:* Pays Meadow, South Harting, Petersfield, Hants. *T:* Harting 278.

**WACHER, David Mure;** Metropolitan Stipendiary Magistrate since 1962; *b* 9 Oct. 1909; *s* of late Dr Harold Wacher, FSA, and Violet Amy Wacher (*née* Peebles); *m* 1935, Kathleen Margaret Roche, *yr d* of late Rev. George Ralph Melvyrn Roche; one *s* one *d*. *Educ:* Charterhouse. Called to Bar, Middle Temple, 1935. Served in Royal Artillery, 1939-43. Acting Attorney-General, Gibraltar, 1943; Stipendiary Magistrate, Gibraltar, 1943-49; Acting Chief Justice, Gibraltar, 1948. Vice-Chairman, Mental Health Review Tribunal for SW Metropolitan RHB Area, 1960-62. *Recreations:* music and the theatre. *Address:* The Platt, Elsted, Midhurst, Sussex. *T:* Harting 261. *Club:* Bath.

**WACKETT, Air Vice-Marshal Ellis Charles,** CB 1957; CBE 1951 (OBE 1941); psa; Royal Australian Air Force; *b* 13 Aug. 1901; *yr s* of James Wackett, Townsville, Queensland; *m* 1928, Doreen I., *d* of Thomas S. Dove, Mildura, Victoria; two *s* one *d*. *Educ:* Jervis Bay Royal Australian Naval Coll.; Keyham Engineering College, England; Imperial College of Science and Technology, London. Joined Australian Navy, 1915; commissioned, 1921. Transferred to Royal Australian Air Force, 1923; graduated RAF Staff Coll., 1933. Air Vice-Marshal, 1948. Air Member for Engineering and Maintenance, 1942; Air Member for Technical Service, RAAF, 1948. *Recreation:* angling. *Address:* Yaralla, Eltham Road, Panton Hill, Victoria, Australia. *Club:* Naval and Military (Victoria).

**WACKETT, Sir Lawrence (James),** Kt 1954; DFC 1918, AFC 1919; BSc; CEng, FRAeS; Manager and a Director of Commonwealth Aircraft Corporation Ltd, 1936-61, retired; Director, Joseph Lucas (Australia) Ltd, 1960-69; *b* 2 Jan. 1896; *s* of James Wackett, Townsville, Queensland; *m* 1919, Letitia Emily Florence, *d* of Fred B. Wood, Townsville, Queensland; one *d* (one *s* decd). *Educ:* Royal Military Coll. (Duntroon); Melbourne University (BSc). Officer, Australian Regular Army, 1913-20; served in Australian Flying Corps in France and Palestine (despatches twice); Officer, RAAF, 1921, retired a Wing Commander, 1930; Aeronautical Engineer, 1930-35. Commodore, Beaumaris Motor Yacht Squadron, 1962-68. Kernot Memorial Medallist, 1959; Finlay National Award, 1967. *Publications:* My Hobby is Trout Fishing, 1944; Studies of an Angler, 1949. *Recreations:* trout fishing, motor boating. *Address:* 31 Tramway Parade, Beaumaris, Melbourne, Victoria, Australia.

**WADDAMS, Rev. Canon Herbert Montague,** MA (Cantab); Canon Residentiary of Canterbury Cathedral and Examining Chaplain to the Archbishop of Canterbury since 1962; *b* 15 Nov. 1911; *s* of William Henry Waddams, CBE, and late Ruby Waddams; *m* 1940, Margaret Mary Burgess; one *s* one *d*. *Educ:* King's Sch., Bruton; King's Coll., Cambridge; Cuddesdon College; Lund Univ., Sweden. Deacon, 1935; Priest, 1936, Dio. of Southwark; Asst Missioner, Corpus Christi Coll., Cambridge Mission, 1935-37; Asst Priest, Grosvenor Chapel, and Chaplain of Liddon House, 1937-41; CF (TA), 1938-41; Priest Vicar and Sub-Dean of Chichester Cathedral, 1941-42; Religious Div., Ministry of Information, 1942-45; Hon. Chaplain, Bishop of Gloucester, 1943-46; Gen. Secretary, C. of E. Council on Foreign Relations, 1945-59; Guild Vicar of St Michael, Paternoster Royal, 1954-59; Hon. Canon of Canterbury, 1955-62; Rector of Manotick, Ont., Canada, 1959-62; Lecturer in Ascetical Theology, General Theological Seminary, New York, 1964; Select Preacher, Oxford Univ., 1965. Chm., Hansard Soc. for Parly Govt, 1970-. Knight of Order of Orange Nassau, 1954; Vardapet's Cross from Armenian Patriarch of Jerusalem, 1955; Archpriest's Cross from Orthodox Patriarch of Rumania, 1958. *Publications:* The Swedish Church, 1946; Communism and the Churches, 1950; Believing, 1958; Meeting of Orthodox Churches, 1964; Life and Fire of Love, 1964; A New Introduction to Moral Theology, 1964; Companion to the Book of Common Prayer, 1966; The Church and Man's Struggle for Unity, 1968; Illustrated Guide to Canterbury, 1968; Basic Questions of Life and Death, 1968; The Life of the Spirit, 1969; Illustrated Life of St Thomas Becket, 1969. Contributor: Christian Counter Attack, 1943; English Church and the Continent, 1959; The Church in the 60's, 1962; numerous articles. *Recreations:* hearing and making music. *Address:* 15 The Precincts, Canterbury, Kent. *T:* Canterbury 64764. *Club:* Athenæum.

**WADDELL, Sir Alexander (Nicol Anton),** KCMG 1959 (CMG 1955); DSC 1944; United Kingdom Commissioner, British Phosphate Commissioners, since 1965; *b* 8 Nov. 1913; *yr s* of late Rev. Alexander Waddell, Eassie, Angus, Scotland, and late Effie Thompson Anton Waddell; *m* 1949, Jean Margot Lesbia, *d* of late W. E. Masters. *Educ:* Fettes Coll., Edinburgh; Edinburgh Univ. (MA); Gonville and Caius Coll., Cambridge. Colonial Administrative Service, 1937; British Solomon Islands Protectorate: Cadet, 1937; District Officer, 1938; District Commissioner, 1945; Acting Resident Commissioner, 1945; Malayan Civil Service, 1946; Principal Asst Secretary, North Borneo, 1947-52 (Acting Dep. Chief Secretary, periods, 1947-51). Colonial Secretary, Gambia, 1952-56; Colonial Secretary, Sierra Leone, 1956-58; Dep. Governor, Sierra Leone, 1958-60; Governor and Commander-in-Chief of Sarawak, 1960-63. On Naval Service, 1942-44. Lieut, RANVR; on Military Service, 1945-47, Lt-Col, Gen. List (British Mil. Administration). *Recreations:* golf, gardening. *Address:* Pilgrim Cottage, Ashton Keynes, Wilts. *Clubs:* RNVR, Royal Commonwealth Society, East India and Sports.

**WADDELL, James Henderson,** CB 1960; Deputy Under-Secretary, Home Office, since 1966; *b* 5 Oct. 1914; *s* of D. M. Waddell and J. C. Fleming; *m* 1940, Dorothy Abbie Wright; one *s* one *d*. *Educ:* George Heriot's Sch.; Edinburgh Univ. Assistance Board, 1936; Ministry of Information, 1940; Reconnaissance Corps, 1942; Ministry of Housing and Local Government, 1946; Under-Secretary, 1955; Under-Secretary, Cabinet Office, 1961-63; Dep.-Secretary, Min. of Housing and Local Government, 1963-66. *Recreation:* sailing. *Address:* 89 Onslow Square, SW7. *T:* 01-584 5312. *Club:* Athenæum.

**WADDINGTON, Professor Conrad Hal,** CBE 1958; MA; ScD; FRS 1947; Buchanan Professor of Animal Genetics, University of Edinburgh, since 1947; *b* 8 Nov. 1905; *s* of Hal Waddington, Coimbatore, S India; *m* 1st, 1926, Cecil Elizabeth Lascelles; one *s*; 2nd, 1934, Margaret Justin Blanco White; two *d*. *Educ:* Clifton Coll.; Sidney Sussex Coll., Cambridge. 1st Class, Nat. Sc. Trip. Part II (Geology) 1926; Gerstenberg Studentship in Philosophy, 1927; Senior Student, Exhibition of 1851; Travelling Fellow, Rockefeller Foundation, 1932 and 1938; Lecturer in Zoology and Embryologist, Strangeways Research Laboratory, Cambridge, 1933-45; Fellow of Christ's Coll., Cambridge, 1934-45; Hon. Fellow, 1966. Hon. Director, MRC's Research Group on Epigenetics; Vis. Einstein Prof., State Univ. of New York at Buffalo, 1969-. President, International Union of Biological Sciences, 1961-67. Albert Brachet Prize for embryology, awarded by Royal Academy of Belgium, 1936; Foreign Hon. Member: American Academy of Arts and Sciences, 1960; Finnish Acad., 1967. Hon. DSc (Montréal) 1958, (Dublin), 1965, (Prague) 1966, (Geneva), 1968. Hon. LLD (Aberdeen) 1966. Operational research in Coastal Command, Royal Air Force, 1942-45; Scientific Adviser to Commander-in-Chief, 1944-45. *Publications:* Introduction to Modern Genetics, 1939; Organisers and Genes, 1940; The Scientific Attitude, 1941; Science and Ethics (ed), 1942; Epigenetics of Birds, 1952; Principles of Embryology, 1956; The Strategy of the Genes, 1957; The Ethical Animal, 1960; The Nature of Life, 1961; New Patterns in Genetics and Development, 1962; Principles of Development and Differentiation, 1966; (ed) Towards a Theoretical Biology, Vol. I, 1968, Vol. II, 1969, Vol. III, 1970; Behind Appearance, 1970; many articles in scientific journals. *Recreation:* painting. *Address:* Institute of Animal Genetics, West Mains Road, Edinburgh 9. *T:* 031-667 1011; Center for Theoretical Biology, State University of New York at Buffalo, Ridgelea, Amherst, NY 14226, USA. *Club:* Athenæum.

**WADDINGTON, David Charles;** MP (C) for Nelson and Colne since 1968; *b* 2 Aug. 1929; *o s* of late Charles Waddington and of Mrs Minnie Hughan Waddington; *m* 1958, Gillian Rosemary, *d* of Alan Green, *qv*; three *s* one *d*. *Educ:* Sedbergh; Hertford Coll., Oxford. President, Oxford Univ. Conservative Assoc., 1950. 2nd Lieut, XII Royal Lancers, 1951-53. Barrister, 1951-. Contested (C): Farnworth Div., General Election, 1955; Nelson and Colne Div., General Election, 1964; Heywood and Royton Div., General Election, 1966. *Address:* Whins House, Sabden, near Blackburn. *T:* Padiham 71070; Flat 125, 4 Whitehall Court, SW1. *T:* 01-930 3160 (Ext. 125). *Club:* St James's (Manchester).

**WADDINGTON, Gerald Eugene;** Attorney General of the Cayman Islands, since 1970; *b* 31 Jan. 1909; *o s* of Walter George Waddington and Una Blanche Waddington (*née* Hammond); *m* 1935, Hylda Kathleen (*née* Allen); one *s* one *d*. *Educ:* Jamaica Coll.; Wolmer's Schl., Jamaica. Solicitor, Supreme Court, Jamaica, 1932; LLB (London) 1949; Solicitor, Supreme Court, England, 1950; called to the Bar, Gray's Inn, 1957. Deputy Clerk of Courts, Jamaica, 1939; Asst Crown Solicitor, Jamaica, 1943-48; Resident Magistrate, 1948-58; Puisne Judge, 1959-64; Judge of the Court of Appeal, Jamaica, 1964-70, retired. Joint ed. West Indian Law Reports. Vice-Pres. Nat. Rifle Assoc. Chm. St John Council for Jamaica. CStJ 1962, KStJ 1970. *Recreation:* shooting (Member of Jamaica Rifle Team to Bisley, 1937, 1950, 1953, 1956, 1957, 1960, 1963, 1965, 1967, 1968; Captain, 1950, 1953, 1957, 1967; Captain, WI Rifle Team, 1960). *Address:* Attorney General's Chambers, PO Box 495, Grand Cayman, Cayman Islands, West Indies. *Clubs:* Royal Commonwealth Society, Royal Over-Seas League.

**WADDINGTON, Very Rev. John Albert Henry,** MBE 1945; TD 1951; MA (Lambeth) 1959; Provost of St Edmundsbury and Ipswich since 1958; *b* 10 Feb. 1910; *s* of H. Waddington, Tooting Graveney, Surrey; *m* 1938, Marguerite Elisabeth, *d* of F. Day, Wallington, Surrey; two *d*. *Educ:* Wandsworth Sch.; London Univ.; London College of Divinity. BCom London Univ., 1929. Deacon, 1933; priest, 1934; Curate of St Andrew's, Streatham, 1933-35; Curate of St Paul's, Furzedown, 1935-38; Rector of Great Bircham, 1938-45; Vicar of St Peter Mancroft, Norwich, 1945; Chaplain to High Sheriff of Norfolk, 1950; Proctor in Convocation of Canterbury, 1950; Hon. Canon of Norwich, 1951. Chaplain to Forces (TA) 1935-58; Staff Chaplain, Eighth Army, 1943 (despatches twice); DACG XIII Corps, 1945, Eastern Command TA, 1951. *Recreations:* Rotary, travel, theatre and cinema, religious journalism. *Address:* The Provost's House, Bury St Edmunds, Suffolk. *T:* 4852.

**WADDY, Rev. Lawrence Heber;** Lecturer, University of California, San Diego, since 1970; Vicar of St James' Mission, University City, since 1970; *b* 5 Oct. 1914; *s* of late Archdeacon Stacy Waddy, Secretary of SPG, and Etheldred (*née* Spittal). *Educ:* Marlborough Coll.; Balliol Coll., Oxford. Domus Exhibitioner in Classics, Balliol, 1933; 1st Class Hon. Mods., Oxford, 1935; de Paravicini Scholar, 1935; Craven Scholar,

1935; 2nd Class Lit. Hum., 1937; BA 1937; MA 1945; Asst Master: Marlborough Coll., 1937-38; Winchester Coll., 1938-42 and 1946-49 (Chaplain, 1946). Headmaster, Tonbridge Sch., 1949-62. Select Preacher, Cambridge Univ., 1951; Oxford Univ., 1954-56. Examining Chaplain to the Bishop of Rochester, 1959-63; Hon. Canon of Rochester, 1961-63; Hon. Chaplain to the Bishop of Rochester, 1963. Deacon, 1940; Priest, 1941; Chaplain, RNVR, 1942-46. Lecturer in Classics, University of California, 1961. Education Officer, School Broadcasting Council, 1962-63; Chaplain to The Bishop's School, La Jolla, California, 1963-67; Headmaster, Santa Maria Internat. Acad., Chula Vista, Calif, 1967-70. *Publications:* Pax Romana and World Peace, 1950; The Prodigal Son (Musical play), 1963. *Recreations:* cricket and other games. *Address:* 866 Prospect Street, La Jolla, California 92037, USA.

**WADE,** family name of **Baron Wade.**

**WADE,** Baron, *cr* 1964 (Life Peer); **Donald William Wade,** DL; MA, LLB; *b* 16 June 1904; *s* of William Mercer and Beatrice Hemington Wade; *m* 1932, Ellenora Beatrice (*née* Bentham); two *s* two *d. Educ:* Mill Hill; Trinity Hall, Cambridge. Admitted Solicitor, 1929. MP (L) Huddersfield West, 1950-64; Liberal Whip, 1956-62; Deputy Leader, Liberal Parliamentary Party, 1962-64; Deputy Liberal Whip, House of Lords, 1965-67; President, Liberal Party, 1967-68. DL, W. Riding, Yorks, 1967. *Publications:* Democracy, 1944; Way of the West, 1945; Our Aim and Purpose, 1961. *Address:* 1 Ashleigh Road, Leeds 16. *T:* Leeds 55173; High Houses, Wath, near Pateley Bridge, Yorks. *T:* Pateley Bridge 431. *Clubs:* National Liberal, Reform.

**WADE, Major-General Douglas Ashton Lofft,** CB 1946; OBE 1941; MC 1918; BA; CEng; MIEE; *b* 13 March 1898; 2nd *s* of C. S. D. Wade, Solicitor, Saffron Walden, Essex; *m* 1926, Heather Mary Patricia Bulmer (*d* 1968), Sowerby, Thirsk, Yorkshire; one *d. Educ:* St Lawrence Coll., Ramsgate; Royal Military Acad., Woolwich; Clare Coll., Cambridge. Commnd into Royal Artillery, 1916; served European War, France and Italy; seconded RE 1918-21; transferred to Royal Signals, 1921; Staff Coll., Camberley, 1933-34; DAQMG India, 1937-40; GSO 1, GHQ, BEF and GHQ Home Forces, 1940-41; AA and QMG 2nd Division, 1941-42; Dep. Ajt.-General, India, 1942-44; Comdr, Madras Area, India, 1944-47; GOC Malaya District, 1947-48; Special Appointment War Office, 1948-49; retired, 1950; Telecommunications Attaché, British Embassy, Washington, 1951-54; Sen. Planning Engineer, Independent Television Authority, 1954-60; Regional Officer, East Anglia, Independent Television Authority, 1960-64. Technical Consultant: Inter-University Research Unit, Cambridge, 1965-69; WRVS Headquarters, 1970-. Chairman Royal Signals Institute, 1957-63; National Vice-Chairman Dunkirk Veterans' Association, 1962-67, National Chairman, 1967-. *Publications:* contributed to various Services publications, including RUSI Journal, United Services Journal (India), and Brassey's Annual. *Recreations:* gardening, acting. *Address:* Phœnix Cottage, Old Catton, Norwich, NOR 74N. *T:* Norwich 45755.

**WADE, Emlyn Capel Stewart,** QC 1959; MA, LLD (Cantab); Hon. DCL (Durham); FBA; Downing Professor of the Laws of England, Cambridge University, 1945-62, Professor Emeritus, since 1962; Fellow of Gonville and Caius College since 1931; Reader in Constitutional Law, Council of Legal Education, 1945-66; Member of the Law Reform Committee, 1952-63; Hinkley Visiting Professor, Johns Hopkins University, Baltimore, 1962-63; Barrister-at-Law; Hon. Bencher, Inner Temple; *b* 31 Aug. 1895; *er s* of late Charles Stewart Douglas Wade; *m* 1924, Mary Esmé, *yr d* of late Rev. W. B. Cardew; four *d. Educ:* St Lawrence Coll., Ramsgate; Gonville and Caius Coll., Cambridge. Served with British Salonika Force, and in France, 1916-19; Temp. Major, RA (TA), 1940-42; employed in offices of War Cabinet and Home Office, 1942-45; Lecturer-in-Law, Armstrong Coll., University of Durham, 1923-24; Vice-Principal, 1924-26, Principal, 1926-28. Law Society's School of Law; Fellow of St John's Coll., Cambridge, 1928-31; Member of the Council of the Senate, Cambridge Univ., 1936-40; Hon. Secretary, Society of Public Teachers of Law, 1925-28, President, 1950-51. Member of Lord Chancellor's Committees on Law of Defamation and Limitation of Actions; Cttee on Electoral Law Reform. *Publications:* (with late G. Godfrey Phillips) Constitutional Law, 1931, 8th edn, 1970; edited Dicey, Law of the Constitution, 10th Ed., 1959; articles in Law Quarterly Review, and various legal publications. *Address:* 17 Sculthorpe Road, Fakenham, Norfolk. *T:* Fakenham 2565.

**WADE, Brigadier Ernest Wentworth,** DSO 1918; OBE 1940; late RAMC; *b* 14 Oct. 1889; *s* of late Major George Augustus Wade, RAMC, and Caroline Oram Ada Corrall; *m* 1st, 1918, Winifred (*d* 1939), *d* of D. McG. Alexander, Rathgar, Dublin; one *s* (two *d* decd); 2nd, 1940, Anna Reaveley, *d* of late T. R. Glover. *Educ:* Stubbington House, Fareham; University College, Bristol (Medical Entrance Scholarship). Augustin Pritchard Anatomy Prize, 1910; 1st Place RAMC Entrance Examination, July 1913; MB BS, London, 1913, MD London, 1921, DPH, RCS 1924, DTM and H RCS 1924; Specialist in Hygiene, 1925; House Physician, Bristol General Hospital, 1913; House Surgeon, Bristol Royal Infirmary, 1914; Joined RAMC 1913; Captain, 1915, Major, 1923; Instructor, Army School of Hygiene, Aldershot, 1925; DADH Lucknow and P. and A. Districts, India, 1927-30; DADH Army Headquarters, India, 1931; DADH South Western Area, Portsmouth, 1932-34; Lieut-Colonel, 1935; Assistant Director of Hygiene, Southern Command, India, 1935-39; ADH Scottish Command, 1939; Colonel, 1938; ADMS Orkney and Shetland Defences, May-Sept. 1940; ADMS 52nd (L) Division, 1940-41; DDMS 3 Corps, Aug.-Dec. 1941; DDMSEF Home Forces, Jan.-June 1942; DDMS 1st Army, June 1942-July 1943; Inspector of Medical Services, War Office, Aug. 1943-April 1944; OC 111 General Hospital, May-Sept. 1944; DDMS Control Commission for Germany, Oct. 1944; retired pay, 1946. Served European War, BEF, Aug. 1914-Oct. 1919. Acting Lieut-Colonel, May 1917-Oct. 1919 (DSO, 1914 Star, General Service and Victory Medals); Coronation Medal, 1937; War of 1939-45 (OBE, 1939-45 Star, Africa Star 1st Army, Defence Medal, War Medal). *Address:* c/o Glyn Mills and Co., Holt's Branch, Kirkland House, Whitehall, SW1.

**WADE, Colonel Sir George Albert,** Kt 1955; MC; JP; Chairman: Wade Potteries Ltd; Wade (Ireland) Ltd; George Wade & Son Ltd; A. J. Wade Ltd; Wade Heath & Co. Ltd; Director, Dalehall Mills Ltd; *b* 1891; *s* of George Wade, JP, Burslem; *m* 1915, Florence, *d* of Samuel Johnson, JP, Burslem; one *s* two *d. Educ:* Newcastle-under-Lyme High Sch., Staffordshire. Served European War, 1914-18, with S. Staffs Regt (MC and Bar); served War of 1939-45, with his Regiment and on General Staff; Colonel (retired) late S Staffs Regiment.

Contested (C) Newcastle-under-Lyme, General Election, 1945. Past President: North Staffordshire Political Union; North Staffs Chamber of Commerce. Chairman: Pottery and Glass Trades Benevolent Institution, 1949-54; Machine Gun Corps Old Comrades Association. Pres. N Staffs Medical Inst. Fellow Corporation of Secretaries. JP Stoke-on-Trent. *Publications:* Minor Tactics Training Manual (issued to Home Guard) and a series of 12 books on Military Training, during War of 1939-45. *Recreations:* painting, photography, ornithology. *Address:* Brand Hall, Norton-in-Hales, Market Drayton, Shropshire. *T:* Norton-in-Hales 206.

**WADE, Professor Henry William Rawson,** QC 1968; FBA 1969; MA; LLD (Cantab); DCL (Oxon); Professor of English Law, Oxford University, since 1961; Fellow of St John's College, Oxford, since 1961; Barrister-at-Law; *b* 16 Jan. 1918; *s* of late Colonel H. O. Wade and of E. L. Rawson-Ackroyd; *m* 1943, Marie, *d* of late G. E. Osland-Hill; two *s. Educ:* Shrewsbury Sch.; Gonville and Caius Coll., Cambridge. Henry Fellow, Harvard Univ., 1939; temp. officer, Treasury, 1940-46. Called to the Bar, Lincoln's Inn, 1946; Hon. Bencher, 1964. Fellow of Trinity Coll., Cambridge, 1946-61; University Lecturer, 1947; Reader, 1959. Lecturer, Council of Legal Education, 1957; British Council lecturer in Scandinavia, 1958, and Turkey, 1959; Cooley Lecturer, Michigan Univ., 1961. Member: Council on Tribunals, 1958; Relationships Commn, Uganda, 1961; Member, Royal Commn on Tribunals of Inquiry, 1966. *Publications:* The Law of Real Property, 1957 (with Hon. Mr Justice Megarry), 3rd edn, 1966; Administrative Law, 1961, 2nd edn, 1967; Towards Administrative Justice, 1963; Editor, Annual Survey of Commonwealth Law; articles in legal journals; broadcast talks. *Recreations:* climbing, gardening. *Address:* The Quarry, East End, Witney, Oxon. *T:* Freeland 239; St John's College, Oxford. *T:* Oxford 47671. *Club:* Alpine.

**WADE, John Charles,** OBE 1959; JP; HM Lieutenant of the County of Cumberland since 1968; *b* 15 Feb. 1908; unmarried. *Educ:* St Bees School. Midland Bank Ltd, 1925-27. West Cumberland Farmers Trading Society Ltd, 1927-68 (General Manager, 1931-64; Managing Director, 1964-68). Director: W Cumberland Farmers Trading Soc. Ltd; Border Television Ltd; Chicpac Ltd; Daniel Robertson (Newcastle) Ltd; Member: Meat and Livestock Commn; Cumberland River Authority. JP Cumberland, 1956. *Recreations:* shooting, fishing. *Address:* Hillcrest, Whitehaven, Cumberland. *T:* Whitehaven 2844. *Clubs:* Public Schools; Cumberland County (Carlisle).

**WADE, John Roland,** CB 1942; retired as Director of Remploy Ltd (1960-63); *b* 11 Oct. 1890; *e s* of late George Alfred Wade; *m* 1928, Penelope Dorothy Haig, *y d* of late Dr Haig Ferguson, Edinburgh; two *s. Educ:* Westminster School (King's Scholar); Queens' Coll., Cambridge (Scholar). Entered War Office, 1914; Director of Establishments, War Office, 1939-53; retired Dec. 1953. Financial Director (part-time), Remploy Ltd, 1954-Oct. 1960. *Address:* 6 Callcott Street, W8.

**WADE, Professor Owen Lyndon,** MD, FRCP; Whitla Professor of Therapeutics and Pharmacology, Queen's Univ., Belfast, since 1957; *b* 17 May 1921; *s* of J. O. D. Wade, MS, FRCS, and Kate Wade, 25 Park Place, Cardiff; *m* 1948, Margaret Burton, LDS; three *d. Educ:* Repton; Cambridge; University College Hospital, London. Senior Scholar, Emmanuel Coll., Cambridge, 1941; Achison and Atkinson Morley Schol., UCH, 1945; Resident Medical Officer, UCH, 1946; Clinical Assistant, Pneumokoniosis Research Unit of the Medical Research Council, 1948-51; Lecturer and Sen. Lecturer in Medicine, Dept of Medicine, University of Birmingham, 1951-57. Rockefeller Travelling Fellowship in Medicine, 1954-55; Research Fellow, Columbia Univ. at Department of Medicine, Presbyterian Hospital, New York, 1954-55; Consultant, WHO. Member: Northern Ireland General Health Services Board; Northern Ireland Hospitals Authority; Chairman, Board of Management, Prescribers' Journal; Member, Cttee on Safety of Drugs and Chairman of Sub-Cttee on adverse reactions of drugs, Ministry of Health, London. *Publications:* (with J. M. Bishop) The cardiac output and regional blood flow, 1962; contrib. to Handbook of Biological Data, National Academy of Sciences, USA, 1957; papers on respiratory and cardio-respiratory research in Journal of Physiology, Clinical Science, Journal of Clinical Investigation, etc. *Recreations:* books, travel and sailing. *Address:* Department of Therapeutics of Queen's University, Institute of Clinical Science, Royal Victoria Hospital, Belfast. *T:* Belfast 40503.

**WADE, R(obert) Hunter;** New Zealand Ambassador to Japan and Korea, since 1969; *b* 14 June 1916; *s* of R. H. Wade, Balclutha, NZ; *m* 1941, Avelda Grace Petersen; two *s* two *d. Educ:* Waitaki; Otago Univ., NZ. NZ Treasury and Marketing Depts, 1939; NZ Govt appts, Delhi, Simla, Sydney, Canberra, 1941-49; Head of Eastern Section, Dept of External Affairs, Wellington, NZ, 1949; First Secretary, NZ Embassy, Washington, 1951; NZ High Commn, Ottawa, 1956; Director of Colombo Plan Bureau, Colombo, 1957; Head of Ext. Aid Div., Dept of External Affairs, Wellington, 1959; Comr for NZ in Singapore and British Borneo, 1962; High Comr for NZ, in Malaya/Malaysia, 1963-67; Dep. High Comr in London, 1967-69. Represented New Zealand at Independence of: Uganda, 1962; Botswana, 1966; Lesotho, 1966. *Address:* New Zealand Embassy, 20 Kamiyama-cho, Shibuya-ku, Tokyo, Japan. *Clubs:* St James'; Wellington (Wellington, NZ).

**WADE, Major-General Ronald Eustace,** CB 1961; CBE 1956; retired; *b* 28 Oct. 1905; *s* of late Rev. E. V. Wade and Marcia Wade; *m* 1933, Doris, *d* of late C. K. Ross, Kojonup, WA; one *s* one *d. Educ:* Melbourne Church of England Grammar Sch.; RMC, Duntroon, ACT. Commissioned, 1927; attached 4/7 DG (India), 1928-29; Adjutant 10 LH and 9 LH, 1930-38; Captain, 1935; Major, 1940; served War of 1939-45, Lieut-Colonel (CO 2/10 Aust. Armd Regt), 1942; Colonel (Colonel A, Adv. LHQ, Morotai), 1945; Colonel Q, AHQ, Melbourne, 1946; idc 1948; Director of Cadets, 1949; Director of Quartering, 1950-51; Director of Personal Services, 1951-52; Military Secretary, 1952-53; Comd 11 Inf. Bde (Brig.), 1953-55; Maj.-General (Head Aust. Joint Service Staff, Washington), 1956-57; Adjutant-General, 1957-60; GOC Northern Command, 1961-62, retired, 1962. *Recreations:* fishing, mechanical handicrafts. *Address:* Albany, Western Australia.

**WADE, Rosalind (Herschel), (Mrs William Kean Seymour);** novelist; Editor, Contemporary Review, since 1970; *d* of Lieut-Colonel H. A. L. H. Wade and Kathleen Adelaide Wade; *m* William Kean Seymour, *qv*; two *s. Educ:* Glendower Sch., London; privately, abroad and Bedford Coll., London. Member: Society of Women Writers and Journalists (Chairman,

1962-64, Vice President, 1965-); Committee West Country Writers Assoc., 1953-65; General and Exec. Councils, The Poetry Society Inc., 1962-64, 1965-66; Guildford Centre of Poetry Soc. (Chm. 1969-); Alresford Historical and Literary Soc. (Chm. 1968-70); conducting Writing and Literary Courses at Moor Park College, Farnham (jointly with William Kean Seymour), 1962-. *Publications: novels:* Children, Be Happy, 1931; Kept Man, 1933; Pity the Child, 1934; Shadow Thy Dream, 1934; A Fawn in a Field, 1935; Men Ask for Beauty, 1936; Treasure in Heaven, 1937; Fairweather Faith, 1940; The Man of Promise, 1941; Bracelet for Julia, 1942; Pride of the Family, 1943; Present Ending, 1946; As the Narcissus, 1946; The Widows, 1948; The Raft, 1950; The Falling Leaves, 1951; Alys at Endon, 1953; The Silly Dove, 1953; Cassandra Calls, 1954; Come Fill The Cup, 1955; Morning Break, 1956; Mrs Jamison's Daughter, 1957; The Grain Will Grow, 1959; The Will of Heaven, 1960; A Small Shower, 1961; The Ramerson Case, 1962; New Pasture, 1964; The Vanished Days, 1966; Ladders, 1968; The Umbrella, 1970; The Golden Bowl, 1970; contrib. to The Fourth Ghost Book, 1965; The Unlikely Ghosts, 1967; Happy Christmas, 1968; Contemporary Review, Poetry Review, Books and Bookmen, Cornish Review, etc. *Recreations:* walking and theatre going. *Address:* White Cottage, Old Alresford, Alresford, Hants. *T:* Alresford 2870. *Club:* PEN.

**WADE-GERY, Henry Theodore,** MC; MA; FBA 1941; Hon. Litt D (Dublin); Wykeham Professor Emeritus, Oxford University; Hon. Fellow of Wadham and New Colleges, Oxford; *b* 2 April 1888; *y s* of Arthur Staunton Wade-Gery, Campton Grange, Shefford, Beds; *m* 1928, Vivian, *yr d* of Richard Whitfield, Kilcormac, King's Co.; one *s* (*see* R. L. Wade-Gery). *Educ:* Winchester; New Coll., Oxford. 1st Class Classical Mods. 1909 and Greats 1911; Home Civil Service (Admiralty), 1912-13; Assistant Master, Sherborne School, 1913-14; Fellow of Wadham, Oxford, 1914-39; served European War in France and Belgium, 1915-18, with 19th Lancs Fusiliers; Member of Institute for Advanced Study, Princeton, USA, 1937-38, 1947-48, 1956-58, 1960-61; Fellow of New College and Wykeham Professor of Ancient History, Oxford Univ., 1939-53; Fellow of Merton Coll., Oxford, 1953-58. Corr. Member, German Archæological Inst. *Publications:* (with C. M. Bowra) Pindar's Pythian Odes, 1928; (with B. D. Meritt and M. F. McGregor) The Athenian Tribute Lists, Vols 1-4, 1939-53; The Poet of the Iliad, 1952; Essays in Greek History, 1958; chapters in Cambridge Ancient History II (1st edn) and III (1st edn), 1924-25. *Address:* The Cottage, Upton, Didcot, Berks. *T:* Blewbury 277.

**WADE-GERY, Robert Lucian;** Counsellor, and Head of Financial Policy and Aid Department, Foreign and Commonwealth Office, since 1969; Fellow of All Souls College, Oxford, since 1951; *b* 22 April 1929; *o s* of Prof. H. T. Wade-Gery, *qv*; *m* 1962, Sarah, *er d* of A. D. Marris, *qv*; one *s* one *d*. *Educ:* Winchester; New Coll., Oxford. 1st cl. Hon. Mods 1949 and Lit. Hum. 1951. Joined HM Foreign (now Diplomatic) Service, 1951; FO (Economic Relations Dept), 1951-54; Bonn, 1954-57; FO (Private Sec. to Perm. Under-Sec., later Southern Dept), 1957-60; Tel Aviv, 1961-64; FO (Planning Staff), 1964-67; Saigon, 1967-68; Cabinet Office (Sec. to Duncan Cttee), 1968-69; Counsellor 1969; on loan to Bank of England, 1969. *Recreations:* walking, sailing, travel. *Address:* 7 Rothwell Street, NW1. *T:* 01-722 4754. *Clubs:* Athenæum, Oxford and Cambridge University.

**WADHAM, Sir Samuel (MacMahon),** Kt 1956; Hon. LLD; Professor of Agriculture, University of Melbourne, 1926-56, now Professor Emeritus; *b* Ealing, 31 Oct. 1891; *s* of Samuel Thomas Wadham; *m* 1919, Dorothy Fanny Baylis; one *s*. *Educ:* Merchant Taylors' Sch., London; Christ's Coll., Cambridge. Cambridge Agricultural Diploma and First Class Hons Nat. Science Tripos, Parts I (1912) and II (1914); Agricultural Department Scholar (England and Wales), 1914; in Signal Service and Durham LI (T) during War; Junior Demonstrator in Botany, Cambridge, 1919; Senior, 1920-26; Member Australian Commonwealth Royal Commission on Wheat Flour and Bread Industries, 1934-35; Member Australian Advisory Council on Nutrition, 1936-38; Member: Rural Reconstruction Commission under Australian Ministry of Post-War Reconstruction, 1943-46; Commonwealth Council Scientific and Industrial Research, 1944-55 and 1959-63; Australian Commonwealth Immigration Planning Council, 1949-62; Commonwealth Council on Tertiary Education, 1961-65; Lay Canon, St Paul's Cathedral, Melbourne, 1954-61; President, ANZAAS, 1960-61. Farrer Memorial Medallist, 1947; Medallist Australian Inst. Agric. Science, 1948. *Publications:* Land Utilization in Australia, with Professor G. L. Wood, 4th edn with Dr R. U. Wilson; Farming in Australia, 1788-1965, 1967; various papers in scientific journals. *Recreation:* talking. *Address:* 220 Park Street West, West Brunswick, Victoria 3055, Australia. *Club:* Australian (Melbourne).

**WADLEY, Sir Douglas,** Kt 1969; solicitor; Senior Partner, O'Shea, Corser & Wadley; *b* 9 Nov. 1904; *s* of John and Honora Wadley; *m* 1928, Vera Joyce Bodman; two *s* two *d*. *Educ:* various state schools in Qld; Central Technical Coll. High Sch., Brisbane. Admitted Solicitor, Supreme Court of Queensland, 1926. Chm. of Dirs, Queensland Brewery Ltd; Chm. of Dirs, Queensland Television Ltd. Pres., Royal National Agricultural and Industrial Assoc. of Queensland. *Recreations:* racing; conducting Jersey cattle stud. *Address:* 18 Nindethana Street, Indooroopilly, Brisbane, Queensland 4068, Australia. *T:* 70-2737. *Clubs:* Brisbane, Tattersalls, Johnsonian, Queensland Turf (Brisbane).

**WADLEY, Walter Joseph Durham,** CMG 1959; *b* 21 June 1903; *o s* of late Joseph Wadley, Stanbrook Croft, Callow End, Worcester; *m* 1946, Marie Ivy Louise, *er d* of late Arthur Dunnett, St Andrew, Jamaica; one *d*. *Educ:* City of London Sch.; Lincoln Coll., Oxford. Classical scholar, Lincoln Coll., Oxford, 1922; BA 1926, MA 1930. Inspector of Schools, Ghana (then Gold Coast), 1926; Senior Education Officer, 1935; Assistant Director of Education, 1944; Deputy Director of Education, Kenya, 1946; Director of Education, Kenya, 1951; retired from Colonial Education Service, 1959. Dep. General Manager, E. Africa Tourist Travel Assoc., 1959-64; Chief Executive Officer of the Association, 1965. Now retired. Coronation Medal, 1953. *Recreations:* travel, photography, woodwork, gardening. *Address:* The Old Brewhouse, Shutford, Banbury, Oxon. *T:* Swalcliffe 478.

**WADSWORTH, George;** *b* 10 Dec. 1902; *s* of Arnold Holroyd Wadsworth, Halifax; *m* 1930, Guinivere Shepherd; one *d*. *Educ:* Heath Grammar Sch., Halifax; Willaston Coll., Nantwich. Director: G. Wadsworth & Sons Ltd, Wadsworth White Lead Co. Ltd., G.

Wadsworth & Son (London) Ltd. Founder Chairman Halifax Round Table. Vice-Chairman Halifax Watch, Safety First, Lighting Committee. Member of Halifax Town Council, 1938-45. MP (L), Buckrose Division of E. Riding of Yorks, 1945-50; Member, Public Accounts Cttee, 1945-49. Past Master Lodge of Probity No. 61. *Recreations:* golf, yachting, swimming. *Address:* 203 Keyes House, Dolphin Square, SW1; Kingston Grange, Halifax, Yorks. *T:* Halifax 61216.

**WADSWORTH, Sir Sidney,** Kt 1946; ICS (retired); *b* 21 Dec. 1888; *s* of late Rev. H. Wadsworth and late Alice Nelstrop; *m* 1916, Olive Florence, MBE 1946 (*d* 1962), *d* of late Sir Robert Clegg, KCIE, Indian Civil Service; one *s* two *d*. *Educ:* Loughborough Grammar Sch.; Sorbonne, Paris; Jesus Coll., Cambridge; Middle Temple. Joined ICS 1913; Sub-Collector; Under-Secretary to Government, Madras; Secretary to Board of Revenue; Registrar, High Court, Madras; District Judge; Judge, High Court, Madras, 1935-47. *Recreations:* gardening, crossword puzzles, bridge. *Address:* Ennore, Ramsey, IOM. *T:* Ramsey 3221.

**WAECHTER, Sir (Harry Leonard) d'Arcy,** 2nd Bt, *cr* 1911; Lieut, RASC; *b* 22 May 1912; *s* of 1st Bt and Josephine (*d* 1955), *o d* of late John d'Arcy, of Corbetstown, Westmeath; *S* father, 1929; *m* 1939, Philippa Margaret (marr. diss. 1957), *y d* of late James Frederick Twinberrow, Suckley, Worcestershire. *Educ:* Pangbourne Nautical School. Lieut, East Yorkshire Regt (SR), 1931-35; Lieut, RASC, 1942-47; Captain, Worcestershire Regt, GSO 3 159 Inf. Bde (TA), 1947-48; Captain, TARO, 1949. Joint MFH North Ledbury. *Heir: b* John d'Arcy Waechter [*b* 16 Nov. 1915; *m* 1952, Caroline Dymond, *yr d* of Ven. E. F. Hall; two *d*]. *Recreation:* hunting.

**WAGNER, Sir Anthony (Richard),** KCVO 1961 (CVO 1953); DLitt, MA, Oxon; FSA; Garter Principal King of Arms, since 1961; Inspector of Regimental Colours, Genealogist of the Order of the Bath and of the Order of St John, since 1961; Kt Principal, Imperial Society of Knights Bachelor, since 1962; Secretary of Order of the Garter, 1952-61; Joint Register of Court of Chivalry, since 1954; Editor, Society of Antiquaries' Dictionary of British Arms, since 1940; *b* 6 Sept. 1908; *o s* of late Orlando Henry Wagner, 90 Queen's Gate, SW, and Monica, *d* of late Rev. G. E. Bell, Henley in Arden; *m* 1953, Gillian Mary Millicent, *e d* of late Major H. A. R. Graham; two *s* one *d*. *Educ:* Eton (King's Scholar); Balliol Coll., Oxford (Robin Holloway Scholar). Portcullis Pursuivant, 1931-43. Richmond Herald, 1943-61; served in WO, 1939-43; Ministry of Town and Country Planning, 1943-46; Private Secretary to Minister, 1944-45; Secretary (1945-46), member, 1947-66, Advisory Cttee on Buildings of special architectural or historic interest. Registrar of College of Arms, 1953-60. President, Chelsea Society, 1967-. KStJ. *Publications:* Catalogue of the Heralds' Commemorative Exhibition, 1934 (compiler); Historic Heraldry of Britain, 1939; Heralds and Heraldry in Britain, 1939; Heralds and Heraldry in the Middle Ages, 1939; Heraldry in England, 1946; Catalogue of English Mediæval Roll of Arms, 1950; articles, Heraldry, Genealogy, etc., Chambers's Encyclopædia; The Records and Collections of the College of Arms, 1952; English Genealogy, 1960; English Ancestry, 1961; Heralds of England, 1967; genealogical and heraldic articles. *Address:* College of Arms, Queen Victoria Street, EC4. *T:* 01-248 4300; 68 Chelsea Square, SW3. *T:* 01-352 0934; Wyndham Cottage, Aldeburgh, Suffolk. *T:* Aldeburgh 2596. *Clubs:* Athenæum, Garrick.

**WAGNER, Professor Franz William;** Professor of Education, and Director of Institute of Education, University of Southampton, 1950-Sept. 1971; *b* 26 Oct. 1905; *s* of Franz Henry and Adelaide Wagner; *m* 1934, Maria Schiller; one *s* one *d*. *Educ:* University of Adelaide, (Rhodes Scholar for S. Austr., 1928) Christ Church, Oxford. Asst Master, Christ's Hospital, 1931-39; Tutor and Lecturer, Oxford Univ., Department of Education, 1939-50. *Recreation:* gardening. *Address:* Avonmore, Southdown, Shawford, Winchester, Hants.

**WAGSTAFF, Charles John Leonard;** *b* 3 March 1875; *s* of late Rev. J. Wagstaff, Rector of Whittonstall, Northumberland; *m* 1913, Marjorie Bloomer; one *s* two *d*. *Educ:* Emmanuel Coll., Cambridge; 16th Wrangler, 1897; 1st Class Natural Sciences Tripos, 1898; Senior Science Master at Bradford Grammar Sch., 1899-1903; Oundle Sch., 1904-09; Headmaster at Haberdashers' Aske's Hampstead Sch., 1910-19; Headmaster King Edward VII Sch., King's Lynn, 1920-39. *Publications:* Electricity; Properties of Matter. *Recreations:* turning ivory, etc. *Address:* 48 The Green, Southwick, Sussex. *T:* 2841.

**WAGSTAFF, Colonel Henry Wynter,** CSI 1945; MC 1917; MInstT; RE (retired); *b* 19 July 1890; *s* of Edward Wynter Wagstaff and Flora de Smidt; *m* 1st, 1918, Jean, MB, BS, *d* of George Frederick Mathieson; two *s*; 2nd, 1967, Margaret, *o d* of late Sir John Hubert Marshall, CIE. *Educ:* Woodbridge; RMA, Woolwich. Commissioned RE 1910; served in India and Mesopotamia in European War, 1914-18 (despatches, MC); Captain, 1916; seconded Indian State Railways, 1921; Major, 1927; Lieut-Colonel, 1934; Colonel, 1940. 1929-46, employed on problems connected with Labour in general and Railway Labour in particular. Member, Railway Board, Government of India, New Delhi, 1942-46; retired, 1948. *Publication:* Operation of Indian Railways in Recent Years, 1931. *Recreations:* reading and writing. *Address:* c/o Lloyds Bank Ltd, 6 Pall Mall, SW1. *Club:* Royal Automobile.

**WAIAPU, NZ, Bishop of;** *see under* New Zealand, Primate and Archbishop of.

**WAIGHTS, Rev. Kenneth (Laws);** Member, Methodist World Council; President, designate, Methodist Conference, 1970, President, June 1971-June 1972; *b* 15 May 1909; *s* of Rev. William Waights and Selina Waights; *m* 1935, Dorothy Margaret Rowe. *Educ:* Stationers' Company Sch.; George Watson's Coll., Edinburgh; Handsworth Theological Coll., Birmingham. Served in the following Methodist Churches: Ilfracombe, Exeter, Birmingham Mission, Winson Green Prison (as Chaplain), Hastings, Liverpool, Scarborough, Nottingham (Chm. of District), Bristol, Sunderland, Newcastle upon Tyne; Chairman, Newcastle District of Methodist Church. *Recreations:* golf, walking, travel; formerly: played Rugby football for Devon County, Moseley and Exeter Rugby Clubs. *Address:* 8 Ancroft Way, Newcastle upon Tyne NE3 2BX. *T:* Newcastle upon Tyne 854163.

**WAIKATO, Bishop of,** since 1969; **Rt. Rev. Allen Howard Johnston,** LTh; *b* Auckland, NZ, 1912; *s* of Joseph Howard Johnston; *m* 1937, Joyce Rhoda, *d* of John A. Grantley, Auckland; four *d*. *Educ:* Seddon Memorial Technical College, St John's College, Auckland Univ. College. Deacon, 1935; Priest, 1936. Assistant Curate of St Mark's, Remuera, 1935-37; Vicar of Dargaville, 1937-42; Vicar of Northern Wairoa, 1942-44; Vicar of Otahuhu, 1944-49; Vicar of Whangarei, 1949-53; Archdeacon of Waimate, 1949-53; Bishop of Dunedin, 1953-69. Hon. LLD Otago. *Address:* Bishop's House, Hamilton, Waikato, NZ.

**WAIN, John Barrington;** Author; *b* 14 March 1925; *e surv. s* of Arnold A. Wain and Anne Wain, Stoke-on-Trent; *m* 1st, 1947, Marianne (marr. diss. 1956), *o d* of Julius Urmston; 2nd, 1960, Eirian, *o d* of late T. E. James; three *s*. *Educ:* The High Sch., Newcastle-under-Lyme; St John's Coll., Oxford. Fereday Fellow, St John's Coll., Oxford, 1946-49; Lecturer in English Literature, University of Reading, 1947-55; resigned to become freelance author and critic. Churchill Visiting Prof., University of Bristol, 1967; Vis. Prof., Centre Universitaire Expérimentale de Vincennes, Paris, 1969. FRSL 1960, resigned 1961. *Publications include: fiction:* Hurry On Down, 1953; Living in the Present, 1955; The Contenders, 1958; A Travelling Woman, 1959; Nuncle and other stories, 1960; Strike the Father Dead, 1962; The Young Visitors, 1965; Death of the Hind Legs and other stories, 1966; The Smaller Sky, 1967; A Winter in the Hills, 1970; *poetry:* A Word Carved on a Sill, 1956; Weep Before God, 1961; Wildtrack, 1965; Letters to Five Artists, 1969; *criticism:* Preliminary Essays, 1957; Essays on Literature and Ideas, 1963; The Living World of Shakespeare, 1964; *autobiography:* Sprightly Running, 1962. *Recreations:* canoeing, walking. *Address:* c/o Macmillan & Co. ltd, Little Essex Street, WC2.

**WAIN, Prof. Ralph Louis,** CBE 1968; FRS 1960; DSc, PhD, FRIC; Professor of Agricultural Chemistry, University of London, since 1950, and Head of Department of Physical Sciences at Wye College (University of London) since 1945; Hon. Director, Agricultural Research Council Unit on Plant Growth Substances and Systemic Fungicides, since 1953; *b* 29 May 1911; 2nd *s* of late G. Wain, Hyde, Cheshire; *m* 1940, Joan Bowker; one *s* one *d*. *Educ:* County Grammar Sch., Hyde, Cheshire; University of Sheffield. First Class Hons Chemistry, Sheffield, 1932; MSc (Sheffield), 1933; PhD (Sheffield), 1935; DSc (London), 1949; Hon. D. Agric. Sci., Ghent, 1963; Town Trustees Fellow, University of Sheffield, 1934; Research Assistant, University of Manchester, 1935-37; Lecturer in Chemistry, Wye Coll., 1937-39; Research Chemist, Long Ashton Research Station (University of Bristol), 1939-45. Vice-President, Royal Institute of Chemistry, 1961-64. Sir Thomas Middleton Memorial Lecturer, London, 1955; Frankland Memorial Lectr, Birmingham, 1965; Benjamin Minge Duggar Memorial Lecturer, Alabama, 1966; Amos Memorial Lectr, E Malling, 1969. Pruthivi Gold Medal, 1957; RASE Research Medal, 1960; John Scott Award, 1963; Flintoff Medal, 1969. *Publications:* numerous research publications in Annals of Applied Biology, Journal of Agric. Science, Journal of Chemical Society, Nature, The Analyst, Berichte der Deutschen Chemischen Gesellschaft, Proc. Royal Society, etc. *Recreations:* painting, travel. *Address:* Staple Farm, Hastingleigh, near Ashford, Kent. *T:* Elmsted 248.

**WAINWRIGHT, Desmond;** *see* Wainwright, E. D.

**WAINWRIGHT, (Edward) Desmond;** Executive Chairman, Army and Navy Stores Ltd, since 1959; *b* 27 Jan. 1902; *s* of late Ernest Harold Wainwright; *m* 1st, 1928, Iris (*d* 1959), *d* of late Rev. Herbert Sheppard; one *s* one *d*; 2nd, 1960, Leonora, *widow* of Maj.-Gen. P. J. Mackesy. *Educ:* Haileybury College; Trinity College, Cambridge. BA, LLB Cantab. 1924; qualified as solicitor, 1927. Lecturer, Law Society's School of Law, 1929-39. *Recreation:* gardening. *Address:* Malmains Manor, Alkham, near Dover, Kent.

**WAINWRIGHT, Edwin,** BEM 1957; MP (Lab.) Dearne Valley Division of Yorkshire West Riding since Oct. 1959; *b* 12 Aug. 1908; *s* of John Wainwright and Ellen (*née* Hodgson); *m* 1938, Dorothy Metcalfe; two *s* two *d*. *Educ:* Darfield Council School; Wombwell and Barnsley Technical Colleges. WEA student for 20 years. Started work at 14, at Darfield Main Colliery; Nat. Union of Mineworkers: Member Branch Cttee, 1933-39; Delegate, 1939-48; Branch Sec., 1948-59; Member, Nat. Exec. Cttee, 1952-59. Member, Wombwell UDC, 1939-59. Sec./Agent, Dearne Valley Labour Party, 1951-59. Sec. Parly Lab. Party Trade Union Gp, 1966-; Sec. Yorkshire Gp of Parly Lab. Party, 1966-. *Recreations:* gardening, reading. *Address:* 34 Dovecliffe Road, Wombwell, near Barnsley, Yorks. *T:* Wombwell 2153.

**WAINWRIGHT, Richard Scurrah;** *b* 11 April 1918; *o s* of late Henry Scurrah and Emily Wainwright; *m* 1948, Joyce Mary Hollis; two *s* two *d*. *Educ:* Shrewsbury Sch.; Clare Coll., Cambridge (Open Scholar). BA Hons Cantab. (History), 1939. Friends Ambulance Unit, NW Europe, 1939-46. Partner, Peat Marwick Mitchell & Co., Chartered Accountants. Pres., Leeds/Bradford Society of Chartered Accountants, 1965-66. Vice-Pres., Liberal Party Organization, 1959-; MP (L) Colne Valley, West Riding, 1966-70; Chm., Liberal Party Research Dept, 1968-. *Recreations:* gardening, swimming. *Address:* The Heath, Adel, Leeds 16. *T:* Leeds 673938. *Clubs:* Reform, National Liberal; Leeds (Leeds).

**WAINWRIGHT, Robert Everard,** CMG 1959; *b* 24 June 1913; *s* of Dr G. B. Wainwright, OBE, MD; *m* 1939, Bridget Alan-Williams; two *s*. *Educ:* Marlborough; Trinity College, Cambridge (BA). District Officer, Kenya, 1935; Provincial Commissioner, Rift Valley Province, 1953-58. Imperial Defence College, 1959. Chief Commissioner, Kenya, 1960-63; Administrator, Turks and Caicos Is, WI, 1967-71. *Recreations:* sailing, tennis, shooting, cabinet-making. *Address:* 42 Cecily Hill, Cirencester, Glos. *Club:* Mombasa (Mombasa).

**WAINWRIGHT, Rear-Adm. Rupert Charles Purchas,** CB 1966; DSC 1943; with Redditch Development Corporation; Vice Naval Deputy to Supreme Allied Commander Europe, 1965-67; retired 1967; *b* 16 Oct. 1913; *s* of late Lieut Comdr O. J. Wainwright and of Mrs S. Wainwright; *m* 1937, Patricia Mary Helen, *d* of late Col F. H. Blackwood, DSO and late Mrs Blackwood; two *s* two *d*. *Educ:* Royal Naval College, Dartmouth. Commanded HM Ships Actaeon, Tintagel Castle, Zephyr, 1952-54; Captain HMS Cambridge, 1955-57; Chief of Staff, S Atlantic and S America Station, 1958-60; Director Naval Recruiting, 1960-62; Commodore Naval Drafting, 1962-64. Comdr 1949; Capt. 1955; Rear-Adm. 1965. MBIM. *Publications:* two Prize Essays, RUSI Jl. *Recreations:* hockey (Combined Services; a Vice-Pres., England Hockey Assoc.), swimming (Royal Navy), tennis. *Address:* Regency Cottage, Maidenhead Road, Stratford-on-Avon, Warwicks. *Clubs:* United Service, Royal Navy.

**WAIT, Air Vice-Marshal George E.,** CBE 1945; CD; RCAF (retired); *b* 26 May 1895; *s* of late

Frank Goodell Wait, Ottawa; *m* 1923, Doris Lilian Browne; one *s*. *Educ:* University of Toronto; Royal College of Science, London. RFC, RAF and RCAF from 1916. *Address:* PO Box 175, St Andrew's, Canada.

**WAITE, Clifford,** CMG 1959; Chairman, International Tin Research Council, since 1963; Director: The Chartered Bank; London Tin Corp. Ltd; Malayan Tin Dredging Ltd; Southern Malayan Tin Dredging Ltd; Southern Kinta Consolidated Ltd; Kamunting Tin Dredging Ltd; *b* 12 Oct. 1896; *s* of late Jasper and Mary Waite; *m* 1920, Mary Isabel Davey; two *s*. *Educ:* Guiseley. Served European War with Royal Engineers, 1914-18. *Recreation:* fishing. *Address:* 61 Albany Manor Road, Bournemouth, Hants. *T:* Bournemouth 23981. *Club:* Oriental.

**WAITE, Air Commodore Reginald Newnham,** CB 1949; CBE 1946; RAF, retired; *b* 30 June 1901; *s* of Alderman Richard Waite, JP, Duffield, Derbyshire; *m* 1940, Jessamy, *d* of late C. F. Lowenthal, KC, Treasurer Middle Temple; one *s* two *d*. *Educ:* Repton; RAF Cadet College, Cranwell. Commissioned, 1921; served War of 1939-45 in First Lord's Operations Room, Admiralty, and Air Ministry, and commanded Coastal Comd Stations at St Eval and Nassau, Bahamas. Supreme Headquarters Allied Exped. Force, 1944; HQ Control Commn, Berlin, for Air matters, until 1949. Conducted Anglo-Russian enquiry into Viking-Yak disaster, 1948. Devised and organised the Air Lift to Berlin in 1948. Assistant Chief of Staff, Allied Air Forces, Central Europe, 1951-53; retd 1953. *Recreations:* yachting, farming. *Address:* Foyers, Woodlands, Southampton.

**WAKE, Sir Hereward,** 14th Bt of Clevedon, *cr* 1621; MC 1942; DL; Major (retired) King's Royal Rifle Corps; *b* 7 Oct. 1916; *e s* of Sir Hereward Wake, 13th Bt, CB, CMG, DSO, and Margaret W., *er d* of R. H. Benson; *S* father, 1963; *m* 1952, Julia Rosemary, JP, *yr d* of late Capt. G. W. M. Lees, Falcutt House, Nr Brackley, Northants; one *s* three *d*. *Educ:* Eton; RMC, Sandhurst. Served War of 1939-45 (wounded, MC). Retired from 60th Rifles, 1947, and studied Estate Management and Agriculture. High Sheriff, 1955, DL 1969, Northants. *Heir: s* Hereward Charles Wake, *b* 22 Nov. 1952. *Address:* Courteenhall, Northampton. *T:* Roade 204; Amhuinnsuidhe Castle, Isle of Harris. *Club:* Brooks's.

**WAKE, Hereward Baldwin Lawrence;** Headmaster of St John's School, Leatherhead, Surrey, 1948-60, retired; *b* Aug. 1900; *s* late Rev. Hereward Eyre Wake and Mary Frances, *d* of late James Sealy Lawrence; *m* 1926, Sheila, *d* of late Captain Henry Harris; two *s*. *Educ:* Marlborough (Classical Scholar); Keble College, Oxford (Classical Scholar). Oxford Rugby XV (blue 1922); Capt. Somerset Rugby XV, 1923-29. Housemaster at Cheltenham Coll., 1934-39 and 1945-48. Lt-Col 5th Bn Gloucestershire Regt (TA), 1939; War Office, 1940-45; GSO1. *Recreations:* ornithology, walking, reading. *Address:* Priory Close, Boxgrove, Chichester, Sussex. *T:* Halnaker 404.

**WAKE, Joan,** CBE 1960; FRHistS; FSA; *b* 29 Feb. 1884; 5th *c* of Sir Herewald Wake, 12th Bt, and of Catherine, *d* of Sir Edward St Aubyn, 1st Bt. *Educ:* at Courteenhall, mainly by Rachel Forester Forbes; London School of Economics (1913-15). Hon. Sec. Northamptonshire District Nursing Assoc., 1916-19. Hon. Sec., Northants Record Society, 1920-63; member of Council and/or committees of British Records Association for 25 years, 1932-55. Hon. MA Oxon, 1953; Hon. LLD, University of Leicester, 1959. Editor, Northamptonshire Past and Present, 1948-59. *Publications:* How to Compile a History and Present-day Record of Village Life; Northampton Vindicated, or Why the Main Line missed the Town; St Peter, Himself a Married Man; A Northamptonshire Rector, The Life of Henry Isham Longden; The Brudenells of Deene, 1953. Editor (for the Northamptonshire Record Society) of: Northamptonshire Quarter Sessions Records, 1630, 1657-8; Musters, Beacons and Subsidies in the County of Northampton, 1586-1623; The Montagu Musters Book, 1602-1623. *Address:* 11 Charlbury Road, Oxford. *T:* Oxford 55397.

**WAKEFIELD,** family name of **Baron Wakefield of Kendal.**

**WAKEFIELD OF KENDAL,** 1st Baron, *cr* 1963, of Kendal; **William Wavell Wakefield,** Kt 1944; Company Director; *b* Beckenham, Kent, 10 March 1898; *s* of late Roger William Wakefield, MB, JP, and Ethel May Knott; *m* 1919, Rowena Doris, *d* of late Llewellyn Lewis, MD, OBE, JP; three *d*. *Educ:* The Craig Preparatory School; Sedbergh School; Pembroke College, Cambridge. In the RNAS then RAF European War (rose to rank of Captain, despatches); retired from the RAF as Flight-Lieutenant, 1923; transferred to Reserve; rejoined RAF at outbreak of war for flying duty; Director of the Air Training Corps, 1942-44; MP (Nat C) Swindon division of Wiltshire, 1935-45; (C) St Marylebone, 1945-63. Parliamentary Private Sec. to the Marquess of Hartington, 1936-38; to Rt Hon. R. H. Hudson, 1939-40; to Capt. Rt Hon. Harold Balfour, 1940-42; Chm. Parliamentary and Scientific Cttee, 1952-55; Director: Transparent Paper Ltd; Lake District Estates Co. Ltd; Rediffusion, Ltd; Redifon Ltd; Shapland & Petter, Ltd; British Domolac Co. Ltd; Skyways Coach Air, Ltd; Skyways Engineering Ltd; Portman Building Society, and other companies; Member of Executive Committee, YMCA; Member Executive Committee and Council, the National Playing Fields Assoc.; formerly Mem. Nature Conservancy; Member, Council of Royal National Mission to Deep Sea Fishermen; President, Metropolitan Assoc. of Building Societies; former Pres., Industrial Transport Assoc.; Vice-Pres., Council of The Roy. Albert Hall. Captained England, Cambridge Univ., Middlesex, Royal Air Force, Harlequins, at Rugby football; Past President of Rugby Football Union. President: Ski Club of Great Britain; British Water Ski Fedn; British Sub-Aqua Club. *Publication:* Rugger. *Recreation:* ski-ing. *Heir:* none. *Address:* 71 Park Street, W1; The Old House, Kendal, Westmorland. *T:* Kendal 20861. *Clubs:* Carlton, MCC.

**WAKEFIELD, Bishop of,** since 1968; **Rt. Rev. Eric Treacy,** MBE 1945; *b* 2 June 1907; *s* of George Treacy, Rangoon; *m* 1932, Mary Leyland, *d* of J. A. Shone, JP, Hoylake; no *c*. *Educ:* Haberdashers' School; King's Coll., London; St Aidan's, Birkenhead. Deacon, 1932, Priest, 1933; Curate of Liverpool Parish Church, 1932-34; Shrewsbury School Missioner, 1930-36; Vicar of Edge Hill, Liverpool, 1936-40; Chaplain to the Forces (EC), 1940-45; Senior Chaplain (NW Europe), 1944 (despatches, MBE); Rector of Keighley, 1945-49; Hon. Canon: of Bradford Cathedral, 1946; of Wakefield Cathedral, 1949; Rural Dean of South Craven, 1946; Proctor in Convocation, 1949; Examining Chaplain to Bishop of Wakefield, 1949; Canon of Wakefield Cathedral, 1956; Archdeacon of Halifax, 1949-61; Vicar and Rural Dean of Halifax, 1950-61;

Bishop Suffragan of Pontefract, 1961-68; Archdeacon of Pontefract, 1961-68. Church Commissioner, 1963. Hon. LLD (Leeds) 1968. *Publications:* Main Lines over the Border, 1960; The Lure of Steam, 1966; Portrait of Steam, 1967; Glory of Steam, 1969. *Recreations:* fell walking, photography, responding for the guests, baiting Yorkshiremen. *Address:* Bishop's Lodge, Woodthorpe Lane, Wakefield, Yorks.

**WAKEFIELD, Asst Bishops of;** *see* Bevan, Rt Rev. K. G., Shearburn, Rt Rev. V. G.

**WAKEFIELD, Arthur John,** CMG 1942; BSc, NDA, NDD; *b* 28 Jan. 1900; *s* of John and Mary Elizabeth Wakefield, Brewood, Staffs; *m* 1927, Winifred Blanche Cook; no *c. Educ:* Brewood Grammar School; Harper Adams Agricultural Coll.; Edinburgh University; Reading University. Artists Rifles, 1918; Stock-Inspector, Veterinary Dept, Northern Rhodesia, 1923; Agricultural Officer, 1924, Deputy Director of Agriculture, 1935, Directory of Agriculture, 1938, Tanganyika Territory; Member of Legislative Council, Tanganyika Territory, 1933 and 1938-40; Member of Makerere College Council; Inspector-General of Agriculture and Agricultural Adviser to Comptroller for Development and Welfare in the West Indies, 1940-46; Acting Director of Agriculture, Jamaica, 1945; Member Anglo-American Caribbean Commission, 1943-45, and Caribbean Research Council, 1944-45; leader East African Groundnuts Mission, 1946; Member Overseas Food Corporation, 1948-49. Member Colonial Advisory Council on Agriculture, Animal Health, and Forestry, 1946-50; Resident Rep. of UN Tech. Assistance Board, Haiti, 1950-52, Burma, 1953-56. *Recreation:* gardening. *Address:* The Croft, Marchamley, Shrewsbury. *T:* Hodnet 282.

**WAKEFIELD, Sir (Edward) Humphry (Tyrrell),** 2nd Bt *cr* 1962; *b* 11 July 1936; *s* of Sir Edward Birkbeck Wakefield, 1st Bt, CIE, and of Constance Lalage, *e d* of late Sir John Perronet Thompson, KCSI, KCIE; *S* father, 1969; *m* 1st, 1960, Priscilla (marr. diss. 1964), *e d* of O. R. Bagot; 2nd, 1966, Hon. Elizabeth Sophia, *e d* of Viscount De L'Isle, *qv*, and former wife of G. S. O. A. Colthurst; one *s. Educ:* Gordonstoun; Trinity Coll., Cambridge. Formerly Lieut, 10th Royal Hussars. *Heir: s* Maximilian Edward Vereker Wakefield, *b* 22 Feb. 1967. *Club:* Cavalry.

**WAKEFIELD, Hubert George;** *see* Wakefield, Hugh.

**WAKEFIELD, Hugh (Hubert George);** MA Cantab; FMA; Keeper of the Department of Circulation, Victoria and Albert Museum, since 1960; *b* 6 March 1915; *o s* of late George Wakefield; *m* 1939, Nora Hilary Inglis; one *s* one *d. Educ:* King Edward's Sch., Birmingham; Trinity Coll., Cambridge. Joined staff of Royal Commission on Historical Monuments (England), 1938. Served War of 1939-45, Temp. Captain (Instructor in Gunnery), RA, 1942-46. Asst Keeper, Victoria and Albert Museum, 1948. Governor of the National Museum of Wales, 1960-; Member, Council of the Museums' Assoc., 1960-63; Sec., Cttee for Museums of Applied Art, Internat. Council of Museums, 1962-; Corresp. Mem., Finnish Soc. of Crafts and Design, 1965-. *Publications:* (ed) Victorian Collector (series): Nineteenth Century British Glass, 1961; Victorian Pottery, 1962; contrib. to Connoisseur Early Victorian Period Guide, 1958, and to Encyc. Brit. *Recreation:* travel. *Address:* 32 Strand-on-the-Green, W4. *T:* 01-994 6355.

**WAKEFIELD, Sir Humphry;** *see* Wakefield, Sir E. H. T.

**WAKEFIELD, Peter George Arthur;** HM Diplomatic Service; Commercial Counsellor, British Embassy, Tokyo, since 1970; *b* 13 May 1922; *s* of John Bunting Wakefield and Dorothy Ina Stace; *m* 1951, Felicity Maurice-Jones; four *s* one *d. Educ:* Cranleigh Sch.; Corpus Christi Coll., Oxford. Army Service, 1942-47; Military Govt, Eritrea, 1946-47; Hulton Press, 1947-49; entered Diplomatic Service, 1949; Middle East Centre for Arab Studies, 1950; 2nd Sec., Amman, 1950-52; Foreign Office, 1953-55; 1st Sec., British Middle East Office, Nicosia, 1955-56; 1st Sec. (Commercial), Cairo, 1956; Administrative Staff Coll., Henley, 1957; 1st Sec. (Commercial), Vienna, 1957-60; 1st Sec. (Commercial), Tokyo, 1960-63; Foreign Office, 1964-66; Consul-General and Counsellor, Benghazi, 1966-69. *Recreations:* restoring ruins; tennis, swimming, squash. *Address:* Lincoln House, Montpelier Row, Twickenham, Mddx; British Embassy, Tokyo, Japan.

**WAKEFIELD, Roger Cuthbert,** CMG 1953; OBE 1950; retired; *b* Cark-in-Cartmel, Lancs, 27 June 1906; 4th and *y s* of late Roger William Wakefield, MB, BCh, Kendal, and Ethel May Knott; *m* 1936, Elizabeth Rhoda, *yr d* of late Sidney R. Davie and Margaret Preston Lawson, West Byfleet, Surrey; one *d. Educ:* Sedbergh School; Trinity College, Cambridge (BA 1928). Joined Sudan Civil Service, 1929; Survey of the Arc of the Thirtieth Meridian, 1935-40. War of 1939-45; Civil Defence Duties and desert navigation, 1940-43; Director of Surveys, Sudan, 1946-54; Survey Consultant to Sudan Government, 1954-55. Director, Equatoria Projects Board, 1949; Chairman, Unclassified Staff Wages Commn, 1951; Councillor without Portfolio on Governor-Gen.'s Exec. Council and Member Legislative Assembly, 1952. Member: British-Argentine Rugby football touring team, 1927; Cambridge East Greenland Exped., 1929; Lake Rudolf Rift Valley Exped., 1934. FRICS, 1949. *Publication:* (with D. F. Munsey) The Arc of the Thirtieth Meridian between the Egyptian Frontier and Latitude 13°45′, 1950. *Recreations:* mountaineering, sailing, fishing. *Address:* Glendrynoch Lodge, Carbost, Isle of Skye. *Club:* Alpine.

**WAKEFIELD-HARREY, Cyril Ogden,** CMG 1953; HM Foreign Service (retired); *b* 16 Sept. 1894; *s* of Captain A. Harrey and Hannah Ogden, Manchester; *m* 1922, Margaret, *d* of late J. H. Wakefield, York, and Elizabeth Curthoys, Bristol; one *s. Educ:* Manchester Grammar School; Caius College, Cambridge (Scholar). Served European War, 1914-18, Manchester Regiment, and Intelligence Corps (French Croix de Guerre). Entered Consular Service, 1920; HM Consul at Florence, 1936; Commercial Secretary, Budapest, 1939-41; Consul at Port Said, 1944-45; Consul-Gen., Zagreb, Yugoslavia, 1945. Permanent UK Representative to the Council of Europe at Strasbourg, 1951-52; Consul-General at Algiers, Oct. 1952-May 1955, retired. *Publications:* The Golden Chain (Poems), 1944; The Everlasting Quest, 1948. *Recreations:* music, travel. *Address:* 98 St Augustine's Avenue, Thorpe Bay, Essex. *T:* Southend-on-Sea 88673.

**WAKEFORD, Edward Felix,** ARA 1968; *b* 1914; *s* of Rev. Robert Wakeford and Felicia Wakeford; *m* 1945, Aileen Mary Rivett-Carnac. *Educ:* King William's Coll., Isle of Man. Studied at Chelsea Sch. of Art, and Royal Coll. of Art. *Exhibitions:* Brook Street Gall., 1946; Hanover Gall., 1953; Wildenstein & Co. (gp exhibns, 1947-62); Ware Gall., 1966. Visiting Teacher at: Chelsea Sch. of Art, 1946-

64; West of England Coll. of Art, 1964-66. Represented in public and private collections in: England; USA; Australia. Lord Mayor's Art Award, 1966. *Publications:* (autobiography) A Prize For Art, 1961. Poetry contributed to: The Observer, The Listener, Poetry Review, etc. *Address:* 108 Beaufort Street, Chelsea, SW3. *T:* 01-352 1618.

**WAKEFORD, John Chrysostom Barnabas,** CMG 1948; *b* 23 Aug. 1898; *o s* of Rev. John Wakeford, Anfield, Liverpool; *m* 1st, 1921, Grace (*d* 1965), *d* of Charles Cooke, Church Coppenhall; one *d*; 2nd, 1970, Dorothy May, *d* of Frederick Ward, Aldeburgh, Suffolk. *Educ:* Malvern College; RMA, Woolwich; Clare College, Cambridge. Commissioned Royal Engineers, 1917; served European War, France and Belgium, 1917-18; N Russia Campaign (despatches). Dep. Dir Transportn, W Africa, 1941-43; Ceylon, 1943-44 (Col); Dir of Transportn, SE Asia, 1944-45 (Brig.). Chief Railway Commissioner, Burma; General Manager, Burma Railways and Technical Adviser to Government of Burma, 1945-48; Chief Engineer, Cameroons Development Corporation, W Africa, 1948-50; with Rendel Palmer & Tritton, 1950-63; FICE, FIMechE, MInstT, FRSA, FRGS. *Address:* 41 South Road, Saffron Walden, Essex. *T:* Saffron Walden 2010.

**WAKEFORD, Major Richard,** VC 1944; MA; JP; Master of Supreme Court of Judicature, Chancery Division, since 1964; late Hampshire Regiment; Solicitor; *b* 23 July 1921; 2nd *s* of late V. D. C. Wakeford, MB, BS, and of Mary Kite; *m* 1951, Denise Elizabeth Corlson. *Educ:* Westminster; Trinity College, Oxford. Governor Haberdashers' Aske's Hatcham Schools, 1961. JP Co. Surrey, 1963. Mem. Civil Judicial Statistics Cttee, 1966-. *Recreation:* shooting. *Address:* Weavers, Elm Drive, Leatherhead, Surrey. *Club:* Leander.

**WAKEFORD, Air Vice-Marshal Richard Gordon,** MVO 1961; OBE 1958; AFC 1952; Commander Northern Maritime Air Region, and Air Officer Scotland and Northern Ireland, since 1970; *b* 20 April 1922; *s* of Charles Edward Augustus Wakeford, property owner; *m* 1948, Anne Butler; two *s* two *d*. *Educ:* Montpelier Sch., Paignton; Kelly Coll., Tavistock. Joined RAF, 1941; flying Catalina flying boats, Coastal Comd, operating out of India, Scotland, N Ireland and Shetland Is, 1942-45; flying Liberator and York transport aircraft on overseas routes, 1945-47; CFS 1947; Flying Instructor, RAF Coll. Cranwell; CFS Examining Wing; ground appts, incl. 2½ years on staff of Dir of Emergency Ops in Malaya, 1952-58; comdg Queen's Flight, 1958-61; Directing Staff, RAF Staff Coll., 1961-64; subseq.: comdg RAF Scampton; SASO, HQ 3 Group Bomber Comd; Asst Comdt (Cadets), RAF Coll. Cranwell; idc 1969. *Recreations:* golf, fishing. *Address:* HQ Northern Maritime Air Region, RAF Pitreavie Castle, Dunfermline, Fife. *T:* Dunfermline 23436. *Club:* Royal Air Force.

**WAKEHURST,** 3rd Baron *cr* 1934, of Ardingly; **(John) Christopher Loder;** Managing Director, Fleming, Suez, Brown Brothers Ltd; Director, London and Manchester Assurance Company Ltd; *b* 23 Sept. 1925; *s* of 2nd Baron Wakehurst, KG, KCMG, and of Lady Wakehurst, *qv*; *S* father, 1970; *m* 1956, Ingeborg Krumbholz-Hess, *d* of Mrs Walther Hess and *step d* of Dr Walther Hess; one *s* one *d*. *Educ:* Eton; King's School, nr Sydney, NSW; Trinity College, Cambridge (BA 1948, LLB 1949, MA 1953). Served War as Sub Lieut RANVR and RNVR; West Pacific, 1943-45. Barrister, Inner Temple, 1950. *Heir: s* Hon. Timothy Walter Loder, *b* 28 March 1958. *Address:* 53 Clabon Mews, SW1.

**WAKEHURST, Lady; Margaret Wakehurst,** DBE; *b* 4 Nov. 1899; *d* of Sir Charles Tennant, Bt and of Marguerite (*née* Miles); *m* 1920, John de Vere Loder (later 2nd Baron Wakehurst, KG, KCMG) (*d* 1970); three *s* one *d*. Vice-Pres., Nat. Assoc. for Mental Health; Founder, Northern Ireland Assoc. for Mental Health; Vice-Pres., Royal College of Nursing. Hon. LLD, Queen's Univ., Belfast. DStJ 1959; GCStJ 1970. *Address:* 31 Lennox Gardens, SW1. *T:* 01-589 4394.

**WAKELEY, Sir Cecil (Pembrey Grey),** 1st Bt *cr* 1952; KBE 1946; CB 1941; DSc (London); MCh; Consulting Surgeon: King's College Hospital; Belgrave Hospital for Children; West End Hospital for Nervous Diseases; Royal Masonic Hospital; Petersfield Hospital; Senior Consulting Surgeon, Royal Navy; Senior Lecturer in Anatomy, King's College, University of London, since 1919; *b* Rainham, Kent, 5 May 1892; *s* of Percy and Mary Wakeley, West Dulwich; *m* 1925, Elizabeth Muriel, *d* of James Nicholson-Smith, Blackheath; three *s*. *Educ:* Dulwich Coll.; King's Coll. Hosp. (Tanner Prizeman, Jelf Medal for surgery and other surgical prizes). Temp. Surgeon, RN, 1915-19, and 1939-46 (Rear-Adm.); Mem., War Wounds and Burns Cttee, MRC. President: Bible League; Chartered Soc. of Physiotherapy; RCS, 1949-54 (formerly Vice-Pres. and Mem. Court of Examiners); Med. Soc. of London; Hunterian Soc. Past President: Harveian Soc. of London; Listerian Soc.; Clinical, United Services and Children's Sections of Roy. Soc. Med.; Royal Life Saving Soc.; Alleyn Club. Vice-President: British Empire Cancer Campaign (also Chm. Council) Imperial Cancer Research Fund; 1949-67. Past Vice-Pres., Council, Med. Defence Union. Chairman: Med. Sickness Finance Corp.; Internat. Wine Soc.; Wakeley Bros, Rainham, Kent. Vice-Chm., Med. Sickness Soc. Member: Cttee of Management, Conjoint Bd, 1942-54; Council (also Treas.), Gen. Med. Council, 1942-55; Council, Med. Defence Union. Treas., Assoc. of Independent Hospitals. Examiner in Surgery to Univs of London, Cambridge, Durham, Sheffield, Glasgow, Wales and Dublin. Royal College of Surgeons: Hunterian Prof., 1929, 1934, 1937, 1940, 1942; Arris and Gale Lectr, 1924, 1925; Erasmus Wilson Lectr, 1928, 1930-33, 1935-36; Bradshaw Lectr, 1947; Hunterian Orator, 1955; Thomas Vicary Lectr, 1957; Arnott Demonstrator, 1934. Harveian Lectr, Harveian Soc., 1934; Sheen Memorial Lectr, Cardiff, 1953. Legg Lectr, King's Coll. Hosp. Med. Sch., 1957; Sir Thomas and Lady Edith Dixon Memorial Lectr, Queen's Univ. of Belfast, 1957. Past Grand Warden, United Grand Lodge of England; Past Master and Mem. Court of Assistants: Worshipful Co. of Barbers; Worshipful Soc. of Apothecaries. Hon. Convener, Professional Nurses and Midwives' Yearly Conference. FRSE, FRCS, FRSA, FKC, FZS. Hon. FRCSE, Hon. FRFPS, Hon. FFR, Hon. FRCSI, Hon. FRACS, Hon. FACS. Hon. LLD: Glasgow; Leeds; Lahore. Hon. DSc: Delhi; Colombo. KStJ; Mem., Chapter Gen., Order of St John; Order of the Nile, 2nd Class, 1938; Legion of Merit (USA), 1946; Chevalier, Légion d'honneur, 1950; Order of Southern Cross, Brazil, 1951. Editorial Sec., British Jl of Surgery, 1940-. *Publications:* A Textbook of Surgical Pathology; The Life of Sir George Buckston Browne; ed Rose and Carless' Manual of Surgery, 1922-; ed Surgical Diagnosis; ed Treeves' and Wakeley's Handbook of Surgical Operations; ed Aids to Surgery; ed The Pineal Gland; ed Neuroradiology; ed Synopsis of Surgery; ed Medical Dictionary; ed Surgery for Nurses; ed Annals of Roy. Coll. of Surgeons, 1947-69; ed Medical Press, 1932; articles on surgery, cancer and cancer research, and surgical subjects, in med. and sci. jls. *Recreations:* gardening and photography. *Heir: s* John Cecil Nicholson Wakeley [*b* 27 Aug. 1926; *m* 1954, June, *d* of D. F. Leney, Shottermill, Haslemere, Surrey; two *s* one *d*]. *Address:* Woodlands, Cold Ash Hill, Liphook, Hants. *T:* Liphook 3343. *Clubs:* Athenæum, Goat.

**WAKELING, Rt. Rev. John Denis;** *see* Southwell, Bishop of.

**WAKELY, Sir Clifford Holland,** KBE, *cr* 1945; *b* 1891; *s* of Charles Wakely. *Educ:* Merchant Taylors' School; St John's College, Oxford. Entered Civil Service, 1914; Deputy Chairman, Board of Inland Revenue, 1942-51. *Address:* The Homestead, Upper Cumberland Walk, Tunbridge Wells, Kent. *T:* Tunbridge Wells 27872.

**WAKELY, Leonard John Dean,** CMG 1965; OBE 1945; *b* 18 June 1909; *s* of Sir Leonard Wakely, KCIE, CB; *m* 1938, Margaret Houssemayne Tinson; two *s. Educ:* Westminster School; Christ Church, Oxford; School of Oriental Studies, London. Indian Civil Service, 1932-47. Served in the Punjab and in the Defence Co-ordination, Defence and Legislative Departments of the Government of India. Appointed to Commonwealth Relations Office, 1947; Office of UK High Commissioner in the Union of South Africa, 1950-52; Dep. UK High Comr in India (Madras), 1953-57; Asst Sec., 1955; Dep. UK High Comr in Ghana, 1957-60; Dep. British High Comr in Canada, 1962-65; British Ambassador in Burma, 1965-67. *Address:* Long Meadow, Forest Road, East Horsley, Surrey.

**WAKEMAN, Captain Sir Offley,** 4th Bt, *cr* 1828; CBE 1957; JP; late Grenadier Guards; *b* 19 Oct. 1887; *s* of 3rd Bt and Catherine Mary (*d* 1925), *d* of Sir Charles Henry Rouse Boughton, 11th Bt; *S* father, 1929; *m* 1st, 1920, Winifred (*d* 1924), 2nd *d* of late Col C. R. Prideaux-Brune; one *s*; 2nd, 1929, Josceline Ethelreda, *widow* of Comm. Walter Leeke, RN, and *e d* of late Maj.-Gen. Bertram Mitford, CB, CMG; one *s. Educ:* Eton; Christ Church, Oxford (MA). Served European War, 1914-15 (wounded); ADC to Governor, New South Wales, 1914; ADC to Viceroy of India, 1918-19; sometime Private Sec. to Sec. for Mines; Member of LCC, 1922-25; Co-opted Member of LCC Education Committee, 1925-30; Member of Shropshire Education Committee, 1926-70, Chm., 1938-40, 1945-67; Mem. Salop County Council since 1928-70 (CA, 1940-70; Chm., 1943-63); Chairman Salop CC Finance Committee, 1940-45; Vice-President County Councils Association (Chairman CCA Education Cttee, 1948-62). Formerly Member Central Board of Finance of Church of England. JP Shropshire, 1927-, Sheriff, 1934; Vice-Lieutenant, for Salop, 1950-69. *Heir: s* Offley David Wakeman [*b* 6 March 1922; *m* 1946, Pamela Rose Arabella, *d* of late Lt-Col C. Hunter Little, DSO, MBE]. *Address:* Grafton Lodge, Montford Bridge, Shrewsbury. *T:* Montford Bridge 262. *Clubs:* Royal Aero; Shropshire (Shrewsbury).

**WAKSMAN, Professor Selman A.;** Professor Emeritus, 1958, Professor of Microbiology, 1940-58 and (first) Director of Institute of Microbiology, 1949-58, Rutgers University; Nobel Prize in Physiology and Medicine, 1952; *b* Priluka, Ukraine, 22 July 1888; *s* of Jacob and Fradia Waksman; became naturalized US citizen, 1916; *m* 1916, Deborah B. Mitnik; one *s. Educ:* Fifth Gymnasium, Odessa; Rutgers Coll. BSc 1915, in Agr., MSc 1916 (Rutgers); PhD 1918, in Biochem. (Univ. of California). Rutgers Univ.: Lectr in Soil Microbiology and Microbiologist at Expt. Station, 1918; Assoc. Prof. 1925; Prof. 1930. Has also served at Woods Hole Oceanographic Instn and is now a Trustee. For limited periods has held industrial positions and been consultant to Govt Organizations. Has isolated (with associates) many antibiotics (streptomycin, neomycin, etc.). Fellow Hon. Mem. and Mem. various scientific socs. Holds several hon. degrees, both Amer. and foreign, in Medicine, Science, Laws, and Hebrew Letters. Has received numerous awards and medals from scientific and other socs. Comdr Legion of Honour (France). *Publications:* My Life With the Microbes (autobiography); has written, alone or with others, 20 books on Soil Microbiology, Actinomycetes, Antibiotics, etc, and over 400 scientific papers. *Address:* c/o Institute of Microbiology, Rutgers, The State University, New Brunswick, NJ, USA.

**WALBANK, Frank William,** FBA 1953; MA; Rathbone Professor of Ancient History and Classical Archæology in the University of Liverpool since 1951; *b* 10 Dec. 1909; *s* of A. J. D. Walbank, Bingley, Yorks; *m* 1935, Mary Woodward, *e d* of O. C. A. Fox, Shipley, Yorks; one *s* two *d. Educ:* Bradford Grammar School; Peterhouse, Cambridge. Scholar of Peterhouse, 1928-31; First Class, Parts I and II Classical Tripos, 1930-31; Hugo de Balsham Research Student, Peterhouse, 1931-32; Senior Classics Master at North Manchester High School, 1932-33; Thirlwall Prize, 1933; Asst Lecturer, 1934-36; Lecturer, 1936-46, in Latin. Professor of Latin, 1946-51, University of Liverpool; Public Orator, 1956-60; Hare Prize, 1939. Andrew Mellon Vis. Prof., Univ. Pittsburgh, 1964; Myres Memorial Lectr, Univ. of Oxford, 1964-65. Mem. of Coun.: Classical Assoc., 1944-48, 1958-61 (Pres. 1969-70); Roman Soc., 1948-51 (Vice-Pres., 1953-; President, 1961-64); Hellenic Soc., 1951-54; 1955-56; Classical Journals Bd, 1948-66; British Acad., 1960-63; J. H. Gray Lecturer, University of Cambridge, 1957; Sather Prof., Univ. of California (Berkeley), 1971. *Publications:* Aratos of Sicyon, 1933; Philip V of Macedon, 1940; Latin Prose Versions contributed to Key to Bradley's Arnold, Latin Prose Composition, ed. J. F. Mountford, 1940; The Decline of the Roman Empire in the West, 1946; Chapters on Greek History, in The Year's Work in Classical Studies, special vol., 1938-45, 1948; vol. 34, 1949; contributions to the Oxford Classical Dictionary, 1949, to Chambers's Encyclopædia, 1950 and to Encyclopædia Britannica, 1960; Chapters in The Cambridge Economic History of Europe, Vol. II, 1952, and A Scientific Survey of Merseyside, 1953; A Historical Commentary on Polybius, Vol. i, 1957, Vol. ii, 1967; The Awful Revolution, 1969; contributor to English and foreign classical books and periodicals. *Address:* Hope Lodge, 5 Poplar Road, Oxton, Birkenhead, Cheshire L43 5TB. *T:* 051-652 2834.

**WALCH, Sir Geoffrey (Archer),** KBE 1954 (CBE 1943); CVO 1954; JP Tasmania; Chairman of J. Walch & Sons Pty Ltd, Publishers and Manufacturing Stationers, Hobart; *b* 8 May 1898; *s* of Richard Crosby and Elvie Mary Walch; *m* 1922, Thelma Fleming; one *s* one *d. Educ:* Hutchins School, Hobart; Clemes College, Hobart. Director of Civil Defence for State of Tasmania, 1940-45. Ex-Pres. of Returned Soldiers' Assoc., Hobart and Hobart Legacy Club; Chairman Tasmanian Veterans Trust; Director: Perpetual Trustees and National Executors Co. Ltd. of Tasmania,

1948; Tasmanian Television Ltd, 1958; Chairman of: Derwent and Tamar Assurance Co. Ltd, Hobart; Oldham, Beddome and Meredith Pty Ltd, Hobart; J. C. McPhee Pty Ltd, Hobart; Australian Landtrusts (Tas.) Ltd; Director: Tasmanian Finance & Agency Co. Ltd; Associated Securities (Tasmania) Ltd. Tasmanian Representative Australian Commonwealth Jubilee Council, 1951; Tasmanian State Director, Commonwealth Jubilee Celebrations, 1951-; State Director, 150th Anniversary Celebrations Committee, 1951-54; Deputy Director for Tasmania Royal Visit, 1954. *Recreation:* gardening. *Address:* 654 Sandy Bay Road, Hobart, Tasmania. *T:* 5-1244. *Club:* Tasmanian (Hobart).

**WALD, Prof. George;** Higgins Professor of Biology, Harvard University, since 1968; *b* 18 Nov. 1906; *s* of Isaac Wald and Ernestine (*née* Rosenmann); *m* 1st, 1931, Frances Kingsley (marr. diss.); two *s*; 2nd, 1958, Ruth Hubbard; one *s* one *d*. *Educ:* Washington Square Coll. of New York Univ. (BS); Columbia Univ. (PhD). Nat. Research Coun. Fellowship, 1932-34. Harvard University: Instr and Tutor in Biology, 1934-39; Faculty Instr, 1939-44; Associate Prof., 1944-48; Prof. of Biology, 1948-68. Nobel Prize in Physiology and Medicine (jointly), 1967. Has many hon. doctorates from univs in USA and abroad. *Publications:* (co-author) General Education in a Free Society; (co-author) Twenty-six Afternoons of Biology. Many sci. papers (on the biochemistry and physiology of vision and on biochem. evolution) in: Jl of Gen. Physiology, Nature, Science, Jl of Opt. Soc. of Amer., etc. *Recreations:* art, archæology, ski-ing, horseback riding. *Address:* Biological Laboratories, Harvard University, Cambridge, Mass 02138, USA. *T:* 868-7600 (Ext. 2311).

**WALDEGRAVE,** family name of **Earl Waldegrave.**

**WALDEGRAVE,** 12th Earl, *cr* 1729, **Geoffrey Noel Waldegrave,** TD; DL; Bt 1643; Baron Waldegrave, 1685; Viscount Chewton, 1729; Member of the Prince's Council of the Duchy of Cornwall, 1951-58 and since 1965, and Lord Warden of the Stannaries, since 1965; Director: Lloyds Bank Ltd (Chairman, Bristol Regional Board); Bristol Waterworks Co.; English Farms Ltd (Chairman); *b* 21 Nov. 1905; *o s* of 11th Earl and Anne Katharine (*d* 1962), *d* of late Rev. W. P. Bastard, Ashburton and Kitley, Devon; *S* father, 1936; *m* 1930, Mary Hermione, *d* of Lt-Col A. M. Grenfell, DSO; two *s* five *d*. *Educ:* Winchester; Trinity Coll., Cambridge (BA). Served War of 1939-45, Major RA (TA). Chm., Som AEC, 1948-51; Liaison Officer to Min. of Agriculture, Fisheries and Food (formerly Min. of Agriculture and Fisheries), for Som, Wilts and Glos, 1952-57; Jt Parly Sec., Min. of Agriculture, Fisheries and Food, 1958-62; Chairman: Forestry Commn, 1963-65; Adv. Cttee on Meat Research, 1969-. Pres., Somerset Trust for Nature Conservation. Member: BBC Gen. Adv. Council, 1963-66; Bristol Univ. Court and Council (Chm., Agricultural Cttee). Mem. Council and Trustee, Bath and W Southern Counties Soc.; Trustee, Partis Coll., Bath; Chm., Friends of Wells Cathedral. Governor: Wells Cathedral Sch.; Nat. Fruit and Cider Inst., Long Ashton. Mem. Som CC, 1937-58; CA, 1949-58; DL Somerset, 1951; Vice-Lieutenant Somerset, 1955-60. Officer, Legion of Merit, USA. *Heir: s* Viscount Chewton, *qv*. *Address:* Chewton House, Chewton Mendip, Bath, Som. *T:* Chewton Mendip 264. *Clubs:* Travellers', Farmers'.

*See also Baron Forteviot, Baron Strathcona and Mount Royal.*

**WALDEN, Brian Alastair;** MP (Lab) Birmingham (All Saints) since 1964; *b* 8 July 1932; *s* of W. F. Walden; *m* 1st, 1957, Sybil Frances Brackstone (marr. diss., 1968); two *s*; 2nd, 1969, Jane, *d* of late Sir Patrick McKerron, KBE, CMG; one *s*. *Educ:* West Bromwich Grammar School; Queen's College and Nuffield College, Oxford. University Lecturer. Joined Labour party, 1951. Member: National Union of General and Municipal Workers; Association of University Teachers; Staff Tutors' Assoc. Contested Oswestry by-election, November 1961. PPS to Chief Secretary to the Treasury and to Financial Secretary to the Treasury, 1964-66. *Recreation:* chess. *Address:* House of Commons, SW1; 277 Chiswick Village, Chiswick, W4.

**WALDEN, Stanley Arthur,** CMG 1956; FRPS(L) 1960; MA Cantab; Secretary, Overseas Service Pensioners' Association; *b* 17 June 1905; *s* of late Alfred Walden. Rotherfield, Henley-on-Thames; unmarried. *Educ:* Royal Grammar Sch., Henley-on-Thames; Selwyn College, Cambridge. Cadet, Colonial Service, Tanganyika, 1929; Assistant District Officer, 1931; District Officer, 1941; Deputy Provincial Comr, 1948; Provincial Commissioner, 1951; Sen. Provincial Commissioner, 1953-59; Provincial Comr in charge of Lake Province, 1954-59; Chm. Wage Structure Cttee of Joint Council of Sisal Industry, Tanganyika, 1960. *Recreations:* philately, music, rowing and tennis. *Address:* Laund, Henley-on-Thames, Oxon RG9 1NN. *T:* 4715. *Clubs:* Royal Commonwealth Society, East India and Sports, Leander.

**WALDER, (Alan) David;** ERD 1965; MP (C) Clitheroe since 1970; Parliamentary Private Secretary to Minister for Trade, since 1970; Barrister and Author; *b* 13 Nov. 1928; *o s* of late James Walder, Chailey, Sussex, and of Helen Walder (*née* McColville); *m* 1956, Elspeth Margaret, *y d* of Rt Hon. Lord Milligan, *qv*; one *s* three *d* (including twin *d*). *Educ:* Latymer School; Christ Church, Oxford (Scholar), MA. Served Malaya, 1948-49; AER of 4th Queen's Own Hussars until 1958, of Queen's Royal Irish Hussars until 1965. Served as a Reservist in Germany, Aden and Borneo, Major. Called to the Bar, Inner Temple, 1956; Forster-Boulton Prize; Paul Methven Scholar; Midland Circuit. Chairman, Wembley South Conservative Assoc., 1959. Contested (C) Leicester SW Division, 1959. MP (C) High Peak Division of Derbyshire, 1961-66. PPS to Jt Under-Secs of State, Scottish Office, 1963-64. Vice-Pres. Derbyshire Naturalists' Trust; Mem. Court of Sheffield University; Mem. Institute of Strategic Studies. Sec. Army sub-cttee, Conservative Defence Cttee. *Publications:* Stability and Survival (with Julian Critchley), 1961; Bags of Swank, 1963; The Short List, 1964; The House Party, 1966; The Gift Bearers (USA), 1967; The Fair Ladies of Salamanca, 1967; The Chanak Affair, 1969; The Short Victorious War, 1971; (contrib.) Purnell's History of the First World War. *Recreations:* shooting, ornithology, opera. *Address:* The White House, Grimsargh, near Preston, Lancs. *T:* Longridge 3618; 45 Courtenay Street, SE11. *T:* 01-735 8281. *Club:* Cavalry.

**WALDER, David;** *see* Walder, A. D.

**WALDER, Ruth Christabel, (Mrs Wesierska),** OBE 1956; Free-lance Consultant, 1968; *b* 15 Jan. 1906; *d* of Rev. Ernest Walder; *m* 1955, Maj.-Gen. George Wesierski (*d* 1967), formerly Judge Advocate General of the Polish Forces. *Educ:* Cheltenham Ladies' College. General Organiser, National Federation of Women's Institutes, 1934-40; Admiralty, 1940-41; Relief Department, Foreign Office, 1942-44; UNRRA, Sec. Food Cttee of Council for Europe, 1944-47; Secretary United Nations Appeal for Children (in the UK), 1948; National General Secretary, YWCA of Great Britain, 1949-67. *Address:* 15 Ennerdale Road, Kew, Surrey; Westhope, Langton Herring, Dorset. *T:* 01-940 0755.

**WALDMAN, Milton;** Author and Publisher; *b* USA, 4 Oct. 1895; *s* of Benjamin Waldman and Ida Spire; *m* 1934, Marguerite David (*d* 1969); one *s* two *d. Educ:* Yale University, USA. Journalist in USA War Service, 1917-19. Assistant Editor London Mercury, 1924-27. Literary Adviser Longmans Green & Co. Ltd, 1919-24; William Collins Sons & Co. Ltd, 1939-52; Joint Managing Director, Rupert Hart-Davis, Ltd, 1952-55; Literary Adviser, William Collins Sons & Co. Ltd, 1955-. Contributor to various periodicals, anthologies, etc. Editor The Golden Hind Series. *Publications:* Americana, 1925; Sir Walter Raleigh, 1928; The Disinherited (a novel), 1929; King, Queen, Jack, 1931; Elizabeth of England, 1933; Joan of Arc, 1935; Biography of a Family, 1936; Three English Dictators, 1940; Elizabeth and Leicester, 1944; Queen Elizabeth (Brief Lives Series), 1952. *Address:* 79 Dorset House, Gloucester Place, NW1. *Club:* Savile.

**WALDMAN, Ronald Hartley;** Managing Director, Visnews Ltd, since 1963; Director: British Commonwealth International Newsfilm Agency Ltd; News Film Services Ltd; *b* 13 May 1914; *e s* of late Michael Ernest Waldman, OBE, JP; *m* 1953, Lana Morris, one *s. Educ:* Owen's School; Pembroke College, Oxford. Actor and Producer, 1935-38. Producer, BBC Variety Dept, 1938; wartime service in RAFVR. Assistant Head of Variety (Productions), 1948; Senior Producer, Television Light Entertainment, 1950; Head of Light Entertainment, BBC Television, 1950; Business Manager, BBC TV Programmes, 1958-60; General Manager, BBC TV Enterprises, 1960-63. *Address:* Visnews Ltd, School Road, NW10. *Clubs:* MCC, Lord's Taverners'.

**WALDOCK, Sir (Claud) Humphrey (Meredith),** Kt 1961; CMG 1946; OBE 1942; QC 1951; DCL; MA; Chichele Professor of Public International Law, Oxford, since 1947; *b* 13 Aug. 1904; *s* of Frederic William Waldock and Lizzie Kyd Souter; *m* 1934, Ethel Beatrice Williams; one *s* one *d. Educ:* Uppingham School; Brasenose Coll., Oxford. Hockey Blue, 1926; BA 1927; BCL 1928; Barrister-at-Law, Gray's Inn, Bencher, 1957; Midland Circuit, 1928-30; Fellow and Lectr in Law, Brasenose, 1930-47; Tutor, 1937; Hon. Fellow, 1960. Lecturer in Law, Oriel College, 1930-39; Pro-Proctor, 1936. Temp. Principal Admiralty, 1940; Assistant-Secretary, 1943; Principal Assistant Secretary, 1944. UK Commissioner on Italo-Yugoslav Boundary Commission; Commission for Free Territory of Trieste, Council of Foreign Ministers, 1946. Trustee, Uppingham Sch., 1947-59. Fellow, All Souls Coll., 1947; Assessor in the Chancellor's Court, 1947; Mem. Hebdomadal Council, 1948-61; European Commn of Human Rights, 1954-61 (Pres. 1955-61); Judge, European Court of Human Rights, 1966- (Vice-Pres., 1968-); Chm., Cttee of Inquiry into Oxford University Press, 1967-70. Editor, British Year Book of International Law, 1955; Member: Inst. of Internat. Law; Swedish-Finnish Conciliation Commn, 1957; Swedish-Swiss Conciliation Commn, 1960; Swedish-Turkish and German-Swiss Conciliation Commns, 1963; US-Danish Conciliation Commn, 1964; Chilean-Italian Conciliation Commn, 1965; Danish-Norwegian Conciliation Commn, 1967; Swedish-Spanish Conciliation Commn, 1968; UN Internat. Law Commn, 1961- (Special Rapporteur on Law of Treaties, 1962-66; President 1967); UN Expert on Law of Treaties, Vienna Conf., 1968, 1969; Member: Permanent Court of Arbitration, 1965-; Council of Legal Education, 1965-. *Publications:* Law of Mortgages; Regulation of the Use of Force by Individual States (Hague Recueil), 1952; General Course on Public International Law (Hague Recueil), 1962; Editor, Brierly's Law of Nations (6th Edn), 1963. Articles on International Law. *Recreations:* cricket, tennis, shooting, fishing. *Address:* 6 Lathbury Road, Oxford. *T:* 58227. *Club:* United University.

**WALDRON, Brig. John Graham Claverhouse,** CBE 1958 (OBE 1944); DSO 1945; *b* 15 Nov. 1909; *s* of William Slade Olver (*d* 1909), Falmouth; *m* 1933, Marjorie, *d* of Arthur Waldron (*d* 1953), Newbury; one *s* one *d. Educ:* Marlborough; RMC, Sandhurst. jssc, psc. 2nd Lieut, Gloucestershire Regt, 1929. Served War of 1939-45 (OBE, DSO): 5 British Division and 1st Bn Green Howards, in India, Middle East, Italy, NW Europe. Lt-Col, 10th Gurkha Rifles, 1951; Brigadier, 1958; ADC to the Queen, 1960-61; retired, 1961. *Address:* La Cañada, Marbella, Spain. *Clubs:* Army and Navy, Royal Cruising.

**WALDRON, Sir John (Lovegrove),** KCVO 1966 (CVO 1959); Commissioner, Metropolitan Police, since 1968; *b* 1909; *s* of late Frederick Waldron, Wargrave, Berkshire; *m* 1937, Joan Elsie, *d* of late P. G. Osborne; two *d. Educ:* Charterhouse; Clare College, Cambridge (BA). Joined Metropolitan Police, 1934; seconded Ceylon Police, 1943-47. Acted as Dep. Inspector-Gen., CID, 1944-47. Asst Chief Constable, Lancashire, 1951-54; Chief Constable, Berkshire, 1954-58; Asst Commissioner, Metropolitan Police, 1959-66; Dep. Commissioner, 1966-68. *Address:* New Scotland Yard, SW1.

**WALES, Archbishop of,** since 1968; **Most Rev. (William) Glyn (Hughes) Simon;** DD (Lambeth), 1954; Bishop of Llandaff since 1957; *b* 1903; *s* of Canon John Simon and Margaret Caroline Simon; *m* 1st, 1942, Sarah Sheila Ellen Roberts (*d* 1963); two *s* one *d*; 2nd, 1970, Camellia, *widow* of Trevor Rees. *Educ:* Christ Coll., Brecon; Jesus Coll., Oxford; St Stephen's House, Oxford. BA 1926, MA 1931; 2nd Cl. Lit. Hum.; 1st Cl. Theol. Ordained Deacon, 1927; Priest, 1928; Asst Priest St Paul, Crewe, 1927-31; Warden Church Hostel, Bangor, Lectr University Coll. N Wales, Bangor, 1931-40; Warden St Michael's College, Llandaff, 1940-48; Canon of Llandaff Cathedral, 1943, Chancellor, 1944. Exam. Chaplain to Bishops of: Bangor, 1931-40; Swansea and Brecon, 1934-38; Llandaff, 1938-48. Dean of Llandaff, 1948-54; Bishop of Swansea and Brecon, 1954-57. Mem., Anglican-RC Preparatory Commn, 1967-. Select Preacher, Univ. of Cambridge, 1958; Univ. of Oxford, 1965, 1966. Sub-Prelate, Order of St John, 1958. FSA 1966. Hon. Fellow Jesus Coll., Oxford, 1967. *Publications:* Torch Commentary I Corinthians, 1959; Bishops (ed. and contrib.), 1961; The Landmark, 1962; Feeding the Flock, 1964; contrib. to Encyclopædia Britannica, 1963. *Address:* Llys Esgob, The Green, Llandaff, Cardiff. *Club:* Cardiff and County (Cardiff).

**WALES, Geoffrey,** RE 1961 (ARE 1948); ARCA 1936; Lecturer, Norwich School of Art, since 1953; Art Critic, Eastern Daily Press, 1958-65; *b* 26 May 1912; *s* of Ernest and Kathleen Wales; *m* 1940, Marjorie Skeeles; two *d. Educ:* Chatham House School, Ramsgate; Thanet School of Art; Royal College of Art. Served War of 1939-45, in Royal Air Force, 1940-46; commissioned, 1943. Member of the Norwich Twenty Group, 1953 (Chairman, 1957). Prints and drawings in Victoria and Albert Museums; Whitworth Gallery, Manchester; Kunsthaus, Graz; and private collections. Exhibits with: Royal Society of Painter Etchers and Engravers; Norwich Twenty Group. Illustrated books for Golden Cockerel Press, Kynoch Press, Folio Soc. and general graphic work. Engravings produced in publications and articles on wood-engraving. *Recreation:* an interest in the seaside. *Address:* 15 Heigham Grove, Norwich, Norfolk NOR 14G. *T:* Norwich 29066.

**WALES, Horace Geoffrey Quaritch,** MA, PhD, LittD; Orientalist and Archæologist; *b* 17 Oct. 1900; *s* of late E. Horace Wales; *g s* of late Bernard Quaritch; *m* 1931, Dorothy Clementina Johnson, LLB. *Educ:* Charterhouse; Queens' College, Cambridge. Siamese Government Service, 1924-28; travelled widely in India, Burma, Indochina and Indonesia in connection with Oriental research; during 1934-36, as Field Director of the Greater-India Research Committee, carried out archæological investigations in Siam, and during 1937-40 in Malaya, excavating ancient sites and exploring early trade routes; conducted excavations at early Buddhist sites in Siam, 1955-56, 1964, 1968. Chairman, Bernard Quaritch Ltd, 1951- ( Director, 1939-); served IA (Gen. Staff), 1940-41; in USA writing and speaking on Pacific affairs and publicising India's war effort, 1942-45. Member Council, Royal Asiatic Society, 1947-58, 1964-68 (Vice-President, 1958-62); Hon. Member Royal Asiatic Soc., Malayan Branch. *Publications:* Siamese State Ceremonies, 1931; Ancient Siamese Government and Administration, 1934; Towards Angkor, 1937; Archæological Researches on Ancient Indian Colonization in Malaya, 1940; The Making of Greater India, 1951; Ancient South-East Asian Warfare, 1952; The Mountain of God, 1953; Prehistory and Religion in South-east Asia, 1957; Angkor and Rome, 1965; The Indianization of China, 1967; Dvāravatī, the Earliest Kingdom of Siam, 1969; contrib. to The Cambridge History of India, many articles in various learned journals. *Club:* Royal Societies.

**WALEY-COHEN, Sir Bernard (Nathaniel),** 1st Bt *cr* 1961; Kt 1957; Director: Bray Gibb (Holdings) Ltd; Lloyds Bank Ltd Central London Region; Burston & Texas Commerce Bank Ltd; Tudor Accessories Ltd; Kleeman Industrial Holdings Ltd, and other companies; *b* 29 May 1914; *er s* of late Sir Robert Waley Cohen, KBE and Alice Violet, *d* of Henry Edward Beddington, London and Newmarket; *m* 1943, Hon. Joyce Constance Ina, MA, JP, *o d* of 1st Baron Nathan of Churt, PC, TD, two *s* two *d. Educ:* HMS Britannia (RNC Dartmouth); Clifton College; Magdalene Coll., Cambridge (MA). Mem. of staff, Duke of York's Camp, Southwold, 1932-36; Mem. of Public School Empire Tour, New Zealand, 1932-33; Liveryman, Clothworkers' Company, 1936; Court 1966; Gunner, HAC, 1937-38; Underwriting Member of Lloyd's 1939; Principal Ministry of Fuel and Power 1940-47. Alderman, City of London Portsoken Ward, 1949; Sheriff, City of London, 1955-56; Lord Mayor of London, 1960-61. Mem. Council and Board of Governors, Clifton Coll., 1952; Mem., College Cttee, University College London, 1953, Treasurer 1962; Vice-Chm. 1970; Mem. Senate, 1962; Court, 1966, London Univ.; Chm., Wellesley House Prep. Sch., 1965. Chm., Devon and Somerset Staghounds, 1953; Mem. Finance and General Purposes Cttee, British Field Sports Soc., 1957, Treasurer 1966; Pres., Bath and West and Southern Counties Show, 1963; Pres., Devon Cattle Breeders' Soc., 1963. Mem., Marshall Aid Commemoration Commn, 1957-60; Treasurer, Jewish Welfare Board, 1948-53; Vice-Pres., United Synagogue, 1952-61; Vice-Pres., Anglo-Jewish Assoc., 1962; Pres., Jewish Museum, 1964; Mem., Nat. Corporation for Care of Old People, 1965; Mem., Executive Cttee and Central Council, Probation and After Care Cttees, 1965-69. Chairman of Simo Securities Trust Ltd 1955-70. Hon. Liveryman of Farmers' Company 1961. Assoc. KStJ 1961. Hon. LLD London, 1961. *Recreations:* hunting and shooting. *Heir: s* Stephen Harry Waley-Cohen [*b* 1946. *Educ:* Eton (Oppidan Scholar); Magdalene Coll., Cambridge (BA 1968). On Staff of Daily Mail City Editor, 1968]. *Address:* 11 Little St James's Street, SW1. *T:* 01-629 1615; Honeymead, Simonsbath, Minehead, Somerset. *T:* Exford 242. *Clubs:* Athenæum, Boodle's, MCC, City Livery; Jockey Club Rooms (Newmarket); University Pitt (Cambridge).

**WALFORD, Major-General Alfred Ernest,** CB 1946; CBE 1944; MM 1916; ED; Legion of Merit (USA); CA; FCIS; Chairman, Tenelux Ltd, since 1969; Director: Triarch Corporation Ltd; The Mercantile Bank of Canada; Montreal Advisory Board of Canada Trust Co. (Chairman); *b* Montreal, 20 Aug. 1896; *s* of Alfred G. S. and Phoebe Anne Walford, Montreal; *m* 1922, Olive Marjorie, *d* of James A. Dyke, Westmount Province of Quebec; one *s. Educ:* Westmount Acad. Served European War, 1914-19, with Royal Canadian Artillery, and War of 1939-45, HQ 1st Canadian Div., 1st Canadian Corps and as DA&QMG 1st Canadian Army in NW Europe; Adjutant-General Canadian Forces, Nat. Defence Headquarters, Ottawa, 1944-46. Partner, Alfred Walford & Sons, Chartered Accountants, 1923-29; Dir, Sec. and Treasurer, of James A. Ogilvy Ltd, 1929-39, of Henry Morgan & Co. Ltd, 1946-61; Pres., Morgan Trust Co., 1946-65; Chairman: E. G. M. Cape & Co. Ltd, 1965-68; Canadian Vickers Ltd, 1959-67. Member Metropolitan Advisory Board, YMCA; Chairman Advisory Board, The Salvation Army; Past President: Fedn Commonwealth Chambers of Commerce; National Cttee, English-Speaking Union; Montreal Board of Trade; Past Chairman, Exec. Development Institute. Fellow, Royal Commonwealth Society; Fellow, Canadian Chartered Inst. of Secretaries; Member Inst. of Chartered Accountants of Quebec. *Address:* (office) Suite 1400, 635 Dorchester Boulevard West, Montreal, PQ, Canada; (home) 728 Upper Belmont Avenue, Westmount, Montreal 217, PQ. *Clubs:* St James's, Mount Royal, Forest and Stream, Royal Montreal Golf (Montreal).

**WALKER, Hon. Lord; James Walker;** one of the Senators of the College of Justice in Scotland since 1954; Chairman Law Reform Committee for Scotland, 1954-64; President of Scottish Universities Law Institute, 1960; *b* Wigtown, 1890; *s* of late A. D. Walker, solicitor; *m* 1918, Ella, *d* of late John Grieve; one *s. Educ:* Ewart Acad., Newton Stewart; Glasgow and Edinburgh Universities. Advocate, 1914; Royal Scots and Machine-Gun Corps in Egypt and France, 1915-19; Member of Rules Council, 1933-48; Junior Counsel to Scottish

Office, 1934-36; Advocate-Depute, 1937-40; Clerk of Justiciary, 1940-48; Vice-Dean of the Faculty of Advocates, 1948-54; Member of Royal Commission on Marriage and Divorce, 1951-55; Sheriff of Inverness, Moray, Nairn and Ross and Cromarty, 1949-53; Sheriff of Aberdeen, Kincardine and Banff, 1953-54. QC (Scotland) 1944. Hon. LLD (Edinburgh), 1961. *Publications:* Intestate Succession in Scotland, 1927. *Recreations:* fishing, shooting. *Address:* 14 Dalrymple Crescent, Edinburgh. *T:* 031-667 1822. *Clubs:* New, Scottish Arts (Edinburgh).

**WALKER, Alan;** *see* Walker, (Horace) Alan.

**WALKER, Sir Allan (Grierson),** Kt 1968; QC (Scotland); Sheriff of Lanarkshire since Oct. 1963; *b* 1 May 1907; *er s* of late Joseph Walker, merchant, London, and Mary Grierson; *m* 1935, Audrey Margaret, *o d* of late Dr T. A. Glover, Doncaster; one *s. Educ:* Whitgift Sch., Croydon; Edinburgh Univ. Practised at Scottish Bar, 1931-39; Sheriff-Substitute of Roxburgh, Berwick, and Selkirk at Selkirk and of the County of Peebles, 1942-45; Sheriff-Substitute of Stirling, Dumbarton and Clackmannan at Dumbarton, 1945-50; Sheriff-Substitute of Lanarkshire at Glasgow, 1950-63; Member, Law Reform Cttee for Scotland, 1964-. Hon. LLD Glasgow, 1967. *Publications:* The Law of Evidence in Scotland (joint author); Purves' Scottish Licensing Laws (7th, 8th edns). *Recreations:* walking, gardening. *Address:* 31 Kersland Street, Glasgow, W2. *T:* 041-339 9828. *Club:* Western (Glasgow).

**WALKER, Arthur Geoffrey,** FRS 1955; Professor of Pure Mathematics, Liverpool University, since 1952; *b* 17 July 1909; 2nd *s* of late A. J. Walker, Watford, Herts; *m* 1939, Phyllis Ashcroft, *d* of late Sterry B. Freeman, CBE. *Educ:* Watford Grammar Sch.; Balliol Coll., Oxford. MA (Oxon); PhD, DSc (Edinburgh); FRSE; Lectr at Imperial Coll. Science and Technology, 1935-36; at Liverpool Univ., 1936-47; Prof. of Mathematics in the Univ. of Sheffield, 1947-52. Mem. of Council, Royal Soc., 1962-63. Pres., London Mathematical Soc., 1963-65. Junior Berwick Prize of London Mathematical Soc., 1947; Keith Medal of Royal Society of Edinburgh, 1950. *Publication:* Harmonic Spaces (with H. S. Ruse and T. J. Willmore), 1962. *Address:* Department of Pure Mathematics, The University, PO Box 147, Liverpool L69 3BX; Thorncroft, Thornton Hough, Wirral, Cheshire L63 4JT. *T:* 051-336 4845.

**WALKER, Air Chief Marshal Sir Augustus;** *see* Walker, Air Chief Marshal Sir G. A.

**WALKER, Sir Baldwin Patrick,** 4th Bt, *cr* 1856; *b* 10 Sept. 1924; *s* of late Comdr Baldwin Charles Walker, *o s* of 3rd Bt and Mary, *d* of F. P. Barnett of Whalton, Northumberland; *S* grandfather, 1928; *m* 1948, Joy Yvonne (marr. diss., 1954); *m* 1954, Sandra Stewart; *m* 1966, Rosemary Ann, *d* of late Henry Hollingdrake; *s* one *d. Educ:* Gordonstoun. Served Royal Navy, Fleet Air Arm, 1943-58. Lieut, RN, retired. *Heir: s* Christopher Robert Baldwin Walker, *b* 25 Oct. 1969. *Address:* Eikerus, Bo Daljosaphat, near Paarl, CP, South Africa.

**WALKER, Sir (Charles) Michael,** KCMG 1963 (CMG 1960); British High Commissioner in Malaysia since 1966; *b* 22 Nov. 1916; *s* of Col C. W. G. Walker, *qv; m* 1945, Enid Dorothy, *d* of late W. A. McAdam, CMG; one *s* one *d. Educ:* Charterhouse; New Coll., Oxford. Clerk of House of Lords, June 1939. Enlisted in Army, Oct. 1939, and served in RA until 1946 when released with rank of Lt-Col. Dominions Office, 1947; First Sec., British Embasssy, Washington, 1949-51; Office of United Kingdom High Comr in Calcutta and New Delhi, 1952-55; Establishment Officer, Commonwealth Relations Office, 1955-58. Imperial Defence Coll., 1958; Asst Under-Sec. of State and Dir of Establishment and Organisation, CRO, 1959-62; British High Comr in Ceylon, 1962-65, concurrently Ambassador to Maldive Islands, July-Nov. 1965. *Recreations:* fishing, gardening, golf. *Address:* c/o Foreign and Commonwealth Office, King Charles Street, SW1; Long Tarrant, Broadwater Road, Burwood Park, Walton-on-Thames, Surrey. *T:* Walton-on-Thames 21165. *Clubs:* Travellers', Oriental.

**WALKER, Vice-Adm. Sir (Charles) Peter (Graham),** KBE 1967; CB 1964; DSC 1944; Director, Cammell Laird & Co. (S & E) Ltd, since 1969; *b* 23 Feb. 1911; *s* of Charles Graham Walker and Lilla Geraldine (*née* Gandy); *m* 1938, Pamela Marcia Hawley, *d* of late George W. Hawley, Cape, SA; one *s* one *d. Educ:* Worksop College. Entered Royal Navy, 1929; Royal Naval Engineering Coll., 1930-34; Advanced Engineering Course at RN Coll., Greenwich, 1935-37. War service in HM Ships Cornwall, Georgetown, Duke of York and Berwick and at the Admiralty; Vice-Admiral, 1965; Dir-Gen., Dockyards and Maintenance, MoD (Navy), 1962-67; Chief Naval Engr Officer, 1963-67; retired 1967. *Recreations:* gardening, golf. *Address:* Brookfield Coach House, Weston Lane, Bath. *T:* Bath 23863. *Clubs:* Army and Navy; Bath and County (Bath).

**WALKER, Col Charles William Garne,** CMG 1933; DSO 1918; *b* 2 July 1882; *s* of late Charles Walker, Bridgend; *m* 1915, Dorothy Frances (*d* 1965), *e d* of late F. Hughes-Gibb, JP, Manor House, Tarrant Gunville, Dorset; one *s. Educ:* King's Sch., Canterbury; Sandhurst. 2nd Lieut, 1902; joined Indian Army, 1903; Captain, 1911; Staff Coll., Camberley, 1912-13; served European War, 1914-18 (despatches twice, DSO, Bt Lt-Col); Col, 1923; Asst Sec. Cttee of Imperial Defence, 1921-25; retired, 1927; Secretary to the Conference of Governors of the East African Dependencies, 1925-36; employed HM Treasury, 1936-40; Principal Officer Southern Civil Defence Region, 1940-42; War Cabinet Office, 1943-47; Secretary: Lord De La Warr's mission to Ethiopia, 1944; Assoc. of Consulting Engineers, 1948-60. *Address:* The Old Vicarage, South Cerney, Cirencester. *Club:* Travellers'.

*See also Sir C. M. Walker.*

**WALKER, David Harry,** MBE 1946; Author; *b* 9 Feb. 1911; *s* of Harry Giles Walker and Elizabeth Bewley (*née* Newsom); *m* 1939, Willa Magee, Montreal; four *s. Educ:* Shrewsbury; Sandhurst. The Black Watch, 1931-47 (retired); ADC to Gov.-Gen. of Canada, 1938-39; Comptroller to Viceroy of India, 1946-47. Member: Royal Company of Archers; Canada Council, 1957-61; Chm., Roosevelt-Campobello Internat. Park Commn, 1970 (Canadian Comr, 1965). Hon. DLitt, Univ. of New Brunswick, 1955. FRSL. *Publications: novels:* The Storm and the Silence, 1950 (USA 1949); Geordie, 1950 (filmed 1955); The Pillar, 1952; Digby, 1953; Harry Black, 1956 (filmed, 1957); Sandy was a Soldier's Boy, 1957; Where the High Winds Blow, 1960; Storms of Our Journey and Other Stories, 1962; Dragon Hill (for children), 1962; Winter of Madness, 1964; Mallabec, 1965; Come Back, Geordie, 1966; Devil's Plunge (USA, Cab-Intersec), 1968; Pirate Rock, 1969; Big Ben (for children), 1970. *Address:* Strathcroix, St Andrews, New Brunswick, Canada. *Club:* Royal and Ancient.

**WALKER, Prof. David Maxwell,** QC; Regius Professor of Law, Glasgow University, since 1958; Dean of the Faculty of Law, 1956-59; Senate Assessor on University Court, 1962-66; *b* 9 April 1920; *o s* of James Mitchell Walker, Branch Manager, Union Bank of Scotland, and Mary Paton Colquhoun Irvine; *m* 1954, Margaret Knox, MA, *yr d* of Robert Knox, yarn merchant, Brookfield, Renfrewshire. *Educ:* High School of Glasgow (Mackindlay Prizeman in Classics); Glasgow, Edinburgh and London Universities. MA (Glasgow) 1946; LLB (Distinction), Robertson Schol., 1948; Faulds Fellow in Law, 1949-52; PhD (Edinburgh), 1952; Blackwell Prize, Aberdeen Univ., 1955; LLB (London), 1957; LLD (Edinburgh), 1960; LLD (London), 1968. Served War of 1939-45, NCO Cameronians; commissioned HLI, 1940; seconded to RIASC, 1941; served with Indian Forces in India, 1942, Middle East, 1942-43, and Italy, 1943-46, in MT companies and as Brigade Supply and Transport Officer (Captain). HQ 21 Ind. Inf. Bde, 8 Ind. Div. Advocate of Scottish Bar, 1948; Barrister-at-law, Middle Temple, 1957; QC (Scotland) 1958; practised at Scottish Bar, 1948-53; studied at Inst. of Advanced Legal Studies, Univ. of London, 1953-54; Prof. of Jurisprudence, Glasgow Univ., 1954-58. Governor Scottish College of Commerce, 1957-64. Hon. Sheriff Substitute of Lanarkshire at Glasgow, 1966-. FSA Scotland. *Publications:* (ed) Faculty Digest of Decisions, 1940-50, Supplements, 1951 and 1952; Law of Damages in Scotland, 1955; The Scottish Legal System, 1959 (3rd edn, 1969); Law of Delict in Scotland, 1966; Scottish Courts and Tribunals, 1969; Principles of Scottish Private Law, 1970; Scottish Part of Topham and Ivamy's Company Law, 12th, 13th, 14th edns; contribs to collaborative works; articles in legal periodicals. *Recreations:* motoring, book collecting, Scottish history. *Address:* 1 Beaumont Gate, Glasgow, W2. *T:* 041-339 2802.

**WALKER, Sir E(dward) Ronald,** Kt 1963; CBE 1956; Australian Ambassador to the Federal Republic of Germany, since 1968; *b* 26 Jan. 1907; *s* of Rev. Frederick Thomas Walker; *m* 1933, Louise Donckers; one *s* one *d. Educ:* Sydney Univ. (MA); Cambridge Univ. (PhD, LittD). Lecturer in Economics, Sydney Univ., 1927-30, 1933-39; Fellow of Rockefeller Foundation, 1931-33; Economic Adviser: NSW Treasury, 1938-39; Govt of Tasmania, 1939-41; Prof. of Economics, Univ. of Tasmania, 1939-46; Chief Economic Adviser and Dep. Dir-Gen., Australian Dept of War Organisation of Industry, 1941-45; UNRRA HQ, Washington, 1945; Counsellor, Australian Embassy, Paris, 1945-50; Exec. Member, Nat. Security Resources Board, Prime Minister's Dept, Canberra, 1950-52; Australian Ambassador to Japan, 1952-55; Ambassador and Permanent Representative of Australia at United Nations, 1956-59; Ambassador to France, 1959-68. Mem. commns and delegate to many confs and assemblies connected with UN, ILO, Unesco, etc; Pres., UN Security Council, 1956, 1957. Pres., UN Economic and Social Council, 1964. *Publications:* An Outline of Australian Economics, 1931; Australia in the World Depression, 1933; Money, 1935; Unemployment Policy, 1936; Wartime Economics, 1939; From Economic Theory to Policy, 1942; The Australian Economy in War and Reconstruction, 1947. *Recreations:* tennis, golf. *Address:* Australian Embassy, Bonn, Federal Republic of Germany. *Club:* University (Sydney, Australia).

**WALKER, Eric Anderson,** MA (Oxon, Cape Town, Cantab); Fellow of St John's College, Cambridge, 1936-68; Vere Harmsworth Professor of Imperial and Naval History, Cambridge, 1936-51, now Emeritus; *b* Streatham, SW, 6 Sept. 1886; *e s* of William and Jessie Walker; *m* 1913, Lucy Stapleton, Rondebosch; two *d. Educ:* Mill Hill Sch.; Merton Coll., Oxford (History Exhibitioner). Lecturer in History in the University of Bristol, 1908-11; King George V Professor of History in University of Cape Town, 1911-36. Hon. DLitt, Witwatersrand, Cape Town. *Publications:* Historical Atlas of South Africa, 1922; Lord de Villiers and his Times, 1925; A Modern History for South Africans, 1926; A History of South Africa, 1928 (2nd edn, 1940, rep. with corrs., 1947); The SA College and the University of Cape Town, 1929; The Frontier Tradition in South Africa, 1930; The Great Trek, 1934, 4th edn, 1960; W. P. Schreiner: A South African, 1937 (shortened edn, 1960); South Africa, 1940 and 1941; Britain and South Africa, 1942; The British Empire, 1943 (2nd and extended edn, 1953); Colonies, 1944; A History of Southern Africa, 1957 (5th reprint 1968); South African Adviser to the Editors of the Cambridge History of the British Empire, Vol. VIII (South Africa); Joint Editor of the Cambridge History of the British Empire, Vol. III and Vol. VIII (2nd edn). *Recreations:* rowing, painting. *Address:* 76 Manning Road, Durban, South Africa. *Club:* Leander (Henley-on-Thames).

**WALKER, Frank Stockdale,** MC 1919; Chairman, Lever Brothers, Port Sunlight Limited, 1954-60, retired; Director, Thames Board Mills Limited (until 1960); Director, Glycerine Limited; *b* 24 June 1895; *s* of Frank and Mary Elizabeth Walker; *m* 1921, Elsie May Nicholas; one *s. Address:* Whitley Close, Bradninch, near Exeter, Devon. *T:* Hele 211.

**WALKER, Geoffrey Basil W.;** *see* Woodd Walker.

**WALKER, Air Chief Marshal Sir (George) Augustus,** GCB 1969 (KCB 1962; CB 1959); CBE 1945; DSO 1941; DFC 1941; AFC 1956; Deputy Commander-in-Chief, Allied Forces, Central Europe, 1967-70; *b* 24 Aug. 1912; *s* of G. H. Walker, Garforth, Leeds; *m* 1942, Brenda Brewis; one *s* one *d. Educ:* St Bees' Sch.; St Catharine's, Cambridge. Entered RAF Univ. Commission, 1934; Air Min. (R&D), 1938-39; commanded Bomber Sqdns, Stations and Base, 1940-45; SASO No. 4 Group, 1945-46; Air Min., Dep. Dir, Operational Training, 1946-48; SASO Rhodesian Air Training Group, 1948-50; JSSC 1950; IDC 1953; Commandant, Royal Air Force Flying Coll., 1954-56; AOC No. 1 Group, 1956-59; Chief Information Officer, Air Min., 1959-61; AOC-in-C, Flying Training Command, 1961-64; Inspector-General, RAF, 1964-67. ADC to the Queen, 1952-56, to King George VI, 1943-52; Air ADC to the Queen, 1968-70. Pres., RFU, 1965-66. *Recreations:* Rugby (played for England, RAF, Blackheath, Yorkshire; Captained RAF, 1936-39), golf, sailing. *Address:* c/o Martin's Bank, 28/30 Park Row, Leeds LS1 1PA. *Club:* Royal Air Force.

**WALKER, George Edward Orr,** MBE 1943; TD 1952; QC (Scotland) 1955; Treasurer of the Faculty of Advocates since 1949 (admitted 1936); *b* 16 Sept. 1909; *s* of Archibald Walker, DL, and Adelaide Orr Thomson; *m* 1935, Margaret Sybil, *d* of George Simpson Orr; one *s* two *d* (and one *s* decd). *Educ:* Winchester Coll.; Trinity Coll., Oxford (BA); Edinburgh Univ. (LLB). Standing Counsel to Scottish Home Dept and to Nat. Art Galleries, 1951-55; Chairman of Medical Appeal Tribunal (Scotland), 1956-. 2nd Lieut, Ayrshire (ECO)

Yeomanry, 1931; served War of 1939-45: Lt-Col North West Europe Campaign, 1945 (despatches). Contested (U) Kilmarnock Burghs, 1945 and 1946. *Recreations:* golf and (formerly) hunting. *Address:* 21 Moray Place, Edinburgh. *T:* 031-225 3622; Newark Castle, Ayr. *T:* Alloway 41204. *Clubs:* Bath; New (Edinburgh); Western (Glasgow).

**WALKER, Major Sir George Ferdinand Forestier-**, 4th Bt, *cr* 1835; Coldstream Guards, retired; *b* 20 May 1899; *o s* of 3rd Bt and Georgina (*d* 1910), *y d* of late Robert D. Chamberlain, 1st Regt; *S* father, 1933. *Educ:* Wellington Coll.; RMC, Sandhurst. *Heir: cousin* Radzivill Clive Forestier-Walker [*b* 23 July 1895; *m* 1921, Kathleen Rose, *d* of late W. G. Tinkler, King's Lynn; one *s* one *d*]. *Address:* Monks Mill, Pilton, Shepton Mallet, Somerset. *T:* Pilton 228.

**WALKER, Col George Gustavus,** CBE 1958; MC and Bar 1917; TD; *b* 4 July 1897; *e s* of Captain George Laurie Walker, Crawfordton, Dumfriesshire; *m* 1924, Sybilla Catherine, 2nd *d* of Charles Hyslop Maxwell, Dalruscan, Dumfriesshire; one *d* decd. *Educ:* Sandroyd; Repton. Joined 3 KOSB, 1914; transferred to Scots Guards, 1916; Captain, 1918; Lt-Col comdg 5 KOSB (TA), 1934; Bt-Col, 1938; Commanded 9 KOSB, 1940-41; Commanded No. 10 Infantry Training Centre, 1942-45. Chairman, Dumfriesshire T&AFA, 1949-62. Hon. Sheriff Substitute of Dumfries and Galloway, 1938. Hon. Colonel, 5 KOSB (TA), 1949-61. DL 1947, JP 1920, County of Dumfries. *Address:* Morrington, Dumfries, Scotland. *T:* Dunscore 349.

**WALKER, Prof. Gilbert James,** MA Oxon, DLitt Birmingham; Professor of Commerce and Head of Department of Industrial Economics and Business Studies, University of Birmingham; Professor of Economics, 1947; Dean of the Faculty of Commerce and Social Science, 1956; Professor of Commerce, 1955; *b* 6 Jan. 1907; *s* of James MacFarlane Walker and Margaret Theresa Burrows; *m* 1943, Mavis Foyle; one *s*. *Educ:* Abbotsholme, Rocester, Staffs; University College Sch., London; New Coll., Oxford. Senior George Webb Medley Schol., Oxford Univ., 1928; Madden Prizeman and Meritorious Disappointed Candidate, TCD, 1930. Asst Lectr in Economics, Birmingham Univ., 1930; Rockefeller Fellow, USA, 1934; Investigator in Transport, Nova Scotia Govt, 1929; Sen. Investigator Man-power Survey, Min. of Labour, 1940; Asst Dir and Dep. Dir of Statistics, Min. of Supply, 1941; Dir of Statistics, British Supply Mission, Washington, DC, 1942; Reader in Economics of Transport, Univ. of Birmingham, 1945. Lectr in Harvard Summer Sch., July 1949 and 1953. Mission to Nigeria, on transport, 1950. Pres. of Section F (Economics and Statistics) of British Assoc. for the Advancement of Science, 1956; Transport Consultant, United Nations, 1957-58. *Publications:* Survey of Transportation in Nova Scotia, 1941; Road and Rail, an enquiry into the economics of competition and state control, 1942, 2nd edn, 1947; Traffic and Transport in Nigeria, 1956; Economic Planning by Programme and Control, 1957. Contrib. to Econ. Jl, Modern Law Review, Economica and Jl of Political Econ.; proc. Inst. Transport; British Transport Review, etc. *Recreation:* continental cycling en famille. *Address:* Department of Industrial Economics and Business Studies, The University, Edgbaston, Birmingham 15. *T:* 021-472 1301. *Club:* Royal Commonwealth Society.

**WALKER, Harold;** MP (Lab) Doncaster, since 1964; *b* 12 July 1927; *s* of Harold and Phyllis Walker; *m* 1956, Barbara Hague; one *d*. *Educ:* Manchester College of Technology. An Assistant Government Whip, 1967-68; Jt Parly Under-Sec. of State, Dept of Employment and Productivity, 1968-70. *Recreations:* reading, gardening. *Address:* House of Commons, SW1. *Clubs:* Westminster, Woodfield, Clay Lane, Doncaster Trades, RN (all Doncaster).

**WALKER, Adm. Sir Harold Thomas Coulthard,** KCB 1946 (CB 1944); *b* 18 March 1891; *yr s* of late Lt-Gen. Sir H. B. Walker, KCB, KCMG, DSO, and late Lady Walker; *m* 1931, Olive Marjory, *yr d* of Major J. A. Berners, Woolverstone Park, Ipswich; one *s* one *d*. *Educ:* St Christopher's, Bath; Royal Naval Colleges, Osborne and Dartmouth. Midshipman, 1908; Sub-Lt, 1911; Lieut, 1913; served European War (wounded, despatches twice); Comdr, 1926; Captain, 1931; Commanded HMS Canterbury, 1932; HMAS Canberra, 1934-36; HMS Hood, 1938-39; HMS Barham, 1939-40; Deputy Director Training and Staff duties, Admiralty, 1936-38; Commodore RNB Portsmouth, 1940-41; Rear-Admiral, 1941; Director of Personal Services, Admiralty, 1941-43; Commanded 5th Crusier Squadron, 1944; 3rd Battle Squadron, 1944-45; Vice-Admiral, 1944; Commanded British Naval Forces in Germany, 1946-47; retired, 1947; Admiral (retired), 1948. *Address:* Pin Mill, Heathfield Road, Woking, Surrey. *T:* Woking 63390. *Club:* United Service.

**WALKER, (Horace) Alan;** Chairman: Bass Charrington Ltd, since 1967; Bass Mitchells & Butlers Ltd; Williams & Humbert Ltd; Director: Eagle Star Insurance Co. Ltd; Wm Cory & Sons Ltd; Canadian Breweries Ltd; Staplegreen Insurance Holdings Ltd. Member, British Railways Board. *Recreations:* fishing, ballet, opera. *Address:* 7 Grosvenor Gardens, SW1. *T:* 01-834 3121; Poachers, Alcester Heath, Warwickshire. *T:* Alcester 2291. *Clubs:* St James', MCC.

**WALKER, Major Sir Hugh (Ronald),** 4th Bt, *cr* 1906; Major, Royal Artillery; 49 Regiment RA, Larkhill. *b* 13 Dec. 1925; *s* of Major Sir Cecil Edward Walker, 3rd Bt, DSO, MC, and Violet (*née* McMaster); *S* father, 1964. *Educ:* Wellington Coll., Berks. Joined Royal Artillery, 1943; commissioned Sept. 1945; 2iC, RA Range, Benbecula, Outer Hebrides; later Commanding Army Information Team, Hong Kong. *Recreation:* horses. *Address:* c/o Lloyds Bank Ltd, Somerton, Somerset.

**WALKER, Sir Hugh Selby N.;** *see* Norman-Walker.

**WALKER, James;** *see* Walker, Hon. Lord.

**WALKER, Prof. James,** BSc, MD, FRCPGlas, FRCOG; Professor of Obstetrics and Gynæcology, University of Dundee, since 1967 (University of St Andrews, 1956-67); Consultant, Eastern Regional Hospital Board, Scotland, since 1956; *b* 8 March 1916; *s* of James Walker, FEIS; *m* 1940, Catherine Clark Johnston, *d* of George R. A. Johnston; one *s* two *d*. *Educ:* High Schs of Falkirk and Stirling; Univ. of Glasgow. BSc 1935; MB, ChB (Hons) 1938; Brunton Memorial Prize; MRCOG 1947; MD (Hons) 1954; FRCOG 1957; MRCPGlas 1963, FRCPGlas 1968. Blair Bell Memorial Lectr, Royal Coll. Obstetrics and Gynæcology, 1953. Served War of 1939-45, RAFVR, UK and India, 1941-46. Hon. Surgeon to Out Patients, Royal Infirmary, Glasgow, Hall Tutor in Midwifery, Univ. Glasgow, 1946; Sen. Lectr in Midwifery and Gynæcology, Univ. of Aberdeen, Consultant NE Regional Hospital Board (Scotland), 1948; Reader in Obst. and Gynæcology, Univ. of

London, Consultant, Hammersmith Hospital, 1955. Visiting Professor: Univ. of New York State, 1957, 1970; Univ. of Florida, 1965, 1970; McGill Univ., 1967. *Publications:* contrib. on Obstetrics and Gynæcology to textbooks and learned journals. *Address:* Strips of Craigie House, 34 Strips of Craigie Road, Dundee. *T:* Dundee 43318. *Club:* Royal Air Force.

**WALKER, James Arthur H.;** *see* Higgs-Walker.

**WALKER, Sir James Heron,** 5th Bt, *cr* 1868; *b* 7 April 1914; *s* of 4th Bt and Synolda, *y d* of late James Thursby-Pelham; *S* father, 1930; *m* 1939, Angela Margaret, *o d* of Victor Alexandre Beaufort; one *s* (one *d* decd). *Educ:* Eton Coll.; Magdalene Coll., Cambridge. *Recreations:* long haired Dachshunds and music. *Heir: s* Victor Stewart Heron Walker [*b* 8 Oct. 1942; *m* 1969, Caroline Louise, *d* of late Lt-Col F. E. B. Wignall.]. *Address:* Ringdale Manor, Faringdon, Berks.
*See also Baron Cornwallis.*

**WALKER, Sir John,** KCMG 1959 (CMG 1951); OBE 1947; *b* 27 June 1906; *s* of late Rupert Walker; *m* 1934, Muriel Winifred, *d* of Henry John Hill; one *s* (and one *s* decd). *Educ:* Ashby Grammar Sch.; London Univ.; Sorbonne. Passed examination and entered Dept of Overseas Trade, 1929; Asst Commercial Sec., Santiago, 1931; transf. to Buenos Aires, 1933; Commercial Sec., Bagdad, 1938, 1943; transf. to Madrid, 1944, Counsellor, (Commercial), 1947; transf. to Tehran, 1948; HM Inspector of Foreign Service Establishments, Foreign Office, 1953-55; Ambassador to Venezuela, 1955-60; Ambassador to Norway, 1961-62. Dir-Gen., Hispanic and Luso-Brazilian Councils, 1963-69. Knight Grand Cross, Order of St Olav (Norway), 1962. Fellow, University College, London, 1968-. *Publications:* Economic Surveys of Iraq and Spain. *Recreations:* golf, shooting, fishing. *Address:* Primrose Cottage, Lodsworth, Petworth, Sussex. *T:* Lodsworth 350.

**WALKER, John;** Director, National Gallery of Art, Washington, DC, 1956-69, now Director Emeritus; *b* 24 Dec. 1906; *s* of Hay Walker and Rebekah Jane Friend; *m* 1937, Lady Margaret Gwendolen Mary Drummond; one *s* one *d*. *Educ:* Harvard Univ. (AB). Associate in charge Dept Fine Arts American Acad., Rome, 1935-39 (now Trustee); Chief Curator, National Gall., Washington DC, 1939-56. Connected with protection and preservation of artistic and historic monuments; John Harvard Fellow, Harvard Univ., 1930-31; American Federation of Arts; Harvard Press; Board of Advisers, Dumbarton Oaks; Trustee: Los Angeles Country Museum of Art; Andrew W. Mellon, Educational and Charitable Trust; American Federation of Arts; Wallace Foundation, NY; National Trust for Historic Preservation; Member Advisory Council: Univ. of Notre Dame; New York Univ.; Hon. Dr Fine Arts: Tufts Univ., 1958; Brown Univ., 1959; La Salle Coll., 1962; LittD: Notre Dame, 1959, Washington and Jefferson Univs, 1960; LHD: Catholic Univ. of America, 1964; Univ. of New York, 1965; Maryland Inst.; Georgetown Univ., 1966; William and Mary Univ., 1967. Holds foreign decorations. *Publications:* (with Mcgill James) Great American Paintings from Smibert to Bellows, 1943; (with Huntington Cairns) Masterpieces of Painting from National Gallery of Art, 1944; Paintings from America, 1951; (with Huntington Cairns) Great Paintings from the National Gallery of Art, 1952; National Gallery of Art, Washington, 1956; Bellini and Titian at Ferrara, 1957; Treasures from the National Gallery of Art, 1963; The National Gallery of Art, Washington, DC, 1964; (with H. Cairns) Pageant of Painting, 1966. *Address:* 2806 N Street, Northwest, Washington, DC 20007, USA. *T:* 965-2253. *Clubs:* Turf; Century Association, The Brook (New York City); Chevy Chase (Washington, DC).

**WALKER, John Henry;** Assistant Secretary, Home Office, since 1950; *b* 14 May 1915; *s* of late Edwin Walker, Nelson, Lancs; *m* 1957, Norma, *d* of late Arthur Griffiths, Hamilton, Ontario, Canada. *Educ:* Grammar Sch., Nelson, Lancs; St John's Coll., Cambridge. Asst Principal, Home Office, 1937. Served War of 1939-45, Captain, East Lancashire Regt, 1940-45. Principal, Home Office, 1945; Asst Secretary, Home Office, 1950; UK Delegate to: UN Narcotics Commission, 1952-56 (Chairman 1956); UN Opium Conference, 1953; Prison Commissioner, 1955-62; Secretary, Prison Commission, 1955-62. *Address:* 24 The Hall, Foxes Dale, Blackheath, SE3. *T:* 01-852 7925.

**WALKER, John Riddell Bromhead,** MVO 1953; MC 1944; Clarenceux King of Arms, since 1968; Lieutenant-Colonel (retired), late 14th Sikhs; *b* 21 June 1913; *s* of late Col P. G. Walker, IA, and Judith Dorothy Gonville, *d* of late Col Sir Benjamin Bromhead, Bt, CB, Thurlby Hall, Lincoln; *m* 1939, Marjorie, *d* of late Col Frank Fleming, DSO, TD; two *s* one *d*. *Educ:* Dover; Royal Military Coll., Sandhurst. Attached 2nd Bn York and Lancaster Regt, 1933; 1/11th Sikh Regt (14th Sikhs) and 7/11th Sikh Regt, 1934-37; adjutant, 1938-41; various staff appointments in India, 1942-47; Instructor Staff Coll., Haifa, 1944-45; NWF (India), Waziristan, 1937; Ahmedzai, 1940; Datta Khel Relief, 1942; Arakan and Imphal, 1944; Rouge Croix Pursuivant of Arms, 1947-53; Lancaster Herald, 1953-68; Registrar of College of Arms, 1960-67. *Address:* College of Arms, Queen Victoria Street, EC4. *T:* 01-236 6231. *Club:* Flyfishers'.

**WALKER, Malcolm Thomas,** CBE 1964; HM Diplomatic Service, retired; *b* 8 April 1915; *s* of late Major Herbert Thomas Walker and Caroline Dorothy Clerk; *m* 1949, Jean Rosemary Edith Mair; two *s* one *d*. *Educ:* Sherborne Sch.; Worcester Coll., Oxford. Entered HM Foreign Service, 1938; served at Beirut, 1938; Jedda, 1940; Bagdad, 1943; First Secretary in Foreign Office, 1947; Benghazi, 1949; Amman, 1950; Foreign Office, 1953; Counsellor at Khartoum, 1956; Consul-General, Hanoi, 1958; Consul–General, Seville, Spain, 1960-63; British Ambassador in Liberia, 1963-67; Consul-General, Cape Town, 1967-70; retd. *Recreations:* sailing and gardening. *Address:* British Consulate General, African Life Centre, St George's Street, Cape Town, South Africa; Plush Manor, Piddletrenthide, Dorchester, Dorset. *T:* Piddletrenthide 280. *Clubs:* Royal Ocean Racing, Royal Automobile.

**WALKER, Sir Michael;** *see* Walker, Sir C. M.

**WALKER, Norman Macdonald Lockhart,** CBE 1960; Sheriff-Substitute of Lanarkshire at Glasgow, 1942-62, retired; *b* 1889; *s* of late Sir Norman Walker, MD, LLD; *m* 1925, Alison, *d* of late Walter W. Blackie, Publisher, Glasgow; two *s*. *Educ:* Edinburgh Academy; St Andrews Univ.; Balliol Coll., Oxford. Glasgow Univ. Served European War, 1914-19; called to Scottish Bar, 1920; Advocate Depute, 1934-36; Sheriff-Substitute of Lanarkshire at Hamilton, 1936-42. Hon. LLD Glasgow, 1955. *Publications:* co-author Walker on Evidence, 1963; co-editor 6th edn of Gloag and Henderson's Introduction to the Law of Scotland, 1956; Digest of Sheriff Court

Practice, 1932. *Address:* Castlelea, East Scores, St Andrews, Fife. *T:* St Andrews 4153. *Clubs:* Western (Glasgow); Royal and Ancient (St Andrews).

**WALKER, Rt. Hon. Patrick C. G.;** *see* Gordon Walker.

**WALKER, Sir Peter;** *see* Walker, Sir C. P. G.

**WALKER, Rt. Hon. Peter Edward,** PC 1970; MBE 1960; MP (C) Worcester since March 1961; Secretary of State for the Environment, since Oct. 1970; *b* 25 March 1932; *s* of Sydney and Rose Walker; *m* 1969, Tessa, *d* of G. I. Pout; one *s*. *Educ:* Latymer Upper Sch. Member, National Executive of Conservative Party, 1956-; Nat. Chairman, Young Conservatives, 1958-60; Parliamentary Candidate (C) for Dartford, 1955 and 1959. Chairman, Walker, Moate, & Co. Ltd, 1956-70, and Rose, Thomson, Young & Co. Ltd (Lloyd's Brokers), 1956-70; Dep. Chairman, Slater, Walker Securities Ltd, 1964-70; Director: Hugh Paul & Co. Ltd, Lloyd's Brokers, 1960; Rodwell London & Provincial Properties Ltd, 1960-69; Adwest Ltd, 1963-70; Annual Subscriber to Lloyd's, 1961. PPS to Leader of House of Commons, 1963-64; Opposition Front Bench Spokesman, Finance and Economics, 1964-66; Shadow Minister: of Transport, 1966-68; of Local Government, Housing, and Land, 1968-70; Minister of Housing and Local Govt, June-Oct. 1970. *Address:* The Old Parsonage, Warndon, Worcester. *Clubs:* Carlton, St Stephen's, Buck's, City of London; Turf; Worcestershire County Cricket, Union (Worcester).

**WALKER, Rev. Peter Knight,** MA; Principal of Westcott House, Cambridge, since 1962; Hon. Canon of Ely Cathedral since 1966; *b* 6 Dec. 1919; *s* of late George Walker and of Eva Muriel Knight; unmarried. *Educ:* Leeds Grammar Sch. (schol.); The Queen's Coll., Oxford (Hastings schol.); Westcott House, Cambridge. Cl. 2 Classical Hon. Mods. 1940, Cl. 1 Lit. Hum. 1947. Served in RN (Seaman and T/Lieut, RNVR), 1940-45. Asst Master: King's Sch., Peterborough, 1947-50; Merchant Taylors' Sch., 1950-56. Ordained, 1954; Curate of Hemel Hempstead, 1956-58; Fellow, Dean of Chapel and Lectr in Theology, Corpus Christi Coll., Cambridge, 1958-62 (Asst Tutor, 1959-62). Select Preacher, Univ. of Cambridge, 1962, Hulsean Preacher, 1967; Examining Chaplain to Bishop of Portsmouth, 1962-. *Publications:* Contrib. to: Classical Quarterly; Theology. *Address:* Westcott House, Cambridge. *T:* 50074.

**WALKER, Philip Gordon,** FCA; Chairman and Chief Executive, Philblack Ltd; Chairman: Philblack (Executive) Ltd; Severn Valley Chemical Industries Ltd; Jones Gas Process Co. Ltd; Deputy Chairman: Sun Life Assurance Society Ltd; Household and General Insurance Co. Ltd; Director: Barclays Bank Ltd (London Local Board); Metal Box Co. Ltd; Metal Box Co. Overseas Ltd; Kentredder Ltd; *b* 9 June 1912; *s* of late William and Kate Blanche Walker; *m* 1st, 1938, Anne May (marr. diss.); one *s* two *d*; 2nd, 1962, Elizabeth Oliver. *Educ:* Epworth Coll., Rhyl, North Wales. Bourner, Bullock & Co., Chartered Accountants, 1929-35; Walkers (Century Oils) Ltd, 1935-40; Layton Bennett, Billingham & Co., Chartered Accountants, 1940, Partner, 1944-51; Reed Paper Group Ltd, Man. Dir, 1951-63. Part-time Mem. Monopolies Commn, 1963-65. *Recreation:* golf. *Address:* Dunwood, East Drive, Wentworth, Virginia Water, Surrey. *T:* Wentworth 2520. *Clubs:* Brooks's; Wildernesse (Sevenoaks); Rye; Royal Jersey.

**WALKER, Raymond St John,** CBE 1970; Director, Administration (formerly of Establishment and Finance), Science Research Council, since 1965; *b* 11 April 1917; *o s* of late William and Sybil MacLaren Walker; *m* 1941, Eva Mary, *e d* of late Walter Lionel and Ethel Marion Dudley; three *s*. *Educ:* Leeds Grammar Sch.; St Peter's Coll., Oxford. Royal Artillery, 1939-46. Min. of Supply, 1947-58 (Private Sec. to Minister, 1950-53); Imperial Defence Coll., 1959; Min. of Aviation, 1960-61; DSIR, 1962-64. *Recreation:* sailing. *Address:* Chanters, Ridgeway, Hutton, Essex. *T:* Brentwood 179.

**WALKER, Robert;** HM Diplomatic Service; Commercial Counsellor, Ankara, since 1970; *b* 1 May 1924; *s* of Young and Gladys Walker, Luddendenfoot, Yorks; *m* 1949, Rita Thomas; one *s* one *d*. *Educ:* Sowerby Bridge Grammar Sch.; Peterhouse, Cambridge. Commissioned RNVR 1944; served in minesweepers in home waters. Cambridge, 1942-43 and 1946-48; BA Hons History, 1948; MA 1963. Joined Commonwealth Relations Office, 1948; served Peshawar and Karachi, 1949-51; New Delhi, 1955-59; Senior First Secretary, Accra, 1962-64; Deputy British High Commissioner, in Ghana, 1964-65; FCO, 1965-68. IDC, 1969. *Recreations:* coarse golf, country wine making, interior decorating. *Address:* British Embassy, Ankara, Turkey. *Clubs:* Naval, Royal Commonwealth Society.

**WALKER, Robert Milnes,** CBE 1964; Director of Surgical Studies, Royal College of Surgeons, since Dec. 1968; Director, Cancer Records Bureau, SW Regional Hospital Board; Professor of Surgery, University of Bristol, 1946-64, Emeritus since 1964; Hon. Surgeon, Bristol Royal Hospital; Member of the Medical Research Council, 1959-63; *b* 2 Aug. 1903; *s* of J. W. Walker, FSA, FRCS, Wakefield, Yorks; *m* 1931, Grace Anna McCormick; two *s* four *d*. *Educ:* Oundle Sch.; University College Hospital, London. Hon. Surgeon, Royal Hospital, Wolverhampton, 1931-46; Rock Carling Fellow, Nuffield Hospital Trust, 1965. Editor, Medical Annual, 1954-. Member Council, RCS, 1953-69; Vice-Pres., 1966-68; President: Assoc. Surgeons of GB, 1961; Surgical Research Soc., 1962-64. Fellow of University Coll., London, 1953. Medical Sub-Cttee, University Grants Cttee, 1959-67. Member Court, Worshipful Co. of Barbers, 1969. Hon. FACS. *Publications:* Portal Hypertension, 1959; Medical Education in Britain, 1965. *Address:* Wergs Copse, Kintbury, Newbury, Berks.

**WALKER, Robert Scott,** FRICS; City Surveyor, City of London Corporation, since 1955; *b* 13 June 1913; *s* of Harold and Mary Walker; *m* 1946, Anne Armstrong; no *c*. *Educ:* West Buckland Sch., North Devon. War Service, 1939-45, Major RA. Assistant City Surveyor, Manchester, 1946-55. *Address:* Guildhall, EC2. *T:* 01-606 3030.

**WALKER, Sir Ronald;** *see* Walker, Sir E. R.

**WALKER, Col Ronald Draycott S.;** *see* Sherbrooke-Walker.

**WALKER, Sir Ronald Fitz-John,** Kt 1953; Chairman, James Walker & Sons Ltd, Mirfield; Chairman, Dewsbury Reporter Group, since 1951; and other directorships; Income Tax Commissioner, 1925-65; Liberal Party (President, 1952); *b* 24 Nov. 1880; *s* of John Ely and Mary Elizabeth Walker; *m* 1916, Edith Mary (*d* 1966). *Educ:* Mill Hill School. On leaving school went into family blanket manufacturing business. Liberal speaker and worker since 1900 and thereafter continually in office; Chairman, Central National Exec.,

1932. Contested (L) NE Leeds, 1922 and 1923, Colne Valley, 1924, Dewsbury, 1929, Royton, 1931 and 1935. First Hon. Life Pres. Yorkshire Liberal Party, 1960 (President, 1947-60). *Publications:* pamphlets on Free Trade, and (against) transport nationalisation. *Recreations:* formerly cliff climbing and golf; now bridge (family type). *Address:* Fir Cottage, Mirfield, Yorks. *T:* Mirfield 2143. *Club:* National Liberal.

**WALKER, Ronald Leslie,** CSI 1946; CIE 1942; *b* 9 April 1896; *m* 1948, Joyce Edwina Collins, OBE, 1946, Kaisar-i-Hind Gold Medal, 1939, *e d* of late G. Turville Brown. *Educ:* Bedford Sch.; Hertford Coll., Oxford. European War, 1914-18, Northamptonshire Regt, 1915; Machine-Gun Corps, 1916-18. Entered Indian Civil Service, 1920; Finance Secretary, Bengal, 1939-45; Adviser to Governor of Bengal, 1945; Chief Secretary, Bengal, 1946. *Address:* Little Coombe, Coombe Hill, East Grinstead. *T:* East Grinstead 25616. *Club:* East India and Sports.

**WALKER, Samuel Richard,** CBE 1955; DL; Founder and Hon. President, Walker & Rice (Walric Fabrics) Ltd; *b* 6 Jan. 1892; *s* of Samuel Reuben Walker; *m* 1923, Marjorie Jackson Clark, *d* of A. J. Clark, Hove, Sussex; one *s* two *d*. *Educ:* William Ellis's. Served European War, 1914-19, in France: 1st King Edward's Horse and RFA. City of London: DL 1951; Member Common Council (Bread Street Ward, 1937-; Deputy, 1951-), Chief Commoner, 1953-54; Chm. Privileges Cttee, 1957-. Sheriff of City of London, 1957-58; Master, Worshipful Company of Farriers, 1954-55; Master, Worshipful Company of Founders, 1962-63, Liveryman of Worshipful Company of Weavers; Chm., Central Criminal Court Extension Cttee. Governor, Bridewell Royal Hosp., 1942-; Life Governor and Vice-Chm., City of London Sheriffs' and Recorders' Fund; Chm., Thomas Carpenter and John Lane Trust; Almoner, Christ's Hosp., 1966-; Trustee and Pres., Seaforth Hall, Warninglid. Commendatore of Order Al Merito della Repubblica (Italy), 1957. *Recreations:* golf, riding. *Address:* Stonewick, Warninglid, Sussex. *Clubs:* City Livery (President, 1955-56, 1957-58), Guildhall, Farmers', Oriental; West Hove Golf (Life Pres.), West Sussex Golf, West Hove Artisans (Pres.).

**WALKER, Air Cdre Sidney George,** CB 1965; OBE 1945; RAF (Retired); *b* 6 Aug. 1911; *s* of late Capt. S. G. Walker, The Sherwood Foresters, and late Katie Rowena (*née* Worley), both of Nottingham; *m* 1939, Laura, *d* of Edward Craig Gorton and of Laura Harriet Matilda (*née* Hayden), Hull; one *s* one *d*. *Educ:* St Edmund's Coll., Shillong, Assam; Nottingham High School. Nottingham City Police, 1929-34; granted perm. commn, Cranwell, on direct entry to Equipment Branch, RAF, 1935; Aden, 1936-38; Arabic Interpretership, Baghdad, 1938; Air Min., 1938-41; Brit. Air Commn, USA, 1941-43; HQ, 2 TAF, 1943-45; HQ, BAFO, 1945-46; RAF Staff Coll., 1946; comd RAF Kemble, 1946-47, and RAF Edzell, 1947; Directing Staff, RAF Staff Coll., 1948-50; Jt Services Staff Coll., 1950-51; Dep. Chief Logistics Div., HQ, Allied Air Forces Central Europe (Fontainebleau), 1951-53; comd RAF Hartlebury, 1953-55; Dep. Dir of Organisation (Aircraft), Air Min., 1955-58; Imp. Def. Coll., 1959; Dep. Dir of Movements, Air Min., Jan.-Oct. 1960; Dir of Movements (RAF) in Min. of Defence (Air), Oct. 1960-July 1965, retd at own request. *Publication:* RUSI Trench Gascoigne Prize Essay, 1947. *Recreations:* Rugby football (RAF representative; founded Ranji Walker's XV), cricket, track athletics. *Address:* 265 Turleigh, Bradford-on-Avon, Wilts. *Clubs:* Royal Air Force; (Life Mem.) Wanderers Football (Dublin); (Life Mem.) Swansea Football (St Helen's).

**WALKER, Susan (Armour),** CBE 1963; Vice-Chairman, Conservative Party Organisation, 1964-68; retired 1969; *d* of James Walker, Bowmont, Dunbar; unmarried. *Educ:* Grammar School, Dunbar. Conservative Central Office Agent, Yorkshire, 1950-56; Deputy Chief Organisation Officer, Conservative Central Office, 1956-64. *Recreations:* golf, walking. *Address:* West Eaton House, West Eaton Place, SW1. *T:* 01-245 9702; Hownam, Kelso, Roxburghshire. *T:* Morebattle 277. *Club:* Constitutional.

**WALKER, Prof. Thomas William,** ARCS; DSc; DIC; Professor of Soil Science, Lincoln College, New Zealand, since 1961; *b* 22 July 1916; *m* 1940, Edith Edna Bott; four *d*. *Educ:* Loughborough Grammar School; Royal College of Science. Royal Scholar and Kitchener Scholar, 1935-39; Salter's Fellow, 1939-41; Lecturer and Adviser in Agricultural Chemistry, Univ. of Manchester, 1941-46. Provincial Advisory Soil Chemist, NAAS, 1946-51; Prof. of Soil Science, Canterbury Agric. Coll., New Zealand, 1952-58; Prof. of Agric., King's Coll., Newcastle upon Tyne, 1958-61. *Publications:* numerous research. *Recreations:* fishing, gardening. *Address:* Lincoln College, Christchurch, New Zealand.

**WALKER, Gen. Sir Walter (Colyear),** KCB 1968 (CB 1964); CBE 1959 (OBE 1949); DSO 1946 and Bars, 1953 and 1965; Commander-in-Chief, Allied Forces Northern Europe, since 1969; *b* 11 Nov. 1912; *s* of late Arthur Colyear Walker; *m* 1938, Beryl Catherine, *d* of late Edward Norman Wybrants Johnston; two *s* one *d*. *Educ:* Blundell's; RMC, Sandhurst. Waziristan, 1939-41 (despatches twice); Burma, 1942, 1944-46 (despatches, DSO); Malaya, 1949-59 (despatches twice, OBE, Bar to DSO, CBE); Borneo, 1962-65 (CB, Bar to DSO); Deputy Chief of Staff, HQ ALFCE, 1965; Acting Chief of Staff, 1966-67; GOC-in-C, Northern Command, 1967-69. jssc 1950; idc 1960. Colonel, 7th Duke of Edinburgh's Own Gurkha Rifles, 1964-. Dato Seri Setia, Order of Paduka Stia Negara, Brunei, 1964; Hon. Panglima Mangku Nagara, Malaysia, 1965. *Address:* Holmenkollen, Oslo 3, Norway. *Club:* United Service.

**WALKER, Sir William (Giles Newsom),** Kt 1959; TD 1942; DL; Chairman, Jute Industries (Holdings) Ltd, (formerly Jute Industries Ltd) Dundee, 1948-70 (Managing Director, 1947-69); *b* 20 Nov. 1905; *e s* of late H. Giles Walker, Over Rankeillour, Cupar, Fife and of late Mrs Elizabeth Bewley Newsom (Walker), Cork, Eire; *m* 1930, Mildred Brenda, 3rd *d* of Sir Michael Nairn, 2nd Bt, Elie House, Fife, and Pitcarmick, Blairgowrie; one *s* two *d*. *Educ:* Shrewsbury Sch.; Jesus Coll., Cambridge (BA). War of 1939-45: Lt-Col comdg 1st Fife and Forfar Yeomanry, 1943-45 (mobilised May 1939; despatches, TD). Jute Industries Ltd, Dundee: entered 1927; rejoined after War, 1945; Director, 1946; Managing Director, 1947; Chairman and Managing Director, 1948. Director: The Dundee, Perth & London Shipping Co. Ltd; Nairn & Williamson (Holdings) Ltd; Clydesdale Bank Ltd; Scottish Television Ltd; Alliance Trust Co. Ltd; Second Alliance Trust Co. Ltd; Dundee Savings Bank (Trustee and Committee of Management). Formerly: Jute Working Party (Employer Mem.); Dundee Chamber of Commerce (Dir); Scottish Industrial Estates Ltd. (Dir); Scottish Board for Industry (Member); Council for Industrial

Design (Scottish Committee); Transport Users Consultative Cttee (Scotland); Internat. Chambers of Commerce (Brit. Nat. Cttee); Assoc. of Chambers of Commerce (Executive Committee); Member, Scottish Railway Bd. Hon. Col Highland Yeomanry (formerly Fife and Forfar Yeomanry/Scottish Horse), 1967. DL Fife, 1958. USA Bronze Star, 1945. *Recreations:* shooting and golf. *Address:* Pitlair, Cupar, Fife. *T:* Ladybank 413. *Clubs:* Cavalry; Eastern (Dundee); Royal and Ancient Golf (Capt. 1962-63) (St Andrews); The Honourable Company of Edinburgh Golfers (Muirfield).

**WALKER LEE, Rev. William;** *see* Lee, Rev. W. W.

**WALKER-OKEOVER, Col Sir Ian Peter Andrew Monro,** 3rd Bt, *cr* 1886; DSO and Bar 1945; TD; JP; HM Lieutenant of Derbyshire since 1951; *b* 30 Nov. 1902; *e s* of Sir Peter Walker, 2nd Bt, and Ethel Blanche, *d* of late H. C. and Hon. Mrs Okeover, *d* of 3rd Baron Waterpark; granted royal licence and authority to use surname of Okeover in addition to that of Walker, 1956; *S* father, 1915; *m* 1938, Dorothy Elizabeth, *yr d* of Capt. Josceline Heber-Percy, Guy's Cliffe, Warwick; one *s* two *d.* Sheriff of Derbyshire, 1934. Served War of 1939-45 (DSO). Formerly Hon. Col, Derbyshire Yeomanry (subsequently Hon. Col Leicestershire and Derbyshire Yeomanry, retired 1962); Col Comdt, Yeomanry, RAC, TA. *Heir: s* Peter Ralph Leopold Walker-Okeover, *b* 22 July 1947. *Address:* Okeover Hall, Ashbourne, Derbyshire; House of Glenmuick, Ballater, Aberdeenshire. *Club:* Boodle's.

**WALKER-SMITH, Rt. Hon. Sir Derek Colclough,** 1st Bt, *cr* 1960; PC 1957; QC 1955; TD; MP (C) East Division of Hertfordshire since 1955 (Hertford Division, 1945-55); *b* April 1910; *y s* of late Sir Jonah Walker-Smith; *m* 1938, Dorothy, *d* of late L. J. W. Etherton, Rowlands Castle, Hants; one *s* two *d. Educ:* Rossall; Christ Church, Oxford. 1st Class Hons Modern History, Oxford Univ., 1931. Called to Bar, 1934; Master of the Bench, Middle Temple, 1963. Chm. Conservative Advisory Cttee on Local Govt, 1954-55; Chm. Conservative Member (1922) Cttee, 1951-55. Parly Sec. to the Board of Trade, 1955-Nov. 1956; Economic Secretary to the Treasury, Nov. 1956-Jan. 1957; Minister of State, Board of Trade, 1957; Minister of Health, 1957-60. Chm., Soc. of Conservative Lawyers. Associate of Royal Institution of Chartered Surveyors. *Heir: s* John Jonah Walker-Smith, *b* 6 Sept. 1939. *Address:* 25 Cavendish Close, NW8. *T:* 01-286 1441; 2 Paper Buildings, Temple, EC4. *T:* 01-353 9394. *Club:* Carlton.

**WALKEY, Maj.-Gen. John Christopher,** CB 1953; CBE 1943; *b* 18 Oct. 1903; *s* of late S. Walkey, Dawlish, Devon; *m* 1947, Beatrice Record Brown; one *d* decd. *Educ:* Newton College, Devon. Commissioned into Royal Engineers from RMA Woolwich, 1923; Chief Engineer, 13 Corps, 1943-47; Asst Comdt, RMA Sandhurst, 1949-51; Chief Engineer, Middle East Land Forces, 1951-54; Engineer-in-Chief, War Office, 1954-57; retired, 1957. Col Comdt RE, 1958-68. Hon. Col RE Resources Units (AER), 1959-64. Officer Legion of Merit (USA), 1945. *Recreations:* usual country pursuits. *Address:* Linden Spinney, Chagford, Devon. *Club:* Naval and Military.

**WALKLEY, Sir William (Gaston),** Kt 1967; CBE 1961; *b* 1 Nov. 1896; *s* of Herbert and Jessie Walkley; *m* 1945, Theresa May Fisher. *Educ:* Wellington, New Zealand. FCIS Australia; FCANZ. *Publication:* Solicitors' Accounts and Audits, 1922. *Recreation:* fishing. *Address:* 3 King Avenue, Balgowlah, NSW, Australia. *T:* 94.6242. *Clubs:* Royal Sydney Yacht Squadron, American National (Sydney).

**WALKLING, Maj.-Gen. Alec Ernest,** OBE 1954; Deputy Master-General of the Ordnance, since 1970; *b* 12 April 1918; *s* of late Ernest George Walkling; *m* 1940, Marian Harris; one *s* one *d. Educ:* Weymouth Grammar School; Keble College, Oxford. BA (Oxon) Mod. Langs, 1939; BA (Oxon) Hons Nat. Science, 1949. Commissioned 2nd Lieut RA, 1940; served War of 1939-45, N Africa and Burma (despatches); Staff Coll., Quetta, 1944; Min. of Supply, 1949-53; British Joint Services Mission, Washington, 1956-58; Comd Regt in BAOR, 1961-63; Comd Brigade (TA), 1963-64; Imperial Defence Coll., 1965; Dep. Commandant, Royal Military Coll. of Science, 1966-68; Dir-Gen. of Artillery, 1969-70. *Recreations:* golf, oil and water colour painting. *Address:* Birchwood, Waverley Drive, Camberley, Surrey. *T:* Camberley 4576. *Club:* Army and Navy.

**WALL, Rt. Rev. Bernard Patrick,** DD; Titular Bishop of Othona; *b* 15 March 1894; *s* of Daniel and Elizabeth Wall. *Educ:* St John's Seminary, Wonersh, Guildford; Institut Catholique, Paris; Collegio Angelico, Rome (DD). Ordained July 1918; curate at English Martyrs' Church, Walworth, SE, 1918-20; postgraduate studies Paris and Rome, 1920-23; Prof. of Humanities, Southwark Junior Seminary, 1923-27; Prof. of Dogmatic Theology, St John's Seminary, Wonersh, 1927-35; Parish Priest of Anerley, SE, 1935-45: of Reigate, 1945-49; Rector of St John's Seminary, Wonersh, 1949-55; Canon of Southwark, 1950; Bishop of Brentwood, 1956-69. Domestic Prelate to HH THE Pope, 1952. *Address:* 18 Bressey Grove, South Woodford, E18.

**WALL, Prof. Charles Terence Clegg,** FRS 1969; Professor of Pure Mathematics, Liverpool University, since 1965; *b* 14 Dec. 1936; *s* of Charles Wall, schoolteacher, Woodfield, Dursley, Glos; *m* 1959, Alexandra Joy, *d* of Prof. Leslie Spencer Hearnshaw, *qv*; two *s* two *d. Educ:* Marlborough Coll.; Trinity Coll., Cambridge. PhD Cantab 1960. Fellow, Trinity Coll., 1959-64; Harkness Fellow, Princeton, 1960-61; Univ. Lectr, Cambridge, 1961-64; Reader in Mathematics, and Fellow of St Catherine's Coll., Oxford, 1964-65. Royal Soc. Leverhulme Vis. Prof., CIEA, Mexico, 1967. *Publications:* Surgery on Compact Manifolds, 1970; papers on various problems in geometric topology, and related algebra. *Address:* 5 Kirby Park, West Kirby, Wirral, Cheshire L48 2HA. *T:* 051-625 5063.

**WALL, David (Richard);** Principal Dancer, Royal Ballet Company; *b* 15 March 1946; *s* of Charles and Dorothy Wall; *m* 1967, Alfreda Thorogood. *Educ:* Royal Ballet Sch. Joined Royal Ballet Co., Aug. 1964. Promotion to: Soloist, Aug. 1966; Junior Principal Dancer, Aug. 1967; Senior Principal Dancer, Aug. 1968. During period of employment has danced all major roles and has had many ballets created for him. *Recreations:* music, theatre. *Address:* 75 Studdridge Street, SW6. *T:* 01-736 1025.

**WALL, Sir (George) Rolande (Percival),** Kt 1946; MC 1917; President Lovell & Christmas Ltd; *b* West Kirby, Cheshire, 9 March 1898; *s* of late Percy T. Wall; *m* 1923, Dorice Katharine Whineray, Neston, Cheshire; one *s* one *d. Educ:* Lockers Park; Winchester College. Served European War, 1914-18. RFA (wounded, MC). Served with Min. of Food from Oct. 1939, starting Asst Dir Imports Dairy Products; Dep. Sec. and Head Supply

Dept until 31 Dec. 1946; Hon. Commercial Adviser to Ministry of Food, 1947-55. *Address:* Fairmead, Greenways, Haywards Heath, Sussex. *Club:* Royal Automobile.

**WALL, Sir John (Edward),** Kt 1968; OBE 1944; Chairman of International Computers (Holdings) Ltd and International Computers Ltd since Oct. 1968; Director: Cunard Steamship Co., since 1966; Laporte Industries (Holdings) Ltd, since 1968; Member (part-time), Sugar Board, since 1964; *b* 15 Feb. 1913; *s* of late Harry Arthur Fitzgerald and Marie Louise Wall; *m* 1939, Gladys Evelyn (*née* Wright); two *s* one *d*. *Educ:* Wandsworth School; London School of Economics. BCom, 1933. O. T. Falk & Co., 1933-39; Min. of Food, 1939-52; Under-Sec., 1948-52. Dep. Head, Finance Dept, Unilever Ltd, 1952-56; Head of Organisation Div., Unilever Ltd, 1956-58; Man. Dir, Electric & Musical Industries, 1960-66 (Dir, 1958); Dep. Chm., Post Office Board, 1966-68. Officer, Order of Orange Nassau, 1947. *Recreation:* golf. *Address:* Wychwood, Coombe End, Kingston-upon-Thames, Surrey. *T:* 01-942 3873. *Club:* Royal Automobile.

**WALL, John William,** CMG 1953; HM Diplomatic Service, retired 1966; *b* 6 Nov. 1910; *m* 1950, Eleanor Rosemary Riesle; one *d*. *Educ:* Secondary Sch., Mexborough; Jesus Coll., Cambridge. Probationer Vice-Consul, Levant Consular Service, 1933; Vice-Consul, Cairo, 1936; in charge of Vice-Consulate, Suez, 1937; transferred to Jedda as 2nd Sec. in Diplomatic Service, 1939; acting Consul, Jedda, 1942, 1943; transferred to Tabriz, 1944, Isfahan, 1946, Casablanca, 1947; Brit. Middle East Office, Cairo: Head of Polit. Div., 1943, in charge 1949, 1950; Oriental Counsellor, Cairo, 1951; Political Agent, Bahrein, 1952-55; Consul-General at Salonika, 1955-57; HM Ambassador and Consul-General to Paraguay, 1957-59; Counsellor, Foreign Office, 1959-63; Consul-General at Alexandria, 1963-66. *Address:* c/o Barclays Bank Ltd, 1 Pall Mall East, SW1. *Club:* Oxford and Cambridge University.

**WALL, Prof. Patrick David,** MA, DM; Professor of Anatomy and Director, Cerebral Functions Research Group, University College, London, since 1967; *b* 5 April 1925; *s* of T. Wall, MC, and R. Wall (*née* Cresswell); *m* 1950, Betty Tucker. *Educ:* St Paul's; Christ Church, Oxford. MA 1947; BM, BCh 1948; DM 1960. Instructor, Yale School of Medicine, 1948-50; Asst Prof., Univ. of Chicago, 1950-53; Instructor, Harvard Univ., 1953-55; Assoc. Prof., 1957-60, Professor 1960-67, Massachusetts Inst. of Technology. *Publications:* many papers on Anatomy and Physiology of the Nervous System; (novel) Trio, The revolting intellectuals' organizations, 1966 (US 1965). *Recreation:* kibbitzing. *Address:* Cerebral Functions Research Group, Department of Anatomy, University College, Gower Street, WC1. *Club:* Athenæum.

**WALL, Major Patrick Henry Bligh,** MC 1945; VRD 1957; MP (C) Haltemprice Division of East Riding of Yorkshire, since 1955 (Haltemprice Division of Hull, (February) 1954-55); *b* 19 Oct. 1916; *s* of Henry Benedict Wall and Gladys Eleanor Finney; *m* 1953, Sheila Elizabeth Putnam; one *d*. *Educ:* Downside. Commissioned in RM 1935 (specialised in naval gunnery). Served in HM Ships, support craft, with RM Commandos and US Navy. Actg Major, 1943; RN Staff Coll., 1945; Joint Services Staff Coll., 1947; Major, 1949. Contested Cleveland Division (Yorks), 1951 and 1952. Parliamentary Private Secretary to: Minister of Agriculture, Fisheries and Food, 1955-57; Chancellor of the Exchequer, 1958-59. Westminster City Council, 1953-62; CO 47 Commando RMFVR, 1951-57; Comr for Sea Scouts for London, 1950-66; Pres. Yorks Area Young Conservatives, 1955-60; Chm. Mediterranean Group of Conservative Commonwealth Council, 1954-67; Chm. Cons. Parly East and Central Africa Cttee, 1956-59; Vice-Chairman: Conservative Commonwealth Affairs Cttee, 1960-68; Cons. Overseas Bureau, 1963-; Cons. Defence Cttee, 1965-; Chairman: Cons. Fisheries Sub-Cttee, 1962-; Africa Centre, 1961-65; Joint East and Central Africa Board, 1965-; British Rep. at 17th General Assembly of UN, 1962. Vice-Pres., British Sub-Aqua Club; Chm., Nat. Underwater Instructors Assoc.; Vice-Pres., Urban District Councils Assoc. Kt, SMO Malta; USA Legion of Merit, 1945. *Publication:* Royal Marine Pocket Book, 1944; Student Power, 1968; Defence Policy, 1969; Overseas Aid, 1969; co-author of a number of political pamphlets. *Recreations:* messing about in boats, ship models, foreign birds. *Address:* 92 Cheyne Walk, SW10. *T:* 01-352 3283; Brantinghamthorp, Brantingham, near Brough, Yorks. *T:* Brough 667248. *Clubs:* United Service; Royal Yacht Squadron; RN Sailing Association.

**WALL, Sir Rolande;** *see* Wall, Sir G. R. P.

**WALL, Ronald George Robert,** CB 1961; Chairman, Sugar Board, since 1970; *b* 25 Jan. 1910; *s* of George Thomas and Sophia Jane Wall; *m* 1st, 1936, Winifred Evans (marr. diss., 1950); one *s*; 2nd, 1960, Mrs Muriel Sorrell (*née* Page). *Educ:* Alleyn's School, Dulwich; St John's College, Oxford (MA). Administrative Civil Service; entered Ministry of Agriculture and Fisheries, 1933; Fisheries Sec., 1952-59. Gwilym Gibbon Research Fellow, Nuffield College, Oxford, 1951-52. President of Permanent Commission under Internat. Fisheries Convention of 1946, 1953-56; Chairman of the International Whaling Commission, 1958-60; Dep. Sec., Min. of Agriculture, Fisheries and Food, 1961-70. *Address:* 201 London Road, Twickenham, Middlesex. *T:* 01-892 7086. *Clubs:* United University, Arts Theatre.

**WALLACE;** *see* Hope-Wallace.

**WALLACE, Very Rev. Alexander Ross;** Dean of Exeter, 1950-60, retired; *b* 27 Sept. 1891; *s* of late Maj.-Gen. Sir Alexander Wallace, KCB; *m* 1915, Winifred, *d* of late Rev. H. C. Sturges; two *s* two *d*. *Educ:* Clifton Coll. (Scholar); Corpus Christi Coll., Cambridge (Scholar). Classical Tripos, 1913, Class II, Div. I; entered ICS, 1914; served in the IARO att. 17th Cavalry; Special Service Officer, Patiala I. S. Lancers; retired from ICS, 1922; Asst Master and Tutor, Wellington Coll., Berks; Headmaster, Cargilfield School, Edinburgh, 1925-30; Blundell's School, Tiverton, 1930-33; Sherborne School, 1934-July 1950; ordained Deacon, 1938; Priest, 1939. Canon and Prebendary of Salisbury Cathedral, 1942-50. *Publications:* The Three Pillars, 1940; Conversation about Christianity, 1946; Christian Focus, 1956. *Recreations:* golf, fishing. *Address;* Bracken Bank, Timber Hill, Lyme Regis, Dorset.

*See also I. A. Wallace.*

**WALLACE, Col the Hon. Clarence,** CBE 1946; CD; LLD; Lieutenant-Governor of British Columbia, Canada, 1950-55; *b* 22 June 1894; *s* of Alfred Wallace and Eliza E. Wallace (*née* Underhill), both of Vancouver, BC; *m* 1916, Charlotte Hazel *d* of Edward Chapman, Vancouver, BC; two *s* (and one *s* killed on active service, RCAF, 1942; one *s* decd 1956). *Educ:* St Andrews Coll., Toronto, Ontario. Trained in various depts of father's business and became Purchasing Agent. Served overseas as Private, 5th Bn, 1914-16; Hon. Col BC Regt (Duke of Connaught's Own Rifles), 13th Armd Regt. President: Burrard Dry Dock Co. Ltd, N Vancouver, BC; Yarrows Ltd, Victoria, BC; Vice-Pres., Cassiar Packing Co. Ltd, Vancouver, BC; Director of companies; Hon. Member of Council, Canadian Industrial Preparedness Association. KStJ 1951. *Recreations:* shooting, golf. *Address:* Plaza del Mar, 1575 Beach Avenue, Vancouver 5, BC, Canada. *T:* MU-2-2300. *Clubs:* Vancouver, Royal Vancouver Yacht, Vancouver Rowing, Capilano Golf (Vancouver); Union (Victoria); Racquet and Tennis (New York); Washington Athletic (Seattle).

**WALLACE, David Mitchell,** OBE 1942; MS, FRCS; Surgeon, St Peter's Hospital; Urologist, Royal Marsden Hospital, Chelsea Hospital for Women, and Manor House Hospitals; Lecturer Institute of Urology; Adviser on Cancer to World Health Organisation; *b* 8 May 1913; *s* of F. David Wallace and M. I. F. Wallace; *m* 1940, Noel Wilson; one *s* three *d*. *Educ:* Mill Hill; University Coll., London, BSc 1934; MB, BS 1938; FRCS 1939; MS 1948. Served War of 1939-45, Wing Comdr, RAF (despatches). Hunterian Prof., Royal Coll. of Surgeons, London, 1956. Mem., Amer. Radium Soc., 1968. *Publications:* Tumours of the Bladder, 1957; contrib. to Cancer, British Jl of Urology, Proc. Royal Soc. Med. *Recreation:* cine photography. *Address:* 56 Cadogan Square, SW1. *T:* 01-584 0251. *Club:* Royal Automobile.

**WALLACE, Doreen, (Mrs D. E. A. Rash),** MA; novelist; *b* 18 June 1897; *d* of R. B. Agnew Wallace and Mary Elizabeth Peebles; *m* 1922, Rowland H. Rash, Wortham, Suffolk; one *s* two *d*. *Educ:* Malvern Girls' College; Somerville College, Oxford. Honours in English 1919; taught English in a grammar school for three years, then married; first novel published, 1931. *Publications:* —Esques (with E. F. A. Geach), 1918; A Little Learning; The Gentle Heart; The Portion of the Levites; Creatures of an Hour; Even Such is Time; Barnham Rectory, 1934; Latter Howe, 1935; So Long to Learn 1936; Going to the Sea, 1936; Old Father Antic, 1937; The Faithful Compass, 1937; The Time of Wild Roses, 1938; A Handful of Silver, 1939; East Anglia, 1939; The Spring Returns, 1940; English Lakeland, 1941; Green Acres, 1941; Land from the Waters, 1944; Carlotta Green, 1944; The Noble Savage, 1945; Billy Potter, 1946; Willow Farm, 1948; How Little We Know, 1949; Only One Life, 1950; (non-fiction) In a Green Shade, 1950; Norfolk (with R. Bagnall-Oakeley), 1951; Root of Evil, 1952; Sons of Gentlemen, 1953; The Younger Son, 1954; Daughters, 1955; The Interloper, 1956; The Money Field, 1957; Forty Years on, 1958; Richard and Lucy, 1959; Mayland Hall, 1960; Lindsay Langton and Wives, 1961; Woman with a Mirror, 1963; The Mill Pond, 1966; Ashbury People, 1968; The Turtle, 1969; Elegy, 1970; An Earthly Paradise, 1971. *Recreations:* politics, gardening. *Address:* Wortham Manor, Diss, Norfolk.

**WALLACE, George Douglas;** MP (Lab) Norwich North since Oct. 1964; *b* 18 April 1906; *e s* of late George Wallace, Cheltenham Spa, Gloucestershire; *m* 1932, Vera Randall, Guildford, Surrey; one *s* one *d*. *Educ:* Central School, Cheltenham Spa. Mem. of Management Cttee, in early years, of YMCA at East Bristol and Guildford; Mem. Chislehurst-Sidcup UDC, 1937-46; has been Divisional Sec. and also Chm., Chislehurst Labour Party; also Chm. of Parks and Cemeteries Cttee of UDC, Schools Manager and Member of Chislehurst, Sidcup and Orpington Divisional Education Executive; Mem., Cray Valley and Sevenoaks Hosp. Management Cttee; Chm., House Cttee, Queen Mary's Hosp. Joined Royal Air Force, reaching rank of Sergeant. Served in No 11 Group Fighter Command, 1941-45. MP (Lab) Chislehurst Div. of Kent, 1945-50; Junior Govt Whip, 1947-50; PPS: to Lord President of the Council, November 1964-65; to Sec. of State for Commonwealth Affairs, 1965; to Minister of State, Min. of Housing and Local Govt, 1967-68. Mem. Kent County Council, 1952-57. Member: Labour Parly Assoc. and Transport and General Workers' Union; Commonwealth Parly Assoc. *Recreations:* interested in Youth Movements and social welfare schemes. *Address:* 44 Shuttle Close, Sidcup, Kent. *T:* 01-300 3634.

**WALLACE, Hon. Sir Gordon,** Kt 1968; **Hon. Mr Justice Wallace;** President, Court of Appeal, New South Wales, since 1966; Acting Chief Justice of New South Wales, Oct. 1968-Feb. 1969; *b* 22 Jan. 1900; *s* of A. C. Isaacs, Sydney; *m* 1927, Marjorie, *d* of A. E. Mullins, Chepstow, Mon.; one *s* one *d*. *Educ:* Sydney High School; RMC Duntroon; Sydney University. Lt, Australian Staff Corps; AMF and AIF, 1939-44 (Col). KC 1940. Judge of Supreme Court, NSW, 1960-. Pres., NSW Bar Assoc., 1957-58; Vice-Pres., Australian Law Council, 1957; Pres., Internat. Law Assoc., Aust. Br., 1961-62. *Publications:* (jtly with Sir Percy Spender) Company Law, 1937; (jtly with J. McI. Young, QC) Australian Company Law, 1965. *Recreations:* bowls, music. *Address:* 6 Lynwood Avenue, Killara, NSW. *Clubs:* University, Pioneers (Sydney); Elanora Country.

**WALLACE, Harry Wright,** CBE 1950; Member of Lambeth Borough Council, 1936-56; Mayor, 1952-53; *b* 11 Sept. 1885; *m* 1924, Margaret Gardiner, BA, *e d* of Edward Gardiner, Laburnum House, Llansamlet, S Wales; one *s*. *Educ:* Public Elementary School. MP (Lab) East Walthamstow, 1929-31 and 1945-55. *Address:* 1 Voss Court, Streatham Common, SW16. *T:* 01-764 5701.

**WALLACE, Ian Alexander;** JP; Headmaster, Canford School, since 1961; *b* 5 Oct. 1917; *s* of Very Rev. A. R. Wallace, *qv*; *m* 1947, Janet Glossop; two *s* two *d*. *Educ:* Clifton; Corpus Christi College, Cambridge (open scholar). Classical Tripos, Part I, 1st Cl.; Theological Tripos Part I, 2nd Cl. Div. One. Served War of 1939-45, Mountain Artillery, NW Frontier, India, 1941; School of Artillery, India, 1942-43; Arakan, 1944; Mandalay, 1945 (despatches). Rossall School: Assistant Master, 1946; Housemaster, 1951-61. JP Poole Borough, 1966. *Address:* Headmaster's House, Canford School, Wimborne, Dorset. *T:* Wimborne 2411.

**WALLACE, Irving;** free-lance author; *b* 19 March 1916; *s* of Alexander Wallace and Bessie (*née* Liss); *m* 1941, Sylvia Kahn Wallace; one *s* one *d*. *Educ:* Kenosha (Wisc.) Central High Sch.; Williams Inst., Berkeley, Calif.; Los Angeles City College. Served USAAF and US Army Signal Corps, 1942-46. Magazine writer, Saturday Evening Post, Reader's Digest, Collier's, etc., 1931-54; film scenarist, 1955-58, Exploration: Honduras jungles, Wisconsin Collegiate Expedn, 1934-35. Member: PEN; Authors League of America. Supreme Award of Merit, George Washington Carver Memorial Inst., Washington, DC, 1964;

Commonwealth Club of Calif. Lit. Award for 1964; Nat. Bestsellers Inst. Paperback of the Year Award, 1965. *Publications:* The Fabulous Originals, 1955; The Square Pegs, 1957; The Fabulous Showman, 1959; The Sins of Philip Fleming, 1959; The Chapman Report, 1960; The Twenty-Seventh Wife, 1961; The Prize, 1962; The Three Sirens, 1963; The Man, 1964; The Sunday Gentleman, 1965; The Plot, 1967; The Writing of One Novel, 1968; The Seven Minutes, 1969; The Nympho and Other Maniacs, 1971; contribs to Collier's Encyclopædia, American Oxford Encyclopædia, Encyclopædia Britannica. *Recreations:* tennis and table tennis, hiking, billiards, travel abroad, collecting autographs, French Impressionist art, canes. *Address:* c/o Paul Gitlin, Counsellor at Law, 5 West 45th Street, New York, NY 10036, USA.

**WALLACE, Air Cdre James,** DSO 1944; MVO 1962; DFC 1942; AFC 1953; *b* 28 July 1918; *s* of late Frederick George Wallace and late Isobel May (*née* Wickham), Limerick, Ireland; *m* 1948, Irene Maria (*née* Heilbuth), Copenhagen; one *s* one *d*. *Educ:* Mountjoy School; Kilkenny College, Ireland. Joined RAF, 1938; served in: Middle East, 1939-41; Desert Air Force, 1941-43; psa 1942; Italy, 1943-44; NE Europe, 1944-48; Fighter Comd, OC 41 Sqdn, 1949-51; Fighter Comd, Duxford wing, 1951-53; jssc 1953; British Joint Staff, Washington, DC, 1954-56; NATO (France), 1956-58; Fighter Comd, 1958-60; Deputy Capt. The Queen's Flight, 1960-63; Director of Public Relations (RAF), Ministry of Defence, 1964-67; retired. Spitfire Productions Ltd, 1967-70; Director, Promoter (Europe) Ltd, 1970. Légion d'Honneur, Croix de Guerre (French), 1945. *Recreations:* shooting, golf. *Address:* 3 Abbotsbury Close, Kensington, W14. *T:* 01-603 9795. *Clubs:* Royal Air Force; St Moritz Tobogganing (Switzerland and London).

**WALLACE, Air Vice-Marshal John Brown,** CB 1963; OBE 1945; RAF retired; Deputy Director-General of Medical Services, Royal Air Force, 1961-66; *b* 4 Sept. 1907; *s* of late James Wallace, Cambuslang, near Glasgow; *m* 1937, Gwendolen Mary Shorthouse; two *d*. *Educ:* Hamilton Academy; Glasgow University. MB, ChB (Glasgow), 1931, MD (Glasgow), 1940. Joined RAF, 1935; served in Southern Rhodesia, 1941-45. Dep. Principal MO, Coastal Command, 1950, appointment in USA, 1950-54; Dep. Principal MO, Home Command, 1955; Principal MO: Fighter Command, 1958; Near East Air Force (Cyprus), 1961. QHS, 1962-66. *Recreation:* gardening. *Address:* 3 Wakehams Hill, Pinner, Mddx. *T:* 01-866 8345.

**WALLACE, John Madder,** CBE 1963; lately Chairman Board Royal Marsden Hospital, London; Director of Companies; *b* 22 July 1887; *s* of late James and Mary Wallace; *m* 1914 (wife *decd* 1949); one *s* two *d*; *m* 1958, Gertrude Florence Mitchell. *Educ:* George Heriot's, Edinburgh. Entered Royal Bank of Scotland, 1904; Toronto-Dominion Bank, 1912; Vice-President: Equitable Trust Co. of NY, 1923; Chase Manhattan Bank, 1930. *Recreations:* golf, fishing. *Address:* Kirklands, Derby Road, Haslemere, Surrey. *T:* Haslemere 2148. *Clubs:* Athenæum, Carlton, City of London.

**WALLACE, Sir Martin (Kelso),** Kt 1963; *b* 3 May 1898; *s* of William Henry and Mary May Wallace; *m* 1926, Eileen Bertha (*née* Marshall); OBE, BA, LLB, HDipEd. *Educ:* Methodist College, Belfast. Served RNVR European War, 1914-18 (General Service and Victory Medals). High Sheriff, 1960, Lord Mayor, 1961-63, Belfast. Rep. Windsor Ward as Councillor, later Alderman, in Belfast Corporation, for 19 years. Serves on various boards, hospital cttees, etc. *Recreation:* angling. *Address:* 23 Cranmore Avenue, Belfast, Northern Ireland. *T:* Belfast 665531; Donaghadee, Co. Down, N Ireland. *T:* Donaghadee 3361. *Club:* Ulster Reform.

**WALLACE, Robert,** CBE 1970; BL; JP; County Clerk, Treasurer and Collector of the County of Inverness, since 1948; *b* 20 May 1911; *s* of John Wallace, Glespin, Lanarkshire and late Elizabeth Brydson; *m* 1940, Jane Maxwell, *d* of late John Smith Rankin, Waulkmill, Thornhill, Dumfriesshire and late Jane Maxwell; no *c*. *Educ:* Sanquhar Sch.; Glasgow University. Solicitor 1932; BL (Dist.) 1933. Private legal practice, 1932-40; Depute Town Clerk, Ayr Burgh, 1940-44; Civil Defence Controller, Ayr Burgh, 1941-44; Depute County Clerk and Treas., Co. Inverness, 1944-48; Hon. Sheriff-Substitute of Inverness, Moray, Nairn and Ross and Cromarty at Inverness, 1967-. JP Co. Inverness, 1951. *Recreations:* fishing, gardening, walking. *Address:* Eildon, 29 Old Edinburgh Road, Inverness. *T:* Inverness 31969. *Club:* Caledonian (Edinburgh).

**WALLACE, Walter Ian James,** CMG 1957; OBE 1943; Assistant Under-Secretary of State, Colonial Office, 1962-Dec. 1966; *b* 18 Dec. 1905; *e s* of late David Wallace, Sandgate, Kent; *m* 1940, Olive Mary, 4th *d* of late Col Charles William Spriggs, Southsea; no *c*. *Educ:* Bedford Modern School; St Catharine's College, Cambridge. Entered ICS 1928, posted to Burma; Dep. Commissioner, 1933; Settlement Officer, 1934-38; Dep. Commissioner, 1939-42; Defence Secretary, 1942-44; Military Administration of Burma (Col and Dep. Director Civil Affairs), 1944-45 (despatches); Commissioner, 1946; Chief Secretary, 1946-47. Joined Colonial Office, 1947, Assistant Secretary, 1949-62. *Publication:* Revision Settlement Operations in the Minbu District of Upper Burma, 1939. *Recreation:* local history. *Address:* Hillside, St Mary's Road, Leatherhead, Surrey. *T:* Leatherhead 3131. *Club:* East India and Sports.

**WALLACE, William,** CBE 1954; MCom; Member: Joseph Rowntree Memorial Trust, 1933-66 (Chairman, 1951-63); Joseph Rowntree Social Service Trust, 1959-69 (Emeritus Trustee, 1969); Acton Society Trust; National Birthday Trust; Court of York University; Vice-President, British Society for International Health Education; resigned as Chairman of Rowntree and Co. Ltd, 31 October 1957; Vice-President, Industrial Co-Partnership Association (Chairman 1954-57); Founder Member, British Institute of Management; *b* 10 May 1891; *s* of late James Wallace; *m* 1918, Nancie E. Hancox; one *s* two *d*. *Educ:* Argyle House Sch.; legal articles; London Univ. Qualified as Solicitor Clements Inn, Daniel Reardon and Clabon prizeman, Scott Scholar, 1912. Ministry of Reconstruction: Secretary of Housing (Rent Restrictions), Housing (Financial Assistance), and Neutral Tonnage Cttees and Asst Secretary Local Government Cttee, 1917-19; an industrial adviser and director, Ministry of Food, 1940-45. Rowntree & Co., Ltd: Executive, 1919; Secretary, 1929-31; Director, 1931-57; Dep.-Chm., 1944-52; Chairman, 1952-57. President, Cocoa, Chocolate and Confectionery Alliance Ltd, 1951-53 (Vice-Pres., 1948-51). Mem. Grand Council, FBI, 1950-57; Lay Member, Restrictive Practices Court, 1958-60. Coronation Medal, 1953. *Publications:* Business Forecasting and its Practical

Application, 1927; We Can Conquer Unemployment, 1929; Enterprise First, 1946; Prescription for Partnership, 1959. Associated with: The Agricultural Dilemma, 1935; British Agriculture, 1938. *Recreations:* travel, gardening and social economics. *Address:* Windrush, Strensall, York. *T:* Strensall 327. *Club:* Reform.

**WALLACE, William,** CMG 1961; Assistant Comptroller of Industrial Property and Copyright Department, Board of Trade (Patent Office), since 1954; *b* 8 July 1911; *s* of A. S. Wallace, Wemyss Bay, Renfrewshire; *m* 1940, Sheila, *d* of Sydney Hopper, Wallington, Surrey; one *s* two *d*. *Educ:* Mill Hill School; St Edmund Hall, Oxford. Barrister, Inner Temple, 1936-39. Served War of 1939-45, Royal Artillery with final rank of Major. Board of Trade legal staff, 1945-54. UK Delegate, Internat. Confs on Copyright and Patents; Chm. Intergovernmental Cttee on Rights of Performers, Record Makers and Broadcasting Orgns, 1967-69. *Address:* Weavers, Capel, Surrey. *T:* Capel 2205. *Clubs'* Athenæum, Oxford and Cambridge University, Old Milhillians.

**WALLACE, William Kay;** historian, United States; *b* NY City, 10 Nov. 1886; *s* of John Wallace and Henriette Clam; *m* M. Karin Joussen. *Educ:* Phillips, Andover; Yale University, BA, MA. Appointed after examination for United States Diplomatic Service, 1908, Third Secretary of Embassy, Tokyo, Japan; Secretary of Legation, Copenhagen, 1909, Chargé d'Affaires, 1909-10; Secretary of Legation, Habana, Cuba, 1911; resigned, 1913; Special Correspondent The Times, 1914-17; volunteered US Army, April 1917; Capt. General Staff, Military Intelligence Division; attached to American Commission to Negotiate Peace of Versailles; Assistant Military Attaché, American Embassy, Rome; Major, USR, 1919; attended First International Economic Conference, Geneva, 1927; President Black Hills Keystone Corp., (Producers of strategic minerals), 1942. *Publications:* Greater Italy, 1917; The Trend of History, 1922; The Passing of Politics, 1924; Thirty Years of Modern History, 1926; The Scientific World View, 1928, 2nd edn 1931; Our Obsolete Constitution, 1932. *Recreations:* lawn tennis and ski-ing. *Address:* Palais Heracles, Boulevard Albert I, Monte Carlo.

**WALLACE-COPLAND, Harold;** Captain late RFA; HM Lieutenant for the County of Stafford, 1949-68; Hon. Colonel; *b* 30 May 1893; *s* of William Wallace-Copland, MVO, and Caroline Sarah Wallace-Copland; *m* 1918, Winifred Hester Sutton (*d* 1961), JP Staffordshire, *d* of Thomas Sutton Lones; one *s*. *Educ:* Coatham, Redcar, Yorks. Solicitor, 1919; Stafford Borough Council, 1922-34 and 1938-49; Staffordshire CC, 1940-50; Mayor of Stafford, 1944-46; Chairman Staffordshire CC, 1946-49. managing Director Duke & Dudley Ltd, Copeway Ltd; and Paramount Building Society. KStJ 1949. *Recreation:* golf. *Address:* Cotteswold, Rowley Park, Stafford. *T:* Stafford 2892.

**WALLACE-HADRILL, John Michael,** DLitt; FBA 1969; Senior Research Fellow, Merton College, Oxford, since 1961; Joint Editor, English Historical Review, since 1967 (Editor, 1965-67); *b* 29 Sept. 1916; *e s* of late Frederic and Norah Wallace-Hadrill, Bromsgrove, Worcs; *m* 1950, Anne, *e d* of late Neville Wakefield, DSO, and of Violet Wakefield; two *s*. *Educ:* Cheltenham College; Corpus Christi College, Oxford (Scholar, Fellow and Librarian). Lothian Prize, 1938. Served War of 1939-45, (Major, Gen. Staff, attached to a dept of Foreign Office). Fellow, Tutor and Librarian of Merton College, Oxford, 1947-55; Professor of Mediæval History, University of Manchester, 1955-61; Sub-Warden, Merton College, Oxford, 1964-66; Ford's Lectr, Oxford, 1969-70. *Publications:* The Barbarian West, 400-1000, 1952; (with J. McManners) France, Government and Society, 1957; The Chronicle of Fredegar, 1960; The Long-Haired Kings, 1962; Early Germanic Kingship, 1971; articles in learned journals. *Address:* Merton College, Oxford.

**WALLEN, Ella Kathleen,** MA (Oxon); Headmistress of Bedford High School, since September 1965; *b* 15 Feb. 1914. *Educ:* Camden School for Girls; St Hugh's College, Oxford. History Mistress, Queen Victoria High School, Stockton-on-Tees, 1937-41; Senior History Mistress, High School for Girls, Gloucester, 1942-59; Headmistress, Queen Victoria High School, Stockton-on-Tees, 1959-65. *Address:* Bedford High School, Bedford.

**WALLER, Hon. Sir George (Stanley),** Kt 1965; OBE 1945; **Hon. Mr Justice Waller;** Judge of the High Court of Justice, Queens Bench Division, since 1965; *b* 3 Aug. 1911; *s* of late James Stanley and late Ann Waller; *m* 1936, Elizabeth Margery, *d* of 1st Baron Hacking; two *s* one *d*. *Educ:* Oundle; Queens' Coll., Cambridge. Called to the Bar, Gray's Inn, 1934, Bencher, 1961. RAFO, 1931-36; served War of 1939-45, in RAFVR, Coastal Command; 502 Sqdn, 1940-41; Wing Comdr, 1943 (despatches). Chm., Northern Dist Valuation Bd, 1948-55; QC 1954; Recorder of Doncaster, 1953-54, of Sunderland, 1954-55, of Bradford, 1955-57, of Sheffield, 1957-61, and of Leeds, 1961-65. Solicitor-General of the County Palatine of Durham, 1957-61; Attorney-General of the County Palatine of Durham, 1961-65; Member: Criminal Injuries Compensation Board, 1964-65; General Council of the Bar, 1958-62 and 1963-65; Parole Bd, 1949-; Adv. Council on the Penal System, 1970-. *Address:* Hatch Hill, Kingsley Green, near Haslemere, Surrey. *T:* Haslemere, 4629. *Clubs:* Oxford and Cambridge University, Army and Navy; Hawks (Cambridge).

**WALLER, Sir (John) Keith,** Kt 1968; CBE 1961 (OBE 1957); Australian Ambassador to United States since 1964; *b* 19 Feb. 1914; *s* of late A. J. Waller, Melbourne; *m* 1943, Alison Irwin Dent; two *d*. *Educ:* Scotch Coll., Melbourne; Melbourne Univ. Entered Dept of External Affairs, Australia, 1936; Private Sec. to Rt Hon. W. M. Hughes, 1937-40; Second Sec., Australian Legation, Chungking, 1941; Sec.-Gen., Australian Delegn, San Francisco Conf., 1945; First Sec., Australian Legation, Rio de Janeiro, 1945; Chargé d'Affaires, 1946; First Sec., Washington, 1947; Consul-Gen., Manila, 1948; Officer-in-Charge, Political Intelligence Div., Canberra, 1950; External Affairs Officer, London, 1951; Asst Sec., Dept of External Affairs, Canberra, 1953-57; Ambassador to Thailand, 1957-60; Ambassador to Moscow, 1960-62; First Asst Sec., Dept of External Affairs, 1963-64. *Address:* Australian Embassy, 3120 Cleveland Avenue NW, Washington, DC, USA. *Clubs:* Travellers'; University (Sydney); Commonwealth (Canberra).

**WALLER, Sir John Stanier,** 7th Bt, *cr* 1815; author, poet, and journalist; *b* 27 July 1917; *s* of Capt. Stanier Edmund William Waller (*d* 1923), and of Alice Amy (who *m* 2nd, 1940, Gerald H. Holiday), *d* of J. W. Harris, Oxford; *S kinsman* Sir Edmund Waller, 6th Bt 1954. *Educ:* Weymouth Coll.; Worcester Coll., Oxford (BA). Founder-Editor of Quarterly,

Kingdom Come, first new literary magazine of war, 1939-41. Served 1940-46 with RASC (in Middle East, 1941-46); Adjt RASC, HQ, Cairo Area; Capt. 1942; Features Editor, Brit. Min. of Inf., Middle East, 1943-45; Chief Press Officer, Brit. Embassy, Bagdad, 1945; News and Features Editor, MIME, Cairo, 1945-46. Dramatic Critic Cairo Weekly, The Sphinx, 1943-46; Founder-Mem. Salamander Soc. of Poets, Cairo, 1942; lectured in Pantheon Theatre, Athens, 1945; Greenwood Award for Poetry, 1947; FRSL 1948; Lectr and Tutor in English and Eng. Lit. at Carlisle and Gregson (Jimmy's), Ltd, 1953-54; Asst Master, London Nautical Sch., May-June 1954; Information Officer, Overseas Press Services Div., Central Office of Information, 1954-59. Director: Literature Ltd, 1940-42; Richard Congreve Ltd, 1948-50; Export Trade Ships Ltd, 1956. *Publications:* The Confessions of Peter Pan, 1941; Fortunate Hamlet, 1941; Spring Legend, 1942; The Merry Ghosts, 1946; Middle East Anthology (Editor), 1946; Crusade, 1946; The Kiss of Stars, 1948; The Collected Poems of Keith Douglas (Editor), 1951 and 1966; Shaggy Dog, 1953; Alamein to Zem Zem by Keith Douglas (Editor), 1966. Contrib. to numerous anthologies and periodicals at home and abroad. *Recreations:* portrait photography, teaching. *Heir: uncle:* Rev. Canon Michael Henry Waller [*b* 29 Sept. 1888; *m* 1923, Eileen Primrose, *d* of Charles Webber, Beckenham]. *Address:* Gaspar Lodge, 50 (A) Courtfield Gardens, Kensington, W8. *T:* 01-373 4609. *Club:* Press.

**WALLER, Vice-Adm. John William Ashley,** CB 1946; *b* 17 Jan. 1892; *s* of John Ashley Waller, Beenham Court, Kingsclere, Hants, and Margaret Priscilla Lavinia Waller. *Educ:* Naval Colleges. Midshipman, 1909; Sub-Lt 1912; Lieutenant 1913; Served in Grand Fleet, 1914-18, King Edward VII, Royal Oak and Marlborough; qualified in torpedoes, 1918; staff college, 1928; Comdr 1926; Capt. 1934; Chief of Intelligence Staff Far East, 1935-36; commanded HMAS Sydney, 1937-39; Naval Assistant to First Sea Lord, 1941-42; commanded HMS Malaya, 1942-44; Rear-Adm. 1944; Red Sea and Suez Canal Area, 1944-45; Washington, USA, 1945-46, on Lend Lease and Administration; Naval Adviser to Netherlands Ministry of Marine, 1946-47; Vice-Admiral, retired list, 1947. *Recreations:* riding, fishing, ornithology. *Address:* Es Mastay, San Cristobal, Menorca, Baleares, Spain; c/o National Westminster Bank Ltd, 14 Sloane Square, SW1.

**WALLER, Sir Keith;** *see* Waller, Sir J. K.

**WALLER, Mervyn Napier,** CMG 1959; OBE 1953; mural painter, stained-glass and mosaic artist; *b* 19 June 1893; *s* of late William and Sarah Waller; *m* 1958, Lorna Marion Reyburn. *Educ:* National Gallery Art School, Melbourne. Served European War, 1914-18 in AIF, 111th Howitzer Battery (loss of right arm at Bullecourt). Served as Trustee, National Art Gallery, Melbourne. Recent major work, stained-glass and mosaic, Hall of Memory, Australian War Memorial, Canberra. *Address:* 9 Crown Road, Ivanhoe, Victoria 3079, Australia. *T:* JX 1014. *Club:* Savage (Melbourne).

**WALLER, Sir Robert William,** 9th Bt, *cr* 1780, of Newport, Co. Tipperary; employed by the General Electric Co. of America as an Industrial Engineer, since 1957; *b* 16 June 1934; *s* of Sir Roland Edgar Waller, 8th Bt, and Helen Madeline, *d* of Joseph Radl, Matawan, New Jersey, USA; *S* father 1958; is a citizen of the United States; *m* 1960, Carol Anne, *d* of John E. Hines, Lynn, Mass; two *s* one *d.* (and one *s* decd). *Educ:* St Peter's Prep. Sch.; Newark Coll. of Engrg; Fairleigh Dickinson University. *Heir: s* John Michael Waller, *b* 14 May 1962. *Address:* 24 Upton Lane, Lynnfield, Mass, USA.

**WALLER, Prof. Ross Douglas,** CBE 1958 (MBE 1945); Director of Extra-Mural Studies, 1937-60, and Professor of Adult Education, 1949-66 (Professor Emeritus, 1966), Manchester University; *b* 21 Jan. 1899; *m* 1928, Isobel May Brown; three *s* one *d. Educ:* Manchester Central High School for Boys; Manchester University. Served European War, KOYLI, and NF, 1917-19. BA, 1920; MA 1921; post-graduate studies in Florence, 1921-22; Schoolmaster, 1922-24; Lecturer in English Literature, Manchester Univ., 1924-37. Chm. North-Western Dist, WEA, 1943-57; President Educational Centre Association, 1948-65; President Manchester Branch, Society of Recorder Players, 1947-, OECD Consultant on Adult Educn in Sardinia, 1961-62. Cavaliere Ufficiale, Order of Merit, Italy, 1956. *Publications:* The Monks and the Giants, 1926; The Rossetti Family, 1932; Marlowe, Edward II (with H. B. Charlton), 1933. Learning to Live, 1947; Harold Pilkington Turner, 1953; Residential College, 1954; Design for Democracy (Introductory Essay), 1956. Articles in Adult Education, Highway, Times Educational Supplement, etc. *Recreations:* recorder playing, painting, and visiting Italy. *Address:* 22 Viceroy Court, Wilmslow Road, Manchester 20. *T:* 061-445 7290.

**WALLEY, Sir John,** KBE 1965; CB 1950; retired as Deputy Secretary, Ministry of Social Security, 1966 (Ministry of Pensions and National Insurance, 1958-66); *b* Barnstaple, Devon, 3 April 1906; *e s* of late R. M. Walley; *m* 1934, Elisabeth Mary, *e d* of late R. H. Pinhorn, OBE; two *s* two *d. Educ:* Hereford High Sch.; Hereford Cathedral Sch.; Merton Coll., Oxford (Postmaster, 1924-28). Ministry of Labour: Asst Principal, 1929; Principal, 1934; Asst Sec., Min. of Labour and National Service, 1941; transf. Min. of National Insurance, 1945; Under Sec., 1946; Chm., Dental Benefit Council, 1945-48. Chm., Hampstead Centre, National Trust, 1969-. *Publications:* contrib. to The Future of the Social Services, ed Robson and Crich, 1970; articles in the press on Social Security matters. *Address:* 46 Rotherwick Road, NW11. *T:* 01-455 6528. *Club:* Oxford and Cambridge University.

**WALLINGER, Sir Geoffrey (Arnold),** GBE 1963; KCMG 1953 (CMG 1947); *b* 2 May 1903; *s* of late William A. Wallinger, OBE, IFS; *m* 1st, 1939, Diana Peel Nelson; one *s*; 2nd, 1950, Alix de la Faye Lamotte (*d* 1956); 3rd, 1958, Stella Irena, *d* of late Konni Zilliacus. *Educ:* Sherborne; Clare Coll., Cambridge. Entered Diplomatic Service, 1926; Secretary: at Cairo, 1927-29, at Vienna, 1929-31, at Foreign Office, 1931-34; Political Sec. to UK High Comr in S Africa, 1935-38; First Sec., Buenos Aires, 1938-42; First Sec., Foreign Office, 1943; Counsellor in China, 1943-47 (Minister–local rank, 1945); Counsellor in Foreign Office, 1947-49; Minister to Hungary, 1949-51; Ambassador to Thailand, 1951-54; Ambassador to Austria, 1954-58; Ambassador to Brazil, 1958-63; retired from Foreign Service, 1963. A Director of Bank of London and South America. *Address:* 10 Moore Street, SW3. *T:* 01-584 2035. *Club:* St James'.

**WALLINGFORD, Air Cdre Sidney,** CB 1951; CBE 1944; RNZAF, retired; *b* 12 July 1898; *s* of late Major Jesse Alfred Wallingford, MC, and Alice Wallingford; *m* 1929, Kathleen

Matilda Jamieson; one *s* one *d*. *Educ:* Auckland Grammar Sch., New Zealand. Served European War, 1916-20, with Artists' Rifles, Rifle Brigade, and RAF; First Commissioned, Dec. 1916; Fiji Constabulary, 1921-23; Royal Air Force, 1924-29; NZ Permanent Air Force, 1929; PSA 1937; NZ Liaison Officer, Air Ministry, 1938-40; Air Force Member for Personnel, Air Dept, Wellington, NZ, 1941-42; RNZAF Staff Officer to Commander Aircraft South Pacific and AOC No. 1 (Islands) Group, RNZAF, 1942-43; AOC Northern Group, RNZAF, 1944; Air Member for Supply at Air Dept, Wellington, NZ, 1945-46; idc 1947; Air Member for Personnel at Air Dept, NZ, 1948-52; AOC HQ Task Force, RNZAF at Hobsonville, Auckland, NZ, 1952-53; retired 1954. Pres. Nat. Rifle Assoc. of NZ, 1954-58. US Legion of Merit (Degree of Officer). *Recreations:* trout fishing, rifle and pistol shooting; winner Queen Mary's Prize at Bisley in 1928; RAF Rifle Championship, 1927, 1929. *Address:* Opito Bay, Whitianga, New Zealand. *Club:* Officers' (Auckland, NZ).

**WALLIS, Captain Arthur Hammond,** CBE 1952; MIEE; RN (retired); Chief of · Naval Information, Admiralty, 1957-64; *b* 16 Sept. 1903; *s* of late Harold T. Wallis; *m* 1940, Lucy Joyce, *er d* of late Lt-Col L. E. Becher, DSO; one *s* one *d*. *Educ:* Wixenford; Osborne and Dartmouth. Entered Royal Navy as Cadet, 1917; specialised as Torpedo Officer, 1930; staff of Rear-Adm. Destroyers, 1936-38; Torpedo Officer, HMS Nelson, 1938-41; Comdr, 1941; i/c Torpedo Experimental Dept, HMS Vernon, 1941-43; Exec. Officer, HMS Illustrious, 1943-45; Captain, 1947; in command HM Underwater Detection Establishment at Portland, 1948-50; Sen. Naval Officer, Persian Gulf and in command HMS Wild Goose, 1950-51; Cdre, HMS Mauritius, 1951; UK Naval Delegate, Military Agency for Standardisation, NATO, 1952-53; Director of Under-water Weapons, Admiralty, 1953-56. Naval ADC to the Queen, 1956. *Recreations:* golf, gardening. *Address:* Compton's Barn, Woodstreet, near Guildford, Surrey. *T:* Normandy 3143. *Clubs:* United Service; Worplesdon Golf.

**WALLIS, Sir Barnes (Neville),** Kt 1968; CBE 1943; FRS 1945; Hon. DSc Eng London and Bristol; Hon. ScD Cambridge; Hon. DSc Loughborough, Oxford and Heriot-Watt; FICE; Hon. MIMechE; Hon. FRAeS; FRSA; FSE; RDI, 1943; Chief of Aeronautical Research and Development, British Aircraft Corporation Ltd, Weybridge Division, Weybridge, Surrey, 1945; *b* 26 Sept. 1887; *s* of Charles George Wallis, BA (Oxon), MRCS, LRCP, and Edith Eyre Ashby; *m* 1925, Mary Frances, *d* of Arthur George Bloxam, FIC; two *s* two *d*. *Educ:* Christ's Hospital. Trained as Marine Engineer at J. S. White & Co. Ltd, Cowes, 1905-1913; Designer, Airship Dept, Vickers Ltd, 1913-15; served European War, Artists' Rifles and RNVR, 1915; Chief Designer, Vickers Ltd, Airship Dept, Barrow-in-Furness, 1916-22; Chief Engineer, Airship Guarantee Co., London and Howden, Yorks, 1923-30; Chief Designer, Structures, Vickers Aviation Ltd, Weybridge, 1930-37; Asst Chief Designer, Vickers-Armstrongs Ltd, Aviation Section, 1937-45. Designer of HMA R100; Inventor of Geodetic Construction; Inventor of weapon which destroyed Moehne and Eder Dams, and penetration bombs, 1940-45; Inventor of Variable Geometry Aircraft in this country. Hon. Fellow, Churchill Coll., Cambridge, 1965-; Senior Fellow, RCA, 1966; Hon. Fellow: UMIST; Manchester Coll. Art and Design. Hon. FRAeS 1967; Hon. Life Mem. and Fellow, Inst. of Patentees and Inventors, 1968. Treasurer, Christ's Hosp., and Chm., Council of Almoners, 1958-70. Freeman and Liveryman, Worshipful Co. of Shipwrights and Guild of Air Pilots and Navigators; Freeman of City of London. Founders' Medal, Air League, 1963; Kelvin Gold Medal, ICE, 1968; Albert Medal, RSA, 1968. *Publications:* Some Technical Aspects of the Commercial Airship (Lloyd's Register of Shipping, 1925); The Design and Construction of HMA R100. *Address:* White Hill House, Effingham, Surrey. *T:* Bookham 2027. *Club:* Athenæum.

**WALLIS, Claude (Edgar),** MBE 1944; retired as Chairman and Managing Director Associated Iliffe Press Ltd (1945-60) and Chairman Kelly's Directories Ltd (1954-60); *b* Madras, India, 21 Jan. 1886; *s* of late Charles and Constance Walder-Wallis. *Educ:* City of Westminster and Emanuel Schools. Associated with motoring journalism for 60 years; joined late Lord Montague in 1905 on staff of Car Illustrated and transf. to Iliffe & Sons Ltd, publishers of The Autocar, Automobile Engineer, and other motoring and aviation journals, 1911; Managing Director Associated Iliffe Press, 1939. Special Reserve of Officers, 1912-20, rank Captain. Served European War: 1st Bn Loyal North Lancashire Regt during retreat from Mons (wounded, prisoner, Sept. 1914; despatches, 1914 Star, GS and Victory Medals); War of 1939-45 (MBE); served on numerous government cttees relating to publishing, paper rationing, etc.; was instrumental in organising special appeals in motor and other industries which raised £250,000 for BRCS. President: Motor & Cycle Trades Bevenolent Fund, 1947-48; Periodical Proprietors Assoc., 1953-56; Fellowship of the Motor Industry; The Camera Club. *Recreations:* motoring, sailing. *Address:* 25 Manchester Square, W1. *T:* 01-935 9375. *Clubs:* Royal Automobile; Royal Motor Yacht (Poole).

**WALLIS, Col Hugh Macdonell,** SM 1969; DSO 1919; OBE 1945; MC, VD, CD; CA; *b* 7 Dec. 1893; *s* of John McCall Wallis, Peterborough, Ont, and Gertrude Thornton, *d* of Lt-Col Samuel Smith Macdonell, QC, LLD, DCL, Windsor, Ont; *m* 1st, 1935, Leslie (marr. diss., 1953), *d* of late Mr and Mrs K. K. Carson, London; 2nd 1969, Corinne de Boucherville, *widow* of Hon. Jean Desy. *Educ:* Lakefield Preparatory Sch.; Toronto Univ. Enlisted 1st CEF, Sept. 1914; served France, Belgium, Germany, 1915-19; Bde Major 4th Can. Inf. Bde, 1918 (DSO, MC, despatches twice); Colonel Comdg The Black Watch, Royal Highlanders of Canada, then Permanent Active Militia, 1930; VD 1930; CD 1967; R of O, 1931; Hon. ADC to Earl of Bessborough, Gov.-Gen. of Canada, 1931-35; Active Service, Canadian Forces, 1940-45; Colonel Asst DAG Nat. Defence HQ (OBE); Hon. Lt-Col 3rd Bn The Black Watch of Canada, 1961-68. Past President: Canadian Citizenship Council, St Andrews Soc. of Montreal, Canadian Club of Montreal, Montreal Museum of Fine Arts. Man. Dir and Pres., Mount Royal Rice Mills Ltd, Montreal, 1924-53. Governor: Lakefield College Sch.; Montreal General Hosp.; Montreal Children's Hosp. (Past Chm. of Exec.); l'Hôpital Marie Enfant; Chm., Adv. Bd, Canadian Centenary (1967) Council (past Chm. Org. and Exec. Cttees). Hon. Sponsor, Trent Univ., Ont., 1963; Associate, McGill Univ. and l'Univ. de Montréal. Member of some 30 other cultural, historical, social, military, educational, etc., associations and societies. FRSA, 1959. Chartered Accountant, with McDonald, Currie & Co., 1923. Outstanding Citizen Award, Montreal Citizenship Council, 1967. Canada Centennial Medal, 1967. *Recreations:* travel, fine arts, golf, Canadiana books and history. *Address:* 1455 Sherbrooke Street West, Montreal, PQ, Canada. *Clubs:* Canadian, St James', United Services (Montreal); Rideau (Ottawa); Braeside Golf (Senneville).

**WALLIS, Leonard G. C.;** *see* Coke Wallis.

**WALLIS, Peter Ralph;** Assistant Chief Scientific Adviser (Research), Ministry of Defence, since 1968; *b* 17 Aug. 1924; *s* of Leonard Francis Wallis and Molly McCulloch Wallis (*née* Jones); *m* 1949, Frances Jean Patricia Cowie; three *s* one *d*. *Educ:* University College Sch., Hampstead; Imperial Coll. of Science and Technology, London (BSc(Eng)). Henrici and Siemens Medals of the College, 1944. Joined Royal Naval Scientific Service 1944; work at Admty Signal and Radar Estab. till 1959, Admty Underwater Weapons Estab. till 1968. Marconi Award of IERE, 1964; ACGI, FIEE, FIMA. *Publications:* articles in Jl of IEE, IERE and Op. Res. Quarterly. *Recreations:* skiing, walking, swimming, tennis, amateur dramatics. *Address:* St Helens, 35 Bincleaves Road, Weymouth, Dorset. *Clubs:* Ski Club of Great Britain; Weymouth Drama.

**WALLIS-JONES, Ewan Perins; His Honour Judge Wallis-Jones;** County Court Judge since 1964; Chairman, Carmarthenshire Quarter Sessions, since 1966; *b* 22 June 1913; *s* of late William James Wallis-Jones, MBE, and late Ethel Perrins Wallis-Jones; *m* 1940, Veronica Mary (*née* Fowler); one *s* two *d*. *Educ:* Mill Hill Sch.; University Coll. of Wales, Aberystwyth; Balliol Coll., Oxford. LLB Hons Wales, 1934; BA Oxon 1936; MA Oxon 1941. Qualified Solicitor, 1935; called to Bar, Gray's Inn, 1938. ARPS. *Recreations:* music, reading and photography. *Address:* 34 Ornan Road, NW3. *T:* 01-794 4707; 28 Quay Street, Carmarthen. *T:* Carmarthen 5106. *Clubs:* New Arts, Royal Photographic Society.

**WALLOP,** family name of **Earl of Portsmouth.**

**WALLS, Prof. Eldred Wright;** S. A. Courtland Professor of Anatomy in the University of London at Middlesex Hospital Medical School, since 1949 (Dean, Medical School, since 1967); *b* 17 Aug. 1912; 2nd *s* of J. T. Walls, Glasgow; *m* 1939, Jessie Vivien Mary Robb, MB, ChB, DPH, *o d* of late R. F. Robb and late M. T. Robb; one *s* one *d*. *Educ:* Hillhead High Sch.; Glasgow Univ. BSc, 1931; MB, ChB (Hons), 1934; MD (Hons), 1947, FRSE, Struthers Medal and Prize, 1942. Demonstrator and Lectr in Anatomy, Glasgow Univ., 1935-41; Senior Lectr in Anatomy, University Coll. of S Wales and Monmouthshire, 1941-47; Reader in Anatomy, Middlesex Hospital Medical Sch. 1947-49. *Publications:* (co-editor) Rest and Pain (by John Hilton) (6th edn), 1950; (co-author) Sir Charles Bell, His Life and Times, 1958; contrib. Blood-vascular and Lymphatic Systems, to Cunningham's Textbook Anat., 1964; contrib. to Journal of Anatomy, Lancet, etc. *Recreations:* golf and gardening. *Address:* 29 St Mary's Avenue, Church End, Finchley, N3. *T:* 01-346 1592. *Club:* Athenæum.

**WALLS, Henry James,** BSc, PhD; Director, Metropolitan Police Laboratory, New Scotland Yard, 1964-68; *b* 1907; *s* of late William Walls, RSA, and late Elizabeth Maclellan Walls; *m* 1940, Constance Mary Butler; one *s* one *d*. *Educ:* George Watson's Boys' Coll., Edinburgh; Melville Coll., Edinburgh; Edinburgh Univ. BSc 1930; PhD 1933. Postgrad. research in physical chemistry, Munich, Edinburgh and Bristol, 1930-35; ICI (Explosives), 1935-36; Staff of Metropolitan Police Lab., 1936-46; Staff Chemist, Home Office Forensic Science Lab., Bristol, 1946-58; Director of Home Office Forensic Science Lab., Newcastle upon Tyne, 1958-64. *Publications:* Forensic Science, 1968; (with Alistair Brownlie) Drink, Drugs and Driving, 1969; two books on photography; papers in journals dealing with forensic science. *Recreations:* reading, plays and films, talking, people. *Address:* c/o David Higham Associates Ltd, 76 Dean Street, W1.

**WALLS, Rev. Roland Charles;** Chaplain of Rosslyn Chapel, Midlothian, since 1962; *b* 7 June 1917; *s* of late Roland William Walls and late Tina Josephine Hayward. *Educ:* Sandown Grammar Sch.; Corpus Christi Coll., Cambridge; Kelham Theological Coll. Curate of St James', Crossgates, Leeds, 1940-42; Curate of St Cecilia's, Parson Cross, Sheffield, 1942-45; Licensed preacher, Diocese of Ely, 1945-48; Fellow of Corpus Christi Coll., Cambridge, 1948-62; Lecturer in Theology, Kelham Theological Coll., 1948-51; Chaplain and Dean of Chapel, Corpus Christi Coll., Cambridge, 1952-58; Canon Residentiary, Sheffield Cathedral, 1958-62. Examining Chaplain to Bishop of Edinburgh. Lecturer at Coates Hall Theological Coll.; Lecturer in Dogmatics Dept, New Coll., Edinburgh. *Publication:* (contrib.) Theological Word Book (ed A. Richardson), 1950. *Recreations:* walking, music, etc. *Address:* The Fraternity, Roslin, Midlothian.

**WALLWORTH, Cyril;** Assistant Under-Secretary of State, Ministry of Defence, since 1964; *b* 6 June 1916; *s* of Albert A. Wallworth and Eva (*née* Taylor); unmarried. *Educ:* Oldham High Sch.; Manchester Univ. BA (Hons) History, 1937. Asst Principal, Admiralty, 1939; Asst Private Secretary to First Lord, 1941-45, Principal, 1943; Asst Secretary, 1951; Under-Secretary, 1964. *Recreations:* music, wine, cooking, photography. *Address:* 5 Leinster Mews, W2. *T:* 01-262 9695. *Club:* Hurlingham.

**WALMSLEY, Arnold Robert,** CMG 1963; MBE 1946; HM Diplomatic Service, retired; *b* 29 Aug. 1912; *s* of late Rev. Canon A. M. Walmsley; *m* 1944, Frances Councell de Mouilpied. *Educ:* Rossall Sch.; Hertford Coll., Oxford. 1st Class Maths Mods, 1st Class Modern Greats. Private Sec. to Julius Meinl, Vienna, 1935-38; Foreign Office, 1939-45; established in Foreign Service, 1946; Foreign Office, 1946-50; British Consul in Jerusalem, 1950-54; Foreign Office, 1954-63; Head of Arabian Dept, 1961; Counsellor, Khartoum, 1963-65; Dir, Middle East Centre of Arab Studies, Lebanon, 1965-69. *Publications:* (as Nicholas Roland) The Great One, 1967; Natural Causes, 1969. *Address:* Manor Farm, Dunmow Road, Bishop's Stortford, Herts. *Club:* Travellers'.

**WALMSLEY, Air Marshal Sir Hugh Sydney Porter,** KCB 1952 (CB 1944); KCIE 1947; CBE 1943 (OBE 1937); MC 1918; DFC 1922; *b* 6 June 1898; 3rd *s* of late James Walmsley, Broughton, near Preston; *m* 1928, Audrey Maude, 3rd *d* of late Dr Pim, Sleaford; three *s*. *Educ:* Old Coll., Windermere; Dover Coll. 2nd Lieut, Loyal North Lancs Regt, 1915-16; seconded to RFC 1916; Captain, RFC, 1917; permanent commission RAF 1919 as Flying Officer; Flt Lt, 1921; Sqdn Ldr, 1931; Wing Comdr, 1937; Gp Capt., 1939; Air Cdre, 1942; Air Vice-Marshal, 1943; Acting Air Marshal, 1947-48; Air Marshal, 1949. 55 Sqdn, BEF, 1917-18 (MC); Iraq, 1921-23; OC 33 Sqdn Bicester, 1933-34, 8 Sqdn, Aden, 1935-37; War of 1939-45 (despatches 5 times); OC 71 Wing AASF, 1939-40; OC RAF Station, Scampton, 1940-41; HQ Bomber Command, 1941-42;

AOC 91 Group, 1942-43; SASO, HQ Bomber Command, 1944-45; AOC 4 Group, Transport Command, 1945-46; Air Officer, Transport Command, SE Asia, 1946; AOC-in-C, Air HQ, India, 1946-47; Deputy Chief of the Air Staff, 1948-50; AOC-in-C, Flying Training Command, 1950-52; Retired from Active List, 1952. Managing Director of Air Service Training Ltd, 1952-59; Principal of College of Air Training, Hamble, 1960, resigned July 1960. *Recreations:* represented RAF Inter-Service Athletics in 1919, 1924 and 1926; all games; gardening, sailing. *Address:* Upwood, Tiptoe, Lymington, Hants. *Club:* Royal Air Force.

**WALMSLEY, Air Commodore John Banks,** CBE 1946; DFC 1918; QC 1955; retired; *b* 9 Oct. 1896; *s* of Thomas James Walmsley; *m* 1926, Dorothy Maud Bleasdale; two *d*. *Educ:* Shrewsbury Sch.; RMC, Sandhurst. Called to Bar, Gray's Inn, 1924. Served European War, 1915-18, as pilot in RFC and RAF. Practised as barrister on Northern Circuit, 1924-33; joined RAF Legal Branch in Office of The Judge Advocate General, 1933; Dep. Judge Advocate General of Army and RAF in Middle East, 1936-40; served in RAF Legal Branch in office of The Judge Advocate General, 1940-48; Director of Legal Services, Air Ministry, 1948-57. Greek Military Cross, 1918. *Recreations:* golf, gardening. *Address:* Littledene, Church Lane, Oxted, Surrey. *T:* Oxted 2942.

**WALMSLEY, Kenneth Maurice,** CMG 1959; OBE 1953; *b* 26 Jan. 1914; *s* of late George Walmsley, Clonskeagh, Dublin, and Ventnor, IoW; *m* 1941, Kathleen Margaret, *d* of late J. R. Patterson, Skeagh House, Brookeborough, Co. Fermanagh; one *s*. *Educ:* St Columba's Coll., Rathfarnham, Co. Dublin; Trinity Coll., Dublin; Christ's Coll., Cambridge. Cadet in Colonial Administrative Service, Nigeria, 1937; District Officer, Nigeria, 1946; Financial Secretary, Somaliland, 1950; Colonial Secretary of the Bahamas, 1956; retired, 1964. *Recreations:* golf and riding. *Address:* c/o PO Box 357, Nassau, Bahamas.

**WALMSLEY, Prof. Robert,** MD; FRCPE, FRCSE, FRSE; Bute Professor of Anatomy, University of St Andrews, since 1946; *b* 24 Aug. 1906; *s* of late Thomas Walmsley, Supt Marine Engr; *m* 1939, Isabel Mary, *e d* of James Mathieson, Aberdeen; two *s*. *Educ:* Greenock Acad.; Univ. of Edinburgh; Carnegie Inst. of Embryology, Baltimore, USA. MB, ChB (Edinburgh); MD (Edinburgh) with Gold Medal Thesis, 1937. Demonstrator, Lectr and Senior Lectr on Anatomy, Univ. of Edinburgh, 1931-46; Goodsir Fellowship in Anatomy, 1933; Rockefeller Fellowship, 1935-36; served as Pathologist in RAMC in UK and MEF, 1939-44. Struthers Lectr, Royal Coll. of Surgeons, Edinburgh, 1952; Fulbright Advanced Scholarship, 1960; Pres., Edinburgh Harveian Soc., 1963-64. Vis. Prof. of Anatomy, Auckland, NZ, 1967. Formerly: Master, St Salvator's Coll.; Chm., Council St Leonard's and St Katherine's Schs; External Examiner in Anatomy, Cantab, Edinburgh, Durham, Glasgow, Aberdeen, Liverpool, Singapore, Kingston (WI), Accra, etc. Member: Anatomical Soc.; Cardiac Soc. *Publications:* Co-author Manual of Surgical Anatomy, 1964. Revised section of Arthrology, Cunningham's Textbook of Anatomy, 1964. Contribs to various jls, on Heart, Bone and Joints, and on Whales. *Recreation:* fishing. *Address:* 45 Kilrymont Road, St Andrews, Fife. *T:* St Andrews 2879.

**WALPOLE,** family name of **Baron Walpole.**

**WALPOLE,** 9th Baron, of Walpole, *cr* 1723; 7th Baron Walpole of Wolterton, *cr* 1756; **Robert Henry Montgomerie Walpole,** TD; Captain, RA; *b* 25 April 1913; *s* of late Horatio Spencer Walpole and of Dorothea Frances, *o d* of Frederick Butler Molyneux Montgomerie; *S* to baronies at the death of his cousin, 5th Earl of Orford, 1931; *m* 1937, Nancy Louisa, *y d* of late Frank Harding Jones, Housham Tye, Harlow, Essex; one *s* one *d* (and one *s* one *d* decd). *Educ:* Eton; South Eastern Agricultural Coll., Wye; Royal Agricultural Coll., Cirencester. *Recreations:* curling, shooting, golf. *Heir:* *s* Hon. Robert Horatio Walpole [*b* 8 Dec. 1938; *m* 1962, Judith, *yr d* of T. T. Schofield, Stockingwood House, Harpenden; two *s* two *d*. *Educ:* Eton; King's Coll., Cambridge]. *Address:* Wolterton Hall, Norwich NOR 44Y. *T:* Hanworth 210, Matlaske 274. *Clubs:* Bath, MCC; Norfolk (Norwich).

**WALPOLE, George Frederick,** CBE 1953; Director-General Department of Lands and Surveys, 1940, Director of Irrigation, 1948, Director of Forests, 1952, in the Jordan Government, retired from the service of the Jordan Government, 1954; *b* 8 Jan. 1892; *o s* of W. J. Walpole, JP, and E. M. Walpole (*née* Russell); *m* 1928, Agnes Letitia Blount-Dinwiddie; two *d*. *Educ:* Bootham Sch., York; Trinity Coll., Dublin (BA, BAI). Served European War, 1914-18, France and Cameroons; commissioned RA, 1914; retired, 1919. Joined Egyptian Civil Service as Inspector of Surveys, 1921; carried out extensive surveys in Sinai, Eastern and Western Deserts of Egypt, 1921-30; discovered and mapped the Qattara Depression, 1926-29; prepared and published the 1/500,000 map of Egypt, 1930-36; resigned from Egyptian service, 1936; Assistant Director of Lands and Surveys, Trans Jordan Government, 1936-40. FRICS 1950; Founder's Medal, Royal Geographical Society, 1950. *Publications:* An Ancient Aqueduct West of Mersa Matruh, 1929; Land Settlement in Trans Jordan, 1942; Land Problems in Trans Jordan, 1947. *Recreation:* gardening.

**WALPOLE, Kathleen Annette,** MA; Head Mistress of Wycombe Abbey School, Bucks, from 1948 until Dec. 1961; *b* Ootacamund, S India, 1899; *e d* of Major A. Walpole, RE. *Educ:* Southlands Sch., Exmouth; Westfield Coll., University of London. BA Hons London, 1921; History Mistress, The Church High Sch., Newcastle upon Tyne, 1922-27; Research Student, Westfield Coll., 1927-28; MA London, 1929; Alexander Prize of RHistSoc, 1931; History Mistress, The Royal Sch., Bath, 1928-34; Head Mistress, The Red Maids Sch., Bristol, 1934-47. *Publications:* articles in the Trans. of Historic Society of Lancashire and Cheshire, and of the RHistSoc, 1929 and 1931, on Emigration to British North America. *Recreations:* gardening, walking, study of antiques. *Address:* Fordley, Charlcombe Lane, Bath. *T:* Bath 2536. *Club:* Royal Commonwealth Society.

**WALSH,** family name of **Baron Ormathwaite.**

**WALSH, Dr Alan,** FRS 1969; Assistant Chief of Division, Division of Chemical Physics, Commonwealth Scientific and Industrial Research Organization; *b* 19 Dec. 1916; *s* of late Thomas Haworth and Betsy Alice Walsh, Hoddlesden, Lancs; *m* 1949, Audrey Dale Hutchinson; two *s*. *Educ:* Darwen Grammar Sch.; Manchester Univ. BSc 1938; MSc (Tech.) 1946; DSc 1960. FAA 1958. British Non-Ferrous Metals Research Assoc., 1939-42 and 1944-46; Min. of Aircraft Production, 1943;

Div. of Chemical Physics, CSIRO, Melbourne, 1946-. Einstein Memorial Lectr, Australian Inst. of Physics, 1967; Pres., Australian Inst. of Physics, 1967-69. Hon. Mem., Soc. of Analytical Chemistry, 1969. Foreign Mem., Royal Acad. of Sciences, Stockholm, 1969. Britannica Australia Science Award, 1966; Research Medal, Royal Soc. of Victoria, 1968; Talanta Gold Medal, 1969. Hon. DSc Monash, 1970. *Publications:* papers in learned jls. *Address:* Division of Chemical Physics, Commonwealth Scientific and Industrial Research Organization, PO Box 160, Clayton, Victoria 3168, Australia. *T:* 544 0633.

**WALSH, Prof. Arthur Donald,** FRS 1964; MA, PhD (Cantab), FRSE, FRIC; Professor of Chemistry, University of Dundee, since 1967 (University of St Andrews, 1955-67); *b* 8 Aug. 1916; *s* of Arthur Thomas and Amy Florence Walsh; *m* 1945, Elin Frances Woolley, MA, *er d* of H. C. Woolley, London; two *s* two *d. Educ:* Loughborough Grammar Sch.; Corpus Christi Coll., Cambridge (Mawson Schol.). Research and teaching: Cambridge Univ., 1938-49; Univ. of Leeds, 1949-54; Visiting Prof., Univ. of California, 1950-51; Reader in Physical Chemistry, Univ. of Leeds, 1953-55. *Publications:* numerous papers in scientific journals. *Recreations:* gardening, bird-watching. *Address:* Department of Chemistry, University of Dundee, Dundee. *T:* Dundee 23181; Groom's Garth, 26 Glamis Drive, Dundee.

**WALSH, Sir Cyril Ambrose,** KBE 1969; Justice of High Court of Australia since 1969; *b* 1909; *s* of late Michael J. and Mary E. Walsh, Sydney; *m* 1942, Mary Agnes Smyth; three *s. Educ:* Parramatta High Sch.; Univ. of Sydney. BA 1930, LLB 1934, Sydney. Admitted Bar of NSW, 1934; Judge of Supreme Court of NSW, 1954; Judge of Appeal, Supreme Court of NSW, 1966. *Address:* 57 Prospect Road, Summer Hill, New South Wales, Australia. *T:* 798-6038. *Club:* University (Sydney).

**WALSH, Sir David (Philip),** KBE 1962; CB 1946; retired as Deputy Secretary, Ministry of Housing and Local Government (1960-63). Formerly: Principal Asst Secretary (Director of Establishments), Admiralty; Under Secretary, Ministry of Town and Country Planning; Under-Secretary, Ministry of Housing and Local Government (formerly Min. of Local Government and Planning), 1951-60. *Address:* Silver Birches, Galley Lane, Barnet, Herts.

**WALSH, Surgeon Rear-Adm. (retired) Dermot Francis,** CB 1960; OBE 1952; FRCSE; QHS 1958; *b* 21 Jan. 1901; *s* of Dr J. A. Walsh. *Educ:* Belvedere Coll., Dublin; Trinity Coll., Dublin. BA 1927; MB, BCh, BAO, 1928; FRCSE 1943. CStJ 1958. *Recreations:* golf, gardening, music. *Address:* Latona, Torquay Road, Foxrock, Co. Dublin. *T:* Dublin 893164. *Clubs:* Naval and Military; Portmarnock Golf (Dublin).

**WALSH, Rt. Rev. Francis,** DD, DPh; Titular Bishop of Birta since 1963; *b* 15 Sept. 1901. *Educ:* Fordyce Academy, Banffshire; Blairs Coll., Aberdeen; Scots Coll., Rome. DPh 1921; DD, 1925. Parish work, Inverness, 1925-29. Joined White Fathers Society (Missionaries of Africa), 1929; founded St Columba's Coll., Newtown St Boswells, 1934; Superior of White Fathers, Heston, Middx, 1949-51. Bishop of Aberdeen, (RC), 1951-63. *Address:* Chapeltown, Braes of Glenlivet, Banffshire.

**WALSH, Maj.-Gen. Francis James,** CB 1948; CBE 1945; psc†; *b* 12 Jan. 1900; *s* of F. J. Walsh, Wexford, Eire; *m* 1931, Marjorie Olive Watney; two *s. Educ:* Clongowes Coll., Eire. RMC, Sandhurst, 1918; Royal Irish Regt, 1918-22; King's African Rifles, 1922-28; South Lancashire Regt, 1928-31; Indian Army, 1931-48; Staff Coll., Camberley, 1933-34; staff employment, India, Burma, Malaya, 1935-48; DA&QMG 33 Corps, 1943; DQMG 11 Army Group, 1943-44; DA&QMG 4 Corps and 14 Army, 1944-45; MGA N Comd, India, 1945-47. Maj.-Gen. (Temp.) 1945; Subst., 1947; retired, 1948. *Recreation:* sailing. *Address:* Orchard House, Turpins Lane, Frinton-on-Sea, Essex. *T:* 4472. *Club:* Naval and Military.

**WALSH, Lt-Gen. Geoffrey,** CBE 1944; DSO 1943; CD; *b* 1909; *s* of H. L. Walsh; *m* 1935, Gwynn Abigail Currie; one *s. Educ:* Royal Military Coll., Kingston; McGill Univ. (BEngEE). Chief Engineer, 1st Canadian Army, 1944-45; DQMG, 1945-46; Comdr Northweast Highway System, 1946-48; Comdr Eastern Ontario Area, 1948-51; Comdr 27 Bde (Europe), 1951-52; DGMT 1953-55; QMG 1955-58; GOC, Western Command, 1958-61; Chief of the General Staff, Canada, 1961-64; Vice Chief of the Defence Staff, Canada, 1964-65. Col Comdt, Royal Canadian Army Cadets and Cadet Services of Canada, 1970-. Legion of Merit (US); Comdr of Orange Order of Nassau (Netherlands). *Recreations:* golf, fishing, philately. *Address:* 201 Northcote Place, Rockcliffe Park, Ottawa, Canada. *Clubs:* RMC, Royal Ottawa Golf (Ottawa); USI (Ottawa and Edmonton).

**WALSH, Maj.-General George Peregrine,** CB 1944; CBE 1943; DSO 1942; late Royal Artillery; *b* 30 June 1899; *s* of late Charles Peregrine Walsh; *m* 1944, Ruth Vaughan Ashe, *yr d* of R. A. Holmes à Court, MC, Manor House, Yetminster; two *s* one *d. Educ:* Felsted; RMA, Woolwich. 2nd Lieut, RA, 1918; served European War, France and Belgium, 1918; Waziristan, 1921-24; Palestine, 1936-39 (despatches); War of 1939-45 (despatches, DSO, CBE, CB); Maj.-General, 1944; Chief of Staff; 8th Army, 1944; ALFSEA 1945; Southern Comd, 1948-49; Director of Weapons and Development, War Office, 1949-52; retired 1954. Assistant Controller of Munitions, Ministry of Supply, 1954-60. *Address:* The Old Rectory, Warmwell, Dorchester, Dorset.

**WALSH, Rt. Rev. Gordon John;** Assistant Bishop of Ely since 1942; *b* 1880; *s* of late John Edward Walsh, BL, JP, Dublin; *m* 1909, Edythe (*d* 1956), *d* of late Archdeacon Spence, DD, Belfast; no *c. Educ:* Sutton Valence Sch., Kent; Trinity Coll., Dublin; BA 1902, MA 1909, DD 1927; MA Jesus Coll., Cambridge, 1945. Ordained, 1903; Curate, Trinity Church, Belfast, 1903, and St Mary's, Belfast, 1905; Association Secretary of the Colonial and Continental Church Society for Ireland, 1909; Rector of St Peter's, Athlone, 1910-13; missionary under the Church Missionary Society at Tokushima, 1914-22; Hakodate, 1922-23; Asahigawa, 1923-27; Secretary to the CMS Hokkaido Mission and Examining Chaplain to the Bishop of the diocese, 1922-27; Bishop in Hokkaido, 1927-40; Vicar of Eastry and Tilmanstone, Kent, 1941-42; Residentiary Canon of Ely Cathedral, 1942-67; Vice-Dean, 1956-67. *Address:* 3 Bishop Wynn Close, Broad Street, Ely, Cambs. *T:* Ely 2764. *Clubs:* Royal Societies, Royal Over-Seas League.

**WALSH, Henry Francis Chester,** OBE 1936; *b* 10 May 1891; *s* of late Richard Walter Walsh and Ismay Chester, Williamstown House, Castlebellingham, Co. Louth; *m* 1st, 1924, Carla (*d* 1955), *d* of Colonel Holger Hedemann, Copenhagen; three *d.* 2nd, 1956, Violet Mary, *d* of late Lt-Col A. T. S. Margan, CMG. *Educ:* Stonyhurst; Exeter Coll., Oxford (MA Mod.

Languages); Inner Temple. Vice-Consul, Surabaya, 1924; Consul at Batavia, 1931; acted at various Consular posts in Siam, French Indo-China and Netherlands East Indies; Acting Consul-General at Batavia in 1935 and 1936; Consul-General at Saigon, 1938-39; at Batavia, 1939-42; Consul–General for Texas and New Mexico, 1942-45; Political Adviser to C-in-C Allied Forces, Netherlands East Indies, 1945-46; retired Oct. 1946. *Recreations:* tennis and golf. *Address:* Williamstown House, Castlebellingham, Co. Louth, Ireland. *Club:* Royal Irish Automobile (Dublin).

**WALSH, James Mark,** CMG 1956; OBE 1948; Consul-General, Zürich, 1962-68; *b* 18 Aug. 1909; *s* of Mark Walsh and Emily (*née* Porter); *m* 1st, 1937, Mireille Loir (*d* 1966); one *s*; 2nd, 1967, Bertha Hoch. *Educ:* Mayfield Coll., Sussex; King's Coll., London; Lincoln's Inn, London. BA (Hons), 1929; LLB, 1932; Barrister, 1932; passed an examination and appointed to Foreign Service, 1932; Vice-Consul: Paris, 1932-33, Rotterdam, 1933-34; Judge of HBM Provincial Court, Alexandria, Egypt, 1934-38; Acting Consul-General, Barcelona, 1939; Vice-Consul, Philadelphia, 1939-44; Consul, Antwerp, 1944-45. First Secretary, British Legation: Helsinki, 1945-46, Budapest, 1946-48; Dep. Consul-General, New York, 1948-50; Counsellor (Commercial), Ankara, 1950-54, and Berne, 1954-59; Consul–General, Jerusalem, 1959-62. *Recreations:* travel, golf. *Address:* Eleonorenstrasse 9, 8032 Zürich, Switzerland.

**WALSH, Dr John James;** Director, National Spinal Injuries Centre, Stoke Mandeville Hospital, Aylesbury, Bucks, since 1966; *b* 4 July 1917; *s* of Dr Thomas Walsh and Margaret O'Sullivan; *m* 1946, Joan Mary, *d* of Henry Teasdale and Nita Birks; three *s* one *d*. *Educ:* Mungret Coll.; University Coll., Cork. MB, BCh 1940; MD 1963; MRCP 1968, FRCS 1969. Various hospital appointments, including Resident Surgical Officer, King George's Hospital, Ilford, 1941-46; Medical Officer, Spinal Injuries Centre, Stoke Mandeville Hospital, Aylesbury, 1947; Deputy Director, National Spinal Injuries Centre, 1957-66. *Publications:* Understanding Paraplegia, 1964; a number of publications on subjects pertaining to paraplegia in medical journals. *Recreation:* shooting. *Address:* Wayside, Station Road, Princes Risborough, Bucks. *T:* Princes Risborough 3347.

**WALSH, Sir John (Patrick),** KBE 1960; Professor of Dentistry and Dean and Director, University of Otago Dental School, since 1946; *b* 5 July 1911; *s* of John Patrick Walsh and Lillian Jane (*née* Burbidge), Vic, Australia; *m* 1934, Enid Morris; one *s* three *d*. *Educ:* Ormond Coll.; Melbourne Univ. BDSc 1st Cl. Hons Melbourne; LDS Victoria, 1936; MB, BS Melbourne, 1943; DDSc Melbourne, 1950; FDSRCS 1950; FDSRCS Edinburgh, 1951; MDS NUI, 1952; FRSNZ 1961; FACD 1962; Hon. FACDS, 1967. Hosp. and teaching appointments in Melbourne till 1946. MO, RAAF, 1945-46. Consultant, WHO Dental Health Seminars: Wellington, 1954; Adelaide, 1959. Speaker: 11th and 12th Internat. Dental Congresses, London and Rome; Centennial Congress of Amer. Dental Assoc., New York, 1959; 12th, 14th and 15th Australian Dental Congresses. Chairman: Dental Council of NZ, 1956-; Mental Health Assoc. of Otago, 1960. Dominion Pres., UNA, 1960-64. Member: MRC of NZ, 1950- (Chm. Dental Cttee, 1947-60); Scientific Commn; Fedn Dentaire Internat., 1954-61; Council, Univ. of Otago, 1958-63; Nat. Commn for UNESCO, 1961-69; Educn Commn, 1961-; Expert Panel on Dental Health, WHO, 1962; Nat. Council, Duke of Edinburgh's Award, 1963-68. CC, Dunedin, 1968-. Pres., Dunedin Rotary Club, 1960, Governor Dist 298, 1966-67. Hon. Mem., American Dental Assoc., 1969-; List of Honour, FDI, 1969-. Holds hon. degrees. *Publications:* A Manual of Stomatology, 1957; Living with Uncertainty, 1968; numerous articles in scientific literature. *Recreations:* gardening, bowls. *Address:* 108 Cannington Road, Dunedin, New Zealand. *T:* Dunedin 69-943. *Club:* Fernhill (Dunedin).

**WALSH, Most Rev. Joseph,** DD, MA; Titular Archbishop of Tubernuca; *b* Newport, Mayo, 1888. *Educ:* St Jarlath's Coll., Tuam; Maynooth. Graduated RUI, 1909; MA 1911; priest, 1914; Prof. of Classics, St Jarlath's Coll., Tuam, 1914-18; Secretary to Archbishop of Tuam, 1918-26; Canon and Vicar General, 1924; Administrator, Tuam, 1926-29; President, St Jarlath's Coll., Tuam, 1929-40; titular Bishop of Cela and Auxiliary to Archbishop of Tuam, 1938; Archbishop of Tuam, 1940-69. *Address:* Shrine House, 6 St Jarlath's Place, Tuam, Eire.

**WALSH, Leslie;** Stipendiary Magistrate, Salford, since 1951; *b* 6 May 1903; *s* of Rt Hon. Stephen and Anne Walsh; *m* 1934, Katharine de Hoghton Birtwell. *Educ:* Wigan Grammar Sch.; Victoria Univ., Manchester (LLB); St John's Coll., Oxford (BCL). Called to Bar, Gray's Inn, 1927; practised Northern Circuit. Deputy Licensing Authority NW Area, 1946-51; Chairman, Salford and District Rent Tribunal, 1946-51. Royal Air Force, 1940-45. *Address:* 4 Grange Road, Urmston, Manchester M31 1HU. *Club:* St James's (Manchester).

**WALSH, Professor William;** Professor of Education and Head of Department of Education, University of Leeds, since 1957; Chairman of the School of Education, and Douglas Grant Fellow in Commonwealth Literature in the School of English, since 1969; Director, Yorkshire Television, since 1967; *b* 23 Feb. 1916; *e s* of William and Elizabeth Walsh; *m* 1945, May Watson; one *s* one *d*. *Educ:* Downing Coll., Cambridge; University of London. Schoolmaster, 1943-51; Senior English Master, Raynes Park County Grammar Sch., 1945-51; Lecturer in Education, University Coll. of N Staffordshire, 1951-53; Lecturer in Education, Univ. of Edinburgh, 1953-57. Chm., Bd of combined Faculties of Arts, Economics, Social Studies and Law, Univ. of Leeds, 1964-66; Pro-Vice-Chancellor, Univ. of Leeds, 1965-67; Vis. Prof., Aust. Nat. Univ., 1968; Chm. Bd of Educn, 1969-; Australian Commonwealth Vis. Fellow, 1970. *Publications:* Use of Imagination, 1959; A Human Idiom, 1964; Coleridge: The Work and the Relevance, 1967; A Manifold Voice, 1970; contributions to: From Blake to Byron, 1957; Young Writers, Young Readers, 1960; Speaking of the Famous, 1962; F. R. Leavis–Some Aspects of his Work, 1963; The Teaching of English Literature Overseas, 1963; papers and essays on literary and educational topics in British and American Journals. *Address:* 27 Moor Drive, Headingley, Leeds. *T:* Leeds 5-5705. *Club:* United University.

**WALSH, Prof. William Henry;** FBA 1969; Professor of Logic and Metaphysics in the University of Edinburgh, since 1960; *b* 10 Dec. 1913; *s* of Fred and Mary Walsh, Leeds; *m* 1938, Frances Beatrix Ruth (*née* Pearson); one *s* two *d*. *Educ:* Leeds Grammar Sch.; Merton Coll., Oxford. Class I, Classical Mods., 1934, Class I, Lit. Hum., 1936; Gaisford Greek Prose Prize, 1934; Junior Research Fellow, Merton Coll., 1936. Served War of 1939-45,

Royal Corps of Signals, 1940-41; subsequently employed in branch of Foreign Office. Lecturer in Philosophy, Univ. Coll., Dundee (University of St Andrews), 1946; Fellow and Tutor in Philosophy, Merton Coll., Oxford, 1947-60. Sub-Warden, 1948-50, Senior Tutor, 1954-60; Lecturer in Philosophy, University of Oxford, 1947-60; Dean of Faculty of Arts, University of Edinburgh, 1966-68. Dawes Hicks Lecturer, British Academy, 1963. Visiting Professor: Ohio State Univ., USA, 1957-58; Dartmouth Coll., NH, USA, 1965; Univ. of Maryland, 1969-70. Pres. Aristotelian Soc., 1964-65. *Publications:* Reason and Experience, 1947; An Introduction to Philosophy of History, 1951; Metaphysics, 1963; Hegelian Ethics, 1969; articles in philosophical periodicals. *Address:* 19 Great Stuart Street, Edinburgh 3. *T:* 031-225 1471.

**WALSH ATKINS, Leonard Brian,** CMG 1962; CVO 1961; *b* 15 March 1915; *o c* of late Leonard George Atkins and Gladys Mary (*née* Griffith); step *s* of late Geoffrey Walsh, CMG, CBE; *m* 1st, 1940, Marguerite Black (marr. diss. 1968); three *s*; 2nd, 1969, Margaret Lady Runcorn. *Educ:* Charterhouse (Scholar); Hertford Coll., Oxford (Scholar). BA, Lit. Hum., Class II, 1937. Asst Principal, India Office, 1937. Served War, Nov. 1940-July 1945, in Fleet Air Arm; Lieut-Comdr (A), RNVR (despatches). Principal, Burma Office, 1945-47; India Office, 1947; Commonwealth Relations Office, 1947; Asst Secretary, 1949; Counsellor, British Embassy, Dublin, 1953-56; Student, Imperial Defence Coll., 1957; Dep. High Comr, Karachi, 1959-61; Asst Under-Sec. of State, 1962; seconded to Civil Service Selection Bd, 1967; retired 1970. *Recreation:* sailing. *Address:* 11 Grove Court, Circus Road, NW8 9EN; Wood Cottage, Mundon, Maldon, Essex. *Club:* United University.

**WALSHAM, Rear-Admiral Sir John Scarlett Warren,** 4th Bt, *cr* 1831; CB 1963; OBE 1944; RN, retired; Admiral Superintendent HM Dockyard, Portsmouth, 1961-64; *b* 29 Nov. 1910; *s* of Sir John S. Walsham, 3rd Bt, and Bessie Geraldine Gundreda (*d* 1941), *e d* of late Vice-Admiral John B. Warren; *S* father, 1940; *m* 1936, Sheila Christina, *o d* of Comdr B. Bannerman, DSO; one *s* two *d*. Rear-Admiral, 1961. *Heir: s* Timothy John Walsham [*b* 26 April 1939. *Educ:* Sherborne]. *Address:* Antioch, Stalbridge, Sturminster Newton, Dorset.

**WALSHE, Sir Francis (Martin Rouse),** Kt 1953; OBE 1919; FRS 1946; MD, DSc, FRCP; Hon. DSc National University of Ireland; Hon. DLittHum University of Cincinnati, USA; Hon. Consulting Physician to University College Hospital and to the National Hospital for Nervous Diseases, Queen Square, WC; Fellow University College, London; *s* of late M. C. Walshe, JP, London; *m* Bertha (*d* 1950), *d* of late Charles Dennehy, FRCSEd, St Lucia, BWI, and Lismore, Co. Cork; two *s*. *Educ:* Prior Park Coll.; University College Sch. and University College and Hospital. Major, RAMC and Consulting Neurologist, MEF and EEF, 1915-19 (despatches, OBE); Welch Lecturer Clinical Physiology, University of Oxford, 1921; Visiting Neurologist Johns Hopkins Hospital, Baltimore, Md, USA, 1925; Oliver Sharpey Lecturer, Royal College of Physicians, 1929, Victor Horsley Lecturer, 1946; Harveian Orator, RCP, 1948; Editor of Brain, 1937-53. Hon. Member Neurological Societies of America, Canada, Denmark, France, Germany, New York, Spain, Uruguay, and of American Academy of Neurology. Thayer Lecturer, Johns Hopkins Hospital, Baltimore, 1952. President: Assoc. British Neurologists, 1950-51; RSM, 1952-54; Royal Soc. Hygiene and Public Health, 1962-64. Fothergillian Gold Medallist, Medical Society of London, 1951; Ferrier Lecturer, Royal Society, 1953; Hughlings Jackson Lecturer and Medallist, 1952, Gowers' Lecturer and Medallist, 1956, RSM, Nuffield Lecturer and Medallist, 1961; Harben Lecturer and Medallist, 1964. *Publications:* Textbook of Nervous Diseases, 11th edn; Critical Studies in Neurology, 1948; Further Critical Studies in Neurology, 1965; On the Structure of Medicine and its Place among the Sciences (Harveian Oration, RCP), 1948; Humanism, History and Natural Science in Medicine (Linacre Lecture); papers on physiology and diseases of nervous system. *Address:* Manor Cottage, Brampton, Hunts.

**WALSINGHAM,** 9th Baron, *cr* 1780; **John de Grey,** MC 1952; Lieut-Colonel, Royal Artillery, retired, 1968; *b* 21 Feb. 1925; *s* of 8th Baron Walsingham, DSO, OBE, and Hyacinth (*d* 1968), *o d* of late Lt-Col Lambart Henry Bouwens, RA; *S* father, 1965; *m* 1963, Wendy, *er d* of E. Hoare, Southwick, Sussex; one *s* two *d*. *Educ:* Wellington Coll.; Aberdeen Univ.; Magdalen Coll., Oxford; RMCS. BA Oxon, 1950; MA 1959. Army in India, 1945-47; Palestine, 1947; Oxford Univ., 1947-50; Foreign Office, 1950; Army in Korea, 1951-52; Hong Kong, 1952-54; Malaya, 1954-56; Cyprus, Suez, 1956; Aden, 1957-58; Royal Military Coll. of Science, 1958; Aden, 1961-63; Malaysia, 1963-65. *Heir: s* Hon. Robert de Grey, *b* 21 June 1969. *Address:* Merton, Thetford, Norfolk. *T:* Watton (Norfolk) 226. *Clubs:* Army and Navy; Norfolk County (Norwich).

**WALSTON,** family name of **Baron Walston.**

**WALSTON,** Baron *cr* 1961 (Life Peer), of Newton; **Henry David Leonard George Walston,** JP; farmer; *b* 16 June 1912; *o s* of late Sir Charles Walston, LittD, LHD, PhD, and Florence, *d* of David Einstein; *m* 1935, Catherine Macdonald, *d* of late D. H. Crompton and of Mrs Charles Tobey; four *s* two *d*. *Educ:* Eton; King's Coll., Cambridge (MA). Research Fellow in Bacteriology, Harvard, USA, 1934-35; Mem., Hunts War Agricultural Cttee, 1939-45; Dir of Agriculture, British Zone of Germany, 1946-47; Agricultural Adviser for Germany to FO, 1947-48; Counsellor, Duchy of Lancaster, 1948-54. Contested: (L) Hunts, 1945; (Lab) Cambridgeshire, 1951 and 1955; (Lab) Gainsborough, 1957 (by-election), and 1959. Parly Under-Sec. of State, FO, 1964-67; Parly Sec., BoT, Jan.-Aug. 1967; Mem., UK Delegn to Council of Europe, 1970. Crown Estate Comr, 1967-; Chm., Inst. of Race Relations, 1968-. Minister of Agriculture's Liaison Officer, 1969-70; Chm., East Anglia Regional Planning Council, 1969-; Member: Cambs Agricultural Cttee, 1948-50; Home Office Cttee on Experiments on Animals, 1961-62. Chm., Harlow Group Hosp. Management Cttee, 1962-64; Dep. Chairman: Council, Royal Commonwealth Soc., 1963-64; Commonwealth Producers Organisation; Trustee, Rural Industries Bureau 1959-64; Governor, Guy's Hosp., 1944-47. JP Cambridge, 1944. *Publications:* From Forces to Farming, 1944; Our Daily Bread, 1952; No More Bread, 1954; Life on the Land, 1954; (with John Mackie) Land Nationalisation, for and against, 1958; Agriculture under Communism, 1961; The Farmer and Europe, 1962; The Farm Gate to Europe, 1970; contribs to Proc. of Experimental Biology and Medicine, Jl of Hygiene, Observer, Economist, New Statesmanm Spectator. *Recreations:* shooting, sailing. *Address:* Town's End Springs, Thriplow, near Royston, Herts;

A14 Albany, Piccadilly, W1; Marquis Estates, St Lucia, West Indies. *Clubs:* Brooks's, MCC; County (Cambridge); House of Lords Yacht.

**WALTARI, Mika;** Author since 1928, Finland; Member of Academy of Finland since 1957; *b* 19 Sept. 1908; *s* of Toimi Armas Waltari and Olga Maria (*née* Johansson); *m* 1931, Marjatta Luukkonen; one *d. Educ:* Helsinki Univ. (MA). Literary critic for Maaseudun Tulevaisuus, 1932-42; Literary reviewer for Finnish Broadcasting Company, 1937-38; Editor for Suomen Kuvalehti, weekly illustrated magazine, 1936-38; with editorial office of Finnish State Information Bureau, 1939-40 and 1941-44. DrPhil *hc* 1970. Awarded literary prizes, Finland 1934, 1935, 1950 and 1954; Pro Finlandia, 1952; Commander of Finnish Lion, 1960. *Publications:* The Egyptian, 1949; Michael the Finn, 1950; The Sultan's Renegade, 1951; The Dark Angel, 1953; A Nail Merchant at Nightfall, 1954; Moonscape, 1955; The Etruscan, 1957; The Secret of the Kingdom, 1961; The Roman, 1966. *Recreation:* detective stories. *Address:* Tunturikatu 13, Helsinki 10, Finland. *Club:* PEN (Finland).

**WALTER, Keith McNeil C.;** *see* Campbell-Walter.

**WALTER, Captain Philip Norman,** DSO 1940; RN; Commandant, Corps of Commissionaires, 1950-60; Director of The Times, 1958-64; *b* 12 Dec. 1898; *s* of Captain Philip Walter, RN, and *g s* of John Walter III, of The Times; *m* 1946, Sylvia, *d* of J. C. M. Ogilvie-Forbes, Boyndlie, Aberdeenshire; one *s. Educ:* RN Colleges Osborne and Dartmouth. Served European War, 1914-18, Dardanelles and North Sea; Commander, 1932; Captain, 1940; War of 1939-45, Norway; commanded Inshore Squadron, N Africa, 1942; wounded, PoW; Assistant Chief of Staff to Allied Naval Commander-in-Chief, 1944; invalided, 1948. Chevalier of Légion d'Honneur, Croix de Guerre (France). *Address:* c/o Barclays Bank Ltd, 1 Pall Mall East, SW1. *Club:* United Service.

**WALTER, W(illiam) Grey,** MA, ScD; Head of Research, Burden Neurological Institute, Bristol, since 1939; *b* Kansas City, Mo, USA, 19 Feb. 1910; *s* of Karl Walter and Margaret Hardy; *m* 1st, 1934, Monica Ratcliffe (divorced, 1947); two *s*; 2nd, 1947, Vivian Joan Dovey; one *s*; 3rd, 1960, Lorraine Josephine Aldridge (*née* Donn). *Educ:* Westminster Sch.; King's Coll., Cambridge. BA Hons 1st class Part II Physiology, 1931; Harold Fry and Michael Foster Student, 1931; MA 1934; ScD 1947; Rockefeller Fellow, Maudsley Hosp., 1935. Founder and Foreign Sec., Electroencephalographic Soc., 1942; Co-Founder and Hon. Pres., Internat. Fedn of Socs for Electroencephalography and Clinical Neurophysiology, 1947; Co-founder and co-Editor of Electroencephalography and Clinical Neurophysiology, 1947. Maudsley Lectr, Royal Medico-Psychological Assoc., 1949. Mem. WHO Study Group on Psychobiological Develt of the Child, 1953-56. Co-Founder and Council Mem. Internat. Assoc. of Cybernetics, 1956. Adolf Meyer Lectr, American Psychiatric Assoc., 1959. Prof. and Dr hc, Univ. of Aix-Marseille, 1949. *Publications:* The Living Brain, 1953; Further Outlook (The Curve of the Snowflake), 1956; papers on neurophysiology, electronics and cybernetics in Jl of Physiology, EEG Jl, Jl of Mental Science, Proc. Royal Soc. Medicine, etc. *Recreations:* tennis, skin diving, gliding. *Address:* 35 Mariner's Drive, Bristol 9. *T:* 68-2412.

**WALTERS, Rev. David John,** MC, MA; *b* Ammanford, Carmarthenshire, 13 Jan. 1893; *s* of T. Watkyn Walters, Tirydail, Neath; *m* 1917, Frances, *d* of Mrs F. Atkinson, Daleside, Sleights, Yorks; one *s* one *d. Educ:* Christ College, Brecon; Brasenose College, Oxford (Junior Hulme Scholar), 2nd Class Hons School of Natural Science. Assistant Master at Haileybury College, 1914-19; Assistant Master and Housemaster at Uppingham School, 1919-31; Headmaster of Bromsgrove School, 1931-53; Vicar of Lindridge, dio. of Worcester, 1953-57; Rector of All Saints', Worcester, 1957-64; Rural Dean of Worcester, 1960-64. On active service as Lieutenant in RGA, 1915-18 (despatches, MC). *Publication:* (Joint) History of 135th Siege Battery, RGA. *Recreation:* walking. *Address:* The Cottage, South Parade, Ledbury, Herefordshire.

**WALTERS, Dennis,** MBE 1960; MP (C) Westbury Division of Wiltshire since 1964; *b* Nov. 1928; *s* of late Douglas L. Walters; *m* 1st, 1955, Vanora (marr. diss. 1969), *yr d* of late Sir Archibald McIndoe; one *s* one *d*; 2nd, 1970, Mrs Celia Kennedy, *yr d* of Rt Hon. Duncan Sandys, *qv*, and of late Mrs Diana Churchill. *Educ:* Downside; St Catharine's College (Exhibitioner), Cambridge (MA). War of 1939-45: interned in Italy; served with Italian Resistance Movement behind German lines after Armistice; repatriated and continued normal educn, 1944. Chm., Fedn of Univ. Conservative and Unionist Assocs, 1950; Personal Asst to Lord Hailsham throughout his Chairmanship of Conservative Party; Chm., Coningsby Club, 1959. Contested (C) Blyth, 1959 and Nov. 1960. Jt Hon. Sec., Conservative Parly Foreign Affairs Cttee, 1965-. Director: Eric Garrott Associates; Specialised Travel Service Ltd; Chm., Asthma Research Council, 1969-. *Address:* 15 Wilton Street, SW1. *T:* 01-235 7750; Orchardleigh, Corton, Warminster, Wilts. *T:* Codford St Mary 369. *Clubs:* Carlton, Hurlingham.

**WALTERS, Francis Paul;** *b* 1888; *s* of late Rev. F. B. Walters, King William's College, Isle of Man, and Cecilia Beales; *m* 1921, Louise Roux-Bourgeois; two *d. Educ:* Eton; University Coll., Oxford. Fellow and Tutor of University Coll., Oxford, 1912, Hon. Fellow, 1938; served European War, in Oxford and Bucks Light Infantry (Special Reserve) (Captain) and General Staff; joined Secretariat of League of Nations, 1919; Deputy-Secretary-General of the League of Nations, 1939-40. *Publication:* A History of the League of Nations, 1951. *Address:* 10 Rue Cortot, Paris 18.

**WALTERS, Peter Ernest,** CMG 1965; Staff Manager, Courage, Barclay and Simonds Ltd, SE1, since 1967; *b* 9 Oct. 1913; *s* of Ernest Helm Walters and Kathleen Walters (*née* Farrer-Baynes); *m* 1943, Ayesha Margaret, *d* of Alfred and Winifred Bunker; three *d. Educ:* Windlesham House Sch. Emigrated to Kenya, 1931. Army Service, 1939-45; commissioned KAR, 1940; Major 1944. Cadet, Colonial Admin. Service, Kenya, 1945; Dist Comr, 1948; Provincial Comr, Northern Prov., 1959; Civil Sec., Eastern Region, Kenya, 1963-65; retd from Colonial Service, 1965. Principal, Min. of Aviation (London), 1965-67. *Address:* Cherry Orchard, Ockley, near Dorking, Surrey. *T:* Capel 3219. *Club:* Nairobi (Kenya).

**WALTERS, Peter (Hugh Bennetts) Ensor,** OBE 1957; MIPR; FInstD; Public Relations and Fund Raising Consultant since 1959; *b* 18 July 1912; *yr s* of late Rev. C. Ensor Walters, a President of the Methodist Conference, and late Muriel Havergal, *d* of late Alderman J. H. Bennetts, JP, Penzance; *m* 1936, Ella Marcia, *er d* of Percival Burdle Hayter; no *c. Educ:*

Manor House Sch.; St Peter's Coll., Oxford. On staff of late Rt Hon. David Lloyd George, 1935-39; enlisted as volunteer in Army, 1940; commissioned in Royal Army Pay Corps, 1942; National Organizer, National Liberal Organization, 1944-51. General Sec., National Liberal Organization, Hon. Sec. and Treas., National Liberal Party Council, and Dir, National Liberal Forum, 1951-58. *Recreation:* travel. *Address:* 51 Richmond Hill Court, Richmond, Surrey. *T:* 01-940 1493. *Clubs:* National Liberal; Union (Oxford).

**WALTERS, Roger Talbot,** CBE 1965; FRIBA, FIStructE; Controller General, Ministry of Public Building and Works, since 1969; *b* 31 March 1917; 3rd *s* of Alfred Bernard Walters, Sudbury, Suffolk; *m*; no *c*. *Educ:* Oundle; Architectural Association School of Architecture; Liverpool University. Diploma in Architecture, 1939. Served in Royal Engineers, 1943-46. Office of Sir E. Owen Williams, KBE, 1936; Directorate of Constructional Design, Min. of Works, 1941-43; Architect to Timber Development Assoc., 1946-49; Principal Asst Architect, Eastern Region, British Railways, 1949-59; Chief Architect (Development), Directorate of Works, War Office, 1959-62; Dep. Dir-Gen., R&D, MPBW, 1962-67; Dir-Gen., Production, 1967-69. *Address:* 40 Farley Court, Allsop Place, NW1. *T:* 01-486 4128. *Club:* Reform.

**WALTHER, Prof. David Philippe;** Professor of Orthodontics, University of London, since 1961; *b* 18 Sept. 1909; *s* of Dr David Walther and Miriam Walther; *m* 1939, Barbara Brook; one *s* one *d*. *Educ:* St Edward's School, Oxford; Guy's Hospital Medical and Dental School. LDS; RCS 1934; MRCS, LRCP, 1941; DOrth, RCS 1954; MDS Univ. London, 1964; FDS, RCS 1965. House Surgeon in Children's Dentistry, including Surgery and Orthodontics, Guy's Hospital, 1934-35; private practice, Hampstead, 1935-49. Served War of 1939-45, Captain, RAMC, 1942-46. Registrar in Dental Department for Children and Orthodontics, Guy's Hospital, 1946-48; half-time Senior Orthodontic Registrar, Hospital for Sick Children, Gt Ormond St, 1948-50. Sen. Hosp. Dental Officer, Orthodontist in Charge of Orthodontic Clinic Dept, Eastman Dental Hosp., 1949-54; Consultant in Orthodontics, Eastman Dental Hosp., and Hosp. for Sick Children, Gt Ormond St, 1952-54. Reader in Orthodontics, Univ. of London and Director and Head of Orthodontic Dept, Royal Dental Hosp. of London School of Dental Surgery, 1954-61. *Publications:* Orthodontic Notes, 1960; (ed) Current Orthodontics, 1966; contrib. to scientific journals. *Recreations:* gardening, farming. *Address:* Cantreyn, Bridgnorth, Salop.

**WALTON, Anthony Michael,** QC 1970; *b* 4 May 1925; *y s* of Henry Herbert Walton and Clara Martha Walton, Dulwich; *m* 1955, Jean Frederica, *o d* of William Montague Hey, Bedford; one *s*. *Educ:* Dulwich College (sometime Scholar); Hertford College, Oxford (sometime Scholar); pupil to W. L. Ferrar (maths) and C. H. S. Fifoot (law). BA 1946; BCL 1950; MA 1950. Pres., Oxford Union Society, Trinity Term 1945. Nat. Service as physicist. Called to the Bar, Middle Temple, 1950; pupil to Lord Justice Winn. Interested in education. Freeman, City of London, 1968. *Publications:* (ed) (Asst to Hon. H. Fletcher-Moulton) Digest of the Patent, Design, Trade Mark and Other Cases, 1959; (ed) Russell on Arbitration, 17th edn, 1963, 18th edn, 1970. *Address:* 62 Kingsmead Road, SW2.

**WALTON, Arthur Halsall,** FCA; Partner in Lysons, Haworth & Sankey since 1949; *b* 13 July 1916; *s* of Arthur Walton and Elizabeth Leeming (*née* Halsall); *m* 1958, Kathleen Elsie Abram; three *s*. *Educ:* The Leys School. Articled in Lysons & Talbot, 1934; ACA 1940. Military Service, 1939-48: commnd Lancs Fusiliers, 1940. Inst. of Chartered Accountants: Mem. Council 1959; Vice-Pres., 1969; Dep. Pres. 1970. *Recreation:* reading. *Address:* 17 Gorsey Road, Wilmslow, Cheshire SK9 5DU. *Club:* St James's (Manchester).

**WALTON, Ernest Thomas Sinton,** MA, MSc, PhD; Fellow of Trinity College, Dublin, 1934, Senior Fellow since 1960; Erasmus Smith's Professor of Natural and Experimental Philosophy since 1946; *b* 6 October 1903; *s* of Rev. J. A. Walton, MA; *m* 1934, Winifred Isabel Wilson; two *s* two *d*. *Educ:* Methodist College, Belfast; Trinity College, Dublin; Cambridge University. 1851 Overseas Research Scholarship, 1927-30; Senior Research Award of Dept of Scientific and Industrial Research, 1930-34; Clerk Maxwell Scholar, 1932-34; Awarded Hughes Medal by Royal Society, 1938. (With Sir John Cockcroft) Nobel prize for physics, 1951. Hon. DSc, Queen's Univ. of Belfast, 1959. *Publications:* Papers on hydrodynamics, nuclear physics and micro-waves. *Address:* Trinity College, Dublin; 26 St Kevin's Park, Dartry Road, Dublin 6. *T:* 971328.

**WALTON, Brig. Sir George (Hands),** KBE 1958 (CBE 1937); CB 1953; TD 1942; DL Co. Durham; JP Northumberland; Director: Morganite Resistors Ltd; Chairman: Newcastle Board, Commercial Union Assurance Co. Ltd; Industrial Management Research Association, 1954-63; Durham County T&AF Association, 1948-58; North Region Re-settlement Committee (Regular Services); *s* of James Walton, JP, North Shields; *m* Winifred, *d* of W. J. Arkle, Stocksfield; one *s* one *d*. Chartered Accountant; served European War, 1914-18; served in Territorial Army between wars and commanded 50th Divisional Signal Regiment, 1930-36. Colonel 1934; Deputy Chief Signal Officer, Northern Command, 1937-39. Served throughout War of 1939-45 as Chief Signal Officer, Northern Command, York; also 10th Corps and 13th Corps, and BTE; Brig. 1942 (despatches twice); 4 years Middle East Command; in 1943 seconded by Army to serve as a Director on Middle East Board of the United Kingdom Commercial Corporation, Ltd (British Government war organisation); 1945, released to return to civil occupation. Hon. Colonel 50th Divisional Signal Regt TA, 1953-58; Chm. Finance Cttee, Member, Corps Cttee, Royal Corps of Signals. OStJ. *Recreations:* shooting, hunting, golf, etc. *Address:* Letton Lodge, Alnmouth, Northumberland. *T:* 270. *Clubs:* Army and Navy; Union (Newcastle upon Tyne); County (Durham).

**WALTON, Col Granville,** CMG 1953; OBE 1919; late Royal Engineers; DL 1950; JP 1942, CC 1931; *b* 1888; *s* of late F. T. G. Walton, CIE, MInstCE, 34 St George's Ct, SW7; *m* 1924, Isabel Joan (MFH Old Berks Hunt 1939-42), *y d* of late Sir Robert McCraken, 23 Kensington Palace Gardens, W8; three *s*. *Educ:* Marlborough; RMA, Woolwich. 2nd Lieut RE 1907; NW State Railway of India, 1912-14 and 1920-28; retd as Asst Chief Operating Supt and Lt-Col, RE, 1928. RE Railway Troops in France and Greece, and on War Office Missions to Middle East, Russia and Rumania (despatches twice), 1914-20. Hon. Sec. World Scout Jamboree, 1929; Member Council Scouts Assoc. 1929-; HQ Commissioner Boy

Scouts Assoc., 1929-40; Group Comdr (Col) Berks HG, 1940-43. Re-employed War Office Directorate of Transportation, 1943-45; Overseas Comr, Boy Scouts Assoc., 1945-54. Chairman Faringdon RDC, 1948-50; High Sheriff of Berkshire, 1949; Transport Users Consultative Committee (SE Area), 1951-53; Member Thames Conservancy Board, 1951-57; Chairman, Faringdon Bench, 1951-57; CA 1949-63; Vice-Chairman Berkshire Standing Joint Cttee, 1955-63; Chairman County Council of Royal County of Berkshire, 1957-60; Chief Scout's Commissioner, 1954-59. Silver Wolf (British Scouting), 1929; Bronze Wolf (International Scouting), 1955. Officier L'Instruction Publique (France); St Anne and St Stanislas with swords (Russia); Commander Crown and Officer Star, with swords (Rumania). *Address:* Longworth Manor, near Abingdon, Berkshire. *T:* Longworth 223.

**WALTON, James Ratcliffe,** CBE 1943; *b* 12 July 1898; *m* 1925, Daisy Elizabeth Outram, Wanstead, Essex; no *c. Educ:* King Henry VIII, Coventry. Pupil with Alfred Herbert Ltd, Machine Tool Makers, Coventry; in India for same company, 1919-23; in 1924 joined staff of John Brown & Co. Ltd, Sheffield and Clydebank (now Thos Firth & John Brown Ltd, Sheffield) as Special Representative in India and the East; seconded to Govt of India as Controller of Steel Imports, 1940-46. *Recreation:* golf. *Address:* 4 Nelson House, Birkdale, Bexhill-on-Sea, Sussex. *T:* Cooden 3598. *Clubs'* Royal Bombay Yacht; Punjab, Lahore, etc.

**WALTON, John,** MA, ScD (Cantab); DSc (Manchester); Hon. LLD (McMaster University); Hon. DèsSc (Universities of Montpellier and Lille); FRSE; Regius Professor of Botany, University of Glasgow, 1930-62, retired; Dean of Faculties, University of Glasgow, 1967-70; *b* London, 1895; *s* of late E. A. Walton, PRSW, RSA; *m* Dorothy, *d* of late Sir Albert C. Seward, FRS; one *s* one *d*. *Educ:* Daniel Stewart's College, Edinburgh; St John's College, Cambridge (Hutchinson Research Student). Junior Demonstrator in Botany, Cambridge University, 1922-23; Lecturer in Botany, University of Manchester, 1923-30; Botanist to 1st Oxford Expedition to Spitsbergen, 1921; Forestry Commissioner, 1949-54; Member of Scottish Cttee, Nature Conservancy, 1949-54; Pres. Botanical Soc. of Edinburgh, 1962-64. Corresp. mem., Botanical Soc. of America, 1957-, and Geological Soc. of Belgium, 1963-; Foreign mem., Botanical Soc. of Poland, 1961. *Publications:* An Introduction to the Study of Fossil Plants and various on Palæobotany in the Trans. Royal Soc. London and Edinburgh and in Annals of Botany; Editor and part-author, four Scottish National Forest Park Guidebooks, since 1938. *Address:* 9 Windsor Street, Dundee, Angus. *T:* Dundee 68411.

**WALTON, Raymond Henry,** QC 1963; *b* 9 Sept. 1915; *e s* of Henry Herbert Walton and Clara Martha Walton, Dulwich; *m* 1940, Helen Alexandra, *e d* of Alexander Dingwall, Jedburgh; one *s* two *d. Educ:* Dulwich College; Balliol College, Oxford. Open Math. Schol., Balliol, 1933; BA 1937; MA 1942. Pres., Oxford Union Soc., Feb. 1938; BCL 1938. Called to Bar, 1939. War service in Anti-Aircraft Artillery (including Instructor in Gunnery and Experimental Officer), 1940-46. Contested (Lib) North Lambeth, 1945. Returned to practice at Bar, 1946-. Member, Lord Chancellor's Law Reform Cttee, 1959. Church Comr for England, 1969-. *Publications:* An introduction to the law of Sales of Land, 1949, 2nd edn 1957; (edited) Kerr on Receivers, 12th edn (with A. W. Sarson) and 13th edn; Adkin's Law of Landlord and Tenant, 13th, 14th and (with Michael Essayan) 15th and 16th edns. *Recreation:* philately. *Address:* 8 Ernle Road, SW20.

**WALTON, Sir Richmond,** KBE 1946; CB 1944; *b* 16 May 1888; *s* of late Rev. Octavius F. Walton; *m* 1912, Emily Gladys Dibben (*d* 1962); one *s* three *d. Educ:* Wolverhampton; Caius Coll., Cambridge (scholar). First Class Classical Tripos, 1910; entered Admiralty, 1911; Assistant Secretary, Admiralty, 1932; Principal Assistant Secretary, Admiralty, 1941; Under-Secretary, Admiralty, 1943; Deputy Secretary of the Admiralty, 1944-48. *Address:* North Lodge, Matfen, Northumberland.

**WALTON, Prof. William Stanley,** GM; MD, BHy; Emeritus Professor of Public Health, London School of Hygiene and Tropical Medicine, University of London; *b* 9 Nov. 1901; *s* of William and Mary Walton; *m* 1930, Anne Dorothy Margaret, *e d* of Edward Robson, Hexham. *Educ:* Gateshead Grammar Sch.; Univ. of Durham. MB, BS, Durham, 1925; BHy and DPH, 1927; MD (Commend.), 1932. Medical Officer of Health, West Bromwich; Dep. Medical Officer of Health for the City and Port of Plymouth; Dep. MOH, Middlesbrough; Medical Officer and School Medical Officer for the City of Newcastle upon Tyne, and Head of Department of Public Health, Durham University; also sometime External Examiner in Public Health to 12 British universities; Consultant to WHO; Fellow of the Society of Medical Officers of Health; Member of Council, RSH; Member Soc. Middle Temple. *Publications:* (joint) A Thousand Families in Newcastle upon Tyne, 1954; One Hundred Years in History of The Society of Medical Officers of Health, 1956; (joint) Growing up in Newcastle upon Tyne, 1960. *Address:* Kingstreet End, Little Missenden, Amersham, Bucks. *T:* Great Missenden 2857. *Club:* Athenæum.

**WALTON, Sir William (Turner),** OM 1967; Kt 1951; MusD; Composer; *b* 29 March 1902; *s* of Charles Alexander and Louisa Maria Walton; *m* 1949, Susana Gil Passo. *Educ:* Cathedral Choir School and Christ Church, Oxford. Hon. Student Christ Church, Oxford; Hon. MusD (Oxon, Dunelm, TCD, Manchester); Hon. DMus (Cantab, London); Hon. FRCM; Hon. FRAM; Gold Medal Royal Philharmonic Society, 1947; Gold Medal Worshipful Company of Musicians 1947. Mem. Royal Swedish Acad. of Music; Accademico onorario di Santa Cecilia, Rome. *Compositions:* Pianoforte Quartet (Carnegie award), 1918; String Quartet (unpublished), 1921; Façade (with Edith Sitwell), 1923 and 1926, Siesta for small orchestra, 1926; Portsmouth Point, 1926; Sinfonia Concertante for piano and orchestra, 1928; Viola Concerto, 1929; Belshazzar's Feast, 1931; Three Songs for Soprano, 1932; Symphony, 1935; Crown Imperial (Coronation March), 1937; In Honour of the City of London, 1937; Violin Concerto, 1939; Music for Children, 1940; Scapino (comedy overture), 1940; Quest (ballet), 1943; Henry V (film), 1945; Quartet, 1947; Hamlet (film), 1948; Sonata for Violin and Pianoforte, 1949; Te Deum, 1953; Orb and Sceptre (Coronation March), 1953; Troilus and Cressida (opera), 1954; Richard III (film), 1955; Johannesburg Overture, 1956; Violoncello Concerto, 1956; Partita, 1957; Anon in Love, 1960; Symphony No. 2, 1960; Gloria, 1961; A Song for the Lord Mayor's Table, 1962; Variations on a Theme by Hindemith, 1963; The Twelve (anthem), 1964; Missa Brevis, 1966; The Bear (comic opera) 1967; Capriccio Burlesco, 1968;

Improvisations on an Impromptu by Benjamin Britten, 1970. *Address:* c/o Oxford University Press, 44 Conduit Street, W1. *Clubs:* Savile, Garrick.

**WALWYN, Lady; (Eileen Mary),** DBE 1947; DStJ; *d* of late Maj.-Gen. T. van Straubenzee, CB, Spennithorne House, Leyburn, Yorks; *m* 1912, Vice-Adm. Sir Humphrey Walwyn, KCSI, KCMG, CB, DSO (*d* 1957), Governor and C-in-C of Newfoundland, 1936-46; one *s*. *Educ:* privately. *Address:* 42 Jubilee Place, SW3.

*See also Rear-Adm. J. H. Walwyn.*

**WALWYN, Rear-Adm. James Humphrey,** CB 1964; OBE 1944; Chief Executive, Personnel, The British Oxygen Co., since 1965; *b* 21 Aug. 1913; *o s* of late Vice-Admiral Sir Humphrey Walwyn, KCSI, KCMG, CB, DSO and of Lady Walwyn, *qv*; *m* 1945, Pamela Digby Bell; one *s* two *d*. *Educ:* The Old Malthouse and RN College, Dartmouth. Entered RN, 1931; Lieut 1935; ADC to Governor of Newfoundland, 1936-37; specialised in Gunnery, 1938; HMS Renown, 1939-41; HMS Newcastle, 1942-44; Staff of C-in-C Home Fleet, 1945-47; Comdr 1948; Naval Staff Course, 1948; Admiralty, 1948-50; Comdg HMS Chevron, 1951-52; Captain 1953; Staff of SHAPE, Paris, 1954-56; Captain Inshore Flotilla, Mediterranean, 1956-58; Dir, RN Tactical School, 1958-59; Dir of Officer Appts, Admiralty, 1960-62; Rear-Adm. 1962; Flag Officer Flotillas, Mediterranean, 1962-65; retired, 1965. Member: Inst. Business Management; Inst. Personnel Management. *Recreations:* fishing, tennis, riding, water-ski-ing. *Address:* 40 Jubilee Place, SW3. *T:* 01-352 7802. *Clubs:* United Service, Hurlingham.

**WALZER, Richard Rudolf,** MA (Oxford); Dr phil (Berlin); FBA; Reader in Arabic and Greek Philosophy, University of Oxford, 1960-70, now Emeritus; Fellow, St Catherine's College, Oxford, 1962-70, now Emeritus; *b* 14 July 1900; *s* of M. Walzer, Berlin; *m* Martha Sofie, *d* of Bruno Cassirer, Berlin. *Educ:* Werner Siemens Realgymnasium, Berlin-Schoeneberg; Univ. of Berlin. Asst, Berlin Univ., 1927; Privatdocent in Classics, 1932; Lectr in Greek Philosophy, Univ. of Rome, 1933-38; Lectr in Medieval Philosophy (Arabic and Hebrew), Univ. of Oxford, 1945; Senior Lectr in Arabic and Greek Philosophy, 1950. Hon. Prof., Univ. of Hamburg, 1952; Member Inst. for Advanced Study, Princeton, New Jersey, 1953-54; Corr. Mem., Academy of Science and Literature, Mainz, 1962. FBA 1956. *Publications:* Magna Moralia und Aristotelische Ethik, 1929; Aristotelis Dialogorum Fragmenta, 1934; Eraclito, 1939; (with F. Rosenthal) Plato Arabus II, 1943; Galen on Medical Experience, 1944; Galen on Jews and Christians, 1949; (with P. Kraus) Plato Arabus I, 1951; Greek into Arabic, 1961; articles on Greek and Arabic subjects in periodicals. *Address:* 2 Bladon Close, Oxford.

**WANAMAKER, Sam;** Actor; Director, Theatrical Producer; *b* Chicago, 14 June 1919; *s* of Morris Wanamaker and Molly (*née* Bobele); *m* 1940, Charlotte Holland; three *d*. *Educ:* Drake University, Iowa, USA. Studied for the stage at Goodman Theatre, Chicago. Appeared in summer theatres, Chicago (acting and directing), 1936-39; joined Globe Shakespearian Theatre Group; first New York Appearance, Café Crown, 1941; Counter Attack, 1942. Served in United States Armed Forces, 1943-46. In several parts on New York stage, 1946-49; appeared in This, Too, Shall Pass, 1946; directed and played in: Joan of Lorraine, 1946-47; Goodbye My Fancy, 1948-49; directed: Caeser and Cleopatra, 1950; The Soldier and the Lady, 1954; created Festival Repertory Theatre, New York, 1950. First performance (also producer) on London stage as Bernie Dodd, in Winter Journey, St James's, 1952; presented and appeared in The Shrike, Prince's, 1953; produced: Purple Dust, Glasgow, 1953; Foreign Field, Birmingham, 1954; directed and appeared in One More River, Cat on a Hot Tin Roof, and The Potting Shed, 1957. In Liverpool, 1957, created New Shakespeare Theatre Cultural Center, where produced (appearing in some): Tea and Sympathy, A View from the Bridge, 1957; The Rose Tattoo, Finian's Rainbow, Bus Stop, The Rainmaker, and Reclining Figure (all in 1958). Presented, prod and appeared in The Big Knife, Duke of York's, 1954; prod The World of Sholom Aleichem, Embassy, 1955; presented, prod and appeared in: The Lovers, Winter Garden, 1955; The Rainmaker, St Martin's 1956; A Hatful of Rain, Prince's, 1957; The Rose Tattoo, New, 1959. Played Iago, Stratford-on-Avon, 1959; Dr Breuer, in A Far Country, New York, 1961; prod King Priam, Coventry Theatre and Royal Opera House, Covent Garden, 1962; and again 1967; prod Verdi's La Forza del Destino, Royal Opera House, Covent Garden, 1962; directed: Children from their Games, New York, 1963; A Case of Libel, New York, 1963; A Murder Among Us, New York, 1964; Defenders, 1964; The File of the Golden Goose, 1968; The Executioner, 1969; acted and directed Macbeth, Goodman Theater, Chicago, 1964; acted (films): Give Us This Day; Taras Bulba; those Magnificent Men in Their Flying Machines, 1964; The Winston Affair, 1964; The Spy Who Came in from the Cold, 1964; Warning Shot; File of the Golden Goose; Kyle. Directs and acts in TV productions, in UK and USA. *Address:* Canada House, Norfolk Street, The Strand, WC2.

**WAND, Rt. Rev. and Rt. Hon. John William Charles,** PC, KCVO 1955; MA, Hon. DD Oxford and London; Canon and Treasurer of St Paul's 1956-69; Editor Church Quarterly Review 1956-69; Dean of the Chapels Royal, 1945-56; Chaplain and Sub-Prelate Order of St John of Jerusalem, 1936; Prelate Order of British Empire, 1946-57; Prelate Emeritus, 1957; STP (Columbia), 1947; STD (Tor.), 1947; DLitt (Ripon, USA), 1949; DD (W Ontario), 1957; *b* 25 Jan. 1885; *s* of Arthur James Henry Wand and Elizabeth Ann Ovelin Turner; *m* 1911, Amy Agnes Wiggins (*d* 1966); one *d*. *Educ:* King's Sch., Grantham; St Edmund Hall, Oxford; Bishop Jacob Hostel, Newcastle upon Tyne. BA (1st Class Theology), 1907; MA 1911; Curate of Benwell, 1908-11; Lanc., 1911-14; Vicar-Choral of Sarum, 1914-19; TCF, 1915-19; Hon. CF, 1919-22 and since 1925; Hon. Chaplain, Royal Naval Volunteer Reserve, 1947; Vicar of St Mark, Sarum, 1919-25; Chaplain RAF, 1922-25; Lectr, Sarum Theol. Coll., 1914-20; Tutor, 1920–24; Fellow, Dean and Tutor Oriel Coll. Oxford, 1925-34; Lectr in Theol. St Edmund Hall, Oxford, 1928-31; Select Preacher, Oxford, 1930-32; Univ. Lectr in Church History, 1931-34; Examiner, Hon. Sch. Theology, Oxford, 1932-34; Archbishop of Brisbane and Metropolitan of Queensland, 1934-43; Bishop of Bath and Wells, 1943-45; Bishop of London, 1945-55, retired 1955; Senior Chaplain (Anglican) 1st Military District, Australian Military Forces, 1935-43; Warburton Lectr, Lincoln's Inn, for 1956-58; Hon. Fellow, St Edmund Hall, Oxford, and Oriel Coll., Oxford; Hon. Fellow, King's Coll., London. *Publications:* The Golden String, 1926; Development of Sacramentalism, 1928; History of the Modern Church, 1930; The Old Faith and the New Age, 1933; Westminster

Commentary on I, II Peter and Jude, 1934; History of the Early Church, 1937; First Century Christianity (Moorhouse Lectures), 1937; New Testament Letters, 1944; God and Goodness, 1947; The Spirit of Church History, 1948; The Latin Doctors, 1948; The Authority of the Scriptures, 1949; White of Carpentaria, 1949; The Church, its Nature, Structure and Function, 1949; The Greek Doctors, 1950; The Four Councils, 1950; The High Church Schism, 1951; What the Church of England stands for, 1951; What St Paul said, 1952; The Second Reform, 1953; The Mystery of the Kingdom, 1953; The Life of Christ, 1954; The Four Heresies, 1955; The Road to Happiness, 1957; True Lights, 1958; The Church To-day, 1960; Anglicanism in History and Today, 1961; Atonement, 1962; Seven Words, Seven Virtues, 1962; St Augustine's City of God, 1963; Reflections on the Collects, 1964; The Temptation, 1964; Changeful Page (Autobiography), 1965; Reflections on the Epistles, 1966; Transfiguration, 1967; What St Paul Really Said, 1968; Reflections on the Gospels, 1969; (ed) The Anglican Communion, 1948; (jointly) Oxford and the Groups, 1934; (jointly) European Civilisation, 1937; (jointly) Union of Christendom, 1938. *Recreations:* reading and writing. *Address:* Maplehurst Cottage, Maplehurst, near Horsham, Sussex. *T:* Cowfold 228. *Clubs:* Athenæum; County (Bath).

*See also Viscount Addison.*

**WAND, Dr Solomon;** Treasurer of British Medical Association since 1963 (Chairman of Council, 1956-61); *b* 14 January 1899; *s* of Louis and Jane Wand; *m* 1st, 1921, Claire Cohen (*d* 1951); one *s* one *d*; 2nd, 1960, Shaunagh Denison Crew, *o d* of Major Robert Douglas Crew and Irene Crew, Milford-on-Sea, Hants. *Educ:* Manchester Grammar School; Manchester University. Qualified 1921, MB, ChB (Manchester), with distinction in medicine; in general practice in Birmingham. Member of: Council BMA, 1935- (Pres. Midland Branch, 1969-70); Gen. Medical Council, 1961-; Advertising Advisory Cttee of ITA, 1961-; Court of Governors, Univ. of Birmingham; Board, General Practice Finance Corporation; Chairman: Gen. Medical Services Cttee, BMA, 1948-52; Representative Body, BMA, 1951-54; Gold Medallist, BMA, 1954; formerly Member Central Health Services Council, Medical Advisory Cttee of Min. of Health; formerly Mem. Health Education Cttee. Hon. Vice-Pres. British Medical Students Assoc., 1959; Chm., British Medical Students Trust, 1968; Mem. Study Cttee of World Medical Assoc., 1959; Mem. Management Cttee, Medical Insurance Agency, 1964. Mem. Royal Coll. of General Practitioners. Hon. DCL, Durham, 1957; Hon. LLD Queen's Univ., Belfast, 1962. *Publications:* contribs to Encyclopædia of General Practice. *Address:* D 5 Kenilworth Court, Hagley Road, Edgbaston, Birmingham. *T:* 021-454 3997.

**WANGARATTA, Bishop of,** since 1969; **Rt. Rev. Keith Rayner;** *b* 22 Nov. 1929; *s* of Sydney and Gladys Rayner, Brisbane; *m* 1963, Audrey Fletcher; one *s* two *d*. *Educ:* C of E Grammar Sch., Brisbane; Univ. of Queensland. BA 1951; PhD 1964. Deacon, 1953; Priest, 1953. Chaplain, St Francis' Theol Coll., Brisbane, 1954; Mem., Brotherhood of St John, Dalby, 1955-58; Vice-Warden, St John's Coll., Brisbane, 1958; Rotary Foundn Fellow, Harvard Univ., 1958-59; Vicar, St Barnabas', Sunnybank, 1959-63; Rector, St Peter's, Wynnum, 1963-69. *Recreation:* tennis. *Address:* Bishop's Lodge, Wangaratta, Victoria 3677, Australia. *T:* 21-3643.

**WANSBROUGH, George,** MA; CompIEE; Director, Mercantile Credit Co. Ltd, since 1934; *b* Oxford, 23 April 1904; *s* of Rev. H. A. Wansbrough, Rector of South Warnborough, and of Uliana, *d* of Bishop Tufnell; *m* 1st, 1928, Elizabeth (who obtained a divorce, 1938), *d* of Sir George Lewis, 2nd Bt; one *s* one *d*; 2nd, 1939, Kathleen Barbara Rawdon (marriage dissolved, 1955), *d* of C. G. H. R. Macnamara, Indian Civil Service; one *s*; 3rd, 1955, Nancy, *d* of F. D. H. Joy, of Marelands, Bentley, Hampshire. *Educ:* Cheam School; Eton (King's Scholar, Capt. of the School); King's College, Cambridge (Minor Scholar). Class I Mathematical Tripos Part I, 1924; Class II Div. I Economics Tripos Part II, 1926; Second Winchester Reading Prize, 1926; stroked Cambridge VIII, 1925; with Selfridge & Co. Ltd, intermittently, 1923-27; played rôle of The Poet in Anmer Hall's production of Sierra's Cradle Song, Little Theatre and Fortune Theatre, 1926-27; Robert Benson & Co. Ltd, Merchant Bankers, 1927-35, Dir, 1932-35; Sec., Anglo-French Timber Production Cttee, 1939-40; Member of Pottery Working Party, 1946; Cttee of Inquiry into Tudor Aircraft, 1947; Cttee to advise Govt on methods of purchase of aircraft for airways corporations, 1948; Dir A. Reyrolle & Co. Ltd, 1934-49, Chm. 1945-59; Dir, Bank of England, 1946-49; Chm., Morphy-Richards Ltd, 1943-54; Member of: National Advisory Council for Motor Manufacturing Industry, 1946-49; Development Areas Treasury Advisory Cttee, 1945-49; Mem. of Public Works Loan Bd; Mem. of Council, Institution of Electrical Engineers, 1946-49; Mem. of St Marylebone Borough Council, 1934-37; Holborn Borough Council, 1937-38. Financial Adviser to New Philharmonia Orchestra, 1968-69. Joint Treas. Fabian Soc., 1936-37; contested (Lab) West Woolwich, 1935. Mem. Governing Body, Bedales Sch., 1965-. MSAE 1967. *Publications:* various articles, reviews, etc., signed and unsigned in The Times, Economist, Economic Journal, motoring and yachting press, etc. *Recreations:* yachting, music. *Address:* Hinton House, King's Worthy, Winchester. *T:* Winchester 2932. *Clubs:* Hampshire (Winchester); Royal Thames Yacht; Leander.

**WANSBROUGH-JONES, Maj.-Gen. Llewelyn,** CB 1946; CVO 1966; CBE 1944; MInstT; General Manager, National Association for Employment of Regular Sailors, Soldiers and Airmen, since October 1965; *b* 2 July 1900; 2nd *s* of late A. Wansbrough-Jones, BA, LLB, Long Stratton, Norfolk; *m* 1939, Laura Skelton, *d* of late J. J. Prest, JP, Hardwick Hall, Castle Eden, Co. Durham; one *s*. *Educ:* Malvern College; RMA, Woolwich. 2nd Lieut Royal Engineers, 1920; served in England, 1920-27; Singapore, 1927-30; Nigerian Survey, 1930-31; Johore Colonial Survey, 1932-33; India, QVO Madras Sappers and Miners, 1934-40 (Waziristan Campaign, 1936-38); War Office, 1940-42; British Joint Staff Mission, Washington, 1942-43; War Office, 1943-44; DQMG (Movements and Transportation) 21 Army Group, 1944-46; DQMG BAOR, 1946-47 (despatches thrice); Dir of Administrative Planning, WO, 1947-48; Chief Admin Officer and Chief of Staff CCG, 1948-51; Chief of Staff, Western Command, 1951-52; Principal Staff Officer to Deputy Supreme Allied Comdr, SHAPE, 1952-54; Maj.-Gen., 1949. Sec.-Gen. to British Transport Commn, May 1955-Dec. 1962, Sec. to British Railways Bd, 1963-65. US Legion of Merit (Officer) and Bronze Star; Croix de Guerre (France). *Recreations:* sailing, shooting, ski-ing. *Address:* Goat Hall, Galleywood, Chelmsford, Essex. *T:* Chelmsford 52809. *Club:* United Service.

**WANSBROUGH-JONES, Sir Owen (Haddon),** KBE 1955 (OBE 1946; MBE 1942); CB 1950; MA, PhD (Cantab); FRIC; Chairman, Albright & Wilson Ltd, 1967-69 (Executive Vice-Chairman, 1965-67); Director, British Oxygen Co. Ltd, since 1960; *b* 25 March 1905; *y s* of late Arthur Wansbrough-Jones, BA, LLB, Long Stratton, Norfolk, and Beatrice, *d* of late Thomas Slipper, JP, Bradeston Hall, Norfolk; unmarried. *Educ:* Gresham's School, Holt; Trinity Hall, Cambridge (Open Schol.). 1st Cl., Natural Sciences Tripos Part I and Part II (Chemistry); Research Student of Trinity Hall, and of Goldsmiths' & Salters' Company; Ramsay Memorial Fellow; studied Physical Chemistry at Cambridge under Prof. Sir Eric Rideal, and in Berlin under Professor Fritz Haber; Fellow of Trinity Hall, 1930-46; Assistant Tutor, 1932-34; Tutor, 1934-40; Hon. Fellow, 1957; Departmental Demonstrator, Dept of Colloid Science, University of Cambridge, 1932-40; Emergency Commission, 1940; France, 1940; Brig. 1945; Dir of Special Weapons and Vehicles, War Office, 1946; Scientific Adviser to Army Council, 1946-51; Principal Dir of Scientific Research (Defence) Min. of Supply, 1951-53; Chief Scientist of Min. of Supply, 1953-59. Mem., Natural Environment Research Council, 1968-. Treasurer of Faraday Soc., 1949-60; Pres., Jesters Club, 1958-. Prime Warden, Goldsmiths' Company, 1967. *Publications:* scientific papers on physical chemistry in British and German scientific journals, 1929-38. *Recreations:* gardening, shooting. *Address:* 7 King Street, St James's, SW1; The Guild House, Long Stratton, Norfolk NOR 72W. *T:* Long Stratton 410. *T:* 01-930 8608. *Club:* Oxford and Cambridge University.

**WARBEY, William Noble;** Executive Director, Organisation for World Political and Social Studies, since 1965; Secretary, World Studies Trust, since 1966; Chairman, Rossetti House Group, since 1968; *b* 16 August 1903; *s* of Charles Noble Warbey and Alice May Symons; *m* 1931, Audrey Grace Wicks; no *c*. *Educ:* Grocers' Company's School, Hackney Downs; King's College, London; London School of Economics. Language Teacher and Interpreter, France and Germany, 1925-26; Secondary School Master, Derby Municipal Secondary School, 1927-28; Secretary and Tutor, University Tutorial College, London, 1929-37; Tutor-Organiser, National Council of Labour Colls, 1937-40; Chief English Press Officer to Norwegian Govt (London), 1941-45. MP (Lab) for Luton Div. of Beds, 1945-50; Broxtowe Div. of Notts (Sept.), 1953-55; Ashfield Div. of Notts, 1955-66, resigned. Travel organiser, 1950-51; Editor of Look and Listen, 1952-55. *Publications:* Look to Norway, 1945; (jt) Modern Norway, 1950; Vietnam: The Truth, 1965; Ho Chi Minh: Life and Achievements, 1970. *Recreations:* music, travel, organic horticulture. *Address:* c/o Merlin Press, 11 Fitzroy Square, W1.

**WARBURG, Fredric John;** Chairman, Secker and Warburg Ltd, Publishers, since 1936; *b* 27 Nov. 1898; *s* of late John Cimon Warburg and Violet Amalia Warburg; *m*; three *s*; *m* 1933, Pamela de Bayou; (one *s* decd). *Educ:* Westminster School; Christ Church, Oxford (Exhibnr). 2nd Cl. Lit. Hum. (Greats); MA 1922. Served as 2nd Lieut with 184th Siege Battery, Belgium and France, 1917-19. Joined George Routledge & Sons Ltd as apprentice, 1922; Joint Man. Dir, 1931; resigned, 1935. Bought publishing firm Martin Secker, Ltd, 1936; name changed to Martin Secker & Warburg, 1936, with himself as Chairman. Served as Corporal in St John's Wood Co., Home Guard under Sergeant George Orwell (Eric Blair), 1941-45. Joined Heinemann Group of Publishers, 1951. Tried at Central Criminal Court (Old Bailey) for publishing an allegedly obscene novel, and acquitted, 1954. Elected Director of Heinemann Group of Publishers, 1961. *Publications:* An Occupation for Gentlemen, 1959; A Slight Case of Obscenity (9000 words) in New Yorker Magazine, 20 April 1957. *Recreations:* replaying chess games of the masters, window box gardening, reading, writing when time available. *Address:* 29 St Edmund's Court, Regent's Park, NW8. *T:* 01-722 5641.

**WARBURG, Sir Siegmund G(eorge),** Kt 1966; President, S. G. Warburg & Co. Ltd, London, since 1970 (Director, 1946-69); *b* 30 Sept. 1902; *s* of George S. Warburg and Lucie (*née* Kaulla); *m* 1926, Eva Maria Philipson; one *s* one *d*. *Educ:* Gymnasium, Reutlingen, Germany; Humanistic Seminary, Urach, Germany, 1920-30; training periods in Hamburg, London, Boston and new York; Partner M. M. Warburg & Co., Hamburg, 1930-38; Director, New Trading Co. Ltd, London, 1938-46. *Recreations:* reading and walking. *Address:* 95 Eaton Square, SW1. *T:* 01-235 4198.

**WARBURTON, Col Alfred Arthur,** CBE 1961; DSO 1945; DL; JP; Chairman, SHEF Engineering Ltd, since 1970; Company Director since 1953; *b* 12 April 1913; *s* of late A. V. Warburton. *Educ:* Sedbergh. Served War of 1939-45, with Essex Yeomanry; Lt-Col comdg South Notts Hussars Yeomanry, 1953-58; Hon. Col 1966; Col DCRA 49th Inf. Div. TA, 1958-60; ADC to the Queen, 1961-66; Chm., Notts Cttee TA&VR Assoc. for E. Midlands. Director, John Shaw Ltd, Worksop, 1953-66. DL 1966, High Sheriff 1968, JP 1968, Notts. *Recreations:* shooting, fishing. *Address:* Wigthorpe House, near Worksop, Notts. *T:* North Carlton 357. *Clubs:* Cavalry; Nottinghamshire County (Nottingham).

**WARBURTON, Eric John Newnham,** CBE 1966; a Vice-Chairman, Lloyds Bank Ltd, since 1967 (Director since 1965); Deputy Chairman, Bank of London & South America Ltd, since 1968 (Director since 1965); Director: Lloyds Bank Europe Ltd, since 1962; Lloyds Bank Unit Trust Managers Ltd, since 1966; *b* 22 Nov. 1904; *o s* of late E. and H. R. Warburton, Bexhill-on-Sea, Sussex; *m* 1933, Louise, *er d* of late C. J. and L. R. Martin, Crowborough, Sussex; one *s* one *d*. *Educ:* Eastbourne Grammar School. Entered Lloyds Bank Ltd, 1922; Jt General Man., 1953; Dep. Chief Gen. Man., 1958; Chief Gen. Man., 1959-66. Director: Lewis's Bank Ltd, 1967-; Bowmaker Ltd, 1967-70; Intercontinental Banking Services Ltd, 1968-; Chairman: Exec. Cttee, Banking Information Service, 1965-; Bank Education Service, 1966-; Dep. Chairman: City of London Savings Cttee, 1962-; Exports Credit Guarantee Dept Adv. Council, 1968- (Member, 1966-); Member: Decimal Currency Bd, 1967-; Nat. Savings Cttee, 1963-; Member Board: Trinity Coll. of Music, 1968-; Management, East Sussex Housing Assoc. for the Aged, 1970-; American Bankers Assoc. Internat. Banking Conf., 1970-. FRSA 1970; Hon. FTCL 1969. *Recreations:* golf, gardening, music. *Address:* Hurstmead, 22 Lewes Road, Haywards Heath, Sussex. *T:* Haywards Heath 51168. *Club:* Bath.

**WARBURTON, Prof. Geoffrey Barratt;** Professor of Applied Mechanics, University of Nottingham, since 1961; *b* 9 June 1924; *s* of Ernest McPherson and Beatrice Warburton; *m* 1952, Margaret Coan; three *d*. *Educ:* William Hulme's Grammar School, Manchester; Peterhouse, Cambridge. Cambridge: Open Exhibition in Mathematics, 1942; 1st cl. Hons in Mechanical Sciences Tripos, 1944; BA 1945; MA 1949; Junior Demonstrator, 1944-46. Asst Lecturer in Engineering, Univ. Coll. of Swansea, 1946-47; Dept of Engineering, Univ. of Edinburgh; Assistant, 1947-48, Lecturer, 1948-50 and 1953-56; ICI Research Fellow, 1950-53; Head of Post-graduate School of Applied Dynamics, 1956-61; PhD (Edinburgh) 1949. FRSE 1960; FIMechE 1968. *Publications:* The Dynamical Behaviour of Structures, 1964; research on mechanical vibrations, in several scientific journals. *Address:* University of Nottingham, Nottingham.

**WARD,** family name of **Earl of Dudley,** and of **Viscounts Bangor** and **Ward of Witley.**

**WARD OF WITLEY,** 1st Viscount, *cr* 1960; **George Reginald Ward,** PC 1957; *b* 20 Nov. 1907; 4th *s* (twin) of 2nd Earl of Dudley; *m* 1st, 1940, Anne Capel (marr. diss., 1951); one *s* one *d*; 2nd, 1962, Hon. Mrs Barbara Astor (who *m* 1st, 1942. Hon. Michael Langhorne Astor, *qv*). *Educ:* Eton; Christ Church, Oxford. AAF, 1929; RAF, 1932-37 and 1939-45. MP (C) for Worcester City, 1945-60. Parly Under-Sec. of State, Air Min., 1952-55; Parly and Financial Sec., Admiralty, Dec. 1955-Jan. 1957; Secretary of State for Air, 1957-60. *Heir:* *s* Hon. Anthony Giles Humble Ward, *b* 10 June 1943. *Address:* 25 Chelsea Square, SW3. *Clubs:* White's, Pratt's.

**WARD, Prof. Alan Gordon,** OBE 1959; Procter Professor of Food and Leather Science, Leeds University, since 1961; *b* 18 April 1914; *s* of Lionel Howell Ward and Lily Maud Ward (*née* Morgan); *m* 1938, Cicely Jean Chapman; one *s* two *d*. *Educ:* Queen Elizabeth's Grammar Sch., Wimborne; Trinity Coll., Cambridge (schol.). BA (Cantab) 1935; MA (Cantab) 1940; FInstP 1946; FIFST 1966. Lectr in Physics and Mathematics, N Staffs Technical Coll., 1937-40; Experimental Officer, Min. of Supply, 1940-46; Sen. Scientific Officer, Building Research Station, 1946-48; Principal Scientific Officer, 1948-49; Dir of Research, The British Gelatine and Glue Research Assoc., 1949-59; Prof. of Leather Industries, Leeds Univ., 1959-61. Chm., Food Standards Cttee set up by Minister of Agriculture, 1965-. *Publications:* Nature of Crystals, 1938; Colloids, Their Properties and Applications, 1945; papers in Trans. Far. Soc., Jl Sci. Instr, Biochem. JL, etc. *Recreation:* music. *Address:* Oaklea, 8 Thornfield Road, West Park, Leeds LS16 5AR. *T:* Leeds 52025.

**WARD, Ven. Arthur Frederick,** BA; Archdeacon of Exeter and a Canon Residentiary of Exeter Cathedral since 1970; *b* 23 April 1912; *s* of William Thomas and Annie Florence Ward, Corbridge, Northumberland; *m* 1937, Margaret Melrose, Tynemouth, Northumberland; two *d*. *Educ:* Durham Choir School; Newcastle upon Tyne Royal Grammar School; Durham University; Ridley Hall, Cambridge. Curate, Byker Parish Church, Newcastle, 1935-40; Rector of Harpurhey, North Manchester, 1940-44; Vicar of Nelson, 1944-55; Vicar of Christ Church, Paignton, 1955-62; Archdeacon of Barnstaple and Rector of Shirwell with Loxhore, Devon, 1962-70. *Recreations:* gardening, cricket, touring. *Address:* 12 The Close, Exeter EX1 1EZ. *T:* Exeter 75745.

**WARD, Sir Aubrey (Ernest),** Kt 1967; DL, JP; Chairman, Buckinghamshire County Council, since 1963; *b* 17 April 1899; *s* of Edward Alfred Ward; *m* 1919, Mary Jane Davidson Rutherford, MB, ChB; one *d*. *Educ:* Royal Veterinary College, London. Veterinary Practice, 1923-66. JP Bucks, 1957; DL Bucks, 1963. *Address:* 54 Pound Lane, Marlow, Bucks. *T:* Marlow 5250.

**WARD, Barbara;** *see* Jackson, Lady (Robert).

**WARD, Basil Robert,** FRIBA; Hon. FRCA; first Lethaby Professor of Architecture, Royal College of Art, 1950-53; in private practice, The Basil Ward Partnership; Visiting Lecturer, University of Lancaster; Lieutenant-Commander, RNVR (Special Branch), retired; *b* Wellington, New Zealand, 1902; 2nd *s* of late Louis Ernest Ward, Civil Servant New Zealand Government and Secretary Geographic Board, and Theresa Kilgour; *m* 1930, Beatrix Douglas, *d* of late Nigel Douglas Connell, Taranaki, New Zealand; two *d*. *Educ:* Napier Boys High School, New Zealand. Served as architect's pupil; studied London University Atelier of Architecture; studied and travelled extensively abroad, 1924-28; worked way round Cape Horn; Henry Jarvis Studentship (2nd prize Rome Scholarship), 1927; studied at British School at Rome, and was employed in carrying out works for Government of Burma, 1928-31; from 1931 until outbreak of war, 1939, in practice in London in firm of Connell & Ward, and Connell, Ward & Lucas; principally concerned with modern forms of planning and construction. Recent and current practice includes: High Altitude Test Facilities bldgs for Rolls Royce; Plan for new science area, Oxford Univ.; numerous laboratories for Oxford Univ.; Electrostatic generator bldg for Cambridge Univ.; HQ Offices for Provincial Insurance Co. Ltd, Kendal; premises for Soc. for Chemical Industries, London; Linear Accelerator, Cyclotron and Radiobiology bldg, Hammersmith, for MRC; Inst. of Experimental Surgery, laboratories and offices, Hammersmith, for Postgrad. Medical Sch., London Univ.; Metabolic Ward, Refectory, laboratories for Hammersmith Hosp.; extensions and alterations for various depts of Royal Coll. of Art, Kensington; cricket pavilion for E Molesey Cricket Club; Lakeland Theatre Project. *Publications:* contrib. Architectural Jls. *Relevant publications:* Bibliog. in Sources of Modern Architecture, 1967; Planning and Architecture, 1967. *Recreations:* food and travel. *Address:* Beachwood House, Arnside via Carnforth, Lancs. *T:* Arnside 218; The Basil Ward Partnership, Martins Bank Chambers, Windermere, Westmorland. *T:* Windermere 2224; Lancaster University, Bailrigg, Lancaster. *T:* Lancaster 65201.

**WARD, Christopher John Ferguson;** *b* 26 Dec. 1942; *m* Elizabeth Ward; two *s* one *d*. *Educ:* Magdalen College Sch.; Law Society Sch. of Law. Solicitor, Reading, 1965-. MP (C) Swindon, Oct. 1969-June 1970. Member: Berks CC, 1965-; Standing Conf. on London and SE Regional Planning; Mem., Young Conservatives, 1958- (former Chm., Young Cons Western Adv. Cttee). Governor, E Berks Coll. of Further Educn. *Address:* 2 Pinkneys Road, Maidenhead, Berks. *T:* Maidenhead 24819.

**WARD, David;** Opera Singer; *b* 3 July 1922; *s* of James Ward and Catherine Bell; *m* 1960, Susan E. V. Rutherford; no *c*. *Educ:* St Patrick's School, Dumbarton; Royal College of Music. Royal Navy, 1940-43; Royal Indian Navy, 1943-46. Sadler's Wells, 1953-59; Covent Garden, 1960-64; now international free-lance singer, Germany, USA, Italy, France, etc. *Recreation:* golf. *Address:* 14 Clarence Terrace, Regent's Park, NW1.

**WARD, Denzil Anthony Seaver,** CMG 1967; Counsel to the Law Drafting Office and

Compiler of Statutes, New Zealand, since 1966; *b* Nelson, NZ, 26 March 1909; 3rd *s* of late Louis Ernest Ward, Civil Servant NZ Government and Secretary Geographic Board, and Theresa Ward (*née* Kilgour); *m* 1938, Mary Iredale Garland, *d* of late John Edwin Garland, Christchurch, NZ; three *d. Educ:* Christ's College and Cathedral Grammar Sch., Christchurch, NZ; Victoria Univ. of Wellington, NZ. BA 1928; LLB 1938; practised law as barrister and solicitor, 1938-42; Asst Law Draftsman, Law Drafting Office, 1942; First Asst, 1947; Law Draftsman, 1958-66. Lecturer in law subjects, Victoria Univ. of Wellington, NZ, 1944-45, 1949-55. Member: NZ Law Revision Commn, 1958-; Public and Administrative Law Reform Cttee, 1966-; Vice-Patron, Legal Research Foundation, 1965-68. Mem. Otaki and Porirua Trusts Bd, 1952-, Chm., 1965-; Mem. Papawai and Kaikokirikiri Trusts Bd, 1965-, Dep. Chm., 1967-. Foundation mem. and mem. Council, NZ Founders Soc., 1939-42; elected hon. life mem., 1941. Chm., Royal Wellington Choral Union, 1949-50; mem. Schola Cantorum, 1951-55. *Publications:* (jointly) Ward and Wild's Mercantile Law in New Zealand, 1947; (ed) NZ Statutes Reprint, 1908-57, vols 3-16; articles in legal periodicals. *Recreations:* music, reading, gardening, watching rugby and cricket. *Address:* 15 Plymouth Street, Karori, Wellington 5, New Zealand. *T:* 768-096.

**WARD, General Sir Dudley,** GCB 1959 (KCB 1957; CB 1945); KBE 1953 (CBE 1945); DSO 1944; DL; *b* 27 Jan. 1905; *s* of L. H. Ward, Wimborne, Dorset; *m* 1st, 1933, Beatrice Constance (*d* 1962), *d* of Rev. T. F. Griffith, The Bourne, Farnham, Surrey; one *d*; 2nd, 1963, Joan Elspeth de Pechell, *d* of Colonel D. C. Scott, CBE, Primrose Cottage, Netherbury, Dorset. *Educ:* Wimborne Grammar Sch.; Royal Military Coll., Sandhurst. 2nd Lieut, Dorset Regt, 1929; Captain, The King's Regt, 1937. Served War of 1939-45 (DSO, CBE, CB); Director of Military Operations, War Office, 1947-48; Commandant, Staff Coll., Camberley, 1948-51; Commander of the 1st Corps, 1951-52; Deputy Chief of Imperial General Staff, 1953-56; Commander, Northern Army Group and Commander-in-Chief, British Army of the Rhine, 1957-Dec. 1959; Comdr in Chief, British Forces, Near East, 1960-62; Governor and Commander in Chief of Gibraltar, 1962-65. Colonel, King's Regt, 1947-57; Colonel Commandant, REME, 1958-63; ADC General to the Queen, 1959-61. DL Suffolk, 1968. *Recreations:* sailing, golf. *Address:* Wynney's Farmhouse, Dennington, Woodbridge, Suffolk. *T:* Badingham 663. *Club:* United Service.

**WARD, Edward;** *see* Bangor, 7th Viscount.

**WARD, Edward Rex,** CMG 1948; *b* 19 May 1902; *y s* of late Daniel Ward, FSI, Tavistock; *m* 1st, 1934, Mary Neil (from whom he obtained a divorce, 1941); 2nd, 1947, Molly Owen Jones (*née* Money), *widow* of Flying Officer Owen Jones, RAF; one *s* two step *d. Educ:* King's Coll., Taunton; Coll. of Estate Management, Lincoln's Inn Fields, WC1. Colonial Administrative Service, Nigeria, 1926; transferred to The Gambia, 1942; Actg Governor on several occasions since 1945; Colonial Secretary, The Gambia, 1945-52; retired, 1952. *Recreation:* gardening. *Address:* Moorings, Lane End, Bembridge, Isle of Wight. *T:* Bembridge 2438.

**WARD, Ven. Edwin James Greenfield,** MVO 1963; Archdeacon of Sherborne since 1967; Rector of West Stafford since 1967; *b* 26 Oct. 1919; *er s* of Canon F. G. Ward, MC, lately of Canberra, Australia; *m* 1946, Grizell Evelyn Buxton; one *s* two *d. Educ:* St John's, Leatherhead; Christ's Coll., Cambridge (MA). Served King's Dragoon Guards, 1940; Reserve, 1946. Ordained 1948; Vicar of North Elmham, Norfolk, 1950-55; Chaplain to the Queen, 1955; Chaplain, Royal Chapel, Windsor Great Park, 1955-67. *Recreations:* shooting, fishing, golf. *Address:* The Rectory, West Stafford, Dorchester, Dorset. *T:* Dorchester 4637. *Club:* Norfolk (Norwich).

**WARD, Air Cdre Ellacott Lyne Stephens,** CB 1954; DFC 1939; RAF, retired; *b* 22 Aug. 1905; *s* of late Lt-Col E. L. Ward, CBE, IMS; *m* 1929, Sylvia Winifred Constance (*née* Etheridge), *d* of late Lt-Col F. Etheridge, DSO, IA, and late Mrs Etheridge; one *s* one *d. Educ:* Bradfield; Cranwell. No. 20 Sqdn, India, 1926-30; Engineering Course, and Engineering duties, UK, 1930-34; student, Army Staff Coll., Quetta, 1936-37; comd No. 28 Sqdn, RAF, 1938-39; MAP, 1940-42; Instructor, RAF Staff Coll., 1942-43; Bomber Comd, 1943-44; Dep. Head, RAF Mission to Chinese Air Force Staff Coll., Chengtu, China, 1945-46; SASO, Burma, 1946-47; Air Ministry, 1947-49; Flying Training Comd, 1949-52; Head of British Services Mission to Burma, 1952-54; AOC No. 64 (N) Group, Royal Air Force, 1954-57. Chinese Cloud and Banner, 1946; Chinese Chenyuan, 1946. *Recreation:* bookbinding. *Address:* Carousel, 37 Brownsea Road, Sandbanks, Poole, Dorset. *T:* Canford Cliffs 79455.

**WARD, Erskine Rueul La Tourette;** Chief Justice, British Honduras, 1954-57; retired; *b* Barbados, 3 Jan. 1900; 3rd *s* of Edmund L. Ward, Planter; *m* 1922, Madeleine Dunn; one *s*; *m* 1947, Winifred Phillips. *Educ:* Harrison Coll., Barbados; St Edmund Hall, Oxford; Middle Temple. Barrister-at-Law, 1924; Member House of Assembly, Barbados, 1929-31; Sub-Editor, Advocate Newspaper, 1925-30; Magistrate, Barbados, 1931-36; Judge Petty Debt Court, 1936; Registrar, 1939; Judge Assistant, Court of Appeal, 1944; Puisne Judge, British Guiana, 1949; Puisne Judge, Trinidad, 1952. King George V Jubilee Medal, 1935; Coronation Medal, 1937; Coronation Medal, 1953. *Recreations:* cricket, gardening. *Clubs:* West Indian; Corona, Georgetown Cricket (British Guiana); Queen's Park Cricket (Trinidad).

**WARD, Francis Alan Burnett,** CBE 1964; PhD; Keeper, Department of Physics, Science Museum, London, SW7, 1945-March 1970; *b* 5 March 1905; *o s* of late Herbert Ward, CBE, and late Eva Caroline (*née* Burnett); *m* 1953, E. Marianne Brown, Ilkley. *Educ:* Highgate Sch.; Sidney Sussex Coll., Cambridge. MA, PhD (Cantab), 1931. Research on atomic physics at Cavendish Laboratory, Cambridge, 1927-31; Asst Keeper, The Science Museum, 1931; seconded to Air Ministry (Meteorological Office), 1939. Flt-Lieut, RAFVR (Meteorological Branch), 1943-45. In charge of Atomic Physics and Time Measurement sections, Science Museum, 1931-70. FBHI; FInstP; FMA. *Publications:* official Science Museum Handbooks on Time Measurement, 1936 and 1937, and later edns. Various papers on atomic physics in Proc. Royal Society and Proc. Physical Soc. *Recreations:* bird-watching, gardening, photography, music. *Address:* Wendover, 8 Parkgate Avenue, Hadley Wood, Barnet, Herts. *T:* 01-449 6880.

**WARD, Frederick John;** Under-Secretary, Ministry of Housing and Local Government, since 1968. *Address:* 29 Groveside, Great Bookham, Leatherhead, Surrey. *T:* Bookham 2282. *Club:* MCC.

**WARD, Hubert;** Headmaster of the King's School, Ely, since 1970; *b* 26 Sept. 1931; *s* of Allan Miles Ward and Joan Mary Ward; *m* 1958, Elizabeth Cynthia Fearn Bechervaise; one *s* two *d*. *Educ:* Westminster Sch.; Trinity Coll., Cambridge. Asst Master (Maths), Geelong C of E Grammar Sch., Victoria, 1955-66; Asst Master (Maths), Westminster Sch., London, 1966-69. *Publication:* (with K. Lewis) Starting Statistics, 1969. *Recreations:* rowing, sailing, bird-watching. *Address:* The King's School, Ely, Cambridgeshire. *T:* Ely 2824.

**WARD, Dame Irene (Mary Bewick),** DBE 1955 (CBE 1929); MP (C) Tynemouth, since 1950; JP; *d* of late Alfred Ward, London, and late Elvina Mary Ward. MP (C) Wallsend-on-Tyne, 1931-45; contested (C) Morpeth, 1924 and 1929, Wallsend, 1945. *Publication:* FANY Invicta, 1955. *Address:* 4 Roseworth Terrace, Gosforth, Newcastle upon Tyne 3. *T:* 51863.

**WARD, Rt. Rev. James;** Bishop-Auxiliary of Glasgow, (RC), since 1960; Vicar General of Glasgow; Protonotary Apostolic; *b* Dumbarton, 4 Sept. 1905; *s* of James Ward and Catherine (*née* Bell). *Educ:* St Aloysius' Coll., Glasgow; St Peter's Coll., Bearsden, Glasgow. Ordained 1929; Secretary, Archdiocese of Glasgow, 1929; Chancellor, Archdiocese of Glasgow, 1947; Vicar General, Archdiocese of Glasgow, Diocesan Treasurer and Member of Diocesan Curia, 1948; Titular Bishop of Sita, 1960; Vicar Capitular, 1963. *Address:* Holy Cross, 113 Dixon Avenue, Glasgow, S2. *T:* 041-423 0105.

**WARD, Prof. John Clive,** FRS 1965; Professor, Macquarie University, Sydney, NSW, since 1967; *b* 1 Aug. 1924; *s* of Joseph William Ward and Winifred Palmer. *Educ:* Bishops Stortford Coll.; Merton Coll., Oxford. Member, Inst. for Advanced Study, Princeton, 1951-52, 1955-56, 1960-61; Professor of Physics, Carnegie Inst. of Technology, Pittsburgh, 1959-60; The Johns Hopkins University, Baltimore, 1961-66. *Publications:* various articles on particle theory and statistical mechanics. *Recreations:* ski-ing, music. *Address:* School of Mathematics and Physics, Macquarie University, 171-7 Epping Road, Eastwood, NSW, Australia; 16 Fern Street, Pymble, NSW.

**WARD, Sir John (Guthrie),** GCMG 1967 (KCMG 1956; CMG 1947); *b* 3 March 1909; *o s* of late Herbert John Ward and Alice Ward (*née* Guthrie); *m* 1st, 1933, Bettine (*d* 1941), *d* of late Col Sydney Hankey; one *s* one *d*; 2nd, 1942, Daphne, *d* of late Captain Hon. A. S. E. Mulholland; two *d*. *Educ:* Wellington Coll.; Pembroke Coll., Cambridge (History Schol.). BA 1929; Member of University Air Squadron. Entered Diplomatic Service, 1931; served Foreign Office and British Embassies, Baghdad (1932-34) and Cairo (1938-40); British Representative on League of Nations Cttee for settlement of Assyrians, 1935-37. Second Sec., 1936; First Sec., 1941; Mem. of UK Delegns to Moscow confs, 1943-44-45 and Potsdam conf., 1945; Counsellor and Head of UN Dept, Foreign Office, 1946; Counsellor, British Embassy, Rome, 1946-49; Civilian Member of Directing Staff of Imperial Defence Coll., London, 1950; Dep. UK High Comr in Germany, 1951-54; Dep. Under-Sec. of State, Foreign Office, 1954-56; British Ambassador to Argentina, 1957-61; British Ambassador to Italy, 1962-66; retired from HM Diplomatic Service, 1967. Chairman, British-Italian Society. Mem. Council, RSPCA. *Recreations:* travel, history, archæology. *Address:* Lenox, St Margarets Bay, near Dover; 31 Knightsbridge Court, Sloane Street, SW1. *Clubs:* Brooks's, Royal Automobile.

**WARD, John Stanton,** RA 1965 (ARA 1956); RP 1953; RWS 1952; NEAC 1950; *b* 10 Oct. 1917; *s* of Russell Stanton and Jessie Elizabeth Ward; *m* 1950, Alison Christine Mary Williams; three *s* twin *d*. *Educ:* St Owen's School, Hereford; Royal College of Art. Royal Engineers, 1939-46. Travelling Schol., RCA, 1947. Vogue Magazine, 1948-52. Has held exhibitions at Trafford Gallery and Arthur Jeffress Gallery. *Address:* Bilting Court, Bilting, Ashford, Kent. *T:* Wye 478. *Club:* Chelsea Arts.

**WARD, Sir Joseph James Laffey,** 4th Bt *cr* 1911; *b* 11 Nov. 1946; *s* of Sir Joseph George Davidson Ward, 3rd Bt, and of Joan Mary Haden, *d* of Major Thomas J. Laffey, NZSC; *S* father, 1970; *m* 1968, Robyn Allison, *d* of William Maitland Martin, Rotorua, NZ. *Heir: b* Roderic Anthony Ward, *b* 23 April 1948. *Address:* Westbrook, 75 Harakeke Street, Christchurch 1, New Zealand.

**WARD, Leslie M.;** *see* Ward, Philip Leslie M.

**WARD, Commander Sir Melvill Willis,** 3rd Bt, *cr* 1914; DSC; RN, retired; *b* 25 May 1885; 2nd *s* of 1st Bt, and Florence Caroline, *d* of H. M. Simons; *S* brother, 1930; *m* 1965, Mrs Margaret Mary Risley, *widow* of Captain Ralph Risley, USN (author of House of Healing, 1962). *Heir:* none. *Recreation:* racing. *Address:* Oenoke Ridge, New Canaan, Connecticut, USA. *Clubs:* St James'; Travellers' (Paris).

**WARD, Sir Michael B.;** *see* Barrington-Ward.

**WARD, (Philip) Leslie Moffat,** RE 1936 (ARE 1916); Artist; formerly Senior Assistant, Southern College of Art, Bournemouth; retired, 1953; *b* 2 April 1888; *s* of Charles James and Charlotte Ward, Worcester; *m* 1st, 1925, Nellie Ethel Robinson; one *s*; 2nd, 1939, Eleanor Glassford Roberts. Gold Medallist (Pictorial Composition and Illustration) National Competition of School of Art, 1909-10. Hon. Member Society of Graphic Art; exhibitor at RA in most years since 1915. Pictures in public art galleries: Southampton, Rochdale, Bournemouth, Eastbourne, Hastings; also at Worcester, Mass, USA, and at Los Angeles, California, USA. One man shows, Red House Art Gallery, Christchurch, Hants, and Eastbourne and Hastings Municipal Galleries, 1956. Senior Fellow, Royal Society of Painter Etchers, 1963. *Address:* 22 Grants Avenue, Bournemouth, Hants.

**WARD, Lt-Gen. Richard Erskine,** CB 1969; DSO 1943 and Bar, 1943; MC 1942; Commander British Forces, Hong Kong, since 1970; *b* 15 Oct. 1917; *o s* of late John Petty Ward and Gladys Rose Ward (*née* Marsh-Dunn); *m* 1947, Stella Elizabeth, 2nd *d* of late Brig. P. N. Ellis, RA, and Mrs Rachel Ellis; two *s* two *d*. *Educ:* Marlborough Coll.; RMC, Sandhurst. Commissioned Royal Tank Corps, 1937; served War of 1939-45 (despatches thrice); 5th Royal Tank Regt, 1939-43; Staff Coll., Camberley, 1944; Bde Major, 4th Armoured Bde, 1944; CO Westminster Dragoons, 1945; Korea with 1st Royal Tank Regt, 1952 (despatches); Lt-Col Chiefs of Staff Secretariat, 1955; CO 3 Royal Tank Regt, 1957; idc 1961; on staff of Chief of Defence Staff, 1962; comd 20 Armoured Bde, 1963; GOC 1st Division 1965-67; Vice-Adjutant-General, 1968-70. Maj.-Gen., 1965; Col Comdt RTR, 1970-. Croix de Guerre, with palm, 1940; Chevalier, Order of Leopold II, with palm, 1945. *Address:* c/o Glyn, Mills & Co.,

Kirkland House, Whitehall, SW1. *Club:* Army and Navy.

**WARD, Ronald,** FRIBA; PPIAnb; FRSH; AIStructE; architect; *b* 20 April 1909; *o s* of Elisha Ward and Elsie M. (*née* Broadway); *m* 1939, Muriel Pemberton (actress, as Muriel Walker). *Educ:* Peter Symonds' Sch., Winchester; Royal Acad. Schools, London. Served War of 1939-45: Lt-Col, RE, France and Africa. Created Ronald Ward & Partners, 1936; architects of works for: Assurance cos: Legal & General; Norwich Union; Pearl; Phœnix; Royal Exchange; Banks: Barclays; Glyn Mills; Martins; Pakistan; Standard of W Africa; English Industrial Estates Corp.; Barham Court Housing Assoc.; Borough Councils of Ilford, Islington, and Reigate; County Councils of London and Herts; Develt Corps of Basildon, Hatfield, Harlow, and Welwyn; HM Comr for Office of Works; Governments of Gambia, Germany, and Portugal; Metropolitan Regional Hosp. Bds (NE, SW and SE); British Transport Commn; NFU; Church Comrs of England; Corp. of Trinity House; Inst. of Marine Engineers; Livery cos: Cutlers; Plaisterers; Associated-Rediffusion Ltd; British-American Tobacco Co. Ltd; British & Commonwealth Shipping Co. Ltd; Diamond Corp. of Sierra Leone; Daily Mirror Group; Nestle Co. Ltd; Remploy Ltd; United Africa Co. Ltd; Vickers Ltd, and many private cos in British Isles, Eire and W Africa. Consultant Architect, Royal Borough of Kingston upon Thames; Hon. Architect to: Church of St Peter-upon-Cornhill; Albert Hall. Director: Abbey Nat. Bldg Soc.; S Eastern Counties Housing Soc.; W End London Dir, Phoenix Assurance Co. Underwriting Mem. of Lloyd's. Member: Housing Study Mission for GB to Canada, 1967; Adv. Panel, Timber Research and Develt Assoc., 1968-; Council, Nat. Assoc. of Property Owners; W Africa Cttee (Mem. Council, 1957-60); British Humane Assoc. (Hon. Dir, 1960-63); Internat. Cultural Exchange (Mem. Central Council, 1960-62); Inst. of Hosp. Administrators (Examiner, 1955-57); St John Ambulance Assoc. (Founder Chm., City of Westminster Branch, 1957-60); Inst. of Royal Engrs (Lt-Col); Hon. Soc. of Knights of Round Table, 1938- (Keeper of Muniments and Chattels of the Knights); Guild of Freemen (Master, 1963-64); Greenhithe Ward Club (Chm., 1950-51 and 1954-55); United Wards Club (Mem. Governing Body, 1950-53); City Pickwick Club (Angelo Cyrus Bantam); City of London Soc.; Old Symondians Assoc.; Winchester City FC (Life Mem.). Hon. Mem., Bldg Society Assoc. Freeman, City of London, 1935-. Liveryman, Worshipful Co. of Horners (Plastics Lectr, 1957; Master, 1967-68); Past Asst Grand Supt of Works, 1969. Governor, Hythe Cricket Club. *Publications:* Design and Equipment of Hospitals, 1949; Historical Survey 1769-1969 of the Royal Athelstan Lodge No 19, 1969; regular contribs to jls and press. *Recreations:* science of building, gardening, golf. *Address:* 29 Chesham Place, Belgrave Square, SW1. *T:* 01-235 3361; The Martello Tower, Hythe, Kent. *T:* Hythe 66246. *Clubs:* City Livery (Pres., 1958-59); Hythe Golf.

**WARD, Ronald Ogier,** DSO 1919; OBE 1940; MC 1918; TD; MCh (Oxon); FRCS; retired as Consulting Surgeon to Miller General Hospital, Greenwich; late Surgeon: St Peter's and St Philip's Hospitals; *b* 6 March 1886; *s* of Allan Ogier Ward; *m* 1928, Elsie Antoinette, *e d* of David Jones; two *s*. *Educ:* Magdalen College Sch. and Queen's Coll., Oxford; St Bartholomew's Hospital. Fellow, Royal Society of Medicine; Ex-President of Section of Urology; Ex-President British Assoc. of Urological Surgeons; served as Surgeon with British Red Cross in Balkan War, 1912-13; European War, HAC Artillery, 1914-18 (DSO, MC, despatches); Officer i/c Surgical Division, BEF, 1939-40 (OBE) and MEF, 1940-42; Consulting Surgeon, East Africa Command, 1942-44. Hon. DSc, Leeds. *Address:* Cuckmere Cottage, Seaford, Sussex. *T:* Seaford 2147.

**WARD, Prof. Stacey George;** Professor and Head of Department of Minerals Engineering, University of Birmingham, since 1948; *b* 3 Sept. 1906; *s* of George Richard Ward; *m* 1950, Helen, *d* of Samuel Thomas Windsor. *Educ:* Queen Elizabeth's Grammar Sch., Kingston-upon-Thames; Imperial College of Science, London. PhD, MSc, DIC. Research Dept, Powell Duffryn Associated Collieries Ltd, 1930-34; Field Research and Liaison Officer, British Iron and Steel Federation, 1935-37; University of Birmingham; Lecturer, Mining Dept, 1937-42; Acting Prof. of Mining, 1942-46 and 1947-48; Prof. of Chemical Engineering, 1946-48; Dean of the Faculty of Science, 1960-63. *Publications:* various technical papers connected with coal, fuel, minerals, engineering and rheology of suspensions. *Address:* The University of Birmingham, PO Box 363, Birmingham 15.

**WARD, Terence George,** CBE 1961 (MBE 1945); Dean of the Faculty of Dental Surgery, Royal College of Surgeons, 1965-68; *b* 16 Jan. 1906; *m* 1931, Elizabeth Ambrose Wilson; one *s* one *d*. *Educ:* Edinburgh. Mem., SE Metropolitan Regional Hosp. Bd; Exmr, DSRCSEd, FDRCSIre. Pres., Internat. Assoc. Oral Surgeons; Past Pres., British Association of Oral Surgeons; Consulting Oral Surgeon to the Royal Navy; Consulting Dental Surgeon: to the British Army; to the Royal Air Force; to the Ministry of Health; to the Queen Victoria Hospital, East Grinstead. LRCP, LRCSEd 1928; LRFPS, 1930; LDS (Edinburgh) 1928; FDSRCS 1948; FACD (USA) 1959; FACDSurgeons; FFDRCS Ire., 1964; Hon. FDSRCSE, 1966; Hon. FRCCD, 1966. DDSc, Melbourne, 1963. Mem., SA Dental Assoc.; Hon. Member: Amer. Soc. Oral Surgeons; Dutch Soc. Oral Surgeons; Hon. Fellow: Scandinavian Assoc. Oral Surgeons; Spanish Assoc. Oral Surgeons. *Publication:* The Dental Treatment of Maxillo-facial Injuries, 1956. *Recreation:* golf. *Address:* 22 Marina Court Avenue, Bexhill-on-Sea, Sussex. *T:* Bexhill-on-Sea 4760.

**WARD, Thomas William,** RE 1955; RWS 1957; Engraver and Painter in water colour and oil colour since 1946; lecturer and teacher, since 1950; *b* 8 Nov. 1918; *s* of John B. Ward, Master Stationer, and Lillie B. Ward (*née* Hunt), Sheffield; *m* 1949, Joan Palmer, ARCA, *d* of Nelson Palmer, Blackheath; one *s* one *d*. *Educ:* Nether Edge Grammar Sch., Sheffield; Royal College of Art, London. Cadet, Merchant Service, 1935-36; stationer, W. H. Smith & Son Ltd, 1937-39. Military service: non-commissioned, 1939-42; commissioned, 1942-46: with N Staffs Regt, 7th Bn, and Royal Welch Fusiliers, 1st Bn, 1944-45; General Staff, 12th Army, Burma Area (GSO III), 1945-46. Royal College of Art, 1946-49, Diploma of Associateship, 1949, 4th year Schol., Dept Engraving, 1949-50. Group Exhibitions: Leicester Galls, 1951; Kensington Galls, 1953; Zwemmers, 1955; one-man Exhibitions: Walker's Gall., 1957, 1960; Wakefield City Art Gall., 1962; Shipley Art Gall.; Gateshead, Newcastle upon Tyne, 1962; Middlesbrough Art Gall., 1963. Work purchased by: S London Art Gall.; National Gall., NZ; Leicester Univ.; Oxford Univ. Illus. Heyday of Sail, D. MacGregor, 1968.

*Recreation:* painting. *Address:* 20 The Grove, W5.

**WARD, Sir (V.) M. B.;** *see* Barrington-Ward.

**WARD, Wilfrid Arthur,** CMG 1948; MC 1918; *b* 9 May 1892; *s* of late Arthur Henry Ward; *m* 1922, Norah Anne Phelps; one *s*. *Educ:* Christ's Hospital. Served European War; mobilised with Civil Service Rifles, 1914, France; commissioned in Lancashire Fusiliers (SR) 1915, France, Salonika, Palestine; Captain, 1917. Cadet Malayan Civil Service, 1920; various District posts in FMS, Kedah and Kelantan; Secretary to Resident, Selangor, 1936; Under-Secretary, Straits Settlements, 1941; interned in Singapore, 1942-45; Resident Commissioner, Selangor, 1946-48; Commissioner for Malaya in the UK, 1948-53. *Address:* Beckleys, Lymington, Hants.

**WARD, William Ernest Frank,** CMG, 1945; *b* 24 Dec. 1900; *s* of W. H. Ward, Borough Treasurer, Battersea; *m* 1926, Sylvia Grace, *d* of Arthur Clayton Vallance, Mansfield, Notts; no *c*. *Educ:* LCC elementary school; Mercers' Sch.; Dulwich Coll.; Lincoln Coll., Oxford (BLitt, MA); Ridley Hall, Cambridge (Diploma in Education). Master, Achimota Coll., Gold Coast, 1924; Director of Education, Mauritius, 1940; Deputy Educational Adviser, Colonial Office, 1945-56. Editor, Oversea Education, 1946-63. Member of UK delegation to seven general conferences of UNESCO and many other international meetings on education. *Publications:* History of Ghana, 1967 (originally published as History of the Gold Coast, 1948); Educating Young Nations, 1959; Fraser of Trinity and Achimota, 1965; The Royal Navy and the Slavers, 1969; various historical works and educational textbooks. *Recreations:* music, walking. *Address:* 59 Beresford Road, Cheam, Surrey. *T:* 01-642 1749.

**WARD, Mrs William J.;** *see* Ward, Sarah A.

**WARD, William Kenneth;** Under-Secretary, Ministry of Technology, since 1969; *b* 20 Jan. 1918; *e s* of late Harold and Emily Ward; *m* 1949, Victoria Emily, *d* of late Ralph Perkins, Carcavelos, Portugal; three *s* one *d*. *Educ:* Queen Elizabeth's Grammar Sch., Ashbourne; Trinity Coll., Cambridge. 1st class Hons Modern and Medieval Langs Tripos. Entered Ministry of Supply, 1939; Board of Trade, 1955; HM Principal Trade Commissioner, Vancouver, BC, 1959-63; Under-Sec., BoT, 1966-69. *Recreation:* gardening. *Address:* 31 Plough Lane, Purley, Surrey. *T:* 01-660 2462.

**WARD-HARRISON, Maj.-Gen. John Martin Donald,** OBE 1962; MC and bar 1945; Chief of Staff, HQ Northern Command, since 1970; *b* 18 April 1918; *s* of Commander S. J. Ward-Harrison, Haughley House, Suffolk; *m* 1945, June Amoret, *d* of late Major C. A. Fleury Teulon, Inniskilling Dragoons; one *s* one *d*. *Educ:* Shrewsbury Sch. Commnd Suffolk and Norfolk Yeomanry, 1936-39; 5th Royal Inniskilling Dragoon Guards, 1939-45; Staff Coll., S Africa, 1945; Staff appts and regimental duty, 1946-56; GSO1, 7 Armoured Div., 1956-58; comd 10th Royal Hussars (PWO), 1959-62; Col Gen. Staff, 1962-63; Brig., Royal Armoured Corps, E and S Commands, 1964; Imperial Defence Coll., 1965; Dep. Comdt, Staff Coll., Camberley, 1966-68; GOC Northumbrian District, 1968-70. *Recreations:* all field sports and polo. *Address:* Hazel Bush House, Stockton-on-the-Forest, York. *T:* Flaxton Moor 239. *Club:* Cavalry.

**WARD-JACKSON, Mrs (Audrey) Muriel;** Finance Director, John Lewis Partnership Ltd, since 1969 (Dir 1957); Director: John Lewis Properties Ltd, since 1969; John Lewis Partnership Pensions Trust (Chairman); *b* 30 Oct. 1914; *d* of William James Jenkins and Alice Jenkins (*née* Glyde); *m* 1946, George Ralph Norman Ward-Jackson; no *c*. *Educ:* Queenswood, Hatfield, Herts; Lady Margaret Hall, Oxford (MA). Home Civil Service: Asst Principal, 1937; Principal, 1942; Asst Sec., 1946-55. John Lewis Partnership: Director of Personnel, 1955-56; Financial Adviser, 1956-67; Gen. Inspector, 1967-69. On Civil Service Arbitration Tribunal, 1959-64; a Governor, British Film Inst., 1962-65; a Governor and Council Member, Bedford College, London University. *Recreations:* swimming, gardening. *Address:* 45 Connaught Square, Hyde Park, W2. *T:* 01-262 2922; John Lewis, Oxford Street, W1. *T:* 01-629 7711. *Clubs:* Oxford and Cambridge, Cowdray.

**WARD-PERKINS, John Bryan,** CBE 1955; MA; FBA 1951; FSA; Director of the British School at Rome; *b* 1912; *s* of late Bryan Ward–Perkins, Indian Civil Service (retired); *m* 1943, Margaret Sheilah Long; three *s* one *d*. *Educ:* Winchester (Schol.); New Coll., Oxford; Senior Demy of Magdalen Coll., Oxford; Craven Travelling Fellow, 1934-36. Asst, London Museum, 1936-38; Prof. of Archæology, Royal Univ. of Malta, 1939; war service (TA), 1939-45, England, Africa, and Italy (despatches); Lt-Col, Royal Artillery; organised military government antiquities dept in Tripoli and Cyrenaica; Dir of Monuments and Fine Arts Subcommission in Italy. Directed archæological excavations at Welwyn, 1937, Ightham, Kent, 1938, Tripolitania, 1948-53, Istanbul, 1953, and Italy, 1957-68. Mem. Pontificia Accademia Romana di Archeologia. Corresp. Member: Royal Acad. of History, Antiquity and Letters, Stockholm; German Archæological Institute. President: Internat. Union of Institutes, Rome, 1953, 1964; Tabula Imperii Romani. Visiting Prof., New York Univ., 1957; Carl Newell Jackson Lectr, Harvard Univ., 1957; Rhind Lectr, Soc. of Antiquaries of Scotland, 1960; Myres Memorial Lectr, Oxford Univ., 1963; M. V. Taylor Memorial Lectr, 1968; Jerome Lectr, Rome and Ann Arbor, 1969. Hon. DLitt, Birmingham; Hon. LLD Alberta, 1969. Medaglia d'oro per i Benemeriti della Cultura (Italian Govt), 1958; Serena Medallist of the British Academy, 1962. *Publications:* London Museum Medieval Catalogue; Inscriptions of Roman Tripolitania, 1952; The Shrine of St Peter, 1955; (jointly) The Great Palace of the Byzantine Emperors, 1959; The Historical Topography of Veii, 1961; The Northeastern Ager Veieintanus, 1969; Roman Architecture, 1970; papers on archæological subjects. *Address:* British School at Rome, 61 Via Gramsci, 00197 Roma, Italy. *T:* 870513. *Club:* Athenæum.

**WARD THOMAS, Gwyn Edward,** DFC; Managing Director, Yorkshire Television Limited, since 1967; *b* 1 Aug. 1923; *o s* of William J. and Constance Thomas; *m* 1945, Patricia Cornelius; one *d*. *Educ:* Bloxham Sch.; The Lycée, Rouen. Served RAF, 1 Group Bomber Command and 229 Group Transport Command, 1941-46 (Flt Lt). Swissair, Zurich, 1946-50; Advertising Executive, SM Bryde & Co., 1951-55; Group Sales Manager, Granada Television, 1955-61; Man. Dir, Grampian Television, 1961-67. British Bureau of Television Advertising: Dir, 1966; Chm., 1968-; Dir, Prowest Electronics, 1967-; Chm., Yorkshire Marketing Services, 1969-; Pres., Independent Television Enterprises SA, 1969-.

Mem. Council, Independent Television Companies Assoc.; former Chm., TV Industry Labour Relations Cttee. *Recreations:* ski-ing, water ski-ing, boats, tennis, golf, theatre, photography. *Address:* Sefton, Old Avenue, St George's Hill, Weybridge, Surrey; Moor Close, Menston in Wharfedale, Yorks.

**WARDALE, Geoffrey Charles;** Under-Secretary (Finance), Ministry of Transport, since 1967; *b* 29 Nov. 1919; *yr s* of late Harry Wardale and Rebecca (*née* Wilkinson), Altrincham, Chesire; *m* 1944, Rosemary Octavia Dyer; one *s* one *d*. *Educ:* Altrincham Grammar Sch.; Queens' Coll., Cambridge (Schol.). Army Service, 1940-41. Joined Ministry of War Transport as Temp. Asst Princ., 1942; Private Sec. to Perm. Sec., 1946; Princ., 1948; Asst Sec., 1957; Under-Sec. (Dir. of Lands and Contracts), 1966. *Recreations:* transport history, painting, listening to music. *Address:* 4 Cranedown, Lewes, Sussex. *T:* Lewes 3468.

**WARDE, Rt. Rev. Geoffrey Hodgson;** *b* 23 Aug. 1889; *s* of Rev. Henry John and Eleanor Harriett Warde; *m* 1915, Eileen Margaret (*d* 1957), *er d* of Rev. F. K. Hodgkinson; no *c*. *Educ:* Tonbridge Sch.; Keble Coll., Oxford; Oxford House, Bethnal Green; Cheshunt Theological Coll. Deacon, 1914; Priest, 1915; Curate of St Pancras, 1914-16; Temp. CF 1916-19. Hon CF 1919; Priest-in-Charge All Saints, Grosvenor Road, Pimlico, 1919-24; Vicar of St Mark's, Regent's Park, 1924-28; Deputy Priest-in-Ordinary to the King, 1922-28; Dean of Gibraltar, 1928-33; Vicar of Grantham, Rural Dean of North Grantham, 1933-39; Vicar of Brighton and Rural Dean, 1939-44; Archdeacon of Carlisle and Canon of Carlisle, 1944-46; Suffragan Bishop of Lewes, 1946-Oct. 1959; Hon. Canon of Chichester, 1947-63. *Recreations:* cricket, golf, lawn tennis. *Address:* The Lodge, Southdown Road, Seaford, Sussex. *T:* Seaford 3355.

**WARDER, John Arthur,** CBE 1957; General Managing Director, Oil Operating Companies in Iran, 1963-67, retired; *b* 13 Nov. 1909; *s* of John William Warder and Blanche Longstaffe, Bournemouth; *m* 1936, Sylvia Mary Hughes; two *s* one *d*. *Educ:* Kent Coll., Canterbury. Joined Asiatic Petroleum Co., 1927; practical training in oilfields and refinery operations in Argentina. Pres. and Gen. Man., Cia. Mexicana de Petroleo El Aguila, 1950; Gen. Man., Shell Cos in Colombia, 1953; Vice-Pres., Cia. Shell de Venezuela, 1957, Pres., 1959; Shell's Regional Co-ordinator (Oil), Middle East, 1961-63; Dir, Shell Internat. Petroleum Co. Ltd, and Mem. of Bds, Iranian Oil Participants Ltd and Iraq Petroleum Co. Ltd, 1961-63. Officer, Order of Arts and Culture (France), 1966; Order of Taj, 3rd degree (Iran), 1966. *Recreations:* yachting, golf. *Address:* Byways, Village de Putron, Guernsey, CI. *T:* 36935. *Clubs:* American; Parkstone Yacht (Poole); Larchmont Yacht (New York); Chapultepec Golf (Mexico); Royal Channel Islands Yacht; Royal Guernsey Golf.

*See also W. J. M. Shelton.*

**WARDINGTON,** 2nd Baron, *cr* 1936, of Alnmouth in the County of Northumberland; **Christopher Henry Beaumont Pease;** *b* 22 Jan. 1924; *s* of 1st Baron and Hon. Dorothy Charlotte, *er d* of 1st Baron Forster; *S* father, 1950; *m* 1964, Margaret Audrey Dunfee, *d* of John and Eva White; one *s* two *d* (adopted). *Educ:* Eton. Served War of 1939-45, in Scots Guards, 1942-47, Captain. Partner in Stockbroking firm of Hoare & Co. Alderman of Broad Street Ward, City of London, 1960-63. Comr, Public Works Loan Bd, 1969-. *Recreations:* cricket, golf, squash racquets. *Heir:* *b* Hon. William Simon Pease [*b* 15 Oct. 1925; *m* 1962, Hon. Elizabeth Jane Ormsby-Gore, *d* of 4th Baron Harlech, KG, PC, GCMG]. *Address:* Wardington Manor, Banbury, Oxon. *T:* Cropredy 202; 29 Moore Street, SW3. *T:* 01-584 5245. *Clubs:* Turf, Royal Automobile.

**WARDLAW, Rear-Admiral A. L. P. M.;** *see* Mark-Wardlaw.

**WARDLAW, Claude Wilson,** PhD, DSc, MSc, FRSE; FLS; George Harrison Professor of Botany, University of Manchester, 1958-66, now Emeritus Professor; *b* 4 Feb. 1901; *s* of Major J. Wardlaw, HLI, and Mary Hood Wardlaw; *m* 1928, Jessie Connell; two *s*. *Educ:* Paisley Grammar Sch.; Glasgow Univ. Demonstrator and Lecturer in Botany, Glasgow Univ., 1921-28; Pathologist and Officer-in-Charge, Low Temperature Research Station, Imperial College of Tropical Agriculture, Trinidad, BWI, 1928-40; Professor of Cryptogamic Botany, University of Manchester, 1940-58; wide travel in United States, Central and South America and in West Indies, Africa and East Indies. Prather Lecturer, Harvard Univ.; Hon. Foreign Mem., American Academy of Arts and Sciences; Hon. Foreign Correspondent, Académie d'Agriculture de la France; Hon. For. Associate, Royal Academy of Belgium; Corresp. Mem., American Botanical Soc., 1967; Sen. For. Scientist Fellowship, Nat. Sci. Foundation, Univ. of California, 1968. Lt-Col TA, retired. Hon. DSc (McGill). *Publications:* Diseases of the Banana, 1935; Green Havoc, 1935; Phylogeny and Morphogenesis; Morphogenesis in Plants, 1952; Embryogenesis in Plants, 1955; Banana Diseases, 1961; Organization and Evolution in Plants, 1965; Morphogenesis in Plants: A Contemporary Study, 1968; Essays on Form in Plants, 1968; Cellular Differentiation in Plants and Other Essays, 1969; Scientific Papers published in Phil. Trans. Royal Society Edinburgh, Royal Soc., Annals of Botany, Nature, etc. *Address:* 6 Robins Close, Bramhall, Cheshire.

**WARDLAW, Sir Henry,** 20th Bt of Pitreavie, *cr* 1631; *b* 30 Aug. 1894; *o s* of Sir Henry Wardlaw, 19th Bt, and Janet Montgomerie, *d* of James Wylie; *S* father 1954; *m* 1929, Ellen, *d* of John Francis Brady; four *s* one *d*. *Heir:* *s* Henry John Wardlaw, *b* 30 Nov. 1930. *Address:* Wamba, 57 Kinkora Road, Hawthorn, Victoria, Australia.

**WARDLE, Air Cdre Alfred Randles,** CBE 1945; AFC 1929; AFRAeS; RAF, retired; *b* 29 Oct. 1898; *s* of William Wardle, Stafford; *m* 1926, Sarah, *d* of David Brindley, Cotes Heath; one *s* one *d*. Joined Hon. Artillery Co., 1916; RFC 1917; RAF 1918; Director of Operational Requirements, Air Ministry, 1943-46; AOC Ceylon, 1947-49; AOC No. 66 (Scottish) Group, 1950-52. Air Commodore, 1943; retired 1952. Secretary: Corby Development Corp., 1954-67; Milton Keynes Development Corp., 1967-68; Peterborough Development Corp., 1968-69; Northampton Development Corp., 1969. *Address:* 88 Gipsy Lane, Kettering, Northants. *T:* Kettering 5780. *Club:* Royal Air Force.

**WARDLE, Sir Thomas (Edward Jewell),** Kt 1970; Lord Mayor of Perth, Western Australia, since 1967; *b* 18 Aug. 1912; *s* of Walter Wardle and Lily Wardle (*née* Jewell); *m* 1940, Hulda May Olson; one *s* one *d*. *Educ:* Perth Boys' Sch., Western Australia. Commendator, Order of Merit (Italy), 1970. *Recreations:* boating, fishing. *Address:* 3 Kent Street, Bicton, Western Australia 6157. *Clubs:* Tattersalls, WA Italian, Commercial

Travellers', Perth, Returned Services League, Western Australian (all in Western Australia).

**WARDLE, Ven. Walter Thomas;** Archdeacon of Gloucester since 1949; Canon Residentiary of Gloucester Cathedral, since 1948; *b* 22 July 1900; *s* of late James Thomas Wardle, Southsea, Hants; unmarried. *Educ:* Pembroke Coll., Oxford; Ripon Hall, Oxford. 3rd Class History BA 1924, MA 1932. Deacon, 1926; Priest, 1927; Curate of Weeke, Winchester, 1926-28; SPG Chaplain, Montana, Switzerland, 1928; Rector of Wolferton with Babingley, Norfolk, 1929-38; Vicar of Great and Little Barrington with Taynton, 1938-43; Vicar of Charlton Kings, Cheltenham, 1943-48. *Address:* 7 College Green, Gloucester. *T:* Gloucester 24948.

**WARDS, Brig. George Thexton,** CMG 1943; OBE 1935; late IA; Historian, Cabinet Office, since 1951. *Educ:* Heversham Sch., Westmorland. Served European War, 1914-18, with 7 London Regt, France and Belgium, 1917-18; 2nd Lieut, Indian Army, 1918; attached to HM Embassy, Tokyo, 1923-28; NW Frontier of India, 1930; Bt Major, 1933; Staff Officer to British Troops in North China, 1932-36; Lt-Col and Asst Military Attaché, Tokyo, 1937-41; Brig., Military Attaché, Tokyo, 1941; GSO1, GHQ India, 1942; Commandant Intelligence Sch., India, 1943-45; Commandant Intelligence Corps, Training Centre, India, 1945-47. Lt-Col, 1944; Col, 1945. Official Interpreter in Japanese to Govt of India, 1928-32, 1936, and 1944-47. Information Officer, Min. of Food, 1949; Chief Enforcement Officer, Min. of Food, 1950. Chm., Nat. Anti-Vivisection Soc., 1954-57; Mem. Council, RSPCA, 1956-67; Official visit to Japan, 1966. *Publications:* Joint author, Official History, The War against Japan, Vol. I 1955, Vol. II 1958, Vol. III 1962, Vol. IV 1965, Vol. V 1969. *Club:* Army and Navy.

**WARE, Henry Gabriel;** Deputy Treasury Solicitor, since 1969; *b* 23 July 1912; *o s* of late Charles Martin Ware and Dorothy Anne Ware (*née* Gwyn Jeffreys); *m* 1939, Gloria Harriet Platt; three *s* (and one *s* decd). *Educ:* Marlborough; St John's Coll., Oxford. Admitted solicitor, 1938; entered Treasury Solicitor's Dept, 1939. Served War of 1939-45 with Royal Artillery. *Recreations:* fly fishing, gardening. *Address:* The Little House, Tilford, Farnham, Surrey. *T:* Frensham 2151. *Clubs:* Athenæum; Frensham Fly Fishers (Frensham).

**WARE, Martin,** MB, FRCP; Editor, British Medical Journal, since 1966; *b* 1 Aug. 1915; *o s* of late Canon Martin Stewart Ware and late Margaret Isabel (*née* Baker, later Baker Wilbraham); *m* 1938, Winifred Elsie Boyce; two *s* three *d*. *Educ:* Eton; St Bartholomew's Hospital. MB, BS (London) 1939; MRCP 1945; FRCP 1967. Editor, St Bartholomew's Hosp. Jl, 1937-38. House-surgeon, St Bartholomew's Hosp., 1939; served with RAMC, attached to Royal W African Frontier Force (Captain, graded physician), 1940-45; Publications Officer, Medical Research Council, 1946-50; Asst Editor, British Medical Jl, 1950; Dep. Editor, 1964; Editor, 1966. Council of Research Defence Soc., 1960-65; Vice-Pres. and Treas., Soc. for Relief of Widows and Orphans of Medical Men, 1961-; Vice-Pres., Internat. Union of Med. Press; Mem., Med. Panel of British Council, 1966-. *Recreations:* golf, travel. *Address:* 99 Nottingham Terrace, Regent's Park, NW1 4QE. *T:* 01-486 5768. *Club:* Athenæum.

**WAREHAM, Arthur George;** Chairman, Arthur Wareham Associates group of companies; *b* 24 April 1908; *y s* of late George Wareham and of Elizabeth Wareham; *m* 1936, Kathleen Mary, *d* of H. E. and Mabel Tapley; one *s* one *d*. *Educ:* Queen's Coll., Taunton. Joined Western Morning News, 1926; Daily Mail, 1935; Editor, Daily Mail, 1954-59. *Address:* Three Corners, Forest Ridge, Keston, Kent. *T:* Farnborough (Kent) 53606. *Club:* Garrick.

**WAREING, Prof. Philip Frank,** PhD, DSc London; FRS 1969, FLS; Professor of Botany, University College of Wales, Aberystwyth, since 1958; *b* 27 April 1914; *e s* of late Frank Wareing; *m* 1939, Helen Clark; one *s* one *d* (and one *d* decd). *Educ:* Watford Grammar School; Birkbeck Coll., Univ. of London. Exec. Officer, Inland Revenue, 1931-41. Captain, REME, 1942-46. Lectr, Bedford Coll., Univ. of London, 1947-50; Lectr, then Sen. Lectr, Univ. of Manchester, 1950-58. Member: Nature Conservancy, 1965-68; Water Resources Board, 1968-. *Publications:* Control of Plant Growth and Differentiation, 1970; various papers on plant physiology in scientific journals. *Recreations:* gardening, hill walking. *Address:* Brynrhedyn, Cae Melyn, Aberystwyth, Cards. *T:* Aberystwyth 3910. *Club:* Royal Commonwealth Society.

**WARHURST, Alan;** Director, Ulster Museum, since 1970; *b* 6 Feb. 1927; *s* of W. Warhurst; *m* 1953, Sheila Lilian Bradbury; one *s* two *d*. *Educ:* Canon Slade Grammar Sch., Bolton; Manchester Univ. BA Hons History 1950. Asst, Grosvenor Museum, Chester, 1950-51; Asst Curator, Maidstone Museum and Art Gallery, 1951-55; Curator, Northampton Museum and Art Gallery, 1955-60; Director, City Museum, Bristol, 1960-70. FSA, 1958; FMA, 1958. *Publications:* various archaeological contribs to learned jls. *Address:* The Ulster Museum, Stranmillis, Belfast 9, Northern Ireland. *T:* Belfast 668251; 30 Myrtlefield Park, Malone, Belfast 9.

**WARING, Sir Alfred Harold,** 2nd Bt, *cr* 1935; BA, BSc, AMIMechE; *b* 14 Feb. 1902; *o s* of Sir Holburt Jacob Waring, 1st Bt, CBE, MS, FRCS, and Annie Cassandra (*d* 1948), *d* of Charles Johnston Hill, Holland Park, W; *S* father, 1953; *m* 1930, Winifred, *d* of late Albert Boston, Stockton-on-Tees; one *s* two *d*. *Educ:* Winchester; Trinity Coll., Cambridge; London Univ. BA Cambridge, 1924; BSc(Eng) London, 1924. AMIMechE 1932. *Heir: s* Alfred Holburt Waring [*b* 2 Aug. 1933; *m* 1958, Anita, *d* of late Valentin Medinilla, Madrid; one *s* two *d*]. *Address:* 10 Fieldfare Lane, Norton-on-Tees, Co. Durham. *T:* Stockton-on-Tees 53253; Pen Moel, Tidenham, near Chepstow, Mon. *T:* Chepstow 2448.

**WARING, Sir (Arthur) Bertram,** Kt 1960; DL; first Hon. President, Joseph Lucas (Industries) Ltd, electrical engineers, Birmingham, since 1969 (Chairman, 1951-69); Past Director of Lloyds Bank Ltd; *b* 12 June 1893; *s* of B. M. Waring, Manchester; *m* 1927, Muriel, *d* of E. H. Collumbell, Derby; one *s*. Chartered Accountant, 1920. Past President: Motor Industry Research Assoc.; Inst. Industrial Supervisors; Soc. of Motor Manufactureres and Traders; Birmingham and district Engineering and Allied Employers' Assoc.; Birmingham Chamber of Commerce; Past Chm., British Productivity Council; Vice-Pres., Engineering and Allied Employers' National Federation; Past Pres., Institution of Works Managers; Pres., Birmingham Productivity Assoc.; Mem. Council, FBI; Life Mem. Court of Governors, Birmingham Univ. Hon. Colonel, TA; Mem. Warwickshire TA Assoc.; Past-President Birmingham CC British Legion. Hon. LLD Birmingham, 1963. DL Warwickshire, 1952. *Address:* Heath

Lodge, Ullenhall, Warwickshire. *T:* Tanworth-in-Arden 227. *Club:* Royal Automobile.

**WARING, Sir Bertram;** *see* Waring, Sir A. B.

**WARING, Sir Douglas (Tremayne),** Kt 1957; CBE 1953; Chairman, London Tin Corporation, since 1961 (Deputy Chairman, 1958); *b* 16 April 1904; *s* of late Rev. C. T. Waring, Oxted, Surrey. *Educ:* Rossall Sch. Chartered Accountant, 1927. Joined London Tin Corp., London, 1927; Director, Anglo-Oriental (Malaya) Ltd, 1934; Chairman of Anglo-Oriental (Malaya) Ltd, 1952-59, and of other Tin Mining Companies operating and registered in Malaya. Pres., FMS Chamber of Mines, Ipoh, Malaya, 1952, 1955, and 1956. Served with FMS Volunteer Force, 1939-46 (POW Malaya and Siam, 1942-45). MLC and Mem. Exec. Council, Federation of Malaya, 1948-59; Chairman: Malayan Chamber of Mines, London, 1963-; Amalgamated Tin Mines of Nigeria, Ltd, 1961-. Ampat Tin Dredging Ltd, 1961-; Southern Kinta Consolidated Ltd, 1961; Kamunting Tin Dredging Ltd, 1966-; Dir, Consolidated Tin Smelters Ltd; Past Pres., Overseas Mining Assoc. Hon. Panglima Mangku Negara (Malaya), 1961. *Recreation:* horse racing. *Address:* 93 Whitehall Court, SW1. *T:* 01-930 5073. *Clubs:* City of London, East India and Sports; Roehampton; Singapore (Singapore); Selangor (Kuala Lumpur); Penang.

**WARK, Sir Ian (William),** Kt 1969; CMG 1967; CBE 1963; PhD (London); DSc (Melbourne); Chairman, Commonwealth Advisory Committee on Advanced Education, since 1965; *b* 8 May 1899; *s* of William John Wark and Florence Emily (*née* Walton); *m* 1927, Elsie Evelyn, *d* of late W. E. Booth; one *d.* *Educ:* Scotch Coll., Melbourne; Univs of Melbourne, London and California (Berkeley). Exhibn of 1851 Science Research Scholarship, 1921-24; Lectr in Chemistry, Univ. of Sydney, 1925; Research Chemist, Electrolytic Zinc Co. of Australasia Ltd, 1926-39; CSIRO: Chief, Div. of Industrial Chemistry, 1940-58; Dir, Chemical Research Laboratories, 1958-60; Mem. Exec., 1961-65. Gen. Pres., Royal Australian Chem. Inst., 1957-58; Treas., Australian Acad. of Science, 1959-63. FAA 1954-; Hon. Mem., Australasian Inst. of Mining and Metallurgy, 1960-; Fellow, UCL, 1965. *Publications:* (monograph) Principles of Flotation, 1938 (revised, with K. L. Sutherland, 1955); Why Research?, 1968; numerous papers in scientific jls. *Recreations:* golf, fishing. *Address:* 31 Linum Street, Blackburn, Victoria 3130, Australia. *T:* Melbourne, 89-1878. *Club:* Melbourne (Melbourne).

**WARMAN, Ven. Francis Frederic Guy;** Archdeacon of Aston since 1965; Canon Residentiary of Birmingham since 1965; *b* 1 Dec. 1904; *er s* of Frederic Sumpter Guy Warman, one time Bishop of Manchester, and Gertrude Warman (*née* Earle); *m* 1932, Kathleen Olive, *d* of O. C. Phillips; one *s* one *d.* *Educ:* Weymouth Coll.; Worcester Coll., Oxford; Ridley Hall, Cambridge. Ordained as Curate of Radford, Coventry, 1927; Curate of Chilvers Coton, Nuneaton, 1930; Vicar of: St James, Selby, 1932; Beeston, Leeds, 1936; Ward End, Birmingham, 1943; Aston-juxta-Birmingham, 1946. Rural Dean of East Birmingham, 1944-46; Proctor in Convocation, 1945-; Hon. Canon of Birmingham, 1948-65. *Recreations:* music, golf. *Address:* 88 Farquhar Road, Birmingham B15 2Q. *T:* 021-454 0247. *Club:* Royal Over-Seas League.

**WARMINGTON, Eric Herbert,** MA; FRHistS; Professor Emeritus of Classics, University of London; Fellow of Birkbeck College; Vice-Master, Birkbeck College, 1954-65, Vice-President, since 1966; Acting Master, 1950-51, 1965-66; *b* 15 March 1898; *s* of John Herbert Warmington, MA, and Maud Lockhart; *m* 1922, Marian Eveline Robertson, Kinsale, Co. Cork; one *s* two *d.* *Educ:* Perse School, Cambridge; Peterhouse, Cambridge (Scholar). Served in Garrison Artillery and King's Own Yorkshire Light Infantry, 1917-19; Cambridge University, 1919-22; First Class, Classical Tripos, Part I, 1921; First Class, Part II, 1922; BA 1922; Assistant master at Charterhouse, 1922-23; Classical Sixth Form master, Mill Hill School, 1923-25; Reader in Ancient History, University of London, 1925-35; Le Bas Prize, Cambridge University, 1925; MA 1925; FRHistS, 1928; Editor of the Loeb Classical Library. Dean of Faculty of Arts, University of London, 1951-56; Member of Senate, University of London, 1956-66; Acting Director Univ. of London Inst. of Education, 1957-58; Chairman, Goldsmiths' College Delegacy; President London Branch Classical Assoc. 1963-66. *Publications:* The Commerce between the Roman Empire and India, 1928; Athens, 1928; The Ancient Explorers (with M. Cary), 1929; Greek Geography, 1934; Africa in Ancient and Medieval Times, in the Cambridge History of the British Empire, 1936; Remains of Old Latin, Vol. I, 1935; Vol. II. 1936; Vol. III. 1938; Vol. IV. 1940; articles in The Oxford Classical Dictionary, 1949; A History of Birkbeck College, University of London, during the second World War, 1939-1945, 1954; (ed) Great Dialogues of Plato (trans. by W. H. D. Rouse), 1956; various articles and reviews. *Recreations:* music, gardening and natural history. *Address:* 48 Flower Lane, Mill Hill, NW7. *T:* 01-959 1905.

**WARMINGTON, Lt-Comdr Sir Marshall George Clitheroe,** 3rd Bt, *cr* 1908; Royal Navy, retired; *b* 26 May 1910; *o s* of Sir Marshall Denham Warmington, 2nd Bt, and Alice Daisy Ing; *S* father, 1935; *m* 1st, 1933, Mollie (from whom he obtained a divorce, 1941), *er d* of late Capt. M. A. Kennard, RN (retired); one *s* one *d*; 2nd, 1942, Eileen Mary (*d* 1969), *o d* of late P. J. Howes; two *s.* *Educ:* Charterhouse. *Heir:* *s* Marshall Denham Malcolm Warmington, *b* 5 Jan. 1934. *Address:* Carpenters Cottage, Forton, Longparish, Hants. *T:* Longparish 389. *Clubs:* Army and Navy; MCC.
*See also Sir H. H. Trusted.*

**WARNE, Rear-Adm. Robert Spencer,** CB 1953; CBE 1945; retired; *b* 26 June 1903; *s* of E. S. Warne, London; *m* 1925, Dorothy Hadwen Wheelwright; three *s.* *Educ:* RN Colleges, Osborne and Dartmouth. Joined Submarine Branch, 1925; Commander, 1936; Captain, 1941; Rear-Admiral 1951; Deputy Chief of Naval Personnel, Admiralty, 1951-53; Flag Officer, Germany and Chief British Naval Representative in the Allied Control Commission, 1953-55; retired 1955. *Recreations:* sailing, golf. *Address:* 56 Hill Rise, Richmond, Surrey. *T:* 01-940 2556. *Clubs:* Army and Navy; Royal Naval (Portsmouth).

**WARNER, Sir (Edward Courtenay) Henry,** 3rd Bt, *cr* 1910; Bishop of Chelmsford's Commissioner, since 1968; *b* 3 Aug. 1922; *s* of Colonel Sir Edward Courtenay Thomas Warner, 2nd Bt, DSO, MC, and Hon. Nesta Douglas-Pennant (*d* 1970), *yr d* of 2nd Baron Penrhyn; *S* father, 1955; *m* 1949, Jocelyn Mary, *d* of Commander Sir Thomas Beevor, 6th Bt, RN, Hargham Hall, Norfolk, and of Mrs Robert Currie, and *sister* of Sir Thomas Beevor, 7th Bt, *qv*; three *s.* *Educ:* Eton; Christ Church, Oxford. Served War of 1939-45 in

France, Lieut Scots Guards (wounded). *Heir: s* Philip Courtenay Thomas Warner, *b* 3 April 1951. *Address:* The Grove, Great Baddow, Essex. *Club:* Guards.

**WARNER, Sir Edward (Redston),** KCMG 1965 (CMG 1955); OBE 1948; *b* 23 March 1911; *s* of Sir George Redston Warner, *qv*; *m* 1943, Grizel Margaret Clerk Rattray; three *s* one *d*. *Educ:* Oundle; King's College, Cambridge. Entered Foreign Office and Diplomatic Service, 1935; Athens, 1937; Foreign Office, 1940; Minister of State's Office, Cairo, 1942; Embassy to Greek Govt, Cairo, 1943; Athens, 1944; FO 1945; UK Deleg. to UN, Geneva, 1947; Internat. Ruhr Authority, Düsseldorf, 1949; FO 1951-56; UK Delegation to OEEC, Paris, 1956-59; Minister at HM Embassy, Tokyo, 1959-62; Ambassador to the Federal Republic of Cameroon, 1963-66; UK Rep., Econ. and Social Council of UN, 1966-67; Ambassador to Tunisia, 1968-70. *Address:* 16 Lennox Street, Edinburgh 4. *Clubs:* Oxford and Cambridge University, Royal Commonwealth Society.

**WARNER, Frederick Archibald,** CMG 1963; Ambassador and Deputy Permanent UK Representative to United Nations, since 1969; *b* 2 May 1918; *s* of Frederick A. Warner, Chaguanas, Trinidad, and Marjorie Miller Winants, New Jersey, USA. *Educ:* Wixenford; RNC Dartmouth; Magdalen Coll., Oxford. Served War of 1939-45. Asst Principal, Foreign Office, Feb. 1946; Member of Foreign Service, April 1946; promoted 2nd Sec., May 1946; promoted 1st Sec., and transferred to Moscow, 1950; Foreign Office, Dec. 1951; Rangoon, 1956 (acted as Chargé d'Affaires, 1956); transferred to Athens, 1958; Head of South-East Asia Dept, Foreign Office, 1960; Imperial Defence College, 1964; Ambassador to Laos, 1965-67; Minister, NATO, 1968; Under-Secretary of State, FCO, 1969. *Address:* L6, Albany, Piccadilly, W1. *T:* 01-734 2856; Laverstock, Bridport, Dorset. *T:* Broadwindsor 230; 510 Park Avenue, New York, NY 10022, USA. *Clubs:* Travellers', Turf.

**WARNER, Sir Frederick (Edward),** Kt 1968; Senior Partner, Cremer and Warner, since 1963; Visiting Professor in Environmental Studies, University College London; *b* 31 March 1910; *s* of Frederick Warner; *m* 1st, Margaret Anderson McCrea; two *s* two *d*; 2nd, Barbara Ivy Reynolds. *Educ:* Bancrofts Sch.; University Coll., London. Pres., Univ. of London Union, 1933. Chemical Engr with various cos, 1934-56; self-employed, 1956-. Inst. of Chemical Engrs: Hon. Sec., 1953; Pres., 1966; Mem. Council, Engrg Instns, 1962; Pres., Fedn Européenne d'Assocs nationales d'Ingénieurs, 1968. Missions and Consultations in India, Russia, Iran, UAR, Greece, France. Chm., Adv. Cttee on Process Engrg; Member: Council, Open University; Court, Cranfield Inst. of Technology. Fellow UCL, 1967. Ordinario, Accademia Tiberina, 1969. Hon. DTech, Bradford, 1969; Hon. DSc, Aston, 1970. Gold Medal, Czecho-Slovak Soc. for Internat. Relations, 1969; Medal, Insinööriliitto, Finland, 1969. *Publications:* Problem in Chemical Engineering Design (with J. M. Coulson), 1949. Papers on nitric acid, heat transfer, underground gasification of coal, air and water pollution, contracts, planning. *Recreations:* monumental brasses, ceramics, gardens. *Address:* 140 Buckingham Palace Road, SW1. *T:* 01-730 0777. *Clubs:* Athenæum, Anglo-Belgian, Chemical.

**WARNER, Frederick Sydney,** LDS RCS, 1926; LRCP, MRCS, 1928; FDS RCS, 1947; Dental Surgeon, Guy's Hospital, 1949-68, Emeritus since 1968; Sub-Dean, 1946-65; Lecturer in Oral Surgery, 1954-61, Guy's Hospital Dental School, SE1; Dean of Dental Studies, 1965-68; Member of Board of Examiners in Dental Surgery, Royal College of Surgeons of England, 1947-64, and University of London, 1953-57. Member of Council of Governors, Guy's Hospital Medical and Dental Schools, since 1966; *b* 14 April 1903; *s* of Frederick Watkin Warner; *m* 1937, Cicely Florence Michelson. *Educ:* Guy's Hospital Medical School. Asst Dental Surgeon, Guy's Hospital, 1936-49. Member of Board of Faculty of Dental Surgery, Royal College of Surgeons of England, 1946-65; Vice-Dean, 1954-55. Fellow of Royal Society of Medicine, 1930. *Recreations:* philately, photography. *Address:* (professional) 88 Harley Street, W1. *T:* 01-580 1939; (home) 6 Leeward Gardens, SW19.

**WARNER, Sir George (Redston),** KCVO 1934; CMG 1927; *b* 18 July 1879; *s* of late Sir Joseph Warner; *m* 1910, Margery Catherine (*d* 1963), *e d* of late W. E. Nicol, Ballogie, Aberdeenshire; three *s*. *Educ:* Eton; Balliol College, Oxford. Entered Foreign Office, 1903; served at HM Legations at Tangier and Oslo; Minister at Berne, 1935-39. *Address:* Appleshaw House, Compton, nr Winchester, Hants. *Club:* Travellers'.

*See also Sir Edward Redston Warner.*

**WARNER, Sir Henry;** *see* Warner, Sir E. C. H.

**WARNER, Jack (Jack Waters),** OBE 1965; film and variety artiste; appearing on television: Dixon of Dock Green; *b* 24 Oct. *Educ:* Coopers' Company School; University of London. Films include: The Captive Heart; Hue and Cry; Dear Murderer; Holiday Camp; It Always Rains on Sunday; Against the Wind; Easy Money; My Brother's Keeper; Here Come the Huggetts; Vote for Huggett; The Huggetts Abroad; Train of Events; Boys in Brown; The Blue Lamp; Scrooge; Emergency Call; Meet Me To-night; The Final Test; The Square Ring; Now and forever; Carve Her Name with Pride. RAF Meritorious Service Medal, 1918. *Recreations:* golf, tennis, swimming. *Address:* Porsea Cottage, Kingsgate, Thanet. *Clubs:* Savage, Green Room, Royal Automobile.

**WARNER, Rt. Rev. Kenneth Charles Harman,** DSO 1919; DD (Edinburgh) 1950; Assistant Bishop in Diocese of Canterbury, since 1962; *b* 6 April 1891; *e s* of late Charles Edward Warner and Ethel Constantia Catharine Cornfoot, Tonbridge, Kent; *m* 1916, Constance Margaret (*d* 1968), 2nd *d* of Arnold F. Hills, Penshurst, Kent; two *s* two *d*; *m* 1970, Angela Margaret, *widow* of Rev. Edward Prescott-Decie. *Educ:* Tonbridge Sch.; Trinity Coll., Oxford; Cuddesdon Theological Coll. 2nd Cl. Jurisp., 1912; MA 1921; Solicitors' Articles, 1912; served European War, 1914-19; Major, Kent Cyclist Bn, 1917 (DSO); partner in firm of Warner Sons and Brydone, Solicitors, Tonbridge, Kent, 1912-22; Cuddesdon, 1923; Deacon, 1923; Priest, 1924; Curate of St George's, Ramsgate, 1923-26; Chaplain Royal Air Force, 1927-33; Rector and Provost of St Mary's Cathedral, Glasgow, 1933-38; Archdeacon of Lincoln and 4th Canon in Lincoln Cathedral; Prebendary of Gretton, 1938-47; Bishop of Edinburgh, 1947-61, retired. Select Preacher: Cambridge University, 1939; Oxford University, 1950-51. *Address:* 1 South Close, The Precincts, Canterbury, Kent. *T:* Canterbury 63990.

**WARNER, Oliver;** writer; *b* 28 Feb. 1903; *s* of Richard Cromwell and Grace Rankin Warner; *m* 1st, 1925, Dorothea Blanchard (*d* 1937); one *d*; 2nd, Elizabeth Strahan; one *s* one *d*. *Educ:* Denstone; Caius College, Cambridge. Gold

Medal, Royal Asiatic Society, 1920. BA (Cantab), 1925, MA 1946. Reader to Chatto and Windus, 1926-41, and again temp., 1964-65; Admiralty, 1941-47; Secretary, Naval Honours and Awards Committee, 1946-47; War Artists Advisory Committee, 1944-46; British Council, Deputy Director of Publications, 1947-63. Member: Council of Soc. for Nautical Research, 1955-60, 1970-71; Coun. of Navy Records Soc., 1960-63, 1967-68, 1970-72; Advisory Board, Buckler's Hard Maritime Museum. Book Critic, the Tatler, 1964-65. FRSL Society of Bookmen, 1949-62. *Publications:* A Secret of the Marsh, 1927; Hero of the Restoration, 1936; Uncle Lawrence, 1939; Captains and Kings, 1947; An Introduction to British Marine Painting, 1948;; Joseph Conrad, 1951; The Crown Jewels, 1951; Captain Marryat, 1953; Battle Honours of the Royal Navy, 1956; A Portrait of Lord Nelson, 1958; Trafalgar, 1959; Emma Hamilton and Sir William, 1960; The Battle of the Nile, 1960; Great Seamen, 1961; The Glorious First of June, 1961; Wilberforce, 1962; A History of the Inn-holders' Company, 1962; Great Sea Battles, 1963; A History of the Tin-Plate Workers' Company, 1964; English Literature: a Portrait Gallery, 1964; The Sea and the Sword, the Baltic, 1630-1945, 1965; Best Sea Stories (ed) 1965; Portsmouth and the Royal Navy, 1965; Nelson's Battles, 1965; Cunningham of Hyndhope, Admiral of the Fleet, 1967; Marshal Mannerheim and the Finns, 1967; The Navy, 1968; The Life and Letters of Lord Collingwood, 1968; A Journey to the Northern Capitals, 1968; Admiral of the Fleet: the Life of Sir Charles Lambe, 1969; Introduction to Centenary History of Chatto and Windus, 1955; (with Margaret Meade-Featherstonhaugh) Uppark and its People, 1964. *Recreation:* numismatics. *Address:* The Old Manor Cottage, Haslemere, Surrey. *T:* Haslemere 2691.

**WARNER, Rex;** author; University Professor, University of Connecticut, since 1964; *b* 9 March 1905; *s* of Rev. F. E. Warner and Kathleen Luce; *m* 1929, Frances Chamier Grove; two *s* one *d*; *m* 1949, Barbara, Lady Rothschild; one *d*; *m* 1966, Frances Chamier Warner. *Educ:* St George's Harpenden; Wadham College, Oxford (Open Classical Scholar, First Class Classical Hon. Mods, degree in English Literature). Schoolmaster in Egypt and in England; Director of The British Institute, Athens, 1945-47. Tallman Prof., Bowdoin Coll., 1962-63. Has written poems, novels, and critical essays; also has done work on films and broadcasting. Hon. DLitt Rider Coll., 1968. Comdr, Royal Order of Phœnix (Greece), 1963. *Publications:* Poems, 1937; The Wild Goose Chase, 1937; The Professor, 1938; The Aerodrome, 1941; Why was I killed?, 1943; Translation of the Medea of Euripides, 1944; English Public Schools, 1945; The Cult of Power, 1946; Translation of Aeschylus' Promethus Bound, 1947; Xenophon's Anabasis, 1949; Men of Stones, 1949; John Milton, 1949; Translation of Euripides' Hippolytus, 1950; Men and Gods, 1950; Translation of Euripides' Helen, 1951; Greeks and Trojans, 1951; Views of Attica, 1951; Escapade, 1953; (with Martin Hürlimann) Eternal Greece, 1953 (new edn 1962); Translation of Thucydides, 1954; The Vengeance of the Gods, 1954; The Young Cæsar, 1958; The Greek Philosophers, 1958; The Fall of the Roman Republic (trans. from Plutarch), 1958; Cæsar's War Commentaries (trans.), 1959; Poems of Seferis (trans.), 1960; Imperial Cæsar, 1960; Confessions of St Augustine (trans.), 1962; Pericles the Athenian, 1963; History of my Times (Hellenica), Xenophon (trans.), 1966; The Greek Style, by Seferis (trans.), 1966; The Converts, 1967; Athens at War, 1970. *Club:* Savile.

**WARNER, Sydney Jeannetta,** CBE 1946 (OBE 1918); Director Dominion and Foreign Relations Department British Red Cross, retired 1949; *b* 13 June 1890; *d* of Frederick Ashton Warner, FRCS, and Sydney Anne Grove. *Educ:* home and in Germany. British Red Cross Commandant, 1910-17; Area VAD Commandant in France, 1915-17; Dep. Asst Dir Personnel in WRNS (OBE), 1917-19. Worked for LNU, rep. them at Geneva at various cttees of the League of Nations, 1919-28; Mem. staff of Internat. Office of World Assoc. of Girl Guides and Girl Scouts, 1928-36; rejoined British Red Cross for the War, 1939. 1st Class Knight of Order of St Olav (Norwegian), 1946; Chevalier de la Légion d'Honneur, 1946; Danish Médaille Royale de Récompense de première classe avec couronne, avec l'autorisation de la porter dans le ruban de l'ordre de Dannebrog, 1947; Commander of Order of Orange Nassau (Netherlands), 1948; Commander or Order of Phœnix (Greece), 1950. *Recreations:* travelling, fishing; Mem. since 1923 of Roy. Inst. of International Affairs, Chatham House. *Address:* 33 Moore Street, Cadogan Square, SW3. *T:* 01-589 6816; The Small House, Upton Grey, Basingstoke, Hants. *T:* Long Sutton 317.

**WARNER, Sylvia Townsend,** FRSL; Author; *b* 1893. *Publications:* The Espalier, 1925; Lolly Willowes, 1926; Mr Fortune's Maggot, 1927; Time Importuned, 1928; The True Heart, 1929; Opus 7, 1931; The Salutation, 1932; Whether a Dove or Seagull (with Valentine Ackland), 1934; Summer Will Show, 1936; After the Death of Don Juan, 1938; A Garland of Straw, 1943; The Museum of Cheats, 1947; The Corner That Held Them, 1948; The Flint Anchor, 1954; Winter in the Air, 1956; Boxwood, 1960; The Cat's Cradle Book, 1960; A Spirit Rises, 1962; A Stranger with a Bag, 1966; T. H. White: a biography, 1967. *Address:* c/o Chatto & Windus, 40 William IV Street, WC2.

**WARNOCK, Rt. Hon. Edmond,** PC (N Ireland) 1944; QC 1932; DL Belfast; *b* 8 May 1887; *m* 1913, Jessie M. Cleland; three *d*. *Educ:* Methodist College, Belfast; Trinity College, Dublin. Called Irish Bar, 1911. MP St Anne's Div. of Belfast, NI Parliament, 1938-69; Parliamentary Secretary to Minister of Home Affairs, 1939-40; Minister of Home Affairs, 1944-49; Attorney-Gen., 1949-56, resigned. *Address:* The Glebe House, Ballee, Downpatrick, Co. Down, N Ireland. *Club:* Ulster Reform (Belfast).

**WARNOCK, Prof. Frederick Victor,** OBE 1955; PhD (QUB), MSc (NUI), FRCScI, CEng; FIMechE; Professor of Mechanical Engineering, Queen's University, 1955-59, now Emeritus Professor (Professor of Mechanical Engineering, College of Technology, Belfast, 1937-55); *b* 11 Feb. 1893; *s* of Samuel and Margaret Warnock; *m* 1920, Mary Ferguson; two *s*. *Educ:* Coll. of Technology, Belfast; Royal Coll. of Science, Ireland. Apprenticeship with Messrs Portadown Foundry Co., Ltd 1909-13; student, Royal Coll. of Science, Dublin, 1914-18; Lecturer in Mechanical Engineering, Londonderry Tech. Coll., 1918-20; Senior Lecturer in Mechanical Engineering, Queen's Univ. and College of Technology, Belfast, 1920-37. *Publications:* Strength of Materials, 1927; Mechanics of Solids and Strength of Materials, 1965. Contribs to: Proc. Iron and Steel Inst., Engrg, and Instn of Mech. Engrs.

*Address:* 43 Balmoral Avenue, Belfast BT9 6NX. *T:* 667324.

**WARNOCK, Geoffrey James;** Fellow and Tutor in Philosophy, Magdalen College, Oxford, since 1953; *b* 16 Aug. 1923; *s* of James Warnock, OBE, MD; *m* 1949, Helen Mary Wilson (*see* Mrs H. M. Warnock); two *s* three *d*. *Educ:* Winchester Coll.; New Coll., Oxford. Served War of 1939-45: Irish Guards, 1942-45 (Captain). Fellow by Examination, Magdalen Coll., 1949; Fellow and Tutor, Brasenose Coll., 1950-53. Visiting Lectr, Univ. of Illinois, 1957; Visiting Professor: Princeton Univ., 1962; Univ. of Wisconsin, 1966. *Publications:* Berkeley, 1953; English Philosophy since 1900, 1958; Contemporary Moral Philosophy, 1967; articles in: Mind, Proc. Aristotelian Soc., etc. *Recreations:* golf, cricket. *Address:* 9 Chadlington Road, Oxford. *T:* Oxford 55470.

**WARNOCK, Mrs Helen Mary;** Headmistress of Oxford High School, GPDST, since 1966; *b* 14 April 1924; *d* of late Archibald Edward Wilson, Winchester; *m* 1949, Geoffrey James Warnock, *qv*; two *s* three *d*. *Educ:* St Swithun's, Winchester; Lady Margaret Hall, Oxford. Fellow and Tutor in Philosophy, St Hugh's Coll., Oxford, 1949-66. *Publications:* Ethics since 1900, 1960; J.-P. Sartre, 1963; Existentialist Ethics, 1966; Existentialism, 1970. *Recreations:* music, golf. *Address:* 9 Chadlington Road, Oxford. *T:* Oxford 55470.
*See also Sir A. D. Wilson.*

**WARNOCK, Rt. Hon. (John) Edmond;** *see* Warnock, Rt Hon. Edmond.

**WARNOCK, William Robertson Lyon;** Chartered Accountant; Chairman, Charterhouse Group Ltd, since 1968; *b* 27 July 1916; *s* of Robert Baillie Lyon Warnock, East India Merchant, and Elizabeth Warnock; *m* 1940, Beryl Atkinson, *d* of Shera Atkinson, LLD and Agnes Atkinson; one *d*. *Educ:* University College Sch. With Brown, Fleming & Murray, CA, 1934-39. Served Royal Artillery (Captain), 1940-44. Lines Brothers Ltd, 1945-48; Charterhouse Group Ltd (and subsidiaries), 1948-. *Recreation:* golf. *Address:* Flat 5, 3 Templewood Avenue, NW3. *T:* 01-435 7377. *Club:* Junior Carlton.

**WARR, George Michael,** CBE 1966; HM Diplomatic Service, retired; *b* 22 Jan. 1915; *s* of late Sir Godfrey Warr, and of Lady Warr; *m* 1950, Gillian Addis (*née* Dearmer); one *s* two *d* (one *step s*). *Educ:* Winchester; Christ Church, Oxford. Entered Foreign Service, 1938; served in Chile, Germany, Soviet Union, Uruguay. Counsellor, British Embassy, Brussels, 1959-62; British Consul-General, Istanbul, Turkey, 1962-67; Ambassador to Nicaragua, 1967-70. *Recreations:* gardening, golf. *Address:* Woodside, Frant, near Tunbridge Wells. *T:* Frant 202. *Club:* Boodle's.

**WARRACK, Guy Douglas Hamilton;** Hon. ARCM; Composer; Conductor; *b* Edinburgh, 8 Feb. 1900; *s* of John Warrack, LLD, and Jean Hamilton (*née* Dunlop); *m* 1st, 1926, Jacynth Ellerton (marriage dissolved); one *s* one *d*; 2nd, 1933, Valentine Clair Jeffrey; two *s*. *Educ:* Winchester; Magdalen College, Oxford; Royal College of Music. BA Oxon, 1923; Hon. ARCM, 1926. Teaching staff of RCM, 1925-35; Examiner for Associated Board of Royal Schools of Music, 1926-; Conductor: Oxford Orchestral Society and Oxford City Concerts for Children, 1926-30; Handel Society, 1934-35; BBC Scottish Orchestra, 1936-45; Musical Director, Sadler's Wells Theatre Ballet, 1948-51; Chairman of Composers' Guild of Great Britain, 1952, 1956; Pres. Internat. Council of Composers, 1955-59; General Council of PRS, 1958-. Chairman: Sherlock Holmes Soc. of London, 1955-57; Intimate Opera Soc. Ltd, 1969-; Conducted Concerts, Opera, Ballet, etc in London, Ceylon, New Zealand, South Africa and Provinces. Compositions include: Variations for Orchestra, 1924; Symphony in C minor (The "Edinburgh"), 1932; Divertimento Pasticciato, 1938; music for many films, including Theirs is the Glory, 1946; XIVth Olympiad, 1948; The Story of Time, 1949; A Queen is Crowned, 1953; also many arrangements. *Publications:* Sherlock Holmes and Music, 1947. Articles in The Times, Daily Telegraph, Music and Letters, Musical Times, etc. *Address:* 72 Courtfield Gardens, SW5. *T:* 01-370 1758. *Clubs:* Savile; New (Edinburgh).

**WARRELL, Ernest Herbert;** Organist and Director of Music, Southwark Cathedral, London, SE1, since 1968; Lecturer in Music, King's College, London, since 1953; Musical Director, Gregorian Association, since 1969; *b* 23 June 1915; *er s* of Herbert Henry Warrell and Edith Peacock; *m* 1952, Jean Denton Denton; two *s* one *d*. *Educ:* Loughborough School. Articled pupil (Dr E. T. Cook), Southwark Cath., 1938; Asst Organist, Southwark Cath., 1946-54; Organist, St Mary's, Primrose Hill, 1954-57; Lectr in Plainsong, Royal Sch. of Church Music, 1954-59; Organist, St John the Divine, Kennington, SW9, 1961-68. *Publications:* Accompaniments to the Psalm Tones, 1942; Plainsong and the Anglican Organist, 1943. *Recreation:* walking. *Address:* 41 Beechhill Road, Eltham, SE9. *T:* 01-850 7800. *Clubs:* Special Forces; Royal Scots (Edinburgh).

**WARREN, Alastair Kennedy,** TD 1953; Editor of The Glasgow Herald since 1965; *b* 17 July 1922; *s* of John Russell Warren, MC, and Jean Cousin Warren; *m* 1952, Ann Lindsay Maclean; two *s*. *Educ:* Glasgow Acad.; Loretto; Glasgow Univ. (MA Hons). Served War of 1939-45; HLI, 1940-46; Major, 1946. Served 5/6th Bn HLI (TA) 1947-63. Sales Clerk, Stewarts & Lloyds Ltd, 1950-53; joined editorial staff of The Glasgow Herald as Sub-Editor, 1954; Leader Writer, 1955-58; Features Editor, 1958-59; Commercial Editor, 1960-64; City Editor, 1964-65. *Publications:* contribs to various periodicals. *Recreations:* swimming, hill walking. *Address:* 20 Glasgow Street, Glasgow, W2. *T:* 041-339 5398. *Club:* Western (Glasgow).

**WARREN, Alec Stephen,** CMG 1950; *b* 27 June 1894; *s* of James Herbert Warren, Hatch End, Middlesex; *m* 1958, Beryl May Cheese. *Educ:* Aldenham School. Director, Warren Sons & Co. Ltd, 1920; Chairman, Warren & Reynolds Ltd, 1935. Joined Ministry of Food, 1939; Director of Canned Fish, Fruit and Vegetables Division, Ministry of Food, 1944-52; Director of Bacon and Ham Division, 1952-56; Mem. Potato Marketing Board, 1956-59. *Publication:* The Warren Code, 1964. *Recreation:* billiards. *Address:* Maison Pommier, Sark, Channel Isles. *T:* Sark 35.

**WARREN, Rt. Rev. Alwyn Keith,** CMG 1967; MC 1945; *b* 23 Sept. 1900; 2nd *s* of Major T. J. C. Warren, JP, Penlee House, Te Aute, Hawkes Bay, NZ, and Lucy, *d* of Ven. Samuel Williams, Archdeacon of Hawkes Bay, NZ; *m* 1928, Doreen Eda, *d* of Capt. C. F. Laws; one *s* two *d*. *Educ:* Marlborough College; Magdalen College, Oxford (BA 1922, Hons Nat. Sci.; MA 1926); Cuddesdon Theological College. Ordained, 1925; Curate of Ashford, Kent, 1925-29; Vicar of Ross and South Westland, NZ, 1929-32; Vicar of Waimate, South Canterbury, NZ, 1932-34; Vicar of St Mary's,

Merivale, Christchurch, NZ, 1934-40; Archdeacon of Christchurch, 1937-44; Dean of Christchurch, 1940-51; Vicar-General, 1940-44 and 1946-51; Bishop of Christchurch, 1951-66. Chaplain to 2nd NZ Exped. Force (NZ Divisional Cavalary), Italy, 1944-45 (wounded, MC). Member Council, University Canterbury, 1946-, Pro-Chancellor, 1961, Chancellor, 1965-69; Member Senate, University of New Zealand, 1948-61; Warden or Chm. Bds various colleges, schools and social service organisations. Chairman National Council of Churches of NZ, 1949-51; Member Central Committee of World Council of Churches, 1954-66. Chap. and Sub-Prelate, Order St John; Chaplain, Priory of St John in NZ; President: Canterbury and West Coast Centre, St John Ambulance Assoc.; Royal Christchurch Musical Soc.; Trustee, NZ National Library. *Publications:* Prayers in Time of War, 1940; Christianity Today: section on Churches in NZ, 1947. Contrib. to Stimmen aus der ökumene, 1963 (Berlin). *Recreations:* music, gardening. *Address:* Littlecourt, 193 Memorial Avenue, Christchurch 5, New Zealand. *Clubs:* Leander; Christchurch, University of Canterbury (NZ).

**WARREN, Mrs Brian;** *see* Barnes, A. J. M. T.

**WARREN, Sir Brian (Charles Pennefather),** 9th Bt *cr* 1784; *b* 4 June 1923; *o s* of Sir Thomas Richard Pennefather Warren, 8th Bt, CBE; *S* father, 1961. *Educ:* Wellington College. Served War of 1939-45; Lt, 1943-45, 2nd Bn Irish Guards, RARO. *Recreations:* hunting, squash. *Heir: uncle,* William Robert Vaughton Warren, OBE, MC [*b* 23 Feb. 1889; *m* 1st, 1914, M. M. Briggs (marr. diss., 1926); two *s* one *d*; 2nd, 1926, V. E. Gill]. *Address:* Woodville, Dunmore East, County Waterford, Eire. *T:* Waterford 83188. *Club:* Guards.

**WARREN, Douglas Daintry,** CSI 1947; CIE 1945; MC 1918; late ICS; *b* 17 Jan. 1897; *s* of Charles Warren, Royston, Herts; *m* 1922, Nora Mary, *d* of Major J. O'C. Phelan; one *s*. *Educ:* King's School, Worcester; Corpus Christi College, Cambridge. Served in European War with Bedfordshire Regt, 1915-19 (MC); entered ICS 1920; Secretary to Govt of Madras, Public Works Dept, 1940-43; Joint Sec. to Govt of India, Transport Dept, 1943, Sec. in 1946 and 1947. *Address:* 18 Cedar Crescent, Royston, Herts.

**WARREN, Earl;** Chief Justice of the United States, 1953-69; *b* Los Angeles, Calif, 19 March 1891; *s* of Methias H. Warren and Chrystal Hernlund; *m* 1925, Nina E. Meyers; three *s* three *d*. *Educ:* public schools, Bakersfield, Calif; University of California, Berkeley, Calif (Bachelor of Letters, 1912; JD 1914). Admitted to California Bar, 1914; practised in San Francisco and Oakland, Calif, 1914-17; Deputy City Attorney, Oakland 1919-20; Dep. Dist Attorney, Alameda County, Calif, 1920-25, Dist Attorney, 1925-39; Attorney-Gen. of Calif, 1939-43; President Nat. Assoc. of Attorneys-General, 1940-41. Alternate Delegate, Republican Nat. Convention, 1928, deleg., 1932; Chm. Republican State Central Cttee, 1934-36; Republican nat. cttee-man from Calif, and member nat. exec. cttee, 1936-38; Governor of California, 1943-53; temp. chm. and keynote speaker, Republican National Convention, 1944; Republican nominee for US vice-presidency, 1948; Candidate for Republican nomination for US Presidency, 1952. Special US Ambassador to Coronation, 1953. Chm., President's Commn on the Assassination of President Kennedy, 1963-64. Hon. Chm., World Association of Judges, 1969-. Entered US Army, as private, 1917, discharged as 1st Lt 1918 (Capt. Reserve until 1935). Hon. Master of the Bench, Gray's Inn, 1965. *Hon. degrees:* LLD University of California and other universities and colleges. Holds various foreign decorations. *Publications:* various articles on legal subjects. *Recreations:* hunting, fishing. *Address:* Supreme Court Building, Washington, DC 20543, USA. *Clubs:* Olympic, Bohemian (San Francisco); Athens Athletic, Claremont Country (Oakland).

**WARREN, Hon. Sir Edward (Emerton),** KCMG 1969 (CMG 1956); KBE 1959; MSM 1918; Member Legislative Council, New South Wales Parliament, since 1954; *b* Broken Hill, NSW, 26 Aug. 1895; *s* of John T. Warren, Derbyshire, England; *m* 1926, Doris, *d* of Charles F. Schultz; two *s*. *Educ:* Broken Hill, NSW. Served European War, 1914-18: 18th Bn AIF, Gallipoli and France. Chairman: NSW Combined Colliery Proprietors' Assoc., 1949; Northern Colliery Proprietors' Assoc., 1949; Aust. Coal Assoc., 1956; Aust. Coal Assoc. (Research) Ltd, 1956; Aust. Coal Industry Research Laboratories Ltd, 1965; Brown's Coal Pty Ltd (Victoria); Coal & Allied (Sales) Pty Ltd; Dowsett Engineering (Australia) Pty Ltd. Man. Dir, The Wallarah Coal Co. Ltd; Governing Dir., Thomas Brown Ltd (Wellington, NZ). Director and Chief General Manager: Coal & Allied Industries Ltd; Coal & Allied Industries KK (Tokyo-Japan); J. & A. Brown & Abermain Seaham Collieries Ltd; Caledonian Collieries Ltd; Cessnock Collieries Ltd; Liddell Collieries Pty Ltd; Durham Coal Mines Pty Ltd; South Maitland Railways Pty Ltd; Hexham Engineering Pty Ltd; Jones Bros Coal Pty Ltd; Director: Westinghouse Brake (A/sia) Pty Ltd; McKenzie & Holland (Australia) Pty Ltd. Member: Coal Conservation Cttee, NSW Govt, 1951; C'wealth Govt Mission investigating overseas coal-mining methods, 1952; Dep. Chm., Aust. Nat. Cttee, World Power Conf., 1960; Vice-Chm., Internat. Exec. Council, World Power Conf., 1962; Chm., Coal Trades Section, Aust. Trade Mission to S America, 1962; Pres., Australia/Japan Business Co-operation Cttee, 1964-; rep. Aust. Employers, ILO, Geneva, 1964; Mem., Nat. Coal Research Adv. Cttee, 1965; launched Malaysia/Australia Business Co-operation Cttee, Kuala Lumpur, 1965; led Aust. Delegn, Hawaii, 1968 (resulted in Pacific Basin Econ. Co-op. Cttee); Mem., C'wealth Govt Adv. Cttee, Expo 70, 1968; Pres., Australia/Korea Business Co-operation Cttee, 1969. Has travelled extensively. Member: Council, Univ. of NSW, 1965-; Med. Foundn, Univ. of NSW, 1968-. Rising Sun with Grand Cordon, Japan, 1967. *Address:* 16 Morella Road, Clifton Gardens, NSW 2088, Australia. *T:* (home) 969 4662; (office) 27 8641. *Clubs:* American, Tattersall's, New South Wales, Royal Automobile of Australia, NSW Sports, Manly Golf (Sydney); Newcastle (Newcastle, NSW).

**WARREN, Brig. Edward Galwey,** CBE 1940; *b* 3 May 1893; *y s* of Deputy Inspector-General T. R. Warren, RN, and Harriet Lavinia Warren, Kylenahoory, Ballyhooly, Co. Cork; *m* 1914, Gwendolyn Agnes, *yr d* of Brooke Brasier, JP, Ballygarrett, Mallow, Co. Cork. *Educ:* Royal Naval School, Eltham; RMC, Sandhurst. Gazetted to Northamptonshire Regt 1912; Commanded 2nd Northamptonshire Regt 1939; 4th Inf. Bde 1940-41; has served in BEF France, 1914, Sudan, Sierra Leone, Iraq, India, and BEF France, 1939-40; retired 1946. *Address:* Stradbally, Castle Connell, Co. Limerick, Ireland.

**WARREN, Frederick Lloyd,** MA, BSc (Oxon), PhD, DSc (London); Professor of

Biochemistry, London Hospital Medical College, since 1952; *b* 2 Oct. 1911; *s* of Frederick James and Edith Agnes Warren; *m* 1st, 1949, Natalia Vera Peierls (*née* Ladan) (marriage dissolved, 1958); two *s* one *d*; 2nd, 1961, Ruth Natalle Jacobs. *Educ:* Bristol Grammar Sch.; Exeter Coll., Oxford. Demonstrator, Biochem. Dept, Oxford, 1932-34; Sir Halley Stewart Res. Fellow, Chester Beatty Research Institute, Royal Cancer Hospital, 1934-46; Laura de Saliceto Student, University of London, 1937-42; Anna Fuller Research Student, 1942-46; Senior Lecturer in Biochemistry, St Mary's Hospital Medical School, 1946-48; Reader in Biochemistry, University College, London, 1948-52. *Publications:* papers and articles in scientific journals. *Address:* London Hospital Medical College, Turner Street, E1. *T:* 01-247 0644.

**WARREN, Ian Scott;** Master of the Supreme Court (Queen's Bench Division) since 1970; *b* 30 March 1917; *e s* of Arthur Owen Warren and Margaret Cromarty Warren; *m* 1943, Barbara, *er d* of Walter Myrick; four *s* one *d. Educ:* Charterhouse; Magdalene Coll., Cambridge. Colonial Administrative Service, 1938-41; RAF, 1942-46. Called to Bar, Lincoln's Inn, 1947, Bencher 1967. *Recreations:* ski-ing, poetry. *Address:* 26 Parthenia Road, SW6. *T:* 01-736 1632. *Club:* MCC.

**WARREN, Lt-Col John Leighton Byrne L.;** *see* Leicester-Warren.

**WARREN, Kenneth Robin;** MP (C) Hastings since 1970; Consultant in Aeronautical Engineering, Warren Woodfield Associates Ltd, since 1970; *b* 15 Aug. 1926; *s* of Edward Charles Warren and Ella Mary Warren (*née* Adams); *m* 1962, Elizabeth Anne Chamberlain, BA Hons Cantab; one *s* one *d. Educ:* Midsomer Norton; Aldenham; London Univ.; De Havilland Aeronautical Technical Sch. Research Engineer, BOAC, 1951-57; Personal Asst to Gen. Manager, Smiths Aircraft Instruments Ltd, 1957-60; Elliott Automation Ltd, 1960-69; Military Flight Systems: Manager, 1960-63; Divisional Manager, 1963-66; Marketing Manager, 1966-69. *Publications:* various papers to technical confs on aeronautical engineering and operations, in USA, UK, Netherlands and Japan. *Recreations:* mountaineering, flying, gardening. *Address:* Woodfield House, Goudhurst, Kent. *T:* Goudhurst 590.

**WARREN, Rev. Canon Max Alexander Cunningham;** Sub-Dean and Canon of Westminster since 1963; *b* 13 Aug. 1904; *s* of Rev. J. A. F. Warren; *m* 1932, Mary Collett; two *d. Educ:* Marlborough College; Jesus College, Cambridge (Rustat Scholar). BA 1926; CMS Missionary, Northern Nigeria, 1927; MA 1931; deacon 1932, priest 1933, Winchester Diocese; Curate of St John's, Boscombe, and Joint Secretary for Youth Work in Diocese of Winchester, 1932-36; Vicar of Holy Trinity Church, Cambridge, and Secretary of the Cambridge Pastorate, 1936-42; General Secretary, Church Missionary Society, 1942-63. Hon. Fellow, Jesus College, Cambridge, 1967. Hon. DD: Wycliffe Coll., Toronto, 1944; St Paul's Univ., Tokyo, 1959; Glasgow Univ., 1963; Huron College, Ontario, 1963; Univ. of Sierra Leone, 1969. *Publications:* Loyalty, 1935; Interpreters, 1936; Master of Time, 1943; The Calling of God, 1944; Strange Victory, 1946; The Truth of Vision, 1948; The Christian Mission, 1951; (Ed.) The Triumph of God, 1948; Revival, 1954; The Christian Imperative, 1955; Caesar the Beloved Enemy, 1955; The Gospel of Victory, 1955; Partnership, 1956; Challenge and Response, 1959; Letters on Purpose, 1963; Perspective in Mission, 1964; The Missionary Movement from Britain in Modern History, 1965; Social History and Christian Mission, 1967. *Recreations:* reading, travel, stamp collecting. *Address:* 3 Little Cloister, Westminster, SW1. *T:* 01-222 7314. *Club:* Royal Commonwealth Society.

**WARREN, Sir Mortimer (Langton),** Kt 1959; FCA; Director: Trustees Corporation Ltd, Great Portland Estates Ltd, Ellis (Kensington) Ltd, Achille Serre, and other companies; *b* 27 Oct. 1903; *o c* of late Mortimer Warren and Mary (*née* Langton); *m* 1929, Dorothea Ann Burns; one *d. Educ:* Cranleigh. Chartered Accountant, 1927; Queen Anne's Bounty: Asst Accountant, 1927; Asst Sec. and Finance Officer, 1942; Church Commissioners for England: Financial Secretary, 1948-54; Secretary, 1954-64, retired. A Governor of Guy's Hospital, of Cranleigh School and of Francis Holland Schools. *Publication:* Investment for the Ordinary Man, 1958. *Address:* 7 Strathearn Place, Hyde Park, W2. *T:* 01-262 9715. *Club:* Athenæum.

**WARREN, Robert Penn;** writer; Member of: American Academy of Arts and Letters; American Philosophical Society; Professor of English, Yale University, since 1961; *b* 24 April 1905; *s* of Robert Franklin Warren and Anna Ruth Penn; *m* 1952, Eleanor Clark; two *c. Educ:* Vanderbilt University of California; Yale University; Oxford University. Asst Professor: Southwestern Coll., Tennessee, 1930-31; Vanderbilt Univ., 1931-34; Assoc. Prof., Univ. of Louisiana, 1934-42; Founder and an editor Southern Review, 1935-42; Prof., Univ. of Minnesota, 1942-50; Prof. of Drama, Yale University, 1951-56. Houghton Mifflin Fellow (fiction), 1936; Guggenheim Fellow 1939, 1947; Shelley Memorial Award (poetry), 1942; Chair of Poetry, Library of Congress, 1944-45; Pulitzer Prize (fiction), 1947; Meltzer Award for screen play, 1949; Sidney Hillman Award for Journalism, 1957; Millay Prize (Amer. Poetry Society), 1958; National Book Award (Poetry), 1958; Pulitzer Prize (poetry), 1958; Irita Van Doren Award (Herald Tribune), 1965; Bollingen Prize for Poetry, 1967; Nat. Arts Foundn Award, 1968; Nat. Medal for Literature, 1970. Hon. DLitt: University of Louisville, 1949; Kenyon College, 1952; Colby College, 1956; University of Kentucky, 1957; Swarthmore College, 1959; Yale University, 1960; Fairfield Univ., 1969; Wesleyan Univ., 1970; Hon. LLD, Univ. of Bridgeport, 1965. *Publications:* John Brown: Making of a Martyr, 1929; XXXVI Poems, 1936; Night Rider (novel), 1939; At Heaven's Gate (novel), 1943; Eleven Poems on Same Theme, 1942; Selected Poems, 1944; All the King's Men (novel), 1946 (film, 1949); Coleridge's Ancient Mariner, 1947; Blackberry Winter (Novelette), 1947; Circus in the Attic (stories), 1947; World Enough and Time (novel), 1950; Brother to Dragons (poem), 1953; Band of Angels (novel), 1955, (film, 1957); Segregation: The Inner Conflict of the South, 1956; Promises: Poems 1954-56, 1957; Selected Essays, 1958; The Cave (novel), 1959; You, Emperors, and Others: Poems 1957-60, 1960; Legacy of the Civil War: A meditation on the centennial, 1961; Wilderness (novel), 1961; Flood: a romance of our time (novel), 1964; Who Speaks for the Negro?, 1965; Selected Poems, Old and New, 1923-1966, 1966; Incarnations: Poems 1966-68, 1968; Audubon: a vision (poems), 1969. Various collections and anthologies. *Recreations:* swimming, walking. *Address:* 2495 Redding Road, Fairfield, Conn, USA. *Club:* Century (New York).

**WARRENDER,** family name of **Baron Bruntisfield.**

**WARRINGTON, Suffragan Bishop of,** since 1970; **Rt. Rev. John Monier Bickersteth;** *b* 6 Sept. 1921; *yr s* of Rev. Canon Edward Monier Bickersteth, *qv*; *m* 1955, Rosemary, *yr d* of late Edward and Muriel Cleveland-Stevens, Gaines, Oxted; three *s* one *d*. *Educ:* Rugby; Christ Church, Oxford; Wells Theol College. MA Oxon 1953. Captain, Buffs and Royal Artillery, 1941-46, Normandy and India. Priest, 1951; Curate, St Matthew, Moorfields, Bristol, 1950-53; Vicar, St John's, Hurst Green, Oxted, 1954-62; St Stephen's, Chatham, 1962-70. C of E Delegate to 4th Assembly of World Council of Churches, Uppsala, 1968. *Recreations:* walking, gardening. *Address:* Martinsfield, Elm Avenue, Great Crosby, Liverpool L23 2SX. *T:* 051-924 7004. *Club:* Travellers'.

**WARTER, Sir Philip,** Kt 1944; President, Associated British Picture Corporation Ltd and associated companies; formerly Chairman: Thames Television; Transport Holding Co.; Director Thomas Cook and Son; *b* 31 Dec. 1903; 3rd *s* of W. H. Warter, Folkestone; *m* 1929, Katherine Scott Maxwell; one *d* (decd). *Address:* 30 Golden Square, W1.

**WARTIOVAARA, Otso Uolevi,** Hon. GCVO; Ambassador of Finland to the Court of St James's since 1968; *b* Helsinki, 16 Nov. 1908; *s* of J. V. Wartiovaara, Dir-Gen. of Finnish Govt Accounting Office, and Siiri Nystén; *m* 1936, Maine Alanen, three *s*. *Educ:* Helsinki Univ. Master of Law, 1932; Asst Judge, 1934. Entered Foreign Service, 1934; Attaché, Paris, 1936-39; Sec. and Head of Section, Min. for For. Affairs, 1939-42; Counsellor, Stockholm, 1942-44; Consul, Haaparanta, Sweden, 1944-45; Head of Section, Min. for For. Affairs, 1945-49; Counsellor, Washington, 1949-52; Head of Admin. Dept, Min. for For. Affairs, 1952-54; Envoy and Minister, 1954; Head of Legal Dept, Min. for For. Affairs, 1954-56; Minister, Belgrade and Athens, 1956-58; Ambassador, Belgrade, and Minister to Athens, 1958-61; Ambassador to Vienna, 1961-68, and to Holy See, 1966-68, also Perm. Rep. to Internat. Atomic Energy Organization, 1961-68. Kt Comdr, Order of White Rose and Order of Lion of Finland; Cross of Freedom; Silver Cross of Sport, Finland. Grand Gold Cross of Austria; Grand Cross, Orders of Phœnix (Greece), Pius IX, Flag (Yugoslavia); Comdr, Orders of Northern Star (Sweden), St Olav (Norway) and Vasa (Sweden). *Recreations:* golf, shooting. *Address:* 14 Kensington Palace Gardens, W8. *T:* 01-229 6242. *Club:* Travellers'.

**WARTNABY, John;** Keeper, Department of Astronomy and Geophysics, Science Museum, South Kensington, since 1969; *b* 6 Jan. 1926; *o s* of Ernest John and Beatrice Hilda Wartnaby; *m* 1962, Kathleen Mary Barber, MD, MRCP; one *s* one *d*. *Educ:* Chiswick Grammar Sch.; Imperial Coll. of Science and Technology; University Coll., London. BSc 1946; DIC 1950; MSc 1967; AInstP 1956. Asst Keeper, Dept of Astronomy and Geophysics, Science Museum, 1951; Deputy Keeper, 1960. Dir, E. & B. Wartnaby Ltd. *Publications:* Seismology, 1957; The International Geophysical Year, 1957; Surveying, 1968; papers in learned jls. *Recreations:* reading, painting, the Irish language. *Address:* Greenway, Greenhurst Lane, Oxted, Surrey. *T:* Oxted 4461.

**WARWICK,** 7th Earl of, *cr* 1759; **Charles Guy Fulke Greville;** Baron Brooke, 1621; Earl Brooke, 1746; Lieut, Reserve of Officers, Grenadier Guards; *b* 4 March 1911, *e s* of 6th Earl and Marjorie (*d* 1943), *d* of Sir W. Eden, 7th Bt; *S* father, 1928; *m* 1st, 1933, Rose (from whom he obtained a divorce, 1938), *d* of late D. C. Bingham, Coldstream Guards, and Lady Rosabelle Brand; one *s*; 2nd, 1942, Mary (from whom he obtained a divorce, 1949), *d* of P. C. Hopkinson, Kingston Gorse, Sussex; 3rd, 1963, Mme Janine Angele Josephine Detry de Marès. Merchant Navy, Admiralty Small Vessels Pool, 1943. Warwickshire CC, 1934-36; a Governor of Birmingham Univ.; Mayor of Warwick, 1951. Alderman 1952; DL, Warwickshire. Governor: Warwick Kings Schools; Royal Shakespeare Theatre. *Heir: s* Lord Brooke, *qv*. *Address:* Warwick Castle.

**WARWICK, Archdeacon of;** *see* Proctor, Ven. J. H.

**WARWICK, Cyril Walter;** Chairman, Houlder Bros & Co. Ltd, 1962-69, President since 1970; *b* 30 Sept. 1899; 2nd *s* of late J. J. W. Warwick; *m* 1925, Dorothy Fitzgerald, *d* of late John Miller; one *s* one *d*. *Educ:* Tollington Sch.; King's Coll., London Univ. Served RFC and RAF, 1917-19. Joined Kaye Son & Co., shipbrokers, 1919; elected Baltic Exchange, 1920; joined Houlder Bros & Co. Ltd, 1938; Director Hadley Shipping Co. Ltd, 1938, Chm. 1962; Director: Houlder Line, 1944-69; Furness Withy & Co. Ltd, 1962-69; Royal Mail Lines Ltd, 1965; and various other shipping companies; Dep. Chairman, Houlder Bros, 1957; Director, Baltic Mercantile and Shipping Exchange, 1951; Vice-Chairman, 1959; Chairman, 1961-63; Hon. Mem., 1970. President, Cereals and Baltic Friendly Society, 1966-68; Member of Council: Chamber of Shipping of UK; Fellow, Inst. Chartered Shipbrokers; Liveryman, Worshipful Company of Shipwrights. Freight Market Rep. of Ministry of Transport, 1958-67. *Recreations:* riding, ski-ing, fishing. *Address:* Walmar, Beech Hill, Hadley Wood, Herts. *T:* 01-449 0491. *Clubs:* Bath, Canning.

**WARWICK, Richard Trevor T.;** *see* Turner-Warwick.

**WARWICK, Prof. Roger;** Professor of Anatomy and Director of Department of Anatomy, Guy's Hospital Medical School, University of London, since 1955. *Educ:* Victoria University of Manchester. BSc, 1935; MB, ChB, Manchester, 1937; MD (Gold Medal), 1952; PhD, 1955. House Physician and House Surgeon, Professorial Unit, Manchester Royal Infirmary, 1938-39; Surgeon Lieut, RNVR, 1939-45; Demonstrator and Lecturer in Anatomy, University of Manchester, 1945-55. Member Anatomical Society of Great Britain (Symington Memorial Prize, 1953); Scientific Fellow of Zoological Society; Member Society for Human Biology, etc. *Publications:* (ed) Gray's Anatomy; contributions to Brain, Journal Anat., Journal Comp. Neurol., etc. *Recreations:* Natural history, especially Lepidoptera, radio communication, archæology. *Address:* Department of Anatomy, Guy's Hospital Medical School, St Thomas's Street, London Bridge, SE1.

**WARWICK, Captain William Eldon,** RD, RNR (Retired); Commodore, Cunard Line Ltd, since 1970; Master, RMS Queen Elizabeth 2, since 1966; *b* 12 Nov. 1912; *e s* of Eldon Warwick, architect and Gertrude Florence Gent; *m* 1939, Evelyn King (*née* Williams); three *s*. *Educ:* Birkenhead Sch.; HMTS Conway. Joined Merchant Service, 1928, serving in Indian Ocean and Red Sea; awarded Master Mariner's Certificate, 1936; joined Cunard White Star as Jun. Officer (Lancastria), 1937; commissioned in RNR, 1937. Mobilized in RN War Service, 1939, in

Coastal Forces and Corvettes in North Atlantic, Russian Convoys and Normandy Landings, 1939-46 (despatches, 1946). First cargo command, Alsatia, 1954; first passenger command, Carinthia, 1958; followed by command of almost all the passenger liners in Cunard fleet. Promoted Captain RNR, 1960; retd RNR, 1965. Younger Brother of Trinity House; Liveryman and Mem. Court of Assistants, Hon. Co. of Master Mariners; Freeman of City of London; MIN. *Recreations:* reading, music, walking. *Address:* Greywell Cottage, Callow Hill, Virginia Water, Surrey. *T:* Wentworth 3361. *Clubs:* United Service, RNVR Officers; Master Mariners (Southampton).

**WASHBOURN, Rear-Admiral Richard Everley,** CB 1961; DSO 1940; OBE 1950; Chief of Naval Staff, RNZN, 1963-65, retired; *b* 14 Feb. 1910; *s* of H. E. A. Washbourn, Nelson, NZ; *m* 1943, June, *d* of L. M. Herapath, Auckland, NZ; one *s* one *d*. *Educ:* Nelson Coll., New Zealand. Entered Royal Navy by Special Entry from New Zealand, 1927; HMS Erebus, 1928; HMS London, 1929-31; Courses, 1932; HMS Warspite, 1933; HMS Diomede, 1934-35; Specialised in Gunnery, 1936-37; HMS Excellent, 1938; HMS Achilles, 1939-42; Battle of the Plate, 13 Dec. 1939 (DSO); HMS Excellent, 1942; HMS Anson, 1943. Admiralty Gunnery Establishment, 1944-45; Exec. Officer, HMNZS, Bellona, 1946-48; Comdr Supt HMNZ Dockyard, Devonport, 1950; Dep. Director of Naval Ordnance, 1950-53; HMS Manxman, 1953; Chief Staff Officer to Flag Officer (Flotillas), Mediterranean, 1954-55; Director of Naval Ordnance, Admiralty, 1956-58; HMS Tiger, 1959; Director-General, Weapons, 1960-62; retired Royal Navy, 1962; entered RNZN, 1963; retired RNZN, 1965. *Recreation:* beachcombing. *Address:* Onekaka, RD2, Takaka, Golden Bay, Nelson, New Zealand.

**WASS, Dr Charles Alfred Alan;** Director of Safety in Mines Research Establishment, Ministry of Technology, Sheffield, since 1970; *b* 20 July 1911; *s* of William and Louise Wass, Sutton-in-Ashfield, Nottinghamshire; *m* 1936, Alice Elizabeth Carpenter; two *d*. *Educ:* Brunt's Sch., Mansfield; Nottingham Univ. Post Office Radio Research Station, 1934-46; Royal Aircraft Establishment, 1946-55; Safety in Mines Research Establishment, 1955-. *Publications:* Introduction to Electronic Analogue Computers, 1955 (2nd edn, with K. C. Garner, 1965); papers on electrical communication subjects and mine safety. *Recreations:* music making, reed instruments. *Address:* (home) 28 Heather Lea Avenue, Dore, Sheffield S17 3DJ. *T:* Sheffield 363906; (office) Ministry of Technology, Red Hill, off Broad Lane, Sheffield S3 7HQ. *T:* Sheffield 78141.

**WASSERSTEIN, Prof. Abraham;** Professor of Greek, Hebrew University of Jerusalem, since 1969; *b* Frankfurt/Main, Germany, 5 Oct. 1921; *s* of late Berl Bernhard Wasserstein and late Czarna Cilla (*née* Laub); *m* 1942, Margaret Eva (*née* Ecker); two *s* one *d*. *Educ:* Schools in Berlin and Rome; privately in Palestine; Birkbeck Coll., London Univ. BA 1949, PhD 1951. Assistant in Greek, 1951-52, Lecturer in Greek, 1952-60, Glasgow Univ.; Prof. of Classics, Leicester Univ., 1960-69, and Dean of Faculty of Arts, 1966-69. FRAS 1961. *Publications:* contrib. to learned journals. *Recreations:* theatre, travel. *Address:* Department of Classics, The Hebrew University, Jerusalem, Israel.

**WASTIE, Winston Victor,** CB 1962; OBE 1946 (MBE 1937); Under-Secretary, Ministry of Public Building and Works, Scotland, 1959-62, retired; *b* 5 March 1900; *s* of H. Wastie; *m* 1924, Charmbury Billows; one *d*. *Educ:* Greenwich Secondary Sch. Civil Service, New Scotland Yard, 1915-42; Chief Licensing Officer, Civil Building Control, Ministry of Works, 1942-46; Assistant Secretary, Scottish HQ, Ministry of Works, 1946-59; Under-Secretary, 1959. *Recreations:* bridge, gardening and sport. *Address:* Dirleton, Hazlebank Close, Petersfield, Hants.

**WATERER, Sir (Robert) Bernard,** Kt 1955; CB 1951; JP; *b* 12 Feb. 1891; *s* of late Robert Waterer, Chertsey, Surrey. *Educ:* Eastbourne Coll. Enlisted RE, 1914; commissioned, RE, Feb. 1915; invalided out, Oct. 1916. Entered Treasury Solicitor's Dept, 1920; transferred to Solicitor's office, Inland Revenue, 1925. Principal Assistant Solicitor of Inland Revenue, 1946-52; Solicitor of Inland Revenue, 1952-56. Chairman, Standing Cttee under Merchandise Marks Act, 1926 (agricultural etc produce), 1960. JP Hants, 1956; Glos, 1958. *Address:* Parkside, Hatherley Court Road, Cheltenham, Glos. *T:* 54504.

**WATERFALL, William Duncan,** CB 1947; *b* 28 Dec. 1889; *s* of Charles and Louisa Maria Waterfall; *m* 1917, Gertrude Gladys Cornish; one *s* four *d*. *Educ:* Manchester Grammar Sch.; Brasenose Coll., Oxford. Entered Home CS (Secretary's Office, GPO), 1913; Principal, 1924; Dep. Regional Director, London Telecommunications Region, PO, 1936; Dep. Regional Director, NW Region, PO, 1939, and Regional Director, 1942. Director of Savings, General Post Office, 1944-51. *Recreations:* tennis, chess. *Address:* 8 Sauncey Avenue, Harpenden, Herts. *T:* Harpenden 4141.
*See also F. M. Drake.*

**WATERFIELD, John Percival;** Managing Director, The British Electrical and Allied Manufacturers' Association Ltd (BEAMA), since 1970; *b* Dublin, 5 Oct. 1921; *er s* of late Percival Waterfield, KBE, CB; *m* 1950, Margaret Lee Thomas; two *s* one *d*. *Educ:* Dragon Sch.; Charterhouse; Christ Church, Oxford (scholar). Served War of 1939-45: 1st Bn, The King's Royal Rifle Corps (60th Rifles), Western Desert, Tunisia, Italy and Austria (despatches). Entered HM Foreign (subseq. Diplomatic) Service, 1946; Third Secretary, Moscow, 1947; Second Secretary, Tokyo, 1950; Foreign Office, 1952; First Secretary, Santiago, Chile, 1954; HM Consul (Commercial), New York, 1957; FO, 1960; Ambassador to Mali Republic, 1964-65, concurrently to Guinea, 1965; duties connected with NATO, 1966; Counsellor and Head of Chancery, New Delhi, 1966-68; Head of Western Organizations Dept, FCO, 1969. *Address:* 30 Kelso Place, W8. *T:* 01-937 2826; 5 North Street, Somerton, Somerset. *T:* Somerton 389. *Club:* Travellers'.

**WATERFORD,** 8th Marquess of, *cr* 1789; **John Hubert de la Poer Beresford,** Baron La Poer, 1375; Baronet, 1668; Viscount Tyrone, Baron Beresford, 1720; Earl of Tyrone, 1746; Baron Tyrone (Great Britain), 1786; *b* 14 July 1933; *er s* of 7th Marquess and Juliet Mary (who *m* 2nd, 1946, Lieut-Colonel John Silcock), 2nd *d* of late David Lindsay; *S* father, 1934; *m* 1957, Lady Caroline Wyndham-Quin, *yr d* of 6th Earl of Dunraven and Mount-Earl, CB, CBE, MC; three *s* one *d*. *Educ:* Eton. Lieut, RHG Reserve. *Heir:* *s* Earl of Tyrone, *qv*. *Address:* Curraghmore, Portlaw, Co. Waterford. *T:* Portlaw 2. *Clubs:* Turf, White's.

**WATERHOUSE, Captain Rt. Hon. Charles,** PC 1944; MC; *b* 1893; 2nd *surv s* of Thomas Crompton Waterhouse, Lomberdale Hall,

Bakewell; *m* 1917, Beryl (*d* 1970), 2nd *d* of Thomas Ford, New South Wales; two *s* one *d*. *Educ:* Cheltenham; Trinity Hall, Cambridge; MA Economics Tripos, 1914. Served European War, France, 1914-18, 1st Life Guards; contested (C) NE Derbyshire, 1922 and 1923, South Leicester, 1945; MP (C) South Leicester, 1924-45, South-East Division of Leicester, 1950-57. Parliamentary Private Secretary to President of Board of Trade, 1928; to Minister of Labour, 1931-34; Assistant Whip, 1935-36; Junior Lord of the Treasury, 1936; Comptroller of HM Household, 1937-38; Treasurer of HM Household, 1938-39; Assistant Postmaster-General, 1939-41; Parliamentary Secretary Board of Trade, 1941-45; Chairman: East Midlands Area of Conservative and Unionist Associations, 1946-51; Public Accounts Cttee, 1951; Nat. Union of Conservative and Unionist Assocs, 1952; Estimates Cttee, 1953. Chairman, Tanganyika Concessions, 1957-66. DL, JP Derbyshire. *Recreations:* shooting, fishing. *Address:* Middleton Hall, Bakewell, Derbyshire. *Clubs:* Carlton, Turf, Buck's.

**WATERHOUSE, Dr Douglas Frew,** CMG 1970; FRS 1967; FAA 1954; FRACI 1951; Chief of Division of Entomology, Commonwealth Scientific and Industrial Research Organization, since 1960; *b* 3 June 1916; *s* of E. G. Waterhouse, *qv*; *m* 1944, Allison D., *d* of J. H. Calthorpe; three *s* one *d*. *Educ:* Sydney C. of E. Grammar Sch.; Universities of Sydney and Cambridge. BSc Hons, University Medal, MSc, DSc, Sydney. Served War of 1939-45, Captain, AAMC Medical Entomology. Joined Research Staff, CSIRO, 1938; Asst Chief, Div. of Entomology, 1953-59. Biological Secretary, Australian Acad. of Science, 1961-66; Chm. Council, Canberra Coll. of Advanced Educn, 1969-. David Syme Research Prize, 1953. *Publications:* numerous articles on insect physiology, biochemistry, ecology and control of insects. *Recreations:* gardening, fishing, gyotaku. *Address:* 60 National Circuit, Deakin, ACT 2600, Australia. *T:* 731722.

**WATERHOUSE, Eben Gowrie,** OBE 1962; MA, Officier d'Académie; Cavaliere of the Order of the Crown of Italy; Professor of German, Sydney University, 1937-46, now Emeritus Professor; *b* 29 April 1881; *s* of Australian parents; *m* 1912, Janet Frew Kellie, MA, Kilmarnock, Scotland; four *s*. *Educ:* Sydney Grammar Sch.; Sydney Univ.; Leipzig Univ.; Paris. BA (Sydney) with First Class Honours in English, French, German, and MacCallum prize for English; MA with First Class Honours in French; Master of Modern Languages at Sydney Grammar Sch. (for 4 years); Senior Lecturer in Modern Languages at Teachers' Coll., Sydney (for 11 years); acting Professor of French at Sydney Univ., 1921; Associate Professor of German and Comparative Literature, 1925-37; President of the Sydney University Union, 1928; Trustee Art Gallery of New South Wales, 1938-62. President Internat. Camellia Society, 1962. Gold Medal of Goethe Institute, 1957. *Publications:* The Teaching of the French Verb by the Direct Method; (with J. A. Snowden) The Initial Stages in French by the Direct Method, Parts I and II; French Phonetic and Fluency Exercises; Goethe (Centenary lecture), 1932; Camellia Quest, 1947; Camellia Trail, with 21 colour plates, 1952; (with Norman Sparnon) The Magic of Camellias, 1968. *Recreations:* landscape gardening; special hobby: the propagation and cultivation of camellias. *Address:* Eryldene, 17 McIntosh Street, Gordon, Sydney, NSW 2072, Australia. *T:* 49-2271.

*see also D. F. Waterhouse.*

**WATERHOUSE, Ellis Kirkham,** CBE 1956 (MBE 1943); MA (Oxon); AM (Princeton); *b* 16 Feb. 1905; *s* of P. Leslie Waterhouse and Eleanor Margetson; *m* 1949, Helen, *d* of F. W. Thomas; two *d*. *Educ:* Marlborough; New Coll., Oxford (Scholar). Commonwealth Fund Fellow (Department of Art and Archæology, University of Princeton, USA), 1927-29; Assistant, National Gallery, 1929-33; Librarian, British School at Rome, 1933-36; selected and catalogued pictures for RA Exhibition of 17th Century Art (1938), 1937; Fellow of Magdalen Coll., Oxford, 1938-47; served with Army and Foreign Office (mainly in Middle East), 1939-45; temp. editor, Burlington Magazine, 1946; Reader in History of Art, Manchester Univ., 1947-48; Director of National Galleries of Scotland, 1949-52; Slade Professor of Fine Arts, University of Oxford, 1953-55; Clark Visiting Professor, Williams Coll., Mass, 1962-63; Mellon Visiting Professor, University of Pittsburgh, 1967-68; Barber Professor of Fine Arts and Dir of Barber Inst., Birmingham Univ., 1952-70. FBA 1955; FRHistSoc. Hon. DLitt: Nottingham, 1968; Leicester, 1970. Officer of Order Orange Nassau. Cavaliere ufficiale, Ordine al Merito della Repubblica italiana, 1961. *Publications:* El Greco's Italian Period, 1930; Roman Baroque Painting, 1937; Sir Joshua Reynolds, 1941; British Painting, 1530-1790, 1953; Gainsborough, 1958; Italian Baroque Painting, 1962; Jayne Lectures, 1964, 1965; Catalogue of Pictures at Waddesdon Manor, 1967; numerous articles and catalogues. *Address:* Overshot Hinksey Hill, Oxford. *T:* Oxford 35320.

**WATERHOUSE, Major-General George Guy,** CB 1939; MC; *b* 12 June 1886; 3rd *s* of late Thomas Crompton Waterhouse of Lomberdale Hall, Bakewell, and Sarah, *d* of late Jonathan Holden of Reims; *m* 1st, Katherine Louise (*d* 1930), *d* of late Charles Birks, Adelaide; no *c*; 2nd, 1932, Eileen Dendy, *d* of late Dendy Watney. *Educ:* Cheltenham Coll.; RMA, Woolwich. 2nd Lieut, Royal Engineers, 1905; employed on survey in Nigeria, 1910-13; served European War in France and Salonika (wounded, despatches twice, MC, brevets of Major and Lieut-Colonel, Chevalier of the Legion of Honour, White Eagle of Serbia); passed Staff Coll., Camberley, 1919; Instructor of English, Ecole Supérieure de Guerre, Paris, 1922-23; passed Royal Naval Staff Coll., Greenwich, 1928; commanded Training Bn, RE, 1930-31; Military Attaché, Paris, 1931-32; with British Military Mission, Iraq, 1934-37; Maj.-General, 1938; Inspector-General and Head of British Advisory Military Mission, Iraq Army, 1938-41; District Commander UK, 1941-44; retired pay, 1945; Deputy Commissioner, British Red Cross and St John War Organisation, at HQ, SEAC, 1945. Order of Rafidain 3rd Class. *Address:* 9 Hamston House, Kensington Court Place, W8. *T:* 01-937 3397. *Club:* United Service.

**WATERHOUSE, Gilbert,** LittD (Dublin), MA (Cambridge and Dublin); MRIA; FRGS; Professor of German, Queen's University, Belfast, 1933-53; *b* Hipperholme, Yorks, 15 July 1888; *s* of late Harold Waterhouse, Tarleton, Lancs; *m* 1920, Mary Elizabeth, *e d* of late Sir Robert Woods, MCh; three *d*. *Educ:* Manchester Grammar Sch.; St John's Coll., Cambridge; University of Berlin. First Tiarks University German Scholar, Cambridge, 1910; Asst Lecturer in English in the University of Leipzig, 1911-14; Asst Master, Manchester Grammar Sch., 1914-15; Professor of German, University of Dublin, 1915-32; served European War as Lieut TF Unattached List and Lieut, RNVR; Administrator,

Government Scheme of Grants to ex-Service Students (Ireland), 1919-25; Secretary, Royal Commission on the University of Dublin, 1920. Dep. Chief Welfare Officer, Belfast Civil Defence, 1941-45. Exchange Professor of German, University of Illinois, 1950, and University of California (Los Angeles), 1951. Trustee, Magee University College, Londonderry, 1953-67. *Publications:* The Literary Relations of England and Germany in the Seventeenth Century, 1914; The War and the Study of German, 1917; Grillparzer: Weh' dem, der lügt, 1923; The Prince of Peace, 1927; German Literature, 1928; (trans.) Clara Viebig: The Sleeping Army, 1929; (trans.) Gen. v. Seeckt: Thoughts of a Soldier, 1930; Simon van der Stel's Journal of his Expedition to Namaqualand, 1932; A Short History of German Literature, 1942, 3rd edn, 1959. Editor of Year-Book of Modern Languages, 1920. *Address:* 92 Malone Road, Belfast. *Club:* Ulster.

*See also Prof. J. Colhoun.*

**WATERHOUSE, Keith Spencer;** Writer; *b* 6 Feb. 1929; 4th *s* of Ernest and Elsie Edith Waterhouse; *m* 1951, Joan Foster; one *s* two *d. Educ:* Leeds. Journalist in Leeds and London, 1950-58. Films (with Willis Hall) include: Billy Liar; Whistle Down the Wind; A Kind of Loving; Lock Up Your Daughters. *Publications: novels:* There is a Happy Land, 1957; Billy Liar, 1959; Jubb, 1963; The Bucket Shop, 1968; *plays:* (all with Willis Hall) include: Billy Liar, 1960; Celebration, 1961; All Things Bright and Beautiful, 1963; Say Who You Are, 1965; Whoops-a-Daisy, 1968; Children's Day, 1969; *general:* (with Guy Deghy) Café Royal, 1956. *Address:* 11 Upper Wimpole Street, W1. *Club:* PEN.

**WATERHOUSE, Ronald Gough,** QC 1969; Deputy Chairman: Cheshire Quarter Sessions, since 1964; Flintshire Quarter Sessions, since 1966; *b* Holywell, Flintshire, 8 May 1926; *s* of late Thomas Waterhouse, CBE, and of Doris Helena Waterhouse (*née* Gough); *m* 1960, Sarah Selina, *d* of late Captain E. A. Ingram; one *s* one *d. Educ:* Holywell Grammar Sch.; St John's Coll., Cambridge. RAFVR, 1944-48. McMahon Schol., St John's Coll., 1949; Pres., Cambridge Union Soc., 1950; toured Amer. Univs (debating), 1951; MA, LLB; called to Bar, Middle Temple, 1952 (Harmsworth Schol.). Mem. Bar Council, 1961-65. Contested (Lab) West Flintshire, 1959. Chm., Cttee of Inquiry on Rabies, 1970. *Recreations:* music, golf. *Address:* 12 Cavendish Avenue, NW8. *T:* 01-286 7659; Farrar's Building, Temple, EC4. *T:* 01-583 9241. *Clubs:* Garrick; Bristol Channel Yacht (Mumbles).

**WATERLOW, Prof. John Conrad,** CMG 1970; MD, ScD; FRCP; FRGS; Professor of Human Nutrition, London School of Hygiene and Tropical Medicine, since Oct. 1970; *b* 13 June 1916; *o s* of Sir Sydney Waterlow, KCMG, CBE, HM Diplomatic Service; *m* 1939, Angela Pauline Cecil Gray; two *s* one *d. Educ:* Eton Coll.; Trinity Coll., Cambridge (MD, ScD); London Hosp. Med. College. Mem., Scientific Staff, MRC, 1942; Dir, MRC Tropical Metabolism Research Unit, Univ. of the West Indies, 1954-70. Vice-Chm., Adv. Cttee on Medical Research, Pan-American Health Organization, 1969-. *Publications:* numerous papers on protein malnutrition and protein metabolism. *Recreation:* mountain walking. *Address:* 3 Campden Hill Square, W8. *T:* 01-727 6719. *Club:* Savile.

**WATERLOW, (Sir) Philip Alexander,** 4th Bt, *cr* 1873 (but does not use this title); retired as Chairman and Managing Director of Waterlow & Sons Ltd, 1960; *b* 17 March 1897; *s* of Sir Edgar Lutwyche Waterlow, 3rd Bt and Martha (Pattie), *d* of late Robert Carter; *S* father, 1954; *m* 1st, 1923, Gwendoline Iris (marr. diss., 1937), *d* of late Charles Rupert Butler, New Place, Sunningdale (one *s* decd); 2nd, 1937, Annie Catherine (judicial separation, 1951), *e d* of late John Hay. *Educ:* Harrow; RMC, Sandhurst. Formerly Lieut, 3rd King's Own Hussars; served in Ireland and European War, 1914-18, 1916-18; ADC to Military Governor of Cologne, BAOR, 1919-20, RARO; served War of 1939-45 as Captain, Home Guard. Governor of Christ's Hospital and Lloyd Memorial (Caxton) Home, Deal; Liveryman Stationers' and Newspaper Manufacturers' Company; Freeman, City of London. *Heir:* *g s* Christopher Rupert Waterlow, *b* 12 Aug. 1959. *Address:* Chapel Cottage, Nuthurst, Horsham, West Sussex. *Club:* Cavalry.

**WATERLOW, Sir Thomas Gordon,** 3rd Bt *cr* 1930; CBE 1946; Deputy Chairman, Royal Bank of Scotland, since 1967 (Director, since 1951); Deputy Chairman, William Thyne (Holdings) Ltd; Director: Standard Life Assurance Company, since 1948 (Chairman, 1960-63); *b* 2 Jan. 1911; *yr s* of late Sir William A. Waterlow, 1st Bt, KBE, Lord Mayor of London, 1929-30, and late Lady Waterlow; *S* brother, 1969; *m* 1938, Helen Elizabeth (*d* 1970), *yr d* of late Gerard A. H. Robinson, Bix, Henley-on-Thames; three *s. Educ:* Marlborough Coll., Trinity Coll., Cambridge. Joined Whitehead Morris Ltd, 1932; Joint Managing Director, 1937-39. Commissioned in Auxiliary Air Force, 601 (County of London) Squadron, 1937. Served RAF, War of 1939-45 (despatches, Battle of Britain, 1940); released with rank of Group Captain. Chairman, British Carton Assoc., 1953-55; Director: British Investment Trust Ltd, 1960; R. and R. Clark Ltd, 1957-; Deputy Chairman, Livingston Development Corp., 1965-68; Member: Scottish Aerodromes Board, 1947-59; Exec. Cttee Scottish Council (Development and Industry), 1946-48; Scottish Cttee, Council of Industrial Design, 1949-50; Exec. Council, Assoc. of British Chambers of Commerce, 1952-54, 1963-65; President, Edinburgh Chamber of Commerce, 1963-65. Fellow British Institute of Management. *Recreations:* golf, tennis, cricket. *Heir:* *s* (James) Gerard Waterlow [*b* 3 Sept. 1939; *m* 1965, Diana Suzanne, *yr d* of W. T. C. Skyrme, *qv*; one *s* one *d*]. *Address:* 1 Lennox Street, Edinburgh EH4 1QB. *T:* 031-332 2621. *Clubs:* MCC; Caledonian, New (Edinburgh); Hon. Company of Edinburgh Golfers.

**WATERMAN, Sir Ewen McIntyre,** Kt 1963; Chairman, Onkaparinga Woollen Co. Ltd; Director: Elder Smith Goldsbrough Mort Ltd; Waterman Bros (Australasia) Ltd; News Ltd; Southern Television Corporation Ltd; *b* Semaphore, South Australia, 22 Dec. 1901; *s* of late Hugh McIntyre Waterman, Echunga, SA; *m* 1928, Vera, *d* of late J. G. Gibb; one *d. Educ:* Woodville High Sch.; Adelaide School of Mines. Commonwealth Member, Australian Wool Board, 1955-63; Australian Member, International Wool Secretariat, 1948-55 (Chairman, 1952-54); Chairman Exec. Cttee, Wool Bureau Incorp. (USA), 1952-54; Consultant, FAO Livestock Survey, E. Africa, 1965; Chairman, Australian Wool Industry Conference, 1966-; President: Royal Flying Doctor Service of Australia (SA Section), 1960-62; South Australian Adult Deaf and Dumb Society, 1947-; Member Council, South Australian Institute of Technology, 1962-; Member Board of Governors, Adelaide Festival of Arts; Hon. Governor, Postgraduate Foundation in Medicine,

University of Adelaide. *Address:* Blackwood Park, Strathalbyn, South Australia. *Clubs:* Oriental; Adelaide (Adelaide).

**WATERMAN, Rt. Rev. Robert Harold;** *b* 11 March 1894; *s* of Canon Robert B. Waterman and Annabella Hughton; *m* 1921, Frances Isabel Bayne; three *s* two *d* (and one *s* decd). *Educ:* University of Bishop's Coll., Lennoxville, PQ. BA 1914, BD 1933, Deacon, 1920; priest, 1921; Curate of Bearbrook, 1920-21, Rector, 1921-27; Rector of Pembroke, 1927-33; Rector of Smith's Falls, 1933-37; Rector of Christchurch Cathedral, Hamilton, Diocese of Niagara, 1937-48; Dean of Niagara, 1938-48; Bishop Coadjutor of Nova Scotia, 1948-50; Bishop of Nova Scotia, 1950-63, retired. *Address:* PO Box 314, Digby, Nova Scotia, Canada.

**WATERPARK,** 7th Baron *cr* 1792; **Frederick Caryll Philip Cavendish,** Bt 1755; *b* 6 Oct. 1926; *s* of Brig.-General Frederick William Laurence Sheppard Hart Cavendish, CMG, DSO (*d* 1931) and Enid, Countess of Kenmare (she *m* 3rd, 1933, as his 3rd wife, 1st Viscount Furness, who *d* 1940; 4th, as his 2nd wife, 6th Earl of Kenmare), *d* of Charles Lindeman, Sydney, New South Wales, and *widow* of Roderick Cameron, New York; *S* uncle 1948; *m* 1951, Daniele, *e d* of Monsieur Guirche, Paris; one *s* two *d*. *Educ:* Eton. Lieut, 4th and 1st Bn Grenadier Guards, 1944-46. Served as Assistant District Commandant Kenya Police Reserve, 1952-55, during Mau Mau Rebellion. *Heir: s* Hon. Roderick Alexander Cavendish, *b* 10 Oct. 1959. *Address:* 32 Kensington Court, W8. *Clubs:* Guards, Royal Aero.

**WATERS, Major (Hon. Colonel) Sir Arnold (Horace Santo),** VC 1919; Kt 1954; CBE 1949; DSO 1918; MC; JP; DL; FInstCE; FIMechE; FGS; MinstWE; Consulting Engineer; *b* 1886; *y s* of Rev. Richard Waters, Plymouth; *m* 1924, Gladys, *d* of Rev. C. D. Barriball, Birmingham; three *s*. President InstStructE, 1933, 1943; Divisional Food Officer, W Midland Div., 1941-42. JP Sutton Coldfield, 1930; DL Warwicks, 1957. Hon. FInstStructE; Hon. MInstRE; Hon. FInstPHE. Chm., South Staffs Waterworks Co., 1946-59. *Address:* St Winnow, Ladywood Road, Four Oaks, Sutton Coldfield, Warwicks. *T:* Four Oaks 0060.

**WATERS, Frank George,** OBE 1963; Counsellor, Foreign and Commonwealth Office, since 1968; *b* 14 April 1911; *m* 1938, Dulcie Georgina (*née* Burden); two *d*. *Educ:* Woolwich Polytechnic Secondary Sch. Business (Swift & Co. Ltd) London, 1928; Royal Ordnance Factories, Woolwich, 1938; HM Customs and Excise, 1939; entered FO, 1942; British Embassy, Washington, 1945-48; Foreign Office, 1949; HM Consul, Leopoldville, 1950-51; First Secretary, Paris, 1952-53; Foreign Office, 1954-58; HM Consul–General, Berlin, 1959-63; Deputy Consul-General, Los Angeles, 1963-66; HBM Consul–General, Alexandria, UAR, 1966-68. *Recreations:* golf, tennis, philately, fishing. *Address:* 5 Stainmore Close, Chislehurst, Kent. *Clubs:* Royal Automobile; British United Services (Los Angeles).

**WATERS, Jack;** *see* Warner, Jack.

**WATERS, Montague,** QC 1968; *b* 28 Feb. 1917; *s* of Elias Wasserman, BSc, and Rose Waters; *m* 1940, Jessica Freedman; three *s*. *Educ:* Central Foundation Sch., City of London; London University. LLB (Hons) London, 1938. Solicitor of the Supreme Court, 1939. Military Service, KRRC, Intelligence Corps and Dept of HM Judge Advocate General, 1940-46 (Defence and Victory Medals, 1939-45 Star). Called to the Bar, 1946; released from HM Forces with rank of Major (Legal Staff), 1946. Governor, Central Foundation Schools, 1968. Freeman, City of London, 1962. *Recreations:* theatre, sport. *Address:* Arlington, The Bishops Avenue, N2. *T:* 01-883 3255.

**WATERS, William Alexander,** FRS 1954; Professor of Chemistry, Dyson Perrins Laboratory, Oxford University, 1967-70, retired; Fellow, Balliol College, Oxford, 1945-70, now Fellow Emeritus; *b* Cardiff, 8 May 1903; *o s* of William Waters, schoolmaster, Cardiff; *m* 1932, Elizabeth, *y d* of William Dougall, Darlington; no *c*. *Educ:* Cardiff High Sch.; Gonville and Caius Coll., Cambridge. Rhondda Schol.; MA; PhD; ScD; MA Oxon (by incorporation). Lecturer in Chemistry, Durham Univ. (Durham Div.), 1928-45; University Demonstrator in Organic Chemistry, Oxford, 1945-60; Reader in Physical Organic Chemistry, 1960-67; Chemistry Tutor, Balliol Coll., 1945-67. Leverhulme Research Fellow, 1939; Ministry of Supply: Scientific Officer, 1939-42; Senior Scientific Officer, 1942-44. Goldsmiths' Company's Exhibitioner (Chem.) 1923. FRIC (Member, Council 1968-71); Chem. Soc. Council, 1948-51, 1959-62; Member DSIR Road Tar Research Cttee, 1950-60. *Publications:* Physical Aspects of Organic Chemistry, 5th edn, 1954; The Chemistry of Free Radicals, 2nd edn, 1948; (Editor and part author) Methods of Quantitive Micro-analysis, 1949, 2nd edn, 1955; (ed) Vistas in Free Radical Chemistry, 1959; Mechanisms of Oxidation of Organic Compounds, 1964. Publications in Proc. Royal Society, Journal Chem. Society, Trans. and Discussions of Faraday Society. *Address:* 5 Field House Drive, Oxford; Dyson Perrins Laboratory, Oxford. *T:* 59601. *Club:* Athenæum.

**WATERSON, Prof. Anthony Peter,** MD, FRCP; Professor of Virology, Royal Postgraduate Medical School, London, since 1967; *b* 23 Dec. 1923; *m* 1958, Ellen Ware; one *s* two *d*. *Educ:* Epsom Coll.; Emmanuel Coll., Cambridge; London Hospital Medical Coll. MD (Cantab) 1954; MRCP 1950; FRCP 1970. House appointments, London Hospital, 1947-48; MO, Headquarters Unit, BAFO, Germany, 1948-50; Ho. Phys. and Clin. Pathologist, Addenbrooke's Hospital, Cambridge, 1950-52; Demonstrator in Path., 1953-58, Lecturer in Path., 1958-64, University of Cambridge; Fellow of Emmanuel Coll., 1954-64, Asst Tutor, 1957-64; Professor of Med. Microbiology, St Thomas's Hospital Medical Sch., 1964-67. Spent year 1962-63 on sabbatical leave at Max-Planck Institut für Virusforschung, Tübingen. *Publications:* Introduction to Animal Virology, 1961, 2nd edn, 1968. Papers on viruses and virus diseases. *Recreations:* mountain walking; European history; gardens; browsing in Who's Who. *Address:* Department of Virology, Royal Postgraduate Medical School, Ducane Road, W12. *T:* 01-743 2030; Brackendene House, Woburn Hill, Weybridge, Surrey. *T:* Weybridge 46051.

**WATERSON, Hon. Sidney Frank;** *b* 4 June 1896; *er s* of late John Waterson, FRIBA, and Louisa Waterson; *m* 1924, Hilda Maude, *d* of late Major J. A. E. Markus; one *s* one *d*. *Educ:* St Clare, Walmer; Westminster (King's Scholar). Served European War, 1915-19: 2nd Lieut, 3rd (Spec. Res.) Royal Sussex Regt attached Machine Gun Corps, Salonika, 1916, France, 1917-18; MP (Union of S Africa) for South Peninsula Division, 1929-38; Envoy Extraordinary and Minister Plenipotentiary for the Union of South Africa to France, 1939; High Commissioner for Union of S. Africa in

London, 1939-42; Minister of Economic Development, 1943-48, of Mines, 1945-48; Minister of Transport, South Africa, 1948. MP Constantia Division, 1943-70. *Recreations:* golf, fishing. *Address:* Blairbuoy, Summerley Road, Kenilworth, CP, SA. *Clubs:* Beefsteak; City, Civil Service (Capetown).

**WATERSTON, David James,** MBE 1940; FRCS; FRCSE; Consultant Surgeon, Hospital for Sick Children, Great Ormond Street, since 1951; *b* 1910; *s* of late Prof. David Waterston, the University of St Andrews; *m* 1948, Anne, *widow* of Lieut H. C. C. Tanner, RN, and *d* of late Rt Rev. A. A. Markham, sometime Bishop of Grantham; one *s* two *d* (and one *s* decd). Educ: Craigflower Sch.; privately; Universities of St Andrews and Edinburgh. Ho. Surg., Royal Infirmary, Edinburgh, 1934; Ho. Surg., Surgical Registrar and Res. Medical Supt, Hospital for Sick Children, Great Ormond Street, London, 1934-38, 1948-51. Hunterian Professor, RCS, 1961; President British Association Pædiatric Surgeons, 1961. Consulting Pædiatric Surgeon to the Army. Served RAMC, 1939-45 (despatches twice, MBE); Captain, Field Ambulance and Field Transfusion Unit, Major (Surgical Specialist). *Publications:* Chapters in Modern Trends in Cardiac Surgery, 1961; Chapters in Pædiatric Surgery, 1970. Articles in medical journals. *Address:* Richard Reynolds House, Old Isleworth, Middlesex. *T:* 01-560 2873. *Club:* Royal and Ancient (St Andrews).

**WATERTON, Sqdn Leader William Arthur,** GM 1952; AFC 1942, Bar 1946; *b* Edmonton, Canada, 18 March 1916. *Educ:* Royal Military College of Canada; University of Alberta. Cadet Royal Military College of Canada, 1934-37; Subaltern and Lieut, 19th Alberta Dragoons, Canadian Cavalry, 1937-39; served RAF, 1939-46: Fighter Squadrons; Training Command; Transatlantic Ferrying Command; Fighter Command; Meteorological Flight; Fighter Experimental Unit; CFE High Speed Flight World Speed Record. Joined Gloster Aircraft Co. Ltd, 1946. 100 km closed circuit record, 1947; Paris/London record (618.5 mph), 1947; "Hare and Tortoise" Helicopter and jet aircraft Centre of London to Centre of Paris (47 mins), 1948. Chief Test Pilot Gloster Aircraft Co. Ltd, 1946-54. Prototype trials on first Canadian jet fighter, Canuck and British first operational delta wing fighter, the Javelin. *Publications:* The Comet Riddle, 1956; The Quick and The Dead, 1956; aeronautical and meteorological articles. *Recreations:* sailing, riding, photography, motoring, shooting. *Address:* c/o Glyn, Mills & Co., Kirkland House, Whitehall, SW1. *Club:* Royal Military College of Canada (Kingston, Ont.).

**WATHERSTON, Sir David (Charles),** KBE 1956; CMG 1953; Hon. PMN (Malaya), 1958; Group Personnel Adviser, Tube Investments Ltd; *b* 26 Feb. 1907; *s* of late Charles Fell Watherston, CB; *m* 1933, Maude, *d* of W. Hobkirk Noble, Aldwick, Sussex; two *s* two *d*. *Educ:* Westminster Sch. (King's Schol.); Christ Church, Oxford. Cadet, Malayan Civil Service, 1930; seconded to Colonial Office, 1939-44. Malayan Planning Unit, 1944-45. British Military Administration, Malaya, 1945-46. Secretary Constitutional Working Cttee which negotiated Federation of Malaya Agreement, 1946-48; Secretary for Defence and Internal Security, Federation of Malaya, 1948; Chief Secretary, Federation of Malaya, 1952-57 (administered the Government on various occasions); Special Counsellor, Malayan High Commission in the United Kingdom, 1957-59; Member of the Commission of Enquiry, North Borneo and Sarawak, 1962; Chm., Electricity Supply Ind. Trng Bd; Mem. Council, City University. Hon. DSc Aston. Liveryman of the Goldsmiths' Company. CStJ 1956. *Address:* Harbury House, Harbury, Warwickshire. *T:* Harbury 218; 14 Vicarage Gardens, W8. *T:* 01-229 6497. *Clubs:* East India and Sports, Royal Commonwealth Society.

**WATKIN, Rev. Dom Christopher Aelred Paul;** Headmaster of Downside School since 1962; *b* 23 Feb. 1918; *s* of Edward Ingram Watkin and Helena Watkin (*née* Shepheard). *Educ:* Blackfriars Sch., Laxton; Christ's Coll., Cambridge (1st class Parts I and II, historical Tripos). Housemaster at Downside Sch., 1948-62. FRHistS, 1946; FSA, 1950; FRSA, 1969. *Publications:* Wells Cathedral Miscellany, 1943; (ed) Great Chartulary of Glastonbury, 3 vols, 1946-58; (ed) Registrum Archdiaconatus Norwyci, 2 vols, 1946-48; Heart of the World, 1954; The Enemies of Love, 1958; articles in Eng. Hist. Rev., Cambridge Hist. Journal, Victoria County History of Wilts, etc. *Address:* Downside School, Stratton-on-the-Fosse, near Bath. *T:* Stratton-on-the-Fosse 206.

**WATKIN WILLIAMS, Sir Peter,** Kt 1963; *b* 8 July 1911; *s* of late Robert Thesiger Watkin Williams, late Master of the Supreme Court, and Mary Watkin Williams; *m* 1938, Jane Dickinson (*née* Wilkin); two *d*. *Educ:* Sherborne; Pembroke Coll., Cambridge. Partner in Hansons, legal practitioners, Shanghai, 1937-40; served War of 1939-45, Rhodesia and Middle East, 1940-46. Resident Magistrate, Uganda, 1946-55; Puisne Judge, Trinidad and Tobago, 1955-58; Puisne Judge, Sierra Leone, 1958-61; Plebiscite Judge, Cameroons, 1961; Chief Justice of Basutoland, Bechuanaland and Swaziland, and President of the Court of Appeal, 1961-65; High Court Judge, Malawi, 1967-69; Chief Justice of Malawi, 1969-70. *Recreation:* fishing. *Address:* Lower East Horner, Stockland, Honiton, Devon.

**WATKINS, Prof. Arthur Goronwy,** CBE 1967; Professor of Child Health, Welsh National School of Medicine, 1950-68, Emeritus Professor, since 1968; Dean of Clinical and Post-Graduate Studies, 1947-68; *b* 19 March 1903; *s* of Sir Percy Watkins; *m* 1933, Aileen Llewellyn; one *s* three *d*. *Educ:* Sidcot Sch.; University Coll., Cardiff; University Coll. Hospital, London. BSc (Wales) 1925; MD (London) 1930; FRCP 1943. Res. Hosp. appts, University Coll. Hosp., 1927-29, West London Hosp., 1929, Hosp. for Sick Children, Gt Ormond Street, 1930; First Asst, Dept of Pædiatrics, University Coll. Hosp., 1930-32; Lectr In Pædiatrics, Welsh Nat. Sch. of Medicine, 1932-50; Cons. Pædiatrician, Royal Infirmary and Llandough Hosp., Cardiff, 1932. Former Mem. Bd of Govs, United Cardiff Hosps; Consultant and Adviser in Pædiatrics, Welsh Hosp. Bd; Hon. Treas. Brit. Pædiatric Assoc., 1958-63, Pres., 1966-67; Pres. Children's Sect., Roy. Soc. Med., 1953, Hon. Mem. 1970; Pres. Cardiff Div., BMA, 1953; Corr. Mem. Soc. de Pédiatrie, Paris; Hon. Fell., Amer. Academy of Pediatrics, 1967; Mem. Albemarle Cttee on Youth Service; Mem. Central Coun. of Educ. (Wales), 1954-56; External Examr, Univs of Brisol, Birmingham, Manchester, Leeds; Colonial Office Visitor to W Indies, 1956 and Far East, 1959. President Cardiff Medical Soc., 1963-64. *Publications:* (with W. J. Pearson) The Infant, 1932; Pædiatrics for Nurses, 1947; articles in BMJ, Lancet, Archives of Disease in Childhood, etc. *Recreation:* golf. *Address:* 181 Cyncoed Road, Cardiff, S Wales. *T:* 751262.

**WATKINS, Brig. Bernard Springett,** CBE 1946; JP Kent; Ecclesiastical Secretary to the Lord Chancellor, 1950-65; *b* 8 April 1900; *o s* of late Rev. H. S. Watkins, Rector of Morchard Bishop, Devon; *m* 1926, Sybil Eugene, *o d* of late Col A. E. Berry, CIE, IMS; three *d*. *Educ:* King's School, Worcester; RMC, Sandhurst. Joined Indian Army, 1918; transferred Royal Signals, 1929; Capt., 1924; Major, 1938; Lieut-Col, 1944; Col, 1946; Temp. Brig., 1944-46; served, India, 1914-18; served with Royal Signals as Chief Signals Officer, Air Force South East Asia and Air Force Germany, 1942-47; AAG War Office, 1947-50; retired, 1950. *Recreations:* gardening, shooting and fishing. *Address:* Highfield, 26 Pennington Road, Southborough, Tunbridge Wells. *T:* Tunbridge Wells 29089.

**WATKINS, David John;** MP (Lab) Consett since 1966; Engineer; b 27 Aug. 1925; *s* of Thomas George Watkins and Alice Elizabeth (*née* Allen); unmarried. *Educ:* Bristol. Member: Bristol City Coun., 1954-57; Bristol Educn Cttee, 1958-66; Labour Party, 1950-; Amalgamated Engineering Union, 1942-. *Recreations:* reading, motoring, swimming. *Address:* 130 Ashton Drive, Bristol 3. *T:* Bristol 666136.

**WATKINS, Lt-Col Hubert Bromley,** OBE 1945; MC 1917; DCM 1916; Chairman, Radnorshire Co. Ltd, since 1966; Chairman, Bates & Hunt (Agric.) Ltd since 1952; *b* 9 July 1897; *s* of Hubert and Helen Watkins, Ludlow; *m* 1936, Mary (*née* Edwards); one *s* two *d*. *Educ:* Monmouth. King's Shropshire Light Infantry, 1914-19; Radnorshire Rifles (HG), 1940-45. Deputy Lieutenant, Radnorshire, 1948; High Sheriff, 1952; Vice-Lieutenant, 1958. President, National Assoc. Corn and Agricultural Merchants, 1949-50. *Recreations:* fishing, previously Rugby football and cricket. *Address:* Shirley, Knighton, Radnor. *T:* Knighton 685. *Clubs:* Farmers'; Cardiff and County (Cardiff).

**WATKINS, Mary Gwendolen,** MA Oxon; Headmistress, Bedford High School, 1949-65, retired; *b* 1905; *d* of late M. J. Watkins, CBE. *Educ:* Newland High School, Hull; Penrhos College; St Hugh's College, Oxford (open scholar). Headmistress, Erdington Grammar School, Birmingham, 1940-49. Member of Staff of Martyrs Memorial School, Papua/New Guinea, Jan.-Dec. 1966. *Address:* 5 South Avenue, Kidlington, Oxford.

**WATKINS, Tasker,** VC 1944; QC 1965; DL; Major, The Welch Regiment; Deputy Chairman, Radnor Quarter Sessions, since 1962; Deputy Chairman, Carmarthenshire Quarter Sessions, since 1966; Recorder of Merthyr Tydfil since 1968; *b* 18 Nov. 1918; *s* of B. Watkins, Nelson, Glam.; *m* 1941, Eirwen Evans; one *s* one *d*. Barrister-at-law; Master of the Bench, Middle Temple, 1970. Counsel (as Deputy to Attorney-General) to Inquiry into Aberfan Disaster, 1966. Chairman, Mental Health Review Tribunal, Wales Region, since 1960. DL Glamorgan, 1956. *Address:* Fairwater Lodge, Fairwater Road, Llandaff, Glamorgan. *T:* Cardiff 563558.

**WATKINS, Alderman Tudor Elwyn;** Alderman Breconshire CC since 1940; Member, Countryside Commission, since 1970; *b* 9 May 1903; *e s* of late County Councillor Howell Watkins, JP, Abercrave, Swansea Valley; *m* 1936, Bronwen R., 3rd *d* of late T. Stather, Talgarth; no *c*. *Educ:* local elementary schools; evening continuation classes; University Tutorial, WEA and NCLC classes; Coleg Harlech, N Wales (Bursary). Began working at local collieries at age of 13½; miner for 8 years; political agent for Brecon and Radnor, 1928-33. MP (Lab) Brecon and Radnor, 1945-70; PPS to Sec. of State for Wales, 1964-68. General Secretary Breconshire Assoc. of Friendly Societies, 1937-48. Vice-Pres. County Councils Assoc., 1969; Hon. Freeman, Brecon Borough; Chm., Brecon Beacons Nat. Park JAC; Mem., Brecon and Radnor Hospital Management Cttee. *Recreations:* served as Secretary of Abercrave Athletic Club, Cricket Club, Ystalyfera Football League, Hort. Soc. and Show. *Address:* Bronafon, Penyfan Road, Brecon. *T:* 2961.

**WATKINS, Prof. Winifred May,** FRS 1969; Professor of Biochemistry, University of London, since 1968; *b* 6 Aug. 1924; *d* of Albert E. and Annie B. Watkins. *Educ:* Godolphin and Latymer Sch., London; Univ. of London. PhD 1950; DSc 1963. Research Asst in Biochemistry, St Bartholomew's Hosp. Med. Sch., 1948-50; Beit Memorial Research Fellow, 1952-55; Mem. of Staff of Lister Inst. of Preventive Medicine, 1955-; Wellcome Travelling Research Fellow, Univ. of California, 1960-61; Reader in Biochemistry, 1965. Landsteiner Memorial Award (jtly), 1967; Paul Ehrlich-Ludwig Darmstädter Prize (jtly), 1969. *Publications:* various papers in biochemical and immunological jls. *Address:* Lister Institute of Preventive Medicine, Chelsea Bridge Road, SW1.

**WATKINS-PITCHFORD, Dr John,** CB 1968; Chief Medical Adviser, Department of Health and Social Security (formerly Ministry of Social Security and Ministry of Pensions and National Insurance), since 1965; *b* 20 April 1912; *s* of Wilfred Watkins Pitchford, FRCS, first Director of South African Institute of Medical Research, and Olive Mary (*née* Nichol); *m* 1945, Elizabeth Patricia Wright; one *s*. *Educ:* Shrewsbury School; St Thomas's Hospital. MRCS, LRCP 1937; MB, BS 1939 (London); MD 1946 (London); DPH 1946; DIH 1949. Various hosp. appts War of 1939-45: served RAFVR, Sqdn Ldr. Med. Inspector of Factories, 1947-50; Sen. Med. Off., Min. of Nat. Insce, 1950. *Publications:* articles on occupational medicine. *Recreation:* gardening. *Address:* Deepdale, Westerham, Kent. *T:* Westerham 2347. *Club:* Athenæum.

**WATKINSON,** family name of **Viscount Watkinson.**

**WATKINSON,** 1st Viscount *cr* 1964, of Woking; **Harold Arthur Watkinson,** PC 1955; CH 1962; Chairman of Cadbury Schweppes Ltd, since 1969 (Group Managing Director, Schweppes Ltd, 1963-68); Director: Midland Bank Ltd (a Deputy Chairman); British Insulated Callender's Cables; *b* 25 Jan. 1910; *e s* of A. G. Watkinson, Walton-on-Thames; *m* 1939, Vera, *y d* of John Langmead, West Sussex; two *d*. *Educ:* Queen's College, Taunton; King's College, London. Family business, 1929-35; technical and engineering journalism, 1935-39. Served War of 1939-45, active service, Lieut-Comdr RNVR. Chairman Production Efficiency Panel for S England, Machine Tool Trades Association, 1948; Chairman (first) Dorking Div. Conservative Assoc., 1948-49. MP (C) Woking Division of Surrey, 1950-64; Parliamentary Private Secretary to the Minister of Transport and Civil Aviation, 1951-52; Parliamentary Secretary to Ministry of Labour and National Service, 1952-55; Minister of Transport and Civil Aviation, Dec. 1955-59; Minister of Defence, 1959-62; Cabinet Minister, 1957-62. Mem., Brit. Nat. Export Coun. 1964-70; Chairman: Cttee for Exports to the United States, 1964-67; Nat. Advisory Cttee on the Employment of Older Men and Women, 1952-55; Council, BIM,

1968-70. President, Grocers' Inst., 1970-; Member Council, Institute of Directors; Trustee, Industrial, Educational and Research Foundation. *Recreations:* mountaineering, walking, sailing. *Heir:* none. *Address:* 11 Clive House, Connaught Place, W2; Dibbles, West Clandon, Nr Guildford, Surrey. *Clubs:* Carlton, RNVR; Royal Yacht Squadron.

**WATKINSON, Sir (George) Laurence,** KBE 1949; CB 1944; MC; *b* 29 Jan. 1896; *s* of late G. L. Watkinson, Battenhall, Worcester; *m* 1919, Doris, *d* of late Richard Pilling, Bolton; one *d*. *Educ:* Port Charlotte School, Islay, NB; Royal Grammar School, Worcester. Served with Worcs Regt 1915-19, in France and Italy (MC and Bar); Board of Inland Revenue, 1919-31; Board of Trade, 1931-46; Deputy Secretary, Ministry of Fuel and Power, 1947-55. Vice-Chm., Harris Lebus Ltd, 1955-57, and Chairman, 1958-61. Mem. Council, RCVS, 1960-65; Chm., London Electricity Consultative Council and Mem., London Electricity Board, 1960-65; Mem. Monopolies Commn, 1960-68. Hon. ARCVS, 1966. *Recreation:* fishing. *Address:* 15 Newnham House, High Road, Loughton, Essex. *T:* 01-508 7141. *Club:* United Service.

**WATKINSON, Sir Laurence;** *see* Watkinson, Sir G. L.

**WATSON,** family name of **Baron Manton.**

**WATSON, Adam;** *see* Watson, John Hugh A.

**WATSON, Very Rev. Alan Cameron,** CMG 1968; retired; *b* 16 March 1900; *s* of Thomas Watson and Marion Thomson; *m* 1928, Eileen Ballantyne; two *s* one *d*. *Educ:* Otago Univ., Dunedin, NZ (MA). Minister: East Taieri, NZ, 1927-32; St Paul's, Christchurch, NZ, 1932-41; Toorak, Melbourne, Aust., 1942-67. Moderator-General, Presbyterian Church of Australia, 1959-62. President, Australian Council of Churches, 1962-63. *Address:* 35 Herbert Street, Mornington, Victoria 3931, Australia. *T:* 5.3666. *Club:* Melbourne (Aust.).

**WATSON, Sir Andrew;** *see* Watson, Sir J. A.

**WATSON, Anthony Heriot,** CBE 1965; Director of Statistics, Ministry of Transport, since 1965; *b* 13 April 1912; *s* of William Watson and Dora Isabel Watson (*née* Fisher); *m* 1946, Hilary Margaret Fyfe. *Educ:* St Paul's Sch.; Christ Church, Oxford; University Coll., London. Statistical Officer, British Cotton Industry Research Assoc., 1936. Min. of Supply, 1940: Statistician; Asst Dir of Statistics; Min. of Aircraft Production, 1942; Statistician, Dept of Civil Aviation, Air Ministry, 1945; Chief Statistician: Min. of Civil Aviation, 1951; Min. of Transport and Civil Aviation, 1954; Min. of Aviation, 1959; Min. of Transport, 1964. *Recreations:* music, garden. *Address:* South Ridge, The Avenue, Tadworth, Surrey. *T:* 01-823 2331. *Club:* Reform.

**WATSON, Benjamin Philp,** MD, Hon. LLD, Edinburgh University, 1951; FRCSE, FACS, FRCOG; Professor Emeritus of Obstetrics and Gynæcology, Columbia University, New York; *b* Anstruther, Scotland, 1880; 2nd *s* of David Watson, Largo, Scotland; *m* 1917, Angèle, *d* of Paul Hamendt, St Nicolas, Belgium. *Educ:* Waid Academy, Anstruther; Universities of St Andrews and Edinburgh. MB, ChB, University of Edinburgh, 1902; awarded Ettles and Buchanan Scholarships; MD Edinburgh, 1905; Gold Medal for Thesis; University Tutor in Gynæcology, 1905-10; Lecturer in School of Medicine, Royal College, Edinburgh, 1910-12; Professor of Obstetrics and Gynæcology, University of Toronto, 1912-22; Professor of Midwifery and Diseases of Women, University of Edinburgh, 1922-26; served with the CAMC in England and Salonika with rank of Captain, 1915-16. *Publications:* Gynecological Pathology and Diagnosis; Chronic Endometritis; New System of Gynecology; many articles in medical and scientific journals. *Recreations:* golf and travel. *Address:* 21 Long Ridge Road, Danbury, Conn 06810, USA. *Club:* Century (New York).

**WATSON, Vice-Adm. (retd) Bertram Chalmers,** CB 1938; DSO 1917; RN; *b* 1887; *s* of Charles Watson, Slateford; *m* 1915, Isabel, *d* of John Buist, Broughty Ferry; one *s* two *d*. *Educ:* Merchiston; Temple Grove. In Harwich Force throughout European War, 1914-18; HMS Valiant, 1933-34; Dir, RN Staff Coll., 1934-36; Rear-Adm., 1936; Rear-Adm. (Submarines), 1938-40; Flag Officer, Greenock, 1940-42; Commodore of Convoys, 1942-43; Admiral Commanding Iceland, 1943-45. *Recreations:* hunting, fishing, astronomy. *Address:* The Court House, Hambledon, Portsmouth. *T:* Hambledon 727. *Club:* Army and Navy.

**WATSON, Daniel Stewart,** CB 1967; OBE 1958; Deputy Chief Scientist (Naval), Ministry of Defence, since 1968; *b* 30 Dec. 1911; *s* of Reverend Dr William Watson, DD, DLitt, and Mary Macintosh Watson; *m* 1939, Isabel (*née* Gibson); one *s*. *Educ:* Robert Gordon's Coll.; Aberdeen University. Student Apprentice, British Thomson Houston, Rugby, 1933, Research Engr, 1936. Scientific Officer, Admiralty, 1938-; Dir, Admiralty Surface Weapons Establishment, 1961-68. *Publications:* contribs to IEEJ. *Recreations:* thoroughbred cars; caravanning. *Address:* Ministry of Defence, Whitehall, SW1.

**WATSON, David Archibald Beverley;** Chairman and Joint Managing Director, Johannesburg Consolidated Investment Company, since 1963; Director: Anglo-American Corp. of SA Ltd; De Beers Consolidated Mines Ltd; Argus Printing & Publishing Co. Ltd; Rand Selection Corp. Ltd; Standard Bank of SA Ltd, and of numerous S African Companies; Chairman, Rustenburg Platinum Mines, etc; *b* 7 Sept. 1905; *s* of late Archibald Watson and late Beatrice Mary Watson; *m* 1930, Christine Margaret (*née* Innes); two *d*. *Educ:* Oundle; Birmingham University (BSc Hons). Associated with Johannesburg Consolidated Investment Company and its allied companies, 1926-. *Recreation:* gardening. *Address:* Keerweder, Sandown, PO Box 590, Johannesburg, South Africa. *Clubs:* Rand, Country (Johannesburg).

**WATSON, David Meredith Seares,** FRS 1922; LLD, DSc; *b* 18 June 1886; *s* of David Watson, DSc; *m* Katherine (*d* 1969), *d* of Rev. I. Parker; two *d*. *Educ:* Manchester Grammar School; Manchester University. Lecturer in Vertebrate Palæontology, UC, 1912-21; Jodrell Prof. of Zoology and Comparative Anatomy, UC, Univ. of London, 1921-51, Emeritus, 1951-. Alexander Agassiz Prof., Harvard Univ., 1952. Lt RNVR 1916-18; Croonian lecturer, Roy. Soc., 1924; Romanes lecturer, Oxford, 1928; Silliman lecturer, Yale University, 1937; Member Agricultural Research Council, 1931-42; Secretary Scientific Food Policy Committee, 1940. Rainer Medal, 1928; Lyell Medal, Geological Soc. of London, 1935; Thompson Medal, National Academy of Sciences of the USA, 1941; Darwin Medal, Royal Society, 1942; Linnean Medal, Linnean Society, 1949; Darwin Wallace Medal, Linnean Soc., 1958; Wollaston Medal, Geological Soc. of London,

1965. Trustee of the British Museum, 1946-63. Hon. LLD, Aberdeen, 1943; Hon. DSc: Cape Town, 1929; Manchester, 1943; Reading, 1948; Wales, 1948; Witwatersrand, 1949. Hon. Mem. of various foreign scientific societies. *Publications:* many papers on Vertebrate Palæontology and connected subjects in Phil. Trans., Proc. Zoo. Soc., Journ. of Anat., etc. *Recreation:* travel. *Address:* Pendean Convalescent Home, Midhurst, Sussex.
*See also Professor John Sutton.*

**WATSON, Sir (David) Ronald Milne-;** *see* Milne-Watson.

**WATSON, Dennis George,** CIE 1945; *s* of late G. E. Watson; *m* 1934, Dawn, *d* of late Lieutenant-Colonel F. O. Bowen, DSO; one *s* one *d*. *Educ:* Blundell's School. Indian Army (Reserve of Officers), 1917-19; Inspector-General of Police, Indore State, 1929-32 and 1937-41; Inspector-Gen. of Police, CP and Berar, 1944-46. *Address:* c/o National and Grindlay's Bank, Ltd, 13 St James's Square, SW1. *Club:* East India and Sports.

**WATSON, Captain Sir Derrick William Inglefield Inglefield-,** 4th Bt, *cr* 1895; TD 1945; 4th Battalion Queen's Own Royal West Kent Regimental Reserve of Officers (TA); Active List 3 Sept. 1939; now retired; *b* 7 Oct. 1901; *s* of Sir John Watson, 2nd Bt, and Edith Jane, *e d* of W. H. Nott, Liverpool; *S* brother, 1918; changed name by Deed Poll to Inglefield-Watson, Jan. 1946; *m* 1925, Margrett Georgina (who obtained a divorce, 1939), *o d* of late Col T. S. G. H. Robertson-Aikman, CB; one *s* one *d*; *m* 1946, Terezia (Terry), *d* of late Prof. Charles Bodon, Budapest. *Educ:* Eton; Christ Church, Oxford. County Councillor, Kent (No 4 Tonbridge Division), 1931-37. *Heir: s* John Forbes Watson, Lt-Col Royal Engineers, *b* 16 May 1926. *Address:* Ringshill House, Wouldham, near Rochester, Kent. *T:* Medway 61514.
*See also Col Rt Hon. Sir R. H. Dorman-Smith.*

**WATSON, Sir Duncan;** *see* Watson, Sir N. D.

**WATSON, Vice-Adm. Sir Dymock;** *see* Watson, Vice-Adm. Sir R. D.

**WATSON, Francis John Bagott,** CVO 1965 (MVO 1959); BA, MA Oxon 1969, FBA 1969, FSA; Director, Wallace Collection, since 1963; Surveyor of The Queen's Works of Art, since 1963; *b* 24 Aug. 1907; *s* of Hugh Watson, Blakedown, and Helen Marian Bagott, Dudley; *m* 1941, Mary Rosalie Gray (*d* 1969), *d* of George Strong, Bognor. *Educ:* Shrewsbury School; St John's College, Cambridge. Registrar, Courtauld Inst. of Art, 1934-38; Asst Keeper (later Dep. Dir), Wallace Collection, 1938-63; Deputy Surveyor of The Queen's (until 1952 The King's) Works of Art, 1947-63; Trustee, Whitechapel Art Gallery, 1949-; Chairman: Furniture History Society, 1966; Walpole Society, 1970-; Slade Prof. of Fine Art, Oxford, 1969-70; Wrightsman Lectr, NY Univ., 1970-71; Vis. Lectr, Univ. of California, 1970. Uff. del Ord. al Merito della Repubblica Italiana, 1961. New York University Gold Medal, 1966. *Publicatons:* Canaletto, 1949 (rev. 2nd edn, 1954); Southill, A Regency House (part author), 1951; Wallace Collection: Catalogue of Furniture, 1956; Louis XVI Furniture, 1959 (rev. French edn, 1963); The Choiseul Gold Box (Charlton Lecture), 1963; Great Family Collections (pt-auth.), 1965; The Guardi Family of Painters (Fred Cook Memorial Lecture), 1966; Eighteenth Century Gold Boxes (pt-author), 1966; The Wrightsman Collection Catalogue, Vols 1 and 2: Furniture, 1966, Vols 3 and 4: Furniture, Goldsmith's Work and Ceramics, 1970; Giambattista Tiepolo, 1966; Fragonard, 1967; numerous contribs to learned journals, in Europe, America and Asia. *Recreations:* reading, writing and arithmetic. *Address:* 8 Groom Place, Belgrave Square, SW1. *Club:* Beefsteak.

**WATSON, George Hugh Nicholas;** *see* Seton-Watson.

**WATSON, Gilbert,** CBE 1947; HM Senior Chief Inspector of Schools in Scotland, retired; *b* 1882; *er s* of John Watson, Edinburgh; *m* 1911, Annie Macdonald (decd). *Educ:* Royal High School, Edinburgh; Edinburgh and Oxford Universities. Rector, Inverness Royal Academy, 1909; entered inspectorate of Scottish Education Department, 1910; HM Senior Chief Inspector, 1944. *Publications:* Theriac and Mithridatium: a study in Therapeutics (Wellcome Historical Medical Library), 1966; co-author of books on Latin Grammar and Latin prose composition. *Recreation:* golf. *Address:* 38 Granby Road, Edinburgh 9. *T:* 031-667 5744.

**WATSON, Maj.-Gen. Gilbert France,** CB 1945; DSO 1915; OBE 1942; Chairman Board of Governors, Bristol United Hospital, 1962-65; *b* 6 May 1895; *s* of late Charles France Watson, of Banchory, Kincardine; *m* 1st, 1917, Marjorie Wyndham (*d* 1962), 2nd *d* of Dr J. Lewis, Roath, Cardiff; one *s*; 2nd, 1964, Evelyn Gaynor, *widow* of Charles Lund. *Educ:* Berkhampstead; Colchester. Served with Royal Engineers in France, 1915-19 (DSO, despatches twice); entered Royal Welch Fusiliers, 1921; graduated Staff College; Director of Manpower Planning, War Office, 1943-46. Bt Major, 1936; Bt Lt-Col, 1939; Temp. Brig., 1940; Col, 1942; Acting Maj.-Gen., 1943; Temp. Maj.-Gen. 1944, retired pay, 1946. Principal Regional Officer, Min. of Health, SW Region, 1946-60. Officer Fr. Légion d'Honneur. *Address:* Knowle, Edward Road, Walton St Mary, Clevedon, Somerset. *T:* Clevedon 3568.

**WATSON, G(ordon) G(raham) Gibbes,** CMG 1957; Barrister; Chairman of Directors of several New Zealand financial and industrial companies; *b* 21 Oct. 1891; *yr s* of Clement and Ruth Watson, Wellington, NZ; *m* 1929, Edith Jessie, *d* of Harry Beloe Crawford, Barrister, Oamaru, NZ; no *c*. *Educ:* Wellington Coll. and Victoria Univ. Coll., Wellington (MA, LLB). Practice as barrister, 1915; Lecturer in Law, Victoria Univ. Coll., 1915-28; Pres. Wellington Law Society, 1932; Mem. Council NZ Law Society, 1932-46. Acted for many years as Counsel for various companies and financial instns in NZ. Mem. Royal Commission on Banking and Monetary System in NZ, 1955-56; Pres. NZ Acad. of Fine Arts, 1938-49; Chm. Management Cttee, National Art Gallery, NZ, 1944-; Pres. Overseas League, Wellington Br., 1949-56. *Recreations:* Horticulture (Pres. Hutt Valley Hort. Soc.), art, travel. *Address:* Wicklow, Waterloo Road, Lower Hutt, New Zealand. *T:* Wellington 63861. *Club:* Wellington (NZ).

**WATSON, Henry,** CBE 1969; QPM 1963; Chief Constable of Cheshire since 1963; *b* 16 Oct. 1910; *s* of John and Ann Watson, Preston, Lancs; *m* 1933, Nellie Greenhalgh; two *d*. *Educ:* Preston Victoria Junior Technical Coll. Admitted to Inst. of Chartered Accountants, 1934; joined Ashton-under-Lyne Borough Police, 1934; King's Lynn Borough Police, 1942; Norfolk County Constabulary, 1947; Asst Chief Constable, Cumberland and Westmorland, 1955, Chief Constable, 1959. OStJ 1968. *Recreation:* golf. *Address:* The

Mount, Tarvin, Chester. *T:* Tarvin 344. *Club:* Royal Commonwealth Society.

**WATSON, Hon. Sir (Henry) Keith,** Kt 1968; FCIS; Public Accountant at Perth, WA, since 1921; Director since 1933, and Chairman since 1951, of Perth Building Society; Director of various companies; *b* 22 Aug. 1900; *s* of W. H. Watson, Cottesloe, WA; *m* 1926, Edith, *d* of Edwin Symonds; one *s* (one *d* decd). *Educ:* Cottesloe and Claremont State Schs, W Australia. Chairman of Building Societies Assoc. of WA, 1951-68. Mem. of Secession Delegn from people of WA to Parlt of UK, 1934-35; MLC of Western Australia (Metropolitan Province), 1948-68. *Publication:* (jtly) Western Australia's Case for Secession, 1934. *Recreation:* bowls. *Address:* 85 Tyrell Street, Nedlands, Western Australia 6009. *Clubs:* Dalkeith Bowling, Nedlands Golf.

**WATSON, Brig. Henry Neville Grylls,** DSO 1919; OBE 1922; late RASC; *b* Worthing, Sussex, 9 Sept. 1885; *s* of late Rev. Wm Grylls Watson, MA Oxon, Rector of St Margaret's, Canterbury; *m* 1946, Dorothy Marian Jones (*née* Boyton). *Educ:* Dover College. In the City, 1904-8; 2nd Lt 3rd Royal Sussex Regt, 1908; joined RASC 2nd Lt 1909; Lt 1912; Capt. 1915; temp. Major, 1915; Major, 1929; Bt, Lt-Col 1932; Lt-Col 1937; Colonel, 1935; served European War (Mons Star, British and Allied War Medals): France, 1914-15; North Russia EF, 1918-19; Adj. 1st Cavalry Div. RASC 1914; Adj. 1st London Div. Train. TF 1915; DADT War Office, 1918; DADST North Russia EF 1918-19 (DSO, brevet Major, despatches thrice, one mention by Secretary of State for War, 2nd class Order of St Stanislaus with swords, 3rd class Order of St Anna with swords); Adjutant North Midland Div. Train. TF 1920; seconded for duty on the staff of Police Adviser to RIC, 1920-22; Adjutant No. 1 Corps Depôt, 1923; Adjutant RASC Training College, 1924; Assistant Director of Supplies and Transport, British Forces in Palestine and Transjordania, 1938-40 (despatches, General Service Medal); War of 1939-45 (1939-45 Star, Africa Star, Defence Medal, War Medal 1939-45); Acting Brig. Feb. 1940; Temp. Brig. Aug. 1940; Dir of Supplies and Transport, GHQ, Middle East, 1940-41; retired pay, 1942; a Governor of Dover Coll., 1924. Coronation Medal, 1937. *Recreations:* Rugby football and golf. *Address:* Barclays Bank Ltd, Aldershot. *Club:* Public Schools.

**WATSON, Herbert A. G.;** *see* Grant Watson.

**WATSON, Herbert Edmeston,** DSc (London); FRIC; MIChemE; Emeritus Professor of Chemical Engineering, University of London; *b* 17 May 1886; *s* of late A. E. Watson, London; *m* 1917, Margaret Kathleen (*d* 1951), *d* of late William Rowson, Liverpool; one *s* one *d*. *Educ:* Marlborough College; London, Berlin, Geneva, Cambridge Universities. BSc 1st Class Hons Chemistry, 1907; DSc 1912; 1851 Exhibition Scholar, 1909; Fellow University College, London, 1914; Assistant Professor Indian Institute of Science, 1911-16; Professor of Inorganic and Physical Chemistry, Indian Institute of Science, Bangalore, 1916-34; Professor of Chemical Engineering, University College, 1934-51 (services lent to Admiralty, 1939-45); invented neon glow lamp, 1911. *Publications:* numerous papers in scientific journals. *Recreation:* walking. *Address:* Westside, Knowl Hill, Woking, Surrey. *T:* Woking 5411.

**WATSON, Herbert James,** CB 1954; *b* 9 Aug. 1895; *s* of Thomas Francis Watson, Inverness; *m* 1929, Elsie May Carter; two *s* one *d*. *Educ:* Royal Naval College, Greenwich. Entered Royal Corps of Naval Constructors, 1918; Chief Constructor: Admiralty, 1940-43; Chatham, 1943-45; Manager: Malta, 1945-46; Devonport, 1946-47; Asst Director of Dockyards, 1947-49; Deputy Director of Dockyards, 1949-56. *Recreation:* sailing. *Address:* 23 Cygni Street, Mandurah, W Australia 6210, Australia.

**WATSON, Rev. Hubert Luing;** retired as General Superintendent of the Baptist Union, North Western Area (1949-60); President of the Baptist Union of Great Britain and Ireland, 1963 (Vice-President, 1962); Chairman, Baptist Minister Fellowship, 1960-63; *b* 30 Nov. 1892; *s* of Austin and Margaret M. Watson; *m* 1914, Mercy (*née* Harwood); one *d*. *Educ:* Winslow School. Baptist Union Exams, External student, Manchester Coll. Pastor of: Milton and Little Leigh, 1918-23; Enon, Burnley, 1923-29; Ansdell, Lytham, 1929-35; Richmond, Liverpool, 1935-49. *Recreations:* gardening and motoring. *Address:* Cartref, Spurlands End Road, Gt Kingshill, High Wycombe, Bucks. *T:* Holmer Green 2062.

**WATSON, Hugh Gordon;** Barrister-at-Law; one of the Special Commissioners of Income Tax since 1952; *b* 3 Feb. 1912; *o s* of late Andrew Gordon Watson, Physician, 21 The Circus, Bath, and Clementina (*née* Macdonald); *m* 1940, Winefride Frances, *d* of late Clement Brand, Westfield, Reigate, and of Winefride Denise (*née* Casella), Orchard House, Brockenhurst; three *s*. *Educ:* Ampleforth College; Pembroke College, Oxford. Insurance Broker, 1935-39. Served War of 1939-45 in RNVR; at Admiralty, on staff of Supt Demagnetisation, 1939-41; HM Anti-submarine Trawlers, Home Fleet, 1941-45; Sen. Intelligence Officer, No. 1 Naval Fighter School, Yeovilton, 1945-46. Called to the Bar, Lincoln's Inn, 1947. *Address:* Torsonce, Pilgrim's Way, Reigate, Surrey. *Clubs:* United Service, Royal Cruising.

**WATSON, Sir (James) Andrew,** 5th Bt, *cr* 1866; *b* 30 Dec. 1937; *s* of 4th Bt and Ella Marguerite, *y d* of late Sir George Farrar, 1st Bt; *S* father, 1941; *m* 1965, Christabel Mary, *e d* of K. R. M. Carlisle and Hon. Mrs Carlisle; two *s*. *Educ:* Eton. Barrister-at-law. *Heir: s* Roland Victor Watson, *b* 4 Mar. 1966. *Address:* Talton House, Newbold on Stour, Warwickshire. *T:* Alderminster 212. *Club:* Cavalry.

**WATSON, Prof. James Dewey;** Professor of Biology, Harvard University, Cambridge, Mass, since July 1961; Director, Cold Spring Harbour Laboratory for Quantitative Biology, since 1969; *b* 6 April 1928; *s* of James D. and Jean Mitchell Watson; *m* 1968, Elizabeth Lewis; one *s*. *Educ:* Univ. of Chicago (BS); Indiana Univ. (PhD); Clare Coll., Cambridge. Senior Res. Fellow in Biology, California Inst. of Technology, 1953-55; Harvard University: Asst Prof. of Biology, 1955-57; Associate Prof., 1958-61. Mem. US National Acad. Sciences, 1962-; Mem. Amer. Acad. of Arts and Sciences, 1957; Mem. Royal Danish Acad. 1962; Sen. Fellow, Soc. of Fellows, Harvard Univ., 1963. Hon. DSc: Univ. of Chicago, 1961; Indiana Univ., 1963. Hon. LLD, Notre Dame Univ., 1965. Hon. Fellow, Clare Coll., Camb., 1967. Nobel Award in Medicine and Physiology (jointly), 1962. *Publications:* Molecular Biology of the Gene, 1965; The Double Helix, 1968, 2nd edn, 1970; scientific papers on the mechanism of heredity. *Recreation:* mountain walking. *Address:* 10 Appian Way, Cambridge, Mass, USA. *T:* TR 6-7414.

**WATSON, Prof. James Wreford;** Professor of Geography and Head of the Department of

Geography, Edinburgh University, since 1954; *b* 8 Feb. 1915; *s* of Rev. James Watson; *m* 1939, Jessie W. Black; one *s* one *d*. *Educ:* George Watson's College, Edinburgh; Edinburgh Univ. (MA); Toronto Univ. (PhD). Asst Lecturer in Geography, Sheffield Eng., 1937-39; Prof. of Geography, McMaster University, Canada, 1945-49; Chief Geographer, Canada, and Director of the Geographical Branch, Department of Mines and Technical Surveys, Canada, 1949-54. Editor, Scottish Studies, 1957-64. Award of Merit, Amer. Assoc. of Geogrs, 1949; Murchison Award, RGS, 1956; Research Medal, RSGS, 1965; Gov. General's Medal, Canada (literary), 1953. FRSC; FRSE. *Publications: geographical:* General Geography, 1957 (Toronto); North America: Its Countries and Regions, 1963 (London); A Geography of Bermuda, 1965 (London); Canada: Problems and Prospects, 1968 (Toronto); Geographical Essays (co-editor with Prof. R. Miller); (ed) The British Isles, A Systematic Geography, 1964 (London); (ed) Collins-Longmans Advanced Atlas, 1968; articles on historical and social geography in Geography, Scottish Geographical Magazine, Geographical Review, Jl of Geography, Canadian Jl of Economics and Political Science, etc; *literary:* Unit of Five, 1947; Of Time and the Lover, 1953; verse in Canadian and British literary jls. *Address:* Dept of Geography, The University, Edinburgh. *Club:* Scottish Arts.

**WATSON, John,** FRCS, FRCSE; Consultant Plastic Surgeon to: Queen Victoria Hospital, East Grinstead, and Tunbridge Wells Group of Hospitals, since 1950; London Hospital, and NE Metropolitan Hospital Board, since 1963; Florence Nightingale Hospital; *b* 10 Sept. 1914; *s* of late John Watson; *m* 1941, June Christine Stiles; one *s* three *d*. *Educ:* Leighton Park, Reading; Jesus Coll., Cambridge; Guy's Hospital. MRCS, LRCP 1938; MA, MB, BChir (Cantab) 1939; FRCS(Ed.) 1946; FRCS 1963. Served as Sqdn Ldr (temp.) RAF, 1940-46 (despatches twice). Marks Fellow in Plastic Surgery, Queen Victoria Hosp., E Grinstead, 1947-50. Exec. Trustee and Sec., E Grinstead Research Trust for McIndoe Memorial Research Unit; Mem. Brit. Assoc. of Plastic Surgeons (Hon. Sec., 1960-62, Pres., 1969); FRSM. *Publications:* numerous articles on plastic surgery in techn. jls and scientific periodicals. Chapters in: Textbook of Surgery, Plastic Surgery for Nurses, Modern Trends in Plastic Surgery, Clinical Surgery. *Recreations:* fishing, contemplation. *Address:* Clock Court, Hartfield, Sussex. *T:* 412; 122 Harley Street, W1. *T:* 01-935 5608. *Club:* Reform.

**WATSON, John Arthur Fergus,** CBE 1965; PPRICS; JP; Member, Lands Tribunal, 1957-69; retired Juvenile Court Magistrate; *b* 24 July 1903; *s* of late Capt. J. G. Maitland Watson, Royal Artillery, and of Mabel (*née* Weir); *m* 1948, Joan, *d* of late Claude Leigh, Cuckfield, Sussex; one *s* one *d*. *Educ:* Uppingham. Passed into RMA, Woolwich, 1921, but declined Cadetship. Chartered surveyor, 1926; partner in Ferris & Puckridge, 1928-47; and in Alfred Savill & Sons, 1947-56. A Chm., Inner London Juvenile Courts, 1936-68. Member: Central Housing Advisory Cttee to Minister of Health, 1936-47; Inter-departmental Cttee on New Towns, 1945-46; Prime Minister's Cttee on Regent's Park Terraces, 1945-46; Pres., RICS, 1949-50; Mem., Stevenage Development Corp., 1952-56. Worked voluntarily for some years in prisons and borstals; Vice-Pres., Nat. Assoc. of Prison Visitors, 1938- (Hon. Sec., 1928-38; Chm., 1941-44); Mem. Youth Advisory Council to Minister of Education, 1942-45; advised CCG on problems of juvenile delinquency in British Zone, 1947-48; Mem., Royal Commission on Justices of the Peace, 1946-48; Mem. Nat. Adv. Council on Training of Magistrates, 1967-. *Publications:* Meet the Prisoner, 1939; The Child and the Magistrate, 1942 (revd 1950, 1965); British Juvenile Courts, 1948; Which is the Justice?, 1969; The Juvenile Court–1970 Onward, 1970. *Address:* Elmdon Old Vicarage, Saffron Walden, Essex. *T:* Chrishall (via Cambridge) 346. *Clubs:* Carlton, Pratt's.

**WATSON, John Garth,** CB 1965; BScEng; CEng, FICE, FIEE; Rear-Admiral (retired); Secretary, Institution of Civil Engineers, since 1967; *b* 20 February 1914; *er s* of Alexander Henry St Croix Watson and Gladys Margaret Watson (*née* Payne); *m* 1943, Barbara Elizabeth Falloon; two *s* one *d*. *Educ:* Univ. Coll. School, Hampstead; Northampton Engineering Coll., Univ. of London. BSc (Eng.). MIEE 1948; AMICE 1944; MAmerIEE 1946; Amer. Soc. of Naval Engrs 1947. 2nd Lieut, 1st Bn Herts Regt (TA), 1932; resigned on joining Admiralty, 1939; Student and Asst Elec. Engr, Northmet Power Co.; HMS Vernon, 1939; Development of Magnetic Minesweepers, Dec. 1939; wounded, 1941; Warship Electrical Supt, London and SE Area, 1943; BJSM, Washington, DC, 1945; Admlty, 1948; transf. to Naval Elec. Branch, 1949; HMS Collingwood, 1950; 6th Destroyer Flot., HMS Broadsword, Battleaxe, Nov. 1950; Staff of Flag Officer, Flot., Home Fleet, HMS Superb, Switsure, 1951; Admlty, 1952; HM Dockyard Devonport, 1953; Capt. 1955; Staff of C-in-C Home Fleet, Fleet Elec. Officer, HMS Tyne, Maidstone, 1955; Suptg Elec. Engr, HM Dockyard Gibraltar, 1957; Sen. Officers' War Course, 1960; Admlty, 1961; Asst Dir of Elec. Engineering, Admlty, Nov. 1961; Adm. Superintendent, Rosyth, 1963-66. ADC to the Queen, 1962. *Recreations:* sailing and light gardening. *Address:* Little Hall Court, Shedfield, Nr Southampton. *T:* Wickham 3216; 58 Iverna Court, W8. *T:* 01-937 2508. *Club:* United Service.

**WATSON, (John Hugh) Adam,** CMG 1958; Diplomatic Adviser, British Leyland Motor Corporation, since 1968; *b* 10 Aug. 1914; *er s* of Joseph Charlton Watson and Alice (*née* Tate); *m* 1950, Katharine Anne Campbell; two *s* one *d*. *Educ:* Rugby; King's Coll., Camb. Entered the Diplomatic Service, 1937; Brit. Legation, Bucharest, 1939; Brit. Embassy, Cairo, 1940; Brit. Embassy, Moscow, 1944; FO, 1947; Brit. Embassy, Washington, 1950; Head of African Dept, Foreign Office, 1956-59. Appointed British Consul-General at Dakar, 1959; British Ambassador: to the Federation of Mali, 1960-61; to Senegal, Mauritania and Togo, 1960-62; to Cuba, 1963-66. Under-Secretary, Foreign Office, 1966-68. Gwilym Gibbon Fellow, Nuffield Coll., Oxford, Oct. 1962-Oct. 1963. *Publications:* The War of the Goldsmith's Daughter, 1964; Nature and Problems of Third World, 1968. *Address:* 53 Hamilton Terrace, NW8. *T:* 01-286 6330; Sharnden Old Manor, Mayfield, Sussex. Club: St James'.

**WATSON, (John) Steven,** MA; FRSE; FRHistS; JP; Principal, University of St Andrews, since 1966; *b* Hebburn-on-Tyne, 20 March 1916; *o s* of George Watson and Elizabeth Layborn Gall, Newcastle upon Tyne; *m* 1942, Heba Sylvia de Cordova Newbery; two *s*. *Educ:* Merchant Taylors' Sch.; St John's Coll., Oxford (Andrew Schol.). 1st cl. hons Mod. Hist., 1939. Harmsworth Sen. Schol., Merton Coll., 1939-42, for research into Speakership of House of Commons; unfit, owning to loss of leg in road accident, for mil. service. Admin Asst to Controller-General, Min. of Fuel and Power, 1942; Private Sec. to Ministers of Fuel and Power, 1942-45; Lectr, Student and Tutor, Christ Church, Oxford, 1945-66 (Censor, 1955-61); Chm. Bd of Modern History, Oxford, 1956-58; Editor, Oxford Historical series, 1950-66; Chm., Scottish Academic Press. Wiles Lectr, 1968. Mem., Franks Commission of University Inquiry, 1964-66. TV Scripts and Performances. Hon. DLitt, DePauw. *Publications:* (with Dr W. C. Costin) The Law and Working of the Constitution 1660-1914, 2 vols, 1952; The Reign of George III 1760-1815 (vol. XII, Oxf. Hist. of England), 1960; A History of the Salters' Company, 1963; essays in various collections and jls. *Address:* University House, The Scores, St Andrews, Fife. *T:* St Andrews 3117; 33 Willoughby Road, NW3. *Clubs:* Caledonian; Royal and Ancient (St Andrews).

**WATSON, Rev. John T.,** BA (London); LTCL; General Secretary, British and Foreign Bible Society, 1960-69, retired; *b* 13 Jan. 1904; *s* of late F. Watson, Sutton Bridge, Lincs; *m* 1933, Gertrude Emily Crossley, Farsley, Leeds; two *s* one *d*. *Educ:* Moulton Grammar School; Westminster Training College, London; Didsbury Training College, Manchester. School-master, 1924-26. Missionary (under Methodist Missionary Soc.) in Dahomey, W Africa, 1929-34; Methodist Minister: Plymouth, 1935-38; Golders Green, 1938-46; Bible Society: Secretary for Schools and Colleges, 1946-49; Asst Home Sec., 1949-54; Asst Gen. Sec., 1954-60. Hon. DD, West Virginia Wesleyan Coll., 1966. *Publications:* Seen and Heard in Dahomey, 1934; Daily Prayers for the Methodist Church, 1951. *Recreation:* music. *Address:* 16 Beverington Road, Eastbourne, Sussex. *T:* Eastbourne 29838.

**WATSON, Joseph Stanley,** MBE 1946; QC 1955; National Insurance and Industrial Injuries Commissioner since 1965; *b* 13 Sept. 1910; *er s* of late Joseph Watson and late Gertrude Ethel (*née* Catton); *m* 1951, Elizabeth Elliston, *d* of late Col G. Elliston Allen, TD; four *d*. *Educ:* Rossall Sch.; Jesus Coll., Cambridge (MA). Barrister, Inner Temple, 1933. Served War of 1939-45 (MBE): RA (Field), UK, MEF, Force 281, Dodecanese in Unit and on G Staff (Greek Military Cross), rank of Major. No 7 (NW) Legal Aid Area Cttee, 1949-55. Mem. Gen. Council of the Bar, 1959-64; Master of the Bench, Inner Temple, 1961; Recorder of Blackpool, 1961-65. *Address:* 6 Grosvenor Gardens, SW1. *T:* 01-730 9236; The Old Dairy, Mickleham, Surrey. *T:* Leatherhead 4387.

**WATSON, Hon. Sir Keith;** *see* Watson, Hon. Sir (Henry) K.

**WATSON, Air Cdre (retired) Michael,** CB 1952; CBE 1945 (OBE 1942); *b* 12 Aug. 1909; *s* of late William Watson, Kew. *Educ:* St Paul's Prep. School; Saffron Walden School. Joined RAF 1929, and qualified as Pilot; trained as Signals Officer, 1933. Served War of 1939-45 (despatches twice); Air Min. Combined Ops Signals Plans 1942; HQ, AEAF, 1943; SHAEF 1944; HQ Middle East, 1946; Air Ministry, 1947; Comdg RAF Welford, 1949; HQ, Fighter Comd, 1950-53; Director of Signals, Air Ministry, 1953-54; retired from RAF at own request, 1954. Rolls Royce Representative with N American Aviation Inc., Calif., 1956-60; Asst Gen. Man., Sales and Service, Rolls Royce, Ltd, 1961-62; Space Div., N American Rockwell Inc., Calif, 1964-. Chevalier de la Légion d'Honneur, 1944; Officer US Legion of Merit, 1945. *Recreations:* fishing, sailing. *Address:* 6150 Bayshore Walk, Long Beach, California 90803, USA.

**WATSON, Sir Michael M.;** *see* Milne-Watson.

**WATSON, Sir (Noel) Duncan,** KCMG, 1967 (CMG 1960); HM Diplomatic Service; British High Commissioner to Malta, since 1970; *b* 16 Dec. 1915; *s* of late Harry and Mary Noel Watson, Bradford, Yorks; *m* 1951, Aileen Bryans, *d* of late Charles Bell, Dublin. *Educ:* Bradford Grammar School; New College, Oxford. Colonial Administrative Service: Admin. Officer, Cyprus, 1938-43; Assistant Colonial Secretary, Trinidad, 1943-45; Principal, Colonial Office (secondment), 1946; transferred to Home Civil Service, 1947; Principal Private Sec. to Sec. of State for the Colonies, 1947-50; Asst Sec.: CO, 1950-62, Cent. Af. Office, 1962-63; Under-Secretary, 1963; Asst Under-Sec. of State, CO and CRO, 1964-67; Political Adviser to C-in-C Far East, 1967-70. *Address:* British High Commissioner's Office, Malta. *Clubs:* Royal Commonwealth Society; Leander.

**WATSON, Sir Norman James,** 2nd Bt, *cr* 1912; late Flying Officer, RAFVR; late KRRC and RAF; FRGS; *b* 17 March 1897; *er s* of Sir George Watson, 1st Bt, and Bessie, *d* of T. Atkinson; *S* father, 1930. *Educ:* Eton. Sheriff of Berkshire, 1940. *Publication:* (with Edward J. King) Round Mystery Mountain, 1935. *Heir:* none. *Address:* Abesters, nr Haslemere, Surrey. *T:* Fernhurst 215; River House, Tite Street, Chelsea, SW3. *T:* 01-352 1883. *Clubs:* Carlton, Royal Air Force, Alpine.

**WATSON, Maj.-Gen. Norman Vyvyan,** CB 1945; OBE 1940; late Royal Artillery; Managing Director, Army Kinema Corporation, 1957-67, Vice-Chairman since 1967, General Manager since 1952; *b* 26 January 1898; *m* 1927, Madge (decd), *d* of R. P. Randall; one *s*; *m* 1962, Vera, *d* of W. P. Tracy. 2nd Lt RA 1915; served European War, France and Belgium, 1916-18 (despatches); Iraq Operations, 1919-20. Director of Staff Duties, GHQ India, 1943-47; Deputy Quarter-Master-General, War Office, 1949-52; retired pay, 1952. *Address:* Games' Farmhouse, Peldon, Essex. *T:* Peldon 326. *Club:* United Service.

**WATSON, Rear-Adm. Philip Alexander,** MVO 1960; Director General Weapons (Naval), Ministry of Defence, since 1970; *b* 7 Oct. 1919; *yr s* of A. H. St C. Watson; *m* 1948, Jennifer Beatrice Tanner; one *s* two *d*. *Educ:* St Albans School. FIEE 1963; FIERE 1965. Sub-Lt RNVR, 1940; qual. Torpedo Specialist, 1943; transf. to RN, 1946; Comdr 1955; HM Yacht Britannia, 1957-59; Captain 1963; MoD (Ship Dept), 1963; Senior Officers' War Course, 1966; comd HMS Collingwood, 1967; Dep. Dir of Engrg (Ship Dept), MoD, 1969; Rear-Adm. 1970. *Recreations:* sailing, model engineering, woodwork and compulsory gardening. *Address:* Ashley Farm House, Box, Wilts. *T:* Box 353. *Club:* Bath and County (Bath).

**WATSON, Rt. Rev. Richard Charles Challinor;** *see* Burnley, Suffragan Bishop of.

**WATSON, Robert,** CMG 1947; OBE 1944; Country Representative, Ethiopia, Food and Agriculture Organisation of United Nations, since 1957; *b* 9 June 1894; *s* of T. Watson; *m* 1926, E. M. S. Armstrong; one *s* one *d*. *Educ:* Gordon Schools, Huntly; Aberdeen Univ. County Organiser on staff of North of Scotland Coll. of Agriculture, 1915-21 (including war service 1915-19); joined Indian Agric. Service, 1921; Dir of Agriculture, Burma, 1941; held commission in Army Reserve, 1927-41, and as Colonel (agriculture) in Civil Affairs Service (Burma), 1945; Dir of Agriculture, Burma, and (from 1946) Commissioner for Agricultural Rehabilitation; Mem. East Africa Rice Mission, April-Oct. 1948; Department of

Agriculture for Scotland, 1949; Dir of Agriculture, Cyrenaica, 1950. *Address:* c/o FAO, Viale delle Terme di Caracalla, Rome; Drynie Farm, Dingwall, Ross-shire Scotland. *T:* Dingwall 3209.

**WATSON, Vice-Adm. Sir (Robert) Dymock,** KCB 1959 (CB 1956); CBE 1948; DL; *b* 5 April 1904; *e s* of Robert Watson, FRIBA, Farnham, Surrey; *m* 1939, Margaret Lois (*d* 1968), *d* of late Rev. F. R. Gillespy; one *s* three *d*. *Educ:* Royal Naval Colls Osborne and Dartmouth. Captain; Asst Dir of Plans, Joint Planning Staff, Min. of Defence, 1944-46; Capt. (D) 1st Destroyer Flotilla Medit., 1947-48; idc, 1949; Dir of Plans, Admty, 1950-52; CO, HMS Illustrious, 1953; Rear-Adm., 1954; Flag Officer Flotillas, Medit., 1954-55, Vice-Adm. 1957; a Lord Commissioner of the Admiralty, Fourth Sea Lord, Chief of Supplies and Transport, 1955-58; Commander-in-Chief, South Atlantic and South America, 1958-60; retired, 1961. DL County of Brecknock, 1965. *Address:* Trebinshwn House, Nr Brecon, Wales.

**WATSON, Roderick Anthony,** QC 1967. Called to the Bar, Lincoln's Inn, 1949. *Address:* 3 Temple Gardens, Temple, EC4.

**WATSON, Sir Stephen (John),** Kt 1969; CBE 1959; MSc, DSc (Dunelm); FRIC; FRSE; Professor of Agriculture and Rural Economy, Edinburgh University and Principal, Edinburgh and East of Scotland College of Agriculture, 1944-68, now Emeritus Professor; *b* 24 March 1898; *e s* of William Watson, Accountant, Newcastle on Tyne, and Lima, Peru; *m* 1925, May, *yr d* of late Joseph Robinson, JP, Newcastle on Tyne; one *s*. *Educ:* Tynemouth School, Northumberland; Armstrong College, University of Newcastle. Scottish Horse and 1st King Edward's Horse, 1915-19; Demonstrator, Armstrong College, 1920-22; Lecturer in Agricultural Chemistry, Cheshire School of Agriculture, 1922-23, East Anglian Institute of Agriculture, 1923-27; Head of Biochemistry and Animal Nutrition Section and Deputy Head of Research Laboratories, ICI, Agricultural Research Station, Jealott's Hill, 1927-36; Head of Research Laboratories, 1937-44. Member Ministry of Agriculture Advisory Panel (grass and fodder conservation), 1939. Director, Central Agricultural Control, Imperial Chemical Industries Ltd, 1944; Member Agricultural Research Council, 1951-61; Deputy Chairman 1953-58; Chm. Bd of Management, Oatridge Agric. Coll., West Lothian, 1967-. *Publications:* Silage and Crop Preservation, 1938; The Science and Practice of Conservation, 1939, revised 1961; Feeding of Livestock 1949; Grassland and Grassland Products, 1951; Silage (with Dr A. M. Smith), 1951; many papers in various chemical and agricultural journals on the results of research in animal nutrition, and the conservation and utilization of grassland herbage. *Address:* 18 Cluny Drive, Edinburgh. *Club:* Farmers'.

**WATSON, Steven;** *see* Watson, J. S.

**WATSON, Sydney,** OBE 1970; MA; DMus; FRCO; FRCM; Student, Organist and Lecturer in Music, Christ Church, Oxford, 1955-70; Professor, Royal College of Music; *b* Denton, Lancashire, 3 Sept. 1903; *s* of W. T. Watson; unmarried. *Educ:* Warwick Sch.; Royal College of Music; Keble Coll., Oxford (Organ Scholar). Assistant music master, Stowe School, 1925-28; Precentor of Radley Coll., 1929-33; Conductor of Abingdon Madrigal Society, 1931-36; Organist of New Coll., Oxford, 1933-38; Organist of Sheldonian Theatre, Conductor of Oxford Harmonic Society, 1933-38; Oxford Orchestral Society, 1936-38; Director of Concerts, Balliol Coll., 1933-38, 1962-69; Choragus to Oxford Univ., 1963-68; Master of Music, Winchester Coll., and Conductor Winchester Music Club, 1938-45; Precentor and Director of Music, Eton Coll., 1946-55; Conductor Petersfield Festival, 1946-64, Slough Philharmonic Society, 1946-55; Windsor and Eton Choral Society, 1949-55; Conductor, Oxford Bach Choir, 1955-70; Oxford Orchestral Society, 1956-70. *Publications:* Church Music. *Address:* Aynhoe Park, Aynho, Banbury, Oxon. *Club:* Athenæum.

**WATSON, Thomas Yirrell,** CMG 1955; MBE 1943; *b* 27 May 1906; *s* of William Scott Watson and Edith Rose Watson (*née* Yirrell); *m* 1935, Margaret Alice, *d* of late J. J. Watson; one *d*. *Educ:* Aberdeen Grammar Sch.; Aberdeen Univ. (BSc); Cambridge Univ. (Diploma in Agricultural Science); Pretoria Univ., South Africa. Colonial Agricultural Scholar, 1929-31; Agricultural Officer, Kenya, 1931-43; Senior Agricultural Officer, Kenya, 1943-48; Dep. Director of Agriculture, Uganda, 1948-51; Director of Agriculture, Uganda, 1951-53; Secretary for Agriculture and Natural Resources, Uganda, 1954-55; Minister of Natural Resources, 1955-56. General Manager, Uganda Lint Cotton Marketing Board, 1951-53; MEC and MLC, Uganda, 1951-56. Member: Commission of Inquiry into Land and Population Problems, Fiji, 1959-60; Economic Development Commn, Zanzibar, 1961; Commission of Inquiry into Cotton Ginning Industry, Uganda, 1962; Commissioner, Burley Tobacco Industry Inquiry, Malawi, 1964. Coronation Medal, 1953. *Address:* Marchwood, 19 Seafield Road, Southbourne, Bournemouth, Hants.

**WATSON, Sir William,** Kt 1962; Director, Standard Life Assurance Company, since 1941 (Chairman, 1966-69); *b* 23 Nov. 1902; *s* of late Knight Watson, SSC; *m* 1929, Elizabeth Margaret Dods; two *s* one *d*. *Educ:* Edinburgh Institution (now Melville College). Member of the Institute of Chartered Accountants of Scotland (Council, 1950-52). Partner Messrs Baillie Gifford & Co., 1930-47. Director: Bank of Scotland (Treasurer, 1952-66); Standard Life Assurance Co.; Member Edinburgh Southern Hospitals Group Board of Management, 1948, Chairman, 1950-52; Member Jenkins Cttee on Company Law Amendment, 1960; President Inst. of Bankers in Scotland, 1963-65; Member Academic Adv. Cttee, Universities of St Andrews and Dundee, 1964-66. *Recreation:* golf. *Address:* Beech Lodge, 10 Church Hill, Edinburgh, 10. *T:* 031-447 2102. *Clubs:* Caledonian, New (Edinburgh).

**WATSON-ARMSTRONG,** family name of **Baron Armstrong.**

**WATSON-JONES, Sir Reginald,** Kt 1945; FRCS, FACS (Hon.), FRACS (Hon.), FRCSE (Hon.), FRCSC (Hon.); MChOrth, BSc; Orthopædic Surgeon Extra to The Queen, 1952 (Orthopædic Surgeon to King George VI, 1946-52); Consultant in Orthopædic Surgery, RAF; Hon. Consultant in Orthopædic and Accident Department, London Hospital; British Editor, Journal of Bone and Joint Surgery, since 1947; Hon. Consultant, Robert Jones and Agnes Hunt Hospital, Shropshire; Hunterian Professor of Surgery, Royal College of Surgeons of England, 1945; Arthur Sims Commonwealth Travelling Professor of Surgery, 1950; President, British Orthopædic Assoc., 1952-53; Senior Vice-President, Royal College of Surgeons of England, 1953-54; Member Court of Examiners, Hunterian

Orator, 1959; President Orthopædic Section, Royal Society of Medicine, 1956; Hon. Orthopædic Surgeon, Liverpool Royal Infirmary; *b* 1902; *m* 1930, Muriel Cook (*d* 1970); one *s* one *d*. Senior Lyon Jones Scholar, 1921; Mitchell Banks Medallist, 1920; George Holt Medallist, 1921; Robert Gee Prizeman, 1923; George Holt Fellow in Physiology, 1923; Samuel's Research Scholar in Surgery, 1926; Robert Jones Fellow in Orthopædic Surgery, 1928; Gold Medallist in Orthopædic Surgery, 1926; Demonstrator in Anatomy and Physiology, 1923; Senior Surgical Tutor and Registrar, Liverpool Royal Infirmary, 1926-27; House Surgeon, Royal National Orthopædic Hospital, and Clinical Assistant, Great Ormond Street Hospital, 1926; formerly Lecturer in Orthopædic Pathology and Orthopædic Surgery, University of Liverpool; Hon. Lecturer, War Surgery, British Post-Grad. Med. Sch., London; FRSM. Hon. Member: American Orthopædic Assoc., American Acad. Orthopædic Surg., Société Française d'Orthopédie et Traumatologie. Societa Italiana di Ortopedia e Traumatalogia Canadian Med. Assoc., Belgian, Swedish, Latin-American, Ecuadorian and Brazilian Orthop. Societies; Australian and NZ Orthop. Associations, etc; Assoc. of Surgeons of E Africa. KStJ. *Publications:* Fractures and Joint Injuries: 1st edn 1940; fifteen reprints; 5th edn 1969; trans.: Italian, Spanish, Portugese, German, Russian, Greek, French; Pye's Surgical Handicraft, 1938, 15th edn 1953; (British edn) Medicine and Surgery for the Attorney, 1959. *Address:* 82 Portland Place, W1. *T:* 01-580 1378 and 1379; House in the Wood, Golden Valley, Hindhead, Surrey. *T:* Hindhead 600. *Clubs:* Garrick, Crockford's.

**WATSON-WATT, Air Chief Commandant Dame Katherine (Jane Trefusis),** DBE 1944 (CBE 1941); *b* 21 March 1899; *d* of late Edmund Forbes, AMICE, and *g d* of late Principal James David Forbes, DCL, LLD, FRS; *m* 1966, Sir Robert Watson-Watt, *qv*. *Educ:* London. Women's Volunteer Reserve, European War, 1916-18; Founder, 1922, and later Managing Director of Bell Mead Kennels Ltd; retired, 1938; Manager of Building Estate, 1932; retired, 1939; Member of Council of Emergency Service, 1935-39, a Service which undertook the training of women as officers, in preparation for the foundation of Women's Services; Chief Instructor to the Auxiliary Territorial Service, School of Instruction for officers, with rank of Company Comdr, 1938; attached to No. 20 Royal Air Force Company ATS, 1939; Director, Women's Auxiliary Air Force, 1939-43; Missions to North America and Far East, 1943-44; retired 1944; Director/Dep. Director of Welfare for CCG, 1946-48. RAF Association: Vice-President; Member Council; Dep. Chairman Exec. Cttee; Chairman and Member, various sub-cttees. Chairman: Draydonne Properties; Disabled Adv. Cttee, Hammersmith; Member: Nat. Adv. Council for Employment of Disabled; Disabled Training and Employment Cttee; Central Adv. Cttee, Ministry of Social Security; Council, RAF Benevolent Fund; Joint Cttee, Service and Ex-Service Organisations. Hon. LLD St Andrews Univ., 1968. *Address:* 7 Crescent Place, SW3. *T:* 01-589 9982; The Shed, Pitlochry, Perth.

**WATSON-WATT, Sir Robert (Alexander),** Kt 1942; CB 1941; LLD (St Andrews) 1943; DSc (Toronto) 1943; DSc (Laval) 1952; FRS 1941; scientific adviser, author and lecturer; *b* 13 April 1892; *s* of Patrick Watson Watt, Brechin, Angus, Scotland, and Mary Matthew; *m* 1st, 1916, Margaret (marr. diss. 1952), *d* of David Robertson, Perth; 2nd, 1952, Jean (*widow* of Prof. George M. Smith) (*d* 1964); one *step s* one *step d*; 3rd, 1966, Air Chief Commandant Dame Katherine Jane Trefusis Forbes (*see* Air Chief Commandant Dame Katherine Watson-Watt). *Educ:* Brechin High Sch.; UC, Dundee, in University of St Andrews. Asst to Professor of Natural Philosophy, UC, Dundee, 1912-21; various posts in meteorology, radio and radar in Met. Office, DSIR, Air Ministry, Ministries of Aircraft Prod., Supply, Civil Aviation and Transp., 1915-52. Dep. Chairman Radio Board of War Cabinet, 1943-46; US Medal for Merit, 1946. Ex-President, Royal Met. Society for Inst. of Navigation; Ex-Vice-President, Inst. of Radio Engineers, New York. Hughes Medal of Royal Society, Elliott Cresson Medal of Franklyn Institute, etc. *Publications:* The Cathode Ray Oscillograph in Radio Research, 1933; Through the Weather House, 1935; Three Steps to Victory, 1958; The Pulse of Radar, 1959; Man's Means to His End, 1961; various communications to learned societies, etc. *Address:* 7 Crescent, SW3. *Club:* Athenæum.

**WATT, Sir Alan (Stewart),** Kt 1954; CBE 1952; Hon. Fellow, Australian National University, since 1965; Director, The Canberra Times; *b* 13 April 1901; *s* of George Watt and Susan Stewart Robb Gray; *m* 1927, Mildred Mary, Wait; three *s* one *d*. *Educ:* Sydney Boys' High Sch.; Sydney and Oxford Universities. Rhodes Scholar for NSW, 1921; practised as Barrister-at-Law, Sydney; appointed to Dept of External Affairs, Canberra, 1937; First Secretary, Australian Legation, Washington, 1940-45; Adviser, Australian Deleg. to San Francisco, UN Conf., 1945; Alternate Deleg., UN General Assembly, London, 1946; Asst Secretary (Political), Dept of External Affairs, 1946; Del. to UN Gen. Assemblies, New York, 1946 and 1947, Paris, 1948; Leader, Australian Deleg. to Conf. on Freedom of Information, Geneva, 1948. Australian Minister to USSR, 1947-48; Australian Ambassador to USSR, 1949-50; Secretary, Department of External Affairs, Canberra, ACT, 1950-53; Australian Commissioner in SE Asia, 1954-56; Australian Ambassador: to Japan, 1956-60; to Federal Republic of Germany, 1960-62. Australian Delegate, Colombo Plan Cons. Cttee Meeting, Sydney, 1950; Member Deleg. accompanying Prime Minister to Prime Ministers' Conf., London, 1951 and 1953; Member Australian Delegation to ANZUS Council Meeting, Honolulu, 1952, and Geneva, 1954; alternate Leader, Australian Deleg. to Conf. on Indo-China and Korea, Geneva, 1954, Manila Treaty Conf., Manila 1954. Bangkok 1955. Retired from Commonwealth Public Service, July 1962. Visiting Fellow, Australian National Univ., 1963-64; Dir, Australian Inst. of Internat. Affairs, 1963-69. *Publications:* The Evolution of Australian Foreign Policy 1938-1965, 1967; Vietnam, 1968. *Recreation:* lawn tennis. *Address:* 1 Mermaid Street, Red Hill, Canberra, ACT.

**WATT, Alexander Stuart,** PhD; FRS 1957; retired as Lecturer in Forest Botany, Cambridge University (1933-59); *b* 21 June 1892; *s* of George Watt and Maggie Jean Stuart; *m* 1929, Annie Constable Kennaway; two *s* one *d*. *Educ:* Turriff Secondary Sch.; Robert Gordon's Coll., Aberdeen; Aberdeen and Cambridge Universities. BA 1919, PhD 1924, Cambridge. Lecturer in Forest Botany and Forest Zoology, 1915-29; Gurney Lecturer in Forestry, Cambridge, 1929-33. Visiting Lecturer, University of Colorado, 1963; Visiting Prof., University of Khartoum, 1965. *Publications:* papers in Journal of Ecology, New Phytologist, etc. *Recreation:* hill walking. *Address:* 38 Chesterton Hall Crescent, Cambridge. *T:* Cambridge 59371.

**WATT, Andrew,** CBE 1963; Forestry Commissioner, 1965-69; *b* 10 Nov. 1909; 2nd *surv. s* of late James Watt, LLD, WS, and of late Menie Watt; *m* 1943, Helen McGuffog (*d* 1969); two *s* one *d. Educ:* Winchester; Magdalen Coll., Oxford. BA 1931. District Officer, Forestry Commn, 1934; Divisional Officer, 1940; Conservator, 1946; Director of Forestry for Scotland, 1957-63; Director of Forest Research, 1963-65. *Address:* Greenways, Ravelston Dykes Lane, Edinburgh EH4 3NY. *T:* 031-337 7986.

**WATT, Very Rev. Dr Archibald;** Minister, Edzell-Lethnot Parish Church, 1957-69, retired; Moderator of the General Assembly of the Church of Scotland, May 1965-66; *b* 1 Aug. 1901; *s* of Archibald Watt and Elsie Cormack; *m* 1933, Mary Swapp; two *s. Educ:* Robert Gordon's Coll., Aberdeen Univ. (MA) and Christ's Coll., Aberdeen; Union Theolog. Seminary, NY (STM *magna cum laude*). Hugh Black Fellowship for Union Theological Seminary, 1926-27; Assistant Minister: North Church, Aberdeen, 1927-29; St Serf's Church, Almondbank, Perthshire, 1929-34; Chalmers Church, Uddingston, 1934-42; Stonelaw Church, Rutherglen, 1942-57. Convener, Social Service Cttee of Church of Scotland, 1957-62. Hon. DD Aberdeen, 1959. *Publications:* 10 pamphlets on the Reformed Faith. *Recreation:* fishing. *Address:* 44 Springfield Avenue, Aberdeen. *T:* Aberdeen 36059. *Clubs:* Royal Over-Seas League; Caledonian (Edinburgh).

**WATT, Francis Clifford,** QC (Scotland) 1946; Sheriff of Stirling, Dunbarton and Clackmannan since 1961 (Caithness, Sutherland, Orkney and Zetland, 1952-61); *b* 20 July 1896; *s* of late Rev. Charles James Watt, Polwarth, Berwickshire; *m* 1945, Theresa Dorothy, *d* of John M'Quaker, Edinburgh; one *s. Educ:* Berwickshire High Sch.; Edinburgh Univ. Served European War, Argyll and Sutherland Highlanders and King's Own Scottish Borderers; called to Scottish Bar, 1925; Junior Counsel to Treasury for Scotland, 1940-46; MP (C) Central Division of Edinburgh, 1941-45. *Recreation:* golf. *Address:* 52 Inverleith Place, Edinburgh. *T:* 031-552 2932. *Clubs:* Caledonian; Caledonian (Edinburgh).

**WATT, George Percival Norman,** CMG 1957; CBE 1951; Chairman, Glanville Holland Pty Ltd and Greater Pacific Life Assurance (Australia) Ltd; *b* 2 June 1890; *s* of Edmund J. Watt, Melbourne, Australia; *m* 1916, Nellie V. M. Hough (decd); one *s* one *d. Educ:* Wesley Coll., Melbourne, Victoria. Clerk, Victorian Railways and State Treasury, 1905-08; Navy Finance Branch, 1911; Accountant, Navy Department, 1917; Secretary, HMA Naval Establishments, Sydney, 1923; Commonwealth Public Service Inspector, 1928-40; First Assistant Secretary, Defence Division Treasury, Melbourne, 1940; Deputy Secretary, Treasury, Canberra, 1947-48; Secretary, Commonwealth Treasury, Canberra, 1948-51, retired. Chairman, Australian National Airlines Commission, 1950-57; Chairman, British Commonwealth Pacific Airlines, 1950-54; Director, Qantas Empire Airways, 1947-62; Chairman and Director, Volkswagen (Australasia) Ltd, 1959-66. *Recreation:* golf. *Address:* 23 Through Road, Burwood, Victoria, Australia. *Club:* Athenæum (Melbourne).

**WATT, Sir G. S. H.;** *see* Harvie-Watt.

**WATT, Ian Buchanan,** CMG 1967; HM Diplomatic Service; British High Commissioner, Lesotho, 1966-70; *b* 3 Aug. 1916; *s* of John Watt and Margaret Gibson Watt, Perth; *m* 1963, Diana Susan, *d* of Captain R. A. Villiers, Royal Navy (retired) and late Mrs R. A. Villiers; two *s* (one *d* decd). *Educ:* Perth Academy; St Andrews Univ. MA 1939. Asst Principal, Government of N. Ireland, 1939. Naval Service, 1942-46; Lieut, RNVR. Principal, Colonial Office, 1946; Asst Secretary, 1956; Dep. UK Commissioner, Malta, 1962; Dep. High Commissioner, Malta, 1964; transf. to Diplomatic Service, 1964; Counsellor, CRO, 1965. *Recreations:* riding, swimming. *Address:* c/o Foreign and Commonwealth Office, SW1. *Clubs:* Reform, MCC.

**WATT, Surgeon Rear-Adm. James,** MS, FRCS; Dean of Naval Medicine and Medical Officer-in-Charge, Institute of Naval Medicine, Alverstoke, since 1969; *b* 19 Aug. 1914; *s* of Thomas Watt and Sarah Alice Clarkson. *Educ:* King Edward VI Sch., Morpeth; Univ. of Durham. MB, BS 1938; MS 1949; FRCS 1955. Surgical Registrar, Royal Vic. Infirm., Newcastle upon Tyne, 1947; Surgical Specialist: N Ire., 1949; RN Hosp., Hong Kong, 1954; Consultant in Surgery, RN Hospitals: Plymouth, 1956; Haslar, 1959; Malta, 1961; Haslar, 1963. Jt Prof. of Naval Surgery, RCS and RN Hosp., Haslar, 1965. Chm., RN Clin. Research Working Party, 1969; Chm. Bd of Trustees, Naval Christian Fellowship, 1969; QHS 1969. Surg. Comdr 1956; Surg. Captain 1965; Surg. Rear-Adm. 1969. FICS 1964; Fellow, Assoc. of Surgeons of Gt Brit. and Ire.; FRSM; Member: Brit. Soc. for Surgery of the Hand; Internat. Soc. for Burns Injuries; Corr. Mem., Surgical Research Soc.; Mem. Editorial Bds: Brit. Jl of Surgery; RN Med. Jl. Errol-Eldridge Prize, 1968. *Publications:* papers on: burns, cytotoxic agents in surgery, peptic ulceration, hyberbaric oxygen therapy. *Recreations:* photography, mountain walking, music. *Address:* Institute of Naval Medicine, Alverstoke, Hampshire. *Club:* English-Speaking Union.

**WATT, (James) David G.;** *see* Gibson-Watt.

**WATT, Prof. John Mitchell,** ED, MB, ChB (Edinburgh), FRCP (Edinburgh), FRSE, FRSSAf; CStJ; Emeritus Professor of Pharmacology and Therapeutics, University of the Witwatersrand, Johannesburg; Priory Surgeon-in-Chief (Reserve), St John Ambulance Brigade, Southern Africa; *b* Port Elizabeth, South Africa, 1 Dec. 1892; Scottish parentage; *m* 1st, 1920, Yelena T. Nikonova; two *s* two *d;* 2nd, 1942, Betty Gwendoline Lory; one *s* one *d. Educ:* Grey Institute High Sch., Port Elizabeth; Stirling High Sch., Scotland; University of Edinburgh. Graduated MB, ChB 1916; commissioned in the RAMC (Special Reserve) 4 Aug. 1914; on Active Service until 1919; Assistant in Materia Medica to Professor Cushny of Edinburgh Univ.; medical author, and member various medical societies; Foreign Corresponding Member, Royal Flemish Academy of Medicine, Belgium. Twice President of the Royal Medical Society of Edinburgh. Selected by Universities' Bureau of British Empire for a Carnegie Corporation Grant, 1933-34. Served as Head of Section M3 on the staff of Medical Headquarters, Union Defence Forces, South Africa, 1941-45; Major, RAMC (Militia) (retired); Colonel, South African Medical Corps (Retired List). *Publications:* numerous articles on medical and natural history subjects in medical and scientific journals; The Medicinal and Poisonous Plants of Southern and Eastern Africa (with Maria G. Breyer-Brandwijk), 2nd edn, 1962. Editor, Formulary of the South African Railways and Harbours

Sick Fund, 1st edn, 1935, 2nd edn, 1943, 3rd edn, 1952; Practical Notes on Pharmacology, Therapeutics, and Prescription Writing, 1940. Editor with F. J. Todd of The South African Pharmaceutical Formulary, 1943; Practical Pharmacology and Prescription Writing (with Margaret Brown), 1949. *Recreations:* gardening, ornithology, philately. *Address:* 36 Ludlow Street, Kenmore, Qld 4069, Australia.

**WATT, Sir Robert A. W.;** *see* Watson-Watt.

**WATT, Robert Cameron;** Assistant Master, Fettes College, since 1967; *b* 4 Aug. 1898; *s* of Rev. J. Gordon Watt; *m* 1925, Barbara, *d* of late Rt Rev. E. J. Bidwell, former Bishop of Ontario; three *s. Educ:* Fettes Coll., Edinburgh; Oriel Coll., Oxford. Lecturer in History, Queen's Univ., Kingston, Ontario, 1922-24; Asst Master, Clifton Coll., 1924-26; Senior History Master, Rugby Sch., 1926-51, Housemaster, 1944-51; Rector, Edinburgh Acad., 1951-62; Asst Master, St George's Sch., Newport, RI, 1963-66. *Recreations:* gardening, walking. *Address:* 9 Wardie Avenue, Edinburgh EH5 2AB.

**WATT, Prof. W(illiam) Montgomery;** Professor of Arabic and Islamic Studies, University of Edinburgh, since 1964; *b* Ceres, Fife, 14 March 1909; *o c* of late Rev. Andrew Watt; *m* 1943, Jean Macdonald, *er d* of late Prof. Robert Donaldson; one *s* four *d. Educ:* George Watson's Coll., Edinburgh; University of Edinburgh; Balliol Coll., Oxford; University of Jena; Cuddesdon Coll. Warner Exhibition (Balliol), 1930; Ferguson Schol. in Classics, 1931; MA, PhD (Edinburgh); MA, BLitt (Oxon). Asst Lecturer, Moral Philosophy, University of Edinburgh, 1934-38; Curate, St Mary Boltons, London, 1939-41; Curate, Old St Paul's, Edinburgh, 1941-43; Arabic specialist to Bishop in Jerusalem, 1943-46; Lecturer, Ancient Philosophy, University of Edinburgh, 1946-47; Lectr, Sen. Lectr and Reader in Arabic, Univ. of Edinburgh, 1947-64; Visiting Prof. of Islamic Studies, University of Toronto, 1963; Visiting Prof., Collège de France, Paris, 1970. Chairman, Assoc. of British Orientalists, 1964-65. Hon. DD Aberdeen, 1966. *Publications:* Free Will and Predestination in Early Islam, 1949; The Faith and Practice of al-Ghazali, 1953; Muhammad at Mecca, 1953; Muhammad at Medina, 1956; The Reality of God, 1958; The Cure for Human Troubles, 1959; Islam and the Integration of Society, 1961; Muhammad Prophet and Statesman, 1961; Islamic Philosophy and Theology, 1962; Muslim Intellectual, 1963; Truth in the Religions, 1963; Islamic Spain, 1965; Islam (in Propyläen Weltgeschichte, XI), 1965; A Companion to the Qur'an, 1967; What is Islam?, 1968; Islamic Political Thought, 1968; Islamic Revelation and the Modern World, 1970; Bell's Introduction to the Qur'ān, 1970; (ed) Islamic Surveys; contribs learned journals. *Address:* The Neuk, Dalkeith, Midlothian. *T:* 031-663 3197.

**WATT, Professor William Smith,** MA (Glasgow and Oxon); Regius Professor of Humanity in the University of Aberdeen since 1952, Vice-Principal since 1969; *b* 20 June 1913; *s* of John Watt and Agnes Smith; *m* 1944, Dorothea, *e d* of R. J. Codrington Smith; one *s. Educ:* University of Glasgow; Balliol Coll., Oxford (Snell Exhibitioner and Hon. Scholar). First Class Hons in Classics, Glasgow Univ., 1933; Ferguson Schol., 1934; Craven Schol., 1934; First Class, Classical Moderations, 1935; Hertford Schol., 1935; Ireland Schol., 1935; First Class, Lit. Hum., 1937. Lecturer in Greek and Greek History, University of Glasgow, 1937-38; Fellow and Tutor in Classics, Balliol Coll., Oxford, 1938-52. Civilian Officer, Admiralty (Naval Intelligence Div.), 1941-45. *Publications:* (ed) Ciceronis Epistulae ad Quintum fratrem, etc, 1958, 1965; (ed) Ciceronis Epistularum ad Atticum Libri I-VIII, 1965; articles and reviews in Classical periodicals. *Address:* Department of Humanity, King's College, Aberdeen; 38 Woodburn Gardens, Aberdeen. *T:* Aberdeen 34369. *Club:* Business and Professional (Aberdeen).

**WATTIE, Sir James,** Kt 1966; CBE 1963; Chairman and Managing Director, J. Wattie Canneries Ltd, since 1934 (Founder, 1934); *b* 23 March 1902; 3rd *s* of late William John Wattie and late Annie Elizabeth; *m* 1925, Gladys Madeline Henderson; two *s. Educ:* Public Schools, Blenheim and Hastings, NZ. Post Office Messenger, 1916; Junior Clerk, HB Farmers Meat Co. Ltd, 1917, Asst Accountant, 1919-24; Accountant, Roachs Ltd, 1924-25; Secretary, H. B. Fruitgrowers Ltd, 1926-27, Manager, 1927-34. Member: Hastings Chamber of Commerce; Hawke's Bay Medical Research Foundation (Life Member); NZ Trade Promotion Council. Fellow: Royal Arts Soc., NZ, 1970; Inst. of Directors, 1970. *Recreations:* trout fishing, horse racing and breeding, horticulture. *Address:* Mangapapa, PO Box 439, Hastings, Hawke's Bay, New Zealand. *T:* Hastings 85-401. *Clubs:* Wellesley (Wellington); Auckland (Auckland); Poverty Bay (Gisborne); Havelock (Havelock North); Hawke's Bay, Napier (Napier); Hastings, County (Hastings).

**WATTON, Rt. Rev. James Augustus;** *see* Moosonee, Bishop of.

**WATTS, Arthur Francis,** CMG 1964; OBE 1959; Assistant High Commissioner, Aden 1964-66; retired; *b* 15 Aug. 1916; *s* of Frank Godley Watts; *m* 1939, Barbara Mills; four *s. Educ:* Trent Coll. Served War of 1939-45. Famine Relief Officer, Eastern Aden Protectorate, 1944-46; Political Officer (Asst Adviser), E Aden Prot. and W Aden Prot., 1946; Dep. Adv. and British Agent, E Aden Prot. 1955, W Aden Prot., 1958; Resident Adviser and British Agent E Aden Prot. until 1960. *Address:* Ashleigh, Mark Cross, Crowborough, Sussex. *T:* Rotherfield 570.

**WATTS, Hon. Arthur Frederick,** CMG 1949; *b* 26 May 1897; *s* of Arthur Joseph Watts, LDS (Ireland) and Martha Kathleen Watts; *m* 1st, 1924, Dorothy Furness Thomson (*decd*); one *s* one *d*; 2nd, 1948, Ida Gladys O'Halloran. *Educ:* Government Sch., Katanning, WA; Guildford Grammar Sch., WA. MLA for Katanning 1935-50, for Stirling, 1950-62; Leader Country Party and Leader Opposition, 1942-47; one of two WA Reps to Constitutional Convention, Canberra, ACT, 1942, Dep. Premier, Minister for Education, Local Government and Industries, West Australian State Government, 1947-53; Dep. Premier, Minister for Education and Attorney-General, April 1959-resignation Feb. 1962. Chairman of State Licensing Court, WA, 1962-68, retd. SBStJ. *Recreations:* literature, motoring. *Address:* 8 Edna Road, Dalkeith, West Australia.

**WATTS, Gordon Edward,** CBE 1960; MA, PHD (Cantab); BSc (London); FRIC; FRSA; Adviser on Technical Education to Ministry of Overseas Development since 1967; *b* 6 Dec. 1902; *s* of Edward Watts, Dulwich, SE; *m* 1929, Nancy Margaret, *d* of Alfred Charles Playne, Looe, Cornwall; one *s* one *d. Educ:* Alleyn's Sch., Dulwich; Magdalene Coll., Cambridge. Research chemist, ICI, 1927-30; Lecturer in Chem. and Head of Dept, Brighton Technical Coll., 1930-39; Adviser on Technical

Education, Anglo-Iranian Oil Co., 1939-41; Vice-Principal, Brighton Technical Coll., 1941-44; Principal: Brighton Technical Coll., 1944-62; Brighton College of Technology, 1962-67. President, Assoc. of Principals of Techn. Instns, 1953-54; Chairman, Council, Assoc. of Techn. Instns, 1959-60; Vice-Chairman, Nat. Adv. Council for Education for Industry and Commerce, 1959-67; Member Adv. Cttee on Education in the Colonies, 1959-62; Member Council for Overseas Colleges of Arts, Sci. and Technol., 1959-62; Member Council for Techn. Education and Training for Overseas Countries, 1962-; Member Ashby Commn on Higher Education in Nigeria, 1959-60; Member British Delegation to Commonwealth Education Confs: Oxford, 1959, New Delhi, 1962, Lagos, 1968. Chairman, Commonwealth Conf. on Education and Training of Technicians, Huddersfield, 1967. Member: Council for National Academic Awards, 1964-67; Governing Body, Imperial Coll. of Science and Technology, 1970-. Hon. DSc Sussex, 1968. *Recreations:* travel, photography, gardening. *Address:* 1 The Green, Barrowfield, Hove, Sussex BN3 6TH. *T:* Brighton 554894.

**WATTS, Grace Elizabeth;** SRN, SCM, RNT, Hospital Administration (Nursing) Certificate; Chief Nursing Officer, United Leeds Hospitals, since 1969; *b* 4 Dec. 1916; *er d* of late Charles James Watts. *Educ:* Nutana Collegiate, Saskatoon, Canada. Trained: St Bartholomew's Hospital, London, 1936-40; Queen Charlotte's Hospital; King's College of Household and Social Science; The Royal College of Nursing. Theatre Sister and Sister Tutor, St Bartholomew's Hospital; Ward Sister, Luton and Dunstable Hospital; Deputy Matron, The Royal Free Hospital; Matron, General Infirmary, Leeds, 1957-69; Chairman: The General Nursing Council for England and Wales, 1965-; Leeds Area Nurse Training Cttee; Governor: Fulneck Girls' Sch., Pudsey; Leeds Girls' High Sch. hon. LLD, Leeds, 1969. *Recreations:* photography, travel, gardening. *Address:* The General Infirmary, Leeds 1. *T:* Leeds 32799. *Club:* Cowdray.

**WATTS, Colonel John Cadman,** OBE 1959; MC 1946; FRCS 1949; Consultant Surgeon, Bedford General Hospital 1966; *b* 13 April 1913; *s* of John Nixon Watts, solicitor, and Amy Bettina (*née* Cadman); *m* 1938, Joan Lillian (*née* Inwood); three *s* one *d*. *Educ:* Merchant Taylors' Sch.; St Thomas's Hospital. MRCS, LRCP, 1936; MB, BS, 1938. Casualty Officer, Resident Anæsthetist, House Surgeon, St Thomas's Hospital, 1937; Surgical Specialist, RAMC, 1938-60, serving in Palestine, Egypt, Libya, Syria, Tunisia, Italy, France, Holland, Germany, Malaya, Java, Japan, and Cyprus. Hunterian Professor, RCS, 1960; Professor of Military Surgery, RCS, 1960-64. *Publications:* Surgeon at War, 1955; Clinical Surgery, 1964; Exploration Medicine, 1964. *Recreations:* sailing, ski-ing, shooting. *Address:* Dunblane, 1 Rothsay Place, Bedford. *Clubs:* Royal Automobile; United Hospitals Sailing (Burnham).

**WATTS, John Hylton;** President, United Transport Company Ltd, since 1968 (Chairman, 1959-68; Managing Director, 1937); *b* Lydney, 14 March 1890; 2nd *s* of late Joseph Stephen Watts, Lydney, Glos.; *m* 1926, Iris Dyne, *er d* of late W. E. Birt; no *c*. *Educ:* Wycliffe Coll., Stonehouse. Pres., United Transport Overseas Ltd, since 1969 (Chairman, 1949-68); Director: Bulwark United Transport Ltd; Cambrian Airways Ltd; Watts of Lydney Ltd; Lydney Industrial Holdings Ltd; Chepstow Racecourse Co. Ltd; Member S. Wales Cttee of Lloyds Bank Ltd, 1959-67. Chairman, St Pierre Golf and Country Club Ltd. Served European War, 1915-19, 14th Siege Battery and Motor Transport Section (four years in France and Belgium). President 1935-65, now Life Patron, Lydney Branch of British Legion; Governor of Wycliffe Coll., 1952-66, now President; Member, Worshipful Company of Carmen, 1948; Freeman City of London, 1957; Verderer and Inclosure Commissioner of the Royal Forest of Dean, 1961. Member of Inst. of Directors, 1949; MInstT 1950. *Recreations:* croquet, cricket, tennis. *Address:* The Rocklands, Lydney, Glos. *T:* Lydney 2827. *Clubs:* United Service; County (Cardiff); St Pierre Golf and Country (Chepstow).

**WATTS, Ronald George,** CBE 1962; Organizing Secretary, Surrey Association for the Elderly; *b* 15 May 1914; *m* 1940, Ruth Hansen (*d* 1970); one *s* two *d*. *Educ:* Latymer Sch., Edmonton; St John's Coll., Cambridge. Foreign Service from 1937; appointed Counsellor, Foreign Office, 1958; Consul-Gen., Osaka-Kobe, 1958-63; Head of Consular Dept, FO, 1963-65; Consul-Gen., Paris, 1966-67; FCO 1967-69, retired. *Recreation:* music. *Address:* 14 Arlington Road, Petersham, Richmond, Surrey. *T:* 01-940 6137.

**WATTS, Rev. Sidney Maurice,** DD (St Andrews), BD (London); Minister of Union Church, Mill Hill, NW7, 1942-61, retired; Moderator, International Congregational Council, 1953-58; *b* Bishops Stortford, 1892; *y s* of James Watts, Lowestoft; *m* 1917, Winifred Chambers; one *s* two *d*. *Educ:* Lowestoft; Hackney Coll. (University of London). President, London University Debating Society, 1915; Asst Minister, Bromley Congregational Church, 1916-18; Supt Minister (Congregational), Whitefield's Central Mission, Tottenham Court Road, W1, 1918-24; Minister of Warwick Road Congregational Church, Coventry, 1924; of Elgin Place Congregational Church, Glasgow, 1937-42. Chairman Congregational Union of England and Wales, 1948-49; Moderator Free Church Federal Council, 1952-53. *Publications:* The Garden of God, a volume of Sermons; Liberty to the Captives, a short history of Slavery; Thinking Again About the Future Life, 1948. *Recreation:* gardening. *Address:* 1 Gipsy Lane, Balsall Common, Coventry, Warwicks. *T:* Berkswell 2428.

**WATTS, Weldon Patrick Tyrone,** AFC 1918; Hon. Surgeon, Royal Victoria Infirmary, since 1963; Consultant Surgeon: Royal Victoria Infirmary, 1947; Princess Mary Maternity Hospital, 1945; Shotley Bridge General Hospital, 1940; Hospital for Sick Children, 1927; retired, 1962; *b* 30 Oct. 1897; *s* of Joseph Patrick Weldon Watts, Dublin, and Kate Crisp, The Elms, Sunderland; *m* 1933, Sarah Bruce Allan, MB, BS; one *s*. *Educ:* Lake House Preparatory Sch., Bexhill; Sherborne Sch., Dorset; College of Medicine, Durham Univ. Served European War, 1914-18, RFC, 1916; RAF, 1917. MB, BS Durham, 1922; MS Durham, 1928; FRCS Edinburgh, 1927. Resident appointments, Royal Victoria Infirmary, Newcastle upon Tyne, 1922-33; general practice, 1924; Resident Med. Officer, 1925-26, Surgical Registrar, 1926-35, Asst Surgeon, 1935-47, Royal Victoria Infirmary. British Medical Association: joined 1922; Secretary, Newcastle Div., 1936-52; Chairman, Newcastle upon Tyne Div., 1953; President, North of England Branch, 1954; Member Council, 1940-59; President, 1957. Member, General Medical Council, 1961-66. *Publications:* contrib. Newcastle Med. Journal and BMJ. *Recreations:* golf, fishing, shooting, natural history. *Address:* Fenham Hill, Beal,

Berwick-on-Tweed. *T:* Beal 234. *Club:* Northumberland Golf (Gosforth).

**WAUCHOPE, Sir Patrick (George) Don-,** 10th Bt, *cr* 1667; Horticulturist; *b* 7 May 1898; *o s* of late Patrick Hamilton Don-Wauchope (3rd *s* of 8th Bt) and late Georgiana Renira; *S* uncle 1951; *m* 1936, Ismay Lilian Ursula (marr. diss.), *d* of late Sidney Hodges, Edendale, Natal, South Africa; two *s*. *Educ:* The Edinburgh Academy. Served European War, 1914-18, with RFA, France and Belgium (wounded); War of 1939-46, Egypt and Italy. *Recreations:* cricket, golf. *Heir: s* Roger (Hamilton) Don-Wauchope [Chartered Accountant, S Africa; *b* 16 Oct. 1938; *m* 1963, Sallee, *yr d* of Lt-Col H. Mill Colman, OBE, AMICE, Durban; two *s*]. *Address:* 21 Winston Road, Kloof, Natal, South Africa.

**WAUGH, Alec;** *b* Hampstead, 8 July 1898; *er s* of late Arthur Waugh; *m* 1932, Joan (*d* 1969), *d* of Andrew Chirnside, Victoria, Australia; two *s* one *d*; *m* 1969, Virginia Sorensen, *d* of Claude Eggertsen, Springfield, Utah, USA. *Educ:* Sherborne; Sandhurst. Gazetted to Dorset Regt, 1917; BEF France, 1917-18; prisoner of war, 1918; has travelled extensively; rejoined Dorset Regt, 1939; BEF France, 1940; Staff Captain, Ministry of Mines, 1940; MEF, 1941; Paiforce, 1942-45; retired with rank of Major, 1945. Writer in Residence at Central State Coll., Edmond, Oklahoma, 1966-67. *Publications:* has written over forty books which include: The Loom of Youth, 1917; Kept, 1925; Nor Many Waters, 1928; Hot Countries, 1930; Most Women . . ., 1931; So Lovers Dream, 1931; The Balliols, 1934; Jill Somerset, 1936; Eight Short Stories, 1937; Going Their Own Ways, 1938; No Truce with Time, 1941; His Second War, 1944; Unclouded Summer, 1948; The Lipton Story, 1951; Where the Clocks Chime Twice, 1952; Guy Renton, 1953; Island in the Sun, 1956 (produced as film, 1957); The Sugar Islands, 1958; In Praise of Wine, 1959; Fuel for the Flame, 1960;My Place in the Bazaar, 1961; The Early Years of Alec Waugh, 1962; A Family of Islands, 1964; The Mule on the Minaret, 1965; My Brother Evelyn and Other Profiles, 1967; Wines and Spirits of the World, 1968; A Spy in the Family, 1970; Bangkok: the story of a city, 1970. *Recreation:* watching life go by. *Address:* c/o Brandt & Brandt, 101 Park Avenue, NYC, NY, USA. *Clubs:* Athenæum, Beefsteak, Pratt's, Savage; Century, Coffee House (New York).

**WAVERLEY,** 2nd Viscount, *cr* 1952, of Westdean; **Alastair Anderson;** Consultant Physician, Reading Group of Hospitals, since 1951; *b* 18 Feb. 1911; *s* of 1st Viscount Waverley, PC, GCB, OM, GCSI, GCIE, FRS, and Christina Anderson; *S* father, 1958; *m* 1948, Myrtle Ledgerwood; one *s* two *d*. *Educ:* Malvern Coll.; Universities of Frankfurt A/Main and Cambridge (Pembroke Coll.); St Thomas's Hospital, London. MB, BChir (Cantab), 1937; MRCP (London), 1946; FRCP (London), 1957. Appointments at St Thomas's Hospital, 1938-39. Served War of 1939-45, RAF Med. Br. Med. Registrar, Res. Asst Physician and Registrar Dept Clin. Pathology, St Thomas's Hospital, 1946-50. *Publications:* various communications to medical journals. *Recreations:* golf and fishing; formerly athletics and Association football (rep. Cambridge *v* Oxford, in Inter-Varsity Relays, etc). *Heir: s* Hon. John Desmond Forbes Anderson, *b* 31 Oct. 1949. *Address:* Path Hill House, Whitchurch, Oxon. *T:* Pangbourne 2417. *Clubs:* Travellers'; Hawks (Cambridge).

*See also Brig. Hon. Dame Mary Anderson.*

**WAVERLEY, Ava, Viscountess;** *o d* of late J. E. C. Bodley and Evelyn (*née* Bell); *m* 1st, 1925, Ralph Wigram, CMG, Counsellor in HM Diplomatic Service (*d* 1936); one *s* decd; 2nd, 1941, Sir John Anderson, PC, GCB, GCSI, GCIE, FRS, MP (*cr* Viscount Waverley of Westdean, 1952; awarded OM 1957) (*d* 1958). *Educ:* in France. Member of Governing Body, Dockland Settlement; Trustee of Royal Ballet Benevolent Fund; Member of Council, "Friends of Covent Garden"; Bloodhound breeder. *Address:* 4 Lord North Street, Westminster, SW1. *Club:* Kennel (Ladies' Branch).

**WAY, Andrew Greville Parry,** CMG 1963; Assistant Commissioner, Metropolitan Police, 1963-69, retired; *b* 9 Dec. 1909; *s* of late Preb. Charles Parry Way, and Ethel Mary (*née* Danks); *m* 1939, Maureen Molyneux; two *s*. *Educ:* St Edward's and Christ Church, Oxford. Joined Metropolitan Police, 1934; Metropolitan Police Coll., 1934-35. Army (General List), 1943-49. Seconded Police Force of Free Territory of Trieste, 1949-52. Commander, Metropolitan Police, 1958-63. Seconded: Montreal Police Dept (Canada), 1961-62; Anguilla Police Unit, 1969. *Recreations:* motoring, reading, Rugby and cricket. *Address:* Ponda Rosa, Lerryn, near Lostwithiel, Cornwall.

**WAY, Christine Stella;** *b* 26 July 1895; *o c* of late Captain C. M. S. Humphreys, JP, Garthmyl Hall, Montgomeryshire; *m* 1932, Captain H. Bromley Way; one *s* one *d*. *Educ:* Tudor Hall, Chislehurst. County Secretary of Girl Guides for County of Montgomeryshire, 1919; County Commissioner (Girl Guides), 1930-47; Hon. Treasurer, Wales Girl Guides since 1945; JP 1934; High Sheriff of Montgomeryshire, 1943. Chairman of House Cttee for Broneirion (The Welsh Training Centre for Girl Guides), 1947. VAD nurse through European War. *Address:* Garthmyl Hall, Montgomery. *T:* Berriew 283.

**WAY, Sir Richard (George Kitchener),** KCB 1961 (CB 1957); CBE 1952; Chairman, London Transport Executive since 1970; *b* 15 Sept. 1914; *s* of Frederick and Clara Way; *m* 1947, Ursula Joan Starr; one *s* two *d*. *Educ:* Polytechnic Secondary Sch., London. Joined Civil Service as Exec. Officer, 1933; Higher Executive Officer, 1940; Principal, 1942; Asst Secretary, 1946; Asst Under-Secretary of State, 1954; Deputy Under-Secretary of State, War Office, 1955-57; Dep. Secretary, Ministry of Defence, 1957-58; Dep. Secretary, Ministry of Supply, 1958-59; Permanent Under-Secretary of State, War Office, 1960-63; Permanent Secretary, Ministry of Aviation, 1963-66. Dep. Chm., Lansing Bagnall Ltd, 1966-67, Chm. 1967-69. Chairman, EDC Machine Tool Industry, 1967-70; Member (part-time), Board of BOAC, 1967-. Chm., Council of Roedean Sch., 1969-. Coronation Medal, 1953. American Medal of Freedom (with bronze palm), 1946. *Address:* Manor Farm, Shalden, Alton, Hants. *T:* Alton 2383. *Clubs:* Brooks's, MCC.

**WAY, Rt. Rev. Wilfrid Lewis Mark;** Rector of Averham with Kelham, since 1960; *b* 12 May, 1905; *s* of late Rev. C. C. L. Way and Margaret (*née* Corser); *m* 1960, Marion Crosbie, *d* of Sir Robert Robinson, *qv*, and late Lady (Gertrude M.) Robinson; one *s* one *d*. *Educ:* Rossall Sch.; Trinity Coll., Cambridge (Classical Scholar); Westcott House. 1st Cl. Class. Tripos, part I, 1925; BA 2nd Cl. Class. Tripos, part II, 1927; MA 1935; Deacon, 1928; Priest, 1929, Liv. Curate of St Faith, Great Crosby, 1928-34; St Bartholomew, Brighton, 1934-37; UMCA Dio., Zanzibar, 1937; Curate of Korogwe,

1937-38; Priest i/c Zanzibar, 1938-40; Msalabani, 1940-44; Mkuzi, 1944-45; Kideleko, 1948-51; Warden of Kalole Theol. Coll., Dio. of Zanzibar, 1951-52; Bishop of Masasi, 1952-59. *Address:* Averham Rectory, Newark, Notts. *T:* Newark 4530.

**WAYMOUTH, Charity,** BSc (London), PhD (Aberdeen); Senior Staff Scientist and Assistant Director (Training), The Jackson Laboratory, Bar Harbor, Maine, USA, since 1963 (Staff Scientist, 1952-63); *b* 29 April 1915; *o d* of Charles Sydney Herbert Waymouth, Major, The Dorsetshire Regt, and Ada Curror Scott Dalgleish; unmarried. *Educ:* Royal School for Daughters of Officers of the Army, Bath; University of London; University of Aberdeen. Biochemist, City of Manchester General Hospitals, 1938-41; Research Fellow, University of Aberdeen, 1944; Beit Memorial Fellow for Medical Research, 1944-46; Member of scientific staff and head of tissue culture dept, Chester Beatty Research Institute for Cancer Research (University of London), 1947-52; British Empire Cancer Campaign-American Cancer Society Exchange Fellow, 1952-53. Member Tissue Culture Association (President, 1960-62, Editor-in-Chief 1968-). Member of various British and American professional and learned societies; Hon. Life member and Hon. Director, Psora Society (Canada); Member, Diocesan Council, Diocese of Maine, and Exec. Council (1967-), Episcopal Church of the USA. *Publications:* numerous papers in scientific journals, on nucleic acids and on tissue culture and cell nutrition. *Recreations:* reading, gardening; lawn tennis. *Address:* c/o National Westminster Bank Ltd, Old Church Street Branch, SW3; 10 Atlantic Avenue, Bar Harbor, Maine 04609, USA. *T:* 288-4208.

**WAYNE, Sir Edward (Johnson),** Kt 1964; MD, MSc, PhD, FRCP (London and Edinburgh); FRCP (Glasgow); Regius Professor of Practice of Medicine, Glasgow University, 1954-67; Physician to Western Infirmary, Glasgow; Hon. Physician to the Queen in Scotland, 1954-67; *b* 3 June 1902; *s* of late William Wayne, Leeds, Yorks, and late Ellen Rawding, Leadenham, Lincs; *m* 1932, Honora Nancy Halloran; one *s* one *d*. *Educ:* Leeds Univ. and Medical School (Akroyd Scholar and Sir Swire Smith Fellow); Manchester Univ. BSc Leeds (1st Class Hons Chemistry) 1923; MB, ChB (Leeds), 1st Class Hons, 1929; MD 1938; Hey Gold Medallist; Demonstrator in Physiology, University of Leeds, 1930-31; Assistant in Dept Clinical Research, University College Hospital, London, 1931-34; Professor of Pharmacology and Therapeutics, University of Sheffield, 1934-53 (formerly Physician to Royal Infirmary and Children's Hospital, Sheffield). Member Scottish Secretary of State's Advisory Cttee on Medical Research, 1958-67; Member of the Medical Research Council, 1958-62; Chairman, Clinical Research Board, 1960-64; Chairman, British Pharmacopœia Commn, 1958-63; Chairman, Advisory Cttee on Drug Dependence, 1967-69. Sims Commonwealth Travelling Professor, 1959. Bradshaw Lecturer, 1953; Lumleian Lecturer, RCP, 1959; Crookshank Lecturer and Medallist, Faculty of Radiol., 1966. Hon. DSc Sheffield, 1967. *Publications:* Papers in scientific and medical journals. *Recreation:* walking. *Address:* Green Dragon Close, Chipping Campden, Glos. *T:* Campden 453. *Club:* Athenæum.

**WAYNE, Naunton;** Actor; *b* 22 June 1901; *s* of William Thomas Davies, Solicitor, and Annie Elizabeth Davies, Porth (Rhondda Valley), South Wales; changed name by deed-poll from Henry Wayne Davies, 1933; *m* 1927, Gladys Dove; two *s*. *Educ:* Clifton Coll. Started professional career in concert party, 1920; first cabaret engagement, 1927; first Radio performance, 1928; first Music Hall booking, Victoria Palace, 1929; first Revue, Chelsea Follies (as Compère), 1930; first Picture, First Mrs Fraser, 1931; non-stop Variety, London Pavilion (40 weeks), 1932; Pictures, Going Gay and For Love of You, 1933; Compère for Josephine Baker season, Prince Edward Theatre, 1933; Cochran's Streamline, 1934; Compère, 1066 and All That, 1935; All Wave, Revue, 1936; first straight play, Norman, in Wise Tomorrow, Lyric Theatre, 1937; played same part in New York, 1937; Choose Your Time, Piccadilly Theatre, 1938; Caldicott in film The Lady Vanishes, 1938; Film, A Girl Must Live, 1938; Farce, Giving the Bride Away, St Martin's Theatre, 1939; Caldicott in films Night Train to Munich and Crooks Tour, 1940; George Black's Black Vanities, Victoria Palace, 1941; Tristan Sprott in J. B. Priestley's Good Night Children, New Theatre, 1942; Tom Arnold's Sky High Revue, Phœnix Theatre, 1942; Arsenic and Old Lace, Strand Theatre, 1942-46; Clutterbuck, Wyndham's, 1946; Young Wives' Tale, Savoy, 1949; Count Your Blessings, Wyndham's, 1951; Trial and Error, Vaudeville, 1953; Its Different for Men, Duchess Theatre, 1955; One Bright Day, Apollo, 1956; A River Breeze, Phœnix 1956; The Bride and the Bachelor, Duchess Theatre, 1957; A Day in the Life of . . ., Savoy, 1958; From the French, Strand, 1959; film, Operation Bullshine, 1959; The Big Killing, Princes, 1962; Vanity Fair, Queen's, 1962; Let's Be Frank, Vaudeville, 1963; The Reluctant Peer, Duchess, 1964; Justice is a Woman, Vaudeville, 1966; Oh Clarence!, Lyric, 1968. Music Hall engagements between productions. *Recreations:* golf and photography. *Address:* 6 Vicarage Gardens, SW14. *T:* 01-876 1808. *Clubs:* Green Room, Stage Golfing.

**WEARING, John Frederick;** HM Diplomatic Service; UK Alternate Governor, International Atomic Energy Agency, since 1967, and UK Permanent Representative to UN Industrial Development Organisation, since 1968; *b* 5 Oct. 1922; *s* of Walter and Elsie Wearing; *m* 1945, Rose Vacher; one *s* one *d*. *Educ:* Whitehaven Grammar Sch.; St Edmund Hall, Oxford. RAF, 1942-46. Asst Principal, Colonial Office, 1948; Foreign Office, 1949; 2nd Secretary, British Legation, Helsinki, 1950; HM Vice-Consul, Amsterdam, 1953; HM Consul, Hanover, 1955; FO, 1956; 1st Secretary, British Embassy, Djakarta, 1959; FO, 1961; 1st Secretary, UK Delegation to OECD, Paris, 1963; Counsellor and Head of Economic General Department, Commonwealth Office, 1966. *Recreations:* gardening, amateur dramatics, debating. *Address:* 42 The Mead, Beckenham, Kent. *T:* 01-658 6837. *Club:* Travellers'.

**WEATHERALL, Miles,** MA, DM, DSc; Deputy Director, Wellcome Research Laboratories, since 1969; *b* 14 Oct. 1920; *s* of Rev. J. H. and Mary Weatherall; *m* 1944, Josephine A. C. Ogston; three *d*. *Educ:* Dragon School and St Edward's School, Oxford; Oriel College, Oxford. BA, BSc 1941; BM 1943; MA 1945; DM 1951; DSc 1966. Open Schol. in Nat. Sci., Oriel Coll., 1938. Lecturer in Pharmacology, Edinburgh University, 1945; Head of Dept of Pharmacology, London Hosp. Med. Coll., 1949-66; Prof. of Pharmacology, Univ. of London, 1958-66; Head, Therapeutic Div., Wellcome Res. Labs, 1967-. Member: Adv. Cttee on Pesticides and other Toxic Chemicals, 1964-66. Council, Pharmaceutical Soc., 1966-70; Cttee, Internat. Exhibn Coop. Wine Soc., 1964-. Chm., Gov. Body, Chelsea

Coll. of Science and Technology, 1970-. *Publications:* Statistics for Medical Students (jointly with L. Bernstein), 1952; Scientific Method, 1968; papers in scientific and medical journals. *Recreations:* various. *Address:* 17 Tollgate Drive, SE21.

**WEATHERBURN, Prof. Charles Ernest,** MA, DSc, Hon. LLD; Emeritus Professor of Mathematics, University of Western Australia since 1950 (Professor of Mathematics 1929-50); Chairman of the Professorial Board, 1934 and 1942-43; *b* Sydney, NSW, 18 June 1884; *s* of Henry Weatherburn, formerly of Leicester, England; *m* 1909, Lucy May Dartnell, Sydney, NSW; three *s. Educ:* Sydney University (post-graduate travelling scholarship); Trinity College, Cambridge (Major Scholarship). First Class Mathematical Tripos. Lecturer in Mathematics and Natural Philosophy for Ormond College, University of Melbourne, 1911-23; Trinity College, 1916-23; Professor of Mathematics at Canterbury University College, Christchurch, New Zealand, 1923-29; President of Section A, Australian and NZ Association for the Advancement of Science, 1932; awarded Hector Medal and Prize by the Royal Society of New Zealand, 1934. Hon. LLD (Glasgow), 1951. *Publications:* Vector Analysis; Differential Geometry; Riemannian Geometry; Mathematical Statistics, and a large number of original memoirs in Pure and Applied Mathematics. *Recreations:* bowling, motoring, gardening. *Address:* 34 Dalkeith Road, Nedlands, W Australia 6009.

**WEATHERHEAD, Sir Arthur (Trenham),** Kt 1960; CMG 1957; *b* 19 May 1905; *s* of late Canon A. S. Weatherhead; *m* 1938, Sylvia Mary, *d* of late A. Lace, Eastbourne; one *s* two *d. Educ:* St Bees School; Queen's College, Oxford. Sudan Plantations Syndicate, 1927; Colonial Administrative Service, Nigeria, 1930-60. Dep. Governor, Northern Region, Nigeria, 1958-60, retired. *Recreations:* gardening, chess. *Address:* 1 Amberley Court, Amberley, Stroud, Glos. *T:* Amberley 2584.

**WEATHERHEAD, Rev. Leslie D.,** CBE 1959; MA (Manchester); PhD (London); Hon. DD (Edinburgh and California); Hon. DLitt (University Puget Sound, Washington); Minister of The City Temple, London, 1936-October 1960, now Minister Emeritus; President of the Methodist Conference, July 1955-56; Hon. Chaplain to Forces; Freeman of City of London; Hon. Member, Association of Psychotherapists; Member: Society for Psychical Research; Churches' Fellowship for Psychical Study; President Institute of Religion and Medicine, 1966-67; *b* London, 1893; *s* of Andrew Weatherhead, a Scottish Presbyterian, and Elizabeth Mary Weatherhead, London; *m* 1920, Evelyn (*d* 1970), *er d* of Rev. Arthur Triggs, formerly Missionary in Ceylon; two *s* one *d. Educ:* Newton Secondary School Leicester; Richmond Theological Coll.; London Univ.; Manchester Univ. Served European War as 2nd Lieut IARO; Mesopotamian Campaign as Staff Capt.; after the Armistice with Turkey served as Chaplain to 1/4 and 1/6 Devon Regts, took charge of English Methodist Church, Madras, 1919; returned England in 1922; Oxford Road Wesleyan Church, Manchester, 1922-25; Brunswick Methodist Church Leeds, 1925-36; specialized in Psychology; Lecturer in Psychology for the Workers' Educational Association; Certificated Teacher of Psychology under Board of Education; Formerly Examiner in Psychology for Ordination Candidates in Wesleyan Methodist Church. *Publications:* After Death; The Afterworld of the Poets; Psychology in Service of the Soul; Psychology and Life; The Mastery of Sex through Psychology and Religion; The Transforming Friendship; Jesus and Ourselves; His Life and Ours; Discipleship; How can I find God?; Why do men Suffer?; It Happened in Palestine; A Shepherd Remembers; The Eternal Voice; Thinking aloud in Wartime; This is the Victory; Personalities of the Passion; In Quest of a Kingdom; The Will of God; A Plain Man looks at the Cross; The Significance of Silence; When The Lamp Flickers; The Resurrection and the Life; Psychology, Religion and Healing; That Immortal Sea; Over His Own Signature; Prescription for Anxiety; A Private House of Prayer; The Resurrection of Christ in the Light of Modern Science and Psychical Research; Key next Door; The Case for Re-incarnation; Salute to a Sufferer; Wounded Spirits; The Christian Agnostic; Time for God; Life Begins at Death. *Recreations:* bird-watching, gardening and travel. *Address:* 20 Richmond Grove, Bexhill-on-Sea, Sussex. *T:* Bexhill 1719.

**WEATHERILL, (Bruce) Bernard;** MP (C) Croydon North-East since 1964; a Lord Commissioner, HM Treasury, since 1970; *b* 25 Nov. 1920; *s* of late Bernard Weatherill, Spring Hill, Guildford, and Annie Gertrude (*née* Creak); *m* 1949, Lyn, *d* of late H. T. Eatwell; two *s* one *d. Educ:* Malvern College. Served War of 1939-45; commissioned 4/7th Royal Dragoon Guards, 1940; transferred to Indian Army, 1941 and served with 19th King George V's Own Lancers, 1941-45 (Captain). Man. Dir, Bernard Weatherill Ltd, 1957-70. First Chm., Guildford Young Conservatives, 1946-49; Chm., Guildford Cons. Assoc., 1959-63; Vice-Chm., SE Area Prov. Coun., 1962-64; Member National Union of Cons. Party, 1963-64. An Opposition Whip, 1967. Freeman of City of London. *Recreations:* golf, tennis. *Address:* 55 Conduit Street, W1. *T:* 01-734 1344; Tyting Glen, St Martha's, Guildford. *T:* Guildford 4783. *Clubs:* Carlton, St Stephens, City Livery; Conservative (Croydon).

**WEATHERLEY, Prof. Paul Egerton;** Regius Professor of Botany in the University of Aberdeen since Oct. 1959; *b* 6 May 1917; *o s* of Leonard Roger Weatherley and late Ethel Maude (*née* Collin), Leicester; *m* 1942, Margaret Logan, *o d* of John Pirie, JP, Castle of Auchry, Aberdeenshire; one *s* three *d. Educ:* Wyggeston School; Keble College (Open Schol.), Oxford. Final Sch. of Nat. Sci. (Hons Botany) 1939; Keble Research Schol., 1939-40, elected to Colonial Agric. Schol., 1940. Trained in RE, then Colonial Office cadet at Imperial Coll. of Tropical Agric. Trinidad, 1940-42. Govt Botanist in Dept of Agriculture, Uganda Protectorate, 1942-47; Asst Lectr, Univ. of Manchester, 1947-49; Lecturer in Botany, 1949-59 (Sen. Lectr 1956); Univ. of Nottingham. *Publications:* papers in (mainly) botanical journals. *Recreations:* music, sketching. *Address:* 8 The Chanonry, Old Aberdeen.

**WEATHERSTONE, Sir Duncan (Mackay),** Kt 1965; MC 1918; TD 1945; DL; Lord Provost of the City of Edinburgh, May 1963-May 1966; *b* Edinburgh, 10 May 1898; *s* of R. M. Weatherstone and Harriet Mackay; *m* 1920, Janet Pringle Brunton; one *s* one *d. Educ:* Daniel Stewart's College, Edinburgh. Entered Life Assurance 1916; joined Army, 1917; returned to Life Assurance, 1919; Branch Manager, Belfast, 1922; Agency Manager and Executive, Head Office, holding position of second in command of the Company, 1933; retired, 1961. ACII 1922. Hon. DLitt, Heriot-Watt Univ., 1966; Hon. LLD, Edinburgh, 1966. Order of The Two Niles (Sudan), 1964. DL, Edinburgh, 1967. *Recreations:* golf, art and culture. *Address:* 4a Granton Road, Edinburgh 5. *T:* 031-552 3636. *Clubs:* Scottish Conservative; Royal Scots (Edinburgh).

**WEAVER, Tobias Rushton,** CB 1962; Deputy Under Secretary of State, Department of Education and Science; *b* 19 July 1911; *s* of late Sir Lawrence Weaver, KBE, and late Lady Weaver (*née* Kathleen Purcell); *m* 1941, Marjorie, *d* of Rt Hon. Sir Charles Trevelyan, 3rd Bt, PC; one *s* three *d*. *Educ:* Clifton College; Corpus Christi College, Cambridge. Bank clerk, Toronto, 1932; teaching at Barking, 1935, Eton, 1936; Asst Director of Education: Wilts CC 1936, Essex CC 1939. Admiralty, 1941; War Office, 1942; Dept of Education and Science, 1946-; Under-Secretary, 1956; Deputy Secretary, 1962. *Address:* 13 Vicarage Gardens, W8. *T:* 01-229 3217. *Club:* English-Speaking Union.

**WEAVER, Warren;** Medal for Merit (US), 1946; Vice-President, Alfred P. Sloan Foundation until 1964, when resigned, but continues as consultant on scientific affairs; *b* 17 July 1894; *s* of Isaiah and Kittie Belle Stupfell Weaver; *m* 1919, Mary Hemenway; one *s* one *d*. *Educ:* Univ. of Wisconsin. 2nd Lieut Air Service, 1917-19. Asst Prof. Mathematics: Throop Coll., 1917-18; Cal. Inst. of Technology, 1919-20; Univ. of Wisconsin, 1920-25, Assoc. Prof. Mathematics, 1925-28, Prof. of Mathematics and Chairman of Dept, 1928-32; Lecturer, Univ. of Chicago, summer, 1928; Dir, Div. of Natural Sciences: Gen. Educn Bd, 1932-37; Rockefeller Foundation, 1932-55; Vice-Pres., Rockefeller Foundation, 1955-59. Chief, Applied Mathematics Panel, Office of Scientific Research and Devel., 1943-46; Chm., Naval Research Adv. Cttee, 1946-47. Sloan-Kettering Inst.: Trustee, 1954-67; Chairman Board, 1959-60; Vice-President, 1958-59; Trustee: Eastman Fund; Alfred P. Sloan Foundation, 1956-67; Member: Nat. Science Board, Nat. Science Foundation, 1956-60; Board of Directors, Coun. on Library Resources, 1956-59; Nat. Advisory Cancer Council, US Public Health Service, 1957-60; Councillor, Amer. Philos. Soc., 1957-60; Bd of Managers, Memorial Center for Cancer and Allied Diseases, 1958-60; Mem. Bd of Managers and Exec. Cttee, Mem. Hosp. for Cancer and Allied Diseases, 1960-67; Mem. and Vice-Chm., Health Res. Council, C., NY, 1958-60; Mem. Gov. Coun., Courant Inst. of Mathematical Sciences, 1962-; Bd of Dirs, Scientists' Inst. for Public Information, 1963-; Mem., Gov. Rockefeller's Cttee on Hosp. Costs, 1964-65. Fellow Amer. Acad. of Arts and Scis., 1958-; Assoc. Trustee, Univ. of Pennsylvania, 1959-; Acad. of Religion and Mental Health (Mem. Bd of Trustees, 1959-63); Vice-Pres., 1961-63, Hon. Vice-Pres., 1963-); Memorial Sloan-Kettering Cancer Center (Vice-Chm. of Board, 1960-67; Chm. Cttee on Scientific Policy); Public Health Research Inst. of City of New York, Inc. (Pres. 1961-63); Salk Inst. for Biological Studies, San Diego, Calif. (Trustee, Chm. Bd, Non-Res. Fellow, 1962-). Holds several hon. degrees and awards. King's Medal for Service in Cause of Freedom (Gt Brit.), 1948; Public Welfare Medal, National Academy of Sciences, USA, 1957. Kalinga Prize, 1964; Arches of Science Award, 1964. Officer, Legion of Honor (France), 1950. *Publications:* (with Max Mason) The Electromagnetic Field, 1929; (with Claude Shannon) Mathematical Theory of Communication, 1949; Lady Luck–The Theory of Probability, 1963; Alice in Many Tongues, 1964; US Philanthropic Foundations: Their History, Structure, Management and Record, 1967; Science and Imagination, 1967; Scene of Change (autobiography), 1970. Editor: The Scientists Speak, 1947; mathematical and general articles, on science, in journals. *Recreation:* collector of Lewis Carroll. *Address:* Second Hill, New Milford, Conn 06776, USA. *T:* New Milford, Elgin 4-4177. *Club:* Century Association (NY City).

**WEBB, Mrs Allan Bourne;** *see* Gibbons, Stella Dorothea.

**WEBB, Anthony Michael Francis,** CMG 1963; QC (Kenya) 1961; JP; Deputy Secretary of Commissions, since 1969, and Secretary National Advisory Council on the Training of Magistrates, and Training Officer, Lord Chancellor's office, since 1964; *b* 27 Dec. 1914; *s* of late Sir (Ambrose) Henry Webb; *m* 1948, Diana Mary, *e d* of late Capt. Graham Farley, Indian Army, and of Mrs Herbert Browne (*née* Pyper); one *s* one *d*. *Educ:* Ampleforth; Magdalen Coll., Oxford (MA). Barrister-at-Law, Gray's Inn, 1939. Served War, 1939-46, Maj. GSO2, The Queen's Bays. Colonial Legal Service (HMOCS), 1947-64 (Malaya; Kenya; MLC 1958-63; Attorney-General and Minister for Legal Affairs, 1961-63). Member of Council of Kenya Lawn Tennis Association, 1957-63. JP, Kent, 1966. *Publication:* The Natzweiler Trial (ed). *Recreation:* tennis. *Address:* 10 Royal Chase, Tunbridge Wells, Kent. *T:* 30016. *Club:* Special Forces.

**WEBB, Cecil Richard,** OBE 1926; MC; *b* 17 Aug. 1887; *y s* of Rev. S. G. M. Webb, late Rector of Newton Kyme, Yorkshire; *m* 1922, Beatrice Helen Gordon, *y d* of late Charles Gulland Ballingall; one *s* one *d*. *Educ:* St John's School, Leatherhead; North Eastern Railway, 1904-14; Assistant Traffic Manager, Uganda Railway, 1914; war service, British and German East Africa, 1914-19 (despatches, MC); Traffic Manager, Tanganyika Railway, 1919-23; General Manager and Traffic Manager, Sierra Leone Railway, 1923-30; General Manager, Palestine Railways, 1930-42; Ministry of War Transport, Cape Town, 1943-45; Ministry of Transport (London), Railways Maintenance Division, 1945-47. *Address:* 1 Stokes House, Sutherland Avenue, Bexhill-on-Sea, Sussex. *T:* Bexhill 2790.

**WEBB, Clifford,** RBA 1936; RE 1948; Illustrator and Engraver; *b* 14 Feb. 1895; *m* 1924, Ella Monckton; two *s* one *d*. Apprenticed as lithographer in City of London. Served European War, 1914-18, Army. Studied Westminster School of Art. Specializes in animal drawing. Illustrated books for Golden Cockerel Press and many others. Member of Wood Engraving Society, Royal Society of Painters Etchers and Royal Society of British Artists. Author and illustrator of children's books. *Publications:* The Story of Noah; The Thirteenth Pig; Butterwick Farm; Animals from Everywhere. *Recreation:* gardening. *Address:* Dormers, Abinger Hammer, Surrey. *T:* Dorking 730172.

**WEBB, Douglas Edward,** CVO 1961; OBE 1947; Deputy Commissioner of Police of the Metropolis, 1961-66; retired; *b* 8 Oct. 1909; *yr s* of late Supt O. C. Webb, KPM, Metropolitan Police; *m* 1935, Mary McMillan, *yr d* of late Capt. J. S. Learmont, Trinity House; one *s* one *d*. *Educ:* Bordon Grammar School; Devonport High School. Joined Metropolitan Police, 1929; Metropolitan Police Coll., Hendon, 1935-36. Allied Commission, Italy and Austria, 1945-47. Chief Supt, Bow Street, 1952-53, West End Central, 1953-54; Dep. Commander, New Scotland Yard, 1954-55; Commander, No. 3 District (E London), 1955-57; Asst Commissioner (Traffic), 1957-58; Assistant Commissioner, Administration and Operations, New Scotland Yard, Dec. 1958-61.

Officer, Legion of Honour, 1961; Order of Merit, Chile, 1965. *Address:* Windermere, Hurst Green, Etchingham, Sussex. *T:* Hurst Green 363.

**WEBB, James;** Commissioner of Inland Revenue since 1967; *b* 11 Nov. 1918; 2nd *s* of late James Webb and late Lucy Webb (*née* McGorrin); *m* 1957, Kathleen Veronica, 3rd *d* of Catherine Downey (*née* McDaid) and of late James Downey, Londonderry. *Educ:* St Francis Xavier's, Liverpool; King's Coll., London Univ. (LLB 1940). Entered Inland Revenue Dept (Estate Duty Office), 1937. Served War of 1939-45: W Africa, India and Burma; HM Forces, South Lancashire Regt, 1940; Sandhurst, 1942; Nigeria Regt, 1942-45 (Temp. Major, 1945). Assistant Principal Inland Revenue, 1947. *Address:* 3 Avondale Avenue, Hinchley Wood, Esher, Surrey. *T:* 01-398 6330.

**WEBB, Prof. John Stuart;** Professor of Applied Geochemistry in the University of London, at Imperial College of Science and Technology, since 1961; *b* 28 Aug. 1920; *s* of Stuart George Webb and Caroline Rabjohns Webb (*née* Pengelly); *m* 1946, Jean Millicent Dyer; one *s*. *Educ:* Westminster City School; Royal School of Mines, Imperial College of Science and Technology, BSc, ARSM, 1941. Served War of 1939-45, Royal Engineers, 1941-43. Geological Survey of Nigeria, 1943-44; Royal School of Mines, Imperial Coll., 1945-; Beit Scientific Research Fellow, 1945-47; PhD, DIC, in Mining Geology, 1947; Lecturer in Mining Geology, 1947-55; Reader in Applied Geochemistry, 1955-61. DSc, 1967. Mem. Council, Instn of Mining and Metallurgy, 1964-. Consolidated Goldfields of SA Gold Medal, Instn of Mining and Metallurgy, 1953. *Publications:* (with H. E. Hawkes) Geochemistry in Mineral Exploration, 1962; contrib. to scientific and technical jls. *Recreations:* fishing, amateur radio. *Address:* Stone Cottage, Theale, Slinfold, Horsham, Sussex. *T:* Slinfold 243.

**WEBB, Prof. Joseph Ernest,** PhD (London) 1944, DSc (London) 1949; FIBiol; Professor of Zoology, Westfield College, University of London, since 1960; *b* 22 March 1915; *s* of Joseph Webb and Constance Inman Webb (*née* Hickox); *m* 1940, Gwenlilian Clara Coldwell; three *s*. *Educ:* Rutlish School; Birkbeck College, London. Research Entomologist and Parasitologist at The Cooper Technical Bureau, Berkhampsted, Herts, 1940-46; Lecturer, Univ. of Aberdeen, 1946-48; Senior Lecturer, 1948-50, Professor of Zoology, 1950-60, University Coll., Ibadan, Nigeria. FIBiol. *Publications:* various on insect physiology, insecticides, systematics, populations, tropical ecology and marine biology. *Recreations:* art, music, photography. *Address:* 43 Hill Top, NW11. *T:* 01-458 2571. *Club:* Athenæum.

**WEBB, Maysie (Florence),** BSc, ALA; Assistant Director, British Museum, since 1968; *b* 1 May 1923; *d* of Charles and Florence Webb. *Educ:* Kingsbury County School; Northern Polytechnic. Southwark Public Libraries, 1940-45; A. C. Cossor Ltd, 1945-50; British Non-Ferrous Metals Research Assoc., 1950-52; Mullard Equipment Ltd, 1952-55; Morgan Crucible Co. Ltd, 1955-60; Patent Office Library, 1960-66; Keeper, National Reference Library of Science and Invention, 1966-68. *Publications:* articles on scientific libraries. *Recreations:* family and friends. *Address:* British Museum, Bloomsbury, WC1.

**WEBB, Pauline Mary,** AKC; Vice-Chairman, Central Committee of World Council of Churches, since 1968; Director of Lay Training, Methodist Church, since 1967; author; *b* 28 June 1927; *d* of Rev. Leonard F. Webb. *Educ:* King's Coll., London Univ. (BA, AKC); Union Theological Seminary, New York (STM). BA English Hons (King's), 1948; Teacher's Diploma, London Inst. of Educn, 1949. Asst Mistress, Thames Valley Grammar Sch., 1949-52; Educn Sec., Methodist Missionary Soc., 1955-66; Vice-Pres., Methodist Conf., 1965-66; Dir, Lay Training, Methodist Church, 1967-. *Publications:* Women of Our Company, 1958; Women of Our Time, 1960; Operation Healing, 1964; All God's Children, 1964; Are We Yet Alive?, 1966; Agenda for the Churches, 1968. *Address:* 2 Chester House, Page's Lane, N10. *T:* 01-883 4124.

**WEBB, Dr Robert Alexander,** AB (Southwestern, Tenn); MD (Johns Hopkins); MRCS; LRCP; PhD (Cambridge); Demonstrator in Bacteriology, Oxford University; Hon. Consultant Pathologist, Royal Free Hospital; Professor Emeritus University of London since 1956; *b* Charleston, SC, USA, 26 July 1891; *s* of Robert A. Webb, Prof. of Theology, Presbyterian Theological Seminary of Kentucky, and Roberta C. Beck; *m* 1918, May Barrow, Edgbaston; one *s* two *d*. Demonstrator in Pathology, University of Manchester, 1921-22; University Demonstrator in Pathology and MRC Research Grant, Cambridge University, 1922-20; Lecturer in Pathology, Cambridge University, 1929-33; Capt. US Medical Corps (attached RAMC, England and BEF), 1917-18. *Publications:* various papers in scientific journals. *Recreations:* golf, tennis, squash. *Address:* Dunn School of Pathology, Oxford University. *T:* Oxford 57321; Wyck Rissington, Glos. *T:* Bourton-on-The-Water 262.

**WEBB, Lt-Col Wilfred Francis,** CIE 1944; late Indian Political Service; *b* 20 Feb. 1897. Dewan, Bundi State, 1932; Political Agent, Orissa States, Sambalpur, 1937; Chhaltesgarh, Raipur, 1938; Punjab Hill States, 1939; Dewan Cutch, Western India, 1939-41; Political Agent, Malwa and Bhopal States, Central India, 1941-45; Resident in Kashmir, 1945-47. *Address:* c/o Lloyds Bank Ltd (Cox's and King's Branch), 6 Pall Mall, SW1; Odstock Farm, PO Box 304, Umtali, Rhodesia.

**WEBB, Hon. Sir William Flood,** KBE, 1954; Kt 1942; LLD (Hon.) Queensland; Justice of the High Court of Australia, 1946-58, retired; Chairman of Electric Power Transmission Pty Ltd; *b* 1887; *m* Beatrice, *y d* of George Agnew, formerly MP, Queensland; two *s* four *d*. *Educ:* Catholic Schs; Qld Univ. Admitted to Bar 1913; Crown Solicitor of Queensland, 1917-22; Solicitor-General of Queensland, 1922-25; visited England on Privy Council Appeals in 1919 and 1924; Judge of Supreme Court, 1925-46; Chief Justice of Queensland, 1940-46; Pres.: Board of Trade and Arbitration, 1925-30; Industrial Court, 1930-46; Chairman, Central Sugar Cane Prices Board, 1926-42; Chairman, Royal Commission on Transport, 1936, and Sugar Industry, 1939; Chairman, Australian Industrial Relations Council, 1942; Japanese Atrocities Commissioner, 1943; Chm. War Crimes Commn, 1944-46, visited England as such in 1944-45 to appear before United Nations War Crimes Commission presided over by Lord Wright; Communication Censorship Commissioner, 1944 (under National Security Regulations); Member Senate of the University of Queensland, 1944-46; President of the International Military Tribunal for the Far East for the trial of major Japanese War

Criminals (incl. 4 former Prime Ministers of Japan: Tojo, Hirota, Hiranuma and Koiso). 1946-48; Chm. of Cttees to advise on Ministerial and Parliamentary allowances in Tasmania (1960) and Queensland (1961, 1963). *Address:* 223 Cavendish Road, Coorparoo, Brisbane, Qld, Australia. *Clubs:* Queensland, Johnsonian, Tattersall's (Brisbane); University of Qld.

**WEBBER, Fernley Douglas,** CMG 1959; MC 1942; TD 1954; Foreign and Commonwealth Office, since 1969; *b* 12 March 1918; *s* of Herbert Webber; *m* 1947, Veronica Elizabeth Ann, *d* of Major F. B. Hitchcock, MC; two *s* two *d. Educ:* Cotham School, Bristol; Jesus College, Cambridge. Entered Colonial Office after open competition, 1939; Diplomatic Service, 1965. Served War of 1939-45, Burma, 1940-45; Comd 624 LAA Regt RA (RF) TA, 1952-54, Bt-Col, 1954. Principal, CO, 1946; Asst Sec. 1950; Establishment Officer, 1952-58; Head of E Af. Dept, 1958-63; idc 1964; Deputy High Commissioner in Eastern Malaysia during part of 1965; High Commissioner in Brunei, 1965-67; Minister, British High Commn in Canberra, 1967-68. *Address:* c/o Foreign and Commonwealth Office, SW1. *Club:* Essex.

**WEBBER, Sir William (James Percival),** Kt 1968; CBE 1962; MA; Member, National Coal Board, 1963-68; *b* 1901; *s* of James Augustus Webber, Swansea, Glam; *m* 1929, Evelyn May, *d* of Thomas Rees, Swansea; one *s. Educ:* Elementary; Swansea Grammar Sch. Entered Great Western Railway Service, 1917, Clerk until 1944; Divl Sec. Railways Clerks' Assoc. (now Transport Salaried Staffs' Assoc.), 1944, Asst Gen. Sec., 1949. Swansea Borough Councillor, 1932-44, Dept. Mayor, 1942-43; Chm. Nat. Jt Council for Local Authorities Clerical, Administrative, Professional and Technical Grades, 1940-44; Member, Labour Party Nat. Exec., 1949-53. Part-time Member, Nat. Coal Bd, 1958-62; served on Govt Cttees and Courts of Inquiry; Member: Royal Commission on the Press, 1961-62; Transport Advisory Council, 1965; General Secretary, Transport Salaried Staffs Association, 1953-62; Mem., General Council, Trades Union Congress, 1953-62. Visiting Fellow, Nuffield College, Oxford, 1954-62. *Address:* 4 Ashridge Close, Kenton, Middx. *T:* 01-907 2956.

**WEBBER, W(illiam) S(outhcombe) Lloyd,** DMus (London) 1938; FRCM 1963; FRCO 1933; FLCM 1963; Hon. RAM 1966; Director, London College of Music, since 1964; Professor of Theory and Compositions, Royal College of Music, since 1946; Musical Director, Central Hall, Westminster, since 1958; *b* 11 March 1914; *m* 1942, Jean Hermione Johnstone; two *s. Educ:* Mercers' School; Royal College of Music. Organist: Christ Church, Newgate Street, 1929-32; St Cyprian's, Clarence Gate, 1932-39; All Saints, Margaret Street, 1939-48. Examiner to Associated Board of Royal Schools of Music, 1946-64; Vice-Pres., Incorporated Assoc. of Organists; Past Pres. and Hon. Mem., London Assoc. of Organists; Mem. Council, Royal College of Organists, 1946- (Hon. Treas., 1953-64); Mem. Senate, London Univ., 1964-67; *Publications:* many instrumental, choral and educational works; contrib. to Musical Times, Musical Opinion. *Recreations:* chess, bridge. *Address:* 10 Harrington Court, Harrington Road, SW7. *T:* 01-589 8614.

**WEBER, (Edmund) Derek (Craig);** Editor, The Geographical Magazine, since 1967; *b* 29 April 1921; 3rd *s* of late R. J. C. and of B. M. Weber; *m* 1953, Molly Patricia, *d* of the late R. O. and Ellen Podger; one *s* four *d. Educ:* Bristol Grammar School. Journalist on newspapers in Swindon, Bristol and Bath, and on magazines in London from 1937 until 1953, except for War Service in RAF, 1940-46. Art Editor, The Geographical Magazine, 1953; Assoc. Editor, 1965. *Address:* 31 Beeleigh Road, Maldon, Essex. *T:* Maldon 3216. *Club:* Savage.

**WEBSTER, Very Rev. Alan Brunskill;** Dean of Norwich, since 1970; *b* 1918; *s* of Reverend J. Webster; *m* 1951, M. C. F. Falconer; two *s* two *d. Educ:* Shrewsbury School; Queen's College, Oxford. Ordained, 1942; Curate of Attercliffe Parishes, Sheffield, 1942; Curate of St Paul's, Arbourthorne, Sheffield, 1944; Chaplain of Westcott House, 1946; Vicar of Barnard Castle, 1953. *Publications:* Joshua Watson, 1954; Broken Bones May Joy, 1968. Contributor to The Historic Episcopate, 1954. *Recreations:* family life, travel, writing. *Address:* The Deanery, Norwich NOR 16P. *T:* Norwich 23846.

**WEBSTER, Dr Cyril Charles,** CMG 1966; Scientific Adviser, Agricultural Research Council, since 1965; *b* 28 Dec. 1909; *s* of Ernest Webster; *m* 1947, Mary, *d* of H. R. Wimhurst; one *s* one *d. Educ:* Beckenham County Sch.; Wye Coll.; Selwyn Coll., Cambridge; Imperial Coll. of Tropical Agriculture, Trinidad. Colonial Agricultural Service, 1936-57: Nigeria, 1936-38; Nyasaland, 1938-50; Kenya (Chief Research Officer), 1950-55; Malaya (Dep. Dir of Agriculture), 1956-57; Prof. of Agriculture, Imperial Coll. of Tropical Agriculture, Univ. of W Indies, 1957-60; Dir, Rubber Research Inst. of Malaya, 1961-65. JMN, 1965. *Publications:* (with P. N. Wilson) Agriculture in the Tropics, 1966; scientific papers in agricultural jls. *Address:* 5 Shenden Way, Sevenoaks, Kent. *T:* Sevenoaks 53984. *Club:* East India and Sports.

**WEBSTER, Sir David (Lumsden),** KCVO 1970; Kt 1960; BA; FRCM; (Hon.) RAM; General Administrator, Royal Opera House, Covent Garden, Ltd, 1946-70; *b* 3 July 1903; *s* of Robert Lumsden and Mary Webster. *Educ:* Holt Sch.; Liverpool Univ.; Oxford Univ. Pres., Liverpool Guild of Undergraduates, 1924-25. Gen. Man. Bon Marché (Liverpool) Ltd, 1932-40; General Manager Lewis Ltd (Liverpool), 1940-41; Ministry of Supply Ordnance Factories, engaged on special methods of developing production, 1942-44; Administrator Covent Garden Preliminary Committee, 1944-46; Chairman Liverpool Philharmonic Society Ltd, June 1940-Aug. 1945. Chairman Orchestral Employers' Assoc., 1948-65; Governor and Treasurer Royal Ballet, 1957-; Governor and General Administrator of the London Opera Centre, 1962-. Director: Southern Television Ltd, 1957-; Commonwealth Arts Festival Ltd, 1961-; Chairman, London Concerts Board, 1965-. Rockefeller Foundation Lecture, Bristol University, 1955-56; Shute Lecturer, Liverpool University, 1958. Officier de la Légion d'Honneur, France, 1960; Commander: Order of the North Star, Sweden, 1954; Military Order of Christ, Portugal, 1955; Order of Merit, Italy, 1965. *Recreations:* theatre-going, talking, travelling, eating and drinking. *Address:* 39 Weymouth Street, W1. *T:* 01-935 1636.

**WEBSTER, Rev. Canon Douglas,** MA; Canon Residentiary and Precentor of St Paul's Cathedral since 1969; *b* 15 April 1920; *s* of Robert and Annie Webster; unmarried. *Educ:* Dulwich Coll.; St Peter's Coll., Oxford; Wycliffe Hall, Oxford. BA 1942, MA 1946. Curate: St Helens Parish Church, Lancs, 1943-46; Christ Church, Crouch End, London, 1946-47; Lectr, London Coll. of Divinity,

1947-52; Educn Sec., CMS, 1953-61; Theologian-Missioner, CMS, 1961-65; Chavasse Lectr in World Mission, Wycliffe Hall, Oxford, 1963-65; Prof. of Mission, Selly Oak Colls, Birmingham, 1966-69. Hon. Canon of Chelmsford, 1963-69; Exam. Chap. to Bp of Chelmsford, 1962-. Mem. Court, Worshipful Co. of Cutlers. Hon. DD Wycliffe Coll., Toronto, 1967. *Publications:* In Debt to Christ, 1957; What is Evangelism?, 1959; Pentecostalism and Speaking with Tongues, 1964; Local Church and World Mission, 1962; Unchanging Mission, 1965; Yes to Mission, 1966; Not Ashamed, 1970. *Recreations:* walking, music. *Address:* 3 Amen Court, EC4. *T:* 01-248 1817. *Club:* Royal Commonwealth Society.

**WEBSTER, Herman Armour,** RE 1914; (ARE 1907); painter-etcher; *b* New York City, 6 April 1878; *s* of George Huntingdon Webster and Ellen F. Pickford; *m* 1st, 1909, Doriane Delors (*d* 1950), Paris; one *s*; 2nd, 1951, Charlotte Huard. *Educ:* St Paul's School, Concord; PhB Yale Univ., 1900. Editorial Staff of the Chicago Record-Herald, 1902; began study of art in the Académie Julian under Jean-Paul Laurens, 1904; Mem. Corresp. de la Société des Peintres-Graveurs Français, 1909; Mem. Titulaire, 1953; Associé de la Société Nationale des Beaux-Arts, 1912; Sociétaire, 1933; Mem. Soc. of American Graphic Artists; Gold Medal, San Francisco International Exposition, 1915; Noyes Prize, Brooklyn, USA, 1930; Grand Prix (gravure), Paris Exposition, 1937; Co-founder Société des Amis des Vieux Moulins (France); entered French Army, 1914; American Field Service, 1915; transferred to American Expeditionary Force, 1st Lieut, SC, 1917; Captain, 1918; Major, 1919; Croix de Guerre, Verdun, 1916; Médaille de la France Libérée; Officier de la Légion d'Honneur. *Address:* 38 rue Boileau, Paris 16e. *T:* Auteuil 73-43.

**WEBSTER, Prof. Hugh Colin,** CMG 1959; Emeritus Professor of Physics, University of Queensland, since 1970, and Counsellor (Scientific), Australian Embassy, Washington, since 1970; *b* 24 Oct. 1905; *s* of Edwin Herbert Webster and Edith Maud Webster (*née* Hudspeth); unmarried. *Educ:* Hutchins School, Hobart, Universities of Tasmania, Melbourne, and Cambridge. Exhibn of 1851 Sci. Research Scholar, 1928-31; PhD (Cantab), 1932; Research Physicist Radio Research Bd (Australia), 1933-37; Lectr in Biophysics, Univ. of Qld, 1937-45; DSc (Tas) 1941; seconded to CSIR (Australia), 1940-45; Austr. Sci. Research Liaison Officer, London, 1941-43; Lectr (later Associate Prof.) in Radiation Physics, Univ. of Qld, 1945-49; Prof. of Physics, Univ. of Qld, 1949-70. Chm. Radio Research Board, 1963-70. *Publications:* Medical Physics (with D. F. Robertson), 1948; Medical and Biological Physics (with D. F. Robertson), 1961. Several papers in scientific jls. *Recreations:* gardening, bushwalking. *Address:* Apt S825, 3003 Van Ness Street NW, Washington, DC 20008, USA. *T:* Washington 212 362-8046. *Club:* Queensland (Brisbane).

**WEBSTER, Prof. James Mathewson,** CBE 1951; MD, FRCSEd; lately Director, West Midland Forensic Science Laboratory, Birmingham. Home Office; Professor of Forensic Medicine and Toxicology, Birmingham University. *Educ:* St Andrews University. MA, BSc; MB, ChB St Andrews, 1923; FRCSEd 1926; MD Birmingham, 1943. Hon. LLD St Andrews, 1960. *Address:* c/o University, Birmingham; Clovelly, Beacon Hill, Rubery, Worcestershire. *T:* Rubery 110.

**WEBSTER, John Henry Douglas,** MD, ChB, FRCPEd, FFR; Emeritus Consultant, Middlesex Hospital; formerly University Lecturer (late Examiner) in Radiology; *b* Edinburgh, 22 June 1882; *e s* of late Arthur Douglas Webster, OBE, MD, FRCPEd, Edinburgh; *m* Siri Björnström-Steffanson, of Ruda, Sweden; two *d*. *Educ:* Royal High School; University, Edinburgh; Prague. Late Hon. Director Meyerstein Institute of Radiotherapy, Middlesex Hosptial; Captain RAMC; served as Radiologist, British Salonika Army; FRSM (late Pres. Section of Radiology); Mem. Royal Medico-Psychol. Assoc., Mem. Committee of Foundation; for Study of Cycles, Pittsburg; New York; Mem. Soc. for Biol. Ryth. Research, Stockholm; Mem. Brit. Astron. Assoc.; Mem. Cttee, Norman Lockyer Observatory, Sidmouth (Univ. of Exeter); Member: Soc. of Authors; Horatian Soc.; Osler Club. Engaged in research on periodicity in nature, life, mind and diseases. *Publications:* The Periodicity of the Psychoses, 1968; Periodic Inspiration in Poetry and Music (Poetry Rev. 1943); Golden Mean Form in Music (Music and Letters, 1950); The Periodicity of the Sevens in Mind, Man and Nature (Brit. Jour. Med. Psychol., 1951). Poems (pen-name Colin Tolly); Horizons, 1918; Knowledge and Dream, 1926; Janus-Man, 1935. *Address:* 23 Hertford Street, W1. *T:* 01-499 7362. *Clubs:* Athenæum; University (New York).

**WEBSTER, John Lawrence Harvey,** CMG 1963; *b* 10 March 1913; *s* of late Sydney Webster, Hindhead, and of Elsie Gwendoline Webster (*née* Harvey); *m* 1st, 1940, Elizabeth Marshall Gilbertson (marr. diss., 1959); two *d*; 2nd, 1960, Jessie Lillian Simpkin. *Educ:* Rugby; Balliol College, Oxford (MA). District Officer, Colonial Administrative Service, Kenya, 1935-49; Secretary for Development, 1949-54; Administrative Sec., 1954-56; Sec. to Cabinet, 1956-58; Permanent Sec., Kenya, 1958-63; on retirement from HMOCS, with the British Council in Thailand, London, Ceylon and Hong Kong. *Recreations:* badminton, swimming, photography. *Address:* c/o British Council, 65 Davies Street, W1. *Clubs:* Royal Commonwealth Society; Leander; Nairobi (Kenya), Hong Kong (Hong Kong).

**WEBSTER, Margaret;** Theatrical Producer, Director and Actress; *b* New York City, 15 March 1905; *d* of late Ben Webster and late Dame May Whitty (Dame May Webster), DBE. *Educ:* Burlington School, London; Queen Anne's School, Caversham; London Univ. Comes of old theatre family; first professional engagements with Sybil Thorndike in Trojan Women, 1924, and with John Barrymore in Hamlet, 1925; subsequently with Dame Sybil in many productions; with the Macdona Players, 1926; J. B. Fagan's Oxford Company, 1927; Ben Greet Players, 1928; Old Vic. Co., 1929-30; played in many London productions, notably with John Gielgud in Musical Chairs, Richard of Bordeaux and Queen of Scots, 1931-34; several productions in London at the Gate, Embassy, Q, St James's and other theatres; came to America, 1936, to produce Richard II with Maurice Evans, and remained to do a notably successful series of Shakespearian revivals with Evans and others, including Hamlet, Henry IV, Twelfth Night, Macbeth, Othello (with Paul Robeson), The Tempest, etc; Managing Director of Am. Rep. Theatre, which did six classic revivals in repertory, NY, 1946-47; directed and played in many other productions in NY; initiated Margaret Webster Shakespeare Company, 1948, playing Shakespearean repertoire through schools and colleges of US; staged Verdi's Don Carlos,

Metropolitan Opera House, NY, 1950; produced Richard II and Taming of the Shrew, City centre, 1951; played in High Ground, NY, 1951; staged Saint Joan, Cort Theatre, NY, 1951; Aida, Metropolitan Opera House, 1951; An Evening with Will Shakespeare, 1952; The Strong Are Lonely, 1953, London, 1955-56; Troilus and Cressida (opera by William Walton), New York City Opera Co., 1955; The Merchant of Venice, Stratford-on-Avon, 1956; Measure for Measure, Old Vic, 1957; Back to Methuselah, NY, 1958; Simone Boccanegra, Metropolitan Opera House, 1960; Prod. The School for Scandal, Birm. Rep., 1960; Prod. Waiting in the Wings, Duke of York's, 1960. Made two visits to S Africa, 1961, 1962, representing the US Dept of State, producing and lecturing. Prod The Aspern Papers, NY, 1962; 12 Angry Men, London, 1964; wrote and performed one-woman show, The Brontës, London, NY and US Tour, 1963-64. Hon. LittD Lawrence College, 1942, Russell Sage Coll., 1944, and Rutgers Univ., 1947; DHL: Smith College, 1945, Fairfield University, 1964; was member of original Coun. of Brit. Actors' Equity; Coun. mem. of American Actors' Equity Ass., and Board member of American National Theatre and Acad.; elected one of ten outstanding Women of the Year for 1946 by Women's Nat. Press Club of America. *Publications:* Shakespeare Without Tears, 1942 (revised and re-issued, 1955); Shakespeare Today, 1957; The Same Only Different, 1969; many articles and essays in New York Times, Good Housekeeping, Theatre Arts Monthly, etc. *Recreations:* gardening, swimming. *Address:* c/o Spotlight, 43 Cranbourne Street, WC2.

**WEBSTER, Michael George Thomas;** Chairman, Watney Mann Ltd, since 1970 (Vice-Chairman, 1965-70); *b* 27 May 1920; *s* of late J. A. Webster, CB, DSO, and late Constance A. Webster, 2nd *d* of late Richard and Lady Constance Combe; *m* 1947, Mrs Isabel Margaret Bucknill, *d* of late Major J. L. Dent, DSO, MC; three *d*. *Educ:* Stowe; Magdalen Coll., Oxford (MA). Commnd Grenadier Guards, 1940-46: NW Europe Campaign, 1944-45 (despatches); DAAG Guards Div., 1946. Joined Watney Combe Reid & Co. Ltd, 1946; Chm., Watney Combe Reid, 1963-68; Master of Brewers' Co., 1964-65. Vice-Chm., Aldenham School Governing Body, 1968-. *Recreations:* fishing, shooting, golf. *Address:* The Vale, Windsor Forest, Berks; 1 Watney House, Palace Street, SW1. *Clubs:* Guards, MCC.

**WEBSTER, Peter (Edlin),** QC 1967; *b* 16 Feb. 1924; *s* of Herbert Edlin Webster and Florence Helen Webster; *m* 1955, Susan Elizabeth Richards (marr. diss.); one *s* two *d*; *m* 1968, Avril Carolyn Simpson, *d* of Dr John Ernest McCrae Harrisson. *Educ:* Haileybury; Merton Coll., Oxford (MA). RNVR, 1943-46 and 1950, Lieut (A). Imperial Tobacco Co., 1949; Lectr in Law, Lincoln Coll., Oxford, 1950-52; called to Bar, Middle Temple, 1952; Standing Jun. Counsel to Min. of Labour, 1964-67. Member of Bar Council, 1968-70. *Address:* 2 Crown Office Row, EC4. *Club:* Annabel's.

**WEBSTER, Sir Robert (Joseph),** Kt 1963; CMG 1959; CBE 1956; MC; Hon. DSc University NSW; Fellow, International Academy of Management; JP; FASA; Chairman of Directors: Bradmill Industries Ltd; F. & T. Industries Ltd; *b* 10 June 1891; *s* of Alexander J. Webster; *m* 1st, 1921, May (*d* 1949), *d* of Charles Twigg; one *s* three *d* (and one *s* decd); 2nd, 1954, Daphne, *d* of Edward Kingcott. *Educ:* Charters Towers School, Qld. In Commonwealth Public Service, 1906-19. Mem. Manufacturing Industries Advisory Council to Minister of Trade; Dep. Chanc. and Mem. Coun., Univ. of NSW; JP Qld and NSW Gen. Manager, Qld Cotton Board, 1926-36, and Commonwealth Controller of Cotton, 1942-46; President: The Sydney Div. Australian Institute of Management, 1947-50, 1958-62 (Federal Pres., 1962-64); NSW Chamber of Manufactures and Assoc. Chamber of Manufactures of Aust., 1950-51; Textile Council of Australia; Member: Aust. Nat. Airlines Commn, 1952-55; Australia-Japan Business Co-operation Cttee. Served European War, 1914-19, with AIF and on Staff (first Australian to be apptd to Staff at GHQ, France) in Egypt, Gallipoli and France (despatches, MC). *Recreation:* golf. *Address:* 2 Buena Vista Avenue, Clifton Gardens, Sydney, New South Wales, Australia. *T:* (home) 969 6714 (business 51 0477). *Clubs:* Union, Imperial Service; American National, Royal Yacht Squadron (Sydney); Commonwealth (Canberra); Athenæum (Melbourne); Australian Golf.

**WEBSTER, Thomas Bertram Lonsdale,** FBA 1965; Professor of Classics, Stanford University, 1968-70, Emeritus since 1970; *b* July 1905; *s* of Sir T. Lonsdale Webster, KCB, and Esther Dalton; *m* 1944, Amy Marjorie Dale, FBA (*d* 1967). *Educ:* Charterhouse; Christ Church, Oxford; Leipzig University. Ireland Scholar, 1924; Student and tutor of Christ Church, Oxford, 1927-31; Derby Schol., 1928, Cromer Prize, 1929; Hulme Professor of Greek at Manchester University, 1931-48; Professor of Greek, University College, London, 1948-68, Prof. Emeritus, 1968, Hon. Fellow, 1969. Prof. of Ancient Literature, Royal Acad. of Arts and Hon. RA, 1955. FSA 1934. President: Hellenic Soc., 1950; Classical Assoc., 1959 (Vice-Pres., 1948); Jt Assoc., Classical Teachers, 1965. Chm., Gilbert Murray Trust, 1959. Corresp. Mem., German Archæological Inst., 1935, Ord. Mem., 1954; Member: Vetenskapsoc. i Lund, 1949; Norwegian Acad. Science and Letters, 1958; Royal Soc. Arts and Sciences, Gothenburg, 1958; For. Mem., Royal Danish Acad. Sciences and Letters; Corresp. Mem., Austrian Acad. Sciences, 1967. Hon. DLitt: Dublin, 1958; Manchester, 1965. *Publications:* Cicero: pro Flacco, 1931; Forum Romanum (with A. S. Owen), 1930; An Anthology of Greek Prose (with E. S. Forster), 1933; Renan: Prière sur l'Acropole, 1934 (with E. Vinaver); Der Niobidenmaler, 1935; An Anthology of Greek Verse (with E. S. Forster), 1935; An Introduction to Sophocles, 1936, 2nd edn, 1969; Greek Art and Literature, 530-400 BC, 1939; Greek Interpretations, 1942; Political Interpretations in Greek Literature, 1947; Studies in Menander, 1950; Greek Terracottas, 1951; Studies in Later Greek Comedy, 1952, 2nd edn, 1970; Art and Literature in Fourth Century Athens, 1955; Greek Theatre Production, 1956, 2nd edn 1970; From Mycenae to Homer, 1958; Greek Art and Literature, 700-530 BC, 1959; Monuments illustrating Old and Middle Comedy, 1960; Monuments illustrating New Comedy, 1961; Monuments illustrating Tragedy and Satyr Play, 1962; 2nd edn of A. W. Pickard-Cambridge, Dithyramb, Tragedy and Comedy, 1962; Griechische Bühnenaltertümer, 1963; Hellenistic Poetry and Art, 1964; Hellenistic Art, 1967; Tragedies of Euripides, 1967; Everyday Life in Classical Athens, 1968; Sophocles, Philoctetes, 1970; The Greek Chorus, 1970. Articles in classical journals, etc. *Recreation:* walking. *Address:* Dept of Classics, Stanford University, Stanford, California 94305, USA. *Club:* Athenæum.

**WEBSTER, Gen. Sir Thomas Sheridan Riddell-,** GCB, *cr* 1946 (KCB, *cr* 1942; CB 1939); DSO 1915; Vice-Lieutenant of the County of Angus, 1959-67; *b* 12 February 1886; *s* of late John Riddell-Webster and Mrs Riddell-Webster of Priorsgate, St Andrews; *m* 1920, Harriet Hill, *d* of Colonel Sir Alexander Sprot, 1st Baronet; two *s*. *Educ:* Harrow; RMC, Sandhurst. Entered Army; 1905; Capt. 1913; Major and Brevet Lt-Col 1923; Lt-Col 1930; Colonel, 1933; Major-Gen. 1938; Lt-Gen. 1941; Gen. 1942; served European War, 1914-18 (despatches, DSO, Bt Major); commanded 2nd Bn The Cameronians (Scottish Rifles), 1930-33; AQMG, War Office, 1933-34; Commander Poona (Independent) Brigade Area, 1935-38; ADC to the King, 1936-38; Director of Movements and Quartering, War Office, 1938-39; Deputy Quarter-Master General, 1939-40; General Officer Commanding-in-Chief, Southern India, 1941; Lt-Gen. i/c Administration, Middle East, 1941-42 (despatches); QMG to the Forces, War Office, 1942-46; retd pay, 1946. Col, The Cameronians, 1946-51; DL Angus, 1946-. President British Legion (Scotland), 1949-65. *Address:* Lintrose, Coupar-Angus, Perthshire. *Club:* Army and Navy.

**WEDDERBURN;** *see* Scrymgeour-Wedderburn.

**WEDDERBURN, Sir (John) Peter;** *see* Ogilvy-Wedderburn.

**WEDDERBURN, Prof. Kenneth William;** Sir Ernest Cassel Professor of Commercial Law, London School of Economics, University of London, since Oct. 1964; *b* 13 April 1927; *o s* of Herbert J. and Mabel Wedderburn, Deptford; *m* 1st, 1951, Nina Salaman; one *s* two *d*; 2nd 1962, Dorothy E. Cole; 3rd, 1969, Frances Ann Knight. *Educ:* Aske's Hatcham School; Whitgift School; Queens' College, Cambridge. BA 1948; LLB 1949 (Chancellor's Medallist); MA 1951. Royal Air Force, 1949-51. Called to the Bar, Middle Temple, 1953. Fellow, 1952-64, Tutor, 1957-60, Clare College, Cambridge; Asst Lectr, 1953-55, Lectr 1955-64, Faculty of Law, Cambridge University. Vis. Prof., Harvard Law Sch., 1969-70. Staff Panel Mem., Civil Service Arbitration Tribunal; Dep. Independent Chm., London and Provincial Theatre Councils. *Publications:* The Worker and the Law, 1965; Cases and Materials on Labour Law, 1967; (with P. Davies) Employment Grievances and Disputes Procedures in Britain, 1969; (ed) Contracts Sutton and Shannon, 1956, 1963; Asst Editor: Torts, Clerk and Lindsell, 1969; Modern Company Law, Gower, 1969; articles in legal and other jls. *Recreations:* pop and disarmament studies. *Address:* London School of Economics, Aldwych, WC2. *T:* 01-405 7686.

**WEDDERSPOON, Sir Thomas (Adam),** Kt, *cr* 1955; JP; *b* 4 August 1904; *s* of late Thomas and Margaret Wedderspoon; *m* 1936, Helen Catherine Margaret MacKenzie; one *s* two *d*. *Educ:* Seafield House, Broughty Ferry, Angus; Trinity College, Glenalmond, Perthshire; Trinity Hall, Cambridge. *Recreation:* shooting. *Address:* Castleton of Eassie, Forfar, Angus, Scotland. *T:* Eassie 200. *Club:* Farmers'.

**WEDELL, Prof. Eberhard (Arthur Otto) George,** Professor of Adult Education and Director of Extra-Mural Studies, Manchester University, since 1964; *b* 4 April 1927; *er s* of Rev. Dr H. Wedell and Gertrude (*née* Bonhoeffer); *m* 1948, Rosemarie Winckler; three *s* one *d*. *Educ:* Cranbrook; London School of Economics (BSc Econ., 1947). Ministry of Education, 1950-58; Sec., Bd for Social Responsibility, Nat. Assembly of Church of England, 1958-60; Dep. Secretary, Independent Television Authority, 1960-61, Secretary, 1961-64; Educational Adviser, ABC Television, 1964-68; Consultant: ODM, 1968; GPO, 1969; UNESCO, 1970; Vice-President, William Temple Association, 1965-; Dep. Chm. of Governors, Manchester Film Theatre, 1967-; Governor, Centre for Educnl Develt Overseas, 1970-; Director, 69 Theatre Company, 1968-. Hon. MEd Manchester, 1968. *Publications:* (ed) Together in Britain: a Christian Handbook on Race Relations, 1960; The Use of Television in Education, 1963; The Reform of Church Government, 1965; Broadcasting and Public Policy, 1968; (with H. D. Perraton) Teaching at a Distance, 1968; (ed) Structures of Broadcasting, 1970; (with R. Glatter) Study by Correspondence, 1971; Correspondence Education in Europe, 1971. *Recreations:* gardening, theatre, reading. *Address:* 18 Cranmer Road, Didsbury, Manchester M20 0AW. *T:* 061-445 5106. *Clubs:* Reform; Ski.

**WEDGWOOD,** family name of **Baron Wedgwood.**

**WEDGWOOD,** 4th Baron *cr* 1942, of Barlaston; **Piers Anthony Weymouth Wedgwood;** *b* 20 Sept. 1954; *s* of 3rd Baron Wedgwood and of Lady Wedgwood (Jane Weymouth, *d* of W. J. Poulton, Kenjockety, Molo, Kenya); *S* father, 1970. *Educ:* Marlborough College. *Heir: cousin* John Wedgwood, MD, FRCP [*b* 28 Sept. 1919; *m* 1943, Margaret, *d* of A. S. Mason; three *s* two *d*]. *Address:* Drywick, Shear Hill, Petersfield, Hants.

**WEDGWOOD, Dame (Cicely) Veronica,** OM 1969; DBE 1968 (CBE 1956); FRHistS; Hon. LLD Glasgow; Hon. LittD Sheffield; Hon. DLitt: Smith College; Harvard; Oxford; Keele; Historian; Member, Royal Commission on Historical MSS since 1953; Trustee, National Gallery, 1962-68 and since 1969; *b* 20 July 1910; *d* of Sir Ralph Wedgwood, 1st Bt, CB, CMG. *Educ:* privately; Lady Margaret Hall, Oxford. 1st Class Mod. Hist. 1931. Pres., English Assoc., 1955-56; Pres., English Centre of Internat. PEN Club, 1951-57; Member: Arts Council, 1958-61; Arts Council Literature Panel, 1965-67; Institute for Advanced Study, Princeton, 1953-68; Adv. Council, V & A Museum, 1960-69; Hon. Member, American Academy of Arts and Letters, 1966. Special Lecturer, UC Lond., 1962-. Hon. Fellow: Lady Margaret Hall, Oxford, 1962; UC London, 1965. Officer, Order of Orange-Nassau, 1946; Goethe Medal, 1958. *Publications:* Strafford, 1935 (revd edn, as Thomas Wentworth, 1961); The Thirty Years' War, 1938; Oliver Cromwell 1939; Charles V by Carl Brandi (trans.), 1939; William the Silent, 1944 (James Tait Black Prize for 1944); Auto da Fé by Elias Canetti (translation), 1946; Velvet Studies, 1946; Richelieu and the French Monarchy, 1949; Seventeenth Century Literature, 1950; The Last of the Radicals, 1951; Montrose, 1952; The King's Peace, 1955; The King's War, 1958; Truth and Opinion, 1960; Poetry and Politics, 1960; The Trial of Charles I, 1964 (in USA as A Coffin for King Charles, 1964); Milton and his World, 1969. *Recreations:* drama, and sightseeing. *Address:* c/o Messrs Collins, 14 St James's Place, SW1.

*See also Sir John Wedgwood, Bt.*

**WEDGWOOD, Geoffrey H.,** RE 1934; ARCA; Artist Engraver; *b* 16 April 1900; *s* of Frank and Jane Wedgwood. *Educ:* Liverpool Institute; Liverpool School of Art; Royal College of Art; British School at Rome. ARE 1925; ARCA (London) 1925; awarded Rome Scholarship in Engraving; Member of The Chicago Society of Etchers 1926; Exhibitor Royal Academy since 1923; Exhibited Prague, Bucharest, Vienna and Empire Exhibition,

South Africa, 1936; works in the following Permanent Collections: British Museum; Victoria and Albert Museum; Rutherston Collection, Manchester; Walker Art Gallery; Wakefield Collection; several English towns; Art Museum Boston, USA; Art Institute of Chicago, USA. *Publications:* Original Engravings. *Address:* Kingsley, 85 Rupert Road, Roby, Liverpool. *Club:* Sandon Society (Liverpool).

**WEDGWOOD, Senator Dame Ivy Evelyn,** DBE 1967; JP; Senator for Victoria, Australia (first woman elected to the Senate for Victoria), 1950-June 1971; *m* Jack Kearns Wedgwood. Member: Senate House Cttee, 1950-55, 1965-; Jt Cttee of Public Accounts, 1955-; Australian delegn to Commonwealth Parly Assoc. Conf., New Delhi, 1957; Jt Select Cttee on New and Permanent Parliament House, 1965- (Mem. Overseas Delegn, 1968-). Temporary Chm. of Cttees, 1962-; Chm., Select Cttee on Medical and Hosp. Costs, 1968-70. *Address:* Whitehall, 16 Woorigoleen Road, Toorak, Victoria 3142, Australia. *Clubs:* Lyceum, Soroptimist (Melbourne).

**WEDGWOOD, Sir John Hamilton,** 2nd Bt, *cr* 1942; TD 1948; Deputy-Chairman of Josiah Wedgwood and Sons Ltd, until 1966; Member, British National Export Council, 1964-66; *b* 16 Nov. 1907; *s* of Sir Ralph L. Wedgwood, 1st Bt, CB, CMG, TD, and of Iris, Lady Wedgwood (*née* Pawson); *S* father 1956; *m* 1933, Diana Mildred, *d* of late Col Oliver Hawkshaw, Chisenbury Priory, Marlborough; four *s* one *d*. *Educ:* Winchester College; Trinity College, Cambridge; and abroad. Served War of 1939-45, Major GSO2 (1b). FRSA 1968. Hon. LLD Birmingham, 1966. *Recreations:* mountaineering, caving, foreign travel. *Heir: s* (Hugo) Martin Wedgwood [*b* 27 Dec. 1933; *m* 1963, Alexandra Mary Gordon Clark, *er d* of late Judge Alfred Gordon Clark, and of Mrs Gordon Clark, Berry's Croft, Westhumble, Dorking; one *s* one *d*. *Educ:* Eton; Trinity College, Oxford]. *Address:* 54 Cadogan Square, SW1. *Clubs:* Alpine, Beefsteak, Savage.

*See also Dame C. V. Wedgwood.*

**WEDGWOOD, Dame Veronica;** *see* Dame C. V. Wedgwood.

**WEDGWOOD BENN, Rt. Hon. Anthony;** *see* Benn, Rt Hon. A. N. W.

**WEE CHONG JIN, Hon. Mr Justice;** Chief Justice of the Supreme Court, Singapore; *b* 28 Sept. 1917; *s* of Wee Gim Puay and Lim Paik Yew; *m* 1955, Cecilia Mary Henderson; three *s* one *d*. *Educ:* Penang Free Sch.; St John's Coll., Cambridge. Called to Bar, Middle Temple, 1938; admitted Advocate and Solicitor of Straits Settlement, 1940; practised in Penang and Singapore, 1940-57; Puisne Judge, Singapore, 1957, Chief Justice, 1963. *Recreation:* golf. *Address:* c/o Chief Justice's Chambers, Supreme Court, Singapore.

**WEEDON, Prof. Basil Charles Leicester,** DSc; PhD; ARCS; DIC; FRIC; Professor of Organic Chemistry, Queen Mary College, University of London, since 1960; *b* 18 July 1923; *s* of late Charles William Weedon; *m* 1959, Barbara Mary Dawe; one *s* one *d*. *Educ:* Wandsworth Sch.; Imperial Coll. of Science and Technology. Research Chemist, ICI Ltd (Dyestuffs Div.), 1943-47; Lecturer in Organic Chemistry, Imperial Coll., 1947-55. Reader, 1955-60. Tilden Lecturer, Chemical Society, 1966. Meldola Medal, Roy. Inst. of Chemistry, 1952. *Publications:* A Guide to Qualitative Organic Chemical Analysis (with Sir Patrick Linstead), 1956; scientific papers, mainly in Jl Chem. Soc. *Address:* 28 Barham Road, SW20. *T:* 01-946 1898.

**WEEDON, Air Marshal (retired) Sir Colin Winterbotham,** KBE, *cr* 1952 (CBE 1943); CB 1946; MA; *b* 2 July 1901; *s* of H. W. Weedon, Durban, South Africa; *m* 1926, Gladys Frances Marian (*d* 1968), *d* of Col T. P. Lawrenson; two *d*. *Educ:* Royal Naval Colleges, Osborne and Dartmouth; Royal Air Force College, Cranwell; Christ's College, Cambridge (Hons Degree Mechanical Sciences). Royal Navy (serving in HMS Royal Sovereign and HMS Walker), 1915-19; Royal Air Force, 1920; 20 Squadron India, 1923-28; 111 Fighter Squadron, Northolt, 1934-35; RAF Staff College, 1936; Director-General Repair and Maintenance, Ministry of Aircraft Production, 1940-44; HQ Air Command, SE Asia, 1944-46; AOC 41 Group, 1946-48. SASO, HQ Technical Training Command, Brampton, Huntingdon, 1948-50; Dir-Gen. of Technical Services, 1950-51; Controller of Engineering and Equipment, Air Ministry, 1951-52; retired, 1952. Director and Gen. Man. (Commercial), Aero Div., Rolls Royce, 1952-61. *Address:* The Old Post Office, Worplesdon, Surrey. *T:* Worplesdon 2618.

**WEEKES, Ven. Archdeacon Ambrose Walter Marcus,** CB 1970; AKC; Hon. Chaplain to the Queen since 1969; Chaplain of the Fleet, and Archdeacon for the Royal Navy, since 1969; *b* 25 April 1919; *s* of Lt-Comdr William Charles Tinnoth Weekes, DSO, RNVR, and Ethel Sarah Weekes, JP. *Educ:* Cathedral Choir Sch., Rochester; Sir Joseph Williamson's Sch., Rochester; King's Coll., London; Scholae Cancellarii, Lincoln. Chaplain, RNVR, 1944-46, RN 1946-; HMS: Ganges, 1946-48; Ulster, 1948-49; Triumph, 1949-51; Royal Marines, Deal, 1951-53; 3 Commando Bde, RM, 1953-55; HMS: Ganges, 1955-56; St Vincent, 1956-58; Tyne, 1958-60; Ganges, 1960-62; 40 Commando, RM, 1962-63; MoD, 1963-65; HMS: Eagle, 1965-66; Vernon, 1966-67; Terror, and Staff of Comdr Far East Fleet, 1967-68; HMS Mercury, 1968-69. *Recreations:* yachting, music. *Address:* Ministry of Defence, Old Admiralty Building, SW1. *T:* 01-930 9000 (Ext. 1486); Fig Tree House, Queenborough, Kent. *Clubs:* United Service, Royal Automobile.

**WEEKLEY, Charles Montague,** FSA; Officer-in-Charge of Bethnal Green Museum, 1946-64; *b* 15 June 1900; *o s* of late Prof. Ernest Weekley, DLitt and Frieda (afterwards Mrs D. H. Lawrence), 2nd *d* of Baron Friedrich von Richthofen; *m* 1930, Vera (artist), *er d* of late P. Murray Ross, Dornoch, Sutherlandshire; one *s* one *d*. *Educ:* St Paul's School (scholar and leaving exhibitioner); St John's College, Oxford (scholar). BA (Oxon), 1922; MA (Oxon) 1967. Assistant, Department of Circulation, V&A Museum, 1924; Dep. Keeper, 1938; General Finance Branch, Ministry of Supply, 1939-43; Southern Dept, Foreign Office, 1943-44; Ministry of Education, 1944-46; Trustee of Whitechapel Art Gallery, 1946-; a Governor of Parmiter's School, 1946-64; Hon. Mem., Art Workers Guild, 1954. *Publications:* William Morris, 1934; Thomas Bewick, 1953; General Editor of The Library of English Art; (ed) A Memoir of Thomas Bewick, 1961; contributor to Chambers's Encyclopædia, DNB, Times, Country Life, Architectural Review, etc. *Recreations:* Oxford University Athletic Team (1 mile) *v* Cambridge, 1922; Oxford University Relay Team (4 miles) *v* Cambridge, 1920. *Address:* 9 John Spencer Square, Canonbury, N1. *T:* 01-226 6839. *Clubs:* Achilles, Press.

**WEEKS, Edward A.;** Senior Editor and Consultant, Atlantic Monthly Press, since 1966; Trustee: Wellesley College; Universities, Pittsburgh, Rochester, Colonial Williamsburg; United Negro College Fund; American Field Service (Croix de Guerre, 1918); Fellow American Academy Arts and Sciences; *b* 19 Feb. 1898; *s* of Edward Augustus Weeks and Frederika Suydam; *m* 1925, Frederica Watriss; one *s* one *d*. *Educ:* Pingry and Battin High School, Elizabeth, NJ; Cornell Univ.; BS Harvard, 1922; Camb. Univ. (Fiske Schol.). Hon. LittD: Northeastern Univ., Boston, 1938; Lake Forest Coll. (Illinois), 1939; Williams Coll., Mass., 1942; Middlebury College, Vt, 1944; University of Alabama, 1945; Dartmouth Coll., 1950; Bucknell Univ., 1952; Boston Univ., 1953; Hobart Coll., 1956; Univ. of Richmond, 1957; New York Univ., 1958; further hon. degrees from: Clark Univ., Massachusetts, 1958 (Humane Letters); Pomona Coll., Calif., 1958 (LittD); Univ. of Pittsburgh, 1959 (Humane Letters); Univ. of Akron, 1961 (LittD); Northwestern Univ., 1961 (Humane Letters); Rutgers, 1962 (Dr Letters); Union College, 1962 (DCL); Washington and Jefferson, 1962 (Dr Laws). Began as manuscript reader and book salesman with Horace Liveright, Inc., New York City, 1923; Associate Editor, Atlantic Monthly, 1924-28; Editor: Atlantic Monthly Press, 1928-37; Atlantic Monthly, 1938-66. Overseer, Harvard Coll., 1945-51. Henry Johnson Fisher Award, 1968; Irita Van Doren Award, 1970. *Publications:* This Trade of Writing, 1935; The Open Heart, 1955; In Friendly Candour, 1959; Breaking into Print, 1962; Boston, Cradle of Liberty, 1965; The Lowells and their Institute, 1966; Fresh Waters, 1968. Editor, Great Short Novels (Anthology), 1941; Jubilee, One Hundred Years of the Atlantic (with Emily Flint), 1957; contrib. essays, articles, and book reviews to magazines. *Recreations:* fishing, preferably with a light rod; golf; poker. *Address:* 59 Chestnut Street, Boston, USA; 8 Arlington Street, Boston, USA. *Cable address:* Lanticmon. *Clubs:* Tavern (Boston); Myopia Hunt (Hamilton, Mass.); Century (New York).

**WEEKS, Major-Gen. Ernest Geoffrey,** CB 1946; CBE 1944; MC (and bar); MM (and bar); CD; retired; *b* Charlottetown, PEI, 30 May 1896; *s* of William Arthur and Fanny Weeks; *m* 1930, Vivian Rose Scott, Toronto, Canada; one *s*. *Educ:* Prince of Wales Coll., Charlottetown, PEI. Canadian Militia, 1910-14; European War, Belgium and France, 1915-19; Canadian Permanent Force from 1920; War of 1939-45, Italy; Maj.-Gen. i/c Administration Canadian Military, HQ, London, England, 1944-45; Adjutant-General Canadian Army, 1946-49; retired, 1949. *Recreations:* gardening, fishing. *Address:* 46 Prince Charles Drive, Charlottetown, PEI, Canada.

**WEEKS, Sir Hugh (Thomas),** Kt 1966; CMG 1946; Director: Industrial and Commercial Finance Corp. Ltd; Finance Corporation for Industry Ltd; Strip Mill Division, British Steel Corporation, and other companies; Chairman: Leopold Joseph & Sons Ltd; Economic Committee of CBI; *b* 27 April 1904; *m* 1929; one *s* one *d*; *m* 1949, Constance Tomkinson; one *d*. *Educ:* Hendon Secondary and Kilburn Grammar Schools; Emmanuel College, Cambridge (MA). Research and Statistical Manager, Cadbury Bros, till 1939; Director of Statistics, Min. of Supply, 1939-42; Director-General of Statistics and Programmes and Member of Supply Council, 1942-43; Head of Programmes and Planning Division, Ministry of Production, 1943-45. Represented Ministries of Supply and Production on various Missions to N America, 1941-45; Managing Director J. S. Fry & Sons, 1945-47; Mem. Economic Planning Bd, 1947-48, 1959-61; Joint Controller of Colonial Development Corporation, 1948-51. UK Representative, UN Cttee for Industrial Development, 1961-63. Dep. Chm., Richard Thomas & Baldwins, 1965-68. Chm., EDC for Distributive Trades, 1964-70. Medal of Freedom with Silver Palm (US). *Publications:* Market Research (with Paul Redmayne); various articles. *Address:* 8 The Grove, Highgate Village, N6. *T:* 01-340 9517; (office) 01-628 4040. *Club:* United University.

**WEEVERS, Theodoor,** LitD (Leyden); Officier in de Orde van Oranje-Nassau; Professor of Dutch Language and Literature, University of London, since 1945; *b* Amersfoort, 3 June 1904; *e s* of Prof. Theodorus Weevers and Cornelia Jeannette, *d* of J. de Graaff; *m* 1933, Sybil Doreen, 2nd *d* of Alfred Jervis; two *s*. *Educ:* Gymnasia at Amersfoort and Groningen; Universities of Groningen and Leyden; Lecturer in Dutch at University College and Bedford College, London, 1931-36; Reader in Dutch Language and Literature in University of London, 1937-45; Lecturer in Dutch at Birkbeck College (Univ. of London), 1942-45. During War of 1939-45 Language Supervisor and Announcer-Translator in European News Service of BBC (Dutch Section), 1940-44. Corr. mem. Koninklijke Nederlandse Akademie van Wetenschappen te Amsterdam; hon. mem. Koninklijke Vlaamse Academie; mem. Maatschappij der Nederlandse Letterkunde. *Publications:* Coornhert's Dolinghe van Ulysse, 1934; De Dolinge van Ulysse door Dierick Volckertsz Coornhert, 1939; The Idea of Holland in Dutch Poetry, 1948; Poetry of the Netherlands in its European Context, 1170-1930, 1960; Mythe en Vorm in de gedichten van Albert Verwey, 1965. Articles and Reviews in Modern Language Review, Mededelingen Kon. Nederlandse Akademie van Wetenschappen, Tijdschrift v. Nederl. Taal en Letterkunde, De Nieuwe Taalgids, Neophilologus, Journal of English and Germanic Philology, Publications of the English Goethe Society, English Studies. *Recreations:* music, walking. *Address:* 10 Devonshire Road, Harpenden, Herts.

**WEIDENFELD, Sir (Arthur) George,** Kt 1969; Chairman: Weidenfeld & Nicolson Ltd since 1948, and associated comapnies; *b* 13 Sept. 1919; *o s* of late Max and of Rosa Weidenfeld; *m* 1st, 1952, Jane Sieff; one *d*; 2nd, 1956, Barbara Connolly (*née* Skelton) (marriage dissolved, 1961); 3rd, 1966, Sandra Payson Meyer. *Educ:* Piaristen Gymnasium, Vienna; University of Vienna (Law); Konsular Akademie (Diplomatic College). BBC Monitoring Service, 1939-42; BBC News Commentator on European Affairs on BBC Empire & North American service, 1942-46. Lectured at Chatham House and wrote weekly foreign affairs column, News Chronicle, 1943-44; Founder: Contact Magazine and Books, 1945; Weidenfeld & Nicolson Ltd, 1948. One year's leave as Political Adviser and Chief of Cabinet of President Weizmann of Israel. *Publication:* The Goebbels Experiment, 1943 (also publ. USA). *Recreations:* travel, opera. *Address:* Cleeve Lodge, 42 Hyde Park Gate, SW7. *T:* 01-589 9491. *Club:* Reform.

**WEIDLEIN, Edward Ray,** MA, ScD, EngD, LLD; President Mellon Institute, 1921-56, retired; Technical Adviser of Rubber Reserve Company (now Synthetic Rubber Division of National Science Foundation), 1941-70; Director, Allegheny County Council West of the Boy Scouts of America; National Council of the Boy Scouts of America; Advisory Committee, Oakland Office, Mellon National Bank and Trust Co.; President, Regional Industrial Devel. Corp. Fund; registered professional engineer in Pa; *b* Augusta, Kansas, 14 July 1887; *s* of Edward Weidlein and Nettie Lemon; *m* 1915, Hazel Butts; three *s*. *Educ:* University of Kansas. Developed processes for the use of sulphur dioxide in hydrometallurgy; Chief of Chemicals Branch War Production Board, 1940-42; Senior Consultant of Chemical Division of War Production Board, Feb. 1942-Mar. 1946; Head Technical Consultant in War Production Board, Mar. 1942-Mar. 1946; Technical Adviser, R&D Div., Quartermaster Corps, US Army, 1943-46; Member: Special Cttee for examination of enemy raw materials and supplies under War Metallurgy Cttee of Nat. Research Council and Nat. Acad. of Sciences; Research Cttee in Co-operation with Chemical Warfare Service of American Chemical Society; Cttee on Co-operation with National Defense Research Cttee of Office of Sc. Research and Development; Studies, Reports, and Seminars Cttee of Army Ordn. Assoc.; Nat. Engineers Cttee of Engineers Jt Council; Exec. Cttees, Allegheny Conf. on Community Develt and Pittsburgh Regional Planning Assoc.; Board of Directors Western Pennsylvania Hosp.; Bd of Trustees, Rolling Rock Club; Trustee (emer.) Univ. of Pittsburgh and of Shadyside Academy, Pittsburgh. Member, leading chemical and scientific societies. Various awards have been obtained for distinguished service in his field; Edward R. Wedlein Professorship established, 1967, by Bd of Trustees, Univ. of Pittsburgh. Holds numerous hon. degrees in Science, Laws and Engineering. *Publications:* (joint) Science in Action; Glances at Industrial Research; many articles on industrial research. *Recreations:* golf, hunting and fishing. *Address:* Weidacres, PO Box 45, Rector, Pennsylvania 15677, USA. *Clubs:* University, Pitt Faculty, Pittsburgh Golf, Rolling Rock, Duquesne, Authors' (Pittsburgh); Chemists' (New York); Chemists' (Pittsburgh).

**WEIGHT, Prof. Carel Victor Morlais,** CBE 1961; RA 1965 (ARA 1955); RBA 1934; practising artist (painter); Fellow since 1956 and Professor of Painting School since 1957, Royal College of Art (Teacher of Painting, 1947); *b* London, 10 Sept. 1908; *s* of Sidney Louis and Blanche H. C. Weight; British. *Educ:* Sloane School; Goldsmiths' Coll., Univ. of London (Sen. County Scholarship, 1933). First exhibited at Royal Acad., 1931; first one-man show, Cooling Galls, 1934; 2nd and 3rd exhibns, Picture Hire Ltd, 1936 and 1938. Official War Artist, 1945. One-man Shows: Leicester Galls, 1946, 1952, 1968; Zwemmer Gall., 1956, 1959, 1961, 1965; Agnew's, 1959; Russell Cotes Gall., Bournemouth, 1962. Exhibited in: 60 Paintings for 1951; (by invitation) exhibns of Contemporary British Art in provinces and overseas, incl. USSR, 1957. Retrospective exhibn, Reading Museum and Art Gallery, 1970. Work purchased by: Chantry Bequest for Tate Gall., 1955, 1956, 1957, 1963, 1968; Walker Art Gall., Liverpool; Southampton, Hastings and Oldham Art Galls, etc; Art Gall., Melbourne; Nat. Gall., Adelaide; Arts Council; New Coll., Oxford; Contemporary Art Soc.; V & A Museum. Mural for: Festival of Britain, 1951; Manchester Cathedral, 1963. Vice-Pres., Greater London Arts Assoc., 1968. Member: London Group, 1950; West of England Acad.; Fine Arts Panel, Arts Council, 1951-57; Rome Faculty of Art. 1960. *Recreations:* music, reading. *Address:* 33 Spencer Road, SW18. *T:* 01-228 6928. *Club:* Arts.

**WEIGHTMAN, William Henry,** CMG 1946; Assistant Secretary, Post Office, 1938-47; *b* 24 March 1887; *s* of late H. Herbert Weightman, Architect, Liverpool; *m* 1912, Grace E. Howes; four *d*. *Educ:* Liverpool College; St John's College, Cambridge. Post Office HQ 1910. *Address:* 123 North End House, W14. *T:* 01-603 2463. *Clubs:* Hamilton, Anglo-Belgian.

*See also Air Marshal Sir H. N. G. Wheeler.*

**WEILER, Terence Gerard;** Assistant Under-Secretary of State, Home Office, since 1967; *b* 12 Oct. 1919; *s* of Charles and Clare Weiler; *m* 1952, Truda, *d* of Wilfrid and Mary Woollen; two *s* two *d*. *Educ:* Wimbledon College; University College, London. Army (RA and Queen's Royal Regiment), 1940-45; UCL, 1937-39 and 1946-47; Home Office: Asst Principal, 1947; Principal, 1948; Asst Sec., 1958; Mem., Prisons Board, 1962-66; Home Office: Probation and After-Care Dept, 1967; Community Relations Dept, 1969. Chm., Working Party on Habitual Drunken Offenders, 1967-70. *Recreation:* cinema. *Address:* 372 Jersey Road, Osterley, Middlesex. *T:* 01-560 7822.

**WEINSTOCK, Sir Arnold,** Kt 1970; BSc (Econ), FSS; Managing Director, General Electric Co. Ltd since 1963; Director, London Weekend Television Ltd; *b* 29 July 1924; *s* of Simon and Golda Weinstock; *m* 1949, Netta, *d* of Michael Sobell; one *s* one *d*. *Educ:* University of London (in wartime at Cambridge). Degree in Statistics. Junior administrative officer, Admiralty, 1944-47; engaged in finance and property development, group of private companies, 1947-54; Radio & Allied Industries Ltd (later Radio & Allied Holdings Ltd), 1954-63 (Managing Director); General Electric Co. Ltd, Director 1961. *Recreations:* racing and music. *Address:* 7 Grosvenor Square, W1.

**WEIPERS, Prof. Sir William (Lee),** Kt 1966; Director of Veterinary Education, 1949-68; Dean of the Faculty of Veterinary Medicine since 1968, University of Glasgow Veterinary School; *b* 21 Jan. 1904; *s* of Rev. John Weipers, MA, BD and Evelyn Bovelle Lee; *m* 1939, Mary MacLean; one *d*. *Educ:* Whitehill Higher Grade School, Dennistoun, Glasgow; Glasgow Veterinary College (MRCVS). General practice, 1925-27; on staff of Royal (Dick) Veterinary College, 1927-29. DVSM 1927; general practice, 1927-49. Member Council of Royal College of Veterinary Surgeons, 1949-, President, 1963-64. BSc (Glasgow), 1951; FRSE 1953; FRCVS 1958. *Publications:* in professional papers. *Recreation:* yachting. *Address:* Snab, Duntocher, Dunbartonshire. *T:* Duntocher 3216. *Clubs:* Farmers', Caledonian.

**WEIR,** family name of **Baron Inverforth** and **Viscount Weir.**

**WEIR,** 2nd Viscount *cr* 1938; **James Kenneth Weir,** CBE 1944; BA (Cantab); Chairman, The Weir Group Ltd; Director: Royal Bank of Scotland, Ltd; Dunlop Co. Ltd; International Nickel Co. of Canada Ltd; Caledonian Insurance Co.; Scottish Television Ltd; Guardian Assurance Co.; *b* 10 Sept. 1905; *s* of 1st Viscount Weir and Alice Blanche MacConnachie (*d* 1959); *S* father 1959; *m* 1929, Lucy, *o d* of late James F. Crowdy, MVO; four *s* one *d* (and one *d* decd). *Educ:* Oundle School; Trinity College, Cambridge. Hon FRCOG. Hon. LLD Strathclyde, 1967. *Recreations:* golf, fishing, shooting. *Heir:* *s* Hon. William Kenneth James Weir [*b* 9 Nov. 1933; *m* 1964, Diana Lucy, *d* of Peter MacDougall, Montreal, Canada; one *s* one *d*. *Educ:* Eton; Trinity College, Cambridge]. *Address:* Montgreenan, Kilwinning, Ayrshire. *T:* Kilwinning 2666; 28 Roebuck House, Palace Street, SW1. *T:* 01-828

2442. *Clubs:* Boodle's, Carlton; Western, Royal Scottish Automobile (Glasgow); Rideau (Ottawa).

**WEIR, Rev. Andrew John,** MSc, BD; Clerk of Assembly and General Secretary, The Presbyterian Church in Ireland, since 1964; *b* 24 March 1919; *s* of Rev. Andrew Weir and Margaret Weir, Missionaries to Manchuria of the Presbyterian Church in Ireland. *Educ:* Campbell Coll., Belfast; Queen's Univ., Belfast; New Coll., Edinburgh; Presbyterian Coll., Belfast. Ordained, 1944; Missionary to China, 1945-52; Minister, Trinity Presbyterian Church, Letterkenny, Co. Donegal, 1952-62; Asst Clerk of Assembly and Home Mission Convener, The Presbyterian Church in Ireland, 1962-64. *Address:* (official) Church House, Belfast BT1 6DW. *T:* Belfast 22284; (home) 16 Harberton Drive, Belfast BT9 6PF. *T:* Belfast 667901.

**WEIR, Rev. Cecil James Mullo,** MA, DD, DPhil; Professor of Hebrew and Semitic Languages, University of Glasgow, 1937-68; *b* Edinburgh, 4 Dec. 1897; *e s* of late James Mullo Weir, SSC, FSAScot, Solicitor, Edinburgh; unmarried. *Educ:* Royal High School, Edinburgh; Universities of Edinburgh, Marburg, Paris and Leipzig; Jesus College, Oxford. Served European War, 1917-19, with Expeditionary Force in France, Belgium and Germany; Tutor in Hebrew, University of Edinburgh, 1921-22; MA Edinburgh with 1st Class Honours in Classics, 1923; 1st Class Honours in Semitic Languages, 1925; BD Edinburgh, 1926; DPhil Oxford, 1930; Minister of Orwell, Kinross-shire, 1932-34; Rankin Lecturer and Head of Department of Hebrew and Ancient Semitic Languages, University of Liverpool, 1934-37; Lecturer in the Institute of Archæology, Liverpool, 1934-37. President, Glasgow Archæological Soc., 1945-48; Dean of Faculty of Divinity, Univ. of Glasgow, 1951-54; Hon. DD (Edinburgh), 1959; FRAS, FSAScot. *Publications:* A Lexicon of Accadian Prayers in the Rituals of Expiation, 1934; contributed to A Companion to the Bible (ed Manson), 1939; Fortuna Domus, 1952; Documents from Old Testament Times (ed Thomas), 1958; Hastings's Dictionary of the Bible, 1963; A Companion to the Bible (ed Rowley), 1963; Archæology and Old Testament Study (ed Thomas), 1967; edited Transactions of Glasgow University Oriental Soc., Studia Semitica et Orientalia, Transactions of Glasgow Archæological Soc.; articles and reviews of books. *Recreations:* golf, travel. *Address:* 3 Inchgarry Court, North Berwick. *T:* North Berwick 2812.

**WEIR, James George,** CMG 1918; CBE 1919; Chairman Cierva Rotorcraft, Ltd; *b* 1887; *s* of late James Weir, Over Courance, Dumfriesshire; *m* 1915, Mora Morton, *d* of late James Christie, Craigearn, Tayport; one *d* (one *s* decd). *Educ:* Dollar Academy; Glasgow University. Served European War, 1914-19; Major, 77th Highland Brigade, Royal Field Artillery (TF), 1916-21. Was Air Commodore Royal Air Force Reserve. Formerly Director of the Bank of England; one of HM's Lieutenants for the City of London from 1936. Officer of Legion of Honour; Order of Crown of Italy. *Address:* 20 Roebuck House, Palace Street, Westminster, SW1. *T:* 01-828 2949; Skeldon, Dalrymple, Ayrshire. *T:* Dalrymple 223. *Club:* Royal Aero.

**WEIR, Sir John,** GCVO 1939 (KCVO 1932; CVO 1926); Royal Victorian Chain, 1949; Knight Grand Cross of Royal Order of St Olav, 1938; MB, ChB Glasgow, FFHom; Physician to the Queen, 1952-68; Honorary Consulting Physician to Royal London Homœopathic Hospital; *b* 1879; *s* of late James Weir, Glasgow; Physician-in-Ordinary to Prince of Wales, 1923-36; Physician to late Queen of Norway, 1928-38; Physician-in-Ordinary to Duke and Duchess of York, 1936, to late King George VI, 1937-52, and to late Queen Mary, 1936-53. *Address:* Flat 11, 96/100 New Cavendish Street, W1. *T:* 01-935 3491. *Club:* Royal Automobile.

**WEIR, Michael Scott;** Deputy Political Resident, Persian Gulf, since 1968; *b* 28 Jan. 1925; *s* of Archibald and Agnes Weir; *m* 1953, Alison Walker; two *s* two *d*. *Educ:* Dunfermline High School; Balliol College, Oxford. Served RAF (Flt Lt), 1944-47; subseq. HM Diplomatic Service; Foreign Office, 1950; Political Agent, Trucial States, 1952-54; FO, 1954-56; Consul, San Francisco, 1956-58; 1st Secretary: Washington, 1958-61; Cairo, 1961-63; FO, 1963-68; Counsellor, Head of Arabian Dept, 1966; Bahrain, 1968. *Recreations:* golf, music. *Address:* 30 Camden Square, NW1.

**WEIR, Robert Hendry,** CB 1960; Director, National Engineering Laboratory, East Kilbride, Scotland, since 1970; *b* Glasgow, 18 Feb. 1912; *s* of Peter and Malcolmina Weir; *m* 1934, Edna Frances Lewis; three *s*. *Educ:* Allan Glen's Glasgow; Glasgow University (BSc Hons). Engineering Apprenticeship, Wm Denny & Bros, Dumbarton, 1928-33; Royal Aircraft Establishment, 1933-39; Air Ministry HQ, 1939-40; Aircraft and Armament Experimental Establishment, 1940-42; Ministry of Aircraft Production and Ministry of Supply, 1942-; Asst Director, 1948-50; Director of Industrial Gas Turbines, 1950-52; Director of Engine Research and Development, 1952-53; Deputy Director-General, Engine Research and Development, 1954-59 (Min. of Supply); Dir-Gen. of Engine Research and Development 1959-60 (Min. of Aviation); Dir, Nat. Gas Turbine Establishment, Pyestock, near Farnborough, 1960-70. FRAeSoc. Coronation Medal, 1953. *Publications:* various. *Recreations:* golf actively when time allows; bridge, but not an addict; keen interest in Association Football. *Address:* Broom Cliff, 30 Castleton Drive, Newton Mearns, Renfrewshire. *T:* Newton Mearns 5388.

**WEIS-FOGH, Prof. Torkel;** Professor of Zoology, and Head of Department of Zoology, University of Cambridge, since 1966; Fellow of Christ's College, Cambridge; *b* 25 March 1922; *s* of S. Weis-Fogh and Dagmar (*née* Foldager Larsen), Aarhus, Denmark; *m* 1946, Hanne (*née* Heckscher); no *c*. *Educ:* Aarhus Kathedralskole; Univ. of Copenhagen. *Magister scientiarum* in Zoology, 1947, Gold Medal, 1944, *Dr phil* 1952, Univ. of Copenhagen. Asst in Research to late Prof. August Krogh, Denmark, 1947-49; Head of his private laboratory, 1949-53; Assoc. Lectr, Copenhagen Univ., 1953-54; Fellow of Rockefeller Foundn, 1954-55; Balfour Student of Univ. of Cambridge (Dept of Zoology) and Member of Trinity Coll., 1956-59; Prof. of Zoophysiology and Head of Zoophysiological Laboratory B, Univ. of Copenhagen, 1958-66. Prather Lectr in Biology, Harvard Univ., 1961. Mem., Danish State Research Foundn, 1962, Chm. Nat. Sci. Sect., 1963. Fellow, Royal Danish Acad., 1961; Fell., Acad. of Techn. Scis, 1965. *Publications:* articles in learned journals. *Recreations:* travel, mountain walking. *Address:* Department of Zoology, Downing Street, Cambridge CB2 3EJ. *T:* 52578; 7 Almoners' Avenue, Cambridge. *T:* 45783.

**WEISBERG, Hyman,** CMG 1942; retd; *b* 1890; *m* 1930, Ester Riva Cernjack; one *s* one *d*.

*Educ:* Cambridge (Wrangler, mathematical tripos). Cadet, FMS, 1914; Treasurer, SS, 1935; Financial Sec., 1937. Director Finance Div., Allied Commission Austria (British Element), 1946; Finance Dept., Foreign Office (German Section), 1947. *Recreations:* music, chess. *Address:* 21 Hillcroft Crescent, Wembley Park, Middlesex. *T:* 01-902 0652.

**WEISKRANTZ, Lawrence;** Professor of Experimental Psychology, Oxford University, since 1967; Fellow, Magdalen College, Oxford; *b* 28 March 1926; *s* of Dr Benjamin Weiskrantz and Rose (*née* Rifkin); *m* 1954, Barbara Collins; one *s* one *d*. *Educ:* Girard College; Swarthmore; Univs of Oxford and Harvard. Part-time Lectr, Tufts University, 1952; Research Assoc., Inst. of Living, 1952-55; Sen. Postdoctoral Fellow, US Nat. Res. Coun., 1955-56; Research Assoc., Cambridge Univ., 1956-61; Asst Dir of Research, Cambridge Univ., 1961-66; Reader in Physiological Psychology, Cambridge Univ., 1966-67. *Publications:* (jtly) Analysis of Behavioural Change, 1967; articles in Science, Nature, Quarterly Jl of Experimental Psychology, Jl of Comparative and Physiological Psychology, Animal Behaviour, Brain. *Recreations:* music, walking. *Address:* Department of Experimental Psychology, South Parks Road, Oxford.

**WEISS, Prof. Joseph J.,** DEng (Vienna), PhD (London); Professor of Radiation Chemistry in the University of Newcastle upon Tyne (formerly King's College, University of Durham), since 1956; *b* 30 August 1907; *s* of Sandor Simon Weiss and Ernestine (*née* Steinhardt); *m* 1942, Frances Sonia Lawson; two *s* one *d*. *Educ:* Technische Hochschule, Vienna; University of Vienna. Head of Chemistry Department, Textile Institute, Sorau, Germany, 1928-30; Assistant to Professor F. Haber, Kaiser Wilhelm Institut für Physikalische Chemie and Elektrochemie, 1930-33; Research work at University of Cambridge, 1933-34; Research at University College, London, 1934-39; Assistant Lecturer, King's College, University of Durham, 1939-44; Lecturer, King's College, University of Durham, 1944-48; Reader in Mechanism of Chemical Reactions, University of Durham, 1948-55. Marie Curie Medal, 1970. Hon. DSc Tech. Univ. of Berlin. *Publications:* scientific papers in: Z physikal. Chemie, Naturwissenschaften, Proceedings of the Royal Society, Nature, Transactions of the Faraday Society, Journal of the Chemical Society, Annual Reviews of the Chemical Society, Advances in Catalysis, etc. *Recreations:* music, cycling, sailing. *Address:* 12 Glastonbury Grove, Newcastle upon Tyne 2. *T:* Newcastle 810658.

**WEISS, Peter;** writer, painter, film producer; *b* Germany, 8 Nov. 1916; *s* of Eugene and Frieda Weiss; *m* 1964, Gunilla Palmstierna. *Educ:* Art Academy, Prague. Left Germany, 1934, lived Czechoslovakia, 1936-38, Sweden since 1939. Awarded Charles Veillon prize for Literature, 1963, Lessing Prize, Hamburg, 1965, Heinrich Mann Prize, Academy of Arts, East Berlin, 1966. Illustrated Swedish edn of Thousand and One Nights, 1957. *Films:* Hallucinations, 1953; Faces in Shadow, 1956; The Mirage, 1958. *Plays:* The Persecution and Assassination of Marat, 1964 (filmed 1967); Mockinpott, 1964; The Investigation, 1965; The Song of the Lusitanian Bogey, 1966; Vietnam Discourse, 1967; The Song of the Scarecrow, 1968; Trotsky in Exile, 1970. *Publications:* The Shadow of the Coachman's Body, 1960; The Leavetaking, 1961; Point of Escape, 1962; The Conversation of the Three Walkers, 1963; Night with Guests (play), 1963. *Address:* Suhrkamp Verlag, Frankfurt-am-Main, Germany.

**WEISSKOPF, Prof. Victor Frederick;** Professor of Physics at Massachusetts Institute of Technology, Cambridge, Mass, USA, since 1946 (on leave, 1961-65); Chairman, Department of Physics, MIT, since 1967; *b* 19 Sept. 1908; *m* 1934, Ellen Margrete Tvede; one *s* one *d*. *Educ:* Göttingen, Germany. PhD 1931. Research Associate: Berlin Univ., 1932; Eidgenossiche Technische Hochschule (Swiss Federal Institute of Technology), Zürich, 1933-35; Inst. for Theoretical Physics, Copenhagen, 1936; Asst Professor of Physics, Univ. of Rochester, NY, USA, 1937-43; Dep. Division Leader, Manhattan Project, Los Alamos, USA, 1943-45; Director-Gen., CERN, Geneva, 1961-65. Planck Medal, 1956. Mem., Nat. Acad. of Sciences, Washington, 1954; Corr. Mem. French Acad. of Sciences, 1957; Corr. Mem. Royal Danish Scientific Soc., 1961; Hon. Fell. Weitzman Inst., Rehovot, Israel, 1962; Hon. PhD: Manchester, 1961; Uppsala, 1964; Yale, 1964; Chicago, 1967; Hon. DSc: Lyon, 1962; Genève, 1964; Oxford, 1965; Vienna, 1965; Paris, 1966. Cherwell-Simon Memorial Lecturer, Oxford, 1963-64. Légion d'Honneur (France), 1959. *Publications:* Theoretical Nuclear Physics, 1952; papers on theoretical physics in various journals. *Address:* 36 Arlington Street, Cambridge, Mass, USA.

**WEITZ, Prof. Bernard George Felix,** OBE 1965; DSc; MRCVS; Director, National Institute for Research in Dairying, University of Reading, Shinfield, Berks, since 1967; *b* London, 14 Aug. 1919; *m* 1945, Elizabeth Shine; one *s* one *d*. *Educ:* St Andrew, Bruges, Belgium; Royal Veterinary College, London. MRCVS 1942; DSc London 1961. Temp. Research Worker, ARC Field Station, Compton, Berks, 1942; Research Officer, Veterinary Laboratory, Min. of Agric. and Fisheries, 1942-47; Asst Bacteriologist, Lister Inst. of Preventive Medicine, Elstree, Herts, 1947; Head of Serum Dept, 1952. *Publications:* many contribs to scientific journals on Immunology and Tropical Medicine. *Recreation:* music. *Address:* National Institute for Research in Dairying, Shinfield, Reading RG2 9AT. *T:* Reading 883103.

**WEITZMAN, David,** QC 1951; Barrister-at-Law; MP (Lab) for Stoke Newington and Hackney North since 1950 (for Stoke Newington, 1945-50); *b* 18 June 1898; *s* of Percy Weitzman; *m* 1st, 1925 (wife *d* 1950); one *s* one *d*; 2nd, 1955, Lena (*d* 1969), *widow* of Dr S. H. Dundon, Liverpool. *Educ:* Hutchesons' Grammar School, Glasgow; Manchester Central School; Manchester University. Private, 3rd Battalion Manchester Regiment, 1916; BA (History Honours), 1921; called to Bar (Gray's Inn), 1922; member of Northern Circuit. Member of Labour Party since 1923. Contested (Lab) Stoke Newington, 1935. *Recreation:* golf. *Address:* 10 King's Bench Walk, Temple EC4. *T:* 01-353 7534.

**WELBORE KER, Keith R.;** *see* Ker.

**WELBOURN, Prof. Richard Burkewood,** MA, MD, FRCS; Professor of Surgery, University of London; Director, Department of Surgery, Royal Post-graduate Medical School and Hammersmith Hospital, since 1963; *b* 1919; *y s* of late Burkewood Welbourn, MEng, MIEE, and Edith Welbourn, Rainhill, Lancs; *m* 1944, Rachel Mary Haighton, BDS, Nantwich, Cheshire; one *s* four *d*. *Educ:* Rugby School; Emmanuel College, Cambridge; Liverpool University. MB, BChir 1942; FRCS 1948; MA, MD Cambridge, 1953. War of 1939-45:

RAMC. Senior Registrar, Liverpool Royal Infirmary, 1948; Research Asst, Dept of Surgery, Liverpool Univ., 1949. Fellow in Surgical Research, Mayo Foundation, Rochester, Minn., 1951. Professor of Surgical Science, Queen's University of Belfast, 1958-63; Surgeon, Royal Victoria Hospital, Belfast, 1951-63 and Belfast City Hosp., 1962-63. Member: Cttee of Management, Royal Postgraduate Med. Sch.; Board of Governors, Hammersmith and St Mark's Hospitals, 1963-. Hunterian Professor, RCS of England, 1958. Member of Council, Association of Surgeons; Pres., Surgical Research Society; former Chm., Assoc. of Professors of Surgery; Member: Society of Sigma XI; British Medical Association; former Mem. Council, British Soc. of Gastro-enterology; 58th Member King James IV Surgical Association Inc.; FRSM, Vice-Pres., Section of Surgery, former Mem. Council, Section of Endocrinology. Examr in Surgery, Univ. of Newcastle (formerly Glasgow, Oxford, Sheffield, and RCS). James Berry Prize (RCS), 1970. Member: Exec. Cttee, British Journal of Surgery; Editorial Cttee, Gut. *Publications:* (with D. A. D. Montgomery) Clinical endocrinology for Surgeons, 1963. Contrib. chaps to Textbook of British Surgery, ed. Souttar & Goligher; Surgery of Peptic Ulcer, ed. Wells & Kyle; Progress in Clinical Surgery, ed. Rodney Smith; British Surgical Practice, ed. Rock-Carling & Ross; Scientific Basis of Surgery, ed. Wells & Kyle; Recent Advances in Surgery. Papers, mainly on gastric and adrenal surgery and physiology, in med. and surg. jls. *Recreations:* reading, writing, gardening, music. *Address:* 6 Broomfield Road, Kew Gardens, Richmond, Surrey. *T:* 01-940 2906. *Club:* Athenæum.

**WELBY, Euphemia Violet,** CBE 1944; JP Somerset; late Superintendent Women's Royal Naval Service; *b* 28 Sept. 1891; *d* of Admiral H. Lyon, CB; *m* 1917, Lt-Comdr R. M. Welby; two *s* one *d* (and one *d* decd). *Educ:* Private. Hon. Sec. SS&AFA Devonport, 1914-16; Red Cross Cook, Malta, 1916-19; later Hon. Sec. SS&AFA; served in WRNS, 1939-45; social work on committees in Plymouth and Chairman Astor Institute. *Recreation:* riding. *Address:* College Farm, Tintinhull, near Yeovil. *T:* Martock 3536; Milton Lodge, Freshwater Bay, Isle of Wight. *T:* Freshwater 3139. *Club:* Service Women's.

**WELBY, Sir Oliver Charles Earle,** 6th Bt, *cr* 1801; TD; *b* 26 Jan. 1902; *o surv. s* of Sir Charles G. E. Welby, 5th Bt, and Lady Maria Louisa Helen (*d* 1920), *e d* of late Lord Augustus Hervey, and *sister* of 5th Marquess of Bristol, *qv*; *m* 1927, Barbara Angela Mary Lind, *d* of late John Duncan Gregory, CB, CMG; two *s*. *Educ:* Eton; Christ Church, Oxford (MA). Addtl Assistant Private Secretary to Home Sec. (Sir W. Joynson-Hicks), 1925-26; JP parts of Kesteven, Lincs, 1931; High Sheriff of Lincolnshire, 1953; Hon. Capt. RA, TA. *Heir:* *s* Richard Bruno Gregory Welby [*b* 11 March 1928; *m* 1952, Jane Biddulph, *y d* of late Ralph Wilfred Hodder-Williams, MC; two *s* one *d*]. *Address:* Denton Manor, Grantham, Lincs. *TA* and *T:* Knipton 256; 76 Burton Court, SW3. *T:* 01-730 8575. *Club:* Leander.

*See also Marshal of the Royal Air Force Viscount Portal of Hungerford, Baron Saltoun.*

**WELBY-EVERARD, Maj.-Gen. Sir Christopher Earle,** KBE 1965 (OBE 1945); CB 1961; DL; *b* 9 Aug. 1909; *s* of late E. E. E. Welby-Everard, Gosberton House, near Spalding, Lincolnshire; *m* 1938, Sybil Juliet Wake Shorrock; two *s*. *Educ:* Charterhouse; CCC, Oxford. Gazetted The Lincolnshire Regt, 1930; OC 2 Lincolns, 1944; GSO1, 49 (WR) Inf. Div., 1944-46; GSO1 GHQ, MELF, 1946-48; OC 1 Royal Lincolnshire Regt, 1949-51; Comd 264 Scottish Beach Bde and 157 (L) Inf. Bde, 1954-57. BGS (Ops), HQ, BAOR, and HQ Northern Army Group, 1957-59; Chief of Staff, HQ Allied Forces, Northern Europe, 1959-61; GOC Nigerian Army, 1962-65; retd. DL Lincolnshire, 1966. *Recreations:* shooting, cricket. *Address:* The Manor House, Sapperton, Sleaford, Lincolnshire. *T:* Ingoldsby 273. *Clubs:* United Service, MCC; Free Foresters.

**WELCH, Anthony Edward,** CB 1957; CMG 1949; formerly Under-Secretary, Board of Trade, 1946-66 (Ministry of Materials, 1951-54); *b* 17 July 1906; *s* of late Francis Bertram Welch; *m* 1946, Margaret Eileen Strudwick; no *c*. *Educ:* Cheltenham College; New College, Oxford. *Address:* Brandon Lodge, Walberswick, Suffolk.

**WELCH, Sir Cullum;** *see* Welch, Sir G. J. C.

**WELCH, Air Vice-Marshal Edward Lawrence C.;** *see* Colbeck-Welch.

**WELCH, Col Sir (George James) Cullum,** 1st Bt, *cr* 1957; Kt 1952; OBE 1944; MC 1918; Alderman of City of London, Ward of Bridge Within, 1947-70; *b* 20 Oct. 1895; *o s* of late James Reader Welch, Beckenham and Croydon, and late Harriet Welch; *m* 1st, 1921, Gertrude Evelyn Sladin (*d* 1966), *o d* of late John William Harrison, Stubbins, Lancs and Eastbourne, and late Evelyn Harrison; one *s* one *d*; 2nd, 1969, Irene Avril, *d* of late John Foster, OBE. *Educ:* Alleyn's School, Dulwich. Served European War, 1914-18, in France in Royal Berkshire Regt and on Staff of 18th Div. Admitted Solicitor, 1920. Member of Court of Common Council (Ward of Candlewick), 1931-47; Chief Commoner, 1946; Sheriff of the City of London, 1950-51; Lord Mayor of London, 1956-57. War of 1939-45 commanded 3rd HGAA Regt; Member City of London TA&AFA, 1941-65 and City Lieutenancy; Hon. Colonel City of London Battalion Royal Fusiliers (TA), 1956-65; and City of London Army Cadet Force, 1953-65; Liveryman and Member, Court of Assistants, Co. of Haberdashers (Warden, 1963, 1964, 1965, 1966; Master, 1966-67); Liveryman: Co. of Spectaclemakers; Co. of Solicitors of the City of London (Past Master); Co. of Parish Clerks (Past Master); Co. of Paviors (Past Master); Member Council, Law Society, 1951-63; Registrar Archdeaconry of London, 1953-67; Chairman, Florence Nightingale Hosp., 1954-63; Vice-Chm. Bd of Govs, Bethlem Royal Hosp. and Maudsley Hosp., 1953-66; Chm. Lord Mayor of London's Nat. Hungarian and Cent. European Relief Fund, 1956-60; Dep. Chm. George VI Foundn Exec. Cttee; Chm., Cttee of Management, London Homes for the Elderly; Governor, Irish Soc., 1967-70; Hon. Treas., UK Cttee, UN Children's Fund, 1963-67; Chm. of Trustees, Morden Coll.; Trustee, Wakefield (Tower Hill Trinity Sq.) Trust; Pres. City Livery Club, 1943-44. Freedoms: Bangor, County Down, 1957; Chard, Somerset, 1957; London, Ontario, 1957; New Orleans, 1957. K of Justice St J. Order of Mercy; Officer of Orange Nassau (Netherlands); Commander Dannebrog (Denmark). Commander (1st Class) of Order of The Lion of Finland; Grand Ufficiale Al Merito Della Repubblica Italiana. *Heir:* *s* John Reader Welch, OStJ [*b* 26 July 1933; *m* 1962, Margaret Kerry, *o d* of K. Douglass, Killara, NSW; twin *d*]. *Address:* 63 Marsham Court, SW1. *T:* 01-828 7219; 43 St Margarets, Rottingdean, Sussex; 29 Martin Lane, Cannon Street, EC4. *T:* 01-626 5728. *Club:* City Livery.

**WELCH, Rt. Rev. William Neville;** *see* Bradwell, Bishop Suffragan of.

**WELD, Harry Porter,** PhB; PhD; Professor of Psychology, Cornell University, 1919, Emeritus, 1945; *b* 1877; *s* of Theodore Dwight Weld and Matilda Cochran Smith; *m* 1904, Martha Christine, *d* of Aaron Black Robinson and Keziah Wilkins; no *c*. *Educ:* Marysville (Ohio) High School; PhB 1900, Ohio State University, PhD 1911, Clark University; Graduate in Music, 1900, Shepardson College Conservatory of Music. Professor of Music, Peabody Normal School, 1900-10; Fellow in Psychology, 1909-10; Research Assistant, 1910-11, Instructor, 1911-12; Clark University; Assistant Professor of Psychology, Cornell Univ., 1912-19; Chm. of Dept. of Psychology, 1938-45; Visiting Prof., The Rice Inst., Texas, 1947-49, Univ. of Texas, 1953. Co-op. editor of the American Journal of Psychology, 1921-26. *Publications:* Psychology as Science, 1928; Ed. E. B. Titchener, Systematic Psychology; Prolegomena, 1929; Ed. Psychology: A Factual Text-Book, 1935; A Manual of Psychological Experiments, 1937; An Introduction to Psychology, 1939; The Foundations of Psychology, 1948; contributor to psychological journals. *Recreations:* music, motoring, gardening. *Address:* Asbury Towers, Bradenton, Florida, 33505, USA. *Clubs:* Sigma Alpha Epsilon; Statler (Ithaca).

**WELD, Colonel Joseph William,** OBE 1946; TD 1947 (two Bars); JP; Lord Lieutenant of Dorset since 1964; *b* 22 Sept. 1909; *s* of Wilfrid Joseph Weld, Avon Dassett, Warwickshire; *m* 1933, Elizabeth, *d* of E. J. Bellord; one *s* six *d*. *Educ:* Stonyhurst; Balliol College, Oxford. Served with Dorset Regt, TA, 1932-41; Staff College, Camberley, 1941; GSO2, General Headquarters Home Forces, 1942; Instructor, Staff College, Camberley, 1942-43; GSO1, Headquarters SEAC, 1943-46; commanded 4th Battalion Dorset Regt, 1947-51; Colonel, 1951. Hon. Colonel, 4th Battalion Dorset Regiment (TA). Chairman of Dorset Branch, County Landowners' Assoc., 1949-60; Chm. S Dorset Conservative Assoc., 1952-55 (Pres., 1955-59); Privy Chamberlain of Sword and Cape to Pope Pius XII. JP 1938, High Sheriff 1951, DL 1952, CC 1961, Dorset. KStJ 1967. *Address:* Lulworth Manor, Dorset. *T:* West Lulworth 259. *Club:* Royal Dorset Yacht.

**WELD-FORESTER;** *see* Forester, family name of Baron Forester.

**WELDON, Sir Anthony Edward Wolseley,** 7th Bt, *cr* 1723; Squadron Leader, AAF, RAF Regiment; *b* 1 Dec. 1902; *e s* of 6th Bt and Winifred, *d* of late Col Varty Rogers of Broxmore Park, Romsey, and late of the Royal Dublin Fusiliers and HM Bodyguard of Gentlemen-at-Arms; *S* father, 1917. *Heir: b* Thomas Brian Weldon [*b* 19 May 1905; *m* 1942, Marie Isobel, *d* of Hon. W. J. French; one *s* one *d*.]. *Club:* White's.

**WELDON, Brig. Hamilton Edward Crosdill,** CBE 1961 (OBE 1951); DL; Secretary: Greater London TA&VRA, since 1968; County of London T&AFA, 1962-68; *b* 14 September 1910; *s* of late Lt-Col Henry Walter Weldon, DSO, and Helen Louise Victoria Weldon (*née* Cowan); *m* 1st, 1935, Margaret Helen Katharine Passy (whom he divorced, 1946); one *d*; 2nd, 1948, Elwyne Priscilla Chaldecott; two *s* one *d*. *Educ:* Bilton Grange Preparatory School; Charterhouse; Royal Military Academy, Woolwich. Commissioned into RA as 2nd Lieut, 1930; Lieut 1933; Capt. 1938. Served War of 1939-45 (despatches, 1943, 1945): Adjutant, 1939-40; Bde Major, Malta, 1941; GSO1, RA Malta (Lt-Col), 1941-43. Staff Coll., Camberley, 1943-44; Lt-Col on Staff of SHAEF and 21 Army Group and various appointments in BAOR, 1944-47; AQMG (Lt-Col) HQ Southern Command, 1948; BAOR, 1951-52; Col on Staff of SHAPE, 1952-53; Command of 22 LAA Regt in Germany, 1953-55; Administrative Staff Coll., Greenlands, Henley, May-August 1955; Col at WO, 1955-58; Comdr, (Brig.) 33 AA Bde, 1958-60; Commandant, School of Artillery, Manorbier, 1960-62. Appointed Brig. RA, Northern Command, Nov. 1962 but retired from Army on 8 Nov. 1962 to take up appt. ADC to the Queen, 1961-62. Croix-de-Guerre with Palm (Fr.), 1945. Hon. Col: 265 Light Air Defence Regt, RA (TA), 1965-67; London and Kent Regt, RA (T), 1967-69; London and Kent Regt RA Cadre, 1969-. DL Greater London, 1967. *Publications:* Drama in Malta, 1946; compiled Official Administrative History of 21 Army Group in NW Europe, 1945. *Recreations:* racing, shooting, theatre and writing. *Address:* Duke of York's Headquarters, Chelsea, SW3. *T:* 01-730 8131, 7400; Prospect, Highlands Road, Heath End, Farnham. *T:* Aldershot 21131. *Clubs:* Hurlingham, Army and Navy.

**WELENSKY, Rt. Hon. Sir Roy, (Roland),** PC 1960; KCMG 1959 (CMG 1946); Kt 1953; *b* Salisbury, Southern Rhodesia, 20 January 1907; *s* of Michael and Leah Welensky; *m* 1928, Elizabeth Henderson (*d* 1969); one *s* one *d*. *Educ:* Salisbury, S Rhodesia. Joined Railway service, 1924; Member National Council of the Railway Workers Union; Director of Manpower, Northern Rhodesia, 1941-46; formed N Rhodesia Labour Party, 1941; Member of Sir John Forster's commission to investigate the 1940 riots in Copperbelt; Chairman of various conciliation Boards and member of the Strauss (1943) and Grant (1946) Railway Arbitration Tribunals. Member of delegn to London to discuss Mineral Royalties (1949) and Constitution (1950 and 1951); Member of Northern Rhodesia delegation to Closer Association Conference at Victoria Falls, 1951. MLC, N Rhodesia, 1938, MEC 1940-53. Chm. Unofficial Members Assoc. 1946-53. Federation of Rhodesia and Nyasaland: Minister of Transport, Communications and Posts, 1953-56; Leader of the House and Deputy Prime Minister, 1955-56; Prime Minister and Minister of External Affairs, 1956-63 (also Minister of Defence, 1956-59). Heavy-weight boxing champion of the Rhodesias, 1926-28. *Publication:* Welensky's 4000 Days, The Life and Death of the Federation of Rhodesia and Nyasaland, 1964. *Relevant Publications:* The Rhodesian, by Don Taylor; Welensky's Story, by Garry Allighan. *Recreation:* gardening. *Address:* PO Box 804, Salisbury, Rhodesia. *T:* (Office) 23338. *Club:* Farmers'.

**WELLBELOVED, James;** MP (Lab) Erith and Crayford since Nov. 1965; Commercial Consultant; *b* 29 July 1926; *s* of Wilfred Henry Wellbeloved, Sydenham and Brockley (London), and Paddock Wood, Kent; *m* 1948, Mavis Beryl Ratcliff; two *s* one *d*. *Educ:* South East London Technical College. Boy seaman, 1942-46. Publisher, Local Council Digest, a fortnightly information service for local government. Parly Private Secretary: Minister of Defence (Admin), 1967-69; Sec. of State for Foreign and Commonwealth Affairs, 1969-70. *Publication:* Local Government. *Recreations:* camping, travel. *Address:* 345 Bedonwell Road, Belvedere, Kent. *T:* Erith 35668.

**WELLBY, Rear-Adm. Roger Stanley,** CB 1958; DSO 1940; Retired; Deputy Commissioner-in-

Chief, St John Ambulance Brigade, since 1963; lately Head of UK Services Liaison Staff in Australia and Senior Naval Adviser to UK High Commissioner, 1956-59; *b* 28 Apr. 1906; *o s* of Dr Stanley Wellby and Marian Schwann; *m* 1936, Elaine, *d* of late Sir Clifford Heathcote-Smith; three *s*. *Educ:* RNC, Dartmouth. Qualified as Torpedo Officer, 1931; Commander, 1939; Special Service in France, 1940 (DSO, Croix de Guerre); Captain, 1947; Imperial Defence College; Rear-Adm. 1956. KStJ, 1966. *Recreation:* hockey, for Navy. *Address:* Oakengrove, Hastoe, Tring, Herts. *T:* Tring 3233.

**WELLER, Dr Thomas Huckle;** Richard Pearson Strong Professor of Tropical Public Health, and Head, Department of Tropical Public Health, Harvard, since 1954; Director Center for Prevention of Infectious Diseases, Harvard School of Public Health, since 1966; *b* 15 June 1915; *s* of Carl V. and Elsie H. Weller; *m* 1945, Kathleen R. Fahey; two *s* two *d*. *Educ:* University of Michigan (AB, MS); Harvard (MD). Fellow, Departments of Comparative Pathology and Tropical Medicine and Bacteriology, Harvard Medical School, 1940-41; Intern, Children's Hosp., Boston, 1941-42. Served War, 1942-45: 1st Lieut to Major, Medical Corps, US Army. Asst Resident in Medicine, Children's Hosp., 1946; Fellow, Pediatrics, Harvard Medical School, 1947; Instructor, Dept Tropical Public Health, Harvard School of Public Health, 1948; Assistant Professor, 1949; Associate Professor, 1950. Asst Director, Research Div. of Infectious Diseases, Children's Medical Center, Boston, 1949-55; Dir, Commission on Parasitic Diseases, Armed Forces Epidemiological Bd, 1953-59, Mem. 1959-; Mem. Trop. Med. and parasitology study sect., US Public Health Service, 1953-56. Diplomate, American Board of Pediatrics, 1948; Amer. Acad. of Arts and Sciences, 1955; National Academy of Sciences, USA. Mead Johnson Award of Amer. Acad. of Pediatrics (jointly), 1954; Kimble Methodology Award (jointly), 1954; Nobel Prize Physiology or Medicine (jointly), 1954; Ledlie Prize, 1963. LLD (Hon.) Univ. of Michigan, 1956. *Publications:* numerous scientific papers on *in vitro* cultivation of viruses and on helminth infections of man. *Recreations:* gardening, photography. *Address:* (home) 56 Winding River Road, Needham, Mass, USA; (office) 665 Huntington Avenue, Boston, Mass 02115. *Club:* Harvard (Boston).

**WELLES, (George) Orson;** Director, Mercury Productions (films, theatre, radio, play publishing); Columnist; *b* Kenosha, Wisc., 6 May 1915; *s* of Richard Head Welles, inventor-manufacturer, and Beatrice Ives, pianist; *m* Virginia Nicholson, Chicago (whom he divorced, 1940); one *d*; *m* Rita Hayworth (who obtained a divorce, 1947); one *d*; *m* 1955, Paola Mori; one *d*. *Educ:* Todd School, Woodstock, Ill. Directed eight productions a year at Todd School, also doing some scene sketching; studied drawing at Chicago Art Inst., 1931; appeared at Gate Theatre, Dublin, 1931, in Trilby, Jew Suss, and Hamlet; returned to America, 1932; trip to Africa; toured US with Katharine Cornell, 1933; went into radio work as an actor, 1934; produced for Federal Theatre Macbeth with negro cast, Doctor Faustus and Horse Eats Hat; later formed Mercury Theatre, which produced The Cradle Will Rock, Heartbreak House, Shoemakers' Holiday, Danton's Death, Caesar and Five Kings; also made a series of Columbia educational recordings of Shakespearean plays for schoolroom use; came to Hollywood, 1939; produced, directed, wrote, and acted in his first picture, Citizen Kane; wrote, directed, and produced film, The Magnificent Ambersons; co-author, producer, and actor in Journey Into Fear. Produced Native Son in New York, 1939; co-starred Jane Eyre, 1943; appeared in Follow the Boys, 1943; produced, directed, starred in Mercury Wonder Show, a magic show for Army and Navy personnel, 1943; co-starred in Tomorrow is Forever, 1945; wrote, produced, acted and directed, The Lady From Shanghai, 1946; wrote screenplay, produced, directed and acted in screenplay, Macbeth, 1947; acted in Cagliostro (screenplay made in Italy), 1947; produced, and acted name-part in Othello, St James's, 1951; acted in film, Three Cases of Murder, 1955; adapted, produced, and acted in play, Moby Dick, Duke of York's, 1955; wrote, directed, and acted in film, Confidential Report, 1955; produced and acted name-part in King Lear, New York, 1956; adapted, directed and acted in film, Othello, 1956; acted in films: The Long, Hot, Summer, 1958, Compulsion, 1959, Ferry to Hong Kong, 1959, David and Goliath, 1961, The VIP's, 1963; produced and acted in film, The Trial, 1963; acted in films, Oedipus The King, 1968, Catch 22, 1970. Directed The Immortal Story, 1968, Southern Star, 1969 (films); acted in film The Kremlin Letter, 1970. Adapted and acted in play, Chimes at Midnight, 1960 (filmed 1966). Prod play, Rhinoceros, Royal Court Theatre, London, 1960. Associate Editor of Free World Magazine. *Publications:* Illustrated edns of Macbeth, Julius Cæsar, Twelfth Night, and the Merchant of Venice with editing, illustrations, and stage directions (Mercury Shakespeare); Mr Arkadin, 1957. *Recreations:* prestidigitating, cartooning, swimming, reading. *Clubs:* Advertising, Lotos (New York); National Variety (Los Angeles).

**WELLESLEY,** family name of **Earl Cowley** and of **Duke of Wellington.**

**WELLESZ, Egon Joseph,** CBE 1957; FBA 1953; MA (by decree 1939); Hon. Mus. Doc. Oxon 1932; Fellow of Lincoln College, Oxford and Music Tutor, since 1939; University Reader in Byzantine Music, 1948-56; late Professor of Music, University of Vienna; Editor of the Monumenta Musicæ Byzantinæ (publ. Royal Danish Academy, 1932-) Co-Editor of The New Oxford History of Music, since 1947; Corresponding Member American Musicological Society, 1947-; Vice-President, canonised Consociatio Internationalis Musicae Sacrae, 1963; *b* 21 October 1885; *s* of S. Wellesz and Ilona Lövenyi; *m* Emmy Frančiska Stross; two *d*. *Educ:* Vienna Hegel-gymnasium; Summer ext., Cambridge; Univ. of Vienna. Dr 1908, Vienna; Privat-Dozent of History of Music, 1913; first performance of his opera, Die Prinzessin Girnara, at Frankfurt, 1921; first performance of Alkestis, Mannheim, 1924; lectures on music at the Hochschule f. Musik, Köln, 1926; Prof. of History of Music, Univ. Vienna, 1929-38; Director of the "siège scientifique" of the Monumenta Musicae Byzantinae at Vienna, 1931-38; Vice-Pres., Osterreichischer Komponistenbund, 1928-38; first performance of Bacchants, State-opera, Vienna, 1931; Lecturer on Byzantine music, London, Cambridge, Oxford, 1932; on Opera, Univ. of London, 1933. RCM London and Univ. of Cambridge, 1938; lecturing on the History of Music, Univ. of Oxford, since 1940; Univ. Lecturer in the History of Music, 1944-48; Member of Board of Faculty of Music, Univ. of Oxford, since 1944; Chm. of Faculty, 1955-56; Fellow Royal Danish Academy of Science and Letters, 1946; Harvard Visiting Scholar, 1954; Pres. Oxford Univ. Byzantine Soc., 1955-66; Gunning Lecturer, University of Edinburgh, 1956; Harvard Visiting Scholar,

1956. Music Prize of City of Vienna, 1953; Grand Silver Medal of City of Paris, 1957; Austrian Order of Merit, Pro Musica Austriaca Medal, Silver Medal of Honour of City of Vienna, 1960; Austrian Great State Prize for work as a composer, 1961; Apostolic KCSG 1961. *Publications: music, operas*—Die Prinzessin Girnara, 1921; Alkestis, 1924; Die Opferung des Gefangenen, 1926; Scherz, List und Rache, 1928; Die Bakchantinnen, 1931; Incognita, 1951; chamber music, songs, Cantata, 1932; Concerto for piano, op. 49, 1934; Amor timido, Cantata 1933, Mass for choir and organ, 1934; Sonette der Elisabeth Barrett-Browning for soprano and string quartet, 1934; Prosperos Beschwörungen, 1934-35; Mass for female voices and orchestra, 1937; Fifth String quartet op. 60, 1943; Cantata op. 61; Symphony in C op. 63, 1945; Sixth String Quartet op. 67, 1947; Symphony in E flat op. 65, 1948; Seventh String Quartet op. 66, 1948; Octet, 1949; Symphony in A, op. 68, 1951; Symphony in G, op. 70, 1953; Fifth Symphony, 1956; Eighth String Quartet, 1957; Clarinet Quintet, 1959; Violin Concerto, op. 84, 1961; Laus Nocturna, op. 88, 1962; Missa brevis, op. 80, 1963; Duineser Elegie, 1963; Music for Strings, 1964; Sixth Symphony, op. 95, 1965; Ninth String Quartet, op. 97, 1966; Vision for Soprano and orchestra, op. 99, 1966; Magnificat, op. 100, 1967; Mirabile Mysterium, op. 101, 1967; Seventh Symphony, op. 102, 1968; Canticum Sapientiae, op. 104, 1969; Divertimento, op. 107, 1969; Symphonic Epilogue, op. 108, 1970; String Quintet, op. 109, 1970; Eighth Symphony, op. 110, 1970; *books:* Biography on A. Schönberg, 1921, English version, 1924; Aufgaben u. Probleme auf d. Gebiet der byzantin. u. oriental. Kirchenmusik, 1923; Byzantinische Musik, 1927, Spanish version, 1930; Die neue Instrumentation, 2 vols, 1929-30; Trésor de musique byzantine, Vol. I, 1934; Monumenta Musicae Byzantinae, Vol. I, Cod. theol. gr. 181 Palat Vindob. (with H. J. W. Tillyard), 1934; Monumenta Musicae Byzantinae, Transcripta I, Hymni mensis Septembris, 1936; Transcripta VII, The Akathistus Hymnus, 1956; articles for Grove's Dictionary of Music, 1939; Eastern Elements in Western Chant, 1947; A History of Byzantine Music and Hymnography, 1949, 2nd edn 1961; Essays on Opera, 1950. Ed. Vol. I on The New Oxford History of Music, 1957; The Music of the Byzantine Church, Anthology of Music, Vol. I, 1959; J. J. Fux, 1965; (ed) Studies in Eastern Chant, vol. 1 1966, vol II, 1970. *Address:* 51 Woodstock Road, Oxford; Lincoln College, Oxford. *T:* 59857.

**WELLINGS, Jack Alfred,** CBE 1970; Chairman and Managing Director, The George Cohen 600 Group Ltd, since 1968; *b* 16 Aug. 1917; *s* of Edward Josiah and Selina Wellings; *m* 1946, Greta, *d* of late George Tidey; one *s* two *d.* *Educ:* Selhurst Grammar Sch.; London Polytechnic. Vice-Pres., Hawker Siddeley (Canada) Ltd, 1952-62; Dep. Man. Dir, George Cohen 600 Group Ltd, 1962. *Address:* Boundary Meadow, Collum Green Road, Stoke Poges, Bucks. *T:* Fulmer 2978.

**WELLINGTON,** 7th Duke of (*cr* 1814), **Lt-Col Gerald Wellesley,** KG 1951; Baron Mornington, 1746; Earl of Mornington; Viscount Wellesley, 1760; Viscount Wellington of Talavera and Wellington, Somersetshire; Baron Douro, 1809; Earl of Wellington, Feb. 1812; Marquess of Wellington, Oct. 1812; Marquess Douro, 1814; Prince of Waterloo, 1815, Netherlands; Count of Vimeiro, Marquess of Torres Vedras and Duke of Victoria in Portugal; *b* 21 Aug. 1885; 3rd *s* of 4th Duke of Wellington; *S* nephew, 1943; *m* Dorothy Violet (*d* 1956), *d* of late Robert Ashton, Croughton, Cheshire, and late Countess of Scarborough; one *s* one *d.* *Educ:* Eton. Entered HM Diplomatic Service, 1908; retired, 1919, having been Sec. at Petrograd, Constantinople, and Rome; 2nd Lt (Temp. Lt-Col) Grenadier Guards, Sept. 1939; Served with BEF, France, 1939-40; MEF 1942; CMF 1943; Lord Lt of County of London, 1944-49; Lord Lt of Hampshire, 1949-60; a Trustee of National Gallery, 1950-57; Chancellor of the Univ. of Southampton, 1951-62; Governor of the Isle of Wight, 1956-65. *Publications:* The Iconography of the First Duke of Wellington, 1935; (ed, with Francis Bamford) The Journal of Mrs Arbuthnot, 1820-1832 (2 vols), 1950; (ed) The Conversations of the First Duke of Wellington with George William Chad, 1956; (ed) Wellington and his Friends: Letters of the First Duke, 1965. *Heir:* *s* Marquess Douro, *qv.* *Address:* Stratfield Saye House, near Reading, Berks. *T:* Turgis Green 218; Apsley House, 149 Piccadilly, W1. *T:* 01-499 1953.

**WELLINGTON (NZ), Bishop of,** since 1960; **Rt. Rev. Henry Wolfe Baines;** *b* 7 Feb. 1905; *y c* and 3rd *s* of Talbot and Caroline Agnes Baines; *m* 1944, Natalie Elizabeth Bartlett; two *s.* *Educ:* Repton; Balliol Coll., Oxford; Cuddesdon Theological College. Travelling Secretary of Student Christian Movement in England, 1927-29; Deacon, 1930; Asst Curate, St Mary the Virgin, Oxford, 1930; Priest, 1931; Asst Chaplain, later Chaplain-in-Charge, St John's Cathedral, Hongkong, 1934-38; Vicar of St Nicholas, Radford, Coventry, 1938-41; Rector of Rugby (St Andrew), 1941-49; Bishop of Singapore, 1949-60. Hon. Canon of Coventry Cathedral, 1947; Proctor in Convocation, 1946. *Recreations:* cricket, music, bird watching. *Address:* Bishopscourt, Wellington, NZ. *Clubs:* Travellers', MCC, Student Movement House, Wellington.

**WELLINGTON (NZ), Archbishop of, (RC),** since 1954; **His Eminence Cardinal Peter Thomas Bertram McKeefry;** *b* 3 July 1899; 5th *s* of late Michael and Mary McKeefry. *Educ:* Christian Brothers, Dunedin; Holy Cross College, Mosgiel; Propaganda Fide, Rome. Ordained, Rome, 1926. Curate, St Patrick's Cathedral, Auckland, 1926; Secretary to late Bishop Cleary, 1926; Assistant Editor, The Month (NZ), 1926; Editor, 1930; Editor and Manager, Zealandia, 1936; Secretary to Archbishop Liston, 1930; Diocesan Secretary, Auckland, 1935; Titular Archbishop of Dercos and Coadjutor-Archbishop to Wellington, with right of succession, 1947. Cardinal, 1969. *Publications:* miscellaneous historical articles; edited pioneer NZ records. *Address:* 10 Guilford Terrace, Wellington 1, NZ. *T:* 42-166.

**WELLINGTON, Rt. Rev. John;** retired; *b* 28 December 1889; *s* of late Reverend G. Wellington. *Educ:* Wimborne Grammar School; Salisbury Theological College. BDLond; Curate S Martin's, Salisbury, 1913-16; SPG Missionary, Shantung, China, 1917-35; Vicar Holy Trinity, Bedford, 1936-40; Bishop of Shantung, 1940-50. Interned by Japanese in China; released, 1945. Assistant Bishop of Truro and Vicar of St Germans, Cornwall, 1951-60; Hon. Canon of St Constantine in Truro Cathedral, 1951-60. Archdeacon of Bodmin, 1953-56. *Address:* 23 East Street, Wareham, Dorset BH20 4NN. *T:* Wareham 2740.

**WELLINGTON, Sir Lindsay;** *see* Wellington Sir R. E. L.

**WELLINGTON, Peter Scott,** DSC; PhD; ARCS; FLS; Director, National Institute of

Agricultural Botany, since 1970; *b* 20 March 1919; *er s* of late Robert Wellington, MBE, MC; *m* 1947, Kathleen Joyce, *widow* of E. H. Coombe; one *s* one *d*. *Educ:* Kelly Coll.; Imperial Coll. of Science. BSc 1946. Observer, Fleet Air Arm, 1940-45 (Lt-Comdr (A) RNVR). Research Asst 1948-52, Chief Officer 1953-61, Official Seed Testing Stn for England and Wales; Asst Dir 1961-68, Dep. Dir 1968-69, Nat. Inst. of Agricultural Botany. Vice-Pres., Internat. Seed Testing Assoc., 1953-56 (Chm. Germination Cttee, 1956-); Chief Officer, UK Variety Classification Unit, 1965-; Chm., Technical Working Group, Internat. Convention for Protection of Plant Varieties, 1966-68. *Publications:* papers on germination of cereals and weeds, seed-testing and seed legislation. *Recreations:* gardening, walking, reading. *Address:* College Farm, 41 High Street, Teversham, Cambs. *T:* Teversham 2308. *Club:* Farmers'.

**WELLINGTON, Sir (Reginald Everard) Lindsay,** Kt 1963; CBE 1944; Retired from BBC, 1963; *b* 10 August 1901; *s* of Hubert Lindsay Wellington and Nancy Charlotte Boughtwood; *m* 1st, 1928, Evelyn Mary Ramsay; one *s* one *d*; 2nd, 1952, Margot Osborn. *Educ:* Queen Elizabeth Grammar School, Wakefield; The Queen's College, Oxford. BBC Programme Staff since 1924; Director Broadcasting Division, Ministry of Information, 1940-41; N American Director, BBC, 1941-44; Controller (Programmes), BBC, 1944-45; Controller BBC Home Service, 1945-52; Director of Sound Broadcasting, BBC, 1952-63. *Recreations:* reading, music. *Address:* Witheridge, near Henley-on-Thames, Oxon. *T:* Nettlebed 214. *Club:* Savile.

**WELLOCK, Wilfred;** *b* Nelson, Lancs, 2 Jan. 1879; *s* of John Wellock, Nelson, Lancs, and Thirza Punt Barker, Norfolk; *m* 1913, Frances, *d* of James Wilson, Colne, Lancs. *Educ:* Elementary school; night schools; Edinburgh University. Journalist and lecturer; MP (Lab) Stourbridge, 1927-31; member of Select Committee on Future Government of East Africa; spent eight months, 1919-20, in Holland, Germany and Austria investigating economic and other conditions; four months, 1925, lecture tour in America and Canada, on Peace and Socialism; lecture tours in USA, 1946 and 1949; tour of Gandhi Ashrams, India, 1949-50; lecture tours in America, 1954 and 1956. *Publications:* The Spiritual Basis of Democracy; (out of print) India's Awakening, The Way Out, Pacifism, A Modern Idealist (novel); War as viewed by Jesus and the Early Church; Money has Destroyed Your Peace; Which Way, Britain?, 1942; A Mechanistic or a Human Society?, 1944; The Third Way, 1947; Rebuilding Britain, 1949; Power or Peace, Gandhi as a Social Revolutionary, 1950; Annihilation or Creative Revolution, 1951; The Orchard Lea papers, 1952; New Horizons, 1954; Not by Bread Alone, 1955; Which Way, America? and Which Way, Britain?, 1957; From Ghandhi to Vinoba Bhave, 1959; The Crisis in our civilization, 1962; Off the Beaten Track (autobiography), 1962; Beyond These Spiritually Barren Years, 1964; Towards One World, but shall we arrive?, 1967. *Recreations:* spinning, gardening, walking. *Address:* Orchard Lea, Saunders Lane, New Longton, Preston, Lancs. *TA:* Wellock, New Longton, Preston.

**WELLS, Dean of;** *see* Edwards, Very Rev. Irven David.

**WELLS, Archdeacon of;** *see* Lance, Ven. J. du B.

**WELLS, Charles Alexander,** CBE 1963; SPk (Sitara-i-Pakistan) 1961; FRCS, etc; Emeritus Professor of Surgery, University of Liverpool; Hon. Surgeon Royal Liverpool United Hospital and Consultant to Royal Prince Alfred, Sydney, NSW, and other hospitals; Vice-President, Royal College of Surgeons, since 1965 (Bradshaw Lecturer, 1966); FRSocMed (Past President Section of Urology); Corresponding member Société Franc. d'Urologie; *b* 9 Jan, 1898; *o s* of late Percy M. and late Frances L. Wells, Liverpool; *m* 1928, Joyce Mary Rivett Harrington; two *s*. *Educ:* Merchant Taylors', Crosby; Liverpool University (MB, ChB, 1st Hons). Active service, RFA, 1916-18. Lately surgeon and urologist to various hospitals; Resident Surgical Officer Ancoats Hospital, Manchester; Demonstrator in Anatomy McGill University, Montreal; Clinical Assistant St Peter's Hospital, London. Mem. Council RCS; Mem. Med. Adv. Council, ODM, and Chm. Recruitment Panel; Chairman: Merseyside Conf. for Overseas Students; Cttee on Surgical Educn, Internat. Fedn Surgical Colls. Ex-Council of British Association of Urological Surgeons (Home and Overseas); Past President Liverpool Medical Institution; Pakistan Health Reforms Commn, 1960; Adrian Committee (Ministry of Health) on Radiation Hazards, 1958-; Medical Research Council's Committee, Pressure Steam Sterilisation. Hon. FACS 1968. Hon. LLD (Panjab), 1960. *Publications:* Surgery for Nurses, 1938; Text Book of Urology (ed Winsbury-White); Treatment of Cancer in Clinical Practice, 1960; contrib. to textbooks and symposia, various chapters, Prostatectomy (monograph), 1952; (with J. Kyle) Peptic Ulceration, 1960; (ed with J. Kyle) Scientific Foundations of Surgery, 1967; numerous articles in Scientific Journals. *Recreations:* shooting, painting in oils. *Address:* The Gap, Hoylake, Cheshire. *T:* Hoylake 4326; 41 Rodney Street, Liverpool. *T:* 051-709 6951. *Clubs:* Junior Carlton; University (Liverpool).

**WELLS, Sir Charles Maltby,** 2nd Bt *cr* 1944, TD 1960; *b* 24 July 1908; *e s* of 1st Bt, and Mary Dorothy Maltby (*d* 1956); *S* father, 1956; *m* 1935, Katharine Boulton, *d* of Frank Boteler Kenrick, Toronto; two *s*. *Educ:* Bedford School; Pembroke College, Cambridge. Joined RE (TA), 1933; Capt. 1939; served War of 1939-45: 54th (EA) Div., 1939-41; Lt-Col 1941; 76th Div., 1941-43; British Army Staff, Washington, 1943-45. *Heir:* *s* Christopher Charles Wells [*b* 12 Aug. 1936; *m* 1960, Elizabeth Florence Vaughan, *d* of I. F. Griffiths, Outremont, Quebec; one *s* one *d*]. *Address:* 37 Duggan Avenue, Toronto, Canada.

**WELLS, Denys George,** RBA 1910; *b* 1881; 4th *s* of late George Wells, JP, of Bedford; *m* 1905; one *d*. *Educ:* Bedford Grammar School. Studied Art at the Slade School under Professor F. Brown and Wilson Steer. British Empire Medal, 1941; Lazlo Bronze Medal, 1943, for picture Waterloo in Wartime. Works bought by Ministry of Works, LCC and Sutherland Public Art Gallery. Vice-President, RBA, 1955. Pension for work as an Artist, awarded by the Queen, 1968. *Address:* 45A Kingston Road, New Malden, Surrey. *T:* Malden 1312.

**WELLS, Doreen Patricia;** Ballerina of the Royal Ballet; *b* 25 June 1937. *Educ:* Walthamstow; Bush Davies School; Royal Ballet School. Engaged in Pantomime, 1952 and 1953. Joined Royal Ballet, 1955; became Principal Dancer, 1960. Has danced leading roles in Noctambules, Harlequin in April, Dance Concertante, Sleeping Beauty, Coppelia, Swan Lake, Sylvia, La Fille mal Gardée, Two Pigeons, Giselle, Invitation, Rendezvous,

Blood Wedding, Raymonda, Concerto, Nutcracker. Has created leading roles in Toccata, La Création du Monde, Sinfonietta. Adeline Genée Gold Medal. *Recreations:* listening to classical records, theatre-going. *Address:* 87 Elsham Road, W14. *T:* 01-603 5936.

**WELLS, Prof. Frederick Arthur,** OBE 1954; Professor of Industrial Economics, University of Nottingham, 1958-67, now Emeritus; *b* 12 July 1901; *s* of Frederick Wells and Lucy Eliza Wells (*née* Hooton); *m* 1931, Dora Jean Ward; one *d. Educ:* University College Nottingham; London School of Economics. BSc (Econ) 1927; Cassel Scholarship, 1927; PhD 1931. University College, Nottingham: Staff Tutor, Department of Adult Education, 1928-32; Lecturer in Economics, 1932-45; Reader in Applied Economics, 1945; Head of Department of Industrial Economics, 1953-. Board of Trade, 1944-45. Visiting Professor: State University of Pennsylvania, 1950-51; University of Khartoum, 1962; Monash Univ., Australia, 1968. Chairman of Wages Councils, Ministry of Labour, 1952-; Member of Agricultural Wages Board, 1950-59. *Publications:* The British Hosiery Trade, 1935; Productivity in a Printing Firm, 1958; (jt) Studies in Industrialisation: Nigeria and the Cameroons; contrib. to works on industrial economics, and articles in learned journals. *Address:* 3 Manor Court, Bramcote, Nottingham. *T:* 255131.

**WELLS, Prof. George Philip,** FRS 1955; ScD; Emeritus Professor of Zoology in the University of London; *b* 17 July 1901; *er s* of Herbert George and Amy Catherine Wells; *m* 1927, Marjorie Stewart Craig (marr. diss., 1960); one *s* one *d. Educ:* Oundle; Trinity Coll., Cambridge. Temp. Asst, Dept of Zoology, University College, London, 1928; Lecturer, 1931; Reader, 1943; Professor, 1954-68. Hon. Associate, Dept of Zoology, British Museum (Natural History), 1953; Hon. Member, Soc. for Experimental Biology, 1964. Broadcaster. *Publications:* (with H. G. Wells and Julian Huxley), The Science of Life, 1929-30 (in fortnightly parts); (various subseq. revisions). Many scientific papers and popular writings. *Address:* University College, WC1. *Club:* Savile.

**WELLS, Lt-Gen. Sir Henry,** KBE 1956 (CBE 1945; OBE 1941); CB 1954; DSO 1943; idc; psc; retired; *b* 22 March 1898; *s* of Arthur Wells, Kyneton, Victoria; *m* 1926, Lorna, *d* of Nathaniel Skippen; two *s*. Trained in England, 1920-21; 6th Cavalry Bde, 1926; RMC, Duntroon, 1927-30; Small Arms Sch., 1931-33; Staff Coll., Camberley, 1934-35; Bde Major 1 Inf. Bde, 1936-38; Instructor in Tactics, RMC Duntroon, 1939-40; seconded to 7 Australian Division, AIF, 1940; served War of 1939-45: Middle East, South West Pacific (OBE, DSO, CBE); Director of Mil. Operations, AHQ, 1946; Comdt, RMC, Duntroon, 1949-50; GOC Southern Command, 1951-52; C-in-C, British Commonwealth Forces in Korea, 1953-54; CGS, Australia, 1954-58; Chairman, Chiefs of Staffs Cttee, Department of Defence, Australia, 1958-59; retired, 1959. Hon. Col, Royal Victoria Regt, 1962-66. Commander, US Legion of Merit, 1954. *Address:* 12A Heyington Place, Toorak, Victoria 3142, Australia.

**WELLS, Sir Henry Weston,** Kt 1966; CBE 1957; Chairman, The Land Commission, 1967-70; Director: Investment & Merchant Finance Corporation Pty Ltd, South Australia; Town & City Holdings (Australia) Pty Ltd; *b* 28 Feb. 1911; *s* of Sir William Henry Wells and Dorothy Kate Wells (*née* Horne); *m* 1937, Rosemary Haliday Witchurch; two *s* one *d. Educ:* Sherborne Sch., Dorset; Coll. of Estate Management. Dir of Accommodation, War Organisation, Order of St John and Brit. Red Cross Soc., 1939-41, and Dep. Dir of Hosps thereof, 1940-41; Reconstruction Officer and Chief Estates Officer, Min. of Town and Country Planning, 1943-46; Dep. Chm., Bracknell Development Corp., 1949-50; Chm., Hemel Hempstead Development Corp., 1950-62. Partner, Chesterton & Sons, Chartered Surveyors, 1934-66. Chairman: Commn for New Towns (UK), 1964-70 (Dep. Chm., 1961-64); The Land Commn (UK), 1967-70. Director: Abbey National Building Society, 1966-70; Morgan Crucible Company, 1965-70; Coll. of Estate Management, 1968-69. President: RICS, 1965-66. Hon. DLitt Reading, 1968. KStJ 1958. *Address:* (office) 33 King William Street, Adelaide, South Australia 5000; (home) Morden House, Crafers, SA 5152, Australia. *Club:* Boodle's.

**WELLS, Lt-Col Herbert James,** CBE 1958; MC 1918; FCA 1934; JP; DL; *b* 27 March 1897; *s* of late James J. Wells, NSW; *m* 1926, Rose Hamilton, *d* of late H. D. Brown, Bournemouth; no *c. Educ:* NSW. Chartered Accountant; Sen. Partner, Amsdon Cossart & Wells. Surrey CC: Alderman, 1960; Vice-Chm., 1959-62; Chm., 1962-65. JP 1952, DL 1962, Surrey; High Sheriff of Surrey, 1965. A General Comr for Income Tax. Freeman, City of London. Pres. Brit. Red Cross, Carshalton and Sutton Division; former Member, Surrey T&AFA, retired 1968; Chairman, Queen Mary's Hospital for Children, Carshalton, 1958-60; Member, Carshalton UDC, 1945-62 (Chm. 1950-52 and 1955-56). Served European War, 1914-18 with Aust. Inf. and Aust. Flying Corps in Egypt and France (MC); served War of 1939-45. *Recreations:* football, hockey, tennis, squash, now golf. *Address:* 17 Oakhurst Rise, Carshalton Beeches, Surrey. *T:* Melville 4125. *Club:* Royal Automobile.

**WELLS, John Julius;** MP (C) Maidstone since October 1959; *b* 30 March 1925; *s* of A. Reginald K. Wells, Marlands, Sampford Arundel, Som; *m* 1948, Lucinda Meath-Baker; two *s* two *d. Educ:* Eton; Corpus Christi College, Oxford (MA). War of 1939-45: joined RN as ordinary seaman, 1942; commissioned, 1943, served in submarines until 1946. Contested (C) Smethwick Division, General Election, 1955. Chairman: Cons. Party Horticulture Cttee, 1965-; Horticultural sub-Cttee, Select Cttee on Agriculture, 1968; Vice-Chm., Cons. Party Agriculture Cttee, 1970. *Recreations:* country pursuits. *Address:* Mere House, Mereworth, Kent.

**WELLS, Ronald Alfred,** OBE 1965; BSc, FRIC, MIMM; Joint Managing Director, Turner Brothers Asbestos Co. Ltd, since 1970 *b* 11 February 1920; *s* of Alfred John Wells and Winifred Jessie (*née* Lambert); *m* 1953, Anne Brebner Lanshe; two *s. Educ:* Birkbeck College, London; Newport Technical College. Service with Government Chemist, 1939-40; Royal Naval Scientific Service, 1940-47; Joined Nat. Chemical Laboratory, 1947; Mem. UK Scientific Mission, Washington, 1951-52; Head of Radio-chemical Group, 1956; Head of Div. of Inorganic and Mineral Chemistry, 1963; Deputy Director, Nov. 1963; Director of National Chemical Laboratory, 1964; Dir of Research, Turner Bros Asbestos Co. Ltd, 1965. Mem. Council, Royal Inst. Chemistry, 1965-68. *Publications:* numerous contribs to Inorganic Chromatography and Extractive Metallurgy. *Recreations:* gardening, golf. *Address:* Barberton, 4 Moorgate Avenue, Bamford, Rochdale, Lancs. *T:* Rochdale 49940.

**WELLS, Stanley Walter,** MBE 1918; Major; owner and controller laundry businesses in Kent, since 1920; *b* 11 Nov. 1887; *s* of William Malcolm and Kate Madeleine Wells, late of High Dells, Woldingham, Surrey; *m* 1917, Violet, *er d* of Edward Manwaring, late of Elm Lodge, College Road, Dulwich; one *s* one *d*. *Educ:* Mercers' School; Dulwich College. Freedom of City of London, 1912; Livery of Tallow Chandlers' Company, 1912, Master, 1947 and 1953; Member: Court of Guild of Freemen (Dep. Master, 1955, Master, 1956); Master The Company of Launderers, 1960; Court of Common Council for Ward of Cripplegate Within, 1949. Sheriff for City of London, 1949-50. Joint Honorary Treasurer of the Corporation of the Sons of the Clergy; Member of the Council of the People's Dispensary for Sick Animals; Member of the Council of the Royal London Society for the Blind. Sevenoaks Rural District Council (Mem. for Westerham) (10 years); Mem. Kent County Constabulary (21 years). Served European War, 1914-19, London Scottish and RASC Horse Transport (despatches twice, MBE); Army Cadet Force, Royal West Kent Regt, 1925-31, 1940-46. Comdr of Order of Merit (Italy); Order of Grand Cross (West German Federal Republic); Officer of Legion of Honour (France). *Recreations:* gardens and sailing. *Address:* Uplands, Westerham, Kent. *T:* Westerham 3243; Downlands, Aldwick, Sussex. *T:* Bognor Regis 1908. *Clubs:* Royal Automobile, City Livery (Pres. 1958), United Wards.

**WELLS, Thomas Umfrey,** MA; Headmaster, Wanganui Collegiate School, New Zealand, since 1960; *b* 6 Feb. 1927; *s* of Athol Umfrey and Gladys Colebrook Wells; *m* 1953, Valerie Esther Brewis; two *s* one *d*. *Educ:* King's College, Auckland, New Zealand; Auckland University (BA); (Orford Studentship to) King's College, Cambridge. BA 1951; MA 1954. Assistant Master, Clifton College, 1952-60 (Senior English Master, 1957-60). *Recreations:* reading, theatre, cricket (Cambridge Blue, 1950), tennis, fishing; formerly Rugby football (Cambridge Blue, 1951). *Address:* The Collegiate School, Wanganui, New Zealand. *T:* 8097. *Clubs:* MCC; Hawks (Cambridge); Wanganui (NZ).

**WELLS, William Thomas,** QC 1955; MP (Lab) Walsall North since 1955 (Walsall, 1945-55); Deputy Chairman, Hertfordshire Quarter Sessions, since 1961; Recorder of King's Lynn, since 1965; Member, Magistrates Courts Rules Committee; A Governor of Northern Polytechnic and of National College of Rubber Technology; Editorial Adviser on English Law, Encyclopædia Britannica; Director: Provincial Insurance Co. Ltd (London Board); Frank O'Shanohun Associates Ltd; *b* 10 Aug. 1908; *s* of late William Collins Wells (formerly of Clare Coll., Cambridge, and Bexhill-on-Sea) and Gertrude Wells; *m* 1936, Angela, 2nd *d* of late Robert Noble, formerly of HM Colonial Legal Service; two *s* two *d*. *Educ:* Lancing Coll.; Balliol Coll., Oxford. Joined Fabian Society, 1930; called to Bar, Middle Temple, 1932; Master of the Bench, 1963. QC Hong Kong, 1968. Formerly Mem., Internat. Adv. Committee of Labour Party and of Political Committee and Local Government Committee of the Fabian Society. Army, 1940-45: a General Staff Officer, 2nd grade, Directorate of Military Training, War Office, with temp. rank of Major, 1942-45. Member of Lord Chancellor's Cttee on Practice and Procedure of Supreme Court, 1947-53; Mem. of Chm.'s Panel, House of Commons, 1948-50; Mem. Departmental Cttee on Homosexual Offences and Prostitution, 1954-57. *Publications:* How English Law Works, 1947; former contributor to The Fortnightly, Spectator, Times Literary Supplement, etc, mainly on political and military subjects. *Address:* Mymms Hall, South Mimms, Potters Bar, Herts. *T:* Potters Bar 58853; 3 Middle Temple Lane, Temple, EC4. *T:* 01-583 0659. *Club:* Athenæum.

**WELLS-PESTELL,** family name of **Baron Wells-Pestell.**

**WELLS-PESTELL, Baron** *cr* 1965 (Life Peer); **Reginald Alfred Wells-Pestell;** Sociologist; *b* 27 Jan. 1910; *o s* of Robert Pestell and Mary (*née* Manning); *m* 1935, Irene, *y d* of late Arthur Wells; two *s*. *Educ:* elementary and Grammar schs; Univ. of London. LLD. London Probation Service: sometime Sen. Probation Officer, N London Magistrates Court. A Founder, Nat. Marriage Guidance Coun. (now a Vice-Pres.). Magistrate for London, 1946-; a Chm., Chelsea and E London Matrimonial Courts. President, Family Law Association. Mem. LCC, 1946-52; Leader of Council, 1946, Mayor, 1947-49, Stoke Newington Borough; Mem. E Suffolk County Council, 1964-67. Contested (Lab) Taunton, 1955 and 1956, Hornsey, 1950 and 1951. Capt. KRRC, 1940-45. FPhS. *Publications:* articles and pamphlets on marriage and family life, delinquency and social problems for press and jls. *Recreations:* music, opera. *Address:* Murcott, near Islip, Oxon.

**WELLWOOD, William,** MC and Bar; *b* Belfast, N Ireland, 1893; Farmed for a period. Joined Northern Ireland Civil Service, and was private secretary to late Rt Hon. Sir R. Dawson Bates, Bt, DL; late Rt Hon. William Lowry, KC, MP; Rt Hon. Edmond C. Warnock, KC, MP; Rt Hon. W. B. Maginess, KC, MP; resigned from the civil service. MP (UU) for Londonderry, at Westminster, (May) 1951-55; was returned unopposed May 1951, and again in October 1951. Member Orange Order, Lodge 1974 for fifteen years (Master for five years). Served European War, 1914-18, with Royal Marines (MC and Bar). *Address:* 90 Hawthornden Road, Belfast.

**WELMAN, Douglas Pole,** CBE 1966; Chairman and Managing Director, Allspeeds Holdings Ltd, since 1967; Director, English Abrasives Corporation Ltd, since 1968; *s* of late Col Arthur Pole Welman and late Lady (Percy) Scott; *m* 1st, 1929, Denise, *d* of Charles Steers Peel; one *d*; 2nd, 1946, Betty Marjorie, *d* of late Henry Huth. *Educ:* Tonbridge Sch.; Faraday House Engineering Coll. Electrical and Mechanical Engineering career at home and abroad; Consulting Practice, 1932-37; Man. Dir of Foster, Yates and Thom Limited, Heavy Precision Engineers, 1937-50; Chairman or Member of number of wartime committees in Lancashire including Armaments Production, Emergency Services Organisation, and Ministry of Production; went to Ministry of Aircraft Production at request of Minister as Director of Engine Production, 1942; Deputy Director-General, 1943; Control of Directorate-Gen. including Propeller and Accessory Production, 1944; Part Time Member North Western Gas Board, 1949, Chairman, 1950-64; Chairman, Southern Gas Board, 1964-67; Member, Gas Council, 1950-67. Member, Ct of Govs, Univ. of Manchester Inst. of Sci. and Techn., 1956-64, 1968- (Mem. Coun., 1960-64, 1968-). CEng, FIMechE, FIEE, CIGasE. OStJ 1964, CStJ 1968. *Publications:* articles and papers on Company management. *Recreations:* sailing, fishing. *Address:* Yew Tree Cottage, Compton, near Winchester, Hampshire. *Clubs:* Royal Automobile; Royal Thames Yacht; Royal Southern Yacht.

**WELSH, Brig. David,** CBE 1959; DSO 1944; late Royal Artillery; Retired; *b* 10 April 1908; *s* of late Capt. Tom Welsh, Earlshaugh, Peebleshire; *m* 1947, Maud Elinor Mitchell, *d* of late Major M. I. M. Campbell, MC, of Auchmannoch; one *s*. *Educ:* Winchester; RMA. Commissioned 2nd Lieut, RA, 1928. Served War of 1939-45 (DSO): with Royal Horse Artillery and Royal Artillery in France, N Africa and Italy. Lt-Col, 1950; Brigadier, 1958; Brigadier, RA, FarELF, 1957-60; retd, 1961. *Address:* Abbeyfield, Tarvin, Chester. *Club:* Army and Navy.

**WELSH, Prof. Harry Lambert,** FRS 1962; FRSC 1952; Professor of Physics, University of Toronto, since 1954; *b* 23 March 1910, Canadian; *s* of Israel Welsh and Harriet Collingwood; *m* 1942, Marguerite Hazel Ostrander; no *c*. *Educ:* University of Toronto; University of Göttingen. Demonstrator in Physics, Univ. of Toronto, 1935-42; Asst Professor, 1942-48; Assoc. Professor, 1948-54; Chm., Dept of Physics, 1962-68. Lt-Comdr, RCNVR (Operational Research at Navy HQ, Ottawa), 1944-45. Medal of Cdn Assoc. of Physicists, 1961; Tory Medal, Royal Society of Canada, 1963. Hon. DSc: Univ. of Windsor, Ont., 1964; Memorial Univ., St Johns's, Newfoundland, 1968. *Publications:* many papers on infra-red and Raman spectroscopy and high-pressure physics in various scientific jls. *Recreation:* music. *Address:* Department of Physics, University of Toronto, Toronto 5, Ontario, Canada. *T:* 928-2939.

**WELSH, Dame Mary,** DBE 1946; **Ruth Mary Eldridge;** Legion of Merit, USA; *d* of late Dr William Dalzell; *m* 1922, Air Marshal Sir William Welsh, KCB, DSC, AFC (marriage dissolved, 1947; he *d* 1962); one *s*. Director WAAF, 1943-46. Air Chief Comdt, WRAF. *Address:* 3 Webb House, The Bury, Odiham, Hampshire.

**WELTY, Eudora.** *Publications:* A Curtain of Green, 1943; The Robber Bridegroom, 1944; The Wide Net, 1945; Delta Wedding, 1947; Golden Apples, 1950; The Ponder Heart, 1954; The Bride of Innisfallen, 1955; The Shoe Bird, 1964. *Address:* 1119 Pinehurst, Jackson, Miss., USA.

**WEMYSS,** 12th Earl of *cr* 1633, and **MARCH,** 8th Earl of *cr* 1697; **Francis David Charteris,** KT 1966; Lord Wemyss of Elcho, 1628; Lord Elcho and Methil, 1633; Viscount Peebles, Baron Douglas of Neidpath, Lyne and Munard, 1697; Baron Wemyss of Wemyss (UK), 1821; Lord Lieutenant of the County of East Lothian since 1967; Lord High Commissioner to the General Assembly of the Church of Scotland, 1959 and 1960; President, The National Trust for Scotland (Chairman of Council, 1947-69); Chairman of Royal Commission on Ancient and Historical Monuments and Constructions of Scotland; Chairman: Committee for Scotland, the Marie Curie Memorial Foundation; Scottish Churches Coun.; Mem. of Central Cttee of World Council of Churches; President, The Thistle Foundation; Director: Wemyss and March Estates Management Co. Ltd; Standard Life Assce Co.; Scottish Television; *b* 19 Jan. 1912; *s* of late Lord Elcho (killed in action, 1916) and Lady Violet Manners (she *m* 2nd, 1921, Guy Holford Benson, *qv*), 2nd *d* of 8th Duke of Rutland; *S* grandfather, 1937; *m* 1940, Mavis Lynette Gordon, BA, *er d* of late E. E. Murray, Hermanus, Cape Province; one *s* one *d* (and one *s* and one *d* decd). *Educ:* Eton; Balliol College, Oxford. Assistant District Commissioner, Basutoland, 1937-44. Served with Basuto Troops in Middle East, 1941-44. Hon. LLD St Andrews, 1953. *Heir:* *s* Lord Neidpath, *qv*. *Address:* Gosford House, Longniddry, East Lothian. *Clubs:* Turf; New (Edinburgh).

*See also Hon. Sir Martin Charteris.*

**WENBAN-SMITH, William,** CMG 1960; CBE 1957; *b* 8 June 1908; *o s* of Frederick Wenban-Smith, Worthing; *m* 1935, Ruth Orme, *e d* of S. B. B. McElderry, *qv*; three *s* two *d*. *Educ:* Bradfield; King's Coll., Cambridge (MA). Cadet, Zanzibar, 1931; Administrative Officer, Grade II, 1933; Asst DO, Tanganyika, 1935; DO, 1943; Sen. DO, 1951 (acted on various occasions as Resident Magistrate, Comr for Co-op. Development, Provincial Comr, and Sec. for Finance); Dir of Establishments, 1953; Minister for Social Services, 1958; Minister for Education and Labour, 1959; Chairman, Public Service Commission and Speaker, Legislative Council, Nyasaland, 1961-63. Pres., Tanganyika Soc., 1957-60 (Hon. Vice-Pres. 1961-). HM Diplomatic Service, Kuala Lumpur, 1964-69. *Recreations:* music, gardening, walking. *Address:* Crossways, Milford on Sea, Lymington, Hants. *T:* Milford on Sea 3207. *Club:* Royal Commonwealth Society.

**WENGER, Marjorie Lawson;** Senior Tutor, SEN School of Nursing, St Francis Hospital, SE22, 1967-70; *b* 10 Sept. 1910; *d* of late Rev. W. J. L. and Mrs A. M. Wenger. *Educ:* Walthamstow Hall, Sevenoaks, Kent. Nursing training, The Middlesex Hospital, 1930-34, SRN 1933; Midwifery training, SCM, 1935; Ward Sister, Night Sister; Sister Tutor, 1940-47. Editor, Nursing Times (Journal of the Royal College of Nursing), 1948-60; Editor, International Nursing Review (Jl of the International Council of Nurses), 1960-65; Nursing Editor, Pitman Medical Publishing Co., 1965-67. *Recreations:* reading, theatre, travel. *Address:* 5 Donne Court, Burbage Road, SE24. *Club:* Cowdray.

**WENNER, Michael Alfred;** HM Diplomatic Service, retired; *b* 17 March 1921; *s* of Alfred E. Wenner and of Simone Roussel; *m* 1950, Gunilla Cecilia Ståhle, *d* of Envoyé Nils K. Ståhle, CBE, and of Birgit Olsson; four *s*. *Educ:* Stonyhurst; Oriel College, Oxford (Scholar). Served E Yorks Regt, 1940; Lancs Fusiliers and 151 Parachute Bn, India, 1941-42; 156 Bn, N Africa, 1943; No 9 Commando, Italy and Greece, 1944-45. Entered HM Foreign Service, 1947; 3rd Sec., Stockholm, 1948-51; 2nd Sec., Washington, 1951-53; Foreign Office, 1953-55; 1st Sec., Tel Aviv, 1956-59; Head of Chancery, La Paz, 1959-61, and at Vienna, 1961-63; Inspector of Diplomatic Establishments, 1964-67; Ambassador to El Salvador, 1967-70. *Recreations:* fly-fishing, old maps. *Address:* c/o Foreign and Commonwealth Office, SW1.

**WENTWORTH, Maurice Frank Gerard,** CMG 1957; OBE 1946; Appointments Officer, Ministry of Overseas Development, since 1964; *b* 5 Nov. 1908; *s* of F. B. Wentworth, Finchley, N3; *m* 1962, Belinda Margaret, *d* of late B. S. Tatham and Mrs Tatham, Mickleham, Surrey; one *s* one *d*. *Educ:* Haileybury; University Coll., London (BA). Military Service, 1939-46, Lieutenant-Colonel. Gold Coast: Inspector of Schools, 1930; Sen. Education Officer, 1945; Principal, Teacher Training Coll., Tamale, 1946; Administrative Officer Class I, 1951; Permanent Secretary, 1953; Establishment Secretary, 1954-57 (Ghana Civil Service); Chairman: Public Service Commission: Sierra Leone, 1958-61; E African High Commn, 1961-64. *Club:* Public Schools.

**WENTWORTH-FITZWILLIAM;** *see* Fitzwilliam.

**WERE, Cecil Allan Walter,** CMG 1943; *b* 16 June 1889; *e s* of late Captain Walter Were, Dublin Fusiliers; *m* 1930, Elinor Louise Rogers; one *s* two *d.* *Educ:* Kelly College, Tavistock; Pembroke College, Cambridge. Entered Levant Consular Service, 1913; served in Egypt (Port Said and Alexandria), 1914-22, and in Morocco, at Tetuan, Tangier, and Marrakesh, 1922-27; Consul at Constantinople, 1928, and served there and at Trebizond until 1932; Consul at Bagdad, 1932-37; Consul-General at Cairo, 1937-43, for Eritrea, 1942-43 and at Alexandria, 1943-46; Consul-Gen. at Bâle, 1946-50; retd. 1950. *Recreations:* golf, bridge. *Address:* 11 The Esplanade, Fowey, Cornwall. *Club:* Royal Fowey Yacht.

**WERNER, Alfred Emil Anthony;** Keeper, British Museum Research Laboratory, since 1959; *b* 18 June 1911; *o s* of late Professor Emil Alphonse Werner, Dublin; *m* 1939, Marion Jane Davies; two *d.* *Educ:* St Gerard's School, Bray; Trinity College, Dublin. MSc (Dublin Univ.) and ARIC 1936; MA (Dublin) and DPhil (Univ. of Freiburg im Breisgau) 1937. Lecturer in Chemistry, TCD, 1937; Reader in Organic Chemistry, TCD, 1946; Research Chemist, National Gallery, 1948; Principal Scientific Officer, British Museum Research Laboratory, 1954. Prof. of Chemistry, Royal Acad., 1962. FSA 1958; FMA 1959 (President, 1967). FIWSc 1963; MRIA 1963. Hon. Treas., International Institute for the Conservation of Artistic and Historic Works, 1962. *Publications:* The Scientific Examination of Paintings, 1952; (with H. Roosen-Runge) Codex Lindisfarnensis, Part V, 1961; articles in scientific and museum journals. *Recreations:* chess, travelling. *Address:* Tudor Lodge, Redgrave, Diss, Norfolk. *T:* Botesdale 353. *Club:* Athenæum.

**WERNHAM, Prof. Archibald Garden,** MA Aberdeen, BA Oxford; Regius Professor of Moral Philosophy in the University of Aberdeen since 1960; *b* 4 March 1916; *e s* of Archibald Garden Wernham and Christina Noble; *m* 1944, Hilda Frances Clayton; two *s.* *Educ:* Robert Gordon's College, Aberdeen; Aberdeen University; Balliol College, Oxford. 1st Class Hons Classics, Aberdeen, 1938, Croom Robertson Fellow, Aberdeen, 1939; 1st Cl. Hons Classical Mods, Oxford, 1939, 1st Cl. Lit. Hum., Oxford, 1943. Served in RA, 1940-42. Lecturer in Moral and Political Philosophy, St Andrews Univ., 1945-53; Sen. Lecturer, 1953-59; Reader, 1959-60. *Publications:* Benedict de Spinoza–The Political Works, 1958; reviews and articles. *Recreations:* music, swimming, walking. *Address:* Department of Moral Philosophy, King's College, Old Aberdeen. *T:* 40241.

**WERNHAM, Prof. Richard Bruce,** MA Oxon; Professor of Modern History, Oxford University, since 1951; Fellow of Worcester College, Oxford, since 1951; *b* 11 Oct. 1906; *o s* of Richard George and Eleanor Mary Wernham; *m* 1939, Isobel Hendry Macmillan, Vancouver BC; one *d.* *Educ:* Newbury Grammar School; Exeter College, Oxford. Research Asst, Inst. of Historical Research, London Univ., 1929-30; Temp. Asst, Public Record Office, 1930-32; Editor, PRO, State Papers, Foreign Series. 1933-; Lecturer in Modern History, University Coll., London, 1933-34; Fellow of Trinity College, Oxford, 1934-51, Senior Tutor, 1940-41 and 1948-51; University Lecturer in Modern History, Oxford, 1941-51; Examiner in Final Honour School of Modern History, Oxford, 1946-48. Served in RAF, 1941-45. *Publications:* Before the Armada: the Growth of English Foreign Policy 1485-1558, 1966; Calendars of State Papers, Foreign Series, Elizabeth; (ed) Vol III, New Cambridge Modern History: The Counter-Reformation and Price Revolution, 1559-1610, 1968. Articles in English Hist. Review, History, Trans Royal Hist. Soc., Encyclopædia Britannica. *Address:* Worcester College, Oxford.

**WERNHER, Hon. Maj.-Gen. Sir Harold Augustus,** 3rd Bt, *cr* 1905; GCVO 1949 (KCVO 1930); TD; DL; President, Electrolux, Ltd, since 1963 (Chairman, 1926-63); Past Chairman Plessey Company; *b* 16 Jan. 1893; *s* of 1st Bt and Alice S. Mankiewicz (afterwards Lady Ludlow); *S* brother 1948; *m* 1917, Lady Anastasia (Zia) Michaelovna Torby, CBE 1956 (OBE 1946), DStJ (given precedence by royal warrant, 1917, as *d* of an Earl), *d* of Grand Duke Michael of Russia and late Countess de Torby; two *d* (one *s* killed in action, 1942). Served European War, 1914-18 (despatches); Lt-Col 5th Bn Beds and Herts Regt (TF); Col 1928, comdg; retd 1928; re-employed, 1939; Actg Brig. 1941; Actg Maj.-Gen. 1943; Hon. Major-General, 1944; Vice-Patron, University College Hospital, 1951- (Chm., 1945-51); Chairman, King Edward VII's Hosp. for Officers, 1941-69, Life Vice-Pres., 1969. DL Bedfordshire. A Knight Commander of the Swedish Order of Vasa, 1930; Knight Grand Cross of Swedish Order of the Pole Star, 1959; Legion of Merit degree of Officer, US Army, 1946. *Heir:* none. *Address:* 15 Grosvenor Square, W1; Luton Hoo, Luton, Beds.
*See also Major D. H. Butter.*

**WESIERSKA, Mrs George;** *see* Walder, Ruth C.

**WESIL, Dennis;** Director, London Postal Region, since 1970; *b* 18 Feb. 1915; *e s* of Jack and Polly Wesil, London; *m* 1941, Kathleen, *d* of H. S. McAlpine; two *d.* *Educ:* Central Foundation Sch.; University Coll., London. Entered London telephone service as Asst Supt of Traffic, 1937; PO Investigation Branch, 1941; Asst Postal Controller, 1947; Principal, PO Headqrtrs, 1953; Dep. Chief Inspector of Postal Services, 1961; Asst Sec. in charge of Postal Mechanisation Branch (GPO), 1963; Dep. Dir, NE Region (GPO), 1966; Dir, NE Postal Region, 1967. *Recreations:* music, theatre, reading, open air. *Address:* 502 Gilbert House, Barbican, EC2. *T:* 01-638 8201.

**WESKER, Arnold;** playwright; Director of Centre 42 since 1961; *b* 24 May 1932; *s* of Joseph Wesker and Leah Perlmutter; *m* 1958, Dusty Bicker; two *s* one *d.* *Educ:* Upton House School, Hackney. Furniture Maker's Apprentice, Carpenter's Mate, 1948; Bookseller's Asst, 1949 and 1952; Royal Air Force, 1950-52; Plumber's Mate, 1952; Farm Labourer, Seed Sorter, 1953; Kitchen Porter, 1953-54; Pastry Cook, 1954-58. Former Member, Youth Service Council. Author of plays: The Kitchen, produced at Royal Court Theatre, 1959, 1961; (filmed, 1961); Trilogy of plays (Chicken Soup with Barley, Roots, I'm Talking about Jerusalem) produced Belgrade Theatre (Coventry), 1959-60, Royal Court Theatre, 1959-60; Chips with Everything, Royal Court, 1962, Vaudeville, 1962 and Plymouth Theatre, Broadway, 1963; The Four Seasons, Belgrade Theatre (Coventry) and Saville, 1965; Their Very Own and Golden City, Royal Court, 1966; The Friends, Stockholm and London, 1970 (also dir). *Television:* (first play) Menace, 1963. *Publications:* Chicken Soup with Barley, 1959; Roots, 1959; I'm Talking about Jerusalem, 1960; The Wesker Trilogy, 1960; The Kitchen,

1961; Chips with Everything, 1962; The Four Seasons, 1966; Their Very Own and Golden City, 1966 (Marzotto Drama Prize, 1964); Fears of Fragmentation, 1970; The Friends, 1970. *Address:* 27 Bishops Road, N6.

**WESSEL, Robert Leslie,** OBE 1969; *b* 21 Oct. 1912; *s* of late H. L. Wessel, Copenhagen, Denmark; *m* 1936, Dora Elizabeth, *d* of G. C. G. Gee, Rothley, Leics; two *s* two *d. Educ:* Malvern College. Entered N. Corah & Sons Ltd, 1932. Served War of 1939-45, 44th Searchlight Regt RATA, 1939-41. Chairman, Council of Industrial Society; Member Governing Body City of Leicester Polytechnic; Pro-Chancellor, Loughborough University of Technology; Group Chairman, Duke of Edinburgh's Conference, 1956. Vice-Pres., British Assoc. of Industrial Editors; Mem., N and E Midlands Regional Bd, Lloyds Bank Ltd; Mem., E Midlands Electricity Bd. Dir, Loughborough Consultants Ltd. FBIM; FIWM. *Recreations:* painting, photography, music, travel. *Address:* The Mill House, 3 Home Farm Close, Old Woodhouse, Loughborough, Leics. *T:* Woodhouse Eaves 529.

**WEST;** *see* Sackville-West, family name of **Baron Sackville.**

**WEST,** family name of **Baron Granville-West** (Life Peer).

**WEST, Mrs Algernon;** *see* Young, Gladys.

**WEST, Maj.-Gen. Clement Arthur,** CB 1944; DSO 1932; MC 1915; idc; psc; RE; *b* Manmad, India, 13 Aug. 1892; *o s* of late Clement West, GIPR, India and Canterbury, Kent, England; *m* Margaret Elizabeth, *o d* of late Aylward Robert O'Conor, Somerton, Co. Dublin. *Educ:* King's School, Canterbury; RMA Woolwich. Commissioned RE 1912; served European War, France and Belgium, 1914-18 (MC, despatches twice); Captain 1917; Assistant Instructor Survey, SME, Chatham, 1919-22; General Staff War Office, 1923-26; Major, 1928; Brigade-Major, India, 1930-31; Operations, NWF, 1930-31 (DSO, despatches); General Staff, AHQ, India, 1932-34; Bt Lieut-Colonel, 1933; Deputy Assistant Military Secretary, War Office, 1934-36; Lieut-Col, 1936; Col, 1938; Deputy Military Secretary to Secretary of State for War, and Assistant Secretary of the Selection Board, War Office, 1938-39; Brig., General Staff, 1940-42; Delegation to New Zealand Govt, 1941; District Commander, 1942-43; Major-General, General Staff, 1943-45; Maj.-Gen. in charge Administration, Southern Command, 1945-46; retired, Jan. 1947. Gen. Sec., Royal United Kingdom Beneficent Assoc., 1947-57. *Recreations:* gardening, fishing, golf. *Address:* Kingsmal, Cross-in-Hand, Heathfield, Sussex. *Club:* Army and Navy.

**WEST, David Thomson;** Counsellor, HM Diplomatic Service, since 1964; *b* 10 March 1923; *m* 1958, Marie Sellar; one *s* one *d. Educ:* Malvern Coll.; St John's Coll., Oxford. Served in RNVR, 1942-45. Entered HM Foreign Service, 1946; served in Foreign Office, Office of Comr General for UK in SE Asia, HM Embassies, Paris, Lima, Tunis, and Berne, and as Commercial Inspector, Diplomatic Service. *Address:* 1 Thornhill Grove, N1. *T:* 01-607 2066. *Club:* Garrick.

**WEST, Air Commodore Ferdinand,** VC 1918; CBE 1945; MC; retired as Managing Director J. Arthur Rank Overseas Film Distributors (1947-58); Chairman: Hurst Park Syndicate; Continental Shipyard Agencies Ltd; Technical Equipment Supplies Ltd; Director, Tokalon Limited; *b* London, 29 Jan. 1896; *s* of late Francis West and late Countess De la Garde de Saignes; *g s* of Sir John West, Admiral of the Fleet; *m* Winifred, *d* of John Leslie; one *s. Educ:* Xaverian Coll., Brighton; Lycée Berchet; Univ. of Genoa. 2nd Lieutenant, Lieutenant, and Acting Captain in the Royal Munster Fusiliers, 1914-17; attached to the Flying Corps, 1917-18; transferred to the Royal Air Force as a Captain, 1919 (wounded three times, MC, VC, despatches twice, Cavaliere Crown of Italy); Commanded 4 Squadron, RAF, Farnborough, 1933-36; Air Attaché, British Legations, Helsingfors, Riga, Tallin, Kovno, 1936-38; Commanded, RAF Station, Odiham, 1938-40; Air Attaché, British Embassy, Rome, 1940; Air Attaché, British Legation, Berne, 1940; retired from RAF, 1946. Comdr Order of Orange Nassau, 1949; Chevalier Legion of Honour, 1958. First Class Army Interpreter (Italian) Second Class (French). *Address:* Zoar, Devenish Road, Sunningdale, Berks. *T:* Ascot 20579. *Club:* Royal Air Force.

**WEST, Rt. Rev. Francis Horner;** *see* Taunton, Suffragan Bishop of.

**WEST, Sir Frederick (John),** Kt 1960; OBE 1952; JP; *b* 29 March 1897; *s* of Frederick Hargrave and Martha West; *m* 1926, Frances (*née* Taylor); one *s* one *d. Educ:* William Morris School, Walthamstow. Member of London Stock Exchange, 1933; Director of companies. Diocesan Reader (Church of England) for Diocese of Chelmsford; JP Essex. Freeman of City of London; Mem. Bakers' Company and Gold and Silver Wire Drawers' Company. *Recreations:* walking, music, reading. *Address:* 75 Theydon Grove, Epping, Essex. *T:* 01-375 3304. *Clubs:* St Stephen's, City Livery.

**WEST, Rt. Rev. George Algernon,** MM; MA; *b* 17 Dec. 1893; *s* of George Algernon and Marion West; *m* 1st, 1923, Helen Margaret Scott Moncrieff (deceased); 2nd, 1943, Grace Hay. *Educ:* S Bees School; Lincoln College, Oxford. Served in Serbia with Serbian Relief Fund, 1915; in France with Royal Garrison Artillery, Corporal; MM 1918. Went to Burma under SPG 1921; Bishop of Rangoon, 1935-54. Asst Bishop of Durham, 1965-68, resigned. *Publications:* Jungle Folk (with D. C. Atwool); Jungle Friends, 1937; The World that Works, 1944. *Address:* Lever Flat, Sherburn House, Durham. *Club:* Royal Over-Seas League.

**WEST, Rt. Hon. Henry William,** PC (N Ire) 1960; MP (N Ire) Enniskillen since 1954; Minister of Agriculture, 1960-67; *b* 27 March 1917; *s* of late W. H. West, JP; *m* 1956, Maureen Elizabeth Hall; three *s* three *d. Educ:* Enniskillen Model School; Portora Royal School. Farmer; N Ireland representative on British Wool Marketing Board, 1950-58; President, Ulster Farmers' Union, 1955-56. High Sheriff, Co. Fermanagh, 1954. Parliamentary Secretary to Minister of Agriculture (NI), 1958. *Address:* Rossahilly House, Enniskillen. *T:* Killadeas 231.

**WEST, Prof. John Clifford,** PhD, DSc; CEng; FIEE; Professor of Electrical and Control Engineering and Dean of the School of Applied Sciences, University of Sussex, since 1965; Pro-Vice-Chancellor, since 1967; Director of the Philatelic Centre, since 1970; *b* 4 June 1922; *s* of J. H. West and Mrs West (*née* Ascroft); *m* 1946, Winefride Mary Turner; three *d. Educ:* Hindley and Abram Grammar School; Victoria Univ., Manchester. PhD 1953, DSc 1957. Matthew Kirtley Entrance Schol., Manchester Univ., 1940. Electrical Lieutenant, RNVR, 1943-46. Lecturer, University of Manchester, 1946-57; Professor of Electrical Engineering, The Queen's University of Belfast, 1958-65. Director, A. C. E. Machinery Ltd, 1966-. Member: Science Res. Council Cttee on Systems and Electrical Engineering, 1963-67; Technology Sub-Cttee, UGC 1966-; Civil Service Commn Special Merit Promotions Panel, 1966-; Naval Educn Adv. Cttee, 1965-. Chm., Automation and Control Div., IEE, 1970-71 (Vice-Chm., 1967-70). Member: Royal Philatelic Soc., 1960-; Sociedad Filatélica de Chile, 1970-. *Publications:* Textbook of Servomechanisms, 1953; Analytical Techniques for Non-Linear Control Systems, 1960; papers in Proc. IEE, Trans Amer. IEE, Brit. Jl of Applied Physics, Jl of Scientific Instruments, Proc. Soc. of Instrument Technology. *Recreation:* philately. *Address:* 17 Eldred Avenue, Withdean, Brighton, Sussex BN1 5EB. *T:* Brighton 554819. *Club:* Athenæum.

**WEST, Col John Milns,** CBE 1960; TD 1938; DL; Vice-Chairman, Combined Cadet Force Association, since 1950; *b* 30 May 1897; *s* of John Henry West; *m* 1934, Katherine Mary, *d* of Robert Scott, Toronto; two *d. Educ:* Shrewsbury; King's College, Cambridge (choral scholar). Served European War, 1914-19 with Rifle Brigade (SR); Adjutant 2nd Bn Rifle Bde, 1918. Assistant Master, Shrewsbury School, 1922; Housemaster, 1945, retired 1957. Staff Capt. OTC Camps, 1924-28; comd Shrewsbury Sch. OTC, 1928-38. Served War of 1939-45: 9th Bn Royal Welch Fusiliers; comd 70th Bn RWF; Lt-Col 1941; comd Infantry NCOs' Sch., 1942-45; Col 1944; comd NCOs' Wing Sch. of Infantry, 1945. Chm. Shrewsbury Branch, British Legion, 1927-34; Vice-Chm., Shropshire Committee, British Legion, 1930-34, Chm., 1959-61; Comr St John Amb. Bde (Salop), 1956-67; Governor: Royal Normal School for the Blind, 1958-; Shrewsbury School, 1961-. Mem. Salop T&AFA, 1947-68. Mem. Shrewsbury Borough Council, 1930-66; Alderman, 1949; Mayor, 1952; DL Salop, 1955. CStJ. *Recreations:* golf, gardening. *Address:* Dorrington House, Dorrington, Shropshire. *T:* Dorrington 396. *Club:* Public Schools.

**WEST, Gen. Sir Michael (Montgomerie Alston Roberts),** GCB 1964 (KCB 1959; CB 1951); DSO and Bar 1945, 2nd Bar, 1953; *b* 27 Oct. 1905; *s* of Capt. H. C. J. Alston-Roberts-West, RN; *m* 1935, Christine Sybil Oppenheim; one *d. Educ:* Uppingham; Royal Military College, Sandhurst. 2nd Lt Oxford and Bucks Light Infantry, 1925. Served War of 1939-45; Brigade Major, 165 Brigade; Commanding 2nd South Lancashire Regt; Dep. Comdr 72 Indian Infantry Brigade; Commander 5 Infantry Brigade; Commandant, School of Infantry, 1946-48; Dep. Director, Man Power Planning, War Office, 1949-50; GOC-in-C British Troops in Austria, 1950-52; Commander, Commonwealth Division, Korea, 1952-53; Director, Territorial Army, War Office, 1955-57; Commander 1st British Corps, BAOR, 1958-59; GOC-in-C, Northern Command, 1960-62; Head of British Defence Staff, Washington, and UK Representative on the NATO Standing Group, 1962-65. Commander, US Legion of Merit, 1954. *Recreations:* undisclosed. *Address:* 28 Laxford House, Cundy Street, SW1; Hope Cottage, Bembridge, Isle of Wight. *Clubs:* White's, Annabel's.

**WEST, Morris (Langlo);** author; *b* 26 April 1916; *s* of Charles Langlo West and Florence Guilfoyle Hanlon; *m* 1953, Joyce Lawford; three *s* one *d. Educ:* Univ. of Melbourne (BA). Served, Lieutenant, AIF, South Pacific, 1939-43. Secretary to William Morris Hughes, former Prime Minister of Australia. FRSL; Fellow World Acad. of Art and Science. Hon. DLitt, Univ. of Santa Clara. *Publications:* Gallows on the Sand, 1955; Kundu, 1956; Children of the Sun, 1957; The Crooked Road, 1957 (Eng.: The Big Story); Backlash, 1958 (Eng.: Second Victory); The Devil's Advocate, 1959 (National Brotherhood Award, National Council of Christians and Jews 1960; James Tait Black Memorial Prize, 1960; RSL Heinemann Award, 1960); Daughter of Silence, 1961; The Shoes of the Fisherman, 1963; The Ambassador, 1965; The Tower of Babel, 1968; The Heretic (stage drama), 1970; (jt author) Scandal in the Assembly, 1970. *Address:* (office) c/o Paul R. Reynolds & Son, 599 Fifth Avenue, New York, NY 10017, USA. *Club:* Royal Prince Alfred Yacht (Sydney).

**WEST, Dame Rebecca,** DBE 1959 (CBE 1949); CLit 1968; *b* Christmas, 1892; Cicily Isabel, *y d* of late Charles Fairfield, Co. Kerry; *m* 1930, Henry Maxwell Andrews (*d* 1968). *Educ:* George Watson's Ladies' College, Edinburgh. Joined Staff of Freewoman as reviewer, 1911; joined staff of The Clarion as political writer, 1912; has since contributed to many leading English and American newspapers as literary critic and political writer. Member American Academy of Arts and Sciences. Hon. DLitt, New York University, USA. Benson Medal (RSL), 1966. Order of Saint Sava, 1937; Chevalier of the Legion of Honour, 1957. *Publications:* Henry James, 1916; The Return of the Soldier, 1918; The Judge, 1922; The Strange Necessity, 1928; Lions and Lambs (pseudonym Lynx in collaboration with Low); Harriet Hume, 1929; D. H. Lawrence, an Elegy, 1930; Ending in Earnest, 1931 (published in America only); St Augustine, 1933; The Rake's Progress (in collaboration with Low), 1934; The Harsh Voice, 1935; The Thinking Reed, 1936; Black Lamb and Grey Falcon (a book about Yugoslavia), 1942; The Meaning of Treason, 1949; A Train of Powder, 1955; The Fountain Overflows, 1957; The Court and the Castle, 1958; The Vassall Affair, 1963; The New Meaning of Treason, 1964; The Birds Fall Down, 1966. *Address:* 148 Kingston House North, Princes Gate, SW7.

**WEST, Dr Richard Gilbert,** FRS 1968; FGS; Fellow of Clare College, Cambridge, since 1954; Director, Subdepartment of Quaternary Research, University of Cambridge since 1966, and Reader in Quaternary Research since 1967; *b* 31 May 1926; *m* 1958, Janet Abram; one *s. Educ:* King's School, Canterbury; Univ. of Cambridge. Univ. Demonstrator in Botany, 1957-60; Univ. Lecturer in Botany, 1960-67. Darwin Lecturer to the British Association, 1959; Lyell Fund, 1961, Bigsby Medal, 1969, Geological Society of London. *Publication:* Pleistocene Geology and Biology, 1968. *Address:* Woodlands, 3 Woollards Lane, Great Shelford, Cambs. *T:* Shelford 2578; Clare College, Cambridge.

**WEST, Dr William Dixon,** CIE 1947; Director of the Geological Survey of India; *b* 1901; *s* of Arthur Joseph West. *Educ:* King's School, Canterbury; St John's College, Cambridge. *Address:* c/o Geological Dept, Indian Museum, Calcutta.

**WEST AFRICA, Archbishop of,** since 1969, and Bishop of Sierra Leone since 1961; **Most Rev. Moses Nathanael Christopher Omobiala Scott, CBE 1970;** Hon. DD Durham; *b* 18 Aug. 1911; *s* of late Christopher Columbus Scott, Hastings Village, Sierra Leone, and Cleopatra Eliza Scott, York Village; *m* 1941, Cordelia Elizabeth Deborah Maddy, Gloucester Village; three *s* two *d. Educ:* CMS Grammar School and Fourah Bay Coll., Freetown,

Sierra Leone. Deacon 1943; Priest, 1946. Curate of: Lunsar, 1943-44; Yongro, Bullom, 1944-47; Missionary-in-charge of Makeni, 1946-48, of Bo, 1948-50; studied at London College of Divinity for DipTheol, 1950; Curate of Grappenhall, Cheshire, 1951-53; returned to Bo, 1954; Priest in charge, Bo District, 1954-57; Archdeacon of Missions, Sierra Leone, 1957-59; Archdeacon of Bonthe and Bo, 1959-61. Hon. DD Durham, 1962. *Recreations:* playwriting, swimming (sea-side). *Address:* Bishopscourt, Freetown, Sierra Leone. *T:* Freetown 2555.

**WEST INDIES, Archbishop of,** since 1950, and Bishop of Guyana, since 1937; **Most Rev. Alan John Knight,** CMG 1954; DD; Sub-Prelate of The Venerable Order of St John of Jerusalem; *s* of John William Knight and Henrietta E. A. Shillito. *Educ:* Owen's School; Cambridge (MA, LLB). DD (Lambeth) 1950. Asst Master University College School (Junior School), 1923; Bishop's College, Cheshunt, 1924; Deacon, 1925; Priest, 1926; Curate at St James', Enfield Highway, 1925-28; Headmaster of Adisadel College, Gold Coast, 1928-37. FCP 1966. *Address:* Austin House, Georgetown, Guyana. *T:* Georgetown 4239; c/o Westminster Bank Ltd, Felixstowe, Suffolk.

**WEST-RUSSELL, David (Sturrock); His Honour Judge West-Russell;** Deputy Chairman, Inner London Quarter Sessions, since 1966; *b* 17 July 1921; *o s* of late Sir Alexander West-Russell and late Agnes West-Russell; *m* Christine, *y d* of Sidney and Gladys Tyler; one *s* two *d*. *Educ:* Rugby; Pembroke Coll., Cambridge. Commissioned Queen's Own Cameron Highlanders, 1941; Parachute Regt, 1942-46; served in N Africa, Italy, France, Greece, Norway and Palestine (despatches, Maj.). Harmsworth Law Scholar, 1952; called to Bar, Middle Temple, 1953; SE Circuit; Member, Departmental Committee on Legal Aid in Criminal Proceedings, 1964-65. *Address:* Edgehill, Limpsfield, Surrey. *T:* Limpsfield Chart 2164. *Clubs:* Bath, Royal Automobile.

**WESTALL, Gen. Sir John Chaddesley,** KCB 1954 (CB 1952); CBE 1951; *b* 2 July 1901; *s* of late John Chaddesley Westall, Hawkes Bay, NZ; *m* 1930, Maud Marion Bushe; two *s* one *d*. *Educ:* Dulwich College. Entered Royal Marines, Oct. 1919; Capt. 1930; Major 1939; Naval Staff College, 1938. Served War of 1939-45: Malaya, India and Burma; promoted Bt Lt-Col for War Service, 1944. Staff Officer Intelligence, South Africa, 1947. Comd Royal Marine Barracks, Plymouth, 1949; Comd Royal Marines, Deal, 1950; Maj.-Gen. 1951; Chief of Staff, Royal Marines, 1951; Commandant General, Royal Marines, 1952-55; retired, 1955. Col Comdt, Royal Marines, 1961-64. Director: United Dominions Trust Ltd, Haleybridge Investment Trust Ltd, Forbes Campbell & Co. Ltd. *Recreations:* fishing, shooting. *Address:* Gorse Cottage, Petworth Road, Haslemere. *Club:* United Service.

**WESTALL, Rupert Vyvyan Hawksley,** MA Cantab; Lieutenant Commander RN (retired); Head Master, Kelly College, Tavistock, Devon, 1939-59; *b* 27 July 1899; *s* of late Rev. William Hawksley Westall and Adela Clara Pope; *m* 1925, Sylvia G. D. Page; two *s* three *d*. *Educ:* RN Colleges Osborne and Dartmouth; Queens' College, Cambridge. Royal Navy, 1912-22; served European War, 1914-18; served in HMS Goliath, HMS Canada, HMS Ure and four years in The Submarine Service; Service on East African Station and Gallipoli, 1914-15, Jutland, China Station; Queens' College, Cambridge, 1922-26 (Exhibitioner in History, MA 1926, 1st division 2nd class both parts History Tripos); Training College for Schoolmasters, Cambridge, 1925-26; VI form and Careers Master, Blundell's School, 1926-34; Head Master West Buckland School, 1934-38. *Address:* Penrose, Kimberley Place, Falmouth, Cornwall.

**WESTALL, Rt. Rev. W. A. E.;** *see* Crediton, Bishop of.

**WESTAWAY, Katharine Mary,** MA (Cantab), DLit (London); Headmistress, Bedford High School, 1924-49; retd 1949; *b* 1893; *d* of late F. W. Westaway, formerly HMI Secondary Schools. *Educ:* Bedford High School; Newnham College, Cambridge (Open Classical Scholar); Classical Tripos, Parts I and II. University of Leyden. Classical Mistress, Cheltenham Ladies' College, 1917-19; Marion Kennedy Research Student, Newnham College, 1919-20; Staff Lecturer in Classics, Royal Holloway College, University of London; member of University Boards of Studies in Classics and History; University Examiner in Classics, 1920-24; Member of the Bedford Borough Education Committee, 1924-45; Lectr Yorks Fedn of Women's Institutes, 1951-65. *Publications'* Original Element in Plautus; Educational Theory of Plutarch; Selections from Plautus; A History of the Bedford High School (editor and contributor); Old Girls in New Times; Unwillingly to School?; A Year in our Village; Cloudy Summits; A Wonderful Town; Seventy-five Years (editor and contributor). *Recreations:* photography, music. *Address:* 128 Foster Hill Road, Bedford.

**WESTBROOK, Neil Gowanloch;** Director, Trafford Park Estates Ltd; Executive Director, Fore Street Investments Ltd; *b* 21 Jan. 1917; *s* of Frank and Dorothy Westbrook; *m* 1945, Hon. Mary Joan Fraser, *o d* of 1st Baron Strathalmond, CBE; one *s* one *d*. *Educ:* Oundle Sch.; Clare Coll., Cambridge (MA). FRICS, FAI 1939. Served War of 1939-45: Sapper, then 2nd Lieut, RE, 1939; BEF, France, 1939-40; Malta, 1941; WO, 1943-44; Bde Major, 11th Armd Bde, France, Belgium, Holland, Germany, 1944-46; Actg Lt-Col 1946 (despatches twice). Treas., Manchester Area Conservative Assoc., 1964-; Manchester City Council, 1949-70: Alderman 1967; Dep. Leader 1967-69; Lord Mayor 1969-70. Chm., North Western Art Galleries and Museums Service, 1965-68; Mem., Exec. Cttee, Museums Assoc., 1965-69. *Recreations:* football, fishing, horse racing. *Address:* White Gables, Prestbury, Cheshire. *T:* Prestbury 89337. *Clubs:* St James's (Manchester); Lyford Cay (New Providence, Bahamas).

**WESTBROOK, Trevor Cresswell Lawrence,** CBE 1945; AFRAeS; MIPE; MInstM; Production Consultant since 1945; Chairman, Sidney Flavel & Co. Ltd; Director of a number of companies; *b* 14 January 1901; *s* of late Dr Ernest Westbrook; *m* 1942, Shielah Gillham; one *s* one *d*. *Educ:* Epsom College. Gen. Man. Vickers Supermarine, 1929-36; Gen. Man. Vickers Aviation Section, 1937-40; joined MAP 1940, Director of Aircraft Repairs and all American Aircraft Purchases and later in charge of Aircraft Programme; Member of Minister's Council, June 1941; Adviser to Intendant-General, Sept. 1941; Production Adviser to Ministry of Supply, Sept. 1941-Jan. 1942; Member first Churchill mission to USA, 1942; Production Controller de Havilland Aircraft, 1942-45; responsible for production of Schneider Spitfire and Wellington aircraft. Also productionising Mosquito; Production adviser to De Havillands Canada temporary war assignment. *Address:* Flat J, 42 Eaton

Square, SW1. *Clubs:* Royal Thames Yacht, Royal Air Force.

**WESTBURY,** 5th Baron, *cr* 1861, **David Alan Bethell,** MC 1942; *b* 16 July 1922; *s* of Captain The Hon. Richard Bethell (*d* 1929; *o c* of 3rd Baron); *S* brother, 1961; *m* 1947, Ursula Mary Rose James; two *s* one *d. Educ:* Harrow. 2nd Lieut 1940, Capt. 1944, Scots Guards. Equerry to the Duke of Gloucester, 1946-49. *Heir: s* Hon. Richard Nicholas Bethell, *b* 29 May 1950. *Address:* Barton Cottage, Malton, Yorkshire. *T:* Malton 2293. *Club:* Turf.

**WESTBURY, Marjorie;** *see* Westbury, R. M.

**WESTBURY, (Rose) Marjorie;** Singer and Actress; *b* 18 June 1905; *o d* of George and Adella Westbury, Langley, Near Birmingham. Won 4 year scholarship to RCM, London, 1927. Sang Gretel at Old Vic as operatic debut for Lilian Baylis, 1932. Began broadcasting (as singer), 1933; joined BBC Drama Repertory, 1942; Solveig in Peer Gynt; Ylena (Lorca); Miles and Flora in Turn of the Screw; Nora in The Doll's House; Elsa Strauss in the Henry Reed series (Emily Butter); Steve Temple in Paul Temple series. *Recreations:* gardening, cooking, sewing, reading maps. *Address:* The Hundred House, Framfield, near Uckfield, Sussex. *T:* Framfield 377.

**WESTCOTT, George Foss,** MA, MIMechE; freelance, since 1957; *b* 6 Feb. 1893; *e s* of Rev. Arthur Westcott, 2nd *s* of Brooke Foss Westcott, Bishop of Durham; *m* 1938, Anne Esther Anderberg; two *d. Educ:* Sherborne; GNR Locomotive Works, Doncaster (Premium Apprentice); Queens' College, Cambridge (Exhibitioner). Served in European War, 1914-19, in ASC (MT) and RFC; Hons Mechanical Science Tripos, 1920; worked for Scientific and Industrial Research Department, 1920; Assistant at Science Museum, 1921; Keeper, 1937; on loan to Admiralty Engineering Lab., 1939; Emergency Commn in RASC, 1941-42; Science Museum, 1942; Keeper of Dept of Land And Water Transport, 1950; retired 1953; re-engaged as Asst Keeper, 1953; finally retired from Civil Service, 1957; worked for Intercontinental Marketing Services Ltd, 1963; Reader, Acad. of Visual Arts, 1964; founded Basic Ideology Research Unit, 1967. *Publications:* Science Museum Handbooks; Pumping Machinery, 1932; Mechanical and Electrical Engineering, 1955 (New edn, 1960); The British Railway Locomotive, 1803-1853, 1958; Various historical Synopses of Events Charts, 1922-56; The Conflict of Ideas, 1967; Christianity, Freethinking and Sex, 1968. *Recreations:* sociological research, reading. *Address:* 1 Netherlands Court, Eaton Road, Sutton, Surrey. *T:* 01-643 2837.

**WESTENRA,** family name of **Baron Rossmore.**

**WESTERMAN, Sir (Wilfred) Alan,** Kt 1963; CBE 1962 (OBE 1957); EdD; MAEcon; Secretary, Department of Trade and Industry, Canberra, since 1960; *b* NZ, 25 March 1913; *s* of W. J. Westerman, Sydney, NSW. *Educ:* Knox Grammar School; Universities of Tasmania, Melbourne and Columbia. Chairman, Commonwealth Tariff Board, 1958-60. *Recreations:* tennis, squash. *Address:* c/o Department of Trade and Industry, Canberra, ACT, Australia. *Clubs:* Commonwealth (Canberra); Athenæum (Melbourne).

**WESTERN, Prof. John Henry,** BSc, PhD (Wales); Professor of Agricultural Botany in the Department of Agricultural Sciences, University of Leeds, since 1959; *b* Ide, Devon, 29 Sept. 1906; *s* of late Henry Toogood and Emma Western, Dawlish, Devon; *m* 1940, Rachel Elizabeth Harries; one *s. Educ:* University College of Wales, Aberystwyth; University of Minnesota, USA. Research on diseases of pasture plants, Welsh Plant Breeding Station, Aberystwyth, 1937-39; Lecturer and Adviser in Agricultural Botany and Mycology, University of Manchester, 1939-46; Provincial Plant Pathologist, Ministry of Agriculture and Fisheries, Newcastle upon Tyne, 1946-50; Senior Lecturer in Agricultural Botany, University of Leeds, 1951-59. Pres., Assoc. Applied Biologists, 1964-65. *Publications:* papers on mycology, plant pathology and agricultural botany in various scientific journals. *Address:* School of Agricultural Sciences, University of Leeds. *T:* Leeds 31751/ext. 364.

**WESTHOFF, Mrs Robert James;** *see* Sagan, Françoise.

**WESTLAKE, Alan Robert Cecil,** CSI 1947; CIE 1943; *b* 18 July 1894; *s* of late Robert Hole and of Gertrude Westlake; *m* 1916, Dorothy Louise Turner (*d* 1966); one *s* three *d*; *m* 1966, Isabel Flora Beck. *Educ:* at a Council School; University College School; Brasenose College, Oxford. DCLI (TF), 1914-18, retiring with rank of Capt.; Political Dept, Iraq, 1919-21; entered ICS 1921. Collector and District Magistrate. Director of Agriculture, 1948. Secretary Revenue, Development Depts. Member Board of Revenue, Madras; retd. *Address:* Chanctonbury, Fuller's Road, Rowledge, Farnham, Surrey. *T:* Frensham 2658.

*See also P. A. G. Westlake.*

**WESTLAKE, Sir Charles (Redvers),** Kt 1954; *b* 25 April 1900; *s* of Capt. H. Westlake; *m* 1st, 1929, Winifred Lucy Luxton (*d* 1965), *d* of F. W. Western, Biggleswade, Beds; two *d*; 2nd, 1968, Evelyn Isabel, *d* of Christian Aistrup, Capetown. County Electrical Engineer, Dumfriesshire, 1929; Chief Engineer and Manager, Electricity Board for N Ireland, 1931; General Manager and Engineer, Finchley Corporation Electricity Dept, 1936. Member Council IEE 1936-39. GSO1, War Office, 1943-44. Member, Uganda Legislative Council, 1954-55; Chairman Uganda Electricity Board, 1947-55; Chairman: Metal Industries Ltd, 1956-64; Williams & Williams (Reliance Holdings) Ltd, 1963-68; S. W. Wood Group Ltd, 1968-70. *Recreation:* golf. *Address:* Avenue Bartolomeu Dias 131, Cascais, Portugal. *T:* 28.3610. *Clubs:* Athenæum; Royal British (Lisbon).

**WESTLAKE, Prof. Henry Dickinson;** Hulme Professor of Greek in the University of Manchester, since 1949; *b* 4 Sept. 1906; *s* of late C. A. Westlake and late Charlotte M. Manlove; *m* 1940, Mary Helen Sayers; one *s* one *d. Educ:* Uppingham School; St John's College, Cambridge (Scholar). Strathcona Student, 1929; Assistant Lecturer, University College, Swansea, 1930-32; Fellow of St John's College, Cambridge, 1932-35; Assistant Lecturer, University of Bristol, 1936-37; Lecturer, King's College, Newcastle, 1937-46; Administrative Assistant, Ministry of Home Security, 1941-44; Reader in Greek, University of Durham, 1946-49; Dean of the Faculty of Arts, Univ. of Manchester, 1960-61; Pro-Vice-Chancellor, 1965-68. *Publications:* Thessaly in the Fourth Century BC, 1935; Timoleon and his relations with tyrants, 1952; Individuals in Thucydides, 1968; Essays on the Greek Historians and Greek History, 1969. Articles and reviews in learned periodicals. *Recreation:* walking. *Address:* Birk

Crag, Eccles Road, Chapel-en-le-Frith, Stockport. *T:* Chapel-en-le-Frith 3112.

**WESTLAKE, Peter Alan Grant,** MC 1943; Counsellor, British High Commission, Canberra; *b* 2 Feb. 1919; *s* of A. R. C. Westlake, *qv*; *m* 1943, Katherine Spackman; two *s*. *Educ:* Sherborne; Corpus Christi Coll., Oxford; Military College of Science. Served with 1st Regt RHA (Adjt 1942), and on the staff. HM Foreign Service (now Diplomatic Service), 1946; served in Japan and at Foreign Office, Joint Services Staff College, 1954; Israel, 1955; Japan, 1957; Administrative Staff Coll., 1961; Foreign Office, 1961; Washington, 1965. *Address:* c/o 8 Mulberry Court, Goring-by-Sea, Sussex.

**WESTMEATH,** 12th Earl of *cr* 1621, **Gilbert Charles Nugent;** Baron Delvin, by tenure temp. Henry II; by summons, 1486; *b* 9 May 1880; 3rd *s* of 10th Earl and Emily, *d* of Andrew William Blake, JP, DL, Furbough, Co. Galway; *S* brother, 1933; *m* 1915, Doris (*d* 1968), 2nd *d* of C. Imlach, Liverpool; one *s* one *d*. *Heir:* *s* Lord Delvin, *qv*. *Address:* Golden Meadow, Gulval, Penzance, Cornwall. *T:* Penzance 2049.

**WESTMINSTER,** 5th Duke of, *cr* 1874; **Robert George Grosvenor,** TD, DL, JP; Bt 1622; Baron Grosvenor, 1761; Earl Grosvenor and Viscount Belgrave, 1784; Marquess of Westminster, 1831; Senator, Northern Ireland Parliament, 1964-67; *b* 24 April 1910; *yr s* of Captain Lord Hugh William Grosvenor, 1st Life Guards (killed in action, 1914), and Lady Mabel Hamilton-Stubber, MBE (*d* 1944); *S* brother, 4th Duke of Westminster, 1967; *m* 1946, Hon. Viola Maud Lyttelton, *e surv d* of 9th Viscount Cobham, KCB, TD, Hagley Hall, Worcestershire; one *s* two *d*. *Educ:* Eton. 2nd Lt City of London Yeo., 1938; served 1939-45 with RA (Middle East), Lt-Col, 1943; Maj., City of London Yeo., 1946-49; Maj. North Irish Horse, 1949, Lieutenant-Colonel, 1953-56. MP (UU) Fermanagh and South Tyrone, 1955-64; PPS to the Foreign Secretary (Mr Selwyn Lloyd), 1957-59. Freeman: The Goldsmiths' Company; City of London; City of Chester. A Younger Brother of Trinity House, 1970-. Joint Master, Fermanagh Harriers, 1959-62. JP 1950, DL 1953, Co. Fermanagh; High Sheriff, 1952; DL Cheshire, 1970. Hon. ADC to Governor of N Ireland, 1953-55. CStJ. *Recreations:* sailing, shooting, fishing. *Heir:* *s* Earl Grosvenor, *qv*. *Address:* Eaton, Chester; Grosvenor Estate Office, 53 Davies Street, W1. *T:* 01-629 1616; Ely Lodge, Enniskillen, Co. Fermanagh, Northern Ireland. *T:* Springfield 224. *Clubs:* Turf, MCC, Royal Ocean Racing; Royal Yacht Squadron; Ulster (Belfast).

**WESTMINSTER, Cardinal Archbishop of; His Eminence Cardinal John Carmel Heenan,** DD, PhD; Archbishop of Westminster since 1963; Cardinal since 1965; *b* 26 January 1905; *s* of James Carmel and Anne Heenan (*née* Pilkington). *Educ:* Ushaw; English Coll., Rome. Ordained, 1930; work in East End of London, 1931-47; Superior of the Catholic Missionary Society, 1947-51; Bishop of Leeds, 1951-57; Archbishop of Liverpool and Metropolitan of Northern Province with Suffragan Sees, Hexham, Lancaster, Leeds, Middlesbrough and Salford, 1957-63. *Publications:* Priest and Penitent, 1936; Cardinal Hinsley, 1945; Letters from Rush Green, 1948; The People's Priest, 1951; Our Faith, 1957; My Lord and My God, 1958; (co-author) Dialogue: The State of the Church Today, 1968. *Address:* Archbishop's House, Westminster, SW1.

**WESTMINSTER, Auxiliary Bishops of, (RC);** *see* Butler, Rt Rev. B. C., Guazzelli, Rt Rev. V., Mahon, Rt Rev. G. T.

**WESTMINSTER, Dean of;** *see* Abbott, Very Rev. Eric Symes.

**WESTMINSTER, Sub-Dean of;** *see* Warren, Rev. Canon Max Alexander Cunningham.

**WESTMINSTER, Archdeacon of;** *see* Carpenter, Ven. E. F.

**WESTMORLAND,** 15th Earl of *cr* 1624, **David Anthony Thomas Fane,** KCVO 1970; Baron Burghersh, 1624; late RHG; a Lord in Waiting to the Queen since 1955; *b* 31 March 1924; *e s* of 14th Earl of Westmorland and Hon. Diana Lister, *widow* of Capt. Arthur Edward Capel, CBE, and *y d* of 4th Baron Ribblesdale; *S* father 1948; *m* 1950, Jane, *d* of Lt-Col Sir Roland Lewis Findlay, Bt, *qv*; two *s* one *d*. Served War of 1939-45 (wounded); resigned from RHG with hon. rank of Lieut, 1950. *Heir:* *s* Lord Burghersh, *qv*. *Address:* 7 Porchester Terrace, W2.

**WESTMORLAND and FURNESS, Archdeacon of;** *see* Hare, Ven. T. R.

**WESTOLL, James,** DL; JP; *b* 26 July 1918; *s* of late James Westoll, Glingerbank, Longtown; *m* 1946, Sylvia Jane Luxmoore, MBE, *d* of late Lord Justice Luxmoore, Bilsington, Kent; two *s* two *d*. *Educ:* Eton; Trinity College, Cambridge (MA). Served War of 1939-45: Major, The Border Regiment (despatches). Called to Bar, Lincoln's Inn, 1952. Member, NW Electricity Board, 1959-66; Additional Deputy Chm., Cumberland Quarter Sessions, 1960-; Chairman, Cumberland County Council, 1958-; CC 1947, CA 1959, JP 1960, DL 1963, High Sheriff 1964, Cumberland. OStJ 1969. *Recreations:* gardening, shooting, fishing. *Address:* Dykeside, Longtown, Cumberland. *T:* Longtown 235; 5 Royal Avenue, SW3. *T:* 01-730 3046. *Clubs:* Boodle's, Oxford and Cambridge, Farmers', County and Border (Carlisle).

**WESTOLL, Prof. Thomas Stanley,** FRS 1952; FRSE, FGS; BSc, PhD (Dunelm), DSc (Aberdeen); J. B. Simpson Professor of Geology, University of Newcastle upon Tyne (formerly King's College, Newcastle upon Tyne, University of Durham), since 1948; *b* W Hartlepool, Durham, 3 July 1912; *e s* of Horace Stanley Raine Westoll; *m* 1st, 1939, Dorothy Cecil Isobel Wood (marriage dissolved, 1951); one *s*; 2nd, 1952, Barbara Swanson McAdie. *Educ:* West Hartlepool Grammar School; Armstrong (later King's) Coll., Univ. of Durham; University College, London. Senior Research Award, DSIR, 1934-37; Lecturer in Geology, Univ. of Aberdeen, 1937-48; Alexander Agassiz Visiting Professor of Vertebrate Paleontology, Harvard University, 1952; Huxley Lectr, Univ. of Birmingham, 1967. J. B. Tyrell Fund, 1937, and Daniel Pidgeon Fund, 1939, Geological Soc. of London. President: Palæontological Assoc., 1966-68; Section C, British Assoc. for Advancement of Science, Durham, 1970; Mem. Coun., Roy. Soc., 1966-68. Corr. Mem., Amer. Museum of Natural History. Murchison Medal, Geol. Soc. London, 1967. *Publications:* (ed) Studies on Fossil Vertebrates, 1958; (ed., with D. G. Murchison) Coal and Coal-bearing Strata, 1968; numerous papers and monographs on vertebrate anatomy and palæontology and geological topics, in several journals. *Recreations:* photography and numismatics. *Address:* University of Newcastle upon Tyne;

21 Osborne Avenue, Newcastle upon Tyne NE2 1JQ. *T:* 81-1622.

**WESTON, Rev. Arthur Ernest,** MM 1917; ThL 1922; Dean of Adelaide, 1957-66; Honorary Chaplain to Bishop of Adelaide, 1966; *b* New South Wales, 22 Jan. 1890; *s* of Thomas Whitney and Mary Eliza Weston; *m* 1925, Mary E., *d* of Richard Zouch, Moss Vale, New South Wales; one *s*. *Educ:* Gilgandra Public School; St John's College, Armidale (ThL). In business, 1902-16; entered Brotherhood of the Good Shepherd, 1916. Served European War, AIF, 1916-19; 33rd Bn France (MM); commissioned 1918. Deacon and Priest, 1922; Curate of All Saints' Cathedral, Bathurst, 1922-23; locum tenens, George's Plains, 1923-24; Rector of Parkes, 1924-34; Rector of South Bathurst, Archdeacon of Bathurst, and Registrar, 1934-36; Rector of St Bartholomew's, Norwood, SA, 1936-47; Archdeacon of Strathalbyn, 1939-53; Honorary Canon of Adelaide, 1939-53; Rector of St Peters, Glenelg, SA, 1947-57; Archdeacon of Adelaide, 1953-57. *Recreations:* cricket and tennis. *Address:* 100 Farrer Brown, Nuffield Village, Castle Hill, NSW 2154, Australia. *Club:* Commonwealth (Adelaide).

**WESTON, Bertram John,** CMG 1960; OBE 1957; retired from the public service; now Estate Factor to British Union Trust Ltd; *b* 30 March 1907; *o s* of late J. G. Weston, Kennington, Kent; *m* 1932, Irene Carey; two *d*. *Educ:* Ashford Grammar School; Sidney Sussex College, Cambridge (MA); Pretoria University, SA (MSc, Agric); Cornell University, USA (Post Grad.). Horticulturist, Cyprus, 1931; Asst Comr, Nicosia (on secondment), 1937; Administrative Officer, 1939. War Service, 1940-43 (Major). Commissioner for development and post-war construction, Cyprus, 1943; Commissioner, 1946; Administrative Officer Class I, 1951; Senior Administrative Officer, 1954; Senior Commissioner, 1958; Government Sec., St Helena, 1960-63; acted as Governor and C-in-C, St Helena, at various times during this period. *Recreations:* lawn tennis, gardening. *Address:* Marchmont Estate Office, Greenlaw, Berwickshire. *Club:* Royal Commonwealth Society.

**WESTON, Sir Eric,** Kt, *cr* 1954; *b* 8 December 1892; *s* of W. J. Weston, South Shields; *m* 1920, Georgina, *d* of W. J. Cork, Hampstead; three *d*. *Educ:* South Shields High School; St John's Coll., Cambridge. Math. Tripos, Part I, 1912; Part II, 1914; ICS Exam. 1915; Assistant Collector and Judge of various districts Bombay Presidency and Sind District, 1916-29; Judge, 1929; Judge, Aden, 1931; Judicial Commissioner, Rajkot and Ajmer, 1934-35 and 1937-38; Judge Chief Court of Sind, 1938-42; Judge High Court, Bombay, 1943-50; Chief Justice, Punjab High Court, Simla, 1950-52; retired, Dec. 1952. *Recreations:* tennis, golf. *Address:* c/o National & Grindlay's Bank, 13 St James's Square, SW1.

**WESTON, Garfield;** *see* Weston, W. G.

**WESTON, Garfield Howard;** Chairman, Associated British Foods, since Sept. 1967; *b* 28 April 1927; *s* of Willard Garfield Weston, *qv*; *m* 1959, Mary Ruth, *d* of late Major-Gen. Sir Howard Kippenberger; three *s* three *d*. *Educ:* Sir William Borlase School, Marlow; New College, Oxford; Harvard University (Economics). Man. Director: Ryvita Co. Ltd, 1951; Weston Biscuit Co., Aust., 1954; Vice-Chairman, Associated British Foods Ltd, 1960; Chairman, Weston Holdings Pty Ltd, Australia, 1965. *Recreation:* squash. *Address:* Weston Centre, 40 Berkeley Square, W1. *T:* 01-499 8931. *Clubs:* Lansdowne; Royal Sydney Yacht Squadron.

**WESTON, Garry;** *see* Weston, G. H.

**WESTON, Maj.-Gen. Gerald Patrick Linton,** CB 1962; CBE 1960; DSO 1945; Free-lance Cricketing and Ski-ing correspondent; *b* 21 August 1910; *s* of late Donald Weston, ICS (retd) and of Ethel Linton Weston, Clent, Worcs; *m* 1938, Moira Olive Hale, *d* of Major D. B. Hale, RA (retd); one *s* one *d*. *Educ:* Haileybury; RMC Sandhurst. Commnd Middlesex Regt, 1931; seconded RAF, 1936-40; served War of 1939-45; comdg: 18 (Bomber) Sqdn, RAF France, 1939-40; 2nd Bn, Middlesex Regt, France and Germany, 1943-45 (despatches); 161 Indian Infantry Brigade, Burma and Java, 1945-46; 6 Parachute Brigade TA, 1947-49; jssc, 1949; AAG War Office, 1949-52; Senior Operations Officer, Malaya, 1952-53 (despatches); idc, 1954; Asst Comdt School of Land/Air Warfare, 1955-57; Commandant, Army Air Corps Centre, 1957-60; Director of Land/Air Warfare, War Office, 1960-64, retd. Order of Leopold and Belgian Croix de Guerre, 1945. *Recreations:* cricket and ski-ing. *Address:* Whitewater, North Warnborough, Hants. *T:* Odiham 2113.

**WESTON, Dr John Carruthers;** General Manager, Northampton Development Corporation, since 1969; *b* 15 May 1917; *o s* of John Albert and May Carruthers Weston; *m* 1943, Mary Standish Lester; two *s*. *Educ:* Univ. of Nottingham. Admiralty Research, 1940-46; Plessey Co., 1946-47; Building Research Station, 1947-64; Chief Exec. Operational Div., Nat. Building Agency, 1964-65; Dir, Building Research Station, MPBW, 1966-69. *Recreations:* gardening, music, theatre, walking, sailing, reading and living. *Address:* The Bartons, Raynsford Road, Dallington, Northampton NN5 7HP. *T:* Northampton 51033.

**WESTON, Air Vice-Marshal Sir John (Gerard Willsley),** KBE 1964 (OBE 1942); CB 1947; *b* 15 Nov. 1908; *e s* of late Col Edward Thomas Weston and Constance Alice Weston (*née* Turpin); *m* 1932, Eileen Margaret Gwendoline (*d* 1966), *o d* of late H. E. Rose, Bristol; one *s* one *d*. *Educ:* Cranbrook Sch.; RAF Coll., Cranwell. 207 (B) Sqdn, 1929; 60 (B) Sqdn, 1930-32; Signals Specialist Course, 1932-33; 99 (B) Sqdn, 1934; seconded RCAF, 1935-36; Air Ministry staff duties, 1938-41 (despatches, 1940); Chief Signals Officer, Ferry Command, 1941; Dep. Director Signals, Air Ministry, 1942-43; Director of Signals, Air Ministry, 1943-45; Comdt Central Signals Establishment, 1946-47; idc, 1948; Director of Policy (AS), Air Ministry, 1949-51; Commandant RAF, Halton, 1952-53; AOC No 90 (Signals) Group, 1954-55; Assistant Chief of Air Staff (Signals), Air Ministry, 1956-59; Senior Directing Staff, Imperial Defence College, 1959-61; Director-General of Manning, Air Ministry, 1961-64, retd. Chm., National Small-bore Rifle Assoc., 1965-68. *Recreations:* cricket, shooting. *Address:* c/o Glyn, Mills & Co., Whitehall, SW1. *Club:* Royal Air Force.

**WESTON, John William;** Principal Assistant Solicitor, Board of Inland Revenue, since Sept. 1967; *b* 3 Feb. 1915; *s* of Herbert Edward Weston, MA, and Emma Gertrude Weston; *m* 1943, Frances Winifred Weston (*née* Johnson); two *s* one *d*. *Educ:* Berkhamsted Sch., Herts. Solicitor, 1937. Joined Inland Revenue, 1940; Sen. Legal Asst, 1948; Asst Solicitor, 1954. *Recreations:* tennis, golf. *Address:* 5 Dickerage Road, Kingston Hill, Surrey. *T:* 01-942 8130.

**WESTON, Kenneth Southwold,** CMG 1956; OBE 1951; Assistant Secretary, HM Treasury, retired, 1962; *b* 9 Nov. 1899; *s* of late Benjamin Samuel Weston, Bromham, Wilts; *m* 1935, Kathleen Elizabeth, *d* of Arthur Leach, Huntingdon; one *s*. *Educ:* Southend-on-Sea High School. Served War of 1914-18, Lieut Wilts Regt; Home Civil Service from 1921; Financial Adviser, HM Embassy, Madrid, 1943-45; HM Treasury Representative in Canada, 1951-53. *Address:* 5 Lancaster Gardens, SW19.

**WESTON, Laurence; Hon. Mr Justice Weston;** Chief Justice, Botswana (formerly Bechuanaland Protectorate), since 1965; *b* 1909. *Educ:* Pembroke College, Oxford. Called to the Bar (Middle Temple), 1942. Asst Custodian of Enemy Property, Palestine, 1939-43. War Service, 1943-46 (Lieut-Colonel). Magistrate, Nigeria, 1950 (Crown Counsel 1951); Assistant Attorney General, North Borneo, 1952; Attorney-General, The Gambia, 1955; Puisne Judge in Tanganyika, 1961-65. *Address:* Lobatsi, Botswana.

**WESTON, Margaret Kate,** BScEng (London); MIEE; Keeper, Department of Museum Services, The Science Museum, since 1967; *b* 7 March 1926; *o c* of Charles Edward and Margaret Weston. *Educ:* Stroud High School; College of Technology, Birmingham. Engineering apprenticeship with General Electric Co. Ltd, followed in 1949 by development work, very largely on high voltage insulation problems. Joined Science Museum as an Assistant Keeper, Dept of Electrical Engineering and Communications, 1955; Deputy Keeper, 1962. *Address:* 7 Shawley Way, Epsom, Surrey. *T:* Burgh Heath 55885.

**WESTON, Brig.-Gen. Spencer Vaughan Percy,** DSO 1917; MC; Member of the Stock Exchange; *b* 1883; *m* 1913, Henrietta Valerie, *d* of W. Compton-Smith; five *s* four *d*. Served European War (Despatches four times, DSO two bars, MC, French and Belgian Croix de Guerre); rejoined from Officers' Emergency Reserve, 1940-46. FRGS. *Address:* Bente, Carters Hill, Sevenoaks, Kent. *T:* Sevenoaks 61082. *Clubs:* Carlton, United Service, City of London; Wildernesse (Sevenoaks).

**WESTON, (Willard) Garfield;** Chairman: George Weston Holdings, Ltd and its associated companies; Weston Foods, Ltd; Fortnum & Mason Ltd; Director of other companies in Britain; President, Associated British Foods Ltd; Chairman of George Weston Ltd, Toronto, and of its associated companies; also of Weston Bakeries Ltd, Toronto; Wm Paterson, Ltd, Brantford, Ontario, and Weston Biscuit Co., Passaic, New Jersey, USA; *b* Toronto, Ontario, 1898; *e s* of George and Emma Maude Weston; *m* 1921, Reta Lila Howard (*d* 1967); three *s* six *d*. *Educ:* Harbord Collegiate Inst., Toronto. Joined Canadian Engrs on leaving sch. and served in France during European War; with George Weston Ltd (Toronto) since 1919, becoming Vice-President in 1921 and Manager in 1922; came to Great Britain in 1934; founded the Weston Biscuit Companies and erected new plants in many parts of the country; founded Allied Bakeries, Ltd. MP (Nat U) for Macclesfield Division, 1939-45. *Recreations:* riding, tennis. *Address:* Weston Centre, 40 Berkeley Square, W1. *T:* 01-499 8931. *TA:* Garwest, London. *Club:* Carlton. *See also G. H. Weston.*

**WESTON, William Guy,** CMG 1945; Governing Director W. G. Weston Ltd; *b* 30 Jan. 1907; *o s* of late W. H. Weston, Quorn Lodge, Melton Mowbray; *m* 1st, 1930, Joan (marriage dissolved, 1953), *d* of J. P. Chettle, RBA; three *s* one *d*; 2nd, 1955, Evelyn Mary, *er d* of late T. G. Marriott. *Educ:* Melton Mowbray Grammar School; Manchester Univ.; St John's College, Cambridge. Lightfoot Scholar in Ecclesiastical History, Cambridge, 1929; Historical Tripos, 1929-30; Dep. Sec. Minister of Transport, 1946-48; General Manager Marine Dept Anglo-Saxon Petroleum Co., 1948-52. *Recreation:* painting. *Address:* Wyfold Grange, near Reading, Berkshire. *T:* Checkendon 751. *Clubs:* Reform, Travellers'.

**WESTON, Rear-Adm. William Kenneth,** CB 1956; OBE 1945; RN retired; *b* 8 November 1904; *s* of late William Weston; *m* 1934, Mary Ursula Shine; one *s* two *d*. *Educ:* RNC Osborne and Dartmouth. RNEC Keyham; RNC Greenwich. Served on staff of Flag Officer Destroyers, Pacific, 1945-46; Admiralty District Engineer Overseer, NW District, 1951-54; Staff of C-in-C Plymouth, 1954-58; retired, 1958. Court of Assistants of the Worshipful Company of Salters, 1959, Master, 1963. *Address:* Brackleyways, Hartley Wintney, Hants. *T:* Hartley Wintney 2546. *Club:* Naval and Military.

**WESTROP, Brigadier Sidney A.,** CBE 1946; DSO 1917; MC 1915; MIMechE; Consulting Engineer; *b* 20 May 1895; *s* of A. W. Westrop; *m* 1918, Eileen M. Alton; one *s* three *d*. *Educ:* Bridgnorth Grammar School; Birmingham Univ. (BSc). Served European War, 1914-18 (despatches twice, MC, DSO); on active service in France, England, Iraq, India and Burmah, 1939-46 (despatches twice, CBE); Chief Engineer and Brig. 1943; was Director of Open Cut Coal Mining for India, 1944-45. *Recreations:* fishing, shooting. *Address:* Old Rectory, Brattleby, Lincoln, *T:* Scampton 221. *Club:* East India and Sports.

**WESTROPP, Maj.-Gen. Victor John Eric,** CB 1947; CBE 1943; *b* 24 May 1897; *s* of Brigadier-General H. C. E. Westropp and M. F. A. Lowndes; *m* 1923, E. A. Lynch (*d* 1940); one *s* one *d*; *m* 1944, Elspeth, *yr d* of Lt-Col H. A. Duncan, one *s* (one *d* decd). *Educ:* Bradfield; RMA, Woolwich. Commissioned Regular Army, RE, 1916; France, 1917-18; transferred to Royal Signals, 1921; Instructor RMA, Woolwich, 1926-29; Staff College, Quetta, 1931-32; NW Frontier, 1930 and 1933-34 (Frontier Medal); War Office 1934-36; Palestine 1936, and 1938-39 (Palestine medal); War of 1939-45 (CBE, Africa Star, 1939-45 Star, Italian Star, Defence Medal, Commander Legion of Merit, USA); late Deputy Adj.-Gen., India; Dep. Chief of Staff, CCG; UK Commissioner, Military Security Board, CCG, 1947-51; retired, 1951. *Address:* Tenacres, Bracknell, Berks.

**WESTRUP, Sir Jack (Allan),** Kt 1961; MA, BMus, FRCO; Hon. DMus Oxon, 1944; FTCL 1946; FBA 1954; Hon. RAM, 1960; FRCM, 1961; FRSCM, 1963; Heather Professor of Music in the University of Oxford, 1947-71; Fellow of Wadham College, Oxford, since 1947; *b* 26 July 1904; *s* of George Westrup and Harriet Sophia Allan; *m* 1938, Solweig Maria, *d* of Musikdirectör Per Johan Rösell, Linköping, Sweden; three *s* one *d*. *Educ:* Dulwich College (scholar); Balliol College, Oxford (Nettleship scholar). President, Oxford University Musical Club and Union, 1926, 1947; Musical Director, Oxford Opera Club, 1927, 1947-62; Asst Master (Classics), Dulwich College, 1928-34; Assistant Music Critic, Daily Telegraph, 1934-40; Editor, Monthly Musical Record, 1933-45; Lecturer in History of Music, RAM, 1938-40; Collard Fellow, Company of Musicians, 1940-43; Lecturer in Music, King's College, Newcastle upon Tyne, 1941-44; Conductor, Newcastle on Tyne Bach Choir, 1942-44; Peyton and Barber Professor of Music, University of Birmingham, 1944-46. Pres., Union of Graduates in Music, 1949-51; Ferens Lecturer in Fine Art, University College, Hull, 1950-51; President Royal Musical Assoc., 1958-53; President, Incorporated Society of Musicians, 1963; President, Royal College of Organists, 1964-66; Member, BBC General Advisory Council, 1963-; Editor, Music and Letters, 1959-; Edited for performance Monteverdi's Orfeo (Oxford, 1925, Royal College of Music, London, 1926, Scala Theatre, London, 1929), Monteverdi's L'Incoronazione di Poppea (Oxford, 1927), Locke's Cupid and Death (Scala Theatre, London, 1929). Conducted at London Opera Festival, 1929-30, London Theatre Concerts, 1938, Barber Institute Chamber Concerts, Birmingham, 1946, etc; Conductor, Oxford Univ. Orchestra, 1954-63. *Publications:* Purcell, 1937; Handel, 1939; Liszt, 1940; Sharps and Flats (essays on music), 1940; When Israel came out of Egypt (motet for double choir), 1940; British Music, 1943; The Meaning of Musical History (Deneke lecture), 1946; 3rd edn of Ernest Walker's History of Music in England, 1952; Introduction to Musical History, 1955; The Nature of Recitative, 1957; Collins Music Encyclopedia (with F. Ll. Harrison), 1959; Bach Cantatas, 1966; Schubert Chamber Music, 1969; songs, organ music, arrangements, etc. Contributions to: Oxford History of Music, 2nd edn, 1932; Grove's Dictionary, 4th edn, 1940, 5th edn, 1954; Musical Education, 1946; British Music of our Time, 1946; The Character of England, 1947; Schubert–a Symposium, 1947; Die Musik in Geschichte und Gegenwart, 1949-67; Bach-Gedenkschrift, 1950; The Heritage of Music, vol. iii, 1951; New Oxford History of Music, 1954; Fanfare for Ernest Newman, 1955; Music and Western Man, 1958; The Decca Book of Ballet, 1958; Riemann Musiklexikon, 12th ed., 1959; Fellerer Festschrift, 1962; Jeppesen Festschrift, 1962; Blume Festschrift, 1963; Wellesz Festschrift, 1966; Proc. Musical Association, various musical periodicals. *Address:* 226 Woodstock Road, Oxford.

**WESTWOOD,** family name of **Baron Westwood.**

**WESTWOOD,** 2nd Baron, *cr* 1944, of Gosforth; **William Westwood;** Company Director; *b* 25 Dec. 1907; *s* of 1st Baron and Margaret Taylor Young (*d* 1916); *S* father 1953; *m* 1937, Marjorie, *o c* of Arthur Bonwick, Newcastle upon Tyne; two *s*. *Educ:* Glasgow; JP Newcastle upon Tyne, 1949. Chm., Newcastle United Football Co. Ltd. FRSA; FCIS. *Recreations:* golf, football. *Heir:* *s* Hon. William Gavin Westwood [*b* 30 Jan. 1944; *m* 1969, Penelope, *er d* of Dr C. E. Shafto, Newcastle upon Tyne]. *Address:* 12 Westfield Drive, Newcastle upon Tyne NE3 4XU. *T:* Newcastle upon Tyne 857020.

**WESTWOOD, Earle Cathers;** Agent-General for British Columbia in London, Oct. 1964-Oct. 1968; *b* 13 September 1909; *s* of Joseph Arthur Westwood and Mary Smith; *m* 1956, Sheila Blackwood Maxwell; one *d*. *Educ:* Nanaimo and Vancouver, BC, Canada. Pres. of Chamber of Commerce, Nanaimo, 1940; Chm. of Sch. Bd, 1942 and 1943; Mem. City Coun., 1944; Finance Chm. for five years; Mayor of City of Nanaimo, 1950, 1951, 1952, 1956. Provincial politics, 1956-63: Minister of Industrial Development, Trade and Commerce; Minister of Recreation and Conservation; Minister of Commercial Transport. *Recreations:* golf, sailing, fishing. *Address:* 1 Newcastle Avenue, Nanaimo, BC, Canada. *Clubs:* Royal Automobile, East India and Sports; Hendon Golf; Nanaimo Yacht; Union (Victoria, BC).

**WETHERALL, Lt-Gen. Sir (Harry) Edward de Robillard,** KBE, *cr* 1946 (OBE 1937); CB 1941; DSO 1917; MC; 2nd *s* of late Major H. A. Wetherall, Coldstream Guards; *m* 1923, Vera G., *o d* of George de Lisle Bush, of Eastington Park, Stonehouse, Gloucestershire. Gloucester Regt; served European War, 1914-18 (wounded, despatches, MC, DSO); GSO for Weapon Training, Scottish Command, 1930-34; commanded 1st Bn York and Lancaster Regiment, 1936-38; Commander 19th Infantry Brigade, 1938-40; Commander 11th African Div. in Abyssinia, 1941; GOC-in-C E Africa, 1941; GOC Ceylon, 1943-45; C-in-C Ceylon, 1945-46; retired pay, 1946. Colonel, The Gloucestershire Regiment, 1947-54. *Address:* Littlecourt, Bagborough, Taunton, Somerset.

**WETHERALL, Rev. Theodore Sumner;** Vicar of Huddersfield, since 1969; *b* 31 May 1910; *s* of Rev. A. S. Wetherall and Mrs G. V. M. Wetherall (*née* Bennett-Powell); *m* 1939, Caroline, 4th *d* of Dr Charles Milne; one *s* three *d*. *Educ:* St Edward's School, Oxford; Oriel College, Oxford. Exhibitioner at Oriel College, 1929; 1st Class Classical Mods, 1931; BA (2nd Class Lit. Hum.), 1933. Preparatory Schoolmaster, Wellesley House, Broadstairs, 1933-35; MA 1936; Liddon Student, 1936; Cuddesdon College, 1936-37; Asst Curate, St John's, Greengates, Bradford, 1937-39; Fellow and Chaplain, Corpus Christi College, Oxford, 1939-47, Dean, 1940-45, Vice-Pres., 1947; Principal of St Chad's College, Durham, 1948-65. Vicar of St Edward the Confessor, Barnsley, 1965-69. Select Preacher to the Univ. of Oxford, 1945-47; Chaplain in the Univ. of Oxford to Bishop of Derby, 1940-47, Examining Chaplain to Bishop of Oxford, 1946-47, to Bishop of Durham, 1948-65, to Bishop of Bradford, 1949-55; to Bishop of Wakefield, 1969-; Surrogate for Marriages, 1969-; Rural Dean of Huddersfield, 1969-. Hon. Canon of Durham, 1958-65. *Address:* Parish House, Venn Street, Huddersfield, Yorks. *T:* Huddersfield 27964.

**WETHERED, His Honour Ernest Handel Cossham,** OBE; MA, LLB; Special Commissioner for Matrimonial Causes, 1947; *b* 18 July 1878; *s* of Edward Bestbridge Wethered, JP, and Mary Ellen Wright; *m* 1904, Jessie Marian Ward (*d* 1956); one *s* one *d*. *Educ:* Cheltenham Coll.; Pembroke Coll., Cambridge. Barrister-at-law called at Lincoln's Inn, 1899; Tancred Student; Western Circuit; practised at Bristol and in London, 1899-1934; Judge of County Courts, Circuit 57, 1934-37; Circuit 54, 1938-50; retired from County Court Bench, 1950; Chairman of Court of Referees under Unemployment Insurance Acts at Bristol, 1912-34; Chairman of Trade Boards, 1919-34; Hon. Member of National Council of Pottery Industry, 1918-46; Chairman SW Tribunal under National Service (Armed Forces) Acts, 1939-47 and re-appointed 1951-60; Training Officer, Fire Guard Service, Clifton Division, Bristol, 1943-45. Vice-Pres. British Red Cross Bristol Branch, 1946-49; County Civil Defence Officer, 1949-54; Hon. Vice-Pres. Bristol Branch, 1954; Civil Defence Corps, General Instructor (Falfield Special), 1950. *Address:* Gort Lodge, 11 The Avenue, Clifton, Bristol 8. *T:* Bristol 33695. *Club:* Royal Automobile.

**WEYMOUTH, Viscount; Alexander George Thynne;** *b* 6 May 1932; *s* of Marquess of Bath, *qv*; *m* 1969, Anna Gyarmathy. *Educ:* Eton College; Christ Church, Oxford. Lieutenant in the Life Guards, 1951-52, and in Royal Wilts

Yeomanry, 1953-57. *Address:* Longleat, Warminster, Wilts. *T:* Maiden Bradley 300.

**WHALE, Rev. John Seldon,** MA (Oxon); DD (Glasgow); *b* 19 Dec. 1896; *s* of Rev. John Whale and Alice Emily Seldon; *m* Mary, *d* of Rev. H. C. Carter, MA; two *s* two *d* (and one *s* decd). *Educ:* Caterham School, Surrey; St Catherine's Society and Mansfield College, Oxford; 1st Class Hons Sch. of Mod. Hist. 1922; Magdalene College, Cambridge, 1933. Minister of Bowdon Downs Congregational Church, Manchester, 1925-29; Mackennal Professor of Ecclesiastical History, Mansfield College, Oxford, and Tutor in Modern History, St Catherine's, 1929-33; President of Cheshunt College, Cambridge, 1933-44; Headmaster of Mill Hill School, 1944-51; Visiting Professor of Christian Theology, Drew Univ., Madison, NJ, USA, 1951-53. Moderator of Free Church Federal Council, 1942-43; Select Preacher, Univ. of Cambridge, 1943, 1957; Warrack Lecturer, 1944; Russell Lecturer (Auburn and New York), 1936 and 1948; Alden Tuthill Lecturer, Chicago, 1952; Greene Lecturer, Andover, 1952; Currie Lecturer, Austin, Texas, 1953; Hill Lectr, St Olaf Coll., Minnesota, 1954; Visiting Lecturer, Univ. of Toronto, 1957; Danforth Scholar, USA, 1958; Sir D. Owen Evans Lectures, Aberystwyth, 1958. Visiting Professor, Univ. of Chicago, 1959; Senior Fellow of Council of Humanities, Princeton Univ., 1960. *Publications:* The Christian Answer to the Problem of Evil, 1936; What is a Living Church?, 1937; This Christian Faith, 1938; Facing the Facts, 1940; Christian Doctrine, 1941; The Protestant Tradition, 1955; Victor and Victim: the Christian doctrine of Redemption, 1960; Church and Sacrament: our historic divisions reconsidered, 1971. *Address:* Wild Goose, Widecombe-in-the-Moor, Newton Abbot, S Devon. *T:* Widecombe-in-the-Moor 260.

**WHALLEY, Prof. William Basil;** Professor of Chemistry, School of Pharmacy, University of London, since 1961; *b* 17 Dec. 1916; *s* of William and Catherine Lucy Whalley; *m* 1945, Marie Agnes Alston; four *s* one *d*. *Educ:* St Edward's College, Liverpool; Liverpool University. BSc Hons 1938; PhD 1940; DSc 1952; FRIC 1950. MOS and ICI 1940-45. Lecturer, 1946-55, Sen. Lectr, 1955-57, Reader, 1957-61, in Organic Chemistry, at Liverpool University. *Publications:* contrib. on organic chemistry to several books: *eg* Heterocyclic Compounds, Vol. 7, Edited R. C. Elderfield, Wiley (New York); many pubns in Jl of Chem. Soc., Jl Amer. Chem. Soc., etc. *Recreations:* music and mountaineering. *Address:* 9 Peaks Hill, Purley, Surrey. *T:* 01-668 2244.

**WHALLEY-TOOKER, Hyde Charnock,** MA, LLM (Cantab), MA (Oxon); Emeritus Fellow of Downing College, Cambridge (Fellow, 1927-67, and Senior Tutor, 1931-47); University Lecturer in Law, 1931-67; *b* 1 Sept. 1900; *o s* of Edward Whalley-Tooker; *m* 1935, Frances, *er d* of late Thomas Halsted; one *d*. *Educ:* Eton; Trinity Hall, Cambridge; Balliol College, Oxford; Law Tripos Part I, Class I, 1921; Part II, Class I, 1922. *Address:* 5 Wilberforce Road, Cambridge. *T:* Cambridge 50073.

**WHARNCLIFFE,** 4th Earl of, *cr* 1876; **Alan James Montagu-Stuart-Wortley-Mackenzie;** Viscount Carlton, 1876; Baron Wharncliffe, 1826; National Service, RNVR, 1953; *b* 23 March 1935; *o s* of 3rd Earl and Lady Elfrida Wentworth Fitzwilliam, *d* of 7th Earl Fitzwilliam; *S* father 1953; *m* 1957, Aline, *d* of late R. F. D. Bruce, Wharncliffe side, near Sheffield; two *d*. *Educ:* Eton. *Recreation:* shooting. *Heir: cousin,* Alan Ralph Montagu-Scott-Wortley [*b* 27 July 1927; *m* 1952, Virginia Anne, *d* of W. Martin Claybaugh; two *s* one *d*]. *Address:* Carlton House, Wortley, Sheffield. *T:* Stocksbridge 2157. *See also Duke of Newcastle.*

**WHARTON,** Baroness (Barony *cr* 1544-5, called out of abeyance, 1916) (10th in line); **Elizabeth Dorothy Vintcent;** *b* 1906; *d* of 8th Baron Wharton and Dorothy (*d* 1944), *y d* of late Maj.-Gen. Sir Arthur Edward Augustus Ellis, GCVO, CSI; *S* brother, 1969; *m* 1st, 1933, David George Arbuthnot (marr. diss. 1946); two *d*; 2nd, 1946, St John Vintcent (marr. diss. 1958). *Co-heiresses: d* Hon. Myrtle Olive Felix Robertson [*b* 20 Feb. 1934; *m* 1958, Henry MacLeod Robertson; one *s* one *d*] and *d* Hon. Caroline Elizabeth Arbuthnot, *b* 28 Aug. 1935.

**WHATELEY, Dame Leslie Violet Lucy Evelyn Mary,** DBE *cr* 1946 (CBE 1943); TD; *d* of late Ada Lilian Hutton and late Col Evelyn F. M. Wood, CB, DSO, OBE; *m* 1st, 1922, W. J. Balfour; one *s*; 2nd, 1939, H. Raymond Whateley, Squadron-Leader, RAFVR. *Educ:* Convents of Society of HCJ, St Leonards-on-Sea and Cavendish Square. Private Secretary up to marriage, and then Social Welfare Work, including District Nursing Associations and Village Institutes. Director of Auxiliary Territorial Service, 1943-46; Hon. Col 668 (bn) HAA Regt RA (TA), 1948-53. Director World Bureau of Girl Guides/Girl Scouts, 1951-64; Administrator of Voluntary Services, Queen Mary's Hosp., Roehampton, 1965. Chevalier Légion d'Honneur, 1945; Order of Merit (USA), 1946. *Publication:* As Thoughts Survive, 1949. *Recreations:* gardening, reading. *Address:* c/o Lloyds Bank, 6 Pall Mall, SW1. *Club:* Lady Golfers'.

**WHEARE, Sir Kenneth Clinton,** Kt 1966; CMG 1953; FBA 1952; DLitt (Oxon); Rector of Exeter College, Oxford, since 1956; Vice-Chancellor, Oxford Univ., 1964-66; Hon. Fellow of Nuffield, Oriel, University, and Wolfson Colleges; *b* Warragul, Vict., Australia, 26 March 1907; *e s* of Eustace Leonard Wheare and Kathleen Frances Kinahan; *m* 1st, 1934, Helen Mary Allan; one *s*; 2nd, 1943, Joan Randell; two *s* two *d*. *Educ:* Scotch College, Melbourne; University of Melbourne; Oriel College, Oxford. BA Univ. of Melbourne, 1929, MA, 1949; Rhodes Scholar from Victoria, Australia, 1929; Oriel College, Oxford, 1929-32; 1st class Hons, School of Philosophy, Politics and Economics, 1932; BA Oxford, 1932, MA 1935, DLitt 1957; Lecturer, Christ Church, Oxford, 1934-39; Beit Lecturer in Colonial History, Oxford, 1935-44; Fellow of University Coll., Oxford, 1939-44, and Dean, 1942-45; Gladstone Prof. of Government and Public Administration, Univ. of Oxford, and Fellow of All Souls Coll., Oxford, 1944-57; Fellow of Nuffield College, 1944-58. Member of Oxford City Council, 1940-57. Member of Hebdomadal Council, 1947-67; Constitutional Adviser to Nat. Convention of Newfoundland, 1946-47, and to Confs on Central African Federation, 1951, 1952, 1953; a Rhodes Trustee, 1948-; Chm. Departmental Cttee on Children and the Cinema, 1947-50; Mem. Franks Cttee on Administrative Tribunals and Inquiries, 1955-57; Member, University Grants Committee, 1959-63; Pro-Vice-Chancellor, Oxford University, 1958-64, 1966-; Nuffield Trustee, 1966-; Pres. Brit. Acad., 1967-. Rede Lectr, Cambridge, 1967. Hon. LHD Columbia, 1954; Hon. LittD, Cambridge, 1969; Hon. LLD Exeter, 1970. *Publications:* The Statute of Westminster, 1931, 1933; The Statute of Westminster and Dominion Status, 1938 (5th ed., 1953); Federal Government, 1946 (4th ed. 1963); Abraham Lincoln and the United States, 1948; Modern Constitutions, 1951; Government by Committee, 1955; The Constitutional Structure of the Commonwealth, 1960; Legislatures, 1963. *Recreations:* walking, cooking. *Address:* Exeter College, Oxford. *T:* Oxford 44681. *Clubs:* Athenæum, Oxford and Cambridge.

**WHEATCROFT, E. L. E.,** MA, FIMechE, FIEE, FInstF; Consultant with Merz and McLellan, consulting engineers, London; *b* 17 July 1896; *s* of late W. H. Wheatcroft, LLD, Cambridge; *m* Ethel Margaret, *d* of late Dr A. E. L. Wear, Harrogate; three *d. Educ:* Oundle; Cambridge. Switchboard Engineer with the British Thomson-Houston Co.; Calculation Engineer with the Commonwealth Power Corporation of Michigan; Professor of Electrical Engineering at Leeds University, 1926-40; Member of Council: of IEE, 1934-36, 1948-51, and 1954-57; of Hydromechanics Research Association, 1950. Freeman of City of London; Liveryman, Worshipful Co. of Makers of Playing Cards. *Publications:* Gaseous Electrical Conductors, 1938; papers in Phil. Mag., Proceedings of IEE, etc. *Recreation:* motoring. *Address:* Milburn, Esher, Surrey. *Club:* Athenæum.

**WHEATCROFT, George Shorrock Ashcombe,** JP; Professor of English Law, University of London, 1959-68, now Professor Emeritus; Editor of British Tax Review since first publication in 1956; Editor of British Tax Encyclopedia since first publication, 1962; Director: G. S. A. & M. Wheatcroft (Advisory Services) Ltd; Abbey Life Assurance Co. Ltd; Associated Business Programmes Ltd; *b* 29 Oct. 1905; *s* of Hubert Ashcombe Wheatcroft and Jane (*née* Eccles); *m* 1930, Mildred Susan, *d* of late Canon Walter Lock, DD, formerly Warden of Keble College, Oxford; two *s* one *d. Educ:* Rugby; New College, Oxford (MA). Qualified as Solicitor, 1929; partner in Corbin Greener and Cook, Solicitors, of 52 Bedford Row, London, 1930-51; Master of the Supreme Court (Chancery Division), 1951-59. Served as an officer in RASC, 1940-45; released in 1945 with hon. rank of Lt-Col (despatches twice). Fellow and Founder Member of British Institute of Management. Past President British Chess Federation; Fellow, Inst. of Taxation. JP County of London. *Publications:* The Taxation of Gifts and Settlements, 1953 (3rd edn 1958); The Law of Income Tax, Surtax and Profits Tax, 1962; Estate and Gift Taxation, 1965; Capital Gains Tax, 1965; Wheatcroft on Capital Gains Taxes (with A. E. W. Park), 1967; Corporation Tax (with J. E. Talbot), 1968; Sweet & Maxwell's Guide to the Estate Duty Statutes, 1969; titles Discovery, Execution, Judgments and Orders and Practice and Procedure in Halsbury's Laws of England (3rd edn); articles on taxation and legal procedure in periodicals. *Recreations:* golf, bridge, chess (represented England at Stockholm in 1937). *Address:* 41 Holland Street, W8. *Clubs:* Reform; Flempton Golf.

**WHEATLEY,** family name of **Baron Wheatley.**

**WHEATLEY,** Baron *cr* 1970 (Life Peer), of Shettleston, Glasgow; **John Wheatley,** PC 1947; one of the Senators of the College of Justice in Scotland since 1954; *b* 17 Jan. 1908; *s* of Patrick Wheatley and Janet Murphy; *m* 1935, Agnes Nichol; four *s* one *d. Educ:* St Aloysius Coll., Glasgow; Mount St Mary's Coll., Chesterfield; Glasgow Univ. MA 1928; LLB 1930; called to Scottish Bar, 1932; Advocate-Depute, 1945-47. War of 1939-45, RA (Field) and later with Judge Advocate-General's Branch; Chm. Scottish Nurses' Salaries Cttee, 1945-47; Chm. Milk Enquiry in Scotland, 1946-47; Chm., Cttee on Teaching Profession (Scotland), 1961-63; Mem., Royal Commn on Penal Reform (England and Wales), 1964-66; Chairman: Exec. Cttee Royal Scottish Soc. for Prevention of Cruelty to Children; Royal Commn on Local Govt in Scotland, 1966-69; Univ. Court, Univ. of Stirling. Solicitor-General for Scotland, March-Oct. 1947; QC (Scotland) 1947; Lord Advocate, 1947-51; MP (Lab) East Edinburgh, 1947-54. Hon. LLD (Glasgow), 1963; Hon. FEIS. *Recreations:* golf, tennis. *Address:* Braemar House, Whitehouse Terrace, Edinburgh 9. *T:* 031-447 1671.
*See also T. Dalyell.*

**WHEATLEY, Sir Andrew;** *see* Wheatley, Sir G. A.

**WHEATLEY, Dennis Yates,** Bronze Star (Mil., US), 1945; FRSA; FRSL; Novelist, Inventor (with J. G. Links) of Crime Dossier Murder Fiction; *b* 8 January 1897; *o s* of late Albert David Wheatley and Florence, Lady Newton; *m* 1st, 1923, Nancy Madelaine Leslie Robinson; one *s*; 2nd, 1931, Joan Gwendoline, *d* of late Hon. Louis Johnstone. *Educ:* HMS Worcester; Germany. Entered his father's Mayfair wine business, 1914; Commissioned RFA (T), Sept. 1914 (City of London Brigade); President, Old Comrades Association, 1961; transferred to 36th (Ulster) Division, 1917; invalided from the Service, 1919; re-entered his father's business; became sole owner, 1926; bought and dispersed many famous cellars; director of numerous companies; sold business, 1931; commenced writing, 1932. Toured England as member of Sir John Anderson's panel of voluntary speakers on National Service, 1939. Recommissioned in RAFVR Dec. 1941 to fill specially created post; only non-regular officer to be commnd to Joint Planning Staff; worked for following three years in Offices of the War Cabinet; Wing Comdr, 1944. Invented war games, Invasion, 1938, Blockade, 1939, Alibi, 1953. Livery of Vintners' Company, 1918, and of Distillers' Company, 1922. Pres. New Forest Agricultural Show, 1968. *Publications:* The Forbidden Territory (filmed); Such Power is Dangerous; Old Rowley (a Private Life of Charles II), 1933; Black August; The Fabulous Valley, 1934; The Devil Rides Out (filmed); The Eunuch of Stamboul (filmed), 1935; They Found Atlantis; Murder Off Miami (with J. G. Links); Contraband, 1936; The Secret War; Who Killed Robert Prentice (with J. G. Links); Red Eagle (a Life of Marshal Voroshilov), 1937; Uncharted Seas (filmed as The Lost Continent); The Malinsay Massacre (with J. G. Links); The Golden Spaniard, 1938; The Quest of Julian Day; Herewith the Clues! (with J. G. Links); Sixty Days to Live; Those Modern Musketeers, 1939; Three Inquisitive People; The Scarlet Impostor; Faked Passports; The Black Baroness, 1940; Strange Conflict; The Sword of Fate; Total War, 1941; V for Vengeance; Mediterranean Nights (Short Stories), 1942; Gunmen, Gallants and Ghosts (Short Stories), 1943; The Man Who Missed the War, 1945; Codeword Golden Fleece; Come into my Parlour, 1946; The Launching of Roger Brook, 1947; The Shadow of Tyburn Tree; The Haunting of Toby Jugg, 1948 (filmed); The Rising Storm; The Seven Ages of Justerini (privately printed for bi-centenary of firm of Justerini & Brooks), 1949; The Second Seal, 1950; The Man Who Killed the King, 1951; Star of Ill Omen, 1952; To the Devil a Daughter; Curtain of Fear, 1953; The Island where Time Stands Still, 1954; The Dark Secret of Josephine, 1955; The Ka of Gifford Hillary, 1956; The Prisoner in the Mask, 1957; Traitors' Gate, 1958; Stranger than Fiction; The Rape of Venice, 1959; The Satanist, 1960; Saturdays with Bricks, 1960; A Vendetta in Spain, 1961; Mayhem in Greece, 1962; The Sultan's Daughter, 1963; Bill for the Use of a Body, 1964; They Used Dark Forces, 1964; Dangerous Inheritance, 1965; The Wanton Princess, 1966; Unholy Crusade, 1967; The White Witch of the South Seas, 1968; Evil in a Mask, 1969; Gateway to Hell, 1970. Writings published in twenty-seven languages. *Recreations:* collecting books, stamps, coins, Georgian furniture and Oriental rugs; travel, building. *Address:* 60 Cadogan Square, SW1. *Clubs:* St James', Pratt's, Paternosters.

**WHEATLEY, Sir (George) Andrew,** Kt 1967; CBE 1960; DL; MA; BCL; Clerk of the Peace and Clerk of Hampshire County Council, 1946-67; *b* 1908; *s* of late Robert Albert Wheatley; *m* 1937, Mary Vera Hunt; three *s* two *d*. *Educ:* Rugby and Exeter Coll., Oxford. Asst Solicitor: Pembrokeshire CC, 1932-34; East Suffolk CC, 1934-36; N Riding, Yorks, 1936-39; Dep. Clerk of the Peace and Dep. Clerk of Cumberland CC, 1939-42; Clerk of the Peace and Clerk of the Cumberland CC, 1942-46. Hon. Sec.: Society of Clerks of the Peace of Counties and of Clerks of County Councils, 1961; Member: Local Government Advisory Panel, Dept of Technical Co-operation; Home Office Adv. Council on Child Care; Central Training Council in Child Care; Min. of Housing and Local Govt. Departmental Cttee on Management in Local Govt; Royal Commn on Assizes and Quarter Sessions. DL Hants, 1967. *Address:* Woodside, Salcombe, South Devon. *T:* Salcombe 2761. *Club:* Salcombe Yacht.

**WHEATLEY, Grace,** RP 1954; RWS 1952 (ARWS); RBA; RGI; RWEA; Painter and Sculptor; *b* London; 4th *d* of James Wolfe; *m* 1912, Prof. John Wheatley (*d* 1955); one *d*. *Educ:* privately. Studied Art at the Slade and in Paris; has works in the British Museum and at the Tate Gallery; Exhibitor at Royal Academy; works bought for many important collections and by Canada and S Africa; for ten years Lecturer in Painting and Sculpture, University of Cape Town. *Recreations:* reading and writing. *Address:* 2 The Mount, Ifield, Sussex. *T:* Rusper 363.

**WHEATLEY, Major (Hon. Lt-Col) Sir Mervyn James,** KBE 1952 (CBE 1928; OBE 1918); DL; retired; *b* Kinson, Dorset, 24 April 1880; 3rd *s* of Lieutenant-Colonel F. G. Wheatley, VD, JP, Ravenshoe, Poole, Dorset; *m* 1909, Mary Irene (*d* 1952), *er d* of Arthur Cox; one *s* one *d*; *m* 1952, Mrs Eileen Shelley, widow of K. J. Shelley, Trentham. *Educ:* Sutton Valence School. Entered Dorset Regt from 1st V/B Dorset Regt 1900; retired, 1918; served South African War, 1900-2; European War, 1914-18; operations in the Sudan, 1917 (despatches twice); Egyptian Army and Sudan Defence Force and Sudan Political Service, 1907-28; Private Sec. Sirdar & Governor-General, 1916-20; Governor and OC District Bahr-el-Ghazal Province, Sudan, 1921-28; Clothworker and Freeman City of London; Hon. Freeman of Poole; Army Welfare Officer, 1939-45; raised and was Comdg Officer 3rd Dorset Bn Home Guard; was Alderman Borough of Poole; JP, Poole; Mayor of Poole, 1936-37; was Alderman County of Dorset; MP (C) East Dorset, 1945-50, Poole, 1950-51; Conservative Whip, 1948-51. Chm.: E Dorset Conservative Assoc., 1940-45; Wessex Area Conservative and Unionist Assoc., 1944-46; Pres. W Regional Assoc. for the Blind, 1945-62. Pres., Poole Conservative Assoc., 1953-67. DL Dorset, 1952. CStJ 1964. 3rd Class Order of the Nile; 3rd Class Nahda; 4th Class Osmanieh. *Publications:* contributions to Geographical Journal and Journal of the African Society. *Address:* 65 Compton Avenue, Parkstone, Poole, Dorset BH14 8PX. *T:* Canford Cliffs 78453.

**WHEATLEY, Maj.-Gen. Mervyn Savile,** CB 1953; CBE 1945; retired 1957; *b* 18 April 1900; *s* of late Major S. G. Wheatley and of Mrs Savile Wheatley, Parkstone, Dorset; *m* 1936, Iris Veronica Margaret Kenyon; one *d* (by previous marriage). *Educ:* Blundell's; RMC Sandhurst. 2nd Lt Dorset Regt, 1918; Lt Royal Signals, 1925, Adjutant, Captain 1926-29; Instructor, RMA, Woolwich, 1929-33; DAAG War Office (Major), 1939-40; Commander, Royal Signals, 1st Armoured Division (Lieutenant-Colonel), 1940-41; Chief Signal Officer, SE Comd (Colonel), 1941-42; GSO1 Home Forces and 21 Army Group (Colonel), 1942-43; Chief Signal Officer, 13 Corps, Italy (Brig.), 1943-44; DD Signals, War Office, 1944-46; Comdr STC, 1946-47; Comdr Canal South District, 1947-49; Dep. Comdr Mid West District, 1949-51; Maj.-Gen. 1951; Chief Signal Officer, MELF, 1951-54; Signal Officer-in-Chief, War Office, 1954-57. Col Comdt Royal Signals, 1957-62. Hon. Col 41st Signal Regt (Princess Louise's Kensington Regt TA), 1957-62. FIEE. *Recreations:* tennis, golf, sailing. *Address:* Apple Tree Cottage, 4 Upper Old Park Lane, Farnham, Surrey. *Club:* Army and Navy.

**WHEATLEY, Maj.-Gen. Percival Ross,** DSO 1943; RAMC retired; Surgeon, P&O Lines Ltd; *b* Westbury, Wilts, 4 May 1909; *s* of late Rev. Percival Wheatley, Congregational Minister, and late Margaret Lettice Wheatley (*née* Wallis); *m* 1939, Dorothy Joan Fellows (*née* Brock); one *s*. *Educ:* St Dunstan's Coll., Catford; Guy's Hosp. Med. School. MB, BS (London), MRCS, LRCP, 1933; FRCS 1940. Commissioned Lieut RAMC, 1939; BEF as Surgical Specialist, Sept. 1939; 2nd in comd 16 Para. Field Ambulance, 1942, comdg, 1943; N Africa, 1942; Sicily and Italy, 1943; ADMS, 2nd Indian Airborne Div., 1944-46; Surgical Specialist, 1946-60: Catterick, Hamburg, Singapore, Japan, Millbank; seconded to Ghana Army, Surgical Specialist, 1960-61; Consultant Surgeon: FARELF, 1963-66; BAOR, 1966-67; Dir of Army Surgery and Consulting Surgeon to the Army, 1967-69. FRSocMed; Senior Fellow: Brit. Orthopædic Assoc.; Assoc. of Surgeons of Great Britain and Ireland. QHS 1967-69. *Publication:* contrib. to Basic Surgery. *Recreation:* sailing. *Address:* Sherwood, High Park Avenue, East Horsley, Surrey. *T:* East Horsley 2151. *Club:* Army and Navy.

**WHEELDON, Edward Christian,** CBE 1959; Chairman: Westland Engineers Ltd; Coenraets SA; Director, Westland Aircraft Ltd; *b* 12 May 1907; *s* of Edward Wheeldon, Manchester; *m* 1935, Alice Willan; one *s*. *Educ:* Openshaw Technical College; Manchester College of Technology. Served apprenticeship at Metropolitan-Vickers Ltd, Manchester, 1923-28; Process Engineer, 1928-34; Group Production Engineer, Parkinson and Cowan, 1934-38; joined Westland Aircraft Ltd as Planning Engineer, 1938; Works Supt, 1939; Works Manager, 1943; Works Dir 1944; Dep. Man. Dir, 1946; Man. Dir, 1950; Dep. Chm. and Man. Dir, 1960; Dep. Chm. and Chief Executive, 1965; Chm., 1968-70. Pres., Soc. of British Aerospace Cos Ltd, 1964-65, Treasurer, 1968-. FIProdE; FRAeS; FInstD. *Recreations:* golf, Association football. *Address:* Coker Firs, Yeovil, Somerset. *T:* Yeovil 3570. *Clubs:* Golf (Yeovil); Golf (Sherborne).

**WHEELDON, Rt. Rev. Philip William;** *see* Kimberley and Kuruman, Bishop of.

**WHEELER, Burton Kendall;** *b* Hudson, Mass, 27 Feb. 1882; *s* of Asa Leonard Wheeler and Mary Elizabeth Tyler; *m* 1907, Lulu White; three *s* three *d. Educ:* Public Schools; Business College; University of Michigan. LLD 1905; elected to Montana Legislature, 1910 (2-year term); US District Attorney, 1913-19; elected US Senate, 1922--1928-1934-1940; Chm. Indian Cttee (3-year); Chm. Interstate Commerce Committee (12-year); nominated Vice-Pres. on progressive ticket, 1924, with Elder Senator Robt M. La Follette. Practising Law, Southern Bldg, Washington, DC. *Recreations:* golf, fishing. *Address:* 704 Southern Building, Washington, DC 20005, USA. *T:* District 7-7117. *Clubs:* Mason, Burning Tree Golf, Metropolitan, Elks (Washington, DC).

**WHEELER, Sir Charles (Reginald),** KBE 1966 (CBE 1946); Company Director; *b* 5 December 1904; *s* of Henry Wheeler and Nellie Bowdler (*née* Healing); *m* 1929, Frieda Close; one *s* two *d. Educ:* St Paul's School. Joined Baldwins Ltd, 1922, and continued with this and associated Cos. Iron and Steel Control, Min. of Supply, 1939-45, Controller, 1945. Jt Man. Dir, Guest Keen Iron and Steel Co. Ltd, 1946-59; Chairman, 1959-60. Chairman, AEI Ltd, 1964-67; Director: Guest Keen & Nettlefolds Ltd; George Wimpey & Co. Ltd; Phœnix Assurance Co. Ltd; Rudolf Wolff (Holdings) Ltd; Triumph Investment Trust Ltd. President: British Electrical and Allied Manufacturers' Association, 1965; Electrical Research Association, 1966; British Iron and Steel Federation, 1961; Iron and Steel Institute, 1958-59. Member Court of Governors, University College of S Wales and Monmouthshire. Vice Pres., British Olympic Assoc.; Mem. Bd of Governors, and Jt Hon. Treasurer, English-Speaking Union. High Sheriff, Co. of Glamorgan, 1955. Officier Légion d'Honneur, 1966. Hon. DSc Salford, 1967. *Recreations:* beagling, rowing, golf. *Address:* The Old Croft, Bellingdon, near Chesham, Bucks; 1272a, Falconers House, St James' Court, Buckingham Gate, SW1. *Clubs:* Garrick, Leander, London Rowing.

**WHEELER, Sir Charles (Thomas);** KCVO 1958; CBE 1948; PPRA (RA 1940; ARA 1934); FRBS 1935 (President, 1944-49); Hon. FRIBA; Hon. RSA; Hon. RE; Hon. RWS; Hon. RI; sculptor: President of the Royal Academy, 1956-66; *b* Codsall (Freedom of Wolverhampton, 1958), 1892; *s* of S. P. Wheeler; *m* Muriel, *yr d* of A. W. Bourne; one *s* one *d. Educ:* South Kensington Royal Exhibitioner. A trustee, Tate Gallery, 1942-49. Exhibited at Royal Academy since 1914; executed sculptures on Winchester College War Memorial Cloisters, 1924; Bishop Jacob Memorial Church, Ilford; Indian Memorial at Neuve Chapelle, India House, South Africa House, Rhodes House, Oxford, Haileybury College Chapel, Royal Empire Society, The Bank of England, Church House, Jellicoe Memorial Bust and Fountain, Trafalgar Sq., RAF Memorial, Malta, English Electric House, Barclay's Bank, Queens Park, Invercargill, NZ, etc; Bust, Infant Christ, purchased for nation under Chantrey Bequest, 1924; also Bronze Statue, Spring, 1930; Aphrodite II, 1944; Earth and Water, 1952; Merchant Navy Memorial, Tower Hill; Statue of Gen. Katoka, Accra; Poseidon Fountain, George Yard, EC. Member Royal Fine Art Commission, 1946-52. Hon. Corresp. Academician, Royal Acad. of San Fernando, Madrid. Gold Medal Royal Soc. Brit. Sculptors for Distinguished Services to Sculpture, 1949; Gold Medal, USA National Academy of Design, 1963. Hon. DCL (Oxon), 1960. Hon. LLD (TCD) 1961. Officier de la Légion d'Honneur; Knight Comdr of the Crown of Siam; Commendatore Al Merito della Repubblica Italiana. *Publication:* (Autobiography) High Relief, 1968. *Address:* Garden Studio, 22 Cathcart Road, South Kensington, SW10. *T:* 01-352 8234; Woodreed Farmhouse, Five Ashes, Mayfield, Sussex. *T:* Hadlow Down 303. *Clubs:* Athenæum, Arts, Chelsea Arts, Savage.

**WHEELER, Dr Denis Edward,** CBE 1965; BSc, PhD, FRIC; Managing Director of The Wellcome Foundation Ltd, 1948-67, Deputy Chairman, since 1967; *b* 6 Sept. 1910; *s* of late Edward James Wheeler; *m* 1938, Dilys Mary, *d* of late Alfred Evans; one *d. Educ:* Queen Elizabeth's, Bristol; University of Bristol (BSc, PhD); Princeton Univ., USA (Salters Fellow). ICI (Explosives), 1935-40; Research and Development Dir, Hardman & Holden Ltd, 1940-45; Asst Managing Dir, The Wellcome Foundation Ltd, 1946. Member: Economic Development Cttee for Chemical Industry; Council CBI; Mem., Trade Affairs Bd of Chemical Industries Assoc.; Vice-Pres., Spastics Soc., 1967 (Chm. 1963-66); Pres., Assoc. of Brit. Pharmaceutical Industry, 1963 and 1964. Master, Salters' Co., 1969-70. *Recreation:* golf. *Address:* The Wellcome Building, Euston Road, NW1. *T:* 01-387 4477. *Club:* Athenæum.

**WHEELER, Sir Frederick (Henry),** Kt 1967; CBE 1962 (OBE 1952); Chairman, Commonwealth Public Service Board, Canberra, since 1961; *b* 9 Jan. 1914; *s* of late A. H. Wheeler; *m* 1939, Peggy Hilda, *d* of Basil P. Bell; one *s* two *d. Educ:* Scotch College; Melbourne University (BCom). State Savings Bank of Victoria, 1929-39; Treasury: Research Officer, 1939; Economist, 1944; Asst Sec., 1946; First Asst Sec., 1949-52; Treasurer Comptroller, ILO, Geneva, 1952-60. Member: British Commonwealth Finance Ministers' Conferences; Austr. Delegns Bretton Woods Monetary Conf.; UN Civil Service Adv. Bd, 1969-. *Address:* 9 Charlotte Street, Red Hill, ACT, Australia. *T:* 959 888. *Clubs:* (Pres. 1966-69) Commonwealth (Canberra); Royal Canberra Golf.

**WHEELER, Geoffrey,** CB 1952; Principal Establishment Officer, Ministry of Technology, since 1967; *b* 22 Nov. 1909; *s* of late A. E. Wheeler; *m* 1937, Dorothy Mary Wallis; one *s* one *d. Educ:* Clay Cross School, Derbyshire; St John's Coll., Cambridge (Scholar). First Class Part I Historical Tripos, 1930; First Class Part II Historical Tripos, 1931. Entered Civil Service, 1932, and appointed to Board of Customs and Excise; Private Sec. to Sir Evelyn Murray, 1936; Principal, 1937; Assistant Secretary, 1943; Under-Secretary (Ministry of Defence), 1948; on loan to Ministry of Defence, 1947-64; Under-Secretary, Min. of Aviation, 1964-67, Min. of Technology, 1967-. *Recreations:* music; amateur theatre. *Address:* 63 Woodcote Valley Road, Purley, Surrey. *T:* 01-660 2858.

**WHEELER, Lt-Col Geoffrey Edleston,** CIE 1943; CBE 1948; Hon. MA University of Durham, 1955; Director of Central Asian Research Centre, 1953-68; *b* 22 June 1897; *s* of late Capt. Owen Wheeler, Leicestershire Regiment; *m* 1927, Irena Nicolaevna Boulatoff; one *s. Educ:* Eastbourne Coll. Commissioned Queen's Regt 1915; served in France, 1915-17; transferred to Indian Army, 1918, 6th Gurkha Rifles; various Intelligence appointments in Turkey, Malta, and Palestine to 1925; Military Attaché, Meshed, 1926; Intelligence duties in Iraq,

1928-31; 7th Rajput Regt to 1936; General Staff, Army HQ, India, 1936-41; Director, Publications Division, Govt of India, 1941-46; Counsellor, British Embassy, Teheran, 1946-50. Sir Percy Sykes Memorial Medal, RCAS, 1967. *Publications:* Racial Problems in Soviet Muslim Asia; The Modern History of Soviet Central Asia; The Peoples of Soviet Central Asia. *Address:* Inglecroft, The Avenue, Tadworth, Surrey. *Club:* Naval and Military.

**WHEELER, Rt. Rev. Monsignor Gordon;** *see* Wheeler, W. G.

**WHEELER, Air Marshal Sir (Henry) Neil (George),** KCB 1969 (CB 1967); CBE 1957 (OBE 1949); DSO 1943; DFC 1941 (Bar 1943); AFC 1954; Air Member for Supply and Organisation, Ministry of Defence, since Dec. 1970; *b* 8 July 1917; *s* of T. H. Wheeler, South African Police; *m* 1942, Elizabeth, *d* of W. H. Weightman, *qv*; two *s* one *d*. *Educ:* St Helen's College, Southsea, Hants. Entered Royal Air Force College, Cranwell, 1935; Bomber Comd, 1937-40; Fighter and Coastal Comds, 1940-45; RAF and US Army Staff Colls, 1943-44; Directing Staff, RAF Staff Coll., 1945-46; FEAF, 1947-49; Directing Staff, JSSC, 1949-51; Bomber Comd, 1951-53; Air Min., 1953-57. Asst Comdt, RAF Coll., 1957-59; OC, RAF Laarbruch, 1959-60; IDC, 1961; Min. of Defence, 1961-63; Senior Air Staff Officer, HQ, RAF Germany (2nd TAF), Sept. 1963-66; Asst Chief of Defence Staff (Operational Requirements), MoD, 1966-67, Deputy Chief of Defence Staff, 1967-68; Commander, FEAF, 1969-70. ADC to the Queen, 1957-61. *Address:* HQ FEAF, RAF Changi, c/o GPO Singapore, Singapore; Boundary Hall, Cooksbridge, Lewes, Sussex. *Clubs:* Hurlingham, RAF.

*See also Maj.-Gen. T. N. S. Wheeler.*

**WHEELER, Sir John (Hieron),** 3rd Bt *cr* 1920; Chairman, Raithby, Lawrence & Co. Ltd; *b* 22 July 1905; 2nd *s* of Sir Arthur Wheeler, 1st Bt; *S* brother, Sir Arthur (Frederick Pullman) Wheeler, 1964; *m* 1929, Gwendolen Alice (*née* Oram); two *s*. *Educ:* Charterhouse. Engaged in Print. Served War of 1939-45, Trooper, RTR, 1941-45. After the war, returned to printing. *Recreations:* whittling, dry stone walling. *Heir:* *s* John Frederick Wheeler [*b* 3 May 1933; *m* 1963, Barbara Mary, *d* of Raymond Flint, Leicester; two *s* one *d*]. *Address:* 39 Morland Avenue, Leicester. *Club:* Eccentric.

**WHEELER, Michael Mortimer,** QC 1961; *b* Westminster, 8 Jan. 1915; *o s* of Sir Mortimer Wheeler, *qv*, and late Tessa Verney Wheeler, FSA; *m* 1939, Sheila, *e d* of late M. S. Mayou, FRCS; two *d*. *Educ:* Dragon School, Oxford; Rugby School; Christ Church, Oxford. Barrister; Gray's Inn, 1938; Lincoln's Inn, 1946 (Bencher 1967). Served throughout War of 1939-45, with RA (TA) in UK and Italy (Lt-Col 1945; despatches); TD 1961. *Address:* 114 Hallam Street, W1. *T:* 01-580 7284. *Clubs:* Garrick, MCC.

**WHEELER, Sir Mortimer;** *see* Wheeler, Sir R. E. M.

**WHEELER, Sir Neil;** *see* Wheeler, Sir H. N. G.

**WHEELER, Brig. (retd) Ralph Pung,** CBE 1952; late RE; (formerly Deputy Director-General, Ordnance Survey); *b* 21 Nov. 1898; *s* of Charles William Wheeler, Speenhamland, near Newbury; *m* 1931, Norah Cordukes Kitchin, *d* of Frederick Hyland Kitchin, Harrogate; two *s*. *Educ:* Owen's School; RMA Woolwich; Peterhouse, Cambridge. Egypt and Palestine, 1917-18; Waziristan, 1920-23; Gold Coast, 1926-28; France and Belgium (despatches), 1939-40; Tunisia, Sicily and Italy, 1943-44; Palestine, 1945-46; seconded to Ordnance Survey, 1935-39 and 1946-. Capt., 1927; Major, 1937; Lt-Col, 1940; Col 1946; Brigadier, 1950. *Recreation:* golf. *Address:* Woodbine Farm, Brent Knoll, Somerset. *T:* Brent Knoll 388.

**WHEELER, Maj.-Gen. (retd) Richard Henry Littleton,** CB 1960; CBE 1953; Maj.-Gen. RA, HQ, Northern Army Group (Northag), 1958-61; *b* 2 Nov. 1906; *s* of Maj. Henry Littleton Wheeler, CB, DSO, and Vera Gillum Webb; *m* 1941, Iris Letitia Hope; one *d*. *Educ:* Uppingham; RMA, Woolwich. 2nd Lt RA, 1926. Served War of 1939-45, 50th Division. Lt-Col 1942; Brigadier 1950; Temp. Maj.-Gen. 1958; Maj.-Gen. 1959. Col Comdt RA, 1963. *Recreations:* riding, music. *Address:* Manor Farm, Knighton, Sherborne, Dorset. *Club:* Army and navy.

**WHEELER, Sir (Robert Eric) Mortimer,** CH 1967; Kt 1952; CIE 1947; MC, TD; SPk (Sitara-i-Pakistan) 1964; MA, DLit (London), Hon. DLitt (Bristol, Delhi, Ireland, Wales, Oxford and Liverpool); Hon. Brigadier; FRS 1968; FBA 1941 (Sec., 1949-68); FSA (Pres., 1954-59; Vice-Pres., 1935-39; Sec., 1939; Dir, 1940-44 and 1949-54; Gold Medal, 1944); Commissioner, Royal Commission on Historical Monuments (England), 1939-58; Chairman, Ancient Monuments Board for England, 1964-66; Trustee, British Museum, since 1963; Professor of Ancient History to Royal Academy, since 1965; Fellow of University College, London, 1922; *b* 1890; *m* 1st, 1914, Tessa Verney, FSA (*d* 1936); one *s*; 2nd, 1939, Mavis de Vere Cole (marr. diss. 1942; she *d* 1970); 3rd, 1945, Margaret Norfolk. Franks Student in Archæology, 1913; on staff of Royal Commission on Historical Monuments (England), 1913; Major, Royal Field Artillery, 1917, France, Italy, Germany (MC, despatches); Keeper of the Archæological Department, National Museum of Wales, 1920-24; Lecturer in Archæology, University of Wales, 1920-24; Director National Museum of Wales, 1924-26; Keeper and Secretary of the London Museum, 1926-44; Lecturer in British Archæology, University College, London; Hon. Director Institute of Archæology, London University, 1934-44; Dir-Gen. Archæology, India, 1944-48; Adviser in Archæological matters to Dominion of Pakistan, 1948-50; Prof. of the Archæology of the Roman Provinces, University of London, 1948-55. Lieutenant-Colonel RA, TA, 1939, raised and commanded a regiment RA, Brig., 1943 (8th Army in Africa, El Alamein to Tunis; 10th Corps in Italy, Salerno landing). Rhys Lecturer (British Academy), 1929; Norman Lockyer Lecturer (British Association), 1937; Rhind Lecturer (Edinburgh), 1951; Norton Lecturer (Arch. Inst. of America), 1952; Hobhouse Lecturer, Univ. of London, 1955; nominated Queen's Lectr in Berlin, 1968; President: Cambrian Archæological Assoc., 1931; South Eastern Union of Scientific Societies, 1932; Conf. of Delegates, British Assoc., 1933; Museums Assoc., 1937-38; Indian Museums Assoc., 1947-48; Pakistan Museums Association, 1949-50; Royal Archæological Institute, 1951-53; Section H Brit. Assoc., 1954. Hon. MRIA; Hon. Mem., Archæological Inst. of America. Hon. Life Mem., NY Acad. of Sciences, 1963; Corres. Mem., German Archæological Inst. Hon. Fellow, School of Oriental and African Studies, 1970. Led Govt Missions from India to Iran and Afghanistan, 1945-46. Directed archæological excavations at: Colchester, 1917 and 1920; Carnarvon, 1921-23; Brecon, 1924-25; Caerleon, 1926-27; Lydney, 1928-29; St Albans, 1930-33; Maiden Castle (Dorset), 1934-37; Brittany, 1938; Normandy, 1939;

India, 1944-48; Pakistan, 1950 and 1958; Stanwick (Yorks) 1951-52, etc. Petrie Medal, Univ. of London, 1950; Lucy Wharton Drexel Medal, Pennsylvania Univ., 1952. OStJ. *Publications:* books on Segontium and the Roman Occupation of Wales, 1924; Prehistoric and Roman Wales, 1925; The Roman Fort near Brecon, 1926; Prehistoric and Roman Site at Lydney, 1932; The Belgic and Roman Cities of Verulamium, 1936; Maiden Castle, 1943; 5,000 Years of Pakistan, 1950; The Indus Civilisation, 1953, 1962 and 1968; Archæology from the Earth, 1954; Rome beyond the Imperial Frontiers, 1954; The Stanwick Fortifications, 1954; Hill-forts of Northern France, 1957; Early India and Pakistan, 1959; Charsada, 1962; Roman Art and Architecture, 1964; Still Digging (autobiog.), 1955; Alms for Oblivion (collected essays), 1966; Roman Africa (with R. Wood), 1966; Civilizations of the Indus Valley and Beyond, 1966; Flames over Persepolis (Alexander in the East), 1968; and papers on European and Indian archæological subjects. *Address:* British Academy, Burlington House, W1. *T:* 01-734 0457. *Club:* Athenæum.
*See also Michael Mortimer Wheeler.*

**WHEELER, Maj.-Gen. Thomas Norman Samuel,** CB 1967; CBE 1964 (OBE 1958); Chief of Staff, HQ, BAOR, since 1969; *b* 16 June 1915; *e s* of late Thomas Henry Wheeler, S African Police; *m* 1939, Helen Clifford, *y d* of F. H. E. Webber, Emsworth, Hants; one *s* one *d*. *Educ:* South Africa; St Helen's College, Southsea; RMC Sandhurst. Commissioned Royal Ulster Rifles, 1935; Palestine Rebellion, 1937-39 (despatches). Served War of 1939-45 (despatches twice): Bde Major, 38 Irish Bde, 1941-42; MEF, 1942-43; British Military Mission to Albania, 1943-44; 2nd Bn Royal Ulster Rifles, 1944-45. AA & QMG 6th Airborne Div., 1945-46; Airborne Establishment, 1946-47; Mil. Asst to Adj.-Gen. to the Forces, 1949-50; UK Services Liaison Staff, Australia, 1951-52; GSO1 and Col GS, HQ Northern Army Group and HQ, BAOR, 1954-57; comd 1st Bn Royal Ulster Rifles Cyprus Rebellion, 1958-59 (despatches); comd 39 Inf. Bde Group, N Ireland, 1960-62; Chief of Staff 1st (British) Corps, BAOR, 1962-63; General Officer Commanding Second Division, 1964-66; Chief of Staff, Contingencies Planning, SHAPE, 1966-69. *Recreations:* travel, tennis, water skiing. *Address:* c/o Lloyds Bank Ltd, 6 Pall Mall, SW1. *Clubs:* Army and Navy, Airborne.
*See also Sir Neil Wheeler.*

**WHEELER, Rt. Rev. (William) Gordon;** *see* Leeds, Bishop of, (RC).

**WHEELER, William Henry,** CMG 1959; PhD (London); Managing Director since 1961, and Deputy Chairman since 1968, Urquhart Engineering Co. Ltd (formerly Urquharts (1926) Ltd), Perivale and Bristol (Deputy Managing Director, 1959-61); *b* Petersfield, Hants, 5 March 1907; *s* of John William and Ellen Wheeler; *m* 1937, Mary Inkpen; no *c*. *Educ:* St Catharine's Coll., Cambridge (BA); Imperial Coll. of Science (DIC). Beit Memorial Research Fellow, Imperial Coll., 1931. Man. British Automatic Refrigerators, London, 1935; Government Scientific Service, 1937; Head of UK Ministry of Supply Staff, Australia, 1955; Director of Explosives Research, Waltham Abbey, 1959. *Publications:* papers on Combustion and Detonation in Proc. and Trans. Royal Society, and on Rocket Propellants in Nature, Proc. of Inst. of Fuel and Instn of Chemical Engineers; papers on the Mechanism of Cavitation Erosion for DSIR and American Soc. of Mechanical Engineers. *Recreation:* private research laboratory. *Address:* Mark House, Ashmead Lane, Denham, Bucks. *T:* Denham 3263.

**WHEELER-BENNETT, Sir John (Wheeler),** KCVO 1959; CMG 1953; OBE 1946; MA (Oxon), MA (Ch. Ch.), FRSL; Hon. DCL (Oxon), 1960; Hon. Fellow, St Anthony's, 1961; Historian; Historical Adviser, Royal Archives, since 1959; Governor: Cuddesdon Theological Coll.; Lord Williams's Grammar Sch., Thame; Member Council: Ditchley Foundation (Chm., 1961-63); Malvern College (Chairman, 1964-67); Trustee, Imperial War Museum; *b* Keston, Kent, 13 Oct. 1902; 2nd *surv. s* of late John Wheeler Wheeler-Bennett, CBE, JP, and Christina Hill McNutt, of Truro, Nova Scotia; *m* 1945, Ruth Harrison Risher, Charlottesville, Va. *Educ:* Wellington House, Westgate-on-Sea; Malvern Coll. Travelled extensively; Asst Publicity Secretary, League of Nations Union, 1923-24; Founder and Hon. Secretary of the Information Service on International Affairs, 1924-30; Hon. Information Secretary, RIIA, 1927-31; Founder and Editor, 1924-32, Bulletin of International News; Lecturer in International Law and Relations, University of Virginia, 1938-39; attached British Library of Information, New York, 1939-40; Assistant-Director, British Press Service, New York, 1940-41; Special Assistant to Director-General of British Information Services in the United States, 1941-42; Head of New York Office of British Political Warfare Mission in the United States, 1942-44; European Adviser to Political Intelligence Dept of Foreign Office, 1944, Assistant Director-General, 1945; Assistant to British Political Adviser to SHAEF, 1944-45; attached to British Prosecuting Team at War Criminal Trial, Nuremberg, 1946; British Editor-in-Chief of captured German Foreign Ministry Archives, 1946-48; Historical Adviser to Foreign Office Project for publishing GFM Archives, 1948-56; Lecturer in Internat. Politics, New College, Oxford, 1946-50; Fellow of St Anthony's College, Oxford, 1950-57; Governor, Radley College, 1955-67; Member Council, RIIA, 1930-38, 1959-67. Leslie Stephen Lecturer, Cambridge University, 1955; Dance Memorial Lecturer, Virginia Military Inst., Lexington, Virginia, 1960; Visiting Lecturer in Politics and History, Univ. of Arizona, 1964, 1966, 1968, 1969, 1970; Page-Barbour Lectr, Univ. of Virginia, 1966; Vis. Prof. of Modern Hist., NY Univ., 1967, 1968-69, 1969-70, 1971; Scholar-in-Residence, Univ. of Virginia, 1967-68. Hon. Citizen of New Orleans, USA, 1949. *Publications:* Information on the Reduction of Armaments, 1925; Information on the Problem of Security (with F. E. Langermann), 1927; Information on the Renunciation of War, 1928; Information on the World Court, 1918-28 (with Maurice Fanshawe), 1929; Information on the Reparation Settlement (with H. Latimer), 1930; Disarmament and Security since Locarno, 1932; The Wreck of Reparations, 1933; the Disarmament Deadlock, 1934; Hindenburg, the Wooden Titan, 1936; Brest-Litovsk; The Forgotten Peace, March 1918, 1938; Munich, Prologue to Tragedy, 1948; Nemesis of Power: the German Army in Politics, 1918-45, 1953; King George VI, his Life and Reign, 1958; John Anderson, Viscount Waverley, 1962; A Wreath to Clio, 1967; (ed) Action this Day, Working with Churchill, 1968; Semblance of Peace (with Anthony Nicholls), 1971; contributor to Foreign Affairs, Virginia Quarterly Review, History Today, New York Review, Dictionary of National Biography, Encyclopædia Britannica, etc. *Address:* Garsington Manor, near Oxford. *T:* Garsington 234. *Clubs:* Beefsteak, Brooks's, Pratt's; Union

Interalliée (Paris); Colonnade, University of Virginia (Charlottesville, Va); The Brook, Century, New York University (New York).

**WHEEN, Rear-Adm. Charles Kerr Thorneycroft,** CB 1966; *b* 28 Sept. 1912; *s* of F. T. Wheen, Holmbury, Chislehurst, Kent; *m* 1940, Veryan Rosamond, *d* of late William Acworth, Chobham; three *s* one *d*. *Educ:* RN College, Dartmouth. Entered RN as Cadet, 1926. Served War of 1939-45: China, The Nore, Admiralty, Normandy Landings, East Indies. Naval Attaché, Beirut, Amman and Addis Ababa, 1958-60; Director of Officers' Appointments (S), Admiralty, 1960-63; Flag Officer Admiralty Interview Board, 1964-66. Capt. 1956; Rear-Adm. 1964; retd 1966. Director, Cement Makers Fedn, 1967-. *Recreation:* golf. *Address:* Donnystone, Chobham, Surrey. *T:* Chobham 8118. *Club:* Army and Navy.

**WHELAN, Air Cdre James Roger,** CBE 1968; DSO 1944; DFC 1940 (Bar 1943); RAF retired; with Glen Line, EC3, since 1968; *b* Saskatoon, Sask, Canada, 29 April 1914; *s* of James P. Whelan; *m* 1946, Irene, *d* of late P. Rennie, Bathurst, NB, Canada; two *d*. *Educ:* Bathurst High School; Univ. of St Francis Xavier, Antigonish, NS, Canada. Commissioned, RAF, 1937. Served War of 1939-45: France, Egypt, Germany, Italy. Commanded RAF St Eval, 1957-58; Base Comdr, Christmas Island, 1959; Dir of Intelligence (B), Air Min., 1961-64; AO i/c A, HQ Coastal Command, 1965-68. RAF Staff Coll., 1949; jssc, 1952; idc, 1960. *Recreations:* ski-ing, tennis, photography. *Address:* 26 Laburnum Court, Dennis Lane, Stanmore, Middx. *T:* 01-954 2255. *Club:* Royal Air Force.

**WHELDON, Huw Pyrs,** OBE 1952; MC 1944; Managing Director, Television, British Broadcasting Corporation, since 1969; *b* 7 May 1916; *e s* of late Sir Wynn Wheldon, and of Lady Wheldon, Canonbury, Prestatyn, Wales; *m* 1956, Jacqueline Mary (*née* Clarke); one *s* two *d*. *Educ:* Friars Sch., Bangor, Wales; London Sch. of Economics. Kent Educn Cttee staff, 1939. Commnd Royal Welch Fusiliers, 1940; served NW Europe and Middle East with 1st and 6th Airborne Divs (Major, 1st Bn Roy. Ulster Rifles), 1941-45. Arts Coun., Dir for Wales, 1946; Festival of Britain Directorate, 1949; BBC Television, 1952-; Producer of Men in Battle, Orson Welles Sketchbook, Portraits of Power, Monitor, etc, 1953-62; Head of Documentary Programmes, 1962; Head of Music and Documentary Programmes, 1963-65; Controller of Programmes, 1965-68. Mem. Coun., Hon. Soc. of Cymmrodorion. FRSA; Hon. Fellow, Manchester Coll. of Art and Design. *Address:* 120 Richmond Hill, Richmond, Surrey. *Club:* Savile.

**WHELER, Captain Sir Trevor Wood,** 13th Bt, *cr* 1660; late Captain Royal Sussex Regiment, TF, 1914-20, and Royal Engineers, 1940-47; *b* 20 Sept. 1889; *s* of 12th Bt and Mary Leontine, *d* of Sir Richard Wood, GCMG; *S* father, 1903; *m* 1915, Margaret Idris, *y d* of late Sir Ernest Birch, KCMG; one *s* two *d*. *Heir: s* Edward Woodford Wheler, late Capt. Royal Sussex Regt [*b* 13 June 1920; *m* 1945, Molly Ashworth, *e d* of Thomas Lever, Devon; one *s* one *d*]. *Address:* 19 Knole Court, Knole Road, Bexhill-on-Sea, Sussex. *T:* Bexhill 1333.

**WHETTON, Prof. John Thomas,** DSO 1943; OBE 1941; MC 1919; TD 1951; Professor of Mining, University of Leeds, 1945-60, now Emeritus; Private Consultant, Mining, Surveying, Geophysical Surveying, since 1960; *b* 27 Oct. 1894; *m*; no *c*. *Educ:* Universities of Leeds and Durham. MSc (Leeds); MSc (Durham); 1st Class Colliery Manager's Certificate. Practical Mining experience West and South Yorks, Durham, Northumberland, Germany, France, Belgium, Poland and Canada. Visited oil fields of the Middle East, Venezuela and Trinidad. Army service France and Russia, 1914-19. Reader in Mining, King's Coll., Univ. of Durham, 1924-39. Comd 4th Survey Regt RA TA, 1937-48; service in Balkans, Middle East and NW Europe. Mining Advr (Tech.), Ruhr, Germany, 1945. Pro-Vice-Chancellor, University of Leeds, 1955-57. Founder Member, International Organising Mining Committee, 1957. Nuffield Foundn and Research Coun. of Canada Lectr, 1960; Engineers Jt Coun., Lectr, American Inst. of Mining Engineers, 1964. Hon. Col, Leeds Univ. Officers' Training Corps T & AVR, 1968-69. President, Midland Institute of Mining Engineers, 1960-61. Russian Order of St Stanislav 2nd class with swords, 1919; Belgian Order of the Crown with Palm, 1945; Belgian Croix de Guerre, 1945. *Publications:* contrib. Prospecting, Boring, and Sinking sections in Coal Mining Practice, 1958; numerous research and general papers on mining and allied sciences to technical press and instns in UK, Canada, USA, Holland, Poland and Czechoslovakia, from 1925. *Recreations:* cricket and bowls. *Address:* Westbourne House, 16 Westbourne Grove, Scarborough, Yorks. *T:* Scarborough 2432.

**WHEWELL, Prof. Charles Smalley,** PhD; Professor and Head of Department of Textile Industries, University of Leeds, since Oct. 1963 (Professor of Textile Technology, 1954-63); *b* 26 April 1912; *m* 1937, Emma Stott, PhD; one *s*. *Educ:* Grammar School, Darwen, Lancs; University of Leeds (BSc, PhD). Research Chemist, Wool Industries Research Association, 1935-37. University of Leeds, 1937-: Lecturer in Textile Chemistry; Lecturer in Textile Finishing; Senior Lecturer in Textile Chemistry; Reader in Textile Finishing. Textile Institute Medal, 1954; Warner Memorial Medal, 1960. *Publications:* contrib. to: Chambers's Encyclopædia; British Wool Manual; Waterproofing and Water-repellency; Jl Soc. of Dyers and Colourists; Jl Textile Inst. *Recreation:* music (organ). *Address:* Department of Textile Industries, The University of Leeds, Leeds 2. *T:* Leeds 31751.

**WHICKER, Alan Donald;** television broadcaster (Whicker's World); writer; *b* 2 Aug. 1925; *o s* of late Charles Henry Whicker and late Anne Jane Cross. *Educ:* Haberdashers' Aske's Sch. Capt., Devonshire Regt; Dir, Army Film and Photo Section, with 8th Army and US 5th Army. War Corresp. in Korea, For. Corresp., novelist, writer and radio broadcaster before going to BBC. TV (Tonight progr.), 1957; appeared nightly in filmed reports from around the world, studio interviews, outside broadcasts, Eurovision, Telstar. First Series of Whicker's World, 1959-60; Whicker Down Under, 1961; Whicker on Top of the World!, 1962. Wrote and reported The Bombmakers (Los Alamos), etc. Played in film, The Angry Silence; conducted first Telstar two-way transmission, at opening of UN Assembly, NY, 1962. Whicker in Sweden, Whicker in the Heart of Texas, Whicker down Mexico Way, 1963. Alan Whicker Report series: The Solitary Billionaire (J. Paul Getty), etc. In 1965: began to write and appear in own series of monthly documentaries on BBC 2, subseq. repeated on BBC 1, under series title, Whicker's World; 31 Progrs (many in colour) later shown around the world. Various cinema films; BBC radio progrs and articles for The Listener, etc. Mem., consortium for Yorkshire Television, 1967. Left BBC, contrib. a documentary series to ITV, 1968 (originated by Yorks TV).

Completed 16 Documentaries for Yorkshire TV during its first year of operation, inc. Whicker's New World Series, and Specials on Gen. Stroessner of Paraguay, Count von Rosen, and Pres. Duvalier of Haiti; Whicker in Europe; Whicker's Walkabout. Various awards, 1963-, incl. Screenwriters' Guild, best Documentary Script, 1963; Guild of Television Producers and Directors Personality of the Year, 1964; Silver Medal, Royal Television Soc., 1968; Dumont Award, Univ. of California, 1970. FRSA 1970. *Publications:* Some Rise by Sin, 1949; Away–with Alan Whicker, 1963; Sunday newspaper columns; contrib. various internat. pubns. *Recreations:* people, photography, writing, travel, and reading (usually airline timetables). *Address:* Capel House, New Broad Street, EC2.

**WHIFFEN, David Hardy,** FRS 1966; MA, DPhil (Oxon), DSc (Birmingham); Professor of Physical Chemistry, University of Newcastle upon Tyne, since 1968; *s* of Noël H. and Mary Whiffen; *m* Jean P. Bell; four *s*. *Educ:* Oundle School; St John's College, Oxford (Scholar). Sometime Commonwealth Fund Fellow, Sen. Student of Commn for 1851 Exhibition. Formerly: Lectr in Chemistry, Univ. of Birmingham; Supt, Molecular Science Div., NPL. *Publications:* papers in scientific jls. *Address:* Department of Physical Chemistry, The University, Newcastle upon Tyne, NE1 7RU. *T:* Newcastle 28511.

**WHINNEY, Margaret Dickens,** FBA 1967; DLit; *b* 4 Feb. 1897; *d* of Thomas Bostock Whinney and Sydney Margaret Dickens. *Educ:* private schools. Academic Diploma in Hist. of Art, Univ. of London, 1935; DLit, Univ. of London, 1946. Reader in the History of Art, Courtauld Inst. of Art, 1950-64. Hon. Sec. and Ed., Walpole Soc., 1957-; Trustee, Sir John Soane's Museum, 1960-; Mem., Adv. Coun., Victoria and Albert Museum, 1966-; FSA 1944; Vice-Pres., Soc. of Antiquaries, 1960-64. Hon. FRIBA 1969. *Publications:* English Art, 1625-1714 (Oxford History of English Art) (with Oliver Millar), 1957; Sculpture in Britain, 1530-1830 (Pelican History of Art), 1964; Catalogue of Models by John Flaxman at University Coll., London (with late Rupert Gunnis), 1967; Early Flemish Painting, 1968; Home House, 1969; articles in Walpole Soc., Jl of Warburg and Courtauld Insts, Archæological Jl, etc. *Address:* 58 Marlborough Court, Pembroke Road, W8. *T:* 01-937 8568. *Club:* (Lady Assoc. Mem.) Oxford and Cambridge University.

**WHIPPLE, Prof. Fred Lawrence;** Director, Smithsonian Institution Astrophysical Observatory, since 1955; Phillips Professor of Astronomy, Harvard University, since 1968; *b* 5 Nov. 1906; *s* of Harry Lawrence Whipple and Celestia Whipple (*née* MacFarland); *m* 1st, 1928, Dorothy Woods (divorced 1935); one *s*; 2nd, 1946, Babette Frances Samelson; two *d*. *Educ:* Long Beach High School, Calif; UCLA; Univ. of California, Berkeley. Lick Observatory Fellow, 1930-31; Staff Member, Harvard Univ., 1931-; Instructor, 1932-38; Lecturer, 1938-45; Assoc. Prof., 1945-50; Professor, 1950-; Chm. Dept of Astronomy, 1949-56. US Nat. Cttee of Internat. Geophysical Year: Chm. Techn. Panel on Rocketry, 1955-59; Member: Techn. Panel on Earth Satellite Program, 1955-59; Working Group on Satellite Tracking and Computation, 1955-58; Scientific Advisory Bd to USAF, 1953-; Cttee on Meteorology, Nat. Acad. of Sciences, Nat. Research Coun., 1958-; Special Cttees on Space Techn., Nat. Advisory Cttee for Aeronautics, 1958- (now NASA), US; Space Sciences Working Group on Orbiting Astronomical Observatories, Nat. Acad. of Sciences (Mem. Nat. Acad. of Sciences, 1959-); Advisory Panel to Cttee on Sci. and Astronautics of US House of Representatives; Amer. Philosophical Soc., Philadelphia; Amer. Acad. of Arts and Sciences, Boston; New York Acad. of Science, NY; several technical societies. Associate, Royal Astronomical Soc., 1970-. Benjamin Franklin Fellow, RSA, 1968-. Editor: Smithsonian Contributions to Astrophysics, 1956-; Planetary and Space Science, 1958-. Hon. degrees: MA, Harvard Univ., 1945; DSc, Amer. Internat. Coll., 1958; DLitt, Northeastern Univ., 1961; DS, Temple Univ., 1961; LLD, CW Post Coll. of Long Island Univ., 1962. J. Lawrence Smith Medal of Nat. Acad. of Sciences, 1949; Donohue Medals, 1932, 1933, 1937, 1940, 1942 (received two medals that year); Presidential Certificate of Merit, 1948; Exceptional Service Award, US Air Force Scientific Adv. Bd, 1960; Space Flight Award, Amer. Astron. Soc., 1961; President's Award for Distinguished Federal Civilian Service, 1963; Space Pioneers Medallion, 1968; NASA Public Services Award, 1969; also has foreign awards. *Publications:* Earth, Moon and Planets, 1942, 3rd edn 1968. Many technical papers in various astronomical and geophysical journals and books; popular articles in magazines and in Encyclopædia Britannica. *Recreation:* cultivation of roses. *Address:* Harvard College Observatory, or Smithsonian Astrophysical Observatory, 60 Garden Street, Cambridge, Mass 02138, USA. *T:* Boston University 4-7383.

**WHIPPLE, Prof. George Hoyt;** Professor of Pathology, University of Rochester School of Medicine and Dentistry, 1921-55; now Emeritus; Dean, 1921-53, now Emeritus; *b* 28 Aug. 1878; *s* of Ashley Cooper Whipple, MD, and Frances Anna Hoyt; *m* 1914, Katherine Ball Waring; one *s* one *d*. *Educ:* Yale University, AB, MA 1927; Johns Hopkins University, MD, Hon. LLD 1947. Assistant in Pathology, Johns Hopkins Medical School, 1905-06; Instructor, 1906-07; Pathologist, Ancon Hospital, Panama, 1907-08; Associate in Pathology, Johns Hopkins Medical School, 1909-11; Associate Professor, 1911-14; Resident Pathologist, Johns Hopkins Hospital, 1910-14; Professor of Research Medicine, Univ. of California Medical School, and Director of the Hooper Foundation for Medical Research, University of California, 1914-21; Dean of the Univ. of California Medical School, 1920-21; Board of Scientific Directors, The Rockefeller Institute for Medical Research since 1936 and Bd of Trustees, 1939-60, Emer., 1960-; Member: Nat. Acad. of Sciences, American Philosophical Society; Hon. Member: Pathological Society of Gt Brit. and Ireland; Internat. Assoc. for Dental Research; Foreign Corresponding Mem., BMA, 1957. Nobel Prize in Medicine, joint award, 1934; Charles Mickle Fellowship, Univ. of Toronto, 1938; Kober Medal Georgetown Univ., 1939; Gold-Headed Cane Award (Amer. Assoc. of Pathologists and Bacteriologists), 1961; Kovalenko Medal (National Acad. of Sciences), 1962. Hon. LLD Glasgow, 1951; numerous other Hon. doctorates in science and laws from American and foreign universities. *Publications:* 270 medical publications. *Recreations:* fishing, hunting, all outdoor recreation. *Address:* 260 Crittenden Boulevard, Rochester, NY 14620, USA.

**WHISHAW, Sir Charles (Percival Law),** Kt 1969; Senior Partner in Freshfields, Solicitors (Partner since 1943); Trustee, Calouste Gulbenkian Foundation, since 1956; *b* 29 October 1909; 2nd *s* of late Montague Law Whishaw and Erna Louise (*née* Spies); *m* 1936,

Margaret Joan, *e d* of late Col T. H. Hawkins, CMG, RMLI; one *s* two *d*. *Educ:* Charterhouse; Worcester College, Oxford. Barrister, 1938; Solicitor, 1939. Member: Iron and Steel Holding and Realisation Agency, 1953-67; Council, Law Soc. *Address:* Holmwood Cottage, Holmwood, Surrey. *T:* Dorking 6220. *Clubs:* Savile, City of London.

**WHISHAW, Sir Ralph,** Kt 1958; CBE 1957; Consulting Physician, Royal Hobart Hospital, Tasmania, since 1955; Consulting Physician, Repatriation Commission, Tasmania, since 1936; *b* Croydon, 29 March 1895; *s* of late Reginald Robert Whishaw, Croydon; *m* 1921, Violet Mary, *d* of G. Beckley; one *d*. *Educ:* Friends' High School, Hobart; Sydney University. MB, ChM 1918; MRCP 1935; FRACP 1938; FRCP 1954. Physician Royal Hobart Hospital, 1930-55. President BMA, Tasmania Br., 1938; Vice-Pres., Royal Australasian Coll. of Physicians, 1949. Served European War, 1914-18, AIF, 7th Field Ambulance, Gallipoli; served Middle East, 1940-42 (Major). *Publications:* contrib. to Medical Jl of Australia. *Recreations:* cabinet making and photography. *Address:* 650 Sandy Bay Road, Hobart, Tasmania, Australia.

**WHISTLER, Maj.-Gen. Alwyne Michael Webster,** CB 1963; CBE 1959; retired, 1965; *b* 30 Dec. 1909; *s* of Rev. W. W. Whistler and Lilian Whistler (*née* Meade), Elsted, Sussex; *m* 1936, Margaret Louise Michelette, *d* of Brig.-Gen. Malcolm Welch, CB, CMG, JP, Stedham, Sussex; one *s* two *d*. *Educ:* Gresham's Sch., Holt; RMA Woolwich. 2nd Lt Royal Signals, 1929; served in India, 1932-44; War of 1939-45: Staff Coll., Camberley, 1944; Burma Campaign, 19 and 25 Indian Divs and XII Army, 1944-45 (despatches twice). ADPR, Berlin, 1946; GSO1 (Military Adviser), Military Governor of Germany, 1946-48; AQMG, War Office, 1949-50; JSSC 1950; Comdg Royal Signals, 3 Div., 1951-54; Col GS, War Office, 1955-57; Col Q Far ELF, 1957-58; Comdr Corps Royal Signals, 1 (British) Corps, BAOR, 1959-60; Signal Officer-in-Chief, War Office, 1960-62; Chairman, British Joint Communications Board, Ministry of Defence, 1962-64; Assistant Chief of the Defence Staff (Signals), 1964-65. Hon. Col Princess Louise's Kensington Regt (41st Signals) TA, 1963-66; Col Commandant, Royal Corps of Signals, 1964-68; Hon. Col 32nd (Scottish) Signal Regiment (V), 1967. *Recreations:* field sports, particularly fishing. *Address:* Tigh-na-Leven, by Tarbert, Argyll. *T:* Ardpatrick 210.

**WHISTLER, Laurence,** OBE 1955; FRSL; engraver on glass; writer; *b* 21 Jan. 1912; *s* of Henry Whistler and Helen (*née* Ward); *yr b* of late Rex Whistler; *m* 1st, 1939, Jill (*d* 1944), *d* of Sir Ralph Furse; one *s* one *d*; 2nd, 1950, Theresa, *yr sister* of Jill Furse; one *s* one *d*. *Educ:* Stowe; Balliol College, Oxford. BA Oxon. Chancellor's Essay Prize, 1934. Served War of 1939-45: private soldier, 1940; commissioned in The Rifle Brigade, 1941. King's Gold Medal for Poetry, 1935 (first award). Work on glass includes; goblets, etc, in point-engraving, and engraved church windows and panels at Sherborne Abbey and at Moreton, Dorset; Checkendon, Oxon; and Ilton, Som. *Publications include:* Sir John Vanbrugh (biography), 1938; The English Festivals, 1947; Rex Whistler, His Life and His Drawings, 1948; The World's Room (Collected Poems), 1949; The Engraved Glass of Laurence Whistler, 1952; Rex Whistler: The Königsmark Drawings, 1952; The Imagination of Vanbrugh and his Fellow Artists, 1954; The View From This Window (poems), 1956; Engraved Glass, 1952-58; The Work of Rex Whistler (with Ronald Fuller), 1960; Audible Silence (poems), 1961; The Initials in the Heart (autobiography), 1964; To Celebrate Her Living (poems), 1967. *Address:* Little Place, Lyme Regis, Dorset. *T:* Lyme Regis 2355.

**WHITAKER, Benjamin Charles George;** author; *b* 15 Sept. 1934; 3rd *s* of Major-General Sir John Whitaker, 2nd Bt, CB, CBE (*d* 1957), Retford, Notts; *m* 1964, Janet Alison Stewart; one *s* one *d*. *Educ:* Eton; New Coll., Oxford. BA (Modern History). Called to Bar, Inner Temple, 1959 (Yarborough-Anderson Scholar). Vice-Chm., Danilo Dolci Trust, 1960-69; Extra-mural Lectr in Law, London Univ., 1963-64. Practised as Barrister, 1959-67. MP (Lab) Hampstead, 1966-70; PPS to Minister of: Overseas Development, 1966; Housing and Local Govt, 1966-67; Parly Sec., ODM, 1969-70. Member: Council, Westfield Coll., London Univ.; Executive, Fabian Soc. *Publications:* The Police, 1964; (ed) A Radical Future, 1967; Crime and Society, 1967; Participation and Poverty, 1968; Parks for People, 1970; articles in New Society, New Statesman, Spectator, Listener, etc. *Address:* 13 Elsworthy Road, NW3.

*See also Sir James Whitaker, Bt.*

**WHITAKER, Ernest Gillett,** CBE 1967; MInstT; Chairman, Central Transport Consultative Committee, 1962-68; Transport Adviser to the Board of Unilever Ltd, 1958-65; *b* 8 May 1903; *s* of Frederick and Bessie Whitaker; *m* 1929, Cissie Mucklow; one *s* one *d*. *Educ:* Knowbury Sch., Salop. After apprenticeship in motor engrg started own business as haulier and motor repairer, 1924. Later merged with Gupwell Gp of Cos, Birmingham; Dir, 1936-47. Ministry of Food: Area Meat and Livestock Forwarding Officer, Apr.-Dec. 1940; Asst Dir of Transport, Dec. 1940. Joined Unilever Ltd, 1947. Deputy Transport Adviser, Unilever Ltd, 1954; Director, SPD Ltd, 1954 (Chairman, 1956-58); Member: Channel Tunnel Study Gp; Rochdale Cttee of Inquiry into Major Ports of Gt Britain, 1961-62; Transport Advisory Council, 1965; National Ports Council, 1962-67; Founder Member (former Dep. Chm.), Inst. of Materials Handling; Pres. Inst. of Transport, 1962-63. *Recreations:* gardening, music, photography. *Address:* Golden Gables, Cliff Road, Worlebury, Weston-super-Mare, Somerset. *T:* Weston-super-Mare 28211.

**WHITAKER, Frank Howard,** CMG 1969; OBE 1946; Secretary of the Metrication Board, since 1969; *b* 9 Jan. 1909; *er s* of late Frank Harold Whitaker and late Edith Whitaker, Bradford; *m* 1937, Marjorie Firth; no *c*. *Educ:* Thornton Grammar Sch.; Leeds University. LLB (1st cl. hons) 1929; Solicitor (1st cl. hons, D. Reardon and Wakefield and Bradford Prizeman), 1931. Legal Practice until 1939. Royal Air Force, 1940-46 (Sqdn Leader). Entered Civil Service as Principal, Board of Trade, 1946; Asst Sec., 1955; Export Credits Guarantee Dept, 1957, Under-Secretary, 1966. *Recreation:* mountaineering. *Address:* Tavistock, The Rowans, Gerrards Cross, Bucks.

**WHITAKER, Mrs Geoffrey Charles Francis;** *see* Love, Enid Rosamond.

**WHITAKER, Sir James Herbert Ingham,** 3rd Bt, *cr* 1936; High Sheriff of Nottinghamshire, 1969; *b* 27 July 1925; *s* of late Maj.-Gen. Sir John Whitaker, 2nd Bt, CB, CBE, and Lady Whitaker (*née* Snowden); *S* father 1957; *m* 1948, Mary Elisabeth Lander Urling Clark (*née* Johnston), *widow* of Captain D. Urling Clark, MC; one *s* one *d*. *Educ:* Eton. Coldstream Guards, 1944. Served in North West Europe. Retired, 1947. Director: Halifax

Building Society; Barrow Barnsley (Holdings); Barnsley District Coking Co.; Member, Board of Economic Forestry (Holdings), 1965-; Member, Governing Body, Atlantic College. *Recreation:* shooting. *Heir:* *s* John James Ingham Whitaker, *b* 23 October 1952. *Address:* Babworth Hall, Retford, Notts. *T:* Retford 3454; Auchnafree, Dunkeld, Perthshire. *Club:* Boodle's.

*See also B. C. G. Whitaker.*

**WHITBREAD, Major Simon;** Lord Lieutenant and Custos Rotulorum for Bedfordshire, 1957; *b* 12 Oct. 1904; *s* of late Samuel Howard Whitbread, CB, JP, Southill, Biggleswade, Beds; *m* 1936, Helen Beatrice Margaret, *d* of Hon. Robert Trefusis, 27 Coleherne Court, SW7; one *s* one *d*. *Educ:* Eton; Trinity College, Cambridge. Joined KRRC, 1925; Captain, 1937; retired, 1937. Re-employed War of 1939-45, served in Africa and Italy (despatches). Director of Whitbread & Co. Ltd; Gov. and mem. Bd of Management, Middlesex Hosp., 1937-; Mem., General Nursing Council for England and Wales, 1958-65. DL 1946, JP 1939. County Councillor, 1938, CA 1949, Beds. High Sheriff of Beds, 1947; Chm. Bedfordshire CC 1967. Hon. Col 286 Field Regt RA (TA) (The Hertfordshire and Bedfordshire Yeomanry), 1965-67. OStJ 1941. *Recreations:* shooting and fishing. *Address:* The Mallowry, Riseley, Bedford. *T:* Riseley 248; 31 Egerton Gardens, SW3. *T:* 01-584 1763. *Clubs:* Brooks's, MCC.

**WHITBREAD, William Henry,** TD; MA Cantab; Chairman: Whitbread and Company, Ltd (Managing Director, 1927-68); Whitbread Investment Co. Ltd; Whitbread International; Whitbread South Africa (Pty) Ltd. Director: Eagle Star Insurance Co. Ltd; Barclays Bank Ltd; etc; Vice-President of the Brewers' Society (Chairman, 1952-53); Past-Master, Brewers' Company; Vice-Pres. Inst. of Brewing (Chm. Res. Cttee, 1948-52); *b* 22 Dec. 1900; *s* of late Henry William Whitbread, Norton Bavant, Wiltshire; *m* 1st, 1927, Ann Joscelyne (*d* 1936), *d* of late Samuel Howard Whitbread, CB, Southill, Beds; two *s* one *d*; 2nd, 1941, Betty Parr, *d* of Samuel Russell, ICS; one *s* two *d*. *Educ:* Eton; Corpus Christi College, Cambridge. Lovat Scouts, 1920-41; served War of 1939-45: Lovat Scouts, 1939-41; Reconnaissance Corps, 1941-45; Parachutist. Chm. Parliamentary Cttee, Brewers' Society, 1948-52. Member Governing Body Aldenham School, 1929-61 (Chairman, 1948-58). President, BSJA, 1966-68; Member: National Hunt Committee, 1956-68; Jockey Club, 1968-; Hurlingham Club Polo Committee, 1932-45; Master, Trinity Foot Beagles, 1921-23. *Recreations:* shooting, fishing and sailing. *Address:* Warren Mere, Godalming, Surrey; Letterewe, Ross-shire; Farleaze, Near Malmesbury, Wilts. *Clubs:* Brooks's, Pratt's, Turf, Royal Thames Yacht; Royal Yacht Squadron.

*See also Sir H. T. Tollemache, Bt.*

**WHITBY, Suffragan Bishop of,** since Oct. 1961; **Rt. Rev. George D'Oyly Snow;** *b* 2 Nov. 1903; *s* of Lt-Gen. Sir Thomas D'Oyly Snow, KCB, KCMG, and Charlotte Geraldine Coke; *m* 1942, Joan Monica, *y d* of late Maj. Henry J. Way, VD; three *s*. *Educ:* Winchester College; Oriel College, Oxford. Assistant Master at Eton College, 1925-36; ordained, 1933; Chaplain at Charterhouse, 1936-46; Headmaster of Ardingly College, Sussex, 1946-61. Prebend of Chichester Cathedral, 1959-61. Chairman National Society, 1963. *Publications:* A Guide to Prayer, 1932; A Guide to Belief, 1935; A School Service Book, 1936; A Guide to Confirmation, 1936; Our Father, 1938; Letters to a Confirmand, 1946; Into His Presence, 1946; The Public School in the New Age, 1959; Forth in His Name, 1964. *Recreations:* gardening, scouting, caravan camping, music, electronics. *Address:* 60 West Green, Stokesley, Middlesborough, Teesside. *T:* Stokesley 390.

**WHITBY, Anthony Charles;** Controller, BBC Radio 4, since 1969; *b* 19 Nov. 1929; *o s* of Charles Thomas Whitby and Ethel May Whitby (*née* King); *m* 1954, Joy Field; three *s*. *Educ:* Bristol Cathedral Sch.; St Edmund Hall and Nuffield Coll., Oxford. National Service (Gloucestershire Regt and Intell. Corps), 1947-49. Asst Principal and Principal, Colonial Office, 1954-59. Joined BBC as Radio Current Affairs Producer, 1959; transferred BBC Television, 1961; Producer of Gallery, 1963-65; Dep. Editor of 24 Hours, 1965-67, Editor, 1967-68; Secretary of the BBC, 1969. *Recreation:* writing plays. *Address:* 20 Brunswick Gardens, W8. *T:* 01-229 1181.

**WHITBY, Sir Bernard James,** Kt 1947; Chartered Accountant; Partner, A. F. Ferguson & Co., Chartered Accountants, Bombay and elsewhere; *b* 8 March 1892; *s* of late Frank Freeman Whitby, Bridgwater, and Louisa, *d* of late Rev. R. James, Yeovil; *m* 1st, 1919, Louey (*d* 1925), *e d* of late Rev. W. T. Soper, Croyde, Devon; 2nd, 1935, Kathleen Mary, *d* of late Metford Rowe, Bridgwater, Som.; two *s*. *Educ:* Taunton School. Mem. Indian Accountancy Board, 1934-47. JP Bombay, 1930-47. *Recreation:* music. *Address:* Villa Capri, Daddyhole Plain, Torquay, Devon. *T:* 27959. *Club:* Royal Bombay Yacht (Bombay).

**WHITBY, Charles Harley,** QC 1970; a Deputy Recorder of Winchester since 1969; *b* 2 April 1926; *s* of Arthur William Whitby and Florence Whitby. *Educ:* St John's, Leatherhead; Peterhouse, Cambridge. Open Schol., Peterhouse, 1943; served RAFVR, 1944-48; BA (History) 1st cl. 1949, MA 1951. Called to Bar, Middle Temple, 1952; Mem. Bar Council, 1969-. *Publications:* contrib. to Master and Servant in Halsbury's Laws of England, 3rd edn, Vol. 25, 1959 and Master and Servant in Atkin's Encyclopaedia of Court Forms, 2nd edn, Vol. 25, 1962. *Recreations:* golf, swimming, theatre, cinema. *Address:* 12 King's Bench Walk, Temple, EC4. *T:* 01-583 0811. *Clubs:* Oxford and Cambridge University, Royal Automobile.

**WHITBY, G. Stafford,** PhD, DSc, ARCS; FRSC; LLD (Hon.); ScD (Hon.); Professor Emeritus of Rubber Chemistry and Director of Rubber Research, Univ. of Akron, Ohio, USA; *b* 26 May 1887; *s* of late Stafford B. Whitby, MBE, Hull; *m* 1915, Wynne Atkinson (*d* 1955; author of Pilgrim Soul, London, 1961), Hampstead; one *s* one *d*; *m* 1964, Claire Newman. *Educ:* The Royal Coll. of Science, London. Demonstrator, Imp. Coll. of Sci. and Technology, 1906-10; in the rubber-growing countries of the East, as Chief Chemist to the Société Financière des Caoutchoucs, 1910-17; Department of Chemistry, McGill University, Montreal, 1917-29; Professor of Organic Chemistry, 1923-29; Director, Division of Chemistry, National Research Laboratories, Ottawa, 1929-39; Director of Chemical Research Laboratory, Teddington, 1939-42; Chm., Canadian Synthetic Rubber Technical Advisory Committee, 1942-44; Pres. Canadian Chemical Association, 1928-29; Pres. Canadian Institute of Chemistry, 1927-28; Officier d'Académie, 1928; Editor, Rubber Section, International Critical Tables; First Colwyn Gold Medallist, Institution of the Rubber Industry, 1928; Charles Goodyear medal, Amer. Chem. Soc., 1954; Foundn

Lectr, Inst. of the Rubber Industry, 1962; Jt Editor, Series on High Polymers, 1941; Editor (with H. Mark), Scientific Progress in the Field of Rubber and Synthetic Elastomers, 1946; Editor-in-Chief, Synthetic Rubber, 1954. *Publications:* Plantation Rubber and the Testing of Rubber, 1920; numerous scientific papers dealing with the chemistry of rubber, colloid chemistry, etc. *Recreations:* reading, walking. *Address:* University of Akron, Akron, Ohio 44304, USA. *Club:* University (Akron, O).

**WHITBY, Harry,** CB 1965; Secretary, Department of Agriculture and Fisheries for Scotland, since 1968; *b* 19 June 1910; *er s* of Edward Whitby, Hatfield, Herts, and Sarah Alice (*née* Booth); *m* 1937, Ruby Josephine, *yr d* of Charles J. Dyer, East Runton, Norfolk; two *s* two *d*. *Educ:* Ardingly College, Sussex; University of Manitoba. Student Asst, Agricultural Economics Research Institute, Univ. of Oxford, 1933-36; Asst to Advisory Officer in Agricultural Economics, Dept of Agriculture, Univ. of Leeds, 1936-38; Economist, Min. of Agriculture and Fisheries, 1938-47; Adviser on Farm Economics, 1947-50, Asst Sec. 1950-58, Under-Sec., 1958-68, Dept of Agriculture and Fisheries for Scotland. *Recreations:* gardening, cricket. *Address:* 31 Abbotsford Court, 18 Colinton Road, Edinburgh 10. *T:* 031-447 6862. *Club:* Royal Commonwealth Society.

**WHITBY, Professor Lionel Gordon,** FRCPE, FRSE; Professor of Clinical Chemistry, University of Edinburgh, since 1963; Dean of Faculty of Medicine, since 1969; *b* 18 July 1926; *s* of late Sir Lionel Whitby, CVO, MC, MD, FRCP, Regius Prof. of Physic and Master of Downing Coll., Cambridge; *m* 1949, Joan Hunter Sanderson; one *s* two *d*. *Educ:* King's Coll., Cambridge; Middlesex Hosp. MA, PhD, MD, BChir, MRCP, MRCPath. Fellow of King's College, Cambridge, 1951-55; W. A. Meek Schol., Univ. of Cambridge, 1953; Murchison Schol., RCP, 1958; Rockefeller Trav. Res. Fellow, Nat. Insts of Health Bethesda, Md, USA, 1959. Registrar and Asst Lectr in Chem. Path., Hammersmith Hosp. and Postgrad. Med. Sch. of London, 1958-60; Univ. Biochemist to Addenbrooke's Hosp., Cambridge, 1960-63; Member: Standing Adv. Cttee on Laboratory Services, Scottish Home and Health Dept, 1965-; Laboratory Automation Trials Gp, Min. of Health, 1966-. Guest Lectr, Amer. Chem. Soc., 1966. Examr for Coll. of Pathologists, Univ. of St Andrews. *Publications:* scientific papers on flavinglucosides, catecholamines and metabolites, several aspects of clin. chem., and early detection of disease by chemical tests. *Recreations:* gardening, golf, photography. *Address:* 57 Fountainhall Road, Edinburgh. *T:* 031-667 3687; The Royal Infirmary, Edinburgh. *T:* 031-229 2477. *Clubs:* Athenæum; New (Edinburgh).

**WHITCOMBE, Maj.-Gen. Philip Sidney,** CB 1944; OBE 1941; *b* 3 Oct. 1893; *e s* of late Rt Rev. Robert Henry Whitcombe, DD, Bishop of Colchester; *m* 1919, Madeline Lelia Brydges, *d* of Canon Arthur Symonds, Over Tabley, Knutsford; two *s*. *Educ:* Winchester. Gazetted to ASC from Durham LI (Spec. Res.), June 1914; served with BEF in France and Flanders, Aug. 1914-18; DAD Transport, 1918-19; psc 1926; Bde Major, Madras, 1928-32; Bt Major, 1933; DAAG, N Comd, York, 1934-36; GSO 2 War Office, 1936-38; Bt Lt-Col 1939; served in France as ADS and T 1939-40 (despatches); AA and QMG 1940-41 (OBE); Gibraltar, Brig. i/c Admin., 1941-42; Col 1942; DA and QMG, BTNI, 1942-43; MGA Eastern Command, 1943-47; retired, 1947. JP for Wilts, 1948. *Recreations:* cricket, fishing. Played cricket for Essex, 1922, the Army, 1925, and Berkshire, 1925-32. *Address:* The Grange, Lake, Amesbury, Wilts. *T:* Amesbury 3175. *Clubs:* Army and Navy, MCC.

**WHITE;** *see* Blanco White.

**WHITE,** family name of **Baron Annaly** and **Baroness White.**

**WHITE,** Baroness *cr* 1970 (Life Peeress), of Rhymney, Monmouth; **Eirene Lloyd White;** *b* 7 Nov. 1909; *d* of late Dr Thomas Jones, CH; *m* 1948, John Cameron White (*d* 1968). *Educ:* St Paul's Girls' Sch.; Somerville Coll., Oxford. Ministry of Labour officer, 1933-37 and 1941-45; Political Correspondent, Manchester Evening News, 1945-49; contested (Lab) Flintshire, 1945; MP (Lab) East Flint, 1950-70. Nat. Exec. Cttee of the Labour Party, 1947-53, 1958-, Chm. 1968-69; Parly Secretary, Colonial Office, 1964-66; Minister of State for Foreign Affairs, 1966-67; Minister of State, Welsh Office, 1967-70. Governor: National Library of Wales; Brit. Film Inst. and National Film Theatre, 1959-64; Indep. Mem. Cinematograph Films Council, 1946-64. Chairman, Fabian Society, 1958-59; Pres., Nursery School Assoc., 1964-66; Pres. Nat. Council of Women (Wales); Vice-Pres. Nat. Union of Students; Vice-Pres., Brit. Commonwealth League. Hon. Fellow, Somerville College, Oxford, 1966. *Address:* 36 Westminster Gardens, Marsham Street, SW1. *T:* 01-828 3320.

**WHITE, Adrian N. S.;** *see* Sherwin-White.

**WHITE, Prof. Alan Richard,** BA, PhD; Ferens Professor of Philosophy in the University of Hull, since 1961; *b* Toronto, Canada, 9 Oct. 1922; *s* of late George Albert White and Jean Gabriel Kingston; *m* 1948, Eileen Anne Jarvis; one *s* two *d*. *Educ:* Midleton College and Presentation College, Cork; Trinity College, Dublin. Dublin: Schol. and 1st class Moderator in Classics, 1st class Moderator in Mental and Moral Science; Boxing Pink; President of the 'Phil'; Univ. Student in Classics and Dep. Lecturer in Logic, 1945-46; Asst Lecturer, Lecturer, Sen. Lecturer in Philosophy, Univ. of Hull, 1946-61; Visiting Professor, Univ. of Maryland, 1967-68; Secretary, Mind Assoc., 1960-69. 42nd Dublin Rifles (LDF), 1941-45. *Publications:* G. E. Moore: A Critical Exposition, 1958; Attention, 1964; The Philosophy of Mind, 1967; (ed) The Philosophy of Action, 1968; Truth, 1970; articles in philosophical journals. *Recreations:* dilettantism and odd-jobbery. *Address:* The University, Hull. *T:* Hull 408960.

**WHITE, Alexander Hay,** CBE 1959; Deputy Chairman, Lithgows Ltd, Kingston Shipbuilding Yard, Port Glasgow; Part-time Member, Iron and Steel Board, 1962-67; *b* 1898; *m* 1929, Louisa Rowan, *d* of late William Cherry Hay, Jordanhill. Assistant Director of Merchant Shipbuilding, Admiralty, 1941-45. Chairman, Dornoch Shipping Co. Ltd; Director: Tontine Hotel (Greenock) Ltd; Ferguson Bros (Port Glasgow), Ltd. Past President of the Shipbuilding Conference (1961-63). FBIM. *Recreation:* golf. *Address:* Thorndene, Kilmacolm, Renfrewshire. *Clubs:* Caledonian; Conservative (Glasgow).

**WHITE, Hon. Alfred John;** Tasmanian Agent-General in London, since 1959; *b* 2 Feb. 1902; British; *m* 1939, Veronica Louisa White; two *s* two *d*. Elected to Tasmanian Parliament, 1941; Minister for Health and Chief Secretary, 1946-48, then Chief Secretary and Minister for Labour and Industry, Shipping and

Emergency Supplies until Jan. 1959. JP since 1934, and Territorial JP for the State of Tasmania in London, 1959. Appointed Agent-General for Tasmania in London for period of 3 years, Jan. 1959, re-appointed for a further period of 3 years, Jan. 1962; re-appointed 1967; granted title of "Honourable" for life. *Recreations:* ski-ing, gardening, bowls and fishing. *Address:* 458 Strand, WC2. *T:* 01-839 2291.

**WHITE, Antonia,** FRSL; author; *b* 31 Mar. 1899; *d* of Cecil George Botting, MA, and Christine Julia Botting (*née* White); *m* 1930, H. T. Hopkinson (marr. diss., 1938); two *d*. *Educ:* Convent of the Sacred Heart, Roehampton; St Paul's Girls' School. Copywriter, W. S. Crawford Ltd, 1924-31; Assistant Editor, Life and Letters, 1928-29; Freelance Journalist, 1931-34; Copywriter, J. Walter Thomson, 1934-35; Fashion Editor, Daily Mirror, 1935-37; Fashion Editor, Sunday Pictorial, 1937-39; BBC 1940-43; Political Intelligence Dept (French Section), FO, 1943-45. Occupied in writing novels, short stories and occasional critical articles and reviews, also translating from the French. Denyse Clairouin prize for translation, 1950. Visiting Lecturer in English, St Mary's College, Notre Dame, Indiana, 1959. *Publications:* Frost in May, 1933; The Lost Traveller, 1950; The Sugar House, 1952; Beyond the Glass, 1954; Strangers (short stories), 1954; Minka and Curdy, 1957; The Hound and the Falcon, 1966; Life with Minka and Curdy, 1970; over 30 trans from the French including Maupassant's Une Vie, 1949, Colette's La Chatte, 1953, Claudine à L'Ecole, 1956, Claudine à Paris, 1958, Claudine en Ménage, 1960; Claudine s'en va, 1961; Le Tendron (Selected Short Stories), 1959; L'Entrave, 1964; L'Ingénue Libertine, 1968; Loys Masson, Le Notaire des Noirs, 1962; H. Fabre-Luce, Haute Cour, 1963; Christine Arnothy, Le Cardinal Prisonnier, 1964; Mémoires du Chevalier d'Eon, 1970. *Recreations:* conversation and cats. *Address:* 42D Courtfield Gardens, SW5. *T:* 01-370 2661.

**WHITE, Col Archie Cecil Thomas,** VC, MC, BA; *b* 1891; *s* of Thomas White and Jean Finlayson; *m* Jean G. Will, MA (*d* 1960); three *d*. *Educ:* Harrogate Grammar School; King's College, London (Univ. Scholar in English Literature, 1912). Served with the Green Howards, 1914-19; with Army Educational Corps, 1920-47. Principal, City Literary Institute, 1948-56; Member of Senate, University of London, 1953-56. Deputy Colonel-Commandant, Royal Army Educational Corps, 1960-69. Officier d'Académie; FKC. *Address:* Brucklay, Upper Park Road, Camberley. *Club:* Naval and Military.

**WHITE, Arthur John Stanley,** CMG 1947; OBE 1932; *b* 28 Aug. 1896; *s* of A. R. White, DL, OBE, and of Minnie B. White, OBE (*née* Beauchamp); *m* 1932, Joan, *d* of R. O. Davies and *niece* of Lord Waring; four *s* one *d*. *Educ:* Marlborough College; Clare College, Cambridge (Scholar), MA 1930. Served European War, Wiltshire Regt, 1915-20, France and Ireland; Indian Civil Service, Burma, 1922; Under-Secretary, Home and Political Dept, 1924; Deputy Commissioner, 1928 (Burma Rebellion 1931-32, OBE); Secretary to Government of Burma, 1934; appointed to British Council as Dep. Sec.-Gen., 1937, Sec.-Gen. 1940-47, Controller, 1947-62. Retired 1962. Director, OPOS (Office for placing overseas boys and girls in British Schs), 1964-67. *Recreations:* hockey (International Trials, 1921 and 1922), cricket, tennis, shooting. *Address:* The Red House, Burkes Road, Beaconsfield, Bucks. *T:* 3244. *Club:* East India and Sports.

**WHITE, Sir Bruce Gordon,** KBE 1944 (CBE 1943; MBE 1919); FCGI; MInstCE; MInstMechE; MIEE; Senior Partner, Sir Bruce White, Wolfe Barry & Partners, Chartered Civil and Consulting Engineers; *b* 5 Feb. 1885; *m* 1912, Margery Gertrude (*d* 1965), *d* of C. W. Hodson, CSI; one *s* one *d*. *Educ:* Marlborough. Served European War, 1914-18 (MBE); War of 1939-45 as Brig. Director of Ports and IWT, War Office (KBE). *Address:* Reydon, Midway, Walton-on-Thames, Surrey.

**WHITE, Maj.-Gen. Cecil Meadows Frith,** CB 1945; CBE 1943 (OBE 1941); DSO 1940; late Royal Signals; retired; Colonel Commandant, Royal Corps of Signals, 1950-60; *b* 29 Aug. 1897; *s* of late Herbert Meadows Frith White and late Annie Laura Borrett; *m* 1925, Elizabeth Rennie Robertson; one *d*. *Educ:* Eton College; RMA, Woolwich. Commissioned RFA 1915; served 1915-19 in Egypt, Serbia, Greece, and Palestine (despatches); transferred to Royal Signals, 1925; Brigade Major Signal Training Centre, 1934-36; Lt-Col 1939; served War of 1939-45 (despatches five times, DSO, OBE, CBE, CB); commanded 4th Indian Divisional Signals in Wavell's advance in Western Desert, 1940; CSO East Africa during East Africa Campaign, 1941; CSO 8th Army, 1941; Temp. Brig. 1941; Col 1943; acting Maj.-Gen. Jan. 1944 as SO in C 21 Army Group; Temp. Maj.-Gen. 1945; Maj.-Gen. 1949; CSO, GHQ, MELF, Nov. 1945-July 1949; GOC Catterick District, 1949-51; retired, 1951. Deputy Controller, Civil Defence, Southdown Group, 1958. Civil Defence Officer, County Borough of Brighton, 1960-65. *Recreations:* fishing, gardening; formerly polo and rugger, show-jumping, hunting, sailing. *Address:* Bachelors', Laughton, near Lewes, Sussex. *TA* and *T:* Ripe 244. *Club:* Army and Navy.

**WHITE, Prof. Cedric Masey,** DSc(Eng.), PhD; Professor Emeritus, University of London, 1966; Consultant for River and Coastal projects; *b* 19 Oct. 1898; *s* of Joseph Masey White, Nottingham; *m* 1st, 1921, Dorothy F. Lowe; 2nd, 1946, Josephine M. Ramage; one *d*. *Educ:* privately; University College, Nottingham. Served European War, in Tank Corps, 1917-19. Lecturer in Civil Engineering, Univ. of London, King's Coll., 1927-33; Reader in Civil Engineering, and Asst Prof. in Imperial Coll. of Science and Technology, 1933-45; Responsible for work of Hawksley Hydraulic Lab., 1933-66; Professor of Fluid Mechanics and Hydraulic Engineering, 1946-66. Completed various investigations for Admiralty, WO, MAP, etc, during War of 1939-45, and investigations of proposed river-structures for Hydro-Power here and abroad, 1946-56. Founder Member, Hydraulic Research Bd, 1946-51, 1959-; sometime member of Research Committees of Instn of Civil Engineers; delegation on Hydrology to Internat. Union of Geodesy and Geophysics, 1939, 1948, 1951; Member: Council of British Hydromechanics Research Assoc., 1949-59; Internat. Assoc. for Hydraulic Research, 1947-59. Hon. ACGI, 1951. *Publications:* various engineering reports and scientific papers, chiefly on the motion of air and water. *Address:* 65 Woodlands Avenue, New Malden, Surrey. *T:* 01-942 6360.

**WHITE, Cyril Grove C.;** *see* Costley-White.

**WHITE, Cyril Montgomery,** QC 1946; MA; Chairman, Foreign Compensation Commission, 1958; *b* 10 August 1897; *o s* of

William Montgomery White and Mary Augusta Mourilyan; *m* 1950, Jessie Thompson (OBE 1945), *d* of late James Kidd of Linlithgow; one *d. Educ:* Colet Court; St Paul's School; Corpus Christi College, Oxford. Served in European War (Royal Flying Corps and Royal Air Force) July 1916-Jan. 1919. Called to Bar, Lincoln's Inn, 1923; Bencher, 1952. Served War of 1939-45 (RAFVR) Aug. 1939-Jan. 1944; Pres. (except for Scottish Proceedings) Transport Arbitration Tribunal, 1947-57. *Publications:* The Conveyancers' Year Book 1947. Senior Editor, Underhill on Trusts and Trustees, 10th edn, 1950, 11th edn, 1959. Has contributed to Halsbury's Laws of England, 3rd edition (Titles: Landlord and Tenant, 1958; Real Property, 1960). *Recreation:* travel. *Address:* 2 Stone Buildings, Lincoln's Inn, WC2. *T:* 01-242 7637; East House, Sydling St Nicholas, Dorset. *T:* Cerne Abbas 264. *Club:* United University.

**WHITE, Lt-Col David A. P.;** *see* Price-White.

**WHITE, Sir Dennis (Charles),** KBE 1962 (OBE 1953); CMG 1959; Brunei Government Agent in the United Kingdom, since 1967; *b* 30 July 1910; unmarried. *Educ:* Bradfield College. Joined service of HH the Rajah of Sarawak, 1932. Civilian Prisoner of War, Dec. 1941-Sept. 1945. HM Overseas Civil Service: Senior Resident, 1955; British Resident, Brunei, 1958; HM High Comr for Brunei, 1959-63. Star of Sarawak (Officer) 1946. Esteemed Family Order of Brunei, 1st Class. *Recreations:* general. *Address:* Virginia Cottage, Emery Down, Lyndhurst, Hants. *Club:* Travellers'.

**WHITE, Sir Dick (Goldsmith),** KCMG 1960; KBE 1955 (CBE 1950; OBE 1942); attached to Foreign and Commonwealth Office; *b* 20 Dec. 1906; *s* of Percy Hall White and Gertrude White (*née* Farthing); *m* 1945, Kathleen Bellamy. *Educ:* Bishops Stortford Coll.; Christ Church, Oxford; Universities of Michigan and California, USA. US Legion of Merit, Croix de Guerre (France). *Address:* The Leat, Burpham, near Arundel, Sussex. *T:* Arundel 3030. *Club:* Garrick.
*See also J. A. White.*

**WHITE, Prof. Edwin George,** PhD, DSc, BSc (Vet. Sci.), BSc (Physiol.), FRCVS; William Prescott Professor of Veterinary Preventive Medicine, University of Liverpool, since 1950; Pro-Vice-Chancellor, 1966-70, Acting Vice-Chancellor, Oct.-Dec. 1969; *b* 26 March 1911; *s* of Edwin White and Alice Maud White; *m* 1936, Grace Mary Adlington; two *d. Educ:* Newport (Mon.) High School; Royal Veterinary College, London; University College, London. Studentship for Research in Animal Health, 1933-35, for postgraduate study in Germany and England; Lecturer in Pathology, Royal Veterinary College, London, 1935; Reader in Pathology, 1939; Principal Scientific Officer, Rowett Research Inst., Bucksburn, Aberdeenshire, 1946; Director of East African Veterinary Research Organisation, 1947; Dean of Faculty of Vet. Sci., Univ. of Liverpool, 1961-65. Pres., RCVS, 1967-68. Chm. Governing Body, Houghton Poultry Research Station. *Publications:* Veterinary Preventive Medicine, 1963; articles in various scientific journals since 1934. *Recreation:* gardening. *Address:* Blue Haze, Leighton Road, Neston, Wirral, Cheshire. *T:* 051-336 4210. *Club:* Royal Commonwealth Society.

**WHITE, (Elizabeth) Evelyne (McIntosh);** *d* of late J. A. Jardine and Alexandrina, *d* of Alexander McIntosh, Manchester; *m* 1st, 1924, W. Bertram White (*d* 1960); 2nd, 1965, Ernest James Battey. *Educ:* Harris Acad., Dundee; University of Liverpool, BSc, MA. Mathematics Mistress, Runcorn Grammar School; Mathematics Mistress, Wallasey High School for Girls; Vice-Principal, Mistress of Method and Lecturer in Education, National Society's Training College for Teachers of Domestic Subjects, London; Editor of The Schoolmistress, 1926-35 (Director, Schoolmistress Newspaper Co.); Lecturer for the Ministry of Information, 1940; Chairman, YWCA Committee, Mansfield; Member of Panel and Executive of Ministry of Information Anglo-American Panel; Member of Mansfield Hospital Board; Governor of Mansfield Technical College; and of Mansfield Queen Elizabeth's Grammar School for Girls; Chairman of Mansfield Juvenile Court; Chm. of Probation Case Committee; Member Notts Combined Probation Cttee; First Woman Chairman, Mansfield Borough Bench, 1957 (formerly Deputy Chairman); Vice-Chm., Women's Sub-Cttee, Mansfield and Dist Employment Cttee. JP Mansfield, 1942-62. *Publications:* Practical Science for Girls, 1920, now in 4th ed.; Practical Courses in Housecraft, 1924; Section on Domestic Science in Girls' Book of Careers, 1925; Housecraft, Vol. VI of Modern Teaching, 1929; The Household from A-Z, 1931; The White-Watson Menu and Recipe Book, 1937; Teach Yourself to Cook, 1938 (6th new edition, 1951); The Russell Dramatic Readers, 1938; Practical English Revision, 1938; Winifred Holtby as I knew her, 1938; Practical Everyday English for Juniors, Books I and II, 1941; The End Crowns All, 1943; Practical Modern English, Pts I, II, and III, 1947; Full Tide, 1946; Love's Enough; Mock Marriage; Love's Conquest; The Lady Entertains; (joint) Essential Everyday Arithmetic for Girls, 1950; Production Notes for The Russell Dramatic Readers; Second Series, 1951; Twenty Time-Tests in English, 1951; Cook Without Fears, 1951; Come Cooking with me, 1953; The Russell Literary Readers, Bks I, II and III, 1953; Twenty Time Tests in Arithmetic, 1954; English for the Primary School, Books 1-4, 1956; Poetry for the Primary School, Books 1-4, 1957; Women of Devotion and Courage, 6 Books, 1957; Poetry for Today (Books 1-4) 1960; Good Everyday English (books 1-4) 1962; Etiquette for the Teen-ager, 1967; English for Junior Forms, Books 1-5, 1968; Poetry for Junior Forms, Books 1-5, 1968; ed (with E. James Battey), The Spanish Cook Book, 1969, and several other foreign cookery books; short stories to various magazines; books reviewer and contributor to newspapers and magazines. *Recreations:* golf, dancing, fishing, motoring, foreign travel. *Address:* Flat 2, 8 The Leas, Folkestone, Kent. *T:* Folkestone 55718. *Clubs:* Royal Commonwealth Society, National Book League, Vanity Fair.

**WHITE, Elwyn Brooks;** Contributor to The New Yorker; *b* 11 July 1899; *s* of Samuel T. White and Jessie Hart; *m* 1929, Katharine Sergeant Angell; one *s. Educ:* Cornell University, USA. Newspaper reporting, advertising, and editorial work as staff member of New Yorker Magazine, to which he has contributed verse, satirical essays, and editorials; wrote a monthly department for Harper's Magazine called One Man's Meat, 1938-43. Hon. degrees: Dartmouth Coll.; Univs of Maine, Yale, Bowdoin, Hamilton, Harvard, Colby. Fellow, Amer. Acad. of Arts and Sciences. Gold Medal Nat. Inst. of Arts and Letters, 1960; Presidential Medal of Freedom, 1963. *Publications:* The Lady is Cold, 1929; (with J. Thurber) Is Sex Necessary, 1929; Every Day is Saturday, 1934; The Fox of Peapack, 1938; Quo Vadimus?,

1939; One Man's Meat, 1942 (enlarged) 1944; Stuart Little, 1945; The Wild Flag, 1946; Here Is New YOrk, 1949; Charlotte's Web, 1952; The Second Tree from the Corner, 1954; The Points of My Compass, 1962; The Trumpet of the Swan, 1970. (Ed., with Katharine S. White) A Subtreasury of American Humor, 1941; rev. and enl. Strunk, The Elements of Style, 1959. *Address:* North Brooklin, Maine, USA. *TA:* care The New Yorker Magazine, 25 W.43.

**WHITE, Sir (Eric) Richard Meadows,** 2nd Bt, *cr* 1937; *b* 29 June 1910; *s* of Sir Robert Eaton White, 1st Bt, and Rose Dorothy (*d* 1967), *d* of Charles Pearce-Serocold, Taplow Hill, Bucks; *S* father, 1940; *m* 1939, Lady Elisabeth Mary Gladys Townshend (marr. diss. 1947; she *d* 1950), *o d* of 6th Marquess Townshend; one *s*; *m* 1947, Ann Heron, *d* of A. G. Eccles, 16 Sussex Mansions, Old Brompton Rd, SW7. *Educ:* Eton. *Heir: s* Christopher Robert Meadows White [*b* 26 Aug. 1940; *m* 1962, Anne Marie Ghislaine, *yr d* of late Major Tom Brown and of Mrs R. W. Taggart-Browne, Hove, Sussex]. *Address:* The Vine, Presteigne, Radnorshire.

**WHITE, Brig. Eric Stuart,** DSO 1918; late RASC; *b* 15 Nov. 1888; *o s* of late W. W. White of Lee, Kent; *m* 1st, 1914; one *d*; 2nd, 1939, Ysobel Dora (*d* 1959), *d* of Lt-Col W. P. Murray, DSO, Farnham. *Educ:* Felsted; Sandhurst. Served European War, 1914-18, NW Persia, Iraq (DSO, despatches, Officer, Order of Crown of Belgium; Belgian Croix de Guerre, with two palms); retired, 1944. OStJ. *Address:* The Cottage, Donnington, Chichester, Sussex.

**WHITE, Sir Eric (Henry) W.;** *see* Wyndham White.

**WHITE, Erica,** FRBS (retired); Sculptor and Painter; *d* of Frederic Charles White, solicitor and Mildred S. Hutchings. *Educ:* St George's School, Harpenden; Slade School of Art (Sculpture Scholarship two years and Painting Prize); gained London University Diploma in Fine Arts; studied at Central School of Arts and Crafts; gained British Institution Scholarship in Sculpture; studied at Royal Acad. Schools (Silver and Bronze Medallist); awarded Feodora Gleichen Memorial Fund Grant; exhibited at Royal Academy and at Glasgow, Brighton, Bournemouth and other Art Galleries. *Recreations:* outdoor sports and music. *Address:* South Cliff Cottage, 3 South Cliff, Bexhill-on-Sea, Sussex. *T:* Bexhill 1013.

**WHITE, Sir Ernest (Keith),** Kt 1969; CBE 1967; MC; Chairman, R. J. White & Co. (Sydney) Pty Ltd, since 1935; *b* 1892; *s* of late Robert John White; *m* 1915, Pauline Marjory, *d* of J. J. Mason; one *s* two *d*. *Educ:* Gosford Public Sch., NSW. Served European War, 1914-18 (despatches, MC): Captain 4th Bn AIF, in Egypt and France (Ypres, Somme, Broodsiend Ridge, Bullecourt, Sttrozeel). Pres., Liberal Democratic Party, Australia, 1943; Delegate to Prelim. and Plenary Conf. which founded Liberal Party of Australia, and apptd to Provisional State and Federal Council, 1943. Vice-Pres., Australian American Assoc. (Founder and 1st Federal Pres., 1936). *Address:* Baden House, Baden Road, Kurraba Point, Sydney, NSW, Australia. *T:* 29 5741. *Clubs:* Royal Commonwealth Society; Tattersall's; Australian Jockey; American National.

**WHITE, Errol Ivor,** CBE 1960; DSc, PhD (London); FRS 1956; FGS, FLS, FKC; retired as Keeper of Department of Palæontology (formerly of Geology), British Museum (Natural History), 1955-66 (Deputy Keeper, 1938-55); *b* 1901; *y s* of late Felix E. White and Lilian Daniels; *m* 1st, 1933, Barbara Gladwyn Christian (marr. diss. 1940, she *d* 1969); 2nd, 1944, Margaret Clare (Jane), BCom (Leeds), *y d* of late T. C. Fawcett, Bolton Abbey, Yorks; one *s*. *Educ:* Highgate School (Senior Foundationer); King's Coll., London Univ. (Tennant Prizeman). BSc 1921; PhD 1927; DSc 1936. Entered British Museum (Natural History), 1922; Geological Expeditions to Madagascar, 1929-30, and Spitsbergen, 1939; temp. Principal, Min. of Health, 1940-April 1945; Hon. Sec. Ray Society, 1946-51, Vice-Pres., 1951-54, 1959-, Pres., 1956-59; Council, Geological Soc., 1949-53, 1956-60; Vice-Pres., 1957-60 (Murchison Medal, 1962); President, Linnean Soc., 1964-67 (Linnean Gold Medal, 1970); Chm. Systematics Assoc., 1955-58; Coun., Zool. Soc., 1959-63. *Publications:* Technical memoirs and papers in various scientific jls, chiefly relating to extinct agnatha and fishes. *Recreations:* ornithology and bridge. *Address:* Prospect House, North Stoke, Oxon. *T:* Wallingford 3342. *Club:* Royal Societies.

**WHITE, Ethelbert,** RWS; Artist; *b* 26 Feb. 1891; *s* of Bernard Richard White; *m* 1911. *Educ:* St George's College, Weybridge, Surrey. Became a Member of the New English Art Club, 1921, Royal Society of Painters in Water-colours, 1930. Exhibited at Venice International Exhibition, 1929. Work purchased by: Tate Gallery; Contemporary Art Society; Municipal Galleries throughout England and Ireland. *Publications:* Fine Art Prints: 1931, 1936, 1940. *Recreation:* music. *Address:* The Pink Cottage, 14 Hampstead Grove, NW3.

**WHITE, Evelyne;** *see* White, E. E. M.

**WHITE, Sir Frederick William George,** KBE 1962 (CBE 1954); FRS 1966; PhD; Chairman, Commonwealth Scientific and Industrial Research Organization, 1959-70 (Deputy Chairman, 1957, Chief Executive Officer, 1949-57); *b* 26 May 1905; *s* of late William Henry White; *m* 1932, Elizabeth Cooper; one *s* one *d*. *Educ:* Wellington College, New Zealand; Victoria University College, Univ. of New Zealand (MSc 1928); Cambridge Univ. (PhD 1932). Postgrad. Schol. in Science, Univ. of NZ and Strathcona Schol., St John's Coll., Cambridge; Research in Physics, Cavendish Laboratory, 1929-31; Asst Lecturer in Physics, Univ. of London, King's Coll., 1931-36; Professor of Physics, Canterbury University Coll., NZ, 1937; Member, British Empire Cancer Campaign Soc., Canterbury Branch Cttee, 1938; Radio Research Cttee, DSIR NZ, 1937; Advisor to NZ Govt on radar research, 1939; seconded to Aust. CSIR, 1941; Chm., Radiophysics Adv. Bd, 1941; Chief, Div. of Radiophysics, 1942. Exec. Officer, 1945, Mem., Exec. Cttee, 1946, CSIR Aust. Radio Research Bd, 1942; Scientific Adv. Cttee, Aust. Atomic Energy Commn, 1953; FInstP; FAA; Fellow Aust. Instn of Radio Engrs. Hon. DSc: Monash Univ.; ANU. *Publications:* scientific papers on nature of ionosphere over NZ and on propagation of radio waves; Electromagnetic Waves, 1934. *Recreation:* fishing. *Address:* 57 Investigator Street, Red Hill, Canberra, ACT 2603, Australia. *T:* 93424.

**WHITE, Gabriel Ernest Edward Francis,** CBE 1963; Director of Art, Arts Council of Great Britain, 1958-70; *b* 29 Nov. 1902; *s* of late Ernest Arthur White and Alice White; *m* 1st, 1928, Elizabeth Grace (*d* 1958), *d* of late Auguste Ardizzone; two *s*; 2nd, 1963, Jane, *d* of late J. R. Kingdon and of Mrs Kingdon, Minehead; one *s* one *d*. *Educ:* Downside Sch.; Trinity Coll., Oxford. Staff Officer RE

Camouflage, 1940-45; Asst Art Director, Arts Council of Great Britain, 1945-58. Order of the Aztec Eagle, 2nd class (Mexico). *Publication:* Sickert Drawings (in Art and Technics), 1952. *Recreations:* drawing, painting. *Address:* 88 Holmdene Avenue, SE24. *T:* 01-274 9643.

**WHITE, Sir George (Stanley Midelton),** 3rd Bt, *cr* 1904; *b* 11 April 1913; *s* of 2nd Bt and Kate Muriel, *d* of late Thomas Baker, Bristol; *S* father, 1964; *m* 1939, Diane Eleanor, *d* of late Bernard Abdy Collins, CIE; one *s* one *d. Educ:* Harrow; Magdalene College, Cambridge. Member of the firm of George White Evans & Co., Bristol; Chairman and Managing Director, Bristol Cars Ltd. *Heir: s* George Stanley James White, *b* 4 November 1948. *Address:* Pypers, Rudgeway, Glos. *T:* Thornbury 2312. *Clubs:* Royal Aero, Royal Motor Yacht.

**WHITE, Maj.-Gen. Gilbert Anthony,** MBE 1944; Chief, Joint Services Liaison Organization, Bonn, since 1969; *b* 10 June 1916; *s* of Cecil James Lawrence White and Muriel (*née* Collins); *m* 1939, Margaret Isabel Duncan Wallet; two *d. Educ:* Christ's Hosp., Horsham. Member of Lloyd's, 1938. Joined TA Artists Rifles, 1937; TA Commn, E Surrey Regt, 1939; served BEF, 1940, N Africa, 1943-44, Italy, 1944-45; Staff Coll., 1944; Instructor, Staff Coll., Haifa, 1946; with UK Delegn to UN, 1946-48; served on Lord Mountbatten's personal staff in MoD, 1960-61; idc 1965. *Recreations:* golf, racing, sitting in the sun. *Address:* Speedwell, Tekels Avenue, Camberley, Surrey. *T:* Camberley 23812. *Club:* Army and Navy.

**WHITE, Lt-Col Harold Fletcher,** CMG 1919; DSO 1917; *b* 13 June 1883; *s* of F. J. White, Saumarez, Armidale, NSW; *m*; two *s* two *d*. Served European War, 1915-19 (despatches, DSO, Croix de Guerre, CMG); MLC New South Wales, 1932-34. *Address:* Bald Blair, Guyra, NSW, Australia.

**WHITE, Sir Harold (Leslie),** Kt 1970; CBE 1962; MA; FLAA; National Librarian, National Library of Australia, Canberra, 1947-70; *b* Numurkah, Vic, 14 June 1905; *s* of late James White, Canterbury, Vic; *m* 1930, Elizabeth, *d* of Richard Wilson; two *s.* two *d. Educ:* Wesley College, Melbourne; Queen's College, University of Melbourne. Commonwealth Parliamentary Library, 1923-67; National and Parliamentary Librarian, 1947-67. Visited US as Carnegie Scholar, 1939, and as first Australian under "Leaders and Specialists programme" of Smith Mundt Act, 1950. Represented Australia at various overseas Conferences, 1939-64. Chairman, Standing Cttee, Aust. Advisory Council on Bibliographical Services, 1960-70; Member: various Aust. cttees for UNESCO; Aust. Nat. Film Bd; UNESCO Internat. Cttee on Bibliography, Documentation and Terminology, 1961-64. *Publications:* (ed) Canberra: A Nation's Capital; contribs to various jls. *Address:* 27 Mugga Way, Canberra, ACT, Australia 2603.

**WHITE, Sir Headley Dymoke,** 3rd Bt *cr* 1922; *b* 15 April 1914; *s* of Sir Dymoke White, 2nd Bt and Isabelle, *yr d* of James G. MacGowan; *S* father, 1968; *m* 1943, Elizabeth Victoria Mary, *er d* of Wilfrid Wrightson; one *s* two *d. Educ:* Winchester; Trinity Coll., Cambridge. *Heir: s* John Woolmer White, *b* 4 Feb. 1947.

**WHITE, Surg. Rear-Adm. Sir Henry Ellis Yeo,** KCVO, *cr* 1947 (CVO 1927; MVO 1922); OBE 1925; late RN; *b* 1888; *s* of late W. H. White, MD, Airton, Yorks; *m* 1921, Adelaide Beatrice, *d* of late Lt-Col G. F. Napier; one *s* one *d. Educ:* Edinburgh Univ. (MB, ChB); MD, FRCS Edinburgh. Accompanied Prince of Wales, Canada, 1919, Australasia, 1920, the East, 1921-22 in HMS Renown, and Africa and S America in HMS Repulse, 1925, Duke and Duchess of York to New Zealand and Australia, 1927; and the King and Queen to Canada and the United States, 1939, and South Africa, 1947; HMY Victoria and Albert, 1927-39; retired list, 1948. CStJ 1948. *Address:* 36 Lourensford Road, Somerset West, CP, South Africa.

**WHITE, Hugh Fortescue Moresby,** CMG 1943; *b* 15 Sept. 1891; *s* of Lt-Col R. F. Moresby White, OBE, VD, Grantham; *m* Betty Sophia Pennington, *d* of Capt. Frank Brandt, RN; one *s. Educ:* Malvern College; St John's College, Oxford. Administrative Service, Nigeria, 1915-45; Senior Resident, Oyo Province, 1940-44. *Address:* Le Clos D'Avranche, St Mary's, Jersey, Channel Islands. *T:* North 631.

**WHITE, Air Vice-Marshal Hugh Granville,** CB 1952; CBE 1944; FIMechE; retired; *b* 1 Mar. 1898; *s* of Herbert White, The Poplars, Maidstone, Kent; *m* 1926, Mabel Joyce Hickman; two *s* one *d. Educ:* HMS Conway; Eastbourne College; Royal Military College, Sandhurst; Jesus College, Cambridge. Commissioned in East Kent Regt, attached RFC, 1916; served as pilot in France, 1916-18; permanent commission on formation of RAF, 1918; comd Nos 29, 64 and 501 Squadrons; Staff appointments as Technical Officer, Royal Air Force College, Cranwell, 1930-33; HQ Air Defence, Gt Britain, 1933-35; STSO, HQ Far East, 1936-39; SASO No. 24 Group, 1939-42; AOC Halton, 1942-46; STSO, HQ, BAFO, Germany, 1946-48; AOC No. 43 Group, 1948-50; AOC No 41 Group, 1950-53; AOA HQ Maintenace Cmd, 1953-55; retired 1955. *Recreations:* played rugby for RAF, 1922-23; gardening. *Address:* 30 Hillside, Eastdean, Eastbourne, Sussex. *T:* Eastdean 3151. *Club:* Royal Over-Seas League.

**WHITE, Prof. James;** Dyson Professor of Refractories Technology, University of Sheffield, since 1956; Dean of Faculty of Metallurgy, 1958-62; *b* 1 April 1908; *s* of late John White and Margaret E. White (*née* Laidlaw), Langholm, Dumfriesshire; *m* 1936, Elizabeth Kelly, Glasgow; one *s. Educ:* Langholm Acad. (Dux Medallist); Dumfries Acad. (Science Dux); Glasgow University. BSc 1st Cl. Hons Physical Chemistry, 1931. DSIR Research Scholarship, Roy. Technical Coll., Glasgow, 1931; Dr James McKenzie Prize for Research, 1933; Research Asst in Metallurgy, Roy. Technical Coll., 1933; Associateship of Roy. Technical Coll., 1934; PhD (Glas.) 1935; Lectr in Metallurgy, Roy. Tech. Coll., 1935; Andrew Carnegie Research Scholarship of Iron and Steel Inst., 1936-38; Andrew Carnegie Gold Medallist of Iron and Steel Inst., 1939; DSc (Glas.) 1939; Research Technologist in Refractories Industry, 1943; Lectr in Refractory Materials, Sheffield Univ., 1946; Reader in Ceramics, Sheffield Univ., 1952. Pres. of Sheffield Metallurgical Assoc., 1950; Fellow Instn of Metallurgists, 1952; Founder Fellow Inst. of Ceramics, 1955; Pres. Refractories Assoc. of Great Britain, 1959-60; Chm. Clay Minerals Group, Mineralogical Society, 1959-61; First Chm. Basic Science Section, British Ceramic Soc.; Pres., British Ceramic Soc., 1961-62. Visiting Prof., Nat. Research Centre, Cairo, 1962; Student's Trust Fund Visiting Lectr, Univ. of the Witwatersrand, SA, 1964; Visiting Prof., Univ. of Illinois, 1966; Nat. Sci. Foundn Senior Foreign Scientist Fellowship, Univ. of Alfred, NY, 1968. Fellow, Mineralogical Soc.

of America, 1960. *Publications:* numerous scientific papers on ferrous metallurgy and refractory materials (some jointly). *Recreations:* sketching, motor-cars, walking. *Address:* 20 Ranmoor Cliffe Road, Sheffield S10 3HB. *T:* Sheffield 305458.

**WHITE, James;** MP (Lab) Glasgow (Pollok) since 1970; *b* 10 April 1922; *m* 1948, Mary E. Dempsey; one *s* two *d*. *Educ:* Knightsmoor Secondary School. Served War of 1939-45: African and Italian Stars; Defence Medal. Managing Director, Glasgow Car Collection Ltd. *Recreations:* reading, golf, swimming. *Address:* 23 Alder Road, Glasgow, S3. *T:* 041-637 6412.

**WHITE, John Alan;** Deputy Chairman, Associated Book Publishers Ltd, since 1963 (Managing Director, 1946-62); Director: Methuen & Co. Ltd (Chairman); British Publishers Guild Ltd; Eyre & Spottiswoode Ltd; *b* 20 June 1905; *e s* of Percy Hall White and Gertrude (*née* Farthing). *Educ:* Bishops Stortford College. President, Publishers' Association, 1955-57; Chairman, National Book League, 1963-65. *Recreations:* reading, gardening. *Address:* Flat 17, 58 Rutland Gate, SW7. *T:* 01-584 4495; Shorts Farm, Nutbourne, Pulborough, Sussex. *T:* West Chiltington 3211. *Clubs:* Athenæum, Garrick.

*See also Sir Dick Goldsmith White.*

**WHITE, Lieutenant-Colonel John Baker,** TD 1950; JP; *b* West Malling, Kent, 12 Aug. 1902; *s* of late J. W. B. White, Street End House, Canterbury; *m* 1925, Sybil Irene Erica, *d* of late C. B. Graham, Onslow Gardens, SW1; one *s* one *d*. *Educ:* Stubbington House, Fareham; Malvern College. Worked on farms in Kent and Sussex to gain a basic knowledge of agriculture, 1920-22; worked in a circus to gain a wider knowledge of human nature, 1922; studied the structure of industry and social science in London and various industrial centres, 1922-24; worked as a voluntary helper in canteens for the unemployed and among distressed ex-service men; employed in the coal industry, 1924-26; Director Economic League, 1926-45, now Publicity Adviser. Joined Territorial Army, London Rifle Brigade, 1934; served in Army as regimental soldier, on War Office staff with Political Intelligence Dept of FO, and Political Warfare Mission in the Middle East. 1939-45; Lieut-Colonel 1941. MP (C) Canterbury division of Kent, 1945-53. JP Kent, 1954. President: E Kent Fruit Show Soc.; East Kent Fat Stock Show and Sale Assoc. Dep. Pres., Canterbury Soc. *Publications:* Red Russia Arms, 1934; It's Gone for Good, 1941; The Soviet Spy System, 1948; The Red Network, 1953; The Big Lie, 1955; Pattern for Conquest, 1956; Sabotage is Suspected, 1957; True Blue, 1970. *Address:* Street End Place, near Canterbury, Kent. *T:* Petham 265. *Clubs:* MCC, Royal Automobile.

**WHITE, Prof. John Edward Clement Twarowski;** Professor of the History of Art and Chairman of the Department of History of Art, Johns Hopkins University, Baltimore, Maryland, USA; *b* 4 Oct. 1924; *s* of Brigadier A. E. White and Suzanne Twarowska; *m* 1950, Xenia Joannides. *Educ:* Ampleforth College; Trinity College, Oxford; Courtauld Institute of Art, University of London. Served in RAF, 1943-47. BA London 1950; Junior Research Fellow, Warburg Institute, 1950-52; PhD Lond. 1952. Lecturer in History of Art, Courtauld Institute, 1952-58; Alexander White Visiting Professor, University of Chicago, 1958; Reader in History of Art, Courtauld Institute, 1958-59; Pilkington Professor of the History of Art and Director of The Whitworth Art Gallery, University of Manchester, 1959-66. Visiting Ferens Professor of Fine Art, University of Hull, 1961-62. MA Manchester, 1963. *Publications:* Perspective in Ancient Drawings and Painting, 1956; The Birth and Rebirth of Pictorial Space, 1957; Art and Architecture in Italy, 1250-1400, 1966; articles in Burlington Magazine, Jl of Warburg and Courtauld Institutes, Art Bulletin. *Address:* Department of The History of Art, Johns Hopkins University, Baltimore, Md 21218, USA; (home) 4000 N Charles Street, Baltimore, Md 21218.

**WHITE, Leslie Gordon,** CBE 1949; retired; *b* 1889; *s* of late Henry Tom White; *m* 1919, Dorothy Morgan (*d* 1961). *Educ:* Eastbourne Grammar School; Entered Inland Revenue Department, 1908; Dep. Chief Inspector of Taxes, 1947-50; retired 1950. *Address:* Ashdene, 277 Dyke Road, Hove 4BN3 6PB. *T:* Brighton 552954.

**WHITE, Margaret B.;** *see* Bourke-White.

**WHITE, Michael James Denham;** FRS 1961; FAA; Professor of Genetics, University of Melbourne, Australia, since 1964; *b* 20 August 1910; *s* of James Kemp White and Una Theodora Chase; *m* 1938, Isobel Mary Lunn; two *s* one *d*. *Educ:* University College, London. Asst Lecturer, 1933-35, Lecturer, 1936-46, Reader, 1947, University Coll., London; Guest Investigator, Carnegie Instn of Washington, 1947; Professor of Zoology, Univ. of Texas, 1947-53; Senior Research Fellow, CSIRO, Canberra, Australia, 1953-56; Prof. of Zoology, Univ. of Missouri, 1957-58; Prof. of Zoology, Univ. of Melbourne, 1958-64. Foreign Member, Amer. Acad. of Arts and Sciences. Mueller Medallist, Aust. and NZ Assoc. for the Advancement of Science, 1965. *Publications:* (Monograph) The Chromosomes, 1st edn 1937, 2nd edn 1942, 3rd edn 1961 (trans into French, Italian and Spanish); Animal Cytology and Evolution, 1st edn 1945, 2nd edn 1954; many papers in learned journals. *Address:* Department of Genetics, University of Melbourne, Parkville, Victoria 3052, Australia. *T:* 34-0484.

**WHITE, Maj.-Gen. Napier;** *see* White, Maj.-Gen. P. N.

**WHITE, Norman Lewis,** MD, FRCS, FRCOG; Obstetrician, University College Hospital; Gynæcological Surgeon, Royal Northern Hospital; Gynæcologist, Ministry of Pensions Hospital, Roehampton, and West Herts Hospital. *Educ:* University of Cambridge; University College Hospital, London. MRCS Eng., LRCP Lond. 1923; BA Cambridge (1st Cl. Nat. Sci. Tripos), MA, BChir, 1929; FRCS Eng. 1929; MD 1933; FRCOG 1943. Examiner in Midwifery, Society of Apothecaries; Fellow of the Royal Society of Medicine. Formerly: Associate Examiner in Obstetrics and Gynæcology, University of London; First Assistant, Obstetrical Unit, University College Hospital; Examiner, Midwives Conjoint Board. *Address:* 15 Devonshire Place, W1.

**WHITE, Oswald,** CMG 1931; *b* 23 Sept. 1884; *m* 1st, Kathleen Elizabeth (*d* 1937), *d* of J. C. Hall, CMG, ISO; three *d*; 2nd, 1937, Margaret Gourley Anderson (*d* 1968). Student Interpreter in Japan, 1903; Vice-Consul at Osaka, 1914; Consul at Nagasaki, 1920; Dairen, 1925; Consul-General at Seoul, 1927; Osaka, 1931; Mukden, 1938; Tientsin, 1939-41; retired, 1944. *Address:* Leicester Court Hotel, 41 Queen's Gate, SW7.

**WHITE, Patrick Victor Martindale;** Author; *b* 28 May 1912; *s* of Victor Martindale White and

Ruth Withycombe. *Educ:* Cheltenham Coll.; King's Coll., Cambridge. Brought up partly in Australia, partly in England. First published while living in London before War of 1939-45. Served War with RAF, as Intelligence Officer, mainly in Middle East. Returned to Australia after War. *Publications: novels:* Happy Valley, 1939; The Living and the Dead, 1941 (new ed. 1962); The Aunt's Story, 1946; The Tree of Man, 1954; Voss, 1957 (1st annual literary award of £1000 from W. H. Smith & Son, 1959); Riders in the Chariot, 1961; The Solid Mandala, 1966; The Vivisector, 1970; *plays:* The Ham Funeral, 1947; The Season at Sarsaparilla, 1961; A Cheery Soul, 1962; Night on Bald Mountain, 1962; *short stories:* The Burnt Ones, 1964. *Recreations:* friendship, cooking, gardening, listening to music, keeping dogs. *Address:* 20 Martin Road, Centennial Park, Sydney, NSW 2021, Australia.

**WHITE, Paul Dudley;** American physician; cardiac specialist since 1913; *b* Roxbury, Mass, 6 June 1886; *s* of Herbert Warren White; *m* 1924, Ina Reid; one *s* one *d*. *Educ:* Roxbury Latin School; Harvard College. AB Harvard, 1908; MD, 1911. Intern. Mass. General Hosp., Boston, 1911-13; Sheldon travelling fellowship, Univ. Coll. Hospital Medical School, London, 1913-14; teaching fellow, Harvard Medical Sch., 1914-20, to Clin. Prof. Med., Harvard, till 1949. Resident in medicine, Mass. General Hospital, 1914-16; served as medical officer, BEF, France, 1916; Capt. US Army Medical Corps, 1917; with AEF, 1917-19; medical officer, Amer. Red Cross, Macedonia, 1919; returned to Mass. Gen. Hosp., 1919, physician in charge cardiac clinics and laboratory, until 1949, subseq. Consultant in Medicine. A founder of American Heart Assoc., 1923; Vice-Pres., 1939-40; Pres., 1940-42; Sec., section pharmacol. and therapeutics, Amer. Med. Assoc., 1921-24, Chm. 1924-25; Chm. subcttee on cardiovascular diseases, National Research Council, 1940-46; Exec. Dir, Nat. Advis. Heart Coun., 1948-56. Vice-Pres. Internat. Soc. of Cardiology, 1950, Pres., 1954; Pres., Internat. Cardiology Foundation. Member: Amer. Acad. Arts and Sciences, RCP (Eng.), 1962; Roy. Soc. Med. (Eng.); Nat. Acad. of Med. of France; Soviet Academy of Medical Sciences, 1961, etc. Distinguished Service Medal, Amer. Med. Assoc., 1952; Albert Lasker award, 1953; Freedom Medal (USA), 1964. Holds honorary degrees from American and European universities and many decorations. *Publications:* Heart Disease (1st edition, 1931, revised and re-issued 1932, 1937, 1944 and 1951); Heart Disease in General Practice, 1937; (jointly) Electrocardiography in Practice (1st edn, 1941, 3rd, 1952); (jointly) Coronary Heart Disease in Young Adults: A Multi-disciplinary Study, 1954; Clues in the Diagnosis and Treatment of Heart Disease, 1955; Hearts: their long follow-up, 1967; (trans., with Prof. Alfred Boursy) Laucise, De Subitaneis Mortibus, 1970; Autobiography, 1971; contribs to medical jls. *Address:* 264 Beacon Street, Boston, Mass, USA; 115 Juniper Road, Belmont, Mass. *Clubs:* Harvard, St Botolph, Saturday (Boston).

**WHITE, Maj.-Gen. (Percival) Napier,** CB 1951; CBE 1946; psc; late Infantry; *b* 1901; *s* of A. J. White, Norton, Evesham, Worcestershire; *m* 1st, 1928, Dorothy Usticke Kemp (*d* 1946), *d* of Rev. Canon Bater, Derby; one *d* (and one *d* decd); 2nd, 1947, Geraldine Margaret Joan Brooking, *d* of late Captain Guy Lushington Coleridge, Royal Navy; two *s*. *Educ:* Cathedral School, Worcester; Royal Military College, Sandhurst. 2nd Lieutenant Sherwood Foresters, 1921; Lt-Colonel, 1941; acting Brigadier, 1943; Colonel, 1946. Served War of 1939-45: in France, 1939-40. Middle East, 1941-45 (despatches twice). Colonel The Sherwood Foresters, 1947-58. Chief of Staff, Northern Command, 1951-53; Assistant Chief of Staff (Organisation and Training), SHAPE, 1953-55; Commandant Joint Services Staff College, 1956-58, retired. *Address:* Little Langley, Chobham, Surrey. *Club:* Army and Navy.

**WHITE, Rear-Adm. Peter,** CBE 1960 (MBE 1944); Director-General Fleet Services, since 1969; *b* 25 Jan. 1919; *s* of William White, Amersham, Bucks; *m* 1947, Audrey Eileen, *d* of Ernest Wallin, Northampton; two *s*. *Educ:* Dover College. Secretary: to Chief of Staff, Home Fleet, 1942-43; to Flag Officer Comdg 4th Cruiser Sqdn, 1944-45; to Asst Chief of Naval Personnel, 1946-47; to Flag Officer, Destroyers, Mediterranean, 1948-49; to Controller of the Navy, 1949-53; to C-in-C Home Fleet and C-in-C Eastern Atlantic, 1954-55; Naval Asst to Chm. BJSM, Washington, and UK Rep. of Standing Group, NATO, 1956-59; Supply Officer, HMS Adamant, 1960-61; Dep. Dir of Service Conditions and Fleet Supply Duties, Admty, 1961-63; idc 1964; CO HMS Raleigh, 1965-66; Principal Staff Officer to Chief of Defence Staff, 1967-69. *Address:* c/o National Westminster Bank Ltd, 26 Haymarket, SW1. *Club:* Army and Navy.

**WHITE, Sir Richard;** *see* White, Sir E. R. M.

**WHITE, Captain Richard Taylor,** DSO 1940 (Bars 1941 and 1942); RN retired; *b* 29 Jan. 1908; *s* of Sir Archibald White, 4th Bt and *heir-pres.* to Sir Thomas White, *qv*; *m* 1936, Gabrielle Ursula Style; three *s* two *d*. *Educ:* RN College, Dartmouth. Served War of 1939-45 (DSO and two Bars). Retired 1955. *Address:* Wateringbury Place, near Maidstone, Kent. *Club:* United Service.

**WHITE, Robert George,** CBE 1949; MSc; *b* 30 April 1885; *m* 1919, Iola, 2nd *d* of late E. O. Price, MD, Bangor; two *s* two *d*. *Educ:* Archbishop Holgates School, York; Leeds University. Lecturer University College, Bangor, 1905-10; County Agricultural Organiser, Edinburgh and East of Scotland Agricultural College, 1910-12; Ministry of Agriculture, 1912; Professor of Agriculture, University College of North Wales, 1913-45; Director of Animal Breeding and Genetics Research Organisation of the Agricultural Research Council, 1945-50, retired 1950. Gold Medal, Royal Welsh Agricultural Society, 1965. Hon. DSc Univ. of Wales, 1967. *Address:* Cymynod, Bangor, North Wales.

**WHITE, Prof. Robert George,** FRSEd; Gardiner Professor and Head of Department of Bacteriology and Immunology, University of Glasgow, since 1963; Hon. Consultant in Bacteriology, Western Infirmary, Glasgow; *b* 18 July 1917; *s* of Thomas Percy White and Alice Robina Fewkes; *m* 1953, Joan Margaret Horsburgh; one *s* two *d*. *Educ:* King Edward VI Sch., Nuneaton; The Queen's Coll., Oxford (Open Schol.). BA 1939; qual. in med., Oxford and London Hosp., BM, BCh 1942; MA 1953; DM 1953; MRCP 1964; FRSEd 1968. Surg. Lt-Comdr, RNVR, 1945-47; Freedom Research Fellow, Lond. Hosp., 1948-52; MRC Trav. Fellow, Lond. Hosp., 1948-52; MRC Trav. Fellow, at Harvard Med. Sch., USA, 1952-53; Reader in Bacteriology, Lond. Hosp., 1954-63. Trav. Prof., Univ. of Florida, 1960. WHO Adv. in Immuno-pathology, 1964-; Meetings Sec., Br. Soc. for Immunology, 1957-63; Mem. Coun., Hannah Dairy Research Inst., Ayr, 1964-. Past Pres., Sect. Allergy and Clin. Immunology, RSM, 1964-66; Mem., Sci. Adv.

Council, Lady Tata Memorial Trust, 1968-. FRSocMed. *Publications:* Essentials of Bacteriology, 1963; (with J. H. Humphrey) Immunology for Students of Medicine, 1963 (3rd edn 1969); articles in sci. jls: Nature, Jl Exptl Med., Lancet, Immunology, Br. Jl Exptl Path. *Recreations:* skating, ski-ing, sailing, painting in oils. *Address:* Dunarden, Campbell Street, Helensburgh, Scotland. *T:* Helensburgh 2201 and 041-339 8822 (ext. 222). *Club:* RNVR (Scotland).

**WHITE, Roger Lowrey;** MP (C) Gravesend since 1970; JP; *b* 1 June 1928; *o s* of late George Frederick White and Dorothy Jeanette White; *m* 1962, Angela Mary (*née* Orman). *Educ:* St Joseph's Coll., Beulah Hill. National Vice-Chm., Young Conservatives, 1958-59; Founder Mem., Conservative Commonwealth Council; Mem. Council, London Borough of Bromley, 1964-68. Freeman, City of London, 1953; JP, Inner London Area, 1965. *Recreations:* golf, tennis, painting. *Address:* 36 Town Court Lane, Orpington, Kent. *T:* Orpington 24855.

**WHITE, Rt. Rev. Russell Berridge;** MA (Oxon), Dipl. Theology (Oxon); *b* 13 Dec. 1896; *yr s* of late Benjamin Beeson, Poplar, London; *m* 1926, Sarah Margaret, *e d* of Rev. J. A. Bunch, Manby, Lincs; two *s* one *d* (and one *s* decd). *Educ:* City of Oxford School; St Edmund Hall, Oxford (1919-22); Wycliffe Hall, Oxford (1922-23). Served European War, 1914-18 (Mons Star, etc.); Queen's Own Oxfordshire Hussars. Curate St Philemon, Toxteth, 1923-27; Clerical Supt, Liverpool CE Scripture Readers Society, 1927-29, Secretary from 1932; Vicar of St Chrysostom, Everton, 1929-33; Secretary, Evangelical Churchmen's Ordination Council, 1933-59; Curate of St Mary Woolnoth, London and offg Chap. Mercer's Co., 1934-37; Vicar of St Stephen, E Twickenham, 1937-45; Vicar of Tonbridge, 1945-59; Rural Dean of Tonbridge, 1946-59; Suffragan Bishop of Tonbridge, 1959-68. Proctor in Convocation, 1947-64. *Recreations:* music, gardening. *Address:* 11 Sondes Place Drive, Dorking, Surrey. *T:* Dorking 3445. *Club:* National.

**WHITE, Sir Thomas Astley Woollaston,** 5th Bt, *cr* 1802; *b* 13 May 1904; *s* of Sir Archibald Woollaston White, 4th Bt, and late Gladys Becher Love, *d* of Rev. E. A. B. Pitman; *S* father, 1945; *m* 1935, Daphne Margaret, *er d* of late Lt-Col F. R. I. Athill; one *d*. *Educ:* Wellington College. *Heir: b* Capt. Richard T. White, *qv*. *Address:* Torhousemuir, Wigtown, Wigtownshire. *T:* Wigtown 2138.

**WHITE, Prof. Thomas Cyril;** Professor of Orthodontics, since 1961, and Director of Dental Studies, University of Glasgow, since 1964; Director of Dental Hospital, Glasgow, since 1964; Dental Consultant to Royal Navy since 1967; *b* 11 March 1911; *s* of Thomas William White, MPS, and Edith Weldon; *m* 1940, Catherine Elizabeth Hunter, LDS; no *c*. *Educ:* Glasgow Acad.; Glasgow Dental Sch. LDS 1933; LRCP, LRCS (Edin.), LRFPS (Glasgow) 1935; BSc, FRCS, FDS, FFD, DDO. Lectr in Orthodontics, in charge Orthodontic Dept, Glasgow Dental School, 1938-48; Cons. Dental Surgeon, Western Regional Hosp. Bd, 1948-61. External Examr: in Orthodontics to Univ. of Edinburgh and QUB; in Dental Subjects to Welsh Nat. Sch. of Medicine, Univ. of Wales. Past President: Glasgow Odontological Society; W of Scotland Branch, Brit. DA; Member: Royal Odonto-Chirurgical Soc. of Scotland; Gen. Dental Council; Dental Education Adv. Council; Standing Dental Adv. Committee to Scottish Health Services Council; Dental Council, Roy. Coll. of Phys and Surg. of Glasgow. *Publications: Text-Books:* Orthodontics for Dental Students, 1954 (Joint), 2nd edn 1967; Manual de Ortodoncia, 1958 (Joint). Contributions to Dental Journals. *Recreations:* gardening. *Address:* Five Acres, Buchlyvie, Stirlingshire. *T:* Buchlyvie 255. *Clubs:* Royal Commonwealth Society; Royal Scottish Automobile (Glasgow).

**WHITE, Wilfrid H.;** *see* Hyde White.

**WHITE, William Lindsay;** Journalist; *b* 17 June 1900; *s* of William Allen White and Sallie Lindsay; *m* 29 April 1931, Kathrine Klinkenberg; one *d*. *Educ:* Harvard University. Elected to Kansas State Legislature, 1930, and served a term. Staff of Washington Post, 1935, Fortune Magazine, 1937. War Correspondent for various American Newspapers and Columbia Broadcasting System (European correspondent), 1939-40; Roving Editor, Readers Digest, 1942; Editor the Emporia Gazette, 1944. Mem. Board of Overseers of Harvard Univ., 1950-56; Member: American Society of Newspaper Editors; Internat. Press Inst. Director: Theodore Roosevelt Memorial Assoc.; American Cttee for Liberation; American Assoc. of Indian Affairs; American Friends of the Middle East; Freedom House; Member National Committee, American Civil Liberties Union; Fellow American Numismatic Society. *Publications:* What People Said, 1938; Journey for Margaret, 1941 (filmed); They were Expendable, 1942 (filmed); Queens Die Proudly, 1943; Report on the Russians, 1945; Report on the Germans, 1947; Lost Boundaries, 1948 (filmed); Land of Milk and Honey, 1949; Bernard Baruch: Portrait of a Citizen, 1950; Back Down the Ridge, 1953; The Captives of Korea, 1957; The Little Toy Dog, 1962; Report on the Asians, 1969. *Address:* 160 East 66th Street, New York, NY 10021, USA. *Clubs:* Century, Harvard, Overseas Press, Dutch Treat (NY); National Press (Washington).

**WHITE-THOMSON, Very Rev. Ian Hugh;** Dean of Canterbury since 1963; *b* 18 December 1904; *m* 1954, Wendy Ernesta Woolliams; two *s* two *d*. *Educ:* Harrow; Oxford. Deacon, 1929; Priest, 1930; Curacy, St Mary's, Ashford, Kent, 1929-34; Rector of S Martin's with St Paul's, Canterbury, 1934-39; Chaplain to Archbishop of Canterbury, 1939-47; Vicar of Folkestone, 1947-54; Archdeacon of Northumberland and Canon of Newcastle, 1955-63; Chaplain to King George VI, 1947-52, to the Queen, 1952-63; Examining Chaplain to Bishop of Newcastle, 1955-63. Hon. Canon of Canterbury Cathedral, 1950. Governor, Harrow School, 1965-69. *Address:* The Deanery, Canterbury, Kent.

**WHITEFOORD, Maj.-Gen. Philip Geoffrey,** OBE 1940; MC 1918; DL; *b* 24 September 1894; *e s* of late Rev. Philip Whitefoord and late Gertrude Relton Whitefoord; *m* 1930, Helen Marjorie (*d* 1969), *d* of late Arthur Edward Lord, The Mount, Hallow, Worcs; one *d*. *Educ:* Realgymnasium, Stuttgart; St John's, Leatherhead; Staff College, Camberley; Imperial Defence College. 2nd Lt, 3rd Bn Lincolnshire Regt, SR, 1912; 2nd Lt, Royal Field Artillery, 1914. Served European War of 1914-18 (despatches twice): France and Belgium, 1915-19. Barrister-at-Law, Gray's Inn, 1930. Bt Major, 1931; Bt Lt-Col, 1935. Served War of 1939-45: France, 1939-40; GSO1 (Intelligence), GHQ, BEF, 1939-40; GSO1 5 Div., 1940; Col, 1940; Brig., Dep. Dir Mil. Intelligence, War Office, 1941; BGS 8 Corps, 1942; Maj.-Gen. Intelligence COSSAC, 1943; Actg Maj.-Gen., 1943; BGS, GHQ, W Africa, 1944; BGS Scottish Comd and Chief of Staff,

Allied Forces, Norway, 1944-45; retired (Hon. Maj.-Gen.), 1945. Contested (C) Lowestoft Div., General Election, 1950. West Suffolk County Council: Mem. Council, 1946; CA 1958; Chm. of Council, 1957-65; DL Suffolk, 1962. Comdr with Star, Order of St Olav, Norway, 1946. *Recreation:* shooting. *Address:* Falkland House, Long Melford, Sudbury, Suffolk. *T:* Long Melford 456. *Clubs:* Army and Navy; West Suffolk, County (Bury St Edmunds).

**WHITEHEAD, Sir Edgar Cuthbert Fremantle,** KCMG 1954 (CMG 1952); OBE 1944; *b* 1905; *s* of late Sir James Beethom Whitehead, KCMG. *Educ:* University College, Oxford (BA 1926, MA 1929). Served War, 1939-45: W Africa (OBE) and with Air Despatch in United Kingdom. Member of the Legislative Assembly for Southern Rhodesia, 1939-40, 1946-53, 1958-65; Acting High Commissioner for S Rhodesia in the UK, 1945-46; Ministry of Finance, and of Posts and Telegraphs, Southern Rhodesia, 1946-53, retd; Member Council University of Rhodesia and Nyasaland, 1955-58; Minister for the Federation of Rhodesia and Nyasaland in Washington, 1957-58. Elected MP for Salisbury North constituency (United Federal Party) in Southern Rhodesia General Election, June 1958. Minister of Native Affairs, 1958-60; Prime Minister of Southern Rhodesia, Feb. 1958-Dec. 1962; Leader of the Opposition, 1962-65 (United Federal Party); returned to England on retirement, 1965. *Address:* Gardeners Cottage, Newtown, Newbury, Berks.

**WHITEHEAD, Commander Edward,** CBE 1967 (OBE 1961); Chairman: Schweppes (USA) Ltd; L. Rose & Co. (America) Ltd; Director: Cadbury Schweppes Ltd, London; Cunard Steam-Ship Co. Ltd; *b* 20 May 1908; *s* of Walter and Amy Whitehead; *m* 1940, Adinah (known as Tommy); one *s* one *step-d. Educ:* Aldershot County High School. General Accident Assurance Company, 1925-39. Served RNVR, 1939-46. General Secretary, British Assoc. for Commercial and Industrial Educn, 1946; HM Treasury, 1947-50; joined Schweppes Ltd, 1950. *Publications:* various articles. *Recreations:* sailing, swimming, walking, beagling, fox hunting, ski-ing. *Address:* 1099 Pequot Road, Southport, Conn 06490, USA; 1200 High Ridge Road, Stamford, Conn 06905, USA. *Clubs:* Lansdowne; Fairfield County Hunt; Pequot Yacht; RN Sailing Assoc.

**WHITEHEAD, George Sydney,** CMG 1966; MVO 1961; Deputy High Commissioner and Minister (Commercial), Ottawa, since 1969; *b* 15 Nov. 1915; *s* of William George and Annie Sabina Whitehead; *m* 1948, Constance Mary Hart (*née* Vale); one *d* (and one step *d*). Educ: Harrow County Sch.; London Sch. of Economics. India Office, 1934. Armed Forces (Royal Artillery), 1940-45. Private Sec. to Parly Under-Sec. of State for India and Burma, 1945-46; British Embassy, Rangoon, 1947; CRO 1948-52; British High Commn, Canberra, 1952-55; Counsellor, British High Commn, Calcutta, 1958-61; Inspector, Commonwealth Service, 1961-64; Inspector, Diplomatic Service, 1965; Head of Commonwealth Trade Dept, CO, 1967-68; Head of Commodities Dept, FCO, 1968-69. *Recreations:* golf, tennis. *Address:* British High Commission, 80 Elgin Street, Ottawa, Canada. *T:* 237-1530. *Clubs:* Civil Service, Royal Commonwealth Society; Bengal (Calcutta); Rideau (Ottawa).

**WHITEHEAD, Col James Buckley,** CBE 1957; MC; TD; DL; JP; Cotton Spinner; Director: National Westminster Bank Ltd (Northern Board); Textile Paper Tube Co. Ltd; *b* 1898; *s* of Edwin Whitehead, Oldham, Lancs; *m* 1926, Florence, *d* of J. R. Thomason, Oldham; one *s* one *d. Educ:* Oldham High School. Served European War, 1916-19, in France and Flanders with 10th Manchester Regt; War of 1939-45 with Roy. Tank Regt and Yorkshire Hussars. Hon. Col 40/41 Royal Tank Regt. DL for Co. Lancaster; JP WR Yorks. *Address:* Staghurst, Grasscroft, near Oldham, Lancs. *T:* Saddleworth 2112. *Club:* Army and Navy.

**WHITEHEAD, Phillip;** MP (Lab) Derby (North) since 1970; *b* 30 May 1937; adopted *s* of late Harold and Frances Whitehead; *m* 1967, Christine, *d* of T. G. Usborne; one *s. Educ:* Lady Manners' Grammar Sch., Bakewell; Exeter Coll., Oxford. President, Oxford Union, 1961. BBC Producer, 1961-67, and WEA Lecturer, 1961-65; Editor of This Week, Thames TV, 1967-70. Guild of TV Producers Award for Factual Programmes, 1969. Vice-Chm., Young Fabian Group, 1965; a founder of 76 Group for Broadcasting Reform, 1969; Mem., NUJ; Mem., Co-operative Party; contested (Lab) W Derbyshire, Gen. Elec., 1966. *Recreations:* walking, cinema, old model railways. *Address:* 12 Needham Road, W11. *T:* 01-229 5297; Mill House, Rowsley, Matlock, Derbys. *T:* Darley Dale 2659.

**WHITEHEAD, Sir Rowland (John Rathbone),** 5th Bt, *cr* 1889; *b* 24 June 1930; *s* of Major Sir Philip Henry Rathbone Whitehead, 4th Bt, and 1st wife Gertrude, *d* of J. C. Palmer, West Virginia, USA; *S* father, 1953; *m* 1954, Marie-Louise, *d* of Arnold Christian Gausel, Stavanger, Norway; one *s* one *d. Educ:* Radley; Trinity Hall, Cambridge (BA). Late 2nd Lieutenant RA. *Heir: s* Philip Henry Rathbone Whitehead, *b* 13 Oct. 1957. *Recreation:* interested in control and communication in the animal and the machine. *Address:* Sutton House, Chiswick Mall, W4. *T:* 01-994 2710. *Club:* Reform.

**WHITEHEAD, Lieut-Col Wilfrid Arthur,** DSO 1941; IA (retired 1947); *b* 28 Jan. 1898; *e s* of late Rev. Arthur Whitehead, Rector of Keinton-Mandeville; *m* 1930, Constance Dulcie (*d* 1967), *e d* of W. W. Crouch, MA; two *s. Educ:* St John's Leatherhead. Entered IA (76th Punjabis), 1915; Mesopotamia and Palestine, 1917-19; NW Frontier of India, 1924-25, 1929-30, 1937; Western Desert and Eritrea, 1940-41 (severely wounded, despatches twice, DSO); Burma 1943. Comdt 3rd Bn 1st Punjab Regt; GSO1 GHQ(I); Comdt Ind. Small Arms School. Patron of Living of Keinton-Mandeville, Somersetshire. *Address:* The Corner House, Instow, North Devon. *Club:* United Service.

**WHITEHORN, John Roland Malcolm;** Deputy Director-General, Confederation of British Industry, since Aug. 1966; *b* 19 May 1924; *s* of Edith and Alan Whitehorn; *m* 1951, Josephine (*née* Plummer); no *c. Educ:* Rugby Sch. (Exhibnr); Trinity Coll., Cambridge (Exhibnr). Served War, 1943-46, RAFVR (Flying Officer). Joined FBI, 1947; Dep. Overseas Dir, 1960; Overseas Dir, 1963; Overseas Dir, CBI, 1965-68; Director, Industrial and Trade Fairs Internat. Ltd; Member: Exec. Cttee, British Council; Council, RUSI; Cambridge Univ. Appointments Bd. *Recreations:* sailing, bird-watching. *Address:* 12 Park Village East, NW1. *T:* 01-387 2323. *Clubs:* Reform, MCC; West Mersea Yacht.

*See also Katharine Whitehorn.*

**WHITEHORN, Katharine Elizabeth, (Mrs Gavin Lyall);** Columnist, The Observer, since 1960; *b*

London; *d* of A. D. and E. M. Whitehorn; *m* 1958, Gavin Lyall, thriller-writer; two *s*. *Educ:* Blunt House; Roedean; Glasgow High School for Girls, and others; Newnham Coll., Cambridge. Publisher's Reader, 1950-53; Teacher-Secretary in Finland, 1953-54; Grad. Asst, Cornell Univ., USA, 1954-55; Picture Post, 1956-57; Woman's Own, 1958; Spectator, 1959-61. Mem., Latey Cttee on Age of Majority, 1965-67. *Publications:* Cooking in a Bedsitter, 1960; Roundabout, 1961; Only on Sundays, 1966; Whitehorn's Social Survival, 1968; Observations, 1970. *Recreations:* gardening, wine. *Address:* c/o The Observer, 160 Queen Victoria Street, EC4. *T:* 01-236 0202.

*See also J. R. M. Whitehorn.*

**WHITEHORN, Rev. Roy Drummond,** MBE 1918; MA (Cambridge; Oxford by incorporation); Hon. DD: Glasgow, 1946; Knox College, Toronto, 1950; *b* 4 Aug. 1891; *s* of late Joseph Hammond Whitehorn, MVO, Past Prime Warden of the Goldsmiths' Company, and late Jane Elizabeth, *d* of Rev. R. S. Drummond, DD; *m* 1921, Constance Margaret, MA Cambridge, *d* of late J. A. Ryley, Birmingham; two *s* one *d*. *Educ:* St Paul's Sch., London; Trinity Coll. (Scholar) and Westminster College, Cambridge (Barnes, Browne, Waddington, Univ. Classical Scholarships). Class I Div. I Classical Tripos Pt I, 1912; Class II Moral Sciences Tripos Pt II, 1914; Secretary, Army Department, YMCA of India, Burma and Ceylon, 1915-19; Lieut 37th (Presidency) Battn Indian Defence Force; Asst Secretary, Student Christian Movement of GB and I, 1921-23; Ordained, 1923, Presbyterian Church of England; Minister, Selangor, Federated Malay States, 1923-27; York, 1928-33; Presbyterian Chaplain and Minister, St Columba's, Oxford, 1933-38; Balliol and Christ Church, Oxford; Moderator, Free Church Federal Council, 1943-44; Moderator, General Assembly of Presbyterian Church of England, 1950; member of Central Cttee, World Council of Churches, 1948-54; Select Preacher, Cambridge University, 1945, 1949, 1951, 1961 and 1963; Sen. Proctor, 1945-46. Editor: Cambridge Review, 1913-14; Journal of Presbyterian Historical Soc. of England, 1940-47. Liveryman of the Goldsmiths' Company. Principal, Westminster College, Cambridge, 1954-63; Professor of Church History, 1938-63. *Publications:* Hibbert Lecture, Beginnings of Nonconformity, 1964; articles in Chambers's Encyclopædia and various periodicals. *Recreations:* formerly swimming (CUSC 1912-14, Capt. 1913), Rugby football (Old Paulines, Middlesex, Selangor). *Address:* 14 Topcliffe Way, Cambridge. *T:* Cambridge 45421. *Clubs:* Union Society, Hawks, Rotary (Cambridge).

**WHITEHOUSE, Cyril John Arthur,** OBE 1951; Under-Secretary, Ministry of Technology, since 1969; *b* 15 May 1913; *s* of F. A. S. and F. A. Whitehouse; *m* 1st, 1937, Elsie Eleanor Reed (*d* 1949); 2nd, 1950, Isobel Mary Lickley; two *d*. *Educ:* Gillingham County School. Clerical Officer, Air Ministry, 1930; Exec. Officer, Inland Revenue, 1932; Higher Exec. Officer, Air Min., 1939; Min. of Aircraft Production: Sen. Exec. Officer, 1942; Asst Dir, 1945; Min. of Supply: Principal, 1946; Asst Sec., 1951; Controller, Scotland, BoT, 1960; Under-Sec., BoT, 1966-69. *Recreations:* golf, gardening. *Address:* 3 Beverley Close, Camberley, Surrey. *T:* Camberley 24452. *Club:* Camberley Heath Golf.

**WHITEHOUSE, Walter Alexander;** Professor of Theology, University of Kent, since 1965; *b* 27 February 1915; *e s* of Walter and Clara Whitehouse, Shelley, near Huddersfield; *m* 1946, Beatrice Mary Kent Smith. *Educ:* Penistone Gram. Sch.; St John's Coll., Cambridge; Mansfield Coll., Oxford. Minister of Elland Congregational Church, 1940-44; Chaplain at Mansfield College, Oxford, 1944-47; Reader in Divinity, Univ. of Durham, 1947-65. Principal of St Cuthbert's Soc., Univ. of Durham, 1955-60; Pro-Vice-Chancellor of Univ., and Sub-Warden, 1961-64; Master of Eliot Coll., Univ. of Kent, 1965-69. Hon. DD Edinburgh, 1960. *Publications:* Christian Faith and the Scientific Attitude, 1952; Order, Goodness, Glory (Riddell Memorial Lectures), 1959. *Address:* The University, Canterbury, Kent. *T:* Canterbury 66822. *Club:* Authors'.

**WHITELAW, David;** Inventor of Games, Lexicon, Alfa-Cubes, Cross-Sums, 1936, Carlette, Sokka, Picture-Rummey, Drafts, 1938, Les Rois de France (Paris), 1952, and Monarchy. *Publications:* M'Stodger's Affinity, 1896; The Gang; Moon of the Valleys; Princess Galva; The Man with the Red Beard; The Secret of Chauville; Girl from the East; The Little Hour of Peter Wells; The League of Saint Louis; A Castle in Bohemia; The Mystery of Enid Bellairs; The Imposter, 1915; A Flutter in Kings, 1916; The Madgwick Affair, 1917; The Master of Merlains; The Valley of Bells, 1918; Man on the Dover Road, 1919; Ballet-scene Carmagnole (music by Herman Finck); Pirates' Gold, 1920; Little Lady of Arrock, 1922; The Stones of Khor, 1923; For Conduct Unbefitting, 1925; The Villa Petroff, 1926; The Man from Mexico City, 1927; Mystery at Furze Acres; Spanish Heels; Number Fifteen; The Roof; Murder Calling; Hotel Sinister, 1936; Wolfs Crag; The Big Picture; Corpus Delicti; The Feud, 1937; The Face; A Bonfire of Leaves, 1938; Frame-Up, 1939; Blackmail-de-Luxe, 1939; Girl Friday, 1940; The Jackal, 1941; Horace Steps Out, 1941; Black-Out Murder, 1942; The Lexicon Murders, 1944; The Ryecroft Verdict, 1945; Lovers-in-Waiting, 1946; Garments of Repentance, 1948; The Moor, 1949; The House in Cavendish Square, 1950; The Yellow Door, 1951; Legacy in Green, 1953; Murder Besieged, 1953; Presumed Dead, 1955; I Could a Tale Unfold, 1957; *plays:* Murder Calling, Theatre Royal, Norwich; The Yellow Book, BBC; Ships That Pass (Television); The Feud; Murder Calling; late Editor, London Magazine. *Address:* The Old Stables, Courtlands Avenue, Esher, Surrey. *T:* Esher 6344. *Clubs:* Savage, Crimes.

**WHITELAW, Rt. Hon. William (Stephen Ian),** PC 1967; MC; DL; MP (C) Penrith and the Border Division of Cumberland, since 1955; Lord President of the Council and Leader of the House of Commons, since 1970; is a Farmer and Landowner; *b* 28 June 1918; *s* of late W. A. Whitelaw and Mrs W. A. Whitelaw, Monkland, Nairn; *m* 1943, Cecilia Doriel, 2nd *d* of late Major Mark Sprot, Riddell, Melrose, Roxburghshire; four *d*. *Educ:* Winchester Coll.; Trinity Coll., Camb. Reg. Officer, Scots Guards; Emergency Commn, 1939; resigned Commn, 1947. Parliamentary Private Secretary to Chancellor of the Exchequer, 1957-58 (to President of Board of Trade, 1956); Assistant Government Whip, 1959-61; a Lord Commissioner of the Treasury, 1961-62; Parly Sec., Min. of Labour, July 1962-Oct. 1964; Chief Opposition Whip, Nov. 1964-70. Visiting Fellow, Nuffield Coll., Oxford, 1970-. DL Dunbartonshire, 1952-66; DL Cumberland 1967. *Recreations:* golf and shooting. *Address:* Ennim, Penrith, Cumberland. *Clubs:* Carlton; County (Carlisle); Royal and Ancient (Captain 1969-70).

**WHITELEY,** family name of **Baron Marchamley.**

**WHITELEY, Maj.-Gen. Gerald Abson,** CB 1969; OBE 1952; a Deputy Assistant Registrar of Criminal Appeals, Royal Courts of Justice, since 1969; *b* 4 March 1915; *s* of late Harry Whiteley, Walton Park, Bexhill; *m* 1943, Ellen Hanna. *Educ:* Worksop Coll.; Emmanuel Coll., Cambridge (MA). Solicitor, 1938. Commissioned, RA, 1940; Maj., DJAG's Staff, ME, 1942-45. AAG, Mil. Dept, JAG's Office, WO, 1945-48; Asst Dir of Army Legal Services: FARELF, 1948-51; WO, 1952-53; Northern Army Gp, 1953-54; MELF, 1954-57; BAOR, 1957-60; Dep. Dir of Army Legal Services, BAOR, 1960-62; Col, Legal Staff, WO, 1962-64; Dir of Army Legal Services, MoD, 1964-69. *Recreations:* photography, walking. *Address:* 8 Kemnal Park, Haslemere, Surrey. *T:* Haslemere 2803. *Club:* United Service.

**WHITELEY, Captain Sir (Herbert) Maurice Huntington-,** 2nd Bt, *cr* 1918; CEng, MIEE, RN (retired); *b* 25 July 1896; *s* of Sir Herbert James Huntington-Whiteley, 1st Bt and Florence Kate (*d* 1948), *e d* of W. B. Huntington, JP, DL; *S* father, 1936; *m* 1919, Lady (Pamela) Margaret, 3rd *d* of 1st Earl Baldwin of Bewdley, KG, PC, FRS; two *s*. *Educ:* Eton. High Sheriff of County of Worcester, 1968. *Heir: s* Hugo Baldwin Huntington-Whiteley, FCA, RN (Retired) [*b* 31 March 1924; *m* 1959, Jean Marie, *d* of late A. F. Ramsay Bock, Warsash, near Southampton; two adopted *d*]. *Address:* The Old Hill, Astley, Stourport-on-Severn, Worcs. *T:* Stourport 2895. *Club:* United Service.

**WHITELEY, Maj.-Gen. Peter John Frederick,** OBE 1960; Major-General Commando Forces, since 1970; *b* 13 Dec. 1920; *s* of late John George Whiteley; *m* 1948, Nancy Vivian, *d* of late W. Carter Clayden; two *s* two *d*. *Educ:* Bishop's Stortford Coll.; Bembridge Sch.; Ecole des Roches. Joined Royal Marines, 1940; 101 Bde, 1941; HMS: Resolution, 1941; Renown, 1942; HMNZS Gambia, 1942; seconded to Fleet Air Arm, 1946-50; Adjt 40 Commando, 1951; Staff Coll., Camberley, 1954; Bde Major 3rd Commando Bde, 1957; Instructor, Staff Coll., Camberley, 1960-63; CO 42 Commando, 1965-66 (despatches, Malaysia, 1966); Col GS Dept of CGRM, 1966-68; Nato Defence Coll., 1968; Comdr 3rd Commando Bde, 1968-70. MBIM. *Recreations:* music (Mem. Glyndebourne Festival Soc.), photography, painting, wood carving, sailing, dogs. *Address:* 69 St Leonard's Road, Chesham Bois, Bucks. *T:* Amersham 3503.

**WHITELEY, Samuel Lloyd;** Deputy Chief Land Registrar; *b* 30 April 1913; *s* of Rev. Charles Whiteley and Ann Letitia Whiteley; *m* 1939, Kathleen Jones; two *d*. *Educ:* George Dixon Sch.; Birmingham Univ. LLB (Hons) 1933. Admitted Solicitor, 1935; HM Land Registry, 1936; seconded Official Solicitor's Dept, 1939; RAF, 1940-46; HM Land Registry, 1946-. *Recreations:* sport, as a reminiscent spectator; amateur theatre. *Address:* 56 Chiltern Court, Baker Street, NW1. *T:* 01-935 5327.

**WHITELOCK, Prof. Dorothy,** CBE 1964; MA, LittD (Cambridge), MA (Oxford); FBA, FSA, FRHistS; Elrington and Bosworth Professor of Anglo-Saxon, Cambridge University, 1957-69; Professorial Fellow, Newnham College, Cambridge, 1957-69, Hon. Fellow since 1970; Hon. Fellow, St Hilda's College, Oxford, since 1967; *b* 11 Nov. 1901; *d* of Edward Whitelock and Emmeline (*née* Dawson). *Educ:* Leeds Girls' High School; Newnham College, Cambridge. 1st Class, English Tripos, section B, 1923, 2nd Class, section A, 1924; Marion Kennedy Student, Newnham Coll., 1924-26; Cambridge Univ. Student, Univ. of Uppsala, 1927-29; Allen Scholar, Univ. of Cambridge, 1929-30. Lecturer in English Language at St Hilda's College, Oxford, 1930-36, Fellow and Tutor in English Language, 1936-57, Vice-Principal, 1951-57; Lecturer in Old English in the University of Oxford, 1946-55, Senior Lecturer, 1955-57. Leverhulme Fellow, 1939-40; Pres. Viking Soc. for Northern Research, 1939-41; Co-Editor of Saga-Book of the Viking Society, 1940-59; Pres., English Place-Name Soc., 1967-. *Publications:* Anglo-Saxon Wills, 1930; Sermo Lupi ad Anglos, 1939; The Audience of Beowulf, 1950; The Beginnings of English Society (Pelican Books), 1952; The Peterborough Chronicle (Copenhagen), 1954; English Historical Documents, *c* 500-1042, 1955; The Anglo-Saxon Chronicle: A Revised Translation, 1961; The Genuine Asser, 1968; The Will of Æthelgifu (Roxburghe Club), 1968; articles in English Historical Review, Medium Aevum, etc. *Address:* Newnham College, Cambridge. *T:* 62273; 30 Thornton Close, Cambridge. *T:* Cambridge 76592. *Club:* University Women's.

**WHITEMAN, G. W.,** MA Oxon; Editor, The Antique Collector, since 1930; *b* 28 Nov. 1903; *m* 1931, Mary Vernon, *d* of Rowland Walker; three *s* one *d*. *Educ:* Highgate School; Queen's College, Oxford. Asst Editor, The Bazaar, Exchange and Mart, 1926; Editor, 1927-29; editorial posts on The Clarion, 1930, and The Friend, 1932-36. Chief Billeting Officer, Saffron Walden Borough, 1940-42; Personnel Secretary, Friends Service Council, 1945-68. *Publications:* Some Famous English Country Homes, 1951; Halls and Treasures of the City Companies, 1970. *Address:* Dykes End, Gibson Close, Saffron Walden, Essex.

**WHITEMAN, William Meredith;** MA; FRSA; writer, lecturer and broadcaster on caravanning; Vice-President: British Caravanners Club; Camping Club; *b* 29 May 1905; *m* 1931, Patricia Aileen Thornton (*d* 1954); three *d*; *m* 1965, Mary Moore (*née* Hall). *Educ:* St Albans School; St John's College, Cambridge. President National Picture Print Society, 1938. Founder National Caravan Council. Hon. Secretary, 1939-49, Hon. Director, 1949-52. Director, Caravan Club, 1938-60. Organiser, Moveable Dwelling Conference, 1947-49. Editor, The Caravan, 1938-61. Man. Editor, Link House Publications Ltd, 1942-70; Dir, Caravan Commn, 1957-70; Countryside Commn transit site study group, 1969-70; served on more than 50 cttees, working parties etc, on caravanning and camping. Hon. Life Mem., Caravan Club; Hon. Mem., Fédération Internationale de Camping et de Caravanning. *Publications:* Books on camping and caravanning. *Address:* Northfield Cottage, Steep, Petersfield, Hants.

**WHITESIDE, Sir Cuthbert William,** Kt, *cr* 1921; *b* 26 Oct. 1880; *o s* of late Rev. Joe Whiteside; *m* 1909, Janet, *d* of late Edward Humpage; one *s* two *d*. *Educ:* Grey College, Port Elizabeth, SA. Solicitor of the Supreme Court, 1901; practising at Grahamstown; retired, 1944; JP District of Albany, SA; Town Councillor, 1912; Mayor of City of Grahamstown, 1918-22. *Recreation:* tennis. *Address:* Leisure Isle, Knysna, S Africa.

*See also Air Vice-Marshal D. C. Stapleton.*

**WHITFIELD,** family name of **Baron Kenswood.**

**WHITFIELD, George;** poet, artist, and (retired) journalist; former art critic, film critic, and sub-editor Liverpool Echo; *b* 1891; *m* Beatrix, *d* of Jacob and Makrouhi Yanekian, Chanak, Dardanelles; one *d*. *Educ:* privately and at

Jesuit College. Studied art under Fred V. Burridge, RE, in Liverpool. Political, sporting, and comic-strip cartoons in London, provincial and overseas papers; former correspondent motoring journals and film publicity, British and American companies. Served Royal Naval Air Service (aerial and service drawings). Founder-member of one-time Liverpool Pickwickians (their first Mr Pickwick) and Liverpool First-Nighters Society. On selection and hanging committees of World Cartoons Exhibn, first Liverpool Festival. *Publications:* poetry and signed articles on art, architecture, cinema, radio, boxing. *Recreations:* poetry, pictures, and people. *Address:* Rockley House, Rossett, Denbighshire. *Club:* Press.

**WHITFIELD, Rev. George Joshua Newbold;** General Secretary, Church of England Board of Education, since 1969; *b* 2 June 1909; *s* of late Joshua Newbold and Eva Whitfield; *m* 1937, Dr Audrey Priscilla Dence, *d* of late Rev. A. T. Dence; two *s* two *d*. *Educ:* Bede Gram. Sch., Sunderland; King's Coll., Univ. of London; Bishops' Coll., Cheshunt. BA 1st cl. Hons, Engl. and AKC, 1930; MA 1935. Asst Master, Trin. Sch., Croydon, 1931-34; Sen. Engl. Master: Doncaster Gram. Sch., 1934-36; Hymers Coll., Hull, 1937-43; Headmaster: Tavistock Gram. Sch., 1943-46; Stockport Sch., 1946-50; Hampton Gram. Sch., 1950-68. Chief Examr in Engl., Univ. of Durham Sch. Exams Bd, 1940-43. Deacon, 1962; Priest, 1963. Member: Duke of Edinburgh's Award Adv. Cttee, 1960-66; Headmasters' Conf., 1964-68; Pres., Headmasters' Assoc., 1967. *Publications:* (ed) Teaching Poetry, 1937; An Introduction to Drama, 1938; God and Man in the Old Testament, 1949; (ed) Poetry in the Sixth Form, 1950; Philosophy and Religion, 1955. *Recreations:* gardening, photography. *Address:* Chesterfield House, Broad Lane, Hampton, Middx. *T:* 01-979 1259. *Clubs:* Athenæum. royal Commonwealth Society.

**WHITFIELD, Professor John Humphreys;** Serena Professor of Italian Language and Literature in the University of Birmingham since 1946; *b* 2 Oct. 1906; *s* of J. A. Whitfield; *m* 1936, Joan Herrin, ARCA; two *s*. *Educ:* Handsworth Grammar School; Magdalen College, Oxford. William Doncaster Scholar, Magdalen Coll., 1925-29; Double First Class Hons in Mod. Langs, 1928, 1929; Paget Toynbee Prizeman, 1933. Asst Master, King Edward VII School, Sheffield, 1930-36; University Lecturer in Italian, Oxford University, 1936-46; Awarder to Oxford and Cambridge Schools Examination Bd, 1940-68. Part-time Temporary Assistant Civil Officer, Naval Intelligence Department, 1943. Chairman, Society for Italian Studies. Senior editor of Italian Studies. President, Dante Alighieri Society (Comitato di Birmingham). Barlow Lecturer on Dante, University College, London, 1958-59. Edmund G. Gardner Memorial Prize, 1959; Amedeo Maiuri Prize (Rome), 1965. Cavaliere Ufficiale (Ordine al Merito della Repubblica Italiana), 1960. *Publications:* Petrarch and the Renascence, 1943 (NY, 1966); Machiavelli, 1947 (NY, 1966); Petrarca e il Rinascimento (tr. V. Capocci, Laterza), 1949; Dante and Virgil, 1949; Giacomo Leopardi, 1954 (Italian tr. 1964); A Short History of Italian Literature, 1962 (Pelican, 1960, 2nd edn 1970); The Barlow Lectures on Dante, 1960; Leopardi's Canti, trans. into English Verse, 1962; Leopardi's Canti, ed. with Introduction and notes, 1967; Discourses on Machiavelli, 1969; The Charlecote Manuscript of Machiavelli's Prince, facsimile edn with an Essay on the Prince, 1969; Valla, The Donation of Constantine, facsimile edn with an introduction, 1970; articles and reviews contrib. to Modern Language Review, Italian Studies, History, Medium Aevum, Comparative Literature, Problemi della Pedagogia, Le parole e le Idee, Encyclopædia Britannica, Chambers's Encyclopædia, Hutchinson's Encyclopædia, etc. *Address:* 2 Woodbourne Road, Edgbaston, Birmingham 15. *T:* 021-454 1035.

**WHITFIELD, Maj.-Gen. John Yeldham,** CB 1945; DSO 1943 and bar 1944; OBE 1942; psc; retired; Colonel, The Queen's Royal Regiment, 1954-59; *b* 11 October 1899; *y s* of late Rev. F. W. G. Whitfield, Caerleon, Mon, and Roehampton; *m* Sheelagh Norah Dundas, *y d* of late H. C. Quin, Inch, County Wexford, Ireland; no *c*. *Educ:* Monmouth School; RMC Sandhurst. 2nd Lt The Queen's Regt 1918; Capt. 1934; Major, 1938; Temp. Lt-Col 1940; Col 1945; Maj.-Gen. 1946. Employed with Royal West African Frontier Force, 1924-30; employed King's African Rifles (Bde Major), 1937-39; served War of 1939-45 (OBE, DSO and Bar, CB); Commander Legion of Merit (US), Order of Red Star (Russia); Comd 15 Inf. Bde, 1944; GOC 56 (London) Div., 1944-46; GOC 50 Div. and Northumbrian District, 1946-48; Chief of Staff, Northern Command, 1948-51; Inspector of Recruiting, War Office, 1952-55, retired 1955. *Address:* Marden Well, Chiddingfold, Surrey. *T:* Wormley 2027. *Club:* Army and Navy.

**WHITFIELD LEWIS, Herbert John;** *see* Lewis, H. J. W.

**WHITFORD, Hon. Sir John (Norman Keates),** Kt 1970; **Hon. Mr Justice Whitford;** a Judge of the High Court, Chancery Division, since 1970; *b* 24 June 1913; *s* of Harry Whitford and Ella Mary Keates; *m* 1946, Rosemary, *d* of John Barcham Green and Emily Paillard; four *d*. *Educ:* University College School; Munich University; Peterhouse, Cambridge. President, ADC. Called to the Bar, 1935. Served with RAFVR, 1939-44: Wing Comdr, 1942; Chief Radar Officer and Dep. Chief Signals Officer, Air Headquarters Eastern Mediterranean; Advisor on patents and information exchanged for war purposes, HM Embassy, Washington, 1944-45. QC 1965. Member of Bar Council, 1968-70. *Address:* Royal Courts of Justice, WC2.

**WHITHAM, Prof. Gerald Beresford,** FRS 1965; Professor of Applied Mathematics, at the California Institute of Technology, Pasadena, Calif, since 1962; *b* 13 Dec. 1927; *s* of Harry and Elizabeth Ellen Whitham; *m* 1951, Nancy (*née* Lord); one *s* two *d*. *Educ:* Elland Gram. Sch., Elland, Yorks; Manchester University. PhD Maths, Manchester, 1953. Lectr in Applied Mathematics, Manchester Univ., 1953-56; Assoc. Prof., Applied Mathematics, New York Univ., 1956-59; Prof., Mathematics, MIT, 1959-62. FAAAS 1959. *Publications:* research papers in Proc. Roy. Soc., Jl Fluid Mechanics, Communications on Pure and Applied Maths. *Address:* California Institute of Technology, Pasadena, California 91109, USA.

**WHITING, Maurice Henry,** OBE; MA, MB, BCh Cantab; FRCS; Consulting Surgeon, Royal London Ophthalmic Hospital; Emeritus Ophthalmic Surgeon, Middlesex Hospital; *b* 12 Oct. 1885; *s* of William Henry Whiting, CB; *m* 1st, 1916, Blanche Beatrice (*d* 1952), *d* of Edward Aggas; (*o s* killed in action, RAF, 1942); 2nd, 1953, Dorothy Miller, *d* of William Gilford. *Educ:* Mill Hill School; Downing College, Cambridge; The Middlesex Hospital, House Surgeon, Middlesex Hospital; House Surgeon and Pathologist, Royal London Ophthalmic Hospital; Capt. RAMC 1914-19;

at Boulogne as Ophthalmic Specialist, 1915-19 (despatches); engaged in work in London as Ophthalmic surgeon since 1919; late Hon. Sec. Ophthalmological Soc. of the UK; late Ophthalmic Surgeon, Paddington Green Children's Hosp.; Member of Board of Governors Middlesex Hospital; President of Ophthalmological Society of UK, 1950-51; Pres. Old Millhillians Club, 1950-51; Pres. Downing College Assoc., 1953-54. *Publications:* Modern Developments in Cataract Extraction, Montgomery Lecture, RCSI, 1933; Ophthalmic Nursing; Concussion Changes in the Crystalline Lens; Technique of the Haab and Small Magnets, and other articles in medical and ophthalmic journals. *Address:* 109 Harley Street, W1. *T:* 01-935 4748; 32 Abbey Gardens, NW8. *T:* 01-624 8010.

**WHITING, Winifred Ada,** MA (London); retired, 1958; *b* 6 Jan. 1898; *d* of Harry Whiting and Ada Elizabeth Kent. *Educ:* County School, Putney; King's College, London. Teaching posts at Kesteven and Sleaford High School, Lincs; William Gibb's School, Faversham, Kent; St Paul's Girls' School; Headmistress, Girls' County Grammar School, Bromley, Kent; Principal, CF Mott Training College, Liverpool; Principal, Nonington Coll. of Physical Educn, near Dover, Kent, retd.

**WHITLAM, Edward Gough,** QC 1962; Leader of the Opposition in the Australian Parliament since 1967; MP for Werriwa, NSW, since 1952; *b* 11 July 1916; *s* of late H. F. E. Whitlam, Commonwealth Crown Solicitor and Aust. rep. on UN Human Rights Commission; *m* 1942, Margaret Elaine, *d* of late Mr Justice Dovey, NSW Supreme Court; three *s* one *d*. *Educ:* University of Sydney. BA 1938; LLB 1946. RAAF Flight Lieut, 1941-45. Barrister, 1947; Joint Committee on Constitutional Review, 1956-59; Deputy Leader, Aust. Labor Party, 1960, Leader, 1967. *Publications:* The Constitution *versus* Labor, 1957; Australian Foreign Policy, 1963; Socialism within the Constitution, 1965; Australia, Base or Bridge?, 1966; Beyond Vietnam: Australia's Regional Responsibility, 1968; An Urban Nation, 1969. *Address:* Parliament House, Canberra, ACT, Australia. *Clubs:* University (Sydney); Helensburgh Workingmen's.

**WHITLEY, Elizabeth Young, (Mrs H. C. Whitley);** social worker and journalist; *b* 28 Dec. 1915; *d* of Robert Thom and Mary Muir Wilson; *m* 1939, Henry Charles Whitley, *qv*; two *s* two *d* (and one *s* decd). *Educ:* Laurelbank School, Glasgow; Glasgow University. MA 1936; courses: in Italian at Perugia Univ., 1935, in Social Science at London School of Economics and Glasgow School of Social Science, 1938-39. Ran Girls' Clubs in Govan and Plantation, Glasgow, and Young Mothers' Clubs in Partick and Port Glasgow; Vice-Chm. Scottish Association of Girls' Clubs and Mixed Clubs, 1957-61, and Chm. of Advisory Cttee, 1958-59. Broadcast regular programme with BBC (Scottish Home Service), 1953. Member: Faversham Committee on AID, 1958-60; Pilkington Committee on Broadcasting, 1960-62. Columnist, Scottish Daily Express. Adopted as Parly candidate for SNP by West Perth and Kinross, 1968. *Publications:* Plain Mr Knox, 1960; descriptive and centenary articles for Scottish papers, particularly Glasgow Herald and Scotland's Magazine. *Recreations:* reading, gardening. *Address:* St Giles' Manse, 6 West Castle Road, Edinburgh 10. *T:* 031-229 3713.

**WHITLEY, Very Rev. Dr Henry Charles,** MA (Edinburgh), PhD (Edinburgh), Hon. DD (Glasgow); Minister of the High Kirk of Edinburgh, St Giles' Cathedral; Chaplain to the Queen in Scotland since 1963; Dean of the Order of the Thistle, since 1969; *b* 20 March 1906; 2nd *s* of W. E. Whitley; *m* 1939, Elizabeth Young Thom (*see* Elizabeth Young Whitley); two *s* two *d* (and one *s* decd). *Educ:* Daniel Stewart's College; George Heriot's School; Edinburgh University; Glasgow University. Parish Minister, Newark Parish Church, 1935-50; Member of Port Glasgow Town Council, 1945-49; Parish Minister, Old Partick Parish Church, 1950-54. Served War of 1939-45 (wounded) as Chaplain with 7th Seaforth Highlanders. Chaplain to: Kingston Shipyard, Port Glasgow, 1945-50; High School, Glasgow, 1950-54; the Waverley Station; the Edinburgh Evening News; Company of Merchants of the City of Edinburgh, 1969-; Royal Coll. of Surgeons of Edinburgh, 1969-; Pontifex Maximus, Harveian Soc. of Edinburgh, 1970-. Gov. of Fettes Coll., 1957; Mem. Managing Board of Edinburgh Royal Infirmary, 1959; Hon. Chaplain to Society of High Constables of Edinburgh. Trustee, National Library of Scotland; Trustee, Iona Abbey. *Publications:* Blinded Eagle—An Introduction to the Life and Teaching of Edward Irving, 1954; A Pictorial Guide to St Giles' Cathedral, 1959; Laughter in Heaven, 1962. *Address:* St Giles' Manse, 6 West Castle Road, Edinburgh. *T:* 031-229 3713. *Club:* New (Edinburgh).

**WHITLEY, Air Marshal Sir John R.,** KBE 1956 (CBE 1945); CB 1946; DSO 1943; AFC 1937, Bar, 1956; *b* 7 September 1905; *s* of late A. Whitley, Condette, Pas de Calais, France; *m* 1932, Barbara Liscombe (*d* 1965); four *s*; *m* 1967, Mrs Alison Russell. *Educ:* Haileybury. Entered Royal Air Force with a short-service commission, 1926; Permanent Commission, 1931; served in India, 1932-37; served in Bomber Command, 1940-45, as a Squadron Comdr, Station Comdr, Base Comdr and AOC a Group; Director of Organisation (Establishments), Air Ministry, 1948 and 1949; Imperial Defence College, 1950; AOA, 2nd Tactical Air Force, 1951 and 1952; AOC No. 1 (Bomber) Group, 1953-56; Air Member for Personnel, 1957-59; Inspector-General, RAF, 1959-62; Controller, RAF Benevolent Fund, 1962-68, retd. *Address:* Little Salterns, Bucklers Hard, Beaulieu, Hampshire.

**WHITLEY, Oliver John;** Managing Director, External Broadcasting, British Broadcasting Corporation, since 1969; *b* 12 Feb. 1912; *s* of Rt Hon. J. H. Whitley, PC, and Marguerite (*née* Marchetti); *m* 1939, Elspeth Catherine (*née* Forrester-Paton); four *s* one *d*. *Educ:* Clifton Coll.; New Coll., Oxford. Barrister-at-Law, 1935; BBC, 1935-41. Served in RNVR, 1942-46; Coastal Forces and Combined Ops. BBC 1946-: seconded to Colonial Office, 1946-49; Head of General Overseas Service, 1950-54; Assistant Controller, Overseas Services, 1955-57; Appointments Officer, 1957-60; Controller, Staff Training and Appointments, 1960-64; Chief Assistant to Dir-Gen., 1964-68. *Recreations:* reading and gardening. *Address:* Brantwood, High Drive, Woldingham, Surrey. *T:* Woldingham 2324. *Clubs:* Bath, RNVR.

**WHITLOCK, William Charles;** MP (Lab) Nottingham North since October 1959; *b* 20 June 1918; *s* of late George Whitlock and of Sarah Whitlock, Sholing, Southampton; *m* 1943, Jessie Hilda, *d* of George Reardon of Armagh; five *s*. *Educ:* Itchen Gram. Sch.; Southampton Univ. Army Service, 1939-46 (Dunkirk and Airborne Invasion of Holland). Apptd full-time Trade Union Officer, Area Organiser of Union of Shop, Distributive and Allied Workers, 1946. President, Leicester and District Trades Council, 1955-56; President,

Leicester City Labour Party, 1956-57, Vice-President, 1959-60; President, North-East Leicester Labour Party, 1955-56, and 1958-59. Member East Midlands Regional Council of Labour Party, 1955-67. Vice-Chairman 1961-62, Chairman 1962-63. Opposition Whip, House of Commons, 1962-64; Vice-Chamberlain of the Household, 1964-66; Lord Comr of Treasury, March 1966-July 1966; Comptroller of HM Household, July 1966-March 1967; Dep. Chief Whip and Lord Comr of the Treasury, March-July 1967; Under Sec. of State for Commonwealth Affairs, 1967-68; Parly Under-Sec. of State, FCO, 1968-69. *Address:* 51 Stoughton Road, Leicester. *T:* 703367.

**WHITMORE, Francis;** Financial Director, Daily Telegraph; *b* 11 Nov. 1903; *y s* of late Charles Whitmore; *m* 1941, Mary, *e d* of late Charles Cubitt Cooke; one *s* one *d*. *Educ:* Merchant Taylors' Sch., Crosby; Manchester Univ. BCom 1923. Financial News, 1924-28; Evening Standard, 1930-33. City Editor, Daily Telegraph, 1938-65. *Publication:* The Money Machine, 1928. *Recreations:* music, books. *Address:* New Mills, Whitebrook, Monmouth. *T:* Trelleck 269. *Clubs:* Reform, Authors', Hurlingham.

**WHITMORE, Sir John (Henry Douglas),** 2nd Bt *cr* 1954; *b* 16 Oct. 1937; *s* of Col Sir Francis Henry Douglas Charlton Whitmore, 1st Bt, KCB, CMG, DSO, TD, and of Lady Whitmore (*née* Ellis Johnsen); *S* father 1961; *m* 1962, Gunilla, *e d* of Sven A. Hansson, OV, KLH, Danderyd, and *o d* of Mrs Ella Hansson, Stockholm, Sweden; one *d*. *Educ:* Stone House, Kent; Eton; Sandhurst; Cirencester. Occupation: tax exile. *Recreations:* flying, ski-ing, etc. *Address:* 1267 Vich, Vaud, Switzerland. *Club:* British Racing Drivers.

**WHITNEY, John Hay;** Bronze Star and Legion of Merit (US); CBE (Hon.; UK), 1948; Editor-in-Chief, and Publisher New York Herald Tribune, 1961-66; Chairman, The International Herald Tribune; *b* 17 Aug. 1904; *s* of Payne and Helen Hay Whitney; *m* 1942, Betsey Cushing. *Educ:* Groton School; Yale University; Oxford University. BA and MA Yale. Served American Air Force in War, 1941-45 (Colonel). American Ambassador to the Court of St James's, 1957-61. Senior Partner J. H. Whitney & Co.; Chairman: Whitney Communications Corporation; John Hay Whitney Foundation; Governor, New York Hospital; Yale Corporation; Trustee: Museum of Modern Art; Nat. Gallery of Art. Formerly special adviser and consultant on public affairs, Department of State; Commission on Foreign Economic Policy; Secretary of State's Public Committee on Personnel, and President's Committee on Education beyond High School; Steward of Jockey Club; Graduate Mem. Business Council. Mem., Corp. for Public Broadcasting. Private collection of Impressionist and post-Impressionist paintings shown at Tate Gallery, London, 1960-61. Hon. Fellow, New College, Oxford, 1957. Hon. Degrees: MA Yale University; Doctorate of Humane Letters, Kenyon College; Doctor of Laws: Colgate Univ.; Brown Univ.; Exeter College, Oxford; Columbia Univ.; Colby Coll. Benjamin Franklin Medal, 1963. *Address:* 110 West 51st Street, New York, NY 10020, USA. *Clubs:* White's, Buck's; Royal and Ancient.

**WHITNEY, William Dwight;** international lawyer, retired; *b* 26 Aug. 1899; *s* of Mr Justice Edward B. Whitney, New York Supreme Court and Josepha Newcomb; *m* 1939, Adrianne Allen; two *d*. *Educ:* Taft Sch.: Yale Univ., USA; New College, Oxford. Cadet for Pilot RAF, 1918; 2nd Lt (Acting Major) Scots Guards, 1940-41. Various Missions for US Government in Liaison with UK, 1941-45. Called to Bar, Inner Temple. *Publication:* Who are the Americans?, 1941. *Recreation:* travel. *Address:* 48 avenue de Sully, La Tour-de-Peilz, Switzerland. *T:* (021)54-03-37. *Club:* Beefsteak.

**WHITTAKER, Arnold,** CSI 1947; CIE 1938; ICS, retired; Chairman Somerset County Council, 1956-59 (County Alderman, 1953); *b* 27 July 1900; *m* 1934, Hilda Lucy, *d* of late O. W. Street, MA; one *d*. *Educ:* Colne Grammar School; London School of Economics; Christ Church, Oxford. Joined ICS 1924; retired, 1939; Political Adviser to Indian Tea Association and Member, Assam Legislative Assembly; Secretary to Planting and Commerce Group, Assam Legislature, 1939-46. Director: The Assam Company, 1946; Commonwealth Trust Ltd, 1948; Bridgwater Building Society, 1961. *Address:* Dundon Beacon, Somerton, Somerset. *T:* Somerton 351. *Club:* East India and Sports.

**WHITTAKER, John Macnaghten,** FRS 1949; MA, DSc, FRSE; Vice-Chancellor of Sheffield University, Sept. 1952-65, retired; *b* 7 March 1905; *s* of late Sir Edmund Whittaker, FRS; *m* 1933, Iona, *d* of J. S. Elliot; two *s*. *Educ:* Fettes; Edin. Univ.; Trinity College, Cambridge (Scholar). Wrangler, 1927; Smith's Prize, 1929; Adams Prize, 1949; Lecturer in Mathematics, Edinburgh Univ., 1927-29; Fellow and Lecturer, Pembroke Coll., Cambridge, 1929-33; Prof. of Pure Mathematics, Liverpool Univ., 1933-52. Senior Fellow, Birmingham University, 1965-66. Vis. Professor: Ain Shams Univ., Cairo, 1967; Inst. of Mathematics, Teheran, 1968-69; Univ. of West Indies, Barbados, 1970-71. Served in RA, 1940-45 (AA Command, Western Desert, Tunisia, and as GSO1, War Office); Lt-Col RA, 1944; Dep. Scientific Adviser to the Army Council, 1944. Chairman: Joint Standing Cttee of Universities and Accountancy Profession, 1953-64; Commn on Royal University of Malta, 1957. A Capital Burgess of the Town and Parish of Sheffield, 1956-70; Freedom of City of Sheffield, 1965. Hon. LLD (Sheffield). *Publications:* Interpolatory Function Theory, 1935; Les séries de base de polynomes quelconques, 1949; Memoirs in various journals. *Address:* 12 Endcliffe Crescent, Sheffield S10 3ED. *T:* Sheffield 63712.

**WHITTALL, Lionel Harry;** *b* 1907; *s* of late H. A. Whittall of J. W. Whittall & Co.; *m* 1937, Elizabeth Morris; no *c*. *Educ:* privately, in W Europe; Oxford (MA); Inst. of Educ., London; Agric. Dept Grad. Sch. HM Foreign Service, 1929-56; latterly Consul-Gen., Berlin. Then, Foreign Books Buyer, Globe Book Shops, Washington, DC, USA; also 1962-: Researcher and Contract Translator to State Dept, Jt Publns Research Service, Berlitz and IML *Publications:* contrib. to official UK and US surveys of foreign press; unsigned trans. for official use: Rumanian Forces Uniforms; Surinam Pilot, and other manuals. *Recreations:* reading, travel. *Address:* 5410 Connecticut Avenue, Washington, DC 20015, USA. *Clubs:* Old Greshamian (Holt); Union (Oxford).

**WHITTERIDGE, Prof. David,** FRS 1953; Waynflete Professor of Physiology, University of Oxford, since 1968; *b* 22 June 1912; 2nd *s* of Walter and Jeanne Whitteridge; *m* 1938, Gweneth, *d* of S. Hutchings; three *d*. *Educ:* Whitgift School, Croydon; Magdalen College, Oxford (1st cl. Physiology Finals, 1934); King's College Hospital. BSc 1936; BM, BCh 1937; DM 1945; Beit Memorial

Fellowship, 1940; Schorstein Research Fellow, 1944; Fellow by Special Election, Magdalen College, Oxford, 1945-50; University Demonstrator in Physiology, Univ. of Oxford, 1944-50; Prof. in Physiology, Univ. of Edinburgh, 1950-68. Leverhulme Vis. Prof., Univ. Delhi, 1967. Mem. Bd of Trustees, Nat. Lib. of Scotland, 1966-. Feldberg Prize, 1962. FRCP London, 1966. *Publications:* papers on physiological topics in Jl Physiol., Brain, etc. *Address:* University Laboratory of Physiology, Parks Road, Oxford OX1 3PT; Winterslow, Lincombe Lane, Boar's Hill, Oxford OX1 5DZ. *T:* Oxford 35211. *Club:* Athenæum.

*See also R. A. Furtado, Sir G. C. Whitteridge.*

**WHITTERIDGE, Sir Gordon (Coligny),** KCMG 1964 (CMG 1956); OBE 1946; *b* 6 Nov. 1908; *s* of Walter Randall Whitteridge, Croydon; *m* 1938, Margaret Lungley (*d* 1942); (one *s* one *d* decd); 2nd, 1951, Jane, twin *d* of Frederick J. Driscoll, Brookline, Mass, USA; one *s*. *Educ:* Whitgift School, Croydon; University of Cambridge. Joined Consular Service, 1932; one of HM Vice-Consuls, Siam, 1933; Vice-Consul, Batavia, 1936; Acting Consul, Batavia, 1937, 1938, and 1939; Acting Consul, Medan, Sept. 1941-Feb. 1942. Employed at Foreign Office from June, 1942; promoted Consul (Grade II), Foreign Office, 1944, Consul, 1945. 1st Secretary, Moscow, 1948-49; Consul-General Stuttgart, 1949-51; Counsellor/Consul-Gen., 1950; Counsellor, Bangkok, 1951-56 (Chargé d'Affaires in 1952, 1953, 1954, 1955); Consul-Gen., Seattle, Wash, 1956-60; HM Consul-General, Istanbul, 1960-62; Ambassador: to Burma, 1962-65; to Afghanistan, 1965-68; retired, 1968. *Recreations:* tennis, music. *Address:* 13 Grimwade Avenue, Croydon, Surrey. *Club:* East India and Sports.

*See also R. A. Furtado, Prof. D. Whitteridge.*

**WHITTET, Dr Thomas Douglas;** Chief Pharmacist, Department of Health and Social Security, since 1967; *b* 4 Jan. 1915; *s* of late Thomas Douglas Whittet and Ellen Sloan Whittet (*née* Scott); *m* 1942, Doreen Mary Bowes; two *s*. *Educ:* Rosebank Sch., Hartlepool; Sunderland Polytechnic; University Coll., London. PhC (now FPS) 1938; BSc (London) 1953; FRIC 1955; PhD (London) 1958. Chief Chemist, Numol Ltd, 1939-41; hospital pharmacy, 1941-43; Chief Pharmacist and Lectr in Pharmacy: Charing Cross Hosp., 1943-47; University Coll. Hosp. and Med. Sch., 1947-65; Dep. Chief Pharmacist, Min. of Health, 1965-67. Member: Brit. Pharm. Codex Revis. Cttee, 1967-; Joint Formulary Cttee, 1967-; Europ. Pharmacopoeia Commn, 1967-; WHO Expert Adv. Cttee on Internat. Pharmacopoeia, 1948-; Council of Europe (Partial Agreement) Pharmaceutical Cttee, 1967-. Liveryman, Soc. of Apohtecaries of London (Sydenham Lectr, 1965). Hon. Member: Royal Spanish Acad. of Pharmacy, 1958; Internat. Acad. of Pharmacy, 1965. Hon. DSc Bath, 1968. Evans Gold Medal (Guild of Public Pharmacists), 1960. FRSocMed. *Publications:* Hormones, 1946; Diagnostic Agents, 1947; Sterilisation and Disinfection, 1965; many papers on medical and pharmaceutical history; numerous papers in Jl of Pharmacy and Pharmacology and in Pharmaceutical Jl on pyrogens and fever and on drug stability. *Recreations:* overseas travel, especially Commonwealth; medical and pharmaceutical history. *Address:* Woburn Lodge, 8 Lyndhurst Drive, Harpenden, Herts. *T:* Harpenden 4376. *Club:* Royal Commonwealth Society.

**WHITTICK, Richard James;** Assistant Under-Secretary of State, Home Office, since 1967; *b* 21 August 1912; *s* of Ernest G. Whittick and Grace M. Shaw; *m* 1938, Elizabeth Mason; two *s*. *Educ:* George Heriot's School; Edinburgh University. British Museum (Natural History), 1936; Home Office, 1940; Principal Private Secretary to Home Secretary, 1952-53; Assistant Secretary, 1953. *Recreation:* gardening. *Address:* 33 Chestnut Avenue, Chorleywood, Herts. *T:* Rickmansworth 72855.

**WHITTINGHAM, Charles Percival,** BA, PhD Cantab; Head of Department of Botany since 1967, and Professor of Plant Physiology, Imperial College of Science and Technology, London University, since 1964; Dean, Royal College of Science, since 1969; Hon. Director, Agricultural Research Council Unit for Plant Physiology; *b* 1922; *m* 1946, Alison Phillips; two *d*. *Educ:* St John's College, Cambridge. Professor of Botany, London University, at Queen Mary College, 1958-64. *Publications:* Chemistry of Plant Processes, 1964; (with R. Hill) Photosynthesis, 1955; contrib. to scientific journals. *Recreations:* music, travel. *Address:* Imperial College, SW7.

**WHITTINGHAM, Air Marshal Sir Harold (Edward),** KCB 1945; KBE 1941 (CBE 1930); MB, ChB (Glasgow); FRCP; FRCPE; FRFPS, DPH, DTM and H; LLD (Hon.) Glasgow; FRCS (Hon.) Edinburgh; KStJ, 1945; Hon. FRSM; Hon. FRIPHH; Hon. Fellow Aviat. Med., Aero Med. Assoc.: Hon. Mem. Assoc. Mil. Surgeons of USA; Hon. Civil Consultant in Aviation Medicine to RAF; Member, World Health Organisation Expert Advisory Panels on International Quarantine and on Environmental Sanitation, and Member, Expert Committee on Sanitation of International Airports; Chairman, Flying Personnel Research Committee, 1949-67; Medical Adviser to the Commonwealth Development Corp.; Member, Internat. Acad. of Astronautics; *b* 1887; 2nd *s* of late Engineer Rear-Admiral Wm Whittingham, CB; *m* 1st, 1912, Agnes Kerr (*d* 1966), *d* of late William Seright, MD, FRFPS, Greenock; one *s* one *d*; 2nd, 1966, Rita C. J., *d* of late W. Harold White, MPS. *Educ:* Christ's Hosp.; Greenock Acad.; Glasgow Univ. Pathologist and Assistant Director of Research, Royal Cancer Hosp., Glasgow, 1910-15; Scottish National Red Cross, 1914-15; served European War, 1915-18, with RAMC in India and Mesopotamia (despatches); attached Royal Flying Corps, 1917-18; transferred RAF, 1918, as Pathologist; Director of Pathology, RAF, 1925-30; Lecturer, Bio-Chemistry, London School of Tropical Medicine, 1926-30; Consultant in Pathology and Tropical Medicine, RAF, 1930-35; Officer Commanding RAF Central Medical Establishment, 1934-39; Consultant in Hygiene, Pathology and Tropical Medicine, Royal Air Force, 1935-39; Hon. Physician to the King, 1938-46; Director of Hygiene, Air Ministry, 1939-41; Chief Executive Officer, Flying Personnel Research Committee, 1939-41; Director-General Medical Services, RAF, 1941-46; Medical Adviser, British Red Cross Soc., 1946-48; Dir of Medical Services, BOAC, 1948-56. Group Capt., 1932; Air Commodore, 1936; Air Vice-Marshal, 1940; Air Marshal, 1941. N Persian Memorial Medallist, 1923; Chadwick Gold Medal, 1925; John Jeffries Award of Institute of Aeronautical Sciences, USA, 1944. Commander of the Legion of Merit, USA, 1945; Cross and Star of the Order of Polonia Restituta, 1945; Knight Grand Cross of the Order of St Olaf of Norway; Czechoslovak Military Medal, 1st Class. Hon. Freeman of Barber-Surgeon's Co. *Publications:* include numerous scientific papers and reports on aviation medicine, cancer, influenza, malaria, dysentery, sandfly fever, cerebrospinal fever, scarlet fever, diphtheria, tonsillitis and first aid. *Address:* 26 Marlborough Gardens, Lovelace Road, Surbiton, Surrey. *T:* 01-399 8648.

**WHITTINGTON, Charles Richard,** MC 1944; Chamberlain of London since 1964; *b* 8 March 1908; *er s* of late Charles Henry Whittington, Stock Exchange, and of Vera Whittington; *m* 1938, Helen Irene Minnie, *d* of late Lieutenant-Colonel J. E. Hance, RHA; one *s* four *d. Educ:* Uppingham School. Commissioned in Queen's Royal Regiment, TA, 1928; Captain, 1931; TARO, 1937. Served War of 1939-45 with Queen's, East Surrey, and Dorset Regts in Sicily, Italy, and NW Europe (D-Day landing, wounded, MC); demobilised with rank of Captain, 1945. Member of The Stock Exchange, London, 1931-64. Liveryman Mercers' Company, 1931; Mem. of Court of Common Council for Ward of Broad Street, 1939-64; one of HM Lieutenants, City of London. *Recreation:* gardening. *Address:* Park Cottage, Brampton Bryan, Bucknell, Salop. *T:* Bucknell 291.

**WHITTINGTON, Prof. Harry Blackmore;** Woodwardian Professor of Geology, Cambridge University, since 1966; *b* 24 March 1916; *s* of Harry Whittington and Edith M. (*née* Blackmore); *m* 1940, Dorothy E. Arnold; no *c. Educ:* Handsworth Gram. Sch.; Birmingham University. Commonwealth Fund Fellow, Yale Univ., 1938-40; Lectr in Geology, Judson Coll., Rangoon, 1940-42; Prof. of Geography, Ginling Coll., Chengtu, W China, 1943-45; Lectr in Geology, Birmingham Univ., 1945-49; Harvard Univ.: Vis. Lectr, 1949-50; Assoc. Prof. of Geology, 1950-58; Prof. of Geology, 1958-66. Hon. AM, Harvard Univ., 1950. *Publications:* articles in Jl of Paleontology, Bulletin Geol. Soc. of Amer., Quarterly Jl Geol. Soc. London, etc. *Address:* 20 Rutherford Road, Cambridge. *Club:* Geological.

**WHITTINGTON, Sir Richard,** KCMG 1958; CBE 1949 (OBE 1945); *b* 22 June 1905; *o s* of Ernest Storrs Whittington, Manchester; *m* 1937, Muriel Elizabeth Fisher. *Educ:* Manchester Grammar School; Brasenose College, Oxford. Som. Thornhill Schol., BA 1927, MA 1959. Joined Consular Service, 1928; Acting Vice-Consul at Batavia, 1929; one of HM Vice-Consuls in Siam, 1931; in charge of HM Consulate, Chiengmai, 1934; Acting Consul-Gen., Bangkok, 1935; in charge of HM Consulate at Songkhla, 1936-38; Consul (Grade II) and 1st Sec., Bangkok, 1939-42; Consul at Algiers, 1942-44; Actg Consul Gen., Algiers, 1944; Consul at Atlanta Ga, 1945-46; Actg Consul-Gen., Bangkok, 1946, Counsellor and Consul-General Bangkok, 1947-51; Chargé d'Affaires in 1948, 1950 and 1951; Inspector, 1952-54; HM Senior Inspector of Foreign Service Establishments, 1954-57; British Ambassador to Thailand, 1957-61, retired. Order of White Elephant of Thailand, First Class, 1960. *Address:* Overbrow, Upavon, Pewsey, Wilts. *T:* Upavon 263.

**WHITTINGTON-INCE, Captain Edward Watkins,** CBE 1943; Royal Navy (retired); *b* 3 Oct. 1886; *s* of late Rev. E. J. C. Whittington-Ince, late of Marrick Abbey, Yorks; *m* 1919, Rosalind Mary, *er d* of E. L. Baker, Rochester, Kent; one *s* one *d. Educ:* Eastman's, Southsea; Burney's, Gosport. Joined RN 1904; served on staff of Admiral Commanding Eastern Mediterranean during Dardanelles Campaign, 1915-16, in Harwich Force, 1917, staff of C-in-C Mediterranean, 1917-19; Secretary to C-in-C East Indies, 1925-27. Paymaster Capt. 1936; Command Supply Officer, Nore Command, 1941-43; retired, 1941. *Address:* Shorne House, Lyme Road, Axminster, Devon. *T:* Axminster 2133.

**WHITTLE, Dr Claude Howard,** MA, MD Cantab; FRCP; Associate Lecturer in Clinical Medicine, University of Cambridge; Physician, and later Physician to the Skin Department of the United Cambridge Hospitals, 1930-61; Consultant Member, Medical Appeal Tribunal; Consultant Dermatologist, Ministry of Social Security, 1945-72; Hon. Consultant Physician; *b* 2 May 1896; *s* of Tom Whittle and Edith Annie Thompson; *m* 1923, Phyllis Lena Fricker, LRAM; three *s. Educ:* The Masonic School, Bushey, Herts; Queens' College, Cambridge (Foundation Scholar in Natural Science); King's Coll. Hosp., London. Clinical Pathologist, 1923. Pres. Dermatological Sec. RSM, 1961-62, Hon. Sec., 1945-6-7; Pres. British Assoc. of Dermatology, 1953-54, Hon. Mem. 1968; Member: Assoc. of Physicians; Path. Soc. of Gt Britain; British Allergy Soc.; Hon. Mem. British Soc. Mycopath., 1968. *Publications:* Vitamin A in psoriasis, Candida skin infections, Fungous infections in Cambridge, Paronychia, Kerato-acanthoma, in Brit. Jl Dermatology, Lancet, etc.; articles on skin diseases in Modern Treatment in General Practice, 1934 and 1938, and in Progress in Biological Sciences, 1960; many others in Proc. Roy. Soc. Medicine, Brit. Jl Dermatology, BMJ, Sabouraudia, Lancet, etc. *Recreations:* painting, sailing, music. *Address:* 41 Newton Road, Cambridge. *T:* 59237.

**WHITTLE, Air Cdre Sir Frank,** KBE 1948 (CBE 1944); CB 1947; Comdr, US Legion of Merit, 1946; FRS 1947; MA Cantab; RAF, retired; *b* 1 June 1907; *s* of M. Whittle; *m* 1930, Dorothy Mary Lee; two *s. Educ:* Leamington Coll.; No 4 Apprentices' Wing, RAF Cranwell; RAF Coll., Cranwell; Peterhouse, Cambridge (Mechanical Sciences Tripos, BA 1st Cl. Hons). No 4 Apprentices' Wing, RAF Cranwell, 1923-26; Flight Cadet, RAF Coll., Cranwell, 1926-28 (Abdy-Gerrard-Fellowes Memorial Prize); Pilot Officer, 111 (Fighter) Sqdn, 1928-29; Flying Instructors' Course, Central Flying Sch., 1929; Flying Instructor, No 2 Flying Training Sch., RAF Digby, 1930; Test Pilot, Marine Aircraft Experimental Estab., RAF Felixstowe, 1931-32; RAF Sch. of Aeronautical Engrg, Henlow, 1932-34; Officer i/c Engine Test, Engine Repair Section, Henlow, 1934 (6 mths); Cambridge Univ., 1934-37 (Post-Graduate year, 1936-37); Special Duty List, attached Power Jets Ltd for develt of aircraft gas turbine for jet propulsion, 1937-46; War Course, RAF Staff Coll., 1943; Technical Adviser to Controller of Supplies (Air), Min. of Supply, 1946-48; retd RAF, 1948. Hon. Technical Adviser: Jet Aircraft, BOAC, 1948-52; Shell Gp, 1953-57. Partnered late Flt-Lt G. E. Campbell in Crazy Flying RAF Display, Hendon, 1930; 1st flights of Gloster jet-propelled aeroplane with Whittle engine, May 1941. Freeman of Royal Leamington Spa, 1944. Hon. FRAeS; Hon. FAeSI; Hon. FIMechE; Hon. Mem., Franklin Inst.; Hon. FAIAA; Hon. Mem., Société Royale Belge des Ingénieurs; Hon. Fellow, Soc. of Experimental Test Pilots, USA; Hon. MEIC. Hon. Fellow, Peterhouse. Hon. DSc: Oxon; Manchester; Leicester; Bath; Warwick; Hon. LLD Edinburgh; Hon. ScD Cantab; Hon. DTech Trondheim. James Alfred Ewing Medal, ICE, 1944; Gold Medal, RAeS, 1944; James Clayton Prize, IMechE, 1946; Daniel Guggenheim Medal, USA, 1946; Kelvin Gold Medal, 1947; Melchett Medal, 1949; Rumford Medal, Royal Soc., 1950; Gold Medal, Fedn Aeronautique Internat., 1951; Churchill Gold Medal, Soc. of Engineers, 1952; Albert Gold Medal, Soc. of Arts, 1952; Franklin Medal,

USA, 1956; John Scott Award, 1957; Goddard Award, USA, 1965; Coventry Award of Merit, 1966; Christopher Columbus Prize, City of Genoa, 1966; Tony Jannus Award, Greater Tampa Chamber of Commerce, 1969. *Publication:* Jet, 1953.

**WHITTLE, Prof. Peter;** Churchill Professor of Mathematics of Operational Research, University of Cambridge, since 1967; *b* 27 Feb. 1927; *s* of Percy Whittle and Elsie Tregurtha; *m* 1951, Käthe Hildegard Blomquist; three *s* three *d*. *Educ:* Wellington Coll., New Zealand. Docent, Uppsala Univ., 1951-53; employed New Zealand DSIR, 1953-59, rising to Senior Principal Scientifc Officer; Lectr, Univ. of Cambridge, 1959-61; Prof. of Mathematical Statistics, Univ. of Manchester, 1961-67. *Publications:* Hypothesis Testing in Time Series Analysis, 1951; Prediction and Regulation, 1963; Probability, 1970; contribs to Biometrika, Jl Roy. Statistical Soc., Proc. Camb. Phil. Soc., Proc. Roy. Soc. *Recreation:* oboe. *Address:* 268 Queen Edith's Way, Cambridge; Statistical Laboratory, University of Cambridge.

**WHITTOME, Sir Maurice (Gordon),** Kt 1961; CB 1955; Solicitor for the Customs and Excise, 1951-63; *b* 15 Dec. 1902; 3rd *s* of late John Whittome; *m* 1934, Angela Nadine, *yr d* of late A. H. Copeman, MD, DL; two *s*. *Educ:* Eton (King's Scholar); Corpus Christi College, Cambridge (Classical Scholar); 1st Cl., Law Tripos (Part II); MA; LLB. Called to the Bar, Gray's Inn, 1928; entered HM Customs and Excise, 1932. *Address:* Freshfield Place Farm, Scaynes Hill, Sussex. *T:* Scaynes Hill 231.

**WHITTON, Charlotte Elizabeth,** SM 1967; CBE 1934; MA; DCL King's College, Halifax, NS, 1939, Acadia, Wolfville, Nova Scotia, 1948; LLD Queen's University, 1941; LLD University of Rochester (NY) 1952; LLD Smith College (Mass), 1955; *b* 8 March, 1896; *d* of John and Elizabeth Langin Whitton. *Educ:* Queen's Univ., Kingston, Ont. Assistant Secretary, Social Service Council of Canada, 1918-22; Asst Editor, Social Welfare; Private Secy to the Minister of Trade and Commerce for Canada, 1922-26; Executive Director, The Canadian Welfare Council, 1926-41; Delegate, Advisory Commission on Social Questions of the League of Nations; Editor, Canadian Welfare, Canadian Welfare Council Publications, 1926-41; now lecturer, writer, and consultant on welfare questions and general historical and literary subjects. Elected Controller, City of Ottawa, 1950; on death of Mayor, 1951, became first woman Mayor of a Canadian City; re-elected, 1952, 1954, 1960, 1962; elected Alderman, in 1966, for 1967-68-69; re-elected 1969, as Alderman and Regional Councillor for 1970-71-72. *Publications:* A Hundred Years A-Fellin', 1942; The Dawn of Ampler Life, 1943; pamphlets on various forms of social work; regular contributor several periodicals. *Recreations:* paddling, skiing. *Address:* 1 Renfrew Avenue, Ottawa, Canada. *Clubs:* Women's Press; Ladies (Toronto); Chelsea (OttawA); Rideau Curling.

**WHITTON, Cuthbert Henry;** Foreign Compensation Commission, Legal Department, since 1959; *b* 18 Feb. 1905; *s* of Henry and Eleanor Whitton; *m* 1938, Iris Elva Moody; one *d*. *Educ:* St Andrew's College, Dublin; Dublin University. Malayan Civil Service, 1929; Colonial Legal Service, 1939; Puisne Judge, Federation of Malaya, 1951; Puisne Judge, Supreme Court, Singapore, 1954. *Recreations:* golf, gardening. *Address:* Far End, Hill Waye, Gerrard's Cross, Bucks. *T:* 5608. *Clubs:* Royal Commonwealth Society; University (Dublin).

**WHITTUCK, Gerald Saumarez,** CB 1959; Assistant Under-Secretary of State, Ministry of Defence, since 1964; *b* 13 Oct. 1912; *s* of late Francis Gerald Whittuck; *m* 1938, Catherine McCrea; two *s*. *Educ:* Cheltenham; Clare Coll., Cambridge. Air Ministry, 1935; Private Secretary to Secretary of State, 1944-46; Asst Under-Secretary of State: Air Ministry, 1955-63; War Office, 1963-64. *Address:* 15A Greenaway Gardens, NW3. *T:* 01-435 3742.

**WHITWELL, Stephen John,** CMG 1969; MC; HM Diplomatic Service; Foreign Office, since 1970; *b* 30 July 1920; *s* of Arthur Percy Whitwell and Marion Whitwell (*nee* Greenwood). *Educ:* Stowe; Christ Church, Oxford. Coldstream Guards, 1941-47 (demobilised with hon. rank Capt.). Joined HM Foreign Service (now Diplomatic Service), 1947; served: Tehran, 1947; FO, 1949; Belgrade, 1952; New Delhi, 1954; FO, 1958; Seoul, 1961. Polit. Adv. to C-in-C Middle East, Aden, 1964; Counsellor, Belgrade, 1965; Ambassador to Somalia, 1968. *Recreations:* reading, painting, looking at buildings. *Address:* Jervis Cottage, Aston Tirrold, Berks; Foreign and Commonwealth Office, SW1. *Clubs:* Travellers', MCC.

**WHITWORTH, Arthur;** late Director, Bank of England; Lieutenant of City of London; *b* 17 June 1875; *e s* of late William Whitworth, Barrister-at-Law; *m* 1914, Monica, *y d* of late Lt-Col E. M. Dansey. *Educ:* Shrewsbury; New Coll., Oxford (MA). High Sheriff County of London, 1924. *Address:* 38 Normandy House, The Drive, Hove 3, Sussex. *T:* Brighton 773617. *Clubs:* Boodle's, Leander.

**WHITWORTH, Clifford,** MSc; PhD; FRIC; FInstF; Vice-Chancellor of the University of Salford, since 1967; *b* 6 Nov. 1906; *s* of late Joseph and Lucy Whitworth; *m* 1941, Ada Alice Belfit. *Educ:* Manchester Grammar School; Manchester University. Senior Research Assistant to Prof. H. S. Taylor, 1931-33; Industrial Research Chemist, 1933-35; Senior Lecturer in Chemistry, 1935-38, and Head of Dept of Pure and Applied Science, 1939-49, Loughborough College; Asst Education Officer for Further Education, Middlesex CC, 1949-57; Principal, Royal Coll. of Advanced Technology, Salford, 1959-67; Mem., Nat. Coun. for Technological Awards, 1955-60; Mem. Educn Cttee, Inst. of Fuel, 1951-, Chm. 1968-; Chm. NW Section, Inst. of Fuel, 1966-68; Vice-Pres., Inst. of Fuel, 1969-. mem. Coun., Brit. Assoc. for the Advancement of Science, 1963-68; Chm., North-Western Regional Adv. Council Academic Bd, 1969-. Mem., Nat. Adv. Council on Educn for Industry and Commerce, 1970-. Mem. Gov. Body, Hornsey Coll. of Art, 1966-; Vice-Pres., Union of Lancs and Cheshire Insts, 1967-. *Publications:* contrib. to sci. jls. *Address:* The University of Salford, Salford, Lancs M5 4WT. *T:* 061-736 5843. *Club:* Athenæum.

**WHITWORTH, Brig. Dysart Edward,** CBE 1943; MC; INdian Army (retired); *b* 13 July 1890; *s* of Major A. W. Whitworth, Royal Warwickshire Regt, Earls Barton, Northants, and Isabel Hunter, Antons Hill, Berwickshire; *m* 1916, Helena Margherita Powell (*d* 1963); one *s*. *Educ:* Shrewsbury; RMC, Sandhurst. Commn, 1910. Served in 2nd Royal Lancers (Gardner's Horse), 1911-35; European War, France, 1917 (MC); Palestine, 1920 (Bar to MC, despatches); War of 1939-45 (CBE); commanded E Bengal and Assam Area, 1940-42; North Assam Bde 1942; Honorary

Commissioner Boy Scouts Assoc., Sussex. *Address:* 14 Swiss Farm, Henley-on-Thames, Oxfordshire. *Club:* Cavalry.

**WHITWORTH, Eric Edward Allen,** MC; Headmaster, Tonbridge School, 1939-July 1949; 3rd *s* of late Prebendary Allen Whitworth, sometime Fellow of St John's Coll., Cambridge, and Vicar of All Saints, Margaret Street; *m* Evelyn (*d* 1966), *d* of late Capt. B. H. Chevalier, RN, The Lodge, Great Beelings, Suffolk; two *s*. *Educ:* Radley; Trinity College, Cambridge (Exhibitioner). History Tripos, Part I, 1st Class, 1911; Part II, 1st Class, 1912; Lightfoot University Scholar, 1912; Assistant Master Rugby School, 1913-28; House Master, 1924-28; Headmaster, Bradfield College, Berks, 1928-39; Officer Commanding Rugby School OTC, 1919-24; served War of 1914-18 with 2nd and 12th Bns of South Wales Borderers in 29th and 40th Divisions (MC, Croix de Guerre, despatches twice, wounded). *Address:* Long Close, Lyddington, Swindon, Wilts. *Club:* Oxford and Cambridge.

**WHITWORTH, Group Captain Frank,** QC 1965; RAFVR retired; *b* 13 May 1910; *o s* of late Daniel Arthur Whitworth, Didsbury, Manchester; *m* 1939, Mary Lucy, *o d* of late Sir John Holdsworth Robinson, JP, Bingley, Yorks; no *c*. *Educ:* Shrewsbury Sch.; Trinity Hall, Cambridge. Served with RAFVR (Special Duties), 1940-45. Called to Bar, Gray's Inn, 1934. Member of Dorking and Horley RDC, 1939-68. Contested (C) St Helens, 1945. Master, Clockmakers' Co., 1962 and 1971. Trustee, Whiteley Village Homes, 1963. *Publications:* miscellaneous verse and articles. *Recreation:* farming. *Address:* Anstie Grange, South Holmwood, near Dorking, Surrey. *T:* Dorking 67136; Goldsmith Building, Temple, EC4. *T:* 01-353 7881. *Club:* Oxford and Cambridge University.

**WHITWORTH, Hugh Hope Aston,** MBE 1945; Lay Assistant to the Archbishop of Canterbury, since 1969; *b* 21 May 1914; *s* of Sidney Alexander Whitworth and Elsie Hope Aston; *m* 1st, 1944, Elizabeth Jean Boyes (*d* 1961); two *s* one *d*; 2nd, 1961, Catherine Helen Bell. *Educ:* Bromsgrove Sch.; Pembroke Coll., Cambridge (BA). Indian Civil Service, Bombay Province, 1937-47; Administrator, Ahmedabad Municipality, 1942-44; Collector and District Magistrate, Nasik, 1945-46; Board of Trade, 1947-55; Scottish Home Dept, 1955; Asst Sec., 1957; Under-Sec., Scottish Home and Health Dept, 1968-69. *Recreations:* travel, theatre, gardening. *Address:* 47 Orford Gardens, Strawberry Hill, Twickenham, Mddx. *T:* 01-892 4672. *Club:* United University.

**WHITWORTH, Air Commodore John Nicholas Haworth,** CB 1960; DSO 1941; DFC and bar 1940; RAF retired; *b* Buenos Aires, 1912; *er s* of late Walter Haworth Whitworth (killed in action, 1918); *m* 1945, Joan Prevett; one *s* one *d* (both adopted). *Educ:* Oundle; RAF College, Cranwell. Served as Flight Comdr (10 Sqdn), Sqdn Comdr (10, 78 and 35 Sqdns), Station and Base Comdr (Scampton), in Bomber Command, 1939-43 (DFC and bar, DSO, MC (Czechoslovakia), despatches); RAF Staff Coll., Haifa, 1946 (psa); AHQ, New Delhi, 1947; HM Air Attaché, Bangkok, 1948; AOC and Comdt Central Flying Sch., Little Rissington, Glos, 1958; Air Chief of Staff, Ghana Air Force, during 1961; AOC, RAF, Hong Kong, 1962-64. *Address:* The Old Rectory, Rodmarton, near Cirencester, Glos. *T:* Rodmarton 223. *Club:* Royal Air Force.

**WHITWORTH, Maj.-Gen. Reginald Henry,** CB 1969; CBE 1963; Bursar and Official Fellow, Exeter College, Oxford, since 1970; *b* 27 Aug. 1916; 2nd *s* of Aymer William Whitworth and Alice (*née* Hervey), Eton College; *m* 1946, June Rachel, *o d* of Sir Bartle Edwards, *qv*; two *s* one *d* (and one *s* decd). *Educ:* Eton; Balliol College, Oxford (Exhibitioner, MA). 1st cl. Hons, Modern History, Oxford, 1938; Laming Travelling Fellow, Queen's Coll., Oxford, 1938-39. 2nd Lt Grenadier Guards, 1940; GSO2, 78 Division, 1944; Bde Major, 24 Guards Brigade, 1945-46; GSO2, Staff College, Camberley, 1953-55; comdg 1st Bn Grenadier Guards, 1955-57; GSO1, SHAPE, 1958-59; Sen. Army Instructor, Jt Services Staff Coll., 1959-61; Comdr Berlin Infantry Bde Gp, 1961-63; DMS 1, Ministry of Defence, 1964-66; GOC: Yorkshire District, 1966-67; Northumbrian District, 1967-68; Chief of Staff, Southern Command, 1968-70. Bronze Star, USA, 1947. *Publication:* Field Marshal Earl Ligonier, 1958. *Recreations:* riding, fishing, military history. *Address:* The Old Manor, Letcombe Regis, Wantage, Berks. *T:* Wantage 2259. *Club:* Guards.

**WHITWORTH, Thomas;** Master of Hatfield College, Durham, since 1956; *b* 7 April 1917; *o s* of late Leonard and Elizabeth Whitworth, Oldham, Lancs; *m* 1941, Joan Mohene, *er d* of Sir Clifford Agarwala, *qv*; one *s* two *d*. *Educ:* Manchester Grammar School; Oriel College, Oxford. Royal Engineers, 1939-45. Burdett-Coutts Scholar, Oxford University, 1947-49. MA (Oxon) 1947, DPhil (Oxon) 1950. University Demonstrator in geology at Oxford and Lecturer of Oriel College, 1949-56. *Publications:* in various scientific journals. *Recreations:* painting; refereeing (Rugby Union); geological expeditions to East Africa. *Address:* The Master's Lodging, Hatfield College, Durham. *T:* Durham 5008.

**WHITWORTH, Admiral Sir William Jock,** KCB, *cr* 1941 (CB 1938); DSO 1918; *b* 29 June 1884; *s* of late Major A. W. Whitworth, Earls Barton, Northants; *m* 1910, Marguerite (*d* 1970), *d* of late Lieut-Col A. H. Maclean, RA; one *s* one *d* (and one *s* one *d* decd). Served European War, 1914-18 (despatches, DSO); commanded the Physical and Recreational Training School, Portsmouth, 1926-28; in command of HMS Stuart and Second Destroyer Flotilla, Mediterranean Fleet, 1928-31; Capt. (D) Reserve Destroyer Flotilla, 1931; Dir of Physical Training and Sports, and Head of the Naval Personnel Committee, 1931-33; Captain of the Fleet to Commander-in-Chief, Mediterranean, 1933-35; commanded HMS Rodney, 1936; Rear-Admiral, 1936; Naval Secretary to First Lord of the Admiralty, 1937-39; Vice-Admiral commanding Battle Cruiser Squadron, 1939-41; in command in Warspite, 2nd Battle of Narvik, 1940; Second Sea Lord of the Admiralty, 1941-44; Commander-in-Chief, Rosyth, 1944 to July 1946; Admiral, 1943; retired list, 1946. Grand Cross Order of St Olav (Norway). *Address:* 3 Canon Lane, Chichester, Sussex. *T:* Chichester 2926. *Club:* United Service.

**WHYATT, Sir John,** Kt 1957; *b* 13 April 1905; *o s* of late George Whyatt; *m* 1936, Margaret, *er d* of Kenneth Stewart; one *s*. *Educ:* Stonyhurst; Balliol Coll., Oxford. Entered Colonial Legal Service, 1937; Crown Counsel, Hong Kong; Hong Kong Deleg. to Eastern Group Conference, New Delhi, 1940; Secretary, Eastern Group Supply Council, New Delhi, 1941; Adviser to British Representative, UNRRA Council Meeting, Sydney, 1945; Attorney-General, Barbados, 1948; Attorney-General and Minister for Legal Affairs, Kenya,

1951-55; Chief Justice of Singapore, 1955-58, retd. Judge of the Chief Court for the Persian Gulf, 1961-66; Director of Studies, Overseas Government Legal Officers Course, 1966-67. KC (Barbados) 1949; QC (Kenya) 1952. *Recreations:* travel, fishing, walking. *Address:* Boxwood, Amberley, Arundel, Sussex. *Club:* Travellers'.

**WHYTE, Angus H.;** *see* Hedley-Whyte.

**WHYTE, Rev. James Aitken;** Professor of Practical Theology and Christian Ethics, St Mary's College, University of St Andrews, since 1958; Dean of Faculty of Divinity, since 1968; *b* 28 Jan. 1920; 2nd *s* of late Andrew Whyte, Leith, and late Barbara Janet Pittillo Aitken; *m* 1942, Elisabeth, *er d* of Rev. G. S. Mill, MA, BSc, Kalimpong, India; two *s* one *d*. *Educ:* Daniel Stewart's Coll., Edinburgh; University of Edinburgh (Arts and Divinity), MA 1st Cl. Hons Phil., 1942. Ordained, 1945; Chaplain to the Forces, 1945-48; Minister of: Dunollie Road, Oban, 1948-54; Mayfield North, Edinburgh (subseq. Mayfield and Fountainhall, Edinburgh), 1954-58. Guest Lectr, Inst. for the Study of Worship and Religious Architecture, Birmingham, 1965-66; Kerr Lectr, Univ. of Glasgow, 1969-72. *Publications:* Contributor to Towards a Church Architecture, 1962; Preparing for the Ministry of the 1970's, 1965; A Dictionary of Christian Ethics, 1967; articles in journals, etc. *Address:* 56 South Street, St Andrews, Fife.

**WHYTE, Air Commandant Dame Roberta (Mary),** DBE, *cr* 1955; RRC 1949; *b* 6 June 1897; *d* of Robert Whyte and Mary Whyte (formerly Lumsden). Trained at King's College Hospital, SE5, 1923-28. Princess Mary's Royal Air Force Nursing Service, 1929-56; Matron-in-Chief Princess Mary's Royal Air Force Nursing Service, 1952-56, retired, QHNS 1952. *Club:* United Nursing Services.

**WHYTE, William Hamilton,** MA; *b* 15 Jan. 1885; *s* of John Whyte and Elizabeth Alexander; *m* 1925, Janet, *d* of late Dr Williamson, Exmouth; two *s*. *Educ:* Woodside School, Glasgow; Universities of Glasgow and Leeds. Stock Exchange, Glasgow; served European War, Lieut RNVR; Staff of University College of the South-West, Exeter, 1921-25; Professor of Economics, University of Bristol, 1925-50 (Dean, Faculty of Arts, 1939-46); Director, Institute of Social and Economic Research, University Coll., Ibadan, Nigeria, 1950-53; Member Nigerian Government Western Region, Overseas, Public Service Board, 1953-60. Ex-Chairman of following Wages Councils: Wholesale Mantle and Costume; Corset; Coffin; Industrial Canteens; Hairdressers. *Publications:* The Stock Exchange; Decasualisation of Dock Labour; Drink and Industrial Efficiency. *Recreations:* golf, tennis. *Address:* Amberley Court 3, Amberley, near Stroud, Glos. *T:* Amberley 2282. *Club:* National Liberal.

**WICKBERG, Gen. Erik E.;** Comdr of the Order of Vasa (Sweden); Order of Moo-Goong-Wha (Korea); General of the Salvation Army since 1969; *b* 6 July 1904; *s* of David Wickberg, Commissioner, Salvation Army, and Betty (*née* Lundblad); *m* 1932, Captain Margarete Dietrich; two *s* two *d*. *Educ:* Uppsala; Berlin; Stockholm. Salvation Army Internat. Training Coll., 1924-25, and Staff Coll., 1926; commissioned, 1925; appts in Scotland, Berlin, London; Divisional Commander, Uppsala, 1946-48; Chief Secretary, Switzerland, 1948-53; Chief Secretary, Sweden, 1953-57; Territorial Commander, Germany, 1957-61; Chief of the Staff, Internat. HQ, London, 1961-69; elected General of the Salvation Army, July 1969; assumed international leadership, Sept. 1969. *Publications:* articles in Salvation Army periodicals and Year Book. *Recreations:* reading, fishing, chess. *Address:* International Headquarters of the Salvation Army, 101 Queen Victoria Street, EC4. *T:* 01-236 5222.

**WICKHAM, Lt-Col Sir Charles (George),** KCMG 1952; KBE 1945; Kt 1922; DSO 1900; DL; late Norfolk Regiment; *b* 11 Sept. 1879; 4th *s* of W. W. Wickham of Chestnut Grove, Yorks; *m* 1st, 1916, Phyllis Amy (*d* 1924), 2nd *d* of Edward G. Rose; two *d*; 2nd 1925, Fanny Desirée Dyott (*d* 1946), 2nd *d* of Howard Paget, Elford Hall, Tamworth. *Educ:* Harrow; Royal Military College, Sandhurst. Entered Army, 1899; Captain, 1906; Major, 1915; served South Africa, 1900-02 (wounded, despatches, Queen's medal 5 clasps, King's medal 2 clasps, DSO); European War, 1914-16 (despatches thrice, Bt Major); AQMG and GSO1, 1918-20 (Bt Lieut-Col); temp. Lieut-Col with General Knox's Military Mission, Siberia; Divisional Commissioner Royal Irish Constabulary, 1920; Inspector-General Royal Ulster Constabulary, 1922-45; Maj.-Gen. (HG). Head of British Police–Prisons Mission to Greece, June 1945-52. Formed: Ulster Special Constabulary, 1920; Royal Ulster Constabulary, 1922; Ulster Home Guard, 1940. High Sheriff, County Down, 1960; DL Co. Down, 1962. French Legion of Honour; Order of Crown of Italy; Czechoslovak War Cross. *Address:* Ashdene, Comber, Co. Down. *T:* Comber 206. *Clubs:* Army and Navy, United Service.

*See also C. O. I. Ramsden.*

**WICKHAM, Glynne William Gladstone;** Professor of Drama, University of Bristol, since 1960; *b* 15 May 1922; *s* of W. G. and Catherine Wickham; *m* 1954, Marjorie Heseltine (*née* Mudford); two *s* one *d*. *Educ:* Winchester College; New College, Oxford. Entered RAF, 1942; commissioned as Navigator, 1943; discharged as Flt Lt, 1946. BA, 1947; DPhil, 1951 (Oxon); President of OUDS, 1946-47. Asst Lecturer, Drama Dept, Bristol Univ., 1948; Senior Lecturer and Head of Dept, 1955. Worked sporadically as actor, script-writer and critic for BBC, from 1946; attended General Course in Broadcasting, BBC Staff Trg Sch., 1953. Travelled in America on Rockefeller Award, 1953. Visiting Prof., Drama Dept, State Univ. of Iowa, 1960; Ferens Vis. Prof. of Drama, Hull Univ., 1969; Vis. Prof. of Theatre History, Yale Univ., 1970. G. F. Reynolds Memorial Lecturer, Univ. of Colorado, 1960; directed Amer. première, The Birthday Party, for Actors' Workshop, San Francisco, 1960. Judith E. Wilson Lecturer in Poetry and Drama, Cambridge Univ., 1960-61; Consultant to Finnish National Theatre and Theatre School on establishment of Drama Department in Univ. of Helsinki, 1963. Governor of Bristol Old Vic Trust, 1963. Consultant to Univ. of E Africa on establishment of a Sch. of Drama in University Coll., Dar-es-Salaam, Tanzania, 1965; Dir, Theatre Seminar, for Summer Univ., Vaasa, Finland, 1965; External Examr to Sch. of Drama in Univ. of Ibadan, Nigeria, 1965-68. *Publications:* Early English Stages, 1300-60, Vol. I (1300-1576), 1959; Vol. II (1576-1660, Pt 1), 1962; Editor: The Relationship between Universities and Radio, Film and Television, 1954; Drama in a World of Science, 1962; Gen. Introd. to the London Shakespeare, 6 vols (ed J. Munro), 1958; Shakespeare's Dramatic Heritage, 1968. *Recreations:* gardening and travel. *Address:* 6 College Road, Clifton, Bristol 8. *T:* Bristol 34918.

**WICKINS, Brevet-Col (Temp. Brig.) George Cradock,** CB 1945; CBE 1939; TD; DL Greater London Council; Royal Signals, TA; *b* 1884; *s* of George Cradock Wickins; *m* 1918, Mabel English. Served European War, 1914-19, and War of 1939-45. Chief Signal Officer Anti-Aircraft Command until Feb. 1945; on return to Post Office appointed Public Relations Officer, 1945-46; Chm. Cadet Committee, County of London, 1945-49. *Address:* 8 Alderton Court, West Parade, Bexhill-on-Sea, Sussex.

**WICKLOW,** 8th Earl of, *cr* 1793; **William Cecil James Philip John Paul Howard;** Baron of Clonmore; Captain Royal Fusiliers; Director, Patriotic Insurance Company, Dublin; *b* 30 Oct. 1902; *o s* of 7th Earl of Wicklow and Lady Gladys Mary Hamilton (*d* 1917), *y d* of 2nd Duke of Abercorn; *S* father, 1946; *m* 1959, Eleanor, *d* of Prof. R. M. Butler. *Educ:* Eton; Merton College, Oxford (BA Hons). Roman Catholic. Editor, Dublin Review, 1937-40. *Publications:* Pope Pius XI and World Peace, 1937; More about Dom Marmion, 1949; Fireside Fusilier, 1959; and various translations. *Heir: cousin* Cecil Aymar Forward-Howard, *b* 1909. *Address:* Sea Grange, Sandycove, Dun Laoghaire, Co. Dublin. *Clubs:* Kildare Street (Dublin); Royal Irish Yacht (Dun Laoghaire).

**WICKREME, A. S. K.;** *see* Kohoban-Wickreme.

**WICKREMESINGHE, Dr Walter Gerald,** CMG 1954; OBE 1949; *b* 13 Feb. 1897; *s* of Peter Edwin Wickremesinghe and Charlotte Catherine Goonetilleka; *m* 1931, Irene Amelia Goontilleka; two *s* two *d*. *Educ:* Royal College, Colombo; Ceylon Medical College; London University (the London Hospital); Harvard University (School of Public Health). Licentiate in Medicine and Surgery (Ceylon), 1921; MRCS, LRCP, 1923; Master of Public Health (Harvard), 1926; Dr of Public Health (Harvard), 1927. Director of Medical and Sanitary Services, Ceylon, 1948-53. Chief Delegate from Ceylon at WHO. Assembly and Executive board, Geneva, 1952; Mem. UN Health Planning Mission to Korea, 1952; WHO Consultant, Manila, 1965; Chairman, Committee of Inquiry into Mental Health Services, Ceylon, 1966. (Hon.) FAPHA 1952. OStJ. *Publications:* contributions to Brit. Med. Jl; Ceylon Med. Jl; Trans. Soc. of Med. Officers of Health, Ceylon; Amer. Jl of Public Health. *Recreations:* golf, tennis, riding, swimming. *Address:* 48 Buller's Lane, Colombo 7, Ceylon. *T:* Colombo 81374. *Clubs:* Otter Aquatic (Colombo); (Life Mem.) Health Dept Sports.

**WICKS, Allan;** Organist, Canterbury Cathedral, since 1961; *b* 1923; *s* of Edward Kemble Wicks, Priest, and Nancie (*née* Murgatroyd); *m* 1955, Elizabeth Kay Butcher; two *d*. *Educ:* Leatherhead; Christ Church, Oxford. Sub-organist, York Minister, 1947; Organist, Manchester Cathedral, 1954. *Address:* 6 Burgate House, Canterbury, Kent.

**WICKS, David Vaughan,** RE 1961 (ARE 1950); Technical Artist, Bank of England Printing Works, since 1954; *b* 20 Dec. 1918; British; *m* 1948, Margaret Gwyneth Downs; one *s* one *d* (and one *s* decd). *Educ:* Wychwood, Bournemouth; Cranleigh School, Surrey. Polytechnic School of Art, 1936, silver medal for figure composition, 1938, 1939. Radio Officer, Merchant Navy, 1940-46. Royal College of Art, Engraving School, 1946-49, Diploma, ARCA Engraving. Taught Processes of Engraving at RCA, 1949-54. *Recreations:* archery and tennis. *Address:* 56 Rous Road, Buckhurst Hill, Essex. *T:* 01-504 8087.

**WIDDAS, Prof. Wilfred Faraday,** MB, BS; BSc; PhD; DSc; Professor of Physiology in the University of London, Bedford College, since Oct. 1960; *b* 2 May 1916; *s* of late Percy Widdas, BSc, mining engineer, and Annie Maude (*née* Snowdon); *m* 1940, Gladys Green; one *s* two *d*. *Educ:* Durham School; University of Durham College of Medicine and Royal Victoria Infirmary, Newcastle upon Tyne. MB, BS 1938; BSc 1947; PhD 1953; DSc 1958. Assistant in General Practice, 1938-39. Served in RAMC, 1939-47; Deputy Assistant Director-General Army Medical Services, War Office (Major), 1942-47. Research Fellow, St Mary's Hospital Medical School, 1947-49; Lecturer and Sen. Lecturer in Physiology, St Mary's Hospital Medical School, 1949-55; Senior Lecturer in Physiology, King's College, 1955-56; University Reader in Physiology at King's College, 1956-60. FRSocMed. Member: Royal Institution of Gt Britain; Physiological Society; Society of Experimental Biology. *Publications:* Membrane Transport of Sugars, chapter in Carbohydrate Metabolism and its Disorders; Permeability, chapter in Recent Advances in Physiology; also papers on similar topics in (chiefly) Jl of Physiology. *Recreations:* tennis, golf. *Address:* 67 Marksbury Avenue, Kew Gardens, Richmond, Surrey. *T:* 01-876 6374. *Club:* Queen's.

**WIDDECOMBE, James Murray,** CB 1968; OBE 1959; Principal, Management Services, Ministry of Defence; formerly Director-General of Supplies and Transport (Naval), MoD, 1968-70; *b* 7 Jan. 1910; *s* of late Charles Frederick Widdecombe and of Alice Widdecombe; *m* 1936, Rita Noreen Plummer; one *s* one *d*. *Educ:* Devonport High Sch. Asst Naval Armament Supply Officer, Portsmouth, Holton Heath and Chatham, 1929-35; Dep. Naval Armt Supply Officer, Chatham, 1936; OC, RN Armt Depot, Gibraltar, 1936-40; Naval Armt Supply Officer: Admty, 1940-43; Levant, 1943-44. Capt. (SP) RNVR. Sen. Armt Supply Officer: Staff of C-in-C, Med., 1944-46; Admty, 1946-50; Asst Dir of Armt Supply, Admty, 1950-51, and 1956-59; Suptg Naval Armt Supply Officer, Portsmouth, 1951-53; Prin. Naval Armt Supply Officer, Staff of C-in-C, Far East, 1953-56; Dep. Dir of Armt Supply, Admiralty, 1959-61; Dir of Victualling, Admty, 1961-66; Head of RN Supply and Transport Service, MoD, 1966-68. FInstPS; MBIM. *Recreations:* golf, gardening, amateur dramatics. *Address:* 1 Manor Close, Critchmere Lane, Haslemere, Surrey. *T:* Haslemere 2899. *Clubs:* West Hill Golf, Navy Department Golfing Society.

**WIDDICOMBE, David Graham,** QC 1965; *b* 7 Jan. 1924; *s* of Aubrey Guy Widdicombe and Margaret (*née* Puddy); *m* 1961, Anastasia Cecilia (*née* Leech); two *s* one *d*. *Educ:* St Albans Sch.; Queen's Coll., Cambridge. Called to the Bar, 1950. *Address:* 2 Mitre Court Buildings, Temple, EC4. *T:* 01-353 4488; 8 Park Village East, NW1. *T:* 01-387 4288. *Club:* Garrick.

**WIDDOWS, Air Commodore (Stanley) Charles,** CB 1959; DFC 1940; RAF Retired; Company Director since 1959; *b* 4 Oct. 1909; *s* of P. L. Widdows, Southend, Bradfield, Berkshire; *m* 1939, Irene Ethel, *d* of S. H. Rawlings, Ugley, Essex; two *s*. *Educ:* St Bartolomew's School, Newbury; No 1 School of Technical Training, RAF, Halton; Royal Air Force College, Cranwell. Commissioned, 1931; Fighting Area, RAF, 1931-32; RAF Middle East, Sudan and Palestine, 1933-37; Aeroplane and Armament Experimental Estab., 1937-40; OC 29 (Night Fighter) Sqdn, 1940-41; OC RAF West Malling, 1941-42; Gp Capt., Night Ops, HQ 11 and 12 Gp, 1942; SASO, No 85 (Base

Defence) Gp, 1943; Gp Capt. Organisation, Supreme HQ, Allied Expeditionary Force, 1944; OC, RAF Wahn, Germany, 1944-46; RAF Instructor, Sen. Officers War Course, RNC, Greenwich, 1946-48; Fighter Command, 1948-54: SASO HQ No 12 Gp; Chief Instructor, Air Defence Wing, School of Land/Air Warfare; Sector Commander, Eastern Sector. Imperial Defence College, 1955; Director of Operations (Air Defence), Air Ministry, 1956-58. *Address:* Les Granges de Beauvoir, Rohais, St Peter Port, Guernsey, CI. *T:* Guernsey 20219. *Club:* Royal Thames Yacht.

**WIDGERY, Rt. Hon. Sir John Passmore,** PC 1968; Kt 1961; OBE 1945; TD; **Rt. Hon. Lord Justice Widgery;** a Lord Justice of Appeal since 1968; *b* 24 July 1911; *s* of Samuel Widgery, South Molton, Devon; *m* 1948, Ann, *d* of William Edwin Kermode, Peel, Isle of Man. *Educ:* Queen's Coll., Taunton. Solicitor (John Mackrell Prizeman), 1933. Served War of 1939-45, Roy. Artillery, North-West Europe, Lieut-Col, 1942; Brigadier (TA) 1952. Called to Bar, Lincoln's Inn, 1946; practising South-Eastern circuit; QC 1958; Recorder of Hastings, 1959-61; Judge of the High Court of Justice (Queen's Bench Division), 1961-68. Bencher of Lincoln's Inn, 1961. Chairman, Deptl Cttee on Legal Aid in Criminal Cases, 1964-65. First Pres. Senate of the Inns of Court, 1966-70. Vice-Chm. Home Office Adv. Council on the Penal System, 1966-70. DL Co. London, 1951. *Address:* Royal Courts of Justice, WC2.

**WIEN, Hon. Sir Philip,** Kt 1970; **Hon. Mr Justice Wien;** a Judge of the High Court, Queen's Bench Division, since 1970; *b* 7 August 1913; *y s* of Samuel Wien, Cyncoed, Cardiff; *m* 1947, Anita Hermer; two *d. Educ:* Canton High School, Cardiff; University College of S Wales and Monmouthshire; University College, London. Solicitor, 1938-46; LLM Exhibitioner in Law. Served War of 1939-45, North Western Europe with 79 Armd Division; Major, 22nd Dragoons, 1940-46 (despatches). Barrister, Inner Temple, 1946; QC 1961; Master of Bench; Mem. Bar Council, 1969; Leader of Wales and Chester Circuit; Recorder of Birkenhead, 1965-69; Recorder of Swansea, 1969-70. Chairman of Medical Appeals Tribunal, 1961-. *Address:* Royal Courts of Justice, WC2. *Club:* Reform.

**WIESNER, Dr Jerome B.;** Provost of the Massachusetts Institute of Technology, since 1966; *b* 30 May 1915; *s* of Joseph and Ida Freedman Wiesner; *m* 1940, Laya Wainger; three *s* one *d. Educ:* University of Michigan, Ann Arbor, Michigan. PhD in electrical engineering, 1950. Staff, University of Michigan, 1937-40; Chief Engineer, Library of Congress, 1940-42; Staff, MIT Radiation Lab., 1942-45; Staff, Univ. of Calif Los Alamos Lab., 1945-46; Director, Research Laboratory of Electronics, MIT, 1946-61; Special Assistant to the President of the USA, for Science and Technology, The White House, 1961-64; Director, Office of Science and Technology, Exec. Office of the President, 1962-64. Dean of Science, MIT, 1964-66. *Publications:* Where Science and Politics Meet, 1965; contrib.: Modern Physics for the Engineer, 1954; Arms Control, Disarmament and National Security, 1960; Arms Control, issues for the Public, 1961; Lectures on Modern Communications, 1961; technical papers in: Science, Physical Rev., Jl Applied Physics, Scientific American, Proc. Inst. Radio Engineers, etc. *Recreations:* photography, boating. *Address:* Massachusetts Institute of Technology, Cambridge, Mass 02139, USA. *T:* University 4-6900, Ext. 2786. *Clubs:* Cosmos (Washington, DC); St Botolph's, (Boston, USA).

**WIESNER, Prof. Karel František,** FRS 1969; Research Professor, University of New Brunswick, since 1964; *b* 25 Nov. 1919; *s* of Karel Wiesner, industrialist, Chrudim, Czechoslovakia, and Eugenie Storová, Prague; *m* 1942, Blanka Pevná; one *s* (and one *d* decd). *Educ:* Gymnasium Chrudim; Charles Univ., Prague. Asst, Dept of Physical Chem., Charles Univ., Prague, 1945-46; Post-doctoral Fellow, ETH Zürich, 1946-48; Prof. of Organic Chem., Univ. of New Brunswick, 1948-62; Associate Dir of Research, Ayerst Laboratories, Montreal, 1962-64. *Publications:* about 140 research papers in various scientific periodicals. *Recreations:* tennis, ski-ing, hunting. *Address:* 814 Jones Street, Fredericton, New Brunswick, Canada. *T:* 4544007.

**WIGAN, Sir Frederick Adair,** 4th Bt, *cr* 1898; *b* 13 April 1911; *e s* of Sir Roderick Grey Wigan, 3rd Bt, and Ina, *o c* of late Lewis D. Wigan, Glenalmond, Perthshire; *S* father 1954. *Educ:* privately. *Heir: b* Alan Lewis Wigan [*b* 19 Nov. 1913; *m* 1950, Robina, *d* of Lt-Col Sir Iain Colquhoun, 7th Bt, KT, DSO; one *s* one *d. Educ:* Eton; Magdalen Coll., Oxford. Captain, King's Royal Rifle Corps (Reserve of Officers); served War of 1939-45 (prisoner)]. *Address:* Paston Hall, North Walsham, Norfolk. *T:* Mundesley 79; Borrobol, Kinbrace, Sutherland.

**WIGG,** family name of **Baron Wigg.**

**WIGG,** Baron *cr* 1967 (Life Peer), of the Borough of Dudley; **George Edward Cecil Wigg,** PC 1964; Chairman, Horserace Betting Levy Board since Nov. 1967; *b* 28 Nov. 1900; *m*; three *d. Educ:* Fairfields Council Schs and Queen Mary's Sch., Basingstoke, Hants. Served in Regular Army, 1919-37, 1940-46. MP (Lab) Dudley, 1945-67; PPS to Rt Hon. E. Shinwell when Minister of Fuel and Power, Sec. of State for War and Minister of Defence; an Opposition Whip, 1951-54; Paymaster-General, 1964-67. Member: Racecourse Betting Control Bd, 1958-61; Totalisator Bd, 1961-64. *Address:* 117 Newcastle Road, Trent Vale, Stoke-on-Trent.

**WIGGIN, Alfred William, (Jerry Wiggin);** MP (C) Weston-super-Mare since 1969; Parliamentary Private Secretary to the Minister of State for the Ministry of Defence, since 1970; *b* 24 Feb. 1937; *e s* of late Col Sir William H. Wiggin, KCB, DSO, TD, DL, JP, and late Lady Wiggin, Worcestershire; *m* 1964, Rosemary Janet, *d* of David L. D. Orr; two *s. Educ:* Eton; Trinity Coll., Cambridge. 2nd Lieut, Queen's Own Warwickshire and Worcestershire Yeomanry (TA), 1959; Major, 1967; Major, 37th Wessex and Welsh Signal Regt, Royal Signals (V), 1969. Contested (C), Montgomeryshire, Gen. Elections, 1964 and 1966. *Address:* The Court, Axbridge, Somerset. *T:* Axbridge 527; 19 Stafford Mansions, Stafford Place, SW1. *T:* 01-828 6721. *Clubs:* Cavalry, Farmers'; New (Edinburgh).

**WIGGIN, Charles Douglas,** CMG 1968; DFC 1944; AFC 1945; Counsellor, Foreign and Commonwealth Office, since 1969; *b* 26 Sept. 1922; *s* of late Arthur Francis Holme Wiggin, CMG, and late Carmen (*née* Fernandez Vallin); *m* 1948, Marie Thérèse Elizabeth, *e d* of late Sir John H. Leche, KCMG, OBE, Chester; three *d. Educ:* Eton; Christ Church, Oxford. RAFVR, 1941-46 (Flt-Lt). Joined Foreign Service (now Diplomatic Service), 1946; FO, 1946-47; Third Sec., Santiago, 1947-

49; Third/Second Sec., Stockholm, 1949-52; FO, 1952-53; Second/First Sec., Tehran, 1953-56; First Sec., Washington, 1956-61; Private Sec. to Lord Privy Seal, FO, 1961-63, and to Lord Carrington, 1963; IDC, 1964; Counsellor, Tehran, 1965-69. *Address:* 16 Regents Park Terrace, NW1. *T:* 01-485 1647.

**WIGGIN, Sir Charles Richard Henry,** 3rd Bt, *cr* 1892; TD; JP, DL, County Warwick; *b* 21 March 1885; *s* of 2nd Bt and Annie Sarah, *d* of C. R. Cope of Kinnerton Court, Radnors; *S* father, 1917; *m* 1916, Mabel Violet Mary (*d* 1961), *d* of late Sir William Jaffray, 2nd Bt; one *s*. *Educ:* Eton; Trinity Coll., Cambridge; BA 1907. Served in European War, 1914-18; in Egypt, Palestine and Syria, 1915-18 (despatches). Lt-Col and Bt-Col comdg Staffs Yeomanry, 1921-25; Hon. Col Staffs Yeomanry, 1951-54. High Sheriff of Warwickshire, 1942. *Heir:* *s* John Henry Wiggin, MC, Major (retired), Grenadier Guards [*b* 3 Mar. 1921; *m* 1st, 1947, Lady Cecilia Evelyn Anson (marriage dissolved, 1961; she *d* 1963), *yr d* of 4th Earl of Lichfield; two *s*; 2nd, 1963, Sarah, *d* of Brigadier Stewart Forster; two *s*. *Educ:* Eton; Trinity College, Cambridge]. *Address:* Honington Hall, Shipston-on-Stour, Warwickshire. *T:* Shipston 434.

**WIGGIN, Jerry;** *see* Wiggin, A. W.

**WIGGINS, Rt. Rev. Maxwell Lester;** *see* Victoria Nyanza, Bishop of.

**WIGGINS, William Denison Clare,** CMG 1968; OBE 1957; Director of Overseas Surveys and Survey Adviser to Minister of Overseas Development, 1965-68, retired; *b* 7 Feb. 1905; *s* of late Dr Clare Aveling Wiggins and Mrs Ethel Beatrice Wiggins; *m* 1933, Mary Isabel Macnair; two *d*. *Educ:* Dragon Sch., Oxford; King's Sch., Canterbury; Univ. Coll., London. Surveyor, Survey Dept, Nigeria, 1928; Mil. Service, RE, 1939-46 (Lt-Col). Overseas (Geodetic and Topographic) surveys: Asst Dir, 1946; Dep. Dir, 1948. Pres., Brit. Cartographic Soc., 1966-68; Chairman: (Royal Society's) Cartography Sub-Cttee of Brit. Nat. Cttee for Geography, 1966-; Jt Cttee, Nat. Certs in Surveying, Cartography and Planning, 1969-. Murchison Award (of RGS), 1952. *Publications:* contrib. to: Antarctic Research, Empire Survey Review, Geographical Jl, etc. Professional papers at Commonwealth Survey Officers' Confs. *Recreation:* golf. *Address:* Rosemary Cottage, Watersfield, Pulborough, Sussex. *T:* Bury 543. *Club:* West Sussex Golf.

**WIGGLESWORTH, Gordon Hardy;** Director of Building Development, Ministry of Public Building and Works, since 1967; *b* 27 June 1920; *m* 1952, Cherry Diana Heath; three *d*. *Educ:* Highgate; University Coll., London; Architectural Association. ARIBA; AADipl. Served War of 1939-45: Royal Engineers, 1941-46. Architectural Assoc., 1946-48; private practice and Univ. of Hong Kong, 1948-52; private practice: London, 1952-54; Hong Kong, 1954-56; London, 1956-57. Dept of Education and Science, 1957-67; Min. of Public Bldg and Works, 1967-. Mem. Council, Architectural Assoc., 1968-. *Address:* 53 Canonbury Park South, N1 2JL. *T:* 01-226 7734. *Clubs:* Reform, Architectural Association.

**WIGGLESWORTH, Sir (Horace Ernest) Philip,** KBE, *cr* 1946 (CBE 1942); CB 1943; DSC; *b* 11 July 1896; *s* of late George and Mary Wigglesworth; *m* 1963, Florence Elizabeth Hills, *widow* of Alec Percy Hills, Hove. *Educ:* Chesterfield. Served European War, 1914-19, commissioned RNAS 1915. Instructor RAF Staff College, Andover, 1933-36; Deputy Director of Intelligence, Air Ministry, 1936-39; Group Captain, 1939; Combined Planning Staff, ME 1939; Air Commodore, 1941 (despatches); Acting Air Vice-Marshal, 1941; SASO ME Command, 1941-42; AOC E Africa, 1942; Dep. C-in-C Allied Air Forces Mediterranean Command, 1943; SASO AEAF, 1943 (despatches); Dep. Chief of Staff (Air) Supreme Headquarters, AEF (acting Air Marshal), 1944; Air Vice-Marshal, 1945; Deputy Air C-in-C, Germany and Dep. Chief of Air Division, British Control Commission, 1945; AOC-in-C British Air Forces of Occupation (Germany) and Chief of Air Division, CCG (BE), 1946; Air Marshal, 1948; retired, 1948. President, Renault Ltd. Comdr Legion of Merit (USA); Comdr Legion of Honour (Fr.); Croix de Guerre (Fr.); Knight Spanish Order Military Merit; Comdr Order King George of Greece. *Address:* 65 Hove Park Road, Hove 4, Sussex. *T:* Brighton 552524.

**WIGGLESWORTH, Sir Vincent (Brian),** Kt 1964; CBE 1951; FRS 1939; MA, MD, BCh Cantab, FRES; Retired Director, Agricultural Research Council Unit of Insect Physiology (1943-67); Quick Professor of Biology, University of Cambridge, 1952-66; Fellow of Gonville and Caius College; *b* 17 April 1899; *s* of late Sidney Wigglesworth, MRCS; *m* 1928, Mabel Katherine, *d* of late Col Sir David Semple, IMS; three *s* one *d*. *Educ:* Repton; Caius Coll., Cambridge (Scholar); St Thomas' Hosp. 2nd Lt RFA, 1917-18, served in France; Frank Smart Student of Caius College, 1922-24; Lecturer in Medical Entomology in London School of Hygiene and Tropical Medicine, 1926; Reader in Entomology in University of London, 1936-44; Reader in Entomology, in University of Cambridge, 1945-52. Hon. Member: Royal Danish Academy of Science; American Academy of Arts and Sciences; Kaiserliche Deutsche Akademie der Naturforscher, Leopoldina; Deutsche Entomologische Gesellschaft; American Entomol. Soc.; USSR Acad. of Sciences; All-Union Entomol. Soc.; Entomol. Soc. of India; Société Zoologique de France; Société Entomologique de France, Société Entomologique d'Egypte; Entomological Society of the Netherlands; Schweizerische Entomologische Gesellschaft; Indian Academy of Zoology; Corresponding Member: Accademia delle Scienze dell' Istituto di Bologna; Société de Pathologie Exotique; Entomological Soc. of Finland; Dunham Lecturer, Harvard, 1945; Woodward Lecturer, Yale, 1945; Croonian Lecturer, Royal Society, 1948; Messenger Lecturer, Cornell, 1958; Tercentenary Lecturer, Royal Society, 1960. Royal Medal, Royal Society, 1955; Swammerdam Medal, Soc. Med. Chir., Amsterdam, 1966; Gregor Mendel Gold Medal, Czechoslovak Acad. of Science, 1967. DPhil (*hc*) University, Berne; DSc (*hc*): Paris, Newcastle and Cambridge. *Publications:* Insect Physiology, 1934; The Principles of Insect Physiology, 1939; The Physiology of Insect Metamorphosis, 1954; The Life of Insects, 1964; numerous papers on comparative physiology. *Address:* The Chimney House, Lavenham, Suffolk. *T:* Lavenham 293.

**WIGGLESWORTH, Walter Somerville;** Barrister-at-law; Vicar-General of Province of York since 1944; Chancellor of Dioceses of Portsmouth since 1940, Exeter since 1941, Bath and Wells since 1942, Derby and York since 1944, and London since 1954; Conveyancing Counsel to the Board of Trade since 1956; Member of Church Assembly and of its Legal Board; *b* 14 April 1906; *yr s* of late Francis William and Florence Mary

Wigglesworth, Marple, Cheshire; unmarried. *Educ:* Clifton Coll. (Scholar); Magdalene Coll., Cambridge (Exhibitioner). BA 1928; LLB 1929; MA 1931; Called to Bar, 1930, Inner Temple and Lincoln's Inn. Squadron Leader, RAFVR (Air Staff Intelligence, 1940-45). Bronze Star Medal (USA), 1949. Bencher, Lincoln's Inn, 1960. Commissary to the Dean and Chapter of St Paul's Cathedral, 1961; DCL (Lambeth) 1961. *Address:* 54 Swan Court, SW3. *T:* 01-352 8751; 3 New Square, Lincoln's Inn, WC2. *T:* 01-405 1124 and 7515. *Clubs:* Athenæum, United Service, United University.

**WIGHAM, Eric Leonard,** CBE 1967; Labour Correspondent, The Times, 1946-69; *b* 8 Oct. 1904; *s* of Leonard and Caroline Nicholson Wigham; *m* 1929, Jane Dawson; one *d*. *Educ:* Ackworth and Bootham Schools; Birmingham University (MA). Reporter on Newcastle upon Tyne papers, 1925-32; Manchester Evening News, 1932-45; War Correspondent, The Observer and Manchester Evening News, 1944-45; Labour Correspondent, Manchester Guardian, 1945-46. Member, Royal Commission on Trade Unions and Employers' Associations, 1965-68. Order of King Leopold II (Belgium), 1945. *Publications:* Trade Unions, 1956; What's Wrong with the Unions?, 1961. *Recreation:* gardening. *Address:* 51 Hartfield Crescent, West Wickham, Kent. *T:* 01-462 5380. *Club:* National Liberal.

**WIGHT, Prof. (Robert James) Martin;** Professor of History, University of Sussex, since 1961; Dean of School of European Studies, 1961-69; *b* 26 Nov. 1913; 2nd *s* of late Dr Edward Wight, Brighton; *m* 1952, Gabriele, *d* of Peter-Erich Ritzen, Rolandia, Brazil; two *s* four *d*. *Educ:* Bradfield; Hertford College, Oxford (open scholar). 1st class hons Modern History, 1935. On Staff of Chatham House, 1936-38; assistant master, Haileybury Coll., 1938-41; on staff of: Nuffield College Colonial Research, Oxford, 1941-46; Chatham House, 1946-49; The Observer, 1946-47; Reader in International Relations in Univ. of London, 1949-61. Member, Council of Roy. Inst. of Internat. Affairs, 1952-; Vis. Professor, Univ. of Chicago, 1956-57; Mem. Academic Planning Bd, Univ. of Kent. *Publications:* Power Politics, 1946; Development of the Legislative Council, 1946; Gold Coast Legislative Council, 1947; (joint) Attitude to Africa, 1951; British Colonial Constitutions, 1952; (joint) The World in March 1939, 1952; (jt editor with Herbert Butterfield) Diplomatic Investigations, 1966. *Recreations:* gardening, bookshops, travel. *Address:* Harwarton, Speldhurst, Kent. *T:* Langton 3131; University of Sussex, Brighton.

**WIGHTMAN, Ralph;** Free-lance Journalist and Broadcaster since 1948; associated with programme Any Questions; *b* 26 July 1901; *s* of Tom Wightman, Farmer and Butcher, Piddletrenthide, Dorchester, Dorset; *m* 1924, Margaret Dorothy Wiggins. *Educ:* Beaminster Grammar Sch.; Durham University. Lectr in Agriculture, Devon CC, 1923-27; Lecturer in Agriculture, Wilts CC, 1927-30; Senior Agricultural Adviser, Dorset CC, 1930-48. *Publications:* Moss Green Days, 1948; My Homeward Road, 1950; Arable Farming, 1951; Watching the Certain Things, 1951; Livestock Farming, 1952; Days on the Farm, 1952; The Seasons, 1953; The Wessex Heathland, 1953; Rural Rides with Ralph Wightman, 1957; Abiding Things, 1962; Portrait of Dorset, 1965; Take Life Easy, 1968; The Countryside Today, 1970. *Recreations:* retired–hockey and cricket. *Address:* Tudor House, Puddletown, Dorchester, Dorset. *T:* Puddletown 464.

**WIGNER, Prof. Eugene P(aul);** Thomas D. Jones Professor of Mathematical Physics of Princeton University, since 1938; *b* 17 Nov. 1902; *s* of Anthony and Elizabeth Wigner; *m* 1st, 1936, Amelia Z. Frank (*d* 1937); 2nd, 1941, Mary Annette Wheeler; one *s* one *d*. *Educ:* Technische Hochschule, Berlin, Dr Ing. 1925. Mem. Gen. Adv. Cttee to US Atomic Energy Commn, 1952-57, 1959-64; Director: Nat. Acad. of Sciences Harbor Project for Civil Defense, 1963; Civil Defense Project, Oak Ridge Nat. Lab., 1964-65. Pres., Amer. Physical Soc., 1956 (Vice-Pres., 1955); Mem. Royal Netherlands Acad. of Science and Letters, 1960; Foreign Mem., Royal Soc., 1970; Corresp. Mem. Acad. of Science, Göttingen, 1951; Austrian Acad. Sciences, 1968; Nat. Acad. Sci. (US); Amer. Philos. Soc.; Amer. Acad. Sci. US Government Medal for Merit, 1946; Franklin Medal, 1950; Fermi Award, 1958; Atoms for Peace Award, 1960; Max Planck Medal of German Phys. Soc., 1961; Nobel Prize for Physics, 1963; US Nat. Medal for Science, 1969. Holds numerous hon. doctorates. *Publications:* Nuclear Structure (with L. Eisenbud), 1958; The Physical Theory of Neutron Chain Reactors (with A. M. Weinberg), 1958; Group Theory (orig. in German, 1931), English trans., NY, 1959; Symmetries and Reflections, 1967. *Address:* 8 Ober Road, Princeton, NJ 08540, USA. *T:* 609-924-1189. *Club:* Cosmos (Washington, DC).

**WIGODER, Basil Thomas,** QC 1966; *b* 12 Feb. 1921; *s* of Dr P. I. Wigoder, Manchester; *m* 1948, Yoland Levinson; three *s* one *d*. *Educ:* Manchester Gram. Sch.; Oriel Coll., Oxford. Served RA, 1942-45. Pres. Oxford Union, 1946. Called to Bar, Gray's Inn, 1946; Mem., Gen. Council of the Bar, 1970-. BoT Inspector, Pinnock Finance (GB) Ltd, 1967. Chm., Liberal Party Exec., 1963-65; Chm., Liberal Party Organising Cttee, 1965-66. Contested (L): Bournemouth, 1945; Westbury, 1959 and 1964. *Recreation:* cricket. *Address:* 29 Henstridge Place, NW8. *T:* 01-722 1860. *Clubs:* Reform, MCC.

**WIGRAM,** family name of **Baron Wigram.**

**WIGRAM,** 2nd Baron, *cr* 1935, of Clewer; **George Neville Clive Wigram,** MC 1945; JP; DL; *b* 2 Aug. 1915; *s* of Clive, 1st Baron Wigram, PC, GCB, GCVO, CSI, and Nora Mary (*d* 1956), *d* of Sir Neville Chamberlain, KCB, KCVO; *S* father 1960; *m* 1941, Margaret Helen, *yr d* of late General Sir Andrew Thorne, KCB, CMG, DSO; one *s* two *d*. *Educ:* Winchester and Magdalen College, Oxford. Page of Honour to HM King George V, 1925-32; served in Grenadier Guards, 1937-57: Military Secretary and Comptroller to Governor-General of New Zealand, 1946-49; commanded 1st Bn Grenadier Guards, 1955-56. Governor of Westminster Hospital, 1967. JP Gloucestershire, 1959; DL, 1969. *Heir:* *s* Hon. Andrew (Francis Clive) Wigram, *b* 18 March 1949. *Address:* Poulton Fields, Cirencester, Gloucestershire. *T:* Poulton 250. *Club:* Guards.

**WIGRAM, Rev. Sir Clifford Woolmore,** 7th Bt, *cr* 1805; Vicar of Marston S Lawrence with Warkworth in Banbury since 1945; *b* 24 Jan. 1911; *er s* of late Robert Ainger Wigram and Evelyn Dorothy, *d* of C. W. E. Henslowe; *S* uncle, 1935; *m* 1948, Christobel Joan Marriott, *d* of late William Winter Goode. *Educ:* Winchester; Trinity Coll., Cambridge. Assist. Priest at St Ann's, Brondesbury, 1934-37; Chaplain Ely Theological College, 1937. *Heir:* *b* Maj. Edward Robert Wigram, Indian Army [*b* 19 July 1913; *m* 1944, Viva Ann, *d* of late Douglas Bailey, Laughton Lodge, near Lewes,

Sussex; one *d. Educ:* Winchester; Trinity Coll., Cambridge. Attached 2nd Batt. South Staffordshire Regt, Bangalore, 1935; Major, 19th KGO Lancers, Lahore, 1938]. *Address:* The Vicarage, Marston S Lawrence, Northamptonshire.

**WIGRAM, Derek Roland,** MA, BSc (Econ.); Headmaster of Monkton Combe School, near Bath, 1946-68; *b* 18 Mar. 1908; *er s* of late Roland Lewis Wigram and of Mildred Willock; *m* 1944, Catharine Mary, *d* of late Very Rev. W. R. Inge, KCVO, DD, former Dean of St Paul's; one *s* one *d. Educ:* Marlborough Coll.; Peterhouse, Cambridge (Scholar). 1st Class Hons Classical Tripos, 1929; 2nd Class Hons Economics and Political Science, London, 1943; Assistant Master and Careers Master, Whitgift School, Croydon, 1929-36; House Master and Careers Master, Bryanston School, 1936-46. Hon. Associate Mem., Headmasters' Conf. (Chm., 1963-64); Chairman: Oxford Conf. for Schoolmasters; Executive Committee of CMS (also Chm., 1956-58); Member: Council and Exec. of Coll. of Preachers; Council of Lee Abbey; Church of England Schools Council. Inspector of Theological Colls; Selector for Ordination Candidates; Dir of Sch. and Charity Consultants. Governor: Allhallows Sch. (Vice-Chm.); Downs Sch., Colwall; Walhampton Sch. (Chairman); St Brandon's Sch.; Westwood County Primary Sch. *Publication:* (Jt Editor) Hymns for Church and School, 1964. *Recreation:* lawn tennis. *Address:* Housels Field, Westwood, Bradford on Avon, Wilts. *T:* Bradford on Avon 2362.

**WIJEYEWARDENE, Hon. Sir (Edwin) Arthur (Lewis),** Kt, *cr* 1949; Chairman; Official Languages Commission, Ceylon, 1951-; Judicial Service Commission, 1949; Land Tenure and Delimitation Commissions, 1953; Commission on Higher Education, 1954; Land Commission, 1955; President, Arts Council of Ceylon, 1957; *b* 21 March 1887; *s* of D. S. L. Wijeyewardene, Notary Public, and Maria Catherine Perera; *m* 1921, Lilian Beatrice Perera; one *s* (and one *s* one *d* decd). *Educ:* Ananda College, Colombo; St Thomas' College, Colombo. Advocate of the Supreme Court, Ceylon, 1911; Public Trustee, 1935; Solicitor-General, 1936; QC 1937; Acting Attorney-General, 1938; Puisne Justice, 1938. Officer Administering the Government, Ceylon, 1949; Chief Justice of Ceylon, 1949-50. *Recreations:* chess, walking. *Address:* Vajira Road, Colombo, Ceylon.

**WIKELEY, Thomas,** CMG 1955; OBE 1944; *b* 9 Oct. 1902; *s* of late Col J. M. Wikeley (Indian Army, retired) and late Christine Wikeley (*née* Duns); unmarried. *Educ:* Loretto; Pembroke Coll., Cambridge. MA Mod. Langs. Levant Consular Service, 1926. Served at Alexandria, Cairo, Jedda, Rabat, Genoa, Hara, Addis Ababa, Port Said. Transferred to Foreign Office, 1944; Consul-General, Athens, Dec. 1946; Consul-General, Leopoldville, 1948-51; Consul-General, Tetuan (Spanish Morocco), 1952-54; Consul-General, Jerusalem, 1954-57; HM Minister and Consul-Gen., Guatemala, 1957-60; Foreign Office, 1962-69 (British Delegate to Internat. Exhibitions Bureau); retired 1969. *Address:* 19 Cromwell Court, Hove 3, Sussex.

**WILBERFORCE,** family name of **Baron Wilberforce.**

**WILBERFORCE,** Baron, *cr* 1964 (Life Peer); **Richard Orme Wilberforce,** PC 1964; Kt 1961; CMG 1956; OBE 1944; a Lord of Appeal in Ordinary since 1964; *b* 11 Mar. 1907; *s* of late S. Wilberforce; *m* 1947, Yvette, *d* of Roger Lenoan, Judge of Court of Cassation, France; one *s* one *d. Educ:* Winchester; New College, Oxford. 1st Cl. Mods; 1st Cl. Lit. Hum.; Hertford and Ireland scholarships, Univ. of Oxford; Fellow of All Souls College, 1932-; Hon. Fellow, New Coll., 1965; Hon. DCL Oxford, 1968. Called to Bar, 1932; Eldon Law Scholar, 1932. Served War, 1939-46; Chief Legal Division Control Commission, Germany (Brigadier), 1945; Under-Secretary, Control Office, Germany and Austria, 1946; UK Rep., Comité Internat. Technique des Experts Juridiques Aériens, 1946; returned to Bar, 1947; QC 1954; Senior UK Representative on Legal Committee of International Civil Aviation Organisation, 1947-. Judge of the High Court of Justice (Chancery Division), 1961-64. Chm. Exec. Council, Internat. Law Assoc.; Mem., Permanent Court of Arbitration. High Steward of Oxford University, 1967-. Hon. FRCM. Hon. Comp. Royal Aeronautical Society; Chm., London Choral Society. Diplôme d'Honneur, Corp. des Vignerons de Champagne. US Bronze Star, 1944. *Publications:* The Law of Restrictive Trade Practices, 1956; articles and pamphlets on Air Law and International Law. *Recreations:* the turf, travel, opera. *Address:* 8 Cambridge Place, W8. *T:* 01-937 4895. *Club:* Athenæum.

**WILBERFORCE, Robert,** CBE 1924; retired; *b* 8 Dec. 1887; 2nd *s* of late H. E. Wilberforce; *m* 1914, Hope Elizabeth (*d* 1970), *d* of late Schuyler N. Warren, New York. *Educ:* Beaumont and Stonyhurst; Balliol College, Oxford. BA 1912, Honour School of Modern History; War Trade Intelligence Department, 1915-16; Attaché HM Legation to Holy See, 1917-19; called to Bar, Inner Temple, 1921; Member of British Delegation to Washington Disarmament Conference, 1921-22; Carnegie Endowment International Mission to Vatican Library, 1927; British Delegation to Geneva Disarmament Conference, 1932 and 1933; Director British Information Services, New York; retired 1952. *Publications:* The Church and Slavery; Meditations in Verse; articles and reviews in various periodicals. *Address:* St Teresa's, Corston, near Bath. *T:* Newton St Loe 607.

**WILBRAHAM;** *see* Bootle-Wilbraham.

**WILBRAHAM, Sir Randle (John) Baker,** 7th Bt, *cr* 1776; FRICS; DL; JP; partner in firm of John German, Hughes & Wilbraham, Land Agents; Land Agent in general practice and managing own property; *b* 31 March 1906; *o s* of Sir Philip W. Baker Wilbraham, 6th Bt, KBE, DCL; *S* father 1957; *m* 1930, Betty Ann, *e d* of W. Matt Torrens, The Grove, Hayes, Kent; one *s* one *d. Educ:* Harrow; Balliol College, Oxford. Entered the Land Agency profession, 1928; served War of 1939-45 as Squadron-Leader, Royal Auxiliary Air Force; resumed practice, 1945. President of the Chartered Land Agents' Society, 1958-59; High Sheriff, 1953, JP 1954, DL 1959, Cheshire. *Heir: s* Richard Baker Wilbraham, late Lieut Welsh Guards [*b* 5 Feb. 1934; *m* 1962, Anne Christine Peto Bennett; one *s* two *d. Educ:* Harrow. A Dir, Schroder Wagg & Co.]. *Address:* Rode Hall, Scholar Green, Cheshire. *T:* Alsager 555. *Clubs:* MCC, United University.

**WILBY, John Ronald William,** CMG 1961; Professor of International Trade and Finance, Seattle University, since 1967; *b* 1 Sept. 1906; *s* of Thomas Wilby and Gertrude Snowdon; *m* 1944, Winifred Russell Walker; no *c. Educ:* Batley School; University of Leeds. Board of Inland Revenue, 1928-46; Board of Trade (Principal), 1946-49; First Secretary

(Commercial), British Embassy, Washington, 1949-53; British Trade Commissioner, Ottawa, 1953-55; Principal British Trade Commissioner in Ontario, Canada, 1955-64; Consul-General in Seattle, 1964-67. *Recreations:* sailing, music. *Address:* 185 34th Avenue E, Seattle, Wash 98102, USA. *T:* EA5-6999. *Club:* Rainier (Seattle).

**WILCHER, Lewis Charles,** CBE 1955; MA, BLitt; *b* 9 December 1908; *s* of L. G. Wilcher, Middle Swan, W Australia; *m* 1935, Vere Wylie; one *s* one *d*. *Educ:* St Peter's College, Adelaide; University of Adelaide; Balliol College, Oxford (Rhodes Scholar). Dean, Trinity College, Melbourne, 1934-37; Lecturer in Modern History, Univ. of Melbourne, 1935-40; AIF 1940-47; Lieut-Col; Asst Dir of Army Education, 1942-47; Principal, Univ. Coll., Khartoum, 1947-56; Warden, Queen Elizabeth House, Oxford, 1956-68. *Publications:* Education, Press, Radio, 1947. *Recreations:* cricket, tennis. *Address:* 12 Staunton Road, Oxford.

**WILCOCKS, C(harles),** CMG 1952; retired; *b* 10 April 1896; *s* of late F. W. Wilcocks; *m* 1921, Frances Gertrude Bullough, MB, ChB, DPH. *Educ:* Wigan Grammar School; Manchester University. Military Service: Lt, Lancs Fusiliers, attached Northamptonshire Regt, Egypt and Palestine Campaign, 1915-19, wounded Gaza, April 1917. MB, ChB, 1924; MD 1932; DTM&H 1941; FRCP 1950. East African Med. Service, 1927; Tuberculosis Res. Officer, Tanganyika, 1930; Asst Director, Bureau of Hygiene and Tropical Diseases, 1938-42; Director, Bureau of Hygiene and Tropical Diseases, 1942-61. Editor, Tropical Diseases Bulletin and Bulletin of Hygiene, 1938-61, Bulletin of War Medicine, 1942-46. President, Royal Society of Tropical Medicine and Hygiene, 1963-65, Hon. Secretary, 1951-63; Editor, Trans. Roy. Soc. Trop. Med. and Hyg., 1964-; Member, Court of Governors, London School of Hygiene and Tropical Medicine, 1963-; Member Board of Governors, University College Hospital, 1953-56; Examiner, DTM & H (apptd by Royal College of Physicians), 1959-63; Heath Clark Lectr, Univ. of London, 1960; Consultant, The Counties Public Health Laboratories, London, 1962-. *Publications:* Tuberculosis in Tanganyika Territory, 1938; Health and Disease in the Tropics, 1950; Aspects of Medical Investigation in Africa, 1961; Medical Advance, Public Health and Social Evolution, 1965; assisted Sir Philip Manson-Bahr with 16th edition of Manson's Tropical Diseases, 1966; articles in medical journals. *Address:* 24 Randalls Road, Leatherhead, Surrey. *T:* Leatherhead 2928. *Club:* Athenæum.

**WILCOX, Albert Frederick,** CBE 1967; Chief Constable of Hertfordshire, 1947-69, retired; *b* 18 April 1909; *s* of late Albert Clement Wilcox, Ashley Hill, Bristol; *m* 1939, Ethel, *d* of late E. H. W. Wilmott, Manor House, Whitchurch, Bristol; one *s* two *d*. *Educ:* Fairfield Grammar School, Bristol. Joined Bristol City Police, 1929; Hendon Police Coll., 1934; Metropolitan Police, 1934-43. Served Allied Mil. Govt, Italy and Austria (Lt-Col), 1943-46. Asst Chief Constable of Buckinghamshire, 1946. Cropwood Fellowship, Inst. of Criminology, Cambridge, 1969. Pres. Assoc. of Chief Police Officers, Eng. and Wales, 1966-67; Chm. of Management Cttee, Police Dependents' Trust, 1967. Regional Police Commander (designate), 1962-69. Member, Parole Board, 1970-. Mem. Council, Medico-Legal Soc. Barrister-at-Law, Gray's Inn, 1941. Queen's Police Medal, 1957. *Address:* 34 Roundwood Park, Harpenden, Herts. *Club:* Reform.

**WILCOX, Claude Henry Marwood;** *b* 10 January 1908; *s* of late Harry Robert Wilcox, Sherborne; *m* 1934, Winifred, *d* of late William Francis, Diss; two *s* two *d*. *Educ:* Sherborne School; Pembroke College, Cambridge (Scholar). Wrangler, 1929; MA 1947. Entered Ministry of Agriculture and Fisheries through Home Civil Service Administrative Examination, 1930; seconded to HM Treasury, 1939-47; Under-Secretary, Ministry of Agriculture, Fisheries and Food, 1948-68. Hon. Sec., Guildford Br., WEA, 1969-; Mem., Guildford Council of Churches, 1969-. *Address:* Blythburgh, 57 Pewley Hill, Guildford, Surrey. *T:* Guildford 65794.

**WILCOX, Herbert,** CBE 1951; Film Producer, Director, and Author; *b* 19 April 1892; *s* of Joseph John and Mary Healy Wilcox; *m* 1943, Florence Marjorie, *d* of late Herbert William Robertson (*see* Dame Anna Neagle). *Educ:* Brighton. Began as journalist. Served European War, 1914-18: 2nd Lieut, East Kent Regiment; Pilot and Flight-Lieut, Royal Flying Corps, then Royal Air Force. Films prod. and Dir.: Good Night Vienna, The Little Damozel, The Wonderful Story, Bitter Sweet, Chu Chin Chow, Decameron Nights, The Only Way, The Scarlet Pimpernel, Madame Pompadour, Carnival, Walls-Lynn Aldwych Farces, Sorrel and Son, The Speckled Band, Paddy the Next Best Thing, Flames of Passion, Escape Me Never, Brewsters Millions, The Blue Danube, Wolves, Black Waters, Nell Gwyn, Peg of Old Drury, Victoria the Great, Sixty Glorious Years, They Flew Alone, Yellow Canary, I Live in Grosvenor Square, Piccadilly Incident, The Courtneys of Curzon Street, Spring in Park Lane, Elizabeth of Ladymead, Maytime in Mayfair, Odette, The Lady With a Lamp, Derby Day, Trent's Last Case, The Beggar's Opera, Laughing Anne, Trouble in the Glen, Lilacs in the Spring, King's Rhapsody, My Teenage Daughter, Yangtse Incident, These Dangerous Years, The Man Who Wouldn't Talk, The Lady is a Square. In Hollywood: Nurse Edith Cavell, Irene, Sunny, No No Nanette. Hon. Mem., Amer. Inst. Cinematography. Gold Cup, Venice. Nat. Film Award 4 times. Hon. Fellow, British Kinematograph Soc. *Recreations:* theatre and work. *Address:* 117B Hamilton Terrace, NW8. *Clubs:* Naval and Military, Garrick, City Livery.

**WILCOX, Mrs Herbert;** *see* Neagle, Dame Anna.

**WILD, Albert,** DL; JP; Chairman, Co-operative Insce Soc. Ltd, 1962-64, retd; *b* 21 Aug. 1899; *m* 1927, Ella Siddall; one *d*. *Educ:* Manchester High School of Commerce. Director: CWS, 1941-64; CIS, 1944-64; Bridgewater Estates, 1948-; Russo-Brit. Chamber of Commerce, 1949-64; Member: Postmaster General's Advisory Council, 1949-64; Min. of Labour, Transp. Tribunal Gen. Panel, 1949-64; Dir, Co-op. Dental Assoc., 1954-64; Dir, Internat. Co-op. Petroleum Assoc., 1954-64. Mem. Coun., Lancaster Univ. (Vice-Chm. Finance Cttee, 1964); Mem. Coun. (Lancs), Order of St John (Chm. Appeals and Publicity Cttee, 1964-); Mem. Management Cttee, Mary MacArthur Holiday Homes, 1948-. DL Lancs 1967; High Sheriff, County Palatine of Lancaster, 1968-69. *Recreations:* reading, gardening, fishing. *Address:* 8 Marlton Way, Lancaster, Lancs. *T:* Lancaster 67451.

**WILD, Ven. Eric;** Archdeacon of Berkshire since 1967; Rector of Milton since 1967; *b* 6 Nov. 1914; *s* of R. E. and E. S. Wild; *m* 1946, Frances Moyra, *d* of late Archibald and Alice Reynolds; one *s* one *d*. *Educ:* Manchester Grammar School; Keble College, Oxford. Ordained deacon 1937, priest 1938, Liverpool Cathedral; Curate, St Anne, Stanley, 1937-40; Curate, St James, Haydock, 1940-42; Chaplain, RNVR, 1942-46; Vicar, St George, Wigan, 1946-52; Vicar, All Saints, Hindley, 1952-59; Director of Religious Education, Dio. Peterborough, 1959-62; Rector, Cranford with Grafton Underwood, 1959-62; Canon of Peterborough, 1961, Emeritus, 1962; Gen. Sec. of National Society and Secretary of C of E Schools Council, 1962-67. *Publications:* articles in periodicals; reviews, etc. *Recreations:* gardening and walking. *Address:* Milton Rectory, Abingdon, Berks. *T:* Steventon 436. *Club:* United Service.

**WILD, Captain Geoffrey Alan,** CBE 1963; retired as Commodore Captain, P&O Steam Navigation Company (1961-63), and Captain of the Canberra; *b* 21 Feb. 1904; *s* of Rev. Harry Wild, formerly Vicar, St Annes, Clifton, near Manchester, and of Susan Holt; *m* 1932, Dorothy Louisa Bickell; no *c. Educ:* St Bees, Cumberland; Nautical College, Pangbourne. One Year in Barquentine St George, then two years as Cadet, New Zealand Shipping Co. Joined P&O as 4th Officer, 1923; Staff Captain, 1949. First command in Shillong, 1951; commanded Iberia, 1956, also Strathnaver, Canton, Corfu, Chusan, Strathaird, Arcadia and Himalaya. *Recreation:* all sports. *Address:* Canberra, Ersham Park Avenue, Hailsham, Sussex.

**WILD, Major Hon. Gerald Percy,** MBE 1941; Agent-General for Western Australia in London since 1965; *b* 2 Jan. 1908; *m* 1944, Virginia Mary Baxter; two *s* one *d. Educ:* Shoreham Gram. Sch., Sussex; Chivers Acad., Portsmouth, Hants. Served War of 1939-45 (despatches, MBE): Middle East, Greece, Crete, Syria, New Guinea and Moratai, Netherlands East Indies (Major). Elected MLA for Western Australia, 1947; Minister for Housing and Forests, 1950-53; Minister for Works and Water Supplies and Labour (WA), 1959-65. JP Perth (WA), 1953. *Recreations:* golf, tennis, cricket, football. *Address:* Kununurra, 292 Crofton Road, Farnborough Park, Kent. *T:* Farnborough, Kent, 56968. *Clubs:* East India and Sports', Royal Thames Yacht; Naval and Military (WA); Cottesloe Golf (WA).

**WILD, Rt. Hon. Sir (Herbert) Richard (Churton),** PC 1966; KCMG 1966; Chief Justice of New Zealand since 1966; *b* 1912; *s* of Dr L. J. Wild; *m* 1940, Janet Grainger; two *s* two *d. Educ:* Feilding High Sch.; Victoria Univ. Private practice, 1939-57 (absent on War Service with NZ Div. in ME, 1940-45). Apptd Judge Advocate Gen., 1955; QC 1957. Solicitor-Gen., 1957-65. Hon. LLD, Victoria Univ., 1969. *Address:* Chief Justice's Chambers, Supreme Court, Wellington, NZ. *Club:* Wellington (NZ).

**WILD, Ira,** CB 1952; CMG 1947; OBE 1939; *b* 23 May 1895; *s* of Leonard Holt Wild and Mary Hopkinson; *m* 1922, Edith Mary Barbour; one *d. Educ:* Bury Grammar School; London School of Economics. Exchequer and Audit Dept, 1914-34; Comptroller and Auditor-General of Newfoundland, 1934-38; Colonial Office and Ministry of Home Security, 1939; HM Treasury, 1940; Commissioner for Finance, Newfoundland, 1941-46; Director of Finance, Ministry of Transport and Civil Aviation, 1948-57. *Address:* 40 Wood Lane, Ruislip, Middlesex.

**WILD, Very Rev. John Herbert Severn,** MA Oxon; Hon. DD Durham, 1958; Dean of Durham since 1951; *b* 22 Dec. 1904; *e s* of Right Rev. Herbert Louis Wild and Helen Christian, *d* of Walter Severn; *m* 1945, Margaret Elizabeth Everard, *d* of G. B. Wainwright, MB, OBE. *Educ:* Clifton Coll.; Brasenose College, Oxford (Scholar); Westcott House, Cambridge. Curate of St Aidan, Newcastle upon Tyne, 1929-33; Chaplain-Fellow of University College, Oxford, 1933-45; Domestic Bursar, 1936-45; Dean, 1939-42; Vice-Master, 1942-43; Pro-Master, 1943-45; Master, 1945-51; Hon. Fellow, 1951-; Select Preacher, Univ. of Oxford, 1948-49. Church Comr, 1958-. ChStJ, 1966-. Chm. of Govs, Durham Sch. Fellow of Woodard Corporation. *Recreations:* fishing, walking (represented Oxford against Cambridge at Three Miles, 1927). *Address:* The Deanery, Durham. *T:* 2500. *Club:* Oxford and Cambridge.

**WILD, Dr John Paul,** FRS 1970; FAA 1962; Chief Research Scientist, Division of Radiophysics, Commonwealth Scientific and Industrial Research Organization; Director, CSIRO Solar Radio Observatory, Culgoora, NSW; *b* 1923; *s* of late Alwyn Howard Wild and late Bessie Delafield (*née* Arnold); *m* 1948, Elaine Poole Hull; two *s* one *d. Educ:* Whitgift Sch.; Peterhouse, Cambridge. ScD 1962. Radar Officer in Royal Navy, 1943-47; joined Research Staff of Div. of Radiophysics, 1947, working on problems in radio astronomy, esp. of the sun. For. Hon. Mem., Amer. Acad. of Arts and Scis, 1961; For. Mem., Amer. Philos. Soc., 1962; Corresp. Mem., Royal Soc. of Scis, Liège, 1969. Edgeworth David Medal, 1958; Hendryk Arctowski Gold Medal, US Nat. Acad. of Scis; Balthasar van der Pol Gold Medal, Internat. Union of Radio Science, 1969. *Publications:* numerous research papers and reviews on radio astronomy in scientific jls. *Address:* 3 Strathfield Avenue, Strathfield, NSW 2135, Australia. *T:* Sydney 76-6880.

**WILD, John Vernon,** CMG 1960; OBE 1955; Colonial Administrative Service, retired; *b* 26 April 1915; *m* 1942, Margaret Patricia Rendell; one *s* one *d. Educ:* Taunton School; King's College, Cambridge. Senior Optime, Cambridge Univ., 1937. Colonial Administrative Service, Uganda: Assistant District Officer, 1938; Assistant Chief Secretary, 1950; Establishment Secretary, 1951; Administrative Secretary, 1955-60; Chairman, Constitutional Committee, 1959. *Publications:* The Story of the Uganda Agreement; The Uganda Mutiny; Early Travellers in Acholi. *Recreations:* cricket (Cambridge Blue, 1938), golf. *Address:* The Tudor Cottage, Ide, near Exeter.

**WILD, Rt. Hon. Sir Richard;** *see* Wild, Rt Hon. Sir H. R. C.

**WILDE, Derek Edward;** Senior General Manager since 1966, and Director since 1969, Barclays Bank Ltd; *b* 6 May 1912; *s* of late William Henry Wilde and Ethel May Wilde; *m* 1940, Helen, *d* of William Harrison; (one *d* decd). *Educ:* King Edward VII School, Sheffield. Entered Barclays Bank Ltd, Sheffield, 1929; General Manager, 1962. Fellow and Member of Council, Institute of Bankers. *Recreation:* gardening. *Address:* Ranmoor, Smart's Hill, Penshurst, Kent. *T:* Penshurst 228.

**WILDE, Peter Appleton;** HM Consul-General, Lourenço Marques, since 1969; *b* 5 April 1925; *m* 1950, Frances Elisabeth Candida Bayliss; two *s. Educ:* Chesterfield Grammar Sch.; St Edmund Hall, Oxford. Army (National Service), 1943-47; Temp. Asst Lectr, Southampton, 1950; FO, 1950; 3rd Sec., Bangkok, 1951-53; Vice-Consul, Zurich, 1953-54; FO, 1954-57; 2nd Sec., Baghdad, 1957-58; 1st Sec., UK Delegn to OEEC (later OECD), Paris, 1958-61; 1st Sec., Katmandu, 1961-64;

FO (later FCO), 1964-69. *Recreation:* forestry. *Address:* c/o Foreign and Commonwealth Office, SW1; British Consulate-General, CP55, Lourenço Marques, Mozambique.

**WILDER, Thornton Niven;** author; *b* Madison, Wisconsin, 17 April 1897; *s* of Amos Parker Wilder and Isabella Niven. *Educ:* Schools in California, China and Ohio; BA Yale Univ. 1920; MA Princeton, Univ., 1926. Schoolmaster, Lawrenceville, NJ, USA, 1921-28; Faculty Univ. of Chicago, 1930-36; C. E. Norton Professor, Harvard Univ., 1950-51. Hon. degrees: LitD: NY Univ., 1930; Kenyon, 1948; LittD: Yale Univ., 1947; Coll. of Wooster, 1950; North-Eastern Univ., 1951; LLD: Harvard Univ., 1951; Goethe-Univ., Frankfurt a/M, 1957; Zürich Univ., 1961. American Acad. of Arts and Letters; Corresp. Mem.: Bayrische Akademie der Schönen Künste; Akademie der Wissenschaften und der Literatur (Mainz). Served European War and War of 1939-45, commnd in Air Corps, Capt. 1942, advanced through grades to Lt-Col, 1944; served overseas, 1943-45 (Legion of Merit). Chevalier Légion d'Honneur, 1951; Hon. MBE (United Kingdom); Order of Merit (Peru); Pour le Mérite (Bonn), 1957; Peace Prize des Deutschen Buchhandels (Frankfurt-a-M); Goethe-Plakette der Stadt (Frankfurt-a-M), 1959; Ehrenmedaille, of Austria, 1959; US Presidential Medal of Freedom, 1963; National Medal of Literature, 1965. *Publications:* The Cabala, 1926; The Bridge of San Luis Rey (awarded Pulitzer Prize), 1927; The Angel that Troubled the Waters, 1928; The Woman of Andros, 1930; The Long Christmas Dinner (made into opera, music by Hindemith, 1961), and other Plays in one act, 1931; Heaven's My Destination, 1934; Our Town (awarded Pulitzer Prize), 1938; The Merchant of Yonkers, 1938; Skin of Our Teeth (Pulitzer Prize), 1942; The Ides of March, 1948; The Matchmaker (Edinburgh Festival), 1954; A Life in the Sun (Edinburgh Festival), 1955; Plays for Bleecker Street, 1962; The Eighth Day, 1967. *Address:* 50 Deepwood Drive, Hamden, Conn, USA.

**WILDING, Michael;** Actor (stage and films); *b* Westcliff-on-Sea, Essex, 23 July 1912; *s* of late Henry Wilding, MBE and Ethel Thompson; *m* 1937, Kay Young (marr. diss. 1952); *m* 1952, Elizabeth Taylor (marr. diss. 1957); two *s*; *m* 1958, Mrs Susan Nell (marr. diss.); *m* 1964, Margaret Leighton, *qv*. *Educ:* Christ's Hospital. Began career painting portraits and working at commercial art in Brussels. First West End appearance, Daly's, 1935; toured with Fay Compton in Australia and New Zealand, playing leading parts in Victoria Regina, To-Night at 8-30, and George and Margaret; played Denys Royd in Quiet Week-End, Wyndham's, 1941-43; went to Gibraltar and Malta, with John Gielgud and Company, entertaining HM Forces, Jan. 1943; succeeded John Mills as Lew in Men in Shadow, Vaudeville, 1943; played the Earl of Harpenden in While the Sun Shines, Dec. 1943 until 1945; succeeded Sir John Gielgud in Nude With Violin, 1957; Mary Mary, Broadway, 1961. First appeared in films, 1940. Films include: Piccadilly Incident, Carnival, The Courtneys of Curzon Street, An Ideal Husband, Spring in Park Lane, Maytime in Mayfair, Under Capricorn, Stage Fright, The Law and The Lady, The Lady With a Lamp, Derby Day, Trent's Last Case, Torch Song, The Egyptian, The Glass Slipper, The World of Suzie Wong, The Naked Edge, The Two Enemies. *Address:* c/o Actors' Guild, Hollywood, Calif, USA.

**WILDISH, Vice-Adm. Denis Bryan Harvey,** CB 1968; Director General of Personal Services and Training (Naval), since June 1970; *b* 24 Nov. 1914; *s* of Rear-Adm. Sir Henry William Wildish, *qv*; *m* 1941, Leslie Henrietta Jacob; two *d*. *Educ:* RNC Dartmouth; RNEC. Entered Royal Navy, 1927; Comdr 1948; Capt. 1957; Rear-Adm. 1966; Vice-Adm. 1970. Dir of Fleet Maintenance, 1962-64; Commodore Naval Drafting, 1964-66; Adm. Supt, HM Dockyard, Devonport, 1966-70. *Recreations:* cricket, painting. *Address:* Deans Farm, Weston, near Petersfield, Hants. *Clubs:* Army and Navy, MCC.

**WILDISH, Engineer Rear-Adm. Sir Henry William,** KBE, *cr* 1946 (CBE 1939); CB 1942; *b* 25 June 1884; *s* of late J. G. Wildish, Naval Architect; *m* 1911, Elfrida Phyllis, *d* of late H. G. Bryant, Milton Regis, Kent; one *s* one *d*. *Educ:* King's School, Rochester; RNE College, Devonport. Joined Navy, 1900; Eng. Commander 1921; in charge Haslar Fuel Experimental Station, 1926-28; Eng. Capt. 1930; Staff of C-in-C Mediterranean, 1934-36; Eng. Rear-Adm. 1936; Staff of C-in-C Nore, 1937-40; Staff of C-in-C Western Approaches, 1940-45. *Address:* Queensberry Lodge, Hayling Island, Hants. *T:* Hayling Island 3604.
*See also Rear-Adm. D. B. M. Wildish.*

**WILDSMITH, Brian Lawrence;** artist and maker of picture books for young children; *b* 22 Jan. 1930; *s* of Paul Wildsmith and Annie Elizabeth Oxley; *m* 1955, Aurelie Janet Craigie Ithurbide; one *s* three *d*. *Educ:* de la Salle Coll.; Barnsley Sch. of Art; Slade Sch. of Fine Arts. Art Master, Selhurst Grammar School for Boys, 1954-57; freelance artist, 1957-. Kate Greenaway Medal, 1962. *Publications:* ABC, 1962; The Lion and the Rat, 1963; The North Wind and the Sun, 1964; Mother Goose, 1964; The Rich Man and the Shoemaker, 1965; The Hare and the Tortoise, 1966; Birds, 1967; Animals, 1967; Fish, 1968; The Miller the Boy and the Donkey, 1969; The Circus, 1970; Puzzles, 1970. *Recreations:* squash, tennis, music (piano). *Address:* 1 Ferrings, College Road, Dulwich, SE21. *T:* 01-693 3772.

**WILDY, Prof. Peter;** Professor of Virology, University of Birmingham, since 1963; *b* 31 March 1920; *s* of Eric Lawrence and Gwendoline Wildy, Galmpton, Devonshire; *m* 1945, Joan Audrey Kenion; one *s* two *d*. *Educ:* Eastbourne College; Caius Coll., Cambridge; St Thos Hosp., London. MRCS, LRCP 1944; MB, BChir 1948. RAMC, 1945-47. Michael and Sydney Herbert and Leonard Dudgeon Res. Fellow, St Thos Hosp. Med. Sch., 1949-51; Lecturer in Bacteriology, 1952-57; Sen. Lectr in Bacteriology, 1957-58; Brit. Memorial Fellow in Virology, 1953-54; Asst Director, MRC Unit for Experimental Virus Research, Glasgow, 1959-63. FRSE 1962. *Publications:* articles on bacteria and viruses. *Address:* The Town Farm, Abberley, Worcs.

**WILEMAN, Margaret Annie,** MA; Principal, Hughes Hall, Cambridge, since 1953; University Lecturer, and Director of Women Students in the University Department of Education since 1953; *b* 19 July 1908; *e d* of Clement Wileman and Alice (*née* Brinson). *Educ:* Lady Margaret Hall, Oxford, and the University of Paris. Scholar of Lady Margaret Hall, Oxford, 1927; First in Hons School of Mod. Langs, 1930; Zaharoff Travelling Scholar, 1931; Assistant, Abbey School, Reading, 1934; Senior Tutor, Queen's College, Harley Street, 1937; Lecturer, St Katherine's Coll., Liverpool, 1940; Resident Tutor, Bedford College, Univ. of London, 1944. *Address:* Hughes Hall, Cambridge. *T:* Cambridge 52866. *Club:* University Women's.

**WILENSKI, Reginald Howard,** Hon. MA (Manchester), 1938; artist and art critic;

Special Lecturer in the History of Art, Victoria University of Manchester, 1933-46; Special Lecturer in Art, Bristol University, 1929 and 1930; *b* London, 1887; *m* Marjorie Harland, BA (*d* 1965). *Educ:* St Paul's Sch.; Balliol Coll., Oxford. Exhibitor, International Society Sculptors, Painters, and Gravers, Royal Society Portrait Painters, ROI, Paris Autumn Salon, etc. Chevalier, Legion of Honour, 1967. *Publications:* The Modern Movement in Art, 1927 (revised 1957); Dutch Painting, 1929 (revised 1955); French Painting, 1931 (revised 1949); The Meaning of Modern Sculpture, 1932; John Ruskin, 1933; English Painting, 1933 (revised 1963); The Study of Art, 1934; Modern French Painters, 1940 (revised 1963); Flemish Painters (2 vols), 1960; Editor: The Faber Gallery. *Address:* Maldah, Marlow, Bucks. *Club:* Savile.

**WILES, Donald Alonzo,** CMG 1965; OBE 1960; General Manager, Department Store, Da Costa & Musson Ltd, Barbados, since 1965; *b* 8 Jan. 1912; *s* of Donald Alonzo Wiles and Millicent Wiles; *m* 1938, Amelie Elsie Pemberton; two *d. Educ:* Harrison Coll., Barbados; Univs of London, Toronto, Oxford. Member of Staff of Harrison College, Barbados, 1931-45; Public Librarian, Barbados, 1945-50; Asst Colonial Secretary, Barbados, 1950-54; Permanent Secretary, Barbados, 1954-60; Administrator, Montserrat, 1960-64. Member, West Indies Committee. *Recreations:* swimming, hiking, tennis. *Address:* Casa Loma, Pine Gardens, St Michael, Barbados. *T:* 93623. *Clubs:* Barbados Yacht, Summerhayes Tennis, Bridgetown (Barbados).

**WILES, Rev. Prof. Maurice Frank;** Canon of Christ Church, Oxford, and Regius Professor of Divinity, since 1970; *b* 17 Oct. 1923; *s* of late Sir Harold Wiles, KBE, CB, and of Lady Wiles; *m* 1950, Patricia Margaret (*née* Mowll); two *s* one *d. Educ:* Tonbridge School; Christ's College, Cambridge. Curate, St George's, Stockport, 1950-52; Chaplain, Ridley Hall, Cambridge, 1952-55; Lectr in New Testament Studies, Ibadan, Nigeria, 1955-59; Lectr in Divinity, Univ. of Cambridge, and Dean of Clare College, 1959-67; Prof. of Christian Doctrine, King's Coll., Univ. of London, 1967-70. *Publications:* The Spiritual Gospel, 1960; The Christian Fathers, 1966; The Divine Apostle, 1967; The Making of Christian Doctrine, 1967. *Address:* Christ Church, Oxford.

**WILES, Prof. Peter John de la Fosse;** Professor of Russian Social and Economic Studies, University of London, since 1965; *b* 25 Nov. 1919; *m* 1st, 1945, Elizabeth Coppin (marr. diss., 1960); one *s* two *d*; 2nd, 1960, Carolyn Stedman. *Educ:* Lambrook Sch.; Winchester Coll.; New Coll., Oxford. Royal Artillery, 1940-45. Fellow, All Souls Coll., Oxford, 1947-48; Fellow, New Coll., Oxford, 1948-60; Prof., Brandeis Univ., USA, 1960-63; Research Associate, Institutet för Internationell Ekonomi, Stockholm, 1963-64. Vis. Prof.: Columbia Univ., USA, 1958; City Coll. of New York, 1964 and 1967. *Publications:* The Political Economy of Communism, 1962; Price, Cost and Output (2nd edn), 1962; Communist International Economics, 1968. *Recreations:* simple. *Address:* 23 Ridgmount Gardens, WC1.

**WILFORD, (Kenneth) Michael,** CMG 1967; Assistant Under-Secretary of State, Foreign and Commonwealth Office, since 1969; *b* Wellington, New Zealand, 31 Jan. 1922; *yr s* of late George McLean Wilford and late Dorothy Veronica (*née* Wilson); *m* 1944, Joan Mary, *d* of Captain E. F. B. Law, RN; three *d. Educ:* Wrekin College; Pembroke College, Cambridge. Served in Royal Engineers, 1940-46 (despatches). Entered HM Foreign (subseq. Diplomatic) Service, 1947; Third Sec., Berlin, 1947; Asst Private Secretary to Secretary of State, Foreign Office, 1949; Paris, 1952; Singapore, 1955; Asst Private Sec. to Sec. of State, Foreign Office, 1959; Private Sec. to the Lord Privy Seal, 1960; served Rabat, 1962; Counsellor (Office of British Chargé d'Affaires) also Consul-General, Peking, 1964-66; Counsellor, Washington, 1967-69. Visiting Fellow of All Souls, Oxford, 1966-67. *Recreations:* golf, tennis, swimming and gardening. *Address:* Rolvenden, Hook Heath Road, Woking, Surrey. *T:* Woking 3775.

**WILHELM, Most Rev. Joseph Lawrence;** *see* Kingston (Ontario), Archbishop of (RC).

**WILKES, Rev. John Comyn Vaughan,** MA Oxon; Rector of Great Kimble, Aylesbury, since 1967; *b* 30 March 1902; *s* of L. C. Vaughan Wilkes, St Cyprian's, Eastbourne; *m* 1940, Joan, *y d* of late Very Rev. C. A. Alington, DD; six *s* one *d. Educ:* Fonthill, East Grinstead; St Cyprian's, Eastbourne; Eton Coll. (King's Schol.); Trinity Coll. Oxford (Classical Schol.). 1st Class Classical Moderations, 1923; 1st Class Lit. Hum., 1925; Half Blue for Golf (played *v* Cambridge, 1924, 1925); subsequently Assistant Master, Eton College 1925-37; Master in College, Eton College, 1930-37; Warden, Radley College, Abingdon, 1937-54; Vicar of Hunslet, Leeds, 1954-58; Vicar of Marlow, 1958-65; Rector of Preston Bissett, Buckingham, 1965-67. Ordained deacon (C of E) 1945; priest, 1945. *Recreations:* golf, gardening. *Address:* Great Kimble Rectory, Aylesbury, Bucks. *T:* Princes Risborough 5080. *Clubs:* MCC; Sussex Martlets, Eton Ramblers, Oxford and Cambridge Golfing Society.

*See also Rt Hon. Sir Alec Douglas-Home.*

**WILKES, Lyall; His Honour Judge Lyall Wilkes;** Judge of the County Courts (Circuit No 1) since 1965; *b* 19 May 1914; *e s* of George and Doris Wilkes, Newcastle upon Tyne; *m* 1946, Margaret, *d* of Frederick and Mabel Tait, Gateshead upon Tyne; four *d. Educ:* Newcastle Grammar School; Balliol Coll., Oxford (MA). Secretary Oxford Union Society, 1937. Joined Middlesex Regiment 1940; active service North Africa, Italy and German-occupied Greece; Major, 1944 (despatches). Called to Bar, Middle Temple, 1947; practised North-Eastern Circuit, 1947-64; Deputy Chairman, County of Durham Quarter Sessions, 1961-64; Assistant Recorder, Sheffield and Newcastle upon Tyne, 1960-62; Judge of the County Courts (Circuit No 14) 1964-65. MP (Lab) for Newcastle Central, 1945-51. Member, Laing Art Gallery Committee, Newcastle upon Tyne, 1957-64. *Publication:* (with Gordon Dodds) Tyneside Classical: the Newcastle of Grainger, Dobson and Clayton, 1964. *Address:* Dissington Garden House, Dalton, Northumberland. *T:* Stamfordham 352.

**WILKES, Maurice Vincent,** FRS 1956; MA, PhD; FIEE; Head of the Computer Laboratory, Cambridge (formerly Mathematical Laboratory), since 1970; Professor of Computer Technology, 1965; Fellow of St John's College, 1950; *b* 26 June 1913; *s* of Vincent J. Wilkes, OBE; *m* 1947, Nina Twyman; one *s* two *d. Educ:* King Edward's School, Stourbridge; St John's College, Cambridge. Mathematical Tripos (Wrangler). Research in physics at Cavendish Lab.; Univ. Demonstrator, 1937. Served War of 1939-45, Radar and Operational Research. Univ. Lecturer and Acting Dir of Mathematical Laboratory, Cambridge, 1945;

Dir of Mathematical Laboratory, 1946-70. Member Measurement and Control Section Committee, IEE, 1956-59; First President British Computer Soc., 1957-60. Mem. Council International Fedn for Information Processing, 1960-63; Chm. IEE E Anglia Sub-Centre, 1969; Turing Lectr Assoc. for Computing Machinery, 1967; Harry Goode Award, Amer. Fedn of Information Processing Socs, 1968. *Publications:* Oscillations of the Earth's Atmosphere, 1949; (joint) Preparations of Programs for an Electronic Digital Computer, Addison-Wesley (Cambridge, Mass), 1951, 2nd edn 1958; Automatic Digital Computers, 1956; A Short Introduction to Numerical Analysis, 1966; Time-sharing Computer System, 1968; papers in scientific jls. *Address:* The Computer Laboratory, Corn Exchange Street, Cambridge. *T:* Cambridge 52435. *Club:* Constitutional.

**WILKIE, James,** MA, FRSE; Secretary Carnegie United Kingdom Trust, 1939-54; *b* Manchester, 1 June 1896; *er s* of late James Wilkie, Glasgow; *m* 1930, Ethel Susan, *er d* of late W. H. Moore, JP, Killough, Co. Down; three *d. Educ:* Whitgift School; Brasenose College, Oxford (Dist. Litt. Hum. 1920). Served European War, 1914-19 (Captain, Machine Gun Corps, despatches twice, wounded, Order of Crown of Rumania) and War of 1939-45 (Major, Home Guard). Entered Board of Education, 1921 (Asst Private Sec. to President, 1924-27), transferred to Empire Marketing Board, 1927-33; returned to Board of Education, 1933-39 (in charge of Metropolitan Div. and Sec. to Adult Education Cttee). Mem. Exec. Cttee: Newbattle Abbey Coll., 1939-54; Scottish Council of Social Service, 1944-54; Land Settlement Assoc., 1939-48; Nat. Central Library, 1939-50; Scottish Leadership Training Assoc., 1945-50; Member: NHS Executive Council for E Sussex; Advisory Council on Education in Scotland, 1948-51; Council of Nat. Federation of Young Farmers' Clubs, 1939-51; Vice-Pres.: Sussex Rural Community Coun.; Irish Library Assoc., 1940-48; Pres., Library Assoc., 1951. *Address:* The Red Cottage, Fletching Common, Newick, Lewes, Sussex. *T:* Newick 2677.

**WILKINS, Charles Timothy,** OBE 1952; CEng; FRAeS; Director of Hawker Siddeley Dynamics Limited, in charge of Space Projects, 1963; *s* of G. C. A. Wilkins and A. N. Berg; *m* 1940, Gladys Marie Alexander; one *s* one *d. Educ:* Cordwalles; Brighton College. With Vickers Armstrongs Limited, Weybridge, 2 years Shops and 1 year Drawing Office; Drawing Office, de Havilland Aircraft Co. Ltd, 1928-30; Drawing Office of Cierva Autogiro Co. for 1½ years and of Handley Page Ltd for six months; rejoined de Havilland Aircraft Co. Ltd, Drawing Office, 1932; appointed Director, 1958. "A" Licence (Pilot's), 1929. FRAeS 1950. Fellow, British Interplanetary Society. *Address:* Whitehorse Cottage, 37 Freehold Street, Lower Heyford, Oxon.

**WILKINS, Frederick Charles,** CB 1963; *b* 10 July 1901; *s* of Richard Charles Wilkins; *m* 1926, Winifred Bertha Denham; one *d. Educ:* Portsmouth. Entered Admiralty Service, 1917; Naval Store Officer, 1939 (Asst 1923; Dep. 1936); Asst Dir of Stores, 1942; Capt. RNVR (attached to Brit. Pacific Fleet, 1944-46); Dep. Dir of Stores, 1955; Dir of Stores, Admiralty, 1960-64. *Recreation:* reading (Theology). *Address:* 6 Spurwood Road, Turramurra, NSW, Australia.

**WILKINS, Prof. Malcolm Barrett;** Regius Professor of Botany, Glasgow University, since 1970; *b* 27 Feb. 1933; *s* of Barrett Charles Wilkins and Eleanor Mary Wilkins (*née* Jenkins); *m* 1959, Mary Patricia Maltby; one *s* one *d. Educ:* Monkton House Sch., Cardiff; King's Coll., London. BSc 1955; PhD London 1958; AKC 1958. Lectr in Botany, King's Coll., London, 1958-64; Rockefeller Foundn Fellow, Yale Univ., 1961-62; Research Fellow, Harvard Univ., 1962-63; Lectr in Biology, Univ. of East Anglia, 1964-65; Prof. of Biology, Univ. of East Anglia, 1965-67; Prof. of Plant Physiology, Univ. of Nottingham, 1967-70. Darwin Lectr, British Assoc. for Advancement of Science, 1967. *Publications:* (ed) The Physiology of Plant Growth and Development; papers in Jl of Experimental Botany, Plant Physiology, Planta, Nature, Proc. Royal Soc. *Recreation:* gardening. *Address:* Department of Botany, The University, Glasgow W2. *T:* 041-339 8855.

**WILKINS, Maurice Hugh Frederick,** CBE 1963; FRS 1959; MA PhD; Professor of Bio-physics, King's College, University of London, since 1970; Deputy Director, Medical Research Council, Biophysics Unit, since 1955; *b* 15 Dec. 1916; *s* of late Edgar Henry Wilkins and of Eveline Constance Jane (*née* Whittaker), both of Dublin; *m* 1959, Patricia Ann Chidgey; two *s* two *d. Educ:* King Edward's Sch., Birmingham: St John's College, Cambridge. Research on luminescence of solids at Physics Department, Birmingham University, with Ministry of Home Security and Aircraft Production, 1938; PhD 1940; Manhattan Project (Ministry of Supply), Univ. of California (research on separation of uranium isotopes by mass spectrograph), 1944; Lectr in Physics, St Andrews Univ., 1945; MRC Biophysics Unit in Physics Department, King's College, London, 1946; Hon. Lecturer in the sub-department of Biophysics, 1958; Prof. of Molecular Biology, King's Coll., 1963-70. Albert Lasker Award, Amer. Public Health Assoc., 1960. (Jt) Nobel Prize for Medicine, 1962. *Publications:* papers in scientific journals on luminescence and topics in bio-physics, *eg* molecular structure of nucleic acids. *Address:* 30 St John's Park, SE3. *T:* 01-858 1817.

**WILKINS, William Albert,** CBE 1965; *b* 17 Jan. 1899; *m* 1923, Violet Florrie Reed; three *s* one *d. Educ:* Whitehall Elementary School, Bristol. Linotype operator; commenced work at 13½ as an errand boy. Apprenticed to Thos Goulding, Printer, 6 Nelson St, Bristol. Later employed by Bristol Evening Times and Echo and Bristol Evening World. Actively engaged in politics since 1922; MP (Lab) Bristol South, 1945-70; Assistant Govt Whip (unpaid), 1947-50; a Lord Comr of the Treasury, 1950-51. Member Typographical Association (now National Graphical Association), 1919-. Past member of Typographical Association Nat. Executive, Past President Bristol Branch, Past Pres. South-Western Group TA Member of Bristol City Coun., 1936-46. *Address:* 37 King St, Two Mile Hill, Kingswood, Bristol. *T:* 673779.

**WILKINSON, Rev. Alan Bassindale,** PhD; Principal of Chichester Theological College since 1970; *b* 26 Jan. 1931; *s* of Rev. J. T. Wilkinson, DD; *m* 1961, Eva Michelson; two *s* one *d. Educ:* William Hulme's Grammar Sch., Manchester; St Catharine's Coll., Cambridge; College of the Resurrection, Mirfield. MA 1958, PhD 1959 (Cambridge). Deacon, 1959; Priest, 1960; Asst Curate, St Augustine's, Kilburn, 1959-61; Chaplain, St Catharine's Coll., Cambridge, 1961-67; Vicar of Barrow Gurney and Lecturer in Theology, College of St Matthias, Bristol, 1967-70. Hulsean Preacher, 1967-68. *Publications:* contributor to: Cambridge Sermons on Christian Unity, 1966; Catholic Anglicans Today, 1968; also to: Faith and Unity, Sobornost, Preacher's Quarterly, London Quarterly Holborn Review. *Recreations:* gardening, walking. *Address:* The Theological College, Chichester, Sussex. *T:* Chichester 83369.

**WILKINSON, Alexander Birrell;** Sheriff-Substitute of Stirling, Dunbarton and Clackmannan at Stirling and Alloa, since 1969; *b* 2 Feb. 1932; *o s* of late Captain Alexander Wilkinson, MBE, The Black Watch and of Isabella Bell Birrell; *m* 1965, Wendy Imogen, *d* of late Ernest Albert Barrett, Belfast. *Educ:* Perth Academy; Univs of St Andrews and Edinburgh. Walker Trust Scholar 1950, Grieve Prizeman in Moral Philosophy 1952, MA(Hons Classics) 1954, Univ. of St Andrews. National Service, RAEC, 1954-56. Balfour Keith Prizeman in Constitutional Law 1957, LLB (with distinction) 1959, Univ. of Edinburgh. Admitted to Faculty of Advocates, 1959; in practice at Scottish bar, 1959-69; Lecturer in Scots Law, Univ. of Edinburgh, 1965-69. *Publications:* articles in legal periodicals. *Recreations:* collecting books and pictures, reading, travel. *Address:* Seton Lodge, Touch, Stirling. *T:* Stirling 3638. *Club:* New (Edinburgh).

**WILKINSON, Prof. Andrew Wood,** ChM (Edinburgh); FRCSE; FRCS; Nuffield Professor of Pædiatric Surgery, Institute of Child Health, Great Ormond Street, and Surgeon, Hospital for Sick Children, Great Ormond Street, since 1958; Hon. Consultant Pædiatric Surgeon, Post-graduate Medical School, Hammersmith, and Queen Elizabeth Hospital for Children; Civilian Consultant in Pediatric Surgery to RN; *b* 19 April 1914; *s* of Andrew W. and Caroline G. Wilkinson; *m* 1941, Joan Longair Sharp; two *s* two *d*. *Educ:* Univ. of Edinburgh. MB, ChB, Edin., 1937; ChM; (1st cl. hons and gold medal for thesis), 1949; FRCS Edin. 1940; FRCS Eng. 1959. Syme Surgical Fellowship, Univ. of Edinburgh, 1946-49; Senior University Clinical Tutor in Surgery, 1946-51; Lecturer in Surgery, University of Edinburgh and Assistant Surgeon, Deaconess Hosp., Edinburgh, 1951-53; Sen. Lectr in Surgery, Univ.of Aberd. and Asst Surg., Roy. Inf. and Roy. Aberd. Hosp. for Sick Children, 1953-58. Mem. Council, RCS Edin., 1964-; Hunterian Prof., RCSEng, 1965. Examr Primary and Final FRCS Ed., Primary FRCSEng; past Ext. Examr Univ. Glas. DCH Lond. Tisdall Lecturer, Canadian Med. Assoc., 1966. Visiting Prof. Univ. of Alexandria, 1965, Albert Einstein Coll. of Medicine, 1967. Late Temp. Lt-Col RAMC Founder Member: Scottish Surgical Pædiatric Soc.; Neonatal Soc.; Pres., British Assoc. of Pediatric Surgeons. Hon. Fellow, Brasilian Soc. Pædiatric Surgery; Hon. Mem. Peruvian Socs Pediatrics and Pædiatric Surgery. *Publications:* Fluid Balance in Surgery, 1955, 3rd edn, 1968; Recent Advances in Pædiatric Surgery, 1963, 2nd edn, 1969; (jtly) Research in Burns, 1966; chapters, articles and reviews in various books, and surgical and other jls. *Recreations:* fishing and gardening. *Address:* Institute of Child Health, Great Ormond Street, WC1. *T:* 01-242 9789. *Club:* University (Aberdeen).

**WILKINSON, Rev. Arthur Henry,** BA, BD; *b* 8 Sept. 1885; *s* of John Wilkinson, Whitworth, Co. Durham; *m* Edith McQuhae; one *s* one *d*. *Educ:* Privately; Balliol College, Oxford; Egerton Hall, Manchester. Secretary of the Student Christian Movement in Manchester University, 1910; Ordained, 1911; Curate at Christ Church, Bradford, Manchester, 1912; Holy Trinity, Rusholme, 1914; CMS Missionary, 1918; Principal of CMS College in West China University, 1924; Vicar of Poynton, Cheshire, 1929. Formerly Chief Secretary, British and Foreign Bible Society. Travelled extensively. *Recreation:* gardening. *Address:* 1 Spring Court, Church Road, W7. *T:* 01-567 5542.

**WILKINSON, Rt. Rev. (Charles Robert) Heber;** Assistant Bishop of Niagara since 1960; *b* 28 Dec. 1900; *s* of late Rev. Frederick Wilkinson; *m* 1926, Rowena Victoria Stringer; two *s* one *d*. *Educ:* University of Toronto Schools; University of Toronto. MA (Toronto) and grad. Wycliffe Coll., Toronto, 1926. Priest, 1926, and appointed to Kangra Mission, Punjab Missionary Society, C of E in Canada. Secretary-Treasurer, Kangra Mission, 1930; Canon, Lahore Cathedral, 1942; Archdeacon, East Punjab, 1949; Assistant Bishop of Lahore, 1950; first Bishop of Amritsar, 1953-59. Hon. DD. Wycliffe Coll., 1946; Huron Coll., 1962. Jubilee Medal, 1935; Coronation Medal, 1937; Kaisar-i-Hind (Silver), 1942. *Address:* 67 Victoria Avenue South, Hamilton, Ont, Canada.

**WILKINSON, Cyril Theodore Anstruther,** CBE 1954; Registrar, Probate and Divorce Registry, 1936-59; *b* 4 Oct. 1884; *o s* of Anthony John Anstruther Wilkinson, barrister-at-law; unmarried. *Educ:* Blundell's. Entered Probate, Divorce and Admiralty Div., 1906; Asst Registrar, Probate Registry, 1931. Served in Artists' Rifles 1914; 8th London Regt, 1915-19. *Publications:* Consulting Editor: Rayden on Divorce; Tristram and Coote's Probate Practice, 1926-60. *Recreations:* cricket (Surrey County Cricket XI, 1909-20, Captain 1914-20), hockey (played for England and for Great Britain in Olympic Games, 1920). *Address:* Belmont Hotel, Sidmouth, Devon. *T:* Sidmouth 2555. *Clubs:* MCC, Free Foresters; Surrey County Cricket, etc.

**WILKINSON, Sir David;** *see* Wilkinson, Sir (Leonard) David.

**WILKINSON, Prof. Denys Haigh,** FRS 1956; Professor of Experimental Physics in the University of Oxford since 1959, Head of the Department of Nuclear Physics since 1962; Fellow of Jesus Coll., Cambridge, 1944-59, Hon. Fellow, since 1961; Student of Christ Church, Oxford, since 1957; *b* Leeds, Yorks, 5 September 1922; *o s* of Charles and Hilda Wilkinson; *m* 1st, 1947, Christiane Andrée Clavier (marriage dissolved, 1967); three *d*; 2nd, 1967, Helen Sellschop. *Educ:* Loughborough Gram. Sch.; Jesus Coll. Cambridge. British and Canadian Atomic Energy Projects, 1943-46; Univ. Demonstrator, Cambridge, 1947-51; Univ. Lecturer, 1951-56; Reader in Nuclear Physics, Univ. of Cambridge, 1956-57; Professor of Nuclear Physics, Univ. of Oxford, 1957-59. Mem. Governing Board of National Institute for Research in Nuclear Science, 1957-63 and 1964-65; Member, Science Research Council, 1967-70; Chm., Nuclear Physics Board of SRC, 1968-70. Lectures: Scott, Cambridge Univ., 1961; Rutherford Memorial, Brit. Physical Soc., 1962; Graham Young, Glasgow Univ., 1964; Queen's, Berlin, 1966; Silliman, Yale Univ., 1966; Walker Ames Prof., Univ. of Washington, 1968; Battelle Distinguished Prof., Univ. of Washington, 1970-71. Holweck Medallist of the British and French Physical Socs, 1957; Hughes Medallist of the Royal Society, 1965; Bruce-Preller Prize, RSE, 1969. Hon. DSc Univ. of Saskatchewan, 1964. *Publications:* Ionization Chambers and Counters, 1951; (ed) Isospin in Nuclear Physics, 1969; papers on nuclear physics and bird navigation. *Recreations:* mediæval church architecture and watching birds. *Address:* 82 Oxford Street, Woodstock, Oxford.

**WILKINSON, Edgar Riley,** CMG 1956; FIMechE; FIEE; Deputy Chairman (London Board), East African Power & Lighting Co. Ltd, since 1966; Kenya Power Co. Ltd, since 1966; *b* 14 April 1898; *s* of late James Driver Wilkinson, Ashton-on-Ribble, Preston, Lancashire; *m* 1945, Frances Elizabeth, *d* of Dr George Lambright, Shaker Heights, Ohio, USA; two *d. Educ:* Technical College, Preston. Power Station design engineer, English Electric Co., 1919-24; Cons. Engineer, Merz and McLellan, 1924-28; Deputy Commercial Manager, Central Electricity Board, 1928-37. Commercial Manager, 1937-48; Commercial Manager, British Electricity Authority, 1948-55. Dep. Chm. Balfour Beatty & Co. Ltd, 1956-67; Dir, Power Securities Corp. Ltd, 1956-68. Pres. Assoc. of Supervising Electrical Engineers, 1944-46; Technical Adviser, Four-Power Conf., Paris, 1946; Chm. Br. Electrical Develt Assoc., 1950-51; Special rep. of IBRD (Mexico), 1954-55. *Address:* 2 Alington House, Lilliput, Poole, Dorset. *T:* Canford Cliffs 78038. *Club:* Reform.

**WILKINSON, Prof. Frank Clare,** CBE 1956; LLD; MD; ChB, BDS, DDSc, MSc; FRCS, FDS; Hon. Consultant Dental Surgeon, Eastman Dental Hospital, 1959-64, retired; Dean and Dir of Studies of Institute of Dental Surgery in British Post-graduate Medical Federation, Univ. of London, and Dir of Eastman Dental Hospital, 1950-59; Prof. of Dental Surgery, London Univ., 1952-57; Consultant Dental Surgeon to the Royal Navy, 1944; Member, Board of the Faculty of Dental Surgery, Roy. Coll. of Surgeons, 1947, Dean, 1953-56; *b* Cheshire, 31 Aug. 1889; *s* of Frank Wilkinson and Annie A. Clare; *m* 1917, Gladys Eveline Tweedie; one *d. Educ:* Wallasey Grammar School; Univ. of Liverpool. Prizes in Operative Dental Surgery and in Orthodontia; House Surgeon, Liverpool Dental Hospital, 1912; Senior Demonstrator in Operative Dental Surgery, University of Liverpool, 1919-23; Dental Tutor, University of Liverpool, 1923; Hon. Dental Surgeon, David Lewis Northern Hospital; Lecturer for the Dental Board of UK; Member, Board Dental Studies University of Liverpool; Professor of Dental Science, Dean of the Faculty of Dental Science, and Director Dental Research Depart, University of Melbourne; Principal of the Australian College of Dentistry, 1925-33; Captain RAMC, attached Liverpool Merchants Mobile Hosp., France, 1915-19; Hon. Major AMC, 1928-33; Professor of Dental Surgery, Dean of the Turner Dental School, and Director of Dental Hospital, Manchester University, 1933-50; Hon. Adviser in Dental Surgery, Manchester Royal Infirmary, 1934-50, and St Mary's Hospitals, 1946-50; Hon. Consultant Dental Surgeon Christie Hospital and Holt Radium Institute, 1934-50; Director, Maxillo-facial Centre, NW Area, 1939-50; Surgical Specialist, EMS; Member: Dental Advisory Cttee, MEd. Research Council, 1947-60; Standing Dental Services Advisory Cttee, Central Health Council, 1948-60; Medical Sub cttee of Univ. Grants Cttee, 1952-60; Inter-departmental Cttee on Recruitment of Dental Students, 1955; Council Roy. Soc. Med. (Pres. Odont. Sect. 1959-60); General Dental Council (Chm. Educ. Cttee), 1956-59; Mem. NW Metropolitan Regional Hospital Board, 1954-60. Colyer Gold Medal, 1965. Hon. FACDS. *Publications:* numerous articles in British Dental Journal, etc. *Recreations:* yachting. *Address:* 33 Craigmore Tower, Guildford Rd, Woking, Surrey.

**WILKINSON, Frederick,** OBE 1968; MA; Head Master, Latymer Upper School, Hammersmith, 1937-57; *b* 18 Apr. 1891; *m* 1924, Edith Mary Previté (*d* 1968), *e d* of Professor Kennedy Orton, DSc, FRS. *Educ:* Grammar School, Dudley; Sidney Sussex College, Cambridge. Historical Tripos, Second Class; Assistant Master, Laxton School, Oundle; Senior History and House Master, Liverpool College, 1920-26; Head Master, Grammar School, Wallasey, 1927-34; Polytechnic School, W1, 1934-37; Active Service 1914-19 in France, Egypt and Italy; Captain 8th Staffs Regt, Captain and Wing Adjutant RAF (Observers' Badge, R Aero Club Certificate, despatches); Producer of Plays and Operas to various Societies–specialised in the work of Purcell and Holst. Hon. Fellow, Roy. Commonwealth Society. *Publications:* Various articles in English and foreign periodicals on subjects connected with education, drama and film. *Recreation:* walking. *Address:* 5 The Mall, East Sheen, SW14. *T:* 01-876 6186.

**WILKINSON, Prof. Geoffrey,** FRS 1965; Professor of Inorganic Chemistry, University of London, since 1956; *b* 14 July 1921; *s* of Henry and Ruth Wilkinson; *m* 1951, Lise Solver, *o d* of Rektor Prof. Svend Aa. Schou, Copenhagen; two *d. Educ:* Todmorden Gram. Sch.; Imperial Coll., London; USA. Junior Scientific Officer, Nat. Res. Council, Atomic Energy Div., Canada, 1943-46; Research Fellow: Radiation Lab., Univ. of Calif, Berkeley, Calif, USA, 1946-50; Chemistry Dept, Mass Inst. of Technology, Cambridge, Mass, USA, 1950-51; Asst Prof. of Chemistry, Harvard Univ., Cambridge, Mass, 1951-56; Arthur D. Little Visiting Prof., MIT, 1967; William Draper Harkins' Memorial Lectr, Univ. of Chicago, 1968; John Simon Guggenheim Fellow, 1954; Foreign Member: Roy. Danish Acad. of Science and Arts (math.-phys section), 1968; Amer. Acad. of Arts and Sciences, 1970. American Chem. Soc. Award in Inorganic Chemistry, 1965; Lavoisier Medal, Société Chimique de France, 1968. *Publications:* Jt author of Advanced Inorganic Chemistry: a Comprehensive Text, 1962, 2nd edn 1966; numerous in Physical Review, Journal of the American Chemical Society, etc. *Address:* Chemistry Dept, Imperial College, SW7. *T:* 01-589 5111.

**WILKINSON, Sir Harold,** Kt 1964; CMG 1946; Managing Director, the "Shell" Transport & Trading Co. Ltd; Director: The Shell Petroleum Co. Ltd; Shell Petroleum NV; *b* 24 February, 1903; *s* of Charles Robert Wilkinson, MA Oxon, ICS, Ramsey, Isle of Man; *m* 1939, Marie Frances Elie; three *s* one *d* (and one *step-d*). *Educ:* King William's Coll., Isle of Man. Joined Royal Dutch/Shell Group of Cos, 1922; Pres. Asiatic Petroleum Corp. (USA), 1936-42 and 1945-53; Pres. 1936-42 and 1948-53, Chm. 1945-48, Caribbean Petroleum Co. (renamed Shell Caribbean Petroleum Co., 1948) (USA); Dir Shell Union Oil Corp. (renamed Shell Oil Co., 1949) (USA), 1939-42 and 1945-53; Petroleum Rep. in Washington of UK Govt, 1941-45; Pres. Canadian Shell, 1953-57; Dir 1953, Man. Dir 1957-64, The Shell Petroleum Co.; Dir 1954, Princ. Dir 1957-64, Bataafse Petroleum Mij. NV (renamed Shell Petroleum NV); Chm., Shell Tankers, 1957-63; Dir, 1949 Man. Dir, 1961-64, Dep. Chm., 1963-64, The "Shell" Transport & Trading Co.; Chm. Canadian Shell (renamed Shell Western Holdings, 1963), 1961-64; Dir Shell Oil Co., 1961-64; retd 1964. US Medal of Freedom with Bronze Palm, 1951; Kt Comdr Order of Merit, Ecuador; Comdr Order of Orange-Nassau, 1964. *Recreations:* golf, sailing and shooting. *Address:* La Sologne en Ballegue, Epalinges

1066, Vaud, Switzerland. *Clubs:* Hurlingham; Sunningdale; St Andrews; Royal Yacht Squadron; Royal Bermuda Yacht (Bermuda).

**WILKINSON, Rt. Rev. Heber;** *see* Wilkinson, Rt Rev. C. R. H.

**WILKINSON, Hector Russell,** CIE 1927; *b* 11 March 1888; *s* of late Rev. G. G. Wilkinson; *m* 1920, Theodora, *d* of late Robert Daintree, Horam, Sussex; two *s* (and one *s* one *d* decd). *Educ:* Clifton Coll.; Queen's Coll., Oxford. Indian CS 1912-39, Dist Magistrate, Chittagong, 1928-30, Sec., Educn Dept, Bengal, 1931-35, Comr, Dacca Div., 1937-38; Ministry of Food, 1939-45. *Address:* Grange Cottage, Hadlow Down, Uckfield, Sussex. *T:* Hadlow Down 252. *Club:* East India and Sports.

**WILKINSON, Ven. Hubert Seed;** Archdeacon of Liverpool, 1951-70; Residentiary Canon, 1968-70; *e s* of late Rev. John and late Margaret Wilkinson; *m* Frances Elizabeth, 4th *d* of Dr J. Staveley Dick; two *d*. *Educ:* University of Durham. Curate of Colne, 1925-29; Rector of Harpurhey, Manchester, 1926-36; Rector of Chester-le-Street, 1936-40; Rural Dean of Chester-le-Street, 1937-40; Vicar of Allerton, Liverpool, 1940-47; Canon Diocesan of Liverpool Cathedral, 1945-47, and 1951-68; Examining Chaplain to Bishop of Liverpool, 1947-47 and 1955; Vicar of Winster, 1947-48; Archdeacon of Westmorland, 1947-51; Vicar of: Ambleside with Rydal, 1948-50; St Mary's, Grassendale, 1951-68; late Hon. Canon of Carlisle Cathedral and Director of Religious Education. *Address:* 8 Fawley Road, Liverpool 18. *T:* 051-724 1604. *Club:* Royal Commonwealth Society.

**WILKINSON, James Hardy,** FRS 1969; MA Cantab, ScD; Deputy Chief Scientific Officer, National Physical Laboratory, Teddington, since 1962; *b* 27 Sept. 1919; *s* of J. W. and K. C. Wilkinson; *m* 1945, Heather Nora Ware; one *s* one *d*. *Educ:* Sir Joseph Williamson's Mathematical Sch., Rochester; Trinity Coll., Cambridge. Major Scholar (Maths) Trinity Coll., 1935; Pemberton Prize, 1937; Mathison Prize, 1939; BA 1939, MA Cantab 1942; ScD 1962. War service: Mathematical Laboratory, Cambridge, 1940-43; Armament Research Dept, Fort Halstead, 1943-46. Mathematics Div., Nat. Physical Lab. (working on design, construction and use of electronic computers), 1946-. Visiting Professor: Univ. of Michigan, numerous occasions, 1957-68; Stanford Univ., 1961, 1967, 1969. Founder Fellow of Inst. of Mathematics and its Applications, and of British Computer Society. Visited USSR Academy of Sciences, as a leading scientist, 1968. *Publications:* Rounding Errors in Algebraic Processes, 1963; The Algebraic Eigenvalue Problem, 1965; chapters in six books on computers and numerical analysis; numerous papers in learned jls. *Recreations:* music, travel. *Address:* 40 Atbara Road, Teddington, Mddx. *T:* 01-977 1207.

**WILKINSON, John Arbuthnot Ducane;** MP (C) Bradford West, since 1970; *b* 23 Sept. 1940; 2nd *s* of late Denys Wilkinson and Gillian Wilkinson, Eton College; *m* 1969, Paula Adey, *o d* of Joseph Adey, East Herrington, Co. Durham. *Educ:* Eton (King's Scholar); RAF Coll., Cranwell; Churchill Coll., Cambridge (2nd cl. Hons Mod. Hist.; MA). Flight Cadet, RAF Coll., Cranwell, 1959-61 (Philip Sassoon Meml Prize, qualified French Interpreter); commnd 1961; Flying Instructor, No 8 FTS, Swinderby, 1962; resigned Oct. 1962. Churchill Coll., Cambridge, Oct. 1962-65. Trooper, 21st Special Air Service Regt (Artists'), TA, 1963-65; rejoined RAF 1965; Flying Instructor, RAF Coll., Cranwell, 1966-67; Tutor, Stanford Univ.'s British Campus, 1967; ADC to Comdr 2nd Allied Tactical Air Force, Germany, 1967; resigned RAF, 1967. Head of Universities' Dept, Conservative Central Office, 1967-68; Aviation Specialist, Cons. Research Dept, 1969; Senior Administration Officer (Anglo-French Jaguar Project), Preston Div., British Aircraft Corp., 1969-70. *Recreation:* flying. *Address:* 13 Manscombe Road, Allerton, Bradford, Yorks. *T:* Bradford 47293. *Clubs:* Royal Air Force, Royal Aero, Coningsby; Tiger (Redhill).

**WILKINSON, Dr John Frederick,** FRCP, MD (Gold Medal), ChB, BSc (1st Cl. Hons Chem.), MSc, PhD Manchester, FRIC; Consulting Physician; Consulting Physician, United Manchester Hospitals; late Director of Department of Hæmatology, University and Royal Infirmary of Manchester; late Reader in Hæmatology, and Lecturer in Systematic Medicine, Univ. of Manchester; late Hon. Consulting Hæmatologist, The Christie Cancer Hospital, Holt Radium Institute and The Duchess of York Hospital for Babies, manchester; Hon. Editor, Manchester Medical Society; President, European Hæmatological Society; Vice-President, International Hæmatological Society; *b* Oldham, 10 June 1897; *s* of John Frederick Wilkinson, Oldham and Stockport, and Annie, *d* of late Reverend E. Wareham, DD, Rector of Heaton Mersey; *m* 1964, Marion Crossfield, Major, WRAC. *Educ:* Arnold School, Blackpool; University of Manchester; Manchester Royal Infirmary. Served European War, 1916-19, RNAS, RN, and later attached Tank Corps, France; also served on Vindictive at Zeebrugge, 1918, and ballotted for Victoria Cross award; Chemical Research Manchester University, 1919-28; Medical Research since 1929; Regional Transfusion Officer, and Regional Adviser on Resuscitation, Ministry of Health, NW Region, 1940-46. Graduate Scholarship (Chemistry), 1920; Dalton Research Scholarship; Sir Clement Royds Research Fellowship; Medical (Graduate) Scholarship, 1923; Hon. Demonstrator in Crystallography; Research Asst in Physiology; Sidney Renshaw Physiology Prizeman; Gold Medal for Dissertation in Med., 1931, University of Manchester. Oliver Sharpey Lecturer, Royal College Physicians, London 1948; Liveryman Worshipful Society of Apothecaries, London; Freeman City of London. *Publications:* scientific and medical publications since 1920 in English and foreign journals, etc. Sections on Blood Diseases, Anæmias and Leukæmias in British Encyclopædia of Medical Practice, 1936, 1950 and 1951 and yearly Supplements to 1971, and in Encyclopædia of General Practice, 1964; Section on Emergencies in Blood Diseases, in Medical Emergencies, 1948/71; ed Modern Trends in Diseases of the Blood, 1955, 1971; The Diagnosis and Treatment of Blood Diseases, 1971; ed, Section in Clinical Surgery, 1967. *Recreations:* motoring, antiques, travel, zoos, and tropical fish keeping. *Address:* Mobberley Old Hall, Knutsford, Cheshire. *T:* Mobberley 2111; 5 Lorne Street, Manchester M13 0EZ. *T:* 061-273 4253. *Club:* Savage.

**WILKINSON, Brig. John Shann,** CB 1939; DSO 1918; MC; psc; retired; *b* 1884; *s* of Christopher George Wilkinson, Bubwith, E Yorks, and Florence Shann, Ripon, Yorks; *m* 1st, 1918, Gwendoline Mary Brooke Bailey (*d* 1962); 2nd, 1965, Katharine Hutton Wanklyn, *widow* of Endell Wanklyn, Christchurch, New Zealand. *Educ:* privately. Sherwood Foresters, 1906; served East Africa, 1913 (medal with clasp); European War, 1914-18 (despatches, DSO, MC); Somaliland, 1920 (despatches, Bt

Lt-Col, clasp, Somaliland 1920); GSO2, Staff Coll., Camberley; Dep. Dir of Movements, War Office; retired pay, 1938. Re-employed, 1939, in charge Administration Aldershot Command, then as DA and QMG 2nd AA Corps. *Recreation:* fishing. *Address:* 13 Highgate Avenue, Christchurch, New Zealand. *Club:* United Service.

**WILKINSON, (Lancelot) Patrick,** MA; Fellow, King's College, Cambridge; Brereton Reader in Classics, Cambridge, since 1969; Chairman of Classical Faculty, 1969-70; Orator of the University since 1958; *b* 1 June 1907; *s* of late Lancelot George William and Kate Wilkinson; *m* 1944, Sydney Alix, *d* of late Sir Herbert Eason, CB, CMG; two adopted *s*. *Educ:* Charterhouse (Talbot Scholar and Medallist); King's College, Cambridge, 1st Class Classical Tripos, Parts I and II; Craven Scholar, 1929; Chancellor's Classical Medallist, 1930; Craven Student, 1930; Fellow of King:s College, Cambridge, 1932; Dean, 1934-45; attached to Foreign Office, 1939-45; Asst Tutor, 1945-46; Senior Tutor, 1946-56; Vice-Provost, 1961-65; University Lecturer in Classics, 1936-67; Reader in Latin Literature, 1967-69. Secretary to the Cambridge Greek Play Cttee, 1938-63; Dep. for Public Orator, 1950-51, 1957; Member of the Council of the Senate, 1952-56; Foundation Mem. Coun., New Hall, Cambridge, 1954-65; Gov., Queen Mary Coll., London, 1954-57; Mem. Gov. Body, Charterhouse School, 1954-69. Mem. Conseil Consultatif of Fondation Hardt (Geneva, 1959-63). FRSL. *Publications:* Horace and his Lyric Poetry, 1945; Letters of Cicero, 1949; Ovid Recalled, 1955 (abr. as Ovid Surveyed, 1962); Golden Latin Artistry, 1963; (with R. H. Bulmer) Register of King's College, Cambridge, 1919-58, 1963; words for Benjamin Britten's *Cantata Misericordium,* 1963; The Georgics of Virgil, 1969; articles in classical jls. *Recreations:* reading, travel. *Address:* King's College, Cambridge. *T:* 50411; 9 Huntingdon Road, Cambridge. *T:* 54888.

**WILKINSON, Sir (Leonard) David,** 2nd Bt *cr* 1941; DSC 1943; *b* 18 Jan. 1920; *o s* of Sir George Henry Wilkinson, KCVO, 1st Bt and of Lady Wilkinson (*née* Volland); *S* father, 1967; *m* 1946, Sylvia Ruby Eva Anne Gater (marr. diss. 1967); one *s* one *d*. *Educ:* Eton; Christ Church, Oxford. Joined RNVR 1939; served Mediterranean, North Sea, Atlantic and Southern reaches with Fleet Air Arm; comd 801 Sqn, 1944, 803 1st RCN Air Sqn, 1945; Lt-Comdr 1946. Hon. Dir, Thermega Ltd, 1947-56; Hon. Treas., Ex-Services Welfare Soc., 1947-56; Mem. Council, Music in Hospitals, 1948-54; a Governor, Bridewell Royal Hosp., 1958-; Assistant Dir-Gen, St John Ambulance Assoc., 1964-68, Director, 1968-. OStJ 1956, CStJ 1965, KStJ 1968, Mem. of Chapter General 1969-. *Recreations:* ski-ing, sailing. *Heir: s* David Graham Brook Wilkinson [*b* 18 May 1947. *Educ:* Millfield; Christ Church, Oxford]. *Address:* Brook, near Godalming, Surrey.

**WILKINSON, Leslie,** OBE 1969; DLitt 1970; FRIBA; (Life) FRAIA; Emeritus Professor of Architecture, University of Sydney (Professor, 1918-47); in practice; *b* London, 12 Oct. 1882; *s* of Edward Henry and Ellen Wilkinson; *m* 1912, Alice Dorothy Ruston; one *s* two *d*. *Educ:* St Edward's School, Oxford. Articled to J. S. Gibson, FRIBA, 1900; Gold and Silver medallist Royal Academy School; Travelling Student RA Schools; Silver medallist, RIBA; Assistant Professor, School of Architecture, University College, London, 1908; RAIA Gold medallist, 1961. *Publications:* papers on architectural subjects. *Address:* 24 Wentworth Road, Vaucluse, Sydney, NSW 2030, Australia.

**WILKINSON, Sir Martin;** *see* Wilkinson, Sir R. F. M.

**WILKINSON, Norman,** CBE 1948 (OBE 1918); Order of the Crown of Belgium; ROI; Hon. RWS; Past President, Royal Institute of Painters in Water Colours; Lieut-Commander, RNVR; Marine Painter to Royal Yacht Squadron; *b* Cambridge, 24 Nov. 1878; *m* 1st, 1918, Evelyn (*d* 1967), *y d* of Rev. Murdo C. Mackenzie; one *s* one *d*; 2nd, 1968, Joyce Jervis. *Educ:* Berkhamsted School; St Paul's Cathedral Choir Sch. Adviser on Camouflage to Air Ministry, 1939-42 (with rank of Hon. Air Cdre). Originator of Dazzle painting adopted by all the Allied Nations in the European War, 1914-18, for the protection of merchant vessels against submarine attack. Seconded to US Navy to advise on dazzle painting of ships. Presented fifty-four pictures of The War at Sea to the Nation, 1944, now at Imperial Maritime Museum, Greenwich. One-man show, Tryon Gallery, 1970. *Publications:* The Dardanelles; Colour Sketches from Gallipoli, 1915; Ships in Pictures, 1945; Water Colour Sketching out of doors, 1953; A Brush with Life (memoirs), 1969. *Address:* The Studio, Winchfield, near Basingstoke, Hants. *T:* Hartley Wintney 2968; (summer) Seaview House, Seaview, Isle of Wight. *T:* Seaview 3160. *Clubs:* Arts; (Hon. Member) Royal Thames Yacht; (Hon. Member) Royal Yacht Squadron; (Hon. Member) RNVR.

**WILKINSON, Patrick;** *see* Wilkinson, L. P.

**WILKINSON, Peter;** Diplomatic Service Counsellor, on secondment to Board of Trade since 1969; *b* 25 May 1918; *s* of late Fred and Doris Wilkinson; *m* 1944, Anne Sutherland; two *s*. *Educ:* Barnsley Holgate Grammar School. Inland Revenue, 1936-38; Air Min., 1938-40; RAF, 1940-46; Control Office for Germany and Austria, 1946-47; FO, 1947-48; 2nd Sec., British Embassy, Bangkok, 1948-50; Asst Political Adviser to Allied Mil. Govt, Trieste, 1950-52; FO, 1952-55; 1st Sec., Baghdad, 1955-58; FO, 1958-61; 1st Sec., Washington, 1961-64; Counsellor, Tehran, 1964-68; Inspector of Diplomatic Service Establishments, 1968-69. *Recreations:* ski-ing, travel, music. *Address:* 65 Cornwall Gardens, SW7. *T:* 01-937 2936. *Club:* Travellers'.

**WILKINSON, Sir Peter (Allix),** KCMG 1970 (CMG 1960); DSO 1944; OBE 1944; Ambassador to Vienna, since 1970; *b* 15 April 1914; *s* of late Captain Osborn Cecil Wilkinson; *m* 1945, Mary Theresa, *d* of late Algernon Villiers; two *d*. *Educ:* Rugby; Corpus Christi Coll., Cambridge. Commissioned in 2nd Bn Royal Fusiliers, 1935; active service in Poland (despatches), France, Italy and Balkans; retired with rank of Lieut-Colonel, 1947. Entered HM Foreign Service, appointed 1st Secretary at British Legation, Vienna, 1947; 1st Secretary at British Embassy, Washington, 1952; Secretary-General of Heads of Government Meeting at Geneva, 1955; Counsellor, HM Embassy, Bonn, 1955; Counsellor, Foreign Office, 1960-63; Under-Secretary, Cabinet Office, 1963-64; Senior Civilian Instructor at the Imperial Defence Coll., 1964-66; Ambassador to Vietnam, 1966-67; Under-Secretary, Foreign Office, 1967-68; Chief of Administration, HM Diplomatic Service, 1968-70. Cross of Valour (Poland), 1940; Order of White Lion (IV Class) (Czechoslovakia), 1945. *Recreations:* ski-ing, sailing, fishing. *Address:* c/o Foreign and Commonwealth Office, SW1; Mill House,

Charing, Kent. *T:* Charing 306. *Clubs:* White's, Army and Navy.

**WILKINSON, Reginald Warren Hale,** QC; *b* Leamington Spa, Warwicks, 1882; *s* of late Rev. Dr Edward Wilkinson; *m* 1928, Catherine, Countess Troyanovsky (*née* de Danilkiewicz). *Educ:* abroad; Leamington Coll.; Balliol Coll., Oxford; BA (Hons in Classics and Modern History), 1904; MA 1911. Barrister-at-law, Inner Temple, 1907; and of Sierra Leone Bar, 1909; Assistant District Commissioner, Sierra Leone, 1909; Assistant Colonial Secretary and JP, Sierra Leone, 1912; Senior Crown Counsel, Gold Coast, 1914; Solicitor-General, Gold Coast, 1915; attached to Colonial Office (Legal Adviser's Department), 1915; acted for prolonged periods as Attorney-General, Gold Coast, and as legal adviser to the British Military Administration in Togoland, 1915-20; Judge of the Supreme Court of the Gold Coast Colony, 1920; Acting Governor and C-in-C, Gold Coast, 1921, Attorney-General, 1921-28; KC 1924; retired, 1928. Formerly Hon. Corr. Secretary, Royal Empire Society (which is now Royal Commonwealth Society). *Address:* c/o Barclays Bank (France), Ltd, Monte Carlo, Monaco.

**WILKINSON, Richard Edward,** CBE 1966; British Consul-General at Izmir, Turkey, 1960-69, retired; *b* 11 Nov. 1901; *s* of Charles Crosbie Wilkinson and Madeline La Fontaine; *m* 1924, Thelma de Cramer; two *s*. *Educ:* privately. Appointed Vice-Consul at Izmir, 1933; Consul, 1950; Consul-General, 1960. *Recreation:* archæology. *Address:* 16 Hürriyet Caddesi, Bornova, Izmir, Turkey. *T:* 29054.

**WILKINSON, Sir (Robert Francis) Martin,** Kt 1969; Chairman, The Stock Exchange, since 1965 (Deputy Chairman, 1963-65); Chairman, Federation of Stock Exchanges in Great Britain and Ireland, since 1965; Member, Panel on Takeovers and Mergers; *b* 4 June 1911; *e s* of late Sir Robert Pelham Wilkinson and Phyllis Marion Wilkinson; *m* 1936, Dora Esme, *d* of late William John Arendt and late Mrs Arendt; three *d*. *Educ:* Repton. Member, Stock Exchange, 1933; Partner in de Zoete & Gorton, 1936; Member of Council, Stock Exchange, 1959. Served with RAF 1940-45. *Recreations:* cricket, gardening. *Address:* Kixes, Sharpthorne, Sussex. *T:* Sharpthorne 370. *Clubs:* City of London, Gresham.

**WILKINSON, Sydney Frank,** CB 1951; Director of Administration, National Research Development Corporation, 1955-65; *b* 14 Dec. 1894; *s* of Charles James Carey Wilkinson; *m* 1924, Gladys MIllicent Boorsma; one *s*. *Educ:* Strand Sch.; King's Coll., London. Entered Civil Service, National Health Insurance Commission, 1913; Commissioned RFA, 1918; Private Secretary to Minister of Food, 1920; Secretary to Parliamentary Conference on Reform of Licensing Law, 1921; Assistant Private Secretary to Sir Kingsley Wood, 1935; loaned to National Fitness Council, 1937; Private Secretary to Mr Walter Elliot and Mr Malcolm MacDonald, 1938-40; Security Executive, 1940-41; Director of Public Relations, Ministry of Health, 1941-43. Under-Secretary for Housing, Ministry of Housing and Local Government, 1951-54 (Ministry of Local Government and Planning, 1951; Ministry of Health, 1947-51). *Recreation:* golf. *Address:* 51 Cornwall Road, Cheam, Surrey. *T:* 01-642 0374. *Club:* Reform.

**WILKINSON, Sir Thomas Crowe S.;** *see* Spenser-Wilkinson.

**WILKINSON, William Dale,** CB 1949; CBE 1942; DSO 1917; MC; *b* 1893; *e s* of late Rev. W. Wilkinson; *m* 1st, 1924, Margaret Frances (*d* 1932), *e d* of late J. E. Bunting; 2nd, 1934, Mary Devas, *e d* of late R. Marshall. *Educ:* Bradford Grammar Sch.; Magdalen Coll., Oxford; MA. Gazetted to 7th Battalion Yorkshire Regt (The Green Howards), 1914; Captain, 1916; served in France, 1915-18 (MC, DSO, despatches); in India (seconded to Indian Army), 1918-19; entered the Treasury, 1919; Private Secretary to the Financial Secretary, 1921-22; to Controller of Finance, 1922-30; Seconded to Cabinet Offices, 1930-34 and 1935-39; to Imperial Defence College, 1934; transferred to Cabinet Offices, 1939; transferred to Ministry of Aircraft Production, afterwards amalgamated with Ministry of Supply, 1942; Principal Assistant Secretary, 1944; Principal Establishment Officer, 1945; Under Secretary, 1946; retired 1954. *Address:* Hanover House, Curry Rivel, Somerset. *T:* Curry Rivel 372.

**WILKS, Jean Ruth Fraser;** Head Mistress, King Edward VI High School for Girls, Birmingham, since 1965; *b* 14 April 1917; *d* of Mark Wilks. *Educ:* North London Collegiate Sch.; Somerville Coll., Oxford (MA). Assistant Mistress: Truro High Sch., 1940-43; James Allen's Girls' Sch., Dulwich, 1943-51; Head Mistress, Hertfordshire and Essex High Sch., Bishop's Stortford, Hertfordshire, 1951-64. Member Public Schools Commn, 1968-70. *Address:* 26 Weoley Hill, Selly Oak, Birmingham 29.

**WILKS, Stanley David;** Under-Secretary, Export Credits Guarantee Department, since 1969; *b* 1 Aug. 1920; *s* of Walter Arthur and Sarah Wilks; *m* 1947, Dorothy Irene Adamthwaite; one *s* one *d*. *Educ:* Polytechnic Sch., London. Royal Armoured Corps, 1939-46; service with 48th Bn, Royal Tank Regt; 3rd Carabiniers, Imphal, 1944. Home Office, 1946-50; Board of Trade: Asst Principal, 1950; Principal 1951; Asst Sec. 1961; Under-Sec. 1969. *Recreations:* water sports, camping, music. *Address:* 6 Foxgrove Avenue, Beckenham, Kent. *T:* 01-650 7728. *Club:* Medway Yacht.

**WILLAN, Edward Gervase,** CMG 1964; HM Diplomatic Service; Ambassador at Rangoon, since 1970; *b* 17 May 1917; *er s* of late Captain F. G. L. Willan, RNR; *m* 1944, Mary Bickley Joy, *d* of late Lieut-Colonel H. A. Joy, IAOC. *Educ:* Radley; Pembroke Coll., Cambridge (Exhibitioner, MA). Indian Civil Service, 1939-47; 2nd Secretary (from 1948, 1st Secretary) on staff of UK High Commissioner, New Delhi, 1947-49; appointed to HM Diplomatic Service, 1948; Foreign Office, 1949-52; 1st Secretary, HM Embassy, The Hague, 1953-55; 1st Secretary, HM Legation, Bucharest, 1956-58 (Chargé d'Affaires, 1956, 1957 and 1958); Head of Communications Dept, FO, 1958-62; Political Adviser to Hong Kong Government, 1962-65; Head of Scientific Relations Dept, FO, 1966-68; Minister, Lagos, 1968-70. *Recreations:* travel, walking, gardening. *Address:* c/o Foreign and Commonwealth Office, SW1. *Club:* Oxford and Cambridge University.

**WILLAN, Sir Harold Curwen,** Kt 1947; CMG 1946; MC 1917; Commissioner, Foreign Compensation Commission, 1962-68, Vice-Chairman, 1967-68; *b* 29 Feb. 1896; *s* of late Richard Willan, Kendal, Westmorland; *m* 1922, Marjorie Rigg; one *s*. *Educ:* Kendal School; Jesus Coll., Oxford (BA). Barrister-at-Law, Inner Temple (Cert. of Hon.); Inns of Court OTC 1915; Lieut, RA, 1916; BEF France, 1916-17 (MC); Cadet, Malayan Civil

Service, 1920; District Judge, Straits Settlements, 1932; Deputy Legal Adviser, Federated Malay States, 1934; Solicitor-General, Kenya, 1937; Attorney-General, Zanzibar, 1940 (Brilliant Star of Zanzibar); Legal Adviser, Civil Affairs, East Africa Command, and acted as Chief Political Officer, 1941; President, High Court, Ethiopia, 1942; Deputy Chief Civil Affairs Officer, Malay Peninsula, with rank of Brigadier, 1945 (despatches twice); Chief Justice, Malayan Union, 1946, Fed. of Malaya, 1948-50; Chief Justice of the United Kingdom High Commission Territories in S. Africa, 1952-56. *Publications:* Digest of Reported Law Cases, Federated Malay States, 1936; High Commission Territories Law Reports. *Recreations:* golf and bowls. *Address:* 6 Squirrels Way, Epsom, Surrey. *T:* Epsom 21185. *Club:* East India and Sports.

**WILLAN, Professor Thomas Stuart,** MA, BLitt, DPhil; Professor of Economic History, University of Manchester, since 1961; *b* 3 Jan. 1910; 3rd *s* of Matthew Willan and Jane (*née* Stuart); unmarried. *Educ:* Queen Elizabeth's Sch., Kirkby Lonsdale; The Queen's Coll., Oxford. Asst Lecturer, School of Economics and Commerce, Dundee, 1934-35; University of Manchester: Asst Lecturer in History, 1935-45; Lecturer in History, 1945-47; Senior Lecturer in History, 1947-49; Reader in History, 1949-61. *Publications:* River Navigation in England, 1600-1750, 1936; The English Coasting Trade, 1600-1750, 1938; (ed with E. W. Crossley) Three Seventeenth-century Yorkshire Surveys, 1941; The Navigation of the Great Ouse between St Ives and Bedford in the Seventeenth Century, 1946; The Navigation of the River Weaver in the Eighteenth Century, 1951; The Muscovy Merchants of 1555, 1953; The Early History of the Russia Company, 1553-1603, 1956; Studies in Elizabethan Foreign Trade, 1959; (ed) A Tudor Book of Rates, 1962; The Early History of the Don Navigation, 1965; An Eighteenth-Century Shopkeeper, Abraham Dent of Kirkby Stephen, 1970; articles in English Historical Review, Economic History Review, etc. *Address:* 3 Raynham Avenue, Didsbury, Manchester M20 0BW. *T:* 061-445 4771. *Club:* Penn.

**WILLASEY-WILSEY, Maj.-Gen. Anthony Patrick,** CB 1970; MBE 1948; MC 1956; Major-General, Commando Forces Royal Marines, Plymouth, 1968-70, retired; *b* 20 Sept. 1920; *e s* of Colonel F. H. Willasey-Wilsey, MC, 8th Gurkha Rifles; *m* 1948, Dorothy, *y d* of Dr R. B. M. Yates, Market Drayton, Salop; two *s*. *Educ:* Repton Sch. Commissioned in RM, Jan. 1939; HMS Rodney, 1940-42; HMS Howe, 1943; 47 Commando, Belgium and Holland, 1944-45. Instructor, RMA, Sandhurst, 1948-50; 40 Commando, Malayan Emergency, 1951-52 (despatches); Staff Coll., Camberley, 1954; 40 Commando, Cyprus and Suez, 1956-58; DAA and QMG, HQ 3 Commando Bde, ME, 1958; jssc, 1961; CO, 43 Commando, 1962-63; G 1 Plans, MoD, 1964-65; Comdr, 3 Commando Bde, Far East, 1965-66. IDC, 1967. MBIM 1970. *Address:* The Dun Cow Cottage, Market Drayton, Salop. *T:* Market Drayton 2360. *Club:* Army and Navy.

**WILLATT, (Robert) Hugh;** Secretary-General, Arts Council of Great Britain, since 1968; *b* 25 April 1909; *m* 1945, Evelyn Gibbs, ARE, ARCA, (Rome Scholar); no *c*. *Educ:* Repton; Pembroke Coll., Oxford (MA). Admitted a Solicitor, 1934; Partner in family firm of Hunt, Dickins and Willatt, Nottingham, and later Partner in Lewis, Silkin & Partners, Westminster. Served War of 1939-45, in RAF (Sqdn Leader). Member BBC Midland Regional Adv. Council, 1953-58; Member Arts Council Drama Panel, 1955-68 (Chairman, 1960-68); Member, Arts Council, 1958-68; (at various times) Member Board: National Theatre; Mercury Trust Ltd (Ballet Rambert); Nottingham Theatre Trust Ltd. Hon. MA, University of Nottingham. *Address:* 32 Maida Avenue, W2. *Club:* Garrick.

**WILLCOCKS, David Valentine,** MC 1944; MA, MusB, ADCM, ARCM; FRSCM, Hon. RAM; Fellow and Organist of King's College, Cambridge, since 1957; University Lecturer in Music, Cambridge University, since 1957; Conductor of the Bradford Festival Choral Society, since 1957; University Organist, Cambridge University, since 1958; Conductor of the Cambridge University Musical Society, since 1958; Musical Director of the Bach Choir since 1960; *b* 30 Dec. 1919; *s* of late T. H. Willcocks; *m* 1947, Rachel Gordon, *d* of late Rev. A. C. Blyth, Fellow of Selwyn Coll., Cambridge; two *s* two *d*. *Educ:* Clifton Coll.; King's Coll., Cambridge. Chorister, Westminster Abbey, 1929-33; Scholar, Clifton Coll., 1934-38; FRCO, 1938; Scholar at College of St Nicolas (RSCM), 1938-39; Organ Scholar, King's Coll., Cambridge, 1939-40; Open Foundation Scholarship, King's Coll., Cambridge, 1940; Stewart of Rannoch Scholarship, 1940. Served War of 1939-45, 5th Bn DCLI, 1940-45. Organ Scholar, King's Coll., Cambridge, 1945-47; Fellow of King's Coll., Cambridge, 1947-51; Conductor, Cambridge Philharmonic Society, 1947; Organist of Salisbury Cathedral, 1947-50; Master of the Choristers and Organist, Worcester Cathedral, 1950-57; Conductor of the City of Birmingham Choir, 1950-57. President, Royal College of Organists, 1966-68. Hon. Fellow, Royal Canadian College of Organists, 1967. *Recreation:* golf. *Address:* 13 Grange Road, Cambridge. *T:* 59559. *Club:* Athenæum.

**WILLERT, Sir Arthur,** KBE, *cr* 1919; *b* 19 May 1882; *s* of late P. F. Willert of Headington Hill, Oxford; *m* 1908, Ethel Florence McKay (*d* 1955), *er d* of Sir Walter Simpson, 2nd Bt of Balabraes, Ayton, Scotland; one *s*. *Educ:* Eton; Balliol Coll., Oxford. Joined staff of The Times, 1906; worked in Paris, Berlin, and Washington Offices of The Times, 1906-08; Member editorial staff of The Times in London, 1909, and also London correspondent of New York Evening Post; Chief correspondent of The Times in USA, 1910-20, except in 1917-18 when served as Secretary in Washington of the British War Mission in the USA, and as Washington representative of the Ministry of Information; joined the Foreign Office, 1921, where he became head of the News Department and Press Officer; Member of the United Kingdom Delegations to the Washington Naval Conference, 1921-22, to the London Economic Conference, 1924, to the London Naval Conference, 1930, to the Geneva Disarmament Conference, 1932-34, and to meetings of the League of Nations, 1929-34; resigned from Foreign Office, 1935; Head of Ministry of Information Office for the Southern Region, 1939-45. *Publications:* Aspects of British Foreign Policy, 1928; The Frontiers of England, 1935; (joint) The Empire in the World, 1937; The Road to Safety, 1952. *Address:* 37 Eaton Place, SW1. *T:* 01-235 6452. *Clubs:* Brooks's, Beefsteak, National Press; Washington (hon. member).

**WILLESDEN, Bishop Suffragan of,** since 1964; **Rt. Rev. Graham Douglas Leonard;** *b* 8 May 1921; *s* of Rev. Douglas Leonard, MA; *m* 1943, Vivien Priscilla, *d* of late M. B. R. Swann, MD, Fellow of Gonville and Caius Coll.,

Cambridge; two *s.* *Educ:* Monkton Combe Sch.; Balliol Coll., Oxford. Hon. Sch. Nat. Science, shortened course. BA 1943, MA 1947. Served War, 1941-45; Captain, Oxford and Bucks Light Infantry; Army Operational Research Group (Ministry of Supply), 1944-45. Westcott House, Cambridge, 1946-47. Deacon 1947, Priest 1948; Vicar of Ardleigh, Essex, 1952-55; Director of Religious Education, Diocese of St Albans, 1955-58; Hon. Canon of St Albans, 1955-57; Canon Residentiary, 1957-58; Canon Emeritus, 1958; General Secretary, Nat. Society, and Secretary, C of E Schools Council, 1958-62; Archdeacon of Hampstead, Exam. Chaplain to Bishop of London, and Rector of St Andrew Undershaft *w* St Mary Axe, City of London, 1962-64. Chairman, Church of England Cttee for Diocesan Moral and Social Welfare Councils, 1967-. Select Preacher to University of Oxford, 1968. *Publications:* (jt author) Growing into Union, 1970; various pamphlets and reviews. *Recreations:* reading, especially biographies; music. *Address:* 2 Church Road, Highgate, N6. *T:* 01-340 6041.
*See also Prof. M. M. Swann.*

**WILLETT, Archibald Anthony;** Director, Cable & Wireless Ltd and eight subsidiary companies, since 1967; Director, Cable & Wireless/Western Union International Inc., since 1968; *b* 27 Jan. 1924; *s* of Reginald Beckett Willett and Mabel Alice (*née* Plaister); *m* 1948, Doris Marjorie Peat; one *s* one *d.* *Educ:* Oswestry High Sch.; Southall Grammar School. Lloyds Bank Ltd, 1940; Great Western Railway Co., 1941-42 and 1947-48; RAF (Signals Branch), 1942-47; Cable & Wireless Ltd, 1948-: Administrative Asst to Sec., 1948; Asst Sec., 1960; Dep. Sec., 1964; Special Asst to Man. Dir, 1966; Dir, 1967. FCIS 1963 (final exam., 1949); MBIM 1967; MInstM. *Recreations:* home and garden, local community affairs, Scout Association, walking, target shooting. *Address:* (office) Mercury House, Theobalds Road, WC1X 8RX. *T:* 01-242 4433; (home) Kingsbury House, Berks Hill, Chorleywood, Herts. *T:* Chorleywood 3031. *Clubs:* Royal Commonwealth Society; Exiles' (Twickenham).

**WILLETT, Lt-Cmdr William (Basil),** OBE 1964; MVO 1969; DSC 1942; RN retd; Private Secretary and Head of Household to The Duke of Edinburgh, since 1970; *b* 24 Feb. 1919; *s* of late Captain B. R. Willett, CBE, DSC, RN, and of Mrs Willett, OBE; *m* 1946, Anne, *d* of late C. R. Rolland, Montreal, Canada, and of Mrs Rolland; one *s* two *d.* *Educ:* Winchester. Royal Navy, 1937. Served War of 1939-45 (despatches, DSC). Retired from Royal Navy, 1969. Sailing Master, Royal Yacht, Bloodhound, 1967-68. *Recreations:* mainly outdoor. *Address:* The Old House, Prinsted, Emsworth, Hants.

**WILLEY,** family name of **Baron Barnby.**

**WILLEY, Basil,** MA (Cantab); FBA 1947; FRSL 1950; Hon. LittD (Manchester), 1948; King Edward VII Professor of English Literature, University of Cambridge, 1946-64; Hon. Fellow, Pembroke College, 1964 (Fellow, 1935); President, 1958-64; *b* 25 July 1897; *s* of William Herbert Willey and Alice Ann Le Gros; *m* 1923, Zélie Murlis Ricks; two *s* two *d.* *Educ:* University College Sch., Hampstead. History Scholarship at Peterhouse, 1915; Lieut, West Yorkshire Regt, 1916-18; 1st Class Historical Tripos, 1920; 1st Class English Tripos, 1921; Hugo de Balsham Student at Peterhouse and Le Bas Prize, 1922; Lecturer in English at Cambridge from 1923; University Lecturer, 1934. Visiting Professor, Columbia Univ., New York, 1948-49; Cornell Univ., 1953; Hibbert Lecturer, 1959; Chairman, Dove Cottage Trustees, 1961; Ballard Mathews Lecturer, University College of North Wales, 1964; Drew Lecturer, New Coll., University of London, 1967. *Publications:* Tendencies in Renaissance Literary Theory (Le Bas Prize Essay), 1922; The Seventeenth Century Background, 1934; The Eighteenth Century Background, 1940; Collected Essays and Studies by Members of the Eng. Assoc., Vol. XXXII, 1946, XLIV, 1958; Coleridge on Imagination and Fancy (British Acad. Warton Lecture, 1946); Chapter on English Thought in The Character of England (ed Sir Ernest Barker, 1947); Richard Crashaw Memorial Lecture, 1949; Nineteenth Century Studies, 1949; Introduction to Thoreau's Walden, 1951; Christianity Past and Present, 1952; (ed) Bacon and Donne in Major British Writers (New York), 1953; More Nineteenth Century Studies, 1956; The Religion of Nature (Essex Hall Lecture), 1957; Darwin and Butler: Two Versions of Evolution, 1959; The English Moralists, 1964; Centenary Introductions to Newman's Apologia and Quiller-Couch's Troy Town, 1964; Spots of Time, 1965; Cambridge and Other Memories, 1920-1953, 1969; Introduction to Mark Rutherford's Autobiography and Deliverance, 1969; Religion Today, 1969; various articles and reviews. *Relevant publication:* The English Mind (essays presented to Basil Willey, ed by H. S. Davies and G. Watson), 1964. *Recreations:* music; the English countryside. *Address:* 18 Adams Road, Cambridge. *Clubs:* Athenæum., Reform.

**WILLEY, Rt. Hon. Frederick Thomas,** PC 1964; MP (Lab) Sunderland North since 1950 (Sunderland, 1945-50); Member Council, Save the Children Fund; Barrister; *b* 1910; *s* of late Frederick and Mary Willey; *m* 1939, Eleanor, *d* of late William and Elizabeth Snowdon; two *s* one *d.* *Educ:* Johnston Sch.; St John's Coll., Cambridge Univ. (Full blue Soccer; 1st Class Hons Law; Blackstone Prizeman, Harmsworth Studentship, McMahon Studentship, etc.). Called to Bar, Middle Temple, 1936. Member Fabian Society. Parliamentary Private Secretary to Rt Hon. J. Chuter Ede, 1946-50; Chairman, Select Cttee on Estimates and member Select Cttees on Statutory Instruments and Public Accounts until 1950; Parliamentary Secretary to Ministry of Food, 1950-51; Director, North-Eastern Trading Estates Ltd, until 1950; River Wear Commissioner until 1950; Former Member of Consultative Assembly of the Council of Europe and Assembly of Western European Union; Minister of Land and Natural Resources, 1964-67; Minister of State, Ministry of Housing and Local Government, 1967; Chairman, Select Cttee on Education and Science, 1968-. *Publications:* Education, Today and Tomorrow, 1964; articles in various periodicals, legal and political. *Address:* 2 Harcourt Buildings, Temple, EC4. *T:* 01-353 2548; 11 North Square, NW11. *T:* 01-455 1870.

**WILLIAM-POWLETT, Vice-Admiral Sir Peveril (Barton Reibey Wallop),** KCB 1953 (CB 1949); KCMG 1959; CBE 1945; DSO 1942; RN retired; Governor of Southern Rhodesia, Nov. 1954-Dec. 1959; Chairman, Appledore Shipbuilders Ltd; *b* 5 March 1898; 2nd *s* of Major Barton William-Powlett; *m* 1923, Helen Constance (*d* 1965), *d* of James Forbes Crombie, Aberdeen; three *d*; *m* 1966, Mrs Barbara Patience William-Powlett, *widow* of Captain Newton William-Powlett, RN. *Educ:* Cordwalles Sch.; Osborne and Dartmouth. Midshipman, 1914; served European War, 1914-18, Gallipoli, Jutland; Lieut, 1918;

specialised in signals; Commander 1931; Captain, 1938; commanded HMS Frobisher, 1938-39; Director of Manning, 1939-40; comd HMS Fiji, 1941 (DSO); Chief of Staff Force 'H', 1941-42; comd HMS Newcastle, 1942-44; Captain of Fleet, Home Fleet, 1944-45 (CBE); Captain in command of Royal Naval Coll., Dartmouth, 1946-48; Naval Secretary to First Lord of the Admiralty, 1948-50; Flag Officer (destroyers), Mediterranean Fleet, 1950-51; Commander-in-Chief, South Atlantic, 1952-54; retired, 1954; Rear-Admiral, 1948; Vice-Admiral, 1950. KStJ. *Recreations:* Rugby (played for England, 1922); golf, shooting, and fishing. *Address:* 80 Old Church Street, Chelsea, SW3. *T:* 01-352 2624; Cadhay, Ottery St Mary, Devon. *T:* Ottery St Mary 2432. *Clubs:* United Service, Chelsea Arts.
*See also Sir Michael Colman, Bt.*

**WILLIAMS;** *see* Lloyd-Williams.

**WILLIAMS;** *see* Rees-Williams, family name of Baron Ogmore.

**WILLIAMS, A. Franklyn,** CMG 1960; *b* 5 Feb. 1907; *s* of Benjamin Williams and Katherine Williams (*née* Thomas); *m* 1st, Doris May (marr. diss., 1952), *d* of David I. and Sarah Jane Munro; one *s* decd; 2nd, 1952, Nancy, MBE, *d* of Evan John and Edith David. *Educ:* Ferndale Secondary Sch., Rhondda; University College of South Wales and Monmouthshire, Cardiff. BSc University of Wales, 1927. HM Inspector of Taxes, Inland Revenue, 1929-45; Ministry of Power, 1946-. Chairman, Coal Cttee of Economic Commn for Europe (ECE), 1952-55. Petroleum Attaché, HM Embassy, Washington, 1956-60; Senior Officer for Wales, Ministry of Power, 1960-61; Chairman, Welsh Bd of Health, 1962-69. CStJ 1968. *Recreation:* wood turning. *Address:* 45 Cyncoed Road, Cardiff. *T:* Cardiff 32334; *Clubs:* National Liberal, Royal Air Force; Cardiff and County (Cardiff).

**WILLIAMS, Alan John;** MP (Lab) Swansea West since 1964; *b* 14 Oct. 1930; *m* 1957, Mary Patricia Rees, Blackwood, Mon; one *s* one *d*. *Educ:* Cardiff High Sch.; Cardiff College of Technology; University College, Oxford. BSc (London); BA (Oxon). Lecturer in economics, Welsh College of Advanced Technology; Free-lance Journalist. Joined Labour Party, 1950. Member: Association of Teachers at Technical Institutes, 1958-; Fabian Society; Co-operative Party; National Union of Students delegation to Russia, 1954. Contested (Lab) Poole, 1959. PPS to Postmaster General, 1966-67; Parly Under-Sec., DEA, 1967-69; Parly Sec., Min. of Technology, 1969-70. Chairman, Welsh Parly Labour Party, 1966-67; Delegate: Council of Europe; WEU; Mem. Public Accts Cttee, 1966-67. *Address:* House of Commons, SW1; Hill View, Plunch Lane, Limeslade, Swansea. *Club:* Blackwood Golf.

**WILLIAMS, Alan (Lee);** *b* 29 Nov. 1930; *m* Karen Scott Holloway; two *s*. *Educ:* Roan Sch., Greenwich; Ruskin Coll., Oxford. Freeman of Company of Watermen and Lightermen, 1945-51; National Service, RAF, 1951-53; Oxford, 1954-56; National Youth Officer, Labour Party, 1956-62; Head of UNA Youth Dept, 1962-66; Visiting Lecturer (Part-time) in Politics and Economics, College of Further Education in SE London, 1962-66. MP (Lab) Hornchurch, 1966-70; PPS to Sec. of State for Defence, 1969-70; Leader, Govt Delegn to 4th Cttee of UN, NY, 1969; Vice-Chm., Labour Party Foreign Affairs Gp, 1968-70. Chairman, British Nat. Cttee, World Assembly of Youth, 1960-66; Vice-President, Council for European Nat. Youth Cttee, 1965-66; Joint Secretary, Gaitskell Youth Commn report, publ. 1959. Sec., All Party Parly River Thames Group; Vice-Pres., River Thames Soc.; Member: UNA Disarmament Cttee, 1966-; RUSI, 1967-. Freeman, City of London. *Publications:* Radical Essays, 1966; UN Assoc. pamphlet, UN and Warsaw and Nato Pacts; Fabian Soc. pamphlet on East/West Détente. *Recreations:* reading, history and novels, sailing, walking, tennis, cricket. *Address:* 9 Foxwood Road, Blackheath, SE3.

**WILLIAMS, Sir Alan (Meredith),** KCMG 1963 (CMG 1958); Ambassador to Spain, 1966-69; *b* 22 Aug. 1909; *s* of Thomas Charles Williams and Margaret Williams (*née* McGregor); *m* 1946, Masha Poustchine; one *s* one *d*. *Educ:* Berkhamsted Sch.; Pembroke Coll., Cambridge. Entered HM Consular Service, 1932, and served at San Francisco, Reykjavik, Leopoldville, Vienna, Panama, Hamburg, Rotterdam, Baghdad, Tunis and at the Foreign Office; Consul-General, New York, 1960-64; also for St Pierre amd Miquelon, 1961-64; Ambassador and Consul-General to Panama, 1964-66. *Recreations:* golf, walking, gardening. *Address:* 1 Morland Close, NW11; Cae Ffynnon, Llangystenin, Caernarvonshire. *Club:* Travellers'.

**WILLIAMS, (Albert) Clifford,** BEM, JP; *b* 28 June 1905; British; *m* 1929; one *d*. *Educ:* Primary Sch., Blaina, Mon. Trade Union Official, 1935-50. County Councillor, Monmouthshire; Alderman, 1964-; MP (Lab) Abertillery, April 1965-1970. *Recreations:* watching sports, Rugby football. *Address:* Brodawel, Abertillery Road, Blaina, Mon. *T:* Blaina 379.

**WILLIAMS, Sir Alexander (Thomas),** KCMG 1958 (CMG 1950); MBE 1936; *b* 13 July 1903; *s* of late John Williams; *m* 1931, Madeline O'Connor; two *s*. *Educ:* Bishop Foy Sch., Waterford; Trinity Coll., Dublin; Downing Coll., Cambridge. BA (Dublin). Cadet, Northern Rhodesia, 1928; District Officer, 1930; Assistant Chief Secretary, 1944; Administrative Secretary, 1947-52; Chief Secretary and Governor's Deputy, 1952-57; Governor and Commander-in-Chief of the Leeward Islands, 1957-59. Hon. LLD Dublin. KStJ 1958. *Recreation:* golf. *Address:* West Dormers, Cowes, Isle of Wight. *T:* Cowes 3657. *Clubs:* Travellers'; University (Dublin).

**WILLIAMS, Alfred Cecil,** CB 1961; Permanent Secretary, Ministry of Education for Northern Ireland, 1958-64; *b* 11 May 1899; *er s* of Owen R. Williams, Dublin and Holyhead; *m* 1926, Eileen Mary, *o d* of Alexander Poole Wilson, Dublin and Birkenhead; one *s* two *d*. *Educ:* St Andrew's Coll., Dublin; Trinity Coll., Dublin. Sizarship in Maths, 1st Place (TCD); Kidd Entrance Schol. 1st Place (TCD); Foundation Schol. (TCD); Senior Moderatorship in Maths, 1st Place; Senior Moderatorship in Experimental Science, 1st Place in Physics; University Studentship in Maths; Fitzgerald Schol. in Physics; BAI, 1st Place, Alexander Prize. Lecturer in Mathematics, Magee University Coll., Londonderry, 1922; Inspector of Schools, Ministry of Education for Northern Ireland, 1924; Senior Inspector of Schools, 1929; Senior Chief Inspector, 1943. Civil Service Commissioner for Northern Ireland, 1958-64. Hon. LLD (*jure dignitatis*) Dublin University. *Recreations:* gardening, music. *Address:* Delgany, 37 Hawthornden Road, Belfast BT4 3JW. *T:* Belfast 653078.

**WILLIAMS, Alfred Martyn,** CBE 1957; DSC; Commander RN retired; *b* 14 May 1897; *s* of J. C. Williams of Caerhays Castle, Cornwall. *m* 1920, Audrey Hester (*d* 1943), 2nd *d* of C.

Coltman Rogers, Stanage Park, Radnorshire; two *s* one *d*; *m* 1945, Dorothea Veronica, *widow* of Major F. F. Robins and *yr d* of Colonel W. H. Carver; one *s*. *Educ:* RN Colleges, Osborne and Dartmouth. MP (U) North Cornwall, 1924-29; High Sheriff of Cornwall, 1938; DL Cornwall, 1956. *Address:* Werrington Park, Launceston, Cornwall. *Club:* Brooks's.

**WILLIAMS, Prof. Alwyn,** FRS 1967; FRSE, MRIA, FGS, PhD (Wales); Professor of Geology, Queen's University of Belfast, since 1954, Pro-Vice-Chancellor since 1967; *b* 8 June 1921; *s* of D. D. and E. M. Williams; *m* 1949, E. Joan Bevan; one *s* one *d*. *Educ:* Aberdare Boys' Grammar Sch.; University College of Wales, Aberystwyth. Harkness Fund Fellow at US National Museum, Washington, DC, 1948-50; Lecturer in Geology in University of Glasgow, 1950-54. Pres., Palaeontological Assoc., 1968-70. Hon. Fellow, Geol Soc. of America, 1970. Bigsby Medal of Geol. Society of London, 1961. *Publications:* contrib. to Quarterly Journal of Geological Society of London; Geological Magazine; Washington Acad. of Sciences; Geological Society of America; Palaeontology; Journal of Paleontology, etc. *Address:* 8 Richmond Park, Stranmillis, Belfast BT9 5EF. *T:* Belfast 666548.

**WILLIAMS, Anthony James;** HM Ambassador at Phnom Penh, since 1970; *b* 28 May 1923; *s* of late Bernard Warren Williams, FRCS, and of Hon. Muriel B. Buckley. *m* 1955, Hedwig Gabrielle, Gräfin Neipperg; two *s* two *d*. *Educ:* Oundle; Trinity Coll., Oxford. Entered Foreign Service, 1945; served in: Prague; Montevideo; Cairo; UK Permanent Mission to UN, New York; Buenos Aires; UK Permanent Mission to 18 Nation Disarmament Conf., Western, United Nations and South East Asian Depts of Foreign Office. Counsellor, Head of Chancery, Moscow, 1965-67; IDC, 1968; Counsellor (Political), Washington, 1969-70. *Address:* c/o Foreign and Commonwealth Office, SW1; Jolly's, Salehurst, Sussex. *Clubs:* Beefsteak, United University.

**WILLIAMS, Rt. Rev. Anthony Lewis Elliott,** MA; DD; Sub-Prelate, Order of St John of Jerusalem, since 1956; *b* 5 Feb. 1892; *s* of George Robert Williams, MD, and Adelaide Frances Williams (*née* Murray); *m* 1922, Mary Freeman; one *s* three *d*. *Educ:* King's Sch., Worcester; Exeter Coll., Oxford; Salisbury Theological Coll. Curate: St John, Kidderminster, 1915-18; Christchurch, Harrogate, 1918-20; Vicar, North Stainley, Ripon, 1921-25; Rector, Kirkby Wiske, Thirsk, 1925-31; Vicar: Banbury, 1931-46; Bournemouth, 1946-56. Chaplain to the Bishop of Ripon, 1921-31; Dep. Priest-in-Ordinary to: King George VI, 1945-52; Queen Elizabeth II, 1952-56. Chaplain, Order of St John of Jerusalem, 1953-56. Bishop of Bermuda, 1956-62, resigned. Hon. Canon: Christchurch, Oxford, 1940-46; Winchester, 1950-56. *Publications:* The Two Ways, 1937; The Happy Heathen, 1938. *Recreations:* painting in oils, motoring, walking. *Address:* 7 Park Street, Woodstock, Oxon. *Clubs:* Athenæum; Oxford Union.

**WILLIAMS, Ven. Arthur Charles;** Archdeacon of Bodmin, 1962-68; Archdeacon Emeritus and Prebendary Emeritus of St Endellion, since 1969 (Rector, 1965-68); *b* 8 July 1899; *s* of Thomas John and Belle Williams, Truro; *m* 1929, Jessie Lucretia Boggia; one *d*. *Educ:* Truro Cathedral Sch.; College of the Resurrection, Mirfield. Joined Army, 1917 (PoW 1918). College of Resurrection, 1919-22. Curate of S Clements, Barnsbury, London, 1922-26; Curate of S Mary, Penzance, 1926-32; Vicar of Stratton, 1932-45; Rural Dean of Stratton, 1934-39 and 1943-45. CF, 1939-43, SCF 1940, Hon. CF 1943 (TA). Vicar of S Mary the Virgin, Penzance, 1945-62; Rural Dean of Penwith, 1959-62. Hon. Canon of Truro Cathedral, 1952; Fellow of Woodard Corporation, 1945-; Vice-Provost of the Western Division; Proctor in Convocation, 1957. *Address:* 4 Clarence Place, Penzance. *T:* Penzance 2798.

**WILLIAMS, Arthur de Coetlogon,** CSI 1946; CIE 1938; *b* 27 Sept. 1890; *s* of late E. de C. Williams; *m* 1919, Bethea Helen Field; one *s* two *d*. *Educ:* Winchester; Marlborough; Balliol Coll., Oxford. Entered ICS 1915. Army Service, 1916-19. Legislative Secretary and Legal Remembrancer, Bengal, 1935; Secretary, Viceroy's Executive Council, 1936; Secretary to the Governor-General and Government of India, Defence Co-ordination, 1938; Secretary to the Governor of Bengal, 1942; Chief Secretary, Bengal, 1943; Civil Supplies Commissioner, Bengal, 1945; Adviser to Governor of Bengal, retired, 1949. *Address:* Glencoe, Les Camps, St Martin's, Guernsey. *Clubs:* East India and Sports; Bengal (Calcutta).

**WILLIAMS, A(rthur) Emlyn,** VRD 1945; BSc, MB, BCh, FRCS Consultant Surgeon, Royal Free Hospital; Consultant Surgeon, Hampstead General Hospital, since 1948; Teacher in Surgery, Royal Free Hospital Medical School; *b* 11 April 1910; *o s* of late Obadiah and Ruth Williams, Cardiff; *m* 1940, Zoë Irene, *d* of late Major Richard Ralph Baldwin Wall, RA, and of Irene Edna Louisa Wall; four *s*. *Educ:* Cardiff High Sch.; University College, Cardiff; Welsh National School of Medicine; University of London (St Bartholomew's Hospital). Demonstrator and Tutor in Anatomy and Physiology, University College, Cardiff, 1935-36; House Surgeon, British Postgraduate Medical School, London, 1937-38. Surgical Specialist, RN, 1940-46 (Surgeon Lieut-Commander RNVR). Surgical Registrar, Hampstead General Hospital, 1946-48; Clinical Asst, St Peter's Hospital and St Mark's Hospital, London, 1946-50. Marsden travelling professorship to USA, 1953. Examiner in Surgery, London Univ. FRSocMed., Fellow Med. Soc. London, Hunterian Society, Fellow Assoc. of Surg., Great Britain. Freeman, City of London, 1952. *Publications:* contributions to learned journals and Societies; contrib. to official Naval Medical History of the War. *Recreations:* golf, sailing. *Address:* 112 Harley Street, W1. *T:* 01-935 1956; 3 Turner Drive, NW11. *T:* 01-458 1646; Pantyrhedd, Newport, Pembrokeshire. *Club:* RNVR.

**WILLIAMS, Sir (Arthur) Leonard,** GCMG 1968; Governor-General of Mauritius, since 1968; *b* 22 Jan. 1904; *o s* of late George Williams; *m* 1930, Margaret Wiggins. *Educ:* Holy Trinity C of E Elementary Sch., Birkenhead; The Labour Coll., London. Member Liverpool & N Wales District Council, NUR, 1920-21; Secretary, Birkenhead & District Joint Cttee, NUR, 1923-24; Staff Tutor, Liverpool Labour Coll., 1924-26; Tutor-Organiser, National Council of Labour Colleges, 1926-36; contested (Lab): Southport, 1929; Winchester, 1935. Secretary Leeds Labour Party, 1936-42; joined Labour Party Head Office Staff, 1942; Reg. Organiser, E and W Ridings of Yorks, 1942-46; Asst National Agent, 1946-51; National Agent, 1951-59; Nat. Agent and Dep. General Secretary, 1959-62; General Secretary, 1962-68. Editor, Leeds Weekly Citizen, 1937-44; Editor, Labour Organiser, 1952-62. *Recreations:* reading, walking, talking. *Address:* Government House, Le Réduit, Mauritius.

**WILLIAMS, Maj.-Gen. Arthur Nicholl,** CBE 1945 (OBE 1941); *b* 28 Oct. 1894; *y s* of late Rev. Canon W. H. Williams and Mrs Williams, Mathern, Mon; *m* 1919, Effie, *d* of late Englesbe Seon; one *s* one *d*. *Educ:* Stancliffe Hall, Matlock; Hereford Cathedral Sch. Entered RM, 2nd Lieut, 1913; served European War, 1914-18, and War of 1939-45 (despatches); retired, 1946; Manager, Conservative Central Board of Finance, 1951-65. *Address:* 901 Hood House, Dolphin Square, SW1. *T:* 01-834 9701. *Club:* United Service.

**WILLIAMS, Arthur Vivian,** CBE 1969; General Manager and Solicitor Peterlee (New Town) Development Corporation, since 1948, and of Aycliffe (New Town) Development Corporation, since 1954; *b* 2 Jan. 1909; *s* of N. T. and Gwendolen Williams; *m* 1937, Charlotte Moyra, *d* of Dr E. H. M. Milligan; three *s* one *d*. *Educ:* William Hulme's Grammar Sch., Manchester; Jesus Coll., Oxford. BA (Oxon), Final Honour Sch. of Mod. Hist. Admitted as Solicitor, 1936; Dep. Town Clerk of Finchley, 1938-41; Town Clerk of Bilston, 1941-46; Town Clerk and Clerk of the Peace, Dudley, 1946-48. *Recreation:* angling. *Address:* The Bryn, Newton Aycliffe, Co. Durham. *T:* Aycliffe 2987. *Club:* United Service.

**WILLIAMS, Maj.-Gen. Aubrey Ellis,** CBE 1944; DSO 1918; MC; *b* 19 May 1888; *s* of late Lieut-Colonel D. E. Williams, VD, JP, of Griffithstown, Mon; *m* 1922, Sybil (*d* 1966), *d* of late Dr J. R. Essex, The Woodlands, Pontypool, Mon; one *s* one *d*. *Educ:* Monmouth Grammar Sch.; Sandhurst. 2nd Lieut, South Wales Borderers, 1907; Lieut, 1909; Captain, 1914; Bt Major, 1918; Major, 1925; Bt Lieut-Colonel, 1930; Lieut-Colonel, 1934; Colonel, 1938; Maj.-General, 1940; served European War, 1914-19 (MC, DSO, Croix de Guerre, despatches five times); Waziristan, 1937 (Bar to DSO, despatches twice); War of 1939-45 (CBE); retired pay, 1941; re-employed, 1941-44; retired pay, 1944. Civil Defence Officer, Isle of Wight, 1950-60. *Address:* Blackbridge House, Freshwater Bay, IoW. *T:* Freshwater 2159; c/o Glyn, Mills & Co., Kirkland House, Whitehall, SW1. *Club:* Naval and Military.

**WILLIAMS, Barbara M.;** *see* Moray Williams.

**WILLIAMS, Basil Hugh G.;** *see* Garnons Williams.

**WILLIAMS, Prof. Bernard Arthur Owen;** Knightbridge Professor of Philosophy, University of Cambridge, and Fellow of King's College, Cambridge, since 1967; *b* 21 Sept. 1929; *s* of O. P. D. Williams, OBE and H. A. Williams; *m* 1955, Shirley Vivienne Teresa Brittain Catlin (*see* Mrs S. V. T. B. Williams); one *d*. *Educ:* Chigwell Sch., Essex; Balliol Coll., Oxford. BA (Oxon) 1951; MA 1954. Fellow of All Souls Coll., Oxford, 1951-54; RAF (Gen. Duties Br.), 1951-53; Fellow of New Coll., Oxford, 1954-59; Vis. Lectr, Univ. Coll. of Ghana, 1958-59; Lectr in Philosophy, Univ. Coll., London, 1959-64; Professor of Philosophy, Bedford College, London, 1964-67. Vis. Prof., Princeton Univ., USA, 1963; Vis. Fellow, Inst. of Advanced Studies, ANU, 1969; Mem., Institut International de Philosophie. Mem., Public Schools Commn, 1965-70. Trustee of Sadler's Wells. *Publications:* (ed with A. C. Montefiore) British Analytical Philosophy, 1966; Imagination and the Self (British Academy Lecture), 1966; articles in philosophical jls, etc. *Recreation:* music, particularly opera. *Address:* King's College, Cambridge; The Well House, Furneux Pelham, Buntingford, Herts.

**WILLIAMS, Mrs Bernard Arthur Owen;** *see* Williams, Shirley V. T. B.

**WILLIAMS, Sir Brandon M. R.;** *see* Rhys Williams.

**WILLIAMS, Prof. Bruce Rodda;** Vice-Chancellor and Principal of the University of Sydney since 1967; Chairman of the New South Wales State Cancer Council since 1967; Member, Reserve Bank Board, since 1969; *b* 10 January 1919; *s* of late Reverend W. J. Williams; *m* 1942, Roma Olive Hotten; five *d*. *Educ:* Wesley College; Queen's College, University of Melbourne. Lecturer in Economics, University of Adelaide, 1939-46 and at Queen's University of Belfast, 1946-50; Professor of Economics, University College of North Staffordshire, 1950-59; Robert Otley Prof., 1959-63, and Stanley Jevons Prof., 1963-67, Univ. of Manchester; Secretary and Joint Director of Research, Science and Industry Committee, 1952-59. Member National Board for Prices and Incomes, 1966-67; Econ. Adviser to Minister of Technology, 1966-67; Mem. Central Advisory Council on Science and Technology, 1967; Editor, the Sociological Review, 1953-59, and the Manchester Sch., 1949-67. Visiting Prof. of Economics, Univ. of Melbourne, 1962; President Economics Section of British Assoc., 1964; *Publications:* The Socialist Order and Freedom, 1942; (with C. F. Carter): Industry and Technical Progress, 1957, Investment in Innovation, 1958, and Science in Industry, 1959; Investment Behaviour, 1962; Investment Proposals and Decisions, 1965; Investment, Technology and Growth, 1967. Chapters in The Structure of British Industry (ed D. Burn), 1958. *Address:* The University of Sydney, Sydney, NSW 2006, Australia.

**WILLIAMS, Campbell (Sherston);** *see under* Smith, Campbell (Sherston).

**WILLIAMS, Carrington B.,** FRS 1954, MA, ScD (Cambridge); Chief Entomologist, Rothamsted Experimental Station, 1932-55; retired; *b* Liverpool, 7 Oct. 1889; *s* of Alfred and Lilian B. Williams; *m* 1920, Ellen Margaret Bain; three *s*. *Educ:* Birkenhead School; Clare Coll., Cambridge. Entomologist at John Innes Horticultural Institution, Merton, Surrey, 1911-16; Sugar Cane Entomologist, Dept of Agriculture, Trinidad, BWI, 1916-21. Sub-Dir and Dir Entomological Service, Ministry of Agriculture, Egypt, 1921-27; Entomologist to East African Agricultural Research Station, Amani, Tanganyika, 1927-29; Steven Lecturer in Agricultural and Forest Zoology, Edinburgh Univ., 1929-32; Guest Professor of Entomology, University of Minnesota, USA, 1932 and 1958. *Publications:* Migration of Butterflies, 1930; Insect Migration, 1958; Patterns in the Balance of Nature, 1964; numerous scientific papers on Entomology and related Sciences. *Address:* Elm Park Lodge, Selkirk, Scotland.

**WILLIAMS, Charles Frederick Victor,** CIE 1944; late ICS; *b* 1898; Director, National Union of Manufacturers, 1953-56, retired Nov. 1956. *Educ:* Pembroke College, Oxford. Joined ICS 1923; Under-Sec. Madras Govt 1928; Sec., 3rd Round Table Conference, London, 1932; Under-Sec., Govt of India, 1933; Dep. Secretary, Govt of India, 1934; Secretary, Agent-General for India in South Africa, 1935; Home Sec., Madras Govt, 1941; Jt Sec., Home Dept, Govt of India, 1945; Sec. to Governor-General (Public), 1947. *Address:* 16 Egerton Gardens, SW3. *Club:* East India and Sports.

**WILLIAMS, Charles Garrett,** DSc; Director: Ricardo & Co.; Ransomes, Sims and Jefferies; *b* 20 October 1901; *s* of Rev. John Williams; *m* 1926, Winifred, *d* of James Doody; one *s* one *d*. *Educ:* Mundella Sch., Nottingham; Manchester University. BSc London 1922; BSc Manchester 1922; DSc Manchester 1941. Research Engineer with Research Association of British Motor and Allied Manufacturers, 1923-29, Technical Sec., 1929-31; Research Manager of Instn of Automobile Engineers, 1931-34, Dir of Research, 1934-40; Dir of Research of Shell Thornton Aero-Engine Laboratory, 1940-48; Dir of Research of Thornton Research Centre, 1948-52; Director of Research, Shell Petroleum Co. Ltd, London, 1952-54; Director and General Manager, Shell Research Ltd, 1955-61. Chairman Automobile Div., IMechE, 1955-56; Mem., Duke of Edinburgh's Schools Science and Technology Cttee; Member Council, University of Surrey. *Publications:* collected researches on Cylinder Wear, 1940; numerous papers to Instn of Automobile Engineers, IMechE, Institute of Petroleum, etc. on internal combustion engine, fuels, lubricants, wear, etc., and on organisation of industrial research. *Address:* Shortlands, 7 Downside Road, Guildford, Surrey. *T:* Guildford 4775. *Club:* Athenæum.

**WILLIAMS, Charles Harold,** MA; Emeritus Professor of History in the University of London (Head, Department of History, and Assistant Principal, 1945-63, King's College); Fellow of King's College, London; *b* 12 May 1895; *s* of Charles and Margaret Williams; *m* 1930, Clare Ruth, *e d* of Justin E. Pollak; one *s* one *d*. *Educ:* Sidney Sussex Coll., Cambridge; University Coll., London. Asst Lecturer, University Coll., London, 1924; Reader in Constitutional History in the University of London, 1931; Asst Editor of History, 1928, Editor, 1934-47. Member of the Council of the Historical Assoc. *Publications:* England under the Early Tudors, 1925; The Making of the Tudor Despotism, 1928; Year Book 1 Henry VI (Vol. L of the Selden Soc. Publications, 1933); The Yorkist Kings, in Cambridge Medieval History, Vol. VIII, 1936; The Modern Historian, 1938; English Historical Documents, 1485-1558, 1967; William Tyndale, 1969; papers, reviews, etc, in historical periodicals. *Recreations:* walking, music. *Address:* 9 Blackfriars Street, Canterbury, Kent. *T:* Canterbury 63392. *Club:* Athenæum.

**WILLIAMS, Sir Charles Henry Trelease, (Sir Harry),** Kt 1970; CBE 1964; FIMechE, FIProdE; Chairman, Iron and Steel Industry Training Board, since 1964; Director, The Steetley Co. Ltd; *b* 11 May 1898; *s* of James Morgan Williams, Consett, Co. Durham and Letitia, *d* of John Henry and Lavinia Dwight Trelease; *m* 1925, Florence Alice, *d* of John William and Mary Ann Exley. *Educ:* Doncaster Road and South Grove Schs, Rotherham. Entered works of The Park Gate Iron & Steel Co. Ltd, as apprentice electrical fitter, 1912; The Park Gate Iron & Steel Co. Ltd: Engng Draughtsman, 1912; Asst Works Manager, 1928; Works Manager, 1936; Dir and Gen. Manager, 1945; Jt Man. Dir, 1948; Managing Director, 1953; Chm., 1960; Dir, Tube Investments Ltd, 1960; Chairman: Renishaw Iron Co. Ltd, 1960; Round Oak Steel Works Ltd, 1960; retired March 1966. Chm., British Iron and Steel Fedn Training Cttee, 1952-66. Master of The Company of Cutlers in Hallamshire, 1960-61. JP Rotherham, 1948-70. *Recreations:* music, golf, cricket. *Address:* Overdales, 4 Brunswick Road, Rotherham. *T:* Rotherham 2463; Park Gate Works, Rotherham. *T:* Rotherham 2141.

**WILLIAMS, Captain Charles Shrine;** *b* 27 Sept. 1895; *s* of William and Wilhelmina Williams; unmarried. *Educ:* Liverpool Institute. Commenced seafaring career, 1913; joined Cunard Steamship Co. Ltd, 1919; Captain of "Queen Elizabeth" from Nov. 1957; retired from active service, September 1958, as Commodore. *Address:* 64 Higher Road, Hunts Cross (Woolton), Liverpool. *T:* 051-486 1505.

**WILLIAMS, Dr Cicely Delphine,** CMG 1968; retired (except on demand); *b* 2 Dec. 1893; *d* of James Rowland Williams, Kew Park, Jamaica (Dir of Educn, Jamaica) and Margaret E. C. Williams (*née* Farewell). *Educ:* Bath High Sch. for Girls; Somerville Coll., Oxford; King's Coll. Hosp. DM, FRCP, DTM&H. Colonial Med. Service: appts, 1929-48. WHO Adv. in Maternal and Child Health, 1948-51; Research on Vomiting Sickness, 1951-53; Sen. Lectr in Nutrition, London, 1953-55; consulting visits to various countries, 1955-59; Vis. Prof. of Maternal and Child Health, Amer. Univ. of Beirut, 1959-64; Adv. in Trg Progrs, Family Planning Assoc., 1964-67. Milroy Lectr, RCP, 1958; James Spence Meml Medal, Br. Paed. Assoc., 1965; Goldberger Award in Clin. Nutrition, Amer. Med. Assoc., 1967. *Publications:* chapters in: Diseases of Children in the Tropics, 1954; Sick Children, 1956; The Matrix of Medicine, 1958; contrib. to: The Lancet, Archives of Diseases in Childhood, Tropical Pediatrics, etc. *Recreations:* people and solitude. *Address:* 57 Poplar Walk, SE24. *T:* 01-733 1678. *Club:* Royal Commonwealth Society.

**WILLIAMS, Clarence Faithfull M.;** *see* Monier-Williams.

**WILLIAMS, Cyril Herbert,** CMG 1956; OBE 1949; Master, Claremont School, since 1969; *b* 27 Dec. 1908; *s* of T. E. Williams; *m* 1936, Patricia Joy Collyer; one *s* two *d*. *Educ:* Bedford Modern Sch.; Jesus Coll., Camb. (MA). Colonial Service, Kenya, 1931; Provincial Commissioner, Nyanza Province, Kenya, 1951-56, retd; farming in Kenya, 1956-65; Mem., Kenya Council of State, 1961-64; Chm., Naivasha CC, 1961-64; Mem., Nyandarua CC, 1963; Deputy Chairman Appeal Tribunal, 1962-63, apptd under the Public Security (Restriction) Regulations. Master, Westerleigh School, 1965-66, Great Sanders School, 1966-69. *Recreations:* golf, tennis. *Address:* Nortons Farm, New House, Sedlescombe, Sussex. *Club:* East India and Sports.

**WILLIAMS, Cyril Robert,** CBE 1945; JP; *b* 11 May 1895; *s* of Rev. F. J. Williams, MA; *m* 1928, Ethel Winifred Wise; two *d*. *Educ:* Wellington College, Berks; New College, Oxford. Dist Loco. Supt, Khartoum, Sudan Rlys, 1923; Asst Mech. Engineer (Outdoor), 1924; Loco. Running Supt, 1927; Works Manager, 1932; Asst Chief Mech. Engineer, 1936; Deputy General Manager, 1939; General Manager, 1941. *Recreation:* philately. *Address:* Ballacree, Somerton, Som. *T:* Somerton 408.

**WILLIAMS, Sir (Daniel) Thomas,** Kt 1958; OBE 1953; JP 1942; FCIS; Lloyd's Underwriter; *y s* of late D. T. Williams, Civil Servant; *m* 1934, Bertha Mary (*d* 1969) *d* of David Morgan, Monmouthshire. Lord Mayor of Cardiff, 1956-57 (Deputy, 1951-52); Vice-Chairman, Wales and Monmouthshire Conservative Association and Chairman, Glamorgan Conservative Association, 1949-60. Member, Council for Wales and Monmouthshire, 1956-59; Past Chairman: Cardiff Bench of Magistrates; Cardiff and Barry Post Office Advisory Committee; Member, Central Executive Committee, NSPCC; Past

President: Cardiff and District Society of Incorporated Secretaries; Cardiff Incorp. Chamber of Commerce. KStJ; Past Pres. Welsh Amateur Boxing Assoc., and many other public bodies. Served War, 1914-18, RFC and RAF. Chevalier de la Légion d'Honneur. DL Glamorgan, 1955-68. *Address:* Freshwinds, Pleinmont, Guernsey, Channel Islands.

**WILLIAMS, Prof. David;** Professor of Mining Geology in the University of London (Imperial College), 1950-66, Emeritus Professor, since 1966; Geological Consultant; *b* 12 Oct. 1898; *s* of William and Laura Williams, Caernarvonshire, N Wales; *m* 1929, Dorothy Welland Shepard; two *d. Educ:* Holt Secondary School, Liverpool; University of Liverpool; Imperial College, London. DSc 1952, PhD 1925, MSc 1923, BEng 1921, Univ. of Liverpool; DIC. Geophysical Prospecting, N Rhodesia, 1926-28; Geologist, Rio Tinto Company, Spain, 1928-32; Lecturer in Geology, Imperial College, 1932-47, Reader in Mining Geology, 1947-50. Dean, Royal School of Mines, 1952-59. Secretary, Geological Society of London, 1942-51, Vice-Pres., 1951-53, 1964-65, Foreign Secretary, 1970-; Council, Institution of Mining and Metallurgy, 1948-70, Vice-President, 1954-57, President, 1960-61; Pres., Geologists' Assoc., 1958-60. Fellow, Imp. Coll. of Science and Technology, 1968. Lyell Medal, Geological Soc. of London, 1959. *Publications:* (with W. R. Jones) Minerals and Mineral Deposits, 1948; scientific papers in geological and mining journals. *Address:* Downsway, 315 Fir Tree Road, Epsom Downs, Surrey. *T:* Burgh Heath 52655.

**WILLIAMS, Prof. David;** Sir John Williams Professor of Welsh History, University College of Wales, 1945-67, retired, 1967; *b* 9 Feb. 1900; *y s* of David and Anne Williams, Llan-y-cefn, Pembrokeshire; *m* 1st, 1930, Irene Muriel Fothergill (*d* 1942); 2nd, 1952, Hilarie Margaret Waddington. *Educ:* University of Wales; Columbia University; Paris and Berlin. AM (Columbia); MA, DLitt (Wales). Lecturer, University College, Cardiff, 1930-45. Served European War of 1914-18, army; War of 1939-45, Man Power Officer for south-east Wales, Min. of Labour. *Publications:* John Frost: A Study in Chartism, 1939; A History of Modern Wales, 1950; The Rebecca Riots, a Study in Agrarian Discontent, 1955; John Penry: Three Treatises concerning Wales, 1960; contrib. Eng. Hist. Rev., American Hist. Rev., etc. *Address:* 2 Laura Place, Aberystwyth. *T:* 7407.

**WILLIAMS, Rear-Adm. David;** Flag Officer, Second in Command Far East Fleet, since Nov. 1970; *b* 22 Oct. 1921; 3rd *s* of A. E. Williams, Ashford, Kent; *m* 1947, Philippa Beatrice Stevens; two *s. Educ:* Yardley Court Sch., Tonbridge; RN College, Dartmouth. Cadet, Dartmouth, 1935. Served War of 1939-45 at sea in RN. Qual. in Gunnery, 1946; Comdr, 1952; Captain, 1960; Naval Asst to First Sea Lord, 1961-64; HMS Devonshire, 1964-66; Dir of Naval Plans, 1966-68; Captain, BRNC, Dartmouth, 1968-70; Rear-Adm. 1970. Grad. of US Naval War Coll., Newport, RI, USA. *Recreations:* sailing, tennis, gardening. *Address:* Green Meadow, Steep, Petersfield, Hants. *T:* Petersfield 2295. *Clubs:* United Service; Royal Dart Yacht; RN Sailing Assoc.

**WILLIAMS, Rear-Adm. David Apthorp,** CB 1965; DSC, 1942; *b* 27 Jan. 1911; *s* of Thomas Pettit Williams and Vera Frederica Dudley Williams (*née* Apthorp); *m* 1951, Susan Eastlake, 3rd *d* of late Dr W. H. Lamplough and *widow* of Surg. Cdr H. de B. Kempthorne, RN; one *s* two step *d. Educ:* Cheltenham College; Royal Naval Engineering College, Keyham. Joined RN, 1929. Served War, Engineer Officer, HMS Hasty, 1939-42 (DSC, despatches four times), 2nd Destroyer Flotilla, Med. Fleet, S Atlantic Stn, Home Fleet, E Med. Fleet; Sen. Engineer, HMS Implacable, 1942-45, Home Fleet, and 1st Aircraft Carrier Sqdn, British Pacific Fleet, Comdr (E) 1945; Capt. 1955; Rear-Adm. 1963; Dir Gen. Aircraft, Admiralty, 1962-64; Dir Gen., Aircraft (Naval), Ministry of Defence, 1964-65; retired list, 1965. Member, Panel of Chairmen of Interview Boards for Professional, Technical and Draughtsmen Class, Civil Service Commn. CEng, MIMechE. *Recreations:* various. *Address:* 3 Ellachie Gardens, Alverstoke, Hants. *T:* Gosport 83375. *Clubs:* Army and Navy; Royal Naval (Portsmouth).

**WILLIAMS, David Gwynne,** MA; Headmaster, The Crypt School, Gloucester, 1920-50, retired; *b* 4 Jan. 1886; *s* of Rev. John Alexander Williams and Louisa Jane Jones; *m* 1910, Henny, *d* of August Felbecker, Colmar, Alsace; two *s. Educ:* Llandovery College; Corpus Christi College, Oxford (Classical Scholar). 1st Class Lit. Hum. 1909; Classical VIth Form master at Reading, 1910; Durham, 1914; Bradford, 1915. *Publications:* Existentialist Sonnets, 1953; The Ascension of Man, 1966; Love in Escalation, 1968. *Recreation:* gardening. *Address:* 153 Finlay Road, Gloucester. *T:* Gloucester 24028.

**WILLIAMS, D(avid) Innes,** MD, MChir Cambridge, FRCS; Genito-urinary Surgeon, Hospital for Sick Children, Great Ormond Street, Royal Masonic Hospital, and St Peter's and St Paul's Hospitals; Civilian Consulting Urologist to Royal Navy, Urologist to King Edward VII Hospital for Officers; *b* 12 June 1919; *s* of late Gwynne E. O. Williams, MS, FRCS; *m* 1944, Margaret Eileen Harding; two *s. Educ:* Sherborne Sch.; Trinity Hall, Cambridge; Univ. College Hospital. *Publications:* Urology of Childhood, 1958; Paediatric Urology, 1968; various contributions to medical journals. *Address:* 61 Harley House, Marylebone Road, NW1. *T:* 01-935 7926; 9 Kidderpore Avenue, NW3. *T:* 01-435 4926.

**WILLIAMS, David James;** Executive Council Member, South Wales Miners' Federation; *b* 3 Feb. 1897. *Educ:* Elementary School; Central Labour College. Colliery Checkweighman. MP (Lab) Neath Division of Glamorgan, 1945-64. *Publication:* Combination in the Coal Industry, 1924. *Address:* Delfryn, Penscynor, Cilfrew, Neath, Glam. *T:* Neath 832.

**WILLIAMS, David John;** Assistant Secretary of Commissions, Lord Chancellor's Office, since 1966; *b* 10 July 1914; *s* of late James Herbert Williams and of Ethel (*née* Redman); unmarried. *Educ:* Lancing College; Christ Church, Oxford (MA). Called to Bar, Inner Temple, 1939. Served War of 1939-45, Royal Artillery. Practised as Barrister, Norwich, 1946-51; Resident Magistrate, Tanganyika, 1951-56; Senior Resident Magistrate, 1956-60; Judge of High Court of Tanganyika, 1960-62; retired, 1962. Postgrad. Dip. in Social Anthropology, LSE, 1965. *Recreations:* The arts and travelling. *Address:* Hillfield, Crawley Hill, Camberley, Surrey.

**WILLIAMS, David Wakelin,** MSc, PhD, FInstBiol, FRES, MBIM; Director, Department of Agriculture and Fisheries for Scotland, Agricultural Scientific Services, since 1963; *b* 2 Oct. 1913; *e s* of John Thomas

Williams and Ethel (*née* Lock); *m* 1948, Margaret Mary Wills, BSc, *d* of late Rev. R. H. Wills; one *s*. *Educ:* Rhondda Grammar School, Porth; University College, Cardiff. Demonstrator, Zoology Dept, Univ. Coll., Cardiff, 1937-38; Lectr in Zoology and Botany, Tech. Coll., Crumlin, Mon., 1938-39; research work on nematode physiology, etc. (MSc, PhD), 1937-41; biochemical work on enzymes (Industrial Estate, Treforest), 1942-43. Food Infestation Control Inspector (Min. of Food), Glasgow; Sen. Inspector, W Scotland, 1945; Scotland and N Ireland, 1946. Prin. Scientific Officer, Dept Agriculture for Scotland, 1948; Sen. Prin. Scientific Officer, 1961; Dep. Chief Scientific Officer (Director), 1963. Chairman, Potato Trials Advisory Cttee, 1963-; FInstBiol 1966 (Council Mem. Scottish Br., 1966-69). *Publications:* various on nematology and entomology. *Recreations:* music, electronics, photography, golf. *Address:* Agricultural Scientific Services, East Craigs, Edinburgh EH12 8NJ. *T:* 031-334 3361; 8 Hillview Road, Edinburgh EH12 8QN. *T:* 031-334 1108.

**WILLIAMS, Dr Denis (John),** CBE 1955; DSc; MD; FRCP; Senior Neurologist, St George's Hospital; Senior Physician, National Hospital, Queen Square; Senior Neurologist, King Edward VII Hospital for Officers; Hon. Neurologist, Star and Garter Home, Richmond; the Civil Consultant in Neurology, RAF and BOAC; Ministry of Aviation, Civil Consultant in Electro-encephalography, RAF and Army; Lecturer in Neurology, London University; the Consultant Adviser in Neurology, Ministry of Health, since 1966; Editor of Brain and of Modern Trends in Neurology; *b* 4 Dec. 1908; *s* of Rev. Daniel Jenkin Williams, MA, BD, Aberayron; *m* 1937, Joyce Beverley Jewson, JP, MB, BS, DPH; one *s* two *d*. *Educ:* Manchester Univ.; Harvard University. DSc (Physiol.), Manchester 1942 (MSc 1938, BSc 1929); MD (Gold Medal) Manchester 1935 (MB, ChB 1932); FRCP 1943 (MRCP 1937). After resident appts in Manchester and London, Prof. Tom Jones Mem. Fellow in Surgery; Halley Stewart Research Fellow, Med. Research Council; Rockefeller Travelling Fellow in Neurology. Hon. Research Fellow, Harvard Univ. Wing Comdr RAF; Air Crew Research and Clinical Neurology in Royal Air Force, 1939-45, and seconded to Royal Navy; since then Physician, Departments of Applied Electrophysiology, St George's and National Hosps. Chm., Academic Bd, Inst. of Neurology, 1965. Bradshaw Lecturer, Royal College of Physicians, 1955; Scott-Heron Lecturer, Belfast, 1960; Guest Lecturer, Canadian Medical Assoc., 1963; Hugh Cairns Lecturer, Adelaide, 1965; Bruce Hall Lecturer, Sydney, 1965; Guest Lecturer, RACP, 1965. Visiting Professor: Univ. of Cincinnati, 1963, 1969; St Vincent's Hosp. Sydney (Hon. Phys.), 1965. Mem. Council, Royal College of Physicians, London, 1960-63 (Chairman, Cttee on Neurology, 1965-); Pres., Sect. of Neurology, RSM, 1967; Sec. Assoc. of British Neurologists, 1952-60; Hon. Mem., American Neurological Assoc. and Canadian Neurological Assoc. Examr in Neurology: RCP; various Univs. *Publications:* Scientific articles dealing mainly with brain function, epilepsy, abnormal behaviour and electro-encephalography, in Brain, Modern Trends in Neurology, and other journals; Neurology, in Price's Medicine; Contrib. to Handbook of Neurology. *Recreations:* farming, gardening. *Address:* National Hospital, Queen Square, WC1. *T:* 01-837 3611; 11 Frognal Way, Hampstead, NW3. *T:* 01-435 4030; Woodlands House, Mathry, Pembs. *T:* St Nicholas 220. *Clubs:* Wayfarers', Royal Air Force.

**WILLIAMS, Donald;** *see* Williams, W. D.

**WILLIAMS, Captain Douglas,** MC; Special Correspondent of the Daily Telegraph; *b* 7 Oct. 1892; 2nd *s* of late G. D. Williams, Chief Editor of Reuters Agency, and *gs* of late W. J. Skerrett, DL, Finavara, Co. Clare; *m* 1948, Anna Wrenn Fulton, *o d* of late Everts Wrenn, Chicago, USA. *Educ:* Benedictine College, Ealing; privately in France and Germany. Joined Reuters, 1910; served in France, 1915-17, Royal Artillery (wounded); Staff Captain on Murmansk Expedition, 1918-19. Chief Editor of Reuters, 1922; joined Daily Telegraph Staff, 1933, as American Correspondent. War Correspondent for Daily Telegraph, 1939-40, and 1943-45; Lieut RA, July 1940; Director American Division of Ministry of Information, 1940-41; Press Adviser to Minister of State at Cairo, 1941-42. *Clubs:* White's; Racquet and Tennis (NYC).

**WILLIAMS, Douglas,** CVO 1966; Under-Secretary, Ministry of Overseas Development, since 1968; *b* 14 May 1917; *s* of James E. Williams and late Elsie Williams; *m* 1948, Marie Jacquot; no *c*. *Educ:* Wolverhampton Sch.; Exeter Coll., Oxford. Served War, 1939-46 (despatches): Major, RA. Colonial Office, 1947; Principal, 1949; Colonial Attaché, Washington, 1956-60; Asst Sec., Colonial Office, 1961; transferred to Min. of Overseas Development, 1967. *Address:* 14 Gomshall Road, Cheam, Sutton, Surrey. *T:* 01-393 7306.

**WILLIAMS, D(ouglas) Graeme;** Editor, Radio Times, 1954-68; *b* 17 Nov. 1909; *s* of late Graeme Douglas and of Winifred Maude Williams; *m* 1938, Jean Mary Drusilla White; one *d*. *Educ:* Downsend, Leatherhead; Wallingbrook, Chulmleigh. Joined BBC, 1927; successively Sub-Editor, Art Editor, and Dep. Editor, Radio Times. Served War of 1939-45, in Army, 1942-46; during last two years was member of staff, Army Bureau of Current Affairs. Editor, London Calling, 1950-54. *Publication:* Britain's Neighbours, 1948. *Recreations:* painting in oils, photography, gardening, golf. *Address:* 12 Oakley Street, Chelsea, SW3; Birklands, Hayling Island, Hants. *Club:* Hayling Golf.

**WILLIAMS, Sir Dudley;** *see* Dudley-Williams, Sir Rolf Dudley.

**WILLIAMS, E. C.,** DSc London, and MSc Manchester; now retired; Industrial Scientist; *b* 1892; *s* of late T. R. Williams, OBE, Newcastle upon Tyne; *m* 1918, Lilian (*d* 1966), *d* of J. H. Baxter, Crewe; two *s* one *d*. *Educ:* Christ's Hospital; (Grecian and Univ. Exhibr, 1911); Manchester University (Mercer Scholar 1914, Dalton Research Scholar 1917). University Rugby XV, 1911-14 and Lancs County Rugby XV, 1913-14; Capt. East Yorks Regiment, 1914-16; Research Staff and head of Intermediate Products Dept, British Dyestuffs Corporation (later Imperial Chemical Industries), 1916-21; Research Chemist to Joint Research Committee of National Benzole Association and University of Leeds, 1921-23, and member of that committee 1923-27; First Ramsay Memorial Professor of Chemical Engineering, University College, London, 1923-28; Director of Research, 1928-40, and Vice-President, 1935-40, Shell Development Co., California; originated supplies of 100 octane aircraft fuels to RAF and USAF prior to World War II, and took leading part in devel of petrochemical industry; scientific and technical adviser to Air Reduction Company, US Industrial Chemical Co., and American Cyanamid Co., 1940-41; Vice-President and Director of Research, General Mills, Inc.,

Minneapolis, 1941-42; Director, Distillation Products, Inc., 1941-42; Vice-Pres. and Director of Research, General Aniline and Film Corpn, New York (IG Farben's Chemical and Photographic Industry in USA), one of four directors appointed by US Government to reorganise and operate this industry after seizure, 1942-45; Director US Industrial Chemical Co., 1942-45; Vice-President and Director of Research, Schenley Industries Corpn, New York, 1945-50; member of first Council of the Institution of Chemical Engineers, London, also of councils of other British and American societies; member of committees of National Research Council, USA, and American Association for the Advancement of Science; Walker Medallist of American Institute of Chemical Engineers, 1942; Chm. Joint-Engineering Societies' Council Advisory Cttee (Fuels) to US Dept of State on industrial disarmament of Germany. *Publications:* scientific and technical papers. *Recreations:* riding, fishing, gardening. *Address:* Belden Hill, Wilton, Conn 06897, USA. *Clubs:* Athenæum; Century Association (NY).

**WILLIAMS, Edgar Trevor,** CB 1946; CBE 1944; DSO 1943; DL; Rhodes Trust since 1951 (Secretary since 1959); Hon. Fellow of Merton College, Oxford, since 1964; Fellow of Balliol College, Oxford, since 1945; a Pro-Vice-Chancellor, University of Oxford, since 1968; Editor, Dictionary of National Biography, since 1949; Chairman, Nuffield Provincial Hospitals Trust, since 1966; a Radcliffe Trustee; *b* 20 Nov. 1912; *e s* of late Rev. J. E. Williams; *m* 1938, Monica, *d* of late Professor P. W. Robertson; one *d*; *m* 1946, Gillian, *yr d* of Major-General M. D. Gambier-Parry, *qv*; one *s* one *d*. *Educ:* Tettenhall College; KES, Sheffield; Merton College, Oxford (Chambers Postmaster, 1931-34; First Class, Modern History, 1934; Harmsworth Senior Scholar, 1934-35; Junior Research Fellow, 1937-39; MA 1938); Asst Lectr, Univ. of Liverpool, 1936. Served War of 1939-45 (despatches thrice); 2nd Lieut (SRO), 1st King's Dragoon Guards, 1939; Western Desert, 1941; GSO1, Eighth Army (North Africa, 1942-43, Sicily and Italy, 1943); Brig., Gen. Staff I, 21st Army Gp, 1944-45; Rhine Army, 1945-46; Officer, US Legion of Merit, 1945. UN Security Council Secretariat, 1946-47. FRHistS 1947. Hon. Col Southern Comd Intelligence Unit (TA), 1958-61. Mem., Devlin Nyasaland Commn, 1959. DL Oxfordshire, 1964. President, OUCC, 1966-68; a Governor, St Edward's Sch., Oxford. Hon. LLD: Waynesburg Coll., Pa, 1947; Univ. of Windsor, Ontario, 1969; Hon. LHD, Williams Coll., Mass, 1965; Hon. PdD, Franklin and Marshall Coll., Pa, 1966; Hon. DLitt: Warwick, 1967; Hull, 1970; Hon. LittD Swarthmore Coll., Pa, 1969. *Address:* Rhodes House, Oxford. *T:* 55745. *Clubs:* Savile; MCC; Vincent's (Oxford).

**WILLIAMS, Maj.-Gen. Edward Alexander Wilmot,** CB 1962; CBE 1958; MC 1940; DL; *b* 8 June 1910; *s* of late Captain B. C. W. Williams, DL, JP, Herringston, Dorchester and of Hon. Mrs W. M. Williams (*er d* of 2nd Baron Addington); *m* 1943, Sybilla Margaret, *er d* of Colonel O. A. Archdale, MBE, late The Rifle Brigade, West Knighton House, Dorchester; one *s* three *d*. *Educ:* Eton; Royal Military College. 2nd Lieut 60th Rifles, 1930; Adjutant, 2nd Battalion (Calais), 1938-39. Served War of 1939-45; commanded 1st Bn 60th Rifles, 1944. Bt Lieut-Col, 1950; Directing Staff, Joint Services Staff College, 1950-52; commanded 2nd Bn 60th Rifles, 1954-55; Comdr 2nd Infantry Brigade, 1956-57; Imperial Defence College, 1958; Brigadier Author, War Office, 1959. GOC 2nd Div. BAOR, 1960-62: Chief of Staff, GHQ Far East Land Forces, May-Nov. 1962; General Officer Commanding Singapore Base District, 1962-63; Chairman, Vehicle Cttee, Min. of Defence, 1964; retired 1965; Colonel Commandant, 2nd Bn The Royal Green Jackets (The King's Royal Rifle Corps), 1966. DL Dorset, 1965. *Recreations:* fishing, shooting. *Address:* Herringston, Dorchester, Dorset. *T:* Dorchester 122. *Clubs:* Lansdowne, Pratt's; Royal Dorset Yacht.

**WILLIAMS, Brig. Edward Stephen Bruce,** CBE 1943; MA by decree Oxon 1934; *b* 2 Nov. 1892; *s* of late Maj.-Gen. Sir Hugh B. Bruce-Williams, KCB, DSO; *m* 1st, 1925, Elizabeth Frances Chadwyck-Healey (*d* 1934); 2nd, 1938, Evelyn Agnes Clay; two *s* two *d*. *Educ:* Winchester Coll.; (Inf. Coy) RMA Woolwich. 2nd Lt Rifle Bde, 1911; Capt. 1915; served France, Belgium, 1914 and 1917, Gallipoli, Egypt, 1915-16 (wounded twice, despatches, Legion of Honour 5th Class); Iraq operations, 1919-20; Bt Major, 1930; Lt-Col, Cmdg Oxford Univ. OTC, 1930-34; Bt Lt-Col 1934; Comd 2nd Bn Rifle Brigade, 1938-40; Palestine Ops 1939; Col 1940; Temp. Brig. 1940; BGS Scottish Command, 1941-42; BGS East Africa Command, 1943-46; psc; ns; retired pay, 1946. *Address:* The Old Rectory, Bramdean, Alresford, Hants. *T:* Bramdean 208.

**WILLIAMS, Edward Taylor,** CMG 1962; AMICE; retired as General Manager, Malayan Railway; Railway Adviser, Saudi Government Railroad, since August 1963; *b* Bolton, Lancashire, 15 October 1911; *s* of Edward and Harriet Williams; *m* 1940, Ethel Gertrude Bradley; one step *s* one step *d*. *Educ:* Accrington Grammar School; Manchester College of Technology. LMS Rly, pupil engineer, 1929-36; Sudan Rly, Asst Civil Engr, 1936-38; Metropolitan Water Board, Civil Engr, 1939-41; Malayan Rly, 1941-62 (Gen. Man. 1959-62). Interned in Singapore, in Changi and Sime Road, 1941-45. *Recreations:* all ball games, particularly cricket and golf. *Address:* Skerries, Watcombe Heights, Torquay. *T:* Torquay 87988; Dammam, Saudi Arabia.

**WILLIAMS, Emlyn,** CBE 1962; Hon. LLD Bangor; *b* 1905; *m* Molly O'Shann; two *s*. *Educ:* County School, Holywell; Geneva; Christ Church, Oxford (MA). *Plays:* A Murder has been Arranged; Glamour; Full Moon; Vigil; Vessels Departing; Spring, 1600; Night Must Fall; He Was Born Gay; The Corn is Green; The Light of Heart; The Morning Star; adaptation of A Month in the Country; The Druid's Rest; The Wind of Heaven; Trespass; Accolade; Someone Waiting; Beth; adaptation of The Master Builder. In addition to acting in most of these, has acted at the Old Vic, also in The Winslow Boy, Lyric, 1947; The Wild Duck, Saville, 1955; Season at Stratford-on-Avon, 1956. Shadow of Heroes, Piccadilly, 1958. As Charles Dickens (solo performance), Lyric (Hammersmith), Criterion, Duchess, 1951, Golden Theatre (New York), Ambassadors, 1952. As Dylan Thomas (A Boy Growing up: solo performance), Globe, 1955 and 1958, also Long Acre Theatre (New York), Oct. 1957. Acted in: Three, Criterion, 1961; Daughter of Silence, New York, 1961; A Man For All Seasons, New York, 1962; The Deputy, New York, 1964; World Tour as Dickens, 1964-65; as Charles Dickens, Globe, 1965; acted in A Month in the Country, Cambridge, 1965; Forty Years On, Apollo, 1969. *Films include:* The Last Days of Dolwyn (author, co-director, and star), 1948; Ivanhoe, 1950; Deep Blue Sea, 1955; I Accuse, 1957; The Wreck of the Mary Deare, 1959; The L-Shaped Room, 1962; Eye of the Devil, 1966; The

Walking-Stick, 1969; David Copperfield, 1969. *Publications:* (autobiog.) George, 1961; Beyond Belief, 1967. *Address:* 123 Dovehouse Street, SW3. *T:* 01-352 0208.

**WILLIAMS, Eric,** MC 1944; Writer; *b* 13 July 1911; *m* 1st, 1940, Joan Mary Roberts (decd); 2nd, 1948, Sibyl Grain, MBE; no *c. Educ:* Christ's College, Finchley. Served War of 1939-45, RAF, 1940-46; shot down over Germany as Flt Lt Dec. 1942; captured, and imprisoned in Stalag-Luft III; escaped Oct. 1943; returned to England Dec. 1943. Book buyer Lewis's Ltd, 1946-49; Scriptwriter, Wessex Film Productions Ltd, 1949-50. Set out on Twenty-year Slowest Expedition round the World, 1959. *Publications:* Goon in the Block, 1945; The Wooden Horse, 1949; The Tunnel, 1951; The Escapers, 1953; Complete and Free, 1957; Great Escape Stories, 1958, Dragoman Pass, 1959; The Borders of Barbarism, 1961; More Escapers, 1968; Great Air Battles, 1971. *Recreations:* travel, seafaring, fishing, fighting officiousness in all its forms. *Address:* Union Bank of Switzerland, Bern, Switzerland.

**WILLIAMS, Rt. Hon. Eric,** PC 1964; CH 1969; Prime Minister, Trinidad and Tobago, since 1961 (also Minister of External Affairs, 1961-64); *b* Trinidad, 25 Sept. 1911; *e s* of T. H. Williams. *Educ:* Tranquillity Boys' School and Queen's Royal College, Trinidad; St Catherine's Society, Oxford. BA 1932, Cl. I Hist., DPhil 1938. Howard University, Washington, DC; Assistant Professor of Social and Political Science, 1939; Associate Prof., 1944; Prof., 1947. Worked with Caribbean Commn and Research Council (Dep. Chm. latter, 1948-55). Founder and Polit. Leader, Peoples' National Movement, 1956; first Chief Minister and Minister of Finance, 1956; first Premier, 1959; led Trinidad and Tobago Delegns, London (US Bases Talks, 1960; WI Fedn Conf., 1961; Indep. Conf., 1961; Commonwealth PM's Conf., 1962), and at discussions with European Economic Commn, Brussels, 1962. Pro-Chancellor, Univ. of WI; Hon. Fellow, St Catherine's College, Oxford, 1964. Hon. DCL, Oxford, 1965. *Publications:* The Negro in the Caribbean, 1942; (Jt) The Economic Future of the Caribbean, 1943; Capitalism and Slavery, 1944; Education in the British West Indies, 1950; History of the People of Trinidad and Tobago, 1962; Documents of West Indian History, Vol. I, 1492-1655, 1963; Inward Hunger: the Education of a Prime Minister, 1969; From Columbus to Castro: the history of the Caribbean 1492-1969, 1970; articles in learned jls. *Address:* Prime Minister's Residence, La Fantasie Road, Port-of-Spain, Trinidad.

**WILLIAMS, Eric Charles,** CB 1969; Chief Scientist (Energy), Ministry of Technology (formerly Chief Scientist Ministry of Power), since 1968; *b* 15 May 1915; *s* of Charles Henry Williams and Agnes (*née* Turner); *m* 1946, Elisabeth Ruby Alice Bryan; one *s* one *d. Educ:* King Edward VI School, Stratford upon Avon; University of Birmingham. BSc (Hons 1st Cl.) 1935, MSc 1936. Joined Civil Service, 1936, at Bawdsey Research Station, Air Ministry; Hon. Wing Commander, RAF, 1943-45; attended Imperial Defence Coll., 1947; Asst Scientific Adviser, Air Ministry, 1948-49; Director of Operational Research, Admiralty, 1949-54; Scientific Adviser, Intelligence, Min. of Defence, 1955-60; Director, SHAPE Technical Centre, 1960-64; Chief Scientific Adviser, MoT, 1964-67. *Recreations:* cricket, gardening. *Address:* 17 Dealtry Road, Putney, SW15. *T:* 01-788 7187. *Club:* Athenæum.

**WILLIAMS, Brig. Eric Llewellyn Griffith G.;** *see* Griffith-Williams.

**WILLIAMS, Francis John Watkin,** QC 1952; JP; Recorder of Chester since 1958; Chairman, Anglesey Quarter Sessions since 1960 (Deputy Chairman, 1949-60); Chairman Flint Quarter Sessions since 1961 (Deputy Chairman, 1953-61); Deputy Chairman, Cheshire Quarter Sessions, since 1952; *b* Anglesey, 24 Jan. 1905; *s* of Col Lawrence Williams, OBE, DL, JP; *heir-pres.* to *b,* Sir Reginald Lawrence William Williams, 7th Bt, *qv*; *m* 1932, Brenda, *d* of Sir John Jarvis, 1st Bt; four *d. Educ:* Malvern College; Trinity Hall, Cambridge. Barrister of Middle Temple, 1928. Served War of 1939-45; Wing Comdr, RAFVR. Recorder of Birkenhead, 1950-58. JP Denbighshire, 1951; Chm. Medical Appeal Tribunal for N Wales Areas, 1954-57; High Sheriff: of Denbighshire, 1957, of Anglesey, 1963. Chancellor, Diocese of St Asaph, 1966. Freeman of City of Chester, 1960. *Address:* 2 Harcourt Buildings, Temple, EC4. *T:* 01-353 8415; (residence) Llys Meirchion, Denbigh. *T:* 69. *Clubs:* Oxford and Cambridge University; Grosvenor (Chester).
*See also Sir Charles Kimber, Bt.*

**WILLIAMS, Frank Denry Clement,** CMG 1956; *b* 3 May 1913; *s* of Frank Norris Williams and Joanna Esther Williams; *m* 1941, Traute Kahn; no *c. Educ:* Leighton Park School, Reading; London School of Economics (BSc Econ.). Cadet, Colonial Administrative Service, 1946; Asst Financial Sec., Nigeria, 1952; Financial Secretary: Jamaica, 1954; Federation of Nigeria, 1956; Economic Adviser, Federation of Nigeria, 1957-58; Permanent Secretary, Prime Minister's Dept, Fedn of The W Indies, 1958-62; Financial Sec., The Gambia, 1962-65. *Recreations:* walking, languages. *Address:* Siggiewi, Malta, GC.

**WILLIAMS, Prof. Frederic Calland,** CBE 1961 (OBE 1945); FRS 1950; FIEE 1950; FIRE 1957; Professor of Electrical Engineering at Manchester University since 1946; Part-time Member, North-West Electricity Board, since 1963; Director, Granada Television Ltd, since 1968; *b* 26 June 1911; *s* of F. Williams and E. A. Williams (*née* Smith); *m* 1938, Gladys Ward; one *s* one *d. Educ:* Stockport Grammar School; Manchester University; Magdalen College, Oxford. Manchester Univ., 1929-33, BSc 1932, MSc 1933; Metropolitan Vickers Elec. Co. Ltd, College Apprentice, 1933-34; Oxford Univ., 1934-36, DPhil 1936. Assistant Lecturer, Manchester University, 1936-39; DSc 1939. Scientific Civil Service, Bawdsey and Telecommunications Research Estab., Malvern, 1939-46. Rank, on leaving, Principal Scientific Officer. First holder of the Benjamin Franklin Medal, Royal Society of Arts, 1957; John Scott Award, City of Philadelphia, 1960; Hughes Medal, Royal Society, 1963. Hon. DSc Durham, 1964; Hon. DEng Liverpool, 1966. *Publications:* (Collab. ed.) Vols 19 and 20 of Radiation Laboratory Series. Scientific papers in: Jl Institution of Electrical Engineers; Proc. Royal Soc.; Wireless Engineer; Post Office Electrical Engineers' Journal; Proc. Cambridge Philosophical Society. *Address:* Spinney End, The Village, Prestbury, Cheshire.

**WILLIAMS, George W.;** *see* Wynn-Williams.

**WILLIAMS, Gerald Wellington,** JP; *b* 1903; *s* of Wellington Archbold Williams, JP, Shernfold Park, Frant, Sussex; *m* 1930, Mary Katharine Victoria, *d* of Captain Joscelyn Heber-Percy, DL, JP, East Lymden, Ticehurst, Sussex; one *s* two *d. Educ:* Eton; Christ Church, Oxford (MA). RNVR, 1939 (Lt-Comdr 1942). MP (C) Tonbridge division of Kent, 1945-56, resigned.

High Sheriff of Kent, 1968-69. *Address:* Crockham House, Westerham, Kent. *T:* Crockham Hill 215. *Clubs:* Carlton, Pratt's, MCC.

**WILLIAMS, Lady (Gertrude),** CBE 1963; Professor of Social Economics, University of London, 1955, Professor Emeritus since 1964; *b* 11 January 1897; *d* of I. Rosenblum; *m* 1919, Sir William Emrys Williams, *qv*; no *c*. *Educ:* Manchester University; London School of Economics. Apptd to Dept of Social Studies and Economics, Bedford Coll., Univ. of London, 1919, since when has been attached to this dept as: Special Lecturer in Economics, Reader in Social Economics, now Professor, Min. of Home Security and Min. of Labour and Nat. Service, 1940-42. Member of many Govt cttees of Enquiry. Member Central Training Council, 1964. *Publications:* The State and the Standard of Living, 1936; The Price of Social Security, 1946; Women and Work, 1946; Economics of Everyday Life (Pelican), 1950; Recruitment to Skilled Trades, 1957; Apprenticeship in Europe: The Lesson for Britain, 1963; The Coming of the Welfare State, 1967; articles in Economic Jl, etc. *Recreations:* travel; ballet, opera. *Address:* Grenville Paddock, Haddenham, Bucks. *T:* Haddenham 464. *Clubs:* Royal Over-Seas League, Cowdray.

**WILLIAMS, Gilbert Milner,** CB 1956; CBE 1950; retired from Civil Service, 1961; *b* London, 27 May 1898; *o s* of late H. Noel Williams; *m* 1927, Vera, *y d* of Carl Salling; two *d* (one *s* decd). *Educ:* Merchant Taylor's School. Barrister-at-law (Gray's Inn). Served European War, 1915-19 (RE); Admty, 1919-28; Min. of Labour, 1928-44; Assistant Secretary, Ministry of National Insurance, 1945-53; Under-Secretary for Finance and Accountant-General, Ministry fof Pensions and National Insurance, 1953-57, and Director of Establishments and Organisation, 1957-61. *Address:* 61 The Avenue, Watford, Herts. *T:* Watford 26761. *Club:* Royal Commonwealth Society.

**WILLIAMS, Prof. Glanmor;** Professor of History, University College of Swansea since 1957; National Governor of BBC for Wales since 1965; *b* 5 May 1920; *s* of Daniel and Ceinwen Williams, Dowlais, Glam; *m* 1946, Margaret Fay Davies; one *s* one *d*. *Educ:* Cyfarthfa Grammar Sch., Merthyr Tydfil; Univ. Coll. of Wales, Aberystwyth. MA 1947; DLitt 1962. Univ. Coll. of Swansea: Asst Lectr in History, 1945; Sen. Lectr, 1952. FRHistS 1954. *Publications:* Yr Esgob Richard Davies, 1953; The Welsh Church, 1962; Owen Glendower, 1965; Welsh Reformation Essays, 1968. Editor, Glamorgan County History. Contrib. to: History, Welsh History Review, etc. *Recreations:* walking, gramophone, cine-photography. *Address:* 11 Grosvenor Road, Swansea. *T:* Swansea 24213. *Club:* National Liberal.

**WILLIAMS, Glanville Llewelyn,** QC 1968, FBA 1957; Fellow of Jesus College, Cambridge, since 1955, and Rouse Ball Professor of English Law in the University of Cambridge, since 1968 (Reader, 1957-65; Professor, 1966); *b* 15 Feb. 1911; *s* of B. E. Williams, Bridgend, Glam; *m* 1939, Lorna Margaret, *d* of late F. W. Lawfield, Cambridge; one *s*. *Educ:* Cowbridge; University College of Wales, Aberystwyth; St John's Coll., Cambridge. Called to the Bar, 1935; PhD (Cantab), 1936; Research Fellow of St John's Coll., 1936-42; LLD (Cantab), 1946; Reader in English Law and successively Professor of Public Law and Quain Professor of Jurisprudence, University of London, 1945-55; Carpentier Lecturer in Columbia Univ., 1956; Cohen Lecturer in Hebrew University of Jerusalem, 1957; first Walter E. Meyer Visiting Research Professor, New York Univ., 1959-60; Charles Inglis Thompson Guest Professor, University of Colorado, 1965. Special Consultant for the American Law Institute's Model Penal Code, 1956-58; Member: Standing Cttee on Criminal Law Revision, 1959-; Law Commn's Working Party on Codification of Criminal Law, 1967-. Ames Prize, Harvard, 1963; (joint) Swiney Prize, RSA, 1964. Hon. LLD, University of Nottingham, 1963. *Publications:* Liability for Animals, 1939; chapters in McElroy's Impossibility of Performance, 1941; The Law Reform (Frustrated Contracts) Act (1943), 1944; Learning the Law, 1st edn 1945, 8th edn 1969; Crown Proceedings, 1948; Joint Obligations, 1949; Joint Torts and Contributory Negligence, 1950; Criminal Law; The General Part, 1st edn 1953, 2nd edn 1961; The Proof of Guilt, 1st edn 1955, 3rd edn 1963; The Sanctity of Life and the Criminal Law, American edn 1956, English edn 1958; The Mental Element in Crime, 1965; articles in legal periodicals. *Address:* Merrion Gate, Gazeley Road, Cambridge CB2 2HB. *T:* Trumpington 3175.

**WILLIAMS, Rev. Dr Glen Garfield;** General Secretary, Conference of European Churches, since 1968; *b* 14 Sept. 1923; *s* of John Archibald Douglas Williams and Violet May (*née* Tucker); *m* 1945, Velia Christina (*née* Baglio). *Educ:* Newport High Sch.; Universities of Wales (Cardiff), London, Tübingen. Military Service, 1943-47. Univ. studies, 1947-55. Minister, Dagnall Street Baptist Church, St Albans, 1955-59; European Area Secretary, World Council of Churches, Geneva, 1959-68. *Publications:* contrib. to Handbook on Western Europe, 1967, etc.; numerous articles, mainly in Continental journals. *Recreations:* travel, reading, archæology. *Address:* c/o 150 Route de Ferney, 1211 Geneva 20, Switzerland. *T:* (022)33.34.00.

**WILLIAMS, Sir Griffith Goodland,** KBE, *cr* 1949; CB 1945; retired; *b* 20 Sept. 1890; *o* surv. *s* of late Alfred Augustus Williams and late Mrs E. F. Ambrose; unmarried. *Educ:* Westminster; Christ Church, Oxford. Assistant Master at Wellington and Lancing; European War, 1914-18, Captain 4th Dorsets, General Staff Officer AHQ India, Poona Brigade, and GHQ Mes. Exp. Force; Board of Education, 1919; Principal Private Secretary to Earl of Halifax, 1935, Colonel Oliver Stanley, 1935-37; Deputy Secretary Ministry of Education, 1946-Dec. 1953. Comr for Boy Scouts, City of Westminster, 1925-35. Governor of Eastbourne College. Secretary, Churches Main Cttee, 1954-70. *Recreation:* music. *Address:* 52 Crammer Court, Sloane Avenue, SW3. *T:* 01-589 4347. *Club:* Athenæum.

**WILLIAMS, Rt. Rev. Gwilym Owen;** *see* Bangor, Bishop of.

**WILLIAMS, Sir Gwilym (Tecwyn),** Kt 1970; CBE 1966; President, National Farmers' Union, 1966-70 (Member Council, 1948-; Vice-President, 1953, 1954, 1960-62; Deputy President, 1955, 1963-65); *b* 1913; *s* of David and Margaret Williams; *m* 1936, Kathleen, *d* of John and Maria Edwards; two *s* one *d*. *Educ:* Llanfyllin CSS; Llysfasi Farm Inst.; Harper Adams Agric. Coll. Leader, Employers' side, Agricultural Wages Board, 1960-66; Director, FMC Ltd, 1962. Potato Marketing Board: Member, 1954-58; Chairman, 1955-58; Special Member, 1961-66. *Recreations:* trout fishing, shooting. *Address:* Longford Grange,

Newport, Shropshire. *T:* Lilleshall 229. *Club:* Farmers'.

**WILLIAMS, Harley;** *see* Williams (J. H.) H.

**WILLIAMS, Lt-Gen. (Hon.) Sir Harold,** KBE 1956 (CBE 1946); CB 1953; FICE, MIE (Ind.), MIS (Ind.); Major-General (Hon.) late Corps of Royal Engineers, retired; Lieutenant-General (Hon.) Indian Army; Colonel Commandant, Corps of Engineers, IA. 1951-55; *b* 1 June 1897; *e s* of late Hillas Williams. *Educ:* Mountjoy Sch., Dublin; RMA, Woolwich; Gonville and Caius Coll., Cambridge. Joined 1st KGO Bengal Sappers and Miners, 1918. Served European War, 1914-18 Aden Field Force; Adj. King George's Own Bengal Sappers and Miners, 1929-33; Ind. Mil. Acad., 1933-36; Bt Major, 1934; Professor of Civil Engineering, Roorkee Coll., 1936-38; CRE 1st Armd Div., 1940-41; Brig. Eng. Staff, GHQ, India, 1942-43; Chief Engineer, 4 Corps, Assam and Burma (despatches), 1943-44; Comdt SME India, 1945-47; Chief Engineer, Southern Command, 1947; Engineer-in-Chief, Indian Army, 1948-55. Retired from Regular Army, 1956. Director, Central Building Research Institute, India, 1955-62; Adviser to Council of Scientific and Industrial Research, India, 1962-64; Consultant, Planning Commn, Government of India, 1965-67. Member Council, Inst. CE, 1951-54, 1958-61. President Inst. of Engineers (Ind.), 1954-55; President, Inst. of Surveyors (Ind.), 1954-55. MBOU. *Publications:* various papers in scientific and technical journals. *Address:* 5 Greenhill Court, Sherborne, Dorset. *T:* Sherborne 3383. *Clubs:* United Service, Alpine; Himalayan (Calcutta; President, 1960-64).

**WILLIAMS, Very Rev. Harold Claude Noel;** Provost of Coventry Cathedral since 1958; *b* 6 Dec. 1914; *s* of Charles Williams and Elizabeth Malherbe, Grahamstown, S Africa; *m* 1940, Pamela Marguerite Taylor, Southampton; two *s* two *d* (and one *d* decd). *Educ:* Graeme Coll., S Africa; Durham Univ.; Southampton Univ. Ordained, 1938; Curate of Weeke, Winchester, 1938-40; Principal, St Matthew's Coll., S Africa, 1941-49; Vicar of Hyde, Winchester, 1950-54; Rector of St Mary's, Southampton, 1954-58. Hon. LLD Valparaiso Univ., USA. *Publications:* African Folk Songs, 1948; (ed) Vision of Duty, 1963; Twentieth Century Cathedral, 1964; Coventry Cathedral and its Ministry, 1965; Nothing to Fear, 1967; Coventry Cathedral in Action, 1968; Basics and Variables, 1970. *Recreations:* mountaineering and fishing. *Address:* The Provost's House, Coventry. *T:* Coventry 74868. *Club:* Alpine.

**WILLIAMS, Air Vice-Marshal Harold Guy L.;** *see* Leonard-Williams.

**WILLIAMS, Harri Llwyd H.;** *see* Hudson-Williams.

**WILLIAMS, Sir Harry;** *see* Williams, Sir Charles H. T.

**WILLIAMS, Rev. Harry Abbott;** Community of the Resurrection, since 1969; *b* 10 May 1919; *s* of Captain Harry Williams, RN, and Annie Williams. *Educ:* Cranleigh Sch.; Trinity Coll., Cambridge; Cuddesdon Coll., Oxford. BA 1941; MA 1945. Deacon, 1943; Priest, 1944. Curate of St Barnabas, Pimlico, 1943-45; Curate of All Saints, Margaret Street, 1945-48; Chaplain and Tutor of Westcott House, Cambridge, 1948-51; Fellow of Trinity Coll., Cambridge, 1951-69; Dean of Chapel, 1958-69, and Tutor, 1958-68; Exam. Chaplain to Bishop of London, 1948-69; Member, Anglican delegation to Russian Orthodox Church, Moscow, 1956; Select Preacher, University of Cambridge, 1950 and 1958; Hulsean Preacher, 1962. Licensed to officiate in Dio. of Ely, 1948- . *Publications:* Jesus and the Resurrection, 1951; God's Wisdom in Christ's Cross, 1960; The Four Last Things, 1960; The True Wilderness, 1965; contribs to: Soundings, 1962; Objections to Christian Belief, 1963; The God I Want, 1967. *Recreations:* idleness and religion. *Address:* House of the Resurrection, Mirfield, Yorks.

**WILLIAMS, Sir Henry Morton Leech,** Kt 1961; MBE 1945; Managing Director, Guest, Keen, Williams Ltd, 1952-62; President, Bengal Chamber of Commerce and Industry, and President, Associated Chambers of Commerce, India, 1960; *b* 1913; *s* of late O. R. Williams; *m* 1945, Bridget Mary, *d* of late C. G. Dowding; two *s* two *d*. *Educ:* Harrow; Corpus Christi Coll., Cambridge. Served War of 1939-45 (despatches, MBE), becoming Major, REME. CC Berkshire, 1967. *Address:* Stanford Place, Faringdon, Berks.

**WILLIAMS, Ian Malcolm Gordon,** CBE 1960 (OBE 1954; MBE 1945); *b* 7 May 1914; *s* of late Thomas and Mabel Williams. *Educ:* Tatterford Sch., Norfolk; Leeds Univ.; Gonville and Caius Coll., Cambridge. President, Leeds University Students' Union, 1939. Volunteered Military Service, Sept. 1939; Officer Cadet, 123 OCTU; Commnd Royal Regt of Artillery, March 1940; NW Frontier of India and Burma, 1940-45, as Major, RA, and Mountain Artillery, Indian Army (despatches, MBE). Staff Officer, Hong Kong Planning Unit, 1946; Adjutant, Hong Kong Defence Force, 1946. Entered Colonial Administrative Service, 1946; was District Officer and Asst Colonial Secretary, Hong Kong, 1946-49; at Colonial Office, 1949-51; Senior Asst Secretary, Secretariat, Cyprus, 1951-53; Commissioner: of Paphos, 1953-55, of Larnaca, 1955-57, of Limassol, 1957-60; Chief Officer, Sovereign Base Areas of Akrotiri and Dhekelia, 1960-64. Member Administrator's Advisory Board; UK Chairman, Joint Consultative Board, 1960-64. *Recreations:* art, Cypriot archæology, swimming. *Address:* White House, Adderbury, near Banbury, Oxfordshire. *Club:* East India and Sports.

**WILLIAMS, Ivor M. B.;** *see* Bankes-Williams.

**WILLIAMS, (J. H.) Harley,** OBE 1950; MD; Physician and Author; Barrister-at-Law; *s* of John and Lilian Williams; *m* 1941, Elizabeth Mackay Pascoe. *Publications:* A Century of Public Health, 1929; Northern Lights and Western Stars, 1938; The Inheritors, 1939; Fingal's Box, 1941; At Cape Faithful, 1943; Doctors Differ, 1946; Men of Stress, 1948; The Healing Touch, 1949; Between Life and Death, 1951; The Conquest of Fear, 1952 (Swedish trans. 1953); Don Quixote of the Microscope, 1954 (Spanish trans. 1955); A Doctor looks at Miracles, 1959; Great Biologists, 1961; The Will to Health, 1961; Your Heart, 1970. *Recreations:* the arts. *Address:* Cloisters, Temple, EC4. *Club:* Reform.

**WILLIAMS, Ven. John Charles;** Archdeacon of Dudley, since 1968; Vicar of Dodderhill, Droitwich, since 1970; *b* 17 July 1912; *s* of William and Edith Williams; *m* 1940, Agnes Mildred Hutchings, MA; one *s* one *d*. *Educ:* Cowbridge Sch.; St David's, Lampeter; University College, Oxford. Asst Curate, Christ Church, Summerfield, Birmingham, 1937-39; Asst Curate, Hales Owen, in charge of St Margaret's, Hasbury, 1939-43; Vicar: Cradley Heath, Staffs, 1943-48; Redditch,

Worcs, 1948-59. Surrogate, 1951-; Rural Dean of Bromsgrove, 1958-59; Rector, Hales Owen, 1959-70. Hon. Canon, Worcester Cathedral, 1965-; Examng Chaplain to Bishop of Worcester, 1969-. *Publication:* One Hundred Years, 1847-1947; A History of Cradley Heath Parish. *Recreations:* history of architecture, sailing, poultry breeding. *Address:* Archdeacon's House, Dodderhill, Droitwich, Worcs WR9 0BE. *T:* Droitwich 3301. *Clubs:* Oxford University Occasionals, Oxford and Cambridge University.

**WILLIAMS, Sir John (Francis),** Kt 1958; Chairman, The Herald and Weekly Times Ltd, Melbourne, 1964-69; *b* Grafton, New South Wales, 16 June 1901; *s* of Edward and Susan Williams; *m* 1931, Mabel Gwendoline Dawkins, Adelaide, SA; one *s*. *Educ:* Sydney High Sch. Managing Editor, Barrier Miner, Broken Hill, NSW, 1933-35; Managing Director, Queensland Newspapers Pty Ltd, Brisbane, 1937-46; Editor-in-Chief, Herald and Weekly Times Ltd, Melbourne, 1946-55, Managing Director, 1955. *Address:* Herald-Sun Office, Melbourne, Victoria 3000, Australia.

**WILLIAMS, Ven. John Frederick;** Archdeacon of Llandaff since 1969, and Priest-in-charge, Penmark; *b* 9 March 1907; *s* of John Abraham and Lydia Miriam Williams; *m* Millicent Jones (JP 1951); one *d*. *Educ:* Friars' School, Bangor; University of Wales. Curate: Portmadoc, Caerns, 1930; Aberdare, Glam, 1933; Vicar: Miskin, Glam, 1937; Skewen, Glam, 1953; Rector, Neath, Glam, 1962; Canon, Llandaff Cathedral, 1963; Precentor, 1966. *Recreation:* calligraphy. *Address:* The Vicarage, Penmark, Barry, Glam.

**WILLIAMS, (John) Kyffin,** ARA 1970; Senior Art Master, Highgate School, since 1944; *b* 9 May 1918; *s* of Henry Inglis Wynne Williams and Essyllt Mary Williams (*née* Williams). *Educ:* Shrewsbury Sch.; Slade Sch. of Art. One-man shows: Leicester Galleries, 1951, 1953, 1956, 1960, 1966, 1970; Colnaghi Galleries, 1948, 1949, 1965, 1970. Pres., Royal Cambrian Acad., 1969. Winston Churchill Fellow, 1968. *Recreations:* the countryside, sport. *Address:* Cefn Gadlys, Llansadwrn, Anglesey. *T:* Menai Bridge 225; 22 Bolton Studios, 17b Gilston Road, SW10. *T:* 01-352 1712. *Club:* Chelsea Arts.

**WILLIAMS, (John) Leslie,** CBE 1970; Secretary General, Civil Service National Whitley Council (Staff Side); *b* 1 Aug. 1913; *s* of Thomas Oliver Williams and Mary Ellen Williams; *m* 1937, Florrie Read Jones; one *s*. *Educ:* Grove Park Grammar Sch., Wrexham, N. Wales. Civil Servant, 1931-46. Society of Civil Servants: Asst Secretary, 1947-49; Dep. General Secretary, 1949-56; General Secretary, 1956-66. Royal Institute of Public Administration: Executive Council Member, 1955-; Chairman, 1968. Member Board of Governors, Nat. Hospitals for Nervous Diseases, 1962-; Member: NW Metropolitan Regional Hospital Board, 1963-65; (part-time) UKAEA, 1970-; Adv. Council, Civil Service Coll., 1970-. *Recreations:* cricket, gardening, music. *Address:* 26 Russell Green Close, Purley, Surrey. *T:* 01-660 9666. *Club:* Royal Automobile.

**WILLIAMS, Captain Sir John (Protheroe),** Kt 1967; CMG 1960; OBE 1950; Chairman: Australian National Line, since 1956; United Salvage Pty Ltd; Governing Director, John Propert Pty Ltd; Chairman: Fleetways (Holdings) Ltd; Fleet Foye Pty Ltd; Underwriting Member of Lloyd's; *b* Hull, England, 5 March 1896; *s* of J. J. Williams, Pembs, Wales; *m* 1921, Gladys (*d* 1962), *d* of Dr T. A. Grieves; one *s* three *d*; *m* 1964, Mrs Althea Florence Carr (widow). *Educ:* Queen Elizabeth's Grammar Sch., Carmarthen. Officer in Charge Salvage Operations on RMS Niagara on behalf of Bank of England, 1942, when £2,396,000 in gold bullion was recovered from depth of 438 feet of water. *Recreation:* fishing. *Address:* 77 St Georges Road, Toorak, Victoria 3142, Australia. *T:* 24.2440. *Clubs:* Australian (Melbourne and Sydney); Savage, Melbourne (Melbourne).

**WILLIAMS, John Robert;** British High Commissioner, Suva; *b* 15 Sept. 1922; *s* of Sydney James Williams, Salisbury; *m* 1958, Helga Elizabeth, *d* of Frederick Konow Lund, Bergen; two *s* two *d*. *Educ:* Sheen County School; Fitzwilliam House, Cambridge. Served War of 1939-45, with 1st Bn King's African Rifles in East Africa and Burma Campaign (Captain). Joined Colonial Office as Asst Principal, 1949; First Secretary, UK High Commission, New Delhi, 1956; Commonwealth Relations Office, 1958; Deputy High Commissioner in North Malaya, 1959-63; Counsellor, New Delhi, 1963-66; Commonwealth Office, 1966; Private Sec. to Commonwealth Secretary, 1967; Diplomatic Service Inspectorate, 1968. *Recreations:* music, gardening. *Address:* c/o Foreign and Commonwealth Office, SW1. *Club:* Roehampton.

**WILLIAMS, John Trevor;** Counsellor, British Embassy, Dublin, since 1970; *b* 12 Nov. 1921; *yr s* of Dr Griffith Williams and Monica Johnson; *m* 1953, Ena Ferguson Boyd; two *d*. *Educ:* St Paul's Sch.; Jesus Coll., Oxford. Joined Royal Armoured Corps, 1941; served with 14th/20th King's Hussars in Middle East and Italy, 1943-45. Central Land Board and War Damage Commn: Private Sec., 1947-49; Principal, 1949-51; Min. of Supply, 1951-57 (JSSC, 1955); Min. of Defence, 1957-60; Min. of Aviation, 1960-61; Asst Sec., Air Min., 1961-63; Min. of Defence, 1963-67; joined HM Diplomatic Service, 1967; Counsellor, High Commn, Wellington, NZ, 1967-69; Nato Defence Coll., Rome, 1970. *Recreations:* riding, theatre, looking for good restaurants. *Address:* 29 Astell Street, Chelsea, SW3. *T:* 01-352 2782. *Clubs:* Oxford and Cambridge University; Hurlingham.

**WILLIAMS, Maj.-Gen. John William Channing,** CB 1963; DSO 1944; OBE 1951; jssc; psc; *b* 14 Aug. 1908; *s* of late W. A. Williams, Inkpen, Berks; *m* 1936, Margaret Blachford, *d* of late A. J. Wood, Maidenhead, Berks; three *s*. *Educ:* Trent Coll.; RMC Sandhurst. Commissioned 2nd Lieut, N. Staffs Regt, 1929. Served War of 1939-45 (despatches, DSO): BEF, France, 1939-40; Instructor, Senior Officers' School, 1942-43; GSO1, Staff Coll., Camberley, 1943-44; CO 4th Bn Welch Regt, 1944; served in France, 1944-45, India and Burma, 1945-46. Asst Instructor, Imperial Defence Coll., 1946-48; AA and QMG, 40th Inf. Div., Hong Kong, 1949-50; Colonel General Staff, HQ Land Forces, Hong Kong, 1951-52; Colonel, 1954; BGS (Operations and Plans), GHQ, MELF, 1955-58; Director of Quartering, War Office, 1960-61; Director of Movements, War Office, 1961-63; retired; Brigadier, 1957; Maj.-Gen., 1960. *Recreations:* shooting, fishing. *Address:* Hayes Well, Inkpen, Newbury, Berks.

**WILLIAMS, Lieut-Col Kenneth Greville,** OBE 1920; *b* 30 Jan. 1892; *s* of Lewis Greville Williams, *g s* of Charles Greville Williams, FRS; *m* Elia Mary, *d* of Major Cecil Howard, Royal Horse Artillery; one *s* three *d*. *Educ:* Royal Military Coll., Sandhurst. Commissioned Royal Northumberland Fusiliers, 1912; France, Flanders, Salonika,

1915-18; Mesopotamia, Brigade Major, 1919-20 (despatches twice, OBE); Bt Major 1918; retired, 1927. Recalled to Colours, 1939; Sen. Movement Control Officer, Cherbourg, 1939-40 (despatches); Glider Pilot Regt, 1942-45; Lieut-Colonel; President: NE Hants Agricultural Assoc., 1936-39; Gillingham and Shaftesbury Agricultural Society, 1952. High Sheriff of Dorset, 1959. *Recreations:* yachting, racing, coaching. *Address:* Stock Hill, Gillingham, Dorset. *T:* Gillingham, Dorset 206. *Clubs:* Royal Thames Yacht; Coaching; Royal Yacht Squadron (Cowes).

**WILLIAMS, Kyffin;** *see* Williams, John K.

**WILLIAMS, L(aurence) F(rederic) Rushbrook,** CBE 1923 (OBE 1919); MA, BLitt; JP Hampshire; formerly Chairman of Petty Sessions and a Commissioner for Income Tax (Basingstoke); Editor: Murray's Handbook to India, Pakistan, Burma and Ceylon; Adviser to Maharao of Kutch; Membre Associé de l'Académie Diplomatique Internationale; Corresponding Hon. Member of the Institut Historique et Heraldique de France; Fellow, Royal Society of Arts; Vice-President, Indo-British Historical Association; Editorial Department The Times, Nov. 1944-55; formerly Eastern Service Director, BBC; Adviser Middle East Affairs, Ministry of Information; *b* 10 July 1890; *m* 1923, Freda May, *d* of Frederick H. Chance, of Coward, Hawksley Sons and Chance; two *s* one *d*. *Educ:* private; University College, Oxford. Linton Exhibitioner at University College, 1909; Leicester Exhibitioner, 1910; Plumptre Prizeman, 1912; Gladstone Memorial Prizeman, 1912; 1st Class Final Honour School of Modern History, 1912; BLitt 1913; Lecturer in Medieval History at Queen's University, Canada, 1913-14; Fellow of All Souls Coll., Oxford, 1914-21; University Professor of Modern Indian History in the University of Allahabad, India, 1914-19; Royal Society of Arts Silver Medal, 1937; on Special Duty in connection with the Indian Constitutional Reforms, 1918; on Special Duty in the Home Department, Government of India, 1919; Director, Central Bureau of Information, 1920-26; Secretary to the Indian Delegation at the Imperial Conference, 1923; Political Secretary to the Maharaja of Patiala, and Substitute-Delegate, League of Nations Assembly, 1925; Secretary to the Chancellor of the Chamber of Princes, 1926-30; Foreign Minister of Patiala State, India, 1925-31, MLA 1924-25; Joint Director, Indian Princes' Special Organisation, 1929-31; Adviser to Indian States Delegn, Round Table Conf., 1930-31; Delegate Round Table Conf., 1932. *Publications:* (with J. K. Fotheringham, DLitt) Marco Sanudo, or The Conquest of the Archipelago; History of the Abbey of St Albans; Four Lectures on the Handling of Historical Material; Students' Supplement to the Ain Akbari and A Sixteenth-Century Empire-Builder; A Primer of Indian Administration; Moral and Material Progress Reports of India (Parliamentary Papers), 1917-25; Report of Lord Chelmsford's Administration (Official Document); History of the Tour of the Prince of Wales (Official Document); India's Parliament, Vols I-IV *et seq*; A History of India under the Company and the Crown; What About India?; India (Oxford Pamphlet); The State of Israel (World Jewish Congress Book of the Year for 1957). The Black Hills: Kutch in History and Legend; The State of Pakistan, 1962, 1966; contribs to: The Times; The Times Literary Supplement; The Round Table; Encyclopædia Britannica; Journal of Royal Central Asian Society, etc. *Recreation:* motoring. *Address:* Little West Hairshaw, Stewarton, Ayrshire. *T:* Stewarton 2318. *Club:* Athenæum.

**WILLIAMS, Sir Leonard;** *see* Williams, Sir A. L.

**WILLIAMS, Leonard;** Under-Secretary, Ministry of Technology, since 1967; *b* 19 Sept. 1919; *m* Anne Taylor Witherley; three *d*. *Educ:* St Olave's Grammar Sch.; King's Coll., London. Inland Revenue, 1938. War Service (RA), 1940-47, Major. Ministry of Defence: Asst Principal, 1948; Principal, 1949; NATO, 1951-54; Min. of Supply (later Aviation), 1954; Asst Sec., 1959. IDC, 1966. *Address:* 7 Woodspring Road, SW19.

**WILLIAMS, Leonard John;** Director, National Provincial Bank Ltd, 1956-69; Vice-President, Institute of Bankers, 1956-69; Director: Ranks Hovis McDougall Ltd; City of London Real Property Co. Ltd and its subsidiaries, 1956-69; *b* 7 Aug. 1894; *s* of late Charles and Lily Williams; *m* 1923, Doris (*d* 1965), *d* of late Arthur Mayall; two *s*. *Educ:* Bideford Grammar Sch. Entered National Provincial Bank, 1911, retired as Chief General Manager, 1956. Member Court of Patrons, Royal College of Surgeons; Hon. FRCS 1968. *Recreations:* music, reading. *Address:* 4 Woodfield Road, Ealing, W5. *T:* 01-997 4219.

**WILLIAMS, Leslie;** *see* Williams, J. L.

**WILLIAMS, Ven. Leslie Arthur,** MA; Archdeacon of Bristol since 1967; *b* 14 May 1909; *s* of Arthur and Susan Williams; *m* 1937, Margaret Mary, *d* of Richard Crocker; one *s* one *d*. *Educ:* Knutsford; Downing Coll., Cambridge. Curate of Holy Trinity, Bristol, 1934-37; Licensed to officiate, St Andrew the Great, Cambridge, 1937-40; Curate in Charge, St Peter, Lowden, Chippenham, 1940-42; Chaplain, RAFVR, 1942-46; Curate, Stoke Bishop, 1946-47; Vicar: Corsham, Wilts, 1947-53; Bishopston, Bristol, 1953-60; Stoke Bishop, Bristol, 1960-67. Rural Dean of Clifton, 1966-67; Hon. Canon of Bristol, 1958. *Recreation:* gardening. *Address:* 29 Old Sneed Avenue, Stoke Bishop, Bristol BS9 1SD. *T:* 683747. *Clubs:* Royal Commonwealth Society; Hawks (Cambridge); Constitutional, Savage, Rotary (Bristol).

**WILLIAMS, Leslie Harry;** Member, British Railways Board, 1962-66 (Member, British Transport Commission, 1961-62); *b* 30 July 1909; *s* of late Harold Williams; Cosham, Hants, and of late Ivy Williams, Reigate, Surrey; *m* 1946, Margaret, *o d* of late H. T. Gerrard, Goring-by-Sea, Sussex; one *s*. *Educ:* Portsmouth Grammar Sch.; Jesus Coll., Cambridge. Joined Shell Petroleum Co., 1930; served Kenya and Uganda, 1931-41; Adviser on oil supplies to Occupied Enemy Territories Administration, Addis Ababa, 1941; West Africa, 1942-45; General Manager, Shell Chemicals, Johannesburg, 1948-50; Managing Director, Petrochemicals Ltd and Shell Chemical Co. Ltd, London, 1955-60. *Recreations:* fishing, gardening, music. *Address:* 18 Woodland Rise, Sevenoaks, Kent. *T:* Sevenoaks 61166. *Clubs:* East India and Sports, MCC, Catalysts.

**WILLIAMS, Leslie Henry;** Deputy Chairman, Imperial Chemical Industries Ltd, 1960-67; Chairman, ICI Fibres Ltd, 1965-67; *b* 26 Jan. 1903; *s* of late Edward Henry Williams; *m* 1930, Alice, *d* of late Henry Oliver Harrison; one *s*. *Educ:* Highbury County Sch.; London Univ. (BSc). Joined ICI Ltd, Paints Division, 1929; appointed Director, 1943; Managing Director, 1946; Chairman, 1947; Director of ICI Main Board, 1957; Director, British Nylon Spinners Ltd, 1957-64; Director Ilford Ltd, 1958-67.

FRIC 1945; President, Royal Institute of Chemistry, 1967-70. Member, Monopolies Commission, 1967-. *Recreations:* golf, gardening, music. *Address:* Penny Green, West End Lane, Stoke Poges, Bucks. *T:* Farnham Common 3423.

**WILLIAMS, Leslie H. W.,** MD, MS, FRCS, FRCOG; Medical Inspector in Nullity to the High Court; Consulting Gynæcological Surgeon, St Mary's Hospital, Paddington; Consulting Obstetric Surgeon, Queen Charlotte's Hospital; Consulting Gynæcological Surgeon, Samaritan Hospital for Women; Sometime Obstetric Consultant to LCC, etc; sometime Examiner in Gynæcology and Obstetrics to The University of London, the Conjoint Board, Universities of Cambridge, Durham, Wales, etc; *b* 27 Feb. 1893; *s* of late T. Gill Williams, Newport (Mon); *m* 1930, Patrice, *er d* of late Hatton Ronayne Conron, Douglas, County Cork; two *s one d*. *Educ:* University College, Cardiff; University College Hospital, London. Served European War, RAMC, 1914-20; Commanded 110 Indian Field Ambulance, 1919; House appointments at University College Hospital, 1920, 1921; Obstetric Registrar, Radium Registrar and Chief Assistant on Obstetric Unit at University College Hospital, 1921-30; Obstetric Registrar St Mary's Hospital, 1930; appointed to Honorary Staff, 1931; President of Section of Obstetrics and Gynæcology of Royal Society of Medicine, 1949-50 (Secretary, 1935-37); Member of Council, RCOG. First William McIlrath Guest Professor to University of Sydney, 1949. *Publications:* Aids to Obstetrics; Recent Advances in Obstetrics and Gynæcology (with Aleck Bourne); Chapters in Fleming's Penicillin; Surgery by Handfield-Jones and Porritt, etc; various contributions to Medical Journals. *Recreations:* golf, photography, travel. *Address:* 44 Wimpole Street, W1. *T:* 01-935 6174; 8 Clifton Road, Wimbledon. *T:* 01-946 7844. *Clubs:* Savage; Berkshire (Ascot); Royal Wimbledon (Wimbledon).

**WILLIAMS, Leslie Thomas Douglas,** CMG 1962; *b* 20 Jan. 1905; *s* of late Herbert Douglas and Alice Williams, St Aubyns, Hove, Sussex; *m* 1927, Anne Irene de la Bere (*d* 1954); no *c*. *Educ:* Brighton College. Royal College of Science Chemical Defence Research Department, 1925-54; Director, Explosives Research and Development Establishment, Ministry of Supply, 1954-58. Attended Imperial Defence Coll., 1958. Director-General, Defence Research Staff, Washington, DC, USA, 1959-62; Director-General of Space Activities, Ministry of Aviation, 1963-66. Retired from public service, June 1966. *Publications:* Some contributions to Journal of Chemical Society. *Address:* 20 Cleveland Terrace, W2. *T:* 01-723 1957; c/o Lloyds Bank, Salisbury, Wilts. *Clubs:* Reform, Royal Commonwealth Society.

**WILLIAMS, Mary;** *e d* of Rev. John Williams, Aberystwyth; *m* Dr G. Arbour Stephens (*d* 1945). *Educ:* Frances Mary Buss Schools, London; University College, Aberystwyth; Sorbonne (University of Paris); National University of Ireland; Scholar of the University of Wales, BA (Honours Double First); MA; Research Fellow of the University of Wales, Docteur de l'Université de Paris; Officier d'Académie; Chevalier de la Légion d'Honneur; FRAI; Assistant Lecturer in French, University of Manchester; Reader in French and Romance Philology in the University of London; Professor of French Language and Literature, University College, Swansea, until 1948; Acting Professor of French Language and Literature, University of Durham, 1948-52. President, Folk-lore Society, 1961-63. *Publications:* Essai sur le Roman Gallois de Peredur; Mabinogi Iesu Grist-3 unpublished MSS in Revue Celtique, T XXXIII; Life in Wales in Mediæval Times; Perceval le Gallois (mediæval French poem by Chrestien de Troyes); Studies in Romance Languages and Literatures (with J. A. de Rothschild); The Dying God in Welsh Literature (Revue Celtique, T L, 1929); contributor to Speculum, Etudes Celtiques, Folklore, Man, etc. *Recreations:* music, archæology, anthropology, folk-lore, letter-writing. *Address:* 35 Fitzjohn's Avenue, NW3. *T:* 01-435 2788.

**WILLIAMS, Sir Michael O.;** *see* Williams, Sir Osmond.

**WILLIAMS, Sir Michael (Sanigear),** KCMG 1968 (CMG 1954); HM Diplomatic Service, retired 1970; *b* 17 Aug. 1911; *s* of late Rev. F. F. S. Williams; *m* 1942, Joy Katharine Holdsworth Hunt (*d* 1964); two *d*; *m* 1965, Mary Grace Lindon (*née* Harding). *Educ:* Rugby; Trinity Coll., Cambridge. Entered Foreign Office, 1935; served at HM Embassy in Spain, 1938-39; Foreign Office, 1939-47; HM Embassy, Rome, 1947-50; HM Embassy, Rio de Janeiro, 1950-52; Foreign Office, 1952-56; Minister at Bonn, 1956-60; Minister to Guatemala, 1960-62; Ambassador to Guatemala, 1962-63; Assistant Under-secretary of State, Foreign Office, 1963-65; Minister to the Holy See, 1965-70. *Recreations:* golf, gardening, motoring. *Address:* Wentways, Waldron, Sussex. *Club:* St James'.

**WILLIAMS, Nevill G. G.;** *see* Garnons Williams.

**WILLIAMS, Sir Osmond,** 2nd Bt, *cr* 1909; MC 1944; JP 1960; *b* 22 April 1914; *s* of late Captain Osmond T. D. Williams, DSO, 2nd *s* of 1st Bt, and Lady Gladys Margaret Finch-Hatton, *o d* of 13th Earl of Winchilsea; *S* grandfather, 1927; *m* 1947, Benita Mary, *yr d* of late G. Henry Booker, and of Mrs Michael Burn; two *d*. *Educ:* Eton; Freiburg Univ. Royal Scots Greys, 1935-37, and 1939-45. Chevalier, Order of Leopold II with Palm; Croix de Guerre with Palm (Belgium), 1940. *Recreations:* music, travelling. *Heir:* none. *Address:* Borthwen, Penrhyndeudraeth, Merionethshire.

**WILLIAMS, Owen Lenn;** Counsellor, UK Delegation to the Organisation for Economic Development and Co-operation, since 1968; *b* 4 March 1914; *s* of Richard Owen Williams and Frances Daisy Williams (*née* Lenn); *m* 1959, Gisela Frucht. *Educ:* St Albans Sch.; London University. Asst Principal, Export Credit Guarantee Dept, 1938; Asst Principal, Treasury, 1939; UK High Commn, Ottawa, 1941; Principal, Treasury, 1945; Asst Treasury Representative, UK High Commn, New Delhi, 1953; Treasury Rep., UK High Commn, Karachi, 1955; Economic and Financial Adviser, Leeward Islands, 1957; Perm. Sec., Min. of Finance, Eastern Nigeria, 1959; Asst Sec., Treasury, 1962. *Recreations:* music, travel. *Address:* c/o National Westminster Bank Ltd, Caxton House, SW1. *Club:* Reform.

**WILLIAMS, Paul;** Chairman: Mount Charlotte Investments Ltd; Mount Charlotte Catering Ltd; Nuthalls Hotels Ltd; Buxton Palace Hotel Ltd; Knightsbridge Cake (Manchester) Ltd; and all their subsidiary companies; Public Relations (Industrial) Ltd; Public Relations (International) Ltd; Brook House Advisers; Director, Grand Hotel Co. Bristol Ltd; *b* 14 Nov. 1922; *s* of late Samuel O. Williams and Esmée I. Williams (*née* Call); *m* 1947, Barbara Joan Hardy (marr. diss. 1964); two *d*; *m* 1964, Gillian Foote, *e d* of A. G. Howland Jackson,

Elstead, Surrey, and of Mrs E. J. Foote, and *step d* of E. J. Foote, London, SW3; one *d.* *Educ:* Marlborough; Trinity Hall, Cambridge (MA). MP (C) Sunderland South, (C 1953-57, Ind. C 1957-58, C 1958-64). Chairman, Monday Club, 1964-69. FInstD. *Address:* 6 Elm Park Road, SW3. *T:* 01-352 5527. *Club:* Institute of Directors.

**WILLIAMS, Paul H.**; *see* Hodder-Williams.

**WILLIAMS, Dr Peter Orchard,** FRCP; Director, and Secretary to the Trustees, The Wellcome Trust; *b* 23 Sept. 1925; *s* of Robert Orchard Williams, CBE, and Agnes Annie Birkinshaw; *m* 1949, Billie Innes Brown; two *d. Educ:* Caterham Sch.; Queen's Royal College, Trinidad; St John's Coll., Cambridge (MA); St Mary's Hospital Medical School. MB, BChir 1950; MRCP 1952; FRCP 1970. House Physician, St Mary's Hospital, 1950-51; Registrar, Royal Free Hospital, 1951-52; Medical Specialist, RAMC, BMH Iserlohn, 1954; Medical Officer, Headquarters, MRC, 1955-60; Wellcome Trust: Asst and Dep. Scientific Secretary, 1960-64; Scientific Secretary, 1964-65. Member Council, Royal Society of Medicine. *Publications:* Careers in Medicine, 1952; papers in scientific journals. *Recreations:* gardening, decorating, tennis. *Address:* Fairlie House, The Grove, Epsom, Surrey. *T:* Epsom 21403.

**WILLIAMS, Sir Peter W.**; *see* Watkin Williams.

**WILLIAMS, Sir Ralph D. D.**; *see under* Dudley-Williams, Sir Rolf (Dudley).

**WILLIAMS, Raymond Henry**; Fellow of Jesus College, Cambridge, since 1961; University Reader in Drama, since 1967; *b* 31 Aug. 1921; *s* of Henry Joseph Williams and Gwendolene Williams (*née* Bird); *m* 1942, Joyce Mary Dalling; two *s* one *d. Educ:* Abergavenny Grammar Sch.; Trinity Coll., Cambridge; MA, LittD. War service (ending as Captain), 21st Anti-Tank Regt, Guards Armoured Div., 1941-45. Staff Tutor in Literature, Oxford University Extra-Mural Delegacy, 1946-61; General Editor, New Thinkers' Library, 1962. Editor: Politics and Letters, 1946-47; May Day Manifesto, 1968. *Publications:* Reading and Criticism, 1950; Drama from Ibsen to Eliot, 1952; Drama in Performance, 1954 (rev. edn 1968); Culture and Society, 1958; Border Country, 1960; The Long Revolution, 1961; Communications, 1962 (rev. edn, 1966); Second Generation, 1964; Modern Tragedy, 1966; Public Inquiry, 1967; Drama from Ibsen to Brecht, 1968; The English Novel from Dickens to Lawrence; A Letter from the Country, 1970. *Recreation:* gardening. *Address:* White Cottage, Hardwick, Cambridge.

**WILLIAMS, Sir Reginald (Lawrence William),** 7th Bt, *cr* 1798; MBE 1944; ED 1945; mining engineer, retired; *b* 3 May 1900; *s* of Colonel Lawrence Williams and Catherine Elizabeth Anne Phibbs; *S* kinsman, Sir Hugh Grenville Williams, 6th Bt, 1961; *m* 1936, Elinor Meriol Enriqueta Trevor; two *d. Educ:* Malvern Coll.; Camborne School of Mines. Joined Royal Tank Corps (temp. commn), 1918; Camborne School of Mines, 1919; Mining Engineer, N Nigeria, 1922-40 (mining in all W African Colonies). Commnd in W African Frontier Force, 1932; War service: in Nigeria, 1940-42; in Burma and India, 1942-45, Major. Commandant, Army Leave Station, N Nigeria, 1946-48, when demobilized and returned to tin mining his own property until retiring in Oct. 1957. High Sheriff of Caernarvonshire, 1968-69. *Recreations:* shooting, racing. *Heir: b* Francis (John Watkin) Williams, *qv. Address:* Penrhos, Caeathraw, Caernarvon. *T:* Caernarvon 2109. *Club:* Grosvenor (Chester).

**WILLIAMS, Air Marshal Sir Richard,** KBE, *cr* 1954 (CBE 1927; OBE 1919); CB 1935; DSO 1917; RAAF (retired); Director-General of Civil Aviation in Australia, 1946-56, retired; *b* 1890; *s* of late Richard Williams, Grant Avenue, Rose Park, Adelaide; *m* 1950, Lois V. Cross. Served European War, 1914-19 (despatches, DSO, OBE, Order of El Nahda of the Hedjaz). Formerly Chief of Air Staff, RAAF, and later RAAF Representative, Washington, DC. *Address:* 5 Ardgour Street, North Balwyn, Victoria 3104, Australia.

**WILLIAMS, Richard Aelwyn Ellis,** CIE 1945; late ICS; *b* 5 Dec. 1901; *s* of Rev. Richard Ellis Williams; *m* 1933, Fay Muriel Boylan; two *s* one *d. Educ:* Taunton School; University College of Wales, Aberystwyth (graduate); Lincoln Coll., Oxford (graduate). Appointed to ICS 1925; posted to province of Bihar and Orissa; Under-Secretary, Political Department, Bihar and Orissa Government, 1930; District Magistrate, Shahabad, 1933; Rent Settlement Officer, 1937; Secretary to Bihar Government, Revenue Dept and Controller of Prices and Supplies, 1939; Chief Secretary to Orissa Government, 1944; retired from India, 1946; with Ministry of Agriculture, London, 1947-67. *Recreations:* gardening and photography. *Address:* 9 Clareville Road, Caterham, Surrey.

**WILLIAMS, Richard Tecwyn,** FRS 1967; (first) Professor of Biochemistry at St Mary's Hospital Medical School (University of London) since 1948; Deputy Dean, St Mary's Hospital Medical School, since 1970; sometime Examiner, Universities of Wales, the West Indies, and Royal Veterinary College, Universities of Glasgow, Liverpool, St Andrews, Ibadan, Nigeria, Ghana, and Royal College of Physicians; *b* Abertillery, Mon, South Wales, 20 Feb. 1909; *e s* of Richard and Mary Williams, North Wales; *m* 1937, Josephine Teresa Sullivan; two *s* three *d. Educ:* Abertillery County Sch.; University College, Cardiff. BSc (Wales) 1929; Research Assistant to Dr J. Pryde at Physiology Institute, Cardiff, 1930-34; PhD (Wales) 1932; Lecturer in Biochemistry, University of Birmingham, 1934-42; DSc (Birmingham) 1939; Senior Lecturer in Biochemistry, University of Liverpool, 1942-48. Visiting Scientist, National Institute of Health, Bethesda, Md, USA, 1956; Visiting Prof. Toxicol., New York Univ. Medical School, 1965-66; Member, Food Additives and Contaminants Cttee, Min. of Agriculture, 1965-. Howard Fox Meml Lectr, New York Univ. Sch. of Medicine, 1969. Hon. Member, Society of Toxicology (USA), 1966; Hon. Life Member, Pan American Medical Assoc., 1968. Docteur (*hc*) Univ. Paris, 1966. Merit award, Society of Toxicology (USA), 1968. *Publications:* Detoxication Mechanisms–The Metabolism of Drugs and Allied Organic Compounds, 1947 (2nd edn, 1959). Ed. Biochemical Society Symposia, 1947-55. Numerous research papers published mainly in Biochemical Journal and Journal of Chemical Society. *Recreations:* walking on Welsh mountains, Welsh Culture and History. *Address:* 95 Vernon Drive, Stanmore, Middlesex. *T:* 01-427 5554.

**WILLIAMS, Robert Emmanuel**; *b* 1 Jan. 1900; *o s* of David Williams; *m* 1st, 1928, Rosamund May Taylor (*d* 1929); 2nd, 1938, Audrey Forbes Higginson; three *s* one *d. Educ:* Liverpool Institute; Liverpool Univ. (MSc); Brasenose Coll., Oxford (MA). Assistant Master: Ilkeston, Rugby, Lawrence Sheriff

Sch., Repton, 1922-36; Lecturer, Oxford Univ. Department of Education, 1936-39; HM Inspector of Schools, 1939; Staff Inspector, 1945; Chief Inspector of Schools, Ministry of Education, 1952-61; Simon Senior Research Fellow, Manchester Univ., 1961-62; Lecturer in Education, London Univ. Institute of Education, 1962-67. *Publications:* contributions to School Science Review, Religion in Education. *Address:* 28 Hamilton Gardens, NW8. *T:* 01-286 4525.

**WILLIAMS, Sir Robert (Ernest),** 9th Bt, *cr* 1866; *b* 6 June 1924; *e s* of late Ernest Claude Williams and of Theresa Gertrude, *d* of R. Graefer; *S* kinsman Sir William Law Williams, 8th Bt, 1960; *m* 1948, Ruth Margaret, *d* of C. Butcher, Hudson Bay; three *s* one *d.* Employed by Canadian National Railways, 1944-60. *Heir: s* Donald Mark Williams, *b* 7 Nov. 1954. *Address:* Upcott House, Barnstaple, N Devon. *T:* Barnstaple 2498.

**WILLIAMS, Prof. Robert Evan Owen;** MD, FRCP, FRCPath; Professor of Bacteriology, University of London at St Mary's Hospital Medical School, since Oct. 1960, Dean, since Oct. 1967; *b* 30 June 1916; *s* of Gwynne Evan Owen Williams and Cicely Mary (*née* Innes); *m* 1944, Margaret (*née* Lumsden); one *s* two *d. Educ:* Sherborne Sch., Dorset; University College, London and University College Hospital. Assistant Pathologist, EMS, 1941-42; Pathologist, Medical Research Council Unit, Birmingham Accident Hospital, 1942-46; on staff Public Health Laboratory Service, 1946-60 (Director, Streptococcus, Staphylococcus and Air Hygiene Laboratory, 1949-60). Mem. Medical Research Council, 1969-. Fellow, University College, London, 1968. *Publications:* (jt author) Hospital Infection, 1966; numerous publications in journals on bacteriological and epidemiological subjects. *Recreation:* horticulture. *Address:* 26 Brampton Grove, Hendon, NW4. *T:* 01-202 9774; Little Platt, Plush, Dorset.

**WILLIAMS, Robert Martin,** PhD; Vice-Chancellor of University of Otago, Dunedin, since 1967; *b* 30 March 1919; *s* of late Canon Henry Williams; *m* Mary Constance, *d* of late Rev. Francis H. Thorpe; one *s* two *d. Educ:* Christ's Coll., NZ; Canterbury University College, NZ; St John's Coll., Cambridge. MA. 1st Class Hons Mathematics, Univ. Sen. Schol., Shirtcliffe Fellow, NZ, 1940; BA, 1st Class Hons Mathematics Tripos, Cantab, 1947; PhD Math. Statistics, Cantab, 1949. Mathematician at Radar Development Laboratory, DSIR, NZ, 1941-44; Member UK Atomic Group in US, 1944-45; Member, 1949-53, Director, 1953-62, Applied Mathematics Laboratory, DSIR, NZ; Harkness Commonwealth Fellow and Vis. Fellow, at Princeton Univ., 1957-58; State Services Commissioner, NZ Public Service, 1963-67; Mem., NZ Metric Adv. Bd, 1969-. Mem., Internat. Statistical Inst., 1961-. *Publications:* papers mainly on mathematical statistics and related topics. *Address:* University Lodge, St Leonards, Dunedin, New Zealand. *T:* 87241.

**WILLIAMS, Sir (Robert) Philip (Nathaniel),** 4th Bt *cr* 1915; *b* 3 May 1950; *s* of Sir David Philip Williams, 3rd Bt and of Elizabeth Mary Garneys, *d* of late William Ralph Garneys Bond; *S* father, 1970. *Educ:* Marlborough; St Andrews Univ. *Heir: b* David Michael Ralph Williams, *b* 1 Feb. 1955. *Address:* Bridehead, Dorchester, Dorset.

**WILLIAMS, Sir Robin (Philip),** 2nd Bt, *cr* 1953; Insurance Broker since 1952; 2nd Lieut, retired, RA; *b* 27 May 1928; *s* of Sir Herbert Geraint Williams, 1st Bt, MP, MSc, MEngAssoc, MInstCE; *S* father 1954; *m* 1955, Wendy Adèle Marguerite, *o d* of late Felix Joseph Alexander, London and Hong Kong; two *s. Educ:* Eton Coll.; St John's Coll., Cambridge (MA). 2nd Lieut, Royal Artillery, 1947. Vice-Chairman, Federation of Univ. Conservative and Unionist Assocs, 1951-52; Acting Chairman, 1952; Chairman of Bow Group (Conservative Research Society), 1954. Called to Bar, Middle Temple, 1954. Councillor, Haringey, 1968. *Publication:* Whose Public Schools?, 1957. *Heir: s* Anthony Geraint Williams, *b* 22 Dec. 1958. *Address:* 1 Broadlands Close, Highgate, N6.

**WILLIAMS, Sir Rolf D. D.;** *see* Dudley-Williams.

**WILLIAMS, Rt. Rev. Ronald Ralph;** *see* Leicester, bishop of.

**WILLIAMS, Major Ronald Samuel Ainslie;** *b* 1890; 2nd *s* of late Frank Williams of Brasted Hall, Kent; *m* 1918, Cicely, 3rd *d* of late Henry Monro; one *s* two *d. Educ:* Repton; RMA, Woolwich. MP (L) Sevenoaks, 1923-24. JP, 1936-64, Alderman, 1945-52, Co. Wilts. *Address:* Little Bridge House, West Chinnock, Crewkerne, Somerset. *Club:* United Service.

**WILLIAMS, Sir Roy E. H.;** *see* Hume-Williams.

**WILLIAMS, Shirley Vivien Teresa Brittain;** MP (Lab) Hitchin since 1964; *b* 27 July 1930; *d* of Prof. Sir George Catlin, *qv* and late Mrs Catlin (Vera Brittain); *m* 1955, Prof. Bernard Arthur Owen Williams, *qv*; one *d. Educ:* St Paul's Girls' Sch.; Somerville Coll., Oxford (MA); Columbia Univ., New York. General Secretary, Fabian Soc., 1960-64. Contested (Lab) Harwich, Essex, 1954 and 1955, and Southampton Test, 1959; Parliamentary Private Secretary, Minister of Health, 1964-66; Parly Sec., Min. of Labour, 1966-67; Minister of State: Education and Science, 1967-69; Home Office, 1969-70. Mem. Labour Party Nat. Exec. Cttee, 1970-. Visiting Fellow, Nuffield College, Oxford, 1967-. Hon. DEd CNAA, 1969. *Publications:* (with B. A. O. Williams) Chapter in What the Human Race is Up To, 1962; chapter in Christian Order and World Poverty, 1964; *pamphlets:* The Common Market and Its Forerunners, 1958; The Free Trade Area, 1958; Central Africa: The Economics of Inequality, 1960. *Recreations:* music and walking. *Address:* 12 Phillimore Place, W8.

**WILLIAMS, Rev. (Sidney) Austen;** Vicar of St Martin-in-the-Fields, since 1956; Chaplain to the Queen's Household since 1961; *b* 23 Feb. 1912; *s* of Sidney Herbert and Dorothy Williams; *m*1945, Daphne Joan McWilliam; one *s* one *d. Educ:* Bromsgrove School; St Catharine's College, Cambridge (MA); Westcott House, Cambridge. Curate of St Paul, Harringay, 1937-40. Chaplain, Toc H, France and Germany (POW), 1940-48. Curate of: All Hallows, Barking by the Tower, 1945-46; St Martin-in-the-Fields, 1946-51; Vicar of St Albans, Westbury Park, Clifton, Bristol, 1951-56. *Publication:* What Jesus Really Said, 1958. *Recreations:* photography, ornithology. *Address:* 5 St Martin's Place, WC2. *T:* 01-930 1862.

**WILLIAMS, Lt-Col Stanley Price,** CIE 1930; *b* 1885; *s* of C. A. Williams, Ashfield, Builth Wells; *m* 1913, Winifred de L., *d* of late Col E. A. Young, Wykeham Close, Steyning; (only son killed in action in Burma, Mar. 1945), two *d. Educ:* Leys School; Sandhurst. Commissioned in 1st Bn Middlesex Regt 1905; transferred to 51st Sikhs FF 1907; during European War served on NWF in Frontier Militia; 3rd Afghan War, 1919; Commandant,

South Waziristan Scouts, 1924-29; commanded 2nd Bn 14th Punjab Regt (DCO) (Brownlow's), 1930-34; retired 1935; RAFVR, 1939-41; recalled to IA, Nov. 1941, and sent to India; reverted to retired list, 1944. *Address:* 15c Hyde Park Mansions, NW1. *T:* 01-723 2850.

**WILLIAMS, Stuart Graeme,** OBE 1949; Controller, Television Administration, BBC, since 1956; Director, Visnews Ltd, since 1957, Deputy Chairman, since 1962; Chairman, European Broadcasting Union Cost-Sharing Group, since 1965; *b* 5 October 1914; *y s* of late Graeme Douglas Williams, author and journalist, and of Winifred Maud Williams (now Mrs Sydney A. Moseley); *m* 1938, Catherine Anne, *d* of Charles Thomas and Florence Hutchison; one *d. Educ:* Alleyn Court, Westcliff-on-Sea; Wallingbrook, Chulmleigh. Joined BBC as Programme Sub-Editor, Radio Times, 1931; particularly concerned with war-time and post-war development, BBC Overseas, European and Monitoring Services. Principal appointments: Executive: Outside Broadcasting, 1938; Monitoring Service, 1939; Empire Service, 1940; Asst Head, Overseas Programme Admin., 1941; Admin. Officer, Overseas Services, 1942; visited Middle and Far East for negotiations concerning future of British Far Eastern Broadcasting Service, Singapore and Radio SEAC, Ceylon, 1947 and 1948; Head of External Broadcasting Admin., 1948; BBC Staff Admin. Officer, 1952; Asst Controller, Staff Admin., 1955; visited Nigeria to advise Nigeria Govt concerning incorporation of Nigeria Broadcasting Service, 1955; visited Malta as member of a BBC Working Party to report on possible introduction of television in Malta, 1959; advised on organisation of Broadcasting in Singapore, 1968. Mem., Exec. Council, Roy. Inst of Public Administration, 1951-68, Chm., 1957. *Address:* 35 The Cedars, Heronsforde, W13. *T:* 01-997 1101.

**WILLIAMS, Tennessee, (Thomas Lanier Williams);** Playwright; *b* 26 March 1911; *s* of Cornelius Coffin Williams and Edwina Dakin. *Educ:* University of Missouri; University of Iowa; Washington University. Awarded Rockefeller Fellowship 1940 (playwriting); Grant from National Institute of Arts and Letters ($1000), 1943; New York Drama Critics Circle Award, 1944-45, 1947-48, 1955, 1960-61; Pulitzer Prize, 1948, 1955. Member Alpha Tau Omega. *Publications: plays:* Battle of Angels; The Glass Menagerie, 1944; (with Donald Windham) You Touched Me, 1945; A Streetcar Named Desire, 1947; Summer and Smoke, 1948; The Rose Tattoo, 1951; Camino Real, 1953; Cat on a Hot Tin Roof, 1955; Orpheus Descending, 1957; Garden District (2 plays: Suddenly Last Summer and Something Unspoken), 1958; Sweet Bird of Youth, 1959; Period of Adjustment, 1960 (filmed, 1963); The Night of the Iguana, 1961 (filmed, 1964); The Milk Train Doesn't Stop Here Any More, 1963 (revised, 1964; filmed, as Boom, 1968); Slapstick Tragedy, 1966; In the Bar of a Tokyo Hotel, 1969; *film:* Baby Doll, 1957; *screen plays for:* The Glass Menagerie, A Street Car Named Desire, The Rose Tattoo; (with Meade Roberts) The Fugitive King (Orpheus Descending); (with Gore Vidal) Suddenly Last Summer; Boom; *volumes:* volume of one-act plays, 1945; vols of short stories, 1948, 1960 (Three Players of a Summer Game); vol. of verse, 1944; Hard Candy and other Stories, 1954; Dragon Country (plays), 1970; *novel:* The Roman Spring of Mrs Stone, 1950; *novella:* The Knightly Quest, 1966. *Recreations:* swimming, travelling. *Address:* c/o Audrey Wood, International Famous Agency, Inc., 1301 Avenue of the Americas, NYC, NY 10019, USA.

**WILLIAMS, Sir Thomas;** *see* Williams, Sir Daniel T.

**WILLIAMS, Sir Thomas Herbert P.;** *see* Parry-Williams.

**WILLIAMS, Thomas Lanier;** *see* Williams, Tennessee.

**WILLIAMS, Trevor Illtyd,** MA, BSc, DPhil; Editor of Endeavour since 1954 and academic relations adviser, ICI Ltd; *b* 16 July 1921; *s* of Illtyd Williams and Alma Mathilde Sohlberg; *m* 1st, 1945 (marriage dissolved, 1952); 2nd, 1952, Sylvia Irène Armstead; four *s* one *d. Educ:* Clifton College; Queen's College, Oxford. Nuffield Research Scholar, Sir William Dunn Sch. of Pathology, Oxford, 1942-45; Deputy Editor of Endeavour, 1945-54. Chm., Soc. for the Study of Alchemy and Early Chemistry, 1967-; Jt Editor, Annals of Science, 1966-; Chm., World List of Scientific Periodicals, 1966-. *Publications:* An Introduction to Chromatography, 1946; Drugs from Plants, 1947; (ed) The Soil and the Sea, 1949; The Chemical Industry Past and Present, 1953; The Elements of Chromatography, 1954; (ed, jtly) A History of Technology, 1954-58; (with T. K. Derry) A Short History of Technology, 1960; Science and Technology (Ch. III, Vol. XI, New Cambridge Mod. History); (rev. edn) Alexander Findlay's A Hundred Years of Chemistry, 1965; (ed) A Biographical Dictionary of Scientists, 1968; numerous articles on scientific subjects, especially history of science and technology. *Recreations:* fishing, trade tokens. *Address:* 20 Blenheim Drive, Oxford. *T:* Oxford 58591. *Club:* Athenæum.

**WILLIAMS, Maj.-Gen. Walter David Abbott,** CB 1946; CBE 1944; Principal of Staff College for Higher Management, at Woking, 1959-65; *b* 31 December 1897; *c* of late Walter Charles Williams; *m* 1925, Eunice Florence Longley; one *s* one *d. Educ:* Brighton College; Royal Military Academy; Emmanuel College, Cambridge. Commissioned Royal Engineers, 1917; Scholar of Emmanuel College, Cambridge, 1923; graduated, 1924; Graduate of Staff College, Camberley, 1933; Actg Maj.-Gen. as a WO Director, 1943; Director of Movements, WO, 1945-49; retd pay, 1949. Commander, US Legion of Merit, 1945. Formerly Director of Port Emergency Planning, Ministry of Transport; Commissioner for Transport, East Africa High Commission, 1954-58. *Club:* United Service.

**WILLIAMS, Prof. William David,** MA, DPhil; Professor of German, Liverpool University, since 1954; *b* 10 March 1917; *s* of William Williams and Winifred Ethel Williams (*née* Anstey); *m* 1946, Mary Hope Davis; one *s* one *d. Educ:* Merchant Taylors' School; St John's Coll., Oxford (MA, DPhil). Served War of 1939-45, with Sudan Defence Force, Middle East, and as Liaison Officer with Polish Army in Italy; Asst Lecturer in German, Leeds Univ., 1946; Lecturer in German, Oxford Univ., 1948-54; Pro-Vice-Chancellor, Liverpool Univ., 1965-68. *Publications:* Nietzsche and the French, 1952; The Stories of C. F. Meyer, 1962; reviews, etc, in Modern Language Review, and Erasmus. *Recreation:* gardening. *Address:* 20 Menlove Gardens South, Liverpool.

**WILLIAMS, (William) Donald;** *b* 17 Oct. 1919; 2nd *s* of Sidney Williams, Malvern; *m* 1945,

Cecilia Mary (*née* Hirons); one *s*. *Educ:* Royal Grammar Sch., Worcester. Served War of 1939-45: Volunteer, 8th Bn Worcestershire Regt, May 1939; POW 1940 (Germany); escaped to Russia and was repatriated, 1945. Qualified as a Chartered Accountant, 1949. In practice as a Partner of firm Kendall, Wadley & Co., 1950-. Contested (C) Dudley, (Gen. Elec.), 1966; MP (C) Dudley, March 1968-70. *Recreation:* reading. *Address:* Sexton Barns, Cockshot Road, Malvern, Worcs. *T:* Malvern 5635.

**WILLIAMS, Sir William Emrys,** Kt 1955; CBE 1946; BA; Hon. Appeals Secretary, National Art-Collections Fund; Arts Adviser, Institute of Directors; Chairman, National Theatre of Wales; Penguin Books (Chief Editor and Director), 1935-65; Secretary-General, Arts Council, 1951-63 (Founder Member, 1946); *b* 5 Oct. 1896; *m* 1919, Gertrude (*see* Lady Williams); no *c*. *Educ:* elementary and secondary schools in Manchester; Univ. of Manchester. Staff Tutor, University of London Extra-Mural Dept, 1928-34. Sec. of British Institute of Adult Education, 1934-40; Director Army Bureau of Current Affairs, 1941-45. Director Bureau of Current Affairs, 1946-51; a Trustee of the National Gallery, 1949-56; a Trustee of Shakespeare's Birthplace, 1953-68; Chm., Arts Council Theatre Enquiry; a Governor, Yehudi Menuhin School; Hon. Member of the Architectural Association. American Medal of Freedom. Hon. DLitt (Wales). *Publications:* Official Historian of Army Education, 1939-46; regular contributor to several national newspapers, 1937-67. *Address:* Grenville Paddock, Haddenham, Aylesbury, Bucks. *T:* Haddenham 464. *Clubs:* Garrick, Savile.

**WILLIAMS, Lt-Col Sir William (Jones),** KCVO 1969; OBE 1953; QPM; Chief Constable, Gwynedd Constabulary, 1967-70; *b* 31 May 1904; *s* of Thomas Williams, Towyn, Merioneth; *m* 1930, Margaret Enid (*d* 1957), *d* of John Pugh, Aberdovey; one *s* one *d*. *Educ:* Bala and Towyn Grammar Schs; Aberystwyth and Birmingham Univs. BSc Aberystwyth 1926, LLB Birmingham 1933. Birmingham City Police, 1926-46. Served War of 1939-45, Lt-Col, Gen. List, 1945. Chief Constable, Caernarvonshire Constabulary, 1946-50; Chief Constable, Gwynedd Constabulary: Counties of Anglesey, Caernarvon and Merioneth, 1950-67; Counties of Anglesey, Caernarvon, Denbigh, Flint and Merioneth, 1967-70. Queen's Police Medal, 1959; KStJ 1969. *Publications:* (Asst to late Dr C. C. H. Moriarty with): Police Procedure and Administration, 6th edn 1955; also (jointly with him) Police Law, 15th edn 1959; (since the death of Dr Moriarty in 1958) Editor of Moriarty's Police Law, 16th edn 1961-, 17th edn 1963, 18th edn 1965, 19th edn 1968, 20th edn 1970. *Recreation:* golf (Captain Royal St David's Golf, Harlech, 1963). *Address:* Coed-y-Glyn, South Road, Caernarvon, N Wales. *T:* Caernarvon 3015. *Clubs:* National Liberal (non-political Mem.); Royal Welsh Yacht (Caernarvon).

**WILLIAMS, Prof. William Moses;** Staff Tutor, University of Newcastle upon Tyne, since 1948; *b* 28 April 1906; *s* of William Robert and Mary Jane Williams; *m* 1st, 1931, Eileen Josephine Daly; one *d*; 2nd, Elsbeth Owen Evans. *Educ:* Liverpool Institute, Liverpool; Jesus College, Oxford (Classical Scholar). First Class Classical Honours Moderations; First Class Final Honour School of Literae Humaniores; Classical Master, Ipswich School, 1928; Classical Sixth Form Master, King's School, Canterbury, 1929-32; Lecturer in Education, Armstrong College, University of Durham, 1932-34; Prof. of Education, University Coll. of Wales, Swansea, 1934; Professor of Education and Head of the Training Department, University College of N Wales, Bangor and Warden of Neuadd Reichel, University Hall of Residence for Men Students, 1942-47. Member Reconstruction Advisory Council for Wales. *Publications:* Selections from the Welsh Piety, 1938; The Friends of Griffith Jones, 1940; Addysg Cyfres Pobun (Education; Welsh Everyman Series). *Address:* 292 Wingrove Road, Newcastle upon Tyne 4.

**WILLIAMS, William Penry,** JP Caernarvon; Bank Manager, Midland Bank Ltd, Caernarvon, 1938-52; retired 1952; *b* 7 Sept. 1892; *s* of Capt. R. Jones Williams, Gwydryn, Abersoch, Caerns; *m* 1918, Elizabeth, *d* of John Hughes, Liverpool; one *s* one *d*; *m* 1949, Mrs Margaret Ellen Roberts. *Educ:* County Secondary School, Pwllheli. Entered Midland Bank Ltd, 1909. High Sheriff Caernarvonshire, 1944. Certificated Associate Inst. of Bankers. Commission First RWF, European War, 1914-18. Member of Council University Coll. of North Wales, Bangor; Vice-Chm. and Trustee of Port of Caernarvon. *Recreations:* golf and shooting. *Address:* Tyddyn Hen, Clynnog, Caernarvon. *T:* Clynnog 238. *Club:* Royal Welsh Yacht.

**WILLIAMS, Col William Picton B.;** *see* Bradley-Williams.

**WILLIAMS, William Thomas,** ARCS; PhD, DSc (London); DIC; FLS; Senior Principal Research Scientist, CSIRO, Australia, since 1966; *b* 18 Apr. 1913; *o s* of William Thomas and Clara Williams. *Educ:* Stationers' Company's School, London; Imperial College of Science and Technology. Demonstrator in Botany, Imperial College, 1933-36; Lecturer in Biology, Sir John Cass' College, 1936-40. Served War, 1940-46; RA (Sjt), RAOC (2/Lt), REME (T/Major). Lecturer in Botany, Bedford College, London, 1946-51; Professor of Botany, University of Southampton, 1951-65; CSIRO Division of Computing Research, Canberra, Australia, 1966-68. Sometime Secretary of Society for Experimental Biology, and of Sherlock Holmes Society of London. Past Editor, Journal of Experimental Botany. *Publications:* papers on plant physiology and statistical ecology in scientific journals. *Recreations:* music, drinking beer. *Address:* Division of Tropical Pastures, CSIRO, Brisbane, Qld 4067, Australia.

**WILLIAMS, W(illiam) Thomas,** QC 1964; MP (Lab and Co-op) Warrington since 1961; Recorder of Birkenhead, since 1969; *b* 22 Sept. 1915; *s* of David John Williams, Aberdare, and late Edith Williams; *m* 1942, Gwyneth, *d* of Rev. D. G. Harries, Aberdare; one *s* one *d*. *Educ:* University Coll., Cardiff; St Catherine's, Oxford; University of London; Lincoln's Inn. President, Students' Union, University of Wales, 1939. Baptist Minister, 1941-46; Chaplain and Welfare Officer, RAF, 1944-46; Tutor, Manchester College, Oxford, 1946-49. Called to the Bar, Lincoln's Inn, 1951. MP (Lab & Co-op) Barons Court, 1955-59 (Hammersmith South (Feb.), 1949-55). Parliamentary Private Secretary: Minister of Pensions, 1950-51; Minister of Health, 1951; Attorney General, 1965-67. Member: Advisory Council on Public Records, 1965-; SE Metropolitan Regional Hospital Board, 1965-; Governor, King's Coll. Hosp., 1968-; Chm., Cray Valley Hosp. Management Cttee, 1968-69. *Address:* 1A Allison Grove, Dulwich Common, SE21. *T:* 01-693 7566.

**WILLIAMS-BULKELEY, Sir Richard Harry David,** 13th Bt, *cr* 1661; TD; JP; HM Lieutenant for the County of Anglesey since 1947; Member: Anglesey County Council; Mayor of Beaumaris, 1949; *b* 5 Oct. 1911; *s* of late Maj. R. G. W. Williams-Bulkeley, MC, and late Mrs V. Williams-Bulkeley; *S* grand-father, 1942; *m* 1938, Renée Arundell, *yr d* of Sir Thomas L. H. Neave, 5th Bt; two *s*. *Educ:* Eton. Served with 9th and 8th Bns Royal Welch Fusiliers, 1939-44, 2nd in Command of both Battalions and with Allied Land Forces South East Asia, specially employed, 1944-Sept. 1945, Lt-Col Comdt, Anglesey and Caernarvonshire Army Cadet Force, 1946-47 (resigned on appointment as HM Lieut). CStJ. *Recreations:* shooting, golf, hunting. *Heir: s* Richard Thomas Williams-Bulkeley [*b* 25 May 1939; *m* 1964, Sarah Susan, *er d* of Rt Hon. Sir Henry Josceline Phillimore, *qv*; twin *s*]. *Address:* Plâs Meigan, Beaumaris, Anglesey. *T:* Beaumaris 345. *Club:* Royal Anglesey Yacht.

**WILLIAMS-DRUMMOND, Sir W. H. D. W.;** *see* Drummond.

**WILLIAMS-ELLIS, Amabel;** Author and Journalist; *b* Newlands Corner, near Guildford; *d* of late J. St Loe Strachey, of the Spectator; *m* 1915, Clough Williams-Ellis, *qv*; (son killed in action, 1944) two *d*. *Educ:* home. Literary editor Spectator, 1922-23. *Publications:* An Anatomy of Poetry; The Pleasures of Architecture (with Clough Williams-Ellis); But We Know Better; Noah's Ark; The Wall of Glass; How You Began; The Tragedy of John Ruskin; The Beagle in S America; Men Who Found Out; How You Are Made; Volcano; What Shall I Be; To Tell the Truth; History of English Life, Senior and Junior (for children); The Big Firm; Good Citizens; Learn to Love First; Women in War Factories; Princesses and Trolls; A Food and People Geography; The Art of being a Woman; Headlong down the Years; The Art of Being a Parent; Changing the World; Seekers and Finders; Modern Scientists at Work; Darwin's Moon; A Life of Alfred Russel Wallace. *Recreations:* walking, sailing, travel. *Address:* Plâs Brondanw, Llanfrothen, N Wales. *TA:* Penrhyndeudraeth.

**WILLIAMS-ELLIS, Clough,** CBE 1958; MC, JP; FRIBA; architect; Past-President Design and Industry Association; Vice-Pres., Council for the Preservation of Rural Wales; Member Town Planning Institute; Member National Parks Committee; Chairman Glass Industry Working Party; Member National Trust Committee for Wales; Member Government Committee on Art and Industry; Member of Art Committee, University of Wales; Member Grand Council, British Travel Association; Vice-President Institute Landscape Architects; Member Advisory Council for Welsh Reconstruction; First Chairman First New Town Development Corporation (Stevenage); Member Festival of Britain 1951 Committee (Wales); Member Trunk Road Advisory Committee; late Welsh Guards, served in France, 1915-18 (despatches); *b* 1883; *m* 1915, Amabel (*see* Amabel Williams-Ellis), *o d* of late J. St Loe Strachey, Newlands Corner, Surrey; (son Christopher, killed in action–Welsh Guards–1944) two *d*. *Educ:* Oundle; Trinity College, Cambridge. Larger works include sections of the Wembley Exhibitions, Llangoed and Bolesworth Castles, Moynes Park, Oare House, Caversham Place, Kilve Court, Stowe School, Hurtwood School, Bishop's Stortford College Chapel, Great Hundridge Manor, Cornwell Manor and Village, conversion of Ashridge Park (Bonar Law College), Lloyd George Mausoleum and Memorial County College, Rhiwlas, Voelas, Nantclwyd Hall, etc; other works include churches, schools and village schemes in England, Ireland and Wales, a number of smaller houses, hotels, monuments and gardens, several London houses, including Dartmouth House and Ladies' Carlton Club, Oxford and Cambridge Club Annexe, also residences in China, S Africa and New Zealand; owns and is designer and builder of the new model resort of Portmeirion, North Wales; Town Planning Consultant to various municipalities. *Publications:* Cottage Building; England and the Octopus; the Architect; The Face of the Land; Sir Laurence Weaver (with his wife); The Tank Corps (a War History); The Pleasures of Architecture; (with John Summerson) Architecture here and now; (Editor) Britain and the Beast, 1937; (with Lord Rosse) The Protection of Ancient Buildings, 1939; Plan for Living; On Trust for the Nation; (2 Vols) An Artist in North Wales; The Adventure of Building; Town and Country Planning; Portmeirion–the place and its meaning; Trunk Roads in the landscape, etc. *Recreations:* travelling, building. *Address:* Plâs Brondanw, Penrhyndeudraeth, Merioneth. *T:* Penrhyndeudraeth 292. *Clubs:* Athenæum, Lansdowne; Royal Welsh Yacht (Caernarvon).

**WILLIAMS-THOMAS, Lt-Col Reginald Silvers,** DSO 1940; TD; JP; DL; Commander of Crown (Belgium); Croix de Guerre; RA; Queen's Own Worcestershire Hussars; Glass Manufacturer; Director: Stevens and Williams Ltd; Stokes Bomford Ltd; Lloyd:s Underwriter; *b* 11 February 1914; *s* of Hubert Silvers Williams-Thomas, Broome, Stourbridge, Worcestershire; *m* 1938, Esmée Florence Taylor; two *s* one *d*; *m* 1963, Sonia Margot Jewell; *d* of Major M. F. S. Jewell, CBE, DL, Upton-on-Severn, Worcs. *Educ:* Shrewsbury School. DL Worcestershire, 1954. Freeman of the City of London. *Recreations:* shooting, archery, fishing, gardening. *Address:* Yew Tree Cottage, Lawnswood, Wordsley, Nr Stourbridge, Worcestershire. *T:* Kingswinford 3748.

**WILLIAMS-WYNN, Col Sir (Owen) Watkin,** 10th Bt, *cr* 1688; CBE 1969; FRAgSs 1969; Lord Lieutenant of Denbighshire since 1966; *b* 30 Nov. 1904; *s* of Sir Robert William Herbert Watkin Williams-Wynn, 9th Bt, KCB, DSO; *S* father 1951; *m* 1st, 1939, Margaret Jean (*d* 1961), *d* of late Col William Alleyne Macbean, RA, and Hon. Mrs Gerald Scarlett; two *s*; 2nd, 1968, Gabrielle Haden Matheson, *d* of late Herbert Alexander Caffin. *Educ:* Eton; RMA, Woolwich. Commnd RA, 1925; RHA, Instructor at Equitation Sch., Weedon; Adj. 61st (Carnarvon and Denbigh Yeo.) Medium Regt RA (TA), 1936-40; Major, 1940. Served with Regt as 2nd in command, France and Dunkirk; served with 18th Division, Singapore (despatches twice); Prisoner of War, Siam and Burmah Railway; Lt-Col comdg 361st Med. Regt RA (TA), 1946; Hon. Col 361 Med. Regt RA (TA), 1952-57. Master Flint and Denbigh Foxhounds, 1946-61; Joint Master, Sir W. W. Wynn's Hounds, 1957. JP 1937, DL 1947, Denbighshire; High Sheriff of Denbighshire, 1954; Vice-Lieutenant, Denbighshire, 1957-66; Liaison Officer to Ministry of Agriculture for North Wales, 1961-70; Mem. Nature Conservancy Cttee for Wales, 1963-66. *Heir: s* David Watkin Williams-Wynn [*b* 18 Feb. 1940; *m* 1968, Harriet Veryan Elspeth, *d* of Gen. Sir Norman Tailyour, *qv*; one *s*]. *Address:* Llangedwyn, Oswestry, Shropshire. *T:* Llanrhaiadr 269. *Club:* Army and Navy.

**WILLIAMS-WYNNE, Col John Francis,** DSO 1945; JP; FRAgSs; HM Lieutenant of Merioneth since 1957; Constable of Harlech

Castle since 1964; *b* 9 June 1908; *s* of late Major F. R. Williams-Wynn, CB, and late Beatrice (*née* Cooper); *m* 1938, Margaret Gwendolen, *d* of late Rev. George Roper and Mrs G. S. White; one *s* two *d*. *Educ:* Oundle; Magdalene College, Cambridge (MA Mech. Sciences). Commissioned in RA 1929; served NW Frontier, 1936; served War of 1939-45; psc Camberley; Brigade Major, RA 2 Div., 1940-41; GSO2 HQ Ceylon Comd, 1942; comd 160 Jungle Field Regt, RA, 1943-44; GSO1, GHQ India, 1945; GSO1, War Office, 1946-48; retd 1948; comd 636 (R Welch) LAA Regt, RA, TA, 1951-54; Subs. Col 1954. Hon. Col 7th (Cadet) Bn RWF, 1964. JP 1950, DL 1953, VL 1954, Merioneth. Chairman, Advisory Cttee, Min. of Agric. Experimental Husbandry Farm, Trawscoed. Part-time mem., Merseyside and N Wales Electricity Bd, 1953-65; Member: Regional Adv. Cttee N Wales Conservancy Forestry Commission, 1950-63; County Agric. Exec. Cttee, 1955-63 and 1967-; Gwynedd River Board, 1957-63; National Parks Comr, 1961-66. UK Forestry Commissioner, 1963-65; Mem. Forestry Cttee of Gt Britain, 1966 and Home Grown Timber Advisory Cttee, 1966; Pres., Royal Welsh Agric. Soc., 1968. Chairman and Man. Dir, Cross Foxes Ltd. *Recreations:* farming, forestry and flying. *Address:* Peniarth Towyn, Merioneth, Wales. *T:* Towyn 328. *Clubs:* Army and Navy, Pratt's.

**WILLIAMSON,** family name of **Barons Forres** and **Williamson.**

**WILLIAMSON,** Baron *cr* 1962, of Eccleston (Life Peer); **Thomas Williamson,** Kt 1956; CBE 1950; JP Liverpool; General Secretary National Union of General and Municipal Workers, 1946-61; a Director of Securicor Ltd since 1964; (part-time) member, Iron and Steel Board, 1960-67; Member of ITA, 1961-64; Chairman British Productivity Council, 1953-54; Director of the Daily Herald, 1953-62; *b* 2 September 1897; *s* of James and Selina Williamson; *m* 1925, Hilda Hartley, St Helens; one *d*. *Educ:* Knowsley Road, St Helens; Workers' Educational Association, Liverpool University. Member Liverpool City Council, 1929-35; Member National Executive British Labour Party, and Chm. of Finance and General Purposes Cttee, 1940-47; Mem. TUC General Council, 1947-62; Chm. TUC, 1956-57; MP (Lab) Brigg Div. of Lincoln and Rutland, 1945-48. Trustee: Thomson Foundn, 1962-; Liverpool Vic. Friendly Soc., 1967-. Hon. Associate, College of Technology, Birmingham. Served as non-commissioned officer, Royal Engineers, 1915-19, two years' active service, France and Belgium. Hon. LLD (Cambridge), 1959. *Address:* 19 Kingsdowne Road, Surbiton, Surrey. *T:* 01-399 5779.

**WILLIAMSON, Alec,** CMG 1944; late Indian Civil Service; *b* 7 Nov. 1886; *s* of late T. Williamson; *m* 1937, Jessie Cunningham Hofford, *d* of J. Hartley Welsh; no *c*. *Educ:* Kirkcudbright Academy; Edinburgh Univ.; Balliol College, Oxford. Asst Commissioner, Burma, 1910; Lt 3/70th Burma Rifles, 1918; Deputy Commissioner and Settlement Officer, 1919; Dep. Chm., Rangoon Develt Trust, 1925; Chm., Rangoon Develt Trust and Collector of Rangoon, 1933; Excise Comr, 1934; Comr of Settlements and Land Records, 1936; Comr of Arakan, 1938; Financial Comr, Burma, 1940. Now retired. *Recreations:* golf, shooting. *Address:* c/o Chartered Bank of India, Australia and China, 38 Bishopsgate, EC2.

**WILLIAMSON, Sir Alexander,** Kt, *cr* 1952; CBE 1941; BSc, MInstCE. *Educ:* Greenock Collegiate School; Glasgow University. Master of the Cutlers' Company of Hallamshire, 1934-35. Chairman of the Gun Forgings Committee, 1940-45. *Recreations:* golf. *Club:* Sheffield (Sheffield).

**WILLIAMSON, Air Commandant Dame Alice Mary,** DBE 1958; RRC 1948 (ARRC 1941); retired as Matron-in-Chief, Princess Mary's Royal Air Force Nursing Service (1956-59); *d* of John William and Theodosia Williamson (*née* Lewis). *Educ:* Mells Girls Sch., Nr Frome, Somerset. Training Sch., Manchester Royal Infirmary, 1924-27; Post Graduate Courses, SCM, 1928-29; X-Ray Course, 1929-30; PMRAFNS, 1930-59. Promoted to Matron, Dec. 1944; Senior Matron, Wing Officer, 1951; Group Officer, 1952; Air Commandant, 1956; QHNS, 1956-59. Chief Nursing Officer, Kuwait Govt Nursing Service, 1959-62. *Recreations:* tennis, swimming, needlework. *Address:* 4 Essex Place, Westlands, Newcastle-under-Lyme, Staffs. *Club:* United Nursing Services.

**WILLIAMSON, Bruce,** MD Edinburgh; FRCP; Hon. Consulting Physician: Royal Northern Hospital, N7; Prince of Wales General Hospital, N15; Barnet General Hospital; Enfield War Memorial Hospital; Brentwood and District Hospital; Hornsey Central Hospital; Ex-Member Medical Appeals Tribunal; Fellow of Royal Society of Medicine; Trustee Edinburgh University Club; President Scottish Medical Golfing Society; *b* South Shields, 1893; 5th *s* of Captain David Williamson, Ladybank, and Jane Theresa Short, Edinburgh; *m* 1936, Margaret Stewart, *d* of William Gibson, Broughty Ferry; one *s*; *m* 1959, Yvonne, *d* of Arthur Carlebach. *Educ:* Newcastle; Bruges; Royal Colleges and University of Edinburgh. Senior Pres., Royal Medical Society, Edinburgh, 1921; Hons MD Edinburgh University, 1925; Lt, Bucks Bn Oxford and Bucks LI, seconded Machine Gun Corps. *Publications:* Text Books: Diseases of Children, 9th edn 1964; Vital Cardiology: A New Outlook on the Prevention of Heart Failure; Diastole (Honeyman Gillespie lecture, Edin. Univ.); Sense and the Seventies (lay physiology); articles in medical journals; The Future and The Fighting General (political-economy); contrib. to The Statist. *Recreation:* golf. *Address:* Weymouth Court, 1 Weymouth Street, W1. *T:* 01-580 4260. *Club:* Devonshire.

**WILLIAMSON, Colin Martin,** CBE 1920; FRPS; Chairman of Williamson Manufacturing Co. Ltd; *b* 1887; *s* of J. Williamson; *m* 1912, Gertrude, *d* of F. Parsons, Hove, Sussex. Rendered service to RAF in connection with Photography during European War, 1914-18. *Address:* Abney Thatch, Bourne End, Bucks. *T:* Bourne End 440.

**WILLIAMSON, David,** QPM 1968; Chief Constable of Renfrew and Bute Constabulary, since 1967; *b* 16 Jan. 1916; *s* of Walter Williamson, fisherman, Havera, Shetland and Margaret Ann Fraser, Havera; *m* 1944, Mary Gwendoline Price, Warley, Staffs; one *s*. *Educ:* Anderson Educational Inst., Lerwick. Joined Greenock Burgh Police, 1937; Flt-Lt, RAF Bomber Comd, 1941-45; rejoined Greenock Burgh Police, 1945; Chief Constable, Greenock Burgh Police, 1958. *Recreations:* gardening, cabinetmaking, reading. *Address:* Havera, Lawmarnock Crescent, Bridge of Weir, Renfrewshire. *T:* Bridge of Weir 2121; Police Headquarters, Mill Street, Paisley, Renfrewshire. *T:* 041-889 1113.

**WILLIAMSON, David Theodore Nelson,** FRS 1968; Director of Research, Molins Ltd, since 1961; *b* 15 Feb. 1923; *s* of David Williamson and Ellie (*née* Nelson); *m* 1951, Alexandra Janet

Smith Neilson; two *s* two *d*. *Educ:* George Heriot's Sch., Edinburgh; Univ. of Edinburgh. MO Valve Co. Ltd, 1943-46; Ferranti Ltd, Edinburgh, 1946-61; pioneered numerical control of machine tools, 1951-; Manager, Machine Tool Control Div., 1959-61; Work on sound reproduction: Williamson amplifier, 1947, Ferranti pickup, 1949; collab. with P. J. Walker in developt of first wide-range electrostatic loud-speaker, 1951-56. Member: NEL Metrology and Noise Control Sub cttee, 1954-57; NEL Cttee on Automatic Design and Machine Tool Control, 1964-66; Min. of Technology Working Party on Computer-Aided Design, 1967; Penny Cttee on Computer-Aided Design, 1967-69; Steering Cttee, IAMTACT, 1967-69; SRC Mech. and Prod. Engrg Cttee, 1965-69; SRC Control Panel, 1966-69; Mech. Engrg EDC, 1968-; SRC Engrg Bd, 1969-; Adv. Cttee for Mech. Engrg, 1969-; Court, Cranfield Inst. of Technology, 1970-; Council and Exec. Cttee, British Hydrodynamics Research Assoc., 1970-. *Publications:* contrib. to: Electronic Engineers' Reference Book, 1959; Progress in Automation, 1960; Numerical Control Handbook, 1968. Papers and articles on engrg subjects. James Clayton Lecture, Inst. Mech. E, 1968. *Recreations:* music, photography. *Address:* Beaumonts, Four Elms, Edenbridge, Kent. *T:* Four Elms 310.

**WILLIAMSON, Elsie Marjorie,** MSc, PhD (London); Principal, Royal Holloway College, University of London, since Oct. 1962; *b* 30 July 1913; *d* of late Leonard Claude Williamson and Hannah Elizabeth Cary. *Educ:* Wakefield Girls' High School; Royal Holloway College. Demonstrator in Physics, Royal Holloway College, University of London, 1936-39; Lecturer in Physics, University College of Wales, Aberystwyth, 1939-45; Lecturer in Physics, Bedford Coll., Univ. of London, 1945-55; Principal, St Mary's Coll., Univ. of Durham, 1955-62. *Publications:* Papers in various scientific periodicals. *Address:* Royal Holloway College, Englefield Green, Surrey. *T:* Egham 4455. *Club:* University Women's.

**WILLIAMSON, Frank Edger;** HM Inspector of Constabulary since 1967; *b* 24 Feb. 1917; *s* of John and late Mary Williamson; *m* 1943, Margaret Beaumont; one *d*. *Educ:* Northampton Grammar Sch. Manchester City Police, 1936-61; Chief Constable: Carlisle, 1961-63; Cumbria Constabulary, 1963-67. Queen's Police Medal, 1966; OStJ 1967. *Address:* 5 Glenmore House, Richmond Hill, Richmond, Surrey. *T:* 01-940 6827.

**WILLIAMSON, Sir George (Alexander),** Kt 1953; DL; Partner, Messrs Paull & Williamsons, Advocates in Aberdeen, since 1928; *b* Aberdeen, 5 Jan. 1898; *e s* of late Robert M. Williamson, CBE, LLD, of Aberdeen, and late Katharine H. Macrae; *m* 1931, Lucie, *yr d* of late Alexander J. Cran, Aberdeen; two *d*. *Educ:* Aberdeen Gram. Sch.; Clifton Bank, St Andrews; RMC, Wellington, S India; Aberdeen Univ. Indian Army: Nov. 1916-; Capt. Nov. 1920; resigned, 1923. BL (Aberdeen) 1926; Scottish Solicitor, 1927. Lt Aberdeen Univ. OTC, 1927-37. ROC, 1939-; Observer Capt. and Scottish Area Comdt, 1950-58. Scottish Unionist Assoc.; Convener Eastern Divl Council, 1950-51; Pres., 1951-52. Aberdeen Savings Bank: Manager, 1932; Trustee and Mem. of Cttee of Management, 1945; Chm. 1953-70. Director, Scottish Northern Investment Trusts, 1938- (Chm. 1943) and other Investment Trusts; Dir Aberdeen Local Bd, Bank of Scotland, 1947-70. mem. Aberdeen City Council, 1934-37. Mem. Aberdeen T&AFA, 1935-56; Hon. Col 501 (Mob.) HAA Regt RA (TA), 1949-55. DL Aberdeen, 1948. *Recreation:* philately. *Address:* 6 Union Row, Aberdeen. *T:* Aberdeen 26262. *Clubs'* United Service, Royal Northern (Aberdeen).

**WILLIAMSON, Sir Hedworth;** *see* Williamson, Sir N. F. H.

**WILLIAMSON, Henry;** author and journalist; *b* 1 Dec. 1895; *o s* of late William Williamson, Parkstone, Dorset. The author lives in N Devon. *Publications:* The Beautiful Years, Dandelion Days, The Dream of Fair Women, The Pathway which form a tetralogy called The Flax of Dream, and were first published respectively in 1921, 1922, 1924 and 1928; also The Lone Swallows, 1922, The Peregrine's Saga (Sun Brothers in USA), 1923; The Old Stag, 1926; Tarka the Otter, 1927 (Hawthornden Prize); The Wet Flanders Plain, 1929; The Patriot's Progress, 1930; Tales of a Devon Village, and Life in a Devon Village, 1932; The Gold Falcon, 1933 (recast and rewritten in 1943); Salar the Salmon, 1935; Selections from Richard Jefferies, 1937; Hodge and his Masters, by Richard Jefferies (a new edition re-arranged by Henry Williamson, 1945); The Children of Shallowford, 1939; The Story of a Norfolk Farm, 1941; T. E. Lawrence, Genius of Friendship, 1941; The Phasian Bird, 1948; Scribbling Lark, 1949; Tales of Moorland and Estuary, 1953; A Clear Water Stream, 1958; The Henry Williamson Animal Saga, 1959; Collected Nature Stories, 1970; A Chronicle of Ancient Sunlight, a novel of 15 volumes, comprising: The Dark Lantern, 1951; Donkey Boy, 1952; Young Phillip Maddison, 1953; How Dear is Life, 1954; A Fox Under My Cloak, 1955; The Golden Virgin, 1957; Love and the Loveless, 1958; A Test to Destruction, 1960; The Innocent Moon, 1961; It was the Nightingale, 1962; The Power of the Dead, 1963; The Phoenix Generation, 1965; A Solitary War, 1966; Lucifer before Sunrise, 1967; The Gale of the World, 1969. *Clubs:* Savage, National Liberal.

**WILLIAMSON, Group Capt. Hugh Alexander,** CMG 1919; AFC; *b* 1885; *s* of Andrew Williamson. Served European War, 1914-19 (despatches, CMG); Iraq command, 1923-24; retired 1928. Calshot Pembroke Dock and Air Ministry, 1939-43. *Address:* No 1 Newlands Manor, Everton, nr Lymington, Hants. *T:* Milford-on-Sea 530.

**WILLIAMSON, Hugh R.;** *see* Ross Williamson.

**WILLIAMSON, John;** Editor, The Press Association Ltd, 1966-69; *b* 19 April 1915; *s* of late William Williamson and Jemima Williamson; *m* 1942, Queenie Myfanwy Pearl Bennett; two *d*. *Educ:* Holy Trinity School, Ashton-under-Lyne, Lancs. Junior Reporter, Manchester Evening News, 1933-34; Reporter, Morecambe & Heysham Visitor, 1934-36; Chief Reporter, East Ham Echo, 1936-38; News Sub-Editor, Press Assoc., 1938; Army, 1940-46, including service as Official Court Shorthand Writer in JAG's Office at Courts Martial and War Crime Trials; rejoined Press Assoc. as Sub-Editor, 1946; held various editorial appointments until 1958, when became Chief News Editor; Acting Man. Editor, Oct. 1965. *Recreations:* gardening, reading, walking. *Address:* 51 Carbery Avenue, W3. *T:* 01-992 7941. *Club:* Press.

**WILLIAMSON, Malcolm Benjamin Graham Christopher;** composer, pianist, organist; *b* 21 Nov. 1931; *s* of Rev. George Williamson, Sydney, Australia; *m* 1960, Dolores Daniel; one *s* two *d*. *Educ:* Barker Coll., Hornsby, NSW; Sydney Conservatorium. *Publications:* operas, ballets, symphonic, chamber, choral and keyboard works. *Recreations:* reading, children. *Address:* 32 Hertford Avenue, SW14. *T:* 01-876 5138.

**WILLIAMSON, Sir (Nicholas Frederick) Hedworth,** 11th Bt, *cr* 1642; *b* 26 Oct. 1937; *s* of late Maj. William Hedworth Williamson (killed in action, 1942) and Diana Mary, *d* of late Brig.-Gen. Hon. Charles Lambton, DSO (she *m* 2nd, 1945, Baron Hailes, *qv*); *S* uncle, 1946. *Heir: kinsman* Hudleston Noel Hedworth Williamson, DSO, MC [*b* 1886; *m* 1926, Leila Isobel, *d* of Lt-Col R. P. Lodwick; one *d*]. *Address:* Lane House, Mortimer, Berks.

**WILLIAMSON, Thomas Bateson;** Assistant Secretary, Department of Health and Social Security, since 1969; *b* 17 April 1915; *y s* of late George Williamson and Dora May Williamson; *m* 1st, 1944, Winifred Mary Johnstone (decd); two *s*; 2nd, 1953, Pauline Mary Luard; four *d*. *Educ:* Barrow Gram. Sch.; Gonville and Caius Coll., Cambridge. 1st Cl. Hons, Mod. Langs Tripos, 1937. Entered War Office as Asst Principal, 1938. Served with HM Forces, 1940-45. Asst Principal, Min. of Health, 1945; Principal, 1946; Asst Secretary, 1954; Commonwealth Fund Fellowship, 1958-59; Under-Secretary, 1965; retired (health grounds), 1969; Asst Secretary, 1969. *Recreations:* fell-walking, music. *Address:* 1 St Mary's Grove, Barnes, SW13. *T:* 01-788 4274.

**WILLINGDON,** 2nd Marquess of, *cr* 1936, **Inigo Brassey Freeman-Thomas;** Earl of Willingdon, *cr* 1931; Viscount Ratendone of Willingdon, *cr* 1931; Viscount Willingdon, *cr* 1924; Baron Willingdon of Ratton, *cr* 1910; President, Securicor Ltd; Director: Albion Insurance Co. Ltd; Andes Trust Ltd; *b* 25 July 1899; 2nd and *o* surv. *s* of 1st Marquess and Lady Marie Adelaide (*d* 1960) (Marie, Marchioness of Willingdon, CI, GBE), *d* of 1st Earl Brassey; *S* father, 1941; *m* 1943, Daphne, *er d* of late Seymour Cadwell. *Educ:* Eton. President of: St John's, Berkshire; The Fauna Preservation Society; The Feathers Clubs Association. Late Capt. 3rd Skinners Horse, Indian Cavalry; Major Sussex Yeomanry; Sqdn Ldr RAFVR. KStJ. *Address:* Kilbees Farm, Windsor Forest. *T:* Winkfield Row 03447. *Clubs:* Turf, White's.

**WILLINK, Rt. Hon. Sir Henry Urmston,** 1st Bt, *cr* 1957; PC 1943; MC; QC 1935; DCL (Lambeth); MA; Master of Magdalene College, Cambridge, 1948-66, Hon. Fellow since 1966; Vice-Chancellor of the University of Cambridge, 1953-55; Dean of the Arches, Master of the Faculties, Vicar-General of the Province of Canterbury and Auditor of the Chancery Court of York, since 1955; *b* 7 March 1894; *s* of William Edward Willink, FRIBA, and Florence Macan, *d* of Col H. B. Urmston; *m* 1st, 1923, Cynthia Frances (*d* 1959), *d* of H. Morley Fletcher, MD, FRCP; two *s* two *d*; 2nd, 1964, Mrs Doris Campbell Preston, *d* of William Campbell Sharman. *Educ:* Eton College (King's Scholar); Trinity College, Cambridge. Served in RFA (TF), 1914-19, Captain (a/Major) (MC despatches; French Croix de Guerre avec Palme). Called to Bar, Inner Temple, 1920; Bencher, 1942. A Special Commissioner for London Region, 1940-43; MP (Nat C) Croydon (North Divn) 1940-48; Minister of Health, 1943-45. Chancellor of Dioceses of Norwich and St Edmundsbury and Ipswich, 1948-55; High Bailiff of Westminster, 1942-67; Member of the Council of the Senate, Univ. of Cambridge, 1951-60. Chairman: Royal Commn on Betting, etc., 1949; Departmental Cttee on Medical Manpower, 1955; Commn of Enquiry to Examine Problems of Minorities in Nigeria, 1957; Royal Commn on the Police, 1960. Mem., Eastern Area Bd, British Transport Commn, 1955-61; Mem., Archbishops' Commn on Crown Appointments, 1962. A Governor of Wellington Coll., 1955-61; Fellow of Eton Coll., 1946-56; Steward of the Courts, Eton Coll., since 1961. Hon. Fellow, Roy. Coll. of General Practitioners; Hon. ARIBA Hon. LLD (Liverpool, Melb.). Officier de la Légion d'Honneur. *Heir: s* Charles William Willink [*b* 10 Sept. 1929; *m* 1954, Elizabeth Andrewes; one *s* one *d*]. *Address:* 51 Madingley Road, Cambridge. *T:* Cambridge 53539.

**WILLIS,** family name of **Baron Willis.**

**WILLIS,** Baron, *cr* 1963, of Chislehurst (Life Peer); **Edward Henry Willis;** FRSA; playwright (as Ted Willis); Director, World Wide Pictures, since 1967; *b* London, 13 Jan. 1918; *m* 1944, Audrey Hale; one *s* one *d*. *Educ:* Tottenham Central School. *Plays include:* Hot Summer Night, New, 1957; God Bless the Guv'nor, Unity, 1959; Woman in a Dressing Gown, 1962; A Slow Roll of Drums, 1964; Queenie, 1967; TV Scriptwriter: Dixon of Dock Green Series, 1953-; Sergeant Cork, 1963-67; Knock on any Door, 1964; Crime of Passion, 1970. *Films include:* Woman in a Dressing Gown, 1958 (Berlin Award); Flame in the Streets (play, Hot Summer Night), 1961; Bitter Harvest, 1963; A Long Way to Shiloh, 1969. President, Screenwriters' Guild, 1958-68. *Publications:* Woman in a Dressing Gown and other TV plays, 1959; Whatever Happened to Tom Mix (autobiography), 1970. *Recreations:* badminton, tennis, Association football. *Address:* 5 Shepherds Green, Chislehurst, Kent.

**WILLIS, Adm. of the Fleet Sir Algernon Usborne,** GCB, *cr* 1947 (KCB, *cr* 1943; CB 1940); KBE, *cr* 1945; DSO 1920; *b* 17 May 1889; *s* of late Herbert Bourdillon Willis; *m* 1916, Olive Christine (*see* Lady Willis), *d* of late Henry E. Millar, Hampstead; two *d*. *Educ:* Eastbourne College; HMS Britannia. Entered Royal Navy, 1904; Midshipman, 1905; Lt 1909; served European War, 1914-18, present at Battle of Jutland HMS Fearless, took part in operations in Baltic, 1919, HMS Wallace (despatches, DSO); HMS Renown with Prince of Wales to Australia and New Zealand, 1920; Commander, 1922; commanded HMS Warwick, 1927-29; Captain, 1929; Staff RN War College, 1930-32; Flag Captain, HMS Kent, China Fleet, 1933-34; Flag Captain, HMS Nelson, Home Fleet, 1934-35; Capt. HMS Vernon, Torpedo School, Portsmouth, 1935-38; Captain HMS Barham, 1st Battle Squadron, 1938-39; Commodore 1st Class, 1939; Chief of Staff, Med. Fleet, HMS Warspite, 1939-41; Rear-Admiral, 1940; Acting Vice-Admiral, 1941; Commander-in-Chief, South Atlantic Station, 1941-42; Vice-Admiral 2nd in Command, Eastern Fleet, 1942-43; Vice-Admiral, 1943; Flag Officer commanding Force H, Mediterranean, 1943 (despatches twice); Commander-in-Chief, Levant Station, 1943; a Lord Commissioner of the Admiralty and Chief of Naval Personnel (Second Sea Lord), 1944-46; Admiral, 1945; C-in-C Mediterranean Fleet, 1946-48; Commander-in-Chief, Portsmouth Command, 1948-50; Admiral of the Fleet, 1949; KStJ 1948; DL Hampshire, 1952. Grand Cross, Order of Phoenix (Greece), 1946; Greek War Cross, 1944. *Address:* Monks Lea, Petersfield, Hants. *Club:* United Service.

**WILLIS, Anthony Armstrong,** OBE 1944; MC 1916; late Squadron-Leader, RAFVR; late Captain RE; author and playwright (writing as Anthony Armstrong); *b* 2 Jan. 1897; *er s* of late Paymaster Capt. G. H. A. Willis, CB, RN; *m* 1926, Monica, *o d* of Dr A. L. M. Sealy; one *s* two *d*. *Educ:* Uppingham School; Trinity College, Cambridge. Entered Royal Engineers, 1915; served with 34th Division in France, 1916-19 (despatches, MC, wounded); retired to RERO, 1925; began to write for Punch, 1924, and contributed every week (as "A. A."), 1925-33; contributor (articles and short stories) to New Yorker, Strand, Daily Mail, Sunday Chronicle, Country Fair, Evening News, etc.; invalided out of Reserve, 1939; joined RAFVR 1940, and founded Tee Emm, the RAF Training Memorandum. *Publications:* five historical romances between 1920 and 1925; *humourous novels:* Patrick Undergraduate; Patrick Engaged; Patrick Helps; No Dragon, No Damsel; *volumes of humorous articles:* Warriors at Ease; Warriors Still at Ease; Selected Warriors; Easy Warriors; Percival and I; Percival at Play; How to Do It; Me and Frances; Livestock in Barracks; Apple and Percival; Two Legs and Four; Britisher on Broadway; While You Wait; Thoughts on Things; Captain Bayonet and Others; Warriors Paraded (an omnibus); Nothing to do with the War; Warriors at War; Prangmere Mess; Good Egg (with Fred Robinson); *crime novels* (also published in USA); The Trail of Fear; The Secret Trail; The Trail of the Lotto; The Trail of the Black King; The Poison Trail; Ten-Minute Alibi (the story of the play); No Higher Mountain; He Was Found in the Road; Spies in Amber; *country books:* Cottage into House; We Like the Country; Village at War; We Keep Going; The Year at Margarets; *other publications:* Yesterdailies (being Extracts from the Press of the Past); The Prince who Hiccupped and other Stories; Taxi, the book about the London taxi-cab; Laughter Omnibus (a Punch Anthology); The After Breakfast Book; Laughter Parade, an Anthology of Humour; Plonk's Party (with Raff); Prune's Progress (with Raff); Nice Types (with Raff); More Nice Types (with Raff); Goodbye Nice Types (with Raff); Whiskers will Not be Worn (with Raff); The Naughty Princess (humorous fairy stories); When the Bells Rang (with Bruce Graeme); England Our England (with Treyer Evans); Sappers at War (for WO); My Friend Serafin; The Strange Case of Mr Pelham; Saying Your Prayers (a book about learning to pray); *plays:* (produced and unproduced): Well Caught, a criminal comedy; Knight of a Night, a farce; Sitting on a Fence, a farcical comedy; Ten-Minute Alibi, a thriller; Mile-Away Murder, a thriller; Spies in Amber, a thriller; No Higher Mountain, a murder play; Happy Ever After, a mad fairy play; (with Ian Hay) Orders are Orders, a military diversion; (with Harold Simpson) Without Witness, a thriller; (adapted from the German) Business with Royalty; (with Roland Crossley) The Three Pigeons, a drama; (with Arnold Ridley) The Running Man, a comedy thriller, and Bellamy, a farce-comedy; (with Philip King) Here We Come Gathering, a comedy; Eleventh Hour, Jumble Warfare, Horatius (3 plays for the WO), and other one-act plays; *radio plays:* For Love of a Lady, The Black King, Return, The Wide Guy, At Squinty Abbott's, Death Set to Music, The Case of Mr Pelham (filmed, 1970, as The Man Who Haunted Himself). Adaption of own plays, and original work for BBC; broadcast in series These Radio Times; script (with Richard Murdoch and Kenneth Horne) of series Over To You; (with David Climie) of series Home And Away; *film work:* OHMS (treatment); Young and Innocent (treatment); *television work:* Armstrong's Garden (weekly programme on Southern TV); Never Come Back (story). *Recreations:* talking, gardening, reading. *Address:* The Knapp, Grayswood Road, Haslemere, Surrey. *T:* Haslemere 2066. *Club:* Savage.

**WILLIS, Charles Armine,** CBE 1930; MA (Oxon); Sudan Political Service (retired); *b* 1881; *s* of John Armine Willis, late Fellow of King's College, Cambridge, and Senior Inspector HM Education Department; *m* 1st, 1919, Clare (*d* 1935), *y d* of 1st Lord Holmpatrick and *g-gd* of 1st Duke of Wellington; one *s*; 2nd, 1937, Katharine Winifred Nutcombe Barnett (*d* 1960), 3rd *d* of late James Nutcombe Gould. *Educ:* Eton (Scholar, 1894); Newcastle Select, 1899; Magdalen Coll., Oxford (Exhibitioner). Eton Eight, 1899 and 1900; won Ladies Plate, 1899; 2nd Captain of boats, and keeper of wall, 1899-1900; Editor Eton College Chronicle, 1899-1900; rowed in trials, Oxford, 1900-01-02; rowed for Oxford, 1903; President, 1904, but did not row; won Ladies' Plate, 1904, rowing for Magdalen, Grand Challenge in Leander crew, 1901; Sudan Political Service, 1905; various appointments in that service till attached to Intelligence Dept, 1914; Director of Intelligence, 1919-26; Governor, Upper Nile Province, 1926-31; Member of Mui Tsai Commission (Colonial Office), 1936; delegate for the Sarawak Government on the Rubber Regulation Cttee, 1937, 1938; Chairman of Royal London Society for Aid of Discharged Prisoners, 1941-47. JP Berks, 1942-49. *Address:* 69 St James's Street, SW1. *Clubs:* Carlton, Beefsteak, Leander.

**WILLIS, Charles Reginald;** Director, Associated Newspapers Ltd, since 1961; Editorial Director, Harmsworth Publications Ltd, 1967; Member, Press Council, 1967; *b* 11 June 1906; *s* of Charles and Marie Willis, Tiverton, Devon; *m* 1929, Violet Stubbs; one *d*. *Educ:* Tiverton Grammar Sch. Tiverton Gazette, 1922-27; North Western Daily Mail, 1927-29; Evening Chronicle, Newcastle upon Tyne, 1929-1935; Evening Chronicle, Manchester, 1935-42; Empire News, London, 1942-43; The Evening News, London, 1943 (Editor, 1954-66). *Recreation:* cricket. *Address:* 133 Torrington Park, North Finchley, N12. *T:* 01-445 9001. *Clubs:* Garrick, Press.

**WILLIS, Rt. Hon. Eustace George,** PC 1967; *b* 7 March 1903; *s* of Walter Willis and Rose Jane Eaton; *m* 1929, Mary Swan Ramsay Nisbet; one *d*. *Educ:* City of Norwich Sch. Engine Room Artificer, Royal Navy, 1919-30. Served Royal Artillery, 1942-45. Political Organiser, 1930-32; Bookseller and Lecturer for NCLC, 1932-64. MP (Lab), North Edinburgh, 1945-50, East Edinburgh, April 1954-70. Member: Select Cttee on Estimates, 1945-50, 1954-59; Central Adv. Cttee to Min. of Pensions, 1945-50; Mineral Development Cttee, 1946-48. Chairman: Edinburgh City Labour Party, 1952-54; Scottish Labour Party, 1954-55; Scottish Parliamentary Labour Party, 1961-63. Parliamentary Deleg. to Atlantic Congress, 1959, NATO, 1960-62. Minister of State, Scottish Office, 1964-67. Member, NUGMW. *Recreations:* book-collecting, music. *Address:* 31 Great King Street, Edinburgh 3. *T:* 031-556 6941.

**WILLIS, Sir Frank;** *see* Willis, Sir Z. F.

**WILLIS, Rt. Rev. Frederick Roberts,** DD; *b* 10 June 1900; *s* of late Ven. J. R. Willis, BD, Church of Ireland; unmarried. *Educ:* Trinity Coll., Dublin. BA 1923; DipEd 1928; MA 1946; DD (jure dignitatis), 1951. Curate of Sandford Parish, Dublin, 1924-28; Missionary to Chota Nagpur (Dublin University Mission), Hazaribagh, India, 1928-51; Head of the DU Mission, 1946-51; Bishop of Delhi, 1951-66. Retired, and now assisting Rev. Canon R. F. G. Jenkins (Archdeacon of Dublin and Vicar of All Saints' Church, Grangegorman, Dublin). Canon of St Patrick's Cathedral, Dublin,

1966-. *Address:* c/o All Saints' Vicarage, 30 Phibsborough Road, Dublin 7, Eire.

**WILLIS, Harold Infield,** QC 1952; Deputy Chairman, Hampshire Quarter Sessions, since 1966; *b* 28 March 1902; *yr s* of late Sir Frederick James Willis, KBE, CB, and Lady Willis; *m* 1943, Eileen Burnett Murray; three *s*. *Educ:* Berkhamsted; New Coll., Oxford. Called to the Bar, 1926, Middle Temple; Bencher, Middle Temple, 1948, Treasurer, 1969. Served War of 1939-45, RAFVR, 1940-45. Chairman of Governors, Berkhamsted Schools. *Recreations:* gardening and fishing. *Address:* Homington House, Coombe Bissett, near Salisbury, Wilts. *Club:* Flyfishers'.

**WILLIS, Dr Hector Ford,** CB 1960; Scientific Adviser, Ministry of Defence, 1962-70, retired; *b* 3 March 1909; *m* 1936, Marie Iddon (*née* Renwick). *Educ:* Howard Gardens High Sch.; University College, Cardiff; Trinity Coll., Cambridge. British Cotton Industry Research Association, 1935-38; Admiralty, 1938; Chief of the Royal Naval Scientific Service, 1954-62. *Publications:* Papers in Proceedings of Royal Society, Philosophical Magazine, Proceedings of the Faraday Society. *Address:* Fulwood, Eaton Park, Cobham, Surrey.

**WILLIS, John Brooke; His Honour Judge Brooke Willis;** County Court Judge (Circuit 19) since 1967; Barrister-at-law; Deputy Chairman of the West Riding of Yorkshire Quarter Sessions, since 1958; *b* 3 July 1906; *yr s* of William Brooke Willis and Maud Mary Willis, Rotherham; *m* 1929, Mary Margaret Coward (marr. diss., 1946); one *s* one *d*; *m* 1964, Terena Ann Steel (formerly Hood); two *d*. *Educ:* Bedford Modern Sch.; Sheffield Univ. Called to the Bar, Middle Temple, 1938, North Eastern Circuit. Served War of 1939-45. RAFVR, 1940-45, Sqdn Leader. Recorder, Rotherham, 1955-59, Huddersfield, 1959-65; County Court Judge (Circuit 14), 1965-66. Chairman, Medical Appeal Tribunal under the National Insurance (Industrial Injuries) Acts, 1953-65. *Address:* Elmton House, Elmton, near Worksop, Notts.

**WILLIS, John Henry,** RBA, ARCA (London); artist; *b* Tavistock, 9 Oct. 1887; *s* of R. Willis, art dealer; *m* Eleanor Rushton (*née* Claughton); one *s* by a former marriage. *Educ:* Armstrong Coll., Durham Univ.; Royal College of Art, South Kensington. Portrait and Landscape Painter. *Principal works:* Kiwi Hut, on the line RA, 1921; 'Twixt Devon and Cornwall, on the line RA, 1923; The Nant Francon Pass, on the line RA, 1924; *portraits:* M. C. Oliver, RA, 1922; Stanley, son of E. J. Miles, RA, 1923. *Recreations:* tennis, golf. *Address:* 20 Titchfield Gardens, Paignton, Devon.

**WILLIS, Hon. Sir John (Ramsay),** Kt 1966; QC 1956; **Hon. Mr Justice Willis;** Judge of the High Court of Justice, Queen's Bench Division, since 1966; *b* 1908; *s* of Dr and Mrs J. K. Willis, Cranleigh, Surrey; *m* 1st, 1935, Peggy Eileen Branch; two *s*; 2nd, 1959, Mrs Barbara Ringrose, 47 Markham Square, SW3. *Educ:* Lancing; Trinity Coll., Dublin (BA, LLB). Called to Bar, Gray's Inn, 1932. Royal Signals (TA), 1938-45; served War of 1939-45; GSO 1 14th Army. Bencher, Gray's Inn, 1953, Treasurer, 1969. Recorder of Southampton, 1965-66; Dep. Chairman, E Suffolk QS, 1965. *Recreation:* mountaineering. *Address:* 1 Verulam Buildings, Gray's Inn, WC1. *T:* 01-242 7722; Waterfields, Snape, near Saxmundham, Suffolk. *Clubs:* Garrick, Alpine.

**WILLIS, John Robert,** CB 1951; MC 1917; Under Secretary, Ministry of Transport, 1948-57; *b* 28 June 1896; *s* of late Professor A. R. Willis; *m* 1925, Alice Mary, *o d* of late R. F. Clarke; one *s* one *d*. *Educ:* St Paul's Sch.; Balliol Coll., Oxford. Inns of Court OTC, Worcestershire Regt (Lieut) and RAF, 1916-19; entered Board of Trade, 1920; Secretary, Food Council, 1932; Assistant Secretary, Industrial Supplies Dept, 1939; Commercial Relations and Treaties Dept, 1940; British Middle East Office, Cairo, 1946. *Address:* 39 Sheen Common Drive, Richmond, Surrey. *T:* 01-876 6022.

**WILLIS, Joseph Robert McKenzie,** CB 1952; CMG 1946; Deputy Chairman, Board of Inland Revenue, since 1957; *b* 18 March 1909; 2nd *s* of Charles Frederick Willis and Lucy Alice McKenzie; *m* 1945, Elizabeth Browning, *er d* of James Ewing, *qv*; one *s* one *d*. *Educ:* Eton; Christ Church, Oxford. Entered Inland Revenue Dept, 1932; Under Secretary, Central Economic Planning Staff, Treasury, 1948-49; Commissioner of Inland Revenue, 1949; Student of Imperial Defence Coll., 1948. *Address:* 28 Heathgate, NW11. *T:* 01-455 8128. *Club:* Reform.

**WILLIS, Lady; Olive Christine,** CBE 1951; *b* 20 Nov. 1895; *d* of late Henry Edward Millar, Hampstead; *m* 1916, Lieut Algernon Usborne Willis (*see* Admiral of the Fleet, Sir Algernon U. Willis); two *d*. *Educ:* St Felix Sch., Southwold, Suffolk; Newnham Coll., Cambridge. Officer (Sister) Order of St John of Jerusalem, 1948. *Recreation:* gardening. *Address:* Monks Lea, Tilmore, Petersfield, Hampshire. *T:* Petersfield 4135. *Club:* English-Speaking Union.

**WILLIS, Robert William Gaspard,** MA; Founder and Headmaster of Copford Glebe School, 1958-69, Principal since 1969; *b* 22 Nov. 1905; *s* of Rev. W. N. Willis, founder and Headmaster for 38 years, of Ascham St Vincent's, Eastbourne, and Sophia Caroline Baker; *m* 1930, Ernestine Ruth Kimber; two *s* two *d*. *Educ:* Ascham St Vincent's, Eastbourne; Eton Coll. (Foundation Scholar); Corpus Christi Coll., Cambridge (Scholar). Assistant Master at Malvern Coll., Worcs, 1927-39 (Mathematics and Classics); Senior Mathematical Master at The King's School, Macclesfield, Cheshire, 1939-41; Headmaster of Sir William Turner's School (Coatham School), Redcar, 1941-53; Headmaster of English High School for Boys, Istanbul, Turkey, 1953-57. *Recreation:* sailing. *Address:* Copford Glebe, near Colchester, Essex. *T:* Marks Tey 341. *Clubs:* Officers (Colchester); Royal Harwich Yacht.

**WILLIS, Roger Blenkiron,** TD; **His Honour Judge Willis;** County Court Judge since Oct. 1959 (Circuit 39, Shoreditch, since 1965; Circuit 40, Bow, 1963-65; Circuit 42, Bloomsbury, 1959-63); *b* 22 June 1906; *s* of late William Outhwaite Willis, KC, and Margaret Alice (*née* Blenkiron); *m* 1933, Joan Eleanor Amy Good; two *d*. *Educ:* Charterhouse School; Emmanuel Coll., Cambridge. Barrister, Inner Temple, Nov. 1930. Joined Middlesex Yeomanry (TA), 1938. Served War of 1939-45. *Recreation:* golf. *Address:* 18 Turners Reach House, 9 Chelsea Embankment, SW3. *T:* 01-352 6041. *Clubs:* Garrick, MCC.

**WILLIS, Prof. Rupert A.,** DSc, MD, FRCP, FRCS; FRACP; Consultant Pathologist, Imperial Cancer Research Fund, London; Emeritus Professor and Research Fellow in Pathology, University of Leeds; *b* 24 Dec. 1898; Australian; *m* 1924, Alice Margaret Tolhurst; one *s* one *d*. *Educ:* Melbourne Univ.

Medical Superintendent, Austin Hospital, Melbourne, 1927-30; Pathologist: Alfred Hospital, Melbourne, 1930-45; Royal College of Surgeons, London, 1945-48; Royal Cancer Hospital, London, 1948-50. Professor of Pathology, University of Leeds, 1950-55; Macfarlane Professor of Experimental Medicine, University of Glasgow, 1963-64. Hon. LLD (Glasgow), 1962. *Publications:* The Spread of Tumours in the Human Body, 1934; Pathology of Tumours, 1948; Principles of Pathology, 1950; Borderland of Embryology and Pathology, 1958; Pathology of Tumours of Children, 1962; contrib. to Journal Path. Bact., Medical Journal Australia, etc. *Recreation:* gardening. *Address:* Inverdee, Delavor Road, Heswall, Cheshire.

**WILLIS, Ted;** *see* Willis, Baron.

**WILLIS, Comdr William John Adlam,** CBE 1953 (OBE 1937); MVO 1936; KPM; RN retired; DL; HM Inspector of Constabulary, 1953-64, retired; *b* 27 June 1894; *s* of Thomas Willis, RN, retired, Gillingham, Kent; *m* 1929, Kate Constance, *d* of Henry Sanders, Gillingham; two *s* one *d*. *Educ:* Royal Navy Hospital Sch., Greenwich. Chief Constable of Rochester, 1937-40; Chief Constable of Bedfordshire, 1940-53; DL Bedfordshire, 1951-61; Suffolk, 1964-. Conspicuous Gallantry Medal; French Médaille Militaire, 1916; KPM 1944. *Address:* Cross Green Cottage, Cockfield, near Bury St Edmunds, Suffolk. *T:* Cockfield Green 376. *Club:* Reform.

**WILLIS, Sir (Zwinglius) Frank,** Kt, *cr* 1947; CBE 1942 (OBE 1918); General Secretary of the National Council of YMCAs, 1939-55, retired; Hon. Consultant to World Council of YMCAs on Ecumenical Questions and YMCA-Church Relationships; Chairman of Council of Voluntary Welfare Work 1956-62; Chairman of Committee for Overseas Travel Parties for Youth of the South African Aid to Britain Fund, 1948-58; Member Executive Committee, National Council of Social Service, 1941-70; *b* 1890; *s* of late Rev. R. Elgar Willis, Ipswich; *m* 1918, Helen Frances, *d* of late Sir Frederick Walker Mott, KBE, FRS, MD. *Educ:* Northgate Grammar Sch., Ipswich, Ipswich Sch. (Foundation Scholar); King's Coll., Cambridge (Drapers' Exhibitioner). Dep. Organising Secretary, YMCA Services, W. Front, 1915-18; Sen. Tutor, YMCA Training Coll., London, 1919-21; Secretary for Personnel, Training, and Programme, Nat. Council of YMCAs, 1921-30; Commonwealth Representative on staff of World Alliance of YMCAs and Co-Director of YMCA Training Coll., Geneva, 1930-34; Asst General Secretary, Nat. Council of YMCAs, 1934-39. Member World Council of YMCAs and several of its main Cttees and Commissions, 1955-65; Member Exec. Cttee, 1948-55, and Vice-Chairman, Internat. Dept, 1951-55, of British Council of Churches; Member, Adult Education Cttee, Board of Education, 1921-28; Member British Inst. of Adult Education, 1921-39; Chairman of Social Hygiene Cttee, British Social Biology Council, 1935-39; Member Standing Conf. of Nat. Voluntary Youth Organisations, 1936-55. *Address:* 165 West Heath Road, NW3. *T:* 01-455 8544.

**WILLISON, Sir John (Alexander),** Kt 1970; OBE 1964; QPM 1968; DL; Chief Constable of West Mercia Constabulary since 1967; *b* 3 Jan. 1914; *s* of John Willison Gow Willison and Mabel Willison, Dalry, Ayrshire; *m* 1947, Jess Morris Bruce. *Educ:* Sedbergh School. Joined City of London Police, 1933; served with RNVR, 1943-46; Chief Constable: Berwick, Roxburgh and Selkirk, 1952-58; Worcestershire Constabulary, 1958-67. DL Worcs 1968. CStJ 1967. *Address:* Lowhill House, Spetchley, Worcester.

**WILLMER, Prof. Edward Nevill,** ScD; FRS 1960; Emeritus Professor of Histology, University of Cambridge, since 1969; Fellow of Clare College since 1936; *b* 15 Aug. 1902; 5th *s* of Arthur W. Willmer, Birkenhead; *m* 1939, Henrietta Noreen (Penny), 2nd *d* of H. Napier Rowlatt; two *s* two *d*. *Educ:* Birkenhead Sch.; Corpus Christi Coll., Oxford. BA (Oxon) 1924; MA (Oxon) 1965; MSc (Manchester) 1927; ScD (Cambridge) 1944. Demonstrator and Assistant Lecturer in Physiology, Manchester, 1924-29; Lecturer in Histology, Cambridge, 1930-48; Reader, 1948-65, Prof., 1966-69. *Publications:* Tissue Culture, 1934; Retinal Structure and Colour Vision, 1946; Cytology and Evolution, 1960, 2nd edn 1970; (ed) Cells and Tissues in Culture, 1965. Contrib. physiological and biological journals. *Recreations:* painting, gardening, walking. *Address:* Yew Garth, Grantchester, Cambridge. *T:* Trumpington 2360.

**WILLMER, Rt. Hon. Sir (Henry) Gordon,** PC 1958; Kt 1945; OBE 1945; TD; a Lord Justice of Appeal, 1958-Jan. 1969; *b* 1899; 4th *s* of late A. W. Willmer, JP, Birkenhead; *m* 1928, Barbara, *d* of late Sir Archibald Hurd; one *s* two *d*. *Educ:* Birkenhead Sch.; Corpus Christi Coll., Oxford. Hon. Fellow of Corpus Christi Coll., 1949. Called to Bar, 1924; KC 1939. Joined Territorial Army in 1925, and served with 53rd Medium Bde, RA (TA), till 1938, when retired on to TA Reserve of Officers, from which called up for service during the war; served with Coast Artillery, 1940-43, and with AMG, CMF, 1943-45. A Justice of the High Court. Probate, Divorce and Admiralty Division, 1945-58. President, Shipping Claims Tribunal, 1946; Member Supreme Court Cttee on Practice and Procedure, 1947; Member, General Claims Tribunal, 1950; Chairman, inns of Court Mission, 1950-63; Treasurer, Inner Temple, 1969; Chm., Statutory Cttee, Pharmaceutical Soc. of GB, 1970. Hon. LLD Liverpool, 1966. *Recreation:* golf. *Address:* Flat 1, 34 Arkwright Road, Hampstead, NW3. *T:* 01-435 0690.

*See also J. F. Willmer.*

**WILLMER, John Franklin,** QC 1967; *b* 30 May 1930; *s* of Rt Hon. Sir (Henry) Gordon Willmer, *qv; m* 1958, Nicola Ann Dickinson; one *s* three *d*. *Educ:* Winchester; Corpus Christi Coll., Oxford. National Service, 2nd Lieut, Cheshire Regt, 1949-50; TA Cheshire Regt, 1950-51; Middlesex Regt, 1951-57 (Captain). Called to Bar, Inner Temple, 1955. Member: panel of Lloyd's Arbitrators in Salvage Cases, 1967; panel from which Wreck Commissioners appointed, 1967. *Recreation:* walking. *Address:* 11 Park Drive, NW11. *T:* 01-455 2048. *Club:* Oxford and Cambridge University.

**WILLMOTT, Sir Maurice (Gordon),** Kt 1956; MC; Master of the Supreme Court (Chancery Division) since 1931 (Chief Master, 1950-59); *b* Ealing, Middlesex, 25 Feb. 1894; *s* of James William Willmott, Ealing; *m* 1934, Joan Barbara, *o d* of Gervase Edward Newby, OBE, FRCS; two *d*. *Educ:* Privately. Qualified as Solicitor, 1915; Inns of Court, OTC, 1915; 2nd Lieut, KRRC, 1916; Captain, 1917; served in France in European War (wounded, despatches); demobilised, 1919; admitted Solicitor, 1919. *Recreation:* gardening. *Address:* Old Beams, Blackford, Yeovil, Somerset. *T:* North Cadbury 397.

**WILLOCHRA, Bishop of,** since 1970; **Rt. Rev. Stanley Bruce Rosier;** *b* 18 Nov. 1928; *s* of S. C.

and A. Rosier; *m* 1954, Faith Margaret Alice Norwood; one *s* three *d*. *Educ:* Univ. of WA; Christ Church, Oxford. Asst Curate, Ecclesall, Dio. of Sheffield, 1954; Rector of: Wyalkatchem, Dio. of Perth, 1957; Kellerberrin, Dio. of Perth, 1964; Auxiliary Bishop in Diocese of Perth, Western Australia, 1967-70. *Recreation:* natural history. *Address:* Bishop's House, Gladstone, SA 5473, Australia. *T:* 622057.

**WILLOCK, Air Vice-Marshal (retired) Robert Peel,** CB 1943; *b* 17 Dec. 1893; *s* of Canon R. P. Willock; *m* 1919, Dorothy York Liversidge; one *d*. *Educ:* Marlborough Coll. Oxford and Bucks LI and RFC 1914-18; RAF 1918; Staff Coll., Camberley, 1928-30; Air Attaché to British Embassy, China, 1933-36; Imperial Defence Coll., 1937; Director of Staff Duties, Air Ministry, 1938; AOC No. 21 Group RAF, 1940-43; AOC Iraq and Persia, 1943-44. Deputy Head of RAF Delegation, Washington, 1944-46; retired list, 1946; Civil Air Attaché to British Embassy, Washington, 1946-47; Overseas Representative of Minister of Civil Aviation, 1947-49; Civil Aviation Adviser to High Commissioner for UK, Australia, 1949-59. Commander USA Legion of Merit, 1946. *Recreation:* shooting. *Address:* c/o Lloyds Bank Ltd, 6 Pall Mall, SW1. *Club:* Royal Air Force.

**WILLOTT, Lt-Col Roland Lancaster,** DSO 1940; OBE 1945; TD 1946; BSc; CEng, FIMechE; Group Chief Engineer, Shotton Works, British Steel Corporation; Director, John Summers & Sons Ltd; *b* 1 May 1912; *s* of Frederick John Willott and Gertrude May Leese; *m* 1960, Elisabeth Petersen. *Educ:* Wellington Sch. (Somerset); University of Wales. College Apprentice Metropolitan Vickers Electrical Co., Trafford Park, Manchester, 1931-33; Mechanical Engineer Metropolitan Vickers Co., 1933-36; Major RE 1939-41; Lt-Col CRE 1941-45; Colonel Commander Army Group RE, 1945 (despatches, DSO, OBE, Order of Leopold of Belgium, Croix de Guerre). Member, Dee and Clwyd River Authority. *Address:* Shrublands, Groomsdale, Hawarden, Deeside, Flintshire CH5 3EH. *T:* Hawarden 2173.

**WILLOUGHBY,** family name of **Baron Middleton.**

**WILLOUGHBY, HEATHCOTE-DRUMMOND-,** family name of **Earl of Ancaster.**

**WILLOUGHBY, Hon. (Digby) Michael (Godfrey John),** MC 1945; DL; JP; *b* 1 May 1921; *er s* and *heir* of 11th Baron Middleton, *qv*; *m* 1947, Janet, *o d* of General Sir James Marshall-Cornwall, *qv*; three *s*. *Educ:* Eton; Trinity Coll., Cambridge. BA 1950; MA 1958. Served War of 1939-45: Coldstream Guards, 1940-46; NW Europe, 1944-45 (despatches, MC, Croix de Guerre). Land Agent, 1951-. DL 1963, JP 1958, CC 1964-, East Riding of Yorks; Mem., Yorkshire and Humberside Economic Planning Council, 1968-. *Address:* North Grimston House, Malton, Yorks. *T:* North Grimston 204. *Club:* Boodle's.

**WILLOUGHBY, Rear-Admiral Guy;** CB 1955; *b* 7 Nov. 1902; *s* of Rev. Nesbit E. Willoughby, Vicar of Bickington, Devon, and of Marjorie Helen Willoughby (*née* Kaye); *m* 1923, Mary, *d* of J. G. W. Aldridge, AMICE, Wimbledon; one *s* one *d*. *Educ:* Osborne and Dartmouth. Joined Osborne, 1916; Sub-Lieut, 1923; qualified as a naval pilot 1925, and thereafter flew as a pilot in Naval and RAF Squadrons, embarked in various Carriers until 1936; Commander, 1937; Commander (Air) in Glorious, 1938-39; served on naval staff, Admiralty, 1940-41; comd HM Carrier Activity, 1942-43; Captain, 1943; Chief Staff Officer to Admiral Comdg Carriers in Eastern Fleet, 1944; Director of Air Warfare and Training (Naval Staff, Admiralty), 1945-46; Imperial Defence Coll., 1947; 4th Naval Member of Australian Commonwealth Navy Board and Cdre (Air), 1948-50; comd HM Carrier Eagle, 1951-52; Rear-Admiral 1953; Flag Officer, Flying Training, 1953-56, retired, 1956. *Address:* High Croft, South Woodchester, near Stroud, Glos. *T:* Amberley 2594. *Club:* United Service.

**WILLOUGHBY, Maj.-Gen. Sir John (Edward Francis),** KBE 1967 (CBE 1963; OBE 1953); Adviser on Defence to Federation of Arab Amirates, since 1968; *b* 18 June 1913; *s* of Major N. E. G. Willoughby, The Middlesex Regt, and Mrs B. A. M. Willoughby, Heytesbury, Wiltshire; *m* 1938, Muriel Alexandra Rosamund Scott; three *d*. Commissioned, Middlesex Regt, 1933. Served War of 1939-45 with Middlesex Regt, BEF, 1940-41; OC 2 Middlesex Regt, 1943; GSO 1 220 Military Mission, USA, Pacific, Burma and UK, 1943-44; OC 1 Dorsets Regt, NW Europe, 1944; served with Middlesex Regt, FARELF, Korea, 1950-51; GSO1, 3 Inf. Div., UK and MELF, 1951-53; OC 1 Middlesex Regt, British Troops Austria, UK and MELF, 1954-56; Colonel, The Middlesex Regt, 1959-65; Chief of Staff, Land Forces, Hong Kong, 1961; GOC, 48 Inf. Div. (TA) and W Midland District, 1963-65; GOC Land Forces ME Comd, Inspector-Gen. of Federal Regular Army of S Arabia and Security Comdr Aden State, 1965-67. *Address:* c/o Ministry of Defence, Whitehall, SW1; Overton House, Codford St Peter, Wilts. *Club:* United Service.

**WILLOUGHBY, Kenneth James;** Under-Secretary, Management Services, Ministry of Technology, since 1968; *b* 6 Nov. 1922; *y s* of late Frank Albert Willoughby and late Florence Rose (*née* Darbyshire); *m* 1943, Vera May Dickerson; one *s* one *d*. *Educ:* Hackney Downs (Grocers') Sch.; Selwyn Coll., Cambridge. Tax Officer, Inland Revenue, 1939; Royal Engineers, UK, Egypt, Italy, Austria, Greece, 1941-47 (despatches, Captain); Asst Auditor, Exchequer and Audit Dept, 1947; Asst Prin., Min. of Civil Aviation, 1949; Asst Private Sec. to Minister of Civil Aviation, 1950; Private Sec. to Perm. Sec., 1951; Principal, Min. of Transport (and later, Civil Aviation), 1951; Sec., Air Transport Adv. Council, 1957; Asst Sec., Min. of Aviation, 1962. *Address:* 67 Pine Hill, Epsom, Surrey. *T:* Epsom 25107.

**WILLOUGHBY, Leonard Ashley,** MA, DLitt (London), PhD (Vienna); Fellow of University College, London; Hon. Director Institute of Germanic Languages and Literatures, University of London, 1950-53; Emeritus Professor of the University of London; President, English Goethe Society; Founder and Editor of German Life and Letters, 1936-56; a Freeman of the City of London; *b* Bonby, Lincs, 4 June 1885; 2nd *s* of W. H. and F. A. Wlloughby; *m* 1916, Lucie Edith, 2nd *d* of H. E. Berthon; one *s*. *Educ:* Lycée Carnot, Paris; Realschule, Ohligs, Germany; City of London Sch.; University College, London; Universities of Vienna and Bonn. Lecturer in English in the University of Cologne, 1908-10; Senior Taylorian Lecturer in German in the University of Oxford, 1910-19; Lecturer in charge of German in the University of Sheffield, 1919-30; Henry Simon Professor of German Language and Literature in the University of Manchester, 1930-31; Fielden Professor of German, University College,

London, 1931-50; visiting Professor in the University of Toronto, 1949, and Columbia Univ., New York, 1953; Advisory sub-editor, Chambers's Encyclopædia. Member Mixed Commission for cultural relations with Austria, 1953-55. Corr. Member of Deutsche Akademie, Darmstadt, 1956. Served European War as 2nd Lieut, in the 2/4 Loyal North Lancs Regt; Lieut, RNVR in the Naval Intelligence Department; for a few months on the Reparation Commission in Paris, 1920. *Publications:* D. G. Rossetti and German Literature, 1912; Samuel Naylor and Reynard the Fox, 1914; Von dem jungesten Tage, 1918; Schiller's Die Räuber, 1922; The Classical Age of German Literature, 1926; The Romantic Movement in Germany, 1930; Letters of Kerner to Alexander of Württemberg, 1938; Urfaust and Faust ein Fragment, 1943; Kabale und Liebe, 1945; (with E. M. Wilkinson) Goethe, Poet and Thinker, 1962; Schiller's Aesthetic Letters, 1967. Articles and Reviews in literary and linguistic journals, English and foreign. *Recreations:* music, travelling. *Address:* Angle Place Cottage, Montague Road, Berkhamsted, Herts. *T:* 3736.

**WILLOUGHBY, Hon. Michael;** *see* Willoughby, Hon. D. M. G. J.

**WILLOUGHBY DE BROKE,** 20th Baron, *cr* 1492; **John Henry Peyto Verney,** MC 1918; AFC 1940; KStJ 1948; JP; Lord Lieutenant of Warwickshire, 1939-68; Air Commodore, Auxiliary Air Force, retired; *b* 21 May 1896; *o c* of 19th Baron and Marie Frances Lisette, OBE (*d* 1941), *y d* of C. A. Hanbury, Strathgarve, Ross-shire; *S* father, 1923; *m* 1933, Rachel, *d* of Sir Bouchier Wrey, 11th Bt, and Mrs Godfrey Heseltine; one *s* one *d*. *Educ:* Eton; Sandhurst. Served European War (MC); ADC to Governor of Bombay, 1919-22; late Captain, 17-21st Lancers; Adjutant, Warwickshire Yeomanry, 1925-29; Joint Master Warwickshire Hounds, 1929-35; commanded No. 605 (County of Warwick) AAF Squadron, 1936-39 (AFCAEA) Staff Officer 11 Fighter Group, 1940 (despatches); Deputy Director Public Relations, Air Ministry, 1941-44; Director Public Relations, 1945-46. Member: National Hunt Cttee, 1940 (Steward, 1942-44, 1950-53, and 1964-67); Jockey Club, 1941 (Steward, 1944-47 and 1954-56). Chm., Tattersall's Cttee, 1948-53; Chairman and Director: Racecourse Technical Services Ltd, 1946-70; Birmingham Racecourse Co. Ltd, 1932-65; Chairman: The Steeplechase Co. (Cheltenham) Ltd; Wolverhampton Racecourse Co. Ltd. President: Hunters' Improvement Society, 1957-58; Warwickshire Association of Boys' Clubs; Scouts Association; Council for Order of St John, 1946-68. Hon. Colonel, Warwickshire Yeomanry, 1942-63. *Heir: s* Hon. Leopold David Verney [*b* 14 Sept. 1938; *m* 1965, Petra, 2nd *d* of Sir John Aird, 3rd Bt, *qv*; two *s*]. *Address:* 2 Upper Phillimore Gardens, W8. *T:* 01-937 8548; Fox Cottage, Kineton, Warwickshire. *T:* Kineton 318. *Clubs:* White's, Cavalry.

**WILLS,** family name of **Baron Dulverton.**

**WILLS, Lieut-Colonel Sir Edward;** *see* Wills, Lieut-Colonel Sir E. E. de W.

**WILLS, Lieut-Colonel Sir (Ernest) Edward (de Winton),** 4th Bt, *cr* 1904, of Hazlewood and Clapton-in-Gordano; *b* 8 Dec. 1903; *s* of Sir Ernest Salter Wills, 3rd Bt, and Caroline Fanny Maud de Winton (*d* 1953); *S* father 1958; *m* 1st, 1926, Sylvia Margaret (*d* 1946), *d* of late William Barker Ogden; two *d*; 2nd, 1949, Juliet Eve, *d* of late Captain John Eagles Henry Graham-Clarke, JP, Frocester Manor, Glos. *Educ:* Eton. Formerly Lieut, Scots Guards; Lieut-Colonel late Middlesex Regt; Lieut-Colonel Comdg 5th Bn, Manchester Regt; served European War, 1939-45. Is a member of Lloyd's. *Recreations:* stalking, shooting, fishing, yachting. *Heir: b* Major George Seton Wills [*b* 18 May 1911; *m* 1st, 1935, Lilah Mary (marr. diss. 1946), *d* of late Captain Percy Richard Hare; one *s*; 2nd, 1961, Victoria Allbut]. *Address:* Meggernie Castle, Glenlyon, Perthshire. *T:* Bridge of Balgie 205 and 200; Mount Prosperous, Hungerford, Berks. *T:* Hungerford 2624. *Clubs:* Household Brigade Yacht, Lloyd's Yacht.
*See also A. C. N. Hopkins, Viscount Savernake.*

**WILLS, Helen;** *see* Roark, H. W.

**WILLS, John Joseph,** CB 1941; CBE 1933; *b* 1877; *s* of John William Thomas Wills and Mary, *d* of Joseph Barrett; *m* 1905, Mary (Lillie) Clark (*d* 1960). *Educ:* St John's Coll., Cambridge, 14th Wrangler, Mathematical Tripos, 1899. Entered Board of Trade, 1901; Secretary of Miners' Eight Hour Day Cttee, 1906; Secretary of Royal Commission on Railway Conciliation Scheme, 1911; Director of Petroleum Department, 1924-28; Member of Cttee on Registration of Accounts, 1930; Member of Cttee on Industrial Life Assurance, 1931; Comptroller of the Companies Department, 1928-32; Member of UK delegation in numerous commercial treaty negotiations and international conferences; Head of Commercial Relations and Treaties Department, 1935; retired from Board of Trade, 1942; Chairman of certain Local Appeal Boards under Essential Work Orders, 1943-47. *Address:* c/o Westminster Bank, 10 St Martin's Place, WC2.

**WILLS, Sir John Spencer;** Kt 1969; Chairman and Managing Director, British Electric Traction Co. Ltd; Chairman: Birmingham and District Investment Trust Ltd; Electrical & Industrial Investment Co. Ltd; Rediffusion Ltd; Rediffusion Television Ltd; Wembley Stadium Ltd; Deputy Chairman, Monotype Corporation Ltd, and Chairman or Director of numerous other companies; *b* 10 Aug. 1904; *s* of Cedric Spencer Wills and Cécile Charlotte; *m* 1936, Elizabeth Drusilla Alice Clare Garcke; two *s*. *Educ:* Cleobury Mortimer Coll., Shropshire; Merchant Taylors' Sch., London. General Manager of E Yorkshire Motor Services Ltd, 1926-31, Dir 1931, and Chm., 1939-68; Chm., Birmingham & Midland Motor Omnibus Co. Ltd, 1946-68; Director of Public Companies, 1931-. Chairman Hull and Grimsby Section of Incorporated Secretaries' Assoc. (now Chartered Inst. of Secretaries), 1929-31; President, BET Federation Ltd; Member of Council: Public Road Transport Assoc. (formerly Public Transport Assoc.), 1943-68 (Chairman, 1945-46; Hon. Mem., 1969-); Institute of Transport (Henry Spurrier Mem. Lecturer, 1946, President, 1950-51); Chairman, Omnibus Owners' Assoc., 1943-44; Member: Nat. Council for Omnibus Industry, 1940-66 (Chairman, 1944-45); Standing Cttee of Air Transport Sect., London Chamber of Commerce. Vice-Patron, The Theatre Royal Windsor Trust, 1965-; Governor, Royal Shakespeare Theatre, Stratford upon Avon, 1946-; Member, Council, The Society of the Royal Opera House, 1962-; Trustee, The London Symphony Orchestra Trust, 1962-68; Member, UK Council, European Movement, 1966-. *Recreations:* complete idleness; formerly: flying, swimming, ski-ing, tennis, riding, shooting. *Address:* 1 Campden House Terrace, Kensington Church Street, W8. *T:* 01-727 5981; Beech Farm, Battle, Sussex. *T:*

Battle 2950. *Clubs:* United Service, Devonshire.

**WILLS, Sir John Vernon,** 4th Bt, *cr* 1923; TD; FRICS; JP; DL; Lieut-Colonel Commanding North Somerset and Bristol Yeomanry, 1965-67, Bt Colonel, 1967; now TARO; *b* 3 July 1928; *s* of Sir George Vernon Proctor Wills, 2nd Bt, and Lady Nellie Jeannie, ARRC, JP, *y d* of late J. T. Rutherford, Abergavenny; *S* brother 1945; *m* 1953, Diana Veronica Cecil (Jane), *o d* of Douglas R. M. Baker, Litton, Somerset; four *s*. *Educ:* Eton. Served Coldstream Guards, 1946-49. Member of Somerset CC. JP 1962, DL 1968. High Sheriff, 1968, Somerset. *Heir: s* David James Vernon Wills, *b* 2 Jan. 1955. *Address:* Langford Court, near Bristol, Somerset. *T:* Wrington 338. *Club:* Guards.

**WILLS, Joseph Lyttleton; Hon. Mr Justice Wills,** CBE 1965; FSA; Judge, Supreme Court, Windward Islands and Leeward Islands, WI, since 1955; *b* 24 June 1899; *m* 1940, Dorothy Cather; one *d*. *Educ:* Middle School, Georgetown, British Guiana; Queen's Coll., British Guiana; King's Coll., London. Barrister-at-law, Inner Temple, 1928; admitted to practice as Barrister-at-Law, British Guiana, 1930; Magistrate, 1947; Additional Puisne Judge of Supreme Court of British Guiana, 1953-55. Councillor of Georgetown, 1933; Deputy Mayor, 1942-43; Hon. Member of Legislative Council, British Guiana, 1933; President, British Guiana Labour Union and British Guiana Workers League; Chairman and Member of several public committees; Member Judicial Service Commn, British Guiana, 1963; Chairman, Income Tax (Appeal) Board of Review, Guyana, 1966. Chairman of British Guiana Congregational Union, 1949-53. Jubilee Medal, 1935; Coronation Medal, 1953. *Recreations:* horse-riding, motoring and cricket. *Address:* Lyttleton House, 57 Chalmers Place, Stabroek, Georgetown, Guyana. *Clubs:* West Indian (London); Guyana Cricket, Maltenoes Sports (Guyana); Castries (WI).

**WILLS, Brigadier Sir Kenneth Agnew,** KBE 1960 (CBE 1946; OBE 1941); MC; ED; Chairman: G. & R. Wills (Holdings) Ltd, Adelaide; Advertiser Newspapers Ltd; *b* Adelaide, 3 March 1896; *s* of late Richard J. H. Wills; *m* 1st, 1920, Viola Ethel (*d* 1956), *d* of late Albert Crossland, Egyptian Civil Service, Cairo; one *s* one *d*; 2nd, 1959, Mavis Catherine, *d* of late H. H. Marsh, Adelaide, *widow* of Dr W. Gilfillan. *Educ:* University College School, London. Served European War, 1914-18 (despatches, MC); Captain, Royal Northumberland Fusiliers; served in France, Salonika, Palestine and Egypt. Served War of 1939-45 (despatches, OBE, CBE): Brigadier, 2nd AIF; DDMI, and Controller, Allied Intelligence Bureau GHQ, SW Pacific Area; served in N Africa, Greece, Crete, Syria and SW Pacific. Member Australian Universities Commission, 1959-65; Chancellor, Adelaide Univ., 1966-68. Hon. Colonel, Adelaide University Regt, 1955-64. KStJ. *Recreation:* fishing. *Address:* 239 Stanley Street, North Adelaide, SA 5006, Australia. *Clubs:* United Service (London); Adelaide; Weld (Perth).

**WILLS, Leonard Johnston;** MA, ScD (Cambridge), PhD (Birmingham); FGS; Emeritus Professor, formerly Professor of Geology and Geomorphology, Birmingham University (1932-49); *b* 27 Feb. 1884; *s* of W. Leonard Wills; *m* 1910, Maud Janet (*d* 1952), *d* of late Sir Alfred Ewing, KCB; one *s* one *d*. *Educ:* Uppingham Sch.; King's Coll., Cambridge. *Publications:* The Physiographical Evolution of Britain, a Palæogeographical Atlas, Concealed Coalfields, and scientific papers. *Address:* Brockencote, Romsley, Halesowen, Worcs.

**WILLS, Philip Aubrey,** CBE 1945; Chairman: George Wills & Sons (Holdings) Ltd; George Wills & Sons Ltd; *b* 26 May 1907; *s* of C. P. Wills; *m* 1931, Katharine Fisher; three *s* one *d*. *Educ:* Harrow. Learnt to fly 1928, owned a light aeroplane and in 1932 took up gliding. Took part in rapid development of British sail-flying from that date; second British holder of international "Silver C" in 1934, held British records for height and distance on and off since 1934. First British holder of International Gold Badge (No. 3) for flights of over 3000 metres and 300 kms distance on a sailplane. Senior pilot British team at seven World Gliding Championships; World Champion, 1952 (single-seaters), Madrid. Joined ATA in 1939, became 2nd in command and Director of Operations. Qualified to ferry all types of single-, twin and multi-engined aircraft. General Manager (Technical) British European Airways Corporation, 1946-48; President of the British Gliding Association. AFRAeS; Coronation Medal, 1953; British gold medal for aeronautics, 1960. *Publications:* On Being a Bird, 1953; Where No Birds Fly, 1961; contributions to the technical and non-technical press on motorless flight, aircraft accident prevention, etc. *Recreation:* sail-flying. *Address:* 54 Holland Park Mews, W11. *Club:* Royal Aero.

**WILLSON, Douglas James,** CBE 1953; TD; Solicitor for the Customs and Excise since 1963; *b* 30 Oct. 1906; *s* of late Ernest Victor Willson and late Mary Willson; *m* 1942, Morna Josephine, *d* of Stanley Hine; one *d*. *Educ:* Bishop's Stortford Coll., Herts. Admitted Solicitor, 1928; joined Customs and Excise, 1928. Served War, 1939-45, Lieut-Colonel, RA. *Publications:* Titles Purchase Tax and Excise in Halsbury's Encyclopædia of Laws of England, 3rd edn. *Recreations:* gardening and bird watching. *Address:* Smith's Croft, West Farleigh, Kent. *T:* Wateringbury 203.

**WILLSON, Thomas Olaf,** CBE 1918; MA; Chevalier de l'Ordre de la Couronne; Director of Education for the County of Oxford, 1920-45; *b* 1880; *er s* of late Rev. Dr. T. B. Willson; *m* 1st, 1919, Constance Horsburgh (*d* 1946), *d* of late Walter Basil Cowan, St Kilda, Sidmouth; one *s* three *d*; 2nd, 1948, Joan, *d* of late A. J. Livesey, Leyland, Lancs. *Educ:* Westminster Sch.; Keble Coll., Oxford. 2nd Class Hons Modern History, 1901. Assistant Secretary, Higher Education for Berkshire, 1905-19; HAC 1914-15; seconded for duty with Foreign Office, Department and Ministry of Information, 1915-18; Asst Secretary, for Education for Oxfordshire, 1919-20. *Publications:* articles on Scandinavian and educational subjects; List of Books relating to Travel and Sport in Scandinavia, 1908, etc; hon. editor Norwegian Club Year-book, 1907-39. *Address:* 93 Aynho, near Banbury, Oxon.

**WILLWAY, Brig. Alfred Cedric Cowan,** CB 1953; CBE 1944; TD 1940; Chairman, Surrey Quarter Sessions, 1955-69; *b* 1898, *o s* of late Rev. A. P. Willway and late Laura Elizabeth (*née* Cowan); *m* 1922, Frances Mary, *y d* of late C. A. Crane; one *s* one *d*. *Educ:* privately; Oriel Coll., Oxford (BA 1921, 2nd Class Honours Mod Hist.). Barrister, Inner Temple, 1924; practised till 1932; Deputy Clerk of the Peace (Surrey), 1932-46; Member, Social Services Committee (Home Office), 1934-36; Probation Advisory Committee and Probation Training Board, 1936-39; Chm. Surrey Probation Cttee, 1948-69, Magistrates Courts

Cttee, 1957-69; Vice-Chm. Surrey Standing Jt Cttee JP (Surrey) 1946; Chairman, Surrey Quarter Sessions (formerly Deputy Chairman), 1955; DL (Surrey) 1950; CC (Surrey) 1952-59. Mem. Standing Cttee on Criminal Law Revision, 1959-69. Served European War (2nd Lt RE), Palestine; commissioned R Signals TA, 1922; War of 1939-45, comd 56 Div. Signals, 1936-41; Dep. CSO, SE Command, 1941; CSO, 5 Corps (N Africa and Italy), 1942-44 (despatches, CBE); CSO, Northern Command, 1945-46; Hon. Col 56 (Lond.) Armd Div. Sig. Regt, 1945-56; Chairman Surrey T&AFA, 1949-52. *Publication:* Willway's Quarter Sessions Practice, 1940 (Supplement, 1952). *Recreation:* gardening. *Address:* The Gables, Holmbury St Mary, Dorking, Surrey. *T:* Dorking 730139. *Clubs:* Junior Carlton, Army and Navy.

**WILMERS, John Geoffrey,** QC 1965; Deputy Chairman, Hampshire Court of Quarter Sessions, since 1970; *b* 27 Dec. 1920; *m* 1946, June I. K. Mecredy; one *s* two *d. Educ:* Leighton Park Sch., Reading; St John's Coll., Cambridge. Called to the Bar, Inner Temple, 1948. *Recreation:* ski-ing. *Address:* 1 Harcourt Buildings, Temple, EC4. *T:* 01-353 2214.

**WILMOT;** *see* Eardley-Wilmot.

**WILMOT, Sir Robert Arthur,** 8th Bt, *cr* 1759; *b* 8 Oct. 1939; *s* of Major Sir Arthur Wilmot, 7th Bt (killed in action at Alamein, 1942), and Pamela Vera (who *m* 2nd, 1955, Lt-Col Charles Frederick Cathcart, Pitcairlie, Newburgh, Fife), twin *d* of Major Garrard, Welton Place, Daventry; *S* father, 1942; *m* 1965, Juliet Elvira, *e d* of Capt. M. N. Tufnell, RN; two *s. Educ:* Eton. Commissioned Scots Guards, 1958; Capt. retd, 1966. Apptd Equerry to HRH the Duke of Gloucester, 1964. *Heir: s* Henry Robert Wilmot, *b* 10 April 1967. *Address:* Pitcairlie, Newburgh, Fife. *T:* Auchtermuchty 464. *Clubs:* Turf, MCC.

**WILSEY, Maj.-Gen. Anthony Patrick W.;** *see* Willasey-Wilsey.

**WILSON;** *see* McNair-Wilson.

**WILSON,** family name of **Barons Moran, Nunburnholme, Wilson** and **Wilson of Langside.**

**WILSON,** 2nd Baron, *cr* 1946, of Libya and of Stowlangtoft; **Patrick Maitland Wilson;** *b* 14 Sept. 1915; *s* of Field-Marshal 1st Baron Wilson, GCB, GBE, DSO, and Hester Mary, *d* of Philip James Digby Wykeham, Tythrop House, Oxon; *S* father 1964; *m* 1945, Violet Storeen, *d* of late Major James Hamilton Douglas Campbell, OBE. *Educ:* Eton; King's College, Cambridge. Served War of 1939-45 (despatches). Lt-Col, Rifle Brigade. *Heir:* none. *Address:* c/o Barclays Bank Ltd, Cambridge.

**WILSON OF LANGSIDE,** Baron *cr* 1969 (Life Peer); **Henry Stephen Wilson,** PC 1967; QC (Scot.) 1965; *b* 21 March 1916; *s* of James Wilson, Solicitor, Glasgow, and Margaret Wilson (*née* Young); *m* 1942, Jessie Forrester Waters; no *c. Educ:* High School, Glasgow; Univ. of Glasgow (MA, LLB). Joined Army, 1939; Commd 1940; Regl Officer, HLI and RAC, 1940-46; demobilized with rank of Capt. Called to Scottish Bar, 1946; Advocate-Depute, 1948-51. Sheriff-Substitute: Greenock, 1955-56; Glasgow, 1956-65; Solicitor-General for Scotland, 1965-67; Lord Advocate, 1967-70. Contested (Lab) Dunfriesshire, 1950, 1955, W Edinburgh, 1951. *Recreations:* hill walking, gardening. *Address:* 3 South Learmonth Gardens, Edinburgh 4. *T:* 031-332 5821. *Clubs:* Caledonian; Royal Scottish Automobile (Glasgow).

**WILSON, Rear-Adm. Alan Christopher Wyndham;** Head of British Defence Liaison Staff, Canberra, since 1970; *b* 7 Sept. 1919; *s* of Alan Christopher Hill-Wilson and Nancy Green; *m* 1958, Joan Rhoda Landale, Deniliquin, Australia; one step *d. Educ:* St Bee's, Cumberland. Served at sea during War of 1939-45; Malta Dockyard, 1946-49; HMS Diamond, 1949-52; Admty, 1952-55; Australia, 1956-58; HMS Ark Royal, 1959-61; Admty, 1962-64; with Flag Officer, Aircraft Carriers, 1964-66; with Comdr, Far East Fleet, 1966-69; idc 1969. *Recreations:* golf, fishing. *Address:* 61 Mugga Way, Red Hill, Canberra, ACT 2603, Australia. *T:* 957374. *Clubs:* Army and Navy, Royal Automobile.

**WILSON, Sir Alan (Herries),** Kt 1961; FRS 1942; Chairman, Glaxo Group Ltd; Director, International Computers (Holdings) Ltd; Part-time Member and Deputy Chairman, Electricity Council; *b* 2 July 1906; *o s* of H. and A. Wilson; *m* 1934, Margaret Constance Monks (*d* 1961); two *s. Educ:* Wallasey Gram. Sch.; Emmanuel College, Cambridge. Smith's Prize, 1928; Adams Prize, 1931-32; Fellow of Emmanuel College, Cambridge, 1929-33; Fellow and Lecturer of Trinity College, Cambridge, 1933-45; University Lecturer in Mathematics in the University of Cambridge, 1933-45; joined Courtaulds Ltd, 1945; Man. Dir, 1954; Dep. Chm., 1957-62. Chairman: Committee on Coal Derivatives, 1959-60; Committee on Noise, 1960-63; Nuclear Safety Adv. Committee, 1965-66; Central Adv. Water Cttee; Member: Iron and Steel Board, 1960-67; University Grants Committee, 1964-66; President: Inst. of Physics and Physical Soc., 1963-64; Nat. Society for Clean Air, 1965-66. Prime Warden, Goldsmiths Co., 1969-70. Hon. Fellow of Emmanuel College, Cambridge; Hon. DSc (Oxford); Hon. DSc (Edin.). Hon. Fellow, St Catherine's College, Oxford. *Publications:* The Theory of Metals, 1936, 2nd edition 1953; Semi-conductors and Metals, 1939; Thermo-dynamics and Statistical Mechanics, 1957; many papers on atomic physics. *Address:* 65 Oakleigh Park South, Whetstone, N20. *T:* 01-445 3030. *Club:* Athenæum.

**WILSON, Alexander;** MP (Lab) Hamilton since 1970; Member, Scottish National Union of Mineworkers; *b* Wilsontown, Lanarkshire, 5 June 1917; *s* of James and Elizabeth Wilson; *m* 1941; one *s* one *d. Educ:* Forth Grammar School. Became a Miner. Joined Labour Party, 1946. Member, 3rd District Council, Lanarkshire, 11 years. Contested (Lab) Hamilton, by-election 1967. Especially interested in welfare of the disabled, sick and elderly persons, and in Trade Unionism. *Address:* House of Commons, SW1.

**WILSON, Maj.-Gen. Alexander James,** CBE 1966 (MBE 1948); MC 1945; GOC North West District since 1970; *b* 13 April 1921; *s* of Maj.-Gen. Bevil Thomson Wilson, *qv*; *m* 1958, Hon. Jean Margaret Paul, 2nd *d* of 2nd Baron Rankeillour; two *s. Educ:* Winchester Coll.; New Coll., Oxford (BA, Law). Served War of 1939-45, North Africa and Italy, Rifle Bde (despatches); Adjt, IMA Dehra Dun, 1945-47; PS to C-in-C Pakistan, 1948-49; Co. Comdr, 1st Bn Rifle Bde, BAOR 1949 and 1951-52, Kenya 1954-55 (despatches); psc 1950; Bde Major 11th Armd Div., BAOR, 1952-54; Instr, Staff Coll. Camberley, 1955-58; 2nd in comd 3rd Green Jackets, BAOR, 1959-60; GSO1 Sandhurst, 1960-62; CO 1st Bn XX Lancs Fus, 1962-64; Chief of Staff, UN Force in Cyprus,

1964-66 (Actg Force Comdr, 1965-66); Comdr, 147 Inf. Bde TA, 1966-67; Dir of Army Recruiting, MoD, 1967-70. Association Football Correspondent, Sunday Times, 1957- . *Publications:* articles and book reviews on mil. subjects and peacekeeping in Spectator and RUSI Jl. *Recreations:* cricket, association football. *Address:* Cuerden Hall, Bamber Bridge, Preston, Lancs. *T:* Preston 35650. *Clubs:* MCC, United Hunts.

**WILSON, Alfred;** Chief Executive Officer, Co-operative Wholesale Society Ltd, since 1969; *b* 10 June 1909; *s* of late William Barnes Wilson and Jane; *m* 1932, Elsie Hulton; one *d* (one *s* decd). *Educ:* Technical Sch., Newcastle upon Tyne. CWS Ltd: Dep. Sec. and Exec. Officer, 1953; Sec., 1965. Chairman: Co-operative Commercial Bank Ltd; FC Finance Ltd; Director: Bridgewater Estates Ltd; Co-operative City Investments Ltd; Co-operative Pension Fund Unit Trust Managers Ltd. FCIS. *Recreations:* photography, walking, gardening. *Address:* 58 Ringley Road, Whitefield, Manchester.

**WILSON, Alfred Harold,** CB 1949; CBE 1946; *b* 9 March 1895; *er s* of late Alfred Henry Wilson; *m* 1925, Edythe Rose, *d* of late Philip Richard Snewin; no *c*. *Educ:* Tottenham Grammar School. Associate of Assoc. of Certified and Corporate Accountants, 1922. Board of Trade, Central Office for Labour Exchanges, 1913; GPO, Accountant-General's Department, 1914. Served European War, Royal Marine Artillery, 1916-19. Assistant Surveyor, General Post Office, 1923; Principal, Air Ministry, Dept of Civil Aviation, 1937; Assistant Secretary, Air Ministry, i/c Organisation and Methods Division, 1941; Assistant Secretary (with title Director of Home Civil Aviation) Air Ministry, Dept of Civil Aviation, 1943; transferred to new Ministry of Civil Aviation on its formation and promoted Principal Asst Secretary, 1945; Under Secretary, Ministry of Civil Aviation, 1946; during this period was Chairman London Airport lay-out Panel, which was responsible for runway layout design of the Airport; Deputy Secretary, Ministry of Transport and Civil Aviation, 1956-58; Adviser on Commercial Air Transport to the Ministry of Transport and Civil Aviation, 1958-60; Member of the Air Transport Licensing Board, 1960-65. *Address:* Cornerways, Epsom Road, Guildford, Surrey. *T:* Guildford 75046. *Club:* Royal Automobile.

**WILSON, Prof. Andrew,** MD, PhD, FPS, FRCPGlas, MRCP; Professor of Pharmacology, University of Liverpool, since 1951; Consultant Physician, Liverpool Regional Hospital Board; *b* 13 July 1909; *s* of late Hugh and Sarah Wilson, Stepps; *m* 1939, Margaret Hope, *d* of late Rev. Thos Paterson, MA; two *d*. *Educ:* Muirkirk Sch.; Royal Technical Coll. and University, Glasgow. Weir Assistant in Materia Medica, Univ. of Glasgow, 1933-37; Lecturer in Pharmacology and Therapeutics, Univ. of Sheffield and Clinical Assistant, Sheffield Royal Infirmary, 1939-46; Lecturer in Applied Pharmacology, University College, London, and University College Hospital Medical School, 1946-48; Reader in University of London, 1948-51. Chm., Adv. Cttee on Pesticides and other Toxic Chemicals; member of other scientific cttees of Government Depts; Member of British Pharmaceutical Codex Revision Cttee; Chairman: British National Formulary Cttee; Prescribers' Jl Cttee. Examiner in Universities of Aberdeen, Belfast, Birmingham, Bristol, Cambridge, Cardiff, Durham, Glasgow, Liverpool, London and Sheffield; Privy Council Visitor to Examinations of Pharmaceutical Society. *Publications:* (jointly) Applied Pharmacology, 10th edn, 1968; original papers in Nature, Jl Physiol., Jl Clinical Invest., Quart. Jl Med., Lancet, BMJ, Amer. Jl Med., Irish Jl Med. Sci. *Recreations:* climbing, ski-ing, golfing. *Address:* 3 Weston Court, Burbo Bank Road, South, Blundellsands, Liverpool 23. *T:* 051-924 4664. *Club:* Authors'.

**WILSON, Rev. Canon Andrew;** Canon Residentiary of Newcastle, and Director of Ordinands and Post-Ordination Studies, since 1964; *b* 27 April 1920; *o s* of late Stewart and of Isobel Wilson. *Educ:* Salt's High School, Shipley; Univ. of Durham. Scholar of St Chad's Coll., Durham, 1939; BA Hons Mod. Hist., 1941; Lightfoot Scholar, 1941; Dip. Theol. (Dist.), 1943; MA 1944; Deacon, 1943; Priest, 1944. Asst Curate: of St Cuthbert's, Newcastle, 1943-45; of St John's, Wallsend, 1945-48; Priest-in-charge of Backworth, 1948-55; Vicar of Horton, 1955-58; Rector of St John's, Ballachulish, 1958-64. *Address:* 1 Mitchell Avenue, Jesmond, Newcastle upon Tyne 2. *T:* Newcastle 81-2075.

**WILSON, Angus Frank Johnstone,** CBE 1968; FRSL 1958; Author; Professor of English Literature, University of East Anglia, since 1966; *b* 11 August 1913; *s* of William Johnstone-Wilson, Dumfriesshire, and of Maude (*née* Caney), Durban, Natal, South Africa. *Educ:* Westminster School; Merton College, Oxford. Foreign Office, 1942-46. Deputy to Superintendent of Reading Room, British Museum, 1949-55. Began to write in 1946. Lectr, Internat. Assoc. of Professors of English, Lausanne, 1959; Ewing Lectr, Los Angeles, 1960; Bergen Lectr, Yale Univ., 1960; Wm Vaughan Moody Lectr, Chicago, 1960; Northcliffe Lectrs, Lond., 1961; Leslie Stephen Lectr, Cambridge, 1962-63; Lectr, Sch. of Eng. Studies, E Anglia Univ., 1963. Mem. Arts Council, 1967-69. Beckman Prof., Univ. of California, Berkeley, Autumn 1967. *Publications:* (short stories, novels, etc); The Wrong Set, 1949; Such Darling Dodos, 1950; Emile Zola, 1950; Hemlock and After (novel), 1952; For Whom The Cloche Tolls, 1953; The Mulberry Bush (play) (prod Bristol, 1955, Royal Court Theatre, London, 1956); Anglo-Saxon Attitudes (novel), 1956; A Bit off the Map, 1957; The Middle Age of Mrs Eliot (novel), 1958; The Old Men at the Zoo (novel), 1961; The Wild Garden, 1963; Late Call (novel), 1964; No Laughing Matter (novel), 1967; The World of Charles Dickens, 1970. TV plays: After the Show (perf. 1959); The Stranger (perf. 1960); The Invasion (perf. 1963). *Recreations:* reading history and natural history, gardening. *Address:* Felsham Woodside, Bradfield St George, Bury St Edmund's, Suffolk. *T:* Rattlesden 200. *Club:* Athenæum.

**WILSON, Sir (Archibald) Duncan,** KCMG 1965 (CMG 1955); Ambassador to the USSR, since 1968; *b* 12 August 1911; *s* of late Archibald Edward Wilson and late Ethel Mary (*née* Schuster); *m* 1937, Elizabeth Anne Martin Fleming; one *s* two *d*. *Educ:* Winchester; Balliol College, Oxford 1st Class Hon. Mods, Lit. Hum., Oxford; Craven schol., Oxford Univ., Jenkyns Exhibitioner, Balliol Coll.; Laming Fellow, Queen's Coll. Taught at Westminster School, 1936-37; Asst Keeper, British Museum, 1937-39; Min. of Economic Warfare, 1939-41; empl. FO, 1941-45; CCG, 1945-46; entered Foreign Service, 1947; served Berlin, 1947-49; Yugoslavia, 1951-53; Director of Research and Acting Librarian, 1955-57; Chargé d'Affaires, Peking, 1957-59; Assistant Under-Secretary, Foreign Office, 1960-64; Ambassador to Yugoslavia, 1964-68. Fellow,

Center of International Affairs, Harvard Univ. (on Secondment, 1959-60). Jt Hon. Pres., Russo-British Chamber of Commerce, 1969-. *Publication:* Life and Times of Vuk Stefanović Karadzić, 1970. *Recreations:* music, painting, tennis, golf, walking. *Address:* c/o Foreign and Commonwealth Office, SW1. *Club:* Travellers'.

*See also Mrs H. M. Warnock.*

**WILSON, Maj.-Gen. Arthur Gillespie,** CBE 1955; DSO 1946; *b* 29 Sept. 1900; *s* of late Charles Wilson, originally of Glasgow, Scotland; *m* 1st, 1927, Edna D. L. Gibson (*d* 1940); no *c*; 2nd, 1953, Shirley H. Cruickshank, *d* of late Colin Campbell, Queenscliff, Victoria, Australia; no *c*. *Educ:* North Sydney Boys' High School, NSW, Australia; Royal Military College, Duntroon, Australia. Commissioned Aust. Staff Corps, 1921; served India with various Brit. and IA Artillery Units, 1924; commanded Roy. Aust. Artillery, Thursday Island, 1926-28; Staff College, Quetta, 1935-36; GSO3, AHQ 1938; continued to serve in various appts at AHQ until joined AIF 1940; GSO1 HQ AIF UK and then Assistant Mil. Liaison Officer, Australian High Commissioner's Office, UK, until 1943, when returned to Australia; served with AIF New Guinea Philippines and Borneo, 1943-45; DDSD(o) Land Headquarters, 1944-45; commanded British Commonwealth Base BCOF Japan, 1946-47; served various appts AHQ and HQ Eastern Command, 1947-52; Aust. Army Rep., UK, 1953-54; GOC, Central Command, Australia, 1954-57; retired 1957. *Address:* Duncraig, Stirling, South Australia 5152, Australia. *Club:* Naval, Military and Air Force (Adelaide).

**WILSON, Arthur James Cochran,** FRS 1963; Professor of Crystallography, Department of Physics, Birmingham University, since Oct. 1965; *b* 28 November 1914; *o s* of Arthur A. C. and Hildegarde Gretchen (*née* Geldert) Wilson, Springhill, Nova Scotia, Canada; *m* 1946, Harriett Charlotte, BSc, PhD, Sociologist (*née* Friedeberg); two *s* one *d*. *Educ:* King's Collegiate School, Windsor, Nova Scotia, Canada; Dalhousie University, Halifax, Canada (MSc); Massachusetts Institute of Technology (PhD); Cambridge University (PhD). 1851 Exhibition Scholar, 1938-41. Lecturer, 1945, and Senior Lecturer, 1946, in Physics, University College, Cardiff; Professor of Physics, University College, Cardiff, 1954-65. Editor of Structure Reports, 1948-59; Editor of Acta Crystallographica, 1960-. Member Executive Committee, International Union of Crystallography, 1954-60. *Publications:* X-ray Optics, 1949 (Russian edn 1951, 2nd edn 1962); Mathematical Theory of X-ray Power Diffractometry, 1963 (French edn 1964, German edn 1965); Elements of X-ray Crystallography, 1970; numerous papers in Proc. Phys. Soc., Proc. Roy. Soc., Acta Cryst., etc. *Address:* The University, PO Box 363, Birmingham B15 2TT.

**WILSON, Sir Arton,** KBE, *cr* 1948; CB 1946; retired from Civil Service; *b* 16 July 1893; *m* 1920, Enid Beatrice Barnard; two *s* one *d*. *Educ:* Central Foundation School, London. Service in General Post Office and later in Ministry of Agriculture; entered Ministry of Labour, 1919; Chief Inspector, 1938-40; Director of Establishments in Ministry of Economic Warfare, 1940; Director of Organisation and Establishments, Ministry of Labour and National Service, 1941-48; Permanent Secretary, Ministry of Pensions, 1948-53. President, Civil Service Pensioners' Alliance. *Recreations:* tennis, country life. *Club:* Royal Commonwealth Society.

**WILSON, Sir Bertram,** Kt 1952; LRIBA; FRICS; JP; *b* 14 March 1893; *s* of Thomas and Emma Wilson, Hazel House, Tadcaster; *m* 1918, Doris (*d* 1948), *d* of J. Walter Harrison, Tadcaster; one *s*. *Educ:* Tadcaster Grammar School. Articled as Civil Engineer and Surveyor to Bromet and Thorman, Tadcaster. Dir (Past Pres.), Leeds Permanent Building Soc. Mem. of W Riding CC, 1940-55; County Alderman, 1945-55; many local govt and public offices. Governor: St Peter's School, York. *Recreations:* music and reading. *Address:* Number One, Millgates, York.

**WILSON, Maj.-Gen. Bevil Thomson,** CB 1941; DSO 1918; RE; *b* Toronto, 12 December 1885; *s* of Alexander Wilson, FRCS, DL Manchester; *m* 1918, Florence Erica, *d* of Sir John Starkey, 1st Bt, one *s* one *d*. *Educ:* Clifton; RMA, Woolwich. Entered RE, 1905; Captain, 1914; Major, 1922; Lt-Col, 1930; Bt Col, 1932; Col, 1934; Maj.-Gen., 1939; served India, 1907-12; Egyptian Army, 1912-14; European War, 1914-18, Egypt, Gallipoli. France, Italy (despatches, DSO, Italian Silver Medal), General Staff, War Office, 1922-25; DAA and QMG West Riding Div. York, 1927-29; Chief Staff Officer, Sudan Defence Force, 1929-33; Commander Lahore Brigade Area, India, 1935-37; Commander Nowshera Brigade, NWFP, India, 1937-39; Commander 53rd (Welsh) Division, 1939-41; retired pay, 1941. Employed, 1944-50, with UNRRA and CCG in Germany, Member of Council Royal National Institute for the Blind, 1952-65. *Address:* 9 Hasker Street, Chelsea, SW3. *T:* 01-589 8945. *Club:* United Service.

*See also A. J. Wilson.*

**WILSON, Col Campbell Aubrey Kenneth I.;** *see* Innes-Wilson.

**WILSON, Charles Edward;** American Industrialist; *b* 18 Nov. 1886; *s* of George H. Wilson and Hannah Rebecca Stiles; *m* 1907, Elizabeth Maisch; one *d*. *Educ:* public schools of New York City. Sprague Works, Gen. Electric Co., Sept. 1899; Gen. Electric Co.: served successively in accounting, production, engineering, manufacturing and marketing depts; Vice-Pres., 1930-37; Exec. Vice-Pres., 1937-39; President, 1940-42 and 1944-50. Appointed by President Roosevelt as Vice-Chm. War Production Bd, 1942; then Exec. Vice-Chm. until 1944; apptd by President Truman as Director, Office of Defense Mobilization, Dec. 1950-Apr. 1952. Director and Consultant, W. R. Grace & Co., 1952; Chm. Exec. Cttee, 1953-55; Chm. Bd of Directors, 1955-56; Pres., People-to-People Foundation, 1956-58. Has various medals and awards for public service; holds hon. degrees. *Address:* (office) 437 Fifth Avenue, New York City, USA; (residence) 7 Hampton Road, Scarsdale, NY 10583, usa.

**WILSON, Sir Charles Haynes,** Kt 1965; MA Glasgow and Oxon; Principal and Vice-Chancellor of University of Glasgow since 1961; *b* 16 May 1909; 2nd *s* of late George Wilson and Florence Margaret Hannay; *m* 1935, Jessie Gilmour Wilson; one *s* two *d*. *Educ:* Hillhead High School; University of Oxford; Glasgow University Faulds Fellow in Political Philosophy, 1932-34. Lecturer in Political Science, London School of Economics, 1934-39; Fellow and Tutor in Modern History, Corpus Christi College, Oxford, 1939-52. Junior Proctor, 1945; Faculty Fellow, Nuffield College. Visiting Professor in Comparative Government at Ohio State Univ., 1950; Principal, The University College of Leicester, 1952-57; Vice-Chancellor, Univ. of Leicester, 1957-61. Chairman: Commn on Fourah Bay Coll.,

Sierra Leone, 1957; Miners' Welfare Nat. Schol. Scheme Selec. Cttee, 1959-64; Acad. Planning Bd for Univ. of E Anglia, 1960; Member: Academic Planning Cttee and Council of UC of Sussex, 1958; Min. of Educ. Selection Committee for State Studentships in Arts Subjects, 1959; Acad. Adv. Cttee, Royal Coll. of Science and Technology, Glasgow (now Univ. of Strathclyde), 1962; British Cttee of Selection for Harkness Fellowships of Commonwealth Fund, 1962-67; Heyworth Cttee on Social Studies, 1962; Acad. Planning Bd, Univ. of Stirling, 1964; Chairman, Cttee of Vice-Chancellors and Principals, 1964-67; Vice-Chm., Assoc. of Commonwealth Univs, 1967-68. Hon. Fellow: Corpus Christi Coll., Oxford, 1963; London School of Economics and Political Science, 1965. LLD (Hon.): Glasgow, 1957; Leicester, 1961; Rhodes Univ., 1964; Queen's Univ., Kingston, Ont, 1967; Ohio State Univ., 1969; DLitt (Hon.) Strathclyde, 1966; DCL (Hon.) East Anglia, 1966. *Address:* The Principal's Lodging, The University, Glasgow. *T:* 041-339 0383. *Clubs:* United University, United Service.

**WILSON, Prof. Charles Henry;** FBA 1966; Fellow of Jesus College, Cambridge, since 1938; Professor of Modern History, Cambridge University, since 1963 (lately Reader in Modern Economic History); *b* 16 Apr. 1914; *s* of Joseph Edwin Wilson and Louisa Wilson; *m* 1939, Angela, *d* of John Marshman; one *d. Educ:* De Aston Gram. Sch., Lincs; Jesus Coll., Cambridge. Studied in Holland and Germany, 1937-38. Served in RNVR and Admiralty, 1940-45. Bursar of Jesus Coll., 1945-55. Ford Lecturer in English History, Oxford Univ., for 1968-69. British Govt Representative, Anglo-Netherlands Cultural Commn Jt Ed., Econ. Hist. Review, 1960-67. Corres. Fellow, Royal Danish Acad. of Arts and Science, 1970. LittD (*hc*) Univ. of Groningen, 1964. *Publications:* Anglo-Dutch Commerce and Finance in 18th Century, 1940. Holland and Britain, 1945; History of Unilever, 1954; Profit and Power, 1957; (with William Reader) Men and Machines, 1958; England's Apprenticeship 1603-1763, 1965; Unilever, 1945-65, 1968; The Dutch Republic and the Civilization of the Seventeenth Century, 1968; Queen Elizabeth and the Revolt of the Netherlands, 1970; numerous articles. *Recreation:* music. *Address:* Jesus College, Cambridge.

**WILSON, Christopher David,** CBE 1968; MC 1945; Managing Director, Southern Television Ltd, since 1959; *b* 17 Dec. 1916; *s* of late Anthony James Wilson, Highclere, Worplesdon, Surrey; *m* 1947, Jean Barbara Morton Smith; no *c. Educ:* St George's Sch., Windsor; Aldenham. Served War of 1939-45: Captain RA, in India, Middle East and Italy. Business Manager, Associated Newspapers Ltd, 1955-57; Dir, Associated Rediffusion Ltd, 1956-57; Gen. Manager, Southern Television Ltd, 1957-59; FCA 1947. *Recreations:* sailing, music. *Address:* Periwinkle Cottage, Worplesdon, Surrey. *T:* Worplesdon 2633. *Clubs:* MCC; Royal Southern Yacht.

**WILSON, Clifford;** Professor of Medicine, University of London, at the London Hospital since 1946 and Director, Medical Unit, The London Hospital; *b* 27 Jan. 1906; *m* 1936, Kathleen Hebden; one *s* one *d. Educ:* Balliol College, Oxford. Brackenbury Scholar, Balliol Coll., Oxford, 1924; 1st Class Oxford Final Hons School of Nat. Sciences, 1928; House Physician, etc., London Hospital, 1931-34; Rockefeller Travelling Fellow, 1934-35; Research Fellow, Harvard Univ.; Asst Director, Medical Unit, London Hosp., 1938; Univ. Reader in Medicine, London Hosp., 1940; Major RAMC, Medical Research Section, 1942-45. President Renal Association, 1963-64. Examiner MRCP, 1960-; Censor, RCP, 1964-66; Senior Censor and Senior Vice-Pres., 1967-68. Dean, Faculty of Medicine, Univ. of London, 1968-. *Publications:* sections on renal diseases and diseases of the arteries in Price's Text Book of Medicine; section on natural history of nephritis in Black's Renal Disease; papers on renal disease, hypertension, arterial disease and other medical subjects, 1930-70. *Address:* The Medical Unit, London Hospital, E1. *T:* 01-247 5454 (Ext. 151).

**WILSON, Clyde Tabor;** retired Metropolitan Police Magistrate, 1962 (South-Western Police Court, 1935, subsequently Marlborough Street Magistrates Court); *b* 21 September 1889; *s* of Dr Foden Wilson, The Wood, Shrewsbury Road, Birkenhead; unmarried. *Educ:* Rugby School; Trinity College, Cambridge. Called to Bar, Inner Temple, 1913, and practised on North Wales and Chester Circuit; served European War with 5th London Brigade RFA (T); MP (U) West Toxteth Division, Liverpool, 1931-35; Recorder of Birkenhead, 1934-35; member for Central Wandsworth on the London County Council, 1925-35. *Address:* Flat 20, Pearl Court, Eastbourne, Sussex. *Club:* Carlton.

**WILSON, Colin Henry;** author; *b* Leicester, 26 June 1931; *s* of Arthur Wilson and Annetta Jones; *m* 1951, Dorothy Betty Troop; one *s*; *m* 1960, Joy Stewart; one *s* one *d. Educ:* The Gateway Secondary Technical School, Leicester. Left school at 16. Laboratory Asst (Gateway School), 1948-49; Civil Servant (collector of taxes), Leicester and Rugby, 1949-50; national service with RAF, AC2, 1949-50. Various jobs, and a period spent in Paris and Strasbourg, 1950; came to London, 1951; various labouring jobs, long period in plastic factory; returned to Paris, 1953; labouring jobs in London until Dec. 1954, when began writing The Outsider: has since made a living at writing. Visiting Professor: Hollins Coll., Va, 1966-67; Univ. of Washington, Seattle, 1967; Dowling Coll., Majorca, 1969. Plays produced: Viennese Interlude; The Metal Flower Blossom; Strindberg. *Publications:* The Outsider, 1956; Religion and the Rebel, 1957; The Age of Defeat, 1959; Ritual in the Dark, 1960; Adrift in Soho, 1961; An Encyclopædia of Murder, 1961; The Strength to Dream, 1962; Origins of the Sexual Impulse, 1963; The Man without a Shadow, 1963; The World of Violence, 1963; Rasputin and the Fall of the Romanovs, 1964; The Brandy of the Damned (musical essays), 1964; Necessary Doubt, 1964; Beyond the Outsider, 1965; Eagle and Earwig, 1965; The Mind Parasites, 1966; Introduction to The New Existentialism, 1966; The Glass Cage, 1966; Sex and the Intelligent Teenager, 1966; The Philosopher's Stone, 1968; The Strange Genius of David Lindsay (with E. H. Visiak), 1968; Strindberg (play), 1968; Bernard Shaw: A Reassessment, 1969; Voyage to a Beginning, 1969; Poetry and Mysticism, 1970; The Black Room, 1970; A Casebook of Murder, 1970; The God of the Labyrinth, 1970; Lingard, 1970. Contribs to: The London Magazine, Encounter, Reynolds News, Sunday Times, Sunday Telegraph, etc. *Recreations:* collecting gramophone records, mainly opera; mathematics. *Address:* Tetherdown, Trewallock Lane, Gorran Haven, Cornwall. *Clubs:* Savage; Gentleman's (St Austell).

**WILSON, Des;** *b* 5 March 1941; *s* of Albert H. Wilson, Oamaru, New Zealand; *m* 1962, Rita Claire Williams; one *s* one *d. Educ:* Waitaki

Boys' High Sch., New Zealand. Journalist-Broadcaster, 1957-67; Director, Shelter, Nat. Campaign for the Homeless, 1967-71. *Publications:* I Know It Was the Place's Fault, 1970; columnist in The Guardian. *Address:* 25 Weston Park, Thames Ditton, Surrey. *T:* 01-398 5271.

**WILSON, Rt. Rev. Douglas John,** MA; Assistant Bishop of Bath and Wells and Canon Residentiary and Treasurer of Wells Cathedral, since 1956; *b* 22 June 1903; *e s* of late Canon J. K. Wilson, Vicar of Bromley, Kent, and late Mrs E. L. Wilson; *m* 1946, Mary Theodora, *er d* of late Rev. A. F. Bliss; one *s* one *d*. *Educ:* King's School, Rochester; Haileybury College; Queen's College, Cambridge; Westcott House, Cambridge. Hist. Tripos, BA Cantab 1924; MA Cantab 1928; ordained 1927, to Curacy of Dartford Parish Church; Curate Walsall Parish Church, 1931; Vicar of Kingswinford, Staffs, 1935; Asst Bishop of British Honduras, 1938-44; Archdeacon in Central America, 1939-44; Asst Bishop of Southwell, 1944-45; Bishop of British Honduras, 1945-50; Bishop of Trinidad, 1950-56; Proctor in Convocation for Dean and Chapter, Wells Cathedral, 1961-63. Coronation Medal, 1953. Fellow of Woodard Corporation (Western Division) 1958. *Recreation:* reading Who's Who. *Address:* 2 The Liberty, Wells, Somerset. *T:* Wells 3246. *Club:* United University.

**WILSON, Sir Duncan;** *see* Wilson, Sir A. D.

**WILSON, Edmund;** writer; *b* Red Bank, New Jersey, 8 May 1895; *s* of Edmund Wilson and Helen Mather Kimball; *m* 1st, 1923, Mary Blair; one *d*; 2nd, 1930, Margaret Canby; 3rd, 1938, Mary McCarthy; one *s*; 4th, 1946, Elena Thornton; one *d*. *Educ:* Hill School, Pottstown, Pa; Princeton Univ. (AB 1916). Reporter on New York Evening Sun, 1916-17; Managing Editor. Vanity Fair, 1920-21; Associate Editor, New Republic, 1926-31. US Presidential Medal of Freedom, 1963. *Publications:* The Undertaker's Garland (with John Peale Bishop), 1922; Discordant Encounters (dialogues and plays), 1926; I Thought of Daisy (novel), 1929; Poets, Farewell! (verse), 1929; Axel's Castle (literary criticism), 1931; The American Jitters–A Year of the Slump, 1932; Travels in Two Democracies, 1936; This Room and This Gin and These Sandwiches (plays), 1937; The Triple Thinkers, 1938; To the Finland Station, 1940; The Boys in the Back Room, 1941; The Wound and the Bow, 1941; Note-Books of Night, 1942; The Shock of Recognition (anthology), 1943; Memoirs of Hecate County, 1946; Europe Without Baedeker, 1947 (new edn 1967); The Little Blue Light (play), Classics and Commercials, 1950; The Shores of Light, 1952; Five Plays, 1954; The Scrolls from the Dead Sea, 1955; Red, Black, Blond and Olive, 1956; A Piece of My Mind, 1956; The American Earthquake, 1958; Apologies to The Iroquois, 1960; Wilson's Night Thoughts, 1961; Patriotic Gore, 1962; The Cold War and the Income Tax; a Protest, 1964; The Bit between my Teeth, 1966; A Prelude, 1967; The Duke of Palermo, and Other Plays, 1969; The Dead Sea Scrolls: 1947-1969, 1969. *Address:* Wellfleet, Cape Cod, Mass, USA.

**WILSON, Prof. Edward Meryon,** FBA 1964; MA, PhD; Professor of Spanish, Cambridge University, since 1953; Vice-Master of Emmanuel College, 1961-65; *b* Kendal, 1906; *s* of Norman F. Wilson, Kendal, and Henrietta Gwendolyn Meryon Harris. *Educ:* Windermere Grammar School; Trinity Coll., Cambridge. Modern Languages Tripos, Part II, 1928; Esmé Howard Studentship at Residencia de Estudiantes, Madrid, 1929-30; Rouse Ball Studentship at Trinity College, Cambridge, 1930-31; Jane Eliza Proctor Visiting Fellowship at University of Princeton (NJ), 1932-33; PhD Cambridge, 1934; Assistant Lecturer in Spanish at Cambridge, 1933-39; University Lecturer there, 1939-45 (absent on national service, 1941-44); Cervantes Prof. of Spanish, Univ. of London, 1945-53. Fellow of Emmanuel College, Cambridge, Jan.-Sept. 1945. Pres. Assoc. of Hispanists of Great Britain and Ireland, 1961-63; Pres. First Internat. Congress of Hispanists, Oxford, 1962; Corresp. Member: Hispanic Soc. of America, 1963; Roy. Spanish Acad., 1964. *Publications:* The Solitudes of Don Luis de Gongora, 1931, 2nd edn, 1965; (with Jack Sage), Poesias líricas en las obras dramáticas de Calderón, 1964; (with F. J. Norton) Two Spanish Verse Chap-books, 1968; also articles in various reviews. *Address:* Emmanuel College, Cambridge.

**WILSON, Brig. Edward William Gravatt,** CBE 1943; MC; *b* 14 April 1888; *s* of Rev. Alfred Wilson; *m* 1926, Edith Margaret Smith; one *s* one *d*. *Educ:* Charterhouse; RMA, Woolwich. 2nd Lt RA 1908; served in RFA till 1936, then Anti-Aircraft; peace-time service in UK, South Africa, and India; European War, 1914-18, France and Salonika; War of 1939-45, A-A Brigade Commander UK, and A-A Defence Commander, Egypt; retired pay, 1944. *Address:* The Firs, Selkirk. *Club:* United Service.

**WILSON, Edwin J. B.;** *see* Boyd-Wilson.

**WILSON, Eleanora Mary C.;** *see* Carus-Wilson.

**WILSON, Eli Marsden,** ARE; ARCamA; *b* Midsummer Day, 1877; *s* of Alfred Wilson, Ossett, Yorkshire, and Emma, *d* of George Marsden; *m* 1905, Hilda Mary, *d* of F. B. Pemberton. Studied at Wakefield School of Art and at the Royal College of Art, South Kensington. Exhibited at the Royal Academy, the Royal Society of Painter-Etchers, the Royal Scottish and Royal Cambrian Academies, Paris Salon (Soc. des Artistes Français and Soc. Nat. des Beaux Arts), international exhibitions at London, Paris, Rome, etc., and at most of the principal galleries in Europe and America; received diplomas at Ghent and Paris; executed series of paintings for Geological Museum, South Kensington; member of various art societies in England and abroad, Hon. mem. Soc. of Painters in Tempera. *Publications:* Etchings and Mezzotints. *Address:* 9 Faraday Road, Acton, W3.

**WILSON, Ellis;** *see* Wilson, H. E. C.

**WILSON, Lt-Col Eric Charles Twelves,** VC 1940; retired; Controller, London House, since 1966; *b* 2 October 1912; *s* of Rev. C. C. C. Wilson; *m* 1943, Ann (from whom he obtained a divorce, 1953), *d* of Major Humphrey Pleydell-Bouverie, MBE; two *s*; *m* 1953, Angela Joy, *d* of Lt-Col J. McK. Gordon, MC; one *s*. *Educ:* Marlborough; RMC, Sandhurst. Commissioned in East Surrey regt, 1933; seconded to King's African Rifles, 1937; seconded to Somaliland Camel Corps, 1939; Long Range Desert Gp, 1941-42; Burma, 1944; seconded to N Rhodesia Regt, 1946; retd from Regular Army, 1949; Admin Officer, HM Overseas Civil Service, 1949-61; Dep. Controller, London House, 1962. *Recreation:* country life. *Address:* 15 Mecklenburgh Square, WC1; *T:* 01-837 7216; Woodside Cottage, Stowell, Sherborne, Dorset. *T:* Templecombe 264.

**WILSON, Frank Richard,** CMG 1963; OBE 1946; Regional Controller, Commonwealth Development Corporation; retired HMOCS Oct. 1963; *b* 26 Oct. 1920; *er s* of Sir Leonard Wilson, *qv* and the late Muriel Wilson; *m* 1947, Alexandra Dorothy Mary (*née* Haigh); two *s*. *Educ:* Oundle Sch.; Trinity Hall, Cambridge (1939-40 only). Commnd Indian Army, 1941; retired as Lieut-Col, 1946. Joined Colonial Administrative Service (later HMOCS) in Kenya, 1947; District Comr, 1950-56; Private Sec. to the Governor, 1956-59; Provincial Comr, Central Province, 1959-63; Civil Sec., Central Region, 1963; joined CDC, 1964. *Address:* c/o Lloyds Bank, 6 Pall Mall, SW1.

**WILSON, Sir Garnet Douglas,** Kt, *cr* 1944; LLD (St Andrews); JP; Hon. Sheriff-Substitute at Dundee; Chairman; Sir James Caird's Travelling Scholarships Trust; Armitstead Lectures Trust; Deputy Chairman, Dundee Savings Bank; Lord Provost of Dundee, 1940-46; Lord Lieutenant of County of City of Dundee, 1940-46, now DL; *b* 24 March 1885; 2nd *s* of Gavin Laurie Wilson, JP, and Jessie Dunlop McCulloch; *m* 1st, 1925, Gladys Margery Johnson (*d* 1953); two *s* one *d*; 2nd, 1953, Mrs Marguerite Lawson, Newport, *widow* of J. Douglas Lawson, and *d* of late Rev. J. H. Morrison, Kirkmichael, Perthshire. *Educ:* Bell Baxter School, Cupar; Newport School, Fife; High School of Dundee. Dundee Education Authority, 1919-30; Newport (Fife) Town Council, 1919-29; Town Council of Dundee, 1929-35 and 1937-46; Chairman of Education Committee, 1930-35, 1937-40; President, University College, Dundee, 1946-52 (Mem., Coll. Council, 1940-53); Member: Nat. Youth Employment Council, 1948-62; Queen's College (now University of Dundee) Council, 1953-67; Chairman: National Camps Association of Scotland, 1941-65; Advis. Committee on Youth Employment (Scotland), 1946-62; Youth Employment Cttee, 1931-62 and Local Employment Cttee, 1936-62; Glenrothes Develt Corp., 1952-60. Hon. FEIS 1943; Vice-Chm. Adv. Council on Education in Scotland, 1942-46; 1947-51; Member, St Andrews University Court, 1940-49; Rector's Assessor, 1946-49. Chairman, Scottish Special Housing Assoc., 1944-46; Mem., Building Apprenticeship and Training Council (MPBW), 1943-56. Senior Partner, G. L. Wilson, Dundee (drapers). Order of Finnish Lion, 1952. *Publications:* Bachelor's Buttons (privately), 1921; The Making of a Lord Provost, 1966; Overspill, 1970; articles and addresses on Scottish education (advocates Pre-Vocational Courses for Secondary Schools). *Recreations:* reading, football (fan). *Address:* St Colmes, Perth Road, Dundee. *T:* Dundee 67454.

**WILSON, Geoffrey;** *see* Wilson, (H.) G. (B.).

**WILSON, Geoffrey;** Member, British Railways Board, since 1968; *b* 11 July 1929; *m* 1962, Philomena Mary Kavanagh; one *s* one *d*. *Educ:* Bolton County Grammar Sch.; Univ. of Birmingham. PE Consulting Group, 1958-63; British Railways, 1963-. Member: Council, Royal Inst. of Public Administration, 1970-; Council, Inst. of Transport, 1970-. *Recreation:* golf. *Address:* 3 Lauriston Road, Wimbledon, SW19. *Clubs:* Wentworth Golf; Royal Dublin Golf.

**WILSON, Sir Geoffrey Masterman,** KCB 1969 (CB 1968); CMG 1962; Deputy Secretary-General (Economic), Commonwealth Secretariat, since 1971; *b* 7 April 1910; 3rd *s* of late Alexander Cowan Wilson and Edith Jane Brayshaw; *m* 1946, Julie Stafford Trowbridge; two *s* two *d*. *Educ:* Manchester Grammar School; Oriel College, Oxford. Chairman, Oxford Univ. Labour Club, 1930; Pres., Oxford Union, 1931. Harmsworth Law Scholar, Middle Temple, 1931; called to Bar, Middle Temple, 1934. Served in HM Embassy, Moscow, and Russian Dept of Foreign Office, 1940-45. Cabinet Office, 1947; Treasury, 1948; Director, Colombo Plan Technical Co-operation Bureau, 1951-53; Under-Secretary, Treasury, 1956-58; Deputy Head of UK Treasury Delegn and Alternate Exec. Dir for UK, Internat. Bank, Washington, 1958; Vice-President, International Bank, Washington, 1961; Deputy Secretary, ODM, 1966-68, Permanent Secretary, 1968-70; Secretary, Overseas Develt Admin, FCO, Oct. 1970. *Address'* 34 Sheffield Terrace, W8.
*See also Prof. J. E. Meade, Prof. R. C. Wilson and S. S. Wilson.*

**WILSON, Geoffrey Studholme,** CMG 1961; Commissioner of Police, Tanganyika Police Force, 1958-62; *b* 5 June 1913; *s* of late J. E. S. Wilson; *m* 1936, Joy Noel, *d* of Capt. C. st G. Harris-Walker; two *s*. *Educ:* Radley College. Joined Hong Kong Police, 1933; Commissioner of Police, Sarawak Constabulary, 1953-58. King's Police Medal, 1950. OStJ 1961. *Recreations:* golf, fishing, sailing. *Address:* c/o The Hong Kong & Shanghai Banking Corporation, 9 Gracechurch Street, EC3. *Clubs:* Royal Commonwealth Society; Hong Kong (Hong Kong).

**WILSON, Sir George,** KBE 1959; Kt 1944; Hon. LLD; Chairman of Governors of West of Scotland Agricultural College since 1942; Member: Stirling CC since 1930; Herring Industry Board, 1945-63; Member of Council Hannah Dairy Research Institute; *b* 24 Nov. 1900; 3rd *s* of Sir David Wilson, 1st Bt of Carbeth, Killearn; unmarried. *Educ:* Harrow; Trinity College, Cambridge (MA, Nat. Sci. Tripos). Hon. LLD (Glasgow), 1950. Post-graduate study, then farming. Member of Balfour of Burleigh Committee on Hill Sheep Farming in Scotland, 1941-44; Director British Linen Bank. *Recreations:* fishing, walking. *Address:* King's Mile, Killearn, by Glasgow. *TA:* King's Mile, Killearn. *T:* Killearn 363. *Club:* Athenæum.

**WILSON, George Pritchard Harvey,** CMG 1966; JP; President, Royal Agricultural Society of Victoria, since 1964; *b* 10 March 1918; *s* of late G. L. Wilson; *m* 1945, Fay Hobart Duff; two *s* one *d*. *Educ:* Geelong Grammar School. Nuffield Scholar (Farming), 1952. Council Member, Monash University, 1961-69; Royal Agricultural Society of Victoria: Councillor, 1950-; President, 1964-; Trustee, 1968-. Member: Victoria Promotion Cttee, 1968-; Victorian Inland Meat Authority, 1970- (Dep. Chm., 1970-). JP 1957. *Recreation:* fishing. *Address:* Wilson House, Berwick, Victoria 3806, Australia. *T:* Berwick 7071271. *Clubs:* Melbourne, Amateur Sports, Royal Automobile Club of Victoria (all Melbourne).

**WILSON, Gilbert;** *b* 2 March 1908; *s* of J. E. Wilson; *m* 1934, Janet Joy Turner; two *d*. *Educ:* Auckland Grammar School. Served with 2nd NZEF, Middle East, 1940-43. Joined National Bank of New Zealand, 1924; joined Reserve Bank of New Zealand, 1935; Dep. Chief Cashier, 1948-53; Chief Cashier, 1953-56; Dep. Governor, 1956-62; Governor, 1962-67; also Alternate Governor for New Zealand of International Monetary Fund, 1962-67. *Recreations:* golf, gardening. *Address:* 41 Mere Road, Taupo, New Zealand. *Clubs:* Wellington (NZ); Taupo Golf (NZ).

**WILSON, Maj.-Gen. (Hon. Lt-Gen.) Sir Gordon,** KCSI, *cr* 1946; CB 1944; CBE 1940 (OBE

1928); MC; MB, ChB, DPH; *b* 1 Feb. 1887; 3rd *s* of late John Wilson, Cheltenham; *m* Ethel Marian, 4th *d* of late John Loring, Doddington, Nantwich; two *s*. *Educ:* Edinburgh Univ. Joined RAMC 1911; Lt-Col 1934; Bt-Col 1937; Subst 1938; Brig. 1941; Maj.-Gen. 1941; local Lt-Gen. 1943; Hon. Lt-Gen., 1946; retired list 1946. Served European War, 1914-18, Mesopotamia; served in India, Burma, NWF, France, Middle East; DADGAMS WO, 1929-33; DADMS Waziristan Dist, 1934-36; DADMS HQ N Command, India, 1936-38; OC Royal Victoria Hospital, Netley, 1938-39; Commandant Dieppe Sub-Area, 1939-40; DDMS X Corps, 1940-41; DDMS Southern Army, India, 1941-43; DMS India, 1943-46; KHS, 1941-46. CStJ. *Address:* c/o Glyn, Mills & Co., Whitehall, SW1.

**WILSON, Graeme McDonald;** British Civil Aviation Representative (Far East), since 1964; *b* 9 May 1919; *s* of Robert Linton McDonald Wilson and Sophie Hamilton Wilson (*née* Milner); *m* 1968, Yabu Masae; one *s*. *Educ:* Rendcomb Coll., Glos; Schloss Schule Salem, Germany; Lincoln Coll., Oxford; Gray's Inn, London. Served in Fleet Air Arm, 1939-46. Joined Home Civil Service, 1946. Private Sec. to Parly Sec., Min. of Civil Aviation, 1946-49; Planning 1, 1949-53; Dep. UK Rep. on Council of ICAO, 1953-56; Lt-Comdr (A) (O) (Ph) (q) RCNR, 1954; Internat. Relations 1, Min. of Transport and Civil Aviation, 1956-61; Asst Sec. Interdependence, Exports and Electronics, Min. of Aviation, 1961-64; seconded to Foreign Service as Counsellor and Civil Air Attaché, at twelve Far Eastern posts, 1964. *Publications:* Face At The Bottom Of The World: translations of the modern Japanese poetry of Hagiwara Sakutaro, 1969; articles and poems (mostly Japanese and Korean trans) in leading reviews in America, Britain, Japan, Australia, Canada and India. *Address:* E7, Repulse Bay Towers, Repulse Bay, Hong Kong. *T:* Hong Kong 92884. *Clubs:* RNVR; PEN Club of Japan (Tokyo).

**WILSON, Prof. Graham Malcolm;** Regius Professor of Medicine, University of Glasgow, since 1967; *b* 16 April 1917; *er s* of Dr Malcolm Wilson; *m* 1949, Elizabeth Stanfield, *er d* of Dr J. T. Bell Nicoll; two *s* four *d*. *Educ:* Edinburgh Academy. MB, ChB, Edinburgh (hons), 1940; Ettles Scholar; MD (gold medal), 1950; DSc 1964; FRCP, 1956; FRCPE, 1947; FRCPG 1967; FRSE 1969. Royal Air Force Medical Service, 1941-46; Assistant Medical Unit, St Mary's Hospital, 1947-49; Lecturer in Therapeutics, University of Sheffield, 1950-54; Professor of Pharmacology and Therapeutics, 1954-67. Eli Lilly Research Fellow, Harvard Univ. Med. School, 1952-53; Visiting Professor of Medicine, Univ. of Adelaide, 1960. Bradshaw Lectr, RCP, 1962. Managing Trustee, Nuffield Foundn. Member: Cttee on Safety of Medicines; British Pharmacopoeia Commn; Royal Commn on Medical Educn; Nat. Council for Educnl Technology. *Publications:* articles in med. and scientific journals dealing chiefly with the peripheral circulation and with metabolic problems. *Recreations:* boating, fishing. *Address:* 11 Westbourne Gardens, Glasgow, W2. *T:* 041-334 3287. *Club:* Athenæum.

**WILSON, Sir Graham (Selby),** Kt 1962; MD, FRCP, DPH (London); late Captain Royal Army Medical Corps (Special Reserve); Hon. Lecturer, Department of Bacteriology and Immunology, London School of Hygiene and Tropical Medicine; Director of the Public Health Laboratory Service, 1941-63; KHP, 1944-46; *b* 10 Sept. 1895; *m* Mary Joyce, *d* of Alfred Ayrton, Chester; two *s*. *Educ:* Epsom College; King's Coll., London; Charing Cross Hospital, London; Governors' Clinical Gold Medal, Charing Cross Hospital, and Gold Medal, University of London, MB, BS; Specialist in Bacteriology, Royal Army Med. Corps, 1916-20; Demonstrator in Bacteriology, Charing Cross Hospital Medical School, 1919-22; Lecturer in Bacteriology, University of Manchester, 1923-27; Reader in Bacteriology, University of London, 1927-30; Prof. of Bacteriology as applied to Hygiene, London School of Hygiene and Tropical Medicine, 1930-47; William Julius Mickle Fellowship, University of London, 1939. Member: Council, RCP, 1938-40; of several cttees on tuberculosis, poliomyelitis and other infectious diseases; Weber-Parkes prize, RCP 1942; Milroy Lecturer, RCP, 1948; Hon. Fellow: American Public Health Association, 1953; Royal Society of Health, 1960; Czechoslovak Medical Society, Jan Evangelista Purkyně, 1963; Bisset Hawkins Medal, RCP, 1956; Marjory Stephenson Memorial Prize, 1959; Stewart Prize, 1960; Buchanan Medal, Royal Society, 1967; Harben Gold Medal, 1970. Hon. LLD (Glasgow) 1962. *Publications:* The Principles of Bacteriology and Immunity (with late Professor W. W. C. Topley and Sir Ashley Miles), 5th edn 1964; The Hazards of Immunization, 1967; The Bacteriological Grading of Milk (with collaborators), 1935; The Pasteurization of Milk, 1942; numerous papers on bacteriological subjects. *Recreation:* cycling. *Address:* 65 Hillway, N6. *Club:* Athenæum.

**WILSON, Rear-Adm. Guy Austen Moore,** CB 1958; Board of Visitors, Blundeston Prison; Breeder and Voluntary Organiser, Guide Dogs for the Blind Association; *b* 7 June 1906; *s* of Ernest Moore Wilson, Buenos Aires, and Katharine Lawrence; *m* 1932, Dorothy, *d* of Sir Arthur Watson, CBE; two *s* three *d*. *Educ:* Royal Naval Colleges, Osborne and Dartmouth. Joined Royal Navy, 1920; Engineering Specialist Course, 1924-28. Advanced Engineering Course, Royal Naval College, Greenwich, 1928-30; served War of 1939-45, at Admiralty and in HMS Berwick; Portsmouth Dockyard, 1946-49; Comdr, 1940; Captain, 1948; Dep. Director Aircraft Maintenance and Repair, Admiralty, 1950-52; Supt, RN Aircraft Yard, Fleetlands, 1952-55; Rear-Admiral, 1955; Deputy Engineer-in-Chief for Fleet Maintenance and Administration, 1955-57; Rear-Admiral Nuclear Propulsion and Deputy Engineer-in-Chief (Nuclear Propulsion), 1957-59, retired 1960; Chief Executive, Dracone Developments Ltd, 1960-63. *Recreations:* swimming, motoring, gardening. *Address:* Barn Acre, Saxstead Green, Woodbridge, Suffolk. *T:* Earl Soham 365.

**WILSON, Rt. Hon. Harold;** *see* Wilson, Rt Hon. (J.) H.

**WILSON, Rev. Harold;** Principal, Salisbury Theological College, since 1965, and Canon Residentiary of Sarum, since 1968; Canon of Salisbury Cathedral and Prebendary of Winterbourne Earls; *b* 17 Dec. 1919; *s* of late John William and Ada Wilson; unmarried. *Educ:* Bradford Regional Coll. of Art; Selwyn Coll., Cambridge. Served RAMC, 1940-46. Deacon, 1951; Priest, 1952. Curate, St Augustine, Sheffield, 1951-54; Chaplain to Bishop of Sheffield and Diocesan Youth Organiser, 1954-59; Sec., C of E Bd of Educn, 1959-65. Chm., Adult Educn Cttee, British Coun. of Churches, 1964. Member: Bd of Management, World Council of Christian Education; Archbishop of Canterbury's Commn on Roman Catholic Relations, 1969.

Du Bose Lectr, Univ. of the South, Tennessee, 1969; Bradner Lectr in Educn, Virginia, 1969. *Publications'* The Parish Youth Club, 1960; Reading the Bible Together, 1960; Living the Liturgy Together, 1962. *Recreations:* painting, music, theatre. *Address:* 19 The Close, Salisbury, Wilts. *T:* Salisbury 4223. *Club:* Royal Commonwealth Society.

**WILSON, Air Commodore Harold Arthur Cooper B.;** *see* Bird-Wilson.

**WILSON, Harold Fitzhardinge Wilson;** Solicitor and Parliamentary Officer, Greater London Council, since 1970 (Dep. Solicitor and Dep. Parly Officer, 1965); *b* 6 Jan. 1913; *s* of Walter James Wilson and Aileen Wilson (*née* Scrivens), Broadway, Worcs; *m* 1939, Deb Buckland; one *s* one *d.* Law Clerk, LCC, 1935. Company Officer, then Senior Company Officer, Nat. Fire Service, 1939-45. Principal Asst, LCC, 1951; Asst Parly Officer, LCC, 1960. *Recreations:* the theatre, walking, gardening, reading. *Address:* 10 Courtenay Square, SE11. *T:* 01-735 1130.

**WILSON, Harry;** *see* Wilson of Langside, Baron.

**WILSON, (Harry) Ellis (Charter),** MB, ChB; DSc; FRCPGlas; retired as Lecturer in Pathological Biochemistry at Royal Hospital for Sick Children, Glasgow; *b* 26 July 1899; *s* of Harry James and Margaret Williamina Wilson. *Educ:* Glasgow Academy and University. Carnegie Scholar, 1923; studied in Würzburg, 1926; Assistant in Institute of Physiology, Glasgow University, 1924; a Rockefeller Fellowship tenable in USA, 1926; carried out research in New York and the Mayo Clinic, Rochester; Carnegie Teaching Fellow in Institute of Physiology, Glasgow University, 1930; studied (research) in Germany, 1931; Professor of Biochemistry and Nutrition, The All-India Institute of Hygiene and Public Health, Calcutta, 1934-37, and Professor of Chemistry, The Medical College, Calcutta, 1935-37. *Publications:* papers on biochemical subjects in various journals. *Recreations:* golf, travel. *Address:* Redholm, 5 West Chapelton Avenue, Bearsden, Glasgow; The Royal Hospital for Sick Children, Yorkhill, Glasgow.

**WILSON, Harry Lawrence L.;** *see* Lawrence-Wilson.

**WILSON, Henry Braithwaite;** Assistant Under-Secretary of State, Home Office, since 1963; *b* 6 Aug. 1911; *s* of Charles Braithwaite Wilson and Ellen Blanche Hargrove; *m* 1936, Margaret Bodden; two *s* two *d. Educ:* Leighton Park School; Lincoln College, Oxford. Editorial work for Joseph Rowntree Social Service Trust, 1933-40; Sub-Warden, Toynbee Hall, 1940-41; Home Office: Temp. Administrative Asst, 1941-44; Sec., Departmental Cttee on War Damaged Licensed Premises and Reconstruction, 1942-44; Principal, 1944 (estab. 1946); Asst Sec., 1956. *Recreations:* gardening, walking. *Address:* 69 Brookland Rise, NW11. *T:* 01-455 7200. *Club:* Athenæum.

**WILSON, Col Henry James,** CBE 1963 (OBE 1943); TD 1944; Farmer since 1949; Chairman: Organisation Committee, NFU; Industry Panel, Bacon Market Understanding; Member, Production Committee, Meat and Livestock Commission; *b* 10 June 1904; *s* of late James Wilson; *m* 1930, Anita Gertrude Petley; three *s. Educ:* Mercers' School. Westminster Bank, 1921-39. Served London Scottish, 1923-44; Commanded 1st Bn London Scottish, 1941-44; AAG, 8th Army HQ, 1944; DDPS, AFHQ, 1944-45; War Office, 1945-49. Joined NFU, 1947; Council Member, 1954; Vice-Pres., 1958; Dep. Pres., 1959-62. Chairman of Bacon Consultative Council, 1957-64; Mem., Pigs Cttee, Meat and Livestock Commn. *Recreations:* shooting, and fishing. *Address:* Bugsell Farm, Robertsbridge, Sussex. *T:* Robertsbridge 350. *Club:* Farmers'.

**WILSON, Henry Moir,** CB 1969; CMG 1965; MBE 1946; PhD, BSc, FRAeS; Director, SHAPE Technical Centre, since 1970; *b* 3 Sept. 1910; 3rd *s* of late Charles Wilson, Belfast; *m* 1937, Susan Eveline Wilson; one *s* three *d. Educ:* Royal Belfast Academical Institution, Queen's Univ., Belfast. Apprentice in Mech. Eng, Combe Barbour, Belfast, 1927-31; QUB, 1927-31 (part-time) and 1931-34 (full-time); BSc with 1st Class Hons in Elect. Eng, 1932; PhD 1934 (Thesis on High Voltage Transients on Power Transmission Lines). College Apprentice, Metropolitan-Vickers, Manchester, 1934-35. Joined RAF Educational Service, 1935; commissioned RAFVR, 1939; Senior Tutor, RAF Advanced Armament Course, Ft. Halstead, 1943-46; Senior Educ. Officer, Empire Air Armament School, Manby (Acting Wing Comdr), 1946-47. Joined Ministry of Supply, 1947, as Senior Principal Sci. Officer, Supt Servo Div., Guided Projectile Estab., Westcott, 1947; Supt Guidance and Control Div. Guided Weapons Dept, RAE, 1947-49; Head of Armament Dept, RAE, 1949-56. Dep. Chief Sci. Officer, 1952; Chief Scientific Officer, 1956; Director-General, Aircraft Equipment Research and Devel., Ministry of Aviation, 1956-62; Head, Defence Research and Development Staff, British Embassy, Washington, DC, 1962-65; Dep. Chief Scientist (Army), 1965-66, Chief Scientist (Army), 1967-70. *Recreations:* golf, gardening. *Address:* SHAPE Technical Centre, PO Box 174, The Hague, 2076, Netherlands.

**WILSON, Henry Wilcox,** QC 1941; BA; LLB; *b* 19 Jan. 1895; *s* of Cornelius Wilcox and Julia Adèle Wilson; *m* 1931, Muriel Gough Wickenden (*d* 1959). *Educ:* Uppingham; Trinity Coll., Cambridge. Barrister-at-law (Inner Temple) South Eastern Circuit; Kent Sessions; Magistrate, Tanganyika, 1929; Legal Secretary, British Somaliland, 1935; Attorney-General: N. Rhodesia, 1937-44; Trinidad and Tobago, 1944-50; Puisne Judge, Federation of Malaya, 1950-56; first Speaker, Nyasaland Legislative Council, 1958-61. *Club:* Bath.

**WILSON, Sir Horace John,** GCB, *cr* 1937 (KCB, *cr* 1924; CB 1920); GCMG, *cr* 1933; CBE 1918; Hon. LLD (Aberdeen, 1934, Liverpool, 1939); *b* 23 Aug. 1882; 2nd *s* of late Harry Wilson, Bournemouth; *m* 1908, Emily, *d* of late John Sheather, Beckley; one *s* two *d. Educ:* Kurnella Sch., Bournemouth; London School of Economics. Entered Civil Service, 1900; Principal Assistant Secretary, Ministry of Labour, 1919-21; Permanent Secretary, Ministry of Labour, 1921-30; Chief Industrial Adviser to HM Government, 1930-39; seconded to the Treasury for service with the Prime Minister, 1935; Permanent Secretary of HM Treasury and official Head of HM Civil Service, 1939-42. Independent Chairman, National Joint Council for Local Authorities' Administrative, Professional, Technical and Clerical Services, 1944-51. Hon. Fellow, LSE, 1960. *Address:* 8 Byron Road, Boscombe, Bournemouth, Hants. *T:* Bournemouth 33752.

**WILSON, Sir Hubert Guy M. M.;** *see* Maryon-Wilson.

**WILSON, Sir Hugh;** *see* Wilson, Sir L. H.

**WILSON, (Hugh) Geoffrey (Birch);** *b* 11 June 1903; *s* of late F. J. Wilson, CIE, Sidmouth, and of Mary Phoebe, *d* of late Colonel E. Birch, IMS; *m* 1935, Daphne Violet Nona, *d* of late Gordon Astley Wake; two *s* five *d*. *Educ:* Clifton College; Pembroke College, Cambridge (MA). Admitted Solicitor, 1928; Solicitors Department, GWR, 1928-47, finishing as senior Solicitor Assistant, Parliamentary and General section; assistant solicitor, Railway Executive, Western Region, 1948-49; resigned Jan. 1949, for political reasons; MP (C) Truro, 1950-70. Now a partner in a London firm. Associate Inst. Transport. *Address:* 36 Cleaver Square, SE11. *T:* 01-735 7566.

**WILSON, Hon. Ian;** *see* Wilson, Hon. T. I. F.

**WILSON, Ian D.;** *see* Douglas-Wilson.

**WILSON, Isabel Grace Hood,** CBE 1961; MD, FRCP; Principal Medical Officer, Ministry of Health, retired; *b* 16 Sept. 1895; *d* of late Dr George R. Wilson and Susan C. Sandeman. *Educ:* privately; University of Edinburgh. MB, ChB, Edinburgh, 1921; DPM London, 1924; MD, Edinburgh, 1926; MRCP London, 1937, FRCP 1947. Formerly: Asst Medical Officer, Severalls Mental Hospital, Colchester; Physician, Tavistock Square Clinic for Functional Nervous Disorders; Medical Commissioner, Board of Control, 1931-49; Senior Medical Commissioner, Board of Control, 1949-60. Member BMA; President, Royal Medico Psychological Assoc., 1962-63. *Publications:* A Study of Hypoglycæmic Shock Treatment in Schizophrenia (Report), 1936; (jointly) Report on Cardiazol Treatment, 1938; various contributions to journals. *Recreations:* water-colour painting; travel. *Address:* 48 Redcliffe Gardens, SW10. *T:* 01-352 5707.

**WILSON, James,** JP; DSc, BCom, CEng, FIMechE; Industrial Training Consultant; *b* 15 July 1899; *s* of late James Wilson, JP, Lugar and Glasgow; *m* 1930, Jesmar Smith, Clarkston, Glasgow; one *s* two *d*. *Educ:* Cumnock Academy; Kilmarnock Academy; Glasgow Univ.; Royal Technical Coll. Mech. and Electr. Engrg with Andrew Barclay Sons & Co. Ltd, Kilmarnock (sandwiched with University studies) and Gen. Electric Co., Coventry, 1914-21; Assistant and Lecturer: Royal Technical Coll., Glasgow, 1921, Glasgow Univ., 1921-35; part-time supervisor of science and technology classes, Corp. of Glasgow, 1931-35; Coventry Technical Coll., Vice-Principal, 1935-36; Principal, 1936-46; Principal, Birmingham College of Tech., 1946-56; Director of Education and Training, British Motor Corp. Ltd, 1962-65. OC engineer unit, Glasgow Univ., OTC, 1933-35; OC 71st LAA Battery (TAR), 122 LAA Regt, RA, 1939; Army Welfare Officer, Warwicks, TA, 1940-45; Chairman No. 84 (2nd City of Coventry) ATC, 1945-48; estab. Midland Theatre Company at College Theatre, Coventry, 1945 (in co-operation with Arts Council); founded Playgoers Circle. Member Anglo-American Prod. Assoc. Team "Education for Management", 1951; Mem. Council, Birmingham Productivity Assoc.; Chairman: Midland Management Cttee, British Council for Rehabilitation; Exam. Adv. Commn, Nat. Exam. Bd in Supervisory Studies; Member: Board of Governors, Welbeck Coll.; Jt Commn, Nat. Diplomas and Cert. in Business Studies. Ed. The Torch, Glasgow Education Cttee, 1932-35. Hon. MIPlantE; Hon. DSc Aston. *Publications:* (jointly) Gaining Skill; various on education and training, management education, humanism in tech. education. *Recreations:* golf, cinematography, magic. *Address:* 254 Warwick Road, Solihull, Warwicks. *T:* 021-706 1409.

**WILSON, Rt. Hon. (James) Harold,** PC 1947; OBE 1945; FRS 1969; MP (Lab) Huyton Division of Lancs since 1950 (Ormskirk Division, 1945-50); Leader of the Opposition since 1970; Leader Labour Party, since 1963; Chancellor of Bradford University, since 1966; *b* 11 March 1916; *s* of James Herbert and of late Ethel Wilson, Huddersfield, Yorks (formerly of Manchester); *m* 1940, Gladys Mary, *d* of Rev. D. Baldwin, The Manse, Duxford, Cambridge; two *s*. *Educ:* Milnsbridge Council School and Royds Hall School, Huddersfield; Wirral Grammar Sch., Bebington, Cheshire; Jesus Coll., Oxford (Gladstone Memorial Prize, Webb Medley Economics Scholarship, First Class Hons Philosophy, Politics and Economics). Lecturer in Economics, New Coll., Oxford, 1937; Fellow of University College, 1938; Praelector in Economics and Domestic Bursar, 1945. Director of Economics amd Statistics, Ministry of Fuel and Power, 1943-44; Parliamentary Secretary to the Ministry of Works, 1945-March 1947; Secretary for Overseas Trade, March-Oct. 1947; President, Board of Trade, Oct. 1947-April 1951; Chairman Labour Party Exec. Cttee, 1961-62; Chairman, Public Accounts Cttee, 1959-63; Prime Minister and First Lord of the Treasury, 1964-70. An Elder Brother of Trinity House, 1968. Hon. Fellow, Jesus and University Colleges, Oxford, 1963. Hon. LLD: Lancaster, 1964; Liverpool, 1965; Nottingham, 1966; Sussex, 1966; Hon. DCL, Oxford, 1965; Hon. DTech., Bradford, 1966; and DUniv Essex, 1967. *Publications:* New Deal for Coal, 1945; In Place of Dollars, 1952; The War on World Poverty, 1953; The Relevance of British Socialism, 1964; Purpose in Politics, 1964; The New Britain (Penguin), 1964; Purpose in Power, 1966. *Recreation:* golf. *Address:* House of Commons, SW1.

**WILSON, James Noel,** ChM, FRCS; Consultant Orthopædic Surgeon: Royal National Orthopædic Hospital, London, National Hospitals for Nervous Diseases, Queen Square and Maida Vale, since 1962; and Surgeon i/c of Accident Unit, RNOH, Stanmore, since 1955; Teacher of Orthopædics and Director of Training, Institute of Orthopædics, University of London; *b* Coventry, 25 Dec. 1919; *s* of Alexander Wilson and Isobel Barbara Wilson (*née* Fairweather); *m* 1945, Patricia Norah McCullough; two *s* two *d*. *Educ:* King Henry VIII Sch., Coventry; University of Birmingham. Peter Thompson Prize in Anatomy, 1940; Sen. Surgical Prize, 1942; Arthur Foxwell Prize in Clinical Medicine, 1943; MB, ChB 1943; MRCS, LRCP, 1943; FRCS 1948; ChM (Birmingham) 1949; House Surgeon, Birmingham General Hospital, 1943; Heaton Award as Best Resident for 1943. Service in RAMC, Nov. 1943-Oct. 1946, discharged as Captain; qualified as Parachutist and served with 1st Airborne Division. Resident surgical posts, Birmingham General Hospital and Coventry and Warwickshire Hospital, 1947-49; Resident Surgical Officer, Robert Jones and Agnes Hunt Orthopædic Hospital, Oswestry, 1949-52; Consultant Orthopædic Surgeon to Cardiff Royal Infirmary and Welsh Regional Hospital Board, 1952-55. Member BMA; Fellow British Orthopædic Assoc. (BOA Travelling Fellowship to USA, 1954); FRSocMed. *Publications:* Sections in Butterworth's Operative Surgery; articles on orthopædic subjects to various journals. *Recreations:* golf, gardening and photography. *Address:* The Chequers, Waterdale, near Watford, Herts. *T:* Garston 72364. *Club:* Airborne.

**WILSON, Air Vice-Marshal James Stewart,** CBE 1959; Lecturer, Institute of Hygiene, RAF Halton, since 1965; *b* 4 Sept. 1909; *s* of late J. Wilson, Broughty Ferry, Angus, and late Helen Fyffe Wilson; *m* 1937, Elizabeth Elias; one *s* (and one *s* decd). *Educ:* Dundee High Sch.; St Andrews Univ. (MB, ChB). DPH (London) 1948. House Surgeon, Dundee Royal Infirmary, 1933; House Surgeon, Arbroath Infirmary, 1934; Commissioned Royal Air Force, 1935. Served North Africa, 1942-45. Director Hygiene and Research, Air Ministry, London, 1956-59; Principal Medical Officer, Flying Training Command, 1959-61; Director-General of Medical Services, Royal Australian Air Force, 1961-63. QHP 1961; Principal Medical Officer, Bomber Command, 1963-65, retired. *Publications:* articles (jointly) on respiratory virus infections, in medical journals. *Recreations:* golf, fishing, shooting. *Address:* Holmlea, Grove Road, Tring, Herts. *Club:* Royal Air Force.

**WILSON, James Thomas Pither,** CBE 1955; *b* 16 Aug. 1884; *e s* of Alfred Thomas Wilson; *m* 1913, Netia Ling, *o d* of William James Welch, St Peter's Port, Guernsey, CI; one *s* (and one *s* decd). HM Land Registry, 1900; High Court of Justice in Bankruptcy, 1910; Registrar Companies Court and in Bankruptcy, 1947-53; Chief Registrar in Bankruptcy of the High Court of Justice, 1953-57. Served European War, 1914-18, in France. *Address:* 31 Ashley Drive, Walton-on-Thames, Surrey.

**WILSON, Hon. John;** *see* Wilson, Hon. R. J. McM.

**WILSON, John Foster,** CBE 1965 (OBE 1955); Director, Royal Commonwealth Society for the Blind, since 1950; *b* 20 Jan. 1919; *s* of late Rev. George Henry Wilson, Buxton, Derbys; *m* 1944, Chloe Jean McDermid; two *d*. *Educ:* Worcester College for the Blind; St Catherine's, Oxford (MA Jurisprudence, Dipl. Public and Social Administration). Asst Secretary, Royal National Inst. for the Blind, 1941-49; Member, Colonial Office Delegation investigating blindness in Africa and Near East, 1946-47. Proposed formation of Royal Commonwealth Society for Blind; became its first Director, 1950; extensive tours in Africa, Asia, Near and Far East, Caribbean and N. America, 1952-67; world tours, 1958 and 1963; formulated Asian plan for the Blind 1963, and African Plan for the Blind, 1966. Chairman, Ghana Cabinet Cttee on Rehabilitation of Disabled, 1961; Internat. Member of World Council for Welfare of Blind (Chairman, Prevention of Blindness Cttee, 1958-); Member Exec. Cttee of World Braille Council and International Conf. of Educators of Blind Youth; Founder Member, National Fed. of Blind (President, 1955-60). Helen Keller International Award, 1970. *Publications:* Blindness in African and Middle East Territories, 1948; Ghana's Handicapped Citizens, 1961; Travelling Blind, 1963; various on Commonwealth affairs, rehabilitation and blindness. *Recreations:* current affairs, travel, writing, tape-recording, wine-making. *Address:* 22 The Cliff, Roedean, Brighton, Sussex. *T:* Brighton 67667. *Club:* Royal Commonwealth Society.

**WILSON, Prof. John Graham;** Cavendish Professor of Physics, since 1963 (Professor, 1952-63), Pro-Vice-Chancellor, since 1969, University of Leeds; *b* 28 April 1911; *er s* of J. E. Wilson, West Hartlepool, Co. Durham; *m* 1938, Georgiana Brooke, *o d* of Charles W. Bird, Bisley, Surrey; one *s* one *d*. *Educ:* West Hartlepool Secondary Sch.; Sidney Sussex Coll., Cambridge. Member of Teaching staff, University of Manchester, 1938-52; Reader in Physics, 1951. University of York: Member, Academic Planning Board, 1960-63; Member of Council, 1964-; Chairman, Joint Matriculation Board, 1964-67. *Publications:* The Principles of Cloud Chamber Technique, 1951. Editor of Progress in Cosmic Ray Physics, 1952 onwards; (with G. D. Rochester), Cloud Chamber Photographs of the Cosmic Radiation, 1952. Papers on cosmic ray physics, articles in jls. *Recreations:* fell-walking, gardening. *Address:* 420 Otley Road, Leeds LS16 8AD. *T:* 678516.

**WILSON, J(ohn) Greenwood,** MD, FRCP, DPH; Fellow of King's College, University of London; Group Medical Consultant, Health and Hygiene, FMC Ltd; formerly Medical Officer of Health, Port and City of London (first holder of dual appointment; MOH Port of London, 1954, MOH, City of London, in addition, 1956); *b* 27 July 1897; 2nd *s* of late Rev. John Wilson, Woolwich; *m* 1st, 1929, Wenda Margaret Hithersay Smith (marr. diss. 1941); one *s* two *d*; 2nd, 1943, Gwendoline Mary Watkins; one *d*. *Educ:* Colfe Grammar Sch.; Westminster Hospital, University of London. Served European War, S. Lancashire Regt, RFC and RAF, 1916-19 (wounded). Various hospital appointments, London and provinces and some general practice, 1923-28; subseq. MOH and Sch. Medical Officer posts; then MOH City and Port of Cardiff, Sch. MO, Cardiff Education Authority, and Lecturer in Preventive Medicine, Welsh Nat. School of Medicine, 1933-54. President, Welsh Br. Society of Med. Officers of Health, 1940-45, Member Nat. Adv. Council for recruitment of Nurses and Midwives, 1943-56. Governor, St Bart's Hospital Medical College. Lecturer Royal Institute of Public Health. Formerly Examiner in Public Health, RCPS (London); Vice-President (Past Chairman of Council) and Hon. Fellow, Royal Society of Health. Member, Central Housing Advisory Cttee, 1936-56; Member Royal Commission on Mental Health, 1954-57; Chairman, City Division, BMA, 1962-63; Vice-President (Past Chairman), National Housebuilders Registration Council. Hon. Fellow American Public Health Association. OStJ 1953. *Publications:* Diptheria Immunisation Propaganda and Counter Propaganda, 1933; Public Health Law in Question and Answer, 1951; numerous contributions to med., scientific and tech. publications. *Recreations:* theatre, music, swimming. *Address:* Flat 2, 10 Beckenham Grove, Bromley BR2 0JU. *T:* 01-460 1532.

**WILSON, John Martindale,** CB 1960; a Deputy Under-Secretary of State, Ministry of Defence, since 1965; *b* 3 Sept. 1915; *e s* of late John and Kate Wilson; *m* 1941, Penelope Beatrice, *e d* of late Francis A. Bolton, JP, Oakamoor, Staffs; one *s* one *d*. *Educ:* Bradfield Coll.; Gonville and Caius Coll., Cambridge. BA (Cantab), 1st Class Law Trip., 1937; MA 1946. Asst Principal, Dept of Agriculture for Scotland, 1938; Ministry of Supply, 1939; served War, 1939-46 (despatches) with Royal Artillery in India and Burma; Private Secretary to Minister of Supply, 1946-50; Asst Secretary, 1950; Under-Secretary, 1954; Cabinet Office, 1955-58; Ministry of Defence, 1958-60; Dep. Secretary, Ministry of Aviation, 1961-65. *Recreations:* gardening and golf. *Address:* Moledale, Bessels Green, near Sevenoaks, Kent. *T:* Sevenoaks 54502. *Club:* Army and Navy.

**WILSON, Sir John Mitchell Harvey,** 2nd Bt, *cr* 1920; KCVO 1957 (CVO 1950); Barrister; late 2nd Lieutenant Coldstream Guards; Keeper of the Queen's Philatelic Collection, 1952-69; President, Royal Philatelic Society, London,

1934-40; *b* 10 Oct. 1898; *e* surv. *s* of 1st Bt and Susan Main (*d* 1944), *d* of Rev. J. Mitchell Harvey, DD; *S* father, 1930; *m* 1927, Mary Elizabeth, *er d* of William Richards, CBE; three *s*. *Educ:* Harrow; New Coll., Oxford. Keeper of the King's Philatelic Collection, 1938-52. An Extra Gentleman Usher to the Queen, 1969-. *Publication:* The Royal Philatelic Collection, 1952. *Heir:* *s* David Wilson [*b* 30 Oct. 1928; *m* 1955, Eva Margareta, *e d* of Tore Lindell, Malmo, Sweden; two *s* one *d*]. *Address:* Carbeth, Killearn, Stirlingshire. *TA:* Killearn. *Club:* Arts.

*See also Sir George Wilson.*

**WILSON, Prof. John Stuart Gladstone,** MA, DipCom; Professor of Economics and Commerce in the University of Hull, and Head of Department, since Oct. 1959; *b* 18 Aug. 1916; *s* of Herbert Gladstone Wilson and Mary Buchanan Wilson (*née* Wylie); *m* 1943, Beryl Margaret Gibson, *d* of Alexander Millar Gibson and Bertha Noble Gibson; no *c*. *Educ:* University of Western Australia. Lecturer in Economics: University of Tasmania, 1941-43; Sydney, 1944-45; Canberra, 1946-47; London School of Economics, 1948-49. Reader in Economics, with special reference to Money and Banking, in the University of London, 1950-59; Dean, Faculty of Social Sciences and Law, University of Hull, 1962-65; Chairman, Centre for S-E Asian Studies, University of Hull, 1963-66. Hackett Research Student, 1947; Leverhulme Research Award, 1955 (to visit United States and Canada). Economic Survey of New Hebrides on behalf of Colonial Office, 1958-59; Consultant, Trade and Payments Dept, OECD, 1965-66; Consultant with Harvard Advisory Development Service in Liberia, 1967; Committee of Management, Institute of Commonwealth Studies, London, 1960-; Governor, School of Oriental and African Studies, London, 1963-. Member: Yorkshire Council for Further Education, 1963-67; Nat. Advisory Council on Education for Industry and Commerce, 1964-66; Conseil d'Administration, Société Universitaire Européenne de Recherches Financières (Secretary-General, 1968-). Editor, Yorkshire Bulletin of Economic and Social Research, 1964-67. *Publications:* French Banking Structure and Credit Policy, 1957; Economic Environment and Development Programmes, 1960; Monetary Policy and the Development of Money Markets, 1966; Economic Survey of the New Hebrides, 1966; (ed, with C. R. Whittlesey), Essays in Money and Banking in Honour of R. S. Sayers, 1968. Contribs. to Banking in the British Commonwealth (ed R. S. Sayers), 1952 and to Banking in Western Europe (ed R. S. Sayers), 1962; A Decade of the Commonwealth, 1955-64, ed W. B. Hamilton and others, 1966; to Economica, Economic Journal, Journal of Political Econ., Economic Record. *Recreations:* squash rackets, gardening, theatre, art galleries. *Address:* Department of Economics and Commerce, The University, Hull, Yorks.

**WILSON, Prof. John Tuzo,** SM (Canada) 1970; OBE 1946; FRS 1968; FRSC 1949; Principal of Erindale College since 1967, Professor of Geophysics, since 1946, University of Toronto; *b* Ottawa, 24 Oct. 1908; *s* of John Armitstead Wilson, CBE, and Henrietta L. Tuzo; *m* 1938, Isabel Jean Dickson; two *d*. *Educ:* Ottawa; Universities of Toronto (Governor-General's medal, Trinity Coll., 1930; Massey Fellow, 1930), Cambridge (ScD), and Princeton (PhD). Asst Geologist, Geological Survey of Canada, 1936-46. Regimental service and staff appointments, Royal Canadian Engrs, UK and Sicily, 1939-43; Director, Opl. Research, Nat. Defence HQ, Ottawa (Colonel), 1944-46. President, International Union of Geodesy and Geophysics, 1957-60; Visiting Prof.: Australian Nat. Univ., 1950 and 1965; Ohio State Univ., 1968. Member Nat. Research Council of Canada, 1957-63; Member Defence Res. Board, 1958-64. Canadian Delegation to Gen. Ass., UNESCO, 1962, 1964, 1966. Overseas Fellow, Churchill Coll., Cambridge, 1965; Trustee, Nat. Museums of Canada, 1968-. Hon. Fellow, Trinity Coll., University of Toronto, 1962. Foreign Associate, Nat. Acad. of Sciences, USA, 1968; Foreign Hon. Mem., Amer. Acad. of Arts and Sciences. Holds hon. doctorates and hon. or foreign memberships and medals, etc, in Canada and abroad. *Publications:* One Chinese Moon, 1959; Physics and Geology (with J. A. Jacobs and R. D. Russell), 1959; IGY Year of the New Moons, 1961; scientific papers. *Recreations:* travel, sailing, Hong Kong junk. *Address:* Principal's House, Erindale College, University of Toronto, Toronto 5, Canada. *T:* 826-1266. *Clubs:* University, Arts and Letters (Toronto); Explorers' (New York).

**WILSON, Joseph Albert;** Secretary to the Cabinet, Sierra Leone Government, 1968; Barrister-at-Law; *b* 22 Jan. 1922; *e s* of late George Wilson; *m* 1947, Esther Massaquoi; two *s* four *d* (and one *s* decd). *Educ:* St Edward's Secondary Sch., Freetown, Sierra Leone; University of Exeter, (DPA); Middle Temple. Graded Clerical Service, Sierra Leone Government, 1941-47; family business, 1948-51; Secretary, Bonthe District Council, 1951-59; Administrative Officer, Sierra Leone Government, rising to rank of Cabinet Secretary, 1959-; High Comr from Sierra Leone to UK, 1967-68. *Recreation:* tennis. *Address:* 14 Syke Street, Brookfields, Freetown, Sierra Leone. *T:* 2590.

**WILSON, Joseph Vivian;** retired as New Zealand Ambassador to France, 1959; *b* 14 July 1894; *s* of J. H. Wilson; *m* 1929, Valentine, *d* of H. van Muyden, Geneva; two *s*. *Educ:* Christchurch Boys' High Sch.; Canterbury University College, NZ; Trinity Coll., Cambridge (MA). Craven Scholar and Porson Prizeman, Cambridge. Served in first New Zealand Expeditionary Force, 1915-18. International Labour Office, Geneva, 1921-23; Secretariat, League of Nations, Geneva, 1923-40 (Chief of Central section, 1933-40); Assistant Director of Research, Chatham House, London, 1940-44; Member NZ delegation to San Francisco Conference, 1945, and to several sessions of the General Assembly of the United Nations; Assistant Secretary of External Affairs, New Zealand, 1944-56; HM New Zealand Minister at Paris, 1956, Ambassador, 1957. *Address:* Mahina Road, Eastbourne, NZ. *Clubs:* Oxford and Cambridge University; Wellington (Wellington, NZ).

**WILSON, Sir Keith (Cameron),** Kt 1966; Member of House of Representatives for Sturt, South Australia, 1949-54, 1955-66; *b* 3 Sept. 1900; *s* of Algernon Theodore King Wilson; *m* 1930, Elizabeth H., *d* of late Sir Lavington Bonython; two *s* one *d*. *Educ:* Collegiate School of St Peter, Adelaide; University of Adelaide. LLB 1922. Admitted to Bar, 1922. Served War of 1939-45: Gunner, 2nd AIF, 1940; Middle East, 1940-43; Major. Senator for South Australia, 1938-44. Chairman: Aged Cottage Homes Inc., 1952-; War Blinded Welfare Fund; President: Good Neighbour Council of SA, 1968-; Queen Elizabeth Hosp. Research Foundn; Past President Legacy. *Publication:* Wilson-Uppill Wheat Equalization Scheme, 1938. *Address:* 79 Tusmore Avenue, Tusmore, SA 5065,

Australia. *T:* 3-5578. *Club:* Adelaide (Adelaide).

**WILSON, Sir Leonard,** KCIE, *cr* 1945; Kt 1941; BEng; MICE; *b* Birkenhead, 12 March 1888; *s* of late G. R. Wilson, Birkenhead; *m* 1919, Muriel (*d* 1926), *d* of John Smethurst; two *s*; *m* 1947, Annis, *d* of late Rev. J. C. Abdy. *Educ:* Birkenhead Sch.; Liverpool Univ. Went to India, 1910; employed GIP Railway, Chief Engineer, 1930-34; General Manager, 1934-40; Chief Commissioner of Railways, India, 1940-46. *Address:* Lowbury, Compton, Berks. *Club:* East India and Sports.
*See also F. R. Wilson.*

**WILSON, Sir (Leslie) Hugh,** Kt 1967; OBE 1952; FRIBA; MTPI; Architect and Town Planner; Partner, Hugh Wilson & Lewis Womersley, Chartered Architects and Town Planners, since 1962; *b* 1 May 1913; *s* of Frederick Charles Wilson and Ethel Anne Hughes; *m* 1938, Monica Chrysavye Nomico (*d* 1966); one *s* two *d*. *Educ:* Haberdashers' Aske's Sch. Asst Architect, private practices, 1933-39; Asst Architect, Canterbury, 1939-45; City Architect and Planning Officer, Canterbury, 1945-56; Chief Architect and Planning Officer, Cumbernauld New Town, 1956-62. Techn. Adviser on Urban Development to Min. of Housing and Local Government, 1965-67. Works include housing, churches, central area develt; Master Plans for Irvine, Skelmersdale, Redditch, and Northampton New Towns; central area plans for Oxford, Brighton, Exeter and Lewes. Vice-President, RIBA, 1960-61, 1962-64, Sen. Vice-President, 1966-67, President, 1967-69. DisTP, 1956. Hon. FRAIC; Hon. FAIA; Hon. Mem., Akademie der Künste, Berlin. Hon. DSc Aston, 1969. *Recreations:* travel, music. *Address:* 71 Fordington Road, N6. *T:* 01-883 4717. *Club:* Savile.

**WILSON, Canon Leslie Rule;** Vicar of Holmside, since 1970; *b* 19 July 1909; *y s* of Rev. John and Mary Adelaide Wilson. *Educ:* Royal Grammar Sch., Newcastle upon Tyne; University College, Durham; Edinburgh Theological College. Asst Priest, Old St Paul's, Edinburgh, 1934-36; Rector of Fort William, 1936; Canon of Argyll and The Isles, 1940-42; Education Officer, 1942-45; Welfare Officer, SEAC (Toc H), 1945-46; Vicar of Malacca, Malaya, 1946-50; Principal Probation Officer, Federation of Malaya, 1950-52; Vicar of Kuching, Sarawak, 1952-55; Provost and Canon of St Thomas' Cathedral, Kuching, 1955-59; Rector of Geraldton, W Australia, 1960-64; Dean of Geraldton, 1964-66; Rector of Winterbourne Stickland with Turnworth and Winterbourne Houghton, 1967-70. Hon. Canon, Holy Cross Cathedral, Geraldton, 1966. Founder and Chairman, Parson Woodforde Society, 1968. *Recreations:* reading, walking, genealogy. *Address:* Holmside Vicarage, Burnhope, Co. Durham. *T:* Lanchester 520820.

**WILSON, Rt. Rev. Lucian C. U.;** *see* Usher-Wilson.

**WILSON, Sir Martin;** *see* Wilson, Sir M. M.

**WILSON, Sir (Mathew) Martin,** 5th Bt, *cr* 1874; *b* 2 July 1906; *s* of Lieut-Colonel Sir Mathew Richard Henry Wilson, 4th Bt, and Hon. Barbara Lister (*d* 1943), *d* of 4th Baron Ribblesdale; *S* father, 1958. *Educ:* Eton. *Heir:* *b* Anthony Thomas Wilson [*b* 15 Nov. 1908; *m* 1934, Margaret (Motion), *d* of late Alfred Holden; one *s*]. *Address:* 39 Blomfield Road, W9.

**WILSON, Michael Thomond,** MBE 1945; Chief General Manager, Lloyds Bank Ltd, since 1967, Director, since 1968; *b* 7 Feb. 1911; *e s* of late Sir Roy Wilson, Pyrford, near Woking; *m* 1933, Jessie Babette, *o d* of late John Winston Foley Winnington, Malvern, Worcs; two *s* one *d*. *Educ:* Rugby Sch.; Oriel Coll., Oxford. War Service with RA and on Staff in UK and India, 1939-45. Entered Lloyds Bank, 1932; Assistant General Manager, 1958; Dep. Chief General Manager, 1963; Director: Lloyds Bank Europe Ltd; Lloyds & Scottish Ltd. JP Berks, 1952-66. *Address:* Clytha, South Ascot, Berks. *T:* Ascot 20833.

**WILSON, Norman George,** CMG 1966; Managing Director, Fibremakers Ltd; Director: ICI of Australia and NZ Ltd; Fibremakers (NZ) Ltd; *b* 20 Oct. 1911; *s* of P. Wilson; *m* 1939, Dorothy Gwen, *d* of late Sir W. Lennon Raws; one *s* two *d*. *Educ:* Melbourne University (BCE). Joined ICI of Australia and NZ Ltd, 1935; Exec. in Technical and Sales Departments, 1936-48; Controller, Dyes and Plastics Group, 1949-54; Director, 1959-. Man. Director, BALM Paints Ltd, BALM Paints (NZ) Ltd, 1954-62. Business Adviser to Dept of Air, and Member Defence Business Board, Commonwealth Government, 1957-; Chairman Board of Management for Production, Dept of Supply, Commonwealth Government, 1960-. FInstD, FRACI, FAIM. *Recreations:* golf, gardening. *Address:* 5 Tahara Road, Toorak, Victoria 3142, Australia. *T:* Melbourne 24-4438. *Clubs:* Australian (Melbourne); Royal Melbourne Golf, Melbourne Cricket, Frankston Golf, Victoria Racing.

**WILSON, Paul Norman,** OBE 1959; DSC 1945; JP; Lieut-Commander RNVR (retired); HM Lieutenant of Westmorland since 1965; *b* 24 Oct. 1908; *y s* of late Norman Forster Wilson, CE, Kendal and Crosthwaite, and H. G. M. Wilson (*née* Harris); *m* 1935, Valerie Frances Elizabeth, *d* of late William Baron Fletcher, Cape Town; no *c*. *Educ:* Gresham's Sch.; Clare Coll., Cambridge. MA (Mech. Sci.) Cantab, 1934. Served War of 1939-45: mainly at sea in capital ships; temp. Lt-Comdr RN. Worked in S Africa, 1930-34; Gilbert Gilkes & Gordon Ltd, Water Turbine & Pump Manufacturers, Kendall: Man. Dir, 1934-67; Chairman, 1954-. Served on local and Westmorland Youth Employment Cttees and Nat. Youth Employment Council for a number of years. Chairman of Governors, Kendal Coll. of Further Educn; Chairman of Trustees, Abbot Hall Museum, 1967-. Governor of BBC, 1968-. JP 1958, DL 1964, Westmorland. KStJ 1966. *Publications:* various works on watermills; contributions to journals on history of water power and technical matters. *Recreation:* industrial archæology (especially water power). *Address:* Gillinggate House, Kendal, Westmorland. *T:* Kendal 20209. *Clubs:* Oxford and Cambridge University; Royal Windermere Yacht.

**WILSON, Percy,** CB 1955; Director of Education, Bank Education Service, since 1965; *b* 15 Dec. 1904; *s* of Joseph Edwin and Louisa Wilson; *m* 1st, 1929, Beryl Godsell (decd); 2nd, 1943. Dorothy Spiers; one *s* one *d*. *Educ:* Market Rasen Grammar Sch.; Jesus Coll., Cambridge. Schoolmaster, 1927-35; HM Inspector of Schools, 1935-45 (seconded to war duties, 1939-42); Staff Inspector for English, 1945-47; a Chief Inspector, Ministry of Education, 1947-57; Sen. Chief Inspector, Dept of Education and Science, 1957-65. Hon. FCP, 1965. A Governor, Wellington Coll., 1966-. *Recreation:* painting. *Address:* The Cottage, 6 Castlebar Park, W5. *T:* 01-997 5224. *Club:* Athenæum.

**WILSON, Peter Cecil,** CBE 1970; Chairman, Sotheby & Co., since 1958 (Director, since 1938); *b* 8 March 1913; 3rd *s* of Sir Mathew Wilson, 4th Bt, CSI, DSO, Eshton Hall, Gargrave, Yorkshire; *m* 1935, Grace Helen Ranken (marr. diss.); two *s*. *Educ:* Eton; New Coll., Oxford. Benjamin Franklin Medal, RSA 1968. *Address:* Garden Lodge, Logan Place, W8. *T:* 01-373 0373. *Club:* St James'.

**WILSON, Peter Humphrey St John,** CB 1956; CBE 1952; Deputy Under Secretary of State, Department of Employment and Productivity, 1968-69, retired (Deputy Secretary, Ministry of Labour, 1958-68); *b* 1 May 1908; *e s* of late Rt Rev. Henry A. Wilson, CBE, DD; *m* 1939, Catherine Laird (*d* 1963), *d* of late H. J. Bonser, London; three *d*. *Educ:* Cheltenham Coll. (Schol.); Corpus Christi Coll., Cambridge (Foundation Schol.). Assistant Principal, Ministry of Labour, 1930; Principal, 1936; Regional Controller, Northern Region, 1941; Controller, Scotland, 1944; Under Secretary, 1952. *Recreations:* reading, music, sailing. *Address:* Thorntree Cottage, Blackheath, near Guildford, Surrey. *T:* Bramley 3758. *Club:* Oxford and Cambridge University.

**WILSON, Sir Reginald (Holmes),** Kt 1951; BCom; MInstT; Chairman: National Freight Corporation, since 1969; Thos Cook & Sons Ltd, since 1967; Transport Holding Co., since 1967; Partner, Whinney, Murray & Co.; Scottish Chartered Accountant; *b* 1905; *o s* of Alexander Wilson and Emily Holmes Wilson. Partner in Whinney, Murray & Co., 1937 and subsequently in Brown, Fleming & Murray; HM Treasury, 1940; Principal Assistant Secretary, Ministry of Shipping, 1941; Director of Finance, Ministry of War Transport, 1941; Under-Secretary, Ministry of Transport, 1945; returned to City, 1946; Joint Financial Adviser, Ministry of Transport, 1946; Member of Royal Commission on Press, 1946; Vice-Chairman, Hemel Hempstead Development Corporation, 1946-56; Adviser on Special Matters, CCG, 1947. Comptroller BTC, 1947, Member BTC, 1953, Chm. E Area Board, 1955-60, Chm. London Midland Area Board, 1960-62; Award of Merit, Inst. Transport, 1953; President, Inst. Transport, 1957-58. Chairman, Board of Governors: Hospitals for Diseases of the Chest, 1960; National Heart Hospital, 1968. *Publications:* various papers on transport matters. *Recreations:* music, walking. *Address:* c/o National Freight Corporation, Argosy House, 215 Great Portland Street, W1N 6BD. *Clubs:* Devonshire, City.

**WILSON, Hon. (Richard) John (McMoran),** CMG 1970; Head of West African Department, Foreign and Commonwealth Office, since 1968, and concurrently HM Ambassador to Chad, since 1970; *b* 22 Sept. 1924; *er s* and *heir* of Dr C. M. Wilson (later Sir Charles Wilson and 1st Baron Moran, *qv*); *m* 1948, Shirley Rowntree Harris; two *s* one *d*. *Educ:* Eton; King's Coll., Cambridge. Served War of 1939-45; Ord. Seaman in HMS Belfast, 1943; Sub-Lt RNVR in Motor Torpedo Boats and HM Destroyer Oribi, 1944-45. Foreign Office, 1945; Third Sec., Ankara, 1948; Tel-Aviv, 1950; Second Sec., Rio de Janeiro, 1953; First Sec., FO, 1956; Washington, 1959; FO 1961; Counsellor: British Embassy in South Africa, 1965. *Recreations:* fishing, fly-tying, bird-watching. *Address:* 26 Church Row, Hampstead, NW3. *T:* 01-435 8717; Llewelyn House, Aberedw, Radnorshire. *T:* Erwood 257. *Clubs:* Beefsteak, Flyfishers'.

**WILSON, Rev. Richard Mercer,** MA; Rector of St George the Martyr, Queen Square, Holborn (with St Bartholomew and Holy Trinity Gray's Inn Road) and Anglican Chaplain, Hospital for Sick Children, Great Ormond Street, 1944-66, resigned; *b* 9 Dec. 1887; *s* of David Wilson and Jane Mercer; *m* 1914; one *s* (and two killed in action, 1939 and 1944) one *d*. *Educ:* St Patrick's Cathedral and Trinity Coll., Dublin. Curate of Christ Church, Delgany, 1910; Mariners Church, Kingstown, 1913; Incumbent, St John's Church, Cork, 1916; Clerical Secretary, Irish Church Missions, London, 1922; Professor of Church History, Wycliffe Coll., Toronto, 1927; General Secretary United Society for Christian Literature and Lutterworth Press, 1931-40; Vicar of St Philip's, Arlington Square, Islington, 1940-43. *Publications:* Before the Reformation, 1929; Vital Themes, 1932; Protestantism: Its Fundamental Basis, 1932; Fourfold Aspect, 1933; The Book of Books, a fresh translation of the New Testament, 1938; Editor: Lutterworth Library, vols i-xiii; Tyndale Commemoration Volume, etc. *Recreations:* swimming and walking. *Address:* 188 Court Lane, SE21. *T:* 01-693 2864.

**WILSON, Prof. Richard Middlewood;** Professor of English Language, University of Sheffield, since 1955; *b* 20 Sept. 1908; *e s* of late R. L. Wilson, The Grange, Kilham, Driffield, E Yorks; *m* 1938, Dorothy Muriel, *y d* of late C. E. Leeson, Eastgate House, Kilham, Driffield; one *d*. *Educ:* Woodhouse Grove School; Leeds University. Asst Lecturer, Leeds Univ., 1931, Lecturer, 1936; Senior Lecturer and Head of Dept of English Language, Sheffield Univ., 1946. *Publications:* Sawles Warde, 1939; Early Middle English Literature, 1939; (with B. Dickins) Early Middle English Texts, 1951; The Lost Literature of Medieval England, 1952; (with D. J. Price) The Equatorie of the Planetis, 1955; articles and reviews. *Recreation:* cricket. *Address:* 9 Endcliffe Vale Avenue, Sheffield 11. *T:* Sheffield 63431.

**WILSON, Robert Andrew,** CB 1962; Principal Keeper, Department of Printed Books, British Museum, 1959-66; *b* 18 July 1905; *s* of Robert Bruce Wilson; *m* 1967, Rosemary Ann, *d* of Sydney Joseph Norris. *Educ:* Westminster School; Trinity College, Cambridge. Assistant Keeper, Department of Printed Books, British Museum, 1929-48, Deputy Keeper, 1948-52; also Superintendent of the Reading Room, British Museum, 1948-52; Keeper, 1952-59. *Address:* 33 Denmark Avenue, Wimbledon, SW19.

**WILSON, Hon. Sir Robert (Christian),** Kt 1966; CMG 1952; MLC New South Wales, 1949-61; General Manager Grazcos Co-operative Ltd, 1924-61; Chairman, Tooheys Ltd; Director: Bank of New South Wales; Australian Guarantee Corporation Ltd; Scottish Australian Company Ltd, and other companies; *b* 11 Nov. 1896; *s* of late Henry Christian Wilson, Blayney; *m* 1932, Gertrude, *d* of Clayton K. Brooks, Boston, Mass., USA; one *s* two *d*. *Educ:* Fort Street High School, Australia. Served European War, 1914-18; on active service, 1st LH Regt, AIF in Egypt, 1915-18. *Address:* 25 Bushlands Avenue, Gordon, Sydney, NSW 2072, Australia. *Club:* Australian, Elanora Country (Sydney).

**WILSON, Very Rev. Prof.-Emeritus Robert John,** MA, BD, DD; retired as Principal of the Presbyterian College, Belfast (1961-64), and Professor of Old Testament Language, Literature and Theology (1939-64), also Principal of the Presbyterian Theological Faculty, Ireland (1962-64); *b* 23 September 1893; *s* of Robert Wilson; *m* 1917, Margaret Mary Kilpatrick; one *s* two *d*. *Educ:* Mayo St National School, Belfast; Trade Preparatory

School, Municipal Technical Inst.; Kelvin House, Botanic Ave; Methodist Coll.; Queen's Univ. and Presbyterian Coll., Belfast. BA 1913, QUB 1st Hons (Philosophy) with Special Prize; MA 1914; BD 1925 London; BD Hons London, 1930, in Hebrew, Aramaic and Syriac; Univ. of London GCE, Classical Hebrew Advanced Level, Grade A, Special Paper, Grade 1 (Distinction), 1968, Ordinary Level Grade A, 1969. Minister of Presbyterian Churches: Raffrey, Co. Down, 1917, First Donaghadee, Co. Down, 1921; Waterside, Londonderry, 1923; First Carrickfergus, Co. Antrim, 1928. Presbyterian College, Belfast: part-time Lecturer in Hebrew, 1933-34; Warden, 1941-49; Carey Lecturer, 1942; Secretary of Faculty, 1945-61; Convener of Coll. Bd of Management, 1946-62; Vice-Principal of Faculty, 1951-61. Recognised Teacher in Faculty of Theology, in Hebrew and Old Testament Theology, and Internal Examiner for BD, QUB, 1939-64; Internal Examiner for BA in Hebrew, 1948-64; Part-time Lecturer in Hebrew in Faculty of Arts, QUB, 1946-64. Moderator of the General Assembly of the Presbyterian Church in Ireland, 1957-58. Hon. DD Knox College, Toronto, 1961. *Recreations:* walking, motoring, lawn-verging. *Address:* 18 Mount Eden Park, Belfast BT9 6RA. *T:* Belfast 668830.

**WILSON, Prof. Roger Cowan;** Professor of Education, University of Bristol, since 1951; Visiting Professor: University of Malawi, 1966; Harvard University, 1968; *b* 3 August 1906; 2nd *s* of Alexander Cowan Wilson and Edith Jane Brayshaw; *m* 1931, Margery Lilian, *y d* of late Rev. C. W. Emmet, Fellow of University College, Oxford, and Gertrude Weir; one *s* one *d*. *Educ:* Manchester Grammar School; The Queen's College, Oxford (Exhibitioner); Manchester College of Technology. Chairman, OU Labour Club, 1927; President, Oxford Union, 1929; First Cl. in Philosophy, Politics and Economics, 1929. Apprentice in Cotton Industry, 1929-35; Talks Staff of BBC, 1935-40; dismissed from BBC as conscientious objector; General Secretary, Friends Relief Service, 1940-46; head of Dept of Social Studies, University College, Hull, 1946-51. Senior Adviser on Social Affairs, United Nations Operation in the Congo, 1961-62. Chm., Bd of Visitors, Shepton Mallet Prison, 1966-. JP Bristol, 1954-67. Médaille de la Reconnaisance Française, 1948. *Publications:* Frank Lenwood, a biography, 1936; Authority, Leadership and Concern, a study of motive and administration in Quaker relief work, 1948; Quaker Relief, 1940-48, 1952; (with Kuenstler and others) Social Group Work in Gt Britain, 1955; Difficult Housing Estates, 1963; (with Lomas and others) Social Aspects of Urban Development, 1966. *Recreations:* walking, Quaker interests. *Address:* Grove Cottage, Woodbury Lane, Bristol 8. *T:* Bristol 37545.

*See also D. M. Emmet, J. E. Meade, G. M. and S. S. Wilson.*

**WILSON, Rt. Rev. Roger Plumpton;** *see* Chichester, Bishop of.

**WILSON, Sir Roland,** KBE 1965 (CBE 1941); Kt 1955; Chairman: Commonwealth Banking Corporation since 1966; Qantas Airways Ltd, since 1966; Wentworth Hotel, since 1966; Director: ICI Australia and New Zealand Ltd; The MLC Ltd; economic and financial consultant; *b* Ulverstone, Tasmania, 7 April 1904; *s* of Thomas Wilson; *m* 1930, Valeska, *d* of William Thompson. *Educ:* Devonport High School; Univ. of Tasmania; Oriel College, Oxford; Chicago University. Rhodes Scholar for Tasmania, 1925; BCom 1926, Univ. of Tasmania; Dipl. in Economics and Political Science 1926, and DPhil 1929, Oxon; Commonwealth Fund Fellow, 1928, and PhD 1930, Chicago. Pitt Cobbett Lecturer in Economics, Univ. of Tasmania, 1930-32; Director of Tutorial Classes, Univ. of Tasmania, 1931-32; Asst Commonwealth Statistician and Economist, 1932; Economist, Statistician's Branch, Commonwealth Treasury, 1933; Commonwealth Statistician and Economic Adviser to the Treasury, Commonwealth of Australia, 1936-40 and 1946-51; Sec. to Dept Labour and Nat. Service, 1941-46; Chairman Economic and Employment Commission, United Nations, 1948-49. Secretary to Treasury, Commonwealth of Australia, 1951-66; Member Bd: of Reserve Bank of Australia, 1953-66; Qantas Empire Airways, 1954-66; Commonwealth Banking Corp., 1960-66. Hon. LLD Tasmania, 1969. *Publications:* Capital Imports and the Terms of Trade, 1931; Public and Private Investment in Australia, 1939; Facts and Fancies of Productivity, 1946. *Address:* 64 Empire Circuit, Forrest, Canberra, ACT, Australia. *T:* 7-1848. *Clubs:* University (Sydney); Commonwealth (Canberra).

**WILSON, Maj.-Gen. Ronald Dare,** MBE 1949; MC 1945; Director, Land-Air Warfare, Ministry of Defence, since 1968; *b* 3 Aug. 1919. Commissioned into Royal Northumberland Fusiliers, War of 1939-45, MC 1945 (despatches 1946). With Parachute Brigade and Airborne Division, 1945-48; GSO2 Staff College, Camberley, 1953-56; AA and QMG 1958-; Brigadier 1966; Brig. AQ, Middle East Command, 1967-68; Maj.-General 1968. *Address:* Directorate of Land-Air Warfare, Ministry of Defence, Whitehall, SW1.

**WILSON, Sir Roy (Mickel),** Kt 1962; QC; President of the Industrial Court since 1961; *b* 1903; *e s* of late Rev. Robert Wilson and Jessie, *d* of Robert Mickel, JP; *m* 1935, Henrietta Bennett, *d* of late Dean Willard L. Sperry, DD of Harvard University, USA. *Educ:* Glasgow High School; Glasgow University; Balliol Coll., Oxford (Lit. Hum. and BCL). Called to Bar, Gray's Inn, 1931; S-E Circuit. KC 1950. Commissioned QO Cameron Highlanders, 1940; served War of 1939-45; DAAG 2nd Division, 1942; GHQ, India, 1942-45; Lt-Col, 1943; Brigadier, 1944. Recorder of Faversham, 1950-51. Recorder of Croydon, 1957-61; Bencher of Gray's Inn, 1956-; Chairman: Cttee of Inquiry into arrangements at Smithfield Market, 1958; Railway Staff National Tribunal, 1961-62; London Transport Rly Wages Bd, 1961-; Cttee of Inquiry into Provincial Bus Dispute, 1964; Cttee on Immigration Appeals, 1966; Cttee of Inquiry into Bristol Siddeley Contracts, 1967-68. Mem., Race Relations Bd, 1968-. FRSA, 1968. *Recreations:* fishing, golf, bird-watching. *Address:* 4 Gray's Inn Square, WC1. *T:* 01-405 7789; The Cottage on the Green, Plaistow, Sussex. *T:* Plaistow 279. *Clubs:* Reform; Union (Oxford).

**WILSON, Sandy;** composer, lyric writer, playwright; *b* 19 May 1924; *s* of George Walter Wilson and Caroline Elsie (*née* Humphrey). *Educ:* Elstree Preparatory School; Harrow School; Oriel College, Oxford (BA Eng. Lit.). Contributed material to Oranges and Lemons, Slings and Arrows, 1948; wrote lyrics for touring musical play Caprice, 1950; words and music for two revues at Watergate Theatre, 1951 and 1952; (musical comedy) The Boy Friend for Players' Theatre, 1953, later produced in West End and on Broadway, 1954, directed revival (Comedy), 1967; (musical play) The Buccaneer, 1955; Valmouth (musical play, based on Firbank's novel), Lyric, Hammersmith and Savile Theatre, 1959, New York, 1960; songs for Call It Love, Wyndham's Theatre, 1960; Divorce Me, Darling! (musical comedy), Players' Theatre, 1964, Globe, 1965; music for TV series, The World of Wooster, 1965-66; music for As Dorothy Parker Once Said, Fortune, 1969; songs for Danny la Rue's Charley's Aunt (TV), 1969. *Publications:* This is Sylvia (with own illustrs), 1954; The Boy Friend (with own illustrs), 1955; Who's Who for Beginners (with photographs by Jon Rose), 1957; Prince What Shall I Do (illustrations, with Rhoda Levine), 1961; The Poodle from Rome, 1962. *Recreations:* reading, painting, theatre and cinema-going, travel. *Address:* 2 Southwell Gardens, SW7. *T:* 01-373 6172. *Clubs:* Players' Theatre, Buckstone.

**WILSON, Stanley Livingstone,** CMG 1966; DSO 1943; Visiting Surgeon, Dunedin Hospital, 1937-66, Hon. Consulting Surgeon, Dunedin Hospital, since 1966; *b* 17 April 1905; *s* of Robert and Elizabeth Wilson; *m* 1930, Isabel, *d* of William Kirkland; two *s* one *d. Educ:* Dannevirke High School; University of Otago. Univ. Entrance Schol., 1923; MB, ChB 1928; FRCS 1932; FRACS 1937. Resident Surgeon, Dunedin Hosp., Royal Northern and St Mary's Hosps, London, 1929-37. NZ Medical Corps, Middle East; Solomons, 1940-43; OC 2 NZ Casualty Clearing Station, Pacific, 1943-44. President, Otago BMA, 1948; Council, RACS 1951-63 (President, 1961-62). Examiner in Surgery, Univ. of Otago, 1952-65; Court of Examiners, RACS, 1948-60; Mem., Otago Hosp. Bd, 1965-. Hon. Fellow, American Coll. of Surgeons, 1963. *Recreation:* golf. *Address:* 27 Burwood Avenue, Dunedin, NW1, NZ. *T:* 60925; Maypark, Middlemarch, Otago, NZ. *Clubs:* Dunedin (Dunedin); Otago Officers' (Dunedin).

**WILSON, Stanley Reginald;** Portrait Painter; *b* Camberwell, 27 May 1890; *yr s* of late Alfred Wilson; unmarried. *Educ:* Aske's School, Hatcham; University of London. Goldsmiths' College, School of Art; Inns of Court Officers Training Corps; Royal Staff College, Camberley; Gazetted 2/Lt to 3rd 6th Battalion (Territorial) Duke of Wellington's Regt (West Riding), attached 10th Service Bn Duke of Wellington's Regt (West Riding), 23rd Division, on Active Service in Flanders, France and Italy (despatches); represented by works in British Museum, Imperial War Museum, South Kensington Museum, The Museums of Leeds, Liverpool, Manchester, Salford, Charlton, Bradford, Rotherham, Whitworth, National Gallery of Sports and Pastimes, Brooklyn, New York, etc. *Address:* c/o Barclays Bank Ltd, 1 Pall Mall East, SW1.

**WILSON, Stephen Shipley,** CB 1950; Keeper of Public Records, 1960-66; *b* 4 Aug. 1904; *s* of late Alexander Cowan Wilson and Edith Jane Brayshaw; *m* 1933, Martha Mott, *d* of A. B. Kelley and Mariana Parrish, Philadelphia, Pa; two *s* one *d. Educ:* Leighton Park; Queen's Coll., Oxford. Fellow, Brookings Inst., Washington, DC, 1926-27; Instructor, Columbia University, New York City, 1927-28; Public Record Office, 1928-29; Ministry of Transport, 1929-47; Ministry of Supply, 1947-50; Secretary, Iron and Steel Corporation of Great Britain, 1950-53, and Secretary, Iron and Steel Holding and Realisation Agency, 1953-60. *Address:* 3 Willow Road, NW3. *T:* 01-435 0148. *Club:* Reform.

*See also J. E. Meade, G. M. Wilson, R. C. Wilson.*

**WILSON, Sydney Ernest,** MA Cantab; retired as Principal of King William's College, Isle of Man (1935-58); *b* London; *s* of late Arthur Wilson and late Emily Ellen Percival; *m* 1923, Barbara Isabel Ross, *d* of late H. J. Davis, LRAM, Bath; two *s. Educ:* Christ's Hospital; Trinity College, Cambridge (Major Scholar). 1st Class, Mathematical Tripos, Part 1, 1920; 1st Class, Part II, 1922, Wrangler; Sixth Form Master, Blundell's School, 1922-30; Headmaster, Burton-on-Trent Grammar School, 1930-35; served European War, Lieut RGA in France and Flanders. *Recreations:* woodwork, gardening, tapestry, watching TV. *Address:* Keristal House, Port Soderick, Isle of Man. *T:* Douglas 3816.

**WILSON, Prof. Thomas,** CBE 1959; Professor of Tropical Hygiene, Liverpool School of Tropical Medicine, University of Liverpool, since 1962; *b* 5 Nov. 1905; *s* of R. H. Wilson, OBE, Belfast; *m* 1930, Annie Cooley; two *s* one *d. Educ:* Belfast Royal Academy; Queen's Univ., Belfast. MB, BCh, BAO (Belfast) 1927; DPH (Belfast) 1929; DTM, DTH (Liverpool) 1930; MD (Belfast) 1952. MO, Central Health Bd, FMS 1930; Health Officer, Malayan Med. Service, 1931; Lieut and Capt., RAMC (POW in Malaya and Thailand), 1942-45; Sen. Malaria Research Officer, Inst. for Med. Res., Fedn of Malaya, 1949; Dir, Inst. for Med. Res., Fedn of Malaya, 1956; Sen. Lectr in Tropical Hygiene, Liverpool Sch. of Trop. Med., Univ. of Liverpool, 1959. *Publications:* (with T. H. Davey) Davey and Lightbody's Control of Disease in the Tropics, 1965, 1970; contrib. to Hobson's Theory and Practice of Public Health, 1969; articles in medical journals on malaria and filariasis. *Recreation:* golf. *Address:* 88 Lynton Road, Hillside, Southport. *T:* Southport 66688.

**WILSON, Prof. Thomas,** OBE 1945; Adam Smith Professor of Political Economy, University of Glasgow, since 1958; *b* 23 June 1916; *s* of late John Bright and Margaret G. Wilson, Belfast; *m* 1943, Dorothy Joan Parry; one *s* two *d. Educ:* Methodist College, Belfast; Universities of Belfast and London. Civil Servant, 1940-46; Prime Minister's Statistical Branch, 1942-45. Fellow of University College, Oxford, 1946-58; Faculty Fellow of Nuffield College, Oxford, 1950-54; Editor, Oxford Economic Papers, 1948-58. Vice-Chm., Scottish Council's Cttee of Inquiry into the Scottish Economy, 1960-61; Nuffield Foundation Visiting Prof., Univ. of Ibadan, 1962. Economic Consultant to Govt of N Ireland, 1964-65; Shipbuilding Industry Cttee, 1965. *Publications:* Fluctuations in Income and Employment, 1941; Ulster under Home Rule (editor) 1955; Inflation, 1960; Planning and Growth, 1964; Policies for Regional Development, 1964; Regional Development (editor), 1965. *Recreations:* sailing and walking. *Address:* 8 The University, Glasgow, W2. *T:* 041-339 8344. *Club:* Reform.

**WILSON, Captain Sir Thomas (Douglas),** 4th Bt, *cr* 1906; MC 1940; *b* (posthumous) 10 June 1917; *s* of Thomas Douglas Wilson (*s* of 1st Bt), 2nd Lieut 7th Bn Argyll and Sutherland Highlanders (killed in action, 1917), and Kathleen Elsie, *d* of Henry Edward Grey; *S* uncle, 1968; *m* 1947, Pamela Aileen, 2nd *d* of Sir Edward Hanmer, Bt, *qv*; one *s* three *d. Educ:* Marlborough and Sandhurst. Commissioned 15th/19th Hussars, 1937; served in France, 1939-40 (MC); Western Desert, 1942-43; retired, 1947. Contested (C) Dudley and Stourbridge, 1955. *Recreations:* hunting, racing. *Heir: s* James William Douglas Wilson, *b* 8 Oct. 1960. *Address:* Lillingstone Lovell Manor, Buckingham. *T:* Lillingstone Dayrell 237. *Club:* Cavalry.

**WILSON, Thomas Marcus;** Under-Secretary, Ministry of Technology, since 1967 (Ministry of Aviation, 1964-67); *b* 15 April 1913; *s* of Reverend C. Wilson; *m* 1939, Norah Boyes (*née* Sinclair); no *c*. *Educ:* Manchester Grammar School; Jesus College, Cambridge. Asst Principal, Customs and Excise, 1936; Private Secretary: to Board of Customs and Excise, 1939; to Chm. Bd, 1940; Principal, 1941; lent to Treasury, 1942; lent to Office of Lord President of Council, 1946; Asst Sec., 1947; seconded: Min. of Food, 1949; Min. of Supply, 1953, Under-Sec., 1962, and Prin. Scientific and Civil Aviation Adv. to Brit. High Comr in Australia, also Head of Defence Research and Supply Staff, 1962-64. *Recreations:* reading, music, painting and travel, especially in France. *Address:* 5 Fir Tree Close, Coronation Road, South Ascot, Berks. *Club:* United University.

**WILSON, Sir T. George;** *see* Wilson, Sir George.

**WILSON, Hon. Sir (Tom) Ian (Findlay),** KBE 1963; CMG 1957; Politician and Farmer, Rhodesia; *b* 15 Jan. 1904; *m* 1952, Jacqueline Primrose, *d* of J. G. Robinson, Salisbury, S Rhodesia; one *s* one *d*. *Educ:* Morrison's Academy, Crieff, Scotland. MP, S Rhodesia, 1940-52. Elected Speaker, Legislative Assembly, S Rhodesia, 1950-53; first Speaker, Fedn of Rhodesia and Nyasaland, 1953, re-elected, 1959, 1962-63. *Address:* Zengeni Farm, Penhalonga, Rhodesia. *Clubs:* Salisbury, Umtali (Rhodesia).

**WILSON, William;** Head of Central and Southern Africa Department, Foreign and Commonwealth Office, since 1969; *b* 10 March 1920; *s* of Major Noel Wilson, Norton Manor, Malmesbury, Wiltshire and of late Hilda Margaret Wilson (*née* Wiggin); *m* 1st, 1944, Sylvia McLachlan (marriage dissolved, 1961); one *s* one *d*; 2nd, 1961, Monica (*née* Dehn); one step *s* one step *d*. *Educ:* Eton. Joined Foreign Office, 1942; 3rd Sec., Rome, 1945; Information Officer, Venice, 1947; Foreign Office, 1949; Military Govt, Berlin, 1952; Consul, Jerusalem, 1954; FO, 1958; Consul, Elisabethville, 1963; Ambassador and Consul-Gen. to Togo and Dahomey, 1965-66; Head of British Interests Section, Dar-es-Salaam, 1966; Head of W and Central African Dept of FO, 1968. *Recreations:* gardening, riding, tennis, shooting. *Address:* Ash, Stedham, Midhurst, Sussex; 6A Garway Road, W2.

**WILSON, William;** DL; MP (Lab) Coventry South since 1964; *b* 28 June 1913; *s* of Charles and Charlotte Wilson; *m* 1939, Bernice Wilson; one *s*. *Educ:* Wheatley St Sch.; Cheylesmore Sch.; Coventry Jun. Technical School. Qual. as Solicitor, 1939. Entered Army, 1941; served in N Africa, Italy and Greece; demobilised, 1946 (Sergeant). Contested (Lab) Warwick and Leamington, 1951, 1955, March 1957, 1959. Mem. Warwicks CC, 1958-. DL County of Warwick, 1967. *Recreations:* gardening, theatre, watching association football. *Address:* Avonside House, High Street, Barford, Warwickshire. *T:* Barford 278.

**WILSON, William Combe;** Regius Professor of Surgery, University of Aberdeen, 1939-62, now Emeritus; *b* 8 Sept. 1897; *s* of John Wilson and Janet Combe; *m* 1939, Ivy Marian Allan; three *s*. *Educ:* Royal High Sch., Edinburgh; Univ. of Edinburgh. MB, ChB Edinburgh 1924; FRCSE 1927. Served Army, 1915-19: Private, Argyll and Sutherland Highlanders, 2nd Lieut Black Watch. rockefeller Travelling Fellow in USA; Carnegie Foundation Research Fellow; Surgeon Royal Hospital for Sick Children, Edinburgh, 1935-39; Director, Edinburgh Surgical Research Unit of Medical Research Council, 1938-39; Lt-Col RAMC i/c No 1 Medical Research Section in Middle East, 1942-43. Hon. LLD (Aberdeen), 1963. *Publications:* papers in surgical and scientific journals. *Address:* 3 Burnside Gardens, Aberdeen AB2 4QW. *T:* Aberdeen 50198.

**WILSON, William Joseph Robinson,** CMG 1961; Grazier; *b* 2 April 1909; *s* of late Alexander William Wilson and Marion Ferris Wilson; *m* 1937, Mary Weir, *d* of late Arthur Maurice and Elizabeth Reid. *Educ:* Scotch Coll., Melbourne. Member: Faculty of Veterinary Science, Univ. of Melbourne; Australian Cattle and Beef Research Cttee, 1962-64; Australian Woolgrowers' Council, 1952-54 and 1955-60; Graziers' Federal Council, 1954-60; Australian Overseas Transport Assoc., 1955-58; President, Graziers' Assoc. of Victoria, 1958-60; Vice-Pres. Graziers' Federal Council, 1958-60. Major, AIF, Middle East and New Guinea, 1940-44. *Address:* Roseneath, Lancefield, Victoria 3435, Australia. *T:* Lancefield 60. *Clubs:* Australian, Melbourne, Naval and Military, Victorian Racing (Melbourne).

**WILSON, William Lawrence,** CB 1967; OBE 1954; Deputy Secretary, Ministry of Public Building and Works, since 1969; *b* 11 Sept. 1912; *s* of Joseph Osmond and Ann Wilson; *m* C. V. Richards; two *s*. *Educ:* Stockton on Tees Secondary School; Constantine College, Middlesbrough. BSc (London), FIMechE, Whitworth Prizeman. Apprentice, ICI Billingham 1928-33; Technical Asst, ICI, 1933-36; Assistant Engineer, HMOW, 1937; subsequently Engineer, 1939; Superintending Engineer, (MOW) 1945; Assistant Chief Engineer, 1954; Chief Engineer, 1962; Dep. Sec., 1969. Past Pres., Assoc. of Supervising Electrical Engineers. Hon. MIHVE. Coronation Medal. *Publications:* papers on Radioactive Wastes; contrib. to World Power Conference, USSR and USA. *Recreations:* cricket, fishing, watching all forms of sport. *Address:* Oakwood, Chestnut Avenue, Rickmansworth, Herts. *T:* Rickmansworth 74419. *Club:* Civil Service.

**WILSON, Group Captain William Proctor,** CBE 1943; (RAFVR); with Mullard Ltd since 1964; *b* 14 Jan. 1902; *e c* of late Canon C. E. Wilson, MA, BD; *m* 1st, 1926, Evelyne Christiana Cornet-Auquier; two *s*; 2nd, 1947, Agnes Christian Gillan, OBE, MB, ChB; one *s*. *Educ:* St Lawrence College, Ramsgate; City and Guilds, South Kensington (University of London). BSc (Eng); FCGI; CEng, FIEE; RAF (Signals Branch), 1939-45; RAF Supplementary Reserve (Signals Branch), 1946-54; Head of Research Department, BBC, 1950-64. Member, Radio Research Board, 1962-64. Hon. Research Associate, Dept of Electrical Engineering, University College, London, 1964. *Address:* c/o Barclays Bank, Langham Place, W1; Mullard Ltd, Torrington Place, WC1. *Clubs:* Athenæum, RAF Reserves.

**WILSON-HAFFENDEN, Maj.-Gen. Donald James,** CBE 1945; *b* 26 November 1900; *s* of late Rev. L. A. Wilson-Haffenden, Seaford, Sussex; *m* 1923, Isabella Sutherland (*d* 1968); one *d*; *m* 1969, Ruth Lea Douglass, late of CMS. *Educ:* Christ's Hosp.; Victoria Coll., Jersey. Commissioned 91st Punjabis (LI), 1920; served Waziristan, 1921-24; psc 1936; AA and QMG, 1st Division, 1941; DA and QMG 110 Force, 1941-42; DA and QMG 33 Corps, 1943; DQMG, GHQ, India, 1944. *Address:* 200 Rivermead Court, SW6. *T:* 01-736 1465. *Clubs:* Royal Commonwealth Society, Hurlingham.

**WILSON SMITH, Sir Henry,** KCB 1949; KBE 1945; Deputy Chairman, Guest Keen and Nettlefolds Ltd; Director, HAT Group Ltd, since 1969; *b* 30 Dec. 1904; *e s* of J. Wilson Smith, Newcastle upon Tyne; *m* 1931, Molly, *d* of A. W. G. Dyson, Wylam, Northumberland; two *s*. *Educ:* Royal Grammar School, Newcastle upon Tyne; Peterhouse, Cambridge. 1st Class, 1st Div. History Tripos, Parts I and II; Administrative Class, Home Civil Service, 1927; Secretary's Office, General Post Office, 1927-29; HM Treasury, 1930; Asst Private Secretary to Chancellor of Exchequer, 1932, Prin. Private Sec., 1940-42; Under-Sec., HM Treasury, 1942-46; Permnt Sec., Min. of Defence, 1947-48; addtl Second Sec., HM Treasury, 1948-51. Chm. Powell Duffryn Ltd, 1957-69; Chm. Doxford and Sunderland Shipbuilding & Engineering Co. Ltd, 1962-68; Formerly Part-time Mem. Nat. Coal Board; Dir, Bank of England, 1964-70. A Vice-Chm., Council BIM, 1963-67. *Address:* Ashton House, Ashton, Wedmore, Somerset. *T:* Wedmore 372. *Club:* United University.

**WILTON,** 7th Earl of, *cr* 1801; **Seymour William Arthur John Egerton;** Viscount Grey de Wilton, 1801; *b* 29 May 1921; *s* of 6th Earl and Brenda (*d* 1930), *d* of late Sir William Petersen, KBE; *S* father, 1927; *m* 1962, Mrs Diana Naylor Leyland. *Heir:* (by special remainder) *kinsman,* Baron Ebury, *qv*. *Clubs:* White's, Buck's.

**WILTON, Arthur John,** CMG 1967; MC 1945; HM Diplomatic Service; Ambassador to Kuwait, since 1970; *b* 21 Oct. 1921; *s* of late Walter Wilton, and of Annetta Irene Wilton (*née* Perman); *m* 1950, Maureen Elizabeth Alison Meaker; four *s* one *d*. *Educ:* Wanstead High School; St John's Coll., Oxford. Open Schol., St John's Coll., Oxford, 1940. Commissioned, Royal Ulster Rifles, 1942; served with Irish Brigade, N Africa, Italy and Austria, 1943-46. Entered HM Diplomatic Service, 1947; served Lebanon, Egypt, Gulf Shaikhdoms, Roumania, Aden, and Yugoslavia. Director, Middle East Centre for Arabic Studies, Shemlan, 1960-65. *Recreation:* whatever is available. *Address:* c/o Lloyds Bank, 6 Pall Mall, SW1. *Clubs:* Athenæum, Royal Automobile.

**WILTON, Gen. Sir John Gordon Noel,** KBE 1964 (CBE 1954; OBE 1946); CB 1962; DSO 1944; idc; psc; Chairman of Australian Chiefs of Staff Committee since 1966; *b* Sydney, 22 November 1910; *s* of late Noel V. S. Wilton, Grafton, New South Wales; *m* 1938, Helen Thelma, *d* of Robert Marshall; two *s* one *d*. *Educ:* Grafton High School, NSW; RMC, Duntroon, Canberra. Served in British Army, in UK, India and Burma, 1931-39. Served War of 1939-45 (DSO, OBE); AIF; Middle East, 1940-41; New Guinea, 1942-43; GSO Aust. Military Mission to Washington, 1944; Col, Gen. Staff Advance HQ, AMF, SW Pacific Area, 1945. Deputy Director, Military Operations, AHQ, Melbourne, 1946; Director, Military Operations and Plans, 1947-51; Comdg 28th Commonwealth Bde, Korea (CBE), 1953; Brig. i/c Administration, HQ Eastern Command, NSW, 1954-55; Brig. Gen. Staff AHQ, 1955-56; Comdt, RMC, Duntroon, Canberra, 1957-60; Head of SEATO, Military Planning Office, Bangkok, 1960-63; Chief of the Australian General Staff, 1963-66. Has the American Legion of Merit. *Recreations:* golf and tennis. *Address:* c/o Department of Defence, Canberra, ACT 2600, Australia. *Club:* Imperial Service (Sydney).

**WILTSHIRE, Earl of; Christopher John Hilton Paulet;** *b* 30 July 1969; *s* and *heir* of Marquess of Winchester, *qv*.

**WILTSHIRE, Archdeacon of;** *see* Plaxton, Ven. C. A.

**WILTSHIRE, Edward Parr,** CBE 1965; Consul, Le Havre, since 1969; *b* 18 Feb. 1910; 2nd *s* of late Major Percy Wiltshire and Kathleen Olivier Lefroy Parr Wiltshire, Great Yarmouth; *m* 1942, Gladys Mabel Stevens; one *d*. *Educ:* Cheltenham College; Jesus College, Cambridge. Entered Foreign Service, 1932. Served in: Beirut, Mosul, Baghdad, Tehran, Basra, New York (one of HM Vice-Consuls, 1944); promoted Consul, 1945; transf. Cairo, 1946 (Actg Consul-Gen., 1947, 1948); transf. Shiraz (having qual. in Arabic, and subseq. in Persian); Consul, Port Said, 1952; 1st Sec. and Consul: Baghdad, 1952, Rio de Janeiro, 1957; promoted Counsellor, 1959; Political Agent, Bahrain, 1959-63; Consul-General, Geneva, 1963-67; Dir, Diplomatic Service Language Centre, London, 1967-68; worked for Council for Nature (Editor, Habitat), 1968-69. *Publication:* The Lepidoptera of Iraq, 1957. *Recreations:* music, entomology, tennis, swimming. *Address:* 23 Avenue Foch, 76 Le Havre, France.

**WIMBERLEY, Maj.-Gen. Douglas Neil,** CB 1943; DSO 1942; MC 1918; DL Dundee, 1947; Hon. LLD Aberdeen, 1948, Dundee, 1967; *b* 15 Aug. 1896; *s* of late Colonel C. N. Campbell Wimberley, CMG, and Lesmoir Gordon Wimberley; *m* 1925, E. Myrtle L., *d* of late Capt. F. L. Campbell, RN, Achalader, Perthshire, and Lady Dobell; one *s* one *d*. *Educ:* Alton Burn, Nairn; Wellington; Emmanuel College, Cambridge; RMC, Sandhurst. 2nd Lieut Cameron Highlanders, 1915; served European War as Regimental officer, France and Belgium, 1st and 51st Highland Divs, 1915-16 and 1917-18 (wounded, MC), including battles of Loos, Somme, Ypres, Cambrai and St Quentin; Acting Major, 1918-19; North Russia, with MGC, 1919; Adjutant, 1st Camerons, 1921; psc 1927; Bde Major 1st (Ghurkha) Inf. Bde, 1929; Operations NWFP India, 1930; Brevet Major, 1933; DAAG and GSO II, WO, 1934-37; Brevet Lt-Col 1936; Lt-Col Commanding 1st Cameron Highlanders, 1938; France, 1939; GSO1 and Chief Instructor Senior Officers' School, 1940; Temp. Brigadier 1941; Temp. Major-General 1942; Major-General 1943; Brig. Comdr 13th and 152nd Seaforth and Cameron Bde, 1940-41; GOC 46th Div., 1941; Div. Comdr, 51st Highland Div., 1941-43; including battles Alamein, Mareth, Medinine, Akarit, and Adrano; 8th Army campaign N Africa, Sicily, 1942-43 (despatches, slightly wounded, DSO, CB), Comdt Staff Coll., Camberley, 1943-44; Dir of Infantry, WO, 1944-46; retd at own request; Principal of University College, Dundee, in the Univ. of St Andrews, 1946-54. Member Royal Company of Archers, Queen's Body Guard for Scotland; Gentleman Usher of the Scarlet Rod in the Order of the Bath, 1948-54; Registrar and Secretary, 1954-64. Hon. Col St Andrews Univ. OTC 1951-63; Col of the Queen's Own Cameron Highlanders, 1951-61. *Publications:* military articles in service jls and Chambers's Encyclopædia; Army Quarterly prize essay, 1933. *Address:* Foxhall, Coupar Angus, Perthshire. *T:* 384. *Club:* United Service.

**WIMBLE, Ernest Walter,** CBE 1946; *b* 23 Sept. 1887; 4th *s* of Charles Wimble, Old Romney, Kent, and Annie Elizabeth Wimble (*née* Aylward); *m* 1912, Daisy Edith Robarts (*d* 1961); one *s* one *d*. *Educ:* Elementary Sch.; St Dunstan's, Catford; King's College, London. 4 years Civil Service, 1903-06; 6 years Commercial, 1906-12; served European War, 1914-19; 11 years WEA, 1912-23; 25 years Secretary and Gen. Man. Workers' Travel

Assoc. Ltd, 1923-47; Dir of Students Bookshops Ltd, 1924-65; Member Management Committee Travel Assoc. of Great Britain and Northern Ireland, 1945-49; Member British Tourist and Holidays Board, 1947-50. Chm. Creative Tourist Agents Conf., 1947-48; Chm. Home Holidays Division British Tourist and Holidays Board, 1947-50; Pres. International Union of Official Travel Organisations, 1948-49; Chm. Olympic Games (Overseas) Visitors Accommodation Bureau, 1948; Member: Hotels Executive (British Transport), 1948-52; British Travel and Holidays Assoc., 1950; National Parks Commission, 1950-51; Founder-member of Youth Hostels Assoc. *Publications:* European Recovery, 1948-51 and the Tourist Industry, 1948; Western Europe's Tourist Trade, 1948, 1949, 1950. Editor and founder of The Travel Log. *Recreation:* travel. *Address:* 3 Netherlands Court, Eaton Road, Sutton, Surrey.

**WIMBORNE,** 3rd Viscount, *cr* 1918; **Ivor Fox-Strangways Guest;** Baron Wimborne, 1880; Baron Ashby St Ledgers, 1910; Bt 1838; *b* 2 Dec. 1939; *s* of 2nd Viscount and of Dowager Viscountess Wimborne; *S* father, 1967; *m* 1966, Victoria Ann, *o d* of late Col Mervyn Vigors, DSO, MC; one *s*. *Educ:* Eton. Managing Dir, Harris & Dixon Group of Cos. *Heir:* *s* Hon. Ivor Mervyn Vigors Guest, *b* 19 Sept. 1968. *Address:* Ashby St Ledgers, Rugby. *Clubs:* White's, Buck's, Beefsteak.

**WINCHELL, Walter;** TV-Radio Commentator; Columnist, New York Morning Telegraph; *b* New York, 7 April 1897; *m* Elizabeth June Magee. Appeared in own act in Vaudeville, 1917; served European War, 1914-18, with USNR; joined staff of Vaudeville News, 1922; with NY Mirror, Journal-American, World-Journal-Tribune, as columnist, dramatic critic, and dramatic editor; syndicated column in over 100 US papers and in 11 foreign lands; broadcasts talks. Founder-Treasurer, Damon Runyon Cancer Fund. Comdr USNR. *Publications:* contributions to magazines. *Address:* (office) 33 W 56th Street, New York City, USA.

**WINCHESTER,** 18th Marquess of, *cr* 1551; **Nigel George Paulet;** Baron St John of Basing, 1539; Earl of Wiltshire, 1550; Premier Marquess of England; *b* 23 Dec. 1941; *s* of George Cecil Paulet (*g g g s* of 13th Marquess) (*d* 1961), and Hazel Margaret, *o d* of late Major Danvers Wheeler, RA, Salisbury, Rhodesia; *S* kinsman, 1968; *m* 1967, Rosemary Anne, *d* of Major Arbery John Hilton. *Heir:* *s* Earl of Wiltshire, *qv*. *Address:* 35 Whyte Ladies Lane, Borrowdale, Salisbury, Rhodesia.

**WINCHESTER, Bishop of,** since 1961; **Rt. Rev. Sherard Falkner Allison;** MA, DD, LLD; Prelate to the Most Noble Order of the Garter since 1961; *b* 19 Jan. 1907; *s* of Reverend W. S. Allison; *m* 1936, Ruth Hills; one *s* two *d* (and one *s* decd). *Educ:* Dean Close School, Cheltenham; Jesus Coll., Cambridge (Scholar); Ridley Hall, Cambridge. 1st Cl. Classical Tripos, Parts I and II; 2nd Class Theological Tripos, Part I and Jeremie Septuagint Prize; Curate of St James', Tunbridge Wells, 1931-34; Chaplain of Ridley Hall, Cambridge, and Examining Chaplain to Bishop of Bradford, 1934-36; Vicar of Rodbourne Cheney, Swindon, 1936-40; Vicar of Erith, 1940-45; Principal of Ridley Hall, Cambridge, 1945-50; Bishop of Chelmsford, 1951-61. Examining Chaplain to Bishop of Rochester, 1945, and to Bishop of Ely, 1947; Select Preacher: Univ. of Cambridge, 1946, 1955, 1962; Univ. of Oxford, 1953-55, 1963; Proctor in Convocation, Diocese of Ely, 1949. Hon. Fellow, Jesus College, Cambridge, 1963. DD, Lambeth, 1951; Hon. DD: Occidental Coll., Los Angeles, 1959; Wycliffe Coll., Toronto, 1959; Hon. STD, Church Divinity Sch. of the Pacific, 1959; Hon. LLD, Sheffield, 1960. *Publication:* The Christian Life, 1938 (Joint). *Recreations:* sailing, water-colour sketching. *Address:* Wolvesey, Winchester, Hants.

**WINCHESTER, Assistant Bishop of;** *see* Cornwall, Rt Rev. Nigel Edmund.

**WINCHESTER, Dean of;** *see* Stancliffe, Very Rev. M. S.

**WINCHESTER, Archdeacon of;** *see* Beynon, Ven. James Royston.

**WINCHESTER, Clarence;** Editor and Author; *s* of Arthur William and Elizabeth Alice Clark; *m* Constance Katherine Groves; one *s* (and one *d* decd). *Educ:* privately; technical schools. Has been variously associated with stage, aeronautics, and journalism in England and abroad, on newspapers and periodicals; learned to fly, 1913-14; formerly with Allied Newspapers, Daily Mail, etc; special correspondent, Kemsley Newspapers, Ltd; Assistant Chief Editor to Cassell's and Chief Editor of group of Amalgamated Press publications; Assistant Editor The Daily Sketch; edited: Railway Wonders of the World; Wonders of World Engineering; Shipping Wonders of the World; Wonders of World Aviation; World Film Encyclopædia; The King's Navy (in co-operation with Admiralty); The King's Army (in co-operation with War Office); The King's Air Force (in co-operation with Air Ministry); British Legion Poppy Annual, 1941; The Queen Elizabeth, Winchester's Screen Encyclopedia, 1948; Mind and Matter, etc; also formerly Director and Managing Editor, Dropmore Press Ltd; Consulting Editor, Law Society's Gazette; Managing Director and Chief Editor, Winchester Publications, Ltd; correspondent on European affairs to the Argonaut weekly, San Francisco, USA; Editor: England (quarterly). Is an Associate of the Royal Aeronautical Society. *Publications:* Sonnets and Some Others; Aerial Photography (with F. L. Wills); The Devil Rides High; An Innocent in Hollywood; Let's Look at London; Earthquake in Los Angeles; Three Men in a Plane; The Captain Lost his Bathroom; City of Lies; Airman Tomorrow (with Alfred Kerr); The Black Poppy; A Great Rushing of Wings and Other Poems; Editor and designer of The Royal Philatelic Collection, by Sir John Wilson, Bt (by permission of HM King George VI); The Crown Jewels, by Major General H. D. W. Sitwell, CB, MC, Keeper of the Jewel House (by permission of the Lord Chamberlain and the Resident Governor of the Tower), etc. *Address:* 60 Jireh Court, Haywards Heath, Sussex. *T:* Haywards Heath 4804. *Clubs:* Savage, Southern Aero.

**WINCHILSEA,** 16th Earl of, *cr* 1628, **and NOTTINGHAM,** 11th Earl of, *cr* 1675, **Christopher Denys Stormont Finch Hatton,** Bart 1611; Viscount Maidstone, 1623; Bart English, 1660; Baron Finch, 1674; Hereditary Lord of Royal Manor of Wye; *b* 17 Nov. 1936; *er s* of 15th Earl and Countess Gladys Széchényi (who obtained a divorce, 1946; she *m* 1954, Arthur Talbot Peterson), 3rd *d* of Count László Széchényi; *S* father, 1950; *m* 1962, Shirley, *e d* of late Bernard Hatfield, Wylde Green, Sutton Coldfield; one *s* one *d*. *Heir:* *s* Viscount Maidstone, *qv*. *Address:* South Cadbury House, Yeovil, Somerset.
*See also W. W. Straight.*

**WIND, Edgar,** MA, DPhil; Professor Emeritus of the History of Art in the University of Oxford and Honorary Fellow of Trinity College, Oxford; *b* Berlin, Germany, 14 May 1900; *s* of late Maurice Delmar Wind; *m* 1942, Margaret Kellner. *Educ:* Kaiser Friedrich Schule, Berlin; Universities of Berlin, Freiburg, Vienna, Hamburg. DPhil (*summa cum laude*) in History of Art, 1922. Kegan Fellow, Instructor, Assistant Professor of Philosophy, Univ. of N Carolina, 1925-27; Research Asst Bibliothek Warburg, Hamburg, 1928-33; Privatdozent, Univ. of Hamburg, 1930-33; Dep. Dir, Warburg Inst., London, and Hon. Lecturer in Philosophy, University Coll., London, 1934-42; Vis. Lectr, Pierpont Morgan Library and Inst. of Fine Arts, NY Univ., 1940-42; Prof. of Art, Univ. of Chicago, 1942-44; William Allan Neilson Research Prof., 1944-48; Prof. of Philosophy and of Art, 1948-55, Smith Coll.; Prof. of History of Art, Univ. of Oxford, 1955-67; Fellow, Trinity Coll., Oxford, 1955-67. Fellow, American Academy of Arts and Sciences, 1951-; Chichele Lecturer, Oxford, 1954; Rede Lecturer, Cambridge, 1960; Reith Lecturer, BBC, 1960. Serena Medal, British Academy, 1967. Grosses Verdienstkreuz der Bundesrepublik Deutschland, 1966. *Publications:* Aesthetischer und kunstwissenschaftlicher Gegenstand, 1924; Humanitätsidee und heroisiertes Porträt in der englischen Kultur des 18. Jahrhunderts, 1932; Das Experiment und die Metaphysik, 1934; Bellini's Feast of the Gods, 1948; Pagan Mysteries in the Renaissance, 1958; 3rd edn enl. 1967; Art and Anarchy, 1963; Michelangelo's Prophets and Sibyls, 1967; Giorgione's Tempesta, 1969. Jt Editor: A Bibliog. on the Survival of the Classics, 1934, 1938; Jl of Warburg Inst., 1937-42; articles on philosophical and iconographic subjects. *Address:* Trinity College, Oxford.

**WINDER, Col John Lyon C.;** *see* Corbett-Winder.

**WINDEYER, Sir Brian (Wellingham),** Kt 1961; FRCP, FRCS, FRCSE, FRSM, FFR, DMRE; Vice-Chancellor, University of London; Professor of Radiology (Therapeutic), Middlesex Hospital Medical School, University of London, 1942-69; Dean, Middlesex Hospital Medical School, 1954-67; formerly Director: Meyerstein Institute of Radiotherapy, Middlesex Hospital; Radiotherapy Department, Mount Vernon Hospital; Cons. Adviser in Radiotherapy to Ministry of Health; *b* 7 Feb. 1904; *s* of Richard Windeyer, KC, Sydney, Australia; *m* 1st, 1928, Joyce Ziele, *d* of Harry Russell, Sydney; one *s* one *d*; 2nd, 1948, Elspeth Anne, *d* of H. Bowry, Singapore; one *s* two *d. Educ:* Sydney C of E Grammar Sch.; St Andrew's Coll., Univ. of Sydney. Sydney Univ. Rugby Team, 1922-27; combined Australian and NZ Univs Rugby Team, 1923; coll. crew, 1922-26. MB, BS Sydney, 1927; FRCSE 1930; DMRE Cambridge, 1933; FFR 1940; FRCS (ad eundem) 1948; MRCP 1957. Formerly House Physician, House Surgeon and Radium Registrar, Royal Prince Alfred Hosp., Sydney; Asst, Fondation Curie, Paris, 1929-30; Middlesex Hospital: Radium Officer, 1931; MO i/c Radiotherapy Dept, 1936; Medical Comdt, 1940-45; Dir, EMS Radiotherapy Dept, Mt Vernon Hosp., 1940-46; Dean, Faculty of Medicine, Univ. of London, 1964-68. Skinner Lectr, Faculty of Radiologists, 1943 (Pres. of Faculty, 1949-52); Hunterian Prof., RCS, 1951. Pres., Radiology Section, RSM, 1958-59. Chairman: Radio-active Substances Adv. Cttee, 1961-70; Nat. Radiological Protection Bd, 1970-; Academic Council, Univ. of London, 1967-69. Member: Royal Commn on Med. Educn; Grand Council and Exec. Cttee, British Empire Cancer Campaign; British Inst. of Radiology (late Mem. Council); Med. Soc. of London; MRC, 1958-62 and 1968-; Clinical Research Bd, 1954-62 (Chm., 1968). Co-opted Mem. Council, RCS, to rep. radiology, 1948-53. Hon. Mem., Amer. Radium Soc., 1948. Hon. FRACS; Hon. FCRA. Hon. DSc: BC; Wales; Hon. LLD Glasgow, 1968. *Publications:* various articles on cancer and radiotherapy. *Recreations:* golf, gardening. *Address:* Moreton Gap, Thame Park Road, Thame, Oxon. *T:* Thame 2371. *Club:* Athenæum.

**WINDEYER, Rt. Hon. Sir (William John) Victor,** PC 1963; KBE 1958 (CBE 1944); CB 1953; DSO (and bar), 1942; ED; Justice of the High Court of Australia, since 1958; *b* 28 July 1900; *s* of W. A. Windeyer, Sydney, NSW; *m* 1934, Margaret Moor Vicars; three *s* one *d. Educ:* Sydney Grammar Sch., University of Sydney (MA, LLB). Admitted to Bar of NSW, 1925; KC (NSW) 1949; sometime lecturer in Faculty of Law, University of Sydney. Lieut AMF (Militia), 1922; War of 1939-45; Lieut-Colonel comdg 2/48 Bn, AIF, 1940-42 (including siege of Tobruk); Brig. comdg 20th Australian Inf. Bde, AIF, 1942-46 (El Alamein, New Guinea, Borneo); Major-General and CMF Member, Australian Military Board, 1950-53; Retired List, 1957. Member of Senate, University of Sydney, 1949-59, Dep. Chancellor, 1953-58; Member Council Australian National University, 1951-55. Director: Colonial Sugar Refining Co., 1953-58; Mutual Life and Citizens Assurance Co., 1954-58. Chairman Trustees, Gowrie Scholarship Fund, 1964-. Vice-President, Selden Society, 1965; Pres., NSW Branch, Australian Boy Scouts Assoc., 1970-. Hon. Member, Society Public Teachers of Law. *Publications:* Lectures on Legal History, 1938, 2nd edn, 1949, rev. 1957; articles on legal and historical subjects. *Address:* Peroomba, Turramurra, NSW 2074, Australia. *Clubs:* Australian, Pioneers (Sydney); Melbourne (Melbourne).

**WINDHAM, Sir Ralph,** Kt 1960; Commissioner, Foreign Compensation Commission, since 1965, Vice-Chairman, since 1969; *b* 25 March 1905; *er s* of Major Ashe Windham and Cora E. S. Middleton, Waghen Hall, East Yorkshire; *m* 1946, Kathleen Mary, *o d* of Captain Cecil Henry FitzHerbert, DSC, Latimerstown, Wexford, Eire; two *s* two *d. Educ:* Wellington Coll.; Trinity Coll., Cambridge, 1st class Part II, Law Tripos; MA, LLB, 1928; Barrister-at-Law, Lincoln's Inn (Buchanan Prizeman), 1930. Legal Draftsman, Government of Palestine, 1935; Judge of Dist Court, Palestine, 1942; Puisne Judge, Supreme Court, Ceylon, 1947; Puisne Judge, Supreme Court, Kenya, 1950-55; Chief Justice, Zanzibar, 1955-59; Justice of Appeal, Court of Appeal for Eastern Africa, 1959-60; Chief Justice, Tanganyika (later Tanzania), 1960-65. Order of the Brilliant Star of Zanzibar (2nd class), 1959; Grand Commander, Star of Africa (Liberia), 1964. *Recreations:* music and tennis. *Address:* Moreton House, Ongar, Essex. *Club:* Lansdowne.

**WINDHAM, William Evan;** *b* 1 May 1904; *o s* of late Sir William Windham, CBE; *m* 1932, Constance (*d* 1939), *d* of late J. H. Loudon, Olantigh, Wye, Kent; two *d; m* 1962, Dorothy Muir, *widow* of Capt. Davis, Villa Berg, Bishopscourt, Cape Town. *Educ:* Wellington Coll.; London University. Barrister at Law, Gray's Inn, 1936. Served AAF, 1928. Administration, Fiji and Western Pacific, 1930-34; practised on South Eastern circuit, 1936-39. Served War of 1939-45 in Fighter Command, RAFVR (despatches), Sqdn Leader. Sen. Res. Magistrate, N Rhodesia,

1952; Commissioner, Emergency Regulations, 1956-57; Puisne Judge, High Court of Northern Rhodesia, 1956-63. *Recreations:* tennis, golf. *Club:* Royal Air Force.

**WINDHAM, Brig. William Russell S.**; *see* Smijth-Windham.

**WINDLESHAM,** 3rd Baron, *cr* 1937, of Windlesham; **David James George Hennessy;** Bt 1927; Minister of State, Home Office, since 1970; *b* 28 Jan. 1932; *s* of 2nd Baron Windlesham and Angela Mary (*d* 1956), *d* of Julian Duggan; *S* father, 1962; *m* 1965, Prudence L. Glynn, *yr d* of Lieut-Colonel R. T. W. Glynn, MC, Harlesford House, Tetsworth, Oxon; one *s* one *d*. *Educ:* Ampleforth; Trinity Coll., Oxford (MA). Chairman, Bow Group, 1959-60, 1962-63; Member, Westminster City Council, 1958-62. Dir, Rediffusion Television, 1965-67; Man. Dir, Grampian Television, 1967-70. Vice-Pres., British Cancer Council, 1968-70. *Publication:* Communication and Political Power, 1966. *Heir: s* Hon. James Hennessy, *b* 9 Nov. 1968. *Address:* 59 Ridgway Place, SW19. *T:* 01-946 5744. *Clubs:* Carlton, Beefsteak; Royal and Ancient (St Andrews).

**WINDLEY, Sir Edward (Henry),** KCMG 1958 (CMG 1953); KCVO 1961; Director, Yuills Ltd; Chairman, Exchange Travel Agency Ltd, since 1965; *b* 10 March 1909; *s* of late E. C. Windley, S Rhodesia, and late Vicomtesse de Toustain; *m* 1939, Patience, *d* of Lieut-General Sir B. Sergison-Brooke, KCB, KCVO, CMG; one *s* three *d*. *Educ:* Repton; Cambridge Univ. District Officer, Kenya, 1931; Dep. Provincial Commissioner, 1947; Provincial Commissioner, 1948; Chief Native Comr and Min. for African Affairs, Kenya, 1953 (despatches 1957). Governor and Commander-in-Chief of the Gambia, 1958-62. Chairman: Guarantee Fund, Deans Yard, 1962-69; Save the Children Fund, 1962-68. *Recreations:* tennis, fishing, shooting, ski-ing, mountaineering. *Address:* 5 Regency Terrace, Elm Place, SW7. *T:* 01-373 5070; Mawley House, Quenington, Glos. *Clubs:* Turf, Travellers'.

*See also Earl of Portarlington.*

**WINDSOR, Viscount; Ivor Edward Other Windsor-Clive;** *b* 19 Nov. 1951; *s* and *heir* of 3rd Earl of Plymouth, *qv*.

**WINDSOR, Dean of (1962-70);** *see under* Worcester, Bishop of.

[*No new appointment made at time of going to press.*]

**WINDSOR, Bt-Col Arthur Herbert,** CMG 1916; TD 1923; *b* 1880; *s* of late Geo. Patrick Windsor, Salisbury; Served S Africa, 1900 (Queen's medal 5 clasps); European War, 1914-19 (despatches, CMG); commanded 11th Batt. London Regt, TA, 1917-23; Brevet Colonel, 1924; Member of the National Trust; Fellow of Royal Society of St George. Freeman of the City of London. *Address:* 23 Bruton Street, W1.

**WINDSOR, Robert;** Assistant Under Secretary of State, Department of Health and Social Security (formerly Ministry of Social Security), since 1966; *b* 9 April 1916; *s* of late Henry and Alice Windsor; *m* 1939, Eleanor Malone; two *s* one *d*. *Educ:* Liverpool Collegiate Sch.; University of Liverpool. BA 1937, MA 1940. Served in S Lancs Regt and Intelligence Corps, 1940-45. Asst Principal, Assistance Board, 1947; Principal, National Assistance Board, 1949; Asst Secretary, National Assistance Board, 1962; Under-Secretary, National Assistance Board, 1965. *Recreation:* listening to music. *Address:* 52 Church Road, Worcester Park, Surrey. *T:* 01-337 8826.

**WINDSOR-AUBREY, Henry Miles;** Puisne Judge, Supreme Court, Ghana, from 1949, retired; Chairman: Industrial Tribunal; Rent Tribunal; Rent Assessment Panel; *b* 1901; *m* 1928, Dorothy Dagmar Montrose; one *s*. *Educ:* Clifton College. Called to the Bar, Inner Temple, 1925. Served in Uganda, 1934-49. Magistrate, 1934-36; Crown Counsel, 1936-43; Solicitor-General, 1943-49. *Recreations:* golf and gardening. *Address:* Bogside House, Irthington, near Carlisle, Cumberland.

**WINDSOR-CLIVE,** family name of **Earl of Plymouth.**

**WINDWARD ISLANDS, Bishop of,** since 1969; **Rt. Rev. (George) Cuthbert Manning Woodroffe,** MA, LTh; *b* 17 May 1918; *s* of James Manning Woodroffe and Evelyn Agatha (*née* Norton); *m* 1947, Aileen Alice Connell; one *s* one *d* (and one *c* decd). *Educ:* Grenada Boys' Secondary School; Codrington Coll., Barbados. Clerk in Civil Service, 1936-41; Codrington Coll., 1941-44; Deacon 1944; Priest 1945; Asst Priest, St George's Cath., St Vincent, 1944-47; Vicar of St Simon's, Barbados, 1947-50; Rector: St Andrew, 1950-57; St Joseph, 1957-62; St John, 1962-67; Rural Dean of St John, Barbados, 1965-67; Sub-Dean and Rector of St George's Cathedral, St Vincent, Windward Islands, 1967-69. *Recreations:* music, driving, detective tales and novels, gramophone records of military band music. *Address:* Bishop's Court, PO Box 128, St Vincent, West Indies. *T:* St Vincent 2895.

**WINGATE, Henry Smith;** Chairman of the Board and Chief Officer since 1960, Director since 1942, Chairman Executive Committee, and Member Advisory Committee, International Nickel Co. of Canada Ltd; Chairman of the Board and Chief Officer since 1960, Director since 1944, International Nickel Co. Inc., New York; Member of Advisory Committee since 1954, International Nickel Ltd; Director: International Nickel Benelux, SA; International Nickel France, SA; International Nickel Projects Ltd; PT International Nickel Indonesia; Bourget Mining Corp. (NPL); Salaberry Mining Corp. (NPL); United States Steel Corporation; American Standard Inc.; Bank of Montreal; Canadian Pacific Railway Co.; JP Morgan & Co., Inc.; Morgan Guaranty Trust Co. of New York; Peoples' Symphony Concerts, Inc., New York; Downtown-Lower Manhattan Association, Inc.; Société de Chimie Industrielle, Paris; Institut des Hautes Études Scientifiques; American Committee for Institute of Advanced Study–Europe, Inc.; Vice-President and Director, International Copper Research Association Inc.; *b* Talas, Turkey, 8 Oct. 1905; *s* of Henry Knowles Wingate and Jane Caroline Wingate (*née* Smith), US citizens; *m* 1929, Ardis Adeline Swenson; two *s*. *Educ:* Carleton Coll.; University of Michigan. BA Carleton Coll., 1927; JD Michigan 1929. Admitted to New York bar, 1931. Associated with Sullivan & Cromwell, NYC, 1929-35. Internat. Nickel Co. of Canada, Ltd: Asst Secretary, 1935-39; Secretary, 1939-49; Vice-President and Secretary, 1949-52; Vice-President, 1952-54; President, 1954-60. Assistant to the President, International Nickel Co., Inc., NY, 1935-54; President, 1954-60. Trustee: Seamen's Bank for Savings, NY; Carleton Coll., Northfield, Minn; Annuity Fund for Congregational Ministers and Retirement Fund for Lay Workers; Council for Latin America, Inc.; US Council of International Chamber of Commerce; Nat. Industrial Conf. Board Inc.

Member: Assoc. for the Aid of Crippled Children; Executive Cttee American Bureau of Metal Statistics; The Business Council, Washington, DC; Canadian-American Cttee, National Planning Association, Washington, DC, and Private Planning Association of Canada, Montreal; US Steel Foundation, Inc. (also Trustee); Association of Bar of City of NY; Canadian Inst. of Mining and Metallurgy; Canadian Society of NY; Council on Foreign Relations, Inc., NY; Economic Club of NY; Mining and Metallurgical Society of America; American Institute of Mining, Metallurgical and Petroleum Engineers, Inc. Nat. Industrial Conf. Board (Canada); Pilgrims of the United States. Hon. LLD: Manitoba, 1957; Marshall, 1967; York, 1967. *Address:* (business) 67 Wall Street, New York, NY 10005, USA. *T:* 944-1000; (home) 520 East 86th Street, New York, NY 10028. *T:* Regent 4-3568. *Clubs:* City Midday, Pinnacle, Recess, Union, Cold Spring Harbor Beach, Huntington Country (New York); International (Washington); Duquesne (Pittsburgh); Laurel Valley Golf (Ligonier, Pa); Mount Royal (Montreal); Toronto (Toronto).

**WINGATE, Sir Ronald (Evelyn Leslie);** 2nd Bt, *cr* 1920; CB 1959; CMG 1952; CIE 1931; OBE 1945; ICS, retired; *b* 30 Sept. 1889; *o* surv. *s* of Sir F. Reginald Wingate, 1st Bt, GCB, GCVO, GBE, KCMG, DSO; *S* father 1953; *m* 1916, Mary Harpoth, *d* of Lady Vinogradoff, Oxford. *Educ:* Bradfield; Balliol Coll., Oxford (MA). Entered ICS 1912; Indian Political Service; retired, 1939; served Mesopotamia, 1917-19 (despatches). Served War of 1939-45, in Africa, South-East Asia and with Joint Planning Staff in Offices of the War Cabinet. *Publications:* Wingate of the Sudan, 1955; Not in the Limelight, 1959; Lord Ismay, 1970. *Recreations:* shooting, fishing, golf. *Heir:* none. *Address:* Barford Manor, Barford St Martin, Salisbury, Wilts. *T:* Wilton 2252. *Club:* Brooks's.

**WINGATE, William Granville,** QC 1963; **His Honour Judge Wingate;** Deputy Chairman, Essex Quarter Sessions, since 1965; a County Court Judge, Clerkenwell, since 1967; *b* 28 May 1911; *s* of Colonel George and Mary Ethel Wingate; *m* 1960, Judith Rosemary Evatt; one *s* one *d*. *Educ:* Brighton Coll.; Lincoln Coll., Oxford (BA). Called to Bar, Inner Temple, 1933; Western Circuit. Served Army, 1940-46. Member, Bar Council, 1961-67. *Recreation:* sailing. *Address:* 2 Garden Court, Temple, EC4. *T:* 01-353 4741; 7 Campden Hill Square, W8. *Clubs:* Reform; Royal Corinthian Yacht (Commodore, 1965-68).

**WINGATE-SAUL, Bazil Sylvester; His Honour Judge Wingate-Saul;** Judge of County Courts, since 1959; *b* 15 June 1906; *s* of late Sir Ernest Wingate-Saul, KC, and late Violet Annie Wingate-Saul; *m* 1942, Cecily Mary Kingston; two *s* two *d*. *Educ:* Rugby; St John's Coll., Oxford. Called to the Bar, 1928; Recorder of Oldham, 1950-59; Junior Counsel to Ministry of Agriculture, Fisheries and Food, Forestry Commission and Commissioners of Crown Lands, 1949-59; Master of the Bench of the Inner Temple, 1958. Served War of 1939-45 in Army (Royal Berkshire Regt), 1940-45. *Address:* Wrayswood, Horsehills, Horley, Surrey. *T:* Norwood Hill 589.

**WINGFIELD,** family name of **Viscount Powerscourt.**

**WINGFIELD DIGBY;** *see* Digby.

**WINGFIELD DIGBY, Ven. Stephen Basil,** MBE 1944; Archdeacon of Sarum and Canon Residentiary of Salisbury Cathedral, since 1968; *b* 10 Nov. 1910; *m* 1940, Barbara Hatton Budge; three *s* one *d*. *Educ:* Marlborough Coll.; Christ Church, Oxford; Wycliffe Hall, Oxford. Asst Master, Kenton Coll., Kenya, 1933-36; Curate, St Paul's, Salisbury, 1936-38; Priest-in-Charge, St George's, Oakdale, Poole, 1938-47. CF (temp.), 1939-45; SCF, 7th Armoured Div., 1943-45. Vicar of Sherborne with Castleton and Lillington, 1947-68. RD of Sherborne and Canon of Salisbury Cathedral, 1954-68. *Recreations:* fishing, shooting, cricket. *Address:* 23 The Close, Salisbury, Wilts.

**WINGFIELD-STRATFORD, Esmé Cecil,** DSc, MA; *b* 20 Sept. 1882; *s* of late Brig.-Gen. C. V. Wingfield-Stratford, CB; CMG; *m* 1915, Barbara Elizabeth, *d* of Lieut-Colonel F. H. L. Errington and Hon. Mrs Errington; one *d*. *Educ:* Eton; King's Coll., Cambridge. BA, 1904. Research Studentship London School of Economics, 1904; MA and Fellowship King's Coll., Cambridge, 1907; DSc (Econ) University of London, 1913; Gazetted to QORW Kent Regt, Aug. 1914; Captain, 1916. *Publications:* The Call of Dawn, 1908; The History of English Patriotism, 2 vols, 1913; An Appeal to the British People, 1914; India, 1920; The Reconstruction of Mind, 1921; Facing Reality, 1922; Life, 1923; The Reconstruction of Life, 1923; Parent or Pedagogue, 1924; The Grand Young Man, 1926; Until it doth Run Over, 1927; The History of British Civilization, 2 vols, 1928; If Labour Wins, 1929; The Victorian Tragedy, 1930; They that take the Sword, 1931; The Victorian Sunset, 1932; The Victorian Aftermath, 1933; New Minds for Old, 1934; The Harvest of Victory, 1935; Good Talk, 1936; King Charles and the Conspirators, 1937; The Making of a Gentleman, 1938; The Foundations of British Patriotism, 1939; Crusade for Civilization, 1940; Churchill, The Making of a Hero, 1942; The New Patriotism and the Old, 1943; The Price of Liberty, 1944; Before the Lamps went out, 1946; Charles King of England, 1949; King Charles and King Pym, 1949; This was a Man, 1949; King Charles the Martyr, 1950; Truth in Masquerade, 1951; The Unfolding Pattern of British Life, 1953; The Squire and his Relations, 1956; The Lords of Cobham Hall, 1959; Beyond Empire, 1964. *Recreations:* golf, travel. *Address:* The Oaks, Berkhamsted, Herts. *T:* Berkhamsted 433. *Clubs:* Constitutional, MCC.

**WINLAW, Ashley William Edgell,** OBE 1968; TD 1953; English Master, Bishops Senior School, Mukano, Uganda, since 1969; *b* 8 Feb. 1914; *s* of Rev. G. P. K. Winlaw, Morden, Surrey, and Minnie Ashley, Kidlington, Yorks. *Educ:* Winchester Coll.; St John's Coll., Cambridge (MA). Master, Aldenham Sch., 1936-39; Master, Shrewsbury Sch., 1939-40; served War, 1940-46; Intelligence Corps, Special Forces, Airborne (Lt-Col; retired as Hon. Major). Master, Rugby Sch., 1946-54; Master, Kent Sch., Connecticut, USA, 1950-51; Headmaster, Achimota Sch., Accra, Ghana, 1954-59; Principal, Government Cadet Coll., Hasan Abdal, W Pakistan, 1959-65; Director of Studies, British Inst., Santiago, Chile, 1965-66; Principal, Federal Govt Coll., Warri, Nigeria, 1966-69. Tamgha-i-Pakistan (TPk), Pakistan, 1964. *Recreations:* sports, sailing, drama, painting. *Address:* c/o Barclays Bank Ltd, Rugby, Warwickshire. *Clubs:* Special Forces, MCC, Free Foresters, I Zingari.

**WINN,** family name of **Barons Headley** and **St Oswald.**

**WINN, Rt. Hon. Sir (Charles) Rodger (Noel),** PC 1965; Kt 1959; CB (Mil); OBE; **Rt. Hon. Lord**

**Justice Winn;** a Lord Justice of Appeal since 1965; *b* 22 Dec. 1903; *s* of Ernest Winn and Joan Winn (later Martino); *m* 1930, Helen Joyce, *d* of late Colonel E. V. Sydenham, DSO, TD, DL; one *d*. *Educ:* Oundle; Trinity Coll., Cambridge (Classics I; Law II; LLB, firsts). Davison Scholar, Yale Univ., 1925; Choate Fellow, Harvard Univ., 1927; MA, LLM, Cambridge, 1928. Called to Bar (Cert. Hon.), Inner Temple, 1928; Bencher, 1953; formerly Counsel to GPO (common law); Junior Counsel to the Treasury (Common Law), 1954-59; Judge of High Court of Justice, Queen's Bench Div., 1959-65. Lord Chancellor's Law Reform Cttee, 1963-; Criminal Law Revision Cttee, 1964-; Chairman: Permanent Security Commn, 1964-; Cttee on Personal Injury Litigation, 1966-68 (Cmnd 3691). Served War of 1939-45, Naval Intelligence Div., Captain, RNVR. Officer, US Legion of Merit, 1945. Governor of St Thomas' Hospital and Chairman of Council of Medical School, 1965-70. *Address:* 11 Groom Place, SW1. *T:* 01-235 3454. *Clubs:* Garrick, Pratt's.

*See also Godfrey H. Winn.*

**WINN, Godfrey (Herbert);** author, broadcaster, and lecturer; *b* Edgbaston, Birmingham, 15 Oct. 1908; *s* of Ernest Winn and Joan Winn (later Martino); unmarried. *Educ:* St Christopher's, Eastbourne; King Edward's, Birmingham. Started career as a boy-actor in Galsworthy's Old English, Haymarket Theatre, followed by St Joan and Noel Coward's The Marquise, Criterion. First novel published, Dreams Fade, 1928; switched after several more novels to freelance journalism, and became star columnist of Daily Mirror, 1936-38, and Sunday Express, 1938-42. Was first British war correspondent to enter Maginot Line (Autumn 1939); later served in RN on Russian run as Ordinary Seaman. After war, lectured twice across United States, and continued to publish books. Appears on sound radio and television. At present under exclusive contract to International Publishing Corporation and Associated Newspapers. Member of Lloyd's. *Publications:* numerous including: PQ 17, Home from Sea, This Fair Country, The Infirm Glory (autobiog.); The Positive Hour (autobiog.), 1970. *Recreations:* lawn tennis, contract bridge, travelling. *Address:* 115 Ebury Street, SW1; The Mill House, Falmer, Sussex. *Clubs:* Queen's, Crockford's.

*See also Hon. Sir C. R. N. Winn.*

**WINN, Hon. Sir Rodger;** *see* Winn, Hon. Sir C. R. N.

**WINNEKE, Hon. Sir Henry (Arthur),** KCMG 1966; Kt 1957; OBE 1944; QC (Australia); Chief Justice, Supreme Court of Victoria, Australia, since Sept. 1964; *b* 29 Oct. 1908; *s* of Henry Christian Winneke, Judge of County Courts, Victoria, and Ethel Janet Winneke; *m* 1933, Nancy Rae Wilkinson; two *s*. *Educ:* Ballarat Grammar Sch.; Scotch Coll., Melbourne; University of Melbourne. Master of Laws, 1st Class Hons, Melbourne, 1929; Hockey Blue, Melbourne Univ. Called to Victorian Bar, 1931. Served with Royal Australian Air Force, 1939-46, Group Captain, Director of Personal Services. Resumed practice Victorian Bar, 1946; KC 1949; Senior Counsel to Attorney-General and Prosecutor for the King, 1950; Solicitor-General of Victoria, 1951-64. Member: Council Scotch Coll., Melbourne, 1947-56; Council Victoria Bar, 1948, 1949. President: Literary Council of Victoria, 1966; Boy Scouts Assoc., Victoria Br.; Victoria Law Foundn; Victorian Council Legal Educn. *Recreations:* golf, gardening, racing. *Address:* 387a Barkers Road, Kew, Victoria 3101, Australia. *Clubs:* Athenæum, Melbourne Cricket, Savage, Metropolitan Golf (Melbourne); Royal Automobile, Moonee Valley Racing (Victoria).

**WINNER, Dame Albertine (Louise),** DBE 1967 (OBE 1945); Linacre Fellow, Royal College of Physicians, and Deputy Medical Director, St Christopher's Hospice, since 1967; *b* 4 March 1907; *d* of Isidore and Annie Winner, 4k Portman Mansions, W1. *Educ:* Francis Holland Sch., Clarence Gate; University College, London, and University College Hospital. BSc (Hons Physiology) 1929; MRCS, LRCP, 1932; MBBS London, 1933 (University Gold Medal); MD (London), 1934; MRCP (London) 1935; FRCP (London) 1959. Hon. Assistant Physician, Elizabeth Garrett Anderson Hospital, 1937; Hon. Physician, Mothers' Hospital, Clapton, 1937. Service with RAMC, 1940-46 (Lieut-Colonel). Service with Ministry of Health, 1947-67. Hon. Consultant for Women's Services to the Army, 1946-70. Visiting Lecturer, London School of Economics, 1951-63. Fellow, University College, London, 1965. QHP 1965-68. *Publications:* articles in Lancet, Public Health, etc. *Recreations:* gardening, Japanese prints, music, people, opera. *Address:* 35 Gordon Mansions, Torrington Place, WC1. *T:* 01-636 1921. *Clubs:* Lansdowne, New Arts.

**WINNER, Prof. Harold Ivor,** MA, MD, MRCP, FRCPath; Professor of Medical Microbiology (formerly of Bacteriology), University of London, at Charing Cross Hospital Medical School, since 1965; Consultant Bacteriologist, Charing Cross Hospital, since 1954; *b* 1 June 1918; *y s* of late Jacob Davis and Janet Winner; *m* 1945, Nina, *e d* of Jacques and Lily Katz; two *s*. *Educ:* St Paul's Sch.; Downing Coll., Cambridge (Maj. Schol.); University College Hospital Medical School. 1st class hons, Nat. Scis Tripos Cambridge, 1939. House Surgeon, Addenbrooke's Hospital, Cambridge, 1942; served RAMC, 1942-44; Asst Pathologist, EMS, 1945-48 and NW Group Laboratory, Hampstead, 1948-50; Lecturer, Sen. Lecturer, and Reader in Bacteriology, Charing Cross Hospital Medical Sch., 1950-64; Scientific Asst for Pathology Exams, London Univ., 1958-; Examiner: Examining Board in England, 1962-; Univ. of Lagos Med. Sch., 1966-68; Founder Fellow, College of Pathologists; Hon. editor, Section of Pathology, RSM; Guest Lectr and corresp. Mem., various univs and medical insts overseas. *Publications:* Candida albicans (jointly), 1964; Symposium on Candida Infections (jointly), 1966; Microbiology in Modern Nursing, 1969; chapters in medical books; papers in medical, scientific and nursing journals. *Recreations:* listening to music, looking at pictures, gardening, travel. *Address:* Charing Cross Hospital Medical School, WC2. *T:* 01-836 7788; 48 Lyndale Avenue, NW2. *T:* 01-435 5959. *Club:* Savage.

**WINNICK, David Julian;** *b* Brighton, 26 June 1933; *s* of Eugene and Rose Winnick; *m* 1968, Bengi Rona, *d* of Tarik and Zeynep Rona. *Educ:* secondary school. Army National Service, 1951-53. Branch Secretary, Clerical and Administrative Workers' Union, 1956-62; Advertisement Manager, Tribune, 1963-66. Contested (Lab) Harwich, 1964; MP (Lab) Croydon South, 1966-70. Member Willesden Borough Council, 1959-64; Member London Borough of Brent Council, 1964-66 (Chairman, Children Cttee, 1965-66); Exec. Member, Willesden International Friendship Council, 1960-67. *Publication:* contrib. to Essays in Local Government Enterprise. *Recreations:* walking, cinema, theatre, reading.

*Address:* 4 Stanton Court, Birdhurst Rise, South Croydon.

**WINNIFRITH, Sir (Alfred) John (Digby),** KCB 1959 (CB 1950); *b* 16 Oct. 1908; *s* of Rev. B. T. Winnifrith; *m* 1935, Lesbia Margaret, *d* of late Sir Arthur Cochrane, KCVO; two *s* one *d*. *Educ:* Westminster School; Christ Church, Oxford. Entered Board of Trade, 1932; transferred to HM Treasury, 1934; Third Secretary, HM Treasury, 1951-59; Permanent Secretary, Ministry of Agriculture, Fisheries and Food, 1959-67; Dir-Gen., National Trust, 1968-70. Trustee, British Museum (Natural History), 1967-; Member: Royal Commn on Environmental Pollution, 1970-; Hops Marketing Board, 1970-. *Address:* Hallhouse Farm, Appledore, Kent. *T:* Appledore 264. *Club:* Boodle's.

**WINNINGTON, Sir Francis Salwey William,** 6th Bt, *cr* 1755; Lieut, late Welsh Guards; *b* 24 June 1907; *er s* of late Francis Salwey Winnington, *e s* of 5th Bt and Blanch, *d* of Commander William John Casberd-Boteler, RN; *S* grandfather, 1931; *m* 1944, Anne, *o d* of late Captain Lawrence Drury-Lowe; one *d*. *Educ:* Eton. Served War of 1939-45 (wounded, prisoner). Owns 4700 acres. *Heir: b* Major Thomas Foley Churchill Winnington, Grenadier Guards, [*b* 16 Aug. 1910; *m* 1944, Lady Betty Marjorie Anson, *er d* of 4th Earl of Lichfield; two *s* two *d*]. *Address:* Brockhill Court, Shelsley Beauchamp, Worcs. *Club:* Guards.

**WINNINGTON-INGRAM, Prof. Reginald Pepys,** FBA 1958; Professor of Greek Language and Literature in the University of London (King's College) since 1953; Fellow of King's College, since 1969; *b* 22 Jan. 1904; *s* of late Rear-Admiral and late Mrs C. W. Winnington-Ingram; *m* 1938, Mary, *d* of late Thomas Cousins. *Educ:* Clifton Coll., Trinity Coll., Cambridge. BA 1925; MA 1929; Scholar of Trinity Coll., 1922, Fellow, 1928-32; 1st Class Classical Tripos, Part I, 1923; Waddington Schol., 1924; 1st Class Classical Tripos, Part II, 1925; Charles Oldham Classical Schol., 1926. Asst Lecturer and Lecturer, University of Manchester, 1928, 1930 and 1933; Reader in Classics, University of London (Birkbeck College), 1934-48. Temp. Civil Servant, Ministry of Labour and National Service, 1940-45 (Asst Secretary, 1944); Professor of Classics in the University of London (Westfield Coll.) 1948; J. H. Gray Lectures, Cambridge Univ., 1956. President, Society for the Promotion of Hellenic Studies, 1959-62 (Hon. Secretary, 1963). Director, University of London Inst. of Classical Studies, 1964-67. Hon. DLitt Glasgow, 1969. *Publications:* Mode in Ancient Greek Music, 1936; Euripides and Dionysus, 1948. Contributions to classical and musical journals, dictionaries, etc. *Recreation:* music. *Address:* 7 Ladywell Court, East Heath Road, NW3. *T:* 01-435 6843. *Club:* Athenæum.

**WINNIPEG, Archbishop of, (RC),** since 1961; **His Eminence Cardinal George Bernard Flahiff,** CSB, DD; *b* Paris, Ontario, 26 Oct. 1905; *s* of John James Flahiff and Eleanor (*née* Fleming). *Educ:* St Michael's Coll. (BA); St Basil's Seminary; University of Strasbourg; École des Chartes and École des Hautes Études, Paris, 1931-35; Professor of Mediæval History, University of Toronto Graduate School and Pontifical Institute of Mediæval Studies, 1935-54; Superior General, Basilian Fathers, 1954-61; Cardinal, 1969. Member: Sacred Congregation of Religions, Sacred Congregation for Catholic Educn, Rome, 1969; Société de l'École des Chartes (Paris); American Catholic Historical Society; Mediæval Academy of America. Hon. LLD: St John Fisher Coll., Syracuse, NY, 1964; Seattle Univ., Seattle, 1965; Univ. of Notre Dame, 1969; Univ. of Manitoba, 1969. *Address:* 50 Stafford Street, Winnipeg 9, Manitoba, Canada.

**WINSER, (Cyril) Legh,** CMG 1928; MVO; Private Secretary to Governors of South Australia, 1915-40; *b* 27 Nov. 1884; *s* of Rev. C. J. Winser, MA; *m* 1912, Agnes Dorothy Mayura Langhorne; one *s* two *d*. *Educ:* Oundle. *Recreations:* cricket, golf. *Address:* Bostock Avenue, Barwon Heads, Victoria 3227, Australia. *Clubs:* Adelaide, Royal Adelaide Golf (Adelaide).

**WINSKILL, Air Commodore Archie Little,** CBE 1960; DFC 1942 (Bar 1943); Captain of the Queen's Flight since 1968; *b* 24 Jan. 1917; *s* of late James Winskill; *m* 1947, Christiane Amilie Pauline, *d* of M. Bailleux, Calais, France; one *s* one *d*. *Educ:* Carlisle Grammar Sch. Joined RAFVR 1937. Served War of 1939-45. Group Captain, 1958; OC, RAF Duxford, 1960-61; Dep. Director, Personnel, 1961-63; Air Commodore, 1963; Air Attaché, British Embassy, Paris, 1964-67. *Recreation:* golf. *Address:* Brook House, North Stoke, Oxon. *T:* Wallingford 3606. *Club:* Royal Air Force.

**WINSTANLEY, Dr Michael Platt;** TV and radio broadcaster, author, journalist, columnist, medical practitioner; *b* Nantwich, Cheshire, 27 Aug. 1918; *e s* of late Dr Sydney A. Winstanley; *m* 1st, 1945, Nancy Penney (marr. diss. 1952); one *s*; 2nd, 1955, Joyce M. Woodhouse; one *s* one *d*. *Educ:* Manchester Grammar Sch.; Manchester Univ. President, Manchester Univ. Union, 1940-41; Captain, Manchester Univ. Cricket Club, 1940-42; Captain Combined English Univs Cricket Team, 1941; Ed. University magazine, 1941-42. MRCS LRCP, 1944. Resident Surgical Officer, Wigan Infirmary, 1945; Surgical Specialist, RAMC, 1946; GP, Urmston, Manchester, 1948-66; MO, Royal Ordnance Factory, Patricroft, 1950-66; Treasury MO and Admiralty Surgeon and Agent, 1953-66; Member Lancs Local Med. Cttee, 1954-66; Member Lancs Exec. Council, 1956-65. Spokesman for Manchester Div. of BMA, 1957-65. Member Liberal Party Council, 1962-66. Contested (L) Stretford, 1964; MP (L) Cheadle, 1966-70; Chairman Liberal Party Health Cttee, 1965-66; Liberal Party Spokesman on health, Post Office and broadcasting. TV and radio broadcaster, 1957-; own series on Indep. TV and BBC. Mem., BBC Gen. Adv. Council, 1967-70. *Publications:* Home Truths for Home Doctors, 1944; The Anatomy of First-Aid, 1966; The British Ombudsman, 1970; cricket columnist, Manchester Evening News, 1964-65; articles on current affairs, health, etc. *Recreations:* cricket; golf; playing the bagpipes. *Address:* Eaglehurst, Barry Rise, Bowdon, Cheshire. *T:* 061-928 4832. *Clubs:* National Liberal, Authors'.

**WINTER, Rt. Rev. Allen Ernest;** *see* St Arnaud, Bishop of.

**WINTER, James Alexander,** CMG 1942; QC Newfoundland, 1933; Chief Clerk and Registrar of Supreme Court, Newfoundland, 1941-63; retired; *b* St John's, Newfoundland, 20 Dec. 1886; *s* of late Sir James Spearman Winter, KCMG; *m* 1915, Mary Evangeline, *d* of late Elias De Barbazan Arnaud; one *s* two *d* (and one *s* killed in action, in Africa, 1943). *Educ:* Bishop Feild Coll., St John's; Rossall Sch., Lancs. Solicitor, 1910; called to Bar, St John's, 1911; Speaker House of Assembly, Newfoundland, 1933-34; Comr for Home Affairs and Education, Newfoundland, 1936-

61. *Address:* 6 Riverview Avenue, St John's, Newfoundland, Canada.

**WINTER, Keith,** Novelist and Dramatist; *b* 22 Oct. 1906; *s* of Thomas Winter, Professor of Agriculture, Bangor University, N Wales, and Margaret Baron. *Educ:* Berkhamsted Sch.; Lincoln Coll., Oxford. After leaving school spent six months in the American Express Co., London; then became a preparatory school master for two and a half years; went to Oxford and published first novel while still there; has been writing ever since. *Publications: novels:* Other Man's Saucer; The Rats of Norway; Impassioned Pygmies; *plays:* The Rats of Norway; Ringmaster; The Shining Hour; Worse Things happen at Sea; Old Music; Weights and Measures; We at the Cross Roads; Miss Hallelujah; The Passionate Men; Round the Corner; Nell (musical). *Recreations:* tennis, swimming, travel. *Address:* c/o Monica McCall, International Famous Agency, 1301 Sixth Avenue, NYC 10019, USA.

**WINTER, Robert Pearson,** CBE 1958; MC 1918; TD 1934; President of the Institute of Chartered Accountants in England and Wales, 1963-64 (Member, 1921, Vice-President, 1962); *b* 4 March 1897; *s* of Robert Pearson Winter, Newcastle upon Tyne; *m* 1937, Nora Margaret, *d* of Harry Hunter Blair, Newcastle upon Tyne; two *s* (and one *s* decd). *Educ:* Mill Hill Sch. 2nd Lieut, Royal Engineers, TA, 1915; served UK, France, Belgium and Italy, 1915-19. Commanded Regt of Royal Engineers, TA, 1934-38 and served on Staff, 1939-42. Member T&AFA of Northumberland, 1934-64, Vice-Chairman 1950-64. Hon. Colonel, Tyne Electrical Engineers (TA), 1952-60. *Recreation:* walking. *Address:* Old Prior Manor, Corbridge, Northumberland. *T:* Corbridge 2185. *Clubs:* Northern Counties, Union (Newcastle upon Tyne).

**WINTERBOTHAM, Group Captain Frederick William,** CBE 1943; author; *b* 16 April 1897; *s* of late F. Winterbotham, Painswick, Gloucestershire; *m* 1st, 1921; one *s* two *d*; *m* 1947; one *d. Educ:* Charterhouse; Christ Church, Oxon. Royal Gloucestershire Hussars, 1915; RFC and RAF, 1916-19; Pedigree Stock Breeder, 1920-29; Air Staff and Foreign Office, 1929-45; BOAC 1945-48. *Publication:* Secret and Personal, 1969. *Address:* Frittiscombe, Chillington, Kingsbridge, S Devon. *T:* Torcross 281. *Club:* Royal Air Force.

**WINTERBOTTOM,** family name of **Baron Winterbottom.**

**WINTERBOTTOM,** Baron, *cr* 1965 (Life Peer); **Ian Winterbottom;** *b* 6 April 1913; *s* of G. H. Winterbottom, Horton House, Northants; *m*; three *s* one *d. Educ:* Charterhouse; Clare Coll., Cambridge. Worked in Textile and Engineering Trades in Manchester, Derby and Germany. Captain Royal Horse Guards; served War of 1939-45, NW European Campaign; ADC and subsequently Personal Assistant to Regional Commissioner, Hamburg, 1946-49, MP (Lab) Nottingham Central, 1950-55. Parliamentary Under Secretary of State, Royal Navy, MoD, 1966-67; Parliamentary Secretary, Ministry of Public Building and Works, 1967-68; Parly Under-Sec. of State, RAF, MoD, 1968-70. *Address:* The Old House, Clopton, Kettering, Northants. *T:* Clopton 227.

**WINTERTON,** 7th Earl, *cr* 1766 (Ireland); **Robert Chad Turnour;** Baron Winterton, *cr* 1761 (Ireland); Viscount Turnour, 1766 (Ireland); Royal Canadian Air Force; *b* 13 Sept. 1915; *s* of Cecil Turnour (*d* 1953), Saskatoon, Sask.; *S* kinsman, 1962; *m* 1941, Kathleen Ella (*d* 1969), *d* of D. B. Whyte. *Educ:* Nutana Coll., Canada. Joined RCAF, 1940. Resident in Canada. *Heir: b* Noel Cecil Turnour, DFM, CD [*b* 11 Dec. 1919; *m* 1941, Evelyn Isobel, *d* of J. C. A. Oulton; three *s*. Formerly Flt Lieut, RCAF]. *Address:* Apartment 407, 225 Royal Avenue, New Westminster, BC, Canada.

**WINTERTON, Maj.-Gen. Sir John;** *see* Winterton, Maj.-Gen. Sir (Thomas) John.

**WINTERTON, Maj.-Gen. Sir (Thomas) John (Willoughby),** KCB 1955 (CB 1946); KCMG 1950; CBE 1942 (OBE 1940); DL; retired; *b* 13 April 1898; *e s* of H. J. C. Winterton, Lichfield, Staffs; *m* 1921, Helen, *d* of late H. Shepherd Cross, Hamels Park, Herts; three *s*. *Educ:* Oundle; RMA, Woolwich. Served European War, 1917-18; Burma, 1930-32; War of 1939-45; Dep. Comr Allied Commission for Austria, 1945-49; British High Commissioner and C-in-C in Austria, 1950; Military Governor and Commander, British/US Zone Free Territory of Trieste, 1951-54, retired Jan. 1955. ADC to the King, 1948-49. Colonel Comdt 1st Green Jackets 43rd and 52nd (formerly the Oxfordshire and Buckinghamshire Light Infantry), 1955-60. President, S. Berks Conservative and Unionist Assoc. (Chairman, 1958-65). Member St John Council for Berkshire (Chairman, 1962-64); Member Cttee, Royal Humane Society, 1962-. DL, Berkshire, 1966. CStJ 1969. *Address:* Craven Lodge, Speen, Newbury, Berks. *T:* Newbury 525. *Club:* Army and Navy.

**WINTERTON, William Ralph,** FRCS, FRCOG; Gynæcological Surgeon, Middlesex Hospital; Surgeon, Hospital for Women, Soho Square; Obstetric Surgeon, Queen Charlotte's Maternity Hospital; *b* 24 June 1905; *o s* of late Rev. William Charles Winterton; *m* 1934, Kathleen Margaret, 2nd *d* of late Rev. D. Marsden; two *s* two *d. Educ:* Marlborough Coll.; Gonville and Caius Coll., Cambridge; Middlesex Hospital. MA; MB, BChir. House appointments, Middlesex Hospital, 1929-31; Gynæcological Registrar, Middlesex Hospital, 1934-36. Examr in Obstetrics to Universities of Cambridge, London, Glasgow, Ibadan and to Royal College of Obstetricians and Gynæcologists. Fellow of the Royal Society of Medicine, President Obstetric Section, 1960-61. Governor: Bancroft's Sch., Woodford Green; Howell's Sch., Denbigh (Vice-Chairman). Court of Assistants of the Drapers' Company (Master, 1964-65). Past President, Guild of Med. Bellringers. *Publications:* Aids to Gynæcology; (jointly) Queen Charlotte's Textbook of Obstetrics. Contributions to Medical Journals. *Recreations:* fishing, gardening, campanology, and Do-it-yourself. *Address:* 19 Harley Street, W1. *T:* 01-580 3733; 48 Portland Place, W1; Youngloves, Rushden, Herts. *T:* Broadfield 217.

**WINTON, Frank Robert,** MA, MD Cambridge, DSc London; FInstBiol, FIST; Consultant, May and Baker Ltd, Market Investigation Ltd, etc; Emeritus Professor of Pharmacology, University of London, 1961; *b* 1894; *m* 1922, Bessie Rawlins; one *d. Educ:* Oundle Sch.; Clare Coll., Cambridge; St Bartholomew's and University College Hospitals. Assistant, Dept of Pharmacology, University College, London, 1924; Lecturer, Dept of Physiology, University College, London, 1927; Beit Memorial Research Fellow; Lecturer in Physiology, University of Cambridge, 1931; Reader in Physiology,

University of Cambridge, 1933; Professor of Pharmacology, University College, London, 1938-61. Vice-Pres., Inst. of Biology, 1970. Hon. Member, Harvey Society of New York. *Publications:* (joint) Human Physiology, 1930, 6th edn, 1968; Modern Views on the Secretion of Urine (ed F. R. Winton), 1956; Scientific Papers in Journal of Physiology, and other journals on the kidney, plain muscle, etc. *Recreations:* chamber music, wine. *Address:* 32 Arkwright Road, NW3. *T:* 01-435 2412.

**WINTON, Walter;** Keeper of the Department of Road, Rail and Air Transport and Loan Circulation, Science Museum, since 1968; *b* 15 May 1917; *m* 1942, Dorothy Rickard; two *s* one *d*. *Educ:* Glossop Grammar Sch.; Manchester Univ. (BSc and Teacher's Diploma). Royal Ordnance Factories, Chemist, 1940-45. Taught Science, Harrow County and Greenford, 1945-50; Assistant and Deputy Keeper, Science Museum, 1950-67. *Publications:* contrib. to journals. *Recreations:* Scottish dancing and gardening. *Address:* The Old Workhouse, Harefield, Middlesex. *T:* 01-420 2103.

**WINTOUR, Charles Vere,** MBE 1945; Editor of The Evening Standard, since 1959, Chairman, since 1968; Director, Beaverbrook Newspapers Ltd, since 1964; *b* 18 May 1917; *s* of late Maj.-Gen. F. Wintour, CB, CBE; *m* 1940, Eleanor Trego Baker, *er d* of Prof. R. J. Baker, Harvard Univ.; two *s* two *d* (and one *s* decd). *Educ:* Oundle Sch.; Peterhouse, Cambridge. BA 1939; MA 1946. Royal Norfolk Regt, 1940; GSO2 Headquarters of Chief of Staff to the Supreme Allied Commander (Designate) and SHAEF, 1943-45 (despatches). Joined Evening Standard, 1946; Political Editor, Evening Standard, 1952; Assistant Editor, Sunday Express, 1952-54; Deputy Editor, Evening Standard, 1954-57; Managing Editor, Daily Express, 1957-59. Croix de Guerre (France) 1945; Bronze Star (US) 1945. *Address:* 9 Phillimore Gardens, W8. *T:* 01-937 2858.

**WINTRINGHAM, Colonel John Workman,** CBE 1943; MC; DL, JP; *b* 24 Sept. 1894; *s* of late John Fildes Wintringham, LLB, and of late Eliza Mapson; *m* 1920, Caroline Howe; two *s* one *d*. *Educ:* Mill Hill Sch. Lincs Yeomanry, 1913-19, Egypt and Palestine (MC, despatches); retired as Hon. Colonel. JP for Lindsey (Lincs), 1929; Asst County Commissioner, Lincs Boy Scouts, 1934; HG, 1940, Zone Commander, 1941, DL Lincs, 1944. *Recreation:* Boy Scouts Association. *Address:* Oakdene, The Avenue, Humberstone, Lincs. *TA:* Wintringham, Humberstone, Lincs. *T:* Humberstone 2134.

**WIPPELL, Rev. Canon John Cecil,** MA; BD; Hon. DD; Chaplain to Deaconess House, Farquharson House and Nuttall Hospital, 1957-63; Warden, St Peter's Theological College, West Indies, 1961-63 (Tutor, 1956-59); retired; *b* 6 June 1883; *s* of late William Joseph Wippell. *Educ:* Exeter Sch. (Oxford and Cambridge Higher Certificate); Exeter Coll., Oxford (2nd Class Hons Theology); BD (London) Pass 1911, 1st Class Hons, 1913. Tutor of St Boniface Coll., Warminster, 1905-11; Deacon, 1907; Priest, 1908; Assistant Curate of Warminster, 1907-10; Prof. of Theology, Codrington Coll., Barbados, 1911-18; Principal of Codrington Coll., 1918-45; Principal Rawle Training Institute for Elementary Teachers; Chaplain of SPG Estates, Barbados; CF to 4 BWI Regt, France, 1917-18; Hon. CF; Examining Chaplain to the Bishop of Barbados, 1918-45, and to the Bishop of the Windward Islands; Canon of Barbados, 1932; Hon. DD Trinity Coll., Toronto, 1934. General License, Diocese of Jamaica, 1945; Canon Emeritus of Barbados, 1946; Rector of Brown's Town, 1947-49; Rector of St Michael's, Kingston, 1949-52; Asst Master, Kingston Coll., 1952-53; Asst Master and Chaplain, Jamaica Coll., 1954-56. Hon. Chaplain to the University of the West Indies, 1960-; Lecturer, United Theological College of West Indies, 1967-70. Coronation Medal, 1937. *Address:* 1 Seymour Avenue, Kingston 10, Jamaica.

**WIRKKALA, Tapio;** Knight of White Rose of Finland; designer; *b* 2 June 1915; *s* of Ilmari Wirkkala, artist, and Selma Wirkkala; *m* 1945, Rut Bryk, artist; one *s* one *d*. *Educ:* Industrial Art Inst., Helsinki. Mil. rank of Lt, Finish Army. Glass designer for Karhula-Iittala, Finland, 1947-; designer for firms in Finland and abroad, 1955-. Art director, Industrial Art Inst., Helsinki, 1951-54. *One-man exhibitions:* Oslo, 1952; England, Germany, Switzerland, Italy, 1962-64; Czechoslovakia, 1967-, etc. Architect of numerous exhibns (or sections of these) abroad, including Ambulatory Finnish Art and Industrial Arts Exhibn, Gt Brit., 1952. *Works included in:* Museum of Modern Art and Metropolitan Museum of Art, New York; Victoria and Albert Museum, London; Kunstgewerbemuseum, Zürich; National Museum, Stockholm; Nordenfjellske Museum, Trondheim. Cross of Freedom (4th class; twice, once with oak leaves), Finland; Pro Finlandia Medal. SIA Medal, 1958; Cultural Foundn of Finland Honorary Prize, 1968; 7 Grande Premios at Milan Triennale and various other prizes and medals for design (ceramics, glass, wood, bank notes, stamps, etc); Hon. RDI (Gt Brit.), 1964, and other foreign awards. *Recreation:* fishing. *Address:* Itäranta 24, Tapiola, Finland. *T:* 46 44 14.

**WISBECH, Archdeacon of;** *see* Fox, Ven. B. G. B.

**WISDOM, Prof. Arthur John Terence Dibben,** MA; Professor of Philosophy, University of Oregon, since Sept. 1968; Fellow of Trinity College, Cambridge; Member of the Senate; *b* 1904; *s* of Rev. H. C. Wisdom and Edith S. Wisdom. *Educ:* Aldeburgh Lodge School; Fitzwilliam House, Cambridge. BA 1924; MA 1934. Lecturer in Moral Sciences, Trinity Coll., Cambridge. *Publications:* Other Minds, 1952; Philosophy and Psycho-Analysis, 1952; Paradox and Discovery, 1966. Contributions to Mind and to Proceedings of the Aristotelian Society. *Address:* Department of Philosophy, College of Liberal Arts, University of Oregon, Eugene, Oregon 97403, USA.

**WISDOM, Norman;** Actor/Comedian; *b* 4 Feb. 1925; has starred regularly in West End, since 1952. First film in 1953 (winning an Academy Award) since which has starred in 19 major films in both England and America; two Broadway awards for stage musical, Walking Happy; numerous Royal Performances, film and stage. *Recreations:* all sports. *Address:* c/o London Management, Regent House, Regent Street, W1. *Club:* Eccentric.

**WISE,** family name of **Baron Wise.**

**WISE,** 2nd Baron, *cr* 1951, of King's Lynn; **John Clayton Wise;** farmer; *b* 11 June 1923; *s* of 1st Baron Wise and of Kate Elizabeth, *e d* of late John Michael Sturgeon; *S* father, 1968; *m* 1946, Margaret Annie, *d* of Frederick Victor Snead, Banbury; two *s*. *Heir:* *s* Hon. Christopher John Clayton, *b* 19 March 1948. *Address:* Ramsley Farm, North Elmham, Norfolk.

**WISE, Lt-Col Alfred Roy,** MBE 1941; TD 1943; Queen's Royal Regiment (West Surrey); *b* 7 July 1901; *s* of late Alfred Gascoyne Wise, Puisne Judge, Supreme Court of Hong Kong, and Augusta Frances, *d* of A. N. C. R. Nugent; *m* 1942, Cassandra Noel, *o d* of Lt-Col B. E. Coke, OBE; one *s*. *Educ:* Repton; Oriel College, Oxford. Asst District Commissioner, Kenya Colony, 1923-26; MP (C) Smethwick Division of Staffordshire, 1931-45; contested Smethwick Division, Staffs, 1929; MP (C) Rugby Division of Warwickshire, 1959-66. Served with British Intelligence Organization (Germany), 1946-54. Westminster City Council, 1956-59. Upper Warden, Worshipful Company of Pattenmakers, 1967, Master, 1968. *Address:* 43 Boscobel Place, SW1. *T:* 01-235 2565. *Club:* Carlton.

**WISE, Rear-Adm. Cyril Hubert Surtees,** CB; MBE; Principal, Technical Training Institute, Royal Saudi Air Force, Dhahran, Saudi Arabia, since 1968; *b* 20 Feb. 1913, *s* of H. P. S. Wise; *m* 1948, Margaret Isobel Phelps McKenzie; one *s*. *Educ:* RN College, Dartmouth. Student RN Staff College, 1953; Imperial Defence College, 1958; Captain, HMS Collingwood, 1963-65; Inspector-Gen., Fleet Maintenance, and Chief Staff Officer (Technical), Western Fleet, 1965-67, retd. *Address:* c/o National Westminster Bank, Ltd, Broadway, Chesham, Bucks.

**WISE, Sir John (Humphrey)** KCMG, *cr* 1943; CBE 1939; Indian Civil Service, retired; *b* 11 March 1890; *s* of late William Wise, Ashbourne, Derbyshire, and St Servan, France; *m* 1918, Edith Frances Anne, *d* of late Lt-Col L. G. Fischer, IMS; one *s* (one *d* decd). *Educ:* Christ's Hospital; University College, Oxford. Entered ICS, 1914; IARO, 1915-19, served in India, Mesopotamia, Egypt and Palestine (92nd Punjabis) (despatches); Deputy Commissioner, Toungoo, 1924; Secretary Public Service Commission, India, 1926; Deputy Commissioner, Pegu, 1931; Secretary to Govt of Burma, 1932-39; Member of Burma Railway Board, 1937; Controller of Supplies, Burma, 1939; Counsellor to Governor of Burma, 1940-46; Adviser to the Secretary of State for Burma, 1946-47; Leader of British Mission to Brazil, 1948; Deputy Chairman, Raw Cotton Commission, 1949-53. *Recreations:* golf, tennis. *Address:* 5 Cressy House, Queen's Ride, SW13. *T:* 01-789 3745. *Club:* Roehampton.

**WISE, Prof. Michael John,** MC 1945; PhD; FRGS; Professor of Geography in the University of London, at the London School of Economics and Political Science, since Oct. 1958; *b* Stafford, 17 August 1918; *s* of Harry Cuthbert and Sarah Evelyn Wise; *m* 1942, Barbara Mary, *d* of C. L. Hodgetts, Wolverhampton; one *s* one *d*. *Educ:* Saltley Grammar School, Birmingham; University of Birmingham. BA (Hons Geography) Birmingham, and Mercator Prize in Geography, 1939; PhD Birmingham, 1951. Served War, Royal Artillery, 80th LAA Regt, 1941-44, 5th Bn The Northamptonshire Regt, 1944-46, in Middle East and Italy; commissioned, 1941, Major, 1944. Assistant Lecturer, Univ. of Birmingham, 1946-48, Lecturer in Geography, 1948-51; Lecturer in Geography, London School of Economics, 1951-54; Sir Ernest Cassel Reader in Economic Geography, 1954-58. Chm., Departmental Cttee of Inquiry into Statutory Smallholdings, 1963-67. Member, University Grants Cttee for Hong Kong, 1966-. Recorder, Sect. E, Brit. Assoc. for Advancement of Science, 1955-60 (Pres., 1965); Vice-Pres., Internat. Geographical Union, 1968-; Hon. Treasurer, Geographical Assoc.; Mem. Coun., Assoc. of Agriculture; Hon. Sec., RGS, 1963-. Erskine Fellow, Univ. of Canterbury, NZ, 1970. Received Gill Memorial award of RGS, 1958. *Publications:* Hon. Editor, Birmingham and its Regional Setting, 1951; A Pictorial Geography of the West Midlands, 1958; numerous articles on economic and urban geography. *Recreation:* music. *Address:* 45 Oakleigh Avenue, N20. *T:* 01-445 6057. *Club:* Athenæum.

**WISEHAM, Sir Joseph (Angus Lucien),** Kt 1967; Chief Justice of the Supreme Court in the Gambia 1957-68; retired; *b* 13 Dec. 1906; *s* of Osmond Wiseham; *m* 1931, Olive Bell. *Educ:* University Coll., University of London. Called to the Bar, Gray's Inn, 1928. Practised at Rangoon High Court, Burma, 1932; Parliamentary Sec. to Premier and to Judicial Minister, Burma, 1937-42; practised in India, 1942-46; Asst Custodian of Enemy Property, Tanganyika, 1946-51; Resident Magistrate, 1951-56; Senior Resident Magistrate, 1956-57. *Address:* Mabruk, Vicarage Lane, East Preston, Littlehampton, Sussex.

**WISEMAN, C. L.,** MA; Headmaster, Queen's College, Taunton, 1926-53; retired, 1953; *b* 20 April 1893; *s* of late Rev. F. L. Wiseman and Elsie Daniel; *m* 1946, Christine Irene, *d* of Sir William Savage, MD. *Educ:* King Edward's School, Birmingham; Peterhouse, Cambridge (Scholar). Instructor Lt RN, 1915-19; Senior Mathematical Master, Kingswood School, Bath, 1921-26. *Recreation:* music. *Address:* 11 Park Lane, Milford-on-Sea, Lymington, Hants.

**WISEMAN, Prof. Donald John,** OBE 1943; DLit; FBA 1966; FSA; Professor of Assyriology in the University of London since 1961; *b* 25 Oct. 1918; *s* of late Air Cdre Percy John Wiseman, CBE, RAF; *m* 1948, Mary Catherine, *d* of P. O. Ruoff; three *d*. *Educ:* Dulwich College; King's College, London. BA (London); AKC, McCaul Hebrew Prize, 1939. Served War of 1939-45, in RAFVR. Ops, 11 Fighter Group, 1939-41; Chief Intelligence Officer, Mediterranean Allied Tactical Air Forces with Rank of Group Capt., 1942-45. Heap Exhibitioner in Oriental Languages, Wadham Coll., Oxford, 1945-47; MA 1949. Asst Keeper, Dept of Egyptian and Assyrian, later Western Asiatic, Antiquities, British Museum, 1948-61. Epigraphist on archæological excavations at Nimrud, Harran, Rimah; Jt Dir of British School of Archæology in Iraq, 1961-65 (Vice-Chm. 1965-). Corresp. Mem., German Archæological Inst., 1961. Ed. of Journal IRAQ, 1953-; Joint Ed. of Reallexion der Assyriologie, 1959-. Bronze Star (USA), 1944. *Publications:* The Alalakh Tablets, 1953; Chronicles of Chaldaean Kings, 1956; Cuneiform Texts from Cappadocian Tablets in the British Museum, V, 1956; Cylinder-Seals of Western Asia, 1958; Vassal-Treaties of Esarhaddon, 1958; Illustrations from Biblical Archæology, 1958; Catalogue of Western Asiatic Seals in the British Museum, 1963, and journals. *Address:* 16 Downs Side, Belmont, Surrey. *T:* 01-642 4805.

**WISEMAN, Sir John William,** 11th Bt, *cr* 1628; *b* 16 March 1957; *o s* of Sir William George Eden Wiseman, 10th Bt, and Joan Mary, *d* of late Arthur Phelps, Harrow; *S* father, 1962. *Heir: kinsman* Thomas Alan Wiseman [*b* 8 July 1921; *m* 1946, Hildemarie Domnik; (one *s* one *d*. decd)]. *Address:* 1308 Sunnyside Avenue, Mamaroneck, New York, USA; Content; Reading, Jamaica.

**WISEMAN, Prof. Stephen,** MEd, DSc, PhD, FBPsS; Director, National Foundation for Educational Research; *b* 1 Sept. 1907; *s* of Stephen Wiseman and Nellie Wiseman (*née*

Wilcox); *m* 1934, Winifred Agnes Rigby, MA; two *s*. *Educ:* Hatfield College, University of Durham. Teaching in various elementary, central and technical schools, 1929-42. War of 1939-45, RAF education service, 1942-46. Senior Lecturer, Univ. of Manchester, 1946; Reader, 1956; Professor, 1961. Vis. Prof., Univ. of Surrey, 1969-. *Publications:* Reporting Research in Education, 1952; The Devon Interest Tests, 1955; The Manchester General Ability, Reading and Arithmetic Tests, 1959; Preparation for Teaching, 1960; Examinations in English Education, 1961; Education and Environment, 1964; Intelligence and Ability, 1967; contrib. to educational and psychological journals. *Address:* 7 Little Buntings, Windsor, Berks. *T:* Windsor 63040.

**WISHART, John,** CBE 1945; LLD 1947; MA; FEIS; General Secretary, Educational Institute of Scotland, 1941-46, President, 1946-47; *b* 1879; *s* of late Robert Wishart, Glasgow; *m* 1920, Isabella Mary (*d* 1969), *d* of late James Gulliland, Glasgow; one *d*. *Educ:* Crookston Street School, Glasgow; Hutchesons' Grammar School, Glasgow; Glasgow University. Teacher in Glasgow Primary and High Schools; Head Teacher Junior Instruction Centres, Glasgow; Organising Secretary of Educational Institute of Scotland and Editor Scottish Educational Journal, 1926. FCollH (Fellow of the College of Handicraft). *Publications:* Selected English Letters, 1919; articles in various educational journals. *Recreation:* walking. *Address:* 37 Craiglockhart Loan, Edinburgh EH14 1JR. *T:* 031-443 1576.

**WISKEMANN, Elizabeth,** MA, DLitt; writer on modern and contemporary history; *d* of Hugo Wiskemann and Myra Burton. *Educ:* Notting Hill High Sch., London; Newnham Coll., Cambridge (First Class Hons in Historical Tripos), Historical Research and Tutoring at Cambridge; from 1932 travelled in Europe as free lance writer; worked for Royal Institute of International Affairs in Czechoslovakia collecting material for book, 1937; lecturing in USA, 1938; Asst Press Attaché, British Legation, Berne, 1941-45; Rome Correspondent of The Economist, 1946-47; Montague Burton Professor of International Relations, Edinburgh Univ., 1958-61; Tutor in Modern European History, Univ. of Sussex, 1961-64; Former Associate of Newnham College. Hon. DLitt (Oxford), 1965. *Publications:* Czechs and Germans, 1938 (new edn 1967); Undeclared War, 1939 (new edn 1967) (American Title–Prologue to War); Italy (World To-day Series), 1947; The Rome-Berlin Axis, 1949 (rev. edn 1966); (joint) Central and South East Europe, 1945-48, 1950; (joint) Hitler's Europe, 1954; Germany's Eastern Neighbours, 1956; (joint) The Initial Triumph of the Axis, 1958; A Great Swiss Newspaper: the Story of the Neue Zürcher Zeitung, 1959; (joint trans. with Marian Jackson) The Kremlin since Stalin (by W. Leonhard), 1962; Europe of the Dictators, 1966; The Europe I Saw, 1968; Fascism in Italy, 1969. *Address:* 41 Moore Street, SW3. *T:* 01-589 2560.

**WITHERS, Googie, (Mrs John McCallum);** Actress since 1932; *b* Karachi, India, 12 March 1917; *d* of Capt. E. C. Withers, CBE, CIE, RIN, and of Catherine Wilhelmina van Wageningen; *m* 1948, John McCallum; one *s* two *d*. *Educ:* Fredville Park, Nonnington, Kent; Convent of the Holy Family, Kensington. Started as dancer in Musical Comedy. First film contract at age of 17; has acted in over 50 pictures, starring in 30. *Films include:* One of our Aircraft is Missing; The Silver Fleet; On Approval; Loves of Joanna Godden; It Always Rains on Sunday; White Corridors, etc. *Plays include:* They Came to a City; Private Lives; Winter Journey; The Deep Blue Sea; Waiting for Gillian; Janus. Stratford on Avon Season, 1958: Beatrice in Much Ado About Nothing; Gertrude in Hamlet. The Complaisant Lover, New York, 1962; Exit the King, London, 1963; Getting Married, Strand, 1967. Tours: 1959, Australia and NZ with: Roar Like a Dove, The Constant Wife and Woman in a Dressing Gown; 1964, excerpts Shakespeare (Kate, Margaret of Anjou, Beatrice, Portia, Rosalind, Cleopatra); 1965, Australia and NZ, with Beekman Place; 1968, Australia, with Relatively Speaking; 1969-70, Australia and NZ, with Plaza Suite. TV appearances in drama; also broadcasts. *Recreations:* music, travel, reading, interior decorating. *Address:* 1740 Pittwater Road, Bay View, NSW 2104, Australia; c/o Coutts & Co., 440 Strand, WC2.

**WITHERS, John Keppel Ingold D.;** *see* Douglas-Withers.

**WITHERS, Rupert Alfred;** Managing Director, Dalgety Ltd, since 1969; *b* 1913; *o s* of late Herbert Withers, FRAM and Marguerite (*née* Elzy); *m*; three *d*. *Educ:* University College School. Fellow Institute of Chartered Accountants, 1938. Secretary and Chief Accountant, Gloster Aircraft Co. Ltd, 1940-44; a Senior Partner of Urwick Orr & Partners Ltd until 1959; Man. Dir, Ilford Ltd, 1959-64; Chm. and Chief Executive, 1964-68. Member: Council, BIM, 1965; Council, Cheltenham Coll. 1964; Horse Race Totalisator Board, 1969-. *Recreations:* music, books, theatre, golf. *Address:* 21 Connaught Square, W2. *T:* 01-262 7141; Epwell Mill Cottage, Banbury, Oxon. *T:* Swalcliffe 327. *Clubs:* Athenæum, Savile.

**WITNEY, Kenneth Percy;** Assistant Under-Secretary of State, Home Office, since 1969; *b* 19 March 1916; *s* of Rev. Thomas and Dr Myfanwy Witney, S India; *m* 1947, Joan Tait; one *s* one *d*. *Educ:* Eltham Coll.; Wadham Coll., Oxford (Schol.). BA Hons Mod. History, 1938. Min. of Home Security, 1940; Private Sec. to Parly Under-Sec., 1942-44; Home Office, 1945; Asst Private Sec. to Home Sec., 1945-47; Colonial Office (Police Div.), 1955-57; Asst Sec., Home Office, 1957. *Recreations:* local history, gardening. *Address:* 61 Hadlow Road, Tonbridge, Kent. *T:* Tonbridge 2971. *Club:* Oxford and Cambridge University.

**WITT, Rt. Rev. Howell Arthur John;** *see* Australia, North-West, Bishop of.

**WITT, Sir John (Clermont),** Kt 1967; FSA; Solicitor; Senior Partner in firm of Stephenson Harwood & Tatham, Saddlers' Hall, Gutter Lane, Cheapside EC2; Member: Management Committee of Courtauld Institute of Art, since 1952; Standing Commission on Museums and Galleries, since 1958; Arts Council, since 1962 (Vice-Chairman, 1970-); Trustee of the National Gallery, since 1965 (and 1955-62; Chairman, 1959-62, 1967-); Chairman, Equity & Law Life Assurance Society Ltd; *b* 5 November 1907; *s* of Sir Robert Clermont Witt, CBE, and Mary Helene Marten; *m* 1931, Margaret, *d* of Henry S. Bowers, Scotland, Conn, USA; one *s* one *d*. *Educ:* Eton; New Coll., Oxford (BA); Harvard, USA. Admitted Solicitor, 1934. Served War, 1941-45; 1st Bn The Rifle Brigade, Middle East, Italy, France, and Germany (Major; despatches). Independent Member, Reviewing Committee on Export of Works of Art, 1952-59, 1963-67. Trustee of the Tate Gall., 1959-62. Cavaliere, Order of S Gregorio Magno, 1965. *Address:* 15 Dorset Square, NW1. *T:* 01-723 5589; Down

Mead, Boro Marsh, Wargrave, Berks. *Clubs:* Travellers', City University.

**WITT, Maj.-Gen. John Evered,** CB 1952; CBE 1948; MC 1918; retired from Army, 1953; *b* 15 Jan. 1897; *s* of late Rev. A. R. Witt, Royal Army Chaplains' Department; *m* 1st, 1924, Kathleen Phyllis Outram (*d* 1968); one *s*; 2nd, 1969, Mrs Cynthia Myrtle Margaret Reynolds, Littleton, Winchester, *yr d* of late Dr Geoffrey Eden, FRCP. *Educ:* King's Sch., Canterbury; RMC Sandhurst, 1914. 2nd Lt ASC, Dec. 1914; BEF, 1915-19; BAOR, 1919-21; UK, 1921-23; BAOR, 1923-26; UK, 1926; India, 1927; Egypt, 1927-32; UK, 1932-46; Director of Supplies and Transport; BAOR, 1946-48; FarELF, 1948-49 (despatches); Director of Supplies and Transport, Middle East Land Forces, 1950-53. *Recreations:* fishing, golf. *Address:* Trecaven, Rock, Wadebridge, Cornwall. *Club:* United Service.

**WITTE, Prof. William;** Professor of German in the University of Aberdeen since 1951; *b* 18 Feb. 1907; *o s* of W. G. J. and E. O. Witte; *m* 1937, Edith Mary Stenhouse Melvin; one *s* one *d*. *Educ:* Universities of Breslau, Munich, Berlin. MA, DLit (London); PhD (Aberdeen). Assistant, Department of German: Aberdeen, 1931-36; Edinburgh, 1936-37; Lecturer, Department of German, Aberdeen, 1937; Head of Dept, 1945; Reader in German, 1947. *Publications:* Modern German Prose Usage, 1937; Schiller, 1949; ed Schiller's Wallenstein, 1952; ed Two Stories by Thomas Mann, 1957; Schiller and Burns, and Other Essays, 1959; ed Schiller's Wallensteins Tod, 1962; ed Schiller's Maria Stuart, 1965. Articles in Modern Language Review, German Life and Letters, Publications of the English Goethe Society, Schiller-Jahrbuch, Forum for Modern Language Studies, Encyclopædia Britannica, etc. *Recreations:* gardening, motoring. *Address:* 74 Don Street, Old Aberdeen. *T:* 43645.

**WITTEWRONGE, Sir J. C. B. L.;** *see* Lawes, Sir J. C. B.

**WITTKOWER, Rudolf,** FBA 1958; Slade Professor of Fine Art, Cambridge, 1970-71; Professor of Fine Arts, Columbia University, New York, 1956-69, now Avalon Foundation Professor Emeritus in the Humanities; *b* 22 June 1901; *er s* of late Henry Wittkower; *m* 1923, Margot Holzmann; one *s*. *Educ:* Munich and Berlin Univs. Asst, Bibliotheca Hertziana, Rome, 1923-27; Research Fellow, Bibl. Hertziana, 1928-33; Lecturer, Cologne Univ., 1932-33; Staff Member, Warburg Institute, London, 1934-56; Reader in the History of Classical Tradition in Art, Univ. of London, 1946; Durning Lawrence Professor in the History of Art in the University of London, 1949-56. Co-Editor: Jl of Warburg and Courtauld Institutes, 1937-56; Studies in Architecture, 1958-; Editor, Columbia Univ. Studies in Art and Archæology, 1962-. Visiting Prof., Harvard Univ., 1954 and 1955, Columbia University, 1955-56; Kress Prof., Nat. Gallery, Washington, 1969-70. Member Accademia Olimpica, Vicenza; For. Corresp. Mem. Max-Planck-Inst. Bibl. Hertziana, Rome; Hon. Fellow Warburg Inst., London, 1958; FIAL 1958; Fellow American Academy of Arts and Sciences, 1959; Hon. Fellow Accademia di Belle Arti, Venice, 1959; Fellow Accademia dei Lincei, Rome, 1960; Hon. FRIBA, 1965; FRSA 1970, etc. Hon. Dr of Fine Arts, Duke Univ., 1969; Hon. Dr of Humane Letters, Columbia, 1970. Serena Medal of the British Academy, 1957; medal of Gallerie Nazionali, Naples, 1957. *Publications:* (with E. Steinmann) Michelangelo Bibliographie, 1927; Die Zeichnungen des G. L. Bernini, 1931; (with T. Borenius) Sir Robert Mond's Collection of Drawings, 1935; (with F. Saxl) British Art and the Mediterranean, 1948. Architectural Principles in the Age of Humanism, 1949; The Artist and the Liberal Arts, 1952; The Drawings of the Carracci in the Royal Collection at Windsor Castle, 1952; Gian Lorenzo Bernini, 1955; Art and Architecture in Italy 1600-1750, 1958; (with Margot Wittkower) Born under Saturn: The Character and Conduct of Artists, 1962; Disegni de le Ruine di Roma, 1963; (with Margot Wittkower) The Divine Michelangelo: The Florentine Academy's Homage on his Death in 1564, 1964; La Cupola di San Pietro, 1964. Contrib. to: Journal of the Warburg and Courtauld Inst., Art Bulletin, Burlington Mag., Archeological Journal, Town Planning Review, Daedalus, etc. *Address:* 7 Crediton Hill, London, NW6. *T:* 01-435 9329.

**WITTON-DAVIES, Ven. Carlyle;** Archdeacon of Oxford and Canon of Christ Church, Oxford, since 1957; Examining Chaplain to the Bishop of Oxford since 1965; *b* 10 June 1913; *s* of late Prof. T. Witton Davies, DD, and Hilda Mabel Witton Davies (*née* Everett); *m* 1941, Mary Rees, BA, *o d* of Canon W. J. Rees, St Asaph, Flintshire; three *s* four *d*. *Educ:* Friars School, Bangor; University College of N Wales, Bangor; Exeter College, Oxford; Cuddesdon College, Oxford; Hebrew University, Jerusalem. Exhib., University Coll. of N Wales, Bangor, 1930-34; BA (Wales), 1st Cl. Hons Hebrew, 1934; BA (Oxon), 2nd Cl. Hons Theology, 1937; Junior Hall Houghton Septuagint Prize, Oxford, 1938, Senior, 1939; MA (Oxon), 1940; Deacon, 1937, Priest, 1938, St Asaph; Assistant Curate, Buckley, 1937-40; Subwarden, St Michael's College, Llandaff, 1940-44; Examining Chaplain to Bishop of Monmouth, 1940-44; Adviser on Judaica to Anglican Bishop in Jerusalem, 1944-49; Examining Chaplain to Bishop in Jerusalem, 1945-49; Canon Residentiary of Nazareth in St George's Collegiate Church, Jerusalem, 1947-49; Dean and Precentor of St David's Cathedral, 1949-57; Examining Chaplain to Bishop of St David's, 1950-57; Chaplain, Order of St John of Jerusalem, 1954-; Surrogate. Chairman: Council of Christians and Jews, 1957-: Clergy Friendly Society, 1961-63. Member, Archbishops' Commission on Crown Appointments, 1962-64. *Publications:* Journey of a Lifetime, 1962; (part translated) Martin Buber's Hasidism, 1948; (translated) Martin Buber's The Prophetic Faith, 1949; contrib. to Oxford Dictionary of the Christian Church, 1957; contrib. to The Mission of Israel, 1963. *Recreations:* music, lawn tennis, swimming. *Address:* Christ Church, Oxford. *T:* Oxford 43847.

**WITTS, Leslie John,** CBE 1959; MD Manchester; FRCP; DM Oxford; Hon. ScD Dublin; Hon. MD Bristol; Hon. DSc Belfast; Fellow of Magdalen College and Nuffield Professor of Clinical Medicine, Oxford, 1938-65; now Emeritus Fellow and Professor; *b* 1898; *s* of Wyndham John Witts, Warrington, Lancs; *m* 1929, Nancy Grace, *y d* of L. F. Salzman; one *s* three *d*. *Educ:* Boteler Grammar Sch., Warrington; Victoria Univ. of Manchester; Sidney Sussex Coll., Cambridge. Served with Inns of Court OTC and RFA, 1916-18; Dickenson Travelling Scholar, 1925; John Lucas Walker Student, 1926; Edmonds Research Fellow, 1929. Lectures: Goulstonian, RCP, 1932; Frederick Price, Dublin, 1950; Schorstein Meml, London Hosp., 1955; Sidney Watson Smith, Edinburgh, 1956; Gwladys and Olwen Williams, Liverpool, 1957; Shepherd, Montreal, 1959; Lumleian, RCP, 1961; Heath Clark, Univ. of London, 1964; Litchfield,

Oxon, 1969. Late Asst to Med. Unit, London Hospital; Director, Medical Professorial Clinic and Physician St Bartholomew's Hospital; Assistant Physician to Guy's Hospital; Member of Medical Research Council, 1938-42, 1943-47; Hon. Secretary and Treasurer Assoc. Physicians of Great Britain and Ireland, 1933-48; Second Vice-Pres. Royal Coll. of Physicians, 1965-66. Mem., Min. of Health Committee on Safety of Drugs, 1963-68. McIlrath Guest Professor, Sydney, 1956. Hon. Fellow, Royal Coll. of Physicians and Surgeons of Canada. Hon. Member, Assoc. of American Physicians, and Danish Soc. of Internal Med. *Publications:* Anæmia and the Alimentary Tract, 1956; The Stomach and Anaemia, 1966; Hypochromic Anaemia, 1969. Editor of Medical Surveys and Clinical Trials, 2nd Edn, 1964. Contributions to medical and scientific journals. *Recreations:* walking, play-going. *Address:* 293 Woodstock Road, Oxford. *T:* 58843.

**WODEHOUSE,** family name of **Earl of Kimberley.**

**WODEHOUSE, Lord; John Armine Wodehouse;** *b* 15 Jan. 1951; *s* and *heir* of 4th Earl of Kimberley, *qv*.

**WODEHOUSE, Pelham Grenville;** author; *b* 15 Oct. 1881; 3rd *s* of late Henry Ernest Wodehouse, CMG; *m* 1914, Ethel, *widow* of late Leonard Rowley of Dee Bank, Cheshire. Became an American Citizen in 1955. *Educ:* Dulwich College. *Publications:* The Pothunters, 1902; A Prefect's Uncle; Tales of St Austin's, 1903, The Gold Bat, 1904; The Head of Kay's, 1905; Love among the Chickens, 1906; The White Feather, 1907; The Swoop, 1909; Mike, 1909; A Gentleman of Leisure, 1910; The Prince and Betty, 1911; The Little Nugget, 1912; Psmith in the City, 1910; Psmith, Journalist, 1915; Something Fresh, 1915; Uneasy Money, 1917; Piccadilly Jim, 1918; A Damsel in Distress, 1919; Jill, the Reckless, 1920; The Coming of Bill, 1920; Indiscretions of Archie, 1921; The Clicking of Cuthbert, 1922; The Girl on the Boat, 1922; Leave it to Psmith, 1923; The Inimitable Jeeves, 1924; Ukridge, 1924; Bill the Conqueror, 1924; Carry on, Jeeves, 1925; Sam the Sudden, 1925; The Heart of a Goof, 1926; The Small Bachelor, 1927; Meet Mr Mulliner, 1927; Money for Nothing, 1928; Mr Mulliner Speaking, 1929; Summer Lightning, 1929 (film version, 1933); Very Good, Jeeves, 1930; Louder and Funnier, 1932; Doctor Sally, 1932; Hot Water, 1932; Mulliner Nights, 1933; Heavy Weather, 1933; Thank You, Jeeves, 1934; Right Ho, Jeeves, 1934; Blandings Castle, 1935; The Luck of the Bodkins, 1935; Mulliner Omnibus, 1935; The Inside Stand (play), 1935; Young Men in Spats, 1936; Laughing Gas, 1936; Lord Emsworth and Others, 1937; Summer Moonshine, 1938; The Code of the Woosters, 1938; Uncle Fred in the Springtime, 1939; Eggs, Beans and Crumpets, 1940; Quick Service, 1940; Full Moon, 1947; Uncle Dynamite, 1948; Mating Season, 1949; Nothing Serious, 1950; The Old Reliable, 1951; Week-End Wodehouse (anthology), 1951; Barmy in Wonderland, 1952; Pigs Have Wings, 1952; Ring for Jeeves, 1953; Performing Flea (autobiog.), 1953; (with Guy Bolton) Bring on the Girls, 1954; Jeeves and the Feudal Spirit, 1954; French Leave, 1956; Something Fishy, 1956; Over Seventy (autobiog.), 1957; Cocktail Time, 1958; A Few Quick Ones, 1959; Jeeves in the Offing, 1960; Ice in the Bedroom, 1961; Service with a Smile, 1962; Stiff Upper Lip, Jeeves, 1963; Frozen Assets, 1964; Galahad at Blandings, 1965; Company for Henry, 1967; Do Butlers Burgle Banks?, 1968. Part author, also writer of lyrics, 18 musical comedies, mostly produced in America; best known in England: Kissing Time, The Golden Moth, 1921; The Cabaret Girl, 1922; (with Ian Hay) Leave it to Psmith, play produced 1930; (with Guy Bolton) Who's Who (adptd from his book, If I were You) and Anything Goes, plays produced 1934 and 1935. *Relevant publication:* Wodehouse at Work, by Richard Usborne, 1961. *Recreations:* golf, swimming, motoring. *Address:* c/o Herbert Jenkins Ltd, 2 Clement's Inn, WC2. *Club:* Coffee House (New York).

**WODEN, George;** *see* Slaney, G. W.

**WOFINDEN, Prof. Robert Cavill;** Medical Officer of Health, City and County of Bristol; Professor of Public Health, University of Bristol, since 1956; *b* 25 Jan. 1914; British; *m* 1938, Eileen Frances Rachel Sinnamon; one *s* two *d*. *Educ:* Rotherham Grammar School; St Mary's Hospital Medical School, Paddington; London School of Hygiene and Tropical Medicine. County Major Schol. to St Mary's Hosp. Med. School, 1931-37; MD London, MB, BS London (Hons); MRCS, LRCP, 1937, MRCP 1967; DPH London (Hons); DPA London. House Physician, Med. Teaching Unit, St Mary's Hosp.; Asst MOH, Rotherham, 1939-42; Dep. MOH and Sen. Sch. MO, Rotherham, 1943-46; Deputy MOH: Bradford, 1946-47; Bristol, 1947-55. Consultant, WHO; Mem., Internat. Epidemiological Assoc.; Mem. various Govt and Nat. Cttees, etc. FRSH; FRIPH; Fellow, Soc. of Med. Officers of Health (Pres., 1968-69). Hon. Fellow, Eugenics Soc. OStJ. *Publications:* Health Services in England, 1947; Problem Families in Bristol (Eugenics Soc.), 1950; contrib. to Public Health, Medical Officer, Lancet, BMJ and foreign journals. *Recreations:* golf, gardening. *Address:* 2 Church Road, Stoke Bishop, Bristol BS9 1JS. *T:* Bristol 682053.

**WOLEDGE, Brian;** Fielden Professor of French, University College, London, since 1939; *b* 16 Aug. 1904; *m* 1933, Christine Mary Craven; one *s* one *d*. *Educ:* Leeds Boys' Modern School; University of Leeds. BA (Leeds) 1926; MA (Leeds) 1928; Docteur de l'Université de Paris, 1930; Asst Lecturer in French, University College, Hull, 1930-32; Lecturer in French, University of Aberdeen, 1932-39. Visiting Andrew Mellon Professor of French, University of Pittsburg, 1967. Docteur *hc* de l'Université d'Aix-Marseille, 1970. *Publications:* L'Atre périlleux; études sur les Manuscrits, la Langue et l'importance littéraire du poème, 1930; L'Atre périlleux, roman de la Table ronde (Les Classiques français du moyen âge 76), 1935; Bibliographie des romans et nouvelles en prose française antérieurs à 1500, 1954; The Penguin Book of French Verse, Vol. 1, To the Fifteenth Century, 1961; Répertoire des premiers textes en prose française, 842-1210 (with H. P. Clive), 1964. *Address:* 28a Dobbins Lane, Wendover, Aylesbury, Bucks. *T:* Wendover 2188.

**WOLFE, Very Rev. Charles William;** Dean of Cashel, since 1961; *b* 15 July 1914; *s* of Charles and Rose Wolfe, Cork; *m* 1938, Violet Millicent McCollum; one *d*. *Educ:* The King's Hosp. and Trinity Coll., Dublin. Sen. Exhibn, 1934; Schol. of the Hse, 1935; Bernard, Wray and Oratory Prize; Moderatorship, 1936, with Large Gold Medal in Mental and Moral Science. BA 1936; BLitt 1938; MLitt 1960; 1st Cl. Divinity Testimonial, 1937; Theolog. Exhibn, 1938. Deacon, 1938; Priest, 1939; Curate, Kinsale, 1938; Rector: Berehaven, 1940; Fermoy, 1943; Tramore, 1949. Archdeacon of Waterford, 1960. Exam. Chap. to Bp of Cashel. *Publications:* A Memoir of Christ Church, Tramore, 1951; Cashel: its

Cathedrals and Library, 1965. *Address:* The Deanery, Cashel, Co. Tipperary, Ireland. *T:* 43.

**WOLFE, Frederick John;** late Chairman, Anglo-American Oil Co. Ltd (Esso Petroleum Co. Ltd); *b* Brantford, Ont, Canada; *s* of Charles Frederick and Sarah Balfour Wolfe; *m* Marguerite, *d* of late Senator John J. Boyce; one *s* one *d*. Formerly Vice-President, Imperial Oil Ltd, Canada. *Clubs:* Carlton; York, National (Toronto); Metropolitan (New York).

**WOLFENDEN, Sir John (Frederick),** Kt 1956; CBE 1942; Director and Principal Librarian, British Museum, since 1969; Chairman, Carnegie UK Trust; *b* 26 June 1906; *s* of late G. Wolfenden, Halifax; *m* 1932, Eileen Le Messurier, 2nd *d* of late A. J. Spilsbury; one *s* two *d* (one *s* decd). *Educ:* Wakefield School; Queen's College, Oxford (Hastings Scholar, Akroyd Scholar; Hon. Fellow 1959); 2nd Class Classical Mods, 1926; 1st Class Literae Humaniores, 1928; Henry P. Davison Scholar Princeton University, USA, 1928-29; Fellow and Tutor in Philosophy, Magdalen College, Oxford, 1929-34; Headmaster of Uppingham School, 1934-44; Headmaster of Shrewsbury School, 1944-50; Vice-Chancellor of Reading University, 1950-63. Director of Pre-Entry Training, Air Ministry, 1941; Chairman: Ministry of Education's Youth Advisory Council, 1942-45; Headmasters' Conference, 1945, 1946, 1948, 1949; Departmental Cttee on Employment of National Service Men, 1956; Secondary School Examinations Council, 1951-57; Departmental Cttee on Homosexual Offences and Prostitution, 1954-57; National Council of Social Service, 1953-60; CCPR Sport Enquiry, 1957-60; Family Service Units, 1957-63; National Association of Youth Clubs, 1958-63; Local Government Examinations Board, 1958-63; Councils for the Training of Health Visitors and for Training in Social Work, 1962-63; University Grants Cttee, 1963-68; President: Section L British Association, 1955; Aslib, 1969-. Hon. DLitt Reading, 1963; Hon. LLD Hull, 1969. Oxford University Hockey XI, 1927, 1928, English Hockey XI, 1930-33. Provost, Order of the Buffalo Hunt (Manitoba). *Publications:* The Approach to Philosophy, 1932; The Public Schools To-Day, 1948; How to Choose Your School, 1952; Chapters in The Prospect Before Us, 1948; Education in a Changing World, 1951; occasional articles, named lectures, and reviews. *Recreation:* walking about. *Address:* The Director's House, British Museum, WC1. *Clubs:* Athenæum, United University; Vincent's (Oxford).

**WOLFF, Hon. Sir Albert (Asher),** KCMG 1959; Lieutenant-Governor of Western Australia, since 1968; Chief Justice of Western Australia, since 1959; *b* 30 April 1899; *s* of Simon and Bertha Clara Wolff; *m* 1st, 1924, Ida Violet Jackson (*d* 1953); one *s* one *d*; 2nd, 1956, Mary Godwin. *Educ:* Perth Modern School. Admitted Bar Supreme Court of Western Australia, 1921; Crown Prosecutor, 1926; Crown Solicitor and Parliamentary Draughtsman, 1929; KC 1936; Justice Supreme Court of Western Australia, 1938. President Public Library, Museum and Art Gallery Trust, WA, 1954-58. Author and draughtsman W Aust. Matrimonial Causes Code and Rules. Official Visitor Harvey Internment Camp, War of 1939-45. *Address:* Lawson, 6 Esplanade, Perth, WA 6000, Australia. *Club:* Weld (Perth).

**WOLFF, Henry D.;** *see* Drummond-Wolff.

**WOLFF, John Arnold Harrop,** CMG 1963; *b* 14 July 1912; *er s* of late Arnold H. Wolff, Halebarns, Cheshire; *m* 1939, Helen Muriel McCracken, Howth, Co. Dublin; one *s* one *d*. *Educ:* Haileybury College; Peterhouse, Cambridge. Colonial Administrative Service, Kenya: District Officer, 1935-59; Provincial Commissioner, 1959-63; Civil Secretary, Rift Valley Region, 1963; retired, Nov. 1963. *Recreations:* cricket, tennis, golf. *Address:* Wallflowers, Bloxham, Oxon. *Clubs:* MCC; Rift Valley Sports (Kenya).

**WOLFF, Mrs Nat;** *see* Best, Edna.

**WOLFF, Prof. Otto Herbert,** MD, FRCP; Nuffield Professor of Child Health, University of London, since 1965; *b* 10 Jan. 1920; *s* of Dr H. A. J. Wolff; *m* 1952, Dr Jill Freeborough; one *s* one *d*. *Educ:* Peterhouse, Cambridge; University College Hospital, London. Lieut and Capt. RAMC, 1944-47. Resident Medical Officer, Registrar and Sen. Med. Registrar, Birmingham Children's Hospital, 1948-51; Lecturer, Sen. Lectr, Reader, Dept of Pædiatrics and Child Health, Univ. of Birmingham, 1951-64. Member: Royal Society of Medicine; British Pædiatric Association; American Pædiatric Society; New York Academy of Sciences; Corresp. Member: Société Française de Pédiatrie; Société Suisse de Pédiatrie. *Publications:* chapter on Disturbances of Serum Lipoproteins in Endocrine and Genetic Diseases of Childhood (ed Lytt 1, Gardner); articles in Lancet, British Medical Journal, Archives of Disease in Childhood, Quarterly Jl of Medicine, etc. *Recreation:* music. *Address:* 53 Danbury Street, N1. *T:* 01-226 0748.

**WOLFSON, Sir Isaac,** 1st Bt *cr* 1962; FRS 1963; Hon. Fellow: Weizmann Institute of Science, Israel; St Edmund Hall, Oxford; Churchill College, Cambridge; Founder Fellow, Wolfson College, Oxford; Chairman (since 1946), The Great Universal Stores Ltd; *b* 17 Sept. 1897; *m* 1926, Edith Specterman; one *s*. *Educ:* Queen's Park School, Glasgow. Joined The Great Universal Stores Ltd, 1932. President, United Synagogue. Member, Worshipful Company of Pattenmakers; Member, Grand Council, British Empire Cancer Campaign; Hon. Pres., Weizmann Institute of Science Foundation; Trustee, Religious Centre, Jerusalem; Hon. Treasurer, Victoria League for Commonwealth Friendship; Patron, Royal College of Surgeons; Founder Chairman and Trustee, Wolfson Foundation which was created in 1955 mainly for the advancement of health, education and youth activities in the UK and Commonwealth. Hon. FRCP 1959; Hon. FRCS 1969. Hon. DCL Oxford, 1962; Hon. LLD: London, 1959; Glasgow, 1963; Cambridge, 1966; Manchester, 1967; Strathclyde, 1969; Brandeis Univ., US 1969; Hon. PhD Jerusalem, 1970. Einstein Award (US) 1967. *Recreation:* golf. *Heir:* *s* Leonard Wolfson [*b* 11 Nov. 1927; *m* Ruth, *d* of E. A. Sterling; four *d*]. *Address:* 74 Portland Place, W1. *Club:* Reform.

**WOLLASTON, Vice-Adm. Herbert Arthur Buchanan-,** CMG 1919; *b* 13 Oct. 1878; *s* of late S. G. Buchanan-Wollaston and C. E. Harper; *m* 1908, Dora Caroline Chambers (*d* 1961); one *d*. *Educ:* Park House, Reading; Cordwalles, Maidenhead; HMS Britannia. Served European War, 1914-18 (despatches four times); Rear-Adm. and retired list, 1928; Vice-Adm., retired, 1932. *Address:* Woodcote House, Ottery St Mary, Devon EX11 1NS. *T:* Ottery 2385.

**WOLLEN, Sir (Ernest) Russell (Storey),** KBE 1969 (CBE 1962; OBE 1953); retired; *b* 9 June 1902; *s* of Cecil Storey Wollen, Glengariffe, Torquay, Devon; *m* 1924, Maise, *d* of Robert Adamson, Neville's Cross, Co. Durham; two *s* two *d*. *Educ:* Marlborough. Coffee Planter, 1922-39; Chm., Coffee Bd of Kenya, 1933-40; Mem., Kenya Supply Bd, 1940-44; E African Manager, Dalgety & Co., 1944-55; Chm., Kenya Coffee Marketing Bd, 1955-67. Retired to reside in Western Australia, 1967. *Recreations:* sailing, riding, golf. *Address:* 9 Dunkley Avenue, Applecross, Western Australia 6153, Australia. *T:* Perth 643193. *Clubs:* Farmers' (London); Muthaiga Country (Nairobi).

**WOLLEN, Sir Russell;** *see* Wollen, Sir E. R. S.

**WOLLHEIM, Richard Arthur;** Grote Professor of Philosophy of Mind and Logic in the University of London since 1963; *b* 5 May 1923; *s* of Eric Wollheim; *m* 1st, 1950, Anne, *yr d* of Lieutenant-Colonel E. G. H. Powell (marr. diss. 1967); two *s*; 2nd, 1969, Mary Day, *er d* of Robert S. Lanier, NYC. *Educ:* Westminster School; Balliol College, Oxford (MA). Assistant Lecturer in Philosophy, University College, London, 1949; Lecturer, 1951; Reader, 1960; Visiting Professor: Columbia Univ., 1959-60, 1970; Visva-Bharati Univ., Santiniketan, India, 1968. Pres., Aristotelian Soc., 1967-68; Vice-Pres., British Soc. of Aesthetics, 1969-. Served in the Army, Northern Europe, 1942-45 (prisoner of war during August 1944). *Publications:* F. H. Bradley, 1959, rev. edn 1969; Socialism and Culture, 1961; On Drawing an Object (Inaugural Lecture), 1965; Art and its Objects, 1968; A Family Romance (fiction), 1969; edited: F. H. Bradley, Ethical Studies, 1961; Hume on Religion, 1963; F. H. Bradley, Appearance and Reality, 1968; articles in anthologies, philosophical and literary jls. *Address:* 2 Pembroke Studios, Pembroke Gardens, W8.

**WOLLONGONG, Bishop of, (RC),** since 1952; **Most Rev. Thomas McCabe,** DD; *b* 30 June 1902; *s* of John Patrick and Elizabeth McCabe. *Educ:* St Augustine's School, Coffs Harbour, NSW; St Columba's College, Springwood, NSW; St Patrick's College, Manly, NSW; Propaganda College, Rome. Ordained Priest in Rome, 1925; Administrator of St Carthage's Cathedral, Lismore, NSW, 1931-39; Bishop of Port Augusta, 1939. *Address:* Bishop's House, Wollongong, NSW 2500, Australia.

**WOLMER, Viscount; John Roundell Palmer;** *b* 24 March 1940; *er s* of late Viscount Wolmer and of Priscilla (who *m* 1948, Hon. Peter Legh, now 4th Baron Newton, *qv*), *d* of late Captain John Egerton-Warburton; *g s* of 3rd Earl of Selborne, *qv*; *m* 1969, Joanna Van Antwerp, *yr d* of Evan Maitland James, *qv*. *Educ:* Eton; Christ Church, Oxford. Member, Hampshire County Council, 1967-. *Address:* Temple Manor, Selborne, Alton, Hants. *T:* Blackmoor 346. *Club:* Brooks's.

**WOLRIGE-GORDON, Patrick;** MP (C) East Aberdeenshire, since Nov. 1958; *b* 10 Aug. 1935; *s* of Captain Robert Wolrige-Gordon, MC and Joan Wolrige-Gordon; *m* 1962, Anne, *o d* of late Peter D. Howard and Mrs Howard; one *s* one *d*. *Educ:* Eton; New College, Oxford. Liveryman Worshipful Company of Wheelwrights, 1966. *Recreation:* listening. *Address:* Ythan Lodge, Newburgh, Aberdeenshire; 19 Cheyne Place, SW3. *T:* 01-352 0714. *Clubs:* Royal Over-Seas League; Northern (Aberdeen).

**WOLSELEY, Sir Charles Garnet Richard Mark,** 11th Bt, *cr* 1628; *b* 16 June 1944; *s* of Capt. Stephen Garnet Hubert Francis Wolseley, Royal Artillery (*d* 1944, of wounds received in action), and of Pamela, *yr d* of late Capt. F. Barry and of Mrs Power, Old Court, Whitchurch, Ross-on-Wye; *S* grandfather, Sir Edric Charles Joseph Wolseley, 10th Bt, 1954; *m* 1968, Anita Maria, *er d* of H. J. Fried, Epsom, Surrey; one *d*. *Educ:* St Bede's School, Nr Stafford; Ampleforth College, York. Staffs Yeomanry, T&AVR (2nd Lt 1964, Lt 1967). *Recreations:* shooting (game and rifle), fishing. *Heir: uncle* Basil Charles Daniel Rudolph Wolseley [*b* 16 Nov. 1921; *m* 1950, Ruth Key, *d* of Lt-Col William Tom Carter, OBE; four *d*]. *Address:* Wolseley, Stafford. *T:* Rugeley 3586. *Clubs:* Challoner; N London Rifle, English XX Rifle (Bisley Camp, Brookwood).

**WOLSELEY, Sir Garnet,** 12th Bt, *cr* 1745 (Ireland); emigrated to Ontario, Canada, 1951; *b* 27 May 1915; *s* of late Richard Bingham and Mary Alexandra Wolseley; *S* cousin (Rev. Sir William Augustus Wolseley), 1950; *m* 1950, Lillian Mary, *d* of late William Bertram Ellison, Wallasey. *Educ:* New Brighton Secondary Sch. Served War of 1939-45, Northants Regt, Madagascar, Sicily, Italy and Germany. Boot Repairer Manager, 1946. *Heir: cousin,* Noel Cecil Wolseley [*b* 14 Dec. 1889; *m* 1913, Mae Evelyn, *d* of John J. O'Connell; one *d*]. *Address:* 73 Dorothy Street, Brantford, Ontario, Canada. *T:* 753-7957.

**WOLSTENCROFT, Alan,** CB 1961; Secretary of the Post Office, since 1970; *b* 18 Oct. 1914; *yr s* of late Walter and Bertha Wolstencroft; *m* 1951, Ellen, *d* of late W. Tomlinson. *Educ:* Lancaster Royal Grammar Sch.; Caius Coll., Cambridge (MA 1st Cl. Classical Tripos). Assistant Principal, GPO, 1936. Served War of 1939-45: Royal Engineers (Postal Section), France and Middle East. Principal GPO, 1945; Assistant Secretary, GPO, 1949; Secretary, Independent Television Authority, 1954; General Post Office: Director of Personnel, 1955; Director of Postal Services, 1957; Director of Radio Services, 1960-64; Deputy Director General, 1964-67; Man. Dir Posts, 1967, Posts and GIRO, 1968; Adviser on Special Projects to Chm. of Post Office Corporation, 1969-70. *Recreations:* walking, swimming. *Address:* 71 Clarence Road, Bickley, Bromley BR1 2DD. *T:* 01-460 1984.

**WOLSTENHOLME, Gordon Ethelbert Ward,** OBE 1944; MA, MB, BChir; FRCP, FIBiol; Director, the Ciba Foundation, since 1949; Organizer and Adviser, Haile Selassie I Prize Trust, Ethiopia; *b* 28 May 1913; *o s* of G. Ethelbert Wolstenholme and Clementina Ward, Sheffield; *m* 1st; one *s* two *d*; 2nd, two *d*. *Educ:* Repton; Corpus Christi Coll., Cambridge; Middlesex Hosp. Med. Sch. Served with RAMC, 1940-47: France, UK, ME and Central Mediterranean; Specialist and Adviser in Transfusion; later comdg Gen. Hosp. Registrar in Dermatology, Middx Hosp., 1947-49. Editor, Ciba Foundn Symposia, Colloquia, and Study Groups (over 100 vols), 1950-. Chm. of Programme Cttee, 2nd Internat. Congress of Endocrinology, 1964. Co-Founder, Louis Rapkine Assoc., 1956; Founder Member: Renal Assoc., 1950 (Hon. Treasurer, 1956-69); Internat. Assoc. of Human Biologists, 1968. Governor, Assoc. for Advancement of Ageing Research, 1968-; Member: Cttee, Brit. Soc. for Research on Ageing, 1955-69; Leprosy Research Fund, 1954-65; Leprosy Study Centre, 1965-69; Cttee, Nuffield Inst. of Comparative Medicine, 1961-; Exec. Bd, UK Cttee for WHO, 1961-69 (Hon. Treasurer, 1954-61); Council, Zoological Soc. 1962-66 and 1967-70 (Hon. Treasurer, 1954-61); Council,

Zoological Soc., 1962-66 and 1967-70 (Vice-Pres., 1969); Council, Zoological Soc. 1962-66 and 1967-70 (Vice-Pres., 1969); Council, Hunterian Soc., 1963-70; Soc. for Visiting Scientists, 1963-66; Soc. for Educn in Applications of Science, 1966-; Library Cttee, RCP, 1966-69, Editorial Cttee, 1969-; Nat. Kidney Research Fund (Mem. Exec. Cttee, 1967-); Council, Developmental Sciences Trust, 1967- (Chm., 1969); Council, Westfield Coll., London Univ., 1965-70. Trustee, Spastics Trust, 1963-67. Hon. Sec., RSM. Hon. Member: Swedish Soc. of Endocrinology, 1955; Soc. of Endocrinology, 1959; Foreign Mem., Swedish Med. Soc., 1959. Hon. LLD Cambridge, 1968. Gold Medal: Perugia Univ., 1961; Italian Min. of Educn, 1961. Tito Lik, 1945; Chevalier, Légion d'Honneur, 1959; Star of Ethiopia, 1966. *Publication:* (ed) Royal College of Physicians: Portraits, 1964. *Recreations:* walking, simple gardening. *Address:* The Ciba Foundation, 41 Portland Place, W1N 4BN. *T:* 01-636 9456; The Dutch House, 77a Fitzjohn's Avenue, NW3. *T:* 01-435 3074. *Club:* Athenæum.

**WOLTERS, Very Rev. Conrad Clifton;** Vicar of Newcastle and Provost of the Cathedral since 1962; *b*3 April 1909; *e s* of Frederick Charles and Gertrude Elizabeth Wolters; *m* 1937, Joyce Cunnold; one *s*. *Educ:* privately; London College of Divinity; St John's College, Durham. ALCD 1932; LTh 1932; BA 1933; MA 1936. Curate: Christ Church, Gipsy Hill, SE19, 1933-37; Christ Church, Beckenham, 1937-41; Vicar, St Luke's, Wimbledon Park, 1941-49; Rector, Sanderstead, Surrey, 1949-59; Canon of Newcastle, 1959-62. *Publications:* (ed) Cloud of Unknowing, 1960; (ed) Revelations of Divine Love, 1966. *Address:* 23 Montagu Avenue, Newcastle upon Tyne NE3 4HY. *T:* Gosforth 853472.

**WOLVERSON, William Alfred,** CB 1954; a Deputy Director General of the Post Office 1960-65, retired; *b* 13 Oct. 1905; *s* of William Alfred Wolverson and Mary (*née* Johnston); unmarried. General Post Office: Asst Traffic Superintendent, 1928; Asst Surveyor, 1932; Asst Principal, 1935; Principal, 1938; Asst Sec., 1946; Regional Director, N Western Region, 1950; Commandant Management Training Centre, 1951; Director External Telecommunications Executive and United Kingdom Member, Commonwealth Telecommunications Board, 1952; Director, Radio Services Department, General Post Office Headquarters, London, 1955-60; idc, 1949. *Recreation:* gardening. *Address:* 28 North Down, Sanderstead, South Croydon, Surrey. *Club:* Reform.

**WOLVERSON COPE, F.;** *see* Cope, F(rederick) Wolverson.

**WOLVERTON,** 5th Baron *cr* 1869; **Nigel Reginald Victor Glyn;** Captain RA, TA; *b* 23 June 1904; *o* surv. *s* of 4th Baron and Lady Edith Amelia Ward, CBE (*d* 1956), *o d* of 1st Earl of Dudley; *S* father, 1932. *Educ:* Eton. *Heir: kinsman* Jeremy Christopher Glyn [*b* 1 Oct. 1930; *m* 1956, Robina Elspeth, *o d* of Sir George Arthur Harford, 2nd Bt; one *d*]. *Address:* Queensberry House, Newmarket, Suffolk.

*See also Lady Hyde, Baron Rhyl.*

**WOMBWELL, Sir (Frederick) Philip (Alfred William),** 6th Bt, *cr* 1778; MBE 1944; Capt. (temporary Major) RE; *b* 6 July 1910; *s* of late Frederick Adolphus Wombwell, Capt. 16th The Queen's Lancers, and May (*d* 1948), *d* of A. Harrison-Smith, of Carlton Hall, Worksop (who *m* 2nd, Thomas Stamford Booth, of Leam Hall, Derbyshire); *S* great-uncle, 1926; *m* 1936, Ida Elizabeth, *er d* of Frederick J. Leitch, Branksome Park, Bournemouth; one *s* two *d*. *Educ:* Repton. Served War of 1939-45 (MBE); Major, 1946. *Heir: s* George Philip Frederick Wombwell, *b* 21 May 1949. *Address:* Bridge House, West Baldwin, Isle of Man. *Club:* Naval and Military.

*See also Earl of Carnarvon.*

**WOMERSLEY, J(ohn) Lewis,** CBE 1962; FRIBA (Distinction Town Planning); MTPI; Partner, Hugh Wilson and Lewis Womersley, Chartered Architects and Town Planners, since 1964; *b* 12 Dec. 1910; *s* of Norman Womersley and Elizabeth Margaret Lewis; *m* 1936, Jean Roberts; two *s*. *Educ:* Huddersfield College. Asst Architect, private practices in London, 1933-38; Principal Asst, Gornall & Wainwright, St Helens, Lancs, 1938-40; Principal Asst, Herbert J. Rowse, FRIBA, Liverpool, 1941-46; Borough Architect and Town Planning Officer, Northampton, 1946-53; City Architect, Sheffield, 1953-64. Mem., Northwest Economic Planning Council. Member Council, RIBA (Vice-President, 1961-62). Works include housing, further education and central area redevelopment. Hon. LLD Sheffield, 1966. *Recreations:* walking, photography, music. *Address:* 3 Rusholme Gardens, Wilmslow Road, Manchester M14 5LG. *T:* 061-224 0034. *Clubs:* Reform; St James's (Manchester).

**WOMERSLEY, Sir Peter (John Walter),** 2nd Bt *cr* 1945; Personnel Officer, Beecham Group; *b* 10 November 1941; *s* of Capt. John Womersley (*o s* of 1st Bt; killed in action in Italy, 1944), and of Betty, *d* of Cyril Williams, Elstead, Surrey; *S* grandfather, 1961; *m* 1968, Janet Margaret Grant; one *d*. *Educ:* Aldro; Charterhouse; RMA, Sandhurst. Entered Royal Military Academy (Regular Army), 1960; Lt, King's Own Royal Border Regt, 1964, retd 1968. *Heir:* none. *Address:* Chantry Lodge, Littlehampton Road, Worthing, Sussex.

**WONTNER, Hugh Walter Kingwell,** CVO 1969 (MVO 1950); JP; Chairman of The Savoy, Claridge's and Berkeley Hotels, London, and other undertakings associated with The Savoy, since 1948 (Managing Director, since 1941); Clerk of the Royal Kitchens, since 1953, and a Catering Adviser in the Royal Household, since 1938; Chairman of Council, British Hotels and Restaurants Association, since 1969; Alderman of City of London (Broad Street Ward), since 1963; *b* 22 Oct. 1908; *er s* of Arthur Wontner, actor-manager; *m* 1936, Catherine, *o d* of Lieut T. W. Irvin, Gordon Highlanders (*d* of wounds, France, 1916); two *s* one *d*. *Educ:* Oundle and in France. On staff of London Chamber of Commerce, 1927-33; Asst Sec., Home Cttee, Associated Chambers of Commerce of India and Ceylon, 1930-31; Sec., London Cttee, Burma Chamber of Commerce, 1931; Gen. Sec., Hotels and Restaurants Assoc. of Great Britain, 1933-38; Asst to Sir George Reeves-Smith at The Savoy, 1938-41; Director, The Savoy Hotel Ltd, 1940; Sec., Coronation Accommodation Cttee, 1936-37, Chm., 1953; A British delegate, Internat. Hotel Alliance, 1933-38; Pres., Internat. Hotel Assoc., 1961-64, Mem. of Honour, 1965-. Chairman: Exec. Cttee, British Hotels and Rests Assoc., 1957-60 (Vice-Chm., 1952-57; Vice-Chm. of Council, 1961-68; Chm., London Div., 1949-51); London Hotels Information Service, 1952-56; Working Party, Owners of Historic Houses open to the public, 1965-66. Member: Historic Buildings Council, 1968-; Board of BTA (Chm., Historic Houses Cttee, to 1970); Lloyd's, 1937-; LCC Consultative Cttee, Hotel and Restaurant Technical School, 1933-

38; Court of Assistants, Irish Soc., 1967-68; Vis. Cttee, Holloway Prison, 1963-68. Governor: University Coll. Hosp., 1945-53 (Chm., Nutrition Cttee, 1945-52); Christ's Hosp., 1963-. Trustee, D'Oyly Carte Opera Trust; Chm., The Savoy Theatre, 1948-. Liveryman: Worshipful Co. of Feltmakers, 1934- (Master, 1962-63); Clockmakers, 1967-; one of HM Lieuts and a JP for the City of London, Freeman, 1934, Sheriff, 1970. Order of Cisneros, Spain, 1964. *Recreations:* genealogy, acting. *Address:* 1 Savoy Hill, WC2. *T:* 01-836 1533. *Clubs:* Garrick, City Livery.

**WOOD,** family name of **Earl of Halifax.**

**WOOD, Sir Anthony John P.;** *see* Page Wood.

**WOOD, Canon Cecil Thomas;** Senior Chaplain to Archbishop of Cape Town since 1965; *b* 1903; *s* of Henry Mathew Wood and Letitia Maud Cannon. *Educ:* Uppingham Sch.; Lincoln Coll., Oxford; Cuddesdon Theological Coll. MA (Oxford) 1926. Deacon 1927, priest 1928, Southwark diocese. Curate, St John the Divine, Kennington, 1927-32; Chaplain to Archbp of Cape Town, 1933-38; SPG Candidates Sec., 1938-41; actg Archdeacon of Bloemfontein, 1942-46; Warden of St John's Hostel, Cape Town, 1946-51; Director of South African Church Institute, London, 1952-55; Rector of Hermanus, Cape, 1955-58; Archdeacon of Cape Town, 1958-65; Canon Emeritus, 1965. Vicar General of Diocese of Cape Town, 1963, 1968. Hon. Associate in Theology (SA), 1963. Provincial Archivist, 1957-. *Publications:* Short History of Bloemfontein Cathedral, 1945; Cathedral Sermons, 1962. *Recreations:* travel, book collecting. *Address:* Bishopscourt, Claremont, Cape, South Africa. *T:* Cape Town 71-2531. *Clubs:* United University; Vincent's (Oxford); Leander (Henley); Civil Service (Cape Town).

**WOOD, Sir David B. H.;** *see* Hill-Wood.

**WOOD, Prof. Edward James;** Professor of Latin, University of Leeds, 1938-67, Professor Emeritus, 1967; Pro-Vice-Chancellor, University of Leeds, 1957-59; *b* 3 Sept. 1902; *s* of James M. A. Wood, Advocate in Aberdeen; *m* 1933, Marion Grace Chorley; one *s* one *d*. *Educ:* Aberdeen Grammar School; Aberdeen University; Trinity College, Cambridge. Lectr in Classics, Manchester University, 1928; Professor of Latin, Aberystwyth, 1932. *Publications:* contributions to: Classical Review, Gnomon. *Address:* 35 Barleyfields Road, Wetherby, Yorks. *T:* Wetherby 2488.

**WOOD, Eric Rawlinson,** CIE 1939; MC and Bar; *b* 24 March 1893; *m* Madeline, *d* of late P. F. Campbell; (two *s* killed in action, War of 1939-45) two *d*. *Educ:* Denstone Coll.; St Catharine's Coll., Cambridge, BA. Joined Indian Civil Service, 1919; officiating Chief Secretary to Government, Orissa, 1938; Revenue Commissioner, Orissa, 1939-42; Ministry of Supply, 1943-55; retired. *Address:* 143 Barnhorn Road, Little Common, Bexhill, Sussex. *T:* Cooden 2830.

**WOOD, Lt-Gen. Sir Ernest,** KBE, *cr* 1947; CB 1945; CIE 1941; MC 1917; Indian Army (retired); *b* 1894; *m* Grace, *y d* of J. F. Goodliffe; two *d*. Appointments in India: Deputy Secretary Defence Department, 1936-38; Sec. Supply Dept, 1939-40; Dir Gen. of Supply, 1940-42; Administrator Gen. Eastern Frontier Communications, 1942; Sec. Food Dept, 1943; Dir Gen. Munitions Production, 1943-45; Dep. Master Gen. of the Ordnance, 1945-46; QMG, India, 1946-47; Controller of Operations, Colonial Development Corporation, 1948-51; Chief of Staff, Defence Production Board, NATO, 1951-52; Director of Civil Defence, Eastern Region (Cambridge), Sept. 1955-60. *Recreation:* golf. *Address:* Foxton House, Via Royston, Herts. *T:* Harston (Cambs) 530.

**WOOD, Frank,** CB 1960; Secretary, Ministry of Posts and Telecommunications, since 1969; *b* 9 Nov. 1913; *m* 1946, Olive May Wilson; two *s* one *d*. *Educ:* The College, Swindon, Wilts. Exchequer and Audit Dept; Assistant Auditor, 1932; Air Ministry; Asst Principal, 1938. Private Secretary to Secretary of State for Air, 1946; Private Secretary to Minister of Defence, 1947; Dep. Sec., Air Min., 1960-61, MoD 1961-65, Min. of Aviation, 1965-66, BoT (Civil Aviation), 1966-69. *Address:* 16 Woodlands Road, Bickley, Kent. *T:* 01-467 6220. *Club:* Reform.

**WOOD, Franklin Garrett,** MA, MB, BCh, DMRE Cantab; Hon. Consulting Radiologist to: Hospital for Diseases of the Chest, German Hospital, London, and Black Notley Hospital; Fellow of Royal Society of Medicine; 2nd *s* of late James Wood, LLD, Grove House, Southport. *Educ:* Rydal School; Jesus Coll., Cambridge; St Thomas' Hospital, London. Late House Physician and Casualty Officer, St Thomas' Hospital; Temporary Surgeon Lt RN. *Publications:* Contributions to Medical Press. *Recreations:* riding and music. *Address:* 14 Upper Park Road, NW3.

**WOOD, Maj.-Gen. George Neville,** CB 1946; CBE 1945; DSO 1945; MC; *b* 4 May 1898; *o s* of Frederick Wood, Newnham-on-Severn, Glos; *m* 1928, Mary, *d* of Ven. H. C. Izard, late Archdeacon of Singapore; one *s* one *d*. *Educ:* Colston's School; Royal Military College, Sandhurst. First Commission Dorset Regt 1916; active service France, Russia, Turkey, 1916-20 (despatches twice, wounded, OBE, MC); regimental service Near East and Sudan, 1921-25; Staff College, Camberley, 1926-27; Staff employment War Office, and Aldershot, 1928-31; regimental service and Staff employment, India, 1932-38; commanded Oxford University OTC 1938-39; MA Oxon (hon.); Staff employment, home theatre, 1939-40; commanded 12th Bn West Yorkshire Regt 1941; commanded 2nd Bn Dorset Regt 1941-42; commanded 4th Infantry Brigade, 1942; BGS Ceylon Army Command, 1943; BGS 33rd Indian Corps in Assam-Burma operations, 1943-44; GOC 25th Indian Division in Arakan operations and re-occupation of Malaya, 1944-46 (despatches twice, CBE, DSO, CB); President No 6 Reg. Commissions Board, 1946; GOC Mid-West District and 53rd (Welsh) Div. TA, 1947-50; Director of Quartering, War Office, 1951-52; retired 1952. Col, The Devonshire and Dorset Regt, 1952-62. *Recreations:* cricket, gardening. *Address:* 6 Elsworthy Terrace, Hampstead, NW3.

**WOOD, Maj.-Gen. Harry Stewart,** CB 1967; TD 1950; Sales Executive with Miles Group of Companies since 1967; *b* 16 Sept. 1913; *e s* of late Roland and Eva M. Wood; *m* 1939, Joan Gordon, *d* of Gordon S. King; two *s* (and one *s* decd). *Educ:* Nautical Coll., Pangbourne. Civil Engineer (inc. articled trg), 1931-39. Commnd RA (TA), 1937. Served War of 1939-45: Regimental Service, Sept. 1939-June 1944; subseq. Technical Staff. Dep. Dir of Artillery, Min. of Supply (Col), 1958-60; Dep. Dir of Inspection (Brig.), 1960-62; Sen. Mil. Officer, Royal Armament Research and Development Estab. (Brig.), 1962-64; Vice-President, Ordnance Board, 1964-66, President, 1966-67. Maj.-Gen. 1964; retd, 1967. Legion of Merit, degree of Legionnaire (USA), 1947. *Recreations:* home and garden, motor sport.

*Address:* Brook House, Faygate, near Horsham, Sussex. *T:* Faygate 342.

**WOOD, Sir Henry (Peart),** Kt 1967; CBE 1960; Principal, Jordanhill College of Education, Glasgow; *b* 30 Nov. 1908; *s* of T. M. Wood, Bedlington, Northumberland; *m* 1937, Isobel Mary, *d* of W. F. Stamp, Carbis Bay, Cornwall; one *s* two *d*. *Educ:* Morpeth Grammar Sch.; Durham University. BSc 1930, MSc 1934, Durham; MA 1938, MEd 1941, Manchester. Lecturer, Manchester University, 1937-44; Jordanhill College of Education: Principal Lecturer, 1944-46; Vice-Principal, 1947-49; Principal, 1949-. *Address:* 51 Whittinghame Drive, Glasgow, W2. *T:* 041-334 3647.

**WOOD, Hubert Lyon-Campbell,** MS London; FRCS; Professor of Clinical Orthopaedics, Ahmadu Bello University, Kano, Nigeria; Senior Orthopædic Surgeon, King's College Hospital, 1952-68, retired from National Health Service, 1968; Orthopædic Surgeon, Royal Masonic Hospital, since 1952; *b* 3 Nov. 1903; *s* of Dr H. M. Wood and Lola Lyon-Campbell; *m* 1935, Dr Irene Parker Murray, MB, BS London (*d* 1966); two *d*. *Educ:* Marlborough Coll., Wilts; King's Coll., London Univ. MRCS, LRCS, 1926; MB, BS London (Hons), 1927; FRCS 1930; MS London, 1934. Orthopædic Surgeon, EMS, 1939-48; Assistant Surgeon: King's College Hosp., 1932; Evelina Hosp., 1934; Orthopædic Surgeon, Leatherhead Hosp., 1940. *Publications:* Chapters in Post Graduate Surgery, 1937; chapters in Rose and Carless, 1958; Operative Surgery, 1957; articles in Br. Jl Bone and Joint Surgery (past member of editorial board). *Recreations:* gardening, riding, photography. *Address:* Private Wing, King's College Hospital, Denmark Hill, SE5. *T:* 01-274 8570.

**WOOD, Sir John (Arthur Haigh),** 2nd Bt, *cr* 1918; MC 1915; DSC 1917; *b* 22 May 1888; *o s* of Sir John Wood, 1st Bt, of Hengrave, and Estelle, *d* of Henry Benham; *S* father 1951; *m* 1919, Hon. Evelyn Saumarez (*d* 1934), *e d* of 4th Baron de Saumarez; one *d* (and one *d* decd). Barrister, Inner Temple, 1912. Served European War, 1914-18, as Capt. in East Surrey Regt, and Lieut RNVR (despatches, DSC, MC). *Heir:* none. *Address:* Sausmarez House, Les Gravées, St Peter Port, Guernsey, CI.

**WOOD, John Kember,** MC 1944; QC 1969; *b* 8 Aug. 1922; *s* of John Rosskruge Wood; *m* 1952, Kathleen Ann Lowe; one *s* one *d*. *Educ:* Shrewsbury Sch.; Magdalene Coll., Cambridge. Served War of 1939-45: Rifle Brigade, 1941-46. Magdalene Coll., 1946-48. Barrister (Lincolns Inn), 1949. *Recreations:* sport, travel. *Address:* 1 Crown Office Row, Temple, EC4. *T:* 01-353 3372. *Clubs:* MCC; Hawks (Cambridge).

**WOOD, John Laurence;** Keeper, Department of Printed Books, British Museum, since 1966; *b* 27 Nov. 1911; *s* of J. A. Wood and Clara Josephine (*née* Ryan); *m* 1947, Rowena Beatrice Ross; one *s* one *d*. *Educ:* King James I Sch., Bishop Auckland; Merton Coll., Oxford (BA); Besançon; Paris. Lecteur, Univ. of Besançon, 1934-35; Asst Cataloguer, British Museum, 1936; seconded to Foreign Office, 1941-45; Asst Keeper, British Museum, 1946; Deputy Keeper, 1959. *Publications:* (trans.) The French Prisoner, Garneray, 1957; (trans.) Contours of the Middle Ages, Genicot, 1967. *Recreations:* eating, do-it-yourself, reading detective stories, failing to learn Arabic. *Address:* 88 Hampstead Way, NW11. *T:* 01-455 4395.

**WOOD, Joseph Neville;** Deputy Director, The Chamber of Shipping of the UK; *b* 25 October 1916; *o s* of Robert Hind Wood and late Emily Wood, Durham; *m* 1st, 1944, Elizabeth May (*d* 1959); three *d*, 2nd, 1965, Josephine Samuel. *Educ:* Johnston School, Durham; London School of Economics. Entered Civil Service (Board of Trade), 1935; Ministry of War Transport, 1940; jssc 1950; Ministry of Transport: Asst Sec., 1951; Far East Representative, 1952-55; Under-Sec., 1961; Chief of Highway Administration, 1967-68. Joined Chamber of Shipping of the UK, 1968. Officier, Ordre de Mérite Maritime, 1950. *Recreation:* gardening. *Address:* The Brew House, Upper Eashing, Godalming, Surrey. *T:* Godalming 7679.

**WOOD, Kenneth Maynard;** Consultant to Thorn Electrical Industries Ltd and Kenwood Manufacturing Co. Ltd; Managing Director, Hydra-Muscle Hydraulics Ltd, since 1969; Chairman: Forest Mere Ltd, since 1968; Rowlands Castle Hotels Ltd, since 1968; Stocklands Equestrian Ltd, since 1968; Multi-Development Engineering Ltd, since 1969; *b* 4 Oct. 1916; *s* of late Frederick Cavendish Wood and Agnes Maynard; *m* 1944, Laurie Marion McKinlay; two *s* two *d*. *Educ:* Bromley County School. Cadet, Merchant Navy, 1930-34; electrical and mechanical engineering, 1934-37; started own company radio, television and radar development, 1937-39; sold business and joined RAF, transferred for development of electronic equipment, 1939-46; started Kenwood Manufacturing Co. Ltd, 1946; Managing Director, 1946-68. Fellow, Inst. of Ophthalmology; FInstMSM. *Recreations:* golf, riding. *Address:* Old Thorns Farm, Liphook, Hampshire. *T:* Liphook 3108. *Clubs:* Constitutional, Royal Automobile.

**WOOD, Sir Kenneth (Millns),** Kt 1970; FCA; Chairman and Joint Managing Director, Concrete Ltd, Hounslow; *b* 25 April 1909; *s* of Sydney Wood and Edith Wood (*née* Barker); *m* 1939, Julia Mary, *d* of John and Mary Ambrose; one *d*. *Educ:* Barnstaple Grammar Sch.; Trinity Coll., Cambridge (BA). Wrangler in Maths Tripos, Trinity Coll., Cambridge (BA). Wrangler in Maths Tripos, Trinity Coll., 1930. Chartered Accountant, 1933. Served War of 1939-45 (Lt-Col). Concrete Ltd: Dir 1946; Man. Dir 1950; Chm. 1958. Seconded to Min. of Housing and Local Govt as Industrial Adviser on House-Building to Minister, 1966-67; Dir, National Building Agency, 1966. *Recreations:* golf, ski-ing, sailing, tennis. *Address:* Ridge End, Finchampstead, Berks. *T:* Eversley (Hants) 3294. *Clubs:* Devonshire; East Berks Golf; Frensham Sailing.

**WOOD, Norman,** CBE 1965; Director, Associated British Foods Ltd, since 1964; Vice-President, BTA, since 1965 (Deputy Chairman 1964); *b* 2 Oct. 1905; *m* 1933, Ada Entwisle; one *s* one *d*. *Educ:* Bolton Co. Grammar Sch.; Co-operative Coll. Nat. Exec. Co-operative Party, and Central Board of Co-operative Union, 1934; Ministry of Information, North-West Regional Cttee, 1939; Chocolate and Sugar Confectionery War-time Assoc., 1942; British Tourist and Holidays Board, 1947; Horace Plunkett Foundation, 1948; Cake and Biscuit Alliance, 1948; Biscuit Industry Nat. Joint Wages Council, 1951; Wheat Commission, 1950; Coal Merchants Consultative Cttee, 1950; Domestic Coal Consumers Council, 1950; Coronation Accommodation Cttee, 1952. Director: Co-operative Wholesale Society Ltd, 1942-64; Manchester Ship Canal Company, 1954-64; Member: British and Irish Millers, 1950-64; White Fish Authority, 1959-63; Food Research Advisory Committee,

1961. Chairman: Food Committee, British Week, Toronto, 1967; Cttee for Exports to Canada, BNEC, 1967; Food and Drink Cttee, British Week, Tokyo, 1969. *Recreations:* tennis and walking. *Address:* Associated British Foods Ltd, Regent Arcade House, 19-25 Argyll Street, W1. *T:* 01-437 5644. *Club:* Oriental.

**WOOD, Oswald Edward;** Director, Midland Bank Ltd, and Midland Bank Executor and Trustee Co. Ltd, since 1962; *b* 13 December 1899; *s* of James and Flora Wood; *m* 1926, Muriel Hay, Hackensack, New Jersey, USA. *Educ:* Latymer Upper School; Gonville and Caius College, Cambridge (Open Scholar). 1st Cl. Historical Tripos, Pt I, 1920, 1st Cl. Law Tripos, Pt II, 1921; Arden Prize, Gray's Inn, 1921; Barrister, Gray's Inn, 1923. Entered Midland Bank, 1921; various appointments in London and Provinces; Asst Gen. Manager, 1940, Jt Gen. Manager (International and City), 1944; Asst Chief Gen. Manager, 1951; Chief General Manager, 1956-62, retired. Director Belfast Banking Co. Ltd, 1960-70; Vice-Chairman Forward Trust Ltd, 1962-69; Ind. Member Cinematograph Films Council, 1962-69; Pres. Manchester & District Bankers' Inst., 1962-63. Pilot Officer, RAF, 1918. *Recreations:* music, golf. *Address:* 65A Egerton Gardens, Knightsbridge, SW3. *T:* 01-589 0254. *Clubs:* United University; Hurlingham; Royal and Ancient (St Andrews); Royal Mid-Surrey (Richmond).

**WOOD, Peter (Lawrence);** Theatrical and Television Director; *b* 8 Oct. 1928; *s* of Frank Wood and Lucy Eleanor (*née* Meeson). *Educ:* Taunton School; Downing College, Cambridge. Resident Director, Arts Theatre, 1956-57; Iceman Cometh (O'Neill), Arts, 1958; Birthday Party (Pinter), Lyric, Hammersmith, 1958; Maria Stuart (Schiller), Old Vic, 1958; As You Like It, Stratford, Canada, 1959; Winter's Tale, Stratford, England, 1960; The Devils (John Whiting), Stratford, Aldwych, 1961; Hamlet, Stratford, England, 1961; The Private Ear and The Public Eye (Peter Shaffer), Globe, 1962; The Devils, Aldwych, 1962; The Beggar's Opera, Aldwych, 1963; The Private Ear and The Public Eye, Morosco, New York, 1963; Co-Director, History Cycle, Stratford-on-Avon, 1964; The Master Builder (Ibsen), National Theatre, 1964; Carving a Statue (Graham Greene), Haymarket, 1964; Poor Richard (Jean Kerr), Helen Hayes Theatre, New York, 1964; Love for Love (Congreve), Moscow, and National Theatre, 1965; Incident at Vichy (Arthur Miller), Phœnix, 1966; The Prime of Miss Jean Brodie (Muriel Spark), Wyndham's, 1966; White Liars, and Black Comedy (Peter Shaffer), 1968; In Search of Gregory (film), 1968-69; Hamlet, NBC TV, 1970. *Recreations:* swimming, sailing, travelling. *Address:* 11 Warwick Avenue, W9.

**WOOD, Rt. Hon. Richard Frederick,** PC 1959; DL; MP (C) Bridlington Division of Yorkshire since 1950; Minister for Overseas Development, Foreign and Commonwealth Office, since Oct. 1970; *b* 5 Oct. 1920; 2nd surv. *s* of 1st Earl of Halifax, KG, PC, OM, GCSI, GCMG, GCIE, TD; *m* 1947, Diana, *d* of late Col E. O. Kellett, DSO, MP, and of Hon. Mrs W. J. McGowan; one *s* one *d*. *Educ:* Eton; New College, Oxford. Hon. Attaché, British Embassy, Rome, 1940; served War of 1939-45 as 2nd Lieutenant and Lieutenant, KRRC, 1941-43; retired, wounded, 1943; toured US Army hospitals, 1943-45; New College, Oxford, 1945-47; Parliamentary Private Secretary: to Minister of Pensions, 1951-53; to Minister of State, Board of Trade, 1953-54; to Minister of Agriculture and Fisheries, 1954-55; Joint Parliamentary Secretary, Ministry of Pensions and National Insurance, 1955-58; Parliamentary Secretary, Ministry of Labour, 1958-59; Minister of Power, October 1959-63, of Pensions and National Insurance, October 1963-64; Minister of Overseas Develt, June-Oct. 1970. DL, E Riding Yorks, 1967. Hon. LLD Sheffield Univ., 1962; Hon. Colonel: Queen's Royal Rifles, 1962; 4th (Volunteer) Bn Royal Green Jackets, 1967-. *Address:* Flat Top House, Bishop Wilton, York. *T:* Bishop Wilton 266; 14 Eaton Place, SW1.

**WOOD, Prof. Ronald Karslake Starr,** ARCS, BSc, DIC, PhD, FIBiol; Professor of Plant Pathology, Imperial College, University of London, since 1964; *b* 8 April 1919; *s* of Percival Thomas Evans Wood and Florence Dix Starr; *m* 1947, Marjorie Schofield; one *s* one *d*. *Educ:* Ferndale Grammar Sch.; Imperial College. Royal Scholar, 1937; Forbes Medal, 1941; Huxley Medal, 1950. Research Asst to Prof. W. Brown, 1941; Directorate of Aircraft Equipment, Min. of Aircraft Production, 1942; Lectr, Imperial Coll., 1947; Commonwealth Fund Fellow, 1950; Univ. Reader in Plant Pathology, 1955; Research Fellow, Connecticut Agric. Experiment Stn, 1957. Mem. Council, British Mycological Soc., 1948; Sec., Assoc. of Applied Biologists; Mem., Parly and Sci. Cttee; Mem., Biological Council, 1949; Consultant, Nat. Fedn of Fruit and Potato Trades, 1955; Mem. council, Inst. of Biology, 1956; Chm., Plant Pathology Cttee, British Mycological Soc.; Mem. Governing Body, Nat. Fruit and Cider Inst., Barnes Memorial Lectr, 1962; Sec., First Internat. Congress of Plant Pathology, 1965; Mem. governing Body, East Malling Research Stn, 1966; Pres., Internat. Soc. for Plant Pathology, 1968. *Publications:* Physiological Plant Pathology, 1967; numerous papers in Annals of Applied Biology, Annals of Botany, Phytopathology, Trans British Mycological Soc. *Recreation:* gardening. *Address:* Pyrford Woods, Pyrford, near Woking, Surrey. *T:* Byfleet 43827.

**WOOD, Russell Dillon,** VRD 1964; Lt-Comdr, RNR; Deputy Treasurer to the Queen since 1969; *b* 16 May 1922; *s* of William G. S. Wood, Whitstable, Kent, and Alice Wood; *m* 1948, Jean Violet Yelwa Davidson, *d* of Alan S. Davidson, Yalding, Kent; one *s* three *d*. *Educ:* King's Sch., Canterbury. Fleet Air Arm Pilot, 1940-46 (despatches twice). Qual. as Chartered Accountant, 1951; financial Management career with major public companies, 1951-68. *Recreations:* private flying, sailing. *Address:* 10 Westerfield Road, Ipswich, Suffolk. *T:* Ipswich 54874; Cleves Cottage, Westleton, Suffolk. *Clubs:* Naval; Royal Harwich Yacht; East Anglian Flying.

**WOOD, Sam,** MSc; Director of Statistics and Business Research, Post Office; *b* 10 Oct. 1911; *m* 1940, Lucy Greenhalgh Whittaker; two *d*. *Educ:* Glossop Grammar School, Derbyshire; University of Manchester. Gaskell Open Scholarship, Derbyshire Major Scholarship, 1929; BSc (1st cl. Hons) Maths; Bishop Harvey Goodwin Research Scholarship, 1932; MSc 1933. Civil Service: GPO, 1933-34; National Assistance Board, 1934-43; Min. of Aircraft Production, 1943-46; Treasury, 1946-50; GPO: Statistician, 1950; Chief Statistician, 1954; Director, 1965. *Publications:* articles in JL of Inst. of Statisticians, British Jl of Industrial Relations. *Address:* 69 Wembley Park Drive, Wembley, Middlesex. *T:* 01-902 1456.

**WOOD, Thomas Andrew Urquhart;** Sheriff-Substitute of Glasgow since 1961; *b* 26 July 1914; *s* of Victor Cartwright Wood, JP, and Barbara Forbes Urquhart; *m* 1942, Daphne

Eileen Wells Weston; two *s. Educ:* Loretto Sch.; Trinity Coll., Oxford; Edinburgh Univ. Captain, York and Lancaster Regt, War of 1939-45; served in India and Burma. Called to Scots Bar, 1947. Sheriff-Substitute of Lanarkshire at Hamilton, 1955-61. *Recreations:* music, golf, squash. *Address:* 22 Murrayfield Gardens, Edinburgh. *T:* 031-225 3028.

**WOOD, Wilfred William H. H.;** *see* Hill-Wood.

**WOOD, William Alan,** CB 1970; Second Crown Estate Commissioner since 1968; *b* 8 Dec. 1916; *m* 1943, Zoë, *d* of Rev. Dr D. Frazer-Hurst; two *s* two *d. Educ:* Dulwich Coll.; Corpus Christi Coll., Cambridge (Scholar). Ministry of Home Affairs, N. Ireland, 1939. Lieut, RNVR, 1942-46. Ministry of Town and Country Planning, 1946; Minister's Private Secretary, 1951; Principal Regional Officer (West Midlands), Ministry of Housing and Local Government, 1954; Asst Secretary, 1956; Under-Secretary, 1964-68. *Address:* 44 Acacia Road, St John's Wood, NW8. *T:* 01-722 5860.

**WOOD, William Walter,** FRIBA, CEng, FIStructE; MIA; *b* Arnold, Notts, 24 Nov. 1896; *e s* of Uriah and Georgina Maria Wood; *m* 1920, Frances Agnes Irene, *yr d* of Samuel Edwin and Emma Jane Varney, Nottingham; two *s. Educ:* Nottingham High Sch. Articled to late Frederick Ball, Nottingham, and trained at Nottingham University College and School of Art, Architectural Association School of Architecture, London, and in the atelier of the late Fernand Billerey in London; Asst Professor of Architecture and Senior Lecturer in Architectural Design in the Royal School of Engineering, Cairo, 1926-28; Head of the Dept of Architecture at Plymouth Central School of Arts and Crafts, 1928-32; Head of the Dept of Building at Plymouth and Devonport Technical Colleges, 1931-32; Principal, Mid-Essex Technical College and School of Art, Chelmsford, 1932-40; Principal, Delhi Polytechnic, Delhi, 1940-46. Member of the Schools Cttee of the Board of Architectural Education, RIBA, 1929-31; Founder-President, Association of Principals of Technical Institutions (India), 1941-46. Chairman, National Service Labour Tribunal, President Technical Training Selection Cttee and Regional Inspector of Technical Training, Delhi, Ajmer-Merwara and Rajputana, 1941-42; served in Egypt, Palestine, France, Belgium, and Germany, 1915-19; works: University of Rajasthan; Government House of South-West Africa; factories, mills, offices, showrooms, banks, hotels, airports, schools, hostels, flats, houses in England, Egypt, India, Southern Africa. Works exhibited at Royal Academy, RIBA, RSA, and Architectural Association, London, also Salon d'Automne, Paris. *Publications:* articles in technical periodicals, with translations in French and French Colonial architectural reviews; South African (previously English) Correspondent of L'Architecture d'Aujourd'hui. *Recreations:* bowls, photography, and travel. *Address:* 7 Karee Street, Greenhills, Randfontein, Transvaal, South Africa.

**WOODALL,** family name of **Baron Uvedale of North End.**

**WOODALL, Lieut-General Sir John (Dane),** KCMG 1959; KBE 1953 (OBE 1942; MBE 1919); CB 1947; MC 1917; Governor and Commander-in-Chief, Bermuda, 1955-59; *b* 19 April 1897; *s* of late Colonel F. Woodall, CMG; *m* 1st, 1920, Helen, *o d* of late Sir Adam Block, KCMG; one *d*; 2nd, 1935, Marion, CStJ, *d* of late Alfred Aitkin Thom; one *s* two *d. Educ:* St Columba's; RMA, Woolwich; Staff Colleges, Camberley and RAF. Served European War, 1914-18, Captain, Royal Artillery (despatches, MBE, MC); DAAG Turkey, 1922-24; Instructor in Gunnery; Brigade Major; commanded battery RA; Instructor RAF Staff college; commanded regt RA; GSO1; Brigadier, General Staff, 1940; DDSD, War Office; Director Man Power, War Office; served War of 1939-46 (despatches, CB, OBE); Vice-Adjutant-General to the Forces, 1949-52; GOC, N. Ireland, 1952-55; retired, 1955. Colonel Comdt, RA, 1954-62. KStJ 1958. *Recreations:* lawn tennis and squash. *Address:* Whitewell Lodge, near Whitchurch, Shropshire. *Club:* Army and Navy.

**WOODALL, Mary,** CBE 1959; PhD; DLitt; FSA; FMA; London Adviser to Felton Bequest, Melbourne, since 1965; Trustee of the National Gallery, since 1969; *b* 6 March 1901. *Educ:* Cheltenham Ladies' Coll.; Somerville Coll., Oxford. Voluntary, British Museum Dept of Prints and Drawings. WVS Regional Administrator, 1938-42; Temp. Principal, Ministry of Health and Ministry of Supply, 1942-45; Keeper, Dept of Art, 1945-56, Director, 1956-64, City Museum and Art Gallery, Birmingham; Member Council Industrial Design, 1966-. Fellow of University College, London, 1958. *Publications:* Gainsborough's Landscape Drawings, 1939; Thomas Gainsborough, 1949; The Letters of Thomas Gainsborough, 1962. *Recreations:* travelling, painting. *Address:* Red House, Clifton Hampden, Abingdon-on-Thames, Berks. *Club:* University Women's.

**WOODARD, Canon Alfred Lambert;** Hon. Canon of Ely since 1933; *b* 27 April 1880; *s* of late Canon L. Woodard and Emily, *d* of late Henry Perkins of Thriplow Place, Cambs; *g s* of Canon Nathanael Woodard, Founder of Schools; *m* 1905, Fanny Gertrude (*d* 1947), *d* of late Rev. Cyril FitzRoy Wilson; five *s* three *d. Educ:* Lancing; Trinity Coll., Cambridge; Classical Tripos. Curate of Sulhamstead, Reading, 1903-05; St James, Bury St Edmunds, 1905-10; Rector of West Stow with Wordwell; Domestic Chaplain to 5th Earl Cadogan, and Chaplain to Culford Parish, 1910-15; Hon. Chaplain to 6th Earl Cadogan, 1915-34; Rector of St Mary Stoke, Ipswich, 1915-24; Rural Dean of Ipswich, 1921-24; Hon. Canon St Edmundsbury and Ipswich, 1922-24; Vicar of Sutton, Cambs, 1924-41; Proctor in Convocation, 1924 and 1929-50; Founder and Convener Teaching Church Group, 1925; Member of Archbishop's Commission on Religious Education, 1926-29; Delegate, Society for the Propagation of the Gospel to the Episcopal Synod of the West Indies; Convener Joint Conference of Anglicans and Evangelical Free Churchmen, 1937-45; Chairman, Standing Cttee Society for the Propagation of the Gospel, 1936-38; Warden of Central Society of Sacred Study, Diocese of Ely, 1938-52; Treasurer of the Society, 1939-50; Vice-Chairman National Society, 1940-44; Envoy for Central Council of the Church of England for Religious Education, 1941-50; Vicar of St Andrew the Great, Cambridge, 1950-58. Fellow Corporation of SS Mary and Nicolas (Woodard Schools); Chairman of Council for East Anglia. *Publications:* St John in the Isle of Patmos; The Teaching Church (Editor); The Teaching Church Review (Editor); Educational Review in Official Year Book of the Church of England, 1928-44. *Recreations:* cricket, rugger, athletics. *Address:* 6 Luard Road, Cambridge. *T:* 48287. *Club:* Athenæum.

**WOODBINE PARISH, David Elmer;** *see* Parish.

**WOODBURN, Rt. Hon. Arthur,** PC 1947; DLitt; *b* Edinburgh, 25 Oct. 1890; *s* of Matthew Woodburn (Brassfounder) and Janet Brown Woodburn; *m* 1919, Barbara Halliday. *Educ:* Bruntsfield and Boroughmuir Public Schools, Edinburgh; Heriot-Watt Coll., Edinburgh. For 25 years in Engineering and Ironfounding Administration, specialised in languages and costing; Hon. Secretary, Edinburgh Labour College till 1932; Secretary, Scottish Labour College, till 1939; President National Council of Labour Colleges, 1937-; Lectured in History, Economics and Finance in Labour College, 1919 onwards; gave evidence before MacMillan Cttee on Finance and Industry, 1929; contested (Lab) S Edinburgh, 1929, Leith, 1931; Scottish Secretary, Labour Party, 1932-39; MP (Lab) Clackmannan and East Stirling, 1939-70; Parliamentary Private Secretary to Rt Hon. Thomas Johnston, Secretary of State for Scotland, 1941-45; Parliamentary Secretary, Ministry of Supply, 1945-47; Secretary of State for Scotland, 1947-50. Member of Select Cttee on National Expenditure and Chairman Sub-Committee on Finance and Establishments, 1939-45; Administrative Cttee and Front Bench of Parliamentary Labour Party, 1943-45; Member of Speaker's Conference on Electoral Reform, 1944; led first Inter-Parliamentary Union Delegn to West German Bundestag at Bonn; Member: Select Cttee on Clergy Disqualification, 1952-53; Select Cttee on Delegated Legislation, 1952-53; Select Cttee on House of Commons Procedure, 1956-68; Historic Buildings Council for Scotland. Trustee, Scottish National Library, 1962. Led British Inter-Parliamentary Union Delegations to Uruguay, 1957, to Spain, 1960 and House of Commons Delegn to Uganda, 1964, to Kenya, 1966; has visited numerous countries in Europe and S America. *Publications:* Banks and the Workers, 1924; Mystery of Money, 1929; Outline of Finance, 1930 (4 Editions). *Recreation:* golf. *Address:* 83 Orchard Road, Edinburgh. *T:* 031-332 1961.

**WOODCOCK, Eric Charles,** MA; Professor of Latin in the University of Durham (late Durham Colleges), 1948-66; now Professor Emeritus; *b* 20 May 1904; *s* of Charles T. Woodcock; *m* 1933, Ruth Mary Ball; two *s*. *Educ:* King Edward's Sch., Birmingham; St John's Coll., Cambridge. First class in both parts of Classical Tripos, Cambridge (Part I, 1925; Part II, 1927); Instructor in Department of Ancient Languages, Harvard, 1927-28; Asst Lecturer in Classics, University of Reading, 1928-30; Asst Lecturer in Classics, University of Manchester, 1930-32; Lecturer in Latin, 1932-47; Senior Lecturer in Latin, 1947-48. *Publications:* Tacitus, Annals XIV (edited with Introduction and notes), 1939; A New Latin Syntax, 1959; various articles and reviews in Harvard Studies in Classical Philology, in Classical Review and in Greece and Rome. *Recreation:* reading. *Address:* 25 Dingle Road, Boscombe, Bournemouth, Hants.

**WOODCOCK, Rt. Hon. George,** PC 1967; CBE 1953; Chairman, Commission on Industrial Relations, since 1969; *b* 20 Oct. 1904; 2nd *s* of Peter Woodcock, Bamber Bridge, Lancashire; *m* 1933, Laura M. McKernan; one *s* one *d*. *Educ:* Brownedge Elementary; Ruskin College and New Coll., Oxford. Cotton Weaver, 1916-27; 1st Class Hons Philos. and Polit. Economy, Oxford, 1933; Jessie Theresa Rowden Senior Scholarship, New Coll., 1933; Civil Servant, 1934-36; Secretary to TUC Research and Economic Dept, 1936-47; Assistant General Secretary, TUC, 1947-60, General Secretary, 1960-69. Member Royal Commn: on Taxation of Profits and Income, 1950; on Trade Unions and Employers' Assocs, 1965-68; Member British Guiana Constitutional Commission, 1954; Member Committee on the Working of the Monetary System, 1957; Vice-Chairman, National Savings Cttee; Member National Economic Development Council. Hon. Fellow, New Coll., Oxford, 1963; Hon. Fellow, LSE, 1964. Hon. LLD: Sussex, 1963; Manchester, 1968; Lancaster, 1970; London, 1970; Hon. DCL: Oxford Univ., 1964; Kent Univ., 1968; Hon. DSc, University of Aston in Birmingham, 1967. *Address:* Commission on Industrial Relations, GKN House, 22 Kingsway, WC2. *T:* 01-242 6828.

**WOODD WALKER, Geoffrey Basil,** FRCS; retired as a Consultant Surgeon (West London Hospital, 1930-65); *b* 9 June 1900; *s* of Basil Woodd Walker, MD, and Margaret Jane Routledge; *m* 1932, Ulla Troili; two *s*. *Educ:* Rugby Sch.; King's Coll., Cambridge; St Mary's Hospital. MA Cambridge; MB, BCh; MRCS, LRCP London; FRCS 1928. *Recreation:* zoology (FZS). *Address:* 6 Dawson Place, W2. *Club:* Athenæum.

**WOODFIELD, Philip John,** CBE 1963; Assistant Under-Secretary of State, Home Office, since 1967; *b* 30 Aug. 1923; *s* of Ralph Woodfield; *m* 1958, Diana Margaret, *d* of Sydney Herington; three *d*. *Educ:* Alleyn's Sch., Dulwich; King's Coll., London. Served War of 1939-45: Royal Artillery, 1942-47 (captain). Entered Home Office, 1950; Asst Private Secretary to Home Secretary, 1952; Federal Government of Nigeria, 1955-57; Home Office, 1957-60; Private Secretary to the Prime Minister, 1961-65; Assistant Secretary, Home Office, 1965-67. Secretary to Commonwealth Immigration Mission, 1965; Secretary to Lord Mountbatten's inquiry into prison security, Nov.-Dec. 1966. *Recreation:* music. *Address:* 102 Willifield Way, NW11. *T:* 01-458 4655. *Clubs:* Garrick, Beefsteak.

**WOODFIELD, Ven. Samuel Percy,** MA; Rector of Waterval Boven (African and European) since 1964 (Priest-in-charge, Waterval Boven Missions, from 1959); Archdeacon of Barberton, 1960-63, Archdeacon Emeritus from 1964; Canon S Alban's Cathedral, Pretoria, South Africa, 1932-64; Hon. Canon, 1964; *b* 19 April 1889; *s* of Samuel Robinson Woodfield and Emma Utting. *Educ:* Great Yarmouth Grammar Sch.; Selwyn Coll., Cambridge. Asst Priest, St Mary's, Hitchin, 1915-19; Headmaster, Norton Sch., Letchworth, 1917-19; Asst Priest, Sawbridgeworth, 1919-21; Vice-Principal, Diocesan Training Coll., Pietersburg, N Transvaal, 1922-24, Principal, 1924-38, 1954-57; Priest-in-Charge, Pietersburg West Native Mission, 1936-38; Priest-in-charge, Pretoria Native Mission, 1938-53, and Coloured Mission, 1943-53; Archdeacon of Pretoria (City) Native Mission, 1945-53; Archdeacon of W Transvaal, 1953-60; Archdeacon of E Transvaal, 1958-60. Exam. Chaplain to Bishop of Pretoria, 1922-50; Member: Advisory Board for Native Education in the Transvaal, 1924-37, 1940-43, 1946-50; Chaplain Westfort Leper Inst., 1938-53; Div. Pathfinder Scout Commissioner for the Transvaal, 1931-50; Deputy Chief Scouts' African Commissioner for S Africa, 1943-53; Chief Scout's Commissioner for African Scouts, S Africa, 1953-61; Emeritus Comr, 1961. King George V Jubilee Medal; Coronation Medals, 1937, 1953. *Address:* The Mission House, PO Box 34, Waterval Boven, E Transvaal, South Africa. *T:* 221.

**WOODFORD, Brigadier Edward Cecil James,** CBE 1946; DSO 1943; *b* 1901; *s* of late Major Edward Francis Woodford, York and Lancaster Regt; *m* 1st, 1928, Margaret, *d* of

Colonel Arthur Claude Mardon, DSO, Framfield, Sussex; one *d*; *m* 2nd, 1932, Eleanor Waterhouse, *d* of H. M. Brandon, Kingston, Jamaica; one *d*; *m* 3rd, 1949, Joanne Eileen, *d* of Peter Charles Mayer, Washington, DC, USA; one *s* two *d*. *Educ:* Bedford Sch.; RMC Sandhurst. 2nd Lieut, York and Lancaster Regt, 1920. Served War of 1939-45, N. Africa, Iraq, Persia, Sicily, Italy, Burma, French Indo-China; Lieut-Colonel, 1942, Brigadier, 1945. Commander, Lubbecke District, BAOR, 1952-55, retired 1955. *Address:* c/o Ministry of Defence, Whitehall, SW1. *Club:* Royal Fowey Yacht.

**WOODFORD, James,** OBE 1953; RA 1945; FRBS; Sculptor; *b* 25 Sept. 1893; *m* 1929, Rose Harrison; one *s*. *Educ:* Nottingham School of Art; Royal College of Art. Served with 11th Sherwood Foresters, France and Italy, 1915-18 (despatches). Member of Royal Mint Advisory Cttee on Seals and Medals. Camouflage Officer to Air Ministry, 1941-44. *Principal Works:* Bronze Doors, RIBA; 3 Main Double Leaf Bronze Doors, Norwich City Hall; Carved Stone Figures and Panels, Huddersfield New Library and Art Gallery; sculpture on Ministry of Agriculture and Fisheries, Whitehall Place; Bronze Statue Robin Hood, Groups and Reliefs, Robin Hood Lawn, Nottingham; Queen's Beasts, Coronation Annexe, Westminster Abbey; 13-ft. Statue, Memorial to Rt Hon. D. S. Senanayake, First Prime Minister of Ceylon; Sculpture for Imperial War Graves Commission British Cemeteries in Italy. Carved Groups, Thor and Marlborough, RN Engineering Coll., Manadon; 13-ft. Reliefs, etc. for Lloyd's New Building; Carved Doors in wood, etc., Main Hall, Carpenters' Company; Carved Panel and Keystones, Coutts Bank, Lombard Street; Memorial Bust, Canon Wylie Blue, May Street Church, Belfast; BMA War Memorial, Tavistock Place (RBS Medal, best work of year, 1955); 17 ft. Royal Arms in aluminium, New Delhi, UK Diplomatic Compound Offices; 6-ft. Memorial Bronze Figure, Captain Cipriani, Port-of-Spain. New design, Royal Coat of Arms, 1962. Clytie Fountain, Assembly Rooms, Norwich; Memorial Bust on granite plinth to Coxswain Henry Blogg, Cromer; Ebenezer Howard Memorial, Welwyn Garden City; Lion and Unicorn Statues, British Embassy, Teheran. Various Coats of Arms in faience or wood. *Recreation:* billiards. *Address:* 19 St Peter's Square, W6. *T:* 01-748 5040. *Club:* Arts.

**WOODGATE, Joan Mary,** CBE 1964; RRC 1959; Matron-in-Chief, Queen Alexandra's RN Nursing Service, 1962-66, retired; *b* 30 Aug. 1912; *d* of Sir Alfred Woodgate, CBE, and Louisa Alice (*née* Digby). *Educ:* Surbiton High Sch., Surrey. Trained at St George's Hospital, 1932-36, Sister, 1937-38; Queen Charlotte's Hospital, 1936. Joined QARNNS, 1938; served Middle East and Far East; HM Hospital Ship, Empire Clyde, 1945-47; HM Hospital Ship, Maine, 1953-54; Principal Matron: RNH Haslar, 1959-61; RNH Malta, 1961-62. OStJ 1959; QHNS, 1962-64. Member Commonwealth War Graves Commn, 1966-. *Recreations:* gardening, country pursuits. *Address:* Tiptoe, near Lymington, Hants. *Clubs:* English-Speaking Union, Service Women's.

**WOODGER, Professor Joseph Henry;** Emeritus Professor of Biology, University of London; *b* 2 May 1894; *s* of N. L. Woodger, Great Yarmouth, Norfolk; *m* 1921, Doris Eden, *d* of late Major-General C. R. Buckle, CB, CMG, DSO; three *s* one *d*. *Educ:* Felsted Sch.; University College, London. Graduated in Zoology, 1914. 2nd Lieut, Norfolk Regt, 1915; served European War, 2nd Bn Norfolk Regt, in Mesopotamia, 1916-18. Protozoologist in Central Lab. Amara, 1918-19; Derby Scholar, UCL, 1919; Assistant in Zoology Department, University College, London, 1919-22; Reader in Biology, 1922; Professor of Biology, 1947, University of London (Middlesex Hosp. Med. Sch.); retired 1959. Tarner Lecturer, Trinity Coll., Cambridge, 1949-50. *Publications:* Elementary Morphology and Physiology, 1924; Biological Principles, 1929; The Axiomatic Method in Biology, 1937; The Technique of Theory Construction, 1939; Biology and Language, 1952; Physics, Psychology and Medicine, 1956. Papers in Quart. Journal Micro. Sci.; Proc. Arist. Soc., Phil. Trans. Royal Society; Quart. Review Biology, British Journal Phil. Sci., etc. *Recreations:* reading the Bible and Shakespeare; viticulture. *Address:* Tanhurst, Epsom Downs, Surrey. *T:* Ashtead (Surrey) 76469.

**WOODHAM, Professor Ronald Ernest;** Professor of Music, Reading University, since 1951; *b* 8 Feb. 1912; *s* of Ernest Victor Woodham, Beckenham, Kent; *m* 1949, Kathleen Isabel, *e d* of P. J. Malone; three *s*. *Educ:* Sherborne Sch.; Royal College of Music, London; Christ Church, Oxford. BA, DMus; FRCO, ARCM. Assistant Director of Music, Bradfield Coll., 1936. Served in RASC, in Middle East and Italy, 1939-45 (despatches). Acting Director of Music, Bradfield Coll., 1946; Director of Music, Sherborne Sch., 1946; Cramb Lecturer in Music, Glasgow Univ., 1947-51. *Address:* 128 Westwood Road, Tilehurst, Reading. *T:* 27847.

**WOODHAM-SMITH, Cecil,** CBE 1960; Historian; *d* of Colonel James FitzGerald, late Berar Commn, and Blanche Elizabeth FitzGerald (*née* Philipps); *m* 1928, George Ivon Woodham-Smith, Solicitor (*d* 1968); one *s* one *d*. *Educ:* St Hilda's Coll., Oxford. Until marriage wrote articles and short stories; started research into life of Florence Nightingale, 1941. A. C. Benson Medal for contrib. to literature, 1969. Hon. DLitt NUI, 1964; Hon. LLD St Andrews, 1965; Hon. Fellow, St Hilda's Coll., Oxford, 1967. *Publications:* Florence Nightingale (London) 1950 (awarded James Tait Black Memorial Prize, 1950), (New York) 1951; Lonely Crusader, (New York) 1951; Lady in Chief, (London) 1953; The Reason Why, (London) 1953, (New York) 1954; The Great Hunger, (London), 1962, (New York), 1963. *Address:* 44 Mount Street, W1. *T:* 01-499 7986.

**WOODHAMS, Ven. Brian Watson;** Archdeacon of Newark since 1965; Hon. Canon of Southwell Minster since 1960; Vicar of Farndon and Rector of Thorpe-by-Newark, diocese of Southwell, since 1965; Priest in Charge, Staunton with Flawborough and Kilvington, since 1969; *b* 16 Jan. 1911; *s* of Herbert and Florence Osmond Woodhams; *m* 1941, Vera Charlotte White; one *s*. *Educ:* Dover Coll.; Oak Hill Theological Coll.; St John's Coll., University of Durham. LTh 1934, BA 1936, Durham. Deacon, 1936; Priest, 1937. Curate: St Mary Magdalene, Holloway, 1936-39; St James-the-Less, Bethnal Green, 1939-41; Christ Church, New Malden, i/c of St John, New Malden, 1941-43; Vicar: St Mark, Poplar, 1943-45; St James-the-Less, Bethnal Green, 1945-50; St Jude's, Mapperley, Nottingham, 1950-65. Proctor in York Convocation, 1955-65. Chairman, Southwell Diocesan Board of Women's Work, 1966-. *Recreations:* children's and refugee work (Chairman, Nottingham Branch Save the Children Fund); interested in sport (local FA football referee). *Address:* St Peter's Vicarage, Farndon, Newark, Notts. *T:* Newark 2269.

**WOODHEAD, Sir John Ackroyd,** GCIE, *cr* 1946 (CIE 1930); KCSI, *cr* 1934; *b* 19 June 1881; *m* 1908; one *s* one *d. Educ:* Bradford Grammar Sch.; Clare Coll., Cambridge, BA. Entered Indian Civil Service, 1904; posted to Bengal, 1904; transferred to Eastern Bengal and Assam, 1905; Magistrate and Collector, 1909; transferred to Bengal, 1912; District and Sessions Judge, 1917; Special Land Acquisition Collector, 1918; Chairman, Calcutta Improvement Trust, 1924; Secretary, Government of Bengal, Finance Department, 1924; Joint-Secretary, Commerce Department, Government of India, 1927; Secretary, Commerce Department, Government of India, 1929; Temporary Member, Council of the Governor-General of India, 1931; Finance Member, Government of Bengal, 1932-37; Acting Governor of Bengal, Aug.-Dec. 1934; Chairman Palestine Partition Commission, 1938; Governor of Bengal, June-Nov. 1939; Adviser to Secretary of State for India, 1939-44; Chairman Famine Enquiry Commission, Aug. 1944; President, India, Pakistan and Burma Association, 1948-62. *Address:* Chevremont, Hockering Road, Woking, Surrey.

**WOODHOUSE,** family name of **Baron Terrington.**

**WOODHOUSE, Ven. Andrew Henry,** DSC 1945; MA; Archdeacon of Ludlow since 1970; *b* 30 Jan. 1923; *s* of H. A. Woodhouse, Dental Surgeon, Hanover Square, W1, and Woking, Surrey, and Mrs P. Woodhouse; unmarried. *Educ:* Lancing Coll.; The Queen's Coll., Oxford. MA 1949. Served War, RNVR, 1942-46 (Lieut). Oxford, 1941-42 and 1946-47; Lincoln Theological Coll., 1948-50. Deacon, 1950; Priest, 1951; Curate of All Saints, Poplar, 1950-56; Vicar of St Martin, West Drayton, 1956-70; Rural Dean of Hillingdon, 1967-70. *Recreations:* photography, walking. *Address:* Wistanstow Rectory, Craven Arms, Shropshire. *T:* Craven Arms 3244. *Club:* Naval.

**WOODHOUSE, Admiral (retired) Sir Charles (Henry Lawrence),** KCB, *cr* 1949 (CB 1940); *b* 9 July 1893; *s* of Rev. A. P. Woodhouse and F. D. Woodhouse; *m* 1928, Barbara Margaret, *d* of Dr H. M. Brownfield, Petersfield; three *d. Educ:* RN Colleges, Osborne and Dartmouth. Commanded HMS Ajax in Battle of the River Plate 1939 (CB); C-in-C East Indies Station, 1948-50; retired, 1950; Admiral, retired list, 1952. *Address:* Flat 2, 98 Westhall Road, Warlingham, Surrey.

**WOODHOUSE, Hon. (Christopher) Montague,** DSO 1943; OBE 1944; MA (Oxon); MP (C) Oxford, 1959-66 and since 1970; *b* 11 May 1917; 2nd *s* of 3rd Baron Terrington, KBE; *b* and *heir-pres.* to 4th Baron Terrington, *qv*; *m* 1945, Lady Davina, *d* of 2nd Earl of Lytton, KG, PC, GCSI, GCIE, and *widow* of 5th Earl of Erne; two *s* one *d. Educ:* Winchester; New Coll., Oxford (Craven and Hertford Schols, Galsford Prizeman). First Cl. Hon. Mods, 1937; First Class Lit Hum, 1939; MA 1947; Lord Justice Holker Schol. Gray's Inn, 1939; enlisted RA, 1939, commissioned 1940; Colonel, Aug. 1943, in command of Allied Military Mission to Greek Guerillas in German-occupied Greece (despatches twice, DSO, OBE, Officer of Legion of Merit (USA), Commander of Order of the Phoenix, with Swords (Greece)). Served in HM Embassy, Athens, 1945, Tehran, 1951; Secretary-General, Allied Mission for Observing Greek Elections, 1946; worked in industry 1946-48; Asst Secretary, Nuffield Foundation, 1948-50; Foreign Office, 1952; Director-General, Royal Institute of International Affairs and Dir. of Studies, 1955-59; Parliamentary Secretary, Ministry of Aviation, 1961-62; Joint Under-Secretary of State, Home Office, July 1962-Oct. 1964. Dir Educn and Training, CBI, 1966-70. President, Classical Assoc., 1968. Fellow of Trinity Hall, Cambridge, 1950; FRSL, 1951; Visiting Fellow, Nuffield Coll., Oxford, 1956. *Publications:* Apple of Discord, 1948; One Omen, 1950; Dostoievsky, 1951; The Greek War of Independence, 1952; Britain and the Middle East, 1959; British Foreign Policy since the Second World War, 1961; Rhodes (with late J. G. Lockhart), 1963; The New Concert of Nations, 1964; The Battle of Navarino, 1965; Post-War Britain, 1966; The Story of Modern Greece, 1968; The Philhellenes, 1969; numerous articles, translations, broadcasts. *Address:* Bois Mill, Latimer, Bucks. *T:* Little Chalfont 2388.

**WOODHOUSE, Rear-Admiral Hector Roy Mackenzie,** CB 1941; OBE 1919; RN, retired; *b* 15 Feb. 1889; *s* of late Alfred Woodhouse; *m* 1920, Norah Constance Mackenzie (*d* 1967); no *c. Educ:* Bedford Sch. Entered Royal Navy, 1906; retired, 1944; Rear-Admiral, retired, 1946. Chairman, South-Eastern Division of National Coal Board, 1946-55. *Address:* 6 Pembroke Chambers, Penny Street, Portsmouth, Hants. *T:* 25322. *Club:* United Service.

**WOODHOUSE, James Stephen;** Headmaster of Rugby School since 1967; *b* 21 May 1933; *s* of late Rt Rev. J. W. Woodhouse, sometime Bishop of Thetford, and late Mrs K. M. Woodhouse; *m* 1957, Sarah, *d* of Major Hubert Blount, Cley, Norfolk; three *s* one *d. Educ:* St Edward's Sch.; St Catharine's Coll., Cambridge. BA (English) Cantab, 1957; MA 1961. 2nd Lieut, 14th Field Regt RA (Hong Kong), 1953. Asst Master, Westminster Sch., 1957; Under Master and Master of the Queen's Scholars, 1963. *Recreations:* sailing, ski-ing. *Address:* School House, Rugby, Warwickshire.

**WOODHOUSE, Hon. Montague;** *see* Woodhouse, Hon. C. M.

**WOODHOUSE, Ven. Samuel Mostyn Forbes;** Archdeacon of London and Canon Residentiary of St Paul's since 1967; *b* 28 April 1912; *s* of Rev. Major James D. F. Woodhouse, DSO, and Elsie Noel Woodhouse, Water, Manaton, Devon; *m* 1939, Patricia Daniel; two *s* one *d. Educ:* Shrewsbury; Christ Church, Oxford; Wells Theological Coll. BA 1934; MA 1942. Deacon, 1936, Priest, 1937, Diocese of Blackburn; Curate, Lancaster Priory, 1936-39. Chaplain to the Forces (Army), 1939-45 (despatches thrice). Vicar, Holy Trinity, South Shore, Blackpool, 1945-49; Vicar of Leominster, 1949-57; Rural Dean of Leominster, 1956-57; Rector of Bristol City Parish Church (St Stephen's), 1957-67. *Recreations:* golf, fishing, walking, painting, architecture. *Address:* 9 Amen Court, EC4. *T:* 01-248 3312. *Clubs:* Army and Navy; Leander; Vincent's (Oxford).

**WOODIFIELD, Rear-Admiral Anthony,** CB 1965; CBE 1961; MVO 1953; *b* 5 Aug. 1912; *s* of late Colonel A. H. Woodifield, CB, CMG, OBE, St Leonards-on-Sea, Sussex; *m* 1947, Elizabeth, *d* of late E. J. Stevens, Sutton, Surrey; two *s. Educ:* Cheltenham College. Joined RN, 1929. Served 1939-45 in Home Fleet and on East Indies Station. On Staff of Commander-in-Chief, Portsmouth and for Coronation Naval Review, 1951-53; Secretary to Flag Officer, Second-in-Command, Mediterranean, 1954-55; Secretary to Third

Sea Lord and Controller of the Navy, 1956-61; Comdg Officer, HMS Phœnicia, 1961-63; Director General of Naval Personal Services and Officer Appointments, 1964-66. Comdr, 1947; Captain, 1955; Rear-Admiral, 1963; retired list, 1966. *Address:* Arford House, Headley, Hants. *T:* Headley Down 3367. *Club:* Army and Navy.

**WOODING, Rt. Hon. Sir Hugh (Olliviere Beresford),** TC 1969; PC 1967; Kt 1963; CBE 1957; Chief Justice, Trinidad and Tobago, 1962-68; *b* 14 Jan. 1904; *s* of late Iddo A. Reginald Wooding and late Mrs Wooding, Port of Spain, Trinidad; *m* 1928, Anne Marie, *d* of late Charles Louis P. R. Coussey, Gold Coast (now Ghana); two *s* two *d. Educ:* Queen's Royal Coll., Trinidad; Middle Temple, London. KC 1948; Hon. Master of Bench, Inner Temple, 1969. Chairman: Trinidad and Tobago Board of Furness Withy & Co., 1969-; Furness-Smiths Dock (Trinidad), 1969-; Furness and Gordon, 1969-; Continental Telephone Holding Co., 1969-; Continental Communications (Caribbean) Ltd, 1969-. Mayor of Port of Spain, 1943-44. Chm., Commn to consider future of Anguilla, 1969. Hon. LLD University of West Indies, 1967. *Recreation:* racing. *Address:* 2 Champs Elysées, Maraval, Trinidad. *T:* 22477. *Clubs:* West Indian (London); Union, Maple and Arima Race (Trinidad); Jamaica (Jamaica).

**WOODLEY, Sir (Frederick George) Richard,** Kt 1950; *m* 1929, Betsy Maud Hind (*d* 1961); *m* 1961, Joyce Mary Forrest, *d* of late S. O. C. Forrest. Alderman, Nairobi Municipal Council, 1947-63 (Councillor, 1944); County Councillor and Rural Dist Councillor, 1955-63; Charter Mayor and three times (1947-50) Mayor of the City of Nairobi; President of Nairobi Chamber of Commerce, 1949; Chairman, Hotel Control Authority for Kenya, 1945-53; Broadcaster for Kenya Information Office, 1942-46; Past President, Kenya Cultural Centre and of The Kenya National Theatre. Cordwainer and Citizen of London. *Address:* The Glebe House, Checkendon, Reading, Berks. *T:* Checkendon 685. *Clubs:* Royal Commonwealth Society; Surrey County Cricket; Nairobi (Nairobi).

**WOODLEY, Sir Richard;** *see* Woodley, Sir (F. G.) R.

**WOODLOCK, Jack Terence;** Assistant Under-Secretary of State, Department of Health and Social Security, since 1969; *b* 10 July 1919; *s* of late James Patrick and Florence Woodlock; *m* 1941, Joan Mary Taylor; three *s* one *d. Educ:* Bromley Grammar School. Entered Civil Service, 1936; served in Royal Artillery, 1939-45; Ministry of Health, 1945; Asst Principal 1946; Principal 1950; Principal Private Sec. to Minister, 1958-59; Asst Sec. 1959. *Recreations:* gardening, camping. *Address:* 14 Blenheim Road, Bromley, Kent. *T:* 01-467 2712.

**WOODMAN, John,** OBE 1928; BA (Oxon); retired; *b* Newcastle upon Tyne, 21 July 1888; *s* of William Hunter Woodman and Mary Ann Woodman (*née* Millican); *m* 1930, Magdeleine Louise Gardoni; no *c. Educ:* Royal Grammar Sch., Newcastle upon Tyne; Brasenose Coll., Oxford. Hulme Scholar, Brasenose Coll., Oxford; 2nd Class Hon. Mods and Lit. Hum.; Barrister, Inner Temple, 1914. Served as Lieut, ASC, attached S and T Corps, India, 1916-20; Afghan War, 1919-20. Judge in Iraq, 1920-28; International lawyer, Paris, 1929-40; War Damage Insurance Dept, Board of Trade, 1941-43; Chief Justice, Seychelles, 1943-47; Acting Governor, Seychelles, 1946; at times Acting Chief Justice, N Rhodesia; Member, Rhodesia and Nyasaland Court of Appeal, 1947-53; Puisne Judge, Northern Rhodesia, 1947-53; retired from Colonial Legal Service, Nov. 1953. *Recreation:* languages. *Address:* 17 rue de Téhéran, Paris 8e, France.

**WOODNUTT, Mark, (Harold Frederick Martin);** MP (C) Isle of Wight since 1959; Export Director, Charles Churchill Ltd; Chartered Secretary; *b* 23 Nov. 1918; *s* of Harold Frederick Woodnutt, Cowes, IoW; *m* 1945, Gwynneth Alice Lovely; two *s* two *d. Educ:* Isleworth Grammar Sch. Militiaman, 1939; commissioned Royal Artillery, Dec. 1939. Served War of 1939-45: Norway, Egypt, Crete, Germany (despatches, POW). Chartered Secretary, 1945. Isle of Wight County Council: elected 1952; Alderman, 1957; Chairman Highways, 1953-55; Chairman Finance, 1955-61. Chairman IOW Conservative Assoc., 1954-59; Chairman, Bembridge Lifeboat, 1960-. *Address:* Portland House, Bembridge, IOW. *T:* Bembridge 2414; 15 Greycoat Place, SW1. *Clubs:* Constitutional; Bembridge Sailing.

**WOODROFFE, Rt. Rev. George Cuthbert Manning;** *see* Windward Islands, Bishop of.

**WOODROOFE, Ernest George,** PhD, FInstP, MIChemE; Chairman, Unilever Ltd, since 1970 (Vice-Chairman, 1961-70); *b* 6 Jan. 1912; *s* of late Ernest George Woodroofe and Ada (*née* Dickinson); *m* 1st, 1938, Margaret Downes (*d* 1961); one *d*; 2nd, 1962, Enid Grace Hutchinson Arnold. *Educ:* Cockburn High Sch.; Leeds Univ. Staff of Loders & Nucoline Ltd, 1935-44; Staff of British Oil & Cake Mills Ltd, 1944-50; Member of Oil Mills Executive of Unilever Ltd, 1951-55; Director of British Oil & Cake Mills Ltd, 1951-55; Head of Research Division of Unilever Ltd, 1955-61; Director: United Africa Co. Ltd, 1961-63; Unilever Ltd, 1956-; Unilever NV, 1956-. President, International Society for Fat Research, 1962. Member Cttee of Enquiry into the Organisation of Civil Science, 1962-63; A Vice-Pres., Soc. of Chemical Industry, 1963-66; Member: Tropical Products Inst. Cttee, 1964-69; Council for Nat. Academic Awards, 1964-67; Cttee of Award of the Commonwealth Fund, 1965-70; Royal Commn for the Exhbn of 1851, 1968-. Trustee, Leverhulme Trust; Chairman, CBI Research Cttee, 1966-69. Hon. ACT, Liverpool, 1963; Hon. Fellow, University of Manchester Inst. of Science and Technology, 1968; Hon. LLD Leeds, 1968. *Recreations:* shooting, fishing, cinematography. *Address:* The Crest, Berry Lane, Worplesdon, Surrey. *T:* Worplesdon 2666. *Club:* Royal Automobile.

**WOODROW, Maj.-Gen. Albert John,** MBE 1949; General Officer Commanding Wales since 1970; *b* 3 June 1919; *s* of Captain F. H. Woodrow, Portsmouth; *m* 1944, Elizabeth, *d* of late Major Sir John Theodore Prestige, Bourne Park, Bishopsbourne, Kent; two *s* one *d. Educ:* Nunthorpe; Sheffield University. Commnd Royal Signals, 1940; served War of 1939-45 with 43 Div. Sigs and 17 Indian Div. in NW Europe and Burma (despatches twice); British Mission to Burma, 1948-49; exchange duty Canada, 1954-56; CO 1 Div. Sigs, 1961-63; British Army Staff, Washington, 1963-65; Comdr Trng Bde Royal Signals, 1965-68; Dir of Public Relations Army, 1968-70. Bt Lt-Col 1960; Brig. 1965; Maj.-Gen. 1970. Col Comdt, Royal Corps of Signals, 1970-. MBIM 1967. *Recreations:* sailing, shooting. *Address:* Hookers Green, Bishopsbourne, Canterbury, Kent. *T:* Bridge 264; Penbryn, Brecon. *T:* Brecon 3574. *Club:* Army and Navy.

**WOODRUFF, Prof. Alan Waller;** Wellcome Professor of Clinical Tropical Medicine,

London School of Hygiene and Tropical Medicine, University of London, since 1952; Lecturer in Tropical Medicine, Royal Free Hospital School of Medicine, since 1952; Physician, Hospital for Tropical Diseases, University College Hospital, London, since 1952; Hon. Consultant in Tropical Diseases to: the Army, since 1956; BOAC, since 1962; *b* 27 June 1916; *s* of late William Henry Woodruff, Sunderland, and Mary Margaret Woodruff; *m* 1946, Mercia Helen, *d* of late Leonard Frederick Arnold, Dorking, and Amy Elizabeth Arnold; two *s* one *d*. *Educ:* Bede Collegiate Sch., Sunderland; Durham Univ. MB, BS 1939, MD 1941, Durham; DTM&H England, 1946; PhD London, 1952; FRCP 1953; FRCPE 1960. House Physician and House Surgeon, Royal Victoria Infirmary, Newcastle upon Tyne, 1939-40; MO and Med. Specialist, RAFVR, 1940-46; Med. Registrar, Royal Victoria Infirmary, Newcastle upon Tyne, 1946-48; Sen. Lectr in Clinical Tropical Medicine, London Sch. of Hygiene and Trop. Medicine, and First Asst, Hosp. for Tropical Diseases, University Coll. Hosp., London, 1948-52; William Julius Mickle Fellow, Univ. of London, 1959. Lectures: Goulstonian, RCP, 1954; Lettsomian, Med. Soc. of London, 1969; Watson-Smith, RCP, 1970. Member: WHO Expert Adv. Panel on Parasitic Diseases, 1963-; Med. Cttee of Minister of Overseas Develt; Assoc. of Physicians of GB and Ireland. Jt Hon. Sec., Royal Soc. of Tropical Medicine and Hygiene, 1957-. Hon. Mem., Burma Med. Assoc., 1966; Foreign Mem., Société de Pathologie Exotique, Paris; Hon. Associate Mem., Soc. Belge de Médicine Tropicale, 1965. Katherine Bishop Harman Prize, BMA, 1951. *Publications:* (with J. Ungar) Antibiotics and Sulphonamides in Tropical Medicine, 1965; (with S. Bell) A Synopsis of Infectious and Tropical Diseases, 1968; (ed) Alimentary and Haematological Aspects of Tropical Disease, 1970; sections in: Paediatrics for the Practitioner (ed Gaisford and Lightwood); Medicine (ed Richardson); contribs to BMJ, Lancet, Trans Royal Soc. Trop. Medicine and Hygiene, W African Med. Jl, E African Med. Jl, Newcastle Med. Jl, Practitioner, Trans Assoc. Industrial Medical Officers, Proc. Nutrition Soc., etc. *Address:* 157 Denmark Hill, SE5. *T:* 01-274 3578. *Club:* Athenæum.

**WOODRUFF, Douglas;** *see* Woodruff, J. D.

**WOODRUFF, Harry Wells,** CMG 1966; Board of Trade, since 1968; *b* 31 Oct. 1912; *s* of Leonard Wells Woodruff and Rosina Woodruff; *m* 1938, Margaret Bradley; one *d*. *Educ:* Reigate Grammar Sch.; London Univ. Trade Comr, Johannesburg, 1946-51; Trade Comr and Economic Adviser to High Commissioner: Salisbury, 1951-55; Kuala Lumpur, 1957-61; Commercial Counsellor, Canberra, 1962-66; Economic Adviser to Foreign Office, 1966-68. *Publication:* (jointly) Economic Development in Rhodesia and Nyasaland, 1955. *Recreation:* painting. *Address:* 8 Wellesley Close, Warren Road, Crowborough, Sussex.

**WOODRUFF, (John) Douglas,** CBE 1962; Chairman, BOW Holdings, 1959-70; Chairman, Associated Catholic Newspapers, since 1953; Editor of The Tablet, 1936-67; *b* 8 May 1897; *s* of late Cumberland Woodruff, BCL, FSA, of the Public Record Office, and late Emily Louisa, *d* of William Hewett, Norton Fitzwarren, Somerset; *m* 1933, Hon. Marie Immaculée, *d* of 2nd Lord Acton. *Educ:* St Augustine's, Ramsgate; Downside Sch.; New Coll., Oxford (Lothian prizeman, 1921, 1st class Hon. Modern History, 1923, President of the Union). Served under Foreign Office in Holland, 1917-19; Lecturer in History at Sheffield Univ., 1923-24; Editorial staff of The Times, 1926-38; in charge of Press Publicity for Empire Marketing Board, 1931-33; on staff of BBC, 1934-36; Dep. Chairman Burns and Oates, Publishers, 1948-62; Director, Hollis & Carter, 1948-62; Chairman of Allied Circle, 1947-62. Grand Cross, Order of St Gregory the Great, 1968. *Publications:* Plato's American Republic, 1926; The British Empire, 1929; Plato's Britannia, 1930; Charlemagne, 1934; Contributor to Early Victorian England, 1934; Great Tudors, 1935; European Civilisation, The Grand Tour, 1935; (Editor) Dear Sir, 1936; The Story of the British Colonial Empire, 1939; Talking at Random, 1941; More Talking at Random, 1944; Still Talking at Random, 1948; Walrus Talk, 1954; The Tichborne Claimant, 1957; Church and State in History, 1961; contrib. to current periodicals. *Address:* Marcham Priory, Abingdon, Berks. *T:* Frilford Heath 260. *Clubs:* Athenæum, Beefsteak, Pratt's.

**WOODRUFF, Keith Montague Cumberland,** MB, BS (London); MRCS; LRCP; FFARCS; *b* 18 June 1891; *s* of Rev. A. W. Woodruff and Emily (*née* Hamilton), Testwood, Hants; *m* 1934, Beatrice Evelyn, *d* of late Colonel C. C. O. Whiteley and of Mrs Whiteley; one *s*. *Educ:* Eastmans Royal Army and Navy Academy, Winchester; St Edward's Sch., Oxford; Guy's Hospital. Consulting Anæsthetist: Royal National Orthopædic Hospital, 1924; Chelsea Hospital for Women, 1925; Queen Charlotte's Maternity Hospital, 1938; Charing Cross Hospital, 1935; Royal Masonic Hospital, 1937. 1914-15 Medal, 1914-18 Medal, Victory Medal, 1914-18. *Recreations:* golf, sailing. *Address:* Mount Cottage, Rhodes Minnis, Elham, near Canterbury, Kent. *T:* Lyminge 87445.

**WOODRUFF, Prof. Sir Michael (Francis Addison),** Kt 1969; FRS 1968; FRCS; DSc, MS (Melbourne); Professor of Surgical Science, University of Edinburgh, and Surgeon, Edinburgh Royal Infirmary, since 1957; Director, Nuffield Transplantation Surgery Unit, Edinburgh, since 1968; *b* 3 April 1911; *s* of late Prof. Harold Addison Woodruff and Margaret Ada (*née* Cooper); *m* 1946, Hazel Gwenyth Ashby; two *s* one *d*. *Educ:* Wesley Coll., Melbourne; Queen's Coll., University of Melbourne. MB, BS (Melbourne) 1937, MD 1940, MS 1941; FRCS 1946. Captain, Australian Army Medical Corps, 1940-46. Tutor in Surgery, Univ. of Sheffield, 1946-48; Lecturer in Surgery, Univ. of Aberdeen, 1948-52; Hunterian Prof., RCS, 1952; Travelling Fellow, WHO, 1949; Prof. of Surgery, Univ. of Otago, Dunedin, NZ, 1953-56. Associé Etranger, Académie de Chirurgie, 1964; Hon. Member American Surgical Assoc., 1965; Korrespondierendem Mitglied, Deutsche Gesellschaft für Chirurgie. Lister Medal, 1969. *Publications:* (Joint) Deficiency Diseases in Japanese Prison Camps, 1951; Surgery for Dental Students, 1954; Transplantation of Tissues and Organs, 1960; articles on surgical topics and on experimental tissue transplantation. *Recreations:* music, sailing. *Address:* The Bield, Juniper Green, Midlothian; University of Edinburgh. *Clubs:* Athenæum; Dunedin (Dunedin).

**WOODRUFF, Philip;** *see* Mason, Philip.

**WOODS, Maj.-Gen. Charles William,** CB 1970; MBE 1952; MC 1944; Director of Manning (Army), 1967-70; *b* 21 March 1917; *s* of Captain F. W. U. Woods and Mrs M. E. Woods, Gosbrook House, Binfield Heath, Henley-on-Thames; *m* 1940, Angela Helen Clay; one *d* (one *s* decd). *Educ:* Uppingham Sch.; Trinity Coll.,

Cambridge (MA). Commnd into Corps of Royal Engineers, 1938; served War of 1939-45, N Africa, Sicily, Italy, NW Europe (D Landings with 50th Div.); Staff Coll., Camberley, 1946; served in Korea, 1951-52; comd 35 Corps Engineer Regt, BAOR, 1959-60; Dep. Military Secretary, 1964-67. *Recreations:* sailing, ski-ing. *Address:* Chalk Barton, West Horsley, Surrey. *T:* East Horsley 2706. *Clubs:* United Service; Royal Ocean Racing, Royal Corinthian Yacht, Ski Club of Great Britain.

**WOODS, Most Rev. Frank;** *see* Melbourne, Archbishop of.

**WOODS, George David;** banker; President and Chairman of Executive Directors, International Bank for Reconstruction and Development and International Development Association, 1963-68; Chairman of Board and President, International Finance Corporation, 1963-68; *b* 27 July 1901; *s* of John Woods and Laura A. Woods (*née* Rhodes); *m* 1935, Louise Taraldson; no *c*. *Educ:* New York public schools; American Institute of Banking; New York Univ. Investment Banking: Harris Forbes & Co., NY City, 1918-34; The First Boston Corporation, NY City, 1934-62 and 1968- (Chairman of Board, 1951-62). Chairman: Henry J. Kaiser Family Foundation, 1968- (also Trustee); New York State Urban Develt Corp., 1968-; Internat. Executive Service Corps, 1968-. Holds honorary doctorates from Universities and Colleges. Legion of Merit, US Army, 1945. *Address:* 277 Park Avenue, New York, NY 10017, USA; (home) 825 Fifth Avenue, New York, NY 10021, USA. *Clubs:* Links, Pinnacle, Players, Racquet & Tennis (New York); Duquesne, Rolling Rock (Pittsburgh); Federal City (Washington, DC).

**WOODS, Irene Charlotte,** CBE 1946; TD 1951; *b* 4 Jan. 1891; *y d* of late Thomas Pickering, Newcastle, and The Hill House, Gilsland; *m* 1918, R. Salisbury Woods, *qv*; one *s* two *d*. *Educ:* privately. European War, 1914-18, trained at St George's Hospital, and became Staff Nurse. Joined ATS 1938. In War of 1939-45 served ATS, reached rank of Controller; invalided out, 1945. Organiser, City of Cambridge, WRVS, 1954-67. *Address:* 4 Manor Court, Grange Road, Cambridge. *T:* 59451.

**WOODS, Prof. Leslie Colin;** Professor of Mathematics (Theory of Plasma), University of Oxford, and Fellow of Balliol College, Oxford, since 1970; *b* Reporoa; NZ, 6 Dec. 1922; *s* of A. B. Woodhead, Sandringham, NZ; *m* 1943, Gladys Elizabeth Bayley; five *d*. *Educ:* Auckland Univ. Coll.; Merton Coll., Oxford. Fighter pilot, RNZAF, Pacific Area, 1942-45. Rhodes Schol., Merton Coll., Oxford, 1948-51; Scientist (NZ Scientific Defense Corps) with Aerodynamics Div., NPL Mddx, 1951-54; Senior Lectr in Applied Maths, Sydney Univ., 1954-56; Nuffield Research Prof. of Engineering, Univ. of New South Wales, 1956-60; Fellow and Tutor in Engrg Science, Balliol Coll., Oxford, 1960-70; Reader in Applied Maths, Oxford, 1964-70. *Publications:* The Theory of Subsonic Plane Flow, 1961; Introduction to Neutron Distribution Theory, 1964; many research papers in aerodynamics and plasma physics in Proc. Royal Soc., Physics of Fluids, etc. *Recreations:* gardening, sailing. *Address:* St Bedes, Foxcombe Lane, Boars Hill, Oxford. *T:* Oxford 35208.

**WOODS, Oliver Frederick John Bradley,** MC 1943; TD and Bar, 1947; MA; Chief Assistant to Editor-in-Chief, Times Newspapers, since 1967; *b* 21 Nov. 1911; *o s* of late Maurice Woods and late Mrs J. L. Garvin; *m* 1956, Joan Nancy, *widow* of F. H. Waters and *d* of late Colonel C. R. Maude, OBE, MC, and Mrs Maude (Nancy Price). *Educ:* Marlborough; Geneva Univ.; New Coll., Oxford. Senior open classical schol., 1930. Joined editorial staff of The Times as sub-editor, 1935. Served War of 1939-45: Major, 3rd County of London Yeomanry (Sharpshooters); Western Desert, Sicily, Italy, North-West Europe (despatches). Rejoined The Times as special writer, 1946; Colonial Correspondent, 1948; Colonial Editor and Assistant Foreign Editor, 1956; Assistant Editor, 1961; Dep. Managing Editor, 1965. Travelled widely, especially in Africa and the Caribbean. Vice-President, Institute of Race Relations. *Address:* 6 Southover High Street, Lewes. *T:* Lewes 3418. *Clubs:* Travellers', Pratt's, Garrick.

**WOODS, Reginald Salisbury,** MA; MD, BCh (Cantab); FRCS; Médaille d'Honneur de l'Education Physique et des Sports, République Française, 1946; in General Practice; Hon. Life Member, British Association of Sport and Medicine; Surgical Specialist to numerous insurance companies; Cambridgeshire Warden King George's Jubilee Trust; Past Assistant of Glazier's Company, Freeman of City of London; a Patron of Cambridge Branch, Old Contemptibles and of British Legion; Past President, Downing College Association, 1962; *b* London, 15 Oct. 1891; *o s* of late H. T. Woods, Galway; *m* 1918, Irene (*see* Irene C. Woods), *y d* of late T. Pickering; one *s* two *d*. *Educ:* Dulwich Coll.; Downing Coll., Cambridge (Entr. Exh.); St George's Hospital (Senior Univ. Entrance Scholar, Research Exhib., etc.). HS, HP, and Surg. Registrar. Captain, RAMC, BEF, 1916-19 (despatches); late Surg. Spec. Ministry of Pensions; Surg. EMS (Cambridge County Hospital), 1939-43; Major, RAMC 1943-45 (Surg. Spec. E Africa Command). Formerly: Hon. Demonstrator Anatomy, Cambridge University Medical Schools; President, Cambridge Med. Society, County Director BRCS, and Chairman, Nat. Playing Fields Assoc. and Cambs AAA. *Publications:* Cambridge Doctor, 1962; contribs on sports injuries in British and US med. jls. *Recreations:* represented England 1914 and 1920-29; Great Britain at Olympic Games, 1924 and 1928, and British Empire *v* USA, 1924 and 1928, in Putting the Weight. President (1914), Hon. Treasurer (1919-39) and Chairman (1939-52), of CUAC. AAA Champion, 1924 and 1926; Captained Public Schools Past and Present at Rugby Football, 1919; golf, bridge. *Address:* 4 Manor Court, Grange Road, Cambridge; 40 Green Street, Cambridge. *Clubs:* British Sportsman's; Cambridge County, Hawks, Pitt, Achilles (Cambridge); Oxford and Cambridge Golfing Society.

*See also F. W. W. Pemberton.*

**WOODS, Rt. Rev. Robert Wilmer;** *see* Worcester, Bishop of.

**WOODS, Maj.-Gen. (Retired) Thomas Frederic Mackie,** CB 1960; OBE 1945; MD; FRCP(I); *b* 14 July 1904; *s* of Dr Annesley Woods, Birr, Ireland; *m* 1930, Juliet Frances, *d* of D. L. Rogers, Dublin; two *d*. *Educ:* St Paul's Sch.; Trinity Coll., Dublin. BA, MB, Dublin, 1926; MD, Dublin, 1932; MRCP Ireland, 1934. Joined RAMC 1927; served in India, Malta and UK until 1940. Served War of 1939-45: in UK, Madagascar, India, Middle East, Burma, Malaya. Seconded to Ministry of Food, 1946-48, as Chief Health Officer E. African Groundnut Scheme; 2 Div., RAMC Depot, HQ London Dist, HQ 1 (BR) Corps; HQ Southern Command. Brigadier, 1956; Maj.-

Gen., 1957. Colonel Comdt, RAMC, 1965-69. OStJ. *Address:* White Lodge, Berwick St James, near Salisbury, Wilts.

**WOODS, Admiral (Retired) Sir Wilfrid (John Wentworth),** GBE 1963; KCB 1960 (CB 1957); DSO 1942; Bar to DSO 1942; *b* 19 Feb. 1906; *s* of late Sir Wilfrid Woods, KCMG, KBE, and late Ethel Maud Woods (*née* Palmer); *m* 1st, 1930, Murray Auriol Ruth Inglis (*d* 1956); one *d* (one *s* decd); 2nd, 1957, Joan Bridget Constance Eden. *Educ:* Seabrook Lodge, Hythe, Kent; Royal Naval Colleges Osborne and Dartmouth. Midshipman, 1924; Sub-Lieut, 1926; joined Submarines, 1927; Lieut, 1928; First Command, HMS/M Seahorse, 1935; Lieut-Commander, HMS Nelson, 1936; RN Staff Coll., 1939. Served War of 1939-45: Staff of 6th S/M Flotilla, Home Waters, 1939; HMS/M Triumph in Command, Mediterranean, 1940 (DSO and Bar, Order of White Eagle of Yugo-Slavia); Commander 1941; Staff of C-in-C, Mediterranean, 1942; HMS Centurion in Command, Normandy Landings, 1944; Staff of 3rd S/M Flotilla, Home Waters, 1944; HMS Forth in Command, and Captain 3rd S/M Flotilla, 1945. Chief Staff Officer to Flag Officer S/M's, 1947; Admiralty, as Director of Torpedo, Anti-Submarine and Mine Warfare, 1948; idc 1951; HMS Indomitable in Command, 1952; Chief of Staff to C-in-C Mediterranean as Cdre 1st Class, 1953; Rear-Admiral, 1955; Flag Officer (Submarines), Dec. 1955-Nov. 1957; Vice-Admiral, 1958; Deputy Supreme Allied Commander Atlantic, 1958-60; Admiral, 1960; Commander-in-Chief, Home Fleet, and NATO C-in-C Eastern Atlantic Area, 1960-62; Commander-in-Chief, Portsmouth, and Allied Commander-in-Chief, Channel, 1963-65; Principal Naval ADC to the Queen, 1962-65; Cdre RN Sailing Assoc., 1963-66. Member, Cttee of Management, RNLI, 1966, Chairman, 1968-; President, Sea Cadet Corps Sports Council, 1966; Chairman, Foudroyant Trust, 1967. Knight Commander, Order of King George the First of Greece, 1963. *Recreations:* sailing, tennis, gardening, walking. *Address:* Shappen Farm, Burley, Hampshire BH24 4AG. *T:* Burley 2256. *Clubs:* United Service, Royal Cruising; Royal Naval (Portsmouth); Royal Yacht Squadron (Cowes).

**WOODS, Colonel William Talbot,** CB 1950; DSO 1918; MC 1915; TD; JP; MIMinE; Mining Engineer since 1920; Umpire to Conciliation Board, SW Division, National Coal Board, 1947-60; *b* 10 Dec. 1891; *s* of William Woods, FRCVS, MSc, Wigan; *m* 1927, Enid Comer, *d* of Arthur Smith, BA, LLB, Golborne, Wigan; one *s* two *d*. *Educ:* Charterhouse. Served European War, 1914-19, Egypt, Gallipoli and France (despatches three times); comd 4th Bn Welch Regt, TA, 1927-32 (Hon. Colonel, 1953-59); Colonel, 1931; comd 15th Bn Welch Regt, 1939; comd Home Guard Bn, 1940-45; Colonel, TARO, 1932-51; Chairman, Carmarthen TA Assoc., 1945-52. DL Carmarthenshire, 1935-69. KStJ, 1957. *Address:* 17 The Fairway, Post Hill, Tiverton, Devon. *T:* Tiverton 3405.

**WOODS, William Wilson,** LRCP, MRCS; Assistant Director, The Pathological Institute, London Hospital, 1920, retired; Formerly Consulting Pathologist (Morbid Histologist) to the Navy; *b* 10 May 1884; 3rd *s* of late Robert Woods, JP, Stewartstown, Tyrone, and Jane Frances, *d* of late John Cowan, Annahavil, Co. Derry; *m* 1911, Stēphanie (*d* 1967), *y d* of late A. W. Bellmont, Christiania; one *s*. *Educ:* Royal Sch., Dungannon; London Univ.; London Hospital. Pathological Asst, Pathological Institute, London Hospital, 1911; Junior Assistant Director, 1912. *Recreation:* played Rugby football for London Hospital, 1906 (Inter-Hospital Cup Winners), and for Middlesex County. *Address:* Guildown, 10 Lynwood Road, Epsom, Surrey.

**WOODS BALLARD, Lt-Col Basil,** CIE 1943; MBE 1935; *b* 28 Sept. 1900; *s* of Frederick George Ballard; *m* 1931, Eileen Rose Molesworth; two *s*. *Educ:* Dulwich Coll. Commissioned 5th Royal Gurkha Rifles, FF, IA, 1920; Indian Political Service, 1925; Political Agent, Loralai, 1936-39; Secretary to Resident, Punjab States, 1939-41; Political Agent, Quetta, 1941-45; Political Agent, Bhopal, 1945-47; Resident in Kolhapur, 1947; retired, Aug. 1947. Employed in Persian Gulf, 1948-53; served on local councils and managing and governing bodies of schools in E Sussex, 1955-. *Address:* Shepherds Oak, Crawley Down, Sussex. *T:* Copthorne 2314.

**WOODWARD, Arthur Maurice,** MA, FSA; Hon. ARIBA; *b* 29 June 1883; 2nd *s* of late W. H. Woodward; *m* 1925, Jocelyn Mary, 2nd *d* of John Pybus, Newcastle on Tyne. *Educ:* Shrewsbury; Magdalen Coll., Oxford. Student at the British School, Athens, 1906-09; Asst Director, 1909-10 and 1922-23; Director, 1923-29; Assistant Lecturer, University of Liverpool, 1911-12, and Leeds, 1912-22; Lecturer in Ancient History, 1931-45, and Reader in Ancient History and Archæology and Head of Dept of Ancient History, University of Sheffield, 1945-47. Served in Macedonia and Bulgaria with British Salonika Force, Nov. 1915-Jan. 1919 (despatches twice). Officer, Greek Order of the Redeemer, 1924. *Publications:* numerous articles on Greek inscriptions and other archæological subjects in Journal of Hellenic Studies, Annual of the British School at Athens, Numismatic Chronicle, etc. *Recreations:* various. *Address:* Spa Hotel, Tunbridge Wells, Kent.

**WOODWARD, Professor C(omer) Vann;** Sterling Professor of History, Yale University, since 1961; *b* 13 Nov. 1908; *s* of Hugh Allison Woodward and Bess (*née* Vann); *m* 1937, Glenn Boyd MacLeod; one *s*. *Educ:* Emory Univ. (PhB); Universities of Columbia (MA), North Carolina (PhD). Asst Professor of History, University of Florida, 1937-39; Visiting Asst Professor of History, University of Virginia, 1939-40; Assoc. Professor of History, Scripps Coll., 1940-43; Assoc. Professor of History, Johns Hopkins University, 1946; Professor of American History, Johns Hopkins Univ., 1947-61. Served with US Naval Reserve, 1943-46. Commonwealth Lecturer, UCL, 1954; Harold Vyvyan Harmsworth Professor of American History, University of Oxford, 1954-55; Literary Award, Nat. Inst. of Arts and Letters, 1954, etc. Member: American Academy of Arts and Sciences; American Philosophical Society; Nat. INst. of Arts and Letters; American Historical Assoc. (President, 1969); Orgn of American Historians (President, 1968-69). Hon. degrees: MA Oxon, 1954; LLD: N Carolina, 1959; Arkansas, 1961; LittD: Emory, 1963; William and Mary, 1964. *Publications:* Tom Watson: Agrarian Rebel, 1938; The Battle for Leyte Gulf, 1947; Origins of the New South (1877-1913), 1951 (Bancroft Prize, 1952); Reunion and Reaction, 1951; The Strange Career of Jim Crow, 1955; The Burden of Southern History, 1960; (ed) The Comparative Approach to American History, 1968. *Address:* History Department, Yale University, New Haven, Conn 06520, USA.

**WOODWARD, Denys Cuthbert,** CMG 1949; MInstT; *b* 15 March 1902; *s* of Rev. W. E. Woodward, MA, and Mrs Woodward (*née* Richardson); *m* Mary Stuart, *d* of Rev. T. H. Strong (late of Sandy, Bedfordshire); one *s*. *Educ:* St Peter's Court, Broadstairs; Christ's Hospital, Horsham. Joined L and NWR, 1918; Nigerian Railway, 1928; General Manager, 1947-Nov. 1953; Chairman of Nigeria Hotels Ltd, 1949-58. *Recreations:* cricket, golf and sailing. *Address:* 1 Spinola Court, The Gardens, St Julians, Malta.

**WOODWARD, Lieut-Colonel Edward Hamilton Everard,** CBE 1949; MC 1916; TD 1931; FIEE; *b* 4 Feb. 1888; *s* of Colonel J. H. Woodward, CB, VD, JP, and Mary Alice Hamilton, *d* of Admiral T. Fisher, Clifton, Bristol; *m* 1917, Violet Ethel, *d* of Lieut-Commander A. S. Hamilton, RN; two *s* two *d*. *Educ:* Clifton Coll.; Bristol University College. BSc (Eng.) London, BSc (Eng.) Bristol. Assistant Engineer, Newcastle on Tyne Electric Supply Co. Ltd, 1909-14. Served European War, 4th Bn Gloucestershire Regt and Tyne Electrical Engineers, RE, 1914-19. North-Eastern Electric Supply Co. Ltd, 1920-48, ending as General Manager and a Director. In command of Tyne Electrical Engineers, RE, 1929-34. Appointed by Minister of Fuel and Power a member Organising Cttee for Electricity Supply Industry, May 1947, and a member British Electricity Authority, Aug. 1947-Dec. 1957. *Recreation:* flower garden. *Address:* Cherryburn, Kivernell Road, Milford-on-Sea, Hants. *T:* 2374. *Club:* Devonshire.

**WOODWARD, Sir (Ernest) Llewellyn,** Kt, *cr* 1952; MA; Hon. LittD, Princeton; FBA; Hon. Fellow of Worcester College, and of Corpus Christi College, Oxford; Member American Philosophical Society; *b* London, 14 May 1890; *s* of late G. E. Woodward, CBE; *m* 1917, Florence Marie (*d* 1961), *y d* of late Very Rev. R. S. O'Loughlin, DD, Dean of Dromore. *Educ:* Merchant Taylors' Sch.; Corpus Christi Coll., Oxford. Served BEF France and Salonika, 1915-18; Fellow of All Souls Coll., 1919-44 and 1962-, and formerly Lecturer in Modern History, New Coll., Oxford; Professor of International Relations, Oxford, 1944-47; Professor of Modern History, Oxford Univ., 1947-51; Professor at the Institute for Advanced Study, Princeton, 1951-62; Senior Proctor, Oxford University, 1928-29; Rhodes Travelling Fellow, 1931; Editor (with R. D'O. Butler), 1944-55, of Documents on British Foreign Policy, 1919-39. *Publications:* Christianity and Nationalism in the Later Roman Empire; Three Studies in European Conservatism; The Twelve-Winded Sky; War and Peace in Europe, 1815-70; French Revolutions; Gt Britain and the German Navy; The Age of Reform (vol. xiii in the Oxford History of England); Short Journey; British Historians; History of England; British Foreign Policy in the Second World War (Official History); Great Britain and the War of 1914-18. *Address:* The Garden House, 2a Walton Street, Oxford.

**WOODWARD, (Foster) Neville,** CBE 1956; FRSE; Chairman, Management Committee, Inveresk Research International; Managing Director, Arthur D. Little Ltd, 1963-68; Director, Arthur D. Little Research Institute, 1956-70; Senior Scientific Counsellor, Directorate of Scientific Affairs, OECD, Paris, since 1961; *b* 2 May 1905; *s* of Foster Woodward; *m* 1932, Elizabeth Holme Siddall; one *s* one *d*. *Educ:* Bradford; University Coll., London (PhD, gold medallist). After ten years in industry, and two as Res. Asst (to Prof. Sir Robert Robinson, FRS), Oxford Univ., became Head of Res. and Develt Div., HM Chem. Defence Res. Estabt, Sutton Oak, 1937-42. During War of 1939-45 served on Govt Sci. Cttees and Missions; subseq. served on scientific missions to 18 foreign countries concerned with natural resources develt, internat. scientific relations, co-operative and contract research management of R&D and industrial research insts in developing countries. Officer in Charge, Min. of Supply Res. Estabt, Leamington Spa, 1943; Dep. Sci. Adv. to Min. of Production, 1944-46; Dir, Inst. of Seaweed Research, 1946-56 (Mem. Bd Inst., 1956-); seconded to FO as Dir UK Sci. Mission, Washington DC; Attaché for Sci. Questions, Brit. Embassy, Washington DC, and Sci. Adv. to UK High Comr in Canada, 1947-48; Hon. Sci. Adv. to Sec. of State for Scotland, 1951-56; Sci. Attaché to European Productivity Agency, OEEC, Paris, 1956-61. Vice-President: Soc. of Chemical Industry, 1968-, Royal Inst. of Chemistry, 1969-; Chm., Assoc. of Consulting Scientists, 1967-69. *Publications:* A Survey of Agricultural, Forestry and Fishery Products in the United Kingdom and their Utilisation (with J. Maxton and A. B. Stewart), 1953; Structure of Industrial Research Associations, 1964. About 50 publications in scientific press. *Recreations:* mountains, foreign travel, reading, writing. *Address:* St Margaret's, Gullane, East Lothian. *T:* Gullane 2210; Cuil Moss, Ardgour, Argyll. *Clubs:* Savage; New (Edinburgh).

**WOODWARD, Joan, (Mrs L. T. Blakeman);** Professor of Industrial Sociology, Imperial College of Science and Technology, since 1969; *b* 19 June 1916; *d* of Joseph Henry Woodward and Lily Woodward (*née* King); *m* 1951, Leslie Thompson Blakeman, *qv*. *Educ:* Durham and Oxford Universities (MA Durham; BA Oxon). Various Industrial Appointments, 1939-46; Administrative Class, Civil Service, 1946-48; Lecturer, Department of Social Science, Liverpool University, 1948-53; Director, DSIR Research Unit, SE Essex College of Technology, 1953-57; Special Tutor, Industrial Sociology, Dept of Social and Administrative Studies, Oxford, 1957-62; Reader in Industrial Sociology, Imperial Coll., 1962-69. Part-time Mem., Nat. Board for Prices and Incomes, 1968-71. *Publications:* include: Employment Relations in a Group of Hospitals, 1951; The Dockworker, 1954; Management and Technology, 1957; The Saleswoman, 1961; Industrial Organization: theory and practice, 1965; (with Flanders and Pomeranz) Experiment in Industrial Democracy, 1968; (ed) Industrial Organization: behaviour and control, 1970. *Recreation:* re-making houses and gardens. *Address:* 71 Roebuck House, Stag Place, SW1. *T:* 01-828 6203; Fishponds Farm, Brook, near Ashford, Kent. *T:* Wye 514.

**WOODWARD, Joan;** *see* Woodward, (W.) J.

**WOODWARD, Sir Llewellyn;** *see* Woodward, Sir E. L.

**WOODWARD, Rev. Max Wakerley;** Methodist Minister, Bromley, Kent, since 1969; *b* 29 Jan. 1908; *s* of Alfred Woodward, Methodist Minister, and Mabel Woodward; *m* 1934, Kathleen May Beaty; three *s* one *d*. *Educ:* Orme Sch., Newcastle; Kingswood Sch., Bath; Handsworth Coll., Birmingham. Missionary to Ceylon, 1929-42; Chaplain, Royal Navy, 1942-46; Minister: Leamington Spa, 1946-50; Finsbury Park, 1950-54; Harrow, 1954-58; Wesley's Chapel, London, 1958-64; Secretary, World Methodist Council, 1964-69. Exchange Preacher, Univ. Methodist Church, Baton Rouge, La, 1957. *Publication:* One At London, 1966. *Recreations:* gardening, chess. *Address:*

30 Manor Way, Beckenham, Kent. *T:* 01-658 6484.

**WOODWARD, Neville;** *see* Woodward, F. N.

**WOODWARD, Prof. R(obert) B(urns),** BS; PhD; Donner Professor of Science, Harvard University, since 1960; Director of the Woodward Research Institute, Basel, since 1963; Member of Corporation, Massachusetts Institute of Technology, 1966-71; *b* Boston, 10 April 1917; *s* of Arthur Chester Woodward and Margaret (*née* Burns); *m* 1st, 1938, Irja Pullman; two *d*; 2nd, 1946, Eudoxia M. M. Muller; one *s* one *d*. *Educ:* Massachusetts Institute of Technology. BS, 1936; PhD, 1937. Post-Doctoral Fellow, Harvard Univ., 1937-38; Mem., Soc. of Fellows, 1938-40; Instructor in Chemistry, 1941-44; Asst Prof., 1944-46; Assoc. Prof., 1946-50; Prof., 1950-53; Morris Loeb Prof. of Chem., 1953-60. Consultant: Polaroid Corp., 1942-; Cttee on Medical Research, Office of Scientific Research and Development, 1944-45; War Production Bd, 1944-45; Pfizer & Co. Inc., 1951-. Mem. Bd of Governors, Weizmann Inst. of Science, 1968-. Hon. Lecturer to many organisations in America, Europe and Australia. Member, National Academy of Sciences; FAAS; Foreign Member: Royal Society; Accademia Nazionale dei Lincei; Hon. Fellow: Chemical Society; Indian Academy of Sciences; Hon. Member: German Chemical Society; Royal Irish Academy; Belgian Chemical Society; Swiss Chemical Society; Member: American Philosophical Society; Deutsche Akademie der Naturforscher (Leopoldina); Corresp. Mem., Austrian Academy of Sciences. Hon. AM Harvard Univ., 1946; Hon. LLD Glasgow, 1966; holds honorary doctorates in Science at Universities and Colleges in USA, Canada, Gt Britain, Switzerland and Israel. John Scott Medal, 1945; Baekeland Medal, 1955; Ledlie Prize, 1955; Research Corp. Award, 1955; Nichols Medal, 1956; Amer. Chem. Soc. Synthetic Organic Chemistry Award, 1957; T. W. Richards Medal, 1958; Davy Medal, Royal Soc., 1959; Roger Adams Medal, 1961; Pius XI Gold Medal of Poutifical Acad. of Sciences, 1961; Nat. Medal of Science, USA. 1964; Nobel Prize for Chemistry, 1965; Willard Gibbs Medal, 1967; Lavoiser Medal, 1968, etc. Order of the Rising Sun, 2nd cl. (Japan), 1970. *Address:* Dept of Chemistry, Harvard University, 12 Oxford Street, Cambridge, Mass 02138, USA.

**WOODWARD, (Winifred) Joan;** Assistant Principal Probation Officer, Inner London Probation and After-care Service, since 1950; *b* 14 Sept. 1907; *d* of late Brig.-Gen. J. A. H. Woodward, IA, and Winifred Mary Strahan. *Educ:* Princess Helena Coll., Ealing. Appointed to Probation Service, 1936; served at: North London and Edmonton, Apr.-Nov. 1936; Marylebone, Nov. 1936-June 1940; appointed to Bow Street, 1940; Senior Probation Officer, Bow Street Magistrates Court, Nov. 1948. *Address:* 2 Queen Anne's Grove, Ealing, W5. *T:* 01-567 8571.

**WOODWARD-NUTT, Arthur Edgar;** Aeronautical Consultant; *b* 19 Aug. 1902; *o s* of late George Arthur and Edith Ellen Nutt; *m* 1928, Dorothy Muriel, *y d* of late Harry J. Linzell; one *s*. *Educ:* King Edward's, Birmingham; Gonville and Caius Coll., Cambridge (MA). Seely Prizeman, Cambridge, 1923. De Havilland Aircraft Co., 1924-25; at RAE, Farnborough, 1925-27 and 1934-38, A&AEE, Martlesham Heath, 1927-31, MAEE Felixstowe, 1931-34; in charge of Air Defence Research Section, Air Ministry, 1938-41; Sec. to Brit. Technical Mission to the USA, 1940; various directing appointments at Min. of Aircraft Production and Min. of Supply, 1941-58; Director-General of Aircraft General Services, Ministry of Aviation, 1958-65; Technical Adviser (Civil) to the Ministry of Aviation, 1965-66. CEng; FRAeS. *Publications:* various Reports and Memoranda of Aeronautical Research Council, and articles in Technical Press. *Recreations:* lawn tennis, gardening. *Address:* 13 Barnfield Wood Road, Beckenham, Kent. *T:* 01-650 5155.

**WOOF, Robert Edward;** MP (Lab) Blaydon, co. Durham, since Feb. 1956; Member and official, National Union of Mineworkers; *b* 24 Oct. 1911; *m* Mary Bell; one *d*. *Educ:* Elementary School. Began work in the mines at an early age, subsequently coal face worker. Member of the Labour Party, 1937-; Member Durham County Council, 1947-56. *Address:* House of Commons, SW1; Laburnum House, Dipwood Road, Rowlands Gill, Co. Durham.

**WOOKEY, Eric Edgar,** MC 1916; Dental Surgeon in private practice at Wimpole Street, 1933-68, retired, 1968; Senior Dental Surgeon, Royal Free Hospital, 1936-Sept. 1958, Hon. Consulting Dental Surgeon, since 1958; *b* 11 January 1892; *s* of Edgar Wookey, Shipham, Somerset, and Clara (*née* Davidson); *m* 1927, Doris Kathleen Fenner; one *s* two *d*. *Educ:* Haverfordwest Grammar School; Clevedon College; Bristol University; Royal Dental Hospital, London. Bristol Univ. Student, medical and dental, 1909-14; Infantry commission in 4th Glos Regt TF, 1914; served overseas, France (wounded, despatches, MC); Italy, BEF (despatches twice); Bt Major, Comd 4th Glos Regt at Armistice, Nov. 1918. LDS, RCS 1919, and after a period of hospital practice commenced private practice at Hendon, 1920; Asst Dental Surgeon, Royal Free Hosp., 1921; full-time practice in Wimpole Street, 1933. During War of 1939-45, served in EMS. Member of Representative Bd, British Dental Assoc., 1946-54 and 1958-61; Pres. Metropolitan Branch, 1949-50; Founder Member, Past-President, and Past Chm. of Council, Brit. Soc. of Med. and Dental Hypnosis (formerly Dental and Med. Soc. for Study of Hypnosis); Fellow Internat. Soc. of Clinical and Experimental Hypnosis (PP Brit. Section). Member: Council, Soc. for Psychical Research; British Archæological Soc.; Ecclesiological Soc. Silver Medal for Valour (Italy), 1918. *Publications:* articles in British Dental Jl. *Recreations:* music (piano), golf, numismatics (FRNS), philately, horology. *Address:* 51 Lake View, Canons Park, Edgware, Middx. *T:* 01-958 6029.

**WOOLDRIDGE, Henry,** CBE 1964 (OBE 1942); *b* 9 Jan. 1908; *o s* of Alderman Henry Wooldridge and Mrs Emma Wooldridge; *m* 1939, Marjorie, *er d* of Albert Dranfield and Mrs Annie Dranfield; two *s*. *Educ:* Reading Sch.; King's Coll., London. King's Schol.; Univ. Exhibr in Sci.; Sec., Coll. Union Soc., 1929-30; Captain and Vice-Pres., Coll. Boat Club; Univ. Rowing Colours, 1928; BSc (Physics, Special), 1929; AKC 1929; Teacher's Dipl. 1930. Asst Sec., British Assoc., 1930-35; DSIR Headquarters as Scientific Officer, 1935; Private Sec. to Perm. Sec., 1935-43; Princ. in Gen. Div., 1943-45; Asst, later Dep. Estab. Off., 1945-47; Head of Stations Div., 1957; Dep. Dir (Stns), 1958; Asst Controller (Stns and Res. Assocs), Min. of Technology, 1965; Head of Information and Regional Org. Div. (Chief Scientific Officer), 1965-66; Head of Productivity Services and Information Div., 1968. *Recreation:* gardening. *Address:* Highfield, Upper Warren Avenue, Caversham, Reading RG4 7EJ. *T:* Reading 471501. *Club:* Athenæum.

**WOOLF, John Moss;** Commissioner, HM Customs and Excise, since 1970; *b* 5 June 1918; *o s* of Alfred and Maud Woolf; *m* 1940, Phyllis Ada Mary Johnson; one *d*. *Educ:* Drayton Manor Sch.; Honourable Society of Lincoln's Inn. Barrister-at-law, 1948. War Service, 1939-46 (Captain, RA). Inland Revenue, 1937. Asst Principal, Min. of Fuel and Power, 1948; HM Customs and Excise, 1950: Principal, 1951; Asst Sec., 1960; Chm., Valuation Cttee, Customs Cooperation Council, Brussels, 1964-65; National Bd for Prices and Incomes, 1965; Under-Secretary, 1967; Asst Under-Sec. of State, Dept of Employment and Productivity, 1968-70. Assoc. of First Div. Civil Servants: Mem. of Exec. Cttee, 1950-58 and 1961-65; Hon. Sec., 1952-55; Chm., 1955-58 and 1964-65; Mem., Civil Service National Whitley Council (Staff Side), 1953-55. *Publication:* Report on Control of Prices in Trinidad and Tobago (with M. M. Eccleshall), 1968. *Recreations:* reading, gardening. *Address:* West Lodge, 113 Marsh Lane, Stanmore, Mddx HA7 4TH. *T:* 01-952 1373. *Clubs:* Reform, Civil Service.

**WOOLFORD, Harry Russell Halkerston,** OBE 1970; Chief Restorer, National Gallery of Scotland; *b* 23 May 1905; *s* of H. Woolford, engineer; *m* 1932, Nancy Philip; one *d*. *Educ:* Edinburgh. Studied art at Edinburgh Coll. of Art (Painting and Drawing) and RSA Life School (Carnegie Travelling Scholarship, 1928), London, Paris and Italy; afterwards specialized in picture restoration. FMA; FIIC. *Address:* Dean Park, Golf Course Road, Bonnyrigg, Midlothian; The National Gallery of Scotland, Edinburgh. *T:* Lasswade 3249. *Club:* Scottish Arts.

**WOOLFSON, Mark;** Chief Mechanical and Electrical Engineer, Ministry of Public Building and Works, since 1969; *b* 10 Nov. 1911; *s* of Victor Woolfson and Sarah (*née* Kixman); *m* 1940, Queenie Carlis; two *d*. *Educ:* City of London. Student Engr, Lancashire Dynamo & Crypto, until 1936; Engr, ASEA Electric Ltd, 1936-40; War Service, RNVR, 1940-46 (Lt-Comdr); MPBW, 1946-. FIMechE, FIEE, Sen. Mem. IEE. *Publications:* papers in Jls of Instns of Civil, Mechanical and Elect. Engrs. *Recreations:* tennis, gardening, golf. *Address:* 3 Runnelfield, Harrow, Mddx. *T:* 01-422 1599.

**WOOLLAM, John Victor;** Barrister-at-Law; *b* 14 Aug. 1927; *s* of Thomas Alfred and Edie Moss Woollam; *m* 1964, Lavinia Rosamund Ela, *d* of S. R. E. Snow; two *s*. *Educ:* Liverpool Univ. Called to the Bar, Inner Temple. Contested (C) Scotland Div. of Liverpool, 1950; MP (C) W Derby Div. of Liverpool, Nov. 1954-Sept. 1964; Parliamentary Private Sec. to Minister of Labour, 1960-62. *Recreation:* philately. *Address:* Plas Newydd, Llanfair DC, near Ruthin, Denbighshire. *Club:* Carlton.

**WOOLLCOMBE, Dame Jocelyn May,** DBE, *cr* 1950 (CBE 1944); *b* 9 May 1898; *d* of late Admiral Maurice Woollcombe and Ella Margaret Roberts; unmarried. *Educ:* Moorfield, Plymouth. Admiralty, NID as Clerk, 1916-19. Joined WRNS, enrolled as Chief Officer, Aug. 1939; Superintendent, 1940; Deputy Director, 1943-46; Director, 1946-50; Hon. ADC to the King, 1949. General Secretary, British Council for Aid to Refugees (Hungarian Section), 1957-58. Governor, The Sister Trust, 1956-65; Gov., WRNS Benevolent Trust, 1942-67; Pres., Assoc. of Wrens 1959-. *Recreation:* drama. *Address:* 2 Thorn Park, Plymouth. *Club:* Service Women's.

**WOOLLCOMBE, Rt. Rev. Kenneth John;** *see* Oxford, Bishop of.

**WOOLLER, Arthur,** CBE 1967; British High Commissioner in Mauritius, 1968-70; *b* 23 May 1912; *s* of Joseph Edward Wooller and Sarah Elizabeth (*née* Kershaw); *m* 1944, Frances, *e d* of Justice A. L. Blank, ICS; three *s*. *Educ:* Bradford Grammar School; Corpus Christi College, Oxford. ICS, Bengal, 1935; Indian Foreign and Political Service, 1939; UK Trade Comr, New Zealand, 1947; First Sec. (Commercial), Ottawa, 1953; UK Trade Comr, Toronto, 1959; British Trade Comr, Hong Kong, 1960; Principal British Trade Comr, Bombay, 1963; British Deputy High Commissioner in Western India, Bombay, 1965-68. *Recreations:* fishing, golf. *Address:* c/o Foreign and Commonwealth Office, SW1. *Club:* United Universities.

**WOOLLETT, Maj.-Gen. John Castle,** CBE 1957 (OBE 1955); MC 1945; MA Cantab; FICE; retired, 1970; *b* 5 Nov. 1915; *o s* of John Castle Woollett and Lily Bradley Woollett, Bredgar, Kent; *m* 1st, 1941, Joan Eileen Stranks (marr. diss., 1957); two *s* (and one *s* decd); 2nd, 1959, Helen Wendy Willis; two step *s*. *Educ:* St Benedict's Sch.; RMA Woolwich; St John's Coll., Cambridge. Joined RE, 1935; 23 Field Co., 1938-40 (BEF, 1939-40); 6 Commando, 1940-42; Major Comdg 16 Field Sqdn and 16 Assault Sqdn RE, 1942-45 (BLA, 1944-45); Student, Staff Coll., Camberley, 1946; DAAG and GSO2, Brit. Service Mission to Burma, 1947-50; Major Comdg 51 Port Sqdn RE, 1950; Instructor, Staff Coll., Camberley, 1950-53; Lt-Col Comdg 28 Field Engr Regt, 1954-55 (Korea); Bt Lt-Col 1955; Comdr Christmas Is, 1956-57; GSO1, Northern Army Gp, 1957-59; Col GS, US Army Staff Coll., Fort Leavenworth, 1959-61; DQMG (Movements), BAOR, 1962-64; Brig. Comdg Hants Sub District and Transportation Centre, RE, 1964-65; Sch. of Transport, 1965-66; Dep. Engr-in-Chief, 1966-67; Maj.-Gen., Chief Engineer, BAOR, 1967-70. *Recreations:* cruising and ocean racing, ski-ing, shooting. *Address:* 19 Shepherds Way, Liphook, Hants. *Clubs:* Army and Navy, Royal Ocean Racing, Ski Club of Great Britain; Island Sailing (Cowes).

**WOOLLEY,** family name of **Baron Woolley.**

**WOOLLEY,** Baron *cr* 1967 (Life Peer), of Hatton; **Harold Woolley,** Kt 1964; CBE 1958; DL; President of National Farmers' Union of England and Wales 1960-66; *b* 6 Feb. 1905; *s* of William Woolley, JP and Eleanor Woolley; *m* 1st, 1926, Martha Annie Jeffs; 2nd, 1937, Hazel Eileen Archer Jones; four *s* two *d*. *Educ:* Woodhouse Grove School, Yorkshire. Farmer. Cheshire Deleg. to NFU Council, 1943; Chairman: NFU Parliamentary Cttee, 1947-57; Employers' Reps of Agricultural Wages Bd, 1947-57; Agricultural Apprenticeship Council for England and Wales, 1951-60. National Farmers' Union: Vice-Pres. 1948 and 1955; Dep. Pres., 1949-50 and 1956; Director: NFU Mutual Insurance Society, 1965-; NW Regional Adv. Bd, Abbey Nat. Building Soc. Member Nat. Jt Advisory Council to Ministry of Labour, 1950-58. DL Cheshire, 1969. *Recreations:* hunting, golf; interested in all sport. *Address:* Hatton House Farm, Hatton Heath, Chester. *T:* Tattenhall 356.

*See also W. E. Woolley.*

**WOOLLEY, Rev. (Alfred) Russell;** MA; Rector, St Lawrence, IoW, since 1967; *b* 10 Sept. 1899; *e s* of late A. W. Woolley, Moseley, and Margaret A. Russell, Shrewsbury; *m* 1933, Lina Mariana, 3rd *d* of late Prof. Bertram

Hopkinson, CMG, FRS, Fellow of King's College, Cambridge; four *s* three *d*. *Educ:* King Edward's Camp Hill Grammar School; Wadham College, Oxford (Symons Exhibitioner). 2nd Class Hons Modern History, 1922; incorporated MA Cantab. (Trinity College), 1929. One year Inns of Court OTC and 6th OC Bn; Bromsgrove School, 1922-26; Repton School, 1927-28; The Leys School (Chief History Master, House-Master, Librarian, OC, OTC), 1929-33; Headmaster of Scarborough Coll., 1933-37, and of Wellingborough Gram. Sch., 1937-45; Educnl Sec. to the Oxford Univ. Appts Cttee, 1945-62. Ordained 1960. Rector of Gestingthorpe, Essex, 1962-67. Mem. Coun. IAHM, 1945; of Oxfordshire Educn Cttee, 1955-62; of Govng Body of Milton Abbey Sch., 1955-; of Lindisfarne Coll., 1961-; ex-Sec. Oxford Union Soc. *Publications:* Oxford University and City, 1951; Clarendon Guide to Oxford, 1963. *Recreations:* walking, travel. *Address:* The Rectory, St Lawrence, Ventnor, Isle of Wight. *T:* Ventnor 377.
*See also F. J. W. Roughton.*

**WOOLLEY, Sir Charles (Campbell),** GBE 1953 (OBE 1934); KCMG 1943 (CMG 1937); MC; LLD; *b* 1893; 3rd *s* of Henry Woolley; *m* 1921, Ivy, *d* of late David Howells, Cwmbarry, Barry, Glamorgan; two *s*. *Educ:* Univ. Coll., Cardiff. Served European War, 1914-20; Captain S Wales Borderers; various staff appts; Active Service, France, Salonika, Constantinople, Caucasus (despatches, MC); Ceylon Civil Service, 1921-35; Secretary to the Governor; Colonial Secretary, Jamaica, 1935-38; Chief Secretary Nigeria, 1938-41; administered Govt of Jamaica and Nigeria at various times; Governor and C-in-C, Cyprus, 1941-46; Governor and Commander-in-Chief, British Guiana, 1947-53; retired Jan. 1953. Pres., Internat. Soc. for Protection of Animals, 1969-71. KJStJ. *Recreations:* bridge, music. *Address:* Orchard Hill, Liss, Hants. *T:* Liss 2317.

**WOOLLEY, Howard Mark,** CBE 1927; *b* 23 June 1879; *m* 1st, Margaret Marie (*d* 1926), *d* of F. Gaze; 2nd, 1932, Aline Veronica, *o d* of late Sir F. A. Van der Meulen; one *s* one *d*. *Educ:* London. Civil Service, Post Office, 1891; Northern Nigeria Civil Service, 1905; retired as Postmaster-General, Nigeria, 1926; served Cameroons Expeditionary Force, 1914-15; Central Electricity Board, 1928-36. *Address:* Little Barden, Speldhurst, Tunbridge Wells, Kent.

**WOOLLEY, John Maxwell,** MBE 1945; TD 1946; Clerk, Merchant Taylors' Company, and Clerk to The Governors, Merchant Taylor's School, since 1962; *b* 22 March 1917; *s* of Lt-Col Jasper Maxwell Woolley, IMS (Retd) and Kathleen Mary Woolley (*née* Waller); *m* 1952, Esme Adela Hamilton-Cole; two *s*. *Educ:* Cheltenham College; Trinity College, Oxford. BA (Oxon.) 1938, MA (Oxon.) 1962. Practising Solicitor, 1950-55; Asst Clerk, Merchant Taylors' Company, 1955-62. *Address:* 32 Salisbury Road, Hove, Sussex. *T:* Brighton 733200.

**WOOLLEY, Sir Richard (van der Riet),** Kt 1963; OBE 1953; FRS 1953; Astronomer Royal, 1956-Dec. 1971; Director designate (from Jan. 1972), South African Astronomical Observatory; Hon. Fellow, University House, Australian National University, since 1955; Hon. Fellow, Gonville and Caius College, Cambridge, since 1956; *b* Weymouth, Dorset, 24 April 1906; *s* of Paymaster Rear-Admiral Charles E. A. Wooley, CMG, RN; *m* 1932, Gwyneth Jane Margaret (*née* Meyler). *Educ:* Allhallows School, Honiton; University of Cape Town; Gonville and Caius College, Cambridge; MSc Cape Town; MA, ScD Cantab; Hon. LLD Melbourne. Commonwealth Fund Fellow, at Mt Wilson Observatory, California, 1929-31; Isaac Newton Student, Cambridge Univ., 1931-33; Chief Assistant, R Observatory, Greenwich, 1933-37; John Couch Adams Astronomer, Cambridge, 1937-39; Commonwealth Astronomer, 1939-55. Hon. Professor of Astronomy in Australian National University, 1950-. Visiting Prof. of Astronomy, Univ. of Sussex, 1966-. Pres., Royal Astronomical Soc., 1963-65. Vice-Pres., International Astronomical Union, 1952-58; Pres., Australian and New Zealand Assoc. for the Advancement of Science, Melbourne meeting, 1955. Hon. DrPhil Uppsala; Hon. DSc Cape Town. Corresp. mem. de la Société Royale des Sciences de Liège, 1956. Master, Worshipful Co. of Clockmakers, 1969. *Publications:* (with Sir Frank Dyson) Eclipses of the Sun and Moon, 1937; (with D. W. N. Stibbs) The Outer Layers of a Star, 1953. *Address:* Royal Greenwich Observatory, Herstmonceux Castle, Sussex. *T:* Herstmonceux 3171. *Clubs:* Athenæum, Beefsteak.

**WOOLLEY, Russell;** *see* Woolley, A. R.

**WOOLLEY, William Edward;** *b* 17 March 1901; *s* of William Woolley, JP, and Eleanor Woolley; *m* 1929, Marion Elizabeth Aspinall; one *s* one *d*. *Educ:* Woodhouse Grove School, Yorkshire; Edinburgh University. MP (Nat L) for Spen Valley Division of Yorkshire, 1940-45; Parliamentary Private Secretary to Minister of Health, 1943, to Minister of Aircraft Production, 1945. JP; Chairman: Blackburn Borough Magistrates; Gen. Comrs Inland Revenue, Blackburn District; Blackburn and District Hosp. Management Cttee; Manchester Regional Hosp. Staff Cttee; Member, Manchester Regional Hosp. Board. Contested (Nat L) Brighouse and Spenborough, General elections, 1950, 1951. *Address:* Billinge Crest, Billinge End Road, Blackburn, Lancs. *TA* and *T:* Blackburn 53449. *Clubs:* National Liberal; Union (Blackburn).
*See also Baron Woolley.*

**WOOLMER, Rt. Rev. Laurence Henry,** MA; Assistant Bishop of Portsmouth, since 1968; Rector of St Andrew's, Meonstoke, with Corhampton with Exton, since 1968; an Honorary Canon of Portsmouth Cathedral, since 1968; *b* 22 Feb. 1906; *s* of Alfred Henry Woolmer, actuary; *m* 1941, Ruth May, *d* of Rev. Canon W. Hanan, MA, Sligo; two *s*. *Educ:* King Edward's School, Birmingham. Bank of England, 1925-34; passed Intermediate Examination Chartered Institute Secretaries, 1927, Final, 1929; Hons Theology 3rd class, St Peter's Hall, Oxford, 1934-37; Wycliffe Hall, Oxford, 1937-38; Curate, S Paul's Church, Salisbury, 1938-40; Church Missionary Society, Gojra, Lyallpur District, Punjab, 1940-44; Sec., CMS Mission, Punjab, 1944-48; Archdeacon of Lahore, 1948-49; Bishop of Lahore, 1949-68. Hon. Fellow, St Peter's College, Oxford, 1968-. *Address:* Meonstoke Rectory, near Southampton, Hants. *T:* Droxford 499.

**WOOLNER, Maj.-Gen. Christopher Geoffrey,** CB 1942; MC; *b* 18 Oct. 1893; *m* 1923, Anne, *d* of Sydney Pitt; two *d*. *Educ:* Marlborough; RMA, Woolwich. 2nd Lt RE, 1912; Captain, 1917; Bt Major, 1919; Major, 1928; Bt Lt-Col, 1933; Lt-Col, 1936; Col, 1939; Maj.-Gen., 1941. Survey Duty, Gold Coast, 1920-23; Officer Company of Gentlemen Cadets Royal Military Academy, 1924-27; GSO2 India, 1930-32; Bde Major, India, 1932-34; Deputy Inspector and Deputy Comdt School of

Military Engineering, Aug.-Sept. 1939; GSO1, BEF, 1939-40; Bde Comdr, Feb.-Nov. 1940; Comdr, 1940. Served European War, 1914-18 (wounded, despatches twice, Bt Major, MC and two Bars); War of 1939-45 (despatches thrice, CB); Commander 81st (West African) Div.; Commander Mid-West District and 53 (Welsh) Infantry Division TA; retired, 1947. *Club:* United Service.

**WOOLNOUGH, Rev. Canon Howard Frank,** OBE 1957; Canon of Manchester Cathedral, 1934-60, Canon Emeritus since 1960; *b* 28 Feb. 1886; *e s* of Howard James and Fanny Kate Woolnough; unmarried. *Educ:* Christ's Coll., Cambridge (MA). Army, 1914-18; Ridley Hall, Cambridge, 1918; Asst Curate St Paul, Cheltenham, 1919-26; Chaplain Christ's College, Cambridge, 1924-34; Gen. Sec., Central Advisory Council of Training for the Ministry, 1927-34. Chairman, Chaplains' Committee, Air Cadet Council, 1941-67. *Address:* 20 Blackfield Lane, Manchester 7. *T:* 061-792 1769.

**WOOLTON,** 3rd Earl of, *cr* 1956; **Simon Frederick Marquis;** Baron Woolton, 1939; Viscount Woolton, 1953; Viscount Walberton, 1956; *b* 24 May 1958; *s* of 2nd Earl of Woolton and Cecily Josephine (now Lady Forres), *e d* of Sir Alexander Gordon Cumming, 5th Bt; *S* father, 1969. *Address:* 31 Tite Street, SW3.

*See also Baron Forres.*

**WOOLWICH, Bishop Suffragan of,** since Oct. 1969; **Rt. Rev. David Stuart Sheppard;** *b* 6 March 1929; *s* of Stuart Morton Winter Sheppard, Solicitor, and Barbara Sheppard; *m* 1957, Grace Isaac; one *d. Educ:* Sherborne; Trinity Hall, Cambridge (MA); Ridley Hall Theological Coll. Asst Curate, St Mary's, Islington, 1955-57; Warden, Mayflower Family Centre, Canning Town, E16, 1957-69. Cricket: Cambridge Univ., 1950-52 (Captain 1952); Sussex, 1947-62 (Captain 1953); England (played 22 times) 1950-63 (Captain 1954). *Publication:* Parson's Pitch, 1964. *Recreations:* family, reading, music, painting, theatre. *Address:* 12 Asylum Road, Peckham, SE15. *T:* 01-639 1613.

**WOOSTER, Clive Edward Doré,** FRIBA; AMTPI; MBIM; Deputy Chief Architect, Ministry of Housing and Local Government, since 1969; *b* 3 Nov. 1913; *s* of Edward Doré Wooster; *m* 1942, Elisabeth Mary (*née* Lewis) (marr. diss. 1970); two *s*; *m* 1970, Patricia Iris (formerly Dewey). *Educ:* Private School, Southend-on-Sea. Private offices, 1930-40; War Service, Captain RA, 1940-46. Local Authority Offices and LCC, 1946-51; Ministry of Education, 1951-58; University Grants Cttee, 1958-59; Works Directorate, War Office, 1959-63; Dir of Building Management, MPBW, 1963-69. RIBA Technical Standards Cttee, 1960-64; RIBA Building Controls Panel Chairman, 1960-63; RIBA Management Handbook Cttee, 1963-67; RIBA Council, 1970. *Publications:* Lectures on architectural and building management subjects; contrib. to professional journals. *Address:* 141 Harefield Road, Rickmansworth, Herts. *T:* Rickmansworth 75401.

**WOOTTEN, Maj.-Gen. Richard Montague,** CB 1940; MC; *b* 19 June 1889; *s* of William Montague Wootten, Headington House, Oxon.; *m* 1st, 1915, *d* of Sir John Wormald, KBE; two *d*; 2nd, *d* of William Percival. *Educ:* Rugby; RMC Sandhurst; Staff College, Camberley. 2nd Lieut 6th Dragoons, 1909; Major Queens Bays, 1921; served European War, France and Belgium, 1914-18 (MC); Palestine and Egypt, 1936-39; War of 1939-45 (CB, Commander Legion of Merit, USA). Retired, 1945. *Address:* Little Court, Cromwell Gardens, Marlow, Bucks. *T:* 4246.

**WOOTTON OF ABINGER,** Baroness *cr* 1958 (Life Peer), of Abinger Common, (**Barbara Frances**), MA; *b* Cambridge, 1897; *d* of late Dr James Adam, Senior Tutor of Emmanuel Coll., Cambridge and Mrs Adam, sometime Fellow of Girton Coll., Cambridge; *m* 1st, 1917, John Wesley Wootton (*d* of wounds, 1917), Earl of Derby Research Student, Trinity College, Cambridge; 2nd, 1935, George Percival Wright (*d* 1964). *Educ:* Perse High School for Girls, Cambridge; Girton Coll., Cambridge (MA Cantab). Director of Studies and Lecturer in Economics, Girton Coll., 1920-22; Research Officer Trades Union Congress and Labour Party Joint Research Department, 1922-26; Principal, Morley College for Working Men and Women, 1926-27; Director of Studies for Tutorial Classes, University of London, 1927-44; Professor of Social Studies, University of London, 1948-52; Nuffield Research Fellow, Bedford College, University of London, 1952-57. A Governor of the BBC, 1950-56; a Deputy-Speaker in House of Lords, 1967-. Member: Royal Commission on Workmen's Compensation, 1938, Royal Commn on the Press, 1947; Royal Commn on the Civil Service, 1954; Royal Commn on Penal System, 1964-66; Council on Tribunals, 1961-64; Chm., Countryside Commn, 1968-70 (Nat. Parks Commn, 1966-68). JP on the Panel of Chairmen in the Metropolitan Juvenile Courts, 1946-62. Hon. degrees: LHD Columbia; LLD Liverpool, Nottingham, Aberdeen and Hull; DSc, Aston in Birmingham, Bath; DUniv, York. Hon. Fellow: Girton Coll., Cambridge, 1965-; Bedford Coll., London, 1964-. *Publications:* (as *Barbara Wootton*): Twos and Threes, 1933; Plan or No Plan, 1934; London's Burning, 1936; Lament for Economics, 1938; End Social Inequality, 1941; Freedom Under Planning, 1945; Testament for Social Science, 1950; The Social Foundations of Wage Policy, 1955; Social Science and Social Pathology, 1959; Crime and the Criminal Law, 1964; In a World I Never Made, 1967. *Recreation:* country life. *Address:* High Barn, Abinger Common, Dorking, Surrey. *T:* Dorking 730180.

**WOOTTON, Harold Samuel,** CMG 1942; FCIS; JP; Town Clerk of Melbourne, 1935-54, retired; *b* Ballan, Vic, 13 Dec. 1891; *s* of late John Richard Wootton, Tatura, Goulburn Valley, Victoria; *m* 1914, Anne, *d* of late Joseph Biggs; one *s* one *d. Educ:* State School, Waranga, Victoria; Central Business College, Melbourne. Junior Clerk, Melbourne Town Hall, 1909; Deputy Town Clerk, 1923. *Recreation:* bowls. *Address:* 453 St Kilda Road, Melbourne, Victoria, Australia. *Club:* St Kilda Bowling.

**WOOTTON, Ian David Phimester,** MA, MB, BChir, PhD, FRIC, MCPath, MRCP; Professor of Chemical Pathology, Postgraduate Medical School of London, University of London, since 1963; *b* 5 March 1921; *s* of D. Wootton and Charlotte (*née* Phimester); *m* 1946, Veryan Mary Walshe; two *s* two *d. Educ:* Weymouth Grammar School; St John's College, Cambridge; St Mary's Hospital, London. Research Assistant, Postgraduate Med. School, 1945; Lecturer, 1949; Sen. Lecturer, 1959; Reader, 1961. Consultant Pathologist to Hammersmith Hospital, 1952. Member of Medical Research Council Unit, Cairo, 1947-48; Major, RAMC, 1949; Smith-Mundt Fellow, Memorial Hosp., New York, 1951. *Publications:* Microanalysis in Medical Biochemistry, 1964; papers in medical and scientific journals on biochemistry and pathology. *Recreations:* beekeeping, carpentry, boating. *Address:* 4 Pemberton Road, East Molesey, Surrey. *T:* 01-979 6246.

**WOOZLEY, Prof. Anthony Douglas,** MA; Professor of Philosophy, University of Virginia, since 1966; *b* 14 Aug. 1912; *o s* of David Adams Woozley and Kathleen Lucy Moore; *m* 1937, Thelma Suffield, *e d* of late Frank Townshend, Worcester; one *d. Educ:* Haileybury College; Queen's College, Oxford. Open Scholar, Queen's College, 1931-35; 1st Cl. Class. Hon. Mods, 1933; 1st Cl. Lit. Hum., 1935; John Locke Schol., 1935. Fellow of All Souls College, 1935-37; Fellow and Praelector in Philosophy, Queen's Coll., 1937-54; Librarian, 1938-54; Professor of Moral Philosophy, Univ. of St Andrews, 1954-67. Served War, 1940-46 (despatches), in Army; commissioned King's Dragoon Guards, 1941; served North Africa, Italy, Greece, Egypt, Syria, Palestine; Major. Tutor, Queen's College, 1946-54; University Lecturer in Philosophy, 1947-54; Senior Proctor, 1953-54. Editor of The Philosophical Quarterly, Quarterly, 1957-62; Editor, Home University Library, 1962-68. Visiting Professor of Philosophy, University of Rochester, USA, 1965. *Publications:* (ed) Thomas Reid's Essays on the Intellectual Powers of Man, 1941; Theory of Knowledge, 1949; (with R. C. Cross) Plato's Republic: a Philosophical Commentary, 1964; (ed) John Locke's Essay Concerning Human Understanding, 1964. Articles and reviews in Mind, etc. *Address:* RFD 3, Kearsarge, Charlottesville, Va 22901, USA.

**WORCESTER, Bishop of,** since 1970; **Rt. Rev. Robert Wilmer Woods,** MA; *b* 15 Feb. 1914; *s* of late Edward Woods, Bishop of Lichfield, and Clemence (*née* Barclay); *m* 1942, Henrietta Marion (JP 1966), *d* of late K. H. Wilson; two *s* three *d. Educ:* Gresham's Sch., Holt; Trinity Coll., Cambridge. Asst Sec., Student Christian Movement, 1937-42; Chaplain to the Forces, 1942-46 (despatches, 1944); Vicar of South Wigston, Leicester, 1946-51; Archdeacon of Singapore and Vicar of St Andrew's Cathedral, 1951-58; Archdeacon of Sheffield and Rector of Tankersley, 1958-62; Dean of Windsor, 1962-70; Domestic Chaplain to the Queen, 1962-70; Register of the Most Noble Order of the Garter, 1962-70. Secretary, Anglican/Methodist Commn for Unity, 1965; Member: Council, Duke of Edinburgh's Award Scheme, 1968; Public Schools Commn, 1968-70; Governor, Haileybury Coll.; Chairman: Windsor Festival Co., 1969; Churches Television Centre, 1969-; Dir, Christian Aid, 1969. *Recreations:* sailing, shooting, painting. *Address:* Bishop's House, Hartlebury Castle, Kidderminster, Worcs. *Clubs:* Brooks's, English-Speaking Union.

**WORCESTER, Assistant Bishops of;** *see* Allenby, Rt Rev. D. H. N, Vockler, Rt Rev. J. C.

**WORCESTER, Dean of;** *see* Kemp, Very Rev. E. W.

**WORCESTER, Archdeacon of;** *see* Eliot, Ven. P. C.

**WORDSWORTH, Maj.-Gen. Robert Harley,** CB 1945; CBE 1943; late IA; Administrator, Norfolk Island, 1962-64; *b* 21 July 1894; *s* of W. H. Wordsworth; *m* 1928, Margaret Joan Ross-Reynolds; one *s* one *d.* Served European War, 1914-18, AIF (despatches); Waziristan, 1919-21; NW Frontier of India, 1930; Persia-Iraq, 1943 (CBE); Middle East, 1945 (CB); retired, 1947. Senator Commonwealth Govt of Australia, 1949-59. *Recreation:* trout fishing. *Address:* Ankerton, The Esplanade, Perth, Tasmania 7300, Australia. *Club:* Launceston (Launceston, Tasmania).

**WORKMAN, Harold,** RBA, ROI, RSMA, RCA, FPhS; Painter in oil and water colour; Lecturer on colour and pigments, and demonstrator of landscape painting; Visiting master, Sir John Cass College, and Hammersmith School of Arts and Crafts; *b* 3 Oct. 1897; 3rd *s* of Ernest Workman, Decorator and Contractor; *m* 1st, (marr. diss.); 2nd, 1958, Margaret Joan, *d* of E. J. Stokes, Darlington. *Educ:* Private School and Tutor; Oldham and Manchester Schools of Art. Exhibitor at Principal exhibitions in Europe, Toronto, and New York; International Exhibitions, Pittsburg and Ghent; numerous works in permanent collections including Manchester, Salford, Oldham, Northampton and Bournemouth; RBA 1937; ROI 1948; RSMA 1962; RCA 1950; Member Manchester Academy of Fine Arts; Pres. United Society of Artists; formerly Art Master and Lecturer at Architectural Assoc. *Publications:* Polymer Painting, 1967; series of articles on Oil Painting, 1945-46. *Recreations:* motoring, chess, billiards. *Address:* 3 Olney House, 51 Palace Road, East Molesey, Surrey. *T:* 01-979 5139. *Club:* Arts.

**WORKMAN, Robert Little;** Under-Secretary, HM Treasury, since 1967; *b* 30 Oct. 1914; *s* of late Robert Workman and Jesse Little; *m* 1940, Gladys Munroe Foord; two *d. Educ:* Sedbergh Sch.; Clare Coll., Cambridge. Economist, Export Credits Guarantee Dept, 1938-49; HM Treasury: Principal, 1949-59; Asst Secretary, 1959-66. Member, St Pancras Borough Council, 1945-49. *Recreations:* building and the visual arts. *Address:* 89 Swain's Lane, N6. *T:* 01-340 2230.

**WORKMAN, William Thomas,** CBE 1919; MC, BA (Hons); Headmaster Alleyne's Grammar School, Stevenage, retired; 2nd *s* of Charles Workman, RHA, and Elizabeth Wilkes; *m* 1919, Veronica Grace Moore; one *d. Educ:* privately; Clevedon; Paris; Rome. Schoolmaster and Journalist, USA, Canada and England; served with Canadians, European War (despatches, CBE, MC). *Recreations:* cricket and golf; first winner of The Bandit's Driver at Knebworth Golf Club. *Address:* Gaerwen, Grenville Road, Salcombe, Devon.

**WORLEY, Sir Newnham (Arthur),** KBE 1958; Kt 1950; *b* 2 March 1892; *y s* of late Charles Worley, Reigate; *m* 1919, Marie (*d* 1966), *d* of late Rev. R. R. Forlong; two *d. Educ:* Reigate Grammar Sch.; Emmanuel Coll., Cambridge (MA). Barrister-at-law, Inner Temple; Hon. Bencher, Inner Temple, 1959. Malayan CS, 1914-37; Colonial Legal Service, Solicitor General Straits Settlement, 1937; Puisne Judge, Supreme Court, Singapore, 1941-47; interned by Japanese, 1942-45; Chief Justice, British Guiana, and a Member of West Indian Court of Appeal, 1947-51; President, E. African Court of Appeal, Oct. 1955-April 1958 (Vice-President, 1951-55); retired from Overseas Judiciary, 1958; Chief Justice, Bermuda, 1958, resigned 1960. *Address:* Hollyoak, Bell Hill Ridge, Petersfield, Hants. *T:* 3857. *Club:* East India and Sports.

**WORLOCK, Rt. Rev. Derek John Harford;** *see* Portsmouth, Bishop of, (RC).

**WORMALD, Brian Harvey Goodwin,** MA; University Lecturer in History, Cambridge, since 1948; Fellow of Peterhouse since 1938; *b* 24 July 1912; *s* of late Rev. C. O. R. Wormald and Mrs A. W. C. Wormald (*née* Brooks); *m* 1946, Rosemary, *d* of E. J. B. Lloyd; four *s.*

*Educ:* Harrow; Peterhouse, Cambridge (Scholar). BA 1934 (1st Class Hons Hist. Tripos, Parts I and II); Members Prize (English Essay), 1935; Strathcona Research Student, St John's College, 1936-38; Prince Consort Prize, 1938; MA 1938. Chaplain and Catechist, Peterhouse, 1940-48; Dean, 1941-44; Tutor, 1952-62. Select Preacher, Cambridge, 1945 and 1954. Junior Proctor, 1951-52. Received into Catholic Church, 1955. *Publication:* Clarendon: Politics, History and Religion, 1951. *Address:* Peterhouse, Cambridge.

**WORMALD, Maj.-Gen. Derrick Bruce,** DSO 1944; MC 1940, Bar 1945; Director-General of Fighting Vehicles and Engineer Equipment, Ministry of Defence, 1966-70; *b* 28 April 1916; 2nd *s* of Arthur and Veronica Wormald; *m* 1953, Betty Craddock; two *d. Educ:* Bryanston Sch.; RMA Sandhurst. Commnd into 13/18 Royal Hussars (QMO), 1936; served in India, 1936-38, BEF, 1939-40 and BLA, 1944-45; Comd, 25th Dragoons, India, 1945-47; Staff Coll., Quetta, 1947; War Office, 1948-50; Comdr, 1st Armoured Car Regt of Arab Legion, 1951-52; Comdr Arab Legion Armoured Corps, 1953-54; jssc 1955; GSO1, 11th Armoured Div., 1956; Comd, 3rd The King's Own Hussars, 1956, and The Queen's Own Hussars, 1958; Comdr, Aden Protectorate Levies, 1959-61; Comdr, Salisbury Plain Sub District, 1962-65. Order of El Istiqlal (Jordan), 1953. *Recreations:* shooting, fishing, sailing. *Address:* Ballards, Wickham Bishops, Essex. *T:* Wickham Bishops 218. *Club:* Cavalry.

**WORMALD, Dame Ethel (May),** DBE 1968; JP; DL; Lecturer and Adviser in Adult Education; *b* 19 Nov. 1901; *d* of late John Robert Robinson, Journalist, Newcastle upon Tyne; *m* 1923, Stanley Wormald, MA, MEd, BSc (decd); two *s. Educ:* Whitley Bay High Sch.; Leeds Univ. (BA, DipEd). JP, Liverpool, 1948-; Liverpool City Councillor, 1953-67; Lord Mayor of Liverpool, 1967-68. President, Assoc. of Education Cttees, 1961-62; Chairman, Liverpool Education Cttee, 1955-61, and 1963-67. DL Lancaster, 1970. *Recreations:* theatre, foreign travel. *Address:* 39 Ullet Road, Liverpool 17. *T:* 051-733 1331. *Clubs:* Crosby Hall (British Federation of University Women) (Chelsea); Bluecoat (Liverpool).

**WORMALD, Francis,** CBE 1969; MA, LittD, FBA, FSA; President, Society of Antiquaries of London, 1965-70; Hon. Fellow Magdalene Coll., Cambridge, 1961; *b* 1 June 1904; *m* 1935, Honoria Mary Rosamund Yeo. *Educ:* Eton; Magdalene Coll., Cambridge. Asst Keeper, Dept of Manuscripts, British Museum, 1927-49; Prof. of Paleography, London Univ., 1950-60; Prof. of History and Dir, Inst. of Historical Research, London Univ., 1960-67. Member: Inst. for Advanced Study, Princeton, 1955-56; Royal Commn on Historical Monuments, 1957; Advisory Council on Public Records, 1965-67; Trustee, British Museum, 1967. FKC 1964. Membre adhérent de la Société des Bollandistes, 1960; Corresp. Fellow, German Archæol Inst., 1962. Hon. DUniv York, 1969. *Publications:* English Kalendars before AD 1100, 1934, English Benedictine Kalendars after AD 1100, 2 vols, 1939, 1946, English Drawings of the 10th and 11th Centuries, 1952; Miniatures in the Gospels of St Augustine, 1954. Style and Design in the Bayeux Tapestry in Phaidon Press's The Bayeux Tapestry, 1957; Liturgical and Palæographical Appendixes in H. Buchthal's Miniature Painting in the Latin Kingdom of Jerusalem, 1957; with O. Pächt and C. R. Dodwell, The St Albans Psalter, 1960. Articles in Analecta Bollandiana, Archæologia, Antiquaries Journal, Proc. Walpole Society, etc. *Address:* 59 Warwick Square, SW1. *Club:* Reform.

**WORMELL, Prof. Donald Ernest Wilson;** Professor of Latin, University of Dublin, since 1942; Fellow, Trinity College, Dublin, 1939; *b* 5 Jan. 1908; *yr s* of Thomas Wilson and Florence Wormell; *m* 1941, Daphne Dillon Wallace; three *s* one *d. Educ:* Perse School. Schol., St John's Coll., Cambridge, 1926; 1st Class Classical Tripos, Parts I and II; Sandys Student, 1930; Henry Fund Fellow, 1931; Sterling Research Fellow, Yale, 1932; PhD Yale, 1933; Fellow, St John's Coll., Cambridge, 1933-36; Asst Lecturer in Classics, University College, Swansea, 1936-39. Leverhulme Research Fellowship, 1958. Employed by Air Ministry and Foreign Office, 1942-44. Public Orator, University of Dublin, 1952. MRIA; Mem., Inst. for Advanced Study, Princeton, USA, 1967-68. *Publications:* (with H. W. Parke) The Delphic Oracle, 1956; articles on classical literature and ancient history in learned periodicals. *Recreation:* music. *Address:* Gatineau, Sandyford Road, Dundrum, Dublin 14. *T:* Dublin 983932.

**WORRALL, Air Vice-Marshal John,** CB 1963; DFC 1940; retired; Managing Director, The Advertising Agency Poster Bureau Ltd, 1964-65; *b* 9 April 1911; *o s* of late J. R. S. Worrall, Thackers, Bombay, India; *m* 1967, Barbara Jocelyne, *er d* of late Vincent Ronald Robb. *Educ:* Cranleigh; Royal Air Force Coll., Cranwell. Commission Royal Air Force, 1931; flying duties No 1 Sqdn, 1932, No 208 Sqdn, 1933-36; language study, Peking, 1936-39; commanded No 32 (F) Sqdn Biggin Hill, 1940; Fighter Control, Biggin Hill, 1940; Fighter and Transport Staff and Unit, 1941-45; RAF Staff Coll., 1945; Senior Personnel Staff Officer, HQ Transport Command, 1945-48; OC, RAF West Malling and Metropolitan Sector, 1948-49; OC, RAF Kai Tak, Hong Kong, 1949-51; HQ Home Command, 1952-53; Air Ministry, Organisation Branch, 1953-54; OC Eastern Sector, 1954-56; AOA, HQ Flying Training Command, 1956-58; Assistant Chief of Air Staff (Training), 1958-60; SASO, NEAF, 1960-63; retired from RAF, 1963. Chairman RAF Ski and Winter Sports Assoc., 1953-60, Vice-President, 1960-68; Chairman, Battle of Britain Fighter Assoc., 1958-60. *Recreations:* ski-ing, sailing. *Address:* c/o National Westminster Bank Ltd, Woking, Surrey. *Club:* RAF Reserves.

**WORSLEY, Lord; Charles John Pelham;** *b* 5 Nov. 1963; *s* and *heir* of 7th Earl of Yarborough, *qv*.

**WORSLEY, Air Cdre G. N. E. T. C.;** *see* Tindal-Carill-Worsley.

**WORSLEY, Very Rev. Godfrey Stuart Harling;** Dean Emeritus of Gibraltar, and Rector of Pen Selwood, since 1969 *b* 4 Dec. 1906; *o s* of late Rev. A. E. Worsley, Rector of Georgeham; *m* 1933, Stella Mary, *o c* of late H. S. Church, Croyde Manor, N Devon; two *s* one *d. Educ:* Dean Close, Cheltenham; London College of Divinity. Deacon, 1929; Priest, 1931; Asst Curate, Croydon Parish Church, 1930-33; CF, Ireland, Malta, Catterick, 1933-43; SCF, W Africa, Greece, Cyprus, 1943-49; DACG, N Midland District and Malta, 1949-54; Rector of Kingsland, 1954-60; Rural Dean of Leominster, 1956-60; Prebendary de Cublington in Hereford Cathedral, 1959-60; Proctor in Convocation, Diocese of Hereford, 1959-60; Dean of Gibraltar and Rural Dean of Southern Spain, and officiating Chaplain RN,

1960-69. *Address:* Pen Selwood Rectory, Wincanton, Somerset. *Club:* United Service.

**WORSLEY, Lt-Gen. Sir John (Francis),** KBE 1966 (OBE 1951); CB 1963; MC 1945; retired, 1968; *b* 8 July 1912; *s* of Geoffrey Worsley, OBE, ICS, and Elsie Margaret (*née* Macpherson); *m* 1942, Barbara Elizabeth Jarvis (*née* Greenwood); one *s* three *d* (and two step *d*). *Educ:* Radley; Royal Military Coll., Sandhurst. Unattached List, Indian Army (attached Queen's Own Cameron Highlanders), 1933; 3rd Bn 2nd Punjab Regt, 1934; served NW Frontier, India, 1935 and 1936-37; War of 1939-45, Middle East and SE Asia; Staff Coll., Quetta, 1941; Comd 2nd Bn 1st Punjab Regt, 1945; York and Lancaster Regt, 1947; Joint Services Staff Coll., 1951; Comd 1st Bn The South Lancashire Regt (Prince of Wales's Volunteers), 1953; Secretary, Joint Planning Staff, Ministry of Defence, 1956; Comd 6th Infantry Brigade Group, 1957; Imperial Defence Coll., 1960; General Officer Commanding 48 Division (Territorial Army) and West Midland District, 1961-63; Commandant, Staff Coll., Camberley, 1963-66; Commander, British Forces, Hong Kong, 1966-68. *Address:* Marlborough House, West Coker, Yeovil, Somerset. *Clubs:* Army and Navy.

**WORSLEY, Marcus;** *see* Worsley, W. M. J.

**WORSLEY, Rev. Richard,** SJ; MA Oxon; *b* 6 Dec. 1889. *Educ:* Stonyhurst; Oxford. Taught at Mount St Mary's Coll., St Francis Xavier's Coll., Liverpool, and Wimbledon Coll.; Professor of Logic at Heythrop Coll.; Headmaster of Stonyhurst Coll., 1929-32. Served as Army Chaplain, War of 1939-45. *Address:* St Joseph's Priory, Harrow Road West, Dorking, Surrey. *T:* 2824.

**WORSLEY, Colonel Sidney John,** DSO 1919; MC; TD; Hon. MA Oxford; Hon. LLD Exeter; BA (London) 1923; Fellow of King's College, London, 1937; Member of Council of King's College, London, 1939; Member of Senate, University of London, 1946-59; Chairman of External Council, 1948; Adviser to Overseas Students, Institute of Education, London, 1960-65; *b* 1895; *m* 1924, Marie Léodine Versnel, Edgbaston; two *d. Educ:* University College, Nottingham; King's Coll., London. Served European War, 1914-19 (wounded, despatches, MC with two bars, DSO). Senior Secretary and Deputy Academic Registrar University of London, 1923-28; Warden of University College Hall, Ealing, 1923-24; Deputy Education Officer, County of Southampton, 1928-30; Academic Registrar, University of London, 1930-45; Principal, College of Estate Management, 1945-55. Colonel Comdg, University of London Contingent, Senior Division, OTC, 1938-40 and 1947-49; Acting Principal of University of London, 1936-37. Military representative Joint Recruiting Board, London University, 1939-40; General Staff, War Office, 1940-44; Chairman, Military Education Cttee, University of London, 1944-45; Chairman Board of Military Studies, 1946; Almoner, Christ's Hospital, 1946-56; Member, South-East Metropolitan Regional Hospital Board, 1947-49. Governor, Wye Coll., 1946-55; Governor, London School of Economics, 1955; Secretary, Inter-University Council for Higher Education Overseas, 1955-59; Academic Secretary, University College, Ibadan, Nigeria, 1959-60. *Address:* 79 Cloncurry Street, SW6. *Club:* Royal Commonwealth Society.

**WORSLEY, Colonel Sir William Arthington,** 4th Bt, *cr* 1838; late Green Howards; *b* 5 April 1890; *s* of Sir William Worsley, 3rd Bt, and Augusta Mary (*d* 1913), *e d* of Edward Chivers Bower, Broxholme, Scarborough; *S* father, 1936; *m* 1924, Joyce Morgan, *d* of Sir John Brunner, 2nd Bt; three *s* one *d. Educ:* Eton; New Coll., Oxford. Joined Green Howards, 1912; served European War, 1914-19 (wounded and prisoner); retired, 1922; rejoined Green Howards, 1939; retired, 1941. Lord Lieutenant, North Riding of Yorkshire, 1951-65; County Alderman N Riding of Yorks. President: Yorkshire Agricultural Society, 1959; Yorks County Cricket Club, 1960-. President of the MCC, 1961-62. Hon. LLD Leeds, 1967. *Recreations:* cricket, golf, shooting. *Heir: s* William Marcus John Worsley, *qv. Address:* Hovingham Hall, York. *TA:* Hovingham. *T:* Hovingham 206. *Clubs:* Bath, Yorkshire (York).

**WORSLEY, (William) Marcus (John);** MP (C) Chelsea, since 1966; Parliamentary Private Secretary to Lord President of the Council, since 1970; *b* 6 April 1925; *s* of Colonel Sir William Worsley, 4th Baronet, *qv*; *m* 1955, Hon. Bridget Assheton, *d* of 1st Baron Clitheroe, *qv*; three *s* one *d. Educ:* Eton; New Coll., Oxford. Green Howards, 1943-47 (Lieut seconded to Royal West African Frontier Force). BA Hons (Oxford) Modern History, 1949. Programme Assistant, BBC European Service, 1950-53. Contested (C) Keighley, 1955; MP (C) Keighley, 1959-64. Parliamentary Private Secretary: to Minister of Health, 1960-61; to Minister without Portfolio, 1962-64. Second Church Estates Commissioner, 1970-. *Recreations:* shooting, walking, reading. *Address:* Wool Knoll, Hovingham, York. *T:* Hovingham 259; 25 Flood Street, SW3. *T:* 01-352 9821. *Clubs:* Carlton; Yorkshire (York).

**WORSNOP, Bernard Lister,** BSc, PhD, FInstP; *b* Bradford, 11 Nov. 1892; *s* of Julius Worsnop and Marie Aykroyd; *m* 1st, Nellie (*d* 1951), *d* of J. H. Wilkinson, Heaton, Bradford; one *s* one *d*; 2nd, Caryl Boyce Gale, *d* of late A. E. Gale, Farnham, Surrey. *Educ:* Carlton Sch., Bradford; King's Coll., London. BSc (1st Class Hons Physics), 1913; AKC 1914; Jelf Medallist, 1913; Layton Research Scholar, 1914; PhD 1927. Served in European War, 1915-19 (i/c X-ray Department, Military Hospital, Cosham, 1915-16; Sound Ranging in France, 1916-19 (Captain, RE); Lecturer in Physics, King's Coll., London, 1919; later Senior Lecturer and Sub-Dean of the Faculty of Science and Lecturer in Radiology, King's College; Head of Dept of Mathematics and Physics, The Polytechnic, Regent Street, 1933-37; Head of Quintin School, 1937-58. Major commanding LU OTC Survey Co., 1923-35; President of the Field Survey Association, 1930-31. *Publications:* Advanced Practical Physics (with H. T. Flint); X-Rays; originator and general editor of Methuen's Monographs on Physical Subjects; original papers in scientific journals. *Address:* Pennyfarthings, 11 Higher Woolbrook Park, Sidmouth, Devon. *T:* Sidmouth 2068. *Club:* Sidmouth (Sidmouth).

**WORSTER-DROUGHT, Charles,** MA, MD Cantab, FRCP, FCST (Hon.); MRCS, etc.; Hon. Consulting Physician and Neurologist to the Metropolitan Hospital; Hon. Consulting Physician West End Hospital for Neurology, and formerly Director of Department of Speech Disorders; Consulting Neurologist and formerly Lecturer in Neurology, Bethlem Royal Hospital; Hon. Consulting Physician-Neurologist to Royal Marsden Hospital, Leatherhead Hospital, National Institute for the Blind; Hon. Medical Director Moor House School for Speech Disorders, Hurst Green,

Surrey; *s* of Thomas C. W. and Louise W. Drought, County Tyrone; *m* 1st, Lilian (*d* 1953), *d* of William T. Revnell; 2nd, Marjorie, *d* of Rev. A. J. Revnell. *Educ:* Merchant Taylors' Sch.; Downing Coll., Cambridge (Scholar and Prizeman). Natural Science Tripos, 1st Class honours, 1910; Guy's Hospital; MRCS 1911; MB, ChB, 1912; MA 1912; MD Cambridge, MRCP 1919; FRCP 1925; Clinical Assistant, Department for Diseases of Nervous System, Guy's Hospital, 1911-14; Captain, RAMC, 1914-19 (European War); Consulting Neurologist, Woolwich Military District, 1917-19, also Tetanus Officer and other medical offices; Fearnsides Scholar in Organic Neurology, University of Cambridge, 1921; FRSM (sometime President, 1947-49) Neurological Section and Member of Council Neurological, Ophthalmological, Psychiatry and Children's Diseases Sections); Consultant Neurologist in EMS, 1939-44. *Publications:* papers and articles on medical subjects, speech disorders and organic diseases of the nervous system, including monographs on Cerebro-Spinal Fever, 1919, Neurosyphilis, 1941; Residential Speech Therapy, 1952, and chapters on Neurological subjects in Oxford Loose-leaf Medicine, British Encyclopædia of Medical Practice, Modern Trends in Neurology and Medical Evidence in Cases of Personal Injury, etc. *Recreations:* various. *Address:* 96 Harley Street, W1. *T:* 01-935 1887; Rider's Cottage, White Hill, Bletchingley, Surrey. *Club:* United University.

**WORSWICK, George David Norman;** Director, National Institute of Economic and Social Research, since 1965; *b* 18 Aug. 1916; *s* of Thomas Worswick, OBE, and Eveline (*née* Green); *m* 1940, Sylvia, *d* of A. E. Walsh, MBE; one *s* two *d* (and one *s* decd). *Educ:* St Paul's Sch.; New Coll., Oxford (Scholar). 1st class Hon. Mods (Maths), 1935; 1st class Final Hons (Maths), 1937; Dipl. in Economics and Political Science (Distinction), 1938. Research staff, Oxford Univ. Institute of Statistics, 1940-60; Fellow and Tutor in Economics, Magdalen Coll., Oxford, 1945-65 (Sen. Tutor, 1955-57; Vice-President, 1963-65; Emeritus Fellow, 1969). Member UN Technical Assistance Mission to Turkey, 1954. Vis. Prof. of Economics, MIT, 1962-63. Member, Social Science Research Council, 1966. *Publications:* Joint Editor: The British Economy 1945-50, 1952; The British Economy in the 1950's, 1962; (ed) The Free Trade Proposals, 1960; (jt) Profits in the British Economy 1909-1938, 1967; articles in Oxford Economic Papers, etc. *Recreation:* squash. *Address:* 7 Highmore Road, SE3. *T:* 01-858 2238. *Club:* United University.

**WORT, Sir Alfred William Ewart,** Kt, *cr* 1939; Barrister; *b* 17 March 1883; *e s* of Alfred and Annie Elizabeth Wort; *m* 1st, Isabelle Mary (*d* 1954), 3rd *d* of Rev. E. Henderson; two *d* (one *s* decd); 2nd, Nancye, *d* of John James Simpson. Engaged in commerce, City of London; journalist until 1913; called to Bar, Middle Temple, 1914; Judge High Court, Patna, India, 1927-40; Acting Chief Justice, 1933, 1936 and 1938. President, Bihar College, University of Patna, 1928-40; President, Council, High Sch., Patna, 1927-40; Member, Diocesan Conference (Sarum), 1946-; Chairman Medical Appeal Tribunal, 1949-; Divorce Commissioner, 1948. *Recreations:* angling and agriculture. *Address:* 2 Paper Buildings, Temple, EC4.

**WORTH, Abbot of;** *see* Farwell, Rt Rev. G. V.

**WORTH, George Arthur,** MBE; DL; Farmer and Landowner; *b* 3 May 1907; *s* of late Arthur Hovendon Worth; *m* 1935, Janet Maitland, *d* of Air Chief Marshal Sir A. M. Longmore, *qv*; two *s* two *d*. *Educ:* Marlborough Coll.; Sidney Sussex Coll., Cambridge. JP for Parts of Holland, 1939. Served War of 1939-45, RAF. High Sheriff of Lincolnshire, 1948-49. *Address:* The Top Hall, Lyndon, Oakham, Rutland. *T:* Manton 267.

**WORTH, Irene;** actress; *b* 23 June 1916; *Educ:* University of California, Los Angeles (BE). Antoinette Perry Award for distinguished achievement in the Theatre, 1965. First appeared as Fenella in Escape Me Never, New York, 1942; debut on Broadway as Cecily Harden in The Two Mrs Carrolls, Booth Theatre, 1943. Studied for six months with Elsie Fogerty, 1944-45. Subsequently appeared frequently at Mercury, Bolton's, Q, Embassy, etc. Parts include: Anabelle Jones in Love Goes to Press, Duchess Theatre, 1946 (after Embassy); Ilona Szabo in The Play's the Thing, St James's, 1947 (after tour and Lyric, Hammersmith); Eileen Perry in Edward my Son, Lyric, 1948; Lady Fortrose in Home is Tomorrow, Cambridge Theatre, 1948; Olivia Raines in Champagne for Delilah, New, 1949; Celia Coplestone in The Cocktail Party, New, 1950 (after Edinburgh Festival, 1949; Henry Miller Theatre, New York, 1950); Desdemona in Othello, Old Vic, 1951; Helena in Midsummer Night's Dream, Old Vic, 1952; Catherine de Vausselles in The Other Heart, Old Vic, 1952; Lady Macbeth in Macbeth, Desdemona in Othello, Helena in Midsummer Night's Dream, Catherine de Vausselles in The Other Heart, Old Vic tour of S Africa, 1952; Portia in The Merchant of Venice, Old Vic, 1953; Helena in All's Well That Ends Well and Queen Margaret in Richard III, First Season Shakespeare Festival Theatre, Stratford, Ont, Canada, 1953; Frances Farrar in A Day By The Sea, Haymarket, 1953-54; Alcestis in A Life in the Sun, Edinburgh Festival, 1955; leading rôles in: The Queen and the Rebels, Haymarket, 1955; Hotel Paradiso, Winter Garden, 1956; Maria Stuart, Phœnix Theatre, NY, 1957, Old Vic, 1958; The Potting Shed, Globe Theatre, London, 1958; Rosalind in As You Like It, Shakespeare Festival Theatre, Stratford, Ont, 1959; Albertine Prine in Toys in the Attic, Hudson Theatre, New York, 1960 (NY Page One Award); Season at Royal Shakespeare Theatre, Stratford, 1962; Goneril in King Lear, Aldwych, 1962; Doctor Mathilde von Zahnd in The Physicists, Aldwych, 1963; Clodia Pulcher in The Ides of March, Haymarket, 1963; World tour of King Lear for Royal Shakespeare Company, 1964; Alice in Tiny Alice, Billy Rose Theatre, New York, 1965, Aldwych, 1970; Hilde in A Song at Twilight, Queen's, 1966; Anne in Shadows of the Evening; Anna-Mary in Come into the Garden Maud, Queen's, 1966; Hesione Hushabye in Heartbreak House, Chichester and Lyric, 1967; Jocasta in Seneca's Oedipus, National Theatre, 1968; Hedda in Hedda Gabler, Stratford, Ont, 1970. *Films:* Order to Kill, 1957 (National Film Award for Best Woman's Performance, 1958-59); The Scapegoat, 1958; King Lear (Goneril), 1970. Daily Mail National Television Award, 1953-54, and has subseq. appeared on Television and acted with CBC Television in NY. Evening Standard Award, 1966; Whitbread Anglo-American Award for Outstanding Actress, 1967; Variety Club of Great Britain Award, 1967. *Recreation:* music. *Address:* 38 Ladbroke Square, W11.

**WORTHINGTON, Edgar Barton,** CBE 1967; MA, PhD; Scientific Director of International Biological Programme; *b* 13 Jan. 1905; *s* of Edgar Worthington and Amy E. Beale; *m* 1930, Stella Desmond Johnson; three *d*. *Educ:*

Rugby; Gonville and Caius Coll., Cambridge. Expeditions to African Lakes, 1927-31; Balfour Student, 1930-33, and Demonstrator in Zoology, Cambridge Univ., 1933-37; Scientist for the African Research Survey, 1934-37; Director of Laboratories and Secretary of Freshwater Biological Assoc., Wray Castle, Ambleside, 1937-46; Scientific Adviser to Middle East Supply Centre, 1943-45; Development Adviser, Uganda, 1946; Scientific Secretary to Colonial Research Council, 1946-49, to E Africa High Commission, 1950-51; Secretary-General to Scientific Council for Africa South of the Sahara, 1951-55; Deputy Director-General (Scientific) Nature Conservancy, 1957-65. *Publications:* (with Stella Worthington) Inland Waters of Africa, 1933; Science in Africa, 1938; Middle East Science, 1946; Development Plan for Uganda, 1947; (with T. T. Macan) Life in Lakes and Rivers, 1951; Science in the Development of Africa, 1958; official reports and papers in scientific journals. *Recreations:* field sports and farming. *Address:* Colin Godmans, Furner's Green, Uckfield, Sussex. *T:* Chelwood Gate 322. *Club:* Athenæum.

**WORTHINGTON, Air Vice-Marshal (Retired) Sir Geoffrey (Luis),** KBE 1960 (CBE 1945); CB 1957; idc; psa; Director-General of Equipment, Air Ministry, 1958-61, retired; *b* 26 April 1903; *s* of late Commander H. E. F. Worthington, RN; *m* 1931, Margaret Joan, *d* of late Maj.-Gen. A. G. Stevenson, CB, CMG, DSO; two *s* one *d*. *Educ:* HMS Conway; Eastbourne Coll. RAF Coll., Cranwell, 1921. Joined RAF, 1922; resigned 1924; re-joined, 1926, in Stores Branch; RAF Staff Coll., 1934. Served War of 1939-45 (despatches, CBE): HQ Maintenance Comd, 1939-43; Air Cdre, 1943; HQ AEAF, 1944; SHAEF, 1944-45; Air Comd, Far East, 1945-47; Director of Equipment B, Air Ministry, 1948-49; idc 1950; Director of Equipment D, Air Ministry, 1951-53; AOC No 42 Group, Maintenance Comd, 1954-55; Air Vice-Marshal, 1956; AOC No 40 Group, 1955-58. Comdr US Legion of Merit, 1955. *Recreations:* sailing, golf. *Address:* Pear Tree House, Ship Road, Burnham-on-Crouch, Essex. *T:* Burnham-on-Crouch 2388. *Clubs:* Royal Air Force; Royal Burnham Yacht.

**WORTHINGTON-EVANS, Sir (William) Shirley (Worthington),** 2nd Bt, *cr* 1916; **His Honour Judge Worthington-Evans;** a Judge of the County Courts for Brentford and Uxbridge since 1957; *b* 9 June 1904; *o s* of The Rt Hon. Sir Laming Worthington-Evans, 1st Bt, GBE, MP, and late Gertrude Annie, CBE 1939, *d* of William Hale; *S* father, 1931; *m* 1st, 1928, Joan Irene (who obtained a divorce, 1943), *er d* of W. H. K. Pears, New Chapel House, Lingfield, Surrey; two *d*; 2nd, Hazel Wells, *o d* of Fearnley Wells Owen. *Educ:* Eton; Trinity Coll., Cambridge (BA). Called to Bar, 1927. Commissioned in RA, Sept. 1939. *Recreations:* golf, tennis. *Heir:* none. *Address:* 29 Eaton Square, SW1. *T:* 01-235 2870. *Club:* White's.

*See also Baron Blackford, Baron Jeffreys.*

**WORTLEY, Prof. Ben Atkinson,** OBE 1946; QC 1969; LLD (Manchester), LLM (Leeds); Hon. Docteur de l'Univ. de Rennes (1955); Strasbourg (1965); membre de l'Institut de droit international, 1956; Professor of Jurisprudence and International Law, University of Manchester, since 1946; Barrister of Gray's Inn, 1947; *b* 16 Nov. 1907; *o s* of late John Edward Wortley and late Mary Cicely (*née* King), Huddersfield; *m* 1935, Kathleen Mary Prynne; two *s* one *d*. *Educ:* King James's Grammar Sch., Almondbury; Leeds Univ.; France. Law Society Open Schol., 1925; 1st Class Hons LLB, 1928, and at Law Society's Final, 1929, also D. Reardon Prizeman. Practised full-time till 1931. Taught Law, London School Econ., 1931-33; Manchester Univ., 1933-34; Birmingham Univ., 1934-36; Manchester Univ., 1936-; visiting Prof. Tulane Univ., New Orleans, 1959. Ministry of Home Security, 1939-43; Instructor Commander RN (temp.), 1943-46. Represents Manchester Univ. on Court of Birmingham Univ., De la Salle Training Coll., Cheshire CC Ed. Cttee; Member of directing bodies of International Inst. for Unification of Private Law, Rome; Inst. Advanced Legal Studies; British Yearbook of International Law; Society of Public Teachers of Law (President, 1964-65). Member Royal Netherlands Academy, 1960; Commendatore (Italy), 1961; Correspondent Hellenic Inst. for International and Foreign Law, and of Belgian Society for Comparative Law. Representative of HM Government at International Confs at the Hague, 1951, 1956, 1960, 1964, and at New York, 1955 and 1958. Member Lord Chancellor's Cttee on Conflict of Laws. *Publications:* series of lectures, 1939, 1947, 1954 and 1958, published by Hague Academy of International Law; Expropriation in Public International Law, 1959; Jurisprudence, 1967; part editor, Dicey's Conflict of Laws, 1949; ed UN, The First Ten Years, 1957. *Recreations:* languages, literature. *Address:* 24 Gravel Lane, Wilmslow, Cheshire. *T:* Wilmslow 22810; Royal Exchange Building, Manchester; 2 Pump Court, EC4. *Club:* Athenæum.

**WOTHERSPOON, Ralph;** Writer and Journalist; *b* 1897; *o s* of George Wotherspoon, MA (sometime Vice-Master, King's College School) and Juliana Mary, *d* of Henry Norton, JP, Green Hill, Carmarthen, Wales; unmarried. *Educ:* Eastbourne Coll.; Merton Coll., Oxford. BA Distinction Honour School English Literature. War service, 1915-19, 5th Bn Queen's Royal West Surreys (TF) and Royal Garrison Artillery; War Service, 1940-41, AOER, Captain, General List; Embarkation Staff Officer Movement Control Southampton, Liverpool; invalided, Oct. 1941; Ministry of Supply, 1942; Ministry of Information, 1943; Regional Press Officer, London and SE Region, 1944-45; Member original Cherwell Editorial Staff, 1920-21; Editorial Staff, George Newnes & Co. Ltd, 1923; Private Secretary to late Henry Arthur Jones, Dramatist, 1923; to Colonel Hon. Angus McDonnell, 1924; Vice-Chairman Kent Federation Junior Imperial League since inception 1928 until 1933; Secretary of Primrose League, 1935-40; as a writer has contributed extensively in prose and verse to leading humorous journals, magazines, newspapers, etc.; first wrote for Punch, 1924 (Woon, 1928); Member contrib. staff of services paper Blighty, 1939-45; Director, Smith and Whiley Theatrical Productions, 1948-61. *Publications:* Ready-Made Rhymes, 1927; (with Aubrey Hammond) Jack and Jill, the Underground Fairy Tale, 1932-33; (with L. N. Jackson) Some Sports and Pastimes of the English, 1937; (with L. N. Jackson) numerous broadcasts from BBC West Regional, including serial sketches, The Life We Lead; one-act play, All in The Day's Work. *Recreations:* formerly playing, now watching Rugby football; golf, fishing, motoring, railways. *Address:* 54 Coleherne Court, SW5. *T:* 01-373 8919. *Clubs:* Royal Automobile; Middlesex CC; Myrmidon; Richmond Rugby Football (tenant member).

**WOTHERSPOON, Robert Andrew;** Clerk of the Peace and of the County Council of North Riding of Yorkshire since 1960; *b* 18 May 1912; *s* of James A. Wotherspoon, Burnley, Lancs; *m* 1937, Mary Beryl, *d* of Robert Cassson

Jackson, Padiham, Lancs; one *s* one *d*. *Educ:* Burnley Sch.; Manchester Univ. RAF, General Duties, 1940-45. Deputy Clerk of the Peace and of County Council of Derbyshire, 1951-60. *Address:* Cotescue Park, Middleham, Leyburn, Yorks. *T:* Coverdale 269. *Club:* Royal Automobile.

**WOUK, Herman;** author, US; *b* New York, 27 May 1915; *s* of Abraham Isaac Wouk and Esther Wouk (*née* Levine); *m* 1945, Betty Sarah Brown; two *s* (and one *s* decd). *Educ:* Townsend Harris High Sch.; Columbia Univ. (AB). Employed as a writer of comedians' scripts for radio programmes, 1935-41; Visiting Professor of English, Yeshiva Univ., 1952-; Presidential consultative expert to the United States Treasury, 1941. Served United States Naval Reserve, 1942-46, Deck Officer (four campaign stars). Member Officers' Reserve Naval Services. Columbia University Medal for excellence, 1952. Trustee, College of the Virgin Islands, 1963-69. Hon. Doctor of Humane Letters, Yeshiva Univ., New York City, 1955; Hon. Doctor of Letters, Clark Univ., 1959. *Publications: novels:* Aurora Dawn (American Book of the Month), 1947; The City Boy, 1948; The Caine Mutiny (Pulitzer Prize), 1951; Marjorie Morningstar, 1955; Youngblood Hawke, 1962; Don't Stop The Carnival, 1965; *plays:* The Traitor, 1949; The Caine Mutiny Court-Martial, 1953; Nature's Way, 1957; *non-fiction:* This Is My God, 1959. *Address:* c/o Harold Matson Co. Inc., 22 East 40th Street, New York, NY 10016, USA. *Clubs:* Authors' Guild (New York); Cosmos, Metropolitan, National Press (Washington); Bohemian (San Francisco).

**WRAIGHT, John Richard,** CMG 1962; Minister HM Consul-General at Milan since 1968; *b* 4 June 1916; *s* of late Richard George Wraight; *m* 1947, Marquita Elliott. Served War of 1939-45 with Honourable Artillery Company and RHA, Western Desert and Libya; Ministry of Economic Warfare Mission in the Middle East, Cairo, 1944. Economic Warfare Adviser, HQ Mediterranean Allied Air Forces, Italy, June-Dec. 1944. Foreign Office, 1945; Special Assistant to Chief of UNRRA Operations in Europe, 1946. Entered Foreign (subseq. Diplomatic) Service, 1947; British Embassy: Athens, 1948; Tel Aviv, 1950; Washington, 1953; Asst Head of Economic Relations Dept, Foreign Office, 1957; Counsellor (Commercial): Cairo, 1959; Brussels and Luxembourg, 1962. Commander of the Order of the Crown (Belgium), 1966. *Recreations:* music, travel. *Address:* c/o Foreign and Commonwealth Office, SW1. *Club:* Travellers'.

**WRANGHAM, Cuthbert Edward,** CBE 1946; BA 1929; Chairman: Marine & General Mutual Life Assurance Society since 1961; C. Tennant, Sons & Co. Ltd, since 1967; Doxford and Sunderland Ltd, since 1969; *b* 16 Dec. 1907; *yr s* of late W. G. Wrangham and late E. A. F. Wilberforce; *m* 1st, 1935, Teresa Jane, *er d* of late Ralph Cotton; three *s* two *d*; 2nd, 1958, Jean Ursula Margaret Tunstall, *yr d* of late Lt-Col T. T. Behrens. *Educ:* Eton Coll.; King's Coll., Cambridge. Director of C. Tennant, Sons & Co. Ltd, 1937-; Air Ministry and Ministry of Aircraft Production, 1939-45; Monopolies Commission, 1954-56; Chairman, Shelbourne Hotel Ltd, 1950-60; Chairman and Managing Director, The Power-Gas Corporation Ltd, 1960-61; Dep. Chairman, Davy-Ashmore Ltd, 1960-61; Chairman, Short Brothers & Harland Ltd, 1961-67. Hon. DL Wilberforce Coll., Ohio, 1957. *Address:* I 3 Albany, W1. *T:* 01-734 3183; Rosemary House, Catterick, Yorkshire. *T:* Old Catterick 375.

**WRANGHAM, Hon. Sir Geoffrey Walter,** Kt 1958; **Hon. Mr Justice Wrangham;** Judge of High Court of Justice, Probate, Divorce and Admiralty Division, since 1958; Chairman, North Riding Quarter Sessions, 1946-58, Dep. Chairman since 1958; *b* 16 June 1900; *s* of late W. G. Wrangham and late E. A. F. Wilberforce; *m* 1925, Mary (*d* 1933), *d* of late S. D. Winkworth; one *s* one *d*; *m* 1947, Joan, *d* of Col W. Boyle; one *s* one *d*. *Educ:* Eton Coll.; Balliol Coll., Oxford. Called to Bar, 1923; joined North-Eastern Circuit; Gresham Lecturer in Law, 1925-33; Practised in London, 1923-33, thereafter in Bradford; Recorder of York, 1941-50; Judge of County Courts, Circuit 20, 1950-57, Circuit 16, 1957-58; Master of the Bench, Inner Temple, 1958. Served KOYLI and RAC (Lt-Col), 1940-45. *Publications:* Edited (with W. A. Macfarlane) 8th Edition Clerk and Lindsell on Torts, 18th edition Chitty on Contracts. *Address:* Royal Courts of Justice, WC2; The Old Rectory, Holwell, Hitchin, Herts.

**WRATTEN, Donald Peter;** Executive Director, Giro and Remittance Services, Post Office, since 1969; *b* 8 July 1925; *er s* of late Frederick George and Marjorie Wratten; *m* 1947, Margaret Kathleen (*née* Marsh); one *s* one *d*. *Educ:* Morehall Elem. Sch. and Harvey Grammar Sch., Folkestone; London Sch. of Economics. Storehand, temp. clerk, meteorological asst (Air Min.), 1940-43; service with RAF Meteorological Wing, 1943-47. LSE, 1947-50. Joined Post Office, 1950; Private Sec. to Asst Postmaster Gen., 1955-56; seconded to Unilever Ltd, 1959; Private Sec. to Postmaster Gen., 1965-66; Head of Telecommunications Marketing Div., 1966-67; Director: Eastern Telecommunications Region, 1967-69; PO Headquarters 1969; Sen. Director, 1970. *Recreations:* travel, photography, study of human ecology and industrial archaeology. *Address:* 10 Homefield Road, Radlett, Herts. *T:* Radlett 4500.

**WRAXALL,** 2nd Baron, *cr* 1928, of Clyst St George, Co. Devon; **George Richard Lawley Gibbs;** *b* 16 May 1928 (for whom Queen Mary was sponsor); *er s* of 1st Baron and Hon. Ursula Mary Lawley, OBE 1945, RRC, *e d* of 6th Baron Wenlock; *S* father 1931. *Educ:* Eton; RMA Sandhurst. Coldstream Guards, 1948-53; Lieut North Somerset Yeomanry/44 Royal Tank Regt (TA), Dec. 1958; Captain, 1962; Major, 1965; retired 1967. Chm., N Somerset Conservative Assoc., 1970. *Heir: b* Hon. Eustace Hubert Beilby Gibbs [*b* 3 July 1929; *m* 1957, Evelyn Veronica, *d* of late S. K. Scott, Reydon Grove Farm, Southwold, Suffolk; three *s* one *d*]. *Address:* Tyntesfield, Bristol. *T:* Flax Bourton 2923. *Clubs:* Royal Automobile, Cavalry.

**WRAXALL, Sir Morville (William Lascelles),** 8th Bt, *cr* 1813; on staff of a rubber company since 1947; *b* 11 June 1922; *o s* of Sir Charles Wraxall, 7th Bt and Marceline, *d* of O. Cauro, of Cauro, Corsica; *S* father 1951; *m* 1956, Irmgard Wilhelmina Maria Schnidrig, Basle, Switzerland; one *s* one *d*. *Educ:* St Mark's Coll., Alexandria, Egypt. RASC 1940-46 (Africa Star and clasp). *Recreations:* gardening, woodwork, stamp collecting. *Heir: s* Charles Frederick Lascelles Wraxall, *b* 17 Sept. 1961.

**WRAY, Sir Kenneth O. R.;** *see* Roberts-Wray.

**WRAY, Martin Osterfield,** CMG 1956; OBE 1954; *b* 14 June 1912; *s* of late C. N. O. Wray; *m* 1938, Lilian Joyce, *d* of late R. W. Playfair, Nairobi, Kenya; one *s* two *d*. *Educ:* St George's Sch., Harpenden; Wadham Coll., Oxford. Colonial Administrative Service in Uganda, 1935; transferred to Zanzibar as

Administrative Secretary, 1949; trans. to be Administrative Secretary to High Commissioner for Basutoland, the Bechuanaland Protectorate and Swaziland, 1952; Resident Commissioner, Bechuanaland Protectorate, 1955-59; Chief Secretary, Northern Rhodesia, 1959-62. *Address:* Prospect House, East Knoyle, Wilts. *Club:* Royal Commonwealth Society.

**WREFORD, Charles Keith,** CMG 1956; Nigerian CS, retired; *b* 1906. *Educ:* Cranleigh; Clare Coll., Cambridge. Barrister-at-Law, Middle Temple; then cadet, Nigeria, 1928; administrative officer, class III, 1931; class II, 1946; class I, 1949; Staff Grade, 1953; Eastern Region, 1955; Senior Resident in the Northern Region, Federation of Nigeria, 1956-59, retired; re-appointed Administrative Officer, S Cameroons, 1960-61.

**WRENBURY,** 3rd Baron, *cr* 1915; **John Burton Buckley;** *b* 18 June 1927; *s* of 2nd Baron and Helen Malise, 2nd *d* of late His Honour John Cameron Graham of Ballewan, Stirlingshire; *S* father, 1940; *m* 1st, 1956, Carolyn Joan Maule (marr. diss., 1961), *o d* of Lt-Col Ian Burn-Murdoch, OBE, of Gartincaber, Doune, Perthshire; 2nd, 1961, Penelope Sara Frances, *o d* of Edward D. Fort, The White House, Sixpenny Handley, Dorset; one *s* two *d*. *Educ:* Eton Coll.; King's Coll., Cambridge. Deputy Legal Adviser to the National Trust, 1955-56; Partner, Freshfield's, Solicitors, 1956-. *Heir: s* Hon. William Edward Buckley, *b* 19 June 1966. *Address:* Oldcastle, Dallington, near Heathfield, Sussex. *T:* Rushlake Green 375. *Club:* Oriental.

*See also B. W. Williams.*

**WREY, Sir (Castel) Richard Bourchier,** 14th Bt, *cr* 1628; temp. Lieut, RNVR; *b* 27 March 1903; *s* of late Edward Castel Wrey and Katharine Joan, *d* of Rev. John Dene; *S* uncle, 1948; *m* 1946, Alice Sybil, *d* of Dr Lubke, Durban, S Africa; two *s*. *Educ:* Oundle. Served War of 1939-45; 2nd Lieut, RASC (Supp. Res.), France, 1939-40 (invalided); joined RN as ordinary seaman, 1940; Lieut, RNVR, 1942. *Heir: s* George Richard Bourchier Wrey, *b* 2 Oct. 1948. *Address:* Tawstock Court, Barnstaple, Devon; Webbery, near Bideford, N Devon.

**WRIGHT;** *see* Cory-Wright.

**WRIGHT,** family name of **Baron Wright of Ashton under Lyne.**

**WRIGHT OF ASHTON UNDER LYNE,** Baron, *cr* 1968 (Life Peer), of Ashton-under-Lyne; **Lewis Tatham Wright,** CBE 1964; General Secretary, Amalgamated Weavers' Association, 1953-68; Member: Advisory Council on Technology, since 1968; Prices and Incomes Board (part-time) since 1968; Central Electricity Generating Board (part-time) since 1968; *b* 11 Oct. 1903; British; *m* 1933, Kathleen (*née* Firth); two *s*. *Educ:* Elementary and Secondary Schools. Ex-Weaver; Full-Time Trades Union Official since age of 24. Chairman, TUC, 1967-68, President, 1968. Hon. DTech, Loughborough, 1968. *Recreations:* gardening, travel; Member Manchester United FC. *Address:* Brookfield Grove, Ashton-under-Lyne, Lancs. *T:* (home) 061-330 4122.

**WRIGHT, Alec Michael John,** CMG 1967; Administrative Commissioner, Government of Hong Kong in London, since 1969; *b* Hong Kong, 19 Sept. 1912; *s* of Arthur Edgar Wright and Margery Hepworth Chapman; *m* 1948, Ethel Surtees; one *d*. *Educ:* Brentwood Sch. ARICS 1934; ARIBA 1937. Articled pupil followed by private practice in London. Joined Colonial Service, 1938; appointed Architect in Hong Kong, 1938. Commissioned Hong Kong Volunteer Defence Force, 1941; POW in Hong Kong, 1941-45. Chief Architect, Public Works Dept, Hong Kong, 1950; Asst Director of Public Works, 1956; Dep. Director, 1959; Director, 1963-69. *Address:* Mellow Cottage, Keymer Road, Burgess Hill, Sussex. *T:* Burgess Hill 6363; 74 Montrose Court, Exhibition Road, SW7. *T:* 01-584 4293. *Clubs:* Travellers'; Hong Kong (Hong Kong).

**WRIGHT, Sir Andrew Barkworth,** KCMG 1948 (CMG 1941); CBE 1932; MC; MA; *b* 30 Nov. 1895; *er s* of late Rev. H. L. Wright, Church Knowle Rectory, Dorset, and Emma, *d* of Rev. S. M. Barkworth, DD, and Ellen Janson; *m* Rosemary, CStJ, *o d* of late Geoffrey Barrett; one *s* one *d* (and one *d* decd). *Educ:* The Old Ride Prep. Sch.; Haileybury; Jesus Coll., Cambridge (Scholar, 1914). Served European War with Suffolk Regt, 1914-19 (immediate award of MC, Hargicourt, 1917, and of bar to MC, Battle of the Lys, 1918); Platoon Comdr, Somme, 1916; Co. Comdr, Arras, 1917; 2 i/c Bn, 1918; Major, Reserve of Officers, 1920; Civil Administration, Cyprus, from 1922 (CBE for services as acting Colonial Secretary during disturbances, 1931); Colonial Secretary, Cyprus, 1937; re-employed in Army, rank of Lieut-Colonel, and served with Middle East Forces, May 1940-Sept. 1942; Colonial Secretary, Trinidad, 1943-46; Governor and C-in-C of the Gambia, 1946-49; Governor and C-in-C, Cyprus, 1949-54. KStJ 1950. *Address:* c/o Midland Bank, Market Hill, Cambridge. *Club:* Travellers'.

**WRIGHT, A(rthur) Dickson,** MS, MB, FRCS; DTM&H; Hon. Fellow, College of Surgeons of South Africa; Hon. FRCSI; Senior Consulting Surgeon St Mary's Hospital and Prince of Wales Hospital; Consulting Surgeon to Society for Propagation of the Gospel, Concert Artists Assoc. and British Railways; Late Member of Council (late Vice-Pres.) Royal College of Surgeons; late Member of Council: British Medical Association; Examrs, RCS; Examiner, Manchester and Newcastle Univs; Bradshaw Lecturer, Hunterian Orator, RCS; Hunterian Orator, Hunterian Society; Late President, Saints and Sinners Society; Vice-President Royal Institute of Hygiene; Late President of the Osler Club; Fellow of the Royal Society of Medicine; President: Institute of British Surgical Technicians; Harvey Tercentenary Congress, 1957; British Medical Representatives Association; Hon. Treasurer Imperial Cancer Research Fund; Hon. Member Scandinavian Society of Neurosurgery; *s* of late Dr Edward Wright, Dublin; *m* Molly Bath; one *s* three *d*. *Educ:* St Mary's Hosp. Late Assistant Dir of Surgical Unit, St Mary's Hospital; House Surgeon, Assistant in Neurological Department, and Ear, Nose, and Throat Department; House Surgeon, North Middlesex Hospital; Professor of Clinical Surgery, Singapore School of Medicine; Acting Senior Surgeon, Singapore; Hon. Surgeon, St Andrew's Hospital, Singapore. Past President: Brit. Soc. of Neurological Surgeons; Med. Soc. of London; Hunterian Soc.; Harveian Soc.; Past Pres. Clinical, Protological and Surgical Sections, RSM. *Publications:* numerous articles in Proc. RSM and medical press, also articles on Diseases of the Liver and Pancreas, Post-Graduate Surgery (Maingot); article on Infections of the Brain, Penicillin (Fleming). *Recreation:* nil. *Address:* Lister House, 12 Wimpole Street, W1. *T:* 01-580 2511. *Clubs:* Athenæum, Carlton, Garrick, Oriental, Royal Air Force.

**WRIGHT, (Arthur Robert) Donald;** Headmaster of Shrewsbury School since 1963; *b* 20 June 1923; *y s* of late Charles North Wright; *m* 1948, Helen Muryell Buxton, *e d* of late Prof. Patrick Buxton, CMG, FRS; two *s* three *d*. *Educ:* Bryanston School; Queens' College, Cambridge. Commissioned in Royal Artillery and served in France, Germany and India, 1942-46 (despatches). Univ. Coll. Sch., 1948-50; The Hill School, Pennsylvania, 1950; Leighton Park School, 1950-52; Marlborough College (Housemaster), 1953-63. *Address:* The Schools, Shrewsbury.

**WRIGHT, Basil Charles;** Film Producer; *b* 12 June 1907; *s* of Major Lawrence Wright, TD, and Gladys Marsden. *Educ:* Sherborne; Corpus Christi Coll., Cambridge. Mawson Schol., CCC, 1926; BA (Hons), Classics and Economics. Concerned with John Grierson and others in development of Documentary Film, 1929-; directed, among many films: Song of Ceylon (Gold Medal and Prix du Gouvernement, Brussels), 1935; (with Harry Watt) Night Mail, 1936; Waters of Time, 1951; (with Paul Rotha) World Without End, 1953; (with Gladys Wright) took film expedition to Greece and made The Immortal Land, 1957 (Council of Europe Award, 1959) and Greek Sculpture (with Michael Ayrton), 1959; A Place for Gold, 1960; Visiting Lectr on Film Art, Univ. of Calif., Los Angeles, 1962, and 1968. Producer, Crown Film Unit, 1945. Governor: Bryanston School, 1949-; British Film Institute, 1953; Fellow, British Film Academy, 1955; Council Mem., Roy. Coll. of Art, 1954-57. Gold Cross, Royal Order of King George I, Greece, 1963. *Publication:* The Use of the Film, 1948. *Recreations:* opera, ballet, gardening. *Address:* Little Adam Farm, Frieth, Henley-on-Thames, Oxon. *Clubs:* Reform, Savile.

**WRIGHT, Beatrice Frederika;** *b* New Haven, Connecticut; *d* of Mrs F. Roland Clough; *m* 1st, 1932, John Rankin Rathbone (Flight Lieut, RAFVR, MP, killed in action, 1940); one *s* one *d*; 2nd, 1942, Paul Hervé Giraud Wright, *qv*; one *d*. *Educ:* Ethel Walker School, Simsbury, Conn; Radcliffe College, Oxford. MP (U) Bodmin Div. of Cornwall, 1941-45. *Address:* c/o P. H. G. Wright Esq., CMG, OBE, c/o Foreign and Commonwealth Office, SW1.

**WRIGHT, Prof. Bernard Arker;** Professor Emeritus, University of Southampton; *b* 20 June 1893; *s* of Rev. James and Emily Wright (*née* Fisher); *m* 1923, Phyllis Adèle Lebus (*d* 1965); one *s*. *Educ:* Ashville Coll., Harrogate; Univ. of Manchester; Lincoln College, Oxford. Lecturer, Adult Education Department, University College, Nottingham, 1921-22; Lecturer in English, Glasgow Univ., 1922-38; Professor of English, University of Southampton, 1938-57. *Publications:* Milton's Shorter Poems, 1938; ed. Milton's Poems (Everyman edition), 1956, Milton's Paradise Lost, 1962; contrib. to Modern Language Review, Review of English Studies, Notes and Queries, Library. *Address:* 210 Ashley Gardens, SW1. *T:* 01-828 2065.

**WRIGHT, Billy;** *see* Wright, W. A.

**WRIGHT, Sir Charles Seymour,** KCB 1946 (CB 1937); OBE, MC; MA, DSc; retired 1955, as Director, Marine Physical Laboratory, Scripps Institution of Oceanography, San Diego; *b* Toronto, 1887; *s* of Alfred Wright, Toronto, and Katherine Kennedy; *m* 1914, Edith Mary Priestley; one *s* two *d*. *Educ:* Upper Canada College and University, Toronto; Gonville and Caius College, Cambridge University (Wollaston Student 1851 Exhibition Scholar). Research at Cavendish Laboratory 1908-10; Scientist British Antarctic Expedition 1910-13; Royal Engineers, 1914-18; Wireless 5th Corps (MC); OC Wireless II Army (Chevalier Legion of Honour); General Staff (Intelligence) GHQ (OBE); Admiralty Department of Scientific Research and Experiment, 1919-29; Superintendent, Admiralty Research Laboratory 1929-34; Director of Scientific Research, Admiralty, 1934-46; Chief of Royal Naval Scientific Service, 1946-47. Contractor for Defence Research Board of Canada, 1956-. Lecturer in Geophysics, Institute of Earth Sciences, Univ. of British Columbia, 1964-68, retired. *Publications:* Scientific Reports. *Address:* Arbutus Road, Ganges, RR1, British Columbia, Canada.

**WRIGHT, Claud William,** CB 1969; Deputy Under-Secretary of State, Ministry of Defence, since 1968; *b* 9 January 1917; *s* of Horace Vipan Wright and Catherine Margaret Sales; *m* 1947, Alison Violet Readman; one *s* four *d*. *Educ:* Charterhouse; Christ Church, Oxford (MA). Assistant Principal, War Office, 1939; Private, Essex Regiment, 1940; 2nd Lieut, KRRC, 1940; War Office, rising to GSO2, 1942-45; Principal, War Office, 1944; Min. of Defence: Principal, 1947; Asst Sec., 1951; Asst Under-Sec. of State, 1961-68. Mem. Cttee of Enquiry into conditions of service life for young servicemen, 1969-70. Lyell Fund, 1947, R. H. Worth Prize, 1958, Geological Society of London; Foulerton Award, Geologists Association, 1955; Stamford Raffles Award, Zoological Society of London, 1965. President, Geologists Assoc., 1956-58. *Publications:* (with W. J. Arkell *et al*) vol. on Ammonites, 1957, (with W. K. Spencer) on Starfish, 1966, in Treatise on Invertebrate Palaeontology. Papers in geological, palaeontological and archaeological journals. *Recreations:* palaeontology, natural history, Oriental ceramics, gardening, archæology. *Address:* 37 Phillimore Gardens, W8. *T:* 01-937 3884; Old Rectory, Seaborough, Beaminster, Dorset. *T:* Broadwindsor 426. *Club:* Athenæum.

**WRIGHT, Sir Denis (Arthur Hepworth),** KCMG 1961 (CMG 1954); Ambassador to Iran, since 1963; *b* 23 March 1911; *s* of late A. E. Wright, Hong Kong, and Margery Hepworth Chapman, York; *m* 1939, Iona Craig, Bolney, Sussex; no *c*. *Educ:* Brentwood School; St Edmund Hall, Oxford. Asst Advertising Manager to Gallaher & Co. (Tobacco Manufacturers), 1935-39. Employed from outbreak of war as Vice-Consul on economic warfare work at HM Consulate at Constantza (Roumania), 1939-41. Vice-Consul-in-charge of HM Consulate at Trebizond (Turkey), 1941-43; Acting-Consul-in-charge of HM Consulate, Mersin (Turkey), 1943-45; First Secretary (Commercial) to HM Embassy, Belgrade, 1946-48; Superintending Trade Consul at Chicago for Middle-Western Region of USA, 1949-51; Head of Economic Relations Department in the Foreign Office, 1951-53; appointed Chargé d'Affaires, Teheran, on resumption of diplomatic relations with Persia, Dec. 1953; Counsellor, HM Embassy, Teheran, 1954-55; Assistant Under-Secretary, Foreign Office, 1955-59; Ambassador to Ethiopia, 1959-62; Assistant Under-Secretary, Foreign Office, 1962. *Address:* British Embassy, Teheran, Iran. *Club:* Travellers'.

**WRIGHT, Dickson;** *see* Wright, A. D.

**WRIGHT, Donald;** *see* Wright, A. R. D.

**WRIGHT, Prof. Donald Arthur,** MSc, DSc; FInstP; FRAS; FIEE; Professor of Applied

Physics, University of Durham, since 1960; *b* Stoke-on-Trent, 29 March 1911; *m* 1937, Mary Kathleen Rimmer; one *s* one *d*. *Educ:* Orme School, Newcastle-under-Lyme; University of Birmingham. 1st Class Hons BSc 1932; MSc 1934; DSc Birmingham 1955. Research Physicist, GEC, Wembley, 1934-59; Head of Solid Physics Laboratory, Research Labs, GEC, Wembley, 1955-59. Fellow Institute of Physics, 1946. Member of Board, Institute of Physics, 1957-64. Mem. of Council, Physical Society, 1955-58, Hon. Treasurer, 1958-60. *Publications:* Semiconductors, 1950 (revd edn 1965); Thermoelectric Cooling in Progress in Cryogenics, Vol. I, 1959; Thermoelectric Generation in Direct Generation of Electricity, 1965; many papers on electron emission and solid-state physics in learned journals. *Recreations:* tennis, music. *Address:* Department of Applied Physics, South Road, Durham; 16 St Mary's Close, Shincliffe, Durham. *T:* Durham 3408.

**WRIGHT, Mrs Edmund Gordon;** *see* Cross, H. M.

**WRIGHT, Edward Maitland,** MA, DPhil; LLD; FRSE; Principal and Vice-Chancellor, University of Aberdeen, since 1962; *b* 1906; *s* of M. T. Wright, Farnley, Leeds; *m* 1934, Elizabeth Phyllis, *d* of H. P. Harris, Bryn Mally Hall, N Wales; one *s*. *Educ:* Jesus Coll. and Christ Church, Oxford; Univ. of Göttingen. Master, Chard School, Somerset, 1923-26; Scholar, Jesus College, Oxford, 1926-30; Senior Scholar, Christ Church, 1930-33; Lecturer, King's College, London, 1932-33; Lecturer, Christ Church, 1933-35; Principal Scientific Officer, Air Ministry, 1943-45; Prof. of Mathematics, 1935-62, Vice-Principal, 1961-62, Univ. of Aberdeen. Member: Anderson Cttee on Grants to Students, 1958-60; Hale Cttee on Univ. Teaching Methods, 1961-64; Chairman: Scottish Universities Entrance Bd, 1955-62; Royal Commission on Medical Education, 1965-67. Vice-Pres., RUSI, 1969-. Hon. Fellow, Jesus College, Oxford, 1963. *Publications:* Introduction to the Theory of Numbers (with Professor G. H. Hardy), 1938, 2nd edn 1945, 3rd edn 1954, 4th edn 1960; Mathematical papers in scientific journals. *Address:* Chanonry Lodge, Old Aberdeen. *T:* Aberdeen 43074. *Clubs:* University (Aberdeen); Royal Scottish Automobile (Glasgow); Caledonian (Edinburgh).

**WRIGHT, Eric David;** Assistant Under-Secretary, Ministry of Defence, since 1965, on loan to Home Office, since 1970; *b* 12 June 1917; *s* of Charles Henry and Cecelia Wright; *m* 1944, Doris (*née* Nicholls); one *s*. *Educ:* Ealing County Grammar School. Joined War Office, 1935; Principal, 1945; seconded to Dept of the Army, Australia, 1951; Asst Secretary, 1955; Command Secretary, BAOR, 1955-58; Imperial Defence College, 1964. *Address:* Green Shutters, Valley Road, Rickmansworth, Herts. *T:* Rickmansworth 75572.

**WRIGHT, Ernest,** CBE 1936; retired; Secretary Guildford Diocesan Board of Finance, 1940-48, thereafter working part-time at Diocesan House, Guildford, until retirement in 1967; *b* 22 April 1882; *s* of late Thomas Wright and Jane Taylor; *m* 1st, 1908, Irene Marion Bishop Ackerman (*d* 1954); two *s* one *d*; 2nd, 1959, Olive May Moody, *née* Ellis (*d* 1969). *Educ:* Privately; Kendrick Grammar School; University College, Reading. Banking: London and County Bank Ltd, 1900-03; Birmingham District and Counties Bank, 1905-06; Alliance Bank of Egypt, Cairo, 1919; Cox and Co., Cairo, Lloyds Bank Ltd, Cairo 1920-22, 1924-25; Bank of Abyssinia, Addis Ababa, 1926-31; Bank of Ethiopia, Addis Ababa (Sub-Governor and Director), 1931-36. Farming: Canada, Manitoba, 1904; Egypt, Kharga Oasis, Libyan Desert, 1910-15; South Africa, Cape Province, 1922-23; Enemy Licensing Office, Public Custodian's Office, Ministry of Finance, Cairo, 1915-19. Officier, Ordre de Menelik II, 1934. *Recreations:* golf, riding, walking. *Address:* at Ludshott Manor, near Bramshott, Hants.

**WRIGHT, Esmond;** Visiting Professor in the Department of Economic History, Strathclyde University, since 1970; *b* 5 Nov. 1915; *m* 1945, Olive Adamson. *Educ:* King's College, Newcastle, in the University of Durham (Open Entrance Schol., Gladstone Memorial Prizeman, 1st Cl. Hons Modern History); Univ. of Virginia (Commonwealth Fund Fellow). War Service, 1940-46, mainly in Middle East; demobilised as Lt-Col, 1946. Glasgow Univ., 1946-67; Prof. of Modern History, 1957-67. MP (C) Glasgow, Pollok, March 1967-1970. Vis. Prof. in various Amer. Univs. Founder-Mem., British Association for American Studies (Chm., 1965-68). Member: Brit. Nat. Commn for UNESCO; Birsay Cttee on Gen. Med. Services in Highlands and Islands of Scotland, 1965-67; Marshall Aid Commemoration Commn; Exec. Cttee, Automobile Assoc.; House of Commons Select Cttee on Scottish Affairs; House of Commons Select Cttee on Educn and Science; Chm., Scottish Sub-Cttee. Dep. Chm., Conservative and Unionist Party in Scotland, 1970-. Gen. Editor, Hamlyn's World History, 1969-70. *Publications:* A Short History of our own Times, 1951; George Washington and the American Revolution, 1957; Fabric of Freedom, 1961; (ed) Illustrated World History, 1964; Benjamin Franklin and American Independence, 1966; (ed) Causes and Consequences of the American Revolution, 1966; (ed) American Themes, 1967; American Profiles, 1967; (ed) History of the World in Colour, 1969; (ed) Benjamin Franklin, a profile, 1970; Articles in periodicals. *Address:* 15 Beaumont Gate, Glasgow W2. *T:* 041-339 3655. *Clubs:* Athenæum, Constitutional.

**WRIGHT, Frank Joseph Henry,** MBE 1966; Music Director, Greater London Council (formerly London County Council) Parks Department, since 1935; Member of Corporation, and Examiner, Trinity College of Music, London, since 1963; Professor and Examiner, Guildhall School of Music and Drama since 1945; *b* Smeaton, Vic, Australia, 2 Aug. 1901; *s* of late W. Wright and Sarah (*née* Higgins); unmarried. *Educ:* singing, piano, composition and brass instruments at Ballarat and Melbourne. Won Australian Cornet Championship, 1919; Open Diploma Award of Associated Board for highest points in Australia (subject singing), 1930. LRSM (London). Master, Worshipful Co. of Musicians, 1970-71; Exec. Mem., Nat. Music Council of Gt Brit., 1959-; Life Mem., Royal Musical Assoc.; Mem. Internat. Jury, Wereld Muziek-Concours, Holland, 1948-; Guest Conductor: London Symphony Orchestra; Royal Philharmonic Orchestra; Music Adviser, Sth Bank Exhibn, Fest. of Brit., 1951. Adjudicated at Nat. Brass Band Fest. 20 times; also at Championships of Aust. and NZ, and for BBC, Challenging Brass, 1967-69. Hon. Editor, The Conductor, since its inception in 1946; edited Brass Today, 1957. Started GLC open-air symphony concerts at: Kenwood Lakeside, 1951; Holland Park, 1955; Crystal Palace Concert Bowl, 1961. Toured W German Opera Houses as guest of Fed. Republic, 1963. Supt, Corps of Hon. Stewards, Royal Albert

Hall, 1962-. Featured in BBC TV Documentary, The Impresario, 1967. Hon. FTCL, FGSM. *Publications:* compositions, mainly brass band, include: Diversions on Original Theme, Sirius; Trilogy, Threshold; Suite, Old Westminster; Preludio Marziale; Ceremonial March, Whitehall. Music and script of tutorial (record), Voice of the Cornet. Test pieces scored for Nat. Brass Band Fest., incl. works by R. Vaughan Williams, Bliss, Rubbra, Howells; also scored T. Wood's The Rainbow (A Tale of Dunkirk), commissioned by the Arts Counciol for Fest. of Britain, 1951. Altogether over 100 works published. *Recreations:* collecting Melba records and Edison phonographs. *Address:* 14 Highbury Grange, N5. *Club:* City Livery.

**WRIGHT, Frank T. W.;** *see* Wynyard-Wright.

**WRIGHT, Georg Henrik von,** MA; Research Professor in the Academy of Finland, since 1961; Professor at Large, Cornell University, since 1965; Chancellor of Abo Academy, since 1968; *b* Helsingfors, 14 June 1916; *s* of Tor von Wright and Ragni Elisabeth Alfthan; *m* 1941, Maria Elisabeth von Troil; one *s* one *d*. *Educ:* Svenska Normallyceum, Helsingfors; Helsingfors Univ. Helsingfors University: Lectr and Acting Prof. of Philosophy, 1943-46; Prof. of Philosophy, 1946-61 (also in Univ. of Cambridge, 1948-51); Visiting Professor: Cornell Univ., 1954 and 1958; Univ. Calif., Los Angeles, 1963; Univ. Pittsburg, 1966; Lectures: Shearman Meml, University Coll., London, 1956; Gifford, Univ. of St Andrews, 1959-60; Tarner, Trinity Coll., Cambridge, 1969. President: Internat. Union of History and Philosophy of Science, 1963-65; Acad. of Finland, 1968-69. Fellow: Finnish Soc. of Sciences; New Soc. of Letters, Lund; Royal Swedish Academy of Sciences; Royal Soc. of Letters, Lund; British Academy; Royal Swedish Academy of Letters, History and Antiquities; Hon. Foreign Mem., Amer. Acad. of Arts and Sciences. sometime Fellow, Trinity College, Cambridge. Hon. degrees: Helsingfors Univ. (doctor of pol. sci.); Univ. of Liverpool (DLitt); Univ. of Lund (doctor of philosophy); Turku Univ. (doctor of philosophy). *Publications:* The Logical Problem of Induction, 1941, rev. edn 1957; Den Logiska Empirismen, 1943; Uber Wahrscheinlichkeit, 1945; A Treatise on Induction and Probability, 1951; An Essay in Modal Logic, 1951; Logical Studies, 1957; The Varieties of Goodness, 1963; The Logic of Preference, 1963; Norm and Action, 1963; An Essay in Deontic Logic, 1968; Time, Change, and Contradiction, 1969. *Address:* 4 Skepparegatan, Helsingfors, Finland.

**WRIGHT, Prof. H(enry) Myles;** FRIBA; MTPI; Lever Professor of Civic Design, University of Liverpool, since 1954; University Planning Consultant, since 1957; *b* 9 June 1908; *s* of H. T. Wright, Gosforth, Newcastle upon Tyne; *m* 1939, Catharine Noble, *y d* of Very Rev. H. N. Craig, Dean of Kildare; two *d*. *Educ:* Fettes College, Edinburgh (Foundationer); King's College, Newcastle upon Tyne; St John's College, Cambridge. Assistant in various private offices, 1930-35; Asst Editor, The Architects' Journal, and in private practice, 1935-40; Partner in firm of Sir William Holford, 1948-54; principally engaged on planning proposals for Cambridge and Corby New Town. Member British Caribbean Federal Capital Commn, 1956. *Publications:* The Planner's Notebook, 1948; Cambridge Planning Proposals, 1950, and Corby New Town (with Lord Holford), 1952; Land Use in an Urban Environment (Editor and contributor), 1961; The Dublin Region: Preliminary and Final Reports, 1965 and 1967; other technical publications. *Recreations:* walking, reading. *Address:* Department of Civic Design, University of Liverpool, PO Box 147, Liverpool L69 3BX. *T:* 051-709 6022. *Club:* University (Dublin).

**WRIGHT, Lt-Col Herbert James,** CMG 1917; Company Director; *b* 1888; *s* of Thomas Wright; *m* 1910, Winifred Alice Croxon (decd); two *s* two *d*. Served War, 1914-18; War of 1939-45 as Commanding Officer, permanent Ships' Staff, 1941. *Recreation:* bowls. *Address:* 40 Fidden's Wharf Road, Killara, NSW 2071, Australia. *T:* 49.3276.

**WRIGHT, Prof. Jack Clifford,** MA, BA; Professor of Sanskrit in the University of London, at the School of Oriental and African Studies since 1964; *b* 5 Dec. 1933; *s* of Jack and Dorothy Wright, Aberdeen; *m* 1958, Hazel Chisholm (*née* Strachan), Crathes, Kincardine; one *s*. *Educ:* Robert Gordon's Coll., Aberdeen; Univ. of Aberdeen (MA Hons in French and German, 1955); University of Zürich; Univ. of London (BA Hons in Sanskrit, 1959). Lectr in Sanskrit, Sch. of Oriental and African Studies, Univ. of London, 1959-64. *Publication:* Non-classical Sanskrit literature, 1966; articles in Bulletin of the School of Oriental and African Studies and elsewhere. *Address:* School of Oriental and African Studies, University of London, WC1.

**WRIGHT, Adm. Jerauld,** DSM (US) (twice); Silver and Bronze Star Medals; Legion of Merit (US); USN retired; US Ambassador to Nationalist China, 1963-65; *b* Amherst, Mass., 4 June 1898; *s* of Gen. William Mason Wright and Marjorie R. (Jerauld) Wright; *m* 1938, Phyllis B. Thompson; one *s* one *d*. *Educ:* US Naval Academy. Ensign, USN, 1917; promoted through grades to Admiral, 1954. Executive Staff of US Naval Academy; operational staff appointments for N African, Sicilian and Italian landings; Mem., Gen. Mark Clark's Expedition to North Africa. Comdr, USS Santa Fe, Pacific, 1943-44; Comdr Amphibious Group Five, 1944-45; Comdr Cruiser Div. Six, 1945; Asst Chief of Naval Operations for Fleet Readiness, 1945-48; Comdr. Amphibious Force, US Atlantic Fleet, 1949-51; US Rep. NATO Standing Group, Washington, 1951-52; C-in-C US Naval Forces, E Atlantic and Medit., 1952-54; Supreme Allied Commander, Atlantic, and C-in-C Western Atlantic Area, NATO, 1954-60; C-in-C Atlantic (US Unified Command), and C-in-C Atlantic Fleet, 1954-60. Pres. US Naval Inst., 1959. Holds Hon. doctorates in Laws and Science. Awarded foreign decorations. *Address:* (Home) 2706 36th Street NW, Washington, DC 20007, USA. *Clubs:* Metropolitan, Alibi, Chevy Chase (Washington); Knickerbocker, Brooke (New York).

**WRIGHT, Air Cdre John Allan Cecil C.;** *see* Cecil-Wright.

**WRIGHT, Prof. John George,** DSc (Hon.); Dr med. vet. (Hon.); MVSc, FRCVS, DVA; Emeritus Professor of Veterinary Surgery, University of Liverpool, since 1963 (Professor, 1941-63); Dean of Faculty of Veterinary Science, 1952-61; *b* 2 Sept. 1897; *m* 1925, Elsie Lloyd Razey (*d* 1955); one *s* one *d*; *m* 1958, Winefred Mayor Jones. *Educ:* High School, Newport, Monmouthshire; Royal Veterinary College, London. Served European War, 1915-19, RFA; France, Belgium, South Russia. Royal Veterinary College, 1919-23; general veterinary practice, 1923-28; Staff of Royal Veterinary College, ending as Professor of Surgery, 1929-41. Member Inter-Univ. Council for Higher Education in the Colonies.

1945-56; Pres. Royal College of Veterinary Surgeons, 1951 and 1952; Fellow, Royal Veterinary Coll., 1965. *Publications:* Veterinary Anæsthesia, 1941, 1946, 1952, 1956, (with L. W. Hall) 1961; Veterinary Obstetrics (with F. Benesch), 1951 and (with G. H. Arthur), 1964. Numerous contribs to veterinary literature on the subjects of surgery, anæsthesia, obstetrics and diseases of reproduction. *Recreation:* gardening. *Address:* Wendover, Overdale Road, Willaston, Wirral, Cheshire.

**WRIGHT, John Henry,** CBE 1964; HM Diplomatic Service, retired; *b* 6 Dec. 1910; *s* of John Robert Wright and Margaret Leadbetter; *m* 1939, Joan Harvey; two *s*. *Educ:* Barrow Grammar Sch.; Trinity Coll., Cambridge. Vice-Consul, Genoa, 1934; Addis Ababa, 1937; Havana, 1939; 2nd Sec., Quito, 1943; 1st Sec., 1945; transf. to Foreign Office, 1948; 1st Sec. (Commercial), Helsinki, 1950; 1st Sec. (Commercial), Santiago, 1953; Counsellor, at Shanghai, of HM Chargé d'Affaires in China, 1958-60; Counsellor, temporarily employed in Foreign Office, Dec. 1960-61; HM Consul-General at Rotterdam, 1961-63; Ambassador to Honduras, 1963-69. *Recreations:* lawn tennis, walking, bridge, music. *Address:* Horse Inn House, Bourton-on-the-Hill, Glos. *Club:* United University.

**WRIGHT, John Moncrieff,** CBE 1920; ICS retired; *b* 1884; *s* of James Moncrieff Wright; *m* 1912, Leonore Ada Beddall (*d* 1959); one *s* (and one killed in action 1944). *Educ:* Dulwich College; Jesus College, Cambridge. 1st class Honours Classical Tripos, 1906; passed Indian Civil Service Examination, 1907; Assistant Commissioner Burma, 1908; Superintendent Chin Hills, 1913-19; Political Officer Operations, 1917-18; Deputy Commissioner Burma, 1920; Port Blair, 1921-24; Burma, 1925-27; Acting Chief Commissioner Andaman and Nicobar Islands, 1927-28; Bursar Malvern Girls' College, 1929-39; JP Worcestershire, 1938-47; Ministry of Food, 1939-48, retired as Assistant Secretary and Director, Ancillary Materials. *Address:* Brookside, Winfrith, Dorset. *T:* Winfrith 239. *Club:* Oxford and Cambridge University.

**WRIGHT, Prof. John Nicholson;** Professor of Logic and Metaphysics in the United College, the University of St Andrews, 1936-66, now Emeritus; Master of St Salvator's College in the University of St Andrews, 1959-66; Acting Master, 1966-67; retired; General Council Assessor, University Court, since 1969; *b* 21 Aug. 1896; *e s* of John Nicholson Wright and Elizabeth Ann Humble; *m* 1923, Florencia Emilia Cowper (*d* 1966), Pacasmayo, Peru, and Canterbury, Kent; two *d*. *Educ:* Bede Collegiate School, Sunderland; Ryhope Grammar School; St Chad's College, University of Durham (scholar and prizeman). Served 4th Bn Durham Light Infantry, 1916-19. BA 1920, MA 1923. Assistant in Dept of Logic and Metaphysics, Univ. of St Andrews, 1920; Lecturer in Logic and Psychology, Univ. Coll., Dundee, 1924-36; Adviser of Studies in Arts, 1932; Dean of the Faculty of Arts, Univ. of St Andrews, 1937-50. Chairman of Regional Cttee for Adult Education, 1938-50; War Office Lecturer to HM Forces in Middle East, 1945 and 1947, Far East, 1950; Member of Advisory Committee on Education to the War Office, 1945; member Fulbright Commission, 1957. President, Mind Association, 1959. President Scottish Amateur Swimming Assoc., 1935, and on Selection Cttee for British Empire Games. Chairman Council of St Leonards and St Katharines Schools, 1952-67 (Hon. Vice-Pres., 1969). Fellow, Morse College, Yale Univ., 1964. Hon. LLD St Andrews Univ., 1967. Order of Polonia Restituta, 1944; Norwegian Order of Freedom, 1947. *Publications:* articles and reviews in learned journals and on philosophy and logic in Chambers's Encyclopædia. *Recreations:* music, swimming. *Address:* 120 North Street, St Andrews, Fife. *T:* 103. *Club:* Royal and Ancient Golf (St Andrews).

**WRIGHT, (John) Oliver,** CMG 1964; DSC 1944; Chief Clerk, HM Diplomatic Service, since 1970; *b* 6 March 1921; *m* 1942, Lillian Marjory Osborne; three *s*. *Educ:* Solihull School; Christ's College, Cambridge (MA). Served in RNVR, 1941-45. Joined HM Diplomatic Service, Nov. 1945; served: New York, 1946-47; Bucharest, 1948-50; Singapore, 1950-51; Foreign Office, 1952-54; Berlin, 1954-56; Pretoria, 1957-58. Imperial Defence College, 1959. Asst Private Sec. to Sec. of State for Foreign Affairs, 1960; Counsellor and Private Sec., 1963; Private Sec. to the Prime Minister, 1964-66 (to Rt Hon. Sir Alec Douglas-Home, and subseq. to Rt Hon. Harold Wilson); Ambassador to Denmark, 1966-69; Dep. Under-Sec. of State, FCO, 1969-70, seconded to Home Office as UK Rep. to NI Govt, Aug. 1969-March 1970. *Recreations:* theatre and golf. *Address:* Burstow Hall, near Horley, Surrey. *T:* Horley 3494. *Clubs:* Naval, Travellers', Arts Theatre.

**WRIGHT, Judith, (Mrs J. P. McKinney);** writer; *b* 31 May 1915; *d* of late Phillip Arundel Wright, CMG, and Ethel Mabel (*née* Bigg); *m* J. P. McKinney; one *d*. *Educ:* NSW Correspondence Sch.; New England Girls' Sch.; Sydney Univ. Secretarial work, 1938-42; Univ. Statistician (Univ. of Queensland), 1945-48. Dr of Letters (Hon.): Univ. of Queensland, 1962; Univ. of New England, 1963. Encyclopædia Britannica Writer's Award, 1965. FAHA 1970. *Publications: verse:* The Moving Image, 1946; Woman to Man, 1950; The Gateway, 1953; The Two Fires, 1955; Birds, 1960; Five Senses, 1963; The Other Half, 1966; *biographical novel:* The Generations of Men, 1955; *criticism:* Preoccupations in Australian Poetry, 1964; *anthologies:* The Oxford Book of Australian Verse, 1954; New Land New Language, 1956; *short stories:* The Nature of Love, 1966; four books for children; also critical essays and monographs. *Recreation:* gardening. *Address:* Calanthe, Long Road, North Tamborine, Queensland, Australia. *T:* North Tamborine 330.

**WRIGHT, Kenneth Anthony,** OBE 1953; General Manager and Director, Harmony Films, I. R. Maxwell Film Distributors Ltd; Director, Norman McCann Artists' Management; Associate Editor, Music; writer, adjudicator and lecturer; retired as Chief Assistant to Head of Music Productions, BBC Television; *b* 5 June 1899; *o s* of William John and Elizabeth Maria Wright; *m* 1931, Helen (marr. diss., 1946), 2nd *d* of John Crichton and Jeanie Forsyth Connal, Cambuslang; no *c*; *m* 1947, Diana (marr. diss., 1962), *o d* of Lt-Col Newton Stirrett, OBE, MC and Desirée Ellinger; two *s*; *m* 1963, Lilian Dorothy Letitia Calleia, *o d* of John Leslie and Lilian Tompkins, two *d* by previous marriage. *Educ:* City of Norwich Sch.; Sheffield Univ. BEng (Hons Mech. and Elec.), 1920; MEng, 1921; Cadet, RFC, Pte XIX Bn The London Regt, gazetted RE, 1919; Res. Engineer Metropolitan Vickers Co., Manchester, 1920-22, while continuing to pursue music energetically as hobby; after participating in pioneer experiments in Radio Telephony he combined engineering and music as first Director of Manchester Station (2ZY) of BBC 1922; subsequent career entirely in BBC. Asst

Mus. Dir of Corporation, 1937; Overseas Mus. Dir, 1940-43; Dep. Dir of Music, 1944-47; Artists' Manager, 1948; Head of Music Programmes (Television), 1951; responsible for special projects involving television and music, 1956-59; retired Oct. 1959; rep. BBC, from 1930 onwards at many internat. music festivals, confs, etc., in Europe, USA, Canada; Mem. Jury first Salzburg internat. Comp. TV Opera, 1959. Hon. FTCL; co-produced and commentated film, Musicians to Moscow, with L. Kristy in two visits to USSR, 1954 and with O. Gajic, of Filmske Novosti, Summer in Dubrovnik, 1956. Prod. Symphony of Switzerland, 1959. Chevalier de la Légion d'Honneur, 1947. *Compositions:* many works for Brass and Military Bands, including Overture, Glendalough, and Rhapsodies, Irish Merry and Peddar's Way, 1937; Suite, Pride of Race, 1935, for National Festival, Crystal Palace, etc. Composed (1946) Scores for Heart's Beloved (Richard Fisher); Shoemaker's Holiday (Dekker-Richard Fisher); Dear Beast (Joan Murray Simpson); Suite Tobacco, commissioned for BBC Light Music Festival, 1949. *Address:* 77 Ashworth Mansions, W9. *T:* 01-286 7495.

**WRIGHT, Rev. Leslie,** CBE 1952; MA (Lambeth), 1953; Vicar of St John's, Kingston Vale, SW15, 1961-68; Hon. Canon of Southwark Cathedral, 1960-68; Emeritus Canon since 1968; *b* 19 Nov. 1899; *s* of John Wright, Carlisle; *m* 1935, Katrina, *d* of Dr T. B. Gilbart-Smith, Nottingham; two *s. Educ:* St Bees, Cumberland; Royal Military Academy, Woolwich. Commissioned into Royal Artillery, Dec. 1919; retired, 1926. Travelling Secretary Officers' Christian Union, 1928-35; ordained, 1935; Curate St Andrews, Nottingham, 1935-36, when commissioned in RAF Chaplains' Branch; KHC, Chaplain-in-Chief Royal Air Force, 1949-53; Prebendary of St Botolph's in Lincoln Cathedral, 1950-May 1953; retired, 1953; Vicar of Wimbledon, 1953-61; Rural Dean, 1954-60. *Recreation:* golf. *Address:* Queen Oak House, Bourton, Gillingham, Dorset. *T:* Bourton 425.

**WRIGHT, Louis Booker;** Hon. OBE 1968; historian, writer; Director, Folger Shakespeare Library, 1948-68; *b* 1 March 1899; *s* of Thomas Fleming Wright and Lena Booker Wright; *m* 1925, Frances Black; one *s. Educ:* Wofford College; University of North Carolina. AB 1920, Wofford Coll.; MA 1924, PhD 1926, N Carolina. Service in US Army, 1918; newspaper corres. and editor, 1918-23; instructor and associate Prof. of Eng., University of North Carolina, 1926-32; visiting scholar, Huntington Library, 1931-32; member permanent research group, Huntington Library, also Chm., Cttee on Fellowships and Mem. Exec. Cttee, 1932-48; Vis. Professor: Univs of Michigan 1935, Washington 1942, Calif. at Los Angeles 1934-48; Pomona Coll., 1941-48; Calif. Inst. of Technology, 1932-48; Univ. of Minnesota, 1946; Indiana Univ. on the Patten Foundation, 1953. Chm. Advisory Bd, John Simon Guggenheim Memorial Foundation; Vice-Chm., Council on Library Resources, Inc.; Mem. Bd of Directors H. F. duPont Winterthur Museum and Harry S. Truman Library Inst. for Nat. and Internat. Affairs. Trustee: Shakespeare Birthplace Trust; National Geographic Society. Hon. LittD: Wofford, 1941; Mills College, 1947; Princeton, 1948; Amherst, 1948; Occidental College, 1949; Bucknell, 1951; Franklin and Marshall, 1957; Colby Coll., 1959; Univ. of British Columbia, 1960; Leicester Univ., 1965; Hon. LLD: Tulane, 1950; George Washington, 1958; Chattanooga, 1959; Akron, 1961; St Andrews, 1961; Washington and Lee, 1964; Mercer, 1965; LHD: Northwestern, 1948; Univ. of N Carolina, 1950, Yale 1954; Rockford Coll., 1956; Coe Coll., 1959; Georgetown Univ., 1961; California State Coll., 1966; Univ. of California, 1967; Brown Univ., 1968; Hon. DLitt, Birmingham, England, 1964. Benjamin Franklin Medal, RSA, 1969. *Publications:* Middle-Class Culture in Elizabethan England, 1935; Puritans in the South Seas, 1936; The First Gentlemen of Virginia, 1940; Religion and Empire, 1942; The First Americans in North Africa, 1945; The Atlantic Frontier, 1947; Culture on the Moving Frontier, 1955; The Cultural Life of the American Colonies, 1957; Shakespeare for Everyman, 1964; The Dream of Prosperity in Colonial America, 1965; The History of the Thirteen Colonies, 1967; Gold, Glory and the Gospel, 1970. Edited: Letters of Robert Carter, 1940; The Secret Diary of William Byrd of Westover, 1709-12, 1941; Quebec to Carolina in 1785-1786, 1943; An Essay Upon the Government of the English Plantation on the Continent of America, 1701, 1945; The History and Present State of Virginia, 1705 (by Robert Beverley), 1947; The Historie of Travell into Virginia Britania, 1612, (by William Strachey) 1953; The Folger Library General Reader's Shakespeare, 1957-; William Byrd of Virginia: The London Diary 1717-1721, and Other Writings, 1958; The Elizabethans' America, 1965. The Prose Works of William Byrd of Westover, 1966. *Recreation:* fishing. *Address:* 3702 Leland Street, Chevy Chase, Md 20015, USA. *T:* 652-5509. *Clubs:* Cosmos (Washington); Century, Grolier (New York).

**WRIGHT, Sir Michael (Robert),** GCMG 1958 (KCMG 1951; CMG 1945); retired; Chairman, Atlantic Trade Study; UK Delegate: to Conference for Cessation of Nuclear Tests, Geneva, 1959; to (10 Power) Disarmament Conference, Geneva, 1960; and to (18 Power) Disarmament Conference, Geneva, 1962; *b* 3 Dec. 1901; *s* of late Sir Robert Wright; *m* 1934, Esther, *d* of late George Long; two *s. Educ:* Winchester; Balliol Coll., Oxford. Entered HM Diplomatic Service, 1926; Brit. Embassy, Washington, 1926-30; FO, 1930-36; Brit. Embassy, Paris, 1936-40; Cairo, 1940-43; Brit. Embassy, Washington, 1943-46; served on staff of Special Commissioner in South-East Asia, 1946-47; Assistant Under-Secretary of State, Foreign Office, 1947-50; Ambassador to Norway, 1951-54; Ambassador to Iraq, 1954-58. Director, Guinness Mahon Holdings Ltd, 1964-. Member Board, International Movement for Atlantic Union. *Publication:* Disarm and Verify, 1964. *Recreations:* fishing, ski-ing. *Address:* 4 Whitehall Court, SW1. *T:* 01-930 3160. *Club:* St James'.

**WRIGHT, Rear-Adm. Noel,** CB 1946; OBE 1919; retired; *b* 24 Dec. 1890; 4th *s* of late William Wright, JP, Whitby, Yorks; *m* 1921, Phœbe, *o d* of J. Gandon, Smyrna; one *s* one *d. Educ:* St Helen's College, Southsea. Entered Navy, 1908; Paymaster Captain, 1939; acting Rear-Admiral (S), 1944. Fleet Supply Officer, Mediterranean and Levant 1942-43; Command Supply Officer Western Approaches, 1944-45. Sponsored British Cape Britannia Expedition, in hopes of finding a message deposited by Sir John Franklin, 1962. Gave to Prime Minister the "Resolute" bell to present to President of USA, 1965. *Publications:* Glimpses of South Africa; Sun of Memory; New Light on Franklin (privately printed); Quest for Franklin, 1959. *Recreations:* literary research and gardening. *Address:* 33 The Avenue, Alverstoke, Hants. *T:* Gosport 81567. *Club:* Nuffield US Officers' (Portsmouth).

**WRIGHT, Oliver;** *see* Wright, J. O.

**WRIGHT, Paul Hervé Giraud,** CMG 1960; OBE 1952; British Ambassador to Congo (Kinshasa) and to Republic of Burundi, since 1969; *b* 12 May 1915; *o s* of late Richard Hervé Giraud Wright; *m* 1942, Beatrice Frederika Rathbone (*see* Beatrice Wright), *widow* of Flt-Lt J. R. Rathbone, MP; one *d*. *Educ:* Westminster. Employed by John Lewis Partnership Ltd, 1933-39. Served HM Forces, War of 1939-45; Major, KRRC; HQ 21 Army Group, 1944-45 (despatches). Contested (L) NE Bethnal Green, 1945. Asst Dir, Public Relations, National Coal Bd, 1946-48; Dir, Public Relations, Festival of Britain, 1948-51. HM Foreign Service: Paris and New York, 1951-54; Foreign Office, 1954-56; The Hague, 1956-57; Head of Information, Policy Dept in FO, 1957-60; Cairo, 1960-61; UK Delegn to N Atlantic Council, 1961-64; Minister (Information), Washington, 1965-68, and Dir-Gen., British Inf. Services, NY, 1964-68. *Address:* c/o Foreign and Commonwealth Office, SW1. *Clubs:* Garrick, Travellers'; Century (New York).

**WRIGHT, Peter Harold,** VC 1944; late Company Sergeant-Major, Coldstream Guards; *b* 10 Aug. 1916, British; *m* 1946, Mollie Mary Hurren, Wenhaston. *Educ:* Brooke, Norfolk (elementary school). Left school at 14 and worked on father's farm up to the age of 20. Joined Coldstream Guards, 1936; sailed for Egypt, 1937. Served in Egypt, Palestine, Syria and throughout the Libyan campaign and North Africa, took part in the landing at Salerno, Italy, Sept. 1943; demobilised, 1945. *Address:* c/o The VC's Association, 807 Nelson House, Dolphin Square, SW1.

**WRIGHT, Lt-Col Robert Ernest,** CIE 1929; BA (Sen. Mod.), MD, MCh (Hon.), DPH (TCD), IMS retired; late Professor of Ophthalmology Medical College and Superintendent Government Ophthalmic Hospital, Madras, India; *b* 1884; *s* of R. Wright, JP, of Prumplestown, Carlow, Ireland; *m* 1930, Ruby Evelyn Sheldon, *d* of Dr S. T. Pruen, Cheltenham. *Educ:* Trinity College, Dublin. Graduated with Honours in 1906, taking Large Gold Medal and Senior Moderatorship in Natural Science; also Med. Travelling Prize; joined the IMS 1907; served in Burma with the Hpi-maw Expedition, 1910; Assistant Director Pasteur Institute of S India, 1912; served in Mesopotamia European War (despatches); brevet promotion to Major, 1915; Lieut-Col, 1927; retired, 1938; Member Internat. Council of Ophthalmology, 1929-39. Re-employed by W. D. as Ophth. Specialist, 1939-46. *Publications:* various papers in Medical Literature dealing chiefly Clinical Ophthalmology, biological and ophthalmological research. *Recreations:* shooting, fishing. *Address:* c/o National and Grindlay's Bank Ltd, 13 St James's Square, SW1. *Club:* East India and Sports.

**WRIGHT, Rev. Ronald (William Vernon) Selby,** CVO 1968; TD; DD; FRSA; FSA Scotland; JP; Minister at the Canongate (The Kirk of Holyroodhouse), Edinburgh, and of Edinburgh Castle, since 1936; Chaplain to the Queen in Scotland, since 1963 (Extra Chaplain, 1961-63); *b* 12 June 1908; *s* of late Vernon O. Wright, ARCM, and late Anna Gilberta, *d* of Major R. E. Selby; unmarried. *Educ:* Edinburgh Academy; Melville College; Edinburgh University (MA; Hon. DD 1956); New College, Edinburgh. Warden, St Giles' Cathedral Boys' Club, 1927-36, and Canongate Boys' Club (formerly St Giles'), 1937-. Cadet Officer, The Royal Scots, 1927-31; Student-Assistant at St Giles' Cathedral, 1929-36; Assistant Minister of Glasgow Cathedral, 1936; Warden of first Scottish Public Schools' and Clubs' Camp, 1938; Chaplain to 7th/9th (Highlanders) Bn The Royal Scots, 1938-42 (France, 1940), 1947-49; Senior Chaplain 52nd (Lowland) Div., 1942-43; Senior Chaplain Edinburgh Garrison, 1943; Senior Chaplain in Middle East Forces, 1943-44; Senior Chaplain NE London, 1944; Senior Chaplain 10th Indian Division, Central Mediterranean Forces, 1944-45 (despatches); Hon. Senior Chaplain since 1945; Special Preacher, Oxford University, 1944; Visiting Preacher, Aberdeen University, 1946, 1953, 1965; Select Preacher, Cambridge University, 1947; Visiting Preacher: St Andrews Univ., 1951, 1956, 1967; Glasgow Univ., 1955; Edinburgh Univ., 1959; Birmingham Univ., 1959; Hull University, 1967. Hon. Chaplain, Fettes College, 1957-60; Chaplain to the Lord High Comr, 1959, and 1960. Conducted numerous series of religious broadcasts for BBC As Radio Padre, toured for War Office and BBC all Home Commands in 1942 and 1943 and Middle East Forces, 1943-44; toured transit camps etc. in Italy, Austria, South Germany, etc., 1945. Moderator, Presbytery of Edinburgh, 1963. Hon. Chaplain to HM Forces; Chairman, Edinburgh and Leith Old People's Welfare Council, 1956-69; Director and Chaplain of Queensberry House, and of Whitefoord House; Hon. Chaplain: Edinburgh Academy; "The Scotsman"; Scottish Breweries Ltd; Sub-Chaplain, Order of St John; Vice-President: Scottish Assoc. of Boys Clubs; Old Edinburgh Club; Hon. Pres. Scottish Churches FA; Patron, Lothian Amateur FA. Mem. Edinburgh Educn Cttee, 1960-70. Governor: Rannoch Sch.; St George's Sch. JP Edinburgh, 1963. Cross of St Mark, 1970. *Publications:* Asking Why (with A. W. Loos), 1939; The Average Man, 1942; Let's Ask the Padre, 1943; The Greater Victory, 1943; The Padre Presents, 1944; Small Talks, 1945; Whatever the Years, 1947; What Worries Me, 1950; Great Men, 1951; They Looked to Him, 1954; Our Club, 1954; The Kirk in the Canongate, 1956; The Selfsame Miracles, 1957; Our Club and Panmure House, 1958; Roses in December, 1960; The Seven Words, 1964; An Illustrated Guide to the Canongate, 1965; Take up God's Armour, 1967; The Seven Dwarfs, 1968; edited and contributed to Asking Them Questions, 1936; A Scottish Camper's Prayer Book, 1936; I Attack, 1937; Asking Them Questions–Second Series, 1938; Front Line Religion, 1941; Soldiers Also Asked, 1943; Asking Them Questions–Third Series, 1950; Asking Them Questions (a Selection), 1953; The Beloved Captain: Essays by Donald Hankey, 1956; (with L. Menzies and R. A. Knox) St Margaret, Queen of Scotland, 1957; A Manual of Church Doctrine (with T. F. Torrance), 1960; Fathers of the Kirk, 1960; Asking Them Questions, a new series, 1971; contrib. to Chambers's Encyclopædia, etc. Editor, Scottish Forces' Magazine (quarterly), 1941-. *Recreations:* trying to run a Boys' Club since 1927, hut camping, history of old Edinburgh. *Address:* Manse of the Canongate, Edinburgh 8. *T:* 031-556 3515; Lyndene, Bayswell Road, Dunbar. *Clubs:* Athenæum; New, Puffins (Edinburgh).

**WRIGHT, Adm. Sir Royston (Hollis),** GBE 1964; KCB 1961 (CB 1958); DSC 1941 and Bar 1944; *b* 29 September 1908; *s* of Thomas Henry and Lydia Maude Wright; *m* 1945, Betty Lilian (*née* Gladstone), *widow* of Lieutenant (E) J. E. Ackery, DSC, RN; no *c*. *Educ:* Haileybury College, Hertford. Naval Cadet, 1927; Comdr 1940; comd HM Ships: Beagle, 1939-41; Derwent, 1942; Hurworth, 1943; Capt. 1946; commanded HM Ships: Wakeful, 1948-49; Triumph, 1953-54; Director of Manning, Admiralty, 1950-51; Imperial Defence Coll., 1952; Cdre Royal Naval Barracks, Devonport,

1955-56; Promoted Rear-Adm. 1956; Asst Chief of Naval Staff, 1956-58; Vice-Adm., 1959; Flag Officer Flotillas, Home Fleet, 1958-59; Flag Officer, Scotland, Dec. 1959-61; a Lord Comr of the Admiralty, Second Sea Lord and Chief of Naval Personnel, 1961-64; Admiral, 1962; Chief of Naval Personnel and Second Sea Lord, Ministry of Defence, 1964-65; retd 1965. Aristeon Amdrias (Greek Gold Medal for Valour), 1944. *Recreations:* fishing, shooting. *Address:* Danewell House, Downton, Wilts. *Club:* United Service.

**WRIGHT, Samuel,** CB 1949; Lately Director of Establishments, and Under Secretary, Ministry of Power, retired 1959; *b* 1895; *o surv s* of late Samuel Wright, HM Inland Revenue; *m* 1923, Dorothy (*d* 1965), *d* of late G. P. Chapman, Wells, Somerset; one *s*. *Educ:* High Pavement Sch.; University Coll., Nottingham. Entered Civil Service, 1913; National Health Insurance Commission, England, 1913-19; Ministry of Health, 1919-40; Mines and Petroleum Depts, 1940-42; Ministry of Fuel and Power, now Ministry of Power, 1942-59. JP Surrey, 1951. *Address:* 2 Ashley Close, Walton-on-Thames. *T:* Walton-on-Thames 20820.

**WRIGHT, Samuel John,** MA, retired; *b* 14 April 1899; *s* of S. J. Wright, Taunton; *m* 1924, Violet, *d* of W. S. Bond; two *s* two *d*. *Educ:* Wellington, Somerset; Emmanuel Coll., Cambridge. Served European War, 1917-19, Lieut, RE; Engineering Dept National Physical Laboratory, 1923-26 and 1927-29; Director Instituite for Research in Agricultural Engineering, 1937-42; Director, National Institute of Agricultural Engineering, 1942-47; Consulting Engineer to Royal Agricultural Society, 1931-64; Agricultural Adviser to Ford Motor Co. Ltd, 1947-64. *Publications:* many papers on engineering research and mechanized farming. *Address:* 6 College Road, Cheltenham, Glos. *T:* Cheltenham 53158. *Club:* Farmers'.

**WRIGHT, Sewall;** Professor Emeritus of Genetics, University of Wisconsin, since 1960; *b* 21 Dec. 1889; *s* of Philip Green Wright and Elizabeth Quincy Sewall; *m* 1921, Louise Lane Williams; two *s* one *d*. *Educ:* Lombard Coll.; University of Illinois; Harvard Univ. BS Lombard Coll., 1911; MS Illinois, 1912; ScD Harvard, 1915. Senior Animal Husbandman, US Dept of Agriculture, 1915-25; University of Chicago: Assoc. Professor of Zoology, 1926-29; Professor of Zoology, 1930-37; Ernest D. Burton Distinguished Service Professor, 1937-54; Leon J. Cole Professor of Genetics, University of Wisconsin, 1955-60; Hitchcock Professor, University of California, 1943; Fulbright Professor, University of Edinburgh, 1949-50. Hon. Member, Royal Society of Edinburgh; Foreign Member: Royal Society, London; Royal Danish Acad. of Sciences and Letters. Hon. ScD: Rochester, 1942; Yale, 1949; Harvard, 1951; Knox Coll., 1957; Western Reserve, 1958; Chicago, 1959; Illinois, 1961; Wisconsin, 1965; Hon. LLD, Michigan State, 1955. Nat. Medal of Science, 1966. *Publications:* Evolution and the Genetics of Populations, vol. 1, 1968, vol. 2, 1969; numerous papers on genetics of characters of guinea pig, population genetics and theory of evolution. *Recreation:* travel. *Address:* 3905 Council Crest, Madison, Wisconsin 53711, USA. *Clubs:* Quadrangle (Chicago); University (Madison).

**WRIGHT, Thomas Erskine,** MA; Supernumerary Fellow, Queen's College, Oxford, since 1953; *b* 15 Sept. 1902; *s* of Rev. Thomas Wright, MA, Stirling, and Isabel Hamilton Ritchie; unmarried. *Educ:* Stirling High Sch.; Univ. of Glasgow; Balliol Coll., Oxford (Snell Exhibitioner and Hon. Scholar). 1st Class Hons in Classics, Univ. of Glasgow, 1924; Hertford and Craven Scholarships, Chancellor's Prize (Latin Prose), Ferguson Scholarship in Classics, 1925; 1st Class Hons Mods, Chancellor's Prize (Latin Verse), Ireland Scholarship, 1926; 1st Class Lit Hum, 1928. Official Fellow of the Queen's Coll., Oxford, and Praelector in Classics, 1928-48; became Tutor and Senior Tutor amd held various other college offices. Professor of Humanity, Univ. of St Andrews, 1948-62, Dean of the Faculty of Arts, 1951-54; Member of the University Grants Cttee, 1954-63; Sec. and Treas., Carnegie Trust for Univs of Scotland, 1962-69. *Publications:* The Latin Contribution to a Liberal Education, 1949; contributions to Oxford Classical Dictionary, *Veterum Laudes,* Fifty Years of Classical Scholarship, and periodicals. *Address:* 10 Gladstone Place, Stirling. *T:* Stirling 2681. *Club:* Stirling and County (Stirling).

**WRIGHT, Prof. William,** MA; ScD; BSc, PhD, CEng, FInstCE, FInstnProdE; FIEI; FRSE; FTCD; Professor of Engineering, Trinity College, Dublin, since 1957; Director, Graduate School of Engineering Studies since 1963; *b* 3 Dec. 1918; *s* of late Rev. James Wright, DD; *m* 1st, 1944, Mildred Anderson (*d* 1959), *d* of James Robertson, MA; two *s* one *d*; 2nd, Barbara Robinson, MA, PhD, LLB, FTCD, *d* of W. Edward Robinson; one *s*. *Educ:* Inverness Royal Academy; George Watson's Coll.; Glasgow Univ. Civil Engineer with LMSR and Min. of Transport, 1935-39. Served War, 1939-46, Captain, Royal Engineers, Middle East, Italy and Germany. Consulting Engineer, 1946-49. Glasgow Univ., 1938-39 and 1946-49 (John Oliphant Bursar) 1st Class Hons Civil Engineering. Lecturer in Civil Engineering, Aberdeen Univ., 1949-54; Head of Dept of Civil Engineering, Southampton Univ., 1954-57. Mem. Council, Instn of Production Engineers, 1964. AMICE 1949; PhD Aberdeen, 1952; MICEI 1957; MICE 1958; MA Dublin, 1960; ScD Dublin, 1963. *Publications:* papers in learned journals in Britain and America. *Recreations:* fishing, mountaineering. *Address:* Les Trembles, 35 Palmerston Road, Rathmines, Dublin 6. *T:* Dublin 9786.19. *Club:* Athenæum.

**WRIGHT, William Alan,** CIE 1945; AFC; *b* 27 Nov. 1895; *s* of Rev. Thomas Wright and Annie Pedley; *m* 1948, Elizabeth Ada, *d* of A. E. Garrott, Launceston, Tasmania; one *s* one *d*. *Educ:* Oundle. 2nd Lieut, Leicestershire Regt, Jan, 1915; joined the Royal Flying Corps, Sept. 1916; Captain about July 1917 (Chevalier of Crown of Belgium and Belgian Croix de Guerre); transferred to RAF on its formation (AFC); joined Indian Civil Service, 1921, and served in Burma, acting Judge Rangoon High Court in 1939; with Government of India, War Dept, 1942-45, as Deputy Secretary, and then as officiating Joint Secretary; Deputy Director of Civil Affairs, Burma, Brig. 1945; Judge Rangoon High Court, 1945-48. *Address:* 3 Cochran Avenue, Camberwell, Melbourne, Victoria, Australia.

**WRIGHT, William Ambrose, (Billy Wright),** CBE 1959; Head of Sport, ATV Network Ltd, since 1966; *b* 6 Feb. 1924; *m* 1958, Joy Beverley; two *d*, and one step *s*. *Educ:* Madeley Secondary Modern Sch. Professional Footballer; became Captain, Wolverhampton Wanderers Football Club; played for England 105 times; Captain of England 85 times; Manager of Arsenal Football Club, 1962-66. FA Cup Winners medal; 3 Football League Winners Medals. *Publications:* Captain of England; The World's my Football Pitch.

*Recreations:* golf, cricket. *Address:* 87 Lyonsdown Road, New Barnet, Herts. *T:* 01-440 3181.

**WRIGHT, Professor William David,** ARCS, DIC, DSc; Professor of Applied Optics, Imperial College of Science and Technology, South Kensington, since 1951; *b* 6 July 1906; *s* of late William John Wright and Grace Elizabeth Ansell; *m* 1932, Dorothy Mary Hudson; two *s*. *Educ:* Southgate County Sch.; Imperial Coll. Research engineer at Westinghouse Electric and Manufacturing Co., Pittsburgh, USA, 1929-30; research and consultant physicist to Electric and Musical Industries, 1930-39. Lecturer and Reader in Technical Optics Section, Imperial Coll., 1931-51. Chm. Physical Soc. Colour Group, 1941-43; Vice-Pres., Physical Soc., 1948-50; Sec., International Commn for Optics, 1953-66; Chm., Physical Soc. Optical Group, 1956-59; Pres., International Colour Assoc., 1967-69; Chm., British Colour Educn Inst, 1970-. *Publications:* The Perception of Light, 1938; The Measurement of Colour, 4th edn, 1969; Researches on Normal and Defective Colour Vision, 1946; Photometry and the Eye, 1950; The Rays are not Coloured, 1967. About 80 original scientific papers, mainly dealing with colour and vision. *Address:* 19 Chalk Lane, Cockfosters, Barnet, Herts. *T:* 01-440 4181.

**WRIGHT, Most Rev. William Lockridge;** *see* Algoma, Archbishop of, and Metropolitan of Ontario.

**WRIGHTSON, Edmund Harry Paul Garmondsway,** QC 1963; Recorder of Walsall, since 1965; *b* 31 Jan. 1919; *o s* of late Lieut-Commander E. G. Wrightson, DSO, RNR, and of Mrs Rose Wrightson, Horspath Manor, Oxford; *m* 1942, Mary, *o c* of late Major L. C. Dickens, MC, and of Mrs Dickens, Froxfield, Hants; three *d*. *Educ:* Marlborough Coll.; Hertford Coll., Oxford (MA). Called to Bar, Lincoln's Inn, 1942; Buchanan Prize; Oxford Circuit. *Recreations:* wireless telegraphy, astronomy, lawn tennis, golf. *Address:* 5 Paper Buildings, Temple, EC4. *T:* 01-353 7811; 4 Milborne Grove, SW10. *Clubs:* United University, Roehampton.

**WRIGHTSON, Sir John (Garmondsway),** 3rd Bt, *cr* 1900; TD 1948; DL; *b* 18 June 1911; *s* of 2nd Bt and Gwendolin Cotterill (*d* 1964), *d* of G. Harding Neame; *S* father, 1950; *m* 1939, Hon. Rosemary Dawson, *y d* of 1st Viscount Dawson, PC, GCVO, KCB, KCMG; one *s* three *d*. *Educ:* Eton. Late Major, Durham LI (TA). Served War of 1939-45, 6th Airborne Div., France and Germany (despatches). High Sheriff, Durham, 1959, DL 1960. *Heir: s* Charles Mark Garmondsway Wrightson, *b* 18 Feb. 1951. *Address:* Neasham Hall, near Darlington. *T:* Croft 333. *Club:* Carlton.

**WRIGLEY, Arthur Joseph,** CBE 1965; MD (London) Gold Medal; FRCS; FRCOG; retired as Obstetric Physician, St Thomas' Hospital, London; *b* 5 May 1902; *er s* of late Canon Joseph Henry Wrigley, Clitheroe, Lancs; *m* 1930, Ann, *d* of late Colonel J. W. Slater, CMG, Dunscar, Lancs; one *s* one *d*. *Educ:* Rossall Sch.; St Thomas' Hospital. Hon. FCOG S Africa. *Publications:* many medical. *Address:* Bay Gate, Bolton-by-Bowland, Clitheroe, Lancs. *T:* Bolton-by-Bowland 646.

**WRIGLEY, Air Vice-Marshal Henry Bertram,** CB 1962; CBE 1956; DL; Senior Technical Staff Officer, Royal Air Force Fighter Command, 1960-64, retired; Sales Manager Air Weapons, Hawker Siddeley Dynamics Ltd; *b* 24 Nov. 1909; *s* of Frederick William Wrigley and Anne Jeffreys, Seascale, Cumberland; *m* 1935, Audrey, *d* of C. S. Boryer, Portsmouth; one *d*. *Educ:* Whitehaven Grammar Sch.; RAF Coll., Cranwell. 33 Squadron, 1930; HMS Glorious 1931; HMS Eagle, 1933; long Signals Course, 1934; various signals appointments until 1937; RAF Signals Officer, HMS Glorious, 1938; served War of 1939-45, X Force, Norway, 1940; Fighter Command, 1940-43; HQ South East Asia, 1943-46; RAF Staff Coll., 1946; comd Northern Signals Area, 1947-50; jssc 1950; Inspector, Radio Services, 1950-52; Chief Signals Officer, 2nd TAF, 1952-54; Director of: Signals (I), Air Ministry, 1954-57; Guided Weapons (Air), Min. of Aviation, 1957-60. DL, Hertfordshire, 1966. *Recreation:* gardening. *Address:* Boonwood, Turpin's Chase, Oaklands Rise, Welwyn, Herts. *T:* Welwyn 5231. *Club:* Royal Air Force.

**WRIGLEY, Mrs H. L.;** *see* Baillie, Isobel.

**WRIGLEY, Sir John Crompton,** KBE, *cr* 1944; CB 1941; *b* 8 Feb. 1888; *s* of George Wrigley, Bury, Lancs; *m* 1919, Jane Elizabeth Pollard; two *s* one *d*. *Educ:* Bury Grammar Sch., Lancs; Corpus Christi Coll., Cambridge. Entered Local Government Board, 1912; Principal, Ministry of Health, 1919; Assistant Secretary, 1930; Principal Assistant Secretary, 1936; Acting Deputy Secretary, 1941-43, Joint Dep. Secretary, 1943-51; Joint Deputy Secretary, Ministry of Housing and Local Government, 1951-52 (formerly Ministry of Local Government and Planning); retired, 1952. *Address:* Over Chess, Chorleywood, Herts. *T:* Chorleywood 2146.

**WRINCH, Dorothy,** BA, MA (Cantab); MSc, DSc (London); MA, DSc (Oxon); Sophia Smith Fellow of Smith College, USA, 1966 (Visiting Professor, 1954-59; Visiting Research Professor, 1959-66); *e d* of late Hugh Wrinch, MIMechE; *m* 1922, J. W. Nicholson, FRS (marr. diss., 1938; he *d* 1955); one *d*; *m* 1941, Otto Charles Glaser (*d* 1951), Prof. of Biology, Amherst Coll. *Educ:* Girton Coll., Cambridge (Scholar); Mathematical Tripos (Wrangler), and Moral Sciences Tripos; Yarrow Fellow of Girton Coll., 1920-24, Hertha Ayrton Fellow, 1930-34; University and King's Colls, Univ. of London; Univs of Oxford, Vienna and Paris. Lectr in Pure Mathematics, University College London, 1918-20, Mem., Research Staff, 1920-24, Hon. Research Associate, Biochem. Dept, 1960. Mem., Faculty of Physical Sciences, Oxford Univ., 1922-39; Sec. Mathematics sub-section, British Assoc., 1932-38; Res. Fellow, Rockefeller Foundn, 1935-41; Carlisle Res. Fellow, Somerville Coll., Oxford, 1939-41; Lectr in Chemistry, Johns Hopkins Univ., USA, 1939-41; Vis. Lectr at Amherst, Mt Holyoke and Smith Colls, 1941-42; Lectr, Smith Coll., 1942-54; Mem. Corp. of Marine Biol. Lab., Woods Hole, 1943. Fellow, Amer. Phys. Soc., 1942; Member: Amer. Chem. Soc.; Amer. Crystallographic Soc.; Peptide and Crystallography Gp, Chemical Soc., London; X-Ray Analysis Gp, Phys. Soc., London. *Publications:* Fourier Transforms and Structure Factors, 1946 (repr. 1966); Chemical Aspects of the Structure of Small Peptides: an introduction, 1960; Chemical Aspects of Polypeptide Chain Structures and the Cyclol Theory, 1965; papers on epistemology, probability, pure and applied mathematics, physics, chemistry and biology. *Recreations:* playing piano duets, swimming, conversation. *Address:* Clark Science Center, Smith College, Northampton, Mass 01060, USA; Greenhaven, Woods Hole, Mass 02543, USA. *Club:* English-Speaking Union.

**WRISBERG, Lieut-General Sir (Frederick) George,** KBE, *cr* 1949 (CBE 1942); CB 1945;

late Royal Regiment of Artillery; *b* 3 Jan. 1895; *s* of late Captain F. W. Wrisberg, Royal Artillery; *m* 1918, Margaret, *d* of late C. Ward, Swadlincote, Derbyshire; one *d*. 2nd Lieut, RA, 1916; served European War, 1916-17, in France and Belgium (wounded); Experimental Officer, Air Defence Experimental Establishment, 1929-33; Staff Captain, War Office, 1934-36; Deputy Assistant Director of Artillery, War Office, 1936-38; Assistant Director, 1938-40; Director Weapons Production, 1940-43; Director-General of Weapons and Instrument Production, Ministry of Supply, 1943-46; Controller of Supplies, Ministry of Supply, 1946-49; retired 1949. Colonel Commandant RA, 1950-60; Chairman, Linotype and Machinery Ltd, 1960-66. *Address:* 5 Moorlands, Wilderness Road, Chislehurst, Kent. *T:* 01-467 1245. *Clubs:* United Service, Chislehurst Golf.

**WRIXON-BECHER, Major Sir William F.;** *see* Becher.

**WROTTESLEY,** family name of **Baron Wrottesley.**

**WROTTESLEY,** 5th Baron, *cr* 1838; **Richard John Wrottesley,** Bt 1642; MC; Major, Royal Horse Guards (Reserve); *b* 7 July 1918; *s* of Hon. Walter Bennet Wrottesley (*yr s* of 3rd Baron); *S* uncle, 1962; *m* 1st, 1941, Roshnara Barbara (marr. diss., 1949), *o d* of Captain Esmé Cecil Wingfield-Stratford; one *s*; 2nd, 1949, Joyce Marion (marr. diss., 1953), *d* of late Frederick A. Wallace; one *s*; 3rd, 1955, Mary Ada Van Echten, *o d* of Edgar Dryden Tudhope; two *s*. *Educ:* Harrow; RMC, Sandhurst. Served War of 1939-45 (MC). Royal Rhodesia Regt, 1961-66. *Recreations:* fishing, shooting, riding. *Heir: s* Hon. Richard Francis Gerard Wrottesley [*b* 16 Aug. 1942; *m* 1967, Georgina, *d* of Col Peter Clifton; one *s*]. *Address:* Wood End, Mountain Road, Claremont, Cape, South Africa; (Seat) Wrottesley Hall, Wolverhampton, Staffs. *Clubs:* Cavalry, Hurlingham; Civil Service (Cape Town); Seven Seas (Simonstown).

**WUNDERLY, Sir Harry Wyatt,** Kt 1954; MD, FRCP; Director of Tuberculosis, Commonwealth Department of Health, Canberra, 1947-57; retired; *b* Camberwell, Vic, Aust., 30 May 1892; *s* of late James Wunderly; *m* 1919, Alice J. B., *d* of Alfred J. Barker. *Educ:* Wesley Coll., Melbourne; Queen's Coll., Melbourne. MB, ChB, Melbourne, 1915; MRCP 1925; MD Melbourne, 1927; FRACP, 1938; FRCP 1952. Formerly: Assistant Pathologist and Assistant Physician, Royal Adelaide Hospital; Member of Panel of Consultants on Tuberculosis, WHO HQ, 1957-. *Publications:* articles on tuberculosis in medical journals. *Address:* 53 Tasmania Circle, Forrest, ACT 2603, Australia. *T:* 731242. *Club:* Commonwealth (Canberra).

**WYATT, Vice-Admiral Sir (Arthur) Guy (Norris),** KBE, *cr* 1949; CB 1948; Retired; *b* 8 March 1893; *s* of late Arthur Norris Wyatt and May (*née* Reynolds); *m* 1922, Anne Christine, *d* of late Hon. James Hogue, Sydney, NSW; no *c*. *Educ:* Stubbington; RN Colleges, Osborne and Dartmouth. Joined Naval College, Osborne, 1906; Lieut., 1915; Comdr, 1929; Capt, 1936; Rear-Adm., 1945; Vice-Adm., 1948. Served European War, 1914-18; commanded HMTBD Beagle, 1918. Joined Royal Naval Surveying Service, 1918; surveys in Home Waters, Australia, New Zealand, East Africa, West Indies, Mediterranean, East Indies, Persian Gulf and Labrador. Served War of 1939-45, Admiralty, and in command of HMS Challenger, South East Asia and SW Pacific (despatches); Hydrographer of the Navy, 1945-50; retired list, 1948. *Recreations:* yacht crusing, fishing. *Address:* Holly Tree Orchard, Woodbridge, Tasmania 7162, Australia.

**WYATT, Gavin Edward,** CMG 1965; Division Chief, Public Utilities Department, Projects Division, International Bank for Reconstruction and Development, since 1968; *b* 12 Jan. 1914; *s* of Edward A. Wyatt and Blanche M. Muller; *m* 1950, Mary Mackinnon, *d* of John Macdonald, Oban; one *s* one *d*. *Educ:* Newton Abbot Grammar Sch. CEng, FIEE 1951; FIMechE 1962. Engineer and Manager, East African Power & Lighting Co. Ltd, Tanganyika and Kenya, 1939-57; Chief Exec. Officer and General Manager, Electricity Corp. of Nigeria, 1957-62; Man. Director, East Africa Power & Lighting Co. Ltd, 1962-64; Engineer, Public Utilities Dept, Projects Div., IBRD, 1964-68. *Recreations:* gardening, sailing. *Address:* 8006 Park Overlook Drive, Bethesda, Maryland 20034, USA; Holne Bridge Lodge, Ashburton, South Devon. *Club:* East India and Sports.

**WYATT, Vice-Admiral Sir Guy;** *see* Wyatt, Vice-Admiral Sir A. G. N.

**WYATT, Woodrow Lyle;** Chairman, Woodrow Wyatt Holdings Ltd; *b* 4 July 1918; *y s* of Robert Harvey Lyle Wyatt and Ethel Morgan; *m* 1957, Lady Moorea Hastings (marr. diss., 1966), *e d* of 15th Earl of Huntingdon, *qv*; one *s*; *m* 1966, Mrs Veronica Banszky; one *d*. *Educ:* Eastbourne Coll.; Worcester Coll., Oxford, MA. Served throughout War of 1939-45 (despatches for Normandy); Major, 1944. Founder and Editor, English Story, 1940-50; Editorial Staff, New Statesman and Nation, 1947-48; Weekly Columnist: Reynolds News, 1949-61; Daily Mirror, 1965-; began Panorama with Richard Dimbleby, 1955; under contract BBC TV, 1955-59; introduced non-heat-set web offset colour printing to England, 1962. MP (Lab), Aston Div. of Birmingham, 1945-55, Bosworth Div. of Leicester, 1959-70; Member of Parly Delegn to India, 1946; Personal Asst to Sir Stafford Cripps on Cabinet Mission to India, 1946; Parly Under-Sec. of State, and Financial Sec., War Office, May-Oct. 1951. Contested (Lab) Grantham Div. of Lincolnshire, 1955. Mem. Council, Zoological Soc. of London, 1968-. *Publications:* The Jews at Home, 1950; Southwards from China, 1952; Into the Dangerous World, 1952; The Peril in Our Midst, 1956; Distinguished for Talent, 1958. *Address:* 12 Devonshire Street, W1. *T:* 01-580 1691; Conock Old Manor, Devizes, Wilts. *T:* Chirton 214.

**WYBURN, Prof. George McCreath;** Regius Professor of Anatomy, Glasgow University, since 1948; *b* 11 March 1903; *s* of Robert Wyburn, Solicitor; *m* 1935, Jean Sharp; four *s* two *d*. *Educ:* High Sch., Glasgow; University of Glasgow. Graduated from Glasgow Univ., 1925; appointed to staff of Anatomy Dept, University of Glasgow, 1930; Senior Lecturer, Anatomy Dept, 1935. *Publications:* scientific publications in Journal of Anatomy, Proc. and Trans. of Royal Society of Edinburgh, Journal of Endocrinology, Journal of Surgery, Journal of Obstetrics and Gynecology, etc. *Address:* 89 Oakfield Avenue, Glasgow, W2. *T:* 041-334 1083. *Club:* Glasgow Golf.

**WYETH, Paul James Logan,** RP 1958; RBA 1957; ARCA 1947; portrait painter and mural painter; *b* 1 Feb. 1920; *s* of Bob Logan (stage name), comedian; *m* 1948, Tina Vasilakon, Greece; two *d*. *Educ:* Kilburn Polytechnic. Willesden School of Art, 1931-33; Hammersmith School of Arts, 1933-39; RCA, 1939-40 and 1946-47. *Publications:* How to

Paint in Oil Colours, 1955; How to Paint in Water-Colours, 1958. *Recreations:* reading, swimming. *Address:* 19 Burstock Road, Putney, SW15. *T:* 01-788 3284. *Club:* Chelsea Arts.

**WYFOLD,** 3rd Baron, *cr* 1919, of Accrington, **Hermon Robert Fleming Hermon-Hodge;** 3rd Bt, *cr* 1902; Director, Robert Fleming & Co. Ltd, and other companies; *b* 26 June 1915; *s* of 2nd Baron and Dorothy, *e d* of late Robert Fleming, Joyce Grove, Oxford; *S* father, 1942. *Educ:* Eton; Le Rosey, Switzerland. Captain, Grenadier Guards (RARO), 1939-65. *Heir:* none. *Address:* Sarsden House, Churchill, Oxfordshire. *T:* Chipping Norton 51. *Clubs:* Carlton, Pratt's; Metropolitan (New York). *See also R. E. Fleming.*

**WYKEHAM, Air Marshal Sir Peter,** KCB 1965 (CB 1961); DSO 1943 and Bar 1944; OBE 1949; DFC 1940 and Bar 1941; AFC 1951; *b* 13 Sept. 1915; *s* of Guy Vane and Audrey Irene Wykeham-Barnes; family changed name by Deed Poll, 1955, from Wykeham-Barnes to Wykeham; *m* 1949, Barbara, *d* of J. B. Priestley, *qv*; two *s* one *d. Educ:* RAF Halton. Commissioned, 1937; served with fighter sqns, 1937-43 (commanded Nos 73, 257 and 23 sqns); commanded fighter sectors and wings, 1943-45; Air Ministry, 1946-48; Test Pilot, 1948-51; seconded to US Air Force, Korea, 1950; commanded fighter stations, 1951-53; NATO, 1953-56; staff appointments, 1956-59; AOC No 38 Gp, RAF, 1960-62; Dir, Jt Warfare Staff, Min. of Defence, Aug. 1962-64. Comdr, FEAF, 1964-66; Dep. Chief of Air Staff, 1967-69. FRAeS 1968; Fellow, Guild of Air Pilots and Air Navigators; FBIM. Chevalier, Order of Dannebrog, 1945; US Air Medal, 1950. *Publications:* Fighter Command, 1960; Santos-Dumont, 1962. *Recreations:* sailing, writing. *Address:* South Bank, Lower Ham Road, Kingston-on-Thames, Surrey. *Club:* Royal Automobile.

**WYKES, James Cochrane,** MA (Cantab); Director of Television, Inner London Education Authority, since 1966; *b* 19 Oct. 1913; *m* 1938, Cecile Winifred Graham, *e d* of J. Graham Rankin; one *s* one *d. Educ:* Oundle Sch.; Clare Coll., Cambridge (Open Exhibn in Classics). 1st Class Hons, Classical Tripos, Part I, 1934; 2nd Class Hons Classical Tripos, Part II, 1935; Asst Master, Loretto Sch., 1935-51; Headmaster, St Bees Sch., 1951-63; Head of Educational Broadcasting, ATV Network, 1963-66. Chm., Nat. Educnl Closed Circuit Television Assoc. Served War of 1939-45: Black Watch (RHR), 1940-44. *Publication:* Caesar at Alexandria, 1951. *Recreations:* athletic sports, fishing, ornithology, music. *Address:* Educational Television Centre, Tennyson Street, SW8. *T:* 01-622 9966. *Club:* MCC.

**WYLDBORE-SMITH, Maj.-Gen. Francis Brian,** CB 1965; DSO 1943; OBE 1944; General Officer Commanding, 44th Division (TA) and Home Counties District, 1965-68; *b* 10 July 1913; *s* of Rev. W. R. Wyldbore-Smith and Mrs D. Wyldbore-Smith; *m* 1944, Hon. Molly Angela Cayzer, *d* of 1st Baron Rotherwick; one *s* four *d. Educ:* Wellington Coll.; RMA, Woolwich. Served Middle East, Italy, France and Germany, 1941-45; Military Adviser to CIGS, 1947-49; GSO1, 7 Armoured Div., 1951-53; Comd 15/19 King's Royal Hussars, 1954-56; IDC 1959; BGS Combat Development, 1959-62; Chief of Staff to Commander-in-Chief, Far East Command, 1962-64. *Recreations:* polo, shooting. *Address:* 34 Cleveland Square, W2; Grantham House, Grantham, Lincs. *T:* Grantham 4705. *Clubs:* Buck's, Naval and Military.

**WYLER, William;** Legion of Merit (USA), 1945; Legion of Honour (France), 1948; Cavaliere Ufficiale (Italy); Film Producer and Director; *b* Mulhouse, Alsace, 1 July 1902; *s* of Leopold Wyler (Swiss) and Melanie Auerbach (German; Non-Arian); *m* 1st, 1934, Margaret Sullavan (marr. diss., 1936), actress; 2nd, 1938, Margaret Tallichet; one *s* three *d* (one *s* decd). *Educ:* Mulhouse, Alsace; Lausanne; Paris. Directed films since 1926; successes include: Counsellor-at-Law, 1934; The Good Fairy, 1935; These Three, 1936; Dodsworth, 1936; Dead End, 1937; Jezebel, 1937; The Letter, 1938; Wuthering Heights, 1939; The Little Foxes, 1940; Mrs Miniver, 1941 (Academy Award for directing); The Best Years of our Lives, 1946 (Acad. award for directing); The Heiress, 1948; Detective Story, 1951; Carrie, 1952; Roman Holiday, 1953; The Desperate House, 1955; Friendly Persuasion, 1956 (Golden Palm Leaf, Cannes, 1957); The Big Country, 1957; Ben Hur, 1959 (Academy Award for Directing); The Loudest Whisper, 1962; The Collector, 1965; How to Steal a Million, 1966; Funny Girl, 1968; The Liberation of Lord Byron Jones, 1970. Served 1942-45 as Major and Lt-Col in USAF, prod. and directed documentary films: The Memphis Belle, Thunderbolt; Air Medal (USA), 1943. *Recreations:* tennis, ski-ing. *Address:* 1121 Summit Drive, Beverly Hills, California, USA.

**WYLES, Lilian Mary Elizabeth,** BEM 1949; retired (but lectures and broadcasts on police subjects and child welfare); *b* Bourne, Lincs, 1895; *d* of Joseph Wyles, brewer, and Julia Grylls Wyles, Bourne House, Bourne. *Educ:* Thanet Hall, Margate; privately. Joined Metropolitan Police, 1919; Sergeant, 1919; Inspector, 1922; transferred from Uniform Branch to CID, 1922; Chief Inspector, 1932. Organised Women's Branch of CID. Retired, 1949. *Publication:* A Woman at Scotland Yard (autobiography), 1952. *Recreations:* sailing, embroidery, cooking. *Address:* Penhale, Kilynack, St Just, near Penzance, Cornwall.

**WYLIE, Sir Campbell,** Kt 1963; ED; QC; Commissioner for Law Revision and Reform, Seychelles, since 1970; *b* NZ, 14 May 1905; *m* 1933, Leita Caroline Clark; no *c. Educ:* Auckland Grammar Sch.; Univ. of New Zealand. LLM 1st Class hons (Univ. of New Zealand), 1928; Barrister and Solicitor (New Zealand), 1928; Barrister-at-law, Inner Temple, 1950. Was in private practice, New Zealand, until 1940. War service, 1940-46 (despatches). Crown Counsel, Malaya, 1946; Senior Federal Counsel, 1950; Attorney-General: Barbados, 1951; British Guiana, 1955; The West Indies, 1956; Federal Justice, Supreme Court of The West Indies, 1959-62; Chief Justice, Unified Judiciary of Sarawak, N Borneo and Brunei, 1962-63; Chief Justice, High Court in Borneo, 1963-66; Law Revision Commissioner, Tonga, 1966-67; Chief Justice, Seychelles, 1967-69. QC 1952 (Barbados), 1955 (British Guiana). *Address:* 26 Verdala, St George's Park, Dragonara, Malta. *T:* 37-662.

**WYLIE, Sir Francis Verner,** GCIE, *cr* 1947 (CIE 1929); KCSI, *cr* 1938; Commander of the Legion of Honour; *b* 9 Aug. 1891; *s* of late David and Margaret (*née* Hyde) Wylie; *m* Kathleen, Kaisar-i-Hind Gold Medal, *y d* of late L. A. Bryne, FRCSI; two *s. Educ:* Royal Sch., Dungannon; Trinity Coll., Dublin. Entered ICS, 1914; arrived in India, 1915; temporary commission, Indian Army, 1916-19; Indian Political Service, 1919-38; Governor of Central Provinces and Berar, 1938-40; Political Adviser to the Crown Representative, 1940-41 and 1943-45; Minister to Afghanistan, 1941-43; Governor of the

United Provinces, 1945-47. *Address:* 85 Rivermead Court, SW6. *Club:* Athenæum.

**WYLIE, Rt. Hon. Norman Russell,** PC 1970; VRD 1961; QC (Scotland) 1964; MP (C) Pentlands Division of Edinburgh since Oct. 1964; Lord Advocate, since 1970; *b* 26 Oct. 1923; *o s* of late William Galloway Wylie and Mrs Nellie Smart Wylie (*née* Russell), Elderslie, Renfrewshire; *m* 1963, Gillian Mary, *yr d* of Dr R. E. Verney, Edinburgh; three *s*. *Educ:* Paisley Grammar Sch.; St Edmund Hall, Oxford; Univs of Glasgow and Edinburgh. BA (Oxon) 1948; LLB (Glasgow) 1951. Admitted to Faculty of Advocates, 1952. Appointed Counsel to Air Ministry in Scotland, 1956; Advocate-Depute, 1959; Solicitor-General for Scotland, April-Oct. 1964. Served in Fleet Air Arm, 1942-46; subseq. RNR; Lt-Comdr, 1954. *Recreations:* shooting, sailing. *Address:* 30 Lauder Road, Edinburgh 9. *T:* 031-667 8377; (Chambers) 29 Northumberland Street, Edinburgh 3. *Clubs:* Constitutional, New (Edinburgh).

**WYLLIE, Lt-Col Harold,** OBE 1919; VPRSMA; placed in charge of restoration of Implacable, 1932; late The Wiltshire Regt and RAF; Marine artist, sculptor and engraver; *b* 29 June 1880; *s* of late W. L. Wyllie, RA, and Marion Amy Wyllie; *m* Euphans Hilary Strain (*d* 1960), Hillhead of Dunkeld, Perthshire, portrait painter, *d* of late John Strain, Civil Engineer, Cassillis House, Ayrshire. *Educ:* Littlejohn's, Greenwich; Smythe's, Southsea. Destined for Navy; failed to pass examination; took up art; went to New York as special artist to the Graphic, 1898; received commission in the 4th Volunteer Bn, Royal West Kent Regt, 1900; South African War (Queen's Medal, 3 bars); temp. commission 2nd Bn The Buffs, 1902; exhibited in Royal Academy and Royal Institute of Painters in Water-colour; Exhibition Britain in Water Colours; Municipal Art Galleries all over England, by invitation. Served on Victory technical cttee, Council of Society for Nautical Research, and Museum Cttee of RUSI; a Vice-Pres., Soc. for Nautical Research, 1950; served in Royal Flying Corps in France, 1914-18, as pilot; granted permanent commission in Regular Army in the field and posted to Wiltshire Regt, 1916 (despatches, OBE, 1914 Star, war medal, victory medal); granted rank of Lieut-Colonel on retirement from Regular Army, 1920; served in Reserve of Air Force Officers, 1925-30, and re-qualified as Air Pilot, granted Hon. rank of Wing Commander on reaching age limit; temp. commission in RAFVR Oct. 1939; transferred to RNVR as Lieut for special duty, 1943; Acting Lieut-Commander, 1944; demobilised Nov. 1945; received RHS certificate; Hon. Marine painter to RYS, 1934; Member of Council of Society of Marine Artists, 1939, Vice-President, 1958; Assoc. Member Instn of Naval Architects, 1959; Life Hon. Vice-President, The Navy League, 1961. *Recreation:* nautical research. *Address:* Hillhead of Dunkeld, Perthshire. *Clubs:* Royal Corinthian Yacht (Cowes); (Marine artist to), Royal Victoria Yacht (Ryde).

**WYLLIE, Robert Lyon,** CBE 1960; DL; JP; FCA; Senior Partner, R. L. Wyllie & Company, Chartered Accountants, Whitehaven; *b* 4 March 1897; *s* of Rev. Robert Howie Wyllie, MA, Dundee; *m* 1924, Anne, *d* of Thomas Rutherford, Harrington, Cumberland; two *d*. *Educ:* Hermitage Sch., Helensburgh; Queen's Park Sch., Glasgow. Served European War, 1914-18, with Lothians and Border Horse (France). Chartered Accountant, 1920; FCA 1949. Director: Gilbert Gilkes & Gordon Ltd; Eagle Star Insurance Co. Ltd (North of England Board); West Cumberland Silk Mills Ltd; Life Vice-President, Cumberland Development Council Ltd. Formerly Chairman: W. Cumberland Industrial Develt Co. Ltd; Cumberland Develt Council Ltd; Whitehaven & Dist Disablement Advisory Cttee, and Youth Employment Cttee; Vice-Chm. W Cumberland Hosp. Management Cttee; Hon. Treas., NW Div., YMCA. JP 1951. DL 1957, Cumberland. *Recreations:* golf and fishing. *Address:* The Cottage, Papcastle, Cockermouth, Cumberland. *T:* Cockermouth 3292; (business) 34 Lowther Street, Whitehaven, Cumberland. *T:* Whitehaven 2074.

**WYMER, Francis John,** CBE 1943; *b* 6 Dec. 1898; *s* of Daniel William and Jean Renwick Wymer; *m* 1st, 1925, Dorothy Edith Kershaw (marr. diss., 1946); one *s*; 2nd, 1948, Elizabeth Mary Grisell Swanson, *yr d* of late Col J. J. C. Davidson, and Mrs Davidson, Cally, Blairgowrie, Perthshire. *Educ:* Merton Court, Sidcup; Eltham Coll., Mottingham. RGA 1917-19; entered service SE and C Ry, 1920; Asst to Traffic Manager, Southern Ry, 1932; Divisional Marine Manager, Dover, 1934; Asst Continental Supt, 1938; Asst to Gen. Manager, 1942; Asst Docks and Marine Manager, Southern Ry, 1945-47; Asst Chief Regional Officer, Southern Region, British Rys, 1951-55; Pres., Retired, Railway Officers' Soc., 1962-63. MInstT. Photography is now occupation. *Address:* Fairlawn, Kemnal Road, Chislehurst, Kent.

**WYN-HARRIS, Sir Percy,** KCMG 1952 (CMG 1949); MBE 1941; MA (Cantab); *b* 24 Aug. 1903; *e s* of late Percy Martin Harris, JP, and Catherine Mary Davies; *m* 1932, Mary M. Macdonald, *d* of late Ranald Macdonald, CBE, Christchurch, New Zealand; one *s*. *Educ:* Gresham's Sch.; Caius Coll., Cambridge. Colonial Administrative Service, 1926; District Officer, Kenya, 1926-45; Settlement Officer (Kikuyu Land Claims), 1939-40; District Commissioner, Nyeri, 1941-43; Labour Liaison Officer, Kenya, 1943; Labour Comr, 1944-46. Provincial Comr, Kenya, 1945; Chief Native Comr and Mem. for African Affairs on Executive Council, Kenya, 1947-49; Governor and C-in-C of the Gambia, 1949-58; Mem. Devlin Commn of Enquiry into disturbances in Nyasaland, 1959; Administrator, Northern Cameroons, for period of plebiscite under UN supervision, 1960-61; toured Canada, Australia, and New Zealand as Special Representative Overseas of the Duke of Edinburgh's Award, 1962-63. With E. E. Shipton, 2nd ascent of Mt Kenya, 1929; first visit to North Island, Lake Rudolf, 1931; Mem. of Mt Everest expedition, 1933, and took part in first assault with L. R. Wager, reaching height of approx. 28,000 ft; mem. Mt Everest Expedition, 1936. KStJ 1950. *Recreation:* cruising under sail. *Address:* 8 Theatre Street, Woodbridge, Suffolk. *T:* Woodbridge 2911. *Clubs:* Alpine, Savile, Little Ship.

**WYNDHAM,** family name of **Baron Leconfield and Egremont.**

**WYNDHAM, Sir Harold (Stanley),** Kt 1969; CBE 1961; retired from Department of Education, New South Wales; *b* Forbes, NSW, Australia, 27 June 1903; *s* of late Stanley Charles Wyndham; *m* 1936, Beatrice Margaret, *d* of Rt. Rev. A. C. Grieve; three *s*. *Educ:* Fort Street Boys' High Sch.; Univ. of Sydney (MA Hons, Cl. I); Stanford Univ. (EdD). Lectr, Sydney Teachers' Coll., 1925-27 and 1934; Teacher, NSW Dept of Educn, 1928-32; Carnegie Fellow, Stanford, 1932-33; Head of Research and Guidance, NSW Dept of Educn, 1935-40; Inspector of Schools, 1940-

41. Flt Lt (A&SD Br.), RAAF, 1942-43; Commonwealth Dept of Post-War Reconstruction, 1944-46 (Leader, Aust. Delegn, Constituent Meeting for UNESCO, London, 1945); Sec., NSW Dept of Educn, 1945-51; Dep. Dir-Gen. of Educn, 1951-52; Dir-Gen. and Permanent Head, Macquarie Univ. Mem. Aust. Delegn to: UNESCO, 1958 and 1966; Commonwealth Educn Conf., Oxford, 1959. Vis. Fellow to Canada, 1966; Fellow, Royal Inst. of Public Admin.; Fellow and Past-Pres., Aust. Coll. of Educn; Mem., Nat. Library Council of Australia. *Publications:* Class Grouping in the Primary School, 1932; Ability Grouping, 1934; articles in a number of professional jls. *Recreations:* music, gardening. *Address:* 3 Amarna Parade, Roseville, NSW 2069, Australia. *T:* 40-4129. *Club:* University (Sydney).

**WYNDHAM, Horace Cowley;** author; *b* Oxfordshire; *s* of Canon G. J. Cowley-Brown, who assumed by licence name of grandmother (Hannah Cowley, author and playwright). *Educ:* Glenalmond. Proceeded to France as Railway Transport Officer, 1914; graded as Staff Captain, 1914; to Ordnance Corps, 1917; to Army of the Rhine, 1918 (1914-15 Mons Star; Allies Victory Medal and War Medal); Demobilised 1920; Military interviewing Officer (recruiting panel), 1940-42; ARP duties, 1942-45. *Publications:* The Queen's Service; The King's Scarlet; Audrey, the Actress; Reginald Auberon; The Call of the Drum; Roses and Rue; Chetwynd's Career; Hilary Onslow; Following the Drum; Limelight; Soldiers on Service; The Nineteen Hundreds; Famous Trials Retold; The Mayfair Calendar; Blotted 'Scutcheons; Judicial Dramas; Crime on the Continent; Criminology; Feminine Frailty; Romances of the Peerage; Victorian Sensations; Victorian Parade; The Magnificent Montez, Courtesan and Convert; Dramas of the Law; Mr Sludge, biography of Daniel Home; Society Sensations; Consider Your Verdict; This was the News; Speranza, Lady Wilde; Chorus to Coronet; and several other books; contributor to Spectator, etc.; also various Encyclopædic articles, two radio plays, and BBC talks. *Recreations:* play-going, travelling. *Address:* Saxlingham Hall, Saxlingham, Norfolk.

**WYNDHAM-QUIN,** family name of **Earl of Dunraven.**

**WYNDHAM-QUIN, Captain Hon. Valentine Maurice;** RN (retired); *b* 1890; *yr s* of 5th Earl of Dunraven, CB, DSO; *u* and *heir-pres* of 7th Earl of Dunraven and Mount-Earl, *qv*; *m* 1919, Marjorie Elizabeth (*d* 1969), *d* of late Rt Hon. E. G. Pretyman; three *d. Educ:* Eton; HMS Britannia. Served European War, 1914-19, in command of destroyers of the Patrol Flotillas, Grand Fleet and Harwich Force; retired 1934; returned to Active Service, 1939-43, in command of HM Ships in Home Waters, the South Atlantic and Mediterranean Fleet; Naval Attaché, Buenos Aires, 1944-47; retired 1947. Chairman, Royal National Life Boat Institution, 1964-68. *Recreations:* hunting and shooting. *Address:* 66 Cadogan Square, SW1. *T:* 01-584 1364. *Clubs:* White's; Royal Yacht Squadron (Cowes).

*See also Viscount Cranbourne, Baron Leconfield.*

**WYNDHAM WHITE, Sir Eric,** KCMG 1968; Director: International Life Insurance Ltd, UK; Business International SA, Geneva; Chairman of Foundation Centre d'Etudes Industriels, Geneva; Chairman, Investors Overseas Service, since 1970; *b* 26 Jan. 1913; *s* of Henry Wyndham White and Helen White (*née* Peppiatt); *m* 1947, Tina Gibson Thayer, Worcester, Mass, USA; two *d. Educ:* Westminster City Sch.; London Sch. of Economics, Univ. of London. LLB first class hons. Member of the Bar, Middle Temple, 1938; Asst Lectr, LSE, 1938-39; Mem. British delegs, Internat. Chamber of Commerce Congresses, Berlin, 1937, Copenhagen, 1939; Min. of Economic Warfare, 1939-41; First Sec., HM Embassy, Washington, 1942-45; Economic Counsellor, HM Embassy, Paris, 1945-46; Special Asst to European Director, UNRRA, 1945; Sec.-Gen., Emergency Economic Cttee for Europe (EECE), 1946; Exec. Sec. Prep. Cttee for ITO, then Sec.-Gen., UN Conf. on Internat. Trade and Employment (London, Geneva, Havana, 1946-48); Exec. Sec., GATT, 1948-65, Dir-Gen., 1965-68. Hon. Dr *rerum publicarum,* of Sch. of Economics, Business and Public Administration, St Gall (Switzerland), 1963; Hon. Dr Laws; Univ. California, Los Angeles, 1966; Dartmouth Coll., New Hampshire, 1968. *Publications:* numerous articles and addresses in various learned jls (legal and economic) in England and abroad. *Recreations:* gardening, ski-ing, music. *Address:* Case Postale 470, 1200 Geneva 3 Rive, Switzerland. *Club:* Reform.

**WYNFORD,** 8th Baron, *cr* 1829; **Robert Samuel Best;** MBE 1952; Major Royal Welch Fusiliers; *b* 5 Jan. 1917; *e s* of 7th Baron and Evelyn (*d* 1929), *d* of late Maj.-Gen. Sir Edward S. May, KCB, CMG; *S* father, 1943; *m* 1941, Anne Daphne Mametz, *d* of late Maj.-Gen. J. R. Minshull Ford, CB, DSO, MC; one *s* two *d. Educ:* Eton; RMC, Sandhurst. 2nd Lieut, RWF, 1937; served BEF; GHQ Home Forces; North Africa (Croix de Guerre); Egypt; Italy; wounded, 1944; Instructor, Staff College, 1945-46; War Office, 1947-49; OC Depot, RWF, 1955-57; Instructor Joint Service Staff Coll., 1957-60; RARO 1960. *Heir: s* Hon. John Philip Best, *b* 23 Nov. 1950. *Address:* Wynford House, Maiden Newton, Dorset. *TA* and *T:* Maiden Newton 241. *Club:* Anglo-Belgian.

**WYNN,** family name of **Baron Newborough.**

**WYNN, Arthur Henry Ashford;** Adviser to Ministry of Technology since 1965; *b* 22 Jan. 1910; *s* of late Prof. William Henry Wynn, MD, MSc; *m* 1938, Margaret Patricia Moxon; three *s* one *d. Educ:* Oundle Sch.; Trinity Coll., Cambridge (Entrance Scholar, Nat. Science and Mathematics; MA). Barrister-at-Law, Lincoln's Inn, 1939; Director of Safety in Mines Research Establishment, Ministry of Fuel and Power, 1948-55; Scientific Member of National Coal Board, 1955-65; Member: Advisory Council on Research and Development, Ministry of Power, 1955-65; Safety in Mines Research Advisory Board, 1950-65; Exec. Cttee, British Standards Institution, 1966; Advisory Council on Calibration and Measurement, 1967; Chairman: Standing Joint Cttee on Metrication, 1966-69; Adv. Cttee on Legal Units of Measurement, 1969. *Address:* 9 View Road, N6. *T:* 01-348 1470. *Club:* Athenæum.

**WYNN, Hon. Rowland Tempest Beresford,** CBE 1949; MA; CEng; FIEE; Chief Engineer, BBC, 1952-60, retired; *b* 31 Jan. 1898; *y s* of late Hon. Charles Henry Wynn, Rhug, Corwen, N Wales, and uncle of 7th Baron Newborough; *m* 1943, Eleanor Mary Tydfil, *y d* of late A. E. Smith-Thomas and Mrs Rondolph Burden, Five Wells, Brentwood, Essex; no *c. Educ:* Uppingham Sch., Rutland; Trinity Hall, Cambridge (MA). Served European War with RFC and RAF, 1917-18. Engineer, Marconi's Wireless Telegraph Co. Experimental Establishment, Writtle, Chelmsford, 1922-26. Head of Engineering Information Dept, BBC, 1926-35; Senior Superintendent Engineer,

BBC, 1935-43; Asst Chief Engineer and Dep. Chief Engineer, BBC, 1943-52. Chairman, Radio Section of Institution of Electrical Engineers, 1949-50. *Publications:* various technical articles and papers. *Recreations:* golf, sailing. *Address:* Sunningdale, The Heights, Worthing, Sussex. *T:* Worthing 60088.
*See also Baron Newborough.*

**WYNN-WILLIAMS, George,** MB, BS London; FRCS; FRCOG; Surgeon, Chelsea Hospital for Women; Consulting Obstetrician to City of Westminster; Consulting Gynæcologist, Chelsea Hospital for Women; Consulting Obstetric Surgeon, Queen Charlotte's Hospital; Consulting Gynæcologist to the Civil Service; Teacher in Gynæcology and Obstetrics, London University; *b* 10 Aug. 1912; *er s* of William Wynn-Williams, MRCS, LRCP, and Jane Anderson Brymer, Caernarvon, N Wales; *m* 1943, Penelope, *o d* of 1st and last Earl Jowitt of Stevenage, PC, and Lesley McIntyre; two *s* one *d. Educ:* Rossall; King's Coll.; Westminster Hospital. MRCS, LRCP 1937; MB, BS (London) 1938; MRCOG 1941; FRCS 1943; FRCOG 1967. Alfred Hughes Anatomy Prize, King's Coll.; Chadwick Prize in Clinical Surgery, Forensic Medicine and Public Health Prizes, Westminster Hospital. Various appointments 1937-41; Chief Asst and Surgical Registrar and Grade I Surgeon, EMS, 1941-45; Acting Obst. and Gynæcol. Registrar, Westminster Hosp., 1941-46; Surgeon-in-Charge, Mobile Surg. Team to Portsmouth and Southampton, June-Oct. 1944; Chief Asst, Chelsea Hosp. for Women, 1946-47; Obst. Registrar, Queen Charlotte's Hosp., 1946-50; Cons. Obstetrician, Borough of Tottenham; Cons. Gynæcologist, Weir Hosp. Surgical Tutor, Westminster Hosp., 1941-46; Obst. and Gynæcol. Tutor, Westminster Hosp., 1941-48; Lectr and Demonstrator to Postgrad. Students, Queen Charlotte's Hosp., 1946-50; Lectr to Postgrad. Students, Chelsea Women's Hosp., 1946-; Examiner, Central Midwives' Board; Recognized Lectr of London Univ.; Assoc. Examiner in Obst. and Gynæcol., Royal Soc. of Apothecaries. Member: BMA; Soc. for Study of Fertility; The Pilgrims. FRSM. *Publications:* (Jtly) Queen Charlotte's Text Book of Obstetrics; contributions to medical journals. *Recreations:* tennis, shooting, fishing. *Address:* 11-12 Wimpole Street, W1. *T:* 01-580 5360; 39 Hurlingham Court, SW6; The Hall, Wittersham, Kent. *Clubs:* Hurlingham, Chelsea Arts, English-Speaking Union, Oriental.

**WYNNE, Prof. Charles Gorrie,** FRS 1970; BA, PhD; Director of Optical Design Group, Imperial College, London, since 1960; Professor of Optical Design, University of London, since 1969; *b* 18 May 1911; *s* of C. H. and A. E. Wynne; *m* 1937, Jean Richardson; two *s* one *d. Educ:* Wyggeston Grammar Sch., Leicester; Exeter Coll., Oxford (Scholar). Optical Designer, Taylor Taylor & Hobson Ltd, 1935-43; Wray (Optical Works) Ltd, 1943-60, latterly Director. Hon. Sec. (business), Physical Soc., 1947-60; Hon. Sec., Inst. of Physics and Physical Soc., 1960-66. Editor, Optica Acta, 1954-65. *Publications:* scientific papers on aberration theory and optical instruments in Proc. Phys. Soc., Mon. Not. RAS, Astrophys. Jl, Optica Acta, etc. *Address:* 13 Elwill Way, Beckenham, Kent. *T:* 01-650 4994.

**WYNNE, Colonel J. F. W.;** *see* Williams Wynne.

**WYNNE-EDWARDS, Sir Robert (Meredydd),** Kt 1965; CBE 1962 (OBE 1944); DSO 1919; MC; MA; FICE (Past President); *b* 1 May 1897; *s* of late Rev. Canon J. R. Wynne-Edwards; *m* 1924, Hope Elizabeth Day, *d* of late Francis Fletcher, Nelson, British Columbia; one *s* three *d. Educ:* Leeds Grammar Sch.; Christ Church, Oxford. Royal Welch Fusiliers, 1914-19. chairman, Council of Engineering Institutions, 1964-66. Hon. Fellow, Manchester College of Science and Technology, 1965; Hon. DSc Salfrod Univ., 1966. *Address:* The Old House, Blandford Forum, Dorset.

**WYNNE-EDWARDS, Vero Copner,** FRS 1970; MA, DSc, FRSC, FRSE; Regius Professor of Natural History, University of Aberdeen, since 1946; Chairman, Natural Environment Research Council, since 1968; *b* 4 July 1906; 3rd *s* of late Rev. Canon John Rosindale Wynne-Edwards and Lilian Agnes Streatfeild; *m* 1929, Jeannie Campbell, *e d* of late Percy Morris, Devon County Architect; one *s* one *d. Educ:* Leeds Grammar Sch.; Rugby Sch.; New Coll., Oxford. 1st Class Hons in Natural Science (Zoology), Oxford, 1927; Senior Scholar of New Coll., 1927-29; Student Probationer, Marine Biological Laboratory, Plymouth, 1927-29; Assistant Lecturer in Zoology, Univ. of Bristol, 1929-30; Asst Prof. of Zoology, McGill Univ., Montreal, 1930-44; Associate Prof., 1944-46. Canadian representative, MacMillan Baffin Island expedition, 1937; Canadian Fisheries Research Board expeditions to Mackenzie River, 1944, and Yukon Territory, 1945; Baird Expedition to Central Baffin Island, 1950. Visiting Prof. of Conservation, University of Louisville, Kentucky, 1959, Commonwealth Universities Interchange Fellow New Zealand, 1962. Jt Editor, Journal of Applied Ecology, 1963-68. Member: Nature Conservancy, 1954-57; Red Deer Commn (Vice-Chm.), 1959-68; Royal Commn on Environmental Pollution, 1970-; President: British Ornithologists' Union, 1965-70; Scottish Marine Biological Assoc., 1967-. *Publications:* Animal Dispersion in relation to social behaviour, 1962; scientific papers on ornithology (esp. oceanic birds), animal populations. *Recreation:* ski-ing. *Address:* Department of Zoology, The University, Aberdeen AB9 2TN. *Clubs:* United Service; New (Edinburgh).

**WYNNE-EYTON, Mrs Selena Frances,** CBE 1943; *b* 21 Jan. 1898; *m* 1916, Wing Comdr S. Wynne-Eyton, DSO, AFC (whom she divorced 1932; he was killed flying, 1944); no *c. Educ:* Downe House, Kent (now Cold Ash, Newbury). Joined WAAF June 1939; posted to Air Ministry as Assistant Director, Sept. 1939; Commanding Officer of WAAF Officers' Sch., and later Senior WAAF Staff Officer at Technical Training Command, 1941; Senior WAAF Staff Officer, HQ, RAF, MEF, 1943-45; with Control Commission for Germany (British Element), 1945-50. *Address:* Marsh Cottage, Fingringhoe, near Colchester, Essex. *T:* Rowhedge 273.

**WYNNE FINCH, Colonel John Charles;** CBE 1956; HM Lieutenant of County of Denbigh, 1951-66; Member of Welsh Agricultural Land Sub-Commission, 1948, Chairman, 1953-63; Agricultural Land Commission, 1952, Deputy Chairman, 1953-63; *b* 31 Aug. 1891; *e s* of late Lieut-Colonel Charles Arthur Wynne Finch, Scots Guards, and Maud Emily, 2nd *d* of late Hon. Richard Charteris, 2nd *s* of 8th Earl of Wemyss; *m* 1914, Alice Mary Sybil (*d* 1970), 2nd *d* of late Rt Rev. Hon. Edward Carr Glyn and Lady Mary Glyn; one *s* two *d. Educ:* Eton; RMC, Sandhurst. Lord of the Manor of Hieraethog, Denbighshire; patron of 1 living; served European War, 1914-18 (MC). Commanded 3rd Battalion Coldstream Guards, 1932-36; retired pay, 1937. Served

War of 1939-45. JP, DL, Denbighshire and Caernarvonshire; High Sheriff of Denbighshire, 1949. President, Welsh Agricultural Society, 1962. Member, Nature Conservancy, 1957-63; Member, Nature Conservancy, Wales, 1957-66; Chairman, National Trust Cttee for Wales, 1957-69. KStJ 1966. *Address:* Voelas, Betws-y-Coed, Denbighshire. *T:* Pentrevoelas 206. *Club:* Guards.

**WYNNE-JONES,** family name of **Baron Wynne-Jones.**

**WYNNE-JONES,** Baron, *cr* 1964, of Abergele (Life Peer); **William Francis Kenrick Wynne-Jones;** Pro-Vice-Chancellor, 1965-68, Professor of Chemistry, Head of the School of Chemistry, 1956-68, University of Newcastle upon Tyne; *b* 8 May 1903; *y s* of late Rev. T. J. Jones, Shaistaganj, India; *m* 1928, Ann Drummond (*d* 1969); two *d. Educ:* Monkton Combe Sch., Bath; University College of Wales, Aberystwyth; Balliol Coll., Oxford. Research Asst and Lectr in Physical Chemistry, Univ. of Bristol; International Research Fellow, Univ. of Copenhagen; Lectr in Chemistry, Univ. of Reading; Leverhulme Research Fellow, Princeton Univ.; Prof. of Chemistry, University College, Dundee; Head of Chemistry Div., Royal Aircraft Establishment, Farnborough. *Publications:* articles in scientific journals. *Address:* 240 Jesmond Dene Road, Newcastle upon Tyne 2.

**WYNNE-JONES, Major Charles Llewelyn,** DL; JP; Vice-Lieutenant of Merioneth, 1957; *b* 3 Oct. 1890; *s* of late Very Rev. Llewelyn Wynne-Jones, MA, Dean of St Asaph; *m* 1915, Sybil, *o c* of late Lieut-Colonel G. F. Scott, DL, JP; one *s* (two *s* killed in action). *Educ:* Eton; RMC. Commissioned in 17th Lancers, 1910; served in France, 1914-18; Captain, N Somerset Yeomanry, 1928-35; retired as Major. Re-employed, 1940-45; DAQMG War Office, 1940; DAAG London District, 1943. JP for Merioneth, 1919; High Sheriff, 1928; DL 1930. *Recreations:* fishing, shooting. *Address:* Penmaenucha, Dolgellau, North Wales. *T:* Dolgellau 625. *Club:* Cavalry.

**WYNNE-JONES, Tom Neville,** CMG 1954; CBE 1950 (OBE 1943); Architect to the Ceylon University; *b* 19 Nov. 1893; *m* 1920, Mabel Phillips. *Educ:* Technical Coll. and School of Arts and Crafts, Swansea. Articled to Sir Charles Tamlyn Ruthen, OBE, Architect, 1909. War Service, 1915-19, Royal Engineers. Ceylon Government, 1920; PWD: Asst Architect; Chief Architect, 1932, retired 1953. FRIBA, FRSanI, MIStructE. *Publications:* professional papers, magazine articles, etc. *Recreations:* work, golf, writing, travel, sketching, lecturing. *Address:* PWD, Colombo, Ceylon; Westwood, Stanmore Crescent, Colombo. *Clubs:* Queen's, Royal Colombo Golf, Rotary (Colombo); Golf (Nuwara Eliya).

**WYNNE MASON, Walter,** CMG 1967; MC 1941; Director of External Relations and Records, Commonwealth War Graves Commission, since 1956; *b* 21 March 1910; *y s* of late George and Eva Mason, Wellington, NZ; *m* 1945, Freda Miller, *d* of late Frederick and Lilian Miller, Woodford, Essex; two *s* one *d. Educ:* Scots Coll., NZ; Victoria University College, NZ (MA). NZ Govt Education Service 1934-39; served NZ Army, 1939-46; NZ War Histories, 1947-48; NZ Diplomatic Service, 1949-54; Chief, Middle East, Commonwealth War Graves Commission, 1954-56. *Publication:* Prisoners of War, 1954. *Recreations:* lawn tennis, theatre, music. *Address:* Keene House, Hillier Road, Guildford, Surrey. *T:* Guildford 2601. *Club:* Royal Automobile.

**WYNTER, Bryan Herbert;** freelance artist (painter); *b* 8 Sept. 1915; *s* of James Harold Wynter and Dora (*née* Judd); *m* 1st, 1949, Suzanne Lethbridge; one *s* one *d*; 2nd, 1959, Monica Harman; two *s. Educ:* Haileybury; Slade School of Fine Art. One Man Exhibitions: 6 of paintings, Redfern Gall., 1947-57; 3 of paintings, Waddington Galls, 1959-67; Imoos kinetic works, Waddington Galleries, 1965. Work exhibited extensively in all continents. Public acquisitions include: Tate Gallery; Museum of Modern Art, NY; Victoria and Albert Museum; British Council; Arts Council; Contemp. Art Society; Gulbenkian Foundation; Stuyvesant Foundation; City Art Galleries of Bristol, Manchester, Bradford, Birmingham, Lincoln, Plymouth, Coventry; Fitzwilliam Museum, Cambridge; Towner Art Gallery, Eastbourne; Whitworth Art Gallery, Univ. of Manchester; Univ. of Warwick; Rutherstone Collection; CEMA; Ulster Museum; Arts Council of NI, Belfast. *Recreations:* white water canoeing, skin diving. *Address:* Treverven House, St Buryan, Penzance, Cornwall. *T:* St Buryan 280.

**WYNYARD-WRIGHT, Frank Trueman,** MA; *b* 29 Jan. 1884; *s* of Rev. Frank Wynyard-Wright and Annie Grace Trueman; *m* Laura Kathleen Tweed (*d* 1964), Lincoln; one *s. Educ:* Rossall; Emmanuel Coll., Cambridge. Asst Master, Lexden House, Seaford; Headmaster, St Peter's Sch., Sheringham, for 10 years; Headmaster, Thames Nautical Training Coll., HMS Worcester; resigned, 1935. Served Malaya States Regt, 1914-18; world traveller, 1912-21. *Recreations:* photography, lecturing. *Address:* Haughton House, Haslemere, Surrey. *Clubs:* Penn, Alpine.

**WYSE, Marjorie A. E.;** *see* Erskine-Wyse, M.

**WYSS, Sophie;** Concert Singer; *b* 1897; 2nd *d* of Oscar and Helène Wyss, La Neuveille, Switzerland; *m* 1925, Captain Arnold Gyde; two *s. Educ:* Conservatoires de Genève et Bâle. Operatic debut, Geneva, 1922; recitals and chamber concerts for BBC, 1927-; concerts throughout Great Britain, in Europe and in Australia. First performances include: Britten's Les Illuminations, Our Hunting Fathers; all Roberto Gerhard's vocal works; works of Lennox Berkeley, Alan Rawsthorne, Elizabeth Maconchy, Racine Fricker, Matyas Seiber, William Wordsworth and many other composers. Inspired many of these composers to write French as well as English songs and to re-arrange innumerable Folk songs into modern idiom. *Address:* 19 The Mall, Surbiton, Surrey.

# Y

**YAHYA KHAN, General Agha Muhammad,** HPk (Hilal-i-Pakistan); HJ (Hilal-i-Jurat); President of Pakistan, and Chief Martial Law Administrator, since 1969; *b* 4 Feb. 1917; *s* of Khan Bahadur Agha Saadat Ali Khan; *m* 1945, Begum Fakhira Yahya; one *s* one *d. Educ:* Indian Military Academy (King's Cadet). On commissioning, he was attached to 2nd Bn Worcester Regt and later to 3rd Bn Baluch Regt. War of 1939-45: 5 year tour of duty overseas with his Regt in Egypt, Sudan, Libya, Cyprus, Iraq, Italy, etc. Staff Coll., Quetta (grad. 1946); Lt-Col, 1947; Brig. 1951; Maj.-Gen. and CGS, 1957 (associated with modernisation of Army); GOC E Pakistan, Dec. 1962-Aug. 1964; commanded an infantry div. during War with India, 1965; became C-in-C of Army, Sept. 1966; President Ayub Khan called upon him to preserve the integrity of Pakistan, 24 March 1969. *Recreations:* golf, shooting, reading. *Address:* President's House, Rawalpindi, Pakistan.

**YAMEY, Prof. Basil Selig;** Professor of Economics, University of London, since 1960; Member (part-time), Monopolies Commission, since 1966; Member, Cinematograph Films Council, since 1969; *b* 4 May 1919; *s* of Solomon and Leah Yamey; *m* 1948, Helen Bloch; one *s* one *d*. *Educ:* Tulbagh High Sch.; Univ. of Cape Town; LSE. Lectr in Commerce, Rhodes Univ., 1945; Senior Lectr in Commerce, Univ. of Cape Town, 1946; Lectr in Commerce, LSE, 1948; Associate Prof. of Commerce, McGill Univ., 1949; Reader in Economics, Univ. of London, 1950. *Publications:* Economics of Resale Price Maintenance, 1954; (jt editor) Studies in History of Accounting, 1956; (with P. T. Bauer) Economics of Under-developed Countries, 1957; (jt editor) Capital, Saving and Credit in Peasant Societies, 1963; (with H. C. Edey and H. Thomson) Accounting in England and Scotland, 1543-1800, 1963; (with R. B. Stevens) The Restrictive Practices Court, 1965; (ed) Resale Price Maintenance, 1966; (with P. T. Bauer) Markets, Market Control and Marketing Reform: Selected Papers, 1968; articles on economics, economic history and law in learned journals. *Address:* 36 Hampstead Way, London, NW11. *T:* 01-455 5810.

**YANG, Chen Ning;** Einstein Professor and Director, Institute for Theoretical Physics, State University of New York at Stony Brook, New York; *b* Hofei, China, 22 Sept. 1922; *s* of Professor and Mrs Ke-Chuan Yang; *m* 1950, Chih-Li Tu; two *s* one *d*. *Educ:* National Southwest Associated Univ., Kunming, China (BSc); University of Chicago (PhD). Institute for Advanced Study, Princeton, NJ: Member, 1949-55; Prof. of Physics, 1955-65; Hon. DSc Princeton Univ., 1958; Polytechnic Inst. of Brooklyn. Nobel Prize in Physics, 1957. Einstein Award in Sciences, 1957. *Publications:* contrib. to Physical Review, Reviews of Modern Physics. *Address:* State University of New York at Stony Brook, New York 11790, USA.

**YARBOROUGH,** 7th Earl of, *cr* 1837; **John Edward Pelham;** Baron Yarborough, Baron Worsley, 1794; Major Grenadier Guards, retired 1952; Vice-Lieutenant, Co. of Lincolnshire, since 1964; JP; *b* 2 June 1920; *s* of 6th Earl of Yarborough; *S* father, 1966; *m* 1957, Mrs Ann Duffin, *d* of late John Herbert Upton, Ingmire Hall, Yorkshire; one *s* three *d*. *Educ:* Eton; Trinity College, Cambridge. Contested (C) Grimsby, 1955. President: Midland Area, British Legion, 1959-60, East Midland Area, 1960-62; Nat. Exec. Council, British Legion, 1962. High Sheriff of Lincolnshire, 1964; Hon. Col, 440 Light AD Regt, RA (TA), 1965-69, Humber Regt, RA T&AVR, 1969-. JP, Parts of Lindsey, 1965. *Recreations:* shooting, sailing. *Heir:* *s* Lord Worsley, *qv*. *Address:* Brocklesby Park, Habrough, Lincs. *T:* Roxton 242. *Clubs:* Guards, Boodle's; Royal Yacht Squadron.

**YARBURGH-BATESON;** *see* de Yarburgh-Bateson.

**YARDE, Air Vice-Marshal Brian Courtenay,** CVO 1953; CBE 1949; psa; *b* 5 September 1905; *s* of late John Edward Yarde, Crediton, Devon, and Bedford; *m* 1927, Marjorie, *d* of late W. Sydney Smith, Bedford; two *d*. *Educ:* Bedford School; RAF College, Cranwell (Sword of Honour), 1926. Served War of 1939-45 in France, Malaya, Middle East, UK (despatches thrice); Deputy Director of Bomber Operations, Air Ministry, 1945; Senior Director, RAF Staff College, 1946-47; Station Commander, Gatow, 1947-49 (Berlin Airlift); Provost Marshal and Chief of the Royal Air Force Police, 1951-53; Air Officer Commanding No. 62 Group, 1953-54. Air Commodore, 1951; Acting Air Vice-Marshal, 1954; Commandant-General of the Royal Air Force Regiment and Inspector of Ground Combat Training, 1954-57, retired. Chairman, Courtenay Caterers Ltd, Andover. Officer American Legion of Merit. *Address:* Wiremead, East Cholderton, Weyhill, Andover, Hants. *T:* Weyhill 265.

**YARDE-BULLER,** family name of **Baron Churston.**

**YARMOUTH, Earl of; Henry Jocelyn Seymour;** *b* 6 July 1958; *s* and *heir* of 8th Marquess of Hertford, *qv*.

**YARROW, Sir Eric Grant,** 3rd Bt, *cr* 1916; MBE 1946; DL; Chairman: Yarrow (Shipbuilders) Ltd, since 1967; Yarrow & Co. Ltd, since 1962; Vice-Chairman, Water-tube Boilermakers' Association, since 1966; Director: Upper Clyde Shipbuilders Ltd 1967-70; Standard Life Assurance Co., since 1958; Yarrow (Africa) (Pty) Ltd, since 1949; Clydesdale Bank Ltd, since 1962; Croftinloan (Holdings) Ltd, since 1959; The Scottish International Trust, since 1965; *b* 23 April 1920; *o s* of Sir Harold Yarrow, 2nd Bt and 1st wife, Eleanor Etheldreda (*d* 1934); *S* father, 1962; *m* 1st, 1951, Rosemary Ann (*d* 1957), *yr d* of H. T. Young, Roehampton, SW15; one *s*; 2nd, 1959, Annette Elizabeth Françoise, *d* of A. J. E. Steven, Grianach, Ardgay, Ross-shire; three *s* (including twin *s*). *Educ:* Marlborough Coll.; Glasgow Univ. Served apprenticeship, G. & J. Weir Ltd. Served Burma, 1942-45; Major RE, 1945. Asst Manager Yarrow & Co., 1946; Dir, 1948; Man. Dir, 1958-67. Mem., Shipbuilding Board Shipbuilders & Repairers Nat. Assoc., 1967-; Mem. Council, RINA, 1957-; Vice-Pres., 1965; Mem., General Cttee, Lloyd's Register of Shipping, 1960; Prime Warden, Worshipful Co. of Shipwrights, 1970; ex-Deacon, Incorporation of Hammermen of Glasgow. Retired Mem. Council, Institution of Engineers & Shipbuilders in Scotland. Pres., Scottish Convalescent Home for Children; mem. Exec. Cttee Princess Louise Scottish Hospital at Erskine. OStJ. DL Renfrewshire, 1970. *Recreations:* golf, shooting. *Heir:* *e s* Richard Grant Yarrow, *b* 21 March 1953. *Address:* Cloak, Kilmacolm, Renfrewshire. *T:* Kilmacolm 2067. *Clubs:* United Service; Royal Scottish Automobile.

**YARWOOD, Alderman Dame Elizabeth (Ann),** DBE 1969; JP; Alderman, Manchester City Council; *b* 25 Nov. 1900; *d* of Henry and Margaret Gaskell; *m* 1918, Vernon Yarwood; two *s*. *Educ:* Whitworth Street High Sch., Manchester. Councillor, Manchester City Council, 1938-, Alderman, 1955-; Lord Mayor of Manchester, 1967-68. Director: Manchester & Salford Co-operative Society Ltd, 1955; Manchester Ship Canal, 1964. Vice-Pres., Manchester County Girl Guides Assoc. JP Manchester, 1945. *Recreation:* reading. *Address:* 80 Yew Tree Lane, Manchester M23 0DR. *T:* 061-998 3179.

**YASHIRO, Yukio;** Member (Deputy Chairman), Commission for Protection of

Cultural Properties (National Treasures, Monuments and National Museums); Member, The Japan Art Academy; Director, Museum Yamato Bunkakan, Nara; *b* Tokio, Nov. 1890; *s* of Munekatsu Yashiro; *m* Fumi Kimura; one *s*. *Educ:* Tokio Imperial University. Studied art, Tokio, Florence, London, Paris, Berlin. Professor, University of Fine Arts, Tokio, 1917-41; Director, Institute of Art Research, Tokio, 1926-43; Lectr, Harvard Univ., 1933; Consulting Prof., Stanford Univ., 1959. Socio Onorario, Ist Italiano per il Medio ed Estremo Oriente, Roma. Medaglia d'Oro ai Benemeriti della Cultura, 1957. Commendatore Ordine al Merito della Repubblica Italiana, 1954. *Publications:* Sandro Botticelli: 3 vols, 1925; 2nd and revised edition in one volume, 1929; Japanische Malerei der Gegenwart, 1 vol. 1931; Characteristics of Japanese Art, 1943 (2nd, and supplemented edn in 2 vols, 1965); Masterpieces of Far Eastern Arts in European and American Collections, 2 vols 1943; 2000 years of Japanese Art, 1958; Art Treasures of Japan, 2 vols, 1961. *Address:* 1017 Oiso, Kanagawa-Ken, Japan.

**YATES, Lt-Gen. Sir David P.;** *see* Peel Yates.

**YATES, Lt-Col Donald,** CMG 1943; MC; Consulting Engineer; *b* 27 Feb. 1893; *s* of Thomas Yates, Adelaide; *m* 1916, Norah, *d* of J. H. Crowe, Adelaide; one *s* one *d*. *Educ:* St Peter's School Collegiate, Adelaide; Adelaide University (BE); School of Mines, Adelaide (FSASM). Served European War, 1st Tunnelling Co., AIF, Capt. (MC); BHP Pty Ltd, Newcastle, 1919-27; BHAS Pty Ltd, Port Pirie, 1927-44; War of 1939-45; rejoined 2/AIF Sept. 1942, Lt-Col SORE; VDC Bn Comdr (Home Guard), 1940-42. Sen. Mem., Australasian Institute of Mining and Metallurgy (Pres. 1937). *Recreations:* rowing, football in former years; golf and tennis. *Clubs:* Adelaide, Naval and Military (Adelaide).

**YATES, Frances Amelia,** DLit; FBA 1967; Hon. Fellow, Warburg Institute since Oct. 1967; Reader in the History of the Renaissance, Warburg Institute, University of London, 1956-67; *b* 28 Nov. 1899; *d* of James Alfred Yates, Royal Corps of Naval Constructors, and Hannah Eliza Malpas. *Educ:* Laurel Bank School, Glasgow; Birkenhead High School; University College, London. BA London 1924 (First Cl. Hons in French), MA London 1926; DLit London 1965. Private research and writing, some teaching at N London Collegiate School, 1926-39; Ambulance Attendant, 1939-41. Warburg Inst., Univ. of London: Part-time Research Assistant, 1941-44; Lecturer and editor of publications, 1944-56. Awarded Rose Mary Crawshay Prize by British Academy, 1934; FRSL 1943; Fellow, Soc. Humanities, Cornell Univ., 1968. Hon. Fellow, Lady Margaret Hall, Oxford, 1970. Hon. DLitt: Edinburgh, 1969; Oxford, 1970. *Publications:* John Florio, The Life of an Italian in Shakespeare's England, 1934; A Study of Love's Labour's Lost, 1936; The French Academies of the Sixteenth Century (Warburg Inst.), 1947; The Valois Tapestries (Warburg Inst.), 1959; Giordano Bruno and the Hermetic Tradition, 1964; The Art of Memory, 1966; Theatre of the World, 1969; many articles in Jl of Warburg and Courtauld Institutes and elsewhere. *Recreations:* reading, travel. *Address:* 5 Coverts Road, Claygate, Surrey; Warburg Institute, Woburn Square, WC1. *T:* 01-580 9663. *Club:* English-Speaking Union.

**YATES, Frank,** CBE 1963; FRS 1948, ScD; Computer Department, Rothamsted Experimental Station, since 1968 (formerly Head of Statistics Department and Agricultural Research Statistical Service, and Deputy Director); *b* 1902; *s* of Percy and Edith Yates, Didsbury, Manchester; *m* Pauline, *d* of Vladimir Shoubersky. *Educ:* Clifton; St John's Coll., Cambridge. Research Officer and Mathematical Adviser, Gold Coast Geodetic Survey, 1927-31; Rothamsted Experimental Station, 1931, Dept of Statistics, 1933, Agric. Res. Statistical Service, 1947, Dep. Dir, 1958; Scientific Adviser to various Mins, UNO, FAO, 1939-; Wing Comdr (Hon.) RAF, 1943-45; Mem. UN Sub-Commn on Statistical Sampling, 1947-52. Pres., British Computer Society, 1960-61; Pres., Royal Statistical Society, 1967-68. Royal Medal of the Royal Society, 1966. *Publications:* Design and Analysis of Factorial Experiments, 1937; (with R. A. Fisher) Statistical Tables for Biological, Medical and Agricultural Research, 1938 (6th edn 1963); Sampling Methods for Censuses and Surveys, 1949 (3rd edn 1960); Experimental Design: Selected Papers, 1970. Numerous scientific papers. *Recreation:* mountaineering. *Address:* Stackyard, Rothamsted, Harpenden, Herts. *T:* Harpenden 2732. *Club:* Athenæum.

**YATES, Sir Thomas,** Kt 1959; CBE 1951; retired as General Secretary, National Union of Seamen (1947-60) and Chairman of the TUC, (1957-58); Member, Southern Region Railway Board, since 1963; *b* 25 Sept. 1896; *s* of William Yates, Sea View, Wallasey, Cheshire; *m* 1st, 1918, Lilian Grace (*d* 1960), *d* of William K. Church; three *s* one *d*; 2nd, 1962, Mrs Dorothy Kilpatrick. *Educ:* St Mary's Sch., Wallasey. Served European War, 1914-18, with Loyal North Lancashire Regiment. District Secretary for SW Coast, National Union of Seamen, 1940-41, and for Scottish Area, 1941-42, National Organiser, 1942-43, and Asst General-Secretary, 1943-47. Chm. of Merchant Seamen's War Memorial Soc.; Member: Seamen's Welfare Board; Merchant Navy Training Board; Management Cttee of Merchant Navy Comforts Trust; Coastal Advisory Cttee; Gen. Council of King George's Fund for Sailors; Exec. Council of Navy League; Shipping Defence Cttee; Personnel Training Cttee; National Maritime Board; International Labour Office Maritime Commission; Covent Garden Market Authority. Delegate for international seafarers to International Labour Office and World Health Organisation Joint Cttee; Representative of Trades Union Congress on Govt's Colonial Advisory Cttee and on various other Joint Bodies. *Address:* Tomdor, Martin Mill, near Dover, Kent.

**YATES, William;** *b* 15 September 1921; *er s* of late William Yates and of Mrs John T. Renshaw, Burrells, Appleby, Westmorland; *m* 1st, 1946, Hon. Rosemary (marriage dissolved, 1955), *yr d* of 1st Baron Elton; one *s* two *d*; 2nd, 1957, Camilla, *d* of late E. W. D. Tennant, Orford House, Ugley, Bishop's Stortford; four *s*. *Educ:* Uppingham; Hertford Coll., Oxford. Served War, 1940-45, North Africa and Italy; Captain The Bays, 1945. Shropshire Yeomanry, 1956-67. Appointed Legal Officer to report on State lands in Department of Custodian's Office in Tripoli, Libya, 1951. MP (C) The Wrekin Division of Shropshire, 1955-66. Myron Taylor Lectures in International Affairs, Cornell Univ., USA, 1958 and 1966. *Address:* 8 Belle Crescent, Mordialloc, Victoria, Australia. *Clubs:* Cavalry, St Stephen's.

**YATES-BELL, John Geoffrey,** FRCS; Consulting Urological Surgeon, since 1930; *b* 6 Dec. 1902; *s* of John Bell, FRCVS, and Matilda Bell, London; *m* 1932, Winifred Frances

Hordern (*née* Perryman); one *s* one *d. Educ:* St Dunstan's College; King's College, London. MB, BS London 1926; FRCS 1930. King's College Hospital: House Surgeon, 1926-28; Surgical Registrar, 1928-29; Junior Urological Surgeon, 1930; Hon. Urological Surgeon, 1937. President, Urological Section, RSM, 1952 (Vice-Pres. 1939); Fellow Internat. Soc. of Urology, 1934; Founder Member, British Assoc. of Urological Surgeons (Hon. Treas., 1954-56). *Publications:* Kidney and Ureter, Stone (British Surgical Practice), 1950; articles in British Jl of Urology, Jl of Urology, Medical Press, Lancet, etc. *Recreations:* lawn tennis, alpine plants. *Address:* Private Patients Wing, King's College Hospital, Denmark Hill, SE5. *T:* 01-274 8570; Westane, Tyrrells Wood, Leatherhead, Surrey. *T:* Leatherhead 3170. *Club:* Athenæum.

**YEABSLEY, Sir Richard Ernest,** Kt 1950; CBE 1943; FCA, JP; *b* 16 May 1898; *m* 1923, Hilda Maude Wilson; one *d. Educ:* Alperton School. Served European War, 3rd Bn (City of London Regiment) Royal Fusiliers, 1914-19. Independent member of Hosiery Working Party, 1945; Member: Committee to examine the organisation and methods of distribution of Building Materials, 1946; Committee to enquire into the resources of Minerals in the United Kingdom, 1946; Supreme Court Cttee on Practice and Procedure, 1947; Cttee on Resale Price Maintenance, 1947; Monopolies and Restrictive Practices Commn, 1949-56. Accountant Adviser to BoT, 1942-68; formerly Sen. Partner, Hill, Vellacott & Co., and Hill, Vellacott & Bailey, Chartered Accountants, retd March 1963; Pres. Society of Incorporated Accountants, 1956-57. *Address:* 9 Alverton Hall, West Cliff Road, Bournemouth. *T:* Westbourne 66293. *Club:* Royal Automobile.

**YEAMAN, Sir Ian (David),** Kt 1958; President of The Law Society, 1957-58; *b* 20 March 1889; *s* of David Yeaman and Catherine Sanger; *m* 1926, Anne Doris Wood; two *s. Educ:* Dean Close Sch., Cheltenham. Admitted Solicitor, 1911; European War, 1914-18; enlisted Gloucestershire Regt TA, Sept. 1914; commissioned, RFA, 1915; served in France, 1916-18 (wounded); demobilised, 1919. Partner Rickerbys, Cheltenham, 1922. Member of Council of Law Society, 1936-64; Pres. Glos and Wilts Law Soc., 1952; Vice-Pres. Law Soc., 1956-57; Member of Lord Chancellor's Cttee on Land Registration, 1942. Hon. Member, American Bar Assoc., 1957. *Recreation:* gardening. *Address:* The Moat House, Uckington, near Cheltenham. *T:* Combe Hill 254. *Clubs:* East India and Sports; New (Cheltenham).

**YELLOWLEES, Henry,** OBE 1919; MD (Glasgow); FRCPGlas, FRCPE; FRCP; DPM (London); Hon. Consulting Physician, St Thomas' Hospital; *b* 11 June 1888; *yr s* of late David Yellowlees, MD, LLD, Gartnavel, Glasgow, and Federata, *d* of late Rev. H. M. Williamson, DD, Belfast; *m* 1918, Dorothy, *d* of Major A. J. Davis, Pagham, Sussex; two *s* one *d. Educ:* Kelvinside Academy, Glasgow; Glasgow Univ. Senior Resident and Deputy Supt Western Infirmary, Glasgow; Asst Physician and Deputy Supt, Perth District Mental Hosp., and Royal Hosp., Morningside, Edinburgh; served in France, 1915-18 as Capt. RAMC and Mental Specialist, Etaples Hospital Area (despatches twice, OBE); Lecturer and Assistant to Professor of Psychiatry, University of Edinburgh, 1919-22; Physician Superintendent of the Retreat, York, 1922-29; Physician for Mental Diseases and Lectr in Psychological Medicine, St Thomas' Hosp., 1928-48; consulting work in London since 1929, and in Bath from 1956. Examiner in Mental Diseases and Psychology, Univ. of London, 1931-35; Examiner in Psychological Medicine, Royal College of Physicians, 1936-39. Colonel, AMS, and Consulting Psychiatrist to BEF in France, 1939-40. *Publications:* A Manual of Psychotherapy, 1923; Clinical Lectures on Psychological Medicine, 1932; Out of Working Hours, 1942; The Human Approach, 1946; To Define True Madness, 1953; Frames of Mind, 1957; lectures, addresses, and papers. *Address:* 1 Lansdown Place West, Bath. *T:* Bath 60593.

**YEMM, Prof. Edmund William,** BA, DPhil Oxon; Melville Wills Professor of Botany, University of Bristol, since 1955; Pro-Vice-Chancellor, since 1970; *b* 16 July 1909; *s* of William H. Yemm and Annie L. Brett; *m* 1935, Marie Solari; one *s* three *d. Educ:* Wyggeston School, Leicester; Queen's College, Oxford. Foundation, Schol., Queen's Coll., 1928; Christopher Welch Schol., 1931. Research Fellow, Queen's Coll., 1935-38; Lecturer, Univ. of Bristol, 1939-49. Major, REME, 1942-45. Reader in Botany, Univ. of Bristol, 1950-55; Fellowship, Rockefeller Foundation, 1954; Vis. Prof., Western Reserve Univ., 1966-67. *Publications:* scientific papers in Proc. Royal Soc., New Phytologist, Biochemical Jl, Jl of Ecology, Jl of Experimental Botany. *Recreations:* cricket, gardening; formerly football (Oxford Univ. Assoc. Football Blue, 1929-31). *Address:* Stoneleigh, Long Ashton, Bristol BS18 9LE. *T:* Long Ashton 2258. *Club:* English-Speaking Union.

**YENDELL, Rear-Adm. William John,** CB 1957; RN, retired; *b* 29 Dec. 1903; *e s* of late Charles Yendell; *m* 1937, Monica Duncan; one *d. Educ:* RN Colleges Osborne and Dartmouth. Qualified Gunnery Officer, 1929; commanded HM Ships: Bittern, 1938; Shah, 1943-45; Glasgow, 1950; Superb, 1950. Director of Naval Ordnance, 1951-54; Assistant Chief of Naval Staff (Warfare), 1954-57. Naval ADC 1954-. Comdr, 1937; Captain, 1945. *Recreations:* painting and most games. *Address:* The Bell Cottage, Newtonmore, Inverness-shire. *T:* Newtonmore 344. *Club:* Royal Naval (Portsmouth).

**YEO, Douglas;** Director, Shell Research Ltd, Woodstock Agricultural Research Centre, Sittingbourne, Kent, since 1969; *b* 13 June 1925; *s* of Sydney and Hylda Yeo; *m* 1947, Joan Elizabeth Chell; two *d. Educ:* Secondary Sch., St Austell; University Coll., Exeter (BSc London). Expedn on locust control, Kenya, 1945. HMOCS, 1948-63; Tropical Pesticides Research Inst., Uganda and Tanzania, 1948-61 (Scientific Officer, 1948-51, Sen. Scientific Officer, 1951-57, Prin. Scientific Officer, 1957-61). Internat. African Migratory Locust Control Organisation, Mali: on secondment, 1958, 1960; Dir and Sec. Gen., 1961-63. Research Dir Shell Research Ltd, Woodstock Agricultural Research Centre, 1963-69. *Publications:* papers in Bulletin Ent. Res., Bull. WHO Anti-Locust Bull., Quart. Jl Royal Met. Soc., Jl Sci. Fd. Agric., Plant Protection Confs, etc. *Recreations:* sailing, fishing. *Address:* Brewster House, Doddington, near Sittingbourne, Kent. *T:* Doddington 207. *Club:* Royal Corinthian Yacht (Burnham on Crouch).

**YEO, Kok Cheang,** CMG 1956; MD; MB; BS; DPH; DTM&H; *b* 1 April 1903; *s* of Yeo Kim Hong; *m* Florence, *d* of late Sir Robert Hotung, KBE; one *s* two *d. Educ:* Hong Kong University; Cambridge University; London School of Hygiene and Tropical Medicine. MB, BS, Hong Kong, 1925, MD, 1930; DTM&H (England) 1927; DPH, Cambridge, 1928.

Assistant Medical Officer of Health, Hong Kong, 1928; Lecturer and Examiner in public health, Hong Kong University, 1936-37; Official JP 1938; Chinese Health Officer, senior grade, 1939-47; Deputy Director of Health Services, and Vice-Chairman of Urban Council, 1947-50; Deputy Director of Medical and Health Services, 1950-52; member of Legislative Council, Hong Kong, 1951-57; Director of Medical and Health Services, Hong Kong, 1952-58; Professor of Social Medicine, Hong Kong University, 1953-58; retd 1958. *Address:* Brendon Cottage, Station Road, Northiam, Sussex. *T:* Northiam 2269.

**YEO, Sir William,** Kt 1964; CBE 1954; JP; farmer and grazier; Member of New South Wales Council of Returned Services League of Australia (President from 1949); *b* Alectown, 1 May 1896; *s* of late Arthur Plane Yeo; *m* 1925, Eileen Theresa, *d* of Robert Golding. *Educ:* Peak Hill Public School. Served European War, 1914-18: 18th Battalion, Australian Imperial Force, Gallipoli and France. *Address:* Flat 7, Beverley Hall, Elizabeth Bay, New South Wales 2011, Australia.

**YERBURGH,** family name of **Baron Alvingham.**

**YERBURY, Air Vice-Marshal Richard Olyffe,** CBE 1962; Principal Medical Officer, HQ Training Command, RAF, since Sept. 1969; *b* 27 May 1914; *s* of Edgar Olyffe Yerbury and Constance Mary Kelson; *m* 1940, Drusilla Mary Dunn; one *s* two *d*. *Educ:* Epsom Coll.; Guy's Hosp. MRCS, LRCP 1937; MB, BS London 1938; DPH 1956; QHS 1970. Indian Medical Service, 1939-48; transfer to RAF (Medical Branch), 1948. Lady Cade Medal, RCS, 1969. *Address:* c/o Lloyds Bank, 6 Pall Mall, SW1. *Club:* Royal Air Force.

**YERBY, Frank Garvin.** Novelist; *b* 5 September 1916; *s* of Rufus Garvin Yerby and Wilhelmina Smythe; *m* 1956, Blanca Calle Pérez; two *s* two *d* of former marriage. *Educ:* Haines Institute; Paine College; Fisk Univ.; Univ. of Chicago. Teacher, Florida Agricultural and Mechanical Coll., 1939; Southern Univ. (Baton Rouge, Louisiana), 1940-41; War work: laboratory technician, Ford Motor Company, Detroit, 1941-44; Ranger Aircraft, New York, 1944-45; writer since 1944; O. Henry Award for short story, 1944. *Publications:* The Foxes of Harrow, 1946; The Vixens, 1947; The Golden Hawk, 1948; Pride's Castle, 1949; Floodtide, 1950; A Woman Called Fancy, 1951; The Saracen Blade, 1952; The Devil's Laughter, 1953; Benton's Row, 1954; The Treasure of Pleasant Valley, 1955; Captain Rebel, 1956; Fairoaks, 1957; The Serpent and the Staff, 1958; Jarrett's Jade, 1959; Gillian, 1960; The Garfield Honor, 1961; Griffin's Way, 1962; The Old Gods Laugh, 1964; An Odor of Sanctity, 1965; Goat Song, 1967; Judas, My Brother, 1968; Speak Now, 1969. *Recreations:* ski-ing, spear fishing, photography, painting. *Address:* c/o Wm Morris Agency, 1350 Avenue of the Americas, New York, NY 10019, USA. *Clubs:* Authors Guild (New York); Real Sociedad Hipica Española (Madrid).

**YOFFEY, Joseph Mendel,** DSc, MD, FRCS; Professor of Anatomy, University of Bristol, 1942-67, now Professor Emeritus; *b* 10 July 1902; *s* of Rabbi Israel Jacob Yoffey and Pere Jaffe; *m* 1940, Betty Gillis, LLB; three *d*. *Educ:* Manchester Grammar School; Univ. of Manchester. Leech Research Fellow, University of Manchester, 1926-27; Research Scholar, BMA, 1928-29; House Surgeon, Manchester Royal Infirmary, 1929-30; Asst Lectr in Anatomy, Univ. of Manchester, 1930; Senior Lectr in Anatomy, University College of South Wales and Monmouthshire, Cardiff; Hunterian Prof., RCS England, 1933 and 1940; Fellow of Rockefeller Foundn, 1937-39. Visiting Professor: Univ. of Washington, 1958; Univ. of Calif., San Francisco, 1967-68; John Curtin Sch. of Medical Research, ANU, 1968-69; Hebrew Univ. of Jerusalem, 1969-70. John Hunter Triennial Medal, RCS, 1968. Knight First Class of the Order of the Dannebrog (Denmark), 1959. *Publications:* Quantitative Cellular Hæmatology, 1960; Bone Marrow Reactions, 1966; (with Dr F. C. Courtice) Lymphatics, Lymph and the Lymphouryeloid Complex, 1970; numerous scientific papers. *Recreations:* music, walking, modern Hebrew. *Address:* 1 Rehov Degania, Beth Hakerem, Jerusalem, Israel.

**YONGE, Sir (Charles) Maurice,** Kt 1967; CBE 1954; FRS 1946; FRSE; DSc(Ed.); President, Royal Society of Edinburgh; *b* 9 Dec. 1899; *s* of John Arthur Yonge, MA, JP, and Sarah Edith Carr; *m* 1st, Martha Jane (*d* 1945), *d* of R. T. Lennox, Newmilns, Ayrshire; one *s* one *d*; 2nd, Phyllis Greenlaw, *d* of Dr D. M. M. Fraser, Eastry, Kent; one *s*. *Educ:* Silcoates School, Wakefield; Edinburgh Univ. Baxter Natural Science Scholar, 1922-24; Carnegie Research Scholar, 1924-25. Temporary Asst Naturalist, Marine Biological Assoc., Plymouth, 1925-27; Balfour Student, Univ. of Cambridge, 1927-29; leader, Great Barrier Reef Expedition, 1928-29; Physiologist, Marine Biological Assoc., Plymouth, 1930-32; Prof. of Zoology, Univ. of Bristol, 1933-44; Regius Prof. of Zoology, Univ. of Glasgow, 1944-64, Research Fellow in Zoology, 1965-70. Visiting Prof., Univ. of California, 1949; Prather Lecturer, Harvard Univ., 1957; Visiting Prof., Univ. of Washington, 1959, 1969. Mem., Advisory Cttee on Fishery Research to the Development Commission, 1937-56; UK Representative, Pacific Science Council; Pres. and Chm. of Council, Scottish Marine Biological Assoc., 1944-67; Mem., Audio-Visual Aids Cttee of Univ. Grants Cttee; Mem., Natural Environment Research Council, 1965-70; Vice-Pres. and Hon. Mem. Marine Biological Assoc. UK; Vice-Pres. Royal Soc. of Edinburgh, 1953-56 (Makdougall-Brisbane Prize, 1957); Pres., Section D, British Assoc., 1961; Mem. Council, Royal Society, 1952-54, 1968-70. Hon. Mem. Malac. Soc. London. Mem. Royal Danish Acad. of Science and Letters; Hon. Mem. California Academy of Sciences; Hon. Mem. Royal Soc. of NZ. Hon. DSc (Bristol). Darwin Medal, Royal Society, 1968. *Publications:* A Year on the Great Barrier Reef; British Marine Life; The Sea Shore; Oysters; (with F. S. Russell) The Seas; ed., (with K. M. Wilbur) Physiology of Mollusca; numerous scientific papers in standard scientific journals. *Recreations:* travel, reading of history, woodwork. *Address:* 13 Cumin Place, Edinburgh EH9 2JX. *T:* 031-667 3678.

**YOOL, Air Vice-Marshal William Munro,** CB 1946; CBE 1941; RAF, retired list; Director of Auxiliaries, Reserves and Air Cadets, Dec. 1951-54; Acting Air Vice-Marshal and AOA, Technical Training Command, 1944; formerly AOA, HQ, Mediterranean and Middle East; retd 1949. *Address:* Moorlands, Pirbright, Surrey.

**YORK, Archbishop of,** since 1961; **Most Rev. and Rt. Hon. (Frederick) Donald Coggan,** PC 1961; MA; DD; *b* 9 Oct. 1909; *s* of late Cornish Arthur Coggan and late Fannie Sarah Coggan; *m* 1935, Jean Braithwaite Strain; two *d*. *Educ:* Merchant Taylors' School; St John's College, Cambridge; Wycliffe Hall, Oxford. Late Schol. of St John's Coll., Cambridge, 1st cl. Or. Lang. Trip. pt i, 1930; BA (1st cl. Or. Lang. Trip. pt ii) and Jeremie Sep. Prize, 1931, Naden Div.

Student, 1931; Tyrwhitt Hebrew Schol. and Mason Prize, 1932; MA 1935. Asst Lectr in Semitic Languages and Literature, University of Manchester, 1931-34; Curate of St Mary Islington, 1934-37; Professor of New Testament, Wycliffe College, Toronto, 1937-44; Principal of the London College of Divinity, 1944-56; Bishop of Bradford, 1956-61. Chairman of the Liturgical Commission, 1960-64. President, Society for Old Testament Studies, 1967-68. Pro-Chancellor, York Univ., 1962-, Hull Univ., 1968-. Prelate, Order of St John of Jerusalem, 1967-. Wycliffe Coll., Toronto: BD 1941, DD (*hc*) 1944; DD (Lambeth) 1957. Hon. DD: Cambridge, 1962; Leeds, 1958; Aberdeen, 1963; Tokyo, 1963; Saskatoon, 1963; Huron, 1963; Hull, 1963; Hon. DHum: Westminster Choir Coll., Princeton, 1966; Hon. DLitt, Lancaster, 1967; STD (*hc*) Gen. Theol. Sem., New York, 1967. *Publications:* A People's Heritage, 1944; The Ministry of the Word, 1945; The Glory of God, 1950; Stewards of Grace, 1958; Five Makers of the New Testament, 1962; Christian Priorities, 1963; The Prayers of The New Testament, 1967; Sinews of Faith, 1969; contributions to Theology, etc. *Recreations:* gardening, motoring, music. *Address:* Bishopthorpe, York YO2 1QE. *T:* 67021. *Club:* Athenæum.

**YORK, Assistant Bishops of;** *see* Armstrong, Rt Rev. Mervyn, Cockin, Rt Rev. G. E. I.

**YORK, Dean of;** *see* Richardson, Very Rev. Alan.

**YORK, Archdeacon of;** *see* Forder, Ven. C. R.

**YORK, Christopher,** DL; *b* 27 July 1909; *s* of late Col Edward York; *m* 1934, Pauline Rosemary, *d* of late Sir Lionel Fletcher, CBE; one *s* three *d*. *Educ:* Eton; RMC Sandhurst. Joined The Royal Dragoons, India, 1930; retired, 1934, on to Supplementary Reserve; rejoined Regt, 1939, rank Major; joined Land Agents Soc., 1934, and passed examinations, acting as Land Agent until elected MP; MP (U) Harrogate Division, 1950-54 (Ripon Division of the West Riding, 1939-50); DL West Riding of Yorkshire, 1954; High Sheriff of Yorkshire, 1966; *Recreation:* shooting. *Address:* South Park, Long Marston, York. *TA* and *T:* Rufforth 357. *Clubs:* Carlton; Yorkshire (York).

*See also Sir Nicholas Nuttall.*

**YORKE,** family name of **Earl of Hardwicke.**

**YORSTON, Sir Keith,** *see* Yorston, Sir R. K.

**YORSTON, Sir (Robert) Keith,** Kt 1969; CBE 1962 (OBE 1960); FCA, FASA, ACIS; Chairman of Directors, Steadfast Insurance Co. Pty Ltd; *b* 12 Feb. 1902; *s* of late R. Yorston, Shetland Is; *m* 1934, Gwendolen C., *d* of late F. A. Ridley; one *s* one *d*. *Educ:* Caulfield Public Sch.; Univ. of Melbourne (BCom). Principal, Aust. Accountancy Coll., Sydney, 1933-66. In practice as a Chartered Acct, in Sydney, 1933-. Federal Pres., Australian-American Assoc., 1960, 1962-64, 1966-67; NSW Pres., Australian-American Assoc., 1957-63, 1965-70; Pres., Aust. Soc. of Accts, NSW, 1959. Rep. Australia at: Internat. Congress of Accts, 1957, 1962; Internat. Congress of Inst. of Management, 1957. Chm., NSW State Council Metropolitan Opera (New York) Auditions; Member: Australian Auditors Council, for Metropolitan Opera, New York; Council, Scots Coll., Bellevue Hill; (since inception of Annual Report Award) Adjudicating Panel for best Annual Report in Australia; Bd, Scottish Hosp., Sydney. Mem. Adv. Bd, Presbyterian Foundation. Chairman: The Presbyterian Church (NSW) Property Trust, 1964-70; Council, Presbyterian Ladies Coll., Armidale; Mem. Council, Woodstock Presbyterian Ladies Coll.; Albury. Annual Research Lecturer, Aust. Soc. of Accts: Univ. Sydney, 1951; Univ. WA, 1952; Univ. Tas, 1953; Univ. Melb., 1959; Edgar Sabine Memorial Lecture, Adelaide Univ., 1959; Guest Lectr, Jubilee Convention of NZ Soc. of Accts, 1960. FAIM. *Publications:* (several books reproduced in other countries, such as United Kingdom and New Zealand; numerous standard text books (some jointly) on accounting, law and company practice (mostly with 2-6 edns) including: Australian Company Director, 1932; Australian Shareholders Guide, 1958, 2nd edn 1961; Australian Commercial Dictionary, 1945, 4th edn 1964; Limited Liability Companies in Australia, 1956; Twentieth Century Commerce and Book-keeping, 12th edn 1960; Costing Procedures, 1951, 4th edn 1966; Advanced Accounting, 1948, 6th edn 1966; Elementary Accounting, 1952, 4th edn 1966; Company Law in New South Wales, 1947, 2nd edn 1950; Company Law in Victoria, 1955, 2nd edn 1959; Accounting Fundamentals, 1949, 6th edn 1966; Australian Mercantile Law, 1939, 14th edn 1970; Annual Reports of Companies, 1958; Australian Secretarial Practice, 1936, 5th edn 1965; Company Secretary's Guide (NSW), 1946, 2nd edn 1950; Company Secretary's Guide (Victoria), 1948, 2nd edn 1952; Company Secretary's Guide (Queensland), 1947; Company Law, 1962, 3rd edn 1969; Proprietary and Private Companies in Australia, 1939, 2nd edn 1952. *Address:* 29 Trafalgar Avenue, Roseville, NSW 2069, Australia.

**YOST, Charles Woodruff;** Ambassador, and Permanent Representative of the United States to the United Nations since 1969; *b* 6 Nov. 1907; *s* of Nicholas Doxtater and Gertrude (Cooper); *m* 1934, Irena Oldakowska; two *s* one *d*. *Educ:* Hotchkiss Sch.; Princeton Univ. (AB); Univ. of Paris. Entered US Foreign Service, 1930; served: Alexandria, 1930-32; Warsaw, 1932-33. Journalist, 1933-35. Dept of State, 1935-45; Asst to Chm., Dumbarton Oaks Conf., 1945; Sec.-Gen., US Delegn, Berlin Conf., 1945; Political Adviser to Comdg Gen., India-Burma Theatre, 1945; Chargé d'Affaires, Bangkok, 1946; Pol. Adviser to US Delegn to UN, 1946; Prague, 1947; Vienna, 1948-49; Pol. Adviser to US Delegn to UN, 1949; Dir, Office of Eastern European Affairs, 1949-50; Minister in Athens, 1950; Dep. High Comr for Austria, 1953; Laos: Minister, 1954, Ambassador, 1955-56; Minister in Paris, 1956; Amb. to Syria, 1957; Amb. to Morocco, 1958-61; Dep. Rep. to UN Security Council, 1961-65; Career Amb., 1964; Dep. Perm. Rep. to UN, 1965-66; Senior Fellow, Council on Foreign Relations, 1966-69. Hon. LLD: St Lawrence Univ., 1963; Princeton Univ., 1969. Rockefeller Public Service Award, 1964. *Publications:* Age of Triumph and Frustration, 1964; The Insecurity of Nations, 1968. *Recreations:* swimming, riding, literature, arts. *Address:* 799 United Nations Plaza, New York, NY 10017, USA. *T:* 212 YU 6-2424. *Clubs:* Century, River (New York); University (Washington, DC).

**YOUDE, Edward,** CMG 1968; MBE 1949; Imperial Defence College, 1970-71; *b* 19 June 1924; *m* 1951, Pamela Fitt; two *d*. *Educ:* Sch. of Oriental Studies, Univ. of London. RNVR, 1943-46. Joined Foreign Office, 1947. First Secretary: Washington, 1956-59; Peking, 1960-62; Foreign Office, 1962-65; Counsellor and Head of Chancery, UK Mission to UN, 1965-69; a Private Secretary to the Prime Minister,

1969-70. *Recreation:* sailing. *Address:* 14e Avenue Road, NW8.

**YOUDS, Edward Ernest; Hon. Mr Justice Edward Youds;** Puisne Judge, High Court, Uganda, since 1969; *b* 21 Nov. 1910; *s* of late Edward Youds; *m* 1960, Anna Lang Macpherson; two *s* one *d. Educ:* Birkenhead Sch.; Magdalene Coll., Cambridge. BA, LLB (Hons) Cantab. Called to Bar, Gray's Inn, 1936. Practised on Northern Circuit as Barrister-at-law. Served 1940-45, France and Germany (despatches, 1945). Dep. Chm., Lancs County Sessions, 1961-66; County Court Judge, 1966-69. *Address:* 38 Prince Charles Drive, Box 5548, Kampala, Uganda.

**YOUELL, Rev. Canon George;** a Residentiary Canon of Ely Cathedral since 1970; *b* 23 Dec. 1910; *s* of late Herbert Youell, Beccles; *m* 1936, Gertrude Barron, *d* of late J. Irvine, West Hartlepool; two *s* three *d. Educ:* Beccles; St Michaels; Hartley Coll., Manchester; St Stephen's House, Oxford; Univ. of Keele (MA 1969). Ordained, 1933; Curate, St John's, Chester, 1933; Clerical Dir of Industrial Christian Fellowship, 1937; chaplain attached to 2nd Bn Grenadier Guards (BEF and Guards Armoured Div.), 1939; Sen. Chaplain to Forces: Nigeria, 1942; Woolwich and SE London, 1944; Nigeria and Gold Coast, 1945; Rector of Ightfield with Calverhall, Salop, 1947; Rural Dean of Leek, 1952-56; Vicar of Leek, 1952-61; Archdeacon of Stoke-upon-Trent, 1956-70; Vicar of Horton, Leek, 1968-70; Chaplain, Univ. of Keele, 1961-68; Hon. Canon, Lichfield Cathedral, 1967-. *Publications:* Africa Marches, 1949; contributor on colonial and sociological affairs to the Guardian, 1947-51. *Recreation:* fell walking. *Address:* The Almonry, Ely. *Club:* Army and Navy.

**YOUENS, Ven. Archdeacon John Ross,** CB 1970; OBE 1959; MC 1946; Chaplain to the Queen since 1969; Chaplain General to the Forces since 1966; *b* 29 Sept. 1914; *e s* of late Canon F. A. C. Youens; *m* 1940, Pamela Gordon Lincoln (*née* Chandler); one *s* one *d* (and one *d* decd). *Educ:* Buxton Coll.; Kelham Theological Coll. Curate of Warsop, Notts, 1939-40. Commissioned RA Chaplains' Dept, 1940; Aldershot and SE Comd, 1940-42; Sen. Chaplain: 59 Inf. Div., 1942; Chatham, 1943; 2nd Army Troops, June 1944; Guards Armd Div., Nov. 1944-45; 3rd Inf. Div. in Egypt and Palestine, 1945-48; 7th Armd Div. in Germany, 1948-50; Aldershot, 1950-51; DACG, Egypt, 1951-53; Tripoli, 1953-54; Sen. Chaplain, RMA Sandhurst, 1955-58; DACG, Gibraltar, 1958-60; ACG War Office, 1960-61, Rhine Army, 1961-66. *Address:* c/o Glyn, Mills & Co., Holt's Branch, Whitehall, SW1. *Clubs:* United Service, Guards' (Hon. Mem.).

**YOUENS, Sir Peter (William),** Kt 1965; CMG 1962; OBE 1960; *b* 29 April 1916; 2nd *s* of late Canon F. A. C. Youens; *m* 1943, Diana Stephanie, *d* of Edward Hawkins, Southacre, Norfolk; two *d. Educ:* King Edward VII's School, Sheffield; Wadham College, Oxford. BA (Oxon), 1938. Joined Colonial Administrative Service; naval service, 1939-40. Sub-Lt, Cadet S. L., 1939; Asst Dist Comr, 1942; Dist Comr, 1948; Colony Comr and Member, Sierra Leone Legislative Council, 1950; Asst Sec., Nyasaland, 1951; Dep. Chief Sec., 1953-63; Secretary to the Prime Minister and to the Cabinet, Malawi 1964-66 (Nyasaland, 1963-64); Mem., Nyasaland Legislative Council, 1954-61. Retired, 1966. Exec. Dir, Lonrho Ltd, 1966-69; Partner, John Tyzack & Partners Ltd, 1969-. *Address:* Forest House, Rowledge, near Farnham, Surrey. *Clubs:* East India and Sports; Vincent's (Oxford).

**YOUNG,** family name of **Baron Kennet** (who wishes to be known as Wayland Young, author).

**YOUNG;** *see* Hughes-Young.

**YOUNG, Prof. Alec David,** OBE 1964; MA, FRAeS; AFAIAA; Professor and Head of the Department of Aeronautical Engineering Queen Mary College, London University, since Oct. 1954; Vice-Principal, Queen Mary College, 1966; *b* 15 Aug. 1913; *s* of Isaac Young and Katherine (*née* Freeman); *m* 1937, Dora Caplan (*d* 1970); two *s* one *d. Educ:* Caius Coll., Cambridge. Wrangler, Mathematical Tripos, 1935. Research Student in Aeronautics, Cambridge, 1935-36; Mem. of staff, Aerodynamics Dept, Royal Aircraft Estab., 1936-46; College of Aeronautics: Senior Lectr and Dep. Head of Dept of Aerodynamics, 1946-50; Prof. and Head of Dept of Aerodynamics, 1950-54. Dean, Faculty of Engineering, Univ. of London, 1962-66; Mem. Senate, Univ. of London, 1970-. Mem. various Cttees of Aeronautical Research Council, Chm. of Council, 1968-. Chm., Bd of Direction, Von Karman Institute for Fluid Dynamics, 1964; Mem., Advisory Bd, RAF Coll., Cranwell, 1966. Past Chm. Aerodynamics Data Sheets Cttee, Royal Aeronautical Soc., FRAeS, 1951. *Publications:* various, of Aeronautical Research Council, Coll. of Aeronautics Reports series; articles in Aeronautical Quarterly and Jl of Royal Aeronautical Soc. Quarterly Jl of Mechanics and Applied Mathematics, and Aircraft Engineering. Co-author of An Elementary Treatise on the Mechanics of Fluids, 1960. *Recreation:* drama. *Address:* The Sycamores, Whitehall Lane, Buckhurst Hill, Essex. *T:* 01-504 8437.

**YOUNG, Maj.-Gen. Alexander;** Director of Ordnance Services, Ministry of Defence, since 1968; *b* 22 Feb. 1915; *s* of late Alexander and Mary M. K. G. Young, Edinburgh; *m* 1942, Joan Madeline, *d* of late John N. Stephens, London; one *s. Educ:* Daniel Stewart's Coll., Edinburgh. Served, BEF, 1940; WO, 1942-46; HQ, Caribbean Area, 1947-50; WO, 1950-52; HQ Middle East Comd, Egypt and Cyprus, 1954-57; Bt Lt-Col 1955; Comdr RAOC, 4 Inf. Div., 1957-59; HQ, BAOR, 1959-61; WO, 1961-64; Dep. Dir, Ordnance Services, Eastern Comd, 1964-65; Comd COD, Bicester, 1965-67; Comd UK Base Org., 1967-68. FBIM. *Recreations:* travel, golf. *Address:* 2 Crescent Place, SW3. *T:* 01-584 2289. *Club:* Army and Navy.

**YOUNG, Rev. Canon Andrew John,** MA (Edinburgh) 1908; Hon. LLD (Edinburgh) 1951; FRSL; Canon of Chichester Cathedral since 1948; Vicar of Stonegate, Sussex, 1941-59; *b* 1885; *m* 1914, Janet Green; one *s* one *d. Educ:* Royal High Sch., Edinburgh; Edinburgh University. Queen's Medal for Poetry, 1952. *Publications:* A Prospect of Flowers, 1945; A Retrospect of Flowers, 1950; Collected Poems, 1950; Into Hades, 1952; A Prospect of Britain, 1956; Out of the World and Back (poem), 1958; The Collected Poems of Andrew Young, 1960; The Poet and the Landscape, 1962; The New Poly-Olbion, 1967. *Relevant Publication:* Andrew Young: Prospect of a Poet (ed Leonard Clark), 1958. *Address:* Park Lodge, Church Lane, Yapton, Arundel, Sussex.

**YOUNG, Col Sir Arthur (Edwin),** Kt 1965; CMG 1953; CVO 1962; Commissioner, City of London Police, since 1950 (seconded 1969-70 as Chief Constable, Royal Ulster Constabulary); *b* 1907; *s* of Edwin Young; *m* 1st, 1939, Ivy Ada (*d* 1956); one *s*; 2nd, 1957, Margaret Furnival Homan (*née* Dolphin), Sidmouth and Washington (*d* 1966); 3rd, 1970, Mrs Ileen Turner. *Educ:* Portsmouth Grammar Sch. Joined Portsmouth City Police, 1924. Chief Constable, Leamington 1938; Senior Assistant Chief Constable of Birmingham, 1941; Allied Control Commission for Italy (Public Safety), 1943-45; Chief Constable of Hertfordshire, 1945; Assistant Commissioner of Police of the Metropolis, May 1947. Visited the Gold Coast, 1951, to make recommendations to Govt on re-organisation of Gold Coast Police; Commissioner of Federation of Malaya Police, 1952; Commissioner of Kenya Police, 1954. Hon. Commissioner of Police, New York. Director, Police Extended Interviews; Chairman: Police Council for Great Britain; Council Police Athletic Assoc.; Life Saving Federation, 1968. Member: Advisory Council National Police Fund (Chairman Educ. Committee); Board of Governors of the Police Coll. and Atlantic Coll.; Vice-President, Police Mutual Assurance Soc.; King's Police Medal, 1952; King Gustav VI of Sweden's medal of merit, for services to sport, 1962. Vice-Chairman, National Small-Bore Rifle Assoc., 1964. Officer (Brother) Order of St John. Holds many foreign decorations. *Recreation:* walking. *Address:* 26 Old Jewry, EC2. *T:* 01-606 8866. *Club:* Athenæum.

**YOUNG, Arthur Primrose,** OBE; CEng, FIEE, FIMechE, FIWM; Member, Factory and Welfare Advisory Board, Ministry of Labour, 1940-47; Founder Vice-President, Institution of Works Managers; *b* 2 July 1885; 7th *s* of late William Young, Highfield, Ayrshire, and late Mary Potts, *d* of late William Walker, Culmalzie, Wigtownshire; *m* 1st, 1912, Lillie Louisa (*d* 1961), 3rd *d* of late Abel Porter, Rugby; one *d*; 2nd 1962, Winifred Rose, *widow* of George Henry Young, Broadford Bridge, Billingshurst, Sussex. *Educ:* Stanley School, St Pancras; Finsbury Technical College, London. Joined BTH Co. Ltd, 1901; continuous service to retirement in 1945 except for a break of nearly two years, 1906-08, when in USA working with General Electric Co.; Engineer Coventry Works, BTH Co. Ltd, 1915-21; Engineer and Manager, 1921-28; Manager Rugby Works, British Thomson Houston Co. Ltd, 1929-45. Took out in association with Company nearly 150 patents, 1909-31; Member Council IAE, 1928-34; Member Faraday Centenary Committee, IEE, 1931; Member Council IEE, 1938-41; Member Coventry Education Committee, 1928-38; Member Warwickshire National Service Committee, 1939; visited USA, 1939 and 1945, at invitation of Episcopal Church of America to attend private conference, Washington, to survey impact of Christian principles on industrial relations; Visiting Fellow Nuffield College, Oxford, 1939-47; Director of Labour Supply Committee, Ministry of Labour, 1940-41; Chairman: Confederation of Management Associations, 1938-48; Institution of Works Managers, 1934-50; Midland Regional Council, UNA, 1946-53; Spencer Trust, Coventry, 1952-62; Dir, BKL Alloys Ltd, 1945-67. Governor: Birmingham College of Advanced Technology, 1956-61; Coventry Technical College and College of Art, 1960-62; Member Warwickshire Education Committee, 1950-62; Member, Management Committee, South Warwickshire Hospital Group (no 14), 1950-62. Institution of Works Managers inaugurated biennial A. P. Young Lecture, 1962. *Publications:* Magnetos, 1919, 2nd edn, revised 1920; Elements of Electrotechnics, 1921; Automobile Electrical Equipment, 1933 (8th edn rev. 1970) (with L. Griffiths); Forward from Chaos, 1933; Plan and Serve, 1938; Man at the Cross Roads, 1941; The Production Front and You, 1942; The World of Industry, 1946; Lord Kelvin, 1948; Coal, 1948; Report on American Productivity, 1949. *Recreations:* walking, reading, writing and painting. *Address:* 51 Beverley Road, Leamington Spa, Warwickshire. *T:* Leamington Spa 25271; Oakcroft, Mannings Heath, near Horsham, Sussex. *T:* Horsham 5509. *Club:* National Liberal.

**YOUNG, Bertram Alfred;** dramatic critic, The Financial Times, since 1964; *b* 20 Jan. 1912; *y* (twin) *s* of Bertram William Young and Dora Elizabeth Young (*née* Knight); unmarried. *Educ:* Highgate. Served with Lancs Fusiliers, KAR and Staff, 1939-48; Asst Editor, Punch, 1949-62; Dramatic Critic, Punch, 1962-64. *Publications:* Tooth and Claw, 1958; How to Avoid People, 1963; Bechuanaland, 1966; Cabinet Pudding, 1967; author of about 20 radio plays broadcast 1938-49. *Recreation:* music (consumer only). *Address:* 28 Elm Park Gardens, Chelsea, SW10. *T:* 01-352 5423. *Club:* Garrick.

**YOUNG, Air Vice-Marshal Brian Pashley,** CBE 1960 (OBE 1944); Commandant General, Royal Air Force Regiment, and Inspector of Ground Defence, since 1968; *b* 5 May 1918; *s* of Kenneth Noel Young and Flora Elizabeth Young, Natal, S Africa; *m* 1942, Patricia Josephine, *d* of Thomas Edward Cole, Bedford; three *s* two *d*. *Educ:* Michaelhouse, Natal, SA; RAF Coll., Cranwell. Fighter Comd, UK and France, 1938-40 (wounded); Hosp., 1941-42; Coastal Comd, N Ire and Western Isles, 1942-43; Aden and Persian Gulf, 1944; Staff Coll., Haifa, 1945; Middle East, 1946-47; Air Min., 1948-50; Bomber Comd HQ No. 1 Gp, Hemswell/Gaydon, 1951-57; HQ Bomber Comd, 1958-60; NATO, Fontainebleau, Asst Chief of Staff, Intelligence, 1960-62; IDC 1963; AOC, Central Reconnaisance Estabt, 1964-67. *Recreations:* cricket, squash; Rep. RAF: athletics, 1939, Rugby, 1947-48. *Address:* Court Lees, Homefield Road, Warlingham, Surrey. *T:* Upper Warlingham 2207. *Club:* Royal Air Force.

**YOUNG, Brian Walter Mark,** MA; Director-General, Independent Television Authority, since 1970; *b* 23 Aug. 1922; *er s* of Sir Mark Young, *qv*; *m* 1947, Fiona Marjorie, *o d* of late Allan, 16th Stewart of Appin, and of Mrs Stewart; one *s* two *d*. *Educ:* Eton; King's College, Cambridge. Served in RNVR, mainly in destroyers, 1941-45. First class hons in Part I, 1946, and Part II, 1947, of Classical Tripos; Porson Prize, 1946; BA 1947; MA 1952. Assistant Master at Eton, 1947-52; Headmaster of Charterhouse, 1952-64; Dir, Nuffield Foundn, 1964-70. Member: Central Advisory Council for Education, 1956-59 (Crowther Report); UNESCO UK National Commission; Health Educn Council; Governing Body of Rugby Sch. *Publications:* Via Vertendi, 1952; Intelligent Reading (with P. D. R. Gardiner), 1964. *Address:* Nuffield Lodge, Regent's Park, NW1.

**YOUNG, Carmichael Aretas,** MD, FRCP; Physician and Physician i/c Diabetic Clinic, St Mary's Hospital, London, W2, since 1948; Physician Paddington General Hospital, since 1950; Consultant in Chest Diseases, Ministry of Pensions, since 1948; *b* Adelaide, S Australia, 19 Aug. 1913; *e s* of Aretas Henry Young, Adelaide, SA and Isabelle Wilson, Parattah, Tas; *m* 1939, Marie, 2nd *d* of W. H. Lewry, Botley, Hants; three *s* one *d*. *Educ:* Carey Grammar Sch., Kew, Vic.; St Mary's

Hosp. Medical Sch., Univ. of London. MRCS, LRCP 1936, FRCP 1950; MB, BS (London), 1936, MD 1940. House Phys. and House Surg., St Mary's Hosp., 1936-37; House Phys., Asst Resident MO, Brompton Hosp., 1938; Asst, Professorial Medical Unit, St Mary's, 1939; Phys., EMS, 1940-41; Medical Specialist 10th (Brit.) CCS, 1942-43 (despatches); No 1 Gen. Hosp., 1944; Lt-Col RAMC Office i/c Medical Div. 43 Gen. Hosp., 1945; OC 43 Gen. Hosp., Beirut, 1946. Medical Registrar, Prince of Wales' Gen. Hosp., 1946-47; Sub-Dean, St Mary's Hosp. Medical School, 1952-53; Examiner: Soc. of Apothecaries, Medicine, 1964-70; Univ. London, Therapeutics, Medicine, 1957-62; Conj. Bd, Pathology, Medicine, FRCP, 1950 (Chm., 1970-71); Royal Soc. Med. Member: Board of Governors, St Mary's Hosp., 1958-61. Hon. Colonel No. 4 Gen. Hosp. AER, 1961. *Publications:* History of the Otter Swimming Club, 1869-1969, 1969; short articles in medical jls. *Recreations:* swimming, water-polo, golf, reading. *Address:* 38 Devonshire Street, W1. *T:* 01-935 7883; 01-788 0490. *Clubs:* Royal Wimbledon Golf; Otter Swimming (Pres. 1964-67).

**YOUNG, Rev. Canon Charles Edgar,** AFC; MA; Vicar of Thornthwaite, 1957-65; Headmaster, Rossall School, 1937-57, retired; Hon. Canon of Carlisle Cathedral, 1962-65; Canon Emeritus, 1965; *b* Clifton, Bristol, 8 Jan. 1897; *s* of late Prof. Sydney Young; *m* 1928, Dorothy Vere, *d* of late Rt Rev. Harry Vere White, late Bishop of Limerick; one *s* two *d*. *Educ:* Charterhouse (Scholar); Exeter College, Oxford. Lieut RASC 1915-17; Lieut, RFC, 1917-18; Capt. RAF, 1918-19; Exeter College, Oxford, 1919-21; 2nd class Honours Moderations, 1921, BA 1921; MA 1928; Lower Sixth Form Master at Fettes College, Edinburgh, 1921-29; Headmaster Lincoln School, 1929-37. Served with RAF, 1940-42; Flight Lieut, 1942. JP, 1947-56. Made deacon, 1952; ordained priest, 1953. *Address:* Park House, Church Stretton, Shropshire. *Club:* Public Schools.

**YOUNG, (Charles) Kenneth,** FRSL; Political and Literary Adviser to Beaverbrook Newspapers since 1965 and formerly, Editor of the Yorkshire Post; *b* 27 Nov. 1916; *o s* of late Robert William Young, Iron Founder, Middlestown, Wakefield, and late Alice, Jane Young (*née* Ramsden); *m* 1951, Phyllis, *d* of late Lt-Col J. A. Dicker; three *s* two *d*. *Educ:* Queen Elizabeth's Grammar Sch. (Junior Dept), Wakefield; Coatham Sch., Redcar; Leeds Univ. BA (1st Cl. Hons Eng. Lang. and Lit.), 1938. Served War of 1939-45. Royal Corps of Signals, 1940; Intelligence Corps, 1941 (Algeria, Italy, Greece); Foreign Office, 1944. BBC European Service, 1948; Daily Mirror, 1949; Daily Mail, 1950; Permanent Under-Sec. Dept, Cabinet Office, 1950; Daily Telegraph, 1952-60; Editor of The Yorkshire Post, 1960-64. FRSL 1964. Broadcaster: Editor, Television series, The Book Man, 1960. Governor, Welbeck College. *Publications:* D. H. Lawrence, 1952; John Dryden (critical biography), 1954; Ford Madox Ford, 1958; (ed) The Bed Post, 1962; (ed) The Second Bed Post, 1965; A. J. Balfour, authorised biography, 1963; Churchill and Beaverbrook: a Study in friendship and politics, 1966; Rhodesia and Independence: A Study in British Colonial Policy, 1967; Sir Compton Mackenzie, an Essay, 1967; Music's Great Days in the Spas and Watering-places, 1968; The Greek Passion: a study in people and politics, 1969; Sir Alec Douglas-Home, 1970; contrib. to Spectator, Encounter, etc. *Recreations:* being with family, listening to music, talk. *Address:* Amberfield, Chart Sutton, Kent. *T:* Maidstone 43000; 01-353 8000. *Club:* Savile.

**YOUNG, Colin;** Director, National Film School of Great Britain, since 1970; *b* 5 April 1927; *s* of Colin Young and Agnes Holmes Kerr Young; *m* 1960, Kristin Ohman; two *s*. *Educ:* Bellahouston Academy, Glasgow; Univs of Glasgow, St Andrews and California (Los Angeles). Theatre and film critic, Bon Accord, Aberdeen, 1951; cameraman, editor, writer, director, 1953-; producer, 1967-; UCLA (Motion Pictures): Instructor, 1956-59; Asst Prof., 1959-64; Assoc. Prof., 1964-68; Prof., 1968-70, Head, Motion Picture Div., Theater Arts Dept, UCLA, 1964-65; Chm., Dept of Theater Arts, 1965-70. Chm., Cttee on Educational Policy, UCLA, 1968-69. Los Angeles Editor, Film Quarterly, 1958-68. *Publications:* various articles in collections of film essays, 1961-; experimental film essay for Unesco, 1963; ethnographic film essay for Unesco, 1966; contribs to Film Quarterly, Sight and Sound, Jl of Aesthetic Education, Jl of the Producers Guild of America, Kosmorama (Copenhagen), etc. *Recreations:* golf, wine-making. *Address:* National Film School, at The National Film Theatre, SE1.

**YOUNG, Sir Douglas;** *see* Young, Sir J. D.

**YOUNG, Edward Preston,** DSO 1944; DSC 1943; Managing Director, The Rainbird Publishing Group Ltd; *b* 17 Nov. 1913; *m* 1st, 1945, Diana Lilian Graves (marr. diss.); two *d*; 2nd, 1956, Mary Reoch Cressall. *Educ:* Highgate Sch. Served War, 1940-45: RNVR; entered submarine service 1940 (despatches, DSC); first RNVR officer to command operational submarine, 1943 (DSO and Bar, to DSC); temp. Commander RNVR, 1945. *Publications:* One of Our Submarines, 1952; Look at Lighthouses, 1961; The Fifth Passenger, 1962; Look at Submarines, 1964. *Recreation:* gardening. *Address:* Horton Cottage, Monks Horton, Sellindge, Kent. *Club:* Garrick.

**YOUNG, Sir Eric;** *see* Young, Sir T. E. B.

**YOUNG, Eric Edgar;** HM Diplomatic Service, retired; *b* 1 July 1912; *yr s* of late Frank E. Young, Dulwich; *m* 1938, Aurora Corral, San Sebastian, Spain; two *d*. *Educ:* Alleyn's Sch., Dulwich; Jesus Coll., Oxford. Served Army, 1940-46 (Major, RAC). Diplomatic (formerly Foreign) Service, 1946-70; Served at: Buenos Aires, 1946-49; Montevideo, 1950-52; Mexico City, 1952-55; FO, 1955-58; Rangoon, 1958-60; HM Consul, Tamsui (Formosa), 1960-62; FO, 1962-64; Adv. to Kenya Min. of Foreign Affairs, Nairobi, 1964-67; HM Consul-General, Paris, 1967-70. *Publications:* The Bowes Museum, Barnard Castle, Catalogue of Spanish and Italian Paintings, 1970; contrib. to: Apollo, The Connoisseur, Archivo Español de Arte, etc. *Recreations:* art history, tennis. *Address:* 49 Oatlands Drive, Weybridge, Surrey. *Club:* Garrick.

**YOUNG, Eric William,** BEng (Hons); MIMechE, MIEE; *b* 26 March 1896; 2nd *s* of Colonel C. A. Young, CB, CMG; *m* 1936, Mrs Olive Bruce. *Educ:* Epsom Coll.; Shrewsbury Sch.; Liverpool Univ. (BEng Hons, 1922). Served RE (T) (Lieut) 1913-19. Metropolitan Vickers Ltd, 1922-26; Technical Manager, Electrolux Ltd, 1926-39; Rootes Ltd: General Manager, Aero Engine Factories, 1939-45; Director and General Manager, Sunbeam Talbot Ltd, 1945-46; Director, Rootes Export Co. Ltd, 1946-47; Sales Director, Harry Ferguson Ltd, 1947-53; Managing Director, Eastern Hemisphere Division, Massey-Ferguson Ltd, 1953-56; Vice-Chm., Massey-Ferguson Holdings Ltd, 1956-65, Chm., 1965-

70. *Recreations:* golf, gardening. *Address:* Childerstone, Liphook, Hampshire. *T:* Liphook 2125. *Clubs:* Bath; Liphook Golf.

**YOUNG, Frank George,** FRS 1949; DSc, PhD (London), MA (Cantab), FRSM, FRIC; Professor of Biochemistry, University of Cambridge, since 1949; Hon. Consultant Biochemist to United Cambridge Hospitals; (First) Master of Darwin College, Cambridge, since 1964; Hon. Fellow of Trinity Hall, Cambridge, since 1965 (Fellow, 1949-64); Fellow of University College, London; *b* 25 March 1908; *er s* of late Frank E. Young, Dulwich; *m* 1933, Ruth (MB, BS, DPM), *o d* of Thomas Turner, Beckenham, Kent; three *s* one *d*. *Educ:* Alleyn's Sch., Dulwich; University Coll., London. Beit Memorial Fellow at University Coll., London, University of Aberdeen and University of Toronto, 1932-36; Member of Scientific Staff, Medical Research Council, 1936-42; Professor of Biochemistry, University of London, 1942-49. Member: Medical Res. Council, 1950-54; Commission on Higher Educ. for Africans in Central Africa, 1952; Inter-University Council for Higher Education Overseas, 1961-; Commission on new Chinese University in Hong Kong, 1962-63; Medical Sub-Cttee, University Grants Cttee, 1964-; Board of Governors of United Cambridge Hospitals, 1964-68; Royal Commn on Medical Educn, 1965-68. Trustee of Kennedy Memorial Trust, 1964-. President: European Assoc. for the Study of Diabetes, 1965-68; British Nutrition Foundn, 1970-; Internat. Diabetes Fedn, 1970; Vice-Pres., Internat. Council of Scientific Unions, 1970-. Chairman: Smith Kline and French Trustees (UK), 1963-; Clinical Endocrinology Cttee (MRC), 1965-; Adv. Cttee on Irradiation of Food (UK), 1967-; Executive Council and Trustee Ciba Foundation, 1967-. Croonian Lecturer, Royal Society, 1962. Named lectureships held abroad: Renziehausen, Pittsburg, 1939; Sterling, Yale, 1939; Jacobæus, Oslo, 1948; Dohme, Johns Hopkins, 1950; Banting, Toronto, 1950; Banting, San Francisco, 1950; Richardson, Harvard, 1952; Hanna, Western Reserve, 1952; Woodward, Yale, 1958; Brailsford Robertson, Adelaide, 1960; Upjohn, Atlantic City, 1963. Hon. or corresp. member of many foreign medical and scientific bodies. Hon. LLD (Aberdeen); Doctor *hc*: Catholic University of Chile; Univ. Montpellier. *Publications:* scientific papers in Biochemical Journal and other scientific and medical journals on hormonal control of metabolism, diabetes mellitus, and related topics. *Address:* Department of Biochemistry, Tennis Court Road, Cambridge. *Club:* Athenæum.

**YOUNG, Frederick Trestrail Clive,** CBE 1937; *b* 19 March 1887; *y s* of late James Young, Calcutta, and of late L. Z. Young, Rockmount, Helensburgh, Dunbartonshire; *m* 1920, Hope MacLellan Fulton, Findhorn, Helensburgh; two *s* one *d*. *Educ:* Merchiston Castle, Edinburgh (School Captain); Pembroke Coll., Cambridge. BA (Hons Classical Tripos, 1909); Sudan Political Service, 1910, District Commissioner; Commissioner Nomad (Beja) Administration, 1926; Assistant Civil Secretary, 1929-32; Governor: Kassala Province, 1932-34; Blue Nile Province, 1934-36; Retired, 1936; Order of Nile 4th class, 1920, 3rd class, 1930; King George V Jubilee Medal, 1935. *Recreations:* golf, tennis, sailing. *Address:* West Down House, Budleigh Salterton, Devon. *T:* Budleigh Salterton 2762. *Club:* Royal Commonwealth Society.

**YOUNG, Frieda Margaret,** OBE 1969; Consul-General, Rotterdam, since 1968; *b* 9 April 1913; *d* of Arthur Edward Young. *Educ:* Wyggeston Grammar Sch., Leicester; Wycombe Abbey Sch., Bucks; and in France and Germany. Home Office, 1937-39; Min. of Home Security, 1939-41; MOI 1941-44; Paris 1944-48; Tehran 1948-51; Vienna 1951-54; FO 1954-57; First Secretary and Consul, Reykjavik, 1957-59; Consul, Cleveland, 1959-62; FO 1962-65; Consul, Bergen, 1965-68. *Recreations:* travel, photography, bird-watching. *Address:* c/o Foreign and Commonwealth Office, SW1. *Club:* Royal Commonwealth Society.

**YOUNG, George Bell;** General Manager, East Kilbride Development Corporation, since 1968; *b* 17 June 1924; *s* of George Bell Young and Jemima Mackinlay; *m* 1946, Margaret Wylie Boyd; one *s*. *Educ:* Queens Park, Glasgow. MIEx 1958; MInstM 1969; MBIM 1970. RNVR, 1942-45, Lieut (destroyers and mine-sweepers). Journalist and Feature Writer, Glasgow Herald, 1945-48; North of Scotland Hydro Electric Board, 1948-52; London Sec. of Scottish Council (Development and Industry), 1952-68. Dir, Royal Caledonian Schools; Chairman: East Kilbride and District National Savings Cttee; British Heart Foundn East Kilbride Cttee. FRSA 1970. *Recreations:* golf, sailing, beachcombing. *Address:* 42 Fraser River Tower, East Kilbride, Lanarkshire. *T:* Murray 260; Spindrift, Ferry Row, Fairlie, Ayrshire. *T:* Fairlie 293. *Clubs:* Caledonian; Royal Scottish Automobile (Glasgow); Largs (Kelburn) Golf; Fairlie Yacht.

**YOUNG, George Kennedy,** CB 1960; CMG 1955; MBE 1945; Kleinwort, Benson Ltd, since 1961; President, Nuclear Fuel Finance SA; *b* 8 April 1911; *s* of late George Stuart Young and Margaret Kennedy, Moffat, Dumfriesshire; *m* 1939, Géryke, *d* of late Dr M. A. G. Harthoorn, Batavia, Dutch EI. *Educ:* Dumfries Acad.; Univs of St Andrews, Giessen, Dijon, Yale, MA (First Class Hons Mod. Langs) 1934; Commonwealth Fund Fellowship, 1934-36; MA (Political Science), Yale, 1936; Editorial staff The Glasgow Herald, 1936-38; British United Press, 1938-39. Served War of 1939-45; commissioned KOSB 1940 (despatches, E Africa, 1941); specially employed list, Italy and W Europe, 1943-45. Berlin correspondent, British United Press, 1946. Joined HM Foreign Service, 1946; Vienna, 1946; Economic Relations Dept, FO, 1949; British Middle East Office, 1951; Ministry of Defence, 1953-61; Under-Secretary, 1960. Medal of Freedom (Bronze Palm), 1945. *Publications:* Masters of Indecision, 1962; Merchant Banking, 1966; Finance and World Power, 1968; Who Goes Home?, 1969. *Recreations:* music, reading, swimming, walking. *Address:* 37 Abbotsbury House, W14. *T:* 01-603 8432.

**YOUNG, Sir George (Samuel Knatchbull),** 6th Bt, *cr* 1813; *b* 16 July 1941; Economic Adviser, Post Office Corporation, since 1969; *s* of Sir George Young, 5th Bt, CMG, and Elisabeth (*née* Knatchbull-Hugessen); *S* father 1960; *m* 1964, Aurelia Nemon-Stuart, *er d* of Oscar Nemon, *qv*, and of Mrs Nemon-Stuart, Boar's Hill, Oxford; two *s* one *d*. *Educ:* Eton; Christ Church, Oxford (Open Exhibitioner); MA Oxon, MPhil Surrey. Economist, National Economic Development Office, 1966-67; Kobler Research Fellow, University of Surrey, 1967-69. Councillor, London Borough of Lambeth; Mem., GLC, for London Borough of Ealing. *Publication:* Accomodation Services 1970-1980, 1970. *Heir: s* George Horatio Young, *b* 11 Oct. 1966. *Address:* 5 Gauden

Road, SW4. *T:* 01-720 1523; Formosa, Cookham, Berks.

**YOUNG, Gerard Francis,** CBE 1967; JP; CEng, FIMechE; Chairman, Tempered Group Ltd; Member, National Board for Prices and Incomes, since 1968; Chairman, Don Division, General Commissioners of Income Tax; *b* 5 May 1910; *s* of Smelter J. Young, MICE, and Edith, *d* of Sir John Aspinall, Pres. ICE and Pres. IMechE; *m* 1937, Diana Graham Murray, *d* of Charles Graham Murray, MD; two *s* three *d*. *Educ:* Ampleforth College. Engrg Apprentice, LNER, Doncaster. Entered family firm, The Tempered Spring Co. Ltd (later Tempered Group Ltd), 1930; Dir, 1936; Man. Dir, 1942; Chm., 1954-. Dir, 1958, Chm., 1967-, Sheffield area Board, Sun Alliance & London Insurance Group. Director: National Vulcan Engineering Group, 1962-; New Sheffield Theatre Trust Ltd; Trustee: Sheffield Town Trust; J. G. Graves Charitable Fund, etc. Univ. of Sheffield: Mem. Council, 1943; Treas., 1947-51; Pro-Chancellor, 1951-67; Chm., 1956-67. Mem. Bd of Govs, United Sheffield Hosps, 1948-53 (Chm. of Finance Cttee, 1948-50); Chm., Royal Hosp., 1951-53. Master, Company of Cutlers in Hallamshire, 1961-62. Hon. LLD Sheffield, 1962. JP Sheffield, 1950. *Recreations:* things seen; and creative use of public resources in support of private initiative. *Address:* The Ridge, Sandygate, Sheffield S10 4LB. *T:* Sheffield 302834. *Clubs:* Junior Carlton; Sheffield (Sheffield).

**YOUNG, Gladys,** OBE 1951; Radio Artist; *b* Newcastle; *d* of William Michael Young; *m* 1916, Algernon West; one *s*. *Educ:* Sutton High Sch.; Bonn, Germany. Entered RADA, 1912; scholarship; Silver Medal, 1913; Gold Medal, 1914; under Vedrenne and Eadie management, 1914-16. War work, 1916-18; began broadcasting, 1926; BBC Rep. Co. from outbreak of war, 1939-49. Has appeared in many television plays, 1930-. *Recreation:* mountaineering. *Address:* Twitten Bend, Willingdon, Eastbourne.

**YOUNG, Air Vice-Marshal Gordon,** CBE 1963; Chief of Staff No 18 (M) Group, RAF, since 1969; *b* 29 May 1919; *s* of late Robert Young, MBE, and late Emily Florence Young, Doncaster; *m* 1943, Pamela Doris Weatherstone-Smith; two *d*. *Educ:* Maltby Grammar School; Sheffield Univ. Served War of 1939-45, Flying Boat Ops S Atlantic and Western Approaches (despatches); Air Min., 1945-47; Asst Air Attaché, Moscow, 1949-52; OC No 204 Sqdn, 1954-55; RAF Staff Coll., 1956; OC Flying Wing, RAF St Mawgan, 1958-60; Asst Chief, Comdrs-in-Chief Mission to Soviet Forces in Germany, 1960-63; OC RAF Wyton, 1963-65; Air Attaché, Bonn, 1966-68; SASO Coastal Command, 1968-69. *Recreation:* bird-watching; MBOU 1969. *Address:* c/o Midland Bank, Rotherham, Yorks. *Club:* Royal Air Force.

**YOUNG, Most Rev. Guilford;** *see* Hobart, Archbishop of, (RC).

**YOUNG, Maj.-Gen. Hugh A.,** CB 1946; CBE 1945; DSO 1944; CD 1954; Deputy Minister of Department of Public Works, Canada, Nov. 1953-April 1963, retired; Vice-President, Central Mortgage and Housing Corporation since 1947; *b* 3 April 1898; *s* of Andrew and Emily Young, Winnipeg; *m* 1927; one *s* one *d*. *Educ:* Winnipeg Collegiate; University of Manitoba (BSc Elec. Engineering, 1924). RC Signals, 1924; Staff Coll., Camberley, England, 1933-34; various General Staff appointments during the war; commanded Inf. Bde, operations Normandy, 1944; QMG Canadian Army, 1944-47; retired, 1947. Dep. Minister of Department of Resources and Development, and Comr of NW Territories, Canada, 1950-53. *Address:* 220 Sandridge Road, Rockcliffe, Ottawa, Canada. *Clubs:* Rideau, Ottawa Country (Ottawa).

**YOUNG, James;** *b* 1 Oct. 1887; *s* of David S. Young and Henrietta Martin; *m* 1914, Margaret Cowan Smith Finlay; one *s*. *Educ:* George Heriot's Sch., Edinburgh. Apprentice Engineer and Draughtsman, 1904-13, Brown Bros, Rosebank Ironworks, Edinburgh; Draughtsman, 1913-18, John Brown & Co., Shipbuilders, Clydebank; Draughtsman, 1918-20, Barclay Curle & Co., Marine Engineers, Glasgow. Assoc. of Engineering and Shipbuilding Draughtsmen: Asst General Secretary, 1920-29; Divisional Organiser, 1929-45; General Secretary, 1945-52. Member General Council Scottish Trades Union Congress, 1932-45, Chairman, 1935-36 and 1944-45; President, Scottish Trades Union Congress, St Andrews, 1936, and Aberdeen, 1945; Member Labour Research Dept Executive, 1920-29; Regional Production Board, Scotland, 1941-45; Advisory Council of Education, Scotland, 1944-46; Executive Council, Confederation of Shipbuilding and Engineering Unions, 1944-52; Member of Commission appointed to enquire into the advancement of Africans in industry in Northern Rhodesia, 1947; Member of Tribunal set up under the constitution of the National Council for the Omnibus Industry to deal with a claim for National Conditions covering stage carriage operations, 1947; Member Court of Enquiry into Road Haulage Dispute, 1947. President, International Federation Commercial Clerical and Technical Employees, 1949-55. Member London County Council for East Woolwich, 1955-65; Chairman, Education Cttee, LCC, 1964-65; Member Greater London Council (Greenwich), 1964-67; Chairman, Education Cttee, Inner London Education Authority, 1964-67. Member Commn to inquire into causes of Trade disputes in Colony of Aden during March 1956; Member Board of Enquiry into Trade Dispute between Pilots and British West Indian Airways Ltd, 1958; part-time Member SE Gas Board, 1955-58. *Address:* Flat 11, 55 Orchard Brae Gardens, Edinburgh EH4 2HR. *T:* 031-332 8153.

**YOUNG, James Alexander,** CB 1970; Permanent Secretary, Ministry of Agriculture for N Ireland, since 1966; *b* Co. Tyrone, 17 Oct. 1918; *s* of Percy James and Margaret Young; *m* 1945, Margaret Doreen Patterson; two *d*. *Educ:* Royal Sch., Dungannon, Co. Tyrone; Queen's Univ., Belfast (BAgr). Asst Agr. Adviser to UK High Commissioner in Ottawa, Canada, 1946-49; Principal, Loughry Agricultural Coll., Cookstown, Co. Tyrone, 1949-63; Asst Sec., Min. of Agriculture for N Ireland, 1963-66. *Recreations:* Rugby football, gardening, photography. *Address:* Westways, Manse Road, Newtownards, Co. Down, N Ireland. *T:* Newtownards 2029.

**YOUNG, Sir James Reid,** Kt 1951; CA; FCIS; Chartered Accountant (Scotland); *b* 2 Dec. 1888; *s* of late Rev. Dr Young, Paisley, and Janet, *d* of late James Reid, Glasgow; *m* 1918, Margaret Boyd, *d* of late Dr Wm Walker, Grangemouth; one *d* (one *s* decd). *Educ:* Paisley Grammar Sch.; Glasgow Univ. Director, Vickers-Armstrongs Ltd, 1936; Chm., 1952-54; Dir, Vickers Ltd, 1937-59; Man. Dir, 1952-54; Chm., International Combustion (Holdings) Ltd, 1956-67. Chm., Advisory Panel, Organisation and Methods Div. of HM Treasury, 1941-54. *Address:* 65 Eaton Square, SW1. *T:* 01-235 1088.

**YOUNG, Major John Darling,** JP; CC; Lord Lieutenant of Buckinghamshire, since 1969; *b* 4 Jan. 1910; *o s* of late Sir Frederick Young; *m* 1934, Nina, *d* of late Lt-Col H. W. Harris; three *d. Educ:* Eton and Oxford (BA). Commissioned The Life Guards, 1932-46; Middle East and Italy, 1940-44. Member Bucks Agricultural Executive Cttee, 1947-58. dl 1958. High Sheriff, 1960, JP and CA 1964, Buckinghamshire. KStJ 1969. *Recreation:* shooting. *Address:* Thornton Hall, Bletchley, Bucks. *T:* Buckingham 3234; Lethem, Jedburgh, Roxburghshire. *T:* Camptown 208. *Clubs:* Turf, Cavalry.

**YOUNG, Sir (John) Douglas,** Kt, *cr* 1935; Controller of Military Government Courts (President, Military Government General Court), Allied Commission for Austria (British Element), Dec. 1944-Jan. 1948; *b* Helensburgh, 7 April 1883; *s* of James Young; *m* 1912, Joyce Macewen, *d* of William Alexander Smith, Glasgow; two *s. Educ:* Merchiston Castle Sch., Edinburgh; Pembroke Coll., Cambridge, BA. Called to Bar, 1907; Midland Circuit; Hon Counsel to Earl Haig's Officers' Assoc.; served European War, 1915-19; contested (L) Hendon, 1922; Southend, 1923, 1924, and West Lothian, 1928; Judge of the High Court, Allahabad, 1929-34; Chief Justice, High Court of Judicature, Lahore, 1934-43. Founded the College of Physical Education and Scouting at Lahore. *Address:* Ballasalla House, Ballasalla, Isle of Man.

**YOUNG, John Richard Dendy; Hon. Mr Justice Young;** Chief Justice of Botswana, since 1968; *b* 4 Sept. 1907; 5th *s* of James Young and Evelyn Maud Hammond; *m* 1947, Patricia Maureen Mount; four *s* two *d. Educ:* Hankey, Cape Province, SA; Humansdorp, CP, SA; University, South Africa (External). Joined Public Service, S Rhodesia, 1926; resigned to practise at Bar, 1934; joined Military Forces, 1940; active service, North Africa, Sicily and Italy; commissioned in the field; demobilised, 1945. QC 1948; MP Southern Rhodesia, 1948-53; Member Federal Assembly, 1953-56; Judge of the High Court of Rhodesia, 1956-68. *Recreations:* golf and tennis. *Address:* High Court, Lobatse, Botswana. *Club:* Salisbury (Rhodesia).

**YOUNG, John Stirling,** MC; Regius Professor of Pathology, University of Aberdeen, 1937-62, now Emeritus; *b* Symington, Ayrshire, 24 Sept. 1894; *s* of Matthew Young and Mary D. Stirling; *m* 1930, Ruth Muir Whipple; three *s. Educ:* Kilmarnock Academy; Glasgow Univ. MA (Glasgow) 1919; BSc 1920; MB, ChB 1923; MD (Gold Medal) 1928; Reader in Experimental Pathology, University of Leeds, 1927-31; Professor of Pathology, Queen's Univ., Belfast, 1932-37; Member Agricultural Research Council, 1952-56. Hon. LLD (Aberdeen), 1963. *Publications:* various scientific papers in Journal of Pathology and Bacteriology. *Recreation:* golf. *Address:* 16 Rubislaw Den South, Aberdeen.

**YOUNG, Sir John William Roe,** 5th Bt, *cr* 1821; Director, Mancunian Building Society; *b* 28 June 1913; *e s* of Sir Cyril Roe Muston Young, 4th Bt, and Gertrude Annie, *d* of John Elliott, Braunton, N Devon; *S* father, 1955; *m* 1946, Joan Minnie Agnes Aldous (*d* 1958); one *s* one *d. Educ:* Elizabeth Coll., Guernsey, CI. Served with RNVR, 1941-45 (prisoner-of-war, Hong Kong). *Heir: s* John Kenyon Roe Young, *b* 23 April 1947. *Address:* c/o Chartered Bank, Bishopsgate, EC2; Mancunian Building Society, 14 St Peter's Square, Manchester. *Club:* RNVR.

**YOUNG, John Zachary,** FRS 1945; MA; Professor of Anatomy, University College, London, since 1945; *b* 18 March 1907; *s* of Philip Young and Constance Maria Lloyd; *m* 1931, Phyllis Elizabeth, *d* of A. J. Heaney; one *s* one *d. Educ:* Wells House, Malvern Wells; Marlborough Coll.; Magdalen Coll., Oxford (Demy). Senior Demy, Magdalen Coll., 1929, Christopher Welch Scholar, 1928, Naples Biological Scholar, 1928, 1929; Fellow of Magdalen Coll., Oxford, 1931-45; University Demonstrator in Zoology and Comparative Anatomy, Oxford, 1933-45; Rockefeller Fellow, 1936. Fullerton Professor of Physiology, Royal Institution, 1958-61. Royal Medal, Royal Society, 1967. *Publications:* The Life of Vertebrates, 1950; Doubt and Certainty in Science, 1951; The Life of Mammals, 1957; A Model of the Brain, 1964 (lectures); scientific papers, mostly on the nervous system. *Address:* Albany Cottage, Park Village East, NW1. *T:* 01-387 6654.

**YOUNG, Kenneth;** *see* Young, C. K.

**YOUNG, Leslie,** DSc (London), PhD, FRIC; Professor of Biochemistry in the University of London; Head of the Department of Biochemistry, St Thomas's Hospital Medical School, London, SE1, since 1948; Hon. Consultant, St Thomas' Hospital; *b* 27 Feb. 1911; *o c* of John and Ethel Young; *m* 1939, Ruth Elliott; one *s. Educ:* Sir Joseph Williamson's Mathematical Sch., Rochester; Royal College of Science, London; University College, London. Sir Edward Frankland Prize and Medal of Royal Institute of Chemistry, 1932; Bayliss-Starling Memorial Scholar in Physiology, University Coll., London, 1933-34; Asst Lectr in Biochemistry, University College, London, 1934-35; Commonwealth Fund Fellow in Biochemistry at Washington Univ. Medical School and Yale Univ., USA, 1935-37; Lectr in Biochemistry, University Coll., London, 1937-39; Assoc. Prof. of Biochemistry, Univ. of Toronto, 1939-44; chemical warfare research for the Dept of Nat. Defence, Canada, 1940-46; Prof. of Biochemistry, Univ. of Toronto, 1944-47; Reader in Biochemistry, University Coll., London, 1947-48. Hon. Sec., The Biochemical Soc., 1950-53; Vice-Pres., The Royal Institute of Chemistry, 1964-66; Mem., Bd of Governors, St Thomas' Hosp., 1970-. *Publications:* (with G. A. Maw) The Metabolism of Sulphur Compounds, 1958; papers on chem. and biochem. subjects in various scientific journals. *Address:* St Thomas's Hospital Medical School, London, SE1. *T:* 01-928 9292.

**YOUNG, Sir Mark Aitchison,** GCMG, *cr* 1946 (KCMG, *cr* 1934; CMG 1931); KStJ; *b* 30 June 1886; 3rd *s* of late Sir W. Mackworth Young, KCSI; *m* Jospehine Mary, CStJ, *d* of late Walter C. Price; two *s* two *d. Educ:* Eton; King's Coll., Cambridge. Entered Ceylon Civil Service, 1909; served European War from 1915; Principal Assistant Colonial Secretary, Ceylon, 1923-28; Colonial Secretary, Sierra Leone, 1928-30; Chief Secretary to the Government of Palestine, 1930-33; Governor and Commander-in-Chief of Barbados, 1933-38; administered Government of Trinidad and Tobago, Nov. 1937-Feb. 1938; Governor and C-in-C of Tanganyika Territory, 1938-41; assumed duties as Governor and C-in-C, Hong Kong, Sept. 1941; prisoner of war in Japanese hands, Dec. 1941-Aug. 1945; resumed duties in Hong Kong, 1 May 1946; retired, 1947. *Address:* Lang House, Winchester. *T:* Winchester 2480.

*See also B. W. M. Young.*

**YOUNG, Mary Lavinia Bessie,** OBE 1967; Matron of the Westminster Hospital, SW1, 1951-66, retired; *b* 15 Nov. 1911; *d* of late Bennett and Rosalind Young. *Educ:* Girls' High Sch., Shaftesbury, Dorset. SRN, RSCN, SCM. Belgrave Hospital for Sick Children, SW9, 1929-32; KCH, SE5, 1933-36; Chiswick and Ealing Maternity Hospital, 1937; private nursing, 1938. King's College Hospital: Night Sister, 1938-40; Home Sister, 1940-41; Sister, Private Patients' Wing, 1941-44. Asst Matron, Royal Hospital, Richmond Surrey, 1944-45; Asst and Dep. Matron, Westminster Hospital, SW1, 1945-51. *Recreation:* gardening. *Address:* St Martins, Angel Square, Shaftesbury, Dorset. *T:* Shaftesbury 2020.

**YOUNG, Michael,** BSc (Econ), MA, PhD; Director, Institute of Community Studies since 1953; Trustee, Dartington Hall, since 1942; *b* 9 Aug. 1915; father a musician, mother a writer; *m* 1st, 1945, Joan Lawson; two *s* one *d*; 2nd, 1960, Sasha Moorsom; one *s* one *d*. *Educ:* Dartington Hall Sch.; London Univ. Barrister, Gray's Inn. Dir of Political and Economic Planning, 1941-45; Sec., Research Dept, Lab. Party, 1945-51. Chairman: Consumer's Assoc., 1956-65 (Pres., 1965-); Advisory Centre for Education, 1959-; National Extension Coll., 1962-; Social Science Research Council, 1965-68; Dartington Amenity Research Trust, 1967-; Nat. Suggestions Centre, 1968-; Mem., Central Adv. Council for Education, 1963-66; Fellow, Churchill Coll., Cambridge, 1961-66. Hon. LittD, Sheffield. *Publications:* Family and Kinship in East London (with Peter Willmott), 1957; The Rise of the Meritocracy, 1958; Family and Class in a London Suburb (with Peter Willmott), 1960; Innovation and Research in Education, 1965; Learning Begins at Home (with Patrick McGeeney), 1968; (ed) Forecasting and the Social Sciences, 1968. *Recreation:* painting. *Address:* 18 Victoria Park Square, E2. *Club:* Reform.

**YOUNG, Sir Norman (Smith),** Kt 1968; Chairman, Natural Gas Pipelines Authority of South Australia, since 1967; Director: The Bank of Adelaide; Elder Smith Goldsbrough Mort Ltd; South Australian Brewing Co. Ltd (Chairman), and other companies; *b* 24 July 1911; *s* of Thomas and Margaret Young; *m* 1936, Jean Fairbairn Sincock; two *s* one *d*. *Educ:* Norwood High Sch.; University of Adelaide. Member: Adelaide City Council, 1949-60; Municipal Tramways Trust, 1951-67 (Dep. Chairman); Royal Commn on Television, 1953-54; Bankruptcy Law Review Cttee, 1956-62. Fellow, Inst. of Chartered Accountants, 1933; FASA, 1932; Associate in Commerce, University of Adelaide, 1930. *Publication:* Bankruptcy Practice in Australia, 1942. *Recreation:* golf. *Address:* 256 Stanley Street, North Adelaide, South Australia 5006, Australia. *T:* 672262.

**YOUNG, Brig. Peter,** DSO 1942; MC 1942 and two Bars 1943; Editor, Purnell's History of The First World War, since 1970; *b* 28 July 1915; *s* of Dallas H. W. Young, MBE, and Irene Barbara Lushington Mellor; *m* 1950, Joan Duckworth; no *c*. *Educ:* Monmouth Sch.; Trinity Coll., Oxford. 2nd Lieut, Bedfordshire and Hertfordshire Regt, 1939. Served War of 1939-45: BEF Dunkirk (wounded), 1940; No 3 Commando, 1940; raids on Guernsey, 1940; Lofoten and Vaagso, 1941, Dieppe, 1942, Sicily and Italy, 1943; comd No 3 Commando, 1943-44; Normandy, 1944; Arakan, 1944-45; comd 1st Commando Bde, 1945-46. Commanded 9th Regt Arab Legion, 1953-56. Reader in Military History, Royal Military Acad., Sandhurst, 1959-69. Gen. Editor, Military Memoirs series, 1967-. FRHistS; FSA 1960; FRGS 1968. Captain-Generall, The Sealed Knot, Soc. of Cavaliers, 1968. Order of El Istiqlal (Jordan) 3rd Class, 1954. *Publications:* Bedouin Command, 1956; Storm from the Sea, 1958; The Great Civil War (with late Lt-Col Alfred H. Burne, DSO), 1959; Cromwell, 1962; Hastings to Culloden (with John Adair), 1964; World War 1939-45, 1966; Edgehill, 1642: The Campaign and the Battle, 1967; The British Army, 1642-1970, 1967; The Israeli Campaign, 1967, 1967; (ed) Decisive Battles of the Second World War, 1967; Charge (with Col J. P. Lawford), 1967; (jt editor) The Civil War: Richard Atkyns and John Gwyn, 1967; Oliver Cromwell, 1968; Cropredy Bridge, 1644 (with Margaret Toynbee), 1970; Marston Moor, 1644, 1970; numerous articles in Army Historical Research Journal and Chambers's Encyclopædia. *Recreations:* collecting model soldiers and military pictures, war games, equitation. *Address:* Lovel End, Windsor Forest, Berks. *Clubs:* United Service, Savage, The Sette of Odd Volumes.

**YOUNG, Ven. Peter Claude;** Archdeacon of Cornwall and Canon Residentiary of Truro Cathedral, since 1965; *b* 21 July 1916; *s* of Rev. Thomas Young and of Mrs Ethel Ashton Young; *m* 1944, Marjorie Désirée Rose; two *s*. *Educ:* Exeter Sch.; Exeter Coll., Oxford; Wycliffe Hall, Oxford. BA 1938, BLitt 1940, MA 1942, Oxon. Asst Curate of Ottery St Mary, 1940-44; Asst Curate of Stoke Damerel, i/c of St Bartholomew's, Milehouse, Plymouth, 1944-47; Rector of Highweek, Newton Abbot, 1947-59; Vicar of Emmanuel, Plymouth, 1959-65. *Recreations:* motoring, fishing, reading. *Address:* Petherton, Kenwyn Road, Truro, Cornwall. *T:* Truro 2866.

**YOUNG, Maj.-Gen. Peter George Francis,** CB 1965; CBE 1958; retired 1968; *b* 15 July 1912; *s* of late Major Reginald Bradley and Mrs Young; *m* 1949, Patricia FitzGerald, *d* of late Lt-Col A. E. FitzGerald and late Mrs Ronald Beauchamp; one *s* one *d*. *Educ:* Winchester Coll.; Royal Military Coll., Sandhurst. Commissioned Oxford and Bucks Light Inf., 1932; served with Oxford and Bucks Light Inf. and RWAFF, 1932-40; served with Airborne Forces, 1941-48; comd 1st Bn Oxford and Bucks Light Inf., 1952-55; comd 44 Parachute Bde, TA, 1955-58; comd 1st Bde, Royal Nigeria Regt, 1958-61; War Office, 1961-62; GOC Cyprus District, 1962-64; Director of Infantry, MoD, 1965-67. *Recreations:* shooting, polo, bird watching. *Address:* The Lodge, Rushall, Pewsey, Wilts. *T:* Upavon 300. *Club:* Army and Navy.

**YOUNG, Sir Richard (Dilworth),** Kt 1970; BSc, MIMechE; Managing Director and Chairman of Alfred Herbert Ltd since 1966 (Deputy Chairman, 1965-66); Chairman, Herbert BSA, since 1967; Director: Rugby Portland Cement Co.; Commonwealth Finance Development Corp. Ltd; Ingersoll Milling Machine Co., USA; *b* 9 April 1914; *s* of Philip Young and Constance Maria Lloyd; *m* 1951, Jean Barbara Paterson Lockwood, *d* of F. G. Lockwood; four *s*. *Educ:* Bromsgrove; Bristol Univ. Joined Weldless Steel Tube Co. Ltd, 1934; served with various Tube Investments companies in production and engineering capacities until 1944; Representative of TI in S America and Man. Director of Tubos Britanicos (Argentina) Ltda, 1945-50; Man. Director of TI (Export) Ltd, 1950-53; Sales Director of TI Aluminium Ltd, 1953-56; Assistant to Chairman of Tube Investments Ltd, 1957-60; Director, 1958; Asst Man. Director, 1959; Managing Director, 1961-64. Member: Council BIM, 1960-; Council, IMechE, 1969-; Adv. Cttee on Scientific Manpower, 1962;

Council, Warwick Univ., 1966-; Central Adv. Council on Science and Technol., 1967-. *Address:* Bearley Manor, Bearley, near Stratford-on-Avon, Warwickshire. *T:* Snitterfield 220.

**YOUNG, Robert Christopher Mackworth-,** CVO 1968 (MVO 1961); Librarian, Windsor Castle, and Assistant Keeper of The Queen's Archives, since 1958; *b* 12 Feb. 1920; *s* of late Gerard Mackworth-Young; *m* 1953, Rosemarie, *d* of W. C. R. Aue, Menton, France; one *s. Educ:* Eton; King's Coll., Cambridge. Pres., Cambridge Union Soc., 1948. Served in RAF, 1939-46. HM Foreign Service, 1948-55; Deputy Librarian, Windsor Castle, 1955-58. *Address:* Garden House, Windsor Castle. *Club:* Roxburghe.

**YOUNG, Robert Henry;** Consultant Orthopædic Surgeon, St George's Hospital, SW1, since 1946; Hon. Consultant, St Peter's Hospital, Chertsey, since 1939; *b* 6 Oct. 1903; *s* of James Allen Young and Constance Barrow Young; *m* 1st, 1929, Nancy Willcox; 2nd, 1961, Norma, *d* of Leslie Williams. *Educ:* Sherborne Sch.; Emmanuel Coll., Cambridge; St Thomas' Hospital, SE1. *Publications:* numerous articles in leading medical journals. *Recreations:* shooting, fishing, flying. *Address:* 48 Wimpole Street, W1. *T:* 01-935 3987. *Clubs:* St James', Oxford and Cambridge University.

**YOUNG, Robert S.;** Play Producer and Adjudicator; retired; *b* near Manchester, 28 May 1891; *s* of late Alexander Young, Manchester, merchant, and Elizabeth Stevenson, both from Sligo, Ireland; *m* 1923, Doris Lillian Hill, Salisbury; no *c. Educ:* Manchester Grammar Sch. Travelled in South America, South Africa, seven years in New Zealand; invited to stand for NZ Parliament for Labour; joined NZ Forces when war broke out in 1914; saw service at Anzac and in France (twice wounded); after the war joined Sir Frank Benson on the stage, founded the County Players Repertory Theatre at Tonbridge, Kent. MP (Lab) Islington North, 1929-31; actively interested in Labour movement for past 50 years. *Publication:* Cricket on the Green. *Recreations:* lacrosse, keen cricketer. *Address:* Ham Cottage, Albourne Road, Hurstpierpoint, Sussex.

**YOUNG, Roger William,** MA; STh, FRSE; Headmaster of George Watson's College, Edinburgh, since 1958; *b* 15 Nov. 1923; *yr s* of Charles Bowden Young and Dr Ruth Young, *qv*; *m* 1950, Caroline Mary Christie; two *s* two *d. Educ:* Dragon Sch., Oxford; Westminster Sch. (King's Scholar); Christ Church, Oxford (Scholar). Served War of 1939-45, RNVR, 1942-45. Classical Mods, 1946, Lit Hum 1948. Resident Tutor, St Catharine's, Cumberland Lodge, Windsor, 1949-51; Asst Master, The Manchester Grammar Sch., 1951-58. 1st Class in Archbishop's examination in Theology (Lambeth Diploma), 1957. Participant, US State Dept Foreign Leader Program, 1964. Member: Educational Research Bd of SSRC, 1966-70; Court, Edinburgh Univ., 1967-; Public Schools Commn, 1968-70; Edinburgh Festival Council, 1970-; Hon. Sec., Headmasters' Assoc. of Scotland, 1968-. *Publications:* Lines of Thought, 1958; Everybody's Business, 1968; Everybody's World, 1970. *Recreations:* gardening, photography, climbing, golf. *Address:* 27 Merchiston Gardens, Edinburgh EH10 5DD. *T:* 031-337 6880.

**YOUNG, Ruth,** CBE 1941 (MBE 1928); MB, ChB; *b* 26 Jan. 1884; *d* of William B. Wilson, Flax Merchant, Dundee; *m* 1917, C. B. Young, sometime Reader in English, Delhi Univ.; two *s* one *d. Educ:* High Sch., Dundee; St Andrews Univ. BSc 1907, MB, ChB 1909; Postgraduate Study, Vienna and Dresden. Lecturer, Women's Christian Medical Coll., Ludhiana, Punjab, India, 1910-16; Professor of Surgery, Lady Hardinge Medical Coll., Delhi, 1916-17; voluntary work till 1925, chiefly in Maternity and Child Welfare; Personal Assistant to Chief Medical Officer, Women's Medical Service of India, 1925-31; Director, Maternity and Child Welfare Bureau, Indian Red Cross Society, 1931-35; Principal, Lady Hardinge Medical Coll., New Delhi, 1936-40; Rockefeller Fellowship to study Public Health Nursing in China, Japan, Canada and USA, 1934. In Ethiopia, to advise Ethiopian Women's Work Association on Welfare Work, 1943. Medical Adviser, Women's Foreign Mission, Church of Scotland, retired, 1951. Kaisar-i-Hind Gold Medal, 1936; Silver Jubilee and Coronation Medals. *Publications:* The Work of Medical Women in India (with Dr M. I. Balfour), 1929; The Science of Health, 1932; Handbook for Health Visitors (Indian Red Cross Society), 1933; numerous pamphlets on Maternity and Child Welfare, Health, etc., relating to India. *Recreation:* gardening. *Address:* 220 Bruntsfield Place, Edinburgh 10. *T:* 031-229 3103.

*See also Roger William Young.*

**YOUNG, Stephen,** JP; MB, ChB, FRCSGlas; Hon. Consulting Surgeon, Royal Infirmary, Glasgow; Lecturer, Otorhino-Laryngology, University of Glasgow; *b* 16 May 1894; *s* of James Young, Merchant, Glanderstan, Renfrewshire, and Glasgow, and Margaret MacAlister; *m* Jessica Adamson Dickie, Ayrshire. *Educ:* Privately; Allen Glen's Sch.; Glasgow Univ.; Edinburgh Univ. RSO Scottish Branch, British Red Cross, 1917-19; Resident, Dept of Medicine, Western Infirmary, 1919-20; Senior ENT Registrar, Edinburgh Royal Infirmary, 1921; ENT Surgeon, Out-Patient Dept, Royal Infirmary, Glasgow, 1922, later Senior Assistant Surgeon, ENT Dept; Surgeon-in-Charge of ENT Wards, Royal Infirmary, 1947; ENT Consultant, Corporation of Glasgow; Regional ENT Consultant, Lanarkshire; Member: Board of Management, Royal Infirmary Group of Hospitals, 1947-59; General Advisory Council, BBC. Burgess and Freeman of City of Glasgow. *Publications:* numerous scientific publications and contributions to BMJ, Glasgow Medical Jl, Jl of Laryngology and Otology, etc. *Recreations:* chess, beagling, golf, breeding and judging hounds. *Address:* 65 Kelvin Court, Glasgow W2. *T:* 041-334 2302. *Clubs:* Kennel; Royal Scottish Automobile (Glasgow).

**YOUNG, Sir Stephen Stewart Templeton,** 3rd Bt, *cr* 1945; *b* 24 May 1947; *s* of Sir Alastair Young, 2nd Bt, and Dorothy Constance Marcelle (*d* 1964), *d* of late Lt-Col Charles Ernest Chambers, and *widow* of Lt J. H. Grayburn, VC, 43rd LI; *S* father, 1963. *Educ:* Rugby; Trinity Coll., Oxford; Edinburgh Univ. Voluntary Service Overseas, Sudan, 1968-69. *Address:* Auchengare, Rhu, Dunbartonshire.

**YOUNG, Maj.-Gen. Thomas,** CB 1951; OBE 1945; retired, 1953; *b* 4 June 1893; *s* of William Fulton Young, Kilmarnock, and Euphemia Murray Wilson, Crosshouse; *m* 1922, Alison Rowe; no *c. Educ:* University of Glasgow. MB, ChB (Glasgow) 1915; MD 1951; DPH (Cambridge) (Dist. in Principles of Hygiene), 1924; Lieut, RAMC (SR) 1914; served European War, Dardanelles, MEF, EEF, 1915-22 (despatches twice); India, 1925-31 and 1934-39. Major, 1927; Lt-Col, 1941; Temp. Major, 1919 and 1924; Temp. Lt-Col, 1939; Temp. Col, 1941; Dep. Dir of Hygiene, BNAF and CMF, 1942-46 (despatches twice); Col, 1945; Comdt Army School of Hygiene, 1946; Brig., 1947; Dir of Medical Services, FARELF, 1948; Maj.-Gen., 1949; KHP, 1950; QHP, 1952-53. Dir, Army Health, 1949-53; retired, 1953. Col Comdt, RAMC, 1955-61. Legion of Merit (USA) Légionnaire, 1946; Medaille de la Reconnaissance Française, 1945. *Publications:* contributions to Journal of RAMC. *Recreation:* gardening. *Address:* Flat 25, Swallowfield Park, near Reading, Berks. *T:* Reading 882330.

**YOUNG, Thomas,** CBE 1953 (OBE 1948); TD 1955; Sheriff Substitute of Stirling, Dunbarton and Clackmannan at Falkirk, 1964-69 (of Lanarkshire at Airdrie, 1955-64); *b* 7 Nov. 1896; *s* of Thomas Downie Young, Edinburgh; *m* 1924, Lilias Adie, *d* of Andrew Allan, Edinburgh and Leith; one *s. Educ:* George Heriot's Sch. Edinburgh Univ. WS 1927; in practice until 1955. Formerly Member: Schuster Cttee on Legal Aid for the Forces; Royal Commn on Marriage and Divorce; Legal Aid Scheme Making Cttee, Central Cttee and Amending Cttee Scotland (Chm.); Legal Aid Cttee for England and Scotland (Jt Chm.); Rules Council (Court of Session); Council of Law Soc. of Scotland; WS Council; Jt Cttee of Edinburgh Legal Socs; Member of Law Reform Cttee (Scotland). Solicitor in Scotland to Ministry of Pensions; Examiner to Police Examinations (Scotland) Board. JP Edinburgh. Served in TA, 1939-52, in Royal Scots and latterly in command of various units of RA. *Address:* 27 Campbell Road, Edinburgh EH12 6DT. *T:* 031-337 5176.

**YOUNG, Sir (Thomas) Eric (Boswell),** Kt 1949; retired; *b* 6 Feb. 1891; *s* of Dr Moffat Young; *m* 1928, Margaret Mary, *d* of Rev. A. E. Hayward, Emley, Yorks; two *s* one *d. Educ:* Loretto; Durham Univ. Mining Engineer with experience in Durham, Northumberland, Yorkshire, Kent, Nottinghamshire and Derbyshire Coalfields. National Production Director, Ministry of Fuel and Power, 1942-43; Member NCB, 1946-50; former Managing Director, Bolsover Colliery Co. Ltd, re-elected a Director in 1950. *Publication:* Simultaneous Cutter and Loader for Longwall Workings (Trans. Inst. Min. E.). *Recreations:* shooting, yachting. *Address:* Willow Cottage, Phyllis Road, Claremont, Cape Town, South Africa. *T:* 77-9106 Cape Town.

**YOUNG, Wayland;** author; (2nd Baron Kennet, *cr* 1935, of the Dene); *b* 2 Aug. 1923; *s* of 1st Baron Kennet, PC, GBE, DSO, DSC, and of Kathleen (who *m* 1st, Captain Robert Falcon Scott, CVO, RN, and died 1947); *S* father 1960; *m* 1948, Elizabeth Ann, *d* of Captain Bryan Fullerton Adams, *qv*; one *s* five *d. Educ:* Stowe; Trinity Coll., Cambridge; Perugia; Harvard Univ., USA. Served in Royal Navy as Ordinary Seaman, Midshipman and Sub-Lieut, 1942-45. Foreign Office, 1946-47, and 1949-51. Rapporteur, Defence Cttee, Parliamentary Assembly, WEU, 1962-65; Parly Sec., Min. of Housing and Local Govt (in House of Lords), 1966-70. Chm., Adv. Cttee on Oil Pollution of the Sea, 1970-. Hon. FRIBA. Editor of Disarmament and Arms Control, 1962-65. *Publications:* The Italian Left, 1949; The Deadweight, 1952; Now or Never, 1953; Old London Churches (with Elizabeth Young), 1956; The Montesi Scandal, 1957; Still Alive Tomorrow, 1958; Strategy for Survival, 1959; The Socialist Imagination (with Elizabeth Young), 1960; Disarmament: Finnegan's Choice (with Elizabeth Young), 1961; The Profumo Affair, 1963; Eros Denied, 1965; Thirty-Four Articles, 1965; (ed) Existing Mechanisms of Arms Control, 1965. *Heir: s* Hon. William Aldus Young, *b* 24 May 1957. *Address:* c/o A. D. Peters, 10 Buckingham Street, WC2.

**YOUNG, William Hilary,** CMG 1957; Ambassador to Colombia 1966-70; *b* 14 Jan. 1913; *s* of late Rev. Arthur John Christopher Young and Ethel Margaret (*née* Goodwin); *m* 1946, Barbara Gordon Richmond, *d* of Gordon Park Richmond; one *s* one *d. Educ:* Marlborough Coll.; Emmanuel Coll., Cambridge. Entered Consular Service, 1935; served HM Legation, Tehran, 1938-41; Foreign Office, 1941-45; 1st Secretary, 1945; Berlin (Political Division, Control Commission), 1945-48; HM Legation, Budapest, 1948-50; attached to IDC, 1951; Counsellor: UK High Commn, New Delhi, 1952-54; Foreign Office, 1954-57; Minister, Moscow, 1957-60; Senior Civilian Instructor, IDC, 1960-62; Minister, British Embassy, Pretoria and Cape Town, 1962-65; Fellow, Harvard University Center for Internat. Affairs, 1965-66. *Address:* c/o Foreign and Commonwealth Office, SW1.

**YOUNG, Sir William Neil,** 10th Bt, *cr* 1769; stockbroker; *b* 22 Jan. 1941; *s* of Captain William Elliot Young, RAMC (killed in action 27 May 1942), and Mary, *d* of late Rev. John Macdonald; *S* grandfather, 1944; *m* 1965, Christine Veronica Morley, *o d* of R. B. Morley, Buenos Aires; one *s* one *d. Educ:* Wellington Coll.; Sandhurst. Captain, 16th/5th The Queen's Royal Lancers, retired 1970. *Recreations:* helicopter flying, ski-ing, sailing, tennis, shooting. *Heir: s* William Lawrence Elliot Young, *b* 26 May 1970. *Address:* 20 Briantspuddle, Dorset.

**YOUNG-HERRIES, Michael Alexander Robert;** *see* Herries.

**YOUNGER,** family name of **Viscount Younger of Leckie.**

**YOUNGER OF LECKIE,** 3rd Viscount, *cr* 1923; **Edward George Younger;** OBE 1940; 3rd Bt of Leckie, *cr* 1911; Lord Lieutenant, County of Stirling, since 1964; Colonel, Argyll and Sutherland Highlanders (TA); *b* 21 Nov. 1906; *er s* of 2nd Viscount and Maud (*d* 1957), *e d* of Sir John Gilmour, 1st Bt; *S* father 1946; *m* 1930, Evelyn Margaret, *e d* of late Alexander Logan McClure, KC; three *s* one *d. Educ:* Winchester; New Coll., Oxford. Served War of 1939-45 (OBE). *Heir: s* Hon. George (Kenneth Hotson) Younger, *qv. Address:* Leckie, Gargunnock, Stirling. *T:* Gargunnock 281. *Club:* New (Edinburgh).

*See also Rt Hon. K. G. Younger.*

**YOUNGER, Maj.-Gen. Allan Elton,** DSO 1944; OBE 1962; MA; Chief of Staff, HQ Allied Forces Northern Europe, Oslo, since 1970; *b* 4 May 1919; *s* of late Brig. Arthur Allan Shakespear Younger, DSO, and Marjorie Rhoda Younger (*née* Halliley); *m* 1942, Diana Lanyon; three *d. Educ:* Gresham's; RMA Woolwich; Christ's Coll., Cambridge. Commnd RE, 1939; France and Belgium, 1940; France, Holland and Germany, 1944-45; Burma, 1946-47; Malaya, 1948; Korea, 1950-51; RMA Sandhurst, 1954-57; Bt Lt-Col 1959; comd 36 Corps Engineer Regt in UK and Kenya, 1960-62; Instructor US Army Comd and Gen. Staff Coll., Fort Leavenworth, 1963-66; Programme Evaluation Gp, 1966-68; Chief Engr, Army Strategic Comd, 1968-69. Silver Star (US), 1951. *Publications:* contribs to RUSI Jl, Military Review (USA). *Recreations:* ski-ing, writing. *Address:* Southern Haye, Heath Rise, Camberley, Surrey. *T:* Camberley 21214. *Club:* Army and Navy.

**YOUNGER, Charles Frank Johnston,** DSO 1944; TD 1952; Director: Scottish & Newcastle Breweries Ltd; Bank of Scotland; Norwich Union Life and Fire Societies, and other companies; Chairman, Brewers Society, London, 1963-64 (Vice-President, 1965); UK Delegation to EFTA Brewing Industry Council, 1964-; Council of CBI, 1965-; Member of Royal Company of Archers (Queen's Body Guard for Scotland); Lieut-Colonel, RA; *b* 11 Dec. 1908; *s* of late Major Charles Arthur Johnston Younger, King's Dragoon Guards; *m* 1935, Joanna, *e d* of late Rev. John Kyrle Chatfield, BD, MA, LLB; one *d*. *Educ:* Royal Naval Coll., Dartmouth. Served Royal Navy, 1926-37. Joined William Younger & Co. Ltd, Brewers, Edinburgh, 1937. Served War of 1939-45 (despatches, DSO); RA (Field), 15th Scottish Division, 1939-41; 17th Indian Light Div., Burma, 1942-45; Commanded 129th Lowland Field Regt, RA, 1942-45 and 278th Lowland Field Regt RA (TA), 1946-52. *Recreations:* country pursuits. *Address:* Gledswood, near Melrose, Roxburghshire. *T:* Melrose 2234; 41 Portman Square, W1. *T:* 01-486 1948. *Clubs:* Boodle's, Pratt's, Flyfishers'; New (Edinburgh).

**YOUNGER, Hon. George (Kenneth Hotson),** TD 1964; DL; MP (C) Ayr, since 1964; Parliamentary Under-Secretary of State, Scottish Office, since 1970; *b* 22 Sept. 1931; *e s* and *heir* of 3rd Viscount Younger of Leckie, *qv*; *m* 1954, Diana Rhona, *er d* of Captain G. S. Tuck, RN, Little London, Chichester, Sussex; three *s* one *d*. *Educ:* Cargilfield Sch., Edinburgh; Winchester Coll.; New Coll., Oxford. Commnd in Argyll and Sutherland Highlanders, 1950; served BAOR and Korea, 1951; 7th Bn Argyll and Sutherland Highlanders (TA), 1951-65. Director: George Younger & Son Ltd, 1958-68; J. G. Thomson & Co. Ltd, Leith, 1962-66; Maclachlans Ltd, 1968-70. Contested (U) North Lanarkshire, 1959; Unionist Candidate for Kinross and West Perthshire, 1963, but stood down in favour of Sir A. Douglas-Home. Scottish Conservative Whip, 1965-67; Dep. Chairman, Conservative Party in Scotland, 1967-. Member of Queen's Body Guard for Scotland (Royal Company of Archers). DL Stirlingshire, 1968. *Recreations:* music, tennis, golf. *Address:* Easter Leckie, Gargunnock, Stirlingshire. *T:* Gargunnock 274. *Clubs:* Caledonian; Highland Brigade.

**YOUNGER, Sir James (Paton),** Kt 1961; CBE 1945; JP; Chairman: George Younger & Son Ltd, since 1947; Scottish Central Glass Works Ltd, 1947-65; Western Regional Hospital Board, Scotland, 1955-63; United Caledonian Breweries Ltd, 1960-68; President, Tennent Caledonian Breweries Ltd, 1968; Lord Lieutenant, County of Clackmannan, 1955-66; *b* 19 June 1891; *s* of James Younger, LLD, Mount Melville, St Andrews, and Annie, *d* of J. Thomson Paton, Alloa; *m* 1921, Rachel Howard, *d* of Paul Waterhouse, Yattendon Court, Berkshire; three *s* one *d*. *Educ:* Eton; Balliol Coll., Oxford. Captain, 3rd Bn Argyll and Sutherland Highlanders; served European War, 1914-18. Director: United Breweries Ltd; Brewers Food Supply Co. Ltd; Charrington United Breweries Ltd. Member, Royal Company of Archers (Queen's Body Guard for Scotland), 1921. JP County of Clackmannan, 1933. *Recreation:* shooting. *Address:* Arnsbrae, Cambus, Alloa, Clackmannanshire. *T:* Alloa 3516; Mount Melville, St Andrews. *T:* St Andrews 2542. *Clubs:* Carlton; New (Edinburgh).

**YOUNGER, Maj.-Gen. John Edward Talbot,** CB 1945; *b* 2 Nov. 1888; *yr s* of late Colonel J. Younger, Royal Artillery, Langshaw Bush, Moffat, Dumfriesshire; *m* 1919, Harriot Bisset, *d* of late Sir Robert Holmes, KCB, Rathfarnham; (one *s* one *d* decd). *Educ:* Wellington Coll.; RMA, Woolwich. 2nd Lieut, RFA, 1909; France and Belgium, 1914-18 (despatches); School of Artillery, 1919-23; Instructor in Gunnery, Southern Command, 1931-34; Dep. Asst Director of Artillery, War Office, 1934-36; Bt Lt-Col, 1936; Asst Dir of Artillery, War Office, 1938-39; Bt Col, 1938; Commander 57th AA Brigade, 1939-40; Commander 3rd AA Division, 1940-42; General Staff, Washington, USA, 1942-43; retired pay, 1944. Red Cross Comr to USSR, 1945. Sec. Ven. Order of St John of Jerusalem, 1944-50; KStJ. Founder and Vice-Pres. of the Army Ski Assoc.; Vice-Pres., Altus Climbing Club; Pres., Royal Artillery Alpine Club. American Medal of Freedom with Bronze Palm; Médaille de la reconnaissance Française en vermeil. *Recreation:* enjoying old age. *Address:* Gowrie House, Kilmington, Devon. *Clubs:* Army and Navy, Ski Club of Great Britain.

**YOUNGER, Rt. Hon. Kenneth Gilmour,** PC 1951; Director, Royal Institute of International Affairs, since 1959; *b* 15 Dec. 1908; 2nd *s* of 2nd Viscount Younger of Leckie, DSO; *m* 1934, Elizabeth Kirsteen Stewart; one *s* two *d*. *Educ:* Winchester; New Coll., Oxford. Barrister, Inner Temple, 1932. Served Army, 1940-45, Temporary Major, Intelligence Corps; Chairman, UNRRA Cttee of Council for Europe, 1946-47. MP (Lab) Grimsby, 1945-59; Parly Under-Sec., Home Office, 1947-50; Minister of State, 1950-51. Joint Vice-Chm., Royal Inst. of Internat. Affairs, 1953-55, re-elected Vice-Chm., 1958-59. Mem. Cttee of Inquiry into Security Procedures and Practices, 1961; Chm., Cttee of Inquiry on Privacy, 1970-. chairman: Howard League for Penal Reform, 1960-; Bd of Trustees, UN Inst. for Training and Research, 1965-; Advisory Council on the Penal System, 1966-; Council St George's Hosp. Medical Sch., 1965-; Bd of Governors, St George's Hosp., 1966-69. Hon. Doctorate in Law, St John's Univ., 1968. *Publications:* (joint editor) Fabian International Essays, 1957; contrib. to New Fabian Colonial Essays, 1959; The Public Service in New States, 1960; Changing Perspectives in British Foreign Policy, 1964. *Recreations:* walking, music, sailing. *Address:* 3 Clareville Grove, SW7.

**YOUNGER, Maj.-Gen. Ralph,** CB 1957; CBE 1954; DSO 1945; MC 1941; JP; DL; *b* 12 July 1904; *e s* of late William Younger, Ravenswood, Melrose; *m* 1938, Greta Mary, *d* of late A. W. Turnbull, Clifton, Maybank, Yeovil; one *s* one *d*. *Educ:* Charterhouse, Trinity Coll., Cambridge. 2nd Lieut, 7th Hussars, 1926; served War of 1939-45 (MC, DSO), 7th Hussars, Western Desert, 1940-41; Burma, 1942; 3rd Carabineers, India, 1942-43; Burma, 1944; Comdr 255 Ind. Tank Bde, Burma, 1945; Lieut-Colonel comdg Royal Scots Greys, 1947-48; Commander: 30 Lowland Armoured Bde, TA, 1949-50; 7th Armoured Bde, 1950-53; Royal Armoured Corps Centre, 1953-54; GOC North Midland District and Commander 49th Armoured Division, TA, 1954-57; retired, 1958. Colonel, 7th Queen's Own Hussars, 1952-58, of Queen's Own Hussars, 1958-62; Commandant, Army Cadet Force (Scotland), 1959-65; Chairman, T&AFA, Roxburgh, Berwick and Selkirk, 1966-68. Joint Master Duke of Buccleuch's Foxhounds, 1960-66; Member Royal Company of Archers (Queen's Body Guard for Scotland). JP Roxburghshire, 1961; DL Roxburgh, 1962. *Recreations:* hunting, fishing, and shooting. *Address:* Ravenswood, Melrose.

Roxburghshire. *T:* St Boswells 2219. *Clubs:* Cavalry, Army and Navy, MCC.

**YOUNGER, Sir William McEwan,** 1st Bt, *cr* 1964, of Fountainbridge; DSO 1942; DL; Chairman: Scottish & Newcastle Breweries Ltd, 1960-69 (Managing Director, 1960-67); The Second Scottish Investment Trust Company Ltd, since 1965; Director: Scottish Television; British Linen Bank, and other companies; *b* 6 Sept. 1905; *y s* of late William Younger, Ravenswood, Melrose; *m* 1936, Nora Elizabeth Balfour (marr. diss., 1967); one *d. Educ:* Winchester; Balliol Coll., Oxford. Served War of 1939-45 (despatches, DSO); Western Desert, 1941-43; Italy, 1943-45; Lt-Col, RA. Hon. Sec., Scottish Unionist Assoc., 1955-64. Mem. Queen's Body Guard for Scotland. Chm., Highland Tourist (Cairngorm Development) Ltd, 1966-. DL Midlothian, 1956. *Recreations:* mountaineering and fishing. *Heir:* none. *Address:* 29 Moray Place, Edinburgh. *T:* 031-225 8173; 18/39 Hyde Park Gate, SW7. *T:* 01-584 8155; Craignish, Ardfern, by Lochgilphead, Argyll. *T:* Barbreck 208. *Clubs:* Carlton, Alpine; New (Edinburgh).

**YOUNGER, Sir William Robert,** 2nd Bt, *cr* 1911; late Diplomatic Service; *b* 27 Oct. 1888; *s* of Sir William Younger, 1st Bt, and Helen Caroline Benyon (Nellie) (*d* 1925), *e d* of Col Sir Robert Gunter, 1st Bt, MP; *S* father, 1937; *m* 1st, 1915, Joan Gwendoline (from whom he obtained a divorce, 1923), *d* of Hon. Louis Johnstone, Lavington Hall, Ipswich; two *s* two *d*; 2nd, 1930, Nellie Archbold (*d* 1960). *Educ:* Harrow; Christ Church, Oxford. *Heir: s* John William Younger, MBE, 1945, Lieut-Colonel, Coldstream Guards [*b* 18 Nov. 1920; *m* 1st, 1948, Mrs Stella Jane Dodd (who obtained a divorce, 1953); one *s* one *d*; 2nd, 1953, Marcella Granito, Princess Pignatelli Di Belmonte]. *Address:* 4 Belgrave Crescent, Edinburgh.

**YOUNGHUSBAND, Dame Eileen (Louise),** DBE 1964 (CBE 1955; MBE 1946); JP; formerly Chairman Hammersmith Juvenile Court; *b* 1 Jan. 1902; *d* of late Sir Francis Younghusband, KCSI, KCIE. *Educ:* privately; London Univ. Social work in S and E London, 1924-29; JP 1933. Lecturer, London School of Economics, 1929-39 and 1944-57; Adviser, Nat. Institute for Social Work Training, 1961-67; Principal Officer for Employment and Training, Nat. Assoc. of Girls' Clubs, 1939-44; and Director of British Council Social Welfare Courses, 1942-44; Welfare investigation for Nat. Assistance Board, 1944; seconded from time to time to UNRRA and the United Nations, 1945-; co-opted member of McNair Cttee, 1943; member of departmental Cttee on Social Workers in the Mental Health Services, 1948; member Cttee of Enquiry into the Law and Practice Relating to Charitable Trusts; Member Cttee on the Probation Service, 1962; Chairman, Ministry of Health Working Party on Social Workers in the Health and Welfare Services; President, Internat. Assoc. of Schools of Social Work, 1961-68; member numerous Cttees for penal reform, child care, youth service, care of old people, family welfare, social studies, international social work, etc. LLD (*hc*): Univ. of British Columbia, 1955; Univ. of Nottingham, 1963; DLitt (*hc*) Univ. of Bradford, 1968; DUniv. York, 1968. Hon. Fellow LSE, 1961. *Publications:* The Employment and Training of Social Workers (Carnegie, UK Trust), 1946; Social Work in Britain (Carnegie UK Trust), 1951; Third International Survey of Training for Social Work (UN, NY, 1959); Social Work and Social Change (London), 1964. Numerous articles in social service publications. *Recreations:* gardening, reading and travel. *Address:* 24 Lansdowne Road, London, W11. *T:* 01-727 4613; Byworthdean, Petworth, Sussex. *T:* Petworth 2327.

**YOUNGSON, Professor Alexander John;** Professor of Political Economy, University of Edinburgh, since 1963; *b* 28 Sept. 1918; *s* of Alexander Brown, MA, MB, ChB and Helen Youngson; *m* 1948, Elizabeth Gisborne Naylor; one *s* one *d. Educ:* Aberdeen Grammar Sch.; Aberdeen Univ. Pilot, Fleet Air Arm, 1940-45. MA Aberdeen Univ., 1947; Commonwealth Fellow, 1947-48. Lecturer, University of St Andrews, 1948-50; Lecturer, University of Cambridge, 1950-58. DLitt Aberdeen Univ., 1952. *Publications:* The American Economy, 1860-1940, 1951; Possibilities of Economic Progress, 1959; The British Economy, 1920-1957, 1960; The Making of Classical Edinburgh, 1966; Overhead Capital, 1967; contrib. to various journals devoted to economics and economic history. *Recreations:* gardening, fishing. *Address:* 7b Blackford Road, Edinburgh 9. *T:* 031-447 4321.

**YOUNSON, Maj.-Gen. Eric John,** OBE 1952; BSc; CEng, MIEEE, MBIM, FRAeS, FRSA; Vice-President, Ordnance Board, since 1970; *b* 1 March 1919; *o s* of Ernest M. Younson, MLitt, BCom, Jarrow; *m* 1946, Jean Beaumont Carter, BA; three *d. Educ:* Jarrow Grammar Sch.; Univ. of Durham; Royal Military Coll. of Science. Served War of 1939-45: commissioned, RA, 1940; UK and NW Europe (despatches). Directing Staff, RMCS, 1953-55; Atomic Weapons Research Estab., 1957-58; Attaché (Washington) as rep. of Chief Scientific Adviser, 1958-61; Head of Defence Science 3, MoD, 1961-63; Dep. Dir of Artillery, 1964-66; Dir of Guided Weapons Trials and Ranges, Min. of Technology, 1967-69. *Publications:* articles on gunnery and scientific subjects in Service jls. *Recreations:* photography, electronics. *Address:* 7 Pondwick Road, Harpenden, Herts. *T:* Harpenden 5892.

**YOUSUF, Lt-Gen. Mohammed,** Nishan-e-Liaqat; Ambassador for Pakistan to Afghanistan, 1963-68; *b* 14 Oct. 1908; *m* 1936, Zubeida Begum; four *s* two *d. Educ:* Royal Military Coll., Sandhurst. Attached for a year to York and Lancaster Regt; subsequently posted to 7th Light Cavalry. Served War of 1939-45, campaigns in Arakan and Assam. Later posted to 18th Cavalry. Supervised evacuation of refugees from across Indian borders, 1947; Member Pakistan Nationalisation Cttee; in comd Bde, Jan. 1948; Maj.-Gen., 1948; GOC East Pakistan, 1950-51; later Chief of General Staff, Pakistan Army; Lt-Gen., 1954; retired from Army, 1956. High Commissioner for Pakistan in Australia and New Zealand, Dec. 1956-April 1959; High Commissioner for Pakistan in UK, May 1959-Sept. 1963, and Ambassador to Ireland, Aug. 1962-Sept. 1963. *Recreations:* polo and shooting. *Address:* c/o Ministry of Foreign Affairs, Rawalpindi, Pakistan.

**YOXALL, Harry Waldo,** OBE 1966; MC 1916 and Bar 1917; JP; Chairman, The Condé Nast Publications Ltd, 1957-64; President, Periodical Proprietors' Association, 1956-59 (Vice-President, 1959-65); Vice-President, International Federation of the Periodical Press, 1960-65; *b* 4 June 1896; *o s* of late Sir James Yoxall, MA, MP, JP, and late Lady Yoxall, JP (*née* Coles); *m* 1918, Josephine Fairchild Baldwin (*d* 1970); one *s* one *d. Educ:* St Paul's Sch. (captain of the school); Balliol Coll., Oxford (scholar). Served KRRC, 1915-19; British Military Mission to US, 1917-18. Joined The Condé Nast Publications Inc., 1921; appointed Business Manager and

Director, The Condé Nast Publications Ltd, 1924; Managing Director, 1934. Comr of Income Tax for Elmbridge Div. of Surrey, 1944-50. Chairman, General Periodicals' Council, Periodical Proprietors' Assoc., 1947-51. Member Council of Royal College of Art, 1951-54; a Governor of the Star and Garter Home for Disabled Sailors, Soldiers and Airmen, 1943- (Chairman, Finance Cttee, 1964-68). JP Richmond, Surrey, 1941- (Past Chairman of Bench and of Juvenile Court). *Publications:* Modern Love, 1927; All Abroad, 1928; A Respectable Man, 1935; Journey into Faith, 1963; Forty Years in Management, 1964; A Fashion of Life, 1966; The Wines of Burgundy, 1968. *Recreations:* wine, bridge, golf. *Address:* 15 Albert Court, SW7. *T:* 01-589 4475. *Clubs:* Savile, Saintsbury; Richmond Golf (Richmond, Surrey).

**YPRES,** 3rd Earl of, *cr* 1922; Viscount, *cr* 1916; of Ypres and of High Lake; **John Richard Charles Lambart French;** *b* 30 Dec. 1921; *o s* of 2nd Earl and Olivia Mary (*d* 1934), *d* of Maj.-Gen. Thomas John; *S* father, 1958; *m* 1943, Maureen Helena, *d* of Major H. John Kelly, US Foreign Service (retd), and of Mrs Kelly, Stow Bedon Hall, Attleborough, Norfolk; three *d*. *Educ:* Winchester; Trinity Coll., Dublin. Served War of 1939-45 as Captain, King's Royal Rifle Corps. *Heir: u* Lt-Col Hon. (Edward) Gerald French, *qv*.

**YUDKIN, John,** MA, PhD, MD, BCh (Cambridge); BSc (London); MRCP, FRIC; Professor of Nutrition, University of London, at Queen Elizabeth College, since 1954; *b* 8 August 1910; 3rd *s* of Louis and Sarah Yudkin, London; *m* 1933, Emily Himmelweit; three *s*. *Educ:* Hackney Downs (formerly Grocers' Company) School, London; Chelsea Polytechnic; Christ's Coll., Cambridge; London Hospital. Research in Biochemical Laboratory, Cambridge, 1931-36; Research in Nutritional Laboratory, Cambridge, 1938-43; Benn Levy Research Student, 1933-35; Grocers' Company Research Scholar, 1938-39; Sir Halley Stewart Research Fellow, 1940-43; Dir of Medical Studies, Christ's Coll., Cambridge, 1940-43; Prof. of Physiology, Queen Elizabeth Coll., 1945-54. William Julius Mickle Fellow, 1961-62. *Publications:* This Slimming Business, 1958; The Complete Slimmer, 1964; (with J. C. McKenzie) Changing Food Habits, 1964; Our Changing Fare, 1966; numerous articles on biochemistry and nutrition in scientific and medical journals. *Address:* 16 Holly Walk, Hampstead, NW3. *T:* 01-794 3023.

**YUKAWA, Prof. Hideki;** Decoration of Cultural Merit (Japan), 1943; Director, Research Institute for Fundamental Physics, Kyoto University, Japan, since 1953; Professor Emeritus, Osaka University, Japan; *b* 23 Jan. 1907; *s* of Takuji and Koyuki Ogawa; *m* 1932, Sumi Yukawa; two *s*. *Educ:* Kyoto University, Kyoto, Japan. Asst Prof., Osaka Univ., Japan, 1936-39; visited Europe and USA, 1939. Awarded Imperial Prize of Japan Acad., 1940; Member of Japan Acad., 1946-. Visiting Prof., Institute for Advanced Study, Princeton USA, 1948-49; Visiting Prof., Columbia Univ., USA, 1949-51; For. Associate, Nat. Acad. of Sciences, USA, 1949; Foreign Member: Royal Society, London, 1963; Academy of Science, USSR. Nobel Prize for Physics, 1949; Lomonosov Medal, 1964; Order Pour le Merite, W Germany, 1967. *Publications:* Introduction to Quantum Mechanics (in Japanese), 1947; Introduction to Theory of Elementary Particles (in Japanese), 1948; Editor of Progress of Theoretical Physics, (Kyoto, Japan) 1946-; Reference: Physical Review (USA); Reviews of Modern Physics (USA). *Address:* Yukawa Hall, Kyoto University, Kyoto, Japan; Izumikawa, Shimogamo, Sakyo-ku, Kyoto, Japan.

**YUKAWA, Morio;** Japanese Ambassador to the Court of St James's, since 1968; *b* 23 Feb. 1908; *m* 1940, Teiko Kohiyama; two *s*. *Educ:* Tokyo Imperial Univ. (Law Dept). Joined Diplomatic Service, and apptd Attaché, London, 1933; Dir, Trade Bureau of Economic Stabilization Bd (Cabinet), 1950; Dir, Econ. Affairs Bureau (For. Min.), 1951; Counsellor, Paris, 1952; Dir, Internat. Co-op. Bureau (For. Min.), 1954; again Dir, Econ. Affairs Bureau, 1955; Ambassador to The Philippines, 1957-61; Dep. Vice-Minister (For. Min.), 1961-63; Ambassador to Belgium, 1963-68; concurrently Ambassador to Luxembourg and Chief of Japanese Mission to European Economic Community, 1964-68. Holds foreign decorations. *Publications:* articles and brochures, principally on economic subjects. *Recreations:* golf, theatre, history and biography. *Address:* 23 Kensington Palace Gardens, W8. *T:* 01-229 7215. *Clubs:* St James'; Sunningdale Golf; Gakushikai, Tokyo International (Tokyo); Hodogaya Country (Yokohama).

**YUKON, Bishop of,** since 1968; **Rt. Rev. John Timothy Frame,** DD; *b* 8 Dec. 1930; *m*; three *d*. *Educ:* Univ. of Toronto. Burns Lake Mission, Dio. Caledonia, 1957; Hon. Canon of Caledonia, 1965. *Address:* PO Box 547, Whitehorse, Yukon, Canada.

**YUSUF, Sir Mohamad,** Kt, 1915; Indian landowner; *s* of Haji Ismail. Founded Ismail College, first Muslim College in Western India at Bombay; Marine College, Seamen's Orphanage, Hospital, Sanatorium, Schools, etc., on Island of Novha, and other Charitable Institutions in Bombay. Formerly Head of Bombay Steam Navigation Co. Now living in retirement on the Island of Novha which he owns. *Address:* Novha House, Bombay.

**YUTANG, Lin;** *see* Lin Yutang.

# Z

**ZAEHNER, Prof. Robert Charles,** FBA 1966; MA; Spalding Professor of Eastern Religions and Ethics, University of Oxford, since 1952; Fellow of All Souls College, Oxford, since 1952; *b* 8 April 1913; *s* of Edward and Maria Louisa Zaehner. *Educ:* Tonbridge School; Christ Church, Oxford (Scholar); King's Coll., Cambridge. MA Oxon Oriental Languages, First Class. Senior Scholar of Christ Church, 1937-39; Research Lectr of Christ Church, 1939; Asst Press Attaché, then Press Attaché, British Embassy, Teheran, 1943-47; received into Roman Catholic Church, 1946; Lectr in Persian, Univ. of Oxford, 1950; Acting Counsellor, British Embassy, Teheran, 1951-52; Jordan Lectr at SOAS, Univ. of London, 1959; Visiting Lectr, Union Theological Seminary, and Columbia Univ., NY, 1962; Gifford Lectr, Univ. of St Andrews, 1968-69; Riddell Lectr, Univ. of Newcastle upon Tyne, 1969; Westcott Lectr on Teape Foundn, St Stephen's Coll., Delhi, 1969. Hon. DLitt Lancaster, 1970. *Publications:* Foolishness to the Greeks, 1953; Zurvān, a Zoroastrian Dilemma, 1955; The Teachings of the Magi, 1956; Mysticism Sacred and Profane, 1957; At Sundry Times, 1958; The Concise Encyclopædia of Living Faiths (editor and two contributions), 1959; Hindu and Muslim Mysticism, 1960; The Dawn and Twilight of Zoroastrianism, 1961; Hinduism, 1962; The Convergent Spirit, 1963; The Catholic Church and World Religions, 1964; Hindu Scriptures (ed and trans.), 1966; The Bhagavad-Gita, 1968; Concordant Discord, 1970. *Address:* All Souls College, Oxford.

**ZAFRULLA KHAN, Hon. Chaudhri Sir Muhammad,** KCSI 1937; Kt 1935; BA (Hons, Punjab), LLB (Hons, London); Hon. Bencher, Lincoln's Inn; Barrister-at-Law, Lincoln's Inn; President, International Court of Justice, since 1970 (Member, 1954-61 and since 1964); *b* 6 Feb. 1893. *Educ:* Government College, Lahore; King's Coll. and Lincoln's Inn, London. Advocate, Sialkot, Punjab, 1914-16; practised in Lahore High Court, 1916-35; Editor, "Indian Cases", 1916-32. Member, Punjab Legislative Council, 1926-35; Deleg. Indian Round Table Confs, 1930, 1931 and 1932; Deleg. to Joint Select Cttee on Indian Parliamentary Reforms, 1933; Pres. All-India Muslim League, 1931; Mem. Viceroy's Exec. Council, 1935-51; Leader Indian Delegn to Session of Assembly of League of Nations, Dec. 1939; Agent-General to Government of India in China, 1942; Judge, Indian Fedl Court, Oct. 1941-June 1947; Constitutional Adviser to Nawab of Bhopal, June-Dec. 1947; Minister of Foreign Affairs and Commonwealth Relations, Pakistan, 1947-54; Leader Pakistan Delegn: to Annual Sessions of Gen. Assembly of UN, 1947-54; to Security Council of UN, on India-Pakistan dispute, 1948-51; Permanent Rep. of Pakistan at UN, 1961-64; Pres., UN Gen. Assembly, 1962. Hon. LLD: Cantab; Columbia; Denver; California; Hon. FKC London. *Publications:* Indian Cases; the Criminal Law Journal of India; Reprints of Punjab Criminal Rulings, Vol. IV; Fifteen Years' Digest; Islam: Its Meaning for Modern Man, 1962; (ed and trans.) The Quran, 1970. *Address:* International Court of Justice, The Hague, Netherlands.

**ZAHEDI, Ardeshir;** Foreign Minister of Iran, since 1967; *b* Tehran, 17 Oct. 1928; *s* of General Fazlollah and Khadijeh Zahedi; *m* 1957, HIH Princess Shahnaz Pahlavi (marr. diss., 1964); one *d*. *Educ:* American Coll. of Beirut; State Univ. of Utah (BS). Treasurer, Jt Iran-American Commn, and Asst to Dir of Point 4 Program, 1950; took part in revolution led by Gen. Zahedi which overthrew Mossadegh, 1953; Special Adviser to Prime Minister, 1953; Chamberlain to HIM the Shahanshah of Iran, 1954-59; Head of Iranian Students Program, 1959-60; Head of Mission representing Iran at 150th Anniv. Celebrations in Argentina, 1960; Ambassador of Iran to: the United States, 1960-62; Court of St James's, 1962-66; represented Iranian Govt at signing of Treaty Banning Nuclear Tests, London, 1963. Hon. Doctorates: Utah Univ., 1951; Chungang Univ. of Seoul, 1969. Holds numerous Iranian and foreign decorations. *Recreations:* hunting, shooting. *Address:* c/o Imperial Ministry of Foreign Affairs, Tehran, Iran.

**ZAIDI, Bashir Husain, Syed,** CIE 1941; Member of Indian Parliament (Rajya Sabha); Director of several industrial concerns; *b* 1898; *s* of Syed Shaukat Husain Zaidi; *m* 1937, Qudsia Abdullah (*d* 1960); two *s* one *d*. *Educ:* St Stephen's College, Delhi; Cambridge University. Called to Bar, Lincoln's Inn, 1923; served Aligarh Univ., 1923-30; entered Rampur State service, 1930; Chief Minister Rampur State, UP, 1936-39; Member: Indian Constituent Assembly, 1947-49, Indian Parliament, 1950-52; Indian Delegation to Gen. Assembly of UN, 1951; Indian Parliament (Lok Sabha), 1952-57; Govt of India's Commn of Inquiry on Communal Disturbances, 1967-69. Vice-Chancellor, Aligarh Muslim University, 1956-62. Leader, Good Will Mission to 9 Afro-Asian countries, 1964; Leader Cultural Delegn to participate in Afghan Independence Week celebrations, 1965. DLitt hc Aligarh 1964. *Address:* 6 Dr Rajindra Prasad Road, New Delhi, India.

**ZAIMIS, Prof. Eleanor,** MD; MRCP; Professor of Pharmacology in University of London at the Royal Free Hospital School of Medicine, since 1958; *b* 16 June 1915; *d* of late Jean Christides and of Helen Christides; *m* 1st, 1938, Evanghelos Chrysafis, MD; 2nd, 1943, John Zaimis, RHN (marriage dissolved, 1957). *Educ:* Greek Gymnasium; Universities of Bucharest, Roumania and Athens, Greece. MB 1938, MD 1941, BScChem 1947, Athens. Assistant to Professor of Pharmacology, Athens University, 1938-47; Head of Dept of Health, Youth Centres, Municipality of Athens, 1940-45; Member of Greek Government's Penicillin and Streptomycin Cttee, 1945-47. British Council Scholar, 1947-48; MRC Fellow, 1948-50; Research Worker: Dept of Pharmacology, Bristol University, Oct.-Dec. 1947; Depts of Chemistry and Physiology, Nat. Inst. for Med. Research, London, Jan.-Nov. 1948; Dept of Pharmacology, School of Pharmacy, London University, 1948-50. Lecturer in Pharmacology, School of Pharmacy, London University, 1950-54; Reader in Pharmacology, London University, Royal Free Hospital School of Medicine, 1954-58. Visiting Lecturer: Univ. of Rio de Janeiro, 1958; Internat. Anaesthesiology Centre, WHO, Copenhagen, 1959. Cameron Prize, Edinburgh, 1956; Gairdner Foundation International Award, Toronto, 1958; Hon. Member, Rome Acad. Medicine, 1965. Cross of Commander, Greek Royal Order of Benevolence, 1962; N. P. Kravkov Pharmacology Medal, USSR Acad. of Med. Sciences, 1968. *Publications:* Textbook on Hygiene (Greek Academy's Prize, 1948); papers on pharmacological and physiological subjects in scientific journals. *Recreation:* motoring. *Address:* 4 Cambridge Gate, Regent's Park, NW1. *T:* 01-486 3350.

**ZAMBRA, William Warren S.;** *see* Shaw-Zambra.

**ZANGWILL, Prof. Oliver Louis;** Professor of Experimental Psychology, University of Cambridge, since 1952; *b* 29 Oct. 1913; *yr s* of Israel Zangwill, author and dramatist, and Edith Ayrton Zangwill; *m* 1947, Joy Sylvia, *d* of Thomas Moult, *qv*. *Educ:* University College School, London; King's College, Cambridge (BA 1935, MA 1939). Natural Science Tripos, Part I, Class 2, 1934; Moral Science Tripos, Part II, Class 1, with special distinction, 1935. Research Student, Cambridge Psychological Laboratory, 1935-40; Psychologist, Brain Injuries Unit, Edinburgh 1940-45; Asst Director, Institute of Experimental Psychology, Oxford, 1945-52; Senior Lecturer in General Psychology, Univ. of Oxford, 1948-52. Visiting Psychologist, Nat. Hosp. for Nervous Diseases, Queen Square, London, 1947-; Hon. Consulting Psychologist to United Cambridge Hospitals, 1969-. Editor, Quart. Jl Exper. Psychology, 1958-66. President: Sect. J. Brit. Assoc. Adv. Sci., 1963; Experimental Psychology Soc., 1962-63. Mem., Biological Research Board, Medical Research Council, 1962-66. Professorial Fellow, King's College, Cambridge, 1955-. *Publications:* An Introduction to Modern Psychology, 1950; Cerebral Dominance and its relation to psychological function, 1960; (Jt Author and

Jt Editor) Current Problems in Animal Behaviour, 1961; (Jt Author and Jt Editor) Amnesia, 1966; papers in psychological and medical journals. *Recreations:* reading, natural history. *Address:* Psychological Laboratory, Downing Street, Cambridge. *T:* Cambridge 51386.

**ZANUCK, Darryl Francis;** Chairman of the Board and Chief Executive Officer, 20th Century-Fox Film Corporation, since 1969 (formerly President); *b* 5 Sept. 1902; *s* of Frank H. and Louise Torpin Norton Zanuck; *m* 1924, Virginia Ogelsby Fox; one *s* two *d. Educ:* Oakdale, Nebraska; Los Angeles, Calif. Served European War, 1917-18, with 37th Div.; with Warner Bros till 1933 (Producer of Little Caesar, Public Enemy, Five Star Final, I am a Fugitive from a Chain Gang, The Jazz Singer); joined Joseph M. Schenck in 20th Century Pictures (Producer of House of Rothschild, Les Misérables, Cardinal Richelieu and others). Amalgamated 20th Century with Fox, 1935, and became Vice-Pres.; first winner Irving Thalberg Memorial Trophy, again winner in 1944 and 1951. Supervised production training films for defence forces, Lt-Col 1941; Col 1942 (Legion of Merit). *Films:* with 20th Century-Fox include: Wilson, How Green was my Valley, This above all, The Purple Heart, Winged Victory, Grapes of Wrath, The Razor's Edge, Forever Amber, Gentleman's Agreement, The Snake Pit, Pinky, All About Eve. D. F. Zanuck Productions: Island in the Sun, The Sun Also Rises, 1957; The Roots of Heaven, 1958. Produced: Crack in the Mirror, 1959 (Paris); The Big Gamble, 1960 (France, Ireland, Africa); The Longest Day, 1962. Comdr Legion of Honour (France); Comdr of Order of Arts and Letters (France), 1968; Comdr in Order of Merit (Italy), 1969. *Recreations:* big-game hunting, polo, ski-ing. *Address:* 20th Century-Fox Film Corporation, 444 West 56th Street, New York, NY 10019, USA.

**ZARNECKI, George,** CBE 1970; MA, PhD; FSA; FBA 1968; Professor of History of Art, University of London, since 1963 (Reader, 1959-63); Deputy Director, Courtauld Institute of Art, since 1961; *b* 12 Sept. 1915; *m* 1945, Anne Leslie Frith; one *s* one *d. Educ:* Cracow Univ. MA Cracow Univ., 1938; PhD Univ. of London, 1950. Junior Asst, Inst. of History of Art, Cracow Univ., 1936-39. Served war of 1939-45 as lance-corporal in Polish Army; in France, 1939-40 (Polish Cross of Valour and Croix de Guerre, 1940); prisoner of war, 1940-42; interned in Spain, 1942-43; in Polish Army in UK, 1943-45. On staff of Courtauld Institute of Art, Univ. of London, 1945-. Slade Professor of Fine Art, Univ. of Oxford, 1960-61. Vice-Pres., Soc. of Antiquaries of London, 1968-; Member: Conservation Cttee, Council for Care of Churches, 1969-; Inst. for Advanced Study, Princeton, 1966. *Publications:* English Romanesque Sculpture 1066-1140, 1951; Later English Romanesque Sculpture 1140-1210, 1953; English Romanesque Lead Sculpture, 1957; Early Sculpture of Ely Cathedral, 1958; Gislebertus, sculpteur d'Autun, 1960 (English edn, 1961); Romanesque Sculpture at Lincoln Cathedral, 1964; La sculpture a Payerne, Lausanne, 1966; 1066 and Architectural Sculpture (Proceedings of Brit. Acad.), 1966; Romanik (Belser Stilgeschichte, VI), 1970; articles in archaeological journals. *Address:* 22 Essex Park, N3. *T:* 01-346 6497.

**ZEFFIRELLI, G. Franco (Corsi);** opera, film and theatrical producer and designer since 1949; *b* 12 February 1923. *Educ:* Florence. Designer: (in Italy): A Streetcar Named Desire; Troilus and Cressida; Three Sisters. Has produced and designed numerous operas in all the great cities of Italy and at world-famous festivals; also in Great Britain: Lucia di Lammermoor, Cavalleria Rusticana, and Pagliacci (Covent Garden, 1959); Falstaff (Covent Garden, 1961); L'Elisir D'Amore (Glyndebourne, 1961); Don Giovanni, and Alcina (Covent Garden, 1962); Tosca, Rigoletto (Covent Garden, 1964, 1966); Dir and Designer: Romeo and Juliet (Old Vic, 1960); Othello (Stratford-on-Avon), 1961; Amleto (National Theatre), 1964; After the Fall (Rome), 1964; Who's Afraid of Virginia Woolf (Paris), 1964, (Milan) 1965; La Lupa ( Rome), 1965; Much Ado About Nothing (National Theatre), 1966; Black Comedy (Rome), 1967; A Delicate Balance (Rome), 1967; Films: The Taming of the Shrew, 1965-66; Florence, Days of Destruction, 1966; Romeo and Juliet, 1967. Directed and designed, new opera, Antony and Cleopatra, Metropolitan Opera House, New York. *Address:* Via due Macelli 31, Rome.

**ZEHETMAYR, John Walter Lloyd,** VRD 1963; FSFor; Senior Officer for Wales and Conservator South Wales, Forestry Commission, since 1966; *b* 24 Dec. 1921; *s* of late Walter Zehetmayr and Gladys Zehetmayr; *m* 1945, Isabell (Betty) Neill-Kennedy; two *s* one *d. Educ:* St Paul's, Kensington; Keble Coll., Oxford (BA). Served RNVR, 1942-46 (despatches); now Lt Cdr RNR retired. Forestry Commission: Silviculturist, 1948-56; Work Study Officer, 1956-64; Conservator West Scotland, 1964-66. *Publications:* Experiments in Treeplanting on Peat, 1954; Afforestation of Upland Heaths, 1960. *Recreations:* garden, nature, skiing. *Address:* 51 Westbourne Road, Penarth, Glam CF6 2HB. *T:* Penarth 701694.

**ZEPLER, Eric Ernest;** Emeritus Professor of Electronics, Southampton University (Professor, 1949-63); Research Fellow, Institute of Sound and Vibration, Southampton University, since 1963; Past President British IRE; *b* 27 Jan. 1898; *s* of Dr med. M. Zepler and F. Guttfreundt; *m* 1926, Eleanor Fischer; one *s* one *d. Educ:* Realgymnasium Altena (Westphalia); Univ. Bonn, Berlin, Würzburg. Dr Phil., Würzburg, 1922. Research Engineer, Telefunken, 1925; Head of Design of Receivers and Direction Finders, Telefunken, 1932-35; came to England, 1935; Research Engineer, Marconi's Wireless Tel. Co. Ltd, 1936-40; Lecturer University Coll., Southampton, 1941; seconded to Cavendish Laboratory, 1943-46. *Publications:* The Technique of Radio Design, 1943; (contrib. 2 chapters) University Radio Conference Proceedings, 1944; Under the Spell of the Chess Problem, 1951; (co-editor with S. W. Punnett) Electronic Devices and Networks, 1963; Electronic Circuit Techniques, 1963; (with K. G. Nichols) Transients in Electronic Circuits; contrib. to Telefunken Zeitung, Wireless Engr. *Recreations:* music, chess, bridge. *Address:* Avonheath, 6 Saxholm Way, Bassett, Southampton. *T:* Southampton 68020.

**ZETLAND,** 3rd Marquess of; **Lawrence Aldred Mervyn Dundas;** Bt 1762; Baron Dundas, 1794; Earl of Zetland, 1838; Earl of Ronaldshay (UK), 1892; DL; Temporary Major Yorkshire Hussars (TA); *b* 12 Nov. 1908; *er s* of 2nd Marquess of Zetland, KG, PC, GCSI, GCIE, FBA, and of Cicely, *d* of Colonel Mervyn Archdale; *S* father, 1961; *m* 1936, Penelope, *d* of late Col Ebenezer Pike, CBE, MC; three *s* one *d. Educ:* Harrow; Trinity Coll., Cambridge. ADC on Staff of Viceroy of India, 1930-31. DL, North Riding of Yorks, 1965. *Heir: s* Earl of Ronaldshay, *qv. Address:* Aske, Richmond, Yorks. *T:* Richmond (Yorks) 3222;

59 Cadogan Place, SW1. *T:* 01-235 6542. (Seat) Aske, Richmond, Yorkshire. *Clubs:* Queen's, All England Lawn Tennis.

**ZETTERLING, Mai Elizabeth, (Mrs David Hughes);** Actress, films and stage, also film director; *b* 24 May 1925; *d* of Joel and Lina Zetterling; *m* 1st, 1944, Tutte Lemkow; one *s* one *d*; 2nd, 1958, David John Hughes. *Educ:* Stockholm, Sweden. Graduate of Royal Theatre School of Drama, Stockholm. First appeared as Cecilia in Midsummer Dream in the Workhouse, Blanche Theatre, Stockholm, Oct. 1941. Stage successes (all at Royal Theatre, Stockholm) include: Janet in St Mark's Eve; Agnes in the Beautiful People; Bridgid in Shadow and Substance; Maria in Twelfth Night; Nerissa in Merchant of Venice; Electra in Les Mouches; Adela in House of Bernarda. First appearance in London, as Hedwig in The Wild Duck, St Martin's, Nov. 1948; subsequently Nina in The Seagull, Lyric, Hammersmith, and St James's, 1949; Eurydice in Point of Departure, Lyric, Hammersmith and Duke of York's, 1950; Karen in The Trap, Duke of York's, 1952; Nora Helmer in A Doll's House, Lyric, Hammersmith, 1953; Poppy in The Count of Clérambard, Garrick, 1955; Thérèse Tard in Restless Heart, St James's, 1957; Tekla in Creditors, Lyric, Hammersmith, 1959, etc. *Swedish films* include: Frenzy, Iris, Rain Follows Dew, Music in the Dark, A Doll's House, Swinging on a Rainbow. *English films* include: Frieda, The Bad Lord Byron, Quartet, Portrait from Life, Lost People, Blackmailed, Hell is Sold Out, Tall Headlines, Desperate moment, Faces in the Dark, Offbeat, The Main Attraction, and Only Two Can Play. *United States films* include: Knock on Wood, Prize of Gold, and Seven Waves Away. Director of documentary films for BBC; Dir and Prod and co-writer with David Hughes of short film The War Game; 1st Award at Venice for Narrative Shorts, 1963; Director: Swedish full-length films, Alskande Par, (Eng.) Loving Couples, 1965; Night Games, 1966 (and *see infra*); Dr Glas, 1968; Flickorna, 1968; The Girls, 1968. *Publications:* The Cat's Tale (with David Hughes), 1965; Night Games (novel), 1966. *Recreations:* gardening, cooking. *Address:* c/o John Redway, 77 Brook Street, W1.

**ZHUKOV, Georgi Alexandrovich;** Orders of: Lenin; Red Banner of Labour (2); Red Star; Columnist of Pravda; Vice-President Soviet Committee of Peace; MP; Member, Foreign Relations Committee, USSR Supreme Soviet; Chairman, Soviet-French parliamentary group; Vice-President, Soviet-American Institut; *b* 1908. *Educ:* Lomonosov Inst., Moscow. Corresp.: local papers in Lugansk, Kharkov, 1927-32; Komsomolskaya Pravda, 1932-46 (Mem. Editorial Bd); Pravda, 1946-47; Pravda in Paris, 1947-52; Foreign Editor of Pravda, 1952-57; Chairman, USSR Council of Ministers' State Committee for Cultural Relations with Foreign Countries, 1957-62. Lenin Prize (for Journalism); Vorovsky Prize. *Publications:* Border, 1938; Russians and Japan, 1945; Three Months in Geneva, 1954; Soldier's Life, 1946; American Notes (essays) 1947; The West After War, 1948; Taming Tigers, 1961; Japan, 1962; Meetings in Transcarpathia, 1962; One MIG from a Thousand, 1963; These Seventeen Years, 1963; Silent Art, 1964; The People of the Thirties, 1964; Vietnam, 1965; America, 1967; The People of the Forties, 1968; etc. *Address:* 24 Pravda Street, Moscow, USSR.

**ZHUKOV, Marshal Georgi Konstantinovich;** Hero of the Soviet Union (three awards); Order of Lenin (five); Order of Victory (2); Order of Suvorov (2), etc; *b* Kalinin Region, 1896. Joined Red Army, 1918; took part in Civil War; took part in Battle of Khalkin-Gol against Japanese, 1939; during War held posts as Chief of General Staff, Deputy People's Commissar of Defence, C-in-C Leningrad, Western and 1st Ukrainian Fronts, 1941-45; in charge of defence of Moscow, 1941; took part in drawing up plan for defeat of German Army at Stalingrad, 1942; co-ordinator of Leningrad and Volkhov Fronts to break blockade of Leningrad, 1943; co-ordinated activity of 1st and 2nd Ukrainian Fronts and 1st and 2nd Byelorussian Fronts, 1943-44; C-in-C 1st Byelorussian Front, 1944-45; commanded capture of Berlin, 1945; Soviet representative at capitulation of Germans, 1945; Deputy Minister of Defence, 1953-55; Minister of Defence of the USSR, 1955-57. Member of the Presidium, in 1957 (Candidate Mem. 1956). Holds several foreign awards. *Address:* Moscow.

**ZIEGLER, Prof. Dr Karl;** Director, Max Planck Institute (formerly Kaiser Wilhelm Institute) for Coal Research, Mülheim-Ruhr, 1943-69, retired; Hon. Professor, Technische Hochschule, Aachen, since 1949; *b* 26 Nov. 1898; *s* of Karl and Luise Ziegler; *m* 1922, Maria Kurtz; one *s* one *d*. *Educ:* Marburg University. Lecturer, Marburg University, 1923-26; Assistant, Chemical Institute, Heidelberg University, 1926-36; Professor of Chemistry and Director of Chemical Institute, University of Halle-Saale, 1936-43. Visiting Professor, University of Chicago, 1936; Carl Folkers Lecturer, Madison, Wisconsin, and Urbana, Illinois, 1952. Holds numerous awards, including Nobel Prize for Chemistry (jointly), 1963. *Publications:* about 180 contribs learned jls. *Recreations:* astronomy, mountain-climbing. *Address:* c/o Max-Planck-Institut für Kohlenforschung, Kaiser-Wilhelm-Platz 1, Mülheim-Ruhr, Germany. *T:* 3061 (private) 306 290.

**ZIGMOND, Joseph; His Honour Judge Zigmond;** Judge of the County Courts (Circuit No 4) since 1967; *b* 5 Dec. 1914; *s* of John and Dinah Zigmond; *m* 1941, Muriel Lermon; two *s*. *Educ:* Cardiff High School; Welsh National Sch. of Medicine. MRCS, LRCP 1938. Royal Army Medical Corps, 1941-46 (Capt.). Called to the Bar, Gray's Inn, 1946. Assistant Recorder, Salford Quarter Sessions, 1965-67. *Recreations:* reading, music. *Address:* Stanley House, Stanley Drive, Handforth, Wilmslow, Cheshire. *T:* 061-437 2010.

**ZIJLSTRA, Jelle;** Central Banker; President, Netherlands Bank, since 1967; *b* 27 Aug. 1918; *s* of Ane Zijlstra and Pietje Postuma; *m* 1946, Hetty Bloksma; two *s* three *d*. *Educ:* Netherlands Sch. of Economics. Asst, Netherlands Sch. of Economics, 1945; Prof., Theoretical Economics, 1948-52; Prof., Public Finance, 1963-66, Free Univ. of Amsterdam; Minister of Economic Affairs, 1952-58; of Finance, 1959-1963; Prime Minister, 1966-67. Mem., Chm. Board, and Pres., BIS, 1967-; Governor, IMF, 1967-. *Publications:* Planned Economy, 1947; The Velocity of Money and its Significance for the Value of Money and for Monetary Equilibrium, 1948; Economic Order and Economic Policy, 1952. *Recreations:* sailing, ski-ing. *Address:* De Nederlandsche Bank NV, Westeinde 1, Amsterdam, Netherlands; Bavoylaan 14, Den Haag, Netherlands.

**ZIMAN, Herbert David;** Literary Editor of The Daily Telegraph, 1956-68; *b* Hampstead, 21 March 1902; *s* of late David Ziman, Reefton, New Zealand and Lena (*née* Cohen); *m* 1928, Jean Ritchie, *d* of late C. J. Macalister, MD, FRCP, TD, of Liverpool and Bourton-on-the-

Water; two *d* (and one *s* decd). *Educ:* Rugby (Scholar and Senior Leaving Exhibitioner) and University College, Oxford (Senior Scholar). Leader-writer and Asst Literary Editor, Liverpool Daily Post, 1925-26; Film critic of Liverpool Daily Post, 1926-29, and of Glasgow Herald, 1927-29; Museum, Library and Archæological Correspondent, The Times, 1930-33; Leader-writer, Daily Telegraph, 1934-39, and 1946-55. Served in Artists' Rifles, Middlesex Regt and Intelligence Corps (GSO3 South-Eastern Command and Southern Command) and in Political Intelligence Dept, 1939-44. Daily Telegraph War Correspondent in France, Belgium, Holland and Germany with 1st Canadian, 2nd British and 1st US Armies, 1944-45. Special Correspondent of Daily Telegraph subsequently in Western Europe, Greece, Turkey, USSR, Israel, China, Uganda, Kenya, Congo, United States, Canada, Mexico, Chile and Brazil. Hon. Secretary, Friends of the National Libraries, 1931-37, Exec. Cttee FNL, 1937-; Council, Anglo-Belgian Union, 1957-. *Address:* 10 Eton Road, NW3. *T:* 01-722 5526. *Club:* Reform.

**ZIMAN, Prof. John Michael,** FRS 1967; Melville Wills Professor of Physics, University of Bristol, since 1969; *b* 16 May 1925; *s* of late Solomon Netheim Ziman, ICS, retired, and Nellie Frances Ziman (*née* Gaster); *m* 1951, Rosemary Milnes Dixon; two adopted *s* two adopted *d*. *Educ:* Hamilton High Sch., NZ; Victoria University Coll., Wellington, NZ; Balliol Coll., Oxford. Junior Lectr in Mathematics, Oxford Univ., 1951-53; Pressed Steel Co. Ltd Research Fellow, Oxford Univ., 1953-54; Lectr in Physics, Cambridge Univ., 1954-64; Fellow of King's Coll., Cambridge, 1957-64; Editor of Cambridge Review, 1958-59; Tutor for Advanced Students, King's Coll., Cambridge, 1959-63; Prof. of Theoretical Physics, Univ. of Bristol, 1964-69. Rutherford Memorial Lectr in India and Pakistan, 1968. *Publications:* Electrons and Phonons, 1960; Electrons in Metals, 1963; (with Jasper Rose) Camford Observed, 1964; Principles of the Theory of Solids, 1965; Public Knowledge, 1968; Elements of Advanced Quantum Theory, 1969; numerous articles in scientific jls. *Address:* H. H. Wills Physics Laboratory, Tyndall Avenue, Bristol BS8 1TL. *T:* 24161.

**ZIMBALIST, Efrem;** Violinist; Director of The Curtis Institute of Music, Philadelphia, 1941-68; *b* Russia, 1889; *m* 1st, 1914, Alma Gluck, singer; one *s* one *d*; 2nd, 1943, Mary Louise Curtis Bok. Musical training Imperial School, St Petersburg, under Leopold Auer. Has concertized continuously since debut in 1907 in Berlin. Composer of works for orchestra: American Rhapsody; Concerto for violin and orchestra (1st performance with Philadelphia Orchestra, 1947); Landara (Opera Première, Acad. of Music, Phila, 1957); Concerto for piano and orchestra (1st perf. with New Orleans Symph. Orch., 1959); String Quartet in E minor; Violin Sonata; many minor works for voice, violin and piano. *Address:* 866 Skyline Boulevard, Reno, Nevada 89502, USA.

**ZINKEISEN, Anna Katrina,** RP, ROI, RDI; Portrait and Mural Painter; *b* Kilcreggan, Scotland; *d* of Victor Zinkeisen and Clare Bolton Charles; *m* 1928, Colonel Guy R. N. Heseltine, MC. *Educ:* home; Royal Academy Schools. Ambulance Officer in St John Ambulance, nursing at St Mary's Hospital and doing pathological and clinical drawings for surgeons throughout the war. *Address:* 25 Cheyne Court, Chelsea, SW3; Looms Cottage, Burgh, Woodbridge, Suffolk.

**ZINN, Major William Victor,** CEng, FICE, FIStructE; MEIC (Canada), MSCE (France); Principal of W. V. Zinn & Associates, International Consulting Civil and Structural Engineers, since 1934; *b* 7 July 1903; *s* of late Roman Reuben Zinn and Bertha Zinn (*née* Simon); *m* 1st, 1934, Laure (*d* 1960), *d* of Chaim and Fleur Modiano, London; one *s* one *d*; 2nd, 1963, Monica, *d* of late Alan Ribton-Turner and Josephine Ribton-Turner (*née* Carey). *Educ:* University College Sch. and University Coll., London. BSc(Eng), MConsE London. War Service, 14th Army Burma, Major RE (retd), 1939-45. Sen. Partner: Haigh Zinn & Associates, Haigh Zinn & Humphreys, and Airport Development Consultants; New Steelworks, Guest Keen & Nettlefolds, Cardiff, 1932-35; Consultant assisting UKAEA and Min. of Works on Atomic Power Stations at Harwell, Windscale, Capenhurst, Calder Hall, Chapel Cross and Dounreay, 1952-56. *Works:* London Hilton Hotel and Royal Garden Hotel; London Govt Offices: Min. of Transport, Min. of Housing, Min. of Works, Dept of Postmaster-Gen., Central Electricity Authority and Min. of Civil Aviation; County Halls: Devon, Gloucester, Norfolk, Lanarkshire, 1954-66; numerous Housing Projects for many UK Local Authorities, totalling over 53,000 dwellings, 1934-69; overseas: Princes Bldg and Mandarin Hotel, also Brit. Mil. Hosp., Hong Kong, 1965; Feasibility Reports for World Bank: Teesta Barrage, and Chandpur Irrigation Project (East Pakistan), 1960-62; Ceylon Water Supplies and Drainage for World Health Organisation of the UNO, 1968; development of new techniques for deep underground city excavations, 1960-66; Engineering Consultant for Livingston New Town, Scotland, 1968. *Publications:* Economical Construction of Deep Basements, 1968; Detailing by Computer, 1969. *Address:* Longdene, Haslemere, Surrey.

**ZINNEMANN, Fred;** Film Director since 1934; *b* Austria, 29 April 1907; *s* of Dr Oskar Zinnemann, Physician and Anna F. Zinnemann; *m* 1936, Renée Bartlett; one *s*. *Educ:* Vienna Univ. (Law School). First film, The Wave (documentary) directed for Mexican Govt, 1934; initiated, with others, school of neo-realism in American cinema, directing among other films: The Seventh Cross, 1943; The Search, 1948; The Men, 1949; Teresa, 1950; High Noon, 1951; From Here to Eternity, 1953. Later films include: Oklahoma!, 1956; The Nun's Story, 1959; The Sundowners, 1960; Behold a Pale Horse, 1964; A Man for All Seasons, 1966. Member: Bd of Trustees, Amer. Film Inst.; Acad. of Motion Picture Arts; Directors' Guild of America. Awards include: Academy Award, Los Angeles, 1951, 1954, 1967; Film Critics' Award, NY, 1952, 1954, 1960, 1967; Golden Thistle Award, Edinburgh, 1965; Moscow Film Festival Award, 1967; D. W. Griffith Award, 1970. Gold Medal of City of Vienna, 1967. *Publication:* article on directing films, Encyclopædia Britannica. *Recreations:* mountain climbing, chamber music. *Address:* 35 Blomfield Road, W9. *T:* 01-289 0433. *Club:* Federal City (Washington, DC).

**ZOUCHE,** 18th Baron, *cr* 1308, of Haryngworth; **James Assheton Frankland;** Bt 1660; served 15/19th the King's Royal Hussars, 1963-68; *b* 23 Feb. 1943; *s* of Major Hon. Sir Thomas William Assheton Frankland, 11th Bt, and Mrs Michael Barclay, *d* of late Capt. Hon. Edward Kay-Shuttleworth; *S* to father's Btcy 1944; *S* grandmother, 17th Baroness Zouche, 1965. *Educ:* Lycée Jaccard, Lausanne. *Heir:* *u* Hon. Roger Nathaniel Frankland [*b* 11 April 1909;

st, 1931 (marr. diss., 1947); two *s*; 2nd, 47, Olivia, *d* of Rev. Hon. Nigel Campbell and *widow* of Major S. J. R. Bucknill, Irish Guards]. *Address:* Barbon Manor, Kirkby Lonsdale, Carnforth, Lancs. *Club:* Cavalry.

**ZUCKERMAN, Sir Solly,** OM 1968; KCB 1964 (CB 1946); Kt 1956; FRS 1943; MA, MD, DSc; MRCS, FRCP; Chief Scientific Adviser to HM Government; Chairman, Central Advisory Council for Science and Technology; Professor at Large, University of East Anglia; Fellow of University College, London; *b* Cape Town, 1904; *m* 1939, Lady Joan Rufus Isaacs, *er d* of 2nd Marquess of Reading, PC, GCMG, CBE, MC, TD, QC; one *s* one *d*. *Educ:* S African College Sch.; Univ. of Cape Town (Liberman Scholar); University Coll. Hosp., London (Goldsmid Exhibitioner). Demonstrator of Anatomy, Univ. of Cape Town, 1923-25; Union Research Scholar, 1925; Research Anatomist to the Zoological Soc. of London, and Demonstrator of Anatomy, University Coll., London, 1928-32; Research Associate and Rockefeller Research Fellow, Yale Univ., 1933-34; University Demonstrator and Lectr in Human Anatomy Dept, Oxford, 1934-45; Sands Cox Prof. of Anatomy, Univ. of Birmingham, 1943-68. William Julius Mickle Fellow, Univ of London, 1935; Beit Memorial Research Fellow, 1934-37; Hunterian Prof., Royal Coll. of Surgeons, 1937; Agricultural Research Council, 1949-59; Chm., Defence Research Policy Cttee, 1960-64; Chm., Cttee on Scientific Manpower, 1950-64; Chm. Natural Resources (Techn.) Cttee, 1951-64; Dep. Chm. Advisory Council on Scientific Policy, 1948-64; Chief Scientific Adviser to the Sec. of State for Defence, 1960-66. Mem., Royal Commn on Environmental Pollution, 1970-. Visitor, Bedford Coll., 1968-. Lectures: Gregynog, University Coll. of Wales, 1956; Mason, Univ. of Birmingham, 1957; Lees Knowles, Cambridge, 1965; Maurice Lubbock, Oxford, 1967; Maurice Bloch, Glasgow, 1969, Trueman Wood, RSA, 1969. BBC Gen. Adv. Council, 1957-62. Hon. Sec., Zoological Soc., London; Hon. Mem. Acad. das Ciencias de Lisboa; Fellow Commoner, Christ's Coll., Cambridge. Dr (*hc*) Univ. of Bordeaux, 1961. Group Capt. (Hon.) RAF, 1943-46. Scientific Advisory posts, Combined Ops RAF, 1939-46. A Trustee of the British Museum (Natural History), 1967-. Hon. DSc: Univ. of Sussex, 1963; Jacksonville, 1964; Bradford, 1966; Hon. LLD Birmingham, 1970. Hon. Fellow RCS, 1964. Foreign Member: American Philosophical Soc.; Amer. Acad. of Arts and Sciences. medal of Freedom with Silver Palm (US); Chevalier de la Légion d'Honneur (France). *Publications:* The Social Life of Monkeys and Apes, 1932; Functional Affinities of Man, Monkeys and Apes, 1933; A New System of Anatomy, 1961; Scientists and War, 1966; The Image of Technology, 1968; (ed) The Ovary (Vols 1 and 2), 1961; contributions to scientific journals. *Address:* 11 Hasker Street, SW3. *Clubs:* Athenæum, Beefsteak, Brooks's.

**ZUKOR, Adolph;** Chairman of Board Emeritus, Paramount Pictures Corporation; *b* 7 Jan. 1873; *s* of Jacob Zukor and Hannah Liebermann; *m* 1897, Lottie Kaufman (*d* 1956); one *s* one *d*. *Educ:* Hungary; evening schools, New York City. Came to US 1888; engaged in hardware, upholstery and fur business; went to Chicago 1892 where he became successful in fur trade; returned to NY in 1901 and 1903 ventured with the late Marcus Loew in the penny arcade; this was the foundation of the Loew Enterprises of which Loew became the President and Zukor the Treasurer; formed Famous Players Film Company with aid of Daniel Frohman, 1912; the first production of the new company was Queen Elizabeth with Sarah Bernhardt; this was followed by Prisoner of Zenda with James K. Hackett and these two were the first two feature pictures of multiple-reel length produced; Famous Players Film Company and Jesse L. Lasky Feature Play Combined under the name of Famous Players Lasky Corporation, 1916, then absorbed Paramount Pictures Corporation; erected theatres in the key cities of the country; this led to establishment of Publix Theatres Corporation, 1926; corporate name changed to Paramount Famous-Lasky Corporation 1927; to Paramount Publix Corporation 1930; to Paramount Pictures, Inc., 1935. *Recreation:* golf. *Address:* c/o Paramount Pictures Corp., 1 Gulf & Western Plaza, New York, NY 10023, USA. *Clubs:* Masons, Lambs, City Athletic (New York); Hillcrest Country (Los Angeles).

**ZULU, Rt. Rev. Alphaeus Hamilton;** *see* Zululand, Bishop of.

**ZULUETA, Sir Philip Francis de,** Kt 1963; Director, Hill Samuel and Co., and other cos; *b* 2 Jan. 1925; *o s* of late Professor Francis de Zulueta; *m* 1955, Hon. Marie-Louise, *e d* of 2nd Baron Windlesham; one *s* one *d*. *Educ:* Beaumont; New College, Oxford (Scholar). MA. Served Welsh Guards, NW Europe, 1943-47 (Capt., 1945). Entered Foreign Service, 1949: Moscow, 1950-52; Private Sec. to successive Prime Ministers (Lord Avon, Mr Macmillan, Sir A. Douglas-Home), 1955-64. Asst Sec., HM Treas., 1962. Resigned from Foreign Service and joined Philip Hill-Higginson, Erlangers, 1964. Chm., Austral Trust, SA, 1968. Member: Wider Share Ownership Council, 1965-; Adv. Council, BBC, 1967. Kt of Honour and Devotion, SMO Malta, 1965. *Address:* 11 Vicarage Gardens, W8. *T:* 01-229 1177; Combe Row, West Wittering, Sussex. *T:* 2321. *Clubs:* Beefsteak, Pratt's.

**ZULULAND, Bishop of,** since 1968; **Rt. Rev. Alphaeus Hamilton Zulu;** *b* 29 June 1905; *m* 1929, Miriam Adelaide Magwaza; one *s* six *d*. *Educ:* St Chad's Coll., Ladysmith (qual. teacher); Univ. of S Africa. BA (dist. Soc. Anthrop.) 1938; LTh 1940. Deacon, 1940; Priest, 1942. Curate of St Faith's Mission, Durban, 1940-52, Priest-in-charge, 1952-60; Suffragan Bishop of St John's, (formerly St John's, Kaffraria), 1960-66; Bishop of Zululand and Swaziland, 1966-68. *Recreation:* tennis. *Address:* Box 147, Eshowe, Zululand, South Africa. *T:* 147.

**ZUNTZ, Prof. Günther,** FBA 1956; DrPhil (Marburg); Emeritus Professor, Manchester University; Professor of Hellenistic Greek, 1963-69; *b* 28 Jan. 1902; *s* of Dr Leo Zuntz and Edith (*née* Bähring); *m* 1947, M. A. Garratt; two *s* one *d*. *Educ:* Bismarck-Gymnasium, Berlin-Wilmersdorf; Berlin, Marburg, Göttingen and Graz Universities. Teacher, Odenwaldschule, 1924-26; Teacher, Marburg Gymnasium and Kassel Gymnasium, 1926-32; worked for Monumenta Musicae Byzantinae, in Copenhagen, 1935-39, in Oxford, 1939-47; Librarian, Mansfield College, Oxford, 1944-47; Senior Lecturer, Manchester University, 1947-55 (Reader, „ 1955-63). *Publications:* Hölderlins Pindar-Übersetzung, 1928; (with C. Höeg) Prophetologium, i-vi, 1939-70; The Text of the Epistles, 1953; Political Plays of Euripides, 1955; Transmission of Plays of Euripides, 1965; Persephone, 1970. Articles in many learned journals. *Recreation:* music. *Address:* Westbourne, 43 Manchester Road, Buxton, Derbyshire. *T:* Buxton 2805.